2014 Standard C

WOR   DINS

2001 to Da   8th Edition

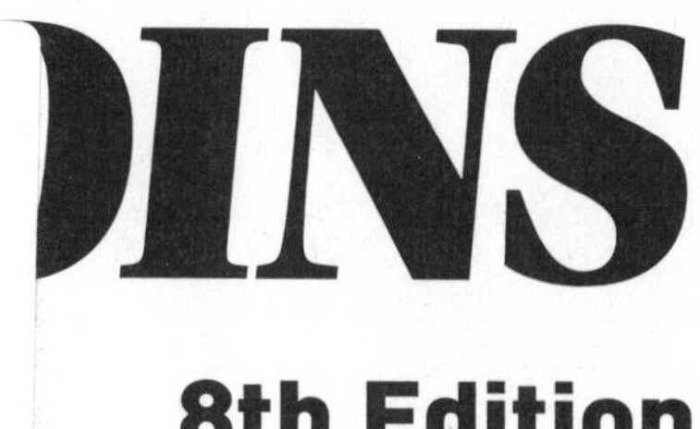

George S. Cuhaj, Editor • **Thomas Michael**, Market Analyst

Harry Miller, U.S. Market Analyst

Deborah McCue, Database Specialist • **Kay Sanders**, Editorial Assistant

Special Contributors

Dylan Arthur • Carmen Fuhiniu

Melvyn Kassenoff • Juri Pschegorlinski

Egon Conti Rossini • Gerhard Schön • Jacek Suchan

Bullion Value (BV) Market Valuations

Valuations for all platinum, gold, palladium and silver coins of the more common, basically bullion types, or those possessing only modest numismatic premiums are presented in this edition based on the market ranges of:

$1,750 per ounce for **platinum** | **$1,750** per ounce for **gold**

$750 per ounce for **palladium** | **$35.00** per ounce for **silver**

Published by

Krause Publications, a division of F+W Media, Inc.
700 East State Street • Iola, WI 54990-0001
715-445-2214 • 888-457-2873
www.krausebooks.com

To order books or other products call toll-free 1-800-258-0929
or visit us online at www.shopnumismaster.com

ISSN: 1935-4339

ISBN-13: 978-1-4402-3568-9
ISBN-10: 1-4402-3568-6

Cover Design by Kevin Ulrich
Designed by Jana Tappa
Edited by George Cuhaj

Printed in The United States of America

INTRODUCTION

Welcome to the 8th edition of the 21st Century Standard Catalog of World Coins. The most recent annual version of our ever growing series of comprehensive reference catalogs is designed to meet the needs of those whose interest in coins exceeds the casual jingle of those in your pants pocket or purse. Perhaps you have traveled overseas and still have some coins that came home with you, maybe you read in the news about the Euro circulating commemoratives or issues from recently formed nations, or you are a long-term collector who wants to wade out into the most current of numismatic trends. In all cases, this book is for you.

This book is arranged in alphabetical fashion by country and with grouping for political structure, coinage type and denomination to better help organize the information. You will find many illustrations, complete listings of metal content, descriptions of the designs and events depicted on the coins as well as date, mint mark varieties and values in multiple grades of preservation. In short, just about all of the information you could want on the most modern coins of the world.

With the information presented in these listings, one can marvel at the ingenuity of today's most inventive world mints, which are striking coins in a variety of shapes, sizes, colors and textures. Enjoy the practicality of coins designed for serious circulation in durable metals. Celebrate the advent of coins made of acrylic materials, those which house precious stones, or display selective gold overlays or are pad-printed in colorful designs. All are here in this 21st Century edition.

The accuracy of the information offered in this volume is assured through the assistance of a vast number of contributing coin dealers, collectors, manufacturers and researchers who have lent their knowledge to the compiling of this reference by providing our staff with information on new issues, new dates to existing types, accurate mintages and up-to-date pricing. To them all, we offer a heartfelt "Thank You" for their generosity and dedication to the advancement of our shared field of coin collecting.

Coins are issued throughout the year. We endeavor to keep pace with this worldwide information flow with updates to the online version of the Standard Catalog series, found at www.numismaster.com. There you will be able to see the latest issues, additional images and for a small monthly or annual subscription fee, price updates of your favorite issues. You may also find additional coin books and supplies at www.shopnumismaster.com. Thanks for using our services.

Finally, to you the reader, we extend our wishes that you may enjoy using this catalog as much as we have enjoyed its production. Look it over, put it to good use and please let us know if you have any comments or questions.

Best Wishes,

The Editorial Staff of the
Standard Catalog of World Coins

ACKNOWLEDGMENTS

Many individuals have contributed countless changes, which have been incorporated into the current edition. While all may not be acknowledged, special appreciation is extended to the following who have exhibited a special enthusiasm for this edition.

Dr. Laurence Adams
Dylan Arthur
Esko Ahlroth
Antonio Alessandrini
Oksana Bandrivska
Albert Beck
Jan Bendix
Richard Benson
Shamik Biswas
Sharon Blocker
Gunta Bluke
Joseph E. Boling
Richard Borek jun.
Al Boulanger
Maruta Brûkle
Mahdi Bseiso
Chris Budesa
John T. Bucek
Juan Cayón
Adolpho Cayón
Fred Colombo
Raymond E. Czahor
Howard A. Daniel III
Konstantinos Dellios
Wilhelm R. Eglseer
Esko Ekman
Andrzej Fischer
Dagmar Flachén
Eugene Freeman
Peter Frei
Arthur Friedburg
Carmen Fuhiniu
Lorraine Gallagher
Tom Galway
J. Halfpenny
Flemming Lyngbeck Hansen
David Harrison
Martin Rodney Hayter
Istvan Hegedus
Emmanuel Henry
Jennifer Hird
Teréz Horváth
Serge Huard
Nelva G. Icaza
Hector Carlos Janson
Alex Kaglyan
Melvyn Kassenoff
Craig Keplinger
Rodolphe Krempp
Alex Lazarovici
Ma Tak Wo
Ranko Mandic
Miguel Angel Pratt Mayans
Bernhard H. Mayer
Juozas Minikevicius
Andy Mirski
Robert Mish
Ing. Benjamin M. Mizrachi R.
Dr. Richard Montrey
Horst-Dieter Müller
Edward Moschetti
Michael G. Nielsen
Alberto Paashaus
Dick Parker
Frank Passic
Martin Peeters
Marc Pelletier
Kirsten F. Petersen
Andreas Pitsillides
Gastone Polacco
Juri Psch
Jordi Puigdemasa
Frank Putrow
Kitty Quan
Yahya Qureshi
Arif Qureshi
Dr. Dennis G. Rainey
Ivan Rakitin
Ilan Rinetzky
William M. Rosenblum
Egon Conti Rossini
Pabitra K. Saha
Remy Said
Leon Saryan
Jacco Scheper
Dr. Andreas Schikora
Gerhard Schön
George Schumacher
Alexander Shapiro
Ole Sjoelund
Mira Spijker
Heimo Steriti
Jacek Suchan
Steven Tan
Mehmet Tolga Taner
Rivka Toledano
Amelia Travaglini
Anthony Tumonis
Erik J. Van Loon
Natanya van Niekerk
Neil Vance
Carmen Viciedo
Wakim Wakim
Paul Welz
J. Brix Westergaard
Hasse Wiersma
J. Hugh Witherow
Joseph Zaffern

AUCTION HOUSES

Dix-Noonan-Webb
Heritage World Coin Auctions
Hess-Divo Ltd.
Gerhard Hirsch
Thomas Høiland Møntauktion
Fritz Rudolf Künker
Leu Numismatik AG
Marudhar Arts
MPO Auctions
Münzenhandlung Harald Möller, GmbH
Noble Numismatics, Pty. Ltd.
Stack's, Bowers and Ponterio
UBS, AG
World Wide Coins of California

WORLD MINTS, CENTRAL BANKS AND DISTRIBUTORS

Austrian Mint
Banco de Mexico
Banque Centrale Du Luxembourg
Black Mountain Coins
Casa de la Moneda de Cuba
Central Bank of D.P.R. Korea - Kumbyol Trading Corp.
Central Bank of the Russian Federation
CIT
Czech National Bank
Downies
Educational Coin Company
Faude & Huguenin
Global Coins & Medals Ltd. - Official Sales Company of the Bulgarian Mint
Imprensa Nacional - Casa da Moeda, S.A.
Israel Coins & Medals Corp.
Istituto Poligrafico e Zecca dello Stato I.p.A.
Jablonex Group - Division of Czech Mint
Japan Mint
JVP Investment Coins
Kazakhstan Mint
KOMSCO - South Korea
Latvijas Banka
Lietuvos Bankas
Lithuanian Mint
Magyar Penzvero Zrt.
Mayer's Mint GmbH
MDM
Mennica Polska
Mincovna Kremnica
Mint of Finland, Ltd.
Mint of Norway
Monnaie de Paris
Moscow Mint
National Bank of the Republic of Belarus
National Bank of Ukraine
New Zealand Mint
Numiscom
Numistrade Gmbh & Co. kg.
Omni Trading B.V.
PandaAmerica
Perth Mint
Pobjoy Mint
Real Casa de la Moneda - Spain
Royal Mint
Royal Australian Mint
Royal Belgian Mint
Royal Canadian Mint
Royal Dutch Mint
Royal Thai Mint
SamlerHuset Group B.V.
Servei D'Emissions Principat D'Andorra
Singapore Mint
SoftSky, Inc.
South African Mint
Staatliche Munze Berlin
Staatliche Munze Baden-Wurttemberg
Talisman Coins
Thailand Treasury Department
Ufficio Filatelico e Numismatico - Vatican
United States Mint

COUNTRY INDEX

HOW TO USE THIS CATALOG

This catalog is designed to serve the needs of both the novice and advanced collectors. It is generally arranged so that persons with no more than a basic knowledge of world history and a casual acquaintance with coin collecting can consult it with confidence and ease. The following explanations summarize the general practices used in preparing this catalog's listings.

ARRANGEMENT

Countries are arranged alphabetically. Political changes within a country are arranged chronologically. In countries where Rulers are the single most significant political entity, a chronological arrangement by Ruler has been employed. Distinctive sub-geographic regions are listed alphabetically following the country's main listings.

Diverse coinage types relating to fabrication methods, revaluations, denomination systems, non-circulating categories and such have been identified, separated and arranged in logical fashion. Chronological arrangement is employed for most circulating coinage. Monetary reforms will flow in order of their institution. Non-circulating types such as Essais, Piefort s, Patterns, Trial Strikes, Mint and Proof sets will follow the main listings.

Within a coinage type coins will be listed by denomination, from smallest to largest. Numbered types within a denomination will be ordered by their first date of issue.

IDENTIFICATION

The most important step in the identification of a coin is the determination of the nation of origin. This is generally easily accomplished where English-speaking lands are concerned, however, use of the country index is sometimes required.

The coins of many countries beyond the English-language realm, such as those of French, Italian or Spanish heritage, are also quite easy to identify through reference to their legends, which appear in the national languages based on Western alphabets. In many instances the name is spelled exactly the same in English as in the national language, such as France; while in other cases it varies only slightly, like Italia for Italy, Belgique or Belgie for Belgium, Brasil for Brazil and Danmark for Denmark.

This is not always the case, however, as in Norge for Norway, Espana for Spain, Sverige for Sweden and Helvetia for Switzerland. Coins bearing Cyrillic lettering are attributable to Bulgaria, Russia, the Slavic states and Mongolia; the Greek script peculiar to Greece, Crete and the Ionian Islands; the Amharic characters of Ethiopia; or Hebrew in the case of Israel.

The toughra monogram, occurs on some of the coins of Afghanistan, Egypt, Sudan, Pakistan, and Turkey. A predominant design feature on the coins of Nepal is the trident; while neighboring Tibet features a lotus blossom or lion on many of their issues.

DATING

Coin dating is the final basic attribution consideration. Here, the problem can be more difficult because the reading of a coin date is subject not only to the vagaries of numeric styling, but to calendar variations caused by the observance of various religious eras or regal periods from country to country, or even within a country. Here again, with the exception of the sphere from North Africa through the Orient, it will be found that most countries rely on Western date numerals and Christian (AD) era reckoning, although in a few instances, coin dating has been tied to the year of a reign or government. The Vatican, for example dates its coinage according to the year of reign of the current pope, in addition to the Christian-era date.

Countries in the Arabic sphere generally date their coins to the Muslim era (AH).

The following table indicates the year dating for the various eras, which correspond to 2009 in Christian calendar reckoning, but it must be remembered that there are overlaps between the eras in some instances.

Christian era (AD)	-2010
Muslim era (AH)	-AH1431
Solar year (SH)	-SH1388
Monarchic Solar era (MS)	-MS2569
Vikrama Samvat (VS)	-VS2067
Saka era (SE)	-SE1932
Buddhist era (BE)	-BE2553
Bangkok era (RS)	-RS229
Chula-Sakarat era (CS)	-CS1372
Ethiopian era (EE)	-EE2003
Korean era	-4343
Javanese Aji Saka era (AS)	-AS1943
Fasli era (FE)	-FE1420
Jewish era (JE)	-JE5770

More detailed guides to less prevalent coin dating systems, which are strictly local in nature, are presented with the appropriate listings.

AH Hejira	AD Christian Date	AH Hejira	AD Christian Date
1420	1999, April 17	1436	2014, October 25
1421	2000, April 6*	1437	2015, October 15*
1422	2001, March 26	1438	2016, October 3
1423	2002, March 15	1439	2017, September 22
1424	2003, March 5	1440	2018, September 12
1425	2004, February 22*	1441	2019, September 11*
1426	2005, February 10	1442	2020, August 20
1427	2006, January 31	1443	2021, August 10
1428	2007, January 20	1444	2022, July 30
1429	2008, January 10*	1445	2023, July 19*
1430	2008, December 29	1446	2024, July 8
1431	2009, December 18	1447	2025, June 27
1432	2010, December 8	1448	2026, June 17
1433	2011, November 27*	1449	2027, June 6*
1434	2012, November 15	1450	2028, May25
1435	2013, November 5		

Some coins carry dates according to both locally observed and Christian eras. This is particularly true in the Arabic world, where the Hejira date may be indicated in Arabic numerals and the Christian date in Western numerals, or both dates in either form.

HEJIRA DATE CONVERSION CHART

HEJIRA (Hijira, Hegira), the name of the Muslim era (A.H. = Anno Hegirae) dates back to the Christian year 622 when Mohammed "fled" from Mecca, escaping to Medina to avoid persecution from the Koreish tribemen. Based on a lunar year the Muslim year is 11 days shorter.

*=Leap Year (Christian Calendar)

The date actually carried on a given coin is generally cataloged here in the first column (Date) to the right of the catalog number. If this date is by a non-Christian dating system, such as 'AH' (Muslim), the Christian equivalent date will appear in parentheses(), for example AH1336(1917). Dates listed alone in the date column which do not actually appear on a given coin, or dates which are known, but do not appear on the coin, are generally enclosed by parentheses with 'ND' at the left, for example ND(2001).

Timing differentials between some era of reckoning, particularly the 354-day Mohammedan and 365-day Christian years, cause situations whereby coins which carry dates for both eras exist bearing two year dates from one calendar combined with a single date from another.

Countermarked Coinage is presented with both 'Countermark Date' and 'Host Coin' date for each type. Actual date representation follows the rules outlined above.

DENOMINATIONS

The second basic consideration to be met in the attribution of a coin is the determination of denomination. Since denominations are usually expressed in numeric rather than word form on a coin, this is usually quite easily accomplished on coins from nations which use Western numerals, except in those instances where issues are devoid of any mention of face value, and denomination must be attributed by size, metallic composition or weight. Coins listed in this volume are generally illustrated in actual size.

The sphere of countries stretching from North Africa through the Orient, on which numeric symbols generally unfamiliar to Westerners are employed, often provide the collector with a much greater challenge. This is particularly true on nearly all pre-20th Century issues. On some of the more modern issues and increasingly so as the years progress, Western-style numerals usually presented in combination with the local numeric system are becoming more commonplace on these coins.

The included table of Standard International Numeral Systems presents charts of the basic numeric designations found on coins of non-Western origin. Although denomination numerals are generally prominently displayed on coins, it must be remembered that these are general representations of characters, which individual coin engravers may have rendered in widely varying styles. Where numeric or script denominations designation forms peculiar to a given coin or country apply, such as the script used on some Persian (Iranian) issues. They are so indicated or illustrated in conjunction with the appropriate listings.

MINTAGES

Quantities minted of each date are indicated where that information is available, generally stated in millions or rounded off to the nearest 10,000 pieces when more exact figures are not available. On quantities of a few thousand or less, actual mintages are generally indicated. For combined mintage figures the abbreviation "Inc. Above" means Included Above, while "Inc. Below" means Included Below. "Est." beside a mintage figure indicates the number given is an estimate or mintage limit.

METALS

Each numbered type listing will contain a description of the coins metallic content. The traditional coinage metals and their symbolic chemical abbreviations sometimes used in this catalog are:

Platinum - (PT)	Copper - (Cu)
Gold - (Au)	Brass -
Silver - (Ag)	Copper-nickel- (CN)
Billion -	Lead - (Pb)
Nickel - (Ni)	Steel -
Zinc - (Zn)	Tin - (Sn)
Bronze - (Ae)	Aluminum - (Al)

Modern commemorative coins have employed still more unusual methods such as bimetallic coins, color applications and precious metal or gem inlays.

PRECIOUS METAL WEIGHTS

Listings of weight, fineness and actual silver (ASW), gold (AGW), platinum or palladium (APW) content of most machine-struck silver, gold, platinum and palladium coins are provided in this edition. This information will be found incorporated in each separate type listing, along with other data related to the coin.

The ASW, AGW or APW figure can be multiplied by the spot price of each precious metal to determine the current intrinsic value of any coin accompanied by these designations.

As the silver and gold bullion markets have advanced and declined sharply over the years, the fineness and total precious metal content of coins has become especially significant where bullion coins - issues which trade on the basis of their intrinsic metallic content rather than numismatic value - are concerned. In many instances, such issues have become worth more in bullion form than their nominal collector values or denominations indicate.

BULLION VALUE

The simplest method for determining the bullion value of a precious metal coin is to multiply the actual precious metal weight by the current spot price for that metal. A silver coin with a .6822 actual silver weight (ASW) would have an intrinsic value of

$8.70 when the spot price of silver is $12.75. If the spot price of silver rose to $17.95 that same coins intrinsic value would rise to $12.25.

PHOTOGRAPHS

To assist the reader in coin identification, every effort has been made to present actual size photographs of every coinage type listed. Obverse and reverse are illustrated, except when a change in design is restricted to one side, and the coin has a diameter of 39mm or larger, in which case only the side required for identification of the type is generally illustrated. All coins up to 60mm are illustrated actual size, to the nearest 1/2mm up to 25mm, and to the nearest 1mm thereafter. Coins larger than 60mm diameter are illustrated in reduced size, with the actual size noted in the descriptive text block. Where slight change in size is important to coin type identification, actual millimeter measurements are stated.

VALUATIONS

Values quoted in this catalog represent the current market and are compiled from recommendations provided and verified through various source documents and specialized consultants. It should be stressed, however, that this book is intended to serve only as an aid for evaluating coins, actual market conditions are constantly changing and additional influences, such as particularly strong local demand for certain coin series, fluctuation of international exchange rates, changes in spot price of precious metals and worldwide collection patterns must also be considered. Publication of this catalog is not intended as a solicitation by the publisher, editors or contributors to buy or sell the coins listed at the prices indicated.

All valuations are stated in U.S. dollars, based on careful assessment of the varied international collector market. Valuations for coins priced below $100.00 are generally stated in full amounts - i.e. 37.50 or 95.00 - while valuations at or above that figure are rounded off in even dollars - i.e. $125.00 is expressed 125. A comma is added to indicate thousands of dollars in value.

For the convenience of overseas collectors and for U.S. collectors doing business with overseas dealers, the base exchange rate for the national currencies of approximately 180 countries are presented in the Foreign Exchange Table.

It should be noted that when particularly select uncirculated or proof-like examples of uncirculated coins become available they can be expected to command proportionately high premiums. Such examples in reference to choice Germanic Thalers are referred to as "erst schlage" or first strikes.

NEW ISSUES

All newly released coins dated up to the year 2006 that have been physically observed by our staff or identified by reliable sources and have been confirmed by press time have been incorporated in this edition. Exceptions exist in some countries where current date coin production lags far behind or information on current issues is less accessible.

SETS

Listings in this catalog for specimen, proof and mint sets are for official, government-produced sets. In many instances privately packaged sets also exist.

Mint Sets/Fleur de Coin Sets: Specially prepared by worldwide mints to provide banks, collectors and government dignitaries with examples of current coinage. Usually subjected to rigorous inspection to insure that top quality specimens of selected business strikes are provided.

Coin Alignment Medal Alignment

COIN vs MEDAL ALIGNMENT

Some coins are struck with obverse and reverse aligned at a rotation of 180 degrees from each other. When a coin is held for vertical viewing with the obverse design aligned upright and the index finger and thumb at the top and bottom, upon rotation from left to right for viewing the reverse, the latter will be upside down. Such alignment is called "coin rotation." Other coins are struck with the obverse and reverse designs mated on an alignment of zero or 360 degrees. If such an example is held and rotated as described, the reverse will appear upright. This is the alignment, which is generally observed in the striking of medals, and for that reason coins produced in this manner are considered struck in "medal rotation". In some instances, often through error, certain coin issues have been struck to both alignment standards, creating interesting collectible varieties, which will be found noted in some listings. In addition, some countries are now producing coins with other designated obverse to reverse alignments which are considered standard for this type.

Specimen Sets: Forerunners of today's proof sets. In most cases the coins were specially struck, perhaps even double struck, to produce a very soft or matte finish on the effigies and fields, along with high, sharp, "wire" rims. The finish is rather dull to the naked eye.

The original purpose of these sets was to provide VIPs, monarchs and mintmasters around the world with samples of the highest quality workmanship of a particular mint. These were usually housed in elaborate velvet-lined leather and metal cases.

Proof-like Sets are relatively new to the field of numismatics. During the mid 1950s the Royal Canadian Mint furnished the hobby with specially selected early business strike coins that exhibited some qualities similar to proof coinage. However, the "proof-like" fields are generally flawed and the edges are rounded. These pieces are not double struck. These are commonly encountered in cardboard holders, later in soft plastic or pliofilm packaging. Of late, the Royal Canadian Mint packages such sets in rigid plastic cases.

Many worldwide officially issued proof sets would in reality fall into this category upon careful examination of the quality of the coin's finish.

Another term encountered in this category is "Special Select," used to describe the crowns of the Union of South Africa and 100-schilling coins produced for collectors in the late 1970s by the Austrian Mint.

Proof Sets: This is undoubtedly among the most misused terms in the hobby, not only by collectors and dealers, but also by many of the world mints.

A true proof set must be at least double-struck on specially prepared polished planchets and struck using dies (often themselves polished) of the highest quality.

Modern-day proof quality consists of frosted effigies surrounded by absolute mirror-like fields.

Listings for proof sets in this catalog are for officially issued proof sets so designated by the issuing authority, and may or may not possess what are considered modern proof quality standards.

It is necessary for collectors to acquire the knowledge to allow them to differentiate true proof sets from would-be proof sets and proof-like sets which may be encountered.

CONDITIONS/GRADING

Wherever possible, coin valuations are given in four or five grades of preservation. For modern commemoratives, which do not circulate, only uncirculated values are usually sufficient. Proof issues are indicated by the word "Proof" next to the date, with valuation proceeded by the word "value" following the mintage. For very recent circulating coins and coins of limited value, one, two or three grade values are presented.

There are almost no grading guides for world coins. What follows is an attempt to help bridge that gap until a detailed, illustrated guide becomes available.

In grading world coins, there are two elements to look for: 1) Overall wear, and 2) loss of design details, such as strands of hair, feathers on eagles, designs on coats of arms, etc.

The age, rarity or type of a coin should not be a consideration in grading.

Grade each coin by the weaker of the two sides. This method appears to give results most nearly consistent with conservative American Numismatic Association standards for U.S. coins. Split grades, i.e., F/VF for obverse and reverse, respectively, are normally no more than one grade apart. If the two sides are more than one grade apart, the series of coins probably wears differently on each side and should then be graded by the weaker side alone.

Grade by the amount of overall wear and loss of design detail evident on each side of the coin. On coins with a moderately small design element, which is prone to early wear, grade by that design alone. For example, the 5-ore (KM#554) of Sweden has a crown above the monogram on which the beads on the arches show wear most clearly. So, grade by the crown alone.

For **Brilliant Uncirculated** (BU) grades there will be no visible signs of wear or handling, even under a 30-power microscope. Full mint luster will be present. Ideally no bags marks will be evident.

For **Uncirculated** (Unc. or MS-60) grades there will be no visible signs of wear or handling, even under a 30-power microscope. Bag marks may be present.

For **Almost Uncirculated** (AU or AU-50), all detail will be visible. There will be wear only on the highest point of the coin. There will often be half or more of the original mint luster present.

On the **Extremely Fine** (EF or XF or XF-40) coin, there will be about 95% of the original detail visible. Or, on a coin with a design with no inner detail to wear down, there will be a light wear over nearly all the coin. If a small design is used as the grading area, about 90% of the original detail will be visible. This latter rule stems from the logic that a smaller amount of detail needs to be present because a small area is being used to grade the whole coin.

The **Very Fine** (VF or VF-20) coin will have about 75% of the original detail visible. Or, on a coin with no inner detail, there will be moderate wear over the entire coin. Corners of letters and numbers may be weak. A small grading area will have about 66% of the original detail.

For **Fine** (F or F-12), there will be about 50% of the original detail visible. Or, on a coin with no inner detail, there will be fairly heavy wear over all of the coin. Sides of letters will be weak. A typically uncleaned coin will often appear as dirty or dull. A small grading area will have just under 50% of the original detail.

On the **Very Good** (VG or VG-8) coin, there will be about 25% of the original detail visible. There will be heavy wear on all of the coin.

The **Good** (G or G-4) coin's design will be clearly outlined but with substantial wear. Some of the larger detail may be visible. The rim may have a few weak spots of wear.

On the **About Good** (AG) coin, there will typically be only a silhouette of a large design. The rim will be worn down into the letters if any.

Strong or weak strikes, partially weak strikes, damage, corrosion, attractive or unattractive toning, dipping or cleaning should be described along with the above grades. These factors affect the quality of the coin just as do wear and loss of detail, but are easier to describe.

STANDARD INTERNATIONAL GRADING TERMINOLOGY AND ABBREVIATIONS

U.S. and ENGLISH SPEAKING LANDS	UNCIRCULATED	EXTREMELY FINE	VERY FINE	FINE	VERY GOOD	GOOD	POOR
Abbreviation	UNC	EF or XF	VF	FF	VG	G	PR
BRAZIL	(1) DW	(3) S	(5) MBC	(7) BC	(8)	(9) R	UTGeG
DENMARK	O	O1	1+	1	1÷	2	3
FINLAND	0	01	1+	1	1?	2	3
FRANCE	NEUF	SUP	TTB or TB	TB or TB	B	TBC	BC
GERMANY	KFR	II / VZGL	III / SS	IV / S	V / S.g.E.	VI / G.e.	G.e.s.
ITALY	FdS	SPL	BB	MB	B	M	—
JAPAN	未使用	極美品	美品	並品	—	—	—
NETHERLANDS	FDC	Pr.	Z.F.	Fr.	Z.g.	G	—
NORWAY	0	01	1+	1	1+	2	3
PORTUGAL	Novo	Soberbo	Muito bo	—	—	—	—
SPAIN	Lujo	SC, IC or EBC	MBC	BC	—	RC	MC
SWEDEN	0	01	1+	1	1?	2	—

BRAZIL

FE — Flor de Estampa
S — Soberba
MBC — Muito Bem Conservada
BC — Bem Conservada
R — Regular
UTGeG — Um Tanto Gasto e Gasto

DENMARK

O — Uncirkuleret
01 — Meget Paent Eksemplar
1+ — Paent Eksemplar
1 — Acceptabelt Eksemplar
1 —Noget Slidt Eksemplar
2 — Darlight Eksemplar
3 — Meget Darlight Eskemplar

FINLAND

00 — Kiiltolyönti
0 — Lyöntiveres
01 — Erittäin Hyvä
1+ — Hyvä
1? — Heikko
2 — Huono

FRANCE

NEUF — New
FDC — Fleur De Coin
SPL — Splendide
SUP — Superbe
TTB — Très Très Beau
TB — Très Beau
B — Beau
TBC — Tres Bien Conserve
BC — Bien Conserve

GERMANY

VZGL — Vorzüglich
SS — Sehr schön
S — Schön
S.g.E. — Sehr gut erhalten
G.e. — Gut erhalten
G.e.S. — Gering erhalten Schlecht

ITALY

Fds — Fior di Stampa
SPL — Splendid
BB — Bellissimo
MB — Molto Bello
B — Bello
M — Mediocre

JAPAN

未使用 — Mishiyo
極美品 — Goku Bihin
美品 — Bihin
並品 — Futuhin

NETHERLANDS

Pr. — Prachtig
Z.F. — Zeer Fraai
Fr. — Fraai
Z.g. — Zeer Goed
G — Goed

NORWAY

0 — Usirkuleret eks
01 — Meget pent eks
1+ — Pent eks
1 — Fullgodt eks
1- — Ikke Fullgodt eks
2 — Darlig eks

ROMANIA

NC — Necirculata (UNC)
FF — Foarte Frumoasa (VF)
F — Frumoasa (F)
FBC — Foarte Bine Conservata (VG)
BC — Bine Conservata (G)
M — Mediocru Conservata (POOR)

SPAIN

EBC — Extraordinariamente Bien Conservada
SC — Sin Circular
IC — Incirculante
MBC — Muy Bien Conservada
BC — Bien Conservada
RC — Regular Conservada
MC — Mala Conservada

SWEDEN

0 — Ocirkulerat
01 — Mycket Vackert
1+ — Vackert
1 — Fullgott
1? — Ej Fullgott
2 — Dalight

STANDARD INTERNATIONAL NUMERAL SYSTEMS

Prepared especially for the *Standard Catalog of World Coins©* 2012 by Krause Publications

Western	0	½	1	2	3	4	5	6	7	8	9	10	50	100	500	1000
Roman			I	II	III	IV	V	VI	VII	VIII	IX	X	L	C	D	M
Arabic-Turkish	٠	١/٢	١	٢	٣	٤	٥	٦	٧	٨	٩	١٠	٥٠	١٠٠	٥٠٠	١٠٠٠
Malay-Persian	٠	١/٢	١	٢	٣	۴	۵	٦ or ۶	٧	٨	٩	١٠	۵٠	١٠٠	۵٠٠	١٠٠٠
Eastern Arabic	۰	۱/۲	۱	۲	۳	۴	۵	۶	۷	۸	۹	۱۰	۵۰	۱۰۰	۵۰۰	۱۰۰۰
Hyderabad Arabic	۰	۱/۲	۱	۲	۳	۴	۵	۶	۷	۸	۹	۱۰	۵۰	۱۰۰	۵۰۰	۱۰۰۰
Indian (Sanskrit)	०	१/२	१	२	३	४	५	६	७	८	९	१०	५०	१००	५००	१०००
Assamese	০	১/২	১	২	৩	৪	৫	৬	৭	৮	৯	১০	৫০	১০০	৫০০	১০০০
Bengali	০	১/২	১	২	৩	৪	৫	৬	৭	৮	৯	১০	৫০	১০০	৫০০	১০০০
Gujarati	૦	૧/૨	૧	૨	૩	૪	૫	૬	૭	૮	૯	૧૦	૫૦	૧૦૦	૫૦૦	૧૦૦૦
Kutch	०	१/२	१	२	३	४	५	६	७	८	९	१०	५०	१००	५००	१०००
Devavnagri	०	१/२	१	२	३	४	५	६ or ६	७	८	९ or ९	१०	५०	१००	५००	१०००
Nepalese	०	१/२	१	२	३	४	५	६	७	८	९	१०	५०	१००	५००	१०००
Tibetan	༠	༡/༢	༡	༢	༣	༤	༥	༦	༧	༨	༩	༡༠	༥༠	༡༠༠	༥༠༠	༡༠༠༠
Mongolian	᠐	᠑/᠒	᠑	᠒	᠓	᠔	᠕	᠖	᠗	᠘	᠙	᠑᠐	᠕᠐	᠑᠐᠐	᠕᠐᠐	᠑᠐᠐᠐
Burmese	၀	၁/၂	၁	၂	၃	၄	၅	၆	၇	၈	၉	၁၀	၅၀	၁၀၀	၅၀၀	၁၀၀၀
Thai-Lao	๐	๑/๒	๑	๒	๓	๔	๕	๖	๗	๘	๙	๑๐	๕๐	๑๐๐	๕๐๐	๑๐๐๐
Lao-Laotian	໐		໑	໒	໓	໔	໕	໖	໗	໘	໙	໑໐				
Javanese	꧐		꧑	꧒	꧓	꧔	꧕	꧖	꧗	꧘	꧙	꧑꧐	꧕꧐	꧑꧐꧐	꧕꧐꧐	꧑꧐꧐꧐
Ordinary Chinese Japanese-Korean	零	半	一	二	三	四	五	六	七	八	九	十	十五	百	百五	千
Official Chinese			壹	貳	叁	肆	伍	陸	柒	捌	玖	拾	拾伍	佰	佰伍	仟
Commercial Chinese			〡	〢	〣	〤	〥	〦	〧	〨	〩	十	〥十	〡百	〥百	〡千
Korean		반	일	이	삼	사	오	육	칠	팔	구	십	오십	백	오백	천
Georgian			ა	ბ	გ	დ	ე	ვ	ზ	ჱ	თ	ი	ნ	რ	ფ	ჩ
			11 [illegible]	20 კ	30 ლ	40 მ	60 ჲ	70 ო	80 პ	90 ჟ	200 ს	300 ტ	400 უ	600 ქ	700 ღ	800 ყ
Ethiopian	◆		፩	፪	፫	፬	፭	፮	፯	፰	፱	፲	፶	፻	፭፻	፲፻
				20 ፳	30 ፴	40 ፵	60 ፷	70 ፸	80 ፹	90 ፺						
Hebrew			א	ב	ג	ד	ה	ו	ז	ח	ט	י	נ	ק	תק	
				20 כ	30 ל	40 מ	60 ס	70 ע	80 פ	90 צ	200 ר	300 ש	400 ת	600 תר	700 תש	800 תת
Greek			Α	Β	Γ	Δ	Ε	Τ	Ζ	Η	Θ	Ι	Ν	Ρ	Φ	Α
				20 Κ	30 Λ	40 Μ	60 Ξ	70 Ο	80 Π		200 Σ	300 Τ	400 Υ	600 Χ	700 Ψ	800 Ω

SILVER BULLION VALUE CHART $25 to $32.50

Oz.	25.00	25.50	26.00	26.50	27.00	27.50	28.00	28.50	29.00	29.50	30.00	30.50	31.00	31.50	32.00	32.50
0.001	0.025	0.026	0.026	0.027	0.027	0.028	0.028	0.029	0.029	0.030	0.030	0.031	0.031	0.032	0.032	0.033
0.002	0.050	0.051	0.052	0.053	0.054	0.055	0.056	0.057	0.058	0.059	0.060	0.061	0.062	0.063	0.064	0.065
0.003	0.075	0.077	0.078	0.080	0.081	0.083	0.084	0.086	0.087	0.089	0.090	0.092	0.093	0.095	0.096	0.098
0.004	0.100	0.102	0.104	0.106	0.108	0.110	0.112	0.114	0.116	0.118	0.120	0.122	0.124	0.126	0.128	0.130
0.005	0.125	0.128	0.130	0.133	0.135	0.138	0.140	0.143	0.145	0.148	0.150	0.153	0.155	0.158	0.160	0.163
0.006	0.150	0.153	0.156	0.159	0.162	0.165	0.168	0.171	0.174	0.177	0.180	0.183	0.186	0.189	0.192	0.195
0.007	0.175	0.179	0.182	0.186	0.189	0.193	0.196	0.200	0.203	0.207	0.210	0.214	0.217	0.221	0.224	0.228
0.008	0.200	0.204	0.208	0.212	0.216	0.220	0.224	0.228	0.232	0.236	0.240	0.244	0.248	0.252	0.256	0.260
0.009	0.225	0.230	0.234	0.239	0.243	0.248	0.252	0.257	0.261	0.266	0.270	0.275	0.279	0.284	0.288	0.293
0.010	0.250	0.255	0.260	0.265	0.270	0.275	0.280	0.285	0.290	0.295	0.300	0.305	0.310	0.315	0.320	0.325
0.020	0.500	0.510	0.520	0.530	0.540	0.550	0.560	0.570	0.580	0.590	0.600	0.610	0.620	0.630	0.640	0.650
0.030	0.750	0.765	0.780	0.795	0.810	0.825	0.840	0.855	0.870	0.885	0.900	0.915	0.930	0.945	0.960	0.975
0.040	1.000	1.020	1.040	1.060	1.080	1.100	1.120	1.140	1.160	1.180	1.200	1.220	1.240	1.260	1.280	1.300
0.050	1.250	1.275	1.300	1.325	1.350	1.375	1.400	1.425	1.450	1.475	1.500	1.525	1.550	1.575	1.600	1.625
0.060	1.500	1.530	1.560	1.590	1.620	1.650	1.680	1.710	1.740	1.770	1.800	1.830	1.860	1.890	1.920	1.950
0.070	1.750	1.785	1.820	1.855	1.890	1.925	1.960	1.995	2.030	2.065	2.100	2.135	2.170	2.205	2.240	2.275
0.080	2.000	2.040	2.080	2.120	2.160	2.200	2.240	2.280	2.320	2.360	2.400	2.440	2.480	2.520	2.560	2.600
0.090	2.250	2.295	2.340	2.385	2.430	2.475	2.520	2.565	2.610	2.655	2.700	2.745	2.790	2.835	2.880	2.925
0.100	2.500	2.550	2.600	2.650	2.700	2.750	2.800	2.850	2.900	2.950	3.000	3.050	3.100	3.150	3.200	3.250
0.110	2.750	2.805	2.860	2.915	2.970	3.025	3.080	3.135	3.190	3.245	3.300	3.355	3.410	3.465	3.520	3.575
0.120	3.000	3.060	3.120	3.180	3.240	3.300	3.360	3.420	3.480	3.540	3.600	3.660	3.720	3.780	3.840	3.900
0.130	3.250	3.315	3.380	3.445	3.510	3.575	3.640	3.705	3.770	3.835	3.900	3.965	4.030	4.095	4.160	4.225
0.140	3.500	3.570	3.640	3.710	3.780	3.850	3.920	3.990	4.060	4.130	4.200	4.270	4.340	4.410	4.480	4.550
0.150	3.750	3.825	3.900	3.975	4.050	4.125	4.200	4.275	4.350	4.425	4.500	4.575	4.650	4.725	4.800	4.875
0.160	4.000	4.080	4.160	4.240	4.320	4.400	4.480	4.560	4.640	4.720	4.800	4.880	4.960	5.040	5.120	5.200
0.170	4.250	4.335	4.420	4.505	4.590	4.675	4.760	4.845	4.930	5.015	5.100	5.185	5.270	5.355	5.440	5.525
0.180	4.500	4.590	4.680	4.770	4.860	4.950	5.040	5.130	5.220	5.310	5.400	5.490	5.580	5.670	5.760	5.850
0.190	4.750	4.845	4.940	5.035	5.130	5.225	5.320	5.415	5.510	5.605	5.700	5.795	5.890	5.985	6.080	6.175
0.200	5.000	5.100	5.200	5.300	5.400	5.500	5.600	5.700	5.800	5.900	6.000	6.100	6.200	6.300	6.400	6.500
0.210	5.250	5.355	5.460	5.565	5.670	5.775	5.880	5.985	6.090	6.195	6.300	6.405	6.510	6.615	6.720	6.825
0.220	5.500	5.610	5.720	5.830	5.940	6.050	6.160	6.270	6.380	6.490	6.600	6.710	6.820	6.930	7.040	7.150
0.230	5.750	5.865	5.980	6.095	6.210	6.325	6.440	6.555	6.670	6.785	6.900	7.015	7.130	7.245	7.360	7.475
0.240	6.000	6.120	6.240	6.360	6.480	6.600	6.720	6.840	6.960	7.080	7.200	7.320	7.440	7.560	7.680	7.800
0.250	6.250	6.375	6.500	6.625	6.750	6.875	7.000	7.125	7.250	7.375	7.500	7.625	7.750	7.875	8.000	8.125
0.260	6.500	6.630	6.760	6.890	7.020	7.150	7.280	7.410	7.540	7.670	7.800	7.930	8.060	8.190	8.320	8.450
0.270	6.750	6.885	7.020	7.155	7.290	7.425	7.560	7.695	7.830	7.965	8.100	8.235	8.370	8.505	8.640	8.775
0.280	7.000	7.140	7.280	7.420	7.560	7.700	7.840	7.980	8.120	8.260	8.400	8.540	8.680	8.820	8.960	9.100
0.290	7.250	7.395	7.540	7.685	7.830	7.975	8.120	8.265	8.410	8.555	8.700	8.845	8.990	9.135	9.280	9.425
0.300	7.500	7.650	7.800	7.950	8.100	8.250	8.400	8.550	8.700	8.850	9.000	9.150	9.300	9.450	9.600	9.750
0.310	7.750	7.905	8.060	8.215	8.370	8.525	8.680	8.835	8.990	9.145	9.300	9.455	9.610	9.765	9.920	10.075
0.320	8.000	8.160	8.320	8.480	8.640	8.800	8.960	9.120	9.280	9.440	9.600	9.760	9.920	10.080	10.240	10.400
0.330	8.250	8.415	8.580	8.745	8.910	9.075	9.240	9.405	9.570	9.735	9.900	10.065	10.230	10.395	10.560	10.725
0.340	8.500	8.670	8.840	9.010	9.180	9.350	9.520	9.690	9.860	10.030	10.200	10.370	10.540	10.710	10.880	11.050
0.350	8.750	8.925	9.100	9.275	9.450	9.625	9.800	9.975	10.150	10.325	10.500	10.675	10.850	11.025	11.200	11.375
0.360	9.000	9.180	9.360	9.540	9.720	9.900	10.080	10.260	10.440	10.620	10.800	10.980	11.160	11.340	11.520	11.700
0.370	9.250	9.435	9.620	9.805	9.990	10.175	10.360	10.545	10.730	10.915	11.100	11.285	11.470	11.655	11.840	12.025
0.380	9.500	9.690	9.880	10.070	10.260	10.450	10.640	10.830	11.020	11.210	11.400	11.590	11.780	11.970	12.160	12.350
0.390	9.750	9.945	10.140	10.335	10.530	10.725	10.920	11.115	11.310	11.505	11.700	11.895	12.090	12.285	12.480	12.675
0.400	10.000	10.200	10.400	10.600	10.800	11.000	11.200	11.400	11.600	11.800	12.000	12.200	12.400	12.600	12.800	13.000
0.410	10.250	10.455	10.660	10.865	11.070	11.275	11.480	11.685	11.890	12.095	12.300	12.505	12.710	12.915	13.120	13.325
0.420	10.500	10.710	10.920	11.130	11.340	11.550	11.760	11.970	12.180	12.390	12.600	12.810	13.020	13.230	13.440	13.650
0.430	10.750	10.965	11.180	11.395	11.610	11.825	12.040	12.255	12.470	12.685	12.900	13.115	13.330	13.545	13.760	13.975
0.440	11.000	11.220	11.440	11.660	11.880	12.100	12.320	12.540	12.760	12.980	13.200	13.420	13.640	13.860	14.080	14.300
0.450	11.250	11.475	11.700	11.925	12.150	12.375	12.600	12.825	13.050	13.275	13.500	13.725	13.950	14.175	14.400	14.625
0.460	11.500	11.730	11.960	12.190	12.420	12.650	12.880	13.110	13.340	13.570	13.800	14.030	14.260	14.490	14.720	14.950

SILVER BULLION VALUE CHART $25 to $32.50

Oz.	25.00	25.50	26.00	26.50	27.00	27.50	28.00	28.50	29.00	29.50	30.00	30.50	31.00	31.50	32.00	32.50
0.470	11.750	11.985	12.220	12.455	12.690	12.925	13.160	13.395	13.630	13.865	14.100	14.335	14.570	14.805	15.040	15.275
0.480	12.000	12.240	12.480	12.720	12.960	13.200	13.440	13.680	13.920	14.160	14.400	14.640	14.880	15.120	15.360	15.600
0.490	12.250	12.495	12.740	12.985	13.230	13.475	13.720	13.965	14.210	14.455	14.700	14.945	15.190	15.435	15.680	15.925
0.500	12.500	12.750	13.000	13.250	13.500	13.750	14.000	14.250	14.500	14.750	15.000	15.250	15.500	15.750	16.000	16.250
0.510	12.750	13.005	13.260	13.515	13.770	14.025	14.280	14.535	14.790	15.045	15.300	15.555	15.810	16.065	16.320	16.575
0.520	13.000	13.260	13.520	13.780	14.040	14.300	14.560	14.820	15.080	15.340	15.600	15.860	16.120	16.380	16.640	16.900
0.530	13.250	13.515	13.780	14.045	14.310	14.575	14.840	15.105	15.370	15.635	15.900	16.165	16.430	16.695	16.960	17.225
0.540	13.500	13.770	14.040	14.310	14.580	14.850	15.120	15.390	15.660	15.930	16.200	16.470	16.740	17.010	17.280	17.550
0.550	13.750	14.025	14.300	14.575	14.850	15.125	15.400	15.675	15.950	16.225	16.500	16.775	17.050	17.325	17.600	17.875
0.560	14.000	14.280	14.560	14.840	15.120	15.400	15.680	15.960	16.240	16.520	16.800	17.080	17.360	17.640	17.920	18.200
0.570	14.250	14.535	14.820	15.105	15.390	15.675	15.960	16.245	16.530	16.815	17.100	17.385	17.670	17.955	18.240	18.525
0.580	14.500	14.790	15.080	15.370	15.660	15.950	16.240	16.530	16.820	17.110	17.400	17.690	17.980	18.270	18.560	18.850
0.590	14.750	15.045	15.340	15.635	15.930	16.225	16.520	16.815	17.110	17.405	17.700	17.995	18.290	18.585	18.880	19.175
0.600	15.000	15.300	15.600	15.900	16.200	16.500	16.800	17.100	17.400	17.700	18.000	18.300	18.600	18.900	19.200	19.500
0.610	15.250	15.555	15.860	16.165	16.470	16.775	17.080	17.385	17.690	17.995	18.300	18.605	18.910	19.215	19.520	19.825
0.620	15.500	15.810	16.120	16.430	16.740	17.050	17.360	17.670	17.980	18.290	18.600	18.910	19.220	19.530	19.840	20.150
0.630	15.750	16.065	16.380	16.695	17.010	17.325	17.640	17.955	18.270	18.585	18.900	19.215	19.530	19.845	20.160	20.475
0.640	16.000	16.320	16.640	16.960	17.280	17.600	17.920	18.240	18.560	18.880	19.200	19.520	19.840	20.160	20.480	20.800
0.650	16.250	16.575	16.900	17.225	17.550	17.875	18.200	18.525	18.850	19.175	19.500	19.825	20.150	20.475	20.800	21.125
0.660	16.500	16.830	17.160	17.490	17.820	18.150	18.480	18.810	19.140	19.470	19.800	20.130	20.460	20.790	21.120	21.450
0.670	16.750	17.085	17.420	17.755	18.090	18.425	18.760	19.095	19.430	19.765	20.100	20.435	20.770	21.105	21.440	21.775
0.680	17.000	17.340	17.680	18.020	18.360	18.700	19.040	19.380	19.720	20.060	20.400	20.740	21.080	21.420	21.760	22.100
0.690	17.250	17.595	17.940	18.285	18.630	18.975	19.320	19.665	20.010	20.355	20.700	21.045	21.390	21.735	22.080	22.425
0.700	17.500	17.850	18.200	18.550	18.900	19.250	19.600	19.950	20.300	20.650	21.000	21.350	21.700	22.050	22.400	22.750
0.710	17.750	18.105	18.460	18.815	19.170	19.525	19.880	20.235	20.590	20.945	21.300	21.655	22.010	22.365	22.720	23.075
0.720	18.000	18.360	18.720	19.080	19.440	19.800	20.160	20.520	20.880	21.240	21.600	21.960	22.320	22.680	23.040	23.400
0.730	18.250	18.615	18.980	19.345	19.710	20.075	20.440	20.805	21.170	21.535	21.900	22.265	22.630	22.995	23.360	23.725
0.740	18.500	18.870	19.240	19.610	19.980	20.350	20.720	21.090	21.460	21.830	22.200	22.570	22.940	23.310	23.680	24.050
0.750	18.750	19.125	19.500	19.875	20.250	20.625	21.000	21.375	21.750	22.125	22.500	22.875	23.250	23.625	24.000	24.375
0.760	19.000	19.380	19.760	20.140	20.520	20.900	21.280	21.660	22.040	22.420	22.800	23.180	23.560	23.940	24.320	24.700
0.770	19.250	19.635	20.020	20.405	20.790	21.175	21.560	21.945	22.330	22.715	23.100	23.485	23.870	24.255	24.640	25.025
0.780	19.500	19.890	20.280	20.670	21.060	21.450	21.840	22.230	22.620	23.010	23.400	23.790	24.180	24.570	24.960	25.350
0.790	19.750	20.145	20.540	20.935	21.330	21.725	22.120	22.515	22.910	23.305	23.700	24.095	24.490	24.885	25.280	25.675
0.800	20.000	20.400	20.800	21.200	21.600	22.000	22.400	22.800	23.200	23.600	24.000	24.400	24.800	25.200	25.600	26.000
0.810	20.250	20.655	21.060	21.465	21.870	22.275	22.680	23.085	23.490	23.895	24.300	24.705	25.110	25.515	25.920	26.325
0.820	20.500	20.910	21.320	21.730	22.140	22.550	22.960	23.370	23.780	24.190	24.600	25.010	25.420	25.830	26.240	26.650
0.830	20.750	21.165	21.580	21.995	22.410	22.825	23.240	23.655	24.070	24.485	24.900	25.315	25.730	26.145	26.560	26.975
0.840	21.000	21.420	21.840	22.260	22.680	23.100	23.520	23.940	24.360	24.780	25.200	25.620	26.040	26.460	26.880	27.300
0.850	21.250	21.675	22.100	22.525	22.950	23.375	23.800	24.225	24.650	25.075	25.500	25.925	26.350	26.775	27.200	27.625
0.860	21.500	21.930	22.360	22.790	23.220	23.650	24.080	24.510	24.940	25.370	25.800	26.230	26.660	27.090	27.520	27.950
0.870	21.750	22.185	22.620	23.055	23.490	23.925	24.360	24.795	25.230	25.665	26.100	26.535	26.970	27.405	27.840	28.275
0.880	22.000	22.440	22.880	23.320	23.760	24.200	24.640	25.080	25.520	25.960	26.400	26.840	27.280	27.720	28.160	28.600
0.890	22.250	22.695	23.140	23.585	24.030	24.475	24.920	25.365	25.810	26.255	26.700	27.145	27.590	28.035	28.480	28.925
0.900	22.500	22.950	23.400	23.850	24.300	24.750	25.200	25.650	26.100	26.550	27.000	27.450	27.900	28.350	28.800	29.250
0.910	22.750	23.205	23.660	24.115	24.570	25.025	25.480	25.935	26.390	26.845	27.300	27.755	28.210	28.665	29.120	29.575
0.920	23.000	23.460	23.920	24.380	24.840	25.300	25.760	26.220	26.680	27.140	27.600	28.060	28.520	28.980	29.440	29.900
0.930	23.250	23.715	24.180	24.645	25.110	25.575	26.040	26.505	26.970	27.435	27.900	28.365	28.830	29.295	29.760	30.225
0.940	23.500	23.970	24.440	24.910	25.380	25.850	26.320	26.790	27.260	27.730	28.200	28.670	29.140	29.610	30.080	30.550
0.950	23.750	24.225	24.700	25.175	25.650	26.125	26.600	27.075	27.550	28.025	28.500	28.975	29.450	29.925	30.400	30.875
0.960	24.000	24.480	24.960	25.440	25.920	26.400	26.880	27.360	27.840	28.320	28.800	29.280	29.760	30.240	30.720	31.200
0.970	24.250	24.735	25.220	25.705	26.190	26.675	27.160	27.645	28.130	28.615	29.100	29.585	30.070	30.555	31.040	31.525
0.980	24.500	24.990	25.480	25.970	26.460	26.950	27.440	27.930	28.420	28.910	29.400	29.890	30.380	30.870	31.360	31.850
0.990	24.750	25.245	25.740	26.235	26.730	27.225	27.720	28.215	28.710	29.205	29.700	30.195	30.690	31.185	31.680	32.175
1.000	25.000	25.500	26.000	26.500	27.000	27.500	28.000	28.500	29.000	29.500	30.000	30.500	31.000	31.500	32.000	32.500

GOLD BULLION VALUE CHART $1,500 to $1,650

Oz.	1500.00	1510.00	1520.00	1530.00	1540.00	1540.00	1550.00	1560.00	1570.00	1580.00	1590.00	1610.00	1620.00	1630.00	1640.00	1650.00
0.001	1.50	1.51	1.52	1.53	1.54	1.54	1.55	1.56	1.57	1.58	1.59	1.61	1.62	1.63	1.64	1.65
0.002	3.00	3.02	3.04	3.06	3.08	3.08	3.10	3.12	3.14	3.16	3.18	3.22	3.24	3.26	3.28	3.30
0.003	4.50	4.53	4.56	4.59	4.62	4.62	4.65	4.68	4.71	4.74	4.77	4.83	4.86	4.89	4.92	4.95
0.004	6.00	6.04	6.08	6.12	6.16	6.16	6.20	6.24	6.28	6.32	6.36	6.44	6.48	6.52	6.56	6.60
0.005	7.50	7.55	7.60	7.65	7.70	7.70	7.75	7.80	7.85	7.90	7.95	8.05	8.10	8.15	8.20	8.25
0.006	9.00	9.06	9.12	9.18	9.24	9.24	9.30	9.36	9.42	9.48	9.54	9.66	9.72	9.78	9.84	9.90
0.007	10.50	10.57	10.64	10.71	10.78	10.78	10.85	10.92	10.99	11.06	11.13	11.27	11.34	11.41	11.48	11.55
0.008	12.00	12.08	12.16	12.24	12.32	12.32	12.40	12.48	12.56	12.64	12.72	12.88	12.96	13.04	13.12	13.20
0.009	13.50	13.59	13.68	13.77	13.86	13.86	13.95	14.04	14.13	14.22	14.31	14.49	14.58	14.67	14.76	14.85
0.010	15.00	15.10	15.20	15.30	15.40	15.40	15.50	15.60	15.70	15.80	15.90	16.10	16.20	16.30	16.40	16.50
0.020	30.00	30.20	30.40	30.60	30.80	30.80	31.00	31.20	31.40	31.60	31.80	32.20	32.40	32.60	32.80	33.00
0.030	45.00	45.30	45.60	45.90	46.20	46.20	46.50	46.80	47.10	47.40	47.70	48.30	48.60	48.90	49.20	49.50
0.040	60.00	60.40	60.80	61.20	61.60	61.60	62.00	62.40	62.80	63.20	63.60	64.40	64.80	65.20	65.60	66.00
0.050	75.00	75.50	76.00	76.50	77.00	77.00	77.50	78.00	78.50	79.00	79.50	80.50	81.00	81.50	82.00	82.50
0.060	90.00	90.60	91.20	91.80	92.40	92.40	93.00	93.60	94.20	94.80	95.40	96.60	97.20	97.80	98.40	99.00
0.070	105.00	105.70	106.40	107.10	107.80	107.80	108.50	109.20	109.90	110.60	111.30	112.70	113.40	114.10	114.80	115.50
0.080	120.00	120.80	121.60	122.40	123.20	123.20	124.00	124.80	125.60	126.40	127.20	128.80	129.60	130.40	131.20	132.00
0.090	135.00	135.90	136.80	137.70	138.60	138.60	139.50	140.40	141.30	142.20	143.10	144.90	145.80	146.70	147.60	148.50
0.100	150.00	151.00	152.00	153.00	154.00	154.00	155.00	156.00	157.00	158.00	159.00	161.00	162.00	163.00	164.00	165.00
0.110	165.00	166.10	167.20	168.30	169.40	169.40	170.50	171.60	172.70	173.80	174.90	177.10	178.20	179.30	180.40	181.50
0.120	180.00	181.20	182.40	183.60	184.80	184.80	186.00	187.20	188.40	189.60	190.80	193.20	194.40	195.60	196.80	198.00
0.130	195.00	196.30	197.60	198.90	200.20	200.20	201.50	202.80	204.10	205.40	206.70	209.30	210.60	211.90	213.20	214.50
0.140	210.00	211.40	212.80	214.20	215.60	215.60	217.00	218.40	219.80	221.20	222.60	225.40	226.80	228.20	229.60	231.00
0.150	225.00	226.50	228.00	229.50	231.00	231.00	232.50	234.00	235.50	237.00	238.50	241.50	243.00	244.50	246.00	247.50
0.160	240.00	241.60	243.20	244.80	246.40	246.40	248.00	249.60	251.20	252.80	254.40	257.60	259.20	260.80	262.40	264.00
0.170	255.00	256.70	258.40	260.10	261.80	261.80	263.50	265.20	266.90	268.60	270.30	273.70	275.40	277.10	278.80	280.50
0.180	270.00	271.80	273.60	275.40	277.20	277.20	279.00	280.80	282.60	284.40	286.20	289.80	291.60	293.40	295.20	297.00
0.190	285.00	286.90	288.80	290.70	292.60	292.60	294.50	296.40	298.30	300.20	302.10	305.90	307.80	309.70	311.60	313.50
0.200	300.00	302.00	304.00	306.00	308.00	308.00	310.00	312.00	314.00	316.00	318.00	322.00	324.00	326.00	328.00	330.00
0.210	315.00	317.10	319.20	321.30	323.40	323.40	325.50	327.60	329.70	331.80	333.90	338.10	340.20	342.30	344.40	346.50
0.220	330.00	332.20	334.40	336.60	338.80	338.80	341.00	343.20	345.40	347.60	349.80	354.20	356.40	358.60	360.80	363.00
0.230	345.00	347.30	349.60	351.90	354.20	354.20	356.50	358.80	361.10	363.40	365.70	370.30	372.60	374.90	377.20	379.50
0.240	360.00	362.40	364.80	367.20	369.60	369.60	372.00	374.40	376.80	379.20	381.60	386.40	388.80	391.20	393.60	396.00
0.250	375.00	377.50	380.00	382.50	385.00	385.00	387.50	390.00	392.50	395.00	397.50	402.50	405.00	407.50	410.00	412.50
0.260	390.00	392.60	395.20	397.80	400.40	400.40	403.00	405.60	408.20	410.80	413.40	418.60	421.20	423.80	426.40	429.00
0.270	405.00	407.70	410.40	413.10	415.80	415.80	418.50	421.20	423.90	426.60	429.30	434.70	437.40	440.10	442.80	445.50
0.280	420.00	422.80	425.60	428.40	431.20	431.20	434.00	436.80	439.60	442.40	445.20	450.80	453.60	456.40	459.20	462.00
0.290	435.00	437.90	440.80	443.70	446.60	446.60	449.50	452.40	455.30	458.20	461.10	466.90	469.80	472.70	475.60	478.50
0.300	450.00	453.00	456.00	459.00	462.00	462.00	465.00	468.00	471.00	474.00	477.00	483.00	486.00	489.00	492.00	495.00
0.310	465.00	468.10	471.20	474.30	477.40	477.40	480.50	483.60	486.70	489.80	492.90	499.10	502.20	505.30	508.40	511.50
0.320	480.00	483.20	486.40	489.60	492.80	492.80	496.00	499.20	502.40	505.60	508.80	515.20	518.40	521.60	524.80	528.00
0.330	495.00	498.30	501.60	504.90	508.20	508.20	511.50	514.80	518.10	521.40	524.70	531.30	534.60	537.90	541.20	544.50
0.340	510.00	513.40	516.80	520.20	523.60	523.60	527.00	530.40	533.80	537.20	540.60	547.40	550.80	554.20	557.60	561.00
0.350	525.00	528.50	532.00	535.50	539.00	539.00	542.50	546.00	549.50	553.00	556.50	563.50	567.00	570.50	574.00	577.50
0.360	540.00	543.60	547.20	550.80	554.40	554.40	558.00	561.60	565.20	568.80	572.40	579.60	583.20	586.80	590.40	594.00
0.370	555.00	558.70	562.40	566.10	569.80	569.80	573.50	577.20	580.90	584.60	588.30	595.70	599.40	603.10	606.80	610.50
0.380	570.00	573.80	577.60	581.40	585.20	585.20	589.00	592.80	596.60	600.40	604.20	611.80	615.60	619.40	623.20	627.00
0.390	585.00	588.90	592.80	596.70	600.60	600.60	604.50	608.40	612.30	616.20	620.10	627.90	631.80	635.70	639.60	643.50
0.400	600.00	604.00	608.00	612.00	616.00	616.00	620.00	624.00	628.00	632.00	636.00	644.00	648.00	652.00	656.00	660.00
0.410	615.00	619.10	623.20	627.30	631.40	631.40	635.50	639.60	643.70	647.80	651.90	660.10	664.20	668.30	672.40	676.50
0.420	630.00	634.20	638.40	642.60	646.80	646.80	651.00	655.20	659.40	663.60	667.80	676.20	680.40	684.60	688.80	693.00
0.430	645.00	649.30	653.60	657.90	662.20	662.20	666.50	670.80	675.10	679.40	683.70	692.30	696.60	700.90	705.20	709.50
0.440	660.00	664.40	668.80	673.20	677.60	677.60	682.00	686.40	690.80	695.20	699.60	708.40	712.80	717.20	721.60	726.00
0.450	675.00	679.50	684.00	688.50	693.00	693.00	697.50	702.00	706.50	711.00	715.50	724.50	729.00	733.50	738.00	742.50

GOLD BULLION VALUE CHART $1,500 to $1,650

Oz.	1500.00	1510.00	1520.00	1530.00	1540.00	1540.00	1550.00	1560.00	1570.00	1580.00	1590.00	1610.00	1620.00	1630.00	1640.00	1650.00
0.460	690.00	694.60	699.20	703.80	708.40	708.40	713.00	717.60	722.20	726.80	731.40	740.60	745.20	749.80	754.40	759.00
0.470	705.00	709.70	714.40	719.10	723.80	723.80	728.50	733.20	737.90	742.60	747.30	756.70	761.40	766.10	770.80	775.50
0.480	720.00	724.80	729.60	734.40	739.20	739.20	744.00	748.80	753.60	758.40	763.20	772.80	777.60	782.40	787.20	792.00
0.490	735.00	739.90	744.80	749.70	754.60	754.60	759.50	764.40	769.30	774.20	779.10	788.90	793.80	798.70	803.60	808.50
0.500	750.00	755.00	760.00	765.00	770.00	770.00	775.00	780.00	785.00	790.00	795.00	805.00	810.00	815.00	820.00	825.00
0.510	765.00	770.10	775.20	780.30	785.40	785.40	790.50	795.60	800.70	805.80	810.90	821.10	826.20	831.30	836.40	841.50
0.520	780.00	785.20	790.40	795.60	800.80	800.80	806.00	811.20	816.40	821.60	826.80	837.20	842.40	847.60	852.80	858.00
0.530	795.00	800.30	805.60	810.90	816.20	816.20	821.50	826.80	832.10	837.40	842.70	853.30	858.60	863.90	869.20	874.50
0.540	810.00	815.40	820.80	826.20	831.60	831.60	837.00	842.40	847.80	853.20	858.60	869.40	874.80	880.20	885.60	891.00
0.550	825.00	830.50	836.00	841.50	847.00	847.00	852.50	858.00	863.50	869.00	874.50	885.50	891.00	896.50	902.00	907.50
0.560	840.00	845.60	851.20	856.80	862.40	862.40	868.00	873.60	879.20	884.80	890.40	901.60	907.20	912.80	918.40	924.00
0.570	855.00	860.70	866.40	872.10	877.80	877.80	883.50	889.20	894.90	900.60	906.30	917.70	923.40	929.10	934.80	940.50
0.580	870.00	875.80	881.60	887.40	893.20	893.20	899.00	904.80	910.60	916.40	922.20	933.80	939.60	945.40	951.20	957.00
0.590	885.00	890.90	896.80	902.70	908.60	908.60	914.50	920.40	926.30	932.20	938.10	949.90	955.80	961.70	967.60	973.50
0.600	900.00	906.00	912.00	918.00	924.00	924.00	930.00	936.00	942.00	948.00	954.00	966.00	972.00	978.00	984.00	990.00
0.610	915.00	921.10	927.20	933.30	939.40	939.40	945.50	951.60	957.70	963.80	969.90	982.10	988.20	994.30	1000.40	1006.50
0.620	930.00	936.20	942.40	948.60	954.80	954.80	961.00	967.20	973.40	979.60	985.80	998.20	1004.40	1010.60	1016.80	1023.00
0.630	945.00	951.30	957.60	963.90	970.20	970.20	976.50	982.80	989.10	995.40	1001.70	1014.30	1020.60	1026.90	1033.20	1039.50
0.640	960.00	966.40	972.80	979.20	985.60	985.60	992.00	998.40	1004.80	1011.20	1017.60	1030.40	1036.80	1043.20	1049.60	1056.00
0.650	975.00	981.50	988.00	994.50	1001.00	1001.00	1007.50	1014.00	1020.50	1027.00	1033.50	1046.50	1053.00	1059.50	1066.00	1072.50
0.660	990.00	996.60	1003.20	1009.80	1016.40	1016.40	1023.00	1029.60	1036.20	1042.80	1049.40	1062.60	1069.20	1075.80	1082.40	1089.00
0.670	1005.00	1011.70	1018.40	1025.10	1031.80	1031.80	1038.50	1045.20	1051.90	1058.60	1065.30	1078.70	1085.40	1092.10	1098.80	1105.50
0.680	1020.00	1026.80	1033.60	1040.40	1047.20	1047.20	1054.00	1060.80	1067.60	1074.40	1081.20	1094.80	1101.60	1108.40	1115.20	1122.00
0.690	1035.00	1041.90	1048.80	1055.70	1062.60	1062.60	1069.50	1076.40	1083.30	1090.20	1097.10	1110.90	1117.80	1124.70	1131.60	1138.50
0.700	1050.00	1057.00	1064.00	1071.00	1078.00	1078.00	1085.00	1092.00	1099.00	1106.00	1113.00	1127.00	1134.00	1141.00	1148.00	1155.00
0.710	1065.00	1072.10	1079.20	1086.30	1093.40	1093.40	1100.50	1107.60	1114.70	1121.80	1128.90	1143.10	1150.20	1157.30	1164.40	1171.50
0.720	1080.00	1087.20	1094.40	1101.60	1108.80	1108.80	1116.00	1123.20	1130.40	1137.60	1144.80	1159.20	1166.40	1173.60	1180.80	1188.00
0.730	1095.00	1102.30	1109.60	1116.90	1124.20	1124.20	1131.50	1138.80	1146.10	1153.40	1160.70	1175.30	1182.60	1189.90	1197.20	1204.50
0.740	1110.00	1117.40	1124.80	1132.20	1139.60	1139.60	1147.00	1154.40	1161.80	1169.20	1176.60	1191.40	1198.80	1206.20	1213.60	1221.00
0.750	1125.00	1132.50	1140.00	1147.50	1155.00	1155.00	1162.50	1170.00	1177.50	1185.00	1192.50	1207.50	1215.00	1222.50	1230.00	1237.50
0.760	1140.00	1147.60	1155.20	1162.80	1170.40	1170.40	1178.00	1185.60	1193.20	1200.80	1208.40	1223.60	1231.20	1238.80	1246.40	1254.00
0.770	1155.00	1162.70	1170.40	1178.10	1185.80	1185.80	1193.50	1201.20	1208.90	1216.60	1224.30	1239.70	1247.40	1255.10	1262.80	1270.50
0.780	1170.00	1177.80	1185.60	1193.40	1201.20	1201.20	1209.00	1216.80	1224.60	1232.40	1240.20	1255.80	1263.60	1271.40	1279.20	1287.00
0.790	1185.00	1192.90	1200.80	1208.70	1216.60	1216.60	1224.50	1232.40	1240.30	1248.20	1256.10	1271.90	1279.80	1287.70	1295.60	1303.50
0.800	1200.00	1208.00	1216.00	1224.00	1232.00	1232.00	1240.00	1248.00	1256.00	1264.00	1272.00	1288.00	1296.00	1304.00	1312.00	1320.00
0.810	1215.00	1223.10	1231.20	1239.30	1247.40	1247.40	1255.50	1263.60	1271.70	1279.80	1287.90	1304.10	1312.20	1320.30	1328.40	1336.50
0.820	1230.00	1238.20	1246.40	1254.60	1262.80	1262.80	1271.00	1279.20	1287.40	1295.60	1303.80	1320.20	1328.40	1336.60	1344.80	1353.00
0.830	1245.00	1253.30	1261.60	1269.90	1278.20	1278.20	1286.50	1294.80	1303.10	1311.40	1319.70	1336.30	1344.60	1352.90	1361.20	1369.50
0.840	1260.00	1268.40	1276.80	1285.20	1293.60	1293.60	1302.00	1310.40	1318.80	1327.20	1335.60	1352.40	1360.80	1369.20	1377.60	1386.00
0.850	1275.00	1283.50	1292.00	1300.50	1309.00	1309.00	1317.50	1326.00	1334.50	1343.00	1351.50	1368.50	1377.00	1385.50	1394.00	1402.50
0.860	1290.00	1298.60	1307.20	1315.80	1324.40	1324.40	1333.00	1341.60	1350.20	1358.80	1367.40	1384.60	1393.20	1401.80	1410.40	1419.00
0.870	1305.00	1313.70	1322.40	1331.10	1339.80	1339.80	1348.50	1357.20	1365.90	1374.60	1383.30	1400.70	1409.40	1418.10	1426.80	1435.50
0.880	1320.00	1328.80	1337.60	1346.40	1355.20	1355.20	1364.00	1372.80	1381.60	1390.40	1399.20	1416.80	1425.60	1434.40	1443.20	1452.00
0.890	1335.00	1343.90	1352.80	1361.70	1370.60	1370.60	1379.50	1388.40	1397.30	1406.20	1415.10	1432.90	1441.80	1450.70	1459.60	1468.50
0.900	1350.00	1359.00	1368.00	1377.00	1386.00	1386.00	1395.00	1404.00	1413.00	1422.00	1431.00	1449.00	1458.00	1467.00	1476.00	1485.00
0.910	1365.00	1374.10	1383.20	1392.30	1401.40	1401.40	1410.50	1419.60	1428.70	1437.80	1446.90	1465.10	1474.20	1483.30	1492.40	1501.50
0.920	1380.00	1389.20	1398.40	1407.60	1416.80	1416.80	1426.00	1435.20	1444.40	1453.60	1462.80	1481.20	1490.40	1499.60	1508.80	1518.00
0.930	1395.00	1404.30	1413.60	1422.90	1432.20	1432.20	1441.50	1450.80	1460.10	1469.40	1478.70	1497.30	1506.60	1515.90	1525.20	1534.50
0.940	1410.00	1419.40	1428.80	1438.20	1447.60	1447.60	1457.00	1466.40	1475.80	1485.20	1494.60	1513.40	1522.80	1532.20	1541.60	1551.00
0.950	1425.00	1434.50	1444.00	1453.50	1463.00	1463.00	1472.50	1482.00	1491.50	1501.00	1510.50	1529.50	1539.00	1548.50	1558.00	1567.50
0.960	1440.00	1449.60	1459.20	1468.80	1478.40	1478.40	1488.00	1497.60	1507.20	1516.80	1526.40	1545.60	1555.20	1564.80	1574.40	1584.00
0.970	1455.00	1464.70	1474.40	1484.10	1493.80	1493.80	1503.50	1513.20	1522.90	1532.60	1542.30	1561.70	1571.40	1581.10	1590.80	1600.50
0.980	1470.00	1479.80	1489.60	1499.40	1509.20	1509.20	1519.00	1528.80	1538.60	1548.40	1558.20	1577.80	1587.60	1597.40	1607.20	1617.00
0.990	1485.00	1494.90	1504.80	1514.70	1524.60	1524.60	1534.50	1544.40	1554.30	1564.20	1574.10	1593.90	1603.80	1613.70	1623.60	1633.50
1.000	1500.00	1510.00	1520.00	1530.00	1540.00	1540.00	1550.00	1560.00	1570.00	1580.00	1590.00	1610.00	1620.00	1630.00	1640.00	1650.00

HEJIRA DATE CONVERSION CHART

HEJIRA (Hijira, Hegira), the name of the Muslim era (A.H. = Anno Hegirae) dates back to the Christian year 622 when Mohammed "fled" from Mecca, escaping to Medina to avoid persecution from the Koreish tribemen. Based on a lunar year the Muslim year is 11 days shorter.

*=Leap Year (Christian Calendar)

AH Hejira	AD Christian Date
1010	1601, July 2
1011	1602, June 21
1012	1603, June 11
1013	1604, May 30
1014	1605, May 19
1015	1606, May 9
1016	1607, April 28
1017	1608, April 17
1018	1609, April 6
1017	1608, April 28
1018	1609, April 6
1019	1610, March 26
1020	1611, March 16
1021	1612, March 4
1022	1613, February 21
1023	1614, February 11
1024	1615, January 31
1025	1616, January 20
1026	1617, January 9
1027	1617, December 29
1028	1618, December 19
1029	1619, December 8
1030	1620, November 26
1031	1621, November 16
1032	1622, November 5
1033	1623, October 25
1034	1624, October 14
1035	1625, October 3
1036	1626, September 22
1037	1627, September 12
1038	1628, August 31
1039	1629, August 21
1040	1630, August 10
1041	1631, July 30
1042	1632, July 19
1043	1633, July 8
1044	1634, June 27
1045	1635, June 17
1046	1636, June 5
1047	1637, May 26
1048	1638, May 15
1049	1639, May 4
1050	1640, April 23
1051	1641, April 12
1052	1642, April 1
1053	1643, March 22
1054	1644, March 10
1055	1645, February 27
1056	1646, February 17
1057	1647, February 6
1058	1648, January 27
1059	1649, January 15
1060	1650, January 4
1061	1650, December 25
1062	1651, December 14
1063	1652, December 2
1064	1653, November 22
1065	1654, November 11
1066	1655, October 31
1067	1656, October 20
1068	1657, October 9
1069	1658, September 29
1070	1659, September 18
1071	1660, September 6
1072	1661, August 27
1073	1662, August 16
1074	1663, August 5
1075	1664, July 25
1076	1665, July 14
1077	1666, July 4
1078	1667, June 23
1079	1668, June 11
1080	1669, June 1
1081	1670, May 21
1082	1671, May 10
1083	1672, April 29
1084	1673, April 18
1085	1674, April 7

AH Hejira	AD Christian Date
1086	1675, March 28
1087	1676, March 16*
1088	1677, March 6
1089	1678, February 23
1090	1679, February 12
1091	1680, February 2*
1092	1681, January 21
1093	1682, January 10
1094	1682, December 31
1095	1683, December 20
1096	1684, December 8*
1097	1685, November 28
1098	1686, November 17
1099	1687, November 7
1100	1688, October 26*
1101	1689, October 15
1102	1690, October 5
1103	1691, September 24
1104	1692, September 12*
1105	1693, September 2
1106	1694, August 22
1107	1695, August 12
1108	1696, July 31*
1109	1697, July 20
1110	1698, July 10
1111	1699, June 29
1112	1700, June 18
1113	1701, June 8
1114	1702, May 28
1115	1703, May 17
1116	1704, May 6*
1117	1705, April 25
1118	1706, April 15
1119	1707, April 4
1120	1708, March 23*
1121	1709, March 13
1122	1710, March 2
1123	1711, February 19
1124	1712, February 9*
1125	1713, January 28
1126	1714, January 17
1127	1715, January 7
1128	1715, December 27
1129	1716, December 16*
1130	1717, December 5
1131	1718, November 24
1132	1719, November 14
1133	1720, November 2*
1134	1721, October 22
1135	1722, October 12
1136	1723, October 1
1137	1724, September 19
1138	1725, September 9
1139	1726, August 29
1140	1727, August 19
1141	1728, August 7*
1142	1729, July 27
1143	1730, July 17
1144	1731, July 6
1145	1732, June 24*
1146	1733, June 14
1147	1734, June 3
1148	1735, May 24
1149	1736, May 12*
1150	1737, May 1
1151	1738, April 21
1152	1739, April 10
1153	1740, March 29*
1154	1741, March 19
1155	1742, March 8
1156	1743, February 25
1157	1744, February 15*
1158	1745, February 3
1159	1746, January 24
1160	1747, January 13
1161	1748, January 2
1162	1748, December 22*
1163	1749, December 11
1164	1750, November 30
1165	1751, November 20
1166	1752, November 8*
1167	1753, October 29
1168	1754, October 18
1169	1755, October 7
1170	1756, September 26*
1171	1757, September 15
1172	1758, September 4
1173	1759, August 25
1174	1760, August 13*
1175	1761, August 2
1176	1762, July 23

AH Hejira	AD Christian Date
1177	1763, July 12
1178	1764, July 1*
1179	1765, June 20
1180	1766, June 9
1181	1767, May 30
1182	1768, May 18*
1183	1769, May 7
1184	1770, April 27
1185	1771, April 16
1186	1772, April 4*
1187	1773, March 25
1188	1774, March 14
1189	1775, March 4
1190	1776, February 21*
1191	1777, February 1
1192	1778, January 30
1193	1779, January 19
1194	1780, January 8*
1195	1780, December 28*
1196	1781, December 17
1197	1782, December 7
1198	1783, November 26
1199	1784, November 14*
1200	1785, November 4
1201	1786, October 24
1202	1787, October 13
1203	1788, October 2*
1204	1789, September 21
1205	1790, September 10
1206	1791, August 31
1207	1792, August 19*
1208	1793, August 9
1209	1794, July 29
1210	1795, July 18
1211	1796, July 7*
1212	1797, June 26
1213	1798, June 15
1214	1799, June 5
1215	1800, May 25
1216	1801, May 14
1217	1802, May 4
1218	1803, April 23
1219	1804, April 12*
1220	1805, April 1
1221	1806, March 21
1222	1807, March 11
1223	1808, February 28*
1224	1809, February 16
1225	1810, February 6
1226	1811, January 26
1227	1812, January 16*
1228	1813, January 6
1229	1813, December 24
1230	1814, December 14
1231	1815, December 3
1232	1816, November 21*
1233	1817, November 11
1234	1818, October 31
1235	1819, October 20
1236	1820, October 9*
1237	1821, September 28
1238	1822, September 18
1239	1823, September 8
1240	1824, August 26*
1241	1825, August 16
1242	1826, August 5
1243	1827, July 25
1244	1828, July 14*
1245	1829, July 3
1246	1830, June 22
1247	1831, June 12
1248	1832, May 31*
1249	1833, May 21
1250	1834, May 10
1251	1835, April 29
1252	1836, April 18*
1253	1837, April 7
1254	1838, March 27
1255	1839, March 17
1256	1840, March 5*
1257	1841, February 23
1258	1842, February 12
1259	1843, February 1
1260	1844, January 22*
1261	1845, January 10
1262	1845, December 30
1263	1846, December 20
1264	1847, December 9
1265	1848, November 27*
1266	1849, November 17
1267	1850, November 6

AH Hejira	AD Christian Date
1268	1851, October 27
1269	1852, October 15*
1270	1853, October 4
1271	1854, September 24
1272	1855, September 13
1273	1856, September 1*
1274	1857, August 22
1275	1858, August 11
1276	1859, July 31
1277	1860, July 20*
1278	1861, July 9
1279	1862, June 29
1280	1863, June 18
1281	1864, June 6*
1282	1865, May 27
1283	1866, May 16
1284	1867, May 5
1285	1868, April 24*
1286	1869, April 13
1287	1870, April 3
1288	1871, March 23
1289	1872, March 11*
1290	1873, March 1
1291	1874, February 18
1292	1875, February 7
1293	1876, January 28*
1294	1877, January 16
1295	1878, January 5
1296	1878, December 26
1297	1879, December 15
1298	1880, December 4*
1299	1881, November 23
1300	1882, November 12
1301	1883, November 2
1302	1884, October 21*
1303	1885, October 10
1304	1886, September 30
1305	1887, September 19
1306	1888, September 7*
1307	1889, August 28
1308	1890, August 17
1309	1891, August 7
1310	1892, July 26*
1311	1893, July 15
1312	1894, July 5
1313	1895, June 24
1314	1896, June 12*
1315	1897, June 2
1316	1898, May 22
1317	1899, May 12
1318	1900, May 1
1319	1901, April 20
1320	1902, April 10
1321	1903, March 30
1322	1904, March 18*
1323	1905, March 8
1324	1906, February 25
1325	1907, February 14
1326	1908, February 4*
1327	1909, January 23
1328	1910, January 13
1329	1911, January 2
1330	1911, December 22
1332	1913, November 30
1333	1914, November 19
1334	1915, November 9
1335	1916, October 28*
1336	1917, October 17
1337	1918, October 7
1338	1919, September 26
1339	1920, September 15*
1340	1921, September 4
1341	1922, August 24
1342	1923, August 14
1343	1924, August 2*
1344	1925, July 22
1345	1926, July 12
1346	1927, July 1
1347	1928, June 20*
1348	1929, June 9
1349	1930, May 29
1350	1931, May 19
1351	1932, May 7*
1352	1933, April 26
1353	1934, April 16
1354	1935, April 5
1355	1936, March 24*
1356	1937, March 14
1357	1938, March 3
1358	1939, February 21
1359	1940, February 10*

AH Hejira	AD Christian Date
1360	1941, January 29
1361	1942, January 19
1362	1943, January 8
1363	1943, December 28
1364	1944, December 17*
1365	1945, December 6
1366	1946, November 25
1367	1947, November 15
1368	1948, November 3*
1369	1949, October 24
1370	1950, October 13
1371	1951, October 2
1372	1952, September 21*
1373	1953, September 10
1374	1954, August 30
1375	1955, August 20
1376	1956, August 8*
1377	1957, July 29
1378	1958, July 18
1379	1959, July 7
1380	1960, June 25*
1381	1961, June 14
1382	1962, June 4
1383	1963, May 25
1384	1964, May 13*
1385	1965, May 2
1386	1966, April 22
1387	1967, April 11
1388	1968, March 31*
1389	1969, March 20
1390	1970, March 9
1391	1971, February 27
1392	1972, February 16*
1393	1973, February 4
1394	1974, January 25
1395	1975, January 14
1396	1976, January 3*
1397	1976, December 23*
1398	1977, December 12
1399	1978, December 2
1400	1979, November 21
1401	1980, November 9*
1402	1981, October 30
1403	1982, October 19
1404	1984, October 8
1405	1984, September 27*
1406	1985, September 16
1407	1986, September 6
1409	1987, August 26
1409	1988, August 14*
1410	1989, August 3
1411	1990, July 24
1412	1991, July 13
1413	1992, July 2*
1414	1993, June 21
1415	1994, June 10
1416	1995, May 31
1417	1996, May 19*
1418	1997, May 9
1419	1998, April 28
1420	1999, April 17
1421	2000, April 6*
1422	2001, March 26
1423	2002, March 15
1424	2003, March 5
1425	2004, February 22*
1426	2005, February 10
1427	2006, January 31
1428	2007, January 20
1429	2008, January 10*
1430	2008, December 29
1431	2009, December 18
1432	2010, December 8
1433	2011, November 27*
1434	2012, November 15
1435	2013, November 5
1436	2014, October 25
1437	2015, October 15*
1438	2016, October 3
1439	2017, September 22
1440	2018, September 12
1441	2019, September 1*
1442	2020, August 20
1443	2021, August 10
1444	2022, July 30
1445	2023, July 19*
1446	2024, July 8
1447	2025, June 27
1448	2026, June 17
1449	2027, June 6*
1450	2028, May25

The Islamic Republic of Afghanistan, which occupies a mountainous region of Southwest Asia, has an area of 251,825 sq. mi. (652,090 sq. km.) and a population of 25.59 million. Presently, about a fifth of the total population lives in exile as refugees, (mostly in Pakistan). Capital: Kabul. It is bordered by Iran, Pakistan, Turkmenistan, Uzbekistan, Tajikistan, and China's Sinkiang Province. Agriculture and herding are the principal industries; textile mills and cement factories add to the industrial sector. Cotton, wool, fruits, nuts, oil, sheepskin coats and hand-woven carpets are normally exported but foreign trade has been interrupted since 1979.

On September 11, 2001, a terrorist attack on the United States, supported by the Taliban, led to retaliatory strikes by the U.S. Military in coalition with Afghans of a Northern Alliance. The Taliban regime was deposed. During a UN-sponsored conference on Afghanistan that was held in Bonn, Germany, in early November 2001, an agreement was reached for an Interim Authority, under the leadership of Hamid Karzai, to be installed in Afghanistan on December 22, 2001 and to hold power for the following four to six months. A "loya jirga" (Grand Council) then established a Transitional Authority with Hamid Karzai as president to prepare for general elections and a new constitution.

The national symbol on most coins of the kingdom is a stylized mosque, within which is seen the *mihrab*, a niche indicating the direction of Mecca, and the *minbar*, the pulpit, with a flight of steps leading up to it. Inscriptions in Pashtu were first used under the rebel Habibullah, but did not become standard until 1950.

ISLAMIC STATE

SH1373-1381 / 1994-2002AD

STANDARD COINAGE

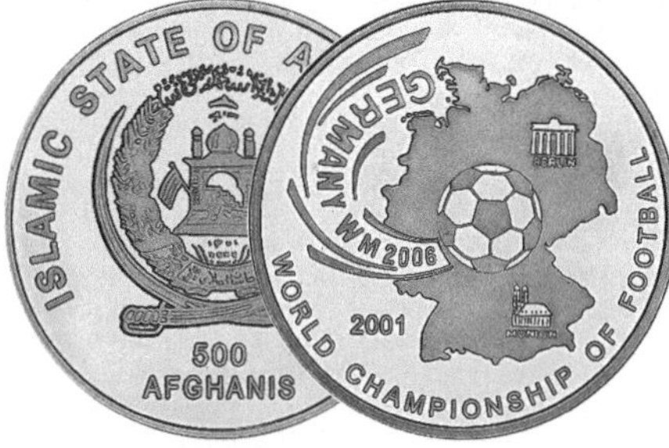

KM# 1043 500 AFGHANIS
19.8700 g., 0.9990 Silver 0.6382 oz. ASW, 37.9 mm. **Subject:** World Championship of Soccer - 2006 - Germany **Obv:** State Emblem **Rev:** Soccer ball on German map **Edge:** Reeded

Date	Mintage	F	VF	XF	Unc	BU
2001 Proof	—	Value: 50.00				

KM# 1048 500 AFGHANIS
15.0000 g., Silver, 35.08 mm. **Subject:** 100th Anniversary Death of Giuseppe Verdi **Obv:** National arms **Rev:** Bust of Verdi 3/4 left, music score below **Edge:** Plain

Date	Mintage	F	VF	XF	Unc	BU
SH1380(2001) Proof	—	Value: 35.00				

REPUBLIC

SH1381- / 2002- AD

DECIMAL COINAGE

100 Pul = 1 Afghani; 20 Afghani = 1 Amani

KM# 1044 AFGHANI
3.2800 g., Copper Plated Steel, 20 mm. **Obv:** Value, legend above, legend and date below **Rev:** Mosque with flags in wreath

Date	Mintage	F	VF	XF	Unc	BU
SH1383(2004)	—	—	—	—	1.50	2.00
SH1384(2005)	—	—	—	—	1.50	2.00

KM# 1045 2 AFGHANIS
4.1000 g., Stainless Steel, 22 mm. **Obv:** Value, legend above, legend and date below **Rev:** Mosque with flags in wreath

Date	Mintage	F	VF	XF	Unc	BU
SH1383(2004)	—	—	—	—	2.00	2.50
SH1384(2005)	—	—	—	—	2.00	2.50

KM# 1046 5 AFGHANIS
5.0800 g., Brass, 24 mm. **Obv:** Value, legend above, legend and date below **Rev:** Mosque with flags in wreath

Date	Mintage	F	VF	XF	Unc	BU
SH1383(2004)	—	—	—	—	2.50	3.00
SH1384(2005)	—	—	—	—	2.50	3.00

The Republic of Albania, a Balkan republic bounded by Macedonia, Greece, Montenegro, and the Adriatic Sea, has an area of 11,100 sq. mi. (28,748 sq. km.) and a population of 3.49 million. Capital: Tirane. The country is predominantly agricultural, although recent progress has been made in the manufacturing and mining sectors. Petroleum, chrome, iron, copper, cotton textiles, tobacco and wood products are exported.

MINT MARKS
L – London
R - Rome
V – Vienna

MONETARY SYSTEM
100 Qindar Leku = 1 Lek
100 Qindar Ari = 1 Frang Ar = 5 Lek

REPUBLIC

STANDARD COINAGE

KM# 75 LEK
3.0000 g., Bronze, 18.1 mm. **Obv:** Dalmatian pelican **Rev:** Denomination **Edge:** Plain

Date	Mintage	F	VF	XF	Unc	BU
2008	—	—	—	0.40	1.50	2.00

KM# 76 5 LEKE
3.1200 g., Nickel Plated Steel, 20 mm. **Obv:** Imperial eagle **Rev:** Olive branch, denomination

Date	Mintage	F	VF	XF	Unc	BU
2011	—	—	—	—	1.00	1.25

KM# 93 10 LEKE
3.6000 g., Aluminum-Bronze, 21.25 mm. **Subject:** 85th Anniversary Tirana as capital **Obv:** Archaic Tomb **Obv. Legend:** SHQIPERI • ALBANIA **Rev:** Outlined bird above value **Edge:** Reeded

Date	Mintage	F	VF	XF	Unc	BU
2005	—	—	—	—	2.00	3.00

KM# 94 10 LEKE
3.6000 g., Aluminum-Bronze, 21.25 mm. **Subject:** Culture **Obv:** Ornate vest **Obv. Legend:** SHQIPERI • ALBANIA **Rev:** Ornate value **Rev. Legend:** OBJEKTE TE TRASHEGIMISE KULTURORE **Edge:** Reeded

Date	Mintage	F	VF	XF	Unc	BU
2005	—	—	—	—	2.00	3.00

KM# 87 20 LEKE
8.5400 g., Brass, 26.1 mm. **Subject:** Prehistoric art **Obv:** Horseman **Rev:** Ancient coin design with Apollo portrait **Edge:** Reeded

Date	Mintage	F	VF	XF	Unc	BU
2002	—	—	—	—	3.00	4.00

KM# 81 50 LEKE
7.5000 g., Copper-Nickel, 28 mm. **Subject:** Michaelangelo's "David", 500th Anniversary **Obv:** Towered building **Rev:** Statue's head and denomination **Edge:** Plain

Date	Mintage	F	VF	XF	Unc	BU
2001	3,000	—	—	—	6.50	8.00

KM# 88 50 LEKE
12.0000 g., Brass, 28 mm. **Subject:** Declaration of Independence, 90th Anniversary **Obv:** Value within circle **Rev:** Bust facing, dates below **Edge:** Reeded

Date	Mintage	F	VF	XF	Unc	BU
2002	20,000	—	—	—	3.00	4.00

KM# 89 50 LEKE
12.0000 g., Brass, 28 mm. **Subject:** Jeronim de Rada, 100th Anniversary of Death **Obv:** Bust 3/4 facing, dates below, circle surrounds **Rev:** Value within box within circle **Edge:** Plain

Date	Mintage	F	VF	XF	Unc	BU
2003	—	—	—	—	3.00	4.00

KM# 86 50 LEKE
5.5000 g., Copper-Nickel, 24.25 mm. **Obv:** Value and legend **Rev:** Ancient Illyrian helmet **Edge:** Reeded

Date	Mintage	F	VF	XF	Unc	BU
2003 (2004)	200,000	—	—	—	6.00	7.50

KM# 90 50 LEKE
5.5000 g., Copper-Nickel, 24.25 mm. **Subject:** The Beauty of Durrës **Obv:** Wheel design **Rev:** Ancient bust above value within circle **Edge:** Reeded

Date	Mintage	F	VF	XF	Unc	BU
2004	200,000	—	—	—	3.00	4.00

KM# 91 50 LEKE
5.5000 g., Copper-Nickel, 24.25 mm. **Obv:** Soldier within circle **Rev:** Value within circle **Edge:** Reeded

Date	Mintage	F	VF	XF	Unc	BU
2004	200,000	—	—	—	3.00	4.00

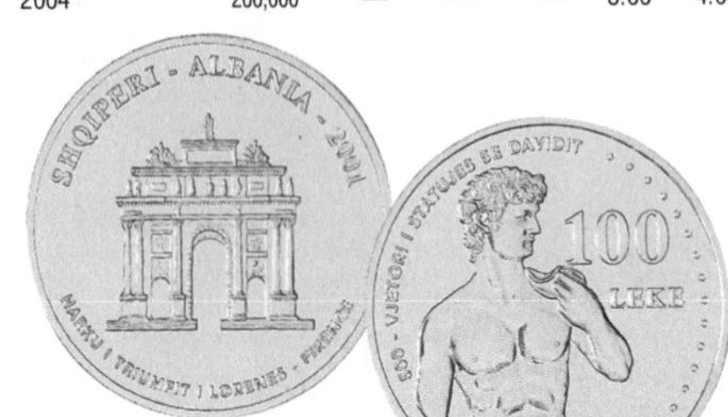

KM# 82 100 LEKE
15.7000 g., 0.9250 Silver 0.4669 oz. ASW, 32.65 mm. **Subject:** Michaelangelo's "David", 500th Anniversary **Obv:** Arch of Triumph **Rev:** Statue's upper half and denomination **Edge:** Plain

Date	Mintage	F	VF	XF	Unc	BU
2001	3,000	—	—	—	32.00	35.00

KM# 84 100 LEKE
15.0000 g., 0.9250 Silver 0.4461 oz. ASW, 32 mm. **Subject:** Albanian-European Integration **Obv:** Dove in flight, stars encircle **Rev:** European and Albanian maps, stars encircle **Edge:** Plain

Date	Mintage	F	VF	XF	Unc	BU
2001	3,000	—	—	—	30.00	32.50

KM# 92 100 LEKE
30.0000 g., 0.9250 Silver 0.8921 oz. ASW, 38 mm. **Subject:** Declaration of Independence, 90th Anniversary **Obv:** Crossed rifle and pistol on manuscript, quill pen **Obv. Legend:** SHQIPERI - ALBANIA **Rev:** Bust of Qemali 3/4 right

Date	Mintage	F	VF	XF	Unc	BU
2002 Proof	7,000	Value: 50.00				

KM# 83 200 LEKE
7.6500 g., 0.9000 Gold 0.2213 oz. AGW, 25.45 mm. **Subject:** Michaelangelo's "David", 500th Anniversary **Obv:** City plaza **Rev:** Statue of "David" and denomination **Edge:** Plain

Date	Mintage	F	VF	XF	Unc	BU
2001	1,000	—	—	—	400	425

KM# 85 200 LEKE
15.0000 g., 0.9250 Silver 0.4461 oz. ASW, 32 mm. **Subject:** Albanian-European Integration **Obv:** Dove in flight within inner circle, stars encircle **Rev:** Adult and infant hand within inner circle, stars encircle **Edge:** Plain

Date	Mintage	F	VF	XF	Unc	BU
2001	1,000	—	—	—	37.50	40.00

MINT SETS

KM#	Date	Mintage	Identification	Issue Price	Mkt Val
MS3	2002-03 (4)	—	KM86, 89 (2003), 87, 88 (2002)	—	22.50

ALDERNEY

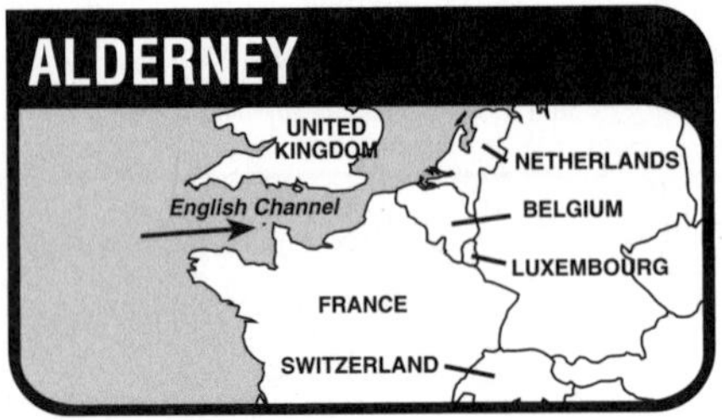

Alderney, the northernmost and third largest of the Channel Islands, separated from the coast of France by the dangerous 8-mile-wide tidal channel, has an area of 3 sq. mi. (8 km.) and a population of 1,686. It is a dependency of the British island of Guernsey, to the southwest. Capital: St. Anne. Principal industries are agriculture and raising cattle.

The Channel Islands have never been subject to the British Parliament and are self-governing units under the direct rule of the Crown acting through the Privy Council. Alderney is one of the nine Channel Islands, the only part of the Duchy of Normandy still belonging to the British Crown, and has been a British possession since the Norman Conquest of 1066. Legislation was only recently introduced for the issue of its own coinage, a right it now shares with Jersey and Guernsey.

RULER
British

MONETARY SYSTEM
100 Pence = 1 Pound Sterling

DEPENDENCY

STANDARD COINAGE

KM# 75 50 PENCE
8.0000 g., 0.9250 Silver 0.2379 oz. ASW **Ruler:** Elizabeth II **Subject:** 50th Anniversary of Coronation **Obv:** Crowned head right **Rev:** Royal coach **Edge:** Plain **Shape:** 7-sided

Date	Mintage	F	VF	XF	Unc	BU
2003 Proof	—	Value: 20.00				

KM# 76 50 PENCE
8.0000 g., 0.9250 Silver 0.2379 oz. ASW **Ruler:** Elizabeth II **Subject:** 50th Anniversary of Coronation **Obv:** Crowned head right **Rev:** St. Edward's crown **Edge:** Plain **Shape:** 7-sided

Date	Mintage	F	VF	XF	Unc	BU
2003 Proof	—	Value: 20.00				

KM# 77 50 PENCE
8.0000 g., 0.9250 Silver 0.2379 oz. ASW **Ruler:** Elizabeth II **Subject:** 50th Anniversary of Coronation **Obv:** Crowned head right **Rev:** Elizabeth II horseback **Edge:** Plain **Shape:** 7-sided

Date	Mintage	F	VF	XF	Unc	BU
2003 Proof	—	Value: 20.00				

KM# 78 50 PENCE
8.0000 g., 0.9250 Silver 0.2379 oz. ASW **Ruler:** Elizabeth II **Subject:** 50th Anniversary of Coronation **Obv:** Crowned head right **Rev:** Elizabeth II seated on throne **Edge:** Plain **Shape:** 7-sided

Date	Mintage	F	VF	XF	Unc	BU
2003 Proof	—	Value: 20.00				

KM# 73 POUND
9.5000 g., 0.9250 Silver 0.2825 oz. ASW **Ruler:** Elizabeth II **Subject:** Queen's 75th Birthday **Obv:** Crowned head right

Date	Mintage	F	VF	XF	Unc	BU
2001 Proof	—	Value: 20.00				

KM# 91 POUND
1.2400 g., 0.9990 Gold 0.0398 oz. AGW, 13.92 mm. **Ruler:** Elizabeth II **Rev:** State arms

Date	Mintage	F	VF	XF	Unc	BU
2002 Proof	Est. 50,000	Value: 80.00				

KM# 119 POUND
1.2400 g., 0.9990 Gold 0.0398 oz. AGW, 13.92 mm. **Ruler:** Elizabeth II **Subject:** Trafalgar - Horatio Nelson **Obv:** Head crowned right **Rev:** Bust right in Navy uniform

Date	Mintage	F	VF	XF	Unc	BU
2005 Proof	Est. 20,000	Value: 85.00				

KM# 122 POUND
1.2400 g., 0.9990 Gold 0.0398 oz. AGW, 13.92 mm. **Ruler:** Elizabeth II **Rev:** Queen Elizabeth I

Date	Mintage	F	VF	XF	Unc	BU
2006 Proof	Est. 20,000	Value: 85.00				

KM# 123 POUND
1.2400 g., 0.9990 Gold 0.0398 oz. AGW, 13.92 mm. **Ruler:** Elizabeth II **Rev:** Sir Isaac Newton

Date	Mintage	F	VF	XF	Unc	BU
2006 Proof	Est. 20,000	Value: 85.00				

KM# 124 POUND
1.2400 g., 0.9990 Gold 0.0398 oz. AGW, 13.92 mm. **Ruler:** Elizabeth II **Rev:** William Shakespeare

Date	Mintage	F	VF	XF	Unc	BU
2006 Proof	20,000	Value: 85.00				

KM# 125 POUND
1.2400 g., 0.9990 Gold 0.0398 oz. AGW, 13.92 mm. **Ruler:** Elizabeth II **Rev:** Charles Dickens

Date	Mintage	F	VF	XF	Unc	BU
2006 Proof	Est. 20,000	Value: 85.00				

KM# 130 POUND
1.2400 g., 0.9990 Gold 0.0398 oz. AGW, 13.92 mm. **Ruler:** Elizabeth II **Rev:** Sir Winston Churchill

Date	Mintage	F	VF	XF	Unc	BU
2006 Proof	Est. 20,000	Value: 85.00				

KM# 131 POUND
1.2400 g., 0.9990 Gold 0.0398 oz. AGW, 13.92 mm. **Ruler:** Elizabeth II **Rev:** Elizabeth II corronation

Date	Mintage	F	VF	XF	Unc	BU
2006 Proof	—	Value: 85.00				

KM# 154 POUND
1.2400 g., 0.9990 Gold 0.0398 oz. AGW, 13.92 mm. **Ruler:** Elizabeth II **Rev:** Capt. James Cook

Date	Mintage	F	VF	XF	Unc	BU
2007 Proof	Est. 20,000	Value: 85.00				

KM# 155 POUND
1.2400 g., 0.9990 Gold 0.0398 oz. AGW, 13.92 mm. **Ruler:** Elizabeth II **Rev:** Sir Edward Elgar

Date	Mintage	F	VF	XF	Unc	BU
2007 Proof	Est. 20,000	Value: 85.00				

KM# 156 POUND
1.2400 g., 0.9990 Gold 0.0398 oz. AGW, 13.92 mm. **Ruler:** Elizabeth II **Rev:** Sir Francis Drake

Date	Mintage	F	VF	XF	Unc	BU
2007 Proof	20,000	Value: 85.00				

KM# 157 POUND
1.2400 g., 0.9990 Gold 0.0398 oz. AGW, 13.92 mm. **Ruler:** Elizabeth II **Rev:** John Constable

Date	Mintage	F	VF	XF	Unc	BU
2007 Proof	Est. 20,000	Value: 85.00				

KM# 174 POUND
1.2400 g., 0.9990 Gold 0.0398 oz. AGW, 13.92 mm. **Ruler:** Elizabeth II **Subject:** Princess Diana, 10th Anniversary of Death **Rev:** Bust 3/4 facing left

Date	Mintage	F	VF	XF	Unc	BU
2007 Proof	Est. 20,000	Value: 85.00				

KM# 175a POUND
28.2800 g., 0.9250 Silver 0.8410 oz. ASW, 38.61 mm. **Ruler:** Elizabeth II

Date	Mintage	F	VF	XF	Unc	BU
2007 Proof	Est. 10,000	Value: 55.00				

KM# 175b POUND

39.9400 g., 0.9160 Gold 1.1762 oz. AGW, 38.61 mm. **Ruler:** Elizabeth II **Subject:** Princess Diana, 10th Anniversary of Death

Date	Mintage	F	VF	XF	Unc	BU
2007 Proof	—	Value: 2,200				

KM# 189 POUND

1.2400 g., 0.9990 Gold 0.0398 oz. AGW, 13.92 mm. **Ruler:** Elizabeth II **Rev:** Concord

Date	Mintage	F	VF	XF	Unc	BU
2008 Proof	Est. 1,000	Value: 85.00				

KM# 84 POUND

1.2400 g., 0.9990 Gold 0.0398 oz. AGW, 13.92 mm. **Ruler:** Elizabeth II **Subject:** Mini Cooper 50th Anniversary **Rev:** Mini Cooper on tiled floor

Date	Mintage	F	VF	XF	Unc	BU
2009 Proof	5,000	Value: 120				

KM# 59 5 POUNDS

28.2800 g., 0.9250 Silver 0.8410 oz. ASW, 38.6 mm. **Ruler:** Elizabeth II **Subject:** Queen's 75th Birthday **Obv:** Queen's portrait right **Rev:** Queen in casual dress surrounded by rose, thistle, daffodil and pimper nickel

Date	Mintage	F	VF	XF	Unc	BU
2001 Proof	—	Value: 50.00				

KM# 60 5 POUNDS

28.2800 g., Copper-Nickel, 38.6 mm. **Ruler:** Elizabeth II **Subject:** Queen's 75th Birrthday **Obv:** Queen's portrait right **Rev:** Queen in casual dress surrounded by rose, thistle, daffodil and primper nickel

Date	Mintage	F	VF	XF	Unc	BU
2001	—	—	—	—	13.50	15.00

KM# 24 5 POUNDS

28.2800 g., Copper-Nickel, 38.6 mm. **Ruler:** Elizabeth II **Subject:** Queen Elizabeth II - 50 Years of Reigh **Obv:** Queen's head right **Rev:** Sword hilt and denomination with royal arms background **Edge:** Reeded

Date	Mintage	F	VF	XF	Unc	BU
2002 Proof	15,000	Value: 15.00				

KM# 24a 5 POUNDS

28.2800 g., 0.9250 Silver 0.8410 oz. ASW, 38.6 mm. **Ruler:** Elizabeth II **Subject:** Queen Elizabeth II - 50 Years of Reign **Obv:** Queen's head right **Rev:** Sword hilt and denomination with royal arms background **Edge:** Reeded

Date	Mintage	F	VF	XF	Unc	BU
2002 Proof	15,000	Value: 45.00				

KM# 25 5 POUNDS

28.2800 g., 0.9250 Silver 0.8410 oz. ASW, 38.6 mm. **Ruler:** Elizabeth II **Subject:** Queen's Golden Jubilee **Obv:** Queen's portrait **Rev:** Honor guard and trumpets **Edge:** Reeded

Date	Mintage	F	VF	XF	Unc	BU
2002 Proof	15,000	Value: 45.00				

KM# 27 5 POUNDS

28.2800 g., Copper-Nickel, 38.6 mm. **Ruler:** Elizabeth II **Subject:** 5th Anniversary Death of Princess Diana **Obv:** Crowned head right **Rev:** Diana accepting flowers from girl **Edge:** Reeded

Date	Mintage	F	VF	XF	Unc	BU
2002	—	—	—	—	13.50	15.00

KM# 27a 5 POUNDS

28.2800 g., 0.9250 Silver 0.8410 oz. ASW, 38.6 mm. **Ruler:** Elizabeth II **Subject:** 5th Anniversary Death of Princess Diana **Obv:** Crowned head right **Rev:** Diana accepting flowers from girl **Edge:** Reeded

Date	Mintage	F	VF	XF	Unc	BU
2002 Proof	20,000	Value: 45.00				

KM# 27b 5 POUNDS

39.9400 g., 0.9167 Gold 1.1771 oz. AGW, 38.6 mm. **Ruler:** Elizabeth II **Subject:** 5th Anniversary Death of Princess Diana **Obv:** Crowned head right **Rev:** Diana accepting flowers from girl **Edge:** Reeded

Date	Mintage	F	VF	XF	Unc	BU
2002 Proof	100	Value: 2,250				

KM# 29 5 POUNDS

28.2800 g., Copper-Nickel, 38.6 mm. **Ruler:** Elizabeth II **Subject:** 150th Anniversary Death of the Duke of Wellington **Obv:** Queen's portrait **Rev:** Coat of arms, castle and portrait **Edge:** Reeded

Date	Mintage	F	VF	XF	Unc	BU
2002	—	—	—	—	13.50	15.00

KM# 29a 5 POUNDS

28.2800 g., 0.9250 Silver 0.8410 oz. ASW, 38.6 mm. **Ruler:** Elizabeth II **Subject:** 150th Anniversary Death of the Duke of Wellington **Obv:** Queen's portrait **Rev:** Multicolor coat of arms, portrait and castle **Edge:** Reeded

Date	Mintage	VG	F	VF	XF	Unc
2002 Proof	15,000	Value: 55.00				

KM# 29b 5 POUNDS

39.9400 g., 0.9167 Gold 1.1771 oz. AGW, 38.6 mm. **Ruler:** Elizabeth II **Subject:** 150th Anniversary Death of the Duke of Wellington **Obv:** Queen's portrait **Rev:** Coat of arms, castle and portrait **Edge:** Reeded

Date	Mintage	VG	F	VF	XF	Unc
2002 Proof	200	Value: 2,200				

KM# 44 5 POUNDS

28.2800 g., Copper-Nickel, 38.6 mm. **Ruler:** Elizabeth II **Obv:** Queen's portrait **Rev:** HMS Mary Rose **Edge:** Reeded

Date	Mintage	F	VF	XF	Unc	BU
2003	—	—	—	—	12.00	13.50

KM# 44a 5 POUNDS

28.2800 g., 0.9250 Silver 0.8410 oz. ASW, 38.6 mm. **Ruler:** Elizabeth II **Obv:** Queen's portrait **Rev:** HMS Mary Rose below multicolor flag **Edge:** Reeded

Date	Mintage	F	VF	XF	Unc	BU
2003 Proof	15,000	Value: 60.00				

KM# 45 5 POUNDS

28.2800 g., Copper-Nickel, 38.6 mm. **Ruler:** Elizabeth II **Obv:** Queen's portrait **Rev:** Alfred the Great on ship **Edge:** Reeded

Date	Mintage	F	VF	XF	Unc	BU
2003	—	—	—	—	12.00	13.50

KM# 45a 5 POUNDS

28.2800 g., 0.9250 Silver 0.8410 oz. ASW, 38.6 mm. **Ruler:** Elizabeth II **Obv:** Queen's portrait **Rev:** Alfred the Great on ship below multicolor flag **Edge:** Reeded

Date	Mintage	F	VF	XF	Unc	BU
2003 Proof	15,000	Value: 60.00				

KM# 45b 5 POUNDS

39.9400 g., 0.9167 Gold 1.1771 oz. AGW, 38.6 mm. **Ruler:** Elizabeth II **Obv:** Queen's portrait **Rev:** Alfred the Great on ship **Edge:** Reeded

Date	Mintage	F	VF	XF	Unc	BU
2003 Proof	500	Value: 2,150				

KM# 31 5 POUNDS

28.2800 g., Copper-Nickel, 38.6 mm. **Ruler:** Elizabeth II **Subject:** Prince William **Obv:** Queen's portrait **Rev:** Portrait with open shirt collar **Edge:** Reeded

Date	Mintage	F	VF	XF	Unc	BU
2003	—	—	—	—	16.50	18.00

KM# 31a 5 POUNDS

28.2800 g., 0.9250 Silver 0.8410 oz. ASW, 38.6 mm. **Ruler:** Elizabeth II **Subject:** Prince William **Obv:** Queen's portrait **Rev:** Portrait with open shirt collar **Edge:** Reeded

Date	Mintage	F	VF	XF	Unc	BU
2003 Proof	—	Value: 47.50				

KM# 31b 5 POUNDS

39.9400 g., 0.9166 Gold 1.1770 oz. AGW, 38.6 mm. **Ruler:** Elizabeth II **Subject:** Prince Willliam **Obv:** Queen's portrait **Rev:** Portrait with open shirt collar **Edge:** Reeded

Date	Mintage	F	VF	XF	Unc	BU
2003 Proof	200	Value: 2,200				

KM# 35 5 POUNDS

28.2800 g., Copper-Nickel, 38.61 mm. **Ruler:** Elizabeth II **Subject:** Last Flight of the Concorde, October 24, 2003 **Obv:** Crowned bust right **Obv. Legend:** ELIZABETH II - ALDERNEY **Rev:** Concorde in flight **Rev. Legend:** CONCORDE 1969 - 2003 **Edge:** Reeded

Date	Mintage	F	VF	XF	Unc	BU
2003	5,000	—	—	—	12.00	15.50

KM# 35a 5 POUNDS

28.2800 g., 0.9250 Silver 0.8410 oz. ASW, 38.61 mm. **Ruler:** Elizabeth II **Subject:** Last Flight of the Concorde, October 24, 2003 **Obv:** Crowned bust right **Obv. Legend:** ELIZABETH II - ALDERNEY **Rev:** Concorde in flight **Rev. Legend:** CONCORDE 1969 - 2003 **Edge:** Reeded

Date	Mintage	F	VF	XF	Unc	BU
2003 Proof	5,000	Value: 50.00				

KM# 35b 5 POUNDS

39.9400 g., 0.9166 Gold 1.1770 oz. AGW, 38.6 mm. **Ruler:** Elizabeth II **Obv:** Queen's portrait **Rev:** Concorde in flight, October 24, 2003 **Edge:** Reeded

Date	Mintage	F	VF	XF	Unc	BU
2003 Proof	500	Value: 2,150				

KM# 38 5 POUNDS

28.2800 g., Copper-Nickel, 38.6 mm. **Ruler:** Elizabeth II **Obv:** Queen's portrait **Rev:** Battleship and transports, HMS Belfast **Edge:** Reeded **Note:** D-Day

Date	Mintage	F	VF	XF	Unc	BU
2004	—	—	—	—	15.00	17.50

KM# 38a 5 POUNDS
28.2800 g., 0.9250 Silver 0.8410 oz. ASW, 38.6 mm. **Ruler:** Elizabeth II **Obv:** Queen's portrait **Rev:** Battleship and transports

Date	Mintage	F	VF	XF	Unc	BU
2004 Proof	10,000	Value: 85.00				

KM# 38b 5 POUNDS
39.9400 g., 0.9167 Gold 1.1771 oz. AGW, 38.6 mm. **Ruler:** Elizabeth II **Obv:** Queen's portrait **Rev:** Battleship and transports

Date	Mintage	F	VF	XF	Unc	BU
2004 Proof	500	Value: 2,150				

KM# 42 5 POUNDS
28.2800 g., Copper-Nickel, 38.6 mm. **Ruler:** Elizabeth II **Obv:** Crowned head right **Rev:** Florence Nightingale **Edge:** Reeded

Date	Mintage	F	VF	XF	Unc	BU
2004	—	—	—	—	18.00	20.00

KM# 42a 5 POUNDS
28.2800 g., 0.9250 Silver 0.8410 oz. ASW, 38.6 mm. **Ruler:** Elizabeth II **Obv:** Queen's portrait **Rev:** Florence Nightingale **Edge:** Reeded

Date	Mintage	F	VF	XF	Unc	BU
2004 Proof	25,000	Value: 70.00				

KM# 43 5 POUNDS
28.2800 g., Copper-Nickel, 38.6 mm. **Ruler:** Elizabeth II **Subject:** 150th Anniversary of the Crimean War **Obv:** Crowned head right **Rev:** Florence Nightingale head above the Battle of Inkerman scene with one multicolor soldier **Edge:** Reeded

Date	Mintage	F	VF	XF	Unc	BU
2004 plain	—	—	—	—	25.00	27.50
2004 partial color	—	—	—	—	25.00	27.50

KM# 43a 5 POUNDS
28.2800 g., 0.9250 Silver 0.8410 oz. ASW, 38.6 mm. **Ruler:** Elizabeth II **Subject:** 150th Anniversary Crimean War **Obv:** Crowned head right **Rev:** Florence Nightingale head above Battle of Inkerman scene with one multicolor soldier **Edge:** Reeded

Date	Mintage	F	VF	XF	Unc	BU
2004 Proof	10,000	Value: 85.00				

KM# 43b 5 POUNDS
39.9400 g., 0.9166 Gold 1.1770 oz. AGW, 38.6 mm. **Ruler:** Elizabeth II **Subject:** 150th Anniversary Crimean War **Obv:** Crowned head right **Rev:** Florence Nightingale head above Battle of Inkerman scene with one multicolor soldier **Edge:** Reeded

Date	Mintage	F	VF	XF	Unc	BU
2004 Proof	500	Value: 2,150				

KM# 94 5 POUNDS
28.2800 g., 0.9250 Silver 0.8410 oz. ASW, 38.61 mm. **Ruler:** Elizabeth II **Subject:** David Beckham **Rev:** Soccer player and ball as background

Date	Mintage	F	VF	XF	Unc	BU
2004 Proof	—	Value: 45.00				

KM# 95 5 POUNDS
28.2800 g., 0.9250 Silver 0.8410 oz. ASW, 38.61 mm. **Ruler:** Elizabeth II **Subject:** Michael Owen **Rev:** Soccer player and ball as background

Date	Mintage	F	VF	XF	Unc	BU
2004 Proof	—	Value: 45.00				

KM# 47 5 POUNDS
28.2800 g., Copper-Nickel, 38.6 mm. **Ruler:** Elizabeth II **Obv:** Queen's portrait **Rev:** Locomotive, The Rocket **Edge:** Reeded

Date	Mintage	F	VF	XF	Unc	BU
2004	—	—	—	—	16.00	18.50

KM# 47a 5 POUNDS
28.2800 g., 0.9250 Silver 0.8410 oz. ASW, 38.6 mm. **Ruler:** Elizabeth II **Obv:** Queen's portrait **Rev:** Locomotive, The Rocket **Edge:** Reeded

Date	Mintage	F	VF	XF	Unc	BU
2004 Proof	20,000	Value: 60.00				

KM# 47b 5 POUNDS
39.9400 g., 0.9167 Gold 1.1771 oz. AGW, 38.6 mm. **Ruler:** Elizabeth II **Obv:** Queen's portrait **Rev:** Locomotive, The Rocket **Edge:** Reeded

Date	Mintage	F	VF	XF	Unc	BU
2004 Proof	500	Value: 2,150				

KM# 48 5 POUNDS
28.2800 g., Copper-Nickel, 38.6 mm. **Ruler:** Elizabeth II **Obv:** Queen's portrait **Rev:** Locomotive, The Royal Scot **Edge:** Reeded

Date	Mintage	F	VF	XF	Unc	BU
2004	—	—	—	—	16.00	18.50

KM# 48a 5 POUNDS
28.2800 g., 0.9250 Silver 0.8410 oz. ASW, 38.6 mm. **Ruler:** Elizabeth II **Obv:** Queen's portrait **Rev:** Locomotive, The Royal Scot **Edge:** Reeded

Date	Mintage	F	VF	XF	Unc	BU
2004 Proof	10,000	Value: 60.00				

KM# 49 5 POUNDS
28.2800 g., Copper-Nickel, 38.6 mm. **Ruler:** Elizabeth II **Obv:** Queen's portrait **Rev:** Locomotive, The Merchant Navy 21C1 **Edge:** Reeded

Date	Mintage	F	VF	XF	Unc	BU
2004	—	—	—	—	16.00	18.50

KM# 49a 5 POUNDS
28.2800 g., 0.9250 Silver 0.8410 oz. ASW, 38.6 mm. **Ruler:** Elizabeth II **Obv:** Queen's portrait **Rev:** Locomotive, The Merchant Navy 21C1 **Edge:** Reeded

Date	Mintage	F	VF	XF	Unc	BU
2004 Proof	10,000	Value: 60.00				

KM# 53a 5 POUNDS
28.2800 g., 0.9250 Silver 0.8410 oz. ASW, 38.6 mm. **Ruler:** Elizabeth II **Subject:** End of WWII **Obv:** Elizabeth II by Maklouf **Rev:** Flag waving crowd **Edge:** Reeded

Date	Mintage	F	VF	XF	Unc	BU
2005 Proof	5,000	Value: 85.00				

KM# 96 5 POUNDS
28.2800 g., 0.9250 Silver 0.8410 oz. ASW **Ruler:** Elizabeth II **Subject:** Locomotives, 200th Anniversary **Rev:** Train station on a branch line

Date	Mintage	F	VF	XF	Unc	BU
2005 Proof	Est. 10,000	Value: 60.00				
2006 Proof	Est. 25,000	Value: 55.00				

KM# 97 5 POUNDS
28.2800 g., 0.9250 Silver 0.8410 oz. ASW **Ruler:** Elizabeth II **Subject:** Locomotives, 200th Anniversary **Rev:** Locomotive Shop

Date	Mintage	F	VF	XF	Unc	BU
2005 Proof	Est. 10,000	Value: 60.00				
2006 proof	Est. 25,000	Value: 55.00				

KM# 98 5 POUNDS
28.2800 g., 0.9250 Silver 0.8410 oz. ASW **Ruler:** Elizabeth II **Subject:** Locomotives, 200th Anniversary **Rev:** Viaduct

Date	Mintage	F	VF	XF	Unc	BU
2005 Proof	Est. 10,000	Value: 60.00				
2006 Proof	Est. 25,000	Value: 55.00				

KM# 53b 5 POUNDS
39.9400 g., 0.9167 Gold 1.1771 oz. AGW, 38.6 mm. **Ruler:** Elizabeth II **Subject:** 60th Anniversary - End of WWII **Obv:** Elizabeth II by Maklouf **Rev:** Flag waving crowd **Edge:** Reeded

Date	Mintage	F	VF	XF	Unc	BU
2005 Proof	150	Value: 2,200				

KM# 54b 5 POUNDS
39.9400 g., 0.9167 Gold 1.1771 oz. AGW, 38.6 mm. **Ruler:** Elizabeth II **Subject:** WWII Liberation **Obv:** Elizabeth II by Maklouf **Rev:** Churchill flashing the "V" sign **Edge:** Reeded

Date	Mintage	F	VF	XF	Unc	BU
2005 Proof	150	Value: 2,200				

KM# 53 5 POUNDS
Copper-Nickel, 38.61 mm. **Ruler:** Elizabeth II **Subject:** End of World War II, 60th Anniversary

Date	Mintage	F	VF	XF	Unc	BU
2005	—	—	—	—	—	15.00

KM# 54 5 POUNDS
28.2800 g., Copper-Nickel, 38.61 mm. **Ruler:** Elizabeth II **Subject:** Winston Churchill

Date	Mintage	F	VF	XF	Unc	BU
2005	Est. 5,000	—	—	—	—	15.00

KM# 54a 5 POUNDS
39.9400 g., 0.9160 Silver 1.1762 oz. ASW, 38.61 mm. **Ruler:** Elizabeth II **Subject:** Sir Winston Churchill

Date	Mintage	F	VF	XF	Unc	BU
2005 Proof	—	Value: 65.00				

KM# 66 5 POUNDS
28.2800 g., Copper-Nickel, 38.6 mm. **Ruler:** Elizabeth II **Subject:** Viscount Samuel Hood on his flagship after the Battle of Saints Passage in 1782 **Obv:** Queen's portrait

Date	Mintage	F	VF	XF	Unc	BU
2005	—	—	—	—	13.50	15.00

KM# 66a 5 POUNDS
28.2800 g., 0.9250 Silver 0.8410 oz. ASW, 38.6 mm. **Ruler:** Elizabeth II **Subject:** Viscount Samuel Hood on his flagship after the Battle of Saints Passage in 1782 **Obv:** Queen's portrait **Note:** Ensign is colored.

Date	Mintage	F	VF	XF	Unc	BU
2005 Proof	—	Value: 50.00				

KM# 68 5 POUNDS
28.2800 g., Copper-Nickel, 38.6 mm. **Ruler:** Elizabeth II **Obv:** Crowned head right **Rev:** HMS Revenge fighting at Azores, 1591

Date	Mintage	F	VF	XF	Unc	BU
2005	—	—	—	—	12.00	14.00

KM# 68a 5 POUNDS
28.2800 g., 0.9250 Silver 0.8410 oz. ASW, 38.6 mm. **Ruler:** Elizabeth II **Obv:** Crowned head right **Rev:** HMS Revenge fighting at Azores, 1591 **Note:** Ensign is colorized.

Date	Mintage	F	VF	XF	Unc	BU
2005 Proof	—	Value: 60.00				

KM# 79 5 POUNDS
28.2800 g., Copper-Nickel, 38.61 mm. **Ruler:** Elizabeth II **Subject:** 200th Anniversary Battle of Trafalgar **Obv:** Crowned head right

Date	Mintage	F	VF	XF	Unc	BU
2005	—	—	—	—	16.00	18.50

KM# 79a 5 POUNDS
28.2800 g., 0.9250 Silver 0.8410 oz. ASW **Ruler:** Elizabeth II **Subject:** 200th Anniversary Battle of Trafalgar **Obv:** Crowned head right

Date	Mintage	F	VF	XF	Unc	BU
2005 Proof	—	Value: 60.00				

KM# 83 5 POUNDS
28.2800 g., Copper-Nickel, 38.61 mm. **Ruler:** Elizabeth II **Subject:** Royal Navy - Admiral Sir John Foster Woodward

Date	Mintage	F	VF	XF	Unc	BU
2005	—	—	—	—	—	15.00

KM# 83a 5 POUNDS
28.2800 g., 0.9250 Silver 0.8410 oz. ASW, 38.61 mm. **Ruler:** Elizabeth II **Subject:** History of the Royal Navy **Obv:** Heraldic shield **Rev:** Admiral John Woodward, partially colored

Date	Mintage	F	VF	XF	Unc	BU
2005 Proof	—	Value: 45.00				

KM# 99 5 POUNDS
28.2800 g., 0.9250 Silver 0.8410 oz. ASW, 38.61 mm. **Ruler:** Elizabeth II **Subject:** Wayne Rooney **Obv:** Shield **Rev:** Soccer player and ball design

Date	Mintage	F	VF	XF	Unc	BU
2005 Proof	—	Value: 45.00				

KM# 100 5 POUNDS
28.2800 g., 0.9250 Silver 0.8410 oz. ASW, 38.61 mm. **Ruler:** Elizabeth II **Subject:** Frank Lampard **Obv:** Shield **Rev:** Soccer player and ball design

Date	Mintage	F	VF	XF	Unc	BU
2005 Proof	—	Value: 45.00				

KM# 101 5 POUNDS
28.2800 g., 0.9250 Silver 0.8410 oz. ASW, 38.61 mm. **Ruler:** Elizabeth II **Obv:** Shield **Rev:** Soccer player and ball design

Date	Mintage	F	VF	XF	Unc	BU
2005 Proof	—	Value: 45.00				

KM# 102 5 POUNDS
28.2800 g., 0.9250 Silver 0.8410 oz. ASW, 38.61 mm. **Ruler:** Elizabeth II **Subject:** Steven Gerrard **Obv:** Shield **Rev:** Soccer player and ball design

Date	Mintage	F	VF	XF	Unc	BU
2005 Proof	—	Value: 45.00				

KM# 103 5 POUNDS
28.2800 g., 0.9250 Silver 0.8410 oz. ASW, 38.61 mm. **Ruler:** Elizabeth II **Obv:** Shield **Rev:** Soccer player and ball design

Date	Mintage	F	VF	XF	Unc	BU
2005 Proof	—	Value: 45.00				

KM# 104 5 POUNDS
28.2800 g., 0.9250 Silver 0.8410 oz. ASW, 38.61 mm. **Ruler:** Elizabeth II **Obv:** Shield **Rev:** Soccer player and ball design

Date	Mintage	F	VF	XF	Unc	BU
2005 Proof	—	Value: 45.00				

KM# 105 5 POUNDS
28.2800 g., 0.9250 Silver 0.8410 oz. ASW, 38.61 mm. **Ruler:** Elizabeth II **Obv:** Shield **Rev:** Soccer player and ball design

Date	Mintage	F	VF	XF	Unc	BU
2005 Proof	—	Value: 45.00				

KM# 106 5 POUNDS
28.2800 g., 0.9250 Silver 0.8410 oz. ASW, 38.61 mm. **Ruler:** Elizabeth II **Obv:** Shield **Rev:** Soccer player and ball design

Date	Mintage	F	VF	XF	Unc	BU
2005 Proof	—	Value: 45.00				

KM# 107 5 POUNDS
28.2800 g., 0.9250 Silver 0.8410 oz. ASW, 38.61 mm. **Ruler:** Elizabeth II **Obv:** Shield **Rev:** Soccer player and ball design

Date	Mintage	F	VF	XF	Unc	BU
2005 Proof	—	Value: 45.00				

KM# 108 5 POUNDS
28.2500 g., 0.9250 Silver 0.8401 oz. ASW, 38.61 mm. **Ruler:** Elizabeth II **Obv:** Shield **Rev:** Soccer player and ball design

Date	Mintage	F	VF	XF	Unc	BU
2005 Proof	—	Value: 45.00				

KM# 113 5 POUNDS
28.2800 g., Copper-Nickel, 38.61 mm. **Ruler:** Elizabeth II **Subject:** Prince William, 21st Birthday

Date	Mintage	F	VF	XF	Unc	BU
2005	—	—	—	—	—	15.00

KM# 113a 5 POUNDS
28.2800 g., 0.9250 Silver 0.8410 oz. ASW, 38.61 mm. **Ruler:** Elizabeth II **Subject:** Prince William, 21st Birthday

Date	Mintage	F	VF	XF	Unc	BU
2005 Proof	Est. 2,500	Value: 60.00				

KM# 113b 5 POUNDS
39.9400 g., 0.9167 Gold 1.1771 oz. AGW, 38.61 mm. **Ruler:** Elizabeth II **Subject:** Prince William, 21st Birthday

Date	Mintage	F	VF	XF	Unc	BU
2005 Proof	Est. 150	Value: 2,200				

KM# 116 5 POUNDS
28.2800 g., Copper-Nickel, 38.61 mm. **Ruler:** Elizabeth II **Subject:** Royal Navy - H.M.S. Warspite

Date	Mintage	F	VF	XF	Unc	BU
2005	—	—	—	—	—	15.00

KM# 116a 5 POUNDS
28.2800 g., 0.9250 Silver 0.8410 oz. ASW, 38.61 mm. **Ruler:** Elizabeth II **Subject:** British Navy - H.M.S. Warspite **Rev:** Multicolor flag

Date	Mintage	F	VF	XF	Unc	BU
2005 Proof	Est. 15,000	Value: 55.00				

KM# 70 5 POUNDS
28.2800 g., 0.9250 Silver 0.8410 oz. ASW, 38.6 mm. **Ruler:** Elizabeth II **Subject:** Queen's 80th Birthday **Obv:** Crowned bust right - gilt **Obv. Legend:** ELIZABETH II - ALDERNEY **Rev:** 1/2 length figures of Queen mother and daughter hugging, facing

Date	Mintage	F	VF	XF	Unc	BU
2006 Proof	—	Value: 45.00				

KM# 126 5 POUNDS
28.2800 g., Copper-Nickel, 38.61 mm. **Ruler:** Elizabeth II **Rev:** Elizabeth I

Date	Mintage	F	VF	XF	Unc	BU
2006	—	—	—	—	—	12.00

KM# 126a 5 POUNDS
28.2800 g., 0.9250 Silver 0.8410 oz. ASW, 38.61 mm. **Ruler:** Elizabeth II **Rev:** Queen Elizabeth I

Date	Mintage	F	VF	XF	Unc	BU
2006 Proof	Est. 25,000	Value: 55.00				

KM# 126b 5 POUNDS
39.9400 g., 0.9160 Gold 1.1762 oz. AGW, 38.61 mm. **Ruler:** Elizabeth II **Rev:** Queen Elizabeth I

Date	Mintage	F	VF	XF	Unc	BU
2006 Proof	—	Value: 2,250				

KM# 127 5 POUNDS
28.2800 g., Copper-Nickel, 38.61 mm. **Ruler:** Elizabeth II **Rev:** Sir Isaac Newton

Date	Mintage	F	VF	XF	Unc	BU
2006	—	—	—	—	—	15.00

KM# 127a 5 POUNDS
28.2800 g., 0.9250 Silver 0.8410 oz. ASW, 38.61 mm. **Ruler:** Elizabeth II **Rev:** Sir Isaac Newton

Date	Mintage	F	VF	XF	Unc	BU
2006 Proof	—	Value: 55.00				

KM# 127b 5 POUNDS
39.9400 g., 0.9167 Gold 1.1771 oz. AGW, 38.61 mm. **Ruler:** Elizabeth II **Rev:** Sir Isaac Newton

Date	Mintage	F	VF	XF	Unc	BU
2006 Proof	—	Value: 2,250				

KM# 128 5 POUNDS
28.2800 g., Copper-Nickel, 38.61 mm. **Ruler:** Elizabeth II **Rev:** William Shakespeare

Date	Mintage	F	VF	XF	Unc	BU
2006	—	—	—	—	—	15.00

KM# 128a 5 POUNDS
28.2800 g., 0.9250 Silver 0.8410 oz. ASW, 38.61 mm. **Ruler:** Elizabeth II **Rev:** William Shakespeare

Date	Mintage	F	VF	XF	Unc	BU
2006 Proof	—	Value: 55.00				

KM# 128b 5 POUNDS
39.9400 g., 0.9160 Gold 1.1762 oz. AGW, 38.61 mm. **Ruler:** Elizabeth II **Rev:** William Shakespeare

Date	Mintage	F	VF	XF	Unc	BU
2006 Proof	—	Value: 2,250				

KM# 129 5 POUNDS
28.2800 g., Copper-Nickel, 38.61 mm. **Ruler:** Elizabeth II **Rev:** Charles Dickens

Date	Mintage	F	VF	XF	Unc	BU
2006	—	—	—	—	—	15.00

KM# 129a 5 POUNDS
28.2800 g., 0.9250 Silver 0.8410 oz. ASW, 38.61 mm. **Ruler:** Elizabeth II **Rev:** Charles Dickens

Date	Mintage	F	VF	XF	Unc	BU
2006 Proof	—	Value: 55.00				

KM# 129b 5 POUNDS
39.9400 g., 0.9160 Gold 1.1762 oz. AGW, 38.61 mm. **Ruler:** Elizabeth II **Rev:** Charles Dickens

Date	Mintage	F	VF	XF	Unc	BU
2006 Proof	—	Value: 2,250				

KM# 132 5 POUNDS
28.2800 g., Copper-Nickel, 38.61 mm. **Ruler:** Elizabeth II **Rev:** Elizabeth II Coronation

Date	Mintage	F	VF	XF	Unc	BU
2006	—	—	—	—	—	15.00

KM# 132a 5 POUNDS
28.2800 g., 0.9250 Silver 0.8410 oz. ASW, 38.61 mm. **Ruler:** Elizabeth II **Rev:** Elizabeth II Corronation

Date	Mintage	F	VF	XF	Unc	BU
2006 Proof	Est. 25,000	Value: 55.00				

KM# 133 5 POUNDS
28.2800 g., Copper-Nickel, 38.61 mm. **Ruler:** Elizabeth II **Obv:** Head in tiara right **Rev:** Bust in tiara right

Date	Mintage	F	VF	XF	Unc	BU
2006	—	—	—	—	—	15.00

KM# 133a 5 POUNDS
28.2800 g., 0.9250 Silver 0.8410 oz. ASW, 38.61 mm. **Ruler:** Elizabeth II **Obv:** Head in tiara right **Rev:** Bust in tiara right

Date	Mintage	F	VF	XF	Unc	BU
2006 Proof	—	Value: 55.00				

KM# 133b 5 POUNDS
39.9400 g., 0.9167 Gold 1.1771 oz. AGW, 38.61 mm. **Ruler:** Elizabeth II **Obv:** Head in tiara right **Rev:** Bust in tiara right

Date	Mintage	F	VF	XF	Unc	BU
2006 Proof	—	Value: 2,250				

KM# 133b.1 5 POUNDS
39.9400 g., 0.9167 Gold with diamonds 1.1771 oz. AGW, 38.61 mm. **Ruler:** Elizabeth II **Obv:** Head in tiara right **Rev:** Bust in tiara right

Date	Mintage	F	VF	XF	Unc	BU
2006 Proof	—	Value: 2,500				

KM# 138 5 POUNDS
28.2800 g., 0.9250 Silver 0.8410 oz. ASW, 38.61 mm. **Ruler:** Elizabeth II **Obv:** Shield **Rev:** Soccer player

Date	Mintage	F	VF	XF	Unc	BU
2006 Proof	—	Value: 55.00				

KM# 139 5 POUNDS
28.2800 g., 0.9250 Silver 0.8410 oz. ASW, 38.61 mm. **Ruler:** Elizabeth II **Obv:** Shield **Rev:** Soccer player

Date	Mintage	F	VF	XF	Unc	BU
2006 Proof	—	Value: 55.00				

KM# 140 5 POUNDS
28.2800 g., 0.9250 Silver 0.8410 oz. ASW, 38.61 mm. **Ruler:** Elizabeth II **Obv:** Shield **Rev:** Soccer player

Date	Mintage	F	VF	XF	Unc	BU
2006 Proof	—	Value: 55.00				

KM# 141 5 POUNDS
28.2800 g., 0.9250 Silver 0.8410 oz. ASW, 38.61 mm. **Ruler:** Elizabeth II **Obv:** Shield **Rev:** Soccer player

Date	Mintage	F	VF	XF	Unc	BU
2006 Proof	—	Value: 55.00				

KM# 142 5 POUNDS
28.2800 g., 0.9250 Silver 0.8410 oz. ASW, 38.61 mm. **Ruler:** Elizabeth II **Obv:** Shield **Rev:** Soccer player

Date	Mintage	F	VF	XF	Unc	BU
2006 Proof	—	Value: 55.00				

KM# 143 5 POUNDS
28.2800 g., 0.9250 Silver 0.8410 oz. ASW, 38.61 mm. **Ruler:** Elizabeth II **Obv:** Shield **Rev:** Soccer player

Date	Mintage	F	VF	XF	Unc	BU
2006 Proof	—	Value: 55.00				

KM# 144 5 POUNDS
28.2800 g., 0.9250 Silver 0.8410 oz. ASW, 38.61 mm. **Ruler:** Elizabeth II **Obv:** Shield **Rev:** Soccer player

Date	Mintage	F	VF	XF	Unc	BU
2006 Proof	—	Value: 55.00				

KM# 145 5 POUNDS

28.2800 g., 0.9250 Silver 0.8410 oz. ASW, 38.61 mm. **Ruler:** Elizabeth II **Obv:** Shield **Rev:** Soccer player

Date	Mintage	F	VF	XF	Unc	BU
2006 Proof	—	Value: 55.00				

KM# 146 5 POUNDS

28.2800 g., 0.9250 Silver 0.8410 oz. ASW, 38.61 mm. **Ruler:** Elizabeth II **Obv:** Shield **Rev:** Soccer player

Date	Mintage	F	VF	XF	Unc	BU
2006 Proof	—	Value: 55.00				

KM# 147 5 POUNDS

28.2800 g., 0.9250 Silver 0.8410 oz. ASW, 38.61 mm. **Ruler:** Elizabeth II **Obv:** Shield **Rev:** Soccer player

Date	Mintage	F	VF	XF	Unc	BU
2006 Proof	—	Value: 55.00				

KM# 148 5 POUNDS

28.2800 g., Copper-Nickel, 38.61 mm. **Ruler:** Elizabeth II **Subject:** Victoria Cross, 150th Anniversary **Rev:** Henry Ramage and Victoria Cross medal

Date	Mintage	F	VF	XF	Unc	BU
2006	—	—	—	—	—	15.00

KM# 148a 5 POUNDS

28.2800 g., 0.9250 Silver 0.8410 oz. ASW, 38.61 mm. **Ruler:** Elizabeth II **Subject:** Victoria Cross, 150th Anniversary **Rev:** Henry Ramage and Victoria Cross medal

Date	Mintage	F	VF	XF	Unc	BU
2006 Proof	Est. 30,000	Value: 55.00				

KM# 149 5 POUNDS

28.2800 g., 0.9250 Silver 0.8410 oz. ASW, 38.61 mm. **Ruler:** Elizabeth II **Subject:** Victoria Cross, 150th Anniversary **Rev:** Charles Lucas, Victoria Cross medal

Date	Mintage	F	VF	XF	Unc	BU
2006 Proof	Est. 30,000	Value: 55.00				

KM# 150 5 POUNDS

28.2800 g., 0.9250 Silver 0.8410 oz. ASW, 38.61 mm. **Ruler:** Elizabeth II **Subject:** Victoria Cross, 150th Anniversary **Rev:** Ernest Smith, Victoria Cross medal

Date	Mintage	F	VF	XF	Unc	BU
2006 Proof	Est. 30,000	Value: 55.00				

KM# 151 5 POUNDS

28.2800 g., 0.9250 Silver 0.8410 oz. ASW, 38.61 mm. **Ruler:** Elizabeth II **Subject:** Victoria Cross, 150th Anniversary **Rev:** Stanley Hollis, Victoria Cross medal

Date	Mintage	F	VF	XF	Unc	BU
2006 Proof	Est. 30,000	Value: 55.00				

KM# 152 5 POUNDS

28.2800 g., 0.9250 Silver 0.8410 oz. ASW, 38.61 mm. **Ruler:** Elizabeth II **Subject:** Victoria Cross, 150th Anniversary **Rev:** Geoffrey Keyes, Victoria Cross medal

Date	Mintage	F	VF	XF	Unc	BU
2006 Proof	Est. 30,000	Value: 55.00				

KM# 153 5 POUNDS

28.2800 g., 0.9250 Silver 0.8410 oz. ASW, 38.61 mm. **Ruler:** Elizabeth II **Subject:** Victoria Cross, 150th Anniversary **Rev:** Daniel Laidlow, Victoria Cross medal

Date	Mintage	F	VF	XF	Unc	BU
2006 Proof	Est. 30,000	Value: 55.00				

KM# 158 5 POUNDS

28.2800 g., Copper-Nickel, 38.61 mm. **Ruler:** Elizabeth II **Rev:** Capt. James Cook

Date	Mintage	F	VF	XF	Unc	BU
2007	—	—	—	—	—	15.00

KM# 158a 5 POUNDS

28.2800 g., 0.9250 Silver 0.8410 oz. ASW, 38.61 mm. **Ruler:** Elizabeth II **Rev:** Capt. Jmes Cook

Date	Mintage	F	VF	XF	Unc	BU
2007 Proof	Est. 25,000	Value: 55.00				

KM# 158b 5 POUNDS

39.9400 g., 0.9160 Gold 1.1762 oz. AGW, 38.61 mm. **Ruler:** Elizabeth II **Rev:** Capt. James Cook

Date	Mintage	F	VF	XF	Unc	BU
2007 Proof	—	Value: 2,250				

KM# 159 5 POUNDS

28.2800 g., Copper-Nickel, 38.61 mm. **Ruler:** Elizabeth II **Rev:** Sir Edward Elgar

Date	Mintage	F	VF	XF	Unc	BU
2007	—	—	—	—	—	15.00

KM# 159a 5 POUNDS

28.2800 g., 0.9250 Silver 0.8410 oz. ASW, 38.61 mm. **Ruler:** Elizabeth II **Rev:** Sir Edward Elgar

Date	Mintage	F	VF	XF	Unc	BU
2007 Proof	Est. 25,000	Value: 55.00				

KM# 159b 5 POUNDS

39.9400 g., 0.9167 Gold 1.1771 oz. AGW, 38.61 mm. **Ruler:** Elizabeth II **Rev:** Sir Edward Elgar

Date	Mintage	F	VF	XF	Unc	BU
2007 Proof	—	Value: 2,250				

KM# 160 5 POUNDS

28.2800 g., Copper-Nickel, 38.61 mm. **Ruler:** Elizabeth II **Rev:** Sir Francis Drake

Date	Mintage	F	VF	XF	Unc	BU
2007	—	Value: 15.00				

KM# 160a 5 POUNDS

28.2800 g., 0.9250 Silver 0.8410 oz. ASW, 38.61 mm. **Ruler:** Elizabeth II **Rev:** Sir Francis Drake

Date	Mintage	F	VF	XF	Unc	BU
2007 Proof	Est. 25,000	Value: 55.00				

KM# 160b 5 POUNDS

39.9400 g., 0.9167 Gold 1.1771 oz. AGW, 38.61 mm. **Ruler:** Elizabeth II **Rev:** Sir Francis Drake

Date	Mintage	F	VF	XF	Unc	BU
2007 Proof	—	Value: 2,250				

KM# 161 5 POUNDS

28.2800 g., Copper-Nickel, 38.61 mm. **Ruler:** Elizabeth II **Rev:** John Constable

Date	Mintage	F	VF	XF	Unc	BU
2007	—	—	—	—	—	15.00

KM# 161a 5 POUNDS

28.2800 g., 0.9250 Silver 0.8410 oz. ASW, 38.61 mm. **Ruler:** Elizabeth II **Rev:** John Constable

Date	Mintage	F	VF	XF	Unc	BU
2007 Proof	Est. 25,000	Value: 55.00				

KM# 162 5 POUNDS

28.2800 g., 0.9250 Silver partially gilt 0.8410 oz. ASW, 38.61 mm. **Ruler:** Elizabeth II **Rev:** Henry VII

Date	Mintage	F	VF	XF	Unc	BU
2007 Proof	Est. 37,500	Value: 55.00				

KM# 161b 5 POUNDS

39.9400 g., 0.9167 Gold 1.1771 oz. AGW, 39.94 mm. **Ruler:** Elizabeth II **Rev:** John Constable

Date	Mintage	F	VF	XF	Unc	BU
2007 Proof	—	Value: 2,250				

KM# 163 5 POUNDS

28.2800 g., 0.9250 Silver partially gilt 0.8410 oz. ASW, 38.61 mm. **Ruler:** Elizabeth II **Rev:** Henry VIII

Date	Mintage	F	VF	XF	Unc	BU
2007 Proof	Est. 37,500	Value: 55.00				

KM# 164 5 POUNDS

28.2800 g., 0.9250 Silver partially gilt 0.8410 oz. ASW, 38.61 mm. **Ruler:** Elizabeth II **Rev:** Edward VI

Date	Mintage	F	VF	XF	Unc	BU
2007 Proof	Est. 37,500	Value: 55.00				

KM# 165 5 POUNDS

28.2800 g., 0.9250 Silver partially gilt 0.8410 oz. ASW, 38.61 mm. **Ruler:** Elizabeth II **Rev:** Mary I

Date	Mintage	F	VF	XF	Unc	BU
2007 Proof	Est. 37,500	Value: 55.00				

KM# 166 5 POUNDS

28.2800 g., 0.9250 Silver 0.8410 oz. ASW, 38.61 mm. **Ruler:** Elizabeth II **Rev:** Elizabeth I

Date	Mintage	F	VF	XF	Unc	BU
2007 Proof	Est. 37,500	Value: 55.00				

KM# 167 5 POUNDS

28.2800 g., 0.9250 Silver partially gilt 0.8410 oz. ASW, 38.61 mm. **Ruler:** Elizabeth II **Rev:** James I

Date	Mintage	F	VF	XF	Unc	BU
2007 Proof	Est. 37,500	Value: 55.00				

KM# 168 5 POUNDS

28.2800 g., 0.9250 Silver 0.8410 oz. ASW, 38.61 mm. **Ruler:** Elizabeth II **Rev:** Charles I

Date	Mintage	F	VF	XF	Unc	BU
2007 Proof	Est. 37,500	Value: 55.00				

KM# 169 5 POUNDS

28.2800 g., 0.9250 Silver partially gilt 0.8410 oz. ASW, 38.61 mm. **Ruler:** Elizabeth II **Rev:** Charles II

Date	Mintage	F	VF	XF	Unc	BU
2007 Proof	Est. 37,500	Value: 55.00				

KM# 170 5 POUNDS

28.2800 g., 0.9160 Silver partially gilt 0.8328 oz. ASW, 38.61 mm. **Ruler:** Elizabeth II **Rev:** James II

Date	Mintage	F	VF	XF	Unc	BU
2007 Proof	Est. 37,500	Value: 55.00				

KM# 171 5 POUNDS

28.2800 g., 0.9250 Silver partially gilt 0.8410 oz. ASW, 38.61 mm. **Ruler:** Elizabeth II **Rev:** William and Mary

Date	Mintage	F	VF	XF	Unc	BU
2007 Proof	Est. 37,500	Value: 55.00				

KM# 172 5 POUNDS

28.2800 g., 0.9250 Silver partially gilt 0.8410 oz. ASW, 38.61 mm. **Ruler:** Elizabeth II **Rev:** William III

Date	Mintage	F	VF	XF	Unc	BU
2007 Proof	37,500	Value: 55.00				

KM# 173 5 POUNDS

28.2800 g., 0.9250 Silver 0.8410 oz. ASW, 38.61 mm. **Ruler:** Elizabeth II **Rev:** Anne

Date	Mintage	F	VF	XF	Unc	BU
2007 Proof	Est. 37,500	Value: 55.00				

KM# 175 5 POUNDS

28.2800 g., Copper-Nickel, 38.61 mm. **Ruler:** Elizabeth II **Subject:** Princess Diana, 10th Anniversary of Death

Date	Mintage	F	VF	XF	Unc	BU
2007	—	—	—	—	—	15.00

KM# 177 5 POUNDS

28.2800 g., Copper-Nickel, 38.61 mm. **Ruler:** Elizabeth II **Subject:** Elizabeth II & Prince Philip, 60th Wedding Anniversary **Rev:** 1947 Wedding Portrait

Date	Mintage	F	VF	XF	Unc	BU
2007	—	—	—	—	—	15.00

KM# 177a 5 POUNDS

28.2800 g., 0.9250 Silver 0.8410 oz. ASW, 38.61 mm. **Ruler:** Elizabeth II **Subject:** Elizabeth II and Prince Philip, 60th Wedding Anniversary **Rev:** 1947 Wedding Portrait

Date	Mintage	F	VF	XF	Unc	BU
2007 Proof	—	Value: 55.00				

KM# 178 5 POUNDS

28.2800 g., Copper-Nickel, 38.61 mm. **Ruler:** Elizabeth II **Subject:** Elizabeth II and Prince Philip, 60th Wedding Anniversary **Rev:** State Carriage

Date	Mintage	F	VF	XF	Unc	BU
2007	—	—	—	—	—	15.00

KM# 178a 5 POUNDS

28.2800 g., 0.9250 Silver 0.8410 oz. ASW, 38.61 mm. **Ruler:** Elizabeth II **Subject:** Elizabeth II and Prince Philip, 60th Wedding Anniversary **Rev:** State Carriage

Date	Mintage	F	VF	XF	Unc	BU
2007 Proof	—	Value: 55.00				

KM# 179 5 POUNDS

28.2800 g., Copper-Nickel, 38.61 mm. **Ruler:** Elizabeth II **Subject:** Elizabeth II and Prince Philip, 60th Wedding Anniversary **Rev:** Honeymoon departure

Date	Mintage	F	VF	XF	Unc	BU
2007	—	—	—	—	—	15.00

KM# 179a 5 POUNDS

28.2800 g., 0.9250 Silver 0.8410 oz. ASW, 38.61 mm. **Ruler:** Elizabeth II **Subject:** Elizabeth II and Prince Philip, 60th Wedding Anniversary **Rev:** Honeymoon departure

Date	Mintage	F	VF	XF	Unc	BU
2007 Proof	—	Value: 55.00				

KM# 180 5 POUNDS

28.2800 g., Copper-Nickel, 38.61 mm. **Ruler:** Elizabeth II **Subject:** Elizabeth II and Prince Philip, 60th Wedding Anniversary **Rev:** Portraits

Date	Mintage	F	VF	XF	Unc	BU
2007	—	—	—	—	—	15.00

KM# 180a 5 POUNDS

28.2800 g., 0.9250 Silver 0.8410 oz. ASW, 38.61 mm. **Ruler:** Elizabeth II **Subject:** Elizabeth II and Prince Philip, 60th Wedding Anniversary **Rev:** Elizabeth II and Philip portraits

Date	Mintage	F	VF	XF	Unc	BU
2007 Proof	—	Value: 55.00				

KM# 181 5 POUNDS

28.2800 g., 0.9250 Silver 0.8410 oz. ASW, 38.61 mm. **Ruler:** Elizabeth II **Subject:** Elizabeth II and Prince Philip, 60th Wedding Anniversary **Rev:** Bridal couple outside Westminster Abbey

Date	Mintage	F	VF	XF	Unc	BU
2007 Proof	Est. 30,000	Value: 55.00				

KM# 182 5 POUNDS

28.2800 g., 0.9250 Silver 0.8410 oz. ASW, 38.61 mm. **Ruler:** Elizabeth II **Subject:** Elizabeth II and Prince Philip, 60th Wedding Anniversary **Rev:** Birth of Prince Charles

Date	Mintage	F	VF	XF	Unc	BU
2007 Proof	Est. 30,000	Value: 55.00				

KM# 183 5 POUNDS

28.2800 g., 0.9250 Silver 0.8410 oz. ASW, 38.61 mm. **Ruler:** Elizabeth II **Subject:** Elizabeth II and Prince Philip, 60th Wedding Anniversary **Rev:** Modern portrait of Elizabeth and Philip

Date	Mintage	F	VF	XF	Unc	BU
2007 Proof	Est. 30,000	Value: 55.00				

KM# 184 5 POUNDS

28.2800 g., 0.9250 Silver 0.8410 oz. ASW, 38.61 mm. **Ruler:** Elizabeth II **Subject:** End of World War I, 90th Anniversary **Rev:** Soldiers and workers, flag in background

Date	Mintage	F	VF	XF	Unc	BU
2008 Proof	Est. 15,000	Value: 55.00				

KM# 184a 5 POUNDS

39.9400 g., 0.9167 Gold 1.1771 oz. AGW, 38.61 mm. **Ruler:** Elizabeth II **Subject:** End of World War I, 90th Anniversary **Rev:** Soldiers and workers, flag in background

Date	Mintage	F	VF	XF	Unc	BU
2008 Proof	Est. 250	Value: 2,200				

KM# 185 5 POUNDS

28.2800 g., 0.9250 Silver 0.8410 oz. ASW, 38.61 mm. **Ruler:** Elizabeth II **Subject:** End of World War I, 90th Anniversary **Rev:** Tank and soldier

Date	Mintage	F	VF	XF	Unc	BU
2008 Proof	Est. 15,000	Value: 55.00				

KM# 185a 5 POUNDS

39.9400 g., 0.9167 Gold 1.1771 oz. AGW, 38.61 mm. **Ruler:** Elizabeth II **Subject:** End of World War I, 90th Anniversary **Rev:** Tank and soldier

Date	Mintage	F	VF	XF	Unc	BU
2008 Proof	Est. 250	Value: 2,200				

KM# 186 5 POUNDS

28.2800 g., 0.9250 Silver 0.8410 oz. ASW, 38.61 mm. **Ruler:** Elizabeth II **Subject:** End of World War I, 90th Anniversary **Rev:** Soldiers and gravesites

Date	Mintage	F	VF	XF	Unc	BU
2008 Proof	Est. 15,000	Value: 55.00				

KM# 186a 5 POUNDS

39.9400 g., 0.9167 Gold 1.1771 oz. AGW, 38.61 mm. **Ruler:** Elizabeth II **Subject:** End of World War I, 90th Anniversary **Rev:** Soldiers and gravesites

Date	Mintage	F	VF	XF	Unc	BU
2008 Proof	Est. 250	Value: 2,200				

KM# 187 5 POUNDS

28.2800 g., 0.9250 Silver 0.8410 oz. ASW, 38.61 mm. **Ruler:** Elizabeth II **Subject:** End of World War I, 90th Anniversary **Rev:** Propaganda

Date	Mintage	F	VF	XF	Unc	BU
2008 Proof	Est. 15,000	Value: 55.00				

KM# 190 5 POUNDS
28.2800 g., Copper-Nickel, 38.61 mm. **Ruler:** Elizabeth II **Rev:** Concorde

Date	Mintage	F	VF	XF	Unc	BU
2008	—	—	—	—	—	15.00

KM# 190a 5 POUNDS
28.2800 g., 0.9250 Silver 0.8410 oz. ASW, 38.61 mm. **Ruler:** Elizabeth II **Rev:** Concorde

Date	Mintage	F	VF	XF	Unc	BU
2008 Proof	—	Value: 55.00				

KM# 190b 5 POUNDS
39.9400 g., 0.9160 Gold 1.1762 oz. AGW, 38.61 mm. **Ruler:** Elizabeth II **Rev:** Concorde

Date	Mintage	F	VF	XF	Unc	BU
2008 Proof	Est. 250	Value: 60,000				

KM# 85 5 POUNDS
28.2800 g., Copper-Nickel, 38.61 mm. **Ruler:** Elizabeth II **Subject:** Mini Cooper 50th Anniversary **Rev:** 1959 Mini Cooper on tiled floor

Date	Mintage	F	VF	XF	Unc	BU
2009	50,000	—	—	—	—	17.50

KM# 86 5 POUNDS
28.2800 g., 0.9250 Silver 0.8410 oz. ASW, 38.61 mm. **Ruler:** Elizabeth II **Subject:** Mini Cooper, 50th Anniversary **Rev:** 1959 Mini Cooper multicolor British flag on roof

Date	Mintage	F	VF	XF	Unc	BU
2009 Proof	—	Value: 75.00				

KM# 87 5 POUNDS
28.2800 g., 0.9250 Silver 0.8410 oz. ASW, 38.61 mm. **Ruler:** Elizabeth II **Subject:** Mini Cooper, 50th Anniversary **Rev:** Mini Cooper, red and pink flowers

Date	Mintage	F	VF	XF	Unc	BU
2009 Proof	2,000	Value: 75.00				

KM# 88 5 POUNDS
28.2800 g., 0.9250 Silver 0.8410 oz. ASW, 38.61 mm. **Ruler:** Elizabeth II **Subject:** Mini Cooper, 50th Anniversary **Rev:** Mini Cooper, 4 views

Date	Mintage	F	VF	XF	Unc	BU
2009 Proof	2,000	Value: 75.00				

KM# 89 5 POUNDS
28.2800 g., 0.9250 Silver 0.8410 oz. ASW, 38.61 mm. **Ruler:** Elizabeth II **Subject:** Mini Cooper, 50th Anniversary **Rev:** Rally Minis

Date	Mintage	F	VF	XF	Unc	BU
2009 Proof	2,000	Value: 75.00				

KM# 193 5 POUNDS
28.2800 g., 0.9250 Silver 0.8410 oz. ASW, 38.61 mm. **Ruler:** Elizabeth II **Subject:** British Automobiles **Rev:** Morris Minor

Date	Mintage	F	VF	XF	Unc	BU
2009 Proof	20,000	Value: 55.00				

KM# 194 5 POUNDS
28.2800 g., 0.9250 Silver 0.8410 oz. ASW, 38.61 mm. **Ruler:** Elizabeth II **Subject:** British Automobiles **Rev:** Land Rover series 1

Date	Mintage	F	VF	XF	Unc	BU
2009 Proof	Est. 20,000	Value: 55.00				

KM# 195 5 POUNDS
28.2800 g., 0.9250 Silver 0.8410 oz. ASW, 38.61 mm. **Ruler:** Elizabeth II **Subject:** British Automobiles **Rev:** Jaguar E type series 1

Date	Mintage	F	VF	XF	Unc	BU
2009 Proof	Est. 20,000	Value: 55.00				

KM# 196 5 POUNDS
28.2800 g., 0.9250 Silver 0.8410 oz. ASW, 38.61 mm. **Ruler:** Elizabeth II **Subject:** British Automobiles **Rev:** Rolls Royce Silver Ghost

Date	Mintage	F	VF	XF	Unc	BU
2009 Proof	Est. 20,000	Value: 55.00				

KM# 197 5 POUNDS
28.2800 g., 0.9250 Silver 0.8410 oz. ASW, 38.61 mm. **Ruler:** Elizabeth II **Subject:** British Automobiles **Rev:** Austrin Seven "Baby Austin"

Date	Mintage	F	VF	XF	Unc	BU
2009 Proof	Est. 20,000	Value: 55.00				

KM# 198 5 POUNDS
28.2800 g., 0.9250 Silver 0.8410 oz. ASW, 38.61 mm. **Ruler:** Elizabeth II **Subject:** British Automobiles **Rev:** Triumph Herald

Date	Mintage	F	VF	XF	Unc	BU
2009 Proof	Est. 20,000	Value: 55.00				

KM# 199 5 POUNDS
28.2800 g., 0.9250 Silver 0.8410 oz. ASW **Ruler:** Elizabeth II **Subject:** British Automobiles **Rev:** Bentley R type Contiental

Date	Mintage	F	VF	XF	Unc	BU
2009 Proof	Est. 20,000	Value: 55.00				

KM# 200 5 POUNDS
28.2800 g., 0.9250 Silver 0.8410 oz. ASW, 38.61 mm. **Ruler:** Elizabeth II **Subject:** British Automobiles **Rev:** Lotus Elite (1957)

Date	Mintage	F	VF	XF	Unc	BU
2009 Proof	Est. 20,000	Value: 55.00				

KM# 202 5 POUNDS
28.2800 g., 0.9250 Silver 0.8410 oz. ASW, 38.61 mm. **Ruler:** Elizabeth II **Subject:** British Automobiles **Rev:** Austin healey Sprint MK 1

Date	Mintage	F	VF	XF	Unc	BU
2009 Proof	Est. 20,000	Value: 55.00				

KM# 203 5 POUNDS
28.2800 g., 0.9250 Silver 0.8410 oz. ASW, 38.61 mm. **Ruler:** Elizabeth II **Subject:** British Automobiles **Rev:** Bentley 4-1/2 Litre

Date	Mintage	F	VF	XF	Unc	BU
2009 Proof	Est. 20,000	Value: 55.00				

KM# 204 5 POUNDS
28.2800 g., 0.9250 Silver 0.8410 oz. ASW, 38.61 mm. **Ruler:** Elizabeth II **Subject:** British Automobiles **Rev:** Hillman Imp

Date	Mintage	F	VF	XF	Unc	BU
2009 Proof	Est. 20,000	Value: 55.00				

KM# 205 5 POUNDS
28.2800 g., 0.9250 Silver 0.8410 oz. ASW, 38.61 mm. **Ruler:** Elizabeth II **Subject:** British Automobiles **Rev:** MGB Roadster MK 1

Date	Mintage	F	VF	XF	Unc	BU
2009 Proof	Est. 20,000	Value: 55.00				

KM# 206 5 POUNDS
28.2800 g., 0.9250 Silver 0.8410 oz. ASW, 38.61 mm. **Ruler:** Elizabeth II **Subject:** British Automobiles **Rev:** MG TC Midget

Date	Mintage	F	VF	XF	Unc	BU
2009 Proof	Est. 20,000	Value: 55.00				

KM# 207 5 POUNDS
28.2800 g., 0.9250 Silver 0.8410 oz. ASW, 38.61 mm. **Ruler:** Elizabeth II **Subject:** British Automobiles **Rev:** BMC Mini

Date	Mintage	F	VF	XF	Unc	BU
2009 Proof	Est. 20,000	Value: 55.00				

KM# 208 5 POUNDS
28.2800 g., 0.9250 Silver 0.8410 oz. ASW, 38.61 mm. **Ruler:** Elizabeth II **Subject:** British Automobiles **Rev:** Morgan Plus Four

Date	Mintage	F	VF	XF	Unc	BU
2009 Proof	Est. 20,000	Value: 55.00				

KM# 209 5 POUNDS
28.2800 g., 0.9250 Silver 0.8410 oz. ASW, 38.61 mm. **Ruler:** Elizabeth II **Subject:** British Automobiles **Rev:** Rover P5B

Date	Mintage	F	VF	XF	Unc	BU
2009 Proof	Est. 20,000	Value: 55.00				

KM# 210 5 POUNDS
28.2800 g., 0.9250 Silver 0.8410 oz. ASW, 38.61 mm. **Ruler:** Elizabeth II **Subject:** British Automobiles **Rev:** Vauhall - Prince Henry

Date	Mintage	F	VF	XF	Unc	BU
2009 Proof	Est. 20,000	Value: 55.00				

KM# 201 5 POUNDS
28.2800 g., 0.9250 Silver 0.8410 oz. ASW, 38.61 mm. **Ruler:** Elizabeth II **Subject:** British Automobiles **Rev:** Aston Martin DB 5 (1963)

Date	Mintage	F	VF	XF	Unc	BU
2009 Proof	Est. 20,000	Value: 55.00				

KM# 218 5 POUNDS
28.2800 g., Copper-Nickel, 38.6 mm. **Ruler:** Elizabeth II **Subject:** Battle of Britain, 1940 **Obv:** Head in tiara right **Rev:** Fighter planes

Date	Mintage	F	VF	XF	Unc	BU
2010 Proof	—	Value: 20.00				

KM# 211 5 POUNDS
28.2800 g., Copper-Nickel, 38.61 mm. **Ruler:** Elizabeth II **Subject:** Engagement - Prince William and Catherine Middleton **Obv:** Head in tiara right **Rev:** Conjoined busts left

Date	Mintage	F	VF	XF	Unc	BU
2010	100,000	—	—	—	—	20.00

KM# 211a 5 POUNDS
28.2800 g., 0.9250 Silver 0.8410 oz. ASW, 38.61 mm. **Ruler:** Elizabeth II **Subject:** Engagement - Prince William and Catherine Middleton **Obv:** Head in tiara right **Rev:** Conjoined busts left

Date	Mintage	F	VF	XF	Unc	BU
2010 Proof	1,500	Value: 120				

KM# 211b 5 POUNDS
39.9400 g., 0.9167 Gold 1.1771 oz. AGW, 38.61 mm. **Ruler:** Elizabeth II **Subject:** Engagement of Prince William and Catherine Middleton **Obv:** Head in tiara right **Rev:** Conjoined busts left

Date	Mintage	F	VF	XF	Unc	BU
2010 Proof	1,000	Value: 2,300				

KM# 212 5 POUNDS
28.2800 g., Copper-Nickel, 38.61 mm. **Ruler:** Elizabeth II **Subject:** Royal Wedding **Obv:** Head with tiara right **Rev:** Catherine and William busts left

Date	Mintage	F	VF	XF	Unc	BU
2011	—	—	—	—	—	17.50

KM# 212a 5 POUNDS
28.2800 g., 0.9250 Silver 0.8410 oz. ASW, 38.61 mm. **Ruler:** Elizabeth II **Subject:** Royal Wedding **Obv:** Head with tiara right **Rev:** Catherine and William busts left

Date	Mintage	F	VF	XF	Unc	BU
2011 Proof	—	Value: 75.00				

KM# 219 5 POUNDS
28.2800 g., Copper-Nickel, 38.61 mm. **Ruler:** Elizabeth II **Subject:** Remembrance Day **Obv:** Head in tiara right **Rev:** Poppy in color

Date	Mintage	F	VF	XF	Unc	BU
2012	—	—	—	—	—	20.00

KM# 220 5 POUNDS
28.2800 g., Copper-Nickel, 38.61 mm. **Ruler:** Elizabeth II **Subject:** Titanic, 100th Anniversary **Obv:** Head with tiara right **Rev:** Female statue from titanic memorial at top left, Ship sailing to left, at right

Date	Mintage	F	VF	XF	Unc	BU
2012	—	—	—	—	—	25.00

KM# 220a 5 POUNDS
28.2800 g., 0.9250 Silver 0.8410 oz. ASW, 38.61 mm. **Ruler:** Elizabeth II **Subject:** Titanic, 100th Anniversary **Obv:** Head with tiara right **Rev:** Part of Titanic memorial at left, ship sailing left, at right

Date	Mintage	F	VF	XF	Unc	BU
2012 Proof	—	Value: 75.00				

KM# 221 5 POUNDS
28.2800 g., Copper-Nickel, 38.61 mm. **Ruler:** Elizabeth II **Subject:** Gold Cup, Ascot **Obv:** Head with tiara right **Rev:** Gold Cup, horse at right

Date	Mintage	F	VF	XF	Unc	BU
2012	—	—	—	—	—	20.00

KM# 221a 5 POUNDS
28.2800 g., 0.9250 Silver 0.8410 oz. ASW, 38.61 mm. **Ruler:** Elizabeth II **Subject:** Gold Cup, Ascot **Obv:** Head with tiara right **Rev:** Gold cup, horse at right

Date	Mintage	F	VF	XF	Unc	BU
2012 Proof	—	Value: 75.00				

KM# 36 10 POUNDS
155.5170 g., 0.9250 Silver 4.6248 oz. ASW, 65.06 mm. **Ruler:** Elizabeth II **Subject:** Last Flight of the Concorde **Obv:** Crowned bust right **Obv. Legend:** ELIIZABETH II - ALDERNEY **Rev:** Concorde in flight **Rev. Legend:** CONCORDE 1969 - 2003 **Edge:** Reeded **Note:** Illustration reduced.

Date	Mintage	F	VF	XF	Unc	BU
2003 Proof	1,969	Value: 200				

KM# 55 10 POUNDS
155.5100 g., 0.9250 Silver 4.6246 oz. ASW, 65 mm. **Ruler:** Elizabeth II **Subject:** WWII Liberation **Obv:** Elizabeth II by Maklouf sign **Rev:** Churchill flashing the "V" **Edge:** Reeded

Date	Mintage	F	VF	XF	Unc	BU
2005 Proof	1,945	Value: 350				

KM# 120 10 POUNDS
155.5000 g., 0.9250 Silver 4.6243 oz. ASW, 65 mm. **Ruler:** Elizabeth II **Subject:** Trafalgar - England espects that every man will do his duty

Date	Mintage	F	VF	XF	Unc	BU
2005 Proof	—	Value: 275				

KM# 82 10 POUNDS
155.5170 g., 0.9250 Silver 4.6248 oz. ASW, 65 mm. **Ruler:** Elizabeth II **Obv:** Crowned bust right **Obv. Legend:** ELIZABETH II - ALDERNEY **Rev:** Four small gilt coinage busts in ornate quadralobe **Rev. Legend:** + HER MAJESTY QUEEN ELIZABETH II + EIGHTIETH BIRTHDAY + **Edge:** Reeded, gilt

Date	Mintage	F	VF	XF	Unc	BU
2006 Proof	1,926	Value: 200				

KM# 135 10 POUNDS
155.5000 g., 0.9250 Silver with diamonds 4.6243 oz. ASW, 65 mm. **Ruler:** Elizabeth II **Obv:** Head in tiara right **Rev:** Bust in tiara right

Date	Mintage	F	VF	XF	Unc	BU
2006 Proof	Est. 1,000	Value: 250				

KM# 176 10 POUNDS
155.5000 g., 0.9250 Silver 4.6243 oz. ASW, 65 mm. **Ruler:** Elizabeth II **Subject:** Princess Diana, 10th Anniversary of Death

Date	Mintage	F	VF	XF	Unc	BU
2007 Proof	Est. 1,500	Value: 275				

KM# 188 10 POUNDS
155.5000 g., 0.9250 Silver 4.6243 oz. ASW, 65 mm. **Ruler:** Elizabeth II **Subject:** End of World War I, 90th Anniversary

Date	Mintage	F	VF	XF	Unc	BU
2008 Proof	Est. 150	Value: 350				

KM# 191 10 POUNDS
155.5000 g., 0.9250 Silver 4.6243 oz. ASW, 65 mm. **Ruler:** Elizabeth II **Rev:** Corcorde

Date	Mintage	F	VF	XF	Unc	BU
2008 Proof	Est. 750	Value: 275				

KM# 213 10 POUNDS
155.5000 g., 0.9250 Silver 4.6243 oz. ASW, 65 mm. **Ruler:** Elizabeth II **Subject:** Royal Wedding - Prince William and Catherine Middleton **Obv:** Head in tiara right **Rev:** Conjoined busts left, rose window in background

Date	Mintage	F	VF	XF	Unc	BU
2011 Proof	500	Value: 200				

KM# 61 25 POUNDS
7.9800 g., 0.9167 Gold 0.2352 oz. AGW, 22 mm. **Ruler:** Elizabeth II **Subject:** Queen's 75th Birthday **Obv:** Queen's portrait right **Rev:** Queen in casual dress surrounded by rose, thistle, daffodil and pimpernel

Date	Mintage	F	VF	XF	Unc	BU
2001 Proof	—	Value: 450				

KM# 74 25 POUNDS
7.9800 g., 0.9166 Gold 0.2352 oz. AGW **Ruler:** Elizabeth II **Subject:** Queen Elizabet II - Golden Jubilee of Reign **Obv:** Crowned head right **Rev:** Honor guard and trumpets

Date	Mintage	F	VF	XF	Unc	BU
2002 Proof	—	Value: 450				

KM# 28 25 POUNDS
7.9800 g., 0.9167 Gold 0.2352 oz. AGW, 22.05 mm. **Ruler:** Elizabeth II **Subject:** 5th Anniversary Death of Princess Diana **Obv:** Queen's portrait **Rev:** Diana's cameo portrait left above denomination **Edge:** Reeded

Date	Mintage	VG	F	VF	XF	Unc
2002 Proof	2,500	Value: 450				

KM# 30 25 POUNDS
7.9800 g., 0.9166 Gold 0.2352 oz. AGW, 22 mm. **Ruler:** Elizabeth II **Subject:** 150th Anniversary Death of the Duke of Wellington **Obv:** Queen's portrait **Rev:** Coat of arms, castle and portrait **Edge:** Reeded

Date	Mintage	VG	F	VF	XF	Unc
2002 Proof	2,500	Value: 450				

KM# 58 25 POUNDS
7.9800 g., 0.9166 Gold 0.2352 oz. AGW, 22 mm. **Ruler:** Elizabeth II **Subject:** Queen Elizabeth II - Golden Jubilee of Reign **Obv:** Crowned head right **Rev:** Sword hilt and denomination with royal arms in background

Date	Mintage	F	VF	XF	Unc	BU
2002 Proof	2,500	Value: 450				

KM# 32 25 POUNDS
7.9800 g., 0.9166 Gold 0.2352 oz. AGW, 22 mm. **Ruler:** Elizabeth II **Subject:** Prince William **Obv:** Queen's portrait **Rev:** Portrait with open shirt collar **Edge:** Reeded

Date	Mintage	F	VF	XF	Unc	BU
2003 Proof	1,500	Value: 450				

KM# 46 25 POUNDS
7.9800 g., 0.9167 Gold 0.2352 oz. AGW, 22 mm. **Ruler:** Elizabeth II **Obv:** Queen's portrait **Rev:** HMS Mary Rose **Edge:** Reeded

Date	Mintage	F	VF	XF	Unc	BU
2003 Proof	2,500	Value: 475				

KM# 93 25 POUNDS
7.9800 g., 0.9160 Gold 0.2350 oz. AGW **Ruler:** Elizabeth II **Subject:** Royal navy - Alfred the Great

Date	Mintage	F	VF	XF	Unc	BU
2003 Proof	Est. 1,000	Value: 500				

KM# 39 25 POUNDS
7.9800 g., 0.9167 Gold 0.2352 oz. AGW, 22 mm. **Ruler:** Elizabeth II **Subject:** D-Day **Obv:** Queen's portrait **Rev:** Battleship and transports **Edge:** Reeded

Date	Mintage	F	VF	XF	Unc	BU
2004 Proof	500	Value: 475				

KM# 50 25 POUNDS
7.9800 g., 0.9167 Gold 0.2352 oz. AGW, 22 mm. **Ruler:** Elizabeth II **Obv:** Queen's portrait **Rev:** Locomotive, The Rocket **Edge:** Reeded

Date	Mintage	F	VF	XF	Unc	BU
2004 Proof	2,500	Value: 475				

KM# 51 25 POUNDS
7.9800 g., 0.9167 Gold 0.2352 oz. AGW, 22 mm. **Ruler:** Elizabeth II **Obv:** Queen's portrait **Rev:** Locomotive, The Merchant Navy 21C1 **Edge:** Reeded

Date	Mintage	F	VF	XF	Unc	BU
2004 Proof	1,500	Value: 475				

KM# 67 25 POUNDS
7.9800 g., 0.9167 Gold 0.2352 oz. AGW, 22 mm. **Ruler:** Elizabeth II **Subject:** Viscount Samuel Hood on his flagship after the Battle of Saints Passage in 1782 **Obv:** Queen's portrait

Date	Mintage	F	VF	XF	Unc	BU
2005 Proof	—	Value: 450				

KM# 69 25 POUNDS
7.9800 g., 0.9167 Gold 0.2352 oz. AGW, 22 mm. **Ruler:** Elizabeth II **Obv:** Queen's portrait right **Rev:** HMS Revenge fighting at Azores, 1591

Date	Mintage	F	VF	XF	Unc	BU
2005 Proof	—	Value: 475				

KM# 109 25 POUNDS
7.9800 g., 0.9160 Gold 0.2350 oz. AGW **Ruler:** Elizabeth II **Subject:** David Beckham **Obv:** Shield **Rev:** Soccer player and ball design

Date	Mintage	F	VF	XF	Unc	BU
2005 Proof	Est. 5,000	Value: 500				

KM# 110 25 POUNDS
7.9800 g., 0.9160 Gold 0.2350 oz. AGW **Ruler:** Elizabeth II **Subject:** Michael Owen **Obv:** Shield **Rev:** Soccer player and ball design

Date	Mintage	F	VF	XF	Unc	BU
2005 Proof	Est. 5,000	Value: 500				

KM# 111 25 POUNDS
7.9800 g., 0.9160 Gold 0.2350 oz. AGW **Ruler:** Elizabeth II **Subject:** Lrank Lampard **Obv:** Shield **Rev:** Soccer player and ball design

Date	Mintage	F	VF	XF	Unc	BU
2005 Proof	Est. 5,000	Value: 500				

KM# 112 25 POUNDS
7.9800 g., 0.9160 Gold 0.2350 oz. AGW **Ruler:** Elizabeth II **Subject:** Jeremiah Campbell **Obv:** Shield **Rev:** Soccer player and ball design.

Date	Mintage	F	VF	XF	Unc	BU
2005 Proof	Est. 5,000	Value: 500				

KM# 117 25 POUNDS
7.9800 g., 0.9160 Gold 0.2350 oz. AGW **Ruler:** Elizabeth II **Subject:** Royal Navy - H.M.S. Warspite

Date	Mintage	F	VF	XF	Unc	BU
2005 Proof	Est. 1,500	Value: 500				

KM# 118 25 POUNDS
7.9800 g., 0.9160 Gold 0.2350 oz. AGW **Ruler:** Elizabeth II **Subject:** Royal Navy - Admiral Sir John Foster Woodward

Date	Mintage	F	VF	XF	Unc	BU
2005 Proof	Est. 1,500	Value: 500				

KM# 121 25 POUNDS
7.9800 g., 0.9160 Gold 0.2350 oz. AGW **Ruler:** Elizabeth II **Series:** Trafalgar - England expects that every man will do his duty

Date	Mintage	F	VF	XF	Unc	BU
2005 Proof	—	Value: 500				

KM# 92 50 POUNDS
1000.0000 g., Bi-Metallic .925 Silver center in .917 Gold ring, 100 mm. **Ruler:** Elizabeth II **Rev:** Coronation at Westminster

Date	Mintage	F	VF	XF	Unc	BU
2002	Est. 2,002	Value: 1,250				

KM# 62 50 POUNDS
1000.0000 g., 0.9250 Silver 29.738 oz. ASW, 100 mm. **Ruler:** Elizabeth II **Subject:** 50th Anniversary of Coronation **Obv:** Queen's portrait right **Rev:** State coach in which the Queen travelled to and from her coronation

Date	Mintage	F	VF	XF	Unc	BU
2003 Proof	—	Value: 1,150				

KM# 33 50 POUNDS
1000.0000 g., 0.9250 Silver 29.738 oz. ASW, 100 mm. **Ruler:** Elizabeth II **Subject:** Prince William **Obv:** Queen's portrait **Rev:** Portrait with open shirt collar **Edge:** Reeded

Date	Mintage	F	VF	XF	Unc	BU
2003 Proof	500	Value: 1,200				

KM# 63 50 POUNDS
1000.0000 g., 0.9250 Silver 29.738 oz. ASW, 100 mm. **Ruler:** Elizabeth II **Subject:** 50th Anniversary of Coronation **Obv:** Queen's portrait right **Rev:** St. Edward's crown, royal scepter, orb of England

Date	Mintage	F	VF	XF	Unc	BU
2003 Proof	—	Value: 1,150				

KM# 64 50 POUNDS
1000.0000 g., 0.9250 Silver 29.738 oz. ASW, 100 mm. **Ruler:** Elizabeth II **Subject:** 50th Anniversary of Coronation **Obv:** Queen's portrait right **Rev:** Queen on horseback dressed in the ceremonial uniform of the Colonel in Chief of the Household Brigade

Date	Mintage	F	VF	XF	Unc	BU
2003 Proof	—	Value: 1,150				

KM# 65 50 POUNDS

1000.0000 g., 0.9250 Silver 29.738 oz. ASW, 100 mm. **Ruler:** Elizabeth II **Subject:** 50th Anniversary of Coronation **Obv:** Queen's portrait right **Rev:** The Queen crowned, seated, holding the orb and scepter

Date	Mintage	F	VF	XF	Unc	BU
2003 Proof	—	Value: 1,150				

KM# 40 50 POUNDS

1000.0000 g., 0.9250 Silver 29.738 oz. ASW, 100 mm. **Ruler:** Elizabeth II **Subject:** D-Day **Obv:** Queen's portrait **Rev:** US and British troops wading ashore **Edge:** Reeded

Date	Mintage	F	VF	XF	Unc	BU
2004 Proof	600	Value: 1,200				

KM# 80 50 POUNDS

1000.0000 g., 0.9250 Silver 29.738 oz. ASW **Ruler:** Elizabeth II **Subject:** 200th Anniversary Battle of Trafalgar **Obv:** Crowned head right

Date	Mintage	F	VF	XF	Unc	BU
2005 Proof	—	Value: 1,200				

KM# 114 50 POUNDS

1000.0000 g., 0.9250 Silver 29.738 oz. ASW, 100 mm. **Ruler:** Elizabeth II **Subject:** Prince William, 21st Birthday

Date	Mintage	F	VF	XF	Unc	BU
2005 Proof	Est. 100	Value: 1,200				

KM# 136 50 POUNDS

1000.0000 g., 0.9250 Silver partially gilt 29.738 oz. ASW, 100 mm. **Ruler:** Elizabeth II **Rev:** Portraits of Elizabeth II and cross of 8 floral emblems

Date	Mintage	F	VF	XF	Unc	BU
2006 Proof	Est. 250	Value: 1,150				

KM# 214 50 POUNDS

1000.0000 g., 0.9250 Silver 29.738 oz. ASW, 100 mm. **Ruler:** Elizabeth II **Subject:** Royal Wedding - Prince William and Catherine Middleton **Obv:** Head in tiara right **Rev:** Conjoined busts left, roase window in background

Date	Mintage	F	VF	XF	Unc	BU
2011 Proof	—	Value: 1,150				

KM# 34 100 POUNDS

1000.0000 g., 0.9166 Gold 29.468 oz. AGW, 100 mm. **Ruler:** Elizabeth II **Subject:** Prince William **Obv:** Queen's portrait **Rev:** Portrait with open shirt collar **Edge:** Reeded

Date	Mintage	F	VF	XF	Unc	BU
2003 Proof	—	Value: 55,000				

KM# 81 100 POUNDS

1000.0000 g., 0.9166 Gold 29.468 oz. AGW **Ruler:** Elizabeth II **Subject:** 200th Anniversary Battle of Trafalgar **Obv:** Crowned head right

Date	Mintage	F	VF	XF	Unc	BU
2005 Proof	—	Value: 55,000				

KM# 37 1000 POUNDS

1090.8600 g., 0.9166 Gold 32.145 oz. AGW, 100 mm. **Ruler:** Elizabeth II **Subject:** Last Flight of the Concorde **Obv:** Queen's portrait **Rev:** Concorde in flight **Edge:** Reeded

Date	Mintage	F	VF	XF	Unc	BU
2003 Proof	34	Value: 60,000				

KM# 41 1000 POUNDS

1000.0000 g., 0.9167 Gold 29.471 oz. AGW, 100 mm. **Ruler:** Elizabeth II **Subject:** D-Day **Obv:** Queen's portrait **Rev:** US and British troops wading ashore **Edge:** Reeded

Date	Mintage	F	VF	XF	Unc	BU
2004 Proof	60	Value: 55,000				

KM# 216 1000 POUNDS

1090.0000 g., 0.9167 Gold 32.123 oz. AGW, 11 mm. **Ruler:** Elizabeth II **Subject:** Trafalgar, 200th Anniversary

Date	Mintage	F	VF	XF	Unc	BU
2005 Proof	—	Value: 60,000				

KM# 115 1000 POUNDS

1098.8600 g., 0.9160 Gold 32.360 oz. AGW, 38.61 mm. **Ruler:** Elizabeth II **Subject:** Prince William, 21st Birthday

Date	Mintage	F	VF	XF	Unc	BU
2005 Proof	Est. 21	Value: 60,000				

KM# 137 1000 POUNDS

1090.8600 g., 0.9160 Gold 32.124 oz. AGW, 100 mm. **Ruler:** Elizabeth II **Rev:** Portraits of Elizabeth II and cross of 8 floral emblems

Date	Mintage	F	VF	XF	Unc	BU
2006 Proof	—	Value: 60,000				

KM# 192 1000 POUNDS

1090.8600 g., 0.9160 Gold 32.124 oz. AGW, 100 mm. **Ruler:** Elizabeth II **Subject:** Prince Charles, 60th Birthday

Date	Mintage	F	VF	XF	Unc	BU
2008 Proof	Est. 30	Value: 60,000				

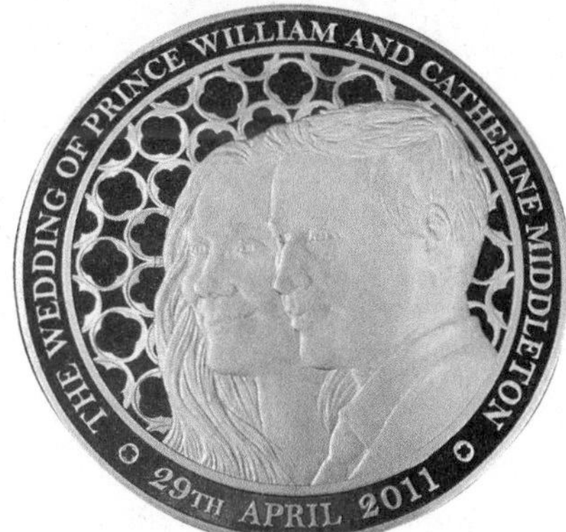

KM# 215 1000 POUNDS

1000.0000 g., 0.9160 Gold 29.448 oz. AGW, 100 mm. **Ruler:** Elizabeth II **Subject:** Royal Wedding - Prince William and Catherine Middleton **Obv:** Head in tiara right **Rev:** Conjoined busts left, rose window in background

Date	Mintage	F	VF	XF	Unc	BU
2011 Proof	—	Value: 57,500				

MINT SETS

KM#	Date	Mintage	Identification	Issue Price	Mkt Val
MS1	2004 (1)	—	Alderney KM#43, Guernsey KM#155, Jersey KM#126, 150th Anniversary of the Crimean War	—	95.00

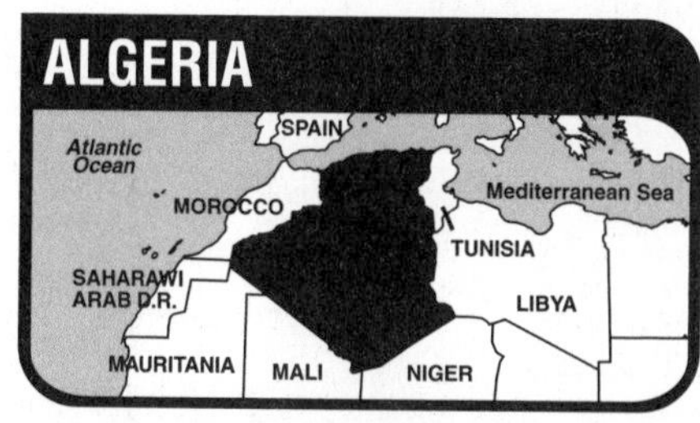

The People's Democratic Republic of Algeria, a North African country fronting on the Mediterranean Sea between Tunisia and Morocco, has an area of 919,595 sq. mi. (2,381,740 sq. km.) and a population of 31.6 million. Capital: Algiers (Alger). Most of the country's working population is engaged in agriculture although a recent industrial diversification, financed by oil revenues, is making steady progress. Wines, fruits, iron and zinc ores, phosphates, tobacco products, liquified natural gas, and petroleum are exported.

MONETARY SYSTEMS

100 Centimes = 1 Franc

REPUBLIC

STANDARD COINAGE

KM# 127 1/4 DINAR

1.1500 g., Aluminum, 16.5 mm. **Subject:** Fennec Fox **Obv:** Value in small circle **Rev:** Head facing

Date	Mintage	F	VF	XF	Unc	BU
2003-AH1423	—	—	1.50	3.00	4.50	5.50

KM# 129 DINAR

4.2400 g., Stainless Steel, 20.6 mm. **Obv:** Value on silhouette of country, within circle **Rev:** African buffalo's head 3/4 left, ancient drawings above **Edge:** Plain

Date	Mintage	F	VF	XF	Unc	BU
AH1422-2002	—	—	1.00	2.00	3.50	6.00
AH1423-2002	—	—	1.00	2.00	3.50	6.00
AH1423-2003	—	—	1.00	2.00	3.50	6.00
AH1424-2003	—	—	1.00	2.00	3.50	6.00
AH1424-2004	—	—	1.00	2.00	3.50	6.00
AH1426-2005	—	—	1.00	2.00	3.50	6.00
AH1427-2006	—	—	1.00	2.00	3.50	6.00
AH1428-2007	—	—	1.00	2.00	3.50	6.00
AH1430-2009	—	—	1.00	2.00	3.50	6.00
AH1431-2010	—	—	1.00	2.00	3.50	6.00

KM# 130 2 DINARS

5.1300 g., Stainless Steel, 22.5 mm. **Obv:** Value on silhouette of country **Rev:** Dromedary camel's head right **Edge:** Plain

Date	Mintage	F	VF	XF	Unc	BU
AH1422-2001	—	—	1.00	2.00	4.00	7.00
AH1422-2002	—	—	1.00	2.00	4.00	7.00
AH1423-2002	—	—	1.00	2.00	4.00	7.00
AH1424-2003	—	—	1.00	2.00	4.00	7.00
AH1424-2004	—	—	1.00	2.00	4.00	7.00
AH1426-2005	—	—	1.00	2.00	4.00	7.00
AH1427-2006	—	—	1.00	2.00	4.00	7.00
AH1428-2007	—	—	1.00	2.00	4.00	7.00
AH1430-2009	—	—	1.00	2.00	4.00	7.00
AH1431-2010	—	—	1.00	2.00	4.00	7.00

KM# 123 5 DINARS
6.2000 g., Stainless Steel, 24.5 mm. **Obv:** Denomination within circle **Rev:** Forepart of African elephant right **Edge:** Plain

Date	Mintage	F	VF	XF	Unc	BU
AH1422-2003	—	—	1.50	3.50	6.50	9.50
AH1423-2003	—	—	1.00	3.50	6.50	9.50
AH1424-2003	—	—	1.00	3.00	5.50	8.00
AH1424-2004	—	—	1.00	3.50	6.50	9.50
AH1426-2005	—	—	1.00	3.00	5.50	8.00
AH1426-2006	—	—	1.00	3.50	6.50	9.50
AH1427-2006	—	—	1.00	3.00	5.50	8.00
AH1428-2007	—	—	1.00	3.00	5.50	8.00
AH1429-2008	—	—	1.00	3.00	5.50	8.00
AH1430-2009	—	—	1.00	3.00	5.50	8.00
AH1431-2010	—	—	1.00	3.00	5.50	8.00
AH1432-2011	—	—	1.00	3.00	5.50	8.00

KM# 124 10 DINARS
4.9500 g., Bi-Metallic Aluminum center in Stainless Steel ring, 26.5 mm. **Obv:** Denomination **Rev:** Barbary falcon's head right **Edge:** Plain

Date	Mintage	F	VF	XF	Unc	BU
AH1422-2002	—	—	1.75	4.00	9.00	—
AH1423-2002	—	—	1.75	4.00	9.00	—
AH1424-2003	—	—	1.75	4.00	9.00	—
AH1425-2004	—	—	1.75	4.00	9.00	—
AH1426-2005	—	—	1.75	4.00	9.00	—
AH1427-2006	—	—	1.75	4.00	9.00	—
AH1428-2007	—	—	1.75	4.00	9.00	—
AH1429-2008	—	—	1.75	4.00	9.00	—
AH1430-2009	—	—	1.75	4.00	9.00	—
AH1431-2010	—	—	1.75	4.00	9.00	—
AH1432-2011	—	—	1.75	4.00	9.00	—
AH1433-2012	—	—	1.75	4.00	9.00	—

KM# 125 20 DINARS
8.6200 g., Bi-Metallic Aluminum-Bronze center in Stainless Steel ring, 27.5 mm. **Subject:** Lion **Obv:** Denomination **Rev:** Head left

Date	Mintage	F	VF	XF	Unc	BU
AH1424-2004	—	—	4.00	8.00	16.50	20.00
AH1426-2005	—	—	4.00	8.00	16.50	20.00
AH1427-2006	—	—	4.00	8.00	16.50	20.00
AH1428-2007	—	—	4.00	8.00	16.50	20.00
AH1430-2009	—	—	4.00	8.00	16.50	20.00
AH1431-2010	—	—	4.00	8.00	16.50	20.00
AH1432-2011	—	—	4.00	8.00	16.50	20.00
AM1433-2012	—	—	4.00	8.00	16.50	20.00

KM# 126 50 DINARS
9.2700 g., Bi-Metallic Stainless Steel center in Aluminum-Bronze ring, 28.5 mm. **Obv:** Denomination **Rev:** Dama gazelle with head left

Date	Mintage	F	VF	XF	Unc	BU
AH1424-2003	—	—	4.00	8.00	16.50	—
AH1425-2004	—	—	4.00	8.00	16.50	—
AH1428-2007	—	—	4.00	8.00	16.50	—
AH1429-2008	—	—	4.00	8.00	16.50	—
AH1430-2009	—	—	4.00	8.00	16.50	—
AH1432-2011	—	—	4.00	8.00	16.50	—

KM# 138 50 DINARS
9.2700 g., Bi-Metallic Stainless Steel center in Aluminum-Bronze ring, 28.5 mm. **Subject:** 50th Anniversary of Liberation **Obv:** Large value **Rev:** Stylized flag and two Moudjahid (revolutionaries)

Date	Mintage	F	VF	XF	Unc	BU
AH1425-2004	3,000,000	—	—	5.00	12.50	15.00
AH1429-2008	—	—	—	5.00	12.50	15.00

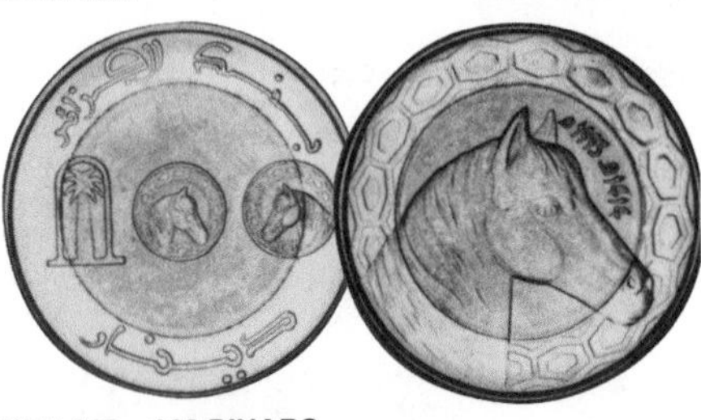

KM# 132 100 DINARS
11.0000 g., Bi-Metallic Copper-Nickel center in Stainless Steel ring, 29.5 mm. **Obv:** Denomination stylized with reverse design **Rev:** Horse head right **Edge:** Reeded

Date	Mintage	F	VF	XF	Unc	BU
AH1422-2002	—	—	6.00	12.00	22.00	26.00
AH1423-2002	—	—	6.00	12.00	22.00	26.00
AH1423-2003	—	—	6.00	12.00	22.00	26.00
AH1425-2004	—	—	6.00	12.00	22.00	26.00
AH1428-2007	—	—	6.00	12.00	22.00	26.00
AH1430-2009	—	—	6.00	12.00	22.00	26.00
AH1431-2010	—	—	6.00	12.00	22.00	26.00
AH1432-2011	—	—	6.00	12.00	22.00	26.00

KM# 137 100 DINARS
11.0000 g., Bi-Metallic Aluminum-Bronze center in Stainless Steel ring, 29.5 mm. **Subject:** 40th Anniversary of Independence **Obv:** Stylized value using palm tree in doorway and two coins depicting horses' heads **Rev:** Number 40 and stylized face **Edge:** Reeded

Date	Mintage	F	VF	XF	Unc	BU
AH1422-2002	—	—	—	—	25.00	28.00

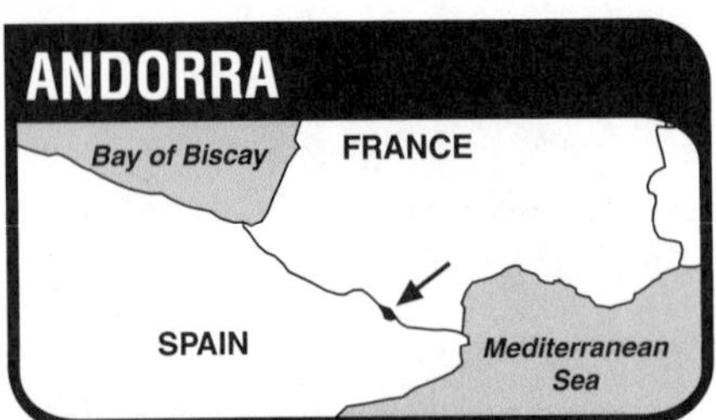

Principality of Andorra (Principat d'Andorra), situated on the southern slopes of the Pyrenees Mountains between France and Spain, has an area of 181 sq. mi. (453 sq. km.) and a population of 80,000. Capital: Andorra la Vella. Tourism is the chief source of income. Timber, cattle and derivatives, and furniture are exported.

RULER
Joan D.M. Bisbe D'Urgell I

MONETARY SYSTEM
100 Centims = 1 Diner
NOTE: The Diners have been struck for collectors while the Euro is used in everyday commerce.

MINT MARK
Crowned M = Madrid

PRINCIPALITY

DECIMAL COINAGE

KM# 176 CENTIM
2.1000 g., Aluminum, 27 mm. **Subject:** Charlemagne **Obv:** National arms, date below **Rev:** Crowned head facing, denomination below **Edge:** Plain

Date	Mintage	F	VF	XF	Unc	BU
2002	—	—	—	—	1.50	2.00

KM# 177 CENTIM
2.1300 g., Aluminum, 27 mm. **Subject:** Isard **Obv:** National arms, date below **Rev:** Chamois left facing, denomination at right **Edge:** Plain

Date	Mintage	F	VF	XF	Unc	BU
2002	—	—	—	—	1.50	2.00

KM# 178 CENTIM
2.1400 g., Aluminum, 27 mm. **Subject:** Agnus Dei **Obv:** National arms **Rev:** Lamb of God **Edge:** Plain

Date	Mintage	F	VF	XF	Unc	BU
2002	—	—	—	—	1.00	1.50

KM# 198 CENTIM
Aluminum-Magnesium, 27 mm. **Obv:** National arms **Rev:** A piece of the wall paintings belonging to the 12th century Romanesque church of St. Marti de la Cortinado

Date	Mintage	F	VF	XF	Unc	BU
2003	—	—	—	—	1.25	1.75

KM# 200 CENTIM
Aluminum-Magnesium, 27 mm. **Obv:** National arms **Rev:** Image of the 12th century Romanesque church of St. Miquel d'Engolasters with its bell tower, the Romanesque apse, the small portico and the large Lombard windows

Date	Mintage	F	VF	XF	Unc	BU
2003	—	—	—	—	1.25	1.75

KM# 199 CENTIM
Aluminum-Magnesium, 27 mm. **Obv:** National arms **Rev:** Pont de la Margineda, reproduction of the bridge

Date	Mintage	F	VF	XF	Unc	BU
2003	—	—	—	—	1.25	1.75

KM# 229 CENTIM
Aluminum **Obv:** Crowned arms **Rev:** Santa Coloma

Date	Mintage	F	VF	XF	Unc	BU
2004	—	—	—	—	0.90	1.20

KM# 230 CENTIM
Aluminum **Obv:** Crowned arms **Rev:** Sant Martí de la Cortinada

Date	Mintage	F	VF	XF	Unc	BU
2004	—	—	—	—	0.90	1.20

KM# 231 CENTIM
Aluminum **Obv:** Crowned arms **Rev:** Altar at Santa Coloma

Date	Mintage	F	VF	XF	Unc	BU
2004	—	—	—	—	0.90	1.20

KM# 236 CENTIM
2.8000 g., Brass, 18 mm. **Subject:** Death of Pope John Paul II **Obv:** National arms **Rev:** Karol Wojtyla as priest **Edge:** Reeded

Date	Mintage	F	VF	XF	Unc	BU
2005	15,000	—	—	0.30	0.80	1.20

KM# 245 CENTIM
2.8000 g., Brass, 18 mm. **Obv:** National arms **Rev:** Findern flower - Poet's Daffodil

Date	Mintage	F	VF	XF	Unc	BU
2005	15,000	—	—	—	0.80	1.20
2006	10,000	—	—	—	0.80	1.20
2007	10,000	—	—	—	0.80	1.20
2008	5,000	—	—	—	0.80	1.20

KM# 290 CENTIM
2.8000 g., Brass, 18 mm. **Obv:** National Arms **Rev:** Portrait of Joseph Ratzinger as priest **Edge:** Reeded

Date	Mintage	F	VF	XF	Unc	BU
2006	15,000	—	—	—	—	1.20

KM# 306 CENTIM
2.8000 g., Brass, 18 mm. **Subject:** Popes of the 20th Century **Obv:** National arms **Rev:** Pope Leo XIII **Edge:** Reeded

Date	Mintage	F	VF	XF	Unc	BU
2007	5,000	—	—	—	—	1.20

KM# 179 2 CENTIMS
Brass, 18 mm. **Subject:** Grandalla **Obv:** National arms **Rev:** Edelweiss flower **Edge:** Plain

Date	Mintage	F	VF	XF	Unc	BU
2002	—	—	—	—	1.50	2.00

KM# 201 2 CENTIMS
Copper-Nickel-Zinc, 18.15 mm. **Obv:** National arms **Rev:** Clavell Deltoide, a flower found in Andorra

Date	Mintage	F	VF	XF	Unc	BU
2003	—	—	—	—	1.75	2.50

KM# 232 2 CENTIMS
Brass **Obv:** Crowned arms **Rev:** West Gothic robe

Date	Mintage	F	VF	XF	Unc	BU
2004	—	—	—	—	1.20	1.60

KM# 237 2 CENTIMS
4.0000 g., Brass, 21.3 mm. **Subject:** Death of Pope John-Paul II **Obv:** National arms **Rev:** Karol Wojtyla as priest

Date	Mintage	F	VF	XF	Unc	BU
2005	15,000	—	—	0.50	1.20	1.60

KM# 246 2 CENTIMS
4.0000 g., Brass, 21.3 mm. **Obv:** National arms **Rev:** Pyrenean Chamois **Edge:** Reeded

Date	Mintage	F	VF	XF	Unc	BU
2005	15,000	—	—	—	1.20	1.60
2006	10,000	—	—	—	1.20	1.60
2007	10,000	—	—	—	1.20	1.60
2008	5,000	—	—	—	1.20	1.60

KM# 291 2 CENTIMS
4.0000 g., Brass, 21.3 mm. **Obv:** National Arms **Rev:** Portrait of Joseph Ratzinger as priest

Date	Mintage	F	VF	XF	Unc	BU
2006	15,000	—	—	—	—	1.60

KM# 307 2 CENTIMS
4.0000 g., Brass, 21.3 mm. **Subject:** Popes of the 20th Century **Obv:** National Arms **Rev:** Pope Pius X

Date	Mintage	F	VF	XF	Unc	BU
2007	5,000	—	—	—	—	1.60

KM# 282 2 CENTIMS
0.7300 g., 0.9990 Gold 0.0234 oz. AGW, 11 mm. **Subject:** Berlin Wall, 20th anniversary **Obv:** Shield **Rev:** Brandenburg Gate and brick wall **Edge:** Reeded

Date	Mintage	F	VF	XF	Unc	BU
2009 Proof	5,000	Value: 75.00				

KM# 180 5 CENTIMS
Brass, 21.8 mm. **Subject:** Squirrel **Obv:** National arms **Rev:** Red Squirrel on tree stump **Edge:** Plain

Date	Mintage	F	VF	XF	Unc	BU
2002	—	—	—	—	2.00	2.50

KM# 181 5 CENTIMS
Brass, 21.8 mm. **Subject:** Gall Fer **Obv:** National arms **Rev:** Male Eurasian Capercaillie (grouse) displaying plumage **Edge:** Plain

Date	Mintage	F	VF	XF	Unc	BU
2002	—	—	—	—	2.00	2.50

KM# 203 5 CENTIMS
Brass, 21.8 mm. **Obv:** National arms **Rev:** Wall painting from the 11th century church of Sant Serni de Nagol showing an eagle

Date	Mintage	F	VF	XF	Unc	BU
2003	—	—	—	—	2.25	2.75

KM# 202 5 CENTIMS
Brass, 21.8 mm. **Obv:** National arms **Rev:** The cross of Seven Arms, traditional Gothic cross

Date	Mintage	F	VF	XF	Unc	BU
2003	—	—	—	—	2.25	2.75

KM# 233 5 CENTIMS
Brass **Obv:** Crowned arms **Rev:** Gothic cross

Date	Mintage	F	VF	XF	Unc	BU
2004	—	—	—	—	1.80	2.40

KM# 234 5 CENTIMS
Brass **Obv:** Crowned arms **Rev:** Lady of Canolic

Date	Mintage	F	VF	XF	Unc	BU
2004	—	—	—	—	1.80	2.40

KM# 238 5 CENTIMS
5.5000 g., Brass, 24.5 mm. **Subject:** Death of Pope John-Paul II **Obv:** National arms **Rev:** Karol Wojtyla as bishop **Edge:** Reeded

Date	Mintage	F	VF	XF	Unc	BU
2005	15,000	—	—	0.70	1.80	2.40

KM# 247 5 CENTIMS
5.5000 g., Brass, 24.5 mm. **Obv:** National arms **Rev:** Wall painting from Santa Coloma church **Edge:** Reeded

Date	Mintage	F	VF	XF	Unc	BU
2005	15,000	—	—	—	1.80	2.40
2006	10,000	—	—	—	1.80	2.40
2007	10,000	—	—	—	1.80	2.40
2008	5,000	—	—	—	1.80	2.40

KM# 292 5 CENTIMS
5.5000 g., Brass, 24.5 mm. **Obv:** National Arms **Rev:** Portrait of Joseph Ratzinger as archbishop

Date	Mintage	F	VF	XF	Unc	BU
2006	15,000	—	—	—	—	2.50

KM# 308 5 CENTIMS
5.5000 g., Brass, 24.5 mm. **Subject:** Popes of the 20th Century **Obv:** National Arms **Rev:** Pope Benedict XV

Date	Mintage	F	VF	XF	Unc	BU
2007	5,000	—	—	—	—	2.40

KM# 182 10 CENTIMS
Brass **Subject:** St. Joan de Caselles **Obv:** National arms **Rev:** Tower and building **Edge:** Plain

Date	Mintage	F	VF	XF	Unc	BU
2002	—	—	—	—	3.00	4.00

KM# 204 10 CENTIMS
Nickel Plated Steel, 27.8 mm. **Obv:** National arms **Rev:** 12th century wood carving image from Our Lady of Meritxell

Date	Mintage	F	VF	XF	Unc	BU
2003	—	—	—	—	3.50	4.50

KM# 235 10 CENTIMS
Nickel Plated Steel **Obv:** Crowned arms **Rev:** Casa de la Vall

Date	Mintage	F	VF	XF	Unc	BU
2004	—	—	—	—	3.00	4.00

KM# 239 10 CENTIMS
6.5000 g., Copper-Nickel, 22.2 mm. **Subject:** Death of Pope John-Paul II **Obv:** National arms **Rev:** Karol Wojtyla as archbishop **Edge:** Reeded

Date	Mintage	F	VF	XF	Unc	BU
2005	15,000	—	—	1.00	2.40	3.20

KM# 248 10 CENTIMS
6.5000 g., Copper-Nickel, 22.2 mm. **Obv:** National arms **Rev:** Saint Vicenç d'Enclar church

Date	Mintage	F	VF	XF	Unc	BU
2005	15,000	—	—	—	2.40	3.20
2006	10,000	—	—	—	2.40	3.20
2007	10,000	—	—	—	2.40	3.20
2008	5,000	—	—	—	2.40	3.20

KM# 293 10 CENTIMS
6.5000 g., Copper-Nickel, 22.2 mm. **Obv:** National Arms **Rev:** Portrait of Joseph Ratzinger as archbishop

Date	Mintage	F	VF	XF	Unc	BU
2006	15,000	—	—	—	—	4.00

KM# 309 10 CENTIMS
6.5000 g., Copper-Nickel, 22.2 mm. **Subject:** Popes of the 20th Century **Obv:** National Arms **Rev:** Pope Pius XI

Date	Mintage	F	VF	XF	Unc	BU
2007	5,000	—	—	—	—	3.40

KM# 240 25 CENTIMS
7.7500 g., Copper-Nickel, 24.2 mm. **Subject:** Death of Pope John-Paul II **Obv:** National arms **Rev:** Karol Wojtyla as cardinal

Date	Mintage	F	VF	XF	Unc	BU
2005	15,000	—	—	1.20	3.00	4.00

KM# 249 25 CENTIMS
7.7500 g., Copper-Nickel, 24.2 mm. **Obv:** National arms **Rev:** Our Lady of Meritxell sanctuary

Date	Mintage	F	VF	XF	Unc	BU
2005	15,000	—	—	—	3.00	4.00
2006	10,000	—	—	—	3.00	4.00
2007	10,000	—	—	—	3.00	4.00
2008	5,000	—	—	—	3.00	4.00

KM# 294 25 CENTIMS
7.7500 g., Copper-Nickel, 24.2 mm. **Obv:** National Arms **Rev:** Portrait of Joseph Ratzinger as cardinal

Date	Mintage	F	VF	XF	Unc	BU
2006	15,000	—	—	—	—	4.00

KM# 310 25 CENTIMS
7.7500 g., Copper-Nickel, 24.2 mm. **Subject:** Popes of the 20th Century **Obv:** National Arms **Rev:** Pope Pius XII

Date	Mintage	F	VF	XF	Unc	BU
2007	5,000	—	—	—	—	4.00

KM# 241 50 CENTIMS
9.0000 g., Copper-Nickel, 25.9 mm. **Subject:** Death of Pope John-Paul II **Obv:** National arms **Rev:** Karol Wojtyla as cardinal

Date	Mintage	F	VF	XF	Unc	BU
2005	15,000	—	—	2.70	3.60	4.80

KM# 250 50 CENTIMS
9.0000 g., Copper-Nickel, 25.9 mm. **Obv:** National arms **Rev:** Map of Andorra, 7 towns highlighted

Date	Mintage	F	VF	XF	Unc	BU
2005	15,000	—	—	—	4.00	5.00
2006	10,000	—	—	—	4.00	5.00
2007	10,000	—	—	—	4.00	5.00
2008	5,000	—	—	—	4.00	5.00

KM# 295 50 CENTIMS
9.0000 g., Copper-Nickel, 25.9 mm. **Obv:** National Arms **Rev:** Portrait of Joseph Ratzinger as cardinal

Date	Mintage	F	VF	XF	Unc	BU
2006	15,000	—	—	—	—	4.80

KM# 311 50 CENTIMS
9.0000 g., Copper-Nickel, 25.9 mm. **Subject:** Popes of the 20th Century **Obv:** National Arms **Rev:** Pope John XXIII

Date	Mintage	F	VF	XF	Unc	BU
2007	5,000	—	—	—	—	6.00

KM# 242 DINER
8.5000 g., Bi-Metallic Brass center in Copper-Nickel ring, 24.5 mm. **Subject:** Death of Pope John-Paul II **Obv:** National arms **Rev:** Karol Wojtyla as pope **Edge:** Reeded

Date	Mintage	F	VF	XF	Unc	BU
2005	15,000	—	—	1.60	4.00	6.00

KM# 251 DINER
8.5000 g., Bi-Metallic Brass center in Copper-Nickel ring, 24.5 mm. **Obv:** National arms **Rev:** Our Lady of Meritxell **Edge:** Reeded

Date	Mintage	F	VF	XF	Unc	BU
2005	15,000	—	—	—	4.50	6.00
2006	10,000	—	—	—	4.50	6.00
2007	10,000	—	—	—	4.50	6.00
2008	5,000	—	—	—	4.50	6.00

KM# 296 DINER
8.5000 g., Bi-Metallic Brass center in Copper-Nickel ring, 24.5 mm. **Obv:** National Arms **Rev:** Portrait of Joseph Ratzinger as Pope Benedict XVI

Date	Mintage	F	VF	XF	Unc	BU
2006	15,000	—	—	—	—	6.00

KM# 299 DINER
11.0000 g., Nickel, 25x25 mm. **Subject:** Chess Set **Obv:** National Arms **Rev:** Pawn **Shape:** Square

Date	Mintage	F	VF	XF	Unc	BU
2006	40,000	—	—	—	—	6.00

KM# 299a DINER
11.0000 g., Brass Gilt, 25x25 mm. **Subject:** Chess Set **Obv:** National Arms **Rev:** Pawn **Shape:** Square

Date	Mintage	F	VF	XF	Unc	BU
2006	40,000	—	—	—	—	6.00

KM# 300 DINER
11.0000 g., Nickel, 25x25 mm. **Subject:** Chess Set **Obv:** National arms **Rev:** Rook **Shape:** Square

Date	Mintage	F	VF	XF	Unc	BU
2006	10,000	—	—	—	—	12.00

KM# 300a DINER
11.0000 g., Brass Gilt, 25x25 mm. **Subject:** Chess Set **Obv:** National Arms **Rev:** Rook **Shape:** Square

Date	Mintage	F	VF	XF	Unc	BU
2006	10,000	—	—	—	—	12.00

KM# 301 DINER
11.0000 g., Nickel, 25x25 mm. **Subject:** Chess Set **Obv:** National Arms **Rev:** Knight **Shape:** Square

Date	Mintage	F	VF	XF	Unc	BU
2006	10,000	—	—	—	—	12.00

KM# 301a DINER
11.0000 g., Brass Gilt, 25x25 mm. **Subject:** Chess Set **Obv:** National Arms **Rev:** Knight **Shape:** Square

Date	Mintage	F	VF	XF	Unc	BU
2006	10,000	—	—	—	—	12.00

KM# 302 DINER
11.0000 g., Nickel, 25x25 mm. **Subject:** Chess Set **Obv:** National Arms **Rev:** Bishop **Shape:** Square

Date	Mintage	F	VF	XF	Unc	BU
2006	10,000	—	—	—	—	12.00

KM# 302a DINER
11.0000 g., Brass Gilt, 25x25 mm. **Subject:** Chess Set **Obv:** National Arms **Rev:** Bishop **Shape:** Square

Date	Mintage	F	VF	XF	Unc	BU
2006	10,000	—	—	—	—	12.00

KM# 303 DINER
11.0000 g., Nickel, 25x25 mm. **Subject:** Chess Set **Obv:** National Arms **Rev:** Queen **Shape:** Square

Date	Mintage	F	VF	XF	Unc	BU
2006	5,000	—	—	—	—	18.00

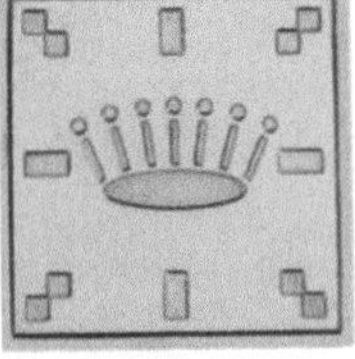

KM# 303a DINER
11.0000 g., Brass Gilt, 25x25 mm. **Subject:** Chess Set **Obv:** National Arms **Rev:** Queen **Shape:** Square

Date	Mintage	F	VF	XF	Unc	BU
2006	5,000	—	—	—	—	18.00

KM# 304 DINER
11.0000 g., Nickel, 25x25 mm. **Subject:** Chess Set **Obv:** National Arms **Rev:** King **Shape:** Square

Date	Mintage	F	VF	XF	Unc	BU
2006	5,000	—	—	—	—	18.00

KM# 304a DINER
11.0000 g., Brass Gilt, 25x25 mm. **Subject:** Chess Set **Obv:** National Arms **Rev:** King **Shape:** Square

Date	Mintage	F	VF	XF	Unc	BU
2006	5,000	—	—	—	—	18.00

KM# 312 DINER
8.5000 g., Bi-Metallic Brass center in Copper-Nickel ring, 24.5 mm. **Subject:** Popes of the 20th Century **Obv:** National Arms **Rev:** Pope Paul VI

Date	Mintage	F	VF	XF	Unc	BU
2007	5,000	—	—	—	—	8.00

KM# 331 DINER
1.2400 g., 0.9990 Gold 0.0398 oz. AGW, 13.92 mm. **Obv:** National arms **Rev:** John Paul II with cross croizer

Date	Mintage	F	VF	XF	Unc	BU
2011 Proof	—	Value: 150				

KM# 243 2 DINERS
11.2500 g., Bi-Metallic Copper-Nickel center in Brass ring, 28.4 mm. **Subject:** Death of Pope John-Paul II **Obv:** National arms **Rev:** Karol Wojtyla as pope **Edge:** Reeded

Date	Mintage	F	VF	XF	Unc	BU
2005	15,000	—	—	2.40	6.00	8.00

KM# 252 2 DINERS
11.2500 g., Bi-Metallic Copper-Nickel center in Brass ring, 28.4 mm. **Obv:** National arms **Rev:** Signing of the Umpirage between the Bishop of Urgell and Count of Foix **Edge:** Reeded

Date	Mintage	F	VF	XF	Unc	BU
2005	15,000	—	—	—	6.00	8.00
2006	10,000	—	—	—	6.00	8.00
2007	10,000	—	—	—	6.00	8.00
2008	5,000	—	—	—	6.00	8.00

KM# 297 2 DINERS
11.2500 g., Bi-Metallic Copper-Nickel center in Brass ring, 28.4 mm. **Obv:** National Arms **Rev:** Portrait of Joseph Ratzinger as Pope Benedict XVI

Date	Mintage	F	VF	XF	Unc	BU
2006	15,000	—	—	—	—	8.00

KM# 313 2 DINERS
6.0000 g., Bi-Metallic Copper-Nickel center in Brass ring, 28.4 mm. **Subject:** Popes of the 20th Century **Obv:** National Arms **Rev:** Pope John Paul I

Date	Mintage	F	VF	XF	Unc	BU
2007	5,000	—	—	—	—	10.00

KM# 269 2 DINERS
0.7300 g., 0.9990 Gold 0.0234 oz. AGW, 11 mm. **Subject:** von Beethoven **Obv:** National arms **Rev:** Beethoven seated at desk

Date	Mintage	F	VF	XF	Unc	BU
2008 Proof	5,000	Value: 80.00				

KM# 281 2 DINERS
0.7300 g., 0.9990 Gold 0.0234 oz. AGW, 11 mm. **Obv:** Shield **Rev:** Charlemagne **Edge:** Reeded

Date	Mintage	F	VF	XF	Unc	BU
2009 Proof	5,000	Value: 80.00				

KM# 193 5 DINERS
1.2400 g., 0.9990 Gold 0.0398 oz. AGW, 13.92 mm. **Obv:** National arms **Rev:** The Escorial Palace in Madrid **Edge:** Reeded

Date	Mintage	F	VF	XF	Unc	BU
2004 Proof	3,000	Value: 75.00				

KM# 194 5 DINERS
1.2400 g., 0.9990 Gold 0.0398 oz. AGW, 13.92 mm. **Obv:** National arms **Rev:** Eiffel Tower **Edge:** Reeded

Date	Mintage	F	VF	XF	Unc	BU
2004 Proof	3,000	Value: 75.00				

KM# 195 5 DINERS
1.2400 g., 0.9990 Gold 0.0398 oz. AGW, 13.92 mm. **Obv:** National arms **Rev:** Atomic model monument **Edge:** Reeded

Date	Mintage	F	VF	XF	Unc	BU
2004 Proof	3,000	Value: 75.00				

KM# 196 5 DINERS
1.2400 g., 0.9990 Gold 0.0398 oz. AGW, 13.92 mm. **Subject:** Andorran membership in the United Nations **Obv:** National arms **Rev:** Seated woman, world globe and UN logo **Edge:** Reeded

Date	Mintage	F	VF	XF	Unc	BU
2004 Proof	3,000	Value: 80.00				

KM# 315 5 DINERS
15.6000 g., 0.9990 Silver 0.5010 oz. ASW, 35 mm. **Rev:** Bear facing

Date	Mintage	F	VF	XF	Unc	BU
2010 Proof	3,000	Value: 90.00				

KM# 324 5 DINERS
20.0000 g., 0.9250 Silver 0.5948 oz. ASW, 38.6 mm. **Subject:** Beautification of Pope John Paul II **Rev:** Hologram with image of John Paul II at left, St. Peter's facade at right

Date	Mintage	F	VF	XF	Unc	BU
2011 Proof	2,500	Value: 135				

KM# 326 5 DINERS
15.5000 g., 0.9250 Silver 0.4609 oz. ASW, 35 mm. **Subject:** Wildlife of the Pyrenees - Golden Eagle **Obv:** National Arms **Rev:** Eagle in flight, eagle on nest

Date	Mintage	F	VF	XF	Unc	BU
2011 Proof	3,000	Value: 125				

KM# 329 5 DINERS
15.6000 g., 0.9990 Silver 0.5010 oz. ASW, 35 mm. **Subject:** Christmas **Obv:** National arms **Rev:** Star over stable with Holy Family, color

Date	Mintage	F	VF	XF	Unc	BU
2011 Proof	—	Value: 90.00				

KM# 337 5 DINERS
0.9250 Silver **Obv:** National arms at center **Rev:** DaVinci's Last supper in color

Date	Mintage	F	VF	XF	Unc	BU
2012 Proof	—	Value: 100				

KM# 333 5 DINERS
20.0000 g., 0.9250 Silver 0.5948 oz. ASW, 38.6 mm. **Subject:** Birds of Andorra **Obv:** National arms **Rev:** Cappercaillie bird left, prism color

Date	Mintage	F	VF	XF	Unc	BU
2012	2,500	—	—	—	—	50.00

KM# 335 5 DINERS
20.0000 g., 0.9250 Silver 0.5948 oz. ASW, 38.6 mm. **Subject:** Birds of Andorra **Obv:** National arms **Rev:** Robin facing left, prism color

Date	Mintage	F	VF	XF	Unc	BU
2012	2,500	—	—	—	—	50.00

KM# 334 5 DINERS
20.0000 g., 0.9250 Silver 0.5948 oz. ASW, 38.61 mm. **Subject:** Birds of Andorra **Obv:** National arms **Rev:** Northern Shoveler in flight right, prism color

Date	Mintage	F	VF	XF	Unc	BU
2012	2,500	—	—	—	—	50.00

KM# 172 10 DINERS
31.4700 g., 0.9250 Silver 0.9359 oz. ASW, 38.6 mm. **Subject:** Europa **Obv:** National arms **Rev:** Europa in chariot **Edge:** Reeded

Date	Mintage	F	VF	XF	Unc	BU
2001 Proof	15,000	Value: 45.00				

KM# 173 10 DINERS
31.4700 g., 0.9250 Silver 0.9359 oz. ASW, 38.6 mm. **Subject:** Concordia Europea **Obv:** National arms **Rev:** Two crowned women holding hands **Edge:** Reeded

Date	Mintage	F	VF	XF	Unc	BU
2001 Proof	15,000	Value: 45.00				

KM# 175 10 DINERS
31.4700 g., 0.9250 Silver 0.9359 oz. ASW, 38.6 mm. **Subject:** Olympics **Obv:** National arms **Rev:** Snowboarder **Edge:** Reeded

Date	Mintage	F	VF	XF	Unc	BU
2002 Proof	15,000	Value: 45.00				

KM# 183 10 DINERS
31.4700 g., 0.9250 Silver 0.9359 oz. ASW, 38.6 mm. **Subject:** Mouflon **Obv:** National arms **Rev:** Mouflon ram **Edge:** Reeded

Date	Mintage	F	VF	XF	Unc	BU
2002 Proof	15,000	Value: 50.00				

KM# 289 10 DINERS
31.4700 g., 0.9250 Silver 0.9359 oz. ASW, 38.61 mm. **Subject:** FIFA World Cup **Obv:** National Arms **Rev:** Soccer ball, names and years of previous World Cup host countries **Edge:** Reeded

Date	Mintage	F	VF	XF	Unc	BU
2003 Proof	50,000	Value: 85.00				

KM# 188 10 DINERS
31.1035 g., 0.9250 Silver 0.9250 oz. ASW, 38.6 mm. **Obv:** National arms **Rev:** Pope with doves **Edge:** Reeded

Date	Mintage	F	VF	XF	Unc	BU
2004 Proof	9,999	Value: 70.00				

KM# 189 10 DINERS
31.1035 g., 0.9250 Silver 0.9250 oz. ASW, 38.6 mm. **Obv:** National arms **Rev:** Pope holding staff with 2 hands **Edge:** Reeded

Date	Mintage	F	VF	XF	Unc	BU
2004 Proof	9,999	Value: 70.00				

KM# 190 10 DINERS
31.1035 g., 0.9250 Silver 0.9250 oz. ASW, 38.6 mm. **Obv:** National arms **Rev:** Pope raising a chalice **Edge:** Reeded

Date	Mintage	F	VF	XF	Unc	BU
2004 Proof	9,999	Value: 70.00				

KM# 191 10 DINERS
31.1035 g., 0.9250 Silver 0.9250 oz. ASW, 38.6 mm. **Obv:** National arms **Rev:** Pope with hammer **Edge:** Reeded

Date	Mintage	F	VF	XF	Unc	BU
2004 Proof	9,999	Value: 70.00				

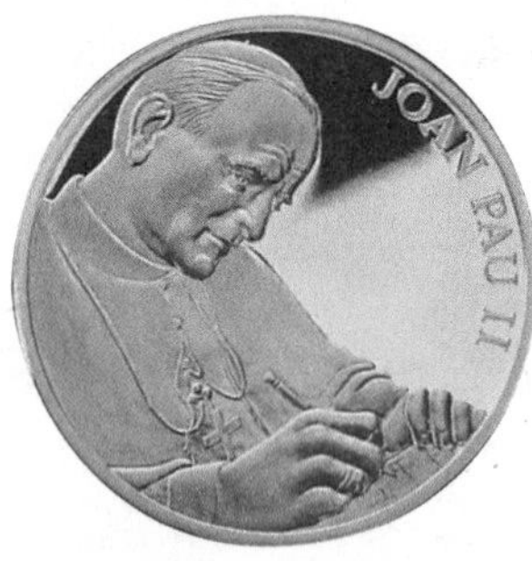

KM# 192 10 DINERS
31.1035 g., 0.9250 Silver 0.9250 oz. ASW, 38.6 mm. **Obv:** National arms **Rev:** Gold-plated Pope writing **Edge:** Reeded

Date	Mintage	F	VF	XF	Unc	BU
2004 Proof	9,999	Value: 70.00				

KM# 205 10 DINERS
31.1000 g., 0.9250 Silver 0.9249 oz. ASW, 38.6 mm. **Rev:** Gold plated Pope John Paul II wearing mitre and holding crucifix staff **Edge:** Reeded

Date	Mintage	F	VF	XF	Unc	BU
2005 Proof	9,999	Value: 70.00				

KM# 206 10 DINERS
31.1000 g., 0.9250 Silver 0.9249 oz. ASW, 38.6 mm. **Obv:** National arms **Rev:** Pope John Paul II with the Holy Virgin in background **Edge:** Reeded

Date	Mintage	F	VF	XF	Unc	BU
2005 Proof	9,999	Value: 70.00				

KM# 207 10 DINERS
31.1000 g., 0.9250 Silver 0.9249 oz. ASW, 38.6 mm. **Obv:** National arms **Rev:** Pope John Paul II in prayer with crucifix at right **Edge:** Reeded

Date	Mintage	F	VF	XF	Unc	BU
2005 Proof	9,999	Value: 70.00				

KM# 208 10 DINERS
31.1000 g., 0.9250 Silver 0.9249 oz. ASW, 38.6 mm. **Obv:** National arms **Rev:** Pope John Paul II blessing Vatican crowd **Edge:** Reeded

Date	Mintage	F	VF	XF	Unc	BU
2005 Proof	9,999	Value: 70.00				

KM# 209 10 DINERS
31.1000 g., 0.9250 Silver 0.9249 oz. ASW, 38.6 mm. **Obv:** National arms **Rev:** Pope John Paul II and Mother Teresa **Edge:** Reeded

Date	Mintage	F	VF	XF	Unc	BU
2005 Proof	9,999	Value: 70.00				

KM# 210 10 DINERS

31.1000 g., 0.9250 Silver 0.9249 oz. ASW, 38.6 mm. **Obv:** National arms **Rev:** Bearded man above Vatican City **Edge:** Reeded

Date	Mintage	F	VF	XF	Unc	BU
2005 Proof	9,999	Value: 60.00				

KM# 211 10 DINERS

31.1000 g., 0.9250 Silver 0.9249 oz. ASW, 38.6 mm. **Obv:** National arms **Rev:** Sad woman above Fatima **Edge:** Reeded

Date	Mintage	F	VF	XF	Unc	BU
2005 Proof	9,999	Value: 60.00				

KM# 212 10 DINERS

31.1000 g., 0.9250 Silver 0.9249 oz. ASW, 38.6 mm. **Obv:** National arms **Rev:** Radiant woman above Guadalupe Cathedral **Edge:** Reeded

Date	Mintage	F	VF	XF	Unc	BU
2005 Proof	9,999	Value: 60.00				

KM# 213 10 DINERS

31.1000 g., 0.9250 Silver 0.9249 oz. ASW, 38.6 mm. **Obv:** National arms **Rev:** Sea shell above Santiago De Compostel-la Cathedral **Edge:** Reeded

Date	Mintage	F	VF	XF	Unc	BU
2005 Proof	9,999	Value: 60.00				

KM# 214 10 DINERS

31.1000 g., 0.9250 Silver 0.9249 oz. ASW, 38.6 mm. **Obv:** National arms **Rev:** Dead man's face with Church of the Holy Sepulchure in the background **Edge:** Reeded

Date	Mintage	F	VF	XF	Unc	BU
2005 Proof	9,999	Value: 60.00				

KM# 215 10 DINERS

28.8000 g., 0.9250 Silver 0.8565 oz. ASW, 38.61 mm. **Obv:** National arms **Rev:** 2006 Olympics freestyle skier **Edge:** Reeded

Date	Mintage	F	VF	XF	Unc	BU
2005 Proof	15,000	Value: 50.00				

KM# 338 10 DINERS

28.2800 g., 0.9250 Silver 0.8410 oz. ASW, 38.61 mm. **Subject:** Benedict XVI election **Obv:** Naitonal arms **Rev:** Benedict XVI with hands raised, gilt; Crystal cross at right

Date	Mintage	F	VF	XF	Unc	BU
2005	—	—	—	—	—	75.00

KM# 217 10 DINERS

3.1100 g., 0.9999 Gold 0.1000 oz. AGW, 20 mm. **Obv:** National arms **Rev:** Jesus carrying the cross **Edge:** Reeded

Date	Mintage	F	VF	XF	Unc	BU
2006 Proof	9,999	Value: 185				

KM# 218 10 DINERS

31.1035 g., 0.9250 Silver 0.9250 oz. ASW, 38.6 mm. **Obv:** National arms **Rev:** Birth of Jesus **Edge:** Reeded

Date	Mintage	F	VF	XF	Unc	BU
2006 Proof	9,999	Value: 60.00				

KM# 219 10 DINERS

31.1035 g., 0.9250 Silver 0.9250 oz. ASW, 38.6 mm. **Obv:** National arms **Rev:** The Last Supper **Edge:** Reeded

Date	Mintage	F	VF	XF	Unc	BU
2006 Proof	9,999	Value: 60.00				

KM# 276 10 DINERS

28.2800 g., 0.9250 Silver 0.8410 oz. ASW, 38.6 mm. **Subject:** Extreme Sports - Mountain Bike **Obv:** Arms **Rev:** Multicolor biker

Date	Mintage	F	VF	XF	Unc	BU
2007 Proof	5,000	Value: 65.00				

KM# 277 10 DINERS

28.2800 g., 0.9250 Silver 0.8410 oz. ASW, 38.6 mm. **Subject:** Extreme Sports - Snowboarding **Obv:** Arms **Rev:** Multicolor snowboarder

Date	Mintage	F	VF	XF	Unc	BU
2007 Proof	5,000	Value: 65.00				

KM# 278 10 DINERS

28.2800 g., 0.9250 Silver 0.8410 oz. ASW, 38.6 mm. **Subject:** Extreme Sports - Heliskiing **Obv:** Arms **Rev:** Multicolor heliskier

Date	Mintage	F	VF	XF	Unc	BU
2007 Proof	5,000	Value: 65.00				

KM# 244 10 DINERS

28.2800 g., 0.9250 Silver 0.8410 oz. ASW, 28x40 mm. **Subject:** Great Painters of the World **Obv:** Mona lisa, national arms at lower left, multicolor **Rev:** Head of Leonardo daVinci at lower left, study of man in background, multicolor **Edge:** Plain **Shape:** Vertical rectangular

Date	Mintage	F	VF	XF	Unc	BU
2008	15,000	—	—	—	—	60.00

KM# 271 10 DINERS

28.2800 g., 0.9250 Silver 0.8410 oz. ASW, 28x40 mm. **Obv:** National arms at left, color painting of ladies at a piano **Rev:** Renoir facing, female portrait in color in artist's pallet shape **Shape:** Vertical rectangle

Date	Mintage	F	VF	XF	Unc	BU
2008 Proof	20,000	Value: 60.00				

KM# 272 10 DINERS

33.0000 g., 0.9250 Silver parially gilt 0.9814 oz. ASW, 38.6 mm. **Subject:** Vikings

Date	Mintage	F	VF	XF	Unc	BU
2008	15,000	—	—	—	—	50.00

KM# 273 10 DINERS

28.2800 g., 0.9250 Silver 0.8410 oz. ASW, 38.6 mm. **Subject:** Cross-country Skiing

Date	Mintage	F	VF	XF	Unc	BU
2008 Proof	10,000	Value: 45.00				

KM# 321 10 DINERS

28.2800 g., 0.9250 Silver 0.8410 oz. ASW, 38.61 mm. **Subject:** Chopin **Rev:** Portrait pair in ovals, Dresden

Date	Mintage	F	VF	XF	Unc	BU
2009 Proof	—	Value: 45.00				

KM# 280 10 DINERS
28.2800 g., 0.9250 Silver 0.8410 oz. ASW, 38.61 mm. **Subject:** World Cup Football, 2010 **Obv:** Shield **Rev:** Linear and shaded player skicking ball **Edge:** Reeded

Date	Mintage	F	VF	XF	Unc	BU
2009 Proof	10,000	Value: 50.00				

KM# 316 10 DINERS
28.2800 g., 0.9250 Silver 0.8410 oz. ASW, 38.61 mm. **Subject:** Chopin **Rev:** Hand and autograph

Date	Mintage	F	VF	XF	Unc	BU
2009 Proof	—	Value: 50.00				

KM# 317 10 DINERS
28.2800 g., 0.9250 Silver 0.8410 oz. ASW **Subject:** Chopin - Vienna **Rev:** Bust at left, house at right

Date	Mintage	F	VF	XF	Unc	BU
2009 Proof	—	Value: 45.00				

KM# 318 10 DINERS
28.2800 g., 0.9250 Silver 0.8410 oz. ASW, 38.61 mm. **Subject:** Chopin - Paris **Rev:** Party scene, Paris

Date	Mintage	F	VF	XF	Unc	BU
2009 Proof	—	Value: 45.00				

KM# 319 10 DINERS
28.2800 g., 0.9250 Silver 0.8410 oz. ASW, 38.6 mm. **Subject:** Chopin **Rev:** Bust at left, memorial stone at right

Date	Mintage	F	VF	XF	Unc	BU
2009 Proof	—	Value: 45.00				

KM# 320 10 DINERS
28.2800 g., 0.9250 Silver 0.8410 oz. ASW, 38.6 mm. **Subject:** Chopin **Rev:** Portrait pair in ovals, Mallorca

Date	Mintage	F	VF	XF	Unc	BU
2009 Proof	—	Value: 45.00				

KM# 322 10 DINERS
28.2800 g., 0.9250 Silver partially gilt 0.8410 oz. ASW, 38.61 mm. **Subject:** Chopin **Rev:** Chopin at piano left, Gilt profile head at right

Date	Mintage	F	VF	XF	Unc	BU
2009 Proof	—	Value: 45.00				

KM# 323 10 DINERS
28.2800 g., 0.9250 Silver 0.8410 oz. ASW, 38.61 mm. **Subject:** Chopin **Rev:** Two portraits, one in color - Wausau

Date	Mintage	F	VF	XF	Unc	BU
2009 Proof	—	Value: 45.00				

KM# 283 10 DINERS
28.2800 g., 0.9250 Silver 0.8410 oz. ASW, 40x28 mm. **Subject:** Albrecht Durer **Obv:** Adama dn even engraving and shield **Rev:** Durer's Adoration of the Holy Trinity

Date	Mintage	F	VF	XF	Unc	BU
2010 Proof	15,000	Value: 50.00				

KM# 284 10 DINERS
28.2800 g., 0.9250 Silver 0.8410 oz. ASW, 38.61 mm. **Obv:** Shield **Rev:** St. Christopher

Date	Mintage	F	VF	XF	Unc	BU
2010 Proof	5,000	Value: 65.00				

KM# 285 10 DINERS
28.2800 g., 0.9250 Silver 0.8410 oz. ASW, 38.61 mm. **Obv:** Shield **Rev:** St. George **Edge:** Reeded

Date	Mintage	F	VF	XF	Unc	BU
2010 Proof	5,000	Value: 65.00				

KM# 286 10 DINERS
28.2800 g., 0.9250 Silver 0.8410 oz. ASW, 38.61 mm. **Obv:** Shield **Rev:** St. Catherine **Edge:** Reeded

Date	Mintage	F	VF	XF	Unc	BU
2010 Proof	5,000	Value: 65.00				

KM# 287 10 DINERS
28.2800 g., 0.9250 Silver 0.8410 oz. ASW, 38.61 mm. **Obv:** Shield **Rev:** St. Barbara **Edge:** Reeded

Date	Mintage	F	VF	XF	Unc	BU
2010 Proof	5,000	Value: 65.00				

KM# 332 10 DINERS
31.1035 g., 0.9990 Silver 0.9990 oz. ASW, 38.6 mm. **Obv:** National arms **Rev:** St. Margaret and dragon

Date	Mintage	F	VF	XF	Unc	BU
2011 Proof	—	Value: 100				

KM# 339 10 DINERS
31.1050 g., 0.9990 Silver 0.9990 oz. ASW, 30x45 mm. **Subject:** Seven Virtures by Pierodel and Antonio Pollaiulo **Obv:** National arms and value **Rev:** Caritas in color **Shape:** Vertical

Date	Mintage	F	VF	XF	Unc	BU
2012 Proof	4,000	Value: 100				

KM# 340 10 DINERS
31.1050 g., 0.9990 Silver 0.9990 oz. ASW, 30x45 mm. **Subject:** Seven Virtures by Pierodel and Antonio Pollaiulo **Obv:** National arms and value **Rev:** Temperantia in color **Shape:** Vertical

Date	Mintage	F	VF	XF	Unc	BU
2012 Proof	4,000	Value: 100				

KM# 341 10 DINERS
31.1050 g., 0.9990 Silver 0.9990 oz. ASW, 30x45 mm. **Subject:** Seven Virtures by Pierodel and Antonio Pollaiulo **Obv:** National arms and value **Rev:** Fides in color **Shape:** Vertical

Date	Mintage	F	VF	XF	Unc	BU
2012 Proof	4,000	Value: 100				

KM# 342 10 DINERS
31.1050 g., 0.9990 Silver 0.9990 oz. ASW, 30x45 mm. **Subject:** Seven Virtures by Pierodel and Antonio Pollaiulo **Obv:** National arms and value **Rev:** Fortitudo in color **Shape:** Vertical

Date	Mintage	F	VF	XF	Unc	BU
2012 Proof	4,000	Value: 100				

KM# 343 10 DINERS
31.1050 g., 0.9990 Silver 0.9990 oz. ASW, 30x45 mm. **Subject:** Seven Virtures by Pierodel and Antonio Pollaiulo **Obv:** National arms and value **Rev:** Iustitia in color **Shape:** Vertical

Date	Mintage	F	VF	XF	Unc	BU
2012 Proof	4,000	Value: 100				

KM# 344 10 DINERS
31.1050 g., 0.9990 Silver 0.9990 oz. ASW, 30x45 mm. **Subject:** Seven Virtures by Pierodel and Antonio Pollaiulo **Obv:** National arms and value **Rev:** Prudentia in color **Shape:** Vertical

Date	Mintage	F	VF	XF	Unc	BU
2012 Proof	4,000	Value: 100				

KM# 345 10 DINERS
31.1050 g., 0.9990 Silver 0.9990 oz. ASW, 30x45 mm. **Subject:** Seven Virtures by Pierodel and Antonio Pollaiulo **Obv:** Naitonal arms and value **Rev:** Spes in color **Shape:** Vertical

Date	Mintage	F	VF	XF	Unc	BU
2012 Proof	4,000	Value: 100				

KM# 327 15 DINERS
Silver **Subject:** Leonardo daVinci painting **Rev:** Madonna **Shape:** Vertical rectangle

Date	Mintage	F	VF	XF	Unc	BU
2011 Proof	—	Value: 150				

KM# 328 15 DINERS
Silver **Subject:** Botticelli painting **Shape:** Vertical rectangle

Date	Mintage	F	VF	XF	Unc	BU
2011 Proof	—	Value: 125				

KM# 346 15 DINERS
50.0000 g., 0.9990 Silver 1.6059 oz. ASW **Subject:** Painting by Lucas Cranche **Rev:** Madonna and Child in color

Date	Mintage	F	VF	XF	Unc	BU
2012 Proof	—	Value: 200				

KM# 174 25 DINERS
12.4414 g., 0.9990 Gold 0.3996 oz. AGW, 26 mm. **Subject:** Christmas **Obv:** National arms **Rev:** Nativity scene **Edge:** Reeded

Date	Mintage	F	VF	XF	Unc	BU
2001 Proof	3,000	Value: 725				

KM# 184 25 DINERS
10.0000 g., 0.9999 Gold 0.3215 oz. AGW, 26 mm. **Subject:** Christmas **Obv:** National arms **Rev:** Standing Christ child **Edge:** Reeded

Date	Mintage	F	VF	XF	Unc	BU
2002 Proof	2,000	Value: 625				

KM# 185 25 DINERS
7.7759 g., 0.9990 Gold 0.2497 oz. AGW, 26 mm. **Subject:** Christmas **Obv:** National arms **Rev:** Madonna-like mother and child **Edge:** Reeded

Date	Mintage	F	VF	XF	Unc	BU
2003 Proof	3,000	Value: 475				

KM# 197 25 DINERS
8.0000 g., 0.9990 Gold 0.2569 oz. AGW, 26 mm. **Subject:** Christmas **Obv:** National arms **Rev:** Nativity scene **Edge:** Reeded

Date	Mintage	F	VF	XF	Unc	BU
2004 Proof	5,000	Value: 475				

KM# 216 25 DINERS
6.0000 g., 0.9999 Gold 0.1929 oz. AGW, 26 mm. **Obv:** National arms **Rev:** St. Joseph holding infant Jesus **Edge:** Reeded

Date	Mintage	F	VF	XF	Unc	BU
2005 Proof	9,999	Value: 385				

KM# 305 25 DINERS
6.0000 g., 0.9990 Gold 0.1927 oz. AGW, 26 mm. **Subject:** Christmas - the Holy Family **Obv:** National Arms **Rev:** St. Joseph, Mary and Jesus

Date	Mintage	F	VF	XF	Unc	BU
2006 Proof	5,000	Value: 575				

KM# 314 25 DINERS
6.0000 g., 0.9990 Gold 0.1927 oz. AGW, 26 mm. **Subject:** Christmas **Obv:** National Arms **Rev:** Angels playing musical instruments

Date	Mintage	F	VF	XF	Unc	BU
2007 Proof	2,000	Value: 575				

KM# 274 25 DINERS
6.0000 g., 0.9990 Gold 0.1927 oz. AGW, 26 mm. **Subject:** Constitution

Date	Mintage	F	VF	XF	Unc	BU
2008 Proof	2,000	Value: 400				

KM# 275 25 DINERS
6.0000 g., 0.9990 Gold 0.1927 oz. AGW, 26 mm. **Subject:** Three Kings **Rev:** Magi following star

Date	Mintage	F	VF	XF	Unc	BU
2008 Proof	2,000	Value: 400				

KM# 279 25 DINERS
6.0000 g., 0.9990 Gold 0.1927 oz. AGW, 26 mm. **Obv:** Shield **Rev:** Madonna and child, star of Bethlehem in backgorund **Edge:** Reeded

Date	Mintage	F	VF	XF	Unc	BU
2009 Proof	1,200	Value: 400				

KM# 288 25 DINERS
6.0000 g., 0.9990 Gold 0.1927 oz. AGW, 26 mm. **Subject:** Christmas **Obv:** Shield **Rev:** Archangel Gabriel telling the good news to Mary

Date	Mintage	F	VF	XF	Unc	BU
2010 Proof	1,200	Value: 400				

KM# 330 25 DINERS
6.0000 g., 0.9990 Gold 0.1927 oz. AGW, 26 mm. **Obv:** National arms **Rev:** Holy family

Date	Mintage	F	VF	XF	Unc	BU
2011 Proof	—	Value: 425				

KM# 186 50 DINERS
159.5000 g., 0.9990 Bi-Metallic .999 Silver 155.5g coin with .999 Gold 4g, 20x50mm insert 5.1227 oz., 65 mm. **Subject:** 10th Anniversary of Constitution **Obv:** National arms **Rev:** Seated allegorical woman holding scrolled constitution **Edge:** Reeded **Note:** Illustration reduced.

Date	Mintage	F	VF	XF	Unc	BU
2003	3,000	—	—	—	325	375

KM# 347 100 DINERS
1000.0000 g., 0.9990 Silver 32.117 oz. ASW, 166x240 mm. **Subject:** Painting by Raffaello **Rev:** Madonna **Shape:** Vertical

Date	Mintage	F	VF	XF	Unc	BU
2012 Proof	—	Value: 1,300				

KM# 336 1000 DINERS
1000.0000 g., 0.9990 Gold 32.117 oz. AGW **Subject:** Pope John Paul II Beautification **Obv:** John Paul II with arms raised, National arms at right **Rev:** Profile at right, looking left

Date	Mintage	F	VF	XF	Unc	BU
2011 Proof	—	Value: 58,000				

BULLION COINAGE

KM# 268 DINER
31.1050 g., 0.9990 Silver 0.9990 oz. ASW, 38.6 mm. **Obv:** Eagle with wings outstretched **Rev:** National Arms **Edge:** Reeded

Date	Mintage	F	VF	XF	Unc	BU
2008	—	—	—	—	—	37.50
2009	—	—	—	—	—	37.50
2010	—	—	—	—	—	37.50
2011	—	—	—	—	—	37.50

KM# 257 5 DINERS
1.5500 g., 0.9990 Gold 0.0498 oz. AGW, 13.92 mm. **Obv:** Eagle with wings outstretched **Rev:** National Arms

Date	Mintage	F	VF	XF	Unc	BU
2009	—	—	—	—	—	100
2010	—	—	—	—	—	100

KM# 258 10 DINERS
3.1100 g., 0.9990 Gold 0.0999 oz. AGW, 16.46 mm. **Obv:** Eagle with wings outstretched **Rev:** National Arms

Date	Mintage	F	VF	XF	Unc	BU
2009	—	—	—	—	—	200
2010	—	—	—	—	—	200

KM# 259 25 DINERS
7.7700 g., 0.9990 Gold 0.2496 oz. AGW, 22.5 mm. **Obv:** Eagle with wings outstretched **Rev:** National Arms

Date	Mintage	F	VF	XF	Unc	BU
2009	—	—	—	—	—	450
2010	—	—	—	—	—	450

KM# 260 50 DINERS
15.5500 g., 0.9990 Gold 0.4994 oz. AGW, 26 mm. **Obv:** Eagle with wings outstretched **Rev:** National Arms

Date	Mintage	F	VF	XF	Unc	BU
2009	—	—	—	—	—	875
2010	—	—	—	—	—	875

KM# 254 50 DINERS
1000.0000 g., 0.9990 Silver 32.117 oz. ASW, 100 mm. **Obv:** Eagle with wings outstretched **Rev:** National Arms

Date	Mintage	F	VF	XF	Unc	BU
2010	—	—	—	—	—	1,200

KM# 298 100 DINERS
31.1035 g., 0.9990 Gold 0.9990 oz. AGW, 35 mm. **Obv:** Eagle with open wings **Rev:** Details of National Arms **Edge:** Reeded

Date	Mintage	F	VF	XF	Unc	BU
2006	1,500	—	—	—	—	2,000

KM# 261 100 DINERS
31.1050 g., 0.9990 Gold 0.9990 oz. AGW, 33 mm. **Obv:** Eagle with wings outstretched **Rev:** National Arms

Date	Mintage	F	VF	XF	Unc	BU
2009	—	—	—	—	—	1,750
2010	—	—	—	—	—	1,750

KM# 255 100 DINERS
3110.5000 g., 0.9990 Silver 99.900 oz. ASW, 120 mm. **Obv:** Eagle with wings outstretched **Rev:** National Arms **Note:** 29mm thick.

Date	Mintage	F	VF	XF	Unc	BU
2010	—	—	—	—	—	5,000

KM# 256 200 DINERS
6221.0000 g., 0.9990 Silver 199.80 oz. ASW, 140 mm. **Obv:** Eagle with wings outstretched **Rev:** National Arms **Note:** 42mm thick

Date	Mintage	F	VF	XF	Unc	BU
2010	—	—	—	—	—	10,000

The Argentine Republic, located in southern South America, has an area of 1,073,518 sq. mi. (3,761,274 sq. km.) and an estimated population of 37.03 million. Capital: Buenos Aires. Its varied topography ranges from the subtropical lowlands of the north to the towering Andean Mountains in the west and the wind-swept Patagonian steppe in the south. The rolling, fertile pampas of central Argentina are ideal for agriculture and grazing, and support most of the republic's population. Meatpacking, flour milling, textiles, sugar refining and dairy products are the principal industries. Oil is found in Patagonia, but most mineral requirements must be imported.

Internal conflict through the first half century of Argentine independence resulted in a provisional national coinage, chiefly of crown-sized silver. Provincial issues mainly of minor denominations supplemented this.

REPUBLIC

REFORM COINAGE

1992; 100 Centavos = 1 Peso

KM# 109 5 CENTAVOS
2.0200 g., Aluminum-Bronze, 17.2 mm. **Obv:** Radiant sunface **Rev:** Large value, date below **Edge:** Reeded **Note:** Prev. KM#84.

Date	Mintage	F	VF	XF	Unc	BU
2004	30,000,000	—	—	—	0.45	0.60
2005	76,000,000	—	—	—	0.45	0.60

KM# 109b 5 CENTAVOS
2.0000 g., Brass Plated Steel, 17.2 mm. **Obv:** Radiant Sunface **Rev:** Large value, date below **Edge:** Plain

Date	Mintage	F	VF	XF	Unc	BU
2006	23,800,000	—	—	—	0.45	0.60
2007	183,000,000	—	—	—	0.45	0.60
2008	114,000,000	—	—	—	0.45	0.60
2009	—	—	—	—	0.45	0.60
2010	—	—	—	—	0.45	0.60
2011	—	—	—	—	0.45	0.60

KM# 107 10 CENTAVOS
2.2500 g., Aluminum-Bronze, 18.2 mm. **Obv:** Argentine arms **Rev:** Value, date below **Edge:** Reeded **Note:** Prev. KM#82.

Date	Mintage	F	VF	XF	Unc	BU
2004	190,000,000	—	—	—	0.65	0.85
2005	114,400,000	—	—	—	0.65	0.85

KM# 107a 10 CENTAVOS
2.2000 g., Brass Plated Steel, 18.2 mm. **Obv:** Argentine arms **Rev:** Large value, date below **Edge:** Plain

Date	Mintage	F	VF	XF	Unc	BU
2006	99,600,000	—	—	—	0.65	0.85
2007	204,000,000	—	—	—	0.65	0.85
2008	317,000,000	—	—	—	0.65	0.85
2009	—	—	—	—	0.65	0.85
2010	—	—	—	—	0.65	0.85
2011	—	—	—	—	0.65	0.85

KM# 110.1 25 CENTAVOS
5.4000 g., Aluminum-Bronze, 24.2 mm. **Obv:** Buenos Aires City Hall, fine lettering **Rev:** Large value, date below **Edge:** Reeded **Note:** Prev. KM#85.1.

Date	Mintage	F	VF	XF	Unc	BU
2009	—	—	—	—	1.25	1.50
2010	—	—	—	—	1.25	1.50

KM# 110a 25 CENTAVOS
6.1000 g., Copper-Nickel, 24.2 mm. **Obv:** Buenos Aires City Hall, bold lettering **Rev:** Large value, date below **Edge:** Reeded **Note:** Prev. KM#85a.

Date	Mintage	F	VF	XF	Unc	BU
2009	—	—	—	—	1.25	1.50

KM# 111.1 50 CENTAVOS
5.8000 g., Aluminum-Bronze, 25.2 mm. **Obv:** Tucuman Province Capital Building; fine lettering **Rev:** Large value, date below **Edge:** Reeded **Note:** Prev. KM#86.1.

Date	Mintage	F	VF	XF	Unc	BU
2009	—	—	—	—	1.75	2.00
2010	—	—	—	—	1.75	2.00

KM# 111.2 50 CENTAVOS
5.8000 g., Aluminum-Bronze, 25.2 mm. **Obv:** Tucuman Province Capital Building; bold lettering **Rev:** Large value, date below **Edge:** Reeded **Note:** Prev. KM#86.2.

Date	Mintage	F	VF	XF	Unc	BU
2009	—	—	—	—	1.75	2.00

KM# 132.1 PESO
6.3500 g., Bi-Metallic Aluninum-Bronze center in Copper-Nickel ring, 23 mm. **Subject:** General Urquiza **Obv:** Stylized portrait facing **Rev:** Church tower and denomination **Edge:** Reeded

Date	Mintage	F	VF	XF	Unc	BU
2001	995,000	—	—	—	3.75	4.50

KM# 132.2 PESO
6.3500 g., Bi-Metallic Aluminum-Bronze center in Copper-Nickel ring, 23 mm. **Subject:** General Urquiza **Obv:** Stylized portrait facing **Rev:** Church tower and denomination **Edge:** Plain

Date	Mintage	F	VF	XF	Unc	BU
2001	5,000	—	—	—	7.50	8.00

KM# 141 PESO
25.0000 g., 0.9000 Silver 0.7234 oz. ASW, 37 mm. **Obv:** Maria Eva Duarte de Peron **Rev:** "EVITA" audience **Edge:** Reeded

Date	Mintage	F	VF	XF	Unc	BU
ND (2004) Proof	5,000	Value: 45.00				

KM# 140 PESO
25.0000 g., 0.9000 Silver 0.7234 oz. ASW, 37 mm. **Subject:** 70th Anniversary of Central Bank **Obv:** Bank building **Rev:** Liberty head in wreath **Edge:** Reeded

Date	Mintage	F	VF	XF	Unc	BU
2005 Proof	2,000	Value: 50.00				

KM# 155 PESO
25.0000 g., 0.9000 Silver 0.7234 oz. ASW, 37 mm. **Subject:** Jorge Luis Borges **Obv:** Stylized bust facing **Rev:** Man walking at street corner

Date	Mintage	F	VF	XF	Unc	BU
2006A	—	—	—	—	—	42.50

KM# 112.1 PESO
6.3500 g., Bi-Metallic Aluminum-Bronze center in Copper-Nickel ring, 23 mm. **Obv:** Argentine arms in circle **Rev:** Design of first Argentine coin in center **Edge:** Plain **Note:** Prev. KM#87.1.

Date	Mintage	F	VF	XF	Unc	BU
2006	30,000,000	—	—	0.50	1.20	1.60
2007	33,000,000	—	—	0.50	1.20	1.60
2008	89,600,000	—	—	0.50	1.20	1.60
2009 D	—	—	—	0.50	1.20	1.60
2010 E	—	—	—	0.50	1.20	1.60

KM# 153 PESO

25.0000 g., 0.9000 Silver 0.7234 oz. ASW, 37 mm. **Subject:** 25th Anniversary Malvinas Islands Occupation - Heroes **Obv:** Soldier's bust facing **Obv. Legend:** REPUBLICA ARGENTINA - 1982 - 2007 - LA NACIÓN A SUS HÉROES **Rev:** Outlined map of islands **Rev. Legend:** MALVINAS ARGENTINAS **Rev. Inscription:** 2 DE APRIL / 1982 **Edge:** Reeded

Date	Mintage	F	VF	XF	Unc	BU
2007 Proof	3,000	Value: 75.00				

KM# 156 PESO

6.3500 g., Bi-Metallic Aluminum-Bronze center in Copper-Nickel ring, 23 mm. **Subject:** Bicentennial - El Palmar **Obv:** Stylized radiant sun **Rev:** Palm trees

Date	Mintage	F	VF	XF	Unc	BU
2010	—	—	—	—	1.20	1.60

KM# 157 PESO

6.3500 g., Bi-Metallic Aluminum-Bronze center in Copper-Nickel ring, 23 mm. **Subject:** Bicentennial - Aconcagua **Obv:** Stylized radiant run **Rev:** Mountains

Date	Mintage	F	VF	XF	Unc	BU
2010	—	—	—	—	1.20	1.60

KM# 158 PESO

6.3500 g., Bi-Metallic Aluminum-Bronze center in Copper-Nickel ring, 23 mm. **Subject:** Bicentennial - Mar del Plata **Obv:** Stylized radiant sun **Rev:** Elephant seal and fishing boat

Date	Mintage	F	VF	XF	Unc	BU
2010	—	—	—	—	1.20	1.60

KM# 159 PESO

6.3500 g., Bi-Metallic Aluminum-Bronze center in Copper-Nickel ring, 23 mm. **Subject:** Bicentennial - Pucara de Tilcara **Obv:** Stylized radiant sun **Rev:** Cactus and mountains

Date	Mintage	F	VF	XF	Unc	BU
2010	—	—	—	—	1.20	1.60

KM# 160 PESO

6.3500 g., Bi-Metallic Aluminum-Bronze center in Copper-Nickel ring, 23 mm. **Subject:** Bicentennial - Glaciar Perito Moreno **Obv:** Stylized radiant sun **Rev:** Glaciar ice bridge and sea

Date	Mintage	F	VF	XF	Unc	BU
2010	—	—	—	—	1.20	1.60

KM# 164 PESO

6.3500 g., Bi-Metallic Aluminum-Bronze center in Copper-Nickel ring, 23 mm. **Subject:** Revolution anniversary

Date	Mintage	F	VF	XF	Unc	BU
2010	—	—	—	—	1.20	1.80

KM# 135.1 2 PESOS

10.4000 g., Copper-Nickel, 30 mm. **Subject:** Eva Peron **Obv:** Head left **Rev:** Stylized crowd scene, value **Rev. Inscription:** EVITA **Edge:** Reeded

Date	Mintage	F	VF	XF	Unc	BU
2002	1,995,000	—	—	0.85	1.85	2.50

KM# 135.2 2 PESOS

10.4000 g., Copper-Nickel, 30 mm. **Subject:** Eva Peron **Obv:** Head left **Rev:** Stylized crowd scene, value **Rev. Inscription:** EVITA **Edge:** Plain

Date	Mintage	F	VF	XF	Unc	BU
2002	5,000	—	—	—	6.00	8.00

KM# 161 2 PESOS

10.4700 g., Copper-Nickel, 30.35 mm. **Subject:** Declaration of Human Rights **Obv:** Legend **Rev:** Female's scarf

Date	Mintage	F	VF	XF	Unc	BU
2006	—	—	—	—	1.85	2.50

KM# 144.1 2 PESOS

10.4000 g., Copper-Nickel, 30 mm. **Subject:** Malvinas Islands War, 25th Anniversary **Obv:** Soldier's bust facing **Obv. Legend:** REPUBLICA ARGENTINA - 1982 - 2007 - LA NACIÓN A SUS HÉROES **Rev:** Outlined map of islands **Rev. Legend:** MALVINAS ARGENTINAS **Rev. Inscription:** 2 DE APRIL / 1982 **Edge:** Reeded

Date	Mintage	F	VF	XF	Unc	BU
2007	1,995,000	—	—	0.85	1.85	2.50

KM# 144.2 2 PESOS

10.4000 g., Copper-Nickel, 30 mm. **Subject:** Malvinas Islands War, 25th Anniversary **Obv:** Soldier's bust facing **Obv. Legend:** REPUBLICA ARGENTINA - 1982 - 2007 - LA NACIÓN A SUS HÉROES **Rev:** Outlined map of islands **Rev. Legend:** MALVINAS ARGENTINAS **Rev. Inscription:** 2 DE APRIL / 1982 **Edge:** Plain

Date	Mintage	F	VF	XF	Unc	BU
2007	5,000	—	—	—	—	9.00

KM# 145 2 PESOS

Copper-Nickel, 30.35 mm. **Subject:** 100th Anniversary First Oil Well **Obv:** Oil well **Obv. Legend:** REPÚBLICA ARGENTINA - DESCUBRIMIENTO DEL PETRÓLEO **Rev:** Modern pump **Rev. Inscription:** CHUBUT **Edge:** Reeded

Date	Mintage	F	VF	XF	Unc	BU
2007	995,000	—	—	—	6.00	8.00

KM# 165 2 PESOS

7.2000 g., Bi-Metallic Copper-Nickel center in Aluminum-Bronze ring, 24.5 mm. **Subject:** 1810 Revolution, 200th Anniversary **Obv:** Sunburst at center of wreath **Rev:** Value at center of wreath **Edge:** Segmented reeding

Date	Mintage	F	VF	XF	Unc	BU
2010	100,000,000	—	—	—	3.00	5.00
2011	—	—	—	—	3.00	5.00

KM# 162 2 PESOS

10.4700 g., Copper-Nickel, 30.35 mm. **Subject:** Central Bank, 75th Anniversary **Obv:** Head at right, facing left **Rev:** Bank's main doors

Date	Mintage	F	VF	XF	Unc	BU
2010	—	—	—	—	1.85	2.50

KM# 133 5 PESOS

8.0640 g., 0.9000 Gold 0.2333 oz. AGW, 22 mm. **Subject:** Gral. Justo Jose de Urquiza **Obv:** Stylized portrait facing **Rev:** Church tower and denomination **Edge:** Reeded

Date	Mintage	F	VF	XF	Unc	BU
2001 Proof	1,000	Value: 450				

KM# 149 5 PESOS

8.0640 g., 0.9000 Gold 0.2333 oz. AGW **Subject:** 100th Anniversary City of Comodoro Rivadavia

Date	Mintage	F	VF	XF	Unc	BU
2001 Proof	750	Value: 475				

KM# 143 5 PESOS

27.0000 g., 0.9250 Silver 0.8029 oz. ASW, 40 mm. **Subject:** FIFA - XVIII World Championship Football - Germany 2006 **Obv:** Football at right on grass, chaff in background **Obv. Legend:** REPÚBLICA ARGENTINA **Rev:** Logo **Rev. Legend:** COPA MUNDIAL DE LA FIFA **Rev. Inscription:** ALEMANIA **Edge:** Reeded

Date	Mintage	F	VF	XF	Unc	BU
2003 Proof	50,000	Value: 55.00				

KM# 146 5 PESOS
27.0000 g., 0.9250 Silver 0.8029 oz. ASW **Subject:** FIFA - XVIII World Football Championship - Germany 2006 **Obv. Legend:** REPÚBLICA ARGENTINA **Rev:** Logo **Edge:** Reeded

Date	Mintage	F	VF	XF	Unc	BU
2004 Proof	50,000	Value: 55.00				

KM# 142 5 PESOS
8.0640 g., 0.9000 Gold 0.2333 oz. AGW, 22 mm. **Obv:** Maria Eva Duarte de Peron **Rev:** "EVITA" and audience

Date	Mintage	F	VF	XF	Unc	BU
ND (2004) Proof	1,000	Value: 450				

KM# 150 5 PESOS
27.0000 g., 0.9250 Silver 0.8029 oz. ASW **Subject:** FIFA - XVIII World Championship Football - Germany 2006 **Obv:** Forward player **Rev:** Logo

Date	Mintage	F	VF	XF	Unc	BU
2005 Proof	—	Value: 65.00				

KM# 154 5 PESOS
8.0640 g., 0.9000 Gold 0.2333 oz. AGW, 22 mm. **Subject:** 25th Anniversary Malvinas Islands Occupation - Heroes **Obv:** Soldier's bust facing **Obv. Legend:** REPUBLICA ARGENTINA - 1982 - 2007 - LA NACIÓN A SUS HÉROES **Rev:** Outlined map of islands **Rev. Legend:** MALVINAS ISLANDS **Rev. Inscription:** 2 DE APRIL / 1982 **Edge:** Reeded

Date	Mintage	F	VF	XF	Unc	BU
2007 Proof	1,000	Value: 450				

KM# 147 10 PESOS
6.7500 g., 0.9990 Gold 0.2168 oz. AGW **Subject:** FIFA - XVIII World Football Championship - Germany 2006 **Obv. Legend:** REPÚBLICA ARGENTINA **Edge:** Reeded

Date	Mintage	F	VF	XF	Unc	BU
2004 Proof	25,000	Value: 400				

KM# 151 10 PESOS
6.7500 g., 0.9990 Gold 0.2168 oz. AGW **Subject:** FIFA - XVIII World Championship Football - Germany 2006 **Obv:** Forward player **Rev:** Logo

Date	Mintage	F	VF	XF	Unc	BU
2005 Proof	—	Value: 400				

KM# 138 25 PESOS
27.0000 g., 0.9250 Silver 0.8029 oz. ASW, 40 mm. **Subject:** IBERO-AMERICA Series **Obv:** Coats of arms **Rev:** Tall ship "Presidente Sarmiento" **Edge:** Reeded

Date	Mintage	F	VF	XF	Unc	BU
2002 Proof	—	Value: 60.00				

KM# 139 25 PESOS
27.0000 g., 0.9250 Silver 0.8029 oz. ASW, 40 mm. **Subject:** Ibero-America **Obv:** National arms in circle of arms **Rev:** Colon Theater building **Edge:** Reeded

Date	Mintage	F	VF	XF	Unc	BU
2005 Proof	15,500	Value: 55.00				

KM# 167 25 PESOS
27.0000 g., 0.9250 Silver 0.8029 oz. ASW, 40 mm. **Obv:** Arms within other national arms **Rev:** Arm dunking basketball

Date	Mintage	F	VF	XF	Unc	BU
2007 Proof	—	Value: 75.00				

KM# 166 25 PESOS
27.0000 g., 0.9250 Silver 0.8029 oz. ASW, 40 mm. **Obv:** National arms within circle of other country's arms **Rev:** 1881 Argentinian coin design at center

Date	Mintage	F	VF	XF	Unc	BU
2010 Proof	—	Value: 75.00				

PROOF SETS

KM#	Date	Mintage	Identification	Issue Price	Mkt Val
PS6	2007 (2)	300	KM#153, 154	475	525

ARMENIA

The Republic of Armenia, formerly Armenian S.S.R., is bordered to the north by Georgia, the east by Azerbaijan and the south and west by Turkey and Iran. It has an area of 11,506 sq. mi. (29,800 sq. km) and an estimated population of 3.66 million. Capital: Yerevan. Agriculture including cotton, vineyards and orchards, hydroelectricity, chemicals - primarily synthetic rubber and fertilizers, vast mineral deposits of copper, zinc and aluminum, and production of steel and paper are major industries.

Fighting between Christians in Armenia and Muslim forces of Azerbaijan escalated in 1992 and continued through early 1994. Each country claimed the Nagorno-Karabakh, an Armenian ethnic enclave, in Azerbaijan. A temporary cease-fire was announced in May 1994.

MONETARY SYSTEM
100 Luma = 1 Dram

MINT NAME
Revan, (Erevan, now Yerevan)

REPUBLIC

STANDARD COINAGE

KM# 112 10 DRAM
1.3000 g., Aluminum, 20 mm. **Obv:** National arms **Rev:** Value **Edge:** Plain

Date	Mintage	F	VF	XF	Unc	BU
2004	—	—	—	—	1.00	1.50

KM# 93 20 DRAM
2.7500 g., Copper Plated Steel, 20.5 mm. **Obv:** National arms **Rev:** Denomination **Edge:** Plain

Date	Mintage	F	VF	XF	Unc	BU
2003	—	—	—	—	1.00	1.50
2005	—	—	—	—	1.00	1.50

KM# 94 50 DRAM
3.5000 g., Brass Plated Steel, 21.5 mm. **Obv:** National arms **Rev:** Value **Edge:** Reeded

Date	Mintage	F	VF	XF	Unc	BU
2003	—	—	—	—	1.25	1.50

KM# 212 50 DRAM
3.5000 g., Brass Plated Steel, 21.5 mm. **Subject:** Aragatsotn region **Edge:** Reeded

Date	Mintage	F	VF	XF	Unc	BU
2012	60,000	—	—	—	1.50	2.50

KM# 213 50 DRAM
3.5000 g., Brass Plated Steel, 21.5 mm. **Subject:** Ararat region **Edge:** Reeded

Date	Mintage	F	VF	XF	Unc	BU
2012	60,000	—	—	—	1.50	2.50

KM# 214 50 DRAM
3.5000 g., Brass Plated Steel, 21.5 mm. **Subject:** Armavir region **Edge:** Reeded

Date	Mintage	F	VF	XF	Unc	BU
2012	—	—	—	—	1.50	2.50

KM# 215 50 DRAM
3.5000 g., Brass Plated Steel, 21.5 mm. **Subject:** Gegharkunik region **Edge:** Reeded

Date	Mintage	F	VF	XF	Unc	BU
2012	60,000	—	—	—	1.50	2.50

KM# 216 50 DRAM
3.5000 g., Brass Plated Steel, 21.5 mm. **Subject:** Kotayk region **Edge:** Reeded

Date	Mintage	F	VF	XF	Unc	BU
2012	60,000	—	—	—	1.50	2.50

KM# 217 50 DRAM
3.5000 g., Brass Plated Steel, 21.5 mm. **Subject:** Lori region **Edge:** Reeded

Date	Mintage	F	VF	XF	Unc	BU
2012	60,000	—	—	—	1.50	2.50

KM# 218 50 DRAM
3.5000 g., Brass Plated Steel, 21.5 mm. **Subject:** Shirak region **Edge:** Reeded

Date	Mintage	F	VF	XF	Unc	BU
2012	60,000	—	—	—	1.50	2.50

KM# 219 50 DRAM
3.5000 g., Brass Plated Steel, 21.5 mm. **Subject:** Syunik region **Edge:** Reeded

Date	Mintage	F	VF	XF	Unc	BU
2012	60,000	—	—	—	1.50	2.50

KM# 220 50 DRAM
3.5000 g., Brass Plated Steel, 21.5 mm. **Subject:** Tavush region **Edge:** Reeded

Date	Mintage	F	VF	XF	Unc	BU
2012	60,000	—	—	—	1.50	2.50

KM# 221 50 DRAM
3.5000 g., Brass Plated Steel, 21.5 mm. **Subject:** Vayots Dzor region **Edge:** Reeded

Date	Mintage	F	VF	XF	Unc	BU
2012	60,000	—	—	—	1.50	2.50

KM# 222 50 DRAM
3.5000 g., Brass Plated Steel, 21.5 mm. **Subject:** Yerevan region **Edge:** Reeded

Date	Mintage	F	VF	XF	Unc	BU
2012	60,000	—	—	—	1.50	2.50

KM# 86 100 DRAM
31.1000 g., 0.9990 Silver 0.9988 oz. ASW, 38 mm. **Obv:** National arms **Rev:** Bust of General Garegin Nzhdeh facing at right **Edge:** Plain **Edge Lettering:** Serial number

Date	Mintage	F	VF	XF	Unc	BU
2001 Proof	170	Value: 1,400				

KM# 86a 100 DRAM
31.1000 g., 0.9990 Silver Gilt 0.9988 oz. ASW, 38 mm. **Obv:** National arms **Obv. Inscription:** Bust of General Garegin Nzhdeh facing at right **Edge:** Plain **Edge Lettering:** Serial number

Date	Mintage	F	VF	XF	Unc	BU
2001 Proof	30	Value: 5,000				

KM# 87 100 DRAM
31.0400 g., 0.9990 Silver 0.9969 oz. ASW, 38 mm. **Subject:** Armenian Membership in the Council of Europe joined January 1, 2001 **Obv:** National arms **Rev:** Spiral design with star circle **Edge:** Plain **Edge Lettering:** Serial number

Date	Mintage	F	VF	XF	Unc	BU
2001 Proof	200	Value: 300				

KM# 98 100 DRAM
31.1000 g., 0.9250 Silver 0.9249 oz. ASW, 40 mm. **Obv:** National arms **Rev:** Aram Khachatryan, Birth Centennial **Edge:** Reeded

Date	Mintage	F	VF	XF	Unc	BU
2002	300	—	—	—	85.00	120

KM# 99 100 DRAM
31.1000 g., 0.9250 Silver 0.9249 oz. ASW, 40 mm. **Obv:** The Book of Sadness **Rev:** Saint Grigor Narekatsi with book and quill millennium of his poem "The Book of Sadness" **Edge:** Reeded

Date	Mintage	F	VF	XF	Unc	BU
2002 Proof	500	Value: 100				

KM# 110 100 DRAM
33.9200 g., 0.9250 Silver 1.0087 oz. ASW, 39 mm. **Subject:** 110th Anniversary of State Banking in Armenia and 10th Year of National Currency October 7 1893 - November 22, 1993 **Obv:** Building above value **Rev:** State Bank emblem **Edge:** Reeded

Date	Mintage	F	VF	XF	Unc	BU
2003 Proof	300	Value: 200				

KM# 95 100 DRAM
4.0000 g., Nickel Plated Steel, 22.5 mm. **Obv:** National arms **Rev:** Value **Edge:** Reeded

Date	Mintage	F	VF	XF	Unc	BU
2003	—	—	—	—	1.50	2.00

KM# 111 100 DRAM
28.2800 g., 0.9250 Silver 0.8410 oz. ASW, 38.6 mm. **Subject:** FIFA World Cup Soccer Games - Germany **Obv:** National arms **Rev:** Three soccer players

Date	Mintage	F	VF	XF	Unc	BU
2004 Proof	300	Value: 150				

KM# 113 100 DRAM
31.1000 g., 0.9990 Silver 0.9988 oz. ASW, 38 mm. **Subject:** Gandzasar Monastery **Obv:** Monastery **Rev:** Folk art crucifix and denomination

Date	Mintage	F	VF	XF	Unc	BU
2004 Proof	500	Value: 100				

KM# 115 100 DRAM

31.1000 g., 0.9250 Silver 0.9249 oz. ASW, 40 mm. **Subject:** Anania Shirakatsi 1400 Anniversary, Scientist **Obv:** Profile of Shirakatsi, deep in thought **Rev:** Planets and stars, denomination

Date	Mintage	F	VF	XF	Unc	BU
2005 Proof	500	Value: 100				

KM# 123 100 DRAM

31.1000 g., 0.9250 Silver 0.9249 oz. ASW, 40.00 mm. **Subject:** Creation of the Armenian alphabet **Obv:** National arms **Rev:** King Vramshapuh standing at left, alphabet at right

Date	Mintage	F	VF	XF	Unc	BU
2005 Proof	500	Value: 150				

KM# 124 100 DRAM

31.1000 g., 0.9250 Silver 0.9249 oz. ASW, 40.00 mm. **Subject:** Creation of the Armenian alphabet **Obv:** National arms **Rev:** Sahak Partev standing at left, alphabet at right

Date	Mintage	F	VF	XF	Unc	BU
2005 Proof	500	Value: 150				

KM# 125 100 DRAM

31.1000 g., 0.9250 Silver 0.9249 oz. ASW, 40.00 mm. **Subject:** 100th Anniversary - Birth of Artem Mikoyan - Inventor of MIG Jet **Obv:** Three jet airplanes **Rev:** Bust of Mikoyan 3/4 left

Date	Mintage	F	VF	XF	Unc	BU
2005 Proof	500	Value: 125				

KM# 127 100 DRAM

28.2800 g., 0.9250 Silver 0.8410 oz. ASW, 38.61 mm. **Subject:** International Polar Year **Obv:** National arms **Obv. Legend:** REPUBLIC OF ARMENIA **Rev:** Bust of Fridtjof Nansen right at left, ship stuck in ice at lower right, multicolor emblem above

Date	Mintage	F	VF	XF	Unc	BU
2006 Proof	10,000	Value: 100				

KM# 129 100 DRAM

28.2800 g., 0.9250 Silver 0.8410 oz. ASW **Subject:** Hovhannes Aivazovsky **Obv:** National arms at lower left, sailing ship listing at center right multicolor **Rev:** Bust of Aivazovsky 3/4 left at lower left, sailing ships at center right **Shape:** Rectangular, 40 x 28 mm

Date	Mintage	F	VF	XF	Unc	BU
2006 Proof	5,000	Value: 500				

KM# 119 100 DRAM

28.2800 g., 0.9250 Silver 0.8410 oz. ASW, 38.61 mm. **Obv:** National arms **Rev:** Brown bear and two red lines **Edge:** Plain

Date	Mintage	F	VF	XF	Unc	BU
2006 Proof	3,000	Value: 170				

KM# 120 100 DRAM

28.2800 g., 0.9250 Silver 0.8410 oz. ASW, 38.61 mm. **Obv:** National arms **Rev:** Long-eared Hedgehog and two red lines **Edge:** Plain

Date	Mintage	F	VF	XF	Unc	BU
2006 Proof	3,000	Value: 170				

KM# 121 100 DRAM

28.2800 g., 0.9250 Silver 0.8410 oz. ASW, 38.6 mm. **Obv:** National arms, date and value **Rev:** Caucasian Forest Cat **Edge:** Plain

Date	Mintage	F	VF	XF	Unc	BU
2006 Proof	3,000	Value: 100				

KM# 122 100 DRAM

28.2800 g., 0.9250 Silver 0.8410 oz. ASW, 38.6 mm. **Obv:** National arms, date and value **Rev:** Armenian Tortoise **Edge:** Plain

Date	Mintage	F	VF	XF	Unc	BU
2006 Proof	3,000	Value: 120				

KM# 135 100 DRAM

28.2400 g., 0.9250 Silver 0.8398 oz. ASW, 38.53 mm. **Subject:** Caucasion Leopard **Obv:** National arms **Obv. Legend:** REPUBLIC OF ARMENIA **Rev:** Leopard walking left **Edge:** Plain

Date	Mintage	F	VF	XF	Unc	BU
2007 Proof	3,000	Value: 100				

KM# 136 100 DRAM

28.2400 g., 0.9250 Silver 0.8398 oz. ASW, 38.5 mm. **Subject:** Northern Shoveler duck **Obv:** National arms **Obv. Legend:** REPUBLIC OF ARMENIA **Rev:** Duck standing left **Edge:** Plain

Date	Mintage	F	VF	XF	Unc	BU
2007 Proof	3,000	Value: 85.00				

KM# 141 100 DRAM

28.2800 g., 0.9250 Silver Zircon crystal attached. 0.8410 oz. ASW, 38.5 mm. **Series:** Signs of the Zodiac **Obv:** National arms within ring of signs of the Zodiac **Obv. Legend:** REPUBLIC OF ARMENIA **Rev:** Capricorn with jeweled star at left, multicolor **Edge:** Plain

Date	Mintage	F	VF	XF	Unc	BU
2007 Proof	12,000	Value: 85.00				

KM# 153 100 DRAM

28.2800 g., 0.9250 Silver 0.8410 oz. ASW, 38.6 mm. **Obv:** National arms **Obv. Legend:** REPUBLIC OF ARMENIA **Rev:** Lake Sevan Salmon

Date	Mintage	F	VF	XF	Unc	BU
2007 Proof	3,000	Value: 85.00				

KM# 154 100 DRAM

28.2800 g., 0.9250 Silver 0.8410 oz. ASW, 38.6 mm. **Obv:** National arms **Obv. Legend:** REPUBLIC OF ARMENIA **Rev:** Armenian viper

Date	Mintage	F	VF	XF	Unc	BU
2007 Proof	3,000	Value: 85.00				

KM# 157 100 DRAM

28.2800 g., 0.9250 Silver 0.8410 oz. ASW, 38.6 mm. **Subject:** Aquarius

Date	Mintage	F	VF	XF	Unc	BU
2007 Proof	—	Value: 80.00				

KM# 158 100 DRAM

28.2800 g., 0.9250 Silver 0.8410 oz. ASW, 38.6 mm. **Subject:** Pisces

Date	Mintage	F	VF	XF	Unc	BU
2007 Proof	—	Value: 80.00				

KM# 155 100 DRAM
28.2800 g., 0.9250 Silver 0.8410 oz. ASW, 39 mm. **Obv:** National Arms **Rev:** Caucasian owl on branch, (Aegolius Funereus Caucasious) red arcs at top and bottom

Date	Mintage	F	VF	XF	Unc	BU
2008 Proof	3,000	Value: 80.00				

KM# 159 100 DRAM
28.2800 g., 0.9250 Silver 0.8410 oz. ASW, 38.6 mm. **Subject:** Aries

Date	Mintage	F	VF	XF	Unc	BU
2008 Proof	—	Value: 80.00				

KM# 160 100 DRAM
28.2800 g., 0.9250 Silver 0.8410 oz. ASW, 38.6 mm. **Subject:** Taurus

Date	Mintage	F	VF	XF	Unc	BU
2008 Proof	—	Value: 80.00				

KM# 161 100 DRAM
28.2800 g., 0.9250 Silver 0.8410 oz. ASW, 38.6 mm. **Subject:** Gemini

Date	Mintage	F	VF	XF	Unc	BU
2008 Proof	—	Value: 80.00				

KM# 162 100 DRAM
28.2800 g., 0.9250 Silver 0.8410 oz. ASW **Subject:** Cancer

Date	Mintage	F	VF	XF	Unc	BU
2008 Proof	—	Value: 80.00				

KM# 163 100 DRAM
28.2800 g., 0.9250 Silver 0.8410 oz. ASW, 38.6 mm. **Subject:** Leo

Date	Mintage	F	VF	XF	Unc	BU
2008 Proof	—	Value: 80.00				

KM# 164 100 DRAM
28.2800 g., 0.9250 Silver 0.8410 oz. ASW, 38.6 mm. **Subject:** Virgo

Date	Mintage	F	VF	XF	Unc	BU
2008 Proof	—	Value: 80.00				

KM# 165 100 DRAM
28.2800 g., 0.9250 Silver 0.8410 oz. ASW, 38.6 mm. **Subject:** Libra

Date	Mintage	F	VF	XF	Unc	BU
2008 Proof	—	Value: 80.00				

KM# 167 100 DRAM
28.2800 g., 0.9250 Silver 0.8410 oz. ASW, 38.6 mm. **Subject:** Bezoar goat

Date	Mintage	F	VF	XF	Unc	BU
2008 Proof	—	Value: 85.00				

KM# 172 100 DRAM
28.2800 g., 0.9250 Silver 0.8410 oz. ASW, 38.6 mm. **Subject:** Scorpio

Date	Mintage	F	VF	XF	Unc	BU
2008 Proof	—	Value: 80.00				

KM# 174 100 DRAM
28.2800 g., 0.9250 Silver 0.8410 oz. ASW, 38.6 mm. **Subject:** Sagittarius

Date	Mintage	F	VF	XF	Unc	BU
2008 Proof	—	Value: 80.00				

KM# 177 100 DRAM
28.2800 g., 0.9250 Silver 0.8410 oz. ASW, 38.6 mm. **Subject:** Armenian Moufflon

Date	Mintage	F	VF	XF	Unc	BU
2008 Proof	—	Value: 75.00				

KM# 178 100 DRAM
28.2800 g., 0.9250 Silver 0.8410 oz. ASW, 38.6 mm. **Subject:** Toad Agama

Date	Mintage	F	VF	XF	Unc	BU
2008 Proof	—	Value: 75.00				

KM# 182 100 DRAM
28.2800 g., 0.9250 Silver 0.8410 oz. ASW, 38.6 mm. **Subject:** Pele

Date	Mintage	F	VF	XF	Unc	BU
2008 Proof	—	Value: 60.00				

KM# 183 100 DRAM
28.2800 g., 0.9250 Silver 0.8410 oz. ASW, 38.6 mm. **Subject:** Eusebio

Date	Mintage	F	VF	XF	Unc	BU
2008 Proof	—	Value: 60.00				

KM# 184 100 DRAM
28.2800 g., 0.9250 Silver 0.8410 oz. ASW, 38.6 mm. **Subject:** Lev Jashin

Date	Mintage	F	VF	XF	Unc	BU
2008 Proof	—	Value: 60.00				

KM# 187 100 DRAM
28.2800 g., 0.9250 Silver 0.8410 oz. ASW, 38.6 mm. **Subject:** Franz Beckenbauer

Date	Mintage	F	VF	XF	Unc	BU
2008 Proof	—	Value: 60.00				

KM# 156 100 DRAM
28.2800 g., 0.9250 Silver 0.8410 oz. ASW, 38.6 mm. **Subject:** Zbigniew Boniek **Rev:** Portrait facing, multicolor flag

Date	Mintage	F	VF	XF	Unc	BU
2009 Proof	50,000	Value: 60.00				

KM# 209 100 DRAM
33.6200 g., 0.9250 Silver 0.9998 oz. ASW, 38.61 mm. **Obv:** Arms with lion supporters **Rev:** Michael Platini, soccer ball and flag in color

Date	Mintage	F	VF	XF	Unc	BU
2011 Proof	—	Value: 100				

KM# 223 100 DRAM
28.2800 g., 0.9250 Silver 0.8410 oz. ASW, 28x40 mm. **Subject:** Sergei Parajanov **Obv:** Artist in studio, painting in color **Rev:** Self portrait **Shape:** Vertical rectangle **Designer:** Urszula Walerzak

Date	Mintage	F	VF	XF	Unc	BU
2012 Proof	Est. 5,555	Value: 100				

KM# 96 200 DRAM
4.5000 g., Brass, 24 mm. **Obv:** National arms **Rev:** Value **Edge:** Reeded

Date	Mintage	F	VF	XF	Unc	BU
2003	—	—	—	—	3.00	4.00

KM# 106 500 DRAM
155.5000 g., 0.9250 Silver 4.6243 oz. ASW, 63 mm. **Subject:** 10th Anniversary of Independence **Obv:** National arms **Rev:** Tower with flag, logo at right 9-21-91

Date	Mintage	F	VF	XF	Unc	BU
2001 Proof	200	Value: 500				

KM# 97 500 DRAM
5.0000 g., Bi-Metallic Copper-Nickel center in a Brass ring, 22 mm. **Obv:** National arms **Rev:** Value **Edge:** Segmented reeding

Date	Mintage	F	VF	XF	Unc	BU
2003	—	—	—	—	6.00	8.00
2004	—	—	—	—	6.00	8.00

KM# 210 500 DRAM
1.2400 g., 0.9990 Gold 0.0398 oz. AGW, 13.92 mm. **Obv:** National arms, value below **Rev:** Pomegranate

Date	Mintage	F	VF	XF	Unc	BU
2011 Proof	Est. 5,000	Value: 150				

KM# 109 1000 DRAM
15.5500 g., 0.5850 Gold 0.2925 oz. AGW, 26 mm. **Obv:** National arms on ancient coin design **Rev:** Tigran the Great ancient coin portrait

Date	Mintage	F	VF	XF	Unc	BU
2003	500	—	—	—	785	1,000

KM# 128 1000 DRAM
33.6000 g., 0.9250 Silver 0.9992 oz. ASW, 38 mm. **Subject:** 100th Anniversary Birth of Marshal Babajanian **Obv:** National arms **Rev:** Bust of Babajanian 3/4 right

Date	Mintage	F	VF	XF	Unc	BU
2006 Proof	500	Value: 150				

KM# 133 1000 DRAM
33.6000 g., 0.9250 Silver 0.9992 oz. ASW, 40 mm. **Subject:** Armenian grapes **Obv:** National arms **Rev:** Large bunch of grapes at left

Date	Mintage	F	VF	XF	Unc	BU
2007 Proof	5,000	Value: 150				

KM# 169 1000 DRAM
33.6000 g., 0.9250 Silver 0.9992 oz. ASW, 40 mm. **Subject:** Viktor Ambartsumian, 100th Anniversary of Birth **Edge:** Reeded

Date	Mintage	F	VF	XF	Unc	BU
2008 Proof	500	Value: 100				

KM# 171 1000 DRAM
33.6000 g., 0.9250 Silver 0.9992 oz. ASW, 40 mm. **Subject:** A. Spendiaryan Theater of Ballet and Opera, 75th Anniversary

Date	Mintage	F	VF	XF	Unc	BU
2008 Proof	—	Value: 100				

KM# 192 1000 DRAM
33.6000 g., 0.9250 Silver 0.9992 oz. ASW, 40 mm. **Subject:** Mkhitar Gosh - The Codex **Edge:** Reeded

Date	Mintage	F	VF	XF	Unc	BU
2009 Proof	500	Value: 100				

KM# 193 1000 DRAM
31.1000 g., 0.9990 Silver 0.9988 oz. ASW, 38 mm. **Subject:** Gladzor University, 750th Anniversary

Date	Mintage	F	VF	XF	Unc	BU
2009 Proof	—	Value: 100				

KM# 199 1000 DRAM
33.6000 g., 0.9250 Silver 0.9992 oz. ASW, 40 mm. **Rev:** Poppy plant and flower in color

Date	Mintage	F	VF	XF	Unc	BU
2011 Proof	—	Value: 75.00				

KM# 201 1000 DRAM
28.2800 g., 0.9250 Silver 0.8410 oz. ASW, 38.61 mm. **Obv:** Berries and flower in color **Rev:** Sorbus Hajastana in color **Designer:** Eduard Kurghinyan

Date	Mintage	F	VF	XF	Unc	BU
2011 Proof	10,000	Value: 75.00				

KM# 202 1000 DRAM
28.2800 g., 0.9250 Silver 0.8410 oz. ASW, 38.61 mm. **Obv:** Two crocus flowers in color **Rev:** Crocus flower open

Date	Mintage	F	VF	XF	Unc	BU
2011 Proof	10,000	Value: 75.00				

KM# 203 1000 DRAM
28.2800 g., 0.9250 Silver 0.8410 oz. ASW, 38.61 mm. **Subject:** WuSu **Obv:** Shaolin Monastery and dragons **Rev:** Three sportsmen

Date	Mintage	F	VF	XF	Unc	BU
2011 Proof	5,000	Value: 80.00				

KM# 204 1000 DRAM
28.2800 g., 0.9250 Silver 0.8410 oz. ASW, 38.61 mm. **Subject:** Judo **Obv:** Eishoji Tempole in Kamakura and lake reflection **Rev:** Two pair of Judo sportsmen, Mt. Fuji and cherry blossom

Date	Mintage	F	VF	XF	Unc	BU
2011 Proof	5,000	Value: 80.00				

KM# 206 1000 DRAM
33.6000 g., 0.9250 Silver 0.9992 oz. ASW, 40 mm. **Subject:** Treaty of Vienna, 200th Anniversary **Obv:** Two partial building façades **Rev:** Treaty with seal, building tower

Date	Mintage	F	VF	XF	Unc	BU
2011 Proof	—	Value: 100				

KM# 207 1000 DRAM
15.6000 g., 0.5850 Gold 0.2934 oz. AGW, 26 mm. **Subject:** Artashat, 2200th Anniversary of Founding **Obv:** Ancient coin at center, Tyche head right **Rev:** Ancient coin at center, Figure standing

Date	Mintage	F	VF	XF	Unc	BU
2011 Antique patina	1,000	—	—	—	—	600

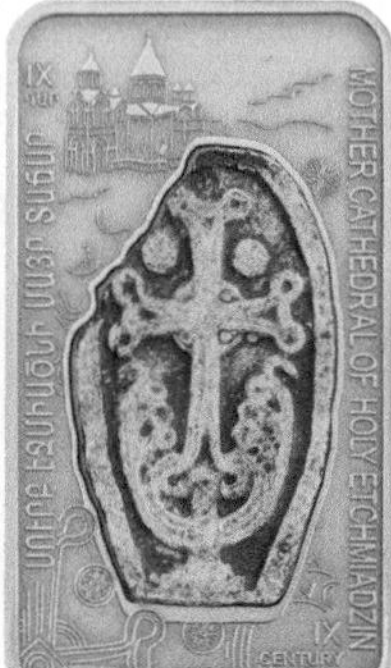

KM# 208 1000 DRAM
Silver, 27x47 mm. **Obv:** National arms, value below **Rev:** Historic fragment and church **Shape:** Vertical rectangle

Date	Mintage	F	VF	XF	Unc	BU
2011 Antique patina	—	—	—	—	—	150

KM# 228 1000 DRAM
33.6000 g., 0.9250 Silver 0.9992 oz. ASW, 40 mm. **Subject:** Army, 20th Anniversary **Rev:** Emblem of the Army and the Order of the Motherland **Shape:** 8-sided

Date	Mintage	F	VF	XF	Unc	BU
2012 Proof	500	Value: 200				

KM# 134 1957 DRAM
33.6000 g., 0.9250 Silver 0.9992 oz. ASW, 40 mm. **Subject:** 50th Anniversay of Matenadaran **Obv:** Small national arms at center surrounded by intricate pattern **Rev:** Building at left center

Date	Mintage	F	VF	XF	Unc	BU
2007 Proof	500	Value: 125				

KM# 117 5000 DRAM
31.1000 g., 0.9250 Silver 0.9249 oz. ASW, 38 mm. **Subject:** Armenian Armed Forces **Obv:** Order of the Combat Cross of the Second Degree and the Emblem of the Ministry of Defense of the Republic of Armenia **Rev:** Arms, date and denomination **Shape:** Octagonal

Date	Mintage	F	VF	XF	Unc	BU
2005 Proof	500	Value: 130				

KM# 126 5000 DRAM
168.1000 g., 0.9250 Silver 4.9990 oz. ASW, 63 mm. **Subject:** 15th Anniversary of Independence **Obv:** National arms **Rev:** Building at center left, multicolor emblem above, mountains in background

Date	Mintage	F	VF	XF	Unc	BU
2006 Proof	300	Value: 400				

KM# 139 5000 DRAM
4.3000 g., 0.9000 Gold 0.1244 oz. AGW, 18 mm. **Subject:** Haik Nahapet **Obv:** Small national arms at upper left, Orion constellation at right **Rev:** 3/4 length classical Archer right

Date	Mintage	F	VF	XF	Unc	BU
2007 Proof	3,000	Value: 400				

KM# 179 5000 DRAM
168.1000 g., 0.9250 Silver partially gold plated 4.9990 oz. ASW, 63 mm. **Subject:** National Currency, 15th Anniversary

Date	Mintage	F	VF	XF	Unc	BU
2008 Proof	—	Value: 150				

KM# 195 5000 DRAM
4.3000 g., 0.9000 Gold 0.1244 oz. AGW, 18 mm. **Subject:** St. Sargis the Commander

Date	Mintage	F	VF	XF	Unc	BU
2009 Proof	—	Value: 400				

KM# 205 5000 DRAM
168.1000 g., 0.9250 Silver 4.9990 oz. ASW, 63 mm. **Subject:** 20th Anniversary of the Republic **Obv:** National arms **Rev:** Two birds in flight, date in color

Date	Mintage	F	VF	XF	Unc	BU
2011 Proof	—	Value: 350				

KM# 107 10000 DRAM
8.6000 g., 0.9990 Gold 0.2762 oz. AGW, 22 mm. **Obv:** Mesrop Mashtots, creator of the Armenian alphabet **Rev:** Armenian alphabet

Date	Mintage	F	VF	XF	Unc	BU
2002 Proof	1,000	Value: 800				

KM# 108 10000 DRAM
8.6000 g., 0.9990 Gold 0.2762 oz. AGW, 22 mm. **Obv:** Building above value **Rev:** Aram Khachatryan left birth centennial

Date	Mintage	F	VF	XF	Unc	BU
2002 Proof	500	Value: 800				

KM# 114 10000 DRAM
8.6000 g., 0.9990 Gold 0.2762 oz. AGW, 22 mm. **Subject:** Arshile Gorky birth April 15, 1904 **Obv:** Bust of Gorky **Rev:** Denomination

Date	Mintage	F	VF	XF	Unc	BU
2004 Proof	1,000	Value: 800				

KM# 116 10000 DRAM
8.6000 g., 0.9990 Gold 0.2762 oz. AGW, 22 mm. **Subject:** Martiros Saryan 125th Anniversary of Birth **Obv:** Bust of Saryan **Rev:** Landscape, denomination

Date	Mintage	F	VF	XF	Unc	BU
2005 Proof	1,000	Value: 800				

KM# 130 10000 DRAM
8.6000 g., 0.9990 Gold 0.2762 oz. AGW, 22 mm. **Subject:** Komitas Vardapet **Obv:** Musical notations and score **Rev:** Bust of Vardapet 3/4 right

Date	Mintage	F	VF	XF	Unc	BU
2006 Proof	1,000	Value: 800				

KM# 131 10000 DRAM
8.6000 g., 0.9000 Gold 0.2488 oz. AGW, 22 mm. **Subject:** 37th Chess Olympiad **Obv:** Chess piece at right **Rev:** National arms within 6 chess pieces in circle

Date	Mintage	F	VF	XF	Unc	BU
2006 Proof	1,000	Value: 800				

KM# 132 10000 DRAM
8.6000 g., 0.9000 Gold 0.2488 oz. AGW, 22 mm. **Subject:** Hakob Gurjian **Obv:** Seated female sculpture **Rev:** Head 3/4 right

Date	Mintage	F	VF	XF	Unc	BU
2006 Proof	1,000	Value: 800				

KM# 137 10000 DRAM
8.6000 g., 0.9000 Gold 0.2488 oz. AGW, 22 mm. **Subject:** Jean Carzou **Obv:** National arms with stylized view of shopping bourse **Rev:** Bust of Carzou 3/4 right at laft center

Date	Mintage	F	VF	XF	Unc	BU
2007 Proof	1,000	Value: 800				

KM# 138 10000 DRAM
8.6000 g., 0.9000 Gold 0.2488 oz. AGW, 22 mm. **Subject:** 15th Anniversary of Armenian Army **Obv:** National arms **Rev:** Military badge

Date	Mintage	F	VF	XF	Unc	BU
2007 Proof	1,000	Value: 800				

KM# 140 10000 DRAM
8.6000 g., 0.9000 Gold 0.2488 oz. AGW, 22 mm. **Subject:** 15th Anniversary Liberation of Shushi **Obv:** Bird with wings outspread above two shields **Rev:** Swirl in background

Date	Mintage	F	VF	XF	Unc	BU
2007 Proof	1,000	Value: 800				

KM# 175 10000 DRAM
8.6000 g., 0.9000 Gold 0.2488 oz. AGW, 22 mm. **Subject:** Sagittarius

Date	Mintage	F	VF	XF	Unc	BU
2008 Proof	—	Value: 700				

KM# 166 10000 DRAM
8.6000 g., 0.9000 Gold 0.2488 oz. AGW, 22 mm. **Subject:** Libra

Date	Mintage	F	VF	XF	Unc	BU
2008 Proof	—	Value: 700				

KM# 168 10000 DRAM
8.6000 g., 0.9000 Gold 0.2488 oz. AGW, 22 mm. **Subject:** Court, 10th Anniversary

Date	Mintage	F	VF	XF	Unc	BU
2008 Proof	—	Value: 700				

KM# 170 10000 DRAM
8.6000 g., 0.9000 Gold 0.2488 oz. AGW, 22 mm. **Subject:** William Saroyan, 100th Anniversary of Birth

Date	Mintage	F	VF	XF	Unc	BU
2008 Proof	—	Value: 700				

KM# 173 10000 DRAM
8.6000 g., 0.9000 Gold 0.2488 oz. AGW, 22 mm. **Subject:** Scorpio

Date	Mintage	F	VF	XF	Unc	BU
2008 Proof	—	Value: 700				

KM# 176 10000 DRAM
8.6000 g., 0.9000 Gold 0.2488 oz. AGW, 22 mm. **Subject:** Capricorn

Date	Mintage	F	VF	XF	Unc	BU
2008 Proof	—	Value: 700				

KM# 180 10000 DRAM
8.6000 g., 0.9000 Gold 0.2488 oz. AGW, 22 mm. **Subject:** Aquarius

Date	Mintage	F	VF	XF	Unc	BU
2008 Proof	—	Value: 700				

KM# 181 10000 DRAM
8.6000 g., 0.9000 Gold 0.2488 oz. AGW, 22 mm. **Subject:** Pisces

Date	Mintage	F	VF	XF	Unc	BU
2008 Proof	—	Value: 700				

KM# 185 10000 DRAM
8.6000 g., 0.9000 Gold 0.2488 oz. AGW, 22 mm. **Subject:** Aries

Date	Mintage	F	VF	XF	Unc	BU
2008 Proof	—	Value: 700				

KM# 186 10000 DRAM
8.6000 g., 0.9000 Gold 0.2488 oz. AGW, 22 mm. **Subject:** Taurus

Date	Mintage	F	VF	XF	Unc	BU
2008 Proof	—	Value: 700				

KM# 188 10000 DRAM
8.6000 g., 0.9000 Gold 0.2488 oz. AGW, 22 mm. **Subject:** Gemini

Date	Mintage	F	VF	XF	Unc	BU
2008 Proof	—	Value: 700				

KM# 189 10000 DRAM
8.6000 g., 0.9000 Gold 0.2488 oz. AGW, 22 mm. **Subject:** Cancer

Date	Mintage	F	VF	XF	Unc	BU
2008 Proof	—	Value: 700				

KM# 190 10000 DRAM
8.6000 g., 0.9000 Gold 0.2488 oz. AGW, 22 mm. **Subject:** Leo

Date	Mintage	F	VF	XF	Unc	BU
2008 Proof	—	Value: 700				

KM# 191 10000 DRAM
8.6000 g., 0.9000 Gold 0.2488 oz. AGW, 22 mm. **Subject:** Virgo

Date	Mintage	F	VF	XF	Unc	BU
2009 Proof	—	Value: 700				

KM# 194 10000 DRAM
8.6000 g., 0.9000 Gold 0.2488 oz. AGW, 22 mm. **Subject:** Khachatour Aboryan, 200th Anniversary of Birth

Date	Mintage	F	VF	XF	Unc	BU
2009 Proof	—	Value: 800				

KM# 200 10000 DRAM
8.6000 g., 0.9000 Gold 0.2488 oz. AGW, 22 mm. **Subject:** Misaq Metsarents, poet, 125th Anniversary of Birth **Edge:** Reeded

Date	Mintage	F	VF	XF	Unc	BU
2011 Proof	1,000	Value: 525				

KM# 211 10000 DRAM

8.6000 g., 0.9000 Gold 0.2488 oz. AGW, 22 mm. **Subject:** Toros Roslin, 800th Anniversary **Edge:** Reeded

Date	Mintage	F	VF	XF	Unc	BU
2011 Proof	1,000	Value: 525				

KM# 229 10000 DRAM

8.6000 g., 0.9000 Gold 0.2488 oz. AGW, 20 mm. **Subject:** Army, 20th Anniversary **Rev:** Army emblem and Order of the Motherland

Date	Mintage	F	VF	XF	Unc	BU
2012 Proof	500	Value: 750				

KM# 118 50000 DRAM

8.6000 g., 0.9990 Gold 0.2762 oz. AGW, 22 mm. **Subject:** Armenian Armed Forces **Obv:** Order of the Combat Cross of the Second Degree and the Emblem of the Ministry of Defense of the Republic of Armenia **Rev:** Arms, date and denomination

Date	Mintage	F	VF	XF	Unc	BU
2005 Proof	1,000	Value: 800				

BULLION COINAGE

KM# 198 100 DRAM

7.7700 g., 0.9990 Silver 0.2496 oz. ASW **Obv:** National arms **Rev:** Noah's Ark

Date	Mintage	F	VF	XF	Unc	BU
2011LEV	—	—	—	—	—	15.00
2012LEV	—	—	—	—	—	15.00

KM# 197 200 DRAM

15.5500 g., 0.9990 Silver 0.4994 oz. ASW **Obv:** National arms **Rev:** Noah's Ark

Date	Mintage	F	VF	XF	Unc	BU
2011LEV	—	—	—	—	—	25.00
2012LEV	—	—	—	—	—	25.00

KM# 196 500 DRAM

31.1050 g., 0.9990 Silver 0.9990 oz. ASW, 38.6 mm. **Obv:** National arms **Rev:** Dove, Noah's Ark and sun rise over Mt. Ararat

Date	Mintage	F	VF	XF	Unc	BU
2011LEV	—	—	—	—	—	50.00
2012LEV	—	—	—	—	—	50.00

KM# 227 1000 DRAM

155.5000 g., 0.9990 Silver 4.9942 oz. ASW, 62.2 mm. **Obv:** National arms **Rev:** Noah's Ark

Date	Mintage	F	VF	XF	Unc	BU
2012LEV	—	—	—	—	—	200

KM# 226 5000 DRAM

311.0500 g., 0.9990 Silver 9.9901 oz. ASW, 75.5 mm. **Obv:** National arms **Rev:** Noah's Ark **Note:** 7.4mm thick.

Date	Mintage	F	VF	XF	Unc	BU
2012LEV	—	—	—	—	—	400

KM# 225 10000 DRAM

1000.0000 g., 0.9990 Silver 32.117 oz. ASW, 100 mm. **Obv:** National arms **Rev:** Noah's Ark **Note:** 14mm thick.

Date	Mintage	F	VF	XF	Unc	BU
2012LEV	—	—	—	—	—	1,200

KM# 224 20000 DRAM

5000.0000 g., 0.9990 Silver 160.58 oz. ASW, 164.6 mm. **Obv:** National arms **Rev:** Noah's Ark **Note:** 29mm thick

Date	Mintage	F	VF	XF	Unc	BU
2012LEV	—	—	—	—	—	6,000

ARUBA

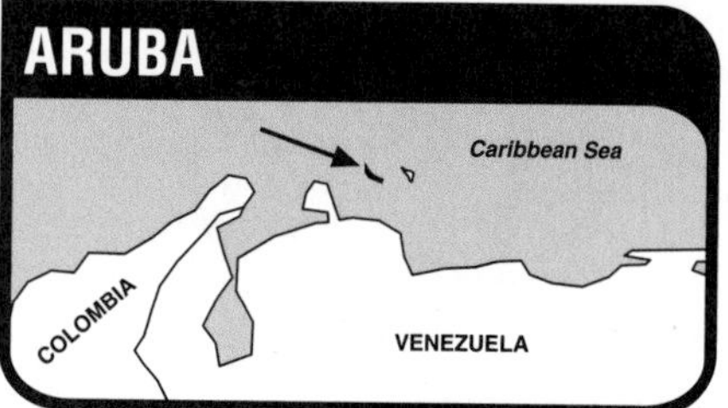

The second largest island of the former Netherlands Antilles, Aruba is situated near the Venezuelan coast. The island has an area of 74-1/2 sq. mi. (193 sq. km.) and a population of 105,000. Capital: Oranjestad, named after the Dutch royal family. Aruba was important in the processing and transportation of petroleum products in the first part of the twentieth century, but today the chief industry is tourism.

For earlier issues see Curacao and the Netherlands Antilles.

RULER

Dutch

MINT MARKS

(u) Utrecht - Privy marks only
Wine tendril with grapes, 2001-
Wine tendril with grapes plus star, 2002-
Sails of a clipper, 2003-

MONETARY SYSTEM

100 Cents = 1 Florin

DUTCH STATE
"Status Aparte"

DECIMAL COINAGE

KM# 1 5 CENTS

2.0000 g., Nickel Bonded Steel, 16 mm. **Ruler:** Beatrix **Obv:** National arms **Rev:** Geometric design with value **Edge:** Plain

Date	Mintage	F	VF	XF	Unc	BU
2001(u)	946,900	—	0.10	0.25	0.50	1.00
2002(u)	1,006,000	—	0.10	0.25	0.50	1.00
2003(u)	1,104,100	—	0.10	0.25	0.50	1.00
2004(u)	502,500	—	0.10	0.25	0.50	1.00
2005(u)	602,500	—	0.10	0.25	0.50	1.00
2006(u)	602,000	—	0.10	0.25	0.50	1.00
2007(u)	1,152,000	—	0.10	0.25	0.50	1.00
2008(u)	1,152,000	—	0.10	0.25	0.50	1.00
2009(u)	—	—	0.10	0.25	0.50	1.00
2010(u)	—	—	0.10	0.25	0.50	1.00
2011(u)	—	—	0.10	0.25	0.50	1.00
2012(u)	—	—	0.10	0.25	0.50	1.00

KM# 2 10 CENTS

3.0000 g., Nickel Bonded Steel, 18 mm. **Ruler:** Beatrix **Obv:** National arms **Rev:** Geometric design with value **Edge:** Reeded

Date	Mintage	F	VF	XF	Unc	BU
2001(u)	1,006,900	—	0.20	0.35	0.60	1.10
2002(u)	1,006,000	—	0.20	0.35	0.60	1.10
2003(u)	1,004,000	—	0.20	0.35	0.60	1.10
2004(u)	402,500	—	0.20	0.35	0.60	1.10
2005(u)	402,500	—	0.20	0.35	0.60	1.10
2006(u)	452,500	—	0.20	0.35	0.60	1.10
2007(u)	1,102,000	—	0.20	0.35	0.60	1.10
2008(u)	1,442,000	—	0.20	0.35	0.60	1.10
2009(u)	—	—	0.20	0.35	0.60	1.10
2009(u)	—	—	0.20	0.35	0.60	1.10
2010(u)	—	—	0.20	0.35	0.60	1.10
2011	—	—	0.20	0.35	0.60	1.10
2012(u)	—	—	0.20	0.35	0.60	1.10

KM# 3 25 CENTS

3.5000 g., Nickel Bonded Steel, 20 mm. **Ruler:** Beatrix **Obv:** National arms **Rev:** Geometric design with value **Edge:** Plain

Date	Mintage	F	VF	XF	Unc	BU
2001(u)	716,900	—	0.20	0.40	0.75	1.50
2002(u)	806,000	—	0.20	0.40	0.75	1.50
2003(u)	804,000	—	0.20	0.40	0.75	1.50
2004(u)	362,500	—	0.20	0.40	0.75	1.50
2005(u)	302,500	—	0.20	0.40	0.75	1.50
2006(u)	302,000	—	0.20	0.40	0.75	1.50
2007(u)	202,000	—	0.20	0.40	0.75	1.50
2008(u)	202,000	—	0.20	0.40	0.75	1.50
2009(u)	—	—	0.20	0.40	0.75	1.50
2010(u)	—	—	0.20	0.40	0.75	1.50
2011(u)	—	—	0.20	0.40	0.75	1.50
2012(u)	—	—	0.20	0.40	0.75	1.50

KM# 4 50 CENTS

5.0000 g., Nickel Bonded Steel, 20 mm. **Ruler:** Beatrix **Obv:** National arms **Rev:** Geometric design with value **Edge:** Plain **Shape:** 4-sided

Date	Mintage	F	VF	XF	Unc	BU
2001(u)	506,900	—	0.30	0.50	1.00	1.50
2002(u)	306,000	—	0.30	0.50	1.00	1.50
2003(u)	279,000	—	0.30	0.50	1.00	1.50
2004(u)	402,500	—	0.30	0.50	1.00	1.50
2005(u)	102,500	—	0.30	0.50	1.00	1.50
2006(u)	102,500	—	0.30	0.50	1.00	1.50
2007(u)	32,000	—	0.30	0.60	1.50	2.50
2008(u)	302,000	—	0.30	0.60	1.50	2.50
2009(u)	—	—	0.30	0.60	1.50	2.50
2010(u)	—	—	0.30	0.60	1.50	2.50
2011(u)	—	—	0.30	0.60	1.50	2.50
2012(u)	—	—	0.30	0.60	1.50	2.50

KM# 5 FLORIN

8.5000 g., Nickel Bonded Steel, 26 mm. **Ruler:** Beatrix **Obv:** Head left **Rev:** National arms and value **Edge:** Lettered **Edge Lettering:** GOD * ZIJ * MET * ONS *

Date	Mintage	F	VF	XF	Unc	BU
2001(u)	406,900	—	0.60	1.00	2.00	3.00
2002(u)	206,000	—	0.60	1.00	2.00	3.00
2003(u)	179,000	—	0.60	1.00	2.00	3.00
2004(u)	410,000	—	0.60	1.00	2.00	3.00
2005(u)	352,500	—	0.60	1.00	2.00	3.00
2006(u)	402,000	—	0.60	1.00	2.00	3.00
2007(u)	502,000	—	0.60	1.00	2.00	3.00
2008(u)	289,000	—	0.60	1.00	2.00	3.00
2009(u)	—	—	0.60	1.00	2.00	3.00
2010(u)	—	—	0.60	1.00	2.00	3.00
2011(u)	—	—	0.60	1.00	2.00	3.00
2012(u)	—	—	0.60	1.00	2.00	3.00

KM# 6 2-1/2 FLORIN

10.3000 g., Nickel Bonded Steel, 30 mm. **Ruler:** Beatrix **Obv:** Head left **Rev:** National arms with value **Edge:** Lettered **Edge Lettering:** GOD * ZIJ * MET * ONS *

Date	Mintage	F	VF	XF	Unc	BU
2001(u) In sets only	6,900	—	—	2.00	3.00	7.00
2002(u) In sets only	6,000	—	—	2.00	3.00	7.00
2003(u) In sets only	4,000	—	—	2.00	3.00	7.00
2004(u) In sets only	2,500	—	—	2.00	3.00	7.00
2005(u) In sets only	2,500	—	—	2.00	3.00	7.00
2006(u) In sets only	2,000	—	—	2.00	3.00	7.00
2007(u) In sets only	2,000	—	—	2.00	3.00	7.00
2008(u) In sets only	2,000	—	—	2.00	3.00	7.00
2009(u) In sets only	2,000	—	—	2.00	3.00	7.00
2010(u) In sets only	—	—	—	2.00	3.00	7.00
2011(u)	—	—	—	2.00	3.00	7.00
2012(u)	—	—	—	2.00	3.00	7.00

KM# 12 5 FLORIN
8.6400 g., Nickel Bonded Steel, 26 mm. **Ruler:** Beatrix **Obv:** Head left **Rev:** National arms with value **Edge:** Plain **Shape:** Square

Date	Mintage	F	VF	XF	Unc	BU
2001(u) In sets only	6,900	—	—	3.00	7.00	9.00
2002(u) In sets only	6,000	—	—	3.00	7.00	9.00
2003(u) In sets only	4,000	—	—	3.00	7.00	9.00
2004(u) In sets only	2,500	—	—	3.00	7.00	9.00
2005(u) In sets only	2,500	—	—	3.00	7.00	9.00

KM# 25 5 FLORIN
11.9000 g., 0.9250 Silver 0.3539 oz. ASW, 29 mm. **Ruler:** Beatrix **Subject:** 50th Anniversary Charter for the Kingdom of the Netherlands including Netherlands Antilles **Obv:** Head left **Rev:** Royal seal **Edge Lettering:** GOD * ZIJ * MET * ONS *

Date	Mintage	F	VF	XF	Unc	BU
2004(u) Proof	4,000	Value: 40.00				

KM# 34 5 FLORIN
11.9000 g., 0.9250 Silver 0.3539 oz. ASW, 29 mm. **Ruler:** Beatrix **Subject:** Queen's Silver Jubilee **Obv:** Head left **Rev:** Flag **Edge:** Lettered **Edge Lettering:** GOD Z'J MET ONS

Date	Mintage	F	VF	XF	Unc	BU
2005(u) Proof	3,100	Value: 32.50				

KM# 38 5 FLORIN
8.4000 g., Aluminum-Bronze, 22.5 mm. **Ruler:** Beatrix **Obv:** Queen with a half crown on face **Rev:** Value and arms **Edge:** Reeded and lettered **Edge Lettering:** GOD * ZIJ * MET * ONS * **Shape:** Round

Date	Mintage	F	VF	XF	Unc	BU
2005(u)	827,500	—	—	—	5.00	8.00
2006(u)	102,000	—	—	—	7.00	10.00
2007(u)	52,000	—	—	—	7.00	10.00
2008(u)	22,000	—	—	—	7.00	15.00
2009(u)	—	—	—	—	7.00	15.00
2010(u)	—	—	—	—	7.00	15.00
2011(u)	—	—	—	—	7.00	15.00
2012(u)	—	—	—	—	7.00	15.00

KM# 41 5 FLORIN
11.9000 g., 0.9250 Silver 0.3539 oz. ASW, 29 mm. **Ruler:** Beatrix **Subject:** Year of the dolphin **Obv:** Head left **Rev:** Two dolphins bounding out of the water **Edge Lettering:** GOD * ZIJ * MET * ONS *

Date	Mintage	F	VF	XF	Unc	BU
2007(u) Proof	1,250	Value: 35.00				

KM# 42 5 FLORIN
11.9000 g., 0.9250 Silver 0.3539 oz. ASW, 29 mm. **Ruler:** Beatrix **Subject:** Fiesta de San Juan **Obv:** Head left **Rev:** Harvesting farmer **Edge Lettering:** GOD * ZIJ * MET * ONS

Date	Mintage	F	VF	XF	Unc	BU
2008(u) Proof	1,250	Value: 40.00				

KM# 43 5 FLORIN
11.9000 g., 0.9250 Silver 0.3539 oz. ASW, 29 mm. **Ruler:** Beatrix **Subject:** Dante at New Year's **Obv:** Head left **Rev:** Dance at New Year's, Hand dropping coins into hat **Edge Lettering:** GOD * ZIJ * MET * ONS

Date	Mintage	F	VF	XF	Unc	BU
2009(u) Proof	1,250	Value: 40.00				

KM# 45 5 FLORIN
11.9000 g., 0.9250 Silver 0.3539 oz. ASW, 29 mm. **Ruler:** Beatrix **Subject:** Olympic Games 2012 **Obv:** Queen Beatrix **Rev:** Two judoka fight men in action **Edge Lettering:** GOD * ZIJ * MET * ONS *

Date	Mintage	F	VF	XF	Unc	BU
2010 Proof	5,000	Value: 35.00				

KM# 46 5 FLORIN
11.9000 g., 0.9250 Silver 0.3539 oz. ASW, 29 mm. **Ruler:** Beatrix **Obv:** Head left **Rev:** California lighthouse and waves **Edge Lettering:** GOD * ZIJ * MET * ONS *

Date	Mintage	F	VF	XF	Unc	BU
2010(u) Proof	1,250	Value: 40.00				

KM# 47 5 FLORIN
11.9000 g., 0.9250 Silver 0.3539 oz. ASW, 29 mm. **Ruler:** Beatrix **Obv:** Shield in wreath above mintmarks **Rev:** 25 years Status Aparte with Parliament building **Edge Lettering:** GOD * ZIJ * MET * ONS *

Date	Mintage	Good	VG	F	VF	XF
2011(u) Proof	1,250	Value: 45.00				

KM# 48 5 FLORIN
11.9000 g., 0.9250 Silver 0.3539 oz. ASW, 29 mm. **Ruler:** Beatrix **Subject:** Royal Vista **Obv:** Shield in wreath above mintmarks **Rev:** Queen Beatrix, Prince Willem-Alexander and Princess Maxima looking left, orange top stripe, blue bottom stripe **Edge Lettering:** GOD * ZIJ * MET * ONS *

Date	Mintage	F	VF	XF	Unc	BU
2011(u) Proof	1,250	Value: 50.00				

KM# 20 10 FLORIN
25.0000 g., 0.9250 Silver 0.7435 oz. ASW, 38 mm. **Ruler:** Beatrix **Subject:** Green Sea Turtles **Obv:** Head left **Rev:** Seven sea turtles **Edge:** Plain **Designer:** E. Fingal

Date	Mintage	F	VF	XF	Unc	BU
2001(u) Prooflike	2,000	—	—	—	—	60.00

KM# 24 10 FLORIN
17.8000 g., 0.9250 Silver 0.5293 oz. ASW, 33 mm. **Ruler:** Beatrix **Subject:** Crown Prince's Wedding **Obv:** Head left **Rev:** Conjoined busts of prince and princess Maxima, right **Edge Lettering:** GOD ZIJ MET ONS **Designer:** G. Colley

Date	Mintage	F	VF	XF	Unc	BU
ND(2002)(u) Prooflike	5,000	—	—	—	—	40.00

KM# 27 10 FLORIN
25.0000 g., 0.9250 Silver 0.7435 oz. ASW, 38 mm. **Ruler:** Beatrix **Obv:** Head left **Rev:** Sea shell **Edge:** Plain

Date	Mintage	F	VF	XF	Unc	BU
2003(u) Proof	2,000	Value: 60.00				

KM# 28 10 FLORIN
25.0000 g., 0.9250 Silver 0.7435 oz. ASW, 38 mm. **Ruler:** Beatrix **Obv:** Head left **Rev:** Arubia Rattlesnake (Crotalus unicolor). **Edge:** Plain

Date	Mintage	F	VF	XF	Unc	BU
2003(u) Proof	2,000	Value: 60.00				

KM# 29 10 FLORIN
25.0000 g., 0.9250 Silver 0.7435 oz. ASW, 38 mm. **Ruler:** Beatrix **Obv:** Head left **Rev:** Burrowing Owl (Athena cunicularia). **Edge:** Plain

Date	Mintage	F	VF	XF	Unc	BU
2003(u) Proof	1,000	Value: 60.00				

KM# 30 10 FLORIN
25.0000 g., 0.9250 Silver 0.7435 oz. ASW, 38 mm. **Ruler:** Beatrix **Obv:** Head left **Rev:** Cuban Tree Frog (Osteopilus septentrionalis). **Edge:** Plain

Date	Mintage	F	VF	XF	Unc	BU
2004(u) Proof	1,000	Value: 50.00				

KM# 31 10 FLORIN
25.0000 g., 0.9250 Silver 0.7435 oz. ASW, 38 mm. **Ruler:** Beatrix **Obv:** Head left **Rev:** Fish right **Edge:** Plain

Date	Mintage	F	VF	XF	Unc	BU
2004(u) Proof	1,000	Value: 50.00				

KM# 26 10 FLORIN
6.7200 g., 0.9000 Gold 0.1944 oz. AGW, 22.5 mm. **Ruler:** Beatrix **Subject:** 20th Anniversary of Autonomy **Obv:** Head left **Rev:** Royal seal **Edge:** Reeded **Designer:** E. Fingal

Date	Mintage	F	VF	XF	Unc	BU
2004(u) Proof	1,000	Value: 375				

KM# 33 10 FLORIN
1.2442 g., 0.9990 Gold 0.0400 oz. AGW, 13.9 mm. **Ruler:** Beatrix **Subject:** Death of Juliana **Obv:** Head left **Rev:** Juliana in center **Edge:** Reeded

Date	Mintage	F	VF	XF	Unc	BU
ND (2005)(u) Proof	10,000	Value: 75.00				

KM# 35 10 FLORIN
6.7200 g., 0.9000 Gold 0.1944 oz. AGW, 22.5 mm. **Ruler:** Beatrix **Subject:** Queen's Silver Jubilee **Obv:** Head left **Rev:** Flag **Edge:** Reeded **Designer:** F.L. Croes

Date	Mintage	F	VF	XF	Unc	BU
2005(u) Proof	750	Value: 375				

KM# 36 10 FLORIN
25.0000 g., 0.9250 Silver 0.7435 oz. ASW, 38 mm. **Ruler:** Beatrix **Subject:** Status Aparte 20th Anniversary - Flag 30th Anniversary **Obv:** Queen's portrait **Rev:** Queen standing next to value and country name **Edge Lettering:** DIOS * TA * CU * NOS *

Date	Mintage	F	VF	XF	Unc	BU
2006(u) Proof	1,250	Value: 45.00				

KM# 44 10 FLORIN
1.2442 g., 0.9990 Gold 0.0400 oz. AGW, 13.9 mm. **Ruler:** Beatrix **Subject:** Carnival **Obv:** Head left **Rev:** Carnival feathered facemask

Date	Mintage	F	VF	XF	Unc	BU
2009 Proof	5,000	Value: 75.00				

KM# 49 10 FLORIN
3.3645 g., 0.9000 Gold 0.0973 oz. AGW, 18.5 mm. **Ruler:** Beatrix **Subject:** Status Aparte **Obv:** Shield in wreath above mintmarks **Rev:** 25 years Status Aparte with Parliament building **Edge:** Reeded

Date	Mintage	F	VF	XF	Unc	BU
2011(u) Proof	1,000	Value: 250				

KM# 22 25 FLORIN
25.0000 g., 0.9250 Silver 0.7435 oz. ASW, 38 mm. **Ruler:** Beatrix **Subject:** 15th Anniversary of Autonomy **Obv:** Head left **Rev:** National arms and inscription **Edge:** Plain

Date	Mintage	F	VF	XF	Unc	BU
2001(u) Proof	3,000	Value: 50.00				

KM# 37 25 FLORIN
6.7200 g., 0.9000 Gold 0.1944 oz. AGW, 22.5 mm. **Ruler:** Beatrix **Subject:** Status Aparte 20th Anniversary - Flag 30th Anniversary **Obv:** Queen's portrait **Rev:** Queen standing next to value and country name **Edge:** Reeded **Note:** Status Aparte

Date	Mintage	F	VF	XF	Unc	BU
2006(u) Proof	1,000	Value: 375				

KM# 23 100 FLORIN
6.7200 g., Gold, 22.5 mm. **Ruler:** Beatrix **Subject:** Independence **Obv:** Arms, treaty name, dates **Rev:** Head left **Edge:** Grained

Date	Mintage	F	VF	XF	Unc	BU
2001(u) Proof	1,000	Value: 400				

MINT SETS

KM#	Date	Mintage	Identification	Issue Price	Mkt Val
MS19	2001 (7)	6,900	KM#1-6, 12	13.25	18.00
MS20	2002 (6)	6,000	KM# 1-6, 12	15.00	20.00
MS21	2003 (7)	4,000	KM# 1-6, 12	15.00	20.00
MS22	2004 (7)	2,500	KM# 1-6, 12	15.00	30.00
MS23	2005 (7)	2,500	KM# 1-6, 12	15.00	30.00
MS24	2006 (7)	2,000	KM# 1-6, 38	15.00	30.00
MS25	2007 (7)	2,500	KM#1-6, 38	20.00	30.00
MS26	2008 (7)	2,000	KM#1-6, 38	26.00	30.00
MS27	2009 (7)	2,000	KM#1-6, 38	26.00	30.00
MS28	2010 (7)	2,000	KM#1-6, 38	26.00	30.00
MS29	2011 (7)	2,000	KM#1-6, 38	26.00	30.00
MS30	2012 (7)	2,000	KM#1-6, 38	28.00	30.00

ASCENSION ISLAND

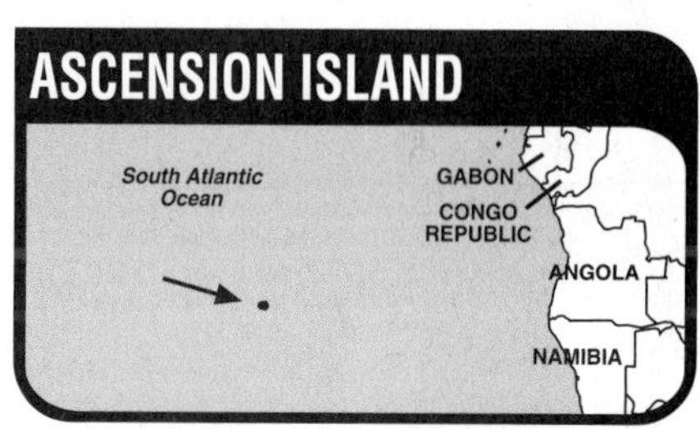

An island of volcanic origin, Ascension Island lies in the South Atlantic, 700 miles (1,100 km.) northwest of St. Helena. It has an area of 34 sq. mi. (88 sq. km.) on an island 9 miles (14 km.) long and 6 miles (10 km.) wide. Approximate population: 1,146. Although having little vegetation and scant rainfall, the island has a very healthy climate. The island is the nesting place for a large number of sea turtles and sooty terns. Phosphates and guano are the chief natural sources of income. Ascension is a dependency of the British Colony of St. Helena.

RULER
British

MINT MARKS
PM - Pobjoy Mint

BRITISH ADMINISTRATION

STANDARD COINAGE

KM# 13 50 PENCE
28.6300 g., Copper-Nickel, 38.6 mm. **Subject:** 75th Birthday of Queen Elizabeth **Obv:** Crowned bust right, denomination below **Rev:** Crowned monogram above flowers within circle, date below **Edge:** Reeded

Date	Mintage	F	VF	XF	Unc	BU
2001	—	—	—	—	8.00	9.50

KM# 13a 50 PENCE
28.2800 g., 0.9250 Silver 0.8410 oz. ASW, 38.6 mm. **Subject:** Queen Elizabeth II's 75th Birthday **Obv:** Crowned bust right, denomination below **Rev:** Crowned monogram above roses within circle, date below **Edge:** Reeded

Date	Mintage	F	VF	XF	Unc	BU
2001 Proof	10,000	Value: 45.00				

KM# 13b 50 PENCE
47.5400 g., 0.9166 Gold 1.4009 oz. AGW, 38.6 mm. **Subject:** Queen Elizabeth II's 75th Birthday **Obv:** Crowned bust right, denomination below **Rev:** Crowned monogram above roses within circle, date below **Edge:** Reeded

Date	Mintage	F	VF	XF	Unc	BU
2001 Proof	75	Value: 2,600				

KM# 14 50 PENCE
28.6300 g., Copper-Nickel, 38.6 mm. **Subject:** Centennial - Queen Victoria's Death **Obv:** Crowned bust right, denomination below **Rev:** Crowned bust left, three dates **Edge:** Reeded

Date	Mintage	F	VF	XF	Unc	BU
2001	—	—	—	—	8.00	9.50

KM# 14a 50 PENCE
28.2800 g., 0.9250 Silver 0.8410 oz. ASW, 38.6 mm. **Subject:** Centennial of Queen Victoria's Death **Obv:** Crowned bust right, denomination below **Rev:** Crowned bust left, three dates **Edge:** Reeded

Date	Mintage	F	VF	XF	Unc	BU
2001 Proof	10,000	Value: 45.00				

KM# 14b 50 PENCE
47.5400 g., 0.9166 Gold 1.4009 oz. AGW, 38.6 mm. **Subject:** Centennial of Queen Victoria's Death **Obv:** Crowned bust right, denomination below **Rev:** Crowned bust left, three dates **Edge:** Reeded

Date	Mintage	F	VF	XF	Unc	BU
2001 Proof	100	Value: 2,600				

KM# 15 50 PENCE
28.3500 g., Copper-Nickel, 38.6 mm. **Subject:** Queen's Golden Jubilee **Obv:** Crowned bust right, denomination below **Rev:** Westminster Abby, monogram at left, circle surrounds, two dates below **Edge:** Reeded

Date	Mintage	F	VF	XF	Unc	BU
ND(2002)	—	—	—	—	8.00	9.50

KM# 15a 50 PENCE
28.2800 g., 0.9250 Silver 0.8410 oz. ASW, 38.6 mm. **Subject:** Queen Elizabeth II's Golden Jubilee **Obv:** Gold-plated crowned bust right, denomination below **Rev:** Monogram and Westminster Abbey within circle, dates below **Edge:** Reeded

Date	Mintage	F	VF	XF	Unc	BU
ND(2002) Proof	10,000	Value: 45.00				

KM# 18 50 PENCE
28.2800 g., Copper-Nickel, 38.6 mm. **Subject:** Death of Queen Mother **Obv:** Crowned bust right, denomination below **Rev:** Queen Mother bust right, between her life dates **Edge:** Reeded

Date	Mintage	F	VF	XF	Unc	BU
ND(2002)	—	—	—	—	10.00	12.00

KM# 18a 50 PENCE
28.2800 g., 0.9250 Silver 0.8410 oz. ASW, 38.6 mm. **Subject:** Death of Queen Mother **Obv:** Crowned bust right, denomination below **Rev:** Queen Mother bust right, between her life dates **Edge:** Reeded

Date	Mintage	F	VF	XF	Unc	BU
ND(2002) Proof	10,000	Value: 45.00				

KM# 16 50 PENCE
28.3600 g., Copper-Nickel, 38.6 mm. **Subject:** Coronation Jubilee **Obv:** Crowned bust right, denomination below **Rev:** Crown, two scepters and the ampula **Edge:** Reeded

Date	Mintage	F	VF	XF	Unc	BU
ND (2003) Prooflike	—	—	—	—	10.00	12.00

KM# 16a 50 PENCE
28.2800 g., 0.9250 Silver 0.8410 oz. ASW, 38.6 mm. **Subject:** Queen Elizabeth II's - 50th Anniversary of Coronation **Obv:** Crowned bust right, denomination below **Rev:** Crown, two scepters and the ampula **Edge:** Reeded

Date	Mintage	F	VF	XF	Unc	BU
ND(2003) Proof	5,000	Value: 50.00				

KM# 16b 50 PENCE
39.9400 g., 0.9166 Gold 1.1770 oz. AGW, 38.6 mm. **Subject:** Queen Elizabeth II's - 50th Anniversary of Coronation **Obv:** Crowned bust right, denomination below **Rev:** Crown, two scepters and the ampula **Edge:** Reeded

Date	Mintage	F	VF	XF	Unc	BU
ND(2003) Proof	50	Value: 2,450				

KM# 17 50 PENCE
28.2800 g., Copper-Nickel, 38.6 mm. **Subject:** Queen Elizabeth II's- 50th Anniversary of Coronation **Obv:** Crowned head right, denomination below **Rev:** Crowned monogram **Edge:** Reeded

Date	Mintage	F	VF	XF	Unc	BU
ND(2003)	—	—	—	—	10.00	12.00

KM# 17a 50 PENCE
28.2800 g., 0.9250 Silver 0.8410 oz. ASW, 38.6 mm. **Subject:** Queen Elizabeth II's- 50th Anniversary of Coronation **Obv:** Crowned head right, denomination below **Rev:** Crowned monogram **Edge:** Reeded

Date	Mintage	F	VF	XF	Unc	BU
ND(2003) Proof	5,000	Value: 50.00				

KM# 17b 50 PENCE
39.9400 g., 0.9166 Gold 1.1770 oz. AGW, 38.6 mm. **Subject:** Queen Elizabeth II's - 50th Anniversary of Coronation **Obv:** Crowned bust right, denomination below **Rev:** Crowned monogram **Edge:** Reeded

Date	Mintage	F	VF	XF	Unc	BU
ND(2003) Proof	50	Value: 2,450				

KM# 19 2 POUNDS
28.2800 g., Copper-Nickel, 38.6 mm. **Subject:** Royal Wedding, Prince William and Catherine Middleton **Obv:** Bust in tiara right **Rev:** Two bells and two doves

Date	Mintage	F	VF	XF	Unc	BU
2011PM	—	—	—	—	10.00	12.50

KM# 19a 2 POUNDS
28.2800 g., 0.9250 Silver 0.8410 oz. ASW **Subject:** Royal Wedding of Prince William and Catherine Middleton **Obv:** Bust in tiara right **Rev:** Two bells and two doves

Date	Mintage	F	VF	XF	Unc	BU
2011PM Proof	—	Value: 65.00				

KM# 20 2 POUNDS
28.2800 g., Copper-Nickel, 38.61 mm. **Subject:** Royal Wedding of Prince William and Catherine Middleton **Obv:** Bust with tiara right **Rev:** Westminster Abbey, profiel portraits conjoined in oval at right

Date	Mintage	F	VF	XF	Unc	BU
2011PM	—	—	—	—	10.00	12.50

KM# 20a 2 POUNDS
28.2800 g., 0.9250 Silver 0.8410 oz. ASW, 38.61 mm. **Subject:** Royal Wedding of Prince William and Catherine Middleton **Obv:** Bust in tiara right **Rev:** Westminster Abbey, portraits in oval at right

Date	Mintage	F	VF	XF	Unc	BU
2011PM Proof	—	Value: 65.00				

KM# 21 2 POUNDS
28.2800 g., Copper-Nickel, 38.61 mm. **Obv:** Conjoined busts right of 1952 and 2012 portraits **Rev:** 1952 era portrait of Elizabeth II **Rev. Legend:** Life of Queen Elizabeth II

Date	Mintage	F	VF	XF	Unc	BU
2012PM	—	—	—	—	—	20.00

KM# 22 2 POUNDS
28.2800 g., Copper-Nickel, 38.61 mm. **Subject:** Life of Queen Elizabeth II **Obv:** Conjoined busts right **Rev:** Elizabeth nursing Prince Charles

Date	Mintage	F	VF	XF	Unc	BU
2012PM	—	—	—	—	—	15.00

KM# 23 5 POUNDS
62.2100 g., 0.9990 Silver 1.9980 oz. ASW, 38.61 mm. **Subject:** Elizabeth II 60th Anniversary **Obv:** Conjoined busts of 2012 and 1952 portraits **Rev:** Young postrait wearing state crown in ultra high relief

Date	Mintage	F	VF	XF	Unc	BU
2012PM Proof	—	Value: 100				

KM# 24 5 POUNDS
31.1050 g., 0.9990 Gold 0.9990 oz. AGW **Obv:** Conjoined busts right of 2012 and 1952 portraits **Rev:** Youthful Elizabeth II wearing state crown in ultra-high relief

Date	Mintage	F	VF	XF	Unc	BU
2012PM Proof	—	Value: 2,000				

KM# 25 60 CROWNS
1866.3000 g., 0.9990 Silver 59.940 oz. ASW **Obv:** Conjoined busts right of 2012 and 1952 portratis **Rev:** Youthful Elizabeth II wearing gilt state crown inset with 60 diamond chips **Note:** Diamond chip inserts total 1 karat in weight.

Date	Mintage	F	VF	XF	Unc	BU
2012PM Proof	—	Value: 3,000				

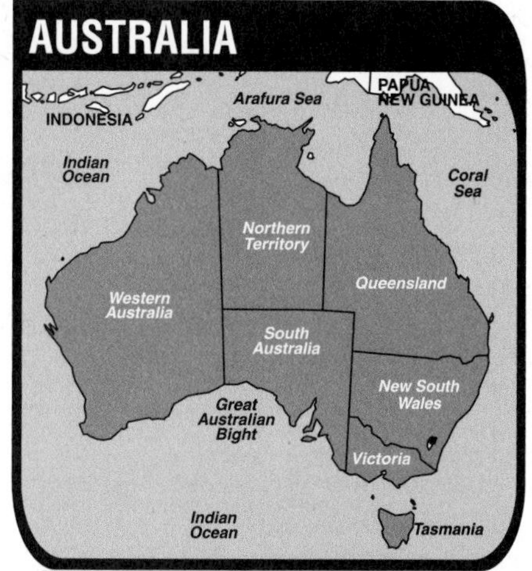

The Commonwealth of Australia, the smallest continent in the world, is located south of Indonesia between the Indian and Pacific oceans. It has an area of 2,967,893 sq. mi. (7,686,850 sq. km.) and an estimated population of 18.84 million. Capital: Canberra. Due to its early and sustained isolation, Australia is the habitat of such curious and unique fauna as the kangaroo, koala, platypus, wombat, echidna and frilled-necked lizard. The continent possesses extensive mineral deposits, the most important of which are iron ore, coal, gold, silver, nickel, uranium, lead and zinc. Raising livestock, mining and manufacturing are the principal industries. Chief exports are wool, meat, wheat, iron ore, coal and nonferrous metals.

Australia is a founding member of the Commonwealth of Nations. Elizabeth II is the Head of State as Queen of Australia; the Prime Minister is Head of Government.

NOTE: Home market grading of Australian coinage is generally stricter than USA practiced standards. The pricing in this catalog reflects strict home market grading standard.

RULER
British until 1942

MONETARY SYSTEM
Decimal Coinage (Commencing 1966)
100 Cents = 1 Dollar

COMMONWEALTH OF AUSTRALIA
DECIMAL COINAGE

KM# 767 CENT
2.6000 g., Bronze, 17.65 mm. **Ruler:** Elizabeth II **Obv:** Head with tiara right **Rev:** Feather-tailed glider and value **Edge:** Plain

Date	Mintage	F	VF	XF	Unc	BU
2006B In sets only	—	—	—	—	—	15.00
2006B Proof	—	Value: 18.00				

KM# 62a CENT
2.6000 g., 0.9990 Silver 0.0835 oz. ASW, 17.53 mm. **Ruler:** Elizabeth II **Obv:** Young bust right **Rev:** Feather-tailed glider and value **Edge:** Plain

Date	Mintage	F	VF	XF	Unc	BU
2006 Proof	6,500	Value: 15.00				

KM# 767b CENT
5.6100 g., 0.9990 Gold 0.1802 oz. AGW, 17.53 mm. **Ruler:** Elizabeth II **Obv:** Head with tiara right **Rev:** Feather-tailed glider **Edge:** Plain

Date	Mintage	F	VF	XF	Unc	BU
2006 Proof	300	Value: 650				

KM# 1249 CENT
2.4300 g., 0.9990 Silver 0.0780 oz. ASW, 17.6 mm. **Ruler:** Elizabeth II **Subject:** 1966 Decimal Pattern **Obv:** Head right **Rev:** Waratah, flower of New South Wales

Date	Mintage	F	VF	XF	Unc	BU
2009P Proof	7,500	Value: 15.00				

KM# 767a CENT
2.9300 g., 0.9990 Silver 0.0941 oz. ASW, 17.53 mm. **Ruler:** Elizabeth II

Date	Mintage	F	VF	XF	Unc	BU
2011B Proof	—	Value: 50.00				

KM# 768 2 CENTS
5.2000 g., Bronze, 21.59 mm. **Ruler:** Elizabeth II **Obv:** Head with tiara right **Rev:** Frill-necked lizard and value

Date	Mintage	F	VF	XF	Unc	BU
2006B	—	—	—	—	15.00	—
2006B Proof	—	Value: 5.00				

KM# 63a 2 CENTS
5.1800 g., 0.9990 Silver 0.1664 oz. ASW, 21.6 mm. **Ruler:** Elizabeth II **Obv:** Young bust right **Rev:** Frill-necked lizard and value **Edge:** Plain

Date	Mintage	F	VF	XF	Unc	BU
2006 Proof	6,500	Value: 15.00				

KM# 768b 2 CENTS
11.3100 g., 0.9990 Gold 0.3632 oz. AGW, 21.6 mm. **Ruler:** Elizabeth II **Obv:** Head with tiara right **Rev:** Frill-necked Lizard and value **Edge:** Plain

Date	Mintage	F	VF	XF	Unc	BU
2006 Proof	300	Value: 700				

KM# 1250 2 CENTS
5.5300 g., 0.9990 Silver 0.1776 oz. ASW, 21.6 mm. **Ruler:** Elizabeth II **Subject:** 1966 Decimal Pattern **Obv:** Head right **Rev:** Wattle, national flower

Date	Mintage	F	VF	XF	Unc	BU
2009P Proof	7,500	Value: 20.00				

KM# 768a 2 CENTS
6.0300 g., 0.9990 Silver 0.1937 oz. ASW, 21.6 mm. **Ruler:** Elizabeth II

Date	Mintage	F	VF	XF	Unc	BU
2011B Proof	—	Value: 100				

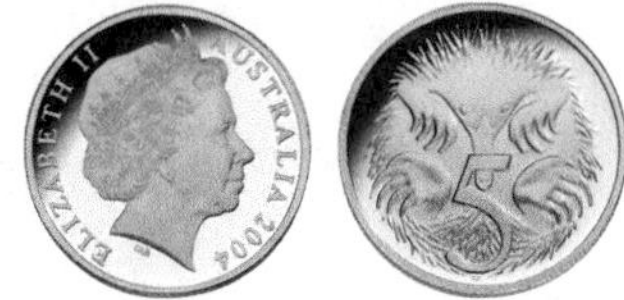

KM# 401 5 CENTS
2.8300 g., Copper-Nickel, 19.41 mm. **Ruler:** Elizabeth II **Obv:** Head with tiara right **Rev:** Echidna and value **Edge:** Reeded

Date	Mintage	F	VF	XF	Unc	BU
2001	174,579,000	—	—	—	2.00	3.00
Note: Large obverse head, IRB spaced						
2001	Inc. above	—	—	—	2.00	3.00
Note: Smaller obverse head, RB joined						
2001 Proof	59,569	Value: 15.00				
2002	148,812,000	—	—	—	2.00	3.00
2002 Proof	39,514	Value: 15.00				

Date	Mintage	F	VF	XF	Unc	BU
2003	115,470,000	—	—	—	2.00	3.00
2003 Proof	39,090	Value: 5.00				
2004	147,658,000	—	—	—	2.00	3.00
Note: Normal sized SD						
2004	Inc. above	—	—	—	2.00	3.00
Note: Smaller SD						
2004 Proof	50,000	Value: 5.00				
2005	194,300,000	—	—	—	2.00	3.00
Note: Normal sized SD						
2005	Inc. above	—	—	—	2.00	3.00
Note: Smaller SD						
2005 Proof	33,520	Value: 5.00				
2006	—	—	—	—	2.00	3.00
2006 Proof	—	Value: 5.00				
2007	—	—	—	—	2.00	3.00
2007 Proof	—	Value: 5.00				
2008	—	—	—	—	2.00	3.00
2008 Proof	—	Value: 5.00				
2009	—	—	—	—	2.00	3.00
2009 Proof	—	Value: 5.00				
2010	—	—	—	—	2.00	3.00
2010 Proof	—	Value: 5.00				
2011	—	—	—	—	2.00	3.00
2011 Proof	—	Value: 5.00				
2012	—	—	—	—	2.00	3.00
2012 Proof	—	Value: 5.00				

KM# 401a 5 CENTS

6.0300 g., 0.9990 Gold 0.1937 oz. AGW, 19.41 mm. **Ruler:** Elizabeth II **Subject:** Federation Centennial **Obv:** Head with tiara right **Rev:** Echidna

Date	Mintage	F	VF	XF	Unc	BU
2001B Proof	650	Value: 650				
2005B Proof	650	Value: 450				
2006B Proof	300	Value: 700				

KM# 401b 5 CENTS

3.2400 g., 0.9999 Silver 0.1042 oz. ASW, 19.41 mm. **Ruler:** Elizabeth II **Obv:** Head with tiara right **Rev:** Echidna **Edge:** Reeded

Date	Mintage	F	VF	XF	Unc	BU
2003B Proof	6,500	Value: 30.00				
2004B Proof	6,500	Value: 20.00				
2005B Proof	6,500	Value: 20.00				
2006B Proof	—	Value: 20.00				
2007B Proof	—	Value: 20.00				
2008B Proof	—	Value: 20.00				
2009B Proof	—	Value: 20.00				
2010B Proof	—	Value: 20.00				
2011B Proof	6,000	Value: 20.00				

KM# 64a 5 CENTS

3.2400 g., 0.9990 Silver 0.1041 oz. ASW, 19.41 mm. **Ruler:** Elizabeth II **Obv:** Young bust right **Rev:** Echidna **Edge:** Reeded

Date	Mintage	F	VF	XF	Unc	BU
2006 Proof	6,500	Value: 20.00				

KM# 1251 5 CENTS

2.7400 g., 0.9990 Silver 0.0880 oz. ASW, 19.6 mm. **Ruler:** Elizabeth II **Subject:** 1966 Decimal Pattern **Obv:** Head right **Rev:** Platypus and yabbie

Date	Mintage	F	VF	XF	Unc	BU
2009P Proof	7,500	Value: 35.00				

KM# 402 10 CENTS

5.6500 g., Copper-Nickel, 23.6 mm. **Ruler:** Elizabeth II **Obv:** Head with tiara right **Rev:** Lyrebird and value **Edge:** Reeded

Date	Mintage	F	VF	XF	Unc	BU
2001	109,357,000	—	—	—	3.00	4.00
Note: Large obverse head, IRB spaced						
2001	Inc. above	—	—	—	3.00	4.00
Note: Smaller obverse head, RB joined						
2001 Proof	59,569	Value: 15.00				
2002	70,329,000	—	—	—	3.00	4.00
2002 Proof	39,514	Value: 5.00				
2003	53,635,000	—	—	—	2.00	3.00
2003 Proof	39,090	Value: 5.00				
2004	89,000,000	—	—	—	3.00	4.00
2004 Proof	50,000	Value: 5.00				
2005	116,700,000	—	—	—	2.00	3.00
2005 Proof	33,520	Value: 5.00				
2006	157,087,000	—	—	—	2.00	3.00
2006 Proof	—	Value: 5.00				
2007	61,096,000	—	—	—	3.00	4.00
2007 Proof	—	Value: 4.00				
2008	82,860,000	—	—	—	3.00	4.00
2008 Proof	—	Value: 5.00				
2009	—	—	—	—	3.00	4.00
2009 Proof	—	Value: 5.00				
2010	—	—	—	—	3.00	4.00
2010 Proof	—	Value: 5.00				
2011	—	—	—	—	3.00	4.00
2011 Proof	—	Value: 5.00				
2012	—	—	—	—	3.00	4.00
2012 Proof	—	Value: 5.00				

KM# 402a 10 CENTS

12.1400 g., 0.9999 Gold 0.3903 oz. AGW, 23.6 mm. **Ruler:** Elizabeth II **Subject:** Federation Centennial **Obv:** Head with tiara right **Rev:** Lyrebird **Edge:** Reeded

Date	Mintage	F	VF	XF	Unc	BU
2001B Proof	650	Value: 750				
2005B Proof	650	Value: 700				
2006B Proof	300	Value: 850				

KM# 402b 10 CENTS

6.5700 g., 0.9999 Silver 0.2112 oz. ASW, 23.6 mm. **Ruler:** Elizabeth II **Obv:** Head with tiara right **Rev:** Lyrebird **Edge:** Reeded

Date	Mintage	F	VF	XF	Unc	BU
2003B Proof	6,500	Value: 20.00				
2004B Proof	6,500	Value: 15.00				
2005B Proof	6,500	Value: 15.00				
2006B Proof	—	Value: 15.00				
2007B Proof	—	Value: 15.00				
2008B Proof	—	Value: 15.00				
2009B Proof	—	Value: 15.00				
2010B Proof	—	Value: 15.00				
2011B Proof	6,000	Value: 15.00				

KM# 65a 10 CENTS

6.5700 g., 0.9990 Silver 0.2110 oz. ASW, 23.6 mm. **Ruler:** Elizabeth II **Obv:** Young bust right **Rev:** Superb Lyrebird **Edge:** Reeded

Date	Mintage	F	VF	XF	Unc	BU
2006 Proof	6,500	Value: 15.00				

KM# 1252 10 CENTS

6.0700 g., 0.9990 Silver 0.1950 oz. ASW, 23.6 mm. **Ruler:** Elizabeth II **Subject:** 1966 Decimal Pattern **Obv:** Head right **Rev:** Kookabura eating snake

Date	Mintage	F	VF	XF	Unc	BU
2009P Proof	7,500	Value: 45.00				

KM# 1789 10 CENTS

3.1200 g., 0.9990 Silver 0.1002 oz. ASW, 21 mm. **Ruler:** Elizabeth II **Obv:** Head with tiara right **Rev:** Koala leaning on and hugging branch

Date	Mintage	F	VF	XF	Unc	BU
2012P	—	—	—	—	—	15.00

KM# 403 20 CENTS

11.3000 g., Copper-Nickel, 28.65 mm. **Ruler:** Elizabeth II **Obv:** Head with tiara right **Rev:** Duckbill Platypus **Edge:** Reeded

Date	Mintage	F	VF	XF	Unc	BU
2001	81,967,000	—	—	—	3.00	4.00
Note: IRB spaced						
2001	Inc. above	—	—	—	3.00	4.00
Note: RB joined						
2001	Inc. above	—	—	—	3.00	4.00
Note: IRB joined						
2001 Proof	59,569	Value: 25.00				
2002	27,244,000	—	—	—	3.00	4.00
2002 Proof	39,514	Value: 2.00				
2004	74,609,000	—	—	—	3.00	4.00
Note: Small obverse head, flat top A						
2004	Est. 400,000	—	—	—	15.00	20.00
Note: Large obverse head, pointed A						
2004 Proof	50,000	Value: 10.00				
Note: Large obverse head, pointed top A						
2004 Proof	Inc. above	Value: 10.00				
Note: Small obverse head, flat top A						
2005	58,600,000	—	—	—	9.00	10.00
2005 Proof	—	Value: 25.00				
2006	102,462,000	—	—	—	3.00	4.00
2006 Proof	—	Value: 6.00				
2007	42,712,000	—	—	—	3.00	4.00
2007 Proof	—	Value: 25.00				
2008	106,220,000	—	—	—	1.00	2.00
2008 Proof	—	Value: 12.00				
2009	—	—	—	—	1.00	2.00
2009 Proof	—	Value: 12.00				
2010	—	—	—	—	1.00	2.00
2010 Proof	—	Value: 12.00				
2011	—	—	—	—	1.00	2.00
2011 Proof	—	Value: 12.00				
2012	—	—	—	—	1.00	2.00
2012 Proof	—	Value: 12.00				

KM# 532 20 CENTS

11.3000 g., Copper-Nickel, 28.65 mm. **Ruler:** Elizabeth II **Subject:** Centenary of Federation - Norfolk Island **Obv:** Head with tiara right **Rev:** Norfolk Pine over map of island **Edge:** Reeded

Date	Mintage	F	VF	XF	Unc	BU
2001B	2,000,000	—	—	—	3.50	5.00
2001B Proof	—	Value: 10.00				

KM# 550 20 CENTS

11.3000 g., Copper-Nickel, 28.65 mm. **Ruler:** Elizabeth II **Series:** Centenary of Federation - New South Wales **Obv:** Head with tiara right **Rev:** Waratah on state map **Edge:** Reeded

Date	Mintage	F	VF	XF	Unc	BU
2001	2,000,000	—	—	—	3.50	5.00
2001 Proof	—	Value: 10.00				

KM# 552 20 CENTS

11.3000 g., Copper-Nickel, 28.65 mm. **Ruler:** Elizabeth II **Series:** Centenary of Federation - Australian Capital Territory **Obv:** Head with tiara right **Rev:** Parliament House, map, flowers **Edge:** Reeded **Note:** Prev. KM#551.

Date	Mintage	F	VF	XF	Unc	BU
2001	2,000,000	—	—	—	5.00	6.00
2001 Proof	—	Value: 20.00				

KM# 554 20 CENTS

11.3000 g., Copper-Nickel, 28.65 mm. **Ruler:** Elizabeth II **Series:** Centenary of Federation - Queensland **Obv:** Head with tiara right **Rev:** Jennifer Gray **Edge:** Reeded

Date	Mintage	F	VF	XF	Unc	BU
2001	2,320,000	—	—	—	6.00	8.00
2001 Proof	—	Value: 20.00				

KM# 556 20 CENTS
11.3000 g., Copper-Nickel, 28.65 mm. **Ruler:** Elizabeth II **Series:** Centenary of Federation - Victoria **Obv:** Head with tiara right **Rev:** Capital building **Edge:** Reeded

Date	Mintage	F	VF	XF	Unc	BU
2001	2,000,000	—	—	—	6.00	8.00
2001 Proof	—	Value: 20.00				

KM# 558 20 CENTS
11.3000 g., Copper-Nickel, 28.65 mm. **Ruler:** Elizabeth II **Series:** Centenary of Federation - Northern Territory **Obv:** Head with tiara right **Rev:** Two brolga cranes in ritual dance **Edge:** Reeded

Date	Mintage	F	VF	XF	Unc	BU
2001	2,100,000	—	—	—	6.00	9.00
2001 Proof	—	Value: 20.00				

KM# 560 20 CENTS
11.3000 g., Copper-Nickel, 28.65 mm. **Ruler:** Elizabeth II **Series:** Centenary of Federation - South Australia **Obv:** Head with tiara right **Rev:** Sturt's Desert Pea, landscape and southern cross **Edge:** Reeded

Date	Mintage	F	VF	XF	Unc	BU
2001	2,320,000	—	—	—	6.00	8.00
2001 Proof	—	Value: 20.00				

KM# 562 20 CENTS
11.3000 g., Copper-Nickel, 28.65 mm. **Ruler:** Elizabeth II **Series:** Centenary of Federation - Western Australia **Obv:** Head with tiara right **Rev:** Rabbit-eared Bandicoot (bilby), plant and map **Edge:** Reeded

Date	Mintage	F	VF	XF	Unc	BU
2001	2,000,000	—	—	—	6.00	10.00
2001 Proof	—	Value: 20.00				

KM# 564 20 CENTS
11.3000 g., Copper-Nickel, 28.65 mm. **Ruler:** Elizabeth II **Series:** Centenary of Federation - Tasmania **Obv:** Head with tiara right **Rev:** Tasmanian Tiger on map **Edge:** Reeded

Date	Mintage	F	VF	XF	Unc	BU
2001	2,000,000	—	—	—	6.00	10.00
2001 Proof	—	Value: 20.00				

KM# 589 20 CENTS
11.3000 g., Copper-Nickel, 28.65 mm. **Ruler:** Elizabeth II **Subject:** Sir Donald Bradman **Obv:** Head with tiara right **Rev:** Sir Donald Bradman **Edge:** Reeded

Date	Mintage	F	VF	XF	Unc	BU
2001B	10,000,000	—	—	—	35.00	40.00

KM# 819 20 CENTS
24.3600 g., 0.9990 Gold 0.7824 oz. AGW, 28.52 mm. **Ruler:** Elizabeth II **Obv:** Head with tiara right **Rev:** Platypus with Federation Star **Edge:** Reeded

Date	Mintage	F	VF	XF	Unc	BU
2001 Proof	650	Value: 1,450				

KM# 403a 20 CENTS
13.3600 g., 0.9999 Silver 0.4295 oz. ASW, 28.52 mm. **Ruler:** Elizabeth II **Obv:** Head with tiara right **Rev:** Platypus **Edge:** Reeded

Date	Mintage	F	VF	XF	Unc	BU
2003B Proof	6,500	Value: 30.00				
2004B Proof	6,500	Value: 25.00				
2006B Proof	6,500	Value: 25.00				
2007B Proof	—	Value: 25.00				
2008B Proof	—	Value: 25.00				
2009B Proof	—	Value: 25.00				
2010B Proof	—	Value: 25.00				
2011B Proof	6,000	Value: 25.00				

KM# 688 20 CENTS
11.3000 g., Copper-Nickel, 28.65 mm. **Ruler:** Elizabeth II **Obv:** Head with tiara right **Rev:** Group of Australian Volunteers **Edge:** Reeded

Date	Mintage	F	VF	XF	Unc	BU
2003B	7,600,000	—	—	—	3.00	4.00
2003B Proof	—	Value: 15.00				

KM# 688a 20 CENTS
11.3000 g., 0.9990 Silver 0.3629 oz. ASW, 28.65 mm. **Ruler:** Elizabeth II **Obv:** Head right **Rev:** Group of Australian Volunteers **Edge:** Reeded

Date	Mintage	F	VF	XF	Unc	BU
2003B Proof	6,500	Value: 35.00				

KM# 688b 20 CENTS
24.3600 g., 0.9990 Gold 0.7824 oz. AGW, 28.65 mm. **Ruler:** Elizabeth II **Obv:** Head with tiara right **Rev:** Group of Australian Volunteers **Edge:** Reeded

Date	Mintage	F	VF	XF	Unc	BU
2003B Proof	650	Value: 1,450				

KM# 745 20 CENTS
11.3000 g., Copper-Nickel, 28.65 mm. **Ruler:** Elizabeth II **Subject:** 60th Anniversary - End of WWII **Obv:** Head right **Rev:** Soldier with wife and child **Edge:** Reeded

Date	Mintage	F	VF	XF	Unc	BU
2005B	33,500,000	—	—	—	2.00	3.00
2005B Proof	—	Value: 10.00				

KM# 745a 20 CENTS
13.3600 g., 0.9990 Silver 0.4291 oz. ASW, 28.65 mm. **Ruler:** Elizabeth II **Obv:** Head right **Rev:** Soldier with wife and child **Edge:** Reeded

Date	Mintage	F	VF	XF	Unc	BU
2005B Proof	6,500	Value: 35.00				

KM# 745b 20 CENTS
24.3600 g., 0.9999 Gold 0.7831 oz. AGW, 28.65 mm. **Ruler:** Elizabeth II **Obv:** Head right **Rev:** Soldier with wife and child **Edge:** Reeded

Date	Mintage	F	VF	XF	Unc	BU
2005B Proof	650	Value: 1,450				

KM# 66a 20 CENTS
13.3600 g., 0.9990 Silver 0.4291 oz. ASW, 28.52 mm. **Ruler:** Elizabeth II **Obv:** Young bust right **Rev:** Platypus **Edge:** Reeded

Date	Mintage	F	VF	XF	Unc	BU
2006 Proof	6,500	Value: 28.00				

KM# 403b 20 CENTS
24.5600 g., 0.9999 Gold 0.7895 oz. AGW, 28.52 mm. **Ruler:** Elizabeth II **Subject:** Federation Centennial **Obv:** Head with tiara right **Rev:** Duckbill Platyus **Edge:** Reeded

Date	Mintage	F	VF	XF	Unc	BU
2006B Proof	300	Value: 1,500				

KM# 820 20 CENTS
11.3000 g., Copper-Nickel, 28.65 mm. **Ruler:** Elizabeth II **Subject:** Year of the Surf Lifesaver **Obv:** Head with tiara right **Rev:** Female lifesaver working line **Edge:** Reeded

Date	Mintage	F	VF	XF	Unc	BU
2007	—	—	—	—	10.00	7.00
2007 Proof	—	Value: 20.00				

KM# 820a 20 CENTS
13.3600 g., 0.9990 Silver 0.4291 oz. ASW, 28.52 mm. **Ruler:** Elizabeth II **Subject:** Year of the Surfer Lifesaver **Rev:** Female with rope line

Date	Mintage	F	VF	XF	Unc	BU
2007B Proof	—	Value: 25.00				

KM# 1058 20 CENTS
11.3000 g., Copper-Nickel, 28.65 mm. **Ruler:** Elizabeth II **Subject:** Planet earth **Rev:** Map of Australia with water and rocks around

Date	Mintage	F	VF	XF	Unc	BU
2008	—	—	—	—	12.00	10.00
2008 Proof	—	Value: 12.00				

KM# 1075 20 CENTS
15.5500 g., Copper-Nickel, 28.52 mm. **Ruler:** Elizabeth II **Subject:** Year of Astronomy **Rev:** Star gazers

Date	Mintage	F	VF	XF	Unc	BU
2009	—	—	—	—	10.00	12.00
2009 Proof	—	Value: 25.00				

KM# 1088 20 CENTS
15.5500 g., Copper-Nickel, 28.52 mm. **Ruler:** Elizabeth II **Rev:** Poppy

Date	Mintage	F	VF	XF	Unc	BU
2009	—	—	—	—	10.00	12.00

KM# 1253 20 CENTS
12.8600 g., 0.9990 Silver 0.4130 oz. ASW, 28.6 mm. **Ruler:** Elizabeth II **Subject:** 1966 Decimal Pattern **Obv:** Head right **Rev:** Black swan in flight

Date	Mintage	F	VF	XF	Unc	BU
2009P Proof	10,000	Value: 200				

KM# 1433 20 CENTS
11.3000 g., Copper-Nickel, 28.65 mm. **Ruler:** Elizabeth II **Subject:** Nurses **Rev:** Nurse looking over serviceman

Date	Mintage	F	VF	XF	Unc	BU
2009C	—	—	—	—	5.00	7.00

KM# 1430 20 CENTS
11.3000 g., Copper-Nickel, 28.65 mm. **Ruler:** Elizabeth II **Subject:** Burke & Wills, 150th Anniversary **Rev:** Burke and Wills on camels

Date	Mintage	F	VF	XF	Unc	BU
2010C	—	—	—	—	5.00	7.00
2010C Proof	—	Value: 10.00				

KM# 1502 20 CENTS
11.3000 g., Copper-Nickel, 28.65 mm. **Ruler:** Elizabeth II **Subject:** Wool Industry **Rev:** Wheel with sheep industry design in spoke wedges

Date	Mintage	F	VF	XF	Unc	BU
2010C	—	—	—	—	2.00	4.00
2010C Proof	—	Value: 12.00				

KM# 1513 20 CENTS
11.3000 g., Copper-Nickel, 28.65 mm. **Ruler:** Elizabeth II **Subject:** Taxation office, 100th Anniversary

Date	Mintage	F	VF	XF	Unc	BU
2010	—	—	—	—	1.50	2.50

KM# 1518 20 CENTS
11.3000 g., Copper-Nickel, 28.65 mm. **Ruler:** Elizabeth II **Subject:** Lost Soldiers of Promelles **Rev:** Soldier carrying another on his shoulder

Date	Mintage	F	VF	XF	Unc	BU
2010	—	—	—	—	1.50	2.50

KM# 1634 20 CENTS
11.3000 g., Copper-Nickel, 28.65 mm. **Ruler:** Elizabeth II **Subject:** Year of the Volunteer **Obv:** Head with tiara right **Rev:** Logo within wreath

Date	Mintage	F	VF	XF	Unc	BU
2011	—	—	—	—	3.00	4.00

KM# 1648 20 CENTS
11.3000 g., Copper-Nickel, 28.65 mm. **Ruler:** Elizabeth II **Subject:** War Historians **Obv:** Head with tiara right **Rev:** Man with tripod taking photograph from atop tank

Date	Mintage	F	VF	XF	Unc	BU
2011	—	—	—	—	3.00	4.00

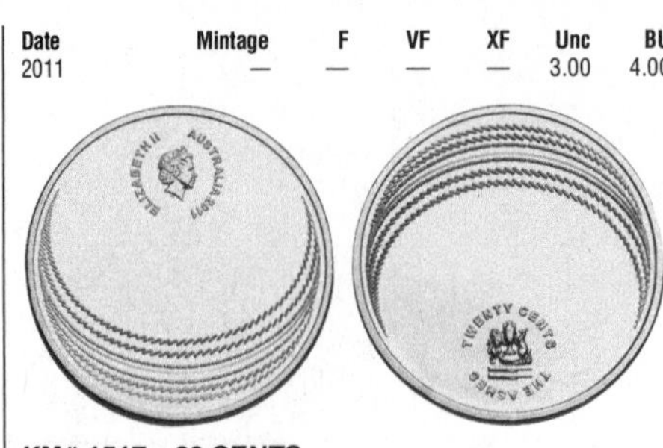

KM# 1517 20 CENTS
11.3000 g., Copper-Nickel, 28.65 mm. **Ruler:** Elizabeth II **Subject:** Ashes Cricket tournament

Date	Mintage	F	VF	XF	Unc	BU
2011	—	—	—	—	1.50	2.50

KM# 1566 20 CENTS
11.3000 g., Copper-Nickel, 28.65 mm. **Ruler:** Elizabeth II **Subject:** Royal Wedding **Rev:** Catherine Middleton and Prince William busts left

Date	Mintage	F	VF	XF	Unc	BU
2011	—	—	—	—	4.00	6.00

KM# 1642 20 CENTS
11.3000 g., Copper-Nickel, 28.65 mm. **Ruler:** Elizabeth II **Subject:** International Womens Day, 100th Anniversary **Obv:** Head with tiara right **Rev:** Three stylized joyful figures

Date	Mintage	F	VF	XF	Unc	BU
2011	—	—	—	—	3.00	4.00

KM# 1625 20 CENTS
11.3000 g., Copper-Nickel, 28.65 mm. **Ruler:** Elizabeth II **Subject:** Australian Wheat **Obv:** Head with tiara right **Rev:** Wheat ear upright

Date	Mintage	F	VF	XF	Unc	BU
2012	—	—	—	—	2.00	2.50
2012 Proof	—	Value: 15.00				

KM# 1742 20 CENTS
11.3000 g., Copper-Nickel, 28.65 mm. **Ruler:** Elizabeth II **Subject:** World War II, Bombing of Australia **Obv:** Head with tiara right **Rev:** People entering air raid shelter

Date	Mintage	F	VF	XF	Unc	BU
2012	—	—	—	—	3.00	4.00

KM# 1743 20 CENTS
11.3000 g., Copper-Nickel, 28.65 mm. **Ruler:** Elizabeth II **Obv:** Head with tiara right **Rev:** Military lookout

Date	Mintage	F	VF	XF	Unc	BU
2012	—	—	—	—	3.00	5.00

KM# 1743a 20 CENTS
13.3600 g., 0.9990 Silver 0.4291 oz. ASW, 28.65 mm. **Ruler:** Elizabeth II **Subject:** Bombing of Australia - World War II **Obv:** Head with tiara right **Rev:** Military lookout

Date	Mintage	F	VF	XF	Unc	BU
2012 Proof	—	Value: 35.00				

KM# 1857 20 CENTS
11.3000 g., Copper-Nickel, 28.65 mm. **Ruler:** Elizabeth II **Subject:** Merchant Navy **Rev:** WWII Freighter sailing left

Date	Mintage	F	VF	XF	Unc	BU
2012	—	—	—	—	4.00	5.00

KM# 599 25 CENTS
7.7750 g., 0.9990 Silver 0.2497 oz. ASW, 24.8 mm. **Ruler:** Elizabeth II **Obv:** Head with tiara right **Rev:** Parliament House **Edge:** Plain **Shape:** 7-pointed star **Note:** "The Dump" portion of the "Holey Dollar" KM#598.

Date	Mintage	F	VF	XF	Unc	BU
2001 Prooflike	30,000	—	—	—	—	28.00

KM# 491.1 50 CENTS
15.5500 g., Copper-Nickel, 31.65 mm. **Ruler:** Elizabeth II **Subject:** Centenary of Federation, 1901-2001 **Obv:** Head with tiara right **Rev:** Commonwealth coat of arms **Edge:** Plain **Shape:** 12-sided **Note:** Prev. KM#491.

Date	Mintage	F	VF	XF	Unc	BU
2001B	43,149,600	—	—	—	5.00	6.00
2001B Proof	—	Value: 40.00				

KM# 491.1a 50 CENTS
33.8800 g., 0.9999 Gold 1.0891 oz. AGW, 31.65 mm. **Ruler:** Elizabeth II **Subject:** Federation Centennial **Obv:** Elizabeth II **Rev:** Commonwealth arms above value

Date	Mintage	F	VF	XF	Unc	BU
2001B Proof	650	Value: 1,950				

KM# 491.2 50 CENTS
15.5500 g., Copper-Nickel, 31.65 mm. **Ruler:** Elizabeth II **Subject:** Federation Centennial **Obv:** Elizabeth II right **Rev:** Multicolor arms above value **Edge:** Plain **Shape:** 12-sided

Date	Mintage	F	VF	XF	Unc	BU
2001B Proof	60,000	Value: 50.00				

KM# 491.2a 50 CENTS
15.5500 g., Copper-Nickel, 31.65 mm. **Ruler:** Elizabeth II **Subject:** Centenary of Federation, 1901-2001 **Obv:** Head with tiara right **Rev:** Multicolored Commonwealth coat of arms **Edge:** Plain **Shape:** 12-sided **Note:** Prev. KM#491a.

Date	Mintage	F	VF	XF	Unc	BU
2001B Proof	—	Value: 50.00				

KM# 533 50 CENTS
15.5500 g., Copper-Nickel, 31.65 mm. **Ruler:** Elizabeth II **Subject:** Centennial - Norfolk Island Federation **Obv:** Head with tiara right **Rev:** Norfolk Island coat of arms **Edge:** Plain **Shape:** 12-sided

Date	Mintage	F	VF	XF	Unc	BU
2001B	2,000,000	—	—	—	6.00	15.00
2001B Proof	—	Value: 70.00				

KM# 535 50 CENTS
16.8860 g., 0.9990 Silver 0.5423 oz. ASW, 32.1 mm. **Ruler:** Elizabeth II **Subject:** Year of the Snake **Obv:** Head right **Rev:** Snake with eggs **Edge:** Plain

Date	Mintage	F	VF	XF	Unc	BU
2001	500,000	—	—	—	—	22.00
2001P Proof	5,000	Value: 65.00				

KM# 551 50 CENTS
15.5500 g., Copper-Nickel, 31.65 mm. **Ruler:** Elizabeth II **Series:** Centenary of Federation - New South Wales **Obv:** Head with tiara right **Rev:** New South Wales state arms **Edge:** Plain **Shape:** 12-sided

Date	Mintage	F	VF	XF	Unc	BU
2001	3,000,000	—	—	—	6.00	7.00
2001 Proof	—	Value: 40.00				

KM# 553 50 CENTS
15.5500 g., Copper-Nickel, 31.65 mm. **Ruler:** Elizabeth II **Series:** Centenary of Federation - Australian Capital Territory **Obv:** Head right **Rev:** Australian Capital Territory arms **Edge:** Plain **Shape:** 12-sided

Date	Mintage	F	VF	XF	Unc	BU
2001	2,000,000	—	—	—	6.00	9.00
2001 Proof	—	Value: 40.00				

KM# 555 50 CENTS
15.5500 g., Copper-Nickel, 31.65 mm. **Ruler:** Elizabeth II **Series:** Centenary of Federation - Queensland **Obv:** Head with tiara right **Rev:** Queensland state arms **Edge:** Plain **Shape:** 12-sided

Date	Mintage	F	VF	XF	Unc	BU
2001	2,300,000	—	—	—	6.00	9.00
2001 Proof	—	Value: 40.00				

KM# 557 50 CENTS
15.5500 g., Copper-Nickel, 31.65 mm. **Ruler:** Elizabeth II **Series:** Centenary of Federation - Victoria **Obv:** Head with tiara right **Rev:** Victoria state arms **Edge:** Plain **Shape:** 12-sided

Date	Mintage	F	VF	XF	Unc	BU
2001	2,800,000	—	—	—	6.00	8.00
2001 Proof	—	Value: 40.00				

KM# 559 50 CENTS
15.5500 g., Copper-Nickel, 31.65 mm. **Ruler:** Elizabeth II **Series:** Centenary of Federation - Northern Territory **Obv:** Head with tiara right **Rev:** Northern Territory state arms **Edge:** Plain **Shape:** 12-sided

Date	Mintage	F	VF	XF	Unc	BU
2001	2,100,000	—	—	—	6.00	10.00
2001 Proof	—	Value: 50.00				

KM# 561 50 CENTS
15.5500 g., Copper-Nickel, 31.65 mm. **Ruler:** Elizabeth II **Series:** Centenary of Federation - South Australia **Obv:** Head with tiara right **Rev:** South Australia state arms **Edge:** Plain **Shape:** 12-sided

Date	Mintage	F	VF	XF	Unc	BU
2001	2,400,000	—	—	—	6.00	20.00
2001 Proof	—	Value: 60.00				

KM# 563 50 CENTS
15.5500 g., Copper-Nickel, 31.65 mm. **Ruler:** Elizabeth II **Series:** Centenary of Federation - Western Australia **Obv:** Head with tiara right **Rev:** Western Australia state arms **Edge:** Plain **Shape:** 12-sided

Date	Mintage	F	VF	XF	Unc	BU
2001	2,400,000	—	—	—	6.00	15.00
2001 Proof	—	Value: 50.00				

KM# 565 50 CENTS
15.5500 g., Copper-Nickel, 31.65 mm. **Ruler:** Elizabeth II **Series:** Centenary of Federation - Tasmania **Obv:** Head with tiara right **Rev:** Tasmania state arms **Edge:** Plain **Shape:** 12-sided

Date	Mintage	F	VF	XF	Unc	BU
2001	2,200,000	—	—	—	6.00	10.00
2001 Proof	—	Value: 50.00				

KM# 694 50 CENTS
15.5500 g., Copper-Nickel, 31.65 mm. **Ruler:** Elizabeth II **Obv:** Head with tiara right **Rev:** Koala, Lorikeet (bird) and Wombat **Edge:** Plain **Shape:** 12-sided

Date	Mintage	F	VF	XF	Unc	BU
2001 Proof	—	Value: 9.00				
2004B	10,577,000	—	—	—	3.00	5.00

KM# 602 50 CENTS
15.5500 g., Copper-Nickel, 31.65 mm. **Ruler:** Elizabeth II **Subject:** The Outback Region **Obv:** Head right **Rev:** Windmill **Edge:** Plain **Shape:** 12-sided

Date	Mintage	F	VF	XF	Unc	BU
2002B	11,507,000	—	—	—	6.00	7.00
2002B Proof	39,000	Value: 25.00				

KM# 645 50 CENTS
15.5500 g., Copper-Nickel, 31.65 mm. **Ruler:** Elizabeth II **Subject:** Queen's 50th Anniversary of Accession **Obv:** Head right **Rev:** Crown and star **Shape:** 12-sided

Date	Mintage	F	VF	XF	Unc	BU
2002B	32,102	—	—	—	30.00	60.00

Note: Issued only in PNC cover

KM# 645a 50 CENTS
18.2400 g., 0.9990 Silver 0.5858 oz. ASW, 31.65 mm. **Ruler:** Elizabeth II **Subject:** Queen's 50th Anniversary of Accession **Obv:** Head right **Rev:** Crown and star **Shape:** 12-sided

Date	Mintage	F	VF	XF	Unc	BU
2002B Proof	13,500	Value: 60.00				

KM# 404a 50 CENTS
18.2400 g., 0.9999 Silver 0.5863 oz. ASW, 31.65 mm. **Ruler:** Elizabeth II **Obv:** Head with tiara right **Rev:** Arms **Edge:** Plain **Shape:** 12-sided

Date	Mintage	F	VF	XF	Unc	BU
2003B Proof	6,500	Value: 35.00				
2004B Proof	6,500	Value: 35.00				

Date	Mintage	F	VF	XF	Unc	BU
2005B Proof	6,500	Value: 35.00				
2006B Proof	—	Value: 35.00				
2007B Proof	—	Value: 35.00				
2008B Proof	—	Value: 35.00				
2009B Proof	—	Value: 35.00				
2010B Proof	—	Value: 35.00				
2011B Proof	6,000	Value: 35.00				

KM# 689 50 CENTS
15.5500 g., Copper-Nickel, 31.65 mm. **Ruler:** Elizabeth II **Obv:** Head right **Rev:** Value within circle of volunteer activities **Edge:** Plain **Shape:** 12-sided

Date	Mintage	F	VF	XF	Unc	BU
2003B	13,927,000	—	—	—	4.50	5.00
2003B Proof	—	Value: 20.00				

KM# 689a 50 CENTS
15.5500 g., 0.9990 Silver 0.4994 oz. ASW, 31.65 mm. **Ruler:** Elizabeth II **Obv:** Head right **Rev:** Value within circle of volunteer activities

Date	Mintage	F	VF	XF	Unc	BU
2003B Proof	6,500	Value: 45.00				

KM# 799 50 CENTS
14.0900 g., Aluminum-Bronze, 31.51 mm. **Ruler:** Elizabeth II **Subject:** 50th Anniversary of the Coronation of Elizabeth II **Obv:** Head with tiara right **Rev:** Crown, Federation star, dates **Edge:** Plain **Shape:** 12-sided

Date	Mintage	F	VF	XF	Unc	BU
2003	65,003	—	—	—	35.00	40.00

KM# 799a 50 CENTS
18.2400 g., 0.9990 Silver 0.5858 oz. ASW, 31.51 mm. **Ruler:** Elizabeth II **Subject:** 50th Anniversary of the Coronation of Elizabeth II **Obv:** Head with tiara right **Rev:** Crown, Federation star, dates **Edge:** Plain **Shape:** 12-sided

Date	Mintage	F	VF	XF	Unc	BU
2003 Proof	6,967	Value: 60.00				

KM# 404 50 CENTS
15.5500 g., Copper-Nickel, 31.65 mm. **Ruler:** Elizabeth II **Obv:** Head with tiara right **Rev:** Australian coat of arms with kangaroo and emu supporters **Edge:** Plain **Shape:** 12-sided

Date	Mintage	F	VF	XF	Unc	BU
2004	17,918,000	—	—	—	9.00	10.00
2004 Proof	—	Value: 25.00				
2005	30,000	—	—	—	25.00	40.00
Note: Issued as part of a PNC only						
2005 Proof	—	Value: 10.00				
2006	—	—	—	—	9.00	10.00
2006 Proof	—	Value: 25.00				
2007	—	—	—	—	1.00	1.50
2007 Proof	—	Value: 10.00				
2008	—	—	—	—	7.00	8.00
2008 Proof	—	Value: 10.00				
2009	—	—	—	—	7.00	8.00
2009 Proof	—	Value: 10.00				
2010	—	—	—	—	7.00	8.00
2010 Proof	—	Value: 10.00				
2011	—	—	—	—	7.00	8.00
2011 Proof	—	Value: 10.00				
2012	—	—	—	—	7.00	8.00

KM# 694a 50 CENTS
18.2400 g., 0.9990 Silver 0.5858 oz. ASW, 31.65 mm. **Ruler:** Elizabeth II **Obv:** Head with tiara right **Rev:** Wombat, lorikeet and koala **Edge:** Plain **Shape:** 12-sided

Date	Mintage	F	VF	XF	Unc	BU
2004B Proof	8,203	Value: 75.00				

KM# 746 50 CENTS
15.5500 g., Copper-Nickel, 31.65 mm. **Ruler:** Elizabeth II **Obv:** Head with tiara right **Rev:** Military cemetery scene **Edge:** Plain **Shape:** 12-sided

Date	Mintage	F	VF	XF	Unc	BU
2005B	11,033,000	—	—	—	3.00	4.00
2005B Proof	—	Value: 20.00				

KM# 746a 50 CENTS
18.2400 g., 0.9990 Silver 0.5858 oz. ASW, 31.65 mm. **Ruler:** Elizabeth II **Obv:** Head with tiara right **Rev:** Military cemetery scene **Edge:** Plain **Shape:** 12-sided

Date	Mintage	F	VF	XF	Unc	BU
2005B Proof	6,500	Value: 38.00				

KM# 746b 50 CENTS
33.6300 g., 0.9999 Gold 1.0811 oz. AGW, 31.65 mm. **Ruler:** Elizabeth II **Obv:** Head with tiara right **Rev:** Military cemetery scene **Edge:** Plain **Shape:** 12-sided

Date	Mintage	F	VF	XF	Unc	BU
2005B Proof	650	Value: 1,950				

KM# 769 50 CENTS
15.5500 g., Copper-Nickel, 31.65 mm. **Ruler:** Elizabeth II **Subject:** Commonweath Games, Secondary School Design Competition **Obv:** Head with tiara right **Rev:** Athletes

Date	Mintage	F	VF	XF	Unc	BU
2005	20,500,000	—	—	—	2.50	3.50
2005 Proof	5,402	Value: 65.00				

KM# 67a 50 CENTS
18.2400 g., 0.9990 Silver 0.5858 oz. ASW, 31.51 mm. **Ruler:** Elizabeth II **Obv:** Young bust right **Rev:** Australian coat of arms **Edge:** Reeded

Date	Mintage	F	VF	XF	Unc	BU
2006 Proof	6,500	Value: 65.00				

KM# 770 50 CENTS
15.5500 g., Copper-Nickel, 31.65 mm. **Ruler:** Elizabeth II **Subject:** Basketball **Obv:** Head with tiara right **Obv. Legend:** ELIZABETH II - AUSTRALIA **Rev:** Basketball player shooting basket, Melbourne 2006 logo at left **Rev. Legend:** XVIII COMMONWEALTH GAMES **Shape:** 12-sided

Date	Mintage	F	VF	XF	Unc	BU
2006	5,002	—	—	—	8.50	10.00

KM# 771 50 CENTS
15.5500 g., Copper-Nickel, 31.65 mm. **Ruler:** Elizabeth II **Subject:** Hockey **Obv:** Head with tiara right **Obv. Legend:** ELIZABETH II - AUSTRALIA **Rev:** Hockey player hitting puck, Melboune 2006 logo at upper left **Rev. Legend:** XVIII COMMONWEALTH GAMES **Shape:** 12-sided

Date	Mintage	F	VF	XF	Unc	BU
2006	4,082	—	—	—	8.50	10.00

KM# 772 50 CENTS
15.5500 g., Copper-Nickel, 31.65 mm. **Ruler:** Elizabeth II **Subject:** Shooting **Obv:** Head with tiara right **Obv. Legend:** ELIZABETH II - AUSTRALIA **Rev:** Shooter, Melbourne 2006 logo at upper right **Rev. Legend:** XVIII COMMONWEALTH GAMES **Shape:** 12-sided

Date	Mintage	F	VF	XF	Unc	BU
2006	21,070	—	—	—	8.50	10.00

KM# 773 50 CENTS
15.5500 g., Copper-Nickel, 31.65 mm. **Ruler:** Elizabeth II **Subject:** Weightlifting **Obv:** Head with tiara right **Obv. Legend:** ELIZABETH II - AUSTRALIA **Rev:** Weightlifter holding barbells above head, Melbourne 2006 logo at left **Rev. Legend:** XVIII COMMONWEALTH GAMES **Shape:** 12-sided

Date	Mintage	F	VF	XF	Unc	BU
2006	22,332	—	—	—	8.50	10.00

KM# 774 50 CENTS
15.5500 g., Copper-Nickel, 31.65 mm. **Ruler:** Elizabeth II **Subject:** Gymnastics **Obv:** Head with tiara right **Obv. Legend:** ELIZABETH II - AUSTRALIA **Rev:** Gymnast standing with right leg up, Melbourne 2006 logo at left **Rev. Legend:** XVIII COMMONWEALTH GAMES **Edge:** Plain **Shape:** 12-sided

Date	Mintage	F	VF	XF	Unc	BU
2006	3,000	—	—	—	8.50	10.00

KM# 775 50 CENTS
15.5500 g., Copper-Nickel, 31.65 mm. **Ruler:** Elizabeth II **Subject:** Rugby 7's **Obv:** Head with tiara right **Obv. Legend:** ELIZABETH II - AUSTRALIA **Rev:** Rugby player running right, Melbourne 2006 logo at upper left **Rev. Legend:** XVIII COMMONWEALTH GAMES **Shape:** 12-sided

Date	Mintage	F	VF	XF	Unc	BU
2006	24,427	—	—	—	8.50	10.00

KM# 776 50 CENTS
15.5500 g., Copper-Nickel, 31.65 mm. **Ruler:** Elizabeth II **Subject:** Cycling **Obv:** Head with tiara right **Obv. Legend:** ELIZABETH II - AUSTRALIA **Rev:** Cyclist heading right, Melbourne 2006 logo at upper right **Rev. Legend:** XVIII COMMONWEALTH GAMES **Shape:** 12-sided

Date	Mintage	F	VF	XF	Unc	BU
2006	22,861	—	—	—	8.50	10.00

KM# 777 50 CENTS
15.5500 g., Copper-Nickel, 31.65 mm. **Ruler:** Elizabeth II **Subject:** Athletics **Obv:** Head with tiara right **Obv. Legend:** ELIZABETH II - AUSTRALIA **Rev:** Runner right, Melbourne 2006 logo at lower right **Rev. Legend:** XVIII COMMONWEALTH GAMES **Shape:** 12-sided

Date	Mintage	F	VF	XF	Unc	BU
2006	22,475	—	—	—	8.50	10.00

KM# 778 50 CENTS
15.5500 g., Copper-Nickel, 31.65 mm. **Ruler:** Elizabeth II **Subject:** Triathlon **Obv:** Head with tiara right **Obv. Legend:** ELIZABETH II - AUSRALIA **Rev:** Bicycle, runner, Melbourne 2006 logo below **Rev. Legend:** XVIII COMMONWEALTH GAMES **Shape:** 12-sided

Date	Mintage	F	VF	XF	Unc	BU
2006	22,302	—	—	—	8.50	10.00

KM# 779 50 CENTS
15.5500 g., Copper-Nickel, 31.65 mm. **Ruler:** Elizabeth II **Subject:** Netball **Obv:** Head with tiara right **Obv. Legend:** ELIZABETH II - AUSTRALIA **Rev:** Player shooting basket, Melbourne 2006 logo at upper left **Rev. Legend:** XVIII COMMONWEALTH GAMES **Shape:** 12-sided

Date	Mintage	F	VF	XF	Unc	BU
2006	22,432	—	—	—	8.50	10.00

KM# 780 50 CENTS
15.5500 g., Copper-Nickel, 31.65 mm. **Ruler:** Elizabeth II **Subject:** Table tennis **Obv:** Head with tiara right **Obv. Legend:** ELIZABETH II - AUSTRALIA **Rev:** Player hitting ball, Melbourne 2006 logo below **Rev. Legend:** XVIII COMMONWEALTH GAMES **Shape:** 12-sided

Date	Mintage	F	VF	XF	Unc	BU
2006	22,070	—	—	—	8.50	10.00

KM# 781 50 CENTS
15.5500 g., Copper-Nickel, 31.65 mm. **Ruler:** Elizabeth II **Subject:** Aquatics **Obv:** Head with tiara right **Obv. Legend:** ELIZABETH II - AUSTRALIA **Rev:** Swimmer, Melbourne 2006 logo **Rev. Legend:** XVIII COMMONWEALTH GAMES **Shape:** 12-sided

Date	Mintage	F	VF	XF	Unc	BU
2006	31,702	—	—	—	8.50	10.00

KM# 801 50 CENTS
15.5500 g., Copper-Nickel, 31.65 mm. **Ruler:** Elizabeth II **Subject:** 80th Birthday of Queen Elizabeth II **Obv:** Head with tiara right **Rev:** Royal Cipher **Shape:** 12-sided

Date	Mintage	F	VF	XF	Unc	BU
2006	28,191	—	—	—	45.00	60.00

KM# 801a 50 CENTS
18.2400 g., 0.9990 Silver partially gilt 0.5858 oz. ASW, 31.65 mm. **Ruler:** Elizabeth II **Subject:** 80th Birthday of Queen Elizabeth II **Obv:** Head with tiara right **Rev:** Crowned Royal Cipher on large 80, border of alternating British and Australian flags **Shape:** 12-sided

Date	Mintage	F	VF	XF	Unc	BU
2006 Proof	7,500	Value: 85.00				

KM# 802 50 CENTS
15.5500 g., Copper-Nickel, 31.65 mm. **Ruler:** Elizabeth II **Subject:** Visit of Queen Elizabeth II **Obv:** Head with tiara right **Rev:** Australian map and world globe **Shape:** 12-sided

Date	Mintage	F	VF	XF	Unc	BU
2006	—	—	—	—	30.00	45.00

KM# 802a 50 CENTS
18.2400 g., 0.9990 Silver partially gilt 0.5858 oz. ASW, 31.65 mm. **Ruler:** Elizabeth II **Subject:** Visit of Queen Elizabeth II **Obv:** Head with tiara right **Rev:** Australian map and world globe **Shape:** 12-sided

Date	Mintage	F	VF	XF	Unc	BU
2006 Proof	7,500	Value: 90.00				

KM# 821 50 CENTS
13.2800 g., 0.8000 Silver 0.3416 oz. ASW, 31.51 mm. **Ruler:** Elizabeth II **Obv:** Head with tiara right **Rev:** Australian coat of arms **Edge:** Reeded

Date	Mintage	F	VF	XF	Unc	BU
2006 Proof	—	Value: 70.00				

KM# 821a 50 CENTS
25.3000 g., 0.9990 Gold 0.8126 oz. AGW, 31.51 mm. **Ruler:** Elizabeth II **Obv:** Head with tiara right **Rev:** Australian coat of arms **Edge:** Reeded

Date	Mintage	F	VF	XF	Unc	BU
2006 Proof	300	Value: 1,500				

KM# 1001 50 CENTS
15.5500 g., Copper-Nickel, 31.65 mm. **Ruler:** Elizabeth II **Subject:** XVIII COMMONWEALTH GAMES **Obv:** Head with tiara right **Obv. Legend:** ELIZABETH II - AUSTRALIA **Rev:** Squash player, Melbourne 2006 logo **Edge:** Plain **Shape:** 12-sided

Date	Mintage	F	VF	XF	Unc	BU
2006	—	—	—	—	12.50	15.00

KM# 1002 50 CENTS
15.5500 g., Copper-Nickel, 31.65 mm. **Ruler:** Elizabeth II **Subject:** XVIII COMMONWEALTH GAMES **Obv:** Head with tiara right **Obv. Legend:** ELIZABETH II - AUSTRALIA **Rev:** Lawn bowler, Melbourne 2006 logo **Edge:** Plain **Shape:** 12-sided

Date	Mintage	F	VF	XF	Unc	BU
2006	22,602	—	—	—	12.50	15.00

KM# 1003 50 CENTS
15.5500 g., Copper-Nickel, 31.65 mm. **Ruler:** Elizabeth II **Subject:** XVIII COMMONWEALTH GAMES **Obv:** Head with tiara right **Obv. Legend:** ELIZABETH II - AUSTRALIA **Rev:** Boxer, Melbourne 2006 logo **Edge:** Plain **Shape:** 12-sided

Date	Mintage	F	VF	XF	Unc	BU
2006	—	—	—	—	12.50	15.00

KM# 1004 50 CENTS
Aluminum-Bronze, 30 mm. **Ruler:** Elizabeth II **Obv:** Head with tiara right **Obv. Legend:** ELIZABETH II - AUSTRALIA **Rev:** Everage head facing, multicolor **Rev. Legend:** DAME EDNA EVERAGE - 50TH ANNIVERSARY

Date	Mintage	F	VF	XF	Unc	BU
ND(2006)P	—	—	—	—	20.00	25.00

KM# 1570 50 CENTS
15.5500 g., Copper-Nickel, 31.65 mm. **Ruler:** Elizabeth II **Subject:** Commonwealth Games **Rev:** Badminton

Date	Mintage	F	VF	XF	Unc	BU
2006	—	—	—	—	8.50	10.00

KM# 1041 50 CENTS
15.5500 g., Copper-Nickel, 31.65 mm. **Ruler:** Elizabeth II **Subject:** Elizabeth and Philip Wedding Anniversary **Rev:** Profile portraits and diamond at center of circle of trumpets

Date	Mintage	F	VF	XF	Unc	BU
2007B	60,030	—	—	—	15.00	18.00

KM# 1049 50 CENTS
15.5500 g., Copper-Nickel, 31.65 mm. **Ruler:** Elizabeth II **Subject:** Scouting Centennial in Australia **Rev:** Australian Scout Emblem

Date	Mintage	F	VF	XF	Unc	BU
2008	49,517	—	—	—	10.00	12.00

KM# 1062 50 CENTS
15.5500 g., Copper-Nickel, 31.65 mm. **Ruler:** Elizabeth II **Subject:** 25th Anniversary Australia's Win of the America's Cup **Rev:** Yacht Australia II sailing left **Shape:** 12-sided

Date	Mintage	F	VF	XF	Unc	BU
2008	32,916	—	—	—	15.00	18.00

KM# 1100 50 CENTS
15.5500 g., 0.9990 Silver 0.4994 oz. ASW, 36.6 mm. **Ruler:** Elizabeth II **Subject:** Great Barrier Reef **Obv:** Head right **Rev:** Lion fish, multicolor **Edge:** reeded

Date	Mintage	F	VF	XF	Unc	BU
2009P Proof	Est. 10,000	Value: 75.00				

KM# 1101 50 CENTS
15.5500 g., 0.9990 Silver 0.4994 oz. ASW, 36.6 mm. **Ruler:** Elizabeth II **Subject:** Great Barrier Reef **Obv:** Head right **Rev:** Leafy Sea Dragon, multicolor **Edge:** Reeded

Date	Mintage	F	VF	XF	Unc	BU
2009P Proof	Est. 10,000	Value: 75.00				

KM# 1102 50 CENTS
15.5500 g., 0.9990 Silver 0.4994 oz. ASW, 36.6 mm. **Ruler:** Elizabeth II **Subject:** Great Barrier Reef **Rev:** Sea turtle, multicolor

Date	Mintage	F	VF	XF	Unc	BU
2009P Proof	—	Value: 75.00				

KM# 1432 50 CENTS
15.5500 g., Copper-Nickel, 31.65 mm. **Ruler:** Elizabeth II **Subject:** Moon Landing 40th Anniversary **Rev:** Earth, moon and orbiter

Date	Mintage	F	VF	XF	Unc	BU
2009C	—	—	—	—	—	10.00

KM# 1328 50 CENTS
15.5500 g., 0.9990 Silver 0.4994 oz. ASW, 36.6 mm. **Ruler:** Elizabeth II **Subject:** Great Barrier Reef **Obv:** Head right **Rev:** Clownfish, multicolor

Date	Mintage	F	VF	XF	Unc	BU
2010P Proof	—	Value: 60.00				

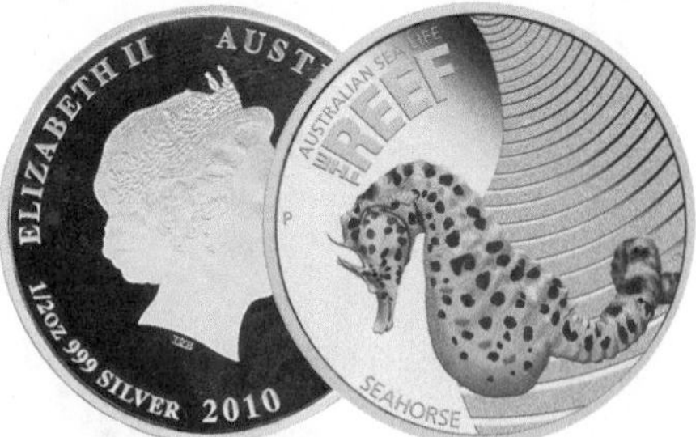

KM# 1329 50 CENTS
15.5730 g., 0.9990 Silver 0.5002 oz. ASW, 36.6 mm. **Ruler:** Elizabeth II **Subject:** Great Barrier Reef **Rev:** Big belly sea horse in multicolor

Date	Mintage	F	VF	XF	Unc	BU
2010P Proof	—	Value: 75.00				

KM# 1389 50 CENTS
15.5500 g., 0.9990 Silver 0.4994 oz. ASW, 36.6 mm. **Ruler:** Elizabeth II **Subject:** Great Barrier Reef - Morey Eel **Obv:** Hear right **Rev:** Tessellate Moray Eel, multicolor

Date	Mintage	F	VF	XF	Unc	BU
2010(p) Proof	—	Value: 86.00				

KM# 1450 50 CENTS
15.5600 g., 0.9990 Silver 0.4997 oz. ASW **Ruler:** Elizabeth II **Rev:** Australian Sugar Glider, multicolor

Date	Mintage	F	VF	XF	Unc	BU
2010P	—	Value: 45.00				

KM# 1456 50 CENTS
15.5600 g., 0.9990 Silver 0.4997 oz. ASW **Ruler:** Elizabeth II **Rev:** Australian kangaroo, multicolor

Date	Mintage	F	VF	XF	Unc	BU
2010P Proof	—	Value: 30.00				

KM# 1493 50 CENTS
15.5000 g., 0.9990 Silver 0.4978 oz. ASW, 36.6 mm. **Ruler:** Elizabeth II **Rev:** Dingo

Date	Mintage	F	VF	XF	Unc	BU
2010 Proof	—	Value: 50.00				

KM# 1500 50 CENTS
15.5500 g., Copper-Nickel, 31.65 mm. **Ruler:** Elizabeth II **Subject:** Australia Day **Shape:** 12-sided

Date	Mintage	F	VF	XF	Unc	BU
2010	—	—	—	—	2.50	4.50

KM# 1501 50 CENTS
15.5500 g., Copper-Nickel, 31.65 mm. **Ruler:** Elizabeth II **Subject:** Melbourne Cup, 150th Anniversary **Rev:** Horses racing right passing finish pole **Shape:** 12-sided

Date	Mintage	F	VF	XF	Unc	BU
2010	—	—	—	—	2.50	4.50

KM# 1519 50 CENTS
18.2400 g., 0.9990 Silver 0.5858 oz. ASW, 31.5 mm. **Ruler:** Elizabeth II **Subject:** Melbourne Cup, 150th race **Rev:** Trophy, partially gilt **Shape:** 12-sided

Date	Mintage	F	VF	XF	Unc	BU
2010 Proof	—	Value: 80.00				

KM# 1520 50 CENTS
18.2400 g., 0.9990 Silver 0.5858 oz. ASW, 31.5 mm. **Ruler:** Elizabeth II **Subject:** Melbourne Cup **Rev:** Horse and rider, partially gilt **Shape:** 12-sided

Date	Mintage	F	VF	XF	Unc	BU
2010 Proof	—	Value: 80.00				

KM# 1571 50 CENTS
15.5500 g., Copper-Nickel, 31.65 mm. **Ruler:** Elizabeth II **Subject:** Prince William and Catherine Middelton engagement **Rev:** Bundle of roses, Royal arms of Prince William below **Shape:** 12-sided

Date	Mintage	F	VF	XF	Unc	BU
2010	—	—	—	—	4.00	5.00

KM# 1571a 50 CENTS
18.2400 g., 0.9990 Silver partially gilt 0.5858 oz. ASW, 31.65 mm. **Ruler:** Elizabeth II **Subject:** Prince William and Catherine Middelton engagement **Rev:** Bunch of roses, gilt; Royal arms of Prince William below **Shape:** 12-sided

Date	Mintage	F	VF	XF	Unc	BU
2010 Proof	—	Value: 60.00				

KM# 1521 50 CENTS
15.5500 g., Copper-Nickel, 31.65 mm. **Ruler:** Elizabeth II **Subject:** National Service, 60th Anniversary **Shape:** 12-sided

Date	Mintage	F	VF	XF	Unc	BU
2011	—	—	—	—	4.00	5.00

KM# 1525 50 CENTS
15.5500 g., Copper-Nickel, 31.5 mm. **Ruler:** Elizabeth II **Subject:** Australia Day **Rev:** Circle of people clasping hands

Date	Mintage	F	VF	XF	Unc	BU
2011	—	—	—	—	4.00	5.00

KM# 1525a 50 CENTS
18.2400 g., Silver, 31.5 mm. **Ruler:** Elizabeth II **Subject:** Australia day **Rev:** Circle of people clasping hands, partially gilt **Shape:** 12-sided

Date	Mintage	F	VF	XF	Unc	BU
2011 Proof	—	Value: 40.00				

KM# 1532 50 CENTS
15.5500 g., 0.9990 Silver 0.4994 oz. ASW **Ruler:** Elizabeth II **Subject:** Bush Baby **Rev:** Dingo in color

Date	Mintage	F	VF	XF	Unc	BU
2011P Proof	—	Value: 65.00				

KM# 1533 50 CENTS
15.5500 g., 0.9990 Silver 0.4994 oz. ASW **Ruler:** Elizabeth II **Subject:** Bush Babies **Rev:** Bilby in color

Date	Mintage	F	VF	XF	Unc	BU
2011P Proof	—	Value: 65.00				

KM# 1567 50 CENTS
15.5500 g., Copper-Nickel, 31.65 mm. **Ruler:** Elizabeth II **Subject:** Royal Wedding **Rev:** Catherine and William busts left **Shape:** 12-sided

Date	Mintage	F	VF	XF	Unc	BU
2011	—	—	—	—	3.50	5.00

KM# 1567a 50 CENTS
18.2400 g., 0.9990 Silver partially gilt 0.5858 oz. ASW, 31.65 mm. **Ruler:** Elizabeth II **Subject:** Royal Wedding **Rev:** Catherine and William busts left, gilt flower at bottom **Shape:** 12-sided

Date	Mintage	F	VF	XF	Unc	BU
2011 Proof	—	Value: 60.00				

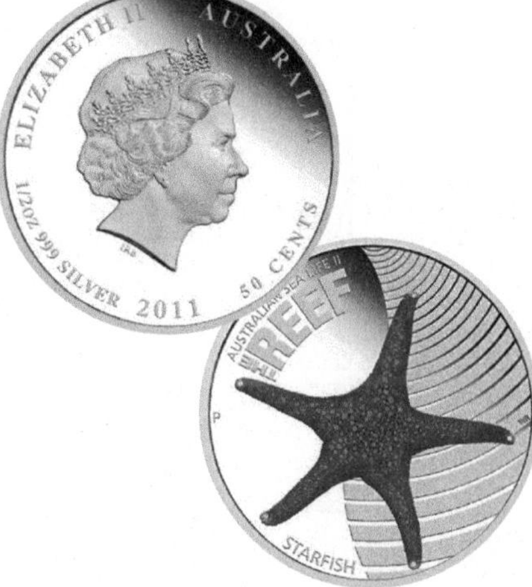

KM# 1577 50 CENTS
15.5910 g., 0.9990 Silver 0.5007 oz. ASW, 36.6 mm. **Ruler:** Elizabeth II **Subject:** Australian Sea Life - Starfish **Rev:** Starfish in color

Date	Mintage	F	VF	XF	Unc	BU
2011P Proof	10,000	Value: 75.00				

KM# 1579 50 CENTS
15.5910 g., 0.9990 Silver 0.5007 oz. ASW, 36.6 mm. **Ruler:** Elizabeth II **Subject:** Australian sea life - Hawksbill Turtle **Rev:** Color turtle swimming right

Date	Mintage	F	VF	XF	Unc	BU
2011P Proof	10,000	Value: 70.00				

KM# 1624 50 CENTS
15.5500 g., Copper-Nickel, 31.65 mm. **Ruler:** Elizabeth II **Subject:** Triple Zero Code for Emergency, 50th Anniversary **Obv:** Head with tiara right **Rev:** Telephone handset and 000, in color **Shape:** 12-sided

Date	Mintage	F	VF	XF	Unc	BU
2011	—	—	—	—	—	20.00

KM# 404b 50 CENTS
15.5500 g., Copper-Nickel with color, 31.65 mm. **Ruler:** Elizabeth II **Obv:** Head with tiara right **Rev:** Australian coat-of-arms with Kangaroo and Emu supporters all in color **Shape:** 12-sided

Date	Mintage	F	VF	XF	Unc	BU
2012	—	—	—	—	—	25.00

KM# 404c 50 CENTS
18.2400 g., 0.9990 Silver partially gilt 0.5858 oz. ASW, 31.65 mm. **Ruler:** Elizabeth II **Obv:** Head with tiara right **Rev:** Australian coat-of-arms with Kangaroo and Emu supporters all gilt **Shape:** 12-sided

Date	Mintage	F	VF	XF	Unc	BU
2012 Proof	—	Value: 75.00				

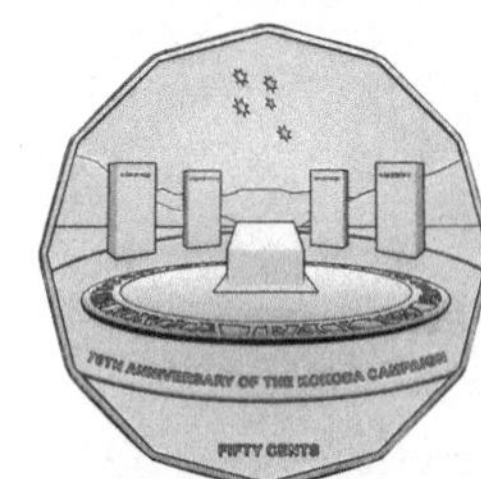

KM# 1855 50 CENTS
15.5000 g., Copper-Nickel, 31.5 mm. **Ruler:** Elizabeth II **Rev:** Kokoda Campaign monument **Shape:** 12-sided

Date	Mintage	F	VF	XF	Unc	BU
2012	—	—	—	—	4.00	5.00

KM# 1578 50 CENTS
15.5910 g., 0.9990 Silver 0.5007 oz. ASW, 36.6 mm. **Ruler:** Elizabeth II **Subject:** Australian sea life - Surgeonfish **Rev:** Surgeonfish in blue, black and yellow colors

Date	Mintage	F	VF	XF	Unc	BU
2012P Proof	10,000	Value: 75.00				

KM# 1697 50 CENTS
15.5910 g., Silver, 36.6 mm. **Ruler:** Elizabeth II **Subject:** Australian 2012 London Olympic Team **Obv:** Head with tiara right **Rev:** Male runner, Syndey Harbor Birdge, Tower of London images

Date	Mintage	F	VF	XF	Unc	BU
2012P Proof	750	Value: 45.00				

KM# 1712 50 CENTS
15.5910 g., 0.9990 Silver 0.5007 oz. ASW, 36.6 mm. **Ruler:** Elizabeth II **Obv:** Head with tiara right **Rev:** Reef Octopus in color

Date	Mintage	F	VF	XF	Unc	BU
2012P Proof	10,000	Value: 50.00				

KM# 1741 50 CENTS
15.5500 g., Copper-Nickel, 31.65 mm. **Ruler:** Elizabeth II **Subject:** Elizabeth II, 60th Anniversary **Obv:** Head with tiara right **Rev:** State Crown and floral design **Shape:** 12-sided

Date	Mintage	F	VF	XF	Unc	BU
2012	—	—	—	—	10.00	15.00

KM# 1741a 50 CENTS
18.2400 g., 0.9990 Silver 0.5858 oz. ASW, 31.65 mm. **Ruler:** Elizabeth II **Subject:** Elizabeth II, 60th Anniversary **Obv:** Head with tiara right **Rev:** State Crown and floral **Shape:** 12-sided **Note:** Illustration reduced.

Date	Mintage	F	VF	XF	Unc	BU
2012 Proof	—	Value: 75.00				

KM# 1744 50 CENTS
15.5500 g., Copper-Nickel, 31.65 mm. **Ruler:** Elizabeth II **Subject:** World War II, Bombing of Australia **Obv:** Head with tiara right **Rev:** Map of Astralia with bombed sites highlighted **Shape:** 12-sided

Date	Mintage	F	VF	XF	Unc	BU
2012	—	—	—	—	7.50	15.00

KM# 1795 50 CENTS
15.5500 g., 0.9990 Silver 0.4994 oz. ASW, 36.6 mm. **Ruler:** Elizabeth II **Subject:** Love Panda **Rev:** Two pandas in color heart shape

Date	Mintage	F	VF	XF	Unc	BU
2012P Proof	7,500	Value: 150				

KM# 1801 50 CENTS
15.5000 g., 0.9990 Silver 0.4978 oz. ASW, 36.6 mm. **Ruler:** Elizabeth II **Subject:** FIFA **Rev:** Soccer player in native costume

Date	Mintage	F	VF	XF	Unc	BU
2012P Proof	—	Value: 60.00				

KM# 1816 50 CENTS
15.5500 g., 0.9990 Silver 0.4994 oz. ASW, 36.6 mm. **Ruler:** Elizabeth II **Subject:** Bush Babies - Lemur

Date	Mintage	F	VF	XF	Unc	BU
2012P Proof	—	Value: 50.00				

KM# 1847 50 CENTS
15.5600 g., 0.9990 Silver 0.4997 oz. ASW, 36.6 mm. **Ruler:** Elizabeth II **Subject:** Australian Sea Life II, The Reef **Rev:** Manta Ray in color

Date	Mintage	F	VF	XF	Unc	BU
2012P Proof	—	Value: 45.00				

KM# 1854 50 CENTS
15.5500 g., Copper-Nickel, 31.5 mm. **Ruler:** Elizabeth II **Subject:** Australian Ballet, 50th Anniversary **Rev:** Two dancers **Shape:** 12-sided

Date	Mintage	F	VF	XF	Unc	BU
2012	—	—	—	—	4.00	5.00

KM# 1854a 50 CENTS
18.2400 g., 0.9990 Silver 0.5858 oz. ASW, 31.5 mm. **Ruler:** Elizabeth II **Subject:** Australian Ballet, 50th Anniversary **Rev:** Two dancers **Shape:** 12-sided

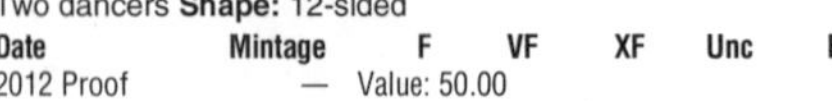

Date	Mintage	F	VF	XF	Unc	BU
2012 Proof	—	Value: 50.00				

KM# 1856 50 CENTS
15.5000 g., Copper-Nickel, 31.5 mm. **Ruler:** Elizabeth II **Subject:** Bathurst Endurance Race **Rev:** Racecar and landscape

Date	Mintage	F	VF	XF	Unc	BU
2012	—	—	—	—	4.00	5.00

KM# 1815 50 CENTS
15.5500 g., 0.9990 Silver 0.4994 oz. ASW, 36.6 mm. **Ruler:** Elizabeth II **Subject:** Birds - Cockatoo

Date	Mintage	F	VF	XF	Unc	BU
2013P Proof	—	Value: 50.00				

KM# 1817 50 CENTS
15.5000 g., 0.9990 Silver 0.4978 oz. ASW, 36.6 mm. **Ruler:** Elizabeth II **Subject:** Bush Babies - Kookaburra

Date	Mintage	F	VF	XF	Unc	BU
2013P Proof	—	Value: 50.00				

KM# 1818 50 CENTS
15.5500 g., Copper-Nickel, 31.65 mm. **Ruler:** Elizabeth II **Subject:** Alesandra Stokic **Rev:** Surfer in wave

Date	Mintage	F	VF	XF	Unc	BU
2013	—	—	—	—	—	9.00

KM# 1254 55 CENTS
15.5500 g., 0.9990 Silver 0.4994 oz. ASW, 26x38 mm. **Ruler:** Elizabeth II **Subject:** Postal Service, 200th Anniversary **Obv:** Head right **Rev:** Early post box **Edge:** Irregular as with a stamp **Shape:** Vertical rectangle

Date	Mintage	F	VF	XF	Unc	BU
2009P Proof	8,700	Value: 90.00				

KM# 1255 55 CENTS
15.5500 g., 0.9990 Silver 0.4994 oz. ASW, 26x38 mm. **Ruler:** Elizabeth II **Subject:** Postal Service, 200th Anniversary **Obv:** Head right **Rev:** Home delivery **Edge:** Irregular as with a stamp **Shape:** Vertical rectangle

Date	Mintage	F	VF	XF	Unc	BU
2009P Proof	8,700	Value: 90.00				

KM# 1803 60 CENTS
Silver **Ruler:** Elizabeth II **Subject:** London Olympics **Rev:** Scenes of London - Double decker bus; Big Ben; St. Paul's Cathedral, Wheel **Shape:** Vertical rectangle

Date	Mintage	F	VF	XF	Unc	BU
2012P	—	Value: 100				

KM# 489 DOLLAR
9.0000 g., Aluminum-Bronze, 25 mm. **Ruler:** Elizabeth II **Obv:** Head with tiara right **Rev:** Circle of 5 kangaroos **Edge:** Segmented reeding

Date	Mintage	F	VF	XF	Unc	BU
2001B Proof	1,001,000	Value: 55.00				
2004B	8,800,000	—	—	—	6.00	7.00
2004B Proof	50,000	Value: 75.00				
2005B	5,792,000	—	—	—	6.00	7.00
2005B Proof	33,520	Value: 85.00				
2006B	38,691,000	—	—	—	4.00	5.00
2006B Proof	—	Value: 45.00				
2006B Special Proof	—	Value: 3,500				
Note: Mintage of 25-35 pieces						
2007B	—	—	—	—	20.00	25.00
2007B Proof	—	Value: 45.00				
2008B	30,106,000	—	—	—	3.00	5.00
2008B Proof	—	Value: 45.00				
2009B	4,682,000	—	—	—	4.00	6.00
2009C Mintmaster mark	—	—	—	—	—	25.00
2009B Proof	—	Value: 45.00				
2010B	—	—	—	—	—	5.00
2010B Proof	—	Value: 45.00				
2011B	—	—	—	—	—	5.00
2011B Proof	—	Value: 45.00				
2012B	—	—	—	—	—	5.00
2012B Proof	—	Value: 45.00				

KM# 588 DOLLAR
9.0000 g., Aluminum-Bronze, 25 mm. **Ruler:** Elizabeth II **Subject:** 90th Anniversary Royal Australian Navy **Obv:** Head with tiara right **Rev:** Navy crest **Edge:** Segmented reeding

Date	Mintage	F	VF	XF	Unc	BU
2001	62,429	—	—	—	60.00	65.00

KM# 530 DOLLAR
9.0000 g., Aluminum-Bronze, 25 mm. **Ruler:** Elizabeth II **Subject:** Army Centennial **Obv:** Head with tiara right **Rev:** Army crest **Edge:** Segmented reeding

Date	Mintage	F	VF	XF	Unc	BU
2001C	125,186	—	—	—	18.00	20.00
Note: Large head, IRB spaced						
2001C	Inc. above	—	—	—	18.00	20.00
Note: Small head, IRB joined						
2001S	38,095	—	—	—	25.00	30.00

KM# 530a DOLLAR
11.6600 g., 0.9990 Silver 0.3745 oz. ASW, 24.9 mm. **Ruler:** Elizabeth II **Subject:** Army Centennial **Obv:** Head with tiara right **Rev:** Army crest **Edge:** Segmented reeding

Date	Mintage	F	VF	XF	Unc	BU
2001 Proof	17,839	Value: 50.00				

KM# 531 DOLLAR
9.0000 g., Aluminum-Bronze, 25 mm. **Ruler:** Elizabeth II **Subject:** 80th Anniversary Royal Australian Air Force **Obv:** Head with tiara right **Rev:** Air Force crest **Edge:** Segmented reeding

Date	Mintage	F	VF	XF	Unc	BU
2001B	99,281	—	—	—	18.00	20.00
Note: IRB spaced						

Date	Mintage	F	VF	XF	Unc	BU
2001B	Inc. above	—	—	—	25.00	30.00
Note: IRB joined						

KM# 534.1 DOLLAR
9.0000 g., Aluminum-Bronze, 25 mm. **Ruler:** Elizabeth II **Subject:** Australian Centenary of Federation - Norfolk Island **Obv:** Head with tiara right **Rev:** Stylized ribbon map of Australia with star **Edge:** Segmented reeding **Note:** Reverse design raised above field. Prev. KM#534.

Date	Mintage	F	VF	XF	Unc	BU
2001B	6,781,200	—	—	—	50.00	55.00
Note: IRB joined						
2001B	Inc. above	—	—	—	50.00	55.00
Note: IRB spaced						
2001B Proof	—	Value: 5.00				

KM# 534.1a DOLLAR
21.7000 g., 0.9999 Gold 0.6976 oz. AGW, 25 mm. **Ruler:** Elizabeth II **Subject:** Federation Centennial **Obv:** Elizabeth II **Rev:** Federation logo

Date	Mintage	F	VF	XF	Unc	BU
2001B Proof	650	Value: 1,300				

KM# 534.2 DOLLAR
9.0000 g., Aluminum-Bronze, 25 mm. **Ruler:** Elizabeth II **Subject:** Australian Centenary of Federation - Norfolk Island **Obv:** Head with tiara right **Rev:** Multicolor ribbon design of Australia with star, printed on the surface. **Edge:** Segmented reeding

Date	Mintage	F	VF	XF	Unc	BU
2001 Proof	—	Value: 12.50				
2001	27,905,000	—	—	—	5.00	—

KM# 594 DOLLAR
31.1035 g., 0.9990 Silver partially gilt 0.9990 oz. ASW, 40 mm. **Ruler:** Elizabeth II **Subject:** Millennium **Obv:** Head with tiara right **Rev:** Gold inset sun on multicolor earth above Egyptian obelisk **Edge:** Reeded

Date	Mintage	F	VF	XF	Unc	BU
2001 Prooflike	30,000	—	—	—	37.00	42.00

KM# 598 DOLLAR
31.1000 g., 0.9990 Silver 0.9988 oz. ASW, 40.4 mm. **Ruler:** Elizabeth II **Subject:** Centenary of Federation "Holey Dollar" **Obv:** Legend around star-shaped center hole **Rev:** Seven coats of arms around star-shaped hole **Edge:** Reeded

Date	Mintage	F	VF	XF	Unc	BU
ND(2001) Prooflike	30,000	—	—	—	35.00	40.00

KM# 682 DOLLAR
9.0000 g., Aluminum-Bronze, 25 mm. **Ruler:** Elizabeth II **Subject:** International Year of Volunteers **Rev:** Volunteers in wreath **Edge:** Segmented reeding

Date	Mintage	F	VF	XF	Unc	BU
2001B	6,000,000	—	—	—	12.00	15.00

KM# 632 DOLLAR
31.1035 g., 0.9990 Silver 0.9990 oz. ASW, 40 mm. **Ruler:** Elizabeth II **Subject:** Queen's Golden Jubilee **Obv:** Head right **Rev:** Queen on horse with multicolor flag background **Edge:** Reeded

Date	Mintage	F	VF	XF	Unc	BU
2002	34,074,000	—	—	—	—	50.00
2002P Proof	40,000	Value: 65.00				

KM# 600.1 DOLLAR
9.0000 g., Aluminum-Bronze, 25 mm. **Ruler:** Elizabeth II **Subject:** Year of the Outback **Obv:** Head with tiara right **Rev:** Stylized map of Australia **Edge:** Segmented reeding **Note:** Prev. KM#600.

Date	Mintage	F	VF	XF	Unc	BU
2002	34,074,000	—	—	—	5.00	7.00
2002 Proof	—	Value: 10.00				
2002C	68,447	—	—	—	7.00	9.00
2002B	32,698	—	—	—	7.00	9.00
2002M	31,694	—	—	—	7.00	9.00
2002S	36,931	—	—	—	7.00	9.00

KM# 600.1a DOLLAR
11.6600 g., 0.9900 Silver 0.3711 oz. ASW, 25 mm. **Ruler:** Elizabeth II **Subject:** Year of the Outback **Obv:** Head with tiara right **Rev:** Stylized map of Australia **Edge:** Segmented reeding

Date	Mintage	F	VF	XF	Unc	BU
2002B Proof	12,500	Value: 65.00				

KM# 600.2 DOLLAR

9.0000 g., Aluminum-Bronze, 25 mm. **Ruler:** Elizabeth II **Subject:** Year of the Outback **Obv:** Head with tiara right **Rev:** Multicolor stylized map of Australia **Edge:** Segmented reeding

Date	Mintage	F	VF	XF	Unc	BU
2002B Proof	39,514	Value: 15.00				

KM# 660 DOLLAR

31.1035 g., 0.9990 Silver partially gilt 0.9990 oz. ASW, 40 mm. **Ruler:** Elizabeth II **Subject:** Melbourne Mint **Obv:** Head with tiara right **Rev:** Mint entrance between two gold foil inserts replicating gold sovereign reverse designs **Edge:** Reeded

Date	Mintage	F	VF	XF	Unc	BU
2002B Proof	13,328	Value: 58.00				

KM# 489a DOLLAR

11.6600 g., 0.9990 Silver 0.3745 oz. ASW, 25 mm. **Ruler:** Elizabeth II **Obv:** Head with tiara right **Rev:** Kangaroos **Edge:** Segmented reeding

Date	Mintage	F	VF	XF	Unc	BU
2003B Proof	6,500	Value: 40.00				
2004B Proof	6,500	Value: 40.00				
2005B Proof	6,500	Value: 40.00				
2006B Proof	—	Value: 40.00				
2007B Proof	—	Value: 40.00				
2008B Proof	—	Value: 40.00				
2009B Proof	—	Value: 40.00				
2010B Proof	—	Value: 40.00				
2011B Proof	6,000	Value: 40.00				

KM# 823 DOLLAR

31.1035 g., 0.9990 Silver 0.9990 oz. ASW, 40 mm. **Ruler:** Elizabeth II **Subject:** 50th Anniversary - Coronation Elizabeth II **Obv:** Head with tiara right **Rev:** Crown in lettered garland **Note:** Colored design.

Date	Mintage	F	VF	XF	Unc	BU
2003P Proof	40,400	Value: 45.00				

KM# 663 DOLLAR

9.0000 g., Aluminum-Bronze, 25 mm. **Ruler:** Elizabeth II **Subject:** 50th Anniversary - End of Korean War **Obv:** Head with tiara right **Rev:** Dove of Peace **Edge:** Segmented reeding

Date	Mintage	F	VF	XF	Unc	BU
2003B	34,949	—	—	—	6.00	8.00
2003C	93,572	—	—	—	6.00	8.00
2003M	36,142	—	—	—	6.00	8.00
2003S	36,091	—	—	—	6.00	8.00

KM# 663a DOLLAR

11.6600 g., 0.9990 Silver 0.3745 oz. ASW, 25 mm. **Ruler:** Elizabeth II **Subject:** Korean War **Obv:** Queens head right **Rev:** Dove of Peace **Edge:** Segmented reeding

Date	Mintage	F	VF	XF	Unc	BU
2003B	15,000	Value: 55.00				

KM# 685 DOLLAR

31.1035 g., 0.9990 Silver 0.9990 oz. ASW, 40.6 mm. **Ruler:** Elizabeth II **Subject:** 21st Birthday of William **Obv:** Head right **Rev:** Multicolor Prince William **Edge:** Segmented reeding

Date	Mintage	F	VF	XF	Unc	BU
ND(2003)P Proof	12,500	Value: 45.00				

KM# 690 DOLLAR

9.0000 g., Aluminum-Bronze, 25 mm. **Ruler:** Elizabeth II **Obv:** Queens head right **Rev:** Australia Volunteers logo **Edge:** Segmented reeding

Date	Mintage	F	VF	XF	Unc	BU
2003B	4,149,000	—	—	—	15.00	17.00

KM# 690a DOLLAR

9.0000 g., 0.9990 Silver 0.2891 oz. ASW, 25 mm. **Ruler:** Elizabeth II **Obv:** Queens head right **Rev:** Australia Volunteers logo

Date	Mintage	F	VF	XF	Unc	BU
2003B Proof	6,500	Value: 30.00				

KM# 690.1 DOLLAR

9.0000 g., Aluminum-Bronze, 25 mm. **Ruler:** Elizabeth II **Subject:** Australia's Volunteers **Obv:** Elizabeth II **Rev:** Multicolor Australia's Volunteers logo **Edge:** Segmented reeding

Date	Mintage	F	VF	XF	Unc	BU
2003B Proof	39,090	Value: 15.00				

KM# 754 DOLLAR

9.0000 g., Aluminum-Bronze, 25 mm. **Ruler:** Elizabeth II **Subject:** Womens Suffrage **Obv:** Queens head right **Rev:** Suffragette talking to Britannia **Edge:** Segmented reeding

Date	Mintage	F	VF	XF	Unc	BU
2003B	10,007,000	—	—	—	5.00	7.00

KM# 763 DOLLAR

13.3600 g., 0.9990 Silver 0.4291 oz. ASW, 28.5 mm. **Ruler:** Elizabeth II **Series:** Masterpieces in Silver - Port Phillip Patterns **Obv:** 1/4 Ounce design **Rev:** Kangaroo design **Edge:** Reeded

Date	Mintage	F	VF	XF	Unc	BU
2003B Proof	10,000	Value: 80.00				

KM# 803 DOLLAR

9.0000 g., Aluminum-Bronze, 25 mm. **Ruler:** Elizabeth II **Subject:** Vietnam War Veterans 1962-1973 **Obv:** Head with tiara right **Rev:** Australian Vietnam Forces National Memorial

Date	Mintage	F	VF	XF	Unc	BU
2003	57,000	—	—	—	45.00	50.00

KM# 822 DOLLAR

54.3000 g., 0.9990 Silver 1.7440 oz. ASW, 50 mm. **Ruler:** Elizabeth II **Obv:** Superimposed head above replica of Holey Dollar **Rev:** Replica of Holey Dollar **Edge:** Reeded **Note:** Holey Dollar replica is embedded in silver collar and comes with replica Dump also in 0.999 silver.

Date	Mintage	F	VF	XF	Unc	BU
2003 Proof	11,000	Value: 90.00				

KM# 824 DOLLAR

31.1035 g., 0.9990 Silver 0.9990 oz. ASW, 40 mm. **Ruler:** Elizabeth II **Subject:** Golden Pipeline **Obv:** Head with tiara right **Rev:** Charles Yelverton O'Connor, innovative engineer, multicolor

Date	Mintage	F	VF	XF	Unc	BU
2003P Proof	5,000	Value: 130				

KM# 725 DOLLAR

56.2300 g., 0.9990 Bi-Metallic Copper center in Silver ring 1.8060 oz., 50 mm. **Ruler:** Elizabeth II **Subject:** The Last Penny **Obv:** 1964 dated penny obverse **Rev:** 1964 date penny reverse **Edge:** Reeded

Date	Mintage	F	VF	XF	Unc	BU
2004B Proof	16,437	Value: 85.00				

KM# 726 DOLLAR

9.0000 g., Aluminum-Bronze, 25 mm. **Ruler:** Elizabeth II **Subject:** Eureka Stockade 1854-2004 **Obv:** Head with tiara right **Rev:** Stockade and stylized soldiers **Edge:** Segmented reeding

Date	Mintage	F	VF	XF	Unc	BU
2004	—	—	—	—	8.00	10.00
2004B	33,835	—	—	—	5.00	6.00
2004C	70,913	—	—	—	5.00	6.00
2004 E	95,948	—	—	—	5.00	6.00
2004S	45,098	—	—	—	5.00	6.00
2004M	37,526	—	—	—	5.00	6.00
2004 3 known	—	—	—	—	—	1,000

KM# 726a DOLLAR

11.6600 g., 0.9990 Silver 0.3745 oz. ASW, 25 mm. **Ruler:** Elizabeth II **Subject:** Eureka Stockade **Obv:** Head with tiara right **Rev:** Stockade and stylized soldiers **Edge:** Segmented reeding

Date	Mintage	F	VF	XF	Unc	BU
2004B Proof	17,697	Value: 38.00				

KM# 733 DOLLAR
9.0000 g., Aluminum-Bronze, 25 mm. **Ruler:** Elizabeth II **Obv:** Head with tiara right **Rev:** Multicolor holographic five kangaroos design **Edge:** Segmented reeding

Date	Mintage	F	VF	XF	Unc	BU
2004B Proof	—	Value: 25.00				

KM# 733.1 DOLLAR
9.0000 g., Aluminum-Bronze, 25 mm. **Ruler:** Elizabeth II **Rev:** Five kangaroos **Edge:** Segmented reeding

Date	Mintage	F	VF	XF	Unc	BU
2004B	—	—	—	—	—	4.50

KM# 733.1a DOLLAR
11.6600 g., 0.9999 Silver 0.3748 oz. ASW, 25 mm. **Ruler:** Elizabeth II **Rev:** Five Kangaroos

Date	Mintage	F	VF	XF	Unc	BU
2004B Proof	6,500	Value: 35.00				

KM# 734 DOLLAR
31.1035 g., 0.9990 Silver 0.9990 oz. ASW, 40 mm. **Ruler:** Elizabeth II **Subject:** First Moon Walk **Obv:** Head with tiara right **Rev:** Multicolor rocket in flight **Edge:** Reeded

Date	Mintage	F	VF	XF	Unc	BU
2004P Proof	40,000	Value: 100				

KM# 735 DOLLAR
31.1035 g., 0.9990 Silver 0.9990 oz. ASW, 40 mm. **Ruler:** Elizabeth II **Subject:** First Moon Walk **Obv:** Head with tiara right **Rev:** Multicolor scene of astronauts planting flag on moon **Edge:** Reeded

Date	Mintage	F	VF	XF	Unc	BU
2004P Proof	40,000	Value: 110				

KM# 736 DOLLAR
31.1035 g., 0.9990 Silver 0.9990 oz. ASW, 40 mm. **Ruler:** Elizabeth II **Subject:** First Moon Walk **Obv:** Head with tiara right **Rev:** Multicolor close up of astronaut on moon **Edge:** Reeded

Date	Mintage	F	VF	XF	Unc	BU
2004P Proof	40,000	Value: 95.00				

KM# 737 DOLLAR
31.1035 g., 0.9990 Silver 0.9990 oz. ASW, 40 mm. **Ruler:** Elizabeth II **Obv:** Head with tiara right **Rev:** Multicolor Antarctic view of Mawson Station and penguins **Edge:** Reeded

Date	Mintage	F	VF	XF	Unc	BU
2004P Proof	7,500	Value: 60.00				

KM# 738 DOLLAR
31.1035 g., 0.9990 Silver partially gilt 0.9990 oz. ASW, 40 mm. **Ruler:** Elizabeth II **Subject:** 50th Anniversary of Royal Visit **Obv:** Queens head right **Rev:** Gilt lion and kangaroo **Edge:** Reeded

Date	Mintage	F	VF	XF	Unc	BU
ND (2004) Proof	12,500	Value: 85.00				

KM# 740 DOLLAR
24.3750 g., 0.9990 Silver Encapsulated gold nuggets in center 0.7829 oz. ASW, 40.6 mm. **Ruler:** Elizabeth II **Obv:** Crowned head right **Rev:** Eureka Stockade leader, miners and flag **Edge:** Reeded

Date	Mintage	F	VF	XF	Unc	BU
2004 Proof	12,500	Value: 145				

KM# 747 DOLLAR
9.0000 g., Aluminum-Bronze, 25 mm. **Ruler:** Elizabeth II **Subject:** 60th Anniversary World War II **Obv:** Head with tiara right **Rev:** Rejoicing serviceman **Edge:** Segmented reeding

Date	Mintage	F	VF	XF	Unc	BU
2005B	31,788,000	—	—	—	3.00	4.00
2005B Proof	—	Value: 35.00				

KM# 747a DOLLAR
11.6600 g., 0.9990 Silver 0.3745 oz. ASW, 25 mm. **Ruler:** Elizabeth II **Obv:** Queen's head right **Rev:** Rejoicing servicemen **Edge:** Segmented reeding

Date	Mintage	F	VF	XF	Unc	BU
2005B Proof	6,500	Value: 45.00				

KM# 747b DOLLAR
21.5200 g., 0.9999 Gold 0.6918 oz. AGW, 25 mm. **Ruler:** Elizabeth II **Obv:** Queen's head right **Rev:** Rejoicing servicemen **Edge:** Segmented reeding

Date	Mintage	F	VF	XF	Unc	BU
2005B Proof	629	Value: 1,300				

KM# 748 DOLLAR
9.0000 g., Aluminum-Bronze, 25 mm. **Ruler:** Elizabeth II **Subject:** 90th Anniversary Gallipoli Landing 1915-2005 **Obv:** Head with tiara right **Rev:** Bugler silhouette **Edge:** Segmented reeding

Date	Mintage	F	VF	XF	Unc	BU
2005	15,000	—	—	—	25.00	30.00
2005B	36,108	—	—	—	5.00	6.00
2005C	76,173	—	—	—	5.00	6.00
2005G	35,452	—	—	—	35.00	40.00
2005M	38,727	—	—	—	5.00	6.00
2005S	39,569	—	—	—	6.00	7.00

KM# 748a DOLLAR
11.6600 g., 0.9990 Silver 0.3745 oz. ASW, 25 mm. **Ruler:** Elizabeth II **Subject:** Gallipoli **Obv:** Queen's head right **Rev:** Bugler silhouette **Edge:** Segmented reeding

Date	Mintage	F	VF	XF	Unc	BU
2005B Proof	17,749	Value: 45.00				
2005B Proof, 2 known	—	Value: 1,500				

KM# 825 DOLLAR
56.4500 g., 0.9990 Silver partially gilt 1.8130 oz. ASW, 50 mm. **Ruler:** Elizabeth II **Obv:** Small head with tiara right superimposed above replica of Sydney Mint Sovereign **Rev:** Replica of Sydney Mint Sovereign **Edge:** Reeded

Date	Mintage	F	VF	XF	Unc	BU
2005 Proof	11,845	Value: 90.00				

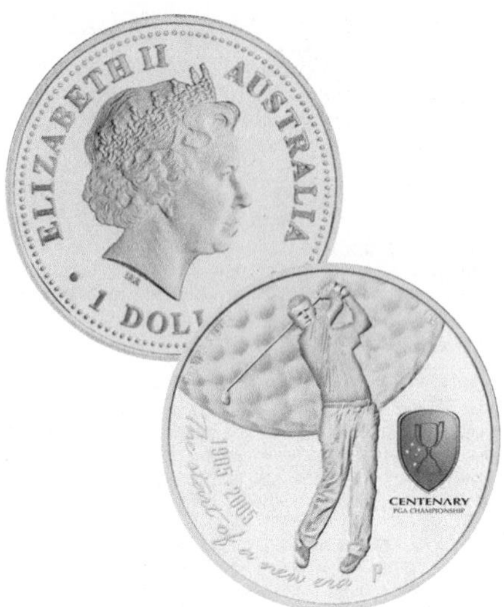

KM# 830 DOLLAR

31.6000 g., 0.9990 Silver 1.0149 oz. ASW, 40 mm. **Ruler:** Elizabeth II **Subject:** Centenary Australian Tennis Open 1905-2005 **Obv:** Head with tiara right **Rev:** Tennis players

Date	Mintage	F	VF	XF	Unc	BU
2005 Proof	10,000	Value: 50.00				

KM# 831 DOLLAR

31.6000 g., 0.9990 Silver 1.0149 oz. ASW, 40 mm. **Ruler:** Elizabeth II **Subject:** Centenary Australian PGA Gold Open 1905-2005 **Obv:** Head with tiara right **Rev:** Golfer

Date	Mintage	F	VF	XF	Unc	BU
2005 Proof	7,500	Value: 85.00				

KM# 832 DOLLAR

31.6000 g., 0.9990 Silver 1.0149 oz. ASW, 40 mm. **Ruler:** Elizabeth II **Subject:** Centenary Rotary 1905-2005 **Obv:** Head with tiara right **Rev:** Rotary International Logo

Date	Mintage	F	VF	XF	Unc	BU
2005 Proof	10,000	Value: 90.00				

KM# 833 DOLLAR

31.1035 g., 0.9990 Silver 0.9990 oz. ASW, 40 mm. **Ruler:** Elizabeth II **Subject:** 90th Anniversary Gallipoli Landings **Obv:** Head with tiara right **Rev:** Multicolor Australian and New Zealand soldiers beneath Australian flag

Date	Mintage	F	VF	XF	Unc	BU
2005 Proof	15,000	Value: 185				

KM# 835 DOLLAR

Aluminum-Bronze, 38.74 mm. **Ruler:** Elizabeth II **Subject:** Living Icons of Australia and New Zealand **Obv:** Head with tiara right **Rev:** Indigenous image of kangaroo

Date	Mintage	F	VF	XF	Unc	BU
2005	20,000	—	—	—	15.00	20.00

KM# 836 DOLLAR

31.1035 g., 0.9990 Silver 0.9990 oz. ASW, 40 mm. **Ruler:** Elizabeth II **Subject:** 21st Birthday Prince Harry of Wales **Obv:** Head with tiara right **Rev:** Prince Harry

Date	Mintage	F	VF	XF	Unc	BU
2005 Proof	12,500	Value: 80.00				

KM# 1015 DOLLAR

31.6000 g., 0.9990 Silver 1.0149 oz. ASW, 40.5 mm. **Ruler:** Elizabeth II **Subject:** 50th Anniversary Australian Territory **Obv:** Head with tiara right **Obv. Legend:** ELIZABETH II • AUSTRALIA **Rev:** Red-footed Booby perched on a branch, multicolor **Rev. Legend:** COCOS (KEELING) ISLANDS **Edge:** Reeded

Date	Mintage	F	VF	XF	Unc	BU
2005P Proof	7,500	Value: 70.00				

KM# 1018 DOLLAR

31.7500 g., 0.9990 Silver 1.0197 oz. ASW, 40.5 mm. **Ruler:** Elizabeth II **Obv:** Head with tiara right **Obv. Legend:** ELIZABETH II - AUSTRALIA **Rev:** Leopard seal with pup on ice, multicolor **Rev. Legend:** Australian Antarctic Territory **Edge:** Reeded

Date	Mintage	F	VF	XF	Unc	BU
2005P Proof	7,500	Value: 60.00				

KM# 838 DOLLAR

31.1035 g., 0.9990 Silver 0.9990 oz. ASW, 40 mm. **Ruler:** Elizabeth II **Subject:** Australain-Japan Year of Exchange **Obv:** Head with tiara right **Rev:** Kangaroo leaping with kangaroo rim decoration

Date	Mintage	F	VF	XF	Unc	BU
2006 Proof	5,000	Value: 50.00				

KM# 77a DOLLAR

11.6600 g., 0.9990 Silver 0.3745 oz. ASW, 25 mm. **Ruler:** Elizabeth II **Obv:** Young bust right **Rev:** Kangaroos **Edge:** Segmented reeding

Date	Mintage	F	VF	XF	Unc	BU
2006 Proof	6,500	Value: 40.00				

KM# 489b DOLLAR

21.5200 g., 0.9990 Gold 0.6912 oz. AGW, 25 mm. **Ruler:** Elizabeth II **Obv:** Head with tiara right **Rev:** Kangaroos **Edge:** Segmented reeding

Date	Mintage	F	VF	XF	Unc	BU
2006 Proof	300	Value: 1,300				

KM# 804 DOLLAR

9.0000 g., Aluminum-Bronze, 25 mm. **Ruler:** Elizabeth II **Subject:** XVIII Commonwealth Games **Obv:** Head with tiara right **Rev:** Graphic at left, logo at right

Date	Mintage	F	VF	XF	Unc	BU
2006	—	—	—	—	3.50	5.00

KM# 805 DOLLAR

9.0000 g., Aluminum-Bronze, 25 mm. **Ruler:** Elizabeth II **Subject:** 50 Years of Television **Obv:** Head with tiara right **Rev:** TV mast and camera **Edge:** Segmented reeding

Date	Mintage	F	VF	XF	Unc	BU
2006B	47,228	—	—	—	5.00	6.00
2006C	135,221	—	—	—	5.00	6.00
2006M	39,600	—	—	—	5.00	6.00
2006S	48,490	—	—	—	5.00	6.00
2006 TV	46,370	—	—	—	15.00	17.00
2006 Without mint mark, 4 known	—	—	—	—	—	1,000

KM# 805a DOLLAR

11.6600 g., 0.9990 Silver 0.3745 oz. ASW, 25 mm. **Ruler:** Elizabeth II **Subject:** 50 Years of Television **Obv:** Head with tiara right **Rev:** TV mast and camera **Edge:** Segmented reeding

Date	Mintage	F	VF	XF	Unc	BU
2006 Proof	10,790	Value: 45.00				
2006A Proof	3,859	Value: 60.00				

KM# 806 DOLLAR

9.0000 g., Aluminum-Bronze Issued in folder., 25 mm. **Ruler:** Elizabeth II **Series:** Colored Oceans **Obv:** Head with tiara right **Rev:** Multicolor jumping Bottlenose dolphins **Edge:** Segmented reeding

Date	Mintage	F	VF	XF	Unc	BU
2006	29,310	—	—	—	—	35.00

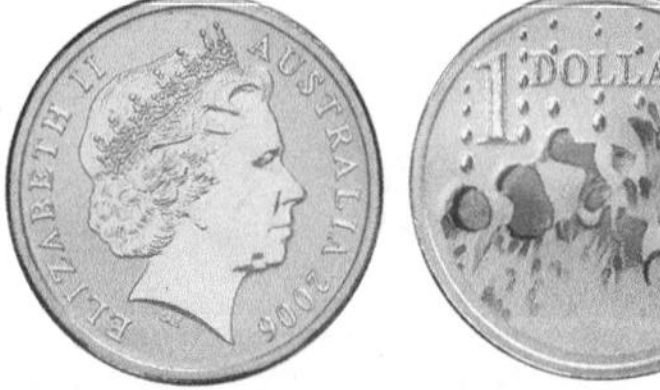

KM# 807 DOLLAR

9.0000 g., Aluminum-Bronze, 25 mm. **Ruler:** Elizabeth II **Series:** Colored Oceans **Obv:** Head with tiara right **Rev:** Multicolor clown fish **Edge:** Segmented reeding **Note:** Issued in folder.

Date	Mintage	F	VF	XF	Unc	BU
2006	29,310	—	—	—	25.00	30.00

KM# 826 DOLLAR
60.5000 g., 0.9990 Silver 1.9431 oz. ASW, 50 mm. **Ruler:** Elizabeth II **Obv:** Replica of 1758 Mexico City Mint 8 Reales **Obv. Legend:** ELIZABETH II (small head right) AUSTRALIA **Rev:** Replica of 1758 Mexico City Mint 8 Reales **Rev. Legend:** PILLAR DOLLAR **Edge:** Reeded

Date	Mintage	F	VF	XF	Unc	BU
2006	9,846	—	—	—	115	—

KM# 841 DOLLAR
31.1035 g., 0.9990 Silver Colorized lenticular display. 0.9990 oz. ASW **Ruler:** Elizabeth II **Subject:** 50 Years of Television in Australia 1956-2006 **Obv:** Head with tiara right **Rev:** SIx different historic TV show images **Shape:** Square with rounded corners

Date	Mintage	F	VF	XF	Unc	BU
2006 Proof	12,500	Value: 95.00				

KM# 842 DOLLAR
31.1035 g., 0.9990 Silver 0.9990 oz. ASW, 40 mm. **Ruler:** Elizabeth II **Subject:** 40th Anniversary of Demise of Pre-Decimal Coins **Obv:** Head with tiara right above transparent locket containing small replicas of pre-decimal currency **Rev:** Rim legend about locket

Date	Mintage	F	VF	XF	Unc	BU
2006P Proof	7,500	Value: 150				

KM# 843 DOLLAR
31.1035 g., 0.9990 Silver 0.9990 oz. ASW, 40 mm. **Ruler:** Elizabeth II **Subject:** 80th Birthday of Queen Elizabeth II **Obv:** Head with tiara right **Rev:** Queen Elizabeth II

Date	Mintage	F	VF	XF	Unc	BU
2006P Proof	12,500	Value: 85.00				

KM# 844 DOLLAR
31.1035 g., 0.9990 Silver 0.9990 oz. ASW, 40 mm. **Ruler:** Elizabeth II **Subject:** Figures of Note **Obv:** Head with tiara right **Rev:** Queen Elizabeth as portrayed on Australia 1 dollar banknote

Date	Mintage	F	VF	XF	Unc	BU
2006P Proof	1,000	Value: 175				

KM# 845 DOLLAR
31.1035 g., 0.9990 Silver 0.9990 oz. ASW, 40 mm. **Ruler:** Elizabeth II **Subject:** Figures of Note **Obv:** Head with tiara right **Rev:** MacArthur and Farrer as portrayed on Australia 2 dollar banknote

Date	Mintage	F	VF	XF	Unc	BU
2006P Proof	1,000	Value: 95.00				

KM# 846 DOLLAR
31.1035 g., 0.9990 Silver 0.9990 oz. ASW, 40 mm. **Ruler:** Elizabeth II **Subject:** Figures of Note **Obv:** Head with tiara right **Rev:** Banks and Chisholm as portrayed on Australia 5 dollar banknote

Date	Mintage	F	VF	XF	Unc	BU
2006P Proof	1,000	Value: 95.00				

KM# 847 DOLLAR
31.1035 g., 0.9990 Silver 0.9990 oz. ASW, 40 mm. **Ruler:** Elizabeth II **Subject:** Figures of Note **Obv:** Head with tiara right **Rev:** Greenway and Lawson as portrayed on Australia 10 dollar banknote

Date	Mintage	F	VF	XF	Unc	BU
2006P Proof	1,000	Value: 95.00				

KM# 848 DOLLAR
31.1035 g., 0.9990 Silver 0.9990 oz. ASW, 40 mm. **Ruler:** Elizabeth II **Subject:** Figures of Note **Obv:** Head with tiara right **Rev:** Kingsford-Smith and Hargrave as portrayed on Australia 20 dollar banknote

Date	Mintage	F	VF	XF	Unc	BU
2006P Proof	1,000	Value: 95.00				

KM# 849 DOLLAR
31.1035 g., 0.9990 Silver 0.9990 oz. ASW, 40 mm. **Ruler:** Elizabeth II **Subject:** 50th Anniversary of Dame Edna Everage **Obv:** Head with tiara right **Rev:** Dame Edna

Date	Mintage	F	VF	XF	Unc	BU
2006P Proof	6,500	Value: 85.00				

KM# 1005 DOLLAR
31.1030 g., 0.9990 Silver 0.9989 oz. ASW, 40 mm. **Ruler:** Elizabeth II **Obv:** Head with tiara right **Obv. Legend:** ELIZABETH II - AUSTRALIA **Rev:** Everage head facing, multicolor **Rev. Legend:** DAME EDNA EVERAGE - 50TH ANNIVERSARY

Date	Mintage	F	VF	XF	Unc	BU
ND(2006)P Proof	6,500	Value: 60.00				

KM# 1008 DOLLAR
31.1030 g., 0.9990 Silver 0.9989 oz. ASW, 40.5 mm. **Ruler:** Elizabeth II **Subject:** Quadricentennial **Obv:** Head with tiara right **Obv. Legend:** ELIZABETH II - AUSTRALIA **Rev:** Sailing ship at left, early map at right **Rev. Legend:** Australia on the Map

Date	Mintage	F	VF	XF	Unc	BU
2006P	—	—	—	—	—	55.00

KM# 1019 DOLLAR
31.3000 g., 0.9990 Silver 1.0053 oz. ASW, 40.5 mm. **Ruler:** Elizabeth II **Subject:** 20th Anniversary of base **Obv:** Head with tiara right **Obv. Legend:** ELIZABETH II - AUSTRALIA **Rev:** Plane above Albatross and chick on ice, multicolor **Rev. Legend:** Australian Antarctic Territory - EDGEWORTH DAVID BASE **Edge:** Reeded

Date	Mintage	F	VF	XF	Unc	BU
2006P Proof	7,500	Value: 60.00				

KM# 808 DOLLAR
9.0000 g., Aluminum-Bronze, 25 mm. **Ruler:** Elizabeth II **Subject:** Ashes Cricket Series 1882-2007 **Obv:** Head with tiara right **Rev:** Urn with supporters **Edge:** Segmented reeding

Date	Mintage	F	VF	XF	Unc	BU
2007	—	—	—	—	3.00	4.00

KM# 809 DOLLAR
9.0000 g., Aluminum-Bronze, 25 mm. **Ruler:** Elizabeth II **Subject:** Year of the Pig **Obv:** Head with tiara right **Rev:** Pig **Edge:** Segmented reeding

Date	Mintage	F	VF	XF	Unc	BU
2007	7,500	—	—	—	95.00	—

KM# 809a DOLLAR
11.6600 g., 0.9990 Silver 0.3745 oz. ASW, 25 mm. **Ruler:** Elizabeth II **Subject:** Year of the Pig **Obv:** Head with tiara right **Rev:** Pig **Edge:** Segmented reeding

Date	Mintage	F	VF	XF	Unc	BU
2007 Proof	—	Value: 28.00				

KM# 828 DOLLAR
9.0000 g., Aluminum-Bronze, 25 mm. **Ruler:** Elizabeth II **Subject:** Year of the Surf Lifesaver **Obv:** Head with tiara right **Rev:** Three lifesavers carrying rescued person **Edge:** Segmented reeding

Date	Mintage	F	VF	XF	Unc	BU
2007 Proof	34,500	Value: 20.00				

KM# 828a DOLLAR
11.6600 g., 0.9990 Silver 0.3745 oz. ASW, 25 mm. **Ruler:** Elizabeth II **Subject:** Year of the Surfer Lifesaver **Rev:** Three men saving fourth

Date	Mintage	F	VF	XF	Unc	BU
2007B	—	Value: 40.00				

KM# 829 DOLLAR
9.0000 g., Aluminum-Bronze, 25 mm. **Ruler:** Elizabeth II **Subject:** Norman Lindsay and his Magic Pudding **Obv:** Head with tiara right **Rev:** Lindsay and Pudding characters **Edge:** Segmented reeding

Date	Mintage	F	VF	XF	Unc	BU
2007	33,690	—	—	—	65.00	—

KM# 850 DOLLAR
27.2200 g., Copper-Nickel, 38.74 mm. **Ruler:** Elizabeth II **Obv:** Head with tiara right **Rev:** Kangaroo mother and joey **Edge:** Reeded

Date	Mintage	F	VF	XF	Unc	BU
2007	5,000	—	—	—	275	300

KM# 1009 DOLLAR
31.1030 g., 0.9990 Silver 0.9989 oz. ASW, 40 mm. **Ruler:** Elizabeth II **Subject:** 75th Anniversary Death of Phar Lap **Obv:** Head with tiara right **Obv. Legend:** ELIZABETH II - AUSTRALIA **Rev:** Horse and rider racing right

Date	Mintage	F	VF	XF	Unc	BU
ND(2007)P Proof	7,500	Value: 95.00				

KM# 1012 DOLLAR
31.1030 g., 0.9990 Silver 0.9989 oz. ASW, 40 mm. **Ruler:** Elizabeth II **Obv:** Bust with tiara right **Obv. Legend:** ELIZABETH II - AUSTRALIA **Rev:** Bridge, multicolor fireworks above **Rev. Legend:** 75th ANNIVERSARY - SYDNEY HARBOUR BRIDGE

Date	Mintage	F	VF	XF	Unc	BU
ND(2007)P Proof	10,000	Value: 85.00				

KM# 1016 DOLLAR

11.6600 g., 0.9990 Silver 0.3745 oz. ASW, 25 mm. **Ruler:** Elizabeth II **Subject:** 75th Anniversary - Sydney Harbor Bridge **Obv:** Head with tiara right **Obv. Legend:** ELIZABETH II _ AUSTRALIA **Rev:** Three men standing at bridge joint **Edge:** Segmented reeding

Date	Mintage	F	VF	XF	Unc	BU
2007B Proof	12,500	Value: 35.00				

KM# 1016a DOLLAR

9.0000 g., Aluminum-Bronze, 25 mm. **Ruler:** Elizabeth II **Subject:** Sydney Harbor Bridge, 75th Anniversary **Obv:** Head with tiara right **Rev:** Three men standing at bridge joint

Date	Mintage	F	VF	XF	Unc	BU
2007S	—	—	—	—	3.00	4.00

KM# 1020 DOLLAR

31.4800 g., 0.9990 Silver 1.0111 oz. ASW, 40.5 mm. **Ruler:** Elizabeth II **Subject:** 50th Anniversary of Station **Obv:** Head with tiara right **Obv. Legend:** ELIZABETH II - AUSTRALIA **Rev:** Ship "Kista Dan", multicolor **Rev. Legend:** Australian Antarctic Territory - DAVIS STATION **Edge:** Reeded

Date	Mintage	F	VF	XF	Unc	BU
2007P Proof	7,500	Value: 60.00				

KM# 1024 DOLLAR

9.0000 g., Aluminum-Bronze, 25 mm. **Ruler:** Elizabeth II **Series:** Colored Oceans **Obv:** Head with tiara right **Rev:** Biscuit Star, multicolor **Edge:** Segmented reeding **Note:** Issued in folder.

Date	Mintage	F	VF	XF	Unc	BU
2007	—	—	—	—	—	22.00

KM# 1025 DOLLAR

9.0000 g., Aluminum-Bronze, 25 mm. **Ruler:** Elizabeth II **Series:** Colored Oceans **Obv:** Head with tiara right **Rev:** Longfin Banner fish, multicolor **Edge:** Segmented reeding

Date	Mintage	F	VF	XF	Unc	BU
2007	25,930	—	—	—	—	22.00

KM# 1026 DOLLAR

9.0000 g., Aluminum-Bronze, 25 mm. **Ruler:** Elizabeth II **Series:** Colored Oceans **Obv:** Head with tiara right **Rev:** White Shark, multicolor **Edge:** Segmented reeding **Note:** Issued in folder.

Date	Mintage	F	VF	XF	Unc	BU
2007	30,416	—	—	—	—	22.00

KM# 1027 DOLLAR

9.0000 g., Aluminum-Bronze, 25 mm. **Ruler:** Elizabeth II **Series:** Colored Oceans **Obv:** Head with tiara right **Rev:** Big Belly seahorse **Edge:** Segmented reeding

Date	Mintage	F	VF	XF	Unc	BU
2007	—	—	—	—	—	22.00

KM# 1040 DOLLAR

9.0000 g., Aluminum-Bronze, 25 mm. **Ruler:** Elizabeth II **Subject:** APEC **Rev:** Multiple stars

Date	Mintage	F	VF	XF	Unc	BU
2007B	20,108,000	—	—	—	3.00	4.00

KM# 1042 DOLLAR

9.0000 g., Aluminum-Bronze, 25 mm. **Ruler:** Elizabeth II **Subject:** 60th Anniversary - Peacekeepers **Rev:** Hand holding globe within wreath, dove above

Date	Mintage	F	VF	XF	Unc	BU
2007B	31,028	—	—	—	—	15.00

KM# 1437 DOLLAR

Silver partially gilt **Ruler:** Elizabeth II **Subject:** Lunar dollar

Date	Mintage	F	VF	XF	Unc	BU
2007 Proof	—	Value: 50.00				

KM# 1438 DOLLAR

Silver partially gilt **Ruler:** Elizabeth II **Subject:** One Johanna

Date	Mintage	F	VF	XF	Unc	BU
2007 Proof	—	Value: 50.00				

KM# 1653 DOLLAR

9.0000 g., Aluminum-Bronze, 25 mm. **Ruler:** Elizabeth II **Subject:** International Polar Year **Obv:** Head with tiara right **Rev:** Sailing ship in ice

Date	Mintage	F	VF	XF	Unc	BU
2007	—	—	—	—	6.00	8.00

KM# 1682 DOLLAR

13.8000 g., Aluminum-Bronze, 30.6 mm. **Ruler:** Elizabeth II **Subject:** World Youth Day **Rev:** Pope Benedict XVI and WYD logo in color

Date	Mintage	F	VF	XF	Unc	BU
2008	—	—	—	—	—	15.00

KM# 1047 DOLLAR

9.0000 g., Aluminum-Bronze, 25 mm. **Ruler:** Elizabeth II **Rev:** First coat of arms

Date	Mintage	F	VF	XF	Unc	BU
2008B	32,500	—	—	—	5.00	6.00
2008M	25,202	—	—	—	5.00	6.00
2008C	104,689	—	—	—	15.00	17.00
2008S	32,500	—	—	—	5.00	6.00

KM# 1063 DOLLAR

9.0000 g., Aluminum-Bronze, 25 mm. **Ruler:** Elizabeth II **Subject:** Saint Sister Mary Mackillop **Rev:** Nun and three children, world map in background

Date	Mintage	F	VF	XF	Unc	BU
2008	29,800	—	—	—	15.00	17.00

KM# 1039 DOLLAR

9.0000 g., Aluminum-Bronze, 25 mm. **Ruler:** Elizabeth II **Subject:** Boy Scouts, 100th Anniversary

Date	Mintage	F	VF	XF	Unc	BU
2008	—	—	—	—	6.00	7.00

KM# 1047a DOLLAR

11.6000 g., 0.9990 Silver 0.3726 oz. ASW, 25 mm. **Ruler:** Elizabeth II **Rev:** First coat of arms

Date	Mintage	F	VF	XF	Unc	BU
2008C Proof	12,500	Value: 45.00				

KM# 1052 DOLLAR

9.0000 g., Aluminum-Bronze, 25 mm. **Ruler:** Elizabeth II **Subject:** Rugby League Centennial **Rev:** Rugby anniversary logo

Date	Mintage	F	VF	XF	Unc	BU
2008	60,400	—	—	—	15.00	17.00

KM# 1056 DOLLAR

9.0000 g., Aluminum-Bronze, 25 mm. **Ruler:** Elizabeth II **Subject:** Year of the Rat

Date	Mintage	F	VF	XF	Unc	BU
2008	—	—	—	—	13.00	15.00

KM# 1056a DOLLAR

11.6600 g., 0.9990 Silver 0.3745 oz. ASW, 25 mm. **Ruler:** Elizabeth II **Subject:** Year of the Rat **Rev:** Mouse at center, flora in arches

Date	Mintage	F	VF	XF	Unc	BU
2008 Proof	10,000	Value: 45.00				

KM# 1059 DOLLAR
9.0000 g., Aluminum-Bronze, 25 mm. **Ruler:** Elizabeth II
Subject: Planet Earth **Rev:** Four hands and elements

Date	Mintage	F	VF	XF	Unc	BU
2008	28,399	—	—	—	20.00	22.00
2008 Proof	—	Value: 25.00				

KM# 1064 DOLLAR
9.0000 g., Aluminum-Bronze, 25 mm. **Ruler:** Elizabeth II
Subject: Centennial of Quarantine **Rev:** Beagle and suitcase like map of Australia

Date	Mintage	F	VF	XF	Unc	BU
2008	30,094	—	—	—	15.00	17.00

KM# 1068 DOLLAR
9.0000 g., Aluminum-Bronze, 25 mm. **Ruler:** Elizabeth II **Rev:** Multicolor Echidna

Date	Mintage	F	VF	XF	Unc	BU
2008	20,589	—	—	—	18.00	22.00

KM# 1069 DOLLAR
9.0000 g., Aluminum-Bronze, 25 mm. **Ruler:** Elizabeth II **Rev:** Multicolor Rock Wallaby

Date	Mintage	F	VF	XF	Unc	BU
2008	24,863	—	—	—	18.00	22.00

KM# 1070 DOLLAR
9.0000 g., Aluminum-Bronze, 25 mm. **Ruler:** Elizabeth II **Rev:** Multicolor koala

Date	Mintage	F	VF	XF	Unc	BU
2008	27,045	—	—	—	18.00	22.00

KM# 1071 DOLLAR
9.0000 g., Aluminum-Bronze, 25 mm. **Ruler:** Elizabeth II **Rev:** Multicolor wombat

Date	Mintage	F	VF	XF	Unc	BU
2008	22,295	—	—	—	18.00	22.00

KM# 1076 DOLLAR
9.0000 g., Aluminum-Bronze, 25 mm. **Ruler:** Elizabeth II
Subject: Year of Astronomy **Rev:** Parkes Telescope

Date	Mintage	F	VF	XF	Unc	BU
2008	—	—	—	—	12.00	14.00
2008 Proof	—	Value: 25.00				

KM# 1090 DOLLAR
13.5000 g., Aluminum-Bronze, 29.5 mm. **Ruler:** Elizabeth II
Subject: Ghost Bat **Obv:** Head right **Rev:** Ghost bat against night sky **Edge:** Reeded

Date	Mintage	F	VF	XF	Unc	BU
2008	—	—	—	—	—	14.00

KM# 1091 DOLLAR
31.1050 g., 0.9990 Silver 0.9990 oz. ASW, 40.6 mm. **Ruler:** Elizabeth II **Subject:** UNESCO Heritage site - Kakadu National Park **Rev:** Saltwater crocodile and multicolor swamp

Date	Mintage	F	VF	XF	Unc	BU
2008P Proof	7,500	Value: 75.00				

KM# 1168 DOLLAR
13.5000 g., Aluminum-Bronze, 29.5 mm. **Ruler:** Elizabeth II
Obv: Head right **Rev:** Common wombat

Date	Mintage	F	VF	XF	Unc	BU
2008P	—	—	—	—	—	14.00

KM# 1169 DOLLAR
13.5000 g., Aluminum-Bronze, 29.5 mm. **Ruler:** Elizabeth II
Obv: Head right **Rev:** Echidna

Date	Mintage	F	VF	XF	Unc	BU
2008P	—	—	—	—	—	14.00

KM# 1170 DOLLAR
13.5000 g., Aluminum-Bronze, 29.5 mm. **Ruler:** Elizabeth II
Obv: Head right **Rev:** Frilled-neck lizard

Date	Mintage	F	VF	XF	Unc	BU
2008P	—	—	—	—	—	14.00

KM# 1171 DOLLAR
13.5000 g., Aluminum-Bronze, 29.5 mm. **Ruler:** Elizabeth II
Obv: Head right **Rev:** Grey kangaroo

Date	Mintage	F	VF	XF	Unc	BU
2008P	—	—	—	—	—	14.00

KM# 1172 DOLLAR
13.5000 g., Aluminum-Bronze, 29.5 mm. **Ruler:** Elizabeth II
Obv: Head right **Rev:** Splendid wren

Date	Mintage	F	VF	XF	Unc	BU
2008P	—	—	—	—	—	14.00

KM# 1173 DOLLAR
13.5000 g., Aluminum-Bronze, 29.5 mm. **Ruler:** Elizabeth II
Obv: Head right **Rev:** Palm cockatoo

Date	Mintage	F	VF	XF	Unc	BU
2008P	—	—	—	—	—	14.00

KM# 1174 DOLLAR
13.5000 g., Aluminum-Bronze, 29.5 mm. **Ruler:** Elizabeth II
Obv: Head right **Rev:** Wedge-tailed eagle

Date	Mintage	F	VF	XF	Unc	BU
2008P	—	—	—	—	—	14.00

KM# 1175 DOLLAR
13.5000 g., Aluminum-Bronze, 29.5 mm. **Ruler:** Elizabeth II
Obv: Head right **Rev:** Whale shark

Date	Mintage	F	VF	XF	Unc	BU
2008P	—	—	—	—	—	14.00

KM# 1176 DOLLAR
13.5000 g., Aluminum-Bronze, 29.5 mm. **Ruler:** Elizabeth II
Obv: Head right **Rev:** Green sea turtle

Date	Mintage	F	VF	XF	Unc	BU
2008P	—	—	—	—	—	14.00

KM# 1177 DOLLAR
13.5000 g., Aluminum-Bronze, 29.5 mm. **Ruler:** Elizabeth II **Obv:** Head right **Rev:** Platypus

Date	Mintage	F	VF	XF	Unc	BU
2008P	—	—	—	—	—	14.00

KM# 1178 DOLLAR
13.5000 g., Aluminum-Bronze, 29.5 mm. **Ruler:** Elizabeth II **Obv:** Head right **Rev:** Australian sea lion

Date	Mintage	F	VF	XF	Unc	BU
2008P	—	—	—	—	—	14.00

KM# 1179 DOLLAR
31.1050 g., 0.9990 Silver 0.9990 oz. ASW, 40.6 mm. **Ruler:** Elizabeth II **Subject:** 90th Anniversary - End of WWI **Obv:** Head right **Rev:** Silhouette of bugler, multicolor poppies below

Date	Mintage	F	VF	XF	Unc	BU
2008P Proof	12,500	Value: 90.00				

KM# 1654 DOLLAR
31.1050 g., 0.9990 Silver 0.9990 oz. ASW, 40.6 mm. **Ruler:** Elizabeth II **Subject:** HMAS Sydney II

Date	Mintage	F	VF	XF	Unc	BU
2008 Proof	—	Value: 90.00				

KM# 1749 DOLLAR
31.1050 g., 0.9990 Silver 0.9990 oz. ASW, 40.6 mm. **Ruler:** Elizabeth II **Subject:** Treasurers of Australia, Opals **Obv:** Small head above container of five opals **Rev:** landscape above container

Date	Mintage	F	VF	XF	Unc	BU
2008P Proof	—	Value: 75.00				

KM# 1428 DOLLAR
13.8000 g., Aluminum-Bronze, 30.6 mm. **Ruler:** Elizabeth II **Subject:** Citizenship **Obv:** Head in tiara right **Rev:** National arms

Date	Mintage	F	VF	XF	Unc	BU
2009P	—	—	—	—	—	14.00
2010P	—	—	—	—	—	14.00
2011P	—	—	—	—	—	14.00
2012P	—	—	—	—	—	14.00

KM# 1429 DOLLAR
9.0000 g., Aluminum-Bronze, 25 mm. **Ruler:** Elizabeth II **Subject:** Steve Irwin **Rev:** Steve Irwin and animal montage

Date	Mintage	F	VF	XF	Unc	BU
2009(p)	—	—	—	—	—	12.00

KM# 1077 DOLLAR
9.0000 g., Aluminum-Bronze, 25 mm. **Ruler:** Elizabeth II **Subject:** Dorothy Wall **Rev:** Portrait and four characters to right

Date	Mintage	F	VF	XF	Unc	BU
2009	—	—	—	—	—	12.00

KM# 1078 DOLLAR
9.0000 g., Aluminum-Bronze, 25 mm. **Ruler:** Elizabeth II **Subject:** Year of the Ox **Rev:** V. Gottwald

Date	Mintage	F	VF	XF	Unc	BU
2009	—	—	—	—	12.00	13.00

KM# 1078a DOLLAR
11.6600 g., 0.9990 Silver 0.3745 oz. ASW, 25 mm. **Ruler:** Elizabeth II **Subject:** Year of the Ox

Date	Mintage	F	VF	XF	Unc	BU
2009 Proof	10,000	Value: 45.00				

KM# 1082 DOLLAR
27.2200 g., Copper-Nickel, 38.74 mm. **Ruler:** Elizabeth II **Rev:** Kangaroo

Date	Mintage	F	VF	XF	Unc	BU
2009	—	—	—	—	—	25.00

KM# 1087 DOLLAR
9.0000 g., Aluminum-Bronze, 25 mm. **Ruler:** Elizabeth II **Subject:** 60th Anniversary - Citizenship **Obv:** Head right **Rev:** Portraits around globe

Date	Mintage	F	VF	XF	Unc	BU
2009C Proof	—	Value: 28.00				

KM# 1087a DOLLAR
11.9000 g., 0.9990 Silver 0.3822 oz. ASW, 25 mm. **Ruler:** Elizabeth II **Subject:** 60th Anniversary - Citizenship **Rev:** Portraits around globe

Date	Mintage	F	VF	XF	Unc	BU
2009C Proof	—	Value: 40.00				

KM# 1089 DOLLAR
Aluminum-Bronze **Ruler:** Elizabeth II **Subject:** Postal Service, 200th Anniversary **Obv:** Head with tiara right **Rev:** Isaac Nichols, first postman

Date	Mintage	F	VF	XF	Unc	BU
2009	—	—	—	—	—	13.00

KM# 1092 DOLLAR
13.3000 g., Aluminum-Bronze, 30.6 mm. **Ruler:** Elizabeth II **Subject:** Celebrate Australia - Western Australia **Rev:** Kangaroo and multicolor Perth city view

Date	Mintage	F	VF	XF	Unc	BU
2009	—	—	—	—	—	13.00

KM# 1093 DOLLAR
13.3000 g., Aluminum-Bronze, 30.6 mm. **Ruler:** Elizabeth II **Series:** Celebrate Australia - Victoria **Rev:** Little Penguin and multicolor Melbourne city view

Date	Mintage	F	VF	XF	Unc	BU
2009	—	—	—	—	—	13.00

KM# 1094 DOLLAR
13.3000 g., Aluminum-Bronze, 30.6 mm. **Ruler:** Elizabeth II **Subject:** Celebrate Australia - Tasmania **Rev:** Tasmanian Devil and multicolor Cradle Mountain National Park

Date	Mintage	F	VF	XF	Unc	BU
2009P	—	—	—	—	—	13.00

KM# 1095 DOLLAR
13.3000 g., Aluminum-Bronze, 30.6 mm. **Ruler:** Elizabeth II **Subject:** Celebrate Australia - South Australia **Rev:** Wombat and multicolor cathedral

Date	Mintage	F	VF	XF	Unc	BU
2009P	—	—	—	—	—	13.00

KM# 1096 DOLLAR
13.3000 g., Aluminum-Bronze, 30.6 mm. **Ruler:** Elizabeth II **Subject:** Celebrate Australia - Queensland **Rev:** Sea Turtle with multicolor skyline of Brisbane

Date	Mintage	F	VF	XF	Unc	BU
2009P	—	—	—	—	—	13.00

KM# 1097 DOLLAR
13.3000 g., Aluminum-Bronze, 30.6 mm. **Ruler:** Elizabeth II **Subject:** Celebrate Australia - Northern Territoty **Rev:** Saltwater crocodile and multicolor Kakadu National Park

Date	Mintage	F	VF	XF	Unc	BU
2009P	—	—	—	—	—	13.00

KM# 1098 DOLLAR
13.3000 g., Aluminum-Bronze, 30.6 mm. **Ruler:** Elizabeth II **Subject:** Celebrate Australia - New South Wales **Rev:** Koala, multicolor Sydney Opera House and Harbor Bridge

Date	Mintage	F	VF	XF	Unc	BU
2009P	—	—	—	—	—	13.00

KM# 1099 DOLLAR
13.3000 g., Aluminum-Bronze, 30.6 mm. **Ruler:** Elizabeth II **Subject:** Celebrate Australia - Capital Territory, Canberra **Rev:** Cockatoo and multicolor design

Date	Mintage	F	VF	XF	Unc	BU
2009P	—	—	—	—	—	13.00

KM# 1211 DOLLAR
31.1050 g., 0.9990 Silver 0.9990 oz. ASW, 40.6 mm. **Ruler:** Elizabeth II **Subject:** Antarctic Territory **Obv:** Head right **Rev:** Douglas Mawson, one of two men standing on magnetic South Pole

Date	Mintage	F	VF	XF	Unc	BU
2009P Proof	7,500	Value: 85.00				

KM# 1245 DOLLAR
31.1050 g., 0.9990 Silver 0.9990 oz. ASW **Ruler:** Elizabeth II **Subject:** 2010 FIFA World Cup, South Africa **Obv:** Head right **Rev:** Soccer player and kangaroo in background

Date	Mintage	F	VF	XF	Unc	BU
2009P Proof	15,000	Value: 100				

KM# 1248 DOLLAR
31.1050 g., 0.9990 Silver 0.9990 oz. ASW, 40.6 mm. **Ruler:** Elizabeth II **Subject:** World Masters Games **Obv:** Head right **Rev:** Sydney Harbor Bridge, multicolor logo

Date	Mintage	F	VF	XF	Unc	BU
2009P Proof	5,000	Value: 100				

KM# 1256 DOLLAR
13.8000 g., Aluminum-Bronze, 31 mm. **Ruler:** Elizabeth II **Subject:** Space Topics - Astronomers **Obv:** Head right **Rev:** Galileo Galilei and telescope

Date	Mintage	F	VF	XF	Unc	BU
2009P	—	—	—	—	—	12.00

KM# 1257 DOLLAR
Aluminum-Bronze, 31 mm. **Ruler:** Elizabeth II **Subject:** Space Topics - Craters **Obv:** Head right **Rev:** Moon crater Daedalus

Date	Mintage	F	VF	XF	Unc	BU
2009P	—	—	—	—	—	12.00

KM# 1258 DOLLAR
Aluminum-Bronze, 31 mm. **Ruler:** Elizabeth II **Subject:** Space Topics - Moons **Obv:** Head right **Rev:** Apollo astronaut on moon walk

Date	Mintage	F	VF	XF	Unc	BU
2009P	—	—	—	—	—	12.00

KM# 1259 DOLLAR
Aluminum-Bronze, 31 mm. **Ruler:** Elizabeth II **Subject:** Space Topics - Observatories **Obv:** Head right **Rev:** Parkes Observatory, New South Wales

Date	Mintage	F	VF	XF	Unc	BU
2009P	—	—	—	—	—	12.00

KM# 1260 DOLLAR
Aluminum-Bronze, 31 mm. **Ruler:** Elizabeth II **Subject:** Space Topics - Rockets **Obv:** Head right **Rev:** Saturn V rocket on launch pad

Date	Mintage	F	VF	XF	Unc	BU
2009P	—	—	—	—	—	12.00

KM# 1261 DOLLAR
Aluminum-Bronze, 31 mm. **Ruler:** Elizabeth II **Subject:** Space Topics - Rovers **Obv:** Head right **Rev:** Mars rover - Spirit and Opportunity

Date	Mintage	F	VF	XF	Unc	BU
2009P	—	—	—	—	—	12.00

KM# 1262 DOLLAR
Aluminum-Bronze, 31 mm. **Ruler:** Elizabeth II **Subject:** Space Topics - Space Shuttles **Obv:** Head right **Rev:** Shuttle Discovery and Space Exploration

Date	Mintage	F	VF	XF	Unc	BU
2009P	—	—	—	—	—	12.00

KM# 1263 DOLLAR
Aluminum-Bronze, 31 mm. **Ruler:** Elizabeth II **Subject:** Space Topics - Probes **Obv:** Head right **Rev:** Deep Space Probes - Pioneer 11 and 11

Date	Mintage	F	VF	XF	Unc	BU
2009P	—	—	—	—	—	12.00

KM# 1264 DOLLAR
Aluminum-Bronze, 31 mm. **Ruler:** Elizabeth II **Subject:** Space Topics - Space Telescope **Obv:** Head right **Rev:** Hubble Space Telescope

Date	Mintage	F	VF	XF	Unc	BU
2009P	—	—	—	—	—	12.00

KM# 1265 DOLLAR
31.1050 g., 0.9990 Silver 0.9990 oz. ASW, 27x48 mm. **Ruler:** Elizabeth II **Subject:** Chinese Mythological Character - Wealth **Obv:** Head right **Rev:** Man standing, multicolor **Shape:** Vertical rectangle

Date	Mintage	F	VF	XF	Unc	BU
2009P	—	—	—	—	—	65.00

KM# 1266 DOLLAR
31.1050 g., 0.9990 Silver 0.9990 oz. ASW, 27x48 mm. **Ruler:** Elizabeth II **Subject:** Chinese Mythological Character - Longevity **Obv:** Head right **Rev:** Man standing with staff, multicolor **Edge Lettering:** Vertical rectangle

Date	Mintage	F	VF	XF	Unc	BU
2009P	—	—	—	—	—	65.00

KM# 1267 DOLLAR
31.1050 g., 0.9990 Silver 0.9990 oz. ASW, 27x48 mm. **Ruler:** Elizabeth II **Subject:** Chinese Mythological Character - Success **Obv:** Head right **Rev:** Man standing with deer, multicolor **Shape:** Vertical rectangle

Date	Mintage	F	VF	XF	Unc	BU
2009P	—	—	—	—	—	65.00

KM# 1268 DOLLAR
31.1050 g., 0.9990 Silver 0.9990 oz. ASW, 27x48 mm. **Ruler:** Elizabeth II **Subject:** Chinese Mythological Character - Fortune **Obv:** Head right **Rev:** Man standing with scroll, multicolor **Shape:** Vertical rectangle

Date	Mintage	F	VF	XF	Unc	BU
2009P	—	—	—	—	—	65.00

KM# 1357 DOLLAR
31.1350 g., 0.9990 Silver 1.0000 oz. ASW, 40.6 mm. **Ruler:** Elizabeth II **Subject:** International Year of Astronomy **Obv:** Head right **Rev:** Youth looking through telescope, pointing at universe

Date	Mintage	F	VF	XF	Unc	BU
2009P	7,500	Value: 60.00				

KM# 1358 DOLLAR
30.6000 g., Aluminum-Bronze, 30.6 mm. **Ruler:** Elizabeth II **Subject:** Swimming **Obv:** Head light **Rev:** Swimmer

Date	Mintage	F	VF	XF	Unc	BU
2009(p) Proof	7,500	Value: 10.00				

KM# 1359 DOLLAR
32.1350 g., 0.9990 Silver 1.0321 oz. ASW, 40 mm. **Ruler:** Elizabeth II **Subject:** Swimming **Obv:** Head right **Rev:** Swimmer with hologram effect added

Date	Mintage	F	VF	XF	Unc	BU
2009(p) Proof	7,500	Value: 70.00				

KM# 1497 DOLLAR
13.8000 g., Aluminum-Bronze, 30.6 mm. **Ruler:** Elizabeth II **Subject:** ANZAC **Rev:** Child on lap of grandfather, bugler in background

Date	Mintage	F	VF	XF	Unc	BU
2009	—	—	—	—	7.50	10.00

KM# 1498 DOLLAR
9.0000 g., Aluminum-Bronze, 25 mm. **Ruler:** Elizabeth II **Subject:** Age pensions, 100th Anniversary **Rev:** Extended family portrait, elder members seated at front center in detail

Date	Mintage	F	VF	XF	Unc	BU
2009	—	—	—	—	7.50	10.00

KM# 1499 DOLLAR
9.0000 g., Aluminum-Bronze, 25 mm. **Ruler:** Elizabeth II **Subject:** Girl Guides, 100th Anniversary

Date	Mintage	F	VF	XF	Unc	BU
2009	—	—	—	—	7.50	10.00

KM# 1655 DOLLAR
9.0000 g., Aluminum-Bronze, 25 mm. **Ruler:** Elizabeth II **Obv:** Head with tiara right **Rev:** Baby bilby in color right

Date	Mintage	F	VF	XF	Unc	BU
2009	—	—	—	—	—	10.00

KM# 1656 DOLLAR
9.0000 g., Aluminum-Bronze, 25 mm. **Ruler:** Elizabeth II **Obv:** Head with tiara right **Rev:** Frilly lizard in color right

Date	Mintage	F	VF	XF	Unc	BU
2009	—	—	—	—	—	10.00

KM# 1657 DOLLAR
9.0000 g., Aluminum-Bronze, 25 mm. **Ruler:** Elizabeth II **Subject:** World Masters Games **Obv:** Head with tiara right **Rev:** Sydney Harbor Bridge, games logo above

Date	Mintage	F	VF	XF	Unc	BU
2009	—	—	—	—	7.00	10.00

KM# 1324 DOLLAR
31.1050 g., 0.9990 Silver 0.9990 oz. ASW, 41 mm. **Ruler:** Elizabeth II **Subject:** Lachen Macquarie, Governor of New South Wales **Obv:** Head right **Rev:** Macquarie, Sydney's "Rum" Hospital, Holey Dollar

Date	Mintage	F	VF	XF	Unc	BU
2010P Proof	7,500	Value: 90.00				

KM# 1325 DOLLAR
31.1050 g., 0.9990 Silver 0.9990 oz. ASW, 41 mm. **Ruler:** Elizabeth II **Subject:** 2010 Australian Olympic Team **Obv:** Head right **Rev:** Downhill skier, multicolor Australian flag

Date	Mintage	F	VF	XF	Unc	BU
2010P Proof	5,000	Value: 100				

KM# 1326 DOLLAR
31.1050 g., 0.9990 Silver 0.9990 oz. ASW, 41 mm. **Ruler:** Elizabeth II **Subject:** Century of Flight in Australia **Obv:** Head right **Rev:** Bi-plane, multicolor

Date	Mintage	F	VF	XF	Unc	BU
2010P Proof	7,500	Value: 90.00				

KM# 1380 DOLLAR
13.8000 g., Aluminum-Bronze, 30.6 mm. **Ruler:** Elizabeth II **Subject:** Anzac Navy **Obv:** Head right **Rev:** Naval crew member and ship

Date	Mintage	F	VF	XF	Unc	BU
2010(p)	—	—	—	—	—	12.00

KM# 1381 DOLLAR
31.1030 g., 0.9990 Silver 0.9989 oz. ASW, 40.5 mm. **Ruler:** Elizabeth II **Subject:** Antarctic - Huskey **Obv:** Head right **Rev:** Huskey in multicolor

Date	Mintage	F	VF	XF	Unc	BU
2010(p) Proof	7,500	Value: 60.00				

KM# 1382 DOLLAR
13.8000 g., Aluminum-Bronze, 30.6 mm. **Ruler:** Elizabeth II **Subject:** Flight Centennial **Obv:** Head right **Rev:** Bi-plane flying right

Date	Mintage	F	VF	XF	Unc	BU
2010(p)	—	—	—	—	—	13.00

KM# 1383 DOLLAR
31.1035 g., 0.9990 Silver 0.9990 oz. ASW, 40 mm. **Ruler:** Elizabeth II **Subject:** Edward VII Coinage **Obv:** Head right **Rev:** Coin designs and Edward VII in multicolor

Date	Mintage	F	VF	XF	Unc	BU
2010(p)	—	—	—	—	—	60.00

KM# 1384 DOLLAR
13.8000 g., Aluminum-Bronze, 30.6 mm. **Ruler:** Elizabeth II **Subject:** Celebrate Australia - Barrier Reef **Obv:** Head right **Rev:** Sea Turtle and multicolor background

Date	Mintage	F	VF	XF	Unc	BU
2010P	—	—	—	—	—	15.00

KM# 1385 DOLLAR
13.8000 g., Aluminum-Bronze, 30.6 mm. **Ruler:** Elizabeth II **Subject:** Celebrate Australia - Blue Mountain **Obv:** Head right **Rev:** Frog and multicolor background

Date	Mintage	F	VF	XF	Unc	BU
2010P	—	—	—	—	—	15.00

KM# 1386 DOLLAR
13.8000 g., Aluminum-Bronze, 30.6 mm. **Ruler:** Elizabeth II **Subject:** Celebrate Australia - Heard Island **Obv:** Head right **Rev:** Penguins and multicolor background

Date	Mintage	F	VF	XF	Unc	BU
2010P	—	—	—	—	—	15.00

KM# 1387 DOLLAR
13.8000 g., Aluminum-Bronze, 30.6 mm. **Ruler:** Elizabeth II **Subject:** Celebrate Australia - Shark Bay **Obv:** Head right

Date	Mintage	F	VF	XF	Unc	BU
2010P	—	—	—	—	—	15.00

KM# 1388 DOLLAR
13.8000 g., Aluminum-Bronze, 30.6 mm. **Ruler:** Elizabeth II **Subject:** Celebrate Australia - Tasmanian Wilderness **Obv:** Head right **Rev:** Animal before multicolor waterfall background

Date	Mintage	F	VF	XF	Unc	BU
2010P	—	—	—	—	—	15.00

KM# 1391 DOLLAR
31.1050 g., 0.9990 Silver 0.9990 oz. ASW **Ruler:** Elizabeth II **Obv:** Head right **Rev:** Panda and koala

Date	Mintage	F	VF	XF	Unc	BU
2010(p)	—	—	—	—	—	45.00

KM# 1392 DOLLAR
31.1050 g., 0.9990 Silver 0.9990 oz. ASW **Ruler:** Elizabeth II **Subject:** World Expo **Obv:** Head right **Rev:** Austrlian Panham

Date	Mintage	F	VF	XF	Unc	BU
2010(p)	—	—	—	—	—	50.00

KM# 1393 DOLLAR
31.1050 g., 0.9990 Silver 0.9990 oz. ASW **Ruler:** Elizabeth II **Obv:** Head right **Rev:** Kookaburra mascot

Date	Mintage	F	VF	XF	Unc	BU
2010(p)	—	—	—	—	—	45.00

KM# 1394 DOLLAR
31.1050 g., 0.9990 Silver 0.9990 oz. ASW **Ruler:** Elizabeth II **Obv:** Head right **Rev:** City scape

Date	Mintage	F	VF	XF	Unc	BU
2010(p)	—	—	—	—	—	45.00

KM# 1395 DOLLAR
Silver, 40x60 mm. **Ruler:** Elizabeth II **Series:** World Expo **Obv:** Head right **Shape:** Australian outline

Date	Mintage	F	VF	XF	Unc	BU
2010(p)	—	—	—	—	—	70.00

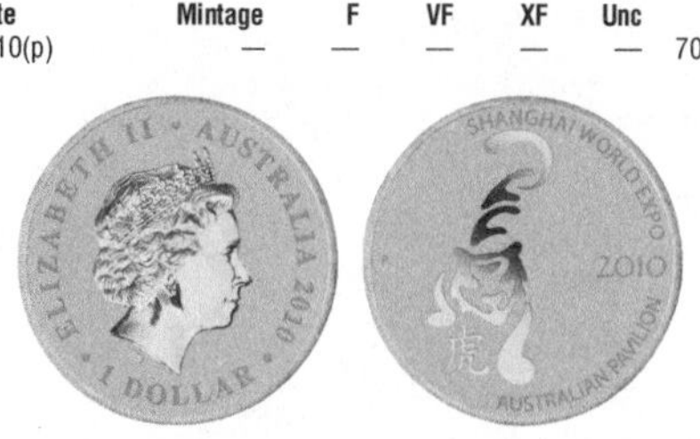

KM# 1396 DOLLAR
13.8000 g., Aluminum-Bronze, 30.6 mm. **Ruler:** Elizabeth II **Subject:** 2010 Shanghai World Expo **Obv:** Head with tiara right **Rev:** Artistic tiger seen from above, advancing forward

Date	Mintage	F	VF	XF	Unc	BU
2010P	—	—	—	—	—	14.00

KM# 1431 DOLLAR
9.0000 g., Aluminum-Bronze, 25 mm. **Ruler:** Elizabeth II **Subject:** Burke and Wills 150th Anniversary **Obv:** Head with tiara right **Rev:** King seated under dig tree

Date	Mintage	F	VF	XF	Unc	BU
2010C	—	—	—	—	—	12.50
2010C Proof	—	Value: 17.50				

KM# 1434 DOLLAR
31.1350 g., 0.9990 Silver 1.0000 oz. ASW **Ruler:** Elizabeth II **Subject:** Burke & Wills expedition **Rev:** Multicolor scene of explorers

Date	Mintage	F	VF	XF	Unc	BU
2010P Proof	7,500	Value: 80.00				

KM# 1435 DOLLAR
31.1350 g., 0.9990 Silver 1.0000 oz. ASW, 40.6 mm. **Ruler:** Elizabeth II **Subject:** Treasures of Australia - Gold **Rev:** Three gold nuggets within insert

Date	Mintage	F	VF	XF	Unc	BU
2010P Proof	—	Value: 135				

KM# 1440 DOLLAR
13.3000 g., Aluminum-Bronze, 30.6 mm. **Ruler:** Elizabeth II **Rev:** Blowfly

Date	Mintage	F	VF	XF	Unc	BU
2010P	—	—	—	—	—	12.00

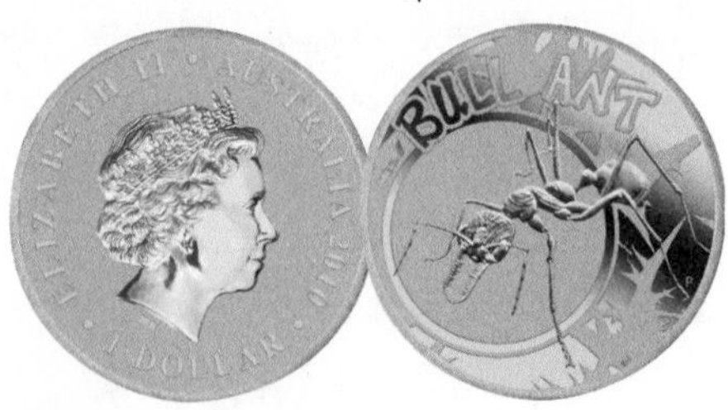

KM# 1441 DOLLAR
13.3000 g., Aluminum-Bronze, 30.6 mm. **Ruler:** Elizabeth II
Rev: Bull Ant

Date	Mintage	F	VF	XF	Unc	BU
2010P	—	—	—	—	—	12.00

KM# 1442 DOLLAR
13.3000 g., Aluminum-Bronze, 30.6 mm. **Ruler:** Elizabeth II
Rev: Burlwing Buttlerfly

Date	Mintage	F	VF	XF	Unc	BU
2010P	—	—	—	—	—	12.00

KM# 1443 DOLLAR
13.3000 g., Aluminum-Bronze, 30.6 mm. **Ruler:** Elizabeth II
Rev: Cicada

Date	Mintage	F	VF	XF	Unc	BU
2010P	—	—	—	—	—	12.00

KM# 1444 DOLLAR
13.3000 g., Aluminum-Bronze, 30.6 mm. **Ruler:** Elizabeth II
Rev: Dragonfly

Date	Mintage	F	VF	XF	Unc	BU
2010P	—	—	—	—	—	12.00

KM# 1445 DOLLAR
13.3000 g., Aluminum-Bronze, 30.6 mm. **Ruler:** Elizabeth II
Rev: Grasshopper

Date	Mintage	F	VF	XF	Unc	BU
2010P	—	—	—	—	—	12.00

KM# 1446 DOLLAR
13.3000 g., Aluminum-Bronze, 30.6 mm. **Ruler:** Elizabeth II
Rev: Ladybug

Date	Mintage	F	VF	XF	Unc	BU
2010P	—	—	—	—	—	12.00

KM# 1447 DOLLAR
13.3000 g., Aluminum-Bronze, 30.6 mm. **Ruler:** Elizabeth II
Rev: Praying mantis

Date	Mintage	F	VF	XF	Unc	BU
2010P	—	—	—	—	—	12.00

KM# 1448 DOLLAR
13.3000 g., Aluminum-Bronze, 30.6 mm. **Ruler:** Elizabeth II
Rev: Red-backed spider

Date	Mintage	F	VF	XF	Unc	BU
2010P	—	—	—	—	—	12.00

KM# 1451 DOLLAR
31.1050 g., 0.9990 Silver 0.9990 oz. ASW **Ruler:** Elizabeth II
Subject: New South Wales - Sidney Coin Show **Rev:** Koala and multicolor opera house and harbor bridge views

Date	Mintage	F	VF	XF	Unc	BU
2010P Proof	—	Value: 45.00				

KM# 1452 DOLLAR
31.1050 g., 0.9990 Silver 0.9990 oz. ASW **Ruler:** Elizabeth II
Subject: Victoria - Melbourne Coin Show **Rev:** Penguin and multicolor tram and building

Date	Mintage	F	VF	XF	Unc	BU
2010P Proof	—	Value: 45.00				

KM# 1490 DOLLAR
13.3000 g., Aluminum-Bronze, 30.6 mm. **Ruler:** Elizabeth II
Rev: Burke & Willis statue

Date	Mintage	F	VF	XF	Unc	BU
2010P	—	—	—	—	—	12.00

KM# 1491 DOLLAR
31.1050 g., 0.9990 Silver 0.9990 oz. ASW, 40.6 mm. **Ruler:** Elizabeth II **Obv:** Head with tiara right **Rev:** Saint Mary Mackillop in color

Date	Mintage	F	VF	XF	Unc	BU
2010 Proof	—	Value: 60.00				

KM# 1494 DOLLAR
31.1050 g., 0.9990 Silver 0.9990 oz. ASW **Ruler:** Elizabeth II
Subject: New South Wales

Date	Mintage	F	VF	XF	Unc	BU
2010 Proof	—	Value: 50.00				

KM# 1495 DOLLAR
9.0000 g., Aluminum-Bronze, 25 mm. **Ruler:** Elizabeth II
Subject: Australian coinage, 100th Anniversary **Obv:** Head with tiara right **Rev:** Coinage portraits of Elizabeth II, George VI, George V and Edward VII

Date	Mintage	F	VF	XF	Unc	BU
2010B	—	—	—	—	4.00	5.00
2010C	—	—	—	—	4.00	5.00
2010M	—	—	—	—	4.00	5.00
2010S	—	—	—	—	4.00	5.00

KM# 1495a DOLLAR
11.6600 g., 0.9990 Silver 0.3745 oz. ASW, 25 mm. **Ruler:** Elizabeth II **Subject:** Centennial of Commonwealth Coins **Obv:** Head in tiara right **Rev:** Four portraits

Date	Mintage	F	VF	XF	Unc	BU
2010 Proof	12,500	Value: 50.00				

KM# 1496 DOLLAR
9.0000 g., Aluminum-Bronze, 25 mm. **Ruler:** Elizabeth II
Subject: Fred Hollows - Inspirational Australians

Date	Mintage	F	VF	XF	Unc	BU
2010	—	—	—	—	3.50	5.00

KM# 1503 DOLLAR
9.0000 g., Aluminum-Bronze, 25 mm. **Ruler:** Elizabeth II **Subject:** Wool Industry **Rev:** Sheep sheering and map of Australia

Date	Mintage	F	VF	XF	Unc	BU
2010	—	—	—	—	5.00	6.00
2010 Proof	—	Value: 25.00				

KM# 1505 DOLLAR
31.1050 g., 0.9990 Silver 0.9990 oz. ASW, 40.6 mm. **Ruler:** Elizabeth II **Subject:** Perth-ANDA Bridge **Rev:** City view

Date	Mintage	F	VF	XF	Unc	BU
2010 Proof	—	Value: 60.00				

KM# 1568 DOLLAR
31.1050 g., 0.9990 Silver 0.9990 oz. ASW, 32.6 mm. **Ruler:** Elizabeth II **Subject:** Sidney Cove Medallion, Wedgewood theme **Obv:** Head with tiara right **Rev:** One female standing on rock facing three others, seascape in backgorund **Edge:** Reeded **Note:** High relief

Date	Mintage	F	VF	XF	Unc	BU
2010P Proof	Est. 5,000	Value: 85.00				

KM# 1659 DOLLAR
9.0000 g., Aluminum-Bronze, 25 mm. **Ruler:** Elizabeth II **Subject:** Year of the Tiger **Rev:** Tiger head at center in circle, floral around

Date	Mintage	F	VF	XF	Unc	BU
2010	—	—	—	—	—	10.00

KM# 1659a DOLLAR
11.6600 g., 0.9990 Silver 0.3745 oz. ASW, 25 mm. **Ruler:** Elizabeth II **Subject:** Year of the Tiger **Obv:** Head with tiara right **Rev:** Tiger head in circle, floral around

Date	Mintage	F	VF	XF	Unc	BU
2010 Proof	—	Value: 30.00				

KM# 1762 DOLLAR
31.1050 g., 0.9990 Silver 0.9990 oz. ASW, 40.6 mm. **Ruler:** Elizabeth II **Obv:** Head with tiara right **Rev:** Kangaroo bounding left at sunset

Date	Mintage	F	VF	XF	Unc	BU
2010 F15	7,000	—	—	—	—	125
2010 F15 Proof	5,000	Value: 125				

KM# 1504 DOLLAR
9.0000 g., Aluminum-Bronze, 25 mm. **Ruler:** Elizabeth II **Subject:** Historical coin designs **Rev:** Sheep head

Date	Mintage	F	VF	XF	Unc	BU
2011C	—	—	—	—	5.00	6.00

KM# 1523 DOLLAR
31.1035 g., 0.9990 Silver 0.9990 oz. ASW, 40.6 mm. **Ruler:** Elizabeth II **Subject:** Australia's Bronze Coinagae, 100th Anniversary **Obv:** Head with tiara right **Rev:** George V and coins, in color

Date	Mintage	F	VF	XF	Unc	BU
2011 Proof	—	Value: 75.00				

KM# 1528 DOLLAR
31.1050 g., 0.9990 Silver 0.9990 oz. ASW, 40.6 mm. **Ruler:** Elizabeth II **Subject:** Famous Battles in Australian History **Rev:** Soldier standing at left, view of Gallipoli, 1915 at right

Date	Mintage	F	VF	XF	Unc	BU
2011P Proof	5,000	Value: 110				

KM# 1529 DOLLAR
13.3000 g., Aluminum-Bronze, 30.6 mm. **Ruler:** Elizabeth II **Subject:** ANZAC Day, RAAF **Rev:** Bugler and plane, two airmen at lower right

Date	Mintage	F	VF	XF	Unc	BU
2011P	—	—	—	—	—	13.00

KM# 1530 DOLLAR
31.1050 g., 0.9990 Silver 0.9990 oz. ASW **Ruler:** Elizabeth II **Subject:** Royal Wedding **Rev:** Catherine Middleton and Prince William in color, Westminster Abbey at left

Date	Mintage	F	VF	XF	Unc	BU
2011P Proof	12,500	Value: 110				

KM# 1531 DOLLAR
31.1050 g., 0.9990 Silver 0.9990 oz. ASW **Ruler:** Elizabeth II **Subject:** Naval Battles **Rev:** Battle of Midway

Date	Mintage	F	VF	XF	Unc	BU
2011P Proof	5,000	Value: 110				

KM# 1564 DOLLAR
31.1050 g., 0.9990 Silver 0.9990 oz. ASW **Ruler:** Elizabeth II **Subject:** Treasures of Australia **Rev:** Keshi pearl engased in mother of pearl locket

Date	Mintage	F	VF	XF	Unc	BU
2011P Proof	—	Value: 185				

KM# 1565 DOLLAR
31.1050 g., 0.9990 Silver 0.9990 oz. ASW, 40.6 mm. **Ruler:** Elizabeth II **Subject:** Antartica **Obv:** Head with tiara right **Rev:** Killer whale in color

Date	Mintage	F	VF	XF	Unc	BU
2011P Proof	7,500	Value: 115				

KM# 1572 DOLLAR
13.0000 g., Aluminum-Bronze, 30.6 mm. **Ruler:** Elizabeth II **Subject:** Bush Babies - Koala **Rev:** Koala lounging at left

Date	Mintage	F	VF	XF	Unc	BU
2011(p)	—	—	—	—	—	15.00

KM# 1573 DOLLAR
13.0000 g., Aluminum-Bronze, 30.6 mm. **Ruler:** Elizabeth II **Subject:** Bush babies - Dingo **Rev:** Dingo seated at left

Date	Mintage	F	VF	XF	Unc	BU
2011(p)	—	—	—	—	—	15.00

KM# 1574 DOLLAR
13.0000 g., Aluminum-Bronze, 30.6 mm. **Ruler:** Elizabeth II **Subject:** Bush babies - Bilby **Rev:** Bilby at left

Date	Mintage	F	VF	XF	Unc	BU
2011(p)	—	—	—	—	—	15.00

KM# 1575 DOLLAR
13.0000 g., Aluminum-Bronze, 30.6 mm. **Ruler:** Elizabeth II **Subject:** Bush babies - Sugar Glider **Rev:** Sugar Glider at left

Date	Mintage	F	VF	XF	Unc	BU
2011(p)	—	—	—	—	—	15.00

KM# 1576 DOLLAR
13.0000 g., Aluminum-Bronze, 30.6 mm. **Ruler:** Elizabeth II **Subject:** Bush babies - Kangaroo **Rev:** Kangaroo seated at left

Date	Mintage	F	VF	XF	Unc	BU
2011(p)	—	—	—	—	—	15.00

KM# 1580 DOLLAR
13.8000 g., Aluminum-Bronze, 30.6 mm. **Ruler:** Elizabeth II **Subject:** Mythical creatures - Dragon

Date	Mintage	F	VF	XF	Unc	BU
2011P	—	—	—	—	—	12.50

KM# 1581 DOLLAR
13.8000 g., Aluminum-Bronze, 30.6 mm. **Ruler:** Elizabeth II **Subject:** Mythical creatures - Fairy

Date	Mintage	F	VF	XF	Unc	BU
2011P	—	—	—	—	—	12.50

KM# 1582 DOLLAR
13.8000 g., Aluminum-Bronze, 30.6 mm. **Ruler:** Elizabeth II **Subject:** Mythical creatures - Goblin

Date	Mintage	F	VF	XF	Unc	BU
2011P	—	—	—	—	—	12.50

KM# 1583 DOLLAR
13.8000 g., Aluminum-Bronze, 30.6 mm. **Ruler:** Elizabeth II **Subject:** Mythical creatures - Griffin

Date	Mintage	F	VF	XF	Unc	BU
2011P	—	—	—	—	—	12.50

KM# 1584 DOLLAR
13.8000 g., Aluminum-Bronze, 30.6 mm. **Ruler:** Elizabeth II **Subject:** Mythical creatures - Mermaid

Date	Mintage	F	VF	XF	Unc	BU
2011P	—	—	—	—	—	12.50

KM# 1585 DOLLAR
13.8000 g., Aluminum-Bronze, 30.6 mm. **Ruler:** Elizabeth II **Subject:** Mythical creatures - Tree ent

Date	Mintage	F	VF	XF	Unc	BU
2011P	—	—	—	—	—	12.50

KM# 1586 DOLLAR
13.8000 g., Aluminum-Bronze, 30.6 mm. **Ruler:** Elizabeth II **Subject:** Mythical creatures - Ogre

Date	Mintage	F	VF	XF	Unc	BU
2011P	—	—	—	—	—	12.50

KM# 1587 DOLLAR
13.8000 g., Aluminum-Bronze, 30.6 mm. **Ruler:** Elizabeth II **Subject:** Mythical creatures - Phoenix

Date	Mintage	F	VF	XF	Unc	BU
2011P	—	—	—	—	—	12.50

KM# 1588 DOLLAR
13.8000 g., Aluminum-Bronze, 30.6 mm. **Ruler:** Elizabeth II **Subject:** Mythical creatures - Unicorn

Date	Mintage	F	VF	XF	Unc	BU
2011P	—	—	—	—	—	12.50

KM# 1589 DOLLAR
13.8000 g., Aluminum-Bronze, 30.6 mm. **Ruler:** Elizabeth II **Obv:** Head in tiara right **Rev:** Christmas tree decorated in color, presents below, stars around, holly at bottom flanking **Rev. Legend:** WISHING YOU A MERRY CHRISTMAS / 2011

Date	Mintage	F	VF	XF	Unc	BU
2011P	—	—	—	—	—	12.50

KM# 1590 DOLLAR
31.1030 g., 0.9990 Silver 0.9989 oz. ASW, 40 mm. **Ruler:** Elizabeth II **Subject:** Dame Nellie Melba **Obv:** Head with tiara right **Rev:** Colored bust right, musical notes below, flowers at left

Date	Mintage	F	VF	XF	Unc	BU
2011P Proof	Est. 5,000	Value: 100				

KM# 1591 DOLLAR
13.8000 g., Aluminum-Bronze, 30.6 mm. **Ruler:** Elizabeth II **Subject:** Dame Nellie Melba **Obv:** Head with tiara right **Rev:** Bust at left facing right, flowers at right

Date	Mintage	F	VF	XF	Unc	BU
2011P	—	—	—	—	—	12.50

KM# 1592 DOLLAR
31.1050 g., 0.9990 Silver 0.9990 oz. ASW, 40 mm. **Ruler:** Elizabeth II **Subject:** Royal Military College - Duntroon; 100th Anniversary **Obv:** Head with tiara right **Rev:** College emblem gilt above images of soldiers

Date	Mintage	F	VF	XF	Unc	BU
2011P Proof	Est. 7,500	Value: 100				

KM# 1593 DOLLAR
13.8000 g., Aluminum-Bronze, 30.6 mm. **Ruler:** Elizabeth II **Subject:** Royal Military College - Duntroon; 100th Anniversary **Obv:** Head with tiara right **Rev:** Military hat badge

Date	Mintage	F	VF	XF	Unc	BU
2011P	—	—	—	—	—	12.50

KM# 1594 DOLLAR

31.1050 g., 0.9990 Silver 0.9990 oz. ASW, 40 mm. **Ruler:** Elizabeth II **Subject:** Australian Antartic Territory, Killer Whale **Obv:** Head with tiara right **Rev:** Killer whale, jumping, and nin the water with a calf

Date	Mintage	F	VF	XF	Unc	BU
2011P Proof	Est. 7,500	Value: 100				

KM# 1597 DOLLAR

Aluminum-Bronze, 40 mm. **Ruler:** Elizabeth II **Subject:** Wiggles, 20th Anniversary **Obv:** Head with tiara right **Rev:** Wiggles characters in Big Red car **Edge:** Reeded

Date	Mintage	F	VF	XF	Unc	BU
2011P	—	—	—	—	—	17.50

KM# 1598 DOLLAR

Aluminum-Bronze, 40 mm. **Ruler:** Elizabeth II **Subject:** Wiggles, 20th Anniversary **Obv:** Head in tiara right **Rev:** Wiggles four band members at instruments **Edge:** Reeded

Date	Mintage	F	VF	XF	Unc	BU
2011P	—	—	—	—	—	17.50

KM# 1599 DOLLAR

Aluminum-Bronze, 40 mm. **Ruler:** Elizabeth II **Subject:** Wiggles, 20th Anniversary **Obv:** Head with tiara right **Rev:** Wiggles Pirate and animal characters

Date	Mintage	F	VF	XF	Unc	BU
2011P	—	—	—	—	—	17.50

KM# 1600 DOLLAR

Aluminum-Bronze, 40 mm. **Ruler:** Elizabeth II **Subject:** Wiggles, 20th Anniversary **Obv:** Head with tiara right **Rev:** Wiggles charactes in starburst

Date	Mintage	F	VF	XF	Unc	BU
2011P	—	—	—	—	—	17.50

KM# 1601 DOLLAR

31.1050 g., 0.9990 Silver 0.9990 oz. ASW, 40 mm. **Ruler:** Elizabeth II **Subject:** Royal Australian Navy, 100th Anniversary **Obv:** Head with tiara right **Rev:** HMAS Yarra, HMAS Anzac and sailors **Edge:** Reeded

Date	Mintage	F	VF	XF	Unc	BU
2011P Proof	—	Value: 120				

KM# 1602 DOLLAR

13.8000 g., Aluminum-Bronze, 30.6 mm. **Ruler:** Elizabeth II **Subject:** Royal Australian Navy, 100th Anniversary **Obv:** Head with tiara right **Rev:** Navy cap badge

Date	Mintage	F	VF	XF	Unc	BU
2011P	—	—	—	—	—	15.00

KM# 1603 DOLLAR

13.8000 g., Aluminum-Bronze, 30.6 mm. **Ruler:** Elizabeth II **Subject:** Elizabeth II's 85th Birthday **Obv:** Head with tiara right **Rev:** Elizabeth II in hat at left, birthday legend and emblem below **Edge:** Reeded

Date	Mintage	F	VF	XF	Unc	BU
2011P	—	—	—	—	—	15.00

KM# 1604 DOLLAR

31.1050 g., 0.9990 Silver 0.9990 oz. ASW, 40 mm. **Ruler:** Elizabeth II **Subject:** Wallabies Rugby team **Obv:** Head with tiara right **Rev:** Wallabies logo in color at left, rugby player at right **Edge:** Reeded

Date	Mintage	F	VF	XF	Unc	BU
2011P Proof	Est. 5,000	Value: 100				

KM# 1606 DOLLAR

31.1050 g., 0.9990 Silver 0.9990 oz. ASW, 40 mm. **Ruler:** Elizabeth II **Subject:** World War II - Siege of Tobruk **Obv:** Head with tiara right **Rev:** Soldier standing at left, image of solder carried on stretcher at right; Campaign ribbon below **Edge:** Reeded

Date	Mintage	F	VF	XF	Unc	BU
2011P Proof	Est. 5,000	Value: 100				

KM# 1607 DOLLAR

31.1050 g., 0.9990 Silver 0.9990 oz. ASW, 40 mm. **Ruler:** Elizabeth II **Subject:** Ginger Meggs, 90th Birthday **Obv:** Head with tiara right **Rev:** Cartoon boy riding kangaroo right **Edge:** Reeded

Date	Mintage	F	VF	XF	Unc	BU
2011P Proof	Est. 3,000	Value: 100				

KM# 1612 DOLLAR

13.8000 g., Aluminum-Bronze, 30.6 mm. **Ruler:** Elizabeth II **Subject:** Wet Tropics of Queensland **Obv:** Head with tiara right **Rev:** Bird walking right and color fauna background **Edge:** Reeded

Date	Mintage	F	VF	XF	Unc	BU
2011P	—	—	—	—	—	15.00

KM# 1613 DOLLAR

13.8000 g., Aluminum-Bronze, 30.6 mm. **Ruler:** Elizabeth II **Subject:** Macquarie Island **Obv:** Bust with tiara right **Rev:** Sea lion and color background **Edge:** Reeded

Date	Mintage	F	VF	XF	Unc	BU
2011P	—	—	—	—	—	15.00

KM# 1614 DOLLAR

13.8000 g., Aluminum-Bronze, 30.6 mm. **Ruler:** Elizabeth II **Subject:** Goondwana Rainforests **Obv:** Head with tiara right **Rev:** Bird left with color fauna background **Edge:** Reeded

Date	Mintage	F	VF	XF	Unc	BU
2011P	—	—	—	—	—	15.00

KM# 1615 DOLLAR

13.8000 g., Aluminum-Bronze, 30.6 mm. **Ruler:** Elizabeth II **Subject:** Australian Fossil Mammal Sites **Obv:** Head with tiara right **Rev:** Dingo left with color landscape in background **Edge:** Reeded

Date	Mintage	F	VF	XF	Unc	BU
2011P	—	—	—	—	—	15.00

KM# 1616 DOLLAR

13.8000 g., Aluminum-Bronze, 30.6 mm. **Ruler:** Elizabeth II **Subject:** Purnululu National Park **Obv:** Head with tiara right **Rev:** Kangaroo right with color background **Edge:** Reeded

Date	Mintage	F	VF	XF	Unc	BU
2011P	—	—	—	—	—	15.00

KM# 1617 DOLLAR

9.0000 g., Aluminum-Bronze, 25 mm. **Ruler:** Elizabeth II **Obv:** Head with tiara right **Rev:** Crimson Rosella in color

Date	Mintage	F	VF	XF	Unc	BU
2011	—	—	—	—	—	15.00

KM# 1618 DOLLAR

9.0000 g., Aluminum-Bronze, 25 mm. **Ruler:** Elizabeth II **Obv:** Head with tiara right **Rev:** Kookaburra in color

Date	Mintage	F	VF	XF	Unc	BU
2011	—	—	—	—	—	15.00

KM# 1619 DOLLAR

9.0000 g., Aluminum-Bronze, 25 mm. **Ruler:** Elizabeth II **Subject:** CHOGM meeting, Perth **Obv:** Head with tiara right **Rev:** Flags around globe

Date	Mintage	F	VF	XF	Unc	BU
2011	—	—	—	—	—	10.00

KM# 1620 DOLLAR

9.0000 g., Aluminum-Bronze, 25 mm. **Ruler:** Elizabeth II **Subject:** President's Cup **Obv:** Head with tiara right **Rev:** Golfer talking swing

Date	Mintage	F	VF	XF	Unc	BU
2011	—	—	—	—	—	10.00

KM# 1620a DOLLAR
11.9000 g., 0.9990 Silver 0.3822 oz. ASW, 25 mm. **Ruler:** Elizabeth II **Subject:** President's Cup **Obv:** Head with tiara right **Rev:** Gopher taking swing

Date	Mintage	F	VF	XF	Unc	BU
2011 Proof	—	Value: 40.00				

KM# 1621 DOLLAR
31.1050 g., 0.9990 Silver 0.9990 oz. ASW, 40 mm. **Ruler:** Elizabeth II **Subject:** President's Cup **Obv:** Head with tiara right **Rev:** Golf Ball and color trophy and logo, players around edge

Date	Mintage	F	VF	XF	Unc	BU
2011 Proof	—	Value: 100				

KM# 1635 DOLLAR
9.0000 g., Aluminum-Bronze, 25 mm. **Ruler:** Elizabeth II **Subject:** Census, 100th Anniversary **Obv:** Head with tiara right **Rev:** Multiple stylized heads at left, geometric Australia outline at right

Date	Mintage	F	VF	XF	Unc	BU
2011	—	—	—	—	7.00	8.00

KM# 1643 DOLLAR
9.0000 g., Aluminum-Bronze, 25 mm. **Ruler:** Elizabeth II **Obv:** Head with tiara right **Rev:** Mitchell Cockatoo in color

Date	Mintage	F	VF	XF	Unc	BU
2011	—	—	—	—	—	10.00

KM# 1644 DOLLAR
9.0000 g., Aluminum-Bronze, 25 mm. **Ruler:** Elizabeth II **Obv:** Head with tiara right **Rev:** Kingfisher in color

Date	Mintage	F	VF	XF	Unc	BU
2011	—	—	—	—	—	10.00

KM# 1645 DOLLAR
9.0000 g., Aluminum-Bronze, 25 mm. **Ruler:** Elizabeth II **Subject:** Dame Joan Sutherland **Obv:** Head with tiara right **Rev:** Sutherland in opera role facing right

Date	Mintage	F	VF	XF	Unc	BU
2011	—	—	—	—	5.00	7.00

KM# 1647 DOLLAR
9.0000 g., Aluminum-Bronze, 25 mm. **Ruler:** Elizabeth II **Obv:** Head with tiara right **Rev:** Flying Fox Bat in color

Date	Mintage	F	VF	XF	Unc	BU
2011	—	—	—	—	—	10.00

KM# 1646 DOLLAR
9.0000 g., Aluminum-Bronze, 25 mm. **Ruler:** Elizabeth II **Obv:** Head with tiara right **Rev:** Birdwing Butterfly in color

Date	Mintage	F	VF	XF	Unc	BU
2011	—	—	—	—	—	10.00

KM# 1661 DOLLAR
9.0000 g., Aluminum-Bronze, 25 mm. **Ruler:** Elizabeth II **Subject:** Year of the Rabbit **Obv:** Head with tiara right **Rev:** Rabbit in circle, floral around

Date	Mintage	F	VF	XF	Unc	BU
2011	—	—	—	—	—	10.00

KM# 1661a DOLLAR
11.6600 g., 0.9990 Silver 0.3745 oz. ASW, 25 mm. **Ruler:** Elizabeth II **Subject:** Year of the rabbit **Obv:** Head with tiara right **Rev:** Rabbit in circle, floral around

Date	Mintage	F	VF	XF	Unc	BU
2011 Proof	—	Value: 30.00				

KM# 1812 DOLLAR
13.3000 g., Aluminum-Bronze, 30.6 mm. **Ruler:** Elizabeth II **Subject:** Animal Athletics - Sailfish

Date	Mintage	F	VF	XF	Unc	BU
2012P	—	—	—	—	—	14.00

KM# 1626 DOLLAR
9.0000 g., Aluminum-Bronze, 25 mm. **Ruler:** Elizabeth II **Subject:** Australian Wheat **Obv:** Head with tiara right **Rev:** Stylized wheat field and combine harvester

Date	Mintage	F	VF	XF	Unc	BU
2012	—	—	—	—	6.00	10.00
2012 Proof	—	Value: 40.00				

KM# 1699 DOLLAR
31.1350 g., 0.9990 Silver 1.0000 oz. ASW, 40.6 mm. **Ruler:** Elizabeth II **Subject:** Battle of Kapyong, Korean War **Obv:** Head with tiara right **Rev:** Soldier walking at left, image of soldiers seated at right **Edge:** Reeded

Date	Mintage	F	VF	XF	Unc	BU
2012P Proof	Est. 5,000	Value: 100				

KM# 1680 DOLLAR
9.0000 g., Aluminum-Bronze, 25 mm. **Ruler:** Elizabeth II **Subject:** Year of the Dragon **Rev:** Dragon head within circle, floral around

Date	Mintage	F	VF	XF	Unc	BU
2012	—	—	—	—	—	10.00

KM# 1680a DOLLAR
11.9000 g., 0.9990 Silver 0.3822 oz. ASW, 25 mm. **Ruler:** Elizabeth II **Subject:** Year of the Dragon **Rev:** Dragon head within circle, floral around

Date	Mintage	F	VF	XF	Unc	BU
2012 Proof	—	Value: 40.00				

KM# 1698 DOLLAR
13.8000 g., Aluminum-Bronze, 30.6 mm. **Ruler:** Elizabeth II **Subject:** Australian 2012 London Olympic Team **Obv:** Head with tiara right **Rev:** Kangaroo with boxing gloves raised

Date	Mintage	F	VF	XF	Unc	BU
2012P	750	—	—	—	—	15.00

KM# 1700 DOLLAR
31.1050 g., 0.9990 Silver 0.9990 oz. ASW, 40.6 mm. **Ruler:** Elizabeth II **Subject:** Battle of Kokoda, World War II **Obv:** Head with tiara right **Rev:** Soldier standing at left, image of soldiers walking over bridge at right **Edge:** Reeded

Date	Mintage	F	VF	XF	Unc	BU
2012P Proof	Est. 5,000	Value: 100				

KM# 1701 DOLLAR
31.1350 g., 0.9990 Silver 1.0000 oz. ASW, 40.5 mm. **Ruler:** Elizabeth II **Subject:** Elizabeth II, 60th Anniversary **Obv:** Head with tiara right **Rev:** Dargie's "wattle painting" of Elizabeth II at left, emblem and signature at right **Edge:** Reeded

Date	Mintage	F	VF	XF	Unc	BU
2012P Proof	7,500	Value: 100				

KM# 1704 DOLLAR
13.8000 g., Aluminum-Bronze, 30.6 mm. **Ruler:** Elizabeth II **Subject:** Year of the Dragon

Date	Mintage	F	VF	XF	Unc	BU
2012P	—	—	—	—	—	15.00

KM# 1705 DOLLAR
31.1350 g., 0.9990 Silver 1.0000 oz. ASW, 36.6 mm. **Ruler:** Elizabeth II **Obv:** Head with tiara right **Rev:** Koala in a gum tree detailed in an opal at center

Date	Mintage	F	VF	XF	Unc	BU
2012P Proof	8,000	Value: 100				

KM# 1711 DOLLAR
9.0000 g., Aluminum-Bronze, 25 mm. **Ruler:** Elizabeth II **Subject:** Ethel C. Pedley **Rev:** Bust facing at left, ncharacters Dot and the Kangaroo at right

Date	Mintage	F	VF	XF	Unc	BU
2012	—	—	—	—	—	12.50

KM# 1714 DOLLAR
13.8000 g., Aluminum-Bronze, 30.6 mm. **Ruler:** Elizabeth II **Subject:** ANZAC Day - Nurses **Obv:** Head with tiara right **Rev:** Nurse tending to soldier

Date	Mintage	F	VF	XF	Unc	BU
2012P	—	—	—	—	—	13.50

KM# 1715 DOLLAR
13.8000 g., Aluminum-Bronze, 30.6 mm. **Ruler:** Elizabeth II **Obv:** Head with tiara right **Rev:** Two boxing kangaroos on color backgorund

Date	Mintage	F	VF	XF	Unc	BU
2012P	7,500	—	—	—	—	15.00

KM# 1732 DOLLAR
9.0000 g., Aluminum-Bronze, 25 mm. **Ruler:** Elizabeth II **Obv:** Head with tiara right **Rev:** Three wheat ears

Date	Mintage	F	VF	XF	Unc	BU
2012B	—	—	—	—	—	5.00
2012C	—	—	—	—	3.00	5.00
2012C bluebell	—	—	—	—	—	20.00
2012M	—	—	—	—	—	5.00
2012S	—	—	—	—	—	5.00

KM# 1732a DOLLAR
11.6000 g., 0.9990 Silver 0.3726 oz. ASW, 25 mm. **Ruler:** Elizabeth II **Obv:** Head with tiara right **Rev:** Three wheat ears

Date	Mintage	F	VF	XF	Unc	BU
2012 Proof	—	Value: 40.00				

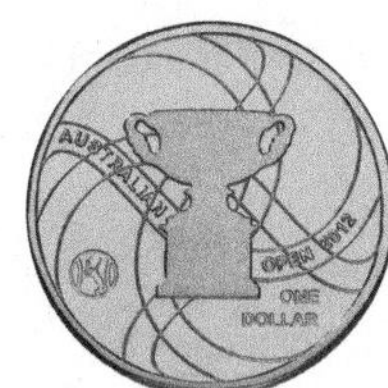

KM# 1734 DOLLAR
9.0000 g., Aluminum-Bronze, 25 mm. **Ruler:** Elizabeth II **Subject:** Australian Open **Obv:** Head with tiara right **Rev:** Men's Trophy

Date	Mintage	F	VF	XF	Unc	BU
2012	—	—	—	—	—	15.00

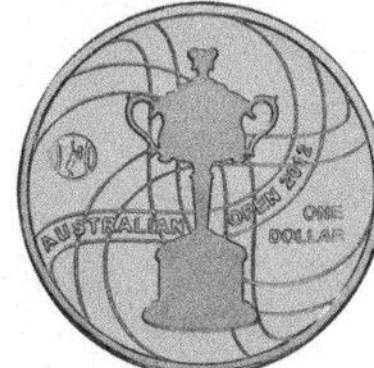

KM# 1735 DOLLAR
9.0000 g., Aluminum-Bronze, 25 mm. **Ruler:** Elizabeth II **Subject:** Australian Open **Obv:** Head with tiara right **Rev:** Women's Trophy

Date	Mintage	F	VF	XF	Unc	BU
2012	—	—	—	—	—	15.00

KM# 1736 DOLLAR
9.0000 g., Aluminum-Bronze, 25 mm. **Ruler:** Elizabeth II **Subject:** International Year of Cooperatives **Obv:** Head with tiara right **Rev:** Stick figures moving blocks into position

Date	Mintage	F	VF	XF	Unc	BU
2012	—	—	—	—	7.00	10.00

KM# 1738 DOLLAR
9.0000 g., Aluminum-Bronze, 25 mm. **Ruler:** Elizabeth II **Subject:** Year of the Farmer **Obv:** Head with tiara right **Rev:** Stylized farm layout with produce and animals

Date	Mintage	F	VF	XF	Unc	BU
2012	—	—	—	—	7.00	10.00

KM# 1745 DOLLAR
9.0000 g., Aluminum-Bronze, 25 mm. **Ruler:** Elizabeth II **Obv:** Head with tiara right **Rev:** Asian Elephant at left in color

Date	Mintage	F	VF	XF	Unc	BU
2012	—	—	—	—	—	15.00

KM# 1746 DOLLAR
9.0000 g., Aluminum-Bronze, 25 mm. **Ruler:** Elizabeth II **Obv:** Head with tiara right **Rev:** Western Lowland Gorilla at right in color

Date	Mintage	F	VF	XF	Unc	BU
2012	—	—	—	—	—	15.00

KM# 1748 DOLLAR
31.1350 g., 0.9990 Silver 1.0000 oz. ASW, 40.6 mm. **Ruler:** Elizabeth II **Subject:** Australian Olympic Team, 2012 London Games **Obv:** Head with tiara right **Rev:** Runner with Big Ben and Sydney Harbor Bridge in color

Date	Mintage	F	VF	XF	Unc	BU
2012P Proof	7,500	Value: 100				

KM# 1780 DOLLAR
Aluminum-Bronze, 30.6 mm. **Ruler:** Elizabeth II **Subject:** 2012 Australian Olympic Team **Obv:** Head with tiara right **Rev:** Runner **Rev. Legend:** FASTER

Date	Mintage	F	VF	XF	Unc	BU
2012P	—	—	—	—	—	14.00

KM# 1781 DOLLAR
Aluminum-Bronze, 30.6 mm. **Ruler:** Elizabeth II **Subject:** 2012 Australian Olympic Team **Obv:** Head with tiara right **Rev:** Pole-vault **Rev. Legend:** HIGHER

Date	Mintage	F	VF	XF	Unc	BU
2012P	—	—	—	—	—	14.00

KM# 1782 DOLLAR
Aluminum-Bronze, 30.6 mm. **Ruler:** Elizabeth II **Subject:** 2012 Australian Olympic Team **Obv:** Head with tiara right **Rev:** Weightlifter **Rev. Legend:** STRONGER

Date	Mintage	F	VF	XF	Unc	BU
2012P	—	—	—	—	—	14.00

KM# 1783 DOLLAR
Aluminum-Bronze, 30.6 mm. **Ruler:** Elizabeth II **Subject:** 2012 Australian Olympic Team **Obv:** Head with tiara right **Rev:** Swimmer with hands raised **Rev. Legend:** VICTORY

Date	Mintage	F	VF	XF	Unc	BU
2012P	—	—	—	—	—	14.00

KM# 1784 DOLLAR
Aluminum-Bronze, 30.6 mm. **Ruler:** Elizabeth II **Subject:** 2012 Australian Olympic Team **Obv:** Head with tiara right **Rev:** Kangaroo with boxing gloves and hands raised **Rev. Legend:** OLYMPIC SPIRIT

Date	Mintage	F	VF	XF	Unc	BU
2012P	—	—	—	—	—	14.00

KM# 1786 DOLLAR
31.1350 g., 0.9990 Silver 1.0000 oz. ASW **Ruler:** Elizabeth II **Subject:** Long Tan, Viet Nam war battle **Obv:** Head with tiara right **Rev:** Line of soldiers in jungle setting

Date	Mintage	F	VF	XF	Unc	BU
2012P Proof	5,000	Value: 100				

KM# 1787 DOLLAR
31.1350 g., 0.9990 Silver 1.0000 oz. ASW, 40.6 mm. **Ruler:** Elizabeth II **Subject:** Elizabeth II's Diamond Jubilee **Obv:** Head with tiara right **Rev:** Elizabeth half-length adjusting shall,gilt royal shield below **Edge:** Reeded

Date	Mintage	F	VF	XF	Unc	BU
2012P Proof	1,000	Value: 100				

KM# 1788 DOLLAR
31.1350 g., 0.9990 Silver 1.0000 oz. ASW, 40.6 mm. **Ruler:** Elizabeth II **Subject:** Elizabeth II's Diamond Jubilee **Obv:** Head with tiara right **Rev:** Elizabeth half-length facing at left, royal trumphants at right **Edge:** Reeded

Date	Mintage	F	VF	XF	Unc	BU
2012P Proof	1,000	Value: 100				

KM# 1791 DOLLAR
31.1050 g., 0.9990 Silver 0.9990 oz. ASW, 40.6 mm. **Ruler:** Elizabeth II **Rev:** Kookaburra in color **Shape:** Irregular, Map of Australia

Date	Mintage	F	VF	XF	Unc	BU
2012P Proof	6,000	Value: 150				

KM# 1792 DOLLAR
31.1050 g., 0.9990 Silver 0.9990 oz. ASW, 40.6 mm. **Ruler:** Elizabeth II **Rev:** Emu in color **Shape:** Irregular, Map of Australia

Date	Mintage	F	VF	XF	Unc	BU
2012P Proof	6,000	Value: 120				

KM# 1796 DOLLAR
31.1050 g., 0.9990 Silver 0.9990 oz. ASW **Ruler:** Elizabeth II **Rev:** Wombat with opal

Date	Mintage	F	VF	XF	Unc	BU
2012P Proof	—	Value: 100				

KM# 1800 DOLLAR
31.1050 g., 0.9990 Silver 0.9990 oz. ASW, 40.6 mm. **Ruler:** Elizabeth II **Subject:** Australia-China Friendship, 40th Anniversary **Rev:** kangaroo and Panda under national flags in color

Date	Mintage	F	VF	XF	Unc	BU
2012P Proof	—	Value: 125				

KM# 1804 DOLLAR
13.5000 g., Aluminum-Bronze, 30 mm. **Ruler:** Elizabeth II **Subject:** London Olympics, 2012 **Rev:** Faster - Runner

Date	Mintage	F	VF	XF	Unc	BU
2012P	—	—	—	—	—	14.00

KM# 1805 DOLLAR
13.5000 g., Aluminum-Bronze, 30 mm. **Ruler:** Elizabeth II **Subject:** London Olympics, 2012 **Rev:** Higher - Pole Vaulter

Date	Mintage	F	VF	XF	Unc	BU
2012P	—	—	—	—	—	14.00

KM# 1807 DOLLAR
13.5000 g., Aluminum-Bronze, 30 mm. **Ruler:** Elizabeth II **Subject:** London Olympics, 2012 **Rev:** Victory - Swimmer, hands raised

Date	Mintage	F	VF	XF	Unc	BU
2012P	—	—	—	—	—	14.00

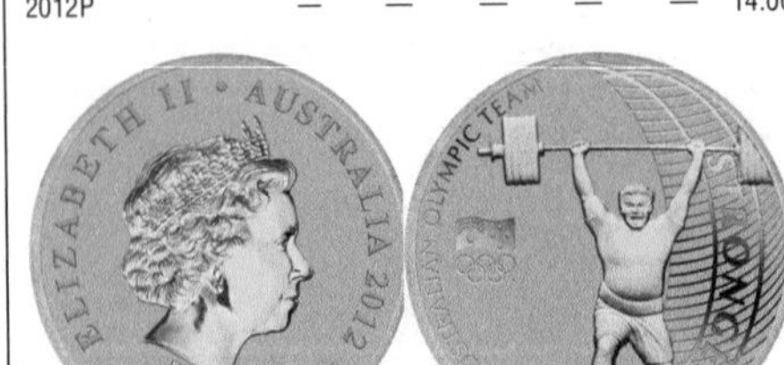

KM# 1806 DOLLAR
13.5000 g., Aluminum-Bronze, 30 mm. **Ruler:** Elizabeth II **Subject:** London Olympics, 2012 **Rev:** Stronger - Weight Lifter

Date	Mintage	F	VF	XF	Unc	BU
2012P	—	—	—	—	—	14.00

KM# 1808 DOLLAR
31.1050 g., 0.9990 Silver 0.9990 oz. ASW, 40.6 mm. **Ruler:** Elizabeth II **Subject:** London Olympics, 2012

Date	Mintage	F	VF	XF	Unc	BU
2012P Proof	—	Value: 100				

KM# 1809 DOLLAR
13.3000 g., Aluminum-Bronze, 30.6 mm. **Ruler:** Elizabeth II **Subject:** Animal Athletics - Cheetah

Date	Mintage	F	VF	XF	Unc	BU
2012P	—	—	—	—	—	14.00

KM# 1810 DOLLAR
13.3000 g., Aluminum-Bronze, 30.6 mm. **Ruler:** Elizabeth II **Subject:** Animal Athletics - Monarch Butterfly

Date	Mintage	F	VF	XF	Unc	BU
2012P	—	—	—	—	—	14.00

KM# 1811 DOLLAR
13.3000 g., Aluminum-Bronze, 30.6 mm. **Ruler:** Elizabeth II **Subject:** Animal Athletics - Kangaroos

Date	Mintage	F	VF	XF	Unc	BU
2012P	—	—	—	—	—	14.00

KM# 1813 DOLLAR
13.3000 g., Aluminum-Bronze, 30.6 mm. **Ruler:** Elizabeth II **Subject:** Animal Athletics - Rhino Beetle

Date	Mintage	F	VF	XF	Unc	BU
2012P	—	—	—	—	—	14.00

KM# 1814 DOLLAR
13.3000 g., Aluminum-Bronze, 30.6 mm. **Ruler:** Elizabeth II **Subject:** Animal Athletics - Rocket Frog

Date	Mintage	F	VF	XF	Unc	BU
2012P	—	—	—	—	—	14.00

KM# 1819 DOLLAR
31.1050 g., 0.9990 Silver 0.9990 oz. ASW, 40.6 mm. **Ruler:** Elizabeth II **Subject:** Famous Battles - Long Tan

Date	Mintage	F	VF	XF	Unc	BU
2012P Proof	—	Value: 100				

KM# 1820 DOLLAR
13.8000 g., Aluminum-Bronze, 30.6 mm. **Ruler:** Elizabeth II **Subject:** Lord Howe Island Group **Rev:** Pair of sparrows in flight, color background

Date	Mintage	F	VF	XF	Unc	BU
2012P	—	—	—	—	—	15.00

KM# 1821 DOLLAR
13.8000 g., Aluminum-Bronze, 30.6 mm. **Ruler:** Elizabeth II **Subject:** Uluru Kata Tyuta National Park **Rev:** Lizard, color background

Date	Mintage	F	VF	XF	Unc	BU
2012P	—	—	—	—	—	15.00

KM# 1822 DOLLAR
13.8000 g., Aluminum-Bronze, 30.6 mm. **Ruler:** Elizabeth II **Subject:** Fraser Island **Rev:** Dingo, color background

Date	Mintage	F	VF	XF	Unc	BU
2012P	—	—	—	—	—	15.00

KM# 1823 DOLLAR
13.8000 g., Aluminum-Bronze, 30.6 mm. **Ruler:** Elizabeth II **Subject:** Kakadu National Park **Rev:** Two storks, color background

Date	Mintage	F	VF	XF	Unc	BU
2012P	—	—	—	—	—	15.00

KM# 1824 DOLLAR
13.8000 g., Aluminum-Bronze, 30.6 mm. **Ruler:** Elizabeth II **Subject:** Willandra Lakes Region **Rev:** Eagle, color background

Date	Mintage	F	VF	XF	Unc	BU
2012P	—	—	—	—	—	15.00

KM# 1858 DOLLAR
9.0000 g., Aluminum-Bronze, 25 mm. **Ruler:** Elizabeth II **Subject:** Southern Corrobreee Frog

Date	Mintage	F	VF	XF	Unc	BU
2012	—	—	—	—	—	10.00

KM# 1860 DOLLAR
9.0000 g., Aluminum-Bronze, 25 mm. **Ruler:** Elizabeth II **Rev:** Monkey in tree

Date	Mintage	F	VF	XF	Unc	BU
2012	—	—	—	—	—	10.00

KM# 1861 DOLLAR
9.0000 g., Aluminum-Bronze, 25 mm. **Ruler:** Elizabeth II **Subject:** Sir Douglas Mawson, explorer

Date	Mintage	F	VF	XF	Unc	BU
2012	—	—	—	—	4.00	5.00

KM# 1859 DOLLAR
9.0000 g., Aluminum-Bronze, 25 mm. **Ruler:** Elizabeth II **Subject:** Sumatran Tiger

Date	Mintage	F	VF	XF	Unc	BU
2012	—	—	—	—	—	10.00

KM# 1826 DOLLAR
31.1050 g., 0.9990 Silver 0.9990 oz. ASW, 40.6 mm. **Ruler:** Elizabeth II **Subject:** Antartic Territories **Rev:** Penguins

Date	Mintage	F	VF	XF	Unc	BU
2013P Proof	—	Value: 100				

KM# 406 2 DOLLARS
6.6000 g., Aluminum-Bronze, 20.5 mm. **Ruler:** Elizabeth II **Obv:** Head with tiara right **Rev:** Aboriginal elder at left, stars above at right **Edge:** Segmented reeding

Date	Mintage	F	VF	XF	Unc	BU
2001	35,650,000	—	—	—	5.00	6.00
Note: Large obverse head, IRB spaced						
2001	Inc. above	—	—	—	—	—
Note: Smaller obverse head, IRB joined						
2001 Proof	59,569	Value: 8.00				
2002	29,689,000	—	—	—	4.00	6.00
2002 Proof	39,514	Value: 8.00				
2003	13,656,000	—	—	—	4.00	6.00
2003 Proof	39,090	Value: 8.00				
2004	20,084,000	—	—	—	3.50	5.00
2004 Proof	50,000	Value: 7.00				
2005	—	—	—	—	3.50	5.00
2005 Proof	33,520	Value: 7.00				
2006	—	—	—	—	3.50	5.00
2006 Proof	—	Value: 7.00				
2007	—	—	—	—	3.00	4.50
2007 Proof	—	Value: 6.00				
2008	—	—	—	—	3.00	4.50
2008 Proof	—	Value: 6.00				
2009	—	—	—	—	3.00	4.50
2009 Proof	—	Value: 6.00				
2010	—	—	—	—	3.00	4.50
2010 Proof	—	Value: 6.00				
2011	—	—	—	—	3.00	4.50
2011 Proof	—	Value: 6.00				
2012	—	—	—	—	3.00	4.50
2012 Proof	—	Value: 6.00				

KM# 406a 2 DOLLARS
15.8800 g., 0.9999 Gold 0.5105 oz. AGW, 20.5 mm. **Ruler:** Elizabeth II **Subject:** Federation Centennial **Obv:** Head with tiara right **Rev:** Aboriginal elder **Edge:** Segmented reeding

Date	Mintage	F	VF	XF	Unc	BU
2001B Proof	350	Value: 925				
2005B Proof	650	Value: 900				
2006B Proof	300	Value: 950				

KM# 406b 2 DOLLARS
8.5500 g., 0.9999 Silver 0.2748 oz. ASW, 20.5 mm. **Ruler:** Elizabeth II **Obv:** Head with tiara right **Rev:** Aboriginal elder **Edge:** Segmented reeding

Date	Mintage	F	VF	XF	Unc	BU
2003B Proof	6,500	Value: 22.00				
2004B Proof	6,500	Value: 22.00				
2005B Proof	6,500	Value: 22.00				

KM# 764 2 DOLLARS
18.2200 g., 0.9990 Silver 0.5852 oz. ASW, 32.5 mm. **Ruler:** Elizabeth II **Series:** Masterpieces in Silver - Port Phillip Patterns **Obv:** 1/2 ounce design **Rev:** Kangaroo design **Edge:** Reeded

Date	Mintage	F	VF	XF	Unc	BU
2003B Proof	10,000	Value: 35.00				

KM# 755 2 DOLLARS
62.2700 g., 0.9990 Silver 1.9999 oz. ASW, 50 mm. **Ruler:** Elizabeth II **Series:** Australian Peacekeepers **Obv:** Queen's head right **Rev:** Australian army and color insignia **Edge:** Reeded

Date	Mintage	F	VF	XF	Unc	BU
2005P Proof	2,500	Value: 90.00				

KM# 756 2 DOLLARS
62.2700 g., 0.9990 Silver 1.9999 oz. ASW, 50.3 mm. **Ruler:** Elizabeth II **Series:** Australian Peacekeepers **Obv:** Queen's head right **Rev:** Australian navy and color insignia **Edge:** Reeded

Date	Mintage	F	VF	XF	Unc	BU
2005P Proof	2,500	Value: 90.00				

KM# 757 2 DOLLARS
62.2700 g., 0.9990 Silver 1.9999 oz. ASW, 50.3 mm. **Ruler:** Elizabeth II **Subject:** Australian Peacekeepers Set **Obv:** Queen's head right **Rev:** Australian airforce and color insignia **Edge:** Reeded

Date	Mintage	F	VF	XF	Unc	BU
2005P Proof	2,500	Value: 90.00				

KM# 758 2 DOLLARS
62.2700 g., 0.9990 Silver 1.9999 oz. ASW, 50.3 mm. **Ruler:** Elizabeth II **Series:** Australian Peacekeepers **Obv:** Queen's head right **Rev:** Australian federal police and color insignia **Edge:** Reeded

Date	Mintage	F	VF	XF	Unc	BU
2005P Proof	2,500	Value: 90.00				

KM# 759 2 DOLLARS
62.2700 g., 0.9990 Silver 1.9999 oz. ASW, 50.3 mm. **Ruler:** Elizabeth II **Series:** Australian Peacekeepers **Obv:** Queen's head right **Rev:** Australian Agency for International Development and color insignia **Edge:** Reeded

Date	Mintage	F	VF	XF	Unc	BU
2005P Proof	2,500	Value: 90.00				

KM# 852 2 DOLLARS
8.8500 g., 0.9990 Silver 0.2842 oz. ASW, 20.5 mm. **Ruler:** Elizabeth II **Obv:** Young bust right **Rev:** Aboriginal elder **Edge:** Segmented reeding

Date	Mintage	F	VF	XF	Unc	BU
2006 Proof	6,500	Value: 22.00				

KM# 853 2 DOLLARS
1.2441 g., 0.9990 Gold 0.0400 oz. AGW **Ruler:** Elizabeth II **Obv:** Head with tiara right **Rev:** FIFA World Cup

Date	Mintage	F	VF	XF	Unc	BU
2006P Proof	50,000	Value: 80.00				

KM# 1246 2 DOLLARS
0.5000 g., 0.9990 Gold 0.0161 oz. AGW, 12 mm. **Ruler:** Elizabeth II **Subject:** 2010 FIFA World Cup, South Africa **Obv:** Head right **Rev:** Dream kangaroo and soccer ball

Date	Mintage	F	VF	XF	Unc	BU
2009P Proof	7,500	Value: 85.00				

KM# 1627 2 DOLLARS
31.1050 g., 0.9990 Silver 0.9990 oz. ASW, 40.6 mm. **Ruler:** Elizabeth II **Subject:** Royal Austrailian Navy, 100th Anniversary **Obv:** Head with tiara right **Rev:** HMAS AE 2 submarine

Date	Mintage	F	VF	XF	Unc	BU
2011 Proof	—	Value: 100				

KM# 1628 2 DOLLARS
31.1050 g., 0.9990 Silver 0.9990 oz. ASW, 40.6 mm. **Ruler:** Elizabeth II **Subject:** Royal Australian Navy, 100th Anniversary **Obv:** Head with tiara right **Rev:** HMAS Australia II

Date	Mintage	F	VF	XF	Unc	BU
2011 Proof	—	Value: 100				

KM# 1629 2 DOLLARS
31.1050 g., 0.9990 Silver 0.9990 oz. ASW, 40.6 mm. **Ruler:** Elizabeth II **Subject:** Royal Australian Navy, 100th Anniversary **Obv:** Head with tiara right **Rev:** HMAS Hobart II

Date	Mintage	F	VF	XF	Unc	BU
2011 Proof	—	Value: 100				

KM# 1630 2 DOLLARS
31.1050 g., 0.9990 Silver 0.9990 oz. ASW, 40.6 mm. **Ruler:** Elizabeth II **Subject:** Royal Australian Navy, 100th Anniversary **Obv:** Head with tiara right **Rev:** HMAS Yarra III

Date	Mintage	F	VF	XF	Unc	BU
2011 Proof	—	Value: 100				

KM# 1631 2 DOLLARS
31.1050 g., 0.9990 Silver 0.9990 oz. ASW, 40.6 mm. **Ruler:** Elizabeth II **Subject:** Royal Australian Navy, 100th Anniversary **Obv:** Head with tiara right **Rev:** HMAS Sydney III

Date	Mintage	F	VF	XF	Unc	BU
2011 Proof	—	Value: 100				

KM# 1632 2 DOLLARS
31.1050 g., 0.9990 Silver 0.9990 oz. ASW, 40.6 mm. **Ruler:** Elizabeth II **Subject:** Royal Australian Navy, 100th Anniversary **Obv:** Head with tiara right **Rev:** HMAS Armidale II

Date	Mintage	F	VF	XF	Unc	BU
2011 Proof	—	Value: 100				

KM# 1740 2 DOLLARS
20.0000 g., 0.9990 Silver partially gilt 0.6423 oz. ASW, 34 mm. **Ruler:** Elizabeth II **Subject:** Australian Open **Obv:** Small Queen's portrait above tennis ball **Rev:** Player serving

Date	Mintage	F	VF	XF	Unc	BU
2012 Proof	10,000	Value: 100				

KM# 1802 2 DOLLARS
0.5000 g., 0.9990 Gold 0.0161 oz. AGW, 11.6 mm. **Ruler:** Elizabeth II **Subject:** FIFA **Rev:** Scoccer player and Australia map

Date	Mintage	F	VF	XF	Unc	BU
2012P Proof	—	Value: 75.00				

KM# 1825 2 DOLLARS
0.5000 g., 0.9990 Gold 0.0161 oz. AGW, 11.6 mm. **Ruler:** Elizabeth II **Subject:** Mini-Roo **Rev:** Kangaroo

Date	Mintage	F	VF	XF	Unc	BU
2012P Proof	—	Value: 50.00				

KM# 591 5 DOLLARS

36.3100 g., 0.9990 Silver 1.1662 oz. ASW, 38.74 mm. **Ruler:** Elizabeth II **Subject:** Centennial of Federation Series Finale **Obv:** Queen's head right **Rev:** Multicolor dual hologram: map and rotunda **Edge:** Reeded

Date	Mintage	F	VF	XF	Unc	BU
2001B Proof	—	Value: 55.00				

KM# 592 5 DOLLARS

36.3100 g., 0.9990 Silver 1.1662 oz. ASW, 38.74 mm. **Ruler:** Elizabeth II **Subject:** Barton and Reid **Obv:** Queen's head right **Rev:** Portraits of Dame Flora Reid and Lady Jean Barton **Edge:** Reeded

Date	Mintage	F	VF	XF	Unc	BU
2001B Proof	5,000	Value: 60.00				

KM# 637 5 DOLLARS

36.3100 g., 0.9990 Silver 1.1662 oz. ASW, 38.74 mm. **Ruler:** Elizabeth II **Subject:** Kingston, Barton and Deakin **Obv:** Queen's head right **Rev:** Three rectangular portraits and value **Edge:** Reeded

Date	Mintage	F	VF	XF	Unc	BU
2001B Proof	5,000	Value: 60.00				

KM# 638 5 DOLLARS

36.3100 g., 0.9990 Silver 1.1662 oz. ASW, 38.74 mm. **Ruler:** Elizabeth II **Subject:** Clark, Parkes and Griffith **Obv:** Queen's head right **Rev:** Three rectangular portraits and value **Edge:** Reeded

Date	Mintage	F	VF	XF	Unc	BU
2001B Proof	5,000	Value: 60.00				

KM# 639 5 DOLLARS

36.3100 g., 0.9990 Silver 1.1662 oz. ASW, 38.74 mm. **Ruler:** Elizabeth II **Subject:** Spence, Nicholls and Anderson **Obv:** Queen's head right **Rev:** Three circular portraits and value **Edge:** Reeded

Date	Mintage	F	VF	XF	Unc	BU
2001B Proof	5,000	Value: 60.00				

KM# 640 5 DOLLARS

36.3100 g., 0.9990 Silver 1.1662 oz. ASW, 38.74 mm. **Ruler:** Elizabeth II **Subject:** Reid, Forrest and Quick **Obv:** Queen's head right **Rev:** Three rectangular portraits and value **Edge:** Reeded

Date	Mintage	F	VF	XF	Unc	BU
2001B Proof	5,000	Value: 60.00				

KM# 641 5 DOLLARS

36.3100 g., 0.9990 Silver 1.1662 oz. ASW, 38.74 mm. **Ruler:** Elizabeth II **Subject:** Bathurst Ladies Organizing Committee **Obv:** Queen's head right **Rev:** Circular design with names above value **Edge:** Reeded

Date	Mintage	F	VF	XF	Unc	BU
2001B Proof	5,000	Value: 60.00				

KM# 662 5 DOLLARS

36.3100 g., 0.9990 Silver 1.1662 oz. ASW, 38.74 mm. **Ruler:** Elizabeth II **Subject:** Year of the Outback **Obv:** Queen's head right **Rev:** Multicolor holographic landscape **Edge:** Reeded

Date	Mintage	F	VF	XF	Unc	BU
2002B Proof	15,000	Value: 100				

KM# 761 5 DOLLARS

36.3100 g., 0.9990 Silver 1.1662 oz. ASW **Ruler:** Elizabeth II **Obv:** Queen's head right **Rev:** Sir Donald Bradman

Date	Mintage	F	VF	XF	Unc	BU
2001 Proof	—	Value: 55.00				

KM# 762 5 DOLLARS

20.0000 g., Aluminum-Bronze, 38.74 mm. **Ruler:** Elizabeth II **Obv:** Queen's head right **Rev:** Sir Donald Bradman

Date	Mintage	F	VF	XF	Unc	BU
2001	—	—	—	—	8.50	9.50

KM# 601 5 DOLLARS

10.5200 g., Bi-Metallic Aluminumn-Bronze center in Stainless Steel ring, 27.8 mm. **Ruler:** Elizabeth II **Subject:** Battle of Sunda Strait **Obv:** Head with tiara right **Rev:** Ships bell from the "USS Houston", denomination below **Shape:** 24-sided **Note:** Demagnetized.

Date	Mintage	F	VF	XF	Unc	BU
2002B	—	—	—	—	7.50	9.50

KM# 647 5 DOLLARS

28.0000 g., Aluminum-Bronze, 38.74 mm. **Ruler:** Elizabeth II **Subject:** Battle of Sunda Strait **Obv:** Queen's head right **Rev:** Two ships; USS Houston and HMS Perth **Edge:** Reeded

Date	Mintage	F	VF	XF	Unc	BU
2002B Proof	15,000	Value: 25.00				

KM# 649 5 DOLLARS

20.0000 g., Aluminum-Bronze, 38.74 mm. **Ruler:** Elizabeth II **Subject:** Commonwealth Games **Obv:** Head with tiara right, denomination below **Rev:** Eight arms, each represents an event of the games **Edge:** Reeded

Date	Mintage	F	VF	XF	Unc	BU
2002B	11,145	—	—	—	8.50	9.50

KM# 650 5 DOLLARS

20.0000 g., Aluminum-Bronze, 38.74 mm. **Ruler:** Elizabeth II **Subject:** Commonwealth Games **Obv:** Head with tiara right, denomination below **Rev:** Eight arms, each represents an event at the games **Edge:** Reeded

Date	Mintage	F	VF	XF	Unc	BU
2002B	11,145	—	—	—	8.50	9.50

KM# 651 5 DOLLARS

20.0000 g., Aluminum-Bronze, 38.74 mm. **Ruler:** Elizabeth II **Subject:** Commonwealth Games **Obv:** Head with tiara right, denomination below **Rev:** Blue games logo; star above tail of stylized kangaroo and torch **Edge:** Reeded

Date	Mintage	F	VF	XF	Unc	BU
2002B	11,145	—	—	—	8.50	9.50

KM# 652 5 DOLLARS

36.3100 g., 0.9990 Silver 1.1662 oz. ASW, 38.74 mm. **Ruler:** Elizabeth II **Subject:** Commonwealth Games **Obv:** Head with tiara right, denomination below **Rev:** Victorious athletes **Edge:** Reeded

Date	Mintage	F	VF	XF	Unc	BU
2002B Proof	7,581	Value: 50.00				

KM# 653 5 DOLLARS
36.3100 g., 0.9990 Silver 1.1662 oz. ASW, 38.74 mm. **Ruler:** Elizabeth II **Obv:** Queen's head right **Rev:** Dutch sailing ship, The Duyfken **Edge:** Reeded

Date	Mintage	F	VF	XF	Unc	BU
2002B Proof	9,096	Value: 47.00				

KM# 654 5 DOLLARS
36.3100 g., 0.9990 Silver 1.1662 oz. ASW, 38.74 mm. **Ruler:** Elizabeth II **Obv:** Queen's head right **Rev:** HMS Endeavour sailing ship **Edge:** Reeded

Date	Mintage	F	VF	XF	Unc	BU
2002B Proof	9,096	Value: 47.00				

KM# 655 5 DOLLARS
36.3100 g., 0.9990 Silver 1.1662 oz. ASW, 38.74 mm. **Ruler:** Elizabeth II **Obv:** Queen's head right **Rev:** HMS Sirius sailing ship **Edge:** Reeded

Date	Mintage	F	VF	XF	Unc	BU
2002B Proof	9,096	Value: 47.00				

KM# 656 5 DOLLARS
36.3100 g., 0.9990 Silver 1.1662 oz. ASW, 38.74 mm. **Ruler:** Elizabeth II **Obv:** Queen's head right **Rev:** HMS Investigator sailing ship **Edge:** Reeded

Date	Mintage	F	VF	XF	Unc	BU
2002B Proof	9,096	Value: 47.00				

KM# 659 5 DOLLARS
31.1035 g., 0.9990 Silver 0.9990 oz. ASW, 40 mm. **Ruler:** Elizabeth II **Subject:** Queen Mother **Obv:** Queen's head right **Rev:** Queen Mother circa 1927 within wreath of roses **Edge:** Reeded

Date	Mintage	F	VF	XF	Unc	BU
2002B Proof	30,000	Value: 40.00				

KM# 765 5 DOLLARS
36.3100 g., 0.9990 Silver 1.1662 oz. ASW, 38.7 mm. **Ruler:** Elizabeth II **Series:** Masterpieces in Silver - Port Phillip Patterns **Obv:** One ounce design **Rev:** Kangaroo design **Edge:** Reeded

Date	Mintage	F	VF	XF	Unc	BU
2003B Proof	10,000	Value: 45.00				

KM# 810 5 DOLLARS
36.3100 g., 0.9950 Silver partially gilt 1.1615 oz. ASW, 40 mm. **Ruler:** Elizabeth II **Subject:** Rugby World Cup **Obv:** Head with tiara right **Rev:** Rugby World Cup and official logos **Edge:** Reeded

Date	Mintage	F	VF	XF	Unc	BU
2003 Proof	20,501	Value: 85.00				

KM# 854 5 DOLLARS
20.0000 g., Aluminum-Bronze, 38.74 mm. **Ruler:** Elizabeth II **Subject:** Rugby World Cup **Obv:** Head with tiara right **Rev:** Player kicking ball at posts, official logo **Edge:** Reeded

Date	Mintage	F	VF	XF	Unc	BU
2003	43,802	—	—	—	15.00	16.50

KM# 1017 5 DOLLARS
36.2100 g., 0.9990 Silver 1.1630 oz. ASW, 38.7 mm. **Ruler:** Elizabeth II **Obv:** Head with tiara right **Obv. Legend:** ELIZABETH II - AUSTRALIA **Rev:** Faces in oval hologram in ornate frame **Rev. Legend:** AUSTRALIA'S VOLUNTEERS - MAKING A DIFFERENCE **Edge:** Reeded

Date	Mintage	F	VF	XF	Unc	BU
2003B Proof	15,000	Value: 45.00				

KM# 727 5 DOLLARS
36.3100 g., 0.9990 Silver 1.1662 oz. ASW, 38.74 mm. **Ruler:** Elizabeth II **Subject:** Olympics **Obv:** Queen's head right **Rev:** Parthenon, Sydney Opera House and shield with multicolor flag and rings **Edge:** Reeded

Date	Mintage	F	VF	XF	Unc	BU
2004B Proof	17,500	Value: 40.00				

KM# 728 5 DOLLARS
36.3100 g., 0.9990 Silver 1.1662 oz. ASW, 38.74 mm. **Ruler:** Elizabeth II **Subject:** Tasmania **Obv:** Queen's head right **Rev:** Ship on island map **Edge:** Reeded

Date	Mintage	F	VF	XF	Unc	BU
2004B Proof	7,500	Value: 47.00				

KM# 728a 5 DOLLARS
20.0000 g., Aluminum-Bronze, 38.74 mm. **Ruler:** Elizabeth II **Subject:** Tasmanian Bicentennial **Obv:** Head with tiara right **Rev:** Ship, map, state flower **Edge:** Reeded

Date	Mintage	F	VF	XF	Unc	BU
2004	18,561	—	—	—	12.00	14.00
2004H	2,841	—	—	—	17.50	20.00

KM# 729 5 DOLLARS
31.1035 g., 0.9990 Silver 0.9990 oz. ASW, 40 mm. **Ruler:** Elizabeth II **Subject:** Adelaide to Darwin Railroad **Obv:** Queen's head right **Rev:** Train, tracks and outline map **Edge:** Reeded

Date	Mintage	F	VF	XF	Unc	BU
2004B Proof	12,500	Value: 40.00				

KM# 730 5 DOLLARS
31.1035 g., 0.9990 Silver 0.9990 oz. ASW, 40 mm. **Ruler:** Elizabeth II **Subject:** 150 Years of Australian Steam Railways **Obv:** Queen's head right **Rev:** Old steam train **Edge:** Reeded

Date	Mintage	F	VF	XF	Unc	BU
2004B Proof	15,000	Value: 37.50				

KM# 812 5 DOLLARS
Aluminum-Bronze, 38.74 mm. **Ruler:** Elizabeth II **Subject:** Olympic Games 2000-2004 **Obv:** Head with tiara right

Date	Mintage	F	VF	XF	Unc	BU
2004	—	—	—	—	15.00	16.50

KM# 855 5 DOLLARS
27.2500 g., Copper-Nickel partially gilt, 38.74 mm. **Ruler:** Elizabeth II **Subject:** Australia's Own Game **Obv:** Head with tiara right **Rev:** Cup and logos **Edge:** Reeded

Date	Mintage	F	VF	XF	Unc	BU
2004 Proof	16,163	Value: 45.00				

KM# 856 5 DOLLARS
20.0000 g., Aluminum-Bronze, 38.74 mm. **Ruler:** Elizabeth II **Subject:** Olympic Games - Sydney To Athens **Obv:** Head with tiara right **Rev:** Silhouettes ancient Greek athlete and Aboriginal **Edge:** Reeded

Date	Mintage	F	VF	XF	Unc	BU
2004	24,376	—	—	—	15.00	16.50

KM# 750 5 DOLLARS
20.0000 g., Aluminum-Bronze, 38.74 mm. **Ruler:** Elizabeth II **Obv:** Queen's head right **Rev:** Tennis player **Edge:** Reeded

Date	Mintage	F	VF	XF	Unc	BU
2005B	—	—	—	—	7.50	8.50

KM# 859 5 DOLLARS
36.3100 g., 0.9990 Silver 1.1662 oz. ASW, 38.74 mm. **Ruler:** Elizabeth II **Subject:** 150 Year of State Government **Obv:** Head with tiara right **Rev:** Outline map of State of Victoria **Edge:** Reeded

Date	Mintage	F	VF	XF	Unc	BU
2006 Proof	12,500	Value: 85.00				

KM# 782 5 DOLLARS
36.3100 g., 0.9999 Silver 1.1672 oz. ASW, 38.74 mm. **Ruler:** Elizabeth II **Subject:** XVIII Commonwealth Games City of Sport **Obv:** Head with tiara right, denomination below **Rev:** City skyline alongside river

Date	Mintage	F	VF	XF	Unc	BU
2006 Proof	10,000	Value: 55.00				

KM# 783 5 DOLLARS
20.0000 g., Aluminum-Bronze, 38.74 mm. **Ruler:** Elizabeth II **Subject:** XVIII Commonwealth Games in Melbourne **Obv:** Head with tiara right, denomination below **Rev:** Games logo and crown surrounded by stylized athletes **Edge:** Reeded

Date	Mintage	F	VF	XF	Unc	BU
2006	—	—	—	—	15.00	16.50

KM# 786 5 DOLLARS
20.0000 g., Aluminum-Bronze, 38.74 mm. **Ruler:** Elizabeth II **Subject:** XVIII Commonwealth Games Queen's Baton Relay **Obv:** Head with tiara right **Rev:** Stylized baton runner **Edge:** Reeded

Date	Mintage	F	VF	XF	Unc	BU
2006	20,488	—	—	—	15.00	16.50

KM# 786a 5 DOLLARS
36.3100 g., 0.9990 Silver 1.1662 oz. ASW, 38.74 mm. **Ruler:** Elizabeth II **Subject:** XVIII Commonwealth Games Queen's Baton Relay **Obv:** Head with tiara right **Rev:** Stylized baton runner **Edge:** Reeded

Date	Mintage	F	VF	XF	Unc	BU
2006 Proof	9,100	Value: 75.00				

KM# 787 5 DOLLARS
36.3100 g., 0.9990 Silver 1.1662 oz. ASW, 38.74 mm. **Ruler:** Elizabeth II **Subject:** Masterpieces in Silver: Australia's Artists **Obv:** Head with tiara right **Rev:** Sidney Nolan: Burke & Wills

Date	Mintage	F	VF	XF	Unc	BU
2006 Proof	10,000	Value: 60.00				

KM# 788 5 DOLLARS
36.3100 g., 0.9990 Silver 1.1662 oz. ASW, 38.74 mm. **Ruler:** Elizabeth II **Subject:** Masters in Art - Siding

Date	Mintage	F	VF	XF	Unc	BU
2006 Proof	10,000	Value: 55.00				

KM# 789 5 DOLLARS
36.3100 g., 0.9990 Silver 1.1662 oz. ASW, 38.74 mm. **Ruler:** Elizabeth II **Subject:** Masterpieces in Silver: Australia's Artists **Obv:** Head with tiara right **Rev:** Brett Whitley: Self Portrait in the Studio

Date	Mintage	F	VF	XF	Unc	BU
2006 Proof	10,000	Value: 60.00				

KM# 790 5 DOLLARS
36.3100 g., 0.9990 Silver 1.1662 oz. ASW, 38.74 mm. **Ruler:** Elizabeth II **Subject:** Masterpieces in Silver: Australia's Artists **Obv:** Head with tiara right **Rev:** Russell Drysdale: The Drover's Wife

Date	Mintage	F	VF	XF	Unc	BU
2006 Proof	10,000	Value: 60.00				

KM# 813 5 DOLLARS
20.0000 g., Aluminum-Bronze, 38.74 mm. **Ruler:** Elizabeth II **Subject:** Voyage of Discovery 1606 **Obv:** Head with tiara right **Rev:** Dutch yacht Duyfken **Edge:** Reeded **Note:** Mint mark: G.

Date	Mintage	F	VF	XF	Unc	BU
2006	—	—	—	—	15.00	16.50

KM# 813a 5 DOLLARS
36.3100 g., 0.9990 Silver 1.1662 oz. ASW, 38.74 mm. **Ruler:** Elizabeth II **Subject:** Voyage of Discovery 1606 **Obv:** Head with tiara right **Rev:** Dutch yacht Duyfken **Edge:** Reeded **Note:** Mint mark: Tulip.

Date	Mintage	F	VF	XF	Unc	BU
2006P Proof	8,500	Value: 125				

KM# 857 5 DOLLARS
36.3100 g., 0.9999 Silver 1.1672 oz. ASW, 38.74 mm. **Ruler:** Elizabeth II **Subject:** 150 Year of State Government **Obv:** Head with tiara right **Rev:** Outline map of State of New South Wales **Edge:** Reeded

Date	Mintage	F	VF	XF	Unc	BU
2006 Proof	12,500	Value: 85.00				

KM# 858 5 DOLLARS
36.3100 g., 0.9990 Silver 1.1662 oz. ASW, 38.74 mm. **Ruler:** Elizabeth II **Subject:** 150 Year of State Government **Obv:** Head with tiara right **Rev:** Outline map of State of Tasmania **Edge:** Reeded

Date	Mintage	F	VF	XF	Unc	BU
2006 Proof	12,500	Value: 85.00				

KM# 860 5 DOLLARS
36.3100 g., 0.9990 Silver 1.1662 oz. ASW, 38.74 mm. **Ruler:** Elizabeth II **Subject:** Masterpieces in Silver: Australia's Artists **Obv:** Ian Rank-Broadley **Rev:** Jeffrey Smart: Keswick Siding

Date	Mintage	F	VF	XF	Unc	BU
2006 Proof	10,000	Value: 60.00				

KM# 1014 5 DOLLARS
1.2441 g., 0.9999 Gold 0.0400 oz. AGW, 19 mm. **Ruler:** Elizabeth II **Obv:** Bust with tiara right **Obv. Legend:** ELIZABETH II - AUSTRALIA **Rev:** Sydney Opera House

Date	Mintage	F	VF	XF	Unc	BU
2006P Proof	100,000	Value: 75.00				

KM# 861 5 DOLLARS
36.3100 g., 0.9990 Silver 1.1662 oz. ASW, 38.74 mm. **Ruler:** Elizabeth II **Subject:** Masterpieces in Silver: Australia's Artists **Obv:** Head with tiara right **Rev:** Grace Cossington-Smith: Curve of the Bridge

Date	Mintage	F	VF	XF	Unc	BU
2007 Proof	10,000	Value: 50.00				

KM# 862 5 DOLLARS
36.3100 g., 0.9990 Silver 1.1662 oz. ASW, 38.74 mm. **Ruler:** Elizabeth II **Subject:** Masterpieces in Silver: Australia's Artists **Obv:** Head with tiara right **Rev:** Clifford Possum Tjpaltjarri: Yuelamu Honey Ant Dreaming

Date	Mintage	F	VF	XF	Unc	BU
2007 Proof	10,000	Value: 50.00				

KM# 863 5 DOLLARS
36.3100 g., 0.9990 Silver 1.1662 oz. ASW, 38.74 mm. **Ruler:** Elizabeth II **Subject:** Masterpieces in Silver: Australia's Artists **Obv:** Head with tiara right **Rev:** William Dobell: Margaret Olley

Date	Mintage	F	VF	XF	Unc	BU
2007 Proof	10,000	Value: 50.00				

KM# 864 5 DOLLARS
36.3100 g., 0.9990 Silver 1.1662 oz. ASW, 38.74 mm. **Ruler:** Elizabeth II **Subject:** Masterpieces in Silver: Australia's Artists **Obv:** Ian Rank-Broadley **Rev:** Margaret Preston: Implement Blue

Date	Mintage	F	VF	XF	Unc	BU
2007 Proof	10,000	Value: 50.00				

KM# 865 5 DOLLARS
36.3100 g., 0.9990 Silver 1.1662 oz. ASW, 38.74 mm. **Ruler:** Elizabeth II **Subject:** Ashes Cricket Series 1882-2007 **Obv:** Head with tiara right **Rev:** Urn with supporters **Edge:** Reeded

Date	Mintage	F	VF	XF	Unc	BU
2007 Proof	12,500	Value: 45.00				

KM# 1013 5 DOLLARS
36.3100 g., 0.9990 Silver 1.1662 oz. ASW, 38.74 mm. **Ruler:** Elizabeth II **Subject:** Sydney Harbour Bridge, 75th Anniversary **Obv:** Bust with tiara right **Obv. Legend:** ELIZABETH II - AUSTRALIA **Rev:** Bridge **Rev. Inscription:** SYDNEY / HARBOUR / BRIDGE

Date	Mintage	F	VF	XF	Unc	BU
2007 Proof	12,500	Value: 50.00				

KM# 1045 5 DOLLARS
36.3100 g., 0.9990 Silver 1.1662 oz. ASW, 38.74 mm. **Ruler:** Elizabeth II **Subject:** Year of the surfer lifesaver **Rev:** Rowboat in rough seas

Date	Mintage	F	VF	XF	Unc	BU
2007B Proof	12,500	Value: 65.00				

KM# 1046 5 DOLLARS
36.3100 g., 0.9990 Silver 1.1662 oz. ASW, 38.74 mm. **Ruler:** Elizabeth II **Subject:** South Australia State Government **Rev:** Australia map and state enlarged

Date	Mintage	F	VF	XF	Unc	BU
2007B Proof	12,500	Value: 65.00				

KM# 1117 5 DOLLARS
1.2400 g., 0.9990 Gold 0.0398 oz. AGW, 14 mm. **Ruler:** Elizabeth II **Subject:** Sydney Harbor Bridge **Obv:** Head right **Rev:** Bridge view

Date	Mintage	F	VF	XF	Unc	BU
2007P Proof	100,000	Value: 110				

KM# 1050 5 DOLLARS
31.1050 g., 0.9990 Silver 0.9990 oz. ASW, 38.74 mm. **Ruler:** Elizabeth II **Subject:** Scouting Centennial in Australia **Rev:** Scout sign and map

Date	Mintage	F	VF	XF	Unc	BU
2008 Proof	5,000	Value: 65.00				

KM# 1053 5 DOLLARS
36.3100 g., 0.9990 Silver 1.1662 oz. ASW, 38.74 mm. **Ruler:** Elizabeth II **Subject:** Rugby League **Rev:** Two players

Date	Mintage	F	VF	XF	Unc	BU
2008 Proof	10,000	Value: 65.00				

KM# 1055 5 DOLLARS
31.1050 g., 0.9990 Silver 0.9990 oz. ASW, 38.74 mm. **Ruler:** Elizabeth II **Rev:** Antarctic skua in flight over map

Date	Mintage	F	VF	XF	Unc	BU
2008 Proof	12,500	Value: 65.00				

KM# 1065 5 DOLLARS
36.3100 g., 0.9990 Silver 1.1662 oz. ASW, 38.74 mm. **Ruler:** Elizabeth II **Subject:** 30th Anniversary - Northern Territorial Government **Rev:** Territory map and Australia map

Date	Mintage	F	VF	XF	Unc	BU
2008 Proof	12,500	Value: 65.00				

KM# 1066 5 DOLLARS
1.1500 g., 0.9990 Gold 0.0369 oz. AGW, 14 mm. **Ruler:** Elizabeth II **Rev:** Kisp Koala

Date	Mintage	F	VF	XF	Unc	BU
2008 Proof	10,000	Value: 110				

KM# 1067 5 DOLLARS
1.1500 g., 0.9990 Gold 0.0369 oz. AGW, 14 mm. **Ruler:** Elizabeth II **Rev:** Binny Bilby

Date	Mintage	F	VF	XF	Unc	BU
2008 Proof	10,000	Value: 110				

KM# 1072 5 DOLLARS
36.3100 g., 0.9990 Silver 1.1662 oz. ASW, 38.74 mm. **Ruler:** Elizabeth II **Rev:** Avro 504K airplane

Date	Mintage	F	VF	XF	Unc	BU
2008 Proof	10,000	Value: 65.00				

KM# 1073 5 DOLLARS
36.3100 g., 0.9990 Silver 1.1662 oz. ASW, 38.74 mm. **Ruler:** Elizabeth II **Rev:** Airbus A380 airplane

Date	Mintage	F	VF	XF	Unc	BU
2008 Proof	10,000	Value: 65.00				

KM# 1084 5 DOLLARS
Aluminum-Bronze, 38.74 mm. **Ruler:** Elizabeth II **Subject:** Sir Donald Bradman 100th Anniversary of Birth **Rev:** Player with cricket bat

Date	Mintage	F	VF	XF	Unc	BU
2008	—	—	—	—	—	10.00

KM# 1080 5 DOLLARS
36.3100 g., 0.9990 Silver 1.1662 oz. ASW, 38.74 mm. **Ruler:** Elizabeth II **Rev:** Three arctic explorers on map

Date	Mintage	F	VF	XF	Unc	BU
2009 Proof	12,500	Value: 65.00				

KM# 1081 5 DOLLARS
36.3100 g., 0.9990 Silver 1.1662 oz. ASW, 38.74 mm. **Ruler:** Elizabeth II **Subject:** Aurora Australis **Obv:** Head right **Rev:** Sailing ship in Antartic ice in hologram

Date	Mintage	F	VF	XF	Unc	BU
2009 Proof	12,500	Value: 50.00				

KM# 1085 5 DOLLARS
1.2000 g., 0.9990 Gold 0.0385 oz. AGW, 14 mm. **Ruler:** Elizabeth II **Obv:** Head right **Rev:** Lilly Pilly full-neck lizard

Date	Mintage	F	VF	XF	Unc	BU
2009 Proof	10,000	Value: 75.00				

KM# 1086 5 DOLLARS
1.2000 g., 0.9990 Gold 0.0385 oz. AGW, 14 mm. **Ruler:** Elizabeth II **Obv:** Head right **Rev:** Petey Platypus

Date	Mintage	F	VF	XF	Unc	BU
2009 Proof	10,000	Value: 75.00				

KM# 1658 5 DOLLARS
36.3100 g., 0.9990 Silver 1.1662 oz. ASW, 38.74 mm. **Ruler:** Elizabeth II **Subject:** Queensland Government **Rev:** Map of Australian states, Queensland highlighted

Date	Mintage	F	VF	XF	Unc	BU
2009 Proof	—	Value: 85.00				

KM# 1509 5 DOLLARS
36.3100 g., 0.9990 Silver 1.1662 oz. ASW, 38.74 mm. **Ruler:** Elizabeth II **Subject:** Aviation - Constellation L749

Date	Mintage	F	VF	XF	Unc	BU
2010 Proof	—	Value: 60.00				

KM# 1510 5 DOLLARS
36.3100 g., 0.9990 Silver 1.1662 oz. ASW, 37.84 mm. **Ruler:** Elizabeth II **Subject:** Aviation - De Havilland DH 86

Date	Mintage	F	VF	XF	Unc	BU
2010 Proof	—	Value: 60.00				

KM# 1511 5 DOLLARS
36.3100 g., 0.9990 Silver 1.1662 oz. ASW, 38.74 mm. **Ruler:** Elizabeth II **Subject:** Aviation - S.25 Sandringham

Date	Mintage	F	VF	XF	Unc	BU
2010 Proof	—	Value: 60.00				

KM# 1512 5 DOLLARS
36.3100 g., 0.9990 Silver 1.1662 oz. ASW, 38.74 mm. **Ruler:** Elizabeth II **Subject:** Aviation - Boeing 747

Date	Mintage	F	VF	XF	Unc	BU
2010 Proof	—	Value: 60.00				

KM# 1633 5 DOLLARS
20.0000 g., Aluminum-Bronze, 38.74 mm. **Ruler:** Elizabeth II **Subject:** Royal Visit **Obv:** Head with tiara right **Rev:** Sixteen crowns

Date	Mintage	F	VF	XF	Unc	BU
2011	—	—	—	—	—	15.00

KM# 1637 5 DOLLARS
1.2400 g., 0.9990 Gold 0.0398 oz. AGW, 14 mm. **Ruler:** Elizabeth II **Subject:** Historic Convict Past - Port Arthur Historic Site

Date	Mintage	F	VF	XF	Unc	BU
2011 Proof	3,000	Value: 125				

KM# 1638 5 DOLLARS
1.2400 g., 0.9990 Gold 0.0398 oz. AGW, 14 mm. **Ruler:** Elizabeth II **Subject:** Historic Convict Past - Cascades Female Factory

Date	Mintage	F	VF	XF	Unc	BU
2011 Proof	3,000	Value: 125				

KM# 1639 5 DOLLARS
1.2400 g., 0.9990 Gold 0.0398 oz. AGW, 14 mm. **Ruler:** Elizabeth II **Subject:** Historic Convict Past - Fremantle Prison

Date	Mintage	F	VF	XF	Unc	BU
2011 Proof	3,000	Value: 125				

KM# 1640 5 DOLLARS
1.2400 g., 0.9990 Gold 0.0398 oz. AGW, 14 mm. **Ruler:** Elizabeth II **Subject:** Historic Convict Past - Coal Mines Historic Site

Date	Mintage	F	VF	XF	Unc	BU
2011 Proof	3,000	Value: 125				

KM# 1641 5 DOLLARS
1.2400 g., 0.9990 Gold 0.0398 oz. AGW, 14 mm. **Ruler:** Elizabeth II **Subject:** Historic Convict Past - Old Government House and Domain

Date	Mintage	F	VF	XF	Unc	BU
2011 Proof	3,000	Value: 125				

KM# 1652 5 DOLLARS
20.0000 g., Aluminum-Bronze, 38.74 mm. **Ruler:** Elizabeth II **Subject:** Remembrance Day, 11.11.11 **Obv:** Head with tiara right **Rev:** Poppy in multicolor

Date	Mintage	F	VF	XF	Unc	BU
2011	—	—	—	—	—	17.50

KM# 1739 5 DOLLARS
20.0000 g., Aluminum-Bronze, 38.74 mm. **Ruler:** Elizabeth II **Subject:** Australian Open **Obv:** Small Queen's head above tennis ball **Rev:** Player serving

Date	Mintage	F	VF	XF	Unc	BU
2012	—	—	—	—	—	20.00

KM# 1747 5 DOLLARS
20.0000 g., Aluminum-Bronze, 38.74 mm. **Ruler:** Elizabeth II **Obv:** Gead with tiara right **Rev:** Perth Town Hall

Date	Mintage	F	VF	XF	Unc	BU
2012 Antique patina	—	—	—	—	20.00	—

KM# 1853 5 DOLLARS
36.3100 g., 0.9990 Silver 1.1662 oz. ASW, 38.74 mm. **Ruler:** Elizabeth II **Rev:** Southen Cross in blue sky **Note:** Concave planchet

Date	Mintage	F	VF	XF	Unc	BU
2012P Proof	—	Value: 125				

KM# 1269 8 DOLLARS
5.0000 g., 0.9990 Gold 0.1606 oz. AGW, 14x23 mm. **Ruler:** Elizabeth II **Subject:** Chinese Mythological Character **Obv:** Head right **Rev:** Man standing, multicolor **Shape:** Vertical rectangle

Date	Mintage	F	VF	XF	Unc	BU
2009P	—	—	—	—	—	435

KM# 1270 8 DOLLARS
5.0000 g., 0.9990 Gold 0.1606 oz. AGW, 14x23 mm. **Ruler:** Elizabeth II **Subject:** Chinese Mythological Character - Longevity **Obv:** Head right **Rev:** Nam standing with staff, multicolor **Shape:** Vertical rectangle

Date	Mintage	F	VF	XF	Unc	BU
2009P	—	—	—	—	—	435

KM# 1271 8 DOLLARS
5.0000 g., 0.9990 Gold 0.1606 oz. AGW, 14x23 mm. **Ruler:** Elizabeth II **Subject:** Chinese Mythological Character - Success **Obv:** Hand right **Rev:** Man standing with deer, multicolor **Shape:** Vertical rectangle

Date	Mintage	F	VF	XF	Unc	BU
2009P	—	—	—	—	—	435

KM# 1272 8 DOLLARS
5.0000 g., 0.9990 Gold 0.1606 oz. AGW, 14x23 mm. **Ruler:** Elizabeth II **Subject:** Mythological Chinese Character - Fortune **Obv:** Head right **Rev:** Man standing with scroll, multicolor **Shape:** Vertical rectangle

Date	Mintage	F	VF	XF	Unc	BU
2009P	—	—	—	—	—	435

KM# 1273 8 DOLLARS
10.0000 g., 0.9990 Gold 0.3212 oz. AGW, 15x25 mm. **Ruler:** Elizabeth II **Subject:** Mythological Chinese Character - Wealth **Obv:** Head right **Rev:** Man standing **Shape:** Vertical rectangle

Date	Mintage	F	VF	XF	Unc	BU
2009P	—	—	—	—	—	800

KM# 593 10 DOLLARS
33.1500 g., Bi-Metallic Gold plated .999 Silver center in Copper ring, 38.74 mm. **Ruler:** Elizabeth II **Subject:** "The Future" **Obv:** Queen's portrait **Rev:** Tree, map and denomination **Edge:** Reeded

Date	Mintage	F	VF	XF	Unc	BU
2001B Proof	20,000	Value: 55.00				

KM# 596 10 DOLLARS
311.0350 g., 0.9990 Silver 9.9896 oz. ASW, 75.5 mm. **Ruler:** Elizabeth II **Subject:** Calendar Evolution **Obv:** Head with tiara right, denomination below **Rev:** Multicolor solar system in center, zodiac symbols in outer circle **Edge:** Segmented reeding **Note:** Illustration reduced.

Date	Mintage	F	VF	XF	Unc	BU
ND(2001) Proof	15,000	Value: 375				

KM# 633 10 DOLLARS
311.0350 g., 0.9990 Silver 9.9896 oz. ASW, 75.5 mm. **Ruler:** Elizabeth II **Subject:** Evolution of Time **Obv:** Queen's portrait right **Rev:** Various time keeping devices **Edge:** Segmented reeding

Date	Mintage	F	VF	XF	Unc	BU
2002P Proof	1,500	Value: 425				

KM# 661 10 DOLLARS
60.5000 g., 0.9990 Silver 1.9431 oz. ASW, 50 mm. **Ruler:** Elizabeth II **Subject:** The Adelaide Pound **Obv:** Queen's portrait above gold-plated coin design **Rev:** Legend around gold-plated coin design **Edge:** Reeded

Date	Mintage	F	VF	XF	Unc	BU
2002B Proof	10,000	Value: 95.00				

KM# 686 10 DOLLARS
311.0000 g., 0.9990 Silver 9.9885 oz. ASW, 75.5 mm. **Ruler:** Elizabeth II **Obv:** Queen's head right **Rev:** Alphabet evolution design **Edge:** Reeded

Date	Mintage	F	VF	XF	Unc	BU
2003P Proof	1,500	Value: 425				

KM# 751 10 DOLLARS
60.5000 g., 0.9990 Silver Partially gilt 1.9431 oz. ASW, 50 mm. **Ruler:** Elizabeth II **Subject:** 150th Anniversary - Sydney Mint **Obv:** Head with tiara right above gilt 1853 Sovereign Pattern of Queen Victoria facing left **Rev:** Gilt reverse of Sovereign Pattern **Edge:** Reeded

Date	Mintage	F	VF	XF	Unc	BU
2003B Proof	10,000	Value: 100				
ND(2005)B Proof	10,000	Value: 80.00				

KM# 766 10 DOLLARS
36.3100 g., 0.9990 Silver 1.1662 oz. ASW, 38.7 mm. **Ruler:** Elizabeth II **Series:** Masterpieces in Silver - Port Phillip Patterns **Obv:** Queen's head right **Rev:** Kangaroo design **Edge:** Reeded

Date	Mintage	F	VF	XF	Unc	BU
2003B Proof	10,000	Value: 90.00				

KM# 1439 10 DOLLARS
Silver partially gilt **Ruler:** Elizabeth II **Subject:** Sydney Mint, 100th Anniversary

Date	Mintage	F	VF	XF	Unc	BU
2003 Proof	10,000	Value: 85.00				

KM# 739 10 DOLLARS
311.0350 g., 0.9990 Silver 9.9896 oz. ASW, 75.5 mm. **Ruler:** Elizabeth II **Subject:** Evolution of Numbers **Obv:** Queen's head right **Rev:** Numbers, symbols, abacus and calculator **Edge:** Reeded

Date	Mintage	F	VF	XF	Unc	BU
2004 Proof	1,500	Value: 425				

KM# 744 10 DOLLARS
311.3460 g., 0.9990 Silver 9.9996 oz. ASW, 75.5 mm. **Ruler:** Elizabeth II **Obv:** Queen's head right **Rev:** Multicolor symbolic design **Edge:** Reeded

Date	Mintage	F	VF	XF	Unc	BU
2005 Proof	1,500	Value: 425				

KM# 866 10 DOLLARS
7.7508 g., 0.9990 Gold 0.2489 oz. AGW, 17.53 mm. **Ruler:** Elizabeth II **Subject:** 90th Anniversary Gallipoli Landings **Obv:** Head with tiara right **Rev:** Australian slouch hat on inverted rifle before memorial

Date	Mintage	F	VF	XF	Unc	BU
2005 Proof	1,000	Value: 750				

KM# 869 10 DOLLARS
7.7759 g., 0.9990 Gold 0.2497 oz. AGW, 17.53 mm. **Ruler:** Elizabeth II **Subject:** FIFA World Cup **Obv:** Head with tiara right **Rev:** Kangaroo and players on football

Date	Mintage	F	VF	XF	Unc	BU
2006P Proof	25,000	Value: 475				

KM# 867 10 DOLLARS
3.1103 g., 0.9990 Gold 0.0999 oz. AGW **Ruler:** Elizabeth II **Subject:** Ashes Cricket Series 1882-2007 **Obv:** Head with tiara right **Rev:** Urn and supporters **Edge:** Reeded

Date	Mintage	F	VF	XF	Unc	BU
2007 Proof	—	Value: 195				

KM# 1000 10 DOLLARS
3.1103 g., 0.9990 Gold 0.0999 oz. AGW, 17.53 mm. **Ruler:** Elizabeth II **Subject:** Year of the Pig **Obv:** Head with tiara right **Rev:** Mother kangaroo with joey **Edge:** Reeded

Date	Mintage	F	VF	XF	Unc	BU
2007 Proof	—	Value: 210				

KM# 1051 10 DOLLARS
3.1000 g., 0.9990 Gold 0.0996 oz. AGW, 17.5 mm. **Ruler:** Elizabeth II **Subject:** Scouting Centennial in Australia **Rev:** Shadow linear portrait of Baden-Powell

Date	Mintage	F	VF	XF	Unc	BU
2008 Proof	1,500	Value: 335				

KM# 1054 10 DOLLARS
3.1100 g., 0.9990 Gold 0.0999 oz. AGW, 17.53 mm. **Ruler:** Elizabeth II **Subject:** Rugby League

Date	Mintage	F	VF	XF	Unc	BU
2008 Proof	3,000	Value: 235				

KM# 1622 10 DOLLARS
31.1050 g., 0.9990 Silver partially gilt 0.9990 oz. ASW, 40 mm. **Ruler:** Elizabeth II **Subject:** President's Cup **Obv:** Head with tiara right **Rev:** Trophy, gilt

Date	Mintage	F	VF	XF	Unc	BU
2011 Proof	—	Value: 120				

KM# 1662 10 DOLLARS
3.1100 g., 0.9990 Gold 0.0999 oz. AGW, 17.53 mm. **Ruler:** Elizabeth II **Subject:** Year of the Rabbit **Rev:** Rabbit seated left within circle, floral around

Date	Mintage	F	VF	XF	Unc	BU
2011 Proof	—	Value: 200				

KM# 1660 10 DOLLARS
3.1100 g., 0.9990 Gold 0.0999 oz. AGW, 17.53 mm. **Ruler:** Elizabeth II **Subject:** Year of the Tiger **Rev:** Tiger head within circle, floral around

Date	Mintage	F	VF	XF	Unc	BU
2012 Proof	—	Value: 200				

KM# 1681 10 DOLLARS
3.1103 g., 0.9990 Gold 0.0999 oz. AGW, 17.53 mm. **Ruler:** Elizabeth II **Subject:** Year of the Dragon **Rev:** Dragon head within circle, floral around

Date	Mintage	F	VF	XF	Unc	BU
2012 Proof	—	Value: 200				

KM# 1492 15 DOLLARS
3.1100 g., 0.9990 Gold 0.0999 oz. AGW, 17.53 mm. **Ruler:** Elizabeth II **Obv:** Head with tiara right **Rev:** Saint Mary Mackillup in color

Date	Mintage	F	VF	XF	Unc	BU
2010 Proof	2,010	Value: 215				

KM# 595 20 DOLLARS
14.0300 g., Bi-Metallic .999 4.5287 Silver center in .9999 9.499 Gold ring, 32.1 mm. **Ruler:** Elizabeth II **Subject:** Gregorian Millennium **Obv:** Head with tiara right **Rev:** Chronograph watch face with observatory in center and three depictions of the earth's rotation **Edge:** Reeded

Date	Mintage	F	VF	XF	Unc	BU
2001 Prooflike	7,500	—	—	—	—	475

KM# 597 20 DOLLARS
19.6300 g., Bi-Metallic .9999 8.8645 Gold center in .9999 10.7618 Silver ring, 32.1 mm. **Ruler:** Elizabeth II **Subject:** Centenary of Federation **Obv:** Head with tiara right within star design **Rev:** National arms on a flowery background **Edge:** Reeded

Date	Mintage	F	VF	XF	Unc	BU
ND(2001) Prooflike	7,500	—	—	—	—	475

KM# 760 20 DOLLARS
Bi-Metallic Gold center in Silver ring **Ruler:** Elizabeth II **Rev:** Sir Donald Bradman portrait

Date	Mintage	F	VF	XF	Unc	BU
2001 Proof	—	Value: 500				

KM# 634 20 DOLLARS
18.3510 g., Bi-Metallic .999 Silver, 4.6655g, breast star shaped center in a .9999 Gold ,13.6855g outer ring, 32.1 mm. **Ruler:** Elizabeth II **Subject:** Queen's Golden Jubilee **Obv:** Queen's head right **Rev:** Queen before Buckingham Palace **Edge:** Reeded

Date	Mintage	F	VF	XF	Unc	BU
2002P Proof	7,500	Value: 675				

KM# 687 20 DOLLARS
13.4056 g., Bi-Metallic .999 Gold 8.3979g Center in a .999 Silver 5.0077g Ring, 32 mm. **Ruler:** Elizabeth II **Subject:** Golden Jubilee of Coronation **Obv:** Head with tiara right **Rev:** Four different coinage portraits of Queen Elizabeth II **Edge:** Reeded

Date	Mintage	F	VF	XF	Unc	BU
2003P Proof	7,500	Value: 625				

KM# 868 25 DOLLARS
7.9881 g., 0.9167 Gold 0.2354 oz. AGW **Ruler:** Elizabeth II **Subject:** 150th Anniversary First Australian Sovereign **Obv:** Head with tiara right

Date	Mintage	F	VF	XF	Unc	BU
2005 Proof	7,500	Value: 475				

KM# 1180 25 DOLLARS
7.7700 g., 0.9990 Gold 0.2496 oz. AGW, 20 mm. **Ruler:** Elizabeth II **Subject:** End of WWI, 90th Anniversary **Obv:** Head right **Rev:** Field cross, multicolor poppies **Rev. Legend:** Ian Rank-Broadley **Edge:** Reeded

Date	Mintage	F	VF	XF	Unc	BU
2008P Proof	1,918	Value: 675				

KM# 1397 25 DOLLARS
7.9880 g., 0.9167 Gold 0.2354 oz. AGW, 22.6 mm. **Ruler:** Elizabeth II **Subject:** Sovereign **Obv:** Head in tiara right **Rev:** National Arms with supporters and flora

Date	Mintage	F	VF	XF	Unc	BU
2009P Proof	2,500	Value: 825				
2010P Proof	—	Value: 825				
2011P Proof	—	Value: 825				
2012P Proof	—	Value: 825				

KM# 1110 25 DOLLARS
10.0000 g., 0.9999 Gold 0.3215 oz. AGW, 15.4x25.4 mm. **Ruler:** Elizabeth II **Rev:** Kangaroo dreaming **Shape:** Vertical rectangle

Date	Mintage	F	VF	XF	Unc	BU
2009 Proof	—	Value: 650				

KM# 1247 25 DOLLARS
7.7700 g., 0.9990 Gold 0.2496 oz. AGW, 21 mm. **Ruler:** Elizabeth II **Subject:** 2010 FIFA World Cup, South Africa **Obv:** Head right **Rev:** Soccer player and kangaroo

Date	Mintage	F	VF	XF	Unc	BU
2009P Proof	7,500	Value: 775				

KM# 1274 25 DOLLARS
10.0000 g., 0.9990 Gold 0.3212 oz. AGW, 15x25 mm. **Ruler:** Elizabeth II **Subject:** Mythological Chinese Character - Longivity **Obv:** Head right **Rev:** Man standing with staff **Shape:** Vertical rectangle

Date	Mintage	F	VF	XF	Unc	BU
2009P	—	—	—	—	—	825

KM# 1275 25 DOLLARS
10.0000 g., 0.9990 Gold 0.3212 oz. AGW, 15x25 mm. **Ruler:** Elizabeth II **Subject:** Mythological Chinese Character - Success **Obv:** Head right **Rev:** Man standing with deer **Shape:** Vertical rectangle

Date	Mintage	F	VF	XF	Unc	BU
2009P	—	—	—	—	—	800

KM# 1276 25 DOLLARS
10.0000 g., 0.9990 Gold 0.3212 oz. AGW, 15x25 mm. **Ruler:** Elizabeth II **Subject:** Mythological Chinese Character - Fortune **Obv:** Head right **Rev:** Man standing with scroll **Shape:** Vertical rectangle

Date	Mintage	F	VF	XF	Unc	BU
2009P	—	—	—	—	—	825

KM# 1623 25 DOLLARS
7.7700 g., 0.9990 Gold 0.2496 oz. AGW, 21 mm. **Ruler:** Elizabeth II **Subject:** President's Cup **Obv:** Head with tiara right **Rev:** Golfer taking swing

Date	Mintage	F	VF	XF	Unc	BU
2011 Proof	—	Value: 600				

KM# 1703 25 DOLLARS
7.7700 g., 0.9999 Gold 0.2498 oz. AGW, 20.6 mm. **Ruler:** Elizabeth II **Subject:** Elizabeth II, 60th Anniversary **Obv:** Head with tiara right **Rev:** Young bust right **Edge:** Reeded

Date	Mintage	F	VF	XF	Unc	BU
2012P Proof	Est. 1,000	Value: 550				

KM# 784 30 DOLLARS
1000.0000 g., 0.9990 Silver 32.117 oz. ASW **Ruler:** Elizabeth II **Subject:** Commonwealth Games **Obv:** Head with tiara right **Rev:** Two figures within circle of all the sports

Date	Mintage	F	VF	XF	Unc	BU
2006 Proof	500	Value: 1,250				

KM# 648 50 DOLLARS
36.5100 g., Tri-Metallic .9999 Gold 7.8g, 13.1 mm center in .999 Silver 13.39g, 26.85mm inner ring within a copper 15.32g, 3, 38.74 mm. **Ruler:** Elizabeth II **Subject:** Commonwealth Games **Obv:** Head with tiara right **Rev:** Victorious athletes within inscriptions and runners **Edge:** Reeded

Date	Mintage	F	VF	XF	Unc	BU
2002B Proof	5,000	Value: 600				

KM# 724 50 DOLLARS
36.5100 g., Tri-Metallic .999 Gold 7.8g center in .999 Silver 13.39g ring within .999 Copper 15.32g outer ring, 38.74 mm. **Ruler:** Elizabeth II **Subject:** Olympics - Sydney to Athens **Obv:** Head with tiara right, denomination below **Rev:** Crossed olive and wattle branches about Australian flag and Olympic ring logo **Edge:** Reeded

Date	Mintage	F	VF	XF	Unc	BU
2004B Proof	2,500	Value: 625				

KM# 785 50 DOLLARS
Tri-Metallic Gold center within Silver ring within Copper outer ring, 38.74 mm. **Ruler:** Elizabeth II **Subject:** Melbourne Commonwealth Games **Obv:** Head with tiara right, denomination below **Rev:** Two stylized athletes on central plug surrounded by Games legend and circle of athletes

Date	Mintage	F	VF	XF	Unc	BU
2006 Proof	5,000	Value: 550				

KM# 1696 60 DOLLARS
10.0000 g., 0.9990 Gold 0.3212 oz. AGW, 22.5 mm. **Ruler:** Elizabeth II **Subject:** Australian 2012 London Olympic Team **Obv:** Head with tiara right **Rev:** Athlete standing on platform with flag

Date	Mintage	F	VF	XF	Unc	BU
2012P Proof	2,012	Value: 675				

KM# 643 100 DOLLARS
10.3678 g., 0.9999 Gold 0.3333 oz. AGW, 25 mm. **Ruler:** Elizabeth II **Subject:** Golden Wattle Flower **Obv:** Queen's head right **Rev:** Flower and denomination **Edge:** Reeded

Date	Mintage	F	VF	XF	Unc	BU
2001B	3,000	—	—	—	600	625
2001B Proof	2,500	Value: 650				

KM# 635 100 DOLLARS
31.1035 g., 0.9999 Gold 0.9999 oz. AGW, 32.1 mm. **Ruler:** Elizabeth II **Subject:** Gold Panning **Obv:** Queen's head right **Rev:** Two prospectors dry panning for gold with color highlighted pans and dust **Edge:** Reeded

Date	Mintage	F	VF	XF	Unc	BU
2002P Proof	1,500	Value: 1,775				

KM# 636 100 DOLLARS
31.1035 g., 0.9995 Platinum 0.9995 oz. APW, 32.1 mm. **Ruler:** Elizabeth II **Subject:** Multiculturalism **Obv:** Head with tiara right **Rev:** Six racially diverse portraits against a blue background **Edge:** Reeded

Date	Mintage	F	VF	XF	Unc	BU
2002 Proof	1,000	Value: 1,850				

KM# 646 100 DOLLARS
31.4000 g., 0.9999 Gold 1.0094 oz. AGW, 34.1 mm. **Ruler:** Elizabeth II **Subject:** Queen's 50th Anniversary of Accession **Obv:** Queen's head right **Rev:** Silhouette of George VI, queen's portrait and denomination **Edge:** Reeded

Date	Mintage	F	VF	XF	Unc	BU
2002B Proof	2,002	Value: 1,775				

KM# 657 100 DOLLARS
10.3678 g., 0.9999 Gold 0.3333 oz. AGW, 25 mm. **Ruler:** Elizabeth II **Obv:** Queen's head right **Rev:** Sturt's Desert Rose **Edge:** Reeded

Date	Mintage	F	VF	XF	Unc	BU
2002B	3,000	—	—	—	600	625
2002B Proof	2,500	Value: 650				

KM# 800 100 DOLLARS
31.1036 g., 0.9990 Gold 0.9990 oz. AGW, 34 mm. **Ruler:** Elizabeth II **Subject:** 50th Anniversary of the Coronation of Elizabeth II **Obv:** Head with tiara right **Rev:** Young portrait of Queen Elizabeth facing left, royal cipher, crown **Edge:** Plain

Date	Mintage	F	VF	XF	Unc	BU
2003 Proof	660	Value: 1,800				

KM# 870 100 DOLLARS
10.3670 g., 0.9990 Gold 0.3330 oz. AGW, 25 mm. **Ruler:** Elizabeth II **Subject:** State Floral Emblems **Obv:** Head with tiara right **Rev:** Royal Blue Bell flowers **Edge:** Reeded

Date	Mintage	F	VF	XF	Unc	BU
2003 Proof	1,383	Value: 650				

KM# 797 100 DOLLARS
31.1070 g., 0.9990 Gold 0.9991 oz. AGW, 25.1 mm. **Ruler:** Elizabeth II **Subject:** 60th Anniversary of end of World War II **Obv:** Head with tiara right **Rev:** Latent news real photographic images of a dancing man celebrating the end of WWII

Date	Mintage	F	VF	XF	Unc	BU
2005P Proof	750	Value: 1,800				

KM# 1243 100 DOLLARS
31.1050 g., 0.9990 Gold 0.9990 oz. AGW, 36 mm. **Ruler:** Elizabeth II **Subject:** Treasures of Australia **Obv:** Head right **Rev:** Mountains **Note:** Insert container with 1 carat of diamonds.

Date	Mintage	F	VF	XF	Unc	BU
2009P Proof	1,000	Value: 2,150				

KM# 1436 100 DOLLARS
Gold **Ruler:** Elizabeth II

Date	Mintage	F	VF	XF	Unc	BU
2010 Proof	—	Value: 1,800				

KM# 1595 100 DOLLARS
31.1050 g., 0.9990 Gold 0.9990 oz. AGW, 36 mm. **Ruler:** Elizabeth II **Subject:** Treasures of Australia **Obv:** Head above pearl container **Rev:** Landscape above pearl container **Edge:** Reeded

Date	Mintage	F	VF	XF	Unc	BU
2011P Proof	Est. 1,000	Value: 2,250				

KM# 1596 100 DOLLARS
31.1050 g., 0.9990 Gold 0.9990 oz. AGW, 32 mm. **Ruler:** Elizabeth II **Subject:** Gold Coin Program, 25th Anniversary **Obv:** Head with tiara right **Rev:** Nugget

Date	Mintage	F	VF	XF	Unc	BU
2011P	Est. 1,500	Value: 1,850				

KM# 644 150 DOLLARS
15.5517 g., 0.9999 Gold 0.4999 oz. AGW, 30 mm. **Ruler:** Elizabeth II **Obv:** Queen's head right **Rev:** Golden Wattle flower, value **Edge:** Reeded

Date	Mintage	F	VF	XF	Unc	BU
2001B Proof	1,500	Value: 900				

KM# 658 150 DOLLARS
15.5517 g., 0.9999 Gold 0.4999 oz. AGW, 30 mm. **Ruler:** Elizabeth II **Subject:** State Floral Emblems **Obv:** Queen's head right **Rev:** Sturt's Desert Rose **Edge:** Reeded

Date	Mintage	F	VF	XF	Unc	BU
2002B Proof	1,500	Value: 900				

KM# 872 150 DOLLARS
15.5510 g., 0.9990 Gold 0.4995 oz. AGW, 30 mm. **Ruler:** Elizabeth II **Subject:** State Floral Emblems **Obv:** Head with tiara right **Rev:** Royal Blue Bell flowers **Edge:** Reeded

Date	Mintage	F	VF	XF	Unc	BU
2003	1,105	Value: 900				

KM# 874 150 DOLLARS
15.5510 g., 0.9990 Gold 0.4995 oz. AGW, 30 mm. **Ruler:** Elizabeth II **Subject:** Rare Australian Birds **Obv:** Head with tiara right **Rev:** Red-tailed black cockatoo **Edge:** Reeded

Date	Mintage	F	VF	XF	Unc	BU
2003 Proof	2,500	Value: 900				

KM# 731 150 DOLLARS
10.3678 g., 0.9990 Gold 0.3330 oz. AGW, 25 mm. **Ruler:** Elizabeth II **Obv:** Queen's head right **Rev:** Cassowary bird **Edge:** Reeded

Date	Mintage	F	VF	XF	Unc	BU
2004B Proof	2,500	Value: 625				

KM# 752 150 DOLLARS
10.3678 g., 0.9999 Gold 0.3333 oz. AGW, 25 mm. **Ruler:** Elizabeth II **Obv:** Queen's head right **Rev:** Malleefowl bird **Edge:** Reeded

Date	Mintage	F	VF	XF	Unc	BU
2005B Proof	2,500	Value: 625				

KM# 873 150 DOLLARS
10.3670 g., 0.9990 Gold 0.3330 oz. AGW, 25 mm. **Ruler:** Elizabeth II **Subject:** Rare Australian Birds **Obv:** Head with tiara right **Rev:** Red-tailed black cockatoo **Edge:** Reeded

Date	Mintage	F	VF	XF	Unc	BU
2006	2,500	Value: 625				

KM# 732 200 DOLLARS
15.5518 g., 0.9990 Gold 0.4995 oz. AGW, 30 mm. **Ruler:** Elizabeth II **Obv:** Queen's head right **Rev:** Cassowary bird **Edge:** Reeded

Date	Mintage	F	VF	XF	Unc	BU
2004B Proof	2,500	Value: 900				

KM# 753 200 DOLLARS
15.5518 g., 0.9999 Gold 0.4999 oz. AGW, 30 mm. **Ruler:** Elizabeth II **Obv:** Queen's head right **Rev:** Malleefowl bird **Edge:** Reeded

Date	Mintage	F	VF	XF	Unc	BU
2005B Proof	2,500	Value: 900				

KM# 1695 200 DOLLARS
62.2140 g., 0.9990 Gold 1.9981 oz. AGW **Ruler:** Elizabeth II **Subject:** Australian 2012 London Olympic Team

Date	Mintage	F	VF	XF	Unc	BU
2012	—	Value: 3,750				

KM# 1702 200 DOLLARS
62.2150 g., 0.9990 Gold 1.9982 oz. AGW, 41.1 mm. **Ruler:** Elizabeth II **Subject:** Elizabeth II, 60th Anniversary **Obv:** Head with tiara right **Rev:** Young head portrait right

Date	Mintage	F	VF	XF	Unc	BU
2012P Proof	60	Value: 4,500				

BULLION - KANGAROO

KM# 1797 50 CENTS
15.5000 g., 0.9990 Silver 0.4978 oz. ASW, 36.6 mm. **Ruler:** Elizabeth II **Rev:** Kangaroo in color

Date	Mintage	F	VF	XF	Unc	BU
2012P Proof	—	Value: 50.00				

KM# 590 DOLLAR
31.1035 g., 0.9990 Silver 0.9990 oz. ASW, 40 mm. **Ruler:** Elizabeth II **Obv:** Queen's portrait **Rev:** Aboriginal-kangaroo design with dots **Edge:** Reeded

Date	Mintage	F	VF	XF	Unc	BU
2001B Frosted Unc	—	—	—	—	—	35.00
2001B Proof	—	Value: 40.00				

KM# 642 DOLLAR
31.1035 g., 0.9990 Silver 0.9990 oz. ASW, 40 mm. **Ruler:** Elizabeth II **Obv:** Head with tiara right, denomination below **Rev:** Aboriginal-style kangaroo with wavy line background **Edge:** Reeded

Date	Mintage	F	VF	XF	Unc	BU
2002B	—	—	—	—	35.00	42.00
2002B Proof	—	Value: 50.00				

KM# 798 DOLLAR
31.1035 g., 0.9990 Silver 0.9990 oz. ASW, 40 mm. **Ruler:** Elizabeth II **Obv:** Head with tiara right **Rev:** Aboriginal-style kangaroo design **Edge:** Reeded

Date	Mintage	F	VF	XF	Unc	BU
2003	35,230	—	—	—	—	40.00
2003 Proof	20,400	Value: 45.00				

KM# 798a DOLLAR
31.1035 g., 0.9990 Silver partially gilt 0.9990 oz. ASW, 40 mm. **Ruler:** Elizabeth II **Obv:** Head with tiara right **Rev:** Aboriginal-style kangaroo design **Edge:** Reeded

Date	Mintage	F	VF	XF	Unc	BU
2003	7,450	—	—	—	—	125

KM# 723 DOLLAR
31.1035 g., 0.9990 Silver 0.9990 oz. ASW, 40 mm. **Ruler:** Elizabeth II **Obv:** Head with tiara right, denomination below **Rev:** Kangaroo with semi-circle background **Edge:** Reeded

Date	Mintage	F	VF	XF	Unc	BU
2004B Frosted Unc	—	—	—	—	—	37.00
2004B Proof	12,500	Value: 42.00				

KM# 723a DOLLAR
31.1035 g., 0.9990 Silver partially gilt 0.9990 oz. ASW, 40 mm. **Ruler:** Elizabeth II **Obv:** Head with tiara right, denomination below **Rev:** Kangaroo with semi-circle background **Edge:** Reeded

Date	Mintage	F	VF	XF	Unc	BU
2004B Frosted Unc	—	—	—	—	—	65.00

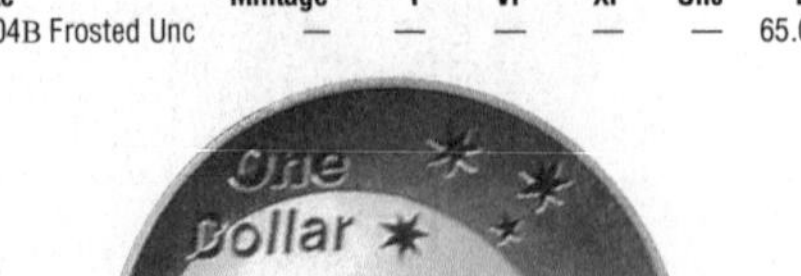

KM# 749 DOLLAR
31.6000 g., 0.9990 Silver 1.0149 oz. ASW, 40 mm. **Ruler:** Elizabeth II **Obv:** Head with tiara right **Rev:** Kangaroo bounding under Southern Cross and above Federation Star **Edge:** Reeded

Date	Mintage	F	VF	XF	Unc	BU
2005	—	—	—	—	35.00	45.00
2005 Proof	12,500	Value: 50.00				

KM# 749a DOLLAR
31.1035 g., 0.9990 Silver Partially Gold Plated 0.9990 oz. ASW, 40 mm. **Ruler:** Elizabeth II **Obv:** Head with tiara right **Rev:** Kangaroo bounding under Southern Cross and above Federation Star **Edge:** Reeded

Date	Mintage	F	VF	XF	Unc	BU
2005 Proof	12,500	Value: 60.00				

KM# 837 DOLLAR
31.6000 g., 0.9990 Silver 1.0149 oz. ASW, 40 mm. **Ruler:** Elizabeth II **Obv:** Head with tiara right **Rev:** Kangaroo bounding under Australian sun **Edge:** Reeded

Date	Mintage	F	VF	XF	Unc	BU
2006	—	—	—	—	—	35.00
2006 Proof	12,500	Value: 42.00				

KM# 837a DOLLAR
31.6000 g., 0.9990 Silver partially gilt 1.0149 oz. ASW, 40 mm. **Ruler:** Elizabeth II **Obv:** Head with tiara right **Rev:** Kangaroo bounding under Australian sun **Edge:** Reeded

Date	Mintage	F	VF	XF	Unc	BU
2006	7,500	—	—	—	—	55.00

KM# 851 DOLLAR
31.6000 g., 0.9990 Silver 1.0149 oz. ASW, 40 mm. **Ruler:** Elizabeth II **Obv:** Head with tiara right **Rev:** Kangaroo mother and joey **Edge:** Reeded

Date	Mintage	F	VF	XF	Unc	BU
2007	15,000	—	—	—	—	45.00
2007 Proof	12,500	Value: 50.00				

KM# 1061 DOLLAR
27.2200 g., Copper-Nickel, 38.74 mm. **Ruler:** Elizabeth II **Rev:** Kangaroo holding football

Date	Mintage	F	VF	XF	Unc	BU
2008	9,234	—	—	—	—	25.00

KM# 1061a DOLLAR
31.1050 g., 0.9990 Silver 0.9990 oz. ASW, 40 mm. **Ruler:** Elizabeth II **Rev:** Kangaroo holding football

Date	Mintage	F	VF	XF	Unc	BU
2008	7,500	—	—	—	—	65.00
2008 Proof	10,000	Value: 50.00				

KM# 1061b DOLLAR
31.1050 g., 0.9990 Silver 0.9990 oz. ASW, 40 mm. **Ruler:** Elizabeth II **Rev:** Kangaroo holding football in color

Date	Mintage	F	VF	XF	Unc	BU
2008 Proof	12,500	Value: 95.00				

KM# 1083 DOLLAR
31.1050 g., 0.9990 Silver 0.9990 oz. ASW, 40 mm. **Ruler:** Elizabeth II **Rev:** Kangaroo

Date	Mintage	F	VF	XF	Unc	BU
2009	20,000	—	—	—	—	50.00
2009 Proof	20,000	Value: 65.00				

KM# 1083a DOLLAR
31.1050 g., 0.9990 Silver Partially gilt 0.9990 oz. ASW, 40 mm. **Ruler:** Elizabeth II **Rev:** Kangaroo

Date	Mintage	F	VF	XF	Unc	BU
2009	—	—	—	—	—	90.00

KM# 1083b DOLLAR
31.1035 g., 0.9990 Silver 0.9990 oz. ASW, 40 mm. **Ruler:** Elizabeth II **Rev:** Kangaroo in color

Date	Mintage	F	VF	XF	Unc	BU
2009 Proof	—	Value: 75.00				

KM# 1457 DOLLAR
31.1050 g., 0.9990 Silver 0.9990 oz. ASW, 40 mm. **Ruler:** Elizabeth II **Rev:** Two kangaroos playing

Date	Mintage	F	VF	XF	Unc	BU
2010P Proof	—	Value: 42.00				

KM# 1514 DOLLAR
31.1050 g., 0.9990 Silver 0.9990 oz. ASW, 40. mm. **Ruler:** Elizabeth II **Rev:** Kangaroo in color

Date	Mintage	F	VF	XF	Unc	BU
2010 Proof	—	Value: 60.00				

KM# 1515 DOLLAR
31.1050 g., 0.9990 Silver 0.9990 oz. ASW, 40 mm. **Ruler:** Elizabeth II **Rev:** Kangaroo in color

Date	Mintage	F	VF	XF	Unc	BU
2010 Proof	—	Value: 60.00				

KM# 1516 DOLLAR
31.1050 g., 0.9990 Silver 0.9990 oz. ASW, 40 mm. **Ruler:** Elizabeth II **Rev:** Kangaroo in color

Date	Mintage	F	VF	XF	Unc	BU
2010 Proof	—	Value: 60.00				

KM# 1758 DOLLAR
31.1050 g., 0.9990 Silver 0.9990 oz. ASW, 40.6 mm. **Ruler:** Elizabeth II **Obv:** Head with tiara right **Rev:** Kangaroo right on rocks

Date	Mintage	F	VF	XF	Unc	BU
2010P	—	—	—	—	—	75.00
2010P Proof	—	Value: 85.00				

KM# 1605 DOLLAR
31.1050 g., 0.9990 Silver 0.9990 oz. ASW, 33 mm. **Ruler:** Elizabeth II **Obv:** Head with tiara right **Rev:** Kangaroo left, sun rays in background **Edge:** Reeded **Note:** Ultra High Relief

Date	Mintage	F	VF	XF	Unc	BU
2011P Proof	Est. 20,000	Value: 110				

KM# 1759 DOLLAR
31.1050 g., 0.9990 Silver 0.9990 oz. ASW, 40.6 mm. **Ruler:** Elizabeth II **Obv:** Head with tiara right **Rev:** Kangaroo and joey

Date	Mintage	F	VF	XF	Unc	BU
2011P	—	—	—	—	—	75.00
2011P Proof	—	Value: 85.00				

KM# 1737 DOLLAR
31.1350 g., 0.9990 Silver 1.0000 oz. ASW, 40 mm. **Ruler:** Elizabeth II **Obv:** Head with tiara right **Rev:** Mareeba Rock Wallaby

Date	Mintage	F	VF	XF	Unc	BU
2012	20,000	—	—	—	—	75.00
2012 Proof	20,000	Value: 100				

KM# 1830 DOLLAR
31.1050 g., 0.9990 Silver 0.9990 oz. ASW, 33 mm. **Ruler:** Elizabeth II **Rev:** Kangaroo **Note:** Ultra High Relief

Date	Mintage	F	VF	XF	Unc	BU
2012P Proof	—	Value: 110				

KM# 1390 2 DOLLARS
0.5000 g., 0.9990 Gold 0.0161 oz. AGW **Ruler:** Elizabeth II **Obv:** Head right **Rev:** Kangaroo

Date	Mintage	F	VF	XF	Unc	BU
2010(p)	—	—	—	—	32.00	35.00

KM# 1527 2 DOLLARS
0.5000 g., 0.9990 Gold 0.0161 oz. AGW, 11.6 mm. **Ruler:** Elizabeth II **Obv:** Head in tiara right **Rev:** Kangaroo bounding left

Date	Mintage	F	VF	XF	Unc	BU
2010P	—	—	—	—	—	50.00

KM# 1649 2 DOLLARS
0.5000 g., 0.9990 Gold 0.0161 oz. AGW, 11.6 mm. **Ruler:** Elizabeth II **Obv:** Head with tiara right **Rev:** Kangaroo left

Date	Mintage	F	VF	XF	Unc	BU
2011 Proof	—	Value: 50.00				

KM# 1790 2 DOLLARS
0.5000 g., 0.9990 Gold 0.0161 oz. AGW, 12 mm. **Ruler:** Elizabeth II **Obv:** Head in tiara right **Rev:** Kangaroo standing right, wind water pump at left

Date	Mintage	F	VF	XF	Unc	BU
2012P	—	—	—	—	—	50.00

KM# 893 5 DOLLARS
1.5710 g., 0.9990 Gold 0.0505 oz. AGW **Ruler:** Elizabeth II **Obv:** Head with tiara right **Rev:** Two kangaroos on map of Australia

Date	Mintage	F	VF	XF	Unc	BU
2001	10,000	—	—	—	—	115

KM# 1776 10 DOLLARS
3.1100 g., 0.9990 Gold 0.0999 oz. AGW, 17.53 mm. **Ruler:** Elizabeth II **Rev:** Kangaroo bounding left at sunset

Date	Mintage	F	VF	XF	Unc	BU
2007P	—	—	—	—	—	225

KM# 1772 10 DOLLARS
3.1100 g., 0.9990 Gold 0.0999 oz. AGW, 17.53 mm. **Ruler:** Elizabeth II **Rev:** Kangaroo bounding right in grassland

Date	Mintage	F	VF	XF	Unc	BU
2008P	—	—	—	—	—	225

KM# 1764 10 DOLLARS
3.1100 g., 0.9990 Gold 0.0999 oz. AGW, 17.53 mm. **Ruler:** Elizabeth II **Obv:** Head with tiara right **Rev:** Kangaroo left, constellation in background

Date	Mintage	F	VF	XF	Unc	BU
2009P	—	Value: 250				

KM# 1768 10 DOLLARS
3.1100 g., 0.9990 Gold 0.0999 oz. AGW, 17.53 mm. **Ruler:** Elizabeth II **Rev:** Kangaroo

Date	Mintage	F	VF	XF	Unc	BU
2010P	—	—	—	—	—	225

KM# 1763 10 DOLLARS
3.1100 g., 0.9990 Gold 0.0999 oz. AGW, 17.53 mm. **Ruler:** Elizabeth II **Obv:** Head with tiara right **Rev:** Kangaroo right on rocks

Date	Mintage	F	VF	XF	Unc	BU
2010P Proof	1,500	Value: 250				

KM# 1522 10 DOLLARS
3.1100 g., 0.9990 Gold 0.0999 oz. AGW, 17.53 mm. **Ruler:** Elizabeth II **Rev:** Two kangaroos

Date	Mintage	F	VF	XF	Unc	BU
2011 Proof	1,500	Value: 265				

KM# 1683 10 DOLLARS

3.1100 g., 0.9990 Gold 0.0999 oz. AGW, 17.53 mm. **Ruler:** Elizabeth II **Rev:** Kangaroo

Date	Mintage	F	VF	XF	Unc	BU
2012P Proof	—	Value: 200				

KM# 894 15 DOLLARS

3.1101 g., 0.9990 Gold 0.0999 oz. AGW **Ruler:** Elizabeth II **Obv:** Head with tiara right **Rev:** Two kangaroos on map of Australia

Date	Mintage	F	VF	XF	Unc	BU
2001	800	—	—	—	—	195

KM# 897 15 DOLLARS

3.1101 g., 0.9990 Gold 0.0999 oz. AGW **Ruler:** Elizabeth II **Obv:** Head with tiara right **Rev:** Kangaroo browsing

Date	Mintage	F	VF	XF	Unc	BU
2002	800	—	—	—	—	195

KM# 902 15 DOLLARS

3.1101 g., 0.9990 Gold 0.0999 oz. AGW **Ruler:** Elizabeth II **Obv:** Head with tiara right **Rev:** Two kangaroos hopping

Date	Mintage	F	VF	XF	Unc	BU
2003	500	—	—	—	—	195

KM# 907 15 DOLLARS

3.1101 g., 0.9990 Gold 0.0999 oz. AGW **Ruler:** Elizabeth II **Obv:** Head with tiara right **Rev:** Crouching kangaroos facing left, Grass tree plant at right

Date	Mintage	F	VF	XF	Unc	BU
2004	500	—	—	—	—	195

KM# 911 15 DOLLARS

3.1101 g., 0.9990 Gold 0.0999 oz. AGW **Ruler:** Elizabeth II **Obv:** Head with tiara right **Rev:** Kangaroo in bush

Date	Mintage	F	VF	XF	Unc	BU
2005	500	—	—	—	—	195

KM# 1362 15 DOLLARS

3.1100 g., 0.9990 Gold 0.0999 oz. AGW **Ruler:** Elizabeth II **Obv:** Head right **Rev:** Kangaroo

Date	Mintage	F	VF	XF	Unc	BU
2010(p)	—	—	—	—	—	195

KM# 895 25 DOLLARS

7.7508 g., 0.9990 Gold 0.2489 oz. AGW **Ruler:** Elizabeth II **Obv:** Head with tiara right **Rev:** Two kangaroos on map of Australia

Date	Mintage	F	VF	XF	Unc	BU
2001	500	—	—	—	—	465

KM# 898 25 DOLLARS

7.7508 g., 0.9990 Gold 0.2489 oz. AGW **Ruler:** Elizabeth II **Obv:** Head with tiara right **Rev:** Kangaroo browsing

Date	Mintage	F	VF	XF	Unc	BU
2002	500	—	—	—	—	465

KM# 903 25 DOLLARS

7.7508 g., 0.9990 Gold 0.2489 oz. AGW **Ruler:** Elizabeth II **Obv:** Head with tiara right **Rev:** Two kangaroos hopping

Date	Mintage	F	VF	XF	Unc	BU
2003	250	—	—	—	—	475

KM# 908 25 DOLLARS

7.7508 g., 0.9990 Gold 0.2489 oz. AGW **Ruler:** Elizabeth II **Obv:** Head with tiara right **Rev:** Crouching kangaroos facing left, Grass tree plant at right

Date	Mintage	F	VF	XF	Unc	BU
2004	250	—	—	—	—	475

KM# 912 25 DOLLARS

7.7508 g., 0.9990 Gold 0.2489 oz. AGW **Ruler:** Elizabeth II **Obv:** Head with tiara right **Rev:** Kangaroo in bush

Date	Mintage	F	VF	XF	Unc	BU
2005	250	—	—	—	—	475

KM# 1777 25 DOLLARS

7.7700 g., 0.9990 Gold 0.2496 oz. AGW **Ruler:** Elizabeth II **Rev:** Kangaroo bounding left at sunset

Date	Mintage	F	VF	XF	Unc	BU
2007P	—	—	—	—	—	475

KM# 1773 25 DOLLARS

7.7700 g., 0.9990 Gold 0.2496 oz. AGW **Ruler:** Elizabeth II **Rev:** Kangaroo bounding right in grassland

Date	Mintage	F	VF	XF	Unc	BU
2008P	—	—	—	—	—	475

KM# 1765 25 DOLLARS

7.7700 g., 0.9990 Gold 0.2496 oz. AGW, 22 mm. **Ruler:** Elizabeth II **Obv:** Head with tiara right **Rev:** Kangaroo left, constellation in background

Date	Mintage	F	VF	XF	Unc	BU
2009P	—	Value: 475				

KM# 1769 25 DOLLARS

7.7700 g., 0.9990 Gold 0.2496 oz. AGW **Ruler:** Elizabeth II **Rev:** Kangaroo

Date	Mintage	F	VF	XF	Unc	BU
2010P	—	—	—	—	—	475

KM# 1363 25 DOLLARS

7.7500 g., 0.9990 Gold 0.2489 oz. AGW **Ruler:** Elizabeth II **Rev:** Two kangaroos playing

Date	Mintage	F	VF	XF	Unc	BU
2010P	—	—	—	—	—	465

KM# 1506 25 DOLLARS

6.2200 g., 0.9990 Gold 0.1998 oz. AGW, 21.69 mm. **Ruler:** Elizabeth II **Obv:** Head with tiara right **Rev:** Kangaroo in outback, windmill at right

Date	Mintage	F	VF	XF	Unc	BU
2010 Proof	1,000	Value: 825				

KM# 1507 25 DOLLARS

6.2200 g., 0.9990 Gold 0.1998 oz. AGW, 21.69 mm. **Ruler:** Elizabeth II **Obv:** Head in tiara right **Rev:** Kangaroo in outback, windmill at center

Date	Mintage	F	VF	XF	Unc	BU
2010 Proof	1,000	Value: 825				

KM# 1508 25 DOLLARS

6.2200 g., 0.9990 Gold 0.1998 oz. AGW, 21.69 mm. **Ruler:** Elizabeth II **Obv:** Head in tiara right **Rev:** Kangaroo in outback, windmill at left

Date	Mintage	F	VF	XF	Unc	BU
2010 Proof	1,000	Value: 825				

KM# 1684 25 DOLLARS

7.7700 g., 0.9990 Gold 0.2496 oz. AGW **Ruler:** Elizabeth II **Rev:** Kangaroo

Date	Mintage	F	VF	XF	Unc	BU
2012P Proof	—	Value: 475				

KM# 899 50 DOLLARS

15.5017 g., 0.9990 Gold 0.4979 oz. AGW **Ruler:** Elizabeth II **Obv:** Head with tiara right **Rev:** Kangaroo browsing

Date	Mintage	F	VF	XF	Unc	BU
2002	650	—	—	—	900	—

KM# 904 50 DOLLARS

15.5017 g., 0.9990 Gold 0.4979 oz. AGW **Ruler:** Elizabeth II **Obv:** Head with tiara right **Rev:** Two kangaroos hopping

Date	Mintage	F	VF	XF	Unc	BU
2003	500	—	—	—	900	—

KM# 909 50 DOLLARS

15.5017 g., 0.9990 Gold 0.4979 oz. AGW **Ruler:** Elizabeth II **Obv:** Head with tiara right **Rev:** Crouching kangaroos facing left, Grass tree plant at right

Date	Mintage	F	VF	XF	Unc	BU
2004	500	—	—	—	900	—

Note: In sets only

KM# 913 50 DOLLARS

15.5017 g., 0.9990 Gold 0.4979 oz. AGW **Ruler:** Elizabeth II **Obv:** Head with tiara right **Rev:** Kangaroo in bush

Date	Mintage	F	VF	XF	Unc	BU
2005	500	—	—	—	900	—

KM# 1778 50 DOLLARS

15.5500 g., 0.9990 Gold 0.4994 oz. AGW **Ruler:** Elizabeth II **Rev:** Kangaroo bounding left in sunset

Date	Mintage	F	VF	XF	Unc	BU
2007P	—	—	—	—	—	950

KM# 1774 50 DOLLARS

15.5500 g., 0.9990 Gold 0.4994 oz. AGW **Ruler:** Elizabeth II **Rev:** Kangaroo bounding right in grassland

Date	Mintage	F	VF	XF	Unc	BU
2008P	—	—	—	—	—	950

KM# 1766 50 DOLLARS

15.5500 g., 0.9990 Gold 0.4994 oz. AGW, 25 mm. **Ruler:** Elizabeth II **Obv:** Head with tiara right **Rev:** Kangaroo left, constellation in background

Date	Mintage	F	VF	XF	Unc	BU
2009P Proof	—	Value: 950				

KM# 1364 50 DOLLARS

15.5600 g., 0.9990 Gold 0.4997 oz. AGW, 25 mm. **Ruler:** Elizabeth II **Obv:** Head right **Rev:** Two kangaroos playing

Date	Mintage	F	VF	XF	Unc	BU
2010(p)	—	—	—	—	—	900

KM# 1770 50 DOLLARS

15.5500 g., 0.9990 Gold 0.4994 oz. AGW, 25 mm. **Ruler:** Elizabeth II **Rev:** Kangaroo

Date	Mintage	F	VF	XF	Unc	BU
2010P	—	—	—	—	—	950

KM# 1685 50 DOLLARS

15.5500 g., 0.9990 Gold 0.4994 oz. AGW, 25 mm. **Ruler:** Elizabeth II **Rev:** Kangaroo

Date	Mintage	F	VF	XF	Unc	BU
2012P Proof	—	Value: 950				

KM# 1779 100 DOLLARS

31.1050 g., 0.9990 Gold 0.9990 oz. AGW, 32 mm. **Ruler:** Elizabeth II **Rev:** Kangaroo bounding left at sunset

Date	Mintage	F	VF	XF	Unc	BU
2007P	—	—	—	—	—	1,850

KM# 1775 100 DOLLARS

31.1050 g., 0.9990 Gold 0.9990 oz. AGW, 32 mm. **Ruler:** Elizabeth II **Rev:** Kangaroo bounding right in grassland

Date	Mintage	F	VF	XF	Unc	BU
2008P	—	—	—	—	—	1,850

KM# 1767 100 DOLLARS

31.1050 g., 0.9990 Gold 0.9990 oz. AGW, 32 mm. **Ruler:** Elizabeth II **Obv:** Head with tiara right **Rev:** Kangaroo left, constellation in background

Date	Mintage	F	VF	XF	Unc	BU
2009P Proof	—	Value: 1,850				

KM# 1365 100 DOLLARS

31.1035 g., 0.9990 Gold 0.9990 oz. AGW, 32 mm. **Ruler:** Elizabeth II **Obv:** Head right **Rev:** Kangaroo

Date	Mintage	F	VF	XF	Unc	BU
2010(p)	—	—	—	—	—	1,850

KM# 1771 100 DOLLARS
31.1050 g., 0.9990 Gold 0.9990 oz. AGW, 32 mm. **Ruler:** Elizabeth II **Rev:** Kangaroo

Date	Mintage	F	VF	XF	Unc	BU
2010P	—	—	—	—	—	1,850

KM# 1686 100 DOLLARS
31.1050 g., 0.9990 Gold 0.9990 oz. AGW, 32 mm. **Ruler:** Elizabeth II **Rev:** Kangaroo

Date	Mintage	F	VF	XF	Unc	BU
2012P Proof	—	Value: 1,850				

KM# 896 200 DOLLARS
62.2140 g., 0.9990 Gold 1.9981 oz. AGW **Ruler:** Elizabeth II **Obv:** Head with tiara right **Rev:** Two kangaroos on map of Australia

Date	Mintage	F	VF	XF	Unc	BU
2001	300	—	—	—	3,500	—

KM# 901 200 DOLLARS
62.2140 g., 0.9990 Gold 1.9981 oz. AGW **Ruler:** Elizabeth II **Obv:** Head with tiara right **Rev:** Kangaroo browsing

Date	Mintage	F	VF	XF	Unc	BU
2002	300	—	—	—	3,500	—

KM# 905 200 DOLLARS
62.2140 g., 0.9990 Gold 1.9981 oz. AGW **Ruler:** Elizabeth II **Obv:** Head with tiara right **Rev:** Two kangaroos hopping

Date	Mintage	F	VF	XF	Unc	BU
2003	200	—	—	—	3,500	—

KM# 910 200 DOLLARS
62.2140 g., 0.9990 Gold 1.9981 oz. AGW **Ruler:** Elizabeth II **Obv:** Head with tiara right **Rev:** Crouching kangaroos facing left, Grass tree plant at right

Date	Mintage	F	VF	XF	Unc	BU
2004	200	—	—	—	3,500	—

KM# 1462 300 DOLLARS
1000.0000 g., 0.9990 Gold 32.117 oz. AGW **Ruler:** Elizabeth II **Obv:** Head with tiara right **Rev:** Two kangaroos playing

Date	Mintage	F	VF	XF	Unc	BU
2010P	—	—	—	—	—	55,500

KM# 1687 3000 DOLLARS
1000.0000 g., 0.9990 Gold 32.117 oz. AGW **Ruler:** Elizabeth II **Rev:** Kangaroo

Date	Mintage	F	VF	XF	Unc	BU
2012P Proof	—	BV+2%				

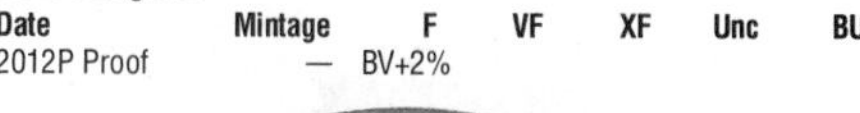

KM# 1569 1000000 DOLLARS
1000000.0000 g., 0.9999 Gold 32146. oz. AGW, 800 mm. **Ruler:** Elizabeth II **Obv:** Head with tiara right **Rev:** Red Kangaroo bounding left **Note:** Cast. 120mm thick. Illustration reduced.

Date	Mintage	F	VF	XF	Unc	BU
2012P	1	—	—	—	—	55,500,000

BULLION - KOOKABURRA

KM# 875 50 CENTS
15.5500 g., 0.9990 Silver 0.4994 oz. ASW, 38.74 mm. **Ruler:** Elizabeth II **Obv:** Head with tiara right **Rev:** Kookaburra on branch, tail above, two leaves **Edge:** Reeded **Shape:** Square **Note:** Lenticular technology makes kookaburra appear to move.

Date	Mintage	F	VF	XF	Unc	BU
2002P Proof	75,350	Value: 35.00				

KM# 684 50 CENTS
15.5500 g., 0.9990 Silver 0.4994 oz. ASW, 32.1x32.1 mm. **Ruler:** Elizabeth II **Obv:** Head with tiara right, denomination below **Rev:** Two kookaburras, one in flight **Edge:** Reeded **Shape:** Square

Date	Mintage	F	VF	XF	Unc	BU
2003P Proof	75,350	Value: 32.00				

KM# 876 50 CENTS
15.5500 g., 0.9990 Silver 0.4994 oz. ASW, 38.74 mm. **Ruler:** Elizabeth II **Obv:** Head with tiara right **Rev:** Kookaburra perched on branch, tail below, four leaves **Edge:** Reeded **Shape:** Square with rounded corners

Date	Mintage	F	VF	XF	Unc	BU
2004P Proof	30,350	Value: 32.00				

KM# 877 50 CENTS
15.5500 g., 0.9990 Silver 0.4994 oz. ASW, 25x25 mm. **Ruler:** Elizabeth II **Obv:** Head with tiara right **Rev:** Two kookaburras on branch, one laughing **Edge:** Reeded **Shape:** Square

Date	Mintage	F	VF	XF	Unc	BU
2005P Proof	30,350	Value: 32.00				

KM# 1799 50 CENTS
15.5000 g., 0.9990 Silver 0.4978 oz. ASW, 36.6 mm. **Ruler:** Elizabeth II **Rev:** Kookaburra in color

Date	Mintage	F	VF	XF	Unc	BU
2012P Proof	—	Value: 50.00				

KM# 691.1 DOLLAR
31.1035 g., 0.9990 Silver 0.9990 oz. ASW, 40 mm. **Ruler:** Elizabeth II **Obv:** Head with tiara right, denomination below **Rev:** Kookaburra flying over map of Australia **Edge:** Reeded

Date	Mintage	F	VF	XF	Unc	BU
2001P Proof	5,000	Value: 42.00				
2002P	—	—	—	—	35.00	37.00

KM# 479 DOLLAR
31.9700 g., 0.9990 Silver 1.0268 oz. ASW **Ruler:** Elizabeth II **Obv:** Head with tiara right, denomination below **Rev:** Two kookaburras back-to-back on branch

Date	Mintage	F	VF	XF	Unc	BU
2001	—	—	—	—	35.00	—
2001	10,000	—	—	—	45.00	—
Note: Federation star privy mark						
2001	50,000	—	—	—	35.00	—
Note: Santa Claus privy mark						
2001	1,000	—	—	—	125	—
Note: Love token personal message						
2001	75,000	—	—	—	42.00	—
Note: New York State Quarter privy mark						
2001	75,000	—	—	—	42.00	—
Note: North Carolina State Quarter privy mark						
2001	75,000	—	—	—	42.00	—
Note: Rhode Island State Quarter privy mark						
2001	75,000	—	—	—	42.00	—
Note: Vermont State Quarter privy mark						
2001	75,000	—	—	—	42.00	—
Note: Kentucky State Quarter privy mark						

KM# 625 DOLLAR
31.1035 g., 0.9990 Silver 0.9990 oz. ASW, 40.4 mm. **Ruler:** Elizabeth II **Subject:** U.S. State Quarter

Date	Mintage	F	VF	XF	Unc	BU
2002	75,000	—	—	—	45.00	—
Note: Tennessee State Quarter privy mark						
2002	75,000	—	—	—	45.00	—
Note: Ohio State Quarter privy mark						
2002	75,000	—	—	—	45.00	—
Note: Louisiana State Quarter privy mark						
2002	75,000	—	—	—	45.00	—
Note: Indiana State Quarter privy mark						
2002	75,000	—	—	—	45.00	—
Note: Mississippi State Quarter privy mark						

KM# 666 DOLLAR
31.6200 g., 0.9990 Silver 1.0155 oz. ASW, 40.3 mm. **Ruler:** Elizabeth II **Obv:** Head with tiara right, denomination below **Rev:** Kookaburra perched on branch **Edge:** Reeded

Date	Mintage	F	VF	XF	Unc	BU
2002	5,000	Value: 37.00				

KM# 691.2 DOLLAR
31.6200 g., 0.9990 Silver 1.0155 oz. ASW, 40.5 mm. **Ruler:** Elizabeth II **Obv:** Head with tiara right, denomination below **Rev:** Multicolor US flag above a kookaburra in flight over Australian map **Edge:** Reeded

Date	Mintage	F	VF	XF	Unc	BU
2002	18,500	—	—	—	35.00	40.00

KM# 683 DOLLAR

31.1035 g., 0.9990 Silver 0.9990 oz. ASW, 40 mm. **Ruler:** Elizabeth II **Obv:** Head with tiara right, denomination below **Rev:** Two kookaburras, one in flight **Edge:** Reeded **Note:** Gilded.

Date	Mintage	F	VF	XF	Unc	BU
2003P Proof	5,000	Value: 37.00				
2004	10,000	—	—	—	—	35.00
2004 Proof	15,000	Value: 45.00				

KM# 1761 DOLLAR

31.1050 g., 0.9990 Silver 0.9990 oz. ASW, 40.6 mm. **Ruler:** Elizabeth II **Obv:** Head with tiara right **Rev:** Kookaburra right on branch

Date	Mintage	F	VF	XF	Unc	BU
2003P	—	—	—	—	—	75.00

KM# 883 DOLLAR

31.1050 g., 0.9990 Silver 0.9990 oz. ASW, 40.5 mm. **Ruler:** Elizabeth II **Obv:** Head with tiara right **Rev:** Kookaburra perched on branch with four leaves **Edge:** Reeded

Date	Mintage	F	VF	XF	Unc	BU
2004P Proof	5,000	Value: 35.00				
2005	5,000	—	—	—	45.00	—
Note: Gemini privy mark						
2005	5,000	—	—	—	45.00	—
Note: Aquarius privy mark						
2005	5,000	—	—	—	45.00	—
Note: Pisces privy mark						
2005	5,000	—	—	—	45.00	—
Note: Aries privy mark						
2005	5,000	—	—	—	45.00	—
Note: Taurus privy mark						
2005	5,000	—	—	—	45.00	—
Note: Cancer privy mark						
2005	5,000	—	—	—	45.00	—
Note: Leo privy mark						
2005	5,000	—	—	—	45.00	—
Note: Virgo privy mark						
2005	5,000	—	—	—	45.00	—
Note: Libra privy mark						
2005	5,000	—	—	—	45.00	—
Note: Scorpio privy mark						
2005	5,000	—	—	—	45.00	—
Note: Sagittarius privy mark						
2005	5,000	—	—	—	45.00	—
Note: Capricorn privy mark						

KM# 883a DOLLAR

31.1035 g., 0.9990 Silver 0.9990 oz. ASW, 40 mm. **Ruler:** Elizabeth II **Obv:** Head with tiara right **Rev:** Kookaburra perched on branch with four leaves **Note:** Gilded.

Date	Mintage	F	VF	XF	Unc	BU
2004	10,000	—	—	—	55.00	—

KM# 720 DOLLAR

1.0350 g., 0.9990 Silver partially gilt 0.0332 oz. ASW, 40 mm. **Ruler:** Elizabeth II **Obv:** Head with tiara right, denomination below **Rev:** Kookabarra, partially gilt **Edge:** Reeded

Date	Mintage	F	VF	XF	Unc	BU
2005 Proof	—	Value: 65.00				

KM# 886 DOLLAR

31.5600 g., 0.9990 Silver 1.0136 oz. ASW, 40.5 mm. **Ruler:** Elizabeth II **Obv:** Head with tiara right **Rev:** Two kookaburras on branch, one laughing **Edge:** Reeded

Date	Mintage	F	VF	XF	Unc	BU
2005P Proof	5,000	Value: 40.00				

KM# 889 DOLLAR

31.5600 g., 0.9990 Silver 1.0136 oz. ASW, 40.5 mm. **Ruler:** Elizabeth II **Obv:** Head with tiara right **Rev:** Kookaburra on branch, no leaves

Date	Mintage	F	VF	XF	Unc	BU
2007	300,000	—	—	—	35.00	38.00

KM# 1760 DOLLAR

31.1050 g., 0.9990 Silver 0.9990 oz. ASW, 40.6 mm. **Ruler:** Elizabeth II **Obv:** Head with tiara right **Rev:** Kookaburra on branch look at spider web at lower left

Date	Mintage	F	VF	XF	Unc	BU
2008P	—	—	—	—	—	75.00

KM# 1277 DOLLAR

31.1050 g., 0.9990 Silver 0.9990 oz. ASW, 40 mm. **Ruler:** Elizabeth II **Subject:** Kookaburra 20th Anniversary **Obv:** Head right **Rev:** Kookaburra standing right

Date	Mintage	F	VF	XF	Unc	BU
2009 P20 Proof	10,000	Value: 47.00				

KM# 1278 DOLLAR

31.1050 g., 0.9990 Silver 0.9990 oz. ASW, 40 mm. **Ruler:** Elizabeth II **Subject:** Kookaburra 20th Anniversary **Obv:** Head right **Rev:** Kookaburra on branch, head right

Date	Mintage	F	VF	XF	Unc	BU
2009 P20 Proof	10,000	Value: 47.00				

KM# 1279 DOLLAR

31.1050 g., 0.9990 Silver 0.9990 oz. ASW, 40 mm. **Ruler:** Elizabeth II **Subject:** Kookaburra 20th Anniversary **Obv:** Head right **Rev:** Kookaburra on branch left, head upwards

Date	Mintage	F	VF	XF	Unc	BU
2009 P20 Proof	10,000	Value: 47.00				

KM# 1280 DOLLAR

31.1050 g., 0.9990 Silver 0.9990 oz. ASW, 40 mm. **Ruler:** Elizabeth II **Subject:** Kookaburra 20th Anniversary **Obv:** Head right **Rev:** Kookaburra feeding young in nest at right

Date	Mintage	F	VF	XF	Unc	BU
2009 P20 Proof	10,000	Value: 47.00				

KM# 1281 DOLLAR

31.1050 g., 0.9990 Silver 0.9990 oz. ASW, 40 mm. **Ruler:** Elizabeth II **Subject:** Kookaburra 20th Anniversary **Obv:** Head right **Rev:** Kookaburra pair on branch

Date	Mintage	F	VF	XF	Unc	BU
2009 P20 Proof	10,000	Value: 47.00				

KM# 1282 DOLLAR

31.1050 g., 0.9990 Silver 0.9990 oz. ASW, 40 mm. **Ruler:** Elizabeth II **Obv:** Head right **Rev:** Kookaburra on branch, head left

Date	Mintage	F	VF	XF	Unc	BU
2009 P20 Proof	10,000	Value: 47.00				

KM# 1283 DOLLAR

31.1050 g., 0.9990 Silver 0.9990 oz. ASW, 40 mm. **Ruler:** Elizabeth II **Subject:** Kookaburra 20th Anniversary **Obv:** Head right **Rev:** Kookaburra in flight right

Date	Mintage	F	VF	XF	Unc	BU
2009 P20 Proof	10,000	Value: 47.00				

KM# 1284 DOLLAR

31.1050 g., 0.9990 Silver 0.9990 oz. ASW, 40 mm. **Ruler:** Elizabeth II **Subject:** Kookaburra 20th Anniversary **Obv:** Head right **Rev:** Kookaburra by nest at left

Date	Mintage	F	VF	XF	Unc	BU
2009 P20 Proof	10,000	Value: 47.00				

KM# 1285 DOLLAR

31.1050 g., 0.9990 Silver 0.9990 oz. ASW, 40 mm. **Ruler:** Elizabeth II **Subject:** Kookaburra 20th Anniversary **Obv:** Head right **Rev:** Kookaburra on fence post

Date	Mintage	F	VF	XF	Unc	BU
2009 P20 Proof	10,000	Value: 47.00				

KM# 1286 DOLLAR

31.1050 g., 0.9990 Silver 0.9990 oz. ASW, 40 mm. **Ruler:** Elizabeth II **Subject:** Kookaburra 20th Anniversary **Obv:** Head right **Rev:** Kookaburra pair on branch left

Date	Mintage	F	VF	XF	Unc	BU
2009 P20 Proof	10,000	Value: 47.00				

KM# 1287 DOLLAR

31.1050 g., 0.9990 Silver 0.9990 oz. ASW, 40 mm. **Ruler:** Elizabeth II **Subject:** Kookaburra 20th Anniversary **Obv:** Head right **Rev:** Kookaburra on leafy branch left

Date	Mintage	F	VF	XF	Unc	BU
2009 P20 Proof	10,000	Value: 47.00				

KM# 1288 DOLLAR

31.1050 g., 0.9990 Silver 0.9990 oz. ASW, 40 mm. **Ruler:** Elizabeth II **Subject:** Kookaburra 20th Anniversary **Obv:** Head right **Rev:** Kookaburra pair on branch, beaks upward

Date	Mintage	F	VF	XF	Unc	BU
2009 P20 Proof	10,000	Value: 47.00				

KM# 1289 DOLLAR

31.1050 g., 0.9990 Silver 0.9990 oz. ASW, 40 mm. **Ruler:** Elizabeth II **Subject:** Kookaburra 20th Anniversary **Obv:** Head right **Rev:** Kookaburra in flight on map of Australia

Date	Mintage	F	VF	XF	Unc	BU
2009 P20 Proof	10,000	Value: 47.00				

KM# 1290 DOLLAR

31.1050 g., 0.9990 Silver 0.9990 oz. ASW, 40 mm. **Ruler:** Elizabeth II **Subject:** Kookaburra 20th Anniversary **Obv:** Head right **Rev:** Kookaburra on branch right

Date	Mintage	F	VF	XF	Unc	BU
2009 P20 Proof	10,000	Value: 47.00				

KM# 1291 DOLLAR

31.1050 g., 0.9990 Silver 0.9990 oz. ASW, 40 mm. **Ruler:** Elizabeth II **Subject:** Kookaburra 20th Anniversary **Obv:** Head right **Rev:** Two kookaburras, one in flight, one on branch

Date	Mintage	F	VF	XF	Unc	BU
2009 P20 Proof	10,000	Value: 47.00				

KM# 1292 DOLLAR

31.1050 g., 0.9990 Silver 0.9990 oz. ASW, 40 mm. **Ruler:** Elizabeth II **Subject:** Kookaburra 20th Anniversary **Obv:** Head right **Rev:** Kookaburra on branch, head right

Date	Mintage	F	VF	XF	Unc	BU
2009 P20 Proof	10,000	Value: 47.00				

KM# 1293 DOLLAR
31.1050 g., 0.9990 Silver 0.9990 oz. ASW, 40 mm. **Ruler:** Elizabeth II **Subject:** Kookaburra 20th Anniversary **Obv:** Head right **Rev:** Kookaburra pair on branch left

Date	Mintage	F	VF	XF	Unc	BU
2009 P20 Proof	10,000	Value: 47.00				

KM# 1294 DOLLAR
31.1050 g., 0.9990 Silver 0.9990 oz. ASW, 40 mm. **Ruler:** Elizabeth II **Subject:** Kookaburra 20th Anniversary **Obv:** Head right **Rev:** Kookaburra on branch left

Date	Mintage	F	VF	XF	Unc	BU
2009 P20 Proof	10,000	Value: 47.00				

KM# 1295 DOLLAR
31.1050 g., 0.9990 Silver 0.9990 oz. ASW, 40 mm. **Ruler:** Elizabeth II **Subject:** Kookaburra 20th Anniversary **Obv:** Head right **Rev:** Kookaburra admiring spider web

Date	Mintage	F	VF	XF	Unc	BU
2009 P20 Proof	10,000	Value: 47.00				

KM# 1296 DOLLAR
31.1050 g., 0.9990 Silver 0.9990 oz. ASW, 40 mm. **Ruler:** Elizabeth II **Subject:** Kookaburra 20th Anniversary **Obv:** Head right **Rev:** Kookaburra on branch, sunburst in background

Date	Mintage	F	VF	XF	Unc	BU
2009 P20 Proof	10,000	Value: 47.00				

KM# 1471 DOLLAR
31.1050 g., 0.9990 Silver 0.9990 oz. ASW, 40 mm. **Ruler:** Elizabeth II **Rev:** Kookabburra on branch

Date	Mintage	F	VF	XF	Unc	BU
2010P	—	—	—	—	—	45.00

KM# 1692 DOLLAR
31.1050 g., 0.9990 Silver 0.9990 oz. ASW, 40.5 mm. **Ruler:** Elizabeth II **Rev:** Kookaburra

Date	Mintage	F	VF	XF	Unc	BU
2012P	—	—	—	—	—	45.00

KM# 1829 DOLLAR
31.1050 g., 0.9990 Silver 0.9990 oz. ASW, 33 mm. **Ruler:** Elizabeth II **Rev:** Kookaburra **Note:** Ultra High Relief

Date	Mintage	F	VF	XF	Unc	BU
2012P Proof	—	Value: 110				

KM# 678 2 DOLLARS
62.2070 g., 0.9990 Silver 1.9979 oz. ASW, 40 mm. **Ruler:** Elizabeth II **Obv:** Head with tiara right, denomination below **Rev:** Kookaburra flying over Australian map **Edge:** Reeded

Date	Mintage	F	VF	XF	Unc	BU
2001P Proof	5,000	Value: 90.00				
2002	1,500	—	—	—	82.00	—
Note: 1661 Spanish cob privy mark						
2002	1,500	—	—	—	82.00	—
Note: 1771 Spanish pillar dollar privy mark						
2002	1,500	—	—	—	82.00	—
Note: 1881 Gold sovereign privy mark						
2002	1,500	—	—	—	82.00	—
Note: 1991 Gold Australian nugget privy mark						

KM# 623.1 2 DOLLARS
62.8500 g., 0.9990 Silver 2.0186 oz. ASW, 50 mm. **Ruler:** Elizabeth II **Obv:** Head with tiara right, denomination below **Rev:** Two kookaburras back to back **Edge:** Reeded

Date	Mintage	F	VF	XF	Unc	BU
2001	—	—	—	—	80.00	85.00

KM# 623.2 2 DOLLARS
62.2070 g., 0.9990 Silver 1.9979 oz. ASW **Ruler:** Elizabeth II **Subject:** USA State Quarters - 2001 **Obv:** Head with tiara right, denomination below **Rev:** Two kookaburras on branch with five U.S. State Quarter designs added **Edge:** Segmented reeding **Note:** Prev. KM#623

Date	Mintage	F	VF	XF	Unc	BU
2001	10,000	—	—	—	145	160

KM# 879 2 DOLLARS
62.8500 g., 0.9990 Silver 2.0186 oz. ASW, 40 mm. **Ruler:** Elizabeth II **Obv:** Head with tiara right **Rev:** Kookaburra on branch plus two leaves **Edge:** Reeded

Date	Mintage	F	VF	XF	Unc	BU
2002P Proof	5,000	Value: 90.00				
2003	1,000	—	—	—	115	—
Note: Boer War privy mark						
2003	1,000	—	—	—	115	—
Note: World War I privy mark						
2003	1,000	—	—	—	115	—
Note: World War II privy mark						
2003	1,000	—	—	—	115	—
Note: Korean War privy mark						
2003	1,000	—	—	—	115	—
Note: Vietnam War privy mark						

KM# 881 2 DOLLARS
62.2070 g., 0.9990 Silver 1.9979 oz. ASW, 50 mm. **Ruler:** Elizabeth II **Obv:** Head with tiara right **Rev:** Two kookaburras, one in flight **Edge:** Reeded

Date	Mintage	F	VF	XF	Unc	BU
2003P Proof	800	Value: 90.00				

KM# 884 2 DOLLARS
62.2070 g., 0.9990 Silver 1.9979 oz. ASW, 50 mm. **Ruler:** Elizabeth II **Obv:** Head with tiara right **Rev:** Kookaburra perched on branch with four leaves **Edge:** Reeded

Date	Mintage	F	VF	XF	Unc	BU
2004P Proof	800	Value: 90.00				

KM# 887 2 DOLLARS
62.2070 g., 0.9990 Silver 1.9979 oz. ASW, 50 mm. **Ruler:** Elizabeth II **Obv:** Head with tiara right **Rev:** Two kookaburras on branch, one laughing **Edge:** Reeded

Date	Mintage	F	VF	XF	Unc	BU
2005P Proof	800	Value: 90.00				

KM# 890 2 DOLLARS
62.2070 g., 0.9990 Silver 1.9979 oz. ASW, 50 mm. **Ruler:** Elizabeth II **Obv:** Head with tiara right **Rev:** Kookaburra on branch, no leaves

Date	Mintage	F	VF	XF	Unc	BU
2007	—	—	—	—	85.00	—

KM# 1297 5 DOLLARS
1.5500 g., 0.9990 Gold 0.0498 oz. AGW, 14 mm. **Ruler:** Elizabeth II **Subject:** Kookaburra 20th Anniversary **Obv:** Head right **Rev:** Kookaburra standing on stump right

Date	Mintage	F	VF	XF	Unc	BU
2009 P20 Proof	2,009	Value: 125				

KM# 1298 5 DOLLARS
1.5500 g., 0.9990 Gold 0.0498 oz. AGW, 14 mm. **Ruler:** Elizabeth II **Subject:** Kookaburra 20th Anniversary **Obv:** Head right **Rev:** Kookaburra on branch, head right

Date	Mintage	F	VF	XF	Unc	BU
2009 P20 Proof	2,009	Value: 125				

KM# 1299 5 DOLLARS
1.5500 g., 0.9990 Gold 0.0498 oz. AGW, 14 mm. **Ruler:** Elizabeth II **Subject:** Kookaburra 20th Anniversary **Obv:** Head right **Rev:** Kookaburra on branch left

Date	Mintage	F	VF	XF	Unc	BU
2009 P20 Proof	2,009	Value: 125				

KM# 1300 5 DOLLARS
1.5500 g., 0.9990 Gold 0.0498 oz. AGW, 14 mm. **Ruler:** Elizabeth II **Subject:** Kookaburra 20th Anniversary **Obv:** Head right **Rev:** Kookaburra on branch feeding young at right

Date	Mintage	F	VF	XF	Unc	BU
2009 P20 Proof	2,009	Value: 125				

KM# 1301 5 DOLLARS
1.5500 g., 0.9990 Gold 0.0498 oz. AGW, 14 mm. **Ruler:** Elizabeth II **Subject:** Kookaburra 20th Anniversary **Obv:** Head right **Rev:** Kookaburra pair on branch, heads opposite

Date	Mintage	F	VF	XF	Unc	BU
2009 P20 Proof	2,009	Value: 125				

KM# 1302 5 DOLLARS
1.5500 g., 0.9990 Gold 0.0498 oz. AGW, 14 mm. **Ruler:** Elizabeth II **Subject:** Kookaburra 20th Anniversary **Obv:** Head right **Rev:** Kookaburra on branch, head left

Date	Mintage	F	VF	XF	Unc	BU
2009 P20 Proof	2,009	Value: 125				

KM# 1303 5 DOLLARS
1.5500 g., 0.9990 Gold 0.0498 oz. AGW, 14 mm. **Ruler:** Elizabeth II **Subject:** Kookaburra 20th Anniversary **Obv:** Head right **Rev:** Kookaburra in flight right

Date	Mintage	F	VF	XF	Unc	BU
2009 P20 Proof	2,009	Value: 125				

KM# 1304 5 DOLLARS
1.5500 g., 0.9990 Gold 0.0498 oz. AGW, 14 mm. **Ruler:** Elizabeth II **Subject:** Kookaburra 20th Anniversary **Obv:** Head right **Rev:** Kookaburra at nest left, head right

Date	Mintage	F	VF	XF	Unc	BU
2009 P20 Proof	2,009	Value: 125				

KM# 1305 5 DOLLARS
1.5500 g., 0.9990 Gold 0.0498 oz. AGW, 14 mm. **Ruler:** Elizabeth II **Subject:** Kookaburra 20th Anniversary **Obv:** Head right **Rev:** Kookaburra on fence post

Date	Mintage	F	VF	XF	Unc	BU
2009 P20 Proof	2,009	Value: 125				

KM# 1306 5 DOLLARS
1.5500 g., 0.9990 Gold 0.0498 oz. AGW, 14 mm. **Ruler:** Elizabeth II **Subject:** Kookaburra 20th Anniversary **Obv:** Head right **Rev:** Kookaburra pair left

Date	Mintage	F	VF	XF	Unc	BU
2009 P20 Proof	2,009	Value: 125				

KM# 1307 5 DOLLARS
1.5500 g., 0.9990 Gold 0.0498 oz. AGW, 14 mm. **Ruler:** Elizabeth II **Subject:** Kookaburra 20th Anniversary **Obv:** Head right **Rev:** Kookaburra left on leafy branch

Date	Mintage	F	VF	XF	Unc	BU
2009 P20 Proof	2,009	Value: 125				

KM# 1308 5 DOLLARS
1.5500 g., 0.9990 Gold 0.0498 oz. AGW, 14 mm. **Ruler:** Elizabeth II **Subject:** Kookaburra 20th Anniversary **Obv:** Head right **Rev:** Kookaburra pair facing opposite

Date	Mintage	F	VF	XF	Unc	BU
2009 P20 Proof	2,009	Value: 125				

KM# 1309 5 DOLLARS
1.5500 g., 0.9990 Gold 0.0498 oz. AGW, 14 mm. **Ruler:** Elizabeth II **Subject:** Kookaburra 20th Anniversary **Obv:** Head right **Rev:** Kookaburra in flight on map of Australia

Date	Mintage	F	VF	XF	Unc	BU
2009 P20 Proof	2,009	Value: 125				

KM# 1310 5 DOLLARS
1.5500 g., 0.9990 Gold 0.0498 oz. AGW, 14 mm. **Ruler:** Elizabeth II **Subject:** Kookaburra 20th Anniversary **Obv:** Head right **Rev:** Kookaburra on branch right

Date	Mintage	F	VF	XF	Unc	BU
2009 P20 Proof	2,009	Value: 125				

KM# 1311 5 DOLLARS
1.5500 g., 0.9990 Gold 0.0498 oz. AGW, 14 mm. **Ruler:** Elizabeth II **Subject:** Kookaburra 20th Anniversary **Obv:** Head right **Rev:** Kookaburras, one in flight, one on branch

Date	Mintage	F	VF	XF	Unc	BU
2009 P20 Proof	2,009	Value: 125				

KM# 1312 5 DOLLARS
1.5500 g., 0.9990 Gold 0.0498 oz. AGW, 14 mm. **Ruler:** Elizabeth II **Subject:** Kookaburra 20th Anniversary **Obv:** Head right **Rev:** Kookaburra on branch, head right

Date	Mintage	F	VF	XF	Unc	BU
2009 P20 Proof	2,009	Value: 125				

KM# 1313 5 DOLLARS
1.5500 g., 0.9990 Gold 0.0498 oz. AGW, 14 mm. **Ruler:** Elizabeth II **Subject:** Kookaburra 20th Anniversary **Obv:** Head right **Rev:** Kookaburra pair on branch, one with head upward

Date	Mintage	F	VF	XF	Unc	BU
2009 P20 Proof	2,009	Value: 125				

KM# 1314 5 DOLLARS
1.5500 g., 0.9990 Gold 0.0498 oz. AGW, 14 mm. **Ruler:** Elizabeth II **Subject:** Kookaburra 20th Anniversary **Obv:** Head right **Rev:** Kookaburra on branch left

Date	Mintage	F	VF	XF	Unc	BU
2009 P20 Proof	2,009	Value: 125				

KM# 1315 5 DOLLARS
1.5500 g., 0.9990 Gold 0.0498 oz. AGW, 14 mm. **Ruler:** Elizabeth II **Subject:** Kookaburra 20th Anniversary **Obv:** Head right **Rev:** Kookaburra on branch admiring spider web

Date	Mintage	F	VF	XF	Unc	BU
2009 P20 Proof	2,009	Value: 125				

KM# 1316 5 DOLLARS
1.5500 g., 0.9990 Gold 0.0498 oz. AGW, 14 mm. **Ruler:** Elizabeth II **Subject:** Kookaburra 20th Anniversary **Obv:** Head right **Rev:** Kookaburra on branch, sunburst in background

Date	Mintage	F	VF	XF	Unc	BU
2009 P20 Proof	2,009	Value: 125				

KM# 603 10 DOLLARS
311.0350 g., 0.9990 Silver 9.9896 oz. ASW, 74.9 mm. **Ruler:** Elizabeth II **Subject:** Kookaburra **Obv:** Head with tiara right, denomination below **Rev:** Flying bird over map **Edge:** Reeded

Date	Mintage	F	VF	XF	Unc	BU
2002 Proof	—	Value: 400				

KM# 891 10 DOLLARS
311.0350 g., 0.9990 Silver 9.9896 oz. ASW, 74.9 mm. **Ruler:** Elizabeth II **Obv:** Head with tiara right **Rev:** Kookaburra on branch, no leaves

Date	Mintage	F	VF	XF	Unc	BU
2007	—	—	—	—	400	—

KM# 1360 10 DOLLARS
311.0350 g., 0.9990 Silver 9.9896 oz. ASW, 75.5 mm. **Ruler:** Elizabeth II **Obv:** Head right **Rev:** Kookaburra

Date	Mintage	F	VF	XF	Unc	BU
2010(p) Proof	—	Value: 425				

KM# 1693 10 DOLLARS
311.0350 g., 0.9990 Silver 9.9896 oz. ASW **Ruler:** Elizabeth II **Rev:** Kookaburra

Date	Mintage	F	VF	XF	Unc	BU
2012P Proof	—	Value: 400				

KM# 630 20 DOLLARS
62.2070 g., 0.9990 Silver 1.9979 oz. ASW **Ruler:** Elizabeth II **Subject:** USA State Quarters - 2002 **Obv:** Head with tiara right, denomination below **Rev:** Kookaburra on branch with five state quarter designs added below **Edge:** Reeded and plain sections

Date	Mintage	F	VF	XF	Unc	BU
2002	10,000	—	—	—	82.00	85.00

KM# 680 30 DOLLARS
1002.5020 g., 0.9990 Silver 32.197 oz. ASW, 101 mm. **Ruler:** Elizabeth II **Obv:** Head with tiara right, denomination below **Rev:** Kookaburra in flight above Australian map **Edge:** Segmented reeding

Date	Mintage	F	VF	XF	Unc	BU
2001P Proof	350	Value: 1,200				
2002	—	—	—	—	—	1,250

KM# 624 30 DOLLARS
1002.5020 g., 0.9990 Silver 32.197 oz. ASW, 101 mm. **Ruler:** Elizabeth II **Subject:** USA State Quarters - 2001 **Obv:** Head with tiara right, denomination below **Rev:** Two kookaburras on branch with five state quarter designs added below **Edge:** Reeded and plain sections

Date	Mintage	F	VF	XF	Unc	BU
2001	1,000	—	—	—	—	1,200

KM# 631 30 DOLLARS
1002.5020 g., 0.9990 Silver 32.197 oz. ASW, 101 mm. **Ruler:** Elizabeth II **Subject:** USA State Quarters - 2002 **Obv:** Head with tiara right, denomination below **Rev:** Kookaburra on branch with five state quarter designs added in gold **Edge:** Reeded and plain sections

Date	Mintage	F	VF	XF	Unc	BU
2002	1,000	—	—	—	—	1,200

KM# 880 30 DOLLARS
1002.5020 g., 0.9990 Silver 32.197 oz. ASW, 101 mm. **Ruler:** Elizabeth II **Obv:** Head with tiara right **Rev:** Kookaburra standing on branch **Edge:** Reeded

Date	Mintage	F	VF	XF	Unc	BU
2002P Proof	350	Value: 1,250				

KM# 882 30 DOLLARS
1002.5020 g., 0.9990 Silver 32.197 oz. ASW, 101 mm. **Ruler:** Elizabeth II **Obv:** Head with tiara right **Rev:** Two kookaburras, one in flight **Edge:** Reeded

Date	Mintage	F	VF	XF	Unc	BU
2003P Proof	350	Value: 1,250				

KM# 885 30 DOLLARS
1002.5020 g., 0.9990 Silver 32.197 oz. ASW, 101 mm. **Ruler:** Elizabeth II **Obv:** Head with tiara right **Rev:** Kookaburra perched on branch with four leaves **Edge:** Reeded

Date	Mintage	F	VF	XF	Unc	BU
2004P Proof	350	Value: 1,250				

KM# 888 30 DOLLARS
1002.5020 g., 0.9990 Silver 32.197 oz. ASW, 101 mm. **Ruler:** Elizabeth II **Obv:** Head with tiara right **Rev:** Two kookaburras on branch, one laughing **Edge:** Reeded

Date	Mintage	F	VF	XF	Unc	BU
2005P Proof	800	Value: 1,250				

KM# 892 30 DOLLARS
1002.5020 g., 0.9990 Silver 32.197 oz. ASW, 101 mm. **Ruler:** Elizabeth II **Obv:** Head with tiara right **Rev:** Kookaburras on branch, no leaves

Date	Mintage	F	VF	XF	Unc	BU
2007	—	—	—	—	1,200	—

KM# 1115 30 DOLLARS
1000.0000 g., 0.9990 Silver 32.117 oz. ASW, 101 mm. **Ruler:** Elizabeth II **Rev:** Kookaburra on branch, sunburst background

Date	Mintage	F	VF	XF	Unc	BU
2009P Proof	—	Value: 1,300				

KM# 1361 30 DOLLARS
1000.0000 g., 0.9990 Silver 32.117 oz. ASW, 100 mm. **Ruler:** Elizabeth II **Obv:** Head right **Rev:** Kookaburra **Note:** Illustration reduced.

Date	Mintage	F	VF	XF	Unc	BU
2010(p)	—	—	—	—	—	1,200

KM# 1694 30 DOLLARS
1000.0000 g., 0.9990 Silver 32.117 oz. ASW **Ruler:** Elizabeth II **Rev:** Kookaburra

Date	Mintage	F	VF	XF	Unc	BU
2012P	—	—	—	—	—	1,200

KM# 878 200 DOLLARS
31.6000 g., 0.9990 Silver 1.0149 oz. ASW, 40 mm. **Ruler:** Elizabeth II **Obv:** Head with tiara right with denomination **Rev:** Kookaburra in flight over map of Australia **Note:** Mule.

Date	Mintage	F	VF	XF	Unc	BU
ND(2001) Proof	Est. 20	Value: 2,500				

BULLION - NUGGET

KM# 692 50 DOLLARS
15.5017 g., 0.9999 Gold 0.4983 oz. AGW, 25.1 mm. **Ruler:** Elizabeth II **Subject:** Tribute to Liberty **Obv:** Head with tiara right, denomination below **Rev:** Two kangaroos on map above silver Liberty Bell insert **Edge:** Reeded

Date	Mintage	F	VF	XF	Unc	BU
2001	650	—	—	—	875	—
2002	1,498	—	—	—	875	—
2002 Proof	—	Value: 900				

KM# 693 100 DOLLARS
31.1035 g., 0.9999 Gold 0.9999 oz. AGW, 32.1 mm. **Ruler:** Elizabeth II **Subject:** Tribute to Liberty **Obv:** Head with tiara right, denomination below **Rev:** Two kangaroos on map above silver Liberty Bell insert, colored image **Edge:** Reeded

Date	Mintage	F	VF	XF	Unc	BU
2001	1,498	—	—	—	1,735	—
2002	—	—	—	—	—	1,735

KM# 900 100 DOLLARS
31.1035 g., 0.9999 Gold 0.9999 oz. AGW, 32 mm. **Ruler:** Elizabeth II **Obv:** Head with tiara right **Rev:** Prospectors dry-blowing gold dust, colored image

Date	Mintage	F	VF	XF	Unc	BU
2002	1,500	—	—	—	1,735	—

KM# 906 100 DOLLARS
31.1035 g., 0.9990 Gold 0.9990 oz. AGW, 32 mm. **Ruler:** Elizabeth II **Obv:** Head with tiara right **Rev:** Prospectors camp, colored image

Date	Mintage	F	VF	XF	Unc	BU
2003	1,500	—	—	—	1,735	—

KM# 741 100 DOLLARS
31.1035 g., 0.9999 Gold 0.9999 oz. AGW, 32 mm. **Ruler:** Elizabeth II **Subject:** Eureka Stockade **Obv:** Head with tiara right, denomination below **Rev:** Eureka Stockade leader Peter Lalor and blue flag, colored image **Edge:** Reeded

Date	Mintage	F	VF	XF	Unc	BU
2004	1,500	—	—	—	1,735	—
2004P Proof	1,500	Value: 1,750				

KM# 915 100 DOLLARS
31.1035 g., 0.9990 Gold 0.9990 oz. AGW, 32 mm. **Ruler:** Elizabeth II **Subject:** Welcome Stranger Nugget **Obv:** Head with tiara right **Rev:** Welcome Stranger Nugget surrounded by Outback setting, colored image

Date	Mintage	F	VF	XF	Unc	BU
2005	1,500	—	—	—	1,735	—

KM# 914 200 DOLLARS
62.2140 g., 0.9990 Gold 1.9981 oz. AGW, 41 mm. **Ruler:** Elizabeth II **Obv:** Head with tiara right **Rev:** Kangaroo in multicolor bush

Date	Mintage	F	VF	XF	Unc	BU
2005	200	—	—	—	3,500	—

BULLION - KOALA

KM# 1838 10 CENTS
3.1100 g., 0.9990 Silver 0.0999 oz. ASW, 30 mm. **Ruler:** Elizabeth II **Rev:** Koala sleeping hugging branch

Date	Mintage	F	VF	XF	Unc	BU
2012P Proof	—	Value: 25.00				

KM# 1366 50 CENTS
15.5500 g., 0.9990 Silver 0.4994 oz. ASW **Ruler:** Elizabeth II **Obv:** Head right **Rev:** Koala

Date	Mintage	F	VF	XF	Unc	BU
2010(p)	—	—	—	—	—	35.00

KM# 1688 50 CENTS
15.5000 g., 0.9990 Silver 0.4978 oz. ASW, 32 mm. **Ruler:** Elizabeth II **Rev:** Koala

Date	Mintage	F	VF	XF	Unc	BU
2012P	—	—	—	—	—	20.00

KM# 1798 50 CENTS
15.5000 g., 0.9990 Silver 0.4978 oz. ASW, 36.6 mm. **Ruler:** Elizabeth II **Rev:** Koala in color

Date	Mintage	F	VF	XF	Unc	BU
2012P Proof	—	Value: 50.00				

KM# 1839 50 CENTS
15.5000 g., 0.9990 Silver 0.4978 oz. ASW, 32 mm. **Ruler:** Elizabeth II **Rev:** Koala sleeping hugging branch

Date	Mintage	F	VF	XF	Unc	BU
2012P	—	—	—	—	—	40.00

KM# 1111 DOLLAR
31.1050 g., 0.9990 Silver 0.9990 oz. ASW, 40.6 mm. **Ruler:** Elizabeth II **Rev:** Koala seated left on branch, shimmer background

Date	Mintage	F	VF	XF	Unc	BU
2009P	—	—	—	—	—	45.00

KM# 1111a DOLLAR
31.1050 g., 0.9999 Silver partially gilt 0.9999 oz. ASW, 40.6 mm. **Ruler:** Elizabeth II **Rev:** Koala seated left on branch, gilt

Date	Mintage	F	VF	XF	Unc	BU
2009P Proof	10,000	Value: 60.00				

KM# 1464 DOLLAR
31.1050 g., 0.9990 Silver 0.9990 oz. ASW, 40 mm. **Ruler:** Elizabeth II **Rev:** Koala on branch

Date	Mintage	F	VF	XF	Unc	BU
2010P	—	—	—	—	—	45.00

KM# 1464a DOLLAR
31.1050 g., 0.9999 Silver partially gilt 0.9999 oz. ASW **Ruler:** Elizabeth II **Rev:** Koala on branch

Date	Mintage	F	VF	XF	Unc	BU
2010P Proof	—	Value: 60.00				

KM# 1689 DOLLAR
31.1050 g., 0.9990 Silver 0.9990 oz. ASW, 40.5 mm. **Ruler:** Elizabeth II **Rev:** Koala

Date	Mintage	F	VF	XF	Unc	BU
2012P	—	—	—	—	—	45.00

KM# 1828 DOLLAR
31.1050 g., 0.9990 Silver 0.9990 oz. ASW, 33 mm. **Ruler:** Elizabeth II **Rev:** Koala **Note:** Ultra High Relief

Date	Mintage	F	VF	XF	Unc	BU
2012P Proof	—	Value: 110				

KM# 1840 DOLLAR
31.1050 g., 0.9990 Silver 0.9990 oz. ASW, 40.6 mm. **Ruler:** Elizabeth II **Rev:** Koala sleeping hugging branch

Date	Mintage	F	VF	XF	Unc	BU
2012P	—	—	—	—	—	55.00

KM# 1840a DOLLAR
31.1050 g., 0.9990 Silver partially gilt 0.9990 oz. ASW, 40.6 mm. **Ruler:** Elizabeth II **Rev:** Gilt Koala sleeping hugging branch

Date	Mintage	F	VF	XF	Unc	BU
2012P	—	—	—	—	—	75.00

KM# 916 5 DOLLARS
1.5710 g., 0.9990 Platinum 0.0505 oz. APW **Ruler:** Elizabeth II **Obv:** Head with tiara right **Rev:** Two koalas on branch

Date	Mintage	F	VF	XF	Unc	BU
2001 Proof	5,000	Value: 125				

KM# 1113 5 DOLLARS
1.2440 g., 0.9999 Gold 0.0400 oz. AGW, 14.1 mm. **Ruler:** Elizabeth II **Rev:** Koala seated left on branch

Date	Mintage	F	VF	XF	Unc	BU
2009P Proof	15,000	Value: 95.00				

KM# 1467 5 DOLLARS
1.2400 g., 0.9990 Gold 0.0398 oz. AGW **Ruler:** Elizabeth II **Rev:** Koala on branch

Date	Mintage	F	VF	XF	Unc	BU
2010P	—	—	—	—	—	90.00

KM# 1843 5 DOLLARS
1.2400 g., 0.9990 Gold 0.0398 oz. AGW, 14.1 mm. **Ruler:** Elizabeth II **Rev:** Koala sleeping hugging branch

Date	Mintage	F	VF	XF	Unc	BU
2012P Proof	—	Value: 150				

KM# 1841 8 DOLLARS
155.5000 g., 0.9990 Silver 4.9942 oz. ASW, 101 mm. **Ruler:** Elizabeth II **Rev:** Koala sleeping hugging branch

Date	Mintage	F	VF	XF	Unc	BU
2012P	—	—	—	—	—	350

KM# 1368 10 DOLLARS
311.3500 g., 0.9990 Silver 9.9997 oz. ASW **Ruler:** Elizabeth II **Obv:** Head right **Rev:** Koala

Date	Mintage	F	VF	XF	Unc	BU
2010P	—	—	—	—	—	400

KM# 1690 10 DOLLARS
311.3500 g., 0.9990 Silver 9.9997 oz. ASW **Ruler:** Elizabeth II **Rev:** Koala

Date	Mintage	F	VF	XF	Unc	BU
2012P	—	—	—	—	—	400

KM# 917 15 DOLLARS
3.1101 g., 0.9990 Platinum 0.0999 oz. APW **Ruler:** Elizabeth II **Obv:** Head with tiara right **Rev:** Two koalas on a branch

Date	Mintage	F	VF	XF	Unc	BU
2001 Proof	650	Value: 210				

KM# 922 15 DOLLARS
3.1101 g., 0.9990 Platinum 0.0999 oz. APW **Ruler:** Elizabeth II **Obv:** Head with tiara right **Rev:** Koala up a gum tree

Date	Mintage	F	VF	XF	Unc	BU
2002 Proof	650	Value: 210				

KM# 926 15 DOLLARS
3.1101 g., 0.9990 Platinum 0.0999 oz. APW **Ruler:** Elizabeth II **Obv:** Head with tiara right **Rev:** Mother and baby koala

Date	Mintage	F	VF	XF	Unc	BU
2003 Proof	500	Value: 210				

KM# 931 15 DOLLARS
3.1101 g., 0.9990 Platinum 0.0999 oz. APW **Ruler:** Elizabeth II **Obv:** Head with tiara right **Rev:** Single koala on branch

Date	Mintage	F	VF	XF	Unc	BU
2004 Proof	500	Value: 210				

KM# 935 15 DOLLARS
3.1101 g., 0.9990 Platinum 0.0999 oz. APW **Ruler:** Elizabeth II **Obv:** Head with tiara right **Rev:** Single koala with gum leaves

Date	Mintage	F	VF	XF	Unc	BU
2005 Proof	500	Value: 210				

KM# 1114 15 DOLLARS
3.1080 g., 0.9999 Gold 0.0999 oz. AGW, 16.1 mm. **Ruler:** Elizabeth II **Rev:** Koala seated left on tree branch

Date	Mintage	F	VF	XF	Unc	BU
2009P Proof	5,000	Value: 190				

KM# 1468 15 DOLLARS
3.1100 g., 0.9990 Gold 0.0999 oz. AGW **Ruler:** Elizabeth II **Rev:** Koala on branch

Date	Mintage	F	VF	XF	Unc	BU
2010P	—	—	—	—	—	190

KM# 1844 15 DOLLARS
3.1100 g., 0.9990 Gold 0.0999 oz. AGW, 16.1 mm. **Ruler:** Elizabeth II **Rev:** Koala sleeping hugging branch

Date	Mintage	F	VF	XF	Unc	BU
2012P Proof	—	Value: 250				

KM# 918 25 DOLLARS
7.7508 g., 0.9990 Platinum 0.2489 oz. APW **Ruler:** Elizabeth II **Obv:** Head with tiara right **Rev:** Two koalas on a branch

Date	Mintage	F	VF	XF	Unc	BU
2001 Proof	275	Value: 485				

KM# 923 25 DOLLARS
7.7508 g., 0.9990 Platinum 0.2489 oz. APW **Ruler:** Elizabeth II **Obv:** Head with tiara right **Rev:** Koala up a gum tree

Date	Mintage	F	VF	XF	Unc	BU
2002 Proof	275	Value: 485				

KM# 927 25 DOLLARS
7.7508 g., 0.9990 Platinum 0.2489 oz. APW **Ruler:** Elizabeth II **Obv:** Head with tiara right **Rev:** Mother and baby koala

Date	Mintage	F	VF	XF	Unc	BU
2003 Proof	200	Value: 485				

KM# 932 25 DOLLARS
7.7508 g., 0.9990 Platinum 0.2489 oz. APW **Ruler:** Elizabeth II **Obv:** Head with tiara right **Rev:** Single koala on branch

Date	Mintage	F	VF	XF	Unc	BU
2004 Proof	200	Value: 485				

KM# 936 25 DOLLARS
7.7508 g., 0.9990 Platinum 0.2489 oz. APW **Ruler:** Elizabeth II **Obv:** Head with tiara right **Rev:** Single koala with gum leaves

Date	Mintage	F	VF	XF	Unc	BU
2005 Proof	200	Value: 485				

KM# 1112 30 DOLLARS
1000.0000 g., 0.9999 Silver 32.146 oz. ASW, 100.6 mm. **Ruler:** Elizabeth II **Rev:** Koala seated left on branch

Date	Mintage	F	VF	XF	Unc	BU
2009P Prooflike	—	—	—	—	—	1,150

KM# 1369 30 DOLLARS
1000.0000 g., 0.9990 Silver 32.117 oz. ASW, 100.6 mm. **Ruler:** Elizabeth II **Obv:** Head light **Rev:** Koala

Date	Mintage	F	VF	XF	Unc	BU
2010(p)	—	—	—	—	—	1,150

KM# 1466 30 DOLLARS
1000.0000 g., 0.9990 Silver 32.117 oz. ASW, 100.6 mm. **Ruler:** Elizabeth II **Rev:** Koala on branch

Date	Mintage	F	VF	XF	Unc	BU
2010P	—	—	—	—	—	1,200

KM# 1691 30 DOLLARS
1000.0000 g., 0.9990 Silver 32.117 oz. ASW, 100.6 mm. **Ruler:** Elizabeth II **Rev:** Koala

Date	Mintage	F	VF	XF	Unc	BU
2012P	—	—	—	—	—	1,200

KM# 1785 30 DOLLARS
1000.0000 g., 0.9990 Silver 32.117 oz. ASW, 100.6 mm. **Ruler:** Elizabeth II **Obv:** Head with tiara right **Rev:** Koala hugging and lying on branch **Edge:** Reeded

Date	Mintage	F	VF	XF	Unc	BU
2012P Proof	—	Value: 1,250				

KM# 1842 30 DOLLARS
1000.0000 g., 0.9990 Silver 32.117 oz. ASW, 101 mm. **Ruler:** Elizabeth II **Rev:** Koala sleeping hugging branch

Date	Mintage	F	VF	XF	Unc	BU
2012P	—	—	—	—	—	1,400

KM# 919 50 DOLLARS
15.5017 g., 0.9990 Platinum 0.4979 oz. APW **Ruler:** Elizabeth II **Obv:** Head with tiara right **Rev:** Two koalas on a branch

Date	Mintage	F	VF	XF	Unc	BU
2001 Proof	350	Value: 960				

KM# 924 50 DOLLARS
15.5017 g., 0.9990 Platinum 0.4979 oz. APW **Ruler:** Elizabeth II **Obv:** Head with tiara right **Rev:** Koala up a gum tree

Date	Mintage	F	VF	XF	Unc	BU
2002 Proof	350	Value: 960				

KM# 928 50 DOLLARS
15.5017 g., 0.9990 Platinum 0.4979 oz. APW **Ruler:** Elizabeth II **Obv:** Head with tiara right **Rev:** Mother and baby koala

Date	Mintage	F	VF	XF	Unc	BU
2003 Proof	350	Value: 960				

KM# 933 50 DOLLARS
15.5017 g., 0.9990 Platinum 0.4979 oz. APW **Ruler:** Elizabeth II **Obv:** Head with tiara right **Rev:** Single koala on branch

Date	Mintage	F	VF	XF	Unc	BU
2004 Proof	350	Value: 960				

KM# 937 50 DOLLARS
15.5017 g., 0.9990 Platinum 0.4979 oz. APW **Ruler:** Elizabeth II **Obv:** Head with tiara right **Rev:** Single koala with gum leaves

Date	Mintage	F	VF	XF	Unc	BU
2005 Proof	350	Value: 960				

KM# 921 100 DOLLARS
31.1035 g., 0.9990 Platinum 0.9990 oz. APW **Ruler:** Elizabeth II **Obv:** Head with tiara right **Rev:** Federation: Sir Henry Parkes, flag, parliament house, colored image

Date	Mintage	F	VF	XF	Unc	BU
2001 Proof	1,000	Value: 1,875				

KM# 930 100 DOLLARS
31.1035 g., 0.9990 Platinum 0.9990 oz. APW **Ruler:** Elizabeth II **Obv:** Head with tiara right **Rev:** The Arts: Dancers, paint brushes, opera house, colored image

Date	Mintage	F	VF	XF	Unc	BU
2003 Proof	1,000	Value: 1,875				

KM# 742 100 DOLLARS
31.1035 g., 0.9995 Platinum 0.9995 oz. APW, 32.1 mm. **Ruler:** Elizabeth II **Obv:** Head with tiara right, denomination below **Rev:** Sports: Australian sportsmen and women, colored image **Edge:** Reeded

Date	Mintage	F	VF	XF	Unc	BU
2004P Proof	1,000	Value: 1,875				

KM# 939 100 DOLLARS
31.1035 g., 0.9990 Platinum 0.9990 oz. APW **Ruler:** Elizabeth II **Obv:** Head with tiara right **Rev:** Two workers and machine, colored image

Date	Mintage	F	VF	XF	Unc	BU
2005 Proof	1,000	Value: 1,875				

KM# 1469 100 DOLLARS
31.1050 g., 0.9990 Gold 0.9990 oz. AGW, 32.1 mm. **Ruler:** Elizabeth II **Rev:** Koala on branch

Date	Mintage	F	VF	XF	Unc	BU
2010P	—	—	—	—	—	1,800

KM# 1608 100 DOLLARS
31.1050 g., 0.9990 Gold 0.9990 oz. AGW, 28 mm. **Ruler:** Elizabeth II **Obv:** Head with tiara right **Rev:** Two pandas seated in fork of a eucalyptus tree **Edge:** Reeded **Note:** Ultra High Relief

Date	Mintage	F	VF	XF	Unc	BU
2011P Proof	2,000	Value: 1,950				

KM# 1845 100 DOLLARS
31.1050 g., 0.9990 Gold 0.9990 oz. AGW, 28 mm. **Ruler:** Elizabeth II **Rev:** Koala sleeping hugging branch **Note:** Ultra High Relief

Date	Mintage	F	VF	XF	Unc	BU
2012P Proof	—	Value: 1,900				

KM# 920 200 DOLLARS
62.2140 g., 0.9990 Platinum 1.9981 oz. APW **Ruler:** Elizabeth II **Obv:** Head with tiara right **Rev:** Two koalas sitting on branch

Date	Mintage	F	VF	XF	Unc	BU
2001	250	Value: 3,800				

KM# 925 200 DOLLARS
62.2140 g., 0.9990 Platinum 1.9981 oz. APW **Ruler:** Elizabeth II **Obv:** Head with tiara right **Rev:** Koala up a gum tree

Date	Mintage	F	VF	XF	Unc	BU
2002 Proof	250	Value: 3,800				

KM# 929 200 DOLLARS
62.2140 g., 0.9990 Platinum 1.9981 oz. APW **Ruler:** Elizabeth II **Obv:** Head with tiara right **Rev:** Mother and baby koala

Date	Mintage	F	VF	XF	Unc	BU
2003 Proof	200	Value: 3,800				

KM# 934 200 DOLLARS
62.2140 g., 0.9990 Platinum 1.9981 oz. APW **Ruler:** Elizabeth II **Obv:** Head with tiara right **Rev:** Single koala on branch

Date	Mintage	F	VF	XF	Unc	BU
2004 Proof	200	Value: 3,800				

KM# 938 200 DOLLARS
62.2140 g., 0.9990 Platinum 1.9981 oz. APW **Ruler:** Elizabeth II **Obv:** Head with tiara right **Rev:** Single koala with multicolor gum leaves

Date	Mintage	F	VF	XF	Unc	BU
2005 Proof	200	Value: 3,800				

KM# 1470 200 DOLLARS
62.2400 g., 0.9990 Gold 1.9990 oz. AGW **Ruler:** Elizabeth II **Rev:** Koala on branch

Date	Mintage	F	VF	XF	Unc	BU
2010P	—	—	—	—	—	3,750

KM# 1846 200 DOLLARS
62.2000 g., 0.9990 Gold 1.9977 oz. AGW, 40.6 mm. **Ruler:** Elizabeth II **Rev:** Koala sleeping hugging branch

Date	Mintage	F	VF	XF	Unc	BU
2012P Proof	—	Value: 3,750				

BULLION - DISCOVER AUSTRALIA

KM# 940 DOLLAR
31.1035 g., 0.9990 Silver 0.9990 oz. ASW **Ruler:** Elizabeth II **Subject:** Australian Landmarks **Obv:** Head with tiara right **Rev:** Melbourne

Date	Mintage	F	VF	XF	Unc	BU
2006 Proof	7,500	Value: 50.00				

KM# 941 DOLLAR
31.1035 g., 0.9990 Silver 0.9990 oz. ASW **Ruler:** Elizabeth II **Subject:** Australian Landmarks **Obv:** Head with tiara right **Rev:** Uluru

Date	Mintage	F	VF	XF	Unc	BU
2006 Proof	7,500	Value: 50.00				

KM# 942 DOLLAR
31.1035 g., 0.9990 Silver 0.9990 oz. ASW **Ruler:** Elizabeth II **Subject:** Australian Landmarks **Obv:** Head with tiara right **Rev:** Canberra

Date	Mintage	F	VF	XF	Unc	BU
2006 Proof	7,500	Value: 50.00				

KM# 943 DOLLAR
31.1035 g., 0.9990 Silver 0.9990 oz. ASW, 40.6 mm. **Ruler:** Elizabeth II **Subject:** Australian Landmarks **Obv:** Head with tiara right **Rev:** Perth

Date	Mintage	F	VF	XF	Unc	BU
2006 Proof	7,500	Value: 50.00				

KM# 944 DOLLAR
31.1035 g., 0.9990 Silver 0.9990 oz. ASW **Ruler:** Elizabeth II **Subject:** Australian Landmarks **Obv:** Head with tiara right **Rev:** Great Barrier Reef

Date	Mintage	F	VF	XF	Unc	BU
2006 Proof	7,500	Value: 50.00				

KM# 949 DOLLAR
31.1035 g., 0.9990 Silver 0.9990 oz. ASW **Ruler:** Elizabeth II **Subject:** Australian Landmarks **Obv:** Head with tiara right **Rev:** Sydney

Date	Mintage	F	VF	XF	Unc	BU
2007	7,500	Value: 60.00				

KM# 945 DOLLAR
31.1035 g., 0.9990 Silver 0.9990 oz. ASW **Ruler:** Elizabeth II **Subject:** Australian Landmarks **Obv:** Head with tiara right **Rev:** Gold Coast

Date	Mintage	F	VF	XF	Unc	BU
2007 Proof	7,500	Value: 60.00				

KM# 946 DOLLAR
31.1035 g., 0.9990 Silver 0.9990 oz. ASW **Ruler:** Elizabeth II **Subject:** Australian Landmarks **Obv:** Head with tiara right **Rev:** Phillip Island

Date	Mintage	F	VF	XF	Unc	BU
2007 Proof	7,500	Value: 60.00				

KM# 947 DOLLAR
31.1035 g., 0.9990 Silver 0.9990 oz. ASW **Ruler:** Elizabeth II **Subject:** Australian Landmarks **Obv:** Head with tiara right **Rev:** Port Arthur

Date	Mintage	F	VF	XF	Unc	BU
2007 Proof	7,500	Value: 60.00				

KM# 948 DOLLAR
31.1035 g., 0.9990 Silver 0.9990 oz. ASW **Ruler:** Elizabeth II **Subject:** Australian Landmarks **Obv:** Head with tiara right **Rev:** Adelaide

Date	Mintage	F	VF	XF	Unc	BU
2007 Proof	7,500	Value: 60.00				

KM# 1021 DOLLAR
31.1050 g., 0.9990 Silver 0.9990 oz. ASW, 40 mm. **Ruler:** Elizabeth II **Subject:** Hobart **Rev:** Buildings and harbor **Rev. Legend:** DISCOVER AUSTRALIA

Date	Mintage	F	VF	XF	Unc	BU
2008P Proof	7,500	Value: 80.00				

KM# 1181 DOLLAR
31.1050 g., 0.9990 Silver 0.9990 oz. ASW, 40 mm. **Ruler:** Elizabeth II **Subject:** Darwin **Obv:** Head right **Rev:** Harbor, multicolor **Rev. Legend:** DISCOVER AUSTRALIA

Date	Mintage	F	VF	XF	Unc	BU
2008P Proof	7,500	Value: 80.00				

KM# 1182 DOLLAR
31.1050 g., 0.9990 Silver 0.9990 oz. ASW, 40 mm. **Ruler:** Elizabeth II **Subject:** Kakadu **Obv:** Head right **Rev:** Crocodile, multicolor **Rev. Legend:** DISCOVER AUSTRALIA

Date	Mintage	F	VF	XF	Unc	BU
2008P Proof	7,500	Value: 80.00				

KM# 1183 DOLLAR
31.1050 g., 0.9990 Silver 0.9990 oz. ASW **Ruler:** Elizabeth II **Subject:** Brisbane **Obv:** Head right **Rev:** Bridge and view **Rev. Legend:** DISCOVER AUSTRALIA

Date	Mintage	F	VF	XF	Unc	BU
2008P Proof	7,500	Value: 80.00				

KM# 1184 DOLLAR
31.1050 g., 0.9990 Silver 0.9990 oz. ASW **Ruler:** Elizabeth II **Subject:** Broome **Obv:** Head right **Rev:** Seascape, pearls, multicolor **Rev. Legend:** DISCOVER AUSTRALIA

Date	Mintage	F	VF	XF	Unc	BU
2008P Proof	7,500	Value: 80.00				

KM# 1185 DOLLAR
31.1050 g., 0.9990 Silver 0.9990 oz. ASW **Ruler:** Elizabeth II **Subject:** Sydney **Obv:** Head right **Rev:** Opera House, Harbor Bridge, multicolor **Rev. Legend:** DISCOVER AUSTRALIA

Date	Mintage	F	VF	XF	Unc	BU
2008P Proof	7,500	Value: 80.00				

KM# 1188 DOLLAR
1.2400 g., 0.9990 Gold 0.0398 oz. AGW, 14 mm. **Ruler:** Elizabeth II **Obv:** Head right **Rev:** Brolga **Rev. Legend:** DISCOVER AUSTRALIA

Date	Mintage	F	VF	XF	Unc	BU
2008P Proof	25,000	Value: 100				

KM# 1103 DOLLAR
31.1050 g., 0.9990 Silver 0.9990 oz. ASW, 27x47 mm. **Ruler:** Elizabeth II **Rev:** Turtle Dreaming **Shape:** Rectangle

Date	Mintage	F	VF	XF	Unc	BU
2009 Proof	—	Value: 75.00				

KM# 1107 DOLLAR
31.1050 g., 0.9999 Silver 0.9999 oz. ASW, 27x47 mm. **Ruler:** Elizabeth II **Rev:** Kangaroo dreaming **Shape:** Vertical rectangle

Date	Mintage	F	VF	XF	Unc	BU
2009 Proof	—	Value: 75.00				

KM# 1212 DOLLAR
31.1050 g., 0.9990 Silver 0.9990 oz. ASW, 40.6 mm. **Ruler:** Elizabeth II **Obv:** Head right **Rev:** Dreaming kangaroo, multicolor **Rev. Legend:** DISCOVER AUSTRALIA

Date	Mintage	F	VF	XF	Unc	BU
2009P Proof	10,000	Value: 90.00				

KM# 1213 DOLLAR
31.1050 g., 0.9990 Silver 0.9990 oz. ASW **Ruler:** Elizabeth II **Obv:** Head right **Rev:** Dreaming dolphin, multicolor **Rev. Legend:** DISCOVER AUSTRALIA **Shape:** 40.6

Date	Mintage	F	VF	XF	Unc	BU
2009P Proof	10,000	Value: 90.00				

KM# 1214 DOLLAR
31.1050 g., 0.9990 Silver 0.9990 oz. ASW, 40.6 mm. **Ruler:** Elizabeth II **Obv:** Head right **Rev:** Dreaming king brown snake, multicolor **Rev. Legend:** DISCOVER AUSTRALIA

Date	Mintage	F	VF	XF	Unc	BU
2009P Proof	10,000	Value: 90.00				

KM# 1215 DOLLAR
31.1050 g., 0.9990 Silver 0.9990 oz. ASW, 40.6 mm. **Ruler:** Elizabeth II **Obv:** Head right **Rev:** Dreaming brolga, multicolor

Date	Mintage	F	VF	XF	Unc	BU
2009P Proof	10,000	Value: 90.00				

KM# 1216 DOLLAR
31.1050 g., 0.9990 Silver 0.9990 oz. ASW, 40.6 mm. **Ruler:** Elizabeth II **Obv:** Head right **Rev:** Dreaming echidna, multicolor

Date	Mintage	F	VF	XF	Unc	BU
2009P Proof	10,000	Value: 90.00				

KM# 1218 DOLLAR
1.2500 g., 0.9990 Gold 0.0401 oz. AGW, 14 mm. **Ruler:** Elizabeth II **Obv:** Head right **Rev:** Dreaming dolphin

Date	Mintage	F	VF	XF	Unc	BU
2009P Proof	25,000	Value: 125				

KM# 1222 DOLLAR
3.1100 g., 0.9990 Gold 0.0999 oz. AGW, 16 mm. **Ruler:** Elizabeth II **Obv:** Head right **Rev:** Dreaming kangaroo

Date	Mintage	F	VF	XF	Unc	BU
2009P Proof	2,500	Value: 175				

KM# 1242 DOLLAR
31.1050 g., 0.9990 Silver 0.9990 oz. ASW, 40.6 mm. **Ruler:** Elizabeth II **Subject:** Treasures of Australia **Obv:** Head right **Rev:** Mountains **Note:** Insert container with 1 carat of diamonds.

Date	Mintage	F	VF	XF	Unc	BU
2009P Proof	7,500	Value: 110				

KM# 1403 DOLLAR
31.1050 g., 0.9990 Silver 0.9990 oz. ASW, 40.6 mm. **Ruler:** Elizabeth II **Obv:** Head right **Rev:** Frill-neck lizard, multicolor

Date	Mintage	F	VF	XF	Unc	BU
2010(p) Proof	—	Value: 90.00				

KM# 1409 DOLLAR
31.1050 g., 0.9990 Silver 0.9990 oz. ASW, 40.6 mm. **Ruler:** Elizabeth II **Obv:** Head right **Rev:** Koala and multicolor

Date	Mintage	F	VF	XF	Unc	BU
2010(p) Proof	—	Value: 90.00				

KM# 1415 DOLLAR
31.1050 g., 0.9990 Silver 0.9990 oz. ASW, 40.6 mm. **Ruler:** Elizabeth II **Obv:** Head right **Rev:** Multicolor platypus

Date	Mintage	F	VF	XF	Unc	BU
2010(p) Proof	—	Value: 90.00				

KM# 1421 DOLLAR
31.1050 g., 0.9990 Silver 0.9990 oz. ASW, 40.6 mm. **Ruler:** Elizabeth II **Obv:** Head right **Rev:** Multicolor salt water crocodile

Date	Mintage	F	VF	XF	Unc	BU
2010(p) Proof	—	Value: 90.00				

KM# 1427 DOLLAR
31.1050 g., 0.9990 Silver 0.9990 oz. ASW, 40.6 mm. **Ruler:** Elizabeth II **Obv:** Head right **Rev:** Multicolor wombat

Date	Mintage	F	VF	XF	Unc	BU
2010(p) Proof	—	Value: 90.00				

KM# 1453 DOLLAR
31.1050 g., 0.9990 Silver 0.9990 oz. ASW, 27x47 mm. **Ruler:** Elizabeth II **Rev:** Dreaming dolphin **Shape:** Vertical rectangle

Date	Mintage	F	VF	XF	Unc	BU
2010P Proof	—	—	—	—	—	80.00

KM# 1534 DOLLAR
31.1050 g., 0.9990 Silver 0.9990 oz. ASW **Ruler:** Elizabeth II **Subject:** Dreaming Emu **Rev:** Linear emu in color

Date	Mintage	F	VF	XF	Unc	BU
2011P Proof	—	Value: 105				

KM# 1540 DOLLAR
31.1050 g., 0.9990 Silver 0.9990 oz. ASW **Ruler:** Elizabeth II **Subject:** Dreaming Tasmanian Devil **Rev:** Linear tasmanian devil in color

Date	Mintage	F	VF	XF	Unc	BU
2011P Proof	—	Value: 105				

KM# 1546 DOLLAR
31.1050 g., 0.9990 Silver 0.9990 oz. ASW **Ruler:** Elizabeth II **Rev:** Linear Kookaburra in color

Date	Mintage	F	VF	XF	Unc	BU
2011P Proof	—	Value: 115				

KM# 1552 DOLLAR
31.1050 g., 0.9990 Silver 0.9990 oz. ASW **Ruler:** Elizabeth II **Subject:** Dreaming Shark **Rev:** Linear shark in color

Date	Mintage	F	VF	XF	Unc	BU
2011P Proof	—	Value: 105				

KM# 1558 DOLLAR
31.1050 g., 0.9990 Silver 0.9990 oz. ASW **Ruler:** Elizabeth II **Subject:** Dreaming Dingo **Rev:** Linear dingo in color

Date	Mintage	F	VF	XF	Unc	BU
2011P Proof	—	Value: 105				

KM# 1609 DOLLAR
31.1050 g., 0.9990 Silver 0.9990 oz. ASW, 27x47 mm. **Ruler:** Elizabeth II **Obv:** Head with tiara right **Rev:** Dearming Platypus **Shape:** Vertical rectangle

Date	Mintage	F	VF	XF	Unc	BU
2011P	—	—	—	—	—	80.00

KM# 1706 DOLLAR
31.1350 g., Silver, 40.6 mm. **Ruler:** Elizabeth II **Obv:** Head with tiara right **Rev:** Green gold bellfrog, background in color **Edge:** Reeded

Date	Mintage	F	VF	XF	Unc	BU
2012P Proof	7,500	Value: 100				

KM# 1707 DOLLAR
31.1350 g., 0.9990 Silver 1.0000 oz. ASW, 40.6 mm. **Ruler:** Elizabeth II **Obv:** Head with tiara right **Rev:** Red kangaroo and color background

Date	Mintage	F	VF	XF	Unc	BU
2012P Proof	7,500	Value: 100				

KM# 1708 DOLLAR
31.1350 g., 0.9990 Silver 1.0000 oz. ASW, 40.6 mm. **Ruler:** Elizabeth II **Obv:** Head with tiara right **Rev:** Kookaburra with color background

Date	Mintage	F	VF	XF	Unc	BU
2012P Proof	7,500	Value: 100				

KM# 1709 DOLLAR
31.1350 g., 0.9990 Silver 1.0000 oz. ASW, 40.6 mm. **Ruler:** Elizabeth II **Obv:** Head with tiara right **Rev:** Goanna on color background

Date	Mintage	F	VF	XF	Unc	BU
2012P Proof	7,500	Value: 100				

KM# 1710 DOLLAR

31.1350 g., 0.9990 Silver 1.0000 oz. ASW, 40.6 mm. **Ruler:** Elizabeth II **Obv:** Head with tiara right **Rev:** Whale shark on color background

Date	Mintage	F	VF	XF	Unc	BU
2012P Proof	—	Value: 100				

KM# 950 5 DOLLARS

1.2441 g., 0.9990 Gold 0.0400 oz. AGW **Ruler:** Elizabeth II **Subject:** Australian Fauna **Obv:** Head with tiara right **Rev:** Salt water crocodile

Date	Mintage	F	VF	XF	Unc	BU
2006 Proof	25,000	Value: 100				

KM# 953 5 DOLLARS

1.2441 g., 0.9990 Gold 0.0400 oz. AGW **Ruler:** Elizabeth II **Subject:** Australian Fauna **Obv:** Head with tiara right **Rev:** Grey kangaroo

Date	Mintage	F	VF	XF	Unc	BU
2006 Proof	25,000	Value: 100				

KM# 956 5 DOLLARS

1.2441 g., 0.9990 Gold 0.0400 oz. AGW **Ruler:** Elizabeth II **Subject:** Australian Fauna **Obv:** Head with tiara right **Rev:** Emu

Date	Mintage	F	VF	XF	Unc	BU
2006 Proof	25,000	Value: 85.00				

KM# 959 5 DOLLARS

1.2441 g., 0.9990 Gold 0.0400 oz. AGW **Ruler:** Elizabeth II **Subject:** Australian Fauna **Obv:** Head with tiara right **Rev:** Koala

Date	Mintage	F	VF	XF	Unc	BU
2006 Proof	25,000	Value: 100				

KM# 962 5 DOLLARS

1.2441 g., 0.9990 Gold 0.0400 oz. AGW **Ruler:** Elizabeth II **Subject:** Australian Fauna **Obv:** Head with tiara right **Rev:** Kookaburra

Date	Mintage	F	VF	XF	Unc	BU
2006 Proof	25,000	Value: 100				

KM# 965 5 DOLLARS

1.2441 g., 0.9990 Gold 0.0400 oz. AGW **Ruler:** Elizabeth II **Subject:** Australian Fauna **Obv:** Head with tiara right **Rev:** Echidna

Date	Mintage	F	VF	XF	Unc	BU
2007 Proof	25,000	Value: 100				

KM# 968 5 DOLLARS

1.2441 g., 0.9990 Gold 0.0400 oz. AGW **Ruler:** Elizabeth II **Subject:** Australian Fauna **Obv:** Head with tiara right **Rev:** Common wombat

Date	Mintage	F	VF	XF	Unc	BU
2007 Proof	25,000	Value: 100				

KM# 971 5 DOLLARS

1.2441 g., 0.9990 Gold 0.0400 oz. AGW **Ruler:** Elizabeth II **Subject:** Australian Fauna **Obv:** Head with tiara right **Rev:** Tasmanian devil

Date	Mintage	F	VF	XF	Unc	BU
2007 Proof	25,000	Value: 95.00				

KM# 974 5 DOLLARS

1.2441 g., 0.9990 Gold 0.0400 oz. AGW **Ruler:** Elizabeth II **Subject:** Australian Fauna **Obv:** Head with tiara right **Rev:** Great white shark

Date	Mintage	F	VF	XF	Unc	BU
2007 Proof	25,000	Value: 100				

KM# 977 5 DOLLARS

1.2441 g., 0.9990 Gold 0.0400 oz. AGW **Ruler:** Elizabeth II **Subject:** Australian Fauna **Obv:** Head with tiara right **Rev:** Platypus

Date	Mintage	F	VF	XF	Unc	BU
2007 Proof	25,000	Value: 100				

KM# 1217 5 DOLLARS

1.2500 g., 0.9990 Gold 0.0401 oz. AGW, 14 mm. **Ruler:** Elizabeth II **Obv:** Head right **Rev:** Dreaming kangaroo

Date	Mintage	F	VF	XF	Unc	BU
2009P Proof	25,000	Value: 125				

KM# 1219 5 DOLLARS

1.2500 g., 0.9990 Gold 0.0401 oz. AGW, 14 mm. **Ruler:** Elizabeth II **Obv:** Head right **Rev:** Dreaming king brown snake

Date	Mintage	F	VF	XF	Unc	BU
2009P Proof	25,000	Value: 125				

KM# 1220 5 DOLLARS

1.2500 g., 0.9990 Gold 0.0401 oz. AGW, 14 mm. **Ruler:** Elizabeth II **Obv:** Head right **Rev:** Dreaming brolga

Date	Mintage	F	VF	XF	Unc	BU
2009P Proof	25,000	Value: 125				

KM# 1221 5 DOLLARS

1.2500 g., 0.9990 Gold 0.0401 oz. AGW, 14 mm. **Ruler:** Elizabeth II **Obv:** Head right **Rev:** Dreaming echidna

Date	Mintage	F	VF	XF	Unc	BU
2009P Proof	25,000	Value: 125				

KM# 1224 5 DOLLARS

3.1100 g., 0.9990 Gold 0.0999 oz. AGW, 14 mm. **Ruler:** Elizabeth II **Obv:** Head right **Rev:** Dreaming brown snake

Date	Mintage	F	VF	XF	Unc	BU
2009P Proof	2,500	Value: 175				

KM# 1402 5 DOLLARS

1.2400 g., 0.9990 Gold 0.0398 oz. AGW, 14 mm. **Ruler:** Elizabeth II **Obv:** Head right **Rev:** Frill-neck lizard

Date	Mintage	F	VF	XF	Unc	BU
2010P Proof	25,000	Value: 130				

KM# 1408 5 DOLLARS

1.2400 g., 0.9990 Gold 0.0398 oz. AGW, 14 mm. **Ruler:** Elizabeth II **Obv:** Head right **Rev:** Koala

Date	Mintage	F	VF	XF	Unc	BU
2010P Proof	25,000	Value: 130				

KM# 1414 5 DOLLARS

1.2400 g., 0.9990 Gold 0.0398 oz. AGW, 14 mm. **Ruler:** Elizabeth II **Obv:** Head right **Rev:** Platypus

Date	Mintage	F	VF	XF	Unc	BU
2010P Proof	25,000	Value: 130				

KM# 1420 5 DOLLARS

1.2400 g., 0.9990 Gold 0.0398 oz. AGW, 14 mm. **Ruler:** Elizabeth II **Obv:** Head right **Rev:** Salt water crocodile

Date	Mintage	F	VF	XF	Unc	BU
2010P Proof	25,000	Value: 130				

KM# 1426 5 DOLLARS

1.2400 g., 0.9990 Gold 0.0398 oz. AGW, 14 mm. **Ruler:** Elizabeth II **Obv:** Head right **Rev:** Wombat

Date	Mintage	F	VF	XF	Unc	BU
2010P Proof	25,000	Value: 130				

KM# 1535 5 DOLLARS

1.2400 g., 0.9990 Gold 0.0398 oz. AGW **Ruler:** Elizabeth II **Subject:** Dreaming Emu **Rev:** Linear emu in color

Date	Mintage	F	VF	XF	Unc	BU
2011P Proof	25,000	Value: 125				

KM# 1541 5 DOLLARS

1.2400 g., 0.9990 Gold 0.0398 oz. AGW **Ruler:** Elizabeth II **Subject:** Dreaming Tasmanian Devil **Rev:** Linear tasmanian devil in color

Date	Mintage	F	VF	XF	Unc	BU
2011P Proof	25,000	Value: 125				

KM# 1547 5 DOLLARS

1.2400 g., 0.9990 Gold 0.0398 oz. AGW **Ruler:** Elizabeth II **Obv:** Dreaming Kookaburra **Edge:** Linear Kookaburra in color

Date	Mintage	F	VF	XF	Unc	BU
2011P Proof	250,000	Value: 125				

KM# 1553 5 DOLLARS

1.2400 g., 0.9990 Gold 0.0398 oz. AGW **Ruler:** Elizabeth II **Subject:** Dreaming shark **Rev:** Linear shark in color

Date	Mintage	F	VF	XF	Unc	BU
2011P Proof	25,000	Value: 125				

KM# 1559 5 DOLLARS

1.2400 g., 0.9990 Gold 0.0398 oz. AGW **Ruler:** Elizabeth II **Subject:** Dreaming Dingo **Rev:** Linear dingo in color

Date	Mintage	F	VF	XF	Unc	BU
2011P Proof	25,000	Value: 125				

KM# 1636 5 DOLLARS

1.2400 g., 0.9990 Gold 0.0398 oz. AGW, 14 mm. **Ruler:** Elizabeth II **Subject:** Historic Convict Past - Hyde Park Barracks

Date	Mintage	F	VF	XF	Unc	BU
2011 Proof	3,000	Value: 125				

KM# 1716 5 DOLLARS

1.2440 g., 0.9990 Gold 0.0400 oz. AGW, 14.6 mm. **Ruler:** Elizabeth II **Rev:** Green and Gold Bell Frog in greass

Date	Mintage	F	VF	XF	Unc	BU
2012P Proof	2,500	Value: 100				

KM# 1717 5 DOLLARS

1.2440 g., 0.9990 Gold 0.0400 oz. AGW, 14.6 mm. **Ruler:** Elizabeth II **Rev:** Kookaburra facing right

Date	Mintage	F	VF	XF	Unc	BU
2012P Proof	2,500	Value: 100				

KM# 1718 5 DOLLARS

1.2440 g., 0.9990 Gold 0.0400 oz. AGW, 14.1 mm. **Ruler:** Elizabeth II **Rev:** Whale shark swimming right

Date	Mintage	F	VF	XF	Unc	BU
2012P Proof	2,500	Value: 100				

KM# 1719 5 DOLLARS

1.2440 g., 0.9990 Gold 0.0400 oz. AGW, 14.6 mm. **Ruler:** Elizabeth II **Rev:** Kangaroo bounding right

Date	Mintage	F	VF	XF	Unc	BU
2012P Proof	2,500	Value: 100				

KM# 1720 5 DOLLARS

1.2440 g., 0.9990 Gold 0.0400 oz. AGW, 14.6 mm. **Ruler:** Elizabeth II **Rev:** Goanna lizard right

Date	Mintage	F	VF	XF	Unc	BU
2012P Proof	2,500	Value: 100				

KM# 1118 10 DOLLARS

1.2400 g., 0.9990 Gold 0.0398 oz. AGW, 14 mm. **Ruler:** Elizabeth II **Obv:** Bust right **Rev:** Salt water crocodile **Rev. Legend:** DISCOVER AUSTRALIA

Date	Mintage	F	VF	XF	Unc	BU
2006P Proof	25,000	Value: 110				

KM# 1119 10 DOLLARS

1.2400 g., 0.9990 Gold 0.0398 oz. AGW, 14 mm. **Ruler:** Elizabeth II **Obv:** Head right **Rev:** Grey kangaroo **Rev. Legend:** DISCOVER AUSTRALIA

Date	Mintage	F	VF	XF	Unc	BU
2006P Proof	25,000	Value: 110				

KM# 1120 10 DOLLARS

1.2400 g., 0.9990 Gold 0.0398 oz. AGW, 14 mm. **Ruler:** Elizabeth II **Obv:** Head right **Rev:** Emu **Rev. Legend:** DISCOVER AUSTRALIA

Date	Mintage	F	VF	XF	Unc	BU
2006P Proof	25,000	Value: 110				

KM# 1121 10 DOLLARS

1.2400 g., 0.9990 Gold 0.0398 oz. AGW, 14 mm. **Ruler:** Elizabeth II **Obv:** Head right **Rev:** Koala **Rev. Legend:** DISCOVER AUSTRALIA

Date	Mintage	F	VF	XF	Unc	BU
2006P Proof	25,000	Value: 110				

KM# 1122 10 DOLLARS
1.2400 g., 0.9990 Gold 0.0398 oz. AGW, 14 mm. **Ruler:** Elizabeth II **Obv:** Head right **Rev:** Kookaburra **Rev. Legend:** DISCOVER AUSTRALIA

Date	Mintage	F	VF	XF	Unc	BU
2006P Proof	25,000	Value: 110				

KM# 1133 10 DOLLARS
3.1000 g., 0.9990 Platinum 0.0996 oz. APW, 16 mm. **Ruler:** Elizabeth II **Obv:** Head right **Rev:** Cooktown orchid, multicolor **Rev. Legend:** DISCOVER AUSTRALIA

Date	Mintage	F	VF	XF	Unc	BU
2006P Proof	2,500	Value: 300				

KM# 1134 10 DOLLARS
3.1000 g., 0.9990 Platinum 0.0996 oz. APW, 16 mm. **Ruler:** Elizabeth II **Obv:** Head right **Rev:** Sturt's desert rose, multicolor **Rev. Legend:** DISCOVER AUSTRALIA

Date	Mintage	F	VF	XF	Unc	BU
2006P Proof	2,500	Value: 300				

KM# 1135 10 DOLLARS
3.1000 g., 0.9990 Platinum 0.0996 oz. APW, 16 mm. **Ruler:** Elizabeth II **Obv:** Head right **Rev:** Royal Bluebell, multicolor **Rev. Legend:** DISCOVER AUSTRALIA

Date	Mintage	F	VF	XF	Unc	BU
2006P Proof	2,500	Value: 300				

KM# 1136 10 DOLLARS
3.1000 g., 0.9990 Platinum 0.0996 oz. APW, 16 mm. **Ruler:** Elizabeth II **Obv:** Head right **Rev:** Red and green kangaroo paw, multicolor **Rev. Legend:** DISCOVER AUSTRALIA

Date	Mintage	F	VF	XF	Unc	BU
2006P Proof	2,500	Value: 300				

KM# 1137 10 DOLLARS
3.1000 g., 0.9990 Platinum 0.0996 oz. APW, 16 mm. **Ruler:** Elizabeth II **Obv:** Head right **Rev:** Common pink heath, multicolor **Rev. Legend:** DISCOVER AUSTRALIA

Date	Mintage	F	VF	XF	Unc	BU
2006P Proof	2,500	Value: 300				

KM# 1143 10 DOLLARS
1.2400 g., 0.9990 Gold 0.0398 oz. AGW, 14 mm. **Ruler:** Elizabeth II **Obv:** Head right **Rev:** Echidna **Rev. Legend:** DISCOVER AUSTRALIA

Date	Mintage	F	VF	XF	Unc	BU
2007P Proof	25,000	Value: 110				

KM# 1144 10 DOLLARS
1.2400 g., 0.9990 Gold 0.0398 oz. AGW, 14 mm. **Ruler:** Elizabeth II **Obv:** Head right **Rev:** Common wombat **Rev. Legend:** DISCOVER AUSTRALIA

Date	Mintage	F	VF	XF	Unc	BU
2007P Proof	25,000	Value: 110				

KM# 1145 10 DOLLARS
1.2400 g., 0.9990 Gold 0.0398 oz. AGW, 14 mm. **Ruler:** Elizabeth II **Obv:** Head right **Rev:** Tasmanian devil **Rev. Legend:** DISCOVER AUSTRALIA

Date	Mintage	F	VF	XF	Unc	BU
2007P Proof	25,000	Value: 110				

KM# 1146 10 DOLLARS
1.2400 g., 0.9990 Gold 0.0398 oz. AGW, 14 mm. **Ruler:** Elizabeth II **Obv:** Head right **Rev:** Great white shark **Rev. Legend:** DISCOVER AUSTRALIA

Date	Mintage	F	VF	XF	Unc	BU
2007P Proof	25,000	Value: 110				

KM# 1147 10 DOLLARS
1.2400 g., 0.9990 Gold 0.0398 oz. AGW, 14 mm. **Ruler:** Elizabeth II **Obv:** Head right **Rev:** Platypus **Rev. Legend:** DISCOVER AUSTRALIA

Date	Mintage	F	VF	XF	Unc	BU
2007P Proof	25,000	Value: 110				

KM# 1159 10 DOLLARS
3.1000 g., 0.9990 Platinum 0.0996 oz. APW, 16 mm. **Ruler:** Elizabeth II **Obv:** Head right **Rev:** Sturt's desert pea, multicolor **Rev. Legend:** DISCOVER AUSTRALIA

Date	Mintage	F	VF	XF	Unc	BU
2007P Proof	2,500	Value: 300				

KM# 1160 10 DOLLARS
3.1000 g., 0.9990 Platinum 0.0996 oz. APW, 16 mm. **Ruler:** Elizabeth II **Obv:** Head right **Rev:** Tasmanian bluegum, multicolor **Rev. Legend:** DISCOVER AUSTRALIA

Date	Mintage	F	VF	XF	Unc	BU
2007P Proof	2,500	Value: 300				

KM# 1161 10 DOLLARS
3.1000 g., 0.9990 Platinum 0.0996 oz. APW, 16 mm. **Ruler:** Elizabeth II **Obv:** Head right **Rev:** Waratah, multicolor **Rev. Legend:** DISCOVER AUSTRALIA

Date	Mintage	F	VF	XF	Unc	BU
2007P Proof	2,500	Value: 300				

KM# 1162 10 DOLLARS
3.1000 g., 0.9990 Platinum 0.0996 oz. APW, 16 mm. **Ruler:** Elizabeth II **Obv:** Head right **Rev:** Golden wattle, multicolor **Rev. Legend:** DISCOVER AUSTRALIA

Date	Mintage	F	VF	XF	Unc	BU
2007P Proof	2,500	Value: 300				

KM# 1186 10 DOLLARS
1.2400 g., 0.9990 Gold 0.0398 oz. AGW, 14 mm. **Ruler:** Elizabeth II **Obv:** Head right **Rev:** Dolphin **Rev. Legend:** DISCOVER AUSTRALIA

Date	Mintage	F	VF	XF	Unc	BU
2008P Proof	25,000	Value: 110				

KM# 1187 10 DOLLARS
1.2400 g., 0.9990 Gold 0.0398 oz. AGW, 14 mm. **Ruler:** Elizabeth II **Obv:** Head right **Rev:** King brown snake **Rev. Legend:** DISCOVER AUSTRALIA

Date	Mintage	F	VF	XF	Unc	BU
2008P Proof	25,000	Value: 110				

KM# 1189 10 DOLLARS
1.2400 g., 0.9990 Gold 0.0398 oz. AGW, 14 mm. **Ruler:** Elizabeth II **Obv:** Head right **Rev:** Dingo **Rev. Legend:** DISCOVER AUSTRALIA

Date	Mintage	F	VF	XF	Unc	BU
2008P Proof	25,000	Value: 110				

KM# 1190 10 DOLLARS
1.2400 g., 0.9990 Gold 0.0398 oz. AGW, 14 mm. **Ruler:** Elizabeth II **Obv:** Head right **Rev:** Frill-neck lizard **Rev. Legend:** DISCOVER AUSTRALIA

Date	Mintage	F	VF	XF	Unc	BU
2008P Proof	25,000	Value: 110				

KM# 1201 10 DOLLARS
3.1000 g., 0.9990 Platinum 0.0996 oz. APW, 16 mm. **Ruler:** Elizabeth II **Obv:** Head right **Rev:** Black anther fax lilly, multicolor **Rev. Legend:** DISCOVER AUSTRALIA

Date	Mintage	F	VF	XF	Unc	BU
2008P Proof	2,500	Value: 300				

KM# 1202 10 DOLLARS
3.1000 g., 0.9990 Platinum 0.0996 oz. APW, 16 mm. **Ruler:** Elizabeth II **Obv:** Head right **Rev:** Native frangipani, multicolor **Rev. Legend:** DISCOVER AUSTRALIA

Date	Mintage	F	VF	XF	Unc	BU
2008P Proof	2,500	Value: 300				

KM# 1203 10 DOLLARS
3.1000 g., 0.9990 Platinum 0.0996 oz. APW, 16 mm. **Ruler:** Elizabeth II **Obv:** Head right **Rev:** Geraldton wax, multicolor

Date	Mintage	F	VF	XF	Unc	BU
2008P Proof	2,500	Value: 300				

KM# 1204 10 DOLLARS
3.1000 g., 0.9990 Platinum 0.0996 oz. APW, 16 mm. **Ruler:** Elizabeth II **Obv:** Head right **Rev:** Red-flowered kurrajong, multicolor **Rev. Legend:** DISCOVER AUSTRALIA

Date	Mintage	F	VF	XF	Unc	BU
2008P Proof	2,500	Value: 300				

KM# 1205 10 DOLLARS
3.1000 g., 0.9990 Platinum 0.0996 oz. APW, 16 mm. **Ruler:** Elizabeth II **Obv:** Head right **Rev:** Small-leaf lily pilly, multicolor **Rev. Legend:** DISCOVER AUSTRALIA

Date	Mintage	F	VF	XF	Unc	BU
2008P Proof	2,500	Value: 300				

KM# 1206 10 DOLLARS
15.5500 g., 0.9990 Gold 0.4994 oz. AGW, 26 mm. **Ruler:** Elizabeth II **Obv:** Head right **Rev:** Black anther flax lily, multicolor **Rev. Legend:** DISCOVER AUSTRALIA

Date	Mintage	F	VF	XF	Unc	BU
2008P Proof	1,000	Value: 1,500				

KM# 980 15 DOLLARS
3.1101 g., 0.9990 Platinum 0.0999 oz. APW **Ruler:** Elizabeth II **Subject:** Australian Flora **Obv:** Head with tiara right **Rev:** Cooktown orchid

Date	Mintage	F	VF	XF	Unc	BU
2006 Proof	2,500	Value: 220				

KM# 982 15 DOLLARS
3.1101 g., 0.9990 Platinum 0.0999 oz. APW **Ruler:** Elizabeth II **Subject:** Australian Flora **Obv:** Head with tiara right **Rev:** Sturt's desert rose

Date	Mintage	F	VF	XF	Unc	BU
2006 Proof	2,500	Value: 220				

KM# 984 15 DOLLARS
3.1101 g., 0.9990 Platinum 0.0999 oz. APW **Ruler:** Elizabeth II **Subject:** Australian Flora **Obv:** Head with tiara right **Rev:** Royal bluebell

Date	Mintage	F	VF	XF	Unc	BU
2006 Proof	2,500	Value: 220				

KM# 986 15 DOLLARS
3.1101 g., 0.9990 Platinum 0.0999 oz. APW **Ruler:** Elizabeth II **Subject:** Australian Flora **Obv:** Head with tiara right **Rev:** Kangaroo paw

Date	Mintage	F	VF	XF	Unc	BU
2006 Proof	2,500	Value: 220				

KM# 988 15 DOLLARS
3.1101 g., 0.9990 Platinum 0.0999 oz. APW **Ruler:** Elizabeth II **Subject:** Australian Flora **Obv:** Head with tiara right **Rev:** Common pink heath

Date	Mintage	F	VF	XF	Unc	BU
2006 Proof	2,500	Value: 220				

KM# 951 15 DOLLARS
3.1101 g., 0.9990 Gold 0.0999 oz. AGW **Ruler:** Elizabeth II **Subject:** Australian Fauna **Obv:** Head with tiara right **Rev:** Saltwater crocodile

Date	Mintage	F	VF	XF	Unc	BU
2006 Proof	2,500	Value: 195				

KM# 954 15 DOLLARS
3.1101 g., 0.9990 Gold 0.0999 oz. AGW **Ruler:** Elizabeth II **Subject:** Australian Fauna **Obv:** Head with tiara right **Rev:** Grey kangaroo

Date	Mintage	F	VF	XF	Unc	BU
2006 Proof	2,500	Value: 195				

KM# 957 15 DOLLARS
3.1101 g., 0.9990 Gold 0.0999 oz. AGW **Ruler:** Elizabeth II **Subject:** Australian Fauna **Obv:** Head with tiara right **Rev:** Emu

Date	Mintage	F	VF	XF	Unc	BU
2006 Proof	2,500	Value: 195				

KM# 960 15 DOLLARS
3.1101 g., 0.9990 Gold 0.0999 oz. AGW **Ruler:** Elizabeth II **Subject:** Australian Fauna **Obv:** Head with tiara right **Rev:** Koala

Date	Mintage	F	VF	XF	Unc	BU
2006 Proof	2,500	Value: 195				

KM# 963 15 DOLLARS
3.1101 g., 0.9990 Gold 0.0999 oz. AGW **Ruler:** Elizabeth II **Subject:** Australian Fauna **Obv:** Head with tiara right **Rev:** Kookaburra

Date	Mintage	F	VF	XF	Unc	BU
2006 Proof	2,500	Value: 195				

KM# 966 15 DOLLARS
3.1101 g., 0.9990 Gold 0.0999 oz. AGW **Ruler:** Elizabeth II **Subject:** Australian Fauna **Obv:** Head with tiara right **Rev:** Echidna

Date	Mintage	F	VF	XF	Unc	BU
2007 Proof	2,500	Value: 195				

KM# 969 15 DOLLARS
3.1101 g., 0.9990 Gold 0.0999 oz. AGW **Ruler:** Elizabeth II **Subject:** Australian Fauna **Obv:** Head with tiara right **Rev:** Common wombat

Date	Mintage	F	VF	XF	Unc	BU
2007 Proof	2,500	Value: 195				

KM# 972 15 DOLLARS
3.1101 g., 0.9990 Gold 0.0999 oz. AGW **Ruler:** Elizabeth II **Subject:** Australian Fauna **Obv:** Head with tiara right **Rev:** Tasmanian devil

Date	Mintage	F	VF	XF	Unc	BU
2007 Proof	2,500	Value: 195				

KM# 975 15 DOLLARS
3.1101 g., 0.9990 Gold 0.0999 oz. AGW **Ruler:** Elizabeth II **Subject:** Australian Fauna **Obv:** Head with tiara right **Rev:** Great white shark

Date	Mintage	F	VF	XF	Unc	BU
2007 Proof	2,500	Value: 195				

KM# 978 15 DOLLARS
3.1101 g., 0.9990 Gold 0.0999 oz. AGW **Ruler:** Elizabeth II **Subject:** Australian Fauna **Obv:** Head with tiara right **Rev:** Platypus

Date	Mintage	F	VF	XF	Unc	BU
2007 Proof	2,500	Value: 195				

KM# 990 15 DOLLARS
3.1101 g., 0.9990 Platinum 0.0999 oz. APW **Ruler:** Elizabeth II **Subject:** Australian Flora **Obv:** Head with tiara right **Rev:** Anemone buttercup

Date	Mintage	F	VF	XF	Unc	BU
2007 Proof	2,500	Value: 220				

KM# 992 15 DOLLARS
3.1101 g., 0.9990 Platinum 0.0999 oz. APW **Ruler:** Elizabeth II **Subject:** Australian Flora **Obv:** Head with tiara right **Rev:** Sturt's desert pea

Date	Mintage	F	VF	XF	Unc	BU
2007 Proof	2,500	Value: 220				

KM# 994 15 DOLLARS
3.1101 g., 0.9990 Platinum 0.0999 oz. APW **Ruler:** Elizabeth II **Subject:** Australian Flora **Obv:** Head with tiara right **Rev:** Tasmanian bluegum

Date	Mintage	F	VF	XF	Unc	BU
2007 Proof	2,500	Value: 220				

KM# 996 15 DOLLARS
3.1101 g., 0.9990 Platinum 0.0999 oz. APW **Ruler:** Elizabeth II **Subject:** Australian Flora **Obv:** Head with tiara right **Rev:** Waratah

Date	Mintage	F	VF	XF	Unc	BU
2007 Proof	2,500	Value: 220				

KM# 998 15 DOLLARS
3.1101 g., 0.9990 Platinum 0.0999 oz. APW **Ruler:** Elizabeth II **Subject:** Australian Flora **Obv:** Head with tiara right **Rev:** Golden wattle

Date	Mintage	F	VF	XF	Unc	BU
2007 Proof	2,500	Value: 220				

KM# 1104 15 DOLLARS
2.5000 g., 0.9999 Gold 0.0804 oz. AGW, 13x22 mm. **Ruler:** Elizabeth II **Rev:** Turtle Dreaming **Shape:** Rectangle

Date	Mintage	F	VF	XF	Unc	BU
2009 Proof	—	Value: 175				

KM# 1108 15 DOLLARS
2.5000 g., 0.9999 Gold 0.0804 oz. AGW, 13x22 mm. **Ruler:** Elizabeth II **Rev:** Kangaroo Dreaming **Shape:** Vertical rectangle

Date	Mintage	Good	VG	F	VF	XF
2009 Proof	—	Value: 175				

KM# 1223 15 DOLLARS
3.1100 g., 0.9990 Gold 0.0999 oz. AGW, 16 mm. **Ruler:** Elizabeth II **Obv:** Head right **Rev:** Dreaming dolphin

Date	Mintage	F	VF	XF	Unc	BU
2009P Proof	2,500	Value: 195				

KM# 1225 15 DOLLARS
3.1100 g., 0.9990 Gold 0.0999 oz. AGW, 16 mm. **Ruler:** Elizabeth II **Obv:** Head right **Rev:** Dreaming brolga

Date	Mintage	F	VF	XF	Unc	BU
2009P Proof	2,500	Value: 195				

KM# 1226 15 DOLLARS
3.1100 g., 0.9990 Gold 0.0999 oz. AGW, 16 mm. **Ruler:** Elizabeth II **Obv:** Head right **Rev:** Dreaming echidna

Date	Mintage	F	VF	XF	Unc	BU
2009P Proof	2,500	Value: 195				

KM# 1228 15 DOLLARS
15.5500 g., 0.9990 Gold 0.4994 oz. AGW, 25 mm. **Ruler:** Elizabeth II **Obv:** Head right **Rev:** Dreaming dolphin

Date	Mintage	F	VF	XF	Unc	BU
2009P Proof	1,000	Value: 1,100				

KM# 1232 15 DOLLARS
3.1100 g., 0.9990 Platinum 0.0999 oz. APW, 16 mm. **Ruler:** Elizabeth II **Obv:** Head right **Rev:** Dreaming kangaroo, multicolor

Date	Mintage	F	VF	XF	Unc	BU
2009P Proof	2,500	Value: 400				

KM# 1233 15 DOLLARS
3.1100 g., 0.9990 Platinum 0.0999 oz. APW, 16 mm. **Ruler:** Elizabeth II **Obv:** Head right **Rev:** Dreaming dolphin, multicolor

Date	Mintage	F	VF	XF	Unc	BU
2009P Proof	2,500	Value: 400				

KM# 1234 15 DOLLARS
3.1100 g., 0.9990 Platinum 0.0999 oz. APW, 16 mm. **Ruler:** Elizabeth II **Obv:** Head right **Rev:** Dreaming king brown snake, multicolor

Date	Mintage	F	VF	XF	Unc	BU
2009P Proof	2,500	Value: 400				

KM# 1235 15 DOLLARS
3.1100 g., 0.9990 Platinum 0.0999 oz. APW, 16 mm. **Ruler:** Elizabeth II **Obv:** Head right **Rev:** Dreaming brolga

Date	Mintage	F	VF	XF	Unc	BU
2009P Proof	2,500	Value: 400				

KM# 1236 15 DOLLARS
3.1100 g., 0.9990 Platinum 0.0999 oz. APW, 16 mm. **Ruler:** Elizabeth II **Obv:** Head right **Rev:** Dreaming echidna, multicolor

Date	Mintage	F	VF	XF	Unc	BU
2009P Proof	2,500	Value: 400				

KM# 1399 15 DOLLARS
3.1100 g., 0.9990 Platinum 0.0999 oz. APW, 17 mm. **Ruler:** Elizabeth II **Obv:** Head right **Rev:** Multicolor frill-neck lizard

Date	Mintage	F	VF	XF	Unc	BU
2010(p)	2,500	Value: 335				

KM# 1401 15 DOLLARS
3.1100 g., 0.9990 Gold 0.0999 oz. AGW, 17 mm. **Ruler:** Elizabeth II **Obv:** Head right **Rev:** Frill-neck lizard

Date	Mintage	F	VF	XF	Unc	BU
2010(p) Proof	2,500	Value: 260				

KM# 1405 15 DOLLARS
3.1100 g., 0.9990 Platinum 0.0999 oz. APW, 17 mm. **Ruler:** Elizabeth II **Obv:** Head right **Rev:** Multicolor koala

Date	Mintage	F	VF	XF	Unc	BU
2010(p) Proof	2,500	Value: 335				

KM# 1407 15 DOLLARS
3.1100 g., 0.9990 Gold 0.0999 oz. AGW, 16 mm. **Ruler:** Elizabeth II **Obv:** Head right **Rev:** Koala

Date	Mintage	F	VF	XF	Unc	BU
2010(p) Proof	2,500	Value: 260				

KM# 1411 15 DOLLARS
3.1100 g., 0.9990 Platinum 0.0999 oz. APW, 17 mm. **Ruler:** Elizabeth II **Obv:** Head right **Rev:** Multicolor platypus

Date	Mintage	F	VF	XF	Unc	BU
2010(p) Proof	2,500	Value: 335				

KM# 1413 15 DOLLARS
0.9990 Gold, 16 mm. **Ruler:** Elizabeth II **Obv:** Head right **Rev:** Platypus

Date	Mintage	F	VF	XF	Unc	BU
2010(p) Proof	2,500	Value: 260				

KM# 1417 15 DOLLARS
0.9990 Platinum APW, 17 mm. **Ruler:** Elizabeth II **Obv:** Head right **Rev:** Muticolor saltwater crocodile

Date	Mintage	F	VF	XF	Unc	BU
2010(p) Proof	2,500	Value: 335				

KM# 1419 15 DOLLARS
3.1100 g., 0.9990 Gold 0.0999 oz. AGW, 16 mm. **Ruler:** Elizabeth II **Obv:** Head right **Rev:** Saltwater crocodile

Date	Mintage	F	VF	XF	Unc	BU
2010(p) Proof	2,500	Value: 260				

KM# 1423 15 DOLLARS
3.1100 g., 0.9990 Platinum 0.0999 oz. APW, 17 mm. **Ruler:** Elizabeth II **Obv:** Head right **Rev:** Multicolor wombat

Date	Mintage	F	VF	XF	Unc	BU
2010(p) Proof	2,500	Value: 335				

KM# 1425 15 DOLLARS
0.9990 Gold, 16 mm. **Ruler:** Elizabeth II **Obv:** Head right **Rev:** Wombat

Date	Mintage	F	VF	XF	Unc	BU
2010(p) Proof	2,500	Value: 260				

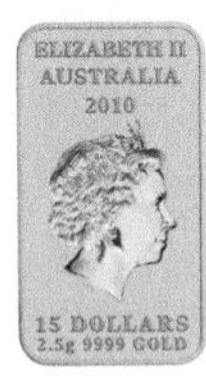

KM# 1454 15 DOLLARS
2.5000 g., 0.9990 Gold 0.0803 oz. AGW, 13x22 mm. **Ruler:** Elizabeth II **Rev:** Dolphin dreaming **Shape:** Vertical rectangle

Date	Mintage	F	VF	XF	Unc	BU
2010P Proof	—	Value: 175				

KM# 1536 15 DOLLARS
3.1100 g., 0.9990 Gold 0.0999 oz. AGW **Ruler:** Elizabeth II **Subject:** Dreaming Emu **Rev:** Linear emu in color

Date	Mintage	F	VF	XF	Unc	BU
2011P Proof	2,500	Value: 250				

KM# 1538 15 DOLLARS
3.1100 g., 0.9990 Platinum 0.0999 oz. APW **Ruler:** Elizabeth II **Subject:** Dreaming Emu **Rev:** Linear emu in color

Date	Mintage	F	VF	XF	Unc	BU
2011P Proof	2,500	Value: 375				

KM# 1542 15 DOLLARS
3.1100 g., 0.9990 Gold 0.0999 oz. AGW **Ruler:** Elizabeth II **Subject:** Dreaming Tasmanian Devil **Rev:** Linear tasmanian devil in color

Date	Mintage	F	VF	XF	Unc	BU
2011P Proof	2,500	Value: 250				

KM# 1544 15 DOLLARS
3.1100 g., 0.9990 Platinum 0.0999 oz. APW **Ruler:** Elizabeth II **Subject:** Dreaming Tasmanian Devil **Rev:** Linear tasmanian devil in color

Date	Mintage	F	VF	XF	Unc	BU
2011P Proof	2,500	Value: 375				

KM# 1548 15 DOLLARS
3.1100 g., 0.9990 Gold 0.0999 oz. AGW **Ruler:** Elizabeth II **Subject:** Dreaming Kookaburra **Rev:** Linear kookaburra in color

Date	Mintage	F	VF	XF	Unc	BU
2011P Proof	2,500	Value: 250				

KM# 1550 15 DOLLARS
3.1100 g., 0.9990 Platinum 0.0999 oz. APW **Ruler:** Elizabeth II **Subject:** Dreaming Kookaburra **Rev:** Linear kookaburra in color

Date	Mintage	F	VF	XF	Unc	BU
2011P Proof	2,500	Value: 375				

KM# 1554 15 DOLLARS
3.1100 g., 0.9990 Gold 0.0999 oz. AGW **Ruler:** Elizabeth II **Subject:** Dreaming Shark **Rev:** Linear shark in color

Date	Mintage	F	VF	XF	Unc	BU
2011P Proof	2,500	Value: 250				

KM# 1556 15 DOLLARS
3.1100 g., 0.9990 Platinum 0.0999 oz. APW **Ruler:** Elizabeth II **Subject:** Dreaming Shark **Rev:** Linear shark in color

Date	Mintage	F	VF	XF	Unc	BU
2011P Proof	2,500	Value: 375				

KM# 1560 15 DOLLARS
3.1100 g., 0.9990 Gold 0.0999 oz. AGW **Ruler:** Elizabeth II **Subject:** Dreaming Dingo **Rev:** Linear dingo in color

Date	Mintage	F	VF	XF	Unc	BU
2011P Proof	2,500	Value: 250				

KM# 1562 15 DOLLARS
3.1100 g., 0.9990 Platinum 0.0999 oz. APW **Ruler:** Elizabeth II **Subject:** Dreaming Dingo **Rev:** Linear dingo in color

Date	Mintage	F	VF	XF	Unc	BU
2011P Proof	2,500	Value: 375				

KM# 1610 15 DOLLARS
2.5000 g., 0.9990 Gold 0.0803 oz. AGW, 13x22 mm. **Ruler:** Elizabeth II **Obv:** Head with tiara right **Rev:** Platypus dreaming **Shape:** Vertical rectangle

Date	Mintage	F	VF	XF	Unc	BU
2011P Proof	—	Value: 175				

KM# 1848 15 DOLLARS
3.1100 g., 0.9990 Platinum 0.0999 oz. APW, 16.6 mm. **Ruler:** Elizabeth II **Rev:** Bell Frog and color background

Date	Mintage	F	VF	XF	Unc	BU
2012P Proof	1,000	Value: 325				

KM# 1721 15 DOLLARS
3.1110 g., 0.9990 Gold 0.0999 oz. AGW, 16.6 mm. **Ruler:** Elizabeth II **Rev:** Green and Gold Bell Frog in grass

Date	Mintage	F	VF	XF	Unc	BU
2012P Proof	1,000	Value: 225				

KM# 1722 15 DOLLARS
3.1110 g., 0.9990 Gold 0.0999 oz. AGW, 16.6 mm. **Ruler:** Elizabeth II **Rev:** Kookaburra standing right

Date	Mintage	F	VF	XF	Unc	BU
2012P Proof	1,000	Value: 225				

KM# 1723 15 DOLLARS
3.1110 g., 0.9990 Gold 0.0999 oz. AGW, 16.6 mm. **Ruler:** Elizabeth II **Rev:** Whale Shark swimming right

Date	Mintage	F	VF	XF	Unc	BU
2012P Proof	1,000	Value: 225				

KM# 1724 15 DOLLARS
3.1110 g., 0.9990 Gold 0.0999 oz. AGW, 16.6 mm. **Ruler:** Elizabeth II **Rev:** Kangaroo bounding right

Date	Mintage	F	VF	XF	Unc	BU
2012P Proof	1,000	Value: 225				

KM# 1725 15 DOLLARS
3.1110 g., 0.9990 Gold 0.0999 oz. AGW, 16.6 mm. **Ruler:** Elizabeth II **Rev:** Goanna lizard right

Date	Mintage	F	VF	XF	Unc	BU
2012P Proof	1,000	Value: 225				

KM# 1849 15 DOLLARS
3.1100 g., 0.9990 Platinum 0.0999 oz. APW, 16.6 mm. **Ruler:** Elizabeth II **Rev:** Kookaburra with color background

Date	Mintage	F	VF	XF	Unc	BU
2012P Proof	1,000	Value: 325				

KM# 1850 15 DOLLARS
3.1100 g., 0.9990 Platinum 0.0999 oz. APW, 16.1 mm. **Ruler:** Elizabeth II **Rev:** Whale shark on color background

Date	Mintage	F	VF	XF	Unc	BU
2012P Proof	1,000	Value: 325				

KM# 1851 15 DOLLARS
3.1100 g., 0.9990 Platinum 0.0999 oz. APW, 16.1 mm. **Ruler:** Elizabeth II **Rev:** Kangaroo on color background

Date	Mintage	F	VF	XF	Unc	BU
2012P Proof	1,000	Value: 325				

KM# 1852 15 DOLLARS
3.1100 g., 0.9990 Platinum 0.0999 oz. APW, 16.1 mm. **Ruler:** Elizabeth II **Rev:** Goanna on color background

Date	Mintage	F	VF	XF	Unc	BU
2012P Proof	1,000	Value: 325				

KM# 1105 20 DOLLARS
5.0000 g., 0.9999 Gold 0.1607 oz. AGW, 14x23.2 mm. **Ruler:** Elizabeth II **Rev:** Turtle Dreaming **Shape:** Rectangle

Date	Mintage	F	VF	XF	Unc	BU
2009 Proof	—	Value: 325				

KM# 1109 20 DOLLARS
5.0000 g., 0.9999 Gold 0.1607 oz. AGW, 14x23.2 mm. **Ruler:** Elizabeth II **Rev:** Kangaroo dreaming **Shape:** Vertical rectangle

Date	Mintage	F	VF	XF	Unc	BU
2009 Proof	—	Value: 325				

KM# 1127 25 DOLLARS
3.1000 g., 0.9990 Gold 0.0996 oz. AGW, 15.5 mm. **Ruler:** Elizabeth II **Obv:** Head right **Rev:** Kookaburra **Rev. Legend:** DISCOVER AUSTRALIA

Date	Mintage	F	VF	XF	Unc	BU
2006P Proof	2,500	Value: 195				

KM# 1123 25 DOLLARS
3.1000 g., 0.9990 Gold 0.0996 oz. AGW, 15.5 mm. **Ruler:** Elizabeth II **Obv:** Head right **Rev:** Saltwater crocodile **Rev. Legend:** DISCOVER AUSTRALIA

Date	Mintage	F	VF	XF	Unc	BU
2006P Proof	2,500	Value: 195				

KM# 1124 25 DOLLARS
3.1000 g., 0.9990 Gold 0.0996 oz. AGW, 15.5 mm. **Ruler:** Elizabeth II **Obv:** Head right **Rev:** Grey kangaroo **Rev. Legend:** DISCOVER AUSTRALIA

Date	Mintage	F	VF	XF	Unc	BU
2006P Proof	2,500	Value: 195				

KM# 1125 25 DOLLARS
3.1000 g., 0.9990 Gold 0.0996 oz. AGW, 15.5 mm. **Ruler:** Elizabeth II **Obv:** Head right **Rev:** Emu **Rev. Legend:** DISCOVER AUSTRALIA

Date	Mintage	F	VF	XF	Unc	BU
2006P Proof	2,500	Value: 195				

KM# 1126 25 DOLLARS
3.1000 g., 0.9990 Gold 0.0996 oz. AGW, 15.5 mm. **Ruler:** Elizabeth II **Obv:** Head right **Rev:** Koala **Rev. Legend:** DISCOVER AUSTRALIA

Date	Mintage	F	VF	XF	Unc	BU
2006P Proof	2,500	Value: 195				

KM# 1148 25 DOLLARS
3.1000 g., 0.9990 Gold 0.0996 oz. AGW, 15.5 mm. **Ruler:** Elizabeth II **Obv:** Head right **Rev:** Echinda **Rev. Legend:** DISCOVER AUSTRALIA

Date	Mintage	F	VF	XF	Unc	BU
2007P Proof	2,500	Value: 195				

KM# 1149 25 DOLLARS
3.1000 g., 0.9990 Gold 0.0996 oz. AGW, 15.5 mm. **Ruler:** Elizabeth II **Obv:** Head right **Rev:** Common wombat **Rev. Legend:** DISCOVER AUSTRALIA

Date	Mintage	F	VF	XF	Unc	BU
2007P Proof	2,500	Value: 195				

KM# 1150 25 DOLLARS
3.1000 g., 0.9990 Gold 0.0996 oz. AGW, 15.5 mm. **Ruler:** Elizabeth II **Obv:** Head right **Rev:** Tasmanian devil **Rev. Legend:** DISCOVER AUSTRALIA

Date	Mintage	F	VF	XF	Unc	BU
2007P Proof	2,500	Value: 195				

KM# 1151 25 DOLLARS
3.1000 g., 0.9990 Gold 0.0996 oz. AGW, 15.5 mm. **Ruler:** Elizabeth II **Obv:** Head right **Rev:** Great white shark **Rev. Legend:** DISCOVER AUSTRALIA

Date	Mintage	F	VF	XF	Unc	BU
2007P Proof	2,500	Value: 195				

KM# 1152 25 DOLLARS
3.1000 g., 0.9990 Gold 0.0996 oz. AGW, 15.5 mm. **Ruler:** Elizabeth II **Obv:** Head right **Rev:** Platypus **Rev. Legend:** DISCOVER AUSTRALIA

Date	Mintage	F	VF	XF	Unc	BU
2007P Proof	2,500	Value: 195				

KM# 1158 25 DOLLARS
3.1000 g., 0.9990 Platinum 0.0996 oz. APW, 16 mm. **Ruler:** Elizabeth II **Obv:** Head right **Rev:** Anemone buttercup, multicolor **Rev. Legend:** DISCOVER AUSTRALIA

Date	Mintage	F	VF	XF	Unc	BU
2007P Proof	2,500	Value: 325				

KM# 1191 25 DOLLARS
3.1000 g., 0.9990 Gold 0.0996 oz. AGW, 15.5 mm. **Ruler:** Elizabeth II **Obv:** Head right **Rev:** Dolphin **Rev. Legend:** DISCOVER AUSTRALIA

Date	Mintage	F	VF	XF	Unc	BU
2008P Proof	2,500	Value: 195				

KM# 1192 25 DOLLARS
3.1000 g., 0.9990 Gold 0.0996 oz. AGW, 15.5 mm. **Ruler:** Elizabeth II **Obv:** Head right **Rev:** King brown snake **Rev. Legend:** DISCOVER AUSTRALIA

Date	Mintage	F	VF	XF	Unc	BU
2008P Proof	2,500	Value: 195				

KM# 1193 25 DOLLARS
3.1000 g., 0.9990 Gold 0.0996 oz. AGW, 15.5 mm. **Ruler:** Elizabeth II **Obv:** Head right **Rev:** Brolga **Rev. Legend:** DISCOVER AUSTRALIA

Date	Mintage	F	VF	XF	Unc	BU
2008P Proof	2,500	Value: 195				

KM# 1194 25 DOLLARS
3.1000 g., 0.9990 Gold 0.0996 oz. AGW, 15.5 mm. **Ruler:** Elizabeth II **Obv:** Head right **Rev:** Dingo **Rev. Legend:** DISCOVER AUSTRALIA

Date	Mintage	F	VF	XF	Unc	BU
2008P Proof	2,500	Value: 195				

KM# 1195 25 DOLLARS
3.1000 g., 0.9990 Gold 0.0996 oz. AGW, 15.5 mm. **Ruler:** Elizabeth II **Obv:** Head right **Rev:** Frill-neck lizard **Rev. Legend:** DISCOVER AUSTRALIA

Date	Mintage	F	VF	XF	Unc	BU
2008P Proof	2,500	Value: 195				

KM# 1106 25 DOLLARS
10.0000 g., 0.9999 Gold 0.3215 oz. AGW, 15.4x25.4 mm. **Ruler:** Elizabeth II **Rev:** Turtle dreaming **Shape:** Verticle rectangle

Date	Mintage	F	VF	XF	Unc	BU
2009 Proof	—	Value: 625				

KM# 1455 25 DOLLARS
10.0000 g., 0.9990 Gold 0.3212 oz. AGW, 15.4x25.4 mm. **Ruler:** Elizabeth II **Rev:** Dolphin dreaming **Shape:** Vertical rectangle

Date	Mintage	F	VF	XF	Unc	BU
2010P Proof	—	Value: 600				

KM# 1611 25 DOLLARS
10.0000 g., 0.9990 Gold 0.3212 oz. AGW, 15.4x25.4 mm. **Ruler:** Elizabeth II **Obv:** Head with tiara right **Rev:** Platypus dreaming **Shape:** Vertical rectangle

Date	Mintage	F	VF	XF	Unc	BU
2011P Proof	—	Value: 625				

KM# 952 50 DOLLARS
15.5017 g., 0.9990 Gold 0.4979 oz. AGW, 25 mm. **Ruler:** Elizabeth II **Subject:** Australian Fauna **Obv:** Head with tiara right **Rev:** Saltwater crocodile

Date	Mintage	F	VF	XF	Unc	BU
2006 Proof	1,000	Value: 900				

KM# 955 50 DOLLARS
15.5017 g., 0.9990 Gold 0.4979 oz. AGW, 25 mm. **Ruler:** Elizabeth II **Subject:** Australian Fauna **Obv:** Head with tiara right **Rev:** Grey kangaroo

Date	Mintage	F	VF	XF	Unc	BU
2006 Proof	1,000	Value: 900				

KM# 958 50 DOLLARS
15.5017 g., 0.9990 Gold 0.4979 oz. AGW, 25 mm. **Ruler:** Elizabeth II **Subject:** Australian Fauna **Obv:** Head with tiara right **Rev:** Emu

Date	Mintage	F	VF	XF	Unc	BU
2006 Proof	1,000	Value: 900				

KM# 961 50 DOLLARS
15.5017 g., 0.9990 Gold 0.4979 oz. AGW, 25 mm. **Ruler:** Elizabeth II **Subject:** Australian Fauna **Obv:** Head with tiara right **Rev:** Koala

Date	Mintage	F	VF	XF	Unc	BU
2006 Proof	1,000	Value: 900				

KM# 964 50 DOLLARS
15.5017 g., 0.9990 Gold 0.4979 oz. AGW, 25 mm. **Ruler:** Elizabeth II **Subject:** Australian Fauna **Obv:** Head with tiara right **Rev:** Kookaburra

Date	Mintage	F	VF	XF	Unc	BU
2006 Proof	1,000	Value: 900				

KM# 981 50 DOLLARS
15.5017 g., 0.9990 Platinum 0.4979 oz. APW **Ruler:** Elizabeth II **Subject:** Australian Flora **Obv:** Head with tiara right **Rev:** Cooktown orchid

Date	Mintage	F	VF	XF	Unc	BU
2006 Proof	1,000	Value: 975				

KM# 983 50 DOLLARS
15.5017 g., 0.9990 Platinum 0.4979 oz. APW **Ruler:** Elizabeth II **Subject:** Australian Flora **Obv:** Head with tiara right **Rev:** Sturt's desert rose

Date	Mintage	F	VF	XF	Unc	BU
2006 Proof	1,000	Value: 975				

KM# 985 50 DOLLARS
15.5017 g., 0.9990 Platinum 0.4979 oz. APW **Ruler:** Elizabeth II **Subject:** Australian Flora **Obv:** Head with tiara right **Rev:** Royal bluebell

Date	Mintage	F	VF	XF	Unc	BU
2006 Proof	1,000	Value: 975				

KM# 987 50 DOLLARS
15.5017 g., 0.9990 Platinum 0.4979 oz. APW **Ruler:** Elizabeth II **Subject:** Australian Flora **Obv:** Head with tiara right **Rev:** Kangaroo paw

Date	Mintage	F	VF	XF	Unc	BU
2006 Proof	1,000	Value: 975				

KM# 989 50 DOLLARS
15.5017 g., 0.9990 Platinum 0.4979 oz. APW **Ruler:** Elizabeth II **Subject:** Australian Flora **Obv:** Head with tiara right **Rev:** Common pink heath

Date	Mintage	F	VF	XF	Unc	BU
2006 Proof	1,000	Value: 975				

KM# 967 50 DOLLARS
15.5017 g., 0.9990 Gold 0.4979 oz. AGW, 25 mm. **Ruler:** Elizabeth II **Subject:** Australian Fauna **Obv:** Head with tiara right **Rev:** Echidna

Date	Mintage	F	VF	XF	Unc	BU
2007 Proof	1,000	Value: 900				

KM# 970 50 DOLLARS
15.5017 g., 0.9990 Gold 0.4979 oz. AGW, 25 mm. **Ruler:** Elizabeth II **Subject:** Australian Fauna **Obv:** Head with tiara right **Rev:** Common wombat

Date	Mintage	F	VF	XF	Unc	BU
2007 Proof	1,000	Value: 900				

KM# 973 50 DOLLARS
15.5017 g., 0.9990 Gold 0.4979 oz. AGW, 25 mm. **Ruler:** Elizabeth II **Subject:** Australian Fauna **Obv:** Head with tiara right **Rev:** Tasmanian devil

Date	Mintage	F	VF	XF	Unc	BU
2007 Proof	1,000	Value: 900				

KM# 976 50 DOLLARS
15.5017 g., 0.9990 Gold 0.4979 oz. AGW, 25 mm. **Ruler:** Elizabeth II **Subject:** Australian Fauna **Obv:** Head with tiara right **Rev:** Great white shark

Date	Mintage	F	VF	XF	Unc	BU
2007 Proof	1,000	Value: 900				

KM# 979 50 DOLLARS
15.5017 g., 0.9990 Gold 0.4979 oz. AGW, 25 mm. **Ruler:** Elizabeth II **Subject:** Australian Fauna **Obv:** Head with tiara right **Rev:** Platypus

Date	Mintage	F	VF	XF	Unc	BU
2007 Proof	1,000	Value: 900				

KM# 991 50 DOLLARS
15.5017 g., 0.9990 Platinum 0.4979 oz. APW, 24 mm. **Ruler:** Elizabeth II **Subject:** Australian Flora **Obv:** Head with tiara right **Rev:** Anemone buttercup

Date	Mintage	F	VF	XF	Unc	BU
2007 Proof	1,000	Value: 975				

KM# 993 50 DOLLARS
15.5017 g., 0.9990 Platinum 0.4979 oz. APW **Ruler:** Elizabeth II **Subject:** Australian Flora **Obv:** Head with tiara right **Rev:** Sturt's desert pea

Date	Mintage	F	VF	XF	Unc	BU
2007 Proof	1,000	Value: 975				

KM# 995 50 DOLLARS
15.5017 g., 0.9990 Platinum 0.4979 oz. APW, 24 mm. **Ruler:** Elizabeth II **Subject:** Australian Flora **Obv:** Head with tiara right **Rev:** Tasmanian Bluegum

Date	Mintage	F	VF	XF	Unc	BU
2007 Proof	1,000	Value: 975				

KM# 997 50 DOLLARS
15.5017 g., 0.9990 Platinum 0.4979 oz. APW **Ruler:** Elizabeth II **Subject:** Australian Flora **Obv:** Head with tiara right **Rev:** Waratah

Date	Mintage	F	VF	XF	Unc	BU
2007 Proof	1,000	Value: 975				

KM# 999 50 DOLLARS
15.5017 g., 0.9990 Platinum 0.4979 oz. APW **Ruler:** Elizabeth II **Subject:** Australian Flora **Obv:** Head with tiara right **Rev:** Golden wattle

Date	Mintage	F	VF	XF	Unc	BU
2007 Proof	1,000	Value: 975				

KM# 1167 50 DOLLARS
15.5500 g., 0.9990 Platinum 0.4994 oz. APW, 25 mm. **Ruler:** Elizabeth II **Subject:** Australian Flora **Rev:** Black-anther flax lily **Rev. Legend:** DISCOVER AUSTRALIA

Date	Mintage	F	VF	XF	Unc	BU
2008 Proof	—	Value: 975				

KM# 1196 50 DOLLARS
15.5500 g., 0.9990 Gold 0.4994 oz. AGW, 25 mm. **Ruler:** Elizabeth II **Obv:** Head right **Rev:** Dolphin **Rev. Legend:** DISCOVER AUSTRALIA

Date	Mintage	F	VF	XF	Unc	BU
2008P Proof	1,000	Value: 900				

KM# 1197 50 DOLLARS
15.5500 g., 0.9990 Gold 0.4994 oz. AGW, 25 mm. **Ruler:** Elizabeth II **Obv:** Head right **Rev:** King brown snake **Rev. Legend:** DISCOVER AUSTRALIA

Date	Mintage	F	VF	XF	Unc	BU
2008P Proof	1,000	Value: 900				

KM# 1198 50 DOLLARS
15.5500 g., 0.9990 Gold 0.4994 oz. AGW, 25 mm. **Ruler:** Elizabeth II **Obv:** Head right **Rev:** Brogla **Rev. Legend:** DISCOVER AUSTRALIA

Date	Mintage	F	VF	XF	Unc	BU
2008P Proof	1,000	Value: 900				

KM# 1199 50 DOLLARS
15.5500 g., 0.9990 Gold 0.4994 oz. AGW, 25 mm. **Ruler:** Elizabeth II **Obv:** Head right **Rev:** Dingo **Rev. Legend:** DISCOVER AUSTRALIA

Date	Mintage	F	VF	XF	Unc	BU
2008P Proof	1,000	Value: 900				

KM# 1200 50 DOLLARS
15.5500 g., 0.9990 Gold 0.4994 oz. AGW, 25 mm. **Ruler:** Elizabeth II **Obv:** Head right **Rev:** Frill-neck lizard **Rev. Legend:** DISCOVER AUSTRALIA

Date	Mintage	F	VF	XF	Unc	BU
2008P Proof	1,000	Value: 900				

KM# 1207 50 DOLLARS
15.5500 g., 0.9990 Platinum 0.4994 oz. APW, 26 mm. **Ruler:** Elizabeth II **Obv:** Head right **Rev:** Native fragipan, multicolor **Rev. Legend:** DISCOVER AUSTRALIA

Date	Mintage	F	VF	XF	Unc	BU
2008P Proof	1,000	Value: 1,500				

KM# 1208 50 DOLLARS
15.5500 g., 0.9990 Platinum 0.4994 oz. APW, 26 mm. **Ruler:** Elizabeth II **Obv:** Head right **Rev:** Geraldton wax, multicolor **Rev. Legend:** DISCOVER AUSTRALIA

Date	Mintage	F	VF	XF	Unc	BU
2008P Proof	1,000	Value: 1,500				

KM# 1209 50 DOLLARS
15.5500 g., 0.9990 Platinum 0.4994 oz. APW, 26 mm. **Ruler:** Elizabeth II **Obv:** Head right **Rev:** Red-flowered kurrajong, multicolor **Rev. Legend:** DISCOVER AUSTRALIA

Date	Mintage	F	VF	XF	Unc	BU
2008P Proof	1,000	Value: 1,500				

KM# 1210 50 DOLLARS
15.5500 g., 0.9990 Platinum 0.4994 oz. APW **Ruler:** Elizabeth II **Obv:** Head right **Rev:** Small-leaf lilly pilly, multicolor **Rev. Legend:** DISCOVER AUSTRALIA

Date	Mintage	F	VF	XF	Unc	BU
2008P Proof	1,500	Value: 1,500				

KM# 1229 50 DOLLARS
15.5500 g., 0.9990 Gold 0.4994 oz. AGW, 25 mm. **Ruler:** Elizabeth II **Obv:** Head right **Rev:** Dreaming king brown snake

Date	Mintage	F	VF	XF	Unc	BU
2009P Proof	1,000	Value: 1,100				

KM# 1227 50 DOLLARS
15.5500 g., 0.9990 Gold 0.4994 oz. AGW, 25 mm. **Ruler:** Elizabeth II **Obv:** Head right **Rev:** Dreaming kangaroo

Date	Mintage	F	VF	XF	Unc	BU
2009P Proof	1,000	Value: 1,100				

KM# 1230 50 DOLLARS
15.5500 g., 0.9990 Gold 0.4994 oz. AGW, 25 mm. **Ruler:** Elizabeth II **Obv:** Head right **Rev:** Dreaming brolga

Date	Mintage	F	VF	XF	Unc	BU
2009P Proof	1,000	Value: 1,100				

KM# 1231 50 DOLLARS
15.5500 g., 0.9990 Gold 0.4994 oz. AGW, 25 mm. **Ruler:** Elizabeth II **Obv:** Head right **Rev:** Dreaming echidna

Date	Mintage	F	VF	XF	Unc	BU
2009P Proof	1,000	Value: 1,100				

KM# 1237 50 DOLLARS
15.5500 g., 0.9990 Platinum 0.4994 oz. APW, 25 mm. **Ruler:** Elizabeth II **Obv:** Head right **Rev:** Dreaming kangaroo, multicolor

Date	Mintage	F	VF	XF	Unc	BU
2009P Proof	1,000	Value: 1,500				

KM# 1238 50 DOLLARS
15.5500 g., 0.9990 Platinum 0.4994 oz. APW, 25 mm. **Ruler:** Elizabeth II **Obv:** Head right **Rev:** Dreaming dolphin, multicolor

Date	Mintage	F	VF	XF	Unc	BU
2009P Proof	1,000	Value: 1,500				

KM# 1239 50 DOLLARS
15.5500 g., 0.9990 Platinum 0.4994 oz. APW, 25 mm. **Ruler:** Elizabeth II **Obv:** Head right **Rev:** Dreaming king brown snake, multicolor

Date	Mintage	F	VF	XF	Unc	BU
2009P Proof	1,000	Value: 1,500				

KM# 1240 50 DOLLARS
15.5500 g., 0.9990 Platinum 0.4994 oz. APW, 25 mm. **Ruler:** Elizabeth II **Obv:** Head right **Rev:** Dreaming brolga, multicolor

Date	Mintage	F	VF	XF	Unc	BU
2009P Proof	1,000	Value: 1,500				

KM# 1241 50 DOLLARS
15.5500 g., 0.9990 Platinum 0.4994 oz. APW, 25 mm. **Ruler:** Elizabeth II **Obv:** Head right **Rev:** Dreaming echidna, multicolor

Date	Mintage	F	VF	XF	Unc	BU
2009P Proof	1,000	Value: 1,500				

KM# 1398 50 DOLLARS
15.5000 g., 0.9990 Platinum 0.4978 oz. APW, 26 mm. **Ruler:** Elizabeth II **Obv:** Head right **Rev:** Multicolor frill-neck lizard

Date	Mintage	F	VF	XF	Unc	BU
2010P Proof	1,000	Value: 1,550				

KM# 1400 50 DOLLARS
15.5000 g., 0.9990 Gold 0.4978 oz. AGW, 26 mm. **Ruler:** Elizabeth II **Obv:** Head right **Rev:** Frill-neck lizard

Date	Mintage	F	VF	XF	Unc	BU
2010P Proof	1,000	Value: 1,250				

KM# 1404 50 DOLLARS
15.5000 g., 0.9990 Platinum 0.4978 oz. APW, 26 mm. **Ruler:** Elizabeth II **Obv:** Head right **Rev:** Multicolor koala

Date	Mintage	F	VF	XF	Unc	BU
2010P Proof	1,000	Value: 1,550				

KM# 1406 50 DOLLARS
15.5000 g., 0.9990 Gold 0.4978 oz. AGW, 26 mm. **Ruler:** Elizabeth II **Obv:** Head right **Rev:** Koala

Date	Mintage	F	VF	XF	Unc	BU
2010P Proof	1,000	Value: 1,250				

KM# 1410 50 DOLLARS
15.5000 g., 0.9990 Platinum 0.4978 oz. APW, 26 mm. **Ruler:** Elizabeth II **Obv:** Head right **Rev:** Multicolor platypus

Date	Mintage	F	VF	XF	Unc	BU
2010P Proof	1,000	Value: 1,550				

KM# 1412 50 DOLLARS
15.5000 g., 0.9990 Gold 0.4978 oz. AGW **Ruler:** Elizabeth II **Obv:** Head right **Rev:** Platypus

Date	Mintage	F	VF	XF	Unc	BU
2010P Proof	1,000	Value: 1,250				

KM# 1416 50 DOLLARS
15.5000 g., 0.9990 Platinum 0.4978 oz. APW, 26 mm. **Ruler:** Elizabeth II **Obv:** Head right **Rev:** Multicolor saltwater crocodile

Date	Mintage	F	VF	XF	Unc	BU
2010P Proof	1,000	Value: 1,550				

KM# 1418 50 DOLLARS
15.5000 g., 0.9990 Gold 0.4978 oz. AGW, 26 mm. **Ruler:** Elizabeth II **Obv:** Head right **Rev:** Saltwater crocodile

Date	Mintage	F	VF	XF	Unc	BU
2010P Proof	1,000	Value: 1,250				

KM# 1422 50 DOLLARS
15.5000 g., 0.9990 Platinum 0.4978 oz. APW, 26 mm. **Ruler:** Elizabeth II **Obv:** Head right **Rev:** Multicolor wombat

Date	Mintage	F	VF	XF	Unc	BU
2010P Proof	1,000	Value: 1,100				

KM# 1424 50 DOLLARS
15.5000 g., 0.9990 Gold 0.4978 oz. AGW, 26 mm. **Ruler:** Elizabeth II **Obv:** Head right **Rev:** Wombat

Date	Mintage	F	VF	XF	Unc	BU
2010P Proof	2,500	Value: 1,250				

KM# 1537 50 DOLLARS
15.5500 g., 0.9990 Gold 0.4994 oz. AGW **Ruler:** Elizabeth II **Subject:** Dreaming Emu **Rev:** Linear emu in color

Date	Mintage	F	VF	XF	Unc	BU
2011P Proof	—	Value: 1,250				

KM# 1539 50 DOLLARS
15.5500 g., 0.9990 Platinum 0.4994 oz. APW **Ruler:** Elizabeth II **Subject:** Dreaming Emu **Rev:** Linear emu in color

Date	Mintage	F	VF	XF	Unc	BU
2011P Proof	1,000	Value: 1,800				

KM# 1543 50 DOLLARS
15.5500 g., 0.9990 Gold 0.4994 oz. AGW **Ruler:** Elizabeth II **Subject:** Dreaming Tasmanian Devil **Rev:** Linear tasmanian devil in color

Date	Mintage	F	VF	XF	Unc	BU
2011P Proof	—	Value: 1,250				

KM# 1545 50 DOLLARS
15.5500 g., 0.9990 Platinum 0.4994 oz. APW **Ruler:** Elizabeth II **Subject:** Dreaming Tasmanian Devil **Rev:** Linear tasmanian devil in color

Date	Mintage	F	VF	XF	Unc	BU
2011P Proof	—	Value: 1,800				

KM# 1549 50 DOLLARS
15.5500 g., 0.9990 Gold 0.4994 oz. AGW **Ruler:** Elizabeth II **Series:** Dreaming Kookaburra **Rev:** Linear kookaburra in color

Date	Mintage	F	VF	XF	Unc	BU
2011P Proof	—	Value: 1,250				

KM# 1551 50 DOLLARS
15.5500 g., 0.9990 Platinum 0.4994 oz. APW **Ruler:** Elizabeth II **Subject:** Dreaming Kookaburra **Rev:** Linear kookaburra in color

Date	Mintage	F	VF	XF	Unc	BU
2011P Proof	1,000	Value: 1,800				

KM# 1555 50 DOLLARS
15.5500 g., 0.9990 Gold 0.4994 oz. AGW **Ruler:** Elizabeth II **Subject:** Dreaming shark **Rev:** Linear shark in color

Date	Mintage	F	VF	XF	Unc	BU
2011P Proof	—	Value: 1,250				

KM# 1557 50 DOLLARS
15.5500 g., 0.9990 Platinum 0.4994 oz. APW **Ruler:** Elizabeth II **Subject:** Dreaming shark **Rev:** Linear shark in color

Date	Mintage	F	VF	XF	Unc	BU
2011P Proof	1,000	Value: 1,800				

KM# 1561 50 DOLLARS
15.5500 g., 0.9990 Gold 0.4994 oz. AGW **Ruler:** Elizabeth II **Subject:** Dreaming Dingo **Rev:** Linear dingo in color

Date	Mintage	F	VF	XF	Unc	BU
2011P Proof	—	Value: 1,250				

KM# 1563 50 DOLLARS
15.5500 g., 0.9990 Platinum 0.4994 oz. APW **Ruler:** Elizabeth II **Subject:** Dreaming Dingo **Rev:** Linear dingo in color

Date	Mintage	F	VF	XF	Unc	BU
2011P Proof	1,000	Value: 1,800				

KM# 1726 50 DOLLARS
15.5540 g., 0.9990 Gold 0.4996 oz. AGW, 25.6 mm. **Ruler:** Elizabeth II **Rev:** Green and Gold Bell Frog in grass

Date	Mintage	F	VF	XF	Unc	BU
2012P Proof	500	Value: 950				

KM# 1727 50 DOLLARS
15.5540 g., 0.9990 Gold 0.4996 oz. AGW, 25.6 mm. **Ruler:** Elizabeth II **Rev:** Kookaburra standing right

Date	Mintage	F	VF	XF	Unc	BU
2012P Proof	500	Value: 950				

KM# 1728 50 DOLLARS
15.5540 g., 0.9990 Gold 0.4996 oz. AGW, 25.6 mm. **Ruler:** Elizabeth II **Rev:** Whale Shark swimming right

Date	Mintage	F	VF	XF	Unc	BU
2012P Proof	500	Value: 950				

KM# 1729 50 DOLLARS
15.5540 g., 0.9990 Gold 0.4996 oz. AGW, 25.6 mm. **Ruler:** Elizabeth II **Rev:** Kangaroo bounding right

Date	Mintage	F	VF	XF	Unc	BU
2012P Proof	500	Value: 950				

KM# 1730 50 DOLLARS
15.5540 g., 0.9990 Gold 0.4996 oz. AGW, 25.6 mm. **Ruler:** Elizabeth II **Rev:** Goanna lizard right

Date	Mintage	F	VF	XF	Unc	BU
2012P Proof	500	Value: 950				

KM# 1731 100 DOLLARS
31.1200 g., 0.9995 Platinum 1.0000 oz. APW, 32.6 mm. **Ruler:** Elizabeth II **Obv:** Head with tiara right **Rev:** Platypus swimming downward **Edge:** Reeded

Date	Mintage	F	VF	XF	Unc	BU
2012P	30,000	Value: 1,750				

BULLION - LUNAR YEAR

KM# 1010 25 CENTS
0.9990 Silver Gilt, 17.8 mm. **Ruler:** Elizabeth II **Obv:** Bust with tiara right **Obv. Legend:** ELIZABETH II - AUSTRALIA **Rev:** 4 Chinese characters **Rev. Legend:** LUNAR NEW YEAR - GOOD FORTUNE & PROSPERITY

Date	Mintage	F	VF	XF	Unc	BU
2007 Proof	8,888	Value: 45.00				

KM# 579 50 CENTS
15.5518 g., 0.9990 Silver 0.4995 oz. ASW, 32.1 mm. **Ruler:** Elizabeth II **Subject:** Year of the Horse **Obv:** Head with tiara right, denomination below **Rev:** Horse running left **Edge:** Reeded

Date	Mintage	F	VF	XF	Unc	BU
2002P Proof	5,000	Value: 35.00				

KM# 664 50 CENTS
16.4000 g., 0.9990 Silver 0.5267 oz. ASW, 31.9 mm. **Ruler:** Elizabeth II **Subject:** Year of the Goat **Obv:** Head with tiara right, denomination below **Rev:** Two goats **Edge:** Reeded

Date	Mintage	F	VF	XF	Unc	BU
2003	—	—	—	—	20.00	25.00
2003 Proof	—	Value: 35.00				

KM# 673 50 CENTS
15.5518 g., 0.9990 Silver 0.4995 oz. ASW, 32.1 mm. **Ruler:** Elizabeth II **Subject:** Year of the Monkey **Obv:** Head with tiara right, denomination below **Rev:** Monkey sitting on branch **Edge:** Reeded

Date	Mintage	F	VF	XF	Unc	BU
2004 Proof	11,000	Value: 35.00				

KM# 791 50 CENTS
15.5680 g., 0.9990 Silver 0.5000 oz. ASW, 32.1 mm. **Ruler:** Elizabeth II **Subject:** Year of the Rooster **Obv:** Elizabeth II **Rev:** Standing Rooster looking backwards **Edge:** Reeded

Date	Mintage	F	VF	XF	Unc	BU
2005P Proof	6,000	Value: 50.00				

KM# 814 50 CENTS
15.5500 g., 0.9990 Silver 0.4994 oz. ASW **Ruler:** Elizabeth II **Subject:** Bullion Lunar Year - Rooster **Obv:** Head with tiara right

Date	Mintage	F	VF	XF	Unc	BU
2005	—	—	—	—	—	20.00

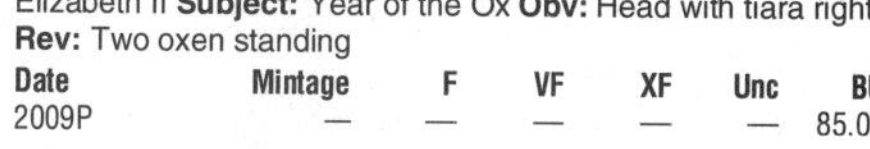

KM# 1750 50 CENTS
15.5500 g., 0.9990 Silver 0.4994 oz. ASW, 32 mm. **Ruler:** Elizabeth II **Subject:** Year of the Ox **Obv:** Head with tiara right **Rev:** Two oxen standing

Date	Mintage	F	VF	XF	Unc	BU
2009P	—	—	—	—	—	85.00

KM# 1750a 50 CENTS
15.5500 g., 0.9990 Silver 0.4994 oz. ASW, 32 mm. **Ruler:** Elizabeth II **Subject:** Year of the Ox **Rev:** Two colored oxen standing

Date	Mintage	F	VF	XF	Unc	BU
2009P	—	—	—	—	—	100

KM# 1370 50 CENTS
15.5500 g., 0.9900 Silver 0.4949 oz. ASW, 32 mm. **Ruler:** Elizabeth II **Subject:** Year of the Tiger **Obv:** Head right **Rev:** Tiger at rest left

Date	Mintage	F	VF	XF	Unc	BU
2010P	—	—	—	—	—	20.00

KM# 1474 50 CENTS
15.5600 g., 0.9990 Silver 0.4997 oz. ASW, 32 mm. **Ruler:** Elizabeth II **Subject:** Year of the Rabbit **Rev:** Mother and baby rabbit nose to nose

Date	Mintage	F	VF	XF	Unc	BU
2011P Proof	—	Value: 30.00				

KM# 1663 50 CENTS
15.5518 g., 0.9990 Silver 0.4995 oz. ASW, 31.9 mm. **Ruler:** Elizabeth II **Subject:** Year of the Dragon

Date	Mintage	F	VF	XF	Unc	BU
2012P Proof	—	Value: 25.00				

KM# 1663a 50 CENTS
15.5518 g., 0.9990 Silver 0.4995 oz. ASW, 32.1 mm. **Ruler:** Elizabeth II **Subject:** Year of the Dragon **Rev:** Dragon in color

Date	Mintage	F	VF	XF	Unc	BU
2012P Proof	—	Value: 30.00				

KM# 1832 50 CENTS
15.5000 g., 0.9990 Silver 0.4978 oz. ASW, 32 mm. **Ruler:** Elizabeth II **Subject:** Year of the Snake

Date	Mintage	F	VF	XF	Unc	BU
2013P Proof	—	Value: 40.00				

KM# 536 DOLLAR
31.1035 g., 0.9990 Silver 0.9990 oz. ASW, 40.6 mm. **Ruler:** Elizabeth II **Subject:** Year of the Snake **Obv:** Head with tiara right, denomination below **Rev:** Snake with eggs **Edge:** Reeded

Date	Mintage	F	VF	XF	Unc	BU
2001	300,000	—	—	—	80.00	100
2001P Proof	2,500	Value: 100				

KM# 536a DOLLAR
31.6350 g., 0.9990 Silver partially gilt 1.0160 oz. ASW, 40.6 mm. **Ruler:** Elizabeth II **Subject:** Year of the Snake **Obv:** Head with tiara right, denomination below **Rev:** Gold-plated snake **Edge:** Reeded

Date	Mintage	F	VF	XF	Unc	BU
2001	50,000	—	—	—	45.00	50.00

KM# 580 DOLLAR
31.1035 g., 0.9990 Silver 0.9990 oz. ASW, 40.6 mm. **Ruler:** Elizabeth II **Subject:** Year of the Horse **Obv:** Head with tiara right, denomination below **Rev:** Horse running left **Edge:** Reeded

Date	Mintage	F	VF	XF	Unc	BU
2002P	—	—	—	—	75.00	80.00
2002P Proof	2,500	Value: 75.00				

KM# 580a DOLLAR
31.6350 g., 0.9990 Silver partially gilt 1.0160 oz. ASW, 40.6 mm. **Ruler:** Elizabeth II **Obv:** Head with tiara right **Rev:** Gold-plated horse **Edge:** Reeded

Date	Mintage	F	VF	XF	Unc	BU
2002	50,000	—	—	—	40.00	45.00

KM# 665 DOLLAR
31.6200 g., 0.9990 Silver 1.0155 oz. ASW, 40.3 mm. **Ruler:** Elizabeth II **Subject:** Year of the Goat **Obv:** Head with tiara right, denomination below **Rev:** Two goats **Edge:** Reeded

Date	Mintage	F	VF	XF	Unc	BU
2003	—	—	—	—	50.00	75.00
2003 Proof	—	Value: 75.00				

KM# 665a DOLLAR
31.6350 g., 0.9990 Silver partially gilt 1.0160 oz. ASW, 40.6 mm. **Ruler:** Elizabeth II **Subject:** Year of the Goat **Obv:** Head with tiara right, denomination below **Rev:** Gold-plated goat **Edge:** Reeded

Date	Mintage	F	VF	XF	Unc	BU
2003	50,000	—	—	—	50.00	55.00

KM# 674 DOLLAR
31.1035 g., 0.9990 Silver 0.9990 oz. ASW, 40.6 mm. **Ruler:** Elizabeth II **Subject:** Year of the Monkey **Obv:** Head with tiara right, denomination below **Rev:** Monkey sitting on branch **Edge:** Reeded

Date	Mintage	F	VF	XF	Unc	BU
2004	—	—	—	—	40.00	45.00
2004 Proof	8,500	Value: 55.00				

KM# 674a DOLLAR

31.6350 g., 0.9990 Silver partially gilt 1.0160 oz. ASW, 40.6 mm. **Ruler:** Elizabeth II **Subject:** Year of the Monkey **Obv:** Head with tiara right, denomination below **Rev:** Monkey, gilt **Edge:** Reeded

Date	Mintage	F	VF	XF	Unc	BU
2004	50,000	—	—	—	50.00	55.00

KM# 695 DOLLAR

31.1050 g., 0.9990 Silver 0.9990 oz. ASW, 40.5 mm. **Ruler:** Elizabeth II **Subject:** Year of the Rooster **Obv:** Head with tiara right, denomination below **Rev:** Rooster **Edge:** Reeded

Date	Mintage	F	VF	XF	Unc	BU
2005	—	—	—	—	75.00	65.00
2005P Proof	3,500	Value: 80.00				

KM# 695a DOLLAR

31.6350 g., 0.9990 Silver partially gilt 1.0160 oz. ASW, 40.5 mm. **Ruler:** Elizabeth II **Subject:** Year of the Rooster **Obv:** Head with tiara right, denomination below **Rev:** Gilt rooster **Edge:** Reeded

Date	Mintage	F	VF	XF	Unc	BU
2005 Polished fields	47,200	—	—	—	45.00	50.00
2005 Matte fields	2,800	—	—	—	175	185

KM# 1011 DOLLAR

31.1050 g., 0.9990 Silver 0.9990 oz. ASW, 40 mm. **Ruler:** Elizabeth II **Obv:** Crowned bust right at top **Obv. Legend:** ELIZABETH II - AUSTRALIA **Rev:** 12 Lunar figures

Date	Mintage	F	VF	XF	Unc	BU
2007 Proof	8,888	Value: 110				

KM# 1755 DOLLAR

31.1050 g., 0.9990 Silver 0.9990 oz. ASW, 40 mm. **Ruler:** Elizabeth II **Subject:** Year of the Mouse **Obv:** Head with tiara right **Rev:** Mouse pair

Date	Mintage	F	VF	XF	Unc	BU
2008P	—	—	—	—	—	75.00

KM# 1755a DOLLAR

31.1050 g., 0.9990 Silver 0.9990 oz. ASW, 40 mm. **Ruler:** Elizabeth II **Subject:** Year of the Mouse **Obv:** Head with tiara right **Rev:** Mouse pair in color

Date	Mintage	F	VF	XF	Unc	BU
2008P	—	—	—	—	—	85.00

KM# 1317 DOLLAR

31.1050 g., 0.9990 Silver 0.9990 oz. ASW, 40.6 mm. **Ruler:** Elizabeth II **Subject:** Year of the Tiger **Obv:** Head right **Rev:** Tiger at rest left

Date	Mintage	F	VF	XF	Unc	BU
2010P	—	—	—	—	—	50.00
2010P Proof	1,000	Value: 75.00				

KM# 1317a DOLLAR

31.1050 g., 0.9990 Silver 0.9990 oz. ASW, 40.6 mm. **Ruler:** Elizabeth II **Subject:** Year of the Tiger **Obv:** Head right **Rev:** Tiger at rest left, partially gilt

Date	Mintage	F	VF	XF	Unc	BU
2010P Proof	50,000	Value: 80.00				

KM# 1317b DOLLAR

31.1050 g., 0.9990 Silver 0.9990 oz. ASW, 40.6 mm. **Ruler:** Elizabeth II **Subject:** Year of the Tiger **Obv:** Head right **Rev:** Multicolor tiger at rest left

Date	Mintage	F	VF	XF	Unc	BU
2010P Proof	170,000	Value: 75.00				

KM# 1475 DOLLAR

31.1050 g., 0.9990 Silver 0.9990 oz. ASW, 40 mm. **Ruler:** Elizabeth II **Subject:** Year of the Rabbit **Rev:** Mother and baby rabbit nose to nose

Date	Mintage	F	VF	XF	Unc	BU
2011P Proof	—	Value: 50.00				

KM# 1475a DOLLAR

31.1050 g., 0.9990 Silver 0.9990 oz. ASW, 40.5 mm. **Ruler:** Elizabeth II **Subject:** Year of the Rabbit **Rev:** Two rabbits, partially gilt

Date	Mintage	F	VF	XF	Unc	BU
2011P Proof	—	Value: 75.00				

KM# 1475b DOLLAR

31.1050 g., 0.9990 Silver 0.9990 oz. ASW, 40.5 mm. **Ruler:** Elizabeth II **Subject:** Year of the Rabbit **Rev:** Two rabbits in color

Date	Mintage	F	VF	XF	Unc	BU
2011P Proof	—	Value: 75.00				

KM# 1664 DOLLAR

31.1050 g., 0.9990 Silver 0.9990 oz. ASW, 40.5 mm. **Ruler:** Elizabeth II **Subject:** Year of the Dragon **Rev:** Dragon

Date	Mintage	F	VF	XF	Unc	BU
2012P	—	—	—	—	—	40.00
2012P Proof	—	Value: 45.00				

KM# 1664.1 DOLLAR

31.1050 g., 0.9990 Silver partially gilt 0.9990 oz. ASW, 40.5 mm. **Ruler:** Elizabeth II **Subject:** Year of the Dragon **Rev:** Dragon gilt

Date	Mintage	F	VF	XF	Unc	BU
2012P Proof	—	Value: 75.00				

KM# 1664.2 DOLLAR

31.1050 g., 0.9990 Silver 0.9990 oz. ASW, 40.5 mm. **Ruler:** Elizabeth II **Subject:** Year of the Dragon **Rev:** Dragon in black collor

Date	Mintage	F	VF	XF	Unc	BU
2012P	—	—	—	—	—	70.00
2012P Proof	—	Value: 75.00				

KM# 1664.3 DOLLAR

31.1050 g., 0.9990 Silver 0.9990 oz. ASW, 40 mm. **Ruler:** Elizabeth II **Subject:** Year of the Dragon **Obv:** Head with tiara right **Rev:** Dragon colored red, brown and yellow

Date	Mintage	F	VF	XF	Unc	BU
2012P	20,000	—	—	—	—	100

M# 1664.4 DOLLAR

31.1050 g., 0.9990 Silver 0.9990 oz. ASW, 40 mm. **Ruler:** Elizabeth II **Subject:** Year of the Dragon **Obv:** Bust with tiara right **Rev:** Dragon colored black and red

Date	Mintage	F	VF	XF	Unc	BU
2012P	—	—	—	—	—	100

KM# 1664.5 DOLLAR

31.1050 g., 0.9990 Silver 0.9990 oz. ASW, 40 mm. **Ruler:** Elizabeth II **Subject:** Year of the Dragon **Obv:** Head with tiara right **Rev:** Dragon colored yellow and lavender

Date	Mintage	F	VF	XF	Unc	BU
2012P	—	—	—	—	—	100

KM# 1664.6 DOLLAR

31.1050 g., 0.9990 Silver 0.9990 oz. ASW, 40 mm. **Ruler:** Elizabeth II **Subject:** Year of the Dragon **Obv:** Head with tiara right **Rev:** Dragon colored blue and yellow

Date	Mintage	F	VF	XF	Unc	BU
2012P	—	—	—	—	—	100

KM# 1664.7 DOLLAR

31.1050 g., 0.9990 Silver 0.9990 oz. ASW, 40 mm. **Ruler:** Elizabeth II **Subject:** Year of the Dragon **Obv:** Head with tiara right **Rev:** Dragon colored purple and yellow

Date	Mintage	F	VF	XF	Unc	BU
2012P	—	—	—	—	—	100

KM# 1664.8 DOLLAR

31.1050 g., 0.9990 Silver 0.9990 oz. ASW, 40 mm. **Ruler:** Elizabeth II **Subject:** Year of the Dragon **Obv:** Head with tiara right **Rev:** Dragon colored orange, brown and yellow

Date	Mintage	F	VF	XF	Unc	BU
2012P	—	—	—	—	—	100

KM# 1664.9 DOLLAR

31.1050 g., 0.9990 Silver 0.9990 oz. ASW, 40 mm. **Ruler:** Elizabeth II **Subject:** Year of the Dragon **Obv:** Head with tiara right **Rev:** Dragon colored white and blue

Date	Mintage	F	VF	XF	Unc	BU
2012P	—	—	—	—	—	100

KM# 1664.10 DOLLAR

31.1050 g., 0.9990 Silver 0.9990 oz. ASW, 40 mm. **Ruler:** Elizabeth II **Subject:** Year of the Dragon **Obv:** Head with tiara right **Rev:** Dragon colored brown and orange

Date	Mintage	F	VF	XF	Unc	BU
2012P	—	—	—	—	—	100

KM# 1664.11 DOLLAR

31.1050 g., 0.9990 Silver 0.9990 oz. ASW, 40 mm. **Ruler:** Elizabeth II **Subject:** Year of the Dragon **Obv:** head with tiara right **Rev:** Dragon colored lavender and grey

Date	Mintage	F	VF	XF	Unc	BU
2012P	—	—	—	—	—	100

KM# 1713 DOLLAR

31.1350 g., 0.9990 Silver 1.0000 oz. ASW, 32.6 mm. **Ruler:** Elizabeth II **Subject:** Year of the Dragon **Obv:** Head with tiara right **Rev:** Dragon **Edge:** Reeded **Note:** High Relief

Date	Mintage	F	VF	XF	Unc	BU
2012P Proof	7,500	Value: 100				

KM# 1793 DOLLAR

31.1050 g., 0.9990 Silver 0.9990 oz. ASW **Ruler:** Elizabeth II **Subject:** Year of the Dragon **Note:** High releif

Date	Mintage	F	VF	XF	Unc	BU
2012P Proof	—	Value: 75.00				

KM# 1827 DOLLAR

31.1050 g., 0.9990 Silver 0.9990 oz. ASW, 33 mm. **Ruler:** Elizabeth II **Subject:** Year of the Snake **Note:** Ultra high relief

Date	Mintage	F	VF	XF	Unc	BU
2013P Proof	—	Value: 110				

KM# 1831 DOLLAR

31.1050 g., 0.9990 Silver 0.9990 oz. ASW, 40.6 mm. **Ruler:** Elizabeth II **Subject:** Year of the Snake

Date	Mintage	F	VF	XF	Unc	BU
2013P	—	—	—	—	—	40.00
2013P Proof	—	Value: 50.00				

KM# 1831a DOLLAR

31.1050 g., 0.9990 Silver partially gilt 0.9990 oz. ASW, 40.6 mm. **Ruler:** Elizabeth II **Subject:** Year of the Snake **Rev:** Gilt snake

Date	Mintage	F	VF	XF	Unc	BU
2013P	—	Value: 75.00				

KM# 537 2 DOLLARS

62.2070 g., 0.9990 Silver 1.9979 oz. ASW, 50.3 mm. **Ruler:** Elizabeth II **Subject:** Year of the Snake **Obv:** Head with tiara right, denomination below **Rev:** Snake with eggs **Edge:** Segmented reeding

Date	Mintage	F	VF	XF	Unc	BU
2001	—	—	—	—	75.00	85.00
2001P Proof	1,000	Value: 110				

KM# 581 2 DOLLARS

62.2070 g., 0.9990 Silver 1.9979 oz. ASW, 50 mm. **Ruler:** Elizabeth II **Subject:** Year of the Horse **Obv:** Head with tiara right, denomination below **Rev:** Horse running left **Edge:** Reeded

Date	Mintage	F	VF	XF	Unc	BU
2002	—	—	—	—	75.00	85.00
2002P Proof	1,000	Value: 110				

KM# 679 2 DOLLARS

62.8500 g., 0.9990 Silver 2.0186 oz. ASW, 50 mm. **Ruler:** Elizabeth II **Subject:** Year of the Goat **Obv:** Head with tiara right, denomination below **Rev:** Two goats **Edge:** Reeded

Date	Mintage	F	VF	XF	Unc	BU
2003	—	—	—	—	75.00	85.00

KM# 675 2 DOLLARS

62.2070 g., 0.9990 Silver 1.9979 oz. ASW, 50 mm. **Ruler:** Elizabeth II **Subject:** Year of the Monkey **Obv:** Head with tiara right, denomination below **Rev:** Monkey sitting on branch **Edge:** Reeded

Date	Mintage	F	VF	XF	Unc	BU
2004	—	—	—	—	75.00	85.00
2004 Proof	7,000	Value: 110				

KM# 793 2 DOLLARS

62.2700 g., 0.9990 Silver 1.9999 oz. ASW, 50.3 mm. **Ruler:** Elizabeth II **Subject:** Year of the Rooster **Obv:** Elizabeth II **Rev:** Standing Rooster looking backwards **Edge:** Reeded

Date	Mintage	F	VF	XF	Unc	BU
2005P Proof	2,000	Value: 150				

KM# 1751 2 DOLLARS

62.2700 g., 0.9990 Silver 1.9999 oz. ASW, 50 mm. **Ruler:** Elizabeth II **Subject:** Year of the Ox **Obv:** Head with tiara right **Rev:** Two oxen standing

Date	Mintage	F	VF	XF	Unc	BU
2009P	—	—	—	—	—	125

KM# 1751a 2 DOLLARS

62.2700 g., 0.9990 Silver 1.9999 oz. ASW, 50 mm. **Ruler:** Elizabeth II **Subject:** Year of the Ox **Obv:** Head with tiara right **Rev:** Two colored oxen standing

Date	Mintage	F	VF	XF	Unc	BU
2009P	—	—	—	—	—	125

KM# 1320 2 DOLLARS
62.2100 g., 0.9990 Silver 1.9980 oz. ASW, 50 mm. **Ruler:** Elizabeth II **Subject:** Year of the Tiger **Obv:** Head right **Rev:** Tiger seated left

Date	Mintage	F	VF	XF	Unc	BU
2010P Proof	1,000	Value: 160				

KM# 1476 2 DOLLARS
62.2000 g., 0.9990 Silver 1.9977 oz. ASW **Ruler:** Elizabeth II **Subject:** Year of the Rabbit **Rev:** Mother and baby rabbit nose to nose

Date	Mintage	F	VF	XF	Unc	BU
2011P Proof	—	Value: 110				

KM# 1665 2 DOLLARS
62.2700 g., 0.9990 Silver 1.9999 oz. ASW, 50.3 mm. **Ruler:** Elizabeth II **Subject:** Year of the Dragon

Date	Mintage	F	VF	XF	Unc	BU
2012P Proof	—	Value: 150				

KM# 1833 2 DOLLARS
62.2000 g., 0.9990 Silver 1.9977 oz. ASW, 50.3 mm. **Ruler:** Elizabeth II **Subject:** Year of the Snake

Date	Mintage	F	VF	XF	Unc	BU
2013P Proof	—	Value: 150				

KM# 538 5 DOLLARS
1.5710 g., 0.9990 Gold 0.0505 oz. AGW, 14.1 mm. **Ruler:** Elizabeth II **Subject:** Year of the Snake **Obv:** Head with tiara right, denomination below **Rev:** Snake in tree **Edge:** Reeded

Date	Mintage	F	VF	XF	Unc	BU
2001	100,000	—	—	—	—	95.00
2001P Proof	100,000	Value: 100				

KM# 582 5 DOLLARS
1.5552 g., 0.9990 Gold 0.0499 oz. AGW, 14.1 mm. **Ruler:** Elizabeth II **Subject:** Year of the Horse **Obv:** Head with tiara right, denomination below **Rev:** Horse galloping left **Edge:** Reeded

Date	Mintage	F	VF	XF	Unc	BU
2002P	100,000	—	—	—	—	95.00

KM# 668 5 DOLLARS
1.5710 g., 0.9999 Gold 0.0505 oz. AGW, 14.1 mm. **Ruler:** Elizabeth II **Subject:** Year of the Monkey **Obv:** Head with tiara right, denomination below **Rev:** Monkey **Edge:** Reeded

Date	Mintage	F	VF	XF	Unc	BU
2004P Proof	100,000	Value: 100				

KM# 1022.1 5 DOLLARS
1.5700 g., 0.9999 Gold 0.0505 oz. AGW, 13.93 mm. **Ruler:** Elizabeth II **Obv:** Head with tiara right **Rev:** Rooster standing right **Edge:** Reeded **Note:** Polished images with matte fields.

Date	Mintage	F	VF	XF	Unc	BU
2005 Proof	28,000	Value: 110				

KM# 1022.2 5 DOLLARS
1.5700 g., 0.9999 Gold 0.0505 oz. AGW, 13.93 mm. **Ruler:** Elizabeth II **Subject:** Year of the Rooster **Obv:** Head with tiara right **Rev:** Rooster standing right, multicolor **Edge:** Reeded

Date	Mintage	F	VF	XF	Unc	BU
2005 Proof	1,000	Value: 120				

KM# 1481 5 DOLLARS
1.5700 g., 0.9999 Gold 0.0505 oz. AGW, 14.1 mm. **Ruler:** Elizabeth II **Subject:** Year of the Rabbit

Date	Mintage	F	VF	XF	Unc	BU
2011P Proof	—	Value: 100				

KM# 1666 5 DOLLARS
155.5175 g., 0.9990 Silver 4.9948 oz. ASW, 65 mm. **Ruler:** Elizabeth II **Subject:** Year of the Dragon

Date	Mintage	F	VF	XF	Unc	BU
2012P Proof	—	Value: 225				

KM# 1670 5 DOLLARS
1.5552 g., 0.9990 Gold 0.0499 oz. AGW, 14.1 mm. **Ruler:** Elizabeth II **Subject:** Year of the Dragon **Rev:** Dragon

Date	Mintage	F	VF	XF	Unc	BU
2012P Proof	—	Value: 110				

KM# 1679 5 DOLLARS
1.5500 g., 0.9990 Gold 0.0498 oz. AGW, 14.1 mm. **Ruler:** Elizabeth II **Subject:** Year of the Dragon **Rev:** Dragon head facing in color

Date	Mintage	F	VF	XF	Unc	BU
2012P Proof	—	Value: 125				

KM# 743 8 DOLLARS
155.5175 g., 0.9990 Silver 4.9948 oz. ASW, 65 mm. **Ruler:** Elizabeth II **Subject:** Year of the Monkey **Obv:** Head with tiara right, denomination below **Rev:** Gold-plated seated monkey and multicolored ornamentation **Edge:** Reeded **Note:** Illustration reduced.

Date	Mintage	F	VF	XF	Unc	BU
2004	6,000	—	—	—	—	220

KM# 1023 8 DOLLARS
155.5150 g., 0.9990 Silver partially gilt 4.9947 oz. ASW, 65 mm. **Ruler:** Elizabeth II **Subject:** Year of the Rooster **Obv:** Head with tiara right **Rev:** Rooster standing left gilt, floral in color **Edge:** Reeded

Date	Mintage	F	VF	XF	Unc	BU
2005 Proof	10,000	Value: 300				

KM# 1754 8 DOLLARS
155.5150 g., 0.9990 Silver 4.9947 oz. ASW, 65 mm. **Ruler:** Elizabeth II **Subject:** Year of the Dog **Rev:** German shepard in color seated

Date	Mintage	F	VF	XF	Unc	BU
2006P	—	—	—	—	—	220

KM# 1756 8 DOLLARS
155.5750 g., 0.9990 Silver 4.9966 oz. ASW, 65 mm. **Ruler:** Elizabeth II **Subject:** Year of the Pig **Obv:** Head with tiara right **Rev:** Pig in color

Date	Mintage	F	VF	XF	Unc	BU
2007P	—	—	—	—	—	225

KM# 1757 8 DOLLARS
155.5750 g., 0.9990 Silver 4.9966 oz. ASW, 65 mm. **Ruler:** Elizabeth II **Subject:** Year of the Mouse **Obv:** Head with tiara right **Rev:** Two mice in color

Date	Mintage	F	VF	XF	Unc	BU
2008P	—	—	—	—	—	225

KM# 1371 8 DOLLARS
155.5175 g., 0.9990 Silver 4.9948 oz. ASW, 65 mm. **Ruler:** Elizabeth II **Subject:** Year of the Tiger **Obv:** Head right **Rev:** Tiger at rest left

Date	Mintage	F	VF	XF	Unc	BU
2010P	—	—	—	—	—	225

KM# 1794 8 DOLLARS
155.5000 g., 0.9990 Silver 4.9942 oz. ASW, 65 mm. **Ruler:** Elizabeth II **Subject:** Year of the Dragon

Date	Mintage	F	VF	XF	Unc	BU
2012P Proof	—	Value: 250				

KM# 539 10 DOLLARS
311.0350 g., 0.9990 Silver 9.9896 oz. ASW, 75.5 mm. **Ruler:** Elizabeth II **Subject:** Year of the Snake **Obv:** Head with tiara right, denomination below **Rev:** Snake with eggs **Edge:** Segmented reeding

Date	Mintage	F	VF	XF	Unc	BU
2001	—	—	—	—	375	400
2001P Proof	250	Value: 475				

KM# 583 10 DOLLARS
311.0350 g., 0.9990 Silver 9.9896 oz. ASW, 75.5 mm. **Ruler:** Elizabeth II **Subject:** Year of the Horse **Obv:** Head with tiara right, denomination below **Rev:** Horse running left **Edge:** Segmented reeding

Date	Mintage	F	VF	XF	Unc	BU
2002	—	—	—	—	375	400
2002P Proof	500	Value: 450				

KM# 710 10 DOLLARS
311.0350 g., 0.9990 Silver 9.9896 oz. ASW, 75.5 mm. **Ruler:** Elizabeth II **Subject:** Year of the Goat **Obv:** Head with tiara right, denomination below **Rev:** Goat

Date	Mintage	F	VF	XF	Unc	BU
2003	—	—	—	—	375	400
2003 Proof	—	Value: 450				

KM# 1339 10 DOLLARS
311.0350 g., 0.9990 Silver 9.9896 oz. ASW, 75.5 mm. **Ruler:** Elizabeth II **Subject:** Year of the Goat **Obv:** Head right

Date	Mintage	F	VF	XF	Unc	BU
2003P	—	—	—	—	400	375
2003P Proof	—	Value: 475				

KM# 676 10 DOLLARS
311.0350 g., 0.9990 Silver 9.9896 oz. ASW, 75.5 mm. **Ruler:** Elizabeth II **Subject:** Year of the Monkey **Obv:** Head with tiara right, denomination below **Rev:** Monkey sitting on branch **Edge:** Segmented reeding

Date	Mintage	F	VF	XF	Unc	BU
2004	—	—	—	—	375	400
2004 Proof	5,000	Value: 475				

KM# 696 10 DOLLARS
311.0350 g., 0.9990 Silver 9.9896 oz. ASW, 75.5 mm. **Ruler:** Elizabeth II **Subject:** Year of the Rooster **Obv:** Head with tiara right, denomination below **Rev:** Rooster

Date	Mintage	F	VF	XF	Unc	BU
2005	—	—	—	—	375	400
2005 Proof	—	Value: 475				

KM# 1057 10 DOLLARS
3.1100 g., 0.9990 Gold 0.0999 oz. AGW, 17.53 mm. **Ruler:** Elizabeth II **Subject:** Year of the Rat

Date	Mintage	F	VF	XF	Unc	BU
2008 Proof	2,500	Value: 200				

KM# 1079 10 DOLLARS
3.1100 g., 0.9990 Gold 0.0999 oz. AGW, 17.53 mm. **Ruler:** Elizabeth II **Subject:** Year of the Ox

Date	Mintage	F	VF	XF	Unc	BU
2009 Proof	2,500	Value: 245				

KM# 1752 10 DOLLARS
311.0350 g., 0.9990 Silver 9.9896 oz. ASW, 75.5 mm. **Ruler:** Elizabeth II **Subject:** Year of the Ox **Obv:** Head with tiara right **Rev:** Two oxen standing

Date	Mintage	F	VF	XF	Unc	BU
2009P	—	—	—	—	—	350

KM# 1752a 10 DOLLARS
311.0350 g., 0.9990 Silver 9.9896 oz. ASW, 75.5 mm. **Ruler:** Elizabeth II **Subject:** Year of the Ox **Obv:** Head with tiara right **Rev:** Two colored oxen standing

Date	Mintage	F	VF	XF	Unc	BU
2009P	—	—	—	—	—	365

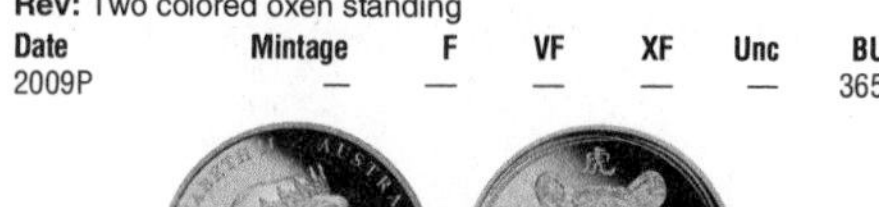

KM# 1321 10 DOLLARS
3.1100 g., 0.9990 Gold 0.0999 oz. AGW, 19 mm. **Ruler:** Elizabeth II **Subject:** Year of the Tiger **Obv:** Head right **Rev:** Tiger head facing

Date	Mintage	F	VF	XF	Unc	BU
2010P Proof	8,000	Value: 260				

KM# 1372 10 DOLLARS
311.0350 g., 0.9990 Silver 9.9896 oz. ASW, 75.5 mm. **Ruler:** Elizabeth II **Subject:** Year of the Tiger **Obv:** Head right **Rev:** Tiger at rest left

Date	Mintage	F	VF	XF	Unc	BU
2010P	—	—	—	—	—	400

KM# 1478 10 DOLLARS
311.0500 g., 0.9990 Silver 9.9901 oz. ASW, 75.5 mm. **Ruler:** Elizabeth II **Subject:** Year of the Rabbit **Rev:** Two rabbits nestled under tree

Date	Mintage	F	VF	XF	Unc	BU
2011P Proof	—	Value: 400				

KM# 1667 10 DOLLARS
311.0350 g., 0.9990 Silver 9.9896 oz. ASW, 75.5 mm. **Ruler:** Elizabeth II **Subject:** Year of the Dragon **Rev:** Dragon

Date	Mintage	F	VF	XF	Unc	BU
2012P Proof	—	Value: 400				

KM# 540 15 DOLLARS
3.1103 g., 0.9990 Gold 0.0999 oz. AGW, 16.1 mm. **Ruler:** Elizabeth II **Subject:** Year of the Snake **Obv:** Head with tiara right, denomination below **Rev:** Snake in tree **Edge:** Reeded

Date	Mintage	F	VF	XF	Unc	BU
2001	80,000	—	—	—	—	175
2001P Proof	7,000	Value: 185				

KM# 584 15 DOLLARS
3.1103 g., 0.9990 Gold 0.0999 oz. AGW, 16.1 mm. **Ruler:** Elizabeth II **Subject:** Year of the Horse **Obv:** Head with tiara right, denomination below **Rev:** Horse galloping half left **Edge:** Reeded

Date	Mintage	F	VF	XF	Unc	BU
2002P	—	—	—	—	—	175
2002P Proof	7,000	Value: 185				

KM# 711 15 DOLLARS
3.1100 g., 0.9999 Gold 0.1000 oz. AGW, 16.1 mm. **Ruler:** Elizabeth II **Subject:** Year of the Goat **Obv:** Head with tiara right, denomination below **Rev:** Goat

Date	Mintage	F	VF	XF	Unc	BU
2003	—	—	—	—	—	175
2003 Proof	—	Value: 185				

KM# 1340 15 DOLLARS
3.1100 g., 0.9990 Gold 0.0999 oz. AGW, 16.1 mm. **Ruler:** Elizabeth II **Subject:** Year of the Goat **Obv:** Head right

Date	Mintage	F	VF	XF	Unc	BU
2003P	—	—	—	—	—	175
2003P Proof	—	Value: 195				

KM# 669 15 DOLLARS

3.1103 g., 0.9999 Gold 0.1000 oz. AGW, 16.1 mm. **Ruler:** Elizabeth II **Subject:** Year of the Monkey **Obv:** Head with tiara right, denomination below **Rev:** Monkey **Edge:** Reeded

Date	Mintage	F	VF	XF	Unc	BU
2004P	—	—	—	—	—	175
2004P Proof	80,000	Value: 185				

KM# 794 15 DOLLARS

3.1103 g., 0.9999 Gold 0.1000 oz. AGW, 16.1 mm. **Ruler:** Elizabeth II **Subject:** Year of the Rooster **Obv:** Elizabeth II **Rev:** Standing rooster right **Edge:** Reeded

Date	Mintage	F	VF	XF	Unc	BU
2005P Proof	7,000	Value: 185				

KM# 794a 15 DOLLARS

31.1030 g., 0.7500 Gold 0.7500 oz. AGW **Ruler:** Elizabeth II **Subject:** Year of the Rooster **Obv:** Head with tiara right **Rev:** Rooster standing right **Edge:** Reeded

Date	Mintage	F	VF	XF	Unc	BU
2005P Proof	15,000	Value: 1,350				

KM# 1373 15 DOLLARS

500.0000 g., 0.9990 Silver 16.058 oz. ASW **Ruler:** Elizabeth II **Subject:** Year of the Tiger **Obv:** Head right **Rev:** Tiger at rest left

Date	Mintage	F	VF	XF	Unc	BU
2010P	—	—	—	—	—	650

KM# 1375 15 DOLLARS

3.1100 g., 0.9990 Gold 0.0999 oz. AGW, 16.1 mm. **Ruler:** Elizabeth II **Subject:** Year of the Tiger **Obv:** Head right

Date	Mintage	F	VF	XF	Unc	BU
2010P	—	—	—	—	—	175

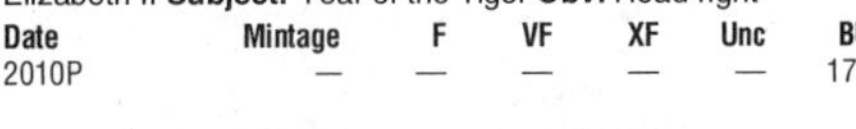

KM# 1482 15 DOLLARS

3.1000 g., 0.9990 Gold 0.0996 oz. AGW, 16.1 mm. **Ruler:** Elizabeth II **Subject:** Year of the Rabbit **Rev:** Rabbit left

Date	Mintage	F	VF	XF	Unc	BU
2011P Proof	—	Value: 185				

KM# 1671 15 DOLLARS

3.1100 g., 0.9990 Gold 0.0999 oz. AGW, 16.1 mm. **Ruler:** Elizabeth II **Subject:** Year of the Dragon

Date	Mintage	F	VF	XF	Unc	BU
2012P Proof	—	Value: 225				

KM# 1671a 15 DOLLARS

3.1100 g., 0.9990 Gold 0.0999 oz. AGW, 16.1 mm. **Ruler:** Elizabeth II **Subject:** Year of the Dragon **Rev:** MUlticolor dragon

Date	Mintage	F	VF	XF	Unc	BU
2012P Proof	—	Value: 225				

KM# 1835 15 DOLLARS

3.1100 g., 0.9990 Gold 0.0999 oz. AGW, 16.1 mm. **Ruler:** Elizabeth II **Subject:** Year of the Snake

Date	Mintage	F	VF	XF	Unc	BU
2013P Proof	—	Value: 250				

KM# 541 25 DOLLARS

7.7508 g., 0.9990 Gold 0.2489 oz. AGW, 20.1 mm. **Ruler:** Elizabeth II **Subject:** Year of the Snake **Obv:** Head with tiara right, denomination below **Rev:** Snake in tree **Edge:** Reeded

Date	Mintage	F	VF	XF	Unc	BU
2001	60,000	—	—	—	—	450
2001P Proof	7,000	Value: 475				

KM# 585 25 DOLLARS

7.7759 g., 0.9990 Gold 0.2497 oz. AGW, 20.1 mm. **Ruler:** Elizabeth II **Subject:** Year of the Horse **Obv:** Head with tiara right, denomination below **Rev:** Horse galloping half left **Edge:** Reeded

Date	Mintage	F	VF	XF	Unc	BU
2002P	—	—	—	—	—	450
2002P Proof	7,000	Value: 475				

KM# 712 25 DOLLARS

7.7500 g., 0.9999 Gold 0.2491 oz. AGW **Ruler:** Elizabeth II **Subject:** Year of the Goat **Obv:** Head with tiara right, denomination below **Rev:** Goat

Date	Mintage	F	VF	XF	Unc	BU
2003	—	—	—	—	—	450
2003 Proof	—	Value: 475				

KM# 1341 25 DOLLARS

7.7600 g., 0.9990 Gold 0.2492 oz. AGW, 20 mm. **Ruler:** Elizabeth II **Subject:** Year of the Goat **Obv:** Head right

Date	Mintage	F	VF	XF	Unc	BU
2003P	—	—	—	—	—	450
2003P Proof	—	Value: 475				

KM# 670 25 DOLLARS

7.7508 g., 0.9999 Gold 0.2492 oz. AGW, 20.1 mm. **Ruler:** Elizabeth II **Subject:** Year of the Monkey **Obv:** Head with tiara right, denomination below **Rev:** Monkey **Edge:** Reeded

Date	Mintage	F	VF	XF	Unc	BU
2004P	—	—	—	—	—	450
2004P Proof	60,000	Value: 475				

KM# 795 25 DOLLARS

7.7759 g., 0.9999 Gold 0.2500 oz. AGW, 20.1 mm. **Ruler:** Elizabeth II **Subject:** Year of the Rooster **Obv:** Elizabeth II **Rev:** Standing rooster right **Edge:** Reeded

Date	Mintage	F	VF	XF	Unc	BU
2005P Proof	7,000	Value: 475				

KM# 1322 25 DOLLARS

7.7700 g., 0.9990 Gold 0.2496 oz. AGW, 22 mm. **Ruler:** Elizabeth II **Subject:** Year of the Tiger **Obv:** Head right **Rev:** Tiger head facing

Date	Mintage	F	VF	XF	Unc	BU
2010P Proof	8,000	Value: 650				

KM# 1483 25 DOLLARS

7.7700 g., 0.9990 Gold 0.2496 oz. AGW **Ruler:** Elizabeth II **Subject:** Year of the Rabbit **Rev:** Rabbit left

Date	Mintage	F	VF	XF	Unc	BU
2011P Proof	—	Value: 475				

KM# 1672 25 DOLLARS

7.7700 g., 0.9990 Gold 0.2496 oz. AGW, 22 mm. **Ruler:** Elizabeth II **Subject:** Year of the Dragon

Date	Mintage	F	VF	XF	Unc	BU
2012P Proof	—	Value: 475				

KM# 1672a 25 DOLLARS

7.7700 g., 0.9990 Gold 0.2496 oz. AGW, 22 mm. **Ruler:** Elizabeth II **Subject:** Year of the Dragon **Rev:** Multicolor dragon

Date	Mintage	F	VF	XF	Unc	BU
2012P Proof	—	Value: 500				

KM# 1836 25 DOLLARS

7.7700 g., 0.9990 Gold 0.2496 oz. AGW, 20 mm. **Ruler:** Elizabeth II **Subject:** Year of the Snake

Date	Mintage	F	VF	XF	Unc	BU
2013P Proof	—	Value: 550				

KM# 542 30 DOLLARS

1002.5020 g., 0.9990 Silver 32.197 oz. ASW, 101 mm. **Ruler:** Elizabeth II **Subject:** Year of the Snake **Obv:** Head with tiara right, denomination below **Rev:** Snake with eggs **Edge:** Segmented reeding

Date	Mintage	F	VF	XF	Unc	BU
2001	—	—	—	—	—	1,150
2001P Proof	250	Value: 1,350				

KM# 586 30 DOLLARS

1002.5020 g., 0.9990 Silver 32.197 oz. ASW, 101 mm. **Ruler:** Elizabeth II **Subject:** Year of the Horse **Obv:** Head with tiara right, denomination below **Rev:** Horse running left **Edge:** Segmented reeding **Note:** Illustration reduced.

Date	Mintage	F	VF	XF	Unc	BU
2002	—	—	—	—	—	1,150
2002P Proof	250	Value: 1,350				

KM# 681 30 DOLLARS

1000.0000 g., 0.9990 Silver 32.117 oz. ASW, 101 mm. **Ruler:** Elizabeth II **Subject:** Year of the Goat **Obv:** Head with tiara right, denomination below **Rev:** Nanny goat and kid **Edge:** Segmented reeding

Date	Mintage	F	VF	XF	Unc	BU
2003	—	—	—	—	—	1,150
2003P Proof	—	Value: 1,350				

KM# 677.1 30 DOLLARS

1000.0000 g., 0.9990 Silver 32.117 oz. ASW, 101 mm. **Ruler:** Elizabeth II **Subject:** Year of the Monkey **Obv:** Head with tiara right, denomination below **Rev:** Monkey sitting on branch **Edge:** Segmented reeding

Date	Mintage	F	VF	XF	Unc	BU
2004	—	—	—	—	—	1,150
2004 Proof	5,250	Value: 1,250				

KM# 677.2 30 DOLLARS

1000.0000 g., 0.9990 Silver 32.117 oz. ASW, 101 mm. **Ruler:** Elizabeth II **Subject:** Year of the Monkey **Obv:** Head with tiara right, denomination below **Rev:** Multicolor ornamentation and monkey with diamond chip eyes sitting on branch **Edge:** Segmented reeding **Note:** Illustration reduced.

Date	Mintage	F	VF	XF	Unc	BU
2004 Proof	5,000	Value: 1,300				

KM# 697 30 DOLLARS

1000.0000 g., 0.9990 Silver 32.117 oz. ASW, 101 mm. **Ruler:** Elizabeth II **Subject:** Year of the Rooster **Obv:** Head with tiara right, denomination below **Rev:** Rooster, partially gilt and colored **Note:** Illustration reduced.

Date	Mintage	F	VF	XF	Unc	BU
2005 Proof	—	Value: 1,300				

KM# 1374 30 DOLLARS

1000.0000 g., 0.9990 Silver 32.117 oz. ASW, 101 mm. **Ruler:** Elizabeth II **Subject:** Year of the Tiger **Obv:** Head right

Date	Mintage	F	VF	XF	Unc	BU
2010P	—	—	—	—	—	1,150

KM# 1319 30 DOLLARS

1000.0000 g., 0.9990 Silver 32.117 oz. ASW, 101 mm. **Ruler:** Elizabeth II **Subject:** Year of the Tiger **Obv:** Head right **Rev:** Tiger at rest left **Note:** Illustration reduced.

Date	Mintage	F	VF	XF	Unc	BU
2010P Proof	5,000	Value: 1,600				

KM# 1479 30 DOLLARS

1000.0000 g., 0.9990 Silver 32.117 oz. ASW, 101 mm. **Ruler:** Elizabeth II **Subject:** Year of the Rabbit **Rev:** Mother and baby rabbit nose to nose **Note:** Illustration reduced.

Date	Mintage	F	VF	XF	Unc	BU
2010P Proof	—	Value: 1,300				

KM# 1668 30 DOLLARS

1000.0000 g., 0.9990 Silver 32.117 oz. ASW, 101 mm. **Ruler:** Elizabeth II **Subject:** Year of the Dragon **Rev:** Dragon

Date	Mintage	F	VF	XF	Unc	BU
2012P Proof	—	Value: 1,250				

KM# 1668a 30 DOLLARS

1000.0000 g., 0.9990 Silver 32.117 oz. ASW, 101 mm. **Ruler:** Elizabeth II **Obv:** Head with tiara right **Rev:** Dragon in color with gemstone

Date	Mintage	F	VF	XF	Unc	BU
2012P Proof	—	Value: 1,400				

KM# 1834 30 DOLLARS

1000.0000 g., 0.9990 Silver 32.117 oz. ASW, 101 mm. **Ruler:** Elizabeth II **Subject:** Year of the Snake

Date	Mintage	F	VF	XF	Unc	BU
2013P Proof	—	Value: 1,500				

KM# 1834a 30 DOLLARS

1000.0000 g., 0.9990 Silver 32.117 oz. ASW, 101 mm. **Ruler:** Elizabeth II **Subject:** Year of the Snake **Rev:** Snake in color with diamond chip as eye

Date	Mintage	F	VF	XF	Unc	BU
2013P Proof	—	Value: 1,750				

KM# 671 50 DOLLARS

15.5940 g., 0.9999 Gold 0.5013 oz. AGW, 25.1 mm. **Ruler:** Elizabeth II **Subject:** Year of the Monkey **Obv:** Head with tiara right, denomination below **Rev:** Monkey **Edge:** Reeded

Date	Mintage	F	VF	XF	Unc	BU
2004P Proof	40,000	Value: 900				

KM# 1376 50 DOLLARS

15.5940 g., 0.9990 Gold 0.5008 oz. AGW, 25 mm. **Ruler:** Elizabeth II **Subject:** Year of the Tiger **Obv:** Head right

Date	Mintage	F	VF	XF	Unc	BU
2010P Proof	—	Value: 900				

KM# 1484 50 DOLLARS

15.5940 g., 0.9990 Gold 0.5008 oz. AGW, 25.1 mm. **Ruler:** Elizabeth II **Subject:** Year of the Rabbit

Date	Mintage	F	VF	XF	Unc	BU
2011P Proof	—	Value: 950				

KM# 1673 50 DOLLARS

15.5500 g., 0.9990 Gold 0.4994 oz. AGW, 25 mm. **Ruler:** Elizabeth II **Subject:** Year of the dragon

Date	Mintage	F	VF	XF	Unc	BU
2012P Proof	—	Value: 950				

KM# 543 100 DOLLARS

31.1035 g., 0.9990 Gold 0.9990 oz. AGW, 32.1 mm. **Ruler:** Elizabeth II **Subject:** Year of the Snake **Obv:** Head with tiara right, denomination below **Rev:** Snake in tree **Edge:** Reeded

Date	Mintage	F	VF	XF	Unc	BU
2001	30,000	—	—	—	—	1,750
2001P Proof	—	Value: 1,800				

KM# 587 100 DOLLARS

31.1035 g., 0.9990 Gold 0.9990 oz. AGW, 32.1 mm. **Ruler:** Elizabeth II **Subject:** Year of the Horse **Obv:** Head with tiara right, denomination below **Rev:** Horse running left **Edge:** Reeded

Date	Mintage	F	VF	XF	Unc	BU
2002	—	—	—	—	—	1,750
2002P Proof	—	Value: 1,800				

KM# 713 100 DOLLARS

31.1035 g., 0.9999 Gold 0.9999 oz. AGW, 32.1 mm. **Ruler:** Elizabeth II **Subject:** Year of the Goat **Obv:** Head with tiara right, denomination below **Rev:** Goat

Date	Mintage	F	VF	XF	Unc	BU
2003	—	—	—	—	—	1,750
2003 Proof	—	Value: 1,800				

KM# 672 100 DOLLARS

31.1035 g., 0.9999 Gold 0.9999 oz. AGW, 32.1 mm. **Ruler:** Elizabeth II **Subject:** Year of the Monkey **Obv:** Head with tiara right, denomination below **Rev:** Monkey walking left on branch **Edge:** Reeded

Date	Mintage	F	VF	XF	Unc	BU
2004	30,000	—	—	—	—	1,750
2004P Proof	—	Value: 1,800				

KM# 796 100 DOLLARS

31.1035 g., 0.9999 Gold 0.9999 oz. AGW, 32.1 mm. **Ruler:** Elizabeth II **Subject:** Year of the Rooster **Obv:** Elizabeth II **Rev:** Standing rooster right **Edge:** Reeded

Date	Mintage	F	VF	XF	Unc	BU
2005P Proof	3,000	Value: 1,800				

KM# 1323 100 DOLLARS

31.1050 g., 0.9990 Gold 0.9990 oz. AGW, 39.34 mm. **Ruler:** Elizabeth II **Subject:** Year of the Tiger **Obv:** Head right **Rev:** Tiger head facing

Date	Mintage	F	VF	XF	Unc	BU
2010P Proof	6,000	Value: 2,650				

KM# 1485 100 DOLLARS

31.1050 g., 0.9990 Gold 0.9990 oz. AGW, 39.34 mm. **Ruler:** Elizabeth II **Subject:** Year of the Rabbit **Rev:** Rabbit seated left

Date	Mintage	F	VF	XF	Unc	BU
2011P Proof	—	Value: 1,800				

KM# 1674 100 DOLLARS

31.1050 g., 0.9990 Gold 0.9990 oz. AGW, 39.34 mm. **Ruler:** Elizabeth II **Subject:** Year of the Dragon

Date	Mintage	F	VF	XF	Unc	BU
2012P Proof	—	Value: 1,850				

KM# 1674a 100 DOLLARS

31.1050 g., 0.9990 Gold 0.9990 oz. AGW, 39.34 mm. **Ruler:** Elizabeth II **Subject:** Year of the Dragon **Rev:** Multicolor dragon

Date	Mintage	F	VF	XF	Unc	BU
2012P Proof	—	Value: 1,875				

KM# 1837 100 DOLLARS

31.1050 g., 0.9990 Gold 0.9990 oz. AGW, 32.1 mm. **Ruler:** Elizabeth II **Subject:** Year of the Snake

Date	Mintage	F	VF	XF	Unc	BU
2013P Proof	—	Value: 1,900				

KM# 704 200 DOLLARS

62.2140 g., 0.9999 Gold 1.9999 oz. AGW, 41.1 mm. **Ruler:** Elizabeth II **Subject:** Year of the Snake **Obv:** Head with tiara right, denomination below **Rev:** Snake

Date	Mintage	F	VF	XF	Unc	BU
2001 Proof	—	Value: 3,500				

KM# 1333 200 DOLLARS

62.2100 g., 0.9990 Gold 1.9980 oz. AGW, 41.1 mm. **Ruler:** Elizabeth II **Subject:** Year of the Snake **Obv:** Head right

Date	Mintage	F	VF	XF	Unc	BU
2001P Proof	—	Value: 3,500				

KM# 707 200 DOLLARS

62.2140 g., 0.9999 Gold 1.9999 oz. AGW, 41.1 mm. **Ruler:** Elizabeth II **Subject:** Year of the Horse **Rev:** Horse

Date	Mintage	F	VF	XF	Unc	BU
2002 Proof	—	Value: 3,500				

KM# 1336 200 DOLLARS

62.2100 g., 0.9990 Gold 1.9980 oz. AGW, 41.1 mm. **Ruler:** Elizabeth II **Subject:** Year of the Horse

Date	Mintage	F	VF	XF	Unc	BU
2002P Proof	—	Value: 3,500				

KM# 714 200 DOLLARS

62.2140 g., 0.9999 Gold 1.9999 oz. AGW, 41.1 mm. **Ruler:** Elizabeth II **Subject:** Year of the Goat **Obv:** Head with tiara right **Rev:** Goat

Date	Mintage	F	VF	XF	Unc	BU
2003 Proof	—	Value: 3,500				

KM# 717 200 DOLLARS

62.2100 g., 0.9999 Gold 1.9998 oz. AGW, 41.1 mm. **Ruler:** Elizabeth II **Subject:** Year of the Monkey **Obv:** Head with tiara right **Rev:** Monkey

Date	Mintage	F	VF	XF	Unc	BU
2004 Proof	—	Value: 3,500				

KM# 698 200 DOLLARS

62.2100 g., 0.9999 Gold 1.9998 oz. AGW, 41.1 mm. **Ruler:** Elizabeth II **Subject:** Year of the Rooster **Obv:** Head with tiara right **Rev:** Rooster

Date	Mintage	F	VF	XF	Unc	BU
2005 Proof	—	Value: 3,500				

KM# 1377 200 DOLLARS

62.2100 g., 0.9990 Gold 1.9980 oz. AGW, 41.1 mm. **Ruler:** Elizabeth II **Obv:** Year of the Tiger **Rev:** Tiger head facing

Date	Mintage	F	VF	XF	Unc	BU
2010P	—	—	—	—	—	3,600

KM# 1486 200 DOLLARS

62.2100 g., 0.9990 Gold 1.9980 oz. AGW, 41.1 mm. **Ruler:** Elizabeth II **Subject:** Year of the Rabbit

Date	Mintage	F	VF	XF	Unc	BU
2011P Proof	—	Value: 3,600				

KM# 1675 200 DOLLARS

62.2140 g., 0.9990 Gold 1.9981 oz. AGW, 41.1 mm. **Ruler:** Elizabeth II **Subject:** Year of the Dragon

Date	Mintage	F	VF	XF	Unc	BU
2012P Proof	—	Value: 3,550				

KM# 1006 300 DOLLARS

10000.0000 g., 0.9990 Silver 321.17 oz. ASW **Ruler:** Elizabeth II **Series:** Lunar year **Subject:** Year of the Dog **Obv:** Head with tiara right **Obv. Legend:** ELIZABETH II - AUSTRALIA **Rev:** Dog sitting, facing right

Date	Mintage	F	VF	XF	Unc	BU
2006	—	—	—	—	—	11,500

KM# 1480 300 DOLLARS

10000.0000 g., 0.9990 Silver 321.17 oz. ASW **Ruler:** Elizabeth II **Subject:** Year of the Rabbit **Rev:** Two rabbits nestled under tree

Date	Mintage	F	VF	XF	Unc	BU
2011P Proof	—	Value: 11,750				

KM# 1669 300 DOLLARS

10000.0000 g., 0.9990 Silver 321.17 oz. ASW **Ruler:** Elizabeth II **Subject:** Year of the Dragon **Rev:** Dragon

Date	Mintage	F	VF	XF	Unc	BU
2012P Proof	—	Value: 11,500				

KM# 705 1000 DOLLARS

311.0480 g., 0.9999 Gold 9.9990 oz. AGW, 75.6 mm. **Ruler:** Elizabeth II **Subject:** Year of the Snake **Obv:** Head with tiara right, denomination below **Rev:** Snake

Date	Mintage	F	VF	XF	Unc	BU
2001	—	—	—	—	—	18,000

KM# 1334 1000 DOLLARS

311.0480 g., 0.9990 Gold 9.9900 oz. AGW, 75.6 mm. **Ruler:** Elizabeth II **Subject:** Year of the Snake **Obv:** Head right

Date	Mintage	F	VF	XF	Unc	BU
2001P	—	—	—	—	—	18,000

KM# 708 1000 DOLLARS

311.0480 g., 0.9999 Gold 9.9990 oz. AGW, 75.6 mm. **Ruler:** Elizabeth II **Subject:** Year of the Horse **Obv:** Head with tiara right, denomination below **Rev:** Horse

Date	Mintage	F	VF	XF	Unc	BU
2002	—	—	—	—	—	18,000

KM# 1337 1000 DOLLARS

311.0480 g., 0.9990 Gold 9.9900 oz. AGW, 75.6 mm. **Ruler:** Elizabeth II **Subject:** Year of the Horse **Obv:** Head right

Date	Mintage	F	VF	XF	Unc	BU
2002P	—	—	—	—	—	18,000

KM# 715 1000 DOLLARS

311.0480 g., 0.9999 Gold 9.9990 oz. AGW, 75.6 mm. **Ruler:** Elizabeth II **Subject:** Year of the Goat **Obv:** Head with tiara right, denomination below **Rev:** Goat

Date	Mintage	F	VF	XF	Unc	BU
2003	—	—	—	—	—	18,000

KM# 718 1000 DOLLARS

311.0480 g., 0.9999 Gold 9.9990 oz. AGW, 75.6 mm. **Ruler:** Elizabeth II **Subject:** Year of the Monkey **Obv:** Head with tiara right, denomination below **Rev:** Monkey

Date	Mintage	F	VF	XF	Unc	BU
2004	—	—	—	—	—	18,000

KM# 699 1000 DOLLARS

311.0480 g., 0.9999 Gold 9.9990 oz. AGW, 75.6 mm. **Ruler:** Elizabeth II **Subject:** Year of the Rooster **Obv:** Head with tiara right, denomination below **Rev:** Rooster

Date	Mintage	F	VF	XF	Unc	BU
2005	—	—	—	—	—	18,000

KM# 1378 1000 DOLLARS

311.0480 g., 0.9990 Gold 9.9900 oz. AGW, 75.6 mm. **Ruler:** Elizabeth II **Subject:** Year of the Tiger **Obv:** Head right

Date	Mintage	F	VF	XF	Unc	BU
2010(p)	—	—	—	—	—	18,000

KM# 1487 1000 DOLLARS

311.0480 g., 0.9990 Gold 9.9900 oz. AGW, 75.6 mm. **Ruler:** Elizabeth II **Subject:** Year of the Rabbit

Date	Mintage	F	VF	XF	Unc	BU
2011P Proof	—	Value: 18,000				

KM# 1676 1000 DOLLARS

311.0500 g., 0.9990 Gold 9.9901 oz. AGW, 75.6 mm. **Ruler:** Elizabeth II **Subject:** Year of the Dragon

Date	Mintage	F	VF	XF	Unc	BU
2012P Proof	—	Value: 18,000				

KM# 706 3000 DOLLARS
1000.0000 g., 0.9999 Gold 32.146 oz. AGW, 100.6 mm. **Ruler:** Elizabeth II **Subject:** Year of the Snake **Obv:** Head with tiara right, denomination below **Rev:** Snake

Date	Mintage	F	VF	XF	Unc	BU
2001	—	—	—	—	—	BV+3%

KM# 1335 3000 DOLLARS
1000.0000 g., 0.9990 Gold 32.117 oz. AGW, 100.6 mm. **Ruler:** Elizabeth II **Subject:** Year of the Snake **Obv:** Head right

Date	Mintage	F	VF	XF	Unc	BU
2001P	—	—	—	—	—	BV+3%

KM# 709 3000 DOLLARS
1000.0000 g., 0.9999 Gold 32.146 oz. AGW, 100.6 mm. **Ruler:** Elizabeth II **Subject:** Year of the Horse **Obv:** Head with tiara right, denomination below **Rev:** Horse

Date	Mintage	F	VF	XF	Unc	BU
2002	—	—	—	—	—	BV+3%

KM# 1338 3000 DOLLARS
1000.0000 g., 0.9990 Gold 32.117 oz. AGW, 100.6 mm. **Ruler:** Elizabeth II **Subject:** Year of the Horse **Obv:** Head right

Date	Mintage	F	VF	XF	Unc	BU
2002P	—	—	—	—	—	BV+3%

KM# 716 3000 DOLLARS
1000.0000 g., 0.9999 Gold 32.146 oz. AGW, 100.6 mm. **Ruler:** Elizabeth II **Subject:** Year of the Goat **Obv:** Head with tiara right, denomination below **Rev:** Goat

Date	Mintage	F	VF	XF	Unc	BU
2003	—	—	—	—	—	BV+3%

KM# 719 3000 DOLLARS
1000.0000 g., 0.9999 Gold 32.146 oz. AGW, 100.6 mm. **Ruler:** Elizabeth II **Subject:** Year of the Monkey **Obv:** Head with tiara right, denomination below **Rev:** Monkey

Date	Mintage	F	VF	XF	Unc	BU
2004	—	—	—	—	—	BV+3%

KM# 700 3000 DOLLARS
1000.0000 g., 0.9999 Gold 32.146 oz. AGW, 100.6 mm. **Ruler:** Elizabeth II **Subject:** Year of the Rooster **Obv:** Head with tiara right, denomination below **Rev:** Rooster

Date	Mintage	F	VF	XF	Unc	BU
2005	—	—	—	—	—	BV+3%

KM# 1379 3000 DOLLARS
1000.0000 g., 0.9990 Gold 32.117 oz. AGW, 100.6 mm. **Ruler:** Elizabeth II **Subject:** Year of the Tiger **Obv:** Head right

Date	Mintage	F	VF	XF	Unc	BU
2010P	—	—	—	—	—	BV+3%

KM# 1488 3000 DOLLARS
1000.0000 g., 0.9990 Gold 32.117 oz. AGW, 100.6 mm. **Ruler:** Elizabeth II **Subject:** Year of the Rabbit

Date	Mintage	F	VF	XF	Unc	BU
2011P Proof	—	BV+3%				

KM# 1677 3000 DOLLARS
1000.0000 g., 0.9990 Gold 32.117 oz. AGW, 100.6 mm. **Ruler:** Elizabeth II **Subject:** Year of the Dragon

Date	Mintage	F	VF	XF	Unc	BU
2012P Proof	—	BV+3%				

KM# 1007 30000 DOLLARS
10000.0000 g., 0.9999 Gold 321.46 oz. AGW, 180.6 mm. **Ruler:** Elizabeth II **Series:** Lunar year **Subject:** Year of the Dog **Obv:** Head with tiara right **Obv. Legend:** ELIZABETH II - AUSTRALIA **Rev:** Dog standing left

Date	Mintage	F	VF	XF	Unc	BU
2006 Proof	100	BV+2%				

KM# 1489 30000 DOLLARS
10000.0000 g., 0.9990 Gold 321.17 oz. AGW, 180.6 mm. **Ruler:** Elizabeth II **Subject:** Year of the Rabbit

Date	Mintage	F	VF	XF	Unc	BU
2011P Proof	100	BV+2%				

KM# 1678 30000 DOLLARS
10000.0000 g., 0.9990 Gold 321.17 oz. AGW, 180.6 mm. **Ruler:** Elizabeth II **Subject:** Year of the Dragon

Date	Mintage	F	VF	XF	Unc	BU
2012P Proof	100	BV+2%				

BABY MINT SETS

KM#	Date	Mintage	Identification	Issue Price	Mkt Val
BMS9	2001 (6)	32,494	KM#401-403, 406, 491.1, 534.1 plus bronze medal	—	110
BMS10	2002 (6)	32,479	KM#401-403, 406, 600.1, 602 plus bronze medal	—	47.50
BMS11	2003 (6)	37,748	KM#401-402, 406, 688-690 plus bronze medal	—	40.00
BMS12	2004 (6)	31,000	KM#401-404, 406, 733.1 plus bronze medal	—	40.00
BMS13	2005 (6)	34,748	KM#401-402, 406, 745-747 plus bronze medal	24.00	27.50
BMS14	2006 (6)	—	KM#401-404, 406, 489 plus bronze medal	24.00	35.00

BABY PROOF SETS

KM#	Date	Mintage	Identification	Issue Price	Mkt Val
BPS7	2001 (6)	15,011	KM#401-403, 406, 491.1, 534.1 plus silver medal	—	165
BPS8	2002 (6)	13,996	KM#401, 403, 406, 600.2, 602 plus silver medal	—	153
BPS9	2003 (6)	14,799	KM#401-402, 406, 688-689, 690.1 plus silver medal	—	125
BPS10	2004 (6)	13,996	KM#401-404, 406, 733 plus silver medal	—	110
BPS11	2005 (6)	—	KM#401-402, 406, 745-747 plus silver medal	—	100
BPS12	2006 (6)	—	KM#401-404, 406, 489 plus silver medal	—	120

MINT SETS

KM#	Date	Mintage	Identification	Issue Price	Mkt Val
MS39	2001 (3)	—	KM532, 533, 534.1	7.80	75.00
MS40	2001 (3)	—	KM534.1, 550, 551	7.80	70.00
MS41	2001 (3)	—	KM534.1, 552, 553	7.80	70.00
MS42	2001 (3)	—	KM534.1, 554, 555	7.80	75.00
MS43	2001 (3)	—	KM534.1, 556, 557	7.80	72.50
MS44	2001 (3)	—	KM534.1, 558, 559	7.80	75.00
MS45	2001 (3)	—	KM534.1, 560, 561	7.80	85.00
MS46	2001 (3)	—	KM534.1, 562, 563	7.80	80.00
MS47	2001 (3)	—	KM534.1, 564, 565	7.80	75.00
MS48	2001 (20)	—	KM532-533, 534.1, 491.1, 550-565	43.68	235
MS49	2001 (6)	—	KM#401-403, 406, 491.1, 534.1	—	80.00
MS50	2002 (6)	—	KM#401-403, 406, 600.1, 602	—	65.00
MS51	2002 (3)	—	KM#691.2, 692, 693	—	2,300
MS52	2003 (5)	—	KM401, 402, 406, 689, 690	—	35.00
MS53	2004 (6)	—	KM401-404, 406, 733.1	—	32.50
MS54	2005 (6)	—	KM#401, 402, 406, 745-747	—	25.00
MS55	2006 (8)	—	KM#401-404, 406, 489, 767-768 40 Years of Decimal Currency	18.50	55.00
MS56	2006 (15)	—	KM#770-781, 1001-1003	80.00	165

PROOF SETS

KM#	Date	Mintage	Identification	Issue Price	Mkt Val
PS107	2001 (3)	—	KM532, 533, 534.2	21.00	95.00
PS108	2001 (3)	—	KM534.2, 550, 551	21.00	65.00
PS109	2001 (3)	—	KM534.2, 552, 553	21.00	75.00
PS110	2001 (3)	—	KM534.2, 554, 555	21.00	75.00
PS111	2001 (3)	—	KM534.2, 556, 557	21.00	75.00
PS112	2001 (3)	—	KM534.2, 558, 559	21.00	85.00
PS113	2001 (3)	—	KM534.2, 560, 561	21.00	95.00
PS114	2001 (3)	—	KM534.2, 562, 563	21.00	85.00
PS115	2001 (3)	—	KM534.2, 564, 565	21.00	85.00
PS116	2001 (20)	—	KM491.2, 532-533, 534.2, 549.2, 550-565	120	665
PS117	2001 (6)	—	KM#401-403, 406, 491.1, 534.1	—	145
PS118	2001 (1)	650	Federation Centennial Set	—	6,000
PS119	2002 (6)	39,513	KM#401-403, 406, 600.2, 602	—	95.00
PS120	2006 (6)	39,090	KM#401-402, 406, 688-689, 690.1	—	70.00
PS121	2003 (6)	6,500	KM#401b, 402b, 406b, 688a, 689a, 690a	—	180
PS122	2003 (4)	10,000	KM763-766	118	250
PS123	2004 (6)	50,000	KM#401-404, 406, 733	—	80.00
PS124	2004 (6)	6,500	KM#401b, 402b, 403b, 404a, 406b, 733.1a	—	150
PS125	2005 (6)	—	KM#401, 402, 406, 745-747	—	85.00
PS126	2005 (6)	6,500	KM#401b, 402b, 406b, 745a, 746a, 747a	—	175
PS127	2005 (6)	650	KM#401a, 402a, 406a, 745b, 746b, 747b	—	5,850
PS129	2006 (8)	6,500	KM#62a, 63a, 64a, 65a, 66a, 77a, 852	180	220
PS128	2006 (8)	—	KM#401-404, 406, 489, 767-768	62.50	120

WEDDING SPECIMEN SETS

KM#	Date	Mintage	Identification	Issue Price	Mkt Val
WSS1	2002 (6)	3,322	KM#401-403, 406, 600.1, 602 Plaque	—	97.50
WSS2	2003 (6)	3,249	KM#401-402, 406, 688-690 Plaque	—	55.00
WSS3	2004 (6)	4,000	KM#401-404, 406, 733.1 Plaque	—	58.50
WSS4	2005 (6)	—	KM#401-402, 406, 745-747 Plaque	60.00	60.00
WSS5	2006 (8)	—	KM#401-404, 406, 489, 767-768 Plaque	60.00	60.00

AUSTRIA

The Republic of Austria, a parliamentary democracy located in mountainous central Europe, has an area of 32,374 sq. mi. (83,850 sq. km.) and a population of 8.08 million. Capital: Wien (Vienna). Austria is primarily an industrial country. Machinery, iron, steel, textiles, yarns and timber are exported.

REPUBLIC

POST WWII DECIMAL COINAGE

100 Groschen - 1 Schilling

KM# 2878 10 GROSCHEN
1.1000 g., Aluminum, 20 mm. **Obv:** Small Imperial Eagle with Austrian shield on breast, at top between numbers, scalloped rim, stylized inscription below **Rev:** Large value above date, scalloped rim **Edge:** Plain **Designer:** Hans Köttenstorfer

Date	Mintage	F	VF	XF	Unc	BU
2001 Special Unc	75,000	—	—	—	—	5.00

KM# 2885 50 GROSCHEN
3.0000 g., Aluminum-Bronze, 19.5 mm. **Obv:** Austrian shield **Rev:** Large value above date **Edge:** Reeded

Date	Mintage	F	VF	XF	Unc	BU
2001 Special Unc	75,000	—	—	—	—	5.00

KM# 2886 SCHILLING
4.2000 g., Aluminum-Bronze, 22.5 mm. **Obv:** Large value above date **Rev:** Edelweiss flower **Edge:** Plain

Date	Mintage	F	VF	XF	Unc	BU
2001 Special Unc	75,000	—	—	—	—	5.00

KM# 2889a 5 SCHILLING
4.8000 g., Copper-Nickel, 23.5 mm. **Obv:** Lippizaner stallion with rider, rearing left **Rev:** Austrian shield divides date, value above, sprays below **Edge:** Plain

Date	Mintage	F	VF	XF	Unc	BU
2001 Special Unc	75,000	—	—	—	—	5.50

KM# 2918 10 SCHILLING
6.2000 g., Copper-Nickel Plated Nickel, 26 mm. **Obv:** Imperial Eagle with Austrian shield on breast, holding hammer and sickle **Rev:** Woman of Wachau left, value and date right of hat **Edge:** Reeded

Date	Mintage	F	VF	XF	Unc	BU
2001 Special Unc	75,000	—	—	—	—	6.00

KM# 3075 20 SCHILLING
8.0000 g., Copper-Aluminum-Nickel, 27.7 mm. **Subject:** Johann Nepomuk Nestroy **Obv:** Denomination within square **Rev:** Bust half left **Edge:** 19 incuse dots **Designer:** Herbert Wähner

Date	Mintage	F	VF	XF	Unc	BU
2001	225,000	—	—	—	4.50	—
2001 Special Unc	75,000	—	—	—	—	10.00

KM# 3076 50 SCHILLING
8.1500 g., Bi-Metallic Copper-Nickel clad Nickel center in Aluminumn-Bronze ring, 26.5 mm. **Subject:** The Schilling Era **Obv:** Denomination and shields **Rev:** Four old coin designs **Edge:** Plain

Date	Mintage	F	VF	XF	Unc	BU
2001	600,000	—	—	—	7.50	—
2001 Special Unc.	100,000	—	—	—	—	9.50

KM# 3073 100 SCHILLING
13.7000 g., 0.2879 Bi-Metallic Titanium center in 9.95g .900 silver ring. 0.1268 oz., 34 mm. **Subject:** Transportation **Obv:** Automobile engine **Rev:** Car, train, truck, and plane **Edge:** Plain

Date	Mintage	F	VF	XF	Unc	BU
2001 Proof	50,000	Value: 40.00				

KM# 3077 100 SCHILLING
20.0000 g., 0.9000 Silver 0.5787 oz. ASW, 34 mm. **Subject:** Charlemagne **Obv:** Holy Roman Emperor's crown above denomination **Rev:** Bust 3/4 facing with scepter, two shields at right **Edge:** Reeded

Date	Mintage	F	VF	XF	Unc	BU
2001 Proof	50,000	Value: 40.00				

KM# 3079 100 SCHILLING
20.0000 g., 0.9000 Silver 0.5787 oz. ASW, 34 mm. **Subject:** Duke Rudolf IV **Obv:** University teaching scene **Rev:** Bust on right looking left, St. Stephen's Cathedral at left **Edge:** Reeded

Date	Mintage	F	VF	XF	Unc	BU
2001 Proof	50,000	Value: 40.00				

KM# 3074 500 SCHILLING
10.1400 g., 0.9860 Gold 0.3214 oz. AGW, 22 mm. **Subject:** 2000 Years of Christianity - Bible **Obv:** Bible and symbols of the saints: Matthew, Luke, Mark, and John **Rev:** St. Paul reading from a scroll to two listeners **Designer:** Thomas Pesendorfer

Date	Mintage	F	VF	XF	Unc	BU
2001 Proof	50,000	Value: 600				

KM# 3078 500 SCHILLING
24.0000 g., 0.9250 Silver 0.7137 oz. ASW, 37 mm. **Subject:** Kufstein Castle **Obv:** Castle view above denomination **Rev:** Emperor Maximilian being shown one of his new cannons **Edge:** Plain with engraved lettering **Designer:** Thomas Pesendorfer

Date	Mintage	F	VF	XF	Unc	BU
2001	50,000	—	—	—	45.00	—
2001 Special Unc.	15,000	—	—	—	—	50.00
2001 Proof	30,000	Value: 60.00				

KM# 3080 500 SCHILLING
24.0000 g., 0.9250 Silver 0.7137 oz. ASW, 37 mm. **Subject:** Schattenburg Castle **Obv:** Castle view **Rev:** Two medieval armourers at work **Edge:** Plain with engraved lettering

Date	Mintage	F	VF	XF	Unc	BU
2001	37,000	—	—	—	42.00	—
2001 Special Unc	15,000	—	—	—	—	50.00
2001 Proof	43,000	Value: 60.00				

KM# 3081 1000 SCHILLING
16.2200 g., 0.9860 Gold 0.5142 oz. AGW, 30 mm. **Subject:** Austrian National Library **Obv:** Archduke Maximilian as a student **Rev:** Library interior view **Edge:** Reeded

Date	Mintage	F	VF	XF	Unc	BU
2001 Proof	30,000	Value: 950				

BULLION COINAGE

Philharmonic Issues

KM# 3004 200 SCHILLING
3.1210 g., 0.9999 Gold 0.1003 oz. AGW, 16 mm. **Series:** Vienna Philharmonic Orchestra **Obv:** The Golden Hall organ **Rev:** Wind and string instruments **Edge:** Reeded **Designer:** Thomas Pesendorfer

Date	Mintage	F	VF	XF	Unc	BU
2001	26,400	—	—	—	BV+13%	—

KM# 2989 500 SCHILLING
7.7760 g., 0.9999 Gold 0.2500 oz. AGW, 22 mm. **Series:** Vienna Philharmonic Orchestra **Obv:** The Golden Hall organ **Rev:** Wind and string instruments **Edge:** Reeded **Designer:** Thomas Pesendorfer

Date	Mintage	F	VF	XF	Unc	BU
2001	25,800	—	—	—	BV+10%	—

KM# 3031 1000 SCHILLING
15.5520 g., 0.9999 Gold 0.4999 oz. AGW, 28 mm. **Series:** Vienna Philharmonic Orchestra **Obv:** The Golden Hall organ **Rev:** Wind and string instruments **Edge:** Reeded **Designer:** Thomas Pesendorfer

Date	Mintage	F	VF	XF	Unc	BU
2001	26,800	—	—	—	BV+8%	—

KM# 2990 2000 SCHILLING
31.1035 g., 0.9999 Gold 0.9999 oz. AGW, 37 mm. **Series:** Vienna Philharmonic Orchestra **Obv:** The Golden Hall organ **Rev:** Wind and string instruments **Edge:** Reeded **Designer:** Thomas Pesendorfer

Date	Mintage	F	VF	XF	Unc	BU
2001	54,700	—	—	—	BV+4%	—

EURO COINAGE

European Union Issues

KM# 3082 EURO CENT

2.3000 g., Copper Plated Steel, 16.25 mm. **Obv:** Gentian flower **Obv. Legend:** EIN EURO CENT **Rev:** Denomination and globe **Edge:** Plain

Date	Mintage	F	VF	XF	Unc	BU
2002	378,400,000	—	—	—	0.35	—
2002 Special Unc	100,000	—	—	—	—	0.50
2002 Proof	10,000	Value: 15.00				
2003	10,800,000	—	—	—	0.35	—
2003 Special Unc	125,000	—	—	—	—	0.50
2003 Proof	25,000	Value: 3.00				
2004	115,000,000	—	—	—	0.35	—
2004 Special Unc	100,000	—	—	—	—	0.50
2004 Proof	20,000	Value: 3.00				
2005	122,900,000	—	—	—	0.35	—
2005 Special Unc	100,000	—	—	—	—	0.50
2005 Proof	20,000	Value: 4.00				
2006	48,300,000	—	—	—	0.35	—
2006 Special Unc	100,000	—	—	—	—	0.50
2006 Proof	20,000	Value: 4.00				
2007	111,900,000	—	—	—	0.35	—
2007 Special Unc	75,000	—	—	—	—	0.50
2007 Proof	20,000	Value: 4.00				
2008	50,900,000	—	—	—	0.35	—
2008 Special Unc	50,000	—	—	—	—	0.50
2008 Proof	15,000	Value: 4.00				
2009	158,900,000	—	—	—	0.35	—
2009 Special Unc	75,000	—	—	—	—	0.50
2009 Proof	15,000	Value: 4.00				
2010	168,500,000	—	—	—	0.35	—
2010 Special Unc	50,000	—	—	—	—	0.50
2010 Proof	15,000	Value: 4.00				
2011	189,600,000	—	—	—	0.35	—
2011 Special Unc	50,000	—	—	—	—	0.50
2011 Proof	15,000	Value: 4.00				
2012	—	—	—	—	0.35	—
2012 Special Unc	50,000	—	—	—	—	0.50
2012 Proof	10,000	Value: 4.00				

KM# 3083 2 EURO CENT

3.0600 g., Copper Plated Steel, 18.75 mm. **Obv:** Edelweiss flower in inner circle, stars in outer circle **Obv. Legend:** ZWEI EURO CENT **Rev:** Denomination and globe **Edge:** Grooved

Date	Mintage	F	VF	XF	Unc	BU
2002	326,400,000	—	—	—	0.50	—
2002 Special Unc	100,000	—	—	—	—	0.65
2002 Proof	10,000	Value: 20.00				
2003	118,500,000	—	—	—	0.50	—
2003 Special Unc	125,000	—	—	—	—	0.65
2003 Proof	25,000	Value: 5.00				
2004	156,400,000	—	—	—	0.50	—
2004 Special Unc	100,000	—	—	—	—	0.65
2004 Proof	20,000	Value: 5.00				
2005	113,000,000	—	—	—	0.50	—
2005 Special Unc	100,000	—	—	—	—	0.65
2005 Proof	20,000	Value: 6.00				
2006	39,800,000	—	—	—	0.35	—
2006 Special Unc	100,000	—	—	—	—	0.65
2006 Proof	20,000	Value: 6.00				
2007	72,200,000	—	—	—	0.35	—
2007 Special Unc	75,000	—	—	—	—	0.65
2007 Proof	20,000	Value: 6.00				
2008	125,100,000	—	—	—	0.35	—
2008 Special Unc	50,000	—	—	—	—	0.65
2008 Proof	15,000	Value: 6.00				
2009	120,400,000	—	—	—	0.35	—
2009 Special Unc	75,000	—	—	—	—	0.65
2009 Proof	15,000	Value: 6.00				
2010	104,200,000	—	—	—	0.35	—
2010 Special Unc	50,000	—	—	—	—	0.65
2010 Proof	15,000	Value: 6.00				
2011	148,600,000	—	—	—	0.35	—
2011 Special Unc	50,000	—	—	—	—	0.65
2011 Proof	15,000	Value: 6.00				
2012	—	—	—	—	0.35	—
2012 Special Unc	50,000	—	—	—	—	0.65
2012 Proof	10,000	Value: 6.00				

KM# 3084 5 EURO CENT

3.9200 g., Copper Plated Steel, 21.25 mm. **Obv:** Alpine prim rose flower in inner ring, stars in outer ring **Obv. Legend:** FUNF EURO CENT **Rev:** Denomination and globe **Edge:** Plain

Date	Mintage	F	VF	XF	Unc	BU
2002	217,000,000	—	—	—	0.75	—
2002 Special Unc	100,000	—	—	—	—	1.00
2002 Proof	10,000	Value: 30.00				
2003	108,500,000	—	—	—	0.75	—
2003 Special Unc	125,000	—	—	—	—	1.00
2003 Proof	25,000	Value: 8.50				
2004	89,300,000	—	—	—	0.75	—
2004 Special Unc	100,000	—	—	—	—	1.00
2004 Proof	20,000	Value: 9.00				
2005	66,100,000	—	—	—	0.75	—
2005 Special Unc	100,000	—	—	—	—	1.00
2005 Proof	20,000	Value: 10.00				
2006	5,600,000	—	—	—	0.75	—
2006 Special Unc	100,000	—	—	—	—	1.00
2006 Proof	20,000	Value: 10.00				
2007	52,700,000	—	—	—	0.75	—
2007 Special Unc	75,000	—	—	—	—	1.00
2007 Proof	20,000	Value: 10.00				
2008	96,700,000	—	—	—	0.75	—
2008 Special Unc	50,000	—	—	—	—	1.00
2008 Proof	15,000	Value: 10.00				
2009	5,800,000	—	—	—	0.75	—
2009 Special Unc	75,000	—	—	—	—	1.00
2009 Proof	15,000	Value: 10.00				
2010	63,700,000	—	—	—	0.75	—
2010 Special Unc	50,000	—	—	—	—	1.00
2010 Proof	15,000	Value: 10.00				
2011	66,600,000	—	—	—	0.75	—
2011 Special Unc	50,000	—	—	—	—	1.00
2011 Proof	15,000	Value: 10.00				
2012	—	—	—	—	0.75	—
2012 Special Unc	50,000	—	—	—	—	1.00
2012 Proof	10,000	Value: 10.00				

KM# 3085 10 EURO CENT

4.1000 g., Brass, 19.75 mm. **Obv:** St. Stephen's Cathedral spires **Rev:** Relief map of European Union at left, denomination at center right **Edge:** Reeded

Date	Mintage	F	VF	XF	Unc	BU
2002	441,600,000	—	—	—	0.75	—
2002 Special Unc	100,000	—	—	—	—	1.00
2002 Proof	10,000	Value: 45.00				
2003 Special Unc	125,000	—	—	—	—	4.00
2003 Proof	35,000	Value: 8.50				
2004	5,200,000	—	—	—	0.80	—
2004 Special Unc	100,000	—	—	—	—	1.00
2004 Proof	20,000	Value: 9.00				
2005	5,200,000	—	—	—	0.80	—
2005 Special Unc	100,000	—	—	—	—	1.00
2005 Proof	20,000	Value: 10.00				
2006	40,000,000	—	—	—	0.75	—
2006 Special Unc	100,000	—	—	—	—	1.00
2006 Proof	20,000	Value: 10.00				
2007	81,300,000	—	—	—	0.75	—
2007 Special Unc	75,000	—	—	—	—	1.00
2007 Proof	20,000	Value: 10.00				

KM# 3139 10 EURO CENT

4.1000 g., Brass, 19.75 mm. **Obv:** St. Stephen's Cathedral spires **Rev:** Relief Map of Western Europe, stars, lines and value **Edge:** Reeded

Date	Mintage	F	VF	XF	Unc	BU
2008	70,200,000	—	—	—	0.75	—
2008 Special Unc	50,000	—	—	—	—	1.00
2008 Proof	15,000	Value: 10.00				
2009	15,900,000	—	—	—	0.75	—
2009 Special Unc	75,000	—	—	—	—	1.00
2009 Proof	15,000	Value: 10.00				
2010	42,800,000	—	—	—	0.75	—
2010 Special Unc	50,000	—	—	—	—	1.00
2010 Proof	15,000	Value: 10.00				
2011	27,600,000	—	—	—	0.75	—
2011 Special Unc	50,000	—	—	—	—	1.00
2011 Proof	15,000	Value: 10.00				
2012	—	—	—	—	0.75	—
2012 Special Unc	50,000	—	—	—	—	1.00
2012 Proof	10,000	Value: 10.00				

KM# 3086 20 EURO CENT

5.7400 g., Brass, 22.25 mm. **Obv:** Belvedere Palace gate **Rev:** Relief map of European Union at left, denomination at center right **Edge:** Notched

Date	Mintage	F	VF	XF	Unc	BU
2002	203,400,000	—	—	—	1.00	—
2002 Special Unc	100,000	—	—	—	—	1.25
2002 Proof	10,000	Value: 60.00				
2003	50,900,000	—	—	—	1.00	—
2003 Special Unc	125,000	—	—	—	—	1.25
2003 Proof	25,000	Value: 10.00				
2004	54,800,000	—	—	—	1.00	—
2004 Special Unc	100,000	—	—	—	—	1.25
2004 Proof	20,000	Value: 11.50				
2005	4,100,000	—	—	—	1.10	—
2005 Special Unc	100,000	—	—	—	—	1.25
2005 Proof	20,000	Value: 12.50				
2006	8,200,000	—	—	—	1.00	—
2006 Special Unc	100,000	—	—	—	—	1.25
2006 Proof	20,000	Value: 12.50				
2007	45,000,000	—	—	—	1.00	—
2007 Special Unc	75,000	—	—	—	—	1.25
2007 Proof	20,000	Value: 12.50				

KM# 3140 20 EURO CENT

5.7400 g., Brass, 22.25 mm. **Obv:** Belvedere Palace gate **Rev:** Expanded relief map of European Union at left, denomination at center right **Edge:** Notched

Date	Mintage	F	VF	XF	Unc	BU
2008	45,300,000	—	—	—	1.00	—
2008 Special Unc.	50,000	—	—	—	—	1.50
2008 Proof	15,000	Value: 12.50				
2009	49,800,000	—	—	—	1.00	—
2009 Special Unc.	75,000	—	—	—	—	1.50
2009 Proof	15,000	Value: 12.50				
2010	4,200,000	—	—	—	1.00	—
2010 Special Unc.	50,000	—	—	—	—	1.50
2010 Proof	15,000	Value: 12.50				
2011	21,300,000	—	—	—	1.00	—
2011 Special Unc.	50,000	—	—	—	—	1.50
2011 Proof	15,000	Value: 12.50				
2012	—	—	—	—	1.00	—
2012 Special Unc.	50,000	—	—	—	—	1.50
2012 Proof	10,000	Value: 12.50				

KM# 3087 50 EURO CENT

7.8000 g., Brass, 24.25 mm. **Obv:** Secession building in Vienna **Rev:** Relief map of European Union at left, denomination at center right **Edge:** Reeded

Date	Mintage	F	VF	XF	Unc	BU
2002	169,100,000	—	—	—	1.25	—
2002 Special Unc	100,000	—	—	—	—	1.50
2002 Proof	10,000	Value: 75.00				
2003	9,100,000	—	—	—	1.25	—
2003 Special Unc	125,000	—	—	—	—	1.50
2003 Proof	25,000	Value: 12.50				
2004	3,100,000	—	—	—	1.25	—
2004 Special Unc	100,000	—	—	—	—	1.50
2004 Proof	20,000	Value: 13.50				
2005	3,100,000	—	—	—	1.25	—
2005 Special Unc	100,000	—	—	—	—	1.50
2005 Proof	20,000	Value: 15.00				
2006	3,200,000	—	—	—	1.25	—
2006 Special Unc	100,000	—	—	—	—	1.50
2006 Proof	20,000	Value: 15.00				
2007	3,000,000	—	—	—	1.25	—
2007 Special Unc	75,000	—	—	—	—	1.50
2007 Proof	20,000	Value: 15.00				

KM# 3141 50 EURO CENT
7.8000 g., Brass, 24.25 mm. **Obv:** Secession building in Vienna **Rev:** Expanded relief map of European Union at left, denomination at right **Edge:** Reeded

Date	Mintage	F	VF	XF	Unc	BU
2008	3,000,000	—	—	—	1.25	—
2008 Special Unc	50,000	—	—	—	—	1.50
2008 Proof	15,000	Value: 15.00				
2009	14,700,000	—	—	—	1.25	—
2009 Special Unc	75,000	—	—	—	—	1.50
2009 Proof	15,000	Value: 15.00				
2010	30,000,000	—	—	—	1.25	—
2010 Special Unc	50,000	—	—	—	—	1.50
2010 Proof	15,000	Value: 15.00				
2011	6,000,000	—	—	—	1.25	—
2011 Special Unc	50,000	—	—	—	—	1.50
2011 Proof	15,000	Value: 15.00				
2012 Special Unc.	50,000	—	—	—	—	1.50
2012 Proof	10,000	Value: 15.00				

KM# 3088 EURO
7.5000 g., Bi-Metallic Copper-Nickel center in Nickel-Brass ring, 23.25 mm. **Obv:** Bust of Mozart right within inner circle, stars in outer circle **Rev:** Value at left, relief map of European Union at right **Edge:** Segmented reeding

Date	Mintage	F	VF	XF	Unc	BU
2002	223,500,000	—	—	—	2.50	—
2002 Special Unc	100,000	—	—	—	—	2.75
2002 Proof	10,000	Value: 100				
2003 Special Unc	125,000	—	—	—	—	5.00
2003 Proof	25,000	Value: 16.50				
2004	2,600,000	—	—	—	2.50	—
2004 Special Unc	100,000	—	—	—	—	2.75
2004 Proof	20,000	Value: 17.50				
2005	2,600,000	—	—	—	2.50	—
2005 Special Unc	100,000	—	—	—	—	2.75
2005 Proof	20,000	Value: 18.50				
2006	7,700,000	—	—	—	2.50	—
2006 Special Unc	100,000	—	—	—	—	2.75
2006 Proof	20,000	Value: 18.50				
2007	41,100,000	—	—	—	2.50	—
2007 Special Unc	75,000	—	—	—	—	2.75
2007 Proof	20,000	Value: 18.50				

KM# 3142 EURO
7.5000 g., Bi-Metallic Copper-Nickel center in Nickel-Brass ring, 23.25 mm. **Obv:** Bust of Mozart right within inner circle, stars in outer circle **Rev:** Value at left, expanded relief map of European Union at right **Edge:** Segmented reeding

Date	Mintage	F	VF	XF	Unc	BU
2008	65,500,000	—	—	—	2.00	—
2008 Special Unc	50,000	—	—	—	—	2.75
2008 Proof	15,000	Value: 15.00				
2009	40,300,000	—	—	—	2.00	—
2009 Special Unc	75,000	—	—	—	—	2.75
2009 Proof	15,000	Value: 15.00				
2010	11,200,000	—	—	—	2.00	—
2010 Special Unc	50,000	—	—	—	—	2.75
2010 Proof	15,000	Value: 15.00				
2011	8,000,000	—	—	—	2.00	—
2011 Special Unc	50,000	—	—	—	—	2.75
2011 Proof	15,000	Value: 15.00				
2012 Special Unc.	50,000	—	—	—	—	2.75
2012 Proof	10,000	Value: 15.00				

KM# 3089 2 EURO
8.5000 g., Bi-Metallic Nickel-Brass center in Copper-Nickel ring, 25.75 mm. **Obv:** Bust of Bertha von Suttner, Novelist and winner of 1905 Peace Prize, facing left within inner circle, stars in outer circle **Rev:** Value at left, relief map of European Union at right **Edge Lettering:** 2 EURO (star) (star) (star) (star)

Date	Mintage	F	VF	XF	Unc	BU
2002	196,400,000	—	—	—	3.75	—
2002 Special Unc	100,000	—	—	—	—	4.00
2002 Proof	10,000	Value: 125				
2003	4,700,000	—	—	—	3.75	—
2003 Special Unc	125,000	—	—	—	—	4.00
2003 Proof	25,000	Value: 25.00				
2004	2,500,000	—	—	—	3.75	—
2004 Special Unc	100,000	—	—	—	—	4.00
2004 Proof	20,000	Value: 27.50				
2006	2,300,000	—	—	—	3.75	—
2006 Special Unc	100,000	—	—	—	—	4.00
2006 Proof	20,000	Value: 27.50				

KM# 3124 2 EURO
8.5000 g., Bi-Metallic Nickel-Brass center in Copper-Nickel ring, 25.75 mm. **Subject:** 50th Anniversary of the State Treaty **Obv:** Treaty seals and signatures **Rev:** Denomination and map **Edge:** Reeding over lettering **Edge Lettering:** "2 EURO" and 3 stars repeated four times

Date	Mintage	F	VF	XF	Unc	BU
2005	6,880,000	—	—	—	5.00	—
2005 Special Unc	100,000	—	—	—	—	6.00
2005 Proof	20,000	Value: 27.50				

KM# 3150 2 EURO
8.5000 g., Bi-Metallic Nickel-Brass center in Copper-Nickel ring, 25.75 mm. **Subject:** 50th Anniversary - Treaty of Rome **Edge:** Reeded and lettered

Date	Mintage	F	VF	XF	Unc	BU
2007	8,905,000	—	—	—	4.00	—
2007 Special Unc	75,000	—	—	—	—	5.00
2007 Proof	20,000	Value: 27.50				

KM# 3143 2 EURO
8.5000 g., Bi-Metallic Nickel-Brass center in Copper-Nickel ring, 25.75 mm. **Obv:** Bust of Bertha von Suttner, Novelist and winner of 1905 Peace Prize, at right facing left in inner circle, stars in outer circle **Rev:** Value at left, expanded relief map of European Union at right **Edge Lettering:** 2 EURO ★ ★ ★

Date	Mintage	F	VF	XF	Unc	BU
2008	2,600,000	—	—	—	5.00	—
2008 Special Unc	50,000	—	—	—	—	6.00
2008 Proof	15,000	Value: 25.00				
2010	17,000,000	—	—	—	5.00	—
2010 Special Unc	50,000	—	—	—	—	6.00
2010 Proof	15,000	Value: 25.00				
2011	27,700,000	—	—	—	5.00	—
2011 Special Unc	50,000	—	—	—	—	6.00
2011 Proof	15,000	Value: 25.00				

KM# 3175 2 EURO
8.5000 g., Bi-Metallic Nickel-Brass center in Copper-Nickel ring, 25.75 mm. **Subject:** 10th Anniversary - European Monetary Union **Edge:** Reeded and lettered

Date	Mintage	F	VF	XF	Unc	BU
2009	4,910,000	—	—	—	6.00	—
2009 Proof	15,000	Value: 25.00				
2009 Special	75,000	—	—	—	—	7.50

KM# 3205 2 EURO
8.5000 g., Bi-Metallic Nickel-Brass center in Copper-Nickel ring, 25.75 mm. **Subject:** Euro Coinage, 10th Anniversary **Obv:** Euro symbol on globe at center, child-like rendering around

Date	Mintage	F	VF	XF	Unc	BU
2012	6,000,000	—	—	—	6.00	8.00
2012 Special Unc.	50,000	—	—	—	—	15.00
2012 Proof	10,000	Value: 25.00				

KM# 3091 5 EURO
10.0000 g., 0.8000 Silver 0.2572 oz. ASW, 28.5 mm. **Subject:** Schoenbrunn Zoo **Obv:** Denomination within sun design at center, provincial arms surround **Rev:** Building and animals **Edge:** Plain **Shape:** 9-sided

Date	Mintage	F	VF	XF	Unc	BU
ND(2002)	500,000	—	—	—	12.50	—
ND(2002) Special Unc	100,000	—	—	—	—	22.50

KM# 3105 5 EURO
10.0000 g., 0.8000 Silver 0.2572 oz. ASW, 28.5 mm. **Subject:** Water Power **Obv:** Denomination within sun design at center, provincial arms surround **Rev:** Dam with turbine, electric power plant and fish **Edge:** Plain **Shape:** 9-sided

Date	Mintage	F	VF	XF	Unc	BU
2003	500,000	—	—	—	11.50	—
2003 Special Unc	100,000	—	—	—	—	15.00

KM# 3122 5 EURO
10.0000 g., 0.8000 Silver 0.2572 oz. ASW, 28.5 mm. **Subject:** Enlargement of the European Union **Obv:** Denomination within sun design at center, provincial arms surround **Rev:** Map of Europe above country names **Edge:** Plain **Shape:** 9-sided

Date	Mintage	F	VF	XF	Unc	BU
2004	275,000	—	—	—	10.00	—
2004 Special Unc	125,000	—	—	—	—	12.50

KM# 3113 5 EURO
10.0000 g., 0.8000 Silver 0.2572 oz. ASW, 28.5 mm. **Obv:** Denomination within sun design at center, provincial arms surround **Rev:** Soccer player scoring a goal **Edge:** Plain **Shape:** 9-sided **Note:** Centennial of Austrian Soccer

Date	Mintage	F	VF	XF	Unc	BU
2004	600,000	—	—	—	10.00	—
2004 Special Unc	100,000	—	—	—	—	12.50

KM# 3117 5 EURO
10.0000 g., 0.8000 Silver 0.2572 oz. ASW, 28.5 mm. **Subject:** Centennial of Sport Skiing **Obv:** Denomination within sun design at center, provincial arms surround **Rev:** Skier within snowflake design **Edge:** Plain **Shape:** 9-sided

Date	Mintage	F	VF	XF	Unc	BU
2005	500,000	—	—	—	10.00	—
2005 Special Unc	100,000	—	—	—	—	14.50

KM# 3120 5 EURO
10.0000 g., 0.8000 Silver 0.2572 oz. ASW, 28.5 mm. **Subject:** 10th Anniversary of Austrian E U Membership **Obv:** Denomination within sun design at center, provincial arms surround **Rev:** Carinthian Gate Theater and Beethoven cameo portrait **Edge:** Plain **Shape:** 9-sided

Date	Mintage	F	VF	XF	Unc	BU
2005	275,000	—	—	—	12.50	—
2005 Special Unc	125,000	—	—	—	—	14.50

KM# 3131 5 EURO
10.0000 g., 0.8000 Silver 0.2572 oz. ASW, 28.5 mm. **Subject:** Mozart **Obv:** Denomination within sun design at center, provincial arms surround **Rev:** Mozart and the Salzburg Cathedral **Edge:** Plain **Shape:** Nine sided

Date	Mintage	F	VF	XF	Unc	BU
2006	375,000	—	—	—	15.00	—
2006 Special Unc	125,000	—	—	—	—	17.50

KM# 3132 5 EURO
10.0000 g., 0.8000 Silver 0.2572 oz. ASW, 28.5 mm. **Subject:** Austrian Presidency of the EU **Obv:** Value in circle of arms **Rev:** Vienna Hofburg and Josefsplatz view **Edge:** Plain **Shape:** Nine sided

Date	Mintage	F	VF	XF	Unc	BU
2006	250,000	—	—	—	12.50	—
2006 Special Unc	100,000	—	—	—	—	14.50

KM# 3144 5 EURO
10.0000 g., 0.8000 Silver 0.2572 oz. ASW, 28.5 mm. **Subject:** Universal Male Suffrage Centennial **Obv:** Value in circle of shields **Rev:** Cameo portraits of Franz Joseph and von Beck on Reichsrat scene **Edge:** Plain **Shape:** 9-sided

Date	Mintage	F	VF	XF	Unc	BU
2007	150,000	—	—	—	13.00	—
2007 Special Unc	100,000	—	—	—	—	15.00

KM# 3145 5 EURO
10.0000 g., 0.8000 Silver 0.2572 oz. ASW, 28.5 mm. **Obv:** Value in circle of shields **Rev:** Mariazell church **Edge:** Plain **Shape:** 9-sided

Date	Mintage	F	VF	XF	Unc	BU
2007	450,000	—	—	—	15.00	—
2007 Special Unc	100,000	—	—	—	—	20.00

KM# 3156 5 EURO
10.0000 g., 0.8000 Silver 0.2572 oz. ASW, 28.5 mm. **Subject:** Herbert Von Karajan, 100th Birth Anniversary **Obv:** Value and nine provincial shields **Rev:** Bust and notes of Beethoven's Ninth Symphony **Shape:** 9-sided

Date	Mintage	F	VF	XF	Unc	BU
2008	150,000	—	—	—	17.00	—
2008 Special Unc	100,000	—	—	—	—	20.00

KM# 3163 5 EURO
10.0000 g., 0.8000 Silver 0.2572 oz. ASW, 28.5 mm. **Obv:** Value within center of nine shields **Rev:** Two soccer players **Shape:** 9-sided

Date	Mintage	F	VF	XF	Unc	BU
2008	225,000	—	—	—	15.00	—
2008 Special Unc	100,000	—	—	—	—	20.00

KM# 3164 5 EURO
10.0000 g., 0.8000 Silver 0.2572 oz. ASW, 28.5 mm. **Obv:** Value within center of nine shields **Rev:** One soccer player **Shape:** 9-sided

Date	Mintage	F	VF	XF	Unc	BU
2008	225,000	—	—	—	15.00	—
2008 Special Unc	100,000	—	—	—	—	20.00

KM# 3170 5 EURO
10.0000 g., 0.8000 Silver 0.2572 oz. ASW, 28.5 mm. **Subject:** Joseph Haydn, 200th Anniversary of Death **Obv:** Value at center of nine shields **Rev:** Bust facing right at left, pair of violins at right **Shape:** 9-sided

Date	Mintage	F	VF	XF	Unc	BU
2009	450,000	—	—	—	15.00	—
2009 Special Unc	100,000	—	—	—	—	20.00

KM# 3177 5 EURO
10.0000 g., 0.8000 Silver 0.2572 oz. ASW, 28.5 mm. **Subject:** Tyrolean Resistance Fighters, 1809 **Shape:** 9-sided

Date	Mintage	F	VF	XF	Unc	BU
2009	250,000	—	—	—	20.00	—
2009 Special Unc	100,000	—	—	—	—	30.00

KM# 3184 5 EURO
10.0000 g., 0.8000 Silver 0.2572 oz. ASW, 28.5 mm. **Subject:** Grossglockner - High Alpine Road **Shape:** 9-sided

Date	Mintage	F	VF	XF	Unc	BU
2010	250,000	—	—	—	15.00	—
2010 Special Unc	50,000	—	—	—	—	20.00

KM# 3192 5 EURO
10.0000 g., 0.8000 Silver 0.2572 oz. ASW, 28.5 mm. **Subject:** Winter sports **Obv:** Nine provincial shields **Rev:** Snowboarding **Shape:** 9-sided

Date	Mintage	F	VF	XF	Unc	BU
2010	225,000	—	—	—	15.00	—
2010 Special Unc	50,000	—	—	—	—	20.00

KM# 3193 5 EURO
10.0000 g., 0.8000 Silver 0.2572 oz. ASW, 28.5 mm. **Subject:** Winter Sports **Obv:** Nine provincial shields **Rev:** Ski jumper **Shape:** 9-sided

Date	Mintage	F	VF	XF	Unc	BU
2010	225,000	—	—	—	15.00	—
2010 Special Unc	50,000	—	—	—	—	20.00

KM# 3195 5 EURO
10.0000 g., 0.8000 Silver 0.2572 oz. ASW, 28.5 mm. **Subject:** Pummerin, Bell, 1711-2011 **Obv:** Value within circle of shields **Rev:** Large bell **Shape:** 9-sided

Date	Mintage	F	VF	XF	Unc	BU
2011	—	—	—	—	15.00	—
2011 Special Unc.	50,000	—	—	—	—	20.00

KM# 3196 5 EURO
10.0000 g., 0.8000 Silver 0.2572 oz. ASW, 28.5 mm. **Subject:** Land of Forests **Shape:** 9-sided **Designer:** H. Andexlinger

Date	Mintage	F	VF	XF	Unc	BU
2011	—	—	—	—	15.00	—
2011 Special Unc.	50,000	—	—	—	—	20.00

KM# 3206 5 EURO
8.9000 g., Copper, 28.5 mm. **Subject:** Society of Music Lovers, 200th Anniversary **Obv:** Value at center of circle of nine shields **Rev:** Interior of the "Golden Hall" in Vienna **Shape:** 9-sided

Date	Mintage	F	VF	XF	Unc	BU
2012	300,000	—	—	—	8.00	—

KM# 3206a 5 EURO
10.0000 g., 0.8000 Silver 0.2572 oz. ASW, 28.5 mm. **Subject:** Society of Music Lovers, 200th Anniversary **Obv:** Value in circle of nine shields **Rev:** Interior of the "Golden Hall" in Vienna **Shape:** 9-sided

Date	Mintage	F	VF	XF	Unc	BU
2012 Special Unc.	50,000	—	—	—	—	28.00

KM# 3215 5 EURO
8.9000 g., Copper, 28.5 mm. **Subject:** Schladming **Rev:** Downhill skier **Shape:** 9-sided

Date	Mintage	F	VF	XF	Unc	BU
2012 Special Unc	300,000	—	—	—	8.00	—

KM# 3215a 5 EURO
10.0000 g., 0.8000 Silver 0.2572 oz. ASW, 28.5 mm. **Subject:** Schladming **Rev:** Downhill skier **Shape:** 9-sided

Date	Mintage	F	VF	XF	Unc	BU
2012 Special Unc	50,000	—	—	—	—	25.00

KM# 3216 5 EURO
8.9000 g., Copper, 28.5 mm. **Subject:** Vienna Waltz **Rev:** Dancers **Shape:** 9-sided

Date	Mintage	F	VF	XF	Unc	BU
2013 Special Unc	—	—	—	—	—	17.50

KM# 3216a 5 EURO
10.0000 g., 0.8000 Silver 0.2572 oz. ASW, 28.5 mm. **Subject:** Vienna Waltz **Rev:** Two dancers

Date	Mintage	F	VF	XF	Unc	BU
2013 Special Unc	—	—	—	—	—	30.00

KM# 3096 10 EURO
17.3000 g., 0.9250 Silver 0.5145 oz. ASW, 32 mm. **Subject:** Ambras Palace **Obv:** Palace, denomination below **Rev:** Three strolling musicians **Edge:** Reeded

Date	Mintage	F	VF	XF	Unc	BU
2002	130,000	—	—	—	20.00	—
2002 Special Unc	20,000	—	—	—	—	30.00
2002 Proof	50,000	Value: 40.00				

KM# 3099 10 EURO
17.3000 g., 0.9250 Silver 0.5145 oz. ASW, 32 mm. **Subject:** Eggenberg Palace and Johannes Kepler **Obv:** Palace, denomination below **Rev:** Half figure seated with tools **Edge:** Reeded

Date	Mintage	F	VF	XF	Unc	BU
2002	130,000	—	—	—	20.00	—
2002 Special Unc	20,000	—	—	—	—	30.00
2002 Proof	50,000	Value: 32.50				

KM# 3103 10 EURO
17.3000 g., 0.9250 Silver 0.5145 oz. ASW, 32 mm. **Subject:** Castle of Schlosshof **Obv:** Baroque fountain and palace, denomination below **Rev:** Two gardeners at work

Date	Mintage	F	VF	XF	Unc	BU
2003	130,000	—	—	—	30.00	—
2003 Special Unc	20,000	—	—	—	—	35.00
2003 Proof	50,000	Value: 40.00				

KM# 3106 10 EURO
17.3000 g., 0.9250 Silver 0.5145 oz. ASW, 32 mm. **Subject:** Schoenbrunn Palace **Obv:** Fountain with palace background, denomination below **Rev:** Palmenhaus greenhouse

Date	Mintage	F	VF	XF	Unc	BU
2003	100,000	—	—	—	30.00	—
2003 Special Unc	40,000	—	—	—	—	35.00
2003 Proof	60,000	Value: 40.00				

KM# 3111 10 EURO
17.3000 g., 0.9250 Silver 0.5145 oz. ASW, 32 mm. **Obv:** Hellbrunn Castle, denomination below **Rev:** Archbishop Marcus Sitticus and Hellbrunn's "Roman Theatre" **Edge:** Reeded

Date	Mintage	F	VF	XF	Unc	BU
2004	130,000	—	—	—	30.00	—
2004 Special Unc	40,000	—	—	—	—	35.00
2004 Proof	60,000	Value: 40.00				

KM# 3115 10 EURO
17.3000 g., 0.9250 Silver 0.5145 oz. ASW, 32 mm. **Obv:** Artstetten Castle, denomination below **Rev:** Crypt entrance behind portraits of Franz Ferdinand and Sophie

Date	Mintage	F	VF	XF	Unc	BU
2004	130,000	—	—	—	30.00	—
2004 Special Unc	40,000	—	—	—	—	35.00
2004 Proof	60,000	Value: 40.00				

KM# 3121 10 EURO
17.3000 g., 0.9250 Silver 0.5145 oz. ASW, 32 mm. **Subject:** 60th Anniversary of the Second Republic **Obv:** Statue of Athena, nine provincial shields and denomination at right **Rev:** Parliament building above broken chain, crowd below

Date	Mintage	F	VF	XF	Unc	BU
2005	130,000	—	—	—	30.00	—
2005 Special Unc	40,000	—	—	—	—	35.00
2005 Proof	60,000	Value: 40.00				

KM# 3125 10 EURO
17.3000 g., 0.9250 Silver 0.5145 oz. ASW, 32 mm. **Subject:** Reopening of the Burg Theater and Opera **Obv:** Two large buildings, denomination at left **Rev:** Comedy and Tragedy Masks

Date	Mintage	F	VF	XF	Unc	BU
2005	130,000	—	—	—	30.00	—
2005 Special Unc	40,000	—	—	—	—	35.00
2005 Proof	60,000	Value: 40.00				

KM# 3129 10 EURO
17.3000 g., 0.9250 Silver 0.5145 oz. ASW, 32 mm. **Subject:** Nonnenberg Abbey **Obv:** Abbey view, denomination below **Rev:** Statue of St. Erentrudis **Edge:** Reeded

Date	Mintage	F	VF	XF	Unc	BU
2006	130,000	—	—	—	30.00	—

Date	Mintage	F	VF	XF	Unc	BU
2006 Special Unc	40,000	—	—	—	—	35.00
2006 Proof	60,000	Value: 40.00				

KM# 3137 10 EURO
17.3000 g., 0.9250 Silver 0.5145 oz. ASW, 32 mm. **Obv:** Gottweig Abby above value **Rev:** Charles VI and staircase

Date	Mintage	F	VF	XF	Unc	BU
2006	130,000	—	—	—	30.00	—
2006 Special Unc	40,000	—	—	—	—	35.00
2006 Proof	60,000	Value: 40.00				

KM# 3146 10 EURO
17.3000 g., 0.9250 Silver 0.5145 oz. ASW, 32 mm. **Obv:** Melk Abbey view **Rev:** Inner view of the Melk Abbey dome

Date	Mintage	F	VF	XF	Unc	BU
2007	130,000	—	—	—	30.00	—
2007 Special Unc	40,000	—	—	—	—	35.00
2007 Proof	60,000	Value: 40.00				

KM# 3148 10 EURO
17.3000 g., 0.9250 Silver 0.5145 oz. ASW, 32 mm. **Obv:** St. Paul's Abbey complex **Obv. Legend:** ST. PAUL IM LAVANTTAL **Obv. Inscription:** REPUBLIK / ÖSTERREICH **Rev:** Entrance facade

Date	Mintage	F	VF	XF	Unc	BU
2007	130,000	—	—	—	30.00	—
2007 Special Unc	60,000	—	—	—	—	35.00
2007 Proof	40,000	Value: 40.00				

KM# 3157 10 EURO
17.3000 g., 0.9250 Silver 0.5145 oz. ASW, 32 mm. **Subject:** Abby of Klosterneuburg **Obv:** Aerial exterior view of church complex **Rev:** Cloister

Date	Mintage	F	VF	XF	Unc	BU
2008	130,000	—	—	—	30.00	—
2008 Special Unc	40,000	—	—	—	—	35.00
2008 Proof	60,000	Value: 45.00				

KM# 3162 10 EURO
17.3000 g., 0.9250 Silver 0.5145 oz. ASW, 32 mm. **Subject:** Seckau Benedictine Abbey **Obv:** Exterior of abby, value, date and inscriptions "BENEDIKTINERABTEI SECKAU" and "REPUBLIK OESTERREICH" **Rev:** Interior of abbey

Date	Mintage	F	VF	XF	Unc	BU
2008	130,000	—	—	—	30.00	—
2008 Special Unc	40,000	—	—	—	—	35.00
2008 Proof	60,000	Value: 45.00				

KM# 3176 10 EURO
17.3000 g., 0.9250 Silver 0.5145 oz. ASW, 32 mm. **Series:** Tales and Legends **Subject:** Basilisk of Vienna

Date	Mintage	F	VF	XF	Unc	BU
2009	130,000	—	—	—	30.00	—
2009 Special Unc	30,000	—	—	—	—	35.00
2009 Proof	40,000	Value: 45.00				

KM# 3180 10 EURO
17.3000 g., 0.9250 Silver 0.5145 oz. ASW, 32 mm. **Series:** Tales and Legends **Subject:** Richard the Lionheart in Dürnstein

Date	Mintage	F	VF	XF	Unc	BU
2009	130,000	—	—	—	30.00	—
2009 Special Unc	30,000	—	—	—	—	35.00
2009 Proof	40,000	Value: 45.00				

KM# 3185 10 EURO
17.3000 g., 0.9250 Silver 0.5145 oz. ASW, 32 mm. **Subject:** Erzberg in Styria **Obv:** Iron Mine **Rev:** Two mermen with cloak

Date	Mintage	F	VF	XF	Unc	BU
2010	130,000	—	—	—	30.00	—
2010 Special Unc	30,000	—	—	—	—	35.00
2010 Proof	40,000	Value: 45.00				

KM# 3186 10 EURO
17.3000 g., 0.9250 Silver 0.5145 oz. ASW, 32 mm. **Subject:** Charlemagne in the Undersberg

Date	Mintage	F	VF	XF	Unc	BU
2010(h)	130,000	—	—	—	30.00	—
2010(h) Special Unc	30,000	—	—	—	—	35.00
2010(h) Proof	40,000	Value: 45.00				

KM# 3197 10 EURO
17.3000 g., 0.9250 Silver 0.5145 oz. ASW, 32 mm. **Subject:** The Lindworm in Klagenfurt

Date	Mintage	F	VF	XF	Unc	BU
2011 Special Unc.	30,000	—	—	—	—	30.00
2011 Proof	40,000	Value: 45.00				

KM# 3198 10 EURO
17.3000 g., 0.9250 Silver 0.5145 oz. ASW, 32 mm. **Subject:** My dear old Augustin

Date	Mintage	F	VF	XF	Unc	BU
2011 Special Unc.	30,000	—	—	—	—	30.00
2011 Proof	40,000	Value: 45.00				

KM# 3208a 10 EURO
17.3000 g., 0.9250 Silver 0.5145 oz. ASW, 32 mm. **Subject:** Falknerei **Obv:** Falconer and bird **Rev:** Child's drawing of countryside

Date	Mintage	F	VF	XF	Unc	BU
2012 Special	40,000	—	—	—	50.00	—
2012 Proof	30,000	Value: 55.00				

KM# 3207 10 EURO
14.9000 g., Copper, 32 mm. **Subject:** Steiermark **Obv:** Graz town view **Rev:** Child's drawing of countryside

Date	Mintage	F	VF	XF	Unc	BU
2012	100,000	—	—	—	15.00	—

KM# 3207a 10 EURO
17.3000 g., 0.9250 Silver 0.5145 oz. ASW, 32 mm. **Subject:** Steiermark **Obv:** Graz town view **Rev:** Child's design of countryside

Date	Mintage	F	VF	XF	Unc	BU
2012 Proof	—	Value: 40.00				

KM# 3208 10 EURO
Copper, 32 mm. **Subject:** Carinthia **Obv:** Falconer with bird **Rev:** Child's drawing of countryside

Date	Mintage	F	VF	XF	Unc	BU
2012	100,000	—	—	—	15.00	—

KM# 3211 10 EURO
20.0000 g., 0.9000 Silver 0.5787 oz. ASW, 34 mm. **Subject:** Rome on the Danube - Brigantium

Date	Mintage	F	VF	XF	Unc	BU
2012 Proof	—	Value: 70.00				

KM# 3097 20 EURO
20.0000 g., 0.9000 Silver 0.5787 oz. ASW, 34 mm. **Subject:** Ferdinand I - Renaissance **Obv:** Hofburg Palace "Swiss Gate" with two guards, denomination below **Rev:** Bust looking left, coat of arms at left, dates at right **Edge:** Reeded

Date	Mintage	F	VF	XF	Unc	BU
2002 Proof	50,000	Value: 37.50				

KM# 3098 20 EURO
20.0000 g., 0.9000 Silver 0.5787 oz. ASW, 34 mm. **Subject:** Prince Eugen - Baroque Period **Obv:** Baroque staircase with statues, denomination below **Rev:** Uniformed bust 1/4 left and dates at right, flags above cannons at left **Edge:** Reeded

Date	Mintage	F	VF	XF	Unc	BU
2002 Proof	50,000	Value: 50.00				

KM# 3104 20 EURO
20.0000 g., 0.9000 Silver 0.5787 oz. ASW, 34 mm. **Subject:** Prince Metternich **Obv:** Early steam locomotive, denomination below **Rev:** Portrait with map background **Edge:** Reeded

Date	Mintage	F	VF	XF	Unc	BU
2003 Proof	50,000	Value: 50.00				

KM# 3107 20 EURO
20.0000 g., 0.9000 Silver 0.5787 oz. ASW, 34 mm. **Obv:** Republic of Austria arms, denomination below **Rev:** Four men in a jeep **Edge:** Reeded **Note:** Post War Austrian Reconstruction

Date	Mintage	F	VF	XF	Unc	BU
2003 Proof	50,000	Value: 50.00				

KM# 3112 20 EURO
20.0000 g., 0.9000 Silver 0.5787 oz. ASW, 34 mm. **Obv:** S.M.S Novara under sail in Chinese waters, denomination below **Rev:** Standing figures behind table with globe and microscope **Edge:** Reeded **Note:** First Global Circumnavigation by an Austrian ship.

Date	Mintage	F	VF	XF	Unc	BU
2004 Proof	50,000	Value: 50.00				

KM# 3114 20 EURO
20.0000 g., 0.9000 Silver 0.5787 oz. ASW, 34 mm. **Obv:** SMS Erzherzog Ferdinand Max sailing to the Battle of Lissa, denomination below **Rev:** Sailors at the wheel with Admiral Tegetthof in background **Edge:** Reeded

Date	Mintage	F	VF	XF	Unc	BU
2004 Proof	50,000	Value: 52.50				

KM# 3126 20 EURO
20.0000 g., 0.9000 Silver 0.5787 oz. ASW, 34 mm. **Obv:** Ship, "Admiral Tegetthoff" in arctic waters, denomination below **Rev:** Expedition leaders, von Payer and Weyprecht with their icebound ship behind them **Edge:** Reeded

Date	Mintage	F	VF	XF	Unc	BU
2005 Proof	50,000	Value: 50.00				

KM# 3127 20 EURO
20.0000 g., 0.9000 Silver 0.5787 oz. ASW, 34 mm. **Obv:** SMS St. George sailing past the Statue of Liberty, denomination below **Rev:** Shipyard at Pola, boat on water **Edge:** Reeded

Date	Mintage	F	VF	XF	Unc	BU
2005 Proof	50,000	Value: 50.00				

KM# 3133 20 EURO
20.0000 g., 0.9000 Silver 0.5787 oz. ASW, 34 mm. **Subject:** Austrian Merchant Marine **Obv:** Two passing steam ships **Rev:** 19th Century Triest harbor view **Edge:** Reeded

Date	Mintage	F	VF	XF	Unc	BU
2006 Proof	50,000	Value: 50.00				

KM# 3134 20 EURO
20.0000 g., 0.9000 Silver 0.5787 oz. ASW, 34 mm. **Obv:** SMS Viribus Unitis, flag ship of the Austrian fleet, and other ships steaming left **Rev:** SMS Viribus Unitis, submarine conning tower and seaplane **Edge:** Reeded

Date	Mintage	F	VF	XF	Unc	BU
2006 Proof	50,000	Value: 50.00				

KM# 3149 20 EURO
20.0000 g., 0.9000 Silver 0.5787 oz. ASW, 34 mm. **Series:** Austrian Railways **Obv:** Steam locomotive 1837 with passenger wagons **Obv. Legend:** REPUBLIK ÖSTERREICH **Obv. Inscription:** DAMPFLOKOMOTIVE / AUSTRIA / 1837 **Rev:** People waving at passenger train crossing a trestle **Rev. Legend:** KAISER - FERDINANDS - NORDBAHN **Edge:** Reeded

Date	Mintage	F	VF	XF	Unc	BU
2007 Proof	50,000	Value: 50.00				

KM# 3151 20 EURO
20.0000 g., 0.9000 Silver 0.5787 oz. ASW, 34 mm. **Series:** Austrian Railways **Obv:** Steam locomotive 1848 standing still, viaduct in background **Obv. Legend:** REPUBLIK ÖSTERREICH **Obv. Inscription:** DAMPF-/ LOKOMOTIVE / STEINBRØCK / 1848 **Rev:** Steam train traveling right through city **Rev. Legend:** K.K. SÜDBAHN WIEN - TRIEST **Edge:** Reeded

Date	Mintage	F	VF	XF	Unc	BU
2007 Proof	50,000	Value: 50.00				

KM# 3154 20 EURO
20.0000 g., 0.9000 Silver 0.5787 oz. ASW, 34 mm. **Subject:** Southern Railways **Obv:** Steam Locomotive on iron railway bridge **Obv. Inscription:** KOK kkStB 306 **Rev:** Statue of Empress Elizabeth and train platform in Vienna's West Railway station **Rev. Inscription:** KAISERIN-/ ELIZABETH-/ WESTBAHN **Edge:** Reeded

Date	Mintage	F	VF	XF	Unc	BU
2008 Proof	50,000	Value: 70.00				

KM# 3161 20 EURO
20.0000 g., 0.9000 Silver 0.5787 oz. ASW, 34 mm. **Subject:** Imperal - Royal State Railway **Obv:** Locomotive steaming left **Obv. Legend:** Nordbahnhof/Wein **Rev:** Female on platform **Edge:** Reeded

Date	Mintage	F	VF	XF	Unc	BU
2008 Proof	50,000	Value: 70.00				

KM# 3178 20 EURO
20.0000 g., 0.9000 Silver 0.5787 oz. ASW, 34 mm. **Subject:** The Electric Railway **Obv:** Locomotive model 1189, the Crocodile **Rev:** Train on the Trisanna Bridge, Wiesburg Castle in background **Edge:** Reeded

Date	Mintage	F	VF	XF	Unc	BU
2009 Proof	50,000	Value: 50.00				

KM# 3179 20 EURO
20.0000 g., 0.9000 Silver 0.5787 oz. ASW, 34 mm. **Subject:** Railways of the Future **Obv:** Railjet highspeed OBB train **Rev:** Electric locomotive of the 1063 class in freight yard **Edge:** Reeded

Date	Mintage	F	VF	XF	Unc	BU
2009 Proof	50,000	Value: 50.00				

KM# 3187 20 EURO
20.0000 g., 0.9000 Silver 0.5787 oz. ASW, 34 mm. **Subject:** Rome on the Danube - Virunum **Obv:** Emperor Claudium, 2-horse wagon, gravestone **Rev:** Street scene, wagon and temple facade **Edge:** Reeded

Date	Mintage	F	VF	XF	Unc	BU
2010 Proof	50,000	Value: 75.00				

KM# 3188 20 EURO
20.0000 g., 0.9000 Silver 0.5787 oz. ASW, 34 mm. **Subject:** Rome on the Danube - Vindovona **Edge:** Reeded

Date	Mintage	F	VF	XF	Unc	BU
2010 Proof	50,000	Value: 75.00				

KM# 3199 20 EURO
20.0000 g., 0.9000 Silver 0.5787 oz. ASW, 34 mm. **Subject:** Rome on the Danube - Carnuntum **Edge:** Reeded

Date	Mintage	F	VF	XF	Unc	BU
2011 Proof	50,000	Value: 70.00				

KM# 3200 20 EURO
20.0000 g., 0.9000 Silver 0.5787 oz. ASW, 34 mm. **Subject:** Rome on the Danube - Aguntum

Date	Mintage	F	VF	XF	Unc	BU
2011 Proof	50,000	Value: 70.00				

KM# 3201 20 EURO
20.0000 g., 0.9000 Silver 0.5787 oz. ASW, 34 mm. **Subject:** Nikolaus Joseph von Jacquin **Obv:** Bust at left, flower at right **Rev:** Karibuk Expedition, Jacquin taking notes of plants in book

Date	Mintage	F	VF	XF	Unc	BU
2011 Proof	50,000	Value: 70.00				

KM# 3209 20 EURO
20.0000 g., 0.9000 Silver 0.5787 oz. ASW, 34 mm. **Series:** European Artists **Subject:** Egon Schiele **Obv:** Portrait of the artist **Rev:** Painting of a female

Date	Mintage	F	VF	XF	Unc	BU
2012 Proof	50,000	Value: 65.00				

KM# 3210 20 EURO
20.0000 g., 0.9000 Silver 0.5787 oz. ASW, 34 mm. **Series:** Rome on the Danube **Subject:** Lauriacum

Date	Mintage	F	VF	XF	Unc	BU
2012 Proof	50,000	Value: 65.00				

KM# 3101 25 EURO
17.1500 g., Bi-Metallic 7.15g pure Niobium (Columbium) blue color center in a 10 g., 0.900 Silver ring, 34 mm. **Subject:** City of Hall in Tyrol **Obv:** Satellite mapping the city from outer space **Rev:** Depiction of the die face used to strike the 1486 guldiner coin **Edge:** Plain

Date	Mintage	F	VF	XF	Unc	BU
2003 Special Unc	50,000	—	—	—	—	125

KM# 3109 25 EURO
17.1500 g., Bi-Metallic 7.15g Niobium center in 10g, 0.900 Silver ring, 34 mm. **Subject:** Semmering Alpine Railway **Obv:** Modern and antique locomotives **Rev:** Steam train **Edge:** Plain

Date	Mintage	F	VF	XF	Unc	BU
2004 Special Unc	50,000	—	—	—	—	100

KM# 3119 25 EURO
17.1500 g., Bi-Metallic Purple color pure Niobium 7.15g center in 10g, 0.900 Silver ring, 34 mm. **Subject:** 50 Years Austrian Television **Obv:** The original test pattern of the 1950's **Rev:** World globe behind "rabbit ear" antenna; television developmental milestones from 7-1 o'clock **Edge:** Plain

Date	Mintage	F	VF	XF	Unc	BU
2005 Special Unc	65,000	—	—	—	—	75.00

KM# 3135 25 EURO
17.1500 g., Bi-Metallic Niobium 7.15g center in 10g, 0.900 Silver ring, 34 mm. **Subject:** European Satellite Navigation **Obv:** Austrian Mint's global location inscribed on a compass face **Rev:** Satellites in orbit around the world globe **Edge:** Plain

Date	Mintage	F	VF	XF	Unc	BU
2006 Special Unc	65,000	—	—	—	—	75.00

KM# 3147 25 EURO
16.5000 g., Bi-Metallic 6.5g Niobium center in 10g, 0.900 Silver ring, 34 mm. **Subject:** Austrian Aviation **Obv:** Interior view of modern cockpit **Rev:** Taube airplane flying above glider and pilot **Edge:** Plain

Date	Mintage	F	VF	XF	Unc	BU
2007 Special Unc	65,000	—	—	—	—	75.00

KM# 3158 25 EURO
16.5000 g., Bi-Metallic 6.5g Niobium center in 10g, 0.900 Silver ring, 34 mm. **Subject:** Carl Baron Auer von Welsbach, 150th Anniversary of Birth **Obv:** Lighting gas lamp before Vienna City Wall **Rev:** Head of Welsbach, development of light bulbs

Date	Mintage	F	VF	XF	Unc	BU
2008 Special Unc	65,000	—	—	—	—	80.00

KM# 3174 25 EURO
16.5000 g., Bi-Metallic 6.5g Niobium center in 10g, 0.900 silver ring, 34 mm. **Subject:** Year of Astronomy **Obv:** Galileo head and instruments **Rev:** Space exploration satellite

Date	Mintage	F	VF	XF	Unc	BU
2009 Special Unc	65,000	—	—	—	—	80.00

KM# 3189 25 EURO
16.5000 g., Bi-Metallic 6.5g Niobium center in 10g, 0.900 Silver ring, 34 mm. **Obv:** Tree and the 4 elements: earth, wind, water, and fire **Rev:** Solar panels, hydroelectric turbine, global thermal energy and wind turbine **Designer:** Helmut Andexlinger

Date	Mintage	F	VF	XF	Unc	BU
2010 Special Unc	65,000	—	—	—	—	80.00

KM# 3204 25 EURO
16.5000 g., Bi-Metallic 6.5g Niobium center in 10g, 0.900 Silver ring, 34 mm. **Subject:** Robotics **Rev:** Mars rover

Date	Mintage	F	VF	XF	Unc	BU
2011 Special Unc.	65,000	—	—	—	—	80.00

KM# 3212 25 EURO
16.5000 g., Bi-Metallic Niobium center in 10g, .900 Silver ring., 34 mm. **Subject:** Bionics

Date	Mintage	F	VF	XF	Unc	BU
2012 Special Unc	65,000	—	—	—	—	75.00

KM# 3090 50 EURO
10.1400 g., 0.9860 Gold 0.3214 oz. AGW, 22 mm. **Subject:** Saints Benedict and Scholastica **Obv:** St. Benedict and his sister St. Scholastica **Rev:** Monk copying a manuscript **Edge:** Reeded

Date	Mintage	F	VF	XF	Unc	BU
2002 Proof	50,000	Value: 600				

KM# 3102 50 EURO
10.1400 g., 0.9860 Gold 0.3214 oz. AGW, 22 mm. **Subject:** Christian Charity **Obv:** Nursing Sister with hospital patient **Rev:** The Good Samaritan **Edge:** Reeded

Date	Mintage	F	VF	XF	Unc	BU
2003 Proof	50,000	Value: 600				

KM# 3110 50 EURO
10.1400 g., 0.9860 Gold 0.3214 oz. AGW, 22 mm. **Subject:** Great Composers - Joseph Haydn (1732-1809) **Obv:** Esterhazy Palace **Rev:** Bust 3/4 right

Date	Mintage	F	VF	XF	Unc	BU
2004 Proof	50,000	Value: 600				

KM# 3118 50 EURO
10.1400 g., 0.9860 Gold 0.3214 oz. AGW, 22 mm. **Subject:** Great Composers - Ludwig Van Beethoven (1770-1827) **Obv:** Lobkowitz Palace above value and document **Rev:** Bust 3/4 facing, dates at left

Date	Mintage	F	VF	XF	Unc	BU
2005 Proof	50,000	Value: 600				

KM# 3130 50 EURO
10.1400 g., 0.9860 Gold 0.3214 oz. AGW, 22 mm. **Subject:** Great Composers - Mozart **Obv:** Mozart's birthplace, denomination below **Rev:** Leopold and Wolfgang Mozart

Date	Mintage	F	VF	XF	Unc	BU
2006 Proof	50,000	Value: 600				

KM# 3138 50 EURO
10.1400 g., 0.9860 Gold 0.3214 oz. AGW, 22 mm. **Obv:** Gerard Van Swieten holding book and facing left **Rev:** Akademie der Wissenschaften building

Date	Mintage	F	VF	XF	Unc	BU
2007 Proof	50,000	Value: 600				

KM# 3153 50 EURO
10.1400 g., 0.9860 Gold 0.3214 oz. AGW, 22 mm. **Subject:** Ignaz Philipp Sammelweis - Personal Hygiene **Obv:** Bust of Sammelweis 3/4 right, staff of Aesculapius at lower right **Obv. Legend:** REPUBLIK ÖSTERREICH **Rev:** Vienna General Hospital, Sammelweis helping patient wash at lower right **Rev. Legend:** ALLGEMEINES KRANKENHAUS WEIN

Date	Mintage	F	VF	XF	Unc	BU
2008 Proof	50,000	Value: 600				

KM# 3171 50 EURO
10.1400 g., 0.9860 Gold 0.3214 oz. AGW, 22 mm. **Subject:** Theodor Billroth **Obv:** Bust and Aesculapius staff **Rev:** Operation scene

Date	Mintage	F	VF	XF	Unc	BU
2009 Proof	50,000	Value: 600				

KM# 3194 50 EURO
10.1400 g., 0.9860 Gold 0.3214 oz. AGW, 22 mm. **Subject:** Baron Clemens von Pirquet **Obv:** Portrait of von Pirquet **Rev:** Facade of Children's Clinic of Vienna

Date	Mintage	F	VF	XF	Unc	BU
2010 Proof	50,000	Value: 600				

KM# 3202 50 EURO
10.1400 g., 0.9860 Gold 0.3214 oz. AGW, 22 mm. **Subject:** Joanneum Museum **Obv:** Exterior of Art Museum **Rev:** Armor display

Date	Mintage	F	VF	XF	Unc	BU
2011 Proof	50,000	Value: 675				

KM# 3213 50 EURO
10.1400 g., 0.9860 Gold 0.3214 oz. AGW, 22 mm. **Subject:** Gustav Klimt **Obv:** Portrait of artist **Rev:** Female subject from painting

Date	Mintage	F	VF	XF	Unc	BU
2012 Proof	30,000	Value: 675				

KM# 3100 100 EURO
16.2270 g., 0.9860 Gold 0.5144 oz. AGW, 30 mm. **Subject:** Raphael Donner **Obv:** Portrait in front of building **Rev:** Providentia Fountain **Edge:** Reeded

Date	Mintage	F	VF	XF	Unc	BU
2002 Proof	30,000	Value: 950				

KM# 3108 100 EURO
16.2270 g., 0.9860 Gold 0.5144 oz. AGW, 30 mm. **Obv:** Gustav Klimt standing **Rev:** Klimt's painting "The Kiss" **Edge:** Reeded

Date	Mintage	F	VF	XF	Unc	BU
2003 Proof	30,000	Value: 950				

KM# 3116 100 EURO
16.2270 g., 0.9860 Gold 0.5144 oz. AGW, 30 mm. **Obv:** Secession Exhibit Hall in Vienna **Rev:** Knight in armor, "strength" with two women, "ambition and sympathy"

Date	Mintage	F	VF	XF	Unc	BU
2004 Proof	30,000	Value: 950				

KM# 3128 100 EURO
16.2270 g., 0.9860 Gold 0.5144 oz. AGW, 30 mm. **Subject:** St. Leopold's Church at Steinhof **Obv:** Domed church building, denomination below **Rev:** Two angels flank stained glass portrait

Date	Mintage	F	VF	XF	Unc	BU
2005 Proof	30,000	Value: 950				

KM# 3136 100 EURO
16.2270 g., 0.9860 Gold 0.5144 oz. AGW, 30 mm. **Subject:** Vienna's River Gate Park **Obv:** Bridge over river scene **Rev:** One of two "sculpted ladies" flanking the park entrance

Date	Mintage	F	VF	XF	Unc	BU
2006 Proof	30,000	Value: 950				

KM# 3155 100 EURO
16.2270 g., 0.9860 Gold 0.5144 oz. AGW, 30 mm. **Obv:** Building at Linke Wienzeile Nr 38 by architect Otto Koloman Wagner **Rev:** Ornate elevator and stairwell

Date	Mintage	F	VF	XF	Unc	BU
2007 Proof	30,000	Value: 950				

KM# 3160 100 EURO
16.2270 g., 0.9860 Gold 0.5144 oz. AGW, 30 mm. **Series:** Crowns of the Habsburgs **Obv:** Crown of the Holy Roman Emperor set upon coronation robe **Rev:** Otto I seated facing and old St. Peter's Bastilica, Rome

Date	Mintage	F	VF	XF	Unc	BU
2008 Proof	30,000	Value: 950				

KM# 3181 100 EURO
16.2270 g., 0.9860 Gold 0.5144 oz. AGW, 30 mm. **Series:** Crowns of the Habsburgs **Subject:** Archducal crown of Austria **Obv:** Crown resting on pillow **Rev:** Procession of the crown, orb and sceptre, Plague memorial column in background

Date	Mintage	F	VF	XF	Unc	BU
2009 Proof	30,000	Value: 950				

KM# 3191 100 EURO
16.2270 g., 0.9860 Gold 0.5144 oz. AGW, 30 mm. **Series:** Crowns of the Habsburgs **Subject:** St. Stephen's Hungarian Crown **Obv:** Crown of St. Stephen **Rev:** Naria Theresa on horseback

Date	Mintage	F	VF	XF	Unc	BU
2010 Proof	30,000	Value: 950				

KM# 3203 100 EURO
16.2270 g., 0.9860 Gold 0.5144 oz. AGW, 30 mm. **Subject:** King Wenceslas

Date	Mintage	F	VF	XF	Unc	BU
2011 Proof	30,000	Value: 950				

KM# 3214 100 EURO
16.2200 g., 0.9860 Gold 0.5142 oz. AGW, 30 mm. **Subject:** Crown's of the Hapsburgs **Obv:** Imperial Crown of Austria **Rev:** Emperor Franz Joseph I

Date	Mintage	F	VF	XF	Unc	BU
2012 Proof	30,000	Value: 950				

EURO BULLION COINAGE

Philharmonic Issues

KM# 3159 1-1/2 EURO
31.1030 g., 0.9990 Silver 0.9989 oz. ASW, 37 mm. **Obv:** Golden Concert Hall **Rev:** Bouquet of Instruments **Edge:** Plain

Date	Mintage	F	VF	XF	Unc	BU
2008	7,800,000	—	—	—	BV	37.50
2009	9,000,000	—	—	—	BV	37.50
2010	11,300,000	—	—	—	BV	37.50
2011	17,873,700	—	—	—	BV	37.50
2012	—	—	—	—	BV	37.50
2013	—	—	—	—	BV	37.50

KM# 3092 10 EURO
3.1210 g., 0.9999 Gold 0.1003 oz. AGW, 16 mm. **Subject:** Vienna Philharmonic **Obv:** The Golden Hall organ **Rev:** Musical instruments **Edge:** Segmented reeding

Date	Mintage	F	VF	XF	Unc	BU
2002	75,789	—	—	—	—	BV+13%
2003	59,654	—	—	—	—	BV+13%
2004	67,994	—	—	—	—	BV+13%
2005	62,071	—	—	—	—	BV+13%
2006	39,892	—	—	—	—	BV+13%
2007	76,325	—	—	—	—	BV+13%
2008	176,700	—	—	—	—	BV+13%
2009	437,700	—	—	—	—	BV+13%
2010	226,700	—	—	—	—	BV+13%
2011	268,200	—	—	—	—	BV+13%
2012	—	—	—	—	—	BV+13%

KM# 3093 25 EURO
7.7760 g., 0.9999 Gold 0.2500 oz. AGW, 22 mm. **Subject:** Vienna Philharmonic **Obv:** The Golden Hall organ **Rev:** Musical instruments **Edge:** Segmented reeding

Date	Mintage	F	VF	XF	Unc	BU
2002	40,807	—	—	—	—	BV+10%
2003	34,019	—	—	—	—	BV+10%
2004	32,449	—	—	—	—	BV+10%
2005	32,817	—	—	—	—	BV+10%
2006	29,609	—	—	—	—	BV+10%
2007	34,631	—	—	—	—	BV+10%
2008	97,100	—	—	—	—	BV+10%
2009	172,000	—	—	—	—	BV+10%
2010	84,900	—	—	—	—	BV+10%
2011	102,000	—	—	—	—	BV+10%
2012	—	—	—	—	—	BV+10%

KM# 3094 50 EURO
15.5520 g., 0.9999 Gold 0.4999 oz. AGW, 28 mm. **Subject:** Vienna Philharmonic **Obv:** The Golden Hall organ **Rev:** Musical instruments **Edge:** Segmented reeding

Date	Mintage	F	VF	XF	Unc	BU
2002	40,922	—	—	—	—	BV+8%
2003	26,848	—	—	—	—	BV+8%
2004	24,269	—	—	—	—	BV+8%
2005	21,049	—	—	—	—	BV+8%
2006	20,085	—	—	—	—	BV+8%
2007	25,091	—	—	—	—	BV+8%
2008	73,800	—	—	—	—	BV+8%
2009	92,300	—	—	—	—	BV+8%
2010	56,600	—	—	—	—	BV+8%

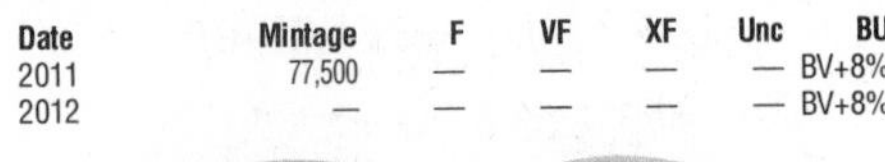

Date	Mintage	F	VF	XF	Unc	BU
2011	77,500	—	—	—	—	BV+8%
2012	—	—	—	—	—	BV+8%

KM# 3095 100 EURO
31.1035 g., 0.9999 Gold 0.9999 oz. AGW, 37 mm. **Subject:** Vienna Philharmonic **Obv:** The Golden Hall organ **Rev:** Musical instruments **Edge:** Segmented reeding

Date	Mintage	F	VF	XF	Unc	BU
2002	164,105	—	—	—	—	BV+4%
2003	179,881	—	—	—	—	BV+4%
2004	176,319	—	—	—	—	BV+4%
2005	158,564	—	—	—	—	BV+4%
2006	82,174	—	—	—	—	BV+4%
2007	108,675	—	—	—	—	BV+4%
2008	715,800	—	—	—	—	BV+4%
2009	903,000	—	—	—	—	BV+4%
2010	512,000	—	—	—	—	BV+4%
2011	586,700	—	—	—	—	BV+4%
2012	—	—	—	—	—	BV+4%

KM# 3182 2000 EURO
622.1000 g., 0.9999 Gold 19.998 oz. AGW, 74 mm. **Subject:** Vienna Philharmonic **Obv:** The Golden Hall Organ **Rev:** Musical instruments **Edge:** Reeded

Date	Mintage	F	VF	XF	Unc	BU
2009	6,027	—	—	—	—	BV+5%

KM# 3123 100000 EURO
31103.5000 g., 0.9999 Gold 999.85 oz. AGW, 370 mm. **Obv:** The Golden Hall organ **Rev:** Musical instruments **Edge:** Reeded

Date	Mintage	F	VF	XF	Unc	BU
2004 Proof	15	BV+5%				

MINT SETS

KM#	Date	Mintage	Identification	Issue Price	Mkt Val
MS10	2001 (6)	75,000	KM#2878, 2885, 2886, 2889a, 2918, 3075	25.00	40.00
MS11	2002 (8)	100,000	KM#3082-3089, Euro	22.50	25.00
MS12	2003 (8)	125,000	KM#3082-3089, Mozart	22.50	25.00
MS13	2004 (8)	100,000	KM#3082-3089, von Suttner	—	25.00
MS14	2005 (8)	100,000	KM#3082-3088, 3124, State treaty	—	25.00
MS15	2006 (8)	100,000	KM#3082-3089, St. Stephan's Cathedral	—	35.00
MS16	2007 (8)	75,000	KM#3082-3088, 3150, Treaty of Rome	—	25.00
MS17	2008 (8)	50,000	KM#3082-3084, 3139-3143, European Map	—	35.00
MS18	2009 (8)	75,000	KM#3082-3084, 3139-3142, 3175	—	25.00
MS19	2010 (8)	50,000	KM#3082-3084, 3139-3143	—	35.00
MS20	2011 (8)	50,000	KM#3082-3084, 3139-3143	—	35.00
MS21	2012 (8)	50,000	KM#3082-3084, 3139-3142, 3205	—	30.00
MS22	2012 (7)	—	KM#3082-3084,3139-3142, 3205 (Baby Mint Set)	—	30.00

PROOF SETS

KM#	Date	Mintage	Identification	Issue Price	Mkt Val
PS53	2002 (8)	10,000	KM#3082-3089	85.00	485
PS54	2003 (8)	25,000	KM#3082-3089	85.00	95.00
PS55	2004 (8)	20,000	KM#3082-3089	—	105
PS56	2005 (8)	20,000	KM#3082-3088, 3124	—	110
PS57	2006 (8)	20,000	KM#3082-3089	—	110
PS58	2007 (8)	20,000	KM#3082-3088, 3150	—	110
PS59	2008 (8)	15,000	KM#3082-3084, 3139-3143	—	120
PS60	2009 (8)	15,000	KM#3082-3084, 3139-3142, 3175	—	120
PS61	2010 (8)	15,000	KM#3082-3084, 3139-3143	—	100
PS62	2011 (8)	15,000	KM#3082-3084, 3139-3142, 3205	—	100
PS63	2012 (8)	10,000	KM#3082-3084, 3139-3142, 3205	—	100

AZERBAIJAN

The Republic of Azerbaijan (formerly Azerbaijan S.S.R.) includes the Nakhichevan Autonomous Republic. Situated in the eastern area of Transcaucasia, it is bordered in the west by Armenia, in the north by Georgia and Dagestan, to the east by the Caspian Sea and to the south by Iran. It has an area of 33,430 sq. mi. (86,600 sq. km.) and a population of 7.8 million. Capital: Baku. The area is rich in mineral deposits of aluminum, copper, iron, lead, salt and zinc, with oil as its leading industry. Agriculture and livestock follow in importance.

MONETARY SYSTEM
100 Qapik = 1 Manat

REPUBLIC

DECIMAL COINAGE

KM# 39 QAPIK
2.8000 g., Copper Plated Steel, 16.25 mm. **Obv:** Map above value **Rev:** Value and musical instruments **Edge:** Plain **Designer:** Robert Kalina

Date	Mintage	F	VF	XF	Unc	BU
ND (2006)	—	—	—	—	—	2.00

KM# 40 3 QAPIK
3.4500 g., Copper Plated Steel, 18 mm. **Obv:** Map above value **Rev:** Value above books **Edge:** Grooved **Designer:** Robert Kalina

Date	Mintage	F	VF	XF	Unc	BU
ND (2006)	—	—	—	—	—	2.50

KM# 41 5 QAPIK
4.8500 g., Copper Plated Steel, 19.75 mm. **Obv:** Map above value **Rev:** The Maiden Tower, Baku, above value **Edge:** Reeded **Designer:** Robert Kalina

Date	Mintage	F	VF	XF	Unc	BU
ND (2006)	—	—	—	—	—	2.75

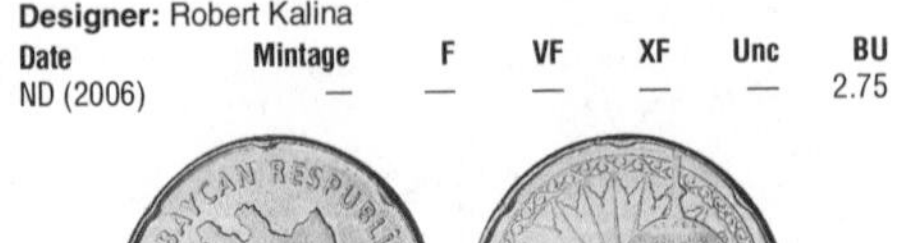

KM# 42 10 QAPIK
5.2500 g., Brass Plated Steel, 22.25 mm. **Obv:** Map above value **Rev:** Value and Military Helmet, Symbolic of desire to regain Nagorno-Karabakh **Edge:** Notched **Designer:** Robert Kalina

Date	Mintage	F	VF	XF	Unc	BU
ND (2006)	—	—	—	—	—	3.00
2010	—	—	—	—	—	3.00

KM# 43 20 QAPIK
6.6000 g., Brass Plated Steel, 24.25 mm. **Obv:** Map above value **Rev:** Value and spiral staircase **Edge:** Segmented reeding **Designer:** Robert Kalina

Date	Mintage	F	VF	XF	Unc	BU
ND (2006)	—	—	—	—	—	4.00

KM# 44 50 QAPIK
7.7000 g., Bi-Metallic Brass plated Steel center in Stainless Steel ring, 25.5 mm. **Obv:** Map above value **Rev:** Two oil wells **Edge:** Reeded and lettered **Designer:** Robert Kalina

Date	Mintage	F	VF	XF	Unc	BU
ND (2006)	—	—	—	—	—	5.00

KM# 37 50 MANAT
28.3400 g., 0.9250 Silver 0.8428 oz. ASW, 38.6 mm. **Subject:** Heydar Aliyev **Obv:** National map **Rev:** Bust 3/4 right **Edge:** Reeded

Date	Mintage	F	VF	XF	Unc	BU
2004 Proof	2,000	Value: 75.00				

KM# 48 50 MANAT
28.2800 g., 0.9250 Silver 0.8410 oz. ASW, 38.6 mm. **Subject:** FIFA World Cup, 2006 **Edge:** Plain

Date	Mintage	F	VF	XF	Unc	BU
2004 Proof	200	Value: 75.00				

KM# 46 100 MANAT
39.9400 g., 0.9167 Gold 1.1771 oz. AGW **Subject:** Heydar Aliyev **Obv:** National map **Rev:** Bust 3/4 right **Edge:** Reeded

Date	Mintage	F	VF	XF	Unc	BU
2004 Proof	1,000	Value: 2,250				

KM# 47 500 MANAT
50.0000 g., 0.9990 Platinum 1.6059 oz. APW **Subject:** Heydar Aliyev **Obv:** National map **Rev:** Bust 3/4 right **Edge:** Reeded

Date	Mintage	F	VF	XF	Unc	BU
2004 Proof	100	Value: 3,500				

MINT SETS

KM#	Date	Mintage	Identification	Issue Price	Mkt Val
MS1	2006 (6)	—	KM#39-44.	—	150

BAHAMAS

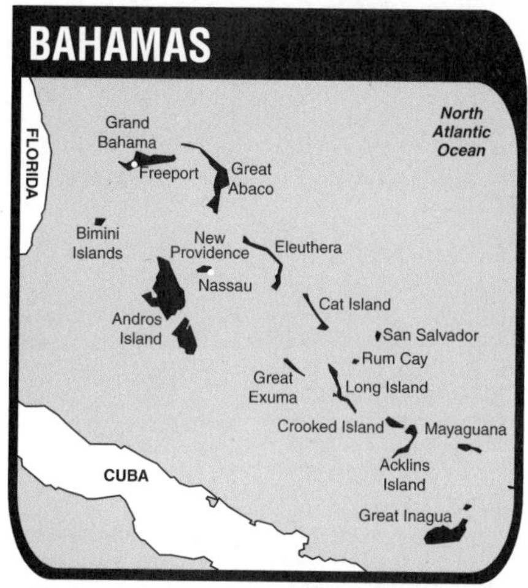

The Commonwealth of the Bahamas is an archipelago of about 3,000 islands, cays and rocks located in the Atlantic Ocean east of Florida and north of Cuba. The total land area of the 800 mile (1,287 km.) long chain of islands is 5,382 sq. mi. (13,935 sq. km.). They have a population of 302,000. Capital: Nassau. The Bahamas import most of their food and manufactured products and export cement, refined oil, pulpwood and lobsters. Tourism is the principal industry. The Bahamas is a member of the Commonwealth of Nations. Elizabeth II is Head of State as Queen of The Bahamas.

The coinage of Great Britain was legal tender in the Bahamas from 1825 to the issuing of a definitive coinage in 1966.

RULER
British

COMMONWEALTH

DECIMAL COINAGE

100 Cents = 1 Dollar

KM# 59a CENT
2.5000 g., Copper Plated Zinc, 19 mm. **Ruler:** Elizabeth II **Obv:** National arms above date **Obv. Legend:** COMMONWEALTH OF THE BAHAMAS **Rev:** Starfish, value at top **Edge:** Plain

Date	Mintage	F	VF	XF	Unc	BU
2000	—	—	—	0.10	0.25	0.75
2001	—	—	—	0.10	0.25	0.75
2004	—	—	—	0.10	0.25	0.75

KM# 218.1 CENT
2.5000 g., Copper Plated Zinc, 19 mm. **Ruler:** Elizabeth II **Obv:** National arms, date below **Rev:** Three starfish

Date	Mintage	F	VF	XF	Unc	BU
2006	—	—	—	—	0.25	0.75
2007	—	—	—	—	0.25	0.75

KM# 218.2 CENT
1.7500 g., Copper Plated Zinc, 17 mm. **Ruler:** Elizabeth II **Obv:** National arms, date below **Rev:** Three starfish

Date	Mintage	F	VF	XF	Unc	BU
2009	—	—	—	—	0.25	0.75

KM# 60 5 CENTS
3.9400 g., Copper-Nickel, 21 mm. **Ruler:** Elizabeth II **Obv:** National arms above date **Obv. Legend:** COMMONWEALTH OF THE BAHAMAS **Rev:** Pineapple above garland divides value at top **Edge:** Smooth

Date	Mintage	F	VF	XF	Unc	BU
2004	—	—	—	0.10	0.25	0.75
2005	—	—	—	0.10	0.25	0.75
2006	—	—	—	0.10	0.25	0.75

KM# 61 10 CENTS
5.1300 g., Copper-Nickel, 23.5 mm. **Ruler:** Elizabeth II **Obv:** National arms, date below, within beaded circle **Rev:** Two bonefish above denomination **Edge:** Plain **Shape:** Scalloped

Date	Mintage	F	VF	XF	Unc	BU
2005	—	—	—	0.25	0.60	0.80

KM# 219 10 CENTS
5.5400 g., Copper-Nickel, 23.5 mm. **Ruler:** Elizabeth II **Obv:** National arms, date below **Rev:** Two fish, value above **Shape:** Scalloped

Date	Mintage	F	VF	XF	Unc	BU
2007	—	—	—	0.25	0.60	0.80

KM# 62 15 CENTS
6.5000 g., Copper-Nickel, 25 mm. **Ruler:** Elizabeth II **Obv:** National arms above date **Rev:** Hibiscus, value divided at bottom **Edge:** Smooth **Shape:** 4-sided

Date	Mintage	F	VF	XF	Unc	BU
2005	—	—	—	0.20	0.50	1.50

KM# 63.2 25 CENTS
5.7500 g., Copper-Nickel, 24.26 mm. **Ruler:** Elizabeth II **Obv:** National arms, date below **Rev:** Bahamian Sloop, value above **Edge:** Reeded

Date	Mintage	F	VF	XF	Unc	BU
2005	—	—	—	0.30	0.50	1.50

KM# 217 DOLLAR
Silver and gold plated ring **Ruler:** Elizabeth II **Subject:** Queen Mother's 100th Birthday

Date	Mintage	F	VF	XF	Unc	BU
2002 Proof	—	Value: 50.00				

BAHRAIN

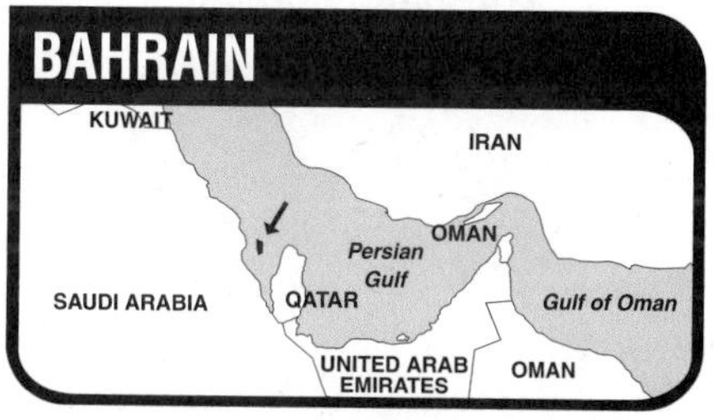

The Kingdom of Bahrain, a group of islands in the Persian Gulf off Saudi Arabia, has an area of 268 sq. mi. (622 sq. km.) and a population of 618,000. Capital: Manama. Prior to the depression of the 1930's, the economy was based on pearl fishing. Petroleum and aluminum industries and transit trade are the vital factors in the economy today.

The coinage of the Kingdom of Bahrain was struck at the Royal Mint, London, England.

RULERS

Al Khalifa Dynasty
Hamed Bin Isa, 1999-

TITLES

State of Bahrain	دولة البحرين
Kingdom of Bahrain	مملكة البحرين

KINGDOM

STANDARD COINAGE

KM# 30 5 FILS
2.5000 g., Brass, 19 mm. **Ruler:** Hamed Bin Isa **Obv:** Palm tree **Obv. Legend:** KINGDOM OF BAHRAIN **Rev:** Denomination in chain link border **Edge:** Plain

Date	Mintage	F	VF	XF	Unc	BU
AH1426-2005	—	—	—	—	0.50	0.75
AH1428-2007	—	—	—	—	0.50	0.75
AH1430-2009	—	—	—	—	0.50	0.75
AH1431-2010	—	—	—	—	0.50	0.75

KM# 30a 5 FILS
2.5000 g., 0.9250 Silver 0.0743 oz. ASW, 19 mm. **Ruler:** Hamed Bin Isa **Obv:** Palm tree **Rev:** Denomination in chain link border

Date	Mintage	F	VF	XF	Unc	BU
AH1431-2010 Proof	500	Value: 15.00				

KM# 28 10 FILS
3.3500 g., Brass, 21 mm. **Ruler:** Hamed Bin Isa **Obv:** Palm tree **Obv. Legend:** KINGDOM OF BAHRAIN **Rev:** Denomination in chain link border **Edge:** Plain

Date	Mintage	F	VF	XF	Unc	BU
AH1423-2002	—	—	—	0.30	0.75	1.00
AH1424-2004	—	—	—	0.30	0.75	1.00
AH1426-2005	—	—	—	0.30	0.75	1.00
AH1428-2007	—	—	—	0.30	0.75	1.00
AH1429-2008	—	—	—	0.30	0.75	1.00
AH1430-2009	—	—	—	0.30	0.75	1.00
AH1431-2010	—	—	—	0.30	0.75	1.00
AH1432-2011	—	—	—	0.30	0.75	1.00

KM# 28a 10 FILS
3.3500 g., 0.9250 Silver 0.0996 oz. ASW, 21 mm. **Ruler:** Hamed Bin Isa **Obv:** Palm tree **Rev:** Denomination in chain link border

Date	Mintage	F	VF	XF	Unc	BU
AH1431-2010 Proof	500	Value: 25.00				

KM# 24 25 FILS
3.5000 g., Copper-Nickel, 20 mm. **Ruler:** Hamed Bin Isa **Obv:** Ancient painting **Obv. Legend:** KINGDOM OF BAHRAIN **Rev:** Denomination in chain link border **Edge:** Reeded

Date	Mintage	F	VF	XF	Unc	BU
AH1423-2002	—	—	—	0.45	1.10	1.50
AH1426-2005	—	—	—	0.45	1.10	1.50
AH1428-2007	—	—	—	0.45	1.10	1.50
AH1429-2008	—	—	—	0.45	1.10	1.50
AH1430-2009	—	—	—	0.45	1.10	1.50

KM# 24a 25 FILS
3.5000 g., 0.9250 Silver 0.1041 oz. ASW, 20 mm. **Ruler:** Hamed Bin Isa **Obv:** Ancient painting **Rev:** Denomination in chain link border

Date	Mintage	F	VF	XF	Unc	BU
AH1431-2010 Proof	500	Value: 25.00				

KM# 25 50 FILS
4.5000 g., Copper-Nickel, 22 mm. **Ruler:** Hamed Bin Isa **Subject:** Kingdom **Obv:** Stylized sailboats **Obv. Legend:** KINGDOM OF BAHRAIN **Rev:** Denomination in chain link border **Edge:** Reeded

Date	Mintage	F	VF	XF	Unc	BU
AH1423-2002	—	—	—	0.60	1.50	2.00
AH1426-2005	—	—	—	0.60	1.50	2.00

Date	Mintage	F	VF	XF	Unc	BU
AH1428-2007	—	—	—	0.60	1.50	2.00
AH1429-2008	—	—	—	0.60	1.50	2.00
AH1430-2009	—	—	—	0.60	1.50	2.00
AH1431-2010	—	—	—	0.60	1.50	2.00

KM# 25a 50 FILS

4.5000 g., 0.9250 Silver 0.1338 oz. ASW, 22 mm. **Ruler:** Hamed Bin Isa **Obv:** Stylized sailboats **Rev:** Denomination in chain link border

Date	Mintage	F	VF	XF	Unc	BU
AH1431-2010 Proof	500	Value: 25.00				

KM# 20 100 FILS

6.0000 g., Bi-Metallic Copper-Nickel center in Brass ring, 24 mm. **Obv:** Coat of arms within circle, dates at either side **Obv. Legend:** STATE OF BAHRAIN **Rev:** Numeric denomination back of boxed denomination within circle, chain surrounds **Edge:** Reeded

Date	Mintage	F	VF	XF	Unc	BU
AH1422-2001	—	—	—	—	3.50	4.00

KM# 26 100 FILS

6.0000 g., Bi-Metallic Copper-Nickel center in Brass ring, 24 mm. **Ruler:** Hamed Bin Isa **Subject:** Kingdom **Obv:** National arms **Obv. Legend:** KINGDOM OF BAHRAIN **Rev:** Denomination in chain link border **Edge:** Reeded

Date	Mintage	F	VF	XF	Unc	BU
AH1423-2002	—	—	—	0.90	2.25	3.00
AH1425-2004	—	—	—	0.90	2.25	3.00
AH1426-2005	—	—	—	0.90	2.25	3.00
AH1427-2006	—	—	—	0.90	2.25	3.00
AH1428-2007	—	—	—	0.90	2.25	3.00
AH1429-2008	—	—	—	0.90	2.25	3.00
AH1430-2009	—	—	—	0.90	2.25	3.00
AH1431-2010	—	—	—	0.90	2.25	3.00

KM# 29 100 FILS

6.0000 g., Bi-Metallic Copper-Nickel center in Brass ring, 24 mm. **Ruler:** Hamed Bin Isa **Subject:** 1st Bahrain Grand Prix **Obv:** Maze design within circle **Rev:** Numeric denomination back of boxed denomination within circle, chain surrounds **Edge:** Reeded

Date	Mintage	F	VF	XF	Unc	BU
AH1425-2004	30,000	—	—	—	30.00	35.00

KM# 26a 100 FILS

6.0000 g., 0.9250 Silver 0.1784 oz. ASW, 24 mm. **Ruler:** Hamed Bin Isa **Obv:** National arms **Rev:** Denomination in chain link border

Date	Mintage	F	VF	XF	Unc	BU
AH1431-2010 Proof	500	Value: 30.00				

KM# 22 500 FILS

9.0000 g., Bi-Metallic Brass center in Copper-Nickel ring, 27 mm. **Ruler:** Hamed Bin Isa **Obv:** Monument and inscription **Obv. Inscription:** STATE OF BAHRAIN **Rev:** Denomination **Edge:** Reeded

Date	Mintage	F	VF	XF	Unc	BU
2001	—	—	—	—	6.00	7.50

KM# 27 500 FILS

9.0000 g., Bi-Metallic Brass center in Copper-Nickel ring, 27 mm. **Ruler:** Hamed Bin Isa **Subject:** Kingdom **Obv:** Monument and inscription **Obv. Legend:** KINGDOM OF BAHRAIN **Rev:** Denomination **Edge:** Reeded

Date	Mintage	F	VF	XF	Unc	BU
2002	—	—	—	—	6.50	8.00

KM# 27a 500 FILS

9.0000 g., 0.9250 Silver 0.2676 oz. ASW, 27 mm. **Ruler:** Hamed Bin Isa **Obv:** Monument and inscription **Rev:** Denomination

Date	Mintage	F	VF	XF	Unc	BU
AH1431-2010 Proof	500	Value: 40.00				

PROOF SETS

KM#	Date	Mintage	Identification	Issue Price	Mkt Val
PS4	2010 (6)	500	KM#30a, 28a, 24a, 25a, 26a, 27a	160	160

BANGLADESH

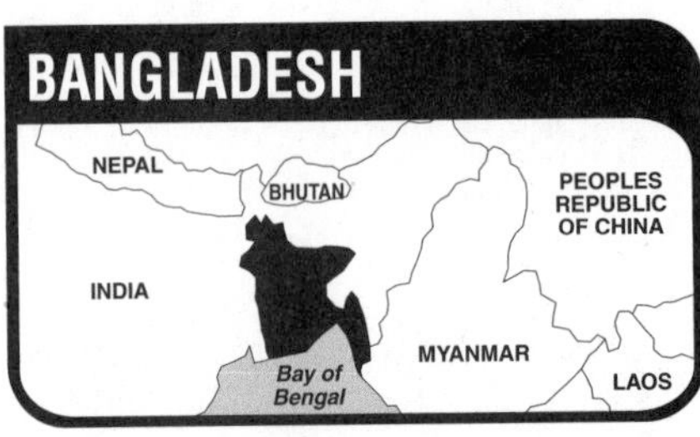

The Peoples Republic of Bangladesh (formerly East Pakistan), a parliamentary democracy located on the Bay of Bengal bordered by India and Burma, has an area of 55,598 sq. mi. (143,998 sq. km.) and a population of 128.1 million. Capital: Dhaka. The economy is predominantly agricultural. Jute products, jute and tea are exported.

Bangladesh is a member of the Commonwealth of Nations. The president is the Head of State and the Government.

MONETARY SYSTEM

100 Poisha = 1 Taka

DATING

Christian era using Bengali numerals.

PEOPLES REPUBLIC

STANDARD COINAGE

KM# 24 50 POISHA

2.6000 g., Stainless Steel, 19.3 mm. **Obv:** National emblem, Shapla (water lily) within wreath above water **Rev:** Fish, chicken and produce within inner circle **Edge:** Plain **Shape:** Octagonal

Date	Mintage	F	VF	XF	Unc	BU
2001	—	—	—	—	1.50	2.50

KM# 9c TAKA

4.2500 g., Stainless Steel, 24.91 mm. **Obv:** National emblem, Shapla (water lily) within wreath above water in octagonal frame **Rev:** Stylized family, value at right within octagonal frame **Edge:** Reeded **Note:** Prev. KM # 9.5.

Date	Mintage	F	VF	XF	Unc	BU
2001	—	—	—	0.80	2.00	3.00
2002	—	—	—	0.80	2.00	3.00
2003	—	—	—	0.80	2.00	3.00
2007	—	—	—	0.80	2.00	3.00

KM# 9b TAKA

4.0000 g., Brass, 25 mm. **Obv:** National emblem, Shapla (water lily) **Rev:** Stylized family, value at right **Edge:** Reeded **Note:** Prev. KM # 9.3.

Date	Mintage	F	VF	XF	Unc	BU
2003	—	—	0.20	0.55	1.20	1.60

KM# 25 2 TAKA

7.0000 g., Stainless Steel, 26.03 mm. **Obv:** State emblem and "TWO 2 TAKA" within beaded border **Rev:** Two children reading, legend within beaded border **Edge:** Plain

Date	Mintage	F	VF	XF	Unc	BU
2004	—	—	—	1.20	3.00	4.00
2008	—	—	—	1.20	3.00	4.00

KM# 31 2 TAKA

5.5000 g., Stainless Steel, 24 mm. **Obv:** State emblem **Rev:** Bust facing

Date	Mintage	F	VF	XF	Unc	BU
2010	—	—	—	—	3.00	4.00

KM# 26 5 TAKA

8.1700 g., Steel, 26.8 mm. **Obv:** National emblem, Shapla (water lily) within wreath above water **Rev:** Bridge, date and denomination below **Note:** Prev. KM#18.3.

Date	Mintage	F	VF	XF	Unc	BU
2006	—	—	—	1.00	2.50	3.50
2008	—	—	—	1.00	2.50	3.50

KM# 27 10 TAKA

0.9250 Silver **Subject:** Cricket World Cup **Obv:** Cricket ball logo **Rev:** Trophy

Date	Mintage	F	VF	XF	Unc	BU
2011 Proof	—	Value: 60.00				

KM# 28 10 TAKA

22.1000 g., 0.9250 Silver 0.6572 oz. ASW, 38 mm. **Subject:** Rabindranath Tagore, 150th Anniversary of Birth **Obv:** Legend **Rev:** Bust right

Date	Mintage	F	VF	XF	Unc	BU
2011 Proof	—	Value: 60.00				

KM# 29 10 TAKA

25.0000 g., 0.9990 Silver 0.8029 oz. ASW, 38 mm. **Subject:** Nationhood, 40th Anniversary **Obv:** Bangabandhu Sheikh Mujibur Rahman at center **Rev:** Six freedom fighters with hands raised

Date	Mintage	F	VF	XF	Unc	BU
2011 Proof	—	Value: 60.00				

KM# 30 10 TAKA

25.0000 g., 0.9990 Silver 0.8029 oz. ASW, 38 mm. **Subject:** Poem: Bidrohi; 90th Anniversary **Obv:** Legend **Rev:** Kazi Nazrul Islam facing

Date	Mintage	F	VF	XF	Unc	BU
2011 Proof	—	Value: 60.00				

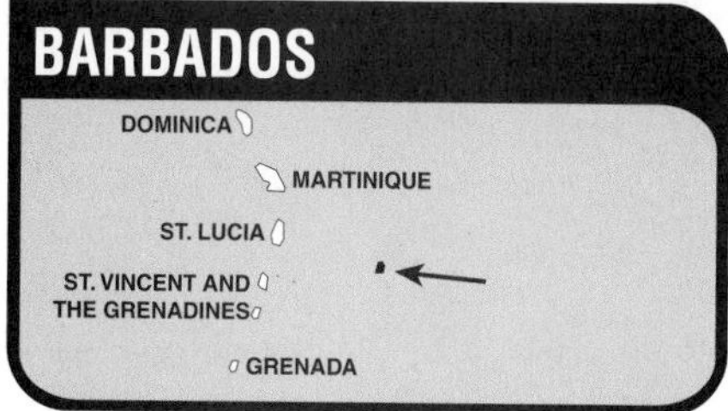

Barbados, a Constitutional Monarchy within the Commonwealth of Nations, is located in the Windward Islands of the West Indies east of St. Vincent. The coral island has an area of 166 sq. mi. (430 sq. km.) and a population of 269,000. Capital: Bridgetown. The economy is based on sugar and tourism. Sugar, petroleum products, molasses, and rum are exported.

MONETARY SYSTEM

100 Cents = 1 Dollar

MINT MARKS

(brm) – British Royal Mint

(O) – Ottawa Royal Canadian Mint

(v) - Valcambi

COMMONWEALTH

DECIMAL COINAGE

KM# 10a CENT

2.5000 g., Copper Plated Zinc, 19 mm. **Obv:** National arms **Rev:** Trident above value **Edge:** Plain

Date	Mintage	F	VF	XF	Unc	BU
2001	—	—	—	0.10	0.25	0.75
2002	—	—	—	—	0.25	0.75
2003	—	—	—	—	0.25	0.75
2004	—	—	—	—	0.25	0.75
2005	—	—	—	—	0.25	0.75
2006	—	—	—	—	0.25	0.75
2007	—	—	—	—	0.25	0.75

KM# 10b CENT

2.7800 g., Copper Plated Steel, 18.86 mm. **Obv:** National arms **Rev:** Trident above value

Date	Mintage	F	VF	XF	Unc	BU
2008	—	—	—	—	0.25	0.50
2009	—	—	—	—	0.25	0.50
2010	—	—	—	—	0.25	0.50
2011	—	—	—	—	0.25	0.50
2012	—	—	—	—	0.25	0.50

KM# 11 5 CENTS

3.7500 g., Brass, 21 mm. **Obv:** National arms **Rev:** South Point Lighthouse, value below **Edge:** Plain

Date	Mintage	F	VF	XF	Unc	BU
2001	—	—	—	—	0.25	0.75
2002	—	—	—	—	0.25	0.75
2004	—	—	—	—	0.25	0.75
2005	—	—	—	—	0.25	0.75
2006	—	—	—	—	0.25	0.75
2007	—	—	—	—	0.25	0.75

KM# 11a 5 CENTS

3.4600 g., Brass Plated Steel, 21 mm. **Obv:** National arms **Rev:** South Point Lighthouse, value below

Date	Mintage	F	VF	XF	Unc	BU
2008	—	—	—	—	0.25	0.75
2009	—	—	—	—	0.25	0.75
2010	—	—	—	—	0.25	0.75
2011	—	—	—	—	0.25	0.75

KM# 12 10 CENTS

2.2900 g., Copper-Nickel, 17.77 mm. **Obv:** National arms **Rev:** Tern flying left, value below **Edge:** Reeded

Date	Mintage	F	VF	XF	Unc	BU
2001	—	—	—	0.15	0.50	1.50
2003	—	—	—	0.15	0.50	1.50
2004	—	—	—	0.15	0.50	1.50
2005	—	—	—	0.15	0.50	1.50

KM# 12a 10 CENTS

2.0900 g., Nickel Plated Steel, 17.77 mm. **Obv:** National arms **Rev:** Tern flying left, value below **Edge:** Reeded

Date	Mintage	F	VF	XF	Unc	BU
2007	—	—	—	—	0.50	1.00
2008	—	—	—	—	0.50	1.00
2009	—	—	—	—	0.50	1.00
2012	—	—	—	—	0.50	1.00

KM# 13 25 CENTS

5.6500 g., Copper-Nickel, 23.66 mm. **Obv:** National arms **Rev:** Morgan Lewis Windmill, value above **Edge:** Reeded **Designer:** Philip Nathan

Date	Mintage	F	VF	XF	Unc	BU
2001	—	—	—	0.30	0.60	1.60
2003	—	—	—	0.30	0.60	1.60
2004	—	—	—	0.30	0.60	1.60
2005	—	—	—	0.30	0.60	1.60
2006	—	—	—	0.30	0.60	1.60

KM# 13a 25 CENTS

5.1000 g., Nickel Plated Steel, 23.66 mm. **Obv:** National arms **Rev:** Morgan Lewis Windmill, value above **Edge:** Reeded

Date	Mintage	F	VF	XF	Unc	BU
2007	—	—	—	0.30	0.60	1.00
2008	—	—	—	0.30	0.60	1.00
2009	—	—	—	0.30	0.60	1.00
2011	—	—	—	0.30	0.60	1.00

KM# 14.2 DOLLAR

5.9500 g., Copper-Nickel, 25.85 mm. **Obv:** National arms **Rev:** Flying fish left, value below **Shape:** 7-sided **Note:** Thinner planchet.

Date	Mintage	F	VF	XF	Unc	BU
2004	—	—	—	—	2.25	3.00
2005	—	—	—	—	2.25	3.00

KM# 14.2a DOLLAR

5.9500 g., Nickel Plated Steel, 25.85 mm. **Obv:** National arms **Rev:** Flying fish left, value below

Date	Mintage	F	VF	XF	Unc	BU
2007	—	—	—	—	2.00	2.50
2008	—	—	—	—	2.25	3.00
2009	—	—	—	—	2.00	2.50
2012	—	—	—	—	2.00	2.50

KM# 69 5 DOLLARS

28.2800 g., 0.9250 Silver 0.8410 oz. ASW, 38.6 mm. **Subject:** UNICEF **Obv:** National arms divide date, denomination below **Rev:** Three boys playing cricket **Edge:** Reeded

Date	Mintage	F	VF	XF	Unc	BU
2001(v) Proof	100	Value: 75.00				

KM# 73 5 DOLLARS

28.2800 g., 0.9250 Silver 0.8410 oz. ASW, 38.61 mm. **Subject:** 375th Anniversary fo the City of Bridgetown **Obv:** Coat of Arms of Barbados **Rev:** Montefiore Fountain (Coleridge Street, Bridgetown)

Date	Mintage	F	VF	XF	Unc	BU
2003(brm) Proof	200	Value: 60.00				

KM# 76 5 DOLLARS

28.2800 g., 0.9250 Silver 0.8410 oz. ASW, 38.61 mm. **Subject:** 3 W's (Sirs Clyde Walcott, Everton Weekes and Frank Worrell) **Obv:** Coat of Arms of Barbados **Rev:** Sirs Clyde Walcott, Everton Weekes and Frank Worrell relaxing together on the cricket field with a cricket bat and ball beside them, legend, their nickname, circumferential legend, denomination **Rev. Legend:** Barbados - Home of the Masters

Date	Mintage	F	VF	XF	Unc	BU
2007 Proof	250	Value: 100				

KM# 78 5 DOLLARS

28.2800 g., 0.9250 Silver 0.8410 oz. ASW, 38.61 mm. **Subject:** The Right Excellent Sir Garfield Sobers **Obv:** Coat of Arms of Barbados **Rev:** Sir Garfield Sobers in action playing a glorious cover drive, legend, circumferential legend, denomination **Rev. Legend:** The Right Excellent Sir Garfield Sobers; Barbados - Home of the Masters

Date	Mintage	F	VF	XF	Unc	BU
2007(brm) Proof	250	Value: 100				

KM# 74 50 DOLLARS

15.9700 g., 0.9167 Gold 0.4707 oz. AGW, 28.4 mm. **Subject:** 375th Anniversary of the City of Bridgetown **Obv:** Coat of Arms of Barbados **Rev:** Montefiore Fountain (Coleridge Street, Bridgetown)

Date	Mintage	F	VF	XF	Unc	BU
2003 Proof	50	Value: 1,000				

KM# 75 50 DOLLARS

15.9700 g., 0.9167 Gold 0.4707 oz. AGW, 28.4 mm. **Subject:** 350th Anniversary of the Bridgetown Synagogue **Obv:** Coat of Arms of Barbados **Rev:** Rum barrel with the initials "mt" on its top (design based on 18th century token used as currency and minted by (and credited with its design) Joseph Tolanto, a Jewish merchant), legend, denomination **Rev. Legend:** 350th ANNIVERSARY OF THE BRIDGETOWN SYNAGOGUE

Date	Mintage	F	VF	XF	Unc	BU
2004 Proof	100	Value: 950				

KM# 77 50 DOLLARS

15.9700 g., 0.9167 Gold 0.4707 oz. AGW, 28.4 mm. **Subject:** Sirs Clyde Walcott, Everton Weekes and Frank Worrell **Obv:** Coat of Arms of Barbados **Rev:** Sirs Clyde Walcott, Everton Weekes and Frank Worrell relaxing together on the cricket field with a cricket bat and ball beside them, legend, their nickname, circumferential legend, denomination **Rev. Legend:** Barbados - Home of the Masters

Date	Mintage	F	VF	XF	Unc	BU
2007(brm) Proof	50	Value: 1,000				

KM# 79 50 DOLLARS

15.9700 g., 0.9167 Gold 0.4707 oz. AGW, 28.4 mm. **Subject:** The Right Excellent Sir Garfield Sobers **Obv:** Coat of Arms of Barbados **Rev:** Sir Garfield Sobers in action playing a glorious cover drive, legend, circumferential legend, denomination **Rev. Legend:** The Right Excellent Sir Garfield Sobers; Barbados - Home of the Masters

Date	Mintage	F	VF	XF	Unc	BU
2007(brm) Proof	50	Value: 1,000				

Belarus (Byelorussia, Belorussia, or White Russia- formerly the Belorussian S.S.R.) is situated along the western Dvina and Dnieper Rivers, bounded in the west by Poland, to the north by Latvia and Lithuania, to the east by Russia and the south by the Ukraine. It has an area of 80,154 sq. mi. (207,600 sq. km.) and a population of 4.8 million. Capital: Minsk. Chief products: peat, salt, and agricultural products including flax, fodder and grasses for cattle breeding and dairy products.

MONETARY SYSTEM

100 Kapeek = 1 Rouble

REPUBLIC

STANDARD COINAGE

KM# 110 ROUBLE

Copper-Nickel, 32 mm. **Subject:** 900th Anniversary of Euphrasinta **Obv:** National arms **Rev:** Euphrasinta of Polatsk **Designer:** S.P. Zaskevich

Date	Mintage	F	VF	XF	Unc	BU
2001	Est. 2,000	—	—	—	50.00	—

KM# 112 ROUBLE

Copper-Nickel, 32 mm. **Subject:** Tower of Kamyantes **Obv:** National arms **Rev:** Kamyanets Tower, seal **Designer:** S.P. Zaskevich

Date	Mintage	F	VF	XF	Unc	BU
2001	2,000	—	—	—	40.00	—

KM# 47 ROUBLE

13.1400 g., Copper-Nickel, 31.9 mm. **Obv:** National arms **Rev:** European Bison **Edge:** Reeded **Designer:** S.P. Zaskevich

Date	Mintage	F	VF	XF	Unc	BU
2001 Proof	5,000	Value: 40.00				

KM# 50 ROUBLE

13.1500 g., Copper-Nickel, 28.7 mm. **Subject:** 2002 Winter Olympics **Obv:** National arms **Rev:** Two freestyle skiers **Edge:** Reeded **Designer:** S.P. Zaskevich

Date	Mintage	F	VF	XF	Unc	BU
2001 Prooflike	2,000	—	—	—	—	35.00

KM# 114 ROUBLE

Copper-Nickel, 32 mm. **Subject:** 200th Birthday of Ignatius Dameika **Obv:** National arms **Rev:** Ignatius Dameika, hammer

Date	Mintage	F	VF	XF	Unc	BU
2002 Prooflike	2,000	—	—	—	—	40.00

KM# 116 ROUBLE

Copper-Nickel, 33 mm. **Subject:** 120th Birthday of Yanka Kupala **Obv:** National arms **Rev:** Yanka Kupala, 1882-1942

Date	Mintage	F	VF	XF	Unc	BU
2002 Prooflike	2,000	—	—	—	—	40.00

KM# 118 ROUBLE

Copper-Nickel, 33 mm. **Subject:** 120th Birthday of Yakub Kolas **Obv:** National arms **Rev:** Yukab Kolas, 1882-1956

Date	Mintage	F	VF	XF	Unc	BU
2002	2,000	—	—	—	40.00	—

KM# 69 ROUBLE

Copper-Nickel, 33 mm. **Subject:** 80th Anniversary of the Savings Bank **Obv:** Folk art design

Date	Mintage	F	VF	XF	Unc	BU
2002 Prooflike	10,000	—	—	—	15.00	—

KM# 106 ROUBLE

Copper-Nickel, 31.9 mm. **Subject:** Jakub Kalas 1881-1956

Date	Mintage	F	VF	XF	Unc	BU
2002 Proof	2,000	Value: 35.00				

KM# 44 ROUBLE

13.1400 g., Copper-Nickel, 31.9 mm. **Obv:** National arms **Rev:** Eurasian Beaver and young **Edge:** Reeded **Designer:** S.P. Zaskevich

Date	Mintage	F	VF	XF	Unc	BU
2002 Proof	5,000	Value: 25.00				

KM# 61 ROUBLE

13.1600 g., Copper-Nickel, 32 mm. **Obv:** National arms **Rev:** Wrestlers **Edge:** Reeded **Designer:** S.P. Zaskevich

Date	Mintage	F	VF	XF	Unc	BU
2003 Prooflike	5,000	—	—	—	—	10.00

KM# 54 ROUBLE

13.1200 g., Copper-Nickel, 31.9 mm. **Obv:** National arms **Rev:** Mute swans on water with reflections **Edge:** Reeded **Designer:** S.P. Zaskevich

Date	Mintage	F	VF	XF	Unc	BU
2003 Proof	5,000	Value: 35.00				

KM# 55 ROUBLE

13.1000 g., Copper-Nickel, 31.9 mm. **Obv:** State arms **Rev:** Herring gull in flight **Edge:** Reeded **Designer:** S.P. Zaskevich

Date	Mintage	F	VF	XF	Unc	BU
2003 Proof	5,000	Value: 25.00				

KM# 56 ROUBLE

13.1000 g., Copper-Nickel, 32 mm. **Obv:** National arms **Rev:** Church of the Savior and Transfiguration **Edge:** Reeded **Designer:** S.P. Zaskevich

Date	Mintage	F	VF	XF	Unc	BU
2003	2,000	—	—	—	35.00	—

KM# 292 ROUBLE

13.1600 g., Copper-Nickel, 32 mm. **Obv:** National arms **Rev:** Church

Date	Mintage	F	VF	XF	Unc	BU
2003 Prooflike	2,000	—	—	—	—	100

KM# 60 ROUBLE

13.1600 g., Copper-Nickel, 32 mm. **Obv:** National arms **Rev:** Two common cranes **Edge:** Reeded **Designer:** S.P. Zaskevich

Date	Mintage	F	VF	XF	Unc	BU
2004 Proof	5,000	Value: 25.00				

KM# 75 ROUBLE

15.9200 g., Copper-Nickel Antiqued Finish, 33 mm. **Subject:** "Kupalle" **Obv:** Folk art cross design **Rev:** Flower above ferns **Edge:** Reeded **Designer:** S.P. Zaskevich

Date	Mintage	F	VF	XF	Unc	BU
2004	5,000	—	—	—	40.00	—

KM# 76 ROUBLE

15.9200 g., Copper-Nickel, 33 mm. **Subject:** "Kalyady" **Obv:** Folk art cross design **Rev:** Stylized sunflower **Edge:** Reeded **Designer:** S.P. Zaskevich

Date	Mintage	F	VF	XF	Unc	BU
2004	5,000	—	—	—	35.00	—

KM# 78 ROUBLE

15.9000 g., Copper-Nickel, 33 mm. **Obv:** National arms **Rev:** Radziwill's Castle in Neswizh **Edge:** Reeded **Designer:** S.P. Zaskevich

Date	Mintage	F	VF	XF	Unc	BU
2004 Prooflike	2,000	—	—	—	—	40.00

KM# 80 ROUBLE

15.9000 g., Copper-Nickel, 33 mm. **Subject:** Defenders of Brest **Obv:** Soviet Patriotic War Order **Rev:** "Courage" monument **Edge:** Reeded **Designer:** S.P. Zaskevich

Date	Mintage	F	VF	XF	Unc	BU
2004	5,000	—	—	—	25.00	—

KM# 85 ROUBLE

Copper-Nickel, 33 mm. **Subject:** Soviet Warriors - Liberators **Obv:** Order of the Patriotric War **Rev:** Partisans with blown up railway track

Date	Mintage	F	VF	XF	Unc	BU
2004	3,000	—	—	—	25.00	—

KM# 83 ROUBLE

Copper-Nickel, 33 mm. **Subject:** Memory of Facist Victims **Obv:** National arms **Rev:** Man holding dead

Date	Mintage	F	VF	XF	Unc	BU
2004	3,000	—	—	—	25.00	—

KM# 62 ROUBLE

Copper-Nickel, 31.9 mm. **Subject:** Sculling **Obv:** National arms **Rev:** Two rowers against a background of stylized oars

Date	Mintage	F	VF	XF	Unc	BU
2004	3,000	—	—	—	15.00	—

KM# 293 ROUBLE

14.3500 g., Copper-Nickel, 33 mm. **Subject:** Mogilev **Obv:** National arms **Rev:** Shield and town view

Date	Mintage	F	VF	XF	Unc	BU
2004 Prooflike	2,000	—	—	—	—	40.00

KM# 294 ROUBLE

14.3500 g., Copper-Nickel, 33 mm. **Subject:** WWII anniversary **Obv:** Order star **Rev:** Soldier and tank

Date	Mintage	F	VF	XF	Unc	BU
2004 Prooflike	3,000	—	—	—	—	40.00

KM# 81 ROUBLE

Copper-Nickel, 33 mm. **Subject:** 60th Anniversary of Victory **Obv:** Order of the Victory **Rev:** Star and arrows

Date	Mintage	F	VF	XF	Unc	BU
2005	2,000	—	—	—	25.00	—

KM# 127 ROUBLE

Copper-Nickel, 32 mm. **Subject:** 1000th Anniversary of Vaukavysk **Obv:** National arms **Rev:** National arms of Vaukavysk

Date	Mintage	F	VF	XF	Unc	BU
2005	2,000	—	—	—	40.00	—

KM# 130 ROUBLE

Copper-Nickel, 32 mm. **Subject:** Jesuit Roman Catholic Church **Obv:** National arms **Rev:** Jesuit Roman Catholic Church in Neswizh **Designer:** S.P. Zaskevich

Date	Mintage	F	VF	XF	Unc	BU
2005	2,000	—	—	—	40.00	—

KM# 104 ROUBLE

Copper-Nickel, 33 mm. **Subject:** Christmas Egg **Obv:** National arms and folk art cross design **Rev:** Easter egg **Designer:** S.P. Zaskevich

Date	Mintage	F	VF	XF	Unc	BU
2005	5,000	—	—	—	35.00	—

KM# 107 ROUBLE

Copper-Nickel, 31.9 mm. **Subject:** Bagach - Candle in Basket **Obv:** National arms and solar symbol **Rev:** Basket of grain, candle, ear, table, tablecloth

Date	Mintage	F	VF	XF	Unc	BU
2005	5,000	—	—	—	35.00	—

KM# 132 ROUBLE

Copper-Nickel, 33 mm. **Subject:** Usyaslau of Polatsk **Obv:** Cathedral of St. Sophia **Rev:** Usyaslav of Polatsk, wolf on a solar disk

Date	Mintage	F	VF	XF	Unc	BU
2005 Proof	5,000	Value: 15.00				

KM# 134 ROUBLE

Copper-Nickel, 33 mm. **Subject:** Tennis **Obv:** National arms **Rev:** Tennis player against racket background

Date	Mintage	F	VF	XF	Unc	BU
2005	5,000	—	—	—	12.00	—

KM# 97 ROUBLE

14.5000 g., Copper-Nickel, 33 mm. **Subject:** Almany Bogs **Obv:** Blooming plant on frosted design **Rev:** Great Grey Owl **Edge:** Lettered **Designer:** S.V. Nekrasova

Date	Mintage	F	VF	XF	Unc	BU
2005 Proof	5,000	Value: 30.00				

KM# 295 ROUBLE

14.3500 g., Copper-Nickel, 33 mm. **Subject:** Grodno **Obv:** National arms **Rev:** Shield and city fortress

Date	Mintage	F	VF	XF	Unc	BU
2005 Prooflike	2,000	—	—	—	—	40.00

KM# 296 ROUBLE

14.3500 g., Copper-Nickel, 33 mm. **Subject:** Brest **Obv:** National arms **Rev:** Shield and city view

Date	Mintage	F	VF	XF	Unc	BU
2005 Prooflike	2,000	—	—	—	—	40.00

KM# 273 ROUBLE

13.2000 g., Copper-Nickel, 32 mm. **Subject:** Skiing **Edge:** Reeded

Date	Mintage	F	VF	XF	Unc	BU
2006	5,000	—	—	—	—	20.00

KM# 274 ROUBLE

15.5000 g., Copper-Nickel, 33 mm. **Subject:** Rogwald

Date	Mintage	F	VF	XF	Unc	BU
2006	5,000	—	—	—	—	20.00

KM# 275 ROUBLE

13.1600 g., Copper-Nickel, 32 mm. **Subject:** Commonwealth of Independent States, 15th Anniversary **Edge:** Reeded

Date	Mintage	F	VF	XF	Unc	BU
2006 Prooflike	5,000	—	—	—	—	20.00

KM# 135 ROUBLE

Copper-Nickel, 32 mm. **Subject:** Vtaselle Wedding **Obv:** National arms, birds, shamrock **Rev:** Loaf of bread, wedding rings, diadem of flowers, background of honeycomb

Date	Mintage	F	VF	XF	Unc	BU
2006	5,000	—	—	—	20.00	25.00

KM# 138 ROUBLE

Copper-Nickel, 33 mm. **Subject:** Sophia of Galshany 600th Anniversary **Obv:** Castle of Galshany **Rev:** National arms and Sophia of Galshany **Designer:** S.P. Zaskevich

Date	Mintage	F	VF	XF	Unc	BU
2006	5,000	—	—	—	20.00	—

KM# 140 ROUBLE

Copper-Nickel, 33 mm. **Subject:** Syomukha **Obv:** National arms, solar symbol **Rev:** Chalice, Chaplet of birch, maple, rowan sweet flag leaves **Designer:** S.P. Zaskevich

Date	Mintage	F	VF	XF	Unc	BU
2006	5,000	—	—	—	25.00	—

KM# 146 ROUBLE

Copper-Nickel, 33 mm. **Subject:** Chyrvomy Bar **Obv:** National arms, blooming plant **Rev:** European Mink **Designer:** S.V. Nekrasova

Date	Mintage	F	VF	XF	Unc	BU
2006 Proof	5,000	Value: 17.50				

KM# 276 ROUBLE

13.2000 g., Copper-Nickel, 32 mm. **Subject:** Cycling **Edge:** Plain

Date	Mintage	F	VF	XF	Unc	BU
2006	5,000	—	—	—	—	20.00

KM# 297 ROUBLE

14.3500 g., Copper-Nickel, 33 mm. **Subject:** Gomel **Obv:** National arms **Rev:** Shield and city view

Date	Mintage	F	VF	XF	Unc	BU
2006 Prooflike	2,000	—	—	—	—	75.00

KM# 298 ROUBLE

15.5000 g., Copper-Nickel, 29x29 mm. **Subject:** Struve-Bogen trail **Obv:** National arms and map **Rev:** Eastern Europe map **Shape:** Square

Date	Mintage	F	VF	XF	Unc	BU
2006 Prooflike	5,000	—	—	—	—	25.00

KM# 417 ROUBLE

15.5500 g., Copper-Nickel, 33 mm. **Subject:** Rogvold of Polotsk and Rogneda **Obv:** Ancient fortress of Izyaslavl **Rev:** Rogvold at left with female **Designer:** S. Zaskevich

Date	Mintage	F	VF	XF	Unc	BU
2006 Prooflike	5,000	—	—	—	—	30.00

KM# 150 ROUBLE

16.0000 g., Copper-Nickel, 33 mm. **Subject:** Holidays and Ceremonies **Obv:** Small arms above quilted star design **Rev:** Food, bowl with spoon - Maslenica

Date	Mintage	F	VF	XF	Unc	BU
2007 Antique	5,000	—	—	—	35.00	—

KM# 151 ROUBLE

13.1600 g., Copper-Nickel, 32 mm. **Obv:** Thrush Nightingale in hands in oval **Obv. Legend:** РЭСПУБЛІКА БЕЛАРУСЬ **Rev:** Thrush Nightingale perched on branch in oval **Edge:** Reeded

Date	Mintage	F	VF	XF	Unc	BU
2007 Prooflike	5,000	—	—	—	—	17.50

KM# 217 ROUBLE

14.3500 g., Copper-Nickel, 33 mm. **Rev:** Sturgeon

Date	Mintage	F	VF	XF	Unc	BU
2007 Proof	5,000	Value: 15.00				

KM# 299 ROUBLE

13.1600 g., Copper-Nickel, 32 mm. **Subject:** Belarus-China relations, 15th anniversary **Obv:** National arms **Rev:** Two archways, with Belerus and China views

Date	Mintage	F	VF	XF	Unc	BU
2007 Prooflike	3,000	—	—	—	—	25.00

KM# 300 ROUBLE

13.1600 g., Copper-Nickel, 32 mm. **Subject:** Naoleon Orda, 200th Anniversary of Birth **Obv:** Three castle views **Rev:** Bust facing, musical notes and sytlized record

Date	Mintage	F	VF	XF	Unc	BU
2007 Prooflike	7,000	—	—	—	—	25.00

KM# 301 ROUBLE

15.5000 g., Copper-Nickel, 33 mm. **Subject:** Gleb Menski **Obv:** Wooden fortress **Rev:** Knight seated left

Date	Mintage	F	VF	XF	Unc	BU
2007 Prooflike	5,000	—	—	—	—	25.00

KM# 302 ROUBLE

13.1600 g., Copper-Nickel, 32 mm. **Subject:** A. Aladawa **Obv:** Building façade **Rev:** Bust and picture frame

Date	Mintage	F	VF	XF	Unc	BU
2007 Prooflike	4,000	—	—	—	—	25.00

KM# 303 ROUBLE

15.5000 g., Copper-Nickel, 33 mm. **Subject:** Legend of the Stork **Obv:** Five stylized storks **Rev:** Large stylized stork

Date	Mintage	F	VF	XF	Unc	BU
2007 Prooflike	5,000	—	—	—	—	25.00

KM# 215 ROUBLE

13.1800 g., Copper-Nickel, 33 mm. **Obv:** Sea chart and compose rose **Rev:** Sailing ship Sedov

Date	Mintage	F	VF	XF	Unc	BU
2008 Proof	7,000	Value: 15.00				

KM# 304 ROUBLE

13.1600 g., Copper-Nickel, 32 mm. **Subject:** Zair Azgur **Obv:** Bust sculpture on pedestal **Rev:** Portrait right

Date	Mintage	F	VF	XF	Unc	BU
2008 Prooflike	3,000	—	—	—	—	25.00

KM# 305 ROUBLE

13.1600 g., Copper-Nickel, 32 mm. **Subject:** Vincent Dunin-Martsynkevich **Obv:** Open stage curtian **Rev:** Bust facing, play names at right

Date	Mintage	F	VF	XF	Unc	BU
2008 Prooflike	3,000	—	—	—	—	25.00

KM# 306 ROUBLE

15.5000 g., Copper-Nickel, 33 mm. **Subject:** Legend **Obv:** Five stylized birds **Rev:** Stylized bird

Date	Mintage	F	VF	XF	Unc	BU
2008 Prooflike	5,000	—	—	—	—	25.00

KM# 307 ROUBLE

13.1600 g., Copper-Nickel, 32 mm. **Subject:** House-warming **Obv:** Cat standing left **Rev:** Key in window, house façade **Edge:** Reeded

Date	Mintage	F	VF	XF	Unc	BU
2008	5,000	—	—	—	—	25.00

KM# 308 ROUBLE

13.1600 g., Copper-Nickel, 32 mm. **Subject:** Great White Egret **Obv:** Bird in hand in horizontal oval **Rev:** Great White Egret standing in vertical oval **Edge:** Reeded

Date	Mintage	F	VF	XF	Unc	BU
2008 Prooflike	5,000	—	—	—	—	30.00

KM# 309 ROUBLE
16.0000 g., Copper-Nickel, 33 mm. **Obv:** Folk embroidery star pattern **Rev:** Two angles with candle above log home entrace with festive table set

Date	Mintage	F	VF	XF	Unc	BU
2008 Antique patina	5,000	—	—	—	—	50.00

KM# 310 ROUBLE
14.3500 g., Copper-Nickel, 33 mm. **Subject:** Minsk **Obv:** EurAsEC logo and graphic **Rev:** Old and new city views in two ovals

Date	Mintage	F	VF	XF	Unc	BU
2008 Prooflike	7,000	—	—	—	—	20.00

KM# 311 ROUBLE
15.5000 g., Copper-Nickel, 33 mm. **Subject:** Davyd of Garadzen **Obv:** Fortress **Rev:** Knight standing facing

Date	Mintage	F	VF	XF	Unc	BU
2008 Prooflike	5,000	—	—	—	—	25.00

KM# 312 ROUBLE
13.1600 g., Copper-Nickel, 32 mm. **Series:** Ministry of Finance, 90th Anniversary **Obv:** National arms **Rev:** Ministry of Finance arms

Date	Mintage	F	VF	XF	Unc	BU
2008 Prooflike	3,000	—	—	—	—	20.00

KM# 313 ROUBLE
14.3500 g., Copper-Nickel, 33 mm. **Subject:** Kingfisher **Obv:** Flower **Rev:** Kingfisher on grass near waterway

Date	Mintage	F	VF	XF	Unc	BU
2008 Prooflike	5,000	—	—	—	—	25.00

KM# 259 ROUBLE
13.1600 g., Copper-Nickel, 32 mm. **Obv:** Compass **Rev:** Dar Parmoza at sail

Date	Mintage	F	VF	XF	Unc	BU
2009	5,000	—	—	—	—	25.00

KM# 218 ROUBLE
13.1600 g., Copper-Nickel, 32 mm. **Subject:** Bialowieza Forest, 600th Anniversary **Obv:** Figures joining hands around tree trunk **Rev:** Stylized nature view **Edge:** Reeded

Date	Mintage	F	VF	XF	Unc	BU
2009 Prooflike	5,000	—	—	—	—	25.00

KM# 219 ROUBLE
13.1600 g., Copper-Nickel, 32 mm. **Subject:** Grey Goose **Obv:** Bird in hand **Rev:** Grey goose in oval **Edge:** Reeded

Date	Mintage	F	VF	XF	Unc	BU
2009 Prooflike	5,000	—	—	—	—	20.00

KM# 220 ROUBLE
15.5000 g., Copper-Nickel, 32 mm. **Subject:** Pakatigaroshak **Rev:** Man clubbing dragon

Date	Mintage	F	VF	XF	Unc	BU
2009 Proof	3,500	Value: 17.50				

KM# 221 ROUBLE
15.5000 g., Copper-Nickel, 33 mm. **Subject:** Legend of the Skylark **Obv:** five stylized birds in flight **Rev:** Stylized skylark, head left

Date	Mintage	F	VF	XF	Unc	BU
2009 Prooflike	5,000	—	—	—	—	13.00

KM# 222 ROUBLE
15.5000 g., Copper-Nickel, 33 mm. **Subject:** Folk Art - Straw Weaving **Rev:** Horse

Date	Mintage	F	VF	XF	Unc	BU
2009 Prooflike	5,000	—	—	—	—	13.00

KM# 314 ROUBLE
13.1600 g., Copper-Nickel, 32 mm. **Subject:** Academy of Science **Obv:** Earth and spaceship orbits **Rev:** Academy building

Date	Mintage	F	VF	XF	Unc	BU
2009 Prooflike	4,000	—	—	—	—	20.00

KM# 315 ROUBLE
13.1600 g., Copper-Nickel, 32 mm. **Subject:** Zodiac - Pisces **Obv:** Sun and moon **Rev:** Two fish **Edge:** Reeded

Date	Mintage	F	VF	XF	Unc	BU
2009	10,000	—	—	—	—	20.00

KM# 316 ROUBLE
13.1600 g., Copper-Nickel, 32 mm. **Subject:** Zodiac - Aries **Obv:** Sun and moon **Rev:** Ram **Edge:** Reeded

Date	Mintage	F	VF	XF	Unc	BU
2009	10,000	—	—	—	—	20.00

KM# 317 ROUBLE
13.1600 g., Copper-Nickel, 32 mm. **Subject:** Zodiac - Taurus **Obv:** Sun and moon **Rev:** Bull

Date	Mintage	F	VF	XF	Unc	BU
2009 Prooflike	10,000	—	—	—	—	20.00

KM# 318 ROUBLE
13.1600 g., Copper-Nickel, 32 mm. **Subject:** Zodiac - Gemini **Obv:** Sun and moon **Rev:** Twins

Date	Mintage	F	VF	XF	Unc	BU
2009 Prooflike	10,000	—	—	—	—	20.00

KM# 319 ROUBLE
13.1600 g., Copper-Nickel, 32 mm. **Subject:** Zodiac - Cancer **Obv:** Sun and moon **Rev:** Crab

Date	Mintage	F	VF	XF	Unc	BU
2009 Prooflike	10,000	—	—	—	—	20.00

KM# 320 ROUBLE
13.1600 g., Copper-Nickel, 32 mm. **Subject:** Christening **Obv:** Stylized stork **Rev:** Child in a baptism gown **Edge:** Reeded

Date	Mintage	F	VF	XF	Unc	BU
2009	5,000	—	—	—	—	20.00

KM# 321 ROUBLE
13.1600 g., Copper-Nickel, 32 mm. **Subject:** Zodiac - Leo **Obv:** Sun and moon **Rev:** Lion standing left **Edge:** Reeded

Date	Mintage	F	VF	XF	Unc	BU
2009	10,000	—	—	—	—	20.00

KM# 322 ROUBLE
14.3500 g., Copper-Nickel, 33 mm. **Series:** Liberationfrom the Nazis, 65th Anniversary **Rev:** Child looking upwards to birds in flight **Edge:** Reeded

Date	Mintage	F	VF	XF	Unc	BU
2009 Prooflike	4,000	—	—	—	—	20.00

KM# 323 ROUBLE
13.1600 g., Copper-Nickel, 32 mm. **Subject:** Zodiac - Virgo **Obv:** Sun and moon **Rev:** Little girl

Date	Mintage	F	VF	XF	Unc	BU
2009 Prooflike	10,000	—	—	—	—	20.00

KM# 324 ROUBLE
13.1600 g., Copper-Nickel, 32 mm. **Subject:** Zodiac - Libra **Obv:** Sun and moon **Rev:** Scales **Edge:** Reeded

Date	Mintage	F	VF	XF	Unc	BU
2009	10,000	—	—	—	—	20.00

KM# 325 ROUBLE
16.0000 g., Copper-Nickel, 33 mm. **Subject:** Harvesttime **Obv:** Star embroidery pattern **Rev:** Apple, honey and grain harvest

Date	Mintage	F	VF	XF	Unc	BU
2009 Antique patina	5,000	—	—	—	—	25.00

KM# 326 ROUBLE
13.1600 g., Copper-Nickel, 32 mm. **Subject:** Zodiac - Scorpio **Obv:** Sun and moon **Rev:** Scorpion

Date	Mintage	F	VF	XF	Unc	BU
2009 Proofilke	10,000	—	—	—	—	20.00

KM# 327 ROUBLE
14.3500 g., Copper-Nickel, 33 mm. **Subject:** White Stork **Obv:** Stork footprint **Rev:** White Stork and nest

Date	Mintage	F	VF	XF	Unc	BU
2009 Prooflike	5,000	—	—	—	—	25.00

KM# 329 ROUBLE
13.1600 g., Copper-Nickel, 32 mm. **Subject:** Zodiac - Sagittarius **Obv:** Sun and moon **Rev:** Girl with bow and arrow

Date	Mintage	F	VF	XF	Unc	BU
2009 Prooflike	10,000	—	—	—	—	20.00

KM# 331 ROUBLE
13.1600 g., Copper-Nickel, 32 mm. **Subject:** Zodiac - Capricorn **Obv:** Sun and moon **Rev:** Ram

Date	Mintage	F	VF	XF	Unc	BU
2009 Prooflike	10,000	—	—	—	—	20.00

KM# 332 ROUBLE
13.1600 g., Copper-Nickel, 32 mm. **Subject:** Zodiac - Aquarius **Obv:** Sun and moon **Rev:** Child in bathtub **Edge:** Reeded

Date	Mintage	F	VF	XF	Unc	BU
2009	10,000	—	—	—	—	20.00

KM# 264 ROUBLE
15.5000 g., Copper-Nickel, 33 mm. **Subject:** Metalsmith **Rev:** Horseshoe, house within, small horsemen flanking

Date	Mintage	F	VF	XF	Unc	BU
2010 Proof	3,500	Value: 17.50				

KM# 223 ROUBLE
14.3500 g., Copper-Nickel, 33 mm. **Subject:** EURASEC, 10th Anniversary **Obv:** Folk embroidery pattern **Rev:** Six flags around globe

Date	Mintage	F	VF	XF	Unc	BU
2010 Proof	3,500	Value: 13.00				

KM# 226 ROUBLE
13.1600 g., Copper-Nickel, 33 mm. **Subject:** 1st Belarus Front **Rev:** Gen. Konstantin Rokossovsky

Date	Mintage	F	VF	XF	Unc	BU
2010 Proof	3,000	Value: 13.00				

KM# 227 ROUBLE
13.1600 g., Copper-Nickel, 33 mm. **Subject:** 2nd Belarus Front **Rev:** Col. Gen. G.F. Zaharov

Date	Mintage	F	VF	XF	Unc	BU
2010 Proof	3,000	Value: 13.00				

KM# 228 ROUBLE
13.1600 g., Copper-Nickel, 33 mm. **Subject:** 3rd Belarus Front **Rev:** Col. Gen. Ivan Chernyakhovsky

Date	Mintage	F	VF	XF	Unc	BU
2010 Proof	3,000	Value: 13.00				

KM# 229 ROUBLE
13.1600 g., Copper-Nickel, 33 mm. **Subject:** 1st Baltic Forces **Rev:** Gen. Hovhannes Bagramayn

Date	Mintage	F	VF	XF	Unc	BU
2010 Proof	3,000	Value: 13.00				

KM# 236 ROUBLE
15.5000 g., Copper-Nickel, 33 mm. **Subject:** Legend of the Tortoise **Obv:** Five stylized turtles **Rev:** Stylized turtle

Date	Mintage	F	VF	XF	Unc	BU
2010 Prooflike	3,000	—	—	—	—	20.00

KM# 240 ROUBLE
Copper-Nickel, 32 mm. **Subject:** Age of Majority **Rev:** Flowers and folk patterns

Date	Mintage	F	VF	XF	Unc	BU
2010 Proof	4,000	Value: 13.00				

KM# 262 ROUBLE
14.3500 g., Copper-Nickel, 33 mm. **Subject:** End of World War II, 65th Anniversary **Obv:** Broken clock face **Rev:** 5 doves in flight, kiting

Date	Mintage	F	VF	XF	Unc	BU
2010 Prooflike	3,000	—	—	—	—	25.00

KM# 263 ROUBLE
13.1600 g., Copper-Nickel, 32 mm. **Obv:** Compass and chart **Rev:** Amergo Vespucci sailing ship

Date	Mintage	F	VF	XF	Unc	BU
2010 Proof	4,000	Value: 17.50				

KM# 265 ROUBLE
15.5500 g., Copper-Nickel, 33 mm. **Subject:** Judaism **Rev:** Valozhyn Yeshiva façade, 1806 date

Date	Mintage	F	VF	XF	Unc	BU
2010 Proof	3,000	Value: 15.00				

KM# 234 ROUBLE
13.1600 g., Copper-Nickel, 32 mm. **Rev:** U.S. Frigate Constitution

Date	Mintage	F	VF	XF	Unc	BU
2010 Proof	3,000	Value: 13.00				

KM# 334 ROUBLE
15.5000 g., Copper-Nickel, 33 mm. **Subject:** Battle of Grunwald, 600th Anniversary **Obv:** Figure in shape of cross **Rev:** Fingerprint **Edge:** Reeded

Date	Mintage	F	VF	XF	Unc	BU
2010 Prooflike	3,000	—	—	—	—	25.00

KM# 336 ROUBLE
13.1600 g., Copper-Nickel, 32 mm. **Obv:** Bird in hand **Rev:** Kestrel in oval **Edge:** Reeded

Date	Mintage	F	VF	XF	Unc	BU
2010 Prooflike	4,000	—	—	—	—	25.00

KM# 337 ROUBLE
14.4800 g., Copper-Nickel, 32 mm. **Subject:** Winter into Springtime **Obv:** Embroidery pattern **Rev:** Bird emerging from snow, into new fields and sunshine **Edge:** Reeded

Date	Mintage	F	VF	XF	Unc	BU
2010 Prooflike	3,000	—	—	—	—	20.00

KM# 338 ROUBLE
15.5000 g., Copper-Nickel, 33 mm. **Subject:** Leu Sapieha **Obv:** Early document **Rev:** Standing figure in robes

Date	Mintage	F	VF	XF	Unc	BU
2010 Prooflike	3,000	—	—	—	—	25.00

KM# 270 ROUBLE
13.1600 g., Copper-Nickel, 32 mm. **Obv:** Compass rose and chart **Rev:** Cutty Sark sailing right

Date	Mintage	F	VF	XF	Unc	BU
2011 Proof	3,000	Value: 13.00				

KM# 287 ROUBLE
13.1600 g., Copper-Nickel, 32 mm. **Subject:** M. Bogdanowicz **Obv:** Embroidery pattern **Rev:** Bust at left center

Date	Mintage	F	VF	XF	Unc	BU
2011 Prooflike	2,000	—	—	—	—	20.00

KM# 288 ROUBLE
20.0000 g., Copper-Nickel, 37 mm. **Subject:** I. Bujnicki **Obv:** Scene of play **Rev:** Bust at left, scene of play

Date	Mintage	F	VF	XF	Unc	BU
2011 Prooflike	2,000	—	—	—	—	25.00

KM# 291 ROUBLE
13.1600 g., Copper-Nickel, 32 mm. **Obv:** National arms **Rev:** Curlew bird standing left, oval background

Date	Mintage	F	VF	XF	Unc	BU
2011 Prooflike	2,000	—	—	—	—	20.00

KM# 339 ROUBLE
20.0000 g., Copper-Nickel, 37 mm. **Subject:** Slavianski Bazaar in Vitebsk **Obv:** Stylized design **Rev:** Historic buildings and stylized designs **Edge:** Reeded

Date	Mintage	F	VF	XF	Unc	BU
2011 Prooflike	2,500	—	—	—	—	25.00

KM# 340 ROUBLE
13.1600 g., Copper-Nickel, 32 mm. **Subject:** Motherhood **Obv:** Embroidery pattern **Rev:** Mother and baby

Date	Mintage	F	VF	XF	Unc	BU
2011 Prooflike	2,000	—	—	—	—	20.00

KM# 341 ROUBLE
13.1600 g., Copper-Nickel, 32 mm. **Subject:** Kruzensztern **Obv:** Compass rose and nautical charts **Rev:** Square-rigged sailing ship

Date	Mintage	F	VF	XF	Unc	BU
2011 Prooflike	2,000	—	—	—	—	50.00

KM# 419 ROUBLE
13.1600 g., Copper-Nickel, 32 mm. **Subject:** Belarus-China Diplomatic Relations, 20th Anniversary **Edge:** Reeded

Date	Mintage	F	VF	XF	Unc	BU
2012 Proof	2,000	Value: 20.00				

KM# 64 10 ROUBLES
16.8200 g., 0.9250 Silver 0.5002 oz. ASW, 32.9 mm. **Obv:** National arms **Rev:** Jakub Kolas (1882-1956) **Edge:** Reeded **Designer:** S.P. Zaskevich

Date	Mintage	F	VF	XF	Unc	BU
2002 Proof	1,000	Value: 150				

KM# 117 10 ROUBLES
15.5500 g., 0.9250 Silver 0.4624 oz. ASW, 33 mm. **Subject:** 120th Birthday of Yanka Kupala **Obv:** National arms **Rev:** Yanka Kupala, 1882-1942

Date	Mintage	F	VF	XF	Unc	BU
2002 Proof	1,000	Value: 150				

KM# 129 10 ROUBLES
1.2400 g., 0.9990 Gold 0.0398 oz. AGW, 13.92 mm. **Subject:** Belarussian Ballet **Obv:** National arms **Rev:** Dancing ballerina

Date	Mintage	F	VF	XF	Unc	BU
2005	25,000	—	—	—	100	130

KM# 342 10 ROUBLES
1.2400 g., 0.9990 Gold 0.0398 oz. AGW, 13.92 mm. **Subject:** Ballet **Obv:** National arms **Rev:** Two ballet performers **Edge:** Reeded

Date	Mintage	F	VF	XF	Unc	BU
2006 Proof	25,000	Value: 150				

KM# 156 10 ROUBLES
16.8100 g., 0.9250 Silver 0.4999 oz. ASW, 32 mm. **Subject:** Alena Aladana **Rev:** Half-length figure facing, picture in background

Date	Mintage	F	VF	XF	Unc	BU
2007 Proof	4,000	Value: 35.00				

KM# 157 10 ROUBLES
16.8100 g., 0.9250 Silver 0.4999 oz. ASW, 32 mm. **Subject:** Thrush Nightingale **Rev:** Bird standing right on branch

Date	Mintage	F	VF	XF	Unc	BU
2007 Proof	5,000	Value: 40.00				

KM# 343 10 ROUBLES
1.2400 g., 0.9990 Gold 0.0398 oz. AGW, 13.92 mm. **Subject:** Ballet **Obv:** National arms **Rev:** Mirror image of ballerina **Edge:** Reeded

Date	Mintage	F	VF	XF	Unc	BU
2007 Proof	10,000	Value: 150				

KM# 172 10 ROUBLES
16.8100 g., 0.9250 Silver 0.4999 oz. ASW, 32 mm. **Subject:** Zair Azgur **Rev:** Profile right

Date	Mintage	F	VF	XF	Unc	BU
2008 Proof	3,000	Value: 40.00				

KM# 173 10 ROUBLES
16.8100 g., 0.9250 Silver 0.4999 oz. ASW, 32 mm. **Subject:** Great White Egret **Rev:** Bird standing left

Date	Mintage	F	VF	XF	Unc	BU
2008 Proof	5,000	Value: 45.00				

KM# 174 10 ROUBLES
16.8100 g., 0.9250 Silver 0.4999 oz. ASW, 32 mm. **Subject:** Vincent Dunin **Rev:** Bust facing

Date	Mintage	F	VF	XF	Unc	BU
2008 Proof	3,000	Value: 35.00				

KM# 175 10 ROUBLES
16.8100 g., 0.9250 Silver 0.4999 oz. ASW, 32 mm. **Subject:** St. Euphrosyne of Polotsk **Rev:** Half-length figure facing within frame

Date	Mintage	F	VF	XF	Unc	BU
2008 Proof	5,000	Value: 40.00				

KM# 176 10 ROUBLES
16.8100 g., 0.9250 Silver 0.4999 oz. ASW, 32 mm. **Subject:** St. Steraphin of Sarov **Rev:** Half-length figure standing within frame

Date	Mintage	F	VF	XF	Unc	BU
2008 Proof	5,000	Value: 40.00				

KM# 177 10 ROUBLES
16.8100 g., 0.9250 Silver 0.4999 oz. ASW, 32 mm. **Subject:** St. Sergii of Radonezh **Rev:** Half-length figure standing within frame

Date	Mintage	F	VF	XF	Unc	BU
2008 Proof	5,000	Value: 40.00				

KM# 178 10 ROUBLES
16.8100 g., 0.9250 Silver 0.4999 oz. ASW, 32 mm. **Subject:** St. Nicholas **Rev:** Half-length figure standing within frame

Date	Mintage	F	VF	XF	Unc	BU
2008 Proof	5,000	Value: 40.00				

KM# 179 10 ROUBLES
16.8100 g., 0.9250 Silver 0.4999 oz. ASW, 32 mm. **Subject:** St. Panteleimon **Rev:** Half-length figure standing within frame

Date	Mintage	F	VF	XF	Unc	BU
2008 Proof	5,000	Value: 40.00				

KM# 194 10 ROUBLES
16.8100 g., 0.9250 Silver 0.4999 oz. ASW, 32 mm. **Subject:** Academy of Science, 80th Anniversary **Rev:** Building

Date	Mintage	F	VF	XF	Unc	BU
2009 Proof	3,000	Value: 40.00				

KM# 195 10 ROUBLES
16.8100 g., 0.9250 Silver 0.4999 oz. ASW, 32 mm. **Subject:** Greylag goose **Rev:** Goose swimming left

Date	Mintage	F	VF	XF	Unc	BU
2009 Proof	5,000	Value: 40.00				

KM# 344 10 ROUBLES
16.8100 g., 0.9250 Silver 0.4999 oz. ASW, 33 mm. **Subject:** Establishment of the Federated State, 10th Anniversary **Obv:** National arms **Rev:** Document and ribbon **Edge:** Reeded

Date	Mintage	F	VF	XF	Unc	BU
2009 Proof	3,000	Value: 50.00				

KM# 260 10 ROUBLES
16.8100 g., 0.9250 Silver 0.4999 oz. ASW, 32 mm. **Obv:** Stylized kestrel in egg **Rev:** Common kestrel

Date	Mintage	F	VF	XF	Unc	BU
2010	2,500	Value: 75.00				

KM# 230 10 ROUBLES
16.8100 g., 0.9250 Silver 0.4999 oz. ASW, 33 mm. **Subject:** 1st Belarus Front **Rev:** Gen. Konstantin Rokosovsky

Date	Mintage	F	VF	XF	Unc	BU
2010 Proof	2,500	Value: 35.00				

KM# 231 10 ROUBLES
16.8100 g., 0.9250 Silver 0.4999 oz. ASW, 33 mm. **Subject:** 2nd Belarus Front **Rev:** Col. Gen. G.F. Zakharov

Date	Mintage	F	VF	XF	Unc	BU
2010 Proof	2,500	Value: 35.00				

KM# 232 10 ROUBLES
16.5500 g., 0.9250 Silver 0.4922 oz. ASW, 33 mm. **Subject:** 3rd Belarus front **Rev:** Col. Gen. Ivan Chernyakovsky

Date	Mintage	F	VF	XF	Unc	BU
2010 Proof	2,500	Value: 35.00				

KM# 233 10 ROUBLES
16.5500 g., 0.9250 Silver 0.4922 oz. ASW, 33 mm. **Subject:** 1st Baltic Front **Rev:** Gen. Hovhannes Bagramgan

Date	Mintage	F	VF	XF	Unc	BU
2010 Proof	2,500	Value: 35.00				

KM# 345 10 ROUBLES
16.8100 g., 0.9250 Silver 0.4999 oz. ASW, 33 mm. **Subject:** Talmudic School **Obv:** Menorah and writings **Rev:** School façade

Date	Mintage	F	VF	XF	Unc	BU
2010 Proof	300	Value: 75.00				

KM# 284 10 ROUBLES
16.8100 g., 0.9250 Silver 0.4999 oz. ASW, 37 mm. **Subject:** I. Bujnicki **Obv:** Play scene **Rev:** Bust at left, place scene

Date	Mintage	F	VF	XF	Unc	BU
2011 Prooflike	2,000	—	—	—	—	75.00

KM# 347 10 ROUBLES
1.0000 g., 0.9000 Gold 0.0289 oz. AGW, 12 mm. **Subject:** M. Oginski **Obv:** National arms **Rev:** Bust facing

Date	Mintage	F	VF	XF	Unc	BU
2011 Proof	2,000	Value: 150				

KM# 348 10 ROUBLES
16.8100 g., 0.9250 Silver 0.4999 oz. ASW, 32 mm. **Subject:** Curlew bird **Obv:** Bird in hand **Rev:** Curlew bird in vertical oval

Date	Mintage	F	VF	XF	Unc	BU
2011 Prooflike	2,000	—	—	—	—	75.00

KM# 349 10 ROUBLES
16.8100 g., 0.9250 Silver 0.4999 oz. ASW, 32 mm. **Subject:** M. Bogdanowicz **Obv:** Embroidery pattern **Rev:** Bust at left, pattern design

Date	Mintage	F	VF	XF	Unc	BU
2011 Prooflike	2,000	—	—	—	—	75.00

KM# 111 20 ROUBLES
31.1000 g., 0.9250 Silver 0.9249 oz. ASW, 38.61 mm. **Subject:** 900th Anniversary of Euphrasinta **Obv:** National arms **Rev:** Euphrasinta of Polatsk, gold cross **Designer:** S.P. Zaskevitch

Date	Mintage	F	VF	XF	Unc	BU
2001 Proof	Est. 2,000	Value: 350				

KM# 113 20 ROUBLES
31.1000 g., 0.9250 Silver 0.9249 oz. ASW, 38.61 mm. **Subject:** Tower of Kamyantes **Obv:** National arms **Rev:** Kamyanets Tower, seal **Designer:** S.P. Zaskevich

Date	Mintage	F	VF	XF	Unc	BU
2001 Proof	2,000	Value: 110				

KM# 46 20 ROUBLES
33.7300 g., 0.9250 Silver 1.0031 oz. ASW, 38.6 mm. **Subject:** Wildlife **Obv:** National arms **Rev:** European Bison **Edge:** Reeded **Designer:** S.P. Zaskevich

Date	Mintage	F	VF	XF	Unc	BU
2001 Proof	2,000	Value: 350				

KM# 49 20 ROUBLES
28.3200 g., 0.9250 Silver 0.8422 oz. ASW, 38.6 mm. **Subject:** 2002 Winter Olympics **Obv:** National arms **Rev:** Marksman aiming at bullseye **Edge:** Reeded **Designer:** S.P. Zaskevich

Date	Mintage	F	VF	XF	Unc	BU
2001 Proof	15,000	Value: 60.00				

KM# 51 20 ROUBLES
33.6500 g., 0.9250 Silver 1.0007 oz. ASW, 38.6 mm. **Subject:** 2002 Winter Olympics **Obv:** National arms **Rev:** Two freestyle skiers **Edge:** Reeded **Designer:** S.P. Zaskevich

Date	Mintage	F	VF	XF	Unc	BU
2001 Proof	2,000	Value: 70.00				

KM# 45 20 ROUBLES
33.7300 g., 0.9250 Silver 1.0031 oz. ASW, 38.8 mm. **Obv:** National arms **Rev:** European beaver and young **Edge:** Reeded **Designer:** S.P. Zaskevich

Date	Mintage	F	VF	XF	Unc	BU
2002 Proof	2,000	Value: 200				

KM# 115 20 ROUBLES
31.1000 g., 0.9250 Silver 0.9249 oz. ASW, 38.61 mm. **Subject:** 200th Birthday of Ignatius Dameika **Obv:** National arms **Rev:** Ignatius Dameika, hammer and inset with a dameikit stone

Date	Mintage	F	VF	XF	Unc	BU
2002 Proof	1,000	Value: 350				

KM# 119 20 ROUBLES
28.2800 g., 0.9250 Silver 0.8410 oz. ASW, 38.61 mm. **Subject:** 2006 World Cup Football **Obv:** National arms **Rev:** Stylized 2006, football **Designer:** S.P. Zaskevich

Date	Mintage	F	VF	XF	Unc	BU
2002 Proof	25,000	Value: 75.00				

KM# 59 20 ROUBLES
28.6300 g., 0.9250 Silver 0.8514 oz. ASW, 38.6 mm. **Obv:** National arms **Rev:** Brown bear with two cubs **Edge:** Reeded

Date	Mintage	F	VF	XF	Unc	BU
2002 Proof	5,000	Value: 120				

KM# 70 20 ROUBLES
33.8500 g., 0.9250 Silver 1.0066 oz. ASW, 38.61 mm. **Obv:** National arms **Rev:** 80th Anniversary - National Savings Bank **Edge:** Reeded

Date	Mintage	F	VF	XF	Unc	BU
2002 Proof	1,000	Value: 225				

KM# 120 20 ROUBLES
31.1000 g., 0.9250 Silver 0.9249 oz. ASW, 38.61 mm. **Subject:** Freestyle Wrestling **Obv:** National arms **Rev:** Two wrestlers **Designer:** S.P. Zaskevich

Date	Mintage	F	VF	XF	Unc	BU
2003 Proof	3,000	Value: 65.00				

KM# 122 20 ROUBLES
31.1000 g., 0.9250 Silver 0.9249 oz. ASW, 38.61 mm. **Obv:** National arms **Rev:** Herring gull in flight **Designer:** S.P. Zaskevitch

Date	Mintage	F	VF	XF	Unc	BU
2003 Proof	2,000	Value: 200				

KM# 149 20 ROUBLES
28.2800 g., 0.9250 Silver 0.8410 oz. ASW, 38.61 mm. **Subject:** 2004 Olympic Games **Obv:** National arms **Rev:** Female shot-putter **Designer:** S.P. Zaskevich

Date	Mintage	F	VF	XF	Unc	BU
2003 Proof	25,000	Value: 65.00				

KM# 53 20 ROUBLES
33.8400 g., 0.9250 Silver 1.0063 oz. ASW, 38.5 mm. **Obv:** State arms **Rev:** Two Mute swans on water with reflections **Edge:** Reeded **Designer:** S.P. Zaskevich

Date	Mintage	F	VF	XF	Unc	BU
2003 Proof	2,000	Value: 250				

KM# 57 20 ROUBLES
31.1000 g., 0.9250 Silver 0.9249 oz. ASW, 38.6 mm. **Obv:** National arms **Rev:** Church of the Savior and Transfiguration **Edge:** Reeded **Designer:** S.P. Zaskevich

Date	Mintage	F	VF	XF	Unc	BU
2003 Proof	2,000	Value: 100				

KM# 86 20 ROUBLES
31.1000 g., 0.9250 Silver 0.9249 oz. ASW, 38.61 mm. **Subject:** Soviet Warriors - Liberators **Obv:** Multicolored Order of the Patriotic War **Rev:** Partisans with blown up railway track

Date	Mintage	F	VF	XF	Unc	BU
2004	2,000	—	—	—	100	—

KM# 84 20 ROUBLES
31.1000 g., 0.9250 Silver 0.9249 oz. ASW, 38.61 mm. **Subject:** Memory of Facist Victims **Obv:** Multicolored Order of the Patriotic War **Rev:** Man holding dead

Date	Mintage	F	VF	XF	Unc	BU
2004	2,000	—	—	—	100	—

KM# 124 20 ROUBLES
31.1000 g., 0.9250 Silver 0.9249 oz. ASW, 38.61 mm. **Subject:** Sculling **Obv:** National arms **Rev:** Two rowers against a background of stylized oars

Date	Mintage	F	VF	XF	Unc	BU
2004	3,000	—	—	—	50.00	—

KM# 71 20 ROUBLES
31.1000 g., 0.9250 Silver 0.9249 oz. ASW, 38.6 mm. **Subject:** "Kupalle" **Obv:** Folk art design **Rev:** Fern flower with inset red synthetic crystal **Edge:** Reeded **Designer:** S.P. Zaskevich

Date	Mintage	F	VF	XF	Unc	BU
2004 Antique finish	3,000	—	—	—	600	—

KM# 72 20 ROUBLES
31.1000 g., 0.9250 Silver 0.9249 oz. ASW, 38.6 mm. **Subject:** Defense of Brest **Obv:** Multicolor Soviet Order of the Patriotic War **Rev:** "Courage" monument **Edge:** Reeded **Designer:** S.P. Zaskevich

Date	Mintage	F	VF	XF	Unc	BU
2004 Proof	3,000	Value: 100				

KM# 73 20 ROUBLES
31.1000 g., 0.9250 Silver 0.9249 oz. ASW, 38.6 mm. **Obv:** National arms **Rev:** Two common cranes **Edge:** Reeded

Date	Mintage	F	VF	XF	Unc	BU
2004 Proof	2,000	Value: 170				

KM# 77 20 ROUBLES
31.1000 g., 0.9250 Silver 0.9249 oz. ASW, 38.6 mm. **Subject:** "Kalyady" **Obv:** Folk art cross design **Rev:** Stylized sunflower with inset blue synthetic crystal **Edge:** Reeded **Designer:** S.P. Zaskevich

Date	Mintage	F	VF	XF	Unc	BU
2004 Antique finish	5,000	—	—	—	350	—

KM# 79 20 ROUBLES
31.1000 g., 0.9250 Silver 0.9249 oz. ASW, 38.6 mm. **Obv:** National arms **Rev:** Radziwill's Castle in Neswizh **Edge:** Reeded **Designer:** S.P. Zaskevich

Date	Mintage	F	VF	XF	Unc	BU
2004 Proof	2,000	Value: 100				

KM# 91 20 ROUBLES
31.1000 g., 0.9250 Silver 0.9249 oz. ASW, 38.61 mm. **Subject:** Trade Union Movement Centennial **Obv:** National arms

Date	Mintage	F	VF	XF	Unc	BU
2004 Proof	1,500	Value: 200				

KM# 350 20 ROUBLES
33.6200 g., 0.9250 Silver 0.9998 oz. ASW, 38.61 mm. **Obv:** Russian Order star **Rev:** Soldier with rifle and tank

Date	Mintage	F	VF	XF	Unc	BU
2004 Proof	2,000	Value: 150				

KM# 351 20 ROUBLES
33.6200 g., 0.9250 Silver 0.9998 oz. ASW, 39 mm. **Subject:** Mogilev **Obv:** National arms **Rev:** Shield and city view

Date	Mintage	F	VF	XF	Unc	BU
2004 Proof	2,000	Value: 200				

KM# 101 20 ROUBLES
25.0000 g., 0.9250 Silver 0.7435 oz. ASW, 38.6 mm. **Subject:** 2006 FIFA World Cup Germany **Obv:** National arms **Rev:** Multicolor Europe, Asia and African maps on soccer ball **Note:** 2006 World Cup Soccer

Date	Mintage	F	VF	XF	Unc	BU
2005 Proof	50,000	Value: 55.00				

KM# 82 20 ROUBLES
28.7200 g., 0.9250 Silver 0.8541 oz. ASW, 38.6 mm. **Subject:** WW II Victory **Obv:** Multicolor Soviet Order of Victory **Rev:** Soviet soldiers raising their flag in the Reichstag in Berlin **Edge:** Reeded

Date	Mintage	F	VF	XF	Unc	BU
2005 Proof	12,000	Value: 60.00				

KM# 92 20 ROUBLES
28.6300 g., 0.9250 Silver 0.8514 oz. ASW, 38.6 mm. **Obv:** Two children sitting on crescent moon **Rev:** Symon the Musician and inset orange color glass crystal **Edge:** Plain **Designer:** S.V. Necrasova

Date	Mintage	F	VF	XF	Unc	BU
2005 Antique finish	20,000	—	—	—	65.00	—

KM# 93 20 ROUBLES
28.2800 g., 0.9250 Silver 0.8410 oz. ASW, 38.61 mm. **Subject:** Kalyady's star **Obv:** Two children sitting on a crescent moon **Rev:** Snow Queen, blue glass crystal inset on forehead, flower **Edge:** Plain **Designer:** S.V. Necrasova

Date	Mintage	F	VF	XF	Unc	BU
2005 Antique finish	20,000	—	—	—	65.00	—

KM# 94 20 ROUBLES
28.6300 g., 0.9250 Silver 0.8514 oz. ASW, 38.6 mm. **Obv:** Two children sitting on a crescent moon **Rev:** White glass crystal inset above landscape with fox, the Little Prince **Edge:** Plain **Designer:** S.V. Necrasova

Date	Mintage	F	VF	XF	Unc	BU
2005 Antique finish	20,000	—	—	—	65.00	—

KM# 95 20 ROUBLES
28.6300 g., 0.9250 Silver 0.8514 oz. ASW, 38.61 mm. **Obv:** Two children sitting on a crescent moon **Rev:** The Stone Flower, Yellow glass crystal inset in flower design, heads flank **Edge:** Plain **Designer:** S.V. Necrasova

Date	Mintage	F	VF	XF	Unc	BU
2005 Antique finish	20,000	—	—	—	65.00	—

KM# 96 20 ROUBLES
33.6600 g., 0.9250 Silver 1.0010 oz. ASW, 38.6 mm. **Subject:** Festivals and Rites - Bogach **Obv:** Small national arms above quilted star design **Rev:** Yellow glass crystal inset in candle flame above basket **Edge:** Reeded **Designer:** S.P. Zaskevich

Date	Mintage	F	VF	XF	Unc	BU
2005 Antique patina	5,000	—	—	—	170	—

KM# 98 20 ROUBLES
33.6300 g., 0.9250 Silver 1.0000 oz. ASW, 38.6 mm. **Subject:** Almany Bogs **Obv:** Blooming plant on frosted design **Rev:** Great grey owl in flight **Edge:** Reeded **Designer:** S.V. Nekrasova

Date	Mintage	F	VF	XF	Unc	BU
2005 Proof	5,000	Value: 70.00				

KM# 99 20 ROUBLES
31.1000 g., 0.9250 Silver 0.9249 oz. ASW, 38.6 mm. **Series:** Easter Egg **Obv:** Quilted cross design **Rev:** Decorated Easter egg with inset pink glass crystal

Date	Mintage	F	VF	XF	Unc	BU
2005 Antique finish	5,000	—	—	—	250	—

KM# 100 20 ROUBLES
33.6200 g., 0.9250 Silver 0.9998 oz. ASW, 38.6 mm. **Obv:** Large church **Rev:** Usyaslau of Polatsk

Date	Mintage	F	VF	XF	Unc	BU
2005 Proof	5,000	Value: 60.00				

KM# 102 20 ROUBLES
33.9400 g., 0.9250 Silver 1.0093 oz. ASW, 39 mm. **Obv:** National arms **Rev:** Female tennis player

Date	Mintage	F	VF	XF	Unc	BU
2005 Proof	7,000	Value: 60.00				

KM# 128 20 ROUBLES
31.1000 g., 0.9250 Silver 0.9249 oz. ASW, 38.61 mm. **Subject:** 1000th Anniversary of Vaukavysk **Obv:** National arms **Rev:** National arms of Vaukavysk

Date	Mintage	F	VF	XF	Unc	BU
2005 Proof	2,000	Value: 100				

KM# 131 20 ROUBLES
31.1000 g., 0.9250 Silver 0.9249 oz. ASW, 38.61 mm. **Subject:** Jesuit Roman Catholic Church **Obv:** National arms **Rev:** Jesuit Roman Catholic Church in Niasvizh **Designer:** S.P. Zaskevich

Date	Mintage	F	VF	XF	Unc	BU
2005 Proof	2,000	Value: 100				

KM# 133 20 ROUBLES
28.2800 g., 0.9250 Silver 0.8410 oz. ASW, 38.61 mm. **Subject:** 2006 Olympic Games **Obv:** National arms **Rev:** Two hockey players

Date	Mintage	F	VF	XF	Unc	BU
2005 Proof	15,000	Value: 60.00				

KM# 352 20 ROUBLES
33.6200 g., 0.9250 Silver 0.9998 oz. ASW, 39 mm. **Subject:** Grodno **Obv:** National arms **Rev:** Shield and fortress

Date	Mintage	F	VF	XF	Unc	BU
2005 Proof	2,000	Value: 150				

KM# 353 20 ROUBLES
33.6200 g., 0.9250 Silver 0.9998 oz. ASW, 39 mm. **Subject:** Brest **Obv:** National arms **Rev:** Shield and fortress

Date	Mintage	F	VF	XF	Unc	BU
2005 Proof	2,000	Value: 150				

KM# 148 20 ROUBLES
28.2800 g., 0.9250 Silver 0.8410 oz. ASW, 38.5 mm. **Subject:** Twelve Months **Obv:** Two children sitting on a crescent moon **Rev:** Campfire with inset amber in a circle of produce **Edge:** Plain **Note:** Antiqued finish. Prev. duplicate of KM #137.

Date	Mintage	F	VF	XF	Unc	BU
2006	20,000	—	—	—	65.00	—

KM# 147 20 ROUBLES
33.6300 g., 0.9250 Silver 1.0000 oz. ASW, 38.61 mm. **Subject:** Chyrvomy Bar **Obv:** National arms, blooming plant **Rev:** European mink **Designer:** S.V. Nekrasova

Date	Mintage	F	VF	XF	Unc	BU
2006 Proof	5,000	Value: 100				

KM# 136 20 ROUBLES
33.6300 g., 0.9250 Silver 1.0000 oz. ASW, 38.61 mm. **Subject:** Vtaselle Wedding **Obv:** National arms, birds, shamrock **Rev:** Loaf of bread, golden wedding rings, diadem of flowers, background of honeycomb

Date	Mintage	F	VF	XF	Unc	BU
2006	25,000	—	—	—	70.00	—

KM# 139 20 ROUBLES
33.6200 g., 0.9250 Silver 0.9998 oz. ASW, 38.61 mm. **Subject:** Sophia of Galshany 600th Anniversary **Obv:** Castle of Galshany **Rev:** National arms and Sophia of Galshany **Designer:** S.P. Zaskevich

Date	Mintage	F	VF	XF	Unc	BU
2006 Proof	5,000	Value: 70.00				

KM# 141 20 ROUBLES
33.6200 g., 0.9250 Silver 0.9998 oz. ASW, 38.61 mm. **Subject:** Festivals and Rites - Syomukha **Obv:** National arms, solar symbol **Rev:** Chalice, Chaplet of birch, maple, rowan, sweet flag leaves inserted in green crystal **Designer:** S.P. Zaskevich

Date	Mintage	F	VF	XF	Unc	BU
2006 Antique patina	5,000	—	—	—	150	—

KM# 155 20 ROUBLES
33.6200 g., 0.9250 Silver 0.9998 oz. ASW, 36x36 mm. **Subject:** Struve Geodetric Arc **Rev:** Map of Eastern Europe **Shape:** Square

Date	Mintage	F	VF	XF	Unc	BU
2006 Proof	5,000	Value: 60.00				

KM# 354 20 ROUBLES
33.6200 g., 0.9250 Silver 0.9998 oz. ASW, 39 mm. **Subject:** Homel **Obv:** National arms **Rev:** Shield and fortress

Date	Mintage	F	VF	XF	Unc	BU
2006 Proof	2,000	Value: 350				

KM# 355 20 ROUBLES
33.6200 g., 0.9250 Silver 0.9998 oz. ASW, 38.61 mm. **Subject:** CIS, 15th Anniversary **Obv:** Building façade **Rev:** Emblem

Date	Mintage	F	VF	XF	Unc	BU
2006 Proof	5,000	Value: 75.00				

KM# 356 20 ROUBLES
33.6200 g., 0.9250 Silver 0.9998 oz. ASW, 38.61 mm. **Subject:** Ski Center in Siliczy **Obv:** Skier **Rev:** Town view

Date	Mintage	F	VF	XF	Unc	BU
2006 Proof	5,000	Value: 75.00				

KM# 357 20 ROUBLES
33.6200 g., 0.9250 Silver 0.9998 oz. ASW, 38.61 mm. **Subject:** Rogwold and Rogneda **Obv:** Fortified circular town **Rev:** Norseman and female, ship

Date	Mintage	F	VF	XF	Unc	BU
2006 Proof	5,000	Value: 85.00				

KM# 358 20 ROUBLES
28.2800 g., 0.9250 Silver 0.8410 oz. ASW, 38.61 mm. **Subject:** Tale of the Thousand and one nights **Obv:** Boy and girl sitting on crescent moon **Rev:** Arabic artistic figure

Date	Mintage	F	VF	XF	Unc	BU
2006 Antique patina	20,000	—	—	—	—	75.00

KM# 359 20 ROUBLES
33.6200 g., 0.9250 Silver 0.9998 oz. ASW, 38.61 mm. **Subject:** Cycling **Obv:** National arms **Rev:** Two bikes on track

Date	Mintage	F	VF	XF	Unc	BU
2006 Proof	5,000	Value: 80.00				

KM# 360 20 ROUBLES
28.2800 g., 0.9250 Silver 0.8410 oz. ASW, 38.61 mm. **Subject:** Beijing Olympics, 2008 **Obv:** National arms **Rev:** Runners around center circle

Date	Mintage	F	VF	XF	Unc	BU
2006 Proof	20,000	Value: 80.00				

KM# 166 20 ROUBLES
33.6200 g., 0.9250 Silver 0.9998 oz. ASW, 38.61 mm. **Subject:** Legend of the Stork **Obv:** Woven basket design **Rev:** Stylized bird

Date	Mintage	F	VF	XF	Unc	BU
2007 Proof	5,000	Value: 65.00				

KM# 158 20 ROUBLES
33.6200 g., 0.9250 Silver 0.9998 oz. ASW, 38.61 mm. **Subject:** Belarus - China diplomatic relations **Rev:** Double arches with country scene

Date	Mintage	F	VF	XF	Unc	BU
2007 Proof	2,000	Value: 100				

KM# 159 20 ROUBLES
33.6200 g., 0.9250 Silver 0.9998 oz. ASW, 38.61 mm. **Subject:** Festivals and Rites - Maslenica **Rev:** Pancake and syrup

Date	Mintage	F	VF	XF	Unc	BU
2007 Antique Patina	5,000	—	—	—	130	—

KM# 160 20 ROUBLES
33.6300 g., 0.9250 Silver 1.0000 oz. ASW, 38.61 mm. **Subject:** Napoleon Orda **Rev:** Bust facing, record and musical notes in background

Date	Mintage	F	VF	XF	Unc	BU
2007 Proof	5,000	Value: 60.00				

KM# 161 20 ROUBLES
28.2800 g., 0.9250 Silver 0.8410 oz. ASW, 38.61 mm. **Subject:** Alice in Wonderland **Obv:** Two children sitting on crescent moon reading book **Rev:** Alice and the March Hare

Date	Mintage	F	VF	XF	Unc	BU
2007 Matte Proof	20,000	Value: 60.00				

KM# 162 20 ROUBLES
28.2800 g., 0.9250 Silver 0.8410 oz. ASW, 38.61 mm. **Subject:** Alice Through the Looking Glass **Obv:** Two children sitting on crescent moon reading book **Rev:** Alice and chess board

Date	Mintage	F	VF	XF	Unc	BU
2007 Matte Proof	20,000	Value: 60.00				

KM# 163 20 ROUBLES
31.1050 g., 0.9990 Silver 0.9990 oz. ASW, 40 mm. **Subject:** Belarusian Ballet **Rev:** Ballerina and mirror view

Date	Mintage	F	VF	XF	Unc	BU
2007 Proof	10,000	Value: 60.00				

KM# 164 20 ROUBLES
31.1000 g., 0.9250 Silver 0.9249 oz. ASW, 38.61 mm. **Subject:** International Polar Year **Obv:** IPY logo **Rev:** Antartic map behind two penguins

Date	Mintage	F	VF	XF	Unc	BU
2007 Proof	10,000	Value: 60.00				

KM# 165 20 ROUBLES
33.6200 g., 0.9250 Silver 0.9998 oz. ASW, 38.61 mm. **Subject:** Prince Gleb of Mensk **Obv:** Wood log building **Rev:** Knight seated left

Date	Mintage	F	VF	XF	Unc	BU
2007 Proof	5,000	Value: 60.00				

KM# 167 20 ROUBLES
31.1050 g., 0.9990 Silver 0.9990 oz. ASW, 38.61 mm. **Subject:** Wolf - Canis Lupus **Rev:** Wolf head facing

Date	Mintage	F	VF	XF	Unc	BU
2007 Proof	7,000	Value: 90.00				

KM# 168 20 ROUBLES
31.1050 g., 0.9990 Silver 0.9990 oz. ASW, 38.61 mm. **Subject:** Wolf - Canis Lupis **Rev:** Wolf standing on rock ledge behind second wolf's head facing

Date	Mintage	F	VF	XF	Unc	BU
2007 Proof	7,000	Value: 90.00				

KM# 169 20 ROUBLES
33.6300 g., 0.9250 Silver 1.0000 oz. ASW, 38.61 mm. **Subject:** Dniepra - Sozhsky **Rev:** Sturgeon fish

Date	Mintage	F	VF	XF	Unc	BU
2007 Proof	5,000	Value: 85.00				

KM# 180 20 ROUBLES
33.6300 g., 0.9250 Silver 1.0000 oz. ASW, 38.61 mm. **Subject:** Minsk **Rev:** Old and new city views

Date	Mintage	F	VF	XF	Unc	BU
2008 Proof	7,000	Value: 60.00				

KM# 181 20 ROUBLES
33.6300 g., 0.9250 Silver 1.0000 oz. ASW, 38.61 mm. **Subject:** Financial System, 90th Anniversary **Rev:** Shield

Date	Mintage	F	VF	XF	Unc	BU
2008 Proof	3,000	Value: 60.00				

KM# 182 20 ROUBLES
33.6300 g., 0.9250 Silver 1.0000 oz. ASW, 38.61 mm. **Subject:** Lipichanskaya Pushcha **Rev:** Kingfisher seated on branch

Date	Mintage	F	VF	XF	Unc	BU
2008 Proof	5,000	Value: 65.00				

KM# 183 20 ROUBLES
33.6200 g., 0.9250 Silver 0.9998 oz. ASW, 38.61 mm. **Subject:** Festivala and Rites - Dzyady **Rev:** Two angels above table

Date	Mintage	F	VF	XF	Unc	BU
2008 Antique patina	5,000	—	—	—	90.00	—

KM# 184 20 ROUBLES
33.6200 g., 0.9250 Silver 0.9998 oz. ASW, 38.61 mm. **Subject:** David of Garadzen **Rev:** Half-length figure of knight

Date	Mintage	F	VF	XF	Unc	BU
2008 Proof	5,000	Value: 60.00				

KM# 185 20 ROUBLES
31.1050 g., 0.9990 Silver 0.9990 oz. ASW, 40 mm. **Rev:** Figure skater

Date	Mintage	F	VF	XF	Unc	BU
2008 Proof	10,000	Value: 55.00				

KM# 186 20 ROUBLES
31.1050 g., 0.9990 Silver 0.9990 oz. ASW, 38.61 mm. **Subject:** Lynx **Rev:** Lynx head facing

Date	Mintage	F	VF	XF	Unc	BU
2008 Proof	8,000	Value: 95.00				

KM# 187 20 ROUBLES
31.1050 g., 0.9990 Silver 0.9990 oz. ASW, 38.61 mm. **Subject:** Lynx **Rev:** Adult lynx with cub

Date	Mintage	F	VF	XF	Unc	BU
2008 Proof	8,000	Value: 95.00				

KM# 188 20 ROUBLES
33.6200 g., 0.9250 Silver 0.9998 oz. ASW, 38.61 mm. **Subject:** Cuckoo Legend **Rev:** Stylized cuckoo

Date	Mintage	F	VF	XF	Unc	BU
2008 Proof	5,000	Value: 60.00				

KM# 189 20 ROUBLES
28.2800 g., 0.9250 Silver 0.8410 oz. ASW, 38.61 mm. **Subject:** Turandot **Rev:** Female opera character

Date	Mintage	F	VF	XF	Unc	BU
2008 Antique	—	—	—	—	65.00	—

KM# 190 20 ROUBLES
33.6310 g., 0.9250 Silver 1.0000 oz. ASW, 38.61 mm. **Subject:** House Warming **Obv:** Cat **Rev:** Plated key within house facade

Date	Mintage	F	VF	XF	Unc	BU
2008 Proof	25,000	Value: 60.00				

KM# 191 20 ROUBLES
28.2800 g., 0.9250 Silver 0.8410 oz. ASW, 38.61 mm. **Subject:** Sedov **Obv:** Compass star, multicolor **Rev:** Sailing ship

Date	Mintage	F	VF	XF	Unc	BU
2008 Proof	25,000	Value: 70.00				

KM# 196 20 ROUBLES
33.6300 g., 0.9250 Silver 1.0000 oz. ASW, 38.61 mm. **Subject:** 65th Anniversary of Liberation **Rev:** Child looking upward to freeded birds

Date	Mintage	F	VF	XF	Unc	BU
2009 Proof	4,000	Value: 60.00				

KM# 197 20 ROUBLES
28.2800 g., 0.9250 Silver 0.8410 oz. ASW, 40x28 mm. **Subject:** Llya Repin **Rev:** Bust and house, artist's palet in corner **Shape:** Rectangle

Date	Mintage	F	VF	XF	Unc	BU
2009 Proof	1,500	Value: 60.00				

KM# 198 20 ROUBLES
28.2800 g., 0.9250 Silver 0.8410 oz. ASW, 38.61 mm. **Subject:** Spasy **Rev:** Bee honey comb, apple tree, grain **Edge:** Reeded

Date	Mintage	F	VF	XF	Unc	BU
2009 Antique finish	5,000	—	—	—	—	80.00

KM# 199 20 ROUBLES
33.6300 g., 0.9990 Silver 1.0801 oz. ASW, 38.61 mm. **Subject:** Christening **Rev:** Child in christening gown

Date	Mintage	F	VF	XF	Unc	BU
2009 Proof	5,000	Value: 80.00				

KM# 200 20 ROUBLES
28.2800 g., 0.9250 Silver 0.8410 oz. ASW, 38.61 mm. **Subject:** Dar Pomorza **Rev:** Sail training vessel

Date	Mintage	F	VF	XF	Unc	BU
2009 Proof	25,000	Value: 60.00				

KM# 201 20 ROUBLES
33.6300 g., 0.9250 Silver 1.0000 oz. ASW, 38.61 mm. **Subject:** White stork **Rev:** Bird and nest

Date	Mintage	F	VF	XF	Unc	BU
2009 Proof	7,000	Value: 70.00				

KM# 202 20 ROUBLES
33.6300 g., 0.9250 Silver 1.0000 oz. ASW, 38.61 mm. **Subject:** Belavezhskaya Pushcha **Rev:** Range animals

Date	Mintage	F	VF	XF	Unc	BU
2009 Proof	8,000	Value: 60.00				

KM# 203 20 ROUBLES
28.2800 g., 0.9250 Silver 0.8410 oz. ASW, 38.61 mm. **Series:** Zodiac - Pisces **Rev:** Two fish

Date	Mintage	F	VF	XF	Unc	BU
2009 Matte Proof	25,000	Value: 55.00				

KM# 204 20 ROUBLES
28.2800 g., 0.9250 Silver 0.8410 oz. ASW, 38.61 mm. **Subject:** Zodiac - Aries **Rev:** Ram

Date	Mintage	F	VF	XF	Unc	BU
2009 Matte Proof	25,000	Value: 55.00				

KM# 205 20 ROUBLES
28.2800 g., 0.9250 Silver 0.8410 oz. ASW, 38.61 mm. **Subject:** Zodiac - Taurus **Rev:** Bull

Date	Mintage	F	VF	XF	Unc	BU
2009 Matte Proof	25,000	Value: 55.00				

KM# 206 20 ROUBLES
28.2800 g., 0.9250 Silver 0.8410 oz. ASW, 38.61 mm. **Subject:** Zodiac - Gemini **Rev:** Twins

Date	Mintage	F	VF	XF	Unc	BU
2009 Matte Proof	25,000	Value: 55.00				

KM# 207 20 ROUBLES
28.2800 g., 0.9250 Silver 0.8410 oz. ASW, 38.61 mm. **Subject:** Zodiac - Cancer **Rev:** Crab

Date	Mintage	F	VF	XF	Unc	BU
2009 Matte Proof	25,000	Value: 55.00				

KM# 208 20 ROUBLES
28.2800 g., 0.9250 Silver 0.8410 oz. ASW, 38.61 mm. **Subject:** Zodiac - Leo **Rev:** Lion

Date	Mintage	F	VF	XF	Unc	BU
2009 Matte Proof	25,000	Value: 55.00				

KM# 209 20 ROUBLES
28.2800 g., 0.9250 Silver 0.8410 oz. ASW, 38.61 mm. **Subject:** Zodiac - Virgo **Rev:** Little girl

Date	Mintage	F	VF	XF	Unc	BU
2009 Matte Proof	25,000	Value: 55.00				

KM# 210 20 ROUBLES
28.2800 g., 0.9250 Silver 0.8410 oz. ASW, 38.61 mm. **Subject:** Zodiac - Libra **Rev:** Balance scales

Date	Mintage	F	VF	XF	Unc	BU
2009 Matte Proof	25,000	Value: 55.00				

KM# 211 20 ROUBLES
28.2800 g., 0.9250 Silver 0.8410 oz. ASW, 38.61 mm. **Rev:** Scorpion

Date	Mintage	F	VF	XF	Unc	BU
2009 Matte Proof	25,000	Value: 55.00				

KM# 242 20 ROUBLES
28.2800 g., 0.9250 Silver 0.8410 oz. ASW, 38.61 mm. **Subject:** 3 Musketeers **Rev:** D'Artagnan, with red stone insert

Date	Mintage	F	VF	XF	Unc	BU
2009	5,000	—	—	—	—	75.00
2009 Proof	10,000	Value: 85.00				

KM# 243 20 ROUBLES
28.2800 g., 0.9250 Silver 0.8410 oz. ASW, 38.61 mm. **Subject:** The Three Musketeers **Rev:** Aramis, light blue stone insert

Date	Mintage	F	VF	XF	Unc	BU
2009	5,000	—	—	—	—	75.00
2009 Proof	10,000	Value: 85.00				

KM# 244 20 ROUBLES
28.2800 g., 0.9250 Silver 0.8410 oz. ASW, 38.61 mm. **Subject:** The Three Musketeers **Rev:** Athos, blue stone insert

Date	Mintage	F	VF	XF	Unc	BU
2009	10,000	—	—	—	—	75.00
2009 Proof	5,000	Value: 85.00				

KM# 245 20 ROUBLES
28.2800 g., 0.9250 Silver 0.8410 oz. ASW, 38.61 mm. **Subject:** The Three Musketeers **Rev:** Porthos, red stone insert

Date	Mintage	F	VF	XF	Unc	BU
2009	5,000	—	—	—	—	75.00
2009 Proof	10,000	Value: 85.00				

KM# 254 20 ROUBLES
28.2800 g., 0.9250 Silver 0.8410 oz. ASW, 45.3x35.3 mm. **Subject:** Pushkin's stories **Rev:** Tale of Tsar Saltan **Shape:** Vertical oval

Date	Mintage	F	VF	XF	Unc	BU
2009 Proof	7,000	Value: 85.00				

KM# 361 20 ROUBLES
28.2800 g., 0.9250 Silver 0.8410 oz. ASW, 38.61 mm. **Subject:** Zodiac - Sagittarius **Obv:** Sun and moon **Rev:** Girl with bow and arrow

Date	Mintage	F	VF	XF	Unc	BU
2009 Matte Proof	25,000	Value: 55.00				

KM# 362 20 ROUBLES
28.2800 g., 0.9250 Silver 0.8410 oz. ASW, 38.61 mm. **Subject:** Zodiac - Capricorn **Obv:** Sun and moon **Rev:** Capricorn

Date	Mintage	F	VF	XF	Unc	BU
2009 Matte Proof	25,000	Value: 55.00				

KM# 363 20 ROUBLES
33.6200 g., 0.9250 Silver 0.9998 oz. ASW, 38.61 mm. **Subject:** Straw Plaiting **Obv:** National arms within floral wreath **Rev:** Straw horse figure **Edge:** Reeded

Date	Mintage	F	VF	XF	Unc	BU
2009 Proof	5,000	Value: 75.00				

KM# 364 20 ROUBLES

28.2800 g., 0.9250 Silver 0.8410 oz. ASW, 38.61 mm. **Subject:** Nutcracker **Obv:** Boy and girl on crescent moon **Rev:** scenes from the Nutcracker ballet

Date	Mintage	F	VF	XF	Unc	BU
2009 Antique patina	25,000	—	—	—	—	75.00

KM# 365 20 ROUBLES

28.2800 g., 0.9250 Silver 0.8410 oz. ASW, 38.61 mm. **Subject:** Zodiac - Aquarius **Obv:** Sun and moon **Rev:** Boy in bathtub

Date	Mintage	F	VF	XF	Unc	BU
2009 Matte Proof	25,000	Value: 55.00				

KM# 366 20 ROUBLES

33.6300 g., 0.9250 Silver 1.0000 oz. ASW, 38.61 mm. **Subject:** Legend of the skylark **Obv:** Five stylized birds in flight **Rev:** Stylized bird, head left

Date	Mintage	F	VF	XF	Unc	BU
2009 Prooflike	5,000	Value: 75.00				

KM# 367 20 ROUBLES

33.6300 g., 0.9250 Silver 1.0000 oz. ASW, 38.61 mm. **Subject:** Pakatigaroshak - Tale of the Dragon **Obv:** Geometric pattern and EURASAC logo **Rev:** Man clubbing dragon

Date	Mintage	F	VF	XF	Unc	BU
2009 Proof	3,000	Value: 75.00				

KM# 368 20 ROUBLES

31.1000 g., 0.9990 Silver 0.9988 oz. ASW, 38.61 mm. **Obv:** National arms **Rev:** Squirrel right eating nut **Edge:** Reeded

Date	Mintage	F	VF	XF	Unc	BU
2009 Proof	5,000	Value: 150				

KM# 369 20 ROUBLES

31.1000 g., 0.9990 Silver 0.9988 oz. ASW, 38.61 mm. **Obv:** National arms **Rev:** Two squirrels on a branch, crystals in eyes **Edge:** Reeded

Date	Mintage	F	VF	XF	Unc	BU
2009 Proof	5,000	Value: 150				

KM# 370 20 ROUBLES

31.1000 g., 0.9250 Silver 0.9249 oz. ASW, 40 mm. **Subject:** London Olympics, 2012 **Obv:** Logo and National arms **Rev:** Two stylized players and Tower Bridge

Date	Mintage	F	VF	XF	Unc	BU
2009 Proof	6,000	Value: 75.00				

KM# 279 20 ROUBLES

31.1000 g., 0.9990 Silver 0.9988 oz. ASW, 38.61 mm. **Obv:** National arms **Rev:** Two eagle owls, crystals in eyes

Date	Mintage	F	VF	XF	Unc	BU
2010 Proof	5,000	Value: 100				

KM# 258 20 ROUBLES

33.6200 g., 0.9250 Silver 0.9998 oz. ASW, 38.61 mm. **Subject:** Expo 2010 **Obv:** Folk pattern **Rev:** Exposition buildings of the past

Date	Mintage	F	VF	XF	Unc	BU
2010 Proof	5,000	Value: 100				

KM# 224 20 ROUBLES

33.6300 g., 0.9250 Silver 1.0000 oz. ASW, 38.61 mm. **Subject:** EURASEC, 10th Anniversary **Obv:** Folk embroidery pattern **Rev:** Six flags around multicolor globe

Date	Mintage	F	VF	XF	Unc	BU
2010 Proof	3,000	Value: 60.00				

KM# 225 20 ROUBLES

33.6300 g., 0.9250 Silver 1.0000 oz. ASW, 38.6 mm. **Subject:** Syarednïaya Pripyat Reserve **Obv:** Eight ferns forming double cross **Rev:** Marsh turtle

Date	Mintage	F	VF	XF	Unc	BU
2010 Proof	3,000	Value: 70.00				

KM# 235 20 ROUBLES

28.2800 g., 0.9250 Silver 0.8410 oz. ASW, 38.61 mm. **Rev:** U.S. Frigate Constitution

Date	Mintage	F	VF	XF	Unc	BU
2010 Proof	7,000	Value: 75.00				

KM# 237 20 ROUBLES

33.6200 g., 0.9250 Silver 0.9998 oz. ASW, 38.61 mm. **Subject:** Legend of the tortoise

Date	Mintage	F	VF	XF	Unc	BU
2010 Proof	3,000	Value: 60.00				

KM# 239 20 ROUBLES

28.2800 g., 0.9250 Silver 0.8410 oz. ASW, 38.6 mm. **Subject:** Battle of Grunwald **Obv:** Figure with outstretched arms **Rev:** Legend within Fingerprint

Date	Mintage	F	VF	XF	Unc	BU
2010 Proof	2,500	Value: 60.00				

KM# 241 20 ROUBLES

33.6300 g., 0.9250 Silver 1.0000 oz. ASW, 38.61 mm. **Subject:** Age of Majority **Rev:** Multicolor flowers within folk patterns

Date	Mintage	F	VF	XF	Unc	BU
2010 Proof	—	Value: 60.00				

KM# 246 20 ROUBLES

28.2800 g., 0.9250 Silver 0.8410 oz. ASW, 38.61 mm. **Subject:** Orthodox Churches **Rev:** Cathedral of the Assumption

Date	Mintage	F	VF	XF	Unc	BU
2010 Proof	3,000	Value: 75.00				

KM# 247 20 ROUBLES
28.2800 g., 0.9250 Silver 0.8410 oz. ASW, 38.61 mm. **Subject:** Orthodox Churches **Rev:** Cathedral of SS Peter and Paul

Date	Mintage	F	VF	XF	Unc	BU
2010 Proof	3,000	Value: 75.00				

KM# 248 20 ROUBLES
28.2800 g., 0.9250 Silver 0.8410 oz. ASW, 38.61 mm. **Subject:** Orthodox Churches **Rev:** Cathedral of Alexander Nevsky

Date	Mintage	F	VF	XF	Unc	BU
2010 Proof	3,000	Value: 75.00				

KM# 249 20 ROUBLES
28.2800 g., 0.9250 Silver 0.8410 oz. ASW, 38.61 mm. **Subject:** Orthodox Churches **Rev:** Cathedral of St. Nicholas

Date	Mintage	F	VF	XF	Unc	BU
2010 Proof	3,000	Value: 75.00				

KM# 250 20 ROUBLES
28.2800 g., 0.9250 Silver 0.8410 oz. ASW, 45.3x35.3 mm. **Subject:** Pushkin's stories **Rev:** Tale of the Golden Cockerel in multicolor **Shape:** Vertical oval

Date	Mintage	F	VF	XF	Unc	BU
2010 Proof	7,000	Value: 85.00				

KM# 251 20 ROUBLES
28.2800 g., 0.9250 Silver 0.8410 oz. ASW, 45.3x35.3 mm. **Subject:** Pushkin's stories **Rev:** Tale of the fisherman and the fish **Shape:** Vertical oval

Date	Mintage	F	VF	XF	Unc	BU
2010 Proof	7,000	Value: 85.00				

KM# 252 20 ROUBLES
28.2800 g., 0.9250 Silver 0.8410 oz. ASW, 45.3x35.3 mm. **Subject:** Pushkin's stories **Rev:** Tale of one Dead Princess and Seven Knights **Shape:** Vertical oval

Date	Mintage	F	VF	XF	Unc	BU
2010 Proof	7,000	Value: 85.00				

KM# 253 20 ROUBLES
28.2800 g., 0.9250 Silver 0.8410 oz. ASW, 45.3x35.3 mm. **Subject:** Pushkin's stories **Rev:** Ruslan and Ludmila **Shape:** Vertical oval

Date	Mintage	F	VF	XF	Unc	BU
2010 Proof	7,000	Value: 85.00				

KM# 256 20 ROUBLES
31.1000 g., 0.9990 Silver 0.9988 oz. ASW, 38.61 mm. **Subject:** Slavic Woman **Rev:** Madonna and child

Date	Mintage	F	VF	XF	Unc	BU
2010 Proof	7,000	—	—	—	—	75.00

KM# 257 20 ROUBLES
28.2800 g., 0.9250 Silver 0.8410 oz. ASW, 28x40 mm. **Subject:** Ivan Khrutsky **Obv:** Color painting of female with fruit basket, arms at lower left **Rev:** Half-length figure of Khrutsky, flowers in vase on table **Shape:** Vertical rectangle

Date	Mintage	F	VF	XF	Unc	BU
2010	4,000	—	—	—	—	75.00

KM# 261 20 ROUBLES
33.6300 g., 0.9250 Silver 1.0000 oz. ASW, 38.61 mm. **Subject:** End of World War II, 65th Anniversary **Rev:** Five doves in flight, kiting

Date	Mintage	F	VF	XF	Unc	BU
2010 Proof	2,000	Value: 75.00				

KM# 266 20 ROUBLES
28.2800 g., 0.9250 Silver 0.8410 oz. ASW, 30x45 mm. **Subject:** Icon of the Most Holy Theotokos of Minsk **Rev:** Madonna icon, partially gilt **Shape:** Vertical rectangle

Date	Mintage	F	VF	XF	Unc	BU
2010 Proof	7,000	Value: 200				

KM# 267 20 ROUBLES
28.2800 g., 0.9250 Silver 0.8410 oz. ASW, 30x45 mm. **Subject:** Icon of the Mold Holy Theotokos of Smolensk **Rev:** Madonna Icon, partially gilt **Shape:** Vertical rectangle

Date	Mintage	F	VF	XF	Unc	BU
2010 Prooflike	7,000	—	—	—	—	150

KM# 268 20 ROUBLES
28.2800 g., 0.9250 Silver 0.8410 oz. ASW, 28x40 mm. **Rev:** Nefertiti bust **Shape:** Vertical rectangle

Date	Mintage	F	VF	XF	Unc	BU
2010 Proof	7,000	Value: 100				

KM# 269 20 ROUBLES
28.2800 g., 0.9250 Silver 0.8410 oz. ASW, 28x40 mm. **Rev:** Cupid & Psyche **Shape:** Vertical rectangle

Date	Mintage	F	VF	XF	Unc	BU
2010 Proof	7,000	Value: 100				

KM# 271 20 ROUBLES
28.2800 g., 0.9250 Silver 0.8410 oz. ASW, 38.6 mm. **Obv:** Compass rose and chart **Rev:** Cutty Sark sailing right

Date	Mintage	F	VF	XF	Unc	BU
2010 Proof	—	Value: 55.00				

KM# 272 20 ROUBLES
28.2800 g., 0.9250 Silver 0.8410 oz. ASW, 38.61 mm. **Obv:** Compass rose and chart **Rev:** Amerigo Vespucci sailing left

Date	Mintage	F	VF	XF	Unc	BU
2010 Proof	—	Value: 75.00				

KM# 278 20 ROUBLES
7.7800 g., 0.9990 Gold 0.2499 oz. AGW, 22 mm. **Subject:** Slavic Women **Obv:** Large lis, national arms at top **Rev:** Madonna and Child

Date	Mintage	F	VF	XF	Unc	BU
2010 Proof	Est. 2,500	Value: 475				

KM# 371 20 ROUBLES
28.2800 g., 0.9250 Silver 0.8410 oz. ASW, 38.61 mm. **Obv:** Heart with butterflies within **Rev:** Heart with vine and crystal

Date	Mintage	F	VF	XF	Unc	BU
2010 Proof	10,000	Value: 125				

KM# 372 20 ROUBLES
5.7600 g., 0.9000 Gold 0.1667 oz. AGW, 19.8 mm. **Subject:** Battle of Grunwald, 600th Anniversary **Obv:** Standard head **Rev:** pellet cross within standard head

Date	Mintage	F	VF	XF	Unc	BU
2010 Proof	500	Value: 400				

KM# 373 20 ROUBLES
28.2800 g., 0.9250 Silver 0.8410 oz. ASW, 28x40 mm. **Subject:** Rodin **Obv:** Portrait facing **Rev:** The Thinker statue

Date	Mintage	F	VF	XF	Unc	BU
2010 Proof	7,000	Value: 125				

KM# 374 20 ROUBLES
28.2800 g., 0.9250 Silver 0.8410 oz. ASW, 28x40 mm. **Subject:** Bernini **Obv:** Portrait facing **Rev:** Ecstasy of St. Theresa

Date	Mintage	F	VF	XF	Unc	BU
2010 Proof	7,000	Value: 125				

KM# 375 20 ROUBLES
31.1000 g., 0.9990 Silver 0.9988 oz. ASW, 38.61 mm. **Obv:** National arms **Rev:** Owl head facing, crystal eyes

Date	Mintage	F	VF	XF	Unc	BU
2010 Proof	5,000	Value: 125				

KM# 376 20 ROUBLES
33.6300 g., 0.9250 Silver 1.0000 oz. ASW, 38.61 mm. **Subject:** Blacksmithing **Obv:** National arms within floral wreath **Rev:** Horseshoe and village church

Date	Mintage	F	VF	XF	Unc	BU
2010 Proof	3,000	Value: 100				

KM# 377 20 ROUBLES
33.6300 g., 0.9250 Silver 1.0000 oz. ASW, 38.61 mm. **Subject:** Candlemas **Obv:** Embroidery pattern **Rev:** Bird rising out of the snow to a flowered field and sunrise **Edge:** Reeded

Date	Mintage	F	VF	XF	Unc	BU
2010 Proof	2,500	Value: 150				

KM# 378 20 ROUBLES
33.6300 g., 0.9250 Silver 1.0000 oz. ASW, 38.61 mm. **Subject:** Lew Sapieha **Obv:** Ancient document **Rev:** Figure standing

Date	Mintage	F	VF	XF	Unc	BU
2010 Proof	3,000	Value: 125				

KM# 255 20 ROUBLES
28.2800 g., 0.9250 Silver 0.8410 oz. ASW, 38.61 mm. **Subject:** My Love **Rev:** Two cats, red heart shaped crystal insert at top

Date	Mintage	F	VF	XF	Unc	BU
2011 Proof	15,000	Value: 100				

KM# 280 20 ROUBLES
28.2800 g., 0.9250 Silver 0.8410 oz. ASW, 38.61 mm. **Subject:** Krusenstern **Obv:** Compass rose and charts, national arms at top **Rev:** Fully-rigged sailing ship left

Date	Mintage	F	VF	XF	Unc	BU
2011 Proof	7,000	Value: 100				

KM# 281 20 ROUBLES
33.6300 g., 0.9250 Silver 1.0000 oz. ASW, 38.61 mm. **Subject:** Motherhood **Obv:** Folk embroidery pattern **Rev:** Mother holding baby, bird

Date	Mintage	F	VF	XF	Unc	BU
2011 Proof	10,000	Value: 90.00				

KM# 281a 20 ROUBLES
33.6300 g., 0.9250 Silver partially gilt 1.0000 oz. ASW, 38.61 mm. **Obv:** Folk embroidery pattern **Rev:** Mother and child, gilt bird

Date	Mintage	F	VF	XF	Unc	BU
2011 Proof	—	Value: 90.00				

KM# 282 20 ROUBLES
31.1000 g., 0.9250 Silver 0.9249 oz. ASW, 30x45 mm. **Subject:** Madonna icon **Obv:** Cross at center of design **Rev:** Icon image, ornate frame

Date	Mintage	F	VF	XF	Unc	BU
2011 Proof	10,000	Value: 250				

KM# 283 20 ROUBLES
31.1000 g., 0.9250 Silver 0.9249 oz. ASW, 30x45 mm. **Subject:** Madonna icon **Obv:** Cross within design **Rev:** Madonna icon, angellic corners

Date	Mintage	F	VF	XF	Unc	BU
2011 Proof	10,000	Value: 250				

KM# 289 20 ROUBLES
28.2800 g., 0.9250 Silver 0.8410 oz. ASW **Subject:** Paleolithic Venus **Obv:** Cave drawing of steer **Rev:** Carved statue of pregnant female **Shape:** Vertical rectangle

Date	Mintage	F	VF	XF	Unc	BU
2011 Proof	Est. 3,500	Value: 90.00				

KM# 290 20 ROUBLES
28.2800 g., 0.9250 Silver 0.8410 oz. ASW **Subject:** Voltaire **Obv:** Carved portrait bust **Rev:** Statue of seated Voltaire **Shape:** Vertical rectangle

Date	Mintage	F	VF	XF	Unc	BU
2011 Proof	Est. 3,500	Value: 90.00				

KM# 379 20 ROUBLES
28.2800 g., 0.9250 Silver 0.8410 oz. ASW, 38.61 mm. **Subject:** Polotsk **Obv:** Map, ship and national arms **Rev:** Shield and city view

Date	Mintage	F	VF	XF	Unc	BU
2011 Proof	7,000	Value: 110				

KM# 380 20 ROUBLES
28.2800 g., 0.9250 Silver 0.8410 oz. ASW, 38.61 mm. **Subject:** Arabic Dance

Date	Mintage	F	VF	XF	Unc	BU
2011 Proof	6,000	Value: 110				

KM# 381 20 ROUBLES
31.1000 g., 0.9990 Silver 0.9988 oz. ASW, 38.61 mm. **Subject:** Hedgehog **Obv:** National arms **Rev:** Hedgehog left, crystal eye

Date	Mintage	F	VF	XF	Unc	BU
2011 Proof	4,000	Value: 125				

KM# 382 20 ROUBLES
31.1000 g., 0.9990 Silver 0.9988 oz. ASW, 38.61 mm. **Subject:** Hedgehog **Obv:** National arms **Rev:** Hedgehog facing, crystal eyes

Date	Mintage	F	VF	XF	Unc	BU
2011 Proof	4,000	Value: 125				

KM# 383 20 ROUBLES
31.1000 g., 0.9250 Silver 0.9249 oz. ASW, 45x30 mm. **Subject:** Akhal-Teke Horses **Obv:** Two horses galloping thru low water right **Rev:** Ancient two-horse carriage, horse walking right **Shape:** Rectangle

Date	Mintage	F	VF	XF	Unc	BU
2011 Proof	6,000	Value: 125				

KM# 416 20 ROUBLES
Silver **Subject:** Icon - Vladmir Madonna

Date	Mintage	F	VF	XF	Unc	BU
2012 Proof	—	Value: 100				

KM# 418 20 ROUBLES
0.9250 Silver **Subject:** Reconstruction of Izyaslavl fortress **Rev:** Regvolod of Polotsk **Edge Lettering:** 38.61 **Designer:** S. Zackevich

Date	Mintage	F	VF	XF	Unc	BU
2012 Proof	5,000	Value: 100				

KM# 121 50 ROUBLES
4.4500 g., 0.9990 Gold 0.1429 oz. AGW, 25 mm. **Subject:** Fox **Obv:** National arms **Rev:** Red fox with inset diamond eyes

Date	Mintage	F	VF	XF	Unc	BU
2002	Est. 2,000	—	—	—	1,000	—

KM# 126 50 ROUBLES
62.2000 g., 0.9250 Silver 1.8497 oz. ASW, 50 mm. **Subject:** 60th Anniversary of Victory **Obv:** Order of the Victory, multicolored **Rev:** Stars and arrows

Date	Mintage	F	VF	XF	Unc	BU
2005	2,000	—	—	—	—	—
2005 Proof	—	Value: 220				

KM# 142 50 ROUBLES
7.7800 g., 0.9990 Gold 0.2499 oz. AGW, 25 mm. **Subject:** Peregrine Falcon **Obv:** National arms **Rev:** Peregrine falcon with inset diamond eye

Date	Mintage	F	VF	XF	Unc	BU
2006	2,000	—	—	750	1,000	—

KM# 143 50 ROUBLES
8.0000 g., 0.9000 Gold 0.2315 oz. AGW, 21 mm. **Subject:** Bison **Obv:** National arms **Rev:** European bison **Designer:** S.P. Zaskevich

Date	Mintage	F	VF	XF	Unc	BU
2006	3,000	Value: 800				

KM# 144 50 ROUBLES
8.0000 g., 0.9000 Gold 0.2315 oz. AGW, 21 mm. **Subject:** Beaver **Obv:** National arms **Rev:** Family of Eurasian beavers **Designer:** S.P. Zaskovich

Date	Mintage	F	VF	XF	Unc	BU
2006 Proof	3,000	Value: 800				

KM# 145 50 ROUBLES
8.0000 g., 0.9000 Gold 0.2315 oz. AGW, 21 mm. **Subject:** Mute Swan **Obv:** National arms **Rev:** Pair of mute swans **Designer:** S.P. Zaskevich

Date	Mintage	F	VF	XF	Unc	BU
2006	3,000	Value: 800				

KM# 123 50 ROUBLES
8.0000 g., 0.9000 Gold 0.2315 oz. AGW, 21 mm. **Subject:** Herring Gull **Obv:** National arms **Rev:** Herring gull in flight **Designer:** S.P. Zaskevitch

Date	Mintage	F	VF	XF	Unc	BU
2006	3,000	Value: 800				

KM# 125 50 ROUBLES
8.0000 g., 0.9000 Gold 0.2315 oz. AGW, 21 mm. **Obv:** National arms **Rev:** Pair of common cranes **Designer:** S.P. Zaskevich

Date	Mintage	F	VF	XF	Unc	BU
2006	3,000	Value: 800				

KM# 384 50 ROUBLES
7.7800 g., 0.9990 Gold 0.2499 oz. AGW, 25 mm. **Obv:** National arms **Rev:** Wolf head facing

Date	Mintage	F	VF	XF	Unc	BU
2007 Proof	2,000	Value: 900				

KM# 385 50 ROUBLES
8.0000 g., 0.9000 Gold 0.2315 oz. AGW, 21 mm. **Obv:** Church within frame **Rev:** Female saint icon

Date	Mintage	F	VF	XF	Unc	BU
2008	14,000	—	—	—	—	700
2008 Proof	1,000	Value: 800				

KM# 386 50 ROUBLES
8.0000 g., 0.9000 Gold 0.2315 oz. AGW, 21 mm. **Obv:** Church within frame **Rev:** Saint Sarowski icon

Date	Mintage	F	VF	XF	Unc	BU
2008	14,000	—	—	—	—	700
2008 Proof	1,000	Value: 800				

KM# 387 50 ROUBLES
8.0000 g., 0.9000 Gold 0.2315 oz. AGW, 21 mm. **Obv:** Church within frame **Rev:** Saint Sergey Radonezski icon

Date	Mintage	F	VF	XF	Unc	BU
2008	14,000	—	—	—	—	700
2008 Proof	1,000	Value: 800				

KM# 388 50 ROUBLES
8.0000 g., 0.9000 Gold 0.2315 oz. AGW, 21 mm. **Obv:** Church within frame **Rev:** Saint Mikplaj the miracle worker icon

Date	Mintage	F	VF	XF	Unc	BU
2008	14,000	—	—	—	—	700
2008 Proof	1,000	Value: 800				

KM# 389 50 ROUBLES
8.0000 g., 0.9000 Gold 0.2315 oz. AGW, 21 mm. **Obv:** Church within frame **Rev:** Saint Pantaleon icon

Date	Mintage	F	VF	XF	Unc	BU
2008	14,000	—	—	—	—	700
2008 Proof	1,000	Value: 800				

KM# 390 50 ROUBLES
7.7800 g., 0.9990 Silver 0.2499 oz. ASW, 25 mm. **Obv:** National arms **Rev:** Lunx head facing

Date	Mintage	F	VF	XF	Unc	BU
2008 Proof	2,000	Value: 850				

KM# 391 50 ROUBLES
7.7800 g., 0.9990 Gold 0.2499 oz. AGW, 25 mm. **Obv:** National arms **Rev:** Squirrel right eating nut

Date	Mintage	F	VF	XF	Unc	BU
2009 Proof	2,000	Value: 900				

KM# 394 50 ROUBLES
155.5000 g., 0.9990 Silver 4.9942 oz. ASW, 65 mm. **Subject:** London Olympics, 2012 **Obv:** National arms and logo **Rev:** Two stylized players and Tower Bridge

Date	Mintage	F	VF	XF	Unc	BU
2009 Prooflike	800	—	—	—	—	250

KM# 277 50 ROUBLES
7.7800 g., 0.9990 Gold 0.2499 oz. AGW, 25 mm. **Obv:** National arms **Rev:** Owl head facing

Date	Mintage	F	VF	XF	Unc	BU
2010 Proof	Est. 2,000	Value: 900				

KM# 392 50 ROUBLES
8.6400 g., 0.9000 Gold 0.2500 oz. AGW, 22 mm. **Subject:** Battle of Grunwald, 600th Anniversary **Obv:** Stylized figure in shape of cross **Rev:** Stylized fingerprint

Date	Mintage	F	VF	XF	Unc	BU
2010 Proof	500	Value: 800				

KM# 393 50 ROUBLES
7.7800 g., 0.9990 Gold 0.2499 oz. AGW, 22 mm. **Subject:** Motherhood **Obv:** Lis **Rev:** Mother and child

Date	Mintage	F	VF	XF	Unc	BU
2010 Proof	2,500	Value: 800				

KM# 286 50 ROUBLES
7.7800 g., 0.9990 Gold 0.2499 oz. AGW, 25 mm. **Obv:** National arms **Rev:** Hedgehog

Date	Mintage	F	VF	XF	Unc	BU
2011 Proof	Est. 1,000	Value: 950				

KM# 58 100 ROUBLES
155.5000 g., 0.9250 Silver 4.6243 oz. ASW, 64 mm. **Obv:** Theater building **Rev:** Two ballet dancers **Edge:** Reeded **Designer:** S.P. Zaskevich **Note:** Illustration reduced.

Date	Mintage	F	VF	XF	Unc	BU
2003 Proof	1,000	Value: 750				

KM# 216 100 ROUBLES
17.2800 g., 0.9000 Gold 0.5000 oz. AGW, 32 mm. **Subject:** China - Belarus relations, 15th Anniversary **Obv:** National arms **Rev:** Two archways, forest in left, Great Wall on right **Edge:** Reeded

Date	Mintage	F	VF	XF	Unc	BU
2007 Proof	1,000	Value: 1,000				

KM# 192 100 ROUBLES
155.5000 g., 0.9990 Silver 4.9942 oz. ASW, 65 mm. **Subject:** Figure skating **Rev:** Pair of skates and snowflakes **Note:** Illustration reduced.

Date	Mintage	F	VF	XF	Unc	BU
2008 Proof	500	Value: 450				

KM# 193 100 ROUBLES
155.5000 g., 0.9990 Silver 4.9942 oz. ASW, 65 mm. **Subject:** White Stork Legend **Rev:** Stylized stork

Date	Mintage	F	VF	XF	Unc	BU
2008 Proof	500	Value: 450				

KM# 395 100 ROUBLES
15.5000 g., 0.9000 Gold 0.4485 oz. AGW, 30 mm. **Subject:** Zodiac - Pisces **Obv:** Sun and moon **Rev:** Two fish

Date	Mintage	F	VF	XF	Unc	BU
2011 Proof	2,000	Value: 1,200				

KM# 396 100 ROUBLES
15.5000 g., 0.9000 Gold 0.4485 oz. AGW, 30 mm. **Subject:** Zodiac - Ram **Obv:** Sun and moon **Rev:** Ram

Date	Mintage	F	VF	XF	Unc	BU
2011 Proof	2,000	Value: 1,200				

KM# 397 100 ROUBLES
15.5000 g., 0.9000 Gold 0.4485 oz. AGW, 30 mm. **Subject:** Zodiac - Taurus **Obv:** Sun and moon **Rev:** Bull

Date	Mintage	F	VF	XF	Unc	BU
2011 Proof	2,000	Value: 1,200				

KM# 398 100 ROUBLES
15.5000 g., 0.9000 Gold 0.4485 oz. AGW, 30 mm. **Subject:** Zodiac - Gemni **Obv:** Sun and moon **Rev:** Twins

Date	Mintage	F	VF	XF	Unc	BU
2011 Proof	2,000	Value: 1,200				

KM# 399 100 ROUBLES
15.5000 g., 0.9000 Gold 0.4485 oz. AGW, 30 mm. **Subject:** Zodiac - Cancer **Obv:** Sun and moon **Rev:** Crab

Date	Mintage	F	VF	XF	Unc	BU
2011 Proof	2,000	Value: 1,200				

KM# 400 100 ROUBLES
15.5000 g., 0.9000 Gold 0.4485 oz. AGW, 30 mm. **Subject:** Zodiac - Leo **Obv:** Sun and moon **Rev:** Lion standing left

Date	Mintage	F	VF	XF	Unc	BU
2011 Proof	2,000	Value: 1,200				

KM# 401 100 ROUBLES
15.5000 g., 0.9000 Gold 0.4485 oz. AGW, 30 mm. **Subject:** Zodiac - Virgo **Obv:** Sun and moon **Rev:** Girl

Date	Mintage	F	VF	XF	Unc	BU
2011 Proof	2,000	Value: 1,200				

KM# 402 100 ROUBLES
15.5000 g., 0.9000 Gold 0.4485 oz. AGW, 30 mm. **Subject:** Zodiac - Libra **Obv:** Sun and moon **Rev:** Balance scales

Date	Mintage	F	VF	XF	Unc	BU
2011 Proof	2,000	Value: 1,200				

KM# 403 100 ROUBLES
15.5000 g., 0.9000 Gold 0.4485 oz. AGW, 30 mm. **Subject:** Zodiac - Scorpion **Obv:** Sun and moon **Rev:** Scorpion

Date	Mintage	F	VF	XF	Unc	BU
2011 Proof	2,000	Value: 1,200				

KM# 404 100 ROUBLES
15.5000 g., 0.9000 Gold 0.4485 oz. AGW, 30 mm. **Subject:** Zodiac - Virgo **Obv:** Sun and moon **Rev:** Girl as angel with bow and arrow

Date	Mintage	F	VF	XF	Unc	BU
2011 Proof	2,000	Value: 1,200				

KM# 405 100 ROUBLES
15.5000 g., 0.9000 Gold 0.4485 oz. AGW, 30 mm. **Subject:** Zodiac - Capricorn **Obv:** Sun and moon **Rev:** Ram standing left

Date	Mintage	F	VF	XF	Unc	BU
2011 Proof	2,000	Value: 1,200				

KM# 406 100 ROUBLES
15.5000 g., 0.9000 Gold 0.4485 oz. AGW, 30 mm. **Subject:** Zodiac - Aquarius **Obv:** Sun and moon **Rev:** Child in bathtub

Date	Mintage	F	VF	XF	Unc	BU
2011 Proof	2,000	Value: 1,200				

KM# 103 200 ROUBLES
31.1050 g., 0.9990 Gold 0.9990 oz. AGW, 40 mm. **Obv:** National arms **Rev:** Belarussian ballerina

Date	Mintage	F	VF	XF	Unc	BU
2005 Proof	1,500	Value: 2,000				

KM# 408 200 ROUBLES
34.5600 g., 0.9000 Gold 1.0000 oz. AGW, 38.61 mm. **Subject:** Ski center in Siliczy **Obv:** Skier **Rev:** Building complex

Date	Mintage	F	VF	XF	Unc	BU
2006 Proof	2,000	Value: 3,000				

KM# 409 200 ROUBLES
31.1000 g., 0.9990 Gold 0.9988 oz. AGW, 40 mm. **Subject:** Ballet **Obv:** National arms **Rev:** Ballet Pair

Date	Mintage	F	VF	XF	Unc	BU
2006 Proof	1,500	Value: 3,250				

KM# 407 200 ROUBLES
31.1000 g., 0.9990 Gold 0.9988 oz. AGW, 40 mm. **Subject:** Ballet **Obv:** National arms **Rev:** Ballerina on point right

Date	Mintage	F	VF	XF	Unc	BU
2007 Proof	1,500	Value: 3,000				

KM# 74 1000 ROUBLES
1000.0000 g., 0.9990 Silver 32.117 oz. ASW, 100 mm. **Subject:** 2004 Olympics **Obv:** National arms **Rev:** Ancient charioteer **Note:** Illustration reduced.

Date	Mintage	F	VF	XF	Unc	BU
2004 Proof	650	Value: 1,500				

KM# 410 1000 ROUBLES

155.5000 g., 0.9990 Gold 4.9942 oz. AGW, 65 mm. **Subject:** Ballet **Obv:** National arms **Rev:** Ballet pair

Date	Mintage	F	VF	XF	Unc	BU
2006 Proof	99	Value: 10,500				

KM# 412 1000 ROUBLES

1000.0000 g., 0.9990 Silver 32.117 oz. ASW, 100 mm. **Subject:** Beijing Olympics, 2008 **Obv:** Naitonal arms **Rev:** Classical runners around center circle

Date	Mintage	F	VF	XF	Unc	BU
2006 Proof	2,000	Value: 2,000				

KM# 170 1000 ROUBLES

1000.0000 g., 0.9990 Silver 32.117 oz. ASW, 100 mm. **Subject:** Belarussian Ballet **Rev:** Ballerina and mirror image **Note:** Illustration reduced.

Date	Mintage	F	VF	XF	Unc	BU
2007 Proof	300	Value: 2,000				

KM# 171 1000 ROUBLES

1000.0000 g., 0.9990 Silver partially gilt 32.117 oz. ASW, 100 mm. **Subject:** Cross of St. Euphrosyne of Polotsk **Obv:** Church facade **Rev:** Gold-plated pectorial cross **Note:** Illustration reduced.

Date	Mintage	F	VF	XF	Unc	BU
2007 Proof-like	2,000	Value: 2,000				

KM# 411 1000 ROUBLES

155.5000 g., 0.9990 Gold 4.9942 oz. AGW, 65 mm. **Subject:** Ballet **Obv:** National arms **Rev:** Mirror image of ballerina

Date	Mintage	F	VF	XF	Unc	BU
2007 Proof	99	Value: 10,500				

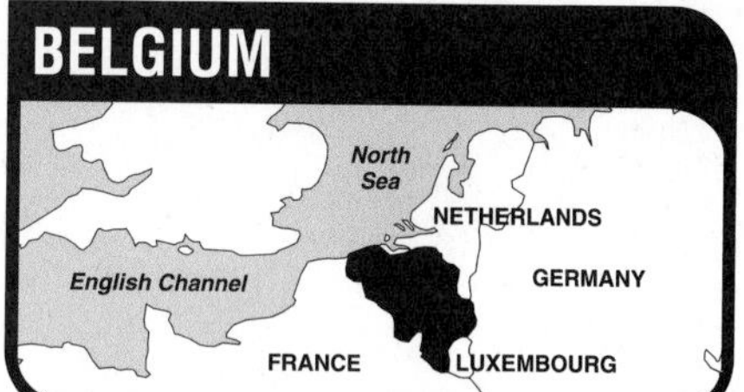

The Kingdom of Belgium, a constitutional monarchy in northwest Europe, has an area of 11,780 sq. mi. (30,519 sq. km.) and a population of 10.1 million, chiefly Dutch-speaking Flemish and French-speaking Walloons. Capital: Brussels. Agriculture, dairy farming, and the processing of raw materials for re-export are the principal industries. Beurs voor Diamant in Antwerp is the world's largest diamond trading center. Iron and steel, machinery motor vehicles, chemicals, textile yarns and fabrics comprise the principal exports.

RULER

Albert II, 1993-

MINT MARK

Angel head - Brussels

MINTMASTERS' INITIALS & PRIVY MARKS

Pair of scales – Romain Coenen (1987 -)
Goose feather – Serge Lesens (2010)

NOTE: Beginning in 1987, the letters "qp" (quality proof) appear on non-circulating coins

MONETARY SYSTEM

100 Centimes = 1 Franc
1 Euro = 100 Cents

LEGENDS

Belgian coins are usually inscribed either in Dutch, French or both. However some modern coins are being inscribed in Latin or German. The language used is best told by noting the spelling of the name of the country.

(Fr) French: BELGIQUE or BELGES
(Du) Dutch: BELGIE or BELGEN
(La) Latin: BELGICA
(Ge) German: BELGIEN

KINGDOM

DECIMAL COINAGE

KM# 148.1 50 CENTIMES

2.7000 g., Bronze, 19 mm. **Ruler:** Baudouin I **Obv:** Crowned denomination divides date, legend in French **Obv. Legend:** BELGIQUE **Rev:** Helmeted mine worker left, miner's lamp at right, large head, tip of neck 1/2 mm from rim **Edge:** Plain **Designer:** Rau

Date	Mintage	F	VF	XF	Unc	BU
2001 In sets only	60,000	—	—	—	2.00	—
2001 Proof	5,000	Value: 25.00				

Note: Medal alignment

KM# 149.1 50 CENTIMES

2.7500 g., Bronze, 19 mm. **Ruler:** Baudouin I **Obv:** Crowned denomination divides date, legend in Dutch **Obv. Legend:** BELGIE **Rev:** Helmeted mine worker left, miner's lamp at right, large head **Edge:** Plain **Designer:** Rau

Date	Mintage	F	VF	XF	Unc	BU
2001 In sets only	60,000	—	—	—	3.00	—
2001 Proof	5,000	Value: 25.00				
Note: Medal alignment						
2007 In sets only	60,000	—	—	—	2.00	—

KM# 148.2 50 CENTIMES

2.7500 g., Bronze, 19 mm. **Ruler:** Baudouin I **Obv:** Crowned denomination divides date, legend in French **Obv. Legend:** BELGIQUE **Rev:** Helmeted mine worker left, miner's lamp at right, large head, tip of neck 1/2 mm from rim **Edge:** Plain **Designer:** Rau **Note:** Medal alignment.

Date	Mintage	F	VF	XF	Unc	BU
2001 Proof	—	Value: 30.00				

KM# 149.2 50 CENTIMES

2.7500 g., Bronze, 19 mm. **Ruler:** Baudouin I **Obv:** Crowned denomination divides date, legend in French **Obv. Legend:** BELGIQUE **Rev:** Helmeted mine worker left, miner's lamp at right, large head, tip of neck 1/2 mm from rim **Edge:** Plain **Designer:** Rau **Note:** Medal alignment.

Date	Mintage	F	VF	XF	Unc	BU
2001 Proof	—	Value: 30.00				

KM# 188 FRANC

2.7500 g., Nickel Plated Iron, 18 mm. **Ruler:** Albert II **Obv:** Head left, outline around back of head **Rev:** Vertical line divides date and large denomination, legend in Dutch **Rev. Legend:** BELGIE **Edge:** Plain

Date	Mintage	F	VF	XF	Unc	BU
2001 In sets only	60,000	—	—	—	3.00	—
2001 Proof	5,000	Value: 25.00				

Note: Medal alignment

KM# 187 FRANC

2.7500 g., Nickel Plated Iron, 18 mm. **Ruler:** Albert II **Obv:** Head left, outline around back of head **Rev:** Vertical line divides date and large denomination, legend in French **Rev. Legend:** BELGIQUE **Note:** Mint mark: angel head. Unknown mintmaster's privy mark: scales.

Date	Mintage	F	VF	XF	Unc	BU
2001 In sets only	60,000	—	—	—	3.00	—
2001 Proof	5,000	Value: 25.00				

Note: Medal alignment

KM# 189 5 FRANCS (5 Frank)

5.5000 g., Aluminum-Bronze, 24 mm. **Ruler:** Albert II **Obv:** Head left, outline around back of head **Rev:** Vertical line divides date and denomination, legend in French **Rev. Legend:** BELGIQUE **Note:** Mint mark: angel head. Mintmaster R. Coenen's privy mark: scale.

Date	Mintage	F	VF	XF	Unc	BU
2001 In sets only	60,000	—	—	—	4.00	—
2001 Proof	5,000	Value: 25.00				

Note: Medal alignment

KM# 190 5 FRANCS (5 Frank)

5.5000 g., Aluminum-Bronze, 24 mm. **Ruler:** Albert II **Obv:** Head left, outline around back of head **Rev:** Vertical line divides date and large denomination, legend in Dutch **Rev. Legend:** BELGIE **Note:** Mint mark: angel head. Mintmaster R. Coenen's privy mark: scale.

Date	Mintage	F	VF	XF	Unc	BU
2001 In sets only	60,000	—	—	—	4.00	—
2001 Proof	5,000	Value: 25.00				

Note: Medal alignment

KM# 191 20 FRANCS (20 Frank)

8.5000 g., Nickel-Bronze, 25.65 mm. **Ruler:** Albert II **Obv:** Head left, outline around back of head **Rev:** Vertical line divides date and large denomination, legend in French **Rev. Legend:** BELGIQUE **Note:** Mint mark: angel head. Mintmaster R. Coenen's privy mark: scale.

Date	Mintage	F	VF	XF	Unc	BU
2001 In sets only	60,000	—	—	—	4.00	—
2001 Proof	5,000	Value: 25.00				

Note: Medal alignment

KM# 192 20 FRANCS (20 Frank)

8.5000 g., Nickel-Bronze, 25.7 mm. **Ruler:** Albert II **Obv:** Head left, outline around back of head **Rev:** Vertical line divides date and large denomination, legend in Dutch **Rev. Legend:** BELGIE **Note:** Mint mark: angel head. Mintmaster R. Coenen's privy mark: scale.

Date	Mintage	F	VF	XF	Unc	BU
2001 In sets only	60,000	—	—	—	5.00	—
2001 Proof	5,000	Value: 25.00				

Note: Medal alignment

KM# 193 50 FRANCS (50 Frank)

7.0000 g., Nickel, 22.7 mm. **Ruler:** Albert II **Obv:** Head left, outline around back of head **Rev:** Vertical line divides large denomination and date, legend in French **Rev. Legend:** BELGIQUE **Note:** Mint mark: angel head. Mintmaster R. Coenen's privy mark: scale.

Date	Mintage	F	VF	XF	Unc	BU
2001 In sets only	60,000	—	—	—	8.00	—
2001 Proof	5,000	Value: 25.00				

Note: Medal alignment

KM# 194 50 FRANCS (50 Frank)

7.0000 g., Nickel, 22.75 mm. **Ruler:** Albert II **Obv:** Head left, outline around back of head **Rev:** Vertical line divides large denomination and date, legend in Dutch **Rev. Legend:** BELGIE **Note:** Mint mark: angel head. Mintmaster R. Coenen's privy mark: scale.

Date	Mintage	F	VF	XF	Unc	BU
2001 In sets only	60,000	—	—	—	8.00	—
2001 Proof	5,000	Value: 25.00				

Note: Medal alignment

KM# 222 500 FRANCS (500 Frank)

22.8500 g., 0.9250 Silver 0.6795 oz. ASW, 37 mm. **Ruler:** Albert II **Subject:** Europe: Europa and the Bull **Obv:** Map and denomination **Rev:** Europa sitting on a bull **Edge:** Plain

Date	Mintage	F	VF	XF	Unc	BU
2001 (qp) Proof	40,000	Value: 50.00				

KM# 223 5000 FRANCS

15.5500 g., 0.9990 Gold 0.4994 oz. AGW, 29 mm. **Ruler:** Albert II **Subject:** Europe: Europa and the Bull **Obv:** Map and denomination **Rev:** Europa sitting on a bull **Edge:** Plain

Date	Mintage	F	VF	XF	Unc	BU
2001 (qp) Proof	2,000	Value: 875				

EURO COINAGE

European Union Issues

KM# 224 EURO CENT

2.3000 g., Copper Plated Steel, 16.25 mm. **Ruler:** Albert II **Obv:** Head left within inner circle, stars 3/4 surround, date below **Rev:** Denomination and globe **Edge:** Plain

Date	Mintage	F	VF	XF	Unc	BU
2001	99,840,000	—	—	0.30	0.75	1.00
2001 Proof	15,000	Value: 12.00				
2002 In sets only	140,000	—	—	—	18.50	25.00
2002 Proof	15,000	Value: 15.00				
2003	10,135,000	—	—	0.25	0.60	0.80
2003 Proof	15,000	Value: 12.00				
2004	180,000,000	—	—	0.25	0.60	0.80
2004 Proof	—	Value: 12.00				
2005 In sets only	—	—	—	—	—	18.50
2005 Proof	3,000	Value: 12.00				
2006	15,000,000	—	—	0.25	0.60	0.80
2006 Proof	—	Value: 12.00				
2007	60,000,000	—	—	0.25	0.60	0.80
2007 Proof	—	Value: 12.00				

KM# 274 EURO CENT

2.3000 g., Copper Plated Steel, 16.25 mm. **Ruler:** Albert II **Obv:** Head of Albert II left, crowned monogram at right, date below

Date	Mintage	F	VF	XF	Unc	BU
2008	50,000,000	—	—	—	0.35	0.75
2008 Proof	—	Value: 12.00				
2009	19,950,000	—	—	—	0.35	0.75
2009 Proof	1,500	Value: 12.00				
2010	30,000,000	—	—	—	0.35	0.75
2010 Proof	1,850	Value: 12.00				
2011	—	—	—	—	—	0.75
2011 Proof	1,850	Value: 12.00				
2012	—	—	—	—	—	0.75
2012 Proof	1,850	Value: 12.00				

KM# 225 2 EURO CENT

3.0600 g., Copper Plated Steel, 18.75 mm. **Ruler:** Albert II **Obv:** Head left within circle, stars 3/4 surround, date below **Rev:** Denomination and globe **Edge:** Grooved

Date	Mintage	F	VF	XF	Unc	BU
2001 In sets only	40,000	—	—	—	—	9.00

Note: Only available in sets at present, circulation strikes not yet released

Date	Mintage	F	VF	XF	Unc	BU
2001 Proof	15,000	Value: 15.00				
2002 In sets only	140,000	—	—	—	—	6.50
2002 Proof	15,000	Value: 12.00				
2003	40,135,000	—	—	0.30	0.75	1.00
2003 Proof	15,000	Value: 12.00				
2004	140,000,000	—	—	0.30	0.75	1.00
2004 Proof	15,000	Value: 12.00				
2005 In sets only	—	—	—	—	—	1.00
2005 Proof	—	Value: 12.00				
2006	30,000,000	—	—	0.30	0.75	1.00
2006 Proof	—	Value: 12.00				
2007	70,000,000	—	—	0.30	0.75	1.00
2007 Proof	—	Value: 12.00				

KM# 275 2 EURO CENT

3.0600 g., Copper Plated Steel, 18.75 mm. **Ruler:** Albert II **Obv:** Head of Albert II left, crowned monogram at right, date below **Edge:** Grooved

Date	Mintage	F	VF	XF	Unc	BU
2008	40,000,000	—	—	—	0.75	1.00
2008 Proof	—	Value: 12.00				
2009	10,000,000	—	—	—	0.75	1.00
2009 Proof	1,500	Value: 12.00				
2010	20,000,000	—	—	—	0.75	1.00
2010 Proof	1,850	Value: 12.00				
2011	—	—	—	—	—	1.00
2011 Proof	1,850	Value: 12.00				
2012	—	—	—	—	—	1.00
2012 Proof	1,850	Value: 12.00				

KM# 226 5 EURO CENT

3.9200 g., Copper Plated Steel, 21.25 mm. **Ruler:** Albert II **Obv:** Head left within circle, stars 3/4 surround, date below **Rev:** Denomination and globe **Edge:** Plain

Date	Mintage	F	VF	XF	Unc	BU
2001 In sets only	40,000	—	—	—	—	12.50
2001 Proof	15,000	Value: 15.00				
2002 In sets only	140,000	—	—	—	—	8.00
2002 Proof	15,000	Value: 15.00				
2003	30,135,000	—	—	0.30	0.80	1.20
2003 Proof	15,000	Value: 12.00				
2004	75,000,000	—	—	0.30	0.80	1.20
2004 Proof	—	Value: 12.00				
2005	110,000,000	—	—	0.30	0.80	1.20
2005 Proof	3,000	Value: 12.00				
2006	35,000,000	—	—	0.30	0.80	1.20
2006 Proof	—	Value: 12.00				
2007 In sets only	—	—	—	—	—	8.00
2007 Proof	—	Value: 12.00				

KM# 276 5 EURO CENT

3.9200 g., Copper Plated Steel, 21.25 mm. **Ruler:** Albert II **Obv:** Redesigned head of Albert II left

Date	Mintage	F	VF	XF	Unc	BU
2008	—	—	—	—	—	2.00
2008 Proof	—	Value: 12.00				
2009	—	—	—	—	—	1.20
2009 Proof	1,500	Value: 12.00				
2010	25,000,000	—	—	—	0.75	1.20
2010 Proof	1,850	Value: 12.00				
2011	—	—	—	—	—	1.20
2011 Proof	1,850	Value: 12.00				
2012	—	—	—	—	—	1.20
2012 Proof	1,850	Value: 12.00				

KM# 227 10 EURO CENT

4.1000 g., Brass, 19.75 mm. **Ruler:** Albert II **Obv:** Head left within inner circle, stars 3/4 surround, date below **Rev:** Denomination and map **Edge:** Reeded

Date	Mintage	F	VF	XF	Unc	BU
2001	145,790,000	—	—	—	0.75	1.25
2001 Proof	15,000	Value: 12.00				
2002 In sets only	140,000	—	—	—	6.00	8.00
2002 Proof	15,000	Value: 15.00				
2003 In sets only	135,000	—	—	—	6.00	8.00
2003 Proof	15,000	Value: 15.00				
2004	20,000,000	—	—	—	1.00	1.50
2004 Proof	—	Value: 12.00				
2005	10,000,000	—	—	—	1.00	1.50
2005 Proof	3,000	Value: 12.00				
2006 In sets only	—	—	—	—	1.00	1.50
2006 Proof	—	Value: 12.00				

KM# 242 10 EURO CENT

4.1000 g., Brass, 19.75 mm. **Ruler:** Albert II **Obv:** King's portrait **Rev:** Relief map of Western Europe, stars, lines and value **Edge:** Reeded

Date	Mintage	F	VF	XF	Unc	BU
2007	—	—	—	—	1.00	1.50
2007 Proof	—	Value: 12.00				

KM# 277 10 EURO CENT

4.1000 g., Brass, 19.75 mm. **Ruler:** Albert II **Obv:** Head of Albert II left, crowned monogram right, date below **Edge:** Reeded

Date	Mintage	F	VF	XF	Unc	BU
2008	—	—	—	—	—	6.00
2008 Proof	—	Value: 12.00				
2009	—	—	—	—	—	1.50
2009 Proof	1,500	Value: 12.00				
2010	20,000,000	—	—	—	1.00	1.50
2010 Proof	1,850	Value: 12.00				
2011	—	—	—	—	1.00	1.50
2011 Proof	1,850	Value: 12.00				
2012	—	—	—	—	—	1.50
2012 Proof	1,850	Value: 12.00				

KM# 228 20 EURO CENT

5.7400 g., Brass, 22.25 mm. **Ruler:** Albert II **Obv:** Head left within circle, stars 3/4 surround, date below **Rev:** Denomination and map **Edge:** Notched

Date	Mintage	F	VF	XF	Unc	BU
2001 In sets only	40,000	—	—	—	10.00	12.50

Note: Only available in sets at present, circulation strikes not yet released

Date	Mintage	F	VF	XF	Unc	BU
2001 Proof	15,000	Value: 15.00				
2002	104,140,000	—	—	—	1.00	1.50
2002 Proof	15,000	Value: 12.00				
2003	30,135,000	—	—	—	1.25	1.75
2003 Proof	15,000	Value: 12.00				
2004	109,550,000	—	—	—	1.25	1.75
2004 Proof	—	Value: 12.00				
2005	10,000,000	—	—	—	1.25	1.75
2005 Proof	3,000	Value: 12.00				
2006	40,000,000	—	—	—	1.25	1.75
2006 Proof	—	Value: 12.00				

KM# 243 20 EURO CENT

5.7400 g., Brass, 22.25 mm. **Ruler:** Albert II **Obv:** King's portrait **Rev:** Relief map of Western Europe, stars, lines and value **Edge:** Notched

Date	Mintage	F	VF	XF	Unc	BU
2007	—	—	—	—	1.25	1.75
2007 Proof	—	Value: 12.00				

KM# 278 20 EURO CENT

5.7400 g., Brass, 22.25 mm. **Ruler:** Albert II **Obv:** Redesigned head of Albert II left **Edge:** Notched

Date	Mintage	F	VF	XF	Unc	BU
2008	—	—	—	—	—	2.00
2008 Proof	—	Value: 12.00				
2009	30,100,000	—	—	—	1.25	1.75
2009 Proof	1,500	Value: 12.00				
2010	15,000,000	—	—	—	1.25	1.75
2010 Proof	1,850	Value: 12.00				
2011	—	—	—	—	1.25	1.75
2011 Proof	1,850	Value: 12.00				
2012	—	—	—	—	—	1.75
2012 Proof	1,850	Value: 12.00				

KM# 229 50 EURO CENT

7.8000 g., Brass, 24.25 mm. **Ruler:** Albert II **Obv:** Head left within circle, stars 3/4 surround, date below **Rev:** Denomination and map **Edge:** Reeded

Date	Mintage	F	VF	XF	Unc	BU
2001 In sets only	40,000	—	—	—	10.00	12.50
2001 Proof	15,000	Value: 15.00				
2002	50,040,000	—	—	—	1.00	1.50
2002 Proof	15,000	Value: 12.00				
2003 In sets only	135,000	—	—	—	—	12.50
2003 Proof	15,000	Value: 12.00				
2004	8,000,000	—	—	—	1.25	1.75
2004 Proof	—	Value: 12.00				
2005 In sets only	—	—	—	—	—	12.50
2005 Proof	3,000	Value: 12.00				
2006 In sets only	—	—	—	—	—	12.50
2006 Proof	—	Value: 12.00				

KM# 244 50 EURO CENT

7.8000 g., Brass, 24.25 mm. **Ruler:** Albert II **Obv:** King's portrait **Rev:** Relief map of Western Europe, stars, lines and value **Edge:** Reeded

Date	Mintage	F	VF	XF	Unc	BU
2007	—	—	—	—	1.25	1.75
2007 Proof	—	Value: 12.00				

KM# 279 50 EURO CENT

7.8000 g., Brass, 24.25 mm. **Ruler:** Albert II **Obv:** Redesigned head of Albert II left **Edge:** Reeded

Date	Mintage	F	VF	XF	Unc	BU
2008	25,000,000	—	—	—	—	4.00
2008 Proof	—	Value: 12.00				
2009	30,000,000	—	—	—	2.00	3.00
2009 Proof	1,500	Value: 12.00				
2010	—	—	—	—	—	3.00
2010 Proof	1,850	Value: 12.00				
2011	—	—	—	—	—	3.00
2011 Proof	1,850	Value: 12.00				
2012	—	—	—	—	—	3.00
2012 Proof	1,850	Value: 12.00				

KM# 230 EURO

7.5000 g., Bi-Metallic Copper-Nickel center in Nickel-Brass ring, 23.25 mm. **Ruler:** Albert II **Obv:** Head left within circle, stars 3/4 surround, date below **Rev:** Denomination and map **Edge:** Segmented reeding

Date	Mintage	F	VF	XF	Unc	BU
2001 In sets only	40,000	—	—	—	—	15.00
Note: Only available in sets at present, circulation strikes not yet released						
2001 Proof	15,000	Value: 18.00				
2002	90,640,000	—	—	—	3.00	5.00
Note: Only a fraction of the mintage released at present						
2002 Proof	15,000	Value: 15.00				
2003	6,000,000	—	—	—	3.00	5.00
2003 Proof	15,000	Value: 15.00				
2004	15,000,000	—	—	—	3.00	5.00
2004 Proof	—	Value: 15.00				
2005 In sets only	—	—	—	—	—	15.00
2005 Proof	3,000	Value: 15.00				
2006 In sets only	—	—	—	—	—	15.00
2006 Proof	—	Value: 15.00				

KM# 245 EURO

7.5000 g., Bi-Metallic Copper-Nickel center in Nickel-Brass ring, 23.25 mm. **Ruler:** Albert II **Obv:** King's portrait **Rev:** Relief map of Western Europe, stars, lines and value **Edge:** Segmented reeding

Date	Mintage	F	VF	XF	Unc	BU
2007	—	—	—	—	3.00	5.00
2007 Proof	—	Value: 15.00				

KM# 280 EURO

7.5000 g., Bi-Metallic Copper-Nickel center in Nickel-Brass ring, 23.25 mm. **Ruler:** Albert II **Obv:** Redesigned head of Albert II left **Edge:** Segmented reeding

Date	Mintage	F	VF	XF	Unc	BU
2008	—	—	—	—	—	6.00
2008 Proof	—	Value: 15.00				
2009	10,000,000	—	—	—	3.00	5.00
2009 Proof	1,500	Value: 15.00				
2010	—	—	—	—	—	5.00
2010 Proof	1,850	Value: 15.00				
2011	—	—	—	—	—	5.00
2011 Proof	1,850	Value: 15.00				
2012	—	—	—	—	—	5.00
2012 Proof	1,850	Value: 15.00				

KM# 231 2 EURO

8.5000 g., Bi-Metallic Nickel-Brass center in Copper-Nickel ring, 25.75 mm. **Ruler:** Albert II **Obv:** Head left within circle, stars 3/4 surround, date below **Rev:** Denomination and map **Edge:** Reeded with 2's and stars

Date	Mintage	F	VF	XF	Unc	BU
2001 In sets only	40,000	—	—	—	12.50	15.00
Note: Only available in sets at present, circulation strikes not yet released						
2001 Proof	15,000	Value: 20.00				
2002	50,140,000	—	—	—	3.75	6.00
2002 Proof	15,000	Value: 18.00				
2003	30,135,000	—	—	—	3.75	6.00
2003 Proof	15,000	Value: 18.00				
2004	65,500,000	—	—	—	3.75	6.00
2004 Proof	—	Value: 18.00				
2005	10,500,000	—	—	—	3.75	6.00
2005 Proof	3,000	Value: 18.00				
2006	20,000,000	—	—	—	3.75	6.00
2006 Proof	—	Value: 18.00				

KM# 240 2 EURO

8.5000 g., Bi-Metallic Nickel-Brass center in Copper-Nickel ring, 25.75 mm. **Ruler:** Albert II **Subject:** Schengen Agreement **Obv:** Albert II of Belgium and Henri of Luxembourg **Rev:** Value and map **Edge:** Reeded with 2's and stars

Date	Mintage	F	VF	XF	Unc	BU
2005	5,977,000	—	—	—	5.00	7.50
2005 Prooflike	20,000	—	—	—	—	20.00
2005 Proof	3,000	Value: 25.00				

KM# 241 2 EURO

8.5000 g., Bi-Metallic Nickel-Brass center in Copper-Nickel ring, 25.75 mm. **Ruler:** Albert II **Obv:** Atomic model **Rev:** Value and map **Edge:** Reeded with 2's and stars

Date	Mintage	F	VF	XF	Unc	BU
2006	4,977,000	—	—	—	4.00	6.00
2006 Prooflike	20,000	—	—	—	—	25.00
2006 Proof	3,000	Value: 100				

KM# 246 2 EURO

8.5000 g., Bi-Metallic Nickel-Brass center in Copper-Nickel ring, 25.75 mm. **Ruler:** Albert II **Obv:** King's portrait **Rev:** Relief map of Western Europe, stars, lines and value **Edge:** Reeded with 2's and stars

Date	Mintage	F	VF	XF	Unc	BU
2007	—	—	—	—	3.75	6.00
2007 Proof	—	Value: 25.00				

KM# 247 2 EURO

8.5000 g., Bi-Metallic Nickel-Brass center in Copper-Nickel ring, 25.75 mm. **Ruler:** Albert II **Subject:** 50th Anniversary Treaty of Rome **Obv:** Open treaty book **Rev:** Large value at left, modified outline of Europe at right **Edge:** Reeded with stars and 2's

Date	Mintage	F	VF	XF	Unc	BU
2007	4,960,000	—	—	—	—	9.00
2007 Prooflike	35,000	—	—	—	—	25.00
2007 Proof	10,000	Value: 75.00				

KM# 248 2 EURO

8.5000 g., Bi-Metallic Nickel-Brass center in Copper-Nickel ring, 25.75 mm. **Ruler:** Albert II **Subject:** Universal Declaration of Human Rights **Obv:** Book in bow **Rev:** Large value "2" at left, modified map of Europe at right **Edge:** Reeded with 2's and stars

Date	Mintage	F	VF	XF	Unc	BU
2008	—	—	—	—	—	6.00

KM# 281 2 EURO

8.5000 g., Bi-Metallic Nickel-Brass center in Copper-Nickel ring, 25.75 mm. **Ruler:** Albert II **Obv:** Head of Albert II left, crowned monogram right, date below **Edge:** Reeded with 2's and stars

Date	Mintage	F	VF	XF	Unc	BU
2008	—	—	—	—	—	7.50
2008 Proof	—	Value: 18.00				
2009	—	—	—	—	4.00	6.00
2009 Proof	—	Value: 18.00				
2010	—	—	—	—	4.00	6.00
2010 Proof	—	Value: 18.00				
2011	—	—	—	—	4.00	6.00
2011 Proof	—	Value: 18.00				
2012	—	—	—	—	4.00	6.00

KM# 282 2 EURO

8.5000 g., Bi-Metallic Nickel-Brass center in Copper-Nickel ring, 25.75 mm. **Ruler:** Albert II **Subject:** 10th Anniversary of EMU **Obv:** Stick figure and E symbol **Edge:** Reeded with 2's and stars

Date	Mintage	F	VF	XF	Unc	BU
2009	5,000,000	—	—	—	15.00	—
2009 Prooflike	—	—	—	—	—	20.00
2009 Proof	—	Value: 70.00				

KM# 288 2 EURO

8.5000 g., Bi-Metallic Nickel-Brass center in Copper-Nickel ring, 25.75 mm. **Ruler:** Albert II **Subject:** Louis Braille, 200th Anniversary of Birth **Obv:** Bust right with braile text **Edge:** Reeded with 2's and stars

Date	Mintage	F	VF	XF	Unc	BU
2009	5,000,000	—	—	—	—	5.00

KM# 289 2 EURO

8.5000 g., Bi-Metallic Nickel-Brass center in Copper-Nickel ring, 25.75 mm. **Ruler:** Albert II **Subject:** EU Council Presidency **Rev:** eu in script **Edge:** Reeded with 2's and stars

Date	Mintage	F	VF	XF	Unc	BU
2010	—	—	—	—	3.00	7.50

KM# 308 2 EURO

8.5000 g., Bi-Metallic Nickel-Brass center in Copper-Nickel ring, 25.75 mm. **Ruler:** Albert II **Subject:** International Women's Day, 100th Anniversary **Obv:** Portraits of I. van Diest and M. Popelin

Date	Mintage	F	VF	XF	Unc	BU
2011	5,000,000	—	—	—	9.00	12.50
2011 Special Unc.	6,000	—	—	—	—	15.00
2011 Proof	7,500	Value: 25.00				

KM# 315 2 EURO

8.5000 g., Bi-Metallic Nickel-Brass center in Copper-Nickel ring, 25.75 mm. **Ruler:** Albert II **Subject:** Euro coinage, 10th Anniversary **Obv:** Euro symbol on globe, child-like rendering around

Date	Mintage	F	VF	XF	Unc	BU
2012	6,000,000	—	—	—	6.00	8.00
2012 Special Unc.	—	—	—	—	—	15.00
2012 Proof	—	Value: 25.00				

KM# 270 5 EURO

14.6000 g., 0.9250 Silver 0.4342 oz. ASW, 30 mm. **Ruler:** Albert II **Subject:** Smurfs - 50th Anniversary **Obv:** Map of Western Europe **Rev:** Smurf

Date	Mintage	F	VF	XF	Unc	BU
2008 Proof	25,000	Value: 50.00				

KM# 270a 5 EURO

14.6000 g., 0.9250 Silver 0.4342 oz. ASW, 30 mm. **Ruler:** Albert II **Subject:** Smurf - 50th Anniversary **Obv:** Map of Western Europe **Rev:** Multicolor 50 and Smurf

Date	Mintage	F	VF	XF	Unc	BU
2008 Proof	—	Value: 75.00				

KM# 303 5 EURO

14.6000 g., 0.9250 Silver 0.4342 oz. ASW, 30 mm. **Ruler:** Albert II **Subject:** Belgian Railways, 175th Anniversary

Date	Mintage	F	VF	XF	Unc	BU
2010 Proof	—	Value: 50.00				

KM# 313 5 EURO

14.6000 g., 0.9250 Silver 0.4342 oz. ASW, 30 mm. **Ruler:** Albert II **Subject:** Helene Dutrieu, Belgium's first female aviator **Obv:** Euro zone map **Rev:** Female portrait at left, biplane at right

Date	Mintage	F	VF	XF	Unc	BU
2011 Proof	—	Value: 50.00				

KM# 233 10 EURO

18.9300 g., 0.9250 Silver 0.5629 oz. ASW, 32.9 mm. **Ruler:** Albert II **Subject:** Belgian Railway System **Obv:** Value, head at right transposed on map **Rev:** Train exiting tunnel **Edge:** Reeded

Date	Mintage	F	VF	XF	Unc	BU
ND (2002) Proof	50,000	Value: 50.00				

KM# 235 10 EURO

18.9300 g., 0.9250 Silver 0.5629 oz. ASW, 32.9 mm. **Ruler:** Albert II **Subject:** "Simenon" **Edge:** Reeded

Date	Mintage	F	VF	XF	Unc	BU
2003 Proof	50,000	Value: 40.00				

KM# 236 10 EURO

18.9300 g., 0.9250 Silver 0.5629 oz. ASW, 32.9 mm. **Ruler:** Albert II **Subject:** "Tintin" **Edge:** Reeded

Date	Mintage	F	VF	XF	Unc	BU
2004 Proof	50,000	Value: 85.00				

KM# 234 10 EURO

18.7500 g., 0.9250 Silver 0.5576 oz. ASW, 33 mm. **Ruler:** Albert II **Obv:** Value **Rev:** Western Europe map and Goddess Europa riding a bull **Edge:** Reeded

Date	Mintage	F	VF	XF	Unc	BU
2004 Proof	50,000	Value: 40.00				

KM# 252 10 EURO

18.7500 g., 0.9250 Silver 0.5576 oz. ASW, 33 mm. **Ruler:** Albert II **Subject:** 60th Anniversary of Liberation **Obv:** Map of Western Europe and stars **Rev:** Phoenix

Date	Mintage	F	VF	XF	Unc	BU
2005 Proof	50,000	Value: 50.00				

KM# 251 10 EURO

18.7500 g., 0.9250 Silver 0.5576 oz. ASW, 33 mm. **Ruler:** Albert II **Subject:** Netherland-Belgium Soccer, 75th Anniversary **Obv:** Map of Western Europe and stars **Rev:** Soccer Player

Date	Mintage	F	VF	XF	Unc	BU
2005 Proof	50,000	Value: 45.00				

KM# 255 10 EURO

18.7500 g., 0.9250 Silver 0.5576 oz. ASW, 33 mm. **Ruler:** Albert II **Subject:** Justus Lipsius, 400th Anniversary of Death **Obv:** Map of Western Europe and stars **Rev:** Half-length figure of Justus Lipsius

Date	Mintage	F	VF	XF	Unc	BU
2006 Proof	50,000	Value: 45.00				

KM# 257 10 EURO

18.7500 g., 0.9250 Silver 0.5576 oz. ASW, 33 mm. **Ruler:** Albert II **Subject:** 50th Anniversary - Mine Accident in Marcinelle **Obv:** Map of Western Europe and stars **Rev:** Male head and industrial mine scene

Date	Mintage	F	VF	XF	Unc	BU
2006 Proof	50,000	Value: 45.00				

KM# 257a 10 EURO

18.7500 g., 0.9250 Silver 0.5576 oz. ASW, 33 mm. **Ruler:** Albert II **Subject:** 50th Anniversary, Mine Accident in Marcinelle **Obv:** Map of Western Europe and stars **Rev:** Multicolor male head and industrial mine scene

Date	Mintage	F	VF	XF	Unc	BU
2006 Proof	2,000	Value: 75.00				

KM# 260 10 EURO

18.7500 g., 0.9250 Silver 0.5576 oz. ASW, 33 mm. **Ruler:** Albert II **Subject:** Treaty of Rome, 50th Anniversary **Obv:** Map of Western Europe **Rev:** Document and feather pen

Date	Mintage	F	VF	XF	Unc	BU
2007 Proof	40,000	Value: 45.00				

KM# 263 10 EURO

18.7500 g., 0.9250 Silver 0.5576 oz. ASW, 33 mm. **Ruler:** Albert II **Subject:** International Polar Year **Obv:** Map of Western Europe **Rev:** Wind farm and polar station

Date	Mintage	F	VF	XF	Unc	BU
2007 Proof	40,000	Value: 50.00				

KM# 266 10 EURO

18.7500 g., 0.9250 Silver 0.5576 oz. ASW, 33 mm. **Ruler:** Albert II **Subject:** 100th Anniversary Maurice Maeterlinck **Obv:** Map of Western Europe **Rev:** Gateway and dome in blue

Date	Mintage	F	VF	XF	Unc	BU
2008 Proof	20,000	Value: 75.00				

KM# 268 10 EURO

18.7500 g., 0.9250 Silver 0.5576 oz. ASW, 33 mm. **Ruler:** Albert II **Subject:** Beijing Olympics **Obv:** Map of Western Europe **Rev:** Sport events, logo and torch

Date	Mintage	F	VF	XF	Unc	BU
2008 Proof	20,000	Value: 50.00				

KM# 284 10 EURO

18.7500 g., 0.9250 Silver 0.5576 oz. ASW **Ruler:** Albert II **Subject:** 75th Birthday of the King **Obv:** Head at left, laurel sprigs

Date	Mintage	F	VF	XF	Unc	BU
2009	—	—	—	—	—	50.00

KM# 285 10 EURO

18.7500 g., 0.9250 Silver 0.5576 oz. ASW **Ruler:** Albert II **Subject:** Erasmus

Date	Mintage	F	VF	XF	Unc	BU
2009	—	—	—	—	—	50.00

KM# 290 10 EURO

18.7500 g., 0.9250 Silver 0.5576 oz. ASW, 33 mm. **Ruler:** Albert II **Subject:** Royal Museum for Central Asia 100th Anniversary

Date	Mintage	F	VF	XF	Unc	BU
2010	—	—	—	—	—	45.00

KM# 291 10 EURO

18.7500 g., 0.9250 Silver 0.5576 oz. ASW, 33 mm. **Ruler:** Albert II **Subject:** Jean Django' Reinhart Birth Centennial

Date	Mintage	F	VF	XF	Unc	BU
2010 Proof	—	Value: 45.00				

KM# 304 10 EURO

18.7500 g., 0.9250 Silver 0.5576 oz. ASW, 33 mm. **Ruler:** Albert II **Subject:** Jean "Django" Reinhardt, 100th Anniversary of Birth

Date	Mintage	F	VF	XF	Unc	BU
2010 Proof	—	Value: 50.00				

KM# 309 10 EURO

18.7500 g., 0.9250 Silver 0.5576 oz. ASW, 33 mm. **Ruler:** Albert II **Subject:** Discovery of the South Pole **Obv:** Euro zone map **Rev:** Map, dog sled, Roald Amundsen

Date	Mintage	F	VF	XF	Unc	BU
2011 Proof	—	Value: 50.00				

KM# 311 10 EURO

18.7500 g., 0.9250 Silver 0.5576 oz. ASW, 33 mm. **Ruler:** Albert II **Obv:** Euro zone map, partially gilt **Rev:** Belgian deep sea exploration

Date	Mintage	F	VF	XF	Unc	BU
2011 Proof	—	Value: 50.00				

KM# 259 12 1/2 EURO

1.2500 g., 0.9990 Gold 0.0401 oz. AGW, 13.92 mm. **Ruler:** Albert II **Subject:** Saxe-Coburg-Gotha, 175th Anniversary **Obv:** Lion and tablet with constitution **Rev:** Head of Leopold I left

Date	Mintage	F	VF	XF	Unc	BU
2006 Proof	15,000	Value: 80.00				

KM# 265 12 1/2 EURO

1.2500 g., 0.9990 Gold 0.0401 oz. AGW, 13.92 mm. **Subject:** 175th Anniversary Saxe-Coburg-Gotha **Obv:** Lion and tablet **Rev:** Leopold II head left

Date	Mintage	F	VF	XF	Unc	BU
2007 Proof	15,000	Value: 80.00				

KM# 271 12 1/2 EURO

1.2500 g., 0.9990 Gold 0.0401 oz. AGW, 13.92 mm. **Ruler:** Albert II **Subject:** 175th Anniversary - Saxe-Coburg-Gotha **Obv:** Lion and tablet **Rev:** Albert I bust right

Date	Mintage	F	VF	XF	Unc	BU
2008 Proof	15,000	Value: 80.00				

KM# 292 12 1/2 EURO

1.2440 g., 0.9990 Gold 0.0400 oz. AGW, 14 mm. **Ruler:** Albert II **Subject:** Leopold III

Date	Mintage	F	VF	XF	Unc	BU
2009 Proof	—	Value: 85.00				

KM# 293 12 1/2 EURO

1.2440 g., 0.9990 Gold 0.0400 oz. AGW, 14 mm. **Ruler:** Albert II

Date	Mintage	F	VF	XF	Unc	BU
2010 Proof	—	Value: 85.00				

KM# 254 20 EURO

22.8500 g., 0.9990 Silver 0.7339 oz. ASW, 37 mm. **Ruler:** Albert II **Subject:** FIFA World Cup in Germany **Obv:** Albert II head left **Rev:** Soccer player with ball

Date	Mintage	F	VF	XF	Unc	BU
2005 Proof	25,000	Value: 65.00				

KM# 262 20 EURO

22.8500 g., 0.9250 Silver 0.6795 oz. ASW, 37 mm. **Ruler:** Albert II **Subject:** Georges Remi, 100th Anniversary of Birth **Obv:** Map of Western Europe and stars **Rev:** Profile of Georges Renir and his character Tin Tin right

Date	Mintage	F	VF	XF	Unc	BU
2007 Proof	50,000	Value: 75.00				

KM# 287 20 EURO

22.8500 g., 0.9250 Silver 0.6795 oz. ASW, 37 mm. **Ruler:** Albert II **Obv:** Value and map of euro countries **Rev:** Fr. Damien and churches in Tremblo and Molokai, date of canionization below

Date	Mintage	F	VF	XF	Unc	BU
2009 Proof	15,000	Value: 75.00				

KM# 305 20 EURO

22.8500 g., 0.9250 Silver 0.6795 oz. ASW, 37 mm. **Ruler:** Albert II **Subject:** A Dog of Flanders

Date	Mintage	F	VF	XF	Unc	BU
2010 Proof	—	Value: 75.00				

KM# 269 25 EURO

3.1100 g., 0.9990 Gold 0.0999 oz. AGW, 18 mm. **Ruler:** Albert II **Subject:** Beijing Olympics **Obv:** Map of Western Europe **Rev:** Sport events, logo, torch

Date	Mintage	F	VF	XF	Unc	BU
2008 Proof	5,000	Value: 225				

KM# 294 25 EURO

3.1100 g., 0.9990 Gold 0.0999 oz. AGW, 18 mm. **Ruler:** Albert II **Subject:** Beijing Olympics

Date	Mintage	F	VF	XF	Unc	BU
2008 Proof	4,050	Value: 250				

KM# 250 50 EURO

6.2200 g., 0.9990 Gold 0.1998 oz. AGW, 21 mm. **Ruler:** Albert II **Subject:** Albert II, 70th Birthday **Obv:** Map of Western Europe and stars **Rev:** Portrait of Albert II

Date	Mintage	F	VF	XF	Unc	BU
2004 Proof	10,000	Value: 350				

KM# 256 50 EURO

6.2200 g., 0.9990 Gold 0.1998 oz. AGW, 21 mm. **Ruler:** Albert II **Subject:** Justus Lipsius, 400th Anniversary of Death **Obv:** Map of Western Europe and stars **Rev:** Half-length figure of Justus Lipius right

Date	Mintage	F	VF	XF	Unc	BU
2006 Proof	2,500	Value: 365				

KM# 261 50 EURO

6.2200 g., 0.9990 Gold 0.1998 oz. AGW, 21 mm. **Ruler:** Albert II **Subject:** Treaty of Rome, 50th Anniversary **Obv:** Map of Western Europe **Rev:** Document and feather pen

Date	Mintage	F	VF	XF	Unc	BU
2007 Proof	2,500	Value: 365				

KM# 267 50 EURO

6.2200 g., 0.9990 Gold 0.1998 oz. AGW, 21 mm. **Ruler:** Albert II **Subject:** 100th Anniversary Maurice Maeterlinck **Obv:** Map of Western Europe **Rev:** Gate and dove

Date	Mintage	F	VF	XF	Unc	BU
2008 Proof	2,500	Value: 400				

KM# 286 50 EURO

8.4500 g., 0.9990 Gold 0.2714 oz. AGW **Ruler:** Albert II **Subject:** Erasmus

Date	Mintage	F	VF	XF	Unc	BU
2009	—	—	—	—	—	475

KM# 306 50 EURO

6.2200 g., 0.9990 Gold 0.1998 oz. AGW, 22 mm. **Ruler:** Albert II **Subject:** Royal Museum for Central Africa

Date	Mintage	F	VF	XF	Unc	BU
2010 Proof	—	Value: 400				

KM# 310 50 EURO

8.4500 g., 0.9990 Gold 0.2714 oz. AGW, 22 mm. **Ruler:** Albert II **Obv:** Euro zone map **Rev:** Four men standing around flag, Roald Amundsen profile at right

Date	Mintage	F	VF	XF	Unc	BU
2011 Proof	—	Value: 550				

KM# 312 50 EURO

6.2200 g., 0.9990 Gold 0.1998 oz. AGW, 22 mm. **Ruler:** Albert II **Obv:** Euro zone map **Rev:** Belgian deep sea exploration

Date	Mintage	F	VF	XF	Unc	BU
2011 Proof	2,500	Value: 550				

KM# 237 100 EURO

15.5500 g., 0.9990 Gold 0.4994 oz. AGW, 29 mm. **Ruler:** Albert II **Subject:** Founding Fathers

Date	Mintage	F	VF	XF	Unc	BU
2002 Proof	5,000	Value: 875				

KM# 238 100 EURO

15.5500 g., 0.9990 Gold 0.4994 oz. AGW, 29 mm. **Ruler:** Albert II **Subject:** 10th Anniversary of Reign

Date	Mintage	F	VF	XF	Unc	BU
2003 Proof	5,000	Value: 875				

KM# 239 100 EURO

15.5500 g., 0.9990 Gold 0.4994 oz. AGW, 29 mm. **Ruler:** Albert II **Subject:** Franc Germinal

Date	Mintage	F	VF	XF	Unc	BU
2004 Proof	5,000	Value: 875				

KM# 253 100 EURO

15.5500 g., 0.9990 Gold 0.4994 oz. AGW, 29 mm. **Ruler:** Albert II **Subject:** 175th Anniversary of Liberty **Obv:** Albert II head left **Rev:** Scene of the 1830 Revolution

Date	Mintage	F	VF	XF	Unc	BU
2005 Proof	5,000	Value: 875				

KM# 258 100 EURO

15.5500 g., 0.9990 Gold 0.4994 oz. AGW, 29 mm. **Ruler:** Albert II **Subject:** Saxe-Coburg-Gotha, 175th Anniversary **Obv:** Map of Western Europe and stars **Rev:** Church in Laeken, Kings monogram around

Date	Mintage	F	VF	XF	Unc	BU
2006 Proof	5,000	Value: 875				

KM# 264 100 EURO

15.5500 g., 0.9990 Gold 0.4994 oz. AGW, 29 mm. **Ruler:** Albert II **Subject:** Belgian Coins, 175th Anniversary **Obv:** Map of Western Europe **Rev:** Screw press, coin designs

Date	Mintage	F	VF	XF	Unc	BU
2007 Proof	5,000	Value: 875				

KM# 272 100 EURO

15.5500 g., 0.9990 Gold 0.4994 oz. AGW, 29 mm. **Ruler:** Albert II **Subject:** 50th Anniversary: Brussels Exposition **Obv:** Map of Western Europe

Date	Mintage	F	VF	XF	Unc	BU
2008 Proof	5,000	Value: 875				

KM# 283 100 EURO

15.5500 g., 0.9990 Gold 0.4994 oz. AGW **Ruler:** Albert II **Subject:** Royal Wedding Anniversary **Obv:** Conjoined leads at right

Date	Mintage	F	VF	XF	Unc	BU
2009 Proof	—	Value: 875				

KM# 307 100 EURO

15.5500 g., 0.9990 Gold 0.4994 oz. AGW, 29 mm. **Ruler:** Albert II **Subject:** Prince Philippe, 50th Birthday

Date	Mintage	F	VF	XF	Unc	BU
2010 Proof	2,000	Value: 900				

KM# 314 100 EURO

15.5500 g., 0.9990 Gold 0.4994 oz. AGW, 29 mm. **Ruler:** Albert II **Subject:** Victor Horta **Obv:** Euro zone map **Rev:** Bust at left, flora

Date	Mintage	F	VF	XF	Unc	BU
2011 Proof	—	Value: 950				

MINT SETS

KM#	Date	Mintage	Identification	Issue Price	Mkt Val
MS14	2001 (10)	60,000	KM#148.1, 149.1, 187-194	15.00	45.00
MS15	1999/2000/ 2001 (24)	40,000	Euro Intro	—	250
MS16	2002 (8)	100,000	KM#224-231, 700th Anniversary	—	62.50
MS17	2002 (8)	20,000	KM#224-231, Cycling	—	62.50
MS18	2002 (8)	20,000	KM#224-231, Euros plus waffle francs	—	62.50
MS19	2003 (8)	100,000	KM#224-231, Television 50th	—	37.50
MS20	2003 (8)	15,000	KM#224-231, Ford Production in Belgium Centennial	—	37.50
MS21	2003 (8)	10,000	KM#224-231, Rose	—	37.50
MS22	2003 (8)	10,000	KM#224-231, Baby	—	37.50
MS23.1	2004 (9)	60,000	KM#224-231, Belgian Red Cross, plain medal	—	25.00
MS23.2	2004 (9)	2,000	KM#224-231, Belgian Red Cross, enameled medal	—	175
MS24	2004 (9)	5,000	KM#224-231, Love, medal for engraving	—	37.50
MS25	2004 (9)	5,000	KM#224-231, Baby, medal for engraving	—	37.50
MS26.1	2005 (9)	38,000	KM#224-231, Grand Palace, UNESCO site, plain medal	—	60.00
MS26.2	2005 (9)	2,000	KM#224-231, Grand Palace, UNESCO site, gilt medal	—	85.00
MS27.1	2006 (9)	38,000	KM#224-231, Flemish Houses, UNESCO site, plain medal	—	40.00
MS27.2	2006 (9)	2,000	KM#224-231, Flemish Houses, UNESCO site, colored medal	—	75.00
MS28.1	2007 (9)	38,000	KM#224-226, 242-246, Canal. UNESCO site, plain medal	—	27.50
MS28.2	2007 (9)	2,000	KM#224-226, 242-246, Canal, UNESCO site, colored medal	—	70.00
MS29.1	2008 (9)	25,000	KM#274-281, Belltower, UNESCO site, plain medal	—	75.00
MS29.2	2008 (9)	2,000	KM#274-281, Belltower, UNESCO site, colored medal	—	85.00
MS30	2009 (8)	25,000	KM#274-281, plus medal	—	45.00
MS31	2010 (8)	30,000	KM#274-281, plus medal	—	45.00
MS32	2011 (8)	30,000	KM#274-281, plus medal	—	45.00

PROOF SETS

KM#	Date	Mintage	Identification	Issue Price	Mkt Val
PS10	2001 (8)	15,000	KM#224-231	80.00	125
PS11	2002 (8)	3,240	KM#224-231	80.00	115
PS12	2003 (8)	3,241	KM#224-231	80.00	110
PS13	2004 (8)	3,006	KM#224-231	80.00	105
PS14	2005 (8)	3,006	KM#224-231	—	110
PS15	2006 (8)	3,006	KM#224-231	—	115
PS17	2007 (8)	3,000	KM#224-226, 242-247	—	175
PS18	2008 (8)	2,500	KM#224-227, 276-278, 280-281	—	100
PS19	2009 (8)	1,500	KM#274-281	—	110
PS20	2010 (8)	1,850	KM#274-281	—	110
PS21	2011 (8)	1,850	KM#274-281	—	110

BELIZE

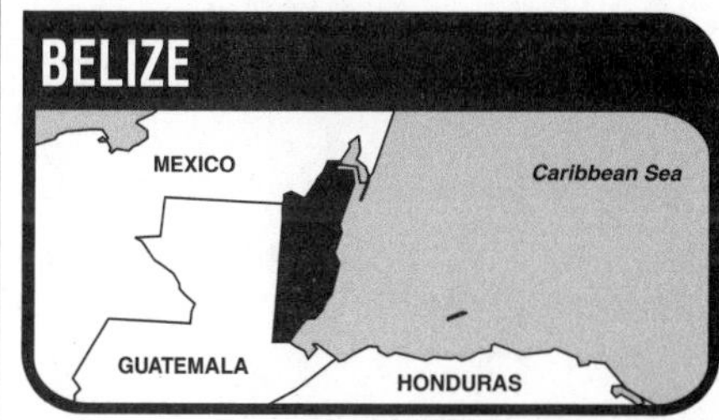

Belize, formerly British Honduras, but now a Constitutional Monarchy within the Commonwealth of Nations, is situated in Central America south of Mexico and east and north of Guatemala, with an area of 8,867 sq. mi. (22,960 sq. km.) and a population of *242,000. Capital: Belmopan. Tourism now augments Belize's economy, in addition to sugar, citrus fruits, chicle and hardwoods, which are exported.

MONETARY SYSTEM

Commencing 1864

100 Cents = 1 Dollar

COMMONWEALTH

DECIMAL COINAGE

KM# 33a CENT

0.8000 g., Aluminum, 19.5 mm. **Obv:** Bust of Queen Elizabeth right **Rev:** Denomination within circle **Edge:** Smooth, scalloped

Date	Mintage	F	VF	XF	Unc	BU
2002	—	—	—	0.10	0.15	0.45
2005	—	—	—	0.10	0.15	0.45
2007	—	—	—	0.10	0.15	0.45
2010	—	—	—	0.10	0.15	0.45

KM# 34a 5 CENTS
1.0400 g., Aluminum, 20.2 mm. **Obv:** Bust of Queen Elizabeth II right **Rev:** Denomination within circle **Edge:** Plain

Date	Mintage	F	VF	XF	Unc	BU
2002	—	—	—	0.10	0.20	0.45
2003	—	—	—	0.10	0.20	0.45
2005	—	—	—	0.10	0.20	0.45
2006	—	—	—	0.10	0.20	0.45
2009	—	—	—	0.10	0.20	0.45

KM# 115 5 CENTS
1.0500 g., Aluminum, 20.2 mm.

Date	Mintage	F	VF	XF	Unc	BU
2002	—	—	—	0.10	0.20	0.40

KM# 36 25 CENTS
5.6550 g., Copper-Nickel, 23.6 mm. **Obv:** Crowned bust of Queen Elizabeth II right **Rev:** Denomination within circle, date below **Edge:** Reeded

Date	Mintage	F	VF	XF	Unc	BU
2003	—	—	—	0.35	0.75	1.50
2007	—	—	—	0.35	0.75	1.50

KM# 37 50 CENTS
9.0700 g., Copper-Nickel, 27.74 mm. **Obv:** Crowned bust of Queen Elizabeth right **Rev:** Denomination within circle, date below **Edge:** Reeded

Date	Mintage	F	VF	XF	Unc	BU
2010	—	—	—	1.00	2.00	3.00

KM# 134 DOLLAR
30.9400 g., 0.9990 Silver 0.9937 oz. ASW, 39.9 mm. **Subject:** Mayan King **Obv:** National arms **Rev:** Mayan portrait in ornate headdress **Edge:** Reeded

Date	Mintage	F	VF	XF	Unc	BU
2002	—	—	—	—	40.00	45.00

KM# 99 DOLLAR
8.9000 g., Nickel-Brass, 27 mm. **Obv:** Crowned bust of Queen Elizabeth II right **Rev:** Columbus' three ships, denomination above, date below **Edge:** Alternating reeded and plain **Shape:** 10-sided

Date	Mintage	F	VF	XF	Unc	BU
2003	—	—	—	—	2.25	3.00
2007	—	—	—	—	2.25	3.00

KM# 136 DOLLAR
8.9000 g., Nickel-Brass, 27 mm. **Subject:** Central Bank, 30th Anniversary **Obv:** Bird in flight left **Rev:** Central Bank building **Shape:** 10-sided

Date	Mintage	F	VF	XF	Unc	BU
2012	—	—	—	—	2.50	3.00

KM# 137 250 DOLLARS
Gold **Subject:** Mayan Heartland **Obv:** Six stones flanked by two Mayans **Rev:** Large carved head

Date	Mintage	F	VF	XF	Unc	BU
2012 Proof	—	Value: 500				

BENIN

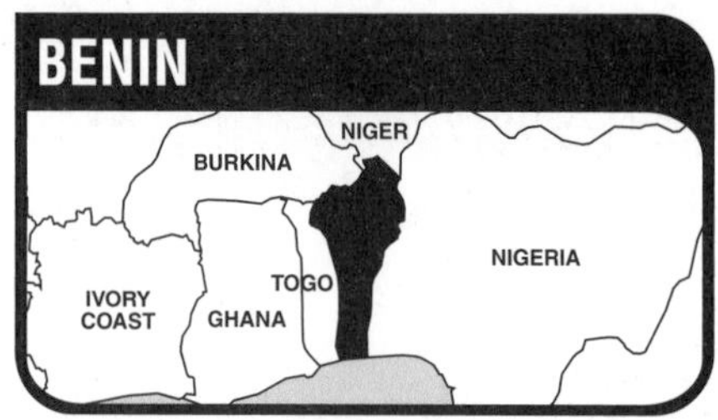

The Republic of Benin (formerly the Republic of Dahomey), located on the south side of the African bulge between Togo and Nigeria, has an area of 43,500 sq. mi. (112,620 sq. km.) and a population of 5.5 million. Capital: Porto-Novo. The principal industry of Benin, one of the poorest countries of West Africa, is the processing of palm oil products. Palm kernel oil, peanuts, cotton, and coffee are exported.

PEOPLES REPUBLIC

STANDARD COINAGE

KM# 53 100 CFA FRANCS
27.0000 g., Copper-Nickel Silver plated, 38.61 mm. **Rev:** Multicolor Cannabis Sativa, Aeromatic

Date	Mintage	F	VF	XF	Unc	BU
2010 Proof	2,500	Value: 65.00				

KM# 53a 100 CFA FRANCS
27.0000 g., Copper-Nickel gilt, 38.61 mm. **Rev:** Multicolor Cannabis Sativa, Aeromatic

Date	Mintage	F	VF	XF	Unc	BU
2010 Proof	2,500	Value: 65.00				

KM# 71 100 FRANCS
20.0000 g., 0.9990 Silver 0.6423 oz. ASW, 36 mm. **Obv:** State arms **Rev:** Steam train in colored forest scene

Date	Mintage	F	VF	XF	Unc	BU
2010 Proof	—	Value: 55.00				

KM# 75 100 FRANCS
Silver Plated Base Metal, 27 mm. **Obv:** National arms **Rev:** Rose in color and fragrant

Date	Mintage	F	VF	XF	Unc	BU
2011 Proof	2,500	Value: 50.00				

KM# 74 100 FRANCS
Silver Plated Base Metal, 38.61 mm. **Subject:** Man in space **Obv:** State arms **Rev:** Gagarin in color

Date	Mintage	F	VF	XF	Unc	BU
2011 Prooflike	961	—	—	—	—	50.00

KM# 76 100 FRANCS
Silver Plated Base Metal, 27 mm. **Obv:** National arms **Rev:** Convallaria majalis, French lilly in color and fragrant

Date	Mintage	F	VF	XF	Unc	BU
2011 Proof	—	Value: 60.00				

KM# 63 500 FRANCS
Silver, 38.61 mm. **Obv:** National arms **Rev:** Euro coin motifs

Date	Mintage	F	VF	XF	Unc	BU
2002	—	Value: 45.00				

KM# 72 500 FRANCS
Silver, 38.6 mm. **Subject:** W.A. Mozart

Date	Mintage	F	VF	XF	Unc	BU
2005 Proof	—	Value: 50.00				

KM# 64 1000 FRANCS
Silver, 38.61 mm. **Obv:** National arms **Rev:** Zebra

Date	Mintage	F	VF	XF	Unc	BU
2001 Proof	—	Value: 45.00				

KM# 65 1000 FRANCS
Silver, 38.61 mm. **Obv:** National arms **Rev:** Giraffe

Date	Mintage	F	VF	XF	Unc	BU
2001 Proof	—	Value: 45.00				

KM# 66 1000 FRANCS
Silver, 38.61 mm. **Obv:** National arms **Rev:** Whale

Date	Mintage	F	VF	XF	Unc	BU
2001 Proof	—	Value: 65.00				

KM# 62 1000 FRANCS
Silver **Rev:** Klaus Stortebeker and ship

Date	Mintage	F	VF	XF	Unc	BU
2002 Proof	—	Value: 37.50				

KM# 54 1000 FRANCS
20.0000 g., 0.9990 Silver 0.6423 oz. ASW, 36 mm. **Rev:** Multicolor Lockheed Orion

Date	Mintage	F	VF	XF	Unc	BU
2002 Proof	—	Value: 35.00				

KM# 55 1000 FRANCS
20.0000 g., 0.9990 Silver 0.6423 oz. ASW, 36 mm. **Rev:** Multicolor Convair 990 Coronado over mountains

Date	Mintage	F	VF	XF	Unc	BU
2002 Proof	—	Value: 35.00				

KM# 60 1000 FRANCS
Silver **Subject:** Sir Francis Drake and the Golden Hind

Date	Mintage	F	VF	XF	Unc	BU
2003 Proof	—	Value: 37.50				

KM# 56 1000 FRANCS
20.0000 g., 0.9990 Silver 0.6423 oz. ASW, 36 mm. **Rev:** Multicolor Douglas DC-8 at airport

Date	Mintage	F	VF	XF	Unc	BU
2003 Proof	—	Value: 35.00				

KM# 57 1000 FRANCS
20.0000 g., 0.9990 Silver 0.6423 oz. ASW, 36 mm. **Rev:** Multicolor Fokker 100 left

Date	Mintage	F	VF	XF	Unc	BU
2003 Proof	—	Value: 35.00				

KM# 58 1000 FRANCS
20.0000 g., 0.9990 Silver 0.6423 oz. ASW, 36 mm. **Rev:** Multicolor Douglas DC-4 right

Date	Mintage	F	VF	XF	Unc	BU
2004 Proof	—	Value: 35.00				

KM# 59 1000 FRANCS
20.0000 g., 0.9990 Silver 0.6423 oz. ASW, 36 mm. **Rev:** Multicolor General Aviation GA-43 against blue sky

Date	Mintage	F	VF	XF	Unc	BU
2004 Proof	—	Value: 45.00				

KM# 67 1000 FRANCS
20.0000 g., 0.9990 Silver 0.6423 oz. ASW, 36 mm. **Obv:** National arms **Rev:** Blue plane at airport in color

Date	Mintage	F	VF	XF	Unc	BU
2005 Proof	—	Value: 45.00				

KM# 68 1000 FRANCS
20.0000 g., 0.9990 Silver 0.6423 oz. ASW, 36 mm. **Obv:** Naitonal arms **Rev:** Red plane in flight with green mountain in background

Date	Mintage	F	VF	XF	Unc	BU
2005 Proof	—	Value: 45.00				

KM# 73 1000 FRANCS
Silver, 16 mm. **Subject:** Cannabis **Rev:** Leaf in green **Shape:** Leaf

Date	Mintage	F	VF	XF	Unc	BU
2011 Proof	—	Value: 50.00				

KM# 77 1000 FRANCS
15.5500 g., 0.9990 Silver 0.4994 oz. ASW **Obv:** National arms **Rev:** Red dragon

Date	Mintage	F	VF	XF	Unc	BU
2012 Proof	—	Value: 25.00				

KM# 78 1000 FRANCS
15.5500 g., 0.9990 Silver 0.4994 oz. ASW, 38.61 mm. **Obv:** National arms **Rev:** Blue dragon

Date	Mintage	F	VF	XF	Unc	BU
2012 Proof	—	Value: 25.00				

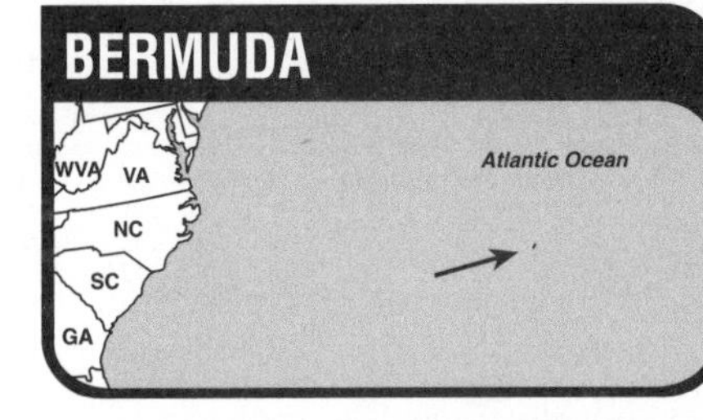

The Parliamentary British Colony of Bermuda, situated in the western Atlantic Ocean 660 miles (1,062 km.) east of North Carolina, has an area of 20.6 sq. mi. (53 sq. km.) and a population of 61,600. Capital: Hamilton. Concentrated essences, beauty preparations, and cut flowers are exported. Most Bermudians derive their livelihood from tourism. The British monarch is the head of state and is represented by a governor. U.S. Currency circulates in common with the Eastern Caribbean Dollar.

RULER
British

BRITISH COLONY

DECIMAL COINAGE

100 Cents = 1 Dollar

KM# 107 CENT
2.5000 g., Copper Plated Zinc, 19 mm. **Ruler:** Elizabeth II **Obv:** Head with tiara right **Rev:** Wild boar left **Edge:** Plain

Date	Mintage	F	VF	XF	Unc	BU
2001	1,600,000	—	—	—	0.50	0.75
2002	1,120,000	—	—	—	0.50	0.75
2003	800,000	—	—	—	0.50	0.75
2004	1,600,000	—	—	—	0.25	0.50
2005	3,200,000	—	—	—	0.25	0.50
2006	800,000	—	—	—	0.25	0.50
2007	—	—	—	—	0.25	0.50
2008	—	—	—	—	0.25	0.50

KM# 107a CENT

2.5000 g., Copper Plated Steel, 19 mm. **Ruler:** Elizabeth II **Obv:** Head with tiara right **Rev:** Wild boar left

Date	Mintage	F	VF	XF	Unc	BU
2008	2,400,000	—	—	—	0.25	0.50
2009	4,000,000	—	—	—	0.25	0.50

KM# 108 5 CENTS

5.0000 g., Copper-Nickel, 21.2 mm. **Ruler:** Elizabeth II **Obv:** Head with tiara right **Rev:** Queen angel fish left **Edge:** Plain

Date	Mintage	F	VF	XF	Unc	BU
2001	1,000,000	—	—	—	0.75	1.00
2002	700,000	—	—	—	0.75	1.00
2003	700,000	—	—	—	0.75	1.00
2004	700,000	—	—	—	0.75	1.00
2005	600,000	—	—	—	0.75	1.00
2008	500,000	—	—	—	0.75	1.00
2009	1,500,000	—	—	—	0.50	0.75

KM# 109 10 CENTS

2.5000 g., Copper-Nickel, 17.8 mm. **Ruler:** Elizabeth II **Obv:** Head with tiara right **Rev:** Bermuda lily **Edge:** Reeded

Date	Mintage	F	VF	XF	Unc	BU
2001	1,400,000	—	—	—	0.85	1.00
2002	800,000	—	—	—	0.85	1.00
2003	600,000	—	—	—	0.85	1.00
2004	800,000	—	—	—	0.85	1.00
2005	800,000	—	—	—	0.85	1.00
2008	2,000,000	—	—	—	0.50	0.75
2009	2,000,000	—	—	—	0.50	0.75

KM# 110 25 CENTS

Copper-Nickel, 24 mm. **Ruler:** Elizabeth II **Obv:** Head with tiara right **Rev:** Yellow-billed tropical bird right **Edge:** Reeded

Date	Mintage	F	VF	XF	Unc	BU
2001	800,000	—	—	—	1.50	2.00
2002	800,000	—	—	—	1.50	2.00
2003	800,000	—	—	—	1.50	2.00
2004	800,000	—	—	—	1.50	2.00
2005	1,440,000	—	—	—	1.50	2.00
2006	320,000	—	—	—	1.50	2.00
2007	—	—	—	—	1.50	2.00
2008	1,200,000	—	—	—	1.00	1.50
2009	2,000,000	—	—	—	1.00	1.50

KM# 111 DOLLAR

Nickel-Brass, 26 mm. **Ruler:** Elizabeth II **Obv:** Head with tiara right **Rev:** Sailboat

Date	Mintage	F	VF	XF	Unc	BU
2001	12,000	—	—	—	3.00	3.50
2002	12,000	—	—	—	3.00	3.50
2003	12,000	—	—	—	3.00	3.50
2004	12,000	—	—	—	3.00	3.50
2005	240,000	—	—	—	2.00	3.00
2008	300,000	—	—	—	2.00	3.00
2009	600,000	—	—	—	2.00	3.00

KM# 139 DOLLAR

28.2800 g., Copper-Nickel, 38.6 mm. **Ruler:** Elizabeth II **Obv:** Head with tiara right **Rev:** 4 Gombey dancers **Edge:** Reeded

Date	Mintage	F	VF	XF	Unc	BU
2001	—	—	—	—	12.00	14.00

KM# 124 DOLLAR

28.4100 g., Copper-Nickel, 38.5 mm. **Ruler:** Elizabeth II **Subject:** Queen's Golden Jubilee **Obv:** Head with tiara right **Rev:** Stylized trumpeters above monogram and date **Edge:** Reeded

Date	Mintage	F	VF	XF	Unc	BU
2002	—	—	—	—	10.00	12.00

KM# 380 2 DOLLARS

31.6040 g., 0.9990 Silver 1.0150 oz. ASW, 38.61 mm. **Ruler:** Elizabeth II **Subject:** Bermuda Hawksbill Turtle **Obv:** Bust right **Rev:** Turtle **Rev. Legend:** BERMUDA HAWKSBILL TURTLE / TWO DOLLARS

Date	Mintage	F	VF	XF	Unc	BU
2008 Proof	2,500	Value: 50.00				

KM# 186 2 DOLLARS

31.6040 g., 0.9990 Silver 1.0150 oz. ASW, 38.61 mm. **Ruler:** Elizabeth II **Subject:** Cahow **Obv:** Head of Queen Elizabeth II with tiara facing right, legend, country name, date **Obv. Legend:** ELIZABETH II **Rev:** Bird over water surrounding outline of Bermuda, denomination

Date	Mintage	F	VF	XF	Unc	BU
2010 Proof	Est. 1,000	Value: 90.00				

KM# 157 3 DOLLARS

33.6300 g., 0.9250 Silver 1.0000 oz. ASW, 35 mm. **Ruler:** Elizabeth II **Subject:** Shipwrecks Series **Obv:** Elizabeth II **Rev:** Gold-plated image of the Hunter Galley **Edge:** Plain

Date	Mintage	F	VF	XF	Unc	BU
2006 Proof	15,000	Value: 90.00				

KM# 158 3 DOLLARS

33.6300 g., 0.9250 Silver 1.0000 oz. ASW, 35 mm. **Ruler:** Elizabeth II **Subject:** Shipwrecks Series **Obv:** Elizabeth II **Rev:** Gold-plated image of the North Carolina **Edge:** Plain

Date	Mintage	F	VF	XF	Unc	BU
2006 Proof	15,000	Value: 90.00				

KM# 159 3 DOLLARS

33.6300 g., 0.9250 Silver 1.0000 oz. ASW, 35 mm. **Ruler:** Elizabeth II **Subject:** Shipwrecks Series **Obv:** Elizabeth II **Rev:** Gold-plated image of the Pollockshields **Edge:** Plain

Date	Mintage	F	VF	XF	Unc	BU
2006 Proof	15,000	Value: 90.00				

KM# 175 3 DOLLARS

31.4890 g., 0.9990 Gold 1.0113 oz. AGW, 35 mm. **Ruler:** Elizabeth II **Series:** Bermuda Shipwrecks **Subject:** The Constellation **Obv:** Head of Queen Elizabeth II with tiara facing right and legend, country name, date **Obv. Legend:** ELIZABETH II **Rev:** The Constellation, legends, denomination **Rev. Legend:** CONSTELLATION Anno Domini 1943 **Shape:** Triangular

Date	Mintage	F	VF	XF	Unc	BU
2006 Proof	Est. 750	Value: 2,400				

KM# 176 3 DOLLARS

31.4890 g., 0.9990 Gold 1.0113 oz. AGW, 35 mm. **Ruler:** Elizabeth II **Series:** Bermuda Shipwrecks **Subject:** The Hunter Galley **Obv:** Head of Queen Elizabeth II with tiara facing right, legend, country name, date **Obv. Legend:** HUNTER GALLEEY Anno Domini 1752 **Rev:** The Hunter Galley, legend, denomination **Shape:** Triangular

Date	Mintage	F	VF	XF	Unc	BU
2006 Proof	Est. 750	Value: 2,400				

KM# 177 3 DOLLARS

31.4890 g., 0.9990 Gold 1.0113 oz. AGW, 35 mm. **Ruler:** Elizabeth II **Series:** Bermuda Shipwrecks **Subject:** The Mary Celestia **Obv:** Head of Queen Elizabeth II with tiara facing right, legend, country name, date **Obv. Legend:** ELIZABETH II **Rev:** The Mary Celestia, legends, denomination **Rev. Legend:** MARY CELESTIA Anno Domini 1864 **Shape:** Triangular

Date	Mintage	F	VF	XF	Unc	BU
2006 Proof	Est. 750	Value: 2,400				

KM# 178 3 DOLLARS

31.4890 g., 0.9990 Gold 1.0113 oz. AGW, 35 mm. **Ruler:** Elizabeth II **Series:** Bemuda Shipwrecks **Subject:** The North Carolina **Obv:** Head of Queen Elizabeth II with tiara facing right, legend, country name, date **Obv. Legend:** ELIZABETH II **Rev:** The North Carolina, legends, denomination **Rev. Legend:** NORTH CAROLINA Anno Domini 1880

Date	Mintage	F	VF	XF	Unc	BU
2006 Proof	Est. 750	Value: 2,400				

KM# 179 3 DOLLARS

31.4890 g., 0.9990 Gold 1.0113 oz. AGW, 35 mm. **Ruler:** Elizabeth II **Series:** Bermuda Shipwrecks **Subject:** The Pollockshields **Obv:** Head of Queen Elizabeth II with tiara facing right, legend, country name, date **Obv. Legend:** ELIZABETH II **Rev:** The Pollockshields, legends, denomination **Rev. Legend:** POLLOCKSHIELD Anno Domini 1915 **Shape:** Triangular

Date	Mintage	F	VF	XF	Unc	BU
2006 Proof	Est. 750	Value: 2,400				

KM# 140 3 DOLLARS

33.6300 g., 0.9250 Silver 1.0000 oz. ASW, 35 mm. **Ruler:** Elizabeth II **Subject:** Shipwreck Series **Obv:** Elizabeth II **Rev:** The Mary Celestia gold-plated image **Edge:** Plain **Shape:** Triangular

Date	Mintage	F	VF	XF	Unc	BU
2006 Proof	15,000	Value: 90.00				

KM# 141 3 DOLLARS

1.5550 g., 0.9990 Gold 0.0499 oz. AGW, 15 mm. **Ruler:** Elizabeth II **Subject:** Shipwreck Series **Obv:** Elizabeth II **Rev:** The Mary Celestia **Edge:** Plain **Shape:** Triangular

Date	Mintage	F	VF	XF	Unc	BU
2006 Proof	15,000	Value: 100				

KM# 148 3 DOLLARS
33.6300 g., 0.9250 Silver 1.0000 oz. ASW, 35 mm. **Ruler:** Elizabeth II **Subject:** Shipwreck Series **Obv:** Elizabeth II **Rev:** The Constellation in gold-plated image **Edge:** Plain **Shape:** Triangular

Date	Mintage	F	VF	XF	Unc	BU
2006 Proof	15,000	Value: 90.00				

KM# 149 3 DOLLARS
1.5550 g., 0.9990 Gold 0.0499 oz. AGW, 15 mm. **Ruler:** Elizabeth II **Subject:** Shipwreck Series **Obv:** Elizabeth II **Rev:** The Constellation **Edge:** Plain **Shape:** Triangular

Date	Mintage	F	VF	XF	Unc	BU
2006 Proof	15,000	Value: 100				

KM# 156 3 DOLLARS
33.6300 g., 0.9250 Silver 1.0000 oz. ASW, 35 mm. **Ruler:** Elizabeth II **Subject:** Shipwrecks Series **Obv:** Elizabeth II **Rev:** Gold-plated image of the Sea Venture **Edge:** Plain

Date	Mintage	F	VF	XF	Unc	BU
2007 Proof	15,000	Value: 90.00				

KM# 180 3 DOLLARS
31.4890 g., 0.9990 Gold 1.0113 oz. AGW, 35 mm. **Ruler:** Elizabeth II **Series:** Bermuda Shipwrecks **Subject:** The Colonel William G. Ball **Obv:** Head of Queen Elizabeth II with tiara facing right, legend, country name, date **Obv. Legend:** ELIZABETH II **Rev:** The colonel William G. Ball, legends, denomination **Rev. Legend:** WILLIAM G. BALL Anno Domini 1943 **Shape:** Triangular

Date	Mintage	F	VF	XF	Unc	BU
2007 Proof	Est. 750	Value: 2,400				

KM# 181 3 DOLLARS
31.4890 g., 0.9990 Gold 1.0113 oz. AGW, 35 mm. **Ruler:** Elizabeth II **Series:** Bermuda Shipwrecks **Subject:** The Chistobal Colon **Obv:** Head of Queen Elizabeth II with tiara facing right, legend, country name, date **Obv. Legend:** ELIZABETH II **Rev:** The Cristobal Colon, legends, denomination **Rev. Legend:** CRISTOBAL COLON Anno Domini 1936 **Shape:** Triangular

Date	Mintage	F	VF	XF	Unc	BU
2007 Proof	Est. 750	Value: 2,400				

KM# 182 3 DOLLARS
31.4890 g., 0.9990 Gold 1.0113 oz. AGW, 35 mm. **Ruler:** Elizabeth II **Series:** Bermuda Shipwrecks **Subject:** The Kate **Obv:** Head of Queen Elizabeth II with tiara facing right and legend, country name, date **Obv. Legend:** ELIZABETH II **Rev:** The Kate, legends, denomination **Rev. Legend:** KATE Anno Domini 1878 **Shape:** Triangular

Date	Mintage	F	VF	XF	Unc	BU
2007 Proof	Est. 750	Value: 2,400				

KM# 183 3 DOLLARS
31.4890 g., 0.9990 Gold 1.0113 oz. AGW, 35 mm. **Ruler:** Elizabeth II **Series:** Bermuda Shipwrecks **Subject:** The San Pedro **Obv:** Head of Queen Elizabeth II with tiara facing right, legend, country name, date **Obv. Legend:** ELIZABETH II **Rev:** The San Pedro, legends, denomination **Rev. Legend:** SAN PEDRO Anno Domini 1595 **Shape:** Triangular

Date	Mintage	F	VF	XF	Unc	BU
2007 Proof	Est. 750	Value: 2,400				

KM# 184 3 DOLLARS
31.4890 g., 0.9990 Gold 1.0113 oz. AGW, 35 mm. **Ruler:** Elizabeth II **Series:** Bermuda Shipwrecks **Subject:** The Santa Lucia **Obv:** Head of Queen Elizabeth II with tiara facing right, legend, country name, date **Obv. Legend:** ELIZABETH II **Rev:** The Santa Lucia, legends, denomination **Rev. Legend:** SANTA LUCIA Anno Domini 1584 **Shape:** Triangular

Date	Mintage	F	VF	XF	Unc	BU
2007 Proof	Est. 750	Value: 2,400				

KM# 185 3 DOLLARS
31.4890 g., 0.9990 Gold 1.0113 oz. AGW, 35 mm. **Ruler:** Elizabeth II **Series:** Bermuda Shipwrecks **Subject:** The Manilla **Obv:** Head of Queen Elizabeth II with tiara facing right, legend, country name, date **Obv. Legend:** ELIZABETH II **Rev:** The Manilla, legends, denomination **Rev. Legend:** MANILLA Anno Domini 1739 **Shape:** Triangular

Date	Mintage	F	VF	XF	Unc	BU
2007 Proof	Est. 750	Value: 2,400				

KM# 164 3 DOLLARS
33.6300 g., 0.9250 Silver 1.0000 oz. ASW, 35 mm. **Ruler:** Elizabeth II **Series:** Bermuda Shipwrecks **Obv:** Head with tiara right, gilt **Rev:** Dutchman sailing ship "Manilla", gilt, 1739 **Edge:** Plain, gilt **Shape:** Triangular

Date	Mintage	F	VF	XF	Unc	BU
2007 Proof	15,000	Value: 85.00				

KM# 165 3 DOLLARS
33.6300 g., 0.9250 Silver 1.0000 oz. ASW, 35 mm. **Ruler:** Elizabeth II **Series:** Bermuda Shipwrecks **Obv:** Head with tiara right, gilt **Rev:** 16th century Spanish sailing ship "Santa Lucia", gilt, 1584 **Edge:** Plain, gilt **Shape:** Triangular

Date	Mintage	F	VF	XF	Unc	BU
2007 Proof	15,000	Value: 85.00				

KM# 166 3 DOLLARS
33.6300 g., 0.9250 Silver 1.0000 oz. ASW **Ruler:** Elizabeth II **Series:** Bermuda Shipwrecks **Obv:** Head with tiara right, gilt **Rev:** Spanish luxury steamship "Cristobal Colon", gilt, 1936 **Edge:** Plain

Date	Mintage	F	VF	XF	Unc	BU
2007 Proof	15,000	Value: 85.00				

KM# 167 3 DOLLARS
33.6300 g., 0.9250 Silver 1.0000 oz. ASW, 35 mm. **Ruler:** Elizabeth II **Series:** Bermuda Shipwrecks **Obv:** Head with tiara right, gilt **Rev:** English iron-hulled steamer with sails "Kate", gilt, 1878 **Edge:** Plain **Shape:** Triangular

Date	Mintage	F	VF	XF	Unc	BU
2007 Proof	15,000	Value: 85.00				

KM# 168 3 DOLLARS
33.6300 g., 0.9250 Silver 1.0000 oz. ASW, 35 mm. **Ruler:** Elizabeth II **Series:** Bermuda Shipwrecks **Obv:** Head with tiara right, gilt **Rev:** 16th century Spanish sailing ship "San Pedro", gilt, 1596 **Edge:** Plain, gilt **Shape:** Triangular

Date	Mintage	F	VF	XF	Unc	BU
2007 Proof	15,000	Value: 85.00				

KM# 169 3 DOLLARS
33.6300 g., 0.9250 Silver 1.0000 oz. ASW, 35 mm. **Ruler:** Elizabeth II **Series:** Bermuda Shipwrecks **Obv:** Head with tiara right, gilt **Rev:** American luxury yacht "Col. William G. Ball", gilt, 1943 **Edge:** Plain, gilt **Shape:** Triangular

Date	Mintage	F	VF	XF	Unc	BU
2007 Proof	15,000	Value: 85.00				

KM# 381 4 DOLLARS
34.0000 g., 0.9250 Silver 1.0111 oz. ASW, 40 mm. **Ruler:** Elizabeth II **Obv:** Bust right **Obv. Legend:** Elizabeth II, Value, BERMUDA **Rev:** Sea venture sailing ship **Rev. Legend:** 1609-2009 400th ANNIVERSARY OF THE SETTLEMENT OF BERMUDA **Shape:** Square

Date	Mintage	F	VF	XF	Unc	BU
ND(2009) Proof	2,000	Value: 55.00				

KM# 120 5 DOLLARS
28.2800 g., 0.9250 Silver 0.8410 oz. ASW, 38.6 mm. **Ruler:** Elizabeth II **Subject:** Gombey Dancers **Obv:** Head with tiara right **Rev:** Multicolor costumed dancers **Edge:** Reeded

Date	Mintage	F	VF	XF	Unc	BU
2001 Proof	3,500	Value: 60.00				

KM# 161 5 DOLLARS
28.2800 g., 0.9250 Silver 0.8410 oz. ASW, 38.6 mm. **Ruler:** Elizabeth II **Obv:** Bust with tiara right **Rev:** Statehouse facade, St. George's **Edge:** Reeded

Date	Mintage	F	VF	XF	Unc	BU
2001 Proof	3,500	Value: 45.00				

KM# 129 5 DOLLARS

28.2800 g., 0.9250 Silver 0.8410 oz. ASW, 38.6 mm. **Ruler:** Elizabeth II **Subject:** Queen's Jubilee **Obv:** Gold-plated head with tiara right, denomination below **Rev:** Trumpeters, monogram and date below **Edge:** Reeded

Date	Mintage	F	VF	XF	Unc	BU
2002 Proof	20,000	Value: 42.00				

KM# 162 5 DOLLARS

28.2800 g., 0.9250 Silver 0.8410 oz. ASW, 38.6 mm. **Ruler:** Elizabeth II **Subject:** 100th Anniversary Cup Match - Cricket **Obv:** Head with tiara right **Rev:** Two players with caps and teams shields below, multicolor **Edge:** Reeded

Date	Mintage	F	VF	XF	Unc	BU
2002 Proof	3,500	Value: 45.00				

KM# 171 5 DOLLARS

28.2800 g., 0.9250 Silver 0.8410 oz. ASW, 38.6 mm. **Ruler:** Elizabeth II **Subject:** Queen's Golden Jubilee **Obv:** Head with tiara right **Rev:** Stylized trumpeters above monogram and date **Edge:** Reeded

Date	Mintage	F	VF	XF	Unc	BU
2002 Proof	3,500	Value: 50.00				

KM# 170 5 DOLLARS

28.2800 g., 0.9250 Silver 0.8410 oz. ASW, 38.6 mm. **Ruler:** Elizabeth II **Subject:** 100th Anniversary Fitted Dinghy Racing **Obv:** Head with tiara right **Rev:** Two dinghies, multicolor sails **Edge:** Reeded

Date	Mintage	F	VF	XF	Unc	BU
ND(2003) Proof	3,500	Value: 50.00				

KM# 130 5 DOLLARS

28.2800 g., 0.9250 Silver 0.8410 oz. ASW, 38.6 mm. **Ruler:** Elizabeth II **Subject:** Queen's Jubilee **Obv:** Gold-plated head with tiara right **Rev:** Royal visit scene **Edge:** Reeded

Date	Mintage	F	VF	XF	Unc	BU
2003 Proof	20,000	Value: 42.00				

KM# 131 5 DOLLARS

28.2800 g., 0.9250 Silver 0.8410 oz. ASW, 38.6 mm. **Ruler:** Elizabeth II **Obv:** Head with tiara right **Rev:** Bermudan stone quarry scene **Edge:** Reeded

Date	Mintage	F	VF	XF	Unc	BU
2004 Proof	3,500	Value: 60.00				

KM# 160 5 DOLLARS

14.5000 g., 0.9250 Silver partially gilt 0.4312 oz. ASW, 30.9 mm. **Ruler:** Elizabeth II **Subject:** Bermuda Quincentennial **Obv:** Head with tiara facing right, partially gold-plated **Rev:** Caravel sailing ship partially gold-plated compass face **Edge:** Plain **Shape:** Pentagonal

Date	Mintage	F	VF	XF	Unc	BU
2005 Proof	2,500	Value: 45.00				

KM# 187 5 DOLLARS

1.5550 g., 0.9990 Gold 0.0499 oz. AGW, 16 mm. **Ruler:** Elizabeth II **Subject:** Cahow **Obv:** Head of Queen Elizabeth II with tiara facing right, legend, country name, date **Obv. Legend:** ELIZABETH II **Rev:** Bird over water surrounding outline of Bermuda, denomination

Date	Mintage	F	VF	XF	Unc	BU
2010 Proof	Est. 500	Value: 150				

KM# 142 9 DOLLARS

155.5200 g., 0.9990 Silver 4.9949 oz. ASW, 65 mm. **Ruler:** Elizabeth II **Subject:** Shipwreck Series **Obv:** Elizabeth II **Rev:** The Mary Celestia **Edge:** Plain **Shape:** Triangular

Date	Mintage	F	VF	XF	Unc	BU
2007 Proof	1,000	Value: 210				

KM# 150 9 DOLLARS

155.5200 g., 0.9990 Silver 4.9949 oz. ASW, 65 mm. **Ruler:** Elizabeth II **Subject:** Shipwreck Series **Obv:** Elizabeth II **Rev:** The Constellation **Edge:** Plain **Shape:** Triangular

Date	Mintage	F	VF	XF	Unc	BU
2007 Proof	1,000	Value: 210				

KM# 143 30 DOLLARS

31.4890 g., 0.9990 Gold 1.0113 oz. AGW, 35 mm. **Ruler:** Elizabeth II **Subject:** Shipwreck Series **Obv:** Elizabeth II **Rev:** The Mary Celestia **Edge:** Plain **Shape:** Triangular

Date	Mintage	F	VF	XF	Unc	BU
2006 Proof	750	Value: 1,850				

KM# 151 30 DOLLARS

31.4890 g., 0.9990 Gold 1.0113 oz. AGW, 35 mm. **Ruler:** Elizabeth II **Subject:** Shipwreck Series **Obv:** Elizabeth II **Rev:** The Constellation **Edge:** Plain **Shape:** Triangular

Date	Mintage	F	VF	XF	Unc	BU
2006 Proof	750	Value: 1,850				

KM# 144 60 DOLLARS

1000.0000 g., 0.9990 Silver 32.117 oz. ASW, 100 mm. **Ruler:** Elizabeth II **Subject:** Shipwreck Series **Obv:** Elizabeth II **Rev:** The Mary Celestia **Edge:** Plain

Date	Mintage	F	VF	XF	Unc	BU
2007 Proof	300	Value: 1,250				

KM# 152 60 DOLLARS

1000.0000 g., 0.9990 Silver 32.117 oz. ASW, 100 mm. **Ruler:** Elizabeth II **Subject:** Shipwreck Series **Obv:** Elizabeth II **Rev:** The Constellation **Edge:** Plain **Shape:** Triangular

Date	Mintage	F	VF	XF	Unc	BU
2007 Proof	300	Value: 1,250				

KM# 145 90 DOLLARS

155.5200 g., 0.9990 Gold 4.9949 oz. AGW, 65 mm. **Ruler:** Elizabeth II **Subject:** Shipwreck Series **Obv:** Elizabeth II **Rev:** The Mary Celestia **Edge:** Plain **Shape:** Triangular

Date	Mintage	F	VF	XF	Unc	BU
2006 Proof	90	Value: 9,100				

KM# 153 90 DOLLARS

155.5200 g., 0.9990 Gold 4.9949 oz. AGW, 65 mm. **Ruler:** Elizabeth II **Subject:** Shipwreck Series **Obv:** Elizabeth II **Rev:** The Constellation **Edge:** Plain **Shape:** Triangular

Date	Mintage	F	VF	XF	Unc	BU
2006 Proof	90	Value: 9,100				

KM# 174 90 DOLLARS

155.5200 g., 0.9990 Gold 4.9949 oz. AGW, 65 mm. **Ruler:** Elizabeth II **Subject:** Sea Venture, 1609 **Obv:** Head with tiara right **Rev:** Sailing ship left **Shape:** Triangle

Date	Mintage	F	VF	XF	Unc	BU
2006 Proof	—	Value: 9,100				

KM# 173 100 DOLLARS

1000.0000 g., 0.9250 Silver selective gold plating 29.738 oz. ASW, 100 mm. **Ruler:** Elizabeth II **Subject:** 500th Anniversary of Discovery **Obv:** Head right **Rev:** Caraval within compass **Shape:** 5-sided

Date	Mintage	F	VF	XF	Unc	BU
2005 Proof	250	Value: 1,150				

KM# 146 300 DOLLARS

155.5200 g., 0.9995 Platinum 4.9974 oz. APW, 65 mm. **Ruler:** Elizabeth II **Subject:** Shipwrecks Series **Obv:** Elizabeth II **Rev:** The Mary Celestia **Edge:** Plain **Shape:** Triangular

Date	Mintage	F	VF	XF	Unc	BU
2006 Proof	60	Value: 9,000				

Note: 9000

KM# 154 300 DOLLARS

155.5200 g., 0.9995 Platinum 4.9974 oz. APW, 65 mm. **Ruler:** Elizabeth II **Subject:** Shipwreck Series **Obv:** Elizabeth II **Rev:** The Constellation **Edge:** Plain **Shape:** Triangular

Date	Mintage	F	VF	XF	Unc	BU
2006 Proof	60	Value: 9,000				

KM# 172 500 DOLLARS

31.1050 g., 0.9990 Gold with selective silver plating 0.9990 oz. AGW, 30.89 mm. **Ruler:** Elizabeth II **Obv:** Queen Elizabeth II **Rev:** Caravel sailing ship in compass face **Edge:** Plain **Shape:** 5-sided **Note:** Bermuda Quincentennial. Prev. KM#160a.

Date	Mintage	F	VF	XF	Unc	BU
2005 Proof	—	Value: 1,850				

KM# 147 600 DOLLARS

1096.0000 g., 0.9180 Gold 32.346 oz. AGW, 100 mm. **Ruler:** Elizabeth II **Subject:** Shipwreck Series **Obv:** Elizabeth II **Rev:** The Mary Celestia **Edge:** Plain **Shape:** Triangular

Date	Mintage	F	VF	XF	Unc	BU
2007 Proof	300	Value: 59,000				

KM# 155 600 DOLLARS

1096.0000 g., 0.9180 Gold 32.346 oz. AGW, 100 mm. **Ruler:** Elizabeth II **Subject:** Shipwreck Series **Obv:** Elizabeth II **Rev:** The Constellation **Edge:** Plain **Shape:** Triangular

Date	Mintage	F	VF	XF	Unc	BU
2007 Proof	300	Value: 59,000				

PIEDFORT

KM#	Date	Mintage	Identification	Mkt Val
P3	2005	250	5 Dollars. 0.9250 Silver. 29.0000 g. 30.89 mm. Gold plated bust and rim. Caravel type sailing ship in partially gold plated compass face and rim. Plain, gold plated edge.	—

MINT SETS

KM#	Date	Mintage	Identification	Issue Price	Mkt Val
MS8	2004 (5)	2,300	KM#107-111.	—	10.00

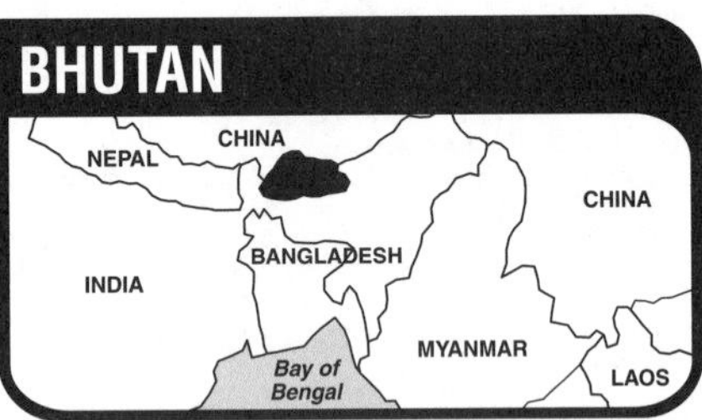

The Kingdom of Bhutan, a landlocked Himalayan country bordered by Tibet and India, has an area of 18,150 sq. mi. (38,394 sq. km.) and a population of 675,000. Capital: Thimphu. Virtually the entire population is engaged in agricultural and pastoral activities. Rice, wheat, barley, and yak butter are produced in sufficient quantity to make the country self-sufficient in food. The economy of Bhutan is primitive and many transactions are conducted on a barter basis.

RULER

Jigme Singye Wangchuck, 1972-2006
King Jigme Khesar Namgyel Wangchuck, 2006-

KINGDOM

REFORM COINAGE

1974 - 100 Chetrums (Paisa) = 1 Ngultrum (Rupee);
100 Ngultrums = 1 Sertum

KM# 105 5 CHETRUMS

3.8600 g., Brass, 21.9 mm. **Obv:** Monkey right, date below **Rev:** Effigy of the old "Ma-tam", value below **Edge:** Plain

Date	Mintage	F	VF	XF	Unc	BU
2003	—	—	—	—	0.25	0.50

KM# 116 NGULTRUM

8.1000 g., Nickel Plated Steel **Ruler:** Jigme Khesar Namgyel Wangchuck

Date	Mintage	F	VF	XF	Unc	BU
2008	—	—	—	—	3.00	4.00

KM# 115 100 NGULTRUMS
20.2000 g., Silver, 38 mm. **Ruler:** Jigme Khesar Namgyel Wangchuck **Subject:** Coronation **Obv:** Portrait left **Rev:** Seal

Date	Mintage	F	VF	XF	Unc	BU
2008 Proof	—	Value: 60.00				

KM# 214 100 NGULTRUMS
0.5000 g., 0.9990 Gold 0.0161 oz. AGW, 11 mm. **Ruler:** Jigme Khesar Namgyel Wangchuck **Subject:** Buddhist Monastery - Taktsang

Date	Mintage	F	VF	XF	Unc	BU
2010 Proof	Est. 5,000	Value: 60.00				

KM# 224 100 NGULTRUMS
0.5000 g., 0.9990 Gold 0.0161 oz. AGW, 11 mm. **Ruler:** Jigme Khesar Namgyel Wangchuck **Subject:** Buddhist Monastery - Chorten Kora

Date	Mintage	F	VF	XF	Unc	BU
2011 Proof	Est. 5,000	Value: 55.00				

KM# 229 100 NGULTRUMS
0.5850 g., 0.5000 Gold with 24Kt plating 0.0094 oz. AGW, 11 mm. **Ruler:** Jigme Khesar Namgyel Wangchuck **Subject:** Traditional Archery **Rev:** Archer

Date	Mintage	F	VF	XF	Unc	BU
2012 Proof	7,000	Value: 25.00				

KM# 208 200 NGULTRUMS
1.2400 g., 0.9990 Gold 0.0398 oz. AGW, 13.92 mm. **Ruler:** Jigme Khesar Namgyel Wangchuck **Subject:** Buddha's of the World - Cambodia **Rev:** Head from Angkor Wat

Date	Mintage	F	VF	XF	Unc	BU
2010 Proof	Est. 30,000	Value: 90.00				

KM# 211 200 NGULTRUMS
1.2400 g., 0.9990 Gold 0.0398 oz. AGW, 13.92 mm. **Ruler:** Jigme Khesar Namgyel Wangchuck **Subject:** Buddha's of the World - Korea **Rev:** Buddha seated

Date	Mintage	F	VF	XF	Unc	BU
2010	Est. 30,000	—	—	—	—	90.00

KM# 217 200 NGULTRUMS
1.2400 g., 0.9990 Gold 0.0398 oz. AGW, 13.92 mm. **Ruler:** Jigme Khesar Namgyel Wangchuck **Subject:** Buddhist World Heritage - Thailand **Rev:** Wat Pho

Date	Mintage	F	VF	XF	Unc	BU
2011	Est. 30,000	—	—	—	—	100

KM# 220 200 NGULTRUMS
1.2400 g., 0.9990 Gold 0.0398 oz. AGW, 13.92 mm. **Ruler:** Jigme Khesar Namgyel Wangchuck **Subject:** Buddhist World Heritage - China **Rev:** Great Buddha in Leshan

Date	Mintage	F	VF	XF	Unc	BU
2011	Est. 30,000	—	—	—	—	80.00

KM# 181 250 NGULTRUMS
31.1050 g., 0.9990 Silver 0.9990 oz. ASW, 38.61 mm. **Ruler:** Jigme Singye Wangchuck **Rev:** Sun Yat-Sen bust facing

Date	Mintage	F	VF	XF	Unc	BU
2003 Proof	Est. 4,999	Value: 70.00				

KM# 185 250 NGULTRUMS
31.1050 g., 0.9990 Silver 0.9990 oz. ASW, 38.61 mm. **Ruler:** Jigme Singye Wangchuck **Subject:** Wonders of the World - Borobudur Temple in Java

Date	Mintage	F	VF	XF	Unc	BU
2003 Proof	Est. 9,999	Value: 70.00				

KM# 189 250 NGULTRUMS
31.1050 g., 0.9990 Silver 0.9990 oz. ASW, 38.61 mm. **Ruler:** Jigme Singye Wangchuck **Subject:** Guanyin, Buddhist godess of mercy

Date	Mintage	F	VF	XF	Unc	BU
2003 Proof	—	Value: 70.00				

KM# 191 250 NGULTRUMS
31.1050 g., 0.9990 Silver 0.9990 oz. ASW, 38.61 mm. **Ruler:** Jigme Singye Wangchuck **Subject:** World Fellowship of Buddhist Youth **Rev:** Lord Buddha, the Enlightenment

Date	Mintage	F	VF	XF	Unc	BU
2003 Proof	Est. 2,999	Value: 70.00				

KM# 170 250 NGULTRUMS
31.1050 g., 0.9990 Silver 0.9990 oz. ASW, 38.61 mm. **Ruler:** Jigme Singye Wangchuck **Subject:** Wonders of the World - Pyramids

Date	Mintage	F	VF	XF	Unc	BU
2004 Proof	Est. 4,999	Value: 70.00				

KM# 172 250 NGULTRUMS
31.1060 g., 0.9990 Silver 0.9990 oz. ASW, 38.61 mm. **Ruler:** Jigme Singye Wangchuck **Subject:** Wonders of the World - Taj Mahal

Date	Mintage	F	VF	XF	Unc	BU
2004 Proof	Est. 4,999	Value: 70.00				

KM# 195 250 NGULTRUMS
31.1050 g., 0.9990 Silver 0.9990 oz. ASW, 38.61 mm. **Ruler:** Jigme Singye Wangchuck **Subject:** Indonesian Games in Palembang **Rev:** Rimau, games mascot

Date	Mintage	F	VF	XF	Unc	BU
2004 Proof	Est. 4,999	Value: 75.00				

KM# 196 250 NGULTRUMS
31.1050 g., 0.9990 Silver 0.9990 oz. ASW, 38.61 mm. **Ruler:** Jigme Singye Wangchuck **Subject:** Indonesian Games in Palembang **Rev:** Bridge card hand

Date	Mintage	F	VF	XF	Unc	BU
2004 Proof	4,999	Value: 75.00				

KM# 197 250 NGULTRUMS
31.1050 g., 0.9990 Silver 0.9990 oz. ASW, 38.61 mm. **Ruler:** Jigme Singye Wangchuck **Subject:** Indonesian Games in Palembang **Rev:** Badminton

Date	Mintage	F	VF	XF	Unc	BU
2004 Proof	Est. 4,999	Value: 75.00				

KM# 198 250 NGULTRUMS
31.1050 g., 0.9990 Silver 0.9990 oz. ASW, 38.61 mm. **Ruler:** Jigme Singye Wangchuck **Subject:** Indonesian Games in Palembang **Rev:** Sailing

Date	Mintage	F	VF	XF	Unc	BU
2004 Proof	Est. 4,999	Value: 75.00				

KM# 199 250 NGULTRUMS
31.1050 g., 0.9990 Silver 0.9990 oz. ASW, 38.61 mm. **Ruler:** Jigme Singye Wangchuck **Subject:** Indonesian Games in Palembang **Rev:** Games logo

Date	Mintage	F	VF	XF	Unc	BU
2004 Proof	Est. 4,999	Value: 75.00				

KM# 200 250 NGULTRUMS
Bi-Metallic 25g .925 Silver and .9g .750 Gold, 38.61 mm. **Ruler:** Jigme Singye Wangchuck **Subject:** Sundial

Date	Mintage	F	VF	XF	Unc	BU
2004	Est. 9,999	—	—	—	—	125

KM# 201 250 NGULTRUMS
Bi-Metallic 25g .925 Silver with 8g Steel, 38.61 mm. **Ruler:** Jigme Singye Wangchuck **Rev:** Compass rose

Date	Mintage	F	VF	XF	Unc	BU
2004	Est. 9,999	—	—	—	—	125

KM# 207 250 NGULTRUMS
31.1050 g., 0.9990 Silver 0.9990 oz. ASW, 40.7 mm. **Ruler:** Jigme Khesar Namgyel Wangchuck **Subject:** Buddha's of the World - Cambodia **Rev:** Head from Angkor Wat, in color

Date	Mintage	F	VF	XF	Unc	BU
2010 Proof	Est. 10,000	Value: 70.00				

KM# 210 250 NGULTRUMS
31.1050 g., 0.9990 Silver 0.9990 oz. ASW, 40.7 mm. **Ruler:** Jigme Khesar Namgyel Wangchuck **Subject:** Buddha's of the World - Korea **Rev:** Buddha seated in color

Date	Mintage	F	VF	XF	Unc	BU
2010 Proof	Est. 10,000	Value: 70.00				

KM# 216 250 NGULTRUMS
31.1050 g., 0.9990 Silver 0.9990 oz. ASW, 40.7 mm. **Ruler:** Jigme Khesar Namgyel Wangchuck **Subject:** Buddhist World heritage - Thailand **Obv:** Dhug in color **Rev:** Wat Pho

Date	Mintage	F	VF	XF	Unc	BU
2011 Proof	Est. 10,000	Value: 70.00				

KM# 219 250 NGULTRUMS
31.1050 g., 0.9990 Silver 0.9990 oz. ASW, 40.7 mm. **Ruler:** Jigme Khesar Namgyel Wangchuck **Subject:** Buddhist World Heritage - China **Obv:** Khorto in color **Rev:** Great Buddha in Leshan

Date	Mintage	F	VF	XF	Unc	BU
2011 Proof	Est. 10,000	Value: 70.00				

KM# 215 300 NGULTRUMS
1.2400 g., 0.9990 Gold 0.0398 oz. AGW, 13.92 mm. **Ruler:** Jigme Khesar Namgyel Wangchuck **Subject:** Buddhist Monastery - Taktsang

Date	Mintage	F	VF	XF	Unc	BU
2010 Proof	Est. 5,000	Value: 100				

KM# 226 300 NGULTRUMS
28.2800 g., 0.9250 Silver 0.8410 oz. ASW, 38.61 mm. **Ruler:** Jigme Khesar Namgyel Wangchuck **Subject:** Olympics 2014 - Cross Country Skiing **Rev:** Two skiers

Date	Mintage	F	VF	XF	Unc	BU
2012 Proof	5,000	Value: 70.00				

KM# 227 300 NGULTRUMS
3.1100 g., 0.9990 Gold 0.0999 oz. AGW, 16.5 mm. **Ruler:** Jigme Khesar Namgyel Wangchuck **Subject:** 2014 FIFA World Cup - Brazil **Rev:** Soccer Player and dragon

Date	Mintage	F	VF	XF	Unc	BU
2012 Proof	1,000	Value: 225				

KM# 228 300 NGULTRUMS
20.0000 g., 0.9250 Silver 0.5948 oz. ASW, 38.61 mm. **Ruler:** Jigme Khesar Namgyel Wangchuck **Subject:** Himalayan Railway **Rev:** Steam Locomotive and outline of mountains

Date	Mintage	F	VF	XF	Unc	BU
2012 Proof	3,000	Value: 60.00				

KM# 203 500 NGULTRUM
62.2000 g., 0.9990 Silver partially gilt 1.9977 oz. ASW **Ruler:** Jigme Singye Wangchuck **Rev:** Zodiac, partially gilt

Date	Mintage	F	VF	XF	Unc	BU
2006 Proof	—	Value: 110				

KM# 205 500 NGULTRUM
31.1050 g., 0.9990 Silver 0.9990 oz. ASW, 38.7 mm. **Ruler:** Jigme Khesar Namgyel Wangchuck **Subject:** Coronation

Date	Mintage	F	VF	XF	Unc	BU
2008 Proof	5,000	Value: 85.00				

KM# 222 500 NGULTRUM
31.1050 g., 0.9990 Silver 0.9990 oz. ASW, 40.7 mm. **Ruler:** Jigme Khesar Namgyel Wangchuck **Subject:** Royal Wedding **Rev:** Couple in color

Date	Mintage	F	VF	XF	Unc	BU
2011 Proof	Est. 20,000	Value: 140				

KM# 173 1000 NGULTRUM
10.0000 g., 0.9990 Gold 0.3212 oz. AGW, 26 mm. **Ruler:** Jigme Singye Wangchuck **Subject:** Wonders of the World - Taj Mahal

Date	Mintage	F	VF	XF	Unc	BU
2002 Proof	Est. 3,000	Value: 700				

KM# 177 1000 NGULTRUM
10.0000 g., 0.9990 Gold 0.3212 oz. AGW, 26 mm. **Ruler:** Jigme Singye Wangchuck **Subject:** World Fellowship of Buddhist Youth

Date	Mintage	F	VF	XF	Unc	BU
2002 Proof	Est. 2,999	Value: 650				

KM# 182 1000 NGULTRUM
6.2200 g., 0.9990 Gold 0.1998 oz. AGW, 26 mm. **Ruler:** Jigme Singye Wangchuck **Rev:** Sun Yat-Sen bust facing

Date	Mintage	F	VF	XF	Unc	BU
2003 Proof	Est. 4,999	Value: 425				

KM# 183 1000 NGULTRUM
10.0000 g., 0.9990 Gold 0.3212 oz. AGW, 26 mm. **Ruler:** Jigme Singye Wangchuck **Subject:** Legends of Sports - Rudy Hartono **Rev:** Bust at left, tennis serve at right

Date	Mintage	F	VF	XF	Unc	BU
2003 Proof	Est. 10,000	Value: 650				

KM# 186 1000 NGULTRUM
10.0000 g., 0.9990 Gold 0.3212 oz. AGW, 26 mm. **Ruler:** Jigme Singye Wangchuck **Subject:** Wonders of the World - Borobudur Temple in Java

Date	Mintage	F	VF	XF	Unc	BU
2003 Proof	Est. 9,999	Value: 650				

KM# 190 1000 NGULTRUM
10.0000 g., 0.9990 Gold 0.3212 oz. AGW, 26 mm. **Ruler:** Jigme Singye Wangchuck **Subject:** Guanyin, Buddhist godess of mercy

Date	Mintage	F	VF	XF	Unc	BU
2003 Proof	—	Value: 650				

KM# 192 1000 NGULTRUM
10.0000 g., 0.9990 Gold 0.3212 oz. AGW, 26 mm. **Ruler:** Jigme Singye Wangchuck **Subject:** World Fellowship of Buddhist Youth **Rev:** Lord Buddha, the Enlightenment

Date	Mintage	F	VF	XF	Unc	BU
2003 Proof	Est. 2,999	Value: 650				

KM# 209 1000 NGULTRUM
7.7800 g., 0.9990 Gold 0.2499 oz. AGW, 22 mm. **Ruler:** Jigme Khesar Namgyel Wangchuck **Subject:** Buddha's of the World - Cambodia **Rev:** Head from Angkor Wat

Date	Mintage	F	VF	XF	Unc	BU
2010 Proof	Est. 6,000	Value: 525				

KM# 212 1000 NGULTRUM
7.7800 g., 0.9990 Gold 0.2499 oz. AGW, 22 mm. **Ruler:** Jigme Khesar Namgyel Wangchuck **Subject:** Buddha's of the World - Korea **Rev:** Buddha seated

Date	Mintage	F	VF	XF	Unc	BU
2010 Proof	Est. 6,000	Value: 525				

KM# 213 1000 NGULTRUM
28.2800 g., 0.9250 Gold 0.8410 oz. AGW, 38.61 mm. **Ruler:** Jigme Khesar Namgyel Wangchuck **Rev:** Charles Lindbergh and Spirit of St. Louis

Date	Mintage	F	VF	XF	Unc	BU
2010 Proof	Est. 5,000	Value: 70.00				

KM# 218 1000 NGULTRUM
7.7800 g., 0.9990 Gold 0.2499 oz. AGW, 22 mm. **Ruler:** Jigme Khesar Namgyel Wangchuck **Subject:** Buddhist World Heritage - Thailand **Rev:** Wat Pho

Date	Mintage	F	VF	XF	Unc	BU
2011 Proof	Est. 6,000	Value: 525				

KM# 221 1000 NGULTRUM
7.7800 g., 0.9990 Gold 0.2499 oz. AGW, 22 mm. **Ruler:** Jigme Khesar Namgyel Wangchuck **Subject:** Buddhist World Heritage - China **Rev:** Great Buddha in Leshan

Date	Mintage	F	VF	XF	Unc	BU
2011 Proof	Est. 6,000	Value: 525				

KM# 202 1500 NGULTRUM
155.5000 g., 0.9990 Silver partially gilt 4.9942 oz. ASW, 65 mm. **Ruler:** Jigme Singye Wangchuck **Subject:** Wonders of the World - Angkor Wat **Rev:** Angkor Wat temple gilt

Date	Mintage	F	VF	XF	Unc	BU
2004 Proof	—	Value: 250				

KM# 204 1500 NGULTRUM
155.5000 g., 0.9990 Silver 4.9942 oz. ASW, 65 mm. **Ruler:** Jigme Singye Wangchuck **Subject:** Year of the Dog

Date	Mintage	F	VF	XF	Unc	BU
2006 Proof	Est. 8,888	Value: 250				

KM# 167 2000 NGULTRUMS
20.0000 g., 0.9990 Gold 0.6423 oz. AGW, 33 mm. **Ruler:** Jigme Singye Wangchuck **Subject:** Year of the Horse

Date	Mintage	F	VF	XF	Unc	BU
2002 Proof	—	Value: 1,250				

KM# 171 2000 NGULTRUMS
Bi-Metallic 31.105 g. .999 Silver and 7.78 g. .999 Gold **Ruler:** Jigme Singye Wangchuck **Subject:** Wonders of the World - Pyramids

Date	Mintage	F	VF	XF	Unc	BU
2002 Proof	Est. 9,999	Value: 550				

KM# 193 2000 NGULTRUMS
20.0000 g., 0.9990 Gold 0.6423 oz. AGW, 26 mm. **Ruler:** Jigme Singye Wangchuck **Subject:** World Fellowship of Buddhist Youth **Rev:** Lord Buddha, the Enlightenment

Date	Mintage	F	VF	XF	Unc	BU
2003 Proof	Est. 2,999	Value: 1,250				

KM# 165 3000 NGULTRUM
31.1050 g., 0.9990 Gold 0.9990 oz. AGW, 38.61 mm. **Ruler:** Jigme Singye Wangchuck **Subject:** Year of the Snake

Date	Mintage	F	VF	XF	Unc	BU
2001 Proof	Est. 18,888	Value: 1,800				

KM# 168 3000 NGULTRUM
31.1050 g., 0.9990 Gold 0.9990 oz. AGW, 38.61 mm. **Ruler:** Jigme Singye Wangchuck **Subject:** Year of the Horse

Date	Mintage	F	VF	XF	Unc	BU
2002 Proof	Est. 18,888	Value: 1,800				

KM# 174 3000 NGULTRUM
31.1050 g., 0.9990 Gold 0.9990 oz. AGW, 38.61 mm. **Ruler:** Jigme Singye Wangchuck **Subject:** Wonders of the World - Taj Mahal

Date	Mintage	F	VF	XF	Unc	BU
2002 Proof	Est. 18,888	Value: 1,800				

KM# 175 3000 NGULTRUM
31.1050 g., 0.9990 Gold 0.9990 oz. AGW, 38.61 mm. **Ruler:** Jigme Singye Wangchuck **Subject:** Royal Society for the Protection of Nature, 15th Anniversary **Rev:** Elephant head

Date	Mintage	F	VF	XF	Unc	BU
2002 Proof	Est. 10,000	Value: 1,800				

KM# 176 3000 NGULTRUM
31.1050 g., 0.9990 Gold 0.9990 oz. AGW, 38.61 mm. **Ruler:** Jigme Singye Wangchuck **Subject:** Royal Society for the Protection of Nature, 15th Anniversary **Rev:** Two tigers

Date	Mintage	F	VF	XF	Unc	BU
2002 Proof	Est. 10,000	Value: 1,800				

KM# 178 3000 NGULTRUM
31.1050 g., 0.9990 Gold 0.9990 oz. AGW, 38.61 mm. **Ruler:** Jigme Singye Wangchuck **Subject:** World Fellowship of Buddhist Youth

Date	Mintage	F	VF	XF	Unc	BU
2002 Proof	Est. 10,000	Value: 1,800				

KM# 179 3000 NGULTRUM
31.1050 g., 0.9990 Gold 0.9990 oz. AGW, 38.61 mm. **Ruler:** Jigme Singye Wangchuck **Subject:** Year of the Goat **Rev:** Three rams

Date	Mintage	F	VF	XF	Unc	BU
2003 Proof	Est. 18,888	—	—	—	—	1,800

KM# 184 3000 NGULTRUM
31.1050 g., 0.9990 Gold 0.9990 oz. AGW, 38.61 mm. **Ruler:** Jigme Singye Wangchuck **Subject:** Legends of Sport - Rudy Hartono **Rev:** Bust at left, tennis serve at right

Date	Mintage	F	VF	XF	Unc	BU
2003 Proof	Est. 10,000	Value: 1,800				

KM# 187 3000 NGULTRUM
31.1050 g., 0.9990 Gold 0.9990 oz. AGW, 38.61 mm. **Ruler:** Jigme Singye Wangchuck **Subject:** Wonders of the World - Borobudur Temple in Java

Date	Mintage	F	VF	XF	Unc	BU
2003 Proof	Est. 30,000	Value: 1,800				

KM# 194 3000 NGULTRUM
31.1050 g., 0.9990 Gold 0.9990 oz. AGW, 38.61 mm. **Ruler:** Jigme Singye Wangchuck **Subject:** World Fellowship of Buddhist Youth **Rev:** Lord Buddha, the Enlightenment

Date	Mintage	F	VF	XF	Unc	BU
2003 Proof	—	Value: 1,800				

KM# 166 20000 NGULTRUM
155.5200 g., 0.9990 Gold 4.9949 oz. AGW, 65 mm. **Ruler:** Jigme Singye Wangchuck **Subject:** Year of the Snake

Date	Mintage	F	VF	XF	Unc	BU
2001 Proof	Est. 88	Value: 9,000				

KM# 169 20000 NGULTRUM
155.5200 g., 0.9990 Gold 4.9949 oz. AGW, 65 mm. **Ruler:** Jigme Singye Wangchuck **Subject:** Year of the Horse

Date	Mintage	F	VF	XF	Unc	BU
2002 Proof	Est. 88	Value: 9,000				

KM# 180 20000 NGULTRUM
155.5200 g., 0.9990 Gold 4.9949 oz. AGW, 65 mm. **Ruler:** Jigme Singye Wangchuck **Subject:** Year of the Goat **Rev:** Three rams

Date	Mintage	F	VF	XF	Unc	BU
2003 Proof	Est. 88	Value: 9,000				

KM# 188 30000 NGULTRUM
155.5200 g., 0.9990 Gold 4.9949 oz. AGW, 65 mm. **Ruler:** Jigme Singye Wangchuck **Subject:** Wonders of the World - Borobudur Temple in Java

Date	Mintage	F	VF	XF	Unc	BU
2003 Proof	—	Value: 9,000				

KM# 223 100000 NGULTRUM
1000.0000 g., 0.9990 Silver 32.117 oz. ASW, 100 mm. **Ruler:** Jigme Khesar Namgyel Wangchuck **Subject:** Royal Wedding **Rev:** Couple

Date	Mintage	F	VF	XF	Unc	BU
2011 Proof	2	Value: 2,000				

KM# 225 5 SERTUMS
7.7800 g., 0.5850 Gold 24Kt plated 0.1463 oz. AGW, 25 mm. **Ruler:** Jigme Khesar Namgyel Wangchuck **Subject:** Olympics, Archery **Rev:** Two archers and target

Date	Mintage	F	VF	XF	Unc	BU
2012 Proof	1,000	Value: 325				

KM# 206 10 SERTUM
31.1050 g., 0.9990 Gold 0.9990 oz. AGW, 38.7 mm. **Ruler:** Jigme Khesar Namgyel Wangchuck **Subject:** Coronation

Date	Mintage	F	VF	XF	Unc	BU
2008 Proof	1,000	Value: 1,800				

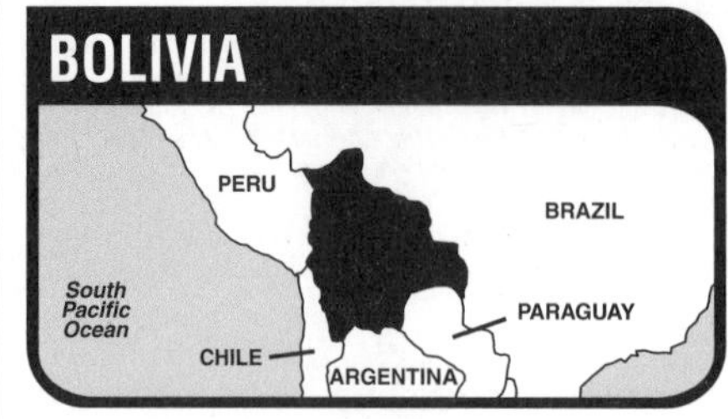

The Plurinational State of Bolivia, a landlocked country in west central South America, has an area of 424,165 sq. mi. (1,098,580 sq. km.) and a population of *8.33 million. Its capitals are: La Paz (administrative) and Sucre (constitutional). Principal exports are tin, zinc, antimony, tungsten, petroleum, natural gas, cotton and coffee.

MINT MARKS
A - Paris
(a) - Paris, privy marks only
CHI - Valcambia
H - Heaton
KN - Kings' Norton

REPUBLIC

REFORM COINAGE

1987-; 1,000,000 Peso Bolivianos = 1 Boliviano;
100 Centavos = 1 Boliviano

KM# 213 10 CENTAVOS
1.8500 g., Copper Clad Steel, 19 mm. **Obv:** National arms **Rev:** Value

Date	Mintage	F	VF	XF	Unc	BU
2001	—	—	—	—	0.50	1.00
2006	—	—	—	—	0.50	1.00
2008	—	—	—	—	0.50	1.00

KM# 202 10 CENTAVOS
1.8500 g., Stainless Steel, 19 mm. **Obv:** National arms, star below **Rev:** Denomination within circle, date below

Date	Mintage	F	VF	XF	Unc	BU
2006	—	—	—	0.20	0.50	0.70

KM# 214 10 CENTAVOS
1.8500 g., Copper Plated Steel, 19 mm. **Obv:** National arms **Obv. Legend:** ESTADO PLURINACIONAL DE BOLIVIA **Rev:** Value

Date	Mintage	F	VF	XF	Unc	BU
2010	—	—	—	—	0.10	0.20

KM# 203 20 CENTAVOS
3.2500 g., Stainless Steel, 22 mm. **Obv:** National arms, star below **Obv. Legend:** REPUBLICA DE BOLIVIA **Rev:** Denomination within circle, date below **Rev. Legend:** LA UNION ES LA FUERZA **Edge:** Plain

Date	Mintage	F	VF	XF	Unc	BU
2001	—	—	—	0.25	0.60	0.80
2006	—	—	—	0.25	0.60	0.80
2008	—	—	—	0.25	0.60	0.80

KM# 215 20 CENTAVOS
3.2500 g., Stainless Steel, 22 mm. **Obv:** National arms **Obv. Legend:** ESTADO PLURINACIONAL DE BOLIVIA **Rev:** Value

Date	Mintage	F	VF	XF	Unc	BU
2010	—	—	—	—	0.15	0.25

KM# 204 50 CENTAVOS
3.7500 g., Stainless Steel, 24 mm. **Obv:** National arms, star below **Obv. Legend:** REPUBLICA DE BOLIVIA **Rev:** Denomination within circle, date below **Rev. Legend:** LA UNION ES LA FUERZA **Edge:** Plain

Date	Mintage	F	VF	XF	Unc	BU
2001	—	—	—	0.30	0.75	1.00
2006	—	—	—	0.30	0.75	1.00
2008	—	—	—	0.30	0.75	1.00

KM# 216 50 CENTAVOS
3.7500 g., Stainless Steel, 24 mm. **Obv:** National arms **Obv. Legend:** ESTADO PLURINACIONAL DE BOLIVIA **Rev:** Value

Date	Mintage	F	VF	XF	Unc	BU
2010	—	—	—	—	0.50	1.00

KM# 205 BOLIVIANO
5.0000 g., Stainless Steel, 27 mm. **Obv:** National arms, star below **Obv. Legend:** REPUBLICA DE BOLIVIA **Rev:** Denomination within circle, date below sprays **Rev. Legend:** LA UNION ES LA FUERZA **Edge:** Plain

Date	Mintage	F	VF	XF	Unc	BU
2001	—	—	—	0.35	0.90	1.20
2004	—	—	—	0.35	0.90	1.20
2008	—	—	—	0.35	0.90	1.20

KM# 217 BOLIVIANO
5.0000 g., Stainless Steel, 27 mm. **Obv:** National arms **Obv. Legend:** ESTADO PLURINACIONAL DE BOLIVIA **Rev:** Value

Date	Mintage	F	VF	XF	Unc	BU
2010	—	—	—	—	1.50	2.00

KM# 206.2 2 BOLIVIANOS
6.2500 g., Stainless Steel, 27 mm. **Obv:** National arms, star below **Rev:** Denomination within circle, date below **Note:** Increased size.

Date	Mintage	F	VF	XF	Unc	BU
2008	—	—	—	—	2.00	3.00

KM# 218 2 BOLIVIANOS
6.2500 g., Stainless Steel, 27 mm. **Obv:** National arms **Obv. Legend:** ESTADO PLURINACIONAL DE BOLIVIA **Rev:** Value

Date	Mintage	F	VF	XF	Unc	BU
2010	—	—	—	—	1.50	2.00
2012	—	—	—	—	1.50	2.00

KM# 212 5 BOLIVIANOS
5.0000 g., Bi-Metallic Bronze Plated Steel center in Stainless Steel ring, 23 mm. **Obv:** National arms **Obv. Legend:** REPUBLICA DE BOLIVIA **Rev:** Denomination **Rev. Legend:** LA UNION ES LA FUERZA **Edge:** Reeded

Date	Mintage	F	VF	XF	Unc	BU
2001	—	—	—	0.90	2.25	3.00
2004	—	—	—	0.90	2.25	3.00

KM# 219 5 BOLIVIANOS
5.0000 g., Bi-Metallic Bronze Plated Steel center in Stainless Steel ring, 23 mm. **Obv:** National arms **Obv. Legend:** ESTADO PLURINACIONAL DE BOLIVIA **Rev:** Value **Edge:** Reeded

Date	Mintage	F	VF	XF	Unc	BU
2010	—	—	—	—	4.00	5.00

BOSNIA - HERZEGOVINA

The Republic of Bosnia and Herzegovina borders Croatia to the north and west, Serbia to the east and Montenegro in the southeast with only 12.4 mi. of coastline. The total land area is 19,735 sq. mi. (51,129 sq. km.). They have a population of *4.34 million. Capital: Sarajevo. Electricity, mining and agriculture are leading industries.

MONETARY SYSTEM
1 Convertible Marka = 100 Convertible Feniga = 1 Deutschemark 1998-

NOTE: German Euros circulate freely.

REPUBLIC

REFORM COINAGE

1998-

KM# 121 5 FENINGA
2.6600 g., Nickel Plated Steel, 18 mm. **Obv:** Denomination on map **Rev:** Triangle and stars **Edge:** Reeded

Date	Mintage	F	VF	XF	Unc	BU
2005	—	—	—	—	1.00	1.25
2008	—	—	—	—	1.00	1.25
2011	—	—	—	—	1.00	1.25

KM# 115 10 FENINGA
3.9000 g., Copper Plated Steel, 20 mm. **Obv:** Denomination on map within circle **Rev:** Triangle and stars, date at left within circle **Edge:** Plain

Date	Mintage	F	VF	XF	Unc	BU
2004	—	—	—	—	0.50	0.75
2007	—	—	—	—	0.50	0.75
2008	—	—	—	—	0.50	0.75
2011	—	—	—	—	0.50	0.75

KM# 116 20 FENINGA
4.5000 g., Copper Plated Steel, 22 mm. **Obv:** Denomination on map within circle **Rev:** Triangle and stars, date at left within circle **Edge:** Reeded

Date	Mintage	F	VF	XF	Unc	BU
2004	—	—	—	—	1.00	1.25
2007	—	—	—	—	1.00	1.25
2008	—	—	—	—	1.00	1.25
2009	—	—	—	—	1.00	1.25

KM# 117 50 FENINGA
5.1500 g., Copper Plated Steel, 24 mm. **Obv:** Denomination on map within circle **Rev:** Triangle and stars, date at left within circle

Date	Mintage	F	VF	XF	Unc	BU
2007	—	—	—	—	—	3.00

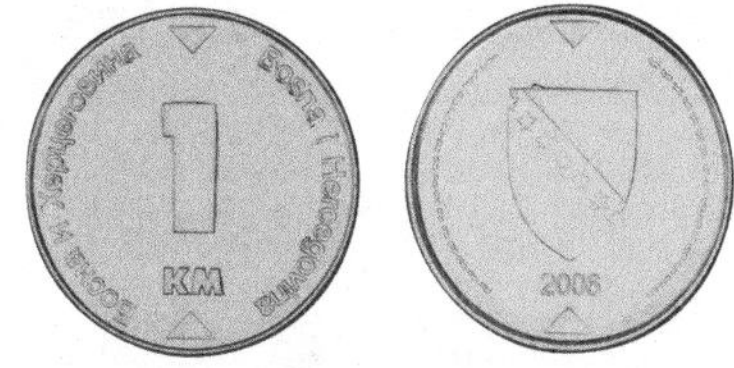

KM# 118 KONVERTIBLE MARKA
4.9500 g., Nickel Plated Steel, 23.23 mm. **Obv:** Denomination **Rev:** Coat of arms above date **Edge:** Segmented reeding

Date	Mintage	F	VF	XF	Unc	BU
2002	—	—	—	—	5.50	6.00
2003	—	—	—	—	5.50	6.00
2004	—	—	—	—	5.50	6.00
2006	—	—	—	—	4.00	5.00
2007	—	—	—	—	4.00	5.00
2008	—	—	—	—	4.00	5.00
2009	—	—	—	—	4.00	5.00

KM# 119 2 KONVERTIBLE MARKA
6.9000 g., Bi-Metallic Copper-Nickel center in Nickel-Brass ring, 25.75 mm. **Obv:** Denomination within circle **Rev:** Dove of Peace, date at right within circle **Edge:** Segmented reeding

Date	Mintage	F	VF	XF	Unc	BU
2002	—	—	—	—	13.50	15.00
2003	—	—	—	—	13.50	15.00
2008	—	—	—	—	13.50	15.00

KM# 120 5 KONVERTIBLE MARKA
10.3500 g., Bi-Metallic Nickel-Brass center in Copper-Nickel ring, 30 mm. **Obv:** Denomination within circle **Rev:** Dove of Peace in flight **Edge:** Reeded

Date	Mintage	F	VF	XF	Unc	BU
2005	—	—	—	—	17.50	20.00
2009	—	—	—	—	17.50	20.00

BOTSWANA

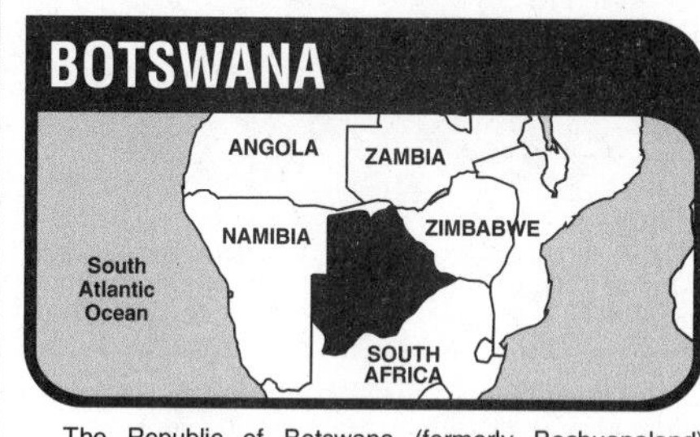

The Republic of Botswana (formerly Bechuanaland), located in south central Africa between Namibia and Zimbabwe, has an area of 224,607 sq. mi. (600,370 sq. km.) and a population of *1.62 million. Capital: Gaborone. Botswana is a member of a Customs Union with South Africa, Lesotho, and Swaziland. The economy is primarily pastoral with a rapidly developing mining industry, of which diamonds, copper and nickel are the chief elements. Meat products and diamonds comprise 85 percent of the exports.

Botswana is a member of the Commonwealth of Nations. The president is Chief of State and Head of government.

MINT MARK
B - Berne

MONETARY SYSTEM
100 Cents = 1 Thebe

REPUBLIC

REFORM COINAGE

100 Thebe = 1 Pula

KM# 26 5 THEBE
2.4100 g., Copper Plated Steel, 16.9 mm. **Obv:** National arms, date below **Rev:** Toko bird left, value above **Edge:** Plain **Shape:** 7-sided

Date	Mintage	F	VF	XF	Unc	BU
2002	—	—	—	0.25	0.50	1.00
2007	—	—	—	0.25	0.50	1.00
2009	—	—	—	0.25	0.50	1.00

KM# 27 10 THEBE
2.8000 g., Nickel Plated Steel, 18 mm. **Obv:** National arms above date **Rev:** South African Oryx right, value above

Date	Mintage	F	VF	XF	Unc	BU
2002	—	—	—	0.30	0.75	1.25
2008	—	—	—	0.30	0.75	1.25

KM# 28 25 THEBE
3.5000 g., Nickel Plated Steel, 21 mm. **Obv:** National arms, date below **Rev:** Zebu left, value above **Shape:** 7-sided

Date	Mintage	F	VF	XF	Unc	BU
2007	—	—	0.30	0.60	1.50	2.00
2009	—	—	0.30	0.60	1.50	2.00

KM# 29 50 THEBE
4.8200 g., Nickel Plated Steel, 21.5 mm. **Obv:** National arms, date below **Rev:** African Fish Eagle left, value above

Date	Mintage	F	VF	XF	Unc	BU
2001	—	—	0.50	1.00	2.00	2.50

KM# 24 PULA

8.7000 g., Nickel-Brass, 23.5 mm. **Obv:** National arms, date below **Rev:** Zebra left, denomination above **Shape:** 7-sided

Date	Mintage	F	VF	XF	Unc	BU
2007	—	—	1.00	1.75	3.50	6.00

KM# 25a 2 PULA

6.0000 g., Brass Plated Steel, 24.5 mm. **Subject:** Wildlife **Obv:** National arms, date below **Rev:** Rhinoceros left, denomination above **Shape:** 7-sided

Date	Mintage	F	VF	XF	Unc	BU
2004	—	—	—	—	2.75	3.50

KM# 30 5 PULA

6.2000 g., Bi-Metallic Copper-Nickel center in Brass ring, 23.4 mm. **Obv:** National arms, date below **Rev:** Mophane worm on a mophane leaf, denomination below within circle **Edge:** Reeded

Date	Mintage	F	VF	XF	Unc	BU
2007	—	—	—	—	6.50	10.00

The Federative Republic of Brazil, which comprises half the continent of South America and is the only Latin American country deriving its culture and language from Portugal, has an area of 3,286,488 sq. mi. (8,511,965 sq. km.) and a population of *169.2 million. Capital: Brasilia. The economy of Brazil is as varied and complex as any in the developing world. Agriculture is a mainstay of the economy, while only 4 percent of the area is under cultivation. Known mineral resources are almost unlimited in variety and size of reserves. A large, relatively sophisticated industry ranges from basic steel and chemical production to finished consumer goods. Coffee, cotton, iron ore and cocoa are the chief exports.

MINT MARKS

(a) - Paris, privy marks only
B - Bahia

REPUBLIC

REFORM COINAGE

1994-present

2750 Cruzeiros Reais = 1 Real; 100 Centavos = 1 Real

KM# 647 CENTAVO

2.4300 g., Copper Plated Steel, 17 mm. **Obv:** Cabral bust at right **Rev:** Denomination on linear design at left, 3/4 globe with sash on right, date below **Edge:** Plain

Date	Mintage	F	VF	XF	Unc	BU
2001	242,924,000	—	—	—	0.10	0.20
2002	161,824,000	—	—	—	0.10	0.20
2003	250,000,000	—	—	—	0.10	0.20
2004	167,232,000	—	—	—	0.10	0.20

KM# 648 5 CENTAVOS

4.1000 g., Copper Plated Steel, 22 mm. **Obv:** Tiradente bust at right, dove at left **Rev:** Denomination on linear design at left, 3/4 globe with sash on right, date below **Edge:** Plain

Date	Mintage	F	VF	XF	Unc	BU
2001	175,940,000	—	—	—	0.45	0.65
2002	153,088,000	—	—	—	0.45	0.65
2003	260,000,000	—	—	—	0.45	0.65
2004	262,656,000	—	—	—	0.45	0.65
2005	230,144,000	—	—	—	0.45	0.65
2006	255,488,000	—	—	—	0.45	0.65
2007	403,968,000	—	—	—	0.45	0.65
2008	28,672,000	—	—	—	0.45	0.65
2009	400,128,000	—	—	—	0.30	0.50
2010	550,144,000	—	—	—	0.30	0.50
2011	437,504,000	—	—	—	0.30	0.50
2012	—	—	—	—	0.30	0.50

KM# 649.2 10 CENTAVOS

4.8000 g., Bronze Plated Steel, 20 mm. **Obv:** Bust of Pedro at right, horseman with sword in right hand at left **Rev:** Denomination on linear design at left, 3/4 globe with sash on right, date below **Edge:** Reeded

Date	Mintage	F	VF	XF	Unc	BU
2001	134,701,000	—	—	—	0.60	0.80
2002	172,032,000	—	—	—	0.60	0.80
2003	252,666,000	—	—	—	0.60	0.80
2004	348,480,000	—	—	—	0.60	0.80
2005	362,112,000	—	—	—	0.60	0.80
2006	265,728,000	—	—	—	0.60	0.80
2007	316,800,000	—	—	—	0.60	0.80
2008	534,412,000	—	—	—	0.50	0.75
2009	205,748,000	—	—	—	0.50	0.75
2010	520,128,000	—	—	—	0.50	0.75
2011	415,104,000	—	—	—	0.50	0.75
2012	—	—	—	—	0.50	0.75

KM# 650 25 CENTAVOS

7.5500 g., Bronze Plated Steel, 25 mm. **Obv:** Deodoro bust at right, national arms at left **Rev:** Denomination on linear design at left, 3/4 globe with sash on right, date below **Edge:** Reeded

Date	Mintage	F	VF	XF	Unc	BU
2001	92,642,000	—	—	—	0.75	1.00
2002	100,096,000	—	—	—	0.75	1.00
2003	147,200,000	—	—	—	0.75	1.00
2004	160,000,000	—	—	—	0.75	1.00
2005	100,096,000	—	—	—	0.75	1.00
2006	110,720,000	—	—	—	0.75	1.00
2007	118,784,000	—	—	—	0.75	1.00
2008	269,031,000	—	—	—	0.60	0.75
2009	200,985,000	—	—	—	0.60	0.75
2010	240,000,000	—	—	—	0.60	0.75
2011	142,592,000	—	—	—	0.60	0.75
2012	—	—	—	—	0.60	0.75

KM# 651 50 CENTAVOS

9.2500 g., Copper-Nickel, 23 mm. **Obv:** Rio Branco bust at right, map at left **Rev:** Denomination on linear design at left, 3/4 globe with sash on right, date below **Edge Lettering:** BRASIL ORDEM E PROGRESSO

Date	Mintage	F	VF	XF	Unc	BU
2001	14,735,000	—	—	—	1.50	1.75

KM# 651a 50 CENTAVOS

6.8000 g., Stainless Steel, 23 mm. **Obv:** Rio Branco bust at right, map at left **Rev:** Denomination on linear design at left, 3/4 globe with sash on right, date below **Edge Lettering:** BRASIL ORDEM E PROGRESSO

Date	Mintage	F	VF	XF	Unc	BU
2002	189,952,000	—	—	—	1.25	1.50
2003	143,696,000	—	—	—	1.25	1.50
2005	122,416,000	—	—	—	1.25	1.50
2006	39,984,000	—	—	—	1.25	1.50
2007	130,032,000	—	—	—	1.25	1.50
2008	290,080,000	—	—	—	1.25	1.50
2009	300,048,000	—	—	—	1.25	1.50
2010	170,016,000	—	—	—	1.25	1.50
2011	116,928,000	—	—	—	1.25	1.50
2012	—	—	—	—	1.25	1.50

KM# 683 50 CENTAVOS

6.8000 g., Stainless Steel, 23 mm. **Obv:** Rio Branco bust at right, map at left **Rev:** Denomination on linear design at left, 3/4 globe with sash on right, date below **Edge Lettering:** BRASIL ORDEM E PROGRESSO **Note:** Mule with the reverse for the 5 centavos coin on the 50 centavos planchet.

Date	Mintage	F	VF	XF	Unc	BU
2012	—	—	—	—	—	250

KM# 652a REAL

7.0000 g., Bi-Metallic Stainless Steel center in Bronze Plated Steel ring, 27 mm. **Obv:** Allegorical portrait **Rev:** Denomination on linear design at left, 3/4 globe with sash on right, date below **Edge:** Segmented reeding

Date	Mintage	F	VF	XF	Unc	BU
2002	54,192,000	—	—	—	3.50	4.50
2003	100,000,000	—	—	—	3.50	4.50
2004	150,016,000	—	—	—	3.50	4.50
2005	43,776,000	—	—	—	3.50	4.50
2006	179,968,000	—	—	—	3.50	4.50
2007	275,712,000	—	—	—	3.50	4.50
2008	664,833,000	—	—	—	3.50	4.50
2009	245,247,000	—	—	—	2.00	2.50
2010	220,032,000	—	—	—	2.00	2.50
2011	140,032,000	—	—	—	2.00	2.50
2012	—	—	—	—	2.00	2.50

KM# 656 REAL

7.0000 g., Bi-Metallic Stainless Steel center in Bronze Plated Steel ring, 27 mm. **Subject:** Centennial of Juscelino Kubitschek, president **Obv:** Head left **Rev:** Denomination on linear design at left, 3/4 globe with sash on right, date below **Edge:** Segmented reeding

Date	Mintage	F	VF	XF	Unc	BU
2002	50,000,000	—	—	—	3.50	4.50

KM# 668 REAL

7.0000 g., Bi-Metallic Stainless Steel center in Bronze Plated Steel ring, 27 mm. **Subject:** 40th Anniversary of Central Bank **Obv:** Monument **Rev:** Value on flag **Edge:** Segmented reeding

Date	Mintage	F	VF	XF	Unc	BU
2005	40,000,000	—	—	—	5.00	6.50

KM# 679 REAL

7.0000 g., Bi-Metallic Stainless Steel center in Bronze Plated Steel ring, 27 mm. **Subject:** Olympic Flag Delivery London 2012 - Rio 2016 **Obv:** Monument **Obv. Legend:** ENTREGA DA BANDEIRA OLIMPICA, LONDRES 2012 - RIO 2016 **Rev:** Value on flag **Edge:** Segmented Reeding

Date	Mintage	F	VF	XF	Unc	BU
2012	2,016,000	—	—	—	5.00	6.50

KM# 657 2 REAIS

28.0000 g., 0.9990 Silver 0.8993 oz. ASW, 40 mm. **Subject:** Centennial - Carlos Drummond de Andrade **Obv:** Denomination and writer **Rev:** Stylized portrait **Edge:** Reeded

Date	Mintage	F	VF	XF	Unc	BU
ND(2002) Proof	6,999	Value: 90.00				

KM# 658 2 REAIS

28.0000 g., 0.9990 Silver 0.8993 oz. ASW, 40 mm. **Subject:** Centennial - Juscelino Kubitschek **Obv:** Bust facing in upper right, initials at left **Rev:** Denomination **Edge:** Reeded

Date	Mintage	F	VF	XF	Unc	BU
2002 Proof	12,999	Value: 90.00				

KM# 663 2 REAIS

27.0000 g., 0.9250 Silver 0.8029 oz. ASW, 40 mm. **Obv:** Value and piano player **Rev:** Ary Barroso singing **Edge:** Reeded

Date	Mintage	F	VF	XF	Unc	BU
2003 Proof	7,000	Value: 90.00				

KM# 665 2 REAIS

27.0000 g., 0.9250 Silver 0.8029 oz. ASW, 40 mm. **Subject:** Centennial - Cándido Con Portinari **Obv:** Starving family scene, value and country name **Rev:** Portinari's portrait, stars in squares design **Edge:** Reeded

Date	Mintage	F	VF	XF	Unc	BU
ND(2003) Proof	2,000	Value: 350				

KM# 666 2 REAIS

27.0000 g., 0.9250 Silver 0.8029 oz. ASW, 40 mm. **Subject:** FIFA Centennial **Obv:** Soccer ball and value **Rev:** Center part of a Brazilian flag and stars **Edge:** Reeded

Date	Mintage	F	VF	XF	Unc	BU
2004 Proof	12,166	Value: 175				

KM# 671 2 REAIS

27.0000 g., 0.9250 Silver 0.8029 oz. ASW, 40 mm. **Subject:** Centennial of Flight 14 bis **Obv:** Image of 14 Bis **Obv. Legend:** "Centenario Do Voo Do 14 Bis Brasil 1906-2006" **Rev:** Image and signature of Santos Dumont and value **Edge:** Reeded

Date	Mintage	F	VF	XF	Unc	BU
2006 Proof	4,000	Value: 110				

KM# 672 2 REAIS

10.1700 g., Copper-Nickel, 30 mm. **Subject:** Pan-American Games XV **Obv:** Official logo of Pan-American Games XV **Rev:** Image of running athlete, XV Jogos Pan-Americanos, value, Brasil and date. **Edge:** Reeded

Date	Mintage	F	VF	XF	Unc	BU
2007	10,000	—	—	—	—	12.00

KM# 675 2 REAIS

10.1700 g., Copper-Nickel, 30 mm. **Subject:** Japanese immigration to Brazil, 100th Anniversary **Obv:** Farmer and persimmon crop **Rev:** Ship "Kasato Maru" **Edge:** Reeded

Date	Mintage	F	VF	XF	Unc	BU
2008	10,000	—	—	—	—	16.00

KM# 661 5 REAIS

28.0000 g., 0.9990 Silver 0.8993 oz. ASW, 40 mm. **Subject:** Brazil's 5th World Cup Championship **Obv:** Soccer player and Brazilian flag **Rev:** Soccer ball and value **Edge:** Reeded

Date	Mintage	F	VF	XF	Unc	BU
2002 Proof	10,149	Value: 90.00				

KM# 673 5 REAIS

27.0000 g., 0.9250 Silver 0.8029 oz. ASW, 40 mm. **Subject:** Pan-American Games XV **Obv:** Official logo of Pan-American Games XV **Rev:** Sugar Loaf, lines of Copacabana sidewalk, "XV Jogos Pan-Americanos", value, Brasil and date. **Edge:** Reeded

Date	Mintage	F	VF	XF	Unc	BU
2007 Proof	4,000	Value: 110				

KM# 674 5 REAIS

27.0000 g., 0.9250 Silver 0.8029 oz. ASW, 40 mm. **Subject:** Royal Family's arrival in Brazil, 200th Anniversary **Obv:** Ship "Martim de Freitas" **Rev:** Names and dates of institutions created by Dom John **Edge:** Reeded

Date	Mintage	F	VF	XF	Unc	BU
2008 Proof	2,000	Value: 300				

KM# 676 5 REAIS

27.0000 g., 0.9250 Silver 0.8029 oz. ASW, 40 mm. **Subject:** World Heritage Sites, Brasilia, 50th Anniversary **Obv:** Schematic city plan **Rev:** Brasilia's architecture montage: Congress, Cathedral, Presidential palace and Warriors sculpture **Edge:** Reeded

Date	Mintage	F	VF	XF	Unc	BU
2010 Proof	6,000	Value: 110				

KM# 677 5 REAIS

27.0000 g., 0.9250 Silver 0.8029 oz. ASW, 40 mm. **Subject:** 2010 World Cup, South Africa **Obv:** Two players with scoccer ball, Brazil flag in background **Rev:** Map of Africa, South african savannah, soccer player at left **Edge:** Reeded

Date	Mintage	F	VF	XF	Unc	BU
2010 Proof	9,000	Value: 110				

KM# 678 5 REAIS

27.0000 g., 0.9250 Silver 0.8029 oz. ASW, 40 mm. **Subject:** UNESCO World Heritage site. 300th Anniversary of the Foundling of the Pilar Vila Rica of Ouro Preto **Obv:** Houses and churches representing the city's architecture **Rev:** Three angels and baroque scrolls **Rev. Legend:** PATRIMONIO DA HUMANIDADE • UNESCO OURO PRETO and BRAZIL **Edge:** Reeded

Date	Mintage	F	VF	XF	Unc	BU
2011 Proof	2,000	Value: 150				

KM# 680 5 REAIS

27.0000 g., 0.9250 Silver 0.8029 oz. ASW, 40 mm. **Subject:** Delivery of Olympic Flag London 2012 - Rio 2016 **Obv:** Olympic flag, logo of 2016 Rio de Janeiro Olympic games, legend, date **Obv. Legend:** ENTREGA DA BANDEIRA OLIMPICA **Rev:** Illustration illuding to London's Tower Bridge, Rio de Janeiro's Christ the Redeemer statue, legend, denomination, country name **Rev. Legend:** LONDRES 2012 - RIO 2016 **Edge:** Reeded

Date	Mintage	F	VF	XF	Unc	BU
2012 Proof	5,000	Value: 110				

KM# 681 5 REAIS

27.0000 g., 0.9250 Silver 0.8029 oz. ASW, 40 mm. **Subject:** International Year of Cooperatives **Obv:** Official logo of International Year of Cooperation, legend, date **Obv. Legend:** ANO INTERNACTIONAL DAS COOPERATIVAS **Rev:** Globe supported by three pairs of hands, legend, denomination, country name **Rev. Legend:** COOPERATIVAS CONSTROEM UM MUNDO MELHOR **Edge:** Reeded

Date	Mintage	F	VF	XF	Unc	BU
2012 Proof	3,500	Value: 100				

KM# 682 5 REAIS
27.0000 g., 0.9250 Silver 0.8029 oz. ASW, 40 mm. **Subject:** UNESCO World Heritage site. City of Goiás **Obv:** House representing the architecture of Goiá City with Cora Coralina's house, an important poetess born in this city, on first view. **Obv. Legend:** GOIÁS 2012 **Rev:** Houses representing the architecture of Goiás City and face value on the left and part of a poem by Cora Coralina ("Eu sou estas casas encostadas cochichando umas com as outras") **Rev. Legend:** PATRIMONIO DA HUMANIDADE • UNESCO **Edge:** Reeded

Date	Mintage	F	VF	XF	Unc	BU
2012 Proof	2,000	Value: 100				

KM# 659 20 REAIS
8.0000 g., 0.9000 Gold 0.2315 oz. AGW, 22 mm. **Obv:** Juscelino Kubitschek de Oliveira's portrait **Rev:** Value **Edge:** Reeded

Date	Mintage	F	VF	XF	Unc	BU
2002 Proof	2,499	Value: 475				

KM# 660 20 REAIS
8.0000 g., 0.9000 Gold 0.2315 oz. AGW, 22 mm. **Obv:** Carlos Drummond de Andrade portrait and value **Rev:** Andrade caricature, name and dates **Edge:** Reeded

Date	Mintage	F	VF	XF	Unc	BU
ND(2002) Proof	2,499	Value: 475				

KM# 662 20 REAIS
8.0000 g., 0.9000 Gold 0.2315 oz. AGW, 22 mm. **Subject:** World Cup 2002 **Obv:** Soccer player **Rev:** Value, inscription and shooting stars **Edge:** Reeded

Date	Mintage	F	VF	XF	Unc	BU
2002 Proof	2,499	Value: 475				

KM# 664 20 REAIS
8.0000 g., 0.9000 Gold 0.2315 oz. AGW, 22 mm. **Subject:** Centennial - Ary Barroso **Obv:** Piano keyboard and musical notes above value **Rev:** Caricature of Ary Barroso **Edge:** Reeded

Date	Mintage	F	VF	XF	Unc	BU
2003 Proof	2,500	Value: 475				

KM# 670 20 REAIS
8.0000 g., 0.9000 Gold 0.2315 oz. AGW, 22 mm. **Subject:** FIFA Centennial **Obv:** Soccer ball, value, date **Obv. Legend:** BRASIL **Rev:** Christ the Redeemer, Sugar Loaf **Rev. Legend:** FUTEBUL MUNDIAL CENTENARIO DA FIFA **Edge:** Reeded

Date	Mintage	F	VF	XF	Unc	BU
2004 Proof	4,060	Value: 700				

BRITISH ANTARCTIC TERRITORY

BRITISH TERRITORY

DECIMAL COINAGE

KM# 1 2 POUNDS
28.2800 g., Copper-Nickel, 38.6 mm. **Ruler:** Elizabeth II **Subject:** 200th Anniversary of the Granting of Letters Patent **Obv:** Elizabeth II bust facing right **Rev:** Arms with denomination below **Rev. Legend:** 1908 . CENTENARY OF GRANTING OF LETTERS PATENT . 2008

Date	Mintage	F	VF	XF	Unc	BU
2008	Est. 50,000	—	—	—	17.50	20.00

KM# 1a 2 POUNDS
28.2800 g., 0.9250 Silver 0.8410 oz. ASW, 38.6 mm. **Ruler:** Elizabeth II **Obv:** Bust right **Rev:** Supported arms

Date	Mintage	F	VF	XF	Unc	BU
2008 Proof	Est. 10,000	Value: 60.00				

KM# 5 2 POUNDS
28.2800 g., Copper-Nickel, 38.6 mm. **Ruler:** Elizabeth II **Subject:** Antartic treaty **Obv:** Bust right **Rev:** Whale and other Antarctic wildlife

Date	Mintage	F	VF	XF	Unc	BU
2009	50,000	—	—	—	15.00	18.00

KM# 5a 2 POUNDS
28.2800 g., 0.9250 Silver 0.8410 oz. ASW, 38.6 mm. **Ruler:** Elizabeth II **Obv:** Bust right **Rev:** Whale and other Antarctic wildlife

Date	Mintage	F	VF	XF	Unc	BU
2009 Proof	10,000	Value: 45.00				

KM# 6 2 POUNDS
28.2800 g., Copper-Nickel, 38.61 mm. **Ruler:** Elizabeth II **Subject:** Scott's Terra Nova Expedition **Obv:** Bust in tiara right **Rev:** Captain scott, ship and men on ice flow

Date	Mintage	F	VF	XF	Unc	BU
2012	—	—	—	—	17.50	20.00

KM# 2 4 POUNDS
1.2400 g., 0.9999 Gold 0.0399 oz. AGW, 13.92 mm. **Ruler:** Elizabeth II **Obv:** Bust right **Rev:** Supported arms

Date	Mintage	F	VF	XF	Unc	BU
2008 Proof	Est. 10,000	Value: 100				

KM# 3 20 POUNDS
6.2200 g., 0.9999 Gold 0.1999 oz. AGW **Ruler:** Elizabeth II **Obv:** Bust right **Rev:** Supported arms

Date	Mintage	F	VF	XF	Unc	BU
2008 Proof	Est. 2,000	Value: 375				

BRITISH INDIAN OCEAN TERRITORY

TERRITORY

DECIMAL COINAGE

KM# 1 2 POUNDS
28.2800 g., Copper-Nickel, 38.61 mm. **Ruler:** Elizabeth II **Obv:** Bust with tiara right **Rev:** Arms with supporters

Date	Mintage	F	VF	XF	Unc	BU
2009PM	—	—	—	—	—	25.00

KM# 1a 2 POUNDS
28.2800 g., 0.9250 Silver 0.8410 oz. ASW, 38.61 mm. **Ruler:** Elizabeth II **Subject:** First commemorative coin

Date	Mintage	F	VF	XF	Unc	BU
2009PM Proof	Est. 10,000	Value: 55.00				

KM# 2 2 POUNDS
22.0000 g., 0.9250 Silver with glass insert 0.6542 oz. ASW, 38.61 mm. **Ruler:** Elizabeth II **Obv:** Small head at top, sea turtle insert **Rev:** Circle of life of the sea turtle

Date	Mintage	F	VF	XF	Unc	BU
2009PM Proof	Est. 5,000	Value: 80.00				

KM# 3 2 POUNDS
28.2800 g., Copper-Nickel, 38.61 mm. **Ruler:** Elizabeth II **Subject:** Engagement **Rev:** Prince William and Catherine Middleton

Date	Mintage	F	VF	XF	Unc	BU
2010PM	—	—	—	—	14.00	17.50

KM# 3a 2 POUNDS
28.2800 g., 0.9250 Silver 0.8410 oz. ASW, 38.61 mm. **Ruler:** Elizabeth II **Subject:** Engagement

Date	Mintage	F	VF	XF	Unc	BU
2011PM Proof	Est. 10,000	Value: 55.00				

KM# 4 2 POUNDS
28.2800 g., Copper-Nickel, 38.61 mm. **Ruler:** Elizabeth II **Subject:** Royal Wedding **Obv:** Bust with tiara right **Rev:** Conjoined busts left of Catherine Middleton and Prince William

Date	Mintage	F	VF	XF	Unc	BU
2011PM	—	—	—	—	10.00	12.50

KM# 4a 2 POUNDS
28.2800 g., 0.9250 Silver 0.8410 oz. ASW, 38.61 mm. **Ruler:** Elizabeth II **Subject:** Royal Wedding

Date	Mintage	F	VF	XF	Unc	BU
2011PM Proof	Est. 10,000	Value: 55.00				

KM# 5 2 POUNDS
28.2800 g., Copper-Nickel, 38.61 mm. **Ruler:** Elizabeth II **Subject:** Prince Philip, 90th Birthday **Obv:** Bust in tiara right **Rev:** Crowned EP cipher within circle of crosses and anchors

Date	Mintage	F	VF	XF	Unc	BU
2011PM	—	—	—	—	17.50	20.00

KM# 5a 2 POUNDS
28.2800 g., 0.9250 Silver 0.8410 oz. ASW **Ruler:** Elizabeth II **Subject:** Prince Philip, 90th Birthday

Date	Mintage	F	VF	XF	Unc	BU
2011PM Proof	Est. 10,000	Value: 55.00				

KM# 6 2 POUNDS
28.2800 g., Copper-Nickel, 38.6 mm. **Ruler:** Elizabeth II **Subject:** Life of Queen Elizabeth II **Obv:** Conjoined busts left **Rev:** Elizabeth and Margaret as children riding a rocking horse

Date	Mintage	F	VF	XF	Unc	BU
2012PM	—	—	—	—	—	15.00

KM# 6a 2 POUNDS
28.2800 g., 0.9250 Silver 0.8410 oz. ASW, 38.61 mm. **Ruler:** Elizabeth II **Subject:** Elizabeth II, 60th Anniversary as Queen **Rev:** Princess Elizabeth and Margaret

Date	Mintage	F	VF	XF	Unc	BU
2012PM Proof	Est. 10,000	Value: 55.00				

KM# 7 2 POUNDS
28.2800 g., Copper-Nickel, 38.61 mm. **Ruler:** Elizabeth II **Subject:** Life of Queen Elizabeth II **Obv:** Conjoined busts right, young and current portraits **Rev:** Queen Mother waving at left, Queen Elizabeth at right

Date	Mintage	F	VF	XF	Unc	BU
2012PM	—	—	—	—	—	20.00

KM# 7a 2 POUNDS
28.2800 g., 0.9250 Silver 0.8410 oz. ASW, 38.61 mm. **Ruler:** Elizabeth II **Subject:** Elizabeth II, 60th Anniversary of reign **Rev:** Queen Mother and Elizabeth

Date	Mintage	F	VF	XF	Unc	BU
2012PM Proof	Est. 10,000	Value: 55.00				

KM# 8 2 POUNDS
28.2800 g., Copper-Nickel, 38.61 mm. **Ruler:** Elizabeth II **Subject:** The Drive, first anniversary **Rev:** Prince William and Kate in Aston Martin DB-6 on wedding day

Date	Mintage	F	VF	XF	Unc	BU
2012PM	—	—	—	—	14.00	17.50

KM# 8a 2 POUNDS
28.2800 g., 0.9250 Silver 0.8410 oz. ASW, 38.61 mm. **Ruler:** Elizabeth II **Subject:** Wedding, 1st Anniversary **Rev:** Duke and Dutchess of Cambridge in Aston Martin DB-6 drive about

Date	Mintage	F	VF	XF	Unc	BU
2012PM Proof	Est. 10,000	Value: 55.00				

BRITISH VIRGIN ISLANDS

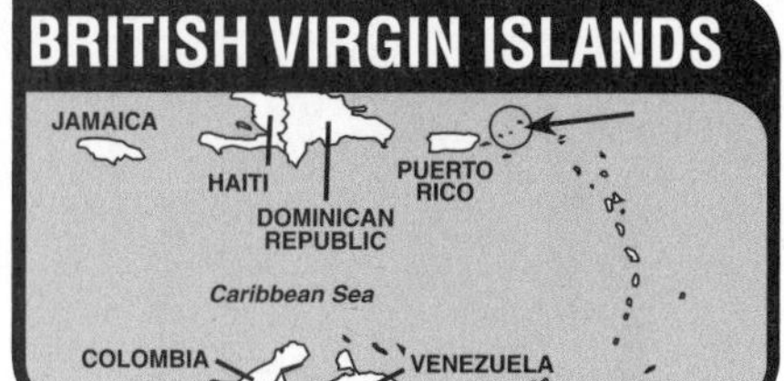

The Colony of the Virgin Islands, a British colony situated in the Caribbean Sea northeast of Puerto Rico and west of the Leeward Islands, has an area of 59 sq. mi. (155 sq. km.) and a population of 13,000. Capital: Road Town. The principal islands of the 36-island group are Tortola, Virgin Gorda, Anegada, and Jost Van Dyke. The chief industries are fishing and stock raising. Fish, livestock and bananas are exported. U.S. currency and Sterling circulate in common with the East Caribbean Dollar.

BRITISH COLONY

STANDARD COINAGE

KM# 196 DOLLAR
28.2800 g., Copper-Nickel, 38.6 mm. **Subject:** Queen's Golden Jubilee **Obv:** Queen's bust right **Rev:** Carnival dancers **Edge:** Reeded

Date	Mintage	F	VF	XF	Unc	BU
2002	—	—	—	—	7.50	9.50

KM# 180 DOLLAR
28.2800 g., Copper-Nickel, 38.6 mm. **Subject:** Sir Francis Drake **Obv:** Queen's bust right **Rev:** Ship, portrait and map **Edge:** Reeded

Date	Mintage	F	VF	XF	Unc	BU
2002	—	—	—	—	7.50	9.50

KM# 183 DOLLAR
28.2800 g., Copper-Nickel, 38.6 mm. **Subject:** Sir Walter Raleigh **Obv:** Queen's bust right **Rev:** Ship, portrait and map **Edge:** Reeded

Date	Mintage	F	VF	XF	Unc	BU
2002	—	—	—	—	7.50	9.50

KM# 187 DOLLAR
28.2800 g., Copper-Nickel, 38.6 mm. **Subject:** Queen's Golden Jubilee **Obv:** Queen's bust right **Rev:** Queen on horse **Edge:** Reeded

Date	Mintage	F	VF	XF	Unc	BU
2002	—	—	—	—	7.50	9.50

KM# 190 DOLLAR
28.2800 g., Copper-Nickel, 38.6 mm. **Subject:** Queen's Golden Jubilee **Obv:** Queen's bust right **Rev:** Queen on throne **Edge:** Reeded

Date	Mintage	F	VF	XF	Unc	BU
2002	—	—	—	—	7.50	9.50

KM# 193 DOLLAR
28.2800 g., Copper-Nickel, 38.6 mm. **Subject:** Queen's Golden Jubilee **Obv:** Queen's bust right **Rev:** Queen with President Ronald Reagan and First Lady Nancy Reagan **Edge:** Reeded

Date	Mintage	F	VF	XF	Unc	BU
2002	—	—	—	—	7.50	9.50

KM# 199 DOLLAR
28.2800 g., Copper-Nickel, 38.6 mm. **Subject:** Teddy Bear Centennial **Obv:** Queen's bust right **Rev:** Teddy bear **Edge:** Reeded

Date	Mintage	F	VF	XF	Unc	BU
2002	—	—	—	—	8.50	15.00

KM# 204 DOLLAR
28.2800 g., Copper-Nickel, 38.6 mm. **Subject:** Princess Diana **Obv:** Queen's bust right **Rev:** Diana's portrait **Edge:** Reeded

Date	Mintage	F	VF	XF	Unc	BU
2002	—	—	—	—	7.50	9.50

KM# 207 DOLLAR
28.2800 g., Copper-Nickel, 38.6 mm. **Subject:** September 11, 2001 **Obv:** Queen's bust right **Rev:** World Trade Center twin towers **Edge:** Reeded

Date	Mintage	F	VF	XF	Unc	BU
2002	—	—	—	—	12.00	13.50

KM# 210 DOLLAR
28.2800 g., Copper-Nickel, 38.6 mm. **Subject:** September 11, 2001 **Obv:** Queen's bust right **Rev:** Statue of Liberty **Edge:** Reeded

Date	Mintage	F	VF	XF	Unc	BU
2002	—	—	—	—	12.00	13.50

KM# 213 DOLLAR
28.2800 g., Copper-Nickel, 38.6 mm. **Subject:** Queen Mother **Obv:** Queen's bust right **Rev:** Queen Mother and a young Prince Charles **Edge:** Reeded

Date	Mintage	F	VF	XF	Unc	BU
2002PM	—	—	—	—	10.00	12.00

KM# 216 DOLLAR
28.2800 g., Copper-Nickel, 38.6 mm. **Subject:** Queen Mother **Obv:** Queen's bust right **Rev:** Queen Mother with four grandchildren **Edge:** Reeded

Date	Mintage	F	VF	XF	Unc	BU
2002PM	—	—	—	—	10.00	12.00

KM# 219 DOLLAR
28.2800 g., Copper-Nickel, 38.6 mm. **Subject:** Queen Mother Series **Obv:** Queen's bust right **Rev:** Queen Mother with uniformed Prince Charles **Edge:** Reeded

Date	Mintage	F	VF	XF	Unc	BU
2002PM	—	—	—	—	10.00	12.00

KM# 222 DOLLAR
28.2800 g., Copper-Nickel, 38.6 mm. **Subject:** Queen Mother Series **Obv:** Queen's bust right **Rev:** Queen Mother's coffin **Edge:** Reeded

Date	Mintage	F	VF	XF	Unc	BU
2002PM	—	—	—	—	10.00	12.00

KM# 225 DOLLAR
28.4400 g., Copper-Nickel, 38.6 mm. **Subject:** Kennedy Assassination **Obv:** Queen's bust right **Rev:** President Kennedy's portrait left **Edge:** Reeded

Date	Mintage	F	VF	XF	Unc	BU
2003	—	—	—	—	10.00	12.00

KM# 229 DOLLAR
28.2800 g., Copper-Nickel, 38.6 mm. **Subject:** Powered Flight Centennial **Obv:** Queen's bust right **Rev:** Three historic airplanes and rocket **Edge:** Reeded

Date	Mintage	F	VF	XF	Unc	BU
2003	—	—	—	—	10.00	12.00

KM# 232 DOLLAR
28.2800 g., Copper-Nickel, 38.6 mm. **Obv:** Queen's bust right **Rev:** Henry VIII and Elizabeth I **Edge:** Reeded

Date	Mintage	F	VF	XF	Unc	BU
2003	—	—	—	—	10.00	12.00

KM# 235 DOLLAR
28.2800 g., Copper-Nickel, 38.6 mm. **Obv:** Queen's bust right **Rev:** Matthew Parker, Archbishop of Canterbury **Edge:** Reeded

Date	Mintage	F	VF	XF	Unc	BU
2003	—	—	—	—	10.00	12.00

KM# 238 DOLLAR
28.2800 g., Copper-Nickel, 38.6 mm. **Obv:** Queen's bust right **Rev:** Sir Francis Drake and ships **Edge:** Reeded

Date	Mintage	F	VF	XF	Unc	BU
2003	—	—	—	—	10.00	12.00

KM# 241 DOLLAR
28.2800 g., Copper-Nickel, 38.6 mm. **Obv:** Queen's bust right **Rev:** Sir Walter Raleigh **Edge:** Reeded

Date	Mintage	F	VF	XF	Unc	BU
2003	—	—	—	—	10.00	12.00

KM# 244 DOLLAR
28.2800 g., Copper-Nickel, 38.6 mm. **Obv:** Queen's bust right **Rev:** Sir William Shakespeare **Edge:** Reeded

Date	Mintage	F	VF	XF	Unc	BU
2003	—	—	—	—	10.00	12.00

KM# 247 DOLLAR
28.2800 g., Copper-Nickel, 38.6 mm. **Obv:** Queen's bust right **Rev:** Elizabeth I above her funeral procession **Edge:** Reeded

Date	Mintage	F	VF	XF	Unc	BU
2003	—	—	—	—	10.00	12.00

KM# 250 DOLLAR
28.2800 g., Copper-Nickel, 38.6 mm. **Subject:** Olympics **Obv:** Queen's bust right **Rev:** Ancient bust, runners and coin **Edge:** Reeded

Date	Mintage	F	VF	XF	Unc	BU
2003	—	—	—	—	10.00	12.00

KM# 253 DOLLAR
28.2800 g., Copper-Nickel, 38.6 mm. **Subject:** Olympics **Obv:** Queen's bust right **Rev:** Ancient bust, charioteer and coin **Edge:** Reeded

Date	Mintage	F	VF	XF	Unc	BU
2003	—	—	—	—	10.00	12.00

KM# 303 DOLLAR
28.2800 g., Copper-Nickel, 38.6 mm. **Subject:** 2004 Athens Olympics **Obv:** Queen's bust right **Rev:** Ancient athlete's bust right, runners at lower right, ancient coin with owl at upper right **Edge:** Reeded

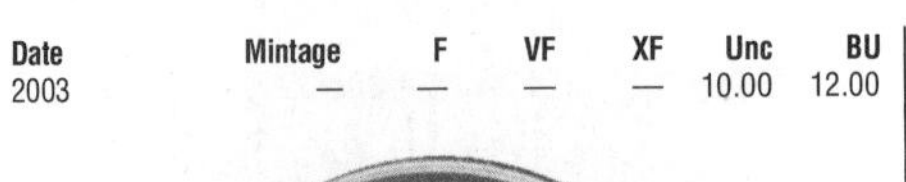

Date	Mintage	F	VF	XF	Unc	BU
2003	—	—	—	—	10.00	12.00

KM# 306 DOLLAR
28.2800 g., Copper-Nickel, 38.6 mm. **Subject:** 2004 Athens Olympics **Obv:** Queen's bust right **Rev:** Ancient athlete bust left, chariot race at lower left, ancient coin at upper left **Edge:** Reeded

Date	Mintage	F	VF	XF	Unc	BU
2003	—	—	—	—	10.00	12.00

KM# 310 DOLLAR
28.2800 g., Copper-Nickel, 38.6 mm. **Subject:** Queen Elizabeth's Golden Coronation Jubilee **Obv:** Elizabeth II **Rev:** Cameo portraits above the ship "Gothic" **Edge:** Reeded

Date	Mintage	F	VF	XF	Unc	BU
2003	—	—	—	—	7.50	9.50

KM# 319 DOLLAR
28.2800 g., Copper-Nickel **Subject:** 50th Anniversary of Coronation **Rev:** Queen riding in automobile

Date	Mintage	F	VF	XF	Unc	BU
2003	—	—	—	—	12.00	15.00

KM# 320 DOLLAR
28.2800 g., Copper-Nickel **Subject:** Golden Jubilee of Coronation **Rev:** Sir. Edmond Hillary on Mt. Everest, Queen II above mountain climbers

Date	Mintage	F	VF	XF	Unc	BU
2003	—	—	—	—	12.00	15.00

KM# 321 DOLLAR
28.2800 g., Copper-Nickel **Rev:** Queen presenting Ascot Horse Racing prize

Date	Mintage	F	VF	XF	Unc	BU
2003	—	—	—	—	10.00	12.00

KM# 265 DOLLAR
28.2800 g., Copper-Nickel, 38.6 mm. **Obv:** Queen's bust right **Rev:** Sir Francis Drake, ship and map **Edge:** Reeded

Date	Mintage	F	VF	XF	Unc	BU
2004	—	—	—	—	10.00	12.00

KM# 267.1 DOLLAR
28.2800 g., Copper-Nickel, 38.6 mm. **Obv:** Queen's bust right **Rev:** Peter Rabbit **Edge:** Reeded

Date	Mintage	F	VF	XF	Unc	BU
2004	—	—	—	—	15.00	17.00

KM# 267.2 DOLLAR
28.2800 g., Copper-Nickel, 38.6 mm. **Obv:** Queen's bust right **Rev:** Multicolor Peter Rabbit **Edge:** Reeded

Date	Mintage	F	VF	XF	Unc	BU
2004	—	—	—	—	20.00	22.00

KM# 268 DOLLAR
3.1100 g., 0.9990 Silver 0.0999 oz. ASW, 18 mm. **Obv:** Queen's bust right **Rev:** Peter Rabbit **Edge:** Reeded

Date	Mintage	F	VF	XF	Unc	BU
2004 Proof	10,000	Value: 25.00				

KM# 281 DOLLAR
28.2800 g., Copper-Nickel, 38.6 mm. **Obv:** Queen's bust right **Rev:** Sailor above two D-Day landing craft **Edge:** Reeded

Date	Mintage	F	VF	XF	Unc	BU
2004	—	—	—	—	10.00	12.00

KM# 286 DOLLAR
28.2800 g., Copper-Nickel, 38.6 mm. **Obv:** Queen's bust right **Rev:** Dolphin **Edge:** Reeded

Date	Mintage	F	VF	XF	Unc	BU
2004	—	—	—	—	12.00	14.00

KM# 297 DOLLAR

28.2800 g., Copper-Nickel, 38.6 mm. **Obv:** Queen's bust right **Rev:** Soldier above tank and jeeps **Edge:** Reeded

Date	Mintage	F	VF	XF	Unc	BU
2004	—	—	—	—	10.00	12.00

KM# 300 DOLLAR

28.2800 g., Copper-Nickel, 38.6 mm. **Obv:** Queen's bust right **Rev:** Pilot and planes above D-Day landing **Edge:** Reeded

Date	Mintage	F	VF	XF	Unc	BU
2004	—	—	—	—	10.00	12.00

KM# 330 DOLLAR

Copper-Nickel **Ruler:** Elizabeth II **Rev:** Battle of Britain

Date	Mintage	F	VF	XF	Unc	BU
2005	—	—	—	—	15.00	17.00

KM# 331 DOLLAR

Copper-Nickel **Ruler:** Elizabeth II **Rev:** Battle of Berlin

Date	Mintage	F	VF	XF	Unc	BU
2005	—	—	—	—	15.00	17.00

KM# 312 DOLLAR

28.2800 g., Copper-Nickel, 38.6 mm. **Obv:** Bust of Queen Elizabeth II right **Rev:** Mother and baby dolphins **Edge:** Reeded

Date	Mintage	F	VF	XF	Unc	BU
2005	—	—	—	—	12.00	14.00

KM# 322 DOLLAR

28.2800 g., Copper-Nickel **Rev:** VJ Day, McArthur and U.S.S. Missiouri Battleship

Date	Mintage	F	VF	XF	Unc	BU
2005	—	—	—	—	10.00	12.00

KM# 323 DOLLAR

28.2800 g., Copper-Nickel **Rev:** Warships near Atlantic coast, West Indies islands

Date	Mintage	F	VF	XF	Unc	BU
2005	—	—	—	—	10.00	12.00

KM# 324 DOLLAR

28.2800 g., Copper-Nickel **Rev:** Death of Nelson

Date	Mintage	F	VF	XF	Unc	BU
2005	—	—	—	—	10.00	12.00

KM# 325 DOLLAR

28.2800 g., Copper-Nickel **Rev:** Nelson and Order Star above ships

Date	Mintage	F	VF	XF	Unc	BU
2005	—	—	—	—	10.00	12.00

KM# 326 DOLLAR

28.2800 g., Copper-Nickel **Rev:** Nelson and Napoleon

Date	Mintage	F	VF	XF	Unc	BU
2005	—	—	—	—	10.00	12.00

KM# 327 DOLLAR

28.2800 g., Copper-Nickel **Rev:** Nelson's Column, statue and ships

Date	Mintage	F	VF	XF	Unc	BU
2005	—	—	—	—	10.00	12.00

KM# 328 DOLLAR

28.2800 g., Copper-Nickel **Rev:** V.E. Day, Montgomery and Eisenhower

Date	Mintage	F	VF	XF	Unc	BU
2005	—	—	—	—	10.00	12.00

KM# 403 DOLLAR

28.2800 g., Copper-Nickel, 38.61 mm. **Ruler:** Elizabeth II **Obv:** Bust in tiara right **Rev:** Inverted Swan postage stamp

Date	Mintage	F	VF	XF	Unc	BU
2005PM	—	—	—	—	17.50	20.00

KM# 349 DOLLAR

28.2800 g., Copper-Nickel, 38.60 mm. **Ruler:** Elizabeth II **Subject:** 5th Anniversary Attack on Twin Towers, New York City **Obv:** Crowned bust right **Obv. Legend:** BRITISH VIRGIN ISLANDS - QUEEN ELIZABETH II **Rev:** Twin Towers in sprays, remembrance ribbon privy mark at upper right **Rev. Inscription:** LEST WE FORGET **Edge:** Reeded

Date	Mintage	F	VF	XF	Unc	BU
2006	—	—	—	—	15.00	17.00

KM# 329 DOLLAR

Copper-Nickel **Rev:** Two dolphins

Date	Mintage	F	VF	XF	Unc	BU
2006	—	—	—	—	10.00	12.00

KM# 332 DOLLAR

28.2800 g., Copper-Nickel, 38.60 mm. **Ruler:** Elizabeth II **Subject:** 400th Anniversary Founding of Jamestown **Obv:** Bust with tiara right **Obv. Legend:** BRITISH VIRGIN ISLANDS - QUEEN ELIZABETH II **Rev:** British lion laying, American eagle perched on sprays **Rev. Legend:** UNITED IN FRIENDSHIP **Edge:** Reeded

Date	Mintage	F	VF	XF	Unc	BU
2007	—	—	—	—	16.50	18.50

KM# 404 DOLLAR

28.2800 g., Copper-Nickel, 38.61 mm. **Ruler:** Elizabeth II **Obv:** Bust in tiara right **Rev:** George Washington 5 cent postage stamp

Date	Mintage	F	VF	XF	Unc	BU
2007PM	—	—	—	—	17.50	20.00

KM# 370 DOLLAR

28.2800 g., Copper-Nickel, 38.6 mm. **Ruler:** Elizabeth II **Obv:** Bust right **Rev:** Two soccer players and leopard

Date	Mintage	F	VF	XF	Unc	BU
2009	—	—	—	—	12.00	15.00

KM# 373 DOLLAR

28.2800 g., Copper-Nickel, 38.6 mm. **Ruler:** Elizabeth II **Obv:** Bust right **Rev:** Queen Elizabeth I aboard ship

Date	Mintage	F	VF	XF	Unc	BU
2009	—	—	—	—	12.00	15.00

KM# 375 DOLLAR

28.2800 g., Copper-Nickel, 38.6 mm. **Ruler:** Elizabeth II **Obv:** Bust right **Rev:** Elizabeth I between two columns

Date	Mintage	F	VF	XF	Unc	BU
2009	—	—	—	—	12.00	15.00

KM# 393 DOLLAR

28.2800 g., Copper-Nickel, 38.6 mm. **Ruler:** Elizabeth II **Subject:** Peanuts 60th Anniversary **Rev:** Snoopy sleeping atop doghouse

Date	Mintage	F	VF	XF	Unc	BU
2010PM	—	—	—	—	—	25.00

KM# 396 DOLLAR

28.2800 g., Bronze with antique patina, 38.6 mm. **Ruler:** Elizabeth II **Subject:** Elgin Marbles **Rev:** Two horsemen

Date	Mintage	F	VF	XF	Unc	BU
2010PM	—	—	—	—	25.00	—

KM# 402 DOLLAR

28.2800 g., Copper-Nickel, 38.61 mm. **Ruler:** Elizabeth II **Subject:** Birth of Venus

Date	Mintage	F	VF	XF	Unc	BU
2010PM	—	—	—	—	—	15.00

KM# 278 2 DOLLARS

58.0000 g., Bronze, 50 mm. **Obv:** Queen's bust right **Rev:** 1896 Olympic medal design **Edge:** Reeded

Date	Mintage	F	VF	XF	Unc	BU
2004 Proof	3,500	Value: 20.00				

KM# 380 2 DOLLARS

Bronze with patina, 50 mm. **Ruler:** Elizabeth II **Rev:** Turtle

Date	Mintage	F	VF	XF	Unc	BU
2008PM	—	—	—	—	—	20.00

KM# 269.1 2.50 DOLLARS

7.7758 g., 0.9990 Silver 0.2497 oz. ASW, 26 mm. **Obv:** Queen's bust right **Rev:** Peter Rabbit **Edge:** Reeded

Date	Mintage	F	VF	XF	Unc	BU
2004 Proof	—	Value: 18.00				

KM# 269.2 2.50 DOLLARS

7.7758 g., 0.9990 Silver 0.2497 oz. ASW, 26 mm. **Obv:** Queen's bust right **Rev:** Multicolor Peter Rabbit **Edge:** Reeded

Date	Mintage	F	VF	XF	Unc	BU
2004 Proof	7,500	Value: 25.00				

KM# 381 4 DOLLARS

Silver **Ruler:** Elizabeth II **Subject:** 400th Anniversary of Settlement

Date	Mintage	F	VF	XF	Unc	BU
2009PM	—	—	—	—	—	35.00

KM# 284 5 DOLLARS

10.0000 g., 0.9900 Titanium 0.3183 oz., 36.1 mm. **Obv:** Queen's bust right **Rev:** British Guiana stamp design **Edge:** Reeded

Date	Mintage	F	VF	XF	Unc	BU
2004 Proof	7,500	Value: 95.00				

KM# 340 5 DOLLARS

0.9999 Bi-Metallic Silver center in Gold ring. **Ruler:** Elizabeth II **Obv:** Conjoined busts with Philip right, within gold ring **Obv. Legend:** BRITISH VIRGIN ISLANDS — QUEEN ELIZABETH II **Rev:** Conjoined busts of Princess Elizabeth and Prince Philip right within gold ring **Rev. Legend:** WITH THIS RING, I THEE WED **Edge:** Reeded

Date	Mintage	F	VF	XF	Unc	BU
2007 Proof	—	Value: 500				

KM# 405 5 DOLLARS

28.2800 g., Copper-Nickel gilt, 38.61 mm. **Ruler:** Elizabeth II **Obv:** Bust in tiara right **Rev:** Benjamin Franklin postage stamp

Date	Mintage	F	VF	XF	Unc	BU
2007PM	—	—	—	—	17.50	20.00

KM# 414 5 DOLLARS

28.2800 g., Copper-Nickel gilt, 38.61 mm. **Ruler:** Elizabeth II **Subject:** Bejing Olympics **Obv:** Bust in tiara right **Rev:** Tennis plays against Great Wall background

Date	Mintage	F	VF	XF	Unc	BU
2008PM Proof	—	Value: 25.00				

KM# 426 5 DOLLARS

28.2800 g., Silver with gilt center, 38.61 mm. **Ruler:** Elizabeth II **Subject:** Bejing Olympics **Obv:** Bust in tiara right **Rev:** Tennis plays against Great Wall background

Date	Mintage	F	VF	XF	Unc	BU
2008PM Proof	—	Value: 50.00				

KM# 383 5 DOLLARS

Titanium **Ruler:** Elizabeth II **Subject:** Bejing Olympics - Tennis

Date	Mintage	F	VF	XF	Unc	BU
2009PM Proof	—	Value: 55.00				

KM# 384 5 DOLLARS

Titanium **Ruler:** Elizabeth II **Subject:** Bejing Olympics - Swimming

Date	Mintage	F	VF	XF	Unc	BU
2009PM Proof	—	Value: 55.00				

KM# 385 5 DOLLARS

Titanium **Ruler:** Elizabeth II **Subject:** Bejing Olympics

Date	Mintage	F	VF	XF	Unc	BU
2009PM Proof	—	Value: 55.00				

KM# 386 5 DOLLARS

Titanium **Ruler:** Elizabeth II **Subject:** Bejing Olympics

Date	Mintage	F	VF	XF	Unc	BU
2009PM Proof	—	Value: 55.00				

KM# 387 5 DOLLARS

Titanium **Ruler:** Elizabeth II **Subject:** Bejing Olympics

Date	Mintage	F	VF	XF	Unc	BU
2009PM Proof	—	Value: 55.00				

KM# 399 5 DOLLARS

7.0000 g., Bi-Metallic Gold and Titanium, 38.6 mm. **Ruler:** Elizabeth II **Subject:** 175th Anniversary of Publication of Hans Christian Anderson's first book **Rev:** Scene from the Little Mermaid

Date	Mintage	F	VF	XF	Unc	BU
2010PM Proof	Est. 5,000	Value: 120				

KM# 400 5 DOLLARS

10.0000 g., Tri-Metallic Silver, Gold and Titanium, 38.6 mm. **Ruler:** Elizabeth II **Subject:** 175th Anniversary of Publication of Hans Christian Andersen's first book **Rev:** Scene from the Little Mermaid

Date	Mintage	F	VF	XF	Unc	BU
2010PM Proof	Est. 7,500	Value: 120				

KM# 181 10 DOLLARS

28.2800 g., 0.9250 Silver 0.8410 oz. ASW, 38.6 mm. **Subject:** Sir Francis Drake **Obv:** Queen's bust right **Rev:** Ship, portrait and map **Edge:** Reeded

Date	Mintage	F	VF	XF	Unc	BU
2002 Proof	—	Value: 45.00				

KM# 184 10 DOLLARS
28.2800 g., 0.9250 Silver 0.8410 oz. ASW, 38.6 mm. **Subject:** Sir Walter Raleigh **Obv:** Queen's bust right **Rev:** Ship, portrait and map **Edge:** Reeded

Date	Mintage	F	VF	XF	Unc	BU
2002 Proof	—	Value: 45.00				

KM# 188 10 DOLLARS
28.2800 g., 0.9250 Gold Clad Silver 0.8410 oz., 38.6 mm. **Subject:** Queen's Golden Jubilee **Obv:** Queen's bust right **Rev:** Queen on horse trotting left **Edge:** Reeded

Date	Mintage	F	VF	XF	Unc	BU
2002 Proof	10,000	Value: 42.50				

KM# 191 10 DOLLARS
28.2800 g., 0.9250 Gold Clad Silver 0.8410 oz., 38.6 mm. **Subject:** Queen's Golden Jubilee **Obv:** Queen's bust right **Rev:** 3/4-length Queen seated on throne **Edge:** Reeded

Date	Mintage	F	VF	XF	Unc	BU
2002 Proof	10,000	Value: 45.00				

KM# 194 10 DOLLARS
28.2800 g., 0.9250 Gold Clad Silver 0.8410 oz., 38.6 mm. **Subject:** Queen's Golden Jubilee **Obv:** Queen's bust right **Rev:** Queen with President Ronald Reagan and First Lady Nancy Reagan **Edge:** Reeded

Date	Mintage	F	VF	XF	Unc	BU
2002 Proof	10,000	Value: 45.00				

KM# 197 10 DOLLARS
28.2800 g., 0.9250 Gold Clad Silver 0.8410 oz., 38.6 mm. **Subject:** Queen's Golden Jubilee **Obv:** Queen's bust right **Rev:** Carnival dancers **Edge:** Reeded

Date	Mintage	F	VF	XF	Unc	BU
2002 Proof	10,000	Value: 45.00				

KM# 200 10 DOLLARS
28.2800 g., 0.9250 Silver 0.8410 oz. ASW, 38.6 mm. **Subject:** Teddy Bear Centennial **Obv:** Queen's bust right **Rev:** Teddy bear **Edge:** Reeded

Date	Mintage	F	VF	XF	Unc	BU
2002 Proof	10,000	Value: 40.00				

KM# 205 10 DOLLARS
28.2800 g., 0.9250 Silver 0.8410 oz. ASW, 38.6 mm. **Subject:** Princess Diana **Obv:** Queen's bust right **Rev:** Diana's portrait **Edge:** Reeded

Date	Mintage	F	VF	XF	Unc	BU
2002 Proof	10,000	Value: 40.00				

KM# 208.1 10 DOLLARS
28.2800 g., 0.9250 Silver 0.8410 oz. ASW, 38.6 mm. **Subject:** September 11, 2001 **Obv:** Queen's bust right **Rev:** World Trade Center twin towers **Edge:** Reeded

Date	Mintage	F	VF	XF	Unc	BU
2002 Proof	10,000	Value: 50.00				

KM# 208.2 10 DOLLARS
28.2800 g., 0.9250 Silver 0.8410 oz. ASW, 38.6 mm. **Subject:** September 11, 2001 **Obv:** Queen's bust right **Rev:** Holographic multicolor World Trade Center twin towers **Edge:** Reeded

Date	Mintage	F	VF	XF	Unc	BU
2002 Proof	10,000	Value: 45.00				

KM# 211 10 DOLLARS
28.2800 g., 0.9250 Silver 0.8410 oz. ASW, 38.6 mm. **Subject:** September 11, 2001 **Obv:** Queen's bust right **Rev:** Statue of Liberty **Edge:** Reeded

Date	Mintage	F	VF	XF	Unc	BU
2002 Proof	10,000	Value: 40.00				

KM# 214 10 DOLLARS
28.2800 g., 0.9250 Silver 0.8410 oz. ASW, 38.6 mm. **Subject:** Queen Mother **Obv:** Queen's bust right **Rev:** Queen Mother with young Prince Charles **Edge:** Reeded

Date	Mintage	F	VF	XF	Unc	BU
2002PM Proof	10,000	Value: 40.00				

KM# 217 10 DOLLARS
28.2800 g., 0.9250 Silver 0.8410 oz. ASW, 38.6 mm. **Subject:** Queen Mother Series **Obv:** Queen's bust right **Rev:** Queen Mother with four grandchildren **Edge:** Reeded

Date	Mintage	F	VF	XF	Unc	BU
2002PM Proof	10,000	Value: 40.00				

KM# 220 10 DOLLARS
28.2800 g., 0.9250 Silver 0.8410 oz. ASW, 38.6 mm. **Subject:** Queen Mother Series **Obv:** Queen's bust right **Rev:** Queen Mother with uniformed Prince Charles **Edge:** Reeded

Date	Mintage	F	VF	XF	Unc	BU
2002PM Proof	10,000	Value: 40.00				

KM# 223 10 DOLLARS
28.2800 g., 0.9250 Silver 0.8410 oz. ASW, 38.6 mm. **Subject:** Queen Mother Series **Obv:** Queen's bust right **Rev:** Queen Mother's coffin **Edge:** Reeded

Date	Mintage	F	VF	XF	Unc	BU
2002PM Proof	10,000	Value: 40.00				

KM# 226 10 DOLLARS
28.2800 g., 0.9250 Silver 0.8410 oz. ASW, 38.6 mm. **Subject:** Kennedy Assassination **Obv:** Queen's bust right **Rev:** President Kennedy's head left **Edge:** Reeded

Date	Mintage	F	VF	XF	Unc	BU
2003 Proof	10,000	Value: 50.00				

KM# 230 10 DOLLARS
28.2800 g., 0.9250 Silver 0.8410 oz. ASW, 38.6 mm. **Subject:** Powered Flight Centennial **Obv:** Queen's bust right **Rev:** Three historic airplanes and rocket **Edge:** Reeded

Date	Mintage	F	VF	XF	Unc	BU
2003 Proof	10,000	Value: 45.00				

KM# 233 10 DOLLARS
28.2800 g., 0.9250 Silver 0.8410 oz. ASW, 38.6 mm. **Obv:** Queen's bust right **Rev:** Henry VIII and Elizabeth I **Edge:** Reeded

Date	Mintage	F	VF	XF	Unc	BU
2003 Proof	10,000	Value: 42.00				

KM# 236 10 DOLLARS
28.2800 g., 0.9250 Silver 0.8410 oz. ASW, 38.6 mm. **Obv:** Queen's bust right **Rev:** Matthew Parker, Archbishop of Canterbury **Edge:** Reeded

Date	Mintage	F	VF	XF	Unc	BU
2003 Proof	10,000	Value: 42.00				

KM# 239 10 DOLLARS
28.2800 g., 0.9250 Silver 0.8410 oz. ASW, 38.6 mm. **Obv:** Queen's bust right **Rev:** Sir Francis Drake and ships **Edge:** Reeded

Date	Mintage	F	VF	XF	Unc	BU
2003 Proof	10,000	Value: 42.00				

KM# 242 10 DOLLARS
28.2800 g., 0.9250 Silver 0.8410 oz. ASW, 38.6 mm. **Obv:** Queen's bust right **Rev:** Sir Walter Raleigh **Edge:** Reeded

Date	Mintage	F	VF	XF	Unc	BU
2003 Proof	10,000	Value: 42.00				

KM# 245 10 DOLLARS
28.2800 g., 0.9250 Silver 0.8410 oz. ASW, 38.6 mm. **Obv:** Queen's bust right **Rev:** Sir William Shakespeare **Edge:** Reeded

Date	Mintage	F	VF	XF	Unc	BU
2003 Proof	10,000	Value: 42.00				

KM# 248 10 DOLLARS
28.2800 g., 0.9250 Silver 0.8410 oz. ASW, 38.6 mm. **Obv:** Queen's bust right **Rev:** Elizabeth I above her funeral procession **Edge:** Reeded

Date	Mintage	F	VF	XF	Unc	BU
2003 Proof	10,000	Value: 42.00				

KM# 251 10 DOLLARS
28.2800 g., 0.9250 Silver 0.8410 oz. ASW, 38.6 mm. **Subject:** Olympics **Obv:** Queen's bust right **Rev:** Ancient bust, runners and coin **Edge:** Reeded

Date	Mintage	F	VF	XF	Unc	BU
2003 Proof	10,000	Value: 42.00				

KM# 254 10 DOLLARS
28.2800 g., 0.9250 Silver 0.8410 oz. ASW, 38.6 mm. **Subject:** Olympics **Obv:** Queen's bust right **Rev:** Ancient bust, charioteer and coin **Edge:** Reeded

Date	Mintage	F	VF	XF	Unc	BU
2003 Proof	10,000	Value: 42.00				

KM# 311 10 DOLLARS
28.3000 g., 0.9250 Gold Clad Silver 0.8416 oz., 38.6 mm. **Subject:** Queen Elizabeth's Golden Coronation Jubilee **Obv:** Elizabeth II **Rev:** Cameo portrait above ship "Gothic" **Edge:** Reeded

Date	Mintage	F	VF	XF	Unc	BU
2003 Proof	—	Value: 50.00				

KM# 266 10 DOLLARS
28.2800 g., 0.9250 Silver 0.8410 oz. ASW, 38.6 mm. **Obv:** Queen's bust right **Rev:** Sir Francis Drake, ship and map **Edge:** Reeded

Date	Mintage	F	VF	XF	Unc	BU
2004 Proof	10,000	Value: 45.00				

KM# 270.1 10 DOLLARS
28.2800 g., 0.9250 Silver 0.8410 oz. ASW, 38.6 mm. **Obv:** Queen's bust right **Rev:** Peter Rabbit **Edge:** Reeded

Date	Mintage	F	VF	XF	Unc	BU
2004 Proof	5,000	Value: 47.50				

KM# 270.2 10 DOLLARS
28.2800 g., 0.9250 Silver 0.8410 oz. ASW, 38.6 mm. **Obv:** Queen's bust right **Rev:** Multicolor Peter Rabbit **Edge:** Reeded

Date	Mintage	F	VF	XF	Unc	BU
2004 Proof	—	Value: 65.00				

KM# 274 10 DOLLARS
1.2440 g., 0.9999 Gold 0.0400 oz. AGW, 14 mm. **Obv:** Queen's bust right **Rev:** Hernando Pizarro **Edge:** Reeded

Date	Mintage	F	VF	XF	Unc	BU
2004 Proof	350	Value: 85.00				

KM# 282 10 DOLLARS
28.2800 g., 0.9250 Silver 0.8410 oz. ASW, 38.6 mm. **Obv:** Queen's bust right **Rev:** Sailor above two D-Day landing craft **Edge:** Reeded

Date	Mintage	F	VF	XF	Unc	BU
2004 Proof	10,000	Value: 50.00				

KM# 287 10 DOLLARS
31.1035 g., 0.9990 Silver 0.9990 oz. ASW, 38.6 mm. **Obv:** Queen's bust right **Rev:** Dolphin **Edge:** Reeded

Date	Mintage	F	VF	XF	Unc	BU
2004 Proof	10,000	Value: 55.00				

KM# 288 10 DOLLARS
1.2440 g., 0.9999 Gold 0.0400 oz. AGW, 14 mm. **Obv:** Queen's bust right **Rev:** Dolphin **Edge:** Reeded

Date	Mintage	F	VF	XF	Unc	BU
2004 Proof	10,000	Value: 75.00				

KM# 298 10 DOLLARS
28.2800 g., 0.9250 Silver 0.8410 oz. ASW, 38.6 mm. **Obv:** Queen's bust right **Rev:** Soldier above tank and jeeps **Edge:** Reeded

Date	Mintage	F	VF	XF	Unc	BU
2004 Proof	10,000	Value: 50.00				

KM# 301 10 DOLLARS
28.2800 g., 0.9250 Silver 0.8410 oz. ASW, 38.6 mm. **Obv:** Queen's bust right **Rev:** Pilot and planes above D-Day landing **Edge:** Reeded

Date	Mintage	F	VF	XF	Unc	BU
2004 Proof	10,000	Value: 50.00				

KM# 304 10 DOLLARS
28.2800 g., 0.9250 Silver 0.8410 oz. ASW, 38.6 mm. **Obv:** Queen's bust right **Rev:** Ancient Olympic bust, runners and owl coin **Edge:** Reeded

Date	Mintage	F	VF	XF	Unc	BU
2004 Proof	10,000	Value: 50.00				

KM# 307 10 DOLLARS
28.2800 g., 0.9250 Silver 0.8410 oz. ASW, 38.6 mm. **Obv:** Queen's bust right **Rev:** Ancient Olympic bust, charioteer and Zeus coin **Edge:** Reeded

Date	Mintage	F	VF	XF	Unc	BU
2004 Proof	10,000	Value: 50.00				

KM# 313 10 DOLLARS
31.1030 g., 0.9990 Silver 0.9989 oz. ASW, 38.6 mm. **Obv:** Bust of Queen Elizabeth II right **Rev:** Mother and baby dolphin **Edge:** Reeded

Date	Mintage	F	VF	XF	Unc	BU
2005 Proof	10,000	Value: 55.00				

KM# 314 10 DOLLARS
1.2440 g., 0.9999 Gold 0.0400 oz. AGW, 13.92 mm. **Obv:** Bust of Queen Elizabeth II right **Rev:** Mother and baby dolphin **Edge:** Reeded

Date	Mintage	F	VF	XF	Unc	BU
2005 Proof	10,000	Value: 75.00				

KM# 350 10 DOLLARS
28.2800 g., 0.9250 Silver 0.8410 oz. ASW, 38.60 mm. **Ruler:** Elizabeth II **Subject:** 5th Anniversary - Attack on Twin Towers, New York City **Obv:** Crowned bust right **Obv. Legend:** BRITISH VIRGIN ISLANDS — QUEEN ELIZABETH II **Rev:** Twin Towers in sprays, remembrance ribbon privy mark at upper right **Rev. Inscription:** LEST WE FORGET **Edge:** Reeded

Date	Mintage	F	VF	XF	Unc	BU
2006 Proof	10,000	Value: 77.50				

KM# 333 10 DOLLARS
28.2800 g., 0.9167 Silver 0.8334 oz. ASW, 38.60 mm. **Ruler:** Elizabeth II **Subject:** 400th Anniversary Founding of Jamestown **Obv:** Bust with tiara right **Obv. Legend:** BRITISH VIRGIN ISLANDS — QUEEN ELIZABETH II **Rev:** British lion laying, American eagle perched on sprays **Rev. Legend:** UNITED IN FRIENDSHIP **Edge:** Reeded

Date	Mintage	F	VF	XF	Unc	BU
2007 Proof	25,000	Value: 75.00				

KM# 334 10 DOLLARS
1.2444 g., 0.9999 Gold 0.0400 oz. AGW, 13.92 mm. **Ruler:** Elizabeth II **Subject:** 400th Anniversary Founding of Jamestown **Obv:** Bust with tiara right **Obv. Legend:** BRITISH VIRGIN ISLANDS — QUEEN ELIZABETH II **Rev:** British lion laying, American eagle perched on sprays **Rev. Legend:** UNITED IN FRIENDSHIP **Edge:** Reeded

Date	Mintage	F	VF	XF	Unc	BU
2007 Proof	20,000	Value: 75.00				

KM# 339 10 DOLLARS
28.2800 g., Copper-Nickel **Ruler:** Elizabeth II **Subject:** 10th Anniversary Death of Princess Diana **Obv:** Bust with tiara right **Obv. Legend:** BRITISH VIRGIN ISLANDS — QUEEN ELIZABETH II **Rev:** Mother Teresa at left, Princess Diana at right **Rev. Legend:** MOTHER TERESA • IN LOVING MEMORY • PRINCESS DIANA **Edge:** Reeded

Date	Mintage	F	VF	XF	Unc	BU
2007	—	—	—	—	18.50	—

KM# 339a 10 DOLLARS
0.9167 Silver **Ruler:** Elizabeth II **Subject:** 10th Anniversary - Death of Princess Diana **Obv:** Bust with tiara right **Obv. Legend:** BRITISH VIRGIN ISLANDS — QUEEN ELIZABETH II **Rev:** Mother Teresa at left, Princess Diana at right **Rev. Legend:** MOTHER TERESA • IN LOVING MEMORY • PRINCESS DIANA **Edge:** Reeded

Date	Mintage	F	VF	XF	Unc	BU
2007 Proof	—	Value: 75.00				

KM# 341 10 DOLLARS
28.2800 g., Copper-Nickel **Ruler:** Elizabeth II **Subject:** Diamond Wedding Anniversary **Obv:** Conjoined busts with Philip right **Obv. Legend:** BRITISH VIRGIN ISLANDS — QUEEN ELIZABETH II **Rev:** Bride to be and King George VI standing facing **Rev. Legend:** Diamond Wedding of H.M. Queen Elizabeth II & H.R.H. Prince Philip **Rev. Inscription:** THE GIVING AWAY **Edge:** Reeded

Date	Mintage	F	VF	XF	Unc	BU
2007	—	—	—	—	16.50	18.50

KM# 341a 10 DOLLARS
28.2800 g., 0.9250 Silver 0.8410 oz. ASW **Ruler:** Elizabeth II **Subject:** Diamond Wedding Anniversary **Obv:** Conjoined busts with Philip right **Obv. Legend:** BRITISH VIRGIN ISLANDS — QUEEN ELIZABETH II **Rev:** Bride to be and King George VI standing facing **Rev. Legend:** Diamond Wedding of H.M. Queen Elizabeth II & H.R.H. Prince Philip **Rev. Inscription:** THE GIVING AWAY **Edge:** Reeded

Date	Mintage	F	VF	XF	Unc	BU
2007 Proof	—	Value: 75.00				

KM# 342 10 DOLLARS
28.2800 g., Copper-Nickel **Ruler:** Elizabeth II **Subject:** Diamond Wedding Anniversary **Obv:** Conjoined busts with Philip right **Obv. Legend:** BRITISH VIRGIN ISLANDS — QUEEN ELIZABETH II **Rev. Legend:** Diamond Wedding of H.M. Queen Elizabeth II & H.R.H. Prince Philip **Rev. Inscription:** THE GLASS COACH **Edge:** Reeded

Date	Mintage	F	VF	XF	Unc	BU
2007	—	—	—	—	16.50	18.50

KM# 342a 10 DOLLARS
28.2800 g., 0.9250 Silver 0.8410 oz. ASW **Ruler:** Elizabeth II **Subject:** Diamond Wedding Anniversary **Obv:** Conjoined busts with Philip right **Obv. Legend:** BRITISH VIRGIN ISLANDS — QUEEN ELIZABETH II **Rev. Legend:** Diamond Wedding of H.M. Queen Elizabeth II & H.R.H. Prince Philip **Rev. Inscription:** THE GLASS COACH **Edge:** Reeded

Date	Mintage	F	VF	XF	Unc	BU
2007 Proof	—	Value: 75.00				

KM# 343 10 DOLLARS
28.2800 g., Copper-Nickel **Ruler:** Elizabeth II **Subject:** Diamond Wedding Anniversary **Obv:** Conjoined busts with Philip right **Obv. Legend:** BRITISH VIRGIN ISLANDS — QUEEN ELIZABETH II **Rev. Legend:** Diamond Wedding of H.M. Queen Elizabeth II & H.R.H. Prince Philip **Rev. Inscription:** THE HONEYMOON **Edge:** Reeded

Date	Mintage	F	VF	XF	Unc	BU
2007	—	—	—	—	16.50	18.50

KM# 343a 10 DOLLARS
28.2800 g., 0.9250 Silver 0.8410 oz. ASW **Ruler:** Elizabeth II **Subject:** Diamond Wedding Anniversary **Obv:** Conjoined busts with Philip right **Obv. Legend:** BRITISH VIRGIN ISLANDS — QUEEN ELIZABETH II **Rev. Legend:** Diamond Wedding of H.M. Queen Elizabeth II & H.R.H. Prince Philip **Rev. Inscription:** THE HONEYMOON **Edge:** Reeded

Date	Mintage	F	VF	XF	Unc	BU
2007 Proof	—	Value: 75.00				

KM# 344 10 DOLLARS
28.2800 g., Copper-Nickel **Ruler:** Elizabeth II **Subject:** Diamond Wedding Anniversary **Obv:** Conjoined busts with Philip right **Obv. Legend:** BRITISH VIRGIN ISLANDS — QUEEN ELIZABETH II **Rev. Legend:** Diamond Wedding of H.M. Queen Elizabeth II & H.R.H. Prince Philip **Rev. Inscription:** THE WEDDING PROGRAM **Edge:** Reeded

Date	Mintage	F	VF	XF	Unc	BU
2007	—	—	—	—	16.50	18.50

KM# 344a 10 DOLLARS
28.2800 g., 0.9250 Silver 0.8410 oz. ASW **Ruler:** Elizabeth II **Subject:** Diamond Wedding Anniversary **Obv:** Conjoined busts with Philip right **Obv. Legend:** BRITISH VIRGIN ISLANDS — QUEEN ELIZABETH II **Rev. Legend:** Diamond Wedding of H.M. Queen Elizabeth II & H.R.H. Prince Philip **Rev. Inscription:** THE WEDDING PROGRAM **Edge:** Reeded

Date	Mintage	F	VF	XF	Unc	BU
2007 Proof	—	Value: 75.00				

KM# 411 10 DOLLARS
28.2800 g., 0.9250 Silver 0.8410 oz. ASW, 38.61 mm. **Ruler:** Elizabeth II **Subject:** Act of Union, 300th Anniversary **Obv:** Bust in tiara right **Rev:** Flags above Queen Anne's portrait, lion and unicorn supporters flanking

Date	Mintage	F	VF	XF	Unc	BU
2007PM Proof	—	Value: 42.00				

KM# 371 10 DOLLARS
28.2800 g., 0.9250 Silver 0.8410 oz. ASW, 38.6 mm. **Ruler:** Elizabeth II **Obv:** Bust right **Rev:** Two soccer players and leopard

Date	Mintage	F	VF	XF	Unc	BU
2009 Proof	10,000	Value: 40.00				
2010	—	Value: 40.00				

KM# 372 10 DOLLARS
1.2400 g., 0.9990 Gold 0.0398 oz. AGW, 13.92 mm. **Ruler:** Elizabeth II **Obv:** Bust right **Rev:** Henry VIII facing

Date	Mintage	F	VF	XF	Unc	BU
2009PM Proof	5,000	Value: 80.00				

KM# 374 10 DOLLARS
28.2800 g., 0.9250 Silver 0.8410 oz. ASW, 38.6 mm. **Ruler:** Elizabeth II **Obv:** Bust right **Rev:** Elizabeth I aboard ship

Date	Mintage	F	VF	XF	Unc	BU
2009 Proof	10,000	Value: 42.00				

KM# 376 10 DOLLARS
28.2800 g., 0.9250 Silver 0.8410 oz. ASW, 38.6 mm. **Ruler:** Elizabeth II **Obv:** Bust right **Rev:** Elizabeth I between two columns

Date	Mintage	F	VF	XF	Unc	BU
2009 Proof	10,000	Value: 42.00				

KM# 382 10 DOLLARS
28.2800 g., Copper-Nickel, 38.6 mm. **Ruler:** Elizabeth II **Subject:** Centennial of Naval Aviation **Rev:** 1936 Fairey Swordfish returning to carrier HMS Fencer

Date	Mintage	F	VF	XF	Unc	BU
2009	—	—	—	—	—	7.50

KM# 382a 10 DOLLARS
28.2800 g., Silver, 38.6 mm. **Ruler:** Elizabeth II **Subject:** Centennial of Naval Aviation **Rev:** 1936 Fairey Swordfish returing to carrier HMS Fencer

Date	Mintage	F	VF	XF	Unc	BU
2009 Proof	10,000	Value: 40.00				

KM# 394 10 DOLLARS
28.2800 g., 0.9250 Silver 0.8410 oz. ASW, 38.6 mm. **Ruler:** Elizabeth II **Subject:** Peanuts 60th Anniversary **Rev:** Multicolor Snoopy asleep atop doghouse

Date	Mintage	F	VF	XF	Unc	BU
2010PM Proof	10,000	Value: 40.00				

KM# 395 10 DOLLARS
1.2400 g., 0.9990 Gold 0.0398 oz. AGW, 13.92 mm. **Ruler:** Elizabeth II **Series:** Peanuts 60th Anniversary **Rev:** Snoopy asleep atop doghouse

Date	Mintage	F	VF	XF	Unc	BU
2010PM Proof	10,000	Value: 100				

KM# 397 10 DOLLARS
31.1060 g., 0.9990 Silver 0.9990 oz. ASW, 38.6 mm. **Ruler:** Elizabeth II **Subject:** Elgin Marbles **Rev:** Two horsemen

Date	Mintage	F	VF	XF	Unc	BU
2010PM Proof	10,000	Value: 50.00				

KM# 398 10 DOLLARS
1.2200 g., 0.9990 Gold 0.0392 oz. AGW, 13.92 mm. **Ruler:** Elizabeth II **Subject:** Birth of Venus

Date	Mintage	F	VF	XF	Unc	BU
2010PM Proof	Est. 10,000	Value: 100				

KM# 401 10 DOLLARS
28.2800 g., 0.9250 Silver 0.8410 oz. ASW, 38.6 mm. **Ruler:** Elizabeth II **Subject:** Birth of Venus

Date	Mintage	F	VF	XF	Unc	BU
2010 Proof	Est. 10,000	Value: 50.00				

KM# 406 10 DOLLARS
28.2800 g., 0.9250 Silver 0.8410 oz. ASW, 38.61 mm. **Ruler:** Elizabeth II **Obv:** Bust in tiara right **Rev:** World Trade Center complex

Date	Mintage	F	VF	XF	Unc	BU
2011PM Proof	—	Value: 45.00				

KM# 407 10 DOLLARS
28.2800 g., 0.9250 Silver 0.8410 oz. ASW, 38.61 mm. **Ruler:** Elizabeth II **Subject:** Queen Elizabeth II's 85th Birthday **Obv:** Older and young busts conjoined right **Rev:** Queen on horseback left

Date	Mintage	F	VF	XF	Unc	BU
2011PM Proof	—	Value: 42.00				

KM# 408 10 DOLLARS
28.2800 g., 0.9250 Silver 0.8410 oz. ASW, 38.61 mm. **Ruler:** Elizabeth II **Subject:** Royal Wedding - Prince William and Catherine Middleton **Obv:** Bust in tiara right **Rev:** Busts of Catherine and William

Date	Mintage	F	VF	XF	Unc	BU
2011PM Proof	—	Value: 42.00				

KM# 409 10 DOLLARS
1.2200 g., 0.9990 Gold 0.0392 oz. AGW, 13.92 mm. **Ruler:** Elizabeth II **Obv:** Bust in tiara right **Rev:** Anne Boylen bust 1/4 left

Date	Mintage	F	VF	XF	Unc	BU
2011PM	—	Value: 100				

KM# 410 10 DOLLARS
28.2800 g., Silver with insert, 38.61 mm. **Ruler:** Elizabeth II **Subject:** Life cycle of a tree frog **Obv:** Frog at center **Rev:** Life cycle of a tree frog

Date	Mintage	F	VF	XF	Unc	BU
2011PM Proof	—	Value: 120				

KM# 417 10 DOLLARS
28.2800 g., 0.9250 Silver 0.8410 oz. ASW, 38.61 mm. **Ruler:** Elizabeth II **Subject:** Life of Queen Elizabeth II **Obv:** Current and young busts conjoined right **Rev:** Half length bust facing wearing Order sash and tiara

Date	Mintage	F	VF	XF	Unc	BU
2012PM Proof	—	Value: 50.00				

KM# 418 10 DOLLARS
28.2800 g., Silver, 38.6 mm. **Ruler:** Elizabeth II **Subject:** Life of Queen Elizabeth II **Obv:** Conjoined busts right **Rev:** Elizabeth II on horseback as if reviewing troops

Date	Mintage	F	VF	XF	Unc	BU
2012PM Proof	—	—	—	—	—	50.00

KM# 419 10 DOLLARS
28.2800 g., Copper-Nickel, 38.6 mm. **Ruler:** Elizabeth II **Subject:** Valentine's day **Obv:** Conjoined busts right **Rev:** Crescent moon and pixi

Date	Mintage	F	VF	XF	Unc	BU
2012PM	—	—	—	—	—	15.00

KM# 420 10 DOLLARS
28.2800 g., 0.9250 Silver 0.8410 oz. ASW, 38.6 mm. **Ruler:** Elizabeth II **Subject:** Summer Olympics, London **Obv:** Conjoined busts right **Rev:** Gymnast on pommel horse, Union Jack in color below

Date	Mintage	F	VF	XF	Unc	BU
2012PM Proof	—	Value: 50.00				

KM# 421 10 DOLLARS

28.2800 g., 0.9250 Silver 0.8410 oz. ASW, 38.6 mm. **Ruler:** Elizabeth II **Subject:** Summer Olympics, London **Obv:** Conjoined busts right **Rev:** Dressage, Union Jack in color below

Date	Mintage	F	VF	XF	Unc	BU
2012PM Proof	—	Value: 50.00				

KM# 422 10 DOLLARS

28.2800 g., 0.9250 Silver 0.8410 oz. ASW, 38.6 mm. **Ruler:** Elizabeth II **Subject:** Summer Olympics, London **Obv:** Conjoined busts right **Rev:** Fencing, Union Jack in color below

Date	Mintage	F	VF	XF	Unc	BU
2012PM Proof	—	Value: 50.00				

KM# 423 10 DOLLARS

28.2800 g., 0.9250 Silver 0.8410 oz. ASW, 38.6 mm. **Ruler:** Elizabeth II **Subject:** Summer Olympics, London **Obv:** Conjoined busts right **Rev:** Soccer players, Union Jack in color below

Date	Mintage	F	VF	XF	Unc	BU
2012PM Proof	—	Value: 50.00				

KM# 424 10 DOLLARS

28.2800 g., Copper-Nickel, 38.61 mm. **Ruler:** Elizabeth II **Rev:** Prince William

Date	Mintage	F	VF	XF	Unc	BU
2012PM	—	—	—	—	—	15.00

KM# 425 10 DOLLARS

28.2800 g., Copper-Nickel, 38.61 mm. **Ruler:** Elizabeth II **Rev:** Duchess of Cambridge

Date	Mintage	F	VF	XF	Unc	BU
2012PM	—	—	—	—	—	15.00

KM# 201 20 DOLLARS

1.2441 g., 0.9999 Gold 0.0400 oz. AGW, 13.92 mm. **Subject:** Teddy Bear Centennial **Obv:** Queen's bust right **Rev:** Teddy bear **Edge:** Reeded

Date	Mintage	F	VF	XF	Unc	BU
2002 Proof	10,000	Value: 75.00				

KM# 227 20 DOLLARS

1.2400 g., 0.9999 Gold 0.0399 oz. AGW, 13.92 mm. **Subject:** Kennedy Assassination **Obv:** Queen's bust right **Rev:** President Kennedy's portrait **Edge:** Reeded

Date	Mintage	F	VF	XF	Unc	BU
2003 Proof	10,000	Value: 75.00				

KM# 279a 20 DOLLARS

63.5900 g., 0.9990 Silver Gilt 2.0423 oz. ASW, 49.93 mm. **Ruler:** Elizabeth II **Subject:** XXVII Olympic Games **Obv:** Bust with tiara right **Rev:** 1896 Olympic medal design **Edge:** Reeded

Date	Mintage	F	VF	XF	Unc	BU
2004PM Proof	—	Value: 100				

KM# 271 20 DOLLARS

1.2440 g., 0.9999 Gold 0.0400 oz. AGW, 14 mm. **Obv:** Queen's bust right **Rev:** Peter Rabbit **Edge:** Reeded

Date	Mintage	F	VF	XF	Unc	BU
2004 Proof	5,000	Value: 80.00				

KM# 279 20 DOLLARS

58.0000 g., 0.9990 Silver 1.8628 oz. ASW, 50 mm. **Subject:** XXVIII Olympic Games **Obv:** Bust with tiara right **Rev:** 1896 Olympic medal design **Edge:** Reeded

Date	Mintage	F	VF	XF	Unc	BU
2004PM Proof	2,004	Value: 90.00				

KM# 345 20 DOLLARS

3.9600 g., 0.7500 Gold 0.0955 oz. AGW, 21.78 mm. **Ruler:** Elizabeth II **Subject:** 500th Anniversary - Death of Columbus **Obv:** Crowned bust right **Obv. Legend:** BRITISH VIRGIN ISLANDS - QUEEN ELIZABETH II **Rev:** Bust of Columbus facing 3/4 left at right, outlined map of the Americas at left **Rev. Legend:** 1451 - CHRISTOPHER COLUMBUS - 1506 **Edge:** Reeded **Note:** Struck in white gold.

Date	Mintage	F	VF	XF	Unc	BU
2006 Proof	1,506	Value: 185				

KM# 346 20 DOLLARS

4.0200 g., 0.7500 Gold 0.0969 oz. AGW, 21.78 mm. **Ruler:** Elizabeth II **Subject:** 500th Anniversary - Death of Columbus **Obv:** Crowned bust right **Obv. Legend:** BRITISH VIRGIN ISLANDS - QUEEN ELIZABETH II **Rev:** Sailing ship "Santa Maria" **Rev. Legend:** 1451 - CHRISTOPHER COLUMBUS - 1506 **Edge:** Reeded **Note:** Struck in rose gold.

Date	Mintage	F	VF	XF	Unc	BU
2006 Proof	1,506	Value: 185				

KM# 347 20 DOLLARS

3.9900 g., 0.7500 Gold 0.0962 oz. AGW, 21.78 mm. **Ruler:** Elizabeth II **Subject:** 500th Anniversary - Death of Columbus **Obv:** Crowned bust right **Obv. Legend:** BRITISH VIRGIN ISLANDS - QUEEN ELIZABETH II **Rev:** Sailing ships "Niña" and "Pinta" **Rev. Legend:** 1451 - CHRISTOPHER COLUMBUS - 1506 **Edge:** Reeded **Note:** Struck in yellow gold.

Date	Mintage	F	VF	XF	Unc	BU
2006 Proof	1,506	Value: 200				

KM# 379 30 DOLLARS

155.5000 g., 0.9990 Silver 4.9942 oz. ASW **Ruler:** Elizabeth II **Subject:** Nelson's Victory at Trafalgar **Rev:** Two ships

Date	Mintage	F	VF	XF	Unc	BU
2008 Proof	—	Value: 250				

KM# 275 25 DOLLARS

3.1100 g., 0.9999 Gold 0.1000 oz. AGW, 18 mm. **Obv:** Queen's bust right **Rev:** Hernando Pizarro portrait and life events pictorial **Edge:** Reeded

Date	Mintage	F	VF	XF	Unc	BU
2004 Proof	350	Value: 185				

KM# 289 25 DOLLARS

3.1100 g., 0.9999 Gold 0.1000 oz. AGW, 18 mm. **Obv:** Queen's bust right **Rev:** Dolphin **Edge:** Reeded

Date	Mintage	F	VF	XF	Unc	BU
2004 Proof	6,000	Value: 180				

KM# 315 25 DOLLARS

3.1100 g., 0.9999 Gold 0.1000 oz. AGW, 18 mm. **Obv:** Bust of Queen Elizabeth II right **Rev:** Mother and baby dolphins **Edge:** Reeded

Date	Mintage	F	VF	XF	Unc	BU
2005 Proof	6,000	Value: 180				

KM# 335 25 DOLLARS

3.1120 g., 0.9999 Gold 0.1000 oz. AGW, 17.95 mm. **Ruler:** Elizabeth II **Subject:** 400th Anniversary Founding of Jamestown **Obv:** Bust with tiara right **Obv. Legend:** BRITISH VIRGIN ISLANDS - QUEEN ELIZABETH II **Rev:** British lion laying, American eagle perched on sprays **Rev. Legend:** UNITED IN FRIENDSHIP **Edge:** Reeded

Date	Mintage	VG	F	VF	XF	Unc
2007 Proof	7,500	Value: 180				

KM# 412 25 DOLLARS

6.2200 g., 0.9990 Gold 0.1998 oz. AGW, 22 mm. **Ruler:** Elizabeth II **Subject:** Nelson's victory at Trafalgar **Obv:** Bust in tiara right **Rev:** Victory crowned Britannia standing on prow

Date	Mintage	F	VF	XF	Unc	BU
2008PM Proof	—	Value: 450				

KM# 202 50 DOLLARS

3.1104 g., 0.9999 Gold 0.1000 oz. AGW, 17.95 mm. **Subject:** Teddy Bear Centennial **Obv:** Queen's bust right **Rev:** Teddy bear **Edge:** Reeded

Date	Mintage	F	VF	XF	Unc	BU
2002 Proof	7,000	Value: 185				

KM# 272 50 DOLLARS

3.1100 g., 0.9999 Gold 0.1000 oz. AGW, 18 mm. **Obv:** Queen's bust right **Rev:** Peter Rabbit **Edge:** Reeded

Date	Mintage	F	VF	XF	Unc	BU
2004 Proof	3,000	Value: 190				

KM# 276 50 DOLLARS

6.2200 g., 0.9999 Gold 0.1999 oz. AGW, 22 mm. **Obv:** Queen's bust right **Rev:** Treasure ship with blue color sail **Edge:** Reeded

Date	Mintage	F	VF	XF	Unc	BU
2004 Proof	350	Value: 400				

KM# 290 50 DOLLARS

6.2200 g., 0.9999 Gold 0.1999 oz. AGW, 22 mm. **Obv:** Queen's bust right **Rev:** Dolphin **Edge:** Reeded

Date	Mintage	F	VF	XF	Unc	BU
2004 Proof	3,500	Value: 350				

KM# 316 50 DOLLARS

6.2200 g., 0.9999 Gold 0.1999 oz. AGW, 22 mm. **Obv:** Bust of Queen Elizabeth II right **Rev:** Large and small dolphins **Edge:** Reeded

Date	Mintage	F	VF	XF	Unc	BU
2005	3,500	Value: 350				

KM# 351 50 DOLLARS

6.2200 g., 0.9999 Gold 0.1999 oz. AGW, 22 mm. **Ruler:** Elizabeth II **Subject:** 5th Anniversary - Attack on Twin Towers, New York City **Obv:** Crowned bust right **Obv. Legend:** BRITISH VIRGIN ISLANDS - QUEEN ELIZABETH II **Rev:** Twin Towers in sprays, remembrance ribbon privy mark at upper right **Rev. Inscription:** LEST WE FORGET **Edge:** Reeded

Date	Mintage	F	VF	XF	Unc	BU
2006 Proof	2,000	Value: 365				

KM# 413 50 DOLLARS

6.2200 g., 0.9990 Gold 0.1998 oz. AGW, 22 mm. **Ruler:** Elizabeth II **Subject:** Color photography, 100th Anniversary **Obv:** Bust in tiara right **Rev:** Conjoined portraits right in photo frame

Date	Mintage	F	VF	XF	Unc	BU
2007PM Proof	—	Value: 450				

KM# 336 50 DOLLARS

6.2230 g., 0.9999 Gold 0.2000 oz. AGW, 22 mm. **Ruler:** Elizabeth II **Subject:** 400th Anniversary Founding of Jamestown **Obv:** Bust with tiara right **Obv. Legend:** BRITISH VIRGIN ISLANDS - QUEEN ELIZABETH II **Rev:** British lion laying, American eagle perched on sprays **Rev. Legend:** UNITED IN FRIENDSHIP **Edge:** Reeded

Date	Mintage	F	VF	XF	Unc	BU
2007 Proof	5,000	Value: 360				

KM# 377 50 DOLLARS

6.2200 g., 0.9990 Gold 0.1998 oz. AGW, 22 mm. **Ruler:** Elizabeth II **Obv:** Bust right **Rev:** Elizabeth II aboard ship with 1mm pearl

Date	Mintage	F	VF	XF	Unc	BU
2009 Proof	750	Value: 375				

KM# 378 50 DOLLARS

6.2200 g., 0.9990 Gold 0.1998 oz. AGW, 22 mm. **Ruler:** Elizabeth II **Obv:** Bust right **Rev:** Elizabeth II between two columns, .01ct ruby insert

Date	Mintage	F	VF	XF	Unc	BU
2009 Proof	750	Value: 375				

KM# 285 75 DOLLARS

11.0000 g., Bi-Metallic .990 Titanium 2g center in .9999 Gold 9g ring, 36.5 mm. **Obv:** Queen's bust right **Rev:** British Guiana stamp design **Edge:** Reeded

Date	Mintage	F	VF	XF	Unc	BU
2004 Proof	2,500	Value: 450				

KM# 389 75 DOLLARS

Bi-Metallic Titanium and gold **Ruler:** Elizabeth II **Subject:** Mozart

Date	Mintage	F	VF	XF	Unc	BU
2006PM Proof	—	Value: 450				

KM# 388 75 DOLLARS

Bi-Metallic Titanium and gold, 36.5 mm. **Ruler:** Elizabeth II **Subject:** Bejing Olympics **Obv:** Bust in tiara right **Rev:** Tennis plays against Great Wall background

Date	Mintage	F	VF	XF	Unc	BU
2009PM Proof	—	Value: 450				

KM# 182 100 DOLLARS

6.2200 g., 0.9990 Gold 0.1998 oz. AGW, 22 mm. **Subject:** Sir Francis Drake **Obv:** Queen's bust right **Rev:** Ship, portrait and map **Edge:** Reeded

Date	Mintage	F	VF	XF	Unc	BU
2002 Proof	5,000	Value: 350				

KM# 185 100 DOLLARS

6.2200 g., 0.9990 Gold 0.1998 oz. AGW, 22 mm. **Subject:** Sir Walter Raleigh **Obv:** Queen's bust right **Rev:** Ship, portrait and map **Edge:** Reeded

Date	Mintage	F	VF	XF	Unc	BU
2002 Proof	5,000	Value: 350				

KM# 189 100 DOLLARS

6.2208 g., 0.9999 Gold 0.2000 oz. AGW, 22 mm. **Subject:** Queen's Golden Jubilee **Obv:** Queen's bust right **Rev:** Queen on horse **Edge:** Reeded

Date	Mintage	F	VF	XF	Unc	BU
2002 Proof	2,002	Value: 365				

KM# 192 100 DOLLARS

6.2208 g., 0.9999 Gold 0.2000 oz. AGW, 22 mm. **Subject:** Queen's Golden Jubilee **Obv:** Queen's bust right **Rev:** Queen on throne **Edge:** Reeded

Date	Mintage	F	VF	XF	Unc	BU
2002 Proof	2,002	Value: 365				

KM# 195 100 DOLLARS

6.2208 g., 0.9999 Gold 0.2000 oz. AGW, 22 mm. **Subject:** Queen's Golden Jubilee **Obv:** Queen's bust right **Rev:** Queen with President Ronald Reagan and Mrs. Nancy Reagan **Edge:** Reeded

Date	Mintage	F	VF	XF	Unc	BU
2002 Proof	2,002	Value: 365				

KM# 198 100 DOLLARS

6.2208 g., 0.9999 Gold 0.2000 oz. AGW, 22 mm. **Subject:** Queen's Golden Jubilee **Obv:** Queen's bust right **Rev:** Carnival dancers **Edge:** Reeded

Date	Mintage	F	VF	XF	Unc	BU
2002 Proof	2,002	Value: 365				

KM# 203 100 DOLLARS

6.2200 g., 0.9999 Gold 0.1999 oz. AGW, 22 mm. **Subject:** Teddy Bear Centennial **Obv:** Queen's bust right **Rev:** Teddy bear **Edge:** Reeded

Date	Mintage	F	VF	XF	Unc	BU
2002 Proof	5,000	Value: 350				

KM# 206 100 DOLLARS

6.2200 g., 0.9999 Gold 0.1999 oz. AGW, 22 mm. **Subject:** Princess Diana **Obv:** Queen's bust right **Rev:** Diana's portrait **Edge:** Reeded

Date	Mintage	F	VF	XF	Unc	BU
2002 Proof	5,000	Value: 350				

KM# 209.1 100 DOLLARS

6.2200 g., 0.9999 Gold 0.1999 oz. AGW, 22 mm. **Subject:** September 11, 2001 **Obv:** Queen's bust right **Rev:** World Trade Center twin towers **Edge:** Reeded

Date	Mintage	F	VF	XF	Unc	BU
2002 Proof	5,000	Value: 350				

KM# 209.2 100 DOLLARS

6.2200 g., 0.9999 Gold 0.1999 oz. AGW, 22 mm. **Subject:** September 11, 2001 **Obv:** Queen's bust right **Rev:** Holographic multicolor World Trade Center twin towers **Edge:** Reeded

Date	Mintage	F	VF	XF	Unc	BU
2002 Proof	5,000	Value: 350				

KM# 212 100 DOLLARS

6.2200 g., 0.9999 Gold 0.1999 oz. AGW, 22 mm. **Subject:** September 11, 2001 **Obv:** Queen's bust right **Rev:** Statue of Liberty **Edge:** Reeded

Date	Mintage	F	VF	XF	Unc	BU
2002 Proof	5,000	Value: 350				

KM# 215 100 DOLLARS

6.2200 g., 0.9999 Gold 0.1999 oz. AGW, 22 mm. **Subject:** Queen Mother Series **Obv:** Queen's bust right **Rev:** Queen Mother with young Prince Charles **Edge:** Reeded

Date	Mintage	F	VF	XF	Unc	BU
2002PM Proof	5,000	Value: 350				

KM# 218 100 DOLLARS

6.2200 g., 0.9999 Gold 0.1999 oz. AGW, 22 mm. **Subject:** Queen Mother Series **Obv:** Queen's bust right **Rev:** Queen Mother with four grandchildren **Edge:** Reeded

Date	Mintage	F	VF	XF	Unc	BU
2002PM Proof	5,000	Value: 350				

KM# 221 100 DOLLARS

6.2200 g., 0.9999 Gold 0.1999 oz. AGW, 22 mm. **Subject:** Queen Mother Series **Obv:** Queen's bust right **Rev:** Queen Mother with uniformed Prince Charles **Edge:** Reeded

Date	Mintage	F	VF	XF	Unc	BU
2002PM Proof	5,000	Value: 350				

KM# 224 100 DOLLARS

6.2200 g., 0.9999 Gold 0.1999 oz. AGW, 22 mm. **Subject:** Queen Mother Series **Obv:** Queen's bust right **Rev:** Queen Mother's coffin **Edge:** Reeded

Date	Mintage	F	VF	XF	Unc	BU
2002PM Proof	5,000	Value: 350				

KM# 228 100 DOLLARS

6.2200 g., 0.9999 Gold 0.1999 oz. AGW, 22 mm. **Subject:** Kennedy Assassination **Obv:** Queen's bust right **Rev:** President Kennedy's portrait **Edge:** Reeded

Date	Mintage	F	VF	XF	Unc	BU
2003 Proof	5,000	Value: 350				

KM# 231 100 DOLLARS

15.5500 g., 0.9999 Gold 0.4999 oz. AGW, 30 mm. **Subject:** Powered Flight Centennial **Obv:** Queen's bust right **Rev:** Three historic airplanes and rocket **Edge:** Reeded

Date	Mintage	F	VF	XF	Unc	BU
2003 Proof	—	Value: 875				

KM# 234 100 DOLLARS

6.2200 g., 0.9999 Gold 0.1999 oz. AGW, 22 mm. **Obv:** Queen's bust right **Rev:** Henry VIII and Elizabeth I **Edge:** Reeded

Date	Mintage	F	VF	XF	Unc	BU
2003 Proof	5,000	Value: 350				

KM# 237 100 DOLLARS

6.2200 g., 0.9999 Gold 0.1999 oz. AGW, 22 mm. **Obv:** Queen's bust right **Rev:** Matthew Parker, Archbishop of Canterbury **Edge:** Reeded

Date	Mintage	F	VF	XF	Unc	BU
2003 Proof	5,000	Value: 350				

KM# 240 100 DOLLARS

6.2200 g., 0.9999 Gold 0.1999 oz. AGW, 22 mm. **Obv:** Queen's bust right **Rev:** Sir Francis Drake and ships **Edge:** Reeded

Date	Mintage	F	VF	XF	Unc	BU
2003 Proof	5,000	Value: 350				

KM# 243 100 DOLLARS

6.2200 g., 0.9999 Gold 0.1999 oz. AGW, 22 mm. **Obv:** Queen's bust right **Rev:** Sir Walter Raleigh **Edge:** Reeded

Date	Mintage	F	VF	XF	Unc	BU
2003 Proof	5,000	Value: 350				

KM# 246 100 DOLLARS

6.2200 g., 0.9999 Gold 0.1999 oz. AGW, 22 mm. **Obv:** Queen's bust right **Rev:** Sir William Shakespeare **Edge:** Reeded

Date	Mintage	F	VF	XF	Unc	BU
2003 Proof	5,000	Value: 350				

KM# 249 100 DOLLARS

6.2200 g., 0.9999 Gold 0.1999 oz. AGW, 22 mm. **Obv:** Queen's bust right **Rev:** Elizabeth I above her funeral procession **Edge:** Reeded

Date	Mintage	F	VF	XF	Unc	BU
2003 Proof	5,000	Value: 350				

KM# 252 100 DOLLARS

6.2200 g., 0.9999 Gold 0.1999 oz. AGW, 22 mm. **Subject:** Olympics **Obv:** Queen's bust right **Rev:** Ancient Olympic bust, runners in background and coin upper right **Edge:** Reeded

Date	Mintage	F	VF	XF	Unc	BU
2003 Proof	5,000	Value: 350				

KM# 255 100 DOLLARS

6.2200 g., 0.9999 Gold 0.1999 oz. AGW, 22 mm. **Subject:** Olympics **Obv:** Queen's bust right **Rev:** Ancient bust, charioteer and coin **Edge:** Reeded

Date	Mintage	F	VF	XF	Unc	BU
2003 Proof	5,000	Value: 350				

KM# 273.1 100 DOLLARS
6.2200 g., 0.9999 Gold 0.1999 oz. AGW, 22 mm. **Obv:** Queen's bust right **Rev:** Peter Rabbit **Edge:** Reeded

Date	Mintage	F	VF	XF	Unc	BU
2004 Proof	2,000	Value: 365				

KM# 273.2 100 DOLLARS
6.2200 g., 0.9999 Gold 0.1999 oz. AGW, 22 mm. **Obv:** Queen's bust right **Rev:** Multicolor Peter Rabbit **Edge:** Reeded

Date	Mintage	F	VF	XF	Unc	BU
2004 Proof	—	Value: 365				

KM# 283 100 DOLLARS
6.2200 g., 0.9999 Gold 0.1999 oz. AGW, 22 mm. **Obv:** Queen's bust right **Rev:** Sailor above two D-Day landing craft **Edge:** Reeded

Date	Mintage	F	VF	XF	Unc	BU
2004 Proof	5,000	Value: 350				

KM# 299 100 DOLLARS
6.2200 g., 0.9999 Gold 0.1999 oz. AGW, 22 mm. **Obv:** Queen's bust right **Rev:** Soldier above tank and jeeps **Edge:** Reeded

Date	Mintage	F	VF	XF	Unc	BU
2004 Proof	5,000	Value: 350				

KM# 302 100 DOLLARS
6.2200 g., 0.9999 Gold 0.1999 oz. AGW, 22 mm. **Obv:** Queen's bust right **Rev:** Pilot and planes above D-Day landing **Edge:** Reeded

Date	Mintage	F	VF	XF	Unc	BU
2004 Proof	5,000	Value: 350				

KM# 305 100 DOLLARS
6.2200 g., 0.9999 Gold 0.1999 oz. AGW, 22 mm. **Obv:** Queen's bust right **Rev:** Ancient Olympic bust, runners and owl coin **Edge:** Reeded

Date	Mintage	F	VF	XF	Unc	BU
2004 Proof	5,000	Value: 350				

KM# 308 100 DOLLARS
6.2200 g., 0.9999 Gold 0.1999 oz. AGW, 22 mm. **Obv:** Queen's bust right **Rev:** Ancient Olympic bust, charioteer and Zeus coin **Edge:** Reeded

Date	Mintage	F	VF	XF	Unc	BU
2004 Proof	5,000	Value: 350				

KM# 317 125 DOLLARS
15.5510 g., 0.9999 Gold 0.4999 oz. AGW, 30 mm. **Obv:** Bust of Queen Elizabeth II right **Rev:** Mother and baby dolphin **Edge:** Reeded

Date	Mintage	F	VF	XF	Unc	BU
2005	1,500	Value: 900				

KM# 337 125 DOLLARS
15.5590 g., 0.9999 Gold 0.5002 oz. AGW, 30 mm. **Ruler:** Elizabeth II **Subject:** 400th Anniversary Founding of Jamestown **Obv:** Bust with tiara right **Obv. Legend:** BRITISH VIRGIN ISLANDS - QUEEN ELIZABETH II **Rev:** British lion laying, American eagle perched on sprays **Rev. Legend:** UNITED IN FRIENDSHIP **Edge:** Reeded

Date	Mintage	F	VF	XF	Unc	BU
2007 Proof	3,000	Value: 875				

KM# 309 250 DOLLARS
15.5517 g., 0.9990 Gold 0.4995 oz. AGW, 30 mm. **Obv:** Queen's bust right **Rev:** Statue of Liberty and the date "11 Sept. 2001" **Edge:** Reeded

Date	Mintage	F	VF	XF	Unc	BU
2002	250	Value: 950				

KM# 280 250 DOLLARS
58.0000 g., 0.5000 Gold 0.9323 oz. AGW, 50 mm. **Obv:** Queen's bust right **Rev:** 1896 Olympic medal design **Edge:** Reeded

Date	Mintage	F	VF	XF	Unc	BU
2004 Proof	1,000	Value: 1,650				

KM# 318 250 DOLLARS
31.1030 g., 0.9999 Gold 0.9998 oz. AGW, 32.7 mm. **Obv:** Bust of Queen Elizabeth II right **Rev:** Mother and baby dolphin **Edge:** Reeded

Date	Mintage	F	VF	XF	Unc	BU
2005 Proof	750	Value: 1,750				

KM# 390 250 DOLLARS
Gold **Ruler:** Elizabeth II **Subject:** Mozart

Date	Mintage	F	VF	XF	Unc	BU
2006PM Proof	—	Value: 1,750				

KM# 338 250 DOLLARS
31.1030 g., 0.9999 Gold 0.9998 oz. AGW, 32.7 mm. **Ruler:** Elizabeth II **Subject:** 400th Anniversary Founding of Jamestown **Obv:** Bust with tiara right **Obv. Legend:** BRITISH VIRGIN ISLANDS - QUEEN ELIZABETH II **Rev:** British lion laying, American eagle perched on sprays **Rev. Legend:** UNITED IN FRIENDSHIP **Edge:** Reeded

Date	Mintage	F	VF	XF	Unc	BU
2007 Proof	1,000	Value: 1,750				

KM# 277 500 DOLLARS
160.7562 g., 0.9990 Gold 5.1630 oz. AGW, 150 mm. **Obv:** Queen's bust right **Rev:** Gold-plated portrait of Hernando Pizarro, small inset emerald above Pizarro's life events pictoral **Edge:** Reeded **Note:** Photo reduced.

Date	Mintage	F	VF	XF	Unc	BU
2004 Proof	500	Value: 9,000				

KM# 348 500 DOLLARS
160.7562 g., 0.9990 Gold 5.1630 oz. AGW, 150 mm. **Ruler:** Elizabeth II **Subject:** 500th Anniversary - Death of Columbus **Obv:** Crowned bust right **Obv. Legend:** BRITISH VIRGIN ISLANDS - QUEEN ELIZABETH II **Rev:** Ship in background at left, Columbus standing at right with right arm outstreched looking right, compass below. **Rev. Legend:** 1451 - DISCOVERER OF AMERICA - CHRISTOPHER COLUMBUS - 1506 **Edge:** Reeded

Date	Mintage	F	VF	XF	Unc	BU
2006 Proof	1,506	Value: 8,900				

KM# 392 500 DOLLARS
160.7560 g., 0.9990 Silver 5.1630 oz. ASW, 150 mm. **Ruler:** Elizabeth II **Subject:** Battle of Trafalgar **Rev:** Two naval ships in battle

Date	Mintage	F	VF	XF	Unc	BU
2008PM Proof	—	Value: 250				

MINT SETS

KM#	Date	Mintage	Identification	Issue Price	Mkt Val
MS12	2007 (4)	—	KM# 341 - 344	65.00	80.00

PROOF SETS

KM#	Date	Mintage	Identification	Issue Price	Mkt Val
PS20	2007 (4)	—	KM# 341a - 344a	300	300

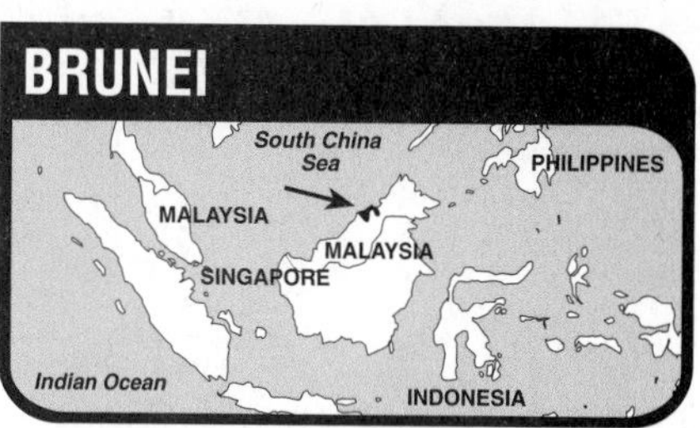

Negara Brunei Darussalam (State of Brunei), an independent sultanate on the northwest coast of the island of Borneo, has an area of 2,226 sq. mi. (5,765 sq. km.) and a population of *326,000. Capital: Bandar Seri Begawan. Crude oil and rubber are exported.

TITLES

نكري بروني

Negri Brunei

RULERS

Sultan Hassanal Bolkiah I, 1967-

SULTANATE

DECIMAL COINAGE

100 Sen = 1 Dollar (Ringgit)

KM# 34 SEN
1.7500 g., Copper Clad Steel, 17.7 mm. **Ruler:** Sultan Hassanal Bolkiah **Obv:** Uniformed bust facing **Rev:** Native design, denomination below, date at right **Edge:** Plain

Date	Mintage	F	VF	XF	Unc	BU
2001	576,000	—	—	0.15	0.40	0.50
2002	804,900	—	—	0.15	0.40	0.50
2004	—	—	—	0.15	0.40	0.50
2005	—	—	—	0.15	0.40	0.50
2006	—	—	—	0.15	0.40	0.50

KM# 34b SEN
1.7000 g., Brass, 17.7 mm. **Ruler:** Sultan Hassanal Bolkiah **Obv:** Uniformed bust facing **Rev:** Native design, denomination below, date at right

Date	Mintage	F	VF	XF	Unc	BU
2008	—	—	—	—	0.40	0.50
2009	—	—	—	—	0.40	0.50
2010	—	—	—	—	0.40	0.50

KM# 35 5 SEN
1.4100 g., Copper-Nickel, 16.26 mm. **Ruler:** Sultan Hassanal Bolkiah **Obv:** Uniformed bust facing **Rev:** Native design, denomination below, date at right **Edge:** Reeded

Date	Mintage	F	VF	XF	Unc	BU
2001	808,000	—	—	0.20	0.50	0.75
2002	1,418,178	—	—	0.20	0.50	0.75
2004	—	—	—	0.20	0.50	0.75
2005	—	—	—	0.20	0.50	0.75
2006	—	—	—	0.20	0.50	0.75
2007	—	—	—	0.20	0.50	0.75
2008	—	—	—	0.20	0.50	0.75
2009	—	—	—	0.20	0.50	0.75
2010	—	—	—	0.20	0.50	0.75

KM# 36 10 SEN
2.8200 g., Copper-Nickel, 19.4 mm. **Ruler:** Sultan Hassanal Bolkiah **Obv:** Uniformed bust facing **Rev:** Native design, denomination below, date at right **Edge:** Reeded

Date	Mintage	F	VF	XF	Unc	BU
2001	164,000	—	—	0.30	0.75	1.00
2002	476,452	—	—	0.30	0.75	1.00
2004	—	—	—	0.30	0.75	1.00
2005	—	—	—	0.30	0.75	1.00
2006	—	—	—	0.30	0.75	1.00
2007	—	—	—	0.30	0.75	1.00
2008	—	—	—	0.30	0.75	1.00
2009	—	—	—	0.30	0.75	1.00

KM# 37 20 SEN
5.6500 g., Copper-Nickel, 23.5 mm. **Ruler:** Sultan Hassanal Bolkiah **Obv:** Uniformed bust facing **Rev:** Native design, denomination below, date at right **Edge:** Reeded

Date	Mintage	F	VF	XF	Unc	BU
2001	270,647	—	—	0.45	1.10	1.50
2002	597,272	—	—	0.45	1.10	1.50
2004	—	—	—	0.45	1.10	1.50
2005	—	—	—	0.45	1.10	1.50
2008	—	—	—	0.45	1.10	1.50
2009	—	—	—	0.45	1.10	1.50
2010	—	—	—	0.45	1.10	1.50

KM# 38 50 SEN
9.3300 g., Copper-Nickel, 27.7 mm. **Ruler:** Sultan Hassanal Bolkiah **Obv:** Uniformed bust facing **Rev:** National arms within circle, denomination below, date at right **Edge:** Security

Date	Mintage	F	VF	XF	Unc	BU
2001	50,000	—	—	1.00	2.50	3.00
2002	1,325	—	—	1.40	3.50	5.00
2004	—	—	—	0.75	1.80	2.50
2005	—	—	—	0.75	1.80	2.50
2006	—	—	—	0.75	1.80	2.50
2007	—	—	—	0.75	1.80	2.50
2008	—	—	—	0.75	1.80	2.50
2009	—	—	—	0.75	1.80	2.50
2010	—	—	—	0.75	1.80	2.50

KM# 80 2 DOLLARS
31.1000 g., Copper-Nickel, 40.7 mm. **Ruler:** Sultan Hassanal Bolkiah **Subject:** 20th Anniversary of Independence **Obv:** Bust 3/4 left, facing **Obv. Legend:** SULTAN HAJI HASSANAL BOLKIAH **Rev:** National arms **Rev. Legend:** NEGARI BRUNEI DARUSSALAM

Date	Mintage	F	VF	XF	Unc	BU
2004 Proof	4,000	Value: 65.00				

KM# 86 2 DOLLARS
31.1000 g., Copper-Nickel, 40.7 mm. **Ruler:** Sultan Hassanal Bolkiah **Subject:** 60th Birthday **Obv:** Bust 3/4 left, facing **Obv. Legend:** SULTAN HAJI HASSANAL BOLKIAH **Rev:** Multicolor 1/2-length figure in civilian clothes, facing

Date	Mintage	F	VF	XF	Unc	BU
2006 Proof	200	Value: 120				

KM# 77 3 DOLLARS
24.0000 g., Copper-Nickel, 40 mm. **Ruler:** Sultan Hassanal Bolkiah **Obv:** Uniformed bust facing **Obv. Legend:** SULTAN HAJI HASSANAL BOLKIAH **Rev:** Logo at center **Rev. Legend:** COMMONWEALTH FINANCE MINISTERS MEETING **Edge:** Reeded

Date	Mintage	F	VF	XF	Unc	BU
2003 Proof	4,000	Value: 40.00				

KM# 83 3 DOLLARS
31.1000 g., Copper-Nickel, 40.7 mm. **Ruler:** Sultan Hassanal Bolkiah **Subject:** Royal Wedding **Obv:** Multicolor portraits of Royal couple

Date	Mintage	F	VF	XF	Unc	BU
2004 Proof	5,000	Value: 50.00				

KM# 81 20 DOLLARS
31.1000 g., 0.9990 Silver 0.9988 oz. ASW, 40.7 mm. **Ruler:** Sultan Hassanal Bolkiah **Subject:** 20th Anniversary of Independence **Obv:** Bust 3/4 left, facing **Obv. Legend:** SULTAN HAJI HASSANAL BOLKIAH **Rev:** National arms **Rev. Legend:** NEGARI BRUNEI DARUSSALAM

Date	Mintage	F	VF	XF	Unc	BU
2004 Proof	1,000	Value: 120				

KM# 87 20 DOLLARS
31.1000 g., 0.9990 Silver 0.9988 oz. ASW, 40.7 mm. **Ruler:** Sultan Hassanal Bolkiah **Subject:** 60th Birthday **Obv:** Bust 3/4 left, facing **Obv. Legend:** SULTAN HAJI HASSANAL BOLKIAH **Rev:** Multicolor 1/2-length figure in civilian clothes, facing

Date	Mintage	F	VF	XF	Unc	BU
2006 Proof	200	Value: 275				

KM# 78 30 DOLLARS
62.2000 g., 0.9990 Silver 1.9977 oz. ASW **Ruler:** Sultan Hassanal Bolkiah **Subject:** Commonwealth Finance Ministers' Meeting **Obv:** Logo at upper left, multicolor bust of Sultan 3/4 left, facing at right **Obv. Legend:** SULTAN HAJI HASSANAL BOLIAH **Rev:** World map at left - center, national arms at upper right **Shape:** Rectangular, 65 x 31 mm

Date	Mintage	F	VF	XF	Unc	BU
2003 Proof	1,000	Value: 210				

KM# 84 30 DOLLARS
31.1000 g., 0.9990 Silver 0.9988 oz. ASW, 40.7 mm. **Ruler:** Sultan Hassanal Bolkiah **Subject:** Royal Wedding **Obv:** Multicolor portraits of Royal couple

Date	Mintage	F	VF	XF	Unc	BU
2004 Proof	1,000	Value: 180				

KM# 82 200 DOLLARS
31.1000 g., 0.9999 Gold 0.9997 oz. AGW, 32.1 mm. **Ruler:** Sultan Hassanal Bolkiah **Subject:** 20th Anniversary of Independence **Obv:** Bust 3/4 left, facing **Obv. Legend:** SULTAN HAJI HASSANAL BOLKIAH **Rev:** National arms **Rev. Legend:** NEGARI BRUNEI DARUSSALAM

Date	Mintage	F	VF	XF	Unc	BU
2004 Proof	200	Value: 2,400				

KM# 85 200 DOLLARS
31.1000 g., 0.9999 Gold 0.9997 oz. AGW, 32 mm. **Ruler:** Sultan Hassanal Bolkiah **Subject:** Royal Wedding **Obv:** Multicolor portraits of Royal couple

Date	Mintage	F	VF	XF	Unc	BU
2004 Proof	200	Value: 2,400				

KM# 88 200 DOLLARS
31.1000 g., 0.9999 Gold 0.9997 oz. AGW, 32.1 mm. **Ruler:** Sultan Hassanal Bolkiah **Subject:** 60th Birthday **Obv:** Bust 3/4 left, facing **Obv. Legend:** SULTAN HAJI HASSANAL BOLKIAH **Rev:** Multicolor 1/2-length figure in civilian clothes, facing

Date	Mintage	F	VF	XF	Unc	BU
2006 Proof	200	Value: 2,500				

PROOF SETS

KM#	Date	Mintage	Identification	Issue Price	Mkt Val
PS20	2003 (2)	500	KM#77-78	—	250
PS21	2004 (3)	200	KM80-82	—	2,600
PS22	2004 (3)	200	KM83-85	—	2,650
PS23	2006 (3)	200	KM86-88	—	2,900

The Republic of Bulgaria, formerly the Peoples Republic of Bulgaria, a Balkan country on the Black Sea in southeastern Europe, has an area of 42,855 sq. mi. (110,910 sq. km.) and a population of *8.31 million. Capital: Sofia. Agriculture remains a key component of the economy but industrialization, particularly heavy industry, has been emphasized since the late 1940s. Machinery, tobacco and cigarettes, wines and spirits, clothing and metals are the chief exports. Bulgaria joined the European Union in January 2007.

MONETARY SYSTEM
100 Stotinki = 1 Lev

REPUBLIC

REFORM COINAGE

KM# 237 STOTINKA
1.8000 g., Aluminum-Bronze, 16 mm. **Obv:** Madara horseman right, animal below **Rev:** Denomination above date **Edge:** Plain

Date	Mintage	F	VF	XF	Unc	BU
2002 Proof	10,000	Value: 1.00				

KM# 237a STOTINKA
1.8000 g., Brass Plated Steel, 16 mm. **Obv:** Madara horseman right **Rev:** Denomination above date

Date	Mintage	F	VF	XF	Unc	BU
2002 Proof	10,000	Value: 1.00				

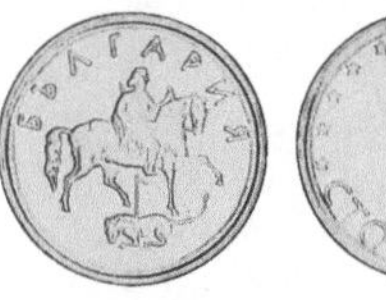

KM# 238 2 STOTINKI
2.5000 g., Aluminum-Bronze, 18 mm. **Obv:** Madara horseman right, animal below **Rev:** Denomination above date **Edge:** Plain

Date	Mintage	F	VF	XF	Unc	BU
2002 Proof	10,000	Value: 1.50				

KM# 238a 2 STOTINKI
2.5000 g., Brass Plated Steel, 18 mm. **Obv:** Madara horseman right **Rev:** Denomination above date

Date	Mintage	F	VF	XF	Unc	BU
2002 Proof	10,000	Value: 1.50				

KM# 239a 5 STOTINKI
3.5000 g., Brass Plated Steel, 20 mm. **Obv:** Madara horseman right **Rev:** Denomination above date

Date	Mintage	F	VF	XF	Unc	BU
2002 Proof	10,000	Value: 2.00				

KM# 239 5 STOTINKI
3.5000 g., Aluminum-Bronze, 20 mm. **Obv:** Madara horseman right, animal below **Rev:** Denomination above date **Edge:** Plain **Note:** Prev. KM#A239.

Date	Mintage	F	VF	XF	Unc	BU
2002 Proof	10,000	Value: 2.00				

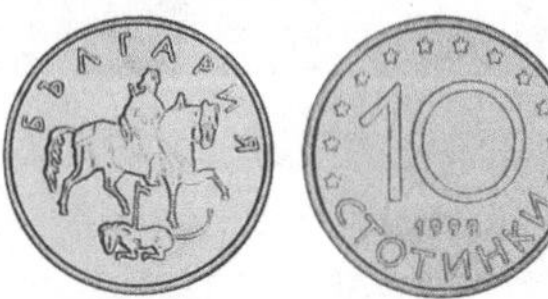

KM# 240 10 STOTINKI
3.0000 g., Copper-Nickel-Zinc, 18.5 mm. **Obv:** Madara horseman right, animal below **Rev:** Denomination above date **Edge:** Reeded

Date	Mintage	F	VF	XF	Unc	BU
2002 Proof	10,000	Value: 2.50				

KM# 241 20 STOTINKI

4.0000 g., Copper-Nickel-Zinc, 20.5 mm. **Obv:** Madara horseman right, animal below **Rev:** Denomination above date **Edge:** Reeded

Date	Mintage	F	VF	XF	Unc	BU
2002 Proof	10,000	Value: 3.00				

KM# 242 50 STOTINKI

5.0000 g., Copper-Nickel-Zinc, 22.5 mm. **Obv:** Madara horseman right, animal below **Rev:** Denomination above date **Edge:** Reeded

Date	Mintage	F	VF	XF	Unc	BU
2002 Proof	10,000	Value: 5.00				

KM# 272 50 STOTINKI

5.0000 g., Copper-Nickel-Zinc, 22.5 mm. **Obv:** Stylized Bulgarian arms, lion left, NATO - 2004 under lion **Rev:** Denomination above date **Edge:** Reeded

Date	Mintage	F	VF	XF	Unc	BU
2004	—	—	—	—	2.00	3.00

KM# 282 50 STOTINKI

5.0000 g., Copper-Nickel-Zinc, 22.5 mm. **Obv:** European Union seated woman allegory **Rev:** Value above date **Edge:** Reeded **Note:** Prev. KM#274.

Date	Mintage	F	VF	XF	Unc	BU
2005	—	—	—	—	1.25	1.75

KM# 291 50 STOTINKI

5.0000 g., Copper-Nickel-Zinc, 22.5 mm. **Obv:** Value **Rev:** Pillar behind open book **Edge:** Reeded **Note:** Prev. KM#276.

Date	Mintage	F	VF	XF	Unc	BU
2007	500,000	—	—	—	—	1.50

KM# 254 LEV

7.0000 g., Bi-Metallic Copper-Nickel center in Brass ring, 24.5 mm. **Obv:** St. Ivan of Rila **Rev:** Denomination **Edge:** Segmented reeding

Date	Mintage	F	VF	XF	Unc	BU
2002	24,842,000	—	—	—	3.00	4.00
2002 Proof	10,000	Value: 10.00				

KM# 257 LEV

15.5500 g., 0.9990 Gold 0.4994 oz. AGW **Obv:** St. Ivan of Rila **Rev:** Large number one **Edge:** Plain

Date	Mintage	F	VF	XF	Unc	BU
2002 Proof	2,000	Value: 875				

KM# 281 1.95583 LEVA

20.0000 g., 0.9990 Silver 0.6423 oz. ASW, 40 mm. **Subject:** Bulgaria - EU **Obv:** National Arms, vlaue below **Rev:** Female seated within stars

Date	Mintage	F	VF	XF	Unc	BU
2005 Proof	14,000	Value: 500				

KM# 290 1.95583 LEVA

20.0000 g., 0.9990 Silver Partially gold plated 0.6423 oz. ASW, 40 mm. **Subject:** Bulgaria in the EU **Obv:** National Arms **Rev:** Column and open window design

Date	Mintage	F	VF	XF	Unc	BU
2007 Proof	14,000	Value: 45.00				

KM# 304 2 LEVA

16.4000 g., 0.9990 Copper 0.5267 oz., 34.2 mm. **Subject:** Dechko, Uzunov 110th Anniversary of Birth **Obv:** National arms **Rev:** Petar Stoikov

Date	Mintage	F	VF	XF	Unc	BU
2009 Proof	8,000	Value: 15.00				

KM# 310 2 LEVA

16.4000 g., Copper-Nickel, 34.2 mm. **Obv:** National arms, value below **Rev:** Zahariy Zograf's self-portriat

Date	Mintage	F	VF	XF	Unc	BU
2010 Proof	—	Value: 25.00				

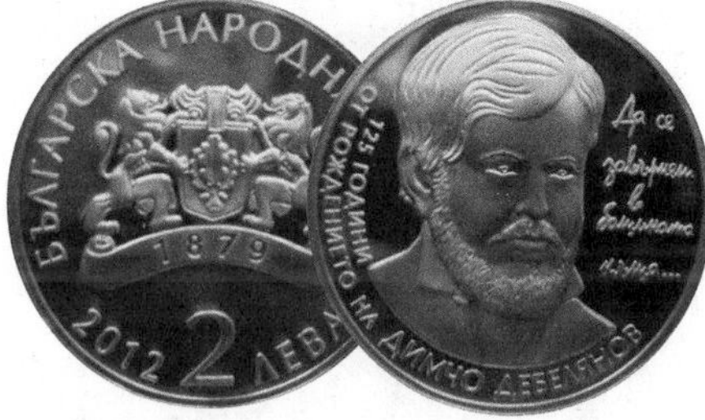

KM# 317 2 LEVA

16.4000 g., Copper, 34.2 mm. **Subject:** Dimcho Debelyanov 125th Anniversary of Birth **Obv:** National arms **Rev:** Portrait facing

Date	Mintage	F	VF	XF	Unc	BU
2012 Proof	5,000	Value: 20.00				

KM# 258 5 LEVA

1.2400 g., 0.9990 Gold 0.0398 oz. AGW **Obv:** Denomination **Rev:** Olympic archer **Edge:** Plain

Date	Mintage	F	VF	XF	Unc	BU
2002 Proof	12,000	Value: 75.00				

KM# 259 5 LEVA

1.2400 g., 0.9990 Gold 0.0398 oz. AGW **Obv:** Denomination **Rev:** Olympic cyclist **Edge:** Plain

Date	Mintage	F	VF	XF	Unc	BU
2002 Proof	12,000	Value: 75.00				

KM# 260 5 LEVA

1.2400 g., 0.9990 Gold 0.0398 oz. AGW **Obv:** Denomination **Rev:** Olympic fencing **Edge:** Plain

Date	Mintage	F	VF	XF	Unc	BU
2002 Proof	12,000	Value: 75.00				

KM# 261 5 LEVA

1.2400 g., 0.9990 Gold 0.0398 oz. AGW **Obv:** Denomination **Rev:** Olympic wrestling **Edge:** Plain

Date	Mintage	F	VF	XF	Unc	BU
2002 Proof	12,000	Value: 75.00				

KM# 262 5 LEVA

1.2400 g., 0.9990 Gold 0.0398 oz. AGW, 14 mm. **Obv:** Denomination **Rev:** Olympic gymnastics **Edge:** Plain

Date	Mintage	F	VF	XF	Unc	BU
2002 Proof	12,000	Value: 75.00				

KM# 263 5 LEVA

1.2400 g., 0.9990 Gold 0.0398 oz. AGW, 14 mm. **Obv:** Denomination **Rev:** Olympics founder Pierre du Coubertin **Edge:** Plain

Date	Mintage	F	VF	XF	Unc	BU
2002 Proof	17,000	Value: 75.00				

KM# 264 5 LEVA

1.2400 g., 0.9990 Gold 0.0398 oz. AGW, 14 mm. **Obv:** Denomination **Rev:** Olympic running **Edge:** Plain

Date	Mintage	F	VF	XF	Unc	BU
2002 Proof	12,000	Value: 75.00				

KM# 265 5 LEVA

1.2400 g., 0.9990 Gold 0.0398 oz. AGW, 14 mm. **Obv:** Denomination **Rev:** Olympic swimming **Edge:** Plain

Date	Mintage	F	VF	XF	Unc	BU
2002 Proof	12,000	Value: 75.00				

KM# 266 5 LEVA

1.2400 g., 0.9990 Gold 0.0398 oz. AGW, 14 mm. **Obv:** Denomination **Rev:** Olympic tennis **Edge:** Plain

Date	Mintage	F	VF	XF	Unc	BU
2002 Proof	12,000	Value: 75.00				

KM# 267 5 LEVA

1.2400 g., 0.9990 Gold 0.0398 oz. AGW, 14 mm. **Obv:** Denomination **Rev:** Olympic weight lifting **Edge:** Plain

Date	Mintage	F	VF	XF	Unc	BU
2002 Proof	12,000	Value: 75.00				

KM# 274 5 LEVA

15.0000 g., Copper-Nickel, 34.2 mm. **Subject:** Sourvakari **Obv:** National arms **Rev:** Multicolor children in winter clothes

Date	Mintage	F	VF	XF	Unc	BU
2002 Proof	5,000	Value: 15.00				

KM# 276 5 LEVA

15.0000 g., Copper-Nickel, 34.2 mm. **Obv:** National arms, date and denomination below **Rev:** Multicolor child on rocking horse **Edge:** Plain **Note:** Prev. KM#275.

Date	Mintage	F	VF	XF	Unc	BU
2003 Proof	10,000	Value: 35.00				

KM# 268 5 LEVA

28.2800 g., 0.9250 Silver 0.8410 oz. ASW, 38.5 mm. **Obv:** Denomination **Rev:** FIFA Soccer trophy cup **Edge:** reeded

Date	Mintage	F	VF	XF	Unc	BU
2003 Proof	50,000	Value: 42.00				

KM# 277 5 LEVA
15.0000 g., Copper-Nickel, 34.2 mm. **Subject:** Palm Sunday **Obv:** National Arms **Rev:** Bogomil Nikolov and Elena Dimitrova

Date	Mintage	F	VF	XF	Unc	BU
2004 Proof	10,000	Value: 15.00				

KM# 279 5 LEVA
15.0000 g., Copper-Nickel, 34.2 mm. **Subject:** Baba Marta **Obv:** National Arms **Rev:** Multicolor flora and butterfly

Date	Mintage	F	VF	XF	Unc	BU
2005 Proof	10,000	Value: 15.00				

KM# 284 5 LEVA
23.3000 g., 0.5000 Silver 0.3745 oz. ASW, 38.6 mm. **Subject:** Bulgaria Crafts - winemaking **Obv:** National Arms **Rev:** Multicolor grapes - wine caraffe

Date	Mintage	F	VF	XF	Unc	BU
2006 Proof	10,000	Value: 30.00				

KM# 296 5 LEVA
23.3000 g., 0.5000 Silver 0.3745 oz. ASW, 38.6 mm. **Subject:** Bulgarian Crafts - Carpet Weaving **Obv:** National Arms **Rev:** Ivan Todorov and Plamen Dzhermanov

Date	Mintage	F	VF	XF	Unc	BU
2007 Proof	7,000	Value: 30.00				

KM# 305 5 LEVA
23.3000 g., 0.9990 Silver 0.7483 oz. ASW, 38.6 mm. **Subject:** Bulgarian National Bank, 130th Anniversary **Obv:** Bank emblem **Rev:** Multicolor lion mozaic, fragment of stained glass

Date	Mintage	F	VF	XF	Unc	BU
2009 Proof	4,000	Value: 45.00				

KM# 306 5 LEVA
0.5000 Silver **Subject:** Traditional Bulgarian Crafts - Pottery **Rev:** Color pot and design

Date	Mintage	F	VF	XF	Unc	BU
2009	—	—	—	—	—	35.00

KM# 247 10 LEVA
23.3300 g., 0.9250 Silver 0.6938 oz. ASW, 38.5 mm. **Subject:** Olympics **Obv:** National arms, date and denomination below **Rev:** Ski jumper **Edge:** Plain with serial number

Date	Mintage	F	VF	XF	Unc	BU
2001 Proof	25,000	Value: 45.00				

KM# 246 10 LEVA
23.6000 g., 0.9250 Silver 0.7018 oz. ASW, 38.5 mm. **Subject:** Higher Education **Obv:** National arms, date and denomination below **Rev:** Graduate before building **Edge:** Plain

Date	Mintage	F	VF	XF	Unc	BU
2001 Proof	10,000	Value: 45.00				

KM# 275 10 LEVA
23.3000 g., 0.9250 Silver 0.6929 oz. ASW, 38.6 mm. **Obv:** National arms **Rev:** Head and Star of David

Date	Mintage	F	VF	XF	Unc	BU
2003 Proof	2,000	Value: 40.00				

KM# 270 10 LEVA
23.3300 g., 0.9990 Silver 0.7493 oz. ASW, 38.6 mm. **Subject:** National Theater Centennial **Edge:** Plain

Date	Mintage	F	VF	XF	Unc	BU
2004 Proof	5,000	Value: 50.00				

KM# 273 10 LEVA
23.2000 g., 0.9250 Silver 0.6899 oz. ASW, 38.5 mm. **Obv:** National arms, date and denomination below **Rev:** St. Nikolay Mirlikiisky Chudofvorez with gold-plated crosses and halo **Edge:** Plain

Date	Mintage	F	VF	XF	Unc	BU
2004 Proof	10,000	Value: 45.00				

KM# 280 10 LEVA
23.3000 g., 0.9250 Silver 0.6929 oz. ASW, 38.6 mm. **Subject:** XX Olympic Games - Turino, Italy **Obv:** National arms **Rev:** Short track speed skater

Date	Mintage	F	VF	XF	Unc	BU
2005 Proof	4,000	Value: 40.00				

KM# 283 10 LEVA
20.0000 g., 0.9990 Silver Partially gold plated 0.6423 oz. ASW, 40 mm. **Obv:** National arms **Rev:** Ancient sculpture

Date	Mintage	F	VF	XF	Unc	BU
2005 Proof	10,000	Value: 45.00				

KM# 285 10 LEVA
23.3000 g., 0.9250 Silver 0.6929 oz. ASW, 38.6 mm. **Subject:** National Parks - Black Sea Coast **Obv:** National arms **Rev:** Map and three circular motifs

Date	Mintage	F	VF	XF	Unc	BU
2006 Proof	7,000	Value: 40.00				

KM# 286 10 LEVA
20.0000 g., 0.9990 Silver 0.6423 oz. ASW, 40 mm. **Subject:** Treasures of Bulgaria - Letnitsa **Obv:** National arms **Rev:** Horseman statue

Date	Mintage	F	VF	XF	Unc	BU
2006 Proof	10,000	Value: 40.00				

KM# 295 10 LEVA
23.3000 g., 0.9250 Silver 0.6929 oz. ASW, 38.6 mm. **Subject:** National Parks - Pirin Mountain **Obv:** National arms **Rev:** Vanya Dimitrova

Date	Mintage	F	VF	XF	Unc	BU
2007 Proof	6,000	Value: 40.00				

KM# 297 10 LEVA
20.0000 g., 0.9990 Silver Partially gold plated 0.6423 oz. ASW, 40 mm. **Subject:** Treasures of Bulgaria - Pegasus from Vayovo **Obv:** National arms **Rev:** Pegasus forepart

Date	Mintage	F	VF	XF	Unc	BU
2007 Proof	10,000	Value: 45.00				

KM# 292 10 LEVA
31.1000 g., 0.9990 Silver 0.9988 oz. ASW, 40 mm. **Subject:** Boris Christov **Obv:** National arms **Obv. Legend:** БЪЛГАРСКА НАРОДНА БАНКА **Rev:** Early regal 1/2-length male figure facing holding orb **Rev. Legend:** ИМЕНИТИ БЪЛГАРСКИ ГЛАСОВЕ **Note:** Prev. KM#277.

Date	Mintage	F	VF	XF	Unc	BU
2007 Proof	10,000	Value: 50.00				

KM# 298 10 LEVA
23.3000 g., 0.9250 Silver 0.6929 oz. ASW, 38.6 mm. **Subject:** 130th Anniversary Bulgarian Liberation **Obv:** National arms **Rev:** Two figures in 19th century coats

Date	Mintage	F	VF	XF	Unc	BU
2008 Proof	10,000	Value: 40.00				

KM# 299 10 LEVA
23.3000 g., 0.9250 Silver 0.6929 oz. ASW, 38.6 mm. **Subject:** Shooting sports **Obv:** National Arms **Rev:** Target, bowhunter, rifleman

Date	Mintage	F	VF	XF	Unc	BU
2008 Proof	5,000	Value: 40.00				

KM# 300 10 LEVA
20.0000 g., 0.9990 Silver Partially gold plated 0.6423 oz. ASW, 40 mm. **Subject:** Treasures of Bulgaria - Sevt III **Obv:** Statue head of King Sevt III **Rev:** Elena Todorova and Todor Todorav

Date	Mintage	F	VF	XF	Unc	BU
2008 Proof	8,000	Value: 45.00				

KM# 301 10 LEVA
23.3000 g., 0.9250 Silver 0.6929 oz. ASW, 38.6 mm. **Subject:** Bulgarian Independence - 100th Anniversary **Rev:** Crowned shield

Date	Mintage	F	VF	XF	Unc	BU
2008 Proof	5,000	Value: 40.00				

KM# 302 10 LEVA
31.1000 g., 0.9990 Silver Partially gold plated 0.9988 oz. ASW, 40 mm. **Subject:** Great Bulgarian Voices: Nikolay Gyaurov **Obv:** National arms **Rev:** Elena Todorov and Todor Todorov

Date	Mintage	F	VF	XF	Unc	BU
2008 Proof	6,000	Value: 50.00				

KM# 308 10 LEVA
31.1050 g., 0.9990 Silver 0.9990 oz. ASW, 40 mm. **Obv:** National arms **Rev:** Belogradchick rock formations

Date	Mintage	F	VF	XF	Unc	BU
2010 Proof	—	Value: 50.00				

KM# 309 10 LEVA
23.3300 g., 0.9250 Silver 0.6938 oz. ASW, 38.61 mm. **Subject:** Unification, 125th Anniversary **Obv:** National arms **Rev:** Document seal gilt

Date	Mintage	F	VF	XF	Unc	BU
2010 Proof	5,000	Value: 50.00				

KM# 312 10 LEVA
23.3300 g., 0.9250 Silver 0.6938 oz. ASW, 38.61 mm. **Obv:** St. George Zograf at right, National arms and value at left **Rev:** St. George Zograf Monastery

Date	Mintage	F	VF	XF	Unc	BU
2011 Proof	6,000	Value: 75.00				

KM# 313 10 LEVA
31.1000 g., 0.9990 Silver 0.9988 oz. ASW, 40 mm. **Obv:** National arms **Rev:** Gena Dimitrova as Princess Turandot

Date	Mintage	F	VF	XF	Unc	BU
2011 Proof	4,000	Value: 75.00				

KM# 314 10 LEVA
23.3300 g., 0.9250 Silver partially gilt 0.6938 oz. ASW, 38.61 mm. **Subject:** Khan Krum **Obv:** Fragment miniture from Constantine Manasses' Chronicle, Khan Krum drinks a toast **Rev:** Khan Krum pursuing the Byzantines

Date	Mintage	F	VF	XF	Unc	BU
2011 Proof	5,000	Value: 75.00				

KM# 318 10 LEVA
23.3300 g., 0.9250 Silver 0.6938 oz. ASW, 38.6 mm. **Subject:** Slavo-Bulgraian History, 250th Anniversary **Obv:** National arms with gilt design above **Rev:** Gilt seal on documnet

Date	Mintage	F	VF	XF	Unc	BU
2012 Proof	—	Value: 75.00				

KM# 319 10 LEVA
23.3300 g., 0.9250 Silver 0.6938 oz. ASW, 38.61 mm. **Subject:** Chudnite Mostove **Obv:** National arms, value below **Rev:** Natural Bridge

Date	Mintage	F	VF	XF	Unc	BU
2012 Proof	—	Value: 75.00				

KM# 269 20 LEVA
1.5500 g., 0.9990 Gold 0.0498 oz. AGW, 16 mm. **Obv:** Denomination **Rev:** Mother of God **Edge:** Plain

Date	Mintage	F	VF	XF	Unc	BU
2003 Proof	20,000	Value: 95.00				

KM# 287 20 LEVA
1.5500 g., 0.9990 Gold 0.0498 oz. AGW, 13.9 mm. **Subject:** Iconography St John the Baptist **Obv:** National arms **Rev:** Saint facing

Date	Mintage	F	VF	XF	Unc	BU
2006 Proof	12,000	Value: 95.00				

KM# 294 20 LEVA
1.5500 g., 0.9990 Gold 0.0498 oz. AGW, 13.9 mm. **Subject:** Iconography - St. George the Victorious **Rev:** St. George slaying dragon

Date	Mintage	F	VF	XF	Unc	BU
2007 Proof	8,000	Value: 100				

KM# 303 20 LEVA
1.5500 g., 0.9990 Gold 0.0498 oz. AGW, 13.9 mm. **Subject:** Tsar Boris I, the Baptist **Obv:** Half-length figure facing **Rev:** Krassimir Angelov, Borislav Kyossev, Razvigov Kolev

Date	Mintage	F	VF	XF	Unc	BU
2008 Proof	8,000	Value: 100				

KM# 316 20 LEVA
1.5500 g., 0.9990 Gold 0.0498 oz. AGW, 13.9 mm. **Obv:** National arms **Rev:** Virgin Mary and Child

Date	Mintage	F	VF	XF	Unc	BU
2011 Proof	—	Value: 100				

KM# 293 100 LEVA
8.6400 g., 0.9990 Gold 0.2775 oz. AGW **Subject:** Iconography - St. George the Victorious **Obv:** National arms **Rev:** Plamen Chernev

Date	Mintage	F	VF	XF	Unc	BU
2007 Proof	1,500	Value: 500				

KM# 307 100 LEVA
7.7700 g., 0.9990 Gold 0.2496 oz. AGW, 22 mm. **Subject:** Bulgarian Iconography - St. Dimitar the Wonder Worker

Date	Mintage	F	VF	XF	Unc	BU
2009 Proof	—	Value: 475				

KM# 311 100 LEVA
8.6400 g., 0.9990 Gold 0.2775 oz. AGW, 24 mm. **Obv:** National arms, value below **Rev:** St. Naum and Monastery of St. Naum in Ohrid

Date	Mintage	F	VF	XF	Unc	BU
2010 Proof	3,000	Value: 500				

KM# 271 125 LEVA
7.7800 g., 0.9990 Gold 0.2499 oz. AGW, 21 mm. **Subject:** Bulgarian National Bank 125th Anniversary

Date	Mintage	F	VF	XF	Unc	BU
2004 Proof	3,000	Value: 475				

PIEDFORT

KM#	Date	Mintage	Identification	Mkt Val
P4	2004	5,000	10 Leva. 0.9990 Silver. 46.6600 g. 100 Years - National Theatre, 38.61mm.	75.00

PROOF SETS

KM#	Date	Mintage	Identification	Issue Price	Mkt Val
PS8	2002 (7)	10,000	KM#237-242, 254	—	25.00

BURUNDI

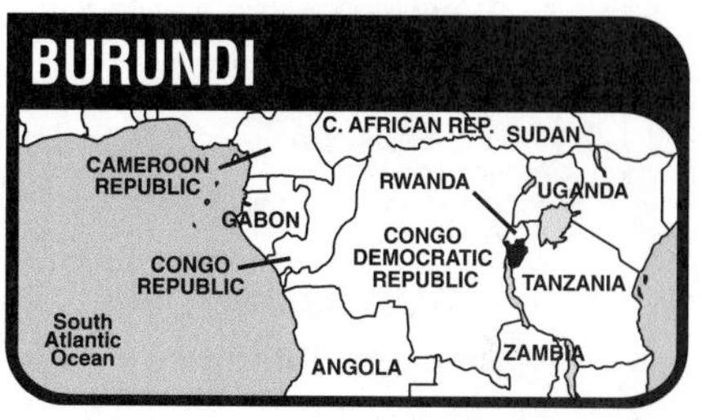

The Republic of Burundi, a landlocked country in central Africa, was a kingdom with a feudalistic society, caste system and Mwami (king) for more than 400 years before independence. It has an area of 10,740 sq. mi. (27,830 sq. km.) and a population of 6.3 million. Capital: Bujumbura. Plagued by poor soil, irregular rainfall and a single-crop economy, coffee, Burundi is barely able to feed itself. Coffee and tea are exported.

Although the area was visited by European explorers and missionaries in the latter half of the 19th century, it wasn't until the 1890s that it, together with Rwanda, fell under European domination as part of German East Africa. Following World War I, the territory was mandated to Belgium by the League of Nations and administered with the Belgian Congo. After World War II it became a U.N. Trust Territory. Limited self-government was established by U.N.-supervised elections in 1961. Burundi gained independence as a kingdom under Mwami Mwambutsa IV on July 1, 1962. The republic was established by military coup in 1966.

NOTE: For earlier coinage see Belgian Congo, and Rwanda and Burundi. For previously listed coinage dated 1966, coins of Mwambutsa IV and Ntare V, refer to *UNUSUAL WORLD COINS*, 5th edition, Krause Publications, 2007.

RULERS
Mwambutsa IV, 1962-1966
Ntare V, 1966

MINT MARKS
PM - Pobjoy Mint
(b) - Privy Marks, Brussels

MONETARY SYSTEM
100 Centimes = 1 Franc

REPUBLIC
1966-
STANDARD COINAGE

KM# 19 FRANC
0.8700 g., Aluminum, 18.91 mm. **Obv:** Denomination **Rev:** Arms above date **Edge:** Reeded

Date	Mintage	F	VF	XF	Unc	BU
2003PM	—	—	—	0.50	1.50	2.00

KM# 21 10 FRANCS
Aluminum **Obv:** Country name in three languages **Rev:** Value at center of wreath of bananas and wheat

Date	Mintage	F	VF	XF	Unc	BU
2011	—	—	—	—	1.00	2.00

KM# 22 50 FRANCS
Aluminum **Obv:** Country name in three languages **Rev:** Drum and drummer

Date	Mintage	F	VF	XF	Unc	BU
2011	—	—	—	—	2.50	3.00

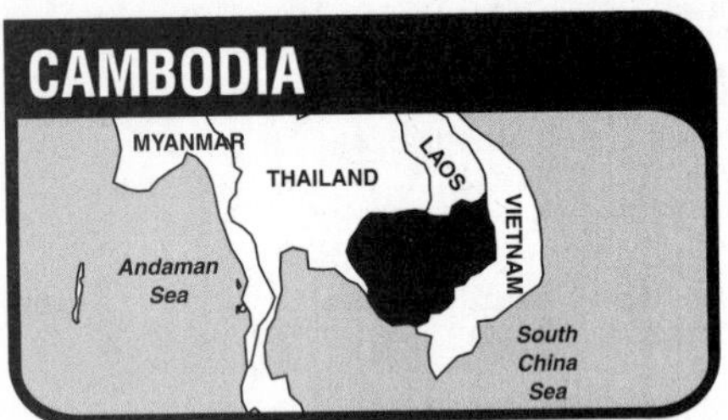

The Kingdom of Cambodia, formerly Democratic Kampuchea and the Khmer Republic, a land of paddy fields and forest-clad hills located on the Indo-Chinese peninsula, fronting on the Gulf of Thailand, has an area of 70,238 sq. mi. (181,040 sq. km.) and a population of *11.21 million. Capital: Phnom Penh. Agriculture is the basis of the economy, with rice the chief crop. Native industries include cattle breeding, weaving and rice milling. Rubber, cattle, corn, and timber are exported.

RULERS

Kings of Cambodia

Norodom Sihanouk, 1991-1993
Chairman, Supreme National Council
King, 1993-2012

KINGDOM

DECIMAL COINAGE

KM# 98 500 RIELS
19.9200 g., Brass, 38.7 mm. **Subject:** Angkor Wat **Obv:** Armless statue of Jayavarman VII **Rev:** View of Angkor Wat in center **Edge:** Reeded

Date	Mintage	F	VF	XF	Unc	BU
2001	28,000	—	—	—	7.50	10.00

KM# 99 3000 RIELS
1.2441 g., 0.9999 Gold 0.0400 oz. AGW, 13.92 mm. **Subject:** Angkor Wat **Obv:** Armless statue of Jayavarman VII **Rev:** View of Angkor Wat in center **Edge:** Reeded

Date	Mintage	F	VF	XF	Unc	BU
2001	28,000	—	—	—	75.00	85.00

KM# 100 3000 RIELS
20.0000 g., 0.9250 Silver 0.5948 oz. ASW, 38.7 mm. **Subject:** Buddha **Obv:** Armless statue of Jayavarman VII **Rev:** Radiant Buddha next to a carved Buddha face **Edge:** Reeded

Date	Mintage	F	VF	XF	Unc	BU
2001 Proof	10,000	Value: 55.00				

KM# 101 3000 RIELS
20.0000 g., 0.9250 Silver 0.5948 oz. ASW, 38.7 mm. **Subject:** Apsara Dance **Obv:** Armless statue of Jayavarman VII **Rev:** Dancer next to multicolor carpet pattern **Edge:** Reeded

Date	Mintage	F	VF	XF	Unc	BU
2001 Proof	10,000	Value: 60.00				

KM# 103 3000 RIELS
20.0000 g., 0.9990 Silver 0.6423 oz. ASW, 38.7 mm. **Obv:** King Jayavarman VII (1162-1201) **Rev:** Multicolor Tutankhamen's mask **Edge:** Reeded

Date	Mintage	F	VF	XF	Unc	BU
2004 Proof	9,100	Value: 65.00				

KM# 104 3000 RIELS
1.2440 g., 0.9990 Gold 0.0400 oz. AGW, 13.92 mm. **Obv:** King Jayavarman VII (1162-1201) **Rev:** Sphinx and pyramid **Edge:** Reeded

Date	Mintage	F	VF	XF	Unc	BU
2004 Proof	27,900	Value: 95.00				

KM# 124 3000 RIELS
1.2400 g., 0.9990 Gold 0.0398 oz. AGW, 13.92 mm. **Rev:** Pyramids

Date	Mintage	F	VF	XF	Unc	BU
2004	—	—	—	—	75.00	85.00

KM# 139 3000 RIELS
31.1050 g., 0.9990 Silver 0.9990 oz. ASW **Subject:** 2006 FIFA World Cup - Germany **Obv:** King Jayayarman VII **Rev:** Temple above half of a soccer ball

Date	Mintage	F	VF	XF	Unc	BU
2004 Proof	—	Value: 80.00				

KM# 126 3000 RIELS
1.2200 g., 0.9990 Gold 0.0392 oz. AGW, 13.92 mm. **Rev:** Taj Mahal

Date	Mintage	F	VF	XF	Unc	BU
2005	—	—	—	—	75.00	85.00

KM# 127 3000 RIELS
31.1050 g., Silver, 38.7 mm. **Rev:** Indian Dancer, multicolor

Date	Mintage	F	VF	XF	Unc	BU
2005	—	Value: 65.00				

KM# 129 3000 RIELS
1.2200 g., 0.9990 Gold 0.0392 oz. AGW, 13.92 mm. **Rev:** Colosseum in Rome

Date	Mintage	F	VF	XF	Unc	BU
2006	—	—	—	—	75.00	85.00

KM# 130 3000 RIELS
Silver, 38.7 mm. **Rev:** Multicolor Roman soldier

Date	Mintage	F	VF	XF	Unc	BU
2006 Proof	—	Value: 80.00				

KM# 110 3000 RIELS
31.1050 g., 0.9990 Silver 0.9990 oz. ASW, 40.7 mm. **Subject:** Year of the Dog **Rev:** Multicolor St. Bernard

Date	Mintage	F	VF	XF	Unc	BU
2006 Prooflike	4,000	—	—	—	—	80.00

KM# 111 3000 RIELS
31.1050 g., 0.9990 Silver 0.9990 oz. ASW, 40.7 mm. **Subject:** Year of the Dog **Rev:** Multicolor Bloodhound

Date	Mintage	F	VF	XF	Unc	BU
2006 Prooflike	4,000	—	—	—	—	80.00

KM# 112 3000 RIELS
31.1050 g., 0.9990 Silver 0.9990 oz. ASW, 40.7 mm. **Subject:** Year of the Dog **Rev:** Multicolor Siberian Husky

Date	Mintage	F	VF	XF	Unc	BU
2006 Prooflike	4,000	—	—	—	—	80.00

KM# 113 3000 RIELS
31.1050 g., 0.9990 Silver 0.9990 oz. ASW, 40.7 mm. **Subject:** Year of the Dog **Rev:** Multicolor Shar Pei

Date	Mintage	F	VF	XF	Unc	BU
2006 Prooflike	4,000	—	—	—	—	80.00

KM# 114 3000 RIELS
31.1050 g., 0.9990 Silver 0.9990 oz. ASW, 40.7 mm. **Subject:** Year of the Dog **Rev:** Multicolor Borzaya

Date	Mintage	F	VF	XF	Unc	BU
2006 Prooflike	51,000	—	—	—	—	80.00

KM# 115 3000 RIELS
31.1050 g., 0.9990 Silver 0.9990 oz. ASW, 40.7 mm. **Subject:** Year of the Dog **Rev:** Multicolor Labrador

Date	Mintage	F	VF	XF	Unc	BU
2006 Prooflike	51,000	—	—	—	—	80.00

KM# 116 3000 RIELS
31.1050 g., 0.9990 Silver 0.9990 oz. ASW, 40.7 mm. **Subject:** Year of the Dog **Rev:** Multicolor Russian Spaniel

Date	Mintage	F	VF	XF	Unc	BU
2006 Prooflike	51,000	—	—	—	—	80.00

KM# 117 3000 RIELS
31.1050 g., 0.9990 Silver 0.9990 oz. ASW, 40.7 mm. **Subject:** Year of the Dog **Rev:** Multicolor Newfoundland

Date	Mintage	F	VF	XF	Unc	BU
2006 Prooflike	51,000	—	—	—	—	80.00

KM# 132 3000 RIELS
1.2200 g., 0.9990 Gold 0.0392 oz. AGW, 13.92 mm. **Rev:** Borobudur Temple, Indonesia

Date	Mintage	F	VF	XF	Unc	BU
2007	28,000	—	—	—	75.00	85.00

KM# 133 3000 RIELS
31.1050 g., 0.9990 Silver 0.9990 oz. ASW, 38.7 mm. **Rev:** Legomo dancer, multicolor

Date	Mintage	F	VF	XF	Unc	BU
2007 Proof	10,000	Value: 80.00				

KM# 118 3000 RIELS
31.1050 g., 0.9990 Silver 0.9990 oz. ASW, 40.7 mm. **Subject:** Year of the Pig **Rev:** Multicolor pig

Date	Mintage	F	VF	XF	Unc	BU
2007 Prooflike	—	—	—	—	—	80.00

KM# 135 3000 RIELS
31.1050 g., 0.9990 Silver 0.9990 oz. ASW, 40.7 mm. **Subject:** Year of the Pig **Rev:** Multicolor pig

Date	Mintage	F	VF	XF	Unc	BU
2007 Prooflike	30,000	—	—	—	—	90.00

KM# 136 3000 RIELS
31.1050 g., 0.9990 Silver 0.9990 oz. ASW, 40.7 mm. **Subject:** Year of the Pig **Rev:** Multicolor pig

Date	Mintage	F	VF	XF	Unc	BU
2007 Prooflike	30,000	—	—	—	—	90.00

KM# 137 3000 RIELS
31.1050 g., 0.9990 Silver 0.9990 oz. ASW, 40.7 mm. **Subject:** Year of the Pig **Rev:** Multicolor pig

Date	Mintage	F	VF	XF	Unc	BU
2007 Prooflike	30,000	—	—	—	—	90.00

KM# 138 3000 RIELS
31.1050 g., 0.9990 Silver 0.9990 oz. ASW, 40.7 mm. **Subject:** Year of the Pig **Rev:** Multicolor pig

Date	Mintage	F	VF	XF	Unc	BU
2007 Prooflike	30,000	—	—	—	—	90.00

KM# 121 3000 RIELS
1.2400 g., 0.9990 Gold 0.0398 oz. AGW, 13.9 mm. **Subject:** Statue torso **Rev:** Shwe Dragon Pagoda, Mynamar

Date	Mintage	F	VF	XF	Unc	BU
2008 Proof	—	Value: 95.00				

KM# 123 3000 RIELS
31.1035 g., 0.9990 Silver 0.9990 oz. ASW, 40.7 mm. **Obv:** Statue torso **Rev:** Multicolor Padaung

Date	Mintage	F	VF	XF	Unc	BU
2009 Proof	—	Value: 75.00				

KM# 102 10000 RIELS
31.1035 g., 0.9990 Bi-Metallic Gold center in silver ring. 0.9990 oz., 40.7 mm. **Subject:** Angkor Wat **Obv:** Armless statue of Jayavarman **Rev:** Multicolor holographic view of Angkor Wat in center **Edge:** Reeded

Date	Mintage	F	VF	XF	Unc	BU
2001 Proof	3,000	Value: 350				

KM# 125 10000 RIELS
31.1050 g., 0.9990 Silver 0.9990 oz. ASW, 40.7 mm. **Rev:** Great Wall of China, holographic insert

Date	Mintage	F	VF	XF	Unc	BU
2003 Proof	—	Value: 300				

KM# 105 10000 RIELS
31.1035 g., 0.9990 Silver 0.9990 oz. ASW, 40.7 mm. **Obv:** King Jayavarman VII (1162-1201) **Rev:** Sphinx and pyramid on holographic gold insert **Edge:** Reeded

Date	Mintage	F	VF	XF	Unc	BU
2004 Proof	2,100	Value: 300				

KM# 119 10000 RIELS
31.1050 g., 0.9990 Silver 0.9990 oz. ASW, 38.7 mm. **Subject:** Zheng He 600th Anniversary **Rev:** Sailing ship with latent image

Date	Mintage	F	VF	XF	Unc	BU
2005 Proof	200	Value: 150				

KM# 120 10000 RIELS
31.1050 g., 0.9990 Silver 0.9990 oz. ASW, 38.7 mm. **Subject:** Zheng He 600th Anniversary **Rev:** Multicolor figure standing

Date	Mintage	F	VF	XF	Unc	BU
2005 Proof	200	Value: 150				

KM# 128 10000 RIELS
31.1050 g., 0.9990 Silver 0.9990 oz. ASW, 40.7 mm. **Rev:** Taj Mahal in multicolor hologram at center

Date	Mintage	F	VF	XF	Unc	BU
2005 Proof	—	Value: 300				

KM# 131 10000 RIELS
31.1050 g., 0.9990 Silver 0.9990 oz. ASW, 40.7 mm. **Rev:** Colosseum in multicolor hologram

Date	Mintage	F	VF	XF	Unc	BU
2006 Proof	—	Value: 300				

KM# 134 10000 RIELS
31.1050 g., 0.9990 Silver 0.9990 oz. ASW, 40.7 mm. **Rev:** Boraburdur temple, Indonesia

Date	Mintage	F	VF	XF	Unc	BU
2007 Proof	300	Value: 300				

KM# 122 10000 RIELS
31.1035 g., 0.9990 Silver 0.9990 oz. ASW, 40.7 mm. **Obv:** Statue torso **Rev:** Hologram of Shwe Dragon Pagoda, Mynamar

Date	Mintage	F	VF	XF	Unc	BU
2009 Proof	—	Value: 150				

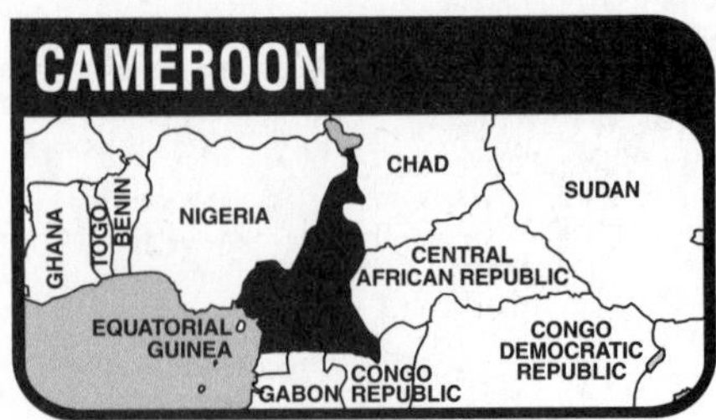

The Republic of Cameroon, located in west-central Africa on the Gulf of Guinea, has an area of 183,569 sq. mi. (475,445 sq. km.) and a population of *15.13 million. Capital: Yaounde. About 90 percent of the labor force is employed on the land; cash crops account for 80 percent of the country's export revenue. Cocoa, coffee, aluminum, cotton, rubber, and timber are exported. Cameroon is a member of the Commonwealth of Nations. The President is the Head of State; the Prime Minister is the Head of Government.

MINT MARKS

(a) - Paris, privy marks only
SA - Pretoria, 1943

MONETARY SYSTEM

100 Centimes = 1 Franc

REPUBLIC

STANDARD COINAGE

KM# 28 500 FRANCS

15.5500 g., 0.9250 Silver 0.4624 oz. ASW, 33 mm. **Subject:** Zodiac - Cancer **Obv:** National arms

Date	Mintage	F	VF	XF	Unc	BU
2010	3,000	—	—	—	—	50.00

KM# 29 500 FRANCS

15.5500 g., 0.9250 Silver 0.4624 oz. ASW **Subject:** Zodiac - Leo **Obv:** National arms

Date	Mintage	F	VF	XF	Unc	BU
2010	3,000	—	—	—	—	50.00

KM# 30 500 FRANCS

15.5500 g., 0.9250 Silver 0.4624 oz. ASW, 33 mm. **Subject:** Zodiac - Virgo **Obv:** National arms

Date	Mintage	F	VF	XF	Unc	BU
2010	3,000	—	—	—	—	50.00

KM# 31 500 FRANCS

15.5500 g., 0.9250 Silver 0.4624 oz. ASW, 33 mm. **Subject:** Zodiac - Libra **Obv:** National arms

Date	Mintage	F	VF	XF	Unc	BU
2010	3,000	—	—	—	—	50.00

KM# 32 500 FRANCS

15.5500 g., 0.9990 Silver 0.4994 oz. ASW, 33 mm. **Subject:** Zodiac - Scorpius **Obv:** National arms

Date	Mintage	F	VF	XF	Unc	BU
2010	3,000	—	—	—	—	50.00

KM# 33 500 FRANCS

15.5500 g., 0.9250 Silver 0.4624 oz. ASW, 33 mm. **Subject:** Zodiac - Sagittarius **Obv:** National arms

Date	Mintage	F	VF	XF	Unc	BU
2010	3,000	—	—	—	—	50.00

KM# 34 500 FRANCS

15.5500 g., 0.9250 Silver 0.4624 oz. ASW, 33 mm. **Subject:** Zodiac - Capricorn **Obv:** National Arms

Date	Mintage	F	VF	XF	Unc	BU
2010	3,000	—	—	—	—	50.00

KM# 35 500 FRANCS

15.5500 g., 0.9250 Silver 0.4624 oz. ASW, 33 mm. **Subject:** Zodiac - Aquarius **Obv:** National arms

Date	Mintage	F	VF	XF	Unc	BU
2010	3,000	—	—	—	—	50.00

KM# 25 500 FRANCS

15.5500 g., 0.9250 Silver 0.4624 oz. ASW, 33 mm. **Subject:** Zodiac - Aries **Obv:** National arms

Date	Mintage	F	VF	XF	Unc	BU
2010	3,000	—	—	—	—	50.00

KM# 26 500 FRANCS

15.5500 g., 0.9250 Silver 0.4624 oz. ASW, 33 mm. **Subject:** Zodiac - Taurus **Obv:** National arms

Date	Mintage	F	VF	XF	Unc	BU
2010	3,000	—	—	—	—	50.00

KM# 36 500 FRANCS

15.5500 g., 0.9250 Silver 0.4624 oz. ASW, 33 mm. **Subject:** Zodiac - Pisces **Obv:** National arms

Date	Mintage	F	VF	XF	Unc	BU
2010	3,000	—	—	—	—	50.00

KM# 27 500 FRANCS

15.5500 g., 0.9250 Silver 0.4624 oz. ASW, 33 mm. **Subject:** Zodiac - Gemini **Obv:** National arms

Date	Mintage	F	VF	XF	Unc	BU
2010	3,000	—	—	—	—	50.00

KM# 24 1000 FRANCS

25.0000 g., 0.9250 Copper-Nickel 0.7435 oz., 38.61 mm. **Obv:** Arms **Rev:** Papillons D'Amour butterfly **Edge:** Reeded

Date	Mintage	F	VF	XF	Unc	BU
2010 Proof	2,500	Value: 65.00				

KM# 37 1000 FRANCS

25.0000 g., 0.9990 Silver 0.8029 oz. ASW, 38.61 mm. **Subject:** Ange de l'amour **Obv:** National arms **Rev:** Cupuid

Date	Mintage	F	VF	XF	Unc	BU
2010 Proof	2,500	Value: 80.00				

KM# 38 1000 FRANCS

20.0000 g., 0.9250 Silver 0.5948 oz. ASW, 38.61 mm. **Obv:** National arms **Rev:** Heat sensetive image of the Shroud of Turin

Date	Mintage	F	VF	XF	Unc	BU
2010 Proof	2,010	Value: 75.00				

KM# 49 1000 FRANCS

25.0000 g., Copper-Nickel, 39 mm. **Obv:** National arms **Rev:** Two swans, hologram between them

Date	Mintage	F	VF	XF	Unc	BU
2011 Antique Finish	—	—	—	—	—	65.00
2011 Proof	—	Value: 50.00				

KM# 50 1000 FRANCS

25.0000 g., Copper-Nickel, 39 mm. **Obv:** National arms **Rev:** Monarch Butterfly in 3-D and color

Date	Mintage	F	VF	XF	Unc	BU
2011 Proof	—	Value: 50.00				

KM# 51 1000 FRANCS

31.1050 g., 0.9990 Silver 0.9990 oz. ASW, 38.61 mm. **Subject:** Year of the Dragon **Obv:** National arms **Rev:** Dragon in color

Date	Mintage	F	VF	XF	Unc	BU
2012 Proof	—	Value: 75.00				

KM# 52 1000 FRANCS

20.0000 g., 0.9990 Silver 0.6423 oz. ASW, 38.61 mm. **Subject:** Year of the Dragon **Obv:** National arms **Rev:** Gilt dragon and Great Wall of China

Date	Mintage	F	VF	XF	Unc	BU
2012 Proof	888	Value: 50.00				

KM# 53 1000 FRANCS

20.0000 g., 0.9990 Silver 0.6423 oz. ASW, 38.61 mm. **Obv:** National arms **Rev:** Unicorn and opal

Date	Mintage	F	VF	XF	Unc	BU
2012 Proof	888	Value: 60.00				

KM# 54 1000 FRANCS

31.1050 g., 0.9990 Silver 0.9990 oz. ASW, 40 mm. **Rev:** Cross River Gorilla

Date	Mintage	F	VF	XF	Unc	BU
2013 Antique patina	1,000	Value: 100				

KM# 40 1500 FRANCS

62.2000 g., 0.9990 Silver 1.9977 oz. ASW, 40x40 mm. **Obv:** National arms **Rev:** Black Rhinoceros head profile facing right

Date	Mintage	F	VF	XF	Unc	BU
2010 Proof	—	Value: 95.00				

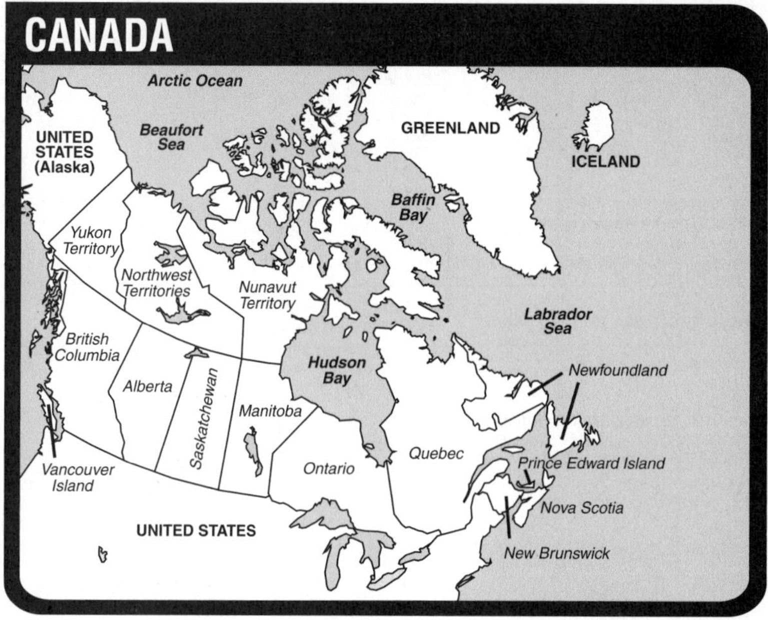

Canada is located to the north of the United States, and spans the full breadth of the northern portion of North America from Atlantic to Pacific oceans, except for the State of Alaska. It has a total area of 3,850,000 sq. mi. (9,971,550 sq. km.) and a population of 30.29 million. Capital: Ottawa.

Canada is a member of the Commonwealth of Nations. Elizabeth II is Head of State as Queen of Canada.

RULER
British 1763-

MONETARY SYSTEM
1 Dollar = 100 Cents

CONFEDERATION

CIRCULATION COINAGE

KM# 289 CENT

2.2500 g., Copper Plated Steel, 19.05 mm. **Ruler:** Elizabeth II **Obv:** Crowned head right **Obv. Designer:** Dora dePédery-Hunt **Rev:** Maple twig design **Rev. Designer:** George E. Kruger-Gray **Edge:** Round and plain

Date	Mintage	MS-63	Proof
2001	919,358,000	0.30	—
2001P Proof	—	—	5.00
2003	92,219,775	0.30	—
2003P Proof	—	—	5.00
2003P	235,936,799	1.50	—

KM# 445 CENT

2.2500 g., Copper Plated Steel, 19.1 mm. **Ruler:** Elizabeth II **Subject:** Elizabeth II Golden Jubilee **Obv:** Crowned head right, Jubilee commemorative dates 1952-2002 **Obv. Designer:** Dora dePédery-Hunt **Rev:** Denomination above maple leaves **Rev. Designer:** George E. Kruger-Gray **Edge:** Plain

Date	Mintage	MS-63	Proof
1952-2002	716,366,000	0.75	—
1952-2002P	114,212,000	1.00	—
1952-2002P Proof	32,642	—	5.00

KM# 445a CENT

0.9250 Silver **Ruler:** Elizabeth II **Subject:** Elizabeth II Golden Jubilee **Obv:** Crowned head right, Jubilee commemorative dates 1952-2002 **Obv. Designer:** Dora dePédery-Hunt **Rev:** Denomination above maple leaves **Rev. Designer:** George E. Kruger-Gray

Date	Mintage	MS-63	Proof
1952-2002	21,537	—	3.00

KM# 490 CENT

2.2500 g., Copper Plated Zinc, 19.05 mm. **Ruler:** Elizabeth II **Obv:** New effigy of Queen Elizabeth II right **Obv. Designer:** Susanna Blunt **Rev:** Two maple leaves **Edge:** Plain

Date	Mintage	MS-63	Proof
2003	56,877,144	0.25	—
2004	653,317,000	0.25	—
2004 Proof	—	—	2.50
2005	759,658,000	0.25	—
2005 Proof	—	—	2.50
2006	886,275,000	0.25	—
2006 Proof	—	—	2.50

KM# 490a CENT

2.2500 g., Copper Plated Steel, 19.05 mm. **Ruler:** Elizabeth II **Obv:** Bust right **Obv. Designer:** Susanna Blunt **Rev:** Two maple leaves **Rev. Designer:** G. E. Kruger-Gray

Date	Mintage	MS-63	Proof
2003P	591,257,000	0.25	—
2003 WP	Inc. above	0.25	—
2004P	134,906,000	0.25	—
2005P	30,525,000	0.25	—
2006P	137,733,000	0.25	—
2006(ml)	Inc. above	0.25	—
2007(ml)	938,270,000	0.25	—
2007(ml) Proof	—	—	2.50
2008(ml)	787,625,000	0.25	—
2008(ml) Proof	—	—	2.50
2009(ml)	455,680,000	0.25	—
2009(ml) Proof	—	—	2.50
2010(ml)	—	0.25	—
2010(ml) Proof	—	—	2.50
2011(ml)	—	0.25	—
2011(ml) Proof	—	—	2.50
2012(ml)	—	0.25	—
2012(ml) Proof	—	—	2.50

KM# 468 CENT

2.5000 g., Copper **Ruler:** Elizabeth II **Subject:** 50th Anniversary of the Coronation of Elizabeth II **Obv:** 1953 Effigy of the Queen, Jubilee commemorative dates 1953-2003 **Obv. Designer:** Mary Gillick

Date	Mintage	MS-63	Proof
1953-2003 Proof	—	—	2.50

KM# 490b CENT

2.2500 g., Copper Plated Zinc **Ruler:** Elizabeth II **Obv:** Head right **Rev:** Maple leaf, selectively gold plated **Note:** Bound into Annual Report.

Date	Mintage	MS-63	Proof
2003 Proof	7,746	—	35.00

KM# 1023 CENT

Copper, 19.1 mm. **Ruler:** Elizabeth II **Obv:** George V bust left **Rev:** Value within wreath, dual dates below

Date	Mintage	MS-63	Proof
1935-2010 Proof	—	—	10.00

KM# 1153 CENT

5.6700 g., Copper, 19.1 mm. **Ruler:** Elizabeth II **Obv:** George V bust **Rev:** Value within wreath

Date	Mintage	MS-63	Proof
1911-2011 Proof	6,000	—	10.00

KM# 410 3 CENTS

3.1100 g., 0.9250 Silver Gilt 0.0925 oz. ASW, 21.3 mm. **Ruler:** Elizabeth II **Subject:** 1st Canadian Postage Stamp **Obv:** Crowned head right **Obv. Designer:** Dora dePédery-Hunt **Rev:** Partial stamp design **Rev. Designer:** Sandford Fleming **Edge:** Plain

Date	Mintage	MS-63	Proof
2001 Proof	59,573	—	12.50

KM# 182 5 CENTS

4.6000 g., Copper-Nickel, 19.55 mm. **Ruler:** Elizabeth II **Obv:** Crowned head right **Obv. Designer:** Dora dePedery-Hunt **Rev:** Beaver on rock divides dates and denomination **Rev. Designer:** George E. Kruger-Gray **Edge:** Plain

Date	Mintage	MS-63	Proof
2001	30,035,000	12.50	—
2001P Proof	—	—	10.00
2003	—	0.30	—

KM# 182b 5 CENTS

3.9000 g., Nickel Plated Steel, 21.2 mm. **Ruler:** Elizabeth II **Obv:** Crowned head right **Obv. Designer:** Dora dePedery-Hunt **Rev:** Beaver on rock divides date and denomination **Rev. Designer:** George E. Kruger-Gray **Edge:** Plain

Date	Mintage	MS-63	Proof
2001 P	136,650,000	0.35	—
2003 P	32,986,921	0.35	—

KM# 182a 5 CENTS

5.3500 g., 0.9250 Silver 0.1591 oz. ASW, 21.2 mm. **Ruler:** Elizabeth II **Obv:** Crowned head right **Obv. Designer:** Dora dePedery-Hunt **Rev:** Beaver on rock divides date and denomination **Rev. Designer:** George E. Kruger-Gray

Date	Mintage	MS-63	Proof
2001 Proof	—	—	8.00
2003 Proof	—	—	8.00

KM# 413 5 CENTS

5.3500 g., 0.9250 Silver 0.1591 oz. ASW, 21.2 mm. **Ruler:** Elizabeth II **Subject:** Royal Military College **Obv:** Crowned head right **Rev:** Marching cadets and arch **Rev. Designer:** Gerald T. Locklin **Edge:** Plain

Date	Mintage	MS-63	Proof
2001 Proof	25,834	—	8.00

KM# 446 5 CENTS

3.9500 g., Nickel Plated Steel, 21.2 mm. **Ruler:** Elizabeth II **Subject:** Elizabeth II Golden Jubilee **Obv:** Crowned head right, Jubilee commemorative dates 1952-2002 **Obv. Designer:** Dora dePedery-Hunt **Rev. Designer:** George E. Kruger-Gray **Note:** Magnetic.

Date	Mintage	MS-63	Proof
1952-2002P	135,960,000	0.45	—
1952-2002P Proof	32,642	—	10.00

KM# 446a 5 CENTS

5.3500 g., 0.9250 Silver 0.1591 oz. ASW, 21.2 mm. **Ruler:** Elizabeth II **Subject:** Elizabeth II Golden Jubilee **Obv:** Queen, Jubilee commemorative dates 1952-2002

Date	Mintage	MS-63	Proof
1952-2002 Proof	21,573	—	11.50

KM# 453 5 CENTS

5.3500 g., 0.9250 Silver 0.1591 oz. ASW, 21.2 mm. **Ruler:** Elizabeth II **Subject:** Vimy Ridge - WWI **Obv:** Crowned head right **Rev:** Vimy Ridge Memorial, allegorical figure and dates 1917-2002 **Rev. Designer:** S. A. Allward

Date	Mintage	MS-63	Proof
2002 Proof	22,646	—	11.50

KM# 491 5 CENTS

3.9500 g., Nickel Plated Steel, 21.2 mm. **Ruler:** Elizabeth II **Obv:** Bare head right **Obv. Designer:** Susanna Blunt **Rev:** Beaver divides date and denomination **Rev. Designer:** George E. Kruger-Gray **Note:** Magnetic.

Date	Mintage	MS-63	Proof
2003P	61,392,180	0.45	—
2004P	132,097,000	0.45	—
2004P Proof	—	—	2.50
2005P	89,664,000	0.45	—
2005P Proof	—	—	2.50
2006P	139,308,000	0.50	—
2006P Proof	—	—	2.50
2006(ml)	184,874,000	0.45	—
2006(ml) Proof	—	—	2.50
2007(ml)	221,472,000	0.45	—
2007(ml) Proof	—	—	2.50
2008(ml)	278,530,000	0.45	—
2008(ml) Proof	—	—	2.50
2009(ml)	266,488,000	0.45	—
2009(ml) Proof	—	—	2.50
2010(ml)	—	0.45	—
2010(ml) Proof	—	—	2.50
2011(ml)	—	0.45	—
2011(ml) Proof	—	—	2.50
2012(ml)	—	0.45	—
2012(ml) Proof	—	—	2.50
2013(ml)	—	0.45	—
2013(ml) Proof	—	—	2.50

KM# 469 5 CENTS

5.3500 g., 0.9250 Silver 0.1591 oz. ASW, 21.2 mm. **Ruler:** Elizabeth II **Subject:** 50th Anniversary of the Coronation of Elizabeth II **Obv:** Crowned head right, Jubilee commemorative dates 1953-2003 **Obv. Designer:** Mary Gillick

Date	Mintage	MS-63	Proof
1953-2003 Proof	21,573	—	11.50

KM# 491a 5 CENTS

5.3500 g., 0.9250 Silver 0.1591 oz. ASW, 21.1 mm. **Ruler:** Elizabeth II **Obv:** Crowned head right **Obv. Designer:** Susanna Blunt **Rev:** Beaver divides date and denomination **Edge:** Plain

Date	Mintage	MS-63	Proof
2004 Proof	—	—	6.50

KM# 506 5 CENTS

5.3500 g., 0.9250 Silver 0.1591 oz. ASW, 21.3 mm. **Ruler:** Elizabeth II **Obv:** Bare head right **Rev:** "Victory " design of the KM-40 reverse **Edge:** Plain **Shape:** 12-sided

Date	Mintage	MS-63	Proof
1944-2004 Proof	20,019	—	15.00

KM# 627 5 CENTS

3.9500 g., Nickel Plated Steel, 21.2 mm. **Ruler:** Elizabeth II **Subject:** 60th Anniversary, Victory in Europe 1945-2005 **Obv:** Head right **Rev:** Large V **Edge:** Plain

Date	Mintage	MS-63	Proof
2005P	59,269,192	4.50	—

KM# 758 5 CENTS

5.3000 g., 0.9250 Silver 0.1576 oz. ASW **Ruler:** Elizabeth II **Obv:** George VI head left **Rev:** Torch and large V

Date	Mintage	MS-63	Proof
2005 Proof	42,792	—	35.00

KM# 758a 5 CENTS

5.3000 g., 0.9250 Silver selectively gold plated 0.1576 oz. ASW **Ruler:** Elizabeth II **Obv:** George VI head left **Rev:** Torch and large V **Note:** Bound into Annual Report.

Date	Mintage	MS-63	Proof
2005 Proof	6,065	—	40.00

KM# 491b 5 CENTS

4.6000 g., Copper-Nickel **Ruler:** Elizabeth II **Obv:** Bust right **Rev:** Beaver

Date	Mintage	MS-63	Proof
2006	43,008,000	5.00	—

KM# 1024 5 CENTS

Nickel, 21.2 mm. **Ruler:** Elizabeth II **Obv:** George V bust left **Rev:** Denomination and 1935-2010 anniversary dates, two maple leaves below

Date	Mintage	MS-63	Proof
1935-2010 Proof	—	—	15.00

KM# 1154 5 CENTS

1.5590 g., 0.9250 Silver 0.0464 oz. ASW, 15.5 mm. **Ruler:** Elizabeth II **Obv:** George V bust **Rev:** Value within wreath

Date	Mintage	MS-63	Proof
1911-2011 Proof	6,000	—	15.00

KM# 412a 10 CENTS

2.4000 g., 0.9250 Silver 0.0714 oz. ASW, 18 mm. **Ruler:** Elizabeth II **Subject:** Year of the Volunteer **Obv:** Crowned head right **Rev:** Three portraits left above banner, radiant sun below **Edge:** Reeded

Date	Mintage	MS-63	Proof
2001P Proof	40,634	—	9.00

KM# 183b 10 CENTS

1.7700 g., Nickel Plated Steel, 18.03 mm. **Ruler:** Elizabeth II **Obv:** Crowned head right **Obv. Designer:** Dora dePedery-Hunt **Rev:** Bluenose sailing left, date at right, denomination below **Rev. Designer:** Emanuel Hahn **Edge:** Reeded

Date	Mintage	MS-63	Proof
2001 P	266,000,000	0.45	—
2003 P	162,398,000	0.20	—

KM# 183a 10 CENTS

2.4000 g., 0.9250 Silver 0.0714 oz. ASW, 18.03 mm. **Ruler:** Elizabeth II **Obv:** Crowned head right **Rev:** Bluenose sailing left, date at right, denomination below

Date	Mintage	MS-63	Proof
2001 Proof	—	—	5.00
2002 Proof	—	—	7.50
2003 Proof	—	—	7.50

KM# 412 10 CENTS

1.7700 g., Nickel Plated Steel, 18 mm. **Ruler:** Elizabeth II **Subject:** Year of the Volunteer **Obv:** Crowned head right **Rev:** Three portraits left and radiant sun **Edge:** Reeded

Date	Mintage	MS-63	Proof
2001P	224,714,000	4.50	—

KM# 447 10 CENTS

1.7700 g., Nickel Plated Steel, 18 mm. **Ruler:** Elizabeth II **Subject:** Elizabeth II Golden Jubilee **Obv:** Crowned head right, Jubilee commemorative dates 1952-2002

Date	Mintage	MS-63	Proof
1952-2002P	252,563,000	1.00	—
1952-2002 Proof	32,642	—	2.50

KM# 447a 10 CENTS

2.3200 g., 0.9250 Silver 0.0690 oz. ASW, 18 mm. **Ruler:** Elizabeth II **Subject:** Elizabeth II Golden Jubilee **Obv:** Crowned head right, Jubilee commemorative dates 1952-2002

Date	Mintage	MS-63	Proof
2002 Proof	21,537	—	12.50

KM# 492 10 CENTS

1.7700 g., Nickel Plated Steel, 18 mm. **Ruler:** Elizabeth II **Obv:** Head right **Obv. Designer:** Susanna Blunt **Rev:** Bluenose sailing left

Date	Mintage	MS-63	Proof
2003P	—	1.25	—
2004P	211,924,000	0.60	—
2004P Proof	—	—	2.50
2005P	212,175,000	0.60	—
2005P Proof	—	—	2.50
2006P	312,122,000	0.60	—
2006P Proof	—	—	2.50
2007(ml) Straight 7	304,110,000	0.60	—
2007(ml) Curved 7	Inc. above	0.60	—
2007(ml) Proof	—	—	2.50
2008(ml)	467,495,000	0.60	—
2008(ml) Proof	—	—	2.50
2009(ml)	370,700,000	0.60	—
2009(ml) Proof	—	—	2.50
2010(ml)	—	0.60	—
2010(ml) Proof	—	—	2.50
2011(ml)	—	0.60	—
2011(ml) Proof	—	—	2.50
2012(ml)	—	0.60	—
2012(ml) Proof	—	—	2.50
2013(ml)	—	0.60	—
2013(ml) Proof	—	—	2.50

KM# 470 10 CENTS

2.3200 g., 0.9250 Silver 0.0690 oz. ASW **Ruler:** Elizabeth II **Subject:** 50th Anniversary of the Coronation of Elizabeth II **Obv:** Head right **Rev:** Bluenose sailing left

Date	Mintage	MS-63	Proof
1953-2003 Proof	21,537	—	12.00

KM# 492a 10 CENTS

2.4000 g., 0.9250 Silver 0.0714 oz. ASW, 18 mm. **Ruler:** Elizabeth II **Obv:** Bare head right **Obv. Designer:** Susanna Blunt **Rev:** Sailboat **Edge:** Reeded

Date	Mintage	MS-63	Proof
2004 Proof	—	—	6.00

KM# 524 10 CENTS

2.4000 g., 0.9250 Silver 0.0714 oz. ASW, 18 mm. **Ruler:** Elizabeth II **Subject:** Golf, Championship of Canada, Centennial. **Obv:** Head right

Date	Mintage	MS-63	Proof
2004	39,486	12.50	—

KM# 1025 10 CENTS

Silver, 18.03 mm. **Ruler:** Elizabeth II **Obv:** George V bust left **Rev:** Value within wreath, dual dates below

Date	Mintage	MS-63	Proof
1935-2010 Proof	—	—	20.00

KM# 1155 10 CENTS

2.4000 g., 0.9250 Silver 0.0714 oz. ASW, 18.03 mm. **Ruler:** Elizabeth II **Obv:** George V bust **Rev:** Value within wreath

Date	Mintage	MS-63	Proof
1911-2011 Proof	6,000	—	20.00

KM# 184 25 CENTS

5.0700 g., Nickel, 23.88 mm. **Ruler:** Elizabeth II **Obv:** Crowned head right **Obv. Designer:** Dora dePedery-Hunt **Rev:** Caribou left, denomination above, date at right **Rev. Designer:** Emanuel Hahn

Date	Mintage	MS-63	Proof
2001	8,415,000	5.00	—
2001 Proof	—	—	7.50

KM# 184b 25 CENTS

4.4000 g., Nickel Plated Steel, 23.88 mm. **Ruler:** Elizabeth II **Obv:** Crowned head right **Rev:** Caribou left, denomination above, date at right

Date	Mintage	MS-63	Proof
2001 P	55,773,000	0.95	—
2001 P Proof	—	—	5.00
2002 P	156,105,000	2.50	—
2002 P Proof	—	—	5.00
2003 P	87,647,000	2.50	—
2003 P Proof	—	—	5.00

KM# 184a 25 CENTS

5.9000 g., 0.9250 Silver 0.1755 oz. ASW, 23.88 mm. **Ruler:** Elizabeth II **Obv:** Crowned head right **Rev:** Caribou left, denomination above, date at right

Date	Mintage	MS-63	Proof
2001 Proof	—	—	9.50
2003 Proof	—	—	9.50

KM# 419 25 CENTS

4.4000 g., Nickel Plated Steel, 23.9 mm. **Ruler:** Elizabeth II **Subject:** Canada Day **Obv:** Crowned head right **Rev:** Maple leaf at center, children holding hands below **Rev. Designer:** Silke Ware **Edge:** Reeded

Date	Mintage	MS-63	Proof
2001	96,352	7.00	—

KM# 448 25 CENTS

4.4000 g., Nickel Plated Steel, 23.9 mm. **Ruler:** Elizabeth II **Subject:** Elizabeth II Golden Jubilee **Obv:** Crowned head right **Rev:** Caribou left

Date	Mintage	MS-63	Proof
1952-2002P	152,485,000	2.00	—
1952-2002P Proof	32,642	—	6.00

KM# 448a 25 CENTS

5.9000 g., 0.9250 Silver 0.1755 oz. ASW, 23.9 mm. **Ruler:** Elizabeth II **Subject:** Elizabeth II Golden Jubilee **Obv:** Crowned head right, Jubilee commemorative dates 1952-2002

Date	Mintage	MS-63	Proof
1952-2002 Proof	100,000	—	12.50

KM# 451 25 CENTS

4.4000 g., Nickel Plated Steel, 23.9 mm. **Ruler:** Elizabeth II **Rev:** Small human figures supporting large maple leaf

Date	Mintage	MS-63	Proof
2002P	30,627,000	5.00	—

KM# 451a 25 CENTS

4.4000 g., Nickel Plated Steel, 23.9 mm. **Ruler:** Elizabeth II **Subject:** Canada Day **Obv:** Crowned head right **Rev:** Human figures supporting large red maple leaf **Edge:** Reeded

Date	Mintage	MS-63	Proof
2002P	49,901	6.00	—

KM# 493 25 CENTS

4.4000 g., Nickel Plated Steel, 23.9 mm. **Ruler:** Elizabeth II **Obv:** Bare head right **Obv. Designer:** Susanna Blunt **Rev:** Caribou left, denomination above, date at right

Date	Mintage	MS-63	Proof
2003P	66,861,633	2.00	—
2003P W	—	—	—
2004P	177,466,000	2.50	—
2004P Proof	—	—	5.00
2005P	206,346,000	2.50	—
2005P Proof	—	—	5.00
2006P	423,189,000	2.50	—
2006P Proof	—	—	5.00
2007(ml)	386,763,000	2.50	—
2007(ml) Proof	—	—	5.00
2008(ml)	387,222,000	2.50	—
2008(ml) Proof	—	—	5.00
2009(ml)	266,766,000	2.50	—
2009(ml) Proof	—	—	5.00
2010(ml)	—	2.50	—
2010(ml) Proof	—	—	5.00
2011(ml)	—	2.50	—
2011(ml) Proof	—	—	5.00
2012(ml)	—	2.50	—
2012(ml) Proof	—	—	5.00
2013(ml)	—	2.50	—
2013(ml) Proof	—	—	5.00

KM# 471 25 CENTS

5.9000 g., 0.9250 Silver 0.1755 oz. ASW, 23.9 mm. **Ruler:** Elizabeth II **Subject:** 50th Anniversary of the Coronation of Elizabeth II **Obv:** 1953 Effigy of the Queen, Coronation Jubilee dates 1953-2003 **Obv. Designer:** Mary Gillick

Date	Mintage	MS-63	Proof
1953-2003 Proof	21,537	—	12.50

KM# 474 25 CENTS

4.4000 g., 0.9250 Silver 0.1308 oz. ASW, 23.9 mm. **Ruler:** Elizabeth II **Subject:** Canada Day **Obv:** Queen's head right **Rev:** Polar bear and red colored maple leaves

Date	Mintage	MS-63	Proof
2003 Proof	63,511	—	12.00

KM# 493a 25 CENTS

5.9000 g., 0.9250 Silver 0.1755 oz. ASW, 23.9 mm. **Ruler:** Elizabeth II **Obv:** Bare head right **Obv. Designer:** Suanne Blunt **Rev:** Caribou **Edge:** Reeded

Date	Mintage	MS-63	Proof
2004 Proof	—	—	6.50

KM# 510 25 CENTS

4.4000 g., Nickel Plated Steel, 23.9 mm. **Ruler:** Elizabeth II **Obv:** Bare head right **Rev:** Red poppy in center of maple leaf **Edge:** Reeded

Date	Mintage	MS-63	Proof
2004	28,500,000	5.00	—

KM# 510a 25 CENTS

5.9000 g., 0.9250 Silver 0.1755 oz. ASW, 23.9 mm. **Ruler:** Elizabeth II **Obv:** Bare head right **Rev:** Poppy at center of maple leaf, selectively gold plated **Edge:** Reeded **Note:** Housed in Annual Report.

Date	Mintage	MS-63	Proof
2004 Proof	12,677	—	20.00

KM# 525 25 CENTS

4.4000 g., Nickel Plated Steel, 23.9 mm. **Ruler:** Elizabeth II **Obv:** Bare head right **Rev:** Maple leaf, colorized

Date	Mintage	MS-63	Proof
2004	16,028	8.00	—

KM# 628 25 CENTS

4.4000 g., Nickel Plated Steel, 23.9 mm. **Ruler:** Elizabeth II **Subject:** First Settlement, Ile Ste Croix 1604-2004 **Obv:** Bare head right **Rev:** Sailing ship Bonne-Renommee

Date	Mintage	MS-63	Proof
2004P	15,400,000	5.00	—

KM# 698 25 CENTS

4.4000 g., Nickel Plated Steel, 23.88 mm. **Ruler:** Elizabeth II **Rev:** Santa, colorized

Date	Mintage	MS-63	Proof
2004	62,777	5.00	—

KM# 699 25 CENTS

4.4000 g., Nickel Plated Steel, 23.9 mm. **Ruler:** Elizabeth II **Series:** Canada Day **Rev:** Moose head, humorous

Date	Mintage	MS-63	Proof
2004	44,752	5.00	—

KM# 529 25 CENTS

4.4000 g., Nickel Plated Steel, 23.9 mm. **Ruler:** Elizabeth II **Subject:** WWII, 60th Anniversary **Obv:** Head right **Rev:** Three soldiers and flag

Date	Mintage	MS-63	Proof
1945-2005	3,500	20.00	—

KM# 530 25 CENTS

4.4000 g., Nickel Plated Steel, 23.9 mm. **Ruler:** Elizabeth II **Subject:** Alberta **Obv:** Head right **Rev:** Oil rig and sunset

Date	Mintage	MS-63	Proof
2005P	20,640,000	7.00	—

KM# 531 25 CENTS

4.4000 g., Nickel Plated Steel, 23.9 mm. **Ruler:** Elizabeth II **Subject:** Canada Day **Obv:** Head right **Rev:** Beaver, colorized

Date	Mintage	MS-63	Proof
2005P	58,370	8.50	—

KM# 532 25 CENTS

4.4000 g., Nickel Plated Steel, 23.9 mm. **Ruler:** Elizabeth II **Subject:** Saskatchewan **Obv:** Head right **Rev:** Bird on fencepost

Date	Mintage	MS-63	Proof
2005P	19,290,000	7.00	—

KM# 533 25 CENTS

4.4000 g., Nickel Plated Steel, 23.9 mm. **Ruler:** Elizabeth II **Obv:** Head right **Rev:** Stuffed bear in Christmas stocking, colorized

Date	Mintage	MS-63	Proof
2005P	72,831	10.00	—

KM# 535 25 CENTS

4.4000 g., Nickel Plated Steel, 23.9 mm. **Ruler:** Elizabeth II **Subject:** Year of the Veteran **Obv:** Head right **Rev:** Conjoined busts of young and veteran left **Edge:** Reeded

Date	Mintage	MS-63	Proof
2005P	29,390,000	7.00	—

KM# 576 25 CENTS

4.4000 g., Nickel Plated Steel, 23.9 mm. **Ruler:** Elizabeth II **Subject:** Quebec Winter Carnival **Obv:** Head right **Rev:** Snowman, colorized

Date	Mintage	MS-63	Proof
2006	8,200	10.00	—

KM# 534 25 CENTS

4.4000 g., Nickel Plated Steel, 23.9 mm. **Ruler:** Elizabeth II **Subject:** Toronto Maple Leafs **Obv:** Head right **Rev:** Colorized team logo

Date	Mintage	MS-63	Proof
2006P	11,765	12.50	—

KM# 575 25 CENTS

4.4000 g., Nickel Plated Steel, 23.9 mm. **Ruler:** Elizabeth II **Subject:** Montreal Canadiens **Obv:** Head right **Rev:** Colorized logo

Date	Mintage	MS-63	Proof
2006P	11,765	12.50	—

KM# 629 25 CENTS
4.4000 g., Nickel Plated Steel, 23.9 mm. **Ruler:** Elizabeth II **Obv:** Head right **Rev:** Medal of Bravery **Edge:** Reeded

Date	Mintage	MS-63	Proof
2006(ml)	20,040,000	2.50	—

KM# 632 25 CENTS
12.6100 g., Nickel Plated Steel, 35 mm. **Ruler:** Elizabeth II **Subject:** Queen Elizabeth II 80th Birthday **Rev:** Crown, colorized

Date	Mintage	MS-63	Proof
1926-2006 Specimen	24,977	25.00	—

KM# 633 25 CENTS
4.4300 g., Nickel Plated Steel, 23.9 mm. **Ruler:** Elizabeth II **Subject:** Canada Day **Obv:** Crowned head right **Rev:** Boy marching with flag, colorized

Date	Mintage	MS-63	Proof
2006P	30,328	6.00	—

KM# 634 25 CENTS
4.4300 g., Nickel Plated Steel, 23.88 mm. **Ruler:** Elizabeth II **Subject:** Breast Cancer **Rev:** Four ribbons, all colorized **Note:** Sold housed in a bookmark.

Date	Mintage	MS-63	Proof
2006P	40,911	10.00	—

KM# 635 25 CENTS
4.4300 g., Nickel Plated Steel, 23.88 mm. **Ruler:** Elizabeth II **Subject:** Breast Cancer **Rev:** Colorized pink ribbon applique in center.

Date	Mintage	MS-63	Proof
2006P	29,798,000	1.50	—

KM# 636 25 CENTS
4.4000 g., Nickel Plated Steel, 23.88 mm. **Ruler:** Elizabeth II **Obv:** Head right **Obv. Designer:** Susana Blunt **Rev:** Medal of Bravery design (maple leaf within wreath)

Date	Mintage	MS-63	Proof
2006	20,045,111	7.00	—

KM# 637 25 CENTS
4.4300 g., Nickel Plated Steel, 23.88 mm. **Ruler:** Elizabeth II **Subject:** Wedding **Rev:** Colorized bouquet of flowers

Date	Mintage	MS-63	Proof
2007(ml)	10,318	5.00	—

KM# 642 25 CENTS
4.4300 g., Nickel Plated Steel, 23.88 mm. **Ruler:** Elizabeth II **Subject:** Ottawa Senators **Obv:** Head right **Rev:** Logo

Date	Mintage	MS-63	Proof
2006P	11,765	12.50	—

KM# 644 25 CENTS
4.4300 g., Nickel Plated Steel, 23.88 mm. **Ruler:** Elizabeth II **Subject:** Calgary Flames **Obv:** Head right **Rev:** Logo

Date	Mintage	MS-63	Proof
2007(ml)	1,082	12.50	—

KM# 645 25 CENTS
4.4300 g., Nickel Plated Steel, 23.88 mm. **Ruler:** Elizabeth II **Subject:** Edmonton Oilers **Obv:** Head right **Rev:** Logo

Date	Mintage	MS-63	Proof
2007(ml)	2,214	12.50	—

KM# 647 25 CENTS
4.4300 g., Nickel Plated Steel **Ruler:** Elizabeth II **Subject:** Santa and Rudolph **Rev:** Colorized Santa in sled lead by Rudolph

Date	Mintage	MS-63	Proof
2006P	99,258	5.00	—

KM# 682 25 CENTS
4.4300 g., Nickel Plated Steel **Ruler:** Elizabeth II **Subject:** Curling **Obv:** Head right

Date	Mintage	MS-63	Proof
2007	22,400,000	7.50	—
2008 Mule	—	—	—

KM# 683 25 CENTS
4.4300 g., Nickel Plated Steel **Ruler:** Elizabeth II **Subject:** Ice Hockey **Obv:** Head right

Date	Mintage	MS-63	Proof
2007	22,400,000	7.50	—
2008 Mule	—	—	—

KM# 684 25 CENTS
4.4300 g., Nickel Plated Steel, 23.8 mm. **Ruler:** Elizabeth II **Subject:** Paraolympic Winter Games **Obv:** Head right **Rev:** Wheelchair curling

Date	Mintage	MS-63	Proof
2007	22,400,000	7.50	—
2008 Mule	—	—	—

KM# 685 25 CENTS
4.4300 g., Nickel Plated Steel **Ruler:** Elizabeth II **Subject:** Biathlon **Obv:** Head right

Date	Mintage	MS-63	Proof
2007	22,400,000	7.50	—
2008 Mule	—	—	—

KM# 638 25 CENTS
4.4300 g., Nickel Plated Steel, 23.88 mm. **Ruler:** Elizabeth II **Subject:** Birthday **Rev:** Colorized balloons

Date	Mintage	MS-63	Proof
2007(ml)	24,531	5.00	—

KM# 639 25 CENTS
4.4300 g., Nickel Plated Steel, 23.88 mm. **Ruler:** Elizabeth II **Subject:** Baby birth **Rev:** Colorized baby rattle **Edge:** Reeded

Date	Mintage	MS-63	Proof
2007(ml)	30,090	5.00	—

KM# 640 25 CENTS
4.4300 g., Nickel Plated Steel, 23.88 mm. **Ruler:** Elizabeth II **Subject:** Oh Canada **Obv:** Head right **Rev:** Maple leaf, colorized

Date	Mintage	MS-63	Proof
2006(ml)	23,582	8.50	—

KM# 641 25 CENTS
4.4300 g., Nickel Plated Steel, 23.88 mm. **Ruler:** Elizabeth II **Subject:** Congratulations **Obv:** Head right **Rev:** Fireworks, colorized

Date	Mintage	MS-63	Proof
2006(ml)	9,671	8.00	—

KM# 643 25 CENTS
4.4300 g., Nickel Plated Steel, 23.88 mm. **Ruler:** Elizabeth II **Subject:** Vancouver Canucks **Obv:** Head right **Rev:** Logo

Date	Mintage	MS-63	Proof
2007(ml)	1,526	12.50	—

KM# 686 25 CENTS
4.4300 g., Nickel Plated Steel, 23.8 mm. **Ruler:** Elizabeth II **Subject:** Alpine Skiing **Obv:** Head right

Date	Mintage	MS-63	Proof
2007	22,400,000	7.50	—
2008 Mule	—	—	—

KM# 701 25 CENTS
4.4300 g., Nickel Plated Steel, 23.88 mm. **Ruler:** Elizabeth II **Subject:** Birthday **Rev:** Party hat, multicolor

Date	Mintage	MS-63	Proof
2007	11,376	8.00	—

KM# 702 25 CENTS
4.4300 g., Nickel Plated Steel, 23.88 mm. **Ruler:** Elizabeth II **Subject:** Congratulations **Rev:** Trophy, multicolor

Date	Mintage	MS-63	Proof
2007	—	8.00	—

KM# 703 25 CENTS
4.4300 g., Nickel Plated Steel, 23.88 mm. **Ruler:** Elizabeth II **Subject:** Wedding **Rev:** Cake, multicolor

Date	Mintage	MS-63	Proof
2007	—	8.00	—

KM# 704 25 CENTS
4.4300 g., Nickel Plated Steel, 23.88 mm. **Ruler:** Elizabeth II **Subject:** Canada Day **Rev:** Mountie, colorized

Date	Mintage	MS-63	Proof
2007(ml)	27,743	8.00	—

KM# 705 25 CENTS
4.4300 g., Nickel Plated Steel, 23.88 mm. **Ruler:** Elizabeth II **Subject:** Christmas **Rev:** Multicolor tree

Date	Mintage	MS-63	Proof
2007	66,267	8.00	—

KM# 706 25 CENTS

12.6100 g., Nickel Plated Steel, 35.0 mm. **Ruler:** Elizabeth II **Subject:** Red-breasted Nuthatch **Obv:** Head right **Obv. Legend:** ELIZABETH II - D • G • REGINA **Obv. Designer:** Susanna Blunt **Rev:** Nuthatch perched on pine branch multicolor **Rev. Legend:** CANADA **Rev. Designer:** Arnold Nogy **Edge:** Plain

Date	Mintage	MS-63	Proof
2007(ml) Specimen	11,909	295	—

KM# 707 25 CENTS

12.6100 g., Nickel Plated Steel, 35 mm. **Ruler:** Elizabeth II **Obv:** Elizabeth II **Rev:** Multicolor ruby-throated hummingbird and flower **Edge:** Plain

Date	Mintage	MS-63	Proof
2007 Specimen	17,174	135	—

KM# 708 25 CENTS

12.6100 g., Nickel Plated Steel, 35 mm. **Ruler:** Elizabeth II **Subject:** Queen's 60th Wedding Anniversary **Rev:** Royal carriage in color

Date	Mintage	MS-63	Proof
1947-2007 Specimen	15,235	25.00	—

KM# 713 25 CENTS

4.4000 g., Nickel Plated Steel **Ruler:** Elizabeth II **Rev:** Toronto Maple Leaf logo, colorized

Date	Mintage	MS-63	Proof
2007(ml)	5,365	5.00	—

KM# 714 25 CENTS

4.4000 g., Nickel Plated Steel **Ruler:** Elizabeth II **Rev:** Ottawa Senators logo, colorized

Date	Mintage	MS-63	Proof
2007(ml)	2,474	5.00	—

KM# 723 25 CENTS

4.4000 g., Nickel Plated Steel **Ruler:** Elizabeth II **Rev:** Montreal Canadiens logo, colorized

Date	Mintage	MS-63	Proof
2007(ml)	4,091	5.00	—

KM# 1039 25 CENTS

4.4300 g., Nickel Plated Steel, 23.9 mm. **Ruler:** Elizabeth II **Subject:** Canada Day **Rev:** Colorized moose head

Date	Mintage	MS-63	Proof
2008	11,538	12.50	—

KM# 760 25 CENTS

4.4300 g., Nickel Plated Steel, 23.88 mm. **Ruler:** Elizabeth II **Subject:** Baby **Rev:** Multicolor blue teddy bear

Date	Mintage	MS-63	Proof
2008	29,639	8.00	—

KM# 761 25 CENTS

4.4300 g., Nickel Plated Steel, 23.88 mm. **Ruler:** Elizabeth II **Subject:** Birthday **Rev:** Multicolor party hat

Date	Mintage	MS-63	Proof
2008	11,376	8.00	—

KM# 762 25 CENTS

4.4300 g., Nickel Plated Steel, 23.88 mm. **Ruler:** Elizabeth II **Subject:** Congratulations **Rev:** Multicolor trophy

Date	Mintage	MS-63	Proof
2008	6,821	8.00	—

KM# 763 25 CENTS

4.4300 g., Nickel Plated Steel, 23.88 mm. **Ruler:** Elizabeth II **Subject:** Wedding **Rev:** Multicolor wedding cake

Date	Mintage	MS-63	Proof
2008	7,407	8.00	—

KM# 764 25 CENTS

4.4300 g., Nickel Plated Steel, 23.88 mm. **Ruler:** Elizabeth II **Subject:** Santa Claus **Rev:** Multicolor Santa

Date	Mintage	MS-63	Proof
2008	42,344	8.00	—

KM# 765 25 CENTS

4.4300 g., Nickel Plated Steel, 23.9 mm. **Ruler:** Elizabeth II **Subject:** Vancouver Olympics **Rev:** Freestyle skiing

Date	Mintage	MS-63	Proof
2008	—	2.00	—

KM# 766 25 CENTS

4.4300 g., Nickel Plated Steel, 23.8 mm. **Ruler:** Elizabeth II **Subject:** Vancouver Olympics **Rev:** Figure skating

Date	Mintage	MS-63	Proof
2008	—	2.00	—

KM# 768 25 CENTS

4.4300 g., Nickel Plated Steel, 23.88 mm. **Ruler:** Elizabeth II **Subject:** Vancouver Olympics **Rev:** Snowboarding

Date	Mintage	MS-63	Proof
2008	—	2.00	—

KM# 769 25 CENTS

4.4300 g., Nickel Plated Steel, 23.88 mm. **Ruler:** Elizabeth II **Subject:** Vancouver Olympics **Rev:** Olympic mascot - Miga

Date	Mintage	MS-63	Proof
2008	—	3.00	—

KM# 770 25 CENTS

4.4300 g., Nickel Plated Steel, 23.88 mm. **Ruler:** Elizabeth II **Subject:** Vancouver Olympics **Rev:** Olympic mascot - Quatchi

Date	Mintage	MS-63	Proof
2008	—	3.00	—

KM# 771 25 CENTS

4.4300 g., Nickel Plated Steel, 23.88 mm. **Ruler:** Elizabeth II **Subject:** Vancouver Olympics **Rev:** Olympic mascot - Sumi

Date	Mintage	MS-63	Proof
2008	—	3.00	—

KM# 772 25 CENTS

4.4300 g., Nickel Plated Steel, 23.88 mm. **Ruler:** Elizabeth II **Subject:** Oh Canada **Rev:** Multicolor red flag

Date	Mintage	MS-63	Proof
2008	—	8.00	—

KM# 773 25 CENTS

12.6100 g., Nickel Plated Steel, 35 mm. **Ruler:** Elizabeth II **Obv:** Bust right **Obv. Designer:** Susanna Blunt **Rev:** Downy woodpecker in tree, multicolor **Rev. Designer:** Arnold Nogy **Edge:** Plain **Note:** Prev. KM#717.

Date	Mintage	MS-63	Proof
2008(ml) Specimen	14,282	275	—

KM# 774 25 CENTS

12.6100 g., Nickel Plated Steel, 35 mm. **Ruler:** Elizabeth II **Obv:** Bust right **Obv. Designer:** Susanna Blunt **Rev:** Northern cardinal perched on branch - multicolor **Rev. Designer:** Arnold Nogy **Edge:** Plain **Note:** Prev. KM#718.

Date	Mintage	MS-63	Proof
2008(ml) Specimen	11,604	275	—

KM# 775 25 CENTS

4.4300 g., Nickel Plated Steel, 23.8 mm. **Ruler:** Elizabeth II **Subject:** End of WWI, 90th Anniversary **Rev:** Multicolor poppy

Date	Mintage	MS-63	Proof
1918-2008	10,167	8.00	—

KM# 776 25 CENTS
12.6100 g., Nickel Plated Steel, 35 mm. **Ruler:** Elizabeth II **Subject:** Anne of Green Gables **Rev:** Image of young girl, multicolor **Rev. Designer:** Ben Stahl

Date	Mintage	MS-63	Proof
1908-2008 Specimen	32,795	20.00	—

KM# 841 25 CENTS
4.4300 g., Nickel Plated Steel, 23.8 mm. **Ruler:** Elizabeth II **Subject:** Vancouver Olympics **Rev:** Bobsleigh

Date	Mintage	MS-63	Proof
2008	—	3.00	—

KM# 1041 25 CENTS
4.4300 g., Nickel Plated Steel **Ruler:** Elizabeth II **Subject:** WWI **Rev:** Three military men standing over tomb

Date	Mintage	MS-63	Proof
2008(ml)	10,167	12.50	—

KM# 840 25 CENTS
4.4300 g., Nickel Plated Steel, 23.8 mm. **Ruler:** Elizabeth II **Subject:** Valcouver 2010 Olympics **Rev:** Cross-country skiing

Date	Mintage	MS-63	Proof
2009	—	3.00	—

KM# 842 25 CENTS
4.4300 g., Nickel Plated Steel, 23.9 mm. **Ruler:** Elizabeth II **Subject:** Edmonton Olympics **Rev:** Speed skating

Date	Mintage	MS-63	Proof
2009	—	3.00	—

KM# 885 25 CENTS
4.4000 g., Nickel Plated Steel, 23.88 mm. **Ruler:** Elizabeth II **Subject:** Canada Day **Rev:** Animals in boat with flag **Rev. Legend:** Canada 25 cents

Date	Mintage	MS-63	Proof
2009	11,091	5.00	—

KM# 886 25 CENTS
12.6100 g., Nickel Plated Steel, 35 mm. **Ruler:** Elizabeth II **Subject:** Notre-Dame-Du-Saguenay **Obv:** Bust right **Obv. Legend:** Elizabeth II DG Regina **Obv. Designer:** Susanna Blunt **Rev:** Color photo of fjord and statue **Rev. Legend:** Canada 25 cents

Date	Mintage	MS-63	Proof
2009 Specimen	16,653	25.00	—

KM# 915 25 CENTS
4.4300 g., Nickel Plated Steel, 23.9 mm. **Ruler:** Elizabeth II **Subject:** Surprise Birthday **Obv:** Bust right **Obv. Designer:** Susanna Blunt **Rev:** Colorized

Date	Mintage	MS-63	Proof
2009	9,663	12.50	—

KM# 916 25 CENTS
4.4300 g., Nickel Plated Steel, 23.9 mm. **Ruler:** Elizabeth II **Subject:** Share the Excitement **Obv:** Bust right **Obv. Designer:** Susanna Blunt **Rev:** Colorized

Date	Mintage	MS-63	Proof
2009	4,126	12.50	—

KM# 917 25 CENTS
4.4300 g., Nickel Plated Steel, 23.9 mm. **Ruler:** Elizabeth II **Subject:** Share the Love **Obv:** Bust right **Obv. Designer:** Susanna Blunt **Rev:** Two doves, coolored

Date	Mintage	MS-63	Proof
2009	7,571	12.50	—

KM# 918 25 CENTS
4.4300 g., Nickel Plated Steel, 23.9 mm. **Ruler:** Elizabeth II **Subject:** Thank You **Obv:** Bust right **Obv. Designer:** Susanna Blunt **Rev:** Colorized

Date	Mintage	MS-63	Proof
2009	4,415	12.50	—

KM# 933 25 CENTS
4.4000 g., Nickel Plated Steel, 23.9 mm. **Ruler:** Elizabeth II **Rev:** Santa Claus, multicolor

Date	Mintage	MS-63	Proof
2009	933	16.50	—

KM# 934 25 CENTS
4.4000 g., Nickel Plated Steel, 23.9 mm. **Ruler:** Elizabeth II **Rev:** Multicolor teddy bear, crescent moon

Date	Mintage	MS-63	Proof
2009	25,182	16.50	—

KM# 935 25 CENTS
4.4000 g., Nickel Plated Steel, 23.9 mm. **Ruler:** Elizabeth II **Subject:** Oh Canada **Rev:** Maple leaves, yellow color

Date	Mintage	MS-63	Proof
2009	14,451	16.50	—

KM# 952 25 CENTS
4.4000 g., Nickel Plated Steel, 23.9 mm. **Ruler:** Elizabeth II **Rev:** Sledge hockey

Date	Mintage	MS-63	Proof
2009	—	3.00	—

KM# 1063 25 CENTS
Nickel Plated Steel **Ruler:** Elizabeth II **Subject:** Men's Hockey **Rev:** Hockey player and maple leaf outline

Date	Mintage	MS-63	Proof
2009	—	2.50	—

KM# 1063a 25 CENTS
Nickel Plated Steel **Ruler:** Elizabeth II **Subject:** Men's Hockey **Rev:** Hockey player and maple leaf outline in red

Date	Mintage	MS-63	Proof
2009	—	7.50	—

KM# 1064 25 CENTS
Nickel Plated Steel, 23.9 mm. **Ruler:** Elizabeth II **Subject:** Women's Hockey **Rev:** Hockey player and maple leaf outline

Date	Mintage	MS-63	Proof
2009	—	2.50	—

KM# 1064a 25 CENTS
Nickel Plated Steel **Ruler:** Elizabeth II **Subject:** Women's Hockey **Rev:** Hockey player and male leaf outline in red

Date	Mintage	MS-63	Proof
2009	—	7.50	—

KM# 1065 25 CENTS
Nickel Plated Steel, 23.9 mm. **Ruler:** Elizabeth II **Subject:** Klassen - Female hockey player **Rev:** Skater and maple leaf outline

Date	Mintage	MS-63	Proof
2009	—	2.50	—

KM# 1065a 25 CENTS
Nickel Plated Steel **Ruler:** Elizabeth II **Subject:** Klassen - female skater **Rev:** Skater and maple leaf outline in red

Date	Mintage	MS-63	Proof
2009	—	7.50	—

KM# 880 25 CENTS
4.4000 g., Nickel Plated Steel, 23.88 mm. **Ruler:** Elizabeth II **Subject:** Miga Mascot Vancouver Olympics **Rev:** Mica Mascot - color **Rev. Legend:** Vancouver 2010 25 cents

Date	Mintage	MS-63	Proof
2010	14,654	3.00	—

KM# 881 25 CENTS
4.4000 g., Nickel Plated Steel, 23.88 mm. **Ruler:** Elizabeth II **Subject:** Quatchi Mascot - Vancouver Olympics **Obv:** Bust right **Rev:** Quatchi Mascot color **Rev. Legend:** Vancouver 2010 25 cents

Date	Mintage	MS-63	Proof
2010	15,310	3.00	—

KM# 882 25 CENTS
4.4000 g., Nickel Plated Steel, 23.88 mm. **Ruler:** Elizabeth II **Subject:** Sumi Mascot **Rev:** Sumi Mascot color **Rev. Legend:** Vancouver 2010 25 cents

Date	Mintage	MS-63	Proof
2010	15,333	3.00	—

KM# 953 25 CENTS
4.4000 g., Nickel Plated Steel, 23.9 mm. **Ruler:** Elizabeth II **Rev:** Ice hockey

Date	Mintage	MS-63	Proof
2010	—	3.00	—

KM# 953a 25 CENTS
4.4000 g., Nickel Plated Steel, 23.9 mm. **Ruler:** Elizabeth II **Rev:** Ice Hockey - red enamel

Date	Mintage	MS-63	Proof
2010	—	8.00	—

KM# 954 25 CENTS
4.4000 g., Nickel Plated Steel, 23.9 mm. **Ruler:** Elizabeth II **Rev:** Curling

Date	Mintage	MS-63	Proof
2010	—	3.00	—

KM# 954a 25 CENTS
4.4000 g., Nickel Plated Steel, 23.9 mm. **Ruler:** Elizabeth II **Rev:** Curling red enamel

Date	Mintage	MS-63	Proof
2010	—	8.00	—

KM# 955 25 CENTS
4.4000 g., Nickel Plated Steel, 23.9 mm. **Ruler:** Elizabeth II **Rev:** Wheelchair curling

Date	Mintage	MS-63	Proof
2010	—	3.00	—

KM# 955a 25 CENTS
4.4000 g., Nickel Plated Steel, 23.9 mm. **Ruler:** Elizabeth II **Rev:** Wheelchair curling - red enamel

Date	Mintage	MS-63	Proof
2010	—	8.00	—

KM# 956 25 CENTS
4.4000 g., Nickel Plated Steel, 23.9 mm. **Ruler:** Elizabeth II **Rev:** Biathlon

Date	Mintage	MS-63	Proof
2010	—	3.00	—

KM# 956a 25 CENTS
4.4000 g., Nickel Plated Steel, 23.9 mm. **Ruler:** Elizabeth II **Rev:** Biathlon - red enamel

Date	Mintage	MS-63	Proof
2010	—	8.00	—

KM# 957 25 CENTS
4.4000 g., Nickel Plated Steel, 23.9 mm. **Ruler:** Elizabeth II **Rev:** Alpine skiing

Date	Mintage	MS-63	Proof
2010	—	3.00	—

KM# 957a 25 CENTS
4.4000 g., Nickel Plated Steel, 23.9 mm. **Ruler:** Elizabeth II **Rev:** Alpine skiing - red enamel

Date	Mintage	MS-63	Proof
2010	—	8.00	—

KM# 958 25 CENTS
4.4000 g., Nickel Plated Steel, 23.9 mm. **Ruler:** Elizabeth II **Rev:** Snowboarding

Date	Mintage	MS-63	Proof
2010	—	3.00	—

KM# 958a 25 CENTS
4.4000 g., Nickel Plated Steel, 23.9 mm. **Ruler:** Elizabeth II **Rev:** Snowboarding - red enamel

Date	Mintage	MS-63	Proof
2010	—	8.00	—

KM# 959 25 CENTS
23.9000 g., Nickel Plated Steel, 23.9 mm. **Ruler:** Elizabeth II **Rev:** Free-style skiing

Date	Mintage	MS-63	Proof
2010	—	3.00	—

KM# 959a 25 CENTS
4.4000 g., Nickel Plated Steel, 23.9 mm. **Ruler:** Elizabeth II **Rev:** Free-style skiing - red enamel

Date	Mintage	MS-63	Proof
2010	—	8.00	—

KM# 960 25 CENTS
4.4000 g., Nickel Plated Steel, 23.9 mm. **Ruler:** Elizabeth II **Rev:** Alpine skiing

Date	Mintage	MS-63	Proof
2010	—	3.00	—

KM# 960a 25 CENTS
4.4000 g., Nickel Plated Steel, 23.9 mm. **Ruler:** Elizabeth II **Rev:** Alpine skiing - red enamel

Date	Mintage	MS-63	Proof
2010	—	8.00	—

KM# 988 25 CENTS
4.4000 g., Nickel Plated Steel, 23.88 mm. **Ruler:** Elizabeth II **Rev:** Blue baby carriage

Date	Mintage	MS-63	Proof
2010	—	10.00	—

KM# 989 25 CENTS
4.4000 g., Nickel Plated Steel, 23.9 mm. **Ruler:** Elizabeth II **Rev:** Purple gift box

Date	Mintage	MS-63	Proof
2010	—	10.00	—

KM# 990 25 CENTS
4.4000 g., Nickel Plated Steel, 23.9 mm. **Ruler:** Elizabeth II **Rev:** Four stars

Date	Mintage	MS-63	Proof
2010	—	10.00	—

KM# 991 25 CENTS
4.4000 g., Nickel Plated Steel, 23.9 mm. **Ruler:** Elizabeth II **Rev:** Three maple leaves

Date	Mintage	MS-63	Proof
2010	—	12.50	—

KM# 992 25 CENTS
4.4000 g., Nickel Plated Steel, 23.9 mm. **Ruler:** Elizabeth II **Rev:** Three zinnias

Date	Mintage	MS-63	Proof
2010	—	12.50	—

KM# 993 25 CENTS
4.4300 g., Nickel Plated Steel, 23.9 mm. **Ruler:** Elizabeth II **Rev:** Pink hearts and roses

Date	Mintage	MS-63	Proof
2010	—	10.00	—

KM# 994 25 CENTS
12.6100 g., Nickel Plated Steel, 35 mm. **Ruler:** Elizabeth II **Rev:** Goldfinch, multicolor **Rev. Designer:** Arnold Nogy

Date	Mintage	MS-63	Proof
2010 Specimen	Est. 14,000	90.00	—

KM# 1001 25 CENTS
12.6100 g., Nickel Plated Steel, 35 mm. **Ruler:** Elizabeth II **Subject:** Blue Jay **Rev:** Multicolor blue jay on yellow maple leaves

Date	Mintage	MS-63	Proof
2010 Specimen	Est. 14,000	90.00	25.00

KM# 1006 25 CENTS
0.5000 g., 0.9990 Gold 0.0161 oz. AGW, 11 mm. **Ruler:** Elizabeth II **Rev:** Caribou head left

Date	Mintage	MS-63	Proof
2010 Proof	15,000	—	80.00

KM# 1021 25 CENTS
Nickel Plated Steel, 23.9 mm. **Ruler:** Elizabeth II **Rev:** Santa Claus in color

Date	Mintage	MS-63	Proof
2010	—	15.00	—

KM# 1026 25 CENTS
Silver, 23.8 mm. **Ruler:** Elizabeth II **Obv:** George V bust left **Rev:** Value within wreath, dual dates below

Date	Mintage	MS-63	Proof
1935-2010 Proof	—	—	25.00

KM# 1028 25 CENTS
4.4000 g., Nickel Plated Steel, 23.9 mm. **Ruler:** Elizabeth II **Rev:** Soldier standing, two red poppies, large maple leaf behind

Date	Mintage	MS-63	Proof
2010	—	15.00	—

KM# 1110 25 CENTS
12.6100 g., Nickel Plated Steel, 35 mm. **Ruler:** Elizabeth II **Subject:** Royal Wedding **Rev:** Colored portraits left of William and Katherine

Date	Mintage	MS-63	Proof
2011 Specimen	—	25.00	—

KM# 1156 25 CENTS
5.9000 g., 0.9250 Silver 0.1755 oz. ASW, 23.8 mm. **Ruler:** Elizabeth II **Obv:** George V bust **Rev:** Value within wreath

Date	Mintage	MS-63	Proof
1911-2011 Proof	6,000	—	25.00

KM# 1079 25 CENTS
12.6100 g., Nickel Plated Steel, 35 mm. **Ruler:** Elizabeth II **Rev:** Barn Swallow in color **Rev. Designer:** Arnold Nagy

Date	Mintage	MS-63	Proof
2011 Specimen	Est. 14,000	55.00	—

KM# 1080 25 CENTS
4.4300 g., Nickel Plated Steel, 23.88 mm. **Ruler:** Elizabeth II **Subject:** Oh Canada! **Rev:** Maple leaf and circular legend

Date	Mintage	MS-63	Proof
2011	—	2.50	—

KM# 1081 25 CENTS
4.4300 g., Nickel Plated Steel, 23.88 mm. **Ruler:** Elizabeth II **Subject:** Wedding **Rev:** Two rings

Date	Mintage	MS-63	Proof
2011	—	2.50	—

KM# 1082 25 CENTS
4.4300 g., Nickel Plated Steel, 23.88 mm. **Ruler:** Elizabeth II **Subject:** Birthday **Rev:** Year in four baloons

Date	Mintage	MS-63	Proof
2011	—	2.50	—

KM# 1083 25 CENTS
4.4300 g., Nickel Plated Steel, 23.88 mm. **Ruler:** Elizabeth II **Subject:** New Baby! **Rev:** Baby's feet

Date	Mintage	MS-63	Proof
2011	—	2.50	—

KM# 1084 25 CENTS
4.4300 g., Nickel Plated Steel, 23.88 mm. **Ruler:** Elizabeth II **Rev:** Tooth Fairy

Date	Mintage	MS-63	Proof
2011	—	2.50	—

KM# 1113 25 CENTS
12.6100 g., Nickel Plated Steel, 35 mm. **Ruler:** Elizabeth II **Rev:** Fantasy Furry Woods creature in color

Date	Mintage	MS-63	Proof
2011	—	20.00	—

KM# 1114 25 CENTS
12.6100 g., Nickel Plated Steel, 35 mm. **Ruler:** Elizabeth II **Rev:** Fantasy sea serpent in color

Date	Mintage	MS-63	Proof
2011	—	20.00	—

KM# 1115 25 CENTS
12.6100 g., Nickel Plated Steel, 35 mm. **Ruler:** Elizabeth II **Rev:** Tulip and ladybug in color

Date	Mintage	MS-63	Proof
2011	—	35.00	—

KM# 1116 25 CENTS
12.6100 g., Nickel Plated Steel, 35 mm. **Ruler:** Elizabeth II **Rev:** Black capped chickadee in color

Date	Mintage	MS-63	Proof
2011 Specimen	—	55.00	—

KM# 1148 25 CENTS
4.4300 g., Nickel Plated Steel, 23.9 mm. **Ruler:** Elizabeth II **Obv:** Bust right **Rev:** Snowflake

Date	Mintage	MS-63	Proof
2011	—	7.50	—

KM# 1168 25 CENTS
4.4000 g., Nickel Plated Steel, 23.9 mm. **Ruler:** Elizabeth II **Obv:** Bust right **Rev:** Stylized bison

Date	Mintage	MS-63	Proof
2011	—	2.50	—

KM# 1168a 25 CENTS
4.4000 g., Nickel Plated Steel with color, 23.9 mm. **Ruler:** Elizabeth II **Obv:** Bust right **Rev:** Stylized bison, green circle in background

Date	Mintage	MS-63	Proof
2011	—	9.50	—

KM# 1169 25 CENTS
4.4000 g., Nickel Plated Steel, 23.9 mm. **Ruler:** Elizabeth II **Obv:** Bust right **Rev:** Stylized falcon

Date	Mintage	MS-63	Proof
2011	—	2.50	—

KM# 1169a 25 CENTS
4.4000 g., Nickel Plated Steel with color, 23.9 mm. **Ruler:** Elizabeth II **Obv:** Bust right **Rev:** Stylized falcon with yellow circle in background

Date	Mintage	MS-63	Proof
2011	—	9.50	—

KM# 1170 25 CENTS
4.4000 g., Nickel Plated Steel, 23.9 mm. **Ruler:** Elizabeth II **Obv:** Bust right **Rev:** Stylized orca whale

Date	Mintage	MS-63	Proof
2011	—	2.50	—

KM# 1170a 25 CENTS
4.4000 g., Nickel Plated Steel with color, 23.9 mm. **Ruler:** Elizabeth II **Obv:** Bust right **Rev:** Stylized orca whale with blue circle in background

Date	Mintage	MS-63	Proof
2011	—	9.50	—

KM# 1171 25 CENTS
0.5000 g., 0.9990 Gold 0.0161 oz. AGW, 11 mm. **Ruler:** Elizabeth II **Obv:** Bust right **Rev:** Cougar head left

Date	Mintage	MS-63	Proof
2011 Proof	—	—	80.00

KM# 1172 25 CENTS
12.6100 g., Copper Plated Silver gold plated, 35 mm. **Ruler:** Elizabeth II **Obv:** Bust right **Rev:** Wayne Greskey in hockey helmet left

Date	Mintage	MS-63	Proof
2011 Specimen	—	35.00	—

KM# 1192 25 CENTS
4.4300 g., Nickel Plated Steel, 23.9 mm. **Ruler:** Elizabeth II **Subject:** Canadian Broadcasting Company, 75th Anniversary **Obv:** Bust right **Rev:** Old-time radio microphone

Date	Mintage	MS-63	Proof
2011	—	2.50	—

KM# 1193 25 CENTS
12.6100 g., Nickel Plated Steel, 35 mm. **Ruler:** Elizabeth II **Subject:** Mythical Creature - Mishepishu **Obv:** Bust right **Rev:** Horned lizard in color

Date	Mintage	MS-63	Proof
2011	—	15.00	—

KM# 1227 25 CENTS
4.4300 g., Nickel Plated Steel, 23.9 mm. **Ruler:** Elizabeth II **Obv:** Bust right **Rev:** Tooth Fairy in flight

Date	Mintage	MS-63	Proof
2012	—	2.50	—

KM# 1228 25 CENTS
4.4300 g., Nickel Plated Steel, 23.9 mm. **Ruler:** Elizabeth II **Subject:** Baby **Rev:** Baby's mobile

Date	Mintage	MS-63	Proof
2012	—	2.50	—

KM# 1229 25 CENTS
4.4300 g., Nickel Plated Steel, 23.9 mm. **Ruler:** Elizabeth II **Subject:** Wedding **Rev:** Two wedding rings with small feet

Date	Mintage	MS-63	Proof
2012	—	2.50	—

KM# 1230 25 CENTS
4.4300 g., Nickel Plated Steel, 23.9 mm. **Ruler:** Elizabeth II **Subject:** Birthday **Rev:** Cone with character face

Date	Mintage	MS-63	Proof
2012	—	2.50	—

KM# 1231 25 CENTS
4.4300 g., Nickel Plated Steel, 23.9 mm. **Ruler:** Elizabeth II **Subject:** Oh, Canada ! **Rev:** Maple leaves with character faces

Date	Mintage	MS-63	Proof
2012	—	2.50	—

KM# 1232 25 CENTS
4.4300 g., Nickel Plated Steel, 23.88 mm. **Ruler:** Elizabeth II **Subject:** Winnipeg Jets **Rev:** Jet superimposed on Maple leaf

Date	Mintage	MS-63	Proof
2012	—	2.50	—

KM# 1233 25 CENTS
12.6100 g., Nickel Plated Steel, 35 mm. **Ruler:** Elizabeth II **Subject:** Titanic, 100th Anniversary **Obv:** Bust right **Rev:** Two views of Titanic, one at dockside, one nighttime at sea

Date	Mintage	MS-63	Proof
2012	—	20.00	—

KM# 1247 25 CENTS
12.6100 g., Nickel Plated Steel, 35 mm. **Ruler:** Elizabeth II **Subject:** Coast Guard, 100th anniversary **Rev:** Rescue craft in rough seas

Date	Mintage	MS-63	Proof
2012	—	30.00	—

KM# 1252 25 CENTS
12.6100 g., Nickel Plated Steel, 35 mm. **Ruler:** Elizabeth II **Subject:** Pachyrhinosaurus Lakusta **Note:** Skelton glows in the dark.

Date	Mintage	MS-63	Proof
2012	—	25.00	—

KM# 1253 25 CENTS
12.6100 g., Nickel Plated Steel, 35 mm. **Ruler:** Elizabeth II **Subject:** Rose Breasted Grosbeak

Date	Mintage	MS-63	Proof
2012	—	35.00	—

KM# 1265 25 CENTS
12.6100 g., Nickel Plated Steel, 35 mm. **Ruler:** Elizabeth II **Subject:** Aster and Bee

Date	Mintage	MS-63	Proof
2012	—	35.00	—

KM# 1313 25 CENTS
0.5000 g., Silver, 35 mm. **Ruler:** Elizabeth II **Subject:** Grey Cup, 100th Anniversary **Obv:** Bust right **Obv. Designer:** Susana Blunt **Rev:** B.C. Lions logo in color

Date	Mintage	MS-63	Proof
2012 Proof	—	—	25.00

KM# 1314 25 CENTS
0.5000 g., Copper-Nickel, 35 mm. **Ruler:** Elizabeth II **Subject:** Grey Cup, 100th Anniversary **Obv:** Bust right **Obv. Designer:** Susana Blunt **Rev:** Calgary Stampeeders logo in color

Date	Mintage	MS-63	Proof
2012 Proof	—	—	25.00

KM# 1315 25 CENTS
0.5000 g., Copper-Nickel, 35 mm. **Ruler:** Elizabeth II **Subject:** Grey Cup, 100th Anniversary **Obv:** Bust right **Obv. Designer:** Susana Blunt **Rev:** Edmonton Eskimos logo in color

Date	Mintage	MS-63	Proof
2012 Proof	—	—	25.00

KM# 1316 25 CENTS
0.5000 g., Copper-Nickel, 35 mm. **Ruler:** Elizabeth II **Subject:** Grey Cup, 100th Anniversary **Obv:** Bust right **Obv. Designer:** Susana Blunt **Rev:** Hamilton Tiger-Cats logo in color

Date	Mintage	MS-63	Proof
2012 Proof	—	—	25.00

KM# 1317 25 CENTS
0.5000 g., Copper-Nickel, 35 mm. **Ruler:** Elizabeth II **Subject:** Grey Cup, 100th Anniversary **Obv:** Bust right **Obv. Designer:** Susana Blunt **Rev:** Montreal Alouettes logo in color

Date	Mintage	MS-63	Proof
2012 Proof	—	—	25.00

KM# 1318 25 CENTS
0.5000 g., Copper-Nickel, 35 mm. **Ruler:** Elizabeth II **Subject:** Grey Cup, 100th Anniversary **Obv:** Bust right **Obv. Designer:** Susana Blunt **Rev:** Saskatchewan Roughriders logo in color

Date	Mintage	MS-63	Proof
2012 Proof	—	—	25.00

KM# 1319 25 CENTS
0.5000 g., Copper-Nickel, 35 mm. **Ruler:** Elizabeth II **Subject:** Grey Cup, 100th Anniversary **Obv:** Bust right **Obv. Designer:** Susana Blunt **Rev:** Toronto Argonauts logo in color

Date	Mintage	MS-63	Proof
2012 Proof	—	—	25.00

KM# 1320 25 CENTS
0.5000 g., Copper-Nickel, 35 mm. **Ruler:** Elizabeth II **Subject:** Grey Cup, 100th Anniversary **Obv:** Bust right **Obv. Designer:** Susana Blunt **Rev:** Winnipeg Blue Bombers logo in color

Date	Mintage	MS-63	Proof
2012 Proof	—	—	25.00

KM# 290 50 CENTS
8.1000 g., Nickel, 27.1 mm. **Ruler:** Elizabeth II **Obv:** Crowned head right **Obv. Designer:** Dora dePedery-Hunt **Rev:** Redesigned arms **Rev. Designer:** Cathy Bursey-Sabourin **Edge:** Reeded

Date	Mintage	MS-63	Proof
2001P	—	1.50	—
2001P Proof	—	—	5.00
2003P	—	1.50	—
2003P Proof	—	—	5.00

KM# 290b 50 CENTS
6.9000 g., Nickel Plated Steel, 27.13 mm. **Ruler:** Elizabeth II **Obv:** Crowned head right **Obv. Designer:** Dora dePedery-Hunt **Rev:** Redesigned arms **Rev. Designer:** Cathy Bursey-Sabourin **Edge:** Reeded

Date	Mintage	MS-63	Proof
2001 P	389,000	1.50	—
2003 P	—	5.00	—

KM# 290a 50 CENTS
11.6640 g., 0.9250 Silver 0.3469 oz. ASW, 27.13 mm. **Ruler:** Elizabeth II **Obv:** Crowned head right **Obv. Designer:** Dora dePedery-Hunt **Rev:** Redesigned arms **Rev. Designer:** Cathy Bursey-Sabourin **Edge:** Reeded

Date	Mintage	MS-63	Proof
2001 Proof	—	—	13.00
2003 Proof	—	—	13.00

KM# 420 50 CENTS
9.3000 g., 0.9250 Silver 0.2766 oz. ASW, 27.13 mm. **Ruler:** Elizabeth II **Series:** Festivals - Quebec **Obv:** Crowned head right **Rev:** Snowman and Chateau Frontenac **Rev. Designer:** Sylvie Daigneault **Edge:** Reeded

Date	Mintage	MS-63	Proof
2001 Proof	58,123	—	8.50

KM# 421 50 CENTS
9.3000 g., 0.9250 Silver 0.2766 oz. ASW, 27.13 mm. **Ruler:** Elizabeth II **Series:** Festivals - Nunavut **Obv:** Crowned head right **Rev:** Dancer, dog sled and snowmobiles **Rev. Designer:** John Mardon **Edge:** Reeded

Date	Mintage	MS-63	Proof
2001 Proof	58,123	—	8.50

KM# 422 50 CENTS
9.3000 g., 0.9250 Silver 0.2766 oz. ASW, 27.13 mm. **Ruler:** Elizabeth II **Series:** Festivals - Newfoundland **Obv:** Crowned head right **Rev:** Sailor and musical people **Rev. Designer:** David Craig **Edge:** Reeded

Date	Mintage	MS-63	Proof
2001 Proof	58,123	—	8.50

KM# 423 50 CENTS
9.3000 g., 0.9250 Silver 0.2766 oz. ASW, 27.13 mm. **Ruler:** Elizabeth II **Series:** Festivals - Prince Edward Island **Obv:** Crowned head right **Rev:** Family, juggler and building **Rev. Designer:** Brenda Whiteway **Edge:** Reeded

Date	Mintage	MS-63	Proof
2001 Proof	58,123	—	8.50

KM# 424 50 CENTS
9.3000 g., 0.9250 Silver 0.2766 oz. ASW, 27.13 mm. **Ruler:** Elizabeth II **Series:** Folklore - The Sled **Obv:** Crowned head right **Rev:** Family scene **Rev. Designer:** Valentina Hotz-Entin **Edge:** Reeded

Date	Mintage	MS-63	Proof
2001 Proof	28,979	—	9.00

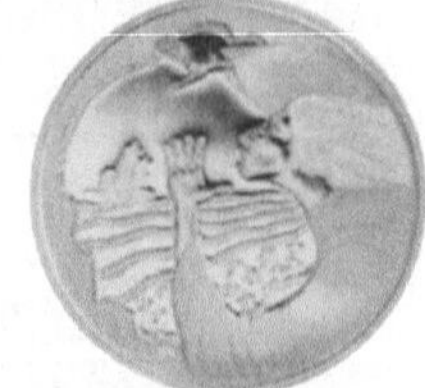

KM# 425 50 CENTS
9.3000 g., 0.9250 Silver 0.2766 oz. ASW, 27.13 mm. **Ruler:** Elizabeth II **Series:** Folklore - The Maiden's Cave **Obv:** Crowned head right **Rev:** Woman shouting **Rev. Designer:** Peter Kiss **Edge:** Reeded

Date	Mintage	MS-63	Proof
2001 Proof	28,979	—	9.00

KM# 426 50 CENTS
9.3000 g., 0.9250 Silver 0.2766 oz. ASW, 27.13 mm. **Ruler:** Elizabeth II **Series:** Folklore - The Small Jumpers **Obv:** Crowned head right **Rev:** Jumping children on seashore **Rev. Designer:** Miynki Tanobe **Edge:** Reeded

Date	Mintage	MS-63	Proof
2001 Proof	28,979	—	9.00

KM# 509 50 CENTS
6.9000 g., Nickel Plated Steel, 27.13 mm. **Ruler:** Elizabeth II **Obv:** Crowned head right **Rev:** National arms **Edge:** Reeded

Date	Mintage	MS-63	Proof
2001 P	—	1.50	—

KM# 444 50 CENTS
6.9000 g., Nickel Plated Steel, 27.13 mm. **Ruler:** Elizabeth II **Subject:** Queen's Golden Jubilee **Obv:** Coronation crowned head right and monogram **Rev:** Canadian arms **Rev. Designer:** Bursey Sabourin **Edge:** Reeded

Date	Mintage	MS-63	Proof
1952-2002P	14,440,000	2.50	—

KM# 444a 50 CENTS
9.3000 g., 0.9250 Silver 0.2766 oz. ASW, 27.13 mm. **Ruler:** Elizabeth II **Subject:** Elizabeth II Golden Jubilee **Obv:** Crowned head right, Jubilee commemorative dates 1952-2002

Date	Mintage	MS-63	Proof
1952-2002 Proof	100,000	—	17.50

KM# 444b 50 CENTS
9.3000 g., 0.9250 Silver Gilt 0.2766 oz. ASW, 27.13 mm. **Ruler:** Elizabeth II **Subject:** Queen's Golden Jubilee **Obv:** Crowned head right and monogram **Rev:** Canadian arms **Edge:** Reeded
Note: Special 24 karat gold-plated issue of KM#444.

Date	Mintage	MS-63	Proof
1952-2002 Proof	32,642	—	35.00

KM# 454 50 CENTS
9.3000 g., 0.9250 Silver 0.2766 oz. ASW, 27.13 mm. **Ruler:** Elizabeth II **Subject:** Nova Scotia Annapolis Valley Apple Blossom Festival **Obv:** Crowned head right **Rev. Designer:** Bonnie Ross

Date	Mintage	MS-63	Proof
2002 Proof	59,998	—	9.50

KM# 455 50 CENTS
9.3000 g., 0.9250 Silver 0.2766 oz. ASW, 27.13 mm. **Ruler:** Elizabeth II **Subject:** Stratford Festival **Obv:** Crowned head right **Rev:** Couple with building in background **Rev. Designer:** Laurie McGaw

Date	Mintage	MS-63	Proof
2002 Proof	59,998	—	9.50

KM# 456 50 CENTS
9.3000 g., 0.9250 Silver 0.2766 oz. ASW, 27.13 mm. **Ruler:** Elizabeth II **Subject:** Folklorama **Obv:** Crowned head right **Rev. Designer:** William Woodruff

Date	Mintage	MS-63	Proof
2002 Proof	59,998	—	9.50

KM# 457 50 CENTS
9.3000 g., 0.9250 Silver 0.2766 oz. ASW, 27.13 mm. **Ruler:** Elizabeth II **Subject:** Calgary Stampede **Obv:** Crowned head right **Rev. Designer:** Stan Witten

Date	Mintage	MS-63	Proof
2002 Proof	59,998	—	9.50

KM# 458 50 CENTS
9.3000 g., 0.9250 Silver 0.2766 oz. ASW, 27.13 mm. **Ruler:** Elizabeth II **Subject:** Squamish Days Logger Sports **Obv:** Crowned head right **Rev. Designer:** Jose Osio

Date	Mintage	MS-63	Proof
2002 Proof	59,998	—	9.50

KM# 459 50 CENTS
9.3000 g., 0.9250 Silver 0.2766 oz. ASW, 27.13 mm. **Ruler:** Elizabeth II **Series:** Folklore and Legends **Obv:** Crowned head right **Rev:** The Shoemaker in Heaven **Rev. Designer:** Francine Gravel

Date	Mintage	MS-63	Proof
2002 Proof	19,267	—	11.00

KM# 460 50 CENTS
9.3000 g., 0.9250 Silver 0.2766 oz. ASW, 27.13 mm. **Ruler:** Elizabeth II **Series:** Folklore and Legends **Subject:** The Ghost Ship **Obv:** Crowned head right **Rev. Designer:** Colette Boivin

Date	Mintage	MS-63	Proof
2002 Proof	19,267	—	11.00

KM# 461 50 CENTS
9.3000 g., 0.9250 Silver 0.2766 oz. ASW, 27.13 mm. **Ruler:** Elizabeth II **Series:** Folklore and Legends **Subject:** The Pig That Wouldn't Get Over the Stile **Obv:** Crowned head right **Rev. Designer:** Laura Jolicoeur

Date	Mintage	MS-63	Proof
2002 Proof	19,267	—	11.00

KM# 494 50 CENTS
6.9000 g., Nickel Plated Steel, 27.13 mm. **Ruler:** Elizabeth II **Obv:** Crowned head right **Obv. Designer:** Susanna Blunt **Rev:** National arms **Rev. Designer:** Cathy Bursey-Sabourin **Edge:** Reeded

Date	Mintage	MS-63	Proof
2003P W	—	5.00	—
2003P W Proof	—	—	7.50
2004P	—	5.00	—
2004P Proof	—	—	7.50
2005P	200,000	1.50	—
2005P Proof	—	—	5.00
2006P	98,000	1.50	—
2006P Proof	—	—	5.00
2007(ml)	250,000	1.50	—
2007(ml) Proof	—	—	5.00
2008(ml)	211,000	1.50	—
2008(ml) Proof	—	—	5.00
2009(ml)	150,000	1.50	—
2009(ml) Proof	—	—	5.00
2010(ml)	—	1.50	—
2010(ml) Proof	—	—	5.00
2011(ml)	—	1.50	—
2011(ml) Proof	—	—	5.00
2012(ml)	—	1.50	—
2012(ml) Proof	—	—	5.00
2013(ml)	—	1.50	—
2013(ml) Proof	—	—	5.00

KM# 472 50 CENTS
11.6200 g., 0.9250 Silver 0.3456 oz. ASW, 27.13 mm. **Ruler:** Elizabeth II **Subject:** 50th Anniversary of the Coronation of Elizabeth II **Obv:** Crowned head right, Jubilee commemorative dates 1952-2002 **Obv. Designer:** Mary Gillick

Date	Mintage	MS-63	Proof
2003 Proof	30,000	—	15.00

KM# 475 50 CENTS
9.3000 g., 0.9250 Silver 0.2766 oz. ASW, 27.13 mm. **Ruler:** Elizabeth II **Obv:** Crowned head right **Obv. Designer:** Dora dePédery-Hunt **Rev:** Golden daffodil **Rev. Designer:** Christie Paquet, Stan Witten

Date	Mintage	MS-63	Proof
2003 Proof	36,293	—	25.00

KM# 476 50 CENTS
9.3000 g., 0.9250 Silver 0.2766 oz. ASW, 27.13 mm. **Ruler:** Elizabeth II **Subject:** Yukon International Storytelling Festival **Obv:** Crowned head right **Obv. Designer:** Dora dePédery-Hunt **Rev. Designer:** Ken Anderson, Jose Oslo

Date	Mintage	MS-63	Proof
2003 Proof	—	—	11.00

KM# 477 50 CENTS
9.3000 g., 0.9250 Silver 0.2766 oz. ASW, 27.13 mm. **Ruler:** Elizabeth II **Subject:** Festival Acadien de Caraquet **Obv:** Crowned head right **Obv. Designer:** Dora dePédery-Hunt **Rev:** Sailboat and couple **Rev. Designer:** Susan Taylor, Hudson Design Group

Date	Mintage	MS-63	Proof
2003 Proof	—	—	11.00

KM# 478 50 CENTS
9.3000 g., 0.9250 Silver 0.2766 oz. ASW, 27.13 mm. **Ruler:** Elizabeth II **Subject:** Back to Batoche **Obv:** Crowned head right **Obv. Designer:** Dora dePédery-Hunt **Rev. Designer:** David Hannan, Stan Witten

Date	Mintage	MS-63	Proof
2003 Proof	—	—	11.00

KM# 479 50 CENTS
9.3000 g., 0.9250 Silver 0.2766 oz. ASW, 27.13 mm. **Ruler:** Elizabeth II **Subject:** Great Northern Arts Festival **Obv:** Crowned head right **Obv. Designer:** Dora dePédery-Hunt **Rev. Designer:** Dawn Oman, Susan Taylor

Date	Mintage	MS-63	Proof
2003 Proof	—	—	11.00

KM# 494a 50 CENTS
9.3000 g., 0.9250 Silver 0.2766 oz. ASW, 27.13 mm. **Ruler:** Elizabeth II **Obv:** Crowned head right **Obv. Designer:** Susanna Blunt **Rev:** Canadian coat of arms **Edge:** Reeded

Date	Mintage	MS-63	Proof
2004 Proof	—	—	7.50

KM# 526 50 CENTS
1.2700 g., 0.9999 Gold 0.0408 oz. AGW, 14 mm. **Ruler:** Elizabeth II **Subject:** Moose **Obv:** Head right **Rev:** Moose head facing right

Date	Mintage	MS-63	Proof
2004 Proof	—	—	85.00

KM# 606 50 CENTS
9.3000 g., 0.9250 Silver 0.2766 oz. ASW, 27.13 mm. **Ruler:** Elizabeth II **Obv:** Head right **Obv. Designer:** Susanna Blunt **Rev:** Clouded Sulphur Butterfly, hologram **Rev. Designer:** Susan Taylor

Date	Mintage	MS-63	Proof
2004 Proof	15,281	—	45.00

KM# 712 50 CENTS
9.3000 g., 0.9250 Silver 0.2766 oz. ASW, 27.13 mm. **Ruler:** Elizabeth II **Rev:** Hologram of Tiger Swallowtail butterfly

Date	Mintage	MS-63	Proof
2004 Proof	20,462	—	45.00

KM# 536 50 CENTS
9.3000 g., 0.9250 Silver with partial gold plating 0.2766 oz. ASW, 27.13 mm. **Ruler:** Elizabeth II **Subject:** Golden rose **Obv:** Head right **Obv. Designer:** Susanna Blunt **Rev. Designer:** Christie Paquet

Date	Mintage	MS-63	Proof
2005 Proof	17,418	—	40.00

KM# 537 50 CENTS
9.3000 g., 0.9250 Silver 0.2766 oz. ASW, 27.13 mm. **Ruler:** Elizabeth II **Obv:** Head right **Obv. Designer:** Susanna Blunt **Rev:** Great Spangled Fritillary butterfly, hologram **Rev. Designer:** Jianping Yan

Date	Mintage	MS-63	Proof
2005 Proof	20,000	—	50.00

KM# 538 50 CENTS
9.3000 g., 0.9250 Silver 0.2766 oz. ASW, 27.13 mm. **Ruler:** Elizabeth II **Subject:** Toronto Maple Leafs **Obv:** Head right **Obv. Designer:** Susanna Blunt **Rev:** Darryl Sittler

Date	Mintage	MS-63	Proof
2005 Specimen	25,000	—	16.00

KM# 539 50 CENTS
9.3000 g., 0.9250 Silver 0.2766 oz. ASW, 27.13 mm. **Ruler:** Elizabeth II **Subject:** Toronto Maple Leafs **Obv:** Head right **Obv. Designer:** Susanna Blunt **Rev:** Dave Keon

Date	Mintage	MS-63	Proof
2005 Specimen	25,000	—	16.00

KM# 540 50 CENTS
9.3000 g., 0.9250 Silver 0.2766 oz. ASW, 27.13 mm. **Ruler:** Elizabeth II **Subject:** Toronto Maple Leafs **Obv:** Head right **Obv. Designer:** Susanna Blunt **Rev:** Jonny Bover, goalie

Date	Mintage	MS-63	Proof
2005 Specimen	25,000	—	16.00

KM# 541 50 CENTS
9.3000 g., 0.9250 Silver 0.2766 oz. ASW, 27.13 mm. **Ruler:** Elizabeth II **Subject:** Toronto Maple Leafs **Obv:** Head right **Obv. Designer:** Susanna Blunt **Rev:** Tim Horton

Date	Mintage	MS-63	Proof
2005 Specimen	25,000	—	16.00

KM# 543 50 CENTS
9.3000 g., 0.9250 Silver 0.2766 oz. ASW **Ruler:** Elizabeth II **Subject:** WWII - Battle of Britain **Obv:** Head right **Rev:** Fighter plane in sky

Date	Mintage	MS-63	Proof
2005 Specimen	20,000	—	22.50

KM# 544 50 CENTS
9.3000 g., 0.9250 Silver 0.2766 oz. ASW, 27.13 mm. **Ruler:** Elizabeth II **Subject:** WWII - Battle of Scheldt **Obv:** Head right **Obv. Designer:** Susanna Blunt **Rev:** Four soldiers walking down road **Rev. Designer:** Peter Mossman

Date	Mintage	MS-63	Proof
2005 Specimen	20,000	—	19.00

KM# 545 50 CENTS
9.3000 g., 0.9250 Silver 0.2766 oz. ASW, 27.13 mm. **Ruler:** Elizabeth II **Subject:** WWII - Battle of the Atlantic **Obv:** Head right **Obv. Designer:** Susanna Blunt **Rev:** Merchant ship sinking **Rev. Designer:** Peter Mossman

Date	Mintage	MS-63	Proof
2005 Specimen	20,000	—	19.00

KM# 546 50 CENTS
9.3000 g., 0.9250 Silver 0.2766 oz. ASW, 27.13 mm. **Ruler:** Elizabeth II **Subject:** WWII - Conquest of Sicily **Obv:** Head right **Obv. Designer:** Susanna Blunt **Rev:** Tank among town ruins **Rev. Designer:** Peter Mossman

Date	Mintage	MS-63	Proof
2005 Specimen	20,000	—	19.00

KM# 547 50 CENTS
9.3000 g., 0.9250 Silver 0.2766 oz. ASW, 27.13 mm. **Ruler:** Elizabeth II **Subject:** WWII - Liberation of the Netherlands **Obv:** Head right **Obv. Designer:** Susanna Blunt **Rev:** Soldiers in parade, one holding flag **Rev. Designer:** Peter Mossman

Date	Mintage	MS-63	Proof
2005 Specimen	20,000	—	19.00

KM# 548 50 CENTS
9.3000 g., 0.9250 Silver 0.2766 oz. ASW, 27.13 mm. **Ruler:** Elizabeth II **Subject:** WWII - Raid of Dieppe **Obv:** Head right **Obv. Designer:** Susanna Blunt **Rev:** Three soldiers exiting landing craft **Rev. Designer:** Peter Mossman

Date	Mintage	MS-63	Proof
2005 Specimen	20,000	—	19.00

KM# 577 50 CENTS
9.3000 g., 0.9250 Silver 0.2766 oz. ASW, 27.13 mm. **Ruler:** Elizabeth II **Subject:** Montreal Canadiens **Obv:** Head right **Obv. Designer:** Susanna Blunt **Rev:** Guy LaFleur

Date	Mintage	MS-63	Proof
2005 Specimen	25,000	—	17.50

KM# 578 50 CENTS

9.3000 g., 0.9250 Silver 0.2766 oz. ASW, 27.13 mm. **Ruler:** Elizabeth II **Subject:** Montreal Canadiens **Obv:** Head right **Obv. Designer:** Susanna Blunt **Rev:** Jaque Plante

Date	Mintage	MS-63	Proof
2005 Specimen	25,000	—	17.50

KM# 579 50 CENTS

9.3000 g., 0.9250 Silver 0.2766 oz. ASW, 27.13 mm. **Ruler:** Elizabeth II **Subject:** Montreal Canadiens **Obv:** Head right **Obv. Designer:** Susanna Blunt **Rev:** Jean Beliveau

Date	Mintage	MS-63	Proof
2005 Specimen	25,000	—	17.50

KM# 580 50 CENTS

9.3000 g., 0.9250 Silver 0.2766 oz. ASW, 27.13 mm. **Ruler:** Elizabeth II **Subject:** Montreal Canadiens **Obv:** Head right **Obv. Designer:** Susanna Blunt **Rev:** Maurice Richard

Date	Mintage	MS-63	Proof
2005 Specimen	25,000	—	17.50

KM# 599 50 CENTS

9.3000 g., 0.9250 Silver 0.2766 oz. ASW, 27.13 mm. **Ruler:** Elizabeth II **Obv:** Head right **Obv. Designer:** Susanna Blunt **Rev:** Monarch butterfly, colorized **Rev. Designer:** Susan Taylor

Date	Mintage	MS-63	Proof
2005 Proof	20,000	—	50.00

KM# 648 50 CENTS

9.3000 g., 0.9250 Silver partially gilt 0.2766 oz. ASW **Ruler:** Elizabeth II **Subject:** Golden Daisy **Obv:** Head right

Date	Mintage	MS-63	Proof
2006 Proof	18,190	—	30.00

KM# 649 50 CENTS

9.3000 g., 0.9250 Silver 0.2766 oz. ASW, 27.13 mm. **Ruler:** Elizabeth II **Subject:** Short-tailed swallowtail **Obv:** Head right **Rev:** Colorized butterfly

Date	Mintage	MS-63	Proof
2006 Proof	24,568	—	45.00

KM# 650 50 CENTS

9.3000 g., 0.9250 Silver 0.2766 oz. ASW, 27.13 mm. **Ruler:** Elizabeth II **Obv:** Head right **Rev:** Butterfly, silvery blue hologram

Date	Mintage	MS-63	Proof
2006 Proof	16,000	—	45.00

KM# 651 50 CENTS

9.3000 g., 0.9250 Silver 0.2766 oz. ASW **Ruler:** Elizabeth II **Subject:** Cowboy **Obv:** Head right

Date	Mintage	MS-63	Proof
2006	—	17.50	—

KM# 494b 50 CENTS

6.9000 g., Nickel Plated Steel partially gilt, 27.13 mm. **Ruler:** Elizabeth II **Rev:** State Arms, gilt **Note:** Housed in Mint Annual Report

Date	Mintage	MS-63	Proof
2006	—	15.00	—

KM# 716 50 CENTS

9.3000 g., 0.9250 Silver 0.2766 oz. ASW **Ruler:** Elizabeth II **Rev:** Multicolor holiday ornaments

Date	Mintage	MS-63	Proof
2006	16,989	17.50	—

KM# 715 50 CENTS

9.3000 g., 0.9250 Silver with partial gold plating 0.2766 oz. ASW, 27.12 mm. **Ruler:** Elizabeth II **Rev:** Forget-me-not flower

Date	Mintage	MS-63	Proof
2007 Proof	22,882	—	29.00

KM# 778 50 CENTS

20.0000 g., 0.9250 Silver colorized green 0.5948 oz. ASW, 34.06 mm. **Ruler:** Elizabeth II **Subject:** Milk delivery **Obv:** Bust right **Rev:** Cow head and milk can **Shape:** Triangle

Date	Mintage	MS-63	Proof
2008 Proof	24,448	—	35.00

KM# 779 50 CENTS

9.3000 g., 0.9250 Silver 0.2766 oz. ASW, 35 mm. **Ruler:** Elizabeth II **Rev:** Multicolor snowman

Date	Mintage	MS-63	Proof
2008	21,679	17.50	—

KM# 780 50 CENTS

9.3000 g., 0.9250 Silver 0.2766 oz. ASW **Ruler:** Elizabeth II **Subject:** Ottawa Mint Centennial 1908-2008

Date	Mintage	MS-63	Proof
2008 Proof	3,248	—	20.00

KM# 845 50 CENTS

9.3000 g., 0.9250 Silver 0.2766 oz. ASW, 27.13 mm. **Ruler:** Elizabeth II **Rev:** Calgary Flames lenticular design, old and new logos

Date	Mintage	MS-63	Proof
2009	—	12.00	—

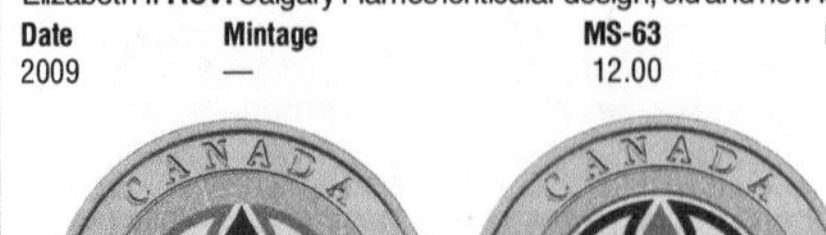

KM# 846 50 CENTS

9.3000 g., 0.9250 Silver 0.2766 oz. ASW, 27.13 mm. **Ruler:** Elizabeth II **Rev:** Edmonton Oiler's lenticular design, old and new logos

Date	Mintage	MS-63	Proof
2009	—	12.00	—

KM# 847 50 CENTS

9.3000 g., 0.9250 Silver 0.2766 oz. ASW, 27.13 mm. **Ruler:** Elizabeth II **Rev:** Montreal Canadiens lenticular design, old and new logos

Date	Mintage	MS-63	Proof
2009	—	12.00	—

KM# 848 50 CENTS

9.3000 g., 0.9250 Silver 0.2766 oz. ASW, 27.13 mm. **Ruler:** Elizabeth II **Rev:** Ottawa Senators lenticular design, old and new logos

Date	Mintage	MS-63	Proof
2009	—	12.00	—

KM# 849 50 CENTS

9.3000 g., 0.9250 Silver 0.2766 oz. ASW, 27.13 mm. **Ruler:** Elizabeth II **Rev:** Toronto Maple Leafs lenticular design, old and new logos

Date	Mintage	MS-63	Proof
2009	—	12.00	—

KM# 850 50 CENTS

9.3000 g., 0.9250 Silver 0.2766 oz. ASW, 27.13 mm. **Ruler:** Elizabeth II **Rev:** Vancouver Canucks lenticular design, old and new logos

Date	Mintage	MS-63	Proof
2009	—	12.00	—

KM# 857 50 CENTS

6.9000 g., Nickel Plated Steel, 35 mm. **Ruler:** Elizabeth II **Rev:** Calgary Flames lenticular old and new logos

Date	Mintage	MS-63	Proof
2009	—	25.00	—

KM# 858 50 CENTS

6.9000 g., Nickel Plated Steel, 35 mm. **Ruler:** Elizabeth II **Rev:** Edmonton Oilers lenticular old and new logos

Date	Mintage	MS-63	Proof
2009	—	25.00	—

KM# 859 50 CENTS

35.0000 g., Nickel Plated Steel, 35 mm. **Ruler:** Elizabeth II **Rev:** Montreal Canadians lenticular old and new logo

Date	Mintage	MS-63	Proof
2009	—	25.00	—

KM# 860 50 CENTS

6.9000 g., Nickel Plated Steel, 35 mm. **Ruler:** Elizabeth II **Rev:** Ottawa Senators lenticular old and new logos

Date	Mintage	MS-63	Proof
2009	—	25.00	—

KM# 861 50 CENTS

6.9000 g., Nickel Plated Steel, 35 mm. **Ruler:** Elizabeth II **Rev:** Toronto Maple Leafs lenticular old and new logos

Date	Mintage	MS-63	Proof
2009	—	25.00	—

KM# 862 50 CENTS

6.9000 g., Nickel Plated Steel, 35 mm. **Ruler:** Elizabeth II **Rev:** Vancouver Canucks lenticular old and new logos

Date	Mintage	MS-63	Proof
2009	—	25.00	—

KM# 887 50 CENTS
19.1000 g., Copper-Nickel, 34.06 mm. **Ruler:** Elizabeth II **Subject:** Six-string national guitar **Obv:** Bust right **Obv. Legend:** Elizabeth II DG Regina **Obv. Designer:** Susanna Blunt **Rev:** Hologram with 6 "strings" **Rev. Legend:** 50 CENTS Canada **Shape:** Triangle

Date	Mintage	MS-63	Proof
2009 Proof	13,602	—	50.00

KM# 936 50 CENTS
9.3000 g., Nickel **Ruler:** Elizabeth II **Rev:** Vancouver Canucks goalie jersey

Date	Mintage	MS-63	Proof
2009	3,563	15.00	—

KM# 937 50 CENTS
6.9000 g., Nickel Plated Steel, 35 mm. **Ruler:** Elizabeth II **Rev:** Calgary Flames player - colorized

Date	Mintage	MS-63	Proof
2009	3,518	15.00	—

KM# 938 50 CENTS
6.9000 g., Nickel Plated Steel, 35 mm. **Ruler:** Elizabeth II **Rev:** Edmonton Oilers player

Date	Mintage	MS-63	Proof
2009	3,562	15.00	—

KM# 939 50 CENTS
6.9000 g., Nickel Plated Steel, 35 mm. **Ruler:** Elizabeth II **Rev:** Toronto Maple Leafs player

Date	Mintage	MS-63	Proof
2009	5,918	15.00	—

KM# 940 50 CENTS
6.9000 g., Nickel Plated Steel, 35 mm. **Ruler:** Elizabeth II **Rev:** Montreal Canadiens player

Date	Mintage	MS-63	Proof
2009	9,865	15.00	—

KM# 941 50 CENTS
6.9000 g., Nickel Plated Steel, 35 mm. **Ruler:** Elizabeth II **Rev:** Ottawa Senators player

Date	Mintage	MS-63	Proof
2009	3,293	15.00	—

KM# 1035 50 CENTS
12.6100 g., Brass Plated Steel, 35 mm. **Ruler:** Elizabeth II **Subject:** Christmas toy train **Rev:** movement from far to close

Date	Mintage	MS-63	Proof
2009	19,103	17.50	—

KM# 961 50 CENTS
6.9000 g., Nickel Plated Steel, 35 mm. **Ruler:** Elizabeth II **Rev:** Bob sleigh

Date	Mintage	MS-63	Proof
2010	—	12.00	—

KM# 961a 50 CENTS
6.9000 g., Nickel Plated Steel, 35 mm. **Ruler:** Elizabeth II **Rev:** Bob sleigh - red enamel

Date	Mintage	MS-63	Proof
2010	—	12.00	—

KM# 962 50 CENTS
6.9000 g., Nickel Plated Steel, 35 mm. **Ruler:** Elizabeth II **Rev:** Speed skating

Date	Mintage	MS-63	Proof
2010	—	12.00	—

KM# 962a 50 CENTS
6.9000 g., Nickel Plated Steel, 35 mm. **Ruler:** Elizabeth II **Rev:** Speed skating - red enamel

Date	Mintage	MS-63	Proof
2010	—	12.00	—

KM# 963 50 CENTS
6.9000 g., Nickel Plated Steel, 35 mm. **Ruler:** Elizabeth II **Rev:** Migaand Quatchi in bob sleigh

Date	Mintage	MS-63	Proof
2010	2,119	12.00	—

KM# 964 50 CENTS
6.9000 g., Nickel Plated Steel, 35 mm. **Ruler:** Elizabeth II **Rev:** Miga in hockey

Date	Mintage	MS-63	Proof
2010	5,275	12.00	—

KM# 965 50 CENTS
6.9000 g., Nickel Plated Steel, 35 mm. **Ruler:** Elizabeth II **Rev:** Quatchi in ice hockey

Date	Mintage	MS-63	Proof
2010	5,614	12.00	—

KM# 966 50 CENTS
6.9000 g., Nickel Plated Steel, 35 mm. **Ruler:** Elizabeth II **Rev:** Sumi Para Sledge

Date	Mintage	MS-63	Proof
2010	3,707	12.00	—

KM# 967 50 CENTS
6.9000 g., Nickel Plated Steel, 35 mm. **Ruler:** Elizabeth II **Rev:** Miga and Quatchi Figure-skating **Edge:** Reeded

Date	Mintage	MS-63	Proof
2010	2,981	12.00	—

KM# 968 50 CENTS
6.9000 g., Nickel Plated Steel, 35 mm. **Ruler:** Elizabeth II **Rev:** Free-style mascot

Date	Mintage	MS-63	Proof
2010	2,114	12.00	—

KM# 969 50 CENTS
6.9000 g., Nickel Plated Steel, 35 mm. **Ruler:** Elizabeth II **Rev:** Skeleton mascot

Date	Mintage	MS-63	Proof
2010	1,672	12.00	—

KM# 970 50 CENTS
6.9000 g., Nickel Plated Steel, 35 mm. **Ruler:** Elizabeth II **Rev:** Parallel giant slalom mascot

Date	Mintage	MS-63	Proof
2010	1,730	12.00	—

KM# 971 50 CENTS
6.9000 g., Nickel Plated Steel, 35 mm. **Ruler:** Elizabeth II **Rev:** Alpine skiing mascot

Date	Mintage	MS-63	Proof
2010	2,309	12.00	—

KM# 972 50 CENTS
6.9000 g., Nickel Plated Steel, 35 mm. **Ruler:** Elizabeth II **Rev:** Para Olympic alpine skiing mascott

Date	Mintage	MS-63	Proof
2010	1,902	12.00	—

KM# 973 50 CENTS
6.9000 g., Nickel Plated Steel, 35 mm. **Ruler:** Elizabeth II **Rev:** Snowboard mascot

Date	Mintage	MS-63	Proof
2010	2,090	12.00	—

KM# 974 50 CENTS
6.9000 g., Nickel Plated Steel, 35 mm. **Ruler:** Elizabeth II **Rev:** Speed-skating mascott

Date	Mintage	MS-63	Proof
2010	1,825	12.00	—

KM# 986 50 CENTS
12.6100 g., Brass Plated Steel, 35 mm. **Ruler:** Elizabeth II **Rev:** Dasplerosaurus Torosus - 3-D lenticular movement

Date	Mintage	MS-63	Proof
2010	—	20.00	—

KM# 1015 50 CENTS
12.6100 g., Brass Plated Steel, 35 mm. **Ruler:** Elizabeth II **Rev:** Sinosauropteryx

Date	Mintage	MS-63	Proof
2010	—	20.00	—

KM# 1016 50 CENTS
12.6100 g., Brass Plated Steel, 35 mm. **Ruler:** Elizabeth II **Rev:** Albertosaurus

Date	Mintage	MS-63	Proof
2010	—	20.00	—

KM# 1043 50 CENTS
Nickel Plated Steel, 34 mm. **Ruler:** Elizabeth II **Rev:** Santa Claus transforms into Rudolf the red-nosed reindeer

Date	Mintage	MS-63	Proof
2010	—	17.50	—

KM# 1157 50 CENTS
11.6200 g., 0.9250 Silver 0.3456 oz. ASW, 29.72 mm. **Ruler:** Elizabeth II **Obv:** George V bust **Rev:** Value within wreath

Date	Mintage	MS-63	Proof
1911-2011 Proof	6,000	—	45.00

KM# 1180 50 CENTS
6.9000 g., Nickel Plated Steel, 27.13 mm. **Ruler:** Elizabeth II **Obv:** Bust right **Rev:** Winnipeg Jets Logo, jet over maple leaf **Edge:** Reeded

Date	Mintage	MS-63	Proof
2011	—	15.00	—

KM# 1191 50 CENTS
12.6100 g., Copper Plated Steel, 35 mm. **Ruler:** Elizabeth II **Obv:** Bust right **Rev:** Santa Claus checking list, and in sled over house

Date	Mintage	MS-63	Proof
2011	—	27.50	—

KM# 1202 50 CENTS
1.2700 g., 0.9999 Gold 0.0408 oz. AGW, 13.92 mm. **Ruler:** Elizabeth II **Rev:** Wood Bison **Rev. Designer:** Corrine Hunt **Edge:** Reeded

Date	Mintage	MS-63	Proof
2011 Proof	Est. 2,500	—	100

KM# 1204 50 CENTS
1.2700 g., 0.9999 Gold 0.0408 oz. AGW, 13.92 mm. **Ruler:** Elizabeth II **Subject:** Boreal Forest **Rev:** Bird and tree **Rev. Designer:** Corrine Hunt **Edge:** Reeded

Date	Mintage	MS-63	Proof
2011 Proof	Est. 2,500	—	100

KM# 1206 50 CENTS
1.2700 g., 0.9999 Gold 0.0408 oz. AGW, 13.92 mm. **Ruler:** Elizabeth II **Rev:** Peregrine Falcon perched on branch **Rev. Designer:** Corrine Hunt

Date	Mintage	MS-63	Proof
2011 Proof	Est. 2,500	—	100

KM# 1208 50 CENTS
1.2700 g., 0.9999 Gold 0.0408 oz. AGW, 13.92 mm. **Ruler:** Elizabeth II **Rev:** Orca Whale **Rev. Designer:** Corrine Hunt **Edge:** Reeded

Date	Mintage	MS-63	Proof
2011 Proof	Est. 2,500	—	100

KM# 1234 50 CENTS
12.6100 g., Nickel Plated Steel, 35 mm. **Ruler:** Elizabeth II **Subject:** Titanic, 100th Anniversary **Obv:** Bust right **Rev:** Titanic sailing forward towards iceberg, colored sea

Date	Mintage	MS-63	Proof
2012 Proof	—	—	65.00

KM# 1264 50 CENTS
1.2700 g., 0.9990 Gold 0.0408 oz. AGW, 13.92 mm. **Ruler:** Elizabeth II **Subject:** Gold Rush

Date	Mintage	MS-63	Proof
2012 Proof	—	—	100

KM# 1293 50 CENTS
9.3000 g., 0.9250 Silver 0.2766 oz. ASW, 27.13 mm. **Ruler:** Elizabeth II **Subject:** Elizabeth II Diamond Jubilee **Rev:** Diamond Jubilee logo in color

Date	Mintage	MS-63	Proof
2012	—	—	—

KM# 186 DOLLAR
7.0000 g., Aureate-Bronze Plated Nickel, 26.5 mm. **Ruler:** Elizabeth II **Obv:** Crowned head right **Obv. Designer:** Dora dePedery-Hunt **Rev:** Loon right, date and denomination **Rev. Designer:** Robert R. Carmichael **Shape:** 11-sided

Date	Mintage	MS-63	Proof
2001	—	2.50	—
2001 Proof	74,194	—	8.00
2002	—	4.50	—
2002 Proof	65,315	—	7.50
2003	—	5.50	—

Note: Mintage of 5,101,000 includes both KM186 and KM495 examples.

Date	Mintage	MS-63	Proof
2003 Proof	—	—	12.00

KM# 414 DOLLAR
25.1750 g., 0.9250 Silver 0.7487 oz. ASW, 36 mm. **Ruler:** Elizabeth II **Subject:** National Ballet **Obv:** Crowned head right **Rev:** Ballet dancers **Rev. Designer:** Scott McKowen **Edge:** Reeded

Date	Mintage	MS-63	Proof
2001	65,000	27.50	—
2001 Proof	225,000	—	35.00

KM# 434 DOLLAR
25.1750 g., 0.9250 Silver 0.7487 oz. ASW, 36 mm. **Ruler:** Elizabeth II **Obv:** Crowned head right **Rev:** Recycled 1911 pattern dollar design: denomination, country name and dates in crowned wreath **Edge:** Reeded

Date	Mintage	MS-63	Proof
1911-2001 Proof	24,996	—	55.00

KM# 186a DOLLAR
Gilt Aureate-Bronze Plated Nickel, 26.5 mm. **Ruler:** Elizabeth II **Subject:** Olympic Win

Date	Mintage	MS-63	Proof
2002 Proof	—	—	40.00

KM# 443 DOLLAR
25.1750 g., 0.9250 Silver 0.7487 oz. ASW, 36 mm. **Ruler:** Elizabeth II **Subject:** Queen's Golden Jubilee **Obv:** Crowned head right, with anniversary date at left **Obv. Designer:** Dora dePédery-Hunt **Rev:** Queen in her coach and a view of the coach, denomination below **Edge:** Reeded

Date	Mintage	MS-63	Proof
1952-2002	65,140	28.50	—
1952-2002 Proof	29,688	—	40.00

KM# 443a DOLLAR
25.1800 g., 0.9250 Silver Gilt 0.7488 oz. ASW, 36 mm. **Ruler:** Elizabeth II **Subject:** Queen's Golden Jubilee **Obv:** Crowned head right with anniversary date **Rev:** Queen in her coach and a view of the coach **Edge:** Reeded **Note:** Special 24 karat gold plated issue of KM#443.

Date	Mintage	MS-63	Proof
2002 Proof	32,642	—	45.00

KM# 462 DOLLAR
7.0000 g., Aureate-Bronze Plated Nickel **Ruler:** Elizabeth II **Obv:** Commemorative dates 1952-2002 **Obv. Designer:** Dora dePédery-Hunt **Rev:** Family of Loons

Date	Mintage	MS-63	Proof
2002 Specimen	67,672	—	35.00

KM# 467 DOLLAR
7.0000 g., Aureate-Bronze Plated Nickel **Ruler:** Elizabeth II **Subject:** Elizabeth II Golden Jubilee **Obv:** Crowned head right, Jubilee commemorative dates 1952-2002 **Obv. Designer:** Dora dePédery-Hunt

Date	Mintage	MS-63	Proof
2002	2,302,000	2.50	—
2002 Proof	—	—	8.00

KM# 467a DOLLAR

Gold **Ruler:** Elizabeth II **Subject:** 50th Anniversary, Accession to the Throne **Obv:** Crowned head right **Note:** Sold on the internet.

Date	Mintage	MS-63	Proof
2002	1	—	55,500

KM# 503 DOLLAR

25.1750 g., 0.9250 Silver 0.7487 oz. ASW, 36 mm. **Ruler:** Elizabeth II **Subject:** Queen Mother **Obv:** Crowned head right **Obv. Designer:** Dora de Pedery-Hunt **Rev:** Queen Mother facing

Date	Mintage	MS-63	Proof
2002 Proof	9,994	—	250

KM# 495 DOLLAR

7.0000 g., Aureate-Bronze Plated Nickel, 26.5 mm. **Ruler:** Elizabeth II **Obv:** Bare head right **Obv. Designer:** Susanna Blunt **Rev:** Loon right **Rev. Designer:** Robert R. Carmichael **Shape:** 11-sided

Date	Mintage	MS-63	Proof
2003	5,102,000	5.50	—
Note: Mintage of 5,101,000 includes both KM 186 and 495 examples.			
2003W Prooflike	—	—	—
2003 Proof	62,507	—	7.50
2004	10,894,000	1.75	—
2004 Proof	—	—	12.00
2005	44,375,000	3.00	—
2005 Proof	—	—	7.50
2006	49,111,000	3.00	—
2006 Proof	—	—	7.50
2006(ml)	49,111,000	3.00	—
2006(ml) Proof	—	—	7.50
2007(ml)	38,045,000	3.00	—
2007(ml) Proof	—	—	7.50
2008(ml)	29,561,000	3.00	—
2008(ml) Proof	—	—	7.50
2009(ml)	39,601,000	3.00	—
2009(ml) Proof	—	—	7.50
2010(ml)	—	3.00	—
2010(ml) Proof	—	—	7.50
2011(ml)	—	3.00	—
2011(ml) Proof	—	—	7.50
2012(ml)	—	3.00	—
2012(ml) Proof	—	—	7.50

KM# 450 DOLLAR

25.1750 g., 0.9999 Silver 0.8093 oz. ASW, 36 mm. **Ruler:** Elizabeth II **Subject:** Cobalt Mining Centennial **Obv:** Queens portrait right **Obv. Designer:** Dora dePédery-Hunt **Rev:** Mine tower and fox **Edge:** Reeded

Date	Mintage	MS-63	Proof
2003	51,130	30.00	—
2003 Proof	88,536	—	45.00

KM# 473 DOLLAR

25.1750 g., 0.9999 Silver 0.8093 oz. ASW **Ruler:** Elizabeth II **Subject:** 50th Anniversary of the Coronation of Elizabeth II **Obv:** 1953 effigy of the Queen, Jubilee dates 1953-2003 **Obv. Designer:** Mary Gillick **Rev:** Voyageur, date and denomination below

Date	Mintage	MS-63	Proof
1953-2003 Proof	21,537	—	45.00

KM# 480 DOLLAR

25.1750 g., 0.9999 Silver 0.8093 oz. ASW **Ruler:** Elizabeth II **Subject:** Coronation of Queen Elizabeth II **Obv:** Head right **Rev:** Voyaguers **Rev. Designer:** Emanuel Hahn

Date	Mintage	MS-63	Proof
1953-2003 Proof	29,586	—	50.00

KM# 480a DOLLAR

Gold **Ruler:** Elizabeth II **Subject:** 50th Anniversary of Coronation **Obv. Designer:** Mary Gilick **Rev:** Voyageur **Note:** Sold on the internet.

Date	Mintage	MS-63	Proof
1953-2003	1	—	62,750

KM# 511 DOLLAR

25.1750 g., 0.9999 Silver 0.8093 oz. ASW, 36 mm. **Ruler:** Elizabeth II **Obv:** Elizabeth II **Rev:** Poppy on maple leaf **Edge:** Reeded

Date	Mintage	MS-63	Proof
2004 Proof	24,527	—	50.00

KM# 507 DOLLAR

7.0000 g., Aureate-Bronze Plated Nickel, 26.5 mm. **Ruler:** Elizabeth II **Obv:** Bare head right, date below **Obv. Designer:** Susanna Blunt **Rev:** Loon **Edge:** Plain **Shape:** 11-sided

Date	Mintage	MS-63	Proof
2004 Proof	25,105	—	75.00

KM# 512 DOLLAR

25.1750 g., 0.9999 Silver 0.8093 oz. ASW, 36 mm. **Ruler:** Elizabeth II **Subject:** First French Settlement in America **Obv:** Crowned head right **Rev:** Sailing ship **Edge:** Reeded

Date	Mintage	MS-63	Proof
2004	42,582	30.00	—
2004 Fleur-dis-lis privy mark	8,315	60.00	—
2004 Proof	106,974	—	50.00

KM# 513 DOLLAR

7.0000 g., Aureate-Bronze Plated Nickel, 26.5 mm. **Ruler:** Elizabeth II **Subject:** Olympics **Obv:** Bare head right **Rev:** Maple leaf, Olympic flame and rings above loon **Edge:** Plain **Shape:** 11-sided

Date	Mintage	MS-63	Proof
2004	6,526,000	8.00	—

KM# 513a DOLLAR

9.3100 g., 0.9250 Silver 0.2769 oz. ASW, 26.5 mm. **Ruler:** Elizabeth II **Subject:** Olympics **Obv:** Bare head right **Rev:** Multicolor maple leaf, Olympic flame and rings above loon **Edge:** Plain **Shape:** 11-sided

Date	Mintage	MS-63	Proof
2004 Proof	19,994	—	50.00

KM# 549 DOLLAR

25.1750 g., 0.9250 Silver 0.7487 oz. ASW, 36.07 mm. **Ruler:** Elizabeth II **Subject:** 40th Anniversary of National Flag **Obv:** Head right **Obv. Designer:** Susanna Blunt **Rev. Designer:** William Woodruff

Date	Mintage	MS-63	Proof
2005	50,948	27.50	—
2005 Proof	95,431	—	40.00

KM# 549a DOLLAR

25.1750 g., 0.9250 Silver partially gilt 0.7487 oz. ASW, 36.07 mm. **Ruler:** Elizabeth II **Subject:** 40th Anniversary of National Flag **Obv:** Head right

Date	Mintage	MS-63	Proof
2005	62,562	75.00	—

KM# 549b DOLLAR

25.1800 g., 0.9250 Silver 0.7488 oz. ASW, 36.07 mm. **Ruler:** Elizabeth II **Subject:** 40th Anniversary National Flag **Rev:** National flag, colorized

Date	Mintage	MS-63	Proof
2005 Proof	4,898	—	350

KM# 552 DOLLAR

7.0000 g., Aureate-Bronze Plated Nickel, 26.5 mm. **Ruler:** Elizabeth II **Obv:** Head right **Rev:** Terry Fox walking left

Date	Mintage	MS-63	Proof
2005	1,290,900	3.50	—

KM# 553 DOLLAR

7.0000 g., Aureate-Bronze Plated Nickel **Ruler:** Elizabeth II **Subject:** Tuffed Puffin **Obv:** Head right **Obv. Designer:** Susanna Blunt

Date	Mintage	MS-63	Proof
2005	39,818	—	30.00

KM# 581 DOLLAR

9.3100 g., 0.9250 Silver 0.2769 oz. ASW **Ruler:** Elizabeth II **Subject:** Lullabies Loonie **Obv:** Head right **Obv. Designer:** Susanna Blunt **Rev:** Loon and moon, teddy bear in stars

Date	Mintage	MS-63	Proof
2006	18,103	4.50	—

KM# 582 DOLLAR

7.0000 g., Aureate-Bronze Plated Nickel, 26.5 mm. **Ruler:** Elizabeth II **Subject:** Snowy owl **Obv:** Head right **Obv. Designer:** Susanna Blunt **Rev:** Snowy owl with year above

Date	Mintage	MS-63	Proof
2006 Specimen	39,935	—	30.00

KM# 583 DOLLAR

25.1750 g., 0.9250 Silver 0.7487 oz. ASW, 36 mm. **Ruler:** Elizabeth II **Obv:** Head right **Rev:** Victoria Cross

Date	Mintage	MS-63	Proof
2006	27,254	25.00	—
2006 Proof	53,822	—	45.00

KM# 583a DOLLAR

25.1750 g., 0.9250 Silver partially gilt 0.7487 oz. ASW, 36 mm. **Ruler:** Elizabeth II **Obv:** Head right **Rev:** Victoria Cross gilt

Date	Mintage	MS-63	Proof
2006 Proof	53,822	—	75.00

KM# 630 DOLLAR

7.0000 g., Aureate Bronze, 26.5 mm. **Ruler:** Elizabeth II **Obv:** Bust right **Rev:** Loon splashing in water

Date	Mintage	MS-63	Proof
2006	—	3.00	—

KM# 630a DOLLAR

9.3100 g., 0.9250 Silver with enamel 0.2769 oz. ASW, 26.5 mm. **Ruler:** Elizabeth II **Subject:** Olympic Games **Obv:** Crowned head right **Rev:** Loon in flight, colored olympic logo above

Date	Mintage	MS-63	Proof
2006	19,956	30.00	—

KM# 654 DOLLAR

7.0000 g., 0.9250 Silver 0.2082 oz. ASW **Ruler:** Elizabeth II **Obv:** Head right **Rev:** Snowflake, colorized **Note:** Sold in a CD package.

Date	Mintage	MS-63	Proof
2006(ml)	34,014	35.00	—

KM# 655 DOLLAR

7.0000 g., 0.9250 Silver 0.2082 oz. ASW **Ruler:** Elizabeth II **Subject:** Baby Rattle **Obv:** Head right **Rev:** Baby rattle

Date	Mintage	MS-63	Proof
2006	3,207	20.00	—

KM# 655a DOLLAR

7.0000 g., 0.9250 Silver 0.2082 oz. ASW **Ruler:** Elizabeth II **Obv:** Bust right **Rev:** Baby Rattle, partially gilt

Date	Mintage	MS-63	Proof
2006	1,911	15.00	—

KM# 656 DOLLAR

28.1750 g., 0.9250 Silver 0.8379 oz. ASW **Ruler:** Elizabeth II **Subject:** Medal of Bravery **Obv:** Head right

Date	Mintage	MS-63	Proof
2006 Proof	8,343	—	50.00

KM# 656a DOLLAR

28.1750 g., 0.9250 Silver with multicolor enamel 0.8379 oz. ASW **Ruler:** Elizabeth II **Subject:** Medal of Bravery **Obv:** Head right **Rev:** Maple leaf within wreath. Colorized.

Date	Mintage	MS-63	Proof
2006 Proof	4,999	—	150

KM# 1287 DOLLAR

7.0000 g., Aureate Bronze, 26.5 mm. **Ruler:** Elizabeth II **Rev:** Goose in flight

Date	Mintage	MS-63	Proof
2006 Proof	—	—	20.00

KM# 688 DOLLAR

7.0000 g., Aureate-Bronze Plated Nickel, 26.5 mm. **Ruler:** Elizabeth II **Obv:** Head right **Rev:** Trumpeter Swan

Date	Mintage	MS-63	Proof
2007(ml)	40,000	20.00	—

KM# 653 DOLLAR

25.1750 g., 0.9250 Silver 0.7487 oz. ASW, 36.07 mm. **Ruler:** Elizabeth II **Subject:** Thayendanegea **Obv:** Head right **Rev:** Bust 3/4 facing right

Date	Mintage	MS-63	Proof
2007	16,378	30.00	—
2007 Proof	—	—	40.00

KM# 653a DOLLAR

25.1750 g., 0.9250 Silver partially gilt 0.7487 oz. ASW, 36.07 mm. **Ruler:** Elizabeth II **Subject:** Thayendanega **Rev:** Bust 3/4 right, partially gold plated

Date	Mintage	MS-63	Proof
2007 Proof	60,000	—	125

KM# 720 DOLLAR

25.1800 g., 0.9250 Silver 0.7488 oz. ASW, 36.07 mm. **Ruler:** Elizabeth II **Obv:** Bust right **Rev:** Thayendanega multicolor

Date	Mintage	MS-63	Proof
2007 Proof	4,760	—	120

KM# 700 DOLLAR

7.0000 g., 0.9250 Silver 0.2082 oz. ASW, 23.88 mm. **Ruler:** Elizabeth II **Rev:** Alphabet Letter Blocks

Date	Mintage	MS-63	Proof
2007	3,207	—	25.00

KM# 719 DOLLAR

25.1800 g., 0.9250 Silver 0.7488 oz. ASW, 36.07 mm. **Ruler:** Elizabeth II **Subject:** Celebration of the Arts **Rev:** Book, TV set, musical instruments, film montage **Rev. Designer:** Friedrich Peter **Edge:** Reeded

Date	Mintage	MS-63	Proof
2007	6,466	—	55.00

KM# A727 DOLLAR

7.0000 g., Aureate-Bronze Plated Nickel, 26.5 mm. **Ruler:** Elizabeth II **Subject:** Vancouver Olympic Games **Rev:** Loon splashing in water, Olympics logo at right

Date	Mintage	MS-63	Proof
2007(ml)	19,973	3.00	—

KM# 721 DOLLAR

7.0000 g., Aureate-Bronze Plated Nickel, 26.5 mm. **Ruler:** Elizabeth II **Obv:** Bust right **Rev:** Calgary flames, multicolor in circle

Date	Mintage	MS-63	Proof
2008	—	25.00	—

KM# 722 DOLLAR

7.0000 g., Aureate-Bronze Plated Nickel, 26.5 mm. **Ruler:** Elizabeth II **Obv:** Bust **Rev:** Edmonton Oilers logo, multicolor in logo

Date	Mintage	MS-63	Proof
2008	1,584	25.00	—

KM# 723A DOLLAR

7.0000 g., Aureate-Bronze Plated Nickel, 26.5 mm. **Ruler:** Elizabeth II **Obv:** Bust right **Rev:** Montreal Canadians, multicolor logo in circle

Date	Mintage	MS-63	Proof
2008	2,659	25.00	—

KM# 724 DOLLAR

7.0000 g., Nickel, 26.5 mm. **Ruler:** Elizabeth II **Rev:** Ottawa Senators, multicolor logo in circle

Date	Mintage	MS-63	Proof
2008	1,633	25.00	—

KM# 725 DOLLAR

7.0000 g., Aureate-Bronze Plated Nickel, 26.5 mm. **Ruler:** Elizabeth II **Obv:** Bust right **Rev:** Toronto Maple Leafs, multicolor logo in circle

Date	Mintage	MS-63	Proof
2008	—	25.00	—

KM# 726 DOLLAR

7.0000 g., Aureate-Bronze Plated Nickel, 26.5 mm. **Ruler:** Elizabeth II **Obv:** Bust left **Rev:** Vancouver Canucks, logo in center

Date	Mintage	MS-63	Proof
2008	1,302	25.00	—

KM# 767 DOLLAR

25.1800 g., 0.9250 Silver 0.7488 oz. ASW, 36.07 mm. **Ruler:** Elizabeth II **Rev:** Poppy at center of large maple leaf

Date	Mintage	MS-63	Proof
2008 Proof	—	—	50.00

KM# 781 DOLLAR

25.1800 g., 0.9250 Silver partially gilt 0.7488 oz. ASW, 36.07 mm. **Ruler:** Elizabeth II **Subject:** Ottawa Mint Centennial 1908-2008 **Rev:** Maple leaf transforming into a common loon, gilt rim and 100 **Rev. Designer:** Jason Bowman

Date	Mintage	MS-63	Proof
2008 Proof	15,000	—	65.00

KM# 784 DOLLAR

7.0000 g., Aureate-Bronze Plated Nickel, 26.5 mm. **Ruler:** Elizabeth II **Rev:** Common elder

Date	Mintage	MS-63	Proof
2008 Specimen	21,227	—	50.00

KM# 785 DOLLAR

25.1800 g., 0.9250 Silver 0.7488 oz. ASW, 36.07 mm. **Ruler:** Elizabeth II **Subject:** Founding of Quebec 400th Anniversary **Rev:** Samuel de Champlain, ship and town view **Rev. Designer:** Susanne Duranceau

Date	Mintage	MS-63	Proof
2008	35,000	25.00	—
2008 Proof	65,000	—	40.00

KM# 785a DOLLAR

25.1800 g., 0.9250 Silver partially gilt. 0.7488 oz. ASW, 36.07 mm. **Ruler:** Elizabeth II **Subject:** Founding of Quebec 400th Anniversary **Rev:** Samuel de Champlain selectively gold plated, ship, town view **Rev. Designer:** Susanne Duranceau

Date	Mintage	MS-63	Proof
2008 Proof	38,630	—	75.00

KM# 787 DOLLAR

7.0000 g., Aureate-Bronze Plated Nickel, 26.5 mm. **Ruler:** Elizabeth II **Subject:** Lucky Loonie **Rev:** Loon splashing and Olympic logo at right **Rev. Designer:** Steve Hepurn

Date	Mintage	MS-63	Proof
2008	—	20.00	—

KM# 787a DOLLAR

9.3100 g., 0.9250 Silver 0.2769 oz. ASW, 26.5 mm. **Ruler:** Elizabeth II **Rev:** Loon splashing with Olympic logo and maple leaf in color above **Rev. Designer:** Steve Hepurn

Date	Mintage	MS-63	Proof
2008 Proof	52,987	—	25.00

KM# 790 DOLLAR

6.5000 g., Nickel, 26.5 mm. **Ruler:** Elizabeth II **Rev:** Calgary Flames

Date	Mintage	MS-63	Proof
2008	—	25.00	—

KM# 791 DOLLAR

6.5000 g., Nickel, 26.5 mm. **Ruler:** Elizabeth II **Rev:** Edmonton Oilers

Date	Mintage	MS-63	Proof
2008	—	25.00	—

KM# 792 DOLLAR

6.5000 g., Nickel, 26.5 mm. **Ruler:** Elizabeth II **Rev:** Montreal Canadiens

Date	Mintage	MS-63	Proof
2008	—	25.00	—

KM# 793 DOLLAR

6.5000 g., Nickel, 26.5 mm. **Ruler:** Elizabeth II **Rev:** Ottawa Senators

Date	Mintage	MS-63	Proof
2008	—	25.00	—

KM# 794 DOLLAR

6.5000 g., Nickel, 26.5 mm. **Ruler:** Elizabeth II **Rev:** Toronto Maple Leafs

Date	Mintage	MS-63	Proof
2008	—	25.00	—

KM# 795 DOLLAR

6.5000 g., Nickel, 26.5 mm. **Ruler:** Elizabeth II **Rev:** Vancouver Canucks

Date	Mintage	MS-63	Proof
2008	—	25.00	—

KM# 851 DOLLAR

33.6500 g., Nickel, 26.5 mm. **Ruler:** Elizabeth II **Rev:** Calgary Flames Road Jersey

Date	Mintage	MS-63	Proof
2009	382	25.00	—

KM# 852 DOLLAR

33.6500 g., Nickel, 26.5 mm. **Ruler:** Elizabeth II **Rev:** Edmonton Oilers Road Jersey

Date	Mintage	MS-63	Proof
2009	472	25.00	—

KM# 853 DOLLAR

33.6500 g., Nickel, 26.5 mm. **Ruler:** Elizabeth II **Rev:** Montreal Canadians Road Jersey

Date	Mintage	MS-63	Proof
2009	4,857	25.00	—

KM# 854 DOLLAR

33.6500 g., Nickel, 26.5 mm. **Ruler:** Elizabeth II **Rev:** Ottawa Senators Road Jersey

Date	Mintage	MS-63	Proof
2009	387	25.00	—

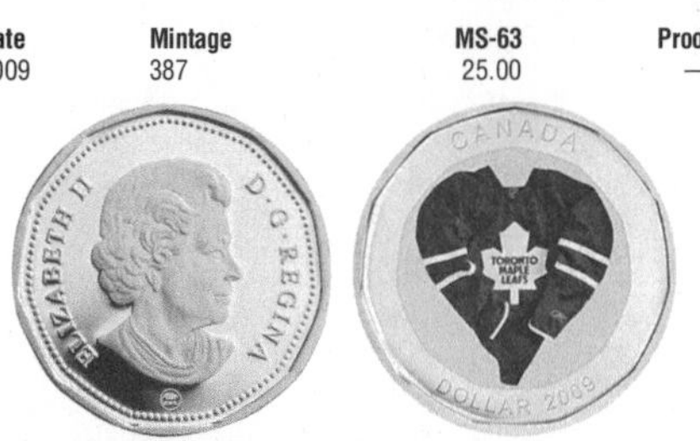

KM# 855 DOLLAR

33.6500 g., Nickel, 26.5 mm. **Ruler:** Elizabeth II **Rev:** Toronto Maple Leafs Road Jersey

Date	Mintage	MS-63	Proof
2009	1,328	25.00	—

KM# 856 DOLLAR

33.6500 g., Nickel, 26.5 mm. **Ruler:** Elizabeth II **Rev:** Vancouver Canucks Road Jersey

Date	Mintage	MS-63	Proof
2009	794	25.00	—

KM# 864 DOLLAR

7.0000 g., Aureate-Bronze Plated Nickel, 26.5 mm. **Ruler:** Elizabeth II **Subject:** Montreal Canadiens, 100th Anniversary **Obv:** Bust right **Rev:** Montreal Canadiens logo and large 100 **Shape:** 11-sided

Date	Mintage	MS-63	Proof
2009	—	25.00	—

KM# 865 DOLLAR

25.1700 g., 0.9250 Silver 0.7485 oz. ASW, 36.07 mm. **Ruler:** Elizabeth II **Subject:** Montreal Canadiens 100th Anniversary **Obv:** Bust right **Obv. Designer:** Susanna Blunt **Rev:** Montreal Canadiens logo partially gilt

Date	Mintage	MS-63	Proof
2009 Proof in black case	15,000	—	75.00
2009 Proof in acrillic stand	5,000	—	150

KM# 889 DOLLAR

25.1800 g., 0.9250 Silver 0.7488 oz. ASW, 36.07 mm. **Ruler:** Elizabeth II **Subject:** 100th Anniversary of flight in Canada **Obv:** Bust right **Obv. Legend:** Elizabeth II DG Regina **Obv. Designer:** Susanna Blunt **Rev:** Silhouette with arms spread, 3 planes, plane cutout **Rev. Legend:** Canada Dollar 1909-2009 **Rev. Designer:** Jason Bouwman

Date	Mintage	MS-63	Proof
2009	13,074	40.00	—
2009 Proof	52,549	—	50.00

KM# 889a DOLLAR
25.1800 g., 0.9250 Silver partially gilt 0.7488 oz. ASW, 36.07 mm. **Ruler:** Elizabeth II **Obv:** Bust right **Rev:** Boy silouette with arms spread, 3 planes, plane shadow partially gilt

Date	Mintage	MS-63	Proof
2009(ml) Proof	27,549	—	65.00

KM# 914 DOLLAR
7.0000 g., Aureate-Bronze Plated Nickel, 26.5 mm. **Ruler:** Elizabeth II **Obv:** Bust right **Obv. Designer:** Susanna Blunt **Rev:** Blue heron in flight

Date	Mintage	MS-63	Proof
2009 Specimen	21,677	50.00	—

KM# 883 DOLLAR
7.0000 g., Aureate-Bronze Plated Nickel, 26.5 mm. **Ruler:** Elizabeth II **Subject:** Lucky Loonie **Obv:** Bust right **Obv. Legend:** Elizabeth II DG Regina **Rev:** Canadian Olympic logo **Rev. Legend:** Canada Dollar

Date	Mintage	MS-63	Proof
2010	12,000	20.00	—

KM# 883a DOLLAR
9.3100 g., 0.9250 Silver 0.2769 oz. ASW, 26.5 mm. **Ruler:** Elizabeth II **Subject:** Lucky Loonie **Obv:** Bust right **Obv. Legend:** Elizabeth II DG Regina **Rev:** Canadian Olympic logo in color **Rev. Legend:** Vancouver 2010 Canada Dollar **Shape:** 11-sided

Date	Mintage	MS-63	Proof
2010 Proof	40,000	—	55.00

KM# 1046 DOLLAR
Aureate-Bronze Plated Nickel, 26.5 mm. **Ruler:** Elizabeth II **Subject:** Roughriders **Rev:** S logo **Shape:** 11-sided

Date	Mintage	MS-63	Proof
2010(ml)	—	7.50	—

KM# 975 DOLLAR
0.9250 Silver, 36 mm. **Ruler:** Elizabeth II **Rev:** Sun mask **Rev. Designer:** Xwa lack Tun

Date	Mintage	MS-63	Proof
2010 Proof	1,278	—	200

KM# 995 DOLLAR
25.1700 g., 0.9250 Silver 0.7485 oz. ASW, 36.07 mm. **Ruler:** Elizabeth II **Rev:** HMCS Sackville **Rev. Designer:** Yves Berube

Date	Mintage	MS-63	Proof
2010 Proof	Est. 50,000	—	55.00

KM# 995a DOLLAR
25.1700 g., 0.9250 Silver partially gilt 0.7485 oz. ASW, 36.07 mm. **Ruler:** Elizabeth II **Subject:** Navy Centennial **Rev:** HMCS Sackville, sea waves in gilt

Date	Mintage	MS-63	Proof
2010	—	—	110

KM# 996 DOLLAR
7.0000 g., Aureate-Bronze Plated Nickel, 26.5 mm. **Ruler:** Elizabeth II **Rev:** Northern Harrier Hawk

Date	Mintage	MS-63	Proof
2010	35,000	30.00	—
2010(ml)	—	—	50.00

KM# 1017 DOLLAR
7.0000 g., Aureate-Bronze Plated Nickel, 26.5 mm. **Ruler:** Elizabeth II **Rev:** Male and female sailors saluting, HMCS Halifax and anchor above

Date	Mintage	MS-63	Proof
2010	—	5.00	—

KM# 1017a DOLLAR
7.0000 g., Aureate Bronze gilt, 26.5 mm. **Ruler:** Elizabeth II **Rev:** Male and female sailors saluting, HMCS Halifax in background and anchor above

Date	Mintage	MS-63	Proof
2010 Proof	—	—	50.00

KM# 1027 DOLLAR
25.1800 g., 0.9250 Silver 0.7488 oz. ASW, 36.07 mm. **Ruler:** Elizabeth II **Obv:** George V bust left **Rev:** Voyaguers, dual dates below

Date	Mintage	MS-63	Proof
2010 Proof	7,500	—	70.00

KM# 1050 DOLLAR
25.1800 g., 0.9250 Silver 0.7488 oz. ASW, 36.07 mm. **Ruler:** Elizabeth II **Rev:** Red poppy in large field of poppies **Edge:** Reeded

Date	Mintage	MS-63	Proof
2010 Proof	5,000	—	150

KM# 1086 DOLLAR
7.0000 g., Aureate-Bronze Plated Nickel, 26.5 mm. **Ruler:** Elizabeth II **Rev:** Great Grey Owl **Rev. Designer:** Arnold Nagy

Date	Mintage	MS-63	Proof
2011	35,000	13.50	—

KM# 1087 DOLLAR
25.1800 g., 0.9250 Silver 0.7488 oz. ASW, 36.07 mm. **Ruler:** Elizabeth II **Subject:** Parks Canada, 100th Anniversary **Rev:** Female head looking downward into hands holding nature scene **Rev. Designer:** Luc Normandin

Date	Mintage	MS-63	Proof
2011	25,000	50.00	—
2011 Proof	—	—	60.00

KM# 1087a DOLLAR
25.1800 g., 0.9250 Silver partially gilt 0.7488 oz. ASW, 36.07 mm. **Ruler:** Elizabeth II **Subject:** Parks Canada, 100th Anniversary **Rev:** Female head looking downward to hands holding nature scene, partially gilt **Rev. Designer:** Luc Normandin

Date	Mintage	MS-63	Proof
2011 Proof	45,000	—	75.00

KM# 1112 DOLLAR
25.1700 g., 0.9250 Silver 0.7485 oz. ASW, 36.07 mm. **Ruler:** Elizabeth II **Obv:** Crowned bust left of George V **Obv. Designer:** E. B. MacKennal **Rev:** Value and date within maple wreath **Rev. Designer:** W.H.J. Blakemore

Date	Mintage	MS-63	Proof
2011 Proof	Est. 15,000	—	115

KM# 1166 DOLLAR
7.0000 g., Aureate-Bronze Plated Nickel, 26.5 mm. **Ruler:** Elizabeth II **Subject:** Canada Parks **Obv:** Bust right **Rev:** Stylized animals

Date	Mintage	MS-63	Proof
2011	—	5.00	—

KM# 1255 DOLLAR
6.2700 g., Brass Plated Steel, 26.5 mm. **Ruler:** Elizabeth II **Rev:** Loon with security feature above **Shape:** 11-sided

Date	Mintage	MS-63	Proof
2012	—	5.00	—
2012 Proof	—	—	7.50
2013	—	5.00	—
2013 Proof	—	—	7.50

KM# 1216 DOLLAR
9.3100 g., 0.9250 Silver 0.2769 oz. ASW, 26.5 mm. **Ruler:** Elizabeth II **Obv:** Bust right, SP/PA below **Rev:** Loon, 1987-2012 below

Date	Mintage	MS-63	Proof
2012 Specimen	—	—	55.00

KM# 1222 DOLLAR
7.0000 g., Aureate-Bronze Plated Nickel, 26.5 mm. **Ruler:** Elizabeth II **Obv:** Bust right **Rev:** Loon and two young, 1987-2012 dates

Date	Mintage	MS-63	Proof
2012 Specimen	—	—	40.00

KM# 1225 DOLLAR
25.1800 g., 0.9250 Silver 0.7488 oz. ASW, 36.07 mm. **Ruler:** Elizabeth II **Subject:** War of 1812, 200th Anniversary **Obv:** Bust right **Rev:** Two soldiers and guide on patrol

Date	Mintage	MS-63	Proof
2012	—	50.00	—
2012 Proof	—	—	60.00

KM# 1225a DOLLAR
25.1800 g., 0.9250 Silver partially gilt 0.7488 oz. ASW, 36.07 mm. **Ruler:** Elizabeth II **Subject:** War of 1812, 200th Anniversary **Obv:** Bust right, gilt rim **Rev:** Two solders and guide, partially gilt

Date	Mintage	MS-63	Proof
2012 Proof	—	—	65.00

KM# 1244 DOLLAR
25.1800 g., 0.9250 Silver 0.7488 oz. ASW, 36.07 mm. **Ruler:** Elizabeth II **Subject:** Calgary Stampede

Date	Mintage	MS-63	Proof
2012	—	—	55.00

KM# 1254 DOLLAR
7.8900 g., 0.9990 Silver 0.2534 oz. ASW, 26.5 mm. **Ruler:** Elizabeth II **Subject:** Loonie, 25th Anniversary **Rev:** Two loons and large 25

Date	Mintage	MS-63	Proof
1987-2012 Proof	15,000	—	35.00

KM# 1256 DOLLAR
6.2700 g., Brass Plated Steel, 26.5 mm. **Ruler:** Elizabeth II **Subject:** Lucky Loonie **Rev:** Loon and Olympic logo **Shape:** 11-sided

Date	Mintage	MS-63	Proof
2012	—	10.00	—

KM# 1256a DOLLAR
12.1600 g., 0.9250 Silver 0.3616 oz. ASW, 26.5 mm. **Ruler:** Elizabeth II **Subject:** Lucky loonie **Rev:** Loon and olympic logo in color

Date	Mintage	MS-63	Proof
2012 Proof	—	—	35.00

KM# 1274 DOLLAR
25.1800 g., 0.9250 Silver 0.7488 oz. ASW, 36.07 mm. **Ruler:** Elizabeth II **Subject:** Artistic Loonie **Rev:** Four Loons in color

Date	Mintage	MS-63	Proof
2012 Proof	—	—	125

KM# 1294 DOLLAR
6.2700 g., Brass Plated Steel, 26.5 mm. **Ruler:** Elizabeth II **Subject:** Grey Cup, 100th Anniversary **Obv:** Bust right **Shape:** 11-sided

Date	Mintage	MS-63	Proof
2012	—	5.00	—

KM# 1295 DOLLAR
25.1800 g., 0.9250 Silver 0.7488 oz. ASW, 36.07 mm. **Ruler:** Elizabeth II **Subject:** Grey Cup, 100th Anniversary

Date	Mintage	MS-63	Proof
2012 Proof	—	—	85.00

KM# 652 DOLLAR (Louis)
1.5000 g., 0.9990 Gold 0.0482 oz. AGW, 14.1 mm. **Ruler:** Elizabeth II **Subject:** Gold Louis **Obv:** Bust right **Obv. Designer:** Susanna Blunt **Rev:** Crowned double L monogram within wreath

Date	Mintage	MS-63	Proof
2006 Proof	5,648	—	110

KM# 756 DOLLAR (Louis)
1.5550 g., 0.9990 Gold 0.0499 oz. AGW, 14.1 mm. **Ruler:** Elizabeth II **Obv:** Bust right **Obv. Designer:** Susanna Blunt **Rev:** Crown above two oval shields

Date	Mintage	MS-63	Proof
2007 Proof	4,023	—	110

KM# 834 DOLLAR (Louis)
1.5550 g., 0.9990 Gold 0.0499 oz. AGW, 14.1 mm. **Ruler:** Elizabeth II **Obv:** Bust right **Obv. Designer:** Susanna Blunt **Rev:** Crowned double L monogram, three lis around

Date	Mintage	MS-63	Proof
2008 Proof	3,793	—	110

KM# 270c 2 DOLLARS
8.8300 g., 0.9250 Silver gold plated center 0.2626 oz. ASW, 28 mm. **Ruler:** Elizabeth II **Obv:** Crowned head right within circle, date below **Rev:** Polar bear right within circle, denomination below **Note:** 1.9mm thick.

Date	Mintage	MS-63	Proof
2001 Proof	—	—	12.00

KM# 270 2 DOLLARS
7.3000 g., Bi-Metallic Aluminum-Bronze center in Nickel ring, 28 mm. **Ruler:** Elizabeth II **Obv:** Crowned head right within circle, date below **Obv. Designer:** Dora dePedery-Hunt **Rev:** Polar bear right within circle, denomination below **Rev. Designer:** Brent Townsend **Edge:** Segmented reeding

Date	Mintage	MS-63	Proof
2001	27,008,000	5.00	—
2001 Proof	74,944	—	12.50
2002	11,910,000	5.00	—
2002 Proof	65,315	—	12.50
2003	7,123,697	5.00	—
2003 Proof	62,007	—	12.50

KM# 449 2 DOLLARS
7.3000 g., Bi-Metallic Aluminum-Bronze center in Nickel ring, 28 mm. **Ruler:** Elizabeth II **Subject:** Elizabeth II Golden Jubilee **Obv:** Crowned head right, jubilee commemorative dates below **Edge:** Segmented reeding

Date	Mintage	MS-63	Proof
1952-2002	27,020,000	4.00	—

KM# 449a 2 DOLLARS
8.8300 g., 0.9250 Silver gold plated center 0.2626 oz. ASW, 28 mm. **Ruler:** Elizabeth II **Subject:** Elizabeth II Golden Jubilee **Obv:** Crowned head right, jubilee commemorative dates below

Date	Mintage	MS-63	Proof
1952-2002 Proof	100,000	—	14.00

KM# 496 2 DOLLARS

7.3000 g., Bi-Metallic Aluminum-Bronze center in Nickel ring, 28 mm. **Ruler:** Elizabeth II **Obv:** Head right **Obv. Designer:** Susanna Blunt **Rev:** Polar bear advancing right **Rev. Designer:** Brent Townsend **Edge:** Segmented reeding

Date	Mintage	MS-63	Proof
2003	11,244,000	5.00	—
2003W	71,142	25.00	—
2004	12,908,000	5.00	—
2004 Proof	—	—	12.50
2005	38,317,000	5.00	—
2005 Proof	—	—	12.50
2006(ml)	35,319,000	5.00	—
2006(ml) Proof	—	—	12.50
2007(ml)	38,957,000	5.00	—
2007(ml) Proof	—	—	12.50
2008(ml)	18,400,000	5.00	—
2008(ml) Proof	—	—	12.50
2009(ml)	38,430,000	5.00	—
2009(ml) Proof	—	—	12.50
2010(ml)	—	5.00	—
2010(ml) Proof	—	—	12.50
2011(ml)	—	5.00	—
2011(ml) Proof	—	—	12.50
2012(ml)	—	5.00	—
2012(ml) Proof	—	—	12.50

KM# 270d 2 DOLLARS

8.8300 g., 0.9250 Silver gold plated center 0.2626 oz. ASW **Ruler:** Elizabeth II **Subject:** 100th Anniversary of the Cobalt Silver Strike **Obv:** Crowned head right, within circle, date below **Rev:** Polar bear right, within circle, denomination below

Date	Mintage	MS-63	Proof
2003 Proof	100,000	—	25.00

KM# 496a 2 DOLLARS

10.8414 g., 0.9250 Bi-Metallic Gold plated Silver center in Silver ring 0.3224 oz., 28 mm. **Ruler:** Elizabeth II **Obv:** Head right **Obv. Designer:** Susanna Blunt **Rev:** Polar Bear **Edge:** Segmented reeding

Date	Mintage	MS-63	Proof
2004 Proof	—	—	25.00

KM# 835 2 DOLLARS

8.8000 g., 0.9250 Silver 0.2617 oz. ASW, 27.95 mm. **Ruler:** Elizabeth II **Rev:** Proud Polar Bear advancing right

Date	Mintage	MS-63	Proof
2004 Proof	12,607	—	40.00

KM# 837 2 DOLLARS

7.3000 g., Bi-Metallic Aluminum-Bronze center in Nickel ring **Ruler:** Elizabeth II **Obv:** Bust left, date at top **Rev:** Polar Bear advancing right

Date	Mintage	MS-63	Proof
2006(ml)	—	7.50	—
2007(ml)	38,957,000	7.50	—

KM# 631 2 DOLLARS

7.3000 g., Bi-Metallic Aluminum-Bronze center in Nickel ring, 28 mm. **Ruler:** Elizabeth II **Subject:** 10th Anniversary of $2 coin **Obv:** Crowned head right **Edge:** Segmented reeding

Date	Mintage	MS-63	Proof
2006(ml)	5,005,000	25.00	—
2006(ml) Proof	—	—	40.00

KM# 631a 2 DOLLARS

Bi-Metallic 22 Kt Gold ring around 4.1 Kt. Gold core **Ruler:** Elizabeth II **Subject:** 10th Anniversary of $2 coin **Obv:** Crowned head right **Rev:** Polar bear

Date	Mintage	MS-63	Proof
2006 Proof	2,068	—	400

KM# 836 2 DOLLARS

7.3000 g., Bi-Metallic Aluminum-Bronze center in Nickel ring, 28 mm. **Ruler:** Elizabeth II **Subject:** $2 coin, 10th Anniversary **Rev:** "Churchill" Polar Bear, northern lights **Edge:** Segmented reeding

Date	Mintage	MS-63	Proof
2006(ml)	31,636	7.50	—

KM# 796 2 DOLLARS

8.8300 g., 0.9250 Silver 0.2626 oz. ASW, 28.07 mm. **Ruler:** Elizabeth II **Rev:** Bear, gold plated center

Date	Mintage	MS-63	Proof
2008	—	25.00	—

KM# 1040 2 DOLLARS

7.3000 g., Bi-Metallic Aluminum-Bronze center in Nickel ring, 28 mm. **Ruler:** Elizabeth II **Subject:** Quebec 400th Anniversary **Rev:** Lis and small sailing ship **Edge:** Segmented reeding

Date	Mintage	MS-63	Proof
2008	—	7.50	—

KM# 1020 2 DOLLARS

7.3000 g., Bi-Metallic Aluminum-Bronze center in Nickel ring, 28 mm. **Ruler:** Elizabeth II **Rev:** Two lynx cubs **Rev. Designer:** Christie Paquet **Edge:** Segmented reeding

Date	Mintage	MS-63	Proof
2010 Specimen	15,000	—	40.00

KM# 1088 2 DOLLARS

7.3000 g., Bi-Metallic Aluminum-Bronze center in Nickel ring, 28 mm. **Ruler:** Elizabeth II **Rev:** Elk Calf **Rev. Designer:** Christine Paquet **Edge:** Segmented reeding

Date	Mintage	MS-63	Proof
2011	—	7.50	—

KM# 1167 2 DOLLARS

7.3000 g., Bi-Metallic Aluminum-Bronze center in Nickel ring, 28 mm. **Ruler:** Elizabeth II **Subject:** Canada Parks **Obv:** Bust right **Rev:** Stylized trees

Date	Mintage	MS-63	Proof
2011	—	7.50	—

KM# 1257 2 DOLLARS

6.9200 g., Bi-Metallic Brass Plated Aluminum-Bronze center in Nickel Plated Steel ring, 28 mm. **Ruler:** Elizabeth II **Rev:** Polar bear with security device above **Edge:** Lettered and segmented reeding

Date	Mintage	MS-63	Proof
2012	—	7.50	—
2012 Proof	—	—	10.00
2013	—	7.50	—
2013 Proof	—	—	10.00

KM# 1258 2 DOLLARS

6.9200 g., Bi-Metallic Brass Plated Aluminum-Bronze center in Nickel Plated Steel ring, 28 mm. **Ruler:** Elizabeth II **Subject:** H.M.S. Shannon **Edge:** Lettered and segmented reeding

Date	Mintage	MS-63	Proof
2012	—	10.00	—

KM# 1263 2 DOLLARS

7.3000 g., Bi-Metallic Aluminum-Bronze center in Nickel ring, 28 mm. **Ruler:** Elizabeth II **Rev:** Wolf cubs

Date	Mintage	MS-63	Proof
2012	—	10.00	—

KM# 657 3 DOLLARS

11.7200 g., 0.9250 Silver gilt 0.3485 oz. ASW, 27x27 mm. **Ruler:** Elizabeth II **Rev:** Beaver within wreath **Shape:** Square

Date	Mintage	MS-63	Proof
2006 Proof	19,963	—	225

KM# 1051 3 DOLLARS

11.6000 g., 0.9250 Silver gilt 0.3450 oz. ASW, 27x27 mm. **Ruler:** Elizabeth II **Subject:** Wildlife conservation **Rev:** Stylized polar bear and northern lights **Shape:** square

Date	Mintage	MS-63	Proof
2010 Specimen	15,000	55.00	—

KM# 978 3 DOLLARS
7.9600 g., Silver Partially Gilt, 27 mm. **Ruler:** Elizabeth II **Rev:** Return of the Tyee (giant salmon)

Date	Mintage	MS-63	Proof
2010 Proof	15,000	—	50.00

KM# 1011 3 DOLLARS
11.6000 g., 0.9250 Silver gilt 0.3450 oz. ASW, 27x27 mm. **Ruler:** Elizabeth II **Rev:** Barn Owl **Rev. Designer:** Jason Bouwman **Shape:** Square

Date	Mintage	MS-63	Proof
2010 Proof	15,000	—	65.00

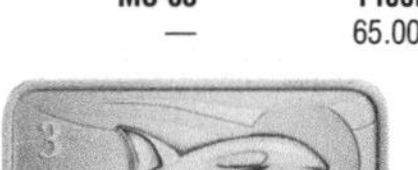

KM# 1089 3 DOLLARS
11.6000 g., 0.9250 Silver gilt 0.3450 oz. ASW, 27x27 mm. **Ruler:** Elizabeth II **Rev:** Orca Whale **Rev. Designer:** Jason Bouwman **Shape:** Square

Date	Mintage	MS-63	Proof
2011 Proof	15,000	—	65.00

KM# 1090 3 DOLLARS
7.9600 g., 0.9990 Silver with red and yellow partial gilding 0.2557 oz. ASW, 27 mm. **Ruler:** Elizabeth II **Obv:** Bust right **Rev:** Eskimo mother kneeling, child on back, partially gilt **Rev. Designer:** Andrew Oappik

Date	Mintage	MS-63	Proof
2011 Proof	10,000	—	65.00

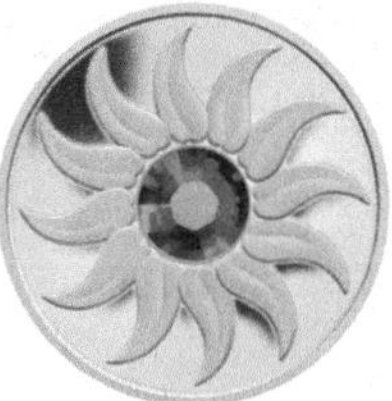

KM# 1117 3 DOLLARS
7.9600 g., 0.9999 Silver 0.2559 oz. ASW, 27 mm. **Ruler:** Elizabeth II **Subject:** January birthstone, Garnet **Obv:** Bust left **Rev:** Birthstone at cener of artistic sunburst **Edge:** Reeded

Date	Mintage	MS-63	Proof
2011 Proof	—	—	45.00

KM# 1118 3 DOLLARS
7.9600 g., 0.9999 Silver 0.2559 oz. ASW, 27 mm. **Ruler:** Elizabeth II **Subject:** February birthstone, Amythest **Obv:** Bust right **Rev:** Birthstone at cener of artistic sunburst **Edge:** Reeded

Date	Mintage	MS-63	Proof
2011 Proof	—	—	45.00

KM# 1119 3 DOLLARS
7.9600 g., 0.9999 Silver 0.2559 oz. ASW, 27 mm. **Ruler:** Elizabeth II **Subject:** March birthstone, Aquamarine **Obv:** Bust right **Rev:** Birthstone at cener of artistic sunburst **Edge:** Reeded

Date	Mintage	MS-63	Proof
2011 Proof	—	—	45.00

KM# 1120 3 DOLLARS
7.9600 g., 0.9999 Silver 0.2559 oz. ASW, 27 mm. **Ruler:** Elizabeth II **Subject:** April birthstone, diamond **Obv:** Bust right **Rev:** Birthstone at cener of artistic sunburst **Edge:** Reeded

Date	Mintage	MS-63	Proof
2011 Proof	—	—	45.00

KM# 1121 3 DOLLARS
7.9600 g., 0.9999 Silver 0.2559 oz. ASW, 27 mm. **Ruler:** Elizabeth II **Subject:** May birthstone **Obv:** Bust right **Rev:** Birthstone at cener of artistic sunburst **Edge:** Reeded

Date	Mintage	MS-63	Proof
2011 Proof	—	—	45.00

KM# 1122 3 DOLLARS
7.9600 g., 0.9999 Silver 0.2559 oz. ASW, 27 mm. **Ruler:** Elizabeth II **Subject:** June birthstone, Alexandrite **Obv:** Bust right **Rev:** Birthstone at cener of artistic sunburst

Date	Mintage	MS-63	Proof
2011 Proof	—	—	45.00

KM# 1123 3 DOLLARS
7.9600 g., 0.9999 Silver 0.2559 oz. ASW, 27 mm. **Ruler:** Elizabeth II **Subject:** July birthstone, Ruby **Obv:** Bust right **Rev:** Birthstone at cener of artistic sunburst

Date	Mintage	MS-63	Proof
2011 Proof	—	—	45.00

KM# 1124 3 DOLLARS
7.9600 g., 0.9999 Silver 0.2559 oz. ASW, 27 mm. **Ruler:** Elizabeth II **Subject:** August birthstone, Priedot **Obv:** Bust right **Rev:** Birthstone at cener of artistic sunburst

Date	Mintage	MS-63	Proof
2011 Proof	—	—	45.00

KM# 1125 3 DOLLARS
7.9600 g., 0.9999 Silver 0.2559 oz. ASW, 27 mm. **Ruler:** Elizabeth II **Subject:** September birhtstone **Obv:** Bust right **Rev:** Birthstone at cener of artistic sunburst **Edge:** Reeded

Date	Mintage	MS-63	Proof
2011 Proof	—	—	45.00

KM# 1126 3 DOLLARS
7.9600 g., 0.9999 Silver 0.2559 oz. ASW, 27 mm. **Ruler:** Elizabeth II **Subject:** October birthstone **Obv:** Bust right **Rev:** Birthstone at cener of artistic sunburst

Date	Mintage	MS-63	Proof
2011 Proof	—	—	45.00

KM# 1127 3 DOLLARS
7.9600 g., 0.9999 Silver 0.2559 oz. ASW, 27 mm. **Ruler:** Elizabeth II **Subject:** November birthstone **Obv:** Bust right **Rev:** Birthstone at cener of artistic sunburst

Date	Mintage	MS-63	Proof
2011 Proof	—	—	45.00

KM# 1128 3 DOLLARS
7.9600 g., 0.9999 Silver 0.2559 oz. ASW, 27 mm. **Ruler:** Elizabeth II **Subject:** December birhtstone **Obv:** Bust right **Rev:** Birthstone at cener of artistic sunburst

Date	Mintage	MS-63	Proof
2011 Proof	—	—	45.00

KM# 1151 3 DOLLARS
11.8000 g., 0.9250 Silver gold plated 0.3509 oz. ASW, 27x27 mm. **Ruler:** Elizabeth II **Obv:** Bust right **Rev:** Black footed ferret

Date	Mintage	MS-63	Proof
2011 Proof	Est. 15,000	—	65.00

KM# 1300 3 DOLLARS
7.9600 g., 0.9999 Silver 0.2559 oz. ASW, 27 mm. **Ruler:** Elizabeth II **Subject:** January birthstone, Garnet **Obv:** Bust right **Obv. Designer:** Susana Blunt **Rev:** Birthstone at center of wreath **Rev. Designer:** Maurice Gervias

Date	Mintage	MS-63	Proof
2013 Proof	—	—	50.00

KM# 1301 3 DOLLARS
7.9600 g., 0.9990 Silver 0.2557 oz. ASW, 27 mm. **Ruler:** Elizabeth II **Subject:** February birthstone, Amythest **Obv:** Bust right **Obv. Designer:** Susana Blunt **Rev:** Birthstone at center of wreath **Rev. Designer:** Maurice Gervais

Date	Mintage	MS-63	Proof
2013 Proof	—	—	65.00

KM# 1302 3 DOLLARS
7.9600 g., 0.9990 Silver 0.2557 oz. ASW, 27 mm. **Ruler:** Elizabeth II **Subject:** March birthstone, Aquamarine **Obv:** Bust right **Obv. Designer:** Susana Blunt **Rev:** Birthstone at center of wreath **Rev. Designer:** Maurice Gervais

Date	Mintage	MS-63	Proof
2013 Proof	—	—	50.00

KM# 1303 3 DOLLARS
7.9600 g., 0.9990 Silver 0.2557 oz. ASW, 27 mm. **Ruler:** Elizabeth II **Subject:** April birthstone, Diamond **Obv:** Bust right **Obv. Designer:** Susana Blunt **Rev:** Birthstone at center of wreath **Rev. Designer:** Maurice Gervais

Date	Mintage	MS-63	Proof
2013 Proof	—	—	50.00

KM# 1304 3 DOLLARS
7.9600 g., 0.9990 Silver 0.2557 oz. ASW, 27 mm. **Ruler:** Elizabeth II **Subject:** May birthstone **Obv:** Bust right **Obv. Designer:** Susana Blunt **Rev:** Birthstone at center of wreath **Rev. Designer:** Maurice Gervais

Date	Mintage	MS-63	Proof
2013 Proof	—	—	50.00

KM# 1305 3 DOLLARS
7.9600 g., 0.9990 Silver 0.2557 oz. ASW, 27 mm. **Ruler:** Elizabeth II **Subject:** June birthstone, Alexandrite **Obv:** Bust right **Obv. Designer:** Susana Blunt **Rev:** Birthstone at center of wreath **Rev. Designer:** Maurice Gervais

Date	Mintage	MS-63	Proof
2013 Proof	—	—	50.00

KM# 1306 3 DOLLARS
7.9600 g., 0.9990 Silver 0.2557 oz. ASW, 27 mm. **Ruler:** Elizabeth II **Subject:** July birthstone - Ruby **Obv:** Bust right **Obv. Designer:** Susana Blunt **Rev:** Birthstone at center of wreath **Rev. Designer:** Maurice Gervais

Date	Mintage	MS-63	Proof
2013 Proof	—	—	50.00

KM# 1307 3 DOLLARS
7.9600 g., 0.9990 Silver 0.2557 oz. ASW, 27 mm. **Ruler:** Elizabeth II **Subject:** August birthstone - Priedot **Obv:** Bust right **Obv. Designer:** Susana Blunt **Rev:** Birthstone at center of wreath **Rev. Designer:** Maurice Gervais

Date	Mintage	MS-63	Proof
2013 Proof	—	—	50.00

KM# 1308 3 DOLLARS
7.9600 g., 0.9990 Silver 0.2557 oz. ASW, 27 mm. **Ruler:** Elizabeth II **Subject:** September birthstone **Obv:** Bust right **Obv. Designer:** Susana Blunt **Rev:** Birthstone at center of wreath **Rev. Designer:** Maruice Gervais

Date	Mintage	MS-63	Proof
2013 Proof	—	—	50.00

KM# 1309 3 DOLLARS
7.9600 g., 0.9990 Silver 0.2557 oz. ASW, 27 mm. **Ruler:** Elizabeth II **Subject:** October birthstone **Obv:** Bust right **Obv. Designer:** Susana Blunt **Rev:** Birthstone at center of wreath **Rev. Designer:** Maurice Gervais

Date	Mintage	MS-63	Proof
2013 Proof	—	—	50.00

KM# 1310 3 DOLLARS
7.9600 g., 0.9990 Silver 0.2557 oz. ASW, 27 mm. **Ruler:** Elizabeth II **Subject:** November birthstone **Obv:** Bust right **Obv. Designer:** Susana Blunt **Rev:** Birthstone at center of wreath **Rev. Designer:** Maurice Gervais

Date	Mintage	MS-63	Proof
2013 Proof	—	—	50.00

KM# 1311 3 DOLLARS
7.9600 g., 0.9990 Silver 0.2557 oz. ASW, 27 mm. **Ruler:** Elizabeth II **Subject:** December birthstone **Obv:** Bust right **Obv. Designer:** Susana Blunt **Rev:** Birthstone at center of wreath **Rev. Designer:** Maurice Gervais

Date	Mintage	MS-63	Proof
2013 Proof	—	—	50.00

KM# 728 4 DOLLARS
15.8700 g., 0.9250 Silver 0.4719 oz. ASW, 34 mm. **Ruler:** Elizabeth II **Subject:** Dinosaur fossil **Obv:** Bust right **Rev:** Parasaurolophus, selective enameling

Date	Mintage	MS-63	Proof
2007 Proof	14,946	—	125

KM# 797 4 DOLLARS

15.8700 g., 0.9990 Silver 0.5097 oz. ASW, 34 mm. **Ruler:** Elizabeth II **Subject:** Dinosaur fossil **Obv:** Bust right **Rev:** Triceratops, enameled **Rev. Designer:** Kerri Burnett

Date	Mintage	MS-63	Proof
2008 Proof	13,046	—	75.00

KM# 890 4 DOLLARS

15.8700 g., 0.9990 Silver 0.5097 oz. ASW, 34 mm. **Ruler:** Elizabeth II **Subject:** Tyrannosaurus Rex **Obv:** Bust right **Obv. Legend:** Elizabeth II DG Regina **Obv. Designer:** Susanna Blunt **Rev:** T-Rex skeleton in selective aging **Rev. Legend:** Canada 4 Dollars **Rev. Designer:** Kerri Burnette

Date	Mintage	MS-63	Proof
2009 Proof	13,572	—	60.00

KM# 942 4 DOLLARS

15.8700 g., Silver, 34 mm. **Ruler:** Elizabeth II **Rev:** Kids hanging stocking on fireplace, Christmas tree on right

Date	Mintage	MS-63	Proof
2009 Proof	6,011	—	45.00

KM# 1014 4 DOLLARS

15.8700 g., 0.9990 Silver selectively plated 0.5097 oz. ASW, 34 mm. **Ruler:** Elizabeth II **Rev:** Euoplocephalus **Rev. Designer:** Kerri Burnett

Date	Mintage	MS-63	Proof
2010 Proof	Est. 13,000	—	60.00

KM# 1022 4 DOLLARS

Silver selective plating **Ruler:** Elizabeth II **Rev:** Dromaeosaurus

Date	Mintage	MS-63	Proof
2010 Proof	8,982	—	85.00

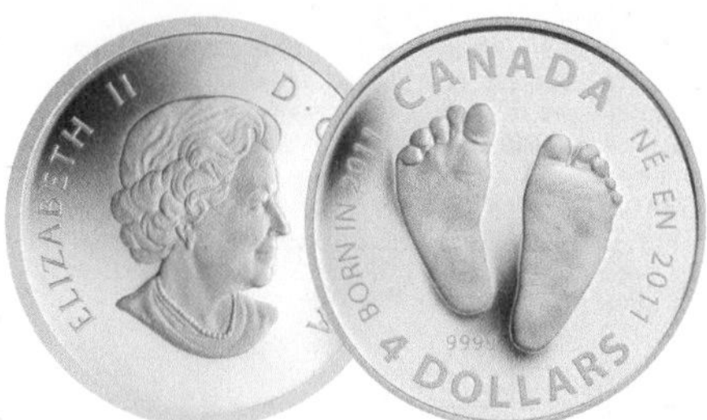

KM# 1129 4 DOLLARS

15.8700 g., 0.9999 Silver 0.5102 oz. ASW, 34 mm. **Ruler:** Elizabeth II **Obv:** Bust right **Rev:** Baby's footprint **Edge:** Reeded

Date	Mintage	MS-63	Proof
2011 Proof	Est. 10,000	—	60.00

KM# 435 5 DOLLARS

16.8600 g., 0.9250 Silver 0.5014 oz. ASW, 28.4 mm. **Ruler:** Elizabeth II **Subject:** Guglielmo Marconi **Obv:** Crowned head right **Rev:** Gold-plated cameo portrait of Marconi **Rev. Designer:** Cosme Saffioti **Edge:** Reeded **Note:** Only issued in two coin set with British 2 pounds KM#1014a.

Date	Mintage	MS-63	Proof
2001 Proof	15,011	—	30.00

KM# 519 5 DOLLARS

8.3600 g., 0.9000 Gold 0.2419 oz. AGW, 21.6 mm. **Ruler:** Elizabeth II **Obv:** Crowned head right **Rev:** National arms **Edge:** Reeded

Date	Mintage	MS-63	Proof
1912-2002 Proof	2,002	—	450

KM# 603 5 DOLLARS

31.1050 g., 0.9999 Silver 0.9999 oz. ASW **Ruler:** Elizabeth II **Obv:** Head right **Rev:** Loon splashing in the water, hologram

Date	Mintage	MS-63	Proof
2002 Satin Proof	30,000	—	45.00

KM# 518 5 DOLLARS

31.1200 g., 0.9999 Silver 1.0004 oz. ASW, 38 mm. **Ruler:** Elizabeth II **Subject:** F.I.F.A. World Cup Soccer , Germany 2006 **Obv:** Crowned head right, denomination **Rev:** Goalie on knees **Edge:** Reeded

Date	Mintage	MS-63	Proof
2003 Proof	21,542	—	40.00

KM# 514 5 DOLLARS

31.1200 g., 0.9999 Silver 1.0004 oz. ASW, 38 mm. **Ruler:** Elizabeth II **Obv:** Crowned head right **Rev:** Moose **Edge:** Reeded

Date	Mintage	MS-63	Proof
2004 Proof	12,822	—	175

KM# 527 5 DOLLARS

31.1200 g., 0.9999 Silver 1.0004 oz. ASW **Ruler:** Elizabeth II **Subject:** Golf, Championship of Canada, Centennial **Obv:** Head right

Date	Mintage	MS-63	Proof
2004 Proof	18,750	—	30.00

KM# 554 5 DOLLARS

31.1200 g., 0.9999 Silver 1.0004 oz. ASW **Ruler:** Elizabeth II **Subject:** Alberta **Obv. Designer:** Head right **Rev. Designer:** Michelle Grant

Date	Mintage	MS-63	Proof
2005 Proof	20,000	—	35.00

KM# 555 5 DOLLARS

31.1200 g., 0.9999 Silver 1.0004 oz. ASW **Ruler:** Elizabeth II **Subject:** Saskatchewan **Obv:** Head right **Obv. Designer:** Susanna Blunt **Rev. Designer:** Paulett Sapergia

Date	Mintage	MS-63	Proof
2005 Proof	20,000	—	35.00

KM# 556.1 5 DOLLARS

31.1200 g., 0.9990 Silver 0.9995 oz. ASW, 38.02 mm. **Ruler:** Elizabeth II **Subject:** 60th Anniversay Victory WWII - Veterans **Obv:** Bust right **Rev:** Large V and heads of sailor, soldier and aviator on large maple leaf **Edge:** Reeded

Date	Mintage	MS-63	Proof
2005	25,000	32.00	—

KM# 556.2 5 DOLLARS

31.1200 g., 0.9999 Silver 1.0004 oz. ASW, 38.02 mm. **Ruler:** Elizabeth II **Subject:** 60th Anniversary Victory WW II - Veterans **Obv:** Bust right **Rev:** Large V and heads of sailor, soldier and aviator on maple leaf with small maple leaf added at left and right **Edge:** Reeded

Date	Mintage	MS-63	Proof
2005	10,000	125	—

KM# 557 5 DOLLARS

31.1200 g., 0.9999 Silver 1.0004 oz. ASW, 36 mm. **Ruler:** Elizabeth II **Subject:** Walrus and calf **Obv:** Head right **Obv. Designer:** Susanna Blunt **Rev:** Two walrusus and calf **Rev. Designer:** Pierre Leduc

Date	Mintage	MS-63	Proof
2005 Proof	5,519	—	45.00

KM# 558 5 DOLLARS

31.1200 g., 0.9999 Silver 1.0004 oz. ASW, 36 mm. **Ruler:** Elizabeth II **Subject:** White tailed deer **Obv:** Head right **Obv. Designer:** Susanna Blunt **Rev:** Two deer standing **Rev. Designer:** Xerxes Irani

Date	Mintage	MS-63	Proof
2005 Proof	6,439	—	45.00

KM# 585 5 DOLLARS
31.1200 g., 0.9999 Silver 1.0004 oz. ASW, 36 mm. **Ruler:** Elizabeth II **Obv:** Head right **Obv. Designer:** Susanna Blunt **Rev:** Peregrine Falcon feeding young ones **Rev. Designer:** Dwayne Harty

Date	Mintage	MS-63	Proof
2006 Proof	7,226	—	50.00

KM# 586 5 DOLLARS
31.1200 g., 0.9999 Silver 1.0004 oz. ASW, 36 mm. **Ruler:** Elizabeth II **Subject:** Sable Island horses **Obv:** Head right **Obv. Designer:** Susanna Blunt **Rev:** Horse and foal standing **Rev. Designer:** Christie Paquet

Date	Mintage	MS-63	Proof
2006 Proof	10,108	—	50.00

KM# 658 5 DOLLARS
31.1200 g., 0.9999 Silver 1.0004 oz. ASW, 36.07 mm. **Ruler:** Elizabeth II **Subject:** Breast Cancer Awareness **Rev:** Colorized pink ribbon

Date	Mintage	MS-63	Proof
2006 Proof	11,048	—	50.00

KM# 659 5 DOLLARS
31.1200 g., 0.9999 Silver 1.0004 oz. ASW **Ruler:** Elizabeth II **Subject:** C.A.F. Snowbirds Acrobatic Jet Flying Team **Rev:** Image of fighter jets and piolt

Date	Mintage	MS-63	Proof
2006 Proof	10,034	—	50.00

KM# 1036 5 DOLLARS
31.1200 g., 0.9990 Silver 0.9995 oz. ASW **Ruler:** Elizabeth II **Subject:** 80th Anniversary **Rev:** Two deer standing, one eating branch

Date	Mintage	MS-63	Proof
2009 Proof	27,872	—	70.00

KM# 1130 5 DOLLARS
8.5000 g., Bi-Metallic Niobium center in .925 Silver ring, 28 mm. **Ruler:** Elizabeth II **Subject:** Summer - Buck Moon **Obv:** Bust right **Rev:** Buck against summer moon

Date	Mintage	MS-63	Proof
2011 Proof	7,500	—	125

KM# 1131 5 DOLLARS
8.5000 g., Bi-Metallic Niobium center in .925 Silver ring, 28 mm. **Ruler:** Elizabeth II **Subject:** Fall Moon **Obv:** Bust right **Rev:** Native American hunter seated tracking prey before Harvest Moon

Date	Mintage	MS-63	Proof
2011 Proof	7,500	—	125

KM# 1132 5 DOLLARS
8.5000 g., Bi-Metallic Niobium center in .925 Silver ring, 28 mm. **Ruler:** Elizabeth II **Subject:** Winter Moon **Obv:** Bust right **Rev:** Wolf howling before Winter Moon

Date	Mintage	MS-63	Proof
2011 Proof	7,500	—	125

KM# 1133 5 DOLLARS
8.5000 g., Bi-Metallic Niobium center in .925 Silver ring, 28 mm. **Ruler:** Elizabeth II **Subject:** Spring Moon **Obv:** Bust right **Rev:** Phlox blossoming agains a Spring Moon

Date	Mintage	MS-63	Proof
2011 Proof	7,500	—	125

KM# 1149 5 DOLLARS
3.1300 g., 0.9999 Gold 0.1006 oz. AGW, 16 mm. **Ruler:** Elizabeth II **Subject:** Norman Bethune **Obv:** Bust right **Rev:** Half-length figure at right, looking left

Date	Mintage	MS-63	Proof
2011 Proof	Est. 5,000	—	300

KM# 1236 5 DOLLARS
8.3600 g., 0.9000 Gold 0.2419 oz. AGW, 21.6 mm. **Ruler:** Elizabeth II **Obv:** Bust right **Rev:** Crowned monogram in wreath

Date	Mintage	MS-63	Proof
1952-2012 Proof	—	—	500

KM# 1194 5 DOLLARS
3.1300 g., 0.9990 Gold 0.1005 oz. AGW, 16 mm. **Ruler:** Elizabeth II **Obv:** Bust right **Rev:** Royal Cypher, wreath below

Date	Mintage	MS-63	Proof
2012 Proof	—	—	200

KM# 1220 5 DOLLARS
3.1300 g., 0.9999 Gold 0.1006 oz. AGW, 16 mm. **Ruler:** Elizabeth II **Subject:** Year of the Dragon **Obv:** Bust right **Rev:** Dragon forpart right

Date	Mintage	MS-63	Proof
2012 Specimen	Est. 38,888	—	225

KM# 1248 5 DOLLARS
31.1200 g., 0.9990 Silver 0.9995 oz. ASW, 36 mm. **Ruler:** Elizabeth II **Subject:** Rich Hansen **Rev:** Wheelchair bound athlethe

Date	Mintage	MS-63	Proof
2012	—	—	75.00

KM# 1261 5 DOLLARS
8.5000 g., Bi-Metallic Niobium center in .925 Silver ring., 28 mm. **Ruler:** Elizabeth II **Rev:** Flowers and moon, field in color

Date	Mintage	MS-63	Proof
2012	—	—	125

KM# 1281 5 DOLLARS
3.1300 g., 0.9990 Gold 0.1005 oz. AGW, 16 mm. **Ruler:** Elizabeth II **Subject:** Year of the Dragon

Date	Mintage	MS-63	Proof
2012 Proof	—	—	200

KM# 1298 5 DOLLARS
3.1300 g., 0.9990 Gold 0.1005 oz. AGW **Ruler:** Elizabeth II **Subject:** Year of the Snake

Date	Mintage	MS-63	Proof
2013 Proof	—	—	225

KM# 515 8 DOLLARS
28.8000 g., 0.9250 Silver 0.8565 oz. ASW, 39 mm. **Ruler:** Elizabeth II **Obv:** Head right **Obv. Designer:** Susanna Blunt **Rev:** Grizzly bear walking left **Edge:** Reeded

Date	Mintage	MS-63	Proof
2004 Proof	12,942	—	85.00

KM# 597 8 DOLLARS
32.1500 g., 0.9999 Silver partially gilt 1.0335 oz. ASW **Ruler:** Elizabeth II **Subject:** Canadian Pacific Railway, 120th Anniversary **Obv:** Head right **Obv. Designer:** Susanna Blunt **Rev:** Railway bridge, center is gilt

Date	Mintage	MS-63	Proof
2005 Proof	9,892	—	65.00

KM# 598 8 DOLLARS
32.1500 g., 0.9999 Silver partially gilt 1.0335 oz. ASW **Ruler:** Elizabeth II **Subject:** Canadian Pacific Railway, 120th Anniversary **Obv:** Head right **Rev:** Railway memorial to the Chinese workers, center gilt

Date	Mintage	MS-63	Proof
2005 Proof	9,892	—	65.00

KM# 730 8 DOLLARS
25.1800 g., 0.9999 Silver 0.8094 oz. ASW, 36.07 mm. **Ruler:** Elizabeth II **Obv:** Queens's head at top in circle, three Chinese characters **Rev:** Dragon and other creatures

Date	Mintage	MS-63	Proof
2007 Proof	19,996	—	50.00

KM# 731 8 DOLLARS
25.1800 g., 0.9990 Silver 0.8087 oz. ASW, 36.1 mm. **Ruler:** Elizabeth II **Rev:** Maple leaf, long life hologram

Date	Mintage	MS-63	Proof
2007	15,000	—	55.00

KM# 943 8 DOLLARS
25.1800 g., 0.9250 Silver 0.7488 oz. ASW, 36.1 mm. **Ruler:** Elizabeth II **Rev:** Hologram maple of wisdom at top left, crystal in center, dragons around

Date	Mintage	MS-63	Proof
2009 Proof	7,273	—	90.00

KM# 1012 8 DOLLARS
25.3000 g., 0.9250 Silver 0.7524 oz. ASW, 36.07 mm. **Ruler:** Elizabeth II **Rev:** Horses around central maple leaf hologram **Rev. Designer:** Simon Ng

Date	Mintage	MS-63	Proof
2010 Proof	8,888	—	100

KM# 520 10 DOLLARS
16.7200 g., 0.9000 Gold 0.4838 oz. AGW, 26.92 mm. **Ruler:** Elizabeth II **Obv:** Crowned head right **Rev:** National arms **Edge:** Reeded

Date	Mintage	MS-63	Proof
1912-2002 Proof	2,002	—	850

KM# 559 10 DOLLARS
25.1750 g., 0.9999 Silver 0.8093 oz. ASW, 36 mm. **Ruler:** Elizabeth II **Subject:** Pope John Paul II **Obv:** Head right

Date	Mintage	MS-63	Proof
2005 Proof	24,716	—	45.00

KM# 757 10 DOLLARS
25.1750 g., 0.9999 Silver 0.8093 oz. ASW **Ruler:** Elizabeth II **Subject:** Year of the Veteran **Rev:** Profile left of young and old veteran

Date	Mintage	MS-63	Proof
2005 Proof	6,549	—	225

KM# 661 10 DOLLARS
25.1750 g., 0.9999 Silver 0.8093 oz. ASW **Ruler:** Elizabeth II **Subject:** National Historic Sites **Obv:** Head right **Rev:** Fortress of Louisbourg

Date	Mintage	MS-63	Proof
2006 Proof	5,544	—	40.00

KM# 1010 10 DOLLARS
15.8700 g., 0.9990 Silver 0.5097 oz. ASW **Ruler:** Elizabeth II **Subject:** 75th Anniversary Canadian Bank Notes **Rev:** Female seated

Date	Mintage	MS-63	Proof
2010 Proof	7,500	—	50.00

KM# 1096 10 DOLLARS
27.7800 g., 0.9250 Silver 0.8261 oz. ASW, 40 mm. **Ruler:** Elizabeth II **Obv:** Bust right **Rev:** Blue whale diving in sea

Date	Mintage	MS-63	Proof
2010 Proof	10,000	—	85.00

KM# 1199 10 DOLLARS
15.8700 g., 0.9999 Silver 0.5102 oz. ASW, 34 mm. **Ruler:** Elizabeth II **Subject:** Winter Scene - Skating **Rev:** Three kids skating on pond, colored holly at left

Date	Mintage	MS-63	Proof
2011 Proof	Est. 8,000	—	40.00

KM# 1198 10 DOLLARS
15.8700 g., 0.9990 Silver 0.5097 oz. ASW, 34 mm. **Ruler:** Elizabeth II **Subject:** Highway of Heroes **Obv:** Bust right **Obv. Designer:** Susanna Blunt **Rev:** Citizens on Highway 401 overpass with signs and flags, large maple leaf in background, Memorial Cross medal at top left. **Rev. Designer:** Stan Witten and Major Carl Gauthier **Edge:** Reeded

Date	Mintage	MS-63	Proof
2011	25,000	—	70.00

KM# 1200 10 DOLLARS
15.8700 g., 0.9999 Silver 0.5102 oz. ASW, 34 mm. **Ruler:** Elizabeth II **Subject:** Winter scene - Two houses **Rev:** Two houses in snowy lane, colored holly flanking

Date	Mintage	MS-63	Proof
2011 Proof	Est. 8,000	—	40.00

KM# 1201 10 DOLLARS
15.8700 g., 0.9999 Silver 0.5102 oz. ASW, 34 mm. **Ruler:** Elizabeth II **Obv:** Bust right **Rev:** Wood Bison **Rev. Designer:** Corrine Hunt

Date	Mintage	MS-63	Proof
2011 Proof	Est. 10,000	—	50.00

KM# 1203 10 DOLLARS
15.8700 g., 0.9999 Silver 0.5102 oz. ASW, 34 mm. **Ruler:** Elizabeth II **Subject:** Boreal Forest **Rev:** Bird and tree **Rev. Designer:** Corrine Hunt

Date	Mintage	MS-63	Proof
2011 Proof	Est. 10,000	—	50.00

KM# 1205 10 DOLLARS
15.8700 g., 0.9999 Silver 0.5102 oz. ASW, 34 mm. **Ruler:** Elizabeth II **Obv:** Bust right **Rev:** Peregrine Falcon perched on branch **Rev. Designer:** Corrine Hunt

Date	Mintage	MS-63	Proof
2011 Proof	Est. 10,000	—	50.00

KM# 1207 10 DOLLARS
15.8700 g., 0.9999 Silver 0.5102 oz. ASW, 34 mm. **Ruler:** Elizabeth II **Obv:** Bust right **Rev:** Orca Whale **Rev. Designer:** Corrine Hunt

Date	Mintage	MS-63	Proof
2011 Proof	Est. 10,000	—	50.00

KM# 1221 10 DOLLARS
15.8700 g., 0.9990 Silver 0.5097 oz. ASW, 34 mm. **Ruler:** Elizabeth II **Subject:** Year of the Dragon **Obv:** Bust right **Rev:** Dragon forepart right

Date	Mintage	MS-63	Proof
2012 Specimen	58,888	—	40.00

KM# 1235 10 DOLLARS
25.1750 g., 0.9990 Silver 0.8086 oz. ASW, 36 mm. **Ruler:** Elizabeth II **Obv:** Bust right **Rev:** Titanic sailing at right, map of Eastern Canada at left

Date	Mintage	MS-63	Proof
2012 Proof	—	—	100

KM# 1249 10 DOLLARS
15.8700 g., 0.9990 Silver 0.5097 oz. ASW, 34 mm. **Ruler:** Elizabeth II **Subject:** H.M.S. Shannon

Date	Mintage	MS-63	Proof
2012	—	—	65.00

KM# 1259 10 DOLLARS
15.8700 g., 0.9990 Silver 0.5097 oz. ASW, 34 mm. **Ruler:** Elizabeth II **Subject:** Praying Mantis

Date	Mintage	MS-63	Proof
2012 Proof	—	—	45.00

KM# 1282 10 DOLLARS
7.7700 g., 0.9990 Gold 0.2496 oz. AGW, 20 mm. **Ruler:** Elizabeth II **Subject:** Year of the Dragon

Date	Mintage	MS-63	Proof
2012 Proof	—	—	450

KM# 1299 10 DOLLARS
31.1050 g., Silver **Ruler:** Elizabeth II **Subject:** Year of the Snake

Date	Mintage	MS-63	Proof
2013 Proof	—	—	50.00

KM# 415 15 DOLLARS
33.6300 g., 0.9250 Silver with gold insert 1.0000 oz. ASW, 40 mm. **Ruler:** Elizabeth II **Subject:** Year of the Snake **Obv:** Crowned head right **Rev:** Snake within circle of lunar calendar signs **Rev. Designer:** Harvey Chain **Edge:** Reeded

Date	Mintage	MS-63	Proof
2001 Proof	60,754	—	85.00

KM# 463 15 DOLLARS
33.6300 g., 0.9250 Silver with gold insert 1.0000 oz. ASW **Ruler:** Elizabeth II **Subject:** Year of the Horse **Obv:** Crowned head right **Obv. Designer:** Dora dePédery-Hunt **Rev:** Horse in center with Chinese Lunar calendar around **Rev. Designer:** Harvey Chain

Date	Mintage	MS-63	Proof
2002 Proof	59,395	—	85.00

KM# 481 15 DOLLARS
33.6300 g., 0.9250 Silver with gold insert 1.0000 oz. ASW, 40 mm. **Ruler:** Elizabeth II **Subject:** Year of the Sheep **Obv:** Crowned head right **Rev:** Sheep in center with Chinese Lunar calendar around **Rev. Designer:** Harvey Chain

Date	Mintage	MS-63	Proof
2003 Proof	53,714	—	85.00

KM# 610 15 DOLLARS
33.6300 g., 0.9250 Silver Gold octagon applique in center 1.0000 oz. ASW **Ruler:** Elizabeth II **Subject:** Year of the Monkey **Obv:** Crowned head right **Rev:** Monkey in center with Chinese Lunar calendar around

Date	Mintage	MS-63	Proof
2004 Proof	46,175	—	150

KM# 560 15 DOLLARS
33.6300 g., 0.9250 Silver with gold insert 1.0000 oz. ASW **Ruler:** Elizabeth II **Subject:** Year of the Rooster **Obv:** Crowned head right **Rev:** Rooster in center with Chinese Lunar calendar around

Date	Mintage	MS-63	Proof
2005 Proof	44,690	—	125

KM# 587 15 DOLLARS
33.6300 g., 0.9250 Silver with gold insert 1.0000 oz. ASW **Ruler:** Elizabeth II **Subject:** Year of the Dog **Obv:** Crowned head left **Rev:** Dog in center with Chinese Lunar calendar around

Date	Mintage	MS-63	Proof
2006 Proof	41,617	—	100

KM# 732 15 DOLLARS
33.6300 g., 0.9250 Silver with gold insert 1.0000 oz. ASW, 40 mm. **Ruler:** Elizabeth II **Subject:** Year of the Pig **Rev:** Pig at center of lunar characters

Date	Mintage	MS-63	Proof
2007 Proof	48,888	—	100

KM# 801 15 DOLLARS
33.6300 g., 0.9250 Silver with gold insert 1.0000 oz. ASW, 40 mm. **Ruler:** Elizabeth II **Subject:** Year of the Rat **Rev:** Rat, gold octagonal insert at center

Date	Mintage	MS-63	Proof
2008 Proof	48,888	—	90.00

KM# 803 15 DOLLARS
30.0000 g., 0.9250 Silver 0.8921 oz. ASW, 36.15 mm. **Ruler:** Elizabeth II **Rev:** Queen Victoria's coinage portrait

Date	Mintage	MS-63	Proof
2008	3,442	100	—

KM# 804 15 DOLLARS
30.0000 g., 0.9250 Silver 0.8921 oz. ASW, 36.15 mm. **Ruler:** Elizabeth II **Rev:** Edward VII coinage portrait **Rev. Designer:** G. W. DeSaulles

Date	Mintage	MS-63	Proof
2008	6,261	100	—

KM# 805 15 DOLLARS
20.0000 g., 0.9250 Silver 0.5948 oz. ASW, 36.15 mm. **Ruler:** Elizabeth II **Rev:** George V coinage portrait

Date	Mintage	MS-63	Proof
2008	—	100	—

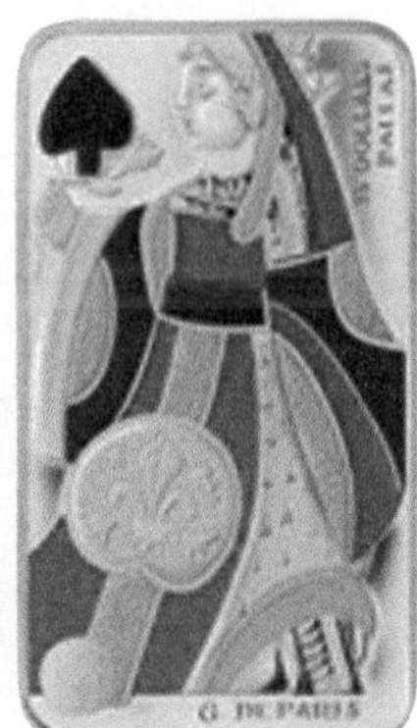

KM# 806 15 DOLLARS
31.5600 g., 0.9250 Silver 0.9385 oz. ASW, 49.8 x 28.6 mm. **Ruler:** Elizabeth II **Rev:** Queen of Spades, multicolor playing card

Date	Mintage	MS-63	Proof
2008 Proof	8,714	—	90.00

KM# 807 15 DOLLARS
31.5600 g., 0.9250 Silver 0.9385 oz. ASW, 28.6x49.8 mm. **Ruler:** Elizabeth II **Rev:** Jack of Hearts, multicolor playing card

Date	Mintage	MS-63	Proof
2008 Proof	11,362	—	85.00

KM# 919 15 DOLLARS
31.5600 g., 0.9250 Silver 0.9385 oz. ASW, 49.8 x 28.6 mm. **Ruler:** Elizabeth II **Obv:** Bust right **Obv. Designer:** Susanna Blunt **Rev:** Ten of spades, multicolor **Shape:** rectangle

Date	Mintage	MS-63	Proof
2009 Proof	5,921	—	150

KM# 920 15 DOLLARS
31.5600 g., 0.9250 Silver 0.9385 oz. ASW, 49.8 x 28.6 mm. **Ruler:** Elizabeth II **Obv:** Bust right **Obv. Designer:** Susanna Blunt **Rev:** King of hearts, multicolor **Shape:** Rectangle

Date	Mintage	MS-63	Proof
2009 Proof	5,798	—	120

KM# 866 15 DOLLARS
33.6300 g., 0.9250 Silver with gold insert 1.0000 oz. ASW, 40 mm. **Ruler:** Elizabeth II **Subject:** Year of the Ox **Rev:** Ox, octagon gold insert

Date	Mintage	MS-63	Proof
2009 Proof	48,888	—	90.00

KM# 922 15 DOLLARS
30.0000 g., 0.9250 Silver 0.8921 oz. ASW, 36.15 mm. **Ruler:** Elizabeth II **Obv:** Bust right **Obv. Designer:** Susanna Blunt **Rev:** Paget portrait of George VI

Date	Mintage	MS-63	Proof
2009(ml) Prooflike	—	100	—

KM# 923 15 DOLLARS
30.0000 g., 0.9250 Silver 0.8921 oz. ASW, 36.15 mm. **Ruler:** Elizabeth II **Obv:** Bust right **Obv. Designer:** Susanna Blunt **Rev:** Gillick portrait of Queen Elizabeth II

Date	Mintage	MS-63	Proof
2009(ml) Prooflike	2,643	100	—

KM# 1038 15 DOLLARS
Silver, 38 mm. **Ruler:** Elizabeth II **Subject:** Year of the tiger **Rev:** Tiger in forest **Shape:** scalloped

Date	Mintage	MS-63	Proof
2009 Proof	10,268	—	85.00

KM# 980 15 DOLLARS
34.0000 g., 0.9250 Silver 1.0111 oz. ASW, 40 mm. **Ruler:** Elizabeth II **Rev:** Tiger in gold insert

Date	Mintage	MS-63	Proof
2010 Proof	48,888	—	100

KM# 1032 15 DOLLARS
0.9990 Silver **Ruler:** Elizabeth II **Subject:** Year of the tiger **Rev:** Tiger walking tiger

Date	Mintage	MS-63	Proof
2010 Proof	9,999	—	85.00

KM# 1055 15 DOLLARS
31.1050 g., 0.9990 Silver 0.9990 oz. ASW, 38 mm. **Ruler:** Elizabeth II **Rev:** Rabbit sitting, head turned left **Shape:** scalloped

Date	Mintage	MS-63	Proof
2011 Proof	19,888	—	85.00

KM# 1091 15 DOLLARS
25.1100 g., 0.9250 Silver 0.7467 oz. ASW, 36.15 mm. **Ruler:** Elizabeth II **Rev:** Prince Charles bust **Rev. Designer:** Laurie McGaw

Date	Mintage	MS-63	Proof
2011 Prooflike	10,000	100	—

KM# 1092 15 DOLLARS
25.1100 g., 0.9250 Silver 0.7467 oz. ASW, 36.15 mm. **Ruler:** Elizabeth II **Rev:** Prince William **Rev. Designer:** Laurie McGaw

Date	Mintage	MS-63	Proof
2011 Prooflike	10,000	100	—

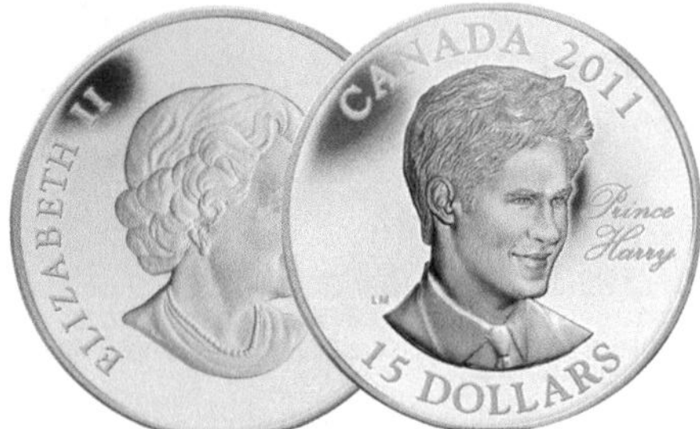

KM# 1093 15 DOLLARS
25.1800 g., 0.9250 Silver 0.7488 oz. ASW, 36.15 mm. **Ruler:** Elizabeth II **Rev:** Prince Harry bust 1/4 right **Rev. Designer:** Laurie McGaw

Date	Mintage	MS-63	Proof
2011 Prooflike	10,000	100	—

KM# 1094 15 DOLLARS
31.3900 g., 0.9990 Silver 1.0082 oz. ASW, 38 mm. **Ruler:** Elizabeth II **Rev:** Rabbit bounding left **Rev. Designer:** Aries Cheung

Date	Mintage	MS-63	Proof
2011 Proof	9,999	—	100

KM# 1152 15 DOLLARS

31.3900 g., 0.9999 Silver 1.0091 oz. ASW, 38 mm. **Ruler:** Elizabeth II **Obv:** Bust right **Rev:** Magpie, bird of happyness in flight at top, lotus flowers at bottom, maple leaf hologram at center

Date	Mintage	MS-63	Proof
2011 Proof	Est. 8,888	—	100

KM# 1183 15 DOLLARS

31.1050 g., 0.9990 Silver 0.9990 oz. ASW, 36.5 mm. **Ruler:** Elizabeth II **Subject:** Year of the Dragon **Obv:** Bust right **Rev:** Dragon right

Date	Mintage	MS-63	Proof
2012 Proof	—	—	75.00

KM# 1186 15 DOLLARS

31.1050 g., 0.9990 Silver 0.9990 oz. ASW, 36.5 mm. **Ruler:** Elizabeth II **Subject:** Year of the Dragon **Obv:** Bust right **Rev:** Dragon left **Shape:** Scalloped

Date	Mintage	MS-63	Proof
2012 Proof	—	—	75.00

KM# 1260 15 DOLLARS

31.3900 g., 0.9990 Silver 1.0082 oz. ASW, 36.5 mm. **Ruler:** Elizabeth II **Subject:** Good Fortune **Rev:** Deer and doe froclicking around central hologram

Date	Mintage	MS-63	Proof
2012 Proof	—	—	75.00

KM# 411 20 DOLLARS

31.1035 g., 0.9250 Silver 0.9250 oz. ASW, 38 mm. **Ruler:** Elizabeth II **Subject:** Transportation - Steam Locomotive **Obv:** Crowned head right **Obv. Designer:** Dora dePédery-Hunt **Rev:** First Canadian Steel Steam Locomotive and cameo hologram **Rev. Designer:** Don Curely **Edge:** Segmented reeding

Date	Mintage	MS-63	Proof
2001 Proof	15,000	—	45.00

KM# 427 20 DOLLARS

31.1030 g., 0.9250 Silver 0.9249 oz. ASW, 38 mm. **Ruler:** Elizabeth II **Series:** Transportation - The Marco Polo **Obv:** Crowned head right **Rev:** Sailship with hologram cameo **Rev. Designer:** J. Franklin Wright **Edge:** Segmented reeding

Date	Mintage	MS-63	Proof
2001 Proof	15,000	—	45.00

KM# 428 20 DOLLARS

31.1030 g., 0.9250 Silver 0.9249 oz. ASW, 38 mm. **Ruler:** Elizabeth II **Series:** Transportation - Russell Touring Car **Obv:** Crowned head right **Rev:** Russell touring car with hologram cameo **Rev. Designer:** John Mardon **Edge:** Segmented reeding

Date	Mintage	MS-63	Proof
2001 Proof	15,000	—	45.00

KM# 464 20 DOLLARS

31.1030 g., 0.9250 Silver 0.9249 oz. ASW **Ruler:** Elizabeth II **Obv:** Crowned head right **Obv. Designer:** Dora dePédery-Hunt **Rev:** Gray-Dort Model 25-SM with cameo hologram **Rev. Designer:** John Mardon

Date	Mintage	MS-63	Proof
2002 Proof	15,000	—	45.00

KM# 465 20 DOLLARS

31.1030 g., 0.9250 Silver 0.9249 oz. ASW **Ruler:** Elizabeth II **Obv:** Crowned head right **Obv. Designer:** Dora dePédery-Hunt **Rev:** Sailing ship William D. Lawrence **Rev. Designer:** Bonnie Ross

Date	Mintage	MS-63	Proof
2002 Proof	15,000	—	45.00

KM# 523 20 DOLLARS

31.3900 g., 0.9990 Silver 1.0082 oz. ASW, 38 mm. **Ruler:** Elizabeth II **Obv:** Crowned head right **Obv. Designer:** Dora dePédery-Hunt **Rev:** Canadian Rockies, multicolor

Date	Mintage	MS-63	Proof
2003 Proof	29,967	—	50.00

KM# 483 20 DOLLARS

31.1030 g., 0.9250 Silver with selective gold plating 0.9249 oz. ASW **Ruler:** Elizabeth II **Subject:** The HMCS Bras d'or (FHE-400) **Obv:** Crowned head right **Obv. Designer:** Dora dePédery-Hunt **Rev:** Ship in water **Rev. Designer:** Donald Curley, Stan Witten

Date	Mintage	MS-63	Proof
2003 Proof	15,000	—	45.00

KM# 482 20 DOLLARS

31.3900 g., 0.9999 Silver 1.0091 oz. ASW, 38 mm. **Ruler:** Elizabeth II **Obv:** Crowned head right **Obv. Designer:** Dora dePédery-Hunt **Rev:** Niagara Falls hologram **Rev. Designer:** Gary Corcoran

Date	Mintage	MS-63	Proof
2003 Proof	29,967	—	75.00

KM# 484 20 DOLLARS

31.1030 g., 0.9250 Silver with selective gold plating 0.9249 oz. ASW **Ruler:** Elizabeth II **Subject:** Canadian National FA-1 diesel-electric locomotive **Obv:** Crowned head right **Obv. Designer:** Dora dePédery-Hunt **Rev. Designer:** John Mardon, William Woodruff

Date	Mintage	MS-63	Proof
2003 Proof	15,000	—	45.00

KM# 485 20 DOLLARS

31.1030 g., 0.9250 Silver with selective gold plating 0.9249 oz. ASW **Ruler:** Elizabeth II **Obv:** Crowned head right **Obv. Designer:** Dora dePédery-Hunt **Rev:** The Bricklin SV-1 **Rev. Designer:** Brian Hughes, José Oslo

Date	Mintage	MS-63	Proof
2003 Proof	15,000	—	45.00

KM# 611 20 DOLLARS

31.3900 g., 0.9999 Silver 1.0091 oz. ASW, 38 mm. **Ruler:** Elizabeth II **Obv:** Head right **Obv. Designer:** Susanna Blunt **Rev:** Iceberg, hologram

Date	Mintage	MS-63	Proof
2004 Proof	24,879	—	45.00

KM# 838 20 DOLLARS

31.3900 g., 0.9999 Silver partially gilt 1.0091 oz. ASW, 38 mm. **Ruler:** Elizabeth II **Rev:** Hopewell Rocks, gilt

Date	Mintage	MS-63	Proof
2004 Proof	16,918	—	45.00

KM# 561 20 DOLLARS

31.3900 g., 0.9999 Silver 1.0091 oz. ASW, 38 mm. **Ruler:** Elizabeth II **Obv:** Head right **Obv. Designer:** Susanna Blunt **Rev:** Three-masted sailing ship, hologram of the sea **Rev. Designer:** Bonnie Ross

Date	Mintage	MS-63	Proof
2005 Proof	18,276	—	55.00

KM# 562 20 DOLLARS

31.3900 g., 0.9999 Silver 1.0091 oz. ASW, 38 mm. **Ruler:** Elizabeth II **Subject:** Northwest Territories Diamonds **Obv:** Head right **Obv. Designer:** Susanna Blunt **Rev:** Multicolor diamond hologram on landscape **Rev. Designer:** José Oslo **Edge:** Reeded

Date	Mintage	MS-63	Proof
2005 Proof	35,000	—	50.00

KM# 563 20 DOLLARS

31.3900 g., 0.9999 Silver 1.0091 oz. ASW **Ruler:** Elizabeth II **Subject:** Mingan Archepelago **Obv:** Head right **Obv. Designer:** Susanna Blunt **Rev:** Cliffs with whale tail out of water **Rev. Designer:** Pierre Leduc

Date	Mintage	MS-63	Proof
2005 Proof	—	—	45.00

KM# 564 20 DOLLARS

31.3900 g., 0.9999 Silver 1.0091 oz. ASW **Ruler:** Elizabeth II **Subject:** Rainforests of the Pacific Northwest **Obv:** Head right **Rev:** Open winged bird **Designer:** Susanna Blunt

Date	Mintage	MS-63	Proof
2005 Proof	—	—	45.00

KM# 565 20 DOLLARS

31.3900 g., 0.9999 Silver 1.0091 oz. ASW, 38 mm. **Ruler:** Elizabeth II **Subject:** Toronto Island National Park **Obv:** Head right **Rev:** Toronto Island Lighthouse, Toronto skyline in background

Date	Mintage	MS-63	Proof
2005 Proof	—	—	55.00

KM# 588 20 DOLLARS

31.3900 g., 0.9999 Silver 1.0091 oz. ASW **Ruler:** Elizabeth II **Subject:** Georgian Bay National Park **Obv:** Head right **Rev:** Canoe and small trees on island

Date	Mintage	MS-63	Proof
2006 Proof	—	—	60.00

KM# 589 20 DOLLARS

31.1000 g., 0.9999 Silver 0.9997 oz. ASW, 38 mm. **Ruler:** Elizabeth II **Obv:** Head right **Rev:** Notre Dame Basilica, Montreal, as a hologram

Date	Mintage	MS-63	Proof
2006 Proof	15,000	—	50.00

KM# 663 20 DOLLARS

31.3900 g., 0.9999 Silver 1.0091 oz. ASW, 38 mm. **Ruler:** Elizabeth II **Subject:** Nahanni National Park **Obv:** Head right **Rev:** Bear walking along sream, cliff in background

Date	Mintage	MS-63	Proof
2006 Proof	—	—	60.00

KM# 664 20 DOLLARS

31.3900 g., 0.9999 Silver 1.0091 oz. ASW, 38 mm. **Ruler:** Elizabeth II **Subject:** Jasper National Park **Obv:** Head right **Rev:** Cowboy on horseback in majestic scene

Date	Mintage	MS-63	Proof
2006 Proof	—	—	60.00

KM# 665 20 DOLLARS

31.1000 g., 0.9999 Silver 0.9997 oz. ASW, 38 mm. **Ruler:** Elizabeth II **Obv:** Head right **Rev:** Holographic rendering of CN Tower

Date	Mintage	MS-63	Proof
2006 Proof	15,000	—	60.00

KM# 666 20 DOLLARS

31.1000 g., 0.9999 Silver 0.9997 oz. ASW **Ruler:** Elizabeth II **Obv:** Head right **Rev:** Holographic view of Pengrowth Saddledome in Calgary

Date	Mintage	MS-63	Proof
2006 Proof	15,000	—	55.00

KM# 667 20 DOLLARS

31.3900 g., 0.9999 Silver 1.0091 oz. ASW **Ruler:** Elizabeth II **Subject:** Tall Ship **Obv:** Head right **Rev:** Ketch and holographic image of thunderstorm in sky

Date	Mintage	MS-63	Proof
2006 Proof	10,299	—	60.00

KM# 734 20 DOLLARS

31.1000 g., 0.9990 Silver 0.9988 oz. ASW, 38 mm. **Ruler:** Elizabeth II **Rev:** Holiday sleigh ride

Date	Mintage	MS-63	Proof
2007 Proof	6,804	—	70.00

KM# 735 20 DOLLARS

31.1000 g., 0.9990 Silver 0.9988 oz. ASW, 38 mm. **Ruler:** Elizabeth II **Rev:** Snowflake, aquamarine crystal

Date	Mintage	MS-63	Proof
2007 Proof	4,989	—	175

KM# 737 20 DOLLARS

31.1000 g., 0.9990 Silver 0.9988 oz. ASW, 38 mm. **Ruler:** Elizabeth II **Subject:** International Polar Year

Date	Mintage	MS-63	Proof
2007 Proof	9,164	—	65.00

KM# 737a 20 DOLLARS

27.7800 g., 0.9250 Silver 0.8261 oz. ASW, 40 mm. **Ruler:** Elizabeth II **Subject:** International Polar Year **Rev:** Blue plasma coating

Date	Mintage	MS-63	Proof
2007 Proof	3,005	—	250

KM# 738 20 DOLLARS

31.3900 g., 0.9999 Silver 1.0091 oz. ASW, 38 mm. **Ruler:** Elizabeth II **Subject:** Tall ships **Rev:** Brigantine in harbor, hologram

Date	Mintage	MS-63	Proof
2007 Proof	16,000	—	60.00

KM# 839 20 DOLLARS

31.3900 g., 0.9999 Silver 1.0091 oz. ASW **Ruler:** Elizabeth II **Rev:** Northern lights in hologram

Date	Mintage	MS-63	Proof
2007	—	35.00	—

KM# 808 20 DOLLARS

31.5000 g., 0.9250 Silver 0.9368 oz. ASW, 38 mm. **Ruler:** Elizabeth II **Subject:** Agriculture trade **Rev:** Team of horses plowing

Date	Mintage	MS-63	Proof
2008 Proof	5,802	—	70.00

KM# 809 20 DOLLARS

31.1050 g., 0.9990 Silver 0.9990 oz. ASW, 38 mm. **Ruler:** Elizabeth II **Rev:** Royal Hudson Steam locomotive

Date	Mintage	MS-63	Proof
2008 Proof	8,345	—	70.00

KM# 810 20 DOLLARS

31.3900 g., 0.9990 Silver 1.0082 oz. ASW, 38 mm. **Ruler:** Elizabeth II **Rev:** Green leaf and crystal raindrop **Rev. Designer:** Stanley Witten

Date	Mintage	MS-63	Proof
2008 Proof	15,000	—	175

KM# 811 20 DOLLARS

31.1050 g., 0.9990 Silver 0.9990 oz. ASW **Ruler:** Elizabeth II **Rev:** Snowflake, amethyst crystal

Date	Mintage	MS-63	Proof
2008 Proof	7,172	—	95.00

KM# 813 20 DOLLARS

31.1050 g., 0.9990 Silver 0.9990 oz. ASW, 38 mm. **Ruler:** Elizabeth II **Rev:** Carolers around tree

Date	Mintage	MS-63	Proof
2008 Proof	10,000	—	70.00

KM# 872 20 DOLLARS

31.1050 g., 0.9990 Silver 0.9990 oz. ASW, 38 mm. **Ruler:** Elizabeth II **Rev:** Snowflake, sapphire crystal

Date	Mintage	MS-63	Proof
2008 Proof	7,765	—	95.00

KM# 893 20 DOLLARS

31.3900 g., 0.9990 Silver 1.0082 oz. ASW, 38 mm. **Ruler:** Elizabeth II **Subject:** Coal mining trade **Obv:** Bust right **Obv. Legend:** Elizabeth II DG Regina **Obv. Designer:** Susanna Blunt **Rev:** Miner pushing cart with coal **Rev. Legend:** Canada 20 Dollars **Rev. Designer:** John Marder

Date	Mintage	MS-63	Proof
2009 Proof	10,000	—	75.00

KM# 891 20 DOLLARS

31.3900 g., 0.9990 Silver 1.0082 oz. ASW, 38 mm. **Ruler:** Elizabeth II **Subject:** Great Canadian Locomotives - Jubilee **Obv:** Bust right **Obv. Legend:** Elizabeth II DG Regina **Obv. Designer:** Susanna Blunt **Rev:** Jubilee locomotive side view **Rev. Legend:** Canada 20 Dollars **Edge Lettering:** Jubilee

Date	Mintage	MS-63	Proof
2009 Proof	6,036	—	70.00

KM# 870 20 DOLLARS

27.7800 g., 0.9250 Silver 0.8261 oz. ASW, 40 mm. **Ruler:** Elizabeth II **Rev:** Calgary Flames goalie mask multicolor on goal net

Date	Mintage	MS-63	Proof
2009 Proof	10,000	—	70.00

KM# 871 20 DOLLARS

27.7800 g., 0.9250 Silver 0.8261 oz. ASW, 40 mm. **Ruler:** Elizabeth II **Rev:** Edmonton Oilers goalie mask, multicolor on goal net

Date	Mintage	MS-63	Proof
2009 Proof	10,000	—	70.00

KM# 872A 20 DOLLARS

27.7800 g., 0.9250 Silver 0.8261 oz. ASW, 40 mm. **Ruler:** Elizabeth II **Rev:** Montreal Canadians goalie mask multicolor

Date	Mintage	MS-63	Proof
2009 Proof	10,000	—	70.00

KM# 873 20 DOLLARS

27.7800 g., 0.9250 Silver 0.8261 oz. ASW, 40 mm. **Ruler:** Elizabeth II **Rev:** Ottawa Senators goalie mask on goal net

Date	Mintage	MS-63	Proof
2009 Proof	10,000	—	70.00

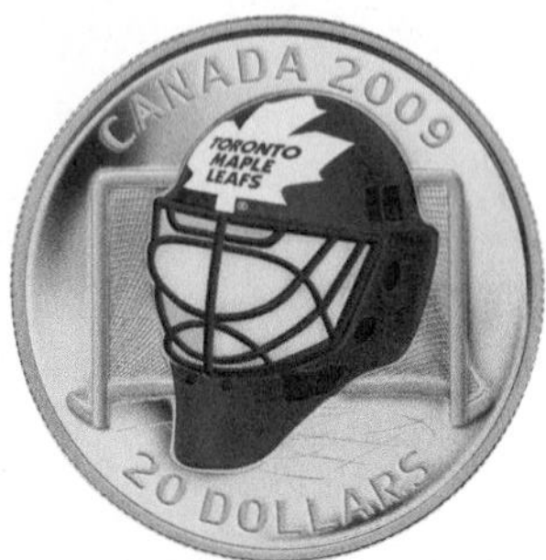

KM# 874 20 DOLLARS

27.7800 g., 0.9250 Silver 0.8261 oz. ASW, 40 mm. **Ruler:** Elizabeth II **Rev:** Toronto Maple Leafs goalie mask, multicolor on goal net

Date	Mintage	MS-63	Proof
2009 Proof	10,000	—	70.00

KM# 875 20 DOLLARS

27.7800 g., 0.9250 Silver 0.8261 oz. ASW, 40 mm. **Ruler:** Elizabeth II **Rev:** Vancouver Canucks goalie mask, multicolor on goal net

Date	Mintage	MS-63	Proof
2009 Proof	10,000	—	70.00

KM# 876 20 DOLLARS

31.5000 g., 0.9250 Silver 0.9368 oz. ASW, 40 mm. **Ruler:** Elizabeth II **Rev:** Summer moon mask

Date	Mintage	MS-63	Proof
2009 Proof	2,834	—	225

KM# 944 20 DOLLARS

31.1050 g., 0.9990 Silver 0.9990 oz. ASW, 38 mm. **Ruler:** Elizabeth II **Rev:** Snowflake - light blue crystal

Date	Mintage	MS-63	Proof
2009 Proof	7,477	—	100

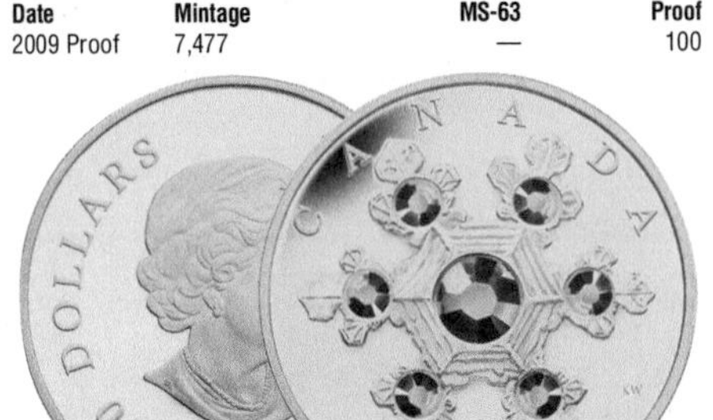

KM# 945 20 DOLLARS

31.1050 g., 0.9990 Silver 0.9990 oz. ASW, 38 mm. **Ruler:** Elizabeth II **Rev:** Snowflake - light red crystal

Date	Mintage	MS-63	Proof
2009 Proof	7,004	—	100

KM# 892 20 DOLLARS

31.3900 g., 0.9990 Silver 1.0082 oz. ASW, 38 mm. **Ruler:** Elizabeth II **Subject:** Crystal raindrop **Obv:** Bust right **Rev:** Maple leaf and rain drop - fall colors **Rev. Designer:** Celia Godkin

Date	Mintage	MS-63	Proof
2009 Proof	9,998	—	85.00

KM# 987 20 DOLLARS

31.3900 g., 0.9999 Silver 1.0091 oz. ASW, 38 mm. **Ruler:** Elizabeth II **Rev:** Lotus Water Lilly in multicolor and crystal **Rev. Designer:** Cladio D'Angelo

Date	Mintage	MS-63	Proof
2010 Proof	10,000	—	120

KM# 1009 20 DOLLARS

31.3900 g., 0.9990 Silver 1.0082 oz. ASW **Ruler:** Elizabeth II **Subject:** 75th Anniversary of Canadian Bank Notes **Rev:** Female and farmer seated

Date	Mintage	MS-63	Proof
2010 Proof	7,500	—	70.00

KM# 1013 20 DOLLARS

31.3900 g., 0.9990 Silver 1.0082 oz. ASW, 38 mm. **Ruler:** Elizabeth II **Rev:** Maple leaf and crystal **Rev. Designer:** Celia Godkin

Date	Mintage	MS-63	Proof
2010 Proof	10,000	—	100

KM# 1018 20 DOLLARS

31.3900 g., 0.9990 Silver 1.0082 oz. ASW, 38 mm. **Ruler:** Elizabeth II **Rev:** Steam Locomotive Selkirk

Date	Mintage	MS-63	Proof
2010 Proof	10,000	—	80.00

KM# 1048 20 DOLLARS
31.1050 g., 0.9999 Silver 0.9999 oz. ASW, 38 mm. **Ruler:** Elizabeth II **Rev:** Snowflake, blue crystals

Date	Mintage	MS-63	Proof
2010 Proof	7,500	—	95.00

KM# 1049 20 DOLLARS
31.1050 g., 0.9999 Silver 0.9999 oz. ASW, 38 mm. **Ruler:** Elizabeth II **Rev:** Snowflake, tanzanite crystals

Date	Mintage	MS-63	Proof
2010 Proof	7,500	—	95.00

KM# 1066 20 DOLLARS
31.9900 g., 0.9990 Silver 1.0274 oz. ASW, 38 mm. **Ruler:** Elizabeth II **Rev:** Pinecone with ruby crystals **Rev. Designer:** Susan Taylor

Date	Mintage	MS-63	Proof
2010 Proof	5,000	—	120

KM# 1067 20 DOLLARS
31.9900 g., 0.9990 Silver 1.0274 oz. ASW, 38 mm. **Ruler:** Elizabeth II **Rev:** Pinecone with moonlight blue crystals **Rev. Designer:** Susan Taylor

Date	Mintage	MS-63	Proof
2010 Proof	5,000	—	120

KM# 1075 20 DOLLARS
27.7800 g., 0.9250 Silver 0.8261 oz. ASW, 40 mm. **Ruler:** Elizabeth II **Subject:** Winter Scene **Rev:** Horse pulling cut Christmas Tree **Rev. Designer:** Rene Clark

Date	Mintage	MS-63	Proof
2011 Proof	8,000	—	70.00

KM# 1111 20 DOLLARS
31.3900 g., 0.9990 Silver 1.0082 oz. ASW, 40 mm. **Ruler:** Elizabeth II **Subject:** Royal Wedding **Rev:** Portraits of Katherine and William facing each other, crystal insert

Date	Mintage	MS-63	Proof
2011 Proof	—	—	80.00

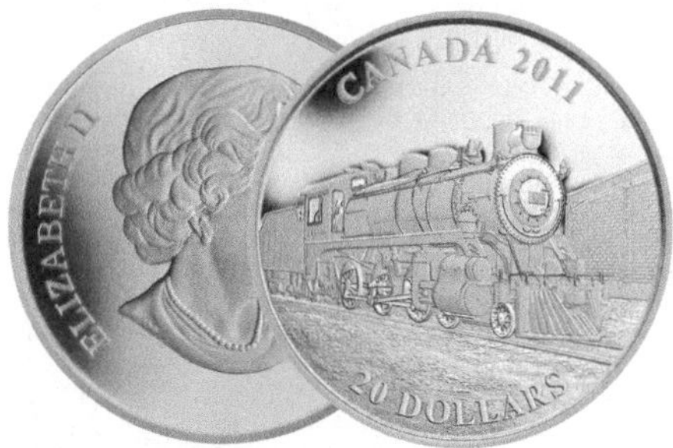

KM# 1134 20 DOLLARS
31.3900 g., 0.9999 Silver 1.0091 oz. ASW, 38 mm. **Ruler:** Elizabeth II **Subject:** Canadian Pacific's D-10 Steam Locomotive **Obv:** Bust right **Rev:** Steam locomotive right **Edge:** Lettered

Date	Mintage	MS-63	Proof
2011 Proof	10,000	—	80.00

KM# 1135 20 DOLLARS
31.3900 g., 0.9999 Silver 1.0091 oz. ASW, 38 mm. **Ruler:** Elizabeth II **Obv:** Bust right **Rev:** Tulip in color and Vienitian glass lady bug

Date	Mintage	MS-63	Proof
2011 Proof	5,000	—	1,000

KM# 1145 20 DOLLARS
31.3900 g., 0.9999 Silver 1.0091 oz. ASW, 38 mm. **Ruler:** Elizabeth II **Obv:** Bust right **Rev:** Wild rose in color, swarovski crystrals

Date	Mintage	MS-63	Proof
2011 Proof	Est. 10,000	—	135

KM# 1147 20 DOLLARS
31.3900 g., 0.9999 Silver 1.0091 oz. ASW, 38 mm. **Ruler:** Elizabeth II **Obv:** Bust right **Rev:** Maple leaves, seeds in color, swarovski crystal drop

Date	Mintage	MS-63	Proof
2011 Proof	—	—	110

KM# 1181 20 DOLLARS
31.3900 g., 0.9990 Silver 1.0082 oz. ASW, 38 mm. **Ruler:** Elizabeth II **Obv:** Bust right **Rev:** Winnipeg Jets Logo, jet over maple leaf

Date	Mintage	MS-63	Proof
2011 Proof	15,000	—	95.00

KM# 1182 20 DOLLARS
31.9900 g., 0.9999 Silver 1.0284 oz. ASW, 38 mm. **Ruler:** Elizabeth II **Obv:** Bust right **Rev:** Christmas tree with six crystals

Date	Mintage	MS-63	Proof
2011 Proof	—	—	75.00

KM# 1187 20 DOLLARS
31.3900 g., 0.9990 Silver 1.0082 oz. ASW, 38 mm. **Ruler:** Elizabeth II **Obv:** Bust right **Rev:** Snowflake with emerald crystals

Date	Mintage	MS-63	Proof
2011 Proof	15,000	—	85.00

KM# 1188 20 DOLLARS
31.8900 g., 0.9990 Silver 1.0242 oz. ASW, 38 mm. **Ruler:** Elizabeth II **Obv:** Bust right **Rev:** Snowflake with topaz crystals

Date	Mintage	MS-63	Proof
2011 Proof	15,000	—	85.00

KM# 1189 20 DOLLARS
31.8900 g., 0.9990 Silver 1.0242 oz. ASW, 38 mm. **Ruler:** Elizabeth II **Obv:** Bust right **Rev:** Three snowflakes with three Hyacinth red crystals

Date	Mintage	MS-63	Proof
2011 Proof	15,000	—	85.00

KM# 1190 20 DOLLARS
31.8900 g., 0.9990 Silver 1.0242 oz. ASW, 38 mm. **Ruler:** Elizabeth II **Obv:** Bust right **Rev:** Three snowflakes with three Montana blue crystals

Date	Mintage	MS-63	Proof
2011 Proof	15,000	—	85.00

KM# 1137 20 DOLLARS
31.3900 g., 0.9990 Silver 1.0082 oz. ASW, 38 mm. **Ruler:** Elizabeth II **Subject:** Elizabeth II, 60th Anniversary of reign **Obv:** Bust right **Rev:** Crowned bust right with swarovski crystal insert **Edge:** Reeded

Date	Mintage	MS-63	Proof
2012 Proof	15,000	—	80.00

KM# 1177 20 DOLLARS
27.7800 g., 0.9250 Silver 0.8261 oz. ASW, 38 mm. **Ruler:** Elizabeth II **Obv:** Bust right **Rev:** Youthful busts right of Elizabeth II and Prince Philip

Date	Mintage	MS-63	Proof
2012 Proof	—	—	85.00

KM# 1178 20 DOLLARS
27.7800 g., 0.9250 Silver 0.8261 oz. ASW, 38 mm. **Ruler:** Elizabeth II **Obv:** Bust right **Rev:** Royal cypher, wreath below

Date	Mintage	MS-63	Proof
2012 Proof	—	—	85.00

KM# 1238 20 DOLLARS
30.7500 g., 0.9999 Silver 0.9885 oz. ASW, 36 mm. **Ruler:** Elizabeth II **Subject:** Elizabeth II, Diamond Jubilee **Obv:** Bust right **Rev:** Elizabeth II profile left, high releif **Rev. Designer:** Laurie McGaw

Date	Mintage	MS-63	Proof
2012 Proof	7,500	—	75.00

KM# 1239 20 DOLLARS
7.9600 g., 0.9990 Silver 0.2557 oz. ASW, 27 mm. **Ruler:** Elizabeth II **Subject:** Elizabeth II, Diamond Jubilee **Obv:** Young portrait right **Obv. Designer:** Mary Gilick **Rev:** Elizabeth II with hat at left **Rev. Designer:** Laurie McGaw

Date	Mintage	MS-63	Proof
1952-2012 Proof	25,000	—	30.00

KM# 1246 20 DOLLARS
27.7800 g., 0.9250 Silver 0.8261 oz. ASW, 38 mm. **Ruler:** Elizabeth II **Subject:** Coast Guard, 50th Anniversary

Date	Mintage	MS-63	Proof
2012	—	—	100

KM# 1250 20 DOLLARS
27.7800 g., 0.9250 Silver 0.8261 oz. ASW, 38 mm. **Ruler:** Elizabeth II **Subject:** F.H. Varley

Date	Mintage	MS-63	Proof
2012	—	—	75.00

KM# 1251 20 DOLLARS
27.7800 g., 0.9250 Silver 0.8261 oz. ASW, 38 mm. **Ruler:** Elizabeth II **Subject:** Arthur Lismer

Date	Mintage	MS-63	Proof
2012 Proof	—	—	75.00

KM# 1266 20 DOLLARS
31.1000 g., 0.9990 Silver 0.9988 oz. ASW, 38 mm. **Ruler:** Elizabeth II **Subject:** Aster and bee

Date	Mintage	MS-63	Proof
2012 Proof	—	—	100

KM# 1269 20 DOLLARS
31.3900 g., 0.9990 Silver 1.0082 oz. ASW, 38 mm. **Ruler:** Elizabeth II **Subject:** Sugar Maple Leaf **Rev:** Leaves in color, crystal

Date	Mintage	MS-63	Proof
2012 Proof	—	—	130

KM# 1270 20 DOLLARS
31.3900 g., 0.9990 Silver 1.0082 oz. ASW, 38 mm. **Ruler:** Elizabeth II **Rev:** Rhododendron

Date	Mintage	MS-63	Proof
2012 Proof	—	—	125

KM# 1280 20 DOLLARS
31.1050 g., 0.9990 Silver 0.9990 oz. ASW, 38 mm. **Ruler:** Elizabeth II **Subject:** Bateman Moose

Date	Mintage	MS-63	Proof
2012 Proof	—	—	135

KM# 1283 20 DOLLARS
15.5500 g., 0.9990 Gold 0.4994 oz. AGW, 25 mm. **Ruler:** Elizabeth II **Subject:** Year of the Dragon

Date	Mintage	MS-63	Proof
2012 Proof	—	—	900

KM# 742 25 DOLLARS
27.7800 g., 0.9250 Silver 0.8261 oz. ASW, 40 mm. **Ruler:** Elizabeth II **Subject:** Vancouver Olympics **Rev:** Alpine skiing, hologram

Date	Mintage	MS-63	Proof
2007 Proof	45,000	—	50.00

KM# 743 25 DOLLARS
27.7800 g., 0.9250 Silver 0.8261 oz. ASW, 40 mm. **Ruler:** Elizabeth II **Subject:** Vancouver Olympics **Rev:** Athletics pride hologram

Date	Mintage	MS-63	Proof
2007 Proof	45,000	—	65.00

KM# 744 25 DOLLARS
27.7500 g., 0.9250 Silver 0.8252 oz. ASW, 40 mm. **Ruler:** Elizabeth II **Subject:** Vancouver Olympics **Rev:** Biathleon hologram

Date	Mintage	MS-63	Proof
2007 Proof	54,000	—	50.00

KM# 745 25 DOLLARS
27.7800 g., 0.9250 Silver 0.8261 oz. ASW, 40 mm. **Ruler:** Elizabeth II **Subject:** Vancouver Olympics **Rev:** Curling hologram

Date	Mintage	MS-63	Proof
2007 Proof	—	—	50.00

KM# 746 25 DOLLARS
27.7800 g., 0.9250 Silver 0.8261 oz. ASW, 40 mm. **Ruler:** Elizabeth II **Subject:** Vancouver Olympics **Rev:** Hockey, hologram

Date	Mintage	MS-63	Proof
2007 Proof	45,000	—	50.00

KM# 814 25 DOLLARS
27.7800 g., 0.9250 Silver 0.8261 oz. ASW, 40 mm. **Ruler:** Elizabeth II **Subject:** Vancouver Olympics **Rev:** Bobsleigh, hologram

Date	Mintage	MS-63	Proof
2008 Proof	45,000	—	50.00

KM# 815 25 DOLLARS
27.7800 g., 0.9250 Silver 0.8261 oz. ASW, 40 mm. **Ruler:** Elizabeth II **Subject:** Vancouver Olympics **Rev:** Figure skating, hologram

Date	Mintage	MS-63	Proof
2008 Proof	45,000	—	50.00

KM# 816 25 DOLLARS
27.7800 g., 0.9250 Silver 0.8261 oz. ASW, 40 mm. **Ruler:** Elizabeth II **Subject:** Vancouver Olympics **Rev:** Freestyle skating, hologram

Date	Mintage	MS-63	Proof
2008 Proof	45,000	—	50.00

KM# 817 25 DOLLARS
27.7800 g., 0.9250 Silver 0.8261 oz. ASW, 40 mm. **Ruler:** Elizabeth II **Subject:** Vancouver Olympics **Rev:** Snowboarding, hologram

Date	Mintage	MS-63	Proof
2008 Proof	45,000	—	50.00

KM# 818 25 DOLLARS
27.7800 g., 0.9250 Silver 0.8261 oz. ASW, 40 mm. **Ruler:** Elizabeth II **Subject:** Vancouver Olympics **Rev:** Home of the 2010 Olympics

Date	Mintage	MS-63	Proof
2008 Proof	45,000	—	50.00

KM# 903 25 DOLLARS
27.7800 g., 0.9250 Silver 0.8261 oz. ASW, 40 mm. **Ruler:** Elizabeth II **Subject:** 2010 Vancouver Olympics **Obv:** Bust right **Obv. Designer:** Susanna Blunt **Rev:** Cross Country Skiing and hologram at left

Date	Mintage	MS-63	Proof
2009 Proof	45,000	—	50.00

KM# 904 25 DOLLARS
27.7800 g., 0.9250 Silver 0.8261 oz. ASW, 40 mm. **Ruler:** Elizabeth II **Subject:** 2010 Vancouver Olympics **Obv:** Bust right **Obv. Designer:** Susanna Blunt **Rev:** Olympians holding torch, hologram at left

Date	Mintage	MS-63	Proof
2009 Proof	45,000	—	50.00

KM# 905 25 DOLLARS
27.7800 g., 0.9250 Silver 0.8261 oz. ASW, 40 mm. **Ruler:** Elizabeth II **Subject:** 2010 Vancouver Olympics **Obv:** Bust right **Obv. Designer:** Susanna Blunt **Rev:** Sled, hologram at left

Date	Mintage	MS-63	Proof
2009 Proof	45,000	—	50.00

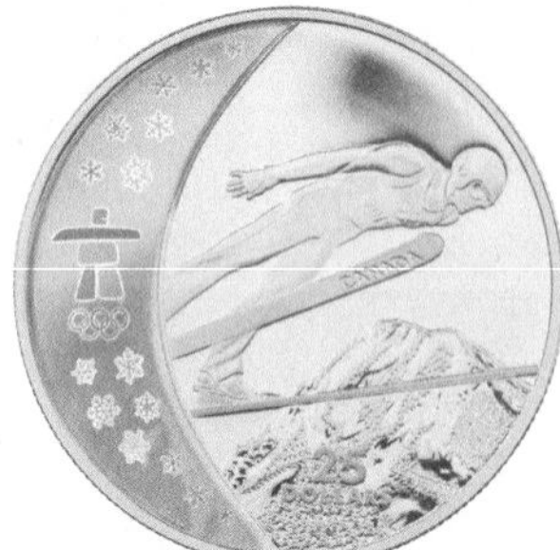

KM# 906 25 DOLLARS
27.7800 g., 0.9250 Silver 0.8261 oz. ASW, 40 mm. **Ruler:** Elizabeth II **Subject:** 2010 Vancouver Olympics **Obv:** Bust right **Obv. Designer:** Susanna Blunt **Rev:** Ski Jumper, hologram at left

Date	Mintage	MS-63	Proof
2009 Proof	45,000	—	50.00

KM# 907 25 DOLLARS
27.7800 g., 0.9250 Silver 0.8261 oz. ASW, 40 mm. **Ruler:** Elizabeth II **Subject:** 2010 Vancouver Olympics **Obv:** Bust right **Obv. Designer:** Susanna Blunt **Rev:** Speed Skaters, hologram at left

Date	Mintage	MS-63	Proof
2009 Proof	45,000	—	50.00

KM# 1146 25 DOLLARS
62.4100 g., 0.9999 Silver selectively gilt 2.0062 oz. ASW, 60 mm. **Ruler:** Elizabeth II **Obv:** Bust right **Rev:** Toronto map and skyline, partilly gilt **Edge:** Reeded

Date	Mintage	MS-63	Proof
2011 Proof	Est. 7,500	—	180

KM# 1173 25 DOLLARS
31.3900 g., 0.9999 Silver 1.0091 oz. ASW, 38 mm. **Ruler:** Elizabeth II **Obv:** Bust right **Rev:** Wayne Greskey skating right, father's portrait in circle at right, 99 in hologram at lower right

Date	Mintage	MS-63	Proof
2011 Proof	—	—	85.00

KM# 590 30 DOLLARS
31.5000 g., 0.9250 Silver 0.9368 oz. ASW **Ruler:** Elizabeth II **Subject:** Pacific Northwest Wood Carvings **Obv:** Head right **Rev:** Welcome figure totem pole

Date	Mintage	MS-63	Proof
2006 Proof	9,904	—	75.00

KM# 668 30 DOLLARS
31.5000 g., 0.9250 Silver 0.9368 oz. ASW **Ruler:** Elizabeth II **Subject:** Canadarm and Col. C. Hadfield **Obv:** Head right **Rev:** Hologram of Canadarm

Date	Mintage	MS-63	Proof
2006 Proof	9,357	—	90.00

KM# 669 30 DOLLARS
31.5000 g., 0.9250 Silver 0.9368 oz. ASW **Ruler:** Elizabeth II **Subject:** National War Memorial **Obv:** Head right **Rev:** Statue of three soldiers

Date	Mintage	MS-63	Proof
2006 Proof	8,876	—	85.00

KM# 670 30 DOLLARS
31.5000 g., 0.9250 Silver 0.9368 oz. ASW **Ruler:** Elizabeth II **Subject:** Beaumont Hamel Newfoundland **Obv:** Head right **Rev:** Caribou statue on rock outcrop

Date	Mintage	MS-63	Proof
2006 Proof	15,325	—	95.00

KM# 671 30 DOLLARS
31.5000 g., 0.9250 Silver 0.9368 oz. ASW **Ruler:** Elizabeth II **Obv:** Head right **Rev:** Dog Sled Team in color

Date	Mintage	MS-63	Proof
2006 Proof	7,384	—	85.00

KM# 739 30 DOLLARS
31.5000 g., 0.9250 Silver 0.9368 oz. ASW, 40 mm. **Ruler:** Elizabeth II **Rev:** Niagra Falls panoramic hologram

Date	Mintage	MS-63	Proof
2007 Proof	7,384	—	85.00

KM# 741 30 DOLLARS
31.5000 g., 0.9250 Silver 0.9368 oz. ASW, 40 mm. **Ruler:** Elizabeth II **Rev:** War Memorial, Vimy Ridge

Date	Mintage	MS-63	Proof
2007 Proof	5,335	—	85.00

KM# 819 30 DOLLARS
31.5000 g., 0.9250 Silver 0.9368 oz. ASW, 40 mm. **Ruler:** Elizabeth II **Subject:** IMAX **Rev:** Youth reaching out to shark on large screen

Date	Mintage	MS-63	Proof
2008 Proof	3,861	—	75.00

KM# 895 30 DOLLARS
33.7500 g., 0.9250 Silver 1.0037 oz. ASW, 40 mm. **Ruler:** Elizabeth II **Subject:** International year of astronomy **Obv:** Bust right **Obv. Legend:** Elizabeth II 30 Dollars DG Regina **Obv. Designer:** Susanna Blunt **Rev:** Observatory with planets and colored sky **Rev. Legend:** Canada **Rev. Designer:** Colin Mayne

Date	Mintage	MS-63	Proof
2009 Proof	7,174	—	90.00

KM# 566 50 DOLLARS

12.0000 g., 0.5833 Gold 0.2250 oz. AGW, 27 mm. **Ruler:** Elizabeth II **Subject:** End of World War II, 60th Anniversary **Obv:** Head right **Rev:** Large V and three portraits

Date	Mintage	MS-63	Proof
2005 Specimen	4,000	—	375

KM# 672 50 DOLLARS

31.1600 g., 0.9995 Palladium 1.0013 oz. **Ruler:** Elizabeth II **Subject:** Constellation in Spring sky position **Rev:** Large Bear at top

Date	Mintage	MS-63	Proof
2006 Proof	297	—	1,250

KM# 673 50 DOLLARS

31.1600 g., 0.9995 Palladium 1.0013 oz. **Ruler:** Elizabeth II **Subject:** Constellation in Summer sky position **Rev:** Large Bear at left

Date	Mintage	MS-63	Proof
2006 Proof	296	—	1,250

KM# 674 50 DOLLARS

31.1600 g., 0.9995 Palladium 1.0013 oz. **Ruler:** Elizabeth II **Subject:** Constellation in Autumn sky position **Rev:** Large Bear towards bottom

Date	Mintage	MS-63	Proof
2006 Proof	296	—	1,250

KM# 675 50 DOLLARS

31.1600 g., 0.9995 Palladium 1.0013 oz. **Ruler:** Elizabeth II **Subject:** Constellation in Winter sky position **Rev:** Large Bear towards right

Date	Mintage	MS-63	Proof
2006 Proof	293	—	1,250

KM# 709 50 DOLLARS

155.5000 g., 0.9999 Silver 4.9987 oz. ASW **Ruler:** Elizabeth II **Subject:** Queen's 60th Wedding Anniversary **Rev:** Coat of Arms and Mascots of Elizabeth and Philip

Date	Mintage	MS-63	Proof
2007 Proof	1,957	—	350

KM# 783 50 DOLLARS

156.7700 g., 0.9990 Silver 5.0350 oz. ASW, 65 mm. **Ruler:** Elizabeth II **Subject:** Ottawa Mint Centennial 1908-2008 **Rev:** Mint building facade **Note:** Photo reduced.

Date	Mintage	MS-63	Proof
2008 Proof	2,078	—	400

KM# 896 50 DOLLARS

156.7700 g., 0.9990 Silver 5.0350 oz. ASW, 65.25 mm. **Ruler:** Elizabeth II **Subject:** 150 Anniversary of the start of construction of the parliament buildings **Obv:** Bust right **Obv. Legend:** Elizabeth II Canada DG Regina **Obv. Designer:** Susanna Blunt **Rev:** Incomplete west block, original architecture **Rev. Legend:** 50 Dollars 1859-2009

Date	Mintage	MS-63	Proof
2009 Proof	910	—	450

KM# 1008 50 DOLLARS

157.6000 g., 0.9990 Silver 5.0617 oz. ASW, 65.25 mm. **Ruler:** Elizabeth II **Subject:** 75th Anniverary of Canadian Bank Notes **Rev:** Female seated speaking into microphone **Note:** Photo reduced.

Date	Mintage	MS-63	Proof
2010 Proof	2,000	—	400

KM# 1243 50 DOLLARS

156.7700 g., 0.9250 Silver 4.6621 oz. ASW, 65.25 mm. **Ruler:** Elizabeth II **Subject:** Calgary Stampede

Date	Mintage	MS-63	Proof
2012	—	—	400

KM# 1284 50 DOLLARS

31.1050 g., 0.9990 Gold 0.9990 oz. AGW, 30 mm. **Ruler:** Elizabeth II **Subject:** Year of the Dragon

Date	Mintage	MS-63	Proof
2012 Proof	—	—	1,750

KM# 1296 50 DOLLARS

Gold **Ruler:** Elizabeth II **Obv:** Bust right **Obv. Designer:** Susana Blunt **Rev:** High relief bust **Note:** Ultra high relief

Date	Mintage	MS-63	Proof
2012	500	—	—

KM# 567 75 DOLLARS

31.4400 g., 0.4166 Gold 0.4211 oz. AGW, 36.07 mm. **Ruler:** Elizabeth II **Subject:** Pope John Paul II **Obv:** Head right **Rev:** Pope giving blessing

Date	Mintage	MS-63	Proof
2005 Proof	1,870	—	825

KM# 747 75 DOLLARS
12.0000 g., 0.5830 Gold 0.2249 oz. AGW, 27 mm. **Ruler:** Elizabeth II **Subject:** Vancouver Olympics - Athletics Pride **Rev:** Athletics celebrating, holding flag aloft

Date	Mintage	MS-63	Proof
2007 Proof	4,524	—	440

KM# 748 75 DOLLARS
12.0000 g., 0.5830 Gold 0.2249 oz. AGW, 27 mm. **Ruler:** Elizabeth II **Obv:** Bust right **Obv. Designer:** Susanna Blunt **Rev:** Canada geese in flight left, multicolor

Date	Mintage	MS-63	Proof
2007 Proof	4,418	—	440

KM# 749 75 DOLLARS
12.0000 g., 0.5830 Gold 0.2249 oz. AGW, 27 mm. **Ruler:** Elizabeth II **Rev:** Mountie, multicolor

Date	Mintage	MS-63	Proof
2007 Proof	6,687	—	440

KM# 820 75 DOLLARS
12.0000 g., 0.5830 Gold partially silver plated 0.2249 oz. AGW, 27 mm. **Ruler:** Elizabeth II **Rev:** 2010 Olympic Inukshuk Stone man, partially silver plated

Date	Mintage	MS-63	Proof
2008 Proof	—	—	420

KM# 821 75 DOLLARS
12.0000 g., 0.5830 Gold 0.2249 oz. AGW, 27 mm. **Ruler:** Elizabeth II **Rev:** Four Host Nations mask emblems, colored **Rev. Designer:** Jody Broomfield

Date	Mintage	MS-63	Proof
2008 Proof	8,000	—	440

KM# 947 75 DOLLARS
12.0000 g., 0.5830 Gold 0.2249 oz. AGW, 27 mm. **Ruler:** Elizabeth II **Subject:** Vancouver Olympics **Rev:** Tent building at Olympic site, color

Date	Mintage	MS-63	Proof
2008 Proof	8,000	—	440

KM# 908 75 DOLLARS
12.0000 g., 0.5830 Gold 0.2249 oz. AGW, 27 mm. **Ruler:** Elizabeth II **Subject:** 2010 Vancouver Olympics **Obv:** Bust right **Obv. Designer:** Susana Blunt **Rev:** Multicolor moose

Date	Mintage	MS-63	Proof
2009 Proof	4,075	—	440

KM# 909 75 DOLLARS
12.0000 g., 0.5830 Gold 0.2249 oz. AGW, 27 mm. **Ruler:** Elizabeth II **Subject:** 2010 Vancouver Olympics **Obv:** Bust right **Obv. Designer:** Susana Blunt **Rev:** Multicolor athletics and torch

Date	Mintage	MS-63	Proof
2009 Proof	4,479	—	440

KM# 910 75 DOLLARS
12.0000 g., 0.5830 Gold 0.2249 oz. AGW, 27 mm. **Ruler:** Elizabeth II **Subject:** 2010 Vancouver Olympics **Obv:** Bust right **Obv. Designer:** Susana Blunt **Rev:** Wolf, multicolor

Date	Mintage	MS-63	Proof
2009 Proof	4,161	—	440

KM# 1002 75 DOLLARS
12.0000 g., 0.5830 Gold 0.2249 oz. AGW, 27 mm. **Ruler:** Elizabeth II **Rev:** Spring color maple leaves

Date	Mintage	MS-63	Proof
2010 Proof	1,000	—	500

KM# 1003 75 DOLLARS
12.0000 g., 0.5830 Gold 0.2249 oz. AGW, 27 mm. **Ruler:** Elizabeth II **Rev:** Summer color maple leaves

Date	Mintage	MS-63	Proof
2010 Proof	1,000	—	500

KM# 1004 75 DOLLARS
12.0000 g., 0.5830 Gold 0.2249 oz. AGW, 27 mm. **Ruler:** Elizabeth II **Rev:** Fall color maple leaves

Date	Mintage	MS-63	Proof
2010 Proof	1,000	—	500

KM# 1005 75 DOLLARS
12.0000 g., 0.5830 Gold 0.2249 oz. AGW, 27 mm. **Ruler:** Elizabeth II **Rev:** Winter color maple leaves

Date	Mintage	MS-63	Proof
2010 Proof	1,000	—	500

KM# 416 100 DOLLARS
13.3375 g., 0.5830 Gold alloyed with 5.5579 g of .999 Silver, .1787 oz ASW 0.2500 oz. AGW, 27 mm. **Ruler:** Elizabeth II **Subject:** Library of Parliament **Obv:** Crowned head right **Obv. Designer:** Dora dePedery-Hunt **Rev:** Statue in domed building **Rev. Designer:** Robert R. Carmichael **Edge:** Reeded

Date	Mintage	MS-63	Proof
2001 Proof	8,080	—	475

KM# 452 100 DOLLARS
13.3375 g., 0.5830 Gold 0.2500 oz. AGW, 27 mm. **Ruler:** Elizabeth II **Subject:** Discovery of Oil in Alberta **Obv:** Crowned head right **Rev:** Oil well with black oil spill on ground **Rev. Designer:** John Marden **Edge:** Reeded

Date	Mintage	MS-63	Proof
2002 Proof	9,994	—	475

KM# 486 100 DOLLARS
13.3375 g., 0.5830 Gold 0.2500 oz. AGW **Ruler:** Elizabeth II **Subject:** 100th Anniversary of the Discovery of Marquis Wheat **Obv:** Head right

Date	Mintage	MS-63	Proof
2003 Proof	9,993	—	475

KM# 528 100 DOLLARS
12.0000 g., 0.5830 Gold 0.2249 oz. AGW **Ruler:** Elizabeth II **Subject:** St. Lawrence Seaway, 50th Anniversary **Obv:** Head right

Date	Mintage	MS-63	Proof
2004 Proof	7,454	—	425

KM# 593 100 DOLLARS
12.0000 g., 0.5833 Gold 0.2250 oz. AGW **Ruler:** Elizabeth II **Subject:** 130th Anniversary, Supreme Court **Obv:** Head right

Date	Mintage	MS-63	Proof
2005 Proof	5,092	—	425

KM# 591 100 DOLLARS
12.0000 g., 0.5833 Gold 0.2250 oz. AGW **Ruler:** Elizabeth II **Subject:** 75th Anniversary, Hockey Classic between Royal Military College and U.S. Military Academy **Obv:** Head right

Date	Mintage	MS-63	Proof
2006 Proof	5,439	—	425

KM# 689 100 DOLLARS
12.0000 g., 0.5833 Gold 0.2250 oz. AGW, 27 mm. **Ruler:** Elizabeth II **Subject:** 140th Anniversary Dominion **Obv:** Head right

Date	Mintage	MS-63	Proof
2007 Proof	4,453	—	425

KM# 823 100 DOLLARS
12.0000 g., 0.5830 Gold 0.2249 oz. AGW, 27 mm. **Ruler:** Elizabeth II **Rev:** Fraser River

Date	Mintage	MS-63	Proof
2008 Proof	3,089	—	425

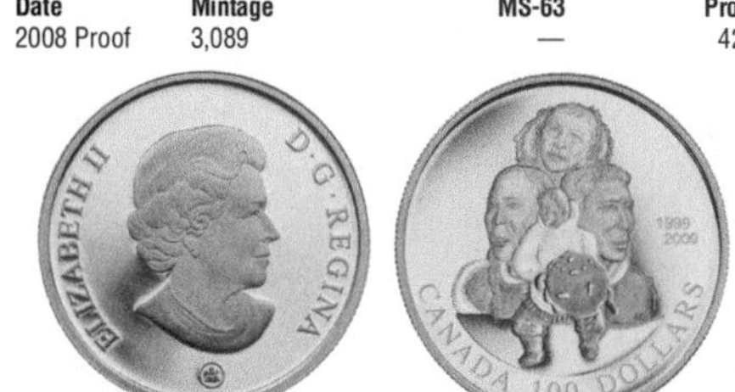

KM# 898 100 DOLLARS
12.0000 g., 0.5830 Gold 0.2249 oz. AGW, 27 mm. **Ruler:** Elizabeth II **Subject:** 10th Anniversary of Nunavut **Obv:** Bust right **Obv. Legend:** Elizabeth II DG Regina **Obv. Designer:** Susanna Blunt **Rev:** Inuit dancer with 3 faces behind **Rev. Legend:** Canada 100 Dollars 1999-2009

Date	Mintage	MS-63	Proof
2009 Proof	2,309	—	425

KM# 997 100 DOLLARS
12.0000 g., 0.5830 Gold 0.2249 oz. AGW, 27 mm. **Ruler:** Elizabeth II **Rev:** Henry Hudson, Map of Hudson's Bay **Rev. Designer:** John Mantha

Date	Mintage	MS-63	Proof
2010 Proof	Est. 5,000	—	425

KM# 1073 100 DOLLARS
12.0000 g., 0.5830 Gold 0.2249 oz. AGW, 27 mm. **Ruler:** Elizabeth II **Subject:** Canadian Railroads, 175th Anniversary **Rev:** Early steam locomotive

Date	Mintage	MS-63	Proof
2011	3,000	—	425

KM# 417 150 DOLLARS
13.6100 g., 0.7500 Gold 0.3282 oz. AGW, 28 mm. **Ruler:** Elizabeth II **Subject:** Year of the Snake **Obv:** Crowned head right **Obv. Designer:** Dora dePedery-Hunt **Rev:** Multicolor snake hologram **Edge:** Reeded

Date	Mintage	MS-63	Proof
2001 Proof	6,571	—	625

KM# 604 150 DOLLARS
13.6100 g., 0.7500 Gold 0.3282 oz. AGW **Ruler:** Elizabeth II **Obv:** Head right **Rev:** Stylized horse left

Date	Mintage	MS-63	Proof
2002 Proof	6,843	—	625

KM# 487 150 DOLLARS
13.6100 g., 0.7500 Gold 0.3282 oz. AGW, 28 mm. **Ruler:** Elizabeth II **Subject:** Year of the Ram **Obv:** Crowned head right **Rev:** Stylized ram left, hologram **Rev. Designer:** Harvey Chan

Date	Mintage	MS-63	Proof
2003 Proof	3,927	—	625

KM# 614 150 DOLLARS
13.6100 g., 0.7500 Gold 0.3282 oz. AGW **Ruler:** Elizabeth II **Obv:** Head right **Rev:** Year of the Monkey, hologram

Date	Mintage	MS-63	Proof
2004 Proof	3,392	—	625

KM# 568 150 DOLLARS
13.6100 g., 0.7500 Gold 0.3282 oz. AGW **Ruler:** Elizabeth II **Subject:** Year of the Rooster **Obv:** Head right **Rev:** Rooster left, hologram

Date	Mintage	MS-63	Proof
2005 Proof	3,731	—	625

KM# 592 150 DOLLARS
13.6100 g., 0.7500 Gold 0.3282 oz. AGW, 28 mm. **Ruler:** Elizabeth II **Subject:** Year of the Dog, hologram **Obv:** Head right **Rev:** Stylized dog left

Date	Mintage	MS-63	Proof
2006 Proof	2,604	—	625

KM# 733 150 DOLLARS
11.8400 g., 0.7500 Gold 0.2855 oz. AGW, 28 mm. **Ruler:** Elizabeth II **Subject:** Year of the Pig **Obv:** Head right **Rev:** Pig in center with Chinese lunar calendar around, hologram

Date	Mintage	MS-63	Proof
2007 Proof	826	—	733

KM# 802 150 DOLLARS
11.8400 g., 0.7500 Gold 0.2855 oz. AGW, 28 mm. **Ruler:** Elizabeth II **Subject:** Year of the Rat **Rev:** Rat, hologram

Date	Mintage	MS-63	Proof
2008 Proof	582	—	550

KM# 899 150 DOLLARS
10.4000 g., 0.9990 Gold 0.3340 oz. AGW, 22.5 mm. **Ruler:** Elizabeth II **Subject:** Blessings of wealth **Obv:** Bust right **Obv. Legend:** Elizabeth II, DG Regina, Fine Gold 99999 or PUR **Obv. Designer:** Susanna Blunt **Rev:** Three goldfish surround peony, clouds **Rev. Legend:** Canada 150 Dollars (Chinese symbols of good fortune) **Rev. Designer:** Harvey Chan **Edge:** Scalloped

Date	Mintage	MS-63	Proof
2009 Proof	1,273	—	650

KM# 867 150 DOLLARS
11.8400 g., 0.7500 Gold 0.2855 oz. AGW, 28 mm. **Ruler:** Elizabeth II **Subject:** Year of the Ox **Rev:** Ox, hologram

Date	Mintage	MS-63	Proof
2009 Proof	486	—	550

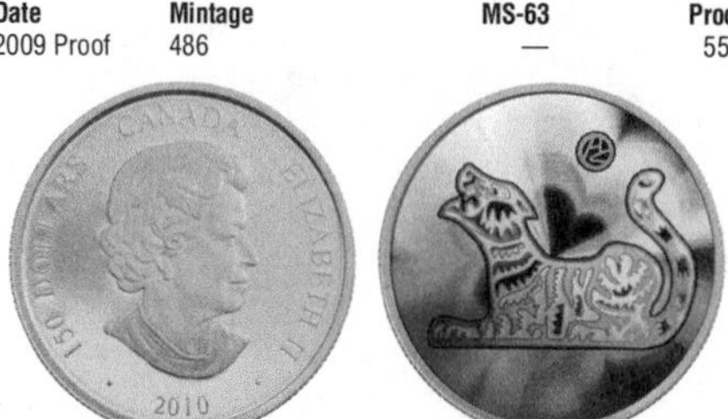

KM# 979 150 DOLLARS
11.8400 g., 0.7500 Gold 0.2855 oz. AGW, 28 mm. **Ruler:** Elizabeth II **Subject:** Year of the Tiger **Rev:** Tiger in hologram

Date	Mintage	MS-63	Proof
2010 Proof	1,507	—	550

KM# 1030 150 DOLLARS
10.4000 g., 0.9999 Gold 0.3343 oz. AGW **Ruler:** Elizabeth II **Subject:** Blessing of Wealth **Shape:** Scalloped

Date	Mintage	MS-63	Proof
2010 Proof	1,388	—	650

KM# 1031 150 DOLLARS
Gold **Ruler:** Elizabeth II **Subject:** Year of the Tiger **Rev:** Tiger walking

Date	Mintage	MS-63	Proof
2010 Proof	2,500	—	600

KM# 1054 150 DOLLARS
Gold **Ruler:** Elizabeth II **Subject:** Year of the rabbit **Rev:** Rabit hopping left, character at left

Date	Mintage	MS-63	Proof
2011 Proof	2,500	—	600

KM# 1053 150 DOLLARS
13.6100 g., 0.7500 Gold 0.3282 oz. AGW, 28 mm. **Ruler:** Elizabeth II **Subject:** Year of the rabbit **Rev:** Rabbit hologram

Date	Mintage	MS-63	Proof
2011 Proof	Est. 4,888	—	600

KM# 1184 150 DOLLARS
13.6100 g., 0.7500 Gold 0.3282 oz. AGW, 28 mm. **Ruler:** Elizabeth II **Subject:** Year of the Dragon **Obv:** Bust right **Rev:** Dragon left

Date	Mintage	MS-63	Proof
2012 Proof	—	—	650

KM# 1262 150 DOLLARS
10.4000 g., 0.9990 Gold 0.3340 oz. AGW, 22.5 mm. **Ruler:** Elizabeth II **Subject:** Good Fortune Panda

Date	Mintage	MS-63	Proof
2012 Proof	—	—	650

KM# 418 200 DOLLARS
17.1350 g., 0.9166 Gold 0.5049 oz. AGW, 29 mm. **Ruler:** Elizabeth II **Subject:** Cornelius D. Krieghoff's "The Habitant farm" **Obv:** Queens head right **Edge:** Reeded

Date	Mintage	MS-63	Proof
2001 Proof	5,406	—	975

KM# 466 200 DOLLARS
17.1350 g., 0.9166 Gold 0.5049 oz. AGW, 29 mm. **Ruler:** Elizabeth II **Subject:** Thomas Thompson "The Jack Pine" (1916-17) **Obv:** Crowned head right

Date	Mintage	MS-63	Proof
2002 Proof	5,264	—	975

KM# 488 200 DOLLARS
17.1350 g., 0.9166 Gold 0.5049 oz. AGW **Ruler:** Elizabeth II **Subject:** Fitzgerald's "Houses" (1929) **Obv:** Crowned head right **Rev:** House with trees

Date	Mintage	MS-63	Proof
2003 Proof	4,118	—	975

KM# 516 200 DOLLARS
16.0000 g., 0.9166 Gold 0.4715 oz. AGW, 29 mm. **Ruler:** Elizabeth II **Subject:** "Fragments" **Obv:** Crowned head right **Rev:** Fragmented face **Edge:** Reeded

Date	Mintage	MS-63	Proof
2004 Proof	3,917	—	900

KM# 569 200 DOLLARS
16.0000 g., 0.9166 Gold 0.4715 oz. AGW **Ruler:** Elizabeth II **Subject:** Fur traders **Obv:** Head right **Rev:** Men in canoe riding wave

Date	Mintage	MS-63	Proof
2005 Proof	3,669	—	900

KM# 594 200 DOLLARS
16.0000 g., 0.9166 Gold 0.4715 oz. AGW **Ruler:** Elizabeth II **Subject:** Timber trade **Obv:** Head right **Rev:** Lumberjacks felling tree

Date	Mintage	MS-63	Proof
2006 Proof	3,218	—	900

KM# 691 200 DOLLARS
16.0000 g., 0.9166 Gold 0.4715 oz. AGW, 29 mm. **Ruler:** Elizabeth II **Subject:** Fishing Trade **Obv:** Head right **Rev:** Two fishermen hauling net

Date	Mintage	MS-63	Proof
2007 Proof	2,137	—	900

KM# 824 200 DOLLARS
16.0000 g., 0.9170 Gold 0.4717 oz. AGW, 29 mm. **Ruler:** Elizabeth II **Subject:** Commerce **Rev:** Horse drawn plow

Date	Mintage	MS-63	Proof
2008 Proof	1,951	—	900

KM# 894 200 DOLLARS
16.0000 g., 0.9160 Gold 0.4712 oz. AGW, 29 mm. **Ruler:** Elizabeth II **Subject:** Coal mining trade **Obv:** Bust right **Obv. Legend:** Elizabeth II DG Regina **Obv. Designer:** Susanna Blunt **Rev:** Miner pushing cart with black coal **Rev. Legend:** Canada 200 Dollars **Rev. Designer:** John Marder

Date	Mintage	MS-63	Proof
2009 Proof	2,241	—	900

KM# 1000 200 DOLLARS
16.0000 g., 0.9160 Gold 0.4712 oz. AGW, 29 mm. **Ruler:** Elizabeth II **Subject:** Petroleum and Oil Trade **Rev:** Oil railcar and well head

Date	Mintage	MS-63	Proof
2010 Proof	Est. 4,000	—	900

KM# 1060 200 DOLLARS
16.0000 g., 0.9167 Gold 0.4715 oz. AGW, 29 mm. **Ruler:** Elizabeth II **Rev:** Olympic athletics with medal, flag and flowers

Date	Mintage	MS-63	Proof
2010 Proof	—	—	900

KM# 1074 200 DOLLARS
16.0000 g., 0.9167 Gold 0.4715 oz. AGW, 29 mm. **Ruler:** Elizabeth II **Rev:** SS Beaver - Seam Sail ship **Rev. Designer:** John Mardon

Date	Mintage	MS-63	Proof
2011 Proof	2,800	—	900

KM# 1143 200 DOLLARS
16.0000 g., 0.9167 Gold 0.4715 oz. AGW, 27 mm. **Ruler:** Elizabeth II **Subject:** Wedding, Prince William and Katherine Middleton **Obv:** Bust right **Rev:** Half-length figures facing, swarovski crystal **Edge:** Reeded

Date	Mintage	MS-63	Proof
2011 Proof	2,000	—	900

KM# 1174 200 DOLLARS
16.0000 g., 0.9160 Gold 0.4712 oz. AGW, 29 mm. **Ruler:** Elizabeth II **Obv:** Bust right **Rev:** Wayne Greskey skating right, father's portrait in circle at right, 99 in color at lower right **Rev. Designer:** Glen Green

Date	Mintage	MS-63	Proof
2011 Proof	999	—	900

KM# 1219 200 DOLLARS
16.0000 g., 0.9167 Gold 0.4715 oz. AGW, 29 mm. **Ruler:** Elizabeth II **Obv:** Bust right **Rev:** Prospector panning for gold in stream

Date	Mintage	MS-63	Proof
2012 Proof	—	—	900

KM# 1223 200 DOLLARS
16.0000 g., 0.9167 Gold 0.4715 oz. AGW, 29 mm. **Ruler:** Elizabeth II **Obv:** Bust right **Rev:** Vikings and ship

Date	Mintage	MS-63	Proof
2012 Proof	—	—	900

KM# 1279 200 DOLLARS
31.1050 g., 0.9990 Gold 0.9990 oz. AGW, 30 mm. **Ruler:** Elizabeth II **Subject:** Bateman Moose

Date	Mintage	MS-63	Proof
2012 Proof	—	—	1,850

KM# 677 250 DOLLARS
45.0000 g., 0.5833 Gold 0.8439 oz. AGW, 40 mm. **Ruler:** Elizabeth II **Rev:** Dog Sled Team

Date	Mintage	MS-63	Proof
2006 Proof	953	—	1,625

KM# 751 250 DOLLARS

1000.0000 g., 0.9999 Silver 32.146 oz. ASW, 101.6 mm. **Ruler:** Elizabeth II **Subject:** Vancouver Olympics, 2010 **Rev:** Early Canada motif **Note:** Illustration reduced.

Date	Mintage	MS-63	Proof
2007 Proof	2,500	—	1,250

KM# 833 250 DOLLARS

1000.0000 g., 0.9990 Silver 32.117 oz. ASW, 101.6 mm. **Ruler:** Elizabeth II **Subject:** Vancouver Olympics 2010 **Rev:** Towards confederation **Note:** Illustration reduced.

Date	Mintage	MS-63	Proof
2008 Proof	2,500	—	1,350

KM# 913 250 DOLLARS

1000.0000 g., 0.9999 Silver 32.146 oz. ASW, 101.5 mm. **Ruler:** Elizabeth II **Obv:** Bust right **Obv. Designer:** Susanna Blunt **Rev:** Mask with fish - Surviving the flood **Note:** Illustration reduced.

Date	Mintage	MS-63	Proof
2009 Proof	815	—	1,350

KM# 949 250 DOLLARS

1000.0000 g., 0.9990 Silver 32.117 oz. ASW, 101.6 mm. **Ruler:** Elizabeth II **Rev:** Modern Canada

Date	Mintage	MS-63	Proof
2009 Proof	905	—	1,350

KM# 981 250 DOLLARS

1000.0000 g., 0.9990 Silver 32.117 oz. ASW, 101.6 mm. **Ruler:** Elizabeth II **Rev:** Eagle head

Date	Mintage	MS-63	Proof
2010 Antique Patina	500	1,350	—
2010 Proof	500	—	1,400

KM# 981a 250 DOLLARS

1000.0000 g., 0.9990 Silver 32.117 oz. ASW, 101.6 mm. **Ruler:** Elizabeth II **Rev:** Eagle head, blue enamel

Date	Mintage	MS-63	Proof
2010 Proof	500	—	1,400

KM# 1044 250 DOLLARS

1000.0000 g., 0.9990 Silver 32.117 oz. ASW, 101.6 mm. **Ruler:** Elizabeth II **Subject:** Baniff, 125th Anniversary of resort founding **Rev:** Features of Baniff

Date	Mintage	MS-63	Proof
2010 Proof	750	—	1,650

KM# 1285 250 DOLLARS

1000.0000 g., 0.9990 Silver 32.117 oz. ASW, 101 mm. **Ruler:** Elizabeth II **Subject:** Olympic views

Date	Mintage	MS-63	Proof
2010 Proof	—	—	1,350

KM# 1150 250 DOLLARS

1000.0000 g., 0.9999 Silver 32.146 oz. ASW, 100 mm. **Ruler:** Elizabeth II **Rev:** Lacrosse

Date	Mintage	MS-63	Proof
2011 Proof	—	—	1,350

KM# 1185 250 DOLLARS

1000.0000 g., 0.9990 Silver 32.117 oz. ASW, 101.6 mm. **Ruler:** Elizabeth II **Subject:** Year of the Dragon **Obv:** Bust left **Rev:** Dragon left

Date	Mintage	MS-63	Proof
2012 Proof	—	—	1,550

KM# 1277 250 DOLLARS
1000.0000 g., 0.9990 Silver 32.117 oz. ASW, 101 mm. **Ruler:** Elizabeth II **Subject:** Bateman Moose

Date	Mintage	MS-63	Proof
2012 Proof	—	—	1,650

KM# 501 300 DOLLARS
60.0000 g., 0.5833 Gold 1.1252 oz. AGW, 50 mm. **Ruler:** Elizabeth II **Obv:** Triple cameo portraits of Queen Elizabeth II by Gillick, Machin and de Pedery-Hunt, each in 14K gold, rose in center **Rev:** Dates "1952-2002" and denomination in legend, rose in center **Note:** Housed in anodized gold-colored aluminum box with cherrywood stained siding

Date	Mintage	MS-63	Proof
1952-2002 Proof	999	—	2,150

KM# 517 300 DOLLARS
60.0000 g., 0.5833 Gold 1.1252 oz. AGW, 50 mm. **Ruler:** Elizabeth II **Obv:** Four coinage portraits of Elizabeth II **Rev:** Canadian arms above value **Edge:** Plain

Date	Mintage	MS-63	Proof
2004 Proof	998	—	2,150

KM# 600 300 DOLLARS
60.0000 g., 0.5833 Gold 1.1252 oz. AGW, 40 mm. **Ruler:** Elizabeth II **Subject:** Welcome Figure Totem Pole **Obv:** Head right **Rev:** Men with totem pole

Date	Mintage	MS-63	Proof
2005 Proof	948	—	2,150

KM# 570.1 300 DOLLARS
45.0000 g., 0.5833 Gold 0.8439 oz. AGW, 40 mm. **Ruler:** Elizabeth II **Subject:** Standard Time - 4 AM Pacific **Obv:** Head right **Rev:** Roman numeral clock with world inside

Date	Mintage	MS-63	Proof
2005 Proof	200	—	1,650

KM# 570.2 300 DOLLARS
45.0000 g., 0.5830 Gold 0.8434 oz. AGW, 40 mm. **Ruler:** Elizabeth II **Subject:** Standard Time - Mountian 5 AM **Obv:** Head right **Rev:** Roman numeral clock with world inside.

Date	Mintage	MS-63	Proof
2005 Proof	200	—	1,650

KM# 570.3 300 DOLLARS
45.0000 g., 0.5830 Gold 0.8434 oz. AGW, 40 mm. **Ruler:** Elizabeth II **Subject:** Standard Time - Central 6 PM **Obv:** Head right **Rev:** Roman numeral clock with world inside

Date	Mintage	MS-63	Proof
2005 Proof	200	—	1,650

KM# 570.4 300 DOLLARS
45.0000 g., 0.5830 Gold 0.8434 oz. AGW, 40 mm. **Ruler:** Elizabeth II **Subject:** Standard Time - Eastern 7 AM **Obv:** Head right **Rev:** Roman numeral clock with world inside

Date	Mintage	MS-63	Proof
2005 Proof	200	—	1,650

KM# 570.5 300 DOLLARS
45.0000 g., 0.5830 Gold 0.8434 oz. AGW, 40 mm. **Ruler:** Elizabeth II **Subject:** Standard Time - Atlantic 8 AM **Obv:** Head right **Rev:** Roman numeral clock with world inside

Date	Mintage	MS-63	Proof
2005 Proof	200	—	1,650

KM# 570.6 300 DOLLARS
45.0000 g., 0.5830 Gold 0.8434 oz. AGW, 40 mm. **Ruler:** Elizabeth II **Subject:** Standard Time - Newfoundland 8:30 **Obv:** Head right **Rev:** Roman numeral clock with world inside

Date	Mintage	MS-63	Proof
2005 Proof	200	—	1,650

KM# 596 300 DOLLARS
60.0000 g., 0.5833 Gold 1.1252 oz. AGW, 50 mm. **Ruler:** Elizabeth II **Subject:** Shinplaster **Obv:** Head right **Rev:** Britannia bust, spear over shoulder

Date	Mintage	MS-63	Proof
2005 Proof	994	—	2,150

KM# 678 300 DOLLARS
45.0000 g., 0.5833 Gold 0.8439 oz. AGW, 40 mm. **Ruler:** Elizabeth II **Rev:** Hologram of Canadarm, Col. C. Hadfield in spacewalk

Date	Mintage	MS-63	Proof
2006 Proof	581	—	1,650

KM# 679 300 DOLLARS
60.0000 g., 0.5833 Gold 1.1252 oz. AGW, 50 mm. **Ruler:** Elizabeth II **Subject:** Queen Elizabeth's 80th Birthday **Rev:** State Crown, colorized

Date	Mintage	MS-63	Proof
2006 Proof	996	—	2,150

KM# 680 300 DOLLARS
60.0000 g., 0.5833 Gold 1.1252 oz. AGW, 50 mm. **Ruler:** Elizabeth II **Subject:** Crystal Snowflake

Date	Mintage	MS-63	Proof
2006 Proof	998	—	2,150

KM# 595 300 DOLLARS
60.0000 g., 0.5833 Gold 1.1252 oz. AGW, 50 mm. **Ruler:** Elizabeth II **Subject:** Shinplaster **Obv:** Head right **Rev:** Seated Britannia with shield

Date	Mintage	MS-63	Proof
2006 Proof	940	—	2,150

KM# 692 300 DOLLARS
60.0000 g., 0.5833 Gold 1.1252 oz. AGW, 50 mm. **Ruler:** Elizabeth II **Subject:** Shinplaster **Rev:** 1923 25 cent bank note

Date	Mintage	MS-63	Proof
2007 Proof	778	—	2,150

KM# 740 300 DOLLARS
45.0000 g., 0.5830 Gold 0.8434 oz. AGW, 40 mm. **Ruler:** Elizabeth II **Rev:** Canadian Rockies panoramic hologram

Date	Mintage	MS-63	Proof
2007 Proof	511	—	1,750

KM# 752 300 DOLLARS
60.0000 g., 0.5830 Gold 1.1246 oz. AGW, 50 mm. **Ruler:** Elizabeth II **Subject:** Vancouver Olympics **Rev:** Olympic ideals, classic figures and torch

Date	Mintage	MS-63	Proof
2007 Proof	953	—	2,150

KM# 825 300 DOLLARS
45.0000 g., 0.5830 Gold 0.8434 oz. AGW, 50 mm. **Ruler:** Elizabeth II **Rev:** Alberta Coat of Arms

Date	Mintage	MS-63	Proof
2008 Proof	344	—	1,750

KM# 826 300 DOLLARS
60.0000 g., 0.5830 Gold 1.1246 oz. AGW, 50 mm. **Ruler:** Elizabeth II **Rev:** Newfoundland and Labrador Coat of Arms

Date	Mintage	MS-63	Proof
2008 Proof	472	—	2,150

KM# 827 300 DOLLARS
45.0000 g., 0.5830 Gold 0.8434 oz. AGW, 40 mm. **Ruler:** Elizabeth II **Subject:** Canadian achievements IMAX **Rev:** Kid in audience reaching out to shark on big screen

Date	Mintage	MS-63	Proof
2008 Proof	—	—	1,650

KM# 828 300 DOLLARS
60.0000 g., 0.5830 Gold 1.1246 oz. AGW, 50 mm. **Ruler:** Elizabeth II **Rev:** Four seasons moon mask in color, blue design in border

Date	Mintage	MS-63	Proof
2008 Proof	544	—	3,800

KM# 830 300 DOLLARS
60.0000 g., 0.5830 Gold 1.1246 oz. AGW, 50 mm. **Ruler:** Elizabeth II **Subject:** Vancouver Olympics **Rev:** Olympic competition, athletics and torch

Date	Mintage	MS-63	Proof
2008 Proof	334	—	2,250

KM# 900 300 DOLLARS
60.0000 g., 0.5830 Gold 1.1246 oz. AGW, 50 mm. **Ruler:** Elizabeth II **Subject:** Yukon Coat of Arms **Obv:** Bust right **Obv. Legend:** Elizabeth II DG Regina **Obv. Designer:** Susanna Blunt **Rev:** Yukon Coat of Arms **Rev. Legend:** Canada 300 Dollars

Date	Mintage	MS-63	Proof
2009 Proof	325	—	2,150

KM# 877 300 DOLLARS
60.0000 g., 0.5830 Gold 1.1246 oz. AGW, 50 mm. **Ruler:** Elizabeth II **Rev:** Summer moon mask, enameled

Date	Mintage	MS-63	Proof
2009 Proof	—	—	2,250

KM# 911 300 DOLLARS
60.0000 g., 0.5830 Gold 1.1246 oz. AGW, 50 mm. **Ruler:** Elizabeth II **Subject:** 2010 Vancouver Olympics **Obv:** Bust right **Obv. Designer:** Susanna Blunt **Rev:** Athletics with torch - Olympic firendship

Date	Mintage	MS-63	Proof
2009 Proof	880	—	2,150

KM# 999 300 DOLLARS
54.0000 g., 0.5830 Gold 1.0121 oz. AGW, 50 mm. **Ruler:** Elizabeth II **Rev:** British Columbia Arms

Date	Mintage	MS-63	Proof
2010 Proof	500	—	1,900

KM# 1047 300 DOLLARS
60.0000 g., 0.5830 Gold 1.1246 oz. AGW, 50 mm. **Ruler:** Elizabeth II **Rev:** Snowflake, white crystals

Date	Mintage	MS-63	Proof
2010 Proof	750	—	2,150

KM# 1078 300 DOLLARS
60.0000 g., 0.5830 Gold 1.1246 oz. AGW, 50 mm. **Ruler:** Elizabeth II **Rev:** New Brunswick Coat of arms

Date	Mintage	MS-63	Proof
2010 Proof	500	—	2,150

KM# 1095 300 DOLLARS
60.0000 g., 0.9167 Gold 1.7683 oz. AGW, 50 mm. **Ruler:** Elizabeth II **Rev:** Manitoba Coat of arms

Date	Mintage	MS-63	Proof
2011 Proof	500	—	3,300

KM# 1215 300 DOLLARS
60.0000 g., 0.9170 Gold 1.7689 oz. AGW, 50 mm. **Ruler:** Elizabeth II **Obv:** Bust right **Rev:** Arms of Nova Scotia

Date	Mintage	MS-63	Proof
2011 Proof	—	—	3,300

KM# 1240 300 DOLLARS
45.0000 g., 0.5830 Gold 0.8434 oz. AGW, 40 mm. **Ruler:** Elizabeth II **Subject:** Elizabeth II, Diamond Jubilee **Obv:** Bust right **Rev:** Youthful bust with crown right, insert crystal at right

Date	Mintage	MS-63	Proof
1952-2012 Proof	—	—	1,600

KM# 1224 300 DOLLARS
60.0000 g., 0.9167 Gold 1.7683 oz. AGW, 50 mm. **Ruler:** Elizabeth II **Obv:** Bust right **Rev:** Shield of Quebec

Date	Mintage	MS-63	Proof
2012 Proof	—	—	3,300

KM# 1242 300 DOLLARS
16.0000 g., 0.9160 Gold 0.4712 oz. AGW, 29 mm. **Ruler:** Elizabeth II **Subject:** Calgary Stampede

Date	Mintage	MS-63	Proof
2012	—	—	900

KM# 1278 300 DOLLARS
31.1090 g., 0.9990 Platinum 0.9991 oz. APW, 30 mm. **Ruler:** Elizabeth II **Subject:** Bateman Moose

Date	Mintage	MS-63	Proof
2012 Proof	—	—	1,750

KM# 433 350 DOLLARS
38.0500 g., 0.9999 Gold 1.2232 oz. AGW, 34 mm. **Ruler:** Elizabeth II **Subject:** The Mayflower Flower **Obv:** Crowned head right **Rev:** Two flowers **Rev. Designer:** Bonnie Ross **Edge:** Reeded

Date	Mintage	MS-63	Proof
2001 Proof	1,988	—	2,350

KM# 502 350 DOLLARS
38.0500 g., 0.9999 Gold 1.2232 oz. AGW, 34 mm. **Ruler:** Elizabeth II **Subject:** The Wild Rose **Obv:** Crowned head right **Obv. Designer:** Dora de Pedery-Hunt **Rev:** Wild rose plant **Rev. Designer:** Dr. Andreas Kare Hellum

Date	Mintage	MS-63	Proof
2002 Proof	2,001	—	2,350

KM# 504 350 DOLLARS
38.0500 g., 0.9999 Gold 1.2232 oz. AGW, 34 mm. **Ruler:** Elizabeth II **Subject:** The White Trillium **Obv:** Crowned head right **Obv. Designer:** Dora de Pedery-Hunt **Rev:** White Trillium

Date	Mintage	MS-63	Proof
2003 Proof	1,865	—	2,350

KM# 601 350 DOLLARS
38.0500 g., 0.9999 Gold 1.2232 oz. AGW **Ruler:** Elizabeth II **Subject:** Western Red Lilly **Obv:** Head right **Rev:** Western Red Lilies

Date	Mintage	MS-63	Proof
2005 Proof	1,634	—	2,350

KM# 626 350 DOLLARS
38.0500 g., 0.9999 Gold 1.2232 oz. AGW, 34 mm. **Ruler:** Elizabeth II **Subject:** Iris Vericolor **Obv:** Crowned head right **Rev:** Iris

Date	Mintage	MS-63	Proof
2006 Proof	1,995	—	2,350

KM# 754 350 DOLLARS
35.0000 g., 0.9999 Gold 1.1251 oz. AGW, 34 mm. **Ruler:** Elizabeth II **Rev:** Purple violet

Date	Mintage	MS-63	Proof
2007 Proof	1,392	—	2,200

KM# 832 350 DOLLARS
35.0000 g., 0.9999 Gold 1.1251 oz. AGW, 34 mm. **Ruler:** Elizabeth II **Rev:** Purple saxifrage

Date	Mintage	MS-63	Proof
2008 Proof	1,313	—	2,200

KM# 901 350 DOLLARS
35.0000 g., 1.0000 Gold 1.1252 oz. AGW, 34 mm. **Ruler:** Elizabeth II **Subject:** Pitcher plant **Obv:** Bust right **Obv. Legend:** Elizabeth II Canada DG Regina Fine Gold 350 Dollars or PUR 99999 **Obv. Designer:** Susana Blunt **Rev:** Cluster of pitcher flowers **Rev. Legend:** Julie Wilson

Date	Mintage	MS-63	Proof
2009 Proof	1,003	—	2,200

KM# 1019 350 DOLLARS
35.0000 g., 0.9990 Gold 1.1241 oz. AGW, 34 mm. **Ruler:** Elizabeth II **Rev:** Praire Crocus **Rev. Designer:** Celia Godkin

Date	Mintage	MS-63	Proof
2010 Proof	Est. 1,400	—	2,200

KM# 1136 350 DOLLARS
35.0000 g., 0.9999 Gold 1.1251 oz. AGW, 34 mm. **Ruler:** Elizabeth II **Obv:** Bust right **Rev:** Mountain Avens in bloom **Edge:** Reeded

Date	Mintage	MS-63	Proof
2011 Proof	1,300	—	2,200

KM# 710 500 DOLLARS
156.5000 g., 0.9999 Gold 5.0309 oz. AGW, 60 mm. **Ruler:** Elizabeth II **Subject:** Queen's 60th Wedding **Rev:** Coat of Arms and Mascots of Elizabeth and Philip

Date	Mintage	MS-63	Proof
2007	198	9,150	—

KM# 782 500 DOLLARS
155.7600 g., 0.9990 Gold 5.0026 oz. AGW, 60 mm. **Ruler:** Elizabeth II **Subject:** Ottawa Mint Centennial 1908-2008 **Rev:** Mint building facade **Note:** Illustration reduced.

Date	Mintage	MS-63	Proof
2008	248	9,150	—

KM# 897 500 DOLLARS
156.0500 g., 0.9990 Gold 5.0119 oz. AGW, 60 mm. **Ruler:** Elizabeth II **Subject:** 150th Anniversary of the start of construction of the Parliament Buildings **Obv:** Bust right **Rev:** Incomplete west block, original architecture **Rev. Legend:** 500 Dollars 1859-2009

Date	Mintage	MS-63	Proof
2009 Proof	77	—	9,150

KM# 1007 500 DOLLARS
156.5000 g., 0.9990 Gold 5.0263 oz. AGW, 60 mm. **Ruler:** Elizabeth II **Subject:** 75th Anniversary of Canadian Bank Notes **Rev:** Abundance seated under tree

Date	Mintage	MS-63	Proof
2010 Proof	200	—	9,150

KM# 1179 500 DOLLARS
156.5000 g., 0.9999 Gold 5.0309 oz. AGW, 60 mm. **Ruler:** Elizabeth II **Obv:** Crowned bust of George V **Rev:** Arms of Canada, dual dates and denomination below **Edge:** Serially numbered

Date	Mintage	MS-63	Proof
1912-2012 Proof	200	—	9,150

KM# 681 2500 DOLLARS
1000.0000 g., 0.9999 Gold 32.146 oz. AGW, 101.6 mm. **Ruler:** Elizabeth II **Subject:** Kilo **Rev:** Common Characters, Early Canada

Date	Mintage	MS-63	Proof
2007	20	57,000	—

KM# 1288 2500 DOLLARS
1000.0000 g., 0.9990 Gold 32.117 oz. AGW, 101 mm. **Ruler:** Elizabeth II **Subject:** Old town view

Date	Mintage	MS-63	Proof
2008 Proof	—	—	57,000

KM# 902 2500 DOLLARS
1000.0000 g., 0.9990 Silver 32.117 oz. ASW, 101.6 mm. **Ruler:** Elizabeth II **Series:** History and Culture Collection **Subject:** Modern Canada **Obv:** Bust right **Obv. Legend:** Vancouver 2010, 2500 Dollars, Elizabeth II **Obv. Designer:** Susanna Blunt **Rev:** Canadian landscape with modern elements

Date	Mintage	MS-63	Proof
2009 Proof	2,500	—	1,250

KM# 902a 2500 DOLLARS
1000.0000 g., 0.9990 Gold 32.117 oz. AGW, 101.6 mm. **Ruler:** Elizabeth II **Series:** History and Culture Collection **Subject:** Modern Canada **Obv:** Bust right **Obv. Legend:** Vancouver 2010, 2500 Dollars, Elizabeth II **Obv. Designer:** Susana Blunt **Rev:** Canadian landscape with modern elements

Date	Mintage	MS-63	Proof
2009 Proof	50	—	57,000

KM# 912 2500 DOLLARS
1000.0000 g., 0.9999 Gold 32.146 oz. AGW, 101 mm. **Ruler:** Elizabeth II **Obv:** Bust right **Obv. Designer:** Susanna Blunt **Rev:** Mask with fish - Surviving the flood

Date	Mintage	MS-63	Proof
2009 Proof	40	—	58,000

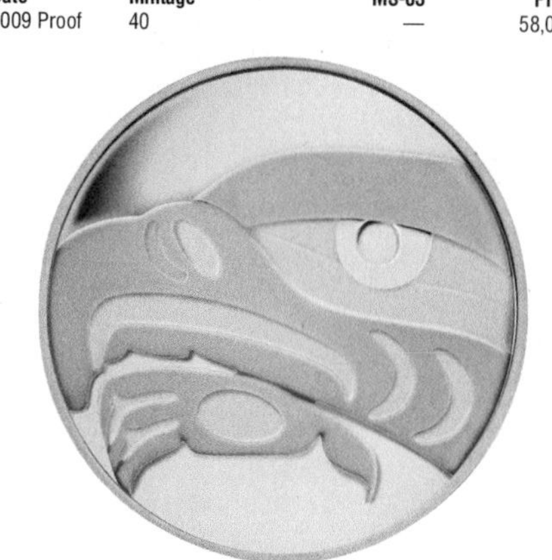

KM# 984 2500 DOLLARS
1000.0000 g., 0.9990 Gold 32.117 oz. AGW, 101 mm. **Ruler:** Elizabeth II

Date	Mintage	MS-63	Proof
2010 Proof	20	—	60,000

KM# 1045 2500 DOLLARS
1000.0000 g., 0.9999 Gold 32.146 oz. AGW, 101 mm. **Ruler:** Elizabeth II **Subject:** Baniff, 125th Anniversary **Rev:** Highlights of Baniff

Date	Mintage	MS-63	Proof
2010	—	—	60,000

KM# 1286 2500 DOLLARS
1000.0000 g., 0.9990 Gold 32.117 oz. AGW, 101 mm. **Ruler:** Elizabeth II **Subject:** Olympic views

Date	Mintage	MS-63	Proof
2010 Proof	—	—	60,000

KM# 1197 2500 DOLLARS
1000.0000 g., 0.9999 Gold 32.146 oz. AGW, 101 mm. **Ruler:** Elizabeth II **Obv:** Bust right **Rev:** Early lacrosse game

Date	Mintage	MS-63	Proof
2011 Proof	35	—	60,000

KM# 1276 2500 DOLLARS
1000.0000 g., 0.9990 Gold 32.117 oz. AGW, 101 mm. **Ruler:** Elizabeth II **Subject:** Bateman Moose

Date	Mintage	MS-63	Proof
2012 Proof	—	—	58,000

SILVER BULLION COINAGE

KM# 617 DOLLAR
1.5550 g., 0.9999 Silver 0.0500 oz. ASW, 16 mm. **Ruler:** Elizabeth II **Obv:** Crowned head right **Rev:** Holographic Maple leaf **Edge:** Reeded

Date	Mintage	MS-63	Proof
2003 Proof	—	—	4.50

KM# 621 DOLLAR
1.5550 g., 0.9999 Silver 0.0500 oz. ASW, 17 mm. **Ruler:** Elizabeth II **Obv:** Crowned head right **Rev:** Maple leaf **Edge:** Reeded

Date	Mintage	MS-63	Proof
2004 Mint logo privy mark Proof	13,859	—	4.50

KM# 718 DOLLAR
15.5500 g., 0.9990 Silver 0.4994 oz. ASW, 32 mm. **Ruler:** Elizabeth II **Obv:** Bust right **Rev:** Grey Wolf standing with moon in background **Rev. Designer:** William Woodruff **Edge:** Reeded

Date	Mintage	MS-63	Proof
2005	106,800	40.00	—
2006	—	40.00	—
2007	—	40.00	—

KM# 618 2 DOLLARS
3.1100 g., 0.9999 Silver 0.1000 oz. ASW, 20.1 mm. **Ruler:** Elizabeth II **Obv:** Crowned head right **Rev:** Holographic Maple leaf **Edge:** Reeded

Date	Mintage	MS-63	Proof
2003 Proof	—	—	7.50

KM# 622 2 DOLLARS
3.1100 g., 0.9999 Silver 0.1000 oz. ASW, 21 mm. **Ruler:** Elizabeth II **Obv:** Crowned head right **Rev:** Maple leaf **Edge:** Reeded

Date	Mintage	MS-63	Proof
2004 Mint logo privy mark Proof	13,859	—	7.50

KM# 571 2 DOLLARS
3.1100 g., 0.9999 Silver 0.1000 oz. ASW, 21 mm. **Ruler:** Elizabeth II **Obv:** Head right **Rev:** Lynx

Date	Mintage	MS-63	Proof
2005 Proof	—	—	7.50

KM# 619 3 DOLLARS
7.7760 g., 0.9999 Silver 0.2500 oz. ASW, 26.9 mm. **Ruler:** Elizabeth II **Obv:** Crowned head right **Rev:** Holographic Maple leaf **Edge:** Reeded

Date	Mintage	MS-63	Proof
2003 Proof	—	—	15.00

KM# 623 3 DOLLARS
7.7760 g., 0.9999 Silver 0.2500 oz. ASW, 27 mm. **Ruler:** Elizabeth II **Obv:** Crowned head right **Rev:** Maple leaf **Edge:** Reeded

Date	Mintage	MS-63	Proof
2004 Mint logo privy mark Proof	13,859	—	12.50

KM# 572 3 DOLLARS
7.7760 g., 0.9999 Silver 0.2500 oz. ASW, 27 mm. **Ruler:** Elizabeth II **Obv:** Head right **Rev:** Lynx

Date	Mintage	MS-63	Proof
2005 Proof	—	—	12.50

KM# 620 4 DOLLARS
15.5500 g., 0.9999 Silver 0.4999 oz. ASW, 33.9 mm. **Ruler:** Elizabeth II **Obv:** Crowned head right **Rev:** Holographic Maple leaf **Edge:** Reeded

Date	Mintage	MS-63	Proof
2003 Proof	—	—	25.00

KM# 624 4 DOLLARS
15.5500 g., 0.9999 Silver 0.4999 oz. ASW, 34 mm. **Ruler:** Elizabeth II **Obv:** Crowned head right **Rev:** Maple leaf **Edge:** Reeded

Date	Mintage	MS-63	Proof
2004 Mint logo privy mark Reverse Proof	13,859	—	22.50

KM# 573 4 DOLLARS
15.5500 g., 0.9999 Silver 0.4999 oz. ASW, 34 mm. **Ruler:** Elizabeth II **Obv:** Head right **Rev:** Lynx

Date	Mintage	MS-63	Proof
2005 Proof	—	—	22.50

KM# 437 5 DOLLARS
31.1035 g., 0.9999 Silver 0.9999 oz. ASW, 38 mm. **Ruler:** Elizabeth II **Obv:** Crowned head right, date and denomination below **Rev:** Radiant maple leaf hologram **Edge:** Reeded

Date	Mintage	MS-63	Proof
2001 Good fortune privy mark	29,906	75.00	—

KM# 187 5 DOLLARS
31.1000 g., 0.9999 Silver 0.9997 oz. ASW **Ruler:** Elizabeth II **Obv:** Crowned head right, date and denomination below **Obv. Designer:** Dora de Pedery-Hunt **Rev:** Maple leaf flanked by 9999

Date	Mintage	MS-63	Proof
2001	398,563	35.00	—
2001 Reverse proof, Snake privy mark	25,000	—	45.00
2002	576,196	35.00	—
2002 Reverse proof, Horse privy mark	25,000	—	45.00
2003	—	35.00	—
2003 Reverse proof, sheep privy mark	25,000	—	45.00

KM# 436 5 DOLLARS

31.1035 g., 0.9999 Silver 0.9999 oz. ASW, 38 mm. **Ruler:** Elizabeth II **Obv:** Crowned head right, date and denomination below **Rev:** Three maple leaves in autumn colors, 9999 flanks **Rev. Designer:** Debbie Adams **Edge:** Reeded

Date	Mintage	MS-63	Proof
2001 Proof	49,709	—	40.00

KM# 505 5 DOLLARS

31.1035 g., 0.9999 Silver 0.9999 oz. ASW, 38 mm. **Ruler:** Elizabeth II **Obv:** Crowned head right, date and denomination below **Rev:** Two maple leaves in spring color (green) **Edge:** Reeded

Date	Mintage	MS-63	Proof
2002	29,509	37.50	—

KM# 521 5 DOLLARS

31.1035 g., 0.9999 Silver 0.9999 oz. ASW **Ruler:** Elizabeth II **Obv:** Head right **Rev:** Maple leaf, summer colors **Rev. Designer:** Stan Witten

Date	Mintage	MS-63	Proof
2003	29,416	37.50	—

KM# 607 5 DOLLARS

31.1200 g., 0.9999 Silver 1.0004 oz. ASW **Ruler:** Elizabeth II **Obv:** Head right **Rev:** Maple leaf, winter colors

Date	Mintage	MS-63	Proof
2004	—	37.50	—

KM# 625 5 DOLLARS

31.1035 g., 0.9999 Silver 0.9999 oz. ASW, 38 mm. **Ruler:** Elizabeth II **Obv:** Bust right **Obv. Designer:** Susanna Blunt **Rev:** Maple leaf **Edge:** Reeded

Date	Mintage	MS-63	Proof
2004 Mint logo privy mark Specimen	13,859	—	37.50
2004 Monkey privy mark Specimen	25,000	—	37.50
2004 D-Day privy mark Specimen	11,698	—	37.50
2004 Desjardins privy mark	15,000	37.50	—
2004 Capricorn privy Mark Reverse proof	5,000	—	37.50
2004 Aquarius privy mark Reverse proof	5,000	—	37.50
2004 Pisces privy mark Reverse proof	5,000	—	37.50
2004 Aries privy mark Reverse proof	5,000	—	37.50
2004 Taurus privy mark Reverse proof	5,000	—	37.50
2004 Gemini privy mark Reverse proof	5,000	—	37.50
2004 Cancer privy mark Reverse proof	5,000	—	37.50
2004 Leo privy mark Reverse proof	5,000	—	37.50
2004 Virgo privy mark Reverse proof	5,000	—	37.50
2004 Libra privy mark Reverse proof	5,000	—	37.50
2004 Scorpio privy mark Reverse proof	5,000	—	37.50
2004 Sagittarius privy mark Reverse proof	5,000	—	50.00
2005	—	35.00	—
2005 Tulip privy mark Reverse proof	3,500	—	50.00
2005 Tank privy mark Reverse proof	7,000	—	60.00
2005 USS Missouri privy mark Reverse proof	7,000	—	60.00
2005 Rooster privy mark Reverse proof	15,000	—	50.00
2006	—	35.00	—
2006 Dog privy mark Reverse proof	—	—	50.00
2007	—	35.00	—
2007 F12 privy mark Reverse proof	—	—	130
2007 Pig privy mark Reverse proof	—	—	50.00
2008	—	35.00	—
2008 F12 privy mark Reverse proof	—	—	130
2008 Rat privy mark Reverse proof	—	—	50.00
2009	—	35.00	—
2009 Brandenberg Gate privy mark Reverse proof	—	—	50.00
2009 Tower Bridge privy mark Reverse proof	—	—	50.00
2009 Ox Privy mark Reverse proof	—	—	50.00
2010	—	35.00	—
2010 Fabulous 15 privy mark Reverse proof	—	—	50.00
2011	—	35.00	—
2012	—	35.00	—
2012 Dragon privy mark Reverse proof	—	—	50.00
2012 Titanic privy mark Reverse proof	—	—	50.00
2012 Pisa privy mark	—	35.00	—
2012 Fabulous 15 privy mark Reverse proof	—	—	75.00
2013	—	35.00	—

KM# 508 5 DOLLARS

31.1035 g., 0.9999 Silver 0.9999 oz. ASW, 38 mm. **Ruler:** Elizabeth II **Obv:** Crowned head right, date and denomination below **Obv. Designer:** Dora de Pedery-Hunt **Rev:** Holographic Maple leaf flanked by 9999 **Edge:** Reeded

Date	Mintage	MS-63	Proof
2003 Proof	—	—	37.50

KM# 522 5 DOLLARS

31.1050 g., 0.9999 Silver 0.9999 oz. ASW **Ruler:** Elizabeth II **Obv:** Head right **Rev:** Maple leaf, winter color **Rev. Designer:** Stan Witten

Date	Mintage	MS-63	Proof
2004	26,763	35.00	—

KM# 574 5 DOLLARS

31.1035 g., 0.9999 Silver 0.9999 oz. ASW, 38 mm. **Ruler:** Elizabeth II **Obv:** Head right **Rev:** Lynx

Date	Mintage	MS-63	Proof
2005 Proof	—	—	37.50

KM# 924 5 DOLLARS

31.1050 g., 0.9999 Silver 0.9999 oz. ASW **Ruler:** Elizabeth II **Rev:** Maple Leaf, laser engraved **Rev. Designer:** Joan Nguyen

Date	Mintage	MS-63	Proof
2005 Proof	25,000	—	60.00

KM# 550 5 DOLLARS

31.1035 g., 0.9999 Silver 0.9999 oz. ASW, 38 mm. **Ruler:** Elizabeth II **Obv:** Head right **Rev:** Big Leaf Maple and seed pod, color **Rev. Designer:** Stan Witten

Date	Mintage	MS-63	Proof
2005	21,233	35.00	—

KM# 660 5 DOLLARS
31.1035 g., 0.9990 Silver 0.9990 oz. ASW **Ruler:** Elizabeth II **Obv:** Bust right **Obv. Designer:** Susanna Blunt **Rev:** Silver maple, colorized **Rev. Designer:** Stan Witten

Date	Mintage	MS-63	Proof
2006	14,157	37.50	—

KM# 625a 5 DOLLARS
31.1050 g., 0.9999 Silver 0.9999 oz. ASW, 38 mm. **Ruler:** Elizabeth II **Rev:** Maple leaf, gilt

Date	Mintage	MS-63	Proof
2007	—	75.00	—
2008	—	75.00	—
2009	—	75.00	—
2009 Tower Bridge Privy Mark	—	75.00	—
2010	—	75.00	—

KM# 729 5 DOLLARS
31.1050 g., 0.9990 Silver 0.9990 oz. ASW, 38 mm. **Ruler:** Elizabeth II **Obv:** Bust right **Rev:** Maple leaf orange multicolor

Date	Mintage	MS-63	Proof
2007 Proof	—	—	45.00

KM# 925 5 DOLLARS
31.1050 g., 0.9990 Silver 0.9990 oz. ASW **Ruler:** Elizabeth II **Obv:** Bust right **Obv. Designer:** Susanna Blunt **Rev:** Sugar maple, colorized **Rev. Designer:** Stan Witten

Date	Mintage	MS-63	Proof
2007	11,495	37.50	—

KM# 928 5 DOLLARS
31.3900 g., 0.9990 Silver 1.0082 oz. ASW, 38 mm. **Ruler:** Elizabeth II **Rev:** Orange sugar maple leaf **Rev. Designer:** Stan Witten

Date	Mintage	MS-63	Proof
2007 Specimen	20,000	—	75.00

KM# 798 5 DOLLARS
31.1050 g., 0.9990 Silver 0.9990 oz. ASW, 38 mm. **Ruler:** Elizabeth II **Subject:** Maple Leaf 20th Anniversary **Rev:** Maple Leaf, selective gold plating

Date	Mintage	MS-63	Proof
2008 Proof	10,000	—	75.00

KM# 799 5 DOLLARS
31.1050 g., 0.9990 Silver 0.9990 oz. ASW, 38 mm. **Ruler:** Elizabeth II **Subject:** Breast Cancer Awareness **Rev:** Multicolor, green maple leaf and pink ribbon

Date	Mintage	MS-63	Proof
2008	11,048	85.00	—

KM# 800 5 DOLLARS
31.1050 g., 0.9990 Silver 0.9990 oz. ASW, 38 mm. **Ruler:** Elizabeth II **Subject:** Vancouver Olympics **Obv:** Bust right **Obv. Designer:** Susanna Blunt **Rev:** Maple leaf, Olympic logo at left, turtle

Date	Mintage	MS-63	Proof
2008	—	37.50	—
2009	—	37.50	—
2010	—	37.50	—

KM# 800a 5 DOLLARS
31.1050 g., 0.9999 Silver partially gilt 0.9999 oz. ASW, 38 mm. **Ruler:** Elizabeth II **Rev:** Maple leaf gilt, olympic logo at left

Date	Mintage	MS-63	Proof
2008	—	50.00	—

KM# 1056 5 DOLLARS
31.1050 g., 0.9999 Silver 0.9999 oz. ASW, 38 mm. **Ruler:** Elizabeth II **Rev:** Maple leaf in brown color, card diamond

Date	Mintage	MS-63	Proof
2008	—	50.00	—

KM# 1057 5 DOLLARS
31.1050 g., 0.9999 Silver 0.9999 oz. ASW, 38 mm. **Ruler:** Elizabeth II **Rev:** Maple Leaf in green color, card heart

Date	Mintage	MS-63	Proof
2008	—	50.00	—

KM# 1058 5 DOLLARS
31.1050 g., 0.9999 Silver 0.9999 oz. ASW, 38 mm. **Ruler:** Elizabeth II **Rev:** Maple leaf in green color, card club

Date	Mintage	MS-63	Proof
2008	—	50.00	—

KM# 1059 5 DOLLARS
31.1050 g., 0.9999 Silver 0.9999 oz. ASW, 38 mm. **Ruler:** Elizabeth II **Rev:** Maple Leaf in red color, card spade

Date	Mintage	MS-63	Proof
2008	—	50.00	—

KM# 863 5 DOLLARS
31.1050 g., 0.9999 Silver 0.9999 oz. ASW, 38 mm. **Ruler:** Elizabeth II **Subject:** Vancouver Olympics **Rev:** Thunderbird Totem **Rev. Designer:** Rick Harry

Date	Mintage	MS-63	Proof
2009	—	50.00	—

KM# 863a 5 DOLLARS
31.1050 g., 0.9999 Silver partially gilt 0.9999 oz. ASW, 38 mm. **Ruler:** Elizabeth II **Rev:** Thunderbird, gilt

Date	Mintage	MS-63	Proof
2009	—	60.00	—

KM# 1061 5 DOLLARS
31.1050 g., 0.9999 Silver 0.9999 oz. ASW, 38 mm. **Ruler:** Elizabeth II **Rev:** Maple leaf in red color, support our troops yellow ribbon

Date	Mintage	MS-63	Proof
2009	—	70.00	—

KM# 998 5 DOLLARS
31.1200 g., 0.9990 Silver 0.9995 oz. ASW, 38 mm. **Ruler:** Elizabeth II **Rev:** Olympic Hockey

Date	Mintage	MS-63	Proof
2010 Proof	—	—	42.50

KM# 998a 5 DOLLARS
31.1050 g., 0.9999 Silver partially gilt 0.9999 oz. ASW, 38 mm. **Ruler:** Elizabeth II **Rev:** Hockey player, gilt maple leaves flanking

Date	Mintage	MS-63	Proof
2010	—	50.00	—

KM# 1077 5 DOLLARS
31.3900 g., 0.9990 Silver 1.0082 oz. ASW, 34 mm. **Ruler:** Elizabeth II **Rev:** Maple leaf on 45 degree angle left **Note:** Piedfort.

Date	Mintage	MS-63	Proof
2010 Reverse Proof	9,000	—	80.00

KM# 1289 5 DOLLARS
31.1050 g., 0.9999 Silver 0.9999 oz. ASW, 38 mm. **Ruler:** Elizabeth II **Rev:** Maple leaf in green with crystal

Date	Mintage	MS-63	Proof
2010	—	65.00	—

KM# 1290 5 DOLLARS
31.1050 g., 0.9990 Silver 0.9990 oz. ASW, 38 mm. **Ruler:** Elizabeth II **Rev:** Maple leaf in red with crystal

Date	Mintage	MS-63	Proof
2010	—	65.00	—

KM# 1291 5 DOLLARS
31.1050 g., 0.9999 Silver 0.9999 oz. ASW, 38 mm. **Ruler:** Elizabeth II **Rev:** Maple leaf in dark green with crystal

Date	Mintage	MS-63	Proof
2010	—	65.00	—

KM# 1292 5 DOLLARS
31.1050 g., 0.9999 Silver 0.9999 oz. ASW, 38 mm. **Ruler:** Elizabeth II **Rev:** Maple leaf in color with crystal

Date	Mintage	MS-63	Proof
2010	—	65.00	—

KM# 1052 5 DOLLARS
31.1050 g., 0.9999 Silver 0.9999 oz. ASW, 38 mm. **Ruler:** Elizabeth II **Rev:** Wolf standing with moonlight in background

Date	Mintage	MS-63	Proof
2011	1,000,000	42.00	—

KM# 1109 5 DOLLARS
31.1050 g., 0.9990 Silver 0.9990 oz. ASW, 38 mm. **Ruler:** Elizabeth II **Rev:** Grizzly Bear walking right

Date	Mintage	MS-63	Proof
2011	1,000,000	40.00	—

KM# 1164 5 DOLLARS
31.1050 g., 0.9990 Silver 0.9990 oz. ASW, 38 mm. **Ruler:** Elizabeth II **Obv. Designer:** Susanna Blunt **Rev:** Cougar **Rev. Designer:** William Woodruff

Date	Mintage	MS-63	Proof
2012	1,000,000	40.00	—

KM# 1241 5 DOLLARS
31.1350 g., 0.9999 Silver 1.0009 oz. ASW, 38 mm. **Ruler:** Elizabeth II **Obv:** Bust right **Obv. Designer:** Susana Blunt **Rev:** Moose left **Rev. Designer:** William Woodruff **Edge:** Reeded

Date	Mintage	MS-63	Proof
2012	1,000,000	42.00	—

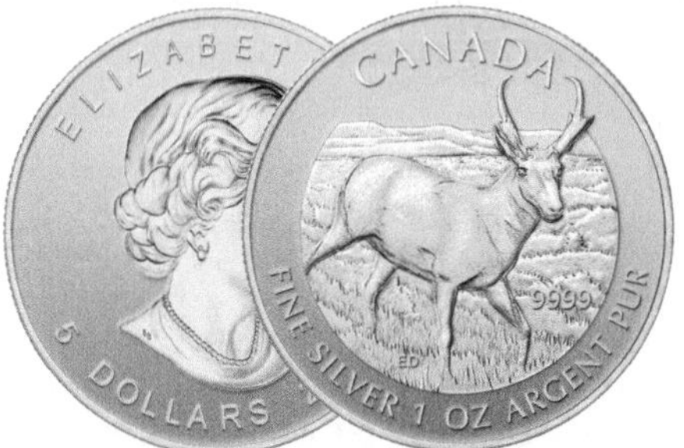

KM# 1297 5 DOLLARS
31.1050 g., 0.9990 Silver 0.9990 oz. ASW, 38 mm. **Ruler:** Elizabeth II **Obv:** Bust right **Rev:** Antelope

Date	Mintage	MS-63	Proof
2013	—	—	—

KM# 1158 10 DOLLARS
31.1050 g., 0.9999 Silver 0.9999 oz. ASW, 38 mm. **Ruler:** Elizabeth II **Obv:** Bust right **Rev:** Branch with three maple leaves

Date	Mintage	MS-63	Proof
2011 Proof	—	—	50.00

KM# 1268 10 DOLLARS
31.1050 g., 0.9990 Silver 0.9990 oz. ASW, 38 mm. **Ruler:** Elizabeth II **Subject:** Maple Leaf Forever

Date	Mintage	MS-63	Proof
2012 Proof	—	—	50.00

KM# 1062 20 DOLLARS
7.9600 g., 0.9999 Silver 0.2559 oz. ASW, 27 mm. **Ruler:** Elizabeth II **Rev:** Five Maple leaves at left **Note:** Thick planchet

Date	Mintage	MS-63	Proof
2011	200,000	25.00	—

KM# 1176 20 DOLLARS
7.9600 g., 0.9999 Silver 0.2559 oz. ASW, 27 mm. **Ruler:** Elizabeth II **Obv:** Bust right **Rev:** Canoe and reflection **Rev. Designer:** Jason Bouwman **Edge:** Reeded **Note:** Thick planchet.

Date	Mintage	MS-63	Proof
2011	200,000	30.00	—

KM# 1226 20 DOLLARS
7.9600 g., 0.9999 Silver 0.2559 oz. ASW, 27 mm. **Ruler:** Elizabeth II **Obv:** Bust right **Rev:** Waterline view of polar bear swimming **Edge:** Reeded

Date	Mintage	MS-63	Proof
2012	250,000	25.00	—

KM# 1237 20 DOLLARS
15.5500 g., 0.9999 Silver 0.4999 oz. ASW, 27 mm. **Ruler:** Elizabeth II **Obv:** Bust right **Rev:** Maple leafs floating on water

Date	Mintage	MS-63	Proof
2012	—	20.00	—

KM# 676 250 DOLLARS
1000.0000 g., 0.9999 Silver 32.146 oz. ASW **Ruler:** Elizabeth II **Subject:** Kilo

Date	Mintage	MS-63	Proof
2006	—	1,350	—

KM# 1160 250 DOLLARS
1000.0000 g., 0.9999 Silver 32.146 oz. ASW, 101 mm. **Ruler:** Elizabeth II **Obv:** Bust right **Obv. Designer:** Susana Blunt **Rev:** Three maple leaves on branch **Rev. Designer:** Debbie Adams

Date	Mintage	MS-63	Proof
2011 Proof	999	—	2,000

KM# 1272 250 DOLLARS
1000.0000 g., 0.9990 Silver 32.117 oz. ASW, 101 mm. **Ruler:** Elizabeth II **Subject:** Maple Leaf Forever

Date	Mintage	MS-63	Proof
2012 Proof	—	—	1,450

KM# 1245 500 DOLLARS
5000.0000 g., 0.9999 Silver 160.73 oz. ASW, 101 mm. **Ruler:** Elizabeth II **Subject:** Haida sculpture

Date	Mintage	MS-63	Proof
2012 Proof	100	—	7,500

GOLD BULLION COINAGE

KM# 542 50 CENTS
1.2700 g., 0.9990 Gold 0.0408 oz. AGW, 13.92 mm. **Ruler:** Elizabeth II **Rev:** Voyagers with northern lights above **Rev. Designer:** Emanuel Hahn

Date	Mintage	MS-63	Proof
2005 Proof	Est. 25,000	—	100

KM# 717 50 CENTS
1.2400 g., 0.9990 Gold 0.0398 oz. AGW, 13.9 mm. **Ruler:** Elizabeth II **Rev:** Wolf

Date	Mintage	MS-63	Proof
2006 Proof	—	—	100

KM# 926 50 CENTS
1.2400 g., 0.9990 Gold 0.0398 oz. AGW, 13.9 mm. **Ruler:** Elizabeth II **Rev:** Cowboy and bronco rider

Date	Mintage	MS-63	Proof
2006 Proof	—	—	100

KM# 927 50 CENTS
1.2400 g., 0.9990 Gold 0.0398 oz. AGW, 13.9 mm. **Ruler:** Elizabeth II **Subject:** Gold Louis

Date	Mintage	MS-63	Proof
2007 Proof	—	—	100

KM# 777 50 CENTS
1.2400 g., 0.9990 Gold 0.0398 oz. AGW, 13.9 mm. **Ruler:** Elizabeth II **Subject:** DeHavilland beaver

Date	Mintage	MS-63	Proof
2008 Proof	20,000	—	100

KM# 888 50 CENTS
1.2700 g., 0.9990 Gold 0.0408 oz. AGW, 13.92 mm. **Ruler:** Elizabeth II **Subject:** Red maple **Obv:** Bust right **Obv. Legend:** Elizabeth II 50 cents **Obv. Designer:** Susanna Blunt **Rev:** Two maple leaves **Rev. Legend:** Canada, Fine gold 1/25 oz or PUR 9999

Date	Mintage	MS-63	Proof
2009 Proof	150,000	—	90.00

KM# 985 50 CENTS
1.2400 g., 0.9990 Gold 0.0398 oz. AGW, 13.92 mm. **Ruler:** Elizabeth II **Subject:** RCMP **Obv:** Bust right **Rev:** Mountie on horseback **Rev. Designer:** Janet Griffin-Scott

Date	Mintage	MS-63	Proof
2010 Proof	Est. 14,000	—	100

KM# 1085 50 CENTS
1.2700 g., 0.9990 Gold 0.0408 oz. AGW, 13.92 mm. **Ruler:** Elizabeth II **Rev:** Geese in flight left **Rev. Designer:** Emily Damstra

Date	Mintage	MS-63	Proof
2011 Proof	10,000	—	90.00

KM# 1214 50 CENTS
1.2700 g., 1.0000 Gold 0.0408 oz. AGW, 13.92 mm. **Ruler:** Elizabeth II **Obv:** Bust right **Rev:** Three maple leaves, 2007-2012 above

Date	Mintage	MS-63	Proof
2012 Proof	—	—	90.00

KM# 1218 50 CENTS
1.2700 g., 0.9999 Gold 0.0408 oz. AGW, 13.92 mm. **Ruler:** Elizabeth II **Obv:** Bust right **Rev:** Schooner sailing left

Date	Mintage	MS-63	Proof
2012 Proof	—	—	90.00

KM# 238 DOLLAR
1.5551 g., 0.9999 Gold 0.0500 oz. AGW **Ruler:** Elizabeth II **Obv:** Crowned head right, denomination and date below **Rev:** Maple leaf flanked by 9999

Date	Mintage	MS-63	Proof
2001	—	BV	—

KM# 438 DOLLAR
1.5810 g., 0.9990 Gold 0.0508 oz. AGW, 14.1 mm. **Ruler:** Elizabeth II **Subject:** Holographic Maple Leaves **Obv:** Crowned head right **Rev:** Three maple leaves multicolor hologram **Edge:** Reeded

Date	Mintage	MS-63	Proof
2001	600	85.00	—

KM# 1138 DOLLAR
1.5600 g., 0.9999 Gold 0.0501 oz. AGW, 14 mm. **Ruler:** Elizabeth II **Obv:** Bust right **Rev:** Maple leaf

Date	Mintage	MS-63	Proof
1911-2011	—	100	—

KM# 1213 DOLLAR
1.5810 g., 1.0000 Gold 0.0508 oz. AGW, 14.1 mm. **Ruler:** Elizabeth II **Obv:** Bust right **Rev:** Three maple leaves, 2007-2012 above

Date	Mintage	MS-63	Proof
2012 Proof	—	—	110

KM# 188 5 DOLLARS
3.1200 g., 0.9999 Gold 0.1003 oz. AGW **Ruler:** Elizabeth II **Obv:** Elizabeth II effigy **Obv. Designer:** Dora dePedery-Hunt **Rev:** Maple leaf

Date	Mintage	MS-63	Proof
2001	—	BV	—

KM# 439 5 DOLLARS
3.1310 g., 0.9999 Gold 0.1006 oz. AGW, 16 mm. **Ruler:** Elizabeth II **Subject:** Holographic Maple Leaves **Obv:** Crowned head right **Rev:** Three maple leaves multicolor hologram **Edge:** Reeded

Date	Mintage	MS-63	Proof
2001	600	200	—

KM# 929 5 DOLLARS
3.1300 g., 0.9990 Gold 0.1005 oz. AGW, 16 mm. **Ruler:** Elizabeth II **Obv. Designer:** Susan Blunt **Rev:** Maple leaf **Rev. Designer:** Walter Ott

Date	Mintage	MS-63	Proof
2007	—	—	200
2008	—	—	200
2009	—	—	200
2010	—	—	200
2011	—	—	200

KM# 1139 5 DOLLARS
3.1300 g., 0.9990 Gold 0.1005 oz. AGW, 16 mm. **Ruler:** Elizabeth II **Obv:** Bust right **Rev:** Maple leaf

Date	Mintage	MS-63	Proof
1911-2011	—	225	—

KM# 1212 5 DOLLARS
3.1300 g., 1.0000 Gold 0.1006 oz. AGW, 16 mm. **Ruler:** Elizabeth II **Obv:** Bust right **Rev:** Three maple leaves, 2007-2012 above

Date	Mintage	MS-63	Proof
2012 Proof	—	—	200

KM# 1267 5 DOLLARS
3.1300 g., 0.9990 Gold 0.1005 oz. AGW, 16 mm. **Ruler:** Elizabeth II **Subject:** Maple Leaf Forever

Date	Mintage	MS-63	Proof
2012 Proof	—	—	200

KM# 189 10 DOLLARS
7.7850 g., 0.9999 Gold 0.2503 oz. AGW **Ruler:** Elizabeth II **Obv:** Crowned head right, date and denomination below **Obv. Designer:** Dora dePedery-Hunt **Rev:** Maple leaf flanked by 9999

Date	Mintage	MS-63	Proof
2001	—	BV	—

KM# 440 10 DOLLARS
7.7970 g., 0.9999 Gold 0.2506 oz. AGW, 20 mm. **Ruler:** Elizabeth II **Subject:** Holographic Maples Leaves **Obv:** Crowned head right **Rev:** Three maple leaves multicolor hologram **Edge:** Reeded

Date	Mintage	MS-63	Proof
2001	15,000	475	—

KM# 1140 10 DOLLARS
7.7970 g., 0.9999 Gold 0.2506 oz. AGW, 20 mm. **Ruler:** Elizabeth II **Obv:** Bust right **Rev:** Maple leaf

Date	Mintage	MS-63	Proof
1911-2011	—	485	—

KM# 1312 10 DOLLARS
6.2200 g., 0.9990 Gold 0.1998 oz. AGW **Ruler:** Elizabeth II **Obv:** Bust right **Rev:** Maple leaf **Note:** Piedfort

Date	Mintage	MS-63	Proof
2011	—	400	—

KM# 1211 10 DOLLARS
7.7970 g., 1.0000 Gold 0.2507 oz. AGW, 20 mm. **Ruler:** Elizabeth II **Obv:** Bust right **Rev:** Three maple leaves, 2007-2012 above

Date	Mintage	MS-63	Proof
2012 Proof	—	—	475

KM# 1275 10 DOLLARS
7.7700 g., 0.9999 Gold 0.2498 oz. AGW, 20 mm. **Ruler:** Elizabeth II **Subject:** War of 1812

Date	Mintage	MS-63	Proof
2012 Proof	—	—	500

KM# 190 20 DOLLARS
15.5515 g., 0.9999 Gold 0.4999 oz. AGW **Ruler:** Elizabeth II **Obv:** Crowned head right, date and denomination below **Obv. Designer:** Dora dePedery-Hunt **Rev:** Maple leaf flanked by 9999

Date	Mintage	MS-63	Proof
2001	—	BV	—

KM# 441 20 DOLLARS
15.5840 g., 0.9999 Gold 0.5010 oz. AGW, 25 mm. **Ruler:** Elizabeth II **Subject:** Holographic Maples Leaves **Obv:** Crowned head right **Rev:** Three maple leaves multicolor hologram **Edge:** Reeded

Date	Mintage	MS-63	Proof
2001	600	925	—

KM# 191 50 DOLLARS
31.1030 g., 0.9999 Gold 0.9998 oz. AGW **Ruler:** Elizabeth II **Obv:** Crowned head right, date and denomination below **Obv. Designer:** Dora dePedery-Hunt **Rev:** Maple leaf flanked by .9999

Date	Mintage	MS-63	Proof
2001	—	BV	—

KM# 442 50 DOLLARS
31.1500 g., 0.9999 Gold 1.0014 oz. AGW, 30 mm. **Ruler:** Elizabeth II **Subject:** Holographic Maples Leaves **Obv:** Crowned head right **Rev:** Three maple leaves multicolor hologram **Edge:** Reeded

Date	Mintage	MS-63	Proof
2001	600	1,850	—

KM# 1042 50 DOLLARS
31.1050 g., 0.9990 Gold 0.9990 oz. AGW, 30 mm. **Ruler:** Elizabeth II **Rev:** Vancouver logo and maple leaf **Edge:** Reeded

Date	Mintage	MS-63	Proof
2008P	—	1,850	—

KM# 1042a 50 DOLLARS
31.1050 g., 0.9999 Gold partially enameled 0.9999 oz. AGW, 30 mm. **Ruler:** Elizabeth II **Rev:** Maple leaf in red enamel, olympic logo at left

Date	Mintage	MS-63	Proof
2008	—	1,850	—

KM# 1037 50 DOLLARS
31.1050 g., 0.9999 Gold 0.9999 oz. AGW, 30 mm. **Ruler:** Elizabeth II **Rev:** Thunderbird **Edge:** Reeded

Date	Mintage	MS-63	Proof
2009	—	1,850	—

KM# 1037a 50 DOLLARS
31.1050 g., 0.9999 Gold 0.9999 oz. AGW, 30 mm. **Ruler:** Elizabeth II **Rev:** Thunderbird, stars in red enamel highlights

Date	Mintage	MS-63	Proof
2009	—	1,850	—

KM# 1029 50 DOLLARS
31.1050 g., 0.9999 Gold 0.9999 oz. AGW, 30 mm. **Ruler:** Elizabeth II **Rev:** Hockey player flanked by maple leaves

Date	Mintage	MS-63	Proof
2010	—	1,850	—

KM# 1029a 50 DOLLARS
31.1050 g., 0.9999 Gold 0.9999 oz. AGW, 30 mm. **Ruler:** Elizabeth II **Rev:** Hockey player, red enameled maple leaves flanking

Date	Mintage	MS-63	Proof
2010	—	1,850	—

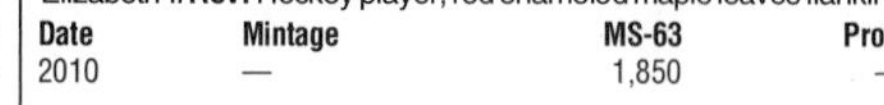

KM# 1141 50 DOLLARS
31.1050 g., 0.9999 Gold 0.9999 oz. AGW, 30 mm. **Ruler:** Elizabeth II **Obv:** Bust right **Rev:** Maple leaf

Date	Mintage	MS-63	Proof
1911-2011	—	1,850	—

KM# 1210 50 DOLLARS
31.1050 g., 1.0000 Gold 100000 oz. AGW, 30 mm. **Ruler:** Elizabeth II **Obv:** Bust right **Rev:** Three maple leaves, 2007-2012 above

Date	Mintage	MS-63	Proof
2012 Proof	—	—	1,850

KM# 750 200 DOLLARS
31.1050 g., 1.0000 Gold 100000 oz. AGW, 30 mm. **Ruler:** Elizabeth II **Rev:** Three maple leaves

Date	Mintage	MS-63	Proof
2007 Proof, T/E privy mark	500	—	1,850

KM# 786 200 DOLLARS
31.1050 g., 1.0000 Gold 100000 oz. AGW, 30 mm. **Ruler:** Elizabeth II **Obv:** Bust right on lathe-work background **Rev:** Two maple leaves on lathe-work background

Date	Mintage	MS-63	Proof
2008 Proof	—	—	1,850

KM# 1162 200 DOLLARS
31.1050 g., 1.0000 Gold 100000 oz. AGW **Ruler:** Elizabeth II **Rev:** Maple leaf with lathe backgound

Date	Mintage	MS-63	Proof
2009 Proof	—	—	1,850

KM# 1163 200 DOLLARS
31.1050 g., 0.9990 Gold 0.9990 oz. AGW **Ruler:** Elizabeth II **Subject:** Celebrating win **Rev:** Three athletics with hands raised

Date	Mintage	MS-63	Proof
2010 Proof	—	—	1,850

KM# 1165 200 DOLLARS
31.1050 g., 1.0000 Gold 100000 oz. AGW, 30 mm. **Ruler:** Elizabeth II **Obv. Designer:** Susanna Blunt **Rev:** Mountie on horseback, lathe backgound **Rev. Designer:** Ago Aarand

Date	Mintage	MS-63	Proof
2011	—	1,850	—

KM# 1161 2500 DOLLARS
1000.0000 g., 0.9999 Gold 32.146 oz. AGW, 101 mm. **Ruler:** Elizabeth II **Rev:** Three maple leaves on branch

Date	Mintage	MS-63	Proof
2011	—	—	56,000

KM# 1271 2500 DOLLARS
1000.0000 g., 0.9990 Gold 32.117 oz. AGW, 101 mm. **Ruler:** Elizabeth II **Subject:** Maple Leaf Forever

Date	Mintage	MS-63	Proof
2012 Proof	—	—	56,000

KM# 1209 100000 DOLLARS
10000.0000 g., 1.0000 Gold 321.49 oz. AGW **Ruler:** Elizabeth II **Obv:** Bust right **Rev:** Bill Reid's sculpture: Spirit of Haida Gwaii **Note:** The sculpture is at the Canadian Embassy in Washington, D.C.

Date	Mintage	MS-63	Proof
2011 Proof	—	—	565,000

KM# 755 1000000 DOLLARS
100000.0000 g., 0.9999 Gold 3214.6 oz. AGW **Ruler:** Elizabeth II **Obv:** Bust right **Rev:** Three maple leaves **Note:** Cast

Date	Mintage	MS-63	Proof
2007	10	5,630,000	—

PLATINUM BULLION COINAGE

KM# 429 30 DOLLARS
3.1100 g., 0.9995 Platinum 0.0999 oz. APW, 16 mm. **Ruler:** Elizabeth II **Obv:** Crowned head right **Rev:** Harlequin duck's head **Rev. Designer:** Cosme Saffioti and Susan Taylor **Edge:** Reeded

Date	Mintage	MS-63	Proof
2001 Proof	448	—	200

KM# 1097 30 DOLLARS
3.1100 g., 0.9995 Platinum 0.0999 oz. APW, 16 mm. **Ruler:** Elizabeth II **Rev:** Great Blue Heron

Date	Mintage	MS-63	Proof
2002 Proof	344	—	200

KM# 1101 30 DOLLARS
3.1100 g., 0.9995 Platinum 0.0999 oz. APW, 16 mm. **Ruler:** Elizabeth II **Rev:** Atlantic Walrus

Date	Mintage	MS-63	Proof
2003	365	—	250

KM# 1105 30 DOLLARS
3.1100 g., 0.9995 Platinum 0.0999 oz. APW, 16 mm. **Ruler:** Elizabeth II **Rev:** Grizzly Bear

Date	Mintage	MS-63	Proof
2004 Proof	380	—	250

KM# 430 75 DOLLARS
7.7760 g., 0.9995 Platinum 0.2499 oz. APW, 20 mm. **Ruler:** Elizabeth II **Obv:** Crowned head right **Rev:** Harlequin duck in flight **Rev. Designer:** Cosme Saffioti and Susan Taylor **Edge:** Reeded

Date	Mintage	MS-63	Proof
2001 Proof	448	—	500

KM# 1098 75 DOLLARS
7.7700 g., 0.9995 Platinum 0.2497 oz. APW, 20 mm. **Ruler:** Elizabeth II **Rev:** Great Blue Heron

Date	Mintage	MS-63	Proof
2002 Proof	344	—	525

KM# 1102 75 DOLLARS
7.7700 g., 0.9995 Platinum 0.2497 oz. APW, 20 mm. **Ruler:** Elizabeth II **Rev:** Atlantic Walrus

Date	Mintage	MS-63	Proof
2003 Proof	365	—	550

KM# 1106 75 DOLLARS
7.7700 g., 0.9995 Platinum 0.2497 oz. APW, 20 mm. **Ruler:** Elizabeth II **Rev:** Grizzly Bear

Date	Mintage	MS-63	Proof
2004 Proof	380	—	550

KM# 431 150 DOLLARS
15.5500 g., 0.9995 Platinum 0.4997 oz. APW, 25 mm. **Ruler:** Elizabeth II **Obv:** Crowned head right **Rev:** Two harlequin ducks **Rev. Designer:** Cosme Saffioti and Susan Taylor **Edge:** Reeded

Date	Mintage	MS-63	Proof
2001 Proof	448	—	1,000

KM# 1099 150 DOLLARS
15.5500 g., 0.9995 Platinum 0.4997 oz. APW, 25 mm. **Ruler:** Elizabeth II **Rev:** Great Blue Heron

Date	Mintage	MS-63	Proof
2002 Proof	344	—	1,000

KM# 1103 150 DOLLARS
15.5500 g., 0.9995 Platinum 0.4997 oz. APW, 25 mm. **Ruler:** Elizabeth II **Rev:** Atlantic Walrus

Date	Mintage	MS-63	Proof
2003 Proof	365	—	1,000

KM# 1107 150 DOLLARS
15.5500 g., 0.9995 Platinum 0.4997 oz. APW, 25 mm. **Ruler:** Elizabeth II **Rev:** Grizzly Bear

Date	Mintage	MS-63	Proof
2004 Proof	380	—	1,000

KM# 432 300 DOLLARS
31.1035 g., 0.9995 Platinum 0.9995 oz. APW, 30 mm. **Ruler:** Elizabeth II **Obv:** Crowned head right **Rev:** Two standing harlequin ducks **Rev. Designer:** Cosme Saffioti and Susan Taylor **Edge:** Reeded

Date	Mintage	MS-63	Proof
2001 Proof	448	—	1,900

KM# 1100 300 DOLLARS
31.1050 g., 0.9995 Platinum 0.9995 oz. APW, 30 mm. **Ruler:** Elizabeth II **Rev:** Great Blue Heron

Date	Mintage	MS-63	Proof
2002 Proof	344	—	1,950

KM# 1104 300 DOLLARS
31.1050 g., 0.9995 Platinum 0.9995 oz. APW, 30 mm. **Ruler:** Elizabeth II **Rev:** Atlantic Walrus

Date	Mintage	MS-63	Proof
2003 Proof	365	—	1,950

KM# 1108 300 DOLLARS
31.1050 g., 0.9995 Platinum 0.9995 oz. APW, 30 mm. **Ruler:** Elizabeth II **Rev:** Grizzly Bear

Date	Mintage	MS-63	Proof
2004 Proof	380	—	1,950

KM# 753 300 DOLLARS
31.1050 g., 0.9999 Platinum 0.9999 oz. APW **Ruler:** Elizabeth II **Rev:** Wooly mammoth

Date	Mintage	MS-63	Proof
2007 Proof	400	—	3,200

KM# 831 300 DOLLARS
31.1050 g., 0.9990 Platinum 0.9990 oz. APW **Ruler:** Elizabeth II **Rev:** Saber Tooth Scimitar cat

Date	Mintage	MS-63	Proof
2008 Proof	200	—	3,500

KM# 951 300 DOLLARS
31.1600 g., 0.9990 Platinum 1.0008 oz. APW, 30 mm. **Ruler:** Elizabeth II **Rev:** Steppe Bison

Date	Mintage	MS-63	Proof
2009 Proof	200	—	3,500

KM# 1159 300 DOLLARS
31.1050 g., 0.9990 Platinum 0.9990 oz. APW, 30 mm. **Ruler:** Elizabeth II **Rev:** Ground Sloth

Date	Mintage	MS-63	Proof
2010 Proof	200	—	1,900

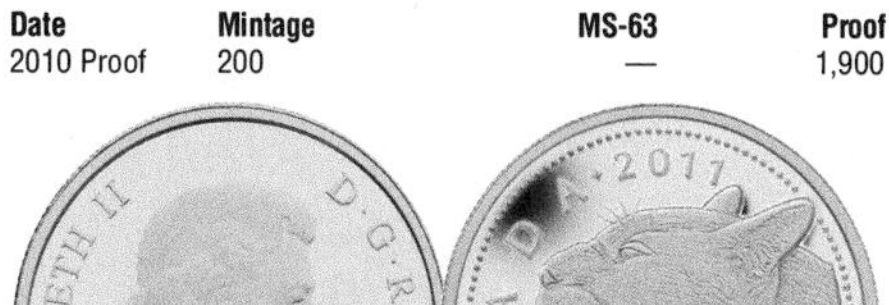

KM# 1175 300 DOLLARS
31.1050 g., 0.9995 Platinum 0.9995 oz. APW, 30 mm. **Ruler:** Elizabeth II **Obv:** Bust right **Rev:** Cougar head left

Date	Mintage	MS-63	Proof
2011 Proof	200	—	1,950

KM# 1273 300 DOLLARS
31.1050 g., 0.9990 Platinum 0.9990 oz. APW, 30 mm. **Ruler:** Elizabeth II **Subject:** Maple Leaf Forever

Date	Mintage	MS-63	Proof
2012 Proof	—	—	1,950

MINT SETS

KM#	Date	Mintage	Identification	Issue Price	Mkt Val
MS8	2001 (5)	600	KM438-442	1,996	2,950
MS9	2002 (7)	135,000	Double-dated 1952-2002, KM#444-449, 467 Elizabeth II Golden Jubilee	11.75	16.00
MS10	2002 (7)	—	KM#444-449, 467, Oh! Canada! 135th Birthday Gift set.	17.00	16.00
MS11	2002 (7)	—	KM#444-449, 467, Tiny Treasures Uncirculated Gift Set	17.00	16.00
MS12	2003 (7)	135,000	KM#289, 182b, 183b, 184b, 290, 186, 270	12.00	16.00
MS13	2003 (7)	75,000	KM490-496	13.25	20.00
MS14	2003 (7)	—	KM289, 182-184, 290, 186, 270, Oh! Canada!	17.75	16.00
MS15	2003 (7)	—	KM289, 182-184, 290, 186, 270, Tiny Treasures Uncirculated Gift Set	17.75	16.00

PROOF SETS

KM#	Date	Mintage	Identification	Issue Price	Mkt Val
PS51	2001 (4)	—	KM429, 430, 431, 432	—	3,600
PS52	2002 (8)	100,000	KM#443, 444a,445,446a-449a, 467 Elizabeth II Golden Jubilee	60.00	125
PS53	2002 (3)	—	KM#459-461 Canadian Folklore and Legends Collection	57.50	35.00
PS54	2002 (2)	—	KM#519, 520	750	1,125
PS55	2003 (8)	100,000	KM#182a,183a,184a, 186, 270d, 289, 290a, 450 100th Anniversary of the Cobalt Silver Strike	62.50	125
PS56	2003 (6)	30,000	KM#468-473 50th Anniversary of the Coronation of Elizabeth II	75.00	100
PS57	2004 (8)	—	KM#490, 491a-494a, 495, 496a, 512	—	115
PS58	2004 (5)	25,000	KM#621-625	—	100

SPECIMEN SETS (SS)

KM#	Date	Mintage	Identification	Issue Price	Mkt Val
SS90	2002 (7)	75,000	KM#444-449,462 Elizabeth II Golden Jubilee	30.00	65.00
SS91	2003 (3)	75,000	KM#(uncertain), 270, 289, 290	30.00	50.00

CAPE VERDE

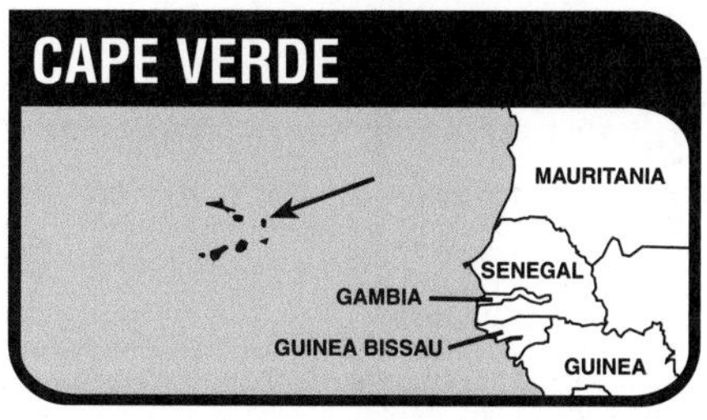

The Republic of Cape Verde, Africa's smallest republic, is located in the Atlantic Ocean, about 370 miles (595 km.) west of Dakar, Senegal, off the coast of Africa. The 14-island republic has an area of 1,557 sq. mi. (4,033 sq. km.) and a population of 435,983. Capital: Praia. The refueling of ships and aircraft is the chief economic function of the country. Fishing is important and agriculture is widely practiced, but the Cape Verdes are not self-sufficient in food. Fish products, salt, bananas, and shellfish are exported.

After 500 years of Portuguese rule, the Cape Verdes became independent on July 5, 1975. At the first general election, all seats of the new national assembly were won by the Party for the Independence of Guinea-Bissau and Cape Verde (PAIGC). The PAIGC linked the two former colonies into one state. Antonio Mascarenhas Monteiro won the first free presidential election in 1991.

RULER
Portuguese, until 1975

MONETARY SYSTEM
100 Centavos = 1 Escudo

REPUBLIC

DECIMAL COINAGE

KM# 46 25 ESCUDOS
15.5517 g., 0.9990 Silver 0.4995 oz. ASW, 30.4 mm. **Obv:** Value above national arms **Rev:** Jesus **Edge:** Plain

Date	Mintage	F	VF	XF	Unc	BU
2006 Proof	—	Value: 40.00				

KM# 47 50 ESCUDOS
1.5550 g., 0.9990 Gold 0.0499 oz. AGW, 16 mm. **Obv:** Value above national arms **Rev:** Jesus **Edge:** Plain

Date	Mintage	F	VF	XF	Unc	BU
2006 Proof	—	Value: 100				

KM# 48 50 ESCUDOS
25.0000 g., 0.9250 Silver 0.7435 oz. ASW, 38.8 mm. **Subject:** 500th Anniversary Death of Christopher Columbus **Obv:** National arms **Obv. Legend:** CABO VERDE **Rev:** Sailing ship "Santa Maria" **Rev. Legend:** A SANTA MARIA DE CHRIST?V?O COLOMBO **Edge:** Reeded

Date	Mintage	F	VF	XF	Unc	BU
2006 Proof	—	Value: 55.00				

KM# 49 50 ESCUDOS
25.0000 g., 0.9250 Silver 0.7435 oz. ASW, 38.6 mm. **Subject:** Appearance in Grotto **Obv:** National arms **Obv. Legend:** CABO VERDE **Rev:** Maria standing facing 3/4 left at right **Rev. Legend:** AVE MARIA - LOURDES **Edge:** Reeded

Date	Mintage	F	VF	XF	Unc	BU
2006 Proof	—	Value: 65.00				

KM# 50 50 ESCUDOS
25.0000 g., 0.9250 Silver 0.7435 oz. ASW **Obv:** National arms **Rev:** Red Kite bird

Date	Mintage	F	VF	XF	Unc	BU
2006 Proof	—	Value: 65.00				

KM# 52 50 ESCUDOS
25.0000 g., 0.9250 Silver 0.7435 oz. ASW, 38.6 mm. **Rev:** East India Company's Princess Louisa and 1/2 real from shipwreck

Date	Mintage	F	VF	XF	Unc	BU
2006 Proof	Est. 1,500	Value: 75.00				

KM# 53 50 ESCUDOS
25.0000 g., 0.9250 Silver 0.7435 oz. ASW, 38.6 mm. **Rev:** Princess Louisa hitting the reef, 1/2 real from shipwreck

Date	Mintage	F	VF	XF	Unc	BU
2006 Proof	Est. 1,500	Value: 75.00				

KM# 45 200 ESCUDOS
7.8000 g., Copper-Nickel, 29.5 mm. **Subject:** 30th Anniversary of Independence **Obv:** National arms in number 2 of 200 **Rev:** Symbolic education design **Edge:** Reeded **Shape:** Round

Date	Mintage	F	VF	XF	Unc	BU
2005	—	—	—	—	8.50	10.00

KM# 45a 200 ESCUDOS

18.2800 g., 0.9250 Silver 0.5436 oz. ASW **Subject:** 30th Anniversary of Independence **Obv:** National arms in number 2 of 200 **Rev:** Symbolic education design **Edge:** Reeded **Shape:** Round

Date	Mintage	F	VF	XF	Unc	BU
2005 Proof	—	Value: 70.00				

KM# 51 250 ESCUDOS

Copper-Nickel **Subject:** Independence, 35th Anniversary **Obv:** Ship sailing forward **Rev:** Arms

Date	Mintage	F	VF	XF	Unc	BU
2010	—	—	—	—	—	15.00

CAYMAN ISLANDS

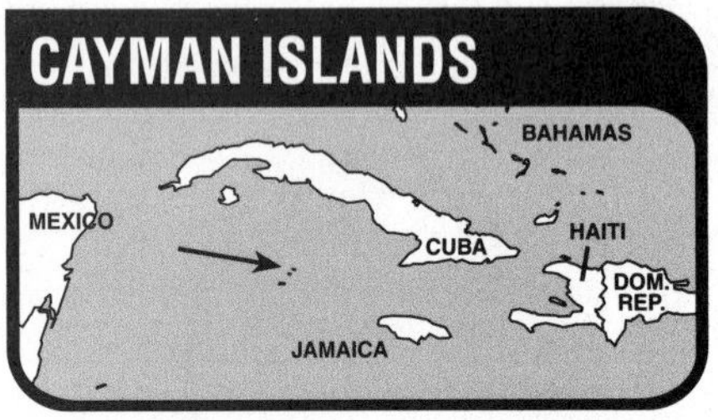

The Cayman Islands are a British Crown Colony situated about 180 miles (280 km) northwest of Jamaica. It consists of three islands: Grand Cayman, Little Cayman, and Cayman Brac. The islands have an area of 102 sq. mi. (259 sq. km.) and a population of 33,200. Capital: George Town. Seafaring, commerce, banking, and tourism are the principal industries. Rope, turtle shells, and sharkskins are exported.

RULER
British

MINT MARKS
CHI - Valcambi

MONETARY SYSTEM
100 Cents = 1 Dollar

BRITISH COLONY

DECIMAL COINAGE

KM# 131 CENT

2.5500 g., Copper Plated Steel, 17 mm. **Ruler:** Elizabeth II **Obv:** Crowned head right **Rev:** Grand Caiman thrush **Edge:** Plain

Date	Mintage	F	VF	XF	Unc	BU
2002	10,000,000	—	—	0.15	0.35	0.75
2005	16,220,000	—	—	0.15	0.35	0.75
2008	12,000,000	—	—	0.15	0.35	0.75

KM# 132 5 CENTS

2.0000 g., Nickel Plated Steel, 18 mm. **Ruler:** Elizabeth II **Obv:** Crowned head right **Rev:** Pink-spotted shrimp **Edge:** Plain

Date	Mintage	F	VF	XF	Unc	BU
2002	2,500,000	—	—	0.15	0.35	1.00
2005	2,500,000	—	—	0.15	0.35	1.00
2008	3,000,000	—	—	0.15	0.35	1.00

KM# 133 10 CENTS

3.4500 g., Nickel Plated Steel, 21 mm. **Ruler:** Elizabeth II **Obv:** Head with tiara right **Rev:** Green turtle surfacing **Edge:** Reeded

Date	Mintage	F	VF	XF	Unc	BU
2002	3,000,000	—	0.25	0.40	1.00	1.25
2005	3,000,000	—	0.25	0.40	1.00	1.25
2008	3,500,000	—	0.25	0.40	1.00	1.25

KM# 134 25 CENTS

5.1000 g., Nickel Plated Steel, 24.26 mm. **Ruler:** Elizabeth II **Obv:** Head with tiara right **Rev:** Schooner sailing right **Edge:** Reeded

Date	Mintage	F	VF	XF	Unc	BU
2002	2,500,000	—	—	0.75	1.25	1.50
2005	2,500,000	—	—	0.75	1.25	1.50
2008	3,000,000	—	—	0.75	1.25	1.50

KM# 136 2 DOLLARS

28.3400 g., 0.9250 Silver 0.8428 oz. ASW, 38.6 mm. **Ruler:** Elizabeth II **Obv:** Gold plated Queen Elizabeth II **Rev:** British crown and value **Edge:** Reeded

Date	Mintage	F	VF	XF	Unc	BU
2002 Proof	—	Value: 45.00				

KM# 135 2 DOLLARS

28.2800 g., 0.9250 Silver 0.8410 oz. ASW, 38.6 mm. **Ruler:** Elizabeth II **Subject:** 500th Anniversary - Christopher Columbus First Recorded Sighting of the Cayman Islands **Obv:** Crowned head right **Rev:** Quincentennial Celebrations Logo in color

Date	Mintage	F	VF	XF	Unc	BU
2003 Proof	1,500	Value: 55.00				

KM# 138 2 DOLLARS

28.2800 g., 0.9250 Silver 0.8410 oz. ASW, 38.61 mm. **Ruler:** Elizabeth II **Subject:** Royal Horticulture Society **Obv:** Head right, gilt portrait **Rev:** RHS Tent and flowers

Date	Mintage	F	VF	XF	Unc	BU
2003 Proof	—	Value: 45.00				

KM# 137 5 DOLLARS

28.2800 g., 0.9250 Silver 0.8410 oz. ASW, 38.6 mm. **Ruler:** Elizabeth II **Subject:** Elizabeth II's 80th Birthday **Obv:** Crowned head right - gilt **Obv. Legend:** CAYMAN ISLANDS - ELIZABETH II **Rev:** Queen crowning Charles as Prince of Wales

Date	Mintage	F	VF	XF	Unc	BU
2006 Proof	25,000	Value: 50.00				

KM# 145 5 DOLLARS

28.2800 g., 0.9250 Silver 0.8410 oz. ASW, 38.61 mm. **Ruler:** Elizabeth II **Subject:** Queen Elizabeth, 80th Birthday **Rev:** Elizabeth and Philip in the state coach

Date	Mintage	F	VF	XF	Unc	BU
2006 Proof	Est. 25,000	Value: 50.00				

KM# 149 5 DOLLARS

28.2800 g., 0.9250 Silver 0.8410 oz. ASW, 38.6 mm. **Ruler:** Elizabeth II **Obv:** Head in tiara right, gilt face and rim **Rev:** Queen and Prince Philip in carriage, gilt 80 above

Date	Mintage	F	VF	XF	Unc	BU
2006 Proof	—	Value: 50.00				

KM# 139 5 DOLLARS

28.2800 g., 0.9250 Silver 0.8410 oz. ASW, 38.61 mm. **Ruler:** Elizabeth II **Subject:** Cayman Islands Monetary Authority, 10th Anniversary **Obv:** Bust right **Rev:** Island's coat of arms

Date	Mintage	F	VF	XF	Unc	BU
2007 Proof	200	Value: 110				

KM# 146 5 DOLLARS

28.2800 g., 0.9250 Silver 0.8410 oz. ASW, 38.61 mm. **Ruler:** Elizabeth II **Subject:** End of World War I, 90th Anniversary

Date	Mintage	F	VF	XF	Unc	BU
2008 Proof	—	Value: 50.00				

KM# 147 5 DOLLARS

28.2800 g., 0.9250 Silver 0.8410 oz. ASW, 38.61 mm. **Ruler:** Elizabeth II **Subject:** End of World War I, 90th Anniversary

Date	Mintage	F	VF	XF	Unc	BU
2008 Proof	—	Value: 50.00				

KM# 141 5 DOLLARS

28.2800 g., 0.9250 Silver 0.8410 oz. ASW, 38.6 mm. **Ruler:** Elizabeth II **Subject:** Constitutional Government, 50th Anniversary **Obv:** Bust right **Rev:** Coat of arms

Date	Mintage	F	VF	XF	Unc	BU
2009 Proof	300	Value: 75.00				

KM# 150 5 DOLLARS

28.2800 g., 0.9250 Silver 0.8410 oz. ASW, 38.61 mm. **Ruler:** Elizabeth II **Subject:** Royal Yacht Britannia, 60th Anniversary **Rev:** HMY Britannia, flags **Rev. Legend:** I NAME THIS SHIP BRITANNIA

Date	Mintage	F	VF	XF	Unc	BU
2012 Proof	Est. 40,000	Value: 110				

KM# 140 10 DOLLARS

7.9880 g., 0.9167 Gold 0.2354 oz. AGW, 22.1 mm. **Ruler:** Elizabeth II **Subject:** Cayman Islands Monetary Authority, 10th Anniversary **Obv:** Bust right **Rev:** Island's coat of arms

Date	Mintage	F	VF	XF	Unc	BU
2007 Proof	75	Value: 475				

KM# 142 10 DOLLARS

7.9880 g., 0.9167 Gold 0.2354 oz. AGW, 22.1 mm. **Ruler:** Elizabeth II **Subject:** Constitutional Government, 50th Anniversary **Obv:** Bust right **Rev:** Coat of Arms

Date	Mintage	F	VF	XF	Unc	BU
2009 Proof	125	Value: 475				

KM# 148 50 DOLLARS

155.5000 g., 0.9250 Silver 4.6243 oz. ASW, 65 mm. **Ruler:** Elizabeth II **Subject:** End of World War I, 90th Anniversary **Rev:** Soldier in the field with barbed wire

Date	Mintage	F	VF	XF	Unc	BU
2008 Proof	Est. 150	Value: 300				

CENTRAL AFRICAN STATES

The Central African States, a monetary union comprised of Equatorial Guinea (a former Spanish possession), the former French possessions and now independent states of the Republic of Congo (Brazzaville), Gabon, Central African Republic, Chad and Cameroon, issues a common currency for the member states from a common central bank. The monetary unit, the African Financial Community franc, is tied to and supported by the French franc.

In 1960, an attempt was made to form a union of the newly independent republics of Chad, Congo, Central Africa and Gabon. The proposal was discarded when Chad refused to become a constituent member. The four countries then linked into an Equatorial Customs Unit, to which Cameroon became an associate member in 1961. A more extensive cooperation of the five republics, identified as the Central African Customs and Economic Union, was entered into force at the beginning of 1966.

In 1974 the Central Bank of the Equatorial African States, which had issued coins and paper currency in its own name and with the names of the constituent member nations, changed its name to the Bank of the Central African States. Equatorial Guinea converted to the CFA currency system issuing its first 100 Franc in 1985.

For earlier coinage see French Equatorial Africa.

MONETARY UNION

STANDARD COINAGE

KM# 8 FRANC
1.3000 g., Aluminum, 23 mm. **Obv:** Three giant eland left, date below **Rev:** Denomination within wreath

Date	Mintage	F	VF	XF	Unc	BU
2003	—	0.20	0.40	0.80	2.00	—

KM# 16 FRANC
1.6100 g., Stainless Steel, 14.9 mm. **Obv:** Value **Rev:** Value above produce **Edge:** Plain

Date	Mintage	F	VF	XF	Unc	BU
2006(a)	—	—	—	—	0.15	0.25

KM# 17 2 FRANCS
2.4300 g., Stainless Steel, 17.9 mm. **Obv:** Value **Rev:** Value above produce **Edge:** Plain

Date	Mintage	F	VF	XF	Unc	BU
2006(a)	—	—	—	—	0.25	0.35

KM# 7 5 FRANCS
3.0000 g., Aluminum-Bronze, 20 mm. **Obv:** Three giant eland left, date below **Rev:** Denomination within wreath

Date	Mintage	F	VF	XF	Unc	BU
2003	—	0.15	0.30	0.60	1.25	—

KM# 18 5 FRANCS
2.4100 g., Brass, 15.9 mm. **Obv:** Value **Rev:** Value above produce **Edge:** Reeded

Date	Mintage	F	VF	XF	Unc	BU
2006(a)	—	—	—	—	0.50	0.65

KM# 9 10 FRANCS
4.0000 g., Aluminum-Bronze, 23 mm. **Obv:** Three giant eland left, date below **Rev:** Denomination within wreath

Date	Mintage	F	VF	XF	Unc	BU
2003(a)	—	0.20	0.35	0.75	1.50	—

KM# 19 10 FRANCS
3.0000 g., Brass, 17.9 mm. **Obv:** Value **Rev:** Value above produce **Edge:** Reeded

Date	Mintage	F	VF	XF	Unc	BU
2006(a)	—	—	—	—	0.75	1.00

KM# 10 25 FRANCS
8.0000 g., Aluminum-Bronze, 27.2 mm. **Obv:** Three giant eland left, date below **Rev:** Denomination within wreath

Date	Mintage	F	VF	XF	Unc	BU
2003(a)	—	0.25	0.50	1.00	2.00	—

KM# 20 25 FRANCS
4.2000 g., Brass, 22.7 mm. **Obv:** Value **Rev:** Value above produce **Edge:** Reeded

Date	Mintage	F	VF	XF	Unc	BU
2006(a)	—	—	—	—	1.00	1.25

KM# 11 50 FRANCS
4.7000 g., Nickel, 21.5 mm. **Obv:** Three giant eland left, date below **Rev:** Denomination within flower design **Edge:** Reeded **Note:** Starting in 1996 an extra flora item was added where the mintmark was formerly located.

Date	Mintage	F	VF	XF	Unc	BU
2003(a)	—	0.75	1.50	3.50	6.00	—

KM# 21 50 FRANCS
4.9000 g., Stainless Steel, 22 mm. **Obv:** Value **Rev:** Value above produce **Edge:** Reeded

Date	Mintage	F	VF	XF	Unc	BU
2006(a)	—	—	—	—	1.25	1.50

KM# 13 100 FRANCS
7.0500 g., Nickel, 25.5 mm. **Obv:** Three giant eland **Rev:** Denomination

Date	Mintage	F	VF	XF	Unc	BU
2003	—	—	—	—	4.50	6.00

KM# 15 100 FRANCS
6.0000 g., Bi-Metallic Stainless Steel center in Brass ring, 23.9 mm. **Obv:** Denomination above initials within beaded circle **Rev:** Value above produce **Edge:** Reeded

Date	Mintage	F	VF	XF	Unc	BU
2006(a)	—	—	—	—	5.00	6.50

KM# 22 500 FRANCS
8.1000 g., Copper-Nickel, 26 mm. **Obv:** Value above produce **Rev:** Value **Edge:** Segmented reeding and lettering

Date	Mintage	F	VF	XF	Unc	BU
2006(a)	—	—	—	—	8.00	10.00

KM# 23 1000 FRANCS
22.2000 g., 0.9000 Silver 0.6423 oz. ASW, 37 mm. **Subject:** FIFA World Cup, England, 2004 **Edge:** Plain

Date	Mintage	F	VF	XF	Unc	BU
2004(a)	—	—	—	—	—	35.00

CHAD

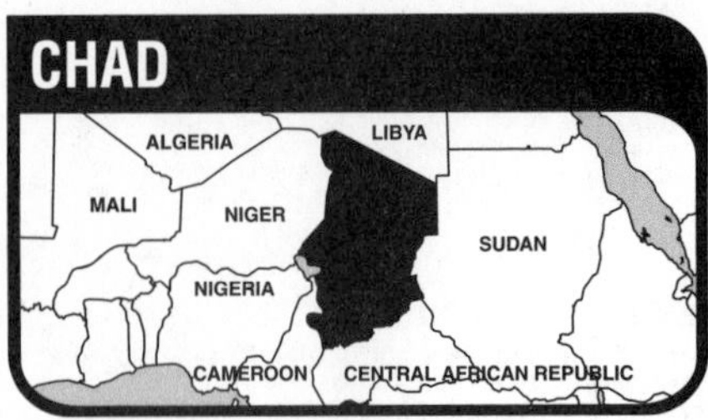

The Republic of Chad, a landlocked country of central Africa, is the largest country of former French Equatorial Africa. It has an area of 495,755 sq. mi. (1,284,000 sq. km.) and a population of *7.27 million. Capital: N'Djamena. An expanding livestock industry produces camels, cattle and sheep. Cotton (the chief product), ivory and palm oil are important exports.

NOTE: For earlier and related coinage see French Equatorial Africa and the Equatorial African States. For later coinage see Central African States.

MINT MARKS

(a) - Paris, privy marks only
(b) = Brussels
NI - Numismatic Italiana, Arezzo, Italy

REPUBLIC

DECIMAL COINAGE

KM# 30 500 FRANCS
Silver, 31 mm. **Obv:** Native portrait within circle **Rev:** Rhino mom and baby

Date	Mintage	F	VF	XF	Unc	BU
2001 Proof	—	Value: 30.00				

KM# 20 1000 FRANCS
15.0000 g., 0.9990 Silver 0.4818 oz. ASW, 35 mm. **Obv:** Native portrait within circle, denomination below **Rev:** Ancient Arabic war ship **Edge:** Plain

Date	Mintage	F	VF	XF	Unc	BU
2001 Proof	—	Value: 40.00				

KM# 21 1000 FRANCS
25.1000 g., 0.9990 Silver 0.8061 oz. ASW, 40 mm. **Obv:** Native portrait within circle, denomination below **Rev:** Soccer player and stadium **Edge:** Reeded

Date	Mintage	F	VF	XF	Unc	BU
2001 Proof	—	Value: 50.00				

KM# 35 1000 FRANCS
20.0000 g., Silver, 40 mm. **Subject:** African Fauna **Obv:** Native portrait within circle **Rev:** Balearica Pavonina (two birds)

Date	Mintage	F	VF	XF	Unc	BU
2001 Proof	—	Value: 45.00				

KM# 29 1000 FRANCS
15.0000 g., 0.9990 Silver 0.4818 oz. ASW, 36 mm. **Obv:** Native portrait within circle **Rev:** Multicolor orang-outan

Date	Mintage	F	VF	XF	Unc	BU
2001 Proof	—	Value: 35.00				

KM# 22 1000 FRANCS
20.0000 g., 0.9990 Silver 0.6423 oz. ASW, 40 mm. **Obv:** Native portrait within circle, denomination below **Rev:** Horizontal soccer player above stadium **Edge:** Reeded

Date	Mintage	F	VF	XF	Unc	BU
2002 Proof	5,000	Value: 45.00				

KM# 23 1000 FRANCS
20.1500 g., 0.9990 Silver 0.6472 oz. ASW, 40 mm. **Obv:** Native portrait within circle, denomination below **Rev:** Soccer player and Arch of Triumph **Edge:** Reeded

Date	Mintage	F	VF	XF	Unc	BU
2002 Proof	—	Value: 40.00				

KM# 31 1000 FRANCS
15.0000 g., 0.9850 Silver 0.4750 oz. ASW, 34 mm. **Rev:** Multicolor McDonnell-Douglass DC-10 landing left

Date	Mintage	F	VF	XF	Unc	BU
2002 Proof	—	Value: 35.00				

KM# 32 1000 FRANCS
15.0000 g., 0.9850 Silver 0.4750 oz. ASW, 34 mm. **Rev:** Multicolor Boeing 747 taking-off right

Date	Mintage	F	VF	XF	Unc	BU
2002 Proof	—	Value: 35.00				

KM# 36 1000 FRANCS
20.0000 g., Silver, 40 mm. **Subject:** Animals in Peril **Obv:** Native portrait within circle **Rev:** Leopard

Date	Mintage	F	VF	XF	Unc	BU
2003 Proof	—	Value: 32.00				

KM# 33 1000 FRANCS
15.0000 g., 0.9850 Silver 0.4750 oz. ASW, 34 mm. **Rev:** Multicolor McDonnell-Douglass DC-9 over mountains

Date	Mintage	F	VF	XF	Unc	BU
2003 Proof	—	Value: 35.00				

KM# 34 1000 FRANCS
15.0000 g., 0.9850 Silver 0.4750 oz. ASW, 34 mm. **Rev:** Multicolor Fokker F-7a top wing

Date	Mintage	F	VF	XF	Unc	BU
2003 Proof	—	Value: 35.00				

The Republic of Chile, a ribbon-like country on the Pacific coast of southern South America, has an area of 292,135 sq. mi. (756,950 sq. km.) and a population of *15.21 million. Capital: Santiago. Historically, the economic base of Chile has been the rich mineral deposits of its northern provinces. Copper has accounted for more than 75 percent of Chile's export earnings in recent years. Other important mineral exports are iron ore, iodine and nitrate of soda. Fresh fruits and vegetables, as well as wine are increasingly significant in inter-hemispheric trade.

MINT MARK

So – Santiago

(ml) – Maple leaf – Royal Canadian Mint (RCM)

REPUBLIC

REFORM COINAGE

100 Centavos = 1 Peso; 1000 Old Escudos = 1 Peso

KM# 231 PESO

0.7000 g., Aluminum, 15.5 mm. **Obv:** Gen. Bernardo O'Higgins bust right **Obv. Legend:** REPUBLICA - DE CHILE **Rev:** Denomination above date within wreath **Edge:** Plain **Shape:** 8-sided **Note:** Varieties exist.

Date	Mintage	F	VF	XF	Unc	BU
2001So Narrow date	—	—	—	—	0.10	0.20
2002So Narrow date	—	—	—	—	0.10	0.20
2003So Narrow date	—	—	—	—	0.10	0.20
2004So Wide date	—	—	—	—	0.10	0.20
2005So Wide date	—	—	—	—	0.10	0.20
2006So Wide date	—	—	—	—	0.10	0.20
2008So Wide date	—	—	—	—	0.10	0.20
2009So Wide date	—	—	—	—	0.10	0.20
2011So Wide date	—	—	—	—	0.10	0.20
2012So Wide date	—	—	—	—	0.10	0.20

KM# 232 5 PESOS

2.2000 g., Aluminum-Bronze, 15.5 mm. **Obv:** Gen. Bernardo O'Higgins bust right **Obv. Legend:** REPUBLICA - DE CHILE **Rev:** Denomination above date within wreath **Edge:** Plain **Shape:** 8-sided **Note:** Varieties exist.

Date	Mintage	F	VF	XF	Unc	BU
2001So Narrow date	—	—	—	0.10	0.35	0.60
2001So (sa) Wide date	—	—	—	0.15	0.50	0.75
Note: Without name of sculptor						
2002So Narrow date	—	—	—	0.15	0.50	0.75
2002So Wide date	—	—	—	0.10	0.35	0.60
2003So	—	—	—	0.10	0.35	0.60
2004So	—	—	—	0.10	0.35	0.60
2005So	—	—	—	0.10	0.35	0.60
2006So	—	—	—	0.10	0.35	0.60
2007So	—	—	—	0.10	0.35	0.60
2008So	—	—	—	0.10	0.35	0.60
2009So	—	—	—	0.10	0.35	0.60
2010So	—	—	—	0.10	0.35	0.60
2011So	—	—	—	0.10	0.35	0.60
2012So (Minted in Madrid	—	—	—	0.10	0.35	0.60

KM# 228.2 10 PESOS

3.5000 g., Aluminum-Bronze, 21 mm. **Obv:** Bust of Gen. Bernardo O'Higgins right **Obv. Legend:** REPUBLICA - DE CHILE **Rev:** Denomination above date within sprays **Edge:** Reeded **Note:** All 9's are curl tail 9's except for the 1999 date, these are straight tail 9's. Normal rim.

Date	Mintage	F	VF	XF	Unc	BU
2001So	—	—	—	0.20	0.50	0.65
2002So	—	—	—	0.20	0.50	0.65
2003So	—	—	—	0.20	0.50	0.65
2004So	—	—	—	0.20	0.50	0.65
2005So	—	—	—	0.20	0.50	0.65
2006So	—	—	—	0.20	0.50	0.65
2007	—	—	—	0.20	0.50	0.65
Note: Struck in Canada						
2008So	—	—	—	0.20	0.50	0.65
2009So	—	—	—	0.20	0.50	0.65
2010So	—	—	—	0.20	0.50	0.65
2011So	—	—	—	0.20	0.50	0.65
2012So	—	—	—	0.20	0.50	0.65

KM# 219.2 50 PESOS

7.0000 g., Aluminum-Bronze, 25 mm. **Obv:** Bust of Gen. Bernardo O'Higgins right **Obv. Legend:** REPUBLICA - DE CHILE **Rev:** Denomination above date within sprays **Edge:** Ornamented **Shape:** 10-sided **Note:** Narrow date.

Date	Mintage	F	VF	XF	Unc	BU
2001So	—	—	—	0.50	1.25	1.50
2002So	—	—	—	0.50	1.25	1.50
2005So	—	—	—	0.50	1.00	1.25
2006So	—	—	—	0.50	1.00	1.25
2007	—	—	—	0.50	1.00	1.25
Note: Struck in Canada						
2009So	—	—	—	0.50	1.00	1.25
2010So	—	—	—	0.50	1.00	1.25
2011So	—	—	—	0.50	1.00	1.25
2012So	—	—	—	0.50	1.00	1.25

KM# 219.3 50 PESOS

7.0000 g., Aluminum-Bronze, 25 mm. **Obv:** Bust of Gen. Bernardo O'Higgins right **Obv. Legend:** REPUBLICA DE CHIIE **Rev:** Denomination above date within sprays **Note:** Error spelling in legend of CHILE.

Date	Mintage	F	VF	XF	Unc	BU
2008	—	—	—	—	1.50	2.50
2009	—	—	—	—	—	2.50

KM# 236 100 PESOS

7.5800 g., Bi-Metallic Copper-Nickel-Zinc center in Aluminum-Bronze ring, 23.5 mm. **Subject:** Native people **Obv:** Bust of native Mapuche girl facing **Obv. Legend:** REPUBLICA DE CHILE - PUEBLOS ORIGINARIOS **Rev:** National arms above denomination **Edge:** Segmented reeding

Date	Mintage	F	VF	XF	Unc	BU
2001So	—	—	0.35	0.90	2.25	3.00
2003So	—	—	0.35	0.90	2.25	3.00
2004So	—	—	0.35	0.90	2.25	3.00
2005So	—	—	0.35	0.90	2.25	3.00
2006So	—	—	0.35	0.90	2.25	3.00
2008So	—	—	0.35	0.90	2.25	3.00
2009So	—	—	0.35	0.90	2.25	3.00
2010So	—	—	0.35	0.90	2.25	3.00
2011So	—	—	0.35	0.90	2.25	3.00
2012So	—	—	0.35	0.90	2.25	3.00

KM# 235 500 PESOS

6.5000 g., Bi-Metallic Aluminum-Bronze center in Copper-Nickel-Zinc ring, 26 mm. **Subject:** Cardinal Raul Silva Henriquez **Obv:** Bust of cardinal within inner ring facing left **Rev:** Denomination above date within wreath **Edge:** Reeded

Date	Mintage	F	VF	XF	Unc	BU
2001So	—	—	—	—	6.00	6.50
2002So 4.1mm date	—	—	—	—	6.00	6.50
2002So 5.2mm date	—	—	—	—	6.00	6.50
2003So	—	—	—	—	6.00	6.50
2008So	—	—	—	—	6.00	6.50
2009So	—	—	—	—	6.00	6.50
2010So	—	—	—	—	6.00	6.50
2011So	—	—	—	—	6.00	6.50
2012So	—	—	—	—	6.00	6.50

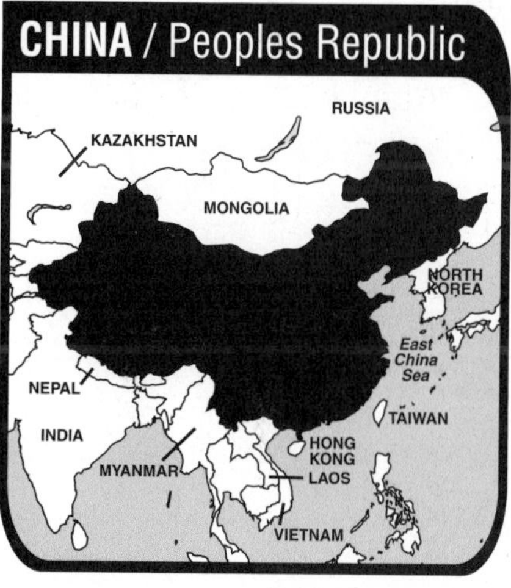

The Peoples Republic of China, located in eastern Asia, has an area of 3,696,100 sq. mi. (9,596,960 sq. km.) (including Manchuria and Tibet) and a population of *1.20 billion. Capital: Peking (Beijing). The economy is based on agriculture, mining, and manufacturing. Textiles, clothing, metal ores, tea and rice are exported.

MONETARY SYSTEM

After 1949

10 Fen (Cents) = 1 Jiao

10 Jiao = 1 Renminbi Yuan

MINT MARKS

(b) - Beijing (Peking)

(s) - Shanghai

(y) - Shenyang (Mukden)

OBVERSE LEGENDS

中华人民共和国

ZHONGHUA RENMIN GONGHEGUO
(Peoples Republic of China)

中国人民银行

ZHONGGUO RENMIN YINHANG
(Peoples Bank of China)

PEOPLES REPUBLIC

STANDARD COINAGE

KM# 1 FEN

0.7000 g., Aluminum, 18 mm. **Obv:** National emblem **Rev:** Value in wreath, date below **Edge:** Reeded **Note:** Prev. Y#1.

Date	Mintage	F	VF	XF	Unc	BU
2005	—	—	—	—	0.15	0.25
2006	—	—	—	—	0.15	0.25
2007	—	—	—	—	0.15	0.25
2008	—	—	—	—	0.15	0.25
2009	—	—	—	—	0.15	0.25
2010	—	—	—	—	0.15	0.25
2011	—	—	—	—	0.15	0.25

KM# 1210 JIAO

1.1200 g., Aluminum, 19 mm. **Obv:** Denomination, date below **Rev:** Orchid **Rev. Legend:** ZHONGGUA RENMIN YINHANG **Edge:** Plain **Note:** Prev. Y#1068.

Date	Mintage	F	VF	XF	Unc	BU
2001	—	—	—	—	0.50	0.75
2002	—	—	—	—	0.50	0.75
2003	—	—	—	—	0.50	0.75

KM# 1210a JIAO

Copper-Nickel, 19 mm. **Obv:** Denomination, date below **Note:** Prev. Y#1068a.

Date	Mintage	F	VF	XF	Unc	BU
2005	—	—	—	—	0.50	0.75

KM# 1210b JIAO

3.2000 g., Stainless Steel, 19 mm. **Obv:** Value, date below **Rev:** Orchid **Rev. Legend:** ZHONGGUA RENMIN YINHANG **Edge:** Plain **Note:** Prev. Y#1068b.

Date	Mintage	F	VF	XF	Unc	BU
2005	—	—	—	—	—	0.25
2006	—	—	—	—	—	0.25
2007	—	—	—	—	—	0.25
2008	—	—	—	—	—	0.25
2009	—	—	—	—	—	0.25
2010	—	—	—	—	—	0.25
2011	—	—	—	—	—	0.25
2012	—	—	—	—	—	0.25

KM# 336 5 JIAO

3.8000 g., Brass, 20.5 mm. **Obv:** National emblem, date below **Rev:** Denomination above flowers **Edge:** Segmented reeding **Note:** Prev. Y#329.

Date	Mintage	F	VF	XF	Unc	BU
2001	—	—	—	—	1.00	1.25

KM# 1411 5 JIAO

3.8000 g., Brass, 20.5 mm. **Obv:** Denomination **Rev:** Flower **Rev. Legend:** ZHONGGUA RENMIN YINHANG **Edge:** Segmented reeding **Note:** Prev. Y#1106.

Date	Mintage	F	VF	XF	Unc	BU
2002	—	—	—	—	1.50	1.75
2003	—	—	—	—	1.50	1.75
2004	—	—	—	—	1.50	1.75
2005	—	—	—	—	1.50	1.75
2006	—	—	—	—	1.50	1.75
2007	—	—	—	—	1.50	1.75
2008	—	—	—	—	1.50	1.75
2009	—	—	—	—	1.50	1.75
2010	—	—	—	—	1.50	1.75
2011	—	—	—	—	1.50	1.75
2012	—	—	—	—	1.50	1.75

KM# 1212 YUAN

6.1000 g., Nickel Plated Steel, 24.9 mm. **Obv:** Denomination, date below **Rev:** Chrysanthemum **Rev. Legend:** ZHONGGUA RENMIN YINHANG **Edge:** "RMB" three times **Note:** Prev. Y#1069.

Date	Mintage	F	VF	XF	Unc	BU
2001	—	—	—	—	2.00	2.50
2002	—	—	—	—	2.00	2.50
2003	—	—	—	—	2.00	2.50
2004	—	—	—	—	2.00	2.50
2005	—	—	—	—	2.00	2.50
2006	—	—	—	—	2.00	2.50
2007	—	—	—	—	2.00	2.50
2008	—	—	—	—	2.00	2.50
2009	—	—	—	—	2.00	2.50
2010	—	—	—	—	2.00	2.50
2011	—	—	—	—	2.00	2.50
2012	—	—	—	—	2.00	2.50

KM# 1465 YUAN

6.8500 g., Brass, 25 mm. **Obv:** Value **Rev:** Celebrating child and ram **Edge:** Lettered **Edge Lettering:** "RMB" three times **Note:** Prev. Y#1125.

Date	Mintage	F	VF	XF	Unc	BU
2003	—	—	—	—	5.00	6.00

KM# 1521 YUAN

Brass **Obv:** Denomination **Rev:** Celebrating Child **Note:** Prev. Y#1247.

Date	Mintage	F	VF	XF	Unc	BU
2004	—	—	—	—	2.50	3.00

KM# 1522 YUAN

6.0000 g., Nickel Clad Steel, 25 mm. **Obv:** Palace **Rev:** Deng Xiao Ping 1904-2004 **Note:** Prev. Y#1248.

Date	Mintage	F	VF	XF	Unc	BU
2004	—	—	—	—	3.50	4.00

KM# 1523 YUAN

Nickel Clad Steel **Subject:** 50th Year of Peoples Congress **Obv:** Congress building **Note:** Prev. Y#1249.

Date	Mintage	F	VF	XF	Unc	BU
2004	—	—	—	—	3.50	4.00

KM# 1574 YUAN

5.9600 g., Nickel Clad Steel, 25 mm. **Obv:** Building **Rev:** Bust of Chenyun **Edge:** Lettered **Note:** Prev. Y#1208.

Date	Mintage	F	VF	XF	Unc	BU
2005	—	—	—	—	3.50	4.00

KM# 1575 YUAN

Brass **Subject:** Year of the Rooster **Obv:** Denomination **Rev:** Celebrating Child **Note:** Prev. Y#1250.

Date	Mintage	F	VF	XF	Unc	BU
2005	—	—	—	—	3.00	3.50

KM# 1650 YUAN

Brass **Subject:** Year of the Dog **Obv:** Denomination **Rev:** Celebrating Child **Note:** Prev. Y#1251.

Date	Mintage	F	VF	XF	Unc	BU
2006	—	—	—	—	7.00	8.00

KM# 1775 YUAN

6.7500 g., Brass, 25 mm. **Subject:** 29th Olympics **Obv:** Stylized Olympics logo **Rev:** Cartoon swimmer **Edge:** Reeded **Note:** Prev. Y#1256.

Date	Mintage	F	VF	XF	Unc	BU
2008 (2006)(y)	—	—	—	—	5.00	6.00

KM# 1776 YUAN

6.7500 g., Brass, 25 mm. **Subject:** 29th Olympics **Obv:** Stylized Olympics logo **Rev:** Cartoon Weight Lifter **Edge:** Reeded **Note:** Prev. Y#1257.

Date	Mintage	F	VF	XF	Unc	BU
2008 (2006)	—	—	—	—	5.00	6.00

KM# 1652 YUAN

6.7500 g., Brass, 25 mm. **Subject:** Year of the Pig

Date	Mintage	F	VF	XF	Unc	BU
2007	10,000,000	—	—	—	—	30.00

KM# 1671 YUAN

6.7500 g., Brass, 25 mm. **Subject:** 29th Summer Olympics, Bejing **Obv:** Olympic Logo **Rev:** Yingying mascot on pomel horse, latent image

Date	Mintage	F	VF	XF	Unc	BU
2008	—	—	—	—	—	7.50

KM# 1672 YUAN

6.7500 g., Brass, 25 mm. **Subject:** 29th Summer Olympics, Bejing **Obv:** Olympic games logo **Rev:** Jingjing mascot with bow and arrow, latent images

Date	Mintage	F	VF	XF	Unc	BU
2008	—	—	—	—	—	7.50

KM# 1673 YUAN

6.7500 g., Brass, 25 mm. **Subject:** 29th Summer Olympics, Bejing **Obv:** Olympics logo **Rev:** Huanhuan mascot playing soccer, latent image

Date	Mintage	F	VF	XF	Unc	BU
2008	—	—	—	—	—	7.50

KM# 1810 YUAN

Brass, 25 mm. **Obv:** Beijing Olympic logo **Rev:** Character playing ping-pong

Date	Mintage	F	VF	XF	Unc	BU
2008	—	—	—	—	2.50	3.00

KM# 1811 YUAN

Brass, 25 mm. **Obv:** Beijing Olympic logo **Rev:** Character fencing with bow and arrow

Date	Mintage	F	VF	XF	Unc	BU
2008	—	—	—	—	2.50	3.00

KM# 1812 YUAN

Brass, 25 mm. **Obv:** Beijing Olympic logo **Rev:** Character on horseback

Date	Mintage	F	VF	XF	Unc	BU
2008	—	—	—	—	2.50	3.00

KM# 1813 YUAN

Brass, 25 mm. **Obv:** Large value **Rev:** Boy with rat pattern chinese knot & cluster of fireworks

Date	Mintage	F	VF	XF	Unc	BU
2008	10,000,000	—	—	—	2.50	3.00

KM# 1790 YUAN

6.7500 g., Brass, 25 mm. **Subject:** Year of the Bull

Date	Mintage	F	VF	XF	Unc	BU
2009	30,000,000	—	—	—	—	7.50

KM# 1791 YUAN

6.7500 g., Brass, 25 mm. **Subject:** Conservation **Rev:** Eye and leaf on globe

Date	Mintage	F	VF	XF	Unc	BU
2009	10,000,000	—	—	—	—	7.50

KM# 1792 YUAN

6.7500 g., Brass, 25 mm. **Subject:** Harmony **Rev:** Haromony in seal script

Date	Mintage	F	VF	XF	Unc	BU
2009	10,000,000	—	—	—	—	7.50

KM# 1988 YUAN

Nickel Plated Brass, 25 mm. **Subject:** Shanghai Expo **Obv:** Expo logo **Rev:** Skyline and expo mascot

Date	Mintage	F	VF	XF	Unc	BU
2010	60,000,000	—	—	—	6.00	8.00

KM# 1989 YUAN

Brass, 25 mm. **Subject:** Year of the Tiger **Obv:** Large value **Rev:** Child dancing

Date	Mintage	F	VF	XF	Unc	BU
2010	60,000,000	—	—	—	5.00	7.50

KM# 1990 YUAN

Brass, 25 mm. **Subject:** Enviornmental protection **Obv:** State emblem **Rev:** Caligraphy - Peace-Harmony

Date	Mintage	F	VF	XF	Unc	BU
2010	10,000,000	—	—	—	6.00	8.00

KM# 1991 YUAN

Brass, 25 mm. **Subject:** Environmental protection **Obv:** National emblem **Rev:** Family dancing, globe

Date	Mintage	F	VF	XF	Unc	BU
2010	10,000,000	—	—	—	6.00	8.00

KM# 1993 YUAN

Brass, 25 mm. **Subject:** Year of the Rabbit **Obv:** Large value **Rev:** Child playing

Date	Mintage	F	VF	XF	Unc	BU
2011	60,000,000	—	—	—	6.00	8.00

KM# 2041 YUAN

6.7500 g., Brass, 25 mm. **Subject:** Year of the Dragon **Obv:** Large numeral value **Rev:** Child dancing with lantern, dragon in background

Date	Mintage	F	VF	XF	Unc	BU
2012	80,000,000	—	—	—	—	5.00

KM# 2058 3 YUAN

7.7800 g., 0.9990 Silver 0.2499 oz. ASW, 25 mm. **Subject:** Panda, 30th Anniversary **Obv:** Temple of Heaven **Rev:** Panda

Date	Mintage	F	VF	XF	Unc	BU
2012 Proof	300,000	Value: 30.00				

KM# 1363 5 YUAN

12.8000 g., Brass, 30 mm. **Subject:** 50th Anniversary - Chinese Occupation of Tibet **Obv:** National emblem **Rev:** Potala Palace, value and two dancers **Edge:** Reeded **Note:** Prev. Y#1126.

Date	Mintage	F	VF	XF	Unc	BU
2001(y)	10,000,000	—	—	—	8.00	—

KM# 1364 5 YUAN

12.8000 g., Brass, 30 mm. **Subject:** Revolution: 90th Anniversary **Obv:** National emblem **Rev:** Battle scene **Edge:** Reeded **Note:** Prev. Y#1109.

Date	Mintage	F	VF	XF	Unc	BU
2001	—	—	—	—	7.50	8.50

KM# 1412 5 YUAN

12.8000 g., Brass, 30 mm. **Subject:** The Great Wall **Obv:** State arms, icroscopic inscription repeated four times on the inner raised rim **Obv. Inscription:** SHI JIE WEN HUA YI CHAN **Rev:** Two views of the Great Wall **Edge:** Reeded **Note:** Prev. Y#1107.

Date	Mintage	F	VF	XF	Unc	BU
2002	—	—	—	—	7.00	8.00

KM# 1413 5 YUAN

12.8000 g., Brass, 30 mm. **Subject:** Terra Cotta Army **Obv:** State arms and the microscopic inscription repeated four times on the raised inner rim. **Obv. Inscription:** SHI JIE WEN HUA YI CHAN **Rev:** Terra Cotta Soldier close-up with many more in background **Edge:** Reeded **Note:** Prev. Y#1108.

Date	Mintage	F	VF	XF	Unc	BU
2002	—	—	—	—	7.00	8.00

KM# 1461 5 YUAN

12.8000 g., Brass, 30 mm. **Obv:** National emblem **Rev:** Chaotian Temple in Beigang Taiwan **Edge:** Reeded **Note:** Prev. Y#1127.

Date	Mintage	F	VF	XF	Unc	BU
2003	10,000,000	—	—	—	7.00	8.00

KM# 1462 5 YUAN

12.8000 g., Brass, 30 mm. **Obv:** National emblem **Rev:** Chikan Tower on Treasure Island Taiwan **Edge:** Reeded **Note:** Prev. Y#1128.

Date	Mintage	F	VF	XF	Unc	BU
2003(y)	10,000,000	—	—	—	7.00	8.00

KM# 1463 5 YUAN

12.8000 g., Brass, 30 mm. **Subject:** Chaotian Temple in Beijing **Obv:** State emblem **Rev:** Buildings **Edge:** Reeded **Note:** Prev. Y#1230.

Date	Mintage	F	VF	XF	Unc	BU
2003	10,000,000	—	—	—	7.00	8.00

KM# 1464 5 YUAN

Brass, 30 mm. **Obv:** National emblem **Rev:** Imperial Palace **Note:** Prev. Y#1252.

Date	Mintage	F	VF	XF	Unc	BU
2003	—	—	—	—	7.00	8.00

KM# 1524 5 YUAN

Brass, 30 mm. **Obv:** National emblem **Rev:** Island scene **Note:** Prev. Y#1253.

Date	Mintage	F	VF	XF	Unc	BU
2004	—	—	—	—	6.00	7.00

KM# 1525 5 YUAN

Brass, 30 mm. **Obv:** National emblem **Rev:** Lighthouse **Note:** Prev. Y#1254.

Date	Mintage	F	VF	XF	Unc	BU
2004	—	—	—	—	6.00	7.00

KM# 1526 5 YUAN

12.7000 g., Brass, 30 mm. **Obv:** National emblem **Rev:** Peking Man bust and discovery site view **Edge:** Reeded **Note:** Prev. Y#1201.

Date	Mintage	F	VF	XF	Unc	BU
2004	6,000,000	—	—	—	6.00	7.00

KM# 1527 5 YUAN

12.7000 g., Brass, 30 mm. **Obv:** National emblem **Rev:** Pavillion and bridge **Edge:** Reeded **Note:** Prev. Y#1202.

Date	Mintage	F	VF	XF	Unc	BU
2004	6,000,000	—	—	—	6.00	7.00

KM# 1068 5 YUAN

22.0000 g., 0.9000 Silver 0.6366 oz. ASW, 36 mm. **Obv:** Great Wall **Rev:** Gymnast, denomination at right **Edge:** Reeded **Note:** Prev. Y#1189.

Date	Mintage	F	VF	XF	Unc	BU
2005(y)	—	—	—	—	75.00	85.00

KM# 1576 5 YUAN

12.9200 g., Brass, 30 mm. **Obv:** National emblem **Rev:** Lijiang building **Edge:** Reeded **Note:** Prev. Y#1209.

Date	Mintage	F	VF	XF	Unc	BU
2005	—	—	—	—	6.00	7.00

KM# 1577 5 YUAN

12.8000 g., Brass, 30 mm. **Subject:** "Taiwan" **Obv:** State emblem **Rev:** Tower and terrace **Edge:** Reeded **Note:** Prev. Y#1231.

Date	Mintage	F	VF	XF	Unc	BU
2005	—	—	—	—	6.00	7.00

KM# 1578 5 YUAN
12.9200 g., Brass, 30 mm. **Obv:** National emblem **Rev:** Green City Hall **Edge:** Reeded **Note:** Prev. Y#1210.

Date	Mintage	F	VF	XF	Unc	BU
2005	—	—	—	—	6.00	7.00

KM# 1651 5 YUAN
12.8000 g., Brass, 30 mm. **Subject:** UNESCO World Heritage site - Summer Palace Pagoda

Date	Mintage	F	VF	XF	Unc	BU
2006	—	—	—	—	6.00	7.00

KM# 1731 5 YUAN
Brass, 30 mm. **Obv:** State emblem **Rev:** Large statue head

Date	Mintage	F	VF	XF	Unc	BU
2006 Proof	10,000,000	Value: 3.00				

KM# 1826 5 YUAN
15.5700 g., 0.9990 Silver 0.5001 oz. ASW, 33 mm. **Subject:** 12th Special Olympics in Shanghai **Obv:** Logo in color

Date	Mintage	F	VF	XF	Unc	BU
2007 Proof	40,000	Value: 60.00				

KM# 1992 5 YUAN
Brass, 30 mm. **Subject:** Chinese Communist Party, 90th Anniversary **Obv:** National emblem **Rev:** Banner, hammer and sythe, stars, birds in flight

Date	Mintage	F	VF	XF	Unc	BU
2011	60,000,000	—	—	—	7.50	9.00

KM# 1395 10 YUAN
31.1035 g., 0.9990 Silver 0.9990 oz. ASW, 40 mm. **Subject:** 2008 Olympics Beijing bid **Obv:** Gold-plated "V" design **Rev:** Radiant Temple of Heaven **Edge:** Reeded **Note:** Prev. Y#1103.

Date	Mintage	F	VF	XF	Unc	BU
2001 Proof	60,000	Value: 50.00				

KM# 1384 10 YUAN
31.1035 g., 0.9990 Silver 0.9990 oz. ASW **Series:** Folk Fairy Tales **Rev:** Heroic figure putting ax to mountains

Date	Mintage	F	VF	XF	Unc	BU
2001 Proof	30,000	Value: 120				

KM# 1385 10 YUAN
31.1035 g., 0.9990 Silver 0.9990 oz. ASW, 40 mm. **Series:** Folk Fairy Tales **Rev:** Multicolor angelic figure

Date	Mintage	F	VF	XF	Unc	BU
2001 Proof	30,000	Value: 120				

KM# 1396 10 YUAN
31.1035 g., 0.9990 Silver 0.9990 oz. ASW, 40 mm. **Series:** Folk customs - Mid Autumn Festival **Rev:** Flora and sun

Date	Mintage	F	VF	XF	Unc	BU
2001 Proof	40,000	Value: 180				

KM# 1397 10 YUAN
31.1035 g., 0.9990 Silver 0.9990 oz. ASW, 32 mm. **Subject:** Bejing International Coin Expo **Obv:** Globe hemisphere view **Rev:** Bejing city view

Date	Mintage	F	VF	XF	Unc	BU
2001 Proof	40,000	Value: 125				

KM# 1398 10 YUAN
31.1035 g., 0.9990 Silver 0.9990 oz. ASW, 40 mm. **Subject:** Bejing opera **Rev:** Two multicolor actors, one with hankie

Date	Mintage	F	VF	XF	Unc	BU
2001 Proof	38,000	Value: 100				

KM# 1399 10 YUAN
31.1035 g., 0.9990 Silver 0.9990 oz. ASW, 40 mm. **Subject:** Bejing opera **Rev:** Two actors, one with blue ribbon

Date	Mintage	F	VF	XF	Unc	BU
2001 Proof	38,000	Value: 120				

KM# 1400 10 YUAN
31.1035 g., 0.9990 Silver 0.9990 oz. ASW, 40 mm. **Subject:** Bejing opera **Rev:** Two multicolor actors, one with tassles

Date	Mintage	F	VF	XF	Unc	BU
2001 Proof	38,000	Value: 60.00				

KM# 1401 10 YUAN
31.1035 g., 0.9990 Silver 0.9990 oz. ASW, 40 mm. **Subject:** Bejing opera **Rev:** Two multicolor actors, white or black beard

Date	Mintage	F	VF	XF	Unc	BU
2001 Proof	38,000	Value: 120				

KM# 1428 10 YUAN
31.1035 g., 0.9990 Silver 0.9990 oz. ASW, 40 mm. **Series:** Folk Fairy Tales **Rev:** Multicolor male figure seated

Date	Mintage	F	VF	XF	Unc	BU
2002 Proof	30,000	Value: 120				

KM# 1429 10 YUAN
31.1035 g., 0.9990 Silver Colorized 0.9990 oz. ASW, 40 mm. **Series:** Folk fairy tails **Rev:** Male figure brandishing sword

Date	Mintage	F	VF	XF	Unc	BU
2002 Proof	30,000	Value: 120				

KM# 1438 10 YUAN
31.1035 g., 0.9990 Silver 0.9990 oz. ASW, 40 mm. **Series:** Folk customs **Rev:** Dragon boat

Date	Mintage	F	VF	XF	Unc	BU
2002 Proof	40,000	Value: 120				

KM# 1441 10 YUAN
31.1035 g., 0.9990 Silver Colorized 0.9990 oz. ASW, 40 mm. **Series:** Classic literature **Rev:** Black and red dressed women seated **Shape:** Octagon

Date	Mintage	F	VF	XF	Unc	BU
2002 Proof	38,000	Value: 100				

KM# 1442 10 YUAN
31.1035 g., 0.9990 Silver 0.9990 oz. ASW, 40 mm. **Series:** Classic literature **Rev:** Multicolor white dressed woman standing **Shape:** Octagon

Date	Mintage	F	VF	XF	Unc	BU
2002 Proof	38,000	Value: 100				

KM# 1443 10 YUAN
31.1035 g., 0.9990 Silver 0.9990 oz. ASW, 40 mm. **Series:** Classic literature **Rev:** Multicolor yellow dressed woman walking left **Shape:** Octagon

Date	Mintage	F	VF	XF	Unc	BU
2002 Proof	38,000	Value: 100				

KM# 1444 10 YUAN
31.1035 g., 0.9990 Silver 0.9990 oz. ASW, 40 mm. **Series:** Classic literature **Obv:** Multicolor purple dressed woman **Shape:** Octagon

Date	Mintage	F	VF	XF	Unc	BU
2002 Proof	38,000	Value: 100				

KM# 1447 10 YUAN
31.1035 g., 0.9990 Silver 0.9990 oz. ASW, 40 mm. **Subject:** Bejing Coin and Stamp Fair **Obv:** Hemisphere map **Rev:** Highway design

Date	Mintage	F	VF	XF	Unc	BU
2002 Proof	40,000	Value: 95.00				

KM# 1448 10 YUAN
31.1035 g., 0.9990 Silver 0.9990 oz. ASW, 40 mm. **Subject:** Table tennis, 50th anniversary **Rev:** Trophies, flag

Date	Mintage	F	VF	XF	Unc	BU
2002 Proof	50,000	Value: 100				

KM# 1449 10 YUAN
31.1035 g., 0.9990 Silver 0.9990 oz. ASW, 40 mm. **Series:** Bejing opera **Rev:** Two multicolor characters, one seated

Date	Mintage	F	VF	XF	Unc	BU
2002 Proof	38,000	Value: 50.00				

KM# 1450 10 YUAN
31.1035 g., 0.9990 Silver 0.9990 oz. ASW, 40 mm. **Series:** Bejing opera **Rev:** Two multicolor characters, white and green

Date	Mintage	F	VF	XF	Unc	BU
2002 Proof	38,000	Value: 125				

KM# 1451 10 YUAN
31.1035 g., 0.9990 Silver 0.9990 oz. ASW, 40 mm. **Series:** Bejing opera **Rev:** Bearded character, black

Date	Mintage	F	VF	XF	Unc	BU
2002 Proof	38,000	Value: 125				

KM# 1452 10 YUAN
31.1035 g., 0.9990 Silver 0.9990 oz. ASW, 40 mm. **Series:** Bejing opera **Rev:** Multicolor bearded character, red

Date	Mintage	F	VF	XF	Unc	BU
2002 Proof	38,000	Value: 125				

KM# A1455 10 YUAN
31.1035 g., 0.9990 Silver 0.9990 oz. ASW, 40 mm. **Subject:** World Expo 2010 **Rev:** Tower

Date	Mintage	F	VF	XF	Unc	BU
2002 Proof	50,000	Value: 100				

KM# 1455 10 YUAN
31.1035 g., 0.9990 Silver 0.9990 oz. ASW, 40 mm. **Subject:** Shanghai World Expo of 2010 **Obv:** Flower design with inset pearl **Rev:** 2010 Logo incorporating a tower **Edge:** Reeded **Note:** Prev. Y#1233.

Date	Mintage	F	VF	XF	Unc	BU
2002 Proof	50,000	Value: 125				

KM# 1507 10 YUAN
31.1035 g., 0.9990 Silver 0.9990 oz. ASW, 40 mm. **Obv:** Stylized forest **Rev:** Cyclists in forest **Edge:** Reeded **Note:** Prev. Y#1132.

Date	Mintage	F	VF	XF	Unc	BU
2003 Proof	30,000	Value: 125				

KM# 1508 10 YUAN
31.1035 g., 0.9990 Silver 0.9990 oz. ASW, 40 mm. **Obv:** Stylized forest **Rev:** Birds flying over forest **Edge:** Reeded **Note:** Prev. Y#1133.

Date	Mintage	F	VF	XF	Unc	BU
2003(y) Proof	30,000	Value: 125				

KM# 1510 10 YUAN
31.1035 g., 0.9990 Silver 0.9990 oz. ASW, 40 mm. **Obv:** Solar system design **Rev:** Multicolor Chinese Astronaut **Edge:** Reeded **Note:** Prev. Y#1134.

Date	Mintage	F	VF	XF	Unc	BU
2003(y) Proof	60,000	Value: 90.00				

KM# 1487 10 YUAN
31.1035 g., 0.9990 Silver 0.9990 oz. ASW, 40 mm. **Rev:** Two Koi

Date	Mintage	F	VF	XF	Unc	BU
2003 Proof	100,000	Value: 90.00				

KM# 1489 10 YUAN
31.1035 g., 0.9990 Silver 0.9990 oz. ASW, 40 mm. **Subject:** Arbor Day **Rev:** Trees with bike riders

Date	Mintage	F	VF	XF	Unc	BU
2003 Proof	30,000	Value: 90.00				

KM# 1490 10 YUAN
31.1035 g., 0.9990 Silver 0.9990 oz. ASW, 40 mm. **Subject:** Arbor Day **Rev:** Close-up of leaves, birds in flight

Date	Mintage	F	VF	XF	Unc	BU
2003 Proof	30,000	Value: 120				

KM# 1491 10 YUAN
31.1035 g., 0.9990 Silver 0.9990 oz. ASW, 40 mm. **Series:** Fairy tails **Rev:** Multicolor blue female

Date	Mintage	F	VF	XF	Unc	BU
2003 Proof	30,000	Value: 120				

KM# 1492 10 YUAN

31.1035 g., 0.9990 Silver 0.9990 oz. ASW, 40 mm. **Subject:** Fairy tails **Rev:** Multicolor red bloused girl

Date	Mintage	F	VF	XF	Unc	BU
2003 Proof	30,000	Value: 120				

KM# 1496 10 YUAN

31.1035 g., 0.9990 Silver 0.9990 oz. ASW, 40 mm. **Series:** Class literature **Rev:** Multicolor purple cloaked man and monkey

Date	Mintage	F	VF	XF	Unc	BU
2003 Proof	38,000	Value: 120				

KM# 1497 10 YUAN

31.1035 g., 0.9990 Silver 0.9990 oz. ASW, 40 mm. **Series:** Classic literature **Rev:** Two multicolor men fighting in clouds

Date	Mintage	F	VF	XF	Unc	BU
2003 Proof	38,000	Value: 120				

KM# 1498 10 YUAN

31.1035 g., 0.9990 Silver 0.9990 oz. ASW, 40 mm. **Rev:** Multicolor female standing, black dress **Shape:** Octagon

Date	Mintage	F	VF	XF	Unc	BU
2003 Proof	38,000	Value: 120				

KM# 1499 10 YUAN

31.1035 g., 0.9990 Silver 0.9990 oz. ASW, 40 mm. **Series:** Classic Literature **Rev:** Multicolor female kneeling **Shape:** Octagon

Date	Mintage	F	VF	XF	Unc	BU
2003 Proof	38,000	Value: 120				

KM# 1500 10 YUAN

31.1035 g., 0.9990 Silver 0.9990 oz. ASW, 40 mm. **Series:** Classic literature **Rev:** Multicolor female walking, rose dress **Shape:** Octagon

Date	Mintage	F	VF	XF	Unc	BU
2003 Proof	—	Value: 120				

KM# 1501 10 YUAN

31.1035 g., 0.9990 Silver 0.9990 oz. ASW, 40 mm. **Series:** Classic literature **Rev:** Multicolor female kneeling, red dress **Shape:** Octagon

Date	Mintage	F	VF	XF	Unc	BU
2003 Proof	—	Value: 120				

KM# 1559 10 YUAN

31.1035 g., 0.9990 Silver 0.9990 oz. ASW, 40 mm. **Obv:** Monkey King leading the Master over bridge **Rev:** Multicolor Monkey King fighting the "Ox Fiend" **Edge:** Reeded **Note:** Prev. Y#1214.

Date	Mintage	F	VF	XF	Unc	BU
2004 Proof	38,000	Value: 110				

KM# 1558 10 YUAN

31.1035 g., 0.9990 Silver 0.9990 oz. ASW, 40 mm. **Obv:** Monkey King leading the Master over bridge **Rev:** Multicolor Pig carrying Monkey King piggy-back style **Edge:** Reeded **Note:** Prev. Y#1215.

Date	Mintage	F	VF	XF	Unc	BU
2004 Proof	38,000	Value: 110				

KM# 1566 10 YUAN

31.1035 g., 0.9990 Silver 0.9990 oz. ASW, 40 mm. **Obv:** Guangan Exposition Hall **Rev:** Deng Xiaoping and value **Edge:** Reeded **Note:** Prev. Y#1240. Photo reduced.

Date	Mintage	F	VF	XF	Unc	BU
2004 Proof	80,000	Value: 90.00				

KM# 1570 10 YUAN

31.1035 g., 0.9990 Silver 0.9990 oz. ASW, 40 mm. **Obv:** National arms above People's Congress Hall and ornamental column **Rev:** Multicolor hologram depicting the hall's overhead lighting **Edge:** Reeded **Note:** Prev. KM#1212.

Date	Mintage	F	VF	XF	Unc	BU
2004 Proof	50,000	Value: 100				

KM# 1539 10 YUAN

31.1035 g., 0.9990 Silver 0.9990 oz. ASW, 40 mm. **Subject:** 20th Anniversary / Bank of China Industrial and Commercial **Rev:** Panda walking with cub

Date	Mintage	F	VF	XF	Unc	BU
2004 Proof	120,000	Value: 90.00				

KM# 1541 10 YUAN

31.1035 g., 0.9990 Silver 0.9990 oz. ASW, 40 mm. **Subject:** 50th Anniversary China Construction Bank **Rev:** Panda walking with cub

Date	Mintage	F	VF	XF	Unc	BU
2004 Proof	170,000	Value: 90.00				

KM# 1543 10 YUAN

31.1035 g., 0.9990 Silver 0.9990 oz. ASW, 40 mm. **Subject:** Bejing International Coin Expo **Rev:** Panda walking with cub, gold plated center

Date	Mintage	F	VF	XF	Unc	BU
2004 Proof	30,000	Value: 120				

KM# 1557 10 YUAN

31.1035 g., 0.9990 Silver 0.9990 oz. ASW, 40 mm. **Series:** Folk customs **Subject:** Lantern Festival **Rev:** Boy holding lantern **Note:** Colorized

Date	Mintage	F	VF	XF	Unc	BU
2004 Proof	60,000	Value: 100				

KM# 1555 10 YUAN

31.1035 g., 0.9990 Silver 0.9990 oz. ASW, 40 mm. **Subject:** 100th Anniversary Red Cross **Obv:** Red Cross within wreath **Rev:** Dove **Note:** Colorized

Date	Mintage	F	VF	XF	Unc	BU
2004 Proof	60,000	Value: 85.00				

KM# 1580 10 YUAN

31.1035 g., 0.9990 Silver 0.9990 oz. ASW, 40 mm. **Subject:** 600th Anniversary of Zheng He's voyage **Obv:** Multicolor stylized sailboat on water **Rev:** Ancient Chinese navigational instruments **Edge:** Reeded **Note:** Prev. Y#1239.

Date	Mintage	F	VF	XF	Unc	BU
2005(y) Proof	—	Value: 100				

KM# 1592 10 YUAN

31.1050 g., 0.9990 Silver gilt rim 0.9990 oz. ASW, 40 mm. **Obv:** Temple of Heaven **Rev:** Panda cub and mom seated in bamboo **Note:** Gilt rim

Date	Mintage	F	VF	XF	Unc	BU
2005 Proof	30,000	Value: 85.00				

KM# 1601 10 YUAN

31.1050 g., 0.9990 Silver 0.9990 oz. ASW, 40 mm. **Subject:** Foundation of Industrial & Commercial Bank **Obv:** Temple of Heaven, gilt rim **Rev:** Panda cub and mom seated in bamboo

Date	Mintage	F	VF	XF	Unc	BU
2005 Proof	100,000	Value: 70.00				

KM# 1603 10 YUAN

31.1050 g., 0.9990 Silver 0.9990 oz. ASW, 40 mm. **Subject:** 100th Anniversary of Bank of Shanghai **Obv:** Temple of Heaven **Rev:** Panda cub and mom seated in bamboo

Date	Mintage	F	VF	XF	Unc	BU
2005 Proof	50,000	Value: 80.00				

KM# 1618 10 YUAN

31.1050 g., 0.9990 Silver 0.9990 oz. ASW, 40 mm. **Subject:** 2006 World Cup - Germany **Obv:** Multicolor logo **Rev:** Classical soccer player and goal net **Note:** Prev - Y1255, KM1670

Date	Mintage	F	VF	XF	Unc	BU
2005 Proof	50,000	Value: 90.00				

KM# 1626 10 YUAN

31.1050 g., 0.9990 Silver 0.9990 oz. ASW, 40 mm. **Subject:** 600th Anniversary - Zheng He's Voyages **Obv:** Multicolor logo **Rev:** Nautical invention

Date	Mintage	F	VF	XF	Unc	BU
2005 Proof	60,000	Value: 85.00				

KM# 1628 10 YUAN

31.1050 g., 0.9990 Silver 0.9990 oz. ASW, 40 mm. **Subject:** Chen Yun Birth Centennial **Obv:** House **Rev:** Half-length figure facing

Date	Mintage	F	VF	XF	Unc	BU
2005 Proof	15,000	Value: 140				

KM# 1629 10 YUAN

31.1050 g., 0.9990 Silver 0.9990 oz. ASW, 40 mm. **Subject:** Chen Yun Birth Centennial **Obv:** House **Rev:** Figure seated in chair, arm outstretched

Date	Mintage	F	VF	XF	Unc	BU
2005 Proof	15,000	Value: 140				

KM# 1631 10 YUAN

31.1050 g., 0.9990 Silver 0.9990 oz. ASW, 40 mm. **Subject:** 60th Anniversary of Victory - War of Resistance **Obv:** Monument **Rev:** People celebrating

Date	Mintage	F	VF	XF	Unc	BU
2005 Proof	30,000	Value: 140				

KM# 1636 10 YUAN

31.1050 g., 0.9990 Silver 0.9990 oz. ASW, 40 mm. **Series:** Classical Literature **Obv:** Horseman on arch bridge **Rev:** Multicolor monkey and female

Date	Mintage	F	VF	XF	Unc	BU
2005 Proof	38,000	Value: 130				

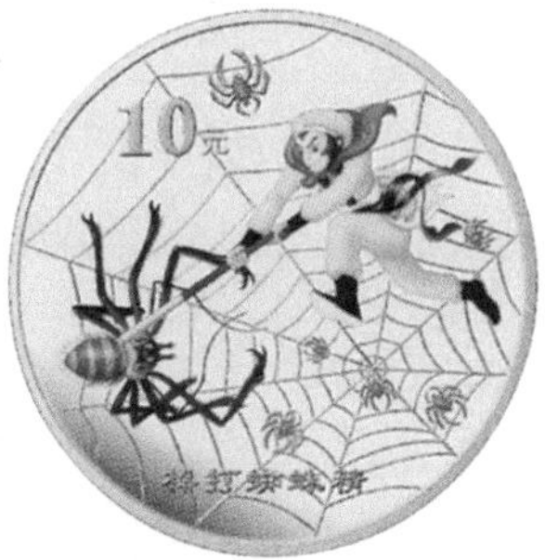

KM# 1637 10 YUAN

31.1050 g., 0.9990 Silver 0.9990 oz. ASW, 40 mm. **Series:** Classical Literature **Obv:** Horseman on arch bridge **Rev:** Multicolor man slaying spider on web

Date	Mintage	F	VF	XF	Unc	BU
2005 Proof	38,000	Value: 130				

KM# 1639 10 YUAN

31.1050 g., 0.9990 Silver 0.9990 oz. ASW, 40 mm. **Subject:** Chinese Movie Centennial **Obv:** Winged column **Rev:** Old time movie camera

Date	Mintage	F	VF	XF	Unc	BU
2005 Proof	60,000	Value: 85.00				

KM# 1670 10 YUAN

31.1035 g., 0.9990 Silver 0.9990 oz. ASW **Subject:** World Cup Soccer **Obv:** Colorized logo **Rev:** Classically dressed athlete scoring goal **Note:** Prev. Y#1255.

Date	Mintage	F	VF	XF	Unc	BU
2006 Proof	—	Value: 100				

KM# 1666 10 YUAN

31.1050 g., 0.9990 Silver 0.9990 oz. ASW, 40 mm. **Obv:** Temple of Heaven **Rev:** Two pandas seated with bamboo

Date	Mintage	F	VF	XF	Unc	BU
2006 Proof	50,000	Value: 75.00				

KM# 1668 10 YUAN

31.1050 g., 0.9990 Silver 0.9990 oz. ASW, 40 mm. **Subject:** 10th Anniversary of China Minsheng Banking Corp **Obv:** Temple of Heaven **Rev:** Two pandas seated with bamboo

Date	Mintage	F	VF	XF	Unc	BU
2006 Proof	70,000	Value: 85.00				

KM# A1670 10 YUAN

31.1050 g., 0.9990 Silver 0.9990 oz. ASW, 40 mm. **Subject:** Shengang Horticultural Expo **Obv:** Temple of Heaven **Rev:** Two pandas seated with bamboo

Date	Mintage	F	VF	XF	Unc	BU
2006 Proof	30,000	Value: 85.00				

KM# 1675 10 YUAN

31.1050 g., 0.9990 Silver 0.9990 oz. ASW, 40 mm. **Subject:** 10th Anniversary Jinan City Commercial Bank **Obv:** Temple of Heaven **Rev:** Two pandas seated with bamboo

Date	Mintage	F	VF	XF	Unc	BU
2006 Proof	20,000	Value: 85.00				

KM# 1676 10 YUAN

31.1050 g., 0.9990 Silver Gold plated outer ring 0.9990 oz. ASW, 40 mm. **Subject:** Beijing International Stamp and Coin Expo **Obv:** Temple of Heaven **Rev:** Two pandas seated with bamboo

Date	Mintage	F	VF	XF	Unc	BU
2006 Proof	20,000	Value: 100				

KM# 1690 10 YUAN

31.1050 g., 0.9990 Silver 0.9990 oz. ASW, 40 mm. **Subject:** Yvelv Academy **Obv:** Front door of Academy **Rev:** Exterior view

Date	Mintage	F	VF	XF	Unc	BU
2006 Proof	40,000	Value: 85.00				

KM# 1691 10 YUAN

31.1050 g., 0.9990 Silver 0.9990 oz. ASW, 40 mm. **Subject:** Qinghai - Tibet Railway Opening **Obv:** Lhasa Railway Station with mountains in background **Rev:** Yvante Bridge over the Yangtze River and tibetan antelope and yak

Date	Mintage	F	VF	XF	Unc	BU
2006 Proof	36,000	Value: 150				

KM# 1693 10 YUAN

31.1050 g., 0.9990 Silver 0.9990 oz. ASW, 40 mm. **Obv:** Map of marches and hammer and sickle **Rev:** Group of marchers in snow

Date	Mintage	F	VF	XF	Unc	BU
2006 Proof	25,000	Value: 110				

KM# 1653 10 YUAN

31.1030 g., 0.9990 Silver 0.9989 oz. ASW, 40 mm. **Subject:** Chengdu multi-purpose warplanes, 10th Anniversary

Date	Mintage	F	VF	XF	Unc	BU
2007 Proof	20,000	Value: 75.00				

KM# 1729 10 YUAN

31.1050 g., 0.9990 Silver 0.9990 oz. ASW, 40 mm. **Subject:** 60th Anniversary - Foundry of Mongolia Autonomous Region **Obv:** Wheel of Mongolian Lele Cart **Rev:** Grassland view of Mongolia, huts and horsemen

Date	Mintage	F	VF	XF	Unc	BU
2007 Proof	20,000	Value: 110				

KM# 1828 10 YUAN

31.1030 g., 0.9990 Silver 0.9989 oz. ASW, 40 mm. **Subject:** Chinese aerospace **Obv:** Solar System **Rev:** Chang'e 1 in lunar orbit

Date	Mintage	F	VF	XF	Unc	BU
2007 Proof	40,000	Value: 75.00				

KM# 1861 10 YUAN

31.1030 g., 0.9990 Silver 0.9989 oz. ASW, 40 mm. **Subject:** Chinese Peoples Liberation Army, 80th Anniversary **Obv:** Military personel saluting, flag in background **Rev:** Ship, tank, plane

Date	Mintage	
	—	Value: 65.00

KM# 1863 10 YUAN

31.1030 g., 0.9990 Silver 0.9989 oz. ASW, 40 mm. **Subject:** Xi'an City Commercial Bank **Obv:** Temple of Heaven **Rev:** Panda

Date	Mintage	F	VF	XF	Unc	BU
2007	20,000	—	—	—	—	300

KM# 1864 10 YUAN

31.1030 g., 0.9990 Silver 0.9989 oz. ASW, 40 mm. **Subject:** China International Trust and Investment Co., 20th Anniversary **Obv:** Temple of Heaven **Rev:** Panda

Date	Mintage	F	VF	XF	Unc	BU
2007	20,000	—	—	—	—	300

KM# 1674 10 YUAN

31.1050 g., 0.9990 Silver 0.9990 oz. ASW, 40 mm. **Subject:** 29th Summer Olympics, Bejing **Rev:** Great Wall, ornament at left in color

Date	Mintage	F	VF	XF	Unc	BU
2008 S Proof	160,000	Value: 75.00				
2008 Y Proof	Inc. above	Value: 75.00				
2008 Z Proof	Inc. above	Value: 75.00				

KM# 1688 10 YUAN

31.1050 g., 0.9990 Silver 0.9990 oz. ASW, 40 mm. **Subject:** 29th Summer Olympics, Bejing **Rev:** Summer Palace, Bejing; flower at left in color

Date	Mintage	F	VF	XF	Unc	BU
2008 S Proof	160,000	Value: 75.00				
2008 Y Proof	Inc. above	Value: 75.00				
2008 Z Proof	Inc. above	Value: 75.00				

KM# 1702 10 YUAN

31.1050 g., 0.9990 Silver 0.9990 oz. ASW, 40 mm. **Subject:** 2007 Summer Olympics **Obv:** Beijing Olympic logo **Rev:** Child with kite, multicolor design **Note:** Issued in 2006

Date	Mintage	F	VF	XF	Unc	BU
2008 S Proof	160,000	Value: 75.00				
2008 Y Proof	Inc. above	Value: 75.00				
2008 Z Proof	Inc. above	Value: 75.00				

KM# 1703 10 YUAN

31.1050 g., 0.9990 Silver 0.9990 oz. ASW, 40 mm. **Subject:** 2007 Summer Olympics **Obv:** Beijing Olympics logo **Rev:** Two children playing leapfrog, multicolor **Note:** Issued in 2006

Date	Mintage	F	VF	XF	Unc	BU
2008 S Proof	160,000	Value: 75.00				
2008 Y Proof	Inc. above	Value: 75.00				
2008 Z Proof	Inc. above	Value: 75.00				

KM# 1704 10 YUAN

31.1050 g., 0.9990 Silver 0.9990 oz. ASW, 40 mm. **Subject:** 2007 Summer Olympics **Obv:** Beijing Olympics logo **Rev:** Child rolling ring with stick, multicolor **Note:** Issued in 2006

Date	Mintage	F	VF	XF	Unc	BU
2008 S Proof	160,000	Value: 75.00				
2008 Y Proof	Inc. above	Value: 75.00				
2008 Z Proof	Inc. above	Value: 75.00				

KM# 1705 10 YUAN

31.1050 g., 0.9990 Silver 0.9990 oz. ASW, 40 mm. **Subject:** 2007 Summer Olympics **Obv:** Beijing Olympic's logo **Rev:** Young girl dancing, multicolor **Note:** Issued in 2006

Date	Mintage	F	VF	XF	Unc	BU
2008 S Proof	160,000	Value: 75.00				
2008 Y Proof	Inc. above	Value: 75.00				
2008 Z Proof	Inc. above	Value: 75.00				

KM# 1732 10 YUAN

31.1050 g., 0.9990 Silver 0.9990 oz. ASW, 40 mm. **Subject:** 29th Summer Games, Beijing **Rev:** White Pagoda, North Sea Park

Date	Mintage	F	VF	XF	Unc	BU
2008 Proof	160,000	Value: 75.00				
2008 Proof	Inc. above	Value: 75.00				
2008 Proof	Inc. above	Value: 75.00				

KM# 1733 10 YUAN

31.1050 g., 0.9990 Silver 0.9990 oz. ASW, 40 mm. **Subject:** 29th Summer Olympics, Beijing **Obv:** Olympics logo **Rev:** Traditonal residence, flower at left in color

Date	Mintage	F	VF	XF	Unc	BU
2008 S Proof	160,000	Value: 75.00				
2008 Y Proof	Inc. above	Value: 75.00				
2008 Z Proof	Inc. above	Value: 75.00				

KM# 1734 10 YUAN

31.1030 g., 0.9990 Silver 0.9989 oz. ASW, 40 mm. **Obv:** Solar system **Rev:** Man walkking in space in color

Date	Mintage	F	VF	XF	Unc	BU
2008 Proof	60,000	Value: 75.00				

KM# 1736 10 YUAN

31.1050 g., 0.9990 Silver 0.9990 oz. ASW, 40 mm. **Subject:** Economic Reform in China, 30th Anniversary **Rev:** Economic Growth

Date	Mintage	F	VF	XF	Unc	BU
2008 Proof	80,000	Value: 55.00				

KM# 1739 10 YUAN

31.1030 g., 0.9990 Silver 0.9989 oz. ASW, 40 mm. **Subject:** Banknote Printing Works, Beijing, 100th Anniversary **Obv:** Temple of Heaven **Rev:** Two pandas

Date	Mintage	F	VF	XF	Unc	BU
2008	20,000	—	—	—	—	275

KM# 1825 10 YUAN

31.1050 g., 0.9990 Silver 0.9990 oz. ASW, 40 mm. **Subject:** Bank of Communications, Centennial

Date	Mintage	F	VF	XF	Unc	BU
2008 Proof	—	Value: 85.00				

KM# 1843 10 YUAN

31.1050 g., 0.9990 Silver 0.9990 oz. ASW, 40 mm. **Subject:** Beijing Olympics **Rev:** Multicolor mask, stall tea scene

Date	Mintage	F	VF	XF	Unc	BU
2008 Proof	160,000	Value: 55.00				

KM# 1844 10 YUAN
31.1050 g., 0.9990 Silver 0.9990 oz. ASW, 40 mm. **Subject:** Beijing Olympics **Rev:** Multicolor mask, lion dancer

Date	Mintage	F	VF	XF	Unc	BU
2008 Proof	160,000	Value: 55.00				

KM# 1845 10 YUAN
31.1050 g., 0.9990 Silver 0.9990 oz. ASW, 40 mm. **Subject:** Beijing Olympics **Rev:** Multicolor mask, Yangtze dancer

Date	Mintage	F	VF	XF	Unc	BU
2008 Proof	160,000	Value: 55.00				

KM# 1846 10 YUAN
31.1050 g., 0.9990 Silver 0.9990 oz. ASW, 40 mm. **Subject:** Beijing Olympics **Rev:** Multicolor mask, Beijing Opera

Date	Mintage	F	VF	XF	Unc	BU
2008 Proof	160,000	Value: 45.00				

KM# 1852 10 YUAN
31.1050 g., 0.9990 Silver 0.9990 oz. ASW, 40 mm. **Subject:** Hainan Special Economic Zone

Date	Mintage	F	VF	XF	Unc	BU
2008 Proof	20,000	Value: 90.00				

KM# 1854 10 YUAN
31.1050 g., 0.9990 Silver 0.9990 oz. ASW, 40 mm. **Subject:** Para Olympics

Date	Mintage	F	VF	XF	Unc	BU
2008 Proof	30,000	Value: 100				

KM# 1856 10 YUAN
31.1050 g., 0.9990 Silver 0.9990 oz. ASW, 40 mm. **Subject:** Ningxia Hui Autonomous Region

Date	Mintage	F	VF	XF	Unc	BU
2008 Proof	20,000	Value: 110				

KM# 1858 10 YUAN
31.1050 g., 0.9990 Silver 0.9990 oz. ASW, 40 mm. **Subject:** Beijing Coin and Stamp Expo

Date	Mintage	F	VF	XF	Unc	BU
2008 Proof	30,000	Value: 75.00				

KM# 1859 10 YUAN
31.1050 g., 0.9990 Silver 0.9990 oz. ASW, 40 mm. **Subject:** Guangxi Zhuang Autonomous Region

Date	Mintage	F	VF	XF	Unc	BU
2008 Proof	20,000	Value: 90.00				

KM# 1907 10 YUAN
31.1050 g., 0.9990 Silver 0.9990 oz. ASW, 40 mm. **Subject:** Shanghai Expo

Date	Mintage	F	VF	XF	Unc	BU
2009 Proof	—	Value: 60.00				

KM# 1891 10 YUAN
31.1050 g., 0.9990 Silver 0.9990 oz. ASW, 40 mm. **Subject:** Precious Metal Commemoratives, 30th Anniversary

Date	Mintage	F	VF	XF	Unc	BU
2009	300,000	—	—	—	—	40.00

KM# 1892 10 YUAN
31.1050 g., 0.9990 Silver 0.9990 oz. ASW, 40 mm. **Subject:** Beijing International Coin & Stamp Show

Date	Mintage	F	VF	XF	Unc	BU
2009	30,000	—	—	—	—	60.00

KM# 1896 10 YUAN
31.1030 g., 0.9990 Silver 0.9989 oz. ASW, 40 mm. **Subject:** Stock Exchange trading in Shenzhen **Obv:** Temple of Heaven **Rev:** Two pandas

Date	Mintage	F	VF	XF	Unc	BU
2009 Proof	30,000	Value: 150				

KM# 1898 10 YUAN
31.1050 g., 0.9990 Silver 0.9990 oz. ASW, 40 mm. **Subject:** P.R.C. 60th Anniversary **Rev:** Multicolor

Date	Mintage	F	VF	XF	Unc	BU
2009 Proof	100,000	Value: 55.00				

KM# 1902 10 YUAN
31.1050 g., 0.9990 Silver 0.9990 oz. ASW, 40 mm. **Subject:** Outlaws of the Marsh, series 1 **Rev:** Multicolor

Date	Mintage	F	VF	XF	Unc	BU
2009 Proof	60,000	Value: 60.00				

KM# 1903 10 YUAN
31.1050 g., 0.9990 Silver 0.9990 oz. ASW, 40 mm. **Subject:** Outlaws of the Marsh, series 1 **Rev:** Multicolor

Date	Mintage	F	VF	XF	Unc	BU
2009 Proof	60,000	Value: 60.00				

KM# 1905 10 YUAN
31.1050 g., 0.9990 Silver 0.9990 oz. ASW, 40 mm. **Subject:** 16th Asian Games

Date	Mintage	F	VF	XF	Unc	BU
2009 Proof	60,000	Value: 48.00				

KM# 1908 10 YUAN
31.1050 g., 0.9990 Silver 0.9990 oz. ASW, 40 mm. **Subject:** Shanghai Expo

Date	Mintage	F	VF	XF	Unc	BU
2009 Proof	—	Value: 48.00				

KM# 1910 10 YUAN
31.1050 g., 0.9990 Silver 0.9990 oz. ASW, 40 mm. **Subject:** China Agricultural Bank

Date	Mintage	F	VF	XF	Unc	BU
2009	100,000	—	—	—	—	45.00

KM# 1793 10 YUAN
31.1050 g., 0.9990 Silver 0.9990 oz. ASW **Subject:** Agricultural Bank, IPO **Obv:** Temple of Heaven **Rev:** Panda

Date	Mintage	F	VF	XF	Unc	BU
2010	70,000	—	—	—	—	275

KM# 1795 10 YUAN
31.1030 g., 0.9990 Silver 0.9989 oz. ASW, 40 mm. **Subject:** Capital Market in the Peoples Republic of China, 20th Anniversary **Obv:** Temple of Heaven **Rev:** Panda

Date	Mintage	F	VF	XF	Unc	BU
2010 Proof	40,000	—	—	—	—	120

KM# 1796 10 YUAN
31.1030 g., 0.9990 Silver 0.9989 oz. ASW, 40 mm. **Subject:** Shanghai Mint, 90th Anniversary **Obv:** Temple of Heaven **Rev:** Panda

Date	Mintage	F	VF	XF	Unc	BU
2010	20,000	—	—	—	—	275

KM# 1939 10 YUAN
31.1050 g., 0.9990 Silver 0.9990 oz. ASW, 40 mm. **Series:** Outlaws of the Marsh, series 2 **Rev:** Multicolor

Date	Mintage	F	VF	XF	Unc	BU
2010 Proof	70,000	Value: 60.00				

KM# 1940 10 YUAN
31.1050 g., 0.9990 Silver 0.9990 oz. ASW, 40 mm. **Series:** Outlaws of the Marsh, series 2 **Rev:** Multicolor

Date	Mintage	F	VF	XF	Unc	BU
2010 Proof	70,000	Value: 60.00				

KM# 1942 10 YUAN
10.3600 g., 0.9990 Gold 0.3327 oz. AGW **Subject:** Shanghai World Expo, 2010

Date	Mintage	F	VF	XF	Unc	BU
2010 Proof	60,000	Value: 600				

KM# 1943 10 YUAN
31.1050 g., 0.9990 Silver 0.9990 oz. ASW, 40 mm. **Subject:** Shanghai World Expo, 2010

Date	Mintage	F	VF	XF	Unc	BU
2010 Proof	80,000	Value: 60.00				

KM# 1944 10 YUAN
31.1050 g., 0.9990 Silver 0.9990 oz. ASW, 40 mm. **Subject:** Shanghai World Expo, 2010

Date	Mintage	F	VF	XF	Unc	BU
2010 Proof	80,000	Value: 60.00				

KM# 1946 10 YUAN
31.1050 g., 0.9990 Silver 0.9990 oz. ASW, 40 mm. **Subject:** Wudang Mountain

Date	Mintage	F	VF	XF	Unc	BU
2010 Proof	60,000	Value: 60.00				

KM# 1953 10 YUAN
31.1050 g., 0.9990 Silver 0.9990 oz. ASW **Subject:** Shenzhen Economic Zone

Date	Mintage	F	VF	XF	Unc	BU
2010 Proof	30,000	Value: 60.00				

KM# 1955 10 YUAN
31.1050 g., 0.9990 Silver 0.9990 oz. ASW, 40 mm. **Subject:** 16th Asian Games

Date	Mintage	F	VF	XF	Unc	BU
2010 Proof	60,000	Value: 60.00				

KM# 1957 10 YUAN
31.1050 g., 0.9990 Silver 0.9990 oz. ASW, 40 mm. **Subject:** Bejing Opera, series 1 **Rev:** Multicolor face mask

Date	Mintage	F	VF	XF	Unc	BU
2010 Proof	50,000	Value: 60.00				

KM# 1958 10 YUAN
31.1050 g., 0.9990 Silver 0.9990 oz. ASW, 40 mm. **Subject:** Bejing Opera, series 1 **Rev:** Multicolor face mask

Date	Mintage	F	VF	XF	Unc	BU
2010 Proof	50,000	Value: 60.00				

KM# 1959 10 YUAN
31.1050 g., 0.9990 Silver 0.9990 oz. ASW, 40 mm. **Subject:** Bejing Stamp & Coin Expo

Date	Mintage	F	VF	XF	Unc	BU
2010 Proof	30,000	Value: 60.00				

KM# 1985 10 YUAN
31.1050 g., 0.9990 Silver 0.9990 oz. ASW, 40 mm. **Subject:** Peking Opera art **Rev:** Lu Zhishen, the "Flowery Monk" character from Water Margin

Date	Mintage	F	VF	XF	Unc	BU
2011 Proof	50,000	Value: 75.00				

KM# 1986 10 YUAN
31.1050 g., 0.9990 Silver 0.9990 oz. ASW, 40 mm. **Subject:** Peking Opera art **Rev:** Shan Ziongxin

Date	Mintage	F	VF	XF	Unc	BU
2011 Proof	50,000	Value: 75.00				

KM# 1798 10 YUAN
31.1030 g., 0.9990 Silver 0.9989 oz. ASW, 40 mm. **Subject:** World Wildlife Fund, 50th Anniversary **Rev:** Tibetian antelope

Date	Mintage	F	VF	XF	Unc	BU
2011 Proof	30,000	Value: 65.00				

KM# 1800 10 YUAN
31.1030 g., 0.9990 Silver 0.9989 oz. ASW, 40 mm. **Subject:** Tsinghua University, 100th Anniversary **Rev:** Old University entrance

Date	Mintage	F	VF	XF	Unc	BU
2011 Proof	Est. 50,000	Value: 75.00				

KM# 1804 10 YUAN
31.1050 g., 0.9990 Silver 0.9990 oz. ASW, 40 mm. **Subject:** 23rd Beijing International Stamp and Coin Exposition **Rev:** Byzantine coin and Song Dynasty coin

Date	Mintage	F	VF	XF	Unc	BU
2011 Proof	Est. 30,000	Value: 125				

KM# 1805 10 YUAN
31.1030 g., 0.9990 Silver 0.9989 oz. ASW, 40 mm. **Subject:** Chinese Literature **Rev:** Archer and geese in color

Date	Mintage	F	VF	XF	Unc	BU
2011 Proof	70,000	Value: 75.00				

KM# 1806 10 YUAN
31.1050 g., 0.9990 Silver 0.9990 oz. ASW, 40 mm. **Subject:** Chinese Literature **Rev:** Li Kui as black wind in color

Date	Mintage	F	VF	XF	Unc	BU
2011 Proof	70,000	Value: 75.00				

KM# 1994 10 YUAN
31.1050 g., 0.9990 Silver 0.9990 oz. ASW, 40 mm. **Subject:** Bejing-Shanghai High Speed Rail **Obv:** Temple of Heaven **Rev:** Two pandas

Date	Mintage	F	VF	XF	Unc	BU
2011 Proof	30,000	Value: 200				

KM# 1996 10 YUAN
31.1050 g., 0.9990 Silver 0.9990 oz. ASW, 40 mm. **Subject:** Xi-an Hortaculture Exposition **Obv:** Temple of Heaven **Rev:** Two pandas

Date	Mintage	F	VF	XF	Unc	BU
2011 Proof	20,000	Value: 235				

KM# 1998 10 YUAN
31.1050 g., 0.9990 Silver 0.9990 oz. ASW, 40 mm. **Subject:** 26th Summer Universade, Shezhuan **Obv:** Colored wreath logo **Rev:** Cubic building

Date	Mintage	F	VF	XF	Unc	BU
2011 Proof	30,000	Value: 200				

KM# 2000 10 YUAN
31.1050 g., 0.9990 Silver 0.9990 oz. ASW, 40 mm. **Subject:** Peaceful liberation, 60th Anniversary **Obv:** National emblem **Rev:** Ornate design

Date	Mintage	F	VF	XF	Unc	BU
2011 Proof	30,000	—	—	—	—	200

KM# 2002 10 YUAN
31.1050 g., 0.9990 Silver 0.9990 oz. ASW, 40 mm. **Subject:** 100th Anniversary of the Revolution **Obv:** National emblem **Rev:** Revolutionary army advancing right - Wuchang Uprising

Date	Mintage	F	VF	XF	Unc	BU
2011 Proof	160,000	Value: 100				

KM# 2004 10 YUAN
31.1050 g., 0.9990 Silver 0.9990 oz. ASW, 40 mm. **Subject:** Avation Industry in the P.R.C., 60th Anniversary **Obv:** Temple of Heaven **Rev:** Two pandas

Date	Mintage	F	VF	XF	Unc	BU
2011 Proof	20,000	Value: 200				

KM# 2007 10 YUAN
31.1050 g., 0.9990 Silver 0.9990 oz. ASW, 40 mm. **Subject:** World Heritage Site **Obv:** National emblem **Rev:** Songyue Temple Pagoda

Date	Mintage	F	VF	XF	Unc	BU
2011 Proof	60,000	Value: 150				

KM# 2034 10 YUAN
31.1030 g., 0.9990 Silver 0.9989 oz. ASW **Subject:** National Committee of the Chinese Financial Workers Union, 60th Anniversary **Rev:** Mother and cub panda

Date	Mintage	F	VF	XF	Unc	BU
2011	30,000	—	—	—	—	200

KM# 2035 10 YUAN
31.1030 g., 0.9990 Silver 0.9989 oz. ASW, 40 mm. **Subject:** Shanghai Gold Exchange, 10th Anniversary **Rev:** Mother and cub panda

Date	Mintage	F	VF	XF	Unc	BU
2011	30,000	—	—	—	—	140

KM# 2037 10 YUAN
31.1030 g., 0.9990 Silver 0.9989 oz. ASW, 40 mm. **Subject:** Xiamen Special Economic Zone, 30th Anniversary **Rev:** Mother and cub panda

Date	Mintage	F	VF	XF	Unc	BU
2011	20,000	—	—	—	—	200

KM# 2039 10 YUAN
31.1030 g., 0.9990 Silver 0.9989 oz. ASW, 40 mm. **Subject:** Rual Credit Cooperatives, 60th Anniversary **Rev:** Mother and cub panda

Date	Mintage	F	VF	XF	Unc	BU
2011	60,000	—	—	—	—	100

KM# 2047 10 YUAN
31.1030 g., 0.9990 Silver 0.9989 oz. ASW, 40 mm. **Subject:** Bejing Opera Masks **Rev:** Zhang Fei mask in color

Date	Mintage	F	VF	XF	Unc	BU
2012 Proof	50,000	Value: 75.00				

KM# 2052 10 YUAN
31.1030 g., 0.9990 Silver 0.9989 oz. ASW, 40 mm. **Subject:** Bronze Age vessels **Rev:** Three water vessels from the Shang Dynasty, Zianwen find

Date	Mintage	F	VF	XF	Unc	BU
2012 Proof	80,000	Value: 80.00				

KM# 2057 10 YUAN
31.1030 g., Silver, 40 mm. **Subject:** Beijing International Stamp and Coin Exposition

Date	Mintage	F	VF	XF	Unc	BU
2012 Proof	30,000	Value: 125				

KM# 2063 10 YUAN
31.1030 g., 0.9990 Silver 0.9989 oz. ASW, 40 mm. **Subject:** Bank of China, 100th Anniversary **Obv:** Temple of Heaven **Rev:** Mother and cub panda seated

Date	Mintage	F	VF	XF	Unc	BU
2012	260,000	—	—	—	—	85.00

KM# 1388 20 YUAN
62.2070 g., 0.9990 Silver 1.9979 oz. ASW, 40 mm. **Subject:** Mogao Grottos **Obv:** 8-story building **Rev:** Buddha-like statue **Edge:** Reeded **Note:** Prev. Y#1082.

Date	Mintage	F	VF	XF	Unc	BU
2001 Proof	30,000	Value: 150				

KM# 1432 20 YUAN
62.2070 g., 0.9990 Silver 1.9979 oz. ASW, 40 mm. **Rev:** Buddha-like statue

Date	Mintage	F	VF	XF	Unc	BU
2002 Proof	30,000	Value: 150				

KM# 1563 20 YUAN
31.1035 g., 0.9990 Silver 0.9990 oz. ASW, 40 mm. **Series:** Maijishan grotto art **Rev:** Two figures standing

Date	Mintage	F	VF	XF	Unc	BU
2004 Proof	20,000	Value: 90.00				

KM# 2042 20 YUAN
62.2700 g., 0.9990 Silver 1.9999 oz. ASW, 40 mm. **Subject:** UNESCO **Rev:** Budda statue in Riwo Tsenga

Date	Mintage	F	VF	XF	Unc	BU
2012 Proof	Est. 100,000	Value: 80.00				

KM# 1390 50 YUAN
155.5175 g., 0.9990 Silver 4.9948 oz. ASW, 70 mm. **Subject:** Mogao Grottoes **Obv:** Eight story building **Rev:** Four musicians **Edge:** Reeded. **Note:** Prev. Y#1083.

Date	Mintage	F	VF	XF	Unc	BU
2001 Proof	8,000	Value: 300				

KM# 1389 50 YUAN
3.1104 g., 0.9990 Gold 0.0999 oz. AGW **Subject:** Mogao Grottoes **Obv:** Eight story building **Rev:** Buddha-like statue **Edge:** Reeded. **Note:** Prev. Y#1084.

Date	Mintage	F	VF	XF	Unc	BU
2001 Proof	50,000	Value: 250				

KM# 1394 50 YUAN
155.5175 g., 0.9990 Silver 4.9948 oz. ASW, 90 x 40 mm. **Subject:** Han Xizai's Dinner Party **Obv:** Tang Dynasty buildings **Rev:** Multicolor "Five Dynasties" painting **Edge:** Plain **Shape:** Rectangular **Note:** Prev. Y#1104.

Date	Mintage	F	VF	XF	Unc	BU
2001 Proof	18,800	Value: 275				

KM# 1386 50 YUAN
155.5175 g., 0.9990 Silver 4.9948 oz. ASW, 90 x 40 mm. **Series:** Folk fairy tails **Rev:** Seven multicolor figures on beach **Shape:** Rectangle

Date	Mintage	F	VF	XF	Unc	BU
2001 Proof	10,000	Value: 300				

KM# 1402 50 YUAN
155.5190 g., 0.9990 Silver 4.9948 oz. ASW, 90 x 50 mm. **Subject:** Bejing opera **Rev:** Four multicolor actors **Shape:** Rectangle

Date	Mintage	F	VF	XF	Unc	BU
2001 Proof	11,800	Value: 300				

KM# 1433 50 YUAN
155.5190 g., 0.9990 Silver 4.9948 oz. ASW, 70 mm. **Series:** Long men grottoes **Rev:** Two figures

Date	Mintage	F	VF	XF	Unc	BU
2002 Proof	8,000	Value: 300				

KM# 1445 50 YUAN
155.5190 g., 0.9990 Silver 4.9948 oz. ASW, 65 x 26 mm. **Series:** Classic literature **Rev:** Multicolor crowd of women **Shape:** Fan-like

Date	Mintage	F	VF	XF	Unc	BU
2002 Proof	11,800	Value: 250				

KM# 1430 50 YUAN
155.7900 g., 0.9990 Silver 5.0035 oz. ASW, 90 x 40 mm. **Series:** Folk fairy tails **Rev:** Multicolor female with red ribbon **Shape:** Rectangle

Date	Mintage	F	VF	XF	Unc	BU
2002 Proof	—	Value: 375				

KM# 1437 50 YUAN
3.1100 g., 0.9990 Gold 0.0999 oz. AGW, 18 mm. **Subject:** Kuan yin

Date	Mintage	F	VF	XF	Unc	BU
2002 Proof	33,000	Value: 225				

KM# 1453 50 YUAN
155.5190 g., 0.9990 Silver 4.9948 oz. ASW, 90 x 40 mm. **Series:** Bejing opera **Rev:** Three multicolor characters one with spikes in costume **Shape:** Rectangle

Date	Mintage	F	VF	XF	Unc	BU
2002 Proof	11,800	Value: 300				

KM# 1493 50 YUAN
155.3500 g., 0.9990 Silver 4.9894 oz. ASW, 90 x 40 mm. **Series:** Fairy tails **Rev:** Multicolor man with two boys in buckets, jenole in flight at left **Shape:** Rectangle

Date	Mintage	F	VF	XF	Unc	BU
2003 Proof	10,000	Value: 350				

KM# 1512 50 YUAN
3.1104 g., 0.9990 Gold 0.0999 oz. AGW, 18 mm. **Obv:** Putuo Mountain Pilgrimage Gate **Rev:** Seated Kuanyin with holographic background **Edge:** Reeded **Note:** Prev. Y#1234.

Date	Mintage	F	VF	XF	Unc	BU
2003 Proof	33,000	Value: 225				

KM# 1502 50 YUAN
155.5000 g., 0.9990 Silver 4.9942 oz. ASW, 80 x 50 mm. **Series:** Class literature **Rev:** Multicolor man lying on couch **Shape:** Rectangle

Date	Mintage	F	VF	XF	Unc	BU
2003 Proof	10,000	Value: 350				

KM# 1503 50 YUAN
155.1500 g., 0.9990 Silver 4.9830 oz. ASW, 65 x 125 mm. **Series:** Class literature **Rev:** Six people **Shape:** Arc **Note:** Colorized

Date	Mintage	F	VF	XF	Unc	BU
2003 Proof	11,800	Value: 350				

KM# 1572 50 YUAN
3.1100 g., 0.9990 Gold 0.0999 oz. AGW, 18 mm. **Obv:** Putuo Mountain Pilgrimage Gate **Rev:** Kuanyin and value **Edge:** Reeded **Note:** Prev. Y#1237.

Date	Mintage	F	VF	XF	Unc	BU
2004 Proof	33,000	Value: 225				

KM# 1560 50 YUAN
155.5175 g., 0.9990 Silver 4.9948 oz. ASW, 80x50 mm. **Obv:** Monkey King leading the Master over bridge **Rev:** Multicolor Monkey King fighting the Pig Demon of Bones **Edge:** Plain **Shape:** Rectangle **Note:** Prev. Y#1216.

Date	Mintage	F	VF	XF	Unc	BU
2004 Proof	10,000	Value: 375				

KM# 1635 50 YUAN
155.0000 g., 0.9990 Silver 4.9782 oz. ASW, 80 x 50 mm. **Series:** Classical Literature **Obv:** Horseman on arch bridge **Rev:** Multicolor female and lion **Shape:** Rectangle **Note:** Illustration reduced.

Date	Mintage	F	VF	XF	Unc	BU
2005 Proof	10,000	Value: 350				

KM# 1901 50 YUAN
155.5000 g., 0.9990 Silver 4.9942 oz. ASW, 80x50 mm. **Subject:** Outlaws of the Marsh, series 1 **Rev:** Multicolor **Shape:** Rectangle

Date	Mintage	F	VF	XF	Unc	BU
2009 Proof	10,000	Value: 250				

KM# 1938 50 YUAN
155.5000 g., 0.9990 Silver 4.9942 oz. ASW, 80x50 mm. **Subject:** Outlaws of the Marsh, series 2 **Rev:** Multicolor **Shape:** Regtangle

Date	Mintage	F	VF	XF	Unc	BU
2010 Proof	12,000	Value: 225				

KM# 1951 50 YUAN
62.1000 g., 0.9990 Silver 1.9945 oz. ASW **Subject:** Yungang Grotto Art

Date	Mintage	F	VF	XF	Unc	BU
2010 Proof	20,000	Value: 120				

KM# 1807 50 YUAN
155.6700 g., 0.9990 Silver 4.9997 oz. ASW, 80x50 mm. **Subject:** Chinese Literature **Rev:** Yan Qing and Ren Yuan in color

Date	Mintage	F	VF	XF	Unc	BU
2011 Proof	12,000	Value: 325				

KM# 2048 50 YUAN
31.1030 g., 0.9990 Silver 0.9989 oz. ASW, 70 mm. **Subject:** Bejing Opera Mask **Rev:** Tao Hong mask in color

Date	Mintage	F	VF	XF	Unc	BU
2012 Proof	50,000	Value: 75.00				

KM# 2049 50 YUAN
155.6700 g., 0.9990 Silver 4.9997 oz. ASW, 70 mm. **Subject:** Beijing Opera Masks **Rev:** Zhong Kui mask in color

Date	Mintage	F	VF	XF	Unc	BU
2012 Proof	10,000	Value: 350				

KM# 2053 50 YUAN
155.6700 g., 0.9990 Silver 4.9997 oz. ASW, 70 mm. **Subject:** Vessels of the Bronze Age **Rev:** Shang Dynasty kettle

Date	Mintage	F	VF	XF	Unc	BU
2012 Proof	10,000	Value: 350				

KM# 2059 50 YUAN
155.6700 g., 0.9990 Silver 4.9997 oz. ASW, 70 mm. **Subject:** Panda, 30th Anniversary **Obv:** Temple of Heaven **Rev:** Panda

Date	Mintage	F	VF	XF	Unc	BU
2012 Proof	30,000	Value: 350				

KM# 2060 50 YUAN
3.1100 g., 0.9990 Gold 0.0999 oz. AGW, 18 mm. **Subject:** Panda, 30th Anniversary **Obv:** Temple of Heaven **Rev:** Panda

Date	Mintage	F	VF	XF	Unc	BU
2012 Proof	100,000	Value: 300				

KM# 1514 100 YUAN
3.1013 g., 0.9990 Platinum 0.0996 oz. APW, 18 mm. **Series:** Guan Yi

Date	Mintage	F	VF	XF	Unc	BU
2003 Proof	33,000	Value: 225				

KM# 1534 100 YUAN
15.5500 g., 0.9990 Palladium 0.4994 oz., 27 mm. **Obv:** Temple of Heaven **Rev:** Panda mother and cub, "kissing pandas" **Edge:** Reeded **Note:** Prev. Y#1211.

Date	Mintage	F	VF	XF	Unc	BU
2004 Proof	8,000	Value: 550				

KM# 1573 100 YUAN
3.1100 g., 0.9995 Platinum 0.0999 oz. APW, 18 mm. **Obv:** Putuo Mountain Pilgrimage Gate **Rev:** Kuanyin and value **Edge:** Reeded **Note:** Prev. Y#1238.

Date	Mintage	F	VF	XF	Unc	BU
2004 Proof	33,000	Value: 225				

KM# 1540 100 YUAN
7.8500 g., 0.9990 Gold 0.2521 oz. AGW, 22 mm. **Subject:** 20th Anniversary / Bank of China Industrial and Commercial **Rev:** Panda walking with cub

Date	Mintage	F	VF	XF	Unc	BU
2004 Proof	50,000	Value: 500				

KM# 1542 100 YUAN
7.8400 g., 0.9990 Gold 0.2518 oz. AGW, 22 mm. **Subject:** 50th Anniversary China Construction Bank **Rev:** Panda walking with cub

Date	Mintage	F	VF	XF	Unc	BU
2004 Proof	60,000	Value: 500				

KM# 1600 100 YUAN
7.7700 g., 0.9990 Gold 0.2496 oz. AGW, 22 mm. **Subject:** Foundation of Industrial & Commercial Bank **Obv:** Temple of Heaven **Rev:** Panda cub and mom seated in bamboo

Date	Mintage	F	VF	XF	Unc	BU
2005 Proof	40,000	Value: 500				

KM# 1602 100 YUAN
7.7700 g., 0.9990 Gold 0.2496 oz. AGW, 22 mm. **Subject:** 100th Anniversary of Bank of Shanghai **Obv:** Temple of Heaven **Rev:** Panda cub and mom seated in bamboo

Date	Mintage	F	VF	XF	Unc	BU
2005 Proof	40,000	Value: 500				

KM# 1616 100 YUAN
7.7000 g., 0.9990 Gold 0.2473 oz. AGW, 22 mm. **Subject:** 2006 World Cup - Germany **Obv:** Multicolor logo **Rev:** Temple of Heaven and soccer ball

Date	Mintage	F	VF	XF	Unc	BU
2005 Proof	10,000	Value: 550				

KM# A979 100 YUAN
8.5000 g., 0.9990 Gold 0.2730 oz. AGW, 22 mm. **Subject:** 10th Anniversary Bank of Beijing **Obv:** Temple of Heaven **Rev:** Two pandas

Date	Mintage	F	VF	XF	Unc	BU
2006	100	—	—	—	—	800

KM# A980 100 YUAN
8.5000 g., 0.9990 Gold 0.2730 oz. AGW, 22 mm. **Subject:** 10th Anniversary China Minsheng Banking Corp. **Obv:** Temple of Heaven **Rev:** Two Pandas munching on bamboo

Date	Mintage	F	VF	XF	Unc	BU
2006	100	—	—	—	—	800

KM# 1665 100 YUAN
7.7700 g., 0.9990 Gold 0.2496 oz. AGW, 22 mm. **Subject:** 10th Anniversary Bank of Beijing **Obv:** Temple of Heaven **Rev:** Two pandas seated with bamboo

Date	Mintage	F	VF	XF	Unc	BU
2006 Proof	150,000	Value: 500				

KM# 1667 100 YUAN
7.7700 g., 0.9990 Silver 0.2496 oz. ASW, 22 mm. **Subject:** 10th Anniversary - China Minsheng Banking Corp **Obv:** Temple of Heaven **Rev:** Two pandas seated with bamboo

Date	Mintage	F	VF	XF	Unc	BU
2006 Proof	20,000	Value: 550				

KM# 1669 100 YUAN
7.7700 g., 0.9990 Gold 0.2496 oz. AGW, 22 mm. **Subject:** Shenyang Horticultural Expo **Obv:** Temple of Heaven **Rev:** Two pandas seated with bamboo

Date	Mintage	F	VF	XF	Unc	BU
2006 Proof	10,000	Value: 550				

KM# 1694 100 YUAN
7.7700 g., 0.9990 Gold 0.2496 oz. AGW, 22 mm. **Subject:** Qinghai - Tibet Railway Opening **Obv:** Map of railway route and track layer **Rev:** Kun Lun Tunnel Portal

Date	Mintage	F	VF	XF	Unc	BU
2006 Proof	16,000	Value: 550				

KM# 1730 100 YUAN
7.7700 g., 0.9990 Gold 0.2496 oz. AGW, 22 mm. **Subject:** 60th Anniversary - Foundry of Mongolia Autonomous Region **Obv:** Wheel of Mongolian Lele Cart **Rev:** Female Mongolian in posture of welcome

Date	Mintage	F	VF	XF	Unc	BU
2007 Proof	10,000	Value: 550				

KM# 1827 100 YUAN
7.7800 g., 0.9990 Gold 0.2499 oz. AGW, 22 mm. **Subject:** 12th Special Olympics in Shanghai **Obv:** Logo in color **Rev:** Runner

Date	Mintage	F	VF	XF	Unc	BU
2007 Proof	20,000	Value: 650				

KM# 1737 100 YUAN
7.7800 g., 0.9990 Gold 0.2499 oz. AGW, 22 mm. **Subject:** Economic Reform in China, 30th Anniversary **Rev:** Flowers and fireworks

Date	Mintage	F	VF	XF	Unc	BU
2008 Proof	30,000	Value: 600				

KM# 1824 100 YUAN
7.7700 g., 0.9990 Gold 0.2496 oz. AGW, 23 mm. **Subject:** Bank of Communications, Centennial **Rev:** Panda

Date	Mintage	F	VF	XF	Unc	BU
2008 Proof	10,000	Value: 550				

KM# 1853 100 YUAN
7.7700 g., 0.9990 Gold 0.2496 oz. AGW **Subject:** Hainan Special Economic Zone

Date	Mintage	F	VF	XF	Unc	BU
2008 Proof	10,000	Value: 550				

KM# 1857 100 YUAN
7.7700 g., 0.9990 Gold 0.2496 oz. AGW **Subject:** Ningxia Hui Autonomous Region

Date	Mintage	F	VF	XF	Unc	BU
2008 Proof	10,000	Value: 550				

KM# 1860 100 YUAN
7.7700 g., 0.9990 Gold 0.2496 oz. AGW **Subject:** Guangzi Zhuang Autonomous Region

Date	Mintage	F	VF	XF	Unc	BU
2008 Proof	10,000	Value: 550				

KM# 1890 100 YUAN
7.7700 g., 0.9990 Gold 0.2496 oz. AGW, 23 mm. **Subject:** Precious Metal Commemoratives, 30th Anniversary **Obv:** Temple of Heaven **Rev:** Two pandas seated

Date	Mintage	F	VF	XF	Unc	BU
2009	10,000	—	—	—	—	550

KM# 1895 100 YUAN
7.7700 g., 0.9990 Gold 0.2496 oz. AGW, 22 mm. **Subject:** P.R.C. 60th Anniversary

Date	Mintage	F	VF	XF	Unc	BU
2009 Proof	100,000	Value: 500				

KM# 1904 100 YUAN
7.7700 g., 0.9990 Gold 0.2496 oz. AGW, 22 mm. **Subject:** 16th Asian Games

Date	Mintage	F	VF	XF	Unc	BU
2009 Proof	30,000	Value: 525				

KM# 1909 100 YUAN
7.7700 g., 0.9990 Gold 0.2496 oz. AGW, 22 mm. **Subject:** China Agricultural Bank

Date	Mintage	F	VF	XF	Unc	BU
2009	100,000	—	—	—	—	500

KM# 1794 100 YUAN
7.7800 g., 0.9990 Gold 0.2499 oz. AGW, 22 mm. **Subject:** Agricultural Bank, IPO **Obv:** Temple of Heaven **Rev:** Panda

Date	Mintage	F	VF	XF	Unc	BU
2010	60,000	—	—	—	—	500

KM# 1797 100 YUAN
7.7800 g., 0.9990 Gold 0.2499 oz. AGW, 22 mm. **Subject:** Shanghai Mint, 90th Anniversary **Obv:** Temple of Heaven **Rev:** Panda

Date	Mintage	F	VF	XF	Unc	BU
2010	5,000	—	—	—	—	500

KM# 1945 100 YUAN
7.7700 g., 0.9990 Gold 0.2496 oz. AGW **Subject:** Wudang Mountain

Date	Mintage	F	VF	XF	Unc	BU
2010 Proof	30,000	Value: 525				

KM# 1952 100 YUAN
7.7700 g., 0.9990 Gold 0.2496 oz. AGW **Subject:** Shenzhen Economic Zone

Date	Mintage	F	VF	XF	Unc	BU
2010 Proof	20,000	Value: 525				

KM# 1954 100 YUAN
7.7700 g., 0.9990 Gold 0.2496 oz. AGW **Subject:** 16th Asian Games

Date	Mintage	F	VF	XF	Unc	BU
2010 Proof	30,000	Value: 525				

KM# 1956 100 YUAN
7.7700 g., 0.9990 Gold 0.2496 oz. AGW **Subject:** Bejing Opera, series 1 **Rev:** Multicolor

Date	Mintage	F	VF	XF	Unc	BU
2010 Proof	30,000	Value: 525				

KM# 1987 100 YUAN
7.7700 g., 0.9990 Gold 0.2496 oz. AGW, 22 mm. **Subject:** Peking Opera art **Rev:** Mask of Guan Yu

Date	Mintage	F	VF	XF	Unc	BU
2011 Proof	30,000	Value: 525				

KM# 1799 100 YUAN
7.7800 g., 0.9990 Gold 0.2499 oz. AGW, 22 mm. **Subject:** World Wildlife Fund, 50th Anniversary **Rev:** Large 50 and WWF logo

Date	Mintage	F	VF	XF	Unc	BU
2011 Proof	10,000	Value: 600				

KM# 1801 100 YUAN
7.7800 g., 0.9990 Gold 0.2499 oz. AGW, 22 mm. **Subject:** Tsinghua University **Rev:** Original main building

Date	Mintage	F	VF	XF	Unc	BU
2011 Proof	Est. 20,000	Value: 550				

KM# 1995 100 YUAN
7.7700 g., 0.9990 Gold 0.2496 oz. AGW, 22 mm. **Subject:** Bejing-Shanghai High Speed Rail **Obv:** Temple of Heaven **Rev:** Two pandas

Date	Mintage	F	VF	XF	Unc	BU
2011 Proof	10,000	Value: 600				

KM# 1997 100 YUAN
7.7700 g., 0.9990 Gold 0.2496 oz. AGW, 22 mm. **Subject:** Xi-an Horticulture Exposition **Obv:** Temple of Heaven **Rev:** Two pandas

Date	Mintage	F	VF	XF	Unc	BU
2011 Proof	3,000	Value: 750				

KM# 1999 100 YUAN
7.7700 g., 0.9990 Gold 0.2496 oz. AGW, 22 mm. **Subject:** 26th Summer Universade, Shezhuan **Obv:** Colored wreath logo **Rev:** Rays and smile face design

Date	Mintage	F	VF	XF	Unc	BU
2011 Proof	20,000	Value: 750				

KM# 2001 100 YUAN
7.7700 g., 0.9990 Gold 0.2496 oz. AGW, 22 mm. **Subject:** Peaceful Liberation, 60th Anniversary **Obv:** National emblem **Rev:** Ornate design

Date	Mintage	F	VF	XF	Unc	BU
2011 Proof	20,000	Value: 750				

KM# 2003 100 YUAN
7.7700 g., 0.9990 Gold 0.2496 oz. AGW, 22 mm. **Subject:** 100th Anniversary of the Revolution **Obv:** National emblem **Rev:** Sun Yat-sen bust facing

Date	Mintage	F	VF	XF	Unc	BU
2011 Proof	100,000	Value: 650				

KM# 2005 100 YUAN
7.7700 g., 0.9990 Gold 0.2496 oz. AGW, 22 mm. **Subject:** Avation Industry in the P.R.C., 60th Anniversary **Obv:** Temple of Heaven **Rev:** Two pandas

Date	Mintage	F	VF	XF	Unc	BU
2011 Proof	5,000	Value: 750				

KM# 2008 100 YUAN
7.7700 g., 0.9990 Gold 0.2496 oz. AGW, 22 mm. **Subject:** World Heritage Site **Obv:** National emblem **Rev:** Gate of the Shaolin Temple

Date	Mintage	F	VF	XF	Unc	BU
2011 Proof	30,000	Value: 650				

KM# 2036 100 YUAN
7.7800 g., 0.9990 Gold 0.2499 oz. AGW, 22 mm. **Subject:** Shanghai Gold Exchange **Rev:** Mother and cub panda

Date	Mintage	F	VF	XF	Unc	BU
2011	6,000	—	—	—	—	550

KM# 2038 100 YUAN
7.7800 g., 0.9990 Gold 0.2499 oz. AGW, 22 mm. **Subject:** Xiamen Special Economic Zone, 30th Anniversary **Rev:** Mother and cub panda

Date	Mintage	F	VF	XF	Unc	BU
2011	5,000	—	—	—	—	550

KM# 2040 100 YUAN
7.7800 g., 0.9990 Gold 0.2499 oz. AGW, 22 mm. **Subject:** Rural Credit Cooperatives, 60th Anniversary **Rev:** Mother and cub panda

Date	Mintage	F	VF	XF	Unc	BU
2011	25,000	—	—	—	—	550

KM# 2044 100 YUAN
7.7800 g., 0.9990 Gold 0.2499 oz. AGW, 22 mm. **Subject:** UNESCO **Rev:** Pusading Temple

Date	Mintage	F	VF	XF	Unc	BU
2012 Proof	60,000	Value: 550				

KM# 2050 100 YUAN
7.7800 g., 0.9990 Gold 0.2499 oz. AGW, 22 mm. **Subject:** Beijing Opera Mask **Rev:** Monkey King in color

Date	Mintage	F	VF	XF	Unc	BU
2012 Proof	30,000	Value: 550				

KM# 2055 100 YUAN
7.7800 g., 0.9990 Gold 0.2499 oz. AGW, 22 mm. **Subject:** Bronze Age vessels **Rev:** Tripod drinking glass, Xia Dynasty, Yanshi find

Date	Mintage	F	VF	XF	Unc	BU
2012 Proof	50,000	Value: 550				

KM# 2064 100 YUAN
7.7800 g., 0.9990 Gold 0.2499 oz. AGW, 22 mm. **Subject:** Bank of China, 100th Anniversary **Obv:** Temple of Heaven **Rev:** Mother and cub panda

Date	Mintage	F	VF	XF	Unc	BU
2012	55,000	—	—	—	—	550

KM# 1488 150 YUAN
10.0500 g., 0.9990 Gold 0.3228 oz. AGW, 23 mm. **Subject:** Spring festival **Obv:** Tree with berries **Rev:** Two Koi in ribbon sea

Date	Mintage	F	VF	XF	Unc	BU
2003 Proof	50,000	Value: 600				

KM# 1511 150 YUAN
10.1300 g., 0.9990 Gold 0.3253 oz. AGW, 23 mm. **Subject:** Space flight **Rev:** Multicolor astronaut and ship

Date	Mintage	F	VF	XF	Unc	BU
2003 Proof	30,000	Value: 625				

KM# 1556 150 YUAN
10.5000 g., 0.9990 Gold 0.3372 oz. AGW, 23 mm. **Series:** Folk customs **Subject:** Lantern Festival **Rev:** Boy holding lantern **Note:** Colorized

Date	Mintage	F	VF	XF	Unc	BU
2004 Proof	20,000	Value: 650				

KM# 1638 150 YUAN
10.0500 g., 0.9990 Gold 0.3228 oz. AGW, 23 mm. **Subject:** Chinese Movie Centennial **Obv:** Winged column **Rev:** Movie clipboard

Date	Mintage	F	VF	XF	Unc	BU
2005 Proof	20,000	Value: 650				

KM# 1654 150 YUAN
10.3600 g., 0.9990 Gold 0.3327 oz. AGW, 23 mm. **Subject:** Chengdu multi-purpose war planes, 10th Anniversary

Date	Mintage	F	VF	XF	Unc	BU
2007 Proof	10,000	Value: 850				

KM# 1829 150 YUAN
10.3600 g., 0.9990 Gold 0.3327 oz. AGW, 23 mm. **Subject:** Chinese aerospace **Obv:** Solar system **Rev:** Chang'e 1 in lunar orbit

Date	Mintage	F	VF	XF	Unc	BU
2007 Proof	20,000	Value: 850				

KM# 1848 150 YUAN
10.1000 g., 0.9990 Gold 0.3244 oz. AGW, 23 mm. **Subject:** Beijing Olympics **Obv:** Beijing Olympics **Rev:** Classical soccer player

Date	Mintage	F	VF	XF	Unc	BU
2008 Proof	60,000	Value: 600				

KM# 1847 150 YUAN
10.1000 g., 0.9990 Gold 0.3244 oz. AGW, 23 mm. **Subject:** Beijing Olympics **Rev:** Classical wrestlers

Date	Mintage	F	VF	XF	Unc	BU
2008 Proof	60,000	Value: 600				

KM# 1696 150 YUAN
10.3600 g., 0.9990 Gold 0.3327 oz. AGW, 23 mm. **Subject:** 29th Summer Olympics, Beijing **Rev:** Swimmer entering water at race start

Date	Mintage	F	VF	XF	Unc	BU
2008 S Proof	60,000	Value: 600				
2008 Y Proof	Inc. above	Value: 600				
2008 Z Proof	Inc. above	Value: 600				

KM# 1697 150 YUAN
10.3600 g., 0.9990 Gold 0.3327 oz. AGW, 23 mm. **Subject:** 29th Summer Olympics, Beijing **Obv:** Olympics Logo **Rev:** Ancient Chinese weightlifter

Date	Mintage	F	VF	XF	Unc	BU
2008 S Proof	60,000	Value: 600				
2008 Y Proof	Inc. above	Value: 600				
2008 Z Proof	Inc. above	Value: 600				

KM# 1700 150 YUAN
10.0500 g., 0.9990 Gold 0.3228 oz. AGW, 23 mm. **Subject:** 29th Summer Olympics **Obv:** Beijing Olympic logo **Rev:** Ancient horsemaid and new logo **Note:** Issued in 2006

Date	Mintage	F	VF	XF	Unc	BU
2008 S Proof	60,000	Value: 600				
2008 Y Proof	Inc. above	Value: 600				
2008 Z Proof	Inc. above	Value: 600				

KM# 1701 150 YUAN

10.0500 g., 0.9990 Gold 0.3228 oz. AGW, 23 mm. **Subject:** 29th Summer Olympics **Obv:** Beijing Olympic logo **Rev:** Ancient archer and new logo **Note:** Issued in 2006

Date	Mintage	F	VF	XF	Unc	BU
2008 S Proof	60,000	Value: 600				
2008 Y Proof	Inc. above	Value: 600				
2008 Z Proof	Inc. above	Value: 600				

KM# 1735 150 YUAN

10.3600 g., 0.9990 Gold 0.3327 oz. AGW, 23 mm. **Obv:** Solar system **Rev:** Man walking in space

Date	Mintage	F	VF	XF	Unc	BU
2008 Proof	30,000	Value: 900				

KM# 1855 150 YUAN

10.1000 g., 0.9990 Gold 0.3244 oz. AGW **Subject:** Para Olympics

Date	Mintage	F	VF	XF	Unc	BU
2008 Proof	15,000	Value: 700				

KM# 1900 150 YUAN

10.3600 g., 0.9990 Gold 0.3327 oz. AGW, 23 mm. **Subject:** Outlaws of the Marsh, series 1 **Rev:** Multicolor

Date	Mintage	F	VF	XF	Unc	BU
2009 Proof	30,000	Value: 650				

KM# 1906 150 YUAN

10.3500 g., 0.9990 Gold 0.3324 oz. AGW **Subject:** Shanghai Expo

Date	Mintage	F	VF	XF	Unc	BU
2009 Proof	—	Value: 650				

KM# 1937 150 YUAN

10.3500 g., 0.9990 Gold 0.3324 oz. AGW **Subject:** Outlaws of the Marsh, series 2 **Rev:** Multicolor

Date	Mintage	F	VF	XF	Unc	BU
2010 Proof	35,000	Value: 650				

KM# 1941 150 YUAN

155.5500 g., 0.9990 Gold 4.9958 oz. AGW **Subject:** Shanghai World Expo, 2010

Date	Mintage	F	VF	XF	Unc	BU
2010 Proof	1,000	Value: 9,500				

KM# 1809 150 YUAN

1036.0000 g., 0.9990 Gold 33.273 oz. AGW, 23 mm. **Subject:** Chinese Literature **Rev:** Wu Yong reviewing the plan in color

Date	Mintage	F	VF	XF	Unc	BU
2011 Proof	35,000	Value: 60,000				

KM# 1387 200 YUAN

15.5519 g., 0.9990 Gold 0.4995 oz. AGW, 27 mm. **Series:** Folk fairy tails **Rev:** Multicolor heroic figure putting ax to clouds

Date	Mintage	F	VF	XF	Unc	BU
2001 Proof	8,800	Value: 1,050				

KM# 1391 200 YUAN

15.5518 g., 0.9990 Gold 0.4995 oz. AGW, 27 mm. **Subject:** Mogao Grottoes **Obv:** Eight story building **Rev:** Dancing drummer **Edge:** Reeded. **Note:** Prev. Y#1085.

Date	Mintage	F	VF	XF	Unc	BU
2001 Proof	8,800	Value: 1,050				

KM# 1393 200 YUAN

15.5518 g., 0.9990 Gold 0.4995 oz. AGW, 27 mm. **Subject:** 50th Anniversary Chinese Occupation of Tibet **Obv:** Five stars **Rev:** Denomination in flower **Edge:** Reeded **Note:** Prev. Y#1087.

Date	Mintage	F	VF	XF	Unc	BU
2001 Proof	15,000	Value: 950				

KM# 1403 200 YUAN

15.5520 g., 0.9990 Gold 0.4995 oz. AGW, 27 mm. **Subject:** Bejing opera **Rev:** Multicolor ribbon dancer

Date	Mintage	F	VF	XF	Unc	BU
2001 Proof	8,000	Value: 1,100				

KM# 1431 200 YUAN

15.5000 g., 0.9990 Gold 0.4978 oz. AGW **Subject:** Art **Rev:** Multicolor male with snake and staff **Note:** Prev. Y#1148.

Date	Mintage	F	VF	XF	Unc	BU
2002 Proof	8,800	Value: 1,050				

KM# 1434 200 YUAN

15.5500 g., 0.9990 Gold 0.4994 oz. AGW, 27 mm. **Subject:** Buddha **Note:** Prev. Y#1145.

Date	Mintage	F	VF	XF	Unc	BU
2002 Proof	8,800	Value: 1,050				

KM# 1439 200 YUAN

15.5190 g., 0.9990 Gold 0.4984 oz. AGW, 27 mm. **Subject:** Sichuan Sanxingdui relics **Obv:** Museum building **Rev:** Face mask

Date	Mintage	F	VF	XF	Unc	BU
2002 Proof	8,800	Value: 1,050				

KM# 1440 200 YUAN

15.5000 g., 0.9990 Gold 0.4978 oz. AGW **Subject:** Ceremonial Mask **Note:** Prev. Y#1149.

Date	Mintage	F	VF	XF	Unc	BU
2002 Proof	5,000	Value: 1,100				

KM# 1446 200 YUAN

15.5000 g., 0.9990 Gold 0.4978 oz. AGW **Subject:** Dream of the Red Mansion **Shape:** Octagon **Note:** Prev. Y#1147.

Date	Mintage	F	VF	XF	Unc	BU
2002 Proof	8,000	Value: 1,100				

KM# 1454 200 YUAN

15.5000 g., 0.9990 Gold 0.4978 oz. AGW **Subject:** Peking Opera **Note:** Prev. Y#1146.

Date	Mintage	F	VF	XF	Unc	BU
2002 Proof	8,000	Value: 1,050				

KM# 1456 200 YUAN

15.5190 g., 0.9990 Gold 0.4984 oz. AGW, 27 mm. **Subject:** World Expo 2010 **Rev:** Skyline

Date	Mintage	F	VF	XF	Unc	BU
2002 Proof	5,000	Value: 1,100				

KM# 1494 200 YUAN

15.5519 g., 0.9999 Gold 0.4999 oz. AGW **Subject:** Chinese Mythical Folk Tales **Note:** Prev. Y#1160.

Date	Mintage	F	VF	XF	Unc	BU
2003 Proof	8,800	Value: 1,050				

KM# 1495 200 YUAN

15.5150 g., 0.9990 Gold 0.4983 oz. AGW, 27 mm. **Subject:** Finger Sarira of Sakyanmunt **Obv:** Tall tower **Rev:** Flora design

Date	Mintage	F	VF	XF	Unc	BU
2003 Proof	12,000	Value: 950				

KM# 1504 200 YUAN

15.5519 g., 0.9999 Gold 0.4999 oz. AGW **Subject:** Pilgrimage to the West **Note:** Prev. Y#1159.

Date	Mintage	F	VF	XF	Unc	BU
2003 Proof	11,800	Value: 950				

KM# 1506 200 YUAN

15.5130 g., 0.9990 Gold 0.4982 oz. AGW, 40 mm. **Series:** Classical literature **Rev:** Multicolor blue seated female **Shape:** Hexagon

Date	Mintage	F	VF	XF	Unc	BU
2003 Proof	8,000	Value: 1,050				

KM# 1509 200 YUAN

15.5150 g., 0.9990 Gold 0.4983 oz. AGW, 27 mm. **Series:** Wulingyan Scenic Resort

Date	Mintage	F	VF	XF	Unc	BU
2003 Proof	8,000	Value: 950				

KM# 1561 200 YUAN

15.5500 g., 0.9990 Gold 0.4994 oz. AGW, 27 mm. **Obv:** Monkey King leading the Master over bridge **Rev:** Multicolor Monkey King on one knee meeting the Master **Edge:** Reeded **Note:** Prev. Y#1217.

Date	Mintage	F	VF	XF	Unc	BU
2004 Proof	11,800	Value: 950				

KM# 1564 200 YUAN

15.5600 g., 0.9990 Gold 0.4997 oz. AGW, 27 mm. **Series:** Maijishan grotto art **Rev:** Buddha statue

Date	Mintage	F	VF	XF	Unc	BU
2004 Proof	8,800	Value: 1,050				

KM# 1567 200 YUAN

15.5518 g., 0.9990 Gold 0.4995 oz. AGW, 27 mm. **Obv:** Guangan Exposition Hall **Rev:** Deng Xiaoping and value **Edge:** Reeded **Note:** Prev. Y#1241.

Date	Mintage	F	VF	XF	Unc	BU
2004 Proof	10,000	Value: 950				

KM# 1571 200 YUAN

15.5500 g., 0.9990 Gold 0.4994 oz. AGW, 27 mm. **Obv:** National arms above People's Congress Hall and ornamental column **Rev:** Multicolor hologram depicting the hall's overhead lighting **Edge:** Reeded **Note:** Prev. Y#1213.

Date	Mintage	F	VF	XF	Unc	BU
2004 Proof	5,000	Value: 1,050				

KM# 1625 200 YUAN

15.5500 g., 0.9990 Gold 0.4994 oz. AGW, 27 mm. **Subject:** 600th Anniversary of Zheng He's Voyages **Obv:** Multicolor logo **Rev:** Zheng He portrait in linear form

Date	Mintage	F	VF	XF	Unc	BU
2005 Proof	6,000	Value: 950				

KM# 1627 200 YUAN

15.5500 g., 0.9990 Gold 0.4994 oz. AGW, 27 mm. **Subject:** Chen Yun Birth Centennial **Obv:** House **Rev:** Head 3/4 right

Date	Mintage	F	VF	XF	Unc	BU
2005 Proof	5,000	Value: 1,100				

KM# 1630 200 YUAN

15.5500 g., 0.9990 Gold 0.4994 oz. AGW, 27 mm. **Subject:** 60th Anniversary of Victory - War of Resistance **Obv:** Monument **Rev:** Mob of Peoples Army

Date	Mintage	F	VF	XF	Unc	BU
2005 Proof	5,000	Value: 1,100				

KM# 1633 200 YUAN

15.5500 g., 0.9990 Gold 0.4994 oz. AGW, 27 mm. **Series:** Classical Literature **Obv:** Horseman on arch bridge **Rev:** Two multicolor women, one with monkey, other with rabbit

Date	Mintage	F	VF	XF	Unc	BU
2005 Proof	11,800	Value: 950				

KM# 1689 200 YUAN
15.5500 g., 0.9990 Gold 0.4994 oz. AGW, 27 mm. **Subject:** Yvelv Academy **Obv:** Front door of Academy **Rev:** Interior room

Date	Mintage	F	VF	XF	Unc	BU
2006 Proof	7,000	Value: 950				

KM# 1692 200 YUAN
15.5500 g., 0.9990 Gold 0.4994 oz. AGW, 27 mm. **Subject:** 70th Anniversary of Long March **Obv:** Route of the marches, hammer and sickle symbol **Rev:** Group of marchers advancing with rifles

Date	Mintage	F	VF	XF	Unc	BU
2006 Proof	10,000	Value: 950				

KM# 1862 200 YUAN
15.5700 g., 0.9990 Gold 0.5001 oz. AGW, 27 mm. **Subject:** Chinese Peoples Liberation Army, 80th Anniversary **Obv:** Three military men saluting, flag in background **Rev:** Ship, tank, plane

Date	Mintage	F	VF	XF	Unc	BU
2007 Proof	10,000	Value: 1,100				

KM# 1949 200 YUAN
15.5500 g., 0.9990 Gold 0.4994 oz. AGW **Subject:** Yungang Grotto Art

Date	Mintage	F	VF	XF	Unc	BU
2010 Proof	10,000	Value: 975				

KM# 1435 300 YUAN
1000.0000 g., 0.9990 Silver 32.117 oz. ASW, 100 mm. **Series:** Long men grottoes **Rev:** Large female statue

Date	Mintage	F	VF	XF	Unc	BU
2002 Proof	8,000	Value: 1,750				

KM# 1513 300 YUAN
1000.0000 g., 0.9990 Silver 32.117 oz. ASW, 100 mm. **Series:** Guan Yi

Date	Mintage	F	VF	XF	Unc	BU
2003 Proof	3,800	Value: 3,500				

KM# 1568 300 YUAN
1000.0000 g., 0.9990 Silver 32.117 oz. ASW, 100 mm. **Obv:** Guangan Exposition Hall **Rev:** Deng Xiaoping and value **Edge:** Reeded **Note:** Prev. Y#1242.

Date	Mintage	F	VF	XF	Unc	BU
2004 Proof	5,000	Value: 1,850				

KM# 1579 300 YUAN
1000.0000 g., 0.9990 Silver 32.117 oz. ASW, 100 mm. **Series:** Kuan Yin **Rev:** Female seated holding flower

Date	Mintage	F	VF	XF	Unc	BU
2004 Proof	3,800	Value: 2,000				

KM# 1617 300 YUAN
1000.0000 g., 0.9990 Silver 32.117 oz. ASW, 100 mm. **Subject:** 2006 World Cup - Germany **Obv:** Multicolor logo **Rev:** World Cup Trophy

Date	Mintage	F	VF	XF	Unc	BU
2005 Proof	3,000	Value: 2,250				

KM# 1634 300 YUAN
1000.0000 g., 0.9990 Silver 32.117 oz. ASW, 100 mm. **Series:** Classical Literature **Obv:** Horseman on arch bridge **Rev:** Multicolor heavenly buddha

Date	Mintage	F	VF	XF	Unc	BU
2005 Proof	5,000	Value: 2,250				

KM# 1695 300 YUAN
1000.0000 g., 0.9990 Silver 32.117 oz. ASW, 100 mm. **Subject:** 29th Summer Olympics, Beijing **Obv:** Olympics Logo **Rev:** Riding and rowing

Date	Mintage	F	VF	XF	Unc	BU
2008 Proof	20,008	Value: 2,000				

KM# 1849 300 YUAN
1000.0000 g., 0.9990 Silver 32.117 oz. ASW, 100 mm. **Subject:** Beijing Olympics **Obv:** Multicolor logo **Rev:** Classical tug of war **Note:** Photo reduced.

Date	Mintage	F	VF	XF	Unc	BU
2008 Proof	20,008	Value: 2,250				

KM# 1897 300 YUAN
1000.0000 g., 0.9990 Silver 32.117 oz. ASW, 100 mm. **Subject:** P.R.C. 60th Anniversary

Date	Mintage	F	VF	XF	Unc	BU
2009 Proof	6,000	Value: 2,100				

KM# 1950 300 YUAN
1000.0000 g., 0.9990 Silver 32.117 oz. ASW **Subject:** Yungang Grotto Art

Date	Mintage	F	VF	XF	Unc	BU
2010 Proof	3,800	Value: 2,100				

KM# 1808 300 YUAN
1000.0000 g., 0.9990 Silver 32.117 oz. ASW, 100 mm. **Subject:** Chinese Literature **Rev:** Meeting of the Heroes in the great hall in color

Date	Mintage	F	VF	XF	Unc	BU
2011 Proof	10,000	Value: 1,650				

KM# 2006 300 YUAN
1000.0000 g., 0.9990 Silver 32.117 oz. ASW, 100 mm. **Subject:** World Heritage Site **Obv:** National emblem **Rev:** Tianzhong Pavillon at the Zhongyue Temple

Date	Mintage	F	VF	XF	Unc	BU
2011 Proof	5,000	Value: 1,750				

KM# 2043 300 YUAN
1000.0000 g., 0.9990 Silver 32.117 oz. ASW, 100 mm. **Subject:** UNESCO **Rev:** Tayuan Temple

Date	Mintage	F	VF	XF	Unc	BU
2012 Proof	—	Value: 1,600				

KM# 2061 500 YUAN
31.1030 g., 0.9990 Gold 0.9989 oz. AGW, 32 mm. **Subject:** Panda, 30th Anniversary **Obv:** Temple of Heaven **Rev:** Panda

Date	Mintage	F	VF	XF	Unc	BU
2012 Proof	30,000	Value: 2,250				

KM# 1392 2000 YUAN
155.5175 g., 0.9990 Gold 4.9948 oz. AGW, 60 mm. **Subject:** Mogao Grottoes **Obv:** Eight story building **Rev:** Two dancers **Edge:** Reeded **Note:** Prev. #Y1086.

Date	Mintage	F	VF	XF	Unc	BU
2001 Proof	288	Value: 25,000				

KM# 1436 2000 YUAN
155.5175 g., 0.9990 Gold 4.9948 oz. AGW, 60 mm. **Subject:** Chinese grottos art - Longmen **Note:** Prev. #Y1151.

Date	Mintage	F	VF	XF	Unc	BU
2002	288	Value: 13,500				

KM# 1505 2000 YUAN
155.5000 g., 0.9990 Gold 4.9942 oz. AGW, 64x40 mm. **Series:** Class literature **Rev:** Two multicolor monkey kings **Shape:** Rectangle **Note:** Illustration reduced.

Date	Mintage	F	VF	XF	Unc	BU
2003 Proof	500	Value: 11,500				

KM# 1562 2000 YUAN
155.5175 g., 0.9990 Gold 4.9948 oz. AGW, 64x40 mm. **Obv:** Monkey King leading Master over bridge **Rev:** Multicolor Monkey King fighting the Pig "Demon of Bones" **Edge:** Plain **Shape:** Ingot **Note:** Prev. #Y1218. Illustration reduced.

Date	Mintage	F	VF	XF	Unc	BU
2004 Proof	500	Value: 11,500				

KM# 1565 2000 YUAN
155.5175 g., 0.9990 Gold 4.9948 oz. AGW, 60 mm. **Subject:** Maijishan Grottos **Obv:** Grotto view **Rev:** Buddha portrait within halo of flying devatas **Edge:** Reeded **Note:** Prev. #Y1206.

Date	Mintage	F	VF	XF	Unc	BU
2004(y) Proof	288	Value: 14,500				

KM# 1569 2000 YUAN
155.5175 g., 0.9990 Gold 4.9948 oz. AGW, 60 mm. **Obv:** Guangan Exposition Hall **Rev:** Deng Xiaoping and value **Edge:** Reeded **Note:** Prev. #Y1243.

Date	Mintage	F	VF	XF	Unc	BU
2004 Proof	600	Value: 13,500				

KM# 1632 2000 YUAN
155.0000 g., 0.9990 Gold 4.9782 oz. AGW, 64x40 mm. **Series:** Classic Literature Pilgrimage To The West **Obv:** Horseback rider on arch bridge **Rev:** Multicolor court scene **Shape:** Rectangle

Date	Mintage	F	VF	XF	Unc	BU
2005 Proof	500	Value: 13,500				

KM# 1698 2000 YUAN
155.5200 g., 0.9990 Gold 4.9949 oz. AGW, 60 mm. **Subject:** 29th Summer Olympics, Beijing **Obv:** Olympics Logo **Rev:** Athletics and team sports

Date	Mintage	F	VF	XF	Unc	BU
2008 Proof	2,008	Value: 9,000				

KM# 1738 2000 YUAN
155.6700 g., 0.9990 Gold 4.9997 oz. AGW, 60 mm. **Subject:** Economic Reform in China, 30th Anniversary **Rev:** Flowers and Fireworks

Date	Mintage	F	VF	XF	Unc	BU
2008 Proof	800	Value: 9,500				

KM# 1850 2000 YUAN
155.5500 g., 0.9990 Gold 4.9958 oz. AGW, 60 mm. **Subject:** Beijing Olympics **Obv:** Multicolor logo **Rev:** Four sports

Date	Mintage	F	VF	XF	Unc	BU
2008 Proof	—	Value: 16,500				

KM# 1894 2000 YUAN
155.5000 g., 0.9990 Gold 4.9942 oz. AGW, 60 mm. **Subject:** P.R.C. 60th Anniversary

Date	Mintage	F	VF	XF	Unc	BU
2009 Proof	600	Value: 12,000				

KM# 1899 2000 YUAN
155.5000 g., 0.9990 Gold 4.9942 oz. AGW, 64c40 mm. **Subject:** Outlaws of the Marsh, series 1 **Rev:** Multicolor **Shape:** Rectangle

Date	Mintage	F	VF	XF	Unc	BU
2009 Proof	800	Value: 12,000				

KM# 1936 2000 YUAN
155.5500 g., 0.9990 Gold 4.9958 oz. AGW, 64x40 mm. **Series:** Outlaws of the Marsh, series 2 **Rev:** Multicolor **Shape:** Rectangle

Date	Mintage	F	VF	XF	Unc	BU
2010 Proof	900	Value: 12,000				

KM# 1948 2000 YUAN
155.5000 g., 0.9990 Gold 4.9942 oz. AGW **Subject:** Yungang Grotto Art

Date	Mintage	F	VF	XF	Unc	BU
2010 Proof	800	Value: 12,000				

KM# 1802 2000 YUAN
155.6700 g., 0.9990 Gold 4.9997 oz. AGW, 90 mm. **Subject:** UNESCO **Rev:** Taishi Que

Date	Mintage	F	VF	XF	Unc	BU
2011 Proof	Est. 1,000	Value: 10,000				

KM# 1819 2000 YUAN
155.6700 g., 0.9990 Gold 4.9997 oz. AGW, 64x40 mm. **Subject:** Chinese Literature **Rev:** Huyan Zhuo and Guan Sheng in color

Date	Mintage	F	VF	XF	Unc	BU
2011 Proof	900	Value: 11,000				

KM# 2045 2000 YUAN
155.6700 g., 0.9990 Gold 4.9997 oz. AGW, 60 mm. **Subject:** UNESCO **Rev:** Xiantong Temple

Date	Mintage	F	VF	XF	Unc	BU
2012 Proof	3,000	Value: 11,000				

KM# 2051 2000 YUAN
155.6700 g., 0.9990 Gold 4.9997 oz. AGW, 60 mm. **Subject:** Beijing Opera Masks **Rev:** Guan Yu mask in color

Date	Mintage	F	VF	XF	Unc	BU
2012 Proof	2,000	Value: 11,000				

KM# 2056 2000 YUAN
155.6700 g., 0.9990 Gold 4.9997 oz. AGW, 40 mm. **Subject:** Bronze Age Containers **Rev:** Storrage vessel from the Shang Dynastie, Zhengzhou find

Date	Mintage	F	VF	XF	Unc	BU
2012 Proof	30,000	Value: 125				

KM# 2062 2000 YUAN
155.6700 g., 0.9990 Gold 4.9997 oz. AGW, 60 mm. **Subject:** Panda, 30th Anniversary **Obv:** Temple of Heaven **Rev:** Panda

Date	Mintage	F	VF	XF	Unc	BU
2012 Proof	3,000	Value: 11,500				

KM# 2054 3000 YUAN
1000.0000 g., 0.9990 Silver 32.117 oz. ASW, 100 mm. **Subject:** Bronze Age Vessels **Rev:** Shang Dynasty wine container

Date	Mintage	F	VF	XF	Unc	BU
2012 Proof	6,000	Value: 1,750				

KM# 1893 10000 YUAN
1000.0000 g., 0.9990 Gold 32.117 oz. AGW, 90 mm. **Subject:** P.R.C. 60th Anniversary

Date	Mintage	F	VF	XF	Unc	BU
2009 Proof	100	Value: 60,000				

KM# 1947 10000 YUAN
1000.0000 g., 0.9990 Gold 32.117 oz. AGW **Subject:** Yungang Grotto Art

Date	Mintage	F	VF	XF	Unc	BU
2010 Proof	100	Value: 60,000				

KM# 1803 10000 YUAN
1000.0000 g., 0.9990 Gold 32.117 oz. AGW, 90 mm. **Subject:** UNESCO **Rev:** Observatory

Date	Mintage	F	VF	XF	Unc	BU
2011 Proof	200	Value: 60,000				

KM# 1869 10000 YUAN
1000.0000 g., 0.9990 Gold 32.117 oz. AGW, 90 mm. **Subject:** Chinese Literature **Rev:** Meeting in the great hall in color

Date	Mintage	F	VF	XF	Unc	BU
2011 Proof	200	Value: 60,000				

KM# 2046 10000 YUAN
1000.0000 g., 0.9990 Gold 32.117 oz. AGW, 90 mm. **Subject:** UNESCO **Rev:** Foguang Temple

Date	Mintage	F	VF	XF	Unc	BU
2012 Proof	300	Value: 60,000				

KM# 1851 100000 YUAN
10000.0000 g., 0.9990 Gold 321.17 oz. AGW, 180 mm. **Subject:** Beijing Olympics **Obv:** Multicolor logo **Rev:** Sports montage, Temple of Heaven

Date	Mintage	F	VF	XF	Unc	BU
2008 Proof	29	Value: 650,000				

SILVER BULLION COINAGE

Lunar Series

KM# 1379 10 YUAN
30.8400 g., 0.9990 Silver 0.9905 oz. ASW, 39.9 mm. **Subject:** Year of the Snake **Obv:** Traditional style building **Rev:** Snake **Shape:** Scalloped **Note:** Prev. Y#1041.

Date	Mintage	F	VF	XF	Unc	BU
2001 Proof	6,800	Value: 165				

KM# 1382 10 YUAN
31.1035 g., 0.9990 Silver 0.9990 oz. ASW **Subject:** Year of the Snake **Shape:** Fan-like **Note:** Prev. Y#1042.

Date	Mintage	F	VF	XF	Unc	BU
2001	66,000	—	—	—	100	115

KM# 1375 10 YUAN
31.1035 g., 0.9990 Silver 0.9990 oz. ASW, 40 mm. **Subject:** Year of the Snake **Rev:** Multicolor

Date	Mintage	F	VF	XF	Unc	BU
2001 Proof	6,800	Value: 150				

KM# 1418 10 YUAN
31.1035 g., 0.9990 Silver 0.9990 oz. ASW, 40 mm. **Subject:** Year of the Horse **Obv:** Da Zheng Hall **Rev:** Stylized horse head **Edge:** Reeded **Note:** Prev. Y#1232.

Date	Mintage	F	VF	XF	Unc	BU
2002	50,000	—	—	—	—	140

KM# 1414 10 YUAN
31.1035 g., 0.9990 Silver 0.9990 oz. ASW, 40 mm. **Subject:** Year of the Horse **Rev:** Multicolor horse prancing right

Date	Mintage	F	VF	XF	Unc	BU
2002 Proof	10,000	Value: 150				

KM# 1423 10 YUAN
31.1035 g., 0.9990 Silver 0.9990 oz. ASW, 40 mm. **Subject:** Year of the Horse **Shape:** Fan-like

Date	Mintage	F	VF	XF	Unc	BU
2002 Proof	50,000	Value: 175				

KM# 1425 10 YUAN
31.1035 g., 0.9990 Silver 0.9990 oz. ASW, 40 mm. **Subject:** Year of the Horse **Shape:** Scalloped

Date	Mintage	F	VF	XF	Unc	BU
2002 Proof	6,800	Value: 400				

KM# A1477 10 YUAN
31.1035 g., 0.9990 Silver 0.9990 oz. ASW, 40 mm. **Subject:** Year of the Sheep

Date	Mintage	F	VF	XF	Unc	BU
2003 Proof	66,000	Value: 150				

KM# 1477 10 YUAN
31.1035 g., 0.9990 Silver 0.9990 oz. ASW, 40 mm. **Subject:** Year of the Sheep **Rev:** Multicolor

Date	Mintage	F	VF	XF	Unc	BU
2003 Proof	6,800	Value: 150				

KM# 1480 10 YUAN
31.1035 g., 0.9990 Silver 0.9990 oz. ASW, 40 mm. **Subject:** Year of the sheep **Shape:** Scalloped

Date	Mintage	F	VF	XF	Unc	BU
2003 Proof	50,000	Value: 70.00				

KM# 1485 10 YUAN
31.1035 g., 0.9990 Silver 0.9990 oz. ASW, 30 x 85 mm. **Subject:** Year of the Sheep **Shape:** Fan-like

Date	Mintage	F	VF	XF	Unc	BU
2003 Proof	66,000	Value: 175				

KM# A1545 10 YUAN
31.1035 g., 0.9990 Silver 0.9990 oz. ASW, 40 mm. **Series:** Lunar New Year **Subject:** Year of the Monkey **Rev:** Multicolor monkey

Date	Mintage	F	VF	XF	Unc	BU
2004 Proof	—	Value: 150				

KM# 1545 10 YUAN
31.1035 g., 0.9990 Silver 0.9990 oz. ASW, 40 mm. **Series:** Lunar New Year **Subject:** Year of the Monkey

Date	Mintage	F	VF	XF	Unc	BU
2004 Proof	80,000	Value: 150				

KM# 1548 10 YUAN
31.1035 g., 0.9990 Silver 0.9990 oz. ASW, 40 mm. **Subject:** Lunar New Year **Rev:** Monkey **Shape:** Scalloped

Date	Mintage	F	VF	XF	Unc	BU
2004 Proof	6,800	Value: 190				

KM# 1553 10 YUAN
31.1035 g., 0.9990 Silver 0.9990 oz. ASW, 30 x 85 mm. **Series:** Lunar New Year **Subject:** Year of the Monkey **Rev:** Monkey **Shape:** Fan-like

Date	Mintage	F	VF	XF	Unc	BU
2004 Proof	66,000	Value: 175				

KM# 1612 10 YUAN
31.1050 g., 0.9990 Silver 0.9990 oz. ASW, 40 mm. **Subject:** Year of the rooster **Obv:** Classical rooster **Rev:** Multicolor rooster

Date	Mintage	F	VF	XF	Unc	BU
2005 Proof	100,000	Value: 190				

KM# 1613 10 YUAN
31.1050 g., 0.9990 Silver 0.9990 oz. ASW, 40 mm. **Subject:** Year of the rooster **Obv:** Classical rooster **Rev:** Rooster, hen and chicks **Shape:** Scallop

Date	Mintage	F	VF	XF	Unc	BU
2005 Proof	60,000	Value: 125				

KM# 1614 10 YUAN
31.1050 g., 0.9990 Silver 0.9990 oz. ASW, 40 mm. **Subject:** Year of the rooster **Obv:** Classical rooster **Rev:** Rooster, hen and chicks

Date	Mintage	F	VF	XF	Unc	BU
2005 Proof	8,000	Value: 150				

KM# 1615 10 YUAN

31.1050 g., 0.9990 Silver 0.9990 oz. ASW, 30 x 85 mm. **Subject:** Year of the rooster **Obv:** Temple **Rev:** Rooster, hen and chicks **Shape:** Fan-like **Note:** Photo reduced.

Date	Mintage	F	VF	XF	Unc	BU
2005 Proof	66,000	Value: 190				

KM# 1684 10 YUAN

31.1035 g., 0.9990 Silver 0.9990 oz. ASW, 40 mm. **Obv:** Dog-shaped belt-hook from ancient Chinese bronze ware, decorative design of dog tail-shaped plant leaves **Rev:** 2 smart dogs **Note:** Prev. Y#1225; 1657.

Date	Mintage	F	VF	XF	Unc	BU
2006	80,000	—	—	—	—	125

KM# 1685 10 YUAN

31.1035 g., 0.9990 Silver 0.9990 oz. ASW, 40 mm. **Obv:** Dog-shaped belt-hook depicted from ancient Chinese bronze ware and a decorative design of dog tail-shaped plant leaves **Rev:** 2 smart dogs **Shape:** Scalloped **Note:** Prev. Y#1223; KM#1655.

Date	Mintage	F	VF	XF	Unc	BU
2006 Proof	60,000	Value: 140				

KM# 1686 10 YUAN

31.1035 g., 0.9990 Silver 0.9990 oz. ASW **Obv:** Qing Yuan Gate of the China Great Wall **Rev:** 2 dogs at play **Shape:** Fan-like **Note:** Prev. Y#1219; KM#1651. Photo reduced.

Date	Mintage	F	VF	XF	Unc	BU
2006 Proof	66,000	Value: 165				

KM# 1687 10 YUAN

31.1035 g., 0.9990 Silver 0.9990 oz. ASW, 40 mm. **Obv:** Belt-hook in dog shape from Chinese ancient bronze ware and a decorative design of dog tail-shaped plant leaves **Rev:** 2 dogs at play **Note:** Prev. Y#1221; KM#1653.

Date	Mintage	F	VF	XF	Unc	BU
2006 Proof	100,000	Value: 125				

KM# 1716 10 YUAN

31.1050 g., 0.9990 Silver 0.9990 oz. ASW, 40 mm. **Subject:** Year of the Pig **Obv:** Classical pig **Rev:** Pig walking right

Date	Mintage	F	VF	XF	Unc	BU
2007 Proof	80,000	Value: 140				

KM# 1717 10 YUAN

31.1050 g., 0.9990 Silver 0.9990 oz. ASW, 40 mm. **Subject:** Year of the Pig **Obv:** Classical pig **Rev:** Multicolor sow and four piglets sucking

Date	Mintage	F	VF	XF	Unc	BU
2007 Proof	100,000	Value: 125				

KM# 1718 10 YUAN

31.1050 g., 0.9990 Silver 0.9990 oz. ASW, 85 x 60 mm. **Subject:** Year of the Pig **Obv:** Temple **Rev:** Sow and four piglets **Shape:** Fan-like

Date	Mintage	F	VF	XF	Unc	BU
2007 Proof	66,000	Value: 190				

KM# 1719 10 YUAN

31.1050 g., 0.9990 Silver 0.9990 oz. ASW, 40 mm. **Subject:** Year of the Pig **Obv:** Classical pig **Rev:** Pig walking right **Shape:** Scalloped

Date	Mintage	F	VF	XF	Unc	BU
2007 Proof	60,000	Value: 140				

KM# 1830 10 YUAN

31.1050 g., 0.9990 Silver 0.9990 oz. ASW, 40 mm. **Rev:** Multicolor

Date	Mintage	F	VF	XF	Unc	BU
2008 Proof	—	Value: 55.00				

KM# 1831 10 YUAN

31.1050 g., 0.9990 Silver 0.9990 oz. ASW, 40 mm. **Subject:** Year of the Rat

Date	Mintage	F	VF	XF	Unc	BU
2008 Proof	—	Value: 140				

KM# 1832 10 YUAN

31.1050 g., 0.9990 Silver 0.9990 oz. ASW, 40 mm. **Subject:** Year of the Rat **Shape:** Scallop

Date	Mintage	F	VF	XF	Unc	BU
2008 Proof	—	Value: 140				

KM# 1833 10 YUAN

31.1050 g., 0.9990 Silver 0.9990 oz. ASW, 85 x 60 mm. **Subject:** Year of the Rat **Shape:** Fan-like

Date	Mintage	F	VF	XF	Unc	BU
2008 Proof	—	Value: 190				

KM# 1875 10 YUAN

31.1050 g., 0.9990 Silver 0.9990 oz. ASW, 40 mm. **Rev:** Multicolor

Date	Mintage	F	VF	XF	Unc	BU
2009 Proof	—	Value: 125				

KM# 1876 10 YUAN

31.1050 g., 0.9990 Silver 0.9990 oz. ASW, 40 mm. **Subject:** Year of the Ox

Date	Mintage	F	VF	XF	Unc	BU
2009 Proof	100,000	Value: 125				

KM# 1877 10 YUAN

31.1050 g., 0.9990 Silver 0.9990 oz. ASW **Subject:** Year of the Ox

Date	Mintage	F	VF	XF	Unc	BU
2009 Proof	66,000	Value: 140				

KM# 1878 10 YUAN

31.1050 g., 0.9990 Silver 0.9990 oz. ASW **Shape:** Fan-like

Date	Mintage	F	VF	XF	Unc	BU
2009 Proof	66,000	Value: 190				

KM# 1922 10 YUAN

31.1050 g., 0.9990 Silver 0.9990 oz. ASW **Subject:** Year of the Tiger **Shape:** Arc

Date	Mintage	F	VF	XF	Unc	BU
2010	66,000	—	—	—	—	100

KM# 1923 10 YUAN

31.1050 g., 0.9990 Silver 0.9990 oz. ASW **Subject:** Year of the Tiger **Shape:** Scalloped

Date	Mintage	F	VF	XF	Unc	BU
2010 Proof	60,000	Value: 100				

KM# 1924 10 YUAN

31.1050 g., 0.9990 Silver 0.9990 oz. ASW **Subject:** Year of the Tiger

Date	Mintage	F	VF	XF	Unc	BU
2010 Proof	100,000	Value: 100				

KM# 1925 10 YUAN

31.1050 g., 0.9990 Silver 0.9990 oz. ASW **Subject:** Year of the Tiger **Rev:** Multicolor

Date	Mintage	F	VF	XF	Unc	BU
2010 Proof	100,000	Value: 125				

KM# 1971 10 YUAN

31.1050 g., 0.9990 Silver 0.9990 oz. ASW **Subject:** Year of the Rabbit **Shape:** Arc

Date	Mintage	F	VF	XF	Unc	BU
2011	66,000	—	—	—	—	100

KM# 1972 10 YUAN

31.1050 g., 0.9990 Silver 0.9990 oz. ASW **Subject:** Year of the Rabbit **Shape:** Scalloped

Date	Mintage	F	VF	XF	Unc	BU
2011 Proof	60,000	Value: 100				

KM# 1973 10 YUAN

31.1050 g., 0.9990 Silver 0.9990 oz. ASW, 40 mm. **Subject:** Year of the Rabbit

Date	Mintage	F	VF	XF	Unc	BU
2011 Proof	100,000	Value: 100				

KM# 1974 10 YUAN
31.1050 g., 0.9990 Silver 0.9990 oz. ASW **Subject:** Year of the Rabbit **Rev:** Multicolor

Date	Mintage	F	VF	XF	Unc	BU
2011 Proof	100,000	Value: 100				

KM# 2020 10 YUAN
31.1050 g., 0.9990 Silver 0.9990 oz. ASW **Subject:** Year of the Dragon **Shape:** Fan

Date	Mintage	F	VF	XF	Unc	BU
2012 Proof	—	Value: 125				

KM# 2021 10 YUAN
31.1050 g., 0.9990 Silver 0.9990 oz. ASW, 40 mm. **Subject:** Year of the Dragon **Shape:** Scalloped

Date	Mintage	F	VF	XF	Unc	BU
2012 proof	—	Value: 100				

KM# 2022 10 YUAN
31.1050 g., 0.9990 Silver 0.9990 oz. ASW, 40 mm. **Subject:** Year of the Dragon

Date	Mintage	F	VF	XF	Unc	BU
2012 Proof	—	Value: 65.00				

KM# 2023 10 YUAN
31.1050 g., 0.9990 Silver 0.9990 oz. ASW **Subject:** Year of the Dragon **Rev:** Colored dragon

Date	Mintage	F	VF	XF	Unc	BU
2012 Proof	—	Value: 100				

KM# 1377 50 YUAN
155.4400 g., 0.9990 Silver 4.9923 oz. ASW, 80.6 x 50.5 mm. **Subject:** Year of the Snake **Obv:** Traditional style building **Rev:** Snake **Edge:** Plain **Shape:** Rectangle **Note:** Illustration reduced. Prev. Y#1040.

Date	Mintage	F	VF	XF	Unc	BU
2001 Proof	1,888	Value: 1,250				

KM# 1421 50 YUAN
155.5190 g., 0.9990 Silver 4.9948 oz. ASW, 80 x 50 mm. **Subject:** Year of the Horse **Rev:** Three horses running left **Shape:** Rectangle

Date	Mintage	F	VF	XF	Unc	BU
2002 Proof	1,888	Value: 2,000				

KM# 1484 50 YUAN
155.5000 g., 0.9990 Silver 4.9942 oz. ASW, 80 x 50 mm. **Subject:** Year of the Sheep **Shape:** Rectangle

Date	Mintage	F	VF	XF	Unc	BU
2003 Proof	1,888	Value: 1,250				

KM# 1551 50 YUAN
155.5000 g., 0.9990 Silver 4.9942 oz. ASW, 80 x 50 mm. **Series:** Lunar New Year **Subject:** Year of the Monkey **Rev:** Monkey **Shape:** Rectangle **Note:** Photo reduced.

Date	Mintage	F	VF	XF	Unc	BU
2004 Proof	1,888	Value: 1,250				

KM# 1611 50 YUAN
155.0000 g., 0.9990 Silver 4.9782 oz. ASW, 80 x 50 mm. **Subject:** Year of the Rooster **Obv:** Classical rooster **Rev:** Rooster, hen and chicks **Shape:** Rectangle **Note:** Photo reduced.

Date	Mintage	F	VF	XF	Unc	BU
2005 Proof	1,888	Value: 1,250				

KM# 1683 50 YUAN
155.4400 g., 0.9990 Silver 4.9923 oz. ASW, 60 x 50 mm. **Subject:** Year of the Dog **Obv:** Classical dog **Rev:** Two dogs **Shape:** Rectangle **Note:** Photo reduced.

Date	Mintage	F	VF	XF	Unc	BU
2006 Proof	1,888	Value: 1,250				

KM# 1720 50 YUAN
155.5500 g., 0.9990 Silver 4.9958 oz. ASW, 80 x 50 mm. **Subject:** Year of the Pig **Obv:** Classical pig **Rev:** Sow and four piglets **Shape:** Rectangle

Date	Mintage	F	VF	XF	Unc	BU
2007 Proof	1,888	Value: 1,250				

KM# 1834 50 YUAN
155.5000 g., 0.9990 Silver 4.9942 oz. ASW, 80 x 50 mm. **Subject:** Year of the Rat **Shape:** Rectangle

Date	Mintage	F	VF	XF	Unc	BU
2008 Proof	—	Value: 1,250				

KM# 1879 50 YUAN
Silver **Subject:** Year of the Ox

Date	Mintage	F	VF	XF	Unc	BU
2009 Proof	1,888	Value: 1,250				

KM# 1920 50 YUAN
155.5000 g., 0.9990 Silver 4.9942 oz. ASW **Subject:** Year of the Tiger **Shape:** Rectangle

Date	Mintage	F	VF	XF	Unc	BU
2010 Proof	1,888	Value: 1,250				

KM# 1921 50 YUAN
155.5000 g., 0.9990 Silver 4.9942 oz. ASW **Subject:** Year of the Tiger

Date	Mintage	F	VF	XF	Unc	BU
2010 Proof	8,800	Value: 850				

KM# 1969 50 YUAN
155.5000 g., 0.9990 Silver 4.9942 oz. ASW, 80x50 mm. **Subject:** Year of the Rabbit **Shape:** Rectangle **Note:** Photo reduced.

Date	Mintage	F	VF	XF	Unc	BU
2011 Proof	1,888	Value: 1,250				

KM# 1970 50 YUAN
155.5000 g., 0.9990 Silver 4.9942 oz. ASW **Subject:** Year of the Rabbit **Rev:** Multicolor

Date	Mintage	F	VF	XF	Unc	BU
2011 Proof	8,800	Value: 750				

KM# 2018 50 YUAN
155.5500 g., 0.9990 Silver 4.9958 oz. ASW, 80x50 mm. **Subject:** Year of the Dragon **Shape:** Rectangle

Date	Mintage	F	VF	XF	Unc	BU
2012 Proof	—	Value: 850				

KM# 2019 50 YUAN
155.5500 g., 0.9990 Silver 4.9958 oz. ASW **Subject:** Year of the Dragon **Rev:** Colored dragon

Date	Mintage	F	VF	XF	Unc	BU
2012 proof	—	Value: 750				

KM# 1420 300 YUAN
1000.0000 g., 0.9990 Silver 32.117 oz. ASW, 100 mm. **Series:** Lunar **Subject:** Year of the Horse

Date	Mintage	F	VF	XF	Unc	BU
2002 Proof	3,800	Value: 6,500				

KM# 1479 300 YUAN
1000.0000 g., 0.9990 Silver 32.117 oz. ASW, 100 mm. **Subject:** Year of the Sheep

Date	Mintage	F	VF	XF	Unc	BU
2003 Proof	3,800	Value: 7,500				

KM# 1547 300 YUAN
1000.0000 g., 0.9990 Silver 32.117 oz. ASW, 100 mm. **Series:** Lunar New Year **Subject:** Year of the Monkey **Rev:** Monkey

Date	Mintage	F	VF	XF	Unc	BU
2004 Proof	3,800	Value: 9,000				

KM# 1610 300 YUAN
1000.0000 g., 0.9990 Silver 32.117 oz. ASW, 100 mm. **Subject:** Year of the Rooster **Obv:** Classical rooster **Rev:** Rooster strutting **Note:** Photo reduced.

Date	Mintage	F	VF	XF	Unc	BU
2005 Proof	3,800	Value: 5,000				

KM# 1682 300 YUAN
1000.0000 g., 0.9990 Silver 32.117 oz. ASW, 100 mm. **Obv:** Dog-shaped belt-hook from ancient Chinese bronze ware, decorative design of dog tail-shaped plant leaves **Rev:** 2 dogs **Note:** Prev. Y#1227; KM#1659. Photo reduced.

Date	Mintage	F	VF	XF	Unc	BU
2006 Proof	3,800	Value: 4,500				

KM# 1725 300 YUAN
1000.0000 g., 0.9990 Silver 32.117 oz. ASW, 100 mm. **Subject:** Year of the Pig **Obv:** Classical pig **Rev:** Three pigs

Date	Mintage	F	VF	XF	Unc	BU
2007 Proof	3,800	Value: 5,000				

KM# 1839 300 YUAN
1000.0000 g., 0.9990 Silver 32.117 oz. ASW, 100 mm. **Subject:** Year of the Rat

Date	Mintage	F	VF	XF	Unc	BU
2008 Proof	—	Value: 5,000				

KM# 1884 300 YUAN
1000.0000 g., 0.9990 Silver 32.117 oz. ASW **Subject:** Year of the Ox

Date	Mintage	F	VF	XF	Unc	BU
2009 Proof	3,800	Value: 5,000				

KM# 1919 300 YUAN
1000.0000 g., 0.9990 Silver 32.117 oz. ASW **Subject:** Year of the Tiger

Date	Mintage	F	VF	XF	Unc	BU
2010 Proof	3,800	Value: 4,500				

KM# 1968 300 YUAN
1000.0000 g., 0.9990 Silver 32.117 oz. ASW, 100 mm. **Subject:** Year of the Rabbit **Note:** Photo reduced.

Date	Mintage	F	VF	XF	Unc	BU
2011 Proof	1,888	Value: 4,500				

KM# 2017 300 YUAN
1000.0000 g., 0.9990 Silver 32.117 oz. ASW, 100 mm. **Subject:** Year of the Dragon

Date	Mintage	F	VF	XF	Unc	BU
2012 Proof	—	Value: 1,250				

SILVER BULLION COINAGE

Panda Series

KM# 1772 3 YUAN
7.7700 g., 0.9990 Silver 0.2496 oz. ASW, 25 mm. **Obv:** Temple of Heaven **Rev:** Panda seated on rock

Date	Mintage	F	VF	XF	Unc	BU
2007 Proof	30,000	Value: 30.00				

KM# 1780 3 YUAN
7.7700 g., 0.9990 Silver 0.2496 oz. ASW, 25 mm. **Obv:** Temple of Heaven **Rev:** Panda looking forward

Date	Mintage	F	VF	XF	Unc	BU
2007 Proof	30,000	Value: 30.00				

KM# 1740 3 YUAN
7.7700 g., 0.9990 Silver 0.2496 oz. ASW, 25 mm. **Obv:** Temple of Heaven **Rev:** Panda seated with branch

Date	Mintage	F	VF	XF	Unc	BU
2007 Proof	30,000	Value: 30.00				

KM# 1742 3 YUAN
7.7700 g., 0.9990 Silver 0.2496 oz. ASW, 25 mm. **Obv:** Temple of Heaven **Rev:** Panda walking right

Date	Mintage	F	VF	XF	Unc	BU
2007 Proof	30,000	Value: 30.00				

KM# 1744 3 YUAN
7.7700 g., 0.9990 Silver 0.2496 oz. ASW, 25 mm. **Obv:** Temple of Heaven **Rev:** Panda seated with bamboo branch

Date	Mintage	F	VF	XF	Unc	BU
2007 Proof	30,000	Value: 30.00				

KM# 1746 3 YUAN
7.7700 g., 0.9990 Silver 0.2496 oz. ASW **Obv:** Temple of Heaven **Rev:** Panda hanging from branch

Date	Mintage	F	VF	XF	Unc	BU
2007 Proof	30,000	Value: 30.00				

KM# 1748 3 YUAN
7.7700 g., 0.9990 Silver 0.2496 oz. ASW, 25 mm. **Obv:** Temple of Heaven **Rev:** Panda walking forward

Date	Mintage	F	VF	XF	Unc	BU
2007 Proof	30,000	Value: 30.00				

KM# 1750 3 YUAN
7.7700 g., 0.9990 Silver 0.2496 oz. ASW, 25 mm. **Obv:** Temple of Heaven **Rev:** Panda drinking water

Date	Mintage	F	VF	XF	Unc	BU
2007 Proof	30,000	Value: 30.00				

KM# 1752 3 YUAN
7.7700 g., 0.9990 Silver 0.2496 oz. ASW, 25 mm. **Obv:** Tample of Heaven **Rev:** Panda seated in oval with branch

Date	Mintage	F	VF	XF	Unc	BU
2007 Proof	30,000	Value: 30.00				

KM# 1754 3 YUAN
7.7700 g., 0.9990 Silver 0.2496 oz. ASW, 25 mm. **Obv:** Temple of Heaven **Rev:** Panda seated on geometric background

Date	Mintage	F	VF	XF	Unc	BU
2007 Proof	30,000	Value: 30.00				

KM# 1756 3 YUAN
7.7700 g., 0.9990 Silver 0.2496 oz. ASW, 10 mm. **Obv:** Temple of Heaven **Rev:** Panda on rock

Date	Mintage	F	VF	XF	Unc	BU
2007 Proof	30,000	Value: 30.00				

KM# 1758 3 YUAN
7.7700 g., 0.9990 Silver 0.2496 oz. ASW, 25 mm. **Obv:** Temple of Heaven **Rev:** Panda seated on river bank

Date	Mintage	F	VF	XF	Unc	BU
2007 Proof	30,000	Value: 30.00				

KM# 1760 3 YUAN
7.7700 g., 0.9990 Silver 0.2496 oz. ASW, 25 mm. **Obv:** Temple of Heaven **Rev:** Panda on tree branch

Date	Mintage	F	VF	XF	Unc	BU
2007 Proof	30,000	Value: 30.00				

KM# 1762 3 YUAN
7.7700 g., 0.9990 Silver 0.2496 oz. ASW, 25 mm. **Obv:** Temple of Heaven **Rev:** Panda on rock ledge

Date	Mintage	F	VF	XF	Unc	BU
2007 Proof	30,000	Value: 30.00				

KM# 1764 3 YUAN
7.7700 g., 0.9990 Silver 0.2496 oz. ASW, 25 mm. **Obv:** Temple of Heaven **Rev:** Panda seated munching bamboo

Date	Mintage	F	VF	XF	Unc	BU
2007 Proof	30,000	Value: 30.00				

KM# 1766 3 YUAN
7.7700 g., 0.9990 Silver 0.2496 oz. ASW, 25 mm. **Obv:** Temple of Heaven **Rev:** Panda pulling bamboo

Date	Mintage	F	VF	XF	Unc	BU
2007 Proof	30,000	Value: 30.00				

KM# 1768 3 YUAN
7.7700 g., 0.9990 Silver 0.2496 oz. ASW, 25 mm. **Obv:** Temple of Heaven **Rev:** Panda in tree

Date	Mintage	F	VF	XF	Unc	BU
2007 Proof	30,000	Value: 30.00				

KM# 1770 3 YUAN
7.7700 g., 0.9990 Silver 0.2496 oz. ASW, 25 mm. **Obv:** Temple of Heaven **Rev:** Panda looking over branch

Date	Mintage	F	VF	XF	Unc	BU
2007 Proof	30,000	Value: 30.00				

KM# 1774 3 YUAN
7.7700 g., 0.9990 Silver 0.2496 oz. ASW, 25 mm. **Obv:** Temple of Heaven **Rev:** Panda looking out over rock

Date	Mintage	F	VF	XF	Unc	BU
2007 Proof	30,000	Value: 30.00				

KM# A1776 3 YUAN
7.7700 g., 0.9990 Silver 0.2496 oz. ASW, 25 mm. **Obv:** Temple of Heaven **Rev:** Panda seated on frosted background

Date	Mintage	F	VF	XF	Unc	BU
2007 Proof	30,000	Value: 30.00				

KM# 1778 3 YUAN
7.7700 g., 0.9990 Silver 0.2496 oz. ASW, 25 mm. **Obv:** Temple of Heaven **Rev:** Panda walking amongst bamboo

Date	Mintage	F	VF	XF	Unc	BU
2007 Proof	30,000	Value: 30.00				

KM# 1782 3 YUAN
7.7700 g., 0.9990 Silver 0.2496 oz. ASW, 25 mm. **Obv:** Temple of Heaven **Rev:** Panda and cub walking right

Date	Mintage	F	VF	XF	Unc	BU
2007 Proof	30,000	Value: 30.00				

KM# 1784 3 YUAN
7.7700 g., 0.9990 Silver 0.2496 oz. ASW, 25 mm. **Obv:** Temple of Heaven **Rev:** Panda seated with cub on left

Date	Mintage	F	VF	XF	Unc	BU
2007 Proof	30,000	Value: 30.00				

KM# 1786 3 YUAN
7.7700 g., 0.9990 Silver 0.2496 oz. ASW, 25 mm. **Obv:** Temple of Heaven **Rev:** Panda seated with cub on right

Date	Mintage	F	VF	XF	Unc	BU
2007 Proof	30,000	Value: 30.00				

KM# 1788 3 YUAN
7.7700 g., 0.9990 Silver 0.2496 oz. ASW, 25 mm. **Obv:** Temple of Heaven **Rev:** Panda seated with cub, both munching bamboo

Date	Mintage	F	VF	XF	Unc	BU
2007 Proof	30,000	Value: 30.00				

KM# 1365 10 YUAN
31.1035 g., 0.9990 Silver 0.9990 oz. ASW, 40.1 mm. **Obv:** Temple of Heaven with incuse legend **Rev:** Panda walking left through bamboo **Edge:** Oblique reeding **Note:** Large and small date varieties exist. Prev. Y#1111.

Date	Mintage	F	VF	XF	Unc	BU
2001	250,000	—	—	—	50.00	45.00
2001 D Proof	—	Value: 75.00				
2002 Proof	—	Value: 75.00				

KM# A1365 10 YUAN
31.2300 g., 0.9990 Silver 1.0030 oz. ASW, 40 mm. **Obv:** Temple of Heaven, incuse legend **Rev:** Multicolor panda walking in bamboo **Edge:** Slanted reeding **Note:** Large and small date varieties exist.

Date	Mintage	F	VF	XF	Unc	BU
2002 Proof	—	Value: 90.00				

Note: Privately colored

KM# 1466 10 YUAN
31.1035 g., 0.9990 Silver 0.9990 oz. ASW, 40 mm. **Obv:** Temple of Heaven **Rev:** Panda eating bamboo in a frosted circle **Edge:** Slant reeded **Note:** Prev. Y#1244.

Date	Mintage	F	VF	XF	Unc	BU
2003 Proof	—	Value: 90.00				

KM# 1528 10 YUAN
31.1035 g., 0.9990 Silver 0.9990 oz. ASW, 40 mm. **Obv:** Temple of Heaven **Rev:** Panda nuzzling her cub **Edge:** Slant reeded **Note:** Prev. Y#1245.

Date	Mintage	F	VF	XF	Unc	BU
2004 Proof	—	Value: 90.00				

KM# 1589 10 YUAN
31.1050 g., 0.9990 Silver 0.9990 oz. ASW, 40 mm. **Obv:** Temple of Heaven **Rev:** Panda cub and mom seated in bamboo

Date	Mintage	F	VF	XF	Unc	BU
2005 Proof	60,000	Value: 90.00				

KM# 1664 10 YUAN
31.1050 g., 0.9990 Silver 0.9990 oz. ASW, 40 mm. **Obv:** Temple of Heaven **Rev:** Two pandas seated with bamboo

Date	Mintage	F	VF	XF	Unc	BU
2006 Proof	600,000	Value: 75.00				

KM# 1706 10 YUAN
31.1050 g., 0.9990 Silver 0.9990 oz. ASW, 40 mm. **Obv:** Temple of Heaven **Rev:** Two pandas, one walking, one seated

Date	Mintage	F	VF	XF	Unc	BU
2007 Proof	600,000	Value: 75.00				

KM# 1865 10 YUAN
31.1050 g., 0.9990 Silver 0.9990 oz. ASW, 40 mm. **Obv:** Temple of Heaven **Rev:** Adult panda at left, facing left, cub on right facing left, cub seated

Date	Mintage	F	VF	XF	Unc	BU
2008 Proof	—	Value: 60.00				

KM# 1814 10 YUAN
31.1050 g., 0.9990 Silver 0.9990 oz. ASW, 40 mm. **Rev:** Panda cub pawing mom

Date	Mintage	F	VF	XF	Unc	BU
2008 Proof	—	Value: 60.00				

KM# 1931 10 YUAN
31.1050 g., 0.9990 Silver 0.9990 oz. ASW, 40 mm. **Obv:** Temple of Heaven **Rev:** Two pandas, one lying on back

Date	Mintage	F	VF	XF	Unc	BU
2010	800,000	—	—	—	—	60.00

KM# 1980 10 YUAN
31.1050 g., 0.9990 Silver 0.9990 oz. ASW, 40 mm.

Date	Mintage	F	VF	XF	Unc	BU
2011	—	—	—	—	—	45.00

KM# 2029 10 YUAN
31.1050 g., 0.9990 Silver 0.9990 oz. ASW, 40 mm.

Date	Mintage	F	VF	XF	Unc	BU
2012	—	—	—	—	—	50.00

KM# 1468 50 YUAN
151.5000 g., 0.9990 Silver 4.8658 oz. ASW, 80 x 50 mm. **Shape:** Rectangle

Date	Mintage	F	VF	XF	Unc	BU
2003 Proof	1,888	Value: 1,150				

KM# 1530 50 YUAN
155.5000 g., 0.9990 Silver 4.9942 oz. ASW, 70 mm. **Rev:** Panda walking with cub **Note:** Illustration reduced.

Date	Mintage	F	VF	XF	Unc	BU
2004 Proof	10,000	Value: 600				

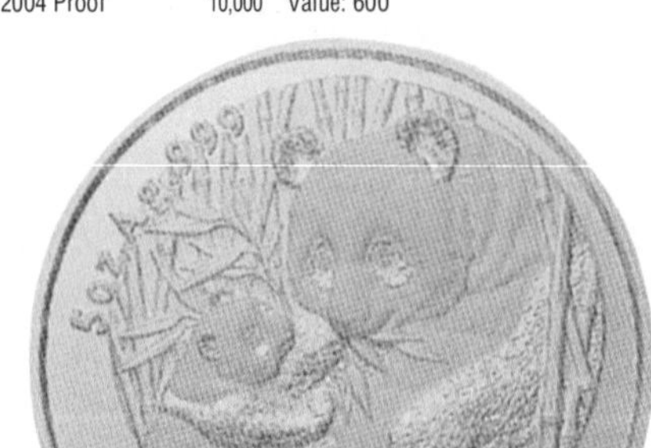

KM# 1588 50 YUAN
155.0000 g., 0.9990 Silver 4.9782 oz. ASW, 70 mm. **Obv:** Temple of Heaven **Rev:** Panda cub and mom seated in bamboo

Date	Mintage	F	VF	XF	Unc	BU
2005 Proof	10,000	Value: 550				

KM# 1663 50 YUAN
155.5500 g., 0.9990 Silver 4.9958 oz. ASW, 70 mm. **Obv:** Temple of Heaven **Rev:** Two pandas seated with bamboo

Date	Mintage	F	VF	XF	Unc	BU
2006 Proof	10,000	Value: 550				

KM# 1708 50 YUAN
155.5500 g., 0.9990 Silver 4.9958 oz. ASW, 70 mm. **Obv:** Temple of Heaven **Rev:** Two pandas, one walking, one seated

Date	Mintage	F	VF	XF	Unc	BU
2007 Proof	10,000	Value: 550				

KM# 1867 50 YUAN
155.5000 g., 0.9990 Silver 4.9942 oz. ASW

Date	Mintage	F	VF	XF	Unc	BU
2008 Proof	—	Value: 550				

KM# 1816 50 YUAN
155.5000 g., Silver, 70 mm. **Rev:** Panda cub pawing mom

Date	Mintage	F	VF	XF	Unc	BU
2008 Proof	—	Value: 550				

KM# 1935 50 YUAN
155.5500 g., 0.9990 Silver 4.9958 oz. ASW **Obv:** Temple of Heaven **Rev:** Two pandas, one lying on back

Date	Mintage	F	VF	XF	Unc	BU
2010 Proof	10,000	Value: 650				

KM# 1984 50 YUAN
155.5500 g., 0.9990 Silver 4.9958 oz. ASW

Date	Mintage	F	VF	XF	Unc	BU
2011 Proof	—	Value: 500				

KM# 2033 50 YUAN
155.5500 g., 0.9990 Silver 4.9958 oz. ASW, 70 mm.

Date	Mintage	F	VF	XF	Unc	BU
2012 Proof	—	Value: 650				

KM# 1370 300 YUAN
1000.0000 g., 0.9990 Silver 32.117 oz. ASW, 100 mm. **Rev:** Panda walking thru bamboo

Date	Mintage	F	VF	XF	Unc	BU
2001 D Proof	2,000	Value: 2,500				

KM# 1416 300 YUAN
1000.0000 g., 0.9990 Silver 32.117 oz. ASW, 100 mm. **Subject:** Panda Coinage 20th Anniversary **Obv:** Temple of Heaven **Rev:** Two gold inserts with the 1982 and 2002 panda designs on bamboo leaves **Edge:** Plain **Note:** Large and small date varieties exist. Prev. Y#1116.

Date	Mintage	F	VF	XF	Unc	BU
2002 Proof	6,000	Value: 3,000				

KM# 1473 300 YUAN
1000.0000 g., 0.9990 Silver 32.117 oz. ASW **Rev:** Panda and bamboo **Shape:** 100

Date	Mintage	F	VF	XF	Unc	BU
2003 Proof	7,500	Value: 2,000				

KM# 1536 300 YUAN
1000.0000 g., 0.9990 Silver 32.117 oz. ASW, 100 mm. **Rev:** Panda walking with cub

Date	Mintage	F	VF	XF	Unc	BU
2004 Proof	4,000	Value: 2,000				

KM# 1587 300 YUAN
1000.0000 g., 0.9990 Silver 32.117 oz. ASW, 100 mm. **Obv:** Temple of Heaven **Rev:** Panda cub and mom seated in bamboo **Note:** Photo reduced.

Date	Mintage	F	VF	XF	Unc	BU
2005 Proof	4,000	Value: 2,250				

KM# 1662 300 YUAN
1000.0000 g., 0.9990 Silver 32.117 oz. ASW, 100 mm. **Obv:** Temple of Heaven **Rev:** Two pandas seated with bamboo **Note:** Photo reduced.

Date	Mintage	F	VF	XF	Unc	BU
2006 Proof	4,000	Value: 2,250				

KM# 1712 300 YUAN
1000.0000 g., 0.9990 Silver 32.117 oz. ASW, 100 mm. **Obv:** Temple of Heaven **Rev:** Two pandas, one walking, one seated

Date	Mintage	F	VF	XF	Unc	BU
2007 Proof	4,000	Value: 2,250				

KM# 1820 300 YUAN
1000.0000 g., 0.9990 Silver 32.117 oz. ASW, 100 mm. **Rev:** Panda cub pawing mom

Date	Mintage	F	VF	XF	Unc	BU
2008 Proof	—	Value: 2,000				

KM# 1871 300 YUAN
1000.0000 g., 0.9990 Silver 32.117 oz. ASW

Date	Mintage	F	VF	XF	Unc	BU
2008 Proof	—	Value: 2,000				

KM# 1934 300 YUAN
1000.0000 g., 0.9990 Silver 32.117 oz. ASW **Obv:** Temple of Heaven **Rev:** Two pandas, one lying on back

Date	Mintage	F	VF	XF	Unc	BU
2010 Proof	4,000	Value: 1,500				

KM# 1983 300 YUAN
1000.0000 g., 0.9990 Silver 32.117 oz. ASW, 100 mm.

Date	Mintage	F	VF	XF	Unc	BU
2011 Proof	—	Value: 1,250				

KM# 2032 300 YUAN
1000.0000 g., 0.9990 Silver 32.117 oz. ASW, 100 mm.

Date	Mintage	F	VF	XF	Unc	BU
2012 Proof	—	Value: 1,500				

GOLD BULLION COINAGE

Panda Series

KM# 1779 15 YUAN
1.2400 g., 0.9990 Gold 0.0398 oz. AGW, 12 mm. **Obv:** Temple of Heaven **Rev:** Panda walking amongst bamboo

Date	Mintage	F	VF	XF	Unc	BU
2007 Proof	18,000	Value: 95.00				

KM# 1741 15 YUAN
1.2400 g., 0.9990 Gold 0.0398 oz. AGW, 12 mm. **Obv:** Temple of Heaven **Rev:** Panda seated with branch

Date	Mintage	F	VF	XF	Unc	BU
2007 Proof	18,000	Value: 95.00				

KM# 1743 15 YUAN
1.2400 g., 0.9990 Gold 0.0398 oz. AGW, 12 mm. **Obv:** Temple of heaven **Rev:** Panda walking right

Date	Mintage	F	VF	XF	Unc	BU
2007 Proof	18,000	Value: 95.00				

KM# 1745 15 YUAN
1.2400 g., 0.9990 Gold 0.0398 oz. AGW, 12 mm. **Obv:** Temple of heaven **Rev:** Panda seated with bamboo branch

Date	Mintage	F	VF	XF	Unc	BU
2007 Proof	18,000	Value: 95.00				

KM# 1747 15 YUAN
1.2400 g., 0.9990 Gold 0.0398 oz. AGW, 12 mm. **Obv:** Temple of Heaven **Rev:** Panda hanging from branch

Date	Mintage	F	VF	XF	Unc	BU
2007 Proof	18,000	Value: 95.00				

KM# 1749 15 YUAN
1.2400 g., 0.9990 Gold 0.0398 oz. AGW, 12 mm. **Obv:** Temple of Heaven **Rev:** Panda walking forward

Date	Mintage	F	VF	XF	Unc	BU
2007 Proof	18,000	Value: 95.00				

KM# 1751 15 YUAN
1.2400 g., 0.9990 Gold 0.0398 oz. AGW, 12 mm. **Obv:** Temple of Heaven **Rev:** Panda drinking water

Date	Mintage	F	VF	XF	Unc	BU
2007 Proof	18,000	Value: 95.00				

KM# 1753 15 YUAN
1.2400 g., 0.9990 Gold 0.0398 oz. AGW, 12 mm. **Obv:** Temple of Heaven **Rev:** Panda seated in oval with branch

Date	Mintage	F	VF	XF	Unc	BU
2007 Proof	18,000	Value: 95.00				

KM# 1755 15 YUAN
1.2400 g., 0.9990 Gold 0.0398 oz. AGW, 12 mm. **Rev:** Panda seated on geometric background

Date	Mintage	F	VF	XF	Unc	BU
2007 Proof	18,000	Value: 95.00				

KM# 1757 15 YUAN
1.2400 g., 0.9990 Gold 0.0398 oz. AGW, 12 mm. **Obv:** Temple of Heaven **Rev:** Panda on rock

Date	Mintage	F	VF	XF	Unc	BU
2007 Proof	18,000	Value: 95.00				

KM# 1759 15 YUAN
1.2400 g., 0.9990 Gold 0.0398 oz. AGW, 12 mm. **Obv:** Temple of Heaven **Rev:** Panda seated on river bank

Date	Mintage	F	VF	XF	Unc	BU
2007 Proof	18,000	Value: 95.00				

KM# 1761 15 YUAN
1.2400 g., 0.9990 Gold 0.0398 oz. AGW, 12 mm. **Obv:** Temple of Heaven **Rev:** Panda on tree branch

Date	Mintage	F	VF	XF	Unc	BU
2007 Proof	18,000	Value: 95.00				

KM# 1763 15 YUAN
1.2400 g., 0.9990 Gold 0.0398 oz. AGW, 12 mm. **Obv:** Temple of Heaven **Rev:** Panda on rock ledge

Date	Mintage	F	VF	XF	Unc	BU
2007 Proof	18,000	Value: 95.00				

KM# 1765 15 YUAN
1.2400 g., 0.9990 Gold 0.0398 oz. AGW, 12 mm. **Obv:** Temple of Heaven **Rev:** Panda seated munching bamboo

Date	Mintage	F	VF	XF	Unc	BU
2007 Proof	18,000	Value: 95.00				

KM# 1767 15 YUAN
1.2400 g., 0.9990 Gold 0.0398 oz. AGW **Obv:** Temple of Heaven **Rev:** Panda pulling bamboo **Shape:** 12

Date	Mintage	F	VF	XF	Unc	BU
2007 Proof	1,800	Value: 95.00				

KM# 1769 15 YUAN
1.2400 g., 0.9990 Gold 0.0398 oz. AGW, 12 mm. **Obv:** Temple of Heaven **Rev:** Panda in tree

Date	Mintage	F	VF	XF	Unc	BU
2007 Proof	18,000	Value: 95.00				

KM# 1771 15 YUAN
1.2400 g., 0.9990 Gold 0.0398 oz. AGW **Obv:** Temple of Heaven **Rev:** Panda looking over branch

Date	Mintage	F	VF	XF	Unc	BU
2007 Proof	18,000	Value: 95.00				

KM# 1773 15 YUAN
1.2400 g., 0.9990 Gold 0.0398 oz. AGW, 12 mm. **Obv:** Temple of Heaven **Rev:** Panda seated on rock

Date	Mintage	F	VF	XF	Unc	BU
2007 Proof	18,000	Value: 95.00				

KM# A1775 15 YUAN
1.2400 g., 0.9990 Gold 0.0398 oz. AGW, 12 mm. **Obv:** Temple of Heaven **Rev:** Panda looking out from rock

Date	Mintage	F	VF	XF	Unc	BU
2007 Proof	18,000	Value: 95.00				

KM# 1777 15 YUAN
1.2400 g., 0.9990 Gold 0.0398 oz. AGW, 12 mm. **Obv:** Temple of Heaven **Rev:** Panda seated on frosted background

Date	Mintage	F	VF	XF	Unc	BU
2007 Proof	18,000	Value: 95.00				

KM# 1781 15 YUAN
1.2400 g., 0.9990 Gold 0.0398 oz. AGW, 12 mm. **Obv:** Temple of Heaven **Rev:** Panda looking forward

Date	Mintage	F	VF	XF	Unc	BU
2007 Proof	18,000	Value: 95.00				

KM# 1783 15 YUAN
1.2400 g., 0.9990 Gold 0.0398 oz. AGW, 12 mm. **Obv:** Temple of Heaven **Rev:** Panda and cub walking right

Date	Mintage	F	VF	XF	Unc	BU
2007 Proof	18,000	Value: 95.00				

KM# 1785 15 YUAN
1.2400 g., 0.9990 Gold 0.0398 oz. AGW, 12 mm. **Obv:** Temple of Heaven **Rev:** Panda seated with cub on left

Date	Mintage	F	VF	XF	Unc	BU
2007 Proof	18,000	Value: 95.00				

KM# 1787 15 YUAN
1.2400 g., 0.9990 Gold 0.0398 oz. AGW, 12 mm. **Obv:** Temple of Heaven **Rev:** Panda seated with cub on right

Date	Mintage	F	VF	XF	Unc	BU
2007 Proof	18,000	Value: 95.00				

KM# 1789 15 YUAN
1.2400 g., 0.9990 Gold 0.0398 oz. AGW, 12 mm. **Obv:** Temple of Heaven **Rev:** Panda seated with cub, both munching bamboo

Date	Mintage	F	VF	XF	Unc	BU
2007 Proof	18,000	Value: 95.00				

KM# 1366 20 YUAN
1.5600 g., 0.9990 Gold 0.0501 oz. AGW, 14 mm. **Obv:** Temple of Heaven **Rev:** Panda walking left through bamboo **Edge:** Reeded **Note:** Large and small date varieties exist. Prev. Y#1112.

Date	Mintage	F	VF	XF	Unc	BU
2001	200,000	—	—	—	100	115
2001 D	Inc. above	—	—	—	100	115
2002	74,601	—	—	—	100	115

KM# 1467 20 YUAN
1.5552 g., 0.9999 Gold 0.0500 oz. AGW, 14.5 mm. **Subject:** Panda **Obv:** Temple of Heaven **Rev:** Panda facing, walking through bamboo **Edge:** Reeded **Note:** Large and small date varieties exist. Prev. Y#1154.

Date	Mintage	F	VF	XF	Unc	BU
2003	117,000	—	—	—	—	110

KM# 1529 20 YUAN
1.5552 g., 0.9999 Gold 0.0500 oz. AGW, 14 mm. **Rev:** Panda walking with cub **Note:** Large and small date varieties exist. Prev. Y#1172.

Date	Mintage	F	VF	XF	Unc	BU
2004	101,000	—	—	—	—	120

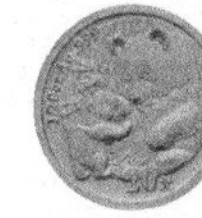

KM# 1586 20 YUAN
1.5500 g., 0.9990 Gold 0.0498 oz. AGW, 14 mm. **Obv:** Temple of Heaven **Rev:** Panda cub and mom seated in bamboo

Date	Mintage	F	VF	XF	Unc	BU
2005 Proof	89,500	Value: 125				

KM# 1661 20 YUAN
1.5552 g., 0.9990 Gold 0.0499 oz. AGW, 14 mm. **Obv:** Temple of Heaven **Rev:** Two pandas seated with bamboo

Date	Mintage	F	VF	XF	Unc	BU
2006 Proof	62,000	Value: 145				

KM# 1707 20 YUAN
1.5552 g., 0.9990 Gold 0.0499 oz. AGW, 14 mm. **Obv:** Temple of Heaven **Rev:** Two pandas, one walking, one seated

Date	Mintage	F	VF	XF	Unc	BU
2007 Proof	200,000	Value: 100				

KM# 1815 20 YUAN
1.5552 g., 0.9990 Gold 0.0499 oz. AGW, 14 mm. **Rev:** Panda cut pawing mom

Date	Mintage	F	VF	XF	Unc	BU
2008 Proof	—	Value: 100				

KM# 1866 20 YUAN
1.5552 g., 0.9990 Gold 0.0499 oz. AGW

Date	Mintage	F	VF	XF	Unc	BU
2008 Proof	—	Value: 100				

KM# 1930 20 YUAN
1.5500 g., 0.9990 Gold 0.0498 oz. AGW **Obv:** Temple of Heaven **Rev:** Two pandas, one lying on back

Date	Mintage	F	VF	XF	Unc	BU
2010	120,000	—	—	—	—	110

KM# 1979 20 YUAN
1.5500 g., 0.9990 Gold 0.0498 oz. AGW, 14 mm.

Date	Mintage	F	VF	XF	Unc	BU
2011	—	—	—	—	—	110

KM# 2028 20 YUAN
1.5500 g., 0.9990 Gold 0.0498 oz. AGW, 14 mm.

Date	Mintage	F	VF	XF	Unc	BU
2012	—	—	—	—	—	110

KM# 1817 30 YUAN
3.1100 g., 0.9990 Gold 0.0999 oz. AGW, 18 mm. **Rev:** Panda cub pawing mom

Date	Mintage	F	VF	XF	Unc	BU
2008 Proof	—	Value: 215				

KM# 1367 50 YUAN
3.1103 g., 0.9990 Gold 0.0999 oz. AGW, 18 mm. **Obv:** Temple of Heaven **Rev:** Panda walking left through bamboo **Edge:** Reeded **Note:** Large and small date varieties exist. Prev. Y#1113.

Date	Mintage	F	VF	XF	Unc	BU
2001	50,000	—	—	—	—	200
2001 D	150,000	—	—	—	—	250

KM# 1457 50 YUAN
3.1103 g., 0.9999 Gold 0.1000 oz. AGW **Subject:** Temple of Heaven **Rev:** Panda walking

Date	Mintage	F	VF	XF	Unc	BU
2002	36,092	—	—	—	—	225

KM# 1469 50 YUAN
3.1103 g., 0.9999 Gold 0.1000 oz. AGW **Subject:** Panda **Note:** Large and small date varieties exist. Prev. Y#1157.

Date	Mintage	F	VF	XF	Unc	BU
2003	47,500	—	—	—	—	215

KM# 1531 50 YUAN
3.1103 g., 0.9999 Gold 0.1000 oz. AGW **Subject:** Panda **Note:** Large and small date varieties exist. Prev. Y#1173.

Date	Mintage	F	VF	XF	Unc	BU
2004	—	—	—	—	—	200

KM# 1585 50 YUAN
3.1100 g., 0.9990 Gold 0.0999 oz. AGW, 18 mm. **Obv:** Temple of Heaven **Rev:** Panda cub and mom seated in bamboo

Date	Mintage	F	VF	XF	Unc	BU
2005	150,000	—	—	—	—	200

KM# 1660 50 YUAN
3.1100 g., 0.9990 Gold 0.0999 oz. AGW, 18 mm. **Obv:** Temple of Heaven **Rev:** Two pandas seated with bamboo

Date	Mintage	F	VF	XF	Unc	BU
2006	150,000	—	—	—	—	200

KM# 1709 50 YUAN
3.1100 g., 0.9990 Gold 0.0999 oz. AGW, 18 mm. **Obv:** Temple of Heaven **Rev:** Two pandas, one walking, one seated

Date	Mintage	F	VF	XF	Unc	BU
2007	150,000	—	—	—	—	200

KM# 1868 50 YUAN
3.1000 g., 0.9990 Gold 0.0996 oz. AGW, 18 mm. **Rev:** Panda cub pawing mom

Date	Mintage	F	VF	XF	Unc	BU
2008	—	—	—	—	—	200

KM# 1929 50 YUAN
3.1100 g., 0.9990 Gold 0.0999 oz. AGW **Obv:** Temple of Heaven **Rev:** Two pandas, one lying on back

Date	Mintage	F	VF	XF	Unc	BU
2010	120,000	—	—	—	—	200

KM# 1978 50 YUAN
3.1100 g., 0.9990 Gold 0.0999 oz. AGW, 18 mm.

Date	Mintage	F	VF	XF	Unc	BU
2011	—	—	—	—	—	200

KM# 2027 50 YUAN
3.1100 g., 0.9990 Gold 0.0999 oz. AGW, 18 mm.

Date	Mintage	F	VF	XF	Unc	BU
2012	—	—	—	—	—	200

KM# 1368 100 YUAN
7.7759 g., 0.9990 Gold 0.2497 oz. AGW, 22 mm. **Obv:** Temple of Heaven **Rev:** Panda walking left through bamboo **Edge:** Reeded **Note:** Large and small date varieties exist. Prev. Y#1114.

Date	Mintage	F	VF	XF	Unc	BU
2001	85,010	—	—	—	—	475
2001 D	Inc. above	—	—	—	—	525

KM# 1458 100 YUAN
7.7759 g., 0.9999 Gold 0.2500 oz. AGW **Obv:** Temple of Heaven **Rev:** Panda walking

Date	Mintage	F	VF	XF	Unc	BU
2002	19,205	—	—	—	—	500

KM# 1471 100 YUAN
7.7759 g., 0.9999 Gold 0.2500 oz. AGW **Subject:** Panda **Note:** Large and small date varieties exist. Prev. Y#1158.

Date	Mintage	F	VF	XF	Unc	BU
2003	28,000	—	—	—	—	475

KM# 1533 100 YUAN
7.7759 g., 0.9999 Gold 0.2500 oz. AGW **Subject:** Panda **Note:** Large and small date varieties exist. Prev. Y#1174. Photo reduced.

Date	Mintage	F	VF	XF	Unc	BU
2004	41,000	—	—	—	—	475

KM# 1584 100 YUAN
7.7700 g., 0.9990 Gold 0.2496 oz. AGW, 22 mm. **Obv:** Temple of Heaven **Rev:** Panda cub and mom seated in bamboo

Date	Mintage	F	VF	XF	Unc	BU
2005	40,000	—	—	—	—	475

KM# 1659 100 YUAN
7.7700 g., 0.9990 Gold 0.2496 oz. AGW, 22 mm. **Obv:** Temple of Heaven **Rev:** Two pandas seated with bamboo

Date	Mintage	F	VF	XF	Unc	BU
2006	28,500	—	—	—	—	500

KM# 1710 100 YUAN
7.7700 g., 0.9990 Gold 0.2496 oz. AGW, 22 mm. **Obv:** Temple of Heaven **Rev:** Two pandas, one walking, one seated

Date	Mintage	F	VF	XF	Unc	BU
2007	60,000	—	—	—	—	475

KM# 1818 100 YUAN
7.7700 g., 0.9990 Gold 0.2496 oz. AGW, 22 mm. **Rev:** Panda cub pawing mom

Date	Mintage	F	VF	XF	Unc	BU
2008	—	—	—	—	—	475

KM# 1928 100 YUAN
7.7700 g., 0.9990 Gold 0.2496 oz. AGW **Obv:** Temple of Heaven **Rev:** Two panda, one lying on back

Date	Mintage	F	VF	XF	Unc	BU
2010	120,000	—	—	—	—	500

KM# 1977 100 YUAN
7.7700 g., 0.9990 Gold 0.2496 oz. AGW, 22 mm.

Date	Mintage	F	VF	XF	Unc	BU
2011	—	—	—	—	—	500

KM# 2026 100 YUAN
7.7700 g., 0.9990 Gold 0.2496 oz. AGW, 22 mm.

Date	Mintage	F	VF	XF	Unc	BU
2012	—	—	—	—	—	450

KM# 1369 200 YUAN
15.5518 g., 0.9990 Gold 0.4995 oz. AGW, 27 mm. **Obv:** Temple of Heaven **Rev:** Panda in bamboo forest **Edge:** Slanted reeding **Note:** Illustration reduced. Large and small date varieties exist. Prev. Y#1105.

Date	Mintage	F	VF	XF	Unc	BU
2001	33,215	—	—	—	—	900
2001 D	100,000	—	—	—	—	875

KM# 1459 200 YUAN
15.5518 g., 0.9999 Gold 0.4999 oz. AGW **Rev:** Panda

Date	Mintage	F	VF	XF	Unc	BU
2002	28,514	—	—	—	—	900

KM# 1472 200 YUAN
15.5519 g., 0.9999 Gold 0.4999 oz. AGW **Subject:** Panda **Note:** Large and small date varieties exist. Prev. Y#1162.

Date	Mintage	F	VF	XF	Unc	BU
2003	25,000	—	—	—	—	900

KM# 1535 200 YUAN
15.5519 g., 0.9990 Gold 0.4995 oz. AGW **Subject:** Panda **Note:** Large and small date varieties exist. Prev. Y#1175.

Date	Mintage	F	VF	XF	Unc	BU
2004	42,000	—	—	—	—	875

KM# 1583 200 YUAN
15.5518 g., 0.9990 Gold 0.4995 oz. AGW, 27 mm. **Obv:** Temple of Heaven **Rev:** Panda cub and mom seated in bamboo

Date	Mintage	F	VF	XF	Unc	BU
2005	36,410	—	—	—	—	875

KM# 1658 200 YUAN
15.5500 g., 0.9990 Gold 0.4994 oz. AGW, 27 mm. **Obv:** Temple of Heaven **Rev:** Two pandas seated with bamboo

Date	Mintage	F	VF	XF	Unc	BU
2006	25,600	—	—	—	—	900

KM# 1711 200 YUAN
15.5500 g., 0.9990 Gold 0.4994 oz. AGW **Obv:** Temple of Heaven **Rev:** Two pandas, one walking, one seated

Date	Mintage	F	VF	XF	Unc	BU
2007	60,000	—	—	—	—	875

KM# 1870 200 YUAN
15.5000 g., 0.9990 Gold 0.4978 oz. AGW

Date	Mintage	F	VF	XF	Unc	BU
2009	—	—	—	—	—	875

KM# 1927 200 YUAN
15.5500 g., 0.9990 Gold 0.4994 oz. AGW **Obv:** Temple of Heaven **Rev:** Two pandas, one lying on back

Date	Mintage	F	VF	XF	Unc	BU
2010	120,000	—	—	—	—	900

KM# 1976 200 YUAN
15.5500 g., 0.9990 Gold 0.4994 oz. AGW

Date	Mintage	F	VF	XF	Unc	BU
2011	—	—	—	—	—	900

KM# 2025 200 YUAN
15.5500 g., 0.9990 Gold 0.4994 oz. AGW, 27 mm.

Date	Mintage	F	VF	XF	Unc	BU
2012	—	—	—	—	—	900

KM# 1371 500 YUAN
31.1035 g., 0.9990 Gold 0.9990 oz. AGW, 32 mm. **Obv:** Temple of Heaven **Rev:** Panda walking through bamboo **Edge:** Reeded **Note:** Prev. Y#1088.

Date	Mintage	F	VF	XF	Unc	BU
2001	—	—	—	—	—	BV+10%
2001 D	150,000	—	—	—	—	BV+10%

KM# 1405 500 YUAN
31.1050 g., 0.9999 Gold 0.9999 oz. AGW **Rev:** Panda

Date	Mintage	F	VF	XF	Unc	BU
2001	41,411	—	—	—	—	BV+10%

KM# 1460 500 YUAN
31.1050 g., 0.9999 Gold 0.9999 oz. AGW **Rev:** Panda

Date	Mintage	F	VF	XF	Unc	BU
2002	28,345	—	—	—	—	BV+15%

KM# 1474 500 YUAN
31.1320 g., 0.9999 Gold 1.0008 oz. AGW **Subject:** Panda **Note:** Large and small date varieties exist. Prev. Y#1164.

Date	Mintage	F	VF	XF	Unc	BU
2003	36,300	—	—	—	—	BV+12%

KM# 1537 500 YUAN
31.1035 g., 0.9999 Gold 0.9999 oz. AGW **Subject:** Panda **Note:** Large and small date varieties exist. Prev. Y#1176.

Date	Mintage	F	VF	XF	Unc	BU
2004	55,000	—	—	—	—	BV+10%

KM# 1582 500 YUAN
31.1050 g., 0.9990 Gold 0.9990 oz. AGW, 32 mm. **Obv:** Temple of Heaven **Rev:** Panda cub and mom seated in bamboo

Date	Mintage	F	VF	XF	Unc	BU
2005	50,300	BV+10%				

KM# 1657 500 YUAN
31.1050 g., 0.9990 Gold 0.9990 oz. AGW, 32 mm. **Obv:** Temple of Heaven **Rev:** Two panda's seated with bamboo

Date	Mintage	F	VF	XF	Unc	BU
2006	115,600	BV+10%				

KM# 1713 500 YUAN
31.1050 g., 0.9990 Gold 0.9990 oz. AGW, 32 mm. **Obv:** Temple of Heaven **Rev:** Two pandas, one walking, one seated

Date	Mintage	F	VF	XF	Unc	BU
2007	150,000	BV+10%				

KM# 1821 500 YUAN
31.1050 g., 0.9990 Gold 0.9990 oz. AGW, 32 mm. **Rev:** Panda cub pawing mom

Date	Mintage	F	VF	XF	Unc	BU
2008	—	BV+10%				

KM# 1872 500 YUAN
31.1050 g., 0.9990 Gold 0.9990 oz. AGW

Date	Mintage	F	VF	XF	Unc	BU
2009	—	BV+10%				

KM# 1926 500 YUAN
31.1050 g., 0.9990 Gold 0.9990 oz. AGW **Obv:** Temple of Heaven **Rev:** Two pandas, one lying on back

Date	Mintage	F	VF	XF	Unc	BU
2010	300,000	—	—	—	—	BV+10%

KM# 1975 500 YUAN
31.1050 g., 0.9990 Gold 0.9990 oz. AGW

Date	Mintage	F	VF	XF	Unc	BU
2011	—	—	—	—	—	BV+10%

KM# 2024 500 YUAN
31.1050 g., 0.9990 Gold 0.9990 oz. AGW, 32 mm.

Date	Mintage	F	VF	XF	Unc	BU
2012	—	—	—	—	—	BV+10%

KM# 1581 2000 YUAN
155.0000 g., 0.9990 Gold 4.9782 oz. AGW, 60 mm. **Obv:** Temple of Heaven **Rev:** Panda cub and mom seated in bamboo **Note:** Photo reduced.

Date	Mintage	F	VF	XF	Unc	BU
2005 Proof	1,000	BV+15%				

KM# 1656 2000 YUAN
155.5500 g., 0.9990 Gold 4.9958 oz. AGW, 60 mm. **Obv:** Temple of Heaven **Rev:** Two pandas seated with bamboo **Note:** Photo reduced.

Date	Mintage	F	VF	XF	Unc	BU
2006 Proof	1,000	BV+15%				

KM# 1714 2000 YUAN
155.5500 g., 0.9990 Gold 4.9958 oz. AGW, 60 mm. **Obv:** Temple of Heaven **Rev:** Two pandas, one walking, one seated

Date	Mintage	F	VF	XF	Unc	BU
2007 Proof	1,000	BV+15%				

KM# 1822 2000 YUAN
155.5000 g., 0.9990 Gold 4.9942 oz. AGW, 60 mm. **Rev:** Panda cub pawing mom

Date	Mintage	F	VF	XF	Unc	BU
2008 Proof	1,000	BV+15%				

KM# 1873 2000 YUAN
155.5000 g., 0.9990 Gold 4.9942 oz. AGW

Date	Mintage	F	VF	XF	Unc	BU
2009 Proof	1,000	BV+15%				

KM# 1914 2000 YUAN
155.5000 g., 0.9990 Gold 4.9942 oz. AGW **Subject:** Year of the Tiger **Rev:** Multicolor

Date	Mintage	F	VF	XF	Unc	BU
2010 Proof	1,800	BV+10%				

KM# 1933 2000 YUAN
155.5000 g., 0.9990 Gold 4.9942 oz. AGW **Obv:** Temple of Heaven **Rev:** Two pandas, one lying on back

Date	Mintage	F	VF	XF	Unc	BU
2010 Proof	1,000	BV+15%				

KM# 1982 2000 YUAN
155.5500 g., 0.9990 Gold 4.9958 oz. AGW, 60 mm.

Date	Mintage	F	VF	XF	Unc	BU
2011 Proof	—	BV+10%				

KM# 1372 10000 YUAN
1000.0000 g., 0.9990 Gold 32.117 oz. AGW **Subject:** Panda **Note:** Large and small date varieties exist. Prev. #Y1138.

Date	Mintage	F	VF	XF	Unc	BU
2001	68	—	—	—	—	BV+25%

KM# A1475 10000 YUAN
1000.0000 g., 0.9999 Gold 32.146 oz. AGW **Subject:** Panda **Note:** Large and small date varieties exist. Prev. #Y1165.

Date	Mintage	F	VF	XF	Unc	BU
2002	68	—	—	—	—	BV+25%

KM# 1475 10000 YUAN
1000.0000 g., 0.9990 Gold 32.117 oz. AGW, 100 mm. **Rev:** Panda and bamboo

Date	Mintage	F	VF	XF	Unc	BU
2003 Proof	68	BV+25%				

KM# 1538 10000 YUAN
1000.0000 g., 0.9999 Gold 32.146 oz. AGW **Subject:** Panda **Note:** Large and small date varieties exist. Prev. #Y1177.

Date	Mintage	F	VF	XF	Unc	BU
2004	68	—	—	—	—	BV+25%

KM# A1580 10000 YUAN
1000.0000 g., 0.9990 Gold 32.117 oz. AGW, 90 mm. **Obv:** Temple of Heaven **Rev:** Panda cub and mom seated in bamboo **Note:** Photo reduced.

Date	Mintage	F	VF	XF	Unc	BU
2005 Proof	100	BV+25%				

KM# 1655 10000 YUAN
1000.0000 g., 0.9990 Gold 32.117 oz. AGW, 90 mm. **Obv:** Temple of Heaven **Rev:** Two pandas seated with bamboo **Note:** Photo reduced.

Date	Mintage	F	VF	XF	Unc	BU
2006 Proof	200	BV+20%				

KM# 1715 10000 YUAN
1000.0000 g., 0.9990 Gold 32.117 oz. AGW **Obv:** Temple of Heaven **Rev:** Two pandas, one walking, one seated

Date	Mintage	F	VF	XF	Unc	BU
2007 Proof	200	BV+20%				

KM# 1823 10000 YUAN
1000.0000 g., 0.9990 Gold 32.117 oz. AGW, 90 mm. **Rev:** Panda cub pawing mom

Date	Mintage	F	VF	XF	Unc	BU
2008 Proof	200	BV+20%				

KM# 1874 10000 YUAN
1000.0000 g., 0.9990 Gold 32.117 oz. AGW

Date	Mintage	F	VF	XF	Unc	BU
2009 Proof	200	BV+20%				

KM# 1932 10000 YUAN
1000.0000 g., 0.9990 Gold 32.117 oz. AGW **Obv:** Temple of Heaven **Rev:** Two pandas, one lying on back

Date	Mintage	F	VF	XF	Unc	BU
2010 Proof	200	BV+20%				

KM# 1981 10000 YUAN
1000.0000 g., 0.9990 Gold 32.117 oz. AGW, 90 mm.

Date	Mintage	F	VF	XF	Unc	BU
2011 Proof	—	BV+20%				

KM# 2030 10000 YUAN
1000.0000 g., 0.9990 Gold 32.117 oz. AGW, 90 mm.

Date	Mintage	F	VF	XF	Unc	BU
2012 Proof	—	BV+20%				

GOLD BULLION COINAGE

Lunar Series

KM# 1967 20 YUAN
3.1100 g., 0.9990 Gold 0.0999 oz. AGW, 18 mm. **Subject:** Year of the Rabbit **Rev:** Multicolor

Date	Mintage	F	VF	XF	Unc	BU
2011 Proof	80,000	Value: 225				

KM# 1374 50 YUAN
3.1103 g., 0.9990 Gold 0.0999 oz. AGW, 18 mm. **Subject:** Year of the Snake **Note:** Prev. Y#1141.1; 1043.

Date	Mintage	F	VF	XF	Unc	BU
2001	48,000	—	—	—	—	265

KM# 1376 50 YUAN
3.1105 g., 0.9999 Gold 0.1000 oz. AGW **Subject:** Year of the Snake **Rev:** Multicolor. **Note:** Prev. Y#1141.2.

Date	Mintage	F	VF	XF	Unc	BU
2001	30,000	—	—	—	—	350

KM# 1419 50 YUAN
3.1050 g., 0.9999 Gold 0.0998 oz. AGW **Subject:** Year of the Horse **Rev:** Dramatic horse profile right **Note:** Prev. Y#1143.1.

Date	Mintage	F	VF	XF	Unc	BU
2002	48,000	—	—	—	—	240

KM# 1417 50 YUAN
3.1050 g., 0.9999 Gold 0.0998 oz. AGW **Subject:** Year of the Horse **Rev:** Multicolor horse prancing forward **Note:** Prev. Y#1143.2.

Date	Mintage	F	VF	XF	Unc	BU
2002	30,000	—	—	—	—	425

KM# 1478 50 YUAN
3.1103 g., 0.9999 Gold 0.1000 oz. AGW **Subject:** Year of the Goat **Note:** Prev. Y#1155.1.

Date	Mintage	F	VF	XF	Unc	BU
2003	48,000	—	—	—	—	275

KM# A1478 50 YUAN
3.1105 g., 0.9999 Gold 0.1000 oz. AGW **Subject:** Year of the Goat **Rev:** Multicolor. **Note:** Prev. Y#1155.2

Date	Mintage	F	VF	XF	Unc	BU
2003	30,000	—	—	—	—	400

KM# 1544 50 YUAN
3.1103 g., 0.9999 Gold 0.1000 oz. AGW, 18 mm. **Subject:** Year of the Monkey **Note:** Prev. Y#1167.1.

Date	Mintage	F	VF	XF	Unc	BU
2004	48,000	—	—	—	—	275

KM# 1546 50 YUAN
3.1103 g., 0.9999 Gold 0.1000 oz. AGW **Subject:** Year of the Monkey **Rev:** Multicolor monkey and baby **Note:** Prev. Y#1167.2

Date	Mintage	F	VF	XF	Unc	BU
2004	30,000	—	—	—	—	425

KM# 1608 50 YUAN
3.1100 g., 0.9990 Gold 0.0999 oz. AGW, 18 mm. **Subject:** Year of the Rooster **Obv:** Classical rooster **Rev:** Multicolor rooster

Date	Mintage	F	VF	XF	Unc	BU
2005 Proof	30,000	Value: 375				

KM# 1609 50 YUAN
3.1100 g., 0.9990 Gold 0.0999 oz. AGW, 18 mm. **Subject:** Year of the Rooster **Obv:** Classical rooster **Rev:** Rooster, hen and chicks

Date	Mintage	F	VF	XF	Unc	BU
2005 Proof	60,000	Value: 300				

KM# 1680 50 YUAN
3.1103 g., 0.9990 Gold 0.0999 oz. AGW, 18 mm. **Obv:** Dog-shaped belt-hook from ancient Chinese bronze ware, decorative design of dog tail-shaped plant leaves **Rev:** 2 smart dogs **Note:** Prev. Y#1226; KM#1658.

Date	Mintage	F	VF	XF	Unc	BU
2006	60,000	—	—	—	—	225

KM# 1681 50 YUAN
3.1103 g., 0.9990 Gold 0.0999 oz. AGW, 18 mm. **Obv:** Dog-shaped belt-hook , an ancient Chinese bronze ware, decorative disign of dog tail-shaped plant leaves **Rev:** 2 dogs at play **Note:** Prev. Y#1222; KM#1654.

Date	Mintage	F	VF	XF	Unc	BU
2006 Proof	30,000	Value: 220				

KM# 1721 50 YUAN
3.1000 g., 0.9990 Gold 0.0996 oz. AGW, 18 mm. **Subject:** Year of the Pig **Obv:** Classical pig **Rev:** Pig walking right

Date	Mintage	F	VF	XF	Unc	BU
2007 Proof	—	Value: 225				

KM# 1722 50 YUAN
3.1000 g., 0.9990 Gold 0.0996 oz. AGW, 18 mm. **Subject:** Year of the Pig **Obv:** Classical pig **Rev:** Multicolor sow and piglets sucking

Date	Mintage	F	VF	XF	Unc	BU
2007 Proof	30,000	Value: 550				

KM# 1835 50 YUAN
3.1100 g., 0.9990 Gold 0.0999 oz. AGW **Subject:** Year of the Rat **Rev:** Multicolor **Shape:** 18

Date	Mintage	F	VF	XF	Unc	BU
2008 Proof	30,000	Value: 350				

KM# 1836 50 YUAN
3.1100 g., 0.9990 Gold 0.0999 oz. AGW, 18 mm. **Subject:** Year of the Rat

Date	Mintage	F	VF	XF	Unc	BU
2008 Proof	60,000	Value: 225				

KM# 1880 50 YUAN
3.1100 g., 0.9990 Gold 0.0999 oz. AGW **Subject:** Year of the Ox colorized

Date	Mintage	F	VF	XF	Unc	BU
2009 Proof	30,000	Value: 400				

KM# 1881 50 YUAN
3.1100 g., 0.9990 Gold 0.0999 oz. AGW **Subject:** Year of the Ox

Date	Mintage	F	VF	XF	Unc	BU
2009 Proof	80,000	Value: 200				

KM# 1917 50 YUAN
3.1100 g., 0.9990 Gold 0.0999 oz. AGW **Subject:** Year of the Tiger

Date	Mintage	F	VF	XF	Unc	BU
2010 Proof	80,000	Value: 225				

KM# 1918 50 YUAN
3.1100 g., 0.9990 Gold 0.0999 oz. AGW **Subject:** Year of the Tiger **Rev:** Multicolor

Date	Mintage	F	VF	XF	Unc	BU
2010 Proof	80,000	Value: 225				

KM# 1966 50 YUAN
3.1100 g., 0.9990 Gold 0.0999 oz. AGW, 18 mm. **Subject:** Year of the Rabbit

Date	Mintage	F	VF	XF	Unc	BU
2011 Proof	80,000	Value: 225				

KM# 2015 50 YUAN
3.1050 g., 0.9990 Gold 0.0997 oz. AGW, 18 mm. **Subject:** Year of the Dragon

Date	Mintage	F	VF	XF	Unc	BU
2012 Proof	—	Value: 225				

KM# 2016 50 YUAN
3.1050 g., 0.9990 Gold 0.0997 oz. AGW, 18 mm. **Subject:** Year of the Dragon **Rev:** Colored

Date	Mintage	F	VF	XF	Unc	BU
2012 Proof	—	Value: 225				

KM# 1380 200 YUAN
15.5518 g., 0.9990 Gold 0.4995 oz. AGW **Subject:** Year of the Snake **Shape:** Flower **Note:** Prev. Y#1045.

Date	Mintage	F	VF	XF	Unc	BU
2001 Proof	2,300	Value: 1,250				

KM# 1383 200 YUAN
15.5518 g., 0.9990 Gold 0.4995 oz. AGW **Subject:** Year of the Snake **Rev:** Fan **Note:** Prev. Y#1044.

Date	Mintage	F	VF	XF	Unc	BU
2001	6,600	—	—	—	—	950

KM# 1424 200 YUAN
15.5500 g., 0.9990 Gold 0.4994 oz. AGW **Subject:** Year of the Horse **Shape:** Fan

Date	Mintage	F	VF	XF	Unc	BU
2002	6,600	—	—	—	—	1,000

KM# 1426 200 YUAN
15.5000 g., 0.9990 Gold 0.4978 oz. AGW **Subject:** Year of the Horse **Shape:** Flower **Note:** Prev. Y#1150.

Date	Mintage	F	VF	XF	Unc	BU
2002	2,300	—	—	—	—	1,350

KM# 1475.1 200 YUAN
15.5517 g., 0.9999 Gold 0.4999 oz. AGW **Subject:** Year of the Goat **Shape:** Fan

Date	Mintage	F	VF	XF	Unc	BU
2003	6,600	—	—	—	—	950

KM# 1481 200 YUAN
15.5519 g., 0.9999 Gold 0.4999 oz. AGW **Subject:** Year of the Goat **Shape:** Flower **Note:** Prev. Y#1161.

Date	Mintage	F	VF	XF	Unc	BU
2003	2,300	—	—	—	—	1,350

KM# 1486 200 YUAN
15.5130 g., 0.9990 Gold 0.4982 oz. AGW, 58 x 30 mm. **Subject:** Year of the Sheep **Shape:** Fan

Date	Mintage	F	VF	XF	Unc	BU
2003 Proof	6,600	Value: 1,100				

KM# 1549 200 YUAN
15.5519 g., 0.9999 Gold 0.4999 oz. AGW **Subject:** Year of the Monkey **Shape:** Flower **Note:** Prev. Y#1169.

Date	Mintage	F	VF	XF	Unc	BU
2004	2,300	—	—	—	—	1,350

KM# 1554 200 YUAN
15.5519 g., 0.9999 Gold 0.4999 oz. AGW **Subject:** Year of the Monkey **Shape:** Fan **Note:** Illustration reduced. Prev. Y#1168.

Date	Mintage	F	VF	XF	Unc	BU
2004	6,600	—	—	—	—	1,100

KM# 1606 200 YUAN
15.5500 g., 0.9990 Gold 0.4994 oz. AGW, 27 mm. **Series:** Classical rooster **Subject:** Year of the Rooster **Obv:** Rooster, hen and chicks **Shape:** Scallops

Date	Mintage	F	VF	XF	Unc	BU
2005 Proof	8,000	Value: 925				

KM# 1607 200 YUAN
15.5500 g., 0.9990 Gold 0.4994 oz. AGW, 58 x 30 mm. **Subject:** Year of the Rooster **Obv:** Temple **Rev:** Rooster, hen and chicks **Shape:** Fan **Note:** Illustration reduced.

Date	Mintage	F	VF	XF	Unc	BU
2005 Proof	6,600	Value: 950				

KM# 1677 200 YUAN
15.6300 g., 0.9990 Gold 0.5020 oz. AGW, 27 mm. **Subject:** Year of the Dog **Obv:** Dog-shaped belt-hook from ancient Chinese bronze ware, decorative design of dog tail-shaped plant leaves **Rev:** 2 smart dogs **Shape:** Scalloped **Note:** Prev. Y#1224; KM#1656.

Date	Mintage	F	VF	XF	Unc	BU
2006 Proof	8,000	Value: 1,350				

KM# 1679 200 YUAN
15.6300 g., 0.9990 Gold 0.5020 oz. AGW **Subject:** Year of the Dog **Obv:** Qing Yuan Gate of the China Great Wall **Rev:** 2 dogs at play **Shape:** 30° Fan **Note:** Prev. Y#1220; KM#1652. Illustration reduced.

Date	Mintage	F	VF	XF	Unc	BU
2006 Proof	6,600	Value: 1,100				

KM# 1723 200 YUAN
15.5000 g., 0.9990 Gold 0.4978 oz. AGW, 58 x 39 mm. **Subject:** Year of the Pig **Obv:** Temple **Rev:** Sow and four piglets **Shape:** Fan

Date	Mintage	F	VF	XF	Unc	BU
2007 Proof	6,600	Value: 1,150				

KM# 1724 200 YUAN
15.5500 g., 0.9990 Gold 0.4994 oz. AGW, 27 mm. **Subject:** Year of the Pig **Obv:** Classical pig **Rev:** Pig walking right **Shape:** Flower

Date	Mintage	F	VF	XF	Unc	BU
2007 Proof	8,000	Value: 950				

KM# 1837 200 YUAN
15.5000 g., 0.9990 Gold 0.4978 oz. AGW, 27 mm. **Subject:** Year of the Rat **Shape:** Flower

Date	Mintage	F	VF	XF	Unc	BU
2008 Proof	8,000	Value: 950				

KM# 1838 200 YUAN
15.5000 g., 0.9990 Gold 0.4978 oz. AGW, 58 x 39 mm. **Subject:** Year of the Rat **Shape:** Fan

Date	Mintage	F	VF	XF	Unc	BU
2008 Proof	6,600	Value: 1,000				

KM# 1883 200 YUAN
15.5000 g., 0.9990 Gold 0.4978 oz. AGW **Subject:** Year of the Ox **Shape:** Fan

Date	Mintage	F	VF	XF	Unc	BU
2009 Proof	6,600	Value: 1,000				

KM# 1882 200 YUAN
15.5000 g., 0.9990 Gold 0.4978 oz. AGW **Subject:** Year of the Ox **Shape:** Flower

Date	Mintage	F	VF	XF	Unc	BU
2009 Proof	8,000	Value: 950				

KM# 1915 200 YUAN
15.5500 g., 0.9990 Gold 0.4994 oz. AGW **Subject:** Year of the Tiger **Shape:** Arc

Date	Mintage	F	VF	XF	Unc	BU
2010	6,600	—	—	—	—	975

KM# 1916 200 YUAN
15.5500 g., 0.9990 Gold 0.4994 oz. AGW **Subject:** Year of the Tiger **Shape:** Scalloped

Date	Mintage	F	VF	XF	Unc	BU
2010 Proof	8,000	Value: 925				

KM# 1964 200 YUAN
15.5000 g., 0.9990 Gold 0.4978 oz. AGW **Subject:** Year of the Rabbit **Shape:** Arc **Note:** Photo reduced.

Date	Mintage	F	VF	XF	Unc	BU
2011	6,600	—	—	—	—	975

KM# 1965 200 YUAN
15.5500 g., 0.9990 Gold 0.4994 oz. AGW, 27 mm. **Subject:** Year of the Rabbit **Shape:** Scallop

Date	Mintage	F	VF	XF	Unc	BU
2011 Proof	8,000	Value: 925				

KM# 2013 200 YUAN
15.5500 g., 0.9990 Gold 0.4994 oz. AGW **Subject:** Year of the Dragon **Shape:** Fan

Date	Mintage	F	VF	XF	Unc	BU
2012 Proof	—	Value: 1,000				

KM# 2014 200 YUAN
15.5500 g., 0.9990 Gold 0.4994 oz. AGW, 27 mm. **Subject:** Year of the Dragon **Shape:** Scalloped

Date	Mintage	F	VF	XF	Unc	BU
2012 Proof	—	Value: 950				

KM# 1378 2000 YUAN
155.5175 g., 0.9990 Gold 4.9948 oz. AGW, 80 x 50 mm. **Subject:** Year of the Snake **Shape:** Rectangle **Note:** Prev. #Y1046.

Date	Mintage	F	VF	XF	Unc	BU
2001 Proof	118	Value: 22,500				

KM# 1422 2000 YUAN
155.5175 g., 0.9999 Gold 4.9993 oz. AGW **Subject:** Year of the Horse **Shape:** Rectangle **Note:** Prev. #Y1152.

Date	Mintage	F	VF	XF	Unc	BU
2002 Proof	118	Value: 22,500				

KM# 1483 2000 YUAN
155.5190 g., 0.9999 Gold 4.9993 oz. AGW **Subject:** Year of the Goat **Note:** Prev. #Y1163.

Date	Mintage	F	VF	XF	Unc	BU
2003 Proof	118	Value: 22,500				

KM# 1552 2000 YUAN
155.1750 g., 0.9999 Gold 4.9883 oz. AGW **Subject:** Year of the Monkey **Note:** Prev. #Y1170. Illustration reduced.

Date	Mintage	F	VF	XF	Unc	BU
2004 Proof	118	Value: 22,500				

KM# 1605 2000 YUAN
155.5500 g., 0.9990 Gold 4.9958 oz. AGW, 64 x 40 mm. **Subject:** Year of the Rooster **Obv:** Classical rooster **Rev:** Rooster, hen and chicks **Shape:** Rectangle **Note:** Photo reduced.

Date	Mintage	F	VF	XF	Unc	BU
2005 Proof	118	Value: 22,500				

KM# 1678 2000 YUAN
155.5500 g., 0.9990 Gold 4.9958 oz. AGW, 64 x 40 mm. **Subject:** Year of the Dog **Obv:** Classical dog **Rev:** Two dogs **Note:** Photo reduced.

Date	Mintage	F	VF	XF	Unc	BU
2006 Proof	118	Value: 22,500				

KM# 1726 2000 YUAN
155.5500 g., 0.9990 Gold 4.9958 oz. AGW, 64 x 40 mm. **Subject:** Year of the Pig **Obv:** Classical pig **Rev:** Sow and four piglets **Shape:** Rectangle

Date	Mintage	F	VF	XF	Unc	BU
2007 Proof	118	Value: 22,500				

KM# 1840 2000 YUAN
155.0000 g., 0.9990 Gold 4.9782 oz. AGW, 64 x 40 mm. **Subject:** Year of the Rat **Shape:** Rectangle

Date	Mintage	F	VF	XF	Unc	BU
2008 Proof	118	Value: 22,500				

KM# 1885 2000 YUAN
155.5000 g., 0.9990 Gold 4.9942 oz. AGW, 64x40 mm. **Subject:** Year of the Ox **Shape:** Rectangle

Date	Mintage	F	VF	XF	Unc	BU
2009 Proof	118	Value: 22,500				

KM# 1913 2000 YUAN
155.2000 g., 0.9990 Gold 4.9846 oz. AGW, 64x40 mm.
Subject: Year of the Tiger **Shape:** Rectangle

Date	Mintage	F	VF	XF	Unc	BU
2010 Proof	118	Value: 20,000				

KM# 1962 2000 YUAN
155.5000 g., 0.9990 Gold 4.9942 oz. AGW, 64x40 mm.
Subject: Year of the Rabbit **Shape:** Rectangle **Note:** Photo reduced.

Date	Mintage	F	VF	XF	Unc	BU
2011 Proof	118	Value: 20,000				

KM# 1963 2000 YUAN
155.5000 g., 0.9990 Gold 4.9942 oz. AGW **Subject:** Year of the Rabbit **Rev:** Multicolor **Note:** Photo reduced.

Date	Mintage	F	VF	XF	Unc	BU
2011 Proof	1,800	Value: 9,500				

KM# 2011 2000 YUAN
155.5500 g., 0.9990 Gold 4.9958 oz. AGW, 64x40 mm.
Subject: Year of the Dragon **Shape:** Rectangle

Date	Mintage	F	VF	XF	Unc	BU
2012 Proof	—	Value: 20,000				

KM# 2012 2000 YUAN
155.5500 g., 0.9990 Gold 4.9958 oz. AGW **Subject:** Year of the Dragon **Rev:** Colored Dragon

Date	Mintage	F	VF	XF	Unc	BU
2012 Proof	—	Value: 9,500				

KM# 2031 2000 YUAN
155.5500 g., 0.9990 Gold 4.9958 oz. AGW, 60 mm.

Date	Mintage	F	VF	XF	Unc	BU
2012 Proof	—	Value: 11,000				

KM# 1381 10000 YUAN
1000.0000 g., 0.9990 Gold 32.117 oz. AGW **Subject:** Year of the Snake **Shape:** Scalloped **Note:** Prev. #Y1047.

Date	Mintage	F	VF	XF	Unc	BU
2001 Proof	15	Value: 125,000				

KM# 1427 10000 YUAN
1000.0000 g., 0.9999 Gold 32.146 oz. AGW **Subject:** Year of the Horse **Shape:** Scalloped **Note:** Prev. #Y1153.

Date	Mintage	F	VF	XF	Unc	BU
2002 Proof	15	Value: 90,000				

KM# 1482 10000 YUAN
1000.0000 g., 0.9999 Gold 32.146 oz. AGW, 100 mm. **Subject:** Year of the Goat **Shape:** Scalloped **Note:** Prev. #Y1166.

Date	Mintage	F	VF	XF	Unc	BU
2003 Proof	15	Value: 75,000				

KM# 1550 10000 YUAN
1000.0000 g., 0.9999 Gold 32.146 oz. AGW, 100 mm. **Subject:** Year of the Monkey **Shape:** Scalloped **Note:** Prev. #Y1171.

Date	Mintage	F	VF	XF	Unc	BU
2004 Proof	15	Value: 90,000				

KM# 1604 10000 YUAN
1000.0000 g., 0.9990 Gold 32.117 oz. AGW, 100 mm. **Obv:** Classical rooster **Rev:** Rooster strutting **Edge:** Scalloped **Note:** Photo reduced.

Date	Mintage	F	VF	XF	Unc	BU
2005 Proof	15	Value: 75,000				

KM# 1727 10000 YUAN
1000.0000 g., 0.9990 Gold 32.117 oz. AGW, 100 mm. **Subject:** Year of the Pig **Obv:** Classical pig **Rev:** Three pigs **Shape:** Scalloped

Date	Mintage	F	VF	XF	Unc	BU
2007 Proof	118	Value: 70,000				

KM# 1841 10000 YUAN
1000.0000 g., 0.9990 Gold 32.117 oz. AGW, 100 mm. **Subject:** Year of the Rat **Shape:** Scalloped

Date	Mintage	F	VF	XF	Unc	BU
2008 Proof	118	Value: 70,000				

KM# 1912 10000 YUAN
1000.0000 g., 0.9990 Gold 32.117 oz. AGW, 100 mm. **Subject:** Year of the Tiger **Shape:** Scalloped

Date	Mintage	F	VF	XF	Unc	BU
2010 Proof	118	Value: 68,000				

KM# 1961 10000 YUAN
1000.0000 g., 0.9990 Gold 32.117 oz. AGW, 100 mm. **Subject:** Year of the Rabbit **Shape:** Scalloped **Note:** Photo reduced.

Date	Mintage	F	VF	XF	Unc	BU
2011 Proof	118	Value: 68,000				

KM# 2010 10000 YUAN
1000.0000 g., 0.9990 Gold 32.117 oz. AGW, 100 mm. **Subject:** Year of the Dragon

Date	Mintage	F	VF	XF	Unc	BU
2012 Proof	—	Value: 75,000				

KM# 1728 100000 YUAN
10000.0000 g., 0.9990 Gold 321.17 oz. AGW, 180 mm. **Subject:** Year of the Pig **Obv:** Classical pig **Rev:** Sow with four pigletts sucking

Date	Mintage	F	VF	XF	Unc	BU
2007 Proof	18	Value: 600,000				

KM# 1842 100000 YUAN
10000.0000 g., 0.9990 Gold 321.17 oz. AGW, 180 mm.

Date	Mintage	F	VF	XF	Unc	BU
2008 Proof	18	Value: 600,000				

KM# 1886 100000 YUAN
1000.0000 g., 0.9990 Gold 32.117 oz. AGW, 180 mm. **Subject:** Year of the Ox

Date	Mintage	F	VF	XF	Unc	BU
2009 Proof	118	Value: 70,000				

KM# 1887 100000 YUAN
10000.0000 g., 0.9990 Gold 321.17 oz. AGW, 180 mm.
Subject: Year of the Ox

Date	Mintage	F	VF	XF	Unc	BU
2009 Proof	—	Value: 700,000				

KM# 1911 100000 YUAN
10000.0000 g., 0.9990 Gold 321.17 oz. AGW, 180 mm.
Subject: Year of the Tiger

Date	Mintage	F	VF	XF	Unc	BU
2010 Proof	18	Value: 700,000				

KM# 1960 100000 YUAN
10000.0000 g., 0.9990 Gold 321.17 oz. AGW, 180 mm.
Subject: Year of the Rabbit **Note:** Photo reduced.

Date	Mintage	F	VF	XF	Unc	BU
2011 Proof	18	Value: 700,000				

KM# 2009 100000 YUAN
10000.0000 g., 0.9990 Gold 321.17 oz. AGW, 180 mm.
Subject: Year of the Dragon

Date	Mintage	F	VF	XF	Unc	BU
2012 Proof	—	Value: 700,000				

PALLADIUM BULLION COINAGE

Panda Series

KM# A1531 100 YUAN
15.5590 g., 0.9990 Palladium 0.4997 oz., 14 mm. **Rev:** Panda walking with cub

Date	Mintage	F	VF	XF	Unc	BU
2004 Proof	8,000	Value: 500				

KM# 1590 100 YUAN
15.5500 g., 0.9990 Palladium 0.4994 oz., 30 mm. **Obv:** Temple of Heaven **Rev:** Panda cub and mom seated in bamboo

Date	Mintage	F	VF	XF	Unc	BU
2005 Proof	8,000	Value: 530				

PLATINUM BULLION COINAGE

Panda Series

KM# 1470 50 YUAN
1.5500 g., 0.9995 Platinum 0.0498 oz. APW, 14.03 mm. **Obv:** Temple of Heaven, incuse legend **Rev:** Panda standing facing eating bamboo **Edge:** Reeded

Date	Mintage	F	VF	XF	Unc	BU
2003 Proof	50,000	Value: 135				

KM# 1532 50 YUAN

1.4500 g., 0.9995 Platinum 0.0466 oz. APW, 14 mm. **Obv:** Temple of Heaven, incuse legend **Rev:** Panda standing facing with cub **Edge:** Reeded

Date	Mintage	F	VF	XF	Unc	BU
2004 Proof	50,000	Value: 135				

KM# 1415 100 YUAN

3.1103 g., 0.9995 Platinum 0.0999 oz. APW, 18 mm. **Subject:** Panda Coinage 20th Anniversary **Obv:** Seated panda design of 1982 **Rev:** Walking panda design of 2002 **Edge:** Reeded **Note:** Prev. Y#1115.

Date	Mintage	F	VF	XF	Unc	BU
2002 Proof	20,000	Value: 250				

KM# 1591 100 YUAN

3.1100 g., 0.9990 Platinum 0.0999 oz. APW, 18 mm. **Obv:** Temple of Heaven **Rev:** Panda cub and mom seated in bamboo

Date	Mintage	F	VF	XF	Unc	BU
2005 Proof	30,000	Value: 200				

CHINA, REPUBLIC OF

TAIWAN

The Republic of China, comprising Taiwan (an island located 90 miles (145 km.) off the southeastern coast of mainland China), the offshore islands of Quemoy and Matsu and nearby islets of the Pescadores chain, has an area of 14,000 sq. mi. (35,980 sq. km.) and a population of 20.2 million. Capital: Taipei. During the past decade, manufacturing has replaced agriculture in importance. Fruits, vegetables, plywood, textile yarns and fabrics and clothing are exported.

The coins of Nationalist China do not carry A.D. dating, but are dated according to the year of the republic, which was established in 1911. However, republican years are added to 1911 to find the western year. Thus republican year 90 plus 1911 equals Gregorian calendar year 2001AD.

REPUBLIC

STANDARD COINAGE

Y# 550 1/2 YUAN

3.0000 g., Bronze, 18 mm. **Obv:** Orchid **Rev:** Value and Chinese symbols **Edge:** Plain

Date	Mintage	F	VF	XF	Unc	BU
90(2001) Proof	—	Value: 10.00				
92(2003)	—	—	—	0.30	1.00	1.25
92(2003) Proof	—	Value: 10.00				
93(2004)	—	—	—	0.30	1.00	1.25

Y# 551 YUAN

3.8000 g., Aluminum-Bronze, 20 mm. **Obv:** Bust of Chiang Kai-shek left **Rev:** Chinese value in center, 1 below **Edge:** Reeded

Date	Mintage	F	VF	XF	Unc	BU
90(2001) Proof	—	Value: 12.50				
92(2003)	—	—	—	0.15	0.30	0.45
92(2003) Proof	—	Value: 12.50				
94 (2005)	—	—	—	0.15	0.30	0.45
95(2006)	—	—	—	0.15	0.30	0.45
96(2007)	—	—	—	0.15	0.30	0.45
97(2008)	—	—	—	0.15	0.30	0.45
98(2009)	—	—	—	0.15	0.30	0.45
99(2010)	—	—	—	0.15	0.30	0.45
100(2011)	—	—	—	0.15	0.30	0.45
101(2012)	—	—	—	0.15	0.30	0.45

Y# 552 5 YUAN

4.4000 g., Copper-Nickel, 22 mm. **Obv:** Bust of Chiang Kai-shek left **Rev:** Chinese value in center, 5 below **Edge:** Reeded

Date	Mintage	F	VF	XF	Unc	BU
90(2001) Proof	—	Value: 12.50				
92(2003)	—	—	—	0.25	0.50	0.75
92(2003) Proof	—	Value: 12.50				
97(2008)	—	—	—	0.25	0.50	0.75
100(2011)	—	—	—	0.25	0.50	0.75
101 (2012)	—	—	—	0.25	0.50	0.75

Y# 553 10 YUAN

7.5000 g., Copper-Nickel, 26 mm. **Obv:** Bust of Chiang Kai-shek left **Rev:** Chinese value in center, 10 below **Edge:** Reeded

Date	Mintage	F	VF	XF	Unc	BU
90(2001) Proof	—	Value: 15.00				
92(2003)	—	—	0.25	0.45	0.75	1.00
92(2003) Proof	—	Value: 15.00				
93(2004)	—	—	—	0.45	0.75	1.00
94(2005)	—	—	—	0.45	0.75	1.00
95(2006)	—	—	—	0.45	0.75	1.00
96(2007)	—	—	—	0.45	0.75	1.00
96(2007) Proof	—	Value: 15.00				
97(2008)	—	—	—	0.45	0.75	1.00
98(2009)	—	—	—	0.45	0.75	1.00
99(2010)	—	—	—	0.45	0.75	1.00

Y# 567 10 YUAN

7.4300 g., Copper-Nickel, 26 mm. **Subject:** 90th Anniversary of the Republic **Obv:** Bust of Sun Yat-sen facing **Rev:** Holographic design and denomination **Edge:** Reeded

Date	Mintage	F	VF	XF	Unc	BU
90 (2001)	30,000,000	—	—	—	2.50	3.00

Y# 572 10 YUAN

7.5000 g., Copper-Nickel, 26 mm. **Subject:** Chiang Ching-kuo, president **Obv:** Portriat facing **Rev:** Two legends in latent format, large value below

Date	Mintage	F	VF	XF	Unc	BU
100 (2010)	—	—	—	—	2.00	3.00

Y# 573 10 YUAN

7.5000 g., Copper-Nickel, 26 mm. **Subject:** Chiang Wei-shui **Obv:** Portrait facing **Rev:** Two legends as latent images, large value below

Date	Mintage	F	VF	XF	Unc	BU
100 (2010)	—	—	—	—	2.00	3.00

Y# 574 10 YUAN

7.5000 g., Copper-Nickel, 26 mm. **Subject:** Dr. Sun Yat-sen **Obv:** Bust facing **Rev:** Two legends as latent images, large value below

Date	Mintage	F	VF	XF	Unc	BU
100 (2011)	—	—	—	—	2.00	3.00
101 (2012)	—	—	—	—	2.00	3.00

Y# 565 20 YUAN

8.5000 g., Bi-Metallic Copper-Nickel center in Aluminum-Bronze ring., 26.85 mm. **Subject:** Mona Rudao, Sediq chieftain **Obv:** Male portrait **Rev:** Three boats **Edge:** Reeded

Date	Mintage	F	VF	XF	Unc	BU
90(2001)	—	—	—	—	3.50	4.50
90(2001) Proof	—	Value: 18.00				
92(2003)	—	—	—	—	3.50	4.50
92(2003) Proof	—	Value: 18.00				
101(2012)	—	—	—	—	3.50	4.50

Y# 568 50 YUAN

10.0000 g., Aluminum-Bronze, 28 mm. **Obv:** Bust **Rev:** Denomination above latent image denomination **Edge:** Reeding and denomination

Date	Mintage	F	VF	XF	Unc	BU
90-2001 Proof	—	Value: 20.00				
91-2002	—	—	—	—	7.50	10.00
92-2003	—	—	—	—	7.50	10.00
92-2003 Proof	—	Value: 20.00				
93-2004	—	—	—	—	7.50	10.00
94-2005	—	—	—	—	7.50	10.00
95-2006	—	—	—	—	7.50	10.00
95-2006 Proof	—	Value: 20.00				
96-2007	—	—	—	—	7.50	10.00
97-2008	—	—	—	—	7.50	10.00
101-2012	—	—	—	—	7.50	10.00

Y# 570 50 YUAN

15.5680 g., 0.9990 Silver 0.5000 oz. ASW, 33 mm. **Subject:** World Cup Baseball **Obv:** Player at bat with ball background **Rev:** Mount Jade above denomination **Edge:** Reeded

Date	Mintage	F	VF	XF	Unc	BU
90(2001)	130,000	—	—	—	25.00	27.50

Y# 569 50 YUAN

15.5680 g., 0.9990 Silver 0.5000 oz. ASW, 33 mm. **Subject:** 90th Anniversary of the Republic **Obv:** Portrait of Sun Yat-sen **Rev:** Latent image above denomination **Edge:** Reeded

Date	Mintage	F	VF	XF	Unc	BU
90(2001)	230,000	—	—	—	25.00	27.50

Y# 571 50 YUAN

31.1035 g., 0.9990 Silver 0.9990 oz. ASW, 38 mm. **Subject:** Third National Expressway **Obv:** Multicolor island map **Rev:** Kao Ping Hsi bridge **Edge:** Reeded

Date	Mintage	F	VF	XF	Unc	BU
93-2004	20,000	—	—	—	45.00	50.00

MINT SETS

KM#	Date	Mintage	Identification	Issue Price	Mkt Val
MS9	92(2003) (6)	—	Y550-553, 565, 568 plus C-N Year of the Goat medal	—	20.00

PROOF SETS

KM#	Date	Mintage	Identification	Issue Price	Mkt Val
PS10	90(2001) (6)	210,000	Y#550-553, 565, 568 plus medal	29.40	90.00
PS12	92(2003) (6)	—	Y550-553, 565, 568 plus silver Year of the Goat Medal	—	100

COLOMBIA

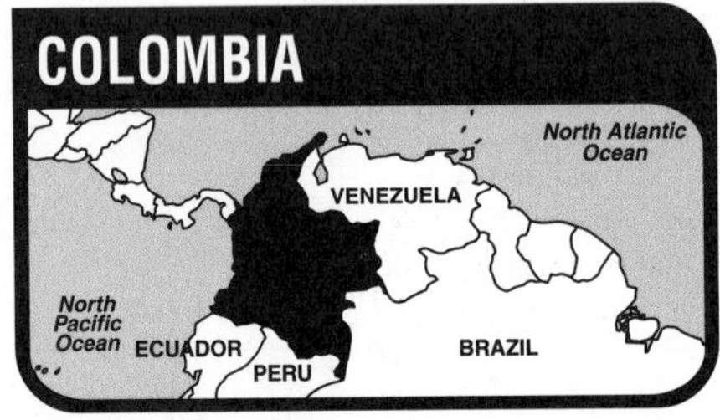

The Republic of Colombia, in the northwestern corner of South America, has an area of 440,831 sq. mi. (1,138,910 sq. km.) and a population of*42.3 million. Capital: Bogota. The economy is primarily agricultural with a mild, rich coffee being the chief crop. Colombia has the world's largest platinum deposits and important reserves of coal, iron ore, petroleum and limestone; other precious metals and emeralds are also mined. Coffee, crude oil, bananas, sugar and emeralds are exported.

MINT MARKS

A, M – Medellin (capital), Antioquia (state)
B - BOGOTA
(D) Denver, USA
H – Birmingham (Heaton & Sons)
(m) - Medellin, w/o mint mark
(Mo) - Mexico City
NI - Numismatica Italiana, Arezzo, Italy mint marks stylized in wreath
(P) - Philadelphia
(S) - San Francisco, USA.
(W) - Waterbury, CT (USA, Scoville mint)

REPUBLIC

DECIMAL COINAGE

100 Centavos = 1 Peso

KM# 282.2 20 PESOS

3.6000 g., Aluminum-Bronze, 20.25 mm. **Obv:** Flagged arms, 68 beads circle around the rim **Rev:** Denomination within wreath

Date	Mintage	F	VF	XF	Unc	BU
2003	15,900,000	—	—	—	0.50	0.75

KM# 294 20 PESOS

2.0000 g., Brass, 17.2 mm. **Obv:** Head of Simon Bolivar left **Rev:** Value **Edge:** Reeded

Date	Mintage	F	VF	XF	Unc	BU
2004	22,700,000	—	—	—	0.15	0.25
2005	56,100,000	—	—	—	0.15	0.25
2006	63,012,500	—	—	—	0.15	0.25
2007	87,300,000	—	—	—	0.15	0.25
2008	5,850,000	—	—	—	0.20	0.30

KM# 283.2 50 PESOS

4.6000 g., Copper-Nickel-Zinc, 21.8 mm. **Obv:** National arms, date below **Rev:** Denomination within wreath, 72 beads circle around rim **Edge:** Reeded

Date	Mintage	F	VF	XF	Unc	BU
2003	59,842,620	—	—	0.30	0.80	1.20
2004	51,700,000	—	—	0.30	0.80	1.20
2005	47,200,000	—	—	0.30	0.80	1.20
2006	22,000,000	—	—	0.30	0.80	1.20
2007	29,324,000	—	—	0.30	0.80	1.20
2008	67,500,000	—	—	0.30	0.80	1.20
2009	3,000,000	—	—	0.40	1.00	1.25
2010	55,100,000	—	—	0.25	0.75	1.00
2011	19,100,000	—	—	0.25	0.75	1.00
2012	—	—	—	0.25	0.75	1.00

KM# 283.2a 50 PESOS

Stainless Steel, 21.8 mm. **Obv:** National Arms **Rev:** Denomination within wreath, 72 beads circle around rim **Edge:** Reeded

Date	Mintage	F	VF	XF	Unc	BU
2007	—	—	—	—	0.80	1.20
2008	—	—	—	—	0.80	1.20
2009	—	—	—	—	0.80	1.20
2010	—	—	—	—	0.80	1.20

KM# 295 50 PESOS

2.0000 g., Nickel Plated Steel, 17 mm. **Obv:** Value at center **Rev:** Spectacled bear (Tremarctos ornatus)

Date	Mintage	F	VF	XF	Unc	BU
2012	—	—	—	—	80.00	1.20

KM# 285.2 100 PESOS

5.3100 g., Aluminum-Bronze, 23 mm. **Obv:** Flagged arms above date **Rev:** Denomination within wreath, numerals 6mm tall **Edge:** Segmented reeding and lettered **Edge Lettering:** CIEN PESOS (twice) **Note:** Edge varieties exist.

Date	Mintage	F	VF	XF	Unc	BU
2006	59,000,000	—	—	0.60	1.50	2.00
2007	55,000,000	—	—	0.60	1.50	2.00
2008	120,200,000	—	—	0.60	1.50	2.00
2009	41,800,000	—	—	0.60	1.50	2.00
2010	85,400,000	—	—	0.50	1.25	1.50
2011	108,500,000	—	—	0.50	1.25	1.50
2012	—	—	—	0.50	1.25	1.50

KM# 296 100 PESOS

3.3400 g., Brass Plated Steel, 20.3 mm. **Obv:** Value at center **Rev:** Colombian fruit frailejon

Date	Mintage	F	VF	XF	Unc	BU
2012	—	—	—	—	1.00	1.50

KM# 287 200 PESOS

7.0800 g., Copper-Nickel-Zinc, 24.4 mm. **Obv:** Denomination within lined circle, date below **Rev:** Quimbaya artwork **Edge Lettering:** MOTIVO QUIMBAYA - 200 PESOS

Date	Mintage	F	VF	XF	Unc	BU
2003	26,600,000	—	—	0.60	1.50	2.00
2004	31,200,000	—	—	0.60	1.50	2.00
2005	49,700,000	—	—	0.60	1.50	2.00
2006	75,462,500	—	—	0.60	1.50	2.00
2007	85,000,000	—	—	0.60	1.50	2.00
2008	110,400,000	—	—	0.60	1.50	2.00
2009	42,200,000	—	—	0.60	1.50	2.00
2010	85,600,000	—	—	0.60	1.50	2.00
2011	104,000,000	—	—	0.60	1.50	2.00
2012	—	—	—	0.60	1.50	2.00

KM# 297 200 PESOS

4.6100 g., Copper-Nickel-Zinc, 22.4 mm. **Obv:** Value at center **Rev:** Scarlet macaw (Ara macao)

Date	Mintage	F	VF	XF	Unc	BU
2012	—	—	—	—	1.50	2.00

KM# 286 500 PESOS

7.1400 g., Bi-Metallic Aluminum-Bronze center in Copper-Zinc-Nickel ring, 23.7 mm. **Obv:** Guacari tree within circle **Rev:** Denomination within circle, date below **Edge:** Segmented reeding

Date	Mintage	F	VF	XF	Unc	BU
2002	38,800,000	—	—	1.20	3.00	4.00
2003	26,410,000	—	—	1.20	3.00	4.00
2004	90,454,000	—	—	1.20	3.00	4.00
2005	97,664,000	—	—	1.20	3.00	4.00
2006	70,700,000	—	—	1.20	3.00	4.00
2007	109,624,000	—	—	1.20	3.00	4.00
2008	132,400,000	—	—	1.20	3.00	4.00
2009	39,700,000	—	—	1.20	3.00	4.00
2010	35,800,000	—	—	1.00	2.00	3.00
2011	76,200,000	—	—	1.00	2.00	3.00
2012	—	—	—	1.00	2.00	3.00

KM# 298 500 PESOS

7.1400 g., Bi-Metallic Aluminum-Bronze center in Copper-Nickel-Zinc ring, 23.7 mm. **Obv:** Value at center **Rev:** Glass frog (Hyalinobatrachium pellucidum) **Edge:** Segmented reeding

Date	Mintage	F	VF	XF	Unc	BU
2012	—	—	—	—	2.00	3.00

KM# 299 1000 PESOS

9.9500 g., Bi-Metallic Copper-Nickel-Zinc center in Aluminum-Bronze ring, 26.7 mm. **Obv:** Value at center with waves below **Rev:** Loggerhead sea turtle (Caretta caretta) and sea waves design **Edge:** Reeded & Security

Date	Mintage	F	VF	XF	Unc	BU
2012	—	—	—	—	5.00	7.50

COMOROS

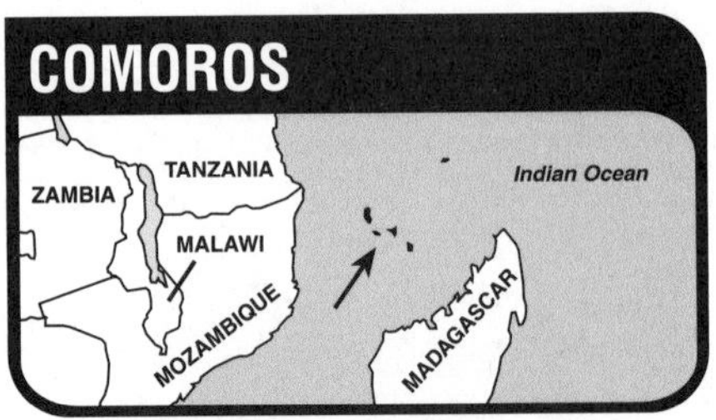

The Federal Islamic Republic of the Comoros, a volcanic archipelago located in the Mozambique Channel of the Indian Ocean 300 miles (483 km.) northwest of Madagascar, has an area of 719 sq. mi. (2,171 sq. km.) and a population of *714,000. Capital: Moroni. The economy of the islands is based on agriculture. There are practically no mineral resources. Vanilla, essence for perfumes, copra, and sisal are exported.

Ancient Phoenician traders were probably the first visitors to the Comoro Islands, but the first detailed knowledge of the area was gathered by Arab sailors. Arab dominion and culture were firmly established when the Portuguese, Dutch, and French arrived in the 16th century. In 1843 a Malagasy ruler ceded the island of Mayotte to France; the other three principal islands of the archipelago-Anjouan, Moheli, and Grand Comore came under French protection in 1886. The islands were joined administratively with Madagascar in 1912. The Comoros became partially autonomous, with the status of a French overseas territory, in 1946, and achieved complete internal autonomy in 1961. On Dec. 31, 1975, after 133 years of French association, the Comoro Islands became the independent Republic of the Comoros.

Mayotte retained the option of determining its future ties and in 1976 voted to remain French. Its present status is that of a French Territorial Collectivity. French currency now circulates there.

MINT MARKS

(a) - Paris, privy marks only
A - Paris

MONETARY SYSTEM

100 Centimes = 1 Franc

FEDERAL ISLAMIC REPUBLIC

BANQUE CENTRAL COINAGE

KM# 19 10 FRANCS

2.4000 g., Steel, 17 mm. **Obv:** Crescent and four stars **Rev:** Value

Date	Mintage	F	VF	XF	Unc	BU
2001(a)	—	—	—	—	7.50	15.00

KM# 14a 25 FRANCS

3.9700 g., Steel, 20 mm. **Series:** F.A.O. **Obv:** Chickens **Rev:** Denomination above date

Date	Mintage	F	VF	XF	Unc	BU
2001(a) Horseshoe	—	0.20	0.40	0.80	2.00	—

KM# 16 50 FRANCS

5.6000 g., Nickel, 23.93 mm. **Obv:** Crescent and stars above denomination, date below **Rev:** Building with tall tower **Edge:** Reeded

Date	Mintage	F	VF	XF	Unc	BU
2001(a) horseshoe	—	—	—	—	2.50	3.50

KM# 16a 50 FRANCS
Nickel Plated Steel, 23.9 mm. **Obv:** Crescent and stars above denomination, date below **Rev:** Building with tall tower **Edge:** Reeded

Date	Mintage	F	VF	XF	Unc	BU
2001(a)	—	0.25	0.50	1.00	2.50	3.50

KM# 18a 100 FRANCS
10.2000 g., Copper-Nickel, 28 mm. **Obv:** Crescent and stars above denomination, date below **Rev:** Boat and fish

Date	Mintage	F	VF	XF	Unc	BU
2003(a)	—	—	—	—	3.50	5.00

KM# 20 1000 FRANCS
22.2000 g., 0.9000 Silver 0.6423 oz. ASW, 37 mm. **Obv:** Crescent and four stars **Rev:** Mosque of the Sultans

Date	Mintage	F	VF	XF	Unc	BU
2002 Proof	500	Value: 100				

CONGO REPUBLIC

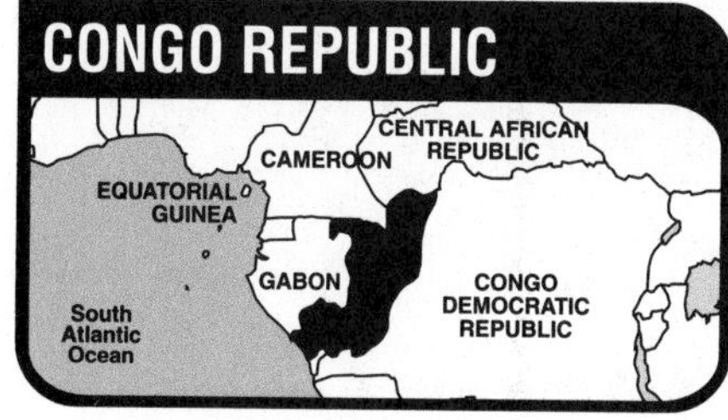

The Republic of the Congo (formerly the Peoples Republic of the Congo), located on the equator in west-central Africa, has an area of 132,047 sq. mi. (342,000 sq. km.) and a population of *2.98 million. Capital: Brazzaville. Agriculture forestry, mining, and food processing are the principal industries. Timber, industrial diamonds, potash, peanuts, and cocoa beans are exported.

NOTE: For earlier and related coinage see French Equatorial Africa and the Equatorial African States. For later coinage see Central African States.

RULER
French until 1960

MINT MARK
(a) - Paris, privy marks only

MONETARY SYSTEM
100 Centimes = 1 Franc

REPUBLIC
Republique du Congo
DECIMAL COINAGE

KM# 110 500 FRANCS
Silver **Subject:** History of aviation **Rev:** Swiss Air jet over mountains, 1931-2001, in color

Date	Mintage	F	VF	XF	Unc	BU
2002 Proof	—	Value: 40.00				

KM# 47 1000 FRANCS
15.0000 g., 0.9990 Silver 0.4818 oz. ASW, 35 mm. **Obv:** Seated woman with tablet **Rev:** Two soccer players and colosseum **Edge:** Plain

Date	Mintage	F	VF	XF	Unc	BU
2001 Proof	—	Value: 40.00				

KM# 48 1000 FRANCS
20.0000 g., 0.9990 Silver 0.6423 oz. ASW, 38 mm. **Obv:** Seated woman with tablet **Rev:** Two soccer players and Mexican pyramid **Edge:** Reeded

Date	Mintage	F	VF	XF	Unc	BU
2001 Proof	—	Value: 45.00				

KM# 112 1000 FRANCS
Silver, 38 mm. **Subject:** Thomas W. Lawson **Obv:** Female holding tablets **Rev:** Seven-masted Great Lakes Sconner sailing right

Date	Mintage	F	VF	XF	Unc	BU
2001 Proof	—	Value: 40.00				

KM# 113 1000 FRANCS
Silver, 38 mm. **Obv:** Female with tablets **Rev:** Hohenzollern castle

Date	Mintage	F	VF	XF	Unc	BU
2002 Proof	—	Value: 40.00				

KM# 114 1000 FRANCS
Silver, 38 mm. **Obv:** Female seated with tablets **Rev:** Nymphenburg palace

Date	Mintage	F	VF	XF	Unc	BU
2002 Proof	—	Value: 40.00				

KM# 109 1000 FRANCS
20.0000 g., 0.9990 Silver 0.6423 oz. ASW, 38.6 mm. **Obv:** Seated woman with tablets **Rev:** Portuguese merchant ship

Date	Mintage	F	VF	XF	Unc	BU
2002 Proof	—	Value: 45.00				

KM# 67 1000 FRANCS
31.1050 g., 0.9990 Silver 0.9990 oz. ASW, 40 mm. **Rev:** Eifle tower and franc coin in color

Date	Mintage	F	VF	XF	Unc	BU
2002 Proof	Est. 2,001	Value: 90.00				

KM# 68 1000 FRANCS
Silver **Subject:** African Wildlife **Shape:** Rectangle

Date	Mintage	F	VF	XF	Unc	BU
2002 Proof	—	—	—	—	—	—

KM# 115 1000 FRANCS
20.0000 g., 0.9990 Silver 0.6423 oz. ASW, 38.6 mm. **Obv:** Seated female with two tablets **Rev:** DC-3 aircraft in clouds

Date	Mintage	F	VF	XF	Unc	BU
2002 Proof	—	Value: 50.00				

KM# 116 1000 FRANCS
20.0000 g., 0.9990 Silver 0.6423 oz. ASW, 38.6 mm. **Obv:** Seated female with two tablets **Rev:** Swiss A-3000 flying over mountains

Date	Mintage	F	VF	XF	Unc	BU
2002 Proof	—	Value: 50.00				

KM# 50 1000 FRANCS
20.2000 g., Silver, 40 mm. **Series:** Endangered Wildlife **Obv:** Seated woman with tablet **Obv. Legend:** REPUBLIQUE DU CONGO **Rev:** Gorilla seated with infant **Rev. Legend:** - LE MONDE ANIMAL EN PERIL **Edge:** Reeded

Date	Mintage	F	VF	XF	Unc	BU
2003 Proof	—	Value: 50.00				

KM# 108 1000 FRANCS
20.0000 g., 0.9990 Silver 0.6423 oz. ASW, 38.6 mm. **Obv:** Seated woman with two tablets **Rev:** James Cook and the Endeavour

Date	Mintage	F	VF	XF	Unc	BU
2003 Proof	—	Value: 45.00				

KM# 117 1000 FRANCS
20.0000 g., 0.9990 Silver 0.6423 oz. ASW, 38.6 mm. **Obv:** Seated female with two tablets **Rev:** MD-11 aircraft on runway

Date	Mintage	F	VF	XF	Unc	BU
2003 Proof	—	Value: 50.00				

KM# 111 1000 FRANCS
Silver, 38 mm. **Subject:** Konrad Duden **Obv:** Female holding tablets **Rev:** Bust facing, writing

Date	Mintage	F	VF	XF	Unc	BU
2004 Proof	—	Value: 40.00				

KM# 118 1000 FRANCS
20.0000 g., 0.9990 Silver 0.6423 oz. ASW, 38.6 mm. **Obv:** Seated female with two tablets **Rev:** BAC-111 on grasy runway

Date	Mintage	F	VF	XF	Unc	BU
2004 Proof	—	Value: 50.00				

KM# 119 1000 FRANCS
20.0000 g., 0.9990 Silver 0.6423 oz. ASW, 38.6 mm. **Obv:** Seated female with two tablets **Rev:** DC-2 in clouds

Date	Mintage	F	VF	XF	Unc	BU
2004 Proof	—	Value: 50.00				

KM# 120 1000 FRANCS
20.0000 g., 0.9990 Silver 0.6423 oz. ASW, 38.6 mm. **Obv:** Seated female with two tablets **Rev:** DC-7 at airport

Date	Mintage	F	VF	XF	Unc	BU
2004 Proof	—	Value: 50.00				

KM# 51 1000 FRANCS
15.5000 g., Silver, 35.02 mm. **Obv:** Seated woman with tablet **Obv. Legend:** REPUBLIQUE DU CONGO **Rev:** Head of Michelangelo 3/4 right **Edge:** Plain

Date	Mintage	F	VF	XF	Unc	BU
2005 Proof	—	Value: 37.50				

KM# 72 1000 FRANCS
0.9990 Silver **Obv:** National Arms **Rev:** Steamlocomotive Limmat and Spanish Bon trasport (1847) from Baden to Zurich

Date	Mintage	F	VF	XF	Unc	BU
2007 Proof	—	Value: 75.00				

KM# 69 1500 FRANCS
1.2400 g., 0.9990 Gold 0.0398 oz. AGW, 13.92 mm. **Rev:** Ferdinand Graf von Zeppelin

Date	Mintage	F	VF	XF	Unc	BU
2005 Proof	—	Value: 100				

KM# 70 1500 FRANCS
1.2400 g., 0.9990 Gold 0.0398 oz. AGW, 13.92 mm. **Rev:** Spinx and Pyramids

Date	Mintage	F	VF	XF	Unc	BU
2005 Proof	—	Value: 100				

KM# 71 1500 FRANCS
1.2400 g., 0.9990 Gold 0.0398 oz. AGW, 13.94 mm. **Rev:** Neuschwanstein castle

Date	Mintage	F	VF	XF	Unc	BU
2005 Proof	—	Value: 100				

CONGO DEMOCRATIC REPUBLIC

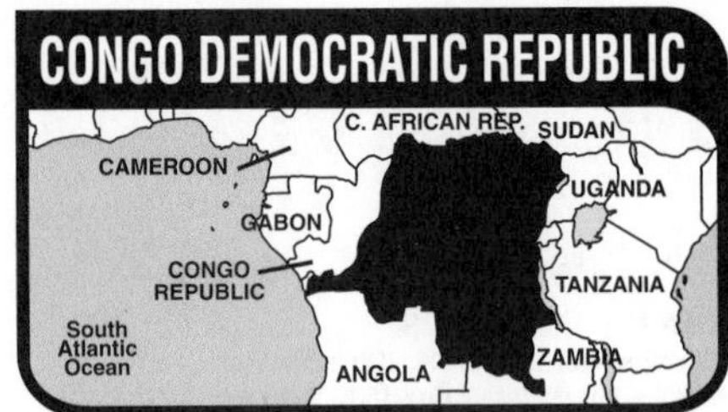

The Democratic Republic of the Congo (formerly the Republic of Zaire, and earlier the Belgian Congo), located in the south-central part of Africa, has an area of 905,568 sq. mi. (2,345,410 sq. km.) and a population of *47.4 million. Capital: Kinshasa. The mineral-rich country produces copper, tin, diamonds, gold, zinc, cobalt and uranium.

DEMOCRATIC REPUBLIC
1998 -
REFORM COINAGE

Congo Francs; July 1998

KM# 76 25 CENTIMES
0.8800 g., Aluminum, 19.90 mm. **Obv:** Lion left **Rev:** Mongoose **Edge:** Plain

Date	Mintage	F	VF	XF	Unc	BU
2002	—	—	—	—	0.75	1.00

KM# 77 25 CENTIMES
0.8500 g., Aluminum, 20 mm. **Obv:** Lion left **Rev:** Ram right, looking left **Edge:** Plain

Date	Mintage	F	VF	XF	Unc	BU
2002	—	—	—	—	0.75	1.00

KM# 83 25 CENTIMES
1.3000 g., Aluminum, 20 mm. **Obv:** Lion left **Rev:** Wild leaping dog right **Edge:** Plain

Date	Mintage	F	VF	XF	Unc	BU
2002	—	—	—	—	0.75	1.00

KM# 75 50 CENTIMES
2.2000 g., Aluminum, 26.97 mm. **Obv:** Lion left **Rev:** Soccer player right, bumping ball with head **Edge:** Plain

Date	Mintage	F	VF	XF	Unc	BU
2002	—	—	—	—	1.25	1.50

KM# 78 50 CENTIMES
2.1600 g., Aluminum, 27 mm. **Obv:** Lion left **Rev:** Giraffe right, looking left **Edge:** Plain

Date	Mintage	F	VF	XF	Unc	BU
2002	—	—	—	—	1.25	1.50

KM# 79 50 CENTIMES
2.2000 g., Aluminum, 26.92 mm. **Obv:** Lion left **Rev:** Gorilla facing, looking left **Edge:** Plain

Date	Mintage	F	VF	XF	Unc	BU
2002	—	—	—	—	1.00	1.25

KM# 80 50 CENTIMES
2.1600 g., Aluminum, 27 mm. **Obv:** Lion left **Rev:** Butterfly **Edge:** Plain

Date	Mintage	F	VF	XF	Unc	BU
2002	—	—	—	—	1.50	1.75

KM# 123 50 CENTIMES
3.9200 g., Stainless Steel, 22.3 mm. **Obv:** Lion left above denomination **Rev:** Verney L. Camereon **Edge:** Plain

Date	Mintage	F	VF	XF	Unc	BU
2002	—	—	—	—	1.00	1.25

KM# 81 FRANC
4.5700 g., Brass, 20.31 mm. **Obv:** Lion left **Rev:** Turtle **Edge:** Plain

Date	Mintage	F	VF	XF	Unc	BU
2002	—	—	—	—	1.25	1.50

KM# 82 FRANC
4.5200 g., Brass, 20.32 mm. **Obv:** Lion left **Rev:** Chicken **Edge:** Plain

Date	Mintage	F	VF	XF	Unc	BU
2002	—	—	—	—	1.50	1.75

KM# 156 FRANC
5.0000 g., Nickel Clad Steel, 24.8 mm. **Subject:** 25th Anniversary - Pope John Paul II's Visit **Obv:** Lion left **Rev:** Pope John Paul II as a priest in 1946 **Edge:** Plain

Date	Mintage	F	VF	XF	Unc	BU
2004	—	—	—	—	2.00	2.50

KM# 157 FRANC
5.0000 g., Nickel Clad Steel, 24.8 mm. **Subject:** 25th Anniversary - Pope John Paul II's Visit **Obv:** Lion left **Rev:** Pope John Paul II as a Cardinal in 1967 **Edge:** Plain

Date	Mintage	F	VF	XF	Unc	BU
2004	—	—	—	—	2.00	2.50

KM# 158 FRANC
5.0000 g., Nickel Clad Steel, 24.8 mm. **Subject:** 25th Anniversary - Pope John Paul II's Visit **Obv:** Lion left **Rev:** Pope John Paul II as newly elected pope in 1978 **Edge:** Plain

Date	Mintage	F	VF	XF	Unc	BU
2004	—	—	—	—	2.00	2.50

KM# 159 FRANC
5.0000 g., Nickel Clad Steel, 24.8 mm. **Subject:** 25th Anniversary - Pope John Paul II's Visit **Obv:** Lion left **Rev:** Pope John Paul II wearing a mitre **Edge:** Plain

Date	Mintage	F	VF	XF	Unc	BU
2004	—	—	—	—	2.00	2.50

KM# 174 FRANC
6.0000 g., Copper-Nickel, 21 mm. **Obv:** Lion left **Rev:** African Golden Cat right **Edge:** Plain

Date	Mintage	F	VF	XF	Unc	BU
2004	5,000	—	—	—	7.25	9.00

KM# 174a FRANC
8.0000 g., 0.9990 Silver 0.2569 oz. ASW, 21 mm. **Obv:** Lion left **Rev:** African Golden Cat right **Edge:** Plain

Date	Mintage	F	VF	XF	Unc	BU
2004	25	—	—	—	270	300

KM# 56 5 FRANCS
22.4000 g., Copper-Nickel, 39.8 mm. **Series:** Wild Life Protection **Obv:** Lion left **Rev:** Multicolor swallowtail butterfly hologram **Edge:** Reeded **Note:** Prev. KM#79.

Date	Mintage	F	VF	XF	Unc	BU
2002(2001)	20,000	—	—	—	35.00	40.00

KM# 57 5 FRANCS
22.4000 g., Copper-Nickel, 39.8 mm. **Series:** Wild Life Protection **Obv:** Lion left **Rev:** Multicolor dark greenish butterfly hologram **Edge:** Reeded **Note:** Prev. KM#80.

Date	Mintage	F	VF	XF	Unc	BU
2002(2001)	20,000	—	—	—	35.00	40.00

KM# 58 5 FRANCS
22.4000 g., Copper-Nickel, 39.8 mm. **Series:** Wild Life Protection **Obv:** Lion left **Rev:** Multicolor red and black butterfly hologram **Edge:** Reeded **Note:** Prev. KM#81.

Date	Mintage	F	VF	XF	Unc	BU
2002(2001)	20,000	—	—	—	35.00	40.00

KM# 170 5 FRANCS
24.3000 g., Copper-Nickel, 38.5 mm. **Obv:** Lion left **Rev:** Multicolor German 1 mark coin dated 2001 **Edge:** Reeded

Date	Mintage	F	VF	XF	Unc	BU
2002	—	—	—	—	15.00	20.00

KM# 198 5 FRANCS
Copper-Nickel, 38.6 mm. **Obv:** Lion left **Rev:** Cameleon on branch in color

Date	Mintage	F	VF	XF	Unc	BU
2003	—	—	—	—	—	25.00

KM# 214 5 FRANCS
22.4000 g., Copper-Nickel, 38.6 mm. **Subject:** Wild Life protection **Obv:** Lion left **Rev:** Loggerhead sea turtle

Date	Mintage	F	VF	XF	Unc	BU
2003	—	—	—	—	—	45.00

KM# 215 5 FRANCS
22.4000 g., Copper-Nickel, 38.6 mm. **Subject:** Wild Life Protection **Obv:** Lion left **Rev:** Dolphin as prism

Date	Mintage	F	VF	XF	Unc	BU
2003	—	—	—	—	—	40.00

KM# 216 5 FRANCS
22.4000 g., Copper-Nickel, 38.6 mm. **Subject:** Wild Life Protection **Obv:** Lion left **Rev:** Orca whale as prism

Date	Mintage	F	VF	XF	Unc	BU
2003	—	—	—	—	—	40.00

KM# 128 5 FRANCS
8.0000 g., Iron, 27.26x14.13 mm. **Obv:** Country name, lion and date in the bowl part of the spoon; value on the handle part **Edge:** Reeded **Note:** This is the Spoon part of the Compass and Spoon set. See also KM#127 (The spoon is the compass needle.)

Date	Mintage	F	VF	XF	Unc	BU
2004	5,000	—	—	—	15.00	—

KM# 164 5 FRANCS
25.4000 g., Copper-Nickel, 38.8 mm. **Subject:** Papal Visit **Obv:** Lion left **Rev:** Pope John Paul II with staff and mitre **Edge:** Reeded

Date	Mintage	F	VF	XF	Unc	BU
ND (2004) Proof	—	Value: 25.00				

KM# 165 5 FRANCS
49.5000 g., Copper-Nickel, 45.1 mm. **Obv:** Lion left **Rev:** Rotating 50 year calender **Edge:** Reeded

Date	Mintage	F	VF	XF	Unc	BU
ND(2004) Matte	—	—	—	—	75.00	—

KM# 146 5 FRANCS
27.0000 g., Copper-Nickel, 38.6 mm. **Obv:** Lion left **Rev:** Multicolor Quetzal bird **Edge:** Reeded

Date	Mintage	F	VF	XF	Unc	BU
2004 Proof	5,000	Value: 45.00				

KM# 147 5 FRANCS
27.0000 g., Copper-Nickel, 38.6 mm. **Obv:** Lion left **Rev:** Multicolor Bird of Paradise **Edge:** Reeded

Date	Mintage	F	VF	XF	Unc	BU
2004 Proof	5,000	Value: 45.00				

KM# 148 5 FRANCS
27.0000 g., Copper-Nickel, 38.6 mm. **Obv:** Lion left **Rev:** Multicolor Kingfisher bird **Edge:** Reeded

Date	Mintage	F	VF	XF	Unc	BU
2004 Proof	5,000	Value: 45.00				

KM# 166 5 FRANCS
2.1600 g., Wood Maple, 39.4 mm. **Obv:** Lion, brown ink **Rev:** Gorilla, brown ink **Edge:** Plain

Date	Mintage	F	VF	XF	Unc	BU
2005	2,000	—	—	—	21.00	—

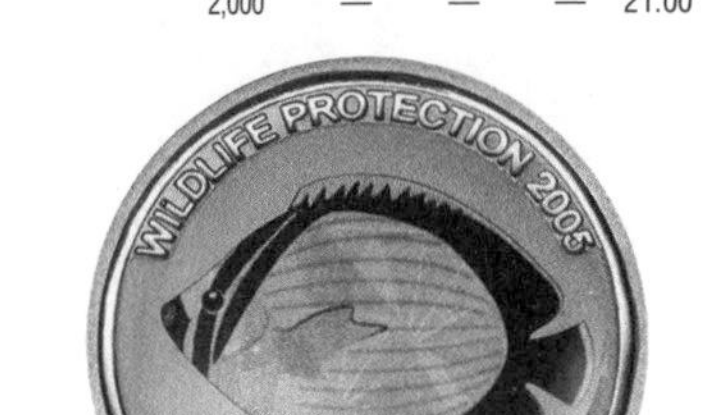

KM# 179 5 FRANCS
25.9200 g., Copper-Nickel, 38.6 mm. **Series:** Wildlife Protection **Obv:** Lion standing left **Obv. Legend:** REPUBLIQUE DEMOCRATIQUE DU CONGO **Rev:** Butterfly Fish, multicolor **Edge:** Reeded

Date	Mintage	F	VF	XF	Unc	BU
2005	5,000	—	—	—	—	26.00

KM# 180 5 FRANCS
25.9200 g., Copper-Nickel, 38.6 mm. **Series:** Wildlife Protection **Obv:** Lion standing left **Obv. Legend:** REPUBLIQUE DEMOCRATIQYE DU CONGO **Rev:** African Moony Fish, multicolor **Edge:** Reeded

Date	Mintage	F	VF	XF	Unc	BU
2005	5,000	—	—	—	—	26.00

KM# 181 5 FRANCS
25.9200 g., Copper-Nickel, 38.6 mm. **Series:** Wildlife Protection **Obv:** Lion standing laft **Obv. Legend:** REPUBLIQUE DENOCRATIQUE DU CONGO **Rev:** Red Perch, multicolor **Edge:** Reeded

Date	Mintage	F	VF	XF	Unc	BU
2005	5,000	—	—	—	—	20.00

KM# 182 5 FRANCS
Copper-Nickel, 38.6 mm. **Obv:** Lion standing left **Rev:** Two cupids embracing, roses - multicolor **Rev. Legend:** *Endless Love* **Edge:** Reeded **Shape:** Heart

Date	Mintage	F	VF	XF	Unc	BU
2005 Proof	5,000	Value: 35.00				

KM# 220 5 FRANCS
Silver, 38.6 mm. **Obv:** Lion standing left **Rev:** Swiss Guard standing at right in hallway

Date	Mintage	F	VF	XF	Unc	BU
2006 Proof	—	Value: 50.00				

KM# 178 5 FRANCS
26.3000 g., Silver Plated Bronze, 38.6 mm. **Obv:** Lion **Rev:** Multicolor Pope John Paul II wearing a mitre **Edge:** Reeded

Date	Mintage	F	VF	XF	Unc	BU
2007 Proof	—	Value: 40.00				

KM# 72 10 FRANCS
20.0000 g., 0.9250 Silver 0.5948 oz. ASW, 40.1 mm. **Series:** Airplanes **Obv:** Lion left **Rev:** Mikoyan-Gurevich Mig 21 fighter flying left **Edge:** Reeded

Date	Mintage	F	VF	XF	Unc	BU
2001 Proof	—	Value: 40.00				

KM# 74 10 FRANCS
31.1035 g., 0.9990 Silver 0.9990 oz. ASW, 40 mm. **Subject:** 2004 Olympics **Obv:** Lion left **Rev:** Convex chariot **Edge:** Reeded

Date	Mintage	F	VF	XF	Unc	BU
2001 Antique Finish	15,000	—	—	—	45.00	—

KM# 167 10 FRANCS
20.0000 g., 0.9250 Silver 0.5948 oz. ASW, 40.1 mm. **Obv:** Lion left **Rev:** SS Bremen ship at sea **Edge:** Reeded

Date	Mintage	F	VF	XF	Unc	BU
2001 Proof	—	Value: 35.00				

KM# 168 10 FRANCS
20.0000 g., 0.9250 Silver 0.5948 oz. ASW, 40.1 mm. **Obv:** Lion left **Rev:** RMS Queen Elizabeth 2 at sea **Edge:** Reeded

Date	Mintage	F	VF	XF	Unc	BU
2001 Proof	—	Value: 35.00				

KM# 169 10 FRANCS
20.0000 g., 0.9250 Silver 0.5948 oz. ASW, 30 mm. **Obv:** Lion left **Rev:** Sail Ship America **Edge:** Reeded

Date	Mintage	F	VF	XF	Unc	BU
2001 Proof	—	Value: 35.00				

KM# 197 10 FRANCS
20.0000 g., 0.5948 Silver 0.3824 oz. ASW, 40.1 mm. **Obv:** LIon left **Rev:** SS Andrea Doria sailing left

Date	Mintage	F	VF	XF	Unc	BU
2001 Proof	—	Value: 45.00				

KM# 199 10 FRANCS
Silver, 40.1 mm. **Obv:** Lion left **Rev:** M.S. Voyager of the Seas sailing left

Date	Mintage	F	VF	XF	Unc	BU
2001 Proof	—	Value: 45.00				

KM# 175 10 FRANCS
25.8300 g., Silver, 40 mm. **Obv:** Lion left **Rev:** 3 players **Edge:** Reeded

Date	Mintage	F	VF	XF	Unc	BU
2001	—	—	—	—	—	50.00

KM# 38 10 FRANCS
31.3000 g., 0.9250 Silver 0.9308 oz. ASW, 27 x 47.1 mm. **Subject:** Illusion **Obv:** Lion left **Rev:** Multicolor couple in flower picture **Edge:** Plain **Shape:** Rectangular **Note:** Prev. KM#61.

Date	Mintage	F	VF	XF	Unc	BU
2001 Proof	—	Value: 50.00				

KM# 59 10 FRANCS
25.9500 g., 0.9250 Silver 0.7717 oz. ASW, 39.9 mm. **Series:** Wild Life Protection **Obv:** Lion left **Rev:** Multicolor swallowtail butterfly hologram **Edge:** Reeded **Note:** Prev. KM#82.

Date	Mintage	F	VF	XF	Unc	BU
2002 (2001) Proof	15,000	Value: 65.00				

KM# 60 10 FRANCS
25.9500 g., 0.9250 Silver 0.7717 oz. ASW, 39.9 mm. **Series:** Wild Life Protection **Obv:** Lion left **Rev:** Multicolor dark greenish butterfly hologram **Edge:** Reeded **Note:** Prev. KM#83.

Date	Mintage	F	VF	XF	Unc	BU
2002 (2001) Proof	15,000	Value: 65.00				

KM# 61 10 FRANCS
25.9500 g., 0.9250 Silver 0.7717 oz. ASW, 39.9 mm. **Series:** Wild Life Protection **Obv:** Lion left **Rev:** Multicolor red and black butterfly hologram **Edge:** Reeded **Note:** Prev. KM#84.

Date	Mintage	F	VF	XF	Unc	BU
2002 (2001) Proof	15,000	Value: 65.00				

KM# 65 10 FRANCS
20.0000 g., 0.9250 Silver 0.5948 oz. ASW, 40.1 mm. **Series:** Airplanes **Obv:** Lion left **Rev:** Vickers Vimy twin engine biplane flying left **Edge:** Reeded **Note:** Prev. KM#88.

Date	Mintage	F	VF	XF	Unc	BU
2001 Proof	—	Value: 40.00				

KM# 66 10 FRANCS
20.0000 g., 0.9250 Silver 0.5948 oz. ASW, 40.1 mm. **Series:** Airplanes **Obv:** Lion left **Rev:** Fokker DR1 triplane flying left **Edge:** Reeded **Note:** Prev. KM#89.

Date	Mintage	F	VF	XF	Unc	BU
2001 Proof	—	Value: 40.00				

KM# 67 10 FRANCS
20.0000 g., 0.9250 Silver 0.5948 oz. ASW, 40.1 mm. **Series:** Airplanes **Obv:** Lion left **Rev:** Lockheed Vega flying left **Edge:** Reeded **Note:** Prev. KM#90.

Date	Mintage	F	VF	XF	Unc	BU
2001 Proof	—	Value: 40.00				

KM# 68 10 FRANCS
20.0000 g., 0.9250 Silver 0.5948 oz. ASW, 40.1 mm. **Series:** Airplanes **Obv:** Lion left **Rev:** Boeing 314 Clipper flying left **Edge:** Reeded **Note:** Prev. KM#91.

Date	Mintage	F	VF	XF	Unc	BU
2001 Proof	—	Value: 40.00				

KM# 69 10 FRANCS
20.0000 g., 0.9250 Silver 0.5948 oz. ASW, 40.1 mm. **Series:** Airplanes **Obv:** Lion left **Rev:** Junkers JU-87 Stuka in a dive **Edge:** Reeded **Note:** Prev. KM#92.

Date	Mintage	F	VF	XF	Unc	BU
2001 Proof	—	Value: 40.00				

KM# 70 10 FRANCS
20.0000 g., 0.9250 Silver 0.5948 oz. ASW, 40.1 mm. **Series:** Airplanes **Obv:** Lion left **Rev:** B-29 Enola Gay flying left **Edge:** Reeded **Note:** Prev. KM#93.

Date	Mintage	F	VF	XF	Unc	BU
2001 Proof	—	Value: 45.00				

KM# 71 10 FRANCS
20.0000 g., 0.9250 Silver 0.5948 oz. ASW, 40.1 mm. **Series:** Airplanes **Obv:** Lion left **Rev:** Bell X-1 rocket plane flying left **Edge:** Reeded **Note:** Prev. KM#94.

Date	Mintage	F	VF	XF	Unc	BU
2001 Proof	—	Value: 40.00				

KM# 91 10 FRANCS
31.1000 g., 0.9990 Silver 0.9988 oz. ASW, 40 mm. **Subject:** Olympics **Obv:** Lion left **Rev:** Ancient athlete incuse design **Edge:** Plain **Note:** Design hubs with the design of the 500 sika coin KM-42 of Ghana

Date	Mintage	F	VF	XF	Unc	BU
2002 Antiqued finish	—	—	—	—	40.00	—

KM# 124 10 FRANCS
26.0000 g., 0.9250 Silver 0.7732 oz. ASW, 40 mm. **Subject:** Field Marshal Erwin Rommel **Obv:** Lion left above value **Rev:** Rommel, tank and map **Edge:** Reeded

Date	Mintage	F	VF	XF	Unc	BU
2002 Proof	15,000	Value: 42.50				

KM# 125 10 FRANCS
26.0000 g., 0.9250 Silver 0.7732 oz. ASW, 40 mm. **Subject:** George S. Patton **Obv:** Lion left above value **Rev:** Patton, tank and map **Edge:** Reeded

Date	Mintage	F	VF	XF	Unc	BU
2002 Proof	15,000	Value: 42.50				

KM# 162 10 FRANCS
20.2000 g., 0.9990 Silver 0.6488 oz. ASW, 40 mm. **Obv:** Lion left **Rev:** Space shuttle and five astronauts **Edge:** Reeded

Date	Mintage	F	VF	XF	Unc	BU
2002 Proof	—	Value: 40.00				

KM# 189 10 FRANCS
26.1500 g., Copper-Nickel, 40.3 mm. **Series:** Automobiles **Obv:** Lion standing left **Rev:** Rolls Royce **Edge:** Reeded

Date	Mintage	F	VF	XF	Unc	BU
2002 Proof	—	Value: 18.00				

KM# 190 10 FRANCS
26.1500 g., Copper-Nickel, 40.3 mm. **Series:** Automobiles **Obv:** Lion standing left **Rev:** Peujeot

Date	Mintage	F	VF	XF	Unc	BU
2002 Proof	—	Value: 18.00				

KM# 191 10 FRANCS
26.1500 g., Copper-Nickel, 40.3 mm. **Series:** Automobiles **Obv:** Lion standing left **Rev:** Opel **Edge:** Reeded

Date	Mintage	F	VF	XF	Unc	BU
2002 Proof	—	Value: 18.00				

KM# 192 10 FRANCS
26.1500 g., Copper-Nickel, 40.3 mm. **Series:** Automobiles **Obv:** Lion standing left **Rev:** Cadillac

Date	Mintage	F	VF	XF	Unc	BU
2002 Proof	—	Value: 18.00				

KM# 93 10 FRANCS
31.2300 g., 0.9990 Silver 1.0030 oz. ASW, 38.7 mm. **Obv:** Lion left **Rev:** Bearded portrait of Verney L. Camereon **Edge:** Reeded

Date	Mintage	F	VF	XF	Unc	BU
2002	—	—	—	—	45.00	50.00

KM# 94 10 FRANCS
26.1500 g., Copper-Nickel, 40.3 mm. **Subject:** Historic Automobiles **Obv:** Lion left **Rev:** 1908 Berliet car **Edge:** Reeded

Date	Mintage	F	VF	XF	Unc	BU
2002 Proof	—	Value: 18.00				

KM# 95 10 FRANCS
26.1500 g., Copper-Nickel, 40.3 mm. **Subject:** Historic Automobiles **Obv:** Lion left **Rev:** 1919 Hispano Suiza H6 car right **Edge:** Reeded

Date	Mintage	F	VF	XF	Unc	BU
2002 Proof	—	Value: 18.00				

KM# 96 10 FRANCS
32.0000 g., Silver Plated Copper, 40 mm. **Subject:** World Cup Soccer **Obv:** Lion left **Rev:** Soccer player and multicolor American flag **Edge:** Reeded

Date	Mintage	F	VF	XF	Unc	BU
2002 Proof	20,000	Value: 50.00				

KM# 97 10 FRANCS
32.0000 g., Silver Plated Copper, 40 mm. **Subject:** World Cup Soccer **Obv:** Lion left **Rev:** Two soccer players and multicolor flag of Ecuador **Edge:** Reeded

Date	Mintage	F	VF	XF	Unc	BU
2002 Proof	20,000	Value: 50.00				

KM# 103 10 FRANCS
19.0000 g., 0.9990 Silver 0.6102 oz. ASW, 40 mm. **Series:** Airplanes **Obv:** Lion left **Rev:** WWI German Gotha Ursinus G bomber flying left at 8 o'clock **Edge:** Reeded

Date	Mintage	F	VF	XF	Unc	BU
2002 Proof	—	Value: 40.00				

KM# 104 10 FRANCS
19.0000 g., 0.9990 Silver 0.6102 oz. ASW, 40 mm. **Series:** Airplanes **Obv:** Lion left **Rev:** WWII ME 109 German fighter plane flying left **Edge:** Reeded

Date	Mintage	F	VF	XF	Unc	BU
2002 Proof	—	Value: 40.00				

KM# 105 10 FRANCS
19.0000 g., 0.9990 Silver 0.6102 oz. ASW, 40 mm. **Series:** Airplanes **Obv:** Lion left **Rev:** Savoia-Marchetti S 55 seaplane flying left **Edge:** Reeded

Date	Mintage	F	VF	XF	Unc	BU
2002 Proof	—	Value: 40.00				

KM# 106 10 FRANCS
19.0000 g., 0.9990 Silver 0.6102 oz. ASW, 40 mm. **Series:** Airplanes **Obv:** Lion left **Rev:** B-58 Hustler Delta wing bomber flying left at 8 o'clock **Edge:** Reeded

Date	Mintage	F	VF	XF	Unc	BU
2002 Proof	—	Value: 40.00				

KM# 107 10 FRANCS
19.0000 g., 0.9990 Silver 0.6102 oz. ASW, 40 mm. **Series:** Airplanes **Obv:** Lion left **Rev:** CF-105 Arrow jet fighter plane flying right, nose up **Edge:** Reeded

Date	Mintage	F	VF	XF	Unc	BU
2002 Proof	—	Value: 40.00				

KM# 108 10 FRANCS
19.0000 g., 0.9990 Silver 0.6102 oz. ASW, 40 mm. **Series:** Airplanes **Obv:** Lion left **Rev:** XB-70 Valkyrie experimental jet bomber flying right **Edge:** Reeded

Date	Mintage	F	VF	XF	Unc	BU
2002 Proof	—	Value: 40.00				

KM# 187 10 FRANCS
26.1500 g., Copper-Nickel, 40.3 mm. **Series:** Automobiles **Obv:** Lion standing left **Rev:** Buick **Edge:** Reeded

Date	Mintage	F	VF	XF	Unc	BU
2002 Proof	—	Value: 18.00				

KM# 188 10 FRANCS
26.1500 g., Copper-Nickel, 40.3 mm. **Series:** Automobiles **Obv:** Lion standing left **Rev:** Land Rover **Edge:** Reeded

Date	Mintage	F	VF	XF	Unc	BU
2002 Proof	—	Value: 18.00				

KM# 193 10 FRANCS
26.1500 g., Copper-Nickel, 40.3 mm. **Series:** Automobiles **Obv:** Lion standing left **Rev:** Benz **Shape:** Reeded

Date	Mintage	F	VF	XF	Unc	BU
2002 Proof	—	Value: 18.00				

KM# 194 10 FRANCS
26.1500 g., Copper-Nickel, 40.3 mm. **Series:** Automobiles **Obv:** Lion standing left **Rev:** Audi **Edge:** Reeded

Date	Mintage	F	VF	XF	Unc	BU
2002 Proof	—	Value: 18.00				

KM# 195 10 FRANCS
26.1500 g., Copper-Nickel, 40.3 mm. **Series:** Automobiles **Obv:** Lion standing left **Rev:** Alfa Romero

Date	Mintage	F	VF	XF	Unc	BU
2002 Proof	—	Value: 18.00				

KM# 196 10 FRANCS
26.1500 g., Copper-Nickel, 40.3 mm. **Series:** Automobiles **Obv:** Lion standing left **Rev:** Ford Model 'T' **Edge:** Reeded

Date	Mintage	F	VF	XF	Unc	BU
2002 Proof	—	Value: 18.00				

KM# 163 10 FRANCS
39.1000 g., Acrylic, 49.9 mm. **Obv:** Old World Swallowtail butterfly above lion and value **Rev:** Rear view of the obverse **Edge:** Plain

Date	Mintage	F	VF	XF	Unc	BU
2003	—	—	—	—	75.00	—

KM# 171 10 FRANCS
39.1000 g., Acrylic, 49.9 mm. **Obv:** Gorch Fock sail ship above lion and value **Rev:** Rear view of the obverse design **Edge:** Plain

Date	Mintage	F	VF	XF	Unc	BU
2003	1,000	—	—	—	75.00	—

KM# 109 10 FRANCS
19.0000 g., 0.9990 Silver 0.6102 oz. ASW, 40 mm. **Obv:** Lion left **Rev:** 14 BIS early aircraft in flight **Edge:** Reeded

Date	Mintage	F	VF	XF	Unc	BU
2003 Proof	—	Value: 40.00				

KM# 110 10 FRANCS
19.0000 g., 0.9990 Silver 0.6102 oz. ASW, 40 mm. **Obv:** Lion left **Rev:** WWI Sopwith Camel fighter plane flying right **Edge:** Reeded

Date	Mintage	F	VF	XF	Unc	BU
2003 Proof	—	Value: 40.00				

KM# 111 10 FRANCS
19.0000 g., 0.9990 Silver 0.6102 oz. ASW, 40 mm. **Obv:** Lion left **Rev:** Curtiss NC-4 early seaplane flying left **Edge:** Reeded

Date	Mintage	F	VF	XF	Unc	BU
2003 Proof	—	Value: 40.00				

KM# 112 10 FRANCS
19.0000 g., 0.9990 Silver 0.6102 oz. ASW, 40 mm. **Obv:** Lion left **Rev:** Macchi-Castoldi MC-72 seaplane flying left at 8 o'clock **Edge:** Reeded

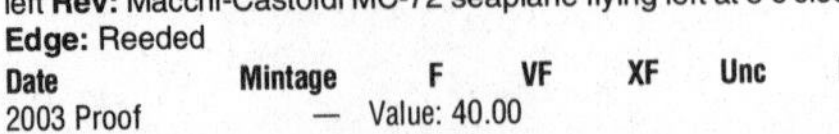

Date	Mintage	F	VF	XF	Unc	BU
2003 Proof	—	Value: 40.00				

KM# 113 10 FRANCS
19.0000 g., 0.9990 Silver 0.6102 oz. ASW, 40 mm. **Obv:** Lion left **Rev:** WWII CA-12 Boomerang fighter plane flying above map at 10 o'clock **Edge:** Reeded

Date	Mintage	F	VF	XF	Unc	BU
2003 Proof	—	Value: 40.00				

KM# 114 10 FRANCS
19.0000 g., 0.9990 Silver 0.6102 oz. ASW, 40 mm. **Obv:** Lion left **Rev:** B-50A Superfortress bomber flying left **Edge:** Reeded

Date	Mintage	F	VF	XF	Unc	BU
2003 Proof	—	Value: 40.00				

KM# 115 10 FRANCS
19.0000 g., 0.9990 Silver 0.6102 oz. ASW, 40 mm. **Obv:** Lion left **Rev:** WWII Heinkel-178 German jet plane flying left **Edge:** Reeded

Date	Mintage	F	VF	XF	Unc	BU
2003 Proof	—	Value: 40.00				

KM# 116 10 FRANCS
19.0000 g., 0.9990 Silver 0.6102 oz. ASW, 40 mm. **Obv:** Lion left **Rev:** Early De Havilland Comet jet liner flying left **Edge:** Reeded

Date	Mintage	F	VF	XF	Unc	BU
2003 Proof	—	Value: 40.00				

KM# 117 10 FRANCS
19.0000 g., 0.9990 Silver 0.6102 oz. ASW, 40 mm. **Obv:** Lion left **Rev:** Panavia Tornado jet fighter-bomber flying left **Edge:** Reeded

Date	Mintage	F	VF	XF	Unc	BU
2003 Proof	—	Value: 40.00				

KM# 118 10 FRANCS
19.0000 g., 0.9990 Silver 0.6102 oz. ASW, 40 mm. **Obv:** Lion left **Rev:** Hindustan HF24 jet fighter flying left **Edge:** Reeded

Date	Mintage	F	VF	XF	Unc	BU
2003 Proof	—	Value: 40.00				

KM# 119 10 FRANCS
19.0000 g., 0.9990 Silver 0.6102 oz. ASW, 40 mm. **Obv:** Lion left **Rev:** Lockheed F-117 Stealth fighter flying left **Edge:** Reeded

Date	Mintage	F	VF	XF	Unc	BU
2003 Proof	—	Value: 40.00				

KM# 120 10 FRANCS
19.0000 g., 0.9990 Silver 0.6102 oz. ASW, 40 mm. **Obv:** Lion left **Rev:** North American X-15 experimental rocket plane flying right at 1 o'clock **Edge:** Reeded

Date	Mintage	F	VF	XF	Unc	BU
2003 Proof	—	Value: 40.00				

KM# 122 10 FRANCS
25.0000 g., 0.9250 Silver 0.7435 oz. ASW, 38.6 mm. **Obv:** Lion left **Rev:** Multicolor 3D hologram view of Victoria Falls **Edge:** Reeded

Date	Mintage	F	VF	XF	Unc	BU
2003 Proof	5,000	Value: 50.00				

KM# 99.1 10 FRANCS
24.9100 g., 0.9250 Silver 0.7408 oz. ASW, 38.6 mm. **Obv:** Lion left **Rev:** Chameleon **Edge:** Reeded

Date	Mintage	F	VF	XF	Unc	BU
2003 Proof	—	Value: 45.00				

KM# 99.2 10 FRANCS
24.9100 g., 0.9250 Silver 0.7408 oz. ASW, 38.6 mm. **Obv:** Lion left **Rev:** Multicolor chameleon **Edge:** Reeded

Date	Mintage	F	VF	XF	Unc	BU
2003 Proof	—	Value: 50.00				

KM# 100 10 FRANCS
24.9100 g., 0.9250 Silver 0.7408 oz. ASW, 38.6 mm. **Obv:** Lion left **Rev:** Striped skunk **Edge:** Reeded

Date	Mintage	F	VF	XF	Unc	BU
2003 Proof	—	Value: 45.00				

KM# 101 10 FRANCS
24.9100 g., 0.9250 Silver 0.7408 oz. ASW, 38.6 mm. **Obv:** Lion left **Rev:** Porcupine on rock, right **Edge:** Reeded

Date	Mintage	F	VF	XF	Unc	BU
2003 Proof	—	Value: 47.50				

LES ANIMAUX D'EXCEPTION
Pangolin géant
2003

KM# 102 10 FRANCS
24.9100 g., 0.9250 Silver 0.7408 oz. ASW, 38.6 mm. **Obv:** Lion left **Rev:** Giant Pangolin on rock right **Edge:** Reeded

Date	Mintage	F	VF	XF	Unc	BU
2003 Proof	—	Value: 45.00				

KM# 132 10 FRANCS
25.0000 g., 0.9000 Silver 0.7234 oz. ASW, 40 mm. **Obv:** Lion left **Rev:** Multicolor dolphin leaping left **Edge:** Reeded

Date	Mintage	F	VF	XF	Unc	BU
2003 Proof	5,000	Value: 50.00				

KM# 133 10 FRANCS
25.0000 g., 0.9000 Silver 0.7234 oz. ASW, 40 mm. **Obv:** Lion left **Rev:** Multicolor sea turtle left **Edge:** Reeded

Date	Mintage	F	VF	XF	Unc	BU
2003 Proof	5,000	Value: 50.00				

KM# 134 10 FRANCS
25.0000 g., 0.9000 Silver 0.7234 oz. ASW, 40 mm. **Obv:** Lion left **Rev:** Multicolor killer whale jumping right **Edge:** Reeded

Date	Mintage	F	VF	XF	Unc	BU
2003 Proof	5,000	Value: 50.00				

KM# 135 10 FRANCS
26.0000 g., 0.9990 Silver 0.8350 oz. ASW, 40 mm. **Obv:** Lion left **Rev:** Pope John Paul II with staff and mitre, waving **Edge:** Reeded

Date	Mintage	F	VF	XF	Unc	BU
2003 Proof	—	Value: 55.00				

KM# 141 10 FRANCS
25.0000 g., 0.9250 Silver 0.7435 oz. ASW, 38.6 mm. **Obv:** Lion left **Rev:** Multicolor Emperor fish swimming left **Edge:** Reeded

Date	Mintage	F	VF	XF	Unc	BU
2004 Proof	5,000	Value: 55.00				

KM# 142 10 FRANCS
25.0000 g., 0.9250 Silver 0.7435 oz. ASW, 38.6 mm. **Obv:** Lion left **Rev:** Multicolor octopus facing **Edge:** Reeded

Date	Mintage	F	VF	XF	Unc	BU
2004 Proof	5,000	Value: 75.00				

KM# 143 10 FRANCS
25.0000 g., 0.9250 Silver 0.7435 oz. ASW, 38.6 mm. **Obv:** Lion left **Rev:** Formula 1 and GT race cars **Edge:** Reeded

Date	Mintage	F	VF	XF	Unc	BU
2004 Proof	5,000	Value: 45.00				

KM# 145 10 FRANCS
25.0000 g., 0.9250 Silver 0.7435 oz. ASW, 27x47 mm. **Obv:** Lion left **Rev:** Pope with crucifix **Edge:** Plain **Shape:** Rectangular

Date	Mintage	F	VF	XF	Unc	BU
2004 Proof	5,000	Value: 50.00				

KM# 149 10 FRANCS
25.0000 g., 0.9250 Silver 0.7435 oz. ASW, 38.6 mm. **Obv:** Lion left **Rev:** Multicolor Quetzal bird **Edge:** Reeded

Date	Mintage	F	VF	XF	Unc	BU
2004 Proof	5,000	Value: 50.00				

KM# 150 10 FRANCS
25.0000 g., 0.9250 Silver 0.7435 oz. ASW, 38.6 mm. **Obv:** Lion left **Rev:** Multicolor Bird of Paradise on branch left **Edge:** Reeded

Date	Mintage	F	VF	XF	Unc	BU
2004 Proof	5,000	Value: 55.00				

KM# 151 10 FRANCS
25.0000 g., 0.9250 Silver 0.7435 oz. ASW, 38.6 mm. **Obv:** Lion left **Rev:** Multicolor Kingfisher bird left **Edge:** Reeded

Date	Mintage	F	VF	XF	Unc	BU
2004 Proof	5,000	Value: 55.00				

KM# 155 10 FRANCS
Acrylic Clear, 50 mm. **Obv:** Etched nine-masted sailing junk above lion, value and country name **Edge:** Plain

Date	Mintage	F	VF	XF	Unc	BU
2004	2,000	—	—	—	55.00	—

KM# 126 10 FRANCS
25.0000 g., 0.9250 Silver 0.7435 oz. ASW, 38.6 mm. **Obv:** Lion left above value **Rev:** Sundial face with collapsible gnomon **Edge:** Reeded

Date	Mintage	F	VF	XF	Unc	BU
2004 Proof	5,000	Value: 50.00				

KM# 127 10 FRANCS
25.0000 g., 0.9250 Silver 0.7435 oz. ASW, 38.6 mm. **Obv:** Lion left above value **Rev:** Compass face **Edge:** Reeded **Note:** Compass part of the compass and spoon set (KM#128)

Date	Mintage	F	VF	XF	Unc	BU
2004 Proof	5,000	Value: 50.00				

KM# 179a 10 FRANCS
25.0000 g., 0.9250 Silver 0.7435 oz. ASW, 38.58 mm. **Series:** Wildlife Protection **Obv:** Lion standing left **Obv. Legend:** REPUBLIQUE DEMOCRATIQUE DU CONGO **Rev:** Butterfly Fish, multicolor **Edge:** Reeded

Date	Mintage	F	VF	XF	Unc	BU
2005 Proof	5,000	Value: 45.00				

KM# 180a 10 FRANCS
25.0000 g., 0.9250 Silver 0.7435 oz. ASW, 38.58 mm. **Series:** Wildlife Protection **Obv:** Lion standing left **Obv. Legend:** REPUBLIQUE DEMOCRATIQUE DU CONGO **Rev:** African Moony Fish, multicolor **Edge:** Reeded

Date	Mintage	F	VF	XF	Unc	BU
2005 Proof	5,000	Value: 45.00				

KM# 181a 10 FRANCS
25.0000 g., 0.9250 Silver 0.7435 oz. ASW, 38.58 mm. **Series:** Wildlife Protection **Obv:** Lion standing left **Obv. Legend:** REPUBLIQUE DEMOCRATIQUE DU CONGO **Rev:** Red Perch, multicolor **Edge:** Reeded

Date	Mintage	F	VF	XF	Unc	BU
2005 Proof	5,000	Value: 45.00				

KM# 172 10 FRANCS
25.0000 g., Silver, 38.6 mm. **Obv:** Lion left **Rev:** Pope waving half facing at left, cross at upper right, Vatican at lower right

Date	Mintage	F	VF	XF	Unc	BU
2005 Proof	3,000	Value: 50.00				

KM# 217 10 FRANCS
39.0000 g., Acrylic, 50 mm. **Obv:** John Paul II, lion and cross

Date	Mintage	F	VF	XF	Unc	BU
2005	—	—	—	—	—	50.00

KM# 218 10 FRANCS
39.1000 g., Acrylic, 50 mm. **Obv:** Sailing training vessel Amergo Vespucci

Date	Mintage	F	VF	XF	Unc	BU
2005	—	—	—	—	—	50.00

KM# 176 10 FRANCS
32.0000 g., 0.9990 Silver 1.0278 oz. ASW, 40 mm. **Obv:** Lion standing left **Obv. Legend:** REPUBLIQUE DEMOCRATIQUE DU CONGO **Rev:** World Trade Center Twin Towers as they were before 9-11 **Edge:** Reeded

Date	Mintage	F	VF	XF	Unc	BU
2006 Proof	—	Value: 50.00				

KM# 219 10 FRANCS
39.0000 g., Acrylic, 50 mm. **Obv:** Sailing ship Shtandart

Date	Mintage	F	VF	XF	Unc	BU
2006	—	—	—	—	—	50.00

KM# 221 10 FRANCS
Silver, 38.6 mm. **Obv:** Lion standing left **Rev:** Swiss Guard standing taking oath on flag

Date	Mintage	F	VF	XF	Unc	BU
2006 Proof	—	Value: 70.00				

KM# 222 10 FRANCS
39.1000 g., Acrylic, 50 mm. **Obv:** Admiral Michiel de Ruyter and sailing ship

Date	Mintage	F	VF	XF	Unc	BU
2007	—	—	—	—	—	50.00

KM# 200 10 FRANCS
Silver Plated Copper, 40 mm. **Subject:** Aviation Centennial 1903-2003 **Obv:** National arms **Rev:** Early aircraft and bust

Date	Mintage	F	VF	XF	Unc	BU
2008 Proof	—	Value: 15.00				

KM# 201 10 FRANCS
Silver Plated Copper, 40 mm. **Subject:** Warriors of the World **Obv:** National arms **Rev:** Spartan standing

Date	Mintage	F	VF	XF	Unc	BU
2010 Proof	—	Value: 20.00				

KM# 202 10 FRANCS
Silver Plated Copper, 40 mm. **Subject:** Warriors of the World **Obv:** National arms **Rev:** Centurian

Date	Mintage	F	VF	XF	Unc	BU
2010 Proof	—	Value: 20.00				

KM# 203 10 FRANCS
Silver Plated Copper, 40 mm. **Subject:** Warriors of the World **Obv:** National arms **Rev:** Gladiator standing

Date	Mintage	F	VF	XF	Unc	BU
2010 Proof	—	Value: 20.00				

KM# 204 10 FRANCS
Silver Plated Copper, 40 mm. **Subject:** Warriors of the World **Obv:** Naitonal arms **Rev:** Chinese warrior

Date	Mintage	F	VF	XF	Unc	BU
2010 Proof	—	Value: 20.00				

KM# 205 10 FRANCS
Silver Plated Copper, 40 mm. **Subject:** Warriors of the World **Obv:** Naitonal Arms **Rev:** Celtic Warrior

Date	Mintage	F	VF	XF	Unc	BU
2010 Proof	—	Value: 20.00				

KM# 206 10 FRANCS
Silver Plated Copper, 40 mm. **Subject:** Warriors of the World **Obv:** National arms **Rev:** Mongolian warrior on horseback

Date	Mintage	F	VF	XF	Unc	BU
2010 Proof	—	Value: 20.00				

KM# 207 10 FRANCS
Silver Plated Copper, 40 mm. **Subject:** Warriors of the World **Obv:** National arms **Rev:** Viking standing

Date	Mintage	F	VF	XF	Unc	BU
2010 Proof	—	Value: 20.00				

KM# 208 10 FRANCS
Silver Plated Copper, 40 mm. **Subject:** Warriors of the World **Obv:** National arms **Rev:** English Archer

Date	Mintage	F	VF	XF	Unc	BU
2010 Proof	—	Value: 20.00				

KM# 209 10 FRANCS
Silver Plated Copper, 40 mm. **Subject:** Warriors of the World **Obv:** National arms **Rev:** Templar Knight on horseback

Date	Mintage	F	VF	XF	Unc	BU
2010 Proof	—	Value: 20.00				

KM# 210 10 FRANCS
Silver Plated Copper, 40 mm. **Subject:** Warriors of the World **Obv:** National arms **Rev:** Ninja standing

Date	Mintage	F	VF	XF	Unc	BU
2010 Proof	—	Value: 20.00				

KM# 211 10 FRANCS
Silver Plated Copper, 40 mm. **Subject:** Warriors of the World **Obv:** National arms **Rev:** Samurai warrior standing

Date	Mintage	F	VF	XF	Unc	BU
2010 Proof	—	Value: 20.00				

KM# 212 10 FRANCS
Silver Plated Copper, 40 mm. **Subject:** Warriors of the World **Obv:** National arms **Rev:** Zulu warrior standing

Date	Mintage	F	VF	XF	Unc	BU
2010 Proof	—	Value: 20.00				

KM# 136 20 FRANCS
1.2440 g., 0.9999 Gold 0.0400 oz. AGW, 13.92 mm. **Obv:** Lion left **Rev:** Pope John Paul II with staff and mitre, waving **Edge:** Plain

Date	Mintage	F	VF	XF	Unc	BU
2003 Proof	—	Value: 75.00				

KM# 137 20 FRANCS
1.2440 g., 0.9999 Gold 0.0400 oz. AGW, 13.92 mm. **Obv:** Lion left **Rev:** Skunk **Edge:** Plain

Date	Mintage	F	VF	XF	Unc	BU
2003 Proof	25,000	Value: 75.00				

KM# 138 20 FRANCS
1.2440 g., 0.9999 Gold 0.0400 oz. AGW, 13.92 mm. **Obv:** Lion left **Rev:** Giant anteater right **Edge:** Plain

Date	Mintage	F	VF	XF	Unc	BU
2003 Proof	25,000	Value: 75.00				

KM# 139 20 FRANCS
1.2440 g., 0.9999 Gold 0.0400 oz. AGW, 13.92 mm. **Obv:** Lion left **Rev:** Porcupine right **Edge:** Plain

Date	Mintage	F	VF	XF	Unc	BU
2003 Proof	25,000	Value: 75.00				

KM# 140 20 FRANCS
1.2440 g., 0.9999 Gold 0.0400 oz. AGW, 13.92 mm. **Obv:** Lion left **Rev:** Chameleon **Edge:** Plain

Date	Mintage	F	VF	XF	Unc	BU
2003 Proof	25,000	Value: 75.00				

KM# 184 20 FRANCS
1.2200 g., 0.9999 Gold 0.0392 oz. AGW, 13.74 mm. **Subject:** XXVIII Summer Olympics - Athens **Obv:** Lion standing right **Rev:** Athenian tetradrachm featuring owl perched **Edge:** Reeded

Date	Mintage	F	VF	XF	Unc	BU
2003 Proof	25,000	Value: 75.00				

KM# 186 20 FRANCS
1.2441 g., 0.9999 Gold 0.0400 oz. AGW, 13.92 mm. **Subject:** Christmas **Obv:** Lion standing left **Rev:** Jesus lying in manger

Date	Mintage	F	VF	XF	Unc	BU
ND(2004) Proof	25,000	Value: 75.00				

KM# 144 20 FRANCS
1.2440 g., 0.9999 Gold 0.0400 oz. AGW, 13.92 mm. **Obv:** Lion left **Rev:** Ferrari coat of arms **Edge:** Plain

Date	Mintage	F	VF	XF	Unc	BU
2004 Proof	5,000	Value: 75.00				

KM# 173 20 FRANCS
1.5300 g., 0.9990 Gold 0.0491 oz. AGW, 13.9 mm. **Obv:** Lion left **Rev:** Pope waving at left, cross at upper right, Vatican at lower right

Date	Mintage	F	VF	XF	Unc	BU
2005 Proof	25,000	Value: 95.00				

KM# 213 25 FRANCS
Acrylic, 50mm mm. **Rev:** H.M. Bark Endeavour at center; Captian James Cook bust at top left, National arms at bottom center

Date	Mintage	F	VF	XF	Unc	BU
2009	—	—	—	—	—	55.00

KM# 223 30 FRANCS
20.0000 g., 0.9990 Silver 0.6423 oz. ASW, 38.61 mm. **Subject:** Big Cats - Lion

Date	Mintage	F	VF	XF	Unc	BU
2011 Proof	3,000	Value: 50.00				

KM# 224 30 FRANCS
20.0000 g., 0.9990 Silver 0.6423 oz. ASW, 38.61 mm. **Subject:** Big cats - Leopard

Date	Mintage	F	VF	XF	Unc	BU
2011 Proof	3,000	Value: 50.00				

KM# 225 30 FRANCS
20.0000 g., 0.9990 Silver 0.6423 oz. ASW, 38.61 mm. **Subject:** Big cats - Chetah

Date	Mintage	F	VF	XF	Unc	BU
2011 Proof	3,000	Value: 50.00				

KM# 226 30 FRANCS
20.0000 g., 0.9990 Silver 0.6423 oz. ASW, 38.61 mm. **Subject:** Big cats - Tiger

Date	Mintage	F	VF	XF	Unc	BU
2011 Proof	3,000	Value: 50.00				

KM# 185 75 FRANCS
15.5500 g., 0.9999 Gold 0.4999 oz. AGW **Subject:** XXVIII Summer Olympics - Athens **Obv:** Lion standing right **Rev:** Athenian tetradrachm featuring owl perched **Edge:** Reeded

Date	Mintage	F	VF	XF	Unc	BU
2003 Proof	500	Value: 900				

KM# 129 100 FRANCS
31.1000 g., 0.9999 Gold 0.9997 oz. AGW, 40 mm. **Series:** Wild Life Protection **Obv:** Lion left **Rev:** Reflective multicolor swallowtail butterfly **Edge:** Reeded

Date	Mintage	F	VF	XF	Unc	BU
2002 Proof	50	Value: 1,800				

KM# 130 100 FRANCS
31.1000 g., 0.9999 Gold 0.9997 oz. AGW, 40 mm. **Series:** Wild Life Protection **Obv:** Lion left **Rev:** Reflective multicolor dark greenish butterfly **Edge:** Reeded

Date	Mintage	F	VF	XF	Unc	BU
2002 Proof	50	Value: 1,800				

KM# 131 100 FRANCS
31.1000 g., 0.9999 Gold 0.9997 oz. AGW, 40 mm. **Series:** Wild Life Protection **Obv:** Lion left **Rev:** Reflective multicolor red and black butterfly **Edge:** Reeded

Date	Mintage	F	VF	XF	Unc	BU
2002 Proof	50	Value: 1,800				

KM# 152 100 FRANCS
31.1035 g., 0.9999 Gold 0.9999 oz. AGW, 38.6 mm. **Obv:** Lion left **Rev:** Multicolor Quetzal bird **Edge:** Reeded

Date	Mintage	F	VF	XF	Unc	BU
2004 Proof	25	Value: 1,800				

KM# 153 100 FRANCS
31.1035 g., 0.9999 Gold 0.9999 oz. AGW, 38.6 mm. **Obv:** Lion left **Rev:** Multicolor Bird of Paradise left **Edge:** Reeded

Date	Mintage	F	VF	XF	Unc	BU
2004 Proof	25	Value: 1,800				

KM# 154 100 FRANCS
31.1035 g., 0.9999 Gold 0.9999 oz. AGW, 38.6 mm. **Obv:** Lion left **Rev:** Multicolor Kingfisher bird **Edge:** Reeded

Date	Mintage	F	VF	XF	Unc	BU
2004 Proof	25	Value: 1,800				

KM# 179b 100 FRANCS
31.1000 g., 0.9990 Gold 0.9988 oz. AGW, 38.58 mm. **Series:** Wildlife Protection **Obv:** Lion standing left **Obv. Legend:** REPUBLIQUE DEMOCRATIQUE DU CONGO **Rev:** Butterfly Fish, multicolor **Edge:** Reeded

Date	Mintage	F	VF	XF	Unc	BU
2005 Proof	25	Value: 1,800				

KM# 180b 100 FRANCS
31.1000 g., 0.9990 Gold 0.9988 oz. AGW, 38.58 mm. **Series:** Wildlife Protection **Obv:** Lion standing left **Obv. Legend:** REPUBLIQUE DEMOCRATIQUE DU CONGO **Rev:** African Mooney Fish, muticolor **Edge:** Reeded

Date	Mintage	F	VF	XF	Unc	BU
2005 Proof	25	Value: 1,800				

KM# 181b 100 FRANCS
31.1000 g., 0.9990 Gold 0.9988 oz. AGW, 38.58 mm. **Series:** Wildlife Protection **Obv:** Lion standing left **Obv. Legend:** REPUBLIQUE DEMOCRATIQUE DU CONGO **Rev:** Red Perch, multicolor **Edge:** Reeded

Date	Mintage	F	VF	XF	Unc	BU
2005 Proof	25	Value: 1,800				

MINT SETS

KM#	Date	Mintage	Identification	Issue Price	Mkt Val
MS2	2004 (4)	—	KM#156-159	—	12.50

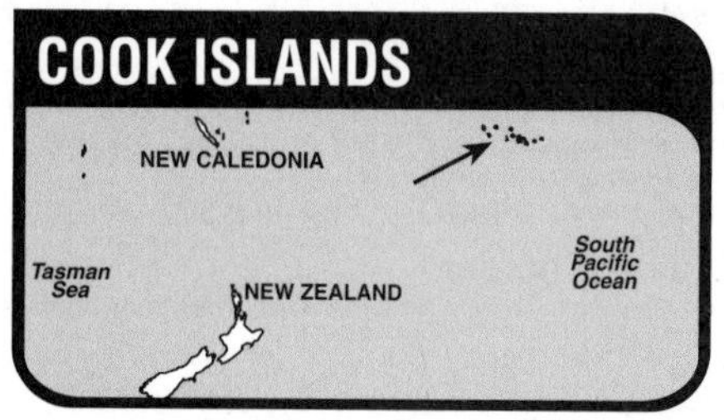

Cook Islands, a self-governing dependency of New Zealand consisting of 15 islands, is located in the South Pacific Ocean about 2,000 miles (3,218 km.) northeast of New Zealand. It has an area of 93 sq. mi. (234 sq. km.) and a population of 17,185. Capital: Avarua. The United States claims the islands of Danger, Manahiki, Penrhyn, and Rakahanga atolls. Citrus and canned fruits and juices, copra, clothing, jewelry, and mother-of-pearl shell are exported.

RULER
British

MINT MARK
PM - Pobjoy Mint

MONETARY SYSTEM
100 Cents = 1 Dollar

DEPENDENCY OF NEW ZEALAND

DECIMAL COINAGE

KM# 419 CENT
1.4400 g., Aluminum, 21.9 mm. **Ruler:** Elizabeth II **Obv:** Crowned head right, date below **Rev:** Bust of Capt. James Cook right, denomination below **Edge:** Plain

Date	Mintage	F	VF	XF	Unc	BU
2003	—	—	—	—	1.25	1.50

KM# 420 CENT
1.4400 g., Aluminum, 21.9 mm. **Ruler:** Elizabeth II **Obv:** Crowned head right, date below **Rev:** Collie dog right, denomination below **Edge:** Plain

Date	Mintage	F	VF	XF	Unc	BU
2003	—	—	—	—	0.75	1.00

KM# 421 CENT
1.4400 g., Aluminum, 21.9 mm. **Ruler:** Elizabeth II **Obv:** Crowned head right, date below **Rev:** Pointer dog right, denomination above **Edge:** Plain

Date	Mintage	F	VF	XF	Unc	BU
2003	—	—	—	—	0.75	1.00

KM# 422 CENT
1.4400 g., Aluminum, 21.9 mm. **Ruler:** Elizabeth II **Obv:** Crowned head right, date below **Rev:** Rooster right, denomination above **Edge:** Plain

Date	Mintage	F	VF	XF	Unc	BU
2003	—	—	—	—	0.75	1.00

KM# 423 CENT
1.4400 g., Aluminum, 22 mm. **Ruler:** Elizabeth II **Obv:** Crowned head right, date below **Rev:** Monkey on branch, denomination at left **Edge:** Plain

Date	Mintage	F	VF	XF	Unc	BU
2003	—	—	—	—	0.75	1.00

KM# 756 CENT
3.6400 g., Brass Plated Steel, 11.8 mm. **Ruler:** Elizabeth II **Obv:** Bust right **Rev:** Female Hula dancer

Date	Mintage	F	VF	XF	Unc	BU
2010	—	—	—	—	0.75	1.00

KM# 757 2 CENTS
5.1000 g., Brass Plated Steel, 19.8 mm. **Ruler:** Elizabeth II **Obv:** Bust right **Rev:** The Endeavor

Date	Mintage	F	VF	XF	Unc	BU
2010	—	—	—	—	0.75	1.00

KM# 758 5 CENTS
6.1500 g., Brass Plated Steel, 21.7 mm. **Ruler:** Elizabeth II **Obv:** Bust right **Rev:** Tiare Maori flower

Date	Mintage	F	VF	XF	Unc	BU
2010	—	—	—	—	1.00	1.50

KM# 759 10 CENTS
11.5000 g., Nickel Plated Steel, 20.5 mm. **Ruler:** Elizabeth II **Obv:** Bust right **Rev:** Yellowfin tuna

Date	Mintage	F	VF	XF	Unc	BU
2010	—	—	—	—	1.00	1.50

KM# 760 20 CENTS
14.1300 g., Nickel Plated Steel, 21.75 mm. **Ruler:** Elizabeth II **Obv:** Bust right **Rev:** Bird

Date	Mintage	F	VF	XF	Unc	BU
2010	—	—	—	—	1.50	2.00

KM# 1116 50 CENTS
28.2800 g., Copper-Nickel, 38.61 mm. **Ruler:** Elizabeth II **Subject:** Elizabeth II Corronation, 50th Anniversary

Date	Mintage	F	VF	XF	Unc	BU
2002	—	—	—	—	—	20.00

KM# 1144 50 CENTS
Copper-Nickel **Ruler:** Elizabeth II **Rev:** Edward "Ned" Kelley in color

Date	Mintage	F	VF	XF	Unc	BU
2004 Proof	Est. 10,000	Value: 15.00				

KM# 761 50 CENTS
Nickel Plated Steel, 34 mm. **Ruler:** Elizabeth II **Obv:** Bust right **Rev:** The Endeavor **Edge Lettering:** Reeded

Date	Mintage	F	VF	XF	Unc	BU
2010	—	—	—	—	2.00	2.50

KM# 1114 DOLLAR
32.0000 g., Copper-Nickel, 40 mm. **Ruler:** Elizabeth II **Subject:** 2002 Winter Olympics, Salt Lake City

Date	Mintage	F	VF	XF	Unc	BU
2001	Est. 20,000	—	—	—	—	15.00

KM# 1115 DOLLAR
9.5000 g., 0.9990 Silver 0.3051 oz. ASW, 22.5 mm. **Ruler:** Elizabeth II **Series:** 2002 Commonwealth Games, Manchester **Rev:** Track field and medals on ribbons

Date	Mintage	F	VF	XF	Unc	BU
2001 Proof	Est. 5,000	Value: 20.00				

KM# 396 DOLLAR
24.8828 g., 0.9990 Silver with Acrylic capsule center containing tiny rubies, sapphires and cubic zirconias 0.7992 oz. ASW, 40.6 mm. **Ruler:** Elizabeth II **Subject:** Crown Jewels **Obv:** Crowned head right, legend **Rev:** Crowns and royal regalia **Edge:** Reeded

Date	Mintage	F	VF	XF	Unc	BU
2002 Proof	50,000	Value: 32.50				

KM# 1117 DOLLAR
0.9990 Silver **Ruler:** Elizabeth II **Subject:** 2002 Winter Olumpics, Salt Lake City **Rev:** Figure skating

Date	Mintage	F	VF	XF	Unc	BU
2002 Proof	—	Value: 37.50				

KM# 1118 DOLLAR
Copper-Nickel **Ruler:** Elizabeth II **Subject:** XVII World Cup, Korea and Japan **Rev:** Soccer player and ball

Date	Mintage	F	VF	XF	Unc	BU
2002 Proof	—	Value: 15.00				

KM# 416 DOLLAR
10.7500 g., Copper-Nickel, 28.5 mm. **Ruler:** Elizabeth II **Obv:** Queen's new portrait **Rev:** Tangaroa statue and value **Shape:** Scalloped

Date	Mintage	F	VF	XF	Unc	BU
2003	—	—	—	—	2.50	3.00
2010	—	—	—	—	2.50	3.00

KM# 455 DOLLAR
23.9000 g., Copper-Nickel, 38.5 mm. **Ruler:** Elizabeth II **Obv:** Queen Elizabeth II **Rev:** 50th Anniversary - Playboy magazine logo **Edge:** Reeded

Date	Mintage	F	VF	XF	Unc	BU
2003	—	—	—	—	7.00	9.00

KM# 455a DOLLAR
25.2700 g., Copper-Nickel partiall gilt, 38.3 mm. **Ruler:** Elizabeth II **Obv:** Elizabeth II **Rev:** Playboy magazine's 50th Anniversary logo **Edge:** Reeded

Date	Mintage	F	VF	XF	Unc	BU
2003 Proof	50,000	Value: 20.00				

KM# 455b DOLLAR
25.2700 g., 0.9990 Silver 0.8116 oz. ASW, 38.3 mm. **Ruler:** Elizabeth II **Obv:** Elizabeth II **Rev:** Playboy magazine's 50th Anniversary logo **Edge:** Reeded

Date	Mintage	F	VF	XF	Unc	BU
2003 Proof	—	Value: 40.00				

KM# 455c DOLLAR
25.2700 g., 0.9990 Silver Gilt 0.8116 oz. ASW, 38.3 mm. **Ruler:** Elizabeth II **Obv:** Elizabeth II **Rev:** Playboy magazine's 50th Anniversary logo **Edge:** Reeded

Date	Mintage	F	VF	XF	Unc	BU
2003 Proof	—	Value: 50.00				

KM# 462 DOLLAR
Copper-Nickel, 41 mm. **Ruler:** Elizabeth II **Rev:** Face of 5 Euro Banknote

Date	Mintage	F	VF	XF	Unc	BU
2003	—	—	—	—	7.00	9.00

KM# 463 DOLLAR
Copper-Nickel, 41 mm. **Ruler:** Elizabeth II **Rev:** Face of 10 Euro Banknote

Date	Mintage	F	VF	XF	Unc	BU
2003	—	—	—	—	7.00	9.00

KM# 464 DOLLAR
Copper-Nickel, 41 mm. **Ruler:** Elizabeth II **Rev:** Face of 20 Euro Banknote

Date	Mintage	F	VF	XF	Unc	BU
2003	—	—	—	—	7.00	9.00

KM# 465 DOLLAR
Copper-Nickel, 41 mm. **Ruler:** Elizabeth II **Rev:** Face of 50 Euro Banknote

Date	Mintage	F	VF	XF	Unc	BU
2003	—	—	—	—	7.00	9.00

KM# 466 DOLLAR
Copper-Nickel, 41 mm. **Ruler:** Elizabeth II **Rev:** Face of 100 Euro Banknote

Date	Mintage	F	VF	XF	Unc	BU
2003	—	—	—	—	7.00	9.00

KM# 467 DOLLAR
Copper-Nickel, 41 mm. **Ruler:** Elizabeth II **Rev:** Face of 500 Euro Banknote

Date	Mintage	F	VF	XF	Unc	BU
2003	—	—	—	—	7.00	9.00

KM# 424 DOLLAR
8.5000 g., 0.9990 Silver 0.2730 oz. ASW, 25.1 mm. **Ruler:** Elizabeth II **Subject:** Zodiac Gemstones - Cancer **Obv:** Crowned head above ornamental center **Rev:** Encapsulated emeralds above Crab (Cancer) **Edge:** Reeded

Date	Mintage	F	VF	XF	Unc	BU
ND(2003) Proof	10,000	Value: 25.00				

KM# 424a DOLLAR
8.5000 g., 0.9990 Silver Gilt 0.2730 oz. ASW, 25.1 mm. **Ruler:** Elizabeth II **Obv:** Crowned head above ornamental center **Rev:** Encapsulated emeralds above Crab (cancer)

Date	Mintage	F	VF	XF	Unc	BU
ND(2003) Proof	10,000	Value: 60.00				

KM# 425 DOLLAR
8.5000 g., 0.9990 Silver 0.2730 oz. ASW, 25.1 mm. **Ruler:** Elizabeth II **Subject:** Zodiac Gemstones - Aquarius **Obv:** Crowned head above ornamental center **Rev:** Encapsulated garnets with Aquarius in background **Edge:** Reeded

Date	Mintage	F	VF	XF	Unc	BU
ND(2004) Proof	10,000	Value: 25.00				

KM# 425a DOLLAR
8.5000 g., 0.9990 Silver Gilt 0.2730 oz. ASW, 25.1 mm. **Ruler:** Elizabeth II **Obv:** Crowned head above ornamental center **Rev:** Encapsulated garnets with Aquarius in background

Date	Mintage	F	VF	XF	Unc	BU
ND(2003) Proof	10,000	Value: 60.00				

KM# 426 DOLLAR
8.5000 g., 0.9990 Silver 0.2730 oz. ASW, 25.1 mm. **Ruler:** Elizabeth II **Subject:** Zodiac Gemstones - Aries **Obv:** Crowned head above ornamental center **Rev:** Encapsulated Bloodstones in center with ram at left **Edge:** Reeded

Date	Mintage	F	VF	XF	Unc	BU
ND(2003) Proof	10,000	Value: 25.00				

KM# 426a DOLLAR
8.5000 g., 0.9990 Silver Gilt 0.2730 oz. ASW, 25.1 mm. **Ruler:** Elizabeth II **Obv:** Crowned head above ornamental center **Rev:** Encapsulated Bloodstones in center with ram at left

Date	Mintage	F	VF	XF	Unc	BU
ND(2003) Proof	10,000	Value: 60.00				

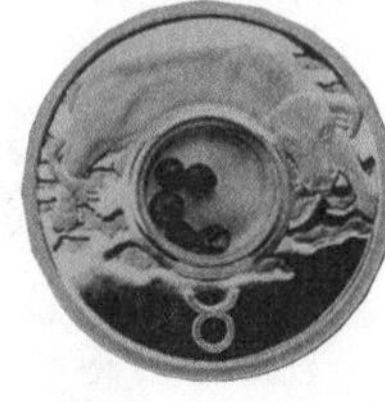

KM# 427 DOLLAR
8.5000 g., 0.9990 Silver 0.2730 oz. ASW, 25.1 mm. **Ruler:** Elizabeth II **Subject:** Zodiac Gemstones - Taurus **Obv:** Crowned head above ornamental center **Rev:** Encapsulated Sapphires with bull in background **Edge:** Reeded

Date	Mintage	F	VF	XF	Unc	BU
ND(2003) Proof	10,000	Value: 25.00				

KM# 427a DOLLAR
8.5000 g., 0.9990 Silver Gilt 0.2730 oz. ASW, 25.1 mm. **Ruler:** Elizabeth II **Subject:** Zodiac Gemstones - Taurus **Obv:** Crowned head above ornamental center **Rev:** Encapsulated Sapphires with bull in background **Edge:** Reeded

Date	Mintage	F	VF	XF	Unc	BU
ND(2003) Proof	10,000	Value: 60.00				

KM# 428 DOLLAR
8.5000 g., 0.9990 Silver 0.2730 oz. ASW, 25.1 mm. **Ruler:** Elizabeth II **Obv:** Crowned head above ornamental center **Rev:** Encapsulated Agates between twins **Edge:** Reeded

Date	Mintage	F	VF	XF	Unc	BU
ND(2003) Proof	10,000	Value: 25.00				

KM# 428a DOLLAR
8.5000 g., 0.9990 Silver Gilt 0.2730 oz. ASW, 25.1 mm. **Ruler:** Elizabeth II **Obv:** Crowned head above ornamental center **Rev:** Encapsulated Agates between twins **Edge:** Reeded

Date	Mintage	F	VF	XF	Unc	BU
ND(2003) Proof	10,000	Value: 60.00				

KM# 429 DOLLAR
8.5000 g., 0.9990 Silver 0.2730 oz. ASW, 25.1 mm. **Ruler:** Elizabeth II **Obv:** Crowned head above ornamental center **Rev:** Encapsulated Onyx stones with lion at right **Edge:** Reeded

Date	Mintage	F	VF	XF	Unc	BU
ND(2003) Proof	10,000	Value: 25.00				

KM# 429a DOLLAR
8.5000 g., 0.9990 Silver Gilt 0.2730 oz. ASW, 25.1 mm. **Ruler:** Elizabeth II **Obv:** Crowned head above ornamental center **Rev:** Encapsulated Onyx stones with lion at right **Edge:** Reeded

Date	Mintage	F	VF	XF	Unc	BU
ND(2003) Proof	10,000	Value: 60.00				

KM# 430 DOLLAR
8.5000 g., 0.9990 Silver 0.2730 oz. ASW, 25.1 mm. **Ruler:** Elizabeth II **Subject:** Zodiac Gemstones - Virgo **Obv:** Crowned head above ornamented center **Rev:** Encapsulated Carnelian stones with woman at right **Edge:** Reeded

Date	Mintage	F	VF	XF	Unc	BU
ND(2003) Proof	10,000	Value: 25.00				

KM# 430a DOLLAR
8.5000 g., 0.9990 Silver Gilt 0.2730 oz. ASW, 25.1 mm. **Ruler:** Elizabeth II **Subject:** Zodiac Gemstones - Virgo **Obv:** Crowned head above ornamented center **Rev:** Encapsulated Carnelian stones with Virgo at right **Edge:** Reeded

Date	Mintage	F	VF	XF	Unc	BU
ND(2003) Proof	10,000	Value: 60.00				

KM# 431 DOLLAR
8.5000 g., 0.9990 Silver 0.2730 oz. ASW, 25.1 mm. **Ruler:** Elizabeth II **Subject:** Zodiac Gemstones - Libra **Obv:** Crowned head above ornamented center **Rev:** Encapsulated Peridot stones with balance scale **Edge:** Reeded

Date	Mintage	F	VF	XF	Unc	BU
ND(2003) Proof	10,000	Value: 25.00				

KM# 431a DOLLAR
8.5000 g., 0.9990 Silver Gilt 0.2730 oz. ASW, 25.1 mm. **Ruler:** Elizabeth II **Subject:** Zodiac Gemstones - Libra **Obv:** Crowned head above ornamented center **Rev:** Encapsulated Peridot stones with balance scale **Edge:** Reeded

Date	Mintage	F	VF	XF	Unc	BU
ND(2003) Proof	10,000	Value: 60.00				

KM# 432 DOLLAR
8.5000 g., 0.9990 Silver 0.2730 oz. ASW, 25.1 mm. **Ruler:** Elizabeth II **Subject:** Zodiac Gemstones - Scorpio **Obv:** Crowned head above ornamented center **Rev:** Encapsulated Aquamarine stones with scorpion at lower right **Edge:** Reeded

Date	Mintage	F	VF	XF	Unc	BU
ND(2003) Proof	10,000	Value: 25.00				

KM# 432a DOLLAR
8.5000 g., 0.9990 Silver Gilt 0.2730 oz. ASW, 25.1 mm. **Ruler:** Elizabeth II **Subject:** Zodiac Gemstones - Scorpio **Obv:** Crowned head above ornamented center **Rev:** Encapsulated Aquamarine stones with scorpion at lower right **Edge:** Reeded

Date	Mintage	F	VF	XF	Unc	BU
ND(2003) Proof	10,000	Value: 60.00				

KM# 433 DOLLAR
8.5000 g., 0.9990 Silver 0.2730 oz. ASW, 25.1 mm. **Ruler:** Elizabeth II **Subject:** Zodiac Gemstones - Sagittarius **Obv:** Crowned head above ornamented center **Rev:** Encapsulated Topaz stones with centaur at right **Edge:** Reeded

Date	Mintage	F	VF	XF	Unc	BU
ND(2003) Proof	10,000	Value: 25.00				

KM# 433a DOLLAR
8.5000 g., 0.9990 Silver Gilt 0.2730 oz. ASW, 25.1 mm. **Ruler:** Elizabeth II **Subject:** Zodiac Gemstones - Sagittarius **Obv:** Crowned head above ornamented center **Rev:** Encapsulated Topaz stones with centaur at right **Edge:** Reeded

Date	Mintage	F	VF	XF	Unc	BU
ND(2003) Proof	10,000	Value: 60.00				

KM# 434 DOLLAR
8.5000 g., 0.9990 Silver 0.2730 oz. ASW, 25.1 mm. **Ruler:** Elizabeth II **Subject:** Zodiac Gemstones - Capricorn **Obv:** Crowned head above ornamental center **Rev:** Encapsulated rubies with goat at right **Edge:** Reeded

Date	Mintage	F	VF	XF	Unc	BU
ND(2003) Proof	10,000	Value: 25.00				

KM# 434a DOLLAR
8.5000 g., 0.9990 Silver Gilt 0.2730 oz. ASW, 25.1 mm. **Ruler:** Elizabeth II **Subject:** Zodiac Gemstones - Capricorn **Obv:** Crowned head above ornamented center **Rev:** Encapsulated Rubies with goat at right **Edge:** Reeded

Date	Mintage	F	VF	XF	Unc	BU
ND(2003) Proof	10,000	Value: 60.00				

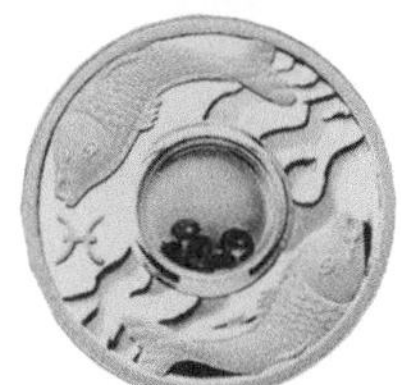

KM# 435 DOLLAR
8.5000 g., 0.9990 Silver 0.2730 oz. ASW, 25.1 mm. **Ruler:** Elizabeth II **Subject:** Zodiac Gemstones - Pices **Obv:** Crowned head above ornamented center **Rev:** Encapsulated Amethyst stones and two fish **Edge:** Reeded

Date	Mintage	F	VF	XF	Unc	BU
ND(2003) Proof	10,000	Value: 25.00				

KM# 435a DOLLAR
8.5000 g., 0.9990 Silver Gilt 0.2730 oz. ASW, 25.1 mm. **Ruler:** Elizabeth II **Subject:** Zodiac Gemstones - Pices **Obv:** Crowned head above ornamented center **Rev:** Encapsulated Amethyst stones and 2 fish **Edge:** Reeded

Date	Mintage	F	VF	XF	Unc	BU
ND(2003) Proof	10,000	Value: 60.00				

KM# 746 DOLLAR
24.9000 g., Copper-Nickel, 38 mm. **Ruler:** Elizabeth II **Subject:** Historic ships - Espusi

Date	Mintage	F	VF	XF	Unc	BU
2003	—	—	—	—	15.00	20.00

KM# 747 DOLLAR
24.9000 g., Copper-Nickel, 38 mm. **Ruler:** Elizabeth II **Subject:** Historic ships - Gorch Foch

Date	Mintage	F	VF	XF	Unc	BU
2003	—	—	—	—	15.00	20.00

KM# 748 DOLLAR
24.9000 g., Copper-Nickel, 38 mm. **Ruler:** Elizabeth II **Subject:** Historic ships - Constitution

Date	Mintage	F	VF	XF	Unc	BU
2003	—	—	—	—	15.00	20.00

KM# 749 DOLLAR
24.9000 g., Copper-Nickel, 38 mm. **Ruler:** Elizabeth II **Subject:** Historic ships - Beagle

Date	Mintage	F	VF	XF	Unc	BU
2003	—	—	—	—	15.00	20.00

KM# 750 DOLLAR
24.9000 g., Copper-Nickel, 38 mm. **Ruler:** Elizabeth II **Subject:** Historic ship - Endeavour

Date	Mintage	F	VF	XF	Unc	BU
2003	—	—	—	—	15.00	20.00

KM# 751 DOLLAR
24.9000 g., Copper-Nickel, 38 mm. **Ruler:** Elizabeth II **Subject:** Historic Ship - Vasa

Date	Mintage	F	VF	XF	Unc	BU
2003	—	—	—	—	15.00	20.00

KM# 1127 DOLLAR
31.6350 g., 0.9990 Silver 1.0160 oz. ASW, 40.5 mm. **Ruler:** Elizabeth II **Rev:** James Cook and sailing ship

Date	Mintage	F	VF	XF	Unc	BU
2003 Proof	Est. 4,999	Value: 50.00				

KM# 1130 DOLLAR
31.1050 g., 0.9990 Silver 0.9990 oz. ASW, 38.6 mm. **Ruler:** Elizabeth II **Subject:** Full Gospel Business Men's Fellowship, 50th Anniversary

Date	Mintage	F	VF	XF	Unc	BU
2003 Proof	Est. 4,999	Value: 55.00				

KM# 1143 DOLLAR
28.2800 g., 0.9250 Silver partially gilt 0.8410 oz. ASW, 38.61 mm. **Ruler:** Elizabeth II **Series:** Elizabeth II, 50th Anniversary of Coronation

Date	Mintage	F	VF	XF	Unc	BU
2003 Proof	Est. 20,000	—	—	—	—	45.00

KM# 454 DOLLAR
27.5300 g., 0.9990 Silver Clad Copper-Nickel 0.8842 oz. ASW, 38.6 mm. **Ruler:** Elizabeth II **Subject:** 60th Anniversary - D-Day Invasion **Obv:** Crowned bust right, new portrait **Rev:** Invasion scene of soldiers storming the beaches (Sword, Gold, Juno, Omaha, and Utah) of Normandy

Date	Mintage	F	VF	XF	Unc	BU
2004	—	—	—	—	15.00	18.00

KM# 438 DOLLAR
31.1035 g., 0.9990 Silver 0.9990 oz. ASW, 40.5 mm. **Ruler:** Elizabeth II **Obv:** Crowned head right **Rev:** Multicolor Deng Xiaoping on Chinese map **Edge:** Plain **Shape:** As a map

Date	Mintage	F	VF	XF	Unc	BU
2004	20,000	—	—	—	50.00	55.00

KM# 1146 DOLLAR
31.6350 g., 0.9990 Silver 1.0160 oz. ASW **Ruler:** Elizabeth II **Subject:** Cobb & Co. 150th Anniversary **Rev:** Hackney Cab in color

Date	Mintage	F	VF	XF	Unc	BU
2004 Proof	Est. 5,000	Value: 60.00				

KM# 1147 DOLLAR
31.6350 g., 0.9990 Silver 1.0160 oz. ASW **Ruler:** Elizabeth II **Subject:** 90th Anniversary, Battle of the Emden and Sydney I

Date	Mintage	F	VF	XF	Unc	BU
2004 Proof	Est. 5,000	Value: 60.00				

KM# 1148 DOLLAR
10.7500 g., Copper-Nickel, 28.28 mm. **Ruler:** Elizabeth II **Rev:** Elvis Presley

Date	Mintage	F	VF	XF	Unc	BU
2004	—	—	—	—	—	15.00

KM# 1150 DOLLAR
31.1050 g., 0.9990 Silver 0.9990 oz. ASW, 45 mm. **Ruler:** Elizabeth II **Subject:** XXVIII Summer Olympics, Athens **Rev:** Cyclist in color

Date	Mintage	F	VF	XF	Unc	BU
2004	Est. 5,000	—	—	—	—	45.00

KM# 1151 DOLLAR
31.1050 g., 0.9990 Silver 0.9990 oz. ASW, 45 mm. **Ruler:** Elizabeth II **Rev:** Gymnast

Date	Mintage	F	VF	XF	Unc	BU
2004	Est. 5,000	—	—	—	—	45.00

KM# 1152 DOLLAR
31.1050 g., 0.9990 Silver 0.9990 oz. ASW, 45 mm. **Ruler:** Elizabeth II **Subject:** XXVIII Summer Olympics, Athens **Rev:** Two basketball players in color

Date	Mintage	F	VF	XF	Unc	BU
2004	Est. 5,000	—	—	—	—	45.00

KM# 1153 DOLLAR
31.1050 g., 0.9990 Silver 0.9990 oz. ASW, 45 mm. **Ruler:** Elizabeth II **Subject:** XVIII Summer Olympics, Athens **Rev:** Sprinter in color

Date	Mintage	F	VF	XF	Unc	BU
2004	Est. 5,000	—	—	—	—	45.00

KM# 1154 DOLLAR
31.1050 g., 0.9990 Silver 0.9990 oz. ASW, 45 mm. **Ruler:** Elizabeth II **Subject:** XXVIII Summer Olympics, Athens **Rev:** Archer in color

Date	Mintage	F	VF	XF	Unc	BU
2004	Est. 5,000	—	—	—	—	45.00

KM# 1155 DOLLAR
31.1050 g., 0.9990 Silver 0.9990 oz. ASW, 45 mm. **Ruler:** Elizabeth II **Subject:** XXVIII Summer Olympics, Athens **Rev:** Weightlifter in color

Date	Mintage	F	VF	XF	Unc	BU
2004 Proof	Est. 5,000	—	—	—	—	45.00

KM# 1156 DOLLAR
24.0000 g., Copper-Nickel, 38 mm. **Ruler:** Elizabeth II **Rev:** Mohandas Ghandhi

Date	Mintage	F	VF	XF	Unc	BU
2004	—	—	—	—	—	15.00

KM# 443 DOLLAR
23.9000 g., Copper-Nickel, 38.5 mm. **Ruler:** Elizabeth II **Subject:** Battle of Trafalgar **Obv:** Crowned bust right, new portrait **Rev:** HMS Victory and color portrait of Nelson **Edge:** Reeded

Date	Mintage	F	VF	XF	Unc	BU
2005	—	—	—	—	12.00	14.00

KM# 470 DOLLAR
31.1600 g., 0.9990 Silver 1.0008 oz. ASW, 39.02 mm. **Ruler:** Elizabeth II **Obv:** Twin Towers and Statue of Liberty, Queens Head below **Obv. Legend:** COOK ISLANDS / WE WILL NEVER FORGET **Rev:** Freedoom Tower and Statue of Liberty **Rev. Inscription:** LET / FREEDOM / RING - FREEDOM TOWER **Edge:** Reeded and plain with lettering **Edge Lettering:** 1 TROY OZ. .999 FINE SILVER

Date	Mintage	F	VF	XF	Unc	BU
2005 Proof	—	Value: 45.00				
2006 Proof	—	Value: 40.00				

KM# 1107 DOLLAR
31.1050 g., 0.9990 Silver partially gilt 0.9990 oz. ASW, 40 mm. **Ruler:** Elizabeth II **Rev:** Pope Benedict XVI partially gilt

Date	Mintage	F	VF	XF	Unc	BU
2005 Proof	—	Value: 45.00				

KM# 1133 DOLLAR
Copper-Nickel, 38.6 mm. **Ruler:** Elizabeth II **Subject:** Star Wars, 30th Anniversary

Date	Mintage	F	VF	XF	Unc	BU
2005 Proof	Est. 9,999	Value: 30.00				

KM# 1157 DOLLAR
31.6350 g., 0.9990 Silver 1.0160 oz. ASW **Ruler:** Elizabeth II **Subject:** Australian Automobiles

Date	Mintage	F	VF	XF	Unc	BU
2005 Proof	Est. 1,500	Value: 60.00				

KM# 1158 DOLLAR
31.6350 g., 0.9990 Silver 1.0160 oz. ASW **Ruler:** Elizabeth II **Subject:** Australian Automobiles

Date	Mintage	F	VF	XF	Unc	BU
2005 Proof	Est. 1,500	Value: 60.00				

KM# 1159 DOLLAR
31.6350 g., 0.9990 Silver 1.0160 oz. ASW **Ruler:** Elizabeth II **Subject:** Australian Automobiles

Date	Mintage	F	VF	XF	Unc	BU
2005 Proof	Est. 1,500	Value: 60.00				

KM# 1160 DOLLAR
31.6350 g., 0.9990 Silver 1.0160 oz. ASW **Ruler:** Elizabeth II **Subject:** Australian Automobiles

Date	Mintage	F	VF	XF	Unc	BU
2005 Proof	Est. 1,500	Value: 60.00				

KM# 1161 DOLLAR
31.6350 g., 0.9990 Silver 1.0160 oz. ASW **Ruler:** Elizabeth II **Subject:** Australian Automobiles

Date	Mintage	F	VF	XF	Unc	BU
2005 Proof	Est. 1,500	Value: 60.00				

KM# 1162 DOLLAR
31.6350 g., 0.9990 Silver 1.0160 oz. ASW **Ruler:** Elizabeth II **Subject:** Australian Automobiles

Date	Mintage	F	VF	XF	Unc	BU
2005 Proof	Est. 1,500	Value: 60.00				

KM# 1163 DOLLAR
31.6350 g., 0.9990 Silver 1.0160 oz. ASW **Ruler:** Elizabeth II **Subject:** Australian Automobiles

Date	Mintage	F	VF	XF	Unc	BU
2005 Proof	Est. 1,500	Value: 60.00				

KM# 1164 DOLLAR
31.6350 g., 0.9990 Silver 1.0160 oz. ASW **Ruler:** Elizabeth II **Subject:** Australian Automobiles

Date	Mintage	F	VF	XF	Unc	BU
2005 Proof	Est. 1,500	Value: 60.00				

KM# 1165 DOLLAR
31.6350 g., 0.9990 Silver 1.0160 oz. ASW **Ruler:** Elizabeth II **Subject:** Australian Automobiles

Date	Mintage	F	VF	XF	Unc	BU
2005 Proof	Est. 1,500	Value: 60.00				

KM# 1166 DOLLAR
31.6350 g., 0.9990 Silver 1.0160 oz. ASW **Ruler:** Elizabeth II **Subject:** Australian Automobiles

Date	Mintage	F	VF	XF	Unc	BU
2005 Proof	1,500	Value: 60.00				

KM# 1167 DOLLAR
31.6350 g., 0.9990 Silver 1.0160 oz. ASW **Ruler:** Elizabeth II **Subject:** Australian Automobiles

Date	Mintage	F	VF	XF	Unc	BU
2005 Proof	Est. 1,500	Value: 60.00				

KM# 1168 DOLLAR
31.6350 g., 0.9990 Silver 1.0160 oz. ASW **Ruler:** Elizabeth II **Subject:** Australian Automobiles

Date	Mintage	F	VF	XF	Unc	BU
2005 Proof	Est. 1,500	Value: 60.00				

KM# 1173 DOLLAR
32.0000 g., Copper-Nickel, 40 mm. **Ruler:** Elizabeth II **Rev:** Snowflake, building tower hockey play and figure skater

Date	Mintage	F	VF	XF	Unc	BU
2005	20,000	—	—	—	—	15.00

KM# 1174 DOLLAR
Copper-Nickel **Ruler:** Elizabeth II **Subject:** Marriage of Prince Charles and Camilla Parker-Bowles

Date	Mintage	F	VF	XF	Unc	BU
2005	Est. 5,000	—	—	—	—	15.00

KM# 1177 DOLLAR
31.6350 g., 0.9990 Silver 1.0160 oz. ASW **Ruler:** Elizabeth II **Rev:** Pope John Paul II in color

Date	Mintage	F	VF	XF	Unc	BU
2005 Proof	5,000	Value: 125				

KM# 479 DOLLAR
Copper-Nickel, 38.6 mm. **Ruler:** Elizabeth II **Subject:** Gun ships of the world **Rev:** HMS Redoutable

Date	Mintage	F	VF	XF	Unc	BU
2006	—	—	—	—	—	25.00

KM# 480 DOLLAR
24.9000 g., Copper-Nickel, 38 mm. **Ruler:** Elizabeth II **Subject:** Gunships of the world **Obv:** Crowned bust right **Rev:** Ark Royal in color **Edge:** Reeded

Date	Mintage	F	VF	XF	Unc	BU
2006	—	—	—	—	—	25.00

KM# 752 DOLLAR
24.9000 g., Copper-Nickel, 38 mm. **Ruler:** Elizabeth II **Subject:** Gun ships - Chesapeak **Rev:** Multicolor naval ship

Date	Mintage	F	VF	XF	Unc	BU
2006	—	—	—	—	15.00	20.00

KM# 753 DOLLAR
24.9000 g., Copper-Nickel, 38 mm. **Ruler:** Elizabeth II **Subject:** Gun ships - Syvende **Rev:** Multicolor naval ship

Date	Mintage	F	VF	XF	Unc	BU
2006	—	—	—	—	15.00	20.00

KM# 754 DOLLAR
24.9000 g., Copper-Nickel, 38 mm. **Ruler:** Elizabeth II **Rev:** Multicolor Naval ship

Date	Mintage	F	VF	XF	Unc	BU
2006	—	—	—	—	15.00	20.00

KM# 755 DOLLAR
24.9000 g., Copper-Nickel, 38 mm. **Ruler:** Elizabeth II **Subject:** Gun Ships - Mary Rose **Rev:** Multicolor Naval ship

Date	Mintage	F	VF	XF	Unc	BU
2006	—	—	—	—	15.00	20.00

KM# 1137 DOLLAR
31.6350 g., 0.9990 Silver 1.0160 oz. ASW **Ruler:** Elizabeth II **Subject:** 1923 New South Wales Garford Fire

Date	Mintage	F	VF	XF	Unc	BU
2006 Proof	Est. 5,000	Value: 55.00				

KM# 1169 DOLLAR
0.5000 g., 0.9990 Gold 0.0161 oz. AGW **Ruler:** Elizabeth II **Rev:** Pope Benedict XVI

Date	Mintage	F	VF	XF	Unc	BU
2006 Proof	—	Value: 45.00				

KM# 1179 DOLLAR
Silver **Ruler:** Elizabeth II **Subject:** David Livingstone

Date	Mintage	F	VF	XF	Unc	BU
2006 Proof	—	Value: 45.00				

KM# 1180 DOLLAR
Silver **Ruler:** Elizabeth II **Subject:** Ferdinanad Magellan

Date	Mintage	F	VF	XF	Unc	BU
2006 Proof	—	Value: 45.00				

KM# 1181 DOLLAR
Silver **Ruler:** Elizabeth II **Subject:** Roald Amundsen

Date	Mintage	F	VF	XF	Unc	BU
2006 Proof	—	Value: 45.00				

KM# 1182 DOLLAR
Silver **Ruler:** Elizabeth II **Subject:** Christopher Columbus

Date	Mintage	F	VF	XF	Unc	BU
2006 Proof	—	Value: 45.00				

KM# 1183 DOLLAR
Silver **Ruler:** Elizabeth II **Subject:** Juan Sebastian de Elcano

Date	Mintage	F	VF	XF	Unc	BU
2006 Proof	—	Value: 45.00				

KM# 1428 DOLLAR
Silver, 38.61 mm. **Ruler:** Elizabeth II **Subject:** Television, 80th anniversary

Date	Mintage	F	VF	XF	Unc	BU
2006	—	—	—	—	—	50.00

KM# 471 DOLLAR
35.8000 g., 0.9990 Silver 1.1498 oz. ASW **Ruler:** Elizabeth II **Subject:** Sputnik 50th Anniversary - 1957-2007 **Obv:** Small bust divides legend above, center globe with color applique **Rev:** Satellite orbiting Earth with color applique **Rev. Legend:** SPUTNIK 50th ANNIVERSARY 1957 - 2007 **Edge:** Plain **Note:** Center piece rotates freely

Date	Mintage	F	VF	XF	Unc	BU
2007 Proof	—	Value: 95.00				

KM# 733 DOLLAR
25.0900 g., Copper-Nickel, 38.8 mm. **Ruler:** Elizabeth II **Rev:** HMS Victory **Rev. Legend:** England expects that every man will do his duty

Date	Mintage	F	VF	XF	Unc	BU
2007	—	—	—	—	—	15.00

KM# 734 DOLLAR
25.0900 g., Copper-Nickel, 38.8 mm. **Ruler:** Elizabeth II **Rev:** Admiral Nelson and two naval vessels **Rev. Legend:** England expects that every man will do his duty

Date	Mintage	F	VF	XF	Unc	BU
2007	—	—	—	—	—	15.00

KM# 735 DOLLAR
0.5000 g., 0.9990 Gold 0.0161 oz. AGW, 11 mm. **Ruler:** Elizabeth II **Rev:** Treaty of Rome - Slovenia

Date	Mintage	F	VF	XF	Unc	BU
2007 Proof	—	Value: 40.00				

KM# 736 DOLLAR
0.5000 g., 0.9990 Gold 0.0161 oz. AGW **Ruler:** Elizabeth II **Rev:** Benedict XVI's 2 Euro Coin

Date	Mintage	F	VF	XF	Unc	BU
2007 Proof	—	Value: 40.00				

KM# 490 DOLLAR
31.1030 g., 0.9990 Silver 0.9989 oz. ASW, 40.6 mm. **Ruler:** Elizabeth II **Subject:** Historical Australian Coins **Obv:** Head with tiara right **Rev:** 1757 New South Wales Holey Dollar **Edge:** Reeded

Date	Mintage	F	VF	XF	Unc	BU
2007 Proof	1,500	Value: 125				

KM# 491 DOLLAR
31.1030 g., 0.9990 Silver 0.9989 oz. ASW, 40.6 mm. **Ruler:** Elizabeth II **Subject:** Historical Australian Coins **Obv:** Head with tiara right **Rev:** Gilt 1857 Sydney Mint Sovereign **Edge:** Reeded

Date	Mintage	F	VF	XF	Unc	BU
2007 Proof	1,500	Value: 125				

KM# 492 DOLLAR
31.1030 g., 0.9990 Silver Selective copper plating 0.9989 oz. ASW, 40.6 mm. **Ruler:** Elizabeth II **Subject:** Historical Australian Coins **Obv:** Head with tiarra right **Rev:** Copper 1937 pattern penny **Edge:** Reeded

Date	Mintage	F	VF	XF	Unc	BU
2007 Proof	1,500	Value: 125				

KM# 1138 DOLLAR
0.5000 g., 0.9990 Gold 0.0161 oz. AGW, 11 mm. **Ruler:** Elizabeth II **Subject:** Treaty of Rome, 50th Anniversary **Rev:** San Marino

Date	Mintage	F	VF	XF	Unc	BU
2007 Proof	Est. 5,000	Value: 50.00				

KM# 1196 DOLLAR
25.0000 g., Copper-Nickel gilt, 38.6 mm. **Ruler:** Elizabeth II **Rev:** Photo of Elizabeth II and Prince Philip in State Crown and uniform

Date	Mintage	F	VF	XF	Unc	BU
2007 Proof	Est. 50,000	Value: 17.50				

KM# 1197 DOLLAR
25.0000 g., Copper-Nickel gilt, 38.6 mm. **Ruler:** Elizabeth II **Rev:** Photo of Elizabeth II and Prince Philip riding in state coach

Date	Mintage	F	VF	XF	Unc	BU
2007 Proof	Est. 50,000	Value: 17.50				

KM# 1198 DOLLAR
25.0000 g., Copper-Nickel gilt, 38.6 mm. **Ruler:** Elizabeth II **Rev:** Photo Elizabeth II in wedding dress and Prince Philip in uniform

Date	Mintage	F	VF	XF	Unc	BU
2007 Proof	Est. 50,000	Value: 17.50				

KM# 1199 DOLLAR
25.0000 g., Copper-Nickel, 38.6 mm. **Ruler:** Elizabeth II **Rev:** Photo of Elizabeth II in wedding dress and Prince Philip in uniform, both waving

Date	Mintage	F	VF	XF	Unc	BU
2007 Proof	Est. 50,000	Value: 17.50				

KM# 1200 DOLLAR
25.0000 g., Copper-Nickel gilt, 38.6 mm. **Ruler:** Elizabeth II **Rev:** Recent photo of Elizabeth in blue hat and Prince Philip in uniform

Date	Mintage	F	VF	XF	Unc	BU
2007 Proof	Est. 50,000	Value: 17.50				

KM# 1445 DOLLAR
25.0000 g., Copper-Nickel gilt, 38.6 mm. **Ruler:** Elizabeth II **Rev:** Modern photo of Elizabeth II in red dress and Prince Philip in suit

Date	Mintage	
	Est. 50,000	Value: 17.50

KM# 1466 DOLLAR
28.2800 g., 0.9250 Silver 0.8410 oz. ASW, 38.61 mm. **Ruler:** Elizabeth II **Rev:** Horatio Nelson and the Battle of Trafalgar

Date	Mintage	F	VF	XF	Unc	BU
2007 Proof	Est. 5,000	Value: 55.00				

KM# 1468 DOLLAR
0.5000 g., 0.9990 Gold 0.0161 oz. AGW, 11 mm. **Ruler:** Elizabeth II **Rev:** Sugar Maple leaf

Date	Mintage	F	VF	XF	Unc	BU
2007 Proof	Est. 5,000	Value: 35.00				

KM# 493 DOLLAR
31.1030 g., 0.9990 Silver 0.9989 oz. ASW, 40.6 mm. **Ruler:** Elizabeth II **Subject:** Historical Australian Coins **Obv:** Head with tiara right **Rev:** 1823 MacIntosh and Degraves Shilling **Edge:** Reeded

Date	Mintage	F	VF	XF	Unc	BU
2008 Proof	1,500	Value: 125				

KM# 494 DOLLAR
31.1030 g., 0.9990 Silver Selective gold plating 0.9989 oz. ASW, 40.6 mm. **Ruler:** Elizabeth II **Subject:** Historic Australian Coins **Obv:** Head with tiara right **Rev:** Gilt 1788 George III Spade Guinea **Edge:** Reeded

Date	Mintage	F	VF	XF	Unc	BU
2008 Proof	1,500	Value: 125				

KM# 495 DOLLAR
31.1030 g., 0.9990 Silver 0.9989 oz. ASW, 40.6 mm. **Ruler:** Elizabeth II **Subject:** Historic Australian Coins **Obv:** Head with tiara right **Rev:** Australian 1910 Florin **Edge:** Reeded

Date	Mintage	F	VF	XF	Unc	BU
2008 Proof	1,500	Value: 125				

KM# 496 DOLLAR
31.1030 g., 0.9990 Silver Selective gold plating 0.9989 oz. ASW, 40.6 mm. **Ruler:** Elizabeth II **Subject:** Historic Australian Coins **Obv:** Head with tiara right **Rev:** Gilt 1808-1815 Gold Pagoda **Edge:** Reeded

Date	Mintage	F	VF	XF	Unc	BU
2008 Proof	1,500	Value: 125				

KM# 497 DOLLAR
31.1030 g., 0.9990 Silver 0.9989 oz. ASW, 40.6 mm. **Ruler:** Elizabeth II **Subject:** Historic Australian Coins **Obv:** Head with tiara right **Rev:** 1850's Taylor's sixpence pattern **Edge:** Reeded

Date	Mintage	F	VF	XF	Unc	BU
2008 Proof	1,500	Value: 125				

KM# 498 DOLLAR

31.1050 g., 0.9990 Silver Selective copper plating 0.9990 oz. ASW, 40.6 mm. **Ruler:** Elizabeth II **Subject:** Historic Australian Coins **Obv:** Head with tiara right **Rev:** Copper Australian WWII Interment Camp Token **Edge:** Reeded

Date	Mintage	F	VF	XF	Unc	BU
2008 Proof	1,500	Value: 125				

KM# 499 DOLLAR

31.1030 g., 0.9990 Silver 0.9989 oz. ASW, 40.6 mm. **Ruler:** Elizabeth II **Subject:** Historic Australian Coins **Obv:** Head with tiara right **Rev:** Australian 1946 Perth Mint Shilling **Edge:** Reeded

Date	Mintage	F	VF	XF	Unc	BU
2008 Proof	1,500	Value: 125				

KM# 500 DOLLAR

31.1030 g., 0.9990 Silver 0.9989 oz. ASW, 40.6 mm. **Ruler:** Elizabeth II **Subject:** Historic Australian Coins **Obv:** Head with tiara right **Rev:** Australian 1938 Crown **Edge:** Reeded

Date	Mintage	F	VF	XF	Unc	BU
2008 Proof	1,500	Value: 125				

KM# 501 DOLLAR

31.1030 g., 0.9990 Silver 0.9989 oz. ASW, 40.6 mm. **Ruler:** Elizabeth II **Subject:** Historic Australian Coins **Obv:** Head with tiara right **Rev:** Copper Australian 1930 Penny **Edge:** Reeded

Date	Mintage	F	VF	XF	Unc	BU
2008 Proof	1,500	Value: 125				

KM# 502 DOLLAR

31.1030 g., 0.9990 Silver 0.9989 oz. ASW, 40.6 mm. **Ruler:** Elizabeth II **Subject:** World War I **Obv:** Head with tiara right **Rev:** Multicolor image of Australian WWI soldier in Europe **Edge:** Reeded

Date	Mintage	F	VF	XF	Unc	BU
2008 Proof	1,918	Value: 85.00				

KM# 504 DOLLAR

31.1030 g., 0.9990 Silver 0.9989 oz. ASW, 40.6 mm. **Ruler:** Elizabeth II **Subject:** WWI **Obv:** Head with tiara right **Rev:** Multicolor image of Australian WWI soldier in Mid-East scene **Edge:** Reeded

Date	Mintage	F	VF	XF	Unc	BU
2008 Proof	1,918	Value: 85.00				

KM# 506 DOLLAR

31.1030 g., 0.9990 Silver 0.9989 oz. ASW, 40.6 mm. **Ruler:** Elizabeth II **Subject:** Captain Cook **Obv:** Head with tiara right **Rev:** Multicolor image of James Cook within letter C **Edge:** Reeded

Date	Mintage	F	VF	XF	Unc	BU
2008 Proof	1,779	Value: 100				

KM# 507 DOLLAR

31.1030 g., 0.9990 Silver 0.9989 oz. ASW, 40.6 mm. **Ruler:** Elizabeth II **Subject:** Captain Cook **Obv:** Head with tiara right **Rev:** Multicolor image of James Cook, Botany Bay all within letter O **Edge:** Reeded

Date	Mintage	F	VF	XF	Unc	BU
2008 Proof	1,779	Value: 100				

KM# 508 DOLLAR

31.1030 g., 0.9990 Silver 0.9989 oz. ASW, 40.6 mm. **Ruler:** Elizabeth II **Subject:** Captain Cook **Obv:** Head with tiara right **Rev:** Multicolor image of James Cook, a new world all within letter O **Edge:** Reeded

Date	Mintage	F	VF	XF	Unc	BU
2008 Proof	1,779	Value: 100				

KM# 509 DOLLAR

31.1030 g., 0.9990 Silver 0.9989 oz. ASW, 40.6 mm. **Ruler:** Elizabeth II **Subject:** Captain Cook **Obv:** Head with tiara right **Rev:** Multicolor image of James Cook, striking the reef, large letter K in background **Edge:** Reeded

Date	Mintage	F	VF	XF	Unc	BU
2008 Proof	1,779	Value: 100				

KM# 765 DOLLAR

35.8000 g., 0.9990 Silver 1.1498 oz. ASW, 40 mm. **Ruler:** Elizabeth II **Subject:** 1961 First man in Space

Date	Mintage	F	VF	XF	Unc	BU
2008 Proof	—	Value: 115				

KM# 801 DOLLAR

31.1050 g., 0.9990 Silver 0.9990 oz. ASW, 40 mm. **Ruler:** Elizabeth II **Rev:** An-2, partially gilt

Date	Mintage	F	VF	XF	Unc	BU
2008 Proof	—	Value: 50.00				

KM# 802 DOLLAR

31.1050 g., 0.9990 Silver 0.9990 oz. ASW, 40 mm. **Ruler:** Elizabeth II **Rev:** An-74, partially gilt

Date	Mintage	F	VF	XF	Unc	BU
2008 Proof	—	Value: 50.00				

KM# 803 DOLLAR

31.1050 g., 0.9990 Silver 0.9990 oz. ASW, 40 mm. **Ruler:** Elizabeth II **Rev:** An-124, partially gilt

Date	Mintage	F	VF	XF	Unc	BU
2008 Proof	—	Value: 50.00				

KM# 804 DOLLAR

31.1050 g., 0.9990 Silver 0.9990 oz. ASW, 40 mm. **Ruler:** Elizabeth II **Rev:** An-148, partially gilt

Date	Mintage	F	VF	XF	Unc	BU
2008 Proof	—	Value: 50.00				

KM# 805 DOLLAR
31.1050 g., 0.9990 Silver 0.9990 oz. ASW, 40 mm. **Ruler:** Elizabeth II **Rev:** An-225, partially gilt

Date	Mintage	F	VF	XF	Unc	BU
2008 Proof	—	Value: 50.00				

KM# 1208 DOLLAR
0.5000 g., 0.9990 Gold 0.0161 oz. AGW, 11 mm. **Ruler:** Elizabeth II **Subject:** British Monarchs - Henry V

Date	Mintage	F	VF	XF	Unc	BU
2008 Proof	Est. 14,500	Value: 35.00				

KM# 1209 DOLLAR
0.5000 g., 0.9990 Gold 0.0161 oz. AGW, 11 mm. **Ruler:** Elizabeth II **Subject:** British Monarchs - Henry VIII

Date	Mintage	F	VF	XF	Unc	BU
2008 Proof	Est. 50,000	Value: 35.00				

KM# 1209a DOLLAR
0.5000 g., 0.9990 Platinum 0.0161 oz. APW, 11 mm. **Ruler:** Elizabeth II **Subject:** British Monarchs - Henry VIII

Date	Mintage	F	VF	XF	Unc	BU
2008 Proof	Est. 50,000	Value: 50.00				

KM# 1210 DOLLAR
0.5000 g., 0.9990 Gold 0.0161 oz. AGW, 11 mm. **Ruler:** Elizabeth II **Subject:** British Monarchs - Elizabeth II

Date	Mintage	F	VF	XF	Unc	BU
2008 Proof	Est. 50,000	Value: 35.00				

KM# 701 DOLLAR
31.1050 g., 0.9990 Silver 0.9990 oz. ASW, 39 mm. **Ruler:** Elizabeth II **Subject:** First Man on the Moon, 40th Anniversary **Obv:** Head right at top, multicolor moon in center **Rev:** Rocket, orbiter, moon walk. moon in multicolor at center

Date	Mintage	F	VF	XF	Unc	BU
2009 Proof	25,000	Value: 110				

KM# 702 DOLLAR
31.1050 g., 0.9990 Silver 0.9990 oz. ASW, 33x33 mm. **Ruler:** Elizabeth II **Subject:** Cook's Cottage, 75th Anniversary of relocation **Obv:** Head right **Rev:** Cottage and multicolor Captain Cook image **Shape:** Square

Date	Mintage	F	VF	XF	Unc	BU
2009 Proof	5,000	Value: 95.00				

KM# 706 DOLLAR
0.5000 g., 0.9990 Gold 0.0161 oz. AGW, 11 mm. **Ruler:** Elizabeth II **Subject:** Pope Benedict XVI visits the Holy Land **Rev:** Dome of the Rock

Date	Mintage	F	VF	XF	Unc	BU
2009 Proof	25,000	Value: 35.00				

KM# 772 DOLLAR
27.0000 g., Copper silver plated, 40 mm. **Ruler:** Elizabeth II **Subject:** Year of Astronomy **Rev:** Sun, multicolor

Date	Mintage	F	VF	XF	Unc	BU
2009	—	—	—	—	—	20.00

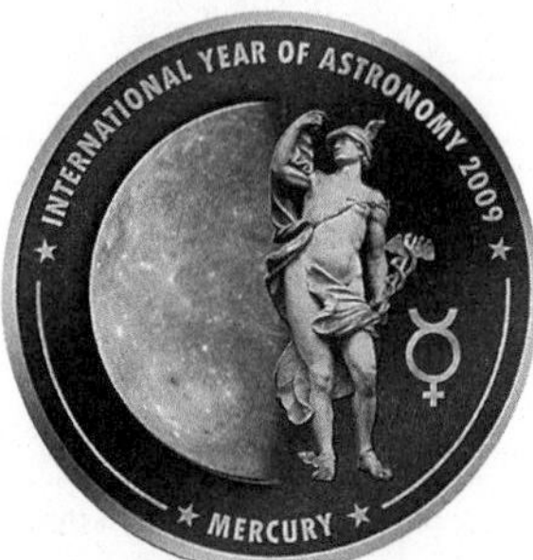

KM# 773 DOLLAR
27.0000 g., Copper silver plated, 40 mm. **Ruler:** Elizabeth II **Subject:** Year of Astronomy **Rev:** Mercury, multicolor

Date	Mintage	F	VF	XF	Unc	BU
2009	—	—	—	—	—	20.00

KM# 774 DOLLAR
27.0000 g., Copper silver plated, 40 mm. **Ruler:** Elizabeth II **Subject:** Year of Astronomy **Rev:** Venus, multicolor

Date	Mintage	F	VF	XF	Unc	BU
2009	—	—	—	—	—	25.00

KM# 775 DOLLAR
27.0000 g., Copper silver plated, 40 mm. **Ruler:** Elizabeth II **Subject:** Year of Astronomy **Rev:** Earth, multicolor

Date	Mintage	F	VF	XF	Unc	BU
2009	—	—	—	—	—	22.00

KM# 776 DOLLAR
27.0000 g., Copper silver plated, 40 mm. **Ruler:** Elizabeth II **Subject:** Year of Astronomy **Rev:** Mars, multicolor

Date	Mintage	F	VF	XF	Unc	BU
2009	—	—	—	—	—	22.00

KM# 777 DOLLAR
27.0000 g., Copper silver plated, 40 mm. **Ruler:** Elizabeth II **Subject:** Year of Astronomy **Rev:** Jupiter, multicolor

Date	Mintage	F	VF	XF	Unc	BU
2009	—	—	—	—	—	22.00

KM# 778 DOLLAR
27.0000 g., Copper silver plated, 40 mm. **Ruler:** Elizabeth II **Subject:** Year of Astronomy **Rev:** Saturn, multicolor

Date	Mintage	F	VF	XF	Unc	BU
2009	—	—	—	—	—	22.00

KM# 779 DOLLAR
27.0000 g., Copper silver plated, 40 mm. **Ruler:** Elizabeth II **Subject:** Year of Astronomy **Rev:** Uranus, multicolor

Date	Mintage	F	VF	XF	Unc	BU
2009	—	—	—	—	—	22.00

KM# 780 DOLLAR
27.0000 g., Copper silver plated, 40 mm. **Ruler:** Elizabeth II **Subject:** Year of Astronomy **Rev:** Neptune, multicolor

Date	Mintage	F	VF	XF	Unc	BU
2009	—	—	—	—	—	22.00

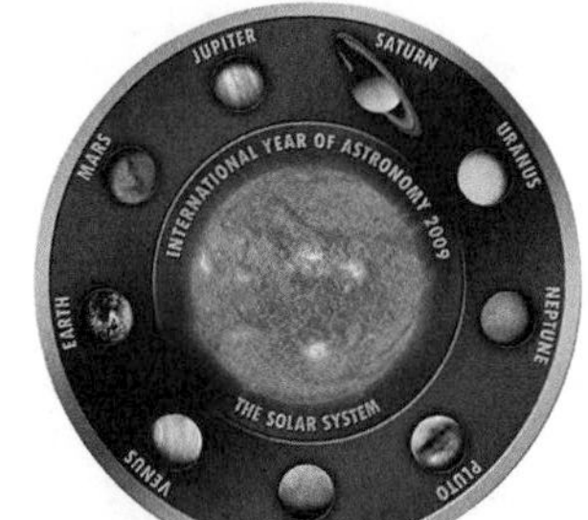

KM# 781 DOLLAR
27.0000 g., Copper silver plated, 40 mm. **Ruler:** Elizabeth II **Subject:** Year of Astronomy **Rev:** Solar System, multicolor

Date	Mintage	F	VF	XF	Unc	BU
2009	—	—	—	—	—	22.00

KM# 794 DOLLAR
Copper-Nickel silver plated, 40 mm. **Ruler:** Elizabeth II **Rev:** Nessie, multicolor

Date	Mintage	F	VF	XF	Unc	BU
2009	—	—	—	—	—	22.00

KM# 795 DOLLAR
Copper-Nickel silver plated, 40 mm. **Ruler:** Elizabeth II **Rev:** Bigfoot, multicolor

Date	Mintage	F	VF	XF	Unc	BU
2009	—	—	—	—	—	22.00

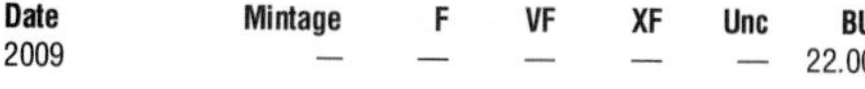

KM# 796 DOLLAR
Copper-Nickel, 40 mm. **Ruler:** Elizabeth II **Rev:** Medussa, multicolor

Date	Mintage	F	VF	XF	Unc	BU
2009	—	—	—	—	—	22.00

KM# 797 DOLLAR
Copper-Nickel, 40 mm. **Ruler:** Elizabeth II **Rev:** Pegasus, multicolor

Date	Mintage	F	VF	XF	Unc	BU
2009	—	—	—	—	—	22.00

KM# 798 DOLLAR
Silver, 40 mm. **Ruler:** Elizabeth II **Rev:** Baba Yaga, multicolor

Date	Mintage	F	VF	XF	Unc	BU
2009	—	—	—	—	—	22.00

KM# 799 DOLLAR
Copper-Nickel, 40 mm. **Ruler:** Elizabeth II **Rev:** Phoenix, multicolor

Date	Mintage	F	VF	XF	Unc	BU
2009	—	—	—	—	—	22.00

KM# 1172 DOLLAR
27.0000 g., Copper-Nickel, 38.6 mm. **Ruler:** Elizabeth II **Subject:** Moon Landing, 40th Anniversary **Rev:** Landing module Eagle and moon in color

Date	Mintage	F	VF	XF	Unc	BU
2009	—	—	—	—	—	17.50

KM# 1231 DOLLAR
25.0000 g., Copper-Nickel partially gilt, 38.6 mm. **Ruler:** Elizabeth II **Subject:** British Monarchs - Henry VIII

Date	Mintage	F	VF	XF	Unc	BU
2009	Est. 50,000	—	—	—	—	17.50

KM# 1241 DOLLAR
31.1350 g., 0.9990 Silver 1.0000 oz. ASW, 38.61 mm. **Ruler:** Elizabeth II **Subject:** Battle of Gettysburg and General Meade **Rev:** Battle scene at left, Meade in color at right

Date	Mintage	F	VF	XF	Unc	BU
2009 Proof	—	Value: 75.00				

KM# 1327 DOLLAR
Silver **Ruler:** Elizabeth II **Subject:** Mystical creatures - Drago **Rev:** Dragon in color

Date	Mintage	F	VF	XF	Unc	BU
2009 Proof	—	Value: 75.00				

KM# 1328 DOLLAR
Copper-Nickel **Ruler:** Elizabeth II **Subject:** Wonders of the World **Rev:** Ayers Rock in color

Date	Mintage	F	VF	XF	Unc	BU
2009	—	—	—	—	—	20.00

KM# 1478 DOLLAR
27.0000 g., Silver Plated Copper, 40 mm. **Ruler:** Elizabeth II **Rev:** Mount Everest in color

Date	Mintage	F	VF	XF	Unc	BU
2009	Est. 5,000	—	—	—	—	25.00

KM# 1479 DOLLAR
27.0000 g., Silver Plated Copper, 40 mm. **Ruler:** Elizabeth II **Rev:** Niagara Falls in color

Date	Mintage	F	VF	XF	Unc	BU
2009	Est. 5,000	—	—	—	—	25.00

KM# 1480 DOLLAR
27.0000 g., Silver Plated Copper, 40 mm. **Ruler:** Elizabeth II **Rev:** Grand Canyon in color

Date	Mintage	F	VF	XF	Unc	BU
2009	Est. 5,000	—	—	—	—	25.00

KM# 1481 DOLLAR
27.0000 g., Silver Plated Copper, 40 mm. **Ruler:** Elizabeth II **Rev:** Mt. Aetna volcano in color

Date	Mintage	F	VF	XF	Unc	BU
2009	Est. 5,000	—	—	—	—	25.00

KM# 1482 DOLLAR
27.0000 g., Silver Plated Copper, 40 mm. **Ruler:** Elizabeth II **Rev:** Northern lights in color

Date	Mintage	F	VF	XF	Unc	BU
2009	Est. 5,000	—	—	—	—	25.00

KM# 1483 DOLLAR
27.0000 g., Silver Plated Copper, 40 mm. **Ruler:** Elizabeth II **Rev:** Strokkur geyser in Iceland

Date	Mintage	F	VF	XF	Unc	BU
2009	Est. 5,000	—	—	—	—	25.00

KM# 1493 DOLLAR
0.5000 g., 0.9990 Gold 0.0161 oz. AGW, 11 mm. **Ruler:** Elizabeth II **Subject:** James Cook, 200th Anniversary of Death **Rev:** H.M.S. Endeavour

Date	Mintage	F	VF	XF	Unc	BU
2009 Proof	Est. 10,000	Value: 35.00				

KM# 762 DOLLAR
10.9300 g., Bi-Metallic Copper Nickel center in Aluminum-Bronze ring. **Ruler:** Elizabeth II **Obv:** Bust right **Rev:** Carved Maori figure (Tangaroa)

Date	Mintage	F	VF	XF	Unc	BU
2010	—	—	—	—	5.00	6.00

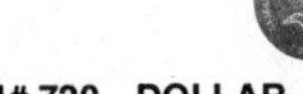

KM# 720 DOLLAR
0.1200 g., 0.9990 Silver 0.0039 oz. ASW, 4 mm. **Ruler:** Elizabeth II **Rev:** Fisherman's God statue **Note:** Illustration enlarged.

Date	Mintage	F	VF	XF	Unc	BU
2010 Prooflike	5,000	—	—	—	—	10.00

KM# 739 DOLLAR
31.1050 g., 0.9990 Silver 0.9990 oz. ASW, 37.65 mm. **Ruler:** Elizabeth II **Subject:** Niko & the way to the stars **Obv:** Head crowned left **Rev:** Multicolor deer **Shape:** 7-sided

Date	Mintage	F	VF	XF	Unc	BU
2010 Proof	3,500	Value: 60.00				

KM# 740 DOLLAR
31.1050 g., 0.9990 Silver 0.9990 oz. ASW, 37.65 mm. **Ruler:** Elizabeth II **Subject:** Niko & the way to the stars **Obv:** Head crowned left **Rev:** Multicolor wolf **Shape:** 7-sided

Date	Mintage	F	VF	XF	Unc	BU
2010 Proof	3,500	Value: 60.00				

KM# 741 DOLLAR
31.1050 g., 0.9990 Silver 0.9990 oz. ASW, 37.65 mm. **Ruler:** Elizabeth II **Subject:** Niko & the way to the stars **Obv:** Head crowned left **Rev:** Multicolor flying squirrel **Shape:** 7-sided

Date	Mintage	F	VF	XF	Unc	BU
2010 Proof	3,500	Value: 60.00				

KM# 742 DOLLAR
31.1050 g., 0.9990 Silver 0.9990 oz. ASW, 37.65 mm. **Ruler:** Elizabeth II **Subject:** Niko and the way to the stars **Obv:** Head crowned right **Rev:** Multicolor Ermine **Shape:** 7-sided

Date	Mintage	F	VF	XF	Unc	BU
2010 Proof	3,500	Value: 60.00				

KM# 743 DOLLAR
31.1050 g., 0.9990 Silver 0.9990 oz. ASW, 37.65 mm. **Ruler:** Elizabeth II **Subject:** Niko and the way to the stars **Obv:** Head crowned right **Rev:** Multicolor deer, flying squirrel and ermine **Shape:** 7-sided

Date	Mintage	F	VF	XF	Unc	BU
2010 Proof	3,500	Value: 60.00				

KM# 744 DOLLAR
31.1350 g., 0.9990 Silver 1.0000 oz. ASW, 40.6 mm. **Ruler:** Elizabeth II **Subject:** Battle of Trafalgar, 1805 **Rev:** Multicolor battle scene, HMS Victory

Date	Mintage	F	VF	XF	Unc	BU
2010 Proof	5,000	Value: 80.00				

KM# 770 DOLLAR
31.1050 g., 0.9990 Silver 0.9990 oz. ASW, 40 mm. **Ruler:** Elizabeth II **Subject:** Battle of Hampton Roads, Va. **Rev:** Monitor, multicolor background

Date	Mintage	F	VF	XF	Unc	BU
2010 Proof	5,000	Value: 80.00				

KM# 771 DOLLAR
31.1050 g., 0.9990 Silver 0.9990 oz. ASW, 40 mm. **Ruler:** Elizabeth II **Subject:** Battle of Salams **Rev:** Trireame, multicolor insert

Date	Mintage	F	VF	XF	Unc	BU
2010 Proof	5,000	Value: 100				

KM# 1243 DOLLAR
31.1350 g., 0.9990 Silver 1.0000 oz. ASW, 40.6 mm. **Ruler:** Elizabeth II **Subject:** Battle of Midway **Rev:** Aircraft carrier

Date	Mintage	F	VF	XF	Unc	BU
2010 Proof	5,000	Value: 100				

KM# 1256 DOLLAR
31.1350 g., 0.9990 Silver 1.0000 oz. ASW, 40.6 mm. **Ruler:** Elizabeth II **Subject:** Battle of Grunwald

Date	Mintage	F	VF	XF	Unc	BU
2010 Proof	—	Value: 50.00				

KM# 1257 DOLLAR
31.1050 g., 0.9990 Silver 0.9990 oz. ASW, 40.6 mm. **Ruler:** Elizabeth II **Subject:** Trafalgar **Rev:** H.M.S. Victory and Battle scene in color

Date	Mintage	F	VF	XF	Unc	BU
2010 Proof	5,000	Value: 80.00				

KM# 1295 DOLLAR
0.5000 g., 0.9990 Gold 0.0161 oz. AGW, 11 mm. **Ruler:** Elizabeth II **Rev:** Martin Luther King

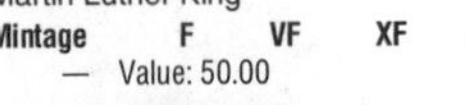

Date	Mintage	F	VF	XF	Unc	BU
2010 Proof	—	Value: 50.00				

KM# 1458 DOLLAR
25.0000 g., Copper-Nickel gilt, 38.61 mm. **Ruler:** Elizabeth II **Rev:** Photo of William and Kate

Date	Mintage	F	VF	XF	Unc	BU
2010 Proof	—	Value: 20.00				

KM# 1313 DOLLAR
27.0000 g., Silver Plated Copper, 38.61 mm. **Ruler:** Elizabeth II **Subject:** Marilyn Monroe, 85th Birthday

Date	Mintage	F	VF	XF	Unc	BU
2011 Proof	2,500	Value: 25.00				

KM# 1283 DOLLAR
31.1000 g., 0.9990 Silver 0.9988 oz. ASW, 40.6 mm. **Ruler:** Elizabeth II **Subject:** Florin - 1927 design

Date	Mintage	F	VF	XF	Unc	BU
2011 Proof	1,500	Value: 75.00				

KM# 1235 DOLLAR
31.1350 g., 0.9990 Silver 1.0000 oz. ASW, 40.6 mm. **Ruler:** Elizabeth II **Subject:** Battle of Jutland, 1916 **Rev:** Multicolor battleship

Date	Mintage	F	VF	XF	Unc	BU
2011 Proof	5,000	Value: 85.00				

KM# 1269 DOLLAR
31.1350 g., 0.9990 Silver 1.0000 oz. ASW, 47.6x27.6 mm. **Ruler:** Elizabeth II **Subject:** Year of the Rabbit **Rev:** Two brown rabbits **Shape:** Rectangle

Date	Mintage	F	VF	XF	Unc	BU
2011 Proof	3,000	Value: 100				

KM# 1270 DOLLAR
31.1350 g., 0.9990 Silver 1.0000 oz. ASW, 47.6x27.6 mm. **Ruler:** Elizabeth II **Subject:** Year of the Rabbit **Rev:** Two white rabbits **Shape:** Rectangle

Date	Mintage	F	VF	XF	Unc	BU
2011 Proof	3,000	Value: 100				

KM# 1271 DOLLAR
31.1350 g., 0.9990 Silver 1.0000 oz. ASW, 47.6x27.6 mm. **Ruler:** Elizabeth II **Subject:** Year of the Rabbit **Rev:** One black rabbit **Shape:** Rectangle

Date	Mintage	F	VF	XF	Unc	BU
2011 Proof	3,000	Value: 100				

KM# 1272 DOLLAR
31.1350 g., 0.9990 Silver 1.0000 oz. ASW, 47.6x27.6 mm. **Ruler:** Elizabeth II **Subject:** Year of the Rabbit **Rev:** One black rabbit **Shape:** Rectangle

Date	Mintage	F	VF	XF	Unc	BU
2011 Proof	3,000	Value: 100				

KM# 1284 DOLLAR
31.1000 g., 0.9990 Silver 0.9988 oz. ASW, 40.6 mm. **Ruler:** Elizabeth II **Subject:** Florin - 1934-35 Centenary

Date	Mintage	F	VF	XF	Unc	BU
2011 Proof	1,500	Value: 75.00				

KM# 1285 DOLLAR
31.1000 g., 0.9990 Silver 0.9988 oz. ASW, 40.6 mm. **Ruler:** Elizabeth II **Subject:** Florin - 1901-51 Jubilee

Date	Mintage	F	VF	XF	Unc	BU
2011 Proof	1,500	Value: 75.00				

KM# 1286 DOLLAR
31.1000 g., 0.9990 Silver 0.9988 oz. ASW, 40.6 mm. **Ruler:** Elizabeth II **Subject:** Florin - 1954 Royal Visit

Date	Mintage	F	VF	XF	Unc	BU
2011 Proof	1,500	Value: 75.00				

KM# 1342 DOLLAR
31.1050 g., 0.9990 Silver 0.9990 oz. ASW, 38.61 mm. **Ruler:** Elizabeth II **Subject:** Planets - Mercury **Rev:** with color

Date	Mintage	F	VF	XF	Unc	BU
2011 Proof	—	Value: 75.00				

KM# 1343 DOLLAR
31.1050 g., 0.9990 Silver 0.9990 oz. ASW, 38.61 mm. **Ruler:** Elizabeth II **Subject:** Plants - Venus **Rev:** with color

Date	Mintage	F	VF	XF	Unc	BU
2011 Proof	—	Value: 75.00				

KM# 1344 DOLLAR
31.1050 g., 0.9990 Silver 0.9990 oz. ASW, 38.61 mm. **Ruler:** Elizabeth II **Subject:** Planets - Earth **Rev:** with color

Date	Mintage	F	VF	XF	Unc	BU
2011 Proof	—	Value: 75.00				

KM# 1345 DOLLAR
31.1050 g., 0.9990 Silver 0.9990 oz. ASW, 38.61 mm. **Ruler:** Elizabeth II **Subject:** Plants - Mars **Rev:** with color

Date	Mintage	F	VF	XF	Unc	BU
2011 Proof	—	Value: 75.00				

KM# 1346 DOLLAR
31.1050 g., 0.9990 Silver 0.9990 oz. ASW, 38.61 mm. **Ruler:** Elizabeth II **Subject:** Planets - Jupiter **Rev:** Jupiter and Sagittarius with color

Date	Mintage	F	VF	XF	Unc	BU
2011 Proof	—	Value: 75.00				

KM# 1347 DOLLAR
31.1050 g., 0.9990 Silver 0.9990 oz. ASW, 38.61 mm. **Ruler:** Elizabeth II **Subject:** Planets - Saturn **Rev:** Saturn and Capricorn with color

Date	Mintage	F	VF	XF	Unc	BU
2011 Proof	—	Value: 75.00				

KM# 1348 DOLLAR
31.1050 g., 0.9990 Silver 0.9990 oz. ASW, 38.61 mm. **Ruler:** Elizabeth II **Subject:** Planets - Uranis **Rev:** Uranis and Aquarius with color

Date	Mintage	F	VF	XF	Unc	BU
2011 Proof	—	Value: 75.00				

KM# 1385 DOLLAR
31.1050 g., 0.9990 Silver 0.9990 oz. ASW, 38.61 mm. **Ruler:** Elizabeth II **Subject:** Marylin Monroe, 80th Birthday **Rev:** Marylin Monroe in color pose

Date	Mintage	F	VF	XF	Unc	BU
2011 Proof	—	Value: 125				

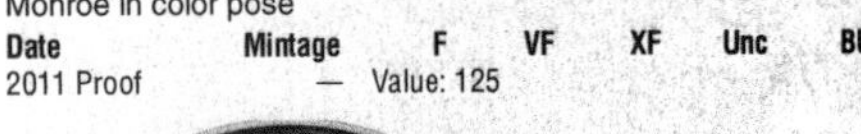

KM# 1396 DOLLAR
31.1050 g., 0.9990 Silver 0.9990 oz. ASW, 38.61 mm. **Ruler:** Elizabeth II **Subject:** Hollywood Legends - Elizabeth Taylor **Rev:** Elizabeth Taylor facing photo

Date	Mintage	F	VF	XF	Unc	BU
2011 Proof	—	Value: 125				

KM# 1459 DOLLAR
25.0000 g., Copper-Nickel gilt, 38.61 mm. **Ruler:** Elizabeth II **Rev:** Photo of William and Kate

Date	Mintage	F	VF	XF	Unc	BU
2011 Proof	—	Value: 25.00				

KM# 1375 DOLLAR
0.5000 g., 0.9990 Gold 0.0161 oz. AGW, 11 mm. **Ruler:** Elizabeth II **Obv:** Head with tiara right **Rev:** Titanic sailing left

Date	Mintage	F	VF	XF	Unc	BU
2012 Proof	—	Value: 50.00				

KM# 1391 DOLLAR
31.1050 g., 0.9990 Silver 0.9990 oz. ASW, 47.6x27.6 mm. **Ruler:** Elizabeth II **Obv:** Head with crown right **Rev:** Orange dragon at right

Date	Mintage	F	VF	XF	Unc	BU
2012 Proof	3,000	Value: 125				

KM# 1392 DOLLAR
31.1050 g., 0.9990 Silver 0.9990 oz. ASW, 47.6x27.6 mm. **Ruler:** Elizabeth II **Obv:** Head with crown right **Rev:** Blue dragon at left center

Date	Mintage	F	VF	XF	Unc	BU
2012 Proof	3,000	Value: 125				

KM# 1393 DOLLAR
31.1050 g., 0.9990 Silver 0.9990 oz. ASW, 47.6x27.6 mm. **Ruler:** Elizabeth II **Obv:** Head with crown right **Rev:** Brown dragon at center

Date	Mintage	F	VF	XF	Unc	BU
2012 Proof	3,000	Value: 125				

KM# 1394 DOLLAR
31.1050 g., 0.9990 Silver 0.9990 oz. ASW, 47.6x27.6 mm. **Ruler:** Elizabeth II **Obv:** Head with crown right **Rev:** Orange dragon at left

Date	Mintage	F	VF	XF	Unc	BU
2012 Proof	3,000	Value: 125				

KM# 1424 DOLLAR
Silver Plated Copper-Nickel, 38.61 mm. **Ruler:** Elizabeth II **Subject:** Ctyrlistek Cartoons **Rev:** Characters in color

Date	Mintage	F	VF	XF	Unc	BU
2012 Proof	100	Value: 35.00				

KM# 1441 DOLLAR
15.5000 g., 0.9990 Silver partially gilt 0.4978 oz. ASW **Ruler:** Elizabeth II **Subject:** Year of the Dragon **Rev:** Blue dragon **Shape:** Arc **Note:** One of four which form circle.

Date	Mintage	F	VF	XF	Unc	BU
2012 Proof	—	Value: 50.00				

KM# 1442 DOLLAR
15.5000 g., 0.9990 Silver partially gilt 0.4978 oz. ASW **Ruler:** Elizabeth II **Subject:** Year of the Dragon **Rev:** Orange dragon **Shape:** Arc **Note:** One of four which form circle.

Date	Mintage	F	VF	XF	Unc	BU
2012 Proof	—	Value: 50.00				

KM# 1443 DOLLAR
15.5000 g., 0.9990 Silver partially gilt 0.4978 oz. ASW **Ruler:** Elizabeth II **Subject:** Year of the Dragon **Rev:** Red dragon **Shape:** Arc **Note:** One of four which form circle.

Date	Mintage	F	VF	XF	Unc	BU
2012 Proof	—	Value: 50.00				

KM# 1444 DOLLAR
15.5000 g., 0.9990 Silver partially gilt 0.4978 oz. ASW **Ruler:** Elizabeth II **Subject:** Year of the Dragon **Rev:** Green dragon **Shape:** Arc **Note:** One of four which form circle.

Date	Mintage	F	VF	XF	Unc	BU
2012 Proof	—	Value: 50.00				

KM# 1449 DOLLAR
Silver Plated Copper, 38.61 mm. **Ruler:** Elizabeth II **Subject:** Abu Simbel **Rev:** Statues in color

Date	Mintage	F	VF	XF	Unc	BU
2012 Proof	—	Value: 40.00				

KM# 1456 DOLLAR
25.0000 g., Copper-Nickel gilt, 38.61 mm. **Ruler:** Elizabeth II **Subject:** Space Walk **Rev:** Photo of Space Walk

Date	Mintage	F	VF	XF	Unc	BU
2012 Proof	—	Value: 60.00				

KM# 1457 DOLLAR
Silver **Ruler:** Elizabeth II **Subject:** Everlasting love **Rev:** Flowers in color **Shape:** Heart

Date	Mintage	F	VF	XF	Unc	BU
2012 Proof	—	Value: 100				

KM# 1460 DOLLAR
31.1050 g., 0.9990 Silver 0.9990 oz. ASW, 27x47 mm. **Ruler:** Elizabeth II **Subject:** Year of the Snake **Rev:** Blue lipped sea snake **Shape:** Rectangle

Date	Mintage	F	VF	XF	Unc	BU
2013 Proof	3,000	Value: 100				

KM# 1461 DOLLAR
31.1050 g., 0.9990 Silver 0.9990 oz. ASW, 27x47 mm. **Ruler:** Elizabeth II **Subject:** Year of the Snake **Rev:** Yellow banded wolf snake **Shape:** Rectangle

Date	Mintage	F	VF	XF	Unc	BU
2013 Proof	3,000	Value: 100				

KM# 1462 DOLLAR
31.1050 g., 0.9990 Silver 0.9990 oz. ASW, 38.61 mm. **Ruler:** Elizabeth II **Subject:** Year of the Snake **Rev:** Red bamboo rat snake

Date	Mintage	F	VF	XF	Unc	BU
2013 Proof	3,000	Value: 100				

KM# 1463 DOLLAR
31.1050 g., 0.9990 Silver 0.9990 oz. ASW, 38.61 mm. **Ruler:** Elizabeth II **Subject:** Year of the Snake **Rev:** Chinese green tree viper

Date	Mintage	F	VF	XF	Unc	BU
2013 Proof	3,000	Value: 100				

KM# 1464 DOLLAR
15.5000 g., 0.9990 Silver 0.4978 oz. ASW, 49x24 mm. **Ruler:** Elizabeth II **Subject:** Year of the Snake **Shape:** Fan

Date	Mintage	F	VF	XF	Unc	BU
2013 Proof	7,500	Value: 75.00				

KM# 554 2 DOLLARS
31.1050 g., 0.9990 Silver 0.9990 oz. ASW, 40.5 mm. **Ruler:** Elizabeth II **Subject:** Asian wildlife **Rev:** Multicolored pheasant-tailed Jacana

Date	Mintage	F	VF	XF	Unc	BU
2001 Proof	3,000	Value: 85.00				

KM# 551 2 DOLLARS
31.1050 g., 0.9990 Silver 0.9990 oz. ASW, 40.5 mm. **Ruler:** Elizabeth II **Subject:** Asian wildlife **Rev:** Multicolor Mikado Pheasant

Date	Mintage	F	VF	XF	Unc	BU
2001 Proof	5,000	Value: 85.00				

KM# 552 2 DOLLARS
31.1050 g., 0.9990 Silver 0.9990 oz. ASW, 40.5 mm. **Ruler:** Elizabeth II **Subject:** Asian wildlife **Rev:** Multicolor black-faced spoonbill

Date	Mintage	F	VF	XF	Unc	BU
2001 Proof	5,000	Value: 85.00				

KM# 553 2 DOLLARS
31.1050 g., 0.9990 Silver 0.9990 oz. ASW, 40.5 mm. **Ruler:** Elizabeth II **Subject:** Asian wildlife **Rev:** Multicolor Indian Pitta

Date	Mintage	F	VF	XF	Unc	BU
2001 Proof	3,000	Value: 85.00				

KM# 468 2 DOLLARS
Copper-Nickel **Ruler:** Elizabeth II **Rev:** Football championship

Date	Mintage	F	VF	XF	Unc	BU
2002	—	—	—	—	5.00	7.00

KM# 1119 2 DOLLARS
Copper-Nickel, 30 mm. **Ruler:** Elizabeth II **Subject:** XXVIII Summer Olympics, Athens **Rev:** Discus thrower

Date	Mintage	F	VF	XF	Unc	BU
2002 Proof	—	Value: 15.00				

KM# 1120 2 DOLLARS
Silver **Ruler:** Elizabeth II **Subject:** Endangered Wildlife **Rev:** Lion family

Date	Mintage	F	VF	XF	Unc	BU
2002 Proof	—	Value: 25.00				

KM# 1282 2 DOLLARS
31.1350 g., 0.9990 Silver 1.0000 oz. ASW, 40.6 mm. **Ruler:** Elizabeth II **Subject:** Taiwan New Koala Family **Obv:** Head crowned right **Rev:** Multicolor Koala seated with leaves

Date	Mintage	F	VF	XF	Unc	BU
2002 Proof	—	Value: 135				

KM# 417 2 DOLLARS
7.5500 g., Copper-Nickel, 26 mm. **Ruler:** Elizabeth II **Obv:** Crowned bust right, new portrait **Rev:** Mortar and pestle from Atiu Island **Shape:** Triangle

Date	Mintage	F	VF	XF	Unc	BU
2003	—	—	—	—	3.00	3.50
2010	—	—	—	—	3.00	3.50

KM# 1123 2 DOLLARS
62.7700 g., 0.9990 Silver 2.0160 oz. ASW, 50 mm. **Ruler:** Elizabeth II **Rev:** Edward "Ned" Kelly in color

Date	Mintage	F	VF	XF	Unc	BU
2003 Proof	Est. 2,500	Value: 125				

KM# 1124 2 DOLLARS
62.7700 g., 0.9990 Silver 2.0160 oz. ASW, 50 mm. **Ruler:** Elizabeth II **Rev:** Daniel Morgan in color

Date	Mintage	F	VF	XF	Unc	BU
2003 Proof	Est. 2,500	Value: 125				

KM# 1125 2 DOLLARS
62.7700 g., 0.9990 Silver 2.0160 oz. ASW **Ruler:** Elizabeth II **Rev:** Ben Hall in color

Date	Mintage	F	VF	XF	Unc	BU
2003 Proof	Est. 2,500	Value: 125				

KM# 1126 2 DOLLARS
62.7700 g., 0.9990 Silver 2.0160 oz. ASW, 50 mm. **Ruler:** Elizabeth II **Rev:** Fred Ward "Captain Thunderbolt" in color

Date	Mintage	F	VF	XF	Unc	BU
2003 Proof	Est. 2,500	Value: 125				

KM# 1139 2 DOLLARS
0.9990 Silver, 30 mm. **Ruler:** Elizabeth II **Subject:** John F. Kennedy, 40th Anniversary of Death

Date	Mintage	F	VF	XF	Unc	BU
2003 Proof	—	Value: 45.00				

KM# 1141 2 DOLLARS
Gold **Ruler:** Elizabeth II **Rev:** Red cardinal in color

Date	Mintage	F	VF	XF	Unc	BU
2003 Proof	Est. 5,000	Value: 85.00				

KM# 1142 2 DOLLARS
Gold **Ruler:** Elizabeth II **Subject:** Love swing **Rev:** Bird in color

Date	Mintage	F	VF	XF	Unc	BU
2003 Proof	Est. 5,000	Value: 85.00				

KM# 536 2 DOLLARS
31.1050 g., 0.9990 Silver 0.9990 oz. ASW, 40.7 mm. **Ruler:** Elizabeth II **Subject:** Birds of New Zealand **Rev:** Multicolor tui

Date	Mintage	F	VF	XF	Unc	BU
2005 Prooflike	8,000	—	—	—	—	90.00

KM# 537 2 DOLLARS
31.1050 g., 0.9990 Silver 0.9990 oz. ASW, 40.7 mm. **Ruler:** Elizabeth II **Subject:** Birds of New Zealand **Rev:** Multicolor bell bird

Date	Mintage	F	VF	XF	Unc	BU
2005 Prooflike	8,000	—	—	—	—	90.00

KM# 538 2 DOLLARS
31.1050 g., 0.9990 Silver 0.9990 oz. ASW, 40.7 mm. **Ruler:** Elizabeth II **Subject:** Birds of New Zealand **Rev:** Multicolor New Zealand Pigeon

Date	Mintage	F	VF	XF	Unc	BU
2005 Prooflike	8,000	—	—	—	—	90.00

KM# 539 2 DOLLARS
31.1050 g., 0.9990 Silver 0.9990 oz. ASW, 40.7 mm. **Ruler:** Elizabeth II **Subject:** Birds of New Zealand **Rev:** Multicolor yellow crowned parakeet

Date	Mintage	F	VF	XF	Unc	BU
2005 Prooflike	8,000	—	—	—	—	90.00

KM# 524 2 DOLLARS
31.1050 g., 0.9990 Silver 0.9990 oz. ASW, 40.7 mm. **Ruler:** Elizabeth II **Subject:** Classic Speedsters from the 1930's **Rev:** Multicolor 1935 Auburn 851 Speedster

Date	Mintage	F	VF	XF	Unc	BU
2006 Prooflike	6,000	—	—	—	—	80.00

KM# 525 2 DOLLARS
31.1050 g., 0.9990 Silver 0.9990 oz. ASW, 40.7 mm. **Ruler:** Elizabeth II **Subject:** Classic Speedsters from the 1930's **Rev:** Multicolor 1935 Bugatti Type 57SC Atlantic Speedster

Date	Mintage	F	VF	XF	Unc	BU
2006 Prooflike	6,000	—	—	—	—	80.00

KM# 526 2 DOLLARS
31.1050 g., 0.9990 Silver 0.9990 oz. ASW, 40.7 mm. **Ruler:** Elizabeth II **Subject:** Speedsters from the 1930's **Rev:** Multicolor 1936 Duesenberg SSJ Speedster

Date	Mintage	F	VF	XF	Unc	BU
2006 Prooflike	—	—	—	—	—	80.00

KM# 527 2 DOLLARS
31.1050 g., 0.9990 Silver 0.9990 oz. ASW, 40.7 mm. **Ruler:** Elizabeth II **Subject:** Speedsters from the 1930's **Rev:** Multicolor 1930 Packard 734 Boattail Speedster

Date	Mintage	F	VF	XF	Unc	BU
2006 Prooflike	6,000	—	—	—	—	80.00

KM# 1170 2 DOLLARS
10.0000 g., 0.9250 Silver 0.2974 oz. ASW, 30 mm. **Ruler:** Elizabeth II **Rev:** Motion Pictures, 100th Anniversary

Date	Mintage	F	VF	XF	Unc	BU
2006	Est. 2,500	—	—	—	—	35.00

KM# 1288 2 DOLLARS
31.1050 g., 0.9990 Silver 0.9990 oz. ASW, 40.7 mm. **Ruler:** Elizabeth II **Rev:** Supermarine S-6B race plane in color

Date	Mintage	F	VF	XF	Unc	BU
2006 Prooflike	6,000	—	—	—	—	75.00

KM# 1289 2 DOLLARS
31.1050 g., 0.9990 Silver 0.9990 oz. ASW, 40.7 mm. **Ruler:** Elizabeth II **Rev:** GeeBee race plane in color

Date	Mintage	F	VF	XF	Unc	BU
2006 Prooflike	6,000	—	—	—	—	75.00

KM# 1290 2 DOLLARS
31.1050 g., 0.9990 Silver 0.9990 oz. ASW, 40.7 mm. **Ruler:** Elizabeth II **Rev:** Hughes H-1 race plane in color

Date	Mintage	F	VF	XF	Unc	BU
2006 Prooflike	6,000	—	—	—	—	75.00

KM# 1291 2 DOLLARS
31.1050 g., 0.9990 Silver 0.9990 oz. ASW, 40.7 mm. **Ruler:** Elizabeth II **Rev:** Polikarpov I-16 race plane in color

Date	Mintage	F	VF	XF	Unc	BU
2006 Prooflike	6,000	—	—	—	—	75.00

KM# 1316 2 DOLLARS
Silver **Ruler:** Elizabeth II **Rev:** Motorcycle - Brough in color

Date	Mintage	F	VF	XF	Unc	BU
2007 Proof	—	Value: 45.00				

KM# 1317 2 DOLLARS
Silver **Ruler:** Elizabeth II **Rev:** Motorcycle - BSA Sloper in color

Date	Mintage	F	VF	XF	Unc	BU
2007 Proof	—	Value: 45.00				

KM# 1318 2 DOLLARS
Silver **Ruler:** Elizabeth II **Rev:** Motorcycle - IZH 8

Date	Mintage	F	VF	XF	Unc	BU
2007 Proof	—	Value: 45.00				

KM# 514 2 DOLLARS
31.1050 g., 0.9990 Silver 0.9990 oz. ASW, 40.7 mm. **Ruler:** Elizabeth II **Subject:** Great Motorcycles from the 1930's **Rev:** Multicolor 1930 BSA Sloper

Date	Mintage	F	VF	XF	Unc	BU
2007 Prooflike	6,000	—	—	—	—	70.00

KM# 515 2 DOLLARS
31.1050 g., 0.9990 Silver 0.9990 oz. ASW, 40.7 mm. **Ruler:** Elizabeth II **Subject:** Great motorcycles from the 1930's **Rev:** Multicolor 1937 Ariel 1000 Squarefour

Date	Mintage	F	VF	XF	Unc	BU
2007 Prooflike	6,000	—	—	—	—	70.00

KM# 516 2 DOLLARS
31.1050 g., 0.9990 Silver 0.9990 oz. ASW, 40.7 mm. **Ruler:** Elizabeth II **Subject:** Great motorcycles from the 1930's **Rev:** Multicolor 1938 12H 8

Date	Mintage	F	VF	XF	Unc	BU
2007 Prooflike	6,000	—	—	—	—	70.00

KM# 517 2 DOLLARS
31.1050 g., 0.9990 Silver 0.9990 oz. ASW, 40.7 mm. **Ruler:** Elizabeth II **Subject:** Great motorcycles from the 1930's **Rev:** Multicolor 1931 Matchless Silver Hawk

Date	Mintage	F	VF	XF	Unc	BU
2007 Prooflike	6,000	—	—	—	—	70.00

KM# 518 2 DOLLARS
31.1050 g., 0.9990 Silver 0.9990 oz. ASW, 40.7 mm. **Ruler:** Elizabeth II **Subject:** Great motocycles from the 1930's **Rev:** Multicolor 1932 Brough Superior SS100

Date	Mintage	F	VF	XF	Unc	BU
2007 Prooflike	6,000	—	—	—	—	70.00

KM# 529 2 DOLLARS
31.1050 g., 0.9990 Silver 0.9990 oz. ASW, 40.7 mm. **Ruler:** Elizabeth II **Subject:** International Women's Day **Rev:** Multicolor tulips, large 8

Date	Mintage	F	VF	XF	Unc	BU
2007 Prooflike	4,000	—	—	—	—	65.00

KM# 532 2 DOLLARS
31.1050 g., 0.9990 Silver 0.9990 oz. ASW, 40.7 mm. **Ruler:** Elizabeth II **Subject:** Sherlock Holmes **Rev:** Multicolor portrait

Date	Mintage	F	VF	XF	Unc	BU
2007 Prooflike	8,000	—	—	—	—	100

KM# 1184 2 DOLLARS
31.1050 g., 0.9990 Silver 0.9990 oz. ASW, 40.7 mm. **Ruler:** Elizabeth II **Subject:** Birds of Fiji **Rev:** Island Thrush in color

Date	Mintage	F	VF	XF	Unc	BU
2007	Est. 4,000	—	—	—	—	45.00

KM# 1185 2 DOLLARS
31.1050 g., 0.9990 Silver 0.9990 oz. ASW, 40.7 mm. **Ruler:** Elizabeth II **Subject:** Birds of Fiji **Rev:** Vampire Bat in color

Date	Mintage	F	VF	XF	Unc	BU
2007	Est. 4,000	—	—	—	—	45.00

KM# 1186 2 DOLLARS
31.1050 g., 0.9990 Silver 0.9990 oz. ASW, 40.7 mm. **Ruler:** Elizabeth II **Subject:** Birds of Fiji **Rev:** Kingfisher in color

Date	Mintage	F	VF	XF	Unc	BU
2007	4,000	—	—	—	—	45.00

KM# 1187 2 DOLLARS
31.1050 g., 0.9990 Silver 0.9990 oz. ASW, 40.7 mm. **Ruler:** Elizabeth II **Subject:** Birds of Fiji **Rev:** Lori in color

Date	Mintage	F	VF	XF	Unc	BU
2007	4,000	—	—	—	—	45.00

KM# 510 2 DOLLARS
31.1050 g., 0.9990 Silver 0.9990 oz. ASW, 40.7 mm. **Ruler:** Elizabeth II **Subject:** Year of the Rat **Rev:** Multicolor scene of little girl from Russian animated cartoon

Date	Mintage	F	VF	XF	Unc	BU
2008 Prooflike	10,000	—	—	—	—	80.00

KM# 511 2 DOLLARS
31.1050 g., 0.9990 Silver 0.9990 oz. ASW, 40.7 mm. **Ruler:** Elizabeth II **Subject:** Year of the Rat **Rev:** Multicolor scene of nutcracker from Russian animated cartoon

Date	Mintage	F	VF	XF	Unc	BU
2008 Prooflike	10,000	—	—	—	—	80.00

KM# 512 2 DOLLARS
39.1050 g., 0.9990 Silver 1.2559 oz. ASW, 40.7 mm. **Ruler:** Elizabeth II **Rev:** Multicolor scene of Adventure of Cat Leopold Russian animated cartoon

Date	Mintage	F	VF	XF	Unc	BU
2008 Prooflike	10,000	—	—	—	—	100

KM# 513 2 DOLLARS
31.1050 g., 0.9990 Silver 0.9990 oz. ASW, 40.7 mm. **Ruler:** Elizabeth II **Subject:** Year of the Rat **Rev:** Multicolor scene of tough toy soldier from Russian animated cartoon

Date	Mintage	F	VF	XF	Unc	BU
2008 Prooflike	10,000	—	—	—	—	80.00

KM# 519 2 DOLLARS
31.1050 g., 0.9990 Silver 0.9990 oz. ASW, 40.7 mm. **Ruler:** Elizabeth II **Subject:** Racers from the 1930's **Rev:** Multicolor Gee Bee

Date	Mintage	F	VF	XF	Unc	BU
2008 Prooflike	6,000	—	—	—	—	70.00

KM# 520 2 DOLLARS
31.1050 g., 0.9990 Silver 0.9990 oz. ASW, 40.7 mm. **Ruler:** Elizabeth II **Subject:** Racers from the 1930's **Rev:** Multicolor, Hughes H-1 Racer

Date	Mintage	F	VF	XF	Unc	BU
2008 Prooflike	6,000	—	—	—	—	70.00

KM# 521 2 DOLLARS
31.1050 g., 0.9990 Silver 0.9990 oz. ASW, 40.7 mm. **Ruler:** Elizabeth II **Subject:** Racers from the 1930's **Rev:** Multicolor Laird Turner LTR-14 Meteor

Date	Mintage	F	VF	XF	Unc	BU
2008 Prooflike	6,000	—	—	—	—	70.00

KM# 522 2 DOLLARS
31.1050 g., 0.9990 Silver 0.9990 oz. ASW, 40.7 mm. **Ruler:** Elizabeth II **Subject:** Racers from the 1930's **Rev:** Multicolor Spuermarine S.6B Floatplane

Date	Mintage	F	VF	XF	Unc	BU
2008 Prooflike	6,000	—	—	—	—	70.00

KM# 523 2 DOLLARS
31.1050 g., 0.9990 Silver 0.9990 oz. ASW, 40.7 mm. **Ruler:** Elizabeth II **Subject:** Racers from the 1930's **Rev:** Multicolor Polikarpov I-16

Date	Mintage	F	VF	XF	Unc	BU
2008 Prooflike	6,000	—	—	—	—	70.00

KM# 528 2 DOLLARS
31.1050 g., 0.9990 Silver 0.9990 oz. ASW, 40.7 mm. **Ruler:** Elizabeth II **Subject:** Valentines (Love) **Rev:** Multicolor pair of swans **Rev. Legend:** Love is precious

Date	Mintage	F	VF	XF	Unc	BU
2008 Prooflike	16,000	—	—	—	—	90.00

KM# 530 2 DOLLARS
31.1050 g., 0.9990 Silver 0.9990 oz. ASW, 40.7 mm. **Ruler:** Elizabeth II **Subject:** Mikhail Kalasknikov **Rev:** Multicolor portrait in uniform with siver gun

Date	Mintage	F	VF	XF	Unc	BU
2008 Prooflike	20,000	—	—	—	—	100

KM# 531 2 DOLLARS
31.1050 g., 0.9990 Silver 0.9990 oz. ASW, 40.7 mm. **Ruler:** Elizabeth II **Subject:** Mikhail Kalashnikov **Rev:** Multicolor red star, soldier and gun

Date	Mintage	F	VF	XF	Unc	BU
2008 Prooflike	20,000	—	—	—	—	100

KM# 533 2 DOLLARS
31.1050 g., 0.9990 Silver 0.9990 oz. ASW, 40.7 mm. **Ruler:** Elizabeth II **Subject:** Sherlock Holmes **Rev:** Multicolor scene from Hound of the Baskervilles

Date	Mintage	F	VF	XF	Unc	BU
2008 Prooflike	8,000	—	—	—	—	100

KM# 534 2 DOLLARS
31.1050 g., 0.9990 Silver 0.9990 oz. ASW, 40.7 mm. **Ruler:** Elizabeth II **Subject:** Sherlock Holmes **Rev:** Multicolor scehe from the Final Problem

Date	Mintage	F	VF	XF	Unc	BU
2008 Prooflike	8,000	—	—	—	—	100

KM# 535 2 DOLLARS
31.1050 g., 0.9990 Silver 0.9990 oz. ASW, 40.7 mm. **Ruler:** Elizabeth II **Subject:** Sherlock Holmes **Rev:** Multicolor scene from the Sign of the Four

Date	Mintage	F	VF	XF	Unc	BU
2008 Prooflike	8,000	—	—	—	—	100

KM# 540 2 DOLLARS
31.1050 g., 0.9990 Silver 0.9990 oz. ASW, 40.7 mm. **Ruler:** Elizabeth II **Subject:** Ballet dancers **Rev:** Multicolor Vasley Nijinnsky

Date	Mintage	F	VF	XF	Unc	BU
2008 Prooflike	8,000	—	—	—	—	85.00

KM# 541 2 DOLLARS

31.1050 g., 0.9990 Silver 0.9990 oz. ASW, 40.7 mm. **Ruler:** Elizabeth II **Subject:** Ballet Dancers **Rev:** Multicolor Matuilda Kshesinskaya

Date	Mintage	F	VF	XF	Unc	BU
2008 Prooflike	8,000	—	—	—	—	85.00

KM# 542 2 DOLLARS

31.1050 g., 0.9990 Silver 0.9990 oz. ASW, 40.7 mm. **Ruler:** Elizabeth II **Subject:** Ballet dancers **Rev:** Multicolor Sergey Lifar

Date	Mintage	F	VF	XF	Unc	BU
2008 Prooflike	8,000	—	—	—	—	85.00

KM# 543 2 DOLLARS

31.1050 g., 0.9990 Silver 0.9990 oz. ASW, 40.7 mm. **Ruler:** Elizabeth II **Subject:** Ballet dancers **Rev:** Multicolor Anna Pavlova

Date	Mintage	F	VF	XF	Unc	BU
2008 Prooflike	—	—	—	—	—	85.00

KM# 544 2 DOLLARS

31.1050 g., 0.9990 Silver 0.9990 oz. ASW, 40.7 mm. **Ruler:** Elizabeth II **Subject:** White Army **Rev:** Multicolor Anton Denkin

Date	Mintage	F	VF	XF	Unc	BU
2008 Prooflike	6,000	—	—	—	—	85.00

KM# 545 2 DOLLARS

31.1050 g., 0.9990 Silver 0.9990 oz. ASW, 40.7 mm. **Ruler:** Elizabeth II **Subject:** White Army **Rev:** Multicolor Pytor Vrangel

Date	Mintage	F	VF	XF	Unc	BU
2008 Prooflike	6,000	—	—	—	—	85.00

KM# 546 2 DOLLARS

31.1050 g., 0.9990 Silver 0.9990 oz. ASW, 40.7 mm. **Ruler:** Elizabeth II **Subject:** White Army **Rev:** Multicolor Alexander Kutepov

Date	Mintage	F	VF	XF	Unc	BU
2008 Prooflike	6,000	—	—	—	—	85.00

KM# 547 2 DOLLARS

31.1050 g., 0.9990 Silver 0.9990 oz. ASW, 40.7 mm. **Ruler:** Elizabeth II **Subject:** White Army **Rev:** Multicolor Alexander Kolchak

Date	Mintage	F	VF	XF	Unc	BU
2008 Prooflike	6,000	—	—	—	—	85.00

KM# 721 2 DOLLARS

0.1200 g., 0.9990 Gold 0.0039 oz. AGW, 4 mm. **Ruler:** Elizabeth II **Rev:** Lady Penrhyn sailing ship **Note:** Illustration enlarged.

Date	Mintage	F	VF	XF	Unc	BU
2010 Prooflike	5,000	—	—	—	—	12.00

KM# 722 2 DOLLARS

0.1200 g., 0.9950 Platinum 0.0038 oz. APW, 4 mm. **Ruler:** Elizabeth II **Rev:** Humpback whale **Note:** Illustration enlarged.

Date	Mintage	F	VF	XF	Unc	BU
2010 Prooflike	5,000	—	—	—	—	15.00

KM# 1294 2 DOLLARS

31.1050 g., 0.9990 Silver 0.9990 oz. ASW, 33 mm. **Ruler:** Elizabeth II **Rev:** Fish with crown partially gilt

Date	Mintage	F	VF	XF	Unc	BU
2010 Proof	—	Value: 55.00				

KM# 1312 2 DOLLARS

15.5500 g., 0.9250 Silver partially gilt 0.4624 oz. ASW, 33 mm. **Ruler:** Elizabeth II **Subject:** Good Luck

Date	Mintage	F	VF	XF	Unc	BU
2010	1,000	—	—	—	—	45.00

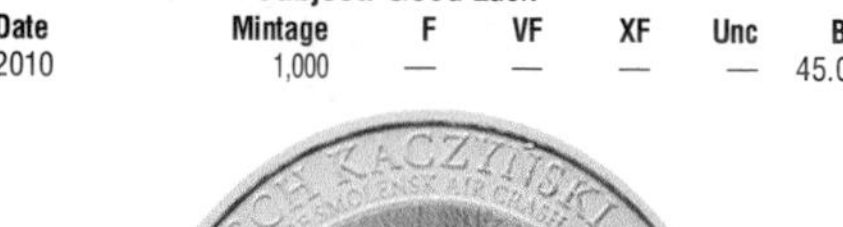

KM# 1384 2 DOLLARS

31.1050 g., 0.9990 Silver 0.9990 oz. ASW, 40.7 mm. **Ruler:** Elizabeth II **Subject:** Polish President's death, 1st Anniversary **Rev:** Portrait at right, plane crash site in color at left

Date	Mintage	F	VF	XF	Unc	BU
2011	—	—	—	—	—	75.00

KM# 1405 2 DOLLARS

15.5000 g., 0.9250 Silver 0.4609 oz. ASW, 15.5x35 mm. **Ruler:** Elizabeth II **Subject:** Hieronymus Bosch, pater **Rev:** Paradise in color **Shape:** Vertical rectangle

Date	Mintage	F	VF	XF	Unc	BU
2011 Proof	500	Value: 150				

KM# 1407 2 DOLLARS

15.5000 g., 0.9250 Silver 0.4609 oz. ASW, 15.5x35 mm. **Ruler:** Elizabeth II **Subject:** Hieronymus Bosch, pater **Rev:** Hell in color **Shape:** Vertical rectangle

Date	Mintage	F	VF	XF	Unc	BU
2011 Proof	500	Value: 150				

KM# 1411 2 DOLLARS

31.1050 g., 0.9990 Silver 0.9990 oz. ASW, 38.61 mm. **Ruler:** Elizabeth II **Subject:** Soyuzmultfilm - Old dog and wolf **Rev:** Wolf in color

Date	Mintage	F	VF	XF	Unc	BU
2011 Proof	2,000	Value: 100				

KM# 1412 2 DOLLARS

31.1080 g., 0.9990 Silver 0.9991 oz. ASW, 38.61 mm. **Ruler:** Elizabeth II **Subject:** Kipling's Jungle Book **Rev:** Mowgli and Aklea in color

Date	Mintage	F	VF	XF	Unc	BU
2011 Proof	2,000	Value: 100				

KM# 1413 2 DOLLARS

31.1050 g., 0.9990 Silver 0.9990 oz. ASW, 38.61 mm. **Ruler:** Elizabeth II **Subject:** Kipling's Jungle Book characters **Rev:** Kaa, snake

Date	Mintage	F	VF	XF	Unc	BU
2011 Proof	2,000	Value: 100				

KM# 1414 2 DOLLARS

31.1050 g., 0.9990 Silver 0.9990 oz. ASW, 38.61 mm. **Ruler:** Elizabeth II **Subject:** Kipling's Jungle Book characters **Rev:** Baloo (bear) in color

Date	Mintage	F	VF	XF	Unc	BU
2011 Proof	2,000	Value: 100				

KM# 1415 2 DOLLARS

31.1050 g., 0.9990 Silver 0.9990 oz. ASW, 38.61 mm. **Ruler:** Elizabeth II **Subject:** Kipling's Jungle Book characters **Rev:** Bagheera and Kaa, panther and crow

Date	Mintage	F	VF	XF	Unc	BU
2011 Proof	2,000	Value: 100				

KM# 1416 2 DOLLARS

31.1050 g., 0.9990 Silver 0.9990 oz. ASW, 38.61 mm. **Ruler:** Elizabeth II **Subject:** Kipling's Jungle Book characters **Rev:** Shere Khan (tiger) in color

Date	Mintage	F	VF	XF	Unc	BU
2011 Proof	2,000	Value: 100				

KM# 1121 5 DOLLARS

Silver **Ruler:** Elizabeth II **Rev:** Sir Francis Drake

Date	Mintage	F	VF	XF	Unc	BU
2002 Proof	—	Value: 35.00				

KM# 1122 5 DOLLARS

Silver **Ruler:** Elizabeth II **Rev:** Kon Tiki and Thor Heyerdahl

Date	Mintage	F	VF	XF	Unc	BU
2002 Proof	—	Value: 45.00				

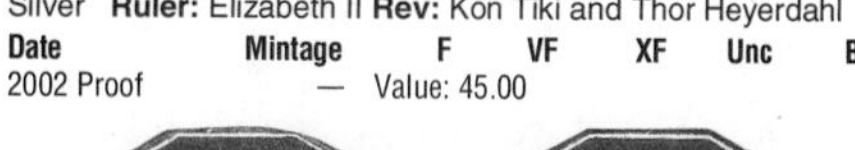

KM# 418 5 DOLLARS

14.0000 g., Aluminum-Bronze, 31.5 mm. **Ruler:** Elizabeth II **Obv:** Crowned bust right, new portrait **Rev:** Conch shell and value **Shape:** 12-sided

Date	Mintage	F	VF	XF	Unc	BU
2003	—	—	—	—	6.00	8.00

KM# 1140 5 DOLLARS

20.0000 g., 0.9990 Silver 0.6423 oz. ASW **Ruler:** Elizabeth II **Subject:** Vincent van Gogh, 150th Anniversary of Birth

Date	Mintage	F	VF	XF	Unc	BU
2003 Proof	Est. 5,000	Value: 35.00				

KM# 469 5 DOLLARS

Copper-Nickel, 40 mm. **Ruler:** Elizabeth II **Obv:** USPS logo, Queens head above **Rev:** 5 cent 1847 Benjamin Franklin stamp

Date	Mintage	F	VF	XF	Unc	BU
2004	—	—	—	—	10.00	12.00

KM# 469a 5 DOLLARS

Silver, 40 mm. **Ruler:** Elizabeth II **Obv:** USPS logo, Queens head above **Rev:** 5 cent 1847 Benjamin Franklin stamp **Edge:** Reeded

Date	Mintage	F	VF	XF	Unc	BU
2004 Proof	—	Value: 40.00				

KM# 1149 5 DOLLARS

31.6350 g., 0.9990 Silver 1.0160 oz. ASW **Ruler:** Elizabeth II **Subject:** Apollo Moon Landing, 35th Anniversary **Rev:** Astronaut in Solar System

Date	Mintage	F	VF	XF	Unc	BU
2004 Proof	Est. 10,000	Value: 55.00				

KM# 1108 5 DOLLARS

25.0000 g., 0.9250 Silver 0.7435 oz. ASW **Ruler:** Elizabeth II **Subject:** Ferrari F2

Date	Mintage	F	VF	XF	Unc	BU
2005 Proof	Est. 8,000	Value: 45.00				

KM# 1109 5 DOLLARS

25.0000 g., 0.9250 Silver 0.7435 oz. ASW **Ruler:** Elizabeth II **Rev:** Ferrari F 2004 in color

Date	Mintage	F	VF	XF	Unc	BU
2005 Proof	Est. 8,000	Value: 45.00				

KM# 1134 5 DOLLARS

31.1050 g., 0.9990 Silver 0.9990 oz. ASW, 38.6 mm. **Ruler:** Elizabeth II **Subject:** Star Wars, 30th Anniversary

Date	Mintage	F	VF	XF	Unc	BU
2005 Proof	Est. 9,999	Value: 50.00				

KM# 1135 5 DOLLARS

31.1050 g., 0.9990 Silver 0.9990 oz. ASW, 38.6 mm. **Ruler:** Elizabeth II **Subject:** Star Wars, 30th Anniversary

Date	Mintage	F	VF	XF	Unc	BU
2005 Proof	Est. 9,999	Value: 50.00				

KM# 1175 5 DOLLARS

25.0000 g., 0.9250 Silver 0.7435 oz. ASW **Ruler:** Elizabeth II **Subject:** Marriage of Prince Charles and Camilla Parker-Bowles

Date	Mintage	F	VF	XF	Unc	BU
2005 Proof	Est. 5,000	Value: 45.00				

KM# 478 5 DOLLARS

Silver Gilt **Ruler:** Elizabeth II **Subject:** Pope Benedict XVI's visit to Valencia, Spain **Obv:** Bust right **Rev:** Valencia Cathedral **Shape:** Cathedral outline **Note:** Jeweled cathedral.

Date	Mintage	F	VF	XF	Unc	BU
2006 Proof	2,500	Value: 100				

KM# 560 5 DOLLARS

25.0000 g., 0.9250 Silver partially gilt 0.7435 oz. ASW, 35x31 mm. **Ruler:** Elizabeth II **Subject:** Benedict XVI Annus Secundus **Rev:** Cross in crystals and gilt Papal Arms **Shape:** 6-sided

Date	Mintage	F	VF	XF	Unc	BU
2006 Proof	5,000	Value: 95.00				

KM# 561 5 DOLLARS
25.0000 g., 0.9990 Silver partially gilt 0.8029 oz. ASW, 42x49 mm. **Ruler:** Elizabeth II **Subject:** Benedict XVI visits Germany **Rev:** Cathedral gilt, crystal inserts **Shape:** oval

Date	Mintage	F	VF	XF	Unc	BU
2006 Proof	5,000	Value: 95.00				

KM# 562 5 DOLLARS
25.0000 g., 0.9990 Silver 0.8029 oz. ASW, 35x35 mm. **Ruler:** Elizabeth II **Subject:** Benedict XVI **Rev:** Profile at left, cross in crystal inserts **Shape:** Square

Date	Mintage	F	VF	XF	Unc	BU
2006 Proof	5,000	Value: 95.00				

KM# 563 5 DOLLARS
25.0000 g., 0.9990 Silver partially gilt 0.8029 oz. ASW, 35x38 mm. **Ruler:** Elizabeth II **Subject:** Christmas in St. Peter's Square **Rev:** St. Peter's partially gilt, star crystal insert **Shape:** Triange

Date	Mintage	F	VF	XF	Unc	BU
2006 Proof	5,000	Value: 95.00				

KM# 564 5 DOLLARS
25.0000 g., 0.9990 Silver 0.8029 oz. ASW, 20x44 mm. **Ruler:** Elizabeth II **Subject:** benedict XVI visits Poland **Rev:** Polish icon, partially gilt, crystal insert **Shape:** Candle

Date	Mintage	F	VF	XF	Unc	BU
2006 Proof	564	Value: 95.00				

KM# 565 5 DOLLARS
25.0000 g., 0.9990 Silver partially gilt 0.8029 oz. ASW, 38.6 mm. **Ruler:** Elizabeth II **Rev:** St. Peter's Basilica, partially gilt, crystals as stars

Date	Mintage	F	VF	XF	Unc	BU
2006 Proof	5,000	Value: 95.00				

KM# 566 5 DOLLARS
25.0000 g., 0.9990 Silver partially gilt 0.8029 oz. ASW, 35x35 mm. **Ruler:** Elizabeth II **Subject:** Swiss Guards, 500th Anniversary **Rev:** Four Swiss guards, partially gilt, crystal insert **Shape:** Diamond

Date	Mintage	F	VF	XF	Unc	BU
2006 Proof	5,000	Value: 95.00				

KM# 567 5 DOLLARS
25.0000 g., 0.9990 Silver 0.8029 oz. ASW, 40x25 mm. **Ruler:** Elizabeth II **Subject:** Benedict XVI visits Turkey **Rev:** Pope and Patrarch, partially gilt, crystal insert **Shape:** Rectangle

Date	Mintage	F	VF	XF	Unc	BU
2006 Proof	5,000	Value: 95.00				

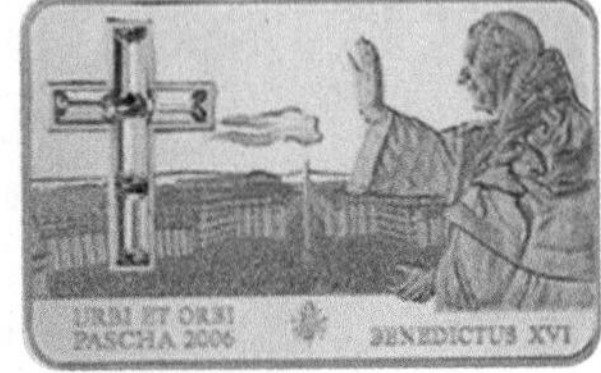

KM# 568 5 DOLLARS
25.0000 g., 0.9990 Silver 0.8029 oz. ASW, 40x25 mm. **Ruler:** Elizabeth II **Subject:** Urbi et Orbi message **Rev:** Benedict XVI giving blessing, partially gilt, crystal insert **Shape:** Rectangle

Date	Mintage	F	VF	XF	Unc	BU
2006 Proof	5,000	Value: 95.00				

KM# 569 5 DOLLARS
0.2500 g., 0.9990 Silver partially gilt 0.0080 oz. ASW, 29x42 mm. **Ruler:** Elizabeth II **Subject:** Benedict XVI visits Vallencia **Rev:** Valencia cathedral façade, partially gilt, crystal inserts **Shape:** Irregular

Date	Mintage	F	VF	XF	Unc	BU
2006 Proof	5,000	Value: 85.00				

KM# 570 5 DOLLARS
31.1000 g., 0.9990 Silver 0.9988 oz. ASW, 38.6 mm. **Ruler:** Elizabeth II **Rev:** Statue of Liberty gilt pop-up

Date	Mintage	F	VF	XF	Unc	BU
2006 Proof	5,000	Value: 100				

KM# 571 5 DOLLARS
31.1000 g., 0.9990 Silver 0.9988 oz. ASW, 38.6 mm. **Ruler:** Elizabeth II **Rev:** Ludwig's castle gilt pop-up

Date	Mintage	F	VF	XF	Unc	BU
2006 Proof	5,000	Value: 100				

KM# 572 5 DOLLARS
25.0000 g., 0.9990 Silver partially gilt 0.8029 oz. ASW, 35x35 mm. **Ruler:** Elizabeth II **Subject:** Benedict XVI visits Marianzell **Rev:** Our Lady or Marianzell, partially gilt, crystal inserts **Shape:** Tablet

Date	Mintage	F	VF	XF	Unc	BU
2007 Proof	5,000	Value: 95.00				

KM# 573 5 DOLLARS
25.0000 g., 0.9990 Silver 0.8029 oz. ASW, 35x35 mm. **Ruler:** Elizabeth II **Rev:** St. Francis, tau cross, partially gilt, crystal insert **Shape:** Dove

Date	Mintage	F	VF	XF	Unc	BU
2007 Proof	5,000	Value: 95.00				

KM# 574 5 DOLLARS
25.0000 g., 0.9990 Silver 0.8029 oz. ASW, 31x40 mm. **Ruler:** Elizabeth II **Rev:** Benedict XVI bust left, partially gilt, crystal insert **Shape:** Irregular

Date	Mintage	F	VF	XF	Unc	BU
2007 Proof	5,000	Value: 95.00				

KM# 575 5 DOLLARS
25.0000 g., 0.9990 Silver 0.8029 oz. ASW, 35x45 mm. **Ruler:** Elizabeth II **Subject:** Benedict XVI visits Brazil **Rev:** Christ statue in Rio, partially gilt, crystal insert **Shape:** Diamond

Date	Mintage	F	VF	XF	Unc	BU
2007 Proof	5,000	Value: 95.00				

KM# 576 5 DOLLARS
25.0000 g., 0.9990 Silver 0.8029 oz. ASW, 37 mm. **Ruler:** Elizabeth II **Subject:** Princess Diana, 10th Anniversary of death **Rev:** Bust at left, multicolored rose **Shape:** Heart

Date	Mintage	F	VF	XF	Unc	BU
2007 Proof	1,997	Value: 75.00				

KM# 577 5 DOLLARS
25.0000 g., 0.9990 Silver partially gilt 0.8029 oz. ASW, 39x24 mm. **Ruler:** Elizabeth II **Subject:** Docrine of the Immaculate Conception **Rev:** Virgin Mary and cathedral, partially gilt, crystal insert **Shape:** Rectangle

Date	Mintage	F	VF	XF	Unc	BU
2007 Proof	5,000	Value: 95.00				

KM# 578 5 DOLLARS
25.0000 g., 0.9990 Silver 0.8029 oz. ASW, 31x35 mm. **Ruler:** Elizabeth II **Subject:** Benedict XVI visits Loredo **Rev:** Pope blessing crowd, cathedral, partially gilt, crystal insert **Shape:** 6-sided

Date	Mintage	F	VF	XF	Unc	BU
2007 Proof	5,000	Value: 95.00				

KM# 579 5 DOLLARS
25.0000 g., 0.9990 Silver 0.8029 oz. ASW, 35x35 mm. **Ruler:** Elizabeth II **Subject:** Santo Subito **Rev:** Pope John Paul II, partially gilt, crystal insert **Shape:** Cross

Date	Mintage	F	VF	XF	Unc	BU
2007 Proof	5,000	Value: 100				

KM# 580 5 DOLLARS
25.0000 g., 0.9990 Silver 0.8029 oz. ASW, 30x45 mm. **Ruler:** Elizabeth II **Subject:** Way of the Cross **Rev:** Benedict XVI holdign cross, collesum in background, partially gilt, crystal insert **Shape:** Vertical oval

Date	Mintage	F	VF	XF	Unc	BU
2007 Proof	5,000	Value: 95.00				

KM# 581 5 DOLLARS
31.1000 g., 0.9990 Silver 0.9988 oz. ASW, 38.6 mm. **Ruler:** Elizabeth II **Rev:** Parthenon gilt pop-up

Date	Mintage	F	VF	XF	Unc	BU
2007 Proof	5,000	Value: 100				

KM# 583 5 DOLLARS
31.1000 g., 0.9990 Silver 0.9988 oz. ASW, 38.6 mm. **Ruler:** Elizabeth II **Rev:** Rio's Christ statue gilt pop-up

Date	Mintage	F	VF	XF	Unc	BU
2007 Proof	5,000	Value: 100				

KM# 584 5 DOLLARS

31.1000 g., 0.9990 Silver 0.9988 oz. ASW, 38.6 mm. **Ruler:** Elizabeth II **Rev:** Collesum gilt pop-up

Date	Mintage	F	VF	XF	Unc	BU
2007 Proof	5,000	Value: 100				

KM# 586 5 DOLLARS

31.1000 g., 0.9990 Silver 0.9988 oz. ASW, 38.6 mm. **Ruler:** Elizabeth II **Rev:** Eifle Tower gilt pop-up

Date	Mintage	F	VF	XF	Unc	BU
2007 Proof	5,000	Value: 100				

KM# 763 5 DOLLARS

20.0000 g., Silver, 38.61 mm. **Ruler:** Elizabeth II **Subject:** Brenham Meteor **Obv:** Bust right **Rev:** Meteorite and fragment inset

Date	Mintage	F	VF	XF	Unc	BU
2007 Proof	2,500	Value: 100				

KM# 1188 5 DOLLARS

20.0000 g., 0.9250 Silver 0.5948 oz. ASW, 38.61 mm. **Ruler:** Elizabeth II **Subject:** Elvis Presley, 30th Anniversary of death

Date	Mintage	F	VF	XF	Unc	BU
2007 Proof	Est. 50,000	Value: 70.00				

KM# 1189 5 DOLLARS

20.0000 g., 0.9250 Silver 0.5948 oz. ASW, 38.61 mm. **Ruler:** Elizabeth II **Subject:** Elvis Presely, 30th Anniversary of Death **Rev:** Love me Tender, 1956

Date	Mintage	F	VF	XF	Unc	BU
2007 Proof	Est. 50,000	Value: 70.00				

KM# 1201 5 DOLLARS

25.0000 g., Copper-Nickel partially gilt, 38.6 mm. **Ruler:** Elizabeth II **Subject:** Lady Diana, 10th Anniversary of Death **Rev:** Diana partially gilt

Date	Mintage	F	VF	XF	Unc	BU
2007 Proof	Est. 50,000	Value: 22.50				

KM# 1202 5 DOLLARS

25.0000 g., Copper-Nickel partially gilt, 38.6 mm. **Ruler:** Elizabeth II **Subject:** Princess Diana, 10th Anniversary of Death **Rev:** Diana in wedding dress, partially gilt

Date	Mintage	F	VF	XF	Unc	BU
2007 Proof	Est. 14,500	Value: 22.50				

KM# 1203 5 DOLLARS

155.5000 g., Copper-Nickel partially gilt, 65 mm. **Ruler:** Elizabeth II **Subject:** Princess Diana, 10th Anniversary of Death **Rev:** Lady Diana, partially gilt

Date	Mintage	F	VF	XF	Unc	BU
2007 Proof	Est. 1,961	Value: 85.00				

KM# 1320 5 DOLLARS

Silver **Ruler:** Elizabeth II **Rev:** Copernicus with solar system, partially gilt

Date	Mintage	F	VF	XF	Unc	BU
2008 Proof	—	Value: 50.00				

KM# 594 5 DOLLARS

25.0000 g., 0.9990 Silver 0.8029 oz. ASW, 35x35 mm. **Ruler:** Elizabeth II **Subject:** Pope John Paul II Election 30th Anniversary **Rev:** John Paul II coat-of-arms, aprtially gilt, crystal insert **Shape:** Diamond

Date	Mintage	F	VF	XF	Unc	BU
2008 Proof	5,000	Value: 120				

KM# 595 5 DOLLARS

25.0000 g., 0.9990 Silver 0.8029 oz. ASW, 30x45 mm. **Ruler:** Elizabeth II **Subject:** Lourdes, 150th Anniversary **Rev:** Statue of Our Lady of Lourdes, partially gilt, crystal insert **Shape:** Vertical oval

Date	Mintage	F	VF	XF	Unc	BU
2008 Proof	5,000	Value: 110				

KM# 596 5 DOLLARS

25.0000 g., 0.9990 Silver 0.8029 oz. ASW, 30x45 mm. **Ruler:** Elizabeth II **Subject:** Lourdes, 150th Anniversary **Rev:** Our Lady of Lourdes, holigram, partially gilt, crystal insert **Shape:** Vertical oval

Date	Mintage	F	VF	XF	Unc	BU
2008 Proof	5,000	Value: 120				

KM# 597 5 DOLLARS

25.0000 g., 0.9990 Silver 0.8029 oz. ASW, 40x25 mm. **Ruler:** Elizabeth II **Subject:** Benedict XVI Annus Novas **Rev:** Benedict XVI and dove **Shape:** Oval

Date	Mintage	F	VF	XF	Unc	BU
2008 Proof	5,000	Value: 100				

KM# 598 5 DOLLARS

25.0000 g., 0.9990 Silver 0.8029 oz. ASW, 32x41 mm. **Ruler:** Elizabeth II **Rev:** St. Peter's Square, cresch and christmas tree, partially gilt, crystal insert **Shape:** Triangle

Date	Mintage	F	VF	XF	Unc	BU
2008 Proof	5,000	Value: 100				

KM# 599 5 DOLLARS

25.0000 g., 0.9990 Silver 0.8029 oz. ASW, 35x35 mm. **Ruler:** Elizabeth II **Subject:** Crufifixio Domini **Rev:** Benedict XVI before cross, partially gilt, crystal inserts **Shape:** Cross

Date	Mintage	F	VF	XF	Unc	BU
2008 Proof	5,000	Value: 100				

KM# 600 5 DOLLARS

25.0000 g., 0.9990 Silver 0.8029 oz. ASW, 29x42 mm. **Ruler:** Elizabeth II **Subject:** Paulus year **Rev:** Benedict XVI in Basicilica, partially gilt, crystal insert **Shape:** Vertical rectangle

Date	Mintage	F	VF	XF	Unc	BU
2008 Proof	5,000	Value: 100				

KM# 601 5 DOLLARS

25.0000 g., 0.9990 Silver 0.8029 oz. ASW, 40x25 mm. **Ruler:** Elizabeth II **Subject:** Sistine Chapel, 500th Anniversary **Rev:** Adam and god, Sistine Chapel ceiling, partially gilt, crystal insert **Shape:** Rectangle

Date	Mintage	F	VF	XF	Unc	BU
2008 Proof	5,000	Value: 120				

KM# 602 5 DOLLARS

25.0000 g., 0.9990 Silver 0.8029 oz. ASW, 40x42 mm. **Ruler:** Elizabeth II **Rev:** St Martin on horseback, partially gilt, crystal insert **Shape:** 8-sided

Date	Mintage	F	VF	XF	Unc	BU
2008 Proof	5,000	Value: 100				

KM# 603 5 DOLLARS

25.0000 g., 0.9990 Silver 0.8029 oz. ASW, 45x34 mm. **Ruler:** Elizabeth II **Subject:** Benedict XVI visits Sydney **Rev:** Sydney Harbor Bridge and Sydney Opera House, partially gilt, crystal insert **Shape:** Irregular oval

Date	Mintage	F	VF	XF	Unc	BU
2008 Proof	5,000	Value: 100				

KM# 604 5 DOLLARS

25.0000 g., 0.9990 Silver 0.8029 oz. ASW, 35x35 mm. **Ruler:** Elizabeth II **Subject:** Tu Es Peterus **Rev:** Cross Keys, Christ handing keys to kneeling St. Peter. Partially gilt, crystal insert. **Shape:** Square

Date	Mintage	F	VF	XF	Unc	BU
2008 Proof	5,000	Value: 120				

KM# 605 5 DOLLARS

25.0000 g., 0.9990 Silver 0.8029 oz. ASW, 38.6 mm. **Ruler:** Elizabeth II **Rev:** Pope blessing crowd, partially gilt, crystal inserts

Date	Mintage	F	VF	XF	Unc	BU
2008 Proof	5,000	Value: 110				

KM# 606 5 DOLLARS

25.0000 g., 0.9990 Silver 0.8029 oz. ASW, 42x29 mm. **Ruler:** Elizabeth II **Subject:** Benedict XVI visits the United States **Rev:** Benedict XVI, the White House, Statue of Liberty, UN Building, partially gilt, crystal inserts **Shape:** Irregular US Map shape

Date	Mintage	F	VF	XF	Unc	BU
2008 Proof	5,000	Value: 110				

KM# 607 5 DOLLARS

25.0000 g., 0.9990 Silver 0.8029 oz. ASW, 40x42 mm. **Ruler:** Elizabeth II **Rev:** St. George slaying dragon, partially gilt, crystal insert **Shape:** 8-sided

Date	Mintage	F	VF	XF	Unc	BU
2008 Proof	5,000	Value: 100				

KM# 608 5 DOLLARS

31.1050 g., 0.9990 Silver 0.9990 oz. ASW, 38.6 mm. **Ruler:** Elizabeth II **Subject:** Conversion of Russia, 1000th Anniversary **Rev:** Baptism scene **Note:** Exclusive to the Russian Market.

Date	Mintage	F	VF	XF	Unc	BU
2008 Proof	500	Value: 120				

KM# 609 5 DOLLARS

31.1050 g., 0.9990 Silver 0.9990 oz. ASW, 47x27 mm. **Ruler:** Elizabeth II **Subject:** Orthodox Communication **Rev:** Patriarch's meeting **Shape:** Rectangle **Note:** Exclusive to the Russian Market.

Date	Mintage	F	VF	XF	Unc	BU
2008 Proof	500	Value: 120				

KM# 610 5 DOLLARS
25.0000 g., 0.9990 Silver 0.8029 oz. ASW, 30x38 mm. **Ruler:** Elizabeth II **Rev:** Icon - Theotokos of Vladimir, wood insert **Shape:** Rectangle **Note:** Exclusive to the Russian Market.

Date	Mintage	F	VF	XF	Unc	BU
2008 Proof	2,500	Value: 120				

KM# 611 5 DOLLARS
31.1050 g., 0.9990 Silver 0.9990 oz. ASW, 38.6 mm. **Ruler:** Elizabeth II **Subject:** Kiev Churches **Rev:** Church of All Saints **Note:** Exclusive to the Russian Market.

Date	Mintage	F	VF	XF	Unc	BU
2008 Proof	500	Value: 120				

KM# 612 5 DOLLARS
31.1050 g., 0.9990 Silver 0.9990 oz. ASW, 38.6 mm. **Ruler:** Elizabeth II **Subject:** Kiev Churches **Rev:** Dormotion of Theotokos **Note:** Exclusive to the Russian Market.

Date	Mintage	F	VF	XF	Unc	BU
2008 Proof	500	Value: 120				

KM# 613 5 DOLLARS
31.1050 g., 0.9990 Silver 0.9990 oz. ASW **Ruler:** Elizabeth II **Subject:** Kiev Churches **Rev:** Refractory of Pechersky **Shape:** 38.6 **Note:** Exclusive to the Russian Market.

Date	Mintage	F	VF	XF	Unc	BU
2008 Proof	500	Value: 120				

KM# 614 5 DOLLARS
31.1050 g., 0.9990 Silver 0.9990 oz. ASW, 38.6 mm. **Ruler:** Elizabeth II **Subject:** Kiev Churches **Rev:** Troitskaya Barbican **Note:** Exclusive to the Russian Market.

Date	Mintage	F	VF	XF	Unc	BU
2008 Proof	500	Value: 120				

KM# 615 5 DOLLARS
25.0000 g., 0.9250 Silver 0.7435 oz. ASW, 37 mm. **Ruler:** Elizabeth II **Rev:** Cupid and roses **Rev. Legend:** My Everlasting Love **Shape:** Heart

Date	Mintage	F	VF	XF	Unc	BU
2008 Proof	2,500	Value: 70.00				

KM# 616 5 DOLLARS
25.0000 g., 0.9250 Silver 0.7435 oz. ASW, 38.6 mm. **Ruler:** Elizabeth II **Subject:** Endangered Wildlife - Arctic **Rev:** Polar bear and cubs, crystal inserts

Date	Mintage	F	VF	XF	Unc	BU
2008 Proof	2,500	Value: 70.00				

KM# 617 5 DOLLARS
25.0000 g., 0.9250 Silver 0.7435 oz. ASW, 38.6 mm. **Ruler:** Elizabeth II **Subject:** Engangered wildlife - Antarctic **Rev:** Penguin, crystal insert

Date	Mintage	F	VF	XF	Unc	BU
2008 Proof	2,500	Value: 70.00				

KM# 618 5 DOLLARS
25.0000 g., 0.9250 Silver 0.7435 oz. ASW, 38.6 mm. **Ruler:** Elizabeth II **Subject:** Pultusk Meteorite **Rev:** Earth and Meteorite fragment insert

Date	Mintage	F	VF	XF	Unc	BU
2008 Proof	2,500	Value: 85.00				

KM# 666 5 DOLLARS
141.4000 g., 0.9990 Silver 4.5414 oz. ASW, 65 mm. **Ruler:** Elizabeth II **Subject:** Tall ships **Obv:** Bust right **Rev:** Germany's Preussen, 5-masted square rigger

Date	Mintage	F	VF	XF	Unc	BU
2008 Proof	—	Value: 285				

KM# 667 5 DOLLARS
141.4000 g., 0.9990 Silver 4.5414 oz. ASW, 65 mm. **Ruler:** Elizabeth II **Subject:** Tall ships **Rev:** France's France II

Date	Mintage	F	VF	XF	Unc	BU
2008 Proof	—	Value: 285				

KM# 668 5 DOLLARS
141.4000 g., 0.9990 Silver 4.5414 oz. ASW, 65 mm. **Ruler:** Elizabeth II **Subject:** Tall Ships **Rev:** America's Thomas W. Lawson, 7-masted schooner

Date	Mintage	F	VF	XF	Unc	BU
2008 Proof	—	Value: 285				

KM# 669 5 DOLLARS
141.4000 g., 0.9990 Silver 4.5414 oz. ASW, 65 mm. **Ruler:** Elizabeth II **Subject:** Tall Ships **Rev:** Russia's Sedov, 4-masted barque

Date	Mintage	F	VF	XF	Unc	BU
2008 Proof	—	Value: 285				

KM# 670 5 DOLLARS
141.4000 g., 0.9990 Silver 4.5414 oz. ASW, 65 mm. **Ruler:** Elizabeth II **Subject:** Tall Ships **Rev:** Norway's Christian Radich

Date	Mintage	F	VF	XF	Unc	BU
2008 Proof	—	Value: 285				

KM# 671 5 DOLLARS
141.4000 g., 0.9990 Silver 4.5414 oz. ASW, 65 mm. **Ruler:** Elizabeth II **Subject:** Tall Ships **Rev:** Russian 4-masted barque Kruzenshtern

Date	Mintage	F	VF	XF	Unc	BU
2008 Proof	—	Value: 285				

KM# 766 5 DOLLARS
31.1050 g., 0.9990 Silver 0.9990 oz. ASW, 40 mm. **Ruler:** Elizabeth II **Subject:** First man on the Moon **Rev:** Moon and rock fragment

Date	Mintage	F	VF	XF	Unc	BU
2008 Proof	—	Value: 120				

KM# 1207 5 DOLLARS
0.5000 g., 0.9990 Gold 0.0161 oz. AGW, 11 mm. **Ruler:** Elizabeth II **Rev:** American Bison

Date	Mintage	F	VF	XF	Unc	BU
2008 Proof	Est. 5,000	Value: 40.00				

KM# 1211 5 DOLLARS
155.5000 g., Copper-Nickel partially gilt, 65 mm. **Ruler:** Elizabeth II **Subject:** British Monarchs - Elizabeth I

Date	Mintage	F	VF	XF	Unc	BU
2008 Proof	Est. 450	Value: 85.00				

KM# 1330 5 DOLLARS
Silver **Ruler:** Elizabeth II **Rev:** European Bison, partially gilt

Date	Mintage	F	VF	XF	Unc	BU
2009 Proof	—	Value: 50.00				

KM# 640 5 DOLLARS
25.0000 g., 0.9990 Silver 0.8029 oz. ASW, 38.6 mm. **Ruler:** Elizabeth II **Rev:** Papal Tiara above crossed keys, partially gilt, crystal inserts

Date	Mintage	F	VF	XF	Unc	BU
2009 Proof	5,000	Value: 120				

KM# 641 5 DOLLARS
25.0000 g., 0.9990 Silver 0.8029 oz. ASW **Ruler:** Elizabeth II **Subject:** Benedict XVI visits Israel **Rev:** Benedict XVI and "Dome of the Rock", partially gilt, crystal inserts **Shape:** Diamond

Date	Mintage	F	VF	XF	Unc	BU
2009 Proof	5,000	Value: 115				

KM# 642 5 DOLLARS
25.0000 g., 0.9990 Silver 0.8029 oz. ASW **Ruler:** Elizabeth II **Subject:** Benedict XVI visits Africa **Rev:** Bust at left, partially gilt, crystal inserts **Shape:** Irregular, Africa shape

Date	Mintage	F	VF	XF	Unc	BU
2009 Proof	5,000	Value: 115				

KM# 643 5 DOLLARS
25.0000 g., 0.9990 Silver 0.8029 oz. ASW **Ruler:** Elizabeth II **Subject:** Easter 2009 **Rev:** Statue of the risen Christ, partially gilt, crystal inserts **Shape:** Fish

Date	Mintage	F	VF	XF	Unc	BU
2009 Proof	5,000	Value: 115				

KM# 644 5 DOLLARS
25.0000 g., 0.9990 Silver 0.8029 oz. ASW, 35 mm. **Ruler:** Elizabeth II **Rev:** Star of the Magi, partially gilt, crystal inserts **Shape:** Star

Date	Mintage	F	VF	XF	Unc	BU
2009 Proof	5,000	Value: 115				

KM# 645 5 DOLLARS
25.0000 g., 0.9990 Silver 0.8029 oz. ASW, 35x35 mm. **Ruler:** Elizabeth II **Rev:** Cathedral of Santiago de Composetla, partially gilt, crystal inserts

Date	Mintage	F	VF	XF	Unc	BU
2009 Proof	5,000	Value: 120				

KM# 646 5 DOLLARS
25.0000 g., 0.9990 Silver 0.8029 oz. ASW, 25x35 mm. **Ruler:** Elizabeth II **Rev:** Michangelo's Pieta, partially gilt, crystal inserts **Shape:** Rectangle

Date	Mintage	F	VF	XF	Unc	BU
2009 Proof	5,000	Value: 115				

KM# 647 5 DOLLARS
25.0000 g., 0.9990 Silver 0.8029 oz. ASW, 30x34 mm. **Ruler:** Elizabeth II **Rev:** St. Christopher, partially gilt, crystal inserts **Shape:** Oval

Date	Mintage	F	VF	XF	Unc	BU
2009 Proof	5,000	Value: 115				

KM# 648 5 DOLLARS
25.0000 g., 0.9990 Silver 0.8029 oz. ASW, 40x25 mm. **Ruler:** Elizabeth II **Subject:** Benedict XVI visits the Czech Republic **Rev:** Benedict XVI in Wenceleses square, partially gilt, crystal inserts **Shape:** Rectangle

Date	Mintage	F	VF	XF	Unc	BU
2009 Proof	5,000	Value: 115				

KM# 649 5 DOLLARS
25.0000 g., 0.9990 Silver 0.8029 oz. ASW **Ruler:** Elizabeth II **Rev:** Christmas, village scene, partially gilt, crystal inserts **Shape:** Diamond

Date	Mintage	F	VF	XF	Unc	BU
2009 Proof	5,000	Value: 115				

KM# 650 5 DOLLARS
31.1050 g., 0.9990 Silver 0.9990 oz. ASW, 38.6 mm. **Ruler:** Elizabeth II **Subject:** Kiev Churches **Rev:** Andreevskaya Church **Note:** Exclusive to the Russian Market.

Date	Mintage	F	VF	XF	Unc	BU
2009 Proof	500	Value: 125				

KM# 651 5 DOLLARS
31.1050 g., 0.9990 Silver 0.9990 oz. ASW, 38.6 mm. **Ruler:** Elizabeth II **Subject:** Kiev Churches **Rev:** Kirillovskaya Church **Note:** Exclusive to the Russian Market.

Date	Mintage	F	VF	XF	Unc	BU
2009 Proof	500	Value: 125				

KM# 652 5 DOLLARS
31.1050 g., 0.9990 Silver 0.9990 oz. ASW, 38.6 mm. **Ruler:** Elizabeth II **Subject:** Kiev Chruches **Rev:** Mikailovsky Monastery **Note:** Exclusive to the Russian Market.

Date	Mintage	F	VF	XF	Unc	BU
2009 Proof	500	Value: 125				

KM# 653 5 DOLLARS
31.1050 g., 0.9990 Silver 0.9990 oz. ASW, 38.6 mm. **Ruler:** Elizabeth II **Subject:** Kiev Churches **Rev:** Cathedral of St. Sophia **Note:** Exclusive to the Russian Market.

Date	Mintage	F	VF	XF	Unc	BU
2009 Proof	500	Value: 125				

KM# 654 5 DOLLARS
31.1050 g., 0.9990 Silver 0.9990 oz. ASW, 38.61 mm. **Ruler:** Elizabeth II **Subject:** Ukraine Landmarks - Bendrological park, Sofiyivka **Rev:** Statue and gardens **Note:** Exclusive to the Russian Market.

Date	Mintage	F	VF	XF	Unc	BU
2009 Proof	500	Value: 120				

KM# 655 5 DOLLARS
31.1050 g., 0.9990 Silver 0.9990 oz. ASW, 38.61 mm. **Ruler:** Elizabeth II **Subject:** Ukraine Landmarks - Holy Dormition Kiev Pechersk Lavra **Rev:** Churches **Note:** Exclusive to the Russian Market.

Date	Mintage	F	VF	XF	Unc	BU
2009 Proof	500	Value: 120				

KM# 656 5 DOLLARS
31.1050 g., 0.9990 Silver 0.9990 oz. ASW, 38.61 mm. **Ruler:** Elizabeth II **Subject:** Ukraine Landmarks - Holy Dormition Pochayiv Lavra **Rev:** Buildings **Note:** Exclusive to the Russian Market.

Date	Mintage	F	VF	XF	Unc	BU
2009 Proof	500	Value: 120				

KM# 657 5 DOLLARS
31.1050 g., 0.9990 Silver 0.9990 oz. ASW, 38.61 mm. **Ruler:** Elizabeth II **Subject:** Ukraine Landmarks - Holy Dormition Sviatohirsk Lavra **Rev:** Virgin Mary and Church **Note:** Exclusive to the Russian Market.

Date	Mintage	F	VF	XF	Unc	BU
2009 Proof	500	Value: 120				

KM# 658 5 DOLLARS
31.1050 g., 0.9990 Silver 0.9990 oz. ASW, 38.61 mm. **Ruler:** Elizabeth II **Subject:** Ukraine Landmarks - Kamyanets National Reserve **Rev:** Fortress **Note:** Exclusive to the Russian Market.

Date	Mintage	F	VF	XF	Unc	BU
2009 Proof	500	Value: 120				

KM# 659 5 DOLLARS
31.1050 g., 0.9990 Silver 0.9990 oz. ASW, 38.6 mm. **Ruler:** Elizabeth II **Subject:** Ukraine Landmarks - Khersones Tavrijsky National Reserve **Rev:** Roman ruins **Note:** Exclusive to the Russian Market.

Date	Mintage	F	VF	XF	Unc	BU
2009 Proof	500	Value: 120				

KM# 660 5 DOLLARS
31.1050 g., 0.9990 Silver 0.9990 oz. ASW, 38.6 mm. **Ruler:** Elizabeth II **Subject:** Ukraine Landmarks - Khortytsia National Reserve **Rev:** Stone carvings and bridge **Note:** Exclusive to the Russian Market.

Date	Mintage	F	VF	XF	Unc	BU
2009 Proof	500	Value: 120				

KM# 661 5 DOLLARS
31.1050 g., 0.9990 Silver 0.9990 oz. ASW, 38.6 mm. **Ruler:** Elizabeth II **Subject:** Ukraine Landmarks - National Theatre of Odessa **Rev:** Opera House **Note:** Exclusive to the Russian Market.

Date	Mintage	F	VF	XF	Unc	BU
2009 Proof	500	Value: 120				

KM# 662 5 DOLLARS
31.1050 g., 0.9990 Silver 0.9990 oz. ASW, 38.6 mm. **Ruler:** Elizabeth II **Subject:** Ukraine Landmarks - Olesko Castle **Rev:** Hillside dwelling **Note:** Exclusive to the Russian Market.

Date	Mintage	F	VF	XF	Unc	BU
2009 Proof	500	Value: 120				

KM# 663 5 DOLLARS
31.1050 g., 0.9990 Silver 0.9990 oz. ASW, 38.6 mm. **Ruler:** Elizabeth II **Subject:** Ukraine Landmarks - Palanok Castle in Mukachevo **Rev:** Hilltop fortress **Note:** Exclusive to the Russian Market.

Date	Mintage	F	VF	XF	Unc	BU
2009 Proof	500	Value: 120				

KM# 664 5 DOLLARS
31.1050 g., 0.9990 Silver 0.9990 oz. ASW, 38.6 mm. **Ruler:** Elizabeth II **Subject:** Ukraine Landmarks - Khotyn Fortress Reserve **Rev:** Road to castle **Note:** Exclusive to the Russian Market.

Date	Mintage	F	VF	XF	Unc	BU
2009 Proof	500	Value: 120				

KM# 665 5 DOLLARS
31.1050 g., 0.9990 Silver 0.9990 oz. ASW, 38.6 mm. **Ruler:** Elizabeth II **Subject:** Ukraine Landmarks - Upper Castle of Lutsk **Rev:** Tower **Note:** Exclusive to the Russian Market.

Date	Mintage	F	VF	XF	Unc	BU
2009 Proof	500	Value: 120				

KM# 672 5 DOLLARS
25.0000 g., 0.9250 Silver 0.7435 oz. ASW, 38.6 mm. **Ruler:** Elizabeth II **Rev:** HMS Endeavour and James Cook portrait

Date	Mintage	F	VF	XF	Unc	BU
2009 Proof	2,500	Value: 45.00				

KM# 673 5 DOLLARS
25.0000 g., 0.5000 Silver 0.4019 oz. ASW, 38.6 mm. **Ruler:** Elizabeth II **Rev:** Ferrari F-2008 Carbon

Date	Mintage	F	VF	XF	Unc	BU
2009 Proof	2,008	Value: 60.00				

KM# 674 5 DOLLARS
20.0000 g., 0.9250 Silver 0.5948 oz. ASW, 38.61 mm. **Ruler:** Elizabeth II **Subject:** Endangered Wildlife **Rev:** Giant Anteater

Date	Mintage	F	VF	XF	Unc	BU
2009 Proof	5,000	Value: 50.00				

KM# 675 5 DOLLARS
31.1050 g., 0.9250 Silver 0.9250 oz. ASW, 38.6 mm. **Ruler:** Elizabeth II **Series:** International Womens Day **Rev:** Roses and butterfly **Note:** Exclusive to the Russian Market

Date	Mintage	F	VF	XF	Unc	BU
2009 Proof	500	Value: 120				

KM# 676 5 DOLLARS
25.0000 g., 0.9250 Silver 0.7435 oz. ASW, 38.6 mm. **Ruler:** Elizabeth II **Rev:** Sir Lancelot, multicolor

Date	Mintage	F	VF	XF	Unc	BU
2009 Proof	2,500	Value: 75.00				

KM# 677 5 DOLLARS
0.9250 Silver **Ruler:** Elizabeth II **Subject:** Masters of Europe - Vermeer **Rev:** Girl with a pearl earing, multicolor **Shape:** Vertical rectangle

Date	Mintage	F	VF	XF	Unc	BU
2009 Proof	—	Value: 85.00				

KM# 678 5 DOLLARS
0.9250 Silver **Ruler:** Elizabeth II **Subject:** Masters of Europe - DaVinci **Rev:** Lady with an ermine, multicolor **Shape:** Vertical rectangle

Date	Mintage	F	VF	XF	Unc	BU
2009 Proof	—	Value: 95.00				

KM# 679 5 DOLLARS
0.9250 Silver **Ruler:** Elizabeth II **Subject:** Masters of Europe - Jan Matejko **Rev:** Wernyhora, multicolor **Shape:** Vertical rectangle

Date	Mintage	F	VF	XF	Unc	BU
2009 Proof	—	Value: 85.00				

KM# 680 5 DOLLARS
Silver **Ruler:** Elizabeth II **Subject:** 50th Anniversary of Space exploration, 40th Anniversary of Apollo 11 **Obv:** Moon **Rev:** Moonscape and moon rock implant

Date	Mintage	F	VF	XF	Unc	BU
2009 Matte	1,969	—	—	—	—	200

KM# 681 5 DOLLARS
25.0000 g., 0.9250 Silver copper plated 0.7435 oz. ASW **Ruler:** Elizabeth II **Subject:** 400th Anniversary of Mars observations **Obv:** Bust with tiara right **Rev:** Mars landscape

Date	Mintage	F	VF	XF	Unc	BU
2009 Matte	2,500	—	—	—	—	175

KM# 682 5 DOLLARS
25.0000 g., 0.9250 Silver 0.7435 oz. ASW, 38.61 mm. **Ruler:** Elizabeth II **Subject:** Year of the Ox **Rev:** Child riding oxen, partially gilt **Note:** Exclusive to the Russian market

Date	Mintage	F	VF	XF	Unc	BU
2009 Proof	1,000	Value: 200				

KM# 683 5 DOLLARS
25.0000 g., 0.9990 Silver 0.8029 oz. ASW **Ruler:** Elizabeth II **Subject:** World of Flowers - Pansey **Rev:** Pansey, multicolor cloisonne

Date	Mintage	F	VF	XF	Unc	BU
2009 Proof	2,500	Value: 85.00				

KM# 684 5 DOLLARS
25.0000 g., 0.9990 Silver 0.8029 oz. ASW, 38.6 mm. **Ruler:** Elizabeth II **Subject:** World of flowers - Poppy **Rev:** Poppy, multicolor closinne

Date	Mintage	F	VF	XF	Unc	BU
2009 Proof	2,500	Value: 85.00				

KM# 685 5 DOLLARS
25.0000 g., 0.9250 Silver 0.7435 oz. ASW, 30x43 mm. **Ruler:** Elizabeth II **Obv:** Bust right **Rev:** Easter chick, thermal image changing **Shape:** Egg

Date	Mintage	F	VF	XF	Unc	BU
2009 Proof	2,500	Value: 70.00				

KM# 686 5 DOLLARS
25.0000 g., 0.9250 Silver 0.7435 oz. ASW, 35x35 mm. **Ruler:** Elizabeth II **Rev:** Season's greetings, rocking horse **Shape:** Square

Date	Mintage	F	VF	XF	Unc	BU
2009 Proof	2,500	Value: 60.00				

KM# 687 5 DOLLARS
25.0000 g., 0.9990 Silver 0.8029 oz. ASW, 30x38 mm. **Ruler:** Elizabeth II **Rev:** Kazan Virgin icon **Shape:** Vertical rectangle **Note:** Exclusive to the Russian market

Date	Mintage	F	VF	XF	Unc	BU
2009 Proof	2,500	Value: 125				

KM# 764 5 DOLLARS
Silver, 25x40 mm. **Ruler:** Elizabeth II **Subject:** Ferrari, the Legend **Rev:** Car and enameled shield **Shape:** Vertical rectangle

Date	Mintage	F	VF	XF	Unc	BU
2009 Proof	—	Value: 125				

KM# 782 5 DOLLARS
20.0000 g., 0.9990 Silver 0.6423 oz. ASW, 40 mm. **Ruler:** Elizabeth II **Subject:** Year of Astronomy **Rev:** Sun, multicolor

Date	Mintage	F	VF	XF	Unc	BU
2009	—	—	—	—	—	50.00

KM# 783 5 DOLLARS
20.0000 g., 0.9990 Silver 0.6423 oz. ASW, 40 mm. **Ruler:** Elizabeth II **Subject:** Year of Astronomy **Rev:** Mercury, multicolor

Date	Mintage	F	VF	XF	Unc	BU
2009	—	—	—	—	—	50.00

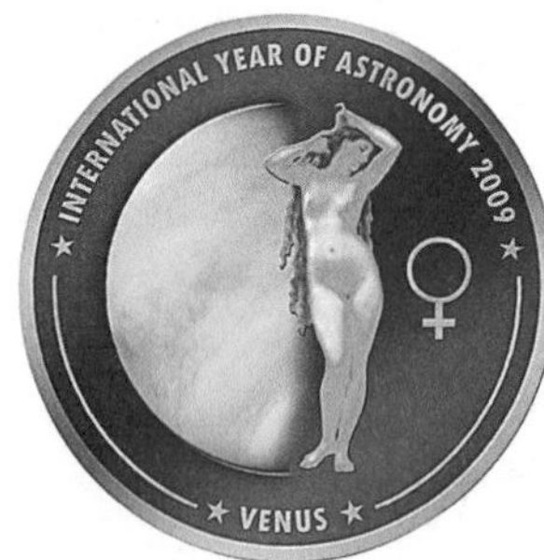

KM# 784 5 DOLLARS
20.0000 g., 0.9990 Silver 0.6423 oz. ASW, 40 mm. **Ruler:** Elizabeth II **Subject:** Year of Astronomy **Rev:** Venus, multicolor

Date	Mintage	F	VF	XF	Unc	BU
2009	—	—	—	—	—	55.00

KM# 785 5 DOLLARS
20.0000 g., 0.9990 Silver 0.6423 oz. ASW, 40 mm. **Ruler:** Elizabeth II **Subject:** Year of Astronomy **Rev:** Earth, multicolor

Date	Mintage	F	VF	XF	Unc	BU
2009	—	—	—	—	—	50.00

KM# 786 5 DOLLARS
20.0000 g., 0.9990 Silver 0.6423 oz. ASW, 40 mm. **Ruler:** Elizabeth II **Subject:** Year of Astronomy **Rev:** Mars, multicolor

Date	Mintage	F	VF	XF	Unc	BU
2009	—	—	—	—	—	50.00

KM# 787 5 DOLLARS
20.0000 g., 0.9990 Silver 0.6423 oz. ASW, 40 mm. **Ruler:** Elizabeth II **Subject:** Year of Astronomy **Rev:** Jupiter, multicolor

Date	Mintage	F	VF	XF	Unc	BU
2009	—	—	—	—	—	50.00

KM# 788 5 DOLLARS
20.0000 g., 0.9990 Silver 0.6423 oz. ASW, 40 mm. **Ruler:** Elizabeth II **Subject:** Year of Astronomy **Rev:** Saturn, multicolor

Date	Mintage	F	VF	XF	Unc	BU
2009	—	—	—	—	—	50.00

KM# 789 5 DOLLARS
20.0000 g., 0.9990 Silver 0.6423 oz. ASW, 40 mm. **Ruler:** Elizabeth II **Subject:** Year of Astronomy **Rev:** Uranus, multicolor

Date	Mintage	F	VF	XF	Unc	BU
2009	—	—	—	—	—	50.00

KM# 790 5 DOLLARS
20.0000 g., 0.9990 Silver 0.6423 oz. ASW, 40 mm. **Ruler:** Elizabeth II **Subject:** Year of Astronomy **Rev:** Neptune, multicolor

Date	Mintage	F	VF	XF	Unc	BU
2009	—	—	—	—	—	50.00

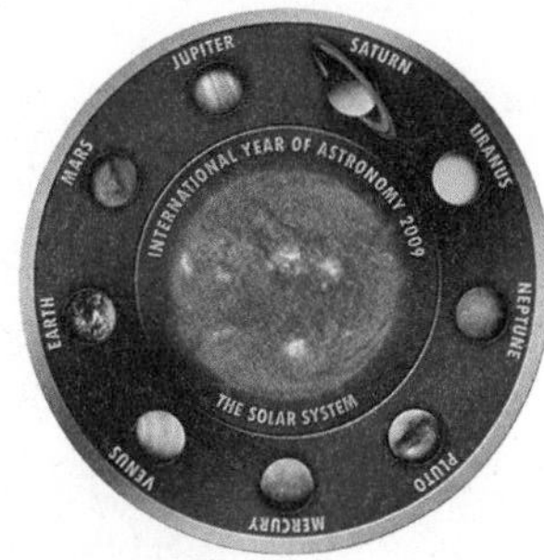

KM# 791 5 DOLLARS
20.0000 g., 0.9990 Silver 0.6423 oz. ASW, 40 mm. **Ruler:** Elizabeth II **Subject:** Year of Astronomy **Rev:** Solar System, multicolor

Date	Mintage	F	VF	XF	Unc	BU
2009	—	—	—	—	—	50.00

KM# 1225 5 DOLLARS
28.2800 g., 0.9250 Silver 0.8410 oz. ASW, 38.6 mm. **Ruler:** Elizabeth II **Subject:** Ikuko Shimizu's Hello Kitty **Rev:** Kitty and London Buss in multicolor

Date	Mintage	F	VF	XF	Unc	BU
2009 Proof	Est. 3,000	Value: 115				

KM# 1226 5 DOLLARS
28.2800 g., 0.9250 Silver 0.8410 oz. ASW, 38.6 mm. **Ruler:** Elizabeth II **Subject:** Ikuko Shimizu's Hello Kitty **Rev:** Kitty playing polo in multicolor

Date	Mintage	F	VF	XF	Unc	BU
2009 Proof	Est. 3,000	Value: 115				

KM# 1227 5 DOLLARS
28.2800 g., 0.9250 Silver 0.8410 oz. ASW, 38.6 mm. **Ruler:** Elizabeth II **Subject:** Ikuko Shimizu's Hello Kitty **Rev:** Kitty and Daniel with Tower Bridge in multicolor

Date	Mintage	F	VF	XF	Unc	BU
2009 Proof	Est. 3,000	Value: 115				

KM# 1236 5 DOLLARS
25.0000 g., 0.9250 Silver 0.7435 oz. ASW, 38.61 mm. **Ruler:** Elizabeth II **Subject:** Lady of the Lake

Date	Mintage	F	VF	XF	Unc	BU
2009 Proof	2,500	Value: 75.00				

KM# 1237 5 DOLLARS
25.0000 g., 0.9250 Silver 0.7435 oz. ASW, 38.61 mm. **Ruler:** Elizabeth II **Rev:** Excalibur set into rock in color

Date	Mintage	F	VF	XF	Unc	BU
2009 Proof	2,500	Value: 75.00				

KM# 1238 5 DOLLARS
25.0000 g., 0.9250 Silver 0.7435 oz. ASW, 38.61 mm. **Ruler:** Elizabeth II **Subject:** King Arthur

Date	Mintage	F	VF	XF	Unc	BU
2009 Proof	2,500	Value: 75.00				

KM# 1239 5 DOLLARS
25.0000 g., 0.9250 Silver 0.7435 oz. ASW, 38.61 mm. **Ruler:** Elizabeth II **Subject:** Sir Galahad

Date	Mintage	F	VF	XF	Unc	BU
2009 Proof	2,500	Value: 75.00				

KM# 1240 5 DOLLARS
25.0000 g., 0.9250 Silver 0.7435 oz. ASW, 38.61 mm. **Ruler:** Elizabeth II **Subject:** Knights of the Round table theme

Date	Mintage	F	VF	XF	Unc	BU
2009 Proof	2,500	Value: 75.00				

KM# 1329 5 DOLLARS
Silver **Ruler:** Elizabeth II **Subject:** Banker's Day **Rev:** Map of Ukraine, locations pinpointed

Date	Mintage	F	VF	XF	Unc	BU
2009 Antique patina	—	—	—	—	—	85.00

KM# 1331 5 DOLLARS
Silver **Ruler:** Elizabeth II **Rev:** Napoleon on horseback in battle in color

Date	Mintage	F	VF	XF	Unc	BU
2009	—	Value: 80.00				

KM# 1430 5 DOLLARS
Copper-Nickel, 38.61 mm. **Ruler:** Elizabeth II **Subject:** First Crusade

Date	Mintage	F	VF	XF	Unc	BU
2009	—	—	—	—	—	25.00

KM# 1490 5 DOLLARS
0.5000 g., 0.9990 Gold 0.0161 oz. AGW, 11 mm. **Ruler:** Elizabeth II **Rev:** Man with golden helmet by Rembrant

Date	Mintage	F	VF	XF	Unc	BU
2009 Proof	—	Value: 40.00				

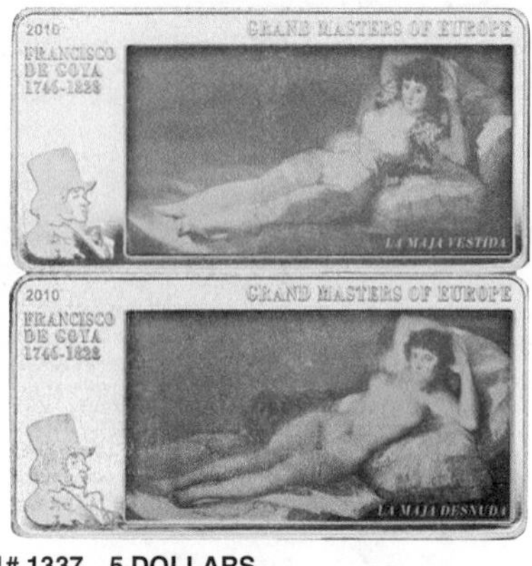

KM# 1337 5 DOLLARS
Silver **Ruler:** Elizabeth II **Subject:** Clothed and nude Maya **Shape:** Rectangle **Note:** Detachable clothing over image.

Date	Mintage	F	VF	XF	Unc	BU
2010 Proof	—	Value: 80.00				

KM# 1340 5 DOLLARS
Silver **Ruler:** Elizabeth II **Subject:** Trafalgar **Rev:** HMS Victory in color

Date	Mintage	F	VF	XF	Unc	BU
2010 Proof	—	Value: 80.00				

KM# 723 5 DOLLARS
31.1050 g., 0.9990 Silver 0.9990 oz. ASW, 24x47 mm. **Ruler:** Elizabeth II **Subject:** War of 1812 **Rev:** Peter Bagraton

Date	Mintage	F	VF	XF	Unc	BU
2010 Antique patina	2,000	—	—	—	—	55.00

KM# 724 5 DOLLARS
31.1050 g., 0.9990 Silver 0.9990 oz. ASW **Ruler:** Elizabeth II **Subject:** War of 1812 **Rev:** Mikhail Kutuzov **Shape:** 24x47

Date	Mintage	F	VF	XF	Unc	BU
2010 Antique patina	2,000	—	—	—	—	55.00

KM# 725 5 DOLLARS
31.1050 g., 0.9990 Silver 0.9990 oz. ASW, 27x47 mm. **Ruler:** Elizabeth II **Subject:** War of 1812 **Rev:** Bikoly Raevsky

Date	Mintage	F	VF	XF	Unc	BU
2010 Antique finish	2,000	—	—	—	—	55.00

KM# 726 5 DOLLARS
20.0000 g., 0.9990 Silver 0.6423 oz. ASW, 30x43 mm. **Ruler:** Elizabeth II **Subject:** Imperial Eggs **Rev:** Blue egg

Date	Mintage	F	VF	XF	Unc	BU
2010 Proof	2,500	Value: 70.00				

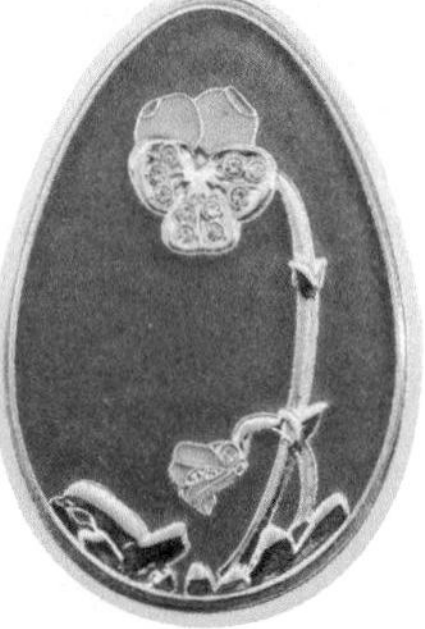

KM# 727 5 DOLLARS
20.0000 g., 0.9990 Silver 0.6423 oz. ASW, 30x43 mm. **Ruler:** Elizabeth II **Subject:** Imperial Egg **Rev:** Green cloisonne

Date	Mintage	F	VF	XF	Unc	BU
2010 Proof	2,500	Value: 70.00				

KM# 728 5 DOLLARS
20.0000 g., 0.9990 Silver 0.6423 oz. ASW, 30x43 mm. **Ruler:** Elizabeth II **Subject:** Imperial Egg **Rev:** Yellow cloisonne and Bohemian crystals

Date	Mintage	F	VF	XF	Unc	BU
2010 Proof	2,500	Value: 70.00				

KM# 729 5 DOLLARS
25.0000 g., 0.9990 Silver 0.8029 oz. ASW, 38.6 mm. **Ruler:** Elizabeth II **Rev:** Martin Luther King, pointing **Note:** Fits together with KM#730.

Date	Mintage	F	VF	XF	Unc	BU
2010 Antique finish	2,500	—	—	—	—	60.00

KM# 730 5 DOLLARS
25.0000 g., 0.9990 Silver 0.8029 oz. ASW, 38.6 mm. **Ruler:** Elizabeth II **Rev:** Barack Obama, pointing **Note:** Fits together with KM#729.

Date	Mintage	F	VF	XF	Unc	BU
2010 Antique finish	2,500	—	—	—	—	60.00

KM# 731 5 DOLLARS
25.0000 g., 0.9250 Silver 0.7435 oz. ASW, 38.6 mm. **Ruler:** Elizabeth II **Subject:** Tender Love **Rev:** Rose in relief hologram

Date	Mintage	F	VF	XF	Unc	BU
2010 Proof	2,500	Value: 50.00				

KM# 732 5 DOLLARS
25.0000 g., 0.9250 Silver 0.7435 oz. ASW, 30x38 mm. **Ruler:** Elizabeth II **Rev:** Holy Trinity icon

Date	Mintage	F	VF	XF	Unc	BU
2010 Proof	2,500	Value: 65.00				

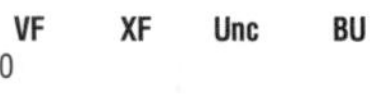

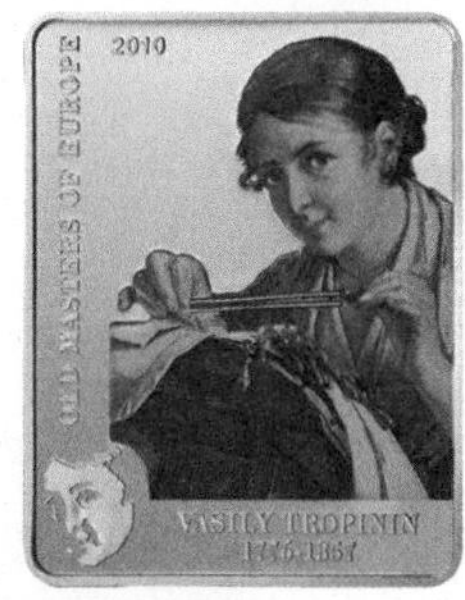

KM# 1244 5 DOLLARS
25.0000 g., 0.9250 Silver 0.7435 oz. ASW, 30x38 mm. **Ruler:** Elizabeth II **Subject:** Vasily Tropinin, 1776-1857 **Rev:** The Lacemaker, multicolor **Shape:** Vertical rectangle

Date	Mintage	F	VF	XF	Unc	BU
2010 Proof	2,500	Value: 65.00				

KM# 1245 5 DOLLARS
25.0000 g., 0.9250 Silver 0.7435 oz. ASW, 40.6 mm. **Ruler:** Elizabeth II **Subject:** Don Juan, Battle of Lepanto

Date	Mintage	F	VF	XF	Unc	BU
2010 Proof	1,000	Value: 75.00				

KM# 1250 5 DOLLARS
26.0000 g., 0.9250 Silver 0.7732 oz. ASW, 30x38 mm. **Ruler:** Elizabeth II **Subject:** Peter Brandl **Shape:** Vertical rectangle

Date	Mintage	F	VF	XF	Unc	BU
2010 Proof	2,500	Value: 60.00				

KM# 1251 5 DOLLARS
25.0000 g., 0.9250 Silver 0.7435 oz. ASW, 30x38 mm. **Ruler:** Elizabeth II **Subject:** Michangelo's David **Shape:** Vertical rectangle

Date	Mintage	F	VF	XF	Unc	BU
2010 Proof	2,500	Value: 55.00				

KM# 1252 5 DOLLARS
25.0000 g., 0.9250 Silver 0.7435 oz. ASW, 38.61 mm. **Ruler:** Elizabeth II **Subject:** Hollywood Stars - Ginger Rogers

Date	Mintage	F	VF	XF	Unc	BU
2010 Proof	2,500	Value: 75.00				

KM# 1254 5 DOLLARS
25.0000 g., 0.9250 Silver 0.7435 oz. ASW, 38.61 mm. **Ruler:** Elizabeth II **Subject:** Hollywood Stars - Clark Gable

Date	Mintage	F	VF	XF	Unc	BU
2010 Proof	• 2,500	Value: 75.00				

KM# 1255 5 DOLLARS
25.0000 g., 0.9250 Silver 0.7435 oz. ASW, 38.61 mm. **Ruler:** Elizabeth II **Subject:** Gdansk **Rev:** Town view, statue in copper **Note:** Antique patina.

Date	Mintage	F	VF	XF	Unc	BU
2010	1,000	Value: 60.00				

KM# 1281 5 DOLLARS
Silver, 27x47 mm. **Ruler:** Elizabeth II **Subject:** Ferrari 250 GTO and 599 GTO **Rev:** Car at top and bottom, yellow logo at center **Shape:** Vertical rectangle

Date	Mintage	F	VF	XF	Unc	BU
2010 Proof	1,010	Value: 135				

KM# 1253 5 DOLLARS
25.0000 g., 0.9250 Silver 0.7435 oz. ASW, 38.61 mm. **Ruler:** Elizabeth II **Subject:** Hollywood Stars - John Wayne

Date	Mintage	F	VF	XF	Unc	BU
2010 Proof	2,500	Value: 75.00				

KM# 1292 5 DOLLARS
25.0000 g., 0.9990 Silver 0.8029 oz. ASW, 30x38 mm. **Ruler:** Elizabeth II **Subject:** Russian Icons **Rev:** Icon of St. Nicolas **Shape:** Vertical rectangle

Date	Mintage	F	VF	XF	Unc	BU
2010 Proof	—	Value: 120				

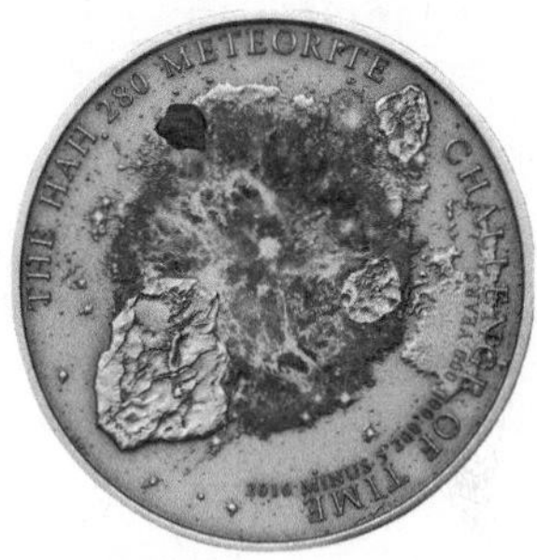

KM# 1299 5 DOLLARS
25.0000 g., 0.9250 Silver 0.7435 oz. ASW, 38.61 mm. **Ruler:** Elizabeth II **Rev:** HAH 280 Meteorite in color

Date	Mintage	F	VF	XF	Unc	BU
2010 Antique Patina	2,500	—	—	—	—	100

KM# 1300 5 DOLLARS
31.1050 g., 0.9250 Silver 0.9250 oz. ASW, 38.61 mm. **Ruler:** Elizabeth II **Subject:** Yugra district **Rev:** Bear

Date	Mintage	F	VF	XF	Unc	BU
2010 Proof	2,000	Value: 75.00				

KM# 1301 5 DOLLARS
31.1050 g., 0.9250 Silver 0.9250 oz. ASW, 38.61 mm. **Ruler:** Elizabeth II **Subject:** Yugra District **Rev:** Crude Oil

Date	Mintage	F	VF	XF	Unc	BU
2010 Proof	2,000	Value: 75.00				

KM# 1302 5 DOLLARS
31.1050 g., 0.9250 Silver 0.9250 oz. ASW, 38.61 mm. **Ruler:** Elizabeth II **Subject:** Yugra District **Rev:** Sledge Jump

Date	Mintage	F	VF	XF	Unc	BU
2010 Proof	2,000	Value: 75.00				

KM# 1303 5 DOLLARS
31.1050 g., 0.9990 Silver 0.9990 oz. ASW, 38.61 mm. **Ruler:** Elizabeth II **Subject:** Day of Prudence

Date	Mintage	F	VF	XF	Unc	BU
2010 Antique patina	500	—	—	—	—	75.00

KM# 1304 5 DOLLARS
25.0000 g., 0.9990 Silver 0.8029 oz. ASW, 30x38 mm. **Ruler:** Elizabeth II **Subject:** Russian Icons **Rev:** The Holy Face of Christ **Shape:** Vertical rectangle

Date	Mintage	F	VF	XF	Unc	BU
2010 Proof	2,500	Value: 75.00				

KM# 1305 5 DOLLARS
25.0000 g., 0.9990 Silver 0.8029 oz. ASW, 30x38 mm. **Ruler:** Elizabeth II **Subject:** Russian Icons **Rev:** St. Sergius of Radonezh **Shape:** Vertical rectangle

Date	Mintage	F	VF	XF	Unc	BU
2010 Proof	2,500	Value: 75.00				

KM# 1307 5 DOLLARS

25.0000 g., 0.9250 Silver 0.7435 oz. ASW, 38.61 mm. **Ruler:** Elizabeth II **Rev:** Wedding day, color and partially gilt

Date	Mintage	F	VF	XF	Unc	BU
2010 Proof	2,000	Value: 75.00				

KM# 1308 5 DOLLARS

31.1050 g., 0.9990 Silver 0.9990 oz. ASW, 38.61 mm. **Ruler:** Elizabeth II **Subject:** Dear Grandmother

Date	Mintage	F	VF	XF	Unc	BU
2010 Proof	500	Value: 75.00				

KM# 1309 5 DOLLARS

25.0000 g., 0.9250 Silver 0.7435 oz. ASW, 38.61 mm. **Ruler:** Elizabeth II **Rev:** Cats at night

Date	Mintage	F	VF	XF	Unc	BU
2010 Proof	2,000	Value: 75.00				

KM# 1310 5 DOLLARS

25.0000 g., 0.9990 Silver 0.8029 oz. ASW, 30x38 mm. **Ruler:** Elizabeth II **Subject:** Patron saints **Rev:** St. Helena **Shape:** Vertical rectangle

Date	Mintage	F	VF	XF	Unc	BU
2010 Proof	2,500	Value: 75.00				

KM# 1311 5 DOLLARS

25.0000 g., 0.9990 Silver 0.8029 oz. ASW, 30x38 mm. **Ruler:** Elizabeth II **Subject:** Patron Saints **Rev:** St. Constantine **Shape:** Vertical rectangle

Date	Mintage	F	VF	XF	Unc	BU
2010 Proof	2,500	Value: 75.00				

KM# 1334 5 DOLLARS

Silver, 40 mm. **Ruler:** Elizabeth II **Subject:** 2nd Crusade

Date	Mintage	F	VF	XF	Unc	BU
2010 Antique patina	—	—	—	—	—	100

KM# 1335 5 DOLLARS

Silver, 40 mm. **Ruler:** Elizabeth II **Subject:** 3rd Crusade

Date	Mintage	F	VF	XF	Unc	BU
2010 Antique patina	—	—	—	—	—	100

KM# 1336 5 DOLLARS

Silver **Ruler:** Elizabeth II **Subject:** 4th Crusade

Date	Mintage	F	VF	XF	Unc	BU
2010 Antique patina	—	—	—	—	—	100

KM# 1338 5 DOLLARS

Silver **Ruler:** Elizabeth II **Subject:** Lubek

Date	Mintage	F	VF	XF	Unc	BU
2010 Antique patina	—	—	—	—	—	100

KM# 1339 5 DOLLARS

Silver **Ruler:** Elizabeth II **Subject:** Zutphen

Date	Mintage	F	VF	XF	Unc	BU
2010 Antque patina	—	—	—	—	—	100

KM# 1429 5 DOLLARS

Silver, 38.61 mm. **Ruler:** Elizabeth II **Rev:** Boticelli's Natalis Domini, partially gilt, crystal inserts above **Shape:** Half-circle

Date	Mintage	F	VF	XF	Unc	BU
2010 Proof	—	Value: 75.00				

KM# 1380 5 DOLLARS

Silver, 30x28.5 mm. **Ruler:** Elizabeth II **Subject:** Seeds of Love **Rev:** Vine and half of a heart shaped red crystal

Date	Mintage	F	VF	XF	Unc	BU
2011 Antique patina	—	Value: 75.00				

KM# 1314 5 DOLLARS

25.0000 g., 0.9250 Silver 0.7435 oz. ASW, 38.61 mm. **Ruler:** Elizabeth II **Subject:** Marilyn Monroe, 85th Birthday

Date	Mintage	F	VF	XF	Unc	BU
2011 Proof	1,926	Value: 75.00				

KM# 1261 5 DOLLARS

25.0000 g., 0.9250 Silver 0.7435 oz. ASW, 38.61 mm. **Ruler:** Elizabeth II **Subject:** Flowers - Daisy

Date	Mintage	F	VF	XF	Unc	BU
2011 Proof	2,500	Value: 60.00				

KM# 1262 5 DOLLARS
25.0000 g., 0.9250 Silver 0.7435 oz. ASW, 38.61 mm. **Ruler:** Elizabeth II **Subject:** Hollywood Stars - Sophia Loren

Date	Mintage	F	VF	XF	Unc	BU
2011 Proof	2,500	Value: 75.00				

KM# 1263 5 DOLLARS
25.0000 g., 0.9250 Silver 0.7435 oz. ASW, 38.61 mm. **Ruler:** Elizabeth II **Subject:** Hollywood Stars - Elizabeth Taylor

Date	Mintage	F	VF	XF	Unc	BU
2011 Proof	2,500	Value: 75.00				

KM# 1264 5 DOLLARS
25.0000 g., 0.9250 Silver 0.7435 oz. ASW, 38.61 mm. **Ruler:** Elizabeth II **Subject:** Hollywood Stars - Marylin Monroe

Date	Mintage	F	VF	XF	Unc	BU
2011 Proof	2,500	Value: 75.00				

KM# 1265 5 DOLLARS
25.0000 g., 0.9250 Silver 0.7435 oz. ASW, 38.61 mm. **Ruler:** Elizabeth II **Subject:** Terminator-2, 20th Anniversary **Rev:** Walking through flames

Date	Mintage	F	VF	XF	Unc	BU
2011 Proof	—	Value: 80.00				

KM# 1266 5 DOLLARS
25.0000 g., 0.9250 Silver 0.7435 oz. ASW, 38.61 mm. **Ruler:** Elizabeth II **Subject:** Terminator-2, 20th Anniversary **Rev:** Riding motorcycle

Date	Mintage	F	VF	XF	Unc	BU
2011 Proof	—	Value: 80.00				

KM# 1267 5 DOLLARS
25.0000 g., 0.9250 Silver 0.7435 oz. ASW **Ruler:** Elizabeth II **Subject:** Terminator-2, 20th Anniversary **Rev:** Head shot **Shape:** 38.61

Date	Mintage	F	VF	XF	Unc	BU
2011 Proof	—	Value: 80.00				

KM# 1287 5 DOLLARS
31.1000 g., 0.9250 Silver 0.9249 oz. ASW, 38.6 mm. **Ruler:** Elizabeth II **Subject:** Scent of Austalia - Eucalyptus **Rev:** Koala, eucalyptus leaves and gum berries

Date	Mintage	F	VF	XF	Unc	BU
2011	2,500	—	—	—	—	100

KM# 1353 5 DOLLARS
25.0000 g., 0.9250 Silver 0.7435 oz. ASW, 30x38 mm. **Ruler:** Elizabeth II **Subject:** Patron Saints **Rev:** St. Mary Magalene **Shape:** Vertical rectangle

Date	Mintage	F	VF	XF	Unc	BU
2011 Proof	—	Value: 75.00				

KM# 1355 5 DOLLARS
25.0000 g., 0.9250 Silver 0.7435 oz. ASW, 30x38 mm. **Ruler:** Elizabeth II **Subject:** Patron Saints **Rev:** St. Catherine Icon **Shape:** Vertical rectangle

Date	Mintage	F	VF	XF	Unc	BU
2011 Proof	—	Value: 75.00				

KM# 1357 5 DOLLARS
25.0000 g., Silver, 30x38 mm. **Ruler:** Elizabeth II **Subject:** Patrol Saints **Rev:** St. Oleg Icon **Shape:** Vertical rectangle

Date	Mintage	F	VF	XF	Unc	BU
2011 Proof	—	Value: 75.00				

KM# 1358 5 DOLLARS
25.0000 g., 0.9250 Silver 0.7435 oz. ASW, 30x38 mm. **Ruler:** Elizabeth II **Subject:** Patron Saints **Rev:** St. Vladimir Icon **Shape:** Vertical rectangle

Date	Mintage	F	VF	XF	Unc	BU
2011 Proof	—	Value: 75.00				

KM# 1361 5 DOLLARS
31.1050 g., 0.9990 Silver 0.9990 oz. ASW, 38.61 mm. **Ruler:** Elizabeth II **Subject:** Soyuzmultfilm 75th Anniversary - Winnie the Pooh **Rev:** Winnie the Pooh in color **Edge:** Reeded

Date	Mintage	F	VF	XF	Unc	BU
2011 Proof	2,000	Value: 100				

KM# 1362 5 DOLLARS
31.1050 g., 0.9990 Silver 0.9990 oz. ASW, 38.61 mm. **Ruler:** Elizabeth II **Subject:** Soyuzmultfilm 75th Anniversary - Winnie the Pooh **Rev:** Piglet in color **Edge:** Reeded

Date	Mintage	F	VF	XF	Unc	BU
2011 Proof	2,000	Value: 95.00				

KM# 1363 5 DOLLARS
31.1050 g., 0.9990 Silver 0.9990 oz. ASW, 38.61 mm. **Ruler:** Elizabeth II **Subject:** Soyuzmultfilm 75th Anniversary - Winnie the Pooh **Rev:** Owl in color **Edge:** Reeded

Date	Mintage	F	VF	XF	Unc	BU
2011 Proof	2,000	Value: 95.00				

KM# 1364 5 DOLLARS
31.1050 g., 0.9990 Silver 0.9990 oz. ASW, 38.61 mm. **Ruler:** Elizabeth II **Subject:** Soyuzmultfilm 75th Anniversary - Winnie the Pooh **Rev:** Eyore in color **Edge:** Reeded

Date	Mintage	F	VF	XF	Unc	BU
2011 Proof	2,000	Value: 95.00				

KM# 1365 5 DOLLARS
31.1050 g., 0.9990 Silver 0.9990 oz. ASW, 38.61 mm. **Ruler:** Elizabeth II **Subject:** Soyuzmultfilm 75th Anniversary - Winnie the Pooh **Rev:** Rabbit in color **Edge:** Reeded

Date	Mintage	F	VF	XF	Unc	BU
2011 Proof	2,000	Value: 95.00				

KM# 1367 5 DOLLARS
31.1050 g., 0.9990 Silver 0.9990 oz. ASW, 38.61 mm. **Ruler:** Elizabeth II **Subject:** Soyuzmultfilm 75th Anniversary - Little Boy and Karlsson-on-the-Roof **Rev:** Little Boy and dog in color **Edge:** Reeded

Date	Mintage	F	VF	XF	Unc	BU
2011 Proof	2,000	Value: 95.00				

KM# 1368 5 DOLLARS
31.1050 g., 0.9990 Silver 0.9990 oz. ASW, 38.61 mm. **Ruler:** Elizabeth II **Subject:** Soyuzmultfilm 75th Anniversary - Little Boy and Karlsson-on-the-Roof **Rev:** Karlsson in color **Edge:** Reeded

Date	Mintage	F	VF	XF	Unc	BU
2011 Proof	2,000	Value: 100				

KM# 1369 5 DOLLARS
31.1050 g., 0.9990 Silver 0.9990 oz. ASW, 38.61 mm. **Ruler:** Elizabeth II **Subject:** Soyuzmultfilm 75th Anniversary - Little Boy and Karlsson-on-the-Roof **Rev:** Freken Bok in color **Edge:** Reeded

Date	Mintage	F	VF	XF	Unc	BU
2011 Proof	2,000	Value: 100				

KM# 1371 5 DOLLARS
31.1050 g., 0.9990 Silver 0.9990 oz. ASW, 38.61 mm. **Ruler:** Elizabeth II **Subject:** Soyuzmultfilm 75th Anniversary - Cheburashka and Crocodile Gena **Rev:** Cheburashka with orange in color **Edge:** Reeded

Date	Mintage	F	VF	XF	Unc	BU
2011 Proof	2,000	Value: 95.00				

KM# 1372 5 DOLLARS
31.1050 g., 0.9990 Silver 0.9990 oz. ASW, 38.61 mm. **Ruler:** Elizabeth II **Subject:** Soyuzmultfilm 75th Anniversary - Cheburashka and Crocodile Gena **Rev:** Madame Shapoklyak and dog in color **Edge:** Reeded

Date	Mintage	F	VF	XF	Unc	BU
2011 Proof	2,000	Value: 100				

KM# 1373 5 DOLLARS
31.1050 g., 0.9990 Silver 0.9990 oz. ASW, 38.61 mm. **Ruler:** Elizabeth II **Subject:** Soyuzmultfilm 75th Anniversary - Cheburashka and Crocodile Gena **Rev:** Crocodile Gena in color **Edge:** Reeded

Date	Mintage	F	VF	XF	Unc	BU
2011 Proof	2,000	Value: 95.00				

KM# 1374 5 DOLLARS
31.1050 g., 0.9990 Silver 0.9990 oz. ASW, 38.61 mm. **Ruler:** Elizabeth II **Subject:** Soyuzmultfilm 75th Anniversary - Hedgehog in a fog **Rev:** Hedgehog in a fog in color **Edge:** Reeded

Date	Mintage	F	VF	XF	Unc	BU
2011 Proof	2,000	Value: 100				

KM# 1381 5 DOLLARS
20.0000 g., 0.9250 Silver 0.5948 oz. ASW, 40 mm. **Ruler:** Elizabeth II **Subject:** Muonionalusta Meteor **Obv:** Head with tiara right **Rev:** View of meteor falling and fragment insert

Date	Mintage	F	VF	XF	Unc	BU
2011 Proof	2,500	Value: 100				

KM# 1386 5 DOLLARS

25.0000 g., 0.9250 Silver 0.7435 oz. ASW, 38.61 mm. **Ruler:** Elizabeth II **Subject:** Marylin Monroe, 80th Birthday **Rev:** Color image of Marylin Monroe

Date	Mintage	F	VF	XF	Unc	BU
2011 Proof	2,500	Value: 125				

KM# 1398 5 DOLLARS

31.1350 g., 0.9990 Silver 1.0000 oz. ASW, 38.61 mm. **Ruler:** Elizabeth II **Subject:** Soyuzmultfilm animation - Cat named Woof **Obv:** Head with crown right **Rev:** Dog and kitten in color **Edge:** Reeded

Date	Mintage	F	VF	XF	Unc	BU
2011 Proof	2,000	Value: 100				

KM# 1399 5 DOLLARS

31.1350 g., 0.9990 Silver 1.0000 oz. ASW, 38.61 mm. **Ruler:** Elizabeth II **Subject:** Soyuzmultfilm animation - Umka **Obv:** Head with crown right **Rev:** Polar bear and cub in color **Edge:** Reeded

Date	Mintage	F	VF	XF	Unc	BU
2011 Proof	2,000	Value: 100				

KM# 1400 5 DOLLARS

31.1350 g., 0.9990 Silver 1.0000 oz. ASW, 38.61 mm. **Ruler:** Elizabeth II **Subject:** Soyuzmultfilm animation - Cat named Woof **Obv:** Head with crown right **Rev:** Cat and dog in color **Edge:** Reeded

Date	Mintage	F	VF	XF	Unc	BU
2011 Proof	2,000	Value: 100				

KM# 1401 5 DOLLARS

31.1350 g., 0.9990 Silver 1.0000 oz. ASW, 38.61 mm. **Ruler:** Elizabeth II **Subject:** Soyuzmultfilm animation - Lion and turtle **Obv:** Head with crown right **Rev:** Turtle and lion **Edge:** Reeded

Date	Mintage	F	VF	XF	Unc	BU
2011 Proof	2,000	Value: 100				

KM# 1406 5 DOLLARS

31.1000 g., 0.9250 Silver 0.9249 oz. ASW, 35x35 mm. **Ruler:** Elizabeth II **Subject:** Hieronymus Bosch, pater **Rev:** The Garden (of Eden), in color **Shape:** Square

Date	Mintage	F	VF	XF	Unc	BU
2011 Proof	500	Value: 300				

KM# 1409 5 DOLLARS

31.1050 g., 0.9990 Silver 0.9990 oz. ASW, 38.61 mm. **Ruler:** Elizabeth II **Subject:** Holidays of Bonifaciya **Rev:** Lion in color

Date	Mintage	F	VF	XF	Unc	BU
2011 Proof	2,000	Value: 100				

KM# 1410 5 DOLLARS

31.1050 g., 0.9990 Silver 0.9990 oz. ASW, 38.61 mm. **Ruler:** Elizabeth II **Subject:** Soyuzmultfilm Anniversary - Old dog and wolf **Rev:** Wolf dog in color

Date	Mintage	F	VF	XF	Unc	BU
2011 Proof	2,000	Value: 100				

KM# 1417 5 DOLLARS

155.5000 g., 0.9990 Silver 4.9942 oz. ASW, 65 mm. **Ruler:** Elizabeth II **Subject:** Brothers Grimm - Bremen Town Musicians **Rev:** Troubador and animals on cart

Date	Mintage	F	VF	XF	Unc	BU
2011 Proof	500	Value: 250				

KM# 1418 5 DOLLARS

31.1050 g., 0.9990 Silver 0.9990 oz. ASW, 38.61 mm. **Ruler:** Elizabeth II **Subject:** Brothers Grimm - Bremen Town Musicians **Rev:** Troubador in color

Date	Mintage	F	VF	XF	Unc	BU
2011 Proof	2,000	Value: 100				

KM# 1419 5 DOLLARS

31.1050 g., 0.9990 Silver 0.9990 oz. ASW, 38.61 mm. **Ruler:** Elizabeth II **Subject:** Brothers Grimm - Bremen Town Musicians **Rev:** Musical coach in color

Date	Mintage	F	VF	XF	Unc	BU
2011 Proof	2,000	Value: 100				

KM# 1420 5 DOLLARS

31.1050 g., 0.9990 Silver 0.9990 oz. ASW, 38.61 mm. **Ruler:** Elizabeth II **Subject:** Brothers Grimm - Bremen Town Musicians **Rev:** Queen and cannoner in color

Date	Mintage	F	VF	XF	Unc	BU
2011 Proof	2,000	Value: 100				

KM# 1421 5 DOLLARS

31.1050 g., 0.9990 Silver 0.9990 oz. ASW, 38.61 mm. **Ruler:** Elizabeth II **Subject:** Brothers Grimm - Bremen Town Musicians **Rev:** Polynesian dancers in color

Date	Mintage	F	VF	XF	Unc	BU
2011 Proof	2,000	Value: 100				

KM# 1422 5 DOLLARS

31.1050 g., 0.9990 Silver 0.9990 oz. ASW, 38.61 mm. **Ruler:** Elizabeth II **Subject:** Brothers Grimm - Bremen Town Musicians **Rev:** Rock and Roll group in color

Date	Mintage	F	VF	XF	Unc	BU
2011 Proof	2,000	Value: 100				

KM# 1427 5 DOLLARS

25.0000 g., 0.9250 Silver 0.7435 oz. ASW, 38.61 mm. **Ruler:** Elizabeth II **Subject:** 5th Crusade **Rev:** John of Brienne

Date	Mintage	F	VF	XF	Unc	BU
2011 Antique patina	1,000	Value: 75.00				

KM# 1431 5 DOLLARS

Silver, 38.61 mm. **Ruler:** Elizabeth II **Subject:** Muonionalusta meteorite **Rev:** Meteorite fragment flying over forest lake

Date	Mintage	F	VF	XF	Unc	BU
2011 Proof	—	Value: 125				

KM# 1503 5 DOLLARS

145.0000 g., Copper Plated Tombac, 65 mm. **Ruler:** Elizabeth II **Subject:** Elizabeth II, 60th anniversary of reign **Rev:** Elizabeth II photo in color by Julian Calder

Date	Mintage	F	VF	XF	Unc	BU
2011	Est. 2,012	Value: 45.00				

KM# 1504 5 DOLLARS

0.5000 g., 0.9990 Gold 0.0161 oz. AGW, 11 mm. **Ruler:** Elizabeth II **Rev:** Tangaroa

Date	Mintage	F	VF	XF	Unc	BU
2011 Proof	—	Value: 40.00				

KM# 1376 5 DOLLARS

25.0000 g., 0.9250 Silver 0.7435 oz. ASW, 45x30 mm. **Ruler:** Elizabeth II **Obv:** Head with tiara right **Rev:** Titanic sailing left in color, coal fragment insert **Shape:** Horizontal oval

Date	Mintage	F	VF	XF	Unc	BU
2012 Proof	2,012	Value: 100				

KM# 1377 5 DOLLARS

20.0000 g., 0.9990 Silver 0.6423 oz. ASW, 30x43 mm. **Ruler:** Elizabeth II **Subject:** Imperial Egg - Swan **Obv:** Head with tiara right **Rev:** Pink coloring

Date	Mintage	F	VF	XF	Unc	BU
2012 Proof	—	Value: 75.00				

KM# 1378 5 DOLLARS

20.0000 g., 0.9990 Silver 0.6423 oz. ASW, 30x43 mm. **Ruler:** Elizabeth II **Subject:** Imperial egg - Elephant **Obv:** Head with tiara right **Rev:** Blue coloring

Date	Mintage	F	VF	XF	Unc	BU
2012 Proof	—	Value: 75.00				

KM# 1379 5 DOLLARS

20.0000 g., 0.9990 Silver 0.6423 oz. ASW, 30x43 mm. **Ruler:** Elizabeth II **Subject:** Imperial egg **Obv:** Head in tiara right **Rev:** Multicolor closonne

Date	Mintage	F	VF	XF	Unc	BU
2012 Proof	—	Value: 75.00				

KM# 1382 5 DOLLARS

31.1050 g., 0.9990 Silver 0.9990 oz. ASW, 38.61 mm. **Ruler:** Elizabeth II **Subject:** History of Egypt **Rev:** Tutankhamun's gold mask in color

Date	Mintage	F	VF	XF	Unc	BU
2012 Proof	—	Value: 125				

KM# 1390 5 DOLLARS
31.1050 g., 0.9990 Silver 0.9990 oz. ASW, 38.61 mm. **Ruler:** Elizabeth II **Subject:** Titanic, 100th Anniversary **Rev:** Titanic side view sailing left, recovered coal fragment insert

Date	Mintage	F	VF	XF	Unc	BU
2012 Proof	—	Value: 125				

KM# 1395 5 DOLLARS
31.1050 g., 0.9990 Silver 0.9990 oz. ASW, 38.61 mm. **Ruler:** Elizabeth II **Obv:** Head with tiara right **Rev:** Cherry Blossom in color

Date	Mintage	F	VF	XF	Unc	BU
2012 Proof	—	Value: 100				

KM# 1425 5 DOLLARS
20.0000 g., 0.9250 Silver 0.5948 oz. ASW, 30x35 mm. **Ruler:** Elizabeth II **Subject:** Love conquers all **Rev:** Roman Cupids by Caravaggio **Shape:** Vertical oval

Date	Mintage	F	VF	XF	Unc	BU
2012 Proof	1,000	Value: 75.00				

KM# 1437 5 DOLLARS
25.0000 g., 0.9250 Silver 0.7435 oz. ASW, 38.61 mm. **Ruler:** Elizabeth II **Subject:** Hollywood Stars - Marlene Dietrich

Date	Mintage	F	VF	XF	Unc	BU
2012 Proof	2,500	Value: 75.00				

KM# 1438 5 DOLLARS
25.0000 g., 0.9250 Silver 0.7435 oz. ASW, 38.61 mm. **Ruler:** Elizabeth II **Subject:** Hollywood Stars - Anita Ekberg

Date	Mintage	F	VF	XF	Unc	BU
2012 Proof	2,500	Value: 75.00				

KM# 1439 5 DOLLARS
25.0000 g., 0.9250 Silver 0.7435 oz. ASW, 38.61 mm. **Ruler:** Elizabeth II **Subject:** Hollywood Stars - Robert Mitchum

Date	Mintage	F	VF	XF	Unc	BU
2012 Proof	2,500	Value: 75.00				

KM# 1440 5 DOLLARS
20.0000 g., 0.9250 Silver 0.5948 oz. ASW, 38.6 mm. **Ruler:** Elizabeth II **Subject:** Seymchan Meteorite **Rev:** Meteorite fragmetn in color scene

Date	Mintage	F	VF	XF	Unc	BU
2012 Proof	2,500	Value: 125				

KM# 1446 5 DOLLARS
31.1050 g., 0.9990 Silver 0.9990 oz. ASW, 38.61 mm. **Ruler:** Elizabeth II **Subject:** Yes of the Dragon **Rev:** Golden dragon

Date	Mintage	F	VF	XF	Unc	BU
2012 Proof	—	Value: 100				

KM# 1447 5 DOLLARS
31.1050 g., 0.9990 Silver 0.9990 oz. ASW, 38.61 mm. **Ruler:** Elizabeth II **Subject:** Year of the Dragon **Rev:** Blue dragon

Date	Mintage	F	VF	XF	Unc	BU
2012 Proof	—	Value: 100				

KM# 1450 5 DOLLARS
20.0000 g., 0.9250 Silver 0.5948 oz. ASW, 38.61 mm. **Ruler:** Elizabeth II **Subject:** PGA Tour - Golf ball insert

Date	Mintage	F	VF	XF	Unc	BU
2012 Proof	2,500	Value: 100				

KM# 1451 5 DOLLARS
20.0000 g., 0.9250 Silver 0.5948 oz. ASW, 38.61 mm. **Ruler:** Elizabeth II **Subject:** Amerigo Vespucci, 500th Anniversary of voyage of discovery **Rev:** Sailing ship

Date	Mintage	F	VF	XF	Unc	BU
2012 Proof	2,500	Value: 75.00				

KM# 1452 5 DOLLARS
25.0000 g., 0.9250 Silver 0.7435 oz. ASW, 30x38 mm. **Ruler:** Elizabeth II **Rev:** Nativity of the Blessed Virgin Mary **Shape:** Vertical rectangle

Date	Mintage	F	VF	XF	Unc	BU
2012 Proof	2,500	Value: 100				

KM# 1453 5 DOLLARS
31.1050 g., 0.9990 Silver 0.9990 oz. ASW, 38.61 mm. **Ruler:** Elizabeth II **Subject:** Year of the Dragon **Rev:** Color dragon

Date	Mintage	F	VF	XF	Unc	BU
2012 Proof	—	Value: 100				

KM# 473 10 DOLLARS
20.1200 g., Silver, 38.62 mm. **Ruler:** Elizabeth II **Subject:** 2004 Summer Olympics - Athens **Obv:** Crowned bust right **Rev:** Male discus thrower **Edge:** Reeded

Date	Mintage	F	VF	XF	Unc	BU
2001 Proof	—	Value: 37.50				

KM# 549 10 DOLLARS
10.0000 g., 0.9999 Gold 0.3215 oz. AGW, 25 mm. **Ruler:** Elizabeth II **Rev:** Multicolored Mikado Pheasant

Date	Mintage	F	VF	XF	Unc	BU
2001 Proof	1,000	Value: 600				

KM# 550 10 DOLLARS
10.0000 g., 0.9999 Gold 0.3215 oz. AGW, 25 mm. **Ruler:** Elizabeth II **Rev:** Multicolor black-faced spoonbill

Date	Mintage	F	VF	XF	Unc	BU
2001 Proof	1,000	Value: 600				

KM# 453 10 DOLLARS
186.8300 g., 0.9990 Silver Gilt 6.0005 oz. ASW, 89 mm. **Ruler:** Elizabeth II **Obv:** Crowned bust right, unique portrait for Cook Is. **Rev:** Queen Victoria standing with lion **Edge:** Reeded

Date	Mintage	F	VF	XF	Unc	BU
2003 Proof	198	Value: 375				

KM# 1110 10 DOLLARS
1.2400 g., 0.9990 Gold 0.0398 oz. AGW **Ruler:** Elizabeth II **Rev:** Emblem

Date	Mintage	F	VF	XF	Unc	BU
2005 Proof	Est. 8,000	Value: 85.00				

KM# 1136 10 DOLLARS
1.2400 g., 0.9990 Gold 0.0398 oz. AGW, 13.92 mm. **Ruler:** Elizabeth II **Subject:** Star Wars, 30th Anniversary

Date	Mintage	F	VF	XF	Unc	BU
2005 Proof	9,999	Value: 85.00				

KM# 1176 10 DOLLARS
1.2400 g., 0.9990 Gold 0.0398 oz. AGW **Ruler:** Elizabeth II **Subject:** Marriage of Prince Charles and Camilla Parker-Bowles

Date	Mintage	F	VF	XF	Unc	BU
2005 Proof	Est. 25,000	Value: 85.00				

KM# 1178 10 DOLLARS
1.2400 g., 0.9990 Gold 0.0398 oz. AGW, 13.92 mm. **Ruler:** Elizabeth II **Rev:** Pope John Paul II

Date	Mintage	F	VF	XF	Unc	BU
2005 Proof	Est. 25,000	Value: 85.00				

KM# 582 10 DOLLARS
31.1000 g., 0.9990 Silver 0.9988 oz. ASW, 38.6 mm. **Ruler:** Elizabeth II **Rev:** Chichen Itza gilt pop-up

Date	Mintage	F	VF	XF	Unc	BU
2007 Proof	5,000	Value: 65.00				

KM# 585 10 DOLLARS
31.1000 g., 0.9990 Silver 0.9988 oz. ASW, 38.6 mm. **Ruler:** Elizabeth II **Rev:** Easter Island status gilt pop-up

Date	Mintage	F	VF	XF	Unc	BU
2007 Proof	5,000	Value: 100				

KM# 587 10 DOLLARS
31.1000 g., 0.9990 Silver 0.9988 oz. ASW, 38.6 mm. **Ruler:** Elizabeth II **Rev:** Pyrmids gilt pop-up

Date	Mintage	F	VF	XF	Unc	BU
2007 Proof	5,000	Value: 65.00				

KM# 588 10 DOLLARS
31.1000 g., 0.9990 Silver 0.9988 oz. ASW, 38.6 mm. **Ruler:** Elizabeth II **Rev:** Golden Gate Bridge gilt pop-up

Date	Mintage	F	VF	XF	Unc	BU
2007 Proof	5,000	Value: 65.00				

KM# 589 10 DOLLARS
31.1000 g., 0.9990 Silver 0.9988 oz. ASW, 38.6 mm. **Ruler:** Elizabeth II **Rev:** Great Wall of China gilt pop-up

Date	Mintage	F	VF	XF	Unc	BU
2007 Proof	5,000	Value: 65.00				

KM# 590 10 DOLLARS
31.1000 g., 0.9990 Silver 0.9988 oz. ASW, 38.6 mm. **Ruler:** Elizabeth II **Rev:** Sydney Harbor Bridge gilt pop-up

Date	Mintage	F	VF	XF	Unc	BU
2007 Proof	5,000	Value: 65.00				

KM# 591 10 DOLLARS
31.1000 g., 0.9990 Silver 0.9988 oz. ASW, 38.6 mm. **Ruler:** Elizabeth II **Rev:** Machu Pichu gilt pop-up

Date	Mintage	F	VF	XF	Unc	BU
2007 Proof	5,000	Value: 65.00				

KM# 592 10 DOLLARS
31.1000 g., 0.9990 Silver 0.9988 oz. ASW, 38.6 mm. **Ruler:** Elizabeth II **Rev:** Petra Treasury gilt pop-up

Date	Mintage	F	VF	XF	Unc	BU
2007 Proof	5,000	Value: 65.00				

KM# 593 10 DOLLARS
31.1000 g., 0.9990 Silver 0.9988 oz. ASW, 38.6 mm. **Ruler:** Elizabeth II **Rev:** Taj mahal gilt pop-up

Date	Mintage	F	VF	XF	Unc	BU
2007 Proof	5,000	Value: 65.00				

KM# 1113 10 DOLLARS
0.5000 g., 0.9990 Gold 0.0161 oz. AGW, 11 mm. **Ruler:** Elizabeth II **Subject:** Treaty of rome, 50th Anniversary **Rev:** Monaco

Date	Mintage	F	VF	XF	Unc	BU
2007 Proof	Est. 5,000	Value: 50.00				

KM# 1171 10 DOLLARS
0.5000 g., 0.9990 Gold 0.0161 oz. AGW, 11 mm. **Ruler:** Elizabeth II **Subject:** Treaty of Rome, 50th Anniversary **Rev:** Vatican City

Date	Mintage	F	VF	XF	Unc	BU
2007 Proof	Est. 5,000	Value: 50.00				

KM# 1192 10 DOLLARS
1.2400 g., 0.9990 Gold 0.0398 oz. AGW, 13.92 mm. **Ruler:** Elizabeth II **Subject:** European Monarchs **Rev:** Elizabeth II

Date	Mintage	F	VF	XF	Unc	BU
2007 Proof	Est. 10,000	Value: 85.00				

KM# 1193 10 DOLLARS
1.2400 g., 0.9990 Gold 0.0398 oz. AGW **Ruler:** Elizabeth II **Subject:** European Monarchs **Rev:** Juan Carlos I

Date	Mintage	F	VF	XF	Unc	BU
2007 Proof	Est. 10,000	Value: 85.00				

KM# 1195 10 DOLLARS
1.2400 g., Gold, 13.92 mm. **Ruler:** Elizabeth II **Subject:** European Monarchs **Rev:** Beatrix

Date	Mintage	F	VF	XF	Unc	BU
2007 Proof	Est. 10,000	Value: 85.00				

KM# 1204 10 DOLLARS
1.2400 g., 0.9990 Gold 0.0398 oz. AGW, 13.92 mm. **Ruler:** Elizabeth II **Subject:** Christmas **Rev:** Cherib seated on rock

Date	Mintage	F	VF	XF	Unc	BU
2007 proof	Est. 15,000	Value: 85.00				

KM# 1194 10 DOLLARS
1.2400 g., 0.9990 Gold 0.0398 oz. AGW **Ruler:** Elizabeth II **Subject:** European Monarchs **Rev:** Carl XVI Gustaf

Date	Mintage	F	VF	XF	Unc	BU
2007 Proof	Est. 10,000	Value: 85.00				

KM# 619 10 DOLLARS
31.1000 g., 0.9990 Silver 0.9988 oz. ASW, 38.6 mm. **Ruler:** Elizabeth II **Rev:** Angor Wat temple gilt pop-up

Date	Mintage	F	VF	XF	Unc	BU
2008 Proof	5,000	Value: 65.00				

KM# 620 10 DOLLARS
31.1000 g., 0.9990 Silver 0.9988 oz. ASW, 38.6 mm. **Ruler:** Elizabeth II **Rev:** Ayer's Rock gilt pop-up

Date	Mintage	F	VF	XF	Unc	BU
2008 Proof	5,000	Value: 65.00				

KM# 621 10 DOLLARS
31.1000 g., 0.9990 Silver 0.9988 oz. ASW, 38.6 mm. **Ruler:** Elizabeth II **Rev:** Parliament Buildings and Big Ben pop-up

Date	Mintage	F	VF	XF	Unc	BU
2008 Proof	5,000	Value: 65.00				

KM# 622 10 DOLLARS
31.1000 g., 0.9990 Silver 0.9988 oz. ASW, 38.6 mm. **Ruler:** Elizabeth II **Rev:** Mt. Rushmore figures gilt pop-up

Date	Mintage	F	VF	XF	Unc	BU
2008 Proof	5,000	Value: 65.00				

KM# 623 10 DOLLARS
31.1000 g., 0.9990 Silver 0.9988 oz. ASW, 38.6 mm. **Ruler:** Elizabeth II **Rev:** Sydney Opera House gilt pop-up

Date	Mintage	F	VF	XF	Unc	BU
2008 Proof	5,000	Value: 65.00				

KM# 624 10 DOLLARS
31.1000 g., 0.9990 Silver 0.9988 oz. ASW, 38.6 mm. **Ruler:** Elizabeth II **Rev:** Malaysian Twin Towers gilt pop-up

Date	Mintage	F	VF	XF	Unc	BU
2008 Proof	5,000	Value: 65.00				

KM# 625 10 DOLLARS
31.1000 g., 0.9990 Silver 0.9988 oz. ASW, 38.6 mm. **Ruler:** Elizabeth II **Rev:** Sphinx gilt pop-up

Date	Mintage	F	VF	XF	Unc	BU
2008 Proof	5,000	Value: 65.00				

KM# 626 10 DOLLARS
31.1000 g., 0.9990 Silver 0.9988 oz. ASW, 38.6 mm. **Ruler:** Elizabeth II **Rev:** Stonehedge gilt pop-up

Date	Mintage	F	VF	XF	Unc	BU
2008 Proof	5,000	Value: 65.00				

KM# 627 10 DOLLARS
62.2050 g., 0.9990 Silver 1.9979 oz. ASW, 50 mm. **Ruler:** Elizabeth II **Rev:** Tsar Alexander II, multicolor **Note:** Exclusive to the Russian Market.

Date	Mintage	F	VF	XF	Unc	BU
2008 Proof	500	Value: 350				

KM# 628 10 DOLLARS
62.2050 g., 0.9990 Silver 1.9979 oz. ASW **Ruler:** Elizabeth II **Rev:** Tsar Alexi, multicolor **Note:** Exclusive to the Russian Market.

Date	Mintage	F	VF	XF	Unc	BU
2008 Proof	500	Value: 350				

KM# 629 10 DOLLARS
62.2050 g., 0.9990 Silver 1.9979 oz. ASW, 50 mm. **Ruler:** Elizabeth II **Rev:** Tsarina Anna, multicolor

Date	Mintage	F	VF	XF	Unc	BU
2008 Proof	500	Value: 350				

KM# 630 10 DOLLARS
62.2050 g., 0.9990 Silver 1.9979 oz. ASW, 50 mm. **Ruler:** Elizabeth II **Rev:** Tsarina Elizabeth, multicolor

Date	Mintage	F	VF	XF	Unc	BU
2008 Proof	500	Value: 350				

KM# 631 10 DOLLARS
62.2050 g., 0.9990 Silver 1.9979 oz. ASW, 50 mm. **Ruler:** Elizabeth II **Rev:** Tsar Mikhail, multicolor

Date	Mintage	F	VF	XF	Unc	BU
2008 Proof	500	Value: 350				

KM# 632 10 DOLLARS
62.2050 g., 0.9990 Silver 1.9979 oz. ASW, 50 mm. **Ruler:** Elizabeth II **Rev:** Tsar Paul I, multicolor

Date	Mintage	F	VF	XF	Unc	BU
2008 Proof	500	Value: 350				

KM# 633 10 DOLLARS
31.1000 g., 0.9990 Silver 0.9988 oz. ASW, 40 mm. **Ruler:** Elizabeth II **Rev:** Nathan Rothschild bust at right, partially gilt

Date	Mintage	F	VF	XF	Unc	BU
2008 Proof	10,000	Value: 55.00				

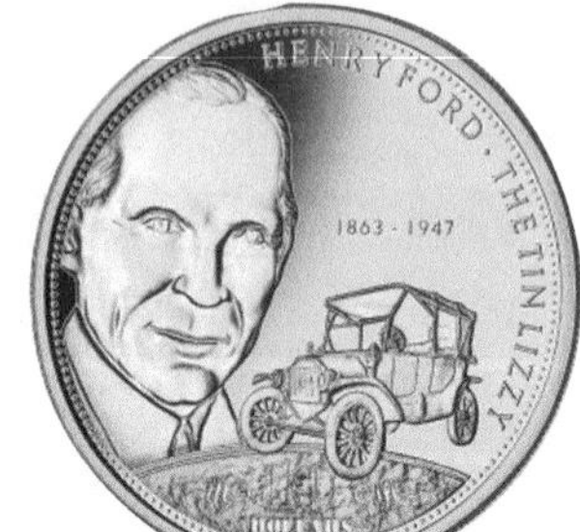

KM# 634 10 DOLLARS
31.1050 g., 0.9990 Silver 0.9990 oz. ASW, 40 mm. **Ruler:** Elizabeth II **Rev:** Henry Ford at left and Model-A car at right, partially gilt

Date	Mintage	F	VF	XF	Unc	BU
2008 Proof	10,000	Value: 55.00				

KM# 635 10 DOLLARS
31.1000 g., 0.9990 Silver 0.9988 oz. ASW, 40 mm. **Ruler:** Elizabeth II **Rev:** John D. Rockefeller Sr., bust right, oil derrick partially gilt.

Date	Mintage	F	VF	XF	Unc	BU
2008 Proof	10,000	Value: 60.00				

KM# 704 10 DOLLARS
1.0000 g., 0.9990 Gold 0.0321 oz. AGW, 13.9 mm. **Ruler:** Elizabeth II **Subject:** Gorch Fock **Rev:** Sailing vessel right

Date	Mintage	F	VF	XF	Unc	BU
2008 Proof	15,000	Value: 70.00				

KM# 705 10 DOLLARS
62.2100 g., 0.9990 Silver 1.9980 oz. ASW, 50 mm. **Ruler:** Elizabeth II **Subject:** Kiev Churches **Rev:** Lavra bell tower

Date	Mintage	F	VF	XF	Unc	BU
2008 Proof	500	—	—	—	—	200

KM# 1205 10 DOLLARS
1.0000 g., 0.9990 Gold 0.0321 oz. AGW, 13.92 mm. **Ruler:** Elizabeth II **Rev:** Gorch Fock I, 1933

Date	Mintage	F	VF	XF	Unc	BU
2008 Proof	—	Value: 70.00				

KM# 1206 10 DOLLARS
1.0000 g., 0.9990 Gold 0.0321 oz. AGW, 13.92 mm. **Ruler:** Elizabeth II **Subject:** Endangered Wildlife **Rev:** Polar Bear

Date	Mintage	F	VF	XF	Unc	BU
2008 Proof	Est. 25,000	Value: 70.00				

KM# 1469 10 DOLLARS
31.1050 g., 0.9990 Silver with gold pop-up 0.9990 oz. ASW, 38.61 mm. **Ruler:** Elizabeth II **Rev:** Koln Cathedral 4 gr. gold pop-up

Date	Mintage	F	VF	XF	Unc	BU
2008	Est. 5,000	—	—	—	—	80.00

KM# 688 10 DOLLARS
31.1050 g., 0.9990 Silver 0.9990 oz. ASW, 38.6 mm. **Ruler:** Elizabeth II **Rev:** Statues of Ramesses II at Abu Simbel gilt pop-up

Date	Mintage	F	VF	XF	Unc	BU
2009 Proof	5,000	Value: 65.00				

KM# 689 10 DOLLARS
31.1050 g., 0.9990 Silver 0.9990 oz. ASW, 38.6 mm. **Ruler:** Elizabeth II **Rev:** Arc de Triumph gilt pop-up

Date	Mintage	F	VF	XF	Unc	BU
2009 Proof	5,000	Value: 65.00				

KM# 690 10 DOLLARS
31.1050 g., 0.9990 Silver 0.9990 oz. ASW, 38.6 mm. **Ruler:** Elizabeth II **Rev:** Hagia Sofia gilt pop-up

Date	Mintage	F	VF	XF	Unc	BU
2009 Proof	5,000	Value: 65.00				

KM# 691 10 DOLLARS
31.1050 g., 0.9990 Silver 0.9990 oz. ASW, 38.6 mm. **Ruler:** Elizabeth II **Rev:** Temple of Heaven gilt pop-up

Date	Mintage	F	VF	XF	Unc	BU
2009 Proof	5,000	Value: 65.00				

KM# 692 10 DOLLARS
31.1050 g., 0.9990 Silver 0.9990 oz. ASW, 38.6 mm. **Ruler:** Elizabeth II **Rev:** Holstein Gate gilt pop-up

Date	Mintage	F	VF	XF	Unc	BU
2009 Proof	5,000	Value: 65.00				

KM# 693 10 DOLLARS
31.1050 g., 0.9990 Silver 0.9990 oz. ASW, 38.6 mm. **Ruler:** Elizabeth II **Rev:** Ruins of Kaiser Church in Berlin, gilt pop-up

Date	Mintage	F	VF	XF	Unc	BU
2009 Proof	5,000	Value: 65.00				

KM# 694 10 DOLLARS
31.1050 g., 0.9990 Silver 0.9990 oz. ASW, 38.6 mm. **Ruler:** Elizabeth II **Rev:** Statue of Peter I gilt pop-up

Date	Mintage	F	VF	XF	Unc	BU
2009 Proof	5,000	Value: 65.00				

KM# 695 10 DOLLARS
31.1050 g., 0.9990 Silver 0.9990 oz. ASW, 38.6 mm. **Ruler:** Elizabeth II **Rev:** Bridge in Venice, gilt pop-up

Date	Mintage	F	VF	XF	Unc	BU
2009 Proof	5,000	Value: 65.00				

KM# 696 10 DOLLARS
31.1050 g., 0.9990 Silver 0.9990 oz. ASW, 38.6 mm. **Ruler:** Elizabeth II **Rev:** Opera house, gilt pop-up

Date	Mintage	F	VF	XF	Unc	BU
2009 Proof	—	Value: 65.00				

KM# 703 10 DOLLARS
25.0000 g., 0.9990 Silver 0.8029 oz. ASW, 38.6 mm. **Ruler:** Elizabeth II **Subject:** Nicolaus Copernicus **Rev:** Bust facing and orbit of the planets, crystal insert, partially gold plated

Date	Mintage	F	VF	XF	Unc	BU
2009 Proof	7,500	Value: 75.00				

KM# 708 10 DOLLARS
1.0000 g., 0.9990 Gold 0.0321 oz. AGW, 13.9 mm. **Ruler:** Elizabeth II **Rev:** Bridge

Date	Mintage	F	VF	XF	Unc	BU
2009 Proof	250	Value: 70.00				

KM# 709 10 DOLLARS
1.0000 g., 0.9990 Gold 0.0321 oz. AGW, 13.9 mm. **Ruler:** Elizabeth II **Rev:** Statue and gardens

Date	Mintage	F	VF	XF	Unc	BU
2009 Proof	250	Value: 70.00				

KM# 710 10 DOLLARS
1.0000 g., 0.9990 Gold 0.0321 oz. AGW, 13.9 mm. **Ruler:** Elizabeth II **Rev:** City Gate tower

Date	Mintage	F	VF	XF	Unc	BU
2009 Proof	250	Value: 70.00				

KM# 711 10 DOLLARS
1.0000 g., 0.9990 Gold 0.0321 oz. AGW, 13.9 mm. **Ruler:** Elizabeth II **Rev:** Virgin Mary statue and church in background

Date	Mintage	F	VF	XF	Unc	BU
2009 Proof	250	Value: 70.00				

KM# 712 10 DOLLARS
1.0000 g., 0.9990 Gold 0.0321 oz. AGW, 13.9 mm. **Ruler:** Elizabeth II **Rev:** Multiple church spires

Date	Mintage	F	VF	XF	Unc	BU
2009 Proof	250	Value: 70.00				

KM# 713 10 DOLLARS

1.0000 g., 0.9990 Gold 0.0321 oz. AGW, 13.9 mm. **Ruler:** Elizabeth II **Rev:** National Theater

Date	Mintage	F	VF	XF	Unc	BU
2009 Proof	250	Value: 70.00				

KM# 714 10 DOLLARS

1.0000 g., 0.9990 Gold 0.0321 oz. AGW, 13.9 mm. **Ruler:** Elizabeth II **Rev:** Castle

Date	Mintage	F	VF	XF	Unc	BU
2009 Proof	250	Value: 70.00				

KM# 715 10 DOLLARS

1.0000 g., 0.9990 Gold 0.0321 oz. AGW, 13.9 mm. **Ruler:** Elizabeth II **Rev:** Castle on a hill

Date	Mintage	F	VF	XF	Unc	BU
2009 Proof	250	Value: 70.00				

KM# 716 10 DOLLARS

1.0000 g., 0.9990 Gold 0.0321 oz. AGW, 13.9 mm. **Ruler:** Elizabeth II **Rev:** Castle

Date	Mintage	F	VF	XF	Unc	BU
2009 Proof	250	Value: 70.00				

KM# 717 10 DOLLARS

1.0000 g., 0.9990 Gold 0.0321 oz. AGW, 13.9 mm. **Ruler:** Elizabeth II **Rev:** Castle

Date	Mintage	F	VF	XF	Unc	BU
2009 Proof	250	Value: 70.00				

KM# 718 10 DOLLARS

1.0000 g., 0.9990 Gold 0.0321 oz. AGW, 13.9 mm. **Ruler:** Elizabeth II **Rev:** Church

Date	Mintage	F	VF	XF	Unc	BU
2009 Proof	250	Value: 70.00				

KM# 719 10 DOLLARS

1.0000 g., 0.9990 Gold 0.0321 oz. AGW, 13.9 mm. **Ruler:** Elizabeth II **Rev:** Ancient ruins

Date	Mintage	F	VF	XF	Unc	BU
2009 Proof	250	Value: 70.00				

KM# 792 10 DOLLARS

31.1050 g., 0.9990 Silver 0.9990 oz. ASW, 40 mm. **Ruler:** Elizabeth II **Subject:** Tycoons - Alfred Nobel **Rev:** Nobel bust at right, Prize Medal partially gilt at right

Date	Mintage	F	VF	XF	Unc	BU
2009 Proof	10,000	Value: 55.00				

KM# 793 10 DOLLARS

31.1050 g., 0.9990 Silver 0.9990 oz. ASW, 40 mm. **Ruler:** Elizabeth II **Subject:** Tycoons **Rev:** Cecil Rhodes, partially gilt

Date	Mintage	F	VF	XF	Unc	BU
2009 Proof	10,000	Value: 55.00				

KM# 1228 10 DOLLARS

155.5000 g., 0.9250 Silver 4.6243 oz. ASW, 65 mm. **Ruler:** Elizabeth II **Subject:** Ikuko Shimizu's Hello Kitty **Rev:** Kitty and Buckingham Palace in multicolor

Date	Mintage	F	VF	XF	Unc	BU
2009 Proof	Est. 1,500	Value: 350				

KM# 1232 10 DOLLARS

1.2400 g., 0.9990 Gold 0.0398 oz. AGW, 13.92 mm. **Ruler:** Elizabeth II **Subject:** Knut Hamsun, 150th Anniversary of Birth

Date	Mintage	F	VF	XF	Unc	BU
2009 Proof	Est. 1,000	Value: 85.00				

KM# 1233 10 DOLLARS

1.2400 g., 0.9990 Gold 0.0398 oz. AGW, 13.92 mm. **Ruler:** Elizabeth II **Subject:** Sweedish King Oscar II

Date	Mintage	F	VF	XF	Unc	BU
2009 Proof	Est. 10,000	Value: 85.00				

KM# 1332 10 DOLLARS

1.2400 g., 0.9990 Gold 0.0398 oz. AGW, 13.92 mm. **Ruler:** Elizabeth II **Subject:** 40th Anniversary of Moon landing

Date	Mintage	F	VF	XF	Unc	BU
2009 Proof	—	Value: 100				

KM# 1333 10 DOLLARS

1.2400 g., 0.9990 Gold 0.0398 oz. AGW, 13.92 mm. **Ruler:** Elizabeth II **Subject:** James Cook and the H.M.S Endeavor

Date	Mintage	F	VF	XF	Unc	BU
2009 Proof	—	Value: 100				

KM# 1484 10 DOLLARS

31.1050 g., 0.9990 Silver with 4 gr. gold insert 0.9990 oz. ASW, 38.61 mm. **Ruler:** Elizabeth II **Rev:** Porta Nigra in Trier

Date	Mintage	F	VF	XF	Unc	BU
2009	Est. 3,000	—	—	—	—	80.00

KM# 1485 10 DOLLARS

31.1050 g., 0.9990 Silver with 4gr gold insert 0.9990 oz. ASW, 38.61 mm. **Ruler:** Elizabeth II **Rev:** Semper Opera House in Dresden

Date	Mintage	F	VF	XF	Unc	BU
2009	Est. 3,000	—	—	—	—	80.00

KM# 1486 10 DOLLARS

31.1050 g., 0.9990 Silver with 4 gr. gold insert 0.9990 oz. ASW, 38.61 mm. **Ruler:** Elizabeth II **Rev:** Battle monument in Leipzig

Date	Mintage	F	VF	XF	Unc	BU
2009	Est. 3,000	—	—	—	—	80.00

KM# 1487 10 DOLLARS

31.1050 g., 0.9990 Silver plus 4 gr. gold insert 0.9990 oz. ASW, 38.61 mm. **Ruler:** Elizabeth II **Rev:** Holy Family Cathedral in Barcelona

Date	Mintage	F	VF	XF	Unc	BU
2009	Est. 3,000	—	—	—	—	80.00

KM# 1488 10 DOLLARS

31.1050 g., 0.9990 Silver with 4 gr. gold insert 0.9990 oz. ASW **Ruler:** Elizabeth II **Rev:** Burj al Arab ni Dubai

Date	Mintage	F	VF	XF	Unc	BU
2009	Est. 3,000	—	—	—	—	80.00

KM# 1489 10 DOLLARS

Silver **Ruler:** Elizabeth II **Rev:** Southern Pacific's GS-4 Daylight Limited

Date	Mintage	F	VF	XF	Unc	BU
2009 Proof	—	Value: 55.00				

KM# 1491 10 DOLLARS

Silver **Ruler:** Elizabeth II **Subject:** Wold Cup Soccer, South Africa

Date	Mintage	F	VF	XF	Unc	BU
2009 Proof	Est. 10,000	Value: 55.00				

KM# 1492 10 DOLLARS

1.0000 g., 0.9990 Gold 0.0321 oz. AGW, 13.92 mm. **Ruler:** Elizabeth II **Subject:** World Cup Soccer in South Africa

Date	Mintage	F	VF	XF	Unc	BU
2009 Proof	Est. 5,000	Value: 70.00				

KM# 1249 10 DOLLARS

31.1350 g., 0.9990 Silver 1.0000 oz. ASW, 45 mm. **Ruler:** Elizabeth II **Subject:** Albert Durer **Rev:** Rabbit illustration with crystals

Date	Mintage	F	VF	XF	Unc	BU
2010 Proof	3,000	Value: 75.00				

KM# 1258 10 DOLLARS

50.0000 g., 0.9250 Silver 1.4869 oz. ASW, 50 mm. **Ruler:** Elizabeth II **Subject:** Windows of Heaven **Rev:** Cologne Cathedral, stained glass windows, facade and ceiling arch plan

Date	Mintage	F	VF	XF	Unc	BU
2010 Proof	2,000	Value: 250				

KM# 1293 10 DOLLARS

31.1050 g., 0.9990 Silver 0.9990 oz. ASW, 45 mm. **Ruler:** Elizabeth II **Subject:** Oberg **Rev:** Rural Russian folk scene

Date	Mintage	F	VF	XF	Unc	BU
2010 Proof	—	Value: 75.00				

KM# 1296 10 DOLLARS

0.5000 g., 0.9990 Gold 0.0161 oz. AGW, 11 mm. **Ruler:** Elizabeth II **Rev:** Barack Obama

Date	Mintage	F	VF	XF	Unc	BU
2010 Proof	—	Value: 50.00				

KM# 1297 10 DOLLARS

1.0000 g., 0.9990 Gold 0.0321 oz. AGW, 13.92 mm. **Ruler:** Elizabeth II **Rev:** Martin Luther King

Date	Mintage	F	VF	XF	Unc	BU
2010 Proof	—	Value: 75.00				

KM# 1298 10 DOLLARS

1.0000 g., 0.9990 Gold 0.0321 oz. AGW, 13.92 mm. **Ruler:** Elizabeth II **Rev:** Barack Obama

Date	Mintage	F	VF	XF	Unc	BU
2010 Proof	—	Value: 75.00				

KM# 1495 10 DOLLARS

31.1050 g., 0.9990 Silver plus 4 gr. gold insert 0.9990 oz. ASW, 38.61 mm. **Ruler:** Elizabeth II **Rev:** Sanssouci Palace in Potsdam

Date	Mintage	F	VF	XF	Unc	BU
2010	Est. 3,000	—	—	—	—	80.00

KM# 1496 10 DOLLARS

31.1050 g., 0.9990 Silver plus 4 gr. gold insert 0.9990 oz. ASW, 38.61 mm. **Ruler:** Elizabeth II **Rev:** Castle in Eisenach

Date	Mintage	F	VF	XF	Unc	BU
2010	Est. 3,000	—	—	—	—	80.00

KM# 1497 10 DOLLARS

31.1050 g., 0.9990 Silver plus 4 gr. gold insert 0.9990 oz. ASW, 38.61 mm. **Ruler:** Elizabeth II **Rev:** The Atomium in Brussels

Date	Mintage	F	VF	XF	Unc	BU
2010	Est. 3,000	—	—	—	—	80.00

KM# 1498 10 DOLLARS

31.1050 g., 0.9990 Silver plus 4 gr. gold insert 0.9990 oz. ASW, 38.61 mm. **Ruler:** Elizabeth II **Rev:** Little Mermaid statue in Copenhagen

Date	Mintage	F	VF	XF	Unc	BU
2010	Est. 3,000	—	—	—	—	80.00

KM# 1499 10 DOLLARS

31.1050 g., 0.9990 Silver plus 4 gr. gold insert 0.9990 oz. ASW, 38.61 mm. **Ruler:** Elizabeth II **Rev:** Comtal castle in Carcassonne

Date	Mintage	F	VF	XF	Unc	BU
2010	Est. 3,000	—	—	—	—	80.00

KM# 1500 10 DOLLARS

31.1050 g., 0.9990 Silver plus 4 gr. gold insert 0.9990 oz. ASW, 38.61 mm. **Ruler:** Elizabeth II **Rev:** Belem tower in Lisbon

Date	Mintage	F	VF	XF	Unc	BU
2010	Est. 3,000	—	—	—	—	80.00

KM# 1501 10 DOLLARS

31.1050 g., 0.9990 Silver 0.9990 oz. ASW, 38.61 mm. **Ruler:** Elizabeth II **Rev:** That Luang in Viet Nam

Date	Mintage	F	VF	XF	Unc	BU
2010	Est. 3,000	—	—	—	—	80.00

KM# 1502 10 DOLLARS

31.1050 g., 0.9990 Silver plus 4 gr. gold insert 0.9990 oz. ASW, 38.61 mm. **Ruler:** Elizabeth II **Rev:** Dala Lama's palace in Tibet

Date	Mintage	F	VF	XF	Unc	BU
2010	Est. 3,000	—	—	—	—	80.00

KM# 1259 10 DOLLARS

50.0000 g., 0.9990 Silver 1.6059 oz. ASW, 50 mm. **Ruler:** Elizabeth II **Subject:** Windows of Heaven **Rev:** Westminister Abbey, stained glass windows, floor plan and facade

Date	Mintage	F	VF	XF	Unc	BU
2011 Proof	2,000	Value: 300				

KM# 1388 10 DOLLARS
50.0000 g., 0.9990 Silver 1.6059 oz. ASW, 50 mm. **Ruler:** Elizabeth II **Subject:** St. Issac's Cathedral, St. Petersburg **Rev:** Stained glass window and floor plan

Date	Mintage	F	VF	XF	Unc	BU
2011 Proof	2,000	Value: 300				

KM# 1389 10 DOLLARS
50.0000 g., 0.9990 Silver 1.6059 oz. ASW, 50 mm. **Ruler:** Elizabeth II **Subject:** Seville Cathedral **Rev:** Stained glass window, floor plan and façade

Date	Mintage	F	VF	XF	Unc	BU
2011 Proof	2,000	Value: 300				

KM# 1505 10 DOLLARS
31.1050 g., 0.9990 Silver 0.9990 oz. ASW, 65 mm. **Ruler:** Elizabeth II **Rev:** Moose before Bandenburg Gate and European Tuscany

Date	Mintage	F	VF	XF	Unc	BU
2011 Proof	Est. 3,000	Value: 80.00				

KM# 1506 10 DOLLARS
31.1050 g., 0.9990 Silver 0.9990 oz. ASW, 65 mm. **Ruler:** Elizabeth II **Rev:** Grizley bear before Statue of Liberty and cattle ranchers in America

Date	Mintage	F	VF	XF	Unc	BU
2011 Proof	Est. 3,000	Value: 80.00				

KM# 1507 10 DOLLARS
31.1050 g., 0.9990 Silver 0.9990 oz. ASW, 65 mm. **Ruler:** Elizabeth II **Rev:** Panda before Taj Mahal and Great Wall of China

Date	Mintage	F	VF	XF	Unc	BU
2011 Proof	Est. 3,000	Value: 80.00				

KM# 1508 10 DOLLARS
31.1050 g., 0.9990 Silver 0.9990 oz. ASW, 65 mm. **Ruler:** Elizabeth II **Rev:** Kangaroo before Harbor Bridge and Ayers Rock in Australia

Date	Mintage	F	VF	XF	Unc	BU
2011 Proof	Est. 3,000	Value: 80.00				

KM# 1509 10 DOLLARS
31.1050 g., 0.9990 Silver 0.9990 oz. ASW, 65 mm. **Ruler:** Elizabeth II **Rev:** Elephant before Great Sphinx and Mt. Kilimanjaro in Africa

Date	Mintage	F	VF	XF	Unc	BU
2011 Proof	Est. 3,000	Value: 80.00				

KM# 1434 10 DOLLARS
50.0000 g., 0.9250 Silver 1.4869 oz. ASW, 50 mm. **Ruler:** Elizabeth II **Subject:** Window's of Heaven - St. Isaac's Cethedral, St. Petersburg, Russia **Rev:** Stained glass window

Date	Mintage	F	VF	XF	Unc	BU
2012 Proof	2,000	Value: 250				

KM# 1433 10 DOLLARS
50.0000 g., 0.9250 Silver 1.4869 oz. ASW, 50 mm. **Ruler:** Elizabeth II **Subject:** Window's of Heaven, Church of St. Francis, Krakow, Poland **Rev:** Stained glass window

Date	Mintage	F	VF	XF	Unc	BU
2012 Proof	2,000	Value: 250				

KM# 1510 10 DOLLARS
31.1050 g., 0.9990 Silver 0.9990 oz. ASW, 65 mm. **Ruler:** Elizabeth II **Subject:** Ancient Cultures - Babylon

Date	Mintage	F	VF	XF	Unc	BU
2012 Proof	—	Value: 80.00				

KM# 1511 10 DOLLARS
31.1060 g., 0.9990 Silver 0.9990 oz. ASW, 65 mm. **Ruler:** Elizabeth II **Subject:** Ancient Cultures - Chinese

Date	Mintage	F	VF	XF	Unc	BU
2012 Proof	—	Value: 80.00				

KM# 1512 10 DOLLARS
31.1050 g., 0.9990 Silver 0.9990 oz. ASW, 65 mm. **Ruler:** Elizabeth II **Subject:** Ancient Cultures - Egyptian

Date	Mintage	F	VF	XF	Unc	BU
2012 Proof	—	Value: 80.00				

KM# 1513 10 DOLLARS
31.1050 g., 0.9990 Silver 0.9990 oz. ASW, 65 mm. **Ruler:** Elizabeth II **Subject:** Ancient Cultures - Greek

Date	Mintage	F	VF	XF	Unc	BU
2012 Proof	—	Value: 80.00				

KM# 1514 10 DOLLARS
31.1050 g., 0.9990 Silver 0.9990 oz. ASW, 65 mm. **Ruler:** Elizabeth II **Subject:** Ancient Cultures - Aztec

Date	Mintage	F	VF	XF	Unc	BU
2012 Proof	—	Value: 80.00				

KM# 1131 12 DOLLARS
10.0000 g., 0.9999 Gold 0.3215 oz. AGW, 26 mm. **Ruler:** Elizabeth II **Subject:** Full Gospel Business Men's Fellowship, 50th Anniversary **Rev:** Jesus Christ

Date	Mintage	F	VF	XF	Unc	BU
2003 Proof	Est. 4,999	Value: 600				

KM# 894 20 DOLLARS
31.1050 g., 0.9250 Silver 0.9250 oz. ASW **Ruler:** Elizabeth II **Rev:** Marco Polo visits the Khubla Khan in China

Date	Mintage	F	VF	XF	Unc	BU
2007 Proof	—	Value: 60.00				

KM# 636 20 DOLLARS
93.3000 g., 0.9990 Silver 2.9965 oz. ASW, 55 mm. **Ruler:** Elizabeth II **Rev:** Michangelo, Creation of Adam, multicolor with crystal inserts

Date	Mintage	F	VF	XF	Unc	BU
2008 Proof	1,000	Value: 700				

KM# 637 20 DOLLARS
93.3000 g., 0.9990 Silver 2.9965 oz. ASW, 55 mm. **Ruler:** Elizabeth II **Rev:** DaVinci, Last Supper, multicolor with crystal inserts

Date	Mintage	F	VF	XF	Unc	BU
2008 Proof	1,000	Value: 750				

KM# 638 20 DOLLARS
93.3000 g., 0.9990 Silver 2.9965 oz. ASW, 55 mm. **Ruler:** Elizabeth II **Rev:** Raffaello, School of Athens, multicolor with crystal inserts

Date	Mintage	F	VF	XF	Unc	BU
2008 Proof	1,000	Value: 650				

KM# 639 20 DOLLARS
93.3000 g., 0.9990 Silver 2.9965 oz. ASW, 55 mm. **Ruler:** Elizabeth II **Rev:** Botticelli, Birth of Venus, multicolor with crystal inserts

Date	Mintage	F	VF	XF	Unc	BU
2008 Proof	1,458	Value: 375				

KM# 1477 20 DOLLARS
93.3000 g., 0.9990 Silver 2.9965 oz. ASW, 55 mm. **Ruler:** Elizabeth II **Rev:** Vatican City 100 Euro design

Date	Mintage	F	VF	XF	Unc	BU
2008 Proof	Est. 960	Value: 225				

KM# 697 20 DOLLARS
93.3150 g., 0.9990 Silver 2.9970 oz. ASW, 55 mm. **Ruler:** Elizabeth II **Subject:** European Masters - DaVinci **Rev:** Mona Lisa, 12 crystals imbedded

Date	Mintage	F	VF	XF	Unc	BU
2009 Proof	999	Value: 1,450				

KM# 698 20 DOLLARS
93.3150 g., 0.9990 Silver 2.9970 oz. ASW, 55 mm. **Ruler:** Elizabeth II **Subject:** European Masters - Rembrandt **Rev:** The Night watch, crystals embedded

Date	Mintage	F	VF	XF	Unc	BU
2009 Proof	1,642	Value: 475				

KM# 699 20 DOLLARS
93.3150 g., 0.9990 Silver 2.9970 oz. ASW, 55 mm. **Ruler:** Elizabeth II **Subject:** European Masters - Raffaelo **Rev:** Sistine Chapel Madonna, crystals embedded

Date	Mintage	F	VF	XF	Unc	BU
2009 Proof	1,512	Value: 475				

KM# 700 20 DOLLARS
93.3150 g., 0.9990 Silver 2.9970 oz. ASW, 55 mm. **Ruler:** Elizabeth II **Subject:** European Masters - Spitzwig **Rev:** The Poor Poet, crystals embedded

Date	Mintage	F	VF	XF	Unc	BU
2009 Proof	—	Value: 425				

KM# 769 20 DOLLARS
93.3150 g., 0.9990 Silver partially gilt 2.9970 oz. ASW, 55 mm. **Ruler:** Elizabeth II **Rev:** Vetruvian man

Date	Mintage	F	VF	XF	Unc	BU
2010 Proof	—	Value: 550				

KM# 1246 20 DOLLARS
93.3000 g., 0.9990 Silver 2.9965 oz. ASW, 55 mm. **Ruler:** Elizabeth II **Subject:** Carlo Maratta **Rev:** Holy Night, color image of Mary and child, crystals

Date	Mintage	F	VF	XF	Unc	BU
2010	1,655	—	—	—	—	450

KM# 1248 20 DOLLARS
93.3000 g., 0.9990 Silver 2.9965 oz. ASW, 55 mm. **Ruler:** Elizabeth II **Subject:** Rembrandt **Rev:** Man in a Golden Helmet, plus crystals

Date	Mintage	F	VF	XF	Unc	BU
2010 Proof	1,655	Value: 450				

KM# 1341 20 DOLLARS
93.1350 g., 0.9990 Silver 2.9912 oz. ASW, 55 mm. **Ruler:** Elizabeth II **Subject:** Van Gogh, Sunflowers

Date	Mintage	F	VF	XF	Unc	BU
2010 Proof	—	Value: 400				

KM# 1494 20 DOLLARS
93.3000 g., 0.9990 Silver plus 7.78 gr. .999 gold inlay 2.9965 oz. ASW, 55 mm. **Ruler:** Elizabeth II **Rev:** Man drawing by DaVinci

Date	Mintage	F	VF	XF	Unc	BU
2010 Proof	Est. 999	Value: 525				

KM# 1387 20 DOLLARS
93.1350 g., 0.9990 Silver 2.9912 oz. ASW, 55 mm. **Ruler:** Elizabeth II **Subject:** Charles LeBrun, painter **Obv:** Head with tiara right **Rev:** Adoration of the Shepards painting **Edge:** Reeded

Date	Mintage	F	VF	XF	Unc	BU
2011 Proof	1,689	Value: 450				

KM# 1402 20 DOLLARS
93.3000 g., 0.9990 Silver 2.9965 oz. ASW, 55 mm. **Ruler:** Elizabeth II **Subject:** Vincent van Gogh **Rev:** Sunflowers

Date	Mintage	F	VF	XF	Unc	BU
2011 Proof	1,655	Value: 400				

KM# 1403 20 DOLLARS
93.3000 g., 0.9990 Silver 2.9965 oz. ASW, 55 mm. **Ruler:** Elizabeth II **Subject:** Franz Marc, painter **Rev:** Blue Horse

Date	Mintage	F	VF	XF	Unc	BU
2011 proof	1,911	Value: 400				

KM# 1404 20 DOLLARS
93.3000 g., 0.9990 Silver 2.9965 oz. ASW, 55 mm. **Ruler:** Elizabeth II **Subject:** Giovanni Canalello Bucentoro **Rev:** St. Mark's and Doge's Palace, Venice

Date	Mintage	F	VF	XF	Unc	BU
2011 Proof	1,732	Value: 450				

KM# 1448 20 DOLLARS
93.3000 g., 0.9990 Silver 2.9965 oz. ASW, 65 mm. **Ruler:** Elizabeth II **Subject:** Vatican Art **Rev:** Giovanni Canaletto's St. Mark's Square and the Doge's palace

Date	Mintage	F	VF	XF	Unc	BU
2011 Proof	—	Value: 450				

KM# 1454 20 DOLLARS
100.0000 g., 0.9990 Silver 3.2117 oz. ASW, 25x36 mm. **Ruler:** Elizabeth II **Subject:** The Luxury lifestyle **Rev:** Large blue crystal insert **Shape:** Vertical rectangle

Date	Mintage	F	VF	XF	Unc	BU
2011 Proof	2,000	Value: 200				

KM# 1397 20 DOLLARS

93.3000 g., 0.9990 Silver 2.9965 oz. ASW, 55 mm. **Ruler:** Elizabeth II **Obv:** Bust with tiara right **Rev:** Nefertiti head in color at center, crystal frame around

Date	Mintage	F	VF	XF	Unc	BU
2012 Proof	—	Value: 350				

KM# 1432 20 DOLLARS

93.3000 g., 0.9990 Silver 2.9965 oz. ASW, 55 mm. **Ruler:** Elizabeth II **Subject:** Portrait of Adele **Rev:** Painting image

Date	Mintage	F	VF	XF	Unc	BU
2012 Proof	1,897	Value: 250				

KM# 1435 20 DOLLARS

93.3000 g., 0.9990 Silver 2.9965 oz. ASW, 55 mm. **Ruler:** Elizabeth II **Subject:** Vatican Art **Rev:** Renoir's Sleeping Bather

Date	Mintage	F	VF	XF	Unc	BU
2012 Proof	—	Value: 375				

KM# 1436 20 DOLLARS

93.3000 g., 0.9990 Silver 2.9965 oz. ASW, 55 mm. **Ruler:** Elizabeth II **Subject:** Vatican Art **Rev:** Neferititi

Date	Mintage	F	VF	XF	Unc	BU
2012 Proof	—	Value: 450				

KM# 1455 20 DOLLARS

93.3000 g., 0.9990 Silver 2.9965 oz. ASW, 65 mm. **Ruler:** Elizabeth II **Subject:** Art - Gustav Klemt **Rev:** Adele 3 in color

Date	Mintage	F	VF	XF	Unc	BU
2012 Proof	—	Value: 550				

KM# 1145 25 DOLLARS

7.8700 g., 0.9999 Gold 0.2530 oz. AGW **Ruler:** Elizabeth II **Rev:** Edward "Ned"Kelley in color

Date	Mintage	F	VF	XF	Unc	BU
2004 proof	Est. 1,000	Value: 500				

KM# 1190 25 DOLLARS

155.5000 g., 0.9250 Silver 4.6243 oz. ASW, 65 mm. **Ruler:** Elizabeth II **Subject:** Elvis Presely, 30th Anniversary of death **Rev:** That's All right, Mama

Date	Mintage	F	VF	XF	Unc	BU
2007 Proof	Est. 1,977	Value: 350				

KM# 1321 25 DOLLARS

Silver **Ruler:** Elizabeth II **Rev:** Christian Radish

Date	Mintage	F	VF	XF	Unc	BU
2008 Proof	—	Value: 85.00				

KM# 1322 25 DOLLARS

Silver **Ruler:** Elizabeth II **Rev:** France II

Date	Mintage	F	VF	XF	Unc	BU
2008 Proof	—	Value: 85.00				

KM# 1325 25 DOLLARS

Silver **Ruler:** Elizabeth II **Rev:** Sedov

Date	Mintage	F	VF	XF	Unc	BU
2008 Proof	—	Value: 85.00				

KM# 1326 25 DOLLARS

Silver **Ruler:** Elizabeth II **Rev:** Thomas Lawson

Date	Mintage	F	VF	XF	Unc	BU
2008 Proof	—	Value: 85.00				

KM# 1423 25 DOLLARS

7.7700 g., 0.9990 Gold 0.2496 oz. AGW **Ruler:** Elizabeth II **Subject:** Pultusk Meteroite

Date	Mintage	F	VF	XF	Unc	BU
2008 Proof	—	Value: 500				

KM# 767 25 DOLLARS

155.5000 g., 0.9990 Silver 4.9942 oz. ASW, 65 mm. **Ruler:** Elizabeth II **Subject:** Year of the Ox **Rev:** Child riding back of ox, partially gilt **Note:** Photo reduced.

Date	Mintage	F	VF	XF	Unc	BU
2009 Proof	—	Value: 675				

KM# 1229 25 DOLLARS

7.9800 g., 0.9160 Gold 0.2350 oz. AGW, 22.05 mm. **Ruler:** Elizabeth II **Subject:** Ikuko Shimizu's Hello Kitty **Rev:** Kitty and Union Jack flag in multicolor

Date	Mintage	F	VF	XF	Unc	BU
2009 Proof	Est. 1,000	Value: 700				

KM# 1242 25 DOLLARS

4.0000 g., 0.9990 Gold 0.1285 oz. AGW, 14x23.3 mm. **Ruler:** Elizabeth II **Subject:** Shroud of Turin **Rev:** Image of the face of Jesus, 3 red crystals

Date	Mintage	F	VF	XF	Unc	BU
2010 Proof	2,000	Value: 500				

KM# 1323 25 DOLLARS

Silver **Ruler:** Elizabeth II **Rev:** Krulzernen

Date	Mintage	F	VF	XF	Unc	BU
2011 Proof	—	Value: 85.00				

KM# 1324 25 DOLLARS

Silver **Ruler:** Elizabeth II **Rev:** Preussen

Date	Mintage	F	VF	XF	Unc	BU
2011 Proof	—	Value: 85.00				

KM# 1360 25 DOLLARS

155.5000 g., 0.9990 Silver 4.9942 oz. ASW, 65 mm. **Ruler:** Elizabeth II **Subject:** Soyuzmultfilm 75th Anniversary - Winnie the Pooh **Rev:** Winnie the Pooh characters in color **Edge:** Reeded **Note:** Photo reduced.

Date	Mintage	F	VF	XF	Unc	BU
2011 Proof	500	Value: 420				

KM# 1366 25 DOLLARS

155.5000 g., 0.9990 Silver 4.9942 oz. ASW, 65 mm. **Ruler:** Elizabeth II **Subject:** Soyuzmultfilm 75th Anniversary - Little Boy and Karlsson-on-the-Roof **Rev:** Little Boy, Karlsson and Freken Bok in color **Edge:** Reeded **Note:** Photo reduced.

Date	Mintage	F	VF	XF	Unc	BU
2011 Proof	500	Value: 425				

KM# 1370 25 DOLLARS

155.5000 g., 0.9990 Silver 4.9942 oz. ASW, 65 mm. **Ruler:** Elizabeth II **Subject:** Soyuzmultfilm 75th Anniversary - Cheburashka and Crocodile Gena **Rev:** Cheburashka, Crocodile Gena and Madame Shapoklyak in color **Edge:** Reeded **Note:** Photo reduced.

Date	Mintage	F	VF	XF	Unc	BU
2011 Proof	500	Value: 420				

KM# 1408 25 DOLLARS

155.5000 g., 0.9990 Silver 4.9942 oz. ASW, 65 mm. **Ruler:** Elizabeth II **Subject:** Kipling's Mowgli story characters **Rev:** Characters in color

Date	Mintage	F	VF	XF	Unc	BU
2011 Proof	Est. 500	Value: 250				

KM# 1426 25 DOLLARS
25.0000 g., 0.9250 Silver 0.7435 oz. ASW, 38.61 mm. **Ruler:** Elizabeth II **Rev:** King Cobra (Ophiophagus hannah)

Date	Mintage	F	VF	XF	Unc	BU
2011 Proof	1,000	Value: 75.00				

KM# 439 30 DOLLARS
10.0000 g., 0.9999 Gold 0.3215 oz. AGW, 16.1 mm. **Ruler:** Elizabeth II **Obv:** Crowned head right, date below **Rev:** Multicolor Peony flower and denomination **Edge:** Reeded

Date	Mintage	F	VF	XF	Unc	BU
2004	10,000	—	—	—	—	600

KM# 1128 35 DOLLARS
10.0210 g., 0.9990 Gold 0.3218 oz. AGW, 25 mm. **Ruler:** Elizabeth II **Rev:** James Cook and sailing ship

Date	Mintage	F	VF	XF	Unc	BU
2003 Proof	Est. 4,999	Value: 625				

KM# 440 35 DOLLARS
10.0000 g., 0.9999 Gold 0.3215 oz. AGW, 16.1 mm. **Ruler:** Elizabeth II **Obv:** Crowned head right, date below **Rev:** Multicolor Chinese man beating a tiger and denomination **Edge:** Reeded

Date	Mintage	F	VF	XF	Unc	BU
2004	6,000	—	—	—	—	600

KM# 441 35 DOLLARS
10.0000 g., 0.9999 Gold 0.3215 oz. AGW, 16.1 mm. **Ruler:** Elizabeth II **Obv:** Crowned head right, date below **Rev:** Multicolor Chinese man riding a horse and denomination **Edge:** Reeded

Date	Mintage	F	VF	XF	Unc	BU
2004	10,000	—	—	—	—	600

KM# 442 35 DOLLARS
10.0000 g., 0.9999 Gold 0.3215 oz. AGW, 25 x 15 mm. **Ruler:** Elizabeth II **Obv:** Crowned head right, date below **Rev:** Multicolor "Eight immortals crossing the sea" and denomination **Edge:** Plain **Shape:** Ingot

Date	Mintage	F	VF	XF	Unc	BU
2004	3,000	—	—	—	—	650

KM# 1132 50 DOLLARS
31.1050 g., 0.9999 Gold 0.9999 oz. AGW, 38.6 mm. **Ruler:** Elizabeth II **Subject:** Full Gospel Business Men's Fellowship, 50th Anniversary **Rev:** Jesus Christ

Date	Mintage	F	VF	XF	Unc	BU
2003 Proof	Est. 2,999	Value: 1,800				

KM# 1319 50 DOLLARS
Silver **Ruler:** Elizabeth II **Subject:** Worlf Wildlife Fund **Rev:** Two deer

Date	Mintage	F	VF	XF	Unc	BU
2007 Proof	—	Value: 100				

KM# 1191 50 DOLLARS
7.7800 g., 0.7500 Gold 0.1876 oz. AGW, 26 mm. **Ruler:** Elizabeth II **Subject:** Elvis Presley, 30th Anniversary of death

Date	Mintage	F	VF	XF	Unc	BU
2007 Proof	500	Value: 420				

KM# 800 50 DOLLARS
155.5000 g., 0.9990 Silver 4.9942 oz. ASW, 65 mm. **Ruler:** Elizabeth II **Subject:** Tales of the Carribean **Rev:** Sea monster atacking Pirate ship

Date	Mintage	F	VF	XF	Unc	BU
2008	500	—	—	—	—	1,500

KM# 1230 50 DOLLARS
15.6100 g., 0.9990 Gold 0.5014 oz. AGW, 26.5 mm. **Ruler:** Elizabeth II **Subject:** Ikuko Shimizu's Hello Kitty **Rev:** Kitty and Daniel in automobile near Westminster and Big Ben in multicolor

Date	Mintage	F	VF	XF	Unc	BU
2009 Proof	Est. 1,000	Value: 950				

KM# 738 50 DOLLARS
31.1050 g., 0.9999 Palladium 0.9999 oz. **Ruler:** Elizabeth II **Rev:** Ship model left

Date	Mintage	F	VF	XF	Unc	BU
2010	—	—	—	—	—	900

KM# 1465 50 DOLLARS
155.5000 g., 0.9990 Silver 4.9942 oz. ASW, 65 mm. **Ruler:** Elizabeth II **Rev:** Airship Hindenburg in flight over New York skyline engraved on mother-of-pearl insert **Note:** Photo reduced.

Date	Mintage	F	VF	XF	Unc	BU
2013 Proof	750	Value: 350				

KM# 397 100 DOLLARS
23.3276 g., 0.9999 Gold Acrylic capsule center containing tiny diamonds, rubies and sapphires 0.7499 oz. AGW, 32.1 mm. **Ruler:** Elizabeth II **Subject:** Crown Jewels **Obv:** Crowned bust right, legend **Rev:** Crowns and royal regalia **Edge:** Reeded

Date	Mintage	F	VF	XF	Unc	BU
2002 Proof	5,000	Value: 1,350				

KM# 1129 100 DOLLARS
31.1620 g., 0.9990 Gold 1.0008 oz. AGW, 32 mm. **Ruler:** Elizabeth II **Rev:** James Cook and sailing ship

Date	Mintage	F	VF	XF	Unc	BU
2003 Proof	Est. 2,999	Value: 1,800				

KM# 503 100 DOLLARS
31.1030 g., 0.9999 Gold 0.9998 oz. AGW, 40.6 mm. **Ruler:** Elizabeth II **Subject:** WWI **Obv:** Head with tiara right **Rev:** Multicolor image of Australian WWI soldier in Europe **Edge:** Reeded

Date	Mintage	F	VF	XF	Unc	BU
2008 Proof	90	Value: 2,000				

KM# 505 100 DOLLARS
31.1030 g., 0.9999 Gold 0.9998 oz. AGW, 40.6 mm. **Ruler:** Elizabeth II **Subject:** WWI **Obv:** Head with tiara right **Rev:** Multicolor image of Australian WWI soldier in Mid-East scene **Edge:** Reeded

Date	Mintage	F	VF	XF	Unc	BU
2008 Proof	90	Value: 2,000				

KM# 737 100 DOLLARS
31.1050 g., 0.9999 Platinum 0.9999 oz. APW **Ruler:** Elizabeth II **Rev:** Ship model left

Date	Mintage	F	VF	XF	Unc	BU
2010	—	—	—	—	—	2,250

KM# 1212 200 DOLLARS
31.1620 g., 0.9999 Gold 1.0017 oz. AGW, 32 mm. **Ruler:** Elizabeth II **Subject:** John Marshall's Cow Parade **Rev:** Cow in multicolor

Date	Mintage	F	VF	XF	Unc	BU
2008	Est. 100	—	—	—	—	1,900

KM# 1213 200 DOLLARS
31.1620 g., 0.9990 Gold 1.0008 oz. AGW, 32 mm. **Ruler:** Elizabeth II **Subject:** John Marshall's Cow Parade **Rev:** African Moonlight Cow in multicolor

Date	Mintage	F	VF	XF	Unc	BU
2008	Est. 100	—	—	—	—	1,900

KM# 1214 200 DOLLARS
31.1650 g., 0.9990 Gold 1.0009 oz. AGW, 32 mm. **Ruler:** Elizabeth II **Subject:** John Marshall's Cow Parade **Rev:** Discownt Motivated in multicolor

Date	Mintage	F	VF	XF	Unc	BU
2008	Est. 100	—	—	—	—	1,900

KM# 1215 200 DOLLARS
31.1650 g., 0.9999 Gold 1.0018 oz. AGW **Ruler:** Elizabeth II **Subject:** John Marshall's Cow Parade **Rev:** Moodonna in multicolor

Date	Mintage	F	VF	XF	Unc	BU
2008	Est. 100	—	—	—	—	1,900

KM# 1216 200 DOLLARS
31.1650 g., 0.9990 Gold 1.0009 oz. AGW, 32 mm. **Ruler:** Elizabeth II **Subject:** John Marshall's Cow Parade **Rev:** Moodiba in multicolor

Date	Mintage	F	VF	XF	Unc	BU
2008	Est. 100	—	—	—	—	1,900

KM# 1217 200 DOLLARS
31.1650 g., 0.9999 Gold 1.0018 oz. AGW, 32 mm. **Ruler:** Elizabeth II **Subject:** John Marshall's Cow Parade **Rev:** Railbow Cowwow in multicolor

Date	Mintage	F	VF	XF	Unc	BU
2008	Est. 100	—	—	—	—	1,900

KM# 1218 200 DOLLARS
31.1650 g., 0.9999 Gold 1.0018 oz. AGW, 32 mm. **Ruler:** Elizabeth II **Subject:** John Marshall's Cow Parade **Rev:** Picowso in multicolor

Date	Mintage	F	VF	XF	Unc	BU
2008	Est. 100	—	—	—	—	1,900

KM# 1219 200 DOLLARS
31.1650 g., 0.9990 Gold 1.0009 oz. AGW, 32 mm. **Ruler:** Elizabeth II **Subject:** John Marshall's Cow Parade **Rev:** Location Cow in multicolor

Date	Mintage	F	VF	XF	Unc	BU
2008	Est. 100	—	—	—	—	1,900

KM# 1220 200 DOLLARS
31.1650 g., 0.9999 Gold 1.0018 oz. AGW, 32 mm. **Ruler:** Elizabeth II **Subject:** John Marshall's Cow Parade **Rev:** Milking in the Farmhouse in multicolor

Date	Mintage	F	VF	XF	Unc	BU
2008	Est. 100	—	—	—	—	1,900

KM# 1221 200 DOLLARS
31.1650 g., 0.9999 Gold 1.0018 oz. AGW, 32 mm. **Ruler:** Elizabeth II **Subject:** John Marshall's Cow Parade **Rev:** Evening Cows in multicolor

Date	Mintage	F	VF	XF	Unc	BU
2008	Est. 100	—	—	—	—	1,900

KM# 1222 200 DOLLARS
31.1650 g., 0.9999 Gold 1.0018 oz. AGW, 32 mm. **Ruler:** Elizabeth II **Subject:** John Marshall's Cow Parade **Rev:** Cultural Moosic Cow in multicolor

Date	Mintage	F	VF	XF	Unc	BU
2008	Est. 100	—	—	—	—	1,900

KM# 1223 200 DOLLARS
31.1650 g., 0.9999 Gold 1.0018 oz. AGW, 32 mm. **Ruler:** Elizabeth II **Subject:** John Marshall's Cow Parade **Rev:** Freedomoo Cow in multicolor

Date	Mintage	F	VF	XF	Unc	BU
2008	Est. 100	—	—	—	—	1,900

KM# 1224 200 DOLLARS
31.1650 g., 0.9999 Gold 1.0018 oz. AGW, 32 mm. **Ruler:** Elizabeth II **Subject:** John Marshall's Cow Parade **Rev:** Bovingham Palace Cow in multicolor

Date	Mintage	F	VF	XF	Unc	BU
2008	Est. 100	—	—	—	—	1,900

KM# 768 200 DOLLARS
31.1050 g., 0.9990 Gold 0.9990 oz. AGW, 40.6 mm. **Ruler:** Elizabeth II **Subject:** Year of the Ox **Rev:** Child riding back of ox

Date	Mintage	F	VF	XF	Unc	BU
2009 Proof	—	Value: 1,850				

KM# 389 500 DOLLARS
2000.0000 g., 0.9990 Silver 64.234 oz. ASW, 105 mm. **Ruler:** Elizabeth II **Subject:** Moby Dick **Obv:** Crowned head right **Rev:** Whale jumping over a six-man rowboat **Edge:** Plain **Note:** Illustration reduced.

Date	Mintage	F	VF	XF	Unc	BU
2001 Proof	—	Value: 2,500				

KM# 548 500 DOLLARS
113.0000 g., 1.0000 Gold 3.6328 oz. AGW, 50 mm. **Ruler:** Elizabeth II **Subject:** Jack Nicklaus **Rev:** Portrait facing - two golf poses flanking

Date	Mintage	F	VF	XF	Unc	BU
2006 Proof	113	Value: 6,850				

BULLION COINAGE

KM# 1473 DOLLAR
31.1050 g., 0.9990 Silver 0.9990 oz. ASW, 39 mm. **Ruler:** Elizabeth II **Rev:** H.M.A.V. Bounty

Date	Mintage	F	VF	XF	Unc	BU
2009	—	—	—	—	—	40.00

KM# 1470 5 DOLLARS
100.0000 g., 0.9990 Silver 3.2117 oz. ASW **Ruler:** Elizabeth II **Rev:** H.M.A.V. Bounty

Date	Mintage	F	VF	XF	Unc	BU
2009	—	—	—	—	—	135

KM# 1474 10 DOLLARS
3.1100 g., 0.9990 Gold 0.0999 oz. AGW **Ruler:** Elizabeth II **Rev:** H.M.A.V. Bounty

Date	Mintage	F	VF	XF	Unc	BU
2009	—	—	—	—	—	185

KM# 1475 25 DOLLARS
7.7800 g., 0.9990 Gold 0.2499 oz. AGW **Ruler:** Elizabeth II **Rev:** H.M.A.V. Bounty

Date	Mintage	F	VF	XF	Unc	BU
2009	—	—	—	—	—	475

KM# 1467 30 DOLLARS
1000.0000 g., 0.9990 Silver 32.117 oz. ASW, 50x105 mm. **Ruler:** Elizabeth II **Shape:** Rectangle

Date	Mintage	F	VF	XF	Unc	BU
2007	—	—	—	—	—	1,200

KM# 1234 50 DOLLARS
31.1050 g., 0.9990 Palladium 0.9990 oz., 38.6 mm. **Ruler:** Elizabeth II **Rev:** H.M.A.V. Bounty, as full hull model

Date	Mintage	F	VF	XF	Unc	BU
2009	—	—	—	—	—	1,000

KM# 1471 100 DOLLARS
3110.0000 g., 0.9990 Silver 99.884 oz. ASW, 89x182 mm. **Ruler:** Elizabeth II **Rev:** H.M.A.V. Bounty

Date	Mintage	F	VF	XF	Unc	BU
2008	—	—	—	—	—	3,500

KM# 1476 100 DOLLARS
31.1050 g., 0.9990 Gold 0.9990 oz. AGW **Ruler:** Elizabeth II **Rev:** H.M.A.V. Bounty

Date	Mintage	F	VF	XF	Unc	BU
2009	—	—	—	—	—	1,900

KM# 1472 150 DOLLARS
5000.0000 g., 0.9990 Silver 160.58 oz. ASW, 89x182 mm. **Ruler:** Elizabeth II **Rev:** H.M.A.V. Bounty

Date	Mintage	F	VF	XF	Unc	BU
2008	—	—	—	—	—	5,500

MAUNDY MONEY

Ceremonial Sterling Pence

KM# 449 PENNY
0.4800 g., 0.9990 Silver 0.0154 oz. ASW, 11.1 mm. **Ruler:** Elizabeth II **Subject:** Maundy **Obv:** Crowned bust right **Rev:** Crowned denomination divides date within wreath **Edge:** Plain

Date	Mintage	F	VF	XF	Unc	BU
2002 Proof	5,000	Value: 8.00				

KM# 450 2 PENCE
0.9400 g., 0.9990 Silver 0.0302 oz. ASW, 13.4 mm. **Ruler:** Elizabeth II **Subject:** Maundy **Obv:** Crowned bust right **Rev:** Crowned denomination divides date within wreath **Edge:** Plain

Date	Mintage	F	VF	XF	Unc	BU
2002 Proof	5,000	Value: 10.00				

KM# 451 3 PENCE
1.4400 g., 0.9990 Silver 0.0462 oz. ASW, 16.1 mm. **Ruler:** Elizabeth II **Subject:** Maundy **Obv:** Crowned bust right **Rev:** Crowned denomination divides date within wreath **Edge:** Plain

Date	Mintage	F	VF	XF	Unc	BU
2002 Proof	5,000	Value: 12.00				

KM# 452 4 PENCE
1.9300 g., 0.9990 Silver 0.0620 oz. ASW, 17.5 mm. **Ruler:** Elizabeth II **Subject:** Maundy **Obv:** Crowned bust right **Rev:** Crowned denomination divides date within wreath **Edge:** Plain

Date	Mintage	F	VF	XF	Unc	BU
2002 Proof	5,000	Value: 15.00				

PROOF SETS

KM#	Date	Mintage	Identification	Issue Price	Mkt Val
PS25	2002 (4)	5,000	KM#449-452 Maundy Set	—	45.00

COSTA RICA

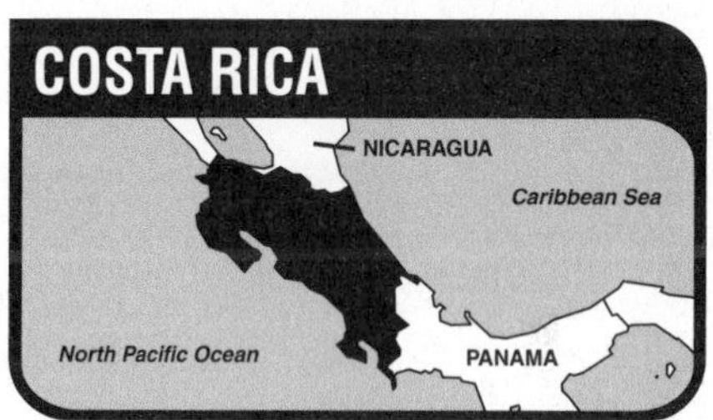

The Republic of Costa Rica, located in southern Central America between Nicaragua and Panama, has an area of 19,730 sq. mi. (51,100 sq. km.) and a population of 3.4 million. Capital: San Jose. Agriculture predominates; tourism and coffee, bananas, beef and sugar contribute heavily to the country's export earnings.

KEY TO MINT IDENTIFICATION

Key Letter	Mint
(a)	Armant Metalurgica, Santiago, Chile
(c)	Casa de Moneda, Mexico City Mint
(cc)	Casa de Moneda, Brazil
(co)	Colombia Republican Banko
(g)	Guatemala Mint
(i)	Italcambio Mint
(p) or (P)	Philadelphia Mint, USA
(r)	RCM – Royal Canadian Mint
(rm)	Royal Mint, London
(s)	San Francisco
(sj)	San Jose
(sm)	Sherrit Mint, Toronto
(v)	Vereingte Deutsche Metallwerke, Karlsruhe
(w)	Westain, Toronto

REPUBLIC

REFORM COINAGE

1920, 100 Centimos = 1 Colon

KM# 227a.2 5 COLONES
4.0000 g., Brass, 21.6 mm. **Obv:** National arms, date below, large letters in legend, large date, shield is not outlined **Rev:** Denomination above spray, B.C.C.R. below, thin '5' **Edge:** Segmented reeding

Date	Mintage	F	VF	XF	Unc	BU
2001(a)	—	—	—	—	0.65	1.00

KM# 227b 5 COLONES
0.9000 g., Aluminum, 21.4 mm. **Obv:** National arms **Obv. Legend:** REPUBLICA DE COSTA RICA **Rev:** Denomination above sprays, B.C.C.R. **Edge:** Plain

Date	Mintage	F	VF	XF	Unc	BU
2005	—	—	—	—	0.35	0.50
2008	—	—	—	—	0.35	0.50

KM# 228.2 10 COLONES
5.0000 g., Brass, 23.5 mm. **Obv:** National arms, date below, large legend and date, shield not outlined **Rev:** Denomination above spray, B.C.C.R. below, thick '1' **Edge:** Segmented reeding

Date	Mintage	F	VF	XF	Unc	BU
2002(a)	—	—	—	—	1.25	1.50

KM# 228b 10 COLONES
1.1300 g., Aluminum, 22.97 mm. **Obv:** National arms **Obv. Legend:** REPUBLICA DE COSTA RICA **Rev:** Denomination above sprays, B.C.C.R. **Edge:** Reeded

Date	Mintage	F	VF	XF	Unc	BU
2005	—	—	—	—	0.50	0.75
2008	—	—	—	—	0.50	0.75

KM# 229a 25 COLONES
7.0000 g., Brass, 25.4 mm. **Obv:** National arms **Obv. Legend:** REPUBLICA DE COSTA RICA **Rev:** Value above sprays, B.C.C.R. below **Edge:** Segmented reeding

Date	Mintage	F	VF	XF	Unc	BU
2001(a)	—	—	—	—	2.50	3.00
2003	—	—	—	—	2.50	3.00
2007	—	—	—	—	2.50	3.00

KM# 229a.1 25 COLONES
7.0000 g., Brass **Obv:** National arms, date below **Rev:** Value above sprays, B.C.C.R. below **Edge:** Plain

Date	Mintage	F	VF	XF	Unc	BU
2005	—	—	—	—	2.50	3.00

KM# 231.1a 50 COLONES
7.9200 g., Aluminum-Bronze, 27.5 mm. **Obv:** National arms, date below **Rev:** Value with spray below **Rev. Legend:** B. C. C. R. **Edge:** Segmented reeding

Date	Mintage	F	VF	XF	Unc	BU
2002	—	—	—	—	3.00	4.00

KM# 231.1b 50 COLONES
7.8400 g., Brass Plated Steel, 27.5 mm. **Obv:** National arms above date **Rev:** Value above sprays, B.C.C.R. below **Edge:** Segmented reeding

Date	Mintage	F	VF	XF	Unc	BU
2006	—	—	—	—	3.50	5.00
2007	—	—	—	—	3.50	5.00
2008	—	—	—	—	3.50	5.00

KM# 230a 100 COLONES
Brass, 29.5 mm. **Obv:** National arms, date below, large letters in legend and date, shield outlined **Rev:** Value above spray, B.C.C.R. below **Edge:** Segmented reeding

Date	Mintage	F	VF	XF	Unc	BU
2006(a)	—	—	—	—	4.50	6.00

KM# 240a 100 COLONES
8.8000 g., Brass Plated Steel, 29.4 mm. **Obv:** National arms above date **Rev:** Value above sprays **Edge:** Reeded

Date	Mintage	F	VF	XF	Unc	BU
2006	—	—	—	—	4.50	6.00
2007	—	—	—	—	4.50	6.00

KM# 239.1 500 COLONES
11.0000 g., Copper-Aluminum-Nickel, 32.9 mm. **Obv:** National arms **Obv. Legend:** REPUBLICA DE COSTA RICA **Rev:** Value above sprays, B.C.C.R. below, thick numerals **Edge:** Segmented reeding

Date	Mintage	F	VF	XF	Unc	BU
2003(a)	—	—	—	2.00	3.00	5.00
2005	—	—	—	2.00	3.00	5.00
2006	—	—	—	2.00	3.00	5.00

KM# 239.2 500 COLONES
Brass, 32.9 mm. **Obv:** National arms, date below **Obv. Legend:** REPUBLICA DE COSTA RICA **Rev:** Denomination above sprays, B.C.C.R. below, thin numerals **Edge:** Segmented reeding

Date	Mintage	F	VF	XF	Unc	BU
2003 Rare	100	—	—	—	—	250

KM# 239.1a 500 COLONES
10.8800 g., Brass Plated Steel, 33 mm. **Obv:** National arms, date below **Rev:** Value above sprays, B.C.C.R. below **Edge:** Segmented reeding

Date	Mintage	F	VF	XF	Unc	BU
2006	—	—	—	—	2.00	5.00
2007	—	—	—	—	2.00	5.00

CREEK NATION

POARCH CREEK INDIANS

SOVEREIGN NATION

MILLED COINAGE

KM# 1 DOLLAR
31.1341 g., 0.9990 Silver 0.9999 oz. ASW, 39 mm. **Subject:** Peace **Obv:** Tribal seal **Obv. Legend:** CREEK NATION OF INDIANS **Rev:** Indian on horseback left **Rev. Legend:** PEACE **Edge:** Reeded

Date	Mintage	F	VF	XF	Unc	BU
2004	20,000	—	—	—	35.00	—
2004 Proof	10,000	Value: 50.00				

KM# 2 DOLLAR
31.1050 g., 0.9990 Silver 0.9990 oz. ASW, 39 mm. **Subject:** 20th Anniversary of Recognition **Obv:** Young sky dancer right, symbol **Obv. Legend:** CREEK NATION OF INDIANS **Rev:** Busts of 5 tribal chiefs, symbol below **Rev. Legend:** SOVEREIGN NATION **Edge:** Reeded

Date	Mintage	F	VF	XF	Unc	BU
2004	20,000	—	—	—	35.00	—
2004 Proof	10,000	Value: 50.00				

KM# 7 DOLLAR
31.1050 g., 0.9990 Silver 0.9990 oz. ASW, 40.52 mm. **Obv:** Tribal seal **Obv. Legend:** CREEK NATION OF INDIANS **Rev:** Bust of Chief Menawa 3/4 left **Rev. Legend:** CHIEF MENAWA "THE GREAT WARRIOR" **Edge:** Reeded

Date	Mintage	F	VF	XF	Unc	BU
2005	20,000	—	—	—	35.00	—
2005 Proof	10,000	Value: 50.00				

KM# 8 DOLLAR

31.1050 g., 0.9990 Silver 0.9990 oz. ASW, 40.55 mm. **Obv:** Tribal seal **Obv. Legend:** CREEK NATION OF INDIANS **Rev:** Tchow-ee-put-o-kaw 3/4 right **Rev. Legend:** TCOW-EE-PUT-O-KAW **Edge:** Reeded

Date	Mintage	F	VF	XF	Unc	BU
2005	20,000	—	—	—	35.00	—
2005 Proof	10,000	Value: 50.00				

KM# 10 DOLLAR

31.1200 g., 0.9990 Silver 0.9995 oz. ASW, 41.61 mm. **Obv:** Dancer left at center right, a tribal seal at lower left **Obv. Legend:** CREEK NATION - OF INDIANS **Rev:** Warrior horseback 3/4 right **Rev. Legend:** SOVEREIGN NATION **Edge:** Reeded

Date	Mintage	F	VF	XF	Unc	BU
2006	20,000	—	—	—	35.00	—
2006 Proof	10,000	Value: 50.00				

KM# 11 DOLLAR

31.1700 g., 0.9990 Silver 1.0011 oz. ASW, 40.58 mm. **Obv:** Tribal seal **Obv. Legend:** CREEK NATION OF INDIANS **Rev:** Facing busts of Chief Tomochichi and his son with eagle **Rev. Legend:** CHIEF TOMOCHICHI **Edge:** Reeded

Date	Mintage	F	VF	XF	Unc	BU
2006	20,000	—	—	—	35.00	—
2006 Proof	10,000	Value: 50.00				

KM# 13 DOLLAR

31.1050 g., 0.9990 Silver 0.9990 oz. ASW, 40.58 mm. **Obv:** Sky Dancer **Obv. Legend:** CREEK NATION OF INDIANS **Rev:** Warrior on horseback **Rev. Legend:** CHIEF OPOTHLE YOHOLO **Edge:** Reeded

Date	Mintage	F	VF	XF	Unc	BU
2007	—	—	—	—	35.00	—
2007 Proof	10,000	Value: 50.00				

KM# 4 5 DOLLARS

6.1700 g., 0.9990 Gold 0.1982 oz. AGW, 22 mm. **Issuer:** Panda America **Subject:** Peace **Obv:** Symbol **Obv. Legend:** CREEK NATION OF INDIANS **Rev:** Indian horseback left **Edge:** Reeded

Date	Mintage	F	VF	XF	Unc	BU
2004 Proof	2,500	Value: 400				

KM# 9 5 DOLLARS

6.1700 g., 0.9990 Gold 0.1982 oz. AGW, 22.18 mm. **Obv:** Tribal seal **Obv. Legend:** CREEK NATION OF INDIANS **Rev:** Busts of Chief Hopothle Mico and George Washington 3/4 left **Rev. Legend:** CHIEF HOPOTHLE MICO • GEORGE WASHINGTON **Edge:** Reeded

Date	Mintage	F	VF	XF	Unc	BU
2005 Proof	2,500	Value: 400				

KM# 12 5 DOLLARS

6.1700 g., 0.9990 Gold 0.1982 oz. AGW, 22.2 mm. **Obv:** Tribal seal **Obv. Legend:** CREEK NATION OF INDIANS **Rev:** Bust of Chief Stee•Chaco•Me•Co **Rev. Legend:** CHIEF STEE • CHACO • ME • CO **Edge:** Reeded

Date	Mintage	F	VF	XF	Unc	BU
2006 Proof	2,500	Value: 400				

KM# 14 5 DOLLARS

6.1700 g., 0.9990 Gold 0.1982 oz. AGW, 22.2 mm. **Obv:** Tribal seal **Obv. Legend:** CREEK NATION OF INDIANS **Rev. Legend:** CHIEF CALVIN MCGHEE **Edge:** Reeded

Date	Mintage	F	VF	XF	Unc	BU
2007 Proof	2,500	Value: 400				

KM# 5 10 DOLLARS

15.5515 g., 0.9995 Palladium 0.4997 oz., 30 mm. **Subject:** 20th Anniversary of Recognition **Obv:** Young sky dancer right, symbol **Obv. Legend:** CREEK NATION OF INDIANS **Rev:** Busts of 5 tribal chiefs, symbol below **Rev. Legend:** SOVEREIGN NATION **Edge:** Reeded

Date	Mintage	F	VF	XF	Unc	BU
2004 Proof	250	Value: 750				

KM# 6 100 DOLLARS

31.1050 g., 0.9990 Gold 0.9990 oz. AGW, 31.94 mm. **Subject:** Treaty for Autonomy, 20th Anniversary **Obv:** Native dancer right at left center, tribal seal at right **Obv. Legend:** CREEK NATION - OF INDIANS **Rev:** Five portraits left to right, tribal seal below **Rev. Legend:** • SOVEREIGN NATION • **Edge:** Reeded

Date	Mintage	F	VF	XF	Unc	BU
2004 Proof	250	Value: 2,000				

CROATIA

The Republic of Croatia, (Hrvatska) bordered on the west by the Adriatic Sea and the northeast by Hungary, has an area of 21,829 sq. mi. (56,538 sq. km.) and a population of 4.7 million. Capital: Zagreb.

NOTE: Coin dates starting with 1994 are followed with a period. Example: 1994.

REPUBLIC

REFORM COINAGE

May 30, 1994 - 1000 Dinara = 1 Kuna; 100 Lipa = 1 Kuna

For the circulating minor coins, the reverse legend (name of item) is in Croatian for odd dated years and Latin for even dated years.

KM# 3 LIPA

0.7000 g., Aluminum, 17 mm. **Obv:** Denomination above crowned arms **Obv. Legend:** REPUBLIKA HRVATSKA **Rev:** Ears of corn, date below **Rev. Legend:** KUKURUZ **Edge:** Plain **Designer:** Kuzma Kovacic

Date	Mintage	F	VF	XF	Unc	BU
2001.	2,000,000	—	—	0.20	0.50	—
2001. Proof	1,000	Value: 2.50				
2003.	1,500,000	—	—	0.20	0.50	—
2003. Proof	1,000	Value: 2.50				
2005.	—	—	—	0.20	0.50	—
2005. Proof	2,000	Value: 2.00				
2007.	—	—	—	0.20	0.50	—
2007. Proof	1,000	Value: 2.00				
2009. In sets only	—	—	—	—	1.00	—
2009. Proof	—	Value: 2.00				
2011. Proof	—	Value: 2.00				

KM# 12 LIPA

0.7000 g., Aluminum, 17 mm. **Obv:** Denomination above crowned arms **Obv. Legend:** REPUBLIKA HRVATSKA **Rev:** Ears of corn, date below **Rev. Legend:** ZEA MAYS **Edge:** Plain

Date	Mintage	F	VF	XF	Unc	BU
2002.	3,000,000	—	—	0.40	1.00	—
2002. Proof	1,000	Value: 2.50				
2004.	2,000,000	—	—	0.40	1.00	—
2004. Proof	2,000	Value: 1.50				
2006.	—	—	—	0.40	1.00	—

Date	Mintage	F	VF	XF	Unc	BU
2006. Proof	1,000	Value: 1.50				
2008.	—	—	—	0.40	1.00	—
2008. Proof	1,000	Value: 1.50				
2010. Proof	—	Value: 1.50				
2012.	—	—	—	0.40	1.00	—
2012. Proof	—	Value: 1.50				

KM# 4 2 LIPE

0.9200 g., Aluminum, 19 mm. **Obv:** Denomination above crowned arms on half braid **Obv. Legend:** REPUBLIKA HRVATSKA **Rev:** Grapevine, date below **Rev. Legend:** VINOVA LOZA **Edge:** Plain

Date	Mintage	F	VF	XF	Unc	BU
2001.	2,986,000	—	—	0.40	1.00	—
2001. Proof	1,000	Value: 3.00				
2003.	2,000,000	—	—	0.40	1.00	—
2003. Proof	1,000	Value: 3.00				
2005.	—	—	—	0.40	1.00	—
2005. Proof	2,000	Value: 3.00				
2007.	—	—	—	0.40	1.00	—
2007. Proof	1,000	Value: 3.00				
2009. In sets only	—	—	—	—	2.00	—
2009. Proof	—	Value: 3.00				
2011. Proof	—	Value: 3.00				

KM# 14 2 LIPE

0.9200 g., Aluminum, 19 mm. **Obv:** Denomination above crowned arms on half braid **Obv. Legend:** REPUBLIKA HRVATSKA **Rev:** Grapevine, date below **Rev. Legend:** VITIS VINIFERA **Edge:** Plain **Designer:** Kuzma Kovacic

Date	Mintage	F	VF	XF	Unc	BU
2002.	2,000,000	—	—	0.80	2.00	—
2002. Proof	1,000	Value: 3.00				
2004.	2,000,000	—	—	0.80	2.00	—
2004. Proof	2,000	Value: 2.50				
2006.	—	—	—	0.80	2.00	—
2006. Proof	1,000	Value: 2.50				
2008.	—	—	—	0.80	2.00	—
2008. Proof	1,000	Value: 2.50				
2010. Proof	—	Value: 2.50				
2012.	—	—	—	0.80	2.00	—
2012. Proof	—	Value: 2.50				

KM# 5 5 LIPA

2.5000 g., Brass Plated Steel, 18 mm. **Obv:** Denomination above crowned arms **Obv. Legend:** REPUBLIKA HRVATSKA **Rev:** Oak leaves, date below **Rev. Legend:** HRAST LUZNJAK **Edge:** Plain **Designer:** Kuzma Kovacic

Date	Mintage	F	VF	XF	Unc	BU
2001.	6,598,000	—	—	0.40	1.00	—
2001. Proof	1,000	Value: 4.00				
2003.	13,000,000	—	—	0.40	1.00	—
2003. Proof	2,000	Value: 3.50				
2005.	—	—	—	0.40	1.00	—
2005. Proof	2,000	Value: 3.50				
2007.	—	—	—	0.40	1.00	—
2007. Proof	1,000	Value: 3.50				
2009.	—	—	—	0.40	1.00	—
2009. Proof	—	Value: 3.50				
2011.	—	—	—	0.40	1.00	—
2011. Proof	—	Value: 3.50				

KM# 15 5 LIPA

2.5000 g., Brass Plated Steel, 18 mm. **Obv:** Denomination above crowned arms **Obv. Legend:** REPUBLIKA HRVATSKA **Rev:** Oak leaves, date below **Rev. Legend:** QUERCUS ROBUR **Edge:** Plain **Designer:** Kuzma Kovacic

Date	Mintage	F	VF	XF	Unc	BU
2002.	3,500,000	—	—	0.80	2.00	—
2002. Proof	1,000	Value: 4.00				
2004.	2,000,000	—	—	0.80	2.00	—
2004. Proof	2,000	Value: 3.00				

Date	Mintage	F	VF	XF	Unc	BU
2006.	—	—	—	0.80	2.00	—
2006. Proof	1,000	Value: 3.00				
2008	—	—	—	0.80	2.00	—
2008. Proof	1,000	Value: 3.00				
2010.	—	—	—	0.80	2.00	—
2010. Proof	—	Value: 3.00				
2012.	—	—	—	0.80	2.00	—
2012. Proof	—	Value: 3.00				

KM# 6 10 LIPA

3.2500 g., Brass Plated Steel, 20 mm. **Obv:** Denomination above crowned arms **Obv. Legend:** REPUBLIKA HRVATSKA **Rev:** Tobacco plant, date below **Rev. Legend:** DUHAN **Edge:** Plain **Designer:** Kuzma Kovacic

Date	Mintage	F	VF	XF	Unc	BU
2001.	31,500,000	—	—	0.40	1.50	—
2001. Proof	1,000	Value: 5.00				
2003.	12,000,000	—	—	0.40	1.50	—
2003. Proof	1,000	Value: 5.00				
2005.	—	—	—	0.40	1.50	—
2005. Proof	2,000	Value: 5.00				
2007.	—	—	—	0.40	1.50	—
2007. Proof	1,000	Value: 5.00				
2009.	—	—	—	0.40	1.50	—
2009. Proof	1,000	Value: 5.00				
2011.	—	—	—	0.40	1.50	—
2011. Proof	—	Value: 5.00				

KM# 16 10 LIPA

3.2500 g., Brass Plated Steel, 20 mm. **Obv:** Denomination above crowned arms on half braid **Obv. Legend:** REPUBLIKA HRVATSKA **Rev:** Tobacco plant, date below **Rev. Legend:** NICOTIANA TABACUM **Edge:** Plain **Designer:** Kuzma Kovacic

Date	Mintage	F	VF	XF	Unc	BU
2002.	2,000,000	—	—	0.80	2.50	—
2002. Proof	1,000	Value: 5.00				
2004.	2,000,000	—	—	0.80	2.50	—
2004. Proof	2,000	Value: 4.50				
2006.	—	—	—	0.80	2.50	—
2006. Proof	1,000	Value: 4.50				
2008.	—	—	—	0.80	2.50	—
2008. Proof	1,000	Value: 4.50				
2010.	—	—	—	0.80	2.50	—
2010. Proof	1,000	Value: 4.50				
2012.	—	—	—	0.80	2.50	—
2012. Proof	—	Value: 4.50				

KM# 7 20 LIPA

2.9000 g., Nickel Plated Steel, 18.5 mm. **Obv:** Denomination above crowned arms on half braid **Obv. Legend:** REPUBLIKA HRVATSKA **Rev:** Olive branch, date below **Rev. Legend:** MASLINA **Edge:** Plain **Designer:** Kuzma Kovacic

Date	Mintage	F	VF	XF	Unc	BU
2001.	23,000,000	—	—	0.45	1.50	—
2001. Proof	1,000	Value: 5.00				
2003.	12,500,000	—	—	0.45	1.50	—
2003. Proof	1,000	Value: 5.00				
2005.	—	—	—	0.45	1.50	—
2005. Proof	2,000	Value: 5.00				
2007.	—	—	—	0.45	1.50	—
2007. Proof	1,000	Value: 5.00				
2009.	—	—	—	0.45	1.50	—
2009. Proof	—	Value: 5.00				
2011.	—	—	—	0.45	1.50	—
2011. Proof	—	Value: 5.00				

KM# 17 20 LIPA

2.9000 g., Nickel Plated Steel, 18.5 mm. **Obv:** Denomination above crowned arms on half braid **Obv. Legend:** REPUBLIKA HRVATSKA **Rev:** Olive branch, date below **Rev. Legend:** OLEA EUROPAEA **Edge:** Plain

Date	Mintage	F	VF	XF	Unc	BU
2002.	2,000,000	—	—	0.80	2.50	—
2002. Proof	1,000	Value: 5.00				
2004.	2,000,000	—	—	0.80	2.50	—
2004. Proof	2,000	Value: 4.50				
2006.	—	—	—	0.80	2.50	—
2006. Proof	1,000	Value: 4.50				
2008.	—	—	—	0.80	2.50	—
2008. Proof	1,000	Value: 4.50				
2010.	—	—	—	0.80	2.50	—
2010. Proof	1,000	Value: 4.50				
2012.	—	—	—	0.80	2.50	—
2012. Proof	—	Value: 4.50				

KM# 8 50 LIPA

3.6500 g., Nickel Plated Steel, 20.5 mm. **Obv:** Denomination above crowned arms on half braid **Obv. Legend:** REPUBLIKA HRVATSKA **Rev:** Flowers, date below **Rev. Legend:** VELEBITSKA DEGENIJA **Edge:** Plain **Designer:** Kuzma Kovacic

Date	Mintage	F	VF	XF	Unc	BU
2001.	5,500,000	—	—	0.60	1.50	—
2001. Proof	1,000	Value: 5.50				
2003.	8,000,000	—	—	0.60	1.50	—
2003. Proof	1,000	Value: 5.50				
2005.	—	—	—	0.60	1.50	—
2005. Proof	2,000	Value: 5.00				
2007.	—	—	—	0.60	1.50	—
2007. Proof	1,000	Value: 5.00				
2009.	—	—	—	0.60	1.50	—
2009. Proof	—	Value: 5.00				
2011.	—	—	—	0.60	1.50	—
2011. Proof	—	Value: 5.00				

KM# 19 50 LIPA

3.6500 g., Nickel Plated Steel, 20.5 mm. **Obv:** Denomination above crowned arms on half braid **Obv. Legend:** REPUBLIKA HRVATSKA **Rev:** Flowers, date below **Rev. Legend:** DEGENIA VELEBITICA **Edge:** Plain **Designer:** Kuzma Kovacic

Date	Mintage	F	VF	XF	Unc	BU
2002.	2,000,000	—	—	0.80	2.50	—
2002. Proof	1,000	Value: 5.00				
2004.	2,000,000	—	—	0.80	2.50	—
2004. Proof	2,000	Value: 4.50				
2006.	—	—	—	0.80	2.50	—
2006. Proof	1,000	Value: 4.50				
2008.	—	—	—	0.80	2.50	—
2008. Proof	1,000	Value: 4.50				
2010.	—	—	—	0.80	2.50	—
2010. Proof	1,000	Value: 4.50				
2012.	—	—	—	0.80	2.50	—
2012. Proof	—	Value: 4.50				

KM# 9.1 KUNA

5.0000 g., Copper-Nickel-Zinc, 22.5 mm. **Obv:** Marten back of numeral, arms divide branches below **Obv. Legend:** REPUBLIKA HRVATSKA **Rev:** Nightingale left, two dates **Rev. Legend:** SLAVUJ **Edge:** Reeded **Designer:** Kusma Kovacic

Date	Mintage	F	VF	XF	Unc	BU
2001.	1,000,000	—	—	0.75	1.65	2.00
2001. Proof	1,000	Value: 4.50				
2003.	2,000,000	—	—	0.75	1.65	2.00
2003. Proof	1,000	Value: 4.50				
2005.	—	—	—	0.75	1.65	2.00
2005. Proof	2,000	Value: 4.50				
2007.	—	—	—	0.75	1.65	2.00
2007. Proof	1,000	Value: 4.50				
2009.	—	—	—	0.75	1.65	2.00
2009. Proof	—	Value: 4.50				
2011.	—	—	—	0.75	1.65	2.00
2011. Proof	—	Value: 4.50				

KM# 9.2 KUNA
5.0000 g., Copper-Nickel-Zinc, 22.5 mm. **Obv:** Crowned arms flanked by sprays, denomination above on marten **Rev:** Nightingale, left, '1994' above, date below **Edge:** Reeded

Date	Mintage	F	VF	XF	Unc	BU
2001 Proof	—	Value: 4.00				

KM# 20.1 KUNA
5.0000 g., Copper-Nickel-Zinc, 22.5 mm. **Obv:** Marten back of numeral, arms divide branches below **Rev:** Nightingale left, date below **Rev. Legend:** Error spelling "LUSCINNIA" MEGARHYNCHOS **Edge:** Reeded **Designer:** Kuzma Kovacic **Note:** Formerly KM-20

Date	Mintage	F	VF	XF	Unc	BU
2002.	—	—	—	—	—	2.00

KM# 20.2 KUNA
5.0000 g., Copper-Nickel-Zinc, 22.5 mm. **Obv:** Marten back of numeral, arms divide branches below **Obv. Legend:** REPUBLIKA HRVATSKA **Rev:** Nightingale left, date below **Rev. Legend:** Correct spelling "LUSCINIA" MEGARHYNCHOS **Edge:** Reeded **Designer:** Kuzma Kovacic

Date	Mintage	F	VF	XF	Unc	BU
2002.	1,000,000	—	—	1.00	3.00	—
2002. Proof	1,000	Value: 5.00				
2006.	—	—	—	1.00	3.00	—
2006. Proof	1,000	Value: 5.00				
2008.	—	—	—	1.00	3.00	—
2008. Proof	1,000	Value: 5.00				
2010.	—	—	—	1.00	3.00	—
2010. Proof	—	Value: 5.00				
2012.	—	—	—	1.00	3.00	—
2012. Proof	—	Value: 5.00				

KM# 79 KUNA
5.0000 g., Copper-Nickel-Zinc, 22.5 mm. **Subject:** 10th Anniversary of National Currency **Obv:** Crowned arms flanked by sprays, denomination above on marten **Obv. Legend:** REPUBLIKA HRVATSKA **Rev:** Nightingale left, date below **Rev. Legend:** MEGARHYNCHOS **Edge:** Reeded

Date	Mintage	F	VF	XF	Unc	BU
ND(2004)	30,000	—	—	1.00	3.00	—
ND(2004) Proof	2,000	Value: 5.00				

KM# 10 2 KUNE
6.2000 g., Copper-Nickel-Zinc, 24.5 mm. **Obv:** Marten back of numeral, arms divide branches below **Obv. Legend:** REPUBLIKA HRVATSKA **Rev:** Bluefin tuna right, date below **Rev. Legend:** TUNJ **Edge:** Reeded **Designer:** Kuzma Kovacic

Date	Mintage	F	VF	XF	Unc	BU
2001.	1,250,000	—	—	1.00	2.00	—
2001. Proof	1,000	Value: 6.50				
2003.	7,250,000	—	—	1.00	2.00	—
2003. Proof	1,000	Value: 6.50				
2005.	—	—	—	1.00	2.00	—
2005. Proof	2,000	Value: 6.50				
2007.	—	—	—	1.00	2.00	—
2007. Proof	1,000	Value: 6.50				
2009.	—	—	—	1.00	2.00	—
2009. Proof	—	Value: 6.50				
2011.	—	—	—	1.00	2.00	—
2011. Proof	—	Value: 6.50				

KM# 21 2 KUNE
6.2000 g., Copper-Nickel-Zinc, 24.5 mm. **Obv:** Marten back of numeral, arms divide branches below **Obv. Legend:** REPUBLIKA HRVATSKA **Rev:** Bluefin tuna right, date below **Rev. Legend:** THUNNUS - THYNNUS **Edge:** Reeded **Designer:** Kuzma Kovacic

Date	Mintage	F	VF	XF	Unc	BU
2002.	1,000,000	—	—	1.50	3.00	—
2002. Proof	1,000	Value: 6.00				
2004.	2,000,000	—	—	1.50	3.00	—
2004. Proof	2,000	Value: 5.50				
2006.	—	—	—	1.50	3.00	—
2006. Proof	1,000	Value: 5.50				
2008.	—	—	—	1.50	3.00	—
2008. Proof	1,000	Value: 5.50				
2010.	—	—	—	1.50	3.00	—
2010. Proof	—	Value: 5.50				
2012.	—	—	—	1.50	3.00	—
2012. Proof	—	Value: 5.50				

KM# 11 5 KUNA
7.4500 g., Copper-Nickel-Zinc, 26.7 mm. **Obv:** Marten back of numeral, arms divide branches below **Obv. Legend:** REPUBLIKA HRVATSKA **Rev:** Brown bear left, date below **Rev. Legend:** MRKI MEDVJED **Edge:** Reeded

Date	Mintage	F	VF	XF	Unc	BU
2001.	17,300,000	—	—	1.50	5.00	10.00
2001. Proof	1,000	Value: 9.00				
2003.	1,000,000	—	—	1.50	5.00	10.00
2003. Proof	1,000	Value: 9.00				
2005.	—	—	—	1.50	5.00	10.00
2005. Proof	2,000	Value: 9.00				
2007.	—	—	—	1.50	5.00	10.00
2007. Proof	1,000	Value: 9.00				
2009.	—	—	—	1.50	5.00	10.00
2009. Proof	—	Value: 9.00				
2011.	—	—	—	1.50	5.00	10.00
2011. Proof	—	Value: 9.00				

KM# 23 5 KUNA
7.4500 g., Copper-Nickel-Zinc, 26.5 mm. **Obv:** Marten back of numeral, arms divide branches below **Obv. Legend:** REPUBLIKA HRVATSKA **Rev:** Brown bear left, date below **Rev. Legend:** URSUS ARCTOS **Edge:** Reeded

Date	Mintage	F	VF	XF	Unc	BU
2002.	2,000,000	—	—	2.00	5.00	9.00
2002. Proof	1,000	Value: 9.00				
2004.	2,000,000	—	—	2.00	5.00	9.00
2004. Proof	2,000	Value: 8.00				
2006.	—	—	—	2.00	5.00	9.00
2006. Proof	1,000	Value: 8.00				
2008.	—	—	—	2.00	5.00	9.00
2008. Proof	1,000	Value: 8.00				
2010.	—	—	—	2.00	5.00	9.00
2010. Proof	—	Value: 8.00				
2012.	—	—	—	2.00	5.00	9.00
2012. Proof	—	Value: 8.00				

KM# 66 25 KUNA
12.7500 g., Bi-Metallic Brass center in Copper-Nickel ring, 32 mm. **Subject:** 10th Anniversary of International Recognition **Obv:** Denomination in 3-D on outlined marten within circle, arms divide sprays below **Rev:** National map **Edge:** Plain **Shape:** 12-sided

Date	Mintage	F	VF	XF	Unc	BU
ND(2002)	200,000	—	—	—	8.50	—

KM# 78 25 KUNA
12.7500 g., Bi-Metallic Brass center in Copper-Nickel ring, 32 mm. **Subject:** Croatian European Union Candidacy **Obv:** Denomination in 3-D on outlined marten within circle, arms divide sprays below **Rev:** Joined squares within circle of stars **Edge:** Plain **Shape:** 12-sided

Date	Mintage	F	VF	XF	Unc	BU
ND (2004)	30,000	—	—	—	10.00	—
ND (2004) Proof	—	Value: 25.00				

KM# 93 25 KUNA
12.7500 g., Bi-Metallic Brass center in Copper-Nickel ring, 32 mm. **Subject:** EBRD Annual Meeting, Zagreb **Obv:** Large value at center **Rev:** Stylized old and new skyline

Date	Mintage	F	VF	XF	Unc	BU
2010	—	—	—	—	—	10.00

KM# 83 150 KUNA
24.0000 g., 0.9250 Silver 0.7137 oz. ASW, 37 mm. **Subject:** 2006 Winter Olympics - Italy **Obv:** National arms below denomination **Rev:** Slalom skiing

Date	Mintage	F	VF	XF	Unc	BU
ND(2006) Proof	15,000	Value: 40.00				

KM# 84 150 KUNA
24.0000 g., 0.9250 Silver 0.7137 oz. ASW, 37 mm. **Subject:** 2006 World Soccer Championship - Germany **Obv:** National arms below denomination **Rev:** Soccer player

Date	Mintage	F	VF	XF	Unc	BU
ND(2006) Proof	50,000	Value: 35.00				

KM# 85 150 KUNA
24.0000 g., 0.9250 Silver 0.7137 oz. ASW, 37 mm. **Subject:** 2006 World Soccer Championship - Germany **Obv:** National arms above denomination **Rev:** Vignette

Date	Mintage	F	VF	XF	Unc	BU
ND(2006) Proof	10,000	Value: 45.00				

KM# 86 150 KUNA
24.0000 g., 0.9250 Silver 0.7137 oz. ASW, 37 mm. **Subject:** 150th Anniversary - Birth of Nikola Tesla **Obv:** National arms above induction motor and denomination **Rev:** Bust of Tesla

Date	Mintage	F	VF	XF	Unc	BU
ND(2006) Proof	5,000	Value: 50.00				

KM# 87 150 KUNA
24.0000 g., 0.9250 Silver 0.7137 oz. ASW, 37 mm. **Issuer:** Croatian National Bank **Subject:** 2008 Olympic Games - Peoples Republic of China **Obv:** National arms, value in laurel wreath **Rev:** T'ai-ho Tien gate in Beijing, athlete **Edge:** Plain **Edge Lettering:** Ag 925/1000 24 g 37 mm PP HNZ

Date	Mintage	F	VF	XF	Unc	BU
ND(2006) Proof	20,000	Value: 40.00				

KM# 88 150 KUNA
24.0000 g., 0.9250 Silver 0.7137 oz. ASW, 37 mm. **Subject:** Ican Mestrovic **Obv:** Squares and shamrocks **Rev:** Female kneeling with Irish harp

Date	Mintage	F	VF	XF	Unc	BU
2007	4,000	—	—	—	—	45.00

KM# 89 150 KUNA
24.0000 g., 0.9250 Silver 0.7137 oz. ASW, 37 mm. **Subject:** Benedikt Kotruljevic **Obv:** Pile of coins **Rev:** Bust right

Date	Mintage	F	VF	XF	Unc	BU
2007	10,000	—	—	—	—	40.00

KM# 90 150 KUNA
24.0000 g., 0.9250 Silver 0.7137 oz. ASW, 37 mm. **Subject:** Historic Ships - Dubrovnik Karaka **Obv:** Sail within compass **Rev:** Ship

Date	Mintage	F	VF	XF	Unc	BU
2007	10,000	—	—	—	—	40.00

KM# 91 1000 KUNA
7.0000 g., 0.9860 Gold 0.2219 oz. AGW, 22 mm. **Subject:** Andrija Monorovicic, 150th Anniversary of Birth **Obv:** Globe bisected showing layers **Rev:** Bust facing

Date	Mintage	F	VF	XF	Unc	BU
2007	2,000	—	—	—	—	425

KM# 92 1000 KUNA
7.0000 g., 0.9860 Gold 0.2219 oz. AGW, 22 mm. **Subject:** Marin Drzic **Obv:** Shield flanked by comedy and tragedy masks **Rev:** Half-length figure right

Date	Mintage	F	VF	XF	Unc	BU
2008	2,000	—	—	—	—	425

MINT SETS

KM#	Date	Mintage	Identification	Issue Price	Mkt Val
MS2	2002 (9)	—	KM#12, 14-17, 19, 20.1, 21, 23	—	25.00

PROOF SETS

KM#	Date	Mintage	Identification	Issue Price	Mkt Val
PS36	2001 (9)	—	KM#3-8, 9.2, 10, 11	—	45.00
PS37	2002 (9)	—	KM#12, 14-17, 19, 20.2, 21, 23	—	45.00
PS38	2003 (9)	—	KM#3-8, 9.1, 10, 11	—	45.00
PS39	2004 (9)	—	KM#12, 14-17, 19, 21, 23, 79	—	40.00
PS40	2005 (9)	—	KM#3-8, 9.1, 10-11	—	45.00
PS41	2006 (9)	—	KM#12, 14-17, 19, 20.2, 21, 23	—	40.00
PS42	2007 (9)	—	KM#3-8, 9.1, 10-11	—	45.00
PS43	2008 (9)	—	KM#12, 14-17, 19, 20.2, 21, 23	—	40.00
PS44	2009 (9)	—	KM#3-8, 9.1, 10-11	—	45.00
PS45	2010 (9)	—	KM#12, 14-17, 19, 20.2, 21, 23	—	45.00
PS46	2011 (9)	—	KM#3-8, 9.1, 10-11	—	45.00
PS47	2012 (9)	—	KM#12, 14-17, 19, 20.2, 21, 23	—	45.00

CUBA

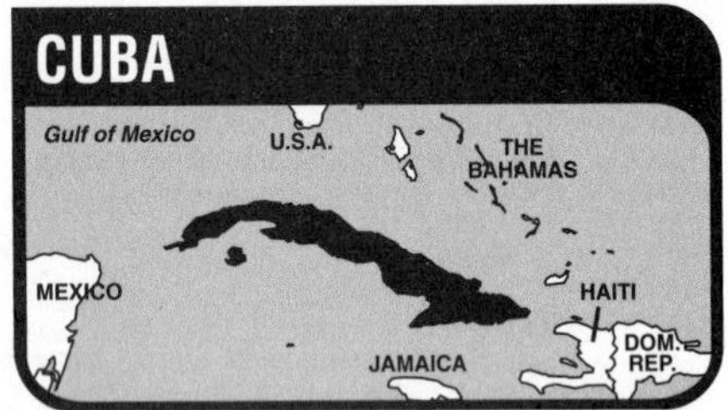

The Republic of Cuba, situated at the northern edge of the Caribbean Sea about 90 miles (145 km.) south of Florida, has an area of 42,804 sq. mi. (110,860 sq. km.) and a population of *11.2 million. Capital: Havana. The Cuban economy is based on the cultivation and refining of sugar, which provides 80 percent of export earnings.

MINT MARK
Key - Havana, 1977-

MONETARY SYSTEM
100 Centavos = 1 Peso

SECOND REPUBLIC
1962 - Present
DECIMAL COINAGE

KM# 33.3 CENTAVO
0.7500 g., Aluminum, 16.76 mm. **Obv:** Cuban arms within wreath, denomination below **Rev:** Roman denomination within circle of star, date below **Edge:** Plain **Note:** Shield varieties exist.

Date	Mintage	F	VF	XF	Unc	BU
2001	—	—	—	0.40	0.80	1.75
2002	—	—	—	0.40	0.80	1.75
2003	—	—	—	0.40	0.80	1.75
2004	—	—	—	0.40	0.80	1.75
2005	—	—	—	0.40	0.80	1.75
2006	—	—	—	0.40	0.80	1.75
2007	—	—	—	0.40	0.80	1.75
2008	—	—	—	—	0.80	1.75
2010	—	—	—	—	0.80	1.75
2012	—	—	—	—	0.80	1.75

KM# 34 5 CENTAVOS
1.5000 g., Aluminum, 21.21 mm. **Obv:** National arms within wreath, denomination below **Rev:** Roman denomination within circle of star, date below **Note:** Shield varieties exist.

Date	Mintage	F	VF	XF	Unc	BU
2001	6,703,331	—	0.10	0.25	0.75	1.50
2002	14,830,000	—	—	0.25	0.75	1.50
Note: High or low dates exist.						
2003	62,520,000	—	—	0.25	0.75	1.50
2004	62,520,000	—	—	0.25	0.75	1.50
2006	62,520,000	—	—	0.25	0.75	1.50
2007	62,520,000	—	—	0.25	0.75	1.50
2008	—	—	—	0.25	0.75	1.50
2009	—	—	—	0.25	0.75	1.50
2010	—	—	—	0.25	0.75	1.50

KM# 35.2 20 CENTAVOS
2.0000 g., Aluminum, 24 mm. **Obv:** National arms, revised shield **Rev:** Roman denomination within circle of star

Date	Mintage	F	VF	XF	Unc	BU
2002	—	4.00	7.00	10.00	15.00	—
Note: Large and small dates exist.						
2003	—	4.00	7.00	10.00	15.00	—
2005	—	4.00	7.00	10.00	15.00	—
2006	—	4.00	7.00	10.00	15.00	—

KM# 35.1 20 CENTAVOS
2.0000 g., Aluminum, 24 mm. **Obv:** Cuban arms within wreath, denomination below **Rev:** Roman denomination within circle of star, date below **Note:** Shield varieties exist.

Date	Mintage	F	VF	XF	Unc	BU
2002	25,000,000	—	0.50	1.00	2.00	4.00
2003	11,911,000	—	0.50	1.00	2.00	4.00
2005	—	—	0.50	1.00	2.00	4.00
2006	—	—	0.50	1.00	2.00	4.00
2007	—	—	0.50	1.00	2.00	4.00

KM# 844 PESO
26.0000 g., Copper-Nickel, 38 mm. **Subject:** Bolivar, 175th Anniversary of Liberation **Rev:** Bust

Date	Mintage	F	VF	XF	Unc	BU
2001	—	—	—	—	—	15.00

KM# 845 PESO
26.0000 g., Copper-Nickel, 38 mm. **Subject:** Bolivar - 175th Anniversary of Liberation **Rev:** Birthplace

Date	Mintage	F	VF	XF	Unc	BU
2001	—	—	—	—	—	15.00

KM# 846 PESO
Copper-Nickel, 38 mm. **Subject:** Boliver, 175th Anniversary of Liberation **Rev:** Battle scene

Date	Mintage	F	VF	XF	Unc	BU
2001	—	—	—	—	—	15.00

KM# 847 PESO
12.7000 g., Nickel Plated Steel, 32.5 mm. **Subject:** Cuban Fauna - Avellaneda Butterfly **Rev:** Butterfly

Date	Mintage	F	VF	XF	Unc	BU
2001	—	—	—	—	—	15.00

KM# 848 PESO
26.0000 g., Copper-Nickel, 38 mm. **Subject:** Global Conference Three

Date	Mintage	F	VF	XF	Unc	BU
2001	200	—	—	—	—	50.00

KM# 849 PESO
26.0000 g., Copper-Nickel, 38 mm. **Subject:** Monuments of Cuba **Rev:** Havana Cathedral

Date	Mintage	F	VF	XF	Unc	BU
2001	—	—	—	—	—	15.00

KM# 850 PESO
26.0000 g., Copper-Nickel, 38 mm. **Subject:** Monuments of Cuba **Rev:** Trinidad Cathedral

Date	Mintage	F	VF	XF	Unc	BU
2001	—	—	—	—	—	15.00

KM# 851 PESO
Copper-Nickel, 38 mm. **Subject:** Monuments of Cuba **Rev:** Templete

Date	Mintage	F	VF	XF	Unc	BU
2001	—	—	—	—	—	15.00

KM# 852 PESO
26.0000 g., Copper-Nickel, 38 mm. **Subject:** Playa Giron

Date	Mintage	F	VF	XF	Unc	BU
2001	—	—	—	—	—	15.00

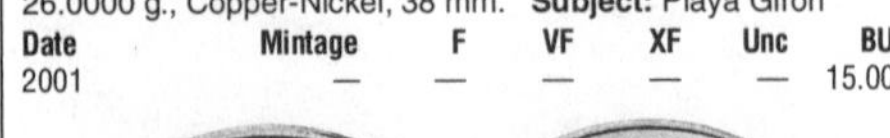

KM# 829 PESO
12.7000 g., Nickel Plated Steel, 32.5 mm. **Obv:** National arms **Rev:** Carpenter bird perched - multicolor **Rev. Legend:** FAUNA CUBANA - PAJERO CARPINTERO **Edge:** Plain

Date	Mintage	F	VF	XF	Unc	BU
2001	—	—	—	—	15.00	—

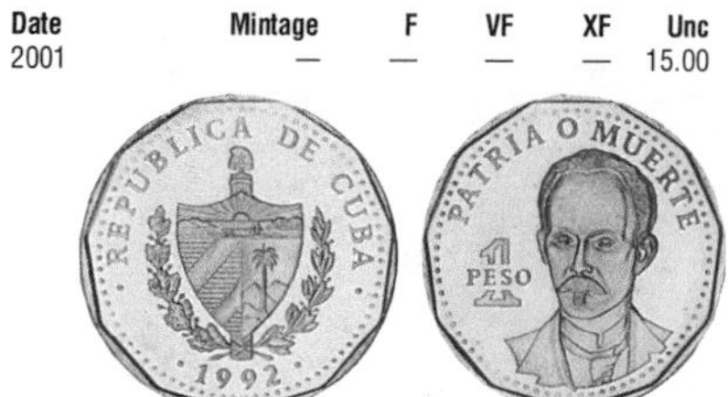

KM# 347 PESO

5.5200 g., Brass Plated Steel, 24.5 mm. **Subject:** Jose Marti **Obv:** National arms within wreath, denomination below **Rev:** Smaller Bust facing, denomination at left **Rev. Legend:** PATRIA O MUERTE **Note:** Rim varieties exist.

Date	Mintage	F	VF	XF	Unc	BU
2001	—	—	—	1.00	2.00	4.00
2002	—	—	—	1.00	2.00	4.00
2012	—	—	—	1.00	2.00	4.00

KM# 830 PESO

12.7000 g., Nickel Plated Steel, 32.5 mm. **Obv:** National arms **Rev:** Parrot perched - multicolor **Rev. Legend:** FAUNA CUBANA - COTORRA **Edge:** Plain

Date	Mintage	F	VF	XF	Unc	BU
2001	—	—	—	—	15.00	—

KM# 831 PESO

12.7000 g., Nickel Plated Steel, 32.5 mm. **Obv:** National arms **Rev:** Pink orchid - multicolor **Rev. Legend:** FLORA CUBANA - ORQUIDEAS **Edge:** Plain

Date	Mintage	F	VF	XF	Unc	BU
2001	—	—	—	—	20.00	—

KM# 832 PESO

12.7000 g., Nickel Plated Steel, 32.5 mm. **Obv:** National arms **Rev:** Yellow orchid - multicolor **Rev. Legend:** FLORA CUBANA - ORQUIDEAS **Edge:** Plain

Date	Mintage	F	VF	XF	Unc	BU
2001	—	—	—	—	20.00	—

KM# 833 PESO

12.7000 g., Nickel Plated Steel, 32.5 mm. **Obv:** National arms **Rev:** White orchid - multicolor **Rev. Legend:** FLORA CUBANA - ORQUIDEAS **Edge:** Plain

Date	Mintage	F	VF	XF	Unc	BU
2001	—	—	—	—	20.00	—

KM# 853 PESO

26.0000 g., Copper-Nickel, 38 mm. **Subject:** Federico Engels

Date	Mintage	F	VF	XF	Unc	BU
2002	—	—	—	—	—	15.00

KM# 854 PESO

26.0000 g., Copper-Nickel, 38 mm. **Subject:** Lenin

Date	Mintage	F	VF	XF	Unc	BU
2002	—	—	—	—	—	15.00

KM# 855 PESO

26.0000 g., Copper-Nickel, 38 mm. **Subject:** Mao Tse Tung

Date	Mintage	F	VF	XF	Unc	BU
2002	—	—	—	—	—	15.00

KM# 856 PESO

26.0000 g., Copper-Nickel, 38 mm. **Subject:** Karl Marx

Date	Mintage	F	VF	XF	Unc	BU
2002	—	—	—	—	—	15.00

KM# 951 PESO

Copper-Nickel **Rev:** Birds in color

Date	Mintage	F	VF	XF	Unc	BU
2002 Proof	—	Value: 60.00				

KM# 953 PESO

20.0000 g., Copper, 38 mm. **Subject:** Ernesto "Che" Guevara, 75th Birthday **Rev:** Bust

Date	Mintage	F	VF	XF	Unc	BU
2003	—	—	—	—	—	50.00

KM# 857 PESO

26.0000 g., Copper-Nickel, 38 mm. **Subject:** Che Guevara, 75th Anniversary of Birth

Date	Mintage	F	VF	XF	Unc	BU
2003	—	—	—	—	—	15.00

KM# 858 PESO

26.0000 g., Copper-Nickel, 38 mm. **Subject:** Che Guevara, 75th Anniversary of Birth

Date	Mintage	F	VF	XF	Unc	BU
2003	—	—	—	—	—	15.00

KM# 728 PESO

Silver **Subject:** Endangered Wildlife **Rev:** Crocodile

Date	Mintage	F	VF	XF	Unc	BU
2003	—	Value: 45.00				

KM# 859 PESO

26.0000 g., Copper-Nickel, 38 mm. **Subject:** Fauna - Hawk Pilgrin

Date	Mintage	F	VF	XF	Unc	BU
2004	—	—	—	—	—	17.00

KM# 860 PESO

26.0000 g., Copper-Nickel, 38 mm. **Subject:** Fauna Iberian Lynx

Date	Mintage	F	VF	XF	Unc	BU
2004	—	—	—	—	—	17.00

KM# 861 PESO

26.0000 g., Copper-Nickel, 38 mm. **Subject:** Fauna - Imperial Eagle

Date	Mintage	F	VF	XF	Unc	BU
2004	—	—	—	—	—	17.00

KM# 862 PESO

26.0000 g., Copper-Nickel, 38 mm. **Subject:** Fauna Lobo Gris

Date	Mintage	F	VF	XF	Unc	BU
2004	—	—	—	—	—	17.00

KM# 863 PESO

26.0000 g., Copper-Nickel, 38 mm. **Subject:** Fauna - Oso Pards

Date	Mintage	F	VF	XF	Unc	BU
2004	—	—	—	—	—	17.00

KM# 864 PESO

26.0000 g., Copper-Nickel, 38 mm. **Subject:** Fauna - Osprey

Date	Mintage	F	VF	XF	Unc	BU
2004	—	—	—	—	—	17.00

KM# 865 PESO

Copper-Nickel, 38 mm. **Subject:** Cuban Tobacco

Date	Mintage	F	VF	XF	Unc	BU
2005	—	—	—	—	—	17.00

KM# 866 PESO

26.0000 g., Nickel Plated Steel, 32.8 mm. **Subject:** Tropical Fish - Pygoplites **Obv:** National arms within wreath **Rev:** Pyglopites dicanthus

Date	Mintage	F	VF	XF	Unc	BU
2005	—	—	—	—	—	15.00

KM# 867 PESO

26.0000 g., Nickel Plated Steel, 32.8 mm. **Subject:** Tropical Fish - Zanclus **Obv:** National arms within wreath **Rev:** Zanclus canescens

Date	Mintage	F	VF	XF	Unc	BU
2005	—	—	—	—	—	15.00

KM# 868 PESO

26.0000 g., Nickel Plated Steel, 32.8 mm. **Subject:** Tropical Fish - Rhinecanthus **Obv:** National arms

Date	Mintage	F	VF	XF	Unc	BU
2005	—	—	—	—	—	15.00

KM# 924 PESO

Nickel Plated Steel **Subject:** Cuban Tobacco, 500th Anniversary **Rev:** Tobacco traders before caraval sailing ship

Date	Mintage	F	VF	XF	Unc	BU
2005 Proof	—	—	—	—	—	10.00

KM# 869 PESO

26.0000 g., Nickel Plated Steel, 38 mm. **Obv:** National arms within wreath **Rev:** Toucan

Date	Mintage	F	VF	XF	Unc	BU
2006	—	—	—	—	—	15.00

KM# 870 PESO

26.0000 g., Copper-Nickel, 38 mm. **Subject:** 29th Summer Olympics

Date	Mintage	F	VF	XF	Unc	BU
2006	—	—	—	—	—	15.00

KM# 871 PESO

26.0000 g., Copper-Nickel, 38 mm. **Subject:** Che Guevara, 40th Anniversary of his Death **Obv:** National arms within wreath **Rev:** Bust facing

Date	Mintage	F	VF	XF	Unc	BU
2007	—	—	—	—	—	15.00

KM# 871a PESO

26.0000 g., Copper, 38 mm. **Obv:** Che Guevara, 40th Anniversary of his Death

Date	Mintage	F	VF	XF	Unc	BU
2007	—	—	—	—	—	15.00

KM# 873 PESO

26.0000 g., Copper-Nickel **Subject:** Fauna - Buitre (Condor)

Date	Mintage	F	VF	XF	Unc	BU
2007	—	—	—	—	—	17.00

KM# 874 PESO

26.0000 g., Copper-Nickel, 38 mm. **Subject:** Fauna - Burro

Date	Mintage	F	VF	XF	Unc	BU
2007	—	—	—	—	—	17.00

KM# 875 PESO

26.0000 g., Copper-Nickel, 38 mm. **Subject:** Fauna - Cobra Montesa

Date	Mintage	F	VF	XF	Unc	BU
2007	—	—	—	—	—	17.00

KM# 876 PESO

26.0000 g., Copper-Nickel **Subject:** Fauna - Gato Montes

Date	Mintage	F	VF	XF	Unc	BU
2007	—	—	—	—	—	17.00

KM# 877 PESO

26.0000 g., Copper-Nickel, 38 mm. **Subject:** Fauma - Mastin Espanol

Date	Mintage	F	VF	XF	Unc	BU
2007	—	—	—	—	—	17.00

KM# 878 PESO

26.0000 g., Copper-Nickel, 26 mm. **Subject:** Fauna - Urogallo

Date	Mintage	F	VF	XF	Unc	BU
2007	—	—	—	—	—	17.00

KM# 879 PESO

26.0000 g., Copper-Nickel, 38 mm. **Subject:** Fortress - El Morro

Date	Mintage	F	VF	XF	Unc	BU
2007	—	—	—	—	—	17.00

KM# 880 PESO

26.0000 g., Copper-Nickel, 38 mm. **Subject:** Fortress - La Fuerza

Date	Mintage	F	VF	XF	Unc	BU
2007	—	—	—	—	—	15.00

KM# 881 PESO

26.0000 g., Copper-Nickel, 38 mm. **Subject:** Fortress - La Punta

Date	Mintage	F	VF	XF	Unc	BU
2007	—	—	—	—	—	15.00

KM# 882 PESO

26.0000 g., Copper-Nickel, 38 mm. **Subject:** Garibaldi

Date	Mintage	F	VF	XF	Unc	BU
2007	—	—	—	—	—	15.00

KM# 883 PESO

26.0000 g., Copper-Nickel, 38 mm. **Subject:** Santa Ana Ship

Date	Mintage	F	VF	XF	Unc	BU
2007	—	—	—	—	—	15.00

KM# 884 PESO

26.0000 g., Copper-Nickel, 38 mm. **Subject:** Sputnik

Date	Mintage	F	VF	XF	Unc	BU
2007	—	—	—	—	—	15.00

KM# 901 PESO

38.0000 g., Copper-Nickel, 38 mm. **Subject:** Ship - Principe Asturias

Date	Mintage	F	VF	XF	Unc	BU
2008	—	—	—	—	15.00	—

KM# 902 PESO

26.0000 g., Copper-Nickel, 38 mm. **Subject:** Ship San Carlos

Date	Mintage	F	VF	XF	Unc	BU
2008	—	—	—	—	15.00	—

KM# 903 PESO

38.0000 g., Copper-Nickel, 38 mm. **Subject:** Ship- San Hermene

Date	Mintage	F	VF	XF	Unc	BU
2008	—	—	—	—	—	15.00

KM# 907 PESO

41.0000 g., Copper, 45 mm. **Subject:** Revolution, 50th Anniversary **Obv:** National arms within wreath **Rev:** Five scenes in medallions

Date	Mintage	F	VF	XF	Unc	BU
2009 Antique patina	2,009	—	—	—	—	15.00

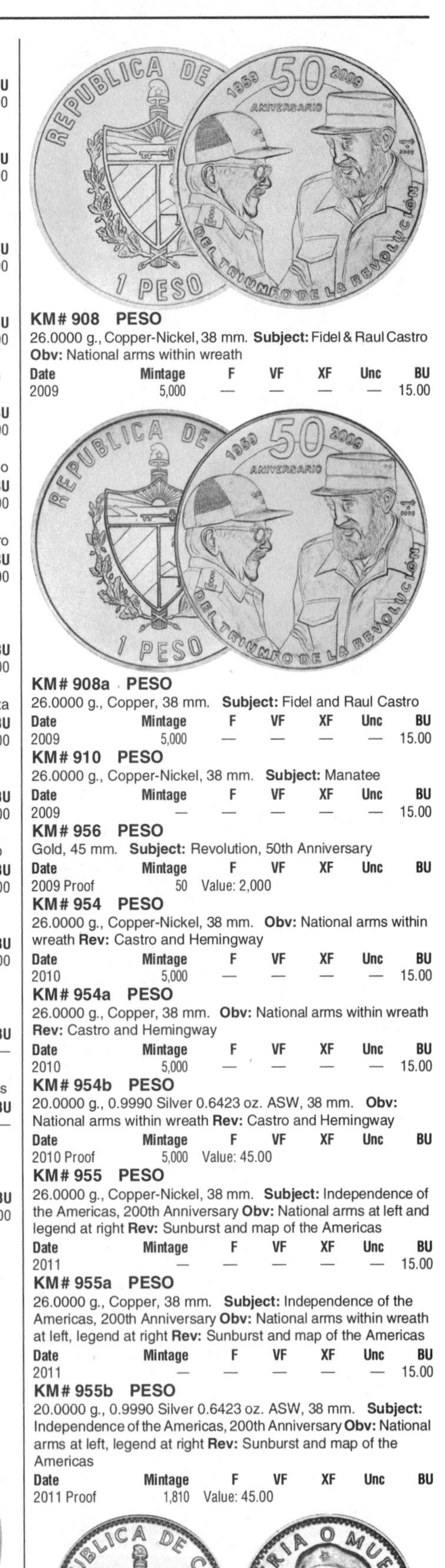

KM# 908 PESO

26.0000 g., Copper-Nickel, 38 mm. **Subject:** Fidel & Raul Castro **Obv:** National arms within wreath

Date	Mintage	F	VF	XF	Unc	BU
2009	5,000	—	—	—	—	15.00

KM# 908a PESO

26.0000 g., Copper, 38 mm. **Subject:** Fidel and Raul Castro

Date	Mintage	F	VF	XF	Unc	BU
2009	5,000	—	—	—	—	15.00

KM# 910 PESO

26.0000 g., Copper-Nickel, 38 mm. **Subject:** Manatee

Date	Mintage	F	VF	XF	Unc	BU
2009	—	—	—	—	—	15.00

KM# 956 PESO

Gold, 45 mm. **Subject:** Revolution, 50th Anniversary

Date	Mintage	F	VF	XF	Unc	BU
2009 Proof	50	Value: 2,000				

KM# 954 PESO

26.0000 g., Copper-Nickel, 38 mm. **Obv:** National arms within wreath **Rev:** Castro and Hemingway

Date	Mintage	F	VF	XF	Unc	BU
2010	5,000	—	—	—	—	15.00

KM# 954a PESO

26.0000 g., Copper, 38 mm. **Obv:** National arms within wreath **Rev:** Castro and Hemingway

Date	Mintage	F	VF	XF	Unc	BU
2010	5,000	—	—	—	—	15.00

KM# 954b PESO

20.0000 g., 0.9990 Silver 0.6423 oz. ASW, 38 mm. **Obv:** National arms within wreath **Rev:** Castro and Hemingway

Date	Mintage	F	VF	XF	Unc	BU
2010 Proof	5,000	Value: 45.00				

KM# 955 PESO

26.0000 g., Copper-Nickel, 38 mm. **Subject:** Independence of the Americas, 200th Anniversary **Obv:** National arms at left and legend at right **Rev:** Sunburst and map of the Americas

Date	Mintage	F	VF	XF	Unc	BU
2011	—	—	—	—	—	15.00

KM# 955a PESO

26.0000 g., Copper, 38 mm. **Subject:** Independence of the Americas, 200th Anniversary **Obv:** National arms within wreath at left, legend at right **Rev:** Sunburst and map of the Americas

Date	Mintage	F	VF	XF	Unc	BU
2011	—	—	—	—	—	15.00

KM# 955b PESO

20.0000 g., 0.9990 Silver 0.6423 oz. ASW, 38 mm. **Subject:** Independence of the Americas, 200th Anniversary **Obv:** National arms at left, legend at right **Rev:** Sunburst and map of the Americas

Date	Mintage	F	VF	XF	Unc	BU
2011 Proof	1,810	Value: 45.00				

KM# 346a 3 PESOS

8.0000 g., Nickel Plated Steel, 26.5 mm. **Obv:** National arms within wreath, denomination below **Rev:** Head facing, date below **Note:** Shield varieties exist.

Date	Mintage	F	VF	XF	Unc	BU
2002	—	—	—	2.50	5.00	7.00

KM# 739 5 PESOS
1.2400 g., Gold, 14 mm. **Subject:** Wonders of the Ancient World **Obv:** Cuban arms **Rev:** Ancient lighthouse of Alexandria

Date	Mintage	F	VF	XF	Unc	BU
2005 Proof	5,000	Value: 85.00				

KM# 740 5 PESOS
1.2400 g., Gold, 14 mm. **Subject:** Wonders of the Ancient World **Obv:** Cuban arms **Rev:** Colossus of Rhodes

Date	Mintage	F	VF	XF	Unc	BU
2005 Proof	5,000	Value: 75.00				

KM# 741 5 PESOS
1.2400 g., Gold, 14 mm. **Subject:** Wonders of the Ancient World **Obv:** Cuban arms **Rev:** Hanging Gardens of Babylon

Date	Mintage	F	VF	XF	Unc	BU
2005 Proof	5,000	Value: 75.00				

KM# 742 5 PESOS
1.2400 g., Gold, 14 mm. **Subject:** Wonders of the Ancient World **Obv:** Cuban arms **Rev:** Egyptian Pyramids

Date	Mintage	F	VF	XF	Unc	BU
2005	5,000	Value: 75.00				

KM# 743 5 PESOS
1.2400 g., Gold, 14 mm. **Subject:** Wonders of the Ancient World **Obv:** Cuban arms **Rev:** Temple of Artemis

Date	Mintage	F	VF	XF	Unc	BU
2005 Proof	5,000	Value: 75.00				

KM# 744 5 PESOS
1.2400 g., Gold, 14 mm. **Subject:** Wonders of the Ancient World **Obv:** Cuban arms **Rev:** Statue of Jupiter

Date	Mintage	F	VF	XF	Unc	BU
2005	5,000	Value: 75.00				

KM# 745 5 PESOS
1.2400 g., Gold, 14 mm. **Subject:** Wonders of the Ancient World **Obv:** Cuban arms **Rev:** Mausoleum of Halicarnas

Date	Mintage	F	VF	XF	Unc	BU
2005 Proof	5,000	Value: 75.00				

KM# 746 5 PESOS
1.2400 g., Gold, 14 mm. **Obv:** Cuban arms **Rev:** Cortes, Montezuma and Aztec Pyramid

Date	Mintage	F	VF	XF	Unc	BU
2005 Proof	15,000	Value: 75.00				

KM# 885 5 PESOS
12.0000 g., Silver, 30 mm. **Subject:** Che Guevara, 40th Anniversary of his Death

Date	Mintage	F	VF	XF	Unc	BU
2007 Proof	—	Value: 45.00				

KM# 763 10 PESOS
20.0000 g., 0.9990 Silver 0.6423 oz. ASW, 38 mm. **Subject:** Third Globalization Conference **Obv:** Cuban arms **Rev:** World map

Date	Mintage	F	VF	XF	Unc	BU
2001 Proof	100	Value: 200				

KM# 764 10 PESOS
20.0000 g., 0.9990 Silver 0.6423 oz. ASW, 38 mm. **Subject:** 40th Anniversary - Battle of Giron **Obv:** Cuban arms **Rev:** Soldiers on tank

Date	Mintage	F	VF	XF	Unc	BU
2001	—	—	—	—	—	30.00
2001 Proof	3,000	Value: 45.00				

KM# 765 10 PESOS
31.1035 g., 0.9990 Silver 0.9990 oz. ASW, 38 mm. **Subject:** 106th Anniversary - Jose Marti's **Obv:** Cuban arms **Rev:** Monument

Date	Mintage	F	VF	XF	Unc	BU
2001 Proof	2,000	Value: 50.00				

KM# 762 10 PESOS
31.1035 g., 0.9990 Silver 0.9990 oz. ASW, 38 mm. **Obv:** Cuban arms **Rev:** Two Bee hummingbirds

Date	Mintage	F	VF	XF	Unc	BU
2001 Proof	20,000	Value: 45.00				

KM# 766 10 PESOS
15.0000 g., 0.9990 Silver 0.4818 oz. ASW, 35 mm. **Subject:** Cuban Fauna **Obv:** Cuban arms **Rev:** Red-splashed Sulphur butterfly

Date	Mintage	F	VF	XF	Unc	BU
2001 Proof	5,000	Value: 40.00				

KM# 767 10 PESOS
15.0000 g., 0.9990 Silver 0.4818 oz. ASW, 35 mm. **Subject:** Cuban Fauna **Obv:** Cuban arms **Rev:** Cuban Parrot

Date	Mintage	F	VF	XF	Unc	BU
2001 Proof	5,000	Value: 40.00				

KM# 768 10 PESOS
15.0000 g., 0.9990 Silver 0.4818 oz. ASW, 35 mm. **Obv:** National arms **Rev:** Cuban (Green) woodpecker

Date	Mintage	F	VF	XF	Unc	BU
2001 Proof	5,000	Value: 40.00				

KM# 769 10 PESOS
15.0000 g., 0.9990 Silver 0.4818 oz. ASW, 35 mm. **Obv:** Cuban arms **Rev:** Multicolor white orchid

Date	Mintage	F	VF	XF	Unc	BU
2001 Proof	5,000	Value: 35.00				

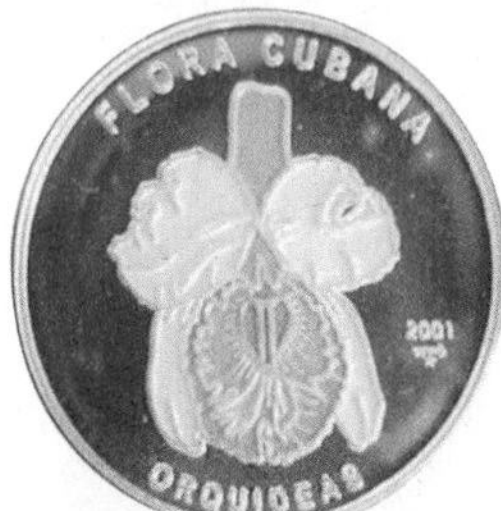

KM# 770 10 PESOS
15.0000 g., 0.9990 Silver 0.4818 oz. ASW, 35 mm. **Subject:** Cuban Flora **Obv:** Cuban arms **Rev:** Multicolor yellow orchid

Date	Mintage	F	VF	XF	Unc	BU
2001 Proof	5,000	Value: 35.00				

KM# 771 10 PESOS
15.0000 g., 0.9990 Silver 0.4818 oz. ASW, 35 mm. **Subject:** Cuban Flora **Obv:** Cuban arms **Rev:** Multicolor pink orchid

Date	Mintage	F	VF	XF	Unc	BU
2001 Proof	5,000	Value: 35.00				

KM# 772 10 PESOS
31.1035 g., 0.9990 Silver 0.9990 oz. ASW, 42 mm. **Obv:** Cuban arms **Rev:** Multicolor Santa Maria

Date	Mintage	F	VF	XF	Unc	BU
2001 Proof	4,000	Value: 55.00				

KM# 773 10 PESOS
15.0000 g., 0.9990 Silver 0.4818 oz. ASW, 35 mm. **Subject:** World Cup Soccer Champions **Obv:** Cuban arms **Rev:** Soccer player and stadium

Date	Mintage	F	VF	XF	Unc	BU
2001 Proof	7,500	Value: 35.00				

KM# 774 10 PESOS
20.0000 g., 0.9990 Silver 0.6423 oz. ASW, 38 mm. **Subject:** Cuban Monuments **Obv:** Cuban arms **Rev:** Trinidad street view

Date	Mintage	F	VF	XF	Unc	BU
2001 Proof	5,000	Value: 45.00				

KM# 775 10 PESOS
20.0000 g., 0.9990 Silver 0.6423 oz. ASW, 38 mm. **Subject:** Cuban Monuments **Obv:** Cuban arms **Rev:** Havana Cathedral

Date	Mintage	F	VF	XF	Unc	BU
2001 Proof	5,000	Value: 45.00				

KM# 776 10 PESOS
20.0000 g., 0.9990 Silver 0.6423 oz. ASW, 38 mm. **Subject:** Cuban Monuments **Obv:** Cuban arms **Rev:** Template building

Date	Mintage	F	VF	XF	Unc	BU
2001 Proof	5,000	Value: 45.00				

KM# 777 10 PESOS
31.1035 g., 0.9990 Silver 0.9990 oz. ASW, 38 mm. **Obv:** Cuban arms **Rev:** Bolivar standing at his birthplace

Date	Mintage	F	VF	XF	Unc	BU
2001 Proof	5,000	Value: 52.00				

KM# 828 10 PESOS
20.0000 g., 0.9990 Silver 0.6423 oz. ASW **Subject:** XVII World Soccer Championship - Korea and Japan 2002 **Obv:** National arms

Date	Mintage	F	VF	XF	Unc	BU
2001 proof	—	Value: 50.00				

KM# 778 10 PESOS
31.1035 g., 0.9990 Silver 0.9990 oz. ASW, 38 mm. **Obv:** Cuban arms **Rev:** Bolivar and map of South America

Date	Mintage	F	VF	XF	Unc	BU
2001 Proof	5,000	Value: 52.00				

KM# 779 10 PESOS
31.1035 g., 0.9990 Silver 0.9990 oz. ASW, 38 mm. **Subject:** 180th Anniversary of the Battle of Carabobo **Obv:** Cuban arms **Rev:** Bolivar leading troops

Date	Mintage	F	VF	XF	Unc	BU
2001 Proof	5,000	Value: 52.00				

KM# 734 10 PESOS
20.0000 g., 0.9990 Silver 0.6423 oz. ASW, 37.9 mm. **Subject:** Olympics **Obv:** Cuban arms **Rev:** Runner and ancient ruins **Edge:** Reeded

Date	Mintage	F	VF	XF	Unc	BU
2002 Proof	—	Value: 40.00				

KM# 780 10 PESOS
20.0000 g., 0.9990 Silver 0.6423 oz. ASW, 38 mm. **Subject:** World Cup Soccer Champions **Obv:** Cuban arms **Rev:** Soccer player and map above "CHILE 1962"

Date	Mintage	F	VF	XF	Unc	BU
2002 Proof	7,500	Value: 40.00				

KM# 781 10 PESOS
20.0000 g., 0.9990 Silver 0.6423 oz. ASW, 38 mm. **Subject:** World Cup Soccer Champions **Obv:** Cuban arms **Rev:** Soccer player and Cuauhtemoc head below MEXICO 1970

Date	Mintage	F	VF	XF	Unc	BU
2002 Proof	7,500	Value: 40.00				

KM# 782 10 PESOS
20.0000 g., 0.9990 Silver 0.6423 oz. ASW, 38 mm. **Obv:** Cuban arms **Rev:** Vasco De Gama and ship

Date	Mintage	F	VF	XF	Unc	BU
2002 Proof	5,000	Value: 45.00				

KM# 783 10 PESOS
20.0000 g., 0.9990 Silver 0.6423 oz. ASW, 38 mm. **Obv:** Cuban arms **Rev:** Americo Vespucio and ship

Date	Mintage	F	VF	XF	Unc	BU
2002 Proof	5,000	Value: 45.00				

KM# 784 10 PESOS
31.1035 g., 0.9990 Silver 0.9990 oz. ASW, 38 mm. **Subject:** Leaders of Communism **Obv:** Cuban arms **Rev:** Head of Mao Tse Tung left

Date	Mintage	F	VF	XF	Unc	BU
2002 Proof	2,000	Value: 55.00				

KM# 785 10 PESOS
31.1035 g., 0.9990 Silver 0.9990 oz. ASW, 38 mm. **Subject:** Leaders of Communism **Obv:** Cuban arms **Rev:** Head of Karl Marx 3/4 left

Date	Mintage	F	VF	XF	Unc	BU
2002 Proof	2,000	Value: 55.00				

KM# 786 10 PESOS
31.1035 g., 0.9990 Silver 0.9990 oz. ASW, 38 mm. **Subject:** Leaders of Communism **Obv:** Cuban arms **Rev:** Head of Vladimir Lenin right

Date	Mintage	F	VF	XF	Unc	BU
2002 Proof	2,000	Value: 65.00				

KM# 787 10 PESOS
31.1035 g., 0.9990 Silver 0.9990 oz. ASW, 38 mm. **Subject:** Leaders of Communism **Obv:** Cuban arms **Rev:** Head of Federico Engels 3/4 right

Date	Mintage	F	VF	XF	Unc	BU
2002 Proof	2,000	Value: 55.00				

KM# 788 10 PESOS
27.0000 g., 0.9990 Silver 0.8672 oz. ASW, 40 mm. **Subject:** IBERO-AMERICA Series **Obv:** Circle of arms around Cuban arms **Rev:** Santisima Trinidad ship

Date	Mintage	F	VF	XF	Unc	BU
2002 Proof	14,000	Value: 50.00				

KM# 952 10 PESOS
27.0000 g., 0.9250 Silver 0.8029 oz. ASW **Obv:** National Arms surrounded by 10 older arms **Rev:** Santisima Trinidad, sailing ship

Date	Mintage	F	VF	XF	Unc	BU
2002 Proof	—	Value: 60.00				

KM# 793 10 PESOS
31.1000 g., 0.9990 Silver 0.9988 oz. ASW, 38 mm. **Subject:** World Cup Soccer - Germany 2006 **Obv:** Cuban arms **Rev:** 5 soccer players

Date	Mintage	F	VF	XF	Unc	BU
2003 Proof	50,000	Value: 48.00				

KM# 789 10 PESOS
31.1035 g., 0.9990 Silver 0.9990 oz. ASW, 38 mm. **Subject:** Jose Marti's 150th Birthday **Obv:** Cuban arms **Rev:** Numbered infield behind head right

Date	Mintage	F	VF	XF	Unc	BU
2003 Proof	150	Value: 150				

KM# 794 10 PESOS
20.0000 g., 0.9990 Silver 0.6423 oz. ASW, 38 mm. **Subject:** Endangered Wildlife **Obv:** Cuban arms **Rev:** Cuban Crocodile

Date	Mintage	F	VF	XF	Unc	BU
2003 Proof	5,000	Value: 50.00				

KM# 795 10 PESOS
20.0000 g., 0.9990 Silver 0.6423 oz. ASW, 38 mm. **Subject:** Endangered Wildlife **Obv:** Cuban arms **Rev:** Ocelot

Date	Mintage	F	VF	XF	Unc	BU
2003 Proof	5,000	Value: 50.00				

KM# 792 10 PESOS
20.0000 g., 0.9990 Silver 0.6423 oz. ASW, 38 mm. **Obv:** Cuban arms **Rev:** Che Guevara, 75th Anniversary of Birth

Date	Mintage	F	VF	XF	Unc	BU
2003 Proof	5,000	Value: 45.00				

KM# 791 10 PESOS
20.0000 g., 0.9990 Silver 0.6423 oz. ASW, 38 mm. **Obv:** Cuban arms **Rev:** Sailing ship, Sovereign of the Seas

Date	Mintage	F	VF	XF	Unc	BU
2003 Proof	5,000	Value: 45.00				

KM# 790 10 PESOS
20.0000 g., 0.9990 Silver 0.6423 oz. ASW, 38 mm. **Obv:** Cuban arms **Rev:** Ferdinand Magellan, ship, and astrolab

Date	Mintage	F	VF	XF	Unc	BU
2003 Proof	5,000	Value: 45.00				

KM# 727 10 PESOS
Silver **Subject:** Endangered wildlife **Rev:** Iguana

Date	Mintage	F	VF	XF	Unc	BU
2003 Proof	—	Value: 45.00				

KM# 921 10 PESOS
Silver **Subject:** World Cup, Germany **Rev:** Five soccer players

Date	Mintage	F	VF	XF	Unc	BU
2003 Proof	50,000	Value: 60.00				

KM# 796 10 PESOS
20.0000 g., 0.9990 Silver 0.6423 oz. ASW, 38 mm. **Obv:** Cuban arms **Rev:** John Cabot's portrait in cameo above ship

Date	Mintage	F	VF	XF	Unc	BU
2004 Proof	5,000	Value: 45.00				

KM# 797 10 PESOS
15.0000 g., 0.9990 Silver 0.4818 oz. ASW, 35 mm. **Subject:** Hippocampus Kuda **Obv:** Cuban arms **Rev:** Spotted seahorse

Date	Mintage	F	VF	XF	Unc	BU
2004 Proof	5,000	Value: 50.00				

KM# 798 10 PESOS
20.0000 g., 0.9990 Silver 0.6423 oz. ASW, 38 mm. **Obv:** Cuban arms **Rev:** Murphy's Petrel bird on rock

Date	Mintage	F	VF	XF	Unc	BU
2004 Proof	5,000	Value: 50.00				

KM# 799 10 PESOS
20.0000 g., 0.9990 Silver 0.6423 oz. ASW, 38 mm. **Obv:** Cuban arms **Rev:** Cuban Rock Iguana on branch

Date	Mintage	F	VF	XF	Unc	BU
2004 Proof	5,000	Value: 50.00				

KM# 800 10 PESOS
31.1000 g., 0.9990 Silver 0.9988 oz. ASW, 38 mm. **Obv:** Cuban arms **Rev:** Imperial eagle perched on branch

Date	Mintage	F	VF	XF	Unc	BU
2004 Proof	1,000	Value: 60.00				

KM# 801 10 PESOS
31.1000 g., 0.9990 Silver 0.9988 oz. ASW, 38 mm. **Obv:** Cuban arms **Rev:** Bearded vulture in flight

Date	Mintage	F	VF	XF	Unc	BU
2004 Proof	1,000	Value: 60.00				

KM# 802 10 PESOS
31.1000 g., 0.9990 Silver 0.9988 oz. ASW, 38 mm. **Obv:** Cuban arms **Rev:** Iberian Lynx

Date	Mintage	F	VF	XF	Unc	BU
2004 Proof	1,000	Value: 60.00				

KM# 803 10 PESOS
31.1000 g., 0.9990 Silver 0.9988 oz. ASW, 38 mm. **Obv:** Cuban arms **Rev:** 2 grey wolves

Date	Mintage	F	VF	XF	Unc	BU
2004 Proof	1,000	Value: 65.00				

KM# 804 10 PESOS
31.1000 g., 0.9990 Silver 0.9988 oz. ASW, 38 mm. **Obv:** Cuban arms **Rev:** Brown bear

Date	Mintage	F	VF	XF	Unc	BU
2004	—	—	—	—	—	40.00
2004 Proof	1,000	Value: 65.00				

KM# 805 10 PESOS
31.1000 g., 0.9990 Silver 0.9988 oz. ASW, 38 mm. **Obv:** Cuban arms **Rev:** Peregrine Falcon perches on branch

Date	Mintage	F	VF	XF	Unc	BU
2004 Proof	1,000	Value: 65.00				

KM# 806 10 PESOS
20.0000 g., 0.9990 Silver 0.6423 oz. ASW, 38 mm. **Subject:** Monuments of Cuba **Obv:** Cuban arms **Rev:** University of Havana building

Date	Mintage	F	VF	XF	Unc	BU
2004 Proof	1,500	Value: 50.00				

KM# 807 10 PESOS
20.0000 g., 0.9990 Silver 0.6423 oz. ASW, 38 mm. **Subject:** Monuments of Cuba **Obv:** Cuban arms **Rev:** Fountain of India

Date	Mintage	F	VF	XF	Unc	BU
2004 Proof	1,500	Value: 50.00				

KM# 808 10 PESOS
20.0000 g., 0.9990 Silver 0.6423 oz. ASW, 38 mm. **Subject:** Monuments of Cuba **Obv:** Cuban arms **Rev:** Plaza building

Date	Mintage	F	VF	XF	Unc	BU
2004 Proof	1,500	Value: 50.00				

KM# 923 10 PESOS
15.0000 g., 0.9990 Silver 0.4818 oz. ASW **Rev:** Sea Horse and coral reef in color

Date	Mintage	F	VF	XF	Unc	BU
2004 Proof	—	Value: 40.00				

KM# 809 10 PESOS
27.0000 g., 0.9250 Silver 0.8029 oz. ASW, 40 mm. **Obv:** Cuban arms within circle of arms **Rev:** Portions of the old Havana Wall

Date	Mintage	F	VF	XF	Unc	BU
2005 Proof	12,000	Value: 75.00				

KM# 810 10 PESOS
20.0000 g., 0.9990 Silver 0.6423 oz. ASW, 38 mm. **Subject:** Tobacco **Obv:** Cuban arms **Rev:** Indian showing tobacco to Columbus, ship in background

Date	Mintage	F	VF	XF	Unc	BU
2005 Proof	2,000	Value: 50.00				

KM# 811 10 PESOS
20.0000 g., 0.9250 Silver 0.5948 oz. ASW, 38 mm. **Subject:** Columbus' Ships **Obv:** Cuban arms **Rev:** The Santa Maria under sail

Date	Mintage	F	VF	XF	Unc	BU
2005 Proof	5,000	Value: 45.00				

KM# 812 10 PESOS
20.0000 g., 0.9250 Silver 0.5948 oz. ASW, 38 mm. **Subject:** Columbus' Ships **Obv:** Cuban arms **Rev:** The Nina under sail

Date	Mintage	F	VF	XF	Unc	BU
2005 Proof	5,000	Value: 45.00				

KM# 813 10 PESOS
20.0000 g., 0.9250 Silver 0.5948 oz. ASW, 38 mm. **Subject:** Columbus' Ships **Obv:** Cuban arms **Rev:** The Pinta under sail

Date	Mintage	F	VF	XF	Unc	BU
2005 Proof	5,000	Value: 45.00				

KM# 814 10 PESOS
20.0000 g., 0.9250 Silver 0.5948 oz. ASW, 38 mm. **Obv:** Cuban arms **Rev:** Cuban Solenodon on branch

Date	Mintage	F	VF	XF	Unc	BU
2005 Proof	5,000	Value: 45.00				

KM# 815 10 PESOS
15.0000 g., 0.9990 Silver 0.4818 oz. ASW, 35 mm. **Obv:** Cuban arms **Rev:** Multicolor Solenodon on branch

Date	Mintage	F	VF	XF	Unc	BU
2005 Proof	5,000	Value: 40.00				

KM# 816 10 PESOS
15.0000 g., 0.9250 Silver 0.4461 oz. ASW, 35 mm. **Subject:** Tropical Fish **Obv:** Cuban arms **Rev:** Picassofish (triggerfish)

Date	Mintage	F	VF	XF	Unc	BU
2005 Proof	2,000	Value: 40.00				

KM# 817 10 PESOS
15.0000 g., 0.9250 Silver 0.4461 oz. ASW, 35 mm. **Subject:** Tropical Fish **Obv:** Cuban arms **Rev:** Moorish Idol fish

Date	Mintage	F	VF	XF	Unc	BU
2005 Proof	2,000	Value: 40.00				

KM# 818 10 PESOS
15.0000 g., 0.9250 Silver 0.4461 oz. ASW, 35 mm. **Subject:** Tropical Fish **Obv:** Cuban arms **Rev:** Regal Angel fish

Date	Mintage	F	VF	XF	Unc	BU
2005 Proof	2,000	Value: 40.00				

KM# 819 10 PESOS
20.0000 g., 0.9990 Silver 0.6423 oz. ASW, 38 mm. **Subject:** Don Quijote, 400th Anniversary **Obv:** Cuban arms **Rev:** Don Quijote and Sancho looking at two windmills

Date	Mintage	F	VF	XF	Unc	BU
2005 Proof	5,000	Value: 50.00				

KM# 820 10 PESOS
31.1000 g., 0.9990 Silver 0.9988 oz. ASW, 38 mm. **Subject:** Maximo Gomez Centennial of Death **Obv:** Cuban arms **Rev:** Bust 3/4 left, numbered behind neck

Date	Mintage	F	VF	XF	Unc	BU
2005 Proof	100	Value: 220				

KM# 925 10 PESOS
27.0000 g., 0.9250 Silver 0.8029 oz. ASW, 40 mm. **Subject:** Ibero American sites **Rev:** Old City Wall

Date	Mintage	F	VF	XF	Unc	BU
2005	—	Value: 60.00				

KM# 821 10 PESOS
20.0000 g., 0.9250 Silver 0.5948 oz. ASW, 38 mm. **Subject:** XXIX Olympics **Obv:** Cuban arms **Rev:** Baseball player with bat, baseball background

Date	Mintage	F	VF	XF	Unc	BU
2006 Proof	15,000	Value: 45.00				

KM# 897 10 PESOS
27.0000 g., 0.9250 Silver 0.8029 oz. ASW, 40 mm. **Subject:** Ibero - American Series - Javelin

Date	Mintage	F	VF	XF	Unc	BU
2007 Proof	—	Value: 45.00				

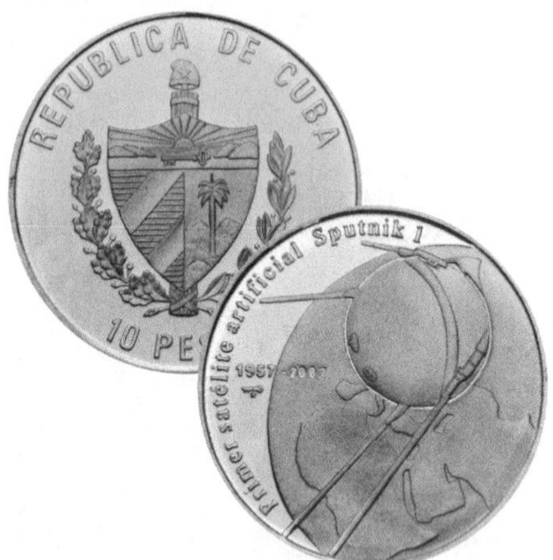

KM# 898 10 PESOS
20.0000 g., Silver, 38 mm. **Subject:** Sputnik

Date	Mintage	F	VF	XF	Unc	BU
2007 Proof	—	Value: 45.00				

KM# 886 10 PESOS
20.0000 g., Silver, 38 mm. **Subject:** Che Guevara, 40th Anniversary of his Death

Date	Mintage	F	VF	XF	Unc	BU
2007 Proof	—	Value: 45.00				

KM# 887 10 PESOS
20.0000 g., Silver, 38 mm. **Subject:** Fauna - Buitre (Condor)

Date	Mintage	F	VF	XF	Unc	BU
2007 Proof	—	Value: 45.00				

KM# 888 10 PESOS
20.0000 g., Silver **Subject:** Fauna Burro

Date	Mintage	F	VF	XF	Unc	BU
2007 Proof	—	Value: 45.00				

KM# 889 10 PESOS
20.0000 g., Silver, 38 mm. **Subject:** Fauna - Cobra Montesa

Date	Mintage	F	VF	XF	Unc	BU
2007 Proof	—	Value: 45.00				

KM# 890 10 PESOS
20.0000 g., Silver, 38 mm. **Subject:** Fauna - Gato Montes

Date	Mintage	F	VF	XF	Unc	BU
2007 Proof	—	—	—	—	—	45.00

KM# 891 10 PESOS
20.0000 g., Silver, 38 mm. **Subject:** Fauna - Mastin Espanol

Date	Mintage	F	VF	XF	Unc	BU
2007 Proof	—	Value: 40.00				

KM# 892 10 PESOS
20.0000 g., Silver, 38 mm. **Subject:** Fauna - Urogallo

Date	Mintage	F	VF	XF	Unc	BU
2007 Proof	—	Value: 45.00				

KM# 893 10 PESOS
20.0000 g., Silver, 38 mm. **Subject:** Fortress - El Morro

Date	Mintage	F	VF	XF	Unc	BU
2007 Proof	—	Value: 45.00				

KM# 894 10 PESOS
20.0000 g., Silver, 38 mm. **Subject:** Fortress - La Fuerza

Date	Mintage	F	VF	XF	Unc	BU
2007 Proof	—	Value: 45.00				

KM# 895 10 PESOS
20.0000 g., Silver, 38 mm. **Subject:** La Punta

Date	Mintage	F	VF	XF	Unc	BU
2007 Proof	—	Value: 45.00				

KM# 896 10 PESOS
20.0000 g., Silver, 38 mm. **Subject:** Garabaldi

Date	Mintage	F	VF	XF	Unc	BU
2007 Proof	—	Value: 45.00				

KM# 899 10 PESOS
20.0000 g., Silver, 38 mm. **Subject:** World Championship Soccer England

Date	Mintage	F	VF	XF	Unc	BU
2007 Proof	—	Value: 45.00				

KM# 904 10 PESOS
20.0000 g., 0.9990 Silver 0.6423 oz. ASW, 38 mm. **Subject:** Ship Principe Asturias

Date	Mintage	F	VF	XF	Unc	BU
2008 Proof	—	Value: 45.00				

KM# 905 10 PESOS
20.0000 g., 0.9990 Silver 0.6423 oz. ASW, 40 mm. **Subject:** Ship - San Carlos **Obv:** National arms within wreath

Date	Mintage	F	VF	XF	Unc	BU
2008 Proof	—	Value: 45.00				

KM# 906 10 PESOS
20.0000 g., 0.9990 Silver 0.6423 oz. ASW, 40 mm. **Subject:** Ship - San Hermene

Date	Mintage	F	VF	XF	Unc	BU
2008 Proof	—	Value: 45.00				

KM# 911 10 PESOS
20.0000 g., 0.9990 Silver 0.6423 oz. ASW, 38 mm. **Subject:** Fidel and Raul Castro

Date	Mintage	F	VF	XF	Unc	BU
2009 Proof	5,000	Value: 45.00				

KM# 912 10 PESOS
20.0000 g., 0.9990 Silver 0.6423 oz. ASW, 38 mm. **Subject:** Manatee **Obv:** National arms in wreath

Date	Mintage	F	VF	XF	Unc	BU
2009 Proof	—	Value: 45.00				

KM# 926 10 PESOS
27.0000 g., 0.9250 Silver 0.8029 oz. ASW, 40 mm. **Subject:** Ibero-American series - Historic coins **Obv:** Cuban arms at center of circle of other national arms **Rev:** Historic coin

Date	Mintage	F	VF	XF	Unc	BU
2010 Proof	12,000	Value: 60.00				

KM# 900 20 PESOS
62.2000 g., 0.9990 Silver 1.9977 oz. ASW, 45 mm. **Subject:** Che Guevara - 40th Anniversary of Death

Date	Mintage	F	VF	XF	Unc	BU
2007 Proof	—	Value: 100				

KM# 913 20 PESOS
62.2100 g., 0.9990 Silver 1.9980 oz. ASW, 45 mm. **Subject:** Revolution 50th Anniversary

Date	Mintage	F	VF	XF	Unc	BU
2009 Proof	1,959	Value: 150				

KM# 922 25 PESOS
7.7800 g., 0.9990 Gold 0.2499 oz. AGW **Subject:** Wold Cup, Germany **Rev:** Socer player and globe

Date	Mintage	F	VF	XF	Unc	BU
2004 Proof	25,000	Value: 475				

KM# 822 100 PESOS
31.1000 g., 0.9990 Gold 0.9988 oz. AGW, 38 mm. **Subject:** 100th Anniversary - Death of Marti **Obv:** Cuban arms **Rev:** Monument

Date	Mintage	F	VF	XF	Unc	BU
2001 Proof	100	Value: 1,850				

PESO CONVERTIBLE SERIES

KM# 733 CENTAVO
0.7500 g., Aluminum, 16.75 mm. **Obv:** Cuban arms **Rev:** Tower and denomination **Edge:** Plain

Date	Mintage	F	VF	XF	Unc	BU
2001	—	—	—	—	2.00	—
2002	—	—	—	—	2.00	—
2003	—	—	—	—	2.00	—
2005	—	—	—	—	2.00	—
2007	—	—	—	—	2.00	—

KM# 729 CENTAVO
1.7000 g., Copper Plated Steel, 15 mm. **Obv:** National arms within wreath, denomination below **Rev:** Tower and denomination **Edge:** Reeded

Date	Mintage	F	VF	XF	Unc	BU
2002	—	—	—	—	3.00	—
2006	—	—	—	—	3.00	—
2007	—	—	—	—	3.00	—

KM# 575.2 5 CENTAVOS
2.6500 g., Nickel Plated Steel, 18 mm. **Obv:** National arms **Rev:** Casa Colonial **Note:** Coin alignment, recut designs.

Date	Mintage	F	VF	XF	Unc	BU
2001	—	—	—	—	1.00	—
2002	—	—	—	—	1.00	—
2003	—	—	—	—	1.00	—
2004	—	—	—	—	1.00	—
2006	—	—	—	—	1.00	—
2007	—	—	—	—	1.00	—
2008	—	—	—	—	1.00	—
2009	—	—	—	—	1.00	—

KM# 576.2 10 CENTAVOS
4.0000 g., Nickel Plated Steel, 20 mm. **Obv:** National arms **Rev:** Castillo de la Fuerza **Note:** Coin alignment, recut designs.

Date	Mintage	F	VF	XF	Unc	BU
2002	—	—	—	—	2.00	—
2003	—	—	—	—	2.00	—
2008	—	—	—	—	2.00	—
2009	—	—	—	—	2.00	—

KM# 577.2 25 CENTAVOS
5.6500 g., Nickel Plated Steel, 23 mm. **Obv:** National arms **Rev:** Trinidad **Note:** Coin alignment.

Date	Mintage	F	VF	XF	Unc	BU
2001	—	—	—	—	3.00	—
2002	—	—	—	—	3.00	—
2003	—	—	—	—	3.00	—
2006	—	—	—	—	3.00	—
2007	—	—	—	—	3.00	—
2008	—	—	—	—	3.00	—

KM# 578.2 50 CENTAVOS
7.5300 g., Nickel Plated Steel, 25 mm. **Obv:** Cuban arms **Rev:** Havana Cathedral **Note:** Coin alignment.

Date	Mintage	F	VF	XF	Unc	BU
2002	—	—	—	—	5.00	—
2007	—	—	—	—	5.00	—

KM# 579.2 PESO
8.5000 g., Nickel Plated Steel, 27 mm. **Obv:** National arms **Rev:** Guama **Edge:** Reeded **Note:** Coin alignment.

Date	Mintage	F	VF	XF	Unc	BU
2001	—	—	—	—	—	5.00
2007	—	—	—	—	—	5.00
2012	—	—	—	—	—	5.00

MINT SETS

KM#	Date	Mintage	Identification	Issue Price	Mkt Val
MS3	2001 (3)	—	KM#831-833	—	62.50

CYPRUS

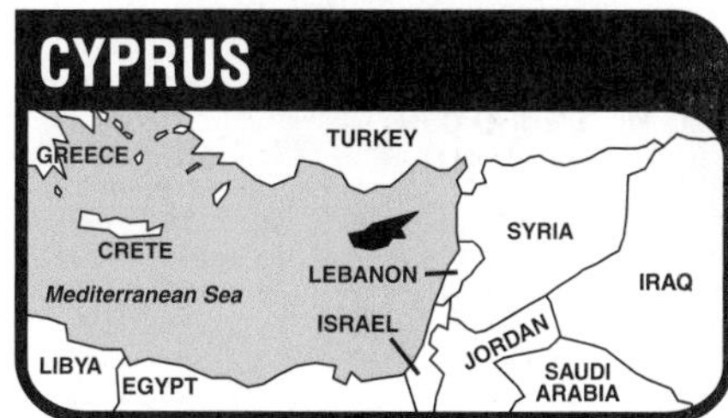

The island of Cyprus lies in the eastern Mediterranean Sea 44 miles (71 km.) south of Turkey and 60 miles (97 km.) off the Syrian coast. It is the third largest island in the Mediterranean Sea, having an area of 3,572 sq. mi. (9,251 sq. km.) and a population of 736,636. Capital: Nicosia. Agriculture, light manufacturing and tourism are the chief industries. Citrus fruit, potatoes, footwear and clothing are exported

Cyprus is a member of the Commonwealth of Nations. The president is Chief of State and Head of Government. Cyprus is also a member of the European Union since May 2004.

MINT MARKS
no mint mark - Royal Mint, London, England
H - Birmingham, England

REPUBLIC

REFORM COINAGE

100 Cents = 1 Pound

KM# 53.3 CENT
2.0000 g., Nickel-Brass, 16.5 mm. **Obv:** Shielded arms within altered wreath, date below **Rev:** Stylized bird on a branch, denomination at left **Edge:** Plain

Date	Mintage	F	VF	XF	Unc	BU
2003	5,000,000	—	—	0.10	0.20	0.30
2004 Narrow figures	12,000,000	—	—	0.10	0.20	0.30

KM# 54.3 2 CENTS
2.5000 g., Nickel-Brass, 19 mm. **Obv:** Shielded arms within altered wreath, date below **Rev:** Stylized goats, denomination upper right **Edge:** Plain

Date	Mintage	F	VF	XF	Unc	BU
2003	5,000,000	—	—	0.15	0.25	0.35
2004	7,000,000	—	—	0.15	0.25	0.35

KM# 55.3 5 CENTS
3.7500 g., Nickel-Brass, 22 mm. **Obv:** Altered wreath around arms **Rev:** Stylized bull's head above denomination **Edge:** Plain

Date	Mintage	F	VF	XF	Unc	BU
2001	15,000,000	—	—	0.20	0.50	0.75
2004	15,000,000	—	—	0.20	0.50	0.75

KM# 56.3 10 CENTS
5.5000 g., Nickel-Brass, 24.5 mm. **Obv:** Altered wreath around arms **Rev:** Decorative vase, denomination above **Edge:** Reeded

Date	Mintage	F	VF	XF	Unc	BU
2002	10,000,000	—	—	0.35	0.75	1.00
2004 Narrow figures	7,000,000	—	—	0.35	0.75	1.00

KM# 62.2 20 CENTS
7.7500 g., Nickel-Brass, 27.25 mm. **Obv:** Altered wreath around arms **Rev:** Head left, denomination at right **Edge:** Reeded

Date	Mintage	F	VF	XF	Unc	BU
2001	15,000,000	—	—	—	1.00	1.50
2004	4,000,000	—	—	—	1.00	1.50

KM# 66 50 CENTS
7.0000 g., Copper-Nickel, 26 mm. **Subject:** Abduction of Europa **Obv:** National arms, date below **Rev:** Female figure riding bull right within square, denomination below **Edge:** Plain **Shape:** 7-sided

Date	Mintage	F	VF	XF	Unc	BU
2002	7,000,000	—	—	—	2.50	3.25
2004	5,000,000	—	—	—	2.50	3.25

KM# 96 POUND
28.2800 g., Copper-Nickel, 38.6 mm. **Obv:** National arms **Rev:** Butterfly on branch

Date	Mintage	F	VF	XF	Unc	BU
2002 Proof	—	Value: 50.00				

KM# 75 POUND
28.2800 g., Copper-Nickel, 38.6 mm. **Subject:** Cyprus Joins the European Union **Obv:** National arms **Rev:** Map in center with Triton trumpeting through a seashell **Edge:** Plain

Date	Mintage	F	VF	XF	Unc	BU
2004	3,000	—	—	—	25.00	50.00

KM# 75a POUND
28.2800 g., 0.9250 Silver 0.8410 oz. ASW, 38.6 mm. **Subject:** Cyprus Joins the European Union **Obv:** National arms **Rev:** Map and Triton trumpeting through a sea shell **Edge:** Plain

Date	Mintage	F	VF	XF	Unc	BU
2004 Proof	3,000	Value: 80.00				

KM# 76 POUND
28.2700 g., Copper-Nickel, 38.5 mm. **Obv:** National arms **Rev:** Mediterranean Monk Seal **Edge:** Plain

Date	Mintage	F	VF	XF	Unc	BU
2005 Proof	4,000	Value: 50.00				

KM# 76a POUND
28.2800 g., 0.9250 Silver 0.8410 oz. ASW, 38.61 mm. **Obv:** National arms **Rev:** Mediterranean Monk Seal **Edge:** Plain

Date	Mintage	F	VF	XF	Unc	BU
2005 Proof	4,000	Value: 60.00				

KM# 77 POUND
28.2800 g., Copper-Nickel, 38.6 mm. **Obv:** National arms **Rev:** Akamas Centaurea flowers **Edge:** Plain

Date	Mintage	F	VF	XF	Unc	BU
2006 Proof	6,000	Value: 30.00				

KM# 77a POUND
28.2800 g., 0.9250 Silver 0.8410 oz. ASW, 38.61 mm. **Obv:** National arms **Rev:** Akamas Centaurea flowers **Edge:** Plain

Date	Mintage	F	VF	XF	Unc	BU
2006 Proof	3,000	Value: 75.00				

KM# 86 POUND
28.2800 g., Copper-Nickel, 38.6 mm. **Subject:** 50th Anniversary Treaty of Rome **Obv:** National arms **Rev:** Open Treaty Book **Edge:** Plain

Date	Mintage	F	VF	XF	Unc	BU
2007 Prooflike	10,000	Value: 28.00				

KM# 87 20 POUNDS
7.9880 g., Gold, 22.05 mm. **Obv:** National arms **Rev:** Greek god Triton, trumpeter (messenger) of the deep sea below outlined map of Cyprus

Date	Mintage	F	VF	XF	Unc	BU
2004 Proof	1,500	Value: 1,000				

EURO COINAGE

European Union Issues

KM# 78 EURO CENT
2.3000 g., Copper Plated Steel, 16.25 mm. **Obv:** Two Mouflons **Rev:** Large value at left, globe at lower right **Edge:** Plain

Date	Mintage	F	VF	XF	Unc	BU
2008	40,000,000	—	—	—	0.35	0.50
2009	20,000,000	—	—	—	0.35	0.50
2010	200,000	—	—	—	0.35	0.50
2011	—	—	—	—	0.35	0.50
2012	—	—	—	—	0.35	0.50

KM# 79 2 EURO CENT
3.0600 g., Copper Plated Steel, 18.75 mm. **Obv:** Two Mouflons **Rev:** Large value at left, globe at lower right **Edge:** Grooved

Date	Mintage	F	VF	XF	Unc	BU
2008	100,000,000	—	—	—	0.50	0.75
2009	1,000,000	—	—	—	0.50	0.75
2010	200,000	—	—	—	0.50	0.75
2011	—	—	—	—	0.50	0.75
2012	—	—	—	—	0.50	0.75

KM# 80 5 EURO CENT
3.9200 g., Copper Plated Steel, 21.25 mm. **Obv:** Two Mouflons **Rev:** Large value at left, globe at lower right **Edge:** Plain

Date	Mintage	F	VF	XF	Unc	BU
2008	60,000,000	—	—	—	1.00	1.25
2009	6,000,000	—	—	—	1.00	1.25
2010	200,000	—	—	—	1.00	1.25
2011	—	—	—	—	1.00	1.25
2012	—	—	—	—	1.00	1.25

KM# 81 10 EURO CENT
4.1000 g., Brass, 19.75 mm. **Obv:** Early sailing boat **Rev:** Modified outline of Europe at left, large value at right **Edge:** Reeded

Date	Mintage	F	VF	XF	Unc	BU
2008	70,000,000	—	—	—	1.25	1.50
2009	1,000,000	—	—	—	1.25	1.50
2010	200,000	—	—	—	1.25	1.50
2011	—	—	—	—	1.25	1.50
2012	—	—	—	—	1.25	1.50

KM# 82 20 EURO CENT
5.7400 g., Brass, 22.25 mm. **Obv:** Early sailing boat **Rev:** Modified outline of Europe at left, large value at right **Edge:** Notched

Date	Mintage	F	VF	XF	Unc	BU
2008	65,000,000	—	—	—	1.50	2.00
2009	1,000,000	—	—	—	1.50	2.00
2010	200,000	—	—	—	1.50	2.00
2011	—	—	—	—	1.50	2.00
2012	—	—	—	—	1.50	2.00

KM# 83 50 EURO CENT
7.8000 g., Brass, 24.25 mm. **Obv:** Early sailing boat **Rev:** Modified outline of Europe at left, large value at right **Edge:** Reeded

Date	Mintage	F	VF	XF	Unc	BU
2008	30,000,000	—	—	—	2.00	2.50
2009	1,000,000	—	—	—	2.00	2.50
2010	200,000	—	—	—	2.00	2.50
2011	—	—	—	—	2.00	2.50
2012	—	—	—	—	2.00	2.50

KM# 84 EURO
7.5000 g., Bi-Metallic Copper-Nickel center in Nickel-Brass ring, 23.25 mm. **Obv:** Ancient cross shaped idol discovered in the village of Pomos in the distrct of Paphos. **Rev:** Large value at left, modified outline of Europe at right **Edge:** Segmented reeding

Date	Mintage	F	VF	XF	Unc	BU
2008	28,000,000	—	—	—	3.50	5.00
2009	4,000,000	—	—	—	3.50	5.00
2010	200,000	—	—	—	3.50	5.00
2011	—	—	—	—	3.50	5.00
2012	—	—	—	—	3.50	5.00

KM# 85 2 EURO
8.5000 g., Bi-Metallic Nickel-Brass center in Copper-Nickel ring, 25.75 mm. **Obv:** Ancient cross shaped idol discovered in the village of Pomos in the distrct of Paphos. **Rev:** Large value at left, modified outline of Europe at right

Date	Mintage	F	VF	XF	Unc	BU
2008	25,000,000	—	—	—	5.00	7.00
2009	5,000,000	—	—	—	5.00	7.00
2010	200,000	—	—	—	5.00	7.00
2011	—	—	—	—	5.00	7.00
2012	—	—	—	—	5.00	7.00

KM# 89 2 EURO
8.5000 g., Bi-Metallic Nickel-Brass center in Copper-Nickel ring, 25.75 mm. **Subject:** 10th Anniversary of Euro **Obv:** Ancient statue wearing a cross found in Solol **Rev:** Childs drawing of a stick figure and 2E

Date	Mintage	F	VF	XF	Unc	BU
2009	980,000	—	—	—	5.00	7.00
2009 Special Unc.	20,000	—	—	—	—	15.00
2009 Proof	—	Value: 25.00				

KM# 97 2 EURO
8.5000 g., Bi-Metallic Nickel-Brass center in Copper-Nickel ring, 25.75 mm. **Subject:** Euro Coinage, 10th Anniversary **Obv:** Euro symbol on globe, child-like rendering around

Date	Mintage	F	VF	XF	Unc	BU
2012	1,000,000	—	—	—	6.00	8.00
2012 Special Unc.	5,000	—	—	—	—	15.00
2012 Proof	8,000	Value: 25.00				

KM# 88 5 EURO
28.2800 g., 0.9250 Silver 0.8410 oz. ASW, 38.61 mm. **Subject:** Entry into Euro Zone **Obv:** National arms **Rev:** Euro band around outlined Europe and Cyprus **Edge:** Reeded

Date	Mintage	F	VF	XF	Unc	BU
2008 Proof	15,000	Value: 75.00				

KM# 94 5 EURO
28.2800 g., 0.9250 Silver 0.8410 oz. ASW, 38.61 mm. **Subject:** Republic of Cyprus, 50th Anniversary **Obv:** National arms **Rev:** Bird in stylized tree **Designer:** Clara Zacharaki-Georgiou

Date	Mintage	F	VF	XF	Unc	BU
2010 Proof	5,000	Value: 65.00				

KM# 95 20 EURO
7.9900 g., 0.9000 Gold 0.2312 oz. AGW, 22 mm. **Subject:** Republic of Cyprus, 50th Anniversary **Obv:** National arms **Rev:** Bird in stylized tree **Edge:** Reeded **Designer:** Clara Zacharaki-Georgiou

Date	Mintage	F	VF	XF	Unc	BU
2010 Proof	750	Value: 450				

MINT SETS

KM#	Date	Mintage	Identification	Issue Price	Mkt Val
MS20	2008 (8)	70,000	KM#78-85	—	50.00
MS21	2009 (9)	15,000	KM#78-85, 89	—	60.00
MS22	2011 (8)	10,000	KM#78-85	—	50.00
MS23	2012 (8)	—	KM#78-85	—	50.00

The Czech Republic was formerly united with Slovakia as Czechoslovakia. It is bordered in the west by Germany, to the north by Poland, to the east by Slovakia and to the south by Austria. It consists of 3 major regions: Bohemia, Moravia and Silesia and has an area of 30,450 sq. mi. (78,864 sq. km.) and a population of 10.4 million. Capital: Prague (Praha). Agriculture and livestock are chief occupations while coal deposits are the main mineral resources.

MINT MARKS
(c) - castle = Hamburg
(cr) - cross = British Royal Mint
(l) - leaf = Royal Canadian
(m) - crowned *b* or *CM* = Jablonec nad Nisou
(mk) - *MK* in circle = Kremnica
(o) - broken circle = Vienna (Wien)

MONETARY SYSTEM
1 Czechoslovak Koruna (Kcs) = 1 Czech Koruna (Kc)
1 Koruna = 100 Haleru

REPUBLIC

STANDARD COINAGE

KM# 6 10 HALERU
0.6000 g., Aluminum, 15.5 mm. **Obv:** Crowned Czech lion left, date below **Rev:** Denomination and stylized river **Edge:** Plain **Designer:** Jiri Pradler **Note:** Two varieties of mint marks exist for 1994.

Date	Mintage	F	VF	XF	Unc	BU
2001(m)	40,525,000	—	—	—	0.20	—
2001(m) Proof	2,500	Value: 10.00				
2002(m)	81,496,000	—	—	—	0.20	—
2002(m) Proof	3,490	Value: 10.00				
2003(m)	3,022,350	—	—	—	0.20	—
2003(m) Proof	3,000	Value: 7.00				
2004(m)	—	—	—	—	0.20	—
2004(m) Proof	—	Value: 7.00				
2005(m)	—	—	—	—	0.20	—

KM# 2.3 20 HALERU
0.7400 g., Aluminum, 17 mm. **Obv:** Crowned Czech lion left, date above **Rev:** Open 2 in denomination, "h" above angle line **Edge:** Reeded **Note:** Medal alignment.

Date	Mintage	F	VF	XF	Unc	BU
2001(m)	44,425,000	—	—	—	0.30	—
2001(m) Proof	2,500	Value: 12.50				
2002(m)	20,000	—	—	—	0.30	—
2002(m) Proof	3,490	Value: 12.50				
2003(m)	22,200	—	—	—	0.30	—
2003(m) Proof	3,000	Value: 7.50				
2004(m)	—	—	—	—	0.30	—
2004(m) Proof	—	Value: 7.50				

KM# 3.2 50 HALERU
0.9000 g., Aluminum, 19 mm. **Obv:** Crowned Czech lion left, date below **Rev:** Large denomination **Edge:** Segmented reeding **Note:** Outlined lettering and larger mint mark

Date	Mintage	F	VF	XF	Unc	BU
2001(m)	21,425,000	—	—	—	0.50	—
2001(m) Proof	2,500	Value: 12.50				
2002(m)	26,246,298	—	—	—	0.50	—
2002(m) Proof	3,490	Value: 12.50				
2003(m)	41,548,000	—	—	—	0.50	—
2003(m) Proof	3,000	Value: 7.50				
2004(m)	931,145	—	—	—	0.50	—
2004(m) Proof	4,000	Value: 7.50				
2005(m)	36,814,000	—	—	—	0.50	—
2005(m) Proof	3,000	Value: 7.50				
2006(m)	40,030,500	—	—	—	0.50	—
2006(m) Proof	2,500	Value: 7.50				
2007(m)	35,020,500	—	—	—	0.50	—
2007(m) Proof	2,500	Value: 7.50				
2008(m)	17,000	—	—	—	0.50	—
2008(m) Proof	2,500	Value: 3.00				
2009(m)	—	—	—	—	0.50	—
2009(m) Proof	2,500	Value: 3.00				

KM# 3.1 50 HALERU
0.9000 g., Aluminum, 19 mm. **Obv:** Crowned Czech lion left, date below **Rev:** Large denomination **Edge:** Segmented reeding **Designer:** Vladimir Oppl **Note:** Prev. KM#3.

Date	Mintage	F	VF	XF	Unc	BU
2001(m)	21,425,000	—	—	—	0.50	—
2001(m) Proof	2,500	Value: 12.50				

KM# 7 KORUNA
3.6000 g., Nickel Plated Steel, 20 mm. **Obv:** Crowned Czech lion left, date below **Rev:** Denomination above crown **Edge:** Reeded **Designer:** Jarmila Truhlikova-Spevakova **Note:** Two varieties of mint marks exist for 1996. 2000-03 have two varieties in the artist monogram.

Date	Mintage	F	VF	XF	Unc	BU
2001(m)	15,938,353	—	—	—	0.60	—
2001(m) Proof	2,500	Value: 20.00				
2002(m)	26,244,666	—	—	—	0.60	—
2002(m) Proof	3,490	Value: 20.00				
2003(m)	36,877,440	—	—	—	0.60	—
2003(m) Proof	3,000	Value: 10.00				
2004(m)	30,500	—	—	—	0.60	—
2004(m) Proof	4,000	Value: 10.00				
2005(m)	14,000	—	—	—	0.60	—
2005(m) Proof	3,000	Value: 10.00				
2006(m)	27,097,500	—	—	—	0.60	—
2006(m) Proof	2,500	Value: 10.00				
2007(m)	14,170,500	—	—	—	0.60	—
2007(m) Proof	2,500	Value: 10.00				
2008(m)	29,617,000	—	—	—	0.60	—
2008(m) Proof	2,500	Value: 6.00				
2009(m)	38,367,400	—	—	—	0.60	—
2009(m) Proof	3,200	Value: 6.00				
2010(m)	15,004,602	—	—	—	0.60	—
2010(m) Proof	3,200	Value: 6.00				
2011(m)	4,000,600	—	—	—	0.60	—
2011(m) Proof	2,500	Value: 6.00				
2012(m)	19,000,000	—	—	—	0.60	—
2013(m)	—	—	—	—	0.60	—

KM# 9 2 KORUNY
3.7000 g., Nickel Plated Steel, 21.5 mm. **Obv:** Crowned Czech lion left, date below **Rev:** Large denomination, pendant design at left **Edge:** Plain **Shape:** 11-sided **Designer:** Jarmila Truhlikova-Spevakova **Note:** Two varieties of designer monograms exist for 2001-04.

Date	Mintage	F	VF	XF	Unc	BU
2001(m)	26,117,000	—	—	—	0.65	—
2001(m) Proof	2,500	Value: 20.00				
2002(m)	20,941,084	—	—	—	0.65	—
2002(m) Proof	3,490	Value: 20.00				
2003(m)	20,955,000	—	—	—	0.65	—
2003(m) Proof	3,000	Value: 12.50				
2004(m)	15,658,556	—	—	—	0.65	—
2004(m) Proof	4,000	Value: 10.00				
2005(m)	14,000	—	—	—	0.65	—
2005(m) Proof	3,000	Value: 7.50				
2006(m)	30,500	—	—	—	0.65	—
2006(m) Proof	2,500	Value: 7.50				
2007(m)	30,020,500	—	—	—	0.65	—
2007(m) Proof	2,500	Value: 7.50				
2008(m)	26,267,000	—	—	—	0.65	—
2008(m) Proof	2,500	Value: 5.00				
2009(m)	25,418,000	—	—	—	0.65	—
2009(m) Proof	3,200	Value: 5.00				
2010(m)	26,054,000	—	—	—	0.65	—
2010(m) Proof	3,200	Value: 5.00				
2011(m)	12,000,000	—	—	—	0.65	—
2011(m) Proof	2,500	Value: 5.00				
2012(m)	—	—	—	—	0.65	—
2012(m)	13,000,000	—	—	—	0.65	—

KM# 8 5 KORUN
4.8000 g., Nickel Plated Steel, 23 mm. **Obv:** Crowned Czech lion left, date below **Rev:** Large denomination, Charles bridge and linden leaf **Edge:** Plain **Designer:** Jiri Harcuba

Date	Mintage	F	VF	XF	Unc	BU
2001(m)	25,000	—	—	—	1.00	—
2001(m) Proof	2,500	Value: 27.50				
2002(m)	21,344,995	—	—	—	1.00	—
2002(m) Proof	3,490	Value: 27.50				
2003(m)	22,000	—	—	—	1.00	—
2003(m) Proof	3,000	Value: 15.00				
2004(m)	34,940	—	—	—	1.00	—
2004(m) Proof	4,000	Value: 12.00				
2005(m)	14,000	—	—	—	1.00	—
2005(m) Proof	3,000	Value: 10.00				
2006(m)	25,030,500	—	—	—	1.00	—
2006(m) Proof	2,500	Value: 10.00				
2007(m)	20,500	—	—	—	1.00	—
2007(m) Proof	2,500	Value: 10.00				
2008(m)	11,617,000	—	—	—	1.00	—

Date	Mintage	F	VF	XF	Unc	BU
2008(m) Proof	2,500	Value: 6.00				
2009(m)	19,911,000	—	—	—	1.00	—
2009(m) Proof	3,200	Value: 6.00				
2010(m)	14,711,000	—	—	—	1.00	—
2010(m) Proof	3,200	Value: 6.00				
2011(m)	—	—	—	—	1.00	—
2011(m) Proof	5,500	Value: 6.00				
2012(m)	—	—	—	—	1.00	—
2013(m)	—	—	—	—	1.00	—

KM# 4 10 KORUN

7.6200 g., Copper Plated Steel, 24.5 mm. **Obv:** Crowned Czech lion left, date below **Rev:** Brno Cathedral, denomination below **Edge:** Reeded **Designer:** Ladislav Kozak **Note:** Position of designer's initials on reverse change during the 1995 strike.

Date	Mintage	F	VF	XF	Unc	BU
2001(m)	25,000	—	—	—	1.50	—
2001(m) Proof	2,500	Value: 28.00				
2002(m)	20,156	—	—	—	1.50	—
2002(m) Proof	3,490	Value: 28.00				
2003(m)	18,747,000	—	—	—	1.50	—
2003(m) Proof	3,000	Value: 17.50				
2004(m)	2,255,740	—	—	—	1.50	—
2004(m) Proof	4,000	Value: 14.00				
2005(m)	14,000	—	—	—	1.50	—
2005(m) Proof	3,000	Value: 10.00				
2006(m)	30,500	—	—	—	1.50	—
2006(m) Proof	2,500	Value: 10.00				
2007(m)	20,500	—	—	—	1.50	—
2007(m) Proof	2,500	Value: 10.00				
2008(m)	10,092,000	—	—	—	1.50	—
2008(m) Proof	2,500	Value: 7.00				
2009(m)	10,511,000	—	—	—	1.50	—
2009(m) Proof	3,200	Value: 7.00				
2010(m)	16,811,000	—	—	—	1.50	—
2010(m) Proof	3,200	Value: 7.00				
2011(m)	—	—	—	—	1.50	—
2011(m) Proof	5,500	Value: 7.00				
2012(m)	—	—	—	—	1.50	—
2013(m)	—	—	—	—	1.50	—

KM# 5 20 KORUN

8.4300 g., Brass Plated Steel, 26 mm. **Obv:** Crowned Czech lion left, date below **Rev:** St. Wenceslas (Duke Vaclav) on horse **Edge:** Plain **Shape:** 13-sided **Designer:** Vladimir Oppl **Note:** Two varieties of mint marks and style of 9's exist for 1997.

Date	Mintage	F	VF	XF	Unc	BU
2001(m)	25,000	—	—	—	2.50	—
2001(m) Proof	2,500	Value: 40.00				
2002(m)	20,996,500	—	—	—	2.50	—
2002(m) Proof	3,490	Value: 40.00				
2003(m)	22,000	—	—	—	2.50	—
2003(m) Proof	3,000	Value: 25.00				
2004(m)	8,249,507	—	—	—	2.50	—
2004(m) Proof	4,000	Value: 22.50				
2005(m)	9,866,778	—	—	—	2.50	—
2005(m) Proof	3,000	Value: 22.50				
2006(m)	2,096,500	—	—	—	2.50	—
2006(m) Proof	2,500	Value: 22.50				
2007(m)	20,500	—	—	—	2.50	—
2007(m) Proof	2,500	Value: 22.50				
2008(m)	17,000	—	—	—	2.50	—
2008(m) Proof	2,500	Value: 10.00				
2009(m)	11,000	—	—	—	2.50	—
2009(m) Proof	3,200	Value: 10.00				
2010(m)	11,000	—	—	—	2.50	—
2010(m) Proof	3,200	Value: 10.00				
2011(m)	8,000,000	—	—	—	2.50	—
2011(m) Proof	5,500	Value: 10.00				
2012(m)	8,000,000	—	—	—	2.50	—
2013	—	—	—	—	2.50	—

KM# 1 50 KORUN

9.7000 g., Bi-Metallic Brass Plated Steel center in Copper Plated Steel ring, 27.5 mm. **Obv:** Crowned Czech lion left **Rev:** Prague city view **Edge:** Plain **Designer:** Ladislav Kozak

Date	Mintage	F	VF	XF	Unc	BU
2001(m)	16,000	—	—	—	9.00	—
2001(m) Proof	2,500	Value: 80.00				
2002(m)	16,771	—	—	—	9.00	—
2002(m) Proof	3,490	Value: 80.00				
2003(m)	22,000	—	—	—	9.00	—
2003(m) Proof	3,000	Value: 50.00				
2004(m)	34,555	—	—	—	9.00	—
2004(m) Proof	4,000	Value: 40.00				
2005(m)	14,000	—	—	—	9.00	—
2005(m) Proof	3,000	Value: 25.00				
2006(m)	30,500	—	—	—	9.00	—
2006(m) Proof	2,500	Value: 25.00				
2007(m)	20,500	—	—	—	9.00	—
2007(m) Proof	2,500	Value: 25.00				
2008(m)	9,528,300	—	—	—	9.00	—
2008(m) Proof	2,500	Value: 20.00				
2009(m)	36,719,050	—	—	—	9.00	—
2009(m) Proof	3,200	Value: 20.00				
2010(m)	17,210,000	—	—	—	9.00	—
2010(m) Proof	32,000	Value: 20.00				
2011(m)	10,000,000	—	—	—	9.00	—
2011(m) Proof	5,500	Value: 20.00				
2012(m)	10,000,000	—	—	—	9.00	—
2013(m)	—	—	—	—	9.00	—

KM# 58 200 KORUN

13.0000 g., 0.9000 Silver 0.3761 oz. ASW, 31 mm. **Subject:** Frantisek Skroup **Obv:** Quartered, elongated arms above date **Rev:** Portrait and name **Designer:** Jiri Harcuba **Note:** 1,480 pieces uncirculated and 13 proof remelted.

Date	Mintage	F	VF	XF	Unc	BU
ND(2001)	11,944	—	—	—	18.00	20.00
Note: Milled edge						
ND(2001) Proof	3,179	Value: 35.00				
Note: Plain edge with CESKA NARODNI BANKA *0.900* 13g						

KM# 51 200 KORUN

13.0000 g., 0.9000 Silver 0.3761 oz. ASW, 31 mm. **Subject:** Jaroslav Seifert **Obv:** Quartered arms above denomination **Rev:** Head right, dates at left **Designer:** Ladislav Kozak **Note:** 1,680 pieces uncirculated and 2 proof remelted.

Date	Mintage	F	VF	XF	Unc	BU
ND(2001)	11,746	—	—	—	18.00	20.00
Note: Milled edge						
ND(2001) Proof	3,186	Value: 35.00				
Note: Plain edge with CESKA NARODNI BANKA *0.900* 13g						

KM# 53 200 KORUN

13.0000 g., 0.9000 Silver 0.3761 oz. ASW, 31 mm. **Subject:** 250th Anniversary - Death of Kilian Ignac Dientzenhofer **Obv:** Quartered arms, denomination at right **Rev:** Doorway and caliper **Designer:** Petr Pyciak **Note:** 1,840 pieces uncirculated and 104 proof remelted.

Date	Mintage	F	VF	XF	Unc	BU
ND(2001)	11,565	—	—	—	18.00	20.00
Note: Milled edge						
ND(2001) Proof	3,282	Value: 35.00				
Note: Plain edge with CESKA NARODNI BANKA *0.900* 13g						

KM# 54 200 KORUN

13.0000 g., 0.9000 Silver 0.3761 oz. ASW, 31 mm. **Subject:** Euro Currency System **Obv:** National arms **Rev:** Prague gros coin design **Designer:** Josef Safarik **Note:** 134 pieces uncirculated and 1 proof remelted.

Date	Mintage	F	VF	XF	Unc	BU
ND(2001)	13,730	—	—	—	18.00	20.00
Note: Milled edge						
ND(2001) Proof	3,995	Value: 35.00				
Note: Plain edge with CESKA NARODNI BANKA *0.900* 13g						

KM# 52 200 KORUN

13.0000 g., 0.9000 Silver 0.3761 oz. ASW, 31 mm. **Subject:** Soccer **Obv:** Quartered arms on square, denomination below **Rev:** Rampant lion on soccer ball **Designer:** Milena Blaskova **Note:** 2,350 pieces uncirculated and 1 proof remelted.

Date	Mintage	F	VF	XF	Unc	BU
ND(2001)	12,050	—	—	—	18.00	20.00
Note: Milled edge						
ND(2001) Proof	3,896	Value: 35.00				
Note: Plain edge with CESKA NARODNI BANKA *0.900* 13g						

KM# 59 200 KORUN

13.0000 g., 0.9000 Silver 0.3761 oz. ASW, 31 mm. **Subject:** Mikolas Ales **Obv:** Four coats of arms above denomination **Rev:** Horse and rider **Note:** 573 pieces uncirculated and 139 proof remelted.

Date	Mintage	F	VF	XF	Unc	BU
ND(2002)	11,879	—	—	—	18.00	20.00
Note: Milled edge						
ND(2002)(m) Proof	4,258	Value: 35.00				
Note: Plain edge with CESKA NARODNI BANKA *0.900* 13g						

KM# 57 200 KORUN

13.0000 g., 0.9000 Silver 0.3761 oz. ASW, 30.9 mm. **Subject:** Jiri of Podebrady **Obv:** Overlapped arms **Rev:** Head right **Designer:** Michal Vitanovsky **Note:** 1,200 pieces uncirculated and 5 proof remelted.

Date	Mintage	F	VF	XF	Unc	BU
ND(2002)	11,729	—	—	—	18.00	20.00
Note: Milled edge						
ND(2002) Proof	3,591	Value: 35.00				
Note: Plain edge with CESKA NARODNI BANKA *0.900* 13g						

KM# 56 200 KORUN

13.0000 g., 0.9000 Silver 0.3761 oz. ASW, 30.9 mm. **Subject:** Emil Holub **Obv:** National arms, eagles and lions, denomination below **Rev:** Traveler and African dancers **Designer:** Ladislav Kozak **Note:** 1,350 pieces uncirculated and 7 proof remelted.

Date	Mintage	F	VF	XF	Unc	BU
ND(2002)	11,602	—	—	—	18.00	20.00
Note: Milled edge						
ND(2002) Proof	3,588	Value: 35.00				
Note: Plain edge with CESKA NARODNI BANKA *0.900* 13g						

KM# 55 200 KORUN

13.0000 g., 0.9000 Silver 0.3761 oz. ASW, 31 mm. **Subject:** St. Zdislava **Obv:** Old and new arms form diamond above denomination **Rev:** Saint feeding sick person **Designer:** Michal Vitanovsky **Note:** 865 pieces uncirculated remelted.

Date	Mintage	F	VF	XF	Unc	BU
ND(2002)	12,083	—	—	—	18.00	20.00
Note: Milled edge						
ND(2002) Proof	3,596	Value: 35.00				
Note: Plain edge with CESKA NARODNI BANKA *0.900* 13g						

KM# 60 200 KORUN

13.0000 g., 0.9000 Silver 0.3761 oz. ASW, 31 mm. **Subject:** Jaroslav Vrchlicky **Obv:** Denomination and quill **Rev:** Bust with hat facing **Note:** 889 pieces unciruclated and 5 proof remelted.

Date	Mintage	F	VF	XF	Unc	BU
ND(2003)	10,583	—	—	—	18.00	20.00
Note: Milled edge						
ND(2003) Proof	3,692	Value: 35.00				
Note: Plain edge with CESKA NARODNI BANKA *0.900* 13g						

KM# 62 200 KORUN

13.0000 g., 0.9000 Silver 0.3761 oz. ASW, 30.9 mm. **Subject:** Josef Thomayer **Obv:** National arms **Rev:** Portrait **Note:** 783 uncirculated and 12 proof were remelted.

Date	Mintage	F	VF	XF	Unc	BU
ND(2003)	10,525	—	—	—	18.00	20.00
Note: Milled edge						
ND(2003) Proof	3,981	Value: 35.00				
Note: Plain edge with CESKA NARODNI BANKA *0.900* 13g						

KM# 63 200 KORUN

13.0000 g., 0.9000 Silver 0.3761 oz. ASW, 31 mm. **Subject:** Tabor-Bechyne Electric Railway **Obv:** Head left **Rev:** Railroad station scene **Designer:** Ladislav Kozak **Note:** 808 Uncirculated were remelted.

Date	Mintage	F	VF	XF	Unc	BU
ND(2003)	10,986	—	—	—	18.00	20.00
Note: Milled edge						
ND(2003) Proof	4,097	Value: 35.00				
Note: Plain edge with CESKA NARODNI BANKA *0.900* 13g						

KM# 64 200 KORUN

13.0000 g., 0.9000 Silver 0.3761 oz. ASW, 31 mm. **Subject:** Bohemian Skiers' Union **Obv:** Head 3/4 left **Rev:** Skier **Designer:** Ladislav Kozak **Note:** 680 Uncirculated and 13 proof were remelted.

Date	Mintage	F	VF	XF	Unc	BU
ND(2003)	10,801	—	—	—	18.00	20.00
Note: Milled edge						
ND(2003) Proof	4,284	Value: 35.00				
Note: Plain edge with CESKA NARODNI BANKA *0.900* 13g						

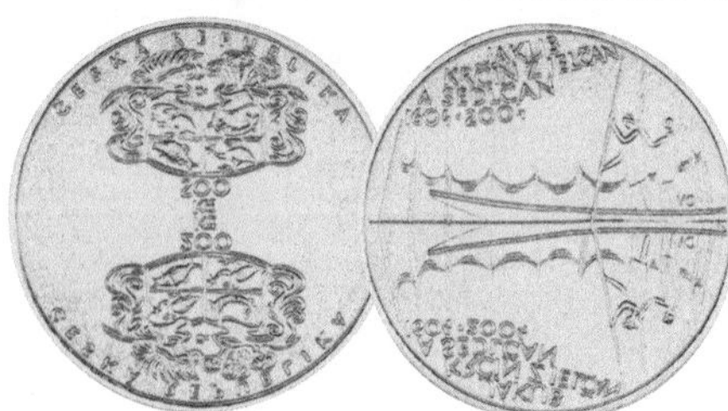

KM# 70 200 KORUN

13.0000 g., 0.9000 Silver 0.3761 oz. ASW, 31 mm. **Subject:** 300th Anniversary - Death of pond builder Jakub Krcin **Obv:** Coat of arms above value with reflected design below **Rev:** Two fishermen in boat with reflection on water below **Designer:** Vladimir Oppl **Note:** 656 uncirculated remelted.

Date	Mintage	F	VF	XF	Unc	BU
ND(2004)(m)	10,685	—	—	—	18.00	20.00
Note: Milled edge						
ND(2004) Proof	3,995	Value: 35.00				
Note: Plain edge with CESKA NARODNI BANKA *0.900* 13g						

KM# 71 200 KORUN

13.0000 g., 0.9000 Silver 0.3761 oz. ASW **Subject:** Entry into the European Union **Rev:** State emblems of 15 members of the European Union

Date	Mintage	F	VF	XF	Unc	BU
2004	13,918	—	—	—	18.00	20.00
Note: Plain edge with codes for EU countries						
2004 Proof	9,994	Value: 32.00				
Note: Plain edge with CESKA NARODNI BANKA *0.900* 13g						

KM# 72 200 KORUN

13.0000 g., 0.9000 Silver 0.3761 oz. ASW, 31 mm. **Subject:** Prokop Diviš **Obv:** Lighting conductor modulator **Rev:** Head of Diviš

Date	Mintage	F	VF	XF	Unc	BU
2004	10,145	—	—	—	18.00	20.00
Note: Milled edge						
2004 Proof	3,897	Value: 35.00				
Note: Plain edge with CESKA NARODNI BANKA *0.900* 13g						

KM# 73 200 KORUN

13.0000 g., 0.9000 Silver 0.3761 oz. ASW **Subject:** Leos Janacek **Rev:** Head of Janacek **Designer:** Jiri Veneck

Date	Mintage	F	VF	XF	Unc	BU
2004	10,143	—	—	—	18.00	20.00
Note: Milled edge						
2004 Proof	4,100	Value: 32.00				
Note: Plain edge with CESKA NARODNI BANKA *0.900* 13g						

KM# 74 200 KORUN

13.0000 g., 0.9000 Silver 0.3761 oz. ASW **Subject:** Kralice Bible **Obv:** Enlargement of bible page **Rev:** Bible page **Designer:** Zbynek Fojtu

Date	Mintage	F	VF	XF	Unc	BU
2004	10,975	—	—	—	18.00	20.00
Note: Reeded						
2004 Proof	5,000	Value: 32.00				

KM# 77 200 KORUN

13.0000 g., 0.9000 Silver 0.3761 oz. ASW, 31 mm. **Obv:** Prokop Divis **Rev:** Lightning conductor

Date	Mintage	F	VF	XF	Unc	BU
2004	14,000	—	—	—	18.00	20.00
Note: Reeded						
2004 Proof	4,600	Value: 32.00				
Note: Plain edge with CESKA NARODNI BANKA * Ag 0.900 * 13g *						

KM# 78 200 KORUN

13.0000 g., 0.9000 Silver 0.3761 oz. ASW, 31 mm. **Subject:** 100th Anniversary of Jan Werich and Jiri Voskovec

Date	Mintage	F	VF	XF	Unc	BU
2005	10,884	—	—	—	18.00	20.00
Note: Milled edge						
2005 Proof	4,997	Value: 32.00				
Note: Plain edge with CESKA NARODNI BANKA *0.900* 13g						

KM# 79 200 KORUN

13.0000 g., 0.9000 Silver 0.3761 oz. ASW, 31 mm. **Subject:** 100th Anniversary of Production of 1st Car in Mlada Boleslav **Rev:** 1st car of LK factory

Date	Mintage	F	VF	XF	Unc	BU
2005	13,225	—	—	—	18.00	20.00
2005 Proof	10,797	Value: 32.00				
Note: Plain edge with CESKA NARODNI BANKA *0.900* 13g						

KM# 80 200 KORUN

13.0000 g., 0.9000 Silver 0.3761 oz. ASW, 31 mm. **Subject:** 450th Anniversary - Birth of Mikulas Dacicky **Obv:** Arms of Dacicky **Rev:** Head of Mikulas Dacicky z Heslova

Date	Mintage	F	VF	XF	Unc	BU
2005	10,076	—	—	—	18.00	20.00
Note: Milled edge						
2005 Proof	5,597	Value: 32.00				
Note: Plain edge with CESKA NARODNI BANKA *0.900* 13g						

KM# 84 200 KORUN

13.0000 g., 0.9000 Silver 0.3761 oz. ASW, 31 mm. **Subject:** 700th Anniversary - Death of Vaclav III **Obv:** Sword between two shields positioned top-to-top **Rev:** King Vaclav III between shields of Bohemia and Moravia **Designer:** Vojtech Dostal

Date	Mintage	F	VF	XF	Unc	BU
2006	10,471	—	—	—	18.00	20.00
Note: Milled edge						
2006 Proof	7,497	Value: 32.00				
Note: Plain edge with CESKA NARODNI BANKA *0.900* 13g						

KM# 85 200 KORUN

13.0000 g., 0.9000 Silver 0.3761 oz. ASW, 31 mm. **Subject:** 100th Anniversary - Birth of Jaroslav Jezek **Obv:** Musical score **Rev:** Caricature looking at score **Designer:** Josef Oplistil

Date	Mintage	F	VF	XF	Unc	BU
2006(m)	10,192	—	—	—	18.00	20.00
Note: Milled edge						
2006(m) Proof	15,442	Value: 30.00				
Note: Plain edge with CESKA NARODNI BANKA *0.900* 13g						

KM# 81 200 KORUN

13.0000 g., 0.9000 Silver 0.3761 oz. ASW, 31 mm. **Subject:** 250th Anniversary - Birth of F.J. Gerstner **Designer:** Vojtich Dostal

Date	Mintage	F	VF	XF	Unc	BU
2006	11,101	—	—	—	18.00	20.00
Note: Milled edge						
2006 Proof	6,194	Value: 32.00				
Note: Plain edge with CESKA NARODNI BANKA *0.900* 13g						

KM# 82 200 KORUN

13.0000 g., 0.9000 Silver 0.3761 oz. ASW, 31 mm. **Subject:** 150th Anniversary - School of Glass Making in Kamenicky Senov **Obv:** Image of National Arms within glass cube **Rev:** Artistic image within glass cube **Designer:** Zuzana Hubena

Date	Mintage	F	VF	XF	Unc	BU
2006	9,546	—	—	—	20.00	22.00
Note: Milled edge						
2006 Proof	6,494	Value: 32.00				
Note: Plain edge with CESKA NARODNI BANKA *0.900* 13g						

KM# 83 200 KORUN

13.0000 g., 0.9000 Silver 0.3761 oz. ASW, 31 mm. **Subject:** 500th Anniversary - Death of Matej Rejsek **Obv:** Pulpit in the church of St. Laurer in Kank **Rev:** Portrait of Rejsek on the Prasna gate in Prague **Designer:** Zbynek Fojtu

Date	Mintage	F	VF	XF	Unc	BU
2006	9,594	—	—	—	20.00	22.00
Note: Milled edge						
2006 Proof	6,494	Value: 32.00				
Note: Plain edge with CESKA NARODNI BANKA *0.900* 13g						

KM# 91 200 KORUN

13.0000 g., 0.9000 Silver 0.3761 oz. ASW, 31 mm. **Subject:** Founding of Jednota Bratrska, 550th Anniversary **Obv:** Emblem of Jednota Bratrska, tree, ram with flag. **Rev:** Chalice with ram with flag **Designer:** Zbynek Fojtu

Date	Mintage	F	VF	XF	Unc	BU
2007	10,471	—	—	—	20.00	22.00
Note: Milled edge						
2007 Proof	8,297	Value: 32.00				
Note: Plain edge with CESKA NARODNI BANKA *0.900* 13g						

KM# 92 200 KORUN

13.0000 g., 0.9000 Silver 0.3761 oz. ASW, 31 mm. **Subject:** Charles Bridge cornerstone, 650th anniversary

Date	Mintage	F	VF	XF	Unc	BU
2007	10,772	—	—	—	20.00	22.00
Note: Milled edge						
2007 Proof	18,746	Value: 32.00				
Note: Plain edge with CESKA NARODNI BANKA *0.900* 13g						

KM# 93 200 KORUN

13.0000 g., 0.9000 Silver 0.3761 oz. ASW, 31 mm. **Subject:** Jarmila Novotná, 100th Anniversary of Birth **Obv:** Names of the operas in which Novotna sang **Rev:** Head of Novotna **Designer:** Vojtech Dostal

Date	Mintage	F	VF	XF	Unc	BU
2007	9,584	—	—	—	20.00	22.00
Note: Milled edge						
2007 Proof	12,788	Value: 32.00				
Note: Plain edge with CESKA NARODNI BANKA *0.900* 13g						

KM# 94 200 KORUN

13.0000 g., 0.9000 Silver 0.3761 oz. ASW, 31 mm. **Subject:** Earth Satelite Launch, 50th Anniversary **Obv:** Satelite and sound signal of satelite **Rev:** Plentary system with satelite **Designer:** Lubos Charsat

Date	Mintage	F	VF	XF	Unc	BU
2007	10,148	—	—	—	20.00	22.00
Note: Milled edge						
2007 Proof	14,797	Value: 32.00				
Note: Plain edge with CESKA NARODNI BANKA *0.900* 13g						

KM# 97 200 KORUN
13.0000 g., 0.9000 Silver 0.3761 oz. ASW, 31 mm. **Subject:** Charles IV Vineyard Planting decree **Designer:** Jiri Veneck

Date	Mintage	F	VF	XF	Unc	BU
2008	9,768	—	—	—	20.00	22.00
Note: Milled edge						
2008 Proof	16,997	Value: 32.00				
Note: Plain edge with CESKA NARODNI BANKA *0.900* 13g						

KM# 98 200 KORUN
13.0000 g., 0.9000 Silver 0.3761 oz. ASW **Subject:** Josef Hlavka, 100th Anniversary of Death **Obv:** Wing over architectural element **Rev:** Facing portrait of Hlavka **Designer:** Vojtech Dostal

Date	Mintage	F	VF	XF	Unc	BU
2008	9,559	—	—	—	20.00	22.00
Note: Milled edge						
2008 Proof	15,976	Value: 32.00				
Note: Plain edge with CESKA NARODNI BANKA *0.900* 13g						

KM# 99 200 KORUN
13.0000 g., 0.9000 Silver 0.3761 oz. ASW, 31 mm. **Subject:** Schengen Convention **Obv:** Arms **Rev:** Opening of the frontiers **Designer:** Zbynek Fojtu

Date	Mintage	F	VF	XF	Unc	BU
2008	9,739	—	—	—	20.00	22.00
Note: Milled edge						
2008 Proof	15,743	Value: 32.00				
Note: Plain edge with CESKA NARODNI BANKA *0.900* 13g						

KM# 100 200 KORUN
13.0000 g., 0.9000 Silver 0.3761 oz. ASW, 31 mm. **Subject:** Viktor Ponrepo,150th Anniversary **Obv:** Tripod camera **Rev:** Mustache and top hat

Date	Mintage	F	VF	XF	Unc	BU
2008	9,572	—	—	—	20.00	22.00
Note: Milled edge						
2008 Proof	14,997	Value: 32.00				
Note: Plain edge with CESKA NARODNI BANKA *0.900* 13g						

KM# 101 200 KORUN
13.0000 g., 0.9000 Silver 0.3761 oz. ASW, 31 mm. **Subject:** National Technical Museum **Obv:** Steam Locomotive and driving wheel **Rev:** Museum façade and clock face **Designer:** Zbynek Fojtu

Date	Mintage	F	VF	XF	Unc	BU
2008	9,972	—	—	—	22.00	25.00
Note: Milled edge						
2008 Proof	14,997	Value: 35.00				
Note: Plain edge with CESKA NARODNI BANKA *0.900* 13g						

KM# 102 200 KORUN
13.0000 g., 0.9000 Silver 0.3761 oz. ASW, 31 mm. **Subject:** Czech Ice Hockey Association - 100th Anniversary **Obv:** Hockey Player **Rev:** Logo **Designer:** Zbynek Fojtu

Date	Mintage	F	VF	XF	Unc	BU
2008	10,272	—	—	—	20.00	22.00
Note: Milled edge						
2008 Proof	15,097	Value: 32.00				
Note: Plain edge with CESKA NARODNI BANKA *0.900* 13g						

KM# 105 200 KORUN
13.0000 g., 0.9000 Silver 0.3761 oz. ASW, 31 mm. **Subject:** Czech Presidency to Council of the European Union **Obv:** Arms in circle **Rev:** Czech flag and circle of stars **Designer:** Josef Oplistil

Date	Mintage	F	VF	XF	Unc	BU
2009	13,172	—	—	—	20.00	22.00
Note: Milled edge						
2009 Proof	19,697	Value: 32.00				
Note: Plain edge with CESKA NARODNI BANKA *0.900* 13g						

KM# 106 200 KORUN
13.0000 g., 0.9000 Silver 0.3761 oz. ASW, 31 mm. **Subject:** Nordic World Ski Championships in Liberec **Obv:** Logo with skis **Rev:** Cross country skiers and ski jumpers

Date	Mintage	F	VF	XF	Unc	BU
2009	10,772	—	—	—	20.00	22.00
Note: Milled edge						
2009 Proof	15,197	Value: 32.00				
Note: Plain edge with CESKA NARODNI BANKA *0.900* 13g						

KM# 107 200 KORUN
13.0000 g., 0.9000 Silver 0.3761 oz. ASW, 31 mm. **Subject:** North Pole Exploration **Obv:** Facing Explorer **Rev:** Sled and Northern Lights **Designer:** Jiri Venecek

Date	Mintage	F	VF	XF	Unc	BU
2009	10,172	—	—	—	20.00	22.00
Note: Milled edge						
2009 Proof	16,767	Value: 32.00				
Note: Plain edge with CESKA NARODNI BANKA *0.900* 13g						

KM# 108 200 KORUN
13.0000 g., 0.9000 Silver 0.3761 oz. ASW, 31 mm. **Subject:** Rabbi Jehuda Löw **Obv:** Star of David and dates **Rev:** Symbols of Rabbi Low

Date	Mintage	F	VF	XF	Unc	BU
2009	11,275	—	—	—	20.00	22.00
Note: Milled edge						
2009 Proof	18,100	Value: 32.00				
Note: Plain edge with CESKA NARODNI BANKA *0.900* 13g						

KM# 109 200 KORUN
13.0000 g., 0.9000 Silver 0.3761 oz. ASW, 31 mm. **Subject:** Kepler's Planetary Motion Laws **Obv:** Kepler's plan of Mars **Rev:** Portrait of Kepler **Designer:** Vojtech Dostal

Date	Mintage	F	VF	XF	Unc	BU
2009	10,472	—	—	—	20.00	22.00
Note: Milled edge						
2009 Proof	19,687	Value: 32.00				
Note: Plain edge with CESKA NARODNI BANKA *0.900* 13g						

KM# 112 200 KORUN
13.0000 g., 0.9000 Silver 0.3761 oz. ASW, 31 mm. **Subject:** Astronomical Clock, Prague **Obv:** Figures of four apostles and rooster **Rev:** Clock works

Date	Mintage	F	VF	XF	Unc	BU
2010	10,372	—	—	—	18.00	20.00
Note: Milled edge						
2010 Proof	16,097	Value: 30.00				
Note: Plain edge with CESKA NARODNI BANKA *0.900* 13g						

KM# 113 200 KORUN
13.0000 g., 0.9000 Silver 0.3761 oz. ASW, 31 mm. **Subject:** Gustav Mahler **Obv:** Part of Mahler's 5th symphony **Rev:** Portrait of Mahler

Date	Mintage	F	VF	XF	Unc	BU
2010	9,672	—	—	—	18.00	20.00
Note: Milled edge						
2010 Proof	15,047	Value: 30.00				
Note: Plain edge with CESKA NARODNI BANKA *0.900* 13g						

KM# 114 200 KORUN

13.0000 g., 0.9000 Silver 0.3761 oz. ASW, 31 mm. **Subject:** Alfons Mucha **Obv:** Print of Music by Mucha **Rev:** Facing portrait of Mucha **Designer:** Ivan Dehak

Date	Mintage	F	VF	XF	Unc	BU
2010	10,072	—	—	—	18.00	20.00
Note: Milled edge						
2010 Proof	15,897	Value: 30.00				
Note: Plain edge with CESKA NARODNI BANKA *0.900* 13g						

KM# 115 200 KORUN

13.0000 g., 0.9000 Silver 0.3761 oz. ASW, 31 mm. **Subject:** John of Luxembourg, 700th Wedding Anniversary **Obv:** Czech lion on tapestry background **Rev:** John and wife standing

Date	Mintage	F	VF	XF	Unc	BU
2010	9,572	—	—	—	18.00	20.00
Note: Milled edge						
2010 Proof	13,897	Value: 32.00				
Note: Plain edge with CESKA NARODNI BANKA *0.900* 13g						

KM# 116 200 KORUN

13.0000 g., 0.9000 Silver 0.3761 oz. ASW, 31 mm. **Subject:** Karel Zeman, 100th Anniversary of Birth **Obv:** Marionettes of Zeman's cinemas **Rev:** Submarine, airship, octopus of Zeman's cinemas

Date	Mintage	F	VF	XF	Unc	BU
2010	9,275	—	—	—	18.00	20.00
Note: Milled edge						
2010 Proof	13,000	Value: 32.00				
Note: Plain edge with CESKA NARODNI BANKA *0.900* 13g						

KM# 119 200 KORUN

13.0000 g., 0.9250 Silver 0.3866 oz. ASW, 31 mm. **Subject:** Prague Conservatory, 200th Anniversary

Date	Mintage	F	VF	XF	Unc	BU
2011	7,777	—	—	—	18.00	20.00
Note: Milled edge						
2011 Proof	11,500	Value: 32.00				
Note: Plain edge with CESKA NARODNI BANKA *0.925* 13g						

KM# 120 200 KORUN

13.0000 g., 0.9250 Silver 0.3866 oz. ASW, 31 mm. **Subject:** Jan Kaspar, 100th Anniversary of First Flight

Date	Mintage	F	VF	XF	Unc	BU
2011	7,777	—	—	—	18.00	20.00
Note: Milled edge						
2011 Proof	11,600	Value: 32.00				
Note: Plain edge with CESKA NARODNI BANKA *0.925* 13g						

KM# 121 200 KORUN

13.0000 g., 0.9250 Silver 0.3866 oz. ASW, 31 mm. **Subject:** Jiri Melantrich, 500th Anniversary of Birth

Date	Mintage	F	VF	XF	Unc	BU
2011	7,877	—	—	—	18.00	20.00
Note: Milled edge						
2011 Proof	11,600	Value: 32.00				
Note: Plain edge with CESKA NARODNI BANKA *0.925* 13g						

KM# 122 200 KORUN

13.0000 g., 0.9250 Silver 0.3866 oz. ASW, 31 mm. **Subject:** Petr Vok, 400th Anniversary of Death

Date	Mintage	F	VF	XF	Unc	BU
2011	8,200	—	—	—	18.00	20.00
Note: Milled edge						
2011 Proof	12,200	Value: 32.00				
Note: Plain edge with CESKA NARODNI BANKA *0.925* 13g						

KM# 126 200 KORUN

13.0000 g., 0.9250 Silver 0.3866 oz. ASW, 31 mm. **Subject:** Emperor Rudolf II, 400th Anniversary of Death **Obv:** Emperor on horseback, Prague city view in backgorund **Rev:** Portrait, signature and arms

Date	Mintage	F	VF	XF	Unc	BU
2012	8,100	—	—	—	—	25.00
Note: Milled edge						
2012 Proof	12,600	Value: 32.00				

KM# 127 200 KORUN

13.0000 g., 0.9250 Silver 0.3866 oz. ASW, 31 mm. **Subject:** Sokol, 150th Anniversary **Obv:** SOKOL logo and stylized gymnasts in background **Rev:** Falcon, stylized gymnasts in background

Date	Mintage	F	VF	XF	Unc	BU
2012	8,000	—	—	—	—	25.00
Note: Milled edge						
2012 Proof	12,200	Value: 32.00				

KM# 128 200 KORUN

13.0000 g., 0.9250 Silver 0.3866 oz. ASW, 31 mm. **Subject:** Czech Scouts - Junak, 100th Anniversary **Obv:** Scouting emblems **Rev:** A. B. Svojsik, founder of Czeck scouting

Date	Mintage	F	VF	XF	Unc	BU
2012	8,000	—	—	—	—	25.00
Note: Milled edge						
2012 Proof	12,200	Value: 32.00				

KM# 129 200 KORUN

13.0000 g., 0.9250 Silver 0.3866 oz. ASW, 31 mm. **Subject:** Kamil Lhoták, 100th Anniversary of Birth

Date	Mintage	F	VF	XF	Unc	BU
2012	7,700	—	—	—	—	25.00
2012 Proof	13,200	Value: 32.00				

KM# 130 200 KORUN

13.0000 g., 0.9250 Silver 0.3866 oz. ASW, 31 mm. **Subject:** Prague Municipal House, 100th Anniversary

Date	Mintage	F	VF	XF	Unc	BU
2012	7,700	—	—	—	—	25.00
2012 Proof	13,600	Value: 32.00				

KM# 123 500 KORUN
25.0000 g., 0.9250 Silver 0.7435 oz. ASW, 40 mm. **Subject:** Karel Jaromir Erben, 200th Anniversary of Birth **Obv:** Floral bouquet **Rev:** Portrait 1/4 left

Date	Mintage	F	VF	XF	Unc	BU
2011	7,300	—	—	—	—	35.00
Note: Milled edge						
2011 Proof	10,800	Value: 45.00				
Note: Plain edge with CESKA NARODNI BANKA *0.925* 13g						

KM# 131 500 KORUN
25.0000 g., 0.9250 Silver 0.7435 oz. ASW, 40 mm. **Subject:** Jiri Trnka, 100th Anniversary of Birth **Rev:** Profile left **Designer:** Josef Oplistil

Date	Mintage	F	VF	XF	Unc	BU
2012	6,800	—	—	—	—	35.00
Note: Milled edge.						
2012 Proof	12,100	Value: 40.00				

GOLD BULLION COINAGE

KM# 65 2000 KORUN
6.2200 g., 0.9999 Gold 0.1999 oz. AGW, 20 mm. **Subject:** Romanesque - Znojmo Rotunda **Obv:** Three heraldic animals **Rev:** Farmer and round building **Designer:** Jiri Harcuba

Date	Mintage	F	VF	XF	Unc	BU
ND(2001)	2,197	—	—	—	—	375
Note: Milled edge						
ND(2001) Proof	2,997	Value: 400				
Note: Plain edge						

KM# 66 2000 KORUN
6.2200 g., 0.9999 Gold 0.1999 oz. AGW, 20 mm. **Subject:** Gothic - Cloister of the Vyssi Brod Monastery **Obv:** Three heraldic animals above Gothic design **Rev:** Man holding church building model **Designer:** Michal Vitanovsky

Date	Mintage	F	VF	XF	Unc	BU
2001	2,195	—	—	—	—	375
Note: Milled edge						
2001 Proof	2,997	Value: 400				
Note: Plain edge						

KM# 67 2000 KORUN
6.2200 g., 0.9999 Gold 0.1999 oz. AGW, 20 mm. **Subject:** Gothic - Fountain in Kutna Hora **Obv:** Three heraldic animals **Rev:** Fountain enclosure **Designer:** Josef Oplistil

Date	Mintage	F	VF	XF	Unc	BU
2002	2,195	—	—	—	—	375
Note: Milled edge						
2002 Proof	2,997	Value: 400				
Note: Plain edge						

KM# 61 2000 KORUN
6.2200 g., 0.9999 Gold 0.1999 oz. AGW, 20 mm. **Subject:** Renaissance - Litomysl Castle **Obv:** Three heraldic animals above mermaid **Rev:** Aerial castle view and mythical creature **Designer:** Jiri Venecek

Date	Mintage	F	VF	XF	Unc	BU
2002	2,094	—	—	—	—	375
Note: Milled edge						
2002 Proof	3,097	Value: 400				
Note: Plain edge						

KM# 68 2000 KORUN
6.2200 g., 0.9999 Gold 0.1999 oz. AGW, 20 mm. **Subject:** Renaissance - Slavonice House Gables **Obv:** Three heraldic animals above city view **Rev:** City arms **Designer:** Jiri Harcuba

Date	Mintage	F	VF	XF	Unc	BU
2003	1,994	—	—	—	—	375
Note: Milled edge						
2003 Proof	2,996	Value: 400				
Note: Plain edge						

KM# 69 2000 KORUN
6.2200 g., 0.9999 Gold 0.1999 oz. AGW, 20 mm. **Subject:** Baroque - Buchlovice Palace **Obv:** Three heraldic animals above palace **Rev:** Palace view **Designer:** Jakub Vlcek

Date	Mintage	F	VF	XF	Unc	BU
2003	1,994	—	—	—	—	375
Note: Milled edge						
2003 Proof	3,197	Value: 400				
Note: Plain edge						

KM# 75 2000 KORUN
6.2200 g., 0.9999 Gold 0.1999 oz. AGW, 20 mm. **Obv:** Ornamental porch below three heraldic animals **Rev:** Hluboka Castle with coat of arms in foreground **Designer:** Jiri Venecek

Date	Mintage	F	VF	XF	Unc	BU
2004	1,994	—	—	—	—	375
Note: Milled edge						
2004 Proof	2,997	Value: 400				
Note: Plain edge						

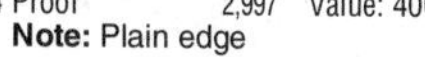

KM# 86 2000 KORUN
6.2200 g., 0.9990 Gold 0.1998 oz. AGW, 20 mm. **Subject:** Kacina Castle **Designer:** Josef Oplistil

Date	Mintage	F	VF	XF	Unc	BU
2004	1,994	—	—	—	—	375
Note: Milled edge						
2004 Proof	2,996	Value: 400				
Note: Plain edge						

KM# 87 2000 KORUN
6.2200 g., 0.9990 Gold 0.1998 oz. AGW, 20 mm. **Subject:** Lazne Bohdanec Spa **Obv:** Gocar Spa Pavillion, full facade **Rev:** Gocar Spa Pavillion central area **Designer:** Jiri Venecek

Date	Mintage	F	VF	XF	Unc	BU
2005	1,997	—	—	—	—	375
Note: Milled edge						
2005 Proof	2,996	Value: 400				
Note: Plain edge						

KM# 88 2000 KORUN
6.2200 g., 0.9990 Gold 0.1998 oz. AGW, 20 mm. **Subject:** Dancing House in Prague **Rev:** Exterior view of Dancing House **Designer:** Vladimir Oppl

Date	Mintage	F	VF	XF	Unc	BU
2005	1,996	—	—	—	—	375
Note: Milled edge						
2005 Proof	3,297	Value: 400				
Note: Plain edge						

KM# 76 2500 KORUN
31.1040 g., Bi-Metallic .9999 Gold 7.776g center in .999 Silver 23.328g ring, 40 mm. **Subject:** Czech entry into the European Union **Obv:** Value within circle of shields **Rev:** "1.5.2004" within circle of dates and text **Edge:** Lettered **Edge Lettering:** CNB * Ag 0.999 * 23,328 g CNB Au 999.9 * 7,776g *

Date	Mintage	F	VF	XF	Unc	BU
ND (2004) Proof	8,117	Value: 500				

KM# 89 2500 KORUN
7.7770 g., 0.9990 Gold 0.2498 oz. AGW, 22 mm. **Subject:** Hand Paper Mill at Velke Losiny **Designer:** Lubos Charvat

Date	Mintage	F	VF	XF	Unc	BU
2006	1,800	—	—	—	1,500	—
Note: Milled edge						
2006	3,000	Value: 3,000				
Note: Plain edge						

KM# 90 2500 KORUN
7.7850 g., 0.9990 Gold 0.2500 oz. AGW, 22 mm. **Subject:** Observatory at Prague Klementinum **Obv:** Sun's rays thru clouds **Rev:** Building tower, rays and moon **Designer:** Josef Oplistil **Note:** Prev. KM #86.

Date	Mintage	F	VF	XF	Unc	BU
2006	1,897	—	—	—	—	700
Note: Milled edge						
2006 Proof	3,797	Value: 1,000				
Note: Plain edge						

KM# 95 2500 KORUN
7.7770 g., 0.9990 Gold 0.2498 oz. AGW, 22 mm. **Subject:** Sevcinsky Mine at Pribram-Brezove Hory **Rev:** Head-gear tower at mine **Designer:** Lubos Charvat

Date	Mintage	F	VF	XF	Unc	BU
2007	2,097	—	—	—	—	475
Note: Milled edge						
2007 Proof	5,097	Value: 500				
Note: Plain edge						

KM# 96 2500 KORUN
7.7770 g., 0.9990 Gold 0.2498 oz. AGW, 22 mm. **Subject:** Water mill at Slup **Obv:** Water Mill **Rev:** Water Mill

Date	Mintage	F	VF	XF	Unc	BU
2007	2,297	—	—	—	—	475
2007 Proof	6,297	Value: 500				

KM# 103 2500 KORUN
7.7800 g., 0.9990 Gold 0.2499 oz. AGW, 22 mm. **Subject:** Stadlec Suspension Bridge **Obv:** Side view of bridge **Rev:** View of bridge thru arch **Designer:** Lubos Charvat

Date	Mintage	F	VF	XF	Unc	BU
2008	3,097	—	—	—	—	475
Note: Milled edge						
2008 Proof	10,897	Value: 500				
Note: Plain edge						

KM# 104 2500 KORUN
7.7800 g., 0.9990 Gold 0.2499 oz. AGW, 22 mm. **Subject:** Plzen Brewery **Obv:** Copper vats **Rev:** Plzen Brewery façade and wooden barrels

Date	Mintage	F	VF	XF	Unc	BU
2008	3,197	—	—	—	—	475
Note: Milled edge						
2008 Proof	10,797	Value: 500				
Note: Plain edge						

KM# 110 2500 KORUN
7.7770 g., 0.9990 Gold 0.2498 oz. AGW, 22 mm. **Subject:** Elbe Sluice under Strekov Castle **Obv:** Turbine in sluice in the Labe (Elbe) river **Rev:** Sluice under Strekov castle **Designer:** Josef Oplistil

Date	Mintage	F	VF	XF	Unc	BU
2009	3,497	—	—	—	—	475
Note: Milled edge						
2009 Proof	10,497	Value: 500				
Note: Plain edge						

KM# 111 2500 KORUN
7.7770 g., 0.9990 Gold 0.2498 oz. AGW, 22 mm. **Subject:** Windmill at Ruprechtov **Designer:** Jiri Harcuba

Date	Mintage	F	VF	XF	Unc	BU
2009	3,497	—	—	—	—	475
2009 Proof	10,497	Value: 500				

KM# 117 2500 KORUN
7.7700 g., 0.9990 Gold 0.2496 oz. AGW, 22 mm. **Subject:** Hammer Mill in Dobriv **Designer:** Jiroslav Veslak

Date	Mintage	F	VF	XF	Unc	BU
2010	3,797	—	—	—	—	475
Note: Milled edge						
2010 Proof	9,997	Value: 500				
Note: Plain edge						

KM# 118 2500 KORUN
7.7700 g., 0.9990 Gold 0.2496 oz. AGW, 22 mm. **Subject:** Michael Mine in Ostrana **Obv:** Turbine **Rev:** Mine shaft

Date	Mintage	F	VF	XF	Unc	BU
2010	3,697	—	—	—	—	475
Note: Milled edge						
2010 Proof	9,097	Value: 500				
Note: Plain edge						

KM# 124 5000 KORUN
15.5530 g., 0.9999 Gold 0.5000 oz. AGW, 28 mm. **Subject:** Gothic Bridge in Pisek

Date	Mintage	F	VF	XF	Unc	BU
2011	2,600	—	—	—	—	900
2011 Proof	6,900	Value: 950				

KM# 125 5000 KORUN
15.5530 g., 0.9999 Gold 0.5000 oz. AGW, 28 mm. **Subject:** Renaissance Bridge in Stribro

Date	Mintage	F	VF	XF	Unc	BU
2011	2,700	—	—	—	—	900
Note: Milled edge						
2011 Proof	7,300	Value: 950				
Note: Plain edge						

KM# 132 5000 KORUN
15.5530 g., 0.9999 Gold 0.5000 oz. AGW, 28 mm. **Subject:** Banocco Bridge in Namest nad Oslavou

Date	Mintage	F	VF	XF	Unc	BU
2012	3,200	—	—	—	—	950
2012 Proof	9,000	Value: 950				

KM# 133 5000 KORUN
15.5530 g., 0.9999 Gold 0.5000 oz. AGW, 28 mm. **Subject:** Negrelli viaduct in Prague

Date	Mintage	F	VF	XF	Unc	BU
2012	3,900	—	—	—	—	900
2012 Proof	12,200	Value: 950				

KM# 134 10000 KORUN
31.1070 g., 0.9999 Gold 1.0000 oz. AGW, 34 mm. **Subject:** Gold Bulla of Sicily, 800th Anniversary

Date	Mintage	F	VF	XF	Unc	BU
2012	3,100	—	—	—	—	1,900
2012 Proof	10,900	Value: 2,000				

MINT SETS

KM#	Date	Mintage	Identification	Issue Price	Mkt Val
MS14	2001 (9)	11,500	KM#1, 2.3, 3.2, 4-9, Tyn Church folder	—	17.50
MS15	2002 (9)	11,885	KM#1, 2.3, 3.2, 4-9, Castles	—	60.00
MS16	2002 (9)	5,115	KM#1, 2.3, 3.2, 4-9, NATO Summit folder	—	17.50
MS17	2003 (9)	22,000	KM#1, 2.3, 3.2, 4-9, CNB 10th Anniversary	—	30.00
MS18	2004 (7)	7,500	KM#1, 3.2, 4-5, 7-9, Football	—	30.00
MS19	2004 (7)	13,000	KM#1, 3.2, 4-5, 7-9, EU Entry	—	40.00
MS20	2004 (7)	10,000	KM#1, 3.2, 4-5, 7-9 IIHF Hockey Year	—	16.00
MS21	2005 (8)	13,015	KM#1, 3.2, 4-5, 7-9, plus Smetna/Dvorak Medal and CD	—	17.50
MS22	2006 (7)	9,000	KM#1, 3.2, 4-5, 7-9. UNESCO Folder	—	16.00
MS23	2006 (7)	5,139	KM#1, 3.2, 4-5, 7-9, Football Championship	—	40.00
MS24	2006 (7)	9,784	KM#1, 3.2, 4-5, 7-9, plus Euro Medal	—	45.00
MS25	2007 (7)	8,500	KM#1, 3.2, 4-5, 7-9, UNESCO Kunta Hora folder	—	25.00
MS26	2007 (14)	10,000	KM#1, 3.2, 4-5, 7-9. Natural beauties with Slovakia coins	—	35.00
MS27	2008 (7)	9,000	KM#1, 3.2, 4-5, 7-9, plus UNESCO Medal	—	30.00
MS28	2008 (8)	6,000	KM#1, 3.2, 4-5, 7-9. Soccer medal and package	—	17.50
MS29	2009 (8)	10,000	KM#1, 3.2, 4-5, 7-9 plus brass Southern Bohemia Medal	—	17.50
MS30	2010 (6)	10,000	KM#1, 3.2, 4-5, 7-9, Zlin Region folder	—	17.50
MS31	2011 (6)	10,000	KM#1, 4-5, 7-9, Plzen Region folder	—	17.50
MS32	2011 (6)	5,000	KM#1, 4-5, 7-9. Baby set.	—	17.50
MS33	2011 (6)	450	KM# 1, 4-5, 7-9. ENA and CNB official distribution	12.00	15.00

PROOF SETS

KM#	Date	Mintage	Identification	Issue Price	Mkt Val
PS6	2001 (9)	2,500	KM#1, 2.3, 3.1, 4-9	35.00	250
PS7	2002 (9)	3,490	KM#1, 2.3, 3.2, 4-9	35.00	250
PS8	2003 (9)	3,000	KM#1, 2.3, 3.2, 4-9	35.00	150
PS9	2004 (7)	4,000	KM#1, 3.2, 4-5, 7-9	35.00	100
PS10	2005 (8)	3,000	KM#1, 3.2, 4-5, 7-9, and silver strike of Czechoslovakia KM#4	—	100
PS11	2006 (8)	2,500	KM#1, 3.2, 4-5, 7-9, and silver strike of Czechoslovakia KM#2	—	120
PS12	2007 (8)	2,500	KM#1, 3.2, 4-5, 7-9, and silver Unesco medal	—	120
PS13	2008 (8)	2,500	KM#1, 3.2, 4-5, 7-9, and silver medal for 15th Anniversary of Republic	—	150
PS14	2009 (8)	3,200	KM#1, 3.2, 4-5, 7-9, and silver medal for the Czech Presidency of the EU	—	85.00
PS15	2010 (7)	3,200	KM#1, 4-5, 7-9, plus silver T. G. Masaryk medal	—	85.00
PS16	2011 (7)	3,500	KM#1, 4-5, 7-9, plus silver Ema Destinnova medal in a velvet case	—	85.00
PS17	2011 (7)	2,000	KM#1, 4-5, 7-9, plus silver Ema Destinnova medal in a leather case	—	120

DENMARK

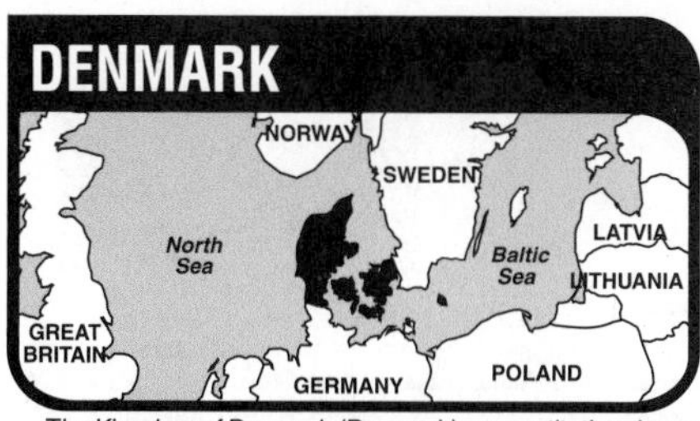

The Kingdom of Denmark (Danmark), a constitutional monarchy located at the mouth of the Baltic Sea, has an area of 16,639 sq. mi. (43,070 sq. km.) and a population of 5.2 million. Capital: Copenhagen. Most of the country is arable. Agriculture is conducted by large farms served by cooperatives. The largest industries are food processing, iron and metal, and shipping. Machinery, meats (chiefly bacon), dairy products and chemicals are exported.

As a result of a referendum held September 28, 2000, the currency of the European Monetary Union, the Euro, will not be introduced in Denmark in the foreseeable future.

RULER

Margrethe II, 1972—

MINT MARKS

(h) - Copenhagen, heart

MINT OFFICIALS' INITIALS

Copenhagen Mint

Letter	Date	Name
LG	1989-2001	Laust Grove

MONEYERS' INITIALS

Copenhagen Mint

Letter	Date	Name
A	1986-	Johan Alkjaer (designer)
HV	1986-	Hanne Varming (sculptor)
JP	1989-	Jan Petersen

MONETARY SYSTEM

100 Øre = 1 Krone

KINGDOM

DECIMAL COINAGE

KM# 868.1 25 ORE

2.8000 g., Bronze, 17.5 mm. **Ruler:** Margrethe II **Obv:** Large crown divides date above, initial to right of country **Rev:** Denomination, small heart above, mint mark and initials LG-JP below **Note:** Beginning in 1996 and ending with 1998, the words "DANMARK" and "ØRE" have raised edges. Heart mint mark under "ØRE"; Prev. KM#868.

Date	Mintage	F	VF	XF	Unc	BU
2001 LG; JP; A	10,530,000	—	—	—	0.15	—

KM# 868.2 25 ORE

2.8000 g., Bronze, 17.5 mm. **Ruler:** Margrethe II **Obv:** Large crown divides date above **Rev:** Denomination, small heart above **Edge:** Plain **Note:** Without initials

Date	Mintage	F	VF	XF	Unc	BU
2002	12,000,000	—	—	—	0.15	—
2003	17,590,000	—	—	—	0.15	—
2004	7,040,304	—	—	—	0.15	1.50
2004 Proof	3,000	Value: 15.00				
2005	19,039,000	—	—	—	0.15	1.50
2005 Proof	2,650	Value: 15.00				
2006	16,796,000	—	—	—	0.15	1.50
2006 Proof	1,800	Value: 15.00				
2007	20,592,000	—	—	—	0.15	1.50
2007 Proof	1,400	Value: 15.00				
2008	2,049,000	—	—	—	1.50	2.25
2008 Proof	1,000	Value: 15.00				

KM# 866.2 50 ORE

4.3000 g., Bronze, 21.5 mm. **Ruler:** Margrethe II **Obv:** Large crown divides date above, initial to right of country name **Rev:** Large heart above value, mint mark and initials LG-JP below **Note:** Beginning in 1996 and ending with 1998, the words "DANMARK" and "ØRE" have raised edges. Heart mint mark under the word "ØRE".

Date	Mintage	F	VF	XF	Unc	BU
2001 LG; JP; A	12,270,000	—	—	—	0.25	—

KM# 866.3 50 ORE

4.3000 g., Bronze, 21.5 mm. **Ruler:** Margrethe II **Obv:** Large crown divides date above **Rev:** Small heart above denomination **Edge:** Plain **Note:** No initials

Date	Mintage	F	VF	XF	Unc	BU
2002	3,900,000	—	—	—	0.20	—
2003	8,817,000	—	—	—	0.15	—
2004	10,040,706	—	—	—	0.15	2.25
2004 Proof	3,000	Value: 15.00				
2005	12,037,000	—	—	—	0.15	2.25
2005 Proof	2,650	Value: 15.00				
2006	14,843,000	—	—	—	0.15	2.25
2006 Proof	1,800	Value: 15.00				
2007	10,198,000	—	—	—	0.15	2.25
2007 Proof	1,400	Value: 15.00				
2008	2,573,000	—	—	—	0.15	2.25
2008 Proof	1,000	Value: 15.00				
2009 In sets only	25,700	—	—	—	—	3.50
2009 Proof	1,050	Value: 15.00				
2010 In sets only	24,300	—	—	—	—	3.50
2010 Proof	1,010	Value: 15.00				
2011 In sets only	—	—	—	—	—	3.50
2011 Proof	—	Value: 15.00				
2012 In sets only	—	—	—	—	—	3.50

KM# 873.1 KRONE

3.6000 g., Copper-Nickel, 20.25 mm. **Ruler:** Margrethe II **Obv:** 3 crowned MII monograms around center hole, date, mint mark, and initials LG-JP-A below **Rev:** Wave design surrounds center hole, value above, hearts flank **Edge:** Reeded **Note:** Prev. KM#873.

Date	Mintage	F	VF	XF	Unc	BU
2001 LG; JP; A	14,640,000	—	—	—	0.50	—

KM# 873.2 KRONE

3.6000 g., Copper-Nickel, 20.25 mm. **Ruler:** Margrethe II **Obv:** 3 crowned MII monograms around center hole, date below **Rev:** Design surounds center hole, value above, hearts flank **Edge:** Reeded **Note:** Without initials

Date	Mintage	F	VF	XF	Unc	BU
2002	9,000,000	—	—	—	0.45	—
2003	5,231,000	—	—	—	0.45	—
2004	16,139,596	—	—	—	0.45	3.00
2004 Proof	3,000	Value: 18.00				
2005	16,757,000	—	—	—	0.45	3.00
2005 Proof	2,650	Value: 18.00				
2006	21,026,000	—	—	—	0.45	3.00
2006 Proof	1,800	Value: 18.00				
2007	11,729,000	—	—	—	0.45	3.00
2007 Proof	1,400	Value: 18.00				
2008	13,339,000	—	—	—	0.45	3.00
2008 Proof	1,000	Value: 18.00				
2009	624,000	—	—	—	1.00	4.00
2009 Proof	1,050	Value: 18.00				
2010 In sets only	26,000	—	—	—	—	6.00
2010 Proof	1,010	Value: 18.00				
2011 In sets only	21,000	—	—	—	—	6.00
2011 Proof	1,000	Value: 18.00				
2012	—	—	—	—	—	6.00
2012 In sets only	—	—	—	—	0.45	—

KM# 874.1 2 KRONER

5.9000 g., Copper-Nickel, 24.5 mm. **Ruler:** Margrethe II **Obv:** 3 crowned MII monograms around center hole, date and initials LG-JP-A below **Rev:** Design surrounds center hole, denomination above, hearts flank **Edge:** Segmented reeding **Note:** Prev. KM#874.

Date	Mintage	F	VF	XF	Unc	BU
2001 LG; JP; A	11,180,000	—	—	—	0.60	—

KM# 874.2 2 KRONER

5.9000 g., Copper-Nickel, 24.5 mm. **Ruler:** Margrethe II **Obv:** 3 crowned MII monograms around center hole, date and initials LGpJP-A below **Rev:** Wave design surrounds center hole, denomination above, hearts flank **Edge:** Segmented reeding **Note:** Without initials

Date	Mintage	F	VF	XF	Unc	BU
2002	60,159,000	—	—	—	0.60	—
2004	7,381,531	—	—	—	0.60	3.00
2004 Proof	3,000	Value: 22.00				
2005	16,681,000	—	—	—	0.60	3.00
2005 Proof	2,650	Value: 22.00				
2006	7,329,000	—	—	—	0.60	3.00
2006 Proof	1,800	Value: 22.00				
2007	22,059,000	—	—	—	0.60	3.00
2007 Proof	1,400	Value: 22.00				
2008	2,622,000	—	—	—	0.60	3.00
2008 Proof	1,000	Value: 22.00				
2009 In sets only	25,700	—	—	—	—	6.00
2009 Proof	1,050	Value: 22.00				
2010 In sets only	24,300	—	—	—	—	6.00
2010 Proof	1,010	Value: 22.00				
2011	919,000	—	—	—	0.80	4.00
2011 Proof	1,000	Value: 22.00				
2012	—	—	—	—	0.80	4.00
2012 In sets only	—	—	—	—	—	6.00

KM# 869.1 5 KRONER

9.2000 g., Copper-Nickel, 28.5 mm. **Ruler:** Margrethe II **Obv:** 3 crowned MII monograms around center hole, date and initials LG-JP-A below **Rev:** Wave design surrounds center hole, denomination above, hearts flank **Edge:** Reeded **Note:** Large and small date varieties exist.

Date	Mintage	F	VF	XF	Unc	BU
2001 LG; JP; A	5,700,000	—	—	—	1.50	—

KM# 869.2 5 KRONER

9.2000 g., Copper-Nickel, 28.5 mm. **Ruler:** Margrethe II **Obv:** 3 crowned MII monograms around center hole, date below **Rev:** Wave design surrounds center hole, denomination above, hearts flank **Edge:** Reeded **Note:** Without initials

Date	Mintage	F	VF	XF	Unc	BU
2002	5,980,000	—	—	—	1.50	—
2004	1,415,925	—	—	—	1.50	4.00
2004 Proof	3,000	Value: 30.00				
2005	7,073,000	—	—	—	1.50	4.00

Date	Mintage	F	VF	XF	Unc	BU
2005 Proof	2,650	Value: 30.00				
2006	3,431,000	—	—	—	1.50	4.00
2006 Proof	1,800	Value: 30.00				
2007	4,983,000	—	—	—	1.50	4.00
2007 Proof	1,400	Value: 30.00				
2008	7,506,000	—	—	—	1.50	4.00
2008 Proof	1,000	Value: 30.00				
2009 In sets only	25,700	—	—	—	—	6.00
2009 Proof	1,050	Value: 30.00				
2010 In sets only	24,300	—	—	—	—	6.00
2010 Proof	1,010	Value: 30.00				
2011 In sets only	19,900	—	—	—	—	8.00
2011 Proof	1,000	Value: 30.00				
2012 In sets only	—	—	—	—	—	6.00
2012 Proof	—	Value: 30.00				

KM# 887.1 10 KRONER

7.0000 g., Aluminum-Bronze, 23.35 mm. **Ruler:** Margrethe II **Obv:** Crowned head right within inner circle, date, initials LG-JP-A below, mint mark after II in title **Obv. Legend:** MARGRETHE II - DANMARKS DRONNING **Rev:** Crowned arms within inner circle above denomination **Edge:** Plain

Date	Mintage	F	VF	XF	Unc	BU
2001(h) LG; JP; A	4,800,000	—	—	—	4.00	—

KM# 887.2 10 KRONER

7.1000 g., Aluminum-Bronze, 23.35 mm. **Ruler:** Margrethe II **Obv:** Crowned bust right, mint mark after II in title **Obv. Legend:** MARGRETHE II - DANMARKS DRONNING **Rev:** Crowned arms and denomination **Edge:** Plain **Note:** Without initials

Date	Mintage	F	VF	XF	Unc	BU
2002(h)	7,299,900	—	—	—	3.50	—

KM# 896 10 KRONER

7.0000 g., Aluminum-Bronze, 23.35 mm. **Ruler:** Margrethe II **Obv:** Crowned bust right within circle, date below **Obv. Legend:** MARGRETHE II - DANMARKS DRONNING **Rev:** Crowned arms above denomination **Edge:** Plain **Designer:** Mogens Moller

Date	Mintage	F	VF	XF	Unc	BU
2004(h)	5,835,426	—	—	—	3.25	5.50
2004(h) Proof	3,000	Value: 35.00				
2005(h)	2,614,000	—	—	—	3.25	5.50
2005(h) Proof	2,650	Value: 35.00				
2006(h)	3,530,000	—	—	—	3.25	5.50
2006(h) Proof	1,800	Value: 35.00				
2007(h)	3,294,000	—	—	—	3.00	5.50
2007(h) Proof	1,400	Value: 35.00				
2008(h)	2,258,000	—	—	—	3.00	5.50
2008(h) Proof	1,000	Value: 35.00				
2009(h)	1,701,000	—	—	—	3.00	5.50
2009(h) Proof	1,050	Value: 35.00				
2010(h) In sets only	—	—	—	—	7.00	12.00
2010(h) Proof	—	Value: 35.00				

KM# 898 10 KRONER

7.0000 g., Aluminum-Bronze, 23.35 mm. **Ruler:** Margrethe II **Series:** Fairy Tales **Subject:** Hans Christian Andersen's Ugly duckling story **Obv:** Crowned bust right within circle, date below **Obv. Legend:** MARGRETHE II - DANMARKS DRONNING **Rev:** Swan and reflection on water within circle, value below **Edge:** Plain

Date	Mintage	F	VF	XF	Unc	BU
2005(h)	1,206,675	—	—	—	3.25	8.00

KM# 906 10 KRONER

31.1000 g., 0.9990 Silver 0.9988 oz. ASW, 38 mm. **Ruler:** Margrethe II **Series:** Fairy Tales **Subject:** Hans Christian Andersen's The Ugly Duckling **Obv:** Crowned bust right **Obv. Legend:** MARGRETHE II - DANMARKS DRONNING **Rev:** Swan and reflection on water

Date	Mintage	F	VF	XF	Unc	BU
2005(h)	75,000	—	—	—	—	40.00

KM# 907 10 KRONER

8.6500 g., 0.9000 Gold 0.2503 oz. AGW, 22 mm. **Ruler:** Margrethe II **Series:** Fairy Tales **Subject:** Hans Christian Andersen's The Ugly Duckling **Obv:** Crowned bust right **Obv. Legend:** MARGRETHE II - DANMARKS DRONNING **Rev:** Swan and reflection on water

Date	Mintage	F	VF	XF	Unc	BU
2005(h)	7,000	—	—	—	—	450

KM# 900 10 KRONER

7.0000 g., Aluminum-Bronze, 23.35 mm. **Ruler:** Margrethe II **Series:** Fairy Tales **Subject:** Hans Christian Andersen's Little Mermaid **Obv:** Crowned bust right within circle, date below **Obv. Legend:** MARGRETHE II - DANMARKS DRONNING **Rev:** Little Mermaid **Edge:** Plain

Date	Mintage	F	VF	XF	Unc	BU
2005(h)	1,206,675	—	—	—	3.25	8.00

KM# 908 10 KRONER

31.1000 g., 0.9990 Silver 0.9988 oz. ASW, 38 mm. **Ruler:** Margrethe II **Series:** Fairy Tales **Subject:** Hans Christian Andersen's Little Mermaid **Obv:** Crowned bust right, date below **Obv. Legend:** MARGRETHE II - DANMARKS DRONNING **Rev:** Little Mermaid

Date	Mintage	F	VF	XF	Unc	BU
2005(h)	40,220	—	—	—	—	40.00

KM# 911 10 KRONER

8.6500 g., 0.9000 Gold 0.2503 oz. AGW, 22 mm. **Ruler:** Margrethe II **Series:** Fairy Tales **Subject:** Hans Christian Andersen's Little Mermaid **Obv:** Crowned bust right **Obv. Legend:** MARGRETHE II - DANMARKS DRONNING **Rev:** Little Mermaid

Date	Mintage	F	VF	XF	Unc	BU
2005(h)	4,220	—	—	—	—	475

KM# 903 10 KRONER

7.1000 g., Aluminum-Bronze, 23.35 mm. **Ruler:** Margrethe II **Series:** Fairy Tales **Subject:** H.C. Andersen's "The Shadow" **Obv:** Crowned bust right within circle, date below **Obv. Legend:** MARGRETHE II - DANMARKS DRONNING **Rev:** Stylized figures **Edge:** Plain

Date	Mintage	F	VF	XF	Unc	BU
2006(h)	1,206,675	—	—	—	3.25	8.00

KM# 909 10 KRONER

31.1000 g., 0.9990 Silver 0.9988 oz. ASW, 38 mm. **Ruler:** Margrethe II **Series:** Fairy Tales **Subject:** H.C. Andersen's "Skyggen" (The Shadow) **Obv:** Crowned bust right **Obv. Legend:** MARGRETHE II - DANMARKS DRONNING **Rev:** Stylized figures

Date	Mintage	F	VF	XF	Unc	BU
2006(h)	22,317	—	—	—	—	40.00

KM# 910 10 KRONER

8.6500 g., 0.9000 Gold 0.2503 oz. AGW, 22 mm. **Ruler:** Margrethe II **Series:** Fairy Tales **Subject:** H.C. Andersen's "Skyggen" (The Shadow) **Obv:** Crowned bust right **Obv. Legend:** MARGRETHE II - DANMARKS DRONNING **Rev:** Stylized figures

Date	Mintage	F	VF	XF	Unc	BU
2006(h)	3,070	—	—	—	—	475

KM# 914a 10 KRONER

31.1000 g., 0.9990 Silver 0.9988 oz. ASW, 38 mm. **Ruler:** Margrethe II **Series:** Fairy Tales **Subject:** Hans Christian Andersen's Snow Queen **Obv:** Crowned bust right **Obv. Legend:** MARGRETHE II - DANMARKS DRONNING **Rev:** Ice pieces

Date	Mintage	F	VF	XF	Unc	BU
2006(h)	25,758	—	—	—	—	40.00

KM# 914b 10 KRONER

8.6500 g., 0.9000 Gold 0.2503 oz. AGW, 22 mm. **Ruler:** Margrethe II **Series:** Fairy Tales **Subject:** The Snow Queen **Obv:** Crowned bust right **Obv. Legend:** MARGRETHE II - DANMARKS DRONNING **Rev:** Ice pieces

Date	Mintage	F	VF	XF	Unc	BU
2006(h)	3,075	—	—	—	—	475

KM# 914 10 KRONER

7.1000 g., Aluminum-Bronze, 23.35 mm. **Ruler:** Margrethe II **Series:** Fairy Tales **Subject:** Hans Christian Andersen's Snow Queen **Obv:** Crowned bust right **Obv. Legend:** MARGRETHE II - DANMARKS DRONNING **Rev:** Ice pieces

Date	Mintage	F	VF	XF	Unc	BU
2006(h)	1,206,675	—	—	—	3.25	10.00

KM# 923a 10 KRONER

31.1000 g., 0.9990 Silver 0.9988 oz. ASW, 38 mm. **Ruler:** Margrethe II **Series:** Fairy Tales **Subject:** H.C. Anderson's 'The Nightengale' **Rev:** Bird

Date	Mintage	F	VF	XF	Unc	BU
2007 Proof	18,117	Value: 40.00				

KM# 916 10 KRONER

7.1000 g., Aluminum-Bronze, 23.35 mm. **Ruler:** Margrethe II **Subject:** International Polar Year 2007-2009 **Obv:** Head with tiara right **Obv. Legend:** MARGRETHE II - DANMARKS DRONNING **Rev:** Polar bear facing, walking on ice flow **Rev. Legend:** POLARÅR 2007-2009 **Edge:** Plain

Date	Mintage	F	VF	XF	Unc	BU
2007(h)	1,200,000	—	—	—	3.25	8.00

KM# 923 10 KRONER

7.1000 g., Aluminum-Bronze, 23.35 mm. **Ruler:** Margrethe II **Series:** Fairy Tales **Subject:** H.C. Anderson's 'The Nightingale' **Rev:** Bird

Date	Mintage	F	VF	XF	Unc	BU
2007	1,206,675	—	—	—	3.25	8.00

KM# 923b 10 KRONER

8.6500 g., 0.9000 Gold 0.2503 oz. AGW, 22 mm. **Ruler:** Margrethe II **Series:** Fairy Tales **Subject:** H.C. Anderson's 'The Nightengale' **Rev:** Bird

Date	Mintage	F	VF	XF	Unc	BU
2007	2,964	—	—	—	—	475

KM# 925 10 KRONER

7.2000 g., Aluminum-Bronze, 23.35 mm. **Ruler:** Margrethe II **Series:** International Polar Year 2007-2009 **Obv:** Head with tiara right **Rev:** Outlined globe **Rev. Legend:** POLARÅR 2007-2009 **Edge:** Plain

Date	Mintage	F	VF	XF	Unc	BU
2008(h)	1,200,000	—	—	—	3.25	8.00

KM# 932 10 KRONER

7.1000 g., Aluminum-Bronze, 23.5 mm. **Ruler:** Margrethe II **Rev:** Ice scape, Northern Lights

Date	Mintage	F	VF	XF	Unc	BU
2009	1,200,000	—	—	—	3.00	10.00

KM# 943 10 KRONER

7.0000 g., Aluminum-Bronze, 23.35 mm. **Ruler:** Margrethe II **Obv:** Head right **Obv. Legend:** MARGRETHE II DANMARKS DRONNING **Rev:** Crowned shield and value **Edge:** Plain

Date	Mintage	F	VF	XF	Unc	BU
2011(h)	2,339,000	—	—	—	4.00	—
2011(h) Proof	1,000	Value: 25.00				
2012 In sets only	—	—	—	—	4.00	—
2012 Proof	—	Value: 25.00				

KM# 888.1 20 KRONER

9.3000 g., Aluminum-Bronze, 27 mm. **Ruler:** Margrethe II **Obv:** Crowned bust right within circle, date and initials LG-JP-A below, mint mark after II in legend **Obv. Legend:** MARGRETHE II - DANMARKS DRONNING **Rev:** Crowned arms within ornaments and value **Edge:** Alternating reeded and plain sections **Designer:** Mogens Moller

Date	Mintage	F	VF	XF	Unc	BU
2001(h) LG; JP; A	2,900,000	—	—	—	5.50	10.00

KM# 889 20 KRONER

9.3000 g., Aluminum-Bronze, 27 mm. **Ruler:** Margrethe II **Series:** Danish Towers **Obv:** Crowned bust right within circle date below, mint mark after II in legend **Obv. Legend:** MARGRETHE II - DANMARKS DRONNING **Rev:** Aarhus City Hall **Edge:** Reeded and plain sections

Date	Mintage	F	VF	XF	Unc	BU
2002(h)	1,208,600	—	—	—	6.50	10.00

KM# 888.2 20 KRONER

9.3000 g., Aluminum-Bronze, 27 mm. **Ruler:** Margrethe II **Obv:** Crowned bust right within circle, mint mark after II in legend **Obv. Legend:** MARGRETHE II - DANMARKS DRONNING **Rev:** Crowned arms within ornaments and value **Edge:** Alternate reeded and plain sections **Designer:** Mogens Møller **Note:** Without initials.

Date	Mintage	F	VF	XF	Unc	BU
2002(h)	5,500,000	—	—	—	6.50	10.00

KM# 890 20 KRONER

9.3000 g., Aluminum-Bronze, 27 mm. **Ruler:** Margrethe II **Series:** Danish towers **Obv:** Crowned bust right within circle, mint mark and date **Obv. Legend:** MARGRETHE II - DANMARKS DRONNING **Rev:** Copenhagen Old Stock Exchange spire with four intertwined dragon tails **Edge:** Alternate reeded and plain sections

Date	Mintage	F	VF	XF	Unc	BU
2003(h)	1,208,600	—	—	—	6.50	10.00

KM# 891 20 KRONER

9.3000 g., Aluminum-Bronze, 27 mm. **Ruler:** Margrethe II **Obv:** Crowned bust right within circle, mint mark and date **Obv. Legend:** MARGRETHE II - DANMARKS DRONNING **Rev:** Crowned arms above denomination **Edge:** Alternate reeded and plain sections

Date	Mintage	F	VF	XF	Unc	BU
2003(h)	5,720,000	—	—	—	6.50	10.00
2004(h)	6,922,182	—	—	—	6.50	10.00
2004(h) Proof	3,000	Value: 50.00				
2005(h)	4,194,000	—	—	—	6.50	10.00
2005(h) Proof	2,650	Value: 50.00				
2006(h)	3,051,000	—	—	—	6.50	10.00
2006(h) Proof	1,800	Value: 50.00				
2007(h)	2,409,000	—	—	—	6.50	10.00
2007(h) Proof	1,400	Value: 50.00				
2008(h)	1,982,000	—	—	—	6.50	10.00
2008(h) Proof	1,000	Value: 50.00				
2009(h)	2,021,000	—	—	—	6.50	10.00
2009(h) Proof	1,050	Value: 50.00				
2010(h) In sets only	—	—	—	—	8.00	10.00
2010(h) Proof	1,010	Value: 50.00				

KM# 892 20 KRONER

9.3100 g., Aluminum-Bronze, 27 mm. **Ruler:** Margrethe II **Series:** Danish towers **Obv:** Crowned bust right within circle, mint mark and date **Obv. Legend:** MARGRETHE II - DANMARKS DRONNING **Rev:** Christiansborg Castle (parliament) tower and Danish flag **Edge:** Alternate reeded and plain sections

Date	Mintage	F	VF	XF	Unc	BU
2003(h)	1,208,600	—	—	—	6.25	10.00

KM# 893 20 KRONER

9.3100 g., Aluminum-Bronze, 27 mm. **Ruler:** Margrethe II **Series:** Danish Towers **Obv:** Crowned bust right within circle, date below **Obv. Legend:** MARGRETHE II - DANMARKS DRONNING **Rev:** Gåsetårnet tower **Edge:** Alternate reeded and plain sections

Date	Mintage	F	VF	XF	Unc	BU
2004(h)	1,208,600	—	—	—	6.00	10.00

KM# 894 20 KRONER

9.3100 g., Aluminum-Bronze, 27 mm. **Ruler:** Margrethe II **Subject:** Crown Prince's Wedding **Obv:** Crowned bust right within circle, date below **Obv. Legend:** MARGRETHE II - DANMARKS DRONNING **Rev:** Crown Prince Frederik and Crown Princess Mary **Edge:** Alternate reeded and plain sections

Date	Mintage	F	VF	XF	Unc	BU
2004(h)	1,200,000	—	—	—	6.50	10.00

KM# 897 20 KRONER

9.3100 g., Aluminum-Bronze, 27 mm. **Ruler:** Margrethe II **Series:** Danish Towers **Obv:** Crowned bust right within circle, date below **Obv. Legend:** MARGRETHE II - DANMARKS DRONNING **Rev:** Svaneke water tower, Bornholm **Edge:** Alternate reeded and plain sections

Date	Mintage	F	VF	XF	Unc	BU
2004(h)	1,208,600	—	—	—	6.25	10.00

KM# 899 20 KRONER

9.3000 g., Aluminum-Bronze, 27 mm. **Ruler:** Margrethe II **Series:** Danish Towers **Obv:** Crowned bust right within circle, date below **Obv. Legend:** MARGRETHE II - DANMARKS DRONNING **Rev:** Landet Kirke, with elements from the story of Elvira Madigan and Sixten Sparre, including a revolver among leaves of chestnut-trees **Edge:** Segmented reeding

Date	Mintage	F	VF	XF	Unc	BU
2005(h)	1,208,600	—	—	—	6.25	10.00

KM# 901 20 KRONER

9.3000 g., Aluminum-Bronze, 27 mm. **Ruler:** Margrethe II **Series:** Danish Towers **Obv:** Crowned bust right within circle, date below **Obv. Legend:** MARGRETHE II - DANMARKS DRONNING **Rev:** Lighthouse of Nolsoy (Faeroe Islands) **Edge:** Alternate plain and reeded segments

Date	Mintage	F	VF	XF	Unc	BU
2005(h)	1,208,600	—	—	—	6.25	10.00

KM# 902 20 KRONER

9.3300 g., Aluminum-Bronze, 27 mm. **Ruler:** Margrethe II **Series:** Danish Towers **Obv:** Crowned bust right within circle, date below **Obv. Legend:** MARGRETHE II - DANMARKS DRONNING **Rev:** Gråsten Castle Bell Tower **Edge:** Segmented reeding

Date	Mintage	F	VF	XF	Unc	BU
2006(h)	1,208,600	—	—	—	6.25	10.00

KM# 913 20 KRONER

9.3000 g., Aluminum-Bronze, 27 mm. **Ruler:** Margrethe II **Series:** Danish Towers **Obv:** Crowned bust right within circle, date below **Obv. Legend:** MARGRETHE II - DANMARKS DRONNING **Rev:** The Greenland Cairns: Nukaritt/Three Brothers **Rev. Legend:** TRE BRØDRE **Edge:** Alternate plain and reeded segments

Date	Mintage	F	VF	XF	Unc	BU
2006(h)	1,208,600	—	—	—	6.25	10.00

KM# 919 20 KRONER

9.3000 g., Aluminum-Bronze, 27 mm. **Ruler:** Margrethe II **Series:** Danish Towers **Obv:** Bust with tiarra right **Obv. Legend:** MARGRETHE II - DANMARKS DRONNING **Rev:** City Hall in Copenhagen **Rev. Legend:** KØBENHAVNS RÅDHUS **Edge:** Alternate plain and reeded segments

Date	Mintage	F	VF	XF	Unc	BU
2007(h)	1,208,600	—	—	—	6.25	10.00

KM# 920 20 KRONER
9.3000 g., Aluminum-Bronze, 27 mm. **Ruler:** Margrethe II **Series:** Danish Ships **Obv:** Crowned bust right **Obv. Legend:** MARGRETHE II - DANMARKS DRONNING **Rev:** Sailing ship Jylland **Rev. Legend:** FREGATTEN - JYLLAND **Edge:** Segmented reeding

Date	Mintage	F	VF	XF	Unc	BU
2007(h)	1,200,000	—	—	—	6.25	10.00

KM# 921 20 KRONER
9.3000 g., Aluminum-Bronze, 27 mm. **Ruler:** Margrethe II **Series:** Danish ships **Subject:** The Galathea 3 expedition **Obv:** Crowned bust right **Obv. Legend:** MARGRETHE II - DANMARKS DRONNING **Rev:** Ship Vaedderen, route map in background **Rev. Legend:** VAEDDEREN **Edge:** Segmented reeding

Date	Mintage	F	VF	XF	Unc	BU
2007(h)	1,200,000	—	—	—	6.25	10.00

KM# 926 20 KRONER
9.3000 g., Aluminum-Bronze, 27 mm. **Ruler:** Margrethe II **Series:** Danish Ships **Obv:** Head with tiara right **Rev:** World's first ocean-going diesel-engine merchant ship, built 1912 **Rev. Legend:** SELANDIA **Edge:** Segmented reeding

Date	Mintage	F	VF	XF	Unc	BU
2008(h)	1,200,000	—	—	—	6.25	9.00
2008(h) Proof	1,500	Value: 85.00				

KM# 927 20 KRONER
9.3000 g., Aluminum-Bronze, 27 mm. **Ruler:** Margrethe II **Series:** Danish Ships **Subject:** Voyage to Dublin, Ireland, with full size replica Viking ship, HAVHINGSTEN **Obv:** Crowned bust right **Obv. Legend:** MARGRETHE II - DANMARKS DRONNING **Rev:** Sailing vessel at sea **Rev. Legend:** HAVHINGSTEN / 20 KRONER **Edge:** Segmented reeding

Date	Mintage	F	VF	XF	Unc	BU
2008	1,200,000	—	—	—	6.00	9.00
2008 Proof	1,500	Value: 85.00				

KM# 928 20 KRONER
9.3000 g., Aluminum-Bronze, 27 mm. **Ruler:** Margrethe II **Series:** Danish Ships **Rev:** Royal Yacht Dannebrog **Edge:** Segmented reeding

Date	Mintage	F	VF	XF	Unc	BU
2008	1,200,000	—	—	—	6.00	9.00
2008 Proof	1,500	Value: 85.00				

KM# 935 20 KRONER
9.3000 g., Aluminum-Bronze, 27 mm. **Ruler:** Margrethe II **Series:** Danish Ships **Obv:** Crowned bust right **Obv. Legend:** MARGRETHE II - DANMARKS DRONNING **Rev:** Lightship XVII (built 1895) on duty **Edge:** Segmented reeding

Date	Mintage	F	VF	XF	Unc	BU
2009	1,100,000	—	—	—	6.00	9.00
2009 Proof	1,500	Value: 85.00				

KM# 936 20 KRONER
9.3000 g., Aluminum-Bronze, 27 mm. **Ruler:** Margrethe II **Series:** Danish Ships **Obv:** Crowned bust facing right **Rev:** FAERØBÅD (Boat of Faeroe Islands) **Edge:** Segmented reeding **Designer:** Hans Pauli Olsen

Date	Mintage	F	VF	XF	Unc	BU
2009	900,000	—	—	—	6.00	9.00
2009 Proof	2,825	Value: 85.00				

KM# 942 20 KRONER
9.3000 g., Aluminum-Bronze, 27 mm. **Ruler:** Margrethe II **Subject:** The Emma Maersk, a container ship **Obv:** Head right **Obv. Legend:** MARGRETHE II DANMARKS DRONNING **Rev:** Emma Maersk, container ship, right **Edge:** Segmented reeding

Date	Mintage	F	VF	XF	Unc	BU
2010 In sets only	—	—	—	—	6.25	—
2011	800,000	—	—	—	6.25	—
2011 Proof	3,810	Value: 30.00				
2012 In sets only	—	—	—	—	6.25	—
2012 Proof	—	Value: 30.00				

KM# 937 20 KRONER
9.3000 g., Aluminum-Bronze, 27 mm. **Ruler:** Margrethe II **Subject:** Queen's 70th Birthday **Obv:** Head right **Rev:** Crowned shield against background of daisies

Date	Mintage	F	VF	XF	Unc	BU
2010	1,440,000	—	—	—	6.00	9.00
2010 Proof	4,100	Value: 25.00				

KM# 940 20 KRONER
9.3000 g., Aluminum-Bronze, 27 mm. **Ruler:** Margrethe II **Series:** Danish Ships **Subject:** Greenland kayak - women's ship **Obv:** Bust facing right **Rev:** Kayak-Umak **Rev. Legend:** "KAJAK • KONEBÅD" **Edge:** Segmented reeding

Date	Mintage	F	VF	XF	Unc	BU
2010	972,000	—	—	—	6.00	—
2010 Proof	1,877	—	—	—	35.00	—

KM# 944 20 KRONER
9.3000 g., Aluminum-Bronze, 27 mm. **Ruler:** Margrethe II **Obv:** Head right **Obv. Legend:** MARGRETHE II DANMARKS DRONNING **Rev:** Crowned shield and value **Edge:** Segmented reeding

Date	Mintage	F	VF	XF	Unc	BU
2011(h)	—	—	—	—	6.25	—
2011(h) Proof	—	Value: 50.00				
2012 In sets only	—	—	—	—	6.25	—

KM# 941 20 KRONER
9.3000 g., Aluminum-Bronze, 27 mm. **Ruler:** Margrethe II **Series:** Danish Ships **Subject:** The Hjejlen, a paddle steamer **Obv:** Head right **Obv. Legend:** MARGRETHE II DANMARKS DRONNING **Rev:** The Hjejlen and value **Edge:** Segmented reeding

Date	Mintage	F	VF	XF	Unc	BU
2011	700,000	—	—	—	6.25	—
2011 Proof	2,662	Value: 30.00				

KM# 945 20 KRONER
9.3000 g., Aluminum-Bronze, 27 mm. **Ruler:** Margrethe II **Subject:** 40th Jubilee of Queen Margrethe II **Obv:** Bust of Queen Margrethe II facing right **Obv. Legend:** MARGRETHE II DANMARKS DRONNING **Rev:** Design, legend 1972 14 JANUAR 2012 and denomination **Edge:** Segmented reeding

Date	Mintage	F	VF	XF	Unc	BU
2012	1,440,000	—	—	—	5.00	—
2012 Proof	3,180	Value: 28.00				

KM# 948 20 KRONER
9.3000 g., Aluminum-Bronze, 27 mm. **Ruler:** Margrethe II **Series:** Danish Ships **Subject:** The Kong Frederik IX, a ferry **Obv:** Bust of Queen Margrethe II facing right **Obv. Legend:** MARGRETHE II DANMARKS DRONNING **Rev:** The Kong Frederik IX, legend KONG FREDERIK IX and denomination **Edge:** Segmented reeding

Date	Mintage	F	VF	XF	Unc	BU
2012	349,000	—	—	—	5.00	—
2012 Proof	2,331	Value: 28.00				

KM# 917 100 KRONER
31.0000 g., 0.9990 Silver 0.9956 oz. ASW, 38 mm. **Ruler:** Margrethe II **Subject:** International Polar Year 2007-2009 **Obv:** Crowned bust right **Obv. Legend:** MARGRETHE II - DANMARKS DRONNING **Rev:** Polar bear facing, walking on ice flow **Rev. Legend:** POLARÅR 2007-2009

Date	Mintage	F	VF	XF	Unc	BU
2007(h)	43,048	—	—	—	—	50.00

KM# 930 100 KRONER
31.1000 g., 0.9990 Silver 0.9988 oz. ASW, 38 mm. **Ruler:** Margrethe II **Subject:** International Polar Year 2007-2009 **Rev:** Globe and dog sled

Date	Mintage	F	VF	XF	Unc	BU
2008	15,631	—	—	—	—	50.00

KM# 933 100 KRONER
31.1000 g., 0.9990 Silver 0.9988 oz. ASW, 38 mm. **Ruler:** Margrethe II **Subject:** International Polar Year 2007-2009 **Rev:** Ice scape, Northern Lights

Date	Mintage	F	VF	XF	Unc	BU
2009	10,600	—	—	—	—	50.00

KM# 895 200 KRONER
31.1000 g., 0.9990 Silver 0.9988 oz. ASW, 38.3 mm. **Ruler:** Margrethe II **Subject:** Wedding of Crown Prince **Obv:** Crowned bust right within circle, date below **Obv. Legend:** MARGRETHE II - DANMARKS DRONNING **Rev:** Crown Prince Frederik and Crown Princess Mary **Edge:** Plain **Note:** No initials.

Date	Mintage	F	VF	XF	Unc	BU
2004(h)	125,000	—	—	—	—	60.00

KM# 929 500 KRONER
31.1000 g., 0.9990 Silver 0.9988 oz. ASW, 38 mm. **Ruler:** Margrethe II **Rev:** Royal Yacht Dannebrog

Date	Mintage	F	VF	XF	Unc	BU
2008	31,700	—	—	—	—	100

KM# 938 500 KRONER
31.1000 g., 0.9990 Silver 0.9988 oz. ASW, 38 mm. **Ruler:** Margrethe II **Subject:** Queen's 70th Birthday **Obv:** Head right **Rev:** Crowned shield against a background of daisies

Date	Mintage	F	VF	XF	Unc	BU
2010	28,336	—	—	—	—	95.00

KM# 946 500 KRONER
31.1000 g., 0.9990 Silver 0.9988 oz. ASW, 38mm mm. **Ruler:** Margrethe II **Subject:** 40th Jubilee of Queen Margrethe II **Obv:** Bust of the Queen Margrethe II facing right **Obv. Legend:** MARGRETHE II DANMARKS DRONNING **Rev:** Design, legend 1972, 14 JANUAR 2012 and denomination

Date	Mintage	F	VF	XF	Unc	BU
2012	16,881	—	—	—	—	95.00

KM# 918 1000 KRONER
8.6500 g., 0.9000 Gold 0.2503 oz. AGW, 22 mm. **Ruler:** Margrethe II **Subject:** International Polar Year 2007-2009 **Obv:** Crowned bust right **Obv. Legend:** MARGRETHE II - DANMARKS DRONNING **Rev:** Polar bear facing, walking on ice flow **Rev. Legend:** POLARÅR 2007-2009 **Note:** Struck from gold from Greenland having a small polar bear to right of denomination.

Date	Mintage	F	VF	XF	Unc	BU
2007(h) Proof	6,000	Value: 475				

KM# 931 1000 KRONER
8.6500 g., 0.9000 Gold 0.2503 oz. AGW, 22 mm. **Ruler:** Margrethe II **Subject:** International Polar Year 2007-2009 **Rev:** Globe and dog sled

Date	Mintage	F	VF	XF	Unc	BU
2008 Proof	3,604	Value: 475				

KM# 934 1000 KRONER
8.6500 g., 0.9000 Gold 0.2503 oz. AGW, 22 mm. **Ruler:** Margrethe II **Subject:** International Polar Year 2007-2009 **Rev:** Ice scape, Northern Lights

Date	Mintage	F	VF	XF	Unc	BU
2009 Proof	2,400	Value: 500				

KM# 939 1000 KRONER
8.6500 g., 0.9000 Gold 0.2503 oz. AGW, 22 mm. **Ruler:** Margrethe II **Subject:** Queen's 70th Birthday **Obv:** Bust right **Rev:** Crowned shield against background of daisies

Date	Mintage	F	VF	XF	Unc	BU
2010	2,689	—	—	—	525	—

KM# 947 3000 KRONER
8.6500 g., 0.9000 Gold 0.2503 oz. AGW, 22 mm. **Ruler:** Margrethe II **Subject:** 40th Jubilee of Queen Margrethe II **Obv:** Bust of Queen Margrethe II facing right **Obv. Legend:** MARGRETHE II DANMARKS DRONNING **Rev:** Design, legend 1972 14 JANUAR 2012 and denomination **Edge:** Segmented reeding

Date	Mintage	F	VF	XF	Unc	BU
2012	2,325	—	—	—	525	—

MINT SETS

KM#	Date	Mintage	Identification	Issue Price	Mkt Val
MS46	2001 (5)	28,000	KM866.2, 868, 869, 873, 874, 887, 888	15.00	37.50
MS47	2002 (7)	28,000	KM866.3, 868.2, 869.2, 873.2, 874.2, 887.2, 888.2	17.50	35.00
MS48	2003 (6)	30,000	KM866.3, 868.2, 873.2, 889, 890, 891	17.50	35.00
MS49	2004 (8)	33,000	KM#866.3, 868.2, 869.2, 873.2, 874.2, 891, 894, 896, plus Battle of Köge Bay medal in Nordic gold	34.50	75.00
MS50	2005 (8)	26,700	KM#866.3, 868.2, 869.2, 873.2, 874.2, 891, 896, 898, plus Battle of Copenhagen medal in Nordic gold	34.50	50.00
MS51	2006 (8)	25,000	KM#866.3, 868.2, 869.2, 873.2, 874.2, 891, 896, plus Floating Dock medal in Copenhagen sound medal in Nordic gold	40.00	42.00
MS52	2006 (8)	5,000	KM#866.3, 868.2, 869.2, 873.2, 874.2, 891, 896 plus children's medal in Nordic gold. (Children's coin set).	—	48.00
MS53	2002-07 (9)	8,600	KM#889, 890, 892, 893, 897, 899, 901, 902, 913, 919. (Tower coin set).	—	100
MS54	2005-07 (6)	6,675	KM#898, 900, 903, 914, 923 plus Hans Christian Anderson medal in Nordic gold (Fairy tale coin set).	—	55.00
MS55	2007 (8)	23,000	KM#866.3, 868.2, 869.2, 873.2, 874.2, 891, 896 plus Galathea medal in Nordic gold.	—	42.00
MS56	2007 (7)	2,700	KM#866.3, 868.2, 869.2, 873.2, 874.2, 891, 896 plus Children's medal in Nordic gold (Children's coin set)	46.00	50.00
MS57	2008 (7)	1,000	KM#866.3, 868.2, 869.2, 873.2, 874.2, 891, 896 plus Children's medal in Nordic gold (Children's coin set).	—	50.00
MS58	2008 (8)	20,350	KM#866.3, 868.2, 869.2, 873.2, 874.2, 891, 896 plus Battle of Kronberg Castle Coast (Elsinore) medal in Nordic gold.	—	45.00
MS59	2009 (6)	1,450	KM#866.3, 869.2, 873.2, 874.2, 891, 896 plus Children's medal in Nordic gold (Children's coin set)	—	65.00
MS60	2009 (7)	24,250	KM#866.3, 869.2, 873.2, 874.2, 891, 896 plus Neptune admiring Naval fleet medal in Nordic gold.	—	60.00
MS61	2010 (7)	1,300	KM#866.3, 869.2, 873.2, 874.2, 891, 896 plus children's medal in Nordic gold (Children's coin set).	—	45.00
MS62	2010 (7)	23,000	KM#866.3, 869.2, 873.2, 874.2, 891, 896 plus Danish Navy's first dry dock medal in Nordic gold	—	45.00
MS63	2011 (6)	1,750	KM#866.3, 869.2, 873.2, 874.2, 943-944 plus children's medal in Nordic gold.	—	45.00
MS64	2011 (6)	17,150	KM#866.3, 869.2, 873.2, 874.2, 943-944	—	40.00
MS65	2012 (6)	—	KM#866.3, 869.2, 873.2, 874.2, 943, 944	—	40.00
MS66	2012 (6)	—	KM#866.3, 869.2, 873.2, 874.2, 943, 944, plus Children's medal in Nordic gold (Children's coin set)	—	45.00

PROOF SETS

KM#	Date	Mintage	Identification	Issue Price	Mkt Val
PS1	2004 (8)	3,000	KM#866.3, 868.2, 869.2, 873.2, 874.2, 891, 896, plus Royal Wedding medal in .925 Silver	150	250
PS2	2005 (8)	2,650	KM866.3, 868.2, 869.2, 873.2, 874.2, 896, 891 plus 1801 Battle of Copenhagen medal in .925 Silver	150	185
PS3	2006 (8)	1,800	KM#866.3, 868.2, 869.2, 873.2, 874.2, 896, 891 plus 1691 Floating Dock medal in .925 Silver	160	185
PS4	2007 (8)	1,400	KM#866.3, 868.2, 869.2, 873.2, 874.2, 896, 891, plus Galathea medal in .925 silver	160	185
PS5	2008 (8)	1,000	KM#866.3, 868.2, 869.2, 873.2, 874.2, 896, 891, plus medal in .925 Silver	—	200
PS6	2009 (7)	1,050	KM#866.3, 869.2, 873.2, 874.2, 891, 896 plus Neptune admiring Naval fleet medal in .925 Silver.	—	250
PS7	2010 (7)	1,010	KM#866.3, 869.2, 873.2, 874.2, 891, 896 plus Danish Navy's first dry dock medal in .925 Silver.	—	185
PS8	2011 (2)	3,010	KM#943-944	—	75.00
PS9	2011 (6)	1,000	KM#866.3, 869.2, 873.2, 874.2, 943-944	—	185

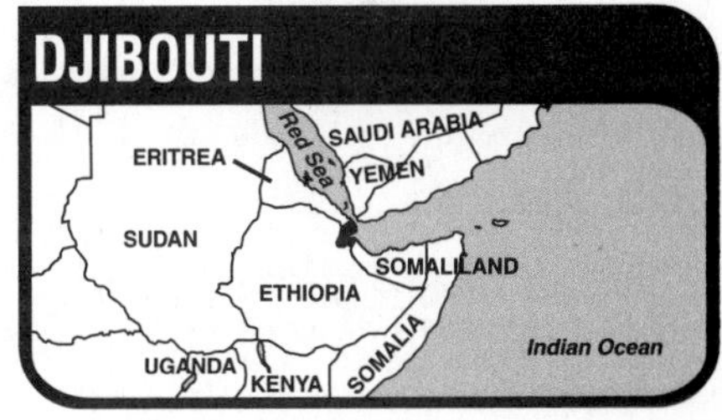

The Republic of Djibouti (formerly French Somaliland and the French Overseas Territory of Afars and Issas), located in northeast Africa at the Bab el Mandeb Strait connecting the Suez Canal and the Red Sea with the Gulf of Aden and the Indian Ocean, has an area of 8,950 sq. mi. (22,000 sq. km.) and a population of 421,320. Capital: Djibouti. The tiny nation has less than one sq. mi. of arable land, and no natural resources except salt, sand, and camels. The commercial activities of the transshipment port of Djibouti and the Addis Abada-Djibouti railroad are the basis of the economy. Salt, fish and hides are exported.

REPUBLIC

STANDARD COINAGE

KM# 34 10 FRANCS
3.4000 g., Copper-Nickel, 20.9 mm. **Obv:** National arms **Rev:** Chimpanzee **Edge:** Plain

Date	Mintage	F	VF	XF	Unc	BU
2003	—	—	—	—	2.00	4.00

KM# 23 10 FRANCS
3.0000 g., Aluminum-Bronze, 20 mm. **Obv:** National arms within wreath, date below **Rev:** Boats on water, denomination above **Note:** Varieties exist.

Date	Mintage	F	VF	XF	Unc	BU
2004(a)	—	—	—	—	2.50	4.50
2007(a)	—	—	—	—	2.50	4.50
2010(a)	—	—	—	—	2.50	4.50

KM# 24 20 FRANCS
4.0000 g., Aluminum-Bronze, 23.5 mm. **Obv:** National arms within wreath, date below **Rev:** Boats on water, denomination above **Note:** Varieties exist.

Date	Mintage	F	VF	XF	Unc	BU
2007(a)	—	—	—	—	2.50	4.50
2010(a)	—	—	—	—	2.50	4.50

KM# 25 50 FRANCS
7.0500 g., Copper-Nickel, 25.7 mm. **Obv:** National arms within wreath, date below **Rev:** Pair of dromedary camels right, denomination above

Date	Mintage	F	VF	XF	Unc	BU
2007(a)	—	—	—	—	6.00	9.00
2010(a)	—	—	—	—	6.00	9.00

KM# 38 100 FRANCS
Nickel Possibly Copper-Nickel-Zinc, confirmation of magnetic quality requested, 35 mm. **Subject:** 25th Anniversary of Independence **Obv:** Small national arms on state flag **Obv. Legend:** REPUBLIQUE DE DJIBOUTI **Rev:** UNITÉ in color **Rev. Legend:** UNITÉ ... ÉGALITÉ ... PAIX

Date	Mintage	F	VF	XF	Unc	BU
ND(2002)	—	—	—	—	—	145

KM# 39 100 FRANCS
Nickel Possibly Copper-Nickel-Zinc, confirmation of magnetic quality requested, 35 mm. **Subject:** 25th Anniversary of Independence **Obv:** Small national arms on state flag **Obv. Legend:** REPUBLIQUE DE DJIBOUTI **Rev:** É/GAL/ITÉ in color **Rev. Legend:** UNITÉ ... ÉGALITÉ ... PAIX

Date	Mintage	F	VF	XF	Unc	BU
AH(2002)	—	—	—	—	—	145

KM# 40 100 FRANCS
Nickel Possibly Copper-Nickel-Zinc, confirmation of magnetic quality requested, 35 mm. **Subject:** 25th Anniversary of Independence **Obv:** Small national arms on state flag **Obv. Legend:** REPUBLIQUE DE DJIBOUTI **Rev:** PAI/X in color **Rev. Legend:** UNITÉ ... ÉGALITÉ ... PAIX

Date	Mintage	F	VF	XF	Unc	BU
ND(2002)	—	—	—	—	—	145

KM# 26 100 FRANCS
12.0000 g., Copper-Nickel, 30 mm. **Obv:** National arms within wreath, date below **Rev:** Pair of dromedary camels right, denomination above

Date	Mintage	F	VF	XF	Unc	BU
2004(a)	—	—	—	2.50	7.00	9.00
2007(a)	—	—	—	2.50	7.00	9.00
2010(a)	—	—	—	2.50	7.00	9.00

KM# 41 250 FRANCS
22.2000 g., 0.9000 Silver 0.6423 oz. ASW **Obv:** National arms **Obv. Legend:** REPUBLIQUE DE DJIBOUTI **Rev:** Two dromedary camels right **Rev. Legend:** UNITÉ - ÉGALITÉ - PAIX

Date	Mintage	F	VF	XF	Unc	BU
2002(a) Proof	—	—	—	—	—	—

Note: Confirmation requested

KM# 27 500 FRANCS
Aluminum-Bronze **Obv:** National arms within wreath, date below **Rev:** Denomination within sprays

Date	Mintage	F	VF	XF	Unc	BU
2010(a)	—	—	—	6.00	12.00	15.00

DOMINICAN REPUBLIC

The Dominican Republic, which occupies the eastern two-thirds of the island of Hispaniola, has an area of 18,704 sq. mi. (48,734 sq. km.) and a population of 7.9 million. Capital: Santo Domingo. The largely agricultural economy produces sugar, coffee, tobacco and cocoa. Tourism and casino gaming are also a rising source of revenue.

REPUBLIC

REFORM COINAGE

1937: 100 Centavos = 1 Peso Oro

KM# 80.2 PESO
6.4900 g., Brass, 25 mm. **Subject:** Juan Pablo Duarte **Obv:** National arms and denomination **Rev:** DUARTE below bust, date below **Note:** Medal die alignment.

Date	Mintage	F	VF	XF	Unc	BU
2002	—	—	—	—	2.00	2.50
2005	—	—	—	—	2.00	2.50
2008	—	—	—	—	2.00	2.50

KM# 90 PESO
12.5000 g., Copper-Nickel, 30.6 mm. **Obv:** Pan American Games logo **Rev:** National arms and denomination **Edge:** Reeded

Date	Mintage	F	VF	XF	Unc	BU
2003 Proof	—	Value: 15.00				

KM# 89 5 PESOS
6.0600 g., Bi-Metallic Stainless Steel center in Brass ring, 23 mm. **Subject:** Sanchez **Obv:** National arms and denomination **Rev:** Portrait facing within circle, date below **Edge:** Segmented reeding

Date	Mintage	F	VF	XF	Unc	BU
2002	—	—	—	—	2.50	3.00
2005	—	—	—	—	2.50	3.00
2007	—	—	—	—	2.50	3.00
2008	—	—	—	—	2.50	3.00

KM# 106 10 PESOS
8.2000 g., Bi-Metallic Brass center in Copper-Nickel ring, 27 mm. **Obv:** Value at left of national arms **Obv. Legend:** • REPUBLICA DOMINICANA • **Rev:** Bust of General Mella facing **Rev. Legend:** BANCO CENTRAL DE LA REPUBLICA DOMINICANA **Edge:** Segmented reeding

Date	Mintage	F	VF	XF	Unc	BU
2005	—	—	—	—	6.00	8.00
2007	—	—	—	—	6.00	8.00
2008	—	—	—	—	6.00	8.00
2010	—	—	—	—	6.00	8.00

KM# 107 25 PESOS
8.5600 g., Copper-Nickel, 28.82 mm. **Obv:** Value at left of national arms **Obv. Legend:** REPUBLICA DOMINICANA **Rev:** Bust of General Luperon facing **Rev. Legend:** BANCO CENTRAL DE LA REPUBLICA DOMINICANA **Rev. Inscription:** HEROE DE LA RESTAURACION **Edge:** Reeded

Date	Mintage	F	VF	XF	Unc	BU
2005	—	—	—	—	5.00	7.00
2008	—	—	—	—	5.00	7.00

EAST CARIBBEAN STATES

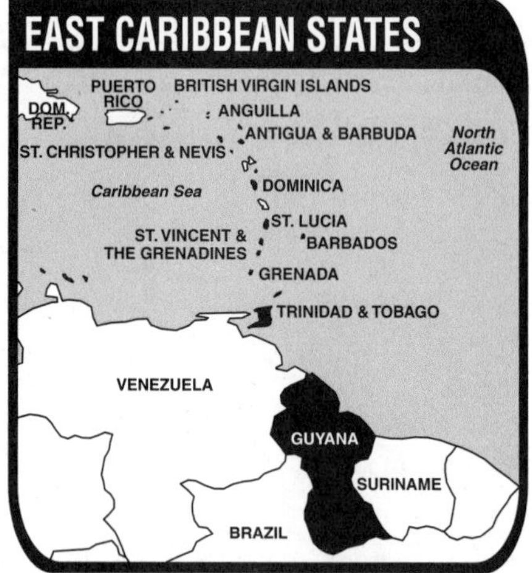

The East Caribbean States, formerly the British Caribbean Territories (Eastern Group), formed a currency board in 1950 to provide the constituent territories of Trinidad & Tobago, Barbados, British Guiana (now Guyana), British Virgin Islands, Anguilla, St. Kitts, Nevis, Antigua, Dominica, St. Lucia, St. Vincent and Grenada with a common currency, thereby permitting withdrawal of the regular British Pound currency. This was dissolved in 1965 and after the breakup, the East Caribbean Territories, a grouping including Barbados, the Leeward and Windward Islands, came into being. Coinage of the dissolved 'Eastern Group' continues to circulate. Paper currency of the East Caribbean Authority was first issued in 1965 and although Barbados withdrew from the group they continued using them prior to 1973 when Barbados issued a decimal coinage.

A series of 4-dollar coins tied to the FAO coinage program were released in 1970 under the name of the Caribbean Development Bank by eight loosely federated island groupings in the eastern Caribbean. These issues are listed individually in this volume under Antigua, Barbados, Dominica, Grenada, Montserrat, St. Kitts, St. Lucia and St. Vincent.

STANDARD COINAGE

100 Cents = 1 Dollar

KM# 10 CENT

0.9000 g., Aluminum, 18.4 mm. **Ruler:** Elizabeth II **Obv:** Young bust right **Rev:** Wreath divides denomination, date upper right **Shape:** Scalloped **Note:** Prev. KM#1.

Date	Mintage	F	VF	XF	Unc	BU
2001	—	—	—	—	0.20	0.30

KM# 34 CENT

1.0300 g., Aluminum, 18.42 mm. **Ruler:** Elizabeth II **Obv:** Crowned head right **Rev:** Denomination **Edge:** Plain

Date	Mintage	F	VF	XF	Unc	BU
2002	—	—	—	—	0.20	0.30
2004	—	—	—	—	0.20	0.30
2008	—	—	—	—	0.20	0.30
2011	—	—	—	—	0.20	0.30

KM# 35 2 CENTS

1.4200 g., Aluminum, 21.46 mm. **Ruler:** Elizabeth II **Obv:** Crowned head right **Rev:** Denomination **Edge:** Plain

Date	Mintage	F	VF	XF	Unc	BU
2002	—	—	—	—	0.25	0.35
2004	—	—	—	—	0.25	0.35
2008	—	—	—	—	0.25	0.35

KM# 36 5 CENTS

1.7400 g., Aluminum, 23.11 mm. **Ruler:** Elizabeth II **Obv:** Crowned head right **Rev:** Denomination **Edge:** Plain

Date	Mintage	F	VF	XF	Unc	BU
2002	—	—	—	—	0.30	0.45
2004	—	—	—	—	0.30	0.45
2008	—	—	—	—	0.30	0.45
2010	—	—	—	—	0.30	0.45

KM# 37 10 CENTS

2.5900 g., Copper-Nickel, 18.06 mm. **Ruler:** Elizabeth II **Obv:** Crowned head right **Rev:** Sir Francis Drake's Golden Hind and denomination **Edge:** Reeded

Date	Mintage	F	VF	XF	Unc	BU
2002	—	—	—	—	0.40	0.60
2004	—	—	—	—	0.40	0.60
2007	—	—	—	—	0.40	0.60

KM# 37a 10 CENTS

Nickel Plated Steel, 18 mm. **Ruler:** Elizabeth II **Obv:** Crowned head right **Rev:** Sir Francis Drake's Golden Hind and denomination **Edge:** Reeded

Date	Mintage	F	VF	XF	Unc	BU
2009	—	—	—	—	0.40	0.60

KM# 38 25 CENTS

6.4800 g., Copper-Nickel, 23.98 mm. **Ruler:** Elizabeth II **Obv:** Crowned head right **Rev:** Sir Francis Drake's Golden Hind and denomination **Edge:** Reeded

Date	Mintage	F	VF	XF	Unc	BU
2002	—	—	—	—	0.50	0.75
2004	—	—	—	—	0.50	0.75
2007	—	—	—	—	0.50	0.75

KM# 38a 25 CENTS

Nickel Plated Steel, 24 mm. **Ruler:** Elizabeth II **Obv:** Crowned head right **Rev:** Sir Francis Drake's Golden Hind and denomination **Edge:** Reeded

Date	Mintage	F	VF	XF	Unc	BU
2010	—	—	—	—	0.50	0.75

KM# 39 DOLLAR

7.9800 g., Copper-Nickel, 26.5 mm. **Ruler:** Elizabeth II **Obv:** Crowned head right **Rev:** Sir Francis Drake's Golden Hind and denomination **Edge:** Segmented reeding

Date	Mintage	F	VF	XF	Unc	BU
2002	—	—	—	—	2.00	3.00
2004	—	—	—	—	2.00	3.00
2007	—	—	—	—	2.00	3.00

KM# 40 DOLLAR

28.2800 g., Copper-Nickel Gilt, 38.6 mm. **Ruler:** Elizabeth II **Subject:** Golden Jubilee Monarchs **Obv:** Crowned head right **Rev:** Henry III (1216-1277) **Edge:** Reeded

Date	Mintage	F	VF	XF	Unc	BU
2002	5,000	—	—	—	22.50	25.00

KM# 42 DOLLAR

28.2800 g., Copper-Nickel Gilt, 38.6 mm. **Ruler:** Elizabeth II **Subject:** Golden Jubilee Monarchs **Obv:** Crowned head right **Rev:** Edward III (1327-1377) **Edge:** Reeded

Date	Mintage	F	VF	XF	Unc	BU
2002	5,000	—	—	—	22.50	25.00

KM# 44 DOLLAR

28.2800 g., Copper-Nickel Gilt, 38.6 mm. **Ruler:** Elizabeth II **Subject:** Golden Jubilee Monarchs **Obv:** Crowned head right **Rev:** George III (1760-1820) **Edge:** Reeded

Date	Mintage	F	VF	XF	Unc	BU
2002	5,000	—	—	—	22.50	25.00

KM# 46 DOLLAR

28.2800 g., Copper-Nickel Gilt, 38.6 mm. **Ruler:** Elizabeth II **Subject:** Golden Jubilee Monarchs **Obv:** Crowned head right **Rev:** Queen Victoria (1837-1901) **Edge:** Reeded

Date	Mintage	F	VF	XF	Unc	BU
2002	5,000	—	—	—	22.50	25.00

KM# 48 DOLLAR

28.2800 g., Copper-Nickel Gilt, 38.6 mm. **Ruler:** Elizabeth II **Subject:** Golden Jubilee Monarchs **Obv:** Crowned head right **Rev:** Queen Elizabeth II (1952-) **Edge:** Reeded

Date	Mintage	F	VF	XF	Unc	BU
2002	5,000	—	—	—	22.50	25.00

KM# 86 DOLLAR

27.7300 g., Copper-Nickel, 38.5 mm. **Ruler:** Elizabeth II **Subject:** Coronation Jubilee **Obv:** Crowned head right **Rev:** Fireworks display above building **Edge:** Reeded

Date	Mintage	F	VF	XF	Unc	BU
2002	—	—	—	—	10.00	12.00

KM# 58 DOLLAR

7.9800 g., Copper-Nickel, 26.5 mm. **Ruler:** Elizabeth II **Subject:** 25th Anniversary **Obv:** Head right **Rev:** Motto within wreath

Date	Mintage	F	VF	XF	Unc	BU
2008	500,000	—	—	—	—	5.00

KM# 51 2 DOLLARS

56.5600 g., Copper-Nickel Gilt, 38.6 mm. **Ruler:** Elizabeth II **Subject:** British Military Leaders **Obv:** Crowned head right **Rev:** Wellington's portrait and battle scene **Edge:** Reeded

Date	Mintage	F	VF	XF	Unc	BU
2002 Proof	10,000	Value: 45.00				

KM# 54 2 DOLLARS

56.5600 g., Copper-Nickel Gilt, 38.6 mm. **Ruler:** Elizabeth II **Subject:** British Military Leaders **Obv:** Crowned head right **Rev:** Admiral Nelson's portrait and naval battle scene **Edge:** Reeded

Date	Mintage	F	VF	XF	Unc	BU
2003 Proof	10,000	Value: 45.00				

KM# 57 2 DOLLARS

56.5600 g., Copper-Nickel Gilt, 38.6 mm. **Ruler:** Elizabeth II **Subject:** British Military Leaders **Obv:** Crowned head right **Rev:** Churchill's portrait and air battle scene **Edge:** Reeded

Date	Mintage	F	VF	XF	Unc	BU
2003 Proof	10,000	Value: 45.00				

KM# 87 2 DOLLARS

11.3500 g., Copper-Nickel, 30 mm. **Ruler:** Elizabeth II **Subject:** Financial Information Month, 10th Anniversary **Rev:** Hands holding tree **Edge:** Reeded

Date	Mintage	F	VF	XF	Unc	BU
2011	—	—	—	—	4.00	4.50

KM# 60 2 DOLLARS

Copper-Nickel, 38.6 mm. **Ruler:** Elizabeth II **Subject:** Financial Information Month **Obv:** Head in tiara right **Rev:** Tree seedling growing in palm of hand

Date	Mintage	F	VF	XF	Unc	BU
2011 Proof	—	Value: 45.00				

KM# 61 8 DOLLARS

Copper-Nickel, 38.61 mm. **Ruler:** Elizabeth II **Subject:** OECS Economic Union **Obv:** Head in tiara right **Rev:** Flags in color

Date	Mintage	F	VF	XF	Unc	BU
2011 Proof	—	Value: 100				

KM# 41 10 DOLLARS

28.2800 g., 0.9250 Silver with gold cameo 0.8410 oz. ASW, 38.6 mm. **Ruler:** Elizabeth II **Subject:** Golden Jubilee Monarchs **Obv:** Crowned head right **Rev:** Henry III (1216-1272) **Edge:** Reeded

Date	Mintage	F	VF	XF	Unc	BU
2002 Proof	10,000	Value: 65.00				

KM# 41a 10 DOLLARS

39.9400 g., 0.9166 Gold 1.1770 oz. AGW, 38.6 mm. **Ruler:** Elizabeth II **Subject:** Golden Jubilee Monarchs **Obv:** Crowned head right **Rev:** Henry III (1216-1272) **Edge:** Reeded

Date	Mintage	F	VF	XF	Unc	BU
2002 Proof	100	Value: 2,200				

KM# 43 10 DOLLARS

28.2800 g., 0.9250 Silver 0.8410 oz. ASW, 38.6 mm. **Ruler:** Elizabeth II **Subject:** Golden Jubile Monarchs **Obv:** Crowned head right **Rev:** Edward III (1327-1377) **Edge:** Reeded

Date	Mintage	F	VF	XF	Unc	BU
2002 Proof	10,000	Value: 65.00				

KM# 43a 10 DOLLARS

39.9400 g., 0.9166 Gold 1.1770 oz. AGW, 38.6 mm. **Ruler:** Elizabeth II **Subject:** Golden Jubilee Monarchs **Obv:** Crowned head right **Rev:** Edward III (1327-1377) **Edge:** Reeded

Date	Mintage	F	VF	XF	Unc	BU
2002 Proof	100	Value: 2,200				

KM# 45 10 DOLLARS

28.2800 g., 0.9250 Silver with gold cameo 0.8410 oz. ASW, 38.6 mm. **Subject:** Golden Jubilee Monarchs **Obv:** Crowned head right **Rev:** George III (1760-1820) **Edge:** Reeded

Date	Mintage	F	VF	XF	Unc	BU
2002 Proof	10,000	Value: 65.00				

KM# 45a 10 DOLLARS

39.9400 g., 0.9166 Gold 1.1770 oz. AGW, 38.6 mm. **Ruler:** Elizabeth II **Subject:** Golden Jubilee Monarchs **Obv:** Crowned head right **Rev:** George III (1760-1820) **Edge:** Reeded

Date	Mintage	F	VF	XF	Unc	BU
2002 Proof	100	Value: 2,200				

KM# 47 10 DOLLARS

28.2800 g., 0.9250 Silver with partial gold plating 0.8410 oz. ASW, 38.6 mm. **Ruler:** Elizabeth II **Subject:** Golden Jubilee Monarchs **Obv:** Crowned head right **Rev:** Queen Victoria (1837-1901) **Edge:** Reeded

Date	Mintage	F	VF	XF	Unc	BU
2002 Proof	10,000	Value: 65.00				

KM# 47a 10 DOLLARS

39.9400 g., 0.9166 Gold 1.1770 oz. AGW, 38.6 mm. **Ruler:** Elizabeth II **Subject:** Golden Jubilee Monarchs **Obv:** Crowned head right **Rev:** Queen Victoria (1837-1901) **Edge:** Reeded

Date	Mintage	F	VF	XF	Unc	BU
2002 Proof	100	Value: 2,200				

KM# 49 10 DOLLARS

28.2800 g., 0.9250 Silver with gold cameo 0.8410 oz. ASW, 38.6 mm. **Ruler:** Elizabeth II **Subject:** Golden Jubilee Monarchs **Obv:** Crowned head right **Rev:** Queen Elizabeth II (1952-) **Edge:** Reeded

Date	Mintage	F	VF	XF	Unc	BU
2002 Proof	10,000	Value: 65.00				

KM# 49a 10 DOLLARS

39.9400 g., 0.9166 Gold 1.1770 oz. AGW, 38.6 mm. **Ruler:** Elizabeth II **Subject:** Golden Jubilee Monarchs **Obv:** Crowned head right **Rev:** Queen Elizabeth II (1952-) **Edge:** Reeded

Date	Mintage	F	VF	XF	Unc	BU
2002 Proof	100	Value: 2,200				

KM# 59 10 DOLLARS

Silver partially gilt, 39 mm. **Ruler:** Elizabeth II **Obv:** Head right, partially gilt **Rev:** Fireworks display above Buckingham Palace

Date	Mintage	F	VF	XF	Unc	BU
2002 Proof	—	Value: 50.00				

EAST TIMOR

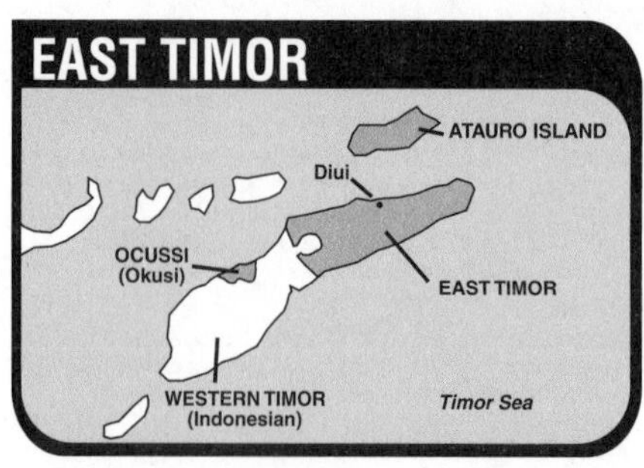

East Timor, population: 522,433, area: 7332 sq. miles, capital: Dili, is primarily located on the eastern half of the island of Timor, just northwest of Australia at the eastern end of the Indonesian archipelago. Formerly a Portuguese colony, Timor declared its independence from Portugal on November 28, 1975. After nine short days of fledgling autonomy, a guerilla faction sympathetic to the Indonesian territorial claim to East Timor seized the government. On July 17, 1976 the Provisional government enacted a law, which dissolved the free republic and made East Timor the 24th province of Indonesia. Violent rule and civil unrest plagued the province, with great loss of life and extreme damage to property and natural resources until independence was again achieved with United Nations assistance during a period from 1999 to 2002. Emerging as the Democratic Republic of Timor-Leste and commonly known as East Timor the country has worked, with international assistance to rebuild its decimated infrastructure. Natural resources waiting to be tapped include rich oil reserves, though current exports are most dependent on coffee, sandalwood and marble. The first coins of the new republic were issued in 2003.

DEMOCRATIC REPUBLIC OF TIMOR-LESTE

DECIMAL COINAGE

KM# 1 CENTAVO

3.1000 g., Nickel Clad Steel, 17 mm. **Obv:** Nautilus above date **Rev:** Denomination within circle **Edge:** Plain **Designer:** Jose Bandeira

Date	Mintage	F	VF	XF	Unc	BU
2003	1,500,000	—	—	—	1.50	2.50
2003 Proof	12,500	Value: 8.00				
2004	1,500,000	—	—	—	1.50	2.50
2005	—	—	—	—	1.50	2.50
2005 Proof	12,500	Value: 8.00				
2012	—	—	—	—	1.50	2.50
2012 Proof	2,000	Value: 8.00				

KM# 2 5 CENTAVOS

4.1000 g., Nickel Clad Steel, 18.75 mm. **Obv:** Rice plant above date **Rev:** Denomination within circle **Edge:** Plain **Designer:** Jose Bandeira

Date	Mintage	F	VF	XF	Unc	BU
2003	1,500,000	—	—	—	2.00	3.00
2003 Proof	12,500	Value: 10.00				
2004	1,500,000	—	—	—	2.00	3.00
2005	—	—	—	—	2.00	3.00
2005 Proof	12,500	Value: 10.00				
2006	—	—	—	—	2.00	3.00
2010	—	—	—	—	2.00	3.00
2012	—	—	—	—	2.00	3.00
2012 Proof	2,000	Value: 10.00				

KM# 3 10 CENTAVOS

5.2000 g., Nickel Clad Steel, 20.75 mm. **Obv:** Rooster left above date **Rev:** Denomination within circle **Edge:** Plain **Designer:** Jose Bandeira

Date	Mintage	F	VF	XF	Unc	BU
2003	2,500,000	—	—	—	2.50	4.00
2003 Proof	12,500	Value: 12.00				
2004	2,500,000	—	—	—	2.50	4.00
2005	—	—	—	—	2.50	4.00
2005 Proof	12,500	Value: 12.00				
2006	—	—	—	—	2.50	4.00
2010	—	—	—	—	2.50	4.00
2011	—	—	—	—	2.50	4.00
2012	—	—	—	—	2.50	2.50
2012 Proof	—	Value: 12.00				

KM# 4 25 CENTAVOS

5.8500 g., Nickel-Brass, 21.25 mm. **Obv:** Sail boat above date **Rev:** Denomination within circle **Edge:** Reeded **Designer:** Jose Bandeira

Date	Mintage	F	VF	XF	Unc	BU
2003	1,500,000	—	—	—	3.50	5.00
2003 Proof	12,500	Value: 16.00				
2004	1,500,000	—	—	—	3.50	5.00
2005	—	—	—	—	3.50	5.00
2005 Proof	12,500	Value: 16.00				
2006	—	—	—	—	3.50	5.00
2011	—	—	—	—	3.50	5.00
2012	—	—	—	—	3.50	5.00
2012 Proof	2,000	Value: 16.00				

KM# 5 50 CENTAVOS

6.5000 g., Nickel-Brass, 25 mm. **Obv:** Coffee plant with beans above date **Rev:** Denomination within circle **Edge:** Reeded **Designer:** Jose Bandeira

Date	Mintage	F	VF	XF	Unc	BU
2003	1,000,000	—	—	—	5.00	7.00
2003 Proof	12,500	Value: 22.00				
2004	1,000,000	—	—	—	5.00	7.00
2005	—	—	—	—	5.00	7.00
2005 Proof	12,500	Value: 22.00				
2006	—	—	—	—	5.00	7.00
2011	—	—	—	—	5.00	7.00
2012	—	—	—	—	5.00	7.00
2012 Proof	2,000	Value: 22.00				

KM# 6 50 CENTAVOS

Nickel-Brass

Date	Mintage	F	VF	XF	Unc	BU
2012	—	—	—	—	10.00	15.00
2012 Proof	2,000	Value: 25.00				

MINT SETS

KM#	Date	Mintage	Identification	Issue Price	Mkt Val
MS1	2003 (5)	25,000	KM#1-5	27.84	35.00
MS2	2004 (5)	25,000	KM#1-5	—	35.00
MS3	2012 (6)	2,000	KM#1-6	—	45.00

PROOF SETS

KM#	Date	Mintage	Identification	Issue Price	Mkt Val
PS1	2003 (5)	12,500	KM#1-5	57.25	70.00
PS2	2005 (5)	12,500	KM#1-5	—	82.00
PS3	2012 (6)	2,000	KM#1-6	—	95.00

ECUADOR

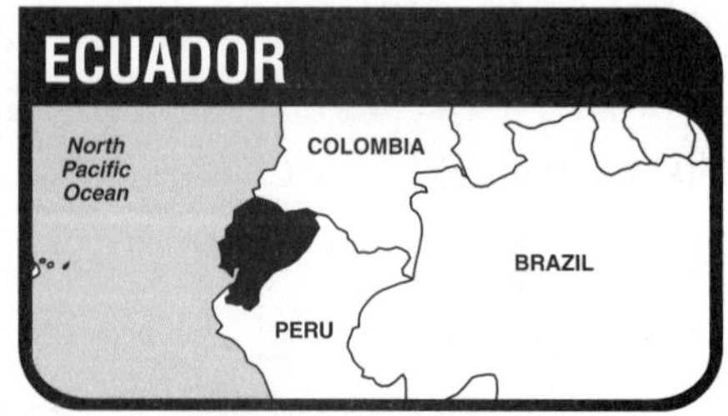

The Republic of Ecuador, located astride the equator on the Pacific Coast of South America, has an area of 105,037 sq. mi. (283,560 sq. km.) and a population of 10.9 million. Capital: Quito. Agriculture is the mainstay of the economy but there are appreciable deposits of minerals and petroleum. It is one of the world's largest exporters of bananas and balsa wood. Coffee, cacao, sugar and petroleum are also valuable exports.

REPUBLIC
REFORM COINAGE

100 Centavos = 1 Dollar

KM# 104 CENTAVO (Un)
2.5200 g., Brass, 19 mm. **Obv:** Map of the Americas within circle **Rev:** Denomination **Edge:** Plain

Date	Mintage	F	VF	XF	Unc	BU
2003	—	—	—	—	0.20	0.40
2004	—	—	—	—	0.20	0.40

KM# 104a CENTAVO (Un)
2.4200 g., Copper Plated Steel, 19 mm. **Obv:** Map of the Americas **Rev:** Denomination **Edge:** Plain

Date	Mintage	F	VF	XF	Unc	BU
2003	—	—	—	—	0.30	0.50

KM# 105 5 CENTAVOS (Cinco)
5.0000 g., Steel, 21.2 mm. **Subject:** Juan Montalvo **Obv:** Bust 3/4 facing and arms **Rev:** Denomination **Edge:** Plain

Date	Mintage	F	VF	XF	Unc	BU
2003	—	—	—	—	0.50	0.75

KM# 115 SUCRE (Un)
8.3600 g., 0.9000 Gold 0.2419 oz. AGW, 22 mm. **Subject:** Homage to Jefferson Pérez Quezada **Obv:** National arms **Obv. Legend:** BANCO CENTRAL DEL ECUADOR **Rev:** 3/4 length figure of Perez running **Rev. Legend:** BICAMPEON MUNDIAL - CAMPEON OLIMPICO ATLANTA 1996

Date	Mintage	F	VF	XF	Unc	BU
2006	—	Value: 450				

KM# 116 SUCRE (Un)
31.1000 g., 0.9990 Silver 0.9988 oz. ASW, 39 mm. **Subject:** Independence 200th Anniversary

Date	Mintage	F	VF	XF	Unc	BU
2009 Proof	200	Value: 75.00				

KM# 117 SUCRE (Un)
Subject: Masacre

Date	Mintage	F	VF	XF	Unc	BU
2010 Proof	—	Value: 100				

KM# 112 25000 SUCRES
27.1000 g., 0.9250 Silver 0.8059 oz. ASW, 40 mm. **Subject:** IBERO-AMERICA Series **Obv:** Coats of arms **Rev:** Balsawood sailing raft **Edge:** Reeded

Date	Mintage	F	VF	XF	Unc	BU
2002 Proof	—	Value: 65.00				

KM# 113 25000 SUCRES
27.0000 g., 0.9250 Silver 0.8029 oz. ASW, 40 mm. **Obv:** National arms **Rev:** Capital building in Quito **Edge:** Reeded

Date	Mintage	F	VF	XF	Unc	BU
2004 Proof	1,000	Value: 60.00				

KM# 114 25000 SUCRES
27.2000 g., 0.9250 Silver 0.8089 oz. ASW, 40 mm. **Subject:** 2006 World Cup Soccer **Obv:** National arms **Rev:** Ecuadorian Soccer player torso holding a soccer ball **Edge:** Reeded

Date	Mintage	F	VF	XF	Unc	BU
ND(2006) Proof	—	Value: 50.00				

EGYPT

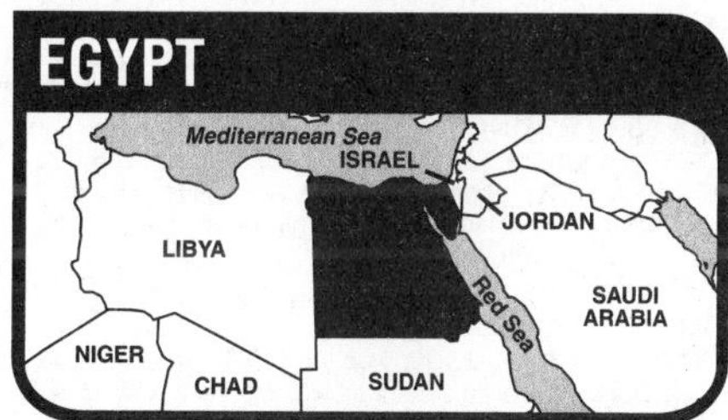

The Arab Republic of Egypt, located on the northeastern corner of Africa, has an area of 385,229 sq. mi. (1,1001,450 sq. km.) and a population of 62.4 million. Capital: Cairo. Although Egypt is an almost rainless expanse of desert, its economy is predominantly agricultural. Cotton, rice and petroleum are exported. Other main sources of income are revenues from the Suez Canal, remittances of Egyptian workers abroad and tourism.

ARAB REPUBLIC
AH1391- / 1971- AD
DECIMAL COINAGE

KM# 941 5 PIASTRES
1.9500 g., Brass, 18 mm. **Obv:** Denomination divides dates below, legend above **Rev:** Antique pottery vase **Edge:** Plain

Date	Mintage	F	VF	XF	Unc	BU
AH1425-2004	—	—	—	—	1.50	2.00

KM# 941a 5 PIASTRES
1.5000 g., Brass Plated Steel, 18 mm. **Obv:** Denomination divides dates below, legend above **Rev:** Antique pottery vase

Date	Mintage	F	VF	XF	Unc	BU
AH1429/2008	—	—	—	—	1.50	2.00

KM# 922 10 PIASTRES
4.5200 g., Copper-Nickel, 24.8 mm. **Subject:** National Women's Council **Obv:** Value **Rev:** Woman standing next to Sphinx **Edge:** Reeded

Date	Mintage	F	VF	XF	Unc	BU
AH1425-2004	—	—	—	—	1.50	2.00

KM# 990 10 PIASTRES
3.4100 g., Nickel Plated Steel, 19.03 mm. **Obv:** Text, date and value **Rev:** Mosque

Date	Mintage	F	VF	XF	Unc	BU
AH1429 (2008)	—	—	—	—	1.00	1.50

KM# 923 20 PIASTRES
6.0000 g., Copper-Nickel, 26.8 mm. **Subject:** National Women's Council **Obv:** Value **Rev:** Woman standing next to Sphinx **Edge:** Reeded

Date	Mintage	F	VF	XF	Unc	BU
AH1425-2004	—	—	—	—	2.50	3.50

KM# 991 25 PIASTRES
4.5000 g., Nickel Plated Steel, 21 mm. **Obv:** Value at center, Arabic legend at top, dates below **Rev:** Value at center, Arabic at top, English value below **Edge:** Reeded

Date	Mintage	F	VF	XF	Unc	BU
AH1429-2008	—	—	—	—	2.50	3.50
AH1430-2009	—	—	—	—	2.50	3.50
AH1431-2010	—	—	—	—	2.50	3.50

KM# 942.1 50 PIASTRES
6.5000 g., Brass, 25 mm. **Obv:** Value **Rev:** Bust of Cleopatra left **Edge:** Reeded **Note:** Non-magnetic.

Date	Mintage	F	VF	XF	Unc	BU
AH1426-2005	—	—	—	1.20	3.00	4.00
AH1427-2006	—	—	—	1.20	3.00	4.00

KM# 942.2 50 PIASTRES
6.5000 g., Brass Plated Steel, 23 mm. **Obv:** Value **Rev:** Bust of Cleopatra left **Edge:** Reeded **Note:** Magnetic

Date	Mintage	F	VF	XF	Unc	BU
AH1428-2007	—	—	—	—	1.00	1.50
AH1429-2008	—	—	—	—	1.00	1.50
AH1430-2009	—	—	—	—	1.00	1.50
AH1431-2010	—	—	—	—	1.00	1.50
AH1433-2012	—	—	—	—	1.00	1.50

KM# 903 1/2 POUND
4.0000 g., 0.8750 Gold 0.1125 oz. AGW, 18 mm. **Subject:** Egyptian Museum Centennial **Obv:** Value **Rev:** Building **Edge:** Reeded

Date	Mintage	F	VF	XF	Unc	BU
AH1423-2002	—	—	—	—	250	270

KM# 930 POUND
15.0000 g., 0.7200 Silver 0.3472 oz. ASW, 35 mm. **Subject:** National Women's Council **Obv:** Value **Rev:** Woman standing next to Sphinx **Edge:** Reeded

Date	Mintage	F	VF	XF	Unc	BU
AH1421-2001	600	—	—	—	45.00	50.00

KM# 936 POUND
8.0000 g., 0.8750 Gold 0.2250 oz. AGW, 24 mm. **Subject:** 50th Anniversary of Egyptian Revolution **Obv:** Value **Rev:** Soldier with flag, pyramids and radiant sun **Edge:** Reeded

Date	Mintage	F	VF	XF	Unc	BU
AH1423-2002	400	—	—	—	415	425

KM# 938 POUND

8.0000 g., 0.8750 Gold 0.2250 oz. AGW, 24 mm. **Subject:** Alexandria Library **Obv:** Cufic text in center **Rev:** Arched inscription above slanted library roof **Edge:** Reeded

Date	Mintage	F	VF	XF	Unc	BU
AH1423-2002	750	—	—	—	415	425

KM# 904 POUND

15.0000 g., 0.7200 Silver 0.3472 oz. ASW, 35 mm. **Subject:** Egyptian Museum Centennial **Obv:** Value **Rev:** Building, centennial numerals in background **Edge:** Reeded

Date	Mintage	F	VF	XF	Unc	BU
AH1423-2002	1,500	—	—	—	35.00	40.00

KM# 905 POUND

8.0000 g., 0.8750 Gold 0.2250 oz. AGW, 24 mm. **Subject:** Egyptian Museum Centennial **Obv:** Value **Rev:** Building, centennial numerals in background **Edge:** Reeded

Date	Mintage	F	VF	XF	Unc	BU
AH1423-2002	300	—	—	—	415	425

KM# 909 POUND

15.0000 g., 0.7200 Silver 0.3472 oz. ASW, 35 mm. **Subject:** International Ear, Nose and Throat Conference **Obv:** King Tut's Gold Mask **Rev:** "IFOS" on world map **Edge:** Reeded

Date	Mintage	F	VF	XF	Unc	BU
AH1423-2002	2,500	—	—	—	30.00	35.00

KM# 910 POUND

15.0000 g., 0.7200 Silver 0.3472 oz. ASW, 35 mm. **Subject:** 50th Anniversary of Egyptian Revolution **Obv:** Value **Rev:** Soldier with flag **Edge:** Reeded

Date	Mintage	F	VF	XF	Unc	BU
AH1423-2002	1,500	—	—	—	35.00	40.00

KM# 912 POUND

15.0000 g., 0.7200 Silver 0.3472 oz. ASW, 35 mm. **Subject:** Alexandria Library **Obv:** Legend and inscription **Rev:** Inscribed arches above library roof **Edge:** Reeded

Date	Mintage	F	VF	XF	Unc	BU
AH1423-2002	8,000	—	—	—	30.00	35.00

KM# 913 POUND

15.0000 g., 0.7200 Silver 0.3472 oz. ASW, 35 mm. **Subject:** Body Building Championships **Obv:** Arabic and English legends **Rev:** Mr. Universe cartoon **Edge:** Reeded

Date	Mintage	F	VF	XF	Unc	BU
AH1423-2002	1,000	—	—	—	30.00	35.00

KM# 955 POUND

8.0000 g., 0.8750 Gold 0.2250 oz. AGW, 24 mm. **Subject:** Golden Jubilee Ein Shams University **Obv:** Value **Rev:** Obelisk with bird standing at left and right **Edge:** Reeded

Date	Mintage	F	VF	XF	Unc	BU
AH1422-2002	400	—	—	—	415	425

KM# 956 POUND

8.0000 g., 0.8750 Gold 0.2250 oz. AGW, 24 mm. **Subject:** Police Day **Obv:** Police eagle with wings spread, value **Rev:** Police badge **Edge:** Reeded

Date	Mintage	F	VF	XF	Unc	BU
AH1422-2002	400	—	—	—	415	425

KM# 957 POUND

8.0000 g., 0.8750 Gold 0.2250 oz. AGW, 24 mm. **Subject:** 30th Anniversary October War Victory **Obv:** Value **Rev:** Soldier holding flag on top of pyramid **Edge:** Reeded

Date	Mintage	F	VF	XF	Unc	BU
AH1424-2003	200	—	—	—	425	435

KM# 958 POUND

8.0000 g., 0.8750 Gold 0.2250 oz. AGW, 24 mm. **Series:** Value **Subject:** Radio and Television Festival **Obv:** Modern abstract design **Edge:** Reeded

Date	Mintage	F	VF	XF	Unc	BU
AH1424-2003	1,000	—	—	—	400	415

KM# 959 POUND

8.0000 g., 0.8750 Gold 0.2250 oz. AGW, 24 mm. **Subject:** 50th Anniversary El Gomhoreya Newspaper - Hosni Mubarak **Obv:** Value **Rev:** Bust facing at left, building in background **Edge:** Reeded

Date	Mintage	F	VF	XF	Unc	BU
AH1424-2003	400	—	—	—	415	425

KM# 915 POUND

15.0000 g., 0.7200 Silver 0.3472 oz. ASW, 35 mm. **Subject:** 30th Anniversary of the October War **Obv:** Value, dates and legend **Rev:** Soldier with flag above pyramids **Edge:** Reeded

Date	Mintage	F	VF	XF	Unc	BU
AH1424-2003	1,000	—	—	—	30.00	35.00

KM# 917 POUND

15.0000 g., 0.7200 Silver 0.3472 oz. ASW, 35 mm. **Subject:** 25th Anniversary of the Commerce Society **Obv:** Value, dates and legend **Rev:** Radiant sun above lattice work **Edge:** Reeded

Date	Mintage	F	VF	XF	Unc	BU
AH1424-2003	1,200	—	—	—	30.00	35.00

KM# 924 POUND

15.0000 g., 0.7200 Silver 0.3472 oz. ASW, 35 mm. **Subject:** 90th Anniversary Scouts **Obv:** Value **Rev:** Combined scouting badge **Edge:** Reeded

Date	Mintage	F	VF	XF	Unc	BU
AH1425-2004	2,000	—	—	—	30.00	35.00

KM# 960 POUND

8.0000 g., 0.8750 Gold 0.2250 oz. AGW, 24 mm. **Subject:** Golden Jubilee Military Production **Obv:** Value **Rev:** Ancient chariot, horse and rider left **Edge:** Reeded

Date	Mintage	F	VF	XF	Unc	BU
AH1425-2004	750	—	—	—	400	415

KM# 934 POUND

15.0000 g., 0.7250 Silver 0.3496 oz. ASW, 35 mm. **Subject:** Golden Jubilee - Military Production **Obv:** Value **Rev:** Ancient chariot, horse and rider **Edge:** Reeded

Date	Mintage	F	VF	XF	Unc	BU
AH1425-2004	1,000	—	—	—	30.00	35.00

KM# 940 POUND

8.5000 g., Bi-Metallic Brass center in Copper-Nickel ring, 25.1 mm. **Obv:** Value **Rev:** King Tutankhaman's gold mask **Edge:** Reeded

Date	Mintage	F	VF	XF	Unc	BU
AH1426-2005	—	—	—	—	3.00	5.00
AH1427-2006	—	—	—	—	3.00	5.00

KM# 965 POUND

15.0000 g., 0.7200 Silver 0.3472 oz. ASW, 35 mm. **Subject:** Golden Jubilee Suez Canal Nationalization **Obv:** Value **Rev:** Large "50" above government buildings **Edge:** Reeded

Date	Mintage	F	VF	XF	Unc	BU
AH1427-2006	1,750	—	—	—	35.00	40.00

KM# 966 POUND

15.0000 g., 0.7200 Silver 0.3472 oz. ASW, 35 mm. **Subject:** 60th Anniversary UNESCO **Obv:** Value **Rev:** Logo **Edge:** Reeded

Date	Mintage	F	VF	XF	Unc	BU
AH1427-2006	800	—	—	—	100	125

KM# 967 POUND

15.0000 g., 0.7200 Silver 0.3472 oz. ASW, 35 mm. **Subject:** 13th General Population Census **Obv:** Value **Rev:** Stylized couple leaning left at left **Edge:** Reeded

Date	Mintage	F	VF	XF	Unc	BU
AH1427-2006	2,000	—	—	—	45.00	50.00

KM# 961 POUND

8.0000 g., 0.8750 Gold 0.2250 oz. AGW, 24 mm. **Subject:** World Environment Day **Obv:** Value **Rev:** Stylized tree, emblem at left, bird standing at right **Edge:** Reeded

Date	Mintage	F	VF	XF	Unc	BU
AH1427-2006	200	—	—	—	415	425

KM# 962 POUND

8.0000 g., 0.8750 Gold 0.2250 oz. AGW, 24 mm. **Subject:** Golden Jubilee Suez Canal Nationalization **Obv:** Value **Rev:** Large "50" above government buildings **Edge:** Reeded

Date	Mintage	F	VF	XF	Unc	BU
AH1427-2006	1,000	—	—	—	400	415

KM# 963 POUND

8.0000 g., 0.8750 Gold 0.2250 oz. AGW, 24 mm. **Subject:** Silver Jubilee Egyptian Enviromental Protection **Obv:** Value **Rev:** World globe **Edge:** Reeded

Date	Mintage	F	VF	XF	Unc	BU
AH1428-2007	300	—	—	—	420	430

KM# 964 POUND

8.0000 g., 0.8750 Gold 0.2250 oz. AGW, 24 mm. **Subject:** Diamond Jubilee Air Force **Obv:** Value **Rev:** Air Force emblem **Edge:** Reeded

Date	Mintage	F	VF	XF	Unc	BU
AH1428-2007	130	—	—	—	550	575

KM# 968 POUND
15.0000 g., 0.7200 Silver 0.3472 oz. ASW, 35 mm. **Subject:** 100th Anniversary Ahly Club **Obv:** Value **Rev:** Large "100" with linked zeroes **Edge:** Reeded

Date	Mintage	F	VF	XF	Unc	BU
AH1428-2007	5,000	—	—	—	45.00	50.00

KM# 940a POUND
8.5000 g., Bi-Metallic Brass Plated Steel center in Nickel Plated Steel ring, 25.1 mm. **Obv:** Value at center **Rev:** King Tutankhaman's gold mask **Edge:** Reeded **Note:** Magnetic

Date	Mintage	F	VF	XF	Unc	BU
AH1428-2007	—	—	—	—	3.00	5.00
AH1429-2008	—	—	—	—	3.00	4.00
AH1430-2009	—	—	—	—	3.00	4.00
AH1431-2010	—	—	—	—	3.00	4.00

KM# 944 POUND
15.0000 g., 0.7200 Silver 0.3472 oz. ASW, 35.00 mm. **Subject:** Air Force Diamond Jubilee **Obv:** Value **Rev:** Air Force insignia **Edge:** Reeded

Date	Mintage	F	VF	XF	Unc	BU
AH1428-2007	—	—	—	—	45.00	50.00

KM# 931 5 POUNDS
17.5000 g., 0.7200 Silver 0.4051 oz. ASW, 37 mm. **Subject:** National Women's Council **Obv:** Value **Rev:** Woman standing next to Sphinx **Edge:** Reeded

Date	Mintage	F	VF	XF	Unc	BU
AH1421-2001	600	—	—	—	55.00	60.00

KM# 932 5 POUNDS
17.5000 g., 0.7200 Silver 0.4051 oz. ASW, 37 mm. **Subject:** 50th Anniversary of the National Police **Obv:** Value and police logo **Rev:** Ceremonial design **Edge:** Reeded

Date	Mintage	F	VF	XF	Unc	BU
AH1422-2002	750	—	—	—	45.00	50.00

KM# 906 5 POUNDS
17.5000 g., 0.7200 Silver 0.4051 oz. ASW, 37 mm. **Subject:** Egyptian Museum Centennial **Obv:** Value **Rev:** Building, centennial numerals in background **Edge:** Reeded

Date	Mintage	F	VF	XF	Unc	BU
AH1423-2002	1,500	—	—	—	45.00	48.00

KM# 907 5 POUNDS
26.0000 g., 0.8750 Gold 0.7314 oz. AGW, 33 mm. **Subject:** Egyptian Museum Centennial **Obv:** Value **Rev:** Building, centennial numerals in background **Edge:** Reeded

Date	Mintage	F	VF	XF	Unc	BU
AH1423-2002	250	—	—	—	1,350	1,400

KM# 911 5 POUNDS
17.5500 g., 0.9250 Silver 0.5219 oz. ASW, 37 mm. **Subject:** 50th Anniversary of the Egyptian Revolution **Obv:** Value **Rev:** Soldier with flag **Edge:** Reeded

Date	Mintage	F	VF	XF	Unc	BU
AH1423-2002	1,500	—	—	—	45.00	48.00

KM# 914 5 POUNDS
17.5000 g., 0.7200 Silver 0.4051 oz. ASW, 37 mm. **Subject:** Body Building Championships **Obv:** Arabic and English legends **Rev:** Mr. Universe cartoon **Edge:** Reeded

Date	Mintage	F	VF	XF	Unc	BU
AH1423-2002	800	—	—	—	40.00	45.00

KM# 916 5 POUNDS
17.5000 g., 0.7200 Silver 0.4051 oz. ASW, 37 mm. **Subject:** 30th Anniversary of the October War **Obv:** Value and legend **Rev:** Soldier with flag above pyramids **Edge:** Reeded

Date	Mintage	F	VF	XF	Unc	BU
AH1424-2003	800	—	—	—	40.00	45.00

KM# 918 5 POUNDS
17.5000 g., 0.7200 Silver 0.4051 oz. ASW, 37 mm. **Obv:** Value and legend **Rev:** Geo-Physical Institute **Edge:** Reeded

Date	Mintage	F	VF	XF	Unc	BU
AH1424-2003	800	—	—	—	40.00	45.00

KM# 919 5 POUNDS
17.5000 g., 0.7200 Silver 0.4051 oz. ASW, 37 mm. **Subject:** 50th Anniversary of the Republic **Obv:** Value and legend **Rev:** Portrait and building **Edge:** Reeded

Date	Mintage	F	VF	XF	Unc	BU
AH1424-2003	3,000	—	—	—	37.00	42.00

KM# 920 5 POUNDS
17.5000 g., 0.7200 Silver 0.4051 oz. ASW, 37 mm. **Subject:** 25th Anniversary of the Delta Bank **Obv:** Value and legend **Rev:** Delta on world globe **Edge:** Reeded

Date	Mintage	F	VF	XF	Unc	BU
AH1424-2004	1,500	—	—	—	37.00	42.00

KM# 925 5 POUNDS
17.5000 g., 0.7200 Silver 0.4051 oz. ASW, 37 mm. **Obv:** Value **Rev:** Balance scale **Edge:** Reeded

Date	Mintage	F	VF	XF	Unc	BU
AH1425-2004	3,300	—	—	—	37.00	42.00

KM# 974 5 POUNDS
17.5000 g., 0.7200 Silver 0.4051 oz. ASW, 37 mm. **Subject:** Golden Jubilee Cairo Mint **Obv:** Value **Rev:** National arms above mint building **Edge:** Reeded

Date	Mintage	F	VF	XF	Unc	BU
AH1425-2004	1,750	—	—	—	45.00	50.00

KM# 933 5 POUNDS
17.5000 g., 0.7200 Silver 0.4051 oz. ASW, 37 mm. **Subject:** 90th Anniversary - Egyptian Scouts Organization - 1914-2004 **Obv:** Value **Rev:** Combined scouting emblem **Edge:** Reeded

Date	Mintage	F	VF	XF	Unc	BU
AH1425-2004	—	—	—	—	37.00	42.00

KM# 935 5 POUNDS
17.5000 g., 0.7200 Silver 0.4051 oz. ASW, 37 mm. **Subject:** Golden Jubilee - Military Production **Obv:** Value **Rev:** Ancient chariot, horse and rider left **Edge:** Reeded

Date	Mintage	F	VF	XF	Unc	BU
AH1425-2004	800	—	—	—	40.00	45.00

KM# 975 5 POUNDS
17.5000 g., 0.7200 Silver 0.4051 oz. ASW, 37 mm. **Subject:** 60th Anniversary Arab League **Obv:** Value **Rev:** Logo in center of ornate background **Edge:** Reeded

Date	Mintage	F	VF	XF	Unc	BU
AH1426-2005	2,000	—	—	—	55.00	60.00

KM# 976 5 POUNDS
17.5000 g., 0.7200 Silver 0.4051 oz. ASW, 37 mm. **Subject:** World Environment Day **Obv:** Value **Rev:** Stylized tree with logo at left, bird at right **Edge:** Reeded

Date	Mintage	F	VF	XF	Unc	BU
AH1427-2006	1,000	—	—	—	70.00	80.00

KM# 977 5 POUNDS
17.5000 g., 0.7200 Silver 0.4051 oz. ASW, 35 mm. **Subject:** Golden jubilee Suez Canal Nationalization **Obv:** Value **Rev:** Large "50" above government buildings **Edge:** Reeded

Date	Mintage	F	VF	XF	Unc	BU
AH1427-2006	1,750	—	—	—	45.00	50.00

KM# 978 5 POUNDS
17.5000 g., 0.7200 Silver 0.4051 oz. ASW, 37 mm. **Subject:** 60th Anniversary UNESCO **Obv:** Value **Rev:** Logo **Edge:** Reeded

Date	Mintage	F	VF	XF	Unc	BU
AH1427-2006	800	—	—	—	100	125

KM# 979 5 POUNDS
17.5000 g., 0.7200 Silver 0.4051 oz. ASW, 37 mm. **Subject:** Diamond Jubilee Academy of Arab Language **Obv:** Value **Rev:** Globe on open book **Edge:** Reeded

Date	Mintage	F	VF	XF	Unc	BU
AH1427-2006	1,000	—	—	—	70.00	80.00

KM# 980 5 POUNDS
17.5000 g., 0.7200 Silver 0.4051 oz. ASW, 37 mm. **Subject:** 13th General Population Census **Obv:** Circle with inscription in center **Rev:** Stylized couple leaning left at left **Edge:** Reeded

Date	Mintage	F	VF	XF	Unc	BU
AH1427-2006	1,500	—	—	—	65.00	75.00

KM# 981 5 POUNDS
17.5000 g., 0.7200 Silver 0.4051 oz. ASW, 37 mm. **Subject:** 100th Anniversary Ahly Club **Obv:** Value **Rev:** Large "100" With linked zeroes **Edge:** Reeded

Date	Mintage	F	VF	XF	Unc	BU
AH1428-2007	3,000	—	—	—	45.00	50.00

KM# 982 5 POUNDS
17.5000 g., 0.7200 Silver 0.4051 oz. ASW, 37 mm. **Subject:** Diamond Jubilee Court of Cassation **Obv:** Balance scale above inscriptions **Rev:** Court building **Edge:** Reeded

Date	Mintage	F	VF	XF	Unc	BU
AH1428-2007	450	—	—	—	125	150

KM# 983 5 POUNDS
17.5000 g., 0.7200 Silver 0.4051 oz. ASW, 37 mm. **Subject:** Silver Jubilee Enviromental Protection Agency **Obv:** Value **Rev:** World globe **Edge:** Reeded

Date	Mintage	F	VF	XF	Unc	BU
AH1428-2007	1,300	—	—	—	55.00	60.00

KM# 984 5 POUNDS
17.5000 g., 0.7200 Silver 0.4051 oz. ASW, 37 mm. **Subject:** 11th Arab Sports Championship - Egypt **Obv:** Value **Rev:** Stylized player on map of Arab countries **Edge:** Reeded

Date	Mintage	F	VF	XF	Unc	BU
AH1428-2007	6,300	—	—	—	45.00	50.00

KM# 943 5 POUNDS
17.5000 g., 0.7200 Silver 0.4051 oz. ASW, 37 mm. **Subject:** 11th Pan-Arab Games **Obv:** Value **Rev:** Logo with outlined map of Arab nations in background **Edge:** Reeded

Date	Mintage	F	VF	XF	Unc	BU
AH1428-2007	6,300	—	—	—	30.00	35.00

KM# 945 5 POUNDS
17.5000 g., 0.7200 Silver 0.4051 oz. ASW, 37 mm. **Subject:** Air Force Diamond Jubilee **Obv:** Value **Rev:** Air Force insignia **Edge:** Reeded

Date	Mintage	F	VF	XF	Unc	BU
AH1428-2007	600	—	—	—	55.00	60.00

KM# 908 10 POUNDS
40.0000 g., 0.8750 Gold 1.1252 oz. AGW, 37 mm. **Subject:** Egyptian Museum Centennial **Obv:** Denomination **Rev:** Building, centennial numerals in background **Edge:** Reeded

Date	Mintage	F	VF	XF	Unc	BU
AH1423-2002	150	—	—	—	2,000	2,100

KM# 989 10 POUNDS
40.0000 g., 0.8750 Gold 1.1252 oz. AGW, 37 mm. **Subject:** Golden Jubilee Police Day **Obv:** Eagle left with wings spread **Rev:** Police emblem **Edge:** Reeded

Date	Mintage	F	VF	XF	Unc	BU
AH1422-2002	150	—	—	—	2,000	2,100

KM# 985 10 POUNDS
40.0000 g., 0.8750 Gold 1.1252 oz. AGW, 37 mm. **Subject:** 50th Anniversary El Gomhoreya News **Obv:** Value **Rev:** Bust of Hosni Mubarak facing at left, building in background **Edge:** Reeded

Date	Mintage	F	VF	XF	Unc	BU
AH1424-2003	50	—	—	—	2,100	2,200

KM# 986 10 POUNDS
40.0000 g., 0.8750 Gold 1.1252 oz. AGW, 37 mm. **Subject:** Golden Jubilee Military Production **Obv:** Value **Rev:** Ancient chariot, horse and rider left **Edge:** Reeded

Date	Mintage	F	VF	XF	Unc	BU
AH1425-2004	85	—	—	—	2,100	2,200

KM# 987 10 POUNDS
40.0000 g., 0.8750 Gold 1.1252 oz. AGW, 37 mm. **Subject:** 60th Anniversary Arab League **Obv:** Value **Rev:** Emblem at center, ornate background **Edge:** Reeded

Date	Mintage	F	VF	XF	Unc	BU
AH1426-2005	50	—	—	—	2,100	2,200

KM# 988 10 POUNDS
40.0000 g., 0.8750 Gold 1.1252 oz. AGW, 37 mm. **Subject:** Diamond Jubilee Air Force **Obv:** Value **Rev:** Air Force emblem **Edge:** Reeded

Date	Mintage	F	VF	XF	Unc	BU
AH1428-2007	25	—	—	—	2,150	2,250

ESTONIA

The Republic of Estonia (formerly the Estonian Soviet Socialist Republic of the U.S.S.R.) is the northernmost of the three Baltic States in Eastern Europe. It has an area of 17,462 sq. mi. (45,100 sq. km.) and a population of 1.6 million. Capital: Tallinn. Agriculture and dairy farming are the principal industries. Butter, eggs, bacon, timber and petroleum are exported.

MODERN REPUBLIC

STANDARD COINAGE

KM# 22 10 SENTI
1.8500 g., Aluminum-Bronze, 17.1 mm. **Obv:** Three lions left divide date **Rev:** Denomination **Rev. Legend:** EESTI VABARIIK **Edge:** Plain

Date	Mintage	F	VF	XF	Unc	BU
2002	30,000,000	—	—	0.20	0.50	0.80
2006	31,000,000	—	—	0.20	0.50	0.80
2008	15,000,000	—	—	0.20	0.50	0.80

KM# 23a 20 SENTI
2.0000 g., Nickel Plated Steel, 18.9 mm. **Obv:** National arms divide date **Rev:** Denomination **Rev. Legend:** EESTI VABARIIK **Edge:** Plain

Date	Mintage	F	VF	XF	Unc	BU
2003	11,100,000	—	—	—	0.60	1.00
2004	20,000,000	—	—	—	0.60	1.00
2006	2,000,000	—	—	—	0.60	1.00
2008	12,000,000	—	—	—	0.60	1.00

KM# 24 50 SENTI
2.9000 g., Aluminum-Bronze, 19.5 mm. **Obv:** National arms divide date **Rev:** Denomination **Rev. Legend:** EESTI VABARIIK **Edge:** Plain

Date	Mintage	F	VF	XF	Unc	BU
2004	10,000,000	—	—	—	1.00	1.50
2006	7,000,000	—	—	—	1.00	1.50
2007	17,000,000	—	—	—	1.00	1.50

KM# 35 KROON
5.0000 g., Aluminum-Bronze, 23.5 mm. **Obv:** National arms **Rev:** Large, thick denomination **Rev. Legend:** EESTI VABARIIK **Edge:** Segmented reeding

Date	Mintage	F	VF	XF	Unc	BU
2001	15,000,000	—	—	0.50	1.50	2.00
2003	15,000,000	—	—	0.50	1.50	2.00
2006	15,170,000	—	—	0.50	1.50	2.00

KM# 44 KROON
4.8000 g., Brass, 23.21 mm. **Obv:** National arms **Rev:** Stylized plant in circle **Rev. Legend:** EESTI VABARIIK **Edge:** Segmented reeding

Date	Mintage	F	VF	XF	Unc	BU
2008	20,000,000	—	—	1.00	2.00	3.00

KM# 38 10 KROONI
28.2800 g., 0.9990 Silver 0.9083 oz. ASW, 38.6 mm. **Subject:** Tartu University **Obv:** National arms **Rev:** Building in oval, value at left **Edge:** Reeded

Date	Mintage	F	VF	XF	Unc	BU
2002 Proof	10,000	Value: 80.00				

KM# 40 10 KROONI
28.2800 g., 0.9990 Silver 0.9083 oz. ASW, 38.6 mm. **Subject:** Estonian Flag **Obv:** National arms **Rev:** Round multicolor flag design **Edge:** Reeded

Date	Mintage	F	VF	XF	Unc	BU
2004 Proof	10,000	Value: 75.00				

KM# 42 10 KROONI
28.2800 g., 0.9990 Silver 0.9083 oz. ASW, 38.6 mm. **Subject:** Torino Winter Olympics **Obv:** National arms **Rev:** Gold inset cross country skier in semi-circle above Olympic flame **Edge:** Reeded

Date	Mintage	F	VF	XF	Unc	BU
2006 Proof	5,000	Value: 150				

KM# 46 10 KROONI
28.2800 g., 0.9990 Silver 0.9083 oz. ASW, 38.61 mm. **Subject:** 90th Anniversary of Independence **Obv:** National arms **Obv. Legend:** EESTI VARBARIIK **Rev:** Wiiralt oak tree **Edge:** Plain **Designer:** Heino Prunsvelt

Date	Mintage	F	VF	XF	Unc	BU
2008 Proof	10,000	Value: 85.00				

KM# 48 10 KROONI
28.2800 g., 0.9990 Silver 0.9083 oz. ASW, 38.61 mm. **Subject:** Olympics **Obv:** Arms **Rev:** Torch and geometric patterns

Date	Mintage	F	VF	XF	Unc	BU
2008 Proof	—	Value: 50.00				

KM# 49 10 KROONI
24.1000 g., 0.9990 Silver 0.7740 oz. ASW, 38.61 mm. **Subject:** National Museum **Obv:** National arms within starburst **Rev:** Design in star

Date	Mintage	F	VF	XF	Unc	BU
2008 Proof	—	Value: 85.00				

KM# 51 10 KROONI
31.1050 g., 0.9990 Silver 0.9990 oz. ASW, 40.6 mm. **Subject:** Song and Dance Festival **Obv:** National Arms **Rev:** Circle of dancers

Date	Mintage	F	VF	XF	Unc	BU
2009 Proof	—	Value: 75.00				

KM# 53 10 KROONI
28.2800 g., 0.9990 Silver 0.9083 oz. ASW, 38.61 mm. **Subject:** Vancouver Winter Olympics **Obv:** National arms within wreath, date below **Rev:** Two stylized cross county skiers right

Date	Mintage	F	VF	XF	Unc	BU
2010 Proof	—	Value: 60.00				

KM# 55 25 KROONI
24.1000 g., 0.9999 Silver 0.7747 oz. ASW, 38.61 mm.

Date	Mintage	F	VF	XF	Unc	BU
2010 Proof	—	Value: 75.00				

KM# 50 50 KROONI
8.6400 g., 0.9990 Gold 0.2775 oz. AGW, 22 mm. **Obv:** National Arms and laurel branch **Rev:** Windmill

Date	Mintage	F	VF	XF	Unc	BU
2008 Proof	—	Value: 650				

KM# 54 50 KROONI
24.5000 g., 0.9990 Silver with Wood insert 0.7869 oz. ASW, 38.61 mm. **Subject:** Estonian Nature **Obv:** Arms and legned

Date	Mintage	F	VF	XF	Unc	BU
2010 Proof	—	Value: 60.00				

KM# 39 100 KROONI
7.7760 g., 0.9999 Gold 0.2500 oz. AGW **Subject:** Monetary Reform **Obv:** National arms **Rev:** Cross design **Edge:** Reeded

Date	Mintage	F	VF	XF	Unc	BU
2002	2,000	—	—	—	—	650

KM# 41 100 KROONI
7.7760 g., 0.9999 Gold 0.2500 oz. AGW, 22 mm. **Subject:** Olympic Games **Obv:** National arms within wreath **Rev:** Olympic flame above rings in center **Edge:** Reeded

Date	Mintage	F	VF	XF	Unc	BU
2004	5,000	—	—	—	—	575

KM# 43 100 KROONI
28.2800 g., 0.9990 Silver 0.9083 oz. ASW, 38.6 mm. **Subject:** National Opera **Obv:** National arms **Rev:** Building front **Edge:** Plain

Date	Mintage	F	VF	XF	Unc	BU
2006 Proof	10,000	Value: 85.00				

KM# 45 100 KROONI
7.7800 g., 0.9999 Gold 0.2501 oz. AGW **Subject:** 15th Anniversary Reintroduction of the Estonian Kroon **Obv:** National arms **Obv. Legend:** EESTI VARBARIIK **Rev:** Cornflower **Rev. Legend:** KROONI TAAS- / KEHTESTAMISE / 15. AASTAPAEV **Edge:** Plain **Shape:** Triangular **Designer:** Ivar Sakk

Date	Mintage	F	VF	XF	Unc	BU
2007 Prooflike	6,000	—	—	—	—	575

KM# 47 100 KROONI
7.7750 g., 0.9990 Platinum 0.2497 oz. APW, 18 mm. **Subject:** 90th Anniversary of Republic **Rev:** Three birds on wire

Date	Mintage	F	VF	XF	Unc	BU
2008 Proof	3,000	Value: 675				

KM# 52 100 KROONI
7.7800 g., 0.9990 Gold 0.2499 oz. AGW, 22 mm. **Subject:** Song and dance festival **Obv:** Arms **Rev:** Stylized chorus on stage

Date	Mintage	F	VF	XF	Unc	BU
2009 Proof	—	Value: 600				

KM# 56 100 KROONI
7.7800 g., 0.9990 Gold 0.2499 oz. AGW, 22 mm.

Date	Mintage	F	VF	XF	Unc	BU
2010 Proof	—	Value: 650				

EURO COINAGE

KM# 61 EURO CENT
2.3000 g., Copper Plated Steel, 16.25 mm. **Obv:** Map of Estonia **Rev:** Denomination and globe

Date	Mintage	F	VF	XF	Unc	BU
2011	—	—	—	—	0.35	0.50
2011 Proof	3,500	Value: 6.00				
2012	25,000,000	—	—	—	0.35	0.50

KM# 62 2 EURO CENT
3.0600 g., Copper Plated Steel, 18.75 mm. **Obv:** Map of Estonia **Rev:** Denomination and globe **Edge:** Grooved

Date	Mintage	F	VF	XF	Unc	BU
2011	—	—	—	—	0.50	0.75
2011 Proof	3,500	Value: 7.00				
2012	25,000,000	—	—	—	0.50	0.75

KM# 63 5 EURO CENT
3.9200 g., Copper Plated Steel, 21.25 mm. **Obv:** Map of Estonia **Rev:** Denomination and globe

Date	Mintage	F	VF	XF	Unc	BU
2011	—	—	—	—	0.75	1.25
2011 Proof	3,500	Value: 7.00				

KM# 64 10 EURO CENT
4.1000 g., Brass, 19.75 mm. **Obv:** Map of Estonia **Rev:** Relief map of Western Europe, stars, line and value **Edge:** Reeded

Date	Mintage	F	VF	XF	Unc	BU
2011	—	—	—	—	1.25	2.00
2011 Proof	3,500	Value: 7.00				

KM# 65 20 EURO CENT
5.7400 g., Brass, 22.25 mm. **Obv:** Map of Estonia **Rev:** Relief map of Western Europe, stars, line and value **Edge:** Notched

Date	Mintage	F	VF	XF	Unc	BU
2011	—	—	—	—	1.00	1.50
2011 Proof	3,500	Value: 9.00				

KM# 66 50 EURO CENT
7.8000 g., Brass, 24.25 mm. **Obv:** Map of Estonia **Rev:** Relief map of Western Europe, stars, line and value **Edge:** Reeded

Date	Mintage	F	VF	XF	Unc	BU
2011	—	—	—	—	1.25	2.00
2011 Proof	3,500	Value: 15.00				

KM# 67 EURO
7.5000 g., Bi-Metallic Copper-Nickel center in Nickel-Brass ring, 23.35 mm. **Obv:** Map of Estonia **Rev:** Relief map of Western Europe, stars, lines and value **Edge:** Segmented reeding

Date	Mintage	F	VF	XF	Unc	BU
2011	—	—	—	—	2.75	4.00
2011 Proof	3,500	Value: 15.00				

KM# 68 2 EURO
8.5000 g., Bi-Metallic Nickel-Brass center in Copper-Nickel ring, 25.75 mm. **Obv:** Map of Estonia **Rev:** Relief map of Western Europe, stars, lines and value **Edge:** Reeded and lettered

Date	Mintage	F	VF	XF	Unc	BU
2011	—	—	—	—	3.75	6.00
2011 Proof	3,500	Value: 30.00				

KM# 70 2 EURO
8.5000 g., Bi-Metallic Nickel-Brass center in Copper-Nickel ring, 25.75 mm. **Subject:** Euro Coinage, 10th Anniversary **Obv:** Euro symbol on globe at center, child-like rendering around

Date	Mintage	F	VF	XF	Unc	BU
2012	2,000,000	—	—	—	3.75	6.00

KM# 71 10 EURO
28.8000 g., 0.9999 Silver 0.9258 oz. ASW, 38.61 mm. **Subject:** Estonia's Future **Obv:** National arms **Rev:** Two dancing figures, value at top **Edge Lettering:** Ag 999.9

Date	Mintage	F	VF	XF	Unc	BU
2011 Proof	30,000	Value: 75.00				

KM# 72 12 EURO
28.2800 g., 0.9990 Silver 0.9083 oz. ASW, 38.61 mm. **Subject:** London Olympics **Obv:** National arms **Rev:** Ribbons, Olympic rings and flame

Date	Mintage	F	VF	XF	Unc	BU
2012 Proof	7,500	Value: 100				

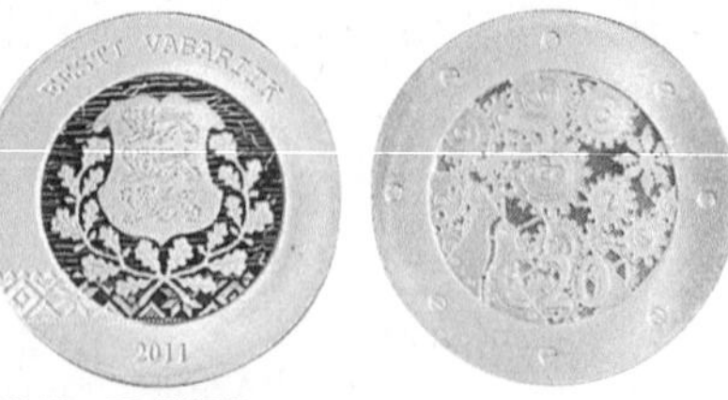

KM# 69 20 EURO
14.6000 g., Bi-Metallic .9999 Gold center in .9999 Silver ring, 27.25 mm. **Subject:** Estonia's entry into Eurozone **Obv:** National arms **Rev:** Lace

Date	Mintage	F	VF	XF	Unc	BU
2011 Proof	10,000	Value: 650				

MINT SETS

KM#	Date	Mintage	Identification	Issue Price	Mkt Val
MS2	2011 (8)	50,000	KM#61-68	—	25.00

PROOF SETS

KM#	Date	Mintage	Identification	Issue Price	Mkt Val
PS1	2011 (8)	3,500	KM#61-68	—	95.00

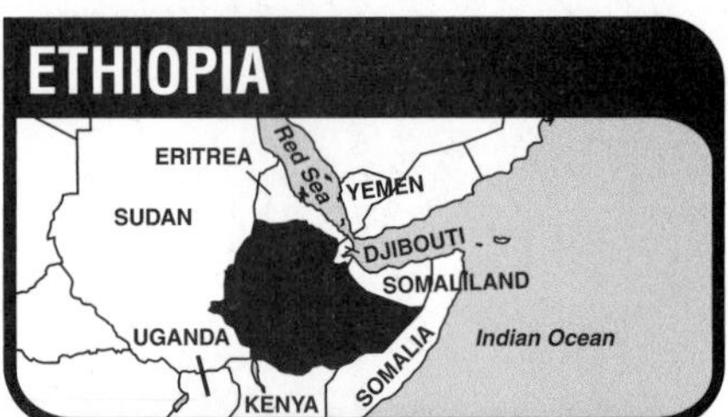

The People's Federal Republic of Ethiopia (formerly the Peoples Democratic Republic and the Empire of Ethiopia), Africa's oldest independent nation, faces the Red Sea in East-Central Africa. The country has an area of 424,214 sq. mi. (1,004,390 sq. km.) and a population of 56 million people who are divided among 40 tribes that speak some 270 languages and dialects. Capital: Addis Ababa. The economy is predominantly agricultural and pastoral. Gold and platinum are mined and petroleum fields are being developed. Coffee, oilseeds, hides and cereals are exported.

DATING

Ethiopian coinage is dated by the Ethiopian Era calendar (E.E.), which commenced 7 years and 8 months after the advent of A.D. dating.

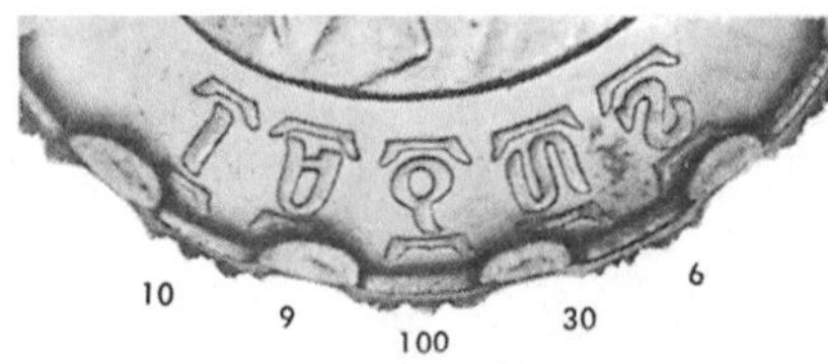

EXAMPLE
1900 (10 and 9 = 19 x 100)
36 (Add 30 and 6)
1936 E.E.
8 (Add)
1943/4 AD

PEOPLES DEMOCRATIC REPUBLIC

DECIMAL COINAGE

100 Santeems (Cents) = 1 Birr (Dollar)
100 Matonas = 100 Santeems

KM# 44.3 5 CENTS
3.0000 g., Brass, 20 mm. **Obv:** Large lion head, right **Rev:** Denomination left of figure **Designer:** Stuart Devlin

Date	Mintage	F	VF	XF	Unc	BU
EE1996 (2004)	—	—	—	—	—	1.00
EE1998 (2006)	—	—	—	—	—	1.00
EE1999 (2007)	—	—	—	—	—	1.00
EE2000 (2008)	—	—	—	—	—	1.00
EE2004 (2012)	—	—	—	—	—	1.00

KM# 45.3 10 CENTS
4.5000 g., Brass, 23 mm. **Obv:** Large lion head right **Rev:** Mountain Nyala, denomination at right **Designer:** Stuart Devlin

Date	Mintage	F	VF	XF	Unc	BU
EE1996 (2004)	—	—	—	—	—	1.25
EE1997 (2005)	—	—	—	—	—	1.25
EE1998 (2006)	—	—	—	—	—	1.25
EE2000 (2008)	—	—	—	—	—	1.25

KM# 46.3 25 CENTS
3.7000 g., Copper-Nickel, 21.45 mm. **Obv:** Large lion head right **Rev:** Man and woman with arms raised divide denomination **Designer:** Stuart Devlin

Date	Mintage	F	VF	XF	Unc	BU
EE1996 (2004)	—	—	—	—	—	1.25
EE1997 (2005)	—	—	—	—	—	1.25
EE2000 (2008)	—	—	—	—	—	1.25
EE2004 (2012)	—	—	—	—	—	1.25

KM# 47.2 50 CENTS

6.0000 g., Copper-Nickel, 25 mm. **Obv:** Small lion head, two long chin whiskers at left nearly touch date **Rev:** People of the republic, denomination above

Date	Mintage	F	VF	XF	Unc	BU
EE1996 (2004)	—	—	—	1.50	3.00	—
EE1997 (2005)	—	—	—	1.50	3.00	—
EE2000 (2008)	—	—	—	1.50	3.00	—

FEDERAL DEMOCRATIC REPUBLIC

DECIMAL COINAGE

100 Santeems (Cents) = 1 Birr (Dollar)
100 Matonas = 100 Santeems

KM# 78 BIRR

6.7500 g., Bi-Metallic Brass Plated Steel center in Nickel Plated Steel ring, 28 mm. **Obv:** Large lion right in center **Rev:** Balance scale

Date	Mintage	F	VF	XF	Unc	BU
EE2002 (2010)	411,600,000	—	—	—	2.25	5.00

KM# 76 20 BIRR

30.0000 g., 0.9000 Silver 0.8680 oz. ASW, 40 mm. **Obv:** Vertical symbol with ribbon **Rev:** Reconstructed skeleton

Date	Mintage	F	VF	XF	Unc	BU
EE2000 (2007) Proof	Est. 50,000	Value: 75.00				

KM# 77 600 BIRR

20.0000 g., Gold, 34 mm. **Rev:** Selam Skull

Date	Mintage	F	VF	XF	Unc	BU
EE2000 (2007) Proof	Est. 1,000	Value: 1,250				

FALKLAND ISLANDS

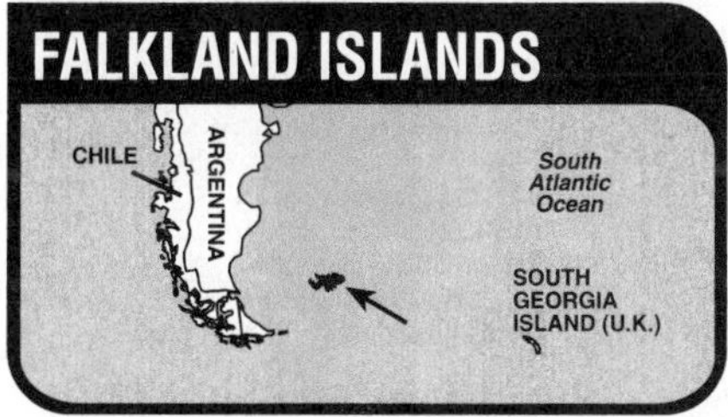

The Colony of the Falkland Islands and Dependencies, a British colony located in the South Atlantic about 500 miles northeast of Cape Horn, has an area of 4,700 sq. mi. (12,170 sq. km.) and a population of 2,121. East Falkland, West Falkland, South Georgia, and South Sandwich are the largest of the 200 islands. Capital: Stanley. Sheep grazing is the main industry. Wool, whale oil, and seal oil are exported.

RULER
British

MONETARY SYSTEM
100 Pence = 1 Pound

BRITISH COLONY

DECIMAL COINAGE

KM# 130 PENNY

3.5600 g., Copper Plated Steel, 20.3 mm. **Ruler:** Elizabeth II **Obv:** Head with tiara right **Obv. Legend:** QUEEN ELIZABETH THE SECOND **Rev:** Two Gentoo penguins flank value **Rev. Legend:** FALKLAND ISLANDS **Edge:** Plain

Date	Mintage	F	VF	XF	Unc	BU
2004	—	—	—	—	0.50	0.75

KM# 131 2 PENCE

7.1200 g., Copper Plated Steel, 25.9 mm. **Ruler:** Elizabeth II **Obv:** Head with tiara right **Obv. Legend:** QUEEN ELIZABETH THE SECOND **Rev:** Upland goose alighting, value above **Rev. Legend:** FALKLAND ISLANDS **Edge:** Plain

Date	Mintage	F	VF	XF	Unc	BU
2004	—	—	—	—	0.50	1.00

KM# 132 5 PENCE

3.2500 g., Copper-Nickel, 18 mm. **Ruler:** Elizabeth II **Obv:** Head with tiara right **Obv. Legend:** QUEEN ELIZABETH THE SECOND **Rev:** Black-browed Albatross in flight, value below **Rev. Legend:** FALKLAND - ISLANDS **Edge:** Reeded

Date	Mintage	F	VF	XF	Unc	BU
2004	—	—	—	—	0.75	1.00

KM# 133 10 PENCE

6.5000 g., Copper-Nickel, 24.5 mm. **Ruler:** Elizabeth II **Obv:** Head with tiara right **Obv. Legend:** QUEEN ELIZABETH THE SECOND **Rev:** Ursine seal with cub, value below **Rev. Legend:** FALKLAND ISLANDS **Edge:** Reeded

Date	Mintage	F	VF	XF	Unc	BU
2004	—	—	—	—	1.50	3.00

KM# 134 20 PENCE

5.0000 g., Copper-Nickel, 21.4 mm. **Ruler:** Elizabeth II **Obv:** Head with tiara right **Obv. Legend:** QUEEN ELIZABETH THE SECOND **Rev:** Romney marsh sheep standing left, value above **Rev. Legend:** FALKLAND ISLANDS **Edge:** Plain **Shape:** 7-sided

Date	Mintage	F	VF	XF	Unc	BU
2004	—	—	—	—	2.00	4.00

KM# 70 50 PENCE

29.1000 g., Copper-Nickel, 38.6 mm. **Ruler:** Elizabeth II **Subject:** Centennial of Queen Victoria's Death **Obv:** Crowned bust right, denomination below **Rev:** Crowned head left, three dates **Edge:** Reeded

Date	Mintage	F	VF	XF	Unc	BU
2001	—	—	—	—	6.00	7.00

KM# 70a 50 PENCE

28.2800 g., 0.9250 Silver 0.8410 oz. ASW, 38.6 mm. **Ruler:** Elizabeth II **Obv:** Crowned bust right, denomination below **Rev:** Crowned head left, three dates **Edge:** Reeded

Date	Mintage	F	VF	XF	Unc	BU
2001 Proof	10,000	Value: 50.00				

KM# 70b 50 PENCE

47.5400 g., 0.9170 Gold 1.4015 oz. AGW, 38.61 mm. **Ruler:** Elizabeth II **Subject:** Centennial of Queen Victoria's Death **Obv:** Crowned bust right, denomination below **Rev:** Victoria's crowned bust left, three dates **Edge:** Reeded

Date	Mintage	F	VF	XF	Unc	BU
2001 Proof	100	Value: 2,500				

KM# 71 50 PENCE

29.1000 g., Copper-Nickel, 38.6 mm. **Ruler:** Elizabeth II **Subject:** Queen Elizabeth's 75th Birthday **Obv:** Crowned bust right, denomination below **Rev:** Bust of Queen Elizabeth II left **Edge:** Reeded

Date	Mintage	F	VF	XF	Unc	BU
2001	—	—	—	—	6.00	7.00

KM# 71b 50 PENCE

47.5400 g., 0.9170 Gold 1.4015 oz. AGW, 38.61 mm. **Ruler:** Elizabeth II **Subject:** Queen Elizabeth's 75th Birthday **Obv:** Crowned bust right, denomination below **Rev:** Bust of Queen Elizabeth II left

Date	Mintage	F	VF	XF	Unc	BU
2001 Proof	Est. 100	Value: 2,500				

KM# 86 50 PENCE

28.2800 g., Copper-Nickel, 38.6 mm. **Ruler:** Elizabeth II **Obv:** Crowned bust right, denomination below **Rev:** Edward IV (1461-83) with Rose Ryal gold coin design **Edge:** Reeded

Date	Mintage	F	VF	XF	Unc	BU
2001	—	—	—	—	9.00	10.00

KM# 86a 50 PENCE

28.2800 g., 0.9250 Silver 0.8410 oz. ASW, 38.6 mm. **Ruler:** Elizabeth II **Obv:** Crowned bust right, denomination below **Rev:** Edward IV (1461-83) with gold-plated Rose Ryal gold coin design **Edge:** Reeded

Date	Mintage	F	VF	XF	Unc	BU
2001 Proof	5,000	Value: 50.00				

KM# 87 50 PENCE

28.2800 g., Copper-Nickel, 38.6 mm. **Ruler:** Elizabeth II **Obv:** Crowned bust right, denomination below **Rev:** Henry VII (1485-1509) with 1489 Gold Sovereign coin design **Edge:** Reeded

Date	Mintage	F	VF	XF	Unc	BU
2001	—	—	—	—	9.00	10.00

KM# 87a 50 PENCE

28.2800 g., 0.9250 Silver 0.8410 oz. ASW, 38.6 mm. **Ruler:** Elizabeth II **Obv:** Crowned bust right, denomination below **Rev:** Henry VII (1485-1509) with gold-plated 1489 gold Sovereign coin design **Edge:** Reeded

Date	Mintage	F	VF	XF	Unc	BU
2001 Proof	5,000	Value: 50.00				

KM# 88 50 PENCE

28.2800 g., Copper-Nickel, 38.6 mm. **Ruler:** Elizabeth II **Obv:** Crowned bust right, denomination below **Rev:** Charles II (1660-85) with 1663 gold Guinea coin design **Edge:** Reeded

Date	Mintage	F	VF	XF	Unc	BU
2001	—	—	—	—	9.00	10.00

KM# 88a 50 PENCE

28.2800 g., 0.9250 Silver 0.8410 oz. ASW, 38.6 mm. **Ruler:** Elizabeth II **Obv:** Crowned bust right, denomination below **Rev:** Charles II (1660-85) with gold-plated Gold Guinea coin design **Edge:** Reeded

Date	Mintage	F	VF	XF	Unc	BU
2001 Proof	5,000	Value: 50.00				

KM# 89 50 PENCE

28.2800 g., Copper-Nickel, 38.6 mm. **Ruler:** Elizabeth II **Obv:** Crowned bust right, denomination below **Rev:** Queen Victoria with Gold Sovereign coin design **Edge:** Reeded

Date	Mintage	F	VF	XF	Unc	BU
2001	—	—	—	—	9.00	10.00

KM# 89a 50 PENCE

28.2800 g., 0.9250 Silver 0.8410 oz. ASW, 38.6 mm. **Ruler:** Elizabeth II **Obv:** Crowned bust right, denomination below **Rev:** Queen Victoria with gold-plated Gold Sovereign coin design **Edge:** Reeded

Date	Mintage	F	VF	XF	Unc	BU
2001 Proof	5,000	Value: 50.00				

KM# 73.1 50 PENCE

28.1300 g., Copper-Nickel, 38.6 mm. **Ruler:** Elizabeth II **Subject:** Queen's Golden Jubilee **Obv:** Crowned head right, denomination below **Rev:** Queen Elizabeth II on throne in inner circle below multicolor bunting **Edge:** Reeded

Date	Mintage	F	VF	XF	Unc	BU
2002(2001) Proof	—	Value: 8.00				

KM# 73.2 50 PENCE

Copper-Nickel **Ruler:** Elizabeth II **Subject:** Queen's Golden Jubilee **Obv:** Crowned bust right, denomination below **Rev:** With plain bunting

Date	Mintage	F	VF	XF	Unc	BU
2002	—	—	—	—	6.00	7.00

KM# 73a.1 50 PENCE

28.2800 g., 0.9250 Silver 0.8410 oz. ASW, 38.6 mm. **Ruler:** Elizabeth II **Subject:** Queen's Golden Jubilee **Obv:** Crowned bust right, denomination below **Rev:** Queen on throne below multicolor bunting **Edge:** Reeded

Date	Mintage	F	VF	XF	Unc	BU
2002 Proof	25,000	Value: 45.00				

KM# 73a.2 50 PENCE

28.2800 g., 0.9250 Silver 0.8410 oz. ASW, 38.61 mm. **Ruler:** Elizabeth II **Obv:** Crowned bust right, denomination below **Rev:** With plain bunting

Date	Mintage	F	VF	XF	Unc	BU
2002 Proof	—	Value: 45.00				

KM# 73b.1 50 PENCE

39.9400 g., 0.9170 Gold 1.1775 oz. AGW, 38.61 mm. **Ruler:** Elizabeth II **Obv:** Crowned bust right, denomination below **Rev:** Crowned queen with scepter and orb below multicolor bunting **Edge:** Reeded

Date	Mintage	F	VF	XF	Unc	BU
2002 Proof	150	Value: 2,100				

KM# 74.1 50 PENCE

28.1300 g., Copper-Nickel, 38.6 mm. **Ruler:** Elizabeth II **Subject:** Queen's Golden Jubilee **Obv:** Crowned bust right, denomination below **Rev:** Queen on horse half left in inner circle below multicolor bunting **Edge:** Reeded

Date	Mintage	F	VF	XF	Unc	BU
2002(2001) Proof	—	Value: 8.00				

KM# 74.2 50 PENCE

Copper-Nickel **Ruler:** Elizabeth II **Subject:** Queen's Golden Jubilee **Obv:** Crowned bust right, denomination below **Rev:** With plain bunting

Date	Mintage	F	VF	XF	Unc	BU
2002	—	—	—	—	7.00	8.00

KM# 74a.1 50 PENCE

28.2800 g., 0.9250 Silver 0.8410 oz. ASW, 38.6 mm. **Ruler:** Elizabeth II **Subject:** Queen's Golden Jubilee **Obv:** Crowned bust right, denomination below **Edge:** Reeded

Date	Mintage	F	VF	XF	Unc	BU
2002 Proof	25,000	Value: 45.00				

KM# 74a.2 50 PENCE

28.2800 g., 0.9250 Silver 0.8410 oz. ASW, 38.61 mm. **Ruler:** Elizabeth II **Subject:** Queen's Golden Jubilee **Obv:** Crowned bust right, denomination below **Rev:** With plain bunting

Date	Mintage	F	VF	XF	Unc	BU
2002 Proof	—	Value: 45.00				

KM# 74b.1 50 PENCE

39.9400 g., 0.9170 Gold 1.1775 oz. AGW, 38.61 mm. **Ruler:** Elizabeth II **Subject:** Queen's Golden Jubilee **Obv:** Crowned bust right, denomination below **Rev:** Queen on horseback below multicolored bunting **Edge:** Reeded

Date	Mintage	F	VF	XF	Unc	BU
2002 Proof	150	Value: 2,050				

KM# 74b.2 50 PENCE

39.9400 g., 0.9170 Gold 1.1775 oz. AGW, 38.61 mm. **Ruler:** Elizabeth II **Subject:** Queen's Golden Jubilee **Obv:** Crowned bust right, denomination below **Rev:** With plain bunting

Date	Mintage	F	VF	XF	Unc	BU
2002 Proof	—	Value: 2,100				

KM# 75.1 50 PENCE

28.1300 g., Copper-Nickel, 38.6 mm. **Ruler:** Elizabeth II **Subject:** Queen's Golden Jubilee **Obv:** Crowned bust right, denomination below **Rev:** Queen Elizabeth II talking into microphone below multicolor bunting **Edge:** Reeded

Date	Mintage	F	VF	XF	Unc	BU
2002(2001) Proof	—	Value: 8.00				

KM# 75.2 50 PENCE

Copper-Nickel **Ruler:** Elizabeth II **Subject:** Queen's Golden Jubilee **Obv:** Crowned bust right, denomination below **Rev:** With plain bunting

Date	Mintage	F	VF	XF	Unc	BU
2002	—	—	—	—	6.00	7.00

KM# 75a.1 50 PENCE

28.2800 g., 0.9250 Silver 0.8410 oz. ASW, 38.6 mm. **Ruler:** Elizabeth II **Subject:** Queen's Golden Jubilee **Obv:** Crowned bust right, denomination below **Rev:** Queen speaking into a radio microphone below multicolored bunting **Edge:** Reeded

Date	Mintage	F	VF	XF	Unc	BU
2002 Proof	25,000	Value: 45.00				

KM# 75a.2 50 PENCE

28.2800 g., 0.9250 Silver 0.8410 oz. ASW, 38.61 mm. **Ruler:** Elizabeth II **Subject:** Queen's Golden Jubilee **Obv:** Crowned bust right, denomination below **Rev:** With plain bunting

Date	Mintage	F	VF	XF	Unc	BU
2002 Proof	—	Value: 45.00				

KM# 75b.1 50 PENCE

39.9400 g., 0.9170 Gold 1.1775 oz. AGW, 38.61 mm. **Ruler:** Elizabeth II **Subject:** Queen's Golden Jubilee **Obv:** Crowned bust right, denomination below **Rev:** Elizabeth speaking into a radio microphone below multicolored bunting **Edge:** Reeded

Date	Mintage	F	VF	XF	Unc	BU
2002 Proof	50	Value: 2,150				

KM# 75b.2 50 PENCE

39.9400 g., 0.9170 Gold 1.1775 oz. AGW, 38.61 mm. **Ruler:** Elizabeth II **Subject:** Queen's Golden Jubilee **Obv:** Crowned bust right, denomination below **Rev:** With plain bunting

Date	Mintage	F	VF	XF	Unc	BU
2002 Proof	—	Value: 2,100				

KM# 76.1 50 PENCE

28.1300 g., Copper-Nickel, 38.6 mm. **Ruler:** Elizabeth II **Subject:** Queen's Golden Jubilee **Obv:** Crowned bust right, denomination below **Rev:** Queen walking to left in front of a crowd below multicolored bunting **Edge:** Reeded

Date	Mintage	F	VF	XF	Unc	BU
2002(2001) Proof	—	Value: 8.00				

KM# 76.2 50 PENCE

Copper-Nickel **Ruler:** Elizabeth II **Subject:** Queen's Golden Jubilee **Obv:** Crowned bust right, denomination below **Rev:** With plain bunting

Date	Mintage	F	VF	XF	Unc	BU
2002	—	—	—	—	6.00	7.00

KM# 76a.1 50 PENCE

28.2800 g., 0.9250 Silver 0.8410 oz. ASW, 38.6 mm. **Ruler:** Elizabeth II **Subject:** Queen's Golden Jubilee **Obv:** Crowned bust right, denomination below **Rev:** Queen standing before crowd below multicolored bunting **Edge:** Reeded

Date	Mintage	F	VF	XF	Unc	BU
2002 Proof	15,000	Value: 45.00				

KM# 76a.2 50 PENCE

28.2800 g., 0.9250 Silver 0.8410 oz. ASW, 38.61 mm. **Ruler:** Elizabeth II **Subject:** Queen's Golden Jubilee **Obv:** Crowned bust right, denomination below **Rev:** With plain bunting

Date	Mintage	F	VF	XF	Unc	BU
2002 Proof	—	Value: 45.00				

KM# 76b.1 50 PENCE

39.9400 g., 0.9170 Gold 1.1775 oz. AGW, 38.61 mm. **Ruler:** Elizabeth II **Subject:** Queen's Golden Jubilee **Obv:** Crowned bust right, denomination below **Rev:** Queen standing before a crowd below multicolored bunting **Edge:** Reeded

Date	Mintage	F	VF	XF	Unc	BU
2002 Proof	50	Value: 2,150				

KM# 76b.2 50 PENCE

39.9400 g., 0.9170 Gold 1.1775 oz. AGW, 38.61 mm. **Ruler:** Elizabeth II **Subject:** Queen's Golden Jubilee **Obv:** Crowned bust right, denomination below **Rev:** With plain bunting

Date	Mintage	F	VF	XF	Unc	BU
2002 Proof	—	Value: 2,100				

KM# 77.1 50 PENCE

28.1300 g., Copper-Nickel, 38.6 mm. **Ruler:** Elizabeth II **Subject:** Queen's Golden Jubilee **Obv:** Crowned bust right, denomination below **Rev:** Conjoined busts of Queen Elizabeth, Prince Charles, Prince William facing left in inner circle below multicolor bunting **Edge:** Reeded

Date	Mintage	F	VF	XF	Unc	BU
2002(2001) Proof	—	Value: 8.00				

KM# 77.2 50 PENCE
Copper-Nickel **Ruler:** Elizabeth II **Subject:** Queen's Golden Jubilee **Obv:** Crowned bust right, denomination below **Rev:** With plain bunting

Date	Mintage	F	VF	XF	Unc	BU
2002	—	—	—	—	6.00	7.00

KM# 77a.1 50 PENCE
28.2800 g., 0.9250 Silver 0.8410 oz. ASW, 38.6 mm. **Ruler:** Elizabeth II **Subject:** Queen's Golden Jubilee **Obv:** Crowned bust right, denomination below **Rev:** Queen, Prince Charles and Prince William below multicolor bunting **Edge:** Reeded

Date	Mintage	F	VF	XF	Unc	BU
2002 Proof	15,000	Value: 45.00				

KM# 77a.2 50 PENCE
28.2800 g., 0.9250 Silver 0.8410 oz. ASW, 38.61 mm. **Ruler:** Elizabeth II **Subject:** Queen's Golden Jubilee **Obv:** Crowned bust right, denomination below **Rev:** With plain bunting

Date	Mintage	F	VF	XF	Unc	BU
2002 Proof	—	Value: 45.00				

KM# 77b.1 50 PENCE
39.9400 g., 0.9170 Gold 1.1775 oz. AGW, 38.61 mm. **Ruler:** Elizabeth II **Subject:** Queen's Golden Jubilee **Obv:** Crowned bust right, denomination below **Rev:** Elizabeth II, Prince Charles and his son William below multicolored bunting **Edge:** Reeded

Date	Mintage	F	VF	XF	Unc	BU
2002 Proof	50	Value: 2,150				

KM# 77b.2 50 PENCE
39.9400 g., 0.9170 Gold 1.1775 oz. AGW, 38.61 mm. **Ruler:** Elizabeth II **Subject:** Queen's Golden Jubilee **Obv:** Crowned bust right, denomination below **Rev:** With plain bunting

Date	Mintage	F	VF	XF	Unc	BU
2002 Proof	—	Value: 2,100				

KM# 78.1 50 PENCE
28.1300 g., Copper-Nickel, 38.6 mm. **Ruler:** Elizabeth II **Subject:** Queen's Golden Jubilee **Obv:** Crowned bust right, denomination below **Rev:** Royal coach below multicolor bunting **Edge:** Reeded

Date	Mintage	F	VF	XF	Unc	BU
2002 Proof	—	Value: 8.00				

KM# 78.2 50 PENCE
Copper-Nickel **Ruler:** Elizabeth II **Subject:** Queen's Golden Jubilee **Obv:** Crowned bust right, denomination below **Rev:** With plain bunting

Date	Mintage	F	VF	XF	Unc	BU
2002	—	—	—	—	6.00	7.00

KM# 78a.1 50 PENCE
28.2800 g., 0.9250 Silver 0.8410 oz. ASW, 38.6 mm. **Ruler:** Elizabeth II **Subject:** Queen's Golden Jubilee **Obv:** Crowned bust right, denomination below **Rev:** Coronation coach below multicolor bunting **Edge:** Reeded

Date	Mintage	F	VF	XF	Unc	BU
2002 Proof	15,000	Value: 45.00				

KM# 78b.1 50 PENCE
39.9400 g., 0.9170 Gold 1.1775 oz. AGW, 38.61 mm. **Ruler:** Elizabeth II **Subject:** Queen's Golden Jubilee **Obv:** Crowned bust right, denomination below **Rev:** Coronation coach below multicolor bunting **Edge:** Reeded

Date	Mintage	F	VF	XF	Unc	BU
2002 Proof	150	Value: 2,150				

KM# 78b.2 50 PENCE
39.9400 g., 0.9170 Gold 1.1775 oz. AGW, 38.61 mm. **Ruler:** Elizabeth II **Subject:** Queen's Golden Jubilee **Obv:** Crowned bust right, denomination below **Rev:** With plain bunting

Date	Mintage	F	VF	XF	Unc	BU
2002 Proof	—	Value: 2,100				

KM# 79.1 50 PENCE
28.1300 g., Copper-Nickel, 38.6 mm. **Ruler:** Elizabeth II **Subject:** Queen's Golden Jubilee **Obv:** Crowned bust right, denomination below **Rev:** Scepter and orb below multicolor bunting **Edge:** Reeded

Date	Mintage	F	VF	XF	Unc	BU
2002 Proof	—	Value: 8.00				

KM# 79.2 50 PENCE
Copper-Nickel **Ruler:** Elizabeth II **Subject:** Queen's Golden Jubilee **Obv:** Crowned bust right, denomination below **Rev:** With plain bunting

Date	Mintage	F	VF	XF	Unc	BU
2002	—	—	—	—	6.00	7.00

KM# 79a.1 50 PENCE
28.2800 g., 0.9250 Silver 0.8410 oz. ASW, 38.6 mm. **Ruler:** Elizabeth II **Subject:** Queen's Golden Jubilee **Obv:** Crowned bust right, denomination below **Rev:** Orb and scepter below multicolor bunting **Edge:** Reeded

Date	Mintage	F	VF	XF	Unc	BU
2002 Proof	15,000	Value: 45.00				

KM# 79a.2 50 PENCE
28.2800 g., 0.9250 Silver 0.8410 oz. ASW, 38.61 mm. **Ruler:** Elizabeth II **Subject:** Queen's Golden Jubilee **Obv:** Crowned bust right, denomination below **Rev:** With plain bunting

Date	Mintage	F	VF	XF	Unc	BU
2002 Proof	—	Value: 45.00				

KM# 79b.1 50 PENCE
39.9400 g., 0.9170 Gold 1.1775 oz. AGW, 38.61 mm. **Ruler:** Elizabeth II **Subject:** Queen's Golden Jubilee **Obv:** Crowned bust right, denomination below **Rev:** Orb and scepter below multicolor bunting **Edge:** Reeded

Date	Mintage	F	VF	XF	Unc	BU
2002 Proof	150	Value: 2,150				

KM# 79b.2 50 PENCE
39.9400 g., 0.9170 Gold 1.1775 oz. AGW, 38.61 mm. **Ruler:** Elizabeth II **Subject:** Queen's Golden Jubilee **Obv:** Crowned bust right, denomination below **Rev:** With plain bunting

Date	Mintage	F	VF	XF	Unc	BU
2002 Proof	—	Value: 2,100				

KM# 80.1 50 PENCE
28.1300 g., Copper-Nickel, 38.6 mm. **Ruler:** Elizabeth II **Subject:** Queen's Golden Jubilee **Obv:** Crowned bust right, denomination below **Rev:** Crown below multicolor bunting **Edge:** Reeded

Date	Mintage	F	VF	XF	Unc	BU
2002 Proof	—	Value: 8.00				

KM# 80.2 50 PENCE
Copper-Nickel **Ruler:** Elizabeth II **Subject:** Queen's Golden Jubilee **Obv:** Crowned bust right, denomination below **Rev:** With plain bunting

Date	Mintage	F	VF	XF	Unc	BU
2002	—	—	—	—	6.00	7.00

KM# 80a.1 50 PENCE
28.2800 g., 0.9250 Silver 0.8410 oz. ASW, 38.6 mm. **Ruler:** Elizabeth II **Subject:** Queen's Golden Jubilee **Obv:** Crowned bust right, denomination below **Rev:** Crown below multicolor bunting **Edge:** Reeded

Date	Mintage	F	VF	XF	Unc	BU
2002 Proof	15,000	Value: 45.00				

KM# 80a.2 50 PENCE
28.2800 g., 0.9250 Silver 0.8410 oz. ASW, 38.61 mm. **Ruler:** Elizabeth II **Subject:** Queen's Golden Jubilee **Obv:** Crowned bust right, denomination below **Rev:** With plain bunting

Date	Mintage	F	VF	XF	Unc	BU
2002 Proof	—	Value: 45.00				

KM# 80b.1 50 PENCE
39.9400 g., 0.9170 Gold 1.1775 oz. AGW, 38.61 mm. **Ruler:** Elizabeth II **Subject:** Queen's Golden Jubilee **Obv:** Crowned bust right, denomination below **Rev:** Crown below multicolor bunting **Edge:** Reeded

Date	Mintage	F	VF	XF	Unc	BU
2002 Proof	150	Value: 2,150				

KM# 80b.2 50 PENCE
39.9400 g., 0.9170 Gold 1.1775 oz. AGW, 38.61 mm. **Ruler:** Elizabeth II **Subject:** Queen's Golden Jubilee **Obv:** Crowned bust right, denomination below **Rev:** With plain bunting

Date	Mintage	F	VF	XF	Unc	BU
2002 Proof	—	Value: 2,100				

KM# 81.1 50 PENCE
28.1300 g., Copper-Nickel, 38.6 mm. **Ruler:** Elizabeth II **Subject:** Queen's Golden Jubilee **Obv:** Crowned bust right, denomination below **Rev:** Throne below multicolor bunting **Edge:** Reeded

Date	Mintage	F	VF	XF	Unc	BU
2002 Proof	—	Value: 8.00				

KM# 81.2 50 PENCE
Copper-Nickel **Ruler:** Elizabeth II **Subject:** Queen's Golden Jubilee **Obv:** Crowned bust right, denomination below **Rev:** With plain bunting

Date	Mintage	F	VF	XF	Unc	BU
2002	—	—	—	—	6.00	7.00

KM# 81a.1 50 PENCE
28.2800 g., 0.9250 Silver 0.8410 oz. ASW, 38.6 mm. **Ruler:** Elizabeth II **Subject:** Queen's Golden Jubilee **Obv:** Crowned bust right, denomination below **Rev:** Coronation throne below multicolor bunting **Edge:** Reeded

Date	Mintage	F	VF	XF	Unc	BU
2002 Proof	15,000	Value: 45.00				

KM# 81a.2 50 PENCE
28.2800 g., 0.9250 Silver 0.8410 oz. ASW, 38.61 mm. **Ruler:** Elizabeth II **Subject:** Queen's Golden Jubilee **Obv:** Crowned bust right, denomination below **Rev:** With plain bunting

Date	Mintage	F	VF	XF	Unc	BU
2002 Proof	—	Value: 45.00				

KM# 81b.1 50 PENCE
39.9400 g., 0.9170 Gold 1.1775 oz. AGW, 38.61 mm. **Ruler:** Elizabeth II **Subject:** Queen's Golden Jubilee **Obv:** Crowned bust right, denomination below **Rev:** Coronation Throne below multicolored bunting **Edge:** Reeded

Date	Mintage	F	VF	XF	Unc	BU
2002 Proof	150	Value: 2,150				

KM# 81b.2 50 PENCE
39.9400 g., 0.9170 Gold 1.1775 oz. AGW, 38.61 mm. **Ruler:** Elizabeth II **Subject:** Queen's Golden Jubilee **Obv:** Crowned bust right, denomination below **Rev:** With plain bunting

Date	Mintage	F	VF	XF	Unc	BU
2002 Proof	—	Value: 2,100				

KM# 82.1 50 PENCE
28.1300 g., Copper-Nickel, 38.6 mm. **Ruler:** Elizabeth II **Subject:** Queen's Golden Jubilee **Obv:** Crowned bust right, denomination below **Rev:** Queen on throne below multicolor bunting **Edge:** Reeded

Date	Mintage	F	VF	XF	Unc	BU
2002 Proof	—	—	—	—	6.00	7.00

KM# 82.2 50 PENCE
Copper-Nickel **Ruler:** Elizabeth II **Subject:** Queen's Golden Jubilee **Obv:** Crowned bust right, denomination below **Rev:** With plain bunting

Date	Mintage	F	VF	XF	Unc	BU
2002	—	—	—	—	6.00	7.00

KM# 82a.1 50 PENCE
28.2800 g., 0.9250 Silver 0.8410 oz. ASW, 38.6 mm. **Ruler:** Elizabeth II **Subject:** Queen's Golden Jubilee **Obv:** Crowned bust right, denomination below **Rev:** Queen on throne below multicolor bunting **Edge:** Reeded

Date	Mintage	F	VF	XF	Unc	BU
2002 Proof	15,000	Value: 45.00				

KM# 82a.2 50 PENCE
28.2800 g., 0.9250 Silver 0.8410 oz. ASW, 38.61 mm. **Ruler:** Elizabeth II **Subject:** Queen's Golden Jubilee **Obv:** Crowned bust right, denomination below **Rev:** With plain bunting

Date	Mintage	F	VF	XF	Unc	BU
2002 Proof	—	Value: 45.00				

KM# 82b.1 50 PENCE
39.9400 g., 0.9170 Gold 1.1775 oz. AGW, 38.61 mm. **Ruler:** Elizabeth II **Subject:** Queen's Golden Jubilee **Obv:** Crowned bust right, denomination below **Rev:** Queen seated on throne below multicolor bunting **Edge:** Reeded

Date	Mintage	F	VF	XF	Unc	BU
2002 Proof	50	Value: 2,150				

KM# 82b.2 50 PENCE
39.9400 g., 0.9170 Gold 1.1775 oz. AGW, 38.61 mm. **Ruler:** Elizabeth II **Subject:** Queen's Golden Jubilee **Obv:** Crowned bust right, denomination below **Rev:** With plain bunting

Date	Mintage	F	VF	XF	Unc	BU
2002 Proof	—	Value: 2,100				

KM# 83.1 50 PENCE
28.1300 g., Copper-Nickel, 38.6 mm. **Ruler:** Elizabeth II **Subject:** Queen's Golden Jubilee **Obv:** Crowned bust right, denomination below **Rev:** Queen and young family below multicolor bunting **Edge:** Reeded

Date	Mintage	F	VF	XF	Unc	BU
2002 Proof	—	—	—	—	6.00	7.00

KM# 83a.1 50 PENCE
28.2800 g., 0.9250 Silver 0.8410 oz. ASW, 38.6 mm. **Ruler:** Elizabeth II **Subject:** Queen's Golden Jubilee **Obv:** Crowned bust right, denomination below **Rev:** Royal family below multicolor bunting **Edge:** Reeded

Date	Mintage	F	VF	XF	Unc	BU
2002 Proof	15,000	Value: 45.00				

KM# 83a.2 50 PENCE
28.2800 g., 0.9250 Silver 0.8410 oz. ASW, 38.61 mm. **Ruler:** Elizabeth II **Subject:** Queen's Golden Jubilee **Obv:** Crowned bust right, denomination below **Rev:** With plain bunting

Date	Mintage	F	VF	XF	Unc	BU
2002 Proof	—	Value: 45.00				

KM# 83b.1 50 PENCE
39.9400 g., 0.9170 Gold 1.1775 oz. AGW, 38.61 mm. **Ruler:** Elizabeth II **Subject:** Queen's Golden Jubilee **Obv:** Crowned bust right, denomination below **Rev:** Royal Family below multicolor bunting **Edge:** Reeded

Date	Mintage	F	VF	XF	Unc	BU
2002 Proof	50	Value: 2,150				

KM# 83b.2 50 PENCE
39.9400 g., 0.9170 Gold 1.1775 oz. AGW, 38.61 mm. **Ruler:** Elizabeth II **Subject:** Queen's Golden Jubilee **Obv:** Crowned bust right, denomination below **Rev:** With plain bunting

Date	Mintage	F	VF	XF	Unc	BU
2002 Proof	—	Value: 2,100				

KM# 84.1 50 PENCE
28.1300 g., Copper-Nickel, 38.6 mm. **Ruler:** Elizabeth II **Subject:** Queen's Golden Jubilee **Obv:** Crowned bust right, denomination below **Rev:** Queens head and tree house below multicolor bunting **Edge:** Reeded

Date	Mintage	F	VF	XF	Unc	BU
2002 Proof	—	Value: 8.00				

KM# 84.2 50 PENCE
Copper-Nickel **Ruler:** Elizabeth II **Subject:** Queen's Golden Jubilee **Obv:** Crowned bust right, denomination below **Rev:** With plain bunting

Date	Mintage	F	VF	XF	Unc	BU
2002	—	—	—	—	6.00	7.00

KM# 84a.1 50 PENCE
28.2800 g., 0.9250 Silver 0.8410 oz. ASW, 38.6 mm. **Ruler:** Elizabeth II **Subject:** Queen's Golden Jubilee **Obv:** Crowned bust right, denomination below **Rev:** Queen and tree house below multicolor bunting **Edge:** Reeded

Date	Mintage	F	VF	XF	Unc	BU
2002 Proof	25,000	Value: 45.00				

KM# 84a.2 50 PENCE
28.2800 g., 0.9250 Silver 0.8410 oz. ASW, 38.61 mm. **Ruler:** Elizabeth II **Subject:** Queen's Golden Jubilee **Obv:** Crowned bust right, denomination below **Rev:** With plain bunting

Date	Mintage	F	VF	XF	Unc	BU
2002 Proof	—	Value: 45.00				

KM# 84b.1 50 PENCE
39.9400 g., 0.9170 Gold 1.1775 oz. AGW, 38.61 mm. **Ruler:** Elizabeth II **Subject:** Queen's Golden Jubilee **Obv:** Crowned bust right, denomination below **Rev:** Queen and tree house below multicolor bunting **Edge:** Reeded

Date	Mintage	F	VF	XF	Unc	BU
2002 Proof	50	Value: 2,150				

KM# 84b.2 50 PENCE
39.9400 g., 0.9170 Gold 1.1775 oz. AGW, 38.61 mm. **Ruler:** Elizabeth II **Subject:** Queen's Golden Jubilee **Obv:** Crowned bust right, denomination below **Rev:** With plain bunting

Date	Mintage	F	VF	XF	Unc	BU
2002 Proof	—	Value: 2,100				

KM# 90 50 PENCE
28.2800 g., Copper-Nickel, 38.6 mm. **Ruler:** Elizabeth II **Obv:** Crowned bust right, denomination below **Rev:** Conjoined busts of Elizabeth and Philip below multicolor bunting **Edge:** Reeded

Date	Mintage	F	VF	XF	Unc	BU
2002	—	—	—	—	6.00	7.00

KM# 90a.1 50 PENCE
28.2800 g., 0.9250 Silver 0.8410 oz. ASW, 38.6 mm. **Ruler:** Elizabeth II **Obv:** Crowned bust right, denomination below **Rev:** Elizabeth and Philip below multicolor bunting **Edge:** Reeded

Date	Mintage	F	VF	XF	Unc	BU
2002 Proof	15,000	Value: 45.00				

KM# 90a.2 50 PENCE
28.2800 g., 0.9250 Silver 0.8410 oz. ASW, 38.6 mm. **Ruler:** Elizabeth II **Obv:** Crowned bust right, denomination below **Rev:** With plain bunting

Date	Mintage	F	VF	XF	Unc	BU
2002 Proof	—	Value: 45.00				

KM# 90b.1 50 PENCE
39.9400 g., 0.9170 Gold 1.1775 oz. AGW, 38.61 mm. **Ruler:** Elizabeth II **Obv:** Crowned bust right, denomination below **Rev:** Elizabeth and Philip below multicolor bunting **Edge:** Reeded

Date	Mintage	F	VF	XF	Unc	BU
2002 Proof	50	Value: 2,150				

KM# 90b.2 50 PENCE
39.9400 g., 0.9170 Gold 1.1775 oz. AGW, 38.61 mm. **Ruler:** Elizabeth II **Obv:** Crowned bust right, denomination below **Rev:** With plain bunting **Edge:** Reeded

Date	Mintage	F	VF	XF	Unc	BU
2002 Proof	—	Value: 2,100				

KM# 91 50 PENCE
28.2800 g., Copper-Nickel, 38.6 mm. **Ruler:** Elizabeth II **Obv:** Crowned bust right, denomination below **Rev:** Queen and Aborigine dancers below multicolor bunting **Edge:** Reeded

Date	Mintage	F	VF	XF	Unc	BU
2002	—	—	—	—	6.00	7.00

KM# 91a.1 50 PENCE
28.2800 g., 0.9250 Silver 0.8410 oz. ASW, 38.6 mm. **Ruler:** Elizabeth II **Obv:** Crowned bust right, denomination below **Rev:** Queen and Aborigine dancers below multicolor bunting **Edge:** Reeded

Date	Mintage	F	VF	XF	Unc	BU
2002 Proof	15,000	Value: 45.00				

KM# 91a.2 50 PENCE
28.2800 g., 0.9250 Silver 0.8410 oz. ASW, 38.6 mm. **Ruler:** Elizabeth II **Obv:** Crowned bust right, denomination below **Rev:** With plain bunting **Edge:** Reeded

Date	Mintage	F	VF	XF	Unc	BU
2002 Proof	—	Value: 45.00				

KM# 91b.1 50 PENCE
39.9400 g., 0.9170 Gold 1.1775 oz. AGW, 38.61 mm. **Ruler:** Elizabeth II **Obv:** Crowned bust right, denomination below **Rev:** Queen and Aborigine dancers below multicolor bunting **Edge:** Reeded

Date	Mintage	F	VF	XF	Unc	BU
2002 Proof	50	Value: 2,150				

KM# 91b.2 50 PENCE
39.9400 g., 0.9170 Gold 1.1775 oz. AGW, 38.61 mm. **Ruler:** Elizabeth II **Obv:** Crowned bust right, denomination below **Rev:** With plain bunting **Edge:** Reeded

Date	Mintage	F	VF	XF	Unc	BU
2002 Proof	—	Value: 2,100				

KM# 92 50 PENCE
28.2800 g., Copper-Nickel, 38.6 mm. **Ruler:** Elizabeth II **Obv:** Crowned bust right, denomination below **Rev:** Queen and St. Paul's Cathedral dome below multicolor bunting **Edge:** Reeded

Date	Mintage	F	VF	XF	Unc	BU
2002	—	—	—	—	6.00	7.00

KM# 92a.1 50 PENCE
28.2800 g., 0.9250 Silver 0.8410 oz. ASW, 38.6 mm. **Ruler:** Elizabeth II **Obv:** Crowned bust right, denomination below **Rev:** Queen and St. Paul's Cathedral dome below multicolor bunting **Edge:** Reeded

Date	Mintage	F	VF	XF	Unc	BU
2002 Proof	15,000	Value: 45.00				

KM# 92a.2 50 PENCE
28.2800 g., 0.9250 Silver 0.8410 oz. ASW, 38.6 mm. **Ruler:** Elizabeth II **Obv:** Crowned bust right, denomination below **Rev:** With plain bunting **Edge:** Reeded

Date	Mintage	F	VF	XF	Unc	BU
2002 Proof	—	Value: 45.00				

KM# 92b.1 50 PENCE
39.9400 g., 0.9170 Gold 1.1775 oz. AGW, 38.61 mm. **Ruler:** Elizabeth II **Obv:** Crowned bust right, denomination below **Rev:** Queen and St. Paul's Cathedral dome below multicolor bunting **Edge:** Reeded

Date	Mintage	F	VF	XF	Unc	BU
2002 Proof	50	Value: 2,150				

KM# 92b.2 50 PENCE
39.9400 g., 0.9170 Gold 1.1775 oz. AGW, 38.61 mm. **Ruler:** Elizabeth II **Obv:** Crowned bust right, denomination below **Rev:** With plain bunting **Edge:** Reeded

Date	Mintage	F	VF	XF	Unc	BU
2002 Proof	—	Value: 2,100				

KM# 93 50 PENCE
28.2800 g., Copper-Nickel, 38.6 mm. **Ruler:** Elizabeth II **Obv:** Crowned bust right, denomination below **Rev:** Elizabeth and Philip in coronation coach below multicolor bunting **Edge:** Reeded

Date	Mintage	F	VF	XF	Unc	BU
2002	—	—	—	—	6.00	7.00

KM# 93a.1 50 PENCE
28.2800 g., 0.9250 Silver 0.8410 oz. ASW, 38.6 mm. **Ruler:** Elizabeth II **Obv:** Crowned bust right, denomination below **Rev:** Elizabeth and Philip in coronation coach below multicolor bunting **Edge:** Reeded

Date	Mintage	F	VF	XF	Unc	BU
2002 Proof	15,000	Value: 45.00				

KM# 93a.2 50 PENCE
28.2800 g., 0.9250 Silver 0.8410 oz. ASW, 38.6 mm. **Ruler:** Elizabeth II **Obv:** Crowned bust right, denomination below **Rev:** With plain bunting **Edge:** Reeded

Date	Mintage	F	VF	XF	Unc	BU
2002 Proof	—	Value: 45.00				

KM# 93b.1 50 PENCE
39.9400 g., 0.9170 Gold 1.1775 oz. AGW, 38.61 mm. **Ruler:** Elizabeth II **Obv:** Crowned bust right, denomination below **Rev:** Elizabeth and Philip in coronation coach below multicolor bunting **Edge:** Reeded

Date	Mintage	F	VF	XF	Unc	BU
2002 Proof	50	Value: 2,150				

KM# 93b.2 50 PENCE
39.9400 g., 0.9170 Gold 1.1775 oz. AGW, 38.61 mm. **Ruler:** Elizabeth II **Obv:** Crowned bust right, denomination below **Rev:** With plain bunting **Edge:** Reeded

Date	Mintage	F	VF	XF	Unc	BU
2002 Proof	—	Value: 2,100				

KM# 94 50 PENCE
28.2800 g., Copper-Nickel, 38.6 mm. **Ruler:** Elizabeth II **Obv:** Crowned bust right, denomination below **Rev:** Elizabeth and Prince Charles at flower show below multicolor bunting **Edge:** Reeded

Date	Mintage	F	VF	XF	Unc	BU
2002	—	—	—	—	6.00	7.00

KM# 94a.1 50 PENCE
28.2800 g., 0.9250 Silver 0.8410 oz. ASW, 38.6 mm. **Ruler:** Elizabeth II **Obv:** Crowned bust right, denomination below **Rev:** Queen and Prince Charles at flower show below multicolor bunting **Edge:** Reeded

Date	Mintage	F	VF	XF	Unc	BU
2002 Proof	15,000	Value: 45.00				

KM# 94a.2 50 PENCE
28.2800 g., 0.9250 Silver 0.8410 oz. ASW, 38.6 mm. **Ruler:** Elizabeth II **Obv:** Crowned bust right, denomination below **Rev:** With plain bunting **Edge:** Reeded

Date	Mintage	F	VF	XF	Unc	BU
2002 Proof	—	Value: 45.00				

KM# 94b.1 50 PENCE
39.9400 g., 0.9170 Gold 1.1775 oz. AGW, 38.61 mm. **Ruler:** Elizabeth II **Obv:** Crowned bust right, denomination below **Rev:** Queen and Prince Charles at flower show below multicolor bunting **Edge:** Reeded

Date	Mintage	F	VF	XF	Unc	BU
2002 Proof	50	Value: 2,150				

KM# 94b.2 50 PENCE
39.9400 g., 0.9170 Gold 1.1775 oz. AGW, 38.61 mm. **Ruler:** Elizabeth II **Obv:** Crowned bust right, denomination below **Rev:** With plain bunting **Edge:** Reeded

Date	Mintage	F	VF	XF	Unc	BU
2002 Proof	—	Value: 2,100				

KM# 95 50 PENCE
28.2800 g., Copper-Nickel, 38.6 mm. **Ruler:** Elizabeth II **Obv:** Crowned bust right, denomination below **Rev:** Elizabeth and Philip on balcony below multicolor bunting **Edge:** Reeded

Date	Mintage	F	VF	XF	Unc	BU
2002	—	—	—	—	6.00	7.00

KM# 95a.1 50 PENCE
28.2800 g., 0.9250 Silver 0.8410 oz. ASW, 38.6 mm. **Ruler:** Elizabeth II **Obv:** Crowned bust right, denomination below **Rev:** Elizabeth and Philip on balcony below colored bunting **Edge:** Reeded

Date	Mintage	F	VF	XF	Unc	BU
2002 Proof	15,000	Value: 45.00				

KM# 95a.2 50 PENCE
28.2800 g., 0.9250 Silver 0.8410 oz. ASW, 38.6 mm. **Ruler:** Elizabeth II **Obv:** Crowned bust right, denomination below **Rev:** With plain bunting **Edge:** Reeded

Date	Mintage	F	VF	XF	Unc	BU
2002 Proof	—	Value: 45.00				

KM# 95b.1 50 PENCE
39.9400 g., 0.9170 Gold 1.1775 oz. AGW, 38.61 mm. **Ruler:** Elizabeth II **Obv:** Crowned bust right, denomination below **Rev:** Elizabeth and Philip on balcony below multicolor bunting **Edge:** Reeded

Date	Mintage	F	VF	XF	Unc	BU
2002 Proof	50	Value: 2,150				

KM# 95b.2 50 PENCE
39.9400 g., 0.9170 Gold 1.1775 oz. AGW, 38.61 mm. **Ruler:** Elizabeth II **Obv:** Crowned bust right, denomination below **Rev:** With plain bunting **Edge:** Reeded

Date	Mintage	F	VF	XF	Unc	BU
2002 Proof	—	Value: 2,100				

KM# 96 50 PENCE
28.2800 g., Copper-Nickel, 38.6 mm. **Ruler:** Elizabeth II **Obv:** Crowned bust right, denomination below **Rev:** Multicolor jets below multicolor bunting **Edge:** Reeded

Date	Mintage	F	VF	XF	Unc	BU
2002	—	—	—	—	6.00	7.00

KM# 96a.1 50 PENCE
28.2800 g., 0.9250 Silver 0.8410 oz. ASW, 38.6 mm. **Ruler:** Elizabeth II **Obv:** Crowned bust right, denomination below **Rev:** Multicolor jets below multicolor bunting **Edge:** Reeded

Date	Mintage	F	VF	XF	Unc	BU
2002 Proof	15,000	Value: 45.00				

KM# 96a.2 50 PENCE
28.2800 g., 0.9250 Silver 0.8410 oz. ASW, 38.6 mm. **Ruler:** Elizabeth II **Obv:** Crowned bust right, denomination below **Rev:** With plain bunting **Edge:** Reeded

Date	Mintage	F	VF	XF	Unc	BU
2002 Proof	—	Value: 45.00				

KM# 96b.1 50 PENCE
39.9400 g., 0.9170 Gold 1.1775 oz. AGW, 38.61 mm. **Ruler:** Elizabeth II **Obv:** Crowned bust right, denomination below **Rev:** Multicolor jets below multicolor bunting **Edge:** Reeded

Date	Mintage	F	VF	XF	Unc	BU
2002 Proof	50	Value: 2,150				

KM# 96b.2 50 PENCE
39.9400 g., 0.9170 Gold 1.1775 oz. AGW, 38.61 mm. **Ruler:** Elizabeth II **Obv:** Crowned bust right, denomination below **Rev:** With plain bunting **Edge:** Reeded

Date	Mintage	F	VF	XF	Unc	BU
2002 Proof	—	Value: 2,100				

KM# 97 50 PENCE
28.2800 g., Copper-Nickel, 38.6 mm. **Ruler:** Elizabeth II **Obv:** Crowned bust right, denomination below **Rev:** Queen and fireworks below multicolor bunting **Edge:** Reeded

Date	Mintage	F	VF	XF	Unc	BU
2002	—	—	—	—	6.00	7.00

KM# 97a.1 50 PENCE
28.2800 g., 0.9250 Silver 0.8410 oz. ASW, 38.61 mm. **Ruler:** Elizabeth II **Obv:** Crowned bust right, denomination below **Rev:** Queen and fireworks below multicolor bunting **Edge:** Reeded

Date	Mintage	F	VF	XF	Unc	BU
2002 Proof	15,000	Value: 45.00				

KM# 97a.2 50 PENCE
28.2800 g., 0.9250 Silver 0.8410 oz. ASW, 38.6 mm. **Ruler:** Elizabeth II **Obv:** Crowned bust right, denomination below **Rev:** With plain bunting **Edge:** Reeded

Date	Mintage	F	VF	XF	Unc	BU
2002 Proof	—	Value: 45.00				

KM# 97b.1 50 PENCE
39.9400 g., 0.9170 Gold 1.1775 oz. AGW, 38.61 mm. **Ruler:** Elizabeth II **Obv:** Crowned bust right, denomination below **Rev:** Queen and fireworks below multicolor bunting **Edge:** Reeded

Date	Mintage	F	VF	XF	Unc	BU
2002 Proof	50	Value: 2,150				

KM# 97b.2 50 PENCE
39.9400 g., 0.9170 Gold 1.1775 oz. AGW, 38.61 mm. **Ruler:** Elizabeth II **Obv:** Crowned bust right, denomination below **Rev:** With plain bunting **Edge:** Reeded

Date	Mintage	F	VF	XF	Unc	BU
2002 Proof	—	Value: 2,100				

KM# 98 50 PENCE
28.2800 g., Copper-Nickel, 38.6 mm. **Ruler:** Elizabeth II **Obv:** Crowned bust right, denomination below **Rev:** UK map and flags below multicolor bunting **Edge:** Reeded

Date	Mintage	F	VF	XF	Unc	BU
2002	—	—	—	—	6.00	7.00

KM# 98a.1 50 PENCE
28.2800 g., 0.9250 Silver 0.8410 oz. ASW, 38.6 mm. **Ruler:** Elizabeth II **Obv:** Crowned bust right, denomination below **Rev:** UK and four flags below multicolor bunting **Edge:** Reeded

Date	Mintage	F	VF	XF	Unc	BU
2002 Proof	15,000	Value: 45.00				

KM# 98a.2 50 PENCE
28.2800 g., 0.9250 Silver 0.8410 oz. ASW, 38.6 mm. **Ruler:** Elizabeth II **Obv:** Crowned bust right, denomination below **Rev:** With plain bunting **Edge:** Reeded

Date	Mintage	F	VF	XF	Unc	BU
2002 Proof	—	Value: 45.00				

KM# 98b.1 50 PENCE
39.9400 g., 0.9170 Gold 1.1775 oz. AGW, 38.61 mm. **Ruler:** Elizabeth II **Obv:** Crowned bust right, denomination below **Rev:** UK map and four flags below multicolor bunting **Edge:** Reeded

Date	Mintage	F	VF	XF	Unc	BU
2002 Proof	50	Value: 2,150				

KM# 98b.2 50 PENCE
39.9400 g., 0.9170 Gold 1.1775 oz. AGW, 38.61 mm. **Ruler:** Elizabeth II **Obv:** Crowned bust right, denomination below **Rev:** With plain bunting **Edge:** Reeded

Date	Mintage	F	VF	XF	Unc	BU
2002 Proof	—	Value: 2,100				

KM# 99 50 PENCE
28.2800 g., Copper-Nickel, 38.6 mm. **Ruler:** Elizabeth II **Obv:** Crowned bust right, denomination below **Rev:** Queen and two Commonwealth Games athletes below multicolor bunting **Edge:** Reeded

Date	Mintage	F	VF	XF	Unc	BU
2002	—	—	—	—	6.00	7.00

KM# 99a.1 50 PENCE
28.2800 g., 0.9250 Silver 0.8410 oz. ASW, 38.6 mm. **Ruler:** Elizabeth II **Obv:** Crowned bust right, denomination below **Rev:** Queen and two Commonwealth Games athletes below multicolor bunting **Edge:** Reeded

Date	Mintage	F	VF	XF	Unc	BU
2002 Proof	15,000	Value: 45.00				

KM# 99a.2 50 PENCE
28.2800 g., 0.9250 Silver 0.8410 oz. ASW, 38.6 mm. **Ruler:** Elizabeth II **Obv:** Crowned bust right, denomination below **Rev:** With plain bunting **Edge:** Reeded

Date	Mintage	F	VF	XF	Unc	BU
2002 Proof	—	Value: 45.00				

KM# 99b.1 50 PENCE
39.9400 g., 0.9170 Gold 1.1775 oz. AGW, 38.61 mm. **Ruler:** Elizabeth II **Obv:** Crowned bust right, denomination below **Rev:** Queen and two Commonwealth Games athletes below multicolor bunting **Edge:** Reeded

Date	Mintage	F	VF	XF	Unc	BU
2002 Proof	50	Value: 2,150				

KM# 99b.2 50 PENCE
39.9400 g., 0.9170 Gold 1.1775 oz. AGW, 38.61 mm. **Ruler:** Elizabeth II **Obv:** Crowned bust right, denomination below **Rev:** With plain bunting **Edge:** Reeded

Date	Mintage	F	VF	XF	Unc	BU
2002 Proof	—	Value: 2,100				

KM# 100 50 PENCE
28.2800 g., Copper-Nickel, 38.6 mm. **Ruler:** Elizabeth II **Obv:** Crowned bust right, denomination below **Rev:** Royal Ascot Carriage scene below multicolor bunting **Edge:** Reeded

Date	Mintage	F	VF	XF	Unc	BU
2002	—	—	—	—	6.00	7.00

KM# 100a.1 50 PENCE
28.2800 g., 0.9250 Silver 0.8410 oz. ASW, 38.6 mm. **Ruler:** Elizabeth II **Obv:** Crowned bust right, denomination below **Rev:** Royal Ascot Carriage scene below multicolor bunting **Edge:** Reeded

Date	Mintage	F	VF	XF	Unc	BU
2002 Proof	15,000	Value: 45.00				

KM# 100a.2 50 PENCE
28.2800 g., 0.9250 Silver 0.8410 oz. ASW, 38.6 mm. **Ruler:** Elizabeth II **Obv:** Crowned bust right, denomination below **Rev:** With plain bunting **Edge:** Reeded

Date	Mintage	F	VF	XF	Unc	BU
2002 Proof	—	Value: 45.00				

KM# 100b.1 50 PENCE
39.9400 g., 0.9170 Gold 1.1775 oz. AGW, 38.61 mm. **Ruler:** Elizabeth II **Obv:** Crowned bust right, denomination below **Rev:** Royal Ascot Carriage scene below multicolor bunting **Edge:** Reeded

Date	Mintage	F	VF	XF	Unc	BU
2002 Proof	50	Value: 2,150				

KM# 100b.2 50 PENCE
39.9400 g., 0.9170 Gold 1.1775 oz. AGW, 38.61 mm. **Ruler:** Elizabeth II **Obv:** Crowned bust right, denomination below **Rev:** With plain bunting **Edge:** Reeded

Date	Mintage	F	VF	XF	Unc	BU
2002 Proof	—	Value: 2,100				

KM# 101 50 PENCE
28.2800 g., Copper-Nickel, 38.6 mm. **Ruler:** Elizabeth II **Obv:** Crowned bust right, denomination below **Rev:** Queen and two hockey players below multicolor bunting **Edge:** Reeded

Date	Mintage	F	VF	XF	Unc	BU
2002	—	—	—	—	6.00	7.00

KM# 101a.1 50 PENCE
28.2800 g., 0.9250 Silver 0.8410 oz. ASW, 38.6 mm. **Ruler:** Elizabeth II **Obv:** Crowned bust right, denomination below **Rev:** Queen and two hockey players below multicolor bunting **Edge:** Reeded

Date	Mintage	F	VF	XF	Unc	BU
2002 Proof	15,000	Value: 45.00				

KM# 101a.2 50 PENCE
28.2800 g., 0.9250 Silver 0.8410 oz. ASW, 38.6 mm. **Ruler:** Elizabeth II **Obv:** Crowned bust right, denomination below **Rev:** With plain bunting **Edge:** Reeded

Date	Mintage	F	VF	XF	Unc	BU
2002 Proof	—	Value: 45.00				

KM# 101b.1 50 PENCE
39.9400 g., 0.9170 Gold 1.1775 oz. AGW, 38.61 mm. **Ruler:** Elizabeth II **Obv:** Crowned bust right, denomination below **Rev:** Queen and two hockey players below multicolor bunting **Edge:** Reeded

Date	Mintage	F	VF	XF	Unc	BU
2002 Proof	50	Value: 2,150				

KM# 101b.2 50 PENCE
39.9400 g., 0.9170 Gold 1.1775 oz. AGW, 38.61 mm. **Ruler:** Elizabeth II **Obv:** Crowned bust right, denomination below **Rev:** With plain bunting **Edge:** Reeded

Date	Mintage	F	VF	XF	Unc	BU
2002 Proof	—	Value: 2,100				

KM# 102 50 PENCE
28.2800 g., Copper-Nickel, 38.6 mm. **Ruler:** Elizabeth II **Obv:** Crowned bust right, denomination below **Rev:** Queen Mother as a young lady and as an elderly lady **Edge:** Reeded

Date	Mintage	F	VF	XF	Unc	BU
ND(2002)	—	—	—	—	9.00	10.00

KM# 102a 50 PENCE
28.2800 g., 0.9250 Silver 0.8410 oz. ASW, 38.6 mm. **Ruler:** Elizabeth II **Obv:** Crowned bust right, denomination below **Rev:** Queen Mother as a young lady and as an elderly lady **Edge:** Reeded

Date	Mintage	F	VF	XF	Unc	BU
ND(2002) Proof	10,000	Value: 45.00				

KM# 135 50 PENCE
8.0000 g., Copper-Nickel, 27.3 mm. **Ruler:** Elizabeth II **Obv:** Crowned bust right **Rev:** Fox standing right **Shape:** 7-sided

Date	Mintage	F	VF	XF	Unc	BU
2004	—	—	—	—	5.00	7.50

KM# 149 50 PENCE
28.2800 g., 0.9250 Silver 0.8410 oz. ASW, 38.6 mm. **Ruler:** Elizabeth II **Subject:** Queen's 80th Birthday **Obv:** Head with tiara right - gilt **Obv. Legend:** QUEEN ELIZABETH II - FALKLAND ISLANDS **Rev:** Elizabeth seated at left, Queen Mother at right holding baby

Date	Mintage	F	VF	XF	Unc	BU
2006 Proof	—	Value: 45.00				

KM# 163 50 PENCE
8.0000 g., Copper-Nickel, 27.3 mm. **Ruler:** Elizabeth II **Subject:** 25th Anniverary of Liberation **Obv:** Head in tiara right **Rev:** Soldier in full gear standing before map of Falklands **Shape:** 7-sided

Date	Mintage	F	VF	XF	Unc	BU
2007PM	—	—	—	—	5.00	7.50

KM# 136 POUND
9.5000 g., Nickel-Brass, 22.5 mm. **Ruler:** Elizabeth II **Obv:** Crowned bust right **Rev:** Shield

Date	Mintage	F	VF	XF	Unc	BU
2004	—	—	—	—	3.50	5.00

KM# 137 2 POUNDS
12.0000 g., Bi-Metallic Copper-Nickel center in Nickel-Brass ring, 28.4 mm. **Ruler:** Elizabeth II **Obv:** Head with tiara right **Obv. Legend:** QUEEN ELIZABETH THE SECOND **Rev:** Sun and map surrounded by wildlife **Edge:** Reeded and lettered **Edge Lettering:** 30 YEARS OF FALKLAND ISLANDS COINAGE

Date	Mintage	F	VF	XF	Unc	BU
2004	—	—	—	5.00	10.00	12.00

KM# 103 25 POUNDS
7.8100 g., 0.9999 Gold 0.2511 oz. AGW, 22 mm. **Ruler:** Elizabeth II **Obv:** Crowned bust right, denomination below **Rev:** Queen Mother as a young lady and as an elderly lady **Edge:** Reeded

Date	Mintage	F	VF	XF	Unc	BU
ND(2002) Proof	1,000	Value: 475				

CROWN COINAGE

KM# 161 1/25 CROWN
0.5000 g., 0.9990 Gold 0.0161 oz. AGW, 11 mm. **Ruler:** Elizabeth II **Subject:** Henry Dunant, Founder, International Red Cross and 1901 Nobel Peace Prize winner **Obv:** Bust with tiara right **Rev:** Dunant bust facing

Date	Mintage	F	VF	XF	Unc	BU
2010PM Proof	—	Value: 80.00				

KM# 141 1/5 CROWN
6.2200 g., 0.9999 Gold 0.1999 oz. AGW **Ruler:** Elizabeth II **Subject:** Diamond Wedding Anniversary **Obv:** Conjoined busts with Prince Philip right **Obv. Legend:** QUEEN ELIZABETH II - FALKLAND ISLANDS **Rev:** Bride and groom standing facing at wedding cake; .01 carat x 1.3mm diamond embedded at top **Rev. Legend:** Diamond Wedding of H.M. Queen Elizabeth II & H.R.H. Prince Philip **Edge:** Reeded

Date	Mintage	F	VF	XF	Unc	BU
2007PM Proof	—	Value: 450				

KM# 129 CROWN
Copper-Nickel **Ruler:** Elizabeth II **Rev:** Nelson and the H.M.S. Victory

Date	Mintage	F	VF	XF	Unc	BU
2005	—	—	—	—	10.00	12.00

KM# 151 CROWN
Copper-Nickel, 38.61 mm. **Ruler:** Elizabeth II **Subject:** I. K. Burnel **Rev:** S. S. Great Britain sailing right

Date	Mintage	F	VF	XF	Unc	BU
2006PM	—	—	—	—	—	15.00

KM# 152 CROWN
Copper-Nickel, 38.61 mm. **Ruler:** Elizabeth II **Subject:** Artic and Antarctic - John Ross and James Clark Ross **Rev:** Ships Victory and Erebus

Date	Mintage	F	VF	XF	Unc	BU
2006PM	—	—	—	—	—	15.00

KM# 143a CROWN
0.9167 Silver **Ruler:** Elizabeth II **Subject:** Diamond Wedding Anniversary **Obv:** Conjoined busts with Prince Philip right **Obv. Legend:** QUEEN ELIZABETH II - FALKLAND ISLANDS **Rev:** Bride and groom standing facing at wedding cake **Rev. Legend:** Diamond Wedding of H.M. Queen Elizabeth II & H.R.H. Prince Philip **Edge:** Reeded

Date	Mintage	VG	F	VF	XF	Unc
2007PM Proof	—	Value: 40.00				

KM# 138 CROWN
Copper-Nickel **Ruler:** Elizabeth II **Rev:** Winston Churchill

Date	Mintage	F	VF	XF	Unc	BU
2007	—	—	—	—	15.00	17.50

KM# 139 CROWN
Copper-Nickel **Ruler:** Elizabeth II **Rev:** Queen Elizabeth I

Date	Mintage	F	VF	XF	Unc	BU
2007	—	—	—	—	15.00	17.50

KM# 140 CROWN
Copper-Nickel **Ruler:** Elizabeth II **Rev:** Charles Darwin

Date	Mintage	F	VF	XF	Unc	BU
2007	—	—	—	—	15.00	17.50

KM# 142 CROWN
Copper-Nickel **Ruler:** Elizabeth II **Subject:** Diamond Wedding Anniversary **Obv:** Conjoined busts with Prince Philip right **Obv. Legend:** QUEEN ELIZABETH II - FALKLAND ISLANDS **Rev:** King George VI standing at left giving Philip standing at right his consent to a contract of matrimony **Rev. Legend:** Diamond Wedding of H.M. Queen Elizabeth II & H.R.H. Prince Philip **Edge:** Reeded

Date	Mintage	F	VF	XF	Unc	BU
2007PM	—	—	—	—	17.00	20.00

KM# 142a CROWN
0.9167 Silver **Ruler:** Elizabeth II **Subject:** Diamond Wedding Anniversary **Obv:** Conjoined busts with Prince Philip right **Obv. Legend:** QUEEN ELIZABETH II - FALKLAND ISLANDS **Rev:** King George VI, standing at left, giving Philip, standing at right, his consent to a contract of matrimony **Rev. Legend:** Diamond Wedding of H.M. Queen Elizabeth II & H.R.H. Prince Philip **Edge:** Reeded

Date	Mintage	F	VF	XF	Unc	BU
2007PM	—	Value: 40.00				

KM# 143 CROWN
Copper-Nickel **Ruler:** Elizabeth II **Subject:** Diamond Wedding Anniversary **Obv:** Conjoined busts with Prince Philip right **Obv. Legend:** QUEEN ELIZABETH II - FALKLAND ISLANDS **Rev:** Bride and groom standing facing at wedding cake **Rev. Legend:** Diamond Wedding of H.M. Queen Elizabeth II & H.R.H. Prince Philip **Edge:** Reeded

Date	Mintage	F	VF	XF	Unc	BU
2007PM	—	—	—	—	17.00	20.00

KM# 144 CROWN
Copper-Nickel **Ruler:** Elizabeth II **Subject:** Diamond Wedding Anniversary **Obv:** Conjoined busts with Prince Philip right **Obv. Legend:** QUEEN ELIZABETH II - FALKLAND ISLANDS **Rev:** Bridesmaids and Page Boys **Rev. Legend:** Diamond Wedding of H.M. Queen Elizabeth II & H.R.H. Prince Philip **Edge:** Reeded

Date	Mintage	F	VF	XF	Unc	BU
2007PM	—	—	—	—	17.00	20.00

KM# 144a CROWN
0.9167 Silver **Ruler:** Elizabeth II **Subject:** Diamond Wedding Anniversary **Obv:** Conjoined busts with Prince Philip right **Obv. Legend:** QUEEN ELIZABETH II - FALKLAND ISLANDS **Rev:** Bridesmaids and Page Boys **Rev. Legend:** Diamond Wedding of H.M. Queen Elizabeth II & H.R.H. Prince Philip **Edge:** Reeded

Date	Mintage	F	VF	XF	Unc	BU
2007PM Proof	—	Value: 40.00				

KM# 145 CROWN
Copper-Nickel **Ruler:** Elizabeth II **Subject:** Diamond Wedding Anniversary **Obv:** Conjoined busts with Prince Philip right **Obv. Legend:** QUEEN ELIZABETH II - FALKLAND ISLANDS **Rev:** Buckingham Palace facade **Rev. Legend:** Diamond Wedding of H.M. Queen Elizabeth II & H.R.H. Prince Philip **Edge:** Reeded

Date	Mintage	F	VF	XF	Unc	BU
2007PM	—	—	—	—	17.00	20.00

KM# 145a CROWN
0.9167 Silver **Ruler:** Elizabeth II **Subject:** Diamond Wedding Anniversary **Obv:** Conjoined busts with Prince Philip right **Obv. Legend:** QUEEN ELIZABETH II - FALKLAND ISLANDS **Rev:** Buckingham Palace facade **Rev. Legend:** Diamond Wedding of H.M. Queen Elizabeth II & H.R.H. Prince Philip **Edge:** Reeded

Date	Mintage	F	VF	XF	Unc	BU
2007PM Proof	—	Value: 40.00				

KM# 146 CROWN
Copper-Nickel **Ruler:** Elizabeth II **Subject:** 10th Anniversary - Death of Princess Diana **Obv:** Bust with tiara right **Obv. Legend:** QUEEN ELIZABETH II - FALKLAND ISLANDS **Rev:** Bust of Princess Diana facing 3/4 right **Rev. Legend:** 1961 - 1997 • DIANA — PRINCESS OF WALES **Edge:** Reeded

Date	Mintage	F	VF	XF	Unc	BU
2007PM	—	—	—	—	17.00	20.00

KM# 146a CROWN
0.9167 Silver **Ruler:** Elizabeth II **Subject:** 10th Anniversary Death of Princess Diana **Obv:** Bust with tiara right **Obv. Legend:** QUEEN ELIZABETH II - FALKLAND ISLANDS **Rev:** Bust of Princess Diana facing 3/4 right **Rev. Legend:** 1961 - 1997 ? DIANA ? PRINCESS OF WALES **Edge:** Reeded

Date	Mintage	F	VF	XF	Unc	BU
2007PM Proof	—	Value: 75.00				

KM# 147 CROWN
Copper-Nickel, 38 mm. **Ruler:** Elizabeth II **Subject:** 20th Anniversary - Falkland Islands Fishery **Obv:** Bust right of Queen Elizabeth II **Rev:** Shortfin Squid (Illex Argentinca) **Edge:** Reeded

Date	Mintage	F	VF	XF	Unc	BU
2007PM	—	—	—	—	17.00	20.00

KM# 148 CROWN
Copper-Nickel, 39 mm. **Ruler:** Elizabeth II **Subject:** Scouting Centennial **Obv:** Crowned bust right **Obv. Legend:** QUEEN ELIZABETH II FALKLAND ISLANDS 2007 **Rev:** Baden-Powell bust 3/4 left, scout saluting, tent flanking within circle on animal tracks **Rev. Legend:** 1857 ROBERT BADEN-POWELL 1941 ONE CROWN **Edge:** Reeded

Date	Mintage	F	VF	XF	Unc	BU
2007PM	—	—	—	—	12.50	15.00

KM# 148a CROWN
28.2800 g., 0.9250 Silver 0.8410 oz. ASW, 38.5 mm. **Ruler:** Elizabeth II **Subject:** Scouting Centennial **Obv:** Crowned bust right **Obv. Legend:** QUEEN ELIZABETH II FALKLAND ISLANDS 2007 **Rev:** Baden-Powell bust 3/4 facing left, scout saluting and tent flanking, within circle of animal tracks and rope **Rev. Legend:** 1857 ROBERT BADEN-POWELL 1941 ONE CROWN **Edge:** Reeded

Date	Mintage	F	VF	XF	Unc	BU
2007PM Proof	10,000	Value: 65.00				

KM# 156 CROWN
28.2800 g., Copper-Nickel, 38.61 mm. **Ruler:** Elizabeth II **Subject:** International Polar Year - Discovery **Obv:** Bust in tiara right **Rev:** Icebound ship

Date	Mintage	F	VF	XF	Unc	BU
2007PM	—	—	—	—	17.50	20.00

KM# 157 CROWN
Copper-Nickel, 38.61 mm. **Ruler:** Elizabeth II **Subject:** 25th Anniversary of Liberation **Obv:** Bust in tiara right **Rev:** Britannia standing before map of the Falkland Islands

Date	Mintage	F	VF	XF	Unc	BU
2007PM	—	—	—	—	17.50	20.00

KM# 158 CROWN
28.2800 g., Copper-Nickel, 38.61 mm. **Ruler:** Elizabeth II **Subject:** Race for the South Pole **Obv:** Bust in tiara right **Rev:** Portrats of Scott and Amundsen, dog-sleds, and man-pulled sleds.

Date	Mintage	F	VF	XF	Unc	BU
2007PM	—	—	—	—	17.50	20.00

KM# 150 CROWN
28.2800 g., Copper-Nickel, 38.6 mm. **Ruler:** Elizabeth II **Subject:** Royal Air Force, 90th anniversary

Date	Mintage	F	VF	XF	Unc	BU
2008	—	—	—	—	—	12.00

KM# 153 CROWN
Copper-Nickel, 38.61 mm. **Ruler:** Elizabeth II **Subject:** Spitfire **Obv:** Bust in tiara right **Rev:** Two planes in flight

Date	Mintage	F	VF	XF	Unc	BU
2008	—	—	—	—	12.50	15.00

KM# 154 CROWN
Copper-Nickel, 38.61 mm. **Ruler:** Elizabeth II **Subject:** Port Louis **Obv:** Bust in tiara right **Rev:** Flag raising over fort

Date	Mintage	F	VF	XF	Unc	BU
2008	—	—	—	—	12.50	15.00

KM# 162 CROWN

Copper-Nickel, 38.61 mm. **Ruler:** Elizabeth II **Obv:** Bust in tiara right **Rev:** Charles Darwin bust left

Date	Mintage	F	VF	XF	Unc	BU
2009PM	—	—	—	—	17.50	20.00

KM# 159 CROWN

Copper-Nickel, 38.61 mm. **Ruler:** Elizabeth II **Subject:** RAF Search and Rescue 70th anniversary **Obv:** Bust in tiara right **Rev:** RAF Search and Rescue Helicopter

Date	Mintage	F	VF	XF	Unc	BU
2011PM	—	—	—	—	17.50	20.00

KM# 160 CROWN

Copper-Nickel, 38.61 mm. **Ruler:** Elizabeth II **Subject:** Royal Wedding - Prince William and Catherine Middleton **Obv:** Bust in tiara right **Rev:** Busts left

Date	Mintage	F	VF	XF	Unc	BU
2011PM	—	—	—	—	17.50	20.00

KM# 164 CROWN

Copper-Nickel, 38.61 mm. **Ruler:** Elizabeth II **Subject:** Elizabeth and Philip 60th Wedding anniversary **Obv:** Bust in tiara right **Rev:** Lion on crown and Plumes

Date	Mintage	F	VF	XF	Unc	BU
2011PM	—	—	—	—	17.50	20.00

KM# 165 CROWN

28.2800 g., Copper-Nickel, 38.6 mm. **Ruler:** Elizabeth II **Subject:** Life of Queen Elizabeth II **Obv:** Conjoined busts right **Rev:** Elizabeth, the Queen mother in robes of the Order of the Garter

Date	Mintage	F	VF	XF	Unc	BU
2012PM	—	—	—	—	—	15.00

KM# 166 CROWN

28.2800 g., Copper-Nickel, 38.6 mm. **Ruler:** Elizabeth II **Subject:** Life of Queen Elizabeth II **Obv:** Conjoined busts right **Rev:** Elizabeth as WWII nurse

Date	Mintage	F	VF	XF	Unc	BU
2012PM	—	—	—	—	—	15.00

KM# 167 CROWN

Silver with glass insert, 38.6 mm. **Ruler:** Elizabeth II **Obv:** Head at top, butterfly in glass **Rev:** Life of the butterfly around central image

Date	Mintage	F	VF	XF	Unc	BU
2012PM Proof	—	Value: 75.00				

PIEDFORT

KM#	Date	Mintage	Identification	Mkt Val
P4	2001	500	50 Pence. 0.9250 Silver. 56.5600 g. 38.6 mm. Reeded edge. Proof KM#86a.	95.00
P5	2001	500	50 Pence. 0.9250 Silver. 56.5600 g. 38.6 mm. Reeded edge. Proof KM#70a.	110
P6	2001	—	50 Pence. 0.9250 Silver. 56.5600 g. 38.6 mm. Queen's portrait. Edward's portrait with two gold plated coin designs. Reeded edge.	—
P7	2001	—	50 Pence. 0.9250 Silver. 56.5600 g. 38.6 mm. Queen's portrait. Henry's portrait with two gold plated coin designs. Reeded edge.	—
P8	2001	—	50 Pence. 0.9250 Silver. 56.5600 g. 38.6 mm. Queen's portrait. Charles' portrait with two gold plated coin designs. Reeded edge.	—
P9	2001	—	50 Pence. 0.9250 Silver. 56.5600 g. 38.6 mm. Queen's portrait. Victoria's portrait with two gold plated coin designs. Reeded edge.	—
P10	2001	500	50 Pence. 0.9250 Silver. 56.5600 g. 38.6 mm. Reeded edge.	90.00
P11	2001	500	50 Pence. 0.9250 Silver. 56.5600 g. 38.6 mm. Reeded edge.	95.00
P12	2001	500	50 Pence. 0.9250 Silver. 56.5600 g. 38.6 mm. Reeded edge.	95.00
P13	2001	500	50 Pence. 0.9250 Silver. 56.5600 g. 38.6 mm. Reeded edge.	110
P14	2002	500	50 Pence. 0.9250 Silver. 56.5600 g. 38.6 mm. Reeded edge. Proof KM#73a.	95.00
P15	2002	500	50 Pence. 0.9250 Silver. 56.5600 g. 38.6 mm. Reeded edge. Proof KM#74a.	110
P16	2002	500	50 Pence. 0.9250 Silver. 56.5600 g. 38.6 mm. Reeded edge. Proof KM#75a.	95.00
P17	2002	500	50 Pence. 0.9250 Silver. 56.5600 g. 38.6 mm. Reeded edge. Proof KM#76a.	95.00
P18	2002	500	50 Pence. 0.9250 Silver. 56.5600 g. 38.6 mm. Reeded edge. Proof KM#77a.	95.00
P19	2002	500	50 Pence. 0.9250 Silver. 56.5600 g. 38.6 mm. Reeded edge. Proof KM#78a.	95.00
P20	2002	500	50 Pence. 0.9250 Silver. 56.5600 g. 38.6 mm. Reeded edge. Proof KM#79a.	95.00
P21	2002	500	50 Pence. 0.9250 Silver. 56.5600 g. 38.6 mm. Reeded edge. Proof KM#80a.	95.00
P22	2002	500	50 Pence. 0.9250 Silver. 56.5600 g. 38.6 mm. Reeded edge. Proof KM#81a.	95.00
P23	2002	500	50 Pence. 0.9250 Silver. 56.5600 g. 38.6 mm. Reeded edge. Proof KM#82a.	95.00
P24	2002	500	50 Pence. 0.9250 Silver. 56.5600 g. 38.6 mm. Reeded edge. Proof KM#83a.	95.00
P25	2002	500	50 Pence. 0.9250 Silver. 56.5600 g. 38.6 mm. Reeded edge. Proof KM#84a.	95.00
P26	ND(2002)	500	50 Pence. 0.9250 Silver. 56.5600 g. 38.6 mm. Reeded edge. Proof KM#102a.	95.00

FIJI

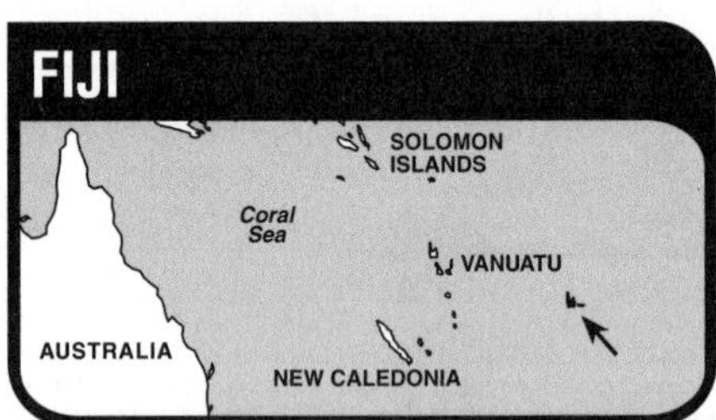

The Republic of Fiji consists of about 320 islands located in the southwestern Pacific 1,100 miles (1,770 km.) north of New Zealand. The islands have a combined area of 7,056 sq. mi. (18,274 sq. km.) and a population of 772,891. Capital: Suva. Fiji's economy is based on agriculture and mining. Sugar, coconut products, manganese, and gold are exported. Fiji is a member of the Commonwealth of Nations, but has been subject to periodic short suspensions.

MINT MARK

(o) - Royal Canadian Mint, Ottawa

REPUBLIC

DECIMAL COINAGE

100 Cents = 1 Dollar

KM# 49a CENT

1.5800 g., Copper Plated Zinc, 17.53 mm. **Ruler:** Elizabeth II **Obv:** Crowned head right, date at right **Rev:** Tanoa kava bowl divides denomination

Date	Mintage	F	VF	XF	Unc	BU
2001(o)	—	—	—	—	0.20	0.65
2002(o)	5,880,000	—	—	—	0.20	0.65
2003(o)	8,030,000	—	—	—	0.20	0.65
2004(o)	8,840,000	—	—	—	0.20	0.65
2005(o)	9,720,000	—	—	—	0.20	0.65

KM# 49b CENT

1.7600 g., Copper Plated Steel, 17.5 mm. **Ruler:** Elizabeth II **Obv:** Crowned head right, date at right **Rev:** Tanoa kava bowl

Date	Mintage	F	VF	XF	Unc	BU
2006(o)	—	—	—	—	0.25	0.50

KM# 50a 2 CENTS

3.1600 g., Copper Plated Zinc, 21.08 mm. **Ruler:** Elizabeth II **Obv:** Crowned head right, date at right **Rev:** Palm fan and denomination

Date	Mintage	F	VF	XF	Unc	BU
2001(o)	2,830,000	—	—	—	0.30	0.85
2002(o)	5,000,000	—	—	—	0.30	0.85
2003(o)	6,410,000	—	—	—	0.30	0.85
2004(o)	7,050,000	—	—	—	0.30	0.85
2005(o)	7,760,000	—	—	—	0.30	0.85

KM# 51a 5 CENTS

2.3400 g., Nickel Plated Steel, 19.41 mm. **Ruler:** Elizabeth II **Obv:** Crowned head right **Rev:** Fijian drum - lali divides denomination **Edge:** Reeded

Date	Mintage	F	VF	XF	Unc	BU
2006(l)	—	—	—	—	0.75	1.00

KM# 119 5 CENTS

2.3400 g., Nickel Plated Steel, 19.5 mm. **Ruler:** Elizabeth II **Obv:** Crowned head right **Rev:** Fijian drum - Lali divides denomination **Edge:** Plain

Date	Mintage	F	VF	XF	Unc	BU
2009	—	—	—	—	0.75	1.00
2010	—	—	—	—	0.75	1.00

KM# 52a 10 CENTS

4.7500 g., Nickel Plated Steel, 23.6 mm. **Ruler:** Elizabeth II **Obv:** Crowned head right **Rev:** Throwing club - ula tava tava divides value **Edge:** Reeded

Date	Mintage	F	VF	XF	Unc	BU
2006	—	—	—	—	1.00	1.25

KM# 120 10 CENTS

3.5500 g., Nickel Plated Steel, 21.5 mm. **Ruler:** Elizabeth II **Obv:** Crowned head right **Rev:** Throwing club - ula tava tava divides value **Edge:** Reeded

Date	Mintage	F	VF	XF	Unc	BU
2009	—	—	—	—	1.00	1.25

KM# 95 20 CENTS

11.2400 g., Copper-Nickel, 28.5 mm. **Ruler:** Elizabeth II **Obv:** Crowned head right, date at right **Rev:** South Pacific Games flame logo **Edge:** Reeded **Note:** Prooflike examples issued in special cards.

Date	Mintage	F	VF	XF	Unc	BU
2003	1,540,000	—	—	—	1.50	2.50
2003 Prooflike	—	—	—	—	—	6.00

KM# 53a 20 CENTS

10.5000 g., Nickel Plated Steel, 28.5 mm. **Ruler:** Elizabeth II **Obv:** Crowned head right **Rev:** Tabua on braided sennit cord divides denomination **Edge:** Reeded

Date	Mintage	F	VF	XF	Unc	BU
2006(l)	—	—	0.20	0.35	1.25	1.50

KM# 121 20 CENTS

4.6800 g., Nickel Plated Steel, 24 mm. **Ruler:** Elizabeth II **Obv:** Crowned head right **Rev:** Tabua, a ceremonial whale's tooth divides denomination **Edge:** Segmented reeding

Date	Mintage	F	VF	XF	Unc	BU
2009	—	—	—	0.35	1.25	1.50
2010	—	—	—	0.35	1.25	1.50

KM# 259 50 CENTS

Copper-Nickel **Ruler:** Elizabeth II **Subject:** Taiwan Wildlife, a Blackfaced Loffler

Date	Mintage	F	VF	XF	Unc	BU
2003	—	—	—	—	—	15.00

KM# 260 50 CENTS

Copper-Nickel **Ruler:** Elizabeth II **Subject:** Taiwan Wildlife - Neon pitta

Date	Mintage	F	VF	XF	Unc	BU
2003	—	—	—	—	—	15.00

KM# 122 50 CENTS

6.5000 g., Nickel Plated Steel, 26.5 mm. **Ruler:** Elizabeth II **Obv:** Crowned head right **Rev:** Sailing canoe - Takia, denomination below **Edge:** Reeded

Date	Mintage	F	VF	XF	Unc	BU
2009	—	—	—	—	1.00	2.00

KM# 164 50 CENTS

27.2200 g., Copper-Nickel, 38.74 mm. **Ruler:** Elizabeth II **Subject:** Year of the Tiger **Obv:** Female goddess facing **Rev:** Multicolor Formosan Tiger

Date	Mintage	F	VF	XF	Unc	BU
2010(c)	6,000	—	—	—	—	50.00

KM# 254 DOLLAR

28.2800 g., Copper-Nickel, 38.61 mm. **Ruler:** Elizabeth II **Subject:** Elizabeth II, 50th Anniversary of Reign **Rev:** Draped sword

Date	Mintage	F	VF	XF	Unc	BU
2002	—	—	—	—	—	20.00

KM# 255 DOLLAR

28.2800 g., Copper-Nickel, 38.61 mm. **Ruler:** Elizabeth II **Subject:** Elizabeth II, 50th Anniversary of Reign **Rev:** Boys Choir in Westminster Abbey

Date	Mintage	F	VF	XF	Unc	BU
2002	—	—	—	—	—	20.00

KM# 261 DOLLAR

31.1050 g., 0.9990 Silver 0.9990 oz. ASW, 38.7 mm. **Ruler:** Elizabeth II **Subject:** Song Meiling, 1st Anniversary of Death **Obv:** National arms **Rev:** Song Meiling and Jiang Jieshi

Date	Mintage	F	VF	XF	Unc	BU
2004 Proof	—	Value: 55.00				

KM# 262 DOLLAR

31.1050 g., 0.9990 Silver 0.9990 oz. ASW, 38.7 mm. **Ruler:** Elizabeth II **Subject:** Song Meiling, 1st Anniversary of Death **Rev:** Song Meiling and Chrysanthemen

Date	Mintage	F	VF	XF	Unc	BU
2004 Proof	—	Value: 55.00				

KM# 114 DOLLAR

31.1050 g., 0.9990 Silver 0.9990 oz. ASW, 40.7 mm. **Ruler:** Elizabeth II **Subject:** Sputnik I, 50th Anniversary **Rev:** Multicolor earth, satellite rocket

Date	Mintage	F	VF	XF	Unc	BU
2007 Prooflike	6,000	—	—	—	—	100

KM# 233 DOLLAR

0.5000 g., 0.9999 Gold 0.0161 oz. AGW, 11 mm. **Ruler:** Elizabeth II **Obv:** Head in tiara right **Rev:** Britannia seated left

Date	Mintage	F	VF	XF	Unc	BU
2007 Proof	15,000	Value: 50.00				

KM# 234 DOLLAR

0.5000 g., 0.9999 Gold 0.0161 oz. AGW, 11 mm. **Ruler:** Elizabeth II **Obv:** Head in tiara right **Rev:** Victory from Mexico's Libertad bullion coinage

Date	Mintage	F	VF	XF	Unc	BU
2007 Proof	15,000	Value: 50.00				

KM# 115 DOLLAR

31.1050 g., 0.9990 Silver 0.9990 oz. ASW **Ruler:** Elizabeth II **Subject:** Birds of Fiji **Rev:** Multicolor - blue crested broadbill

Date	Mintage	F	VF	XF	Unc	BU
2008 Prooflike	4,000	—	—	—	—	90.00

KM# 116 DOLLAR

31.1050 g., 0.9990 Silver 0.9990 oz. ASW **Ruler:** Elizabeth II **Subject:** Birds of Fiji **Rev:** Multicolor collared lory

Date	Mintage	F	VF	XF	Unc	BU
2008 Prooflike	4,000	—	—	—	—	90.00

KM# 117 DOLLAR

31.1050 g., 0.9990 Silver 0.9990 oz. ASW **Ruler:** Elizabeth II **Subject:** Birds of Fiji **Rev:** Multicolor - Island Thrush

Date	Mintage	F	VF	XF	Unc	BU
2008 Prooflike	4,000	—	—	—	—	90.00

KM# 118 DOLLAR

31.1050 g., 0.9990 Silver 0.9990 oz. ASW **Ruler:** Elizabeth II **Subject:** Birds of Fiji **Rev:** Multicolor white collared kingfisher

Date	Mintage	F	VF	XF	Unc	BU
2008 Prooflike	4,000	—	—	—	—	90.00

KM# 237 DOLLAR

28.2800 g., 0.9250 Silver 0.8410 oz. ASW, 38.61 mm. **Ruler:** Elizabeth II **Subject:** History fo Seafaring **Obv:** Head with tiara right **Rev:** Pamir sailing right

Date	Mintage	F	VF	XF	Unc	BU
2008 Proof	1,500	Value: 35.00				

KM# 124 DOLLAR

Copper-Nickel **Ruler:** Elizabeth II **Subject:** Barack Obama elected U.S. President

Date	Mintage	F	VF	XF	Unc	BU
2009	—	—	—	—	—	15.00

KM# 130 DOLLAR

Copper-Nickel partially gilt, 40 mm. **Ruler:** Elizabeth II **Subject:** Pacific Explorers - Sir Francis Drake **Rev:** Ship, portrait in oval

Date	Mintage	F	VF	XF	Unc	BU
2009 Proof	—	Value: 15.00				

KM# 131 DOLLAR

Copper-Nickel partially gilt, 40 mm. **Ruler:** Elizabeth II **Subject:** Pacific Explorers - Ferdinand Magellan **Rev:** Ship, portrait in oval

Date	Mintage	F	VF	XF	Unc	BU
2009 Proof	—	Value: 15.00				

KM# 132 DOLLAR

Copper-Nickel partially gilt, 40 mm. **Ruler:** Elizabeth II **Subject:** Pacific Explorers - James Cook **Rev:** Ship, portrait in oval

Date	Mintage	F	VF	XF	Unc	BU
2009 Proof	—	Value: 15.00				

KM# 133 DOLLAR

Copper-Nickel partially gilt, 40 mm. **Ruler:** Elizabeth II **Subject:** Pacific Explorers - Abel Tasman **Rev:** Ship, portrait in oval

Date	Mintage	F	VF	XF	Unc	BU
2009 Proof	—	Value: 15.00				

KM# 134 DOLLAR

Copper-Nickel partially gilt **Ruler:** Elizabeth II **Subject:** Pacific Explorers - Jacob DeMare & William Schouten **Rev:** Ship, portraits in oval

Date	Mintage	F	VF	XF	Unc	BU
2009 Proof	—	Value: 15.00				

KM# 135 DOLLAR

Copper-Nickel partially gilt **Ruler:** Elizabeth II **Subject:** Pacific Explorers - William Bligh **Rev:** Ship, portrait in oval

Date	Mintage	F	VF	XF	Unc	BU
2009	—	—	—	—	—	15.00

KM# 137 DOLLAR

Copper-Nickel, 38.61 mm. **Ruler:** Elizabeth II **Subject:** Great animals of the World - Panda **Rev:** Panda seated, fur pattern as background

Date	Mintage	F	VF	XF	Unc	BU
2009	—	—	—	—	—	15.00

KM# 137a DOLLAR

Copper-Nickel gilt **Ruler:** Elizabeth II **Subject:** Great animals of the World - Panda

Date	Mintage	F	VF	XF	Unc	BU
2009	—	—	—	—	—	15.00

KM# 138 DOLLAR

Copper-Nickel, 38.61 mm. **Ruler:** Elizabeth II **Subject:** Great animals of the World - Koi **Rev:** Koi fish swimming right, scale pattern as background

Date	Mintage	F	VF	XF	Unc	BU
2009	—	—	—	—	—	15.00

KM# 138a DOLLAR

Copper-Nickel gilt **Ruler:** Elizabeth II **Subject:** Great animals of the World - Koi

Date	Mintage	F	VF	XF	Unc	BU
2009	—	—	—	—	—	15.00

KM# 139 DOLLAR

Copper-Nickel **Ruler:** Elizabeth II **Subject:** Great animals of the World - Zebra

Date	Mintage	F	VF	XF	Unc	BU
2009	—	—	—	—	—	15.00

KM# 139a DOLLAR

Copper-Nickel gilt, 38.61 mm. **Ruler:** Elizabeth II **Subject:** Great animals of the World - Zebra

Date	Mintage	F	VF	XF	Unc	BU
2009	—	—	—	—	—	15.00

KM# 140 DOLLAR

Copper-Nickel **Ruler:** Elizabeth II **Subject:** Great animals of the World - Elephant

Date	Mintage	F	VF	XF	Unc	BU
2009	—	—	—	—	—	15.00

KM# 140a DOLLAR

Copper-Nickel gilt **Ruler:** Elizabeth II **Subject:** Great animals of the World - Elephant

Date	Mintage	F	VF	XF	Unc	BU
2009	—	—	—	—	—	15.00

KM# 141 DOLLAR

Copper-Nickel, 38.61 mm. **Ruler:** Elizabeth II **Subject:** Great animals of the world - Cheeta **Rev:** Cheets standing left, fur pattern background

Date	Mintage	F	VF	XF	Unc	BU
2009	—	—	—	—	—	15.00

KM# 141a DOLLAR

Copper-Nickel gilt **Ruler:** Elizabeth II **Subject:** Great animals of the World - Cheeta

Date	Mintage	F	VF	XF	Unc	BU
2009	—	—	—	—	—	15.00

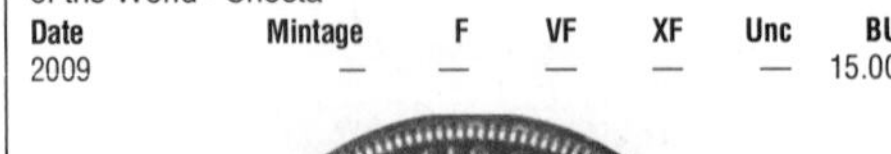

KM# 142 DOLLAR

Copper-Nickel, 38.61 mm. **Ruler:** Elizabeth II **Subject:** Great animals of teh World - Leopard **Rev:** Leopard walking left, leopard skin background

Date	Mintage	F	VF	XF	Unc	BU
2009	—	—	—	—	—	15.00

KM# 142a DOLLAR

Copper-Nickel gilt **Ruler:** Elizabeth II **Subject:** Great animals of the World - Leopard

Date	Mintage	F	VF	XF	Unc	BU
2009	—	—	—	—	—	15.00

KM# 143 DOLLAR

Copper-Nickel **Ruler:** Elizabeth II **Subject:** Great animals of the World - Giraffe

Date	Mintage	F	VF	XF	Unc	BU
2009	—	—	—	—	—	15.00

KM# 143a DOLLAR

Copper-Nickel gilt **Ruler:** Elizabeth II **Subject:** Great animals of the World - Giraffe

Date	Mintage	F	VF	XF	Unc	BU
2009	—	—	—	—	—	15.00

KM# 144 DOLLAR

Copper-Nickel, 38.61 mm. **Ruler:** Elizabeth II **Subject:** Great animals of the World - Tiger **Rev:** Tiger advancing right, fur pattern as background

Date	Mintage	F	VF	XF	Unc	BU
2009	—	—	—	—	—	15.00

KM# 144a DOLLAR

Copper-Nickel gilt **Ruler:** Elizabeth II **Subject:** Great animals of the World - Tiger

Date	Mintage	F	VF	XF	Unc	BU
2009	—	—	—	—	—	15.00

KM# 145 DOLLAR

Copper-Nickel silver plated **Ruler:** Elizabeth II **Subject:** Tropical fish - Yellow pointed nose

Date	Mintage	F	VF	XF	Unc	BU
2009	—	—	—	—	—	15.00

KM# 146 DOLLAR

Copper-Nickel silver plated **Ruler:** Elizabeth II **Subject:** Tropical fish - Albino yellow fish

Date	Mintage	F	VF	XF	Unc	BU
2009	—	—	—	—	—	15.00

KM# 147 DOLLAR

Copper-Nickel silver plated **Ruler:** Elizabeth II **Subject:** Tropical fish - Striped Butterfly fish

Date	Mintage	F	VF	XF	Unc	BU
2009	—	—	—	—	—	15.00

KM# 148 DOLLAR

Copper-Nickel silver plated **Ruler:** Elizabeth II **Subject:** Tropical fish - Damsel fish

Date	Mintage	F	VF	XF	Unc	BU
2009	—	—	—	—	—	15.00

KM# 149 DOLLAR

Copper-Nickel silver plated, 38.6 mm. **Ruler:** Elizabeth II **Subject:** Tropical fish - Surgern fish **Rev:** Colored fish below ship

Date	Mintage	F	VF	XF	Unc	BU
2009	—	—	—	—	—	15.00

KM# 150 DOLLAR

Copper-Nickel silver plated **Ruler:** Elizabeth II **Subject:** Tropical fish - Clown fish

Date	Mintage	F	VF	XF	Unc	BU
2009	—	—	—	—	—	15.00

KM# 293 DOLLAR

25.0000 g., Aluminum-Bronze, 38.61 mm. **Ruler:** Elizabeth II **Rev:** Mary and Christ child

Date	Mintage	F	VF	XF	Unc	BU
2009	—	—	—	—	—	10.00

KM# 126 DOLLAR

Silver **Ruler:** Elizabeth II **Subject:** H.C. Andersen - Steadfast Tin Soldier **Rev:** Multicolor toy soldier in flames

Date	Mintage	F	VF	XF	Unc	BU
2010 Proof	—	Value: 50.00				

KM# 127 DOLLAR

Silver **Ruler:** Elizabeth II **Subject:** H.C. Andersen - The Nightengale **Rev:** Multicolor bird

Date	Mintage	F	VF	XF	Unc	BU
2010 Proof	—	Value: 65.00				

KM# 128 DOLLAR

Silver **Ruler:** Elizabeth II **Subject:** H.C. Andersen - Thumbelina **Rev:** Multicolor Pixi

Date	Mintage	F	VF	XF	Unc	BU
2010 Proof	—	Value: 50.00				

KM# 129 DOLLAR

Silver **Ruler:** Elizabeth II **Subject:** H.C. Andersen - The little match girl **Rev:** Multicolor girl with match

Date	Mintage	F	VF	XF	Unc	BU
2010 Proof	—	Value: 50.00				

KM# 152 DOLLAR

31.1050 g., 0.9990 Silver 0.9990 oz. ASW, 46x29 mm. **Ruler:** Elizabeth II **Subject:** Siberian Tiger **Shape:** Irregular

Date	Mintage	F	VF	XF	Unc	BU
2010 Proof	10,000	Value: 60.00				

KM# 153 DOLLAR

31.1050 g., 0.9990 Silver 0.9990 oz. ASW, 46x29 mm. **Ruler:** Elizabeth II **Subject:** Bengal Tiger **Shape:** Irregular

Date	Mintage	F	VF	XF	Unc	BU
2010 Proof	10,000	Value: 60.00				

KM# 154 DOLLAR

Tri-Metallic Copper center, Brass inner ring, Copper-Nickel outer ring., 40 mm. **Ruler:** Elizabeth II **Subject:** FIAA World Cup - South Africa **Rev:** Pretoria stadium and antelopes

Date	Mintage	F	VF	XF	Unc	BU
2010	—	—	—	—	—	20.00

KM# 155 DOLLAR

Tri-Metallic Copper center, Brass inner ring, Copper-Nickel outer ring., 40 mm. **Ruler:** Elizabeth II **Subject:** FIAA World Cup - South Africa **Rev:** Kapstadt stadium and Zebra

Date	Mintage	F	VF	XF	Unc	BU
2010	—	—	—	—	—	20.00

KM# 156 DOLLAR

Tri-Metallic Copper center, Brass inner ring, Copper-Nickel outer ring., 40 mm. **Ruler:** Elizabeth II **Subject:** FIAA World Cup - South Africa **Rev:** Johannesburg Stadium and Rhinos

Date	Mintage	F	VF	XF	Unc	BU
2010	—	—	—	—	—	20.00

KM# 157 DOLLAR

Tri-Metallic Copper center, Brass inner ring, Copper-Nickel outer ring., 40 mm. **Ruler:** Elizabeth II **Subject:** FIAA World Cup - South Africa **Rev:** Johannesburg Stadium and Leopard

Date	Mintage	F	VF	XF	Unc	BU
2010	—	—	—	—	—	20.00

KM# 158 DOLLAR

Tri-Metallic Copper center, Brass inner ring, Copper-Nickel outer ring., 40 mm. **Ruler:** Elizabeth II **Subject:** FIAA World Cup - South Africa **Rev:** Rustenburg Stadium and Lion

Date	Mintage	F	VF	XF	Unc	BU
2010	—	—	—	—	—	20.00

KM# 159 DOLLAR

Tri-Metallic Copper center, Brass inner ring, Copper-Nickel outer ring., 40 mm. **Ruler:** Elizabeth II **Subject:** FIAA World Cup - South Africa **Rev:** Durban Stadium and Giraffes

Date	Mintage	F	VF	XF	Unc	BU
2010	—	—	—	—	—	20.00

KM# 160 DOLLAR

Tri-Metallic Copper center, Brass inner ring, Copper-Nickel outer ring., 40 mm. **Ruler:** Elizabeth II **Subject:** FIAA World Cup - South Africa **Rev:** Polokwane Stadium and Elephant

Date	Mintage	F	VF	XF	Unc	BU
2010	—	—	—	—	—	20.00

KM# 161 DOLLAR

Tri-Metallic Copper center, Brass inner ring, Copper-Nickel outer ring., 40 mm. **Ruler:** Elizabeth II **Subject:** FIAA World Cup - South Africa **Rev:** Nelspruit stadium and Water buffalo

Date	Mintage	F	VF	XF	Unc	BU
2010	—	—	—	—	—	20.00

KM# 162 DOLLAR

Tri-Metallic Copper center, Brass inner ring, Copper-Nickel outer ring., 40 mm. **Ruler:** Elizabeth II **Subject:** FIAA World Cup - South Africa **Rev:** Bloemfontein stadium and Lemurs

Date	Mintage	F	VF	XF	Unc	BU
2010	—	—	—	—	—	20.00

KM# 163 DOLLAR

Tri-Metallic Copper center, Brass inner ring, Copper-Nickel outer ring., 40 mm. **Ruler:** Elizabeth II **Subject:** FIAA World Cup - South Africa **Rev:** Port Elizabeth stadium and Animal

Date	Mintage	F	VF	XF	Unc	BU
2010	—	—	—	—	—	20.00

KM# 181 DOLLAR

31.1050 g., 0.9990 Silver 0.9990 oz. ASW, 38.61 mm. **Ruler:** Elizabeth II **Subject:** Year of the Tiger **Obv:** Head with crown right **Rev:** Bengal Tiger in color **Shape:** Yin-Yang

Date	Mintage	F	VF	XF	Unc	BU
2010 Proof	—	Value: 50.00				

KM# 182 DOLLAR

31.1050 g., 0.9990 Silver 0.9990 oz. ASW, 38.61 mm. **Ruler:** Elizabeth II **Obv:** Head with crown right **Rev:** Siberian tiger in color **Shape:** Yin-Yang

Date	Mintage	F	VF	XF	Unc	BU
2010 Proof	—	Value: 50.00				

KM# 238 DOLLAR

0.5000 g., 0.9990 Gold 0.0161 oz. AGW, 11 mm. **Ruler:** Elizabeth II **Subject:** Johann Philipp Reis **Obv:** Head in tiara right **Rev:** Reis portrait

Date	Mintage	F	VF	XF	Unc	BU
2010 Proof	5,000	Value: 50.00				

KM# 240 DOLLAR

26.0300 g., Copper Plated Silver, 38.61 mm. **Ruler:** Elizabeth II **Subject:** London Olympics, 2012 **Obv:** Head with tiara right **Rev:** Triathlon sports

Date	Mintage	F	VF	XF	Unc	BU
2010 Proof	10,000	Value: 20.00				

KM# 242 DOLLAR

6.2200 g., 0.9990 Silver 0.1998 oz. ASW, 35 mm. **Ruler:** Elizabeth II **Subject:** Vitus Bering **Obv:** Head with tiara right **Rev:** Vitus J. Bering and ship Saint Peter

Date	Mintage	F	VF	XF	Unc	BU
2010 Proof	5,000	Value: 35.00				

KM# 170 DOLLAR

31.1050 g., 0.9990 Silver 0.9990 oz. ASW, 38.6 mm. **Ruler:** Elizabeth II **Subject:** Year of the Dragon **Obv:** Characters, Filigree center **Rev:** Characters, Filigree center

Date	Mintage	F	VF	XF	Unc	BU
2011 Proof	10,000	Value: 100				

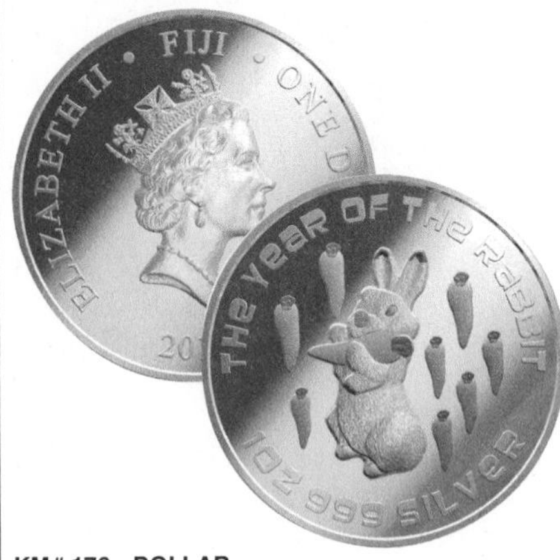

KM# 176 DOLLAR

31.1050 g., 0.9990 Silver 0.9990 oz. ASW, 38.61 mm. **Ruler:** Elizabeth II **Subject:** Year of the Rabbit **Obv:** Head with crown right **Rev:** Rabbit eating carrot, carrots in color

Date	Mintage	F	VF	XF	Unc	BU
2011 Proof	—	Value: 60.00				

KM# 177 DOLLAR

31.1050 g., 0.9990 Silver 0.9990 oz. ASW, 38.61 mm. **Ruler:** Elizabeth II **Subject:** Year of the Rabbit **Obv:** Head at left, rabbit in center cut-out **Rev:** Rabbit in center, leatuce leaves around

Date	Mintage	F	VF	XF	Unc	BU
2011 Proof	—	Value: 120				

KM# 179 DOLLAR

31.1050 g., 0.9990 Silver 0.9990 oz. ASW, 38.61 mm. **Ruler:** Elizabeth II **Subject:** Year of the Rabbit **Obv:** Head in crown right **Rev:** Snow rabbit in color **Shape:** Yin-Yang

Date	Mintage	F	VF	XF	Unc	BU
2011 Proof	—	Value: 90.00				

KM# 180 DOLLAR

31.1050 g., 0.9990 Silver 0.9990 oz. ASW, 38.61 mm. **Ruler:** Elizabeth II **Subject:** Year of the Rabbit **Obv:** Head with crown right **Rev:** Summer rabbit **Shape:** Yin-Yang

Date	Mintage	F	VF	XF	Unc	BU
2011 Proof	—	Value: 90.00				

KM# 183 DOLLAR
Copper-Nickel Silver plated, partially gilt, 38.61 mm. **Ruler:** Elizabeth II **Obv:** Bust right **Rev:** Sun, gilt figure

Date	Mintage	F	VF	XF	Unc	BU
2011	—	—	—	—	—	30.00

KM# 184 DOLLAR
Copper-Nickel Silver plated, partially gilt, 38.61 mm. **Ruler:** Elizabeth II **Obv:** Bust right **Rev:** Mercury, gilt figure

Date	Mintage	F	VF	XF	Unc	BU
2011	—	—	—	—	—	30.00

KM# 185 DOLLAR
Copper-Nickel Silver plated, partially gilt, 38.6 mm. **Ruler:** Elizabeth II **Obv:** Bust right **Rev:** Venus, gilt statue

Date	Mintage	F	VF	XF	Unc	BU
2011	—	—	—	—	—	30.00

KM# 186 DOLLAR
Copper-Nickel Silver plated, partially gilt, 38.61 mm. **Ruler:** Elizabeth II **Obv:** Bust right **Rev:** Earth, gilt statue

Date	Mintage	F	VF	XF	Unc	BU
2011	—	—	—	—	—	30.00

KM# 187 DOLLAR
Copper-Nickel Silver plated, partially gilt, 38.61 mm. **Ruler:** Elizabeth II **Obv:** Bust right **Rev:** Mars, gilt statue

Date	Mintage	F	VF	XF	Unc	BU
2011	—	—	—	—	—	30.00

KM# 188 DOLLAR
Copper-Nickel Silver plated, partially gilt, 38.61 mm. **Ruler:** Elizabeth II **Obv:** Bust right **Rev:** Jupiter, gilt statue

Date	Mintage	F	VF	XF	Unc	BU
2011	—	—	—	—	—	30.00

KM# 189 DOLLAR
Copper-Nickel Silver plated, partially gilt, 38.61 mm. **Ruler:** Elizabeth II **Obv:** Bust right **Rev:** Saturn, gilt statue

Date	Mintage	F	VF	XF	Unc	BU
2011	—	—	—	—	—	30.00

KM# 190 DOLLAR
Copper-Nickel Silver plated, partially gilt, 38.6 mm. **Ruler:** Elizabeth II **Obv:** Bust right **Rev:** Uranus, gilt statue

Date	Mintage	F	VF	XF	Unc	BU
2011	—	—	—	—	—	30.00

KM# 191 DOLLAR
Copper-Nickel Silver plated, partially gilt, 38.61 mm. **Ruler:** Elizabeth II **Obv:** Bust right **Rev:** Nepture, gilt statue

Date	Mintage	F	VF	XF	Unc	BU
2011	—	—	—	—	—	30.00

KM# 192 DOLLAR
Copper-Nickel Silver plated, partially gilt, 38.61 mm. **Ruler:** Elizabeth II **Obv:** Bust right **Rev:** Pluto, gilt statue

Date	Mintage	F	VF	XF	Unc	BU
2011	—	—	—	—	—	30.00

KM# 246 DOLLAR
0.5000 g., 0.9990 Gold 0.0161 oz. AGW, 11 mm. **Ruler:** Elizabeth II **Obv:** Head with tiara right **Rev:** Nero head right

Date	Mintage	F	VF	XF	Unc	BU
2011 Proof	5,000	Value: 50.00				

KM# 171 DOLLAR
15.5500 g., 0.9990 Silver with color. 0.4994 oz. ASW, 38.6 mm. **Ruler:** Elizabeth II **Subject:** Year of the Dragon **Rev:** Red dragon **Shape:** Yin

Date	Mintage	F	VF	XF	Unc	BU
2012 Proof	10,000	Value: 85.00				

KM# 172 DOLLAR
15.5500 g., 0.9990 Silver with color 0.4994 oz. ASW, 38.6 mm. **Ruler:** Elizabeth II **Subject:** Year of the Dragon **Rev:** Blue dragon **Shape:** Yang

Date	Mintage	F	VF	XF	Unc	BU
2012 Proof	—	Value: 85.00				

KM# 200 DOLLAR
20.0000 g., Copper-Nickel Silver plated, 38.61 mm. **Ruler:** Elizabeth II **Subject:** Carnival - Rio

Date	Mintage	F	VF	XF	Unc	BU
2012	2,500	—	—	—	—	40.00

KM# 201 DOLLAR
20.0000 g., Copper-Nickel Silver plated, 38.6 mm. **Ruler:** Elizabeth II **Subject:** Carnival - Venice **Obv:** Head with tiara right

Date	Mintage	F	VF	XF	Unc	BU
2012	2,500	—	—	—	—	50.00

KM# 202 DOLLAR
20.0000 g., Copper-Nickel Silver plated, 38.6 mm. **Ruler:** Elizabeth II **Subject:** Carnival - Nice **Obv:** Head with tiara right

Date	Mintage	F	VF	XF	Unc	BU
2012	2,500	—	—	—	—	50.00

KM# 203 DOLLAR
20.0000 g., Copper-Nickel Silver plated, 38.6 mm. **Ruler:** Elizabeth II **Subject:** Carnival - New Orleans **Obv:** Head with tiara right

Date	Mintage	F	VF	XF	Unc	BU
2012	2,500	—	—	—	—	50.00

KM# 204 DOLLAR
20.0000 g., Copper-Nickel Silver plated, 38.6 mm. **Ruler:** Elizabeth II **Subject:** Carnival - Cologne **Obv:** Head with tiara right

Date	Mintage	F	VF	XF	Unc	BU
2012	2,500	—	—	—	—	50.00

KM# 205 DOLLAR
20.0000 g., Copper-Nickel Silver plated, 38.6 mm. **Ruler:** Elizabeth II **Subject:** Carnival - Basel **Obv:** Head with tiara right

Date	Mintage	F	VF	XF	Unc	BU
2012	2,500	—	—	—	—	50.00

KM# 212 DOLLAR
20.0000 g., Copper-Nickel Silver plated, 38.6 mm. **Ruler:** Elizabeth II **Subject:** Music - Chanson

Date	Mintage	F	VF	XF	Unc	BU
2012 Proof	2,500	Value: 30.00				

KM# 213 DOLLAR
20.0000 g., Copper-Nickel Silver plated, 38.6 mm. **Ruler:** Elizabeth II **Subject:** Music - Bob Marley

Date	Mintage	F	VF	XF	Unc	BU
2012 Proof	2,500	Value: 30.00				

KM# 214 DOLLAR
20.0000 g., Copper-Nickel Silver plated, 38.6 mm. **Ruler:** Elizabeth II **Subject:** Music - Elvis Presley

Date	Mintage	F	VF	XF	Unc	BU
2012 Proof	2,500	Value: 30.00				

KM# 108 2 DOLLARS
10.0000 g., 0.9250 Silver 0.2974 oz. ASW, 30 mm. **Ruler:** Elizabeth II **Subject:** XVIII FIFA World Rootball Championship - Germany 2006 **Obv:** Crowned head right **Obv. Legend:** ELIZABETH II - FIJI **Rev:** World cup

Date	Mintage	F	VF	XF	Unc	BU
2004 Proof	50,000	Value: 22.00				

KM# 193 2 DOLLARS

Silver, 38.61 mm. **Ruler:** Elizabeth II **Obv:** Head crowned right **Rev:** Orthodox church in color

Date	Mintage	F	VF	XF	Unc	BU
2009 Proof	—	Value: 50.00				

KM# 194 2 DOLLARS

Silver, 38.61 mm. **Ruler:** Elizabeth II **Obv:** Head crowned right **Rev:** Nicholas II Romanoff wedding portrait in color

Date	Mintage	F	VF	XF	Unc	BU
2009 Proof	—	Value: 50.00				

KM# 273 2 DOLLARS

0.9990 Silver, 45x31 mm. **Ruler:** Elizabeth II **Rev:** British airship R34 in color **Shape:** Oval

Date	Mintage	F	VF	XF	Unc	BU
2009 Proof	20,000	Value: 100				

KM# 274 2 DOLLARS

0.9990 Silver, 45x31 mm. **Ruler:** Elizabeth II **Rev:** Soviet airship B6 in color **Shape:** Oval

Date	Mintage	F	VF	XF	Unc	BU
2009 Proof	20,000	Value: 100				

KM# 275 2 DOLLARS

0.9990 Silver, 45x31 mm. **Ruler:** Elizabeth II **Rev:** U.S. Airship Akron in color **Shape:** Oval

Date	Mintage	F	VF	XF	Unc	BU
2009 Proof	20,000	Value: 100				

KM# 276 2 DOLLARS

0.9990 Silver, 45x31 mm. **Ruler:** Elizabeth II **Rev:** German airship Hindenburg in color **Shape:** Oval

Date	Mintage	F	VF	XF	Unc	BU
2009 Proof	20,000	Value: 100				

KM# 195 2 DOLLARS

Silver, 38.61 mm. **Ruler:** Elizabeth II **Obv:** Head crowned right **Rev:** Romanoff family portrait in color

Date	Mintage	F	VF	XF	Unc	BU
2009 Proof	—	Value: 50.00				

KM# 166 2 DOLLARS

31.1050 g., 0.9990 Silver 0.9990 oz. ASW, 45x31 mm. **Ruler:** Elizabeth II **Rev:** Submarine Ohio in color **Shape:** Oval

Date	Mintage	F	VF	XF	Unc	BU
2010 Prooflike	15,000	—	—	—	—	90.00

KM# 167 2 DOLLARS

31.1050 g., 0.9990 Silver 0.9990 oz. ASW, 45x31 mm. **Ruler:** Elizabeth II **Rev:** Submarine Triomphant in color **Shape:** Oval

Date	Mintage	F	VF	XF	Unc	BU
2010 Prooflike	15,000	—	—	—	—	90.00

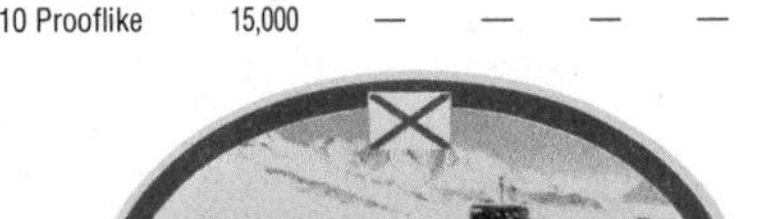

KM# 168 2 DOLLARS

31.1050 g., 0.9990 Silver 0.9990 oz. ASW, 45x31 mm. **Ruler:** Elizabeth II **Rev:** Submarine Typhoon in color **Shape:** Oval

Date	Mintage	F	VF	XF	Unc	BU
2010 Prooflike	15,000	—	—	—	—	90.00

KM# 169 2 DOLLARS

31.1050 g., 0.9990 Silver 0.9990 oz. ASW, 45x31 mm. **Ruler:** Elizabeth II **Rev:** Submarine Vanguard in color **Shape:** Oval

Date	Mintage	F	VF	XF	Unc	BU
2010 Prooflike	15,000	—	—	—	—	90.00

KM# 252 2 DOLLARS

31.1050 g., 0.9990 Silver 0.9990 oz. ASW **Ruler:** Elizabeth II **Rev:** Muhammad Ali, color portrait

Date	Mintage	F	VF	XF	Unc	BU
2012 Proof	7,500	Value: 100				

KM# 93 5 DOLLARS

1.5550 g., 0.9999 Gold 0.0500 oz. AGW **Ruler:** Elizabeth II **Obv:** Crowned head right, date at right **Rev:** Arms

Date	Mintage	F	VF	XF	Unc	BU
2002	3,000	Value: 100				

KM# 115A 5 DOLLARS

1.5600 g., 0.9999 Gold 0.0501 oz. AGW, 13.9 mm. **Ruler:** Elizabeth II **Rev:** Coat of Arms

Date	Mintage	F	VF	XF	Unc	BU
2002 Proof	3,000	Value: 220				

KM# 173 5 DOLLARS

Silver partially gilt, 39 mm. **Ruler:** Elizabeth II **Subject:** Queen Elizabeth II, 80th Birthday

Date	Mintage	F	VF	XF	Unc	BU
2006	—	Value: 50.00				

KM# 265 5 DOLLARS

Silver partially gilt **Ruler:** Elizabeth II **Subject:** Christopher Columbus, 500th Anniversary of Death **Rev:** Santa Maria and Columbus portrait

Date	Mintage	F	VF	XF	Unc	BU
2006 Proof	3,000	Value: 35.00				

KM# 266 5 DOLLARS

1.2400 g., 0.5850 Gold 0.0233 oz. AGW, 13.92 mm. **Ruler:** Elizabeth II **Rev:** Stonehedge

Date	Mintage	F	VF	XF	Unc	BU
2006 Proof	7,500	Value: 50.00				

KM# 267 5 DOLLARS

1.2400 g., 0.5850 Gold 0.0233 oz. AGW, 13.92 mm. **Ruler:** Elizabeth II **Rev:** Easter Island rock sculptures

Date	Mintage	F	VF	XF	Unc	BU
2006 Proof	7,500	Value: 50.00				

KM# 268 5 DOLLARS

1.2400 g., 0.5850 Gold 0.0233 oz. AGW, 13.92 mm. **Ruler:** Elizabeth II **Rev:** Bird glyph on Nazca Plateau

Date	Mintage	F	VF	XF	Unc	BU
2006 Proof	7,500	Value: 50.00				

KM# 269 5 DOLLARS

1.2400 g., 0.5850 Gold 0.0233 oz. AGW, 13.92 mm. **Ruler:** Elizabeth II **Rev:** Seven castles

Date	Mintage	F	VF	XF	Unc	BU
2006 Proof	7,500	Value: 50.00				

KM# 270 5 DOLLARS

1.2400 g., 0.5850 Gold 0.0233 oz. AGW, 13.92 mm. **Ruler:** Elizabeth II **Rev:** Atlantis

Date	Mintage	F	VF	XF	Unc	BU
2006 Proof	7,500	Value: 50.00				

KM# 271 5 DOLLARS

1.2400 g., 0.5850 Gold 0.0233 oz. AGW, 13.92 mm. **Ruler:** Elizabeth II **Rev:** Ayers Rock

Date	Mintage	F	VF	XF	Unc	BU
2006 Proof	7,500	Value: 50.00				

KM# 272 5 DOLLARS

1.2400 g., 0.5850 Gold 0.0233 oz. AGW, 13.92 mm. **Ruler:** Elizabeth II **Rev:** Sailing ship in Bermuda triangle

Date	Mintage	F	VF	XF	Unc	BU
2006 Proof	7,500	Value: 50.00				

KM# 206 5 DOLLARS

62.2000 g., 0.9990 Silver partially gilt 1.9977 oz. ASW, 60 mm. **Ruler:** Elizabeth II **Subject:** Map - New York City, Manhattan Island

Date	Mintage	F	VF	XF	Unc	BU
2011 Proof	5,000	Value: 120				

KM# 207 5 DOLLARS

62.2000 g., 0.9990 Silver partially gilt 1.9977 oz. ASW, 60 mm. **Ruler:** Elizabeth II **Subject:** Map - Paris

Date	Mintage	F	VF	XF	Unc	BU
2011 Proof	5,000	Value: 120				

KM# 208 5 DOLLARS

62.2000 g., 0.9990 Silver partially gilt 1.9977 oz. ASW, 60 mm. **Ruler:** Elizabeth II **Subject:** Map - Tokyo

Date	Mintage	F	VF	XF	Unc	BU
2011 Proof	5,000	Value: 120				

KM# 209 5 DOLLARS
62.2000 g., 0.9990 Silver partially gilt 1.9977 oz. ASW, 60 mm. **Ruler:** Elizabeth II **Subject:** Map - Sidney

Date	Mintage	F	VF	XF	Unc	BU
2011 Proof	5,000	Value: 120				

KM# 210 5 DOLLARS
62.2000 g., 0.9990 Silver partially gilt 1.9977 oz. ASW, 60 mm. **Ruler:** Elizabeth II **Subject:** Map - Berlin

Date	Mintage	F	VF	XF	Unc	BU
2011 Proof	5,000	Value: 120				

KM# 82 10 DOLLARS
31.6200 g., 0.9250 Silver 0.9403 oz. ASW, 38.6 mm. **Ruler:** Elizabeth II **Obv:** Crowned head right, date at right **Rev:** William Bligh's - HMS Providence **Edge:** Reeded

Date	Mintage	F	VF	XF	Unc	BU
2001 Proof	—	Value: 40.00				

KM# 83 10 DOLLARS
28.2800 g., 0.9250 Silver 0.8410 oz. ASW, 38.6 mm. **Ruler:** Elizabeth II **Subject:** Queen Elizabeth II - 50 Years of Reign **Obv:** Queen's head right, gilded **Rev:** Cloth draped sword hilt, legend and denomination **Rev. Legend:** Defender of the Faith... **Edge:** Reeded

Date	Mintage	F	VF	XF	Unc	BU
2002 Proof	15,000	Value: 40.00				

KM# 84 10 DOLLARS
28.2800 g., 0.9250 Silver 0.8410 oz. ASW, 38.6 mm. **Ruler:** Elizabeth II **Subject:** Queen Elizabeth II - 50th Year of Reign **Obv:** Head right, gilded **Rev:** Four man chorus, legend, and denomination **Rev. Legend:** Westminster Abbey June 1953. **Edge:** Reeded

Date	Mintage	F	VF	XF	Unc	BU
2002 Proof	15,000	Value: 40.00				

KM# 94 10 DOLLARS
3.1100 g., 0.9999 Gold 0.1000 oz. AGW **Ruler:** Elizabeth II **Obv:** Crowned head right, date at right **Rev:** Arms **Edge:** Reeded

Date	Mintage	F	VF	XF	Unc	BU
2002 Proof	2,000	Value: 200				

KM# 101 10 DOLLARS
31.1000 g., 0.9990 Silver 0.9988 oz. ASW, 40 mm. **Ruler:** Elizabeth II **Series:** Save the Whales **Obv:** Crowned head right, date at right **Obv. Legend:** ELIZABETH II - FIJI **Rev:** Sperm Whale on mother-of-pearl inset **Edge:** Plain

Date	Mintage	F	VF	XF	Unc	BU
2002 Proof	2,000	Value: 85.00				

KM# 104 10 DOLLARS
28.2800 g., 0.9250 Silver 0.8410 oz. ASW, 38.6 mm. **Ruler:** Elizabeth II **Series:** Endangered Wildlife **Obv:** Crowned head right **Obv. Legend:** ELIZABETH II - FIJI **Rev:** Head of Peregrine Falcon right

Date	Mintage	F	VF	XF	Unc	BU
2002 Proof	—	Value: 45.00				

KM# 105 10 DOLLARS
28.2800 g., 0.9250 Silver 0.8410 oz. ASW, 38.6 mm. **Ruler:** Elizabeth II **Obv:** Crowned head right **Obv. Legend:** ELIZABETH II - FIJI **Rev:** Sailing ship "Vostok"

Date	Mintage	F	VF	XF	Unc	BU
2002 Proof	—	Value: 40.00				

KM# 106 10 DOLLARS
1.2400 g., 0.9999 Gold 0.0399 oz. AGW, 13.88 mm. **Ruler:** Elizabeth II **Obv:** Crowned head right **Obv. Legend:** ELIZABETH II - FIJI **Rev:** Sailing ship at left, naval bust 3/4 left at right **Rev. Legend:** HMS INVESTIGATOR * MATTHEW FLINDERS **Edge:** Reeded

Date	Mintage	F	VF	XF	Unc	BU
2002 Proof	—	Value: 85.00				

KM# 114A 10 DOLLARS
3.1100 g., 0.9999 Gold 0.1000 oz. AGW, 16 mm. **Ruler:** Elizabeth II **Rev:** Coat of Arms

Date	Mintage	F	VF	XF	Unc	BU
2002 Proof	2,000	Value: 350				

KM# 258 10 DOLLARS
31.1050 g., 0.9990 Silver 0.9990 oz. ASW, 40 mm. **Ruler:** Elizabeth II **Subject:** Fairwell to the Irish Pfund **Rev:** Coin motif in color

Date	Mintage	F	VF	XF	Unc	BU
2002 Proof	Est. 2,001	Value: 80.00				

KM# 113 10 DOLLARS
1.2400 g., Gold, 13.91 mm. **Ruler:** Elizabeth II **Subject:** Lost Treasure of King Richard **Obv:** Crowned head right **Rev:** Bust of King Richard facing **Edge:** Reeded

Date	Mintage	F	VF	XF	Unc	BU
2003 Proof	—	Value: 80.00				

KM# 107 10 DOLLARS
28.2600 g., 0.9250 Silver 0.8404 oz. ASW, 38.61 mm. **Ruler:** Elizabeth II **Obv:** Crowned head right **Obv. Legend:** ELIZABETH II - FIJI **Rev:** Sailing ship at left, naval bust 3/4 left at right **Rev. Legend:** HMS INVESTIGATOR * MATTHEW FLINDERS **Edge:** Reeded

Date	Mintage	F	VF	XF	Unc	BU
2003 Proof	—	Value: 40.00				

KM# 109 10 DOLLARS
28.2800 g., 0.9250 Silver 0.8410 oz. ASW, 38.61 mm. **Ruler:** Elizabeth II **Subject:** XXVIII Summer Olympics - Athens 2004 **Obv:** Crowned head right **Obv. Legend:** ELIZABETH II - FIJI **Rev:** Regatta **Edge:** Reeded

Date	Mintage	F	VF	XF	Unc	BU
2004 Proof	—	Value: 40.00				

KM# 110 10 DOLLARS
Copper-Nickel-Zinc, 38.6 mm. **Ruler:** Elizabeth II **Subject:** XVIII FIFA World Football Championship - Germany 2006 **Obv:** Crowned head right **Obv. Legend:** ELIZABETH II - FIJI **Rev:** Digital countdown clock

Date	Mintage	F	VF	XF	Unc	BU
2005	50,000	—	—	—	—	45.00

KM# 263 10 DOLLARS
31.1050 g., 0.9990 Silver with gold inlay 0.9990 oz. ASW, 38.61 mm. **Ruler:** Elizabeth II **Subject:** FIFA World Cup **Rev:** Trophy

Date	Mintage	F	VF	XF	Unc	BU
2005	—	—	—	—	—	80.00

KM# 111 10 DOLLARS
1.2400 g., 0.9999 Gold 0.0399 oz. AGW **Ruler:** Elizabeth II **Subject:** 500th Anniversary Death of Christopher Columbus **Obv:** Crowned head right **Obv. Legend:** ELIZABETH II - FIJI **Rev:** Sailing ship "Santa Maria"

Date	Mintage	F	VF	XF	Unc	BU
2006 Proof	15,000	Value: 80.00				

KM# 235 10 DOLLARS
28.2800 g., 0.9250 Silver 0.8410 oz. ASW, 38.61 mm. **Ruler:** Elizabeth II **Subject:** James Watt **Obv:** Head in tiara right **Rev:** James Watt and steam engine

Date	Mintage	F	VF	XF	Unc	BU
2008 Proof	5,000	Value: 35.00				

KM# 236 10 DOLLARS
1.0000 g., 0.9999 Gold 0.0321 oz. AGW, 13.92 mm. **Ruler:** Elizabeth II **Subject:** Lapita art **Obv:** Head with Tiara right **Rev:** Artistic design

Date	Mintage	F	VF	XF	Unc	BU
2008 Proof	15,000	Value: 75.00				

KM# 125 10 DOLLARS
31.1050 g., 0.9990 Silver 0.9990 oz. ASW **Ruler:** Elizabeth II **Obv:** Crowned head right **Rev:** Yes we can!

Date	Mintage	F	VF	XF	Unc	BU
2009 Proof	—	Value: 50.00				

KM# 178 10 DOLLARS

28.2800 g., 0.9250 Silver 0.8410 oz. ASW, 38.61 mm. **Ruler:** Elizabeth II **Obv:** Head with tiara right **Rev:** Barak Obama at left

Date	Mintage	F	VF	XF	Unc	BU
2009 Proof	—	Value: 50.00				

KM# 277 10 DOLLARS

28.2800 g., 0.9250 Silver 0.8410 oz. ASW, 38.61 mm. **Ruler:** Elizabeth II **Rev:** Butterfly fish in color

Date	Mintage	F	VF	XF	Unc	BU
2009 Proof	—	Value: 45.00				

KM# 277a 10 DOLLARS

39.0000 g., 0.9160 Gold 1.1485 oz. AGW, 38.61 mm. **Ruler:** Elizabeth II **Rev:** Butterfly fish

Date	Mintage	F	VF	XF	Unc	BU
2009 Proof	—	Value: 2,100				

KM# 278 10 DOLLARS

28.2800 g., 0.9250 Silver 0.8410 oz. ASW, 38.61 mm. **Ruler:** Elizabeth II **Rev:** Imperial Angler fish in color

Date	Mintage	F	VF	XF	Unc	BU
2009 Proof	—	Value: 45.00				

KM# 278a 10 DOLLARS

39.0000 g., 0.9160 Gold 1.1485 oz. AGW, 38.61 mm. **Ruler:** Elizabeth II **Rev:** Imperial Angler

Date	Mintage	F	VF	XF	Unc	BU
2009 Proof	—	Value: 2,100				

KM# 279 10 DOLLARS

28.2800 g., 0.9250 Silver 0.8410 oz. ASW, 38.61 mm. **Ruler:** Elizabeth II **Rev:** Clown fish in color

Date	Mintage	F	VF	XF	Unc	BU
2009 Proof	—	Value: 45.00				

KM# 279a 10 DOLLARS

39.0000 g., 0.9160 Gold 1.1485 oz. AGW, 38.61 mm. **Ruler:** Elizabeth II **Rev:** Clown fish

Date	Mintage	F	VF	XF	Unc	BU
2009 Proof	—	Value: 2,100				

KM# 280 10 DOLLARS

28.2800 g., 0.9250 Silver 0.8410 oz. ASW, 38.61 mm. **Ruler:** Elizabeth II **Rev:** Flame dwarf angel fish in color

Date	Mintage	F	VF	XF	Unc	BU
2009 Proof	—	Value: 45.00				

KM# 280a 10 DOLLARS

39.0000 g., 0.9160 Gold 1.1485 oz. AGW, 38.61 mm. **Ruler:** Elizabeth II **Rev:** Flame dwarf angel fish

Date	Mintage	F	VF	XF	Unc	BU
2009 Proof	—	Value: 2,100				

KM# 281 10 DOLLARS

28.2800 g., 0.9250 Silver 0.8410 oz. ASW, 38.61 mm. **Ruler:** Elizabeth II **Rev:** Pallet surgeon fish in color

Date	Mintage	F	VF	XF	Unc	BU
2009 Proof	—	Value: 45.00				

KM# 281a 10 DOLLARS

39.0000 g., 0.9160 Gold 1.1485 oz. AGW, 38.61 mm. **Ruler:** Elizabeth II **Rev:** Pallet surgeon fish

Date	Mintage	F	VF	XF	Unc	BU
2009 Proof	—	Value: 2,100				

KM# 282a 10 DOLLARS

39.0000 g., 0.9160 Gold 1.1485 oz. AGW, 38.61 mm. **Ruler:** Elizabeth II **Rev:** Yellow nose surgeon fish

Date	Mintage	F	VF	XF	Unc	BU
2009 Proof	—	Value: 2,100				

KM# 282 10 DOLLARS

28.2800 g., 0.9250 Silver 0.8410 oz. ASW, 38.61 mm. **Ruler:** Elizabeth II **Rev:** Yellow nose surgeon fish in color

Date	Mintage	F	VF	XF	Unc	BU
2009 Proof	—	—	—	—	—	45.00

KM# 283 10 DOLLARS

28.2800 g., 0.9250 Silver 0.8410 oz. ASW, 38.61 mm. **Ruler:** Elizabeth II **Rev:** Cheetah

Date	Mintage	F	VF	XF	Unc	BU
2009 Proof	—	Value: 45.00				

KM# 283a 10 DOLLARS

39.0000 g., 0.9160 Gold 1.1485 oz. AGW, 38.61 mm. **Ruler:** Elizabeth II **Rev:** Cheetah

Date	Mintage	F	VF	XF	Unc	BU
2009 Proof	—	Value: 2,100				

KM# 284 10 DOLLARS

28.2800 g., 0.9250 Silver 0.8410 oz. ASW, 38.61 mm. **Ruler:** Elizabeth II **Rev:** Elephant

Date	Mintage	F	VF	XF	Unc	BU
2009 Proof	—	Value: 45.00				

KM# 284a 10 DOLLARS

39.0000 g., 0.9160 Gold 1.1485 oz. AGW, 38.61 mm. **Ruler:** Elizabeth II **Rev:** Elephant

Date	Mintage	F	VF	XF	Unc	BU
2009 Proof	—	Value: 2,100				

KM# 285a 10 DOLLARS

39.0000 g., 0.9160 Gold 1.1485 oz. AGW, 38.61 mm. **Ruler:** Elizabeth II **Rev:** Giraffe

Date	Mintage	F	VF	XF	Unc	BU
2009 Proof	—	Value: 2,100				

KM# 285 10 DOLLARS

28.2800 g., 0.9250 Silver 0.8410 oz. ASW, 38.61 mm. **Ruler:** Elizabeth II **Rev:** Giraffe

Date	Mintage	F	VF	XF	Unc	BU
2009 Proof	—	Value: 45.00				

KM# 286 10 DOLLARS

28.2800 g., 0.9250 Silver 0.8410 oz. ASW, 38.61 mm. **Ruler:** Elizabeth II **Rev:** Koi

Date	Mintage	F	VF	XF	Unc	BU
2009 Proof	—	Value: 45.00				

KM# 286a 10 DOLLARS

39.0000 g., 0.9160 Gold 1.1485 oz. AGW, 38.61 mm. **Ruler:** Elizabeth II **Rev:** Koi

Date	Mintage	F	VF	XF	Unc	BU
2009 Proof	—	Value: 2,100				

KM# 287 10 DOLLARS

28.2800 g., 0.9250 Silver 0.8410 oz. ASW, 38.61 mm. **Ruler:** Elizabeth II **Rev:** Leopard

Date	Mintage	F	VF	XF	Unc	BU
2009 Proof	—	Value: 45.00				

KM# 287a 10 DOLLARS

39.0000 g., 0.9160 Gold 1.1485 oz. AGW, 38.61 mm. **Ruler:** Elizabeth II **Rev:** Leopard

Date	Mintage	F	VF	XF	Unc	BU
2009 Proof	—	Value: 2,100				

KM# 288 10 DOLLARS

28.2800 g., 0.9250 Silver 0.8410 oz. ASW, 38.61 mm. **Ruler:** Elizabeth II **Rev:** Panda

Date	Mintage	F	VF	XF	Unc	BU
2009 Proof	—	Value: 45.00				

KM# 288a 10 DOLLARS

39.0000 g., 0.9160 Gold 1.1485 oz. AGW, 38.61 mm. **Ruler:** Elizabeth II **Rev:** Panda

Date	Mintage	F	VF	XF	Unc	BU
2009 Proof	—	Value: 2,100				

KM# 289 10 DOLLARS

28.2800 g., 0.9250 Silver 0.8410 oz. ASW, 38.61 mm. **Ruler:** Elizabeth II **Rev:** Tiger

Date	Mintage	F	VF	XF	Unc	BU
2009 Proof	—	Value: 45.00				

KM# 289a 10 DOLLARS

39.0000 g., 0.9160 Gold 1.1485 oz. AGW, 38.61 mm. **Ruler:** Elizabeth II **Rev:** Tiger

Date	Mintage	F	VF	XF	Unc	BU
2009 Proof	—	Value: 2,100				

KM# 290 10 DOLLARS

28.2800 g., 0.9250 Silver 0.8410 oz. ASW, 38.61 mm. **Ruler:** Elizabeth II **Rev:** Zebra

Date	Mintage	F	VF	XF	Unc	BU
2009 Proof	—	Value: 45.00				

KM# 290a 10 DOLLARS

39.0000 g., 0.9160 Gold 1.1485 oz. AGW, 38.61 mm. **Ruler:** Elizabeth II **Rev:** Zebra

Date	Mintage	F	VF	XF	Unc	BU
2009 Proof	—	Value: 2,100				

KM# 291 10 DOLLARS

Silver **Ruler:** Elizabeth II **Subject:** Wold Cup Soccer, South Africa

Date	Mintage	F	VF	XF	Unc	BU
2009 Proof	Est. 10,000	Value: 55.00				

KM# 292 10 DOLLARS

1.0000 g., 0.9990 Gold 0.0321 oz. AGW, 13.92 mm. **Ruler:** Elizabeth II **Subject:** World Cup Soccer, South Africa

Date	Mintage	F	VF	XF	Unc	BU
2009 Proof	Est. 5,000	Value: 70.00				

KM# 294 10 DOLLARS

28.2800 g., 0.9250 Silver 0.8410 oz. ASW, 38.61 mm. **Ruler:** Elizabeth II **Rev:** Mary and Christ child

Date	Mintage	F	VF	XF	Unc	BU
2009 Proof	—	Value: 45.00				

KM# 294a 10 DOLLARS

39.0000 g., 0.9160 Gold 1.1485 oz. AGW, 38.61 mm. **Ruler:** Elizabeth II **Rev:** Mary and Christ child

Date	Mintage	F	VF	XF	Unc	BU
2009 Proof	—	Value: 2,100				

KM# 216 10 DOLLARS

0.5000 g., 0.9990 Gold 0.0161 oz. AGW, 11 mm. **Ruler:** Elizabeth II **Obv:** Head in tiara right **Rev:** Sun, statue and symbol

Date	Mintage	F	VF	XF	Unc	BU
2010 Proof	2,000	Value: 40.00				

KM# 217 10 DOLLARS

0.5000 g., 0.9990 Gold 0.0161 oz. AGW, 11 mm. **Ruler:** Elizabeth II **Obv:** Head with tiara right **Rev:** Mercury, statue and symbol

Date	Mintage	F	VF	XF	Unc	BU
2010 Proof	2,000	Value: 40.00				

KM# 218 10 DOLLARS

0.5000 g., 0.9990 Gold 0.0161 oz. AGW, 11 mm. **Ruler:** Elizabeth II **Obv:** Head with tiara right **Rev:** Venus, statue and symbol

Date	Mintage	F	VF	XF	Unc	BU
2010 Proof	2,000	Value: 40.00				

KM# 219 10 DOLLARS

0.5000 g., 0.9990 Gold 0.0161 oz. AGW, 11 mm. **Ruler:** Elizabeth II **Obv:** Head with tiara right **Rev:** Earth, statue and symbol

Date	Mintage	F	VF	XF	Unc	BU
2010 Proof	2,000	Value: 40.00				

KM# 220 10 DOLLARS

0.5000 g., 0.9990 Gold 0.0161 oz. AGW, 11 mm. **Ruler:** Elizabeth II **Obv:** Head with tiara right **Rev:** Mars, statue and symbol

Date	Mintage	F	VF	XF	Unc	BU
2010 Proof	2,000	Value: 40.00				

KM# 221 10 DOLLARS

0.5000 g., 0.9990 Gold 0.0161 oz. AGW, 11 mm. **Ruler:** Elizabeth II **Obv:** Head with tiara right **Rev:** Jupiter, statue and symbol

Date	Mintage	F	VF	XF	Unc	BU
2010 Proof	2,000	Value: 40.00				

KM# 222 10 DOLLARS

0.5000 g., 0.9990 Gold 0.0161 oz. AGW, 11 mm. **Ruler:** Elizabeth II **Obv:** Head with tiara right **Rev:** Saturn, statue and symbol

Date	Mintage	F	VF	XF	Unc	BU
2010 Proof	2,000	Value: 40.00				

KM# 223 10 DOLLARS

0.5000 g., 0.9990 Gold 0.0161 oz. AGW, 11 mm. **Ruler:** Elizabeth II **Obv:** Head with tiara right **Rev:** Uranus, statue and symbol

Date	Mintage	F	VF	XF	Unc	BU
2010 Proof	2,000	Value: 40.00				

KM# 224 10 DOLLARS

0.5000 g., 0.9990 Gold 0.0161 oz. AGW, 11 mm. **Ruler:** Elizabeth II **Obv:** Head with tiara right **Rev:** Neptune, statue and symbol

Date	Mintage	F	VF	XF	Unc	BU
2010 Proof	2,000	Value: 40.00				

KM# 225 10 DOLLARS

0.5000 g., 0.9990 Gold 0.0161 oz. AGW, 11 mm. **Ruler:** Elizabeth II **Obv:** Head with tiara right **Rev:** Pluto, statue and symbol

Date	Mintage	F	VF	XF	Unc	BU
2010 Proof	2,000	Value: 40.00				

KM# 239 10 DOLLARS

28.2800 g., 0.9250 Silver 0.8410 oz. ASW, 38.61 mm. **Ruler:** Elizabeth II **Subject:** John Bull, steam locomotive **Obv:** Head with tiara right **Rev:** Steam locomotive left

Date	Mintage	F	VF	XF	Unc	BU
2010 Proof	5,000	Value: 35.00				

KM# 241 10 DOLLARS

28.2800 g., 0.9250 Silver 0.8410 oz. ASW, 38.61 mm. **Ruler:** Elizabeth II **Subject:** London Olympics, 2012 **Obv:** Head with tiara right **Rev:** Triathlon sports

Date	Mintage	F	VF	XF	Unc	BU
2010 Proof	5,000	Value: 35.00				

KM# 295 10 DOLLARS

0.5000 g., 0.9990 Gold 0.0161 oz. AGW, 11 mm. **Ruler:** Elizabeth II **Rev:** Eye of Horus

Date	Mintage	F	VF	XF	Unc	BU
2010 Proof	—	Value: 35.00				

KM# 296 10 DOLLARS

0.5000 g., 0.9990 Gold 0.0161 oz. AGW, 11 mm. **Ruler:** Elizabeth II **Rev:** Gold mask of Tutanchamun

Date	Mintage	F	VF	XF	Unc	BU
2010 Proof	—	Value: 35.00				

KM# 297 10 DOLLARS

0.5000 g., 0.9990 Gold 0.0161 oz. AGW, 11 mm. **Ruler:** Elizabeth II **Rev:** Egyptian dog-headed god

Date	Mintage	F	VF	XF	Unc	BU
2010 Proof	—	Value: 35.00				

KM# 243 10 DOLLARS

28.2800 g., 0.9250 Silver 0.8410 oz. ASW, 38.61 mm. **Ruler:** Elizabeth II **Subject:** Etrich II Taube **Obv:** Head with tiara right **Rev:** Early experimental aircraft

Date	Mintage	F	VF	XF	Unc	BU
2011 Proof	5,000	Value: 35.00				

KM# 245 10 DOLLARS
28.2800 g., 0.9250 Silver partially gilt 0.8410 oz. ASW, 38.6 mm. **Ruler:** Elizabeth II **Subject:** Lady Diana Spencer **Obv:** Head with tiara right **Rev:** Bust at right, gilt rose at left

Date	Mintage	F	VF	XF	Unc	BU
2011 Proof	7,500	Value: 35.00				

KM# 247 10 DOLLARS
28.2800 g., 0.9250 Silver 0.8410 oz. ASW, 38.61 mm. **Ruler:** Elizabeth II **Subject:** London Olympics, 2012 **Obv:** Head with tiara right **Rev:** Rowing

Date	Mintage	F	VF	XF	Unc	BU
2011 Proof	5,000	Value: 35.00				

KM# 249 10 DOLLARS
28.2800 g., 0.9250 Silver selectively gilt 0.8410 oz. ASW, 38.6 mm. **Ruler:** Elizabeth II **Subject:** Lady Diana **Obv:** Head with tiara right **Rev:** Diana with Prince William and Prince Harry

Date	Mintage	F	VF	XF	Unc	BU
2011 Proof	7,500	Value: 35.00				

KM# 250 10 DOLLARS
28.2800 g., 0.9250 Silver partially gilt 0.8410 oz. ASW, 38.6 mm. **Ruler:** Elizabeth II **Subject:** Princess Diana **Obv:** Head with tiara right **Rev:** Diana and AIDS baby, gilt rose at left

Date	Mintage	F	VF	XF	Unc	BU
2011 Proof	7,500	Value: 35.00				

KM# 251 10 DOLLARS
28.2800 g., 0.9250 Silver partially gilt 0.8410 oz. ASW, 38.6 mm. **Ruler:** Elizabeth II **Subject:** Lady Diana **Obv:** Head with tiara right **Rev:** Bust left, gilt rose to left

Date	Mintage	F	VF	XF	Unc	BU
2011 Proof	7,500	Value: 35.00				

KM# 298 10 DOLLARS
0.5000 g., 0.9990 Gold 0.0161 oz. AGW, 11 mm. **Ruler:** Elizabeth II **Rev:** Matterhorn

Date	Mintage	F	VF	XF	Unc	BU
2011 Proof	Est. 5,000	Value: 35.00				

KM# 299 10 DOLLARS
0.5000 g., 0.9990 Gold 0.0161 oz. AGW, 11 mm. **Ruler:** Elizabeth II **Rev:** Bay of Halong, Viet Nam

Date	Mintage	F	VF	XF	Unc	BU
2011 Proof	Est. 5,000	Value: 35.00				

KM# 300 10 DOLLARS
0.5000 g., 0.9990 Gold 0.0161 oz. AGW, 11 mm. **Ruler:** Elizabeth II **Rev:** Amazon in Brazil

Date	Mintage	F	VF	XF	Unc	BU
2011 Proof	Est. 5,000	Value: 35.00				

KM# 301 10 DOLLARS
0.5000 g., 0.9990 Gold 0.0161 oz. AGW, 11 mm. **Ruler:** Elizabeth II **Rev:** Monument Valley in the USA

Date	Mintage	F	VF	XF	Unc	BU
2011 Proof	Est. 5,000	Value: 35.00				

KM# 302 10 DOLLARS
0.5000 g., 0.9990 Gold 0.0161 oz. AGW, 11 mm. **Ruler:** Elizabeth II **Rev:** Pamukkale in Turkey

Date	Mintage	F	VF	XF	Unc	BU
2011 Proof	Est. 5,000	Value: 35.00				

KM# 303 10 DOLLARS
0.5000 g., 0.9990 Gold 0.0161 oz. AGW, 11 mm. **Ruler:** Elizabeth II **Rev:** Mesa in South Africa

Date	Mintage	F	VF	XF	Unc	BU
2011 Proof	Est. 5,000	Value: 35.00				

KM# 304 10 DOLLARS
0.5000 g., 0.9990 Gold 0.0161 oz. AGW, 11 mm. **Ruler:** Elizabeth II **Rev:** Namibia feature

Date	Mintage	F	VF	XF	Unc	BU
2011 Proof	—	Value: 35.00				

KM# 305 10 DOLLARS
0.5000 g., 0.9990 Gold 0.0161 oz. AGW, 11 mm. **Ruler:** Elizabeth II **Subject:** Euro motif **Rev:** Map of Estonia

Date	Mintage	F	VF	XF	Unc	BU
2011 Proof	—	Value: 35.00				

KM# 198 10 DOLLARS
Silver, 38.61 mm. **Ruler:** Elizabeth II **Obv:** Jewels at center **Rev:** Sunset

Date	Mintage	F	VF	XF	Unc	BU
2012 Proof	—	Value: 50.00				

KM# 199 10 DOLLARS
Silver, 38.6 mm. **Ruler:** Elizabeth II **Obv:** Foral with blue jewel insert as cut out **Rev:** Flowers around blue jewel insert

Date	Mintage	F	VF	XF	Unc	BU
2012 Proof	—	Value: 50.00				

KM# 226 10 DOLLARS
20.0000 g., 0.9250 Silver 0.5948 oz. ASW, 54x32 mm. **Ruler:** Elizabeth II **Obv:** Head with tiara right, insert **Rev:** Maya design, insert **Shape:** Horizontal oval

Date	Mintage	F	VF	XF	Unc	BU
2012	1,000	—	—	—	—	75.00

KM# 227 10 DOLLARS
20.0000 g., 0.9250 Silver 0.5948 oz. ASW, 32x54 mm. **Ruler:** Elizabeth II **Obv:** Head in tiara right, insert **Rev:** Atlas holding up world on shoulders, insert **Shape:** Vertical oval

Date	Mintage	F	VF	XF	Unc	BU
2012	1,000	—	—	—	—	75.00

KM# 230 10 DOLLARS
31.1050 g., 0.9990 Silver 0.9990 oz. ASW, 40 mm. **Ruler:** Elizabeth II **Subject:** Year of the Dragon **Obv:** Head with tiara right **Rev:** Gilt dragon and pearl

Date	Mintage	F	VF	XF	Unc	BU
2012 Proof	8,888	Value: 100				

KM# 253 10 DOLLARS
20.0000 g., 0.9990 Silver 0.6423 oz. ASW **Ruler:** Elizabeth II **Subject:** End of World War I **Rev:** Fireworks in color over Kremlin skyline

Date	Mintage	F	VF	XF	Unc	BU
2012 Proof	—	Value: 100				

KM# 307 10 DOLLARS
20.0000 g., 0.9250 Silver 0.5948 oz. ASW, 54x32 mm. **Ruler:** Elizabeth II **Subject:** Aztec Calender **Rev:** Aztec symbols, circle of Chaos in color **Shape:** Oval

Date	Mintage	F	VF	XF	Unc	BU
2012 Proof	Est. 1,000	Value: 125				

KM# 256 20 DOLLARS
Platinum APW **Ruler:** Elizabeth II **Subject:** Elizabeth II, 50th Anniversary of Reign **Rev:** Draped sword

Date	Mintage	F	VF	XF	Unc	BU
2002 Proof	—	—	—	—	—	—

KM# 257 20 DOLLARS
Platinum APW **Ruler:** Elizabeth II **Subject:** Elizabeth II, 50th Anniversary of Reign **Rev:** Boys Choir in Westminister Abbey

Date	Mintage	F	VF	XF	Unc	BU
2002 Proof	—	—	—	—	—	—

KM# 231 20 DOLLARS
62.2000 g., 0.9990 Silver 1.9977 oz. ASW, 50.2 mm. **Ruler:** Elizabeth II **Subject:** Year of the Dragon **Obv:** Head with tiara right **Rev:** Fire Red Dragon with ruby insert

Date	Mintage	F	VF	XF	Unc	BU
2012 Proof	888	Value: 250				

KM# 112 25 DOLLARS
155.5000 g., 0.9990 Silver 4.9942 oz. ASW **Ruler:** Elizabeth II **Obv:** Crowned head right **Obv. Legend:** ELIZABETH II - FIJI **Rev:** Sailing ship "Vostok"

Date	Mintage	F	VF	XF	Unc	BU
2002 Proof	—	Value: 200				

KM# 264 50 DOLLARS
155.0000 g., 0.9990 Silver 4.9782 oz. ASW, 65 mm. **Ruler:** Elizabeth II **Rev:** Marine life - coral reef

Date	Mintage	F	VF	XF	Unc	BU
2005 Proof	500	Value: 275				

KM# 244 50 DOLLARS
7.7800 g., 0.9999 Gold 0.2501 oz. AGW, 22 mm. **Ruler:** Elizabeth II **Subject:** Diana Princess of Wales **Obv:** Head with tiara right **Rev:** Bust right, while colored rose at right

Date	Mintage	F	VF	XF	Unc	BU
2011 Proof	Est. 3,000	Value: 475				

KM# 248 50 DOLLARS
7.7700 g., 0.5833 Gold with a 24 kt. gold plating 0.1457 oz. AGW, 25 mm. **Ruler:** Elizabeth II **Subject:** London Olympics, 2012 **Obv:** Head with tiara right **Rev:** Rowing

Date	Mintage	F	VF	XF	Unc	BU
2011 Proof	1,000	Value: 325				

KM# 196 50 DOLLARS
155.5000 g., 0.9990 Silver 4.9942 oz. ASW, 65 mm. **Ruler:** Elizabeth II **Subject:** Year of the Dragon **Obv:** Head crowned right **Rev:** Dragon etched in mother of pearl

Date	Mintage	F	VF	XF	Unc	BU
2012 Proof	750	Value: 400				

KM# 197 50 DOLLARS
155.5000 g., 0.9990 Silver 4.9942 oz. ASW, 65 mm. **Ruler:** Elizabeth II **Obv:** Head crowned right **Rev:** Titanic etched mother of pearl

Date	Mintage	F	VF	XF	Unc	BU
2012 Proof	750	Value: 450				

KM# 228 50 DOLLARS
62.2000 g., 0.9990 Silver 1.9977 oz. ASW, 65 mm. **Ruler:** Elizabeth II **Obv:** Head in tiara right **Rev:** Tutankhamun in color

Date	Mintage	F	VF	XF	Unc	BU
2012 Proof	999	Value: 200				

KM# 229 50 DOLLARS
62.2000 g., 0.9990 Silver 1.9977 oz. ASW, 65 mm. **Ruler:** Elizabeth II **Obv:** Head in tiara right **Rev:** Neferititi head in color

Date	Mintage	F	VF	XF	Unc	BU
2012 Proof	999	Value: 200				

KM# 306 50 DOLLARS
155.5000 g., 0.9990 Silver 4.9942 oz. ASW, 65 mm. **Ruler:** Elizabeth II **Rev:** Dragon with the pearl of wisdom in gold

Date	Mintage	F	VF	XF	Unc	BU
2012 Proof	888	Value: 250				

KM# 99 100 DOLLARS
7.7800 g., 0.5850 Gold 0.1463 oz. AGW **Ruler:** Elizabeth II **Subject:** 2006 FIFA World Cup - Germany **Obv:** Crowned head right, date at right **Rev:** World Cup **Edge:** Reeded

Date	Mintage	F	VF	XF	Unc	BU
2003 Proof	25,000	Value: 275				

SILVER BULLION COINAGE

KM# 211 DOLLAR
15.5000 g., 0.9990 Silver 0.4978 oz. ASW, 32.5 mm. **Ruler:** Elizabeth II **Obv:** Head with crown right **Rev:** Hawksbill turtle

Date	Mintage	F	VF	XF	Unc	BU
2012 Prooflike	—	—	—	—	—	22.50

KM# 151 2 DOLLARS
31.1050 g., 0.9990 Silver 0.9990 oz. ASW, 40.5 mm. **Ruler:** Elizabeth II **Rev:** Hawksbill Taku Turtle

Date	Mintage	F	VF	XF	Unc	BU
2010 Prooflike	—	—	—	—	—	50.00
2011 Prooflike	—	—	—	—	—	50.00
2012 Prooflike	—	—	—	—	—	50.00

KM# 151a 2 DOLLARS
31.1050 g., 0.9990 Silver partially gilt 0.9990 oz. ASW, 40 mm. **Ruler:** Elizabeth II **Rev:** Hawksbill Taku Turtle, gilt

Date	Mintage	F	VF	XF	Unc	BU
2010 Proof	Est. 5,000	Value: 65.00				
2012 Proof	—	Value: 65.00				

KM# 165 2 DOLLARS
31.1050 g., 0.9990 Silver partially gilt 0.9990 oz. ASW, 40.7 mm. **Ruler:** Elizabeth II **Rev:** Pacific Swordfish gilt

Date	Mintage	F	VF	XF	Unc	BU
2011 Prooflike	5,000	—	—	—	—	80.00

KM# 232 10 DOLLARS
155.5000 g., 0.9990 Silver 4.9942 oz. ASW **Ruler:** Elizabeth II **Obv:** Head with tiara right **Rev:** Hawkbill turtle

Date	Mintage	F	VF	XF	Unc	BU
2012 Prooflike	—	—	—	—	—	185

GOLD BULLION COINAGE

KM# 136 PACIFIC SOVEREIGN
31.1050 g., 0.9990 Gold 0.9990 oz. AGW, 32 mm. **Ruler:** Elizabeth II **Rev:** Beach scene, two palm trees at right

Date	Mintage	F	VF	XF	Unc	BU
2009 Proof-like	—	—	—	—	—	1,850

KM# 215 PACIFIC SOVEREIGN
31.1350 g., 0.9990 Gold 1.0000 oz. AGW, 32.1 mm. **Ruler:** Elizabeth II **Obv:** Head crowned right **Rev:** Beach scene, one palm tree at left

Date	Mintage	F	VF	XF	Unc	BU
2011 Proof	—	Value: 1,850				

FINLAND

The Republic of Finland, the third most northerly state of the European continent, has an area of 130,559 sq. mi. (338,127 sq. km.) and a population of 5.1 million. Capital: Helsinki. Lumbering, shipbuilding, metal and woodworking are the leading industries. Paper, timber, wood pulp, plywood and metal products are exported.

MONETARY SYSTEM
100 Pennia = 1 Markka until 2001
100 Euro Cent = 1 Euro 2001 -

MINT MARKS
H - Birmingham 1921
Heart (h) - Copenhagen 1922
No mm – Helsinki
M – 1987-2006
FI – FINLAND – 2007-
Rampant lion in a circle – 2010-

MINT OFFICIALS' INITIALS

Letter	Date	Name
J-M	2002	Toivo Jaatinen & Raimo Makkonen
L-M	2000-03	Maija Lavonen & Raimo Makkonen
K-M	2004	Heli Kauhanen & Raimo Makkonen
K-M	2005-2006	Tapio Kettunen & Raimo Makkonen
M-M	2002-2006	Pertti Mäkinen & Raimo Makkonen
N-M	2001	Antti Neuvonen & Raimo Makkonen
P-M	2003	Matti Peltokangas & Raimo Makkonen
P-M	2001, 2005-2007	Reijo Paavilainen & Raimo Makkonen
S-M	2003	Anneli Sigriläinen & Raimo Makkonen
VV-M	2002	Erkki Vainio & Hannu Veijalainen & Raimo Makkonen

REPUBLIC

REFORM COINAGE

KM# 65 10 PENNIA
1.8000 g., Copper-Nickel, 16.3 mm. **Obv:** Flower pods and stems, date at right **Rev:** Denomination to right of honeycombs **Designer:** Antti Neuvonen

Date	Mintage	F	VF	XF	Unc	BU
2001 M	25,000,000	—	—	—	1.00	1.50
2001 M Proof	—	Value: 7.00				

KM# 66 50 PENNIA
3.3000 g., Copper-Nickel, 19.7 mm. **Obv:** Polar bear, date below **Rev:** Denomination above flower heads **Edge:** Reeded **Designer:** Antti Neuvonen

Date	Mintage	F	VF	XF	Unc	BU
2001 M	200,000	—	—	0.20	1.00	1.50
2001 M Proof	—	Value: 8.00				

KM# 76 MARKKA

5.0000 g., Aluminum-Bronze, 22.2 mm. **Obv:** Rampant lion left within circle, date below **Rev:** Ornaments flank denomination within circle

Date	Mintage	F	VF	XF	Unc	BU
2001 M	200,000	—	—	0.35	0.75	1.00
2001 M Proof	—	Value: 10.00				

KM# 95 MARKKA

8.6400 g., 0.7500 Gold 0.2083 oz. AGW, 22 mm. **Subject:** Last Markka Coin **Obv:** Rampant lion with sword left **Rev:** Stylized tree with roots **Edge:** Reeded **Designer:** Reijo Paavilainen

Date	Mintage	F	VF	XF	Unc	BU
2001M P-M Proof	55,000	Value: 375				

KM# 106 MARKKA

6.1000 g., Copper-Nickel, 24 mm. **Subject:** Remembrance Markka **Obv:** Rampant lion with sword left **Rev:** Denomination and pine tree **Edge:** Plain **Designer:** Antti Neuvonen **Note:** This coin is encased in acrylic resin and sealed in a display card.

Date	Mintage	F	VF	XF	Unc	BU
2001M N-M	500,000	—	—	—	5.00	6.50

KM# 73 5 MARKKAA

5.5000 g., Copper-Aluminum-Nickel, 24.5 mm. **Obv:** Lake Saimaa ringed seal, date below **Rev:** Denomination, dragonfly and lily pad leaves

Date	Mintage	F	VF	XF	Unc	BU
2001 M	200,000	—	—	—	3.00	4.50
2001 M Proof	—	Value: 12.00				

KM# 77 10 MARKKAA

8.8000 g., Bi-Metallic Brass center in Copper-Nickel ring, 27.25 mm. **Obv:** Capercaillie bird within circle, date above **Rev:** Denomination and branches

Date	Mintage	F	VF	XF	Unc	BU
2001 M	200,000	—	—	3.00	5.00	6.00
2001 M Proof	—	Value: 18.00				

KM# 96 25 MARKKAA

20.2000 g., Bi-Metallic Brass center in Copper-Nickel ring, 35 mm. **Subject:** First Nordic Ski Championship, "Lahti 2001" **Obv:** Stylized woman's face **Rev:** Female torso, landscape **Edge:** Plain **Designer:** Jarkko Roth

Date	Mintage	F	VF	XF	Unc	BU
2001M Prooflike	100,000	—	—	25.00	30.00	35.00

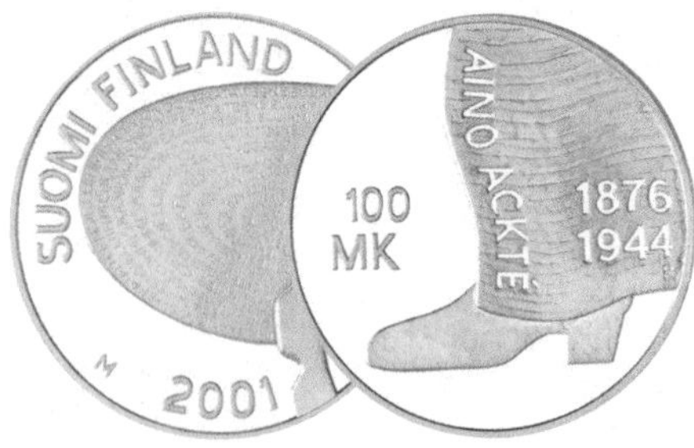

KM# 97 100 MARKKAA

31.0000 g., 0.9250 Silver 0.9219 oz. ASW, 35 mm. **Subject:** Aino Ackte **Obv:** Partial portrait **Rev:** High heel boot and trouser bottom **Edge:** Plain **Designer:** Timo Rytkönen.

Date	Mintage	F	VF	XF	Unc	BU
2001M	33,000	—	—	—	32.00	45.00
2001M Proof	12,000	Value: 60.00				

EURO COINAGE

European Union Issues

KM# 98 EURO CENT

2.3000 g., Copper Plated Steel, 16.25 mm. **Obv:** Rampant lion left surrounded by stars, date at left **Rev:** Denomination and globe **Edge:** Plain

Date	Mintage	F	VF	XF	Unc	BU
2001M	500,000	—	—	—	10.00	—
2001M Proof	15,000	—	—	—	—	—
2002M	659,000	—	—	—	5.00	—
2002M Proof	13,000	Value: 15.00				
2003M	6,790,000	—	—	—	1.00	—
2003M Proof	14,500	Value: 15.00				
2004M	9,690,000	—	—	—	1.00	—
2004M Proof	5,000	Value: 15.00				
2005M	5,800,000	—	—	—	1.00	—
2005M Proof	3,000	Value: 15.00				
2006M	4,000,000	—	—	—	1.00	—
2006M Proof	3,300	Value: 15.00				
2007FI	3,000,000	—	—	—	1.00	—
2007FI Proof	—	Value: 15.00				
2008FI	1,500,000	—	—	—	1.00	—
2008FI Proof	2,500	Value: 15.00				
2009FI	—	—	—	—	1.00	—
2009FI Proof	2,500	Value: 15.00				
2010FI	—	—	—	—	1.00	—
2010FI Proof	2,000	Value: 15.00				
2011FI	—	—	—	—	1.00	—
2011FI Proof	—	Value: 15.00				
2012FI	—	—	—	—	1.00	—
2012FI Proof	—	Value: 15.00				
2013FI	—	—	—	—	1.00	—
2013FI Proof	—	Value: 15.00				

KM# 99 2 EURO CENT

3.0600 g., Copper Plated Steel, 18.75 mm. **Obv:** Rampant lion surrounded by stars, date at left **Rev:** Denomination and globe **Edge:** Grooved

Date	Mintage	F	VF	XF	Unc	BU
2001M	500,000	—	—	—	10.00	—
2001M Proof	15,000	Value: 15.00				
2002M	659,000	—	—	—	5.00	—
2002M Proof	13,000	Value: 15.00				
2003M	6,790,000	—	—	—	2.00	—
2003M Proof	14,500	Value: 15.00				
2004M	8,024,000	—	—	—	2.00	—
2004M Proof	5,000	Value: 15.00				
2005M	5,800,000	—	—	—	2.50	—
2005M Proof	3,000	Value: 15.00				
2006M	4,000,000	—	—	—	2.00	—
2006M Proof	3,300	Value: 15.00				
2007FI	3,000,000	—	—	—	2.00	—
2007FI Proof	—	Value: 15.00				
2008FI	1,500,000	—	—	—	2.00	—
2008FI Proof	2,500	Value: 15.00				
2009FI	—	—	—	—	2.00	—
2009FI Proof	2,500	Value: 15.00				
2010FI	—	—	—	—	2.00	—
2010FI Proof	2,000	Value: 15.00				
2011FI	—	—	—	—	3.00	—
2011FI Proof	—	Value: 15.00				
2012FI	—	—	—	—	3.00	—
2012FI Proof	—	Value: 15.00				
2013FI	—	—	—	—	3.00	—
2013FI Proof	—	Value: 15.00				

KM# 100 5 EURO CENT

3.9200 g., Copper Plated Steel, 21.25 mm. **Obv:** Rampant lion left surrounded by stars, date at left **Rev:** Denomination and globe **Edge:** Plain

Date	Mintage	F	VF	XF	Unc	BU
2001M	213,756,000	—	—	—	0.50	—
2001M Proof	15,000	Value: 15.00				
2002M	101,824,000	—	—	—	0.50	—
2002M Proof	13,000	Value: 15.00				
2003M	790,000	—	—	—	2.00	—
2003M Proof	14,500	Value: 15.00				
2004M	629,000	—	—	—	2.00	—
2004M Proof	5,000	Value: 15.00				
2005M	800,000	—	—	—	2.00	—
2005M Proof	3,000	Value: 15.00				
2006M	1,000,000	—	—	—	1.00	—
2006M Proof	3,000	Value: 15.00				
2007FI	1,000,000	—	—	—	1.00	—
2007FI Proof	—	Value: 15.00				
2008FI	1,000,000	—	—	—	1.00	—
2008FI Proof	2,500	Value: 15.00				
2009FI	—	—	—	—	1.00	—
2009FI Proof	2,500	Value: 15.00				
2010FI	—	—	—	—	1.00	—
2010FI Proof	2,000	Value: 15.00				
2011FI	—	—	—	—	1.00	—
2011FI Proof	—	Value: 15.00				
2012FI	—	—	—	—	1.00	—
2012FI Proof	—	Value: 15.00				
2013FI	—	—	—	—	1.00	—
2013FI Proof	—	Value: 15.00				

KM# 101 10 EURO CENT

4.1000 g., Brass, 19.75 mm. **Obv:** Rampant lion left surrounded by stars, date at left **Rev:** Denomination and map **Edge:** Reeded

Date	Mintage	F	VF	XF	Unc	BU
2001M	14,730,000	—	—	—	10.00	—
2001M Proof	15,000	Value: 18.00				
2002M	1,499,000	—	—	—	10.00	—
2002M Proof	13,000	Value: 18.00				
2003M	790,000	—	—	—	5.00	—
2003M Proof	14,500	Value: 18.00				
2004M	629,000	—	—	—	5.00	—
2004M Proof	5,000	Value: 18.00				
2005M	800,000	—	—	—	3.00	—
2005M Proof	3,000	Value: 18.00				
2006M	1,000,000	—	—	—	3.00	—
2006M Proof	3,300	Value: 18.00				

KM# 126 10 EURO CENT

4.1000 g., Brass, 19.75 mm. **Obv:** Rampant lion surrounded by stars **Rev:** Relief map of Western Europe, stars, lines and value **Edge:** Reeded

Date	Mintage	F	VF	XF	Unc	BU
2007FI	1,000,000	—	—	—	2.50	—
2007FI Proof	—	Value: 18.00				
2008FI	1,000,000	—	—	—	2.50	—
2008FI Proof	2,500	Value: 18.00				
2009FI	—	—	—	—	2.50	—
2009FI Proof	2,500	Value: 18.00				
2010FI	—	—	—	—	2.50	—
2010FI Proof	2,000	Value: 18.00				
2011FI	—	—	—	—	2.50	—
2011FI Proof	—	Value: 18.00				
2012FI	—	—	—	—	2.50	—
2012FI Proof	—	Value: 18.00				
2013FI	—	—	—	—	2.50	—
2013FI Proof	—	Value: 18.00				

KM# 102 20 EURO CENT

5.7400 g., Brass, 22.25 mm. **Obv:** Rampant lion left surrounded by stars, date at left **Rev:** Denomination and map **Edge:** Notched

Date	Mintage	F	VF	XF	Unc	BU
2001M	121,763,000	—	—	—	2.00	—
2001M Proof	15,000	Value: 20.00				

Date	Mintage	F	VF	XF	Unc	BU
2002M	100,759,000	—	—	—	2.00	—
2002M Proof	13,000	Value: 20.00				
2003M	790,000	—	—	—	3.00	—
2003M Proof	14,500	Value: 20.00				
2004M	629,000	—	—	—	3.00	—
2004M Proof	5,000	Value: 20.00				
2005M	800,000	—	—	—	3.00	—
2005M Proof	3,000	Value: 20.00				
2006M	1,000,000	—	—	—	2.00	—
2006M Proof	3,300	Value: 20.00				

KM# 127 20 EURO CENT

5.7400 g., Brass, 22.25 mm. **Obv:** Rampant lion surrounded by stars **Rev:** Relief map of Western Europe, stars, lines and value **Edge:** Notched

Date	Mintage	F	VF	XF	Unc	BU
2007FI	1,000,000	—	—	—	2.00	—
2007FI Proof	—	Value: 20.00				
2008FI	1,000,000	—	—	—	2.00	—
2008FI Proof	2,500	Value: 20.00				
2009FI	—	—	—	—	2.00	—
2009FI Proof	2,500	Value: 20.00				
2010FI	—	—	—	—	1.75	—
2010FI Proof	2,000	Value: 20.00				
2011FI	—	—	—	—	1.75	—
2011FI Proof	—	Value: 20.00				
2012FI	—	—	—	—	1.75	—
2012FI Proof	—	Value: 20.00				
2013FI	—	—	—	—	1.75	—
2013FI Proof	—	Value: 20.00				

KM# 103 50 EURO CENT

7.8000 g., Brass, 24.25 mm. **Obv:** Rampant lion left surrounded by stars, date at left **Rev:** Denomination and map **Edge:** Reeded

Date	Mintage	F	VF	XF	Unc	BU
2001M	4,432,000	—	—	—	5.00	—
2001M Proof	15,000	Value: 22.00				
2002M	1,147,000	—	—	—	10.00	—
2002M Proof	13,000	Value: 22.00				
2003M	790,000	—	—	—	5.00	—
2003M Proof	14,500	Value: 22.00				
2004M	629,000	—	—	—	5.00	—
2004M Proof	5,000	Value: 22.00				
2005M	4,800,000	—	—	—	5.00	—
2005M Proof	3,000	Value: 22.00				
2006M	6,850,000	—	—	—	3.00	—
2006M Proof	3,300	Value: 22.00				

KM# 128 50 EURO CENT

7.8000 g., Brass, 24.25 mm. **Obv:** Rampant lion surrounded by stars **Rev:** Relief map of Western Europe, stars, lines and value **Edge:** Reeded

Date	Mintage	F	VF	XF	Unc	BU
2007FI	1,000,000	—	—	—	3.00	—
2007FI Proof	—	Value: 22.00				
2008FI	8,000,000	—	—	—	3.00	—
2008FI Proof	2,500	Value: 22.00				
2009FI	—	—	—	—	3.00	—
2009FI Proof	2,500	Value: 22.00				
2010FI	—	—	—	—	3.00	—
2010FI Proof	2,000	Value: 22.00				
2011FI	—	—	—	—	5.00	—
2011FI Proof	—	Value: 22.00				
2012FI	—	—	—	—	3.00	—
2012FI Proof	—	Value: 22.00				
2013FI	—	—	—	—	5.00	—
2013FI Proof	—	Value: 22.00				

KM# 104 EURO

7.5000 g., Bi-Metallic Copper-Nickel center in Nickel-Brass ring, 23.25 mm. **Obv:** 2 flying swans, date below, surrounded by stars on outer ring **Rev:** Denomination and map **Edge:** Segmented reeding

Date	Mintage	F	VF	XF	Unc	BU
2001M	13,862,000	—	—	—	5.00	—
2001M Proof	15,000	Value: 25.00				
2002M	14,114,000	—	—	—	5.00	—
2002M Proof	13,000	Value: 25.00				
2003M	790,000	—	—	—	10.00	—
2003M Proof	14,500	Value: 25.00				
2004M	5,529,000	—	—	—	6.50	—
2004M Proof	5,000	Value: 25.00				
2005M	7,935,000	—	—	—	6.50	—
2005M Proof	3,000	Value: 25.00				
2006M	1,705,000	—	—	—	5.00	—
2006M Proof	3,300	Value: 25.00				

KM# 129 EURO

7.5000 g., Bi-Metallic Copper-Nickel center in Nickel-Brass ring, 23.25 mm. **Obv:** 2 flying swans surrounded by stars on outer ring **Rev:** Relief map of western Europe, stars, lines and value **Edge:** Segmented reeding

Date	Mintage	F	VF	XF	Unc	BU
2007FI	1,000,000	—	—	—	5.00	—
2007FI Proof	—	Value: 25.00				
2008FI	1,000,000	—	—	—	5.00	—
2008FI Proof	2,500	Value: 25.00				
2009FI	—	—	—	—	5.00	—
2009FI Proof	2,500	Value: 25.00				
2010FI	—	—	—	—	5.00	—
2010FI Proof	2,000	Value: 25.00				
2011FI	—	—	—	—	6.50	—
2011FI Proof	—	Value: 25.00				
2012FI	—	—	—	—	6.50	—
2012FI Proof	—	Value: 25.00				
2013FI	—	—	—	—	6.50	—
2013FI Proof	—	Value: 25.00				

KM# 105 2 EURO

8.5000 g., Bi-Metallic Nickel-Brass center in Copper-Nickel ring, 25.75 mm. **Obv:** 2 cloudberry flowers surrounded by stars on outer ring **Rev:** Denomination and map **Edge:** Reeded and lettered **Edge Lettering:** SUOMI FINLAND

Date	Mintage	F	VF	XF	Unc	BU
2001M	29,132,000	—	—	—	5.00	—
2001M Proof	15,000	Value: 30.00				
2002M	1,386,000	—	—	—	15.00	—
2002M Proof	13,000	Value: 30.00				
2003M	9,080,000	—	—	—	7.50	—
2003M Proof	14,500	Value: 30.00				
2004M	10,029,000	—	—	—	7.00	—
2004M Proof	5,000	Value: 30.00				
2005M	10,800,000	—	—	—	7.00	—
2005M Proof	3,000	Value: 30.00				
2006M	11,000,000	—	—	—	5.00	—
2006M Proof	3,300	Value: 30.00				

KM# 114 2 EURO

8.5000 g., Bi-Metallic Nickel-Brass center in Copper-Nickel ring, 25.75 mm. **Subject:** EU Expansion **Obv:** Stylized flower **Rev:** Denomination and map **Edge:** Reeded and lettered

Date	Mintage	F	VF	XF	Unc	BU
2004M M	1,000,000	—	—	—	30.00	11.50
2004M M Proof	—	—	—	—	—	—

KM# 119 2 EURO

8.5000 g., Bi-Metallic Nickel-Brass center in Copper-Nickel ring, 25.75 mm. **Subject:** 60th Anniversary - Finland - UN **Obv:** Dove on a puzzle **Rev:** Denomination over map **Edge Lettering:** YK 1945-2005 FN

Date	Mintage	F	VF	XF	Unc	BU
2005M K	2,000,000	—	—	—	6.00	7.50

KM# 125 2 EURO

8.5000 g., Bi-Metallic Nickel-Brass center in Copper-Nickel ring, 25.75 mm. **Subject:** Centennial of Universal Suffrage **Obv:** Two faces **Rev:** Value and map **Edge Lettering:** SUOMI FINLAND

Date	Mintage	F	VF	XF	Unc	BU
2006M M	2,500,000	—	—	—	6.00	7.50

KM# 130 2 EURO

8.5000 g., Bi-Metallic Nickel-Brass center in Copper-Nickel ring, 25.75 mm. **Obv:** 2 cloudberry flowers surrounded by stars on outer ring **Rev:** Relief map of Western Europe, stars, lines and value **Edge:** Reeded and lettered **Edge Lettering:** SUOMI FINLAND

Date	Mintage	F	VF	XF	Unc	BU
2006M Error die pairing	Est. 55,000	—	—	50.00	75.00	100
2007FI	8,600,000	—	—	—	6.00	7.50
2007FI Proof	—	Value: 30.00				
2008FI	9,800,000	—	—	—	6.00	7.50
2008FI Proof	2,500	Value: 30.00				
2009FI	—	—	—	—	6.00	7.50
2009FI Proof	2,500	Value: 30.00				
2010FI	—	—	—	—	6.00	7.50
2010FI Proof	2,000	Value: 30.00				
2011FI	—	—	—	—	6.00	7.50
2011FI Proof	—	Value: 30.00				
2012FI	—	—	—	—	6.00	7.50
2012FI Proof	—	Value: 30.00				
2013FI	—	—	—	—	6.00	7.50
2013FI Proof	—	Value: 30.00				

KM# 138 2 EURO

8.5000 g., Bi-Metallic Nickel-Brass center in Copper-Nickel ring, 25.75 mm. **Subject:** 50th Anniversary Treaty of Rome **Obv:** Open treaty book **Rev:** Large value at left, modified outline of Europe at right **Edge:** Reeded and lettered

Date	Mintage	F	VF	XF	Unc	BU
2007	—	—	—	—	7.00	9.00
2007 Proof	—	Value: 75.00				

KM# 139 2 EURO

8.5000 g., Bi-Metallic Nickel-Brass center in Copper-Nickel ring, 25.75 mm. **Subject:** 90th Anniversary of Independence **Obv:** Longboat rowing together **Edge:** Reeded and lettered

Date	Mintage	F	VF	XF	Unc	BU
2007M	2,000,000	—	—	—	—	6.00
2007M Proof	20,000	Value: 20.00				

KM# 143 2 EURO

8.5000 g., Bi-Metallic Nickel-Brass center in Copper-Nickel ring, 25.75 mm. **Subject:** Universal Declaration of Human Rights **Obv:** Human figure within heart in landscape **Rev:** Segmented reeding

Date	Mintage	F	VF	XF	Unc	BU
2008	2,500,000	—	—	—	6.00	7.50
2008 Proof	2,500	Value: 25.00				

KM# 144 2 EURO

8.5000 g., Bi-Metallic Nickel-Brass center in Copper-Nickel ring, 25.75 mm. **Subject:** EMU 10th Anniversary **Obv:** Stick figure and E symbol **Edge:** Reeded and lettered

Date	Mintage	F	VF	XF	Unc	BU
2009	1,400,000	—	—	—	6.00	7.50
2009 Proof	25,000	Value: 30.00				

KM# 149 2 EURO

8.5000 g., Bi-Metallic Nickel-Brass center in Copper-Nickel ring, 25.75 mm. **Subject:** Finnish Autonomy, 200th Anniversary **Obv:** Classical Pyramid **Edge:** Lettered

Date	Mintage	F	VF	XF	Unc	BU
2009	1,600,000	—	—	—	6.00	7.50
2009 Proof	2,500	Value: 30.00				

KM# 154 2 EURO

8.5000 g., Bi-Metallic Nickel-Brass center in Copper-Nickel ring, 25.75 mm. **Subject:** Finnish Currency, 150th Anniversary

Date	Mintage	F	VF	XF	Unc	BU
2010	1,600,000	—	—	—	6.00	7.50
2010 Proof	25,000	Value: 30.00				

KM# 163 2 EURO

8.5000 g., Bi-Metallic Nickel-Brass center in Copper-Nickel ring, 25.75 mm. **Subject:** Bank of Finland, 200th Anniversary **Obv:** Swan in Flight

Date	Mintage	F	VF	XF	Unc	BU
2011	—	—	—	—	6.00	7.50
2011 Proof	25,000	Value: 30.00				

KM# 178 2 EURO

8.5000 g., Bi-Metallic Nickel-Brass center in Copper-Nickel ring, 25.75 mm. **Subject:** Euro coinage, 10th Anniversary **Obv:** Euro symbol on globe at center, child-like rendering around

Date	Mintage	F	VF	XF	Unc	BU
2012M	1,500,000	—	—	—	6.00	8.00
2012M Special Unc.	—	—	—	—	—	15.00
2012 Proof	25,000	Value: 25.00				

KM# 182 2 EURO

8.5000 g., Bi-Metallic Nickel-Brass center in Copper-Nickel ring, 25.75 mm. **Subject:** Helene Schjerfbeck, 150th Anniversary of Birth **Obv:** Helene Schjerfbeck

Date	Mintage	F	VF	XF	Unc	BU
2012	1,987,000	—	—	—	—	—
2012 Proof	13,000	Value: 30.00				

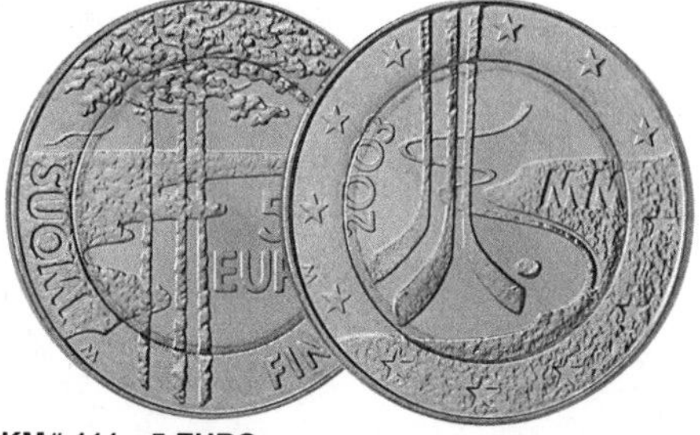

KM# 111 5 EURO

20.1000 g., Bi-Metallic Copper-Nickel center in Brass ring, 34.9 mm. **Subject:** Ice Hockey World Championships **Obv:** Summer landscape and denomination **Rev:** Three hockey sticks and a puck **Edge:** Plain **Designer:** Pertti Mäkinen

Date	Mintage	F	VF	XF	Unc	BU
2003M M-M	150,000	—	—	—	25.00	30.00

KM# 118 5 EURO

19.8000 g., Bi-Metallic Brass center in Copper-Nickel ring, 35 mm. **Subject:** 10th Anniversary - IAAF World Championships in Athletics **Obv:** Female javelin thrower, denomination **Rev:** Running feet **Edge:** Plain **Designer:** Tapio Kettunen

Date	Mintage	F	VF	XF	Unc	BU
2005M K-M	170,000	—	—	—	15.00	20.00
2005M K-M Proof	5,000	Value: 30.00				

KM# 123 5 EURO

18.7000 g., Brass, 35 mm. **Subject:** 150th Anniversary - Demilitarization of Aland **Obv:** Boat, Dove of Peace on the helm **Rev:** Tree **Edge Lettering:** AHVENANMAAN DEMILITARISOINTI 150 VUOTTA* **Designer:** Pertti Mäkinen

Date	Mintage	F	VF	XF	Unc	BU
2006 M-M	55,000	—	—	—	20.00	25.00

KM# 131 5 EURO

9.8100 g., Bi-Metallic Copper-Nickel center in Aluminum-Bronze ring, 27.25 mm. **Subject:** Finland Presidency of European Union **Obv:** Letter decorations with 2006 and SUOMI-FINLAND **Rev:** 5 EURO below letter decoration **Designer:** Reijo Paavilainen

Date	Mintage	F	VF	XF	Unc	BU
2006M P-M	100,000	—	—	—	15.00	20.00

KM# 135 5 EURO

19.8100 g., Bi-Metallic Aluminum-Bronze center in Copper-Nickel ring, 35 mm. **Subject:** 90th Anniversary of Finland's Independence **Designer:** Reijo Paavilainen

Date	Mintage	F	VF	XF	Unc	BU
2007 P	130,000	—	—	—	15.00	20.00
2007 P Proof	20,000	Value: 30.00				

KM# 146 5 EURO

19.8100 g., Bi-Metallic Aluminum-Bronze center in Copper-Nickel ring., 35 mm. **Subject:** Independence, 90th Anniversary **Obv:** Petroglif of a longboat

Date	Mintage	F	VF	XF	Unc	BU
2007P	130,000	—	—	—	—	15.00
2007P Proof	20,000	Value: 35.00				

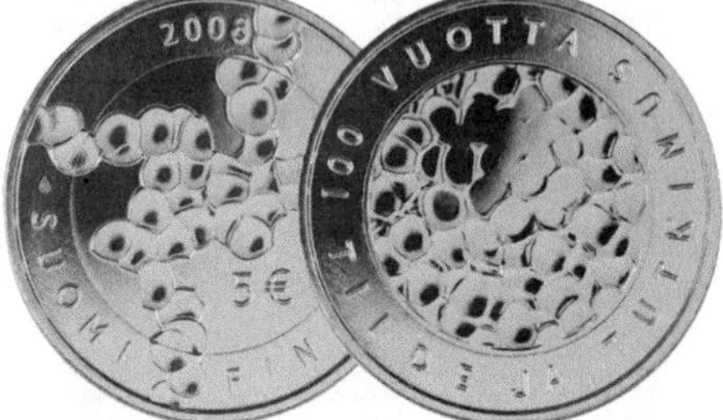

KM# 141 5 EURO

19.8100 g., Bi-Metallic Copper-Nickel center in Aluminum-Bronze ring, 35 mm. **Subject:** Science and Research **Designer:** Tapio Kettunen

Date	Mintage	F	VF	XF	Unc	BU
2008K	25,000	—	—	—	15.00	20.00
2008K Proof	20,000	Value: 30.00				

KM# 158 5 EURO

9.8000 g., Bi-Metallic Copper-Nickel center in Aluminum-Bronze ring, 27.5 mm. **Subject:** Provinces - Finland proper **Designer:** Nora Tapper

Date	Mintage	F	VF	XF	Unc	BU
2010T	90,000	—	—	—	—	15.00
2010T Proof	30,000	Value: 30.00				

KM# 156 5 EURO

9.8000 g., Bi-Metallic Copper-Nickel center in Aluminum-Bronze ring, 27.25 mm. **Subject:** Historical Provinces - Satakunta **Designer:** Nora Tapper

Date	Mintage	F	VF	XF	Unc	BU
2010T	—	—	—	—	—	15.00
2010T	—	Value: 30.00				

KM# 159 5 EURO

9.8000 g., Bi-Metallic Copper-Nickel center in Aluminum-Bronze ring, 27.25 mm. **Subject:** Provinces - Karelia **Rev:** Shield **Designer:** Nora Tapper

Date	Mintage	F	VF	XF	Unc	BU
2011T	100,000	—	—	—	13.00	15.00
2011T Proof	20,000	Value: 30.00				

KM# 160 5 EURO

9.8000 g., Bi-Metallic Copper-Nickel center in Aluminum-Bronze ring, 27.5 mm. **Subject:** Provinces - Uusimaa **Designer:** Nora Tapper

Date	Mintage	F	VF	XF	Unc	BU
2011T	100,000	—	—	—	15.00	20.00
2011T Proof	20,000	Value: 30.00				

KM# 161 5 EURO

9.8000 g., Bi-Metallic Copper-Nickel center in Aluminum-Bronze ring, 27.5 mm. **Subject:** Provinces - Tavastia **Designer:** Nora Tapper

Date	Mintage	F	VF	XF	Unc	BU
2011T	100,000	—	—	—	—	15.00
2011T Proof	20,000	Value: 25.00				

KM# 162 5 EURO

9.8000 g., Bi-Metallic Copper-Nickel center in Aluminum-Bronze ring, 27.5 mm. **Subject:** Provinces - Savonia **Designer:** Nora Tapper

Date	Mintage	F	VF	XF	Unc	BU
2011T	100,000	—	—	—	15.00	20.00
2011T Proof	20,000	Value: 30.00				

KM# 170 5 EURO

9.8000 g., Bi-Metallic Copper-Nickel center in Aluminum-Bronze ring, 27.25 mm. **Subject:** Provinces: Lapland **Obv:** Shield **Rev:** Antler **Designer:** Nora Tapper

Date	Mintage	F	VF	XF	Unc	BU
2011T	100,000	—	—	—	13.00	15.00
2011T Proof	20,000	Value: 30.00				

KM# 171 5 EURO

9.8000 g., Bi-Metallic Copper-Nickel center in Aluminum-Bronze ring, 27.25 mm. **Subject:** Provinces: Ostrobuthnia **Obv:** Shield **Rev:** Wood **Designer:** Nora Tapper

Date	Mintage	F	VF	XF	Unc	BU
2011T	—	—	—	—	—	15.00
2011T Proof	—	Value: 30.00				

KM# 175 5 EURO

9.8000 g., Bi-Metallic Copper-Nickel center in Nickel-Brass ring, 27.25 mm. **Subject:** Provinces - Häme **Rev:** Shield **Designer:** Nora Tapper

Date	Mintage	F	VF	XF	Unc	BU
2011T	100,000	—	—	—	—	25.00
2011T Proof	20,000	Value: 35.00				

KM# 176 5 EURO

9.8000 g., Bi-Metallic Copper-Nickel center in Nickel-Brass ring, 27.25 mm. **Subject:** Provinces Pohjois-Karjalan **Rev:** Shield **Designer:** Nora Tapper

Date	Mintage	F	VF	XF	Unc	BU
2011T	100,000	—	—	—	—	25.00
2011T Proof	20,000	Value: 35.00				

KM# 177 5 EURO

9.8000 g., Bi-Metallic Copper-Nickel center in Aluminum-Bronze ring., 27.25 mm. **Series:** Provinces - Åland **Obv:** Needle sewing fishing net **Rev:** Shield **Designer:** Nora Tapper

Date	Mintage	F	VF	XF	Unc	BU
2011T	100,000	—	—	—	—	25.00
2011T Proof	20,000	Value: 30.00				

KM# 181 5 EURO

9.0000 g., Aluminum-Bronze, 27.25 mm. **Subject:** World Design Capital Helsinki 2012 **Obv:** Angular **Rev:** Angular **Designer:** Henna Lamberg

Date	Mintage	F	VF	XF	Unc	BU
2012	100,000	—	—	—	—	105

KM# 183 5 EURO

9.8000 g., Bi-Metallic Copper-Nickel center in Aluminum-Bronze ring, 27.25 mm. **Subject:** IIHF Ice Hockey World Championship **Obv:** Puck flying into the goal **Rev:** Hockey player **Designer:** Petri Neuvonen

Date	Mintage	F	VF	XF	Unc	BU
2012N	180,000	—	—	—	—	20.00
2012N Proof	20,000	Value: 18.00				

KM# 184 5 EURO

9.8000 g., Bi-Metallic Copper-Nickel center in Aluminum-Bronze ring, 27.25 mm. **Subject:** Northern Nature - Flora **Obv:** Crowfoot framed by moss and lichen **Designer:** Reijo Paavilainen

Date	Mintage	F	VF	XF	Unc	BU
2012P	50,000	—	—	—	—	—
2012P Proof	7,000	Value: 8.00				

KM# 185 5 EURO

9.8000 g., Bi-Metallic Copper-Nickel center in Aluminum-Bronze ring, 27.25 mm. **Subject:** Northern Nature - Fauna **Obv:** Paw trail of the arctic fox **Rev:** 5 EURO SUOMI FINLAND **Designer:** Reijo Paavilainen

Date	Mintage	F	VF	XF	Unc	BU
2012P	50,000	—	—	—	—	—
2012P Proof	7,000	Value: 8.00				

KM# 186 5 EURO

9.8000 g., Bi-Metallic Copper-Nickel center in Aluminum-Bronze ring, 27.25 mm. **Subject:** Northern Nature - Winter **Obv:** Northern lights **Rev:** Animal tracks in the snow **Designer:** Reijo Paavilainen

Date	Mintage	F	VF	XF	Unc	BU
2012P	50,000	—	—	—	—	—
2012P Proof	7,000	Value: 8.00				

KM# 107 10 EURO

27.4000 g., 0.9250 Silver 0.8148 oz. ASW, 38.6 mm. **Subject:** 50th Anniversary - Helsinki Olympics **Obv:** Flames and denomination above globe with map of Finland **Rev:** Tower and partial coin design **Edge:** Plain

Date	Mintage	F	VF	XF	Unc	BU
2002M VV-M	10,000	—	—	—	30.00	32.00
2002M VV-M Proof	34,800	Value: 35.00				

KM# 108 10 EURO
27.4000 g., 0.9250 Silver 0.8148 oz. ASW, 38.6 mm. **Subject:** Elias Lönnrot **Obv:** Ribbon with stars **Rev:** Quill and signature **Edge:** Plain **Designer:** Pertti Mäkinen.

Date	Mintage	F	VF	XF	Unc	BU
2002M M-M	40,000	—	—	—	30.00	32.00
2002M M-M Proof	40,000	Value: 35.00				

KM# 110 10 EURO
27.4000 g., 0.9250 Silver 0.8148 oz. ASW, 38.6 mm. **Subject:** Anders Chydenius **Obv:** Stylized design **Rev:** Name and book **Edge:** Plain **Designer:** Tero Lounas

Date	Mintage	F	VF	XF	Unc	BU
2003M L-M	30,000	—	—	—	32.00	35.00
2003M Proof	30,000	Value: 40.00				

KM# 112 10 EURO
27.4000 g., 0.9250 Silver 0.8148 oz. ASW, 38.6 mm. **Subject:** Mannerheim and St. Petersburg **Obv:** Head 3/4 facing **Rev:** Fortress, denomination at right **Designer:** Anneli Sipiläinen

Date	Mintage	F	VF	XF	Unc	BU
2003 S-M	6,000	—	—	—	35.00	37.50
2003 S-M Proof	29,000	Value: 55.00				

KM# 115 10 EURO
27.4000 g., 0.9250 Silver 0.8148 oz. ASW, 38.6 mm. **Subject:** 200th Birthday of Johan Ludwig Runeberg **Obv:** Head of Runeberg **Rev:** Text of 1831 Helsingfors Tidningar newspaper **Designer:** Heli Kauhanen

Date	Mintage	F	VF	XF	Unc	BU
2004 K-M	5,600	—	—	—	35.00	37.50
2004 K-M Proof	22,750	Value: 55.00				

KM# 116 10 EURO
27.4000 g., 0.9250 Silver 0.8148 oz. ASW, 38.6 mm. **Subject:** Tove Jansson **Obv:** Three "muumi" figures **Rev:** Head of Tove Jansson **Designer:** Pertti Mäkinen

Date	Mintage	F	VF	XF	Unc	BU
2004 M-M	50,000	—	—	—	32.00	60.00
2004 M-M Proof	20,000	Value: 80.00				

KM# 120 10 EURO
25.5000 g., 0.9250 Silver 0.7583 oz. ASW, 38.6 mm. **Subject:** 60 years of Peace **Obv:** Dove of peace **Rev:** Flowering plant **Designer:** Pertti Mäkinen

Date	Mintage	F	VF	XF	Unc	BU
2005 M-M	55,000	—	—	—	32.00	35.00
2005 Proof	5,000	Value: 60.00				

KM# 122 10 EURO
25.5000 g., 0.9250 Silver 0.7583 oz. ASW, 38.6 mm. **Subject:** Unknown Soldier and Finnish Film Art **Obv:** Trench **Rev:** Soldier with helmet on top of a film **Designer:** Reijo Paavilainen

Date	Mintage	F	VF	XF	Unc	BU
2005 P-M	25,000	—	—	—	35.00	37.50
2005 P-M Proof	15,000	Value: 50.00				

KM# 124 10 EURO
25.5000 g., 0.9250 Silver 0.7583 oz. ASW, 38.6 mm. **Subject:** 200th Birthday - Johan Vilhelm Snellman **Obv:** Sun rising over the lake **Rev:** Snellman **Designer:** Tapio Kettunen

Date	Mintage	F	VF	XF	Unc	BU
2006 K-M	—	—	—	—	32.00	35.00
2006 K-M Proof	—	Value: 45.00				

KM# 132 10 EURO
25.5000 g., 0.9250 Silver 0.7583 oz. ASW, 38.6 mm. **Subject:** 100th Anniversary of Parliamentary Reform **Obv:** Two stylist heads female and male with text SUOMI FINLAND 10 EURO **Rev:** Male and female fingers inserting ballot paper into ballot box with text 100V EDUSKUNTAUUDISTUS 2006 **Edge Lettering:** LANTDAGSREFORMEN 1906 **Designer:** Pertti Mäkinen

Date	Mintage	F	VF	XF	Unc	BU
2006M M-M	40,000	—	—	—	35.00	50.00
2006M M-M Proof	20,000	Value: 60.00				

KM# 134 10 EURO
25.5000 g., 0.9250 Silver 0.7583 oz. ASW, 38.6 mm. **Subject:** A.E. Nordenskiöld and the Northeast Passage **Rev:** Sailor at ship's wheel during foul weather **Designer:** Reijo Paavilainen

Date	Mintage	F	VF	XF	Unc	BU
2007M P	7,000	—	—	—	35.00	50.00
2007M P Proof	33,000	Value: 70.00				

KM# 136 10 EURO
25.5000 g., 0.9250 Silver 0.7583 oz. ASW, 38.6 mm. **Subject:** Mikael Agricola - Finnish Language **Obv:** Quill pen and lettering **Rev:** Alphabet Letters **Designer:** Reijo Paavilainen

Date	Mintage	F	VF	XF	Unc	BU
2007 P	6,000	—	—	—	35.00	50.00
2007 P Proof	24,000	Value: 70.00				

KM# 140 10 EURO
25.5000 g., 0.9250 Silver 0.7583 oz. ASW, 38.6 mm. **Subject:** Finnish Flag **Obv:** SUOMI FINLAND 2008 and flag **Rev:** SUOMEN LIPPU 1918-2008-FINLANDS FLAGGA and value **Designer:** Tapio Kettunen

Date	Mintage	F	VF	XF	Unc	BU
2008K	9,000	—	—	—	30.00	32.00
2008K Proof	26,000	Value: 35.00				

KM# 142 10 EURO
25.5000 g., 0.9250 Silver 0.7583 oz. ASW, 38.6 mm. **Subject:** Mika Waltari **Obv:** Signature and 1908-1879 **Rev:** Egyptian pharaoh hound and value **Designer:** Reijo Paavilainen

Date	Mintage	F	VF	XF	Unc	BU
2008P	5,000	—	—	—	30.00	32.00
2008P Proof	15,000	Value: 35.00				

KM# 148 10 EURO
25.5000 g., 0.9250 Silver 0.7583 oz. ASW, 38.6 mm. **Subject:** Fredrik Pacius **Obv:** Opening notes to Kung Karls Jakt, first opera of Pacius **Rev:** Stage curtian opening **Designer:** Pertti Mäkinen

Date	Mintage	F	VF	XF	Unc	BU
2009M	7,000	—	—	—	35.00	58.00
2009M Proof	28,000	Value: 80.00				

KM# 173 10 EURO
25.5000 g., 0.9250 Silver 0.7583 oz. ASW **Subject:** Council of State, 200th Anniversary **Designer:** Reijo Paavilainen

Date	Mintage	F	VF	XF	Unc	BU
2009P	5,000	—	—	—	—	50.00
2009P Proof	15,000	Value: 80.00				

KM# 151 10 EURO
25.5000 g., 0.9250 Silver 0.7583 oz. ASW, 38.6 mm. **Subject:** Eero Saarinen, 100th Anniversary of Birth **Obv:** Tulip chair **Rev:** St. Louis Arch

Date	Mintage	F	VF	XF	Unc	BU
2010K	6,000	—	—	—	—	50.00
2010K Proof	20,000	Value: 80.00				

KM# 152 10 EURO
25.5000 g., 0.9250 Silver 0.7583 oz. ASW, 38.6 mm. **Subject:** Minna Carth, author **Designer:** Reijo Paavilainen

Date	Mintage	F	VF	XF	Unc	BU
2010P	4,000	—	—	—	—	50.00
2010P Proof	16,000	Value: 80.00				

KM# 157 10 EURO
25.5000 g., 0.9250 Silver 0.7583 oz. ASW, 38.6 mm. **Subject:** Konsta Jylhä, 100th Anniversary of Birth **Designer:** Reijo Paavilainen

Date	Mintage	F	VF	XF	Unc	BU
2010P	—	—	—	—	32.00	50.00
2010P Proof	—	Value: 80.00				

KM# 165 10 EURO
25.5000 g., 0.9250 Silver 0.7583 oz. ASW, 38.6 mm. **Subject:** Hella Wuolijoki and Equality **Designer:** Petri Neuvonen

Date	Mintage	F	VF	XF	Unc	BU
2011P	5,000	—	—	—	30.00	70.00
2011P Proof	7,000	Value: 80.00				

KM# 166 10 EURO
25.5000 g., 0.9250 Silver 0.7583 oz. ASW, 38.6 mm. **Subject:** Kaj Franck and industrial art **Obv:** Franck's signature **Designer:** Reijo Paavilainen

Date	Mintage	F	VF	XF	Unc	BU
2011P	5,000	—	—	—	30.00	70.00
2011P Proof	10,000	Value: 80.00				

KM# 167 10 EURO
25.5000 g., 0.9250 Silver 0.7583 oz. ASW, 38.6 mm. **Subject:** Pehr Kalm and European Explorers **Obv:** Mountain laurel - kalmia latifolia **Rev:** Surveyor before Niagara Falls **Designer:** Erkki Vainio

Date	Mintage	F	VF	XF	Unc	BU
2011V	6,000	—	—	—	30.00	35.00
2011V Proof	14,000	Value: 70.00				

KM# 168 10 EURO
25.5000 g., 0.5000 Silver 0.4099 oz. ASW, 38.6 mm. **Subject:** Juhani Aho and Finnish Literature **Rev:** Pen point and manuscript **Designer:** Reijo Paavilainen

Date	Mintage	F	VF	XF	Unc	BU
2011P	8,000	—	—	—	—	50.00

KM# 168a 10 EURO
25.5000 g., 0.9250 Silver 0.7583 oz. ASW, 38.6 mm. **Subject:** Juhani Aho and Finnish Literature **Designer:** Reijo Paavilainen

Date	Mintage	F	VF	XF	Unc	BU
2011P Proof	7,000	Value: 80.00				

KM# 179 10 EURO
25.5000 g., 0.9250 Silver 0.7583 oz. ASW, 38.6 mm. **Subject:** Henrik Wigström, 150th Anniversary of Birth **Obv:** Swan swimming left, lilly pads nearby **Rev:** Floral Easter egg ball **Designer:** Pertti Mäkinen

Date	Mintage	F	VF	XF	Unc	BU
2012M	—	—	—	—	30.00	70.00
2012M Proof	—	Value: 75.00				

KM# 187 10 EURO
25.5000 g., 0.9250 Silver 0.7583 oz. ASW, 38.6 mm. **Subject:** Arvo Ylppö and Medicin **Obv:** Colored alphabet letters **Rev:** Baby nestled in stethoscope **Designer:** Reijo Paavilainen

Date	Mintage	F	VF	XF	Unc	BU
2012M	20,000	—	—	—	—	70.00
2012M Proof	20,000	Value: 80.00				

KM# 188 10 EURO
25.5000 g., 0.9250 Silver 0.7583 oz. ASW, 38.6 mm. **Subject:** Armi Ratia and Industrial Art **Obv:** Armi Ratia 1912-1973 **Rev:** Unikko flower **Designer:** Kari Markkanen

Date	Mintage	F	VF	XF	Unc	BU
2012	20,000	—	—	—	—	70.00
2012 Proof	20,000	Value: 80.00				

KM# 121 20 EURO
1.7300 g., 0.9000 Gold 0.0501 oz. AGW, 13.9 mm. **Subject:** 10th Anniversary - IAAF World Championships in Athletics **Obv:** Helsinki Stadium **Rev:** Two faces **Designer:** Pertti Mäkinen

Date	Mintage	F	VF	XF	Unc	BU
2005 M-M Proof	30,000	Value: 100				

KM# 172 20 EURO
25.5000 g., 0.9250 Silver 0.7583 oz. ASW, 38.6 mm. **Subject:** Peace and security **Obv:** Two peace doves with a twig **Designer:** Tapio Kettunen

Date	Mintage	F	VF	XF	Unc	BU
2009K	3,500	—	—	—	32.00	40.00
2009K Proof	11,500	Value: 120				

KM# 153 20 EURO
33.6200 g., 0.9250 Silver 0.9998 oz. ASW, 38.61 mm. **Subject:** Children's creativity

Date	Mintage	F	VF	XF	Unc	BU
2010M	3,500	—	—	—	—	100
2010M Proof	10,000	Value: 120				

KM# 169 20 EURO
33.6200 g., 0.5000 Silver 0.5404 oz. ASW, 38.6 mm. **Subject:** Protecting Baltic Sea **Obv:** Fishing boat and map of the Baltic Sea **Rev:** Seal and fish **Designer:** Essi Kulju

Date	Mintage	F	VF	XF	Unc	BU
2011K	7,000	—	—	—	—	80.00

KM# 169a 20 EURO
33.6200 g., 0.9250 Silver 0.9998 oz. ASW, 38.6 mm. **Subject:** Protecting the Baltic **Obv:** Fishing boat and map of the Baltic Sea **Rev:** Seal and fish

Date	Mintage	F	VF	XF	Unc	BU
2011K Proof	8,000	Value: 110				

KM# 189 20 EURO
33.6200 g., 0.9250 Silver 0.9998 oz. ASW, 38.6 mm. **Subject:** Equity and Tolerance **Obv:** World map **Rev:** Human faces and value **Designer:** Katri Piri

Date	Mintage	F	VF	XF	Unc	BU
2012P	20,000	—	—	—	—	110
2012P Proof	20,000	Value: 120				

KM# 113 50 EURO
13.2000 g., Bi-Metallic .75 Gold center in .925 Silver ring, 27.25 mm. **Subject:** Finnish art and design **Obv:** Snowflake design within box, beaded circle surrounds **Rev:** Snowflake design within beaded circle **Designer:** Matti Peltokangas

Date	Mintage	F	VF	XF	Unc	BU
2003 P-M Proof	10,600	Value: 375				

KM# 133 50 EURO
12.8000 g., Bi-Metallic .75 Gold center in .925 Silver ring, 27.25 mm. **Subject:** Finland Presidency of European Union **Obv:** Letter decorations with 2006 and SUOMI-FINLAND **Rev:** 50 EURO below letter decoration **Designer:** Reijo Paavilainen

Date	Mintage	F	VF	XF	Unc	BU
2006M P-M Proof	8,000	Value: 400				

KM# 180 50 EURO
10.8000 g., Bi-Metallic 5.75 g gold center in 5.8 g .925 Silver ring, 27.25 mm. **Subject:** World Design Capital Helsinki 2012 **Obv:** WORLD DESIGN CAPITAL HELSINKI around angular patterns **Rev:** 50 above angular patterns **Designer:** Henna Lamberg

Date	Mintage	F	VF	XF	Unc	BU
2012L Proof	5,000	Value: 600				

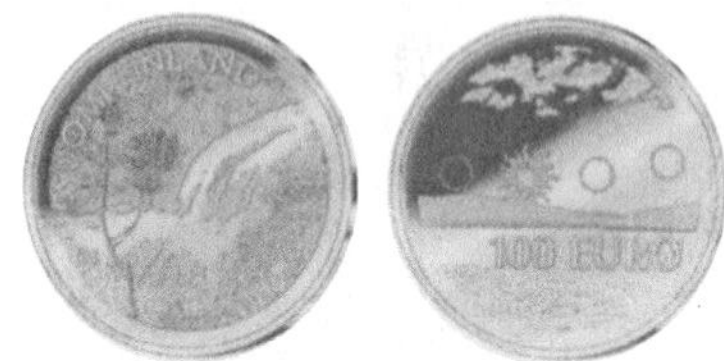

KM# 109 100 EURO
8.6400 g., 0.9000 Gold 0.2500 oz. AGW, 22 mm. **Subject:** Lapland **Obv:** Small tree and mountain stream **Rev:** Lake landscape beneath the midnight sun **Edge:** Plain with serial number **Designer:** Toivo Jaatinen

Date	Mintage	F	VF	XF	Unc	BU
2002M J-M Proof	25,000	Value: 450				

KM# 117 100 EURO
8.6400 g., 0.9000 Gold 0.2500 oz. AGW, 22 mm. **Subject:** 150th Birthday of Albert Edelfelt **Obv:** Flower **Rev:** Head of Edelfelt **Designer:** Pertti Mäkinen

Date	Mintage	F	VF	XF	Unc	BU
2004 M-M Proof	8,500	Value: 475				

KM# 137 100 EURO
8.4800 g., 0.9170 Gold 0.2500 oz. AGW **Subject:** 90th Anniversary of Finland's Independence **Obv:** Finland and the years of independence **Rev:** Abstract composition **Designer:** Reijo Paavilainen

Date	Mintage	F	VF	XF	Unc	BU
2007 P	—	—	—	—	450	465
2007 P Proof	—	Value: 475				

KM# 174 100 EURO
8.4800 g., 0.9170 Gold 0.2500 oz. AGW, 22 mm. **Subject:** Finnish War and the Birth of Autonomy **Obv:** Half of an Eagle at left **Rev:** Half of a Crown at right **Designer:** Reijo Paavilainen

Date	Mintage	F	VF	XF	Unc	BU
2008P Proof	9,000	Value: 625				

KM# 145 100 EURO

6.7800 g., 0.9170 Gold 0.1999 oz. AGW, 22 mm. **Subject:** Diet of Porvoo **Rev:** Porvoo

Date	Mintage	F	VF	XF	Unc	BU
2009P Proof	7,500	Value: 375				

KM# 150 100 EURO

5.6500 g., 0.9170 Gold 0.1666 oz. AGW, 22 mm. **Subject:** Finnish Currency, 150th Anniversary **Obv:** Finnish Lion **Rev:** Composition of figures **Designer:** Reijo Paavilainen

Date	Mintage	F	VF	XF	Unc	BU
2010P Proof	—	Value: 550				

KM# 164 100 EURO

5.6500 g., 0.9170 Gold 0.1666 oz. AGW, 22 mm. **Subject:** Bank of Finland, 200th Anniversary **Obv:** Swan in flight **Rev:** Left wing of swan SUOMI FINLAND value and date **Designer:** Hannu Veijalainen

Date	Mintage	F	VF	XF	Unc	BU
2011V Proof	8,000	Value: 525				

MINT SETS

KM#	Date	Mintage	Identification	Issue Price	Mkt Val
MS58	2001 (5)	20,000	KM#65, 66, 73, 76, 77 plus 1865 coin design medal	18.00	22.50
MS59	2001 (5)	—	KM#65, 66, 73, 76, 77, medal (Johan Vilhelm Snellman)	—	22.50
MS60	2002 (8)	130,000	KM#98-105, Church medal	—	40.00
MS61	2003 (8)	170,000	KM#98-105, Golden Medal, goldpanning in Lappland	—	37.50
MS62	2002 (8)	2,000	KM#98-105, Baby	—	100
MS63	2003 (9)	8,000	KM#98-105, Silver medal, goldpanning in Lappland	—	125
MS64	2003 (8)	15,000	KM#98-105, Ice Hockey	—	60.00
MS65	2003 (9)	3,000	KM#98-105, medal and teddy bear	—	—
MS66	2003 (9)	5,000	KM#98-105, Baby, medal	—	37.50
MS67	2003 (9)	4,000	KM#98-105, Rose, medal	—	60.00
MS68	2003 (9)	30,000	KM#98-105, Christmas, golden medal	—	37.50
MS69	2004 (8)	55,000	KM#98-105, Euro zone, medal	—	40.00
MS70	2004 (8)	5,000	KM#98-105, 114, baby, medal	—	35.00
MS71	2004 (8)	18,000	KM#98-105, Tove Jansson, 90th Birthday	—	42.50
MS72	2004 (9)	4,000	KM#98-105, Music, medal	—	60.00
MS73	2005 (8)	40,000	KM#98-105, Wildlife, medal	—	42.50
MS74	2005 (9)	30,000	KM#98-105, 118, Paraolympics	—	55.00
MS75	2005 (9)	4,000	KM#98-105, Baby, medal	—	45.00
MS76	2005 (9)	3,000	KM#98-105, Music, medal	—	55.00
MS77	2006 (9)	40,000	KM#98-105, 119, Lighthouse	—	45.00
MS78	2006 (9)	20,000	KM#98-105, 125, Centennial of Parlament reform, suffrage	—	55.00
MS79	2006 (9)	3,200	KM#98-105, Music, medal	—	55.00
MS80	2006 (9)	4,000	KM#98-105, Wedding, medal	—	55.00
MS81	2006 (9)	4,600	KM#98-105, Baby, medal	—	55.00
MS82	2006 (9)	4,000	KM#98-105, Aland	—	45.00
MS83	2007 (9)	30,000	KM#98-100, 126-130, Lighthouse, medal	—	30.00
MS84	2007 (9)	3,000	KM#98-100, 126-130, Rose, medal	—	70.00
MS85	2007 (9)	3,000	KM#98-100, 126-130, Marriage, medal	—	55.00
MS86	2007 (9)	4,000	KM#98-100, 126-130, Baby, medal	—	65.00
MS87	2007 (10)	20,000	KM#98-100, 126-130, 138, European Song Festival, medal	—	45.00
MS88	2007 (8)	4,000	KM#98-100, 126-130, Aland	—	40.00
MS89	2007 (9)	20,000	KM#98-100, 126-130, 139, Swans	—	50.00
MS90	2007 (3)	—	KM98-100	—	10.00
MS91	2008 (9)	30,000	KM#98-100, 126-130, Lighthouse, medal	—	35.00
MS92	2008 (9)	3,000	KM#98-100, 126-130, Rose, medal	—	55.00
MS93	2008 (9)	3,000	KM#98-100, 126-130, Wedding, medal	—	45.00
MS94	2008 (9)	4,000	KM#98-100, 126-130, Baby, medal	—	50.00
MS95	2008 (9)	4,000	KM#98-100, 126-130, Aland medal	—	25.00
MS96	2008 (9)	30,000	KM#98-100, 126-130, 143	—	25.00
MS100	2009 (10)	1,500	KM#98-100, 126-130, 149, Wedding, plus medal	—	45.00
MS101	2009 (10)	3,000	KM#98-100, 126-130, 149, Music plus medal	—	45.00
MS102	2009 (10)	4,000	KM#98-100, 126-130, 149, Baby, plus medal	—	45.00
MS97	2009 (10)	20,000	KM#98-100, 126-130, 149 plus medal	—	40.00
MS98	2009 (10)	30,000	KM#98-100, 126-130, 149 plus lighthouse medal	—	45.00
MS99	2009 (10)	2,200	KM#98-100, 126-130, 149 Aland	—	40.00
MS103	2010 (10)	30,000	KM#98-100, 126-130, 154 and Lighthouse medal	—	45.00
MS104	2010 (10)	15,000	KM#98-100, 126-130, 154 plus Biology medal	—	45.00
MS105	2010 (10)	2,500	KM#98-100, 126-130, 154 plus Music medal	—	45.00
MS106	2010 (10)	2	KM#98-100, 126-130, 154 plus Wedding medal	—	45.00
MS107	2010 (10)	3,000	KM#98-100, 126-130, 154 plus Kids medal	—	45.00
MS108	2010 (3)	7,000	KM#98-100	—	12.50
MS109	2011 (10)	20,000	KM#98-100, 126-130, 163 plus Lighthouse medal	—	45.00
MS110	2011 (10)	15,000	KM#98-100, 126-130, 163 plus Nature medal	—	45.00
MS111	2011 (10)	3,000	KM#98-100, 126-130, 163 plus Kids medal	—	45.00
MS112	2011 (10)	2,500	KM#98-100, 126-130, 163 plus Music medal	—	45.00
MS113	2011 (10)	2,500	KM#98-100, 126-130, 163 plus Wedding medal	—	45.00
MS114	2011 (3)	10,000	KM#98-100	—	15.00

PROOF SETS

KM#	Date	Mintage	Identification	Issue Price	Mkt Val
PS9	2001 (6)	—	KM#65-66, 73, 76-77, medal (Suomen Markka 1864-2001)	—	60.00
PS10	2002 (9)	5,000	KM#98-105, European Union gold medal	—	550
PS11	2002 (9)	8,000	KM#98-105, National Theater silver medal	—	185
PS12	2003 (9)	500	KM#98-105, Gold medal	—	350
PS13	2003 (9)	5,000	KM#98-105, Gold medal with diamond chip	—	500
PS14	2003 (9)	1,000	KM#98-105, Silver medal	—	400
PS15	2003 (9)	8,000	KM#98-105, Silver medal with diamond chip	—	150
PS16	2004 (10)	5,000	KM#98-105, 114, Silver medal	—	225
PS17	2005 (10)	3,000	KM#98-105, 118, Silver medal	—	200
PS18	2005 (4)	2,005	KM#118, 121 plus 2 older coins.	—	225
PS19	2006 (10)	3,300	KM#98-105, 125, Salmon medal	—	200
PS20	2007 (10)	2,500	KM#98-100, 126-130, 138, Silver medal.	—	150
PS21	2008 (10)	2,500	KM#98-100, 126-130, 143 plus medal	—	185
PS22	2009 (11)	2,500	KM#98-100, 126-130, 144, 149, plus medal	—	225
PS23	2010 (10)	2,000	KM#98-100, 126-130, 154 plus medal	—	200
PS24	2011 (10)	—	KM#98-100, 126-130, 163 plus medal	—	200
PS25	2010 (3)	7,000	KM#150 plus Russian 1863 Kopek and Finnish 1864 Pennia	—	475

FRANCE

The French Republic, largest of the West European nations, has an area of 210,026 sq. mi. (547,030 sq. km.) and a population of 58.1 million. Capital: Paris. Agriculture, manufacturing, tourist industry and financial services are the most important elements of France's diversified economy. Textiles and clothing, steel products, machinery and transportation equipment, chemicals, pharmaceuticals, nuclear electricity, agricultural products and wine are exported.

ENGRAVER GENERALS' PRIVY MARKS

Mark	Desc.	Date	Name
	Horseshoe	2000-2002	Gérard Buquoy
	SL Heart-shaped monogram	2002-2003	Serge Levet
	French horn w/starfish in water	2003	Hubert Lariviére

MINT DIRECTORS' PRIVY MARKS

Some modern coins struck from dies produced at the Paris Mint have the 'A' mint mark. In the absence of a mint mark, the cornucopia privy mark serves to attribute a coin to Paris design.

A – Paris, Central Mint

MODERN REPUBLICS

1870-present

REFORM COINAGE

Commencing 1960

1 Old Franc = 1 New Centime;
100 New Centimes = 1 New Franc

KM# 928 CENTIME

1.6500 g., Stainless Steel, 15 mm. **Obv:** Cursive legend surrounds grain sprig **Rev:** Cursive denomination, date at top **Edge:** Plain **Designer:** Atelier de Paris **Note:** 1991-1993 dated coins, non-Proof, exist in both coin and medal alignment. Values given here are for medal alignment examples. Pieces struck in coin alignment have been traded for as much as $50.00.

Date	Mintage	F	VF	XF	Unc	BU
2001 In sets only	—	—	—	—	—	1.50
2001 Proof	—	Value: 2.00				

KM# 928a CENTIME

2.5000 g., 0.7500 Gold 0.0603 oz. AGW **Obv:** Cursive legend surrounds grain sprig, medallic alignment **Rev:** Cursive denomination, date above, medallic alignment **Edge:** Plain **Note:** Last Centime.

Date	Mintage	F	VF	XF	Unc	BU
2001	Est. 7,492	—	—	—	—	225

KM# 933 5 CENTIMES

2.0000 g., Aluminum-Bronze, 17 mm. **Obv:** Liberty bust left **Rev:** Denomination above date, grain sprig below, laurel branch at left **Edge:** Plain **Note:** 1991-1993 dated coins, non-Proof exist in both coin and medal alignment.

Date	Mintage	F	VF	XF	Unc	BU
2001 In sets only	—	—	—	—	1.50	2.50
2001 Proof	—	Value: 1.00				

KM# 929 10 CENTIMES

3.0000 g., Aluminum-Bronze, 20 mm. **Obv:** Liberty bust left **Rev:** Denomination above date, grain sprig below, laurel branch at left **Edge:** Plain **Note:** Without mint mark. 1991-1993 dated coins, non-Proof, exist in both coin and medal alignment.

Date	Mintage	F	VF	XF	Unc	BU
2001 In sets only	—	—	—	—	—	3.00
2001 Proof	—	Value: 1.00				

KM# 930 20 CENTIMES

4.0000 g., Aluminum-Bronze, 23.5 mm. **Obv:** Liberty bust left **Rev:** Denomination above date, grain sprig below, laurel branch at left **Edge:** Plain **Note:** Without mint mark. 1991-1993 dated coins, non-Proof, exist in both coin and medal alignment.

Date	Mintage	F	VF	XF	Unc	BU
2001 In sets only	—	—	—	—	—	3.00
2001 Proof	—	Value: 1.00				

KM# 931.1 1/2 FRANC

4.5000 g., Nickel, 19.5 mm. **Obv:** The Seed Sower **Rev:** Laurel divides denomination and date **Edge:** Reeded **Designer:** Louis Oscar Roty **Note:** Without mint mark.

Date	Mintage	F	VF	XF	Unc	BU
2001 In sets only	—	—	—	—	2.00	3.00

KM# 931.2 1/2 FRANC

4.5000 g., Nickel, 19.5 mm. **Obv:** Modified sower, engraver's signature: "O. ROTY" preceded by "D'AP" **Rev:** Laurel divides date and denomination **Edge:** Plain

Date	Mintage	F	VF	XF	Unc	BU
2001	—	—	—	—	0.40	0.60
2001 Proof	—	Value: 1.50				

KM# 925.2 FRANC

6.0000 g., Nickel, 24 mm. **Obv:** Modified sower, engraver's signature: O. ROTY, preceded by D'AP **Rev:** Laurel divides date and denomination **Edge:** Plain

Date	Mintage	F	VF	XF	Unc	BU
2001	—	—	—	—	0.40	0.60
2001 Proof	—	Value: 2.50				

KM# 925.1a FRANC

8.0000 g., 0.7500 Gold 0.1929 oz. AGW, 24 mm. **Obv:** The Seed Sower **Rev:** Laurel divides date and denomination **Edge:** Reeded **Designer:** Louis Oscar Roty **Note:** Medallic alignment.

Date	Mintage	F	VF	XF	Unc	BU
2001	Est. 9,941	—	—	—	BV	365

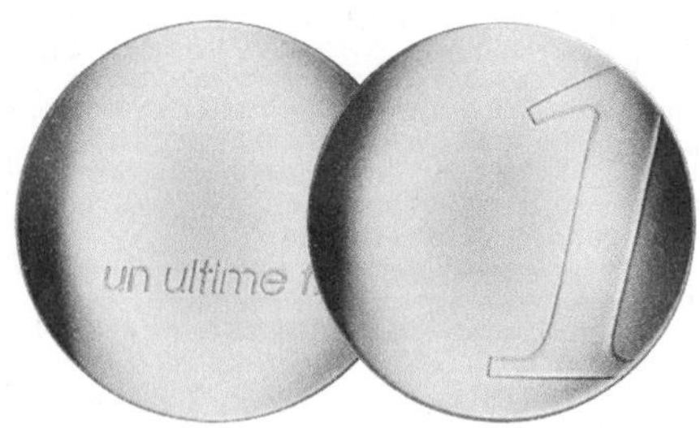

KM# 1290 FRANC

17.7700 g., 0.9800 Silver 0.5599 oz. ASW **Subject:** The Last Franc **Obv:** Legend on polished field **Obv. Legend:** UN ULTIME FRANC **Rev:** Number "1" on polished field **Edge Lettering:** REPUBLIQUE FRANCAISE STARCK LIBERTE EGALITE FRATERNITE (2001). **Note:** The coin is intentionally warped and the edge inscription is very faint. Struck at Paris Mint.

Date	Mintage	F	VF	XF	Unc	BU
2001 Matte	49,838	Value: 110				

KM# 1290a FRANC

26.1000 g., 0.7500 Gold 0.6293 oz. AGW **Subject:** The Last Franc **Obv:** Legend on polished field **Obv. Legend:** UN ULTIME FRANC **Rev:** Number "1" on polished field **Edge Lettering:** REPUBLIQUE FRANCAISE. STARCK. LIBERTE. EGALITE. FRATERNITE (cornucopia) 2001 **Note:** This coin has an intentionally warped surface and the edge inscription is very weak.

Date	Mintage	F	VF	XF	Unc	BU
2001 Matte	4,963	—	—	—	1,250	1,700

KM# 925.1 FRANC

6.0000 g., Nickel, 24 mm. **Obv:** The Seed Sower **Rev:** Laurel branch divides denomination and date **Edge:** Reeded **Note:** Without mint mark.

Date	Mintage	F	VF	XF	Unc	BU
2001	20,000,000	—	—	—	0.40	0.60

KM# 942.1 2 FRANCS

7.5000 g., Nickel, 26.5 mm. **Obv:** The Seed Sower **Rev:** Denomination on branches, date below **Edge:** Wide reeded **Designer:** Louis Oscar Roty

Date	Mintage	F	VF	XF	Unc	BU
2001 Bee	—	—	—	—	0.75	1.25

KM# 942.2 2 FRANCS

7.5000 g., Nickel, 26.5 mm. **Obv:** The Seed Sower **Rev:** Denomination on branches, date below **Edge:** Plain

Date	Mintage	F	VF	XF	Unc	BU
2001	—	—	—	—	0.75	1.25
2001 Proof	—	Value: 3.50				

KM# 926a.1 5 FRANCS

10.0000 g., Nickel Clad Copper-Nickel, 29 mm. **Obv:** The Seed Sower **Rev:** Branches divide denomination and date **Edge:** Reeded **Designer:** Raymond Joly

Date	Mintage	F	VF	XF	Unc	BU
2001 In sets only	—	—	—	—	5.00	7.50

KM# 926a.2 5 FRANCS

10.0000 g., Nickel Clad Copper-Nickel, 29 mm. **Obv:** Modified sower, engraver's signature: "O. ROTY" preceded by "D'AP" **Rev:** Branches divide date and denomination **Edge:** Plain

Date	Mintage	F	VF	XF	Unc	BU
2001	—	—	—	—	1.65	2.50
2001 Proof	—	Value: 6.50				

KM# 1309 5 FRANCS

12.0000 g., 0.9000 Silver 0.3472 oz. ASW, 29 mm. **Subject:** Last Year of the Franc **Obv:** The Seed Sower **Rev:** Denomination and date **Edge:** Lettered **Edge Lettering:** "* LIBERTY * EGALITE * FRATERNITE * "

Date	Mintage	F	VF	XF	Unc	BU
2001	25,000	—	—	—	22.50	25.00

KM# 1265.1 6.55957 FRANCS

13.0000 g., 0.9000 Silver 0.3761 oz. ASW **Subject:** Last Year of the French Franc **Obv:** French and other European euro currency equivalents **Rev:** Europa allegorical portrait, date below, "last year of the franc" logo after the date **Edge:** Reeded

Date	Mintage	F	VF	XF	Unc	BU
2001	Est. 20,000	—	—	—	25.00	35.00

KM# 1265.2 6.55957 FRANCS

22.2000 g., 0.9000 Silver 0.6423 oz. ASW **Obv:** French and other European euro currency equivalents **Rev:** Europa allegorical portrait, date below, "last year of the franc" logo after the date **Edge:** Plain

Date	Mintage	F	VF	XF	Unc	BU
2001 Proof	Est. 10,000	Value: 50.00				

KM# 1276 6.55957 FRANCS

22.2000 g., 0.9000 Silver 0.6423 oz. ASW **Subject:** Mottos **Obv:** Denomination **Rev:** FRATERNITE in red letters **Edge:** Reeded

Date	Mintage	F	VF	XF	Unc	BU
2001 Proof	2,171	Value: 50.00				

KM# 1277 6.55957 FRANCS

22.2000 g., 0.9000 Silver 0.6423 oz. ASW **Subject:** Mottos **Obv:** Denomination **Rev:** EGALITE in white letters

Date	Mintage	F	VF	XF	Unc	BU
2001 Proof	2,190	Value: 50.00				

KM# 1278 6.55957 FRANCS

22.2000 g., 0.9000 Silver 0.6423 oz. ASW **Subject:** Mottos **Obv:** Denomination **Rev:** LIBERTE in white letters

Date	Mintage	F	VF	XF	Unc	BU
2001 Proof	2,259	Value: 50.00				

KM# 964.2 10 FRANCS

Aluminum-Bronze, 23 mm. **Obv:** Winged figure divides RF **Rev:** Patterned denomination above date **Edge:** Plain

Date	Mintage	F	VF	XF	Unc	BU
2001	—	—	—	—	6.00	7.50
2001 Proof	—	Value: 15.00				

KM# 1268 10 FRANCS

22.2000 g., 0.9000 Silver 0.6423 oz. ASW **Subject:** Monuments of France - Palace of Versailles **Obv:** Stylized French map **Rev:** 1/2 bust of Louis XIV at right, internal and external palace views at left **Edge:** Plain

Date	Mintage	F	VF	XF	Unc	BU
2001 Proof	Est. 2,561	Value: 50.00				

KM# 1270 10 FRANCS

22.2000 g., 0.9000 Silver 0.6423 oz. ASW **Subject:** Monuments of France - Arch of Triumph **Obv:** Stylized French map **Rev:** Arch of Triumph on the Champs Elysees partial close up and aerial views

Date	Mintage	F	VF	XF	Unc	BU
2001 Proof	Est. 2,882	Value: 50.00				

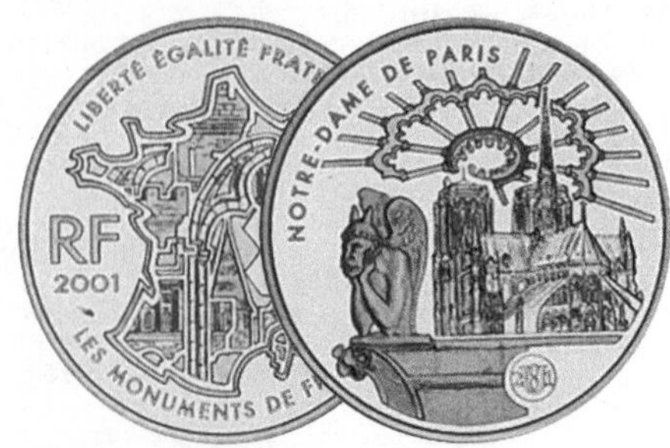

KM# 1272 10 FRANCS
22.2000 g., 0.9000 Silver 0.6423 oz. ASW **Subject:** Monuments of France - Notre Dame Cathedral **Obv:** Stylized French map **Rev:** Gargoyle at left, cathedral views at right

Date	Mintage	F	VF	XF	Unc	BU
2001 Proof	Est. 2,877	Value: 50.00				

KM# 1274 10 FRANCS
22.2000 g., 0.9000 Silver 0.6423 oz. ASW **Subject:** Monuments of France - Eiffel Tower **Obv:** Stylized French map **Rev:** Two tower views

Date	Mintage	F	VF	XF	Unc	BU
2001 Proof	Est. 3,888	Value: 45.00				

KM# 1008.2 20 FRANCS
9.0000 g., Tri-Metallic Copper-Aluminum-Nickel center, Nickel inner ring, Copper-Aluminum-Nickel outer ring, 27 mm. **Obv:** Mont St. Michel **Rev:** Patterned denomination above date **Edge:** 5 milled bands, reeded or plain

Date	Mintage	F	VF	XF	Unc	BU
2001	—	—	—	—	8.00	10.00
2001 Proof	—	Value: 25.00				

KM# 1266 65.5997 FRANCS
8.4500 g., 0.9200 Gold 0.2499 oz. AGW **Subject:** Last Year of the French Franc **Obv:** French and other European euro currency equivalents **Rev:** Europa allegorical portrait, date below, "last year of the franc" logo after the date **Edge:** Reeded

Date	Mintage	F	VF	XF	Unc	BU
2001 Proof	3,000	Value: 650				

KM# 1269 100 FRANCS
17.0000 g., 0.9200 Gold 0.5028 oz. AGW **Subject:** Palace of Versailles **Obv:** Stylized French map **Rev:** Louis XIV with internal and external palace views **Edge:** Plain

Date	Mintage	F	VF	XF	Unc	BU
2001 Proof	105	Value: 875				

KM# 1271 100 FRANCS
17.0000 g., 0.9200 Gold 0.5028 oz. AGW **Obv:** Champs-Elysees **Rev:** Arch of Triumph partial close up and aerial views

Date	Mintage	F	VF	XF	Unc	BU
2001 Proof	115	Value: 875				

KM# 1273 100 FRANCS
17.0000 g., 0.9200 Gold 0.5028 oz. AGW **Obv:** Notre-Dame Cathedral **Rev:** Gargoyle and cathedral views

Date	Mintage	F	VF	XF	Unc	BU
2001 Proof	116	Value: 875				

KM# 1275 100 FRANCS
17.0000 g., 0.9200 Gold 0.5028 oz. AGW **Obv:** Eiffel Tower **Rev:** Two tower views

Date	Mintage	F	VF	XF	Unc	BU
2001 Proof	170	Value: 875				

KM# 1994 100 FRANCS
155.5500 g., 0.9990 Gold 4.9958 oz. AGW **Obv:** Cruved cross with coins **Rev:** Europa facing at right, flags at left

Date	Mintage	F	VF	XF	Unc	BU
2003 Proof	99	Value: 9,500				

KM# 2001 100 FRANCS
155.5500 g., 0.9990 Gold 4.9958 oz. AGW **Subject:** Athletic World Championships **Obv:** Winner Podium before buildings **Rev:** Runner

Date	Mintage	F	VF	XF	Unc	BU
2003 Proof	369	Value: 10,000				

KM# 2002 100 FRANCS
155.5500 g., 0.9990 Gold 4.9958 oz. AGW **Subject:** Louisana Purchase, 200th Anniversary **Obv:** Thomas Jefferson and Napoleon Bonaparte with map of purchase **Rev:** Celebration of Lousiana: plantation mansion, jazz, riverboat

Date	Mintage	F	VF	XF	Unc	BU
2003 Proof	99	Value: 10,000				

KM# 1267 655.957 FRANCS
31.1035 g., 0.9990 Gold 0.9990 oz. AGW **Subject:** Last Year of the French Franc **Obv:** French and other European euro currency equivalents **Rev:** Europa allegorical portrait, date below, "last year of the franc" logo after the date **Edge:** Plain

Date	Mintage	F	VF	XF	Unc	BU
2001 Proof	2,000	Value: 2,100				

KM# 1267.1 655.957 FRANCS
155.5175 g., 0.9990 Gold 4.9948 oz. AGW **Obv:** French and other European euro currency equivalents **Rev:** Europa allegorical portrait, date below, "last year of the franc" after the date **Edge:** Plain

Date	Mintage	F	VF	XF	Unc	BU
2001 Proof	99	Value: 9,500				

KM# 1279 655.957 FRANCS
17.0000 g., 0.9200 Gold 0.5028 oz. AGW **Subject:** Motto Series **Obv:** Denomination **Rev:** FRATERNITE **Edge:** Reeded

Date	Mintage	F	VF	XF	Unc	BU
2001 Proof	62	Value: 900				

KM# 1280 655.957 FRANCS
17.0000 g., 0.9200 Gold 0.5028 oz. AGW **Subject:** Motto Series **Obv:** Denomination **Rev:** EGALITE

Date	Mintage	F	VF	XF	Unc	BU
2001 Proof	64	Value: 900				

KM# 1281 655.957 FRANCS
17.0000 g., 0.9200 Gold 0.5028 oz. AGW **Subject:** Motto Series **Obv:** Denomination **Rev:** LIBERTE

Date	Mintage	F	VF	XF	Unc	BU
2001 Proof	63	Value: 900				

EURO COINAGE

KM# 1282 EURO CENT
2.2700 g., Copper Plated Steel, 16.3 mm. **Obv:** Human face **Rev:** Denomination and globe **Edge:** Plain

Date	Mintage	F	VF	XF	Unc	BU
2001	300,681,580	—	—	—	0.35	0.50
2001 Proof	15,000	Value: 10.00				
2002	200,000	—	—	—	—	10.00
2002 Proof	21,453	Value: 8.00				
2003	160,017,000	—	—	—	1.00	1.50
2003 Proof	40,000	Value: 8.00				
2004	400,032,000	—	—	—	0.35	0.50
2004 Proof	20,000	Value: 10.00				
2005	240,320,000	—	—	—	0.35	0.50
2005 Proof	10,000	Value: 12.00				
2006	343,078,000	—	—	—	0.35	0.50
2006 Proof	10,000	Value: 12.00				
2007	300,058,000	—	—	—	0.35	0.50
2007 Proof	7,500	Value: 14.00				
2008	462,757,000	—	—	—	0.35	0.50
2008 Proof	7,500	Value: 14.00				
2009	404,050,500	—	—	—	0.35	0.50
2009 Proof	7,500	Value: 14.00				
2010	—	—	—	—	0.35	0.50
2010 Proof	—	Value: 15.00				
2011	—	—	—	—	0.35	0.50
2011 Proof	—	Value: 15.00				
2012	—	—	—	—	0.35	0.50
2012 Proof	—	Value: 15.00				
2013	—	—	—	—	0.35	0.50
2013 Proof	—	Value: 15.00				

KM# 1283 2 EURO CENT
3.0300 g., Copper Plated Steel, 18.7 mm. **Obv:** Human face **Rev:** Denomination and globe **Edge:** Grooved

Date	Mintage	F	VF	XF	Unc	BU
2001	249,101,580	—	—	—	0.50	0.75
2001 Proof	15,000	Value: 10.00				
2002 In sets only	100,000	—	—	—	—	12.50
2002 Proof	21,453	Value: 8.00				
2003	160,175,000	—	—	—	1.25	2.00
2003 Proof	40,000	Value: 8.00				
2004	300,024,000	—	—	—	—	1.00
2004 Proof	20,000	Value: 10.00				
2005	2,603,202,000	—	—	—	—	1.00
2005 Proof	10,000	Value: 12.00				
2006	283,278,000	—	—	—	—	1.00
2006 Proof	10,000	Value: 12.00				
2007	213,258,000	—	—	—	—	1.00
2007 Proof	7,500	Value: 14.00				
2008	386,557,000	—	—	—	—	1.00
2008 Proof	7,500	Value: 14.00				
2009	317,050,500	—	—	—	—	1.00
2009 Proof	7,500	Value: 14.00				
2010	—	—	—	—	—	1.00
2010 Proof	—	Value: 14.00				
2011	—	—	—	—	—	1.00
2011 Proof	—	Value: 14.00				
2012	—	—	—	—	—	1.00
2012 Proof	—	Value: 14.00				
2013	—	—	—	—	—	1.00
2013 Proof	—	Value: 14.00				

KM# 1284 5 EURO CENT
3.8600 g., Copper Plated Steel, 21.2 mm. **Obv:** Human face **Rev:** Denomination and globe **Edge:** Plain

Date	Mintage	F	VF	XF	Unc	BU
2001	217,324,477	—	—	—	0.75	1.25
2001 Proof	15,000	Value: 12.00				
2002	186,400,000	—	—	—	0.75	1.25
2002 Proof	21,453	Value: 10.00				
2003	101,175,000	—	—	—	1.00	1.50
2003 Proof	40,000	Value: 10.00				
2004	60,162,000	—	—	—	—	1.25
2004 Proof	20,000	Value: 12.00				
2005	20,320,000	—	—	—	—	1.25
2005 Proof	10,000	Value: 14.00				
2006	132,078,000	—	—	—	—	1.25
2006 Proof	10,000	Value: 14.00				
2007	130,058,000	—	—	—	—	1.25
2007 Proof	7,500	Value: 16.00				
2008	218,257,000	—	—	—	—	1.25
2008 Proof	7,500	Value: 16.00				
2009	184,550,500	—	—	—	—	1.25
2009 Proof	7,500	Value: 16.00				
2010	—	—	—	—	—	1.25
2010 Proof	—	Value: 16.00				
2011	—	—	—	—	—	1.25
2011 Proof	—	Value: 16.00				
2012	—	—	—	—	—	1.25
2012 Proof	—	Value: 16.00				
2013	—	—	—	—	—	1.25
2013 Proof	—	Value: 16.00				

KM# 1285 10 EURO CENT
4.0700 g., Brass, 19.7 mm. **Obv:** The seed sower divides date and RF **Rev:** Denomination and map **Edge:** Reeded

Date	Mintage	F	VF	XF	Unc	BU
2001	144,513,261	—	—	—	1.25	2.00
2001 Proof	15,000	Value: 12.00				
2002	206,700,000	—	—	—	0.75	1.25
2002 Proof	21,453	Value: 10.00				
2003	180,875,000	—	—	—	1.25	2.00
2003 Proof	40,000	Value: 10.00				
2004	5,000,000	—	—	—	—	1.50
2004 In sets only	140,000	—	—	—	—	—
2004 Proof	20,000	Value: 12.00				
2005	45,120,000	—	—	—	—	1.50
2005 Proof	10,000	Value: 14.00				
2006	60,278,000	—	—	—	—	1.50
2006 Proof	10,000	Value: 14.00				

KM# 1410 10 EURO CENT
4.0700 g., Brass, 19.7 mm. **Obv:** Sower **Rev:** Relief map of Western Europe, stars, lines and value **Edge:** Reeded

Date	Mintage	F	VF	XF	Unc	BU
2007	90,158,000	—	—	—	—	1.50
2007 Proof	7,500	Value: 14.00				
2008	178,757,000	—	—	—	—	1.50
2008 Proof	7,500	Value: 14.00				
2009	142,550,500	—	—	—	—	1.50
2009 Proof	7,500	Value: 14.00				
2010	—	—	—	—	—	1.50
2010 Proof	—	Value: 14.00				
2011	—	—	—	—	—	1.50
2011 Proof	—	Value: 14.00				
2012	—	—	—	—	—	1.50
2012 Proof	—	Value: 14.00				
2013	—	—	—	—	—	1.50
2013 Proof	—	Value: 14.00				

KM# 1286 20 EURO CENT

5.7300 g., Brass, 22.2 mm. **Obv:** The seed sower divides date and RF **Rev:** Denomination and map **Edge:** Notched

Date	Mintage	F	VF	XF	Unc	BU
2001	256,342,108	—	—	—	1.00	1.50
2001 Proof	15,000	Value: 14.00				
2002	192,100,000	—	—	—	1.00	1.50
2002 Proof	21,453	Value: 12.00				
2003 In sets only	180,000	—	—	—	—	9.50
2003 Proof	40,000	Value: 12.00				
2004 In sets only	160,000	—	—	—	—	9.50
2004 Proof	20,000	Value: 14.00				
2005 In sets only	120,000	—	—	—	—	9.50
2005 Proof	10,000	Value: 16.00				
2006 In sets only	67,600	—	—	—	—	9.50
2006 Proof	10,000	Value: 16.00				

KM# 1411 20 EURO CENT

5.7300 g., Brass, 22.2 mm. **Obv:** Sower **Rev:** Relief map of Western Europe, stars, lines and value **Edge:** Notched

Date	Mintage	F	VF	XF	Unc	BU
2007	40,258,000	—	—	—	—	1.50
2007 Proof	7,500	Value: 14.00				
2008	25,557,000	—	—	—	—	1.50
2008 Proof	7,500	Value: 14.00				
2009	82,550,500	—	—	—	—	1.50
2009 Proof	7,500	Value: 14.00				
2010	—	—	—	—	—	1.50
2010 Proof	—	Value: 14.00				
2011	—	—	—	—	—	1.50
2011 Proof	—	Value: 14.00				
2012	—	—	—	—	—	1.50
2012 Proof	—	Value: 14.00				
2013	—	—	—	—	—	1.50
2013 Proof	—	Value: 14.00				

KM# 1293 1/4 EURO

12.5000 g., Aluminum-Bronze, 30 mm. **Subject:** Childrens Design **Obv:** Euro globe with children **Rev:** Denomination and stars **Edge:** Plain

Date	Mintage	F	VF	XF	Unc	BU
2002	1,000,000	—	—	—	6.50	8.50

KM# 1300 1/4 EURO

13.0000 g., 0.9000 Silver 0.3761 oz. ASW, 30 mm. **Subject:** Europa **Obv:** Eight French euro coin designs **Rev:** Portrait and flags design of 6.55957 francs coin KM-1265 **Edge:** Reeded

Date	Mintage	F	VF	XF	Unc	BU
2002	20,000	—	—	—	20.00	22.00

KM# 1293a 1/4 EURO

13.0000 g., 0.9000 Silver 0.3761 oz. ASW, 30 mm. **Subject:** Childrens Design **Obv:** Euro globe with children **Rev:** Denomination **Edge:** Plain

Date	Mintage	F	VF	XF	Unc	BU
2002 Proof	10,000	Value: 45.00				

KM# 1331 1/4 EURO

3.1100 g., 0.9990 Gold 0.0999 oz. AGW, 15 mm. **Subject:** Children's Design **Obv:** Euro globe with children **Rev:** Denomination **Edge:** Plain

Date	Mintage	F	VF	XF	Unc	BU
2002 Proof	5,000	Value: 185				

KM# 1983 1/4 EURO

13.0000 g., 0.9000 Silver 0.3761 oz. ASW **Obv:** Soccer ball and syylized map of France **Rev:** Two soccer players and stadium plan

Date	Mintage	F	VF	XF	Unc	BU
2002	9,033	—	—	—	—	35.00

KM# 1350 1/4 EURO

3.1100 g., 0.9999 Gold 0.1000 oz. AGW, 15 mm. **Obv:** Obverse design of first one franc coin **Rev:** Reverse design of first one franc coin **Edge:** Plain

Date	Mintage	F	VF	XF	Unc	BU
2003 Proof	5,000	Value: 185				

KM# 1991 1/4 EURO

13.0000 g., 0.9000 Silver 0.3761 oz. ASW **Obv:** Curved cross pattern with coins **Rev:** Europa head at right, flags at left

Date	Mintage	F	VF	XF	Unc	BU
2003	16,035	—	—	—	—	25.00

KM# 1995 1/4 EURO

13.0000 g., 0.9000 Silver 0.3761 oz. ASW **Subject:** Tour de France, 100th Anniversary

Date	Mintage	F	VF	XF	Unc	BU
2003	71,257	—	—	—	—	20.00

KM# 1372 1/4 EURO

22.2000 g., 0.9000 Silver 0.6423 oz. ASW, 37 mm. **Obv:** Samuel de Champlain **Rev:** Sail ship **Edge:** Plain

Date	Mintage	F	VF	XF	Unc	BU
2004	20,000	—	—	—	27.50	32.50

KM# 1390 1/4 EURO

13.0000 g., 0.9000 Silver 0.3761 oz. ASW, 30 mm. **Subject:** European Union Expansion **Obv:** Partial face and flags **Rev:** Puzzle map **Edge:** Plain

Date	Mintage	F	VF	XF	Unc	BU
2004	20,000	—	—	—	22.00	25.00

KM# 2017 1/4 EURO

22.2000 g., 0.9000 Silver 0.6423 oz. ASW **Subject:** Chinese - French culture **Obv:** Rooster and dragon **Rev:** Temple of Heaven and Eiffel tower

Date	Mintage	F	VF	XF	Unc	BU
2004	10,000	—	—	—	—	100

KM# 1402 1/4 EURO

11.0000 g., Aluminum-Bronze, 30 mm. **Subject:** Jules Verne **Obv:** Various scenes from Jules Verne's novels **Rev:** Jules Verne's portrait left of value and date

Date	Mintage	F	VF	XF	Unc	BU
2005	50,000	—	—	—	—	10.00

KM# 1442 1/4 EURO

22.2000 g., 0.9000 Silver 0.6423 oz. ASW, 37 mm. **Obv:** Bust of Franklin facing slightly right at left, his diplomatic and technical successes at right **Obv. Legend:** BENJAMIN FRANKLIN 1706-2006 **Obv. Inscription:** AMI DE LA FRANCE **Rev:** French flag at left, American flag at right **Rev. Inscription:** PHILOSOPHE / DIPLOMATE / ÉCRIVAIN / SAVANT

Date	Mintage	F	VF	XF	Unc	BU
2006	15,000	—	—	—	32.00	35.00

KM# 1445 1/4 EURO

22.2000 g., 0.9000 Silver 0.6423 oz. ASW, 37 mm. **Subject:** Marshall Bernadotte under Napoleon **Rev:** Military bust facing 3/4 right at left, building in backgound at right **Rev. Legend:** LIBERTÉ / ÉGALITÉ / FRATERNITÉ - KARL XIV JOHAN ROI DE SUÈDE

Date	Mintage	F	VF	XF	Unc	BU
2006 Proof	10,000	—	—	—	32.00	35.00

KM# 1457 1/4 EURO

22.2000 g., 0.9000 Silver 0.6423 oz. ASW, 37 mm. **Subject:** Hèpitaux de France Foundation **Obv:** Foundation logo **Rev:** TGV train, money box on outlined map of France

Date	Mintage	F	VF	XF	Unc	BU
2006	50,000	—	—	—	28.00	30.00

KM# 1415 1/4 EURO

22.2000 g., 0.9000 Silver 0.6423 oz. ASW, 37 mm. **Obv:** Jean de la Fontaine, value, Chinese astrological animals, date, Paris mint privy marks but without national identification **Rev:** Dog in wreath **Edge:** Reeded **Note:** Anonymous coinage

Date	Mintage	F	VF	XF	Unc	BU
2006	10,000	—	—	—	32.00	35.00

KM# 2061 1/4 EURO

22.2000 g., 0.9000 Silver 0.6423 oz. ASW **Subject:** Wolfgang Amadeus Mozart, 250th Anniversary of Birth **Obv:** Youthful bust **Rev:** Hand on piano keys, music above

Date	Mintage	F	VF	XF	Unc	BU
2006	5,000	—	—	—	—	55.00

KM# 1419 1/4 EURO

13.0000 g., 0.9000 Silver 0.3761 oz. ASW, 30 mm. **Obv:** Military bust of Lafayette facing 3/4 left **Obv. Legend:** LA FAYETTE. HÉROS DE LA RÉVOLUTION AMÉRICAINE **Obv. Inscription:** 1757/1854 at left, RF monogram at right **Rev:** Sailing ship L' Hermione **Rev. Legend:** LA FAYETTE, HERO OF THE AMERICAN REVOLUTION **Edge:** Plain

Date	Mintage	F	VF	XF	Unc	BU
2007 (a) Proof-like	5,000	—	—	—	32.00	35.00

KM# 1421 1/4 EURO

15.0000 g., 0.9000 Silver 0.4340 oz. ASW **Subject:** 90th Anniversary Death of Degas **Obv:** Ballerina "The Star" at left **Obv. Inscription:** *Degas* **Rev:** Paint brushes and oils multicolor at left, self portrait at right **Rev. Inscription:** LIBERTÉ / ÉGALITÉ / FRATERNITÉ **Shape:** rectangular, 30 x 21 mm

Date	Mintage	F	VF	XF	Unc	BU
2007	5,000	—	—	—	42.00	45.00

KM# 1417 1/4 EURO

22.2000 g., 0.9000 Silver 0.6423 oz. ASW, 37 mm. **Obv:** Jean de la Fontaine, value, Chinese astrological animals, date, Paris mint privy marks but without national identification **Rev:** Pig in wreath **Edge:** Reeded **Note:** Anonymous issue.

Date	Mintage	F	VF	XF	Unc	BU
2007	10,000	—	—	—	32.00	35.00

KM# 1461 1/4 EURO

13.0000 g., 0.9000 Silver 0.3761 oz. ASW, 30 mm. **Subject:** Sebastien Le Prestre de Vauban, 300th Anniversary of Death **Obv:** Arms above funeral coach, book at left **Rev:** Vauban standing; plans of fortress

Date	Mintage	F	VF	XF	Unc	BU
2007 Proof	5,000	Value: 22.00				

KM# 1483 1/4 EURO

13.0000 g., 0.9000 Silver 0.3761 oz. ASW, 37 mm. **Subject:** 2007 Rugby World Cup **Obv:** Two Rugby players **Rev:** Logo and goal

Date	Mintage	F	VF	XF	Unc	BU
2007	5,000	—	—	—	32.00	35.00

KM# 1570 1/4 EURO

15.0000 g., 0.9000 Silver 0.4340 oz. ASW, 30 x 21 mm. **Subject:** Edward Manet **Obv:** Manet's "Olympia" painting **Rev:** Multicolor paint brushes and Manet's portrait **Shape:** Rectangle

Date	Mintage	F	VF	XF	Unc	BU
2008	10,000	—	—	—	—	65.00

KM# 1572 1/4 EURO

22.2000 g., 0.9000 Silver 0.6423 oz. ASW, 37 mm. **Subject:** Lunar New Year - Year of the Rat **Obv:** Bust of Jean de la Fontaine and twelve awards **Rev:** Rat within border

Date	Mintage	F	VF	XF	Unc	BU
2008	10,000	—	—	—	32.00	35.00

KM# 1287 50 EURO CENT

7.8100 g., Brass, 24.2 mm. **Obv:** The Seed Sower divides date and RF **Rev:** Denomination and map **Edge:** Reeded

Date	Mintage	F	VF	XF	Unc	BU
2001	276,287,274	—	—	—	1.25	2.00
2001 Proof	15,000	Value: 15.00				
2002	226,500,000	—	—	—	1.25	2.00
2002 Proof	21,453	Value: 14.00				
2003 In sets only	180,000	—	—	—	—	11.50
2003 Proof	40,000	Value: 14.00				
2004 In sets only	160,000	—	—	—	—	11.50
2004 Proof	20,000	Value: 15.00				
2005 In sets only	120,000	—	—	—	—	11.50
2005 Proof	10,000	Value: 17.00				
2006 In sets only	67,600	—	—	—	—	11.50
2006 Proof	10,000	Value: 17.00				

KM# 1412 50 EURO CENT

7.8100 g., Brass, 24.2 mm. **Obv:** Sower **Rev:** Relief map of Western Europe, stars, lines and value **Edge:** Reeded

Date	Mintage	F	VF	XF	Unc	BU
2007 In sets only	58,000	—	—	—	—	11.50
2007 Proof	7,500	Value: 16.00				
2008 In sets only	57,000	—	—	—	—	2.00
2008 Proof	7,500	Value: 16.00				
2009 In sets only	50,500	—	—	—	—	2.00
2009 Proof	7,500	Value: 16.00				
2010	—	—	—	—	—	2.00
2010 Proof	—	Value: 16.00				
2011	—	—	—	—	—	2.00
2011 Proof	—	Value: 16.00				
2012	—	—	—	—	—	2.00
2012 Proof	—	Value: 16.00				
2013	—	—	—	—	—	2.00
2013 Proof	—	Value: 16.00				

KM# 1288 EURO

7.5000 g., Bi-Metallic Copper-Nickel center in Nickel-Brass ring, 23.25 mm. **Obv:** Stylized tree divides RF within circle, date below **Rev:** Denomination and map **Edge:** Segmented reeding

Date	Mintage	F	VF	XF	Unc	BU
2001	150,251,624	—	—	—	2.75	4.00
2001 Proof	15,000	Value: 18.00				
2002	129,400,000	—	—	—	2.50	3.75
2002 Proof	21,453	Value: 16.00				
2003 In sets only	100,000	—	—	—	8.00	12.50
2003 Proof	20,000	Value: 18.00				
2004 In sets only	160,000	—	—	—	—	2.50
2004 Proof	20,000	Value: 18.00				
2005 In sets only	120,000	—	—	—	—	2.50
2005 Proof	10,000	Value: 20.00				
2006 In sets only	78,000	—	—	—	—	2.50
2006 Proof	10,000	Value: 20.00				

KM# 1413 EURO

7.5000 g., Bi-Metallic Copper-Nickel center in Nickel-Brass ring, 23.25 mm. **Obv:** Stylized tree **Rev:** Relief map of Western Europe, stars, lines and value **Edge:** Segmented reeding

Date	Mintage	F	VF	XF	Unc	BU
2007 In sets only	58,000	—	—	—	—	11.50
2007 Proof	7,500	Value: 20.00				
2008 In sets only	57,000	—	—	—	—	2.50
2008 Proof	7,500	Value: 20.00				
2009 In sets only	50,500	—	—	—	—	2.50
2009 Proof	7,500	Value: 20.00				
2010	—	—	—	—	—	2.50
2010 Proof	—	Value: 20.00				
2011	—	—	—	—	—	2.50
2011 Proof	—	Value: 20.00				
2012	—	—	—	—	—	2.50
2012 Proof	—	Value: 20.00				
2013	—	—	—	—	—	2.50
2013 Proof	—	Value: 20.00				

KM# 1464 EURO

155.5500 g., 0.9500 Silver 4.7508 oz. ASW, 50 mm. **Subject:** Sebastien Le Prestre de Vauban, 300th Anniversary of Death

Date	Mintage	F	VF	XF	Unc	BU
2007 Proof	500	Value: 325				

KM# 1470 EURO

17.0000 g., 0.9200 Gold 0.5028 oz. AGW, 31 mm. **Subject:** Le Petit Prince, 60th Anniversary **Obv:** Prince standing with rabbit

Date	Mintage	F	VF	XF	Unc	BU
2007 Proof	2,000	Value: 875				

KM# 1486 EURO

17.0000 g., 0.9200 Gold 0.5028 oz. AGW, 31 mm. **Subject:** 2007 Rugby World Cup **Obv:** Two players and goal **Rev:** Logo and goal

Date	Mintage	F	VF	XF	Unc	BU
2007 Proof	500	Value: 875				

KM# 1490 EURO

22.0000 g., 0.9000 Silver 0.6366 oz. ASW **Subject:** Unesco **Obv:** Great Wall of China

Date	Mintage	F	VF	XF	Unc	BU
2007 Proof	5,000	Value: 60.00				

KM# 1491 EURO

8.4500 g., 0.9200 Gold 0.2499 oz. AGW, 22 mm. **Subject:** Unesco **Obv:** Crest Wall of China **Rev:** Unesco Building and emblem

Date	Mintage	F	VF	XF	Unc	BU
2007 Proof	500	Value: 450				

KM# 1492 EURO

22.2000 g., 0.9000 Silver 0.6423 oz. ASW, 37 mm. **Subject:** Point Neuf 400th Anniversary **Obv:** Monuments of France logo **Rev:** Point Neuf Bridge, Paris Mint Museum

Date	Mintage	F	VF	XF	Unc	BU
2007 Proof	3,000	Value: 80.00				

KM# 1493 EURO

8.4500 g., 0.9200 Gold 0.2499 oz. AGW, 22 mm. **Subject:** Point Neuf, 400th Anniversary **Obv:** Monuments of France logo **Rev:** Point Neuf Brudge, Paris Mint Building

Date	Mintage	F	VF	XF	Unc	BU
2007 Proof	500	Value: 450				

KM# 1495 EURO

8.4500 g., 0.9200 Gold 0.2499 oz. AGW, 22 mm. **Subject:** Cannes Film Festival **Obv:** Cinema screen and stage, Golden Palm Award

Date	Mintage	F	VF	XF	Unc	BU
2007 Proof	500	Value: 450				

KM# 1514 EURO

17.0000 g., 0.9200 Gold 0.5028 oz. AGW, 31 mm. **Subject:** Stanislas Lesczynski **Obv:** Bust, shield **Rev:** Palac Stanislas - Nancy

Date	Mintage	F	VF	XF	Unc	BU
2007 Proof	500	Value: 875				

KM# 1587 EURO

8.4500 g., 0.9200 Gold 0.2499 oz. AGW, 22 mm. **Subject:** Court of Human Rights, 50th Anniversary **Obv:** Sower left **Rev:** Text

Date	Mintage	F	VF	XF	Unc	BU
2009P Proof	500	Value: 450				

KM# 1332 1-1/2 EURO

22.2000 g., 0.9000 Silver 0.6423 oz. ASW, 37 mm. **Obv:** Victor Hugo, denomination and map **Rev:** Multicolor "Gavroche" **Edge:** Plain

Date	Mintage	F	VF	XF	Unc	BU
2002 Proof	10,000	Value: 55.00				

KM# 1301 1-1/2 EURO

22.2000 g., 0.9000 Silver 0.6423 oz. ASW, 37 mm. **Subject:** Europa **Obv:** Eight French euro coins design **Rev:** Portrait and flags design of 6.55957 francs KM-1265 **Edge:** Plain

Date	Mintage	F	VF	XF	Unc	BU
2002 Proof	50,000	Value: 45.00				

KM# 1305 1-1/2 EURO

22.2000 g., 0.9000 Silver 0.6423 oz. ASW, 37 mm. **Subject:** French Landmarks **Obv:** French map **Rev:** Le Mont St. Michel **Edge:** Plain

Date	Mintage	F	VF	XF	Unc	BU
2002 Proof	10,000	Value: 50.00				

KM# 1307 1-1/2 EURO

22.2000 g., 0.9000 Silver 0.6423 oz. ASW, 37 mm. **Subject:** French Landmarks **Obv:** French map **Rev:** La Butte Montmartre **Edge:** Plain

Date	Mintage	F	VF	XF	Unc	BU
2002 Proof	10,000	Value: 47.50				

KM# 1310 1-1/2 EURO

22.2000 g., 0.9000 Silver 0.6423 oz. ASW, 37 mm. **Subject:** First West to East Transatlantic Flight **Obv:** Denomination, map and Lindbergh portrait **Rev:** Spirit of St. Louis (airplane) and map **Edge:** Plain

Date	Mintage	F	VF	XF	Unc	BU
2002 Proof	10,000	Value: 50.00				

KM# 1840 1-1/2 EURO

22.2000 g., 0.9000 Silver 0.6423 oz. ASW, 37 mm. **Subject:** Snow White **Rev:** Scenes from the book, color

Date	Mintage	F	VF	XF	Unc	BU
2002 Proof	—	Value: 55.00				

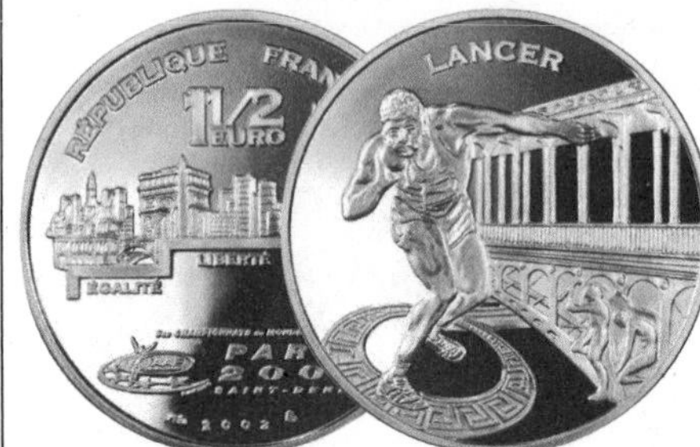

KM# 1843 1-1/2 EURO

22.2000 g., 0.9000 Silver 0.6423 oz. ASW, 37 mm. **Subject:** Athletic Games **Rev:** Shot Put athlete and stadium

Date	Mintage	F	VF	XF	Unc	BU
2002 Proof	—	Value: 55.00				

KM# 1841 1-1/2 EURO

22.2000 g., 0.9000 Silver 0.6423 oz. ASW, 37 mm. **Subject:** Cinderella **Rev:** Scenes from the book, color

Date	Mintage	F	VF	XF	Unc	BU
2002 Proof	—	Value: 55.00				

KM# 1842 1-1/2 EURO
22.2000 g., 0.9000 Silver 0.6423 oz. ASW, 37 mm. **Subject:** Pinocchio **Rev:** Scenes form the book, color

Date	Mintage	F	VF	XF	Unc	BU
2002 Proof	—	Value: 55.00				

KM# 1321 1-1/2 EURO
22.2000 g., 0.9000 Silver 0.6423 oz. ASW, 37 mm. **Obv:** Tour de France logo **Rev:** Cyclist going left **Edge:** Plain

Date	Mintage	F	VF	XF	Unc	BU
2003 Proof	150,000	Value: 50.00				

KM# 1322 1-1/2 EURO
22.2000 g., 0.9000 Silver 0.6423 oz. ASW, 37 mm. **Obv:** Tour de France logo **Rev:** Group of cyclists and Arch de Triumph **Edge:** Plain

Date	Mintage	F	VF	XF	Unc	BU
2003 (Ht) Proof	150,000	Value: 50.00				

KM# 1323 1-1/2 EURO
22.2000 g., 0.9000 Silver 0.6423 oz. ASW, 37 mm. **Obv:** Tour de France logo **Rev:** Two cyclists and spectators **Edge:** Plain

Date	Mintage	F	VF	XF	Unc	BU
2003 (Ht) Proof	150,000	Value: 50.00				

KM# 1324 1-1/2 EURO
22.2000 g., 0.9000 Silver 0.6423 oz. ASW, 37 mm. **Obv:** Tour de France logo **Rev:** Two groups of cyclists **Edge:** Plain

Date	Mintage	F	VF	XF	Unc	BU
2003 (Ht) Proof	150,000	Value: 50.00				

KM# 1325 1-1/2 EURO
22.2000 g., 0.9000 Silver 0.6423 oz. ASW, 37 mm. **Obv:** Tour de France logo **Rev:** Cyclists, stopwatch and gears **Edge:** Plain

Date	Mintage	F	VF	XF	Unc	BU
2003 (Ht) Proof	150,000	Value: 50.00				

KM# 1336 1-1/2 EURO
22.2000 g., 0.9000 Silver 0.6423 oz. ASW, 37 mm. **Obv:** Jefferson and Napoleon with Louisiana Purchase map **Rev:** Jazz musician, mansion and river boat **Edge:** Plain

Date	Mintage	F	VF	XF	Unc	BU
2003 Proof	10,000	Value: 55.00				

KM# 1338 1-1/2 EURO
22.2000 g., 0.9000 Silver 0.6423 oz. ASW, 37 mm. **Obv:** Curved cross design with multiple values **Rev:** Goddess Europa and flags **Edge:** Plain

Date	Mintage	F	VF	XF	Unc	BU
2003 Proof	40,000	Value: 50.00				

KM# 1341 1-1/2 EURO
22.2000 g., 0.9000 Silver 0.6423 oz. ASW, 37 mm. **Obv:** Denomination and compass face **Rev:** SS Normandie and New York City **Edge:** Plain

Date	Mintage	F	VF	XF	Unc	BU
2003 Proof	15,000	Value: 55.00				

KM# 1343 1-1/2 EURO
22.2000 g., 0.9000 Silver 0.6423 oz. ASW, 37 mm. **Obv:** Denomination and compass face **Rev:** Airplane and Tokyo Geisha **Edge:** Plain

Date	Mintage	F	VF	XF	Unc	BU
2003 Proof	15,000	Value: 55.00				

KM# 1345 1-1/2 EURO
22.2000 g., 0.9000 Silver 0.6423 oz. ASW, 37 mm. **Obv:** Paul Gauguin **Rev:** Native woman **Edge:** Plain

Date	Mintage	F	VF	XF	Unc	BU
2003 Proof	15,000	Value: 65.00				

KM# 1351 1-1/2 EURO
22.2000 g., 0.9000 Silver 0.6423 oz. ASW, 37 mm. **Obv:** Obverse design of first one franc coin **Rev:** Reverse design of first one franc coin **Edge:** Plain

Date	Mintage	F	VF	XF	Unc	BU
2003 Proof	15,000	Value: 55.00				

KM# 1353 1-1/2 EURO
22.2000 g., 0.9000 Silver 0.6423 oz. ASW, 37 mm. **Obv:** Mona Lisa **Rev:** Leonardo da Vinci **Edge:** Plain

Date	Mintage	F	VF	XF	Unc	BU
2003 Proof	10,000	Value: 55.00				

KM# 1355 1-1/2 EURO
22.2000 g., 0.9000 Silver 0.6423 oz. ASW, 37 mm. **Obv:** Map and denomination **Rev:** Chateau Chambord **Edge:** Plain

Date	Mintage	F	VF	XF	Unc	BU
2003 Proof	10,000	Value: 50.00				

KM# 1357 1-1/2 EURO
22.2000 g., 0.9000 Silver 0.6423 oz. ASW, 37 mm. **Obv:** Denomination in swirling design **Rev:** Multicolor Hansel and Gretel, witch and house **Edge:** Plain

Date	Mintage	F	VF	XF	Unc	BU
2003 Proof	10,000	Value: 55.00				

KM# 1359 1-1/2 EURO
22.2000 g., 0.9000 Silver 0.6423 oz. ASW, 37 mm. **Obv:** Denomination in swirling design **Rev:** Multicolor Alice in Wonderland **Edge:** Plain

Date	Mintage	F	VF	XF	Unc	BU
2003 Proof	10,000	Value: 55.00				

KM# 1361 1-1/2 EURO
22.2000 g., 0.9000 Silver 0.6423 oz. ASW, 37 mm. **Obv:** Pierre de Coubertin **Rev:** Olympic runners **Edge:** Plain

Date	Mintage	F	VF	XF	Unc	BU
2003 Proof	50,000	Value: 50.00				

KM# 1996 1-1/2 EURO
22.2000 g., 0.9000 Silver 0.6423 oz. ASW **Subject:** Athletic World Championships **Obv:** Winner podium before buildigns **Rev:** Runners by Pont des Arts

Date	Mintage	F	VF	XF	Unc	BU
2003 Proof	4,425	Value: 45.00				

KM# 1997 1-1/2 EURO
22.2000 g., 0.9000 Silver 0.6423 oz. ASW **Subject:** Athletic Wordl Championships **Obv:** Winner podium before buildings **Rev:** High jumper before Pont au Double

Date	Mintage	F	VF	XF	Unc	BU
2003 Proof	4,169	Value: 45.00				

KM# 2003 1-1/2 EURO
22.2000 g., 0.9000 Silver 0.6423 oz. ASW **Obv:** Sower advancing left **Rev:** Stars and map of European Union

Date	Mintage	F	VF	XF	Unc	BU
2003 Proof	6,100	Value: 55.00				

KM# 2006 1-1/2 EURO
22.2000 g., 0.9000 Silver 0.6423 oz. ASW **Subject:** Orient Express, Hagia Sophia in Istanbul

Date	Mintage	F	VF	XF	Unc	BU
2003 Proof	Est. 15,000	Value: 45.00				

KM# 2008 1-1/2 EURO
22.2000 g., 0.9000 Silver 0.6423 oz. ASW **Subject:** Childhood Fairy Tales **Rev:** Sleeping Beauty

Date	Mintage	F	VF	XF	Unc	BU
2003 Proof	3,246	Value: 55.00				

KM# 1364 1-1/2 EURO
22.2000 g., 0.9000 Silver 0.6423 oz. ASW, 37 mm. **Obv:** Map with denomination **Rev:** Avignon Popes Palace **Edge:** Plain

Date	Mintage	F	VF	XF	Unc	BU
2004 Proof	10,000	Value: 50.00				

KM# 1373 1-1/2 EURO
22.2000 g., 0.9000 Silver 0.6423 oz. ASW, 37 mm. **Obv:** Emile Loubet and King Edward VII **Rev:** Marianne and Britannia **Edge:** Plain

Date	Mintage	F	VF	XF	Unc	BU
2004 Proof	10,000	Value: 50.00				

KM# 1374 1-1/2 EURO
22.2000 g., 0.9000 Silver 0.6423 oz. ASW, 37 mm. **Obv:** Soccer ball and denomination **Rev:** Rooster and quill **Edge:** Plain

Date	Mintage	F	VF	XF	Unc	BU
2004 Proof	25,000	Value: 55.00				

KM# 1378 1-1/2 EURO
22.2000 g., 0.9000 Silver 0.6423 oz. ASW, 37 mm. **Obv:** Compass rose **Rev:** Ocean liner **Edge:** Plain

Date	Mintage	F	VF	XF	Unc	BU
2004 Proof	10,000	Value: 50.00				

KM# 1380 1-1/2 EURO
22.2000 g., 0.9000 Silver 0.6423 oz. ASW, 37 mm. **Obv:** Compass rose **Rev:** Trans-Siberian Railroad **Edge:** Plain

Date	Mintage	F	VF	XF	Unc	BU
2004 Proof	10,000	Value: 50.00				

KM# 1382 1-1/2 EURO
22.2000 g., 0.9000 Silver 0.6423 oz. ASW, 37 mm. **Obv:** Compass rose **Rev:** Half-track vehicle **Edge:** Plain

Date	Mintage	F	VF	XF	Unc	BU
2004 Proof	10,000	Value: 47.50				

KM# 1384 1-1/2 EURO
22.2000 g., 0.9000 Silver 0.6423 oz. ASW, 37 mm. **Obv:** Compass rose **Rev:** Biplane airliner **Edge:** Plain

Date	Mintage	F	VF	XF	Unc	BU
2004 Proof	10,000	Value: 47.50				

KM# 1386 1-1/2 EURO
22.2000 g., 0.9000 Silver 0.6423 oz. ASW, 37 mm. **Obv:** F.A. Bartholdi **Rev:** Statue of Liberty **Edge:** Plain

Date	Mintage	F	VF	XF	Unc	BU
2004 Proof	15,000	Value: 47.50				

KM# 1391 1-1/2 EURO
22.2000 g., 0.9000 Silver 0.6423 oz. ASW, 37 mm. **Subject:** European Union Expansion **Obv:** Puzzle map of Europe **Rev:** Partial face and flags **Edge:** Plain

Date	Mintage	F	VF	XF	Unc	BU
2004 Proof	40,000	Value: 42.50				

KM# 1366 1-1/2 EURO
22.2000 g., 0.9000 Silver 0.6423 oz. ASW, 37 mm. **Obv:** Book, eagle and denomination **Rev:** Napoleon and coronation scene in background **Edge:** Plain

Date	Mintage	F	VF	XF	Unc	BU
2004 Proof	20,000	Value: 45.00				

KM# 1369 1-1/2 EURO
22.2000 g., 0.9000 Silver 0.6423 oz. ASW, 37 mm. **Obv:** Soldiers and Normandy invasion scene **Rev:** "D-DAY" above denomination **Edge:** Plain

Date	Mintage	F	VF	XF	Unc	BU
2004 Proof	20,000	Value: 50.00				

KM# 1844 1-1/2 EURO
22.2000 g., 0.9000 Silver 0.6423 oz. ASW, 37 mm. **Obv:** Sower advancing left within stars **Rev:** Head at left, stars at right

Date	Mintage	F	VF	XF	Unc	BU
2004 Proof	—	Value: 55.00				

KM# 2013 1-1/2 EURO
22.2000 g., 0.9000 Silver 0.6423 oz. ASW **Subject:** Childhood stories **Rev:** Aladdin and lamp in color

Date	Mintage	F	VF	XF	Unc	BU
2004 Proof	2,222	Value: 70.00				

KM# 2014 1-1/2 EURO
22.2000 g., 0.9000 Silver 0.6423 oz. ASW **Subject:** Childhood stories **Rev:** Peter Pan in color

Date	Mintage	F	VF	XF	Unc	BU
2004 Proof	2,469	Value: 70.00				

KM# 1423 1-1/2 EURO
22.2000 g., 0.9000 Silver 0.6423 oz. ASW, 37 mm. **Subject:** Biathlon **Rev:** Skier at right facing 3/4 left, mountain peaks in background **Rev. Inscription:** JEUX D'HIVER

Date	Mintage	F	VF	XF	Unc	BU
2005 Proof	30,000	Value: 45.00				

KM# 1425 1-1/2 EURO
22.2000 g., 0.9000 Silver 0.6423 oz. ASW, 37 mm. **Series:** Jules Verne **Subject:** From the Earth to the Moon **Rev:** Crowd observing at lower left, volcano erupting above, moon at upper right, Verne in spaceship at lower right, factory chimneys belching smoke in bachground **Rev. Legend:** DE LA TERRE... LA LUNE

Date	Mintage	F	VF	XF	Unc	BU
2005 Proof	5,000	Value: 65.00				

KM# 1427 1-1/2 EURO
22.2000 g., 0.9000 Silver 0.6423 oz. ASW, 37 mm. **Rev:** Kitty and poodle at table at cafe, multicolor **Rev. Legend:** Hello Kitty

Date	Mintage	F	VF	XF	Unc	BU
2005 Proof	4,000	Value: 65.00				

KM# 1428 1-1/2 EURO
22.2000 g., 0.9000 Silver 0.6423 oz. ASW, 37 mm. **Rev:** Kitty on the Champs-Elysees, multicolor **Rev. Legend:** Hello Kitty

Date	Mintage	F	VF	XF	Unc	BU
2005 Proof	4,000	Value: 65.00				

KM# 1431 1-1/2 EURO
22.2000 g., 0.9000 Silver 0.6423 oz. ASW, 37 mm. **Subject:** Bicentennial Victory at Austerlitz **Rev:** Battle scene **Rev. Legend:** LIBERTÉ ÉGALITÉ FRATERNITÉ

Date	Mintage	F	VF	XF	Unc	BU
2005 Proof	15,000	Value: 50.00				

KM# 1434 1-1/2 EURO
22.2000 g., 0.9000 Silver 0.6423 oz. ASW, 37 mm. **Subject:** 50th Anniversary of the Europe flag **Rev:** Stars at left, partial flag at center right

Date	Mintage	F	VF	XF	Unc	BU
2005 Proof	15,000	Value: 50.00				

KM# 1436 1-1/2 EURO
22.2000 g., 0.9000 Silver 0.6423 oz. ASW, 37 mm. **Subject:** Centenary Law of Dec. 9, 1905 **Obv:** "Sower" left in ring of stars

Date	Mintage	F	VF	XF	Unc	BU
2005 Proof	15,000	Value: 50.00				
2006 Proof	10,000	Value: 50.00				

KM# 1438 1-1/2 EURO
22.2000 g., 0.9000 Silver 0.6423 oz. ASW, 37 mm. **Series:** Jules Verne **Subject:** 20,000 Leagues Under the Sea **Rev:** Submarine above plants and divers **Rev. Legend:** VINGT MILLE LIEUES SOUS LES MERS

Date	Mintage	F	VF	XF	Unc	BU
2005 Proof	5,000	Value: 65.00				

KM# 1440 1-1/2 EURO
22.2000 g., 0.9000 Silver 0.6423 oz. ASW, 37 mm. **Subject:** 150th Anniversary of Classification of Bordeaux Wines **Rev:** Stylized female with grapes between various names of wines at her feet

Date	Mintage	F	VF	XF	Unc	BU
2005 Proof	5,000	Value: 65.00				

KM# 1441 1-1/2 EURO
22.2000 g., 0.9000 Silver 0.6423 oz. ASW, 37 mm. **Subject:** 60th Anniversary - End of World War II **Rev:** Doves in flight **Rev. Inscription:** L'EUROPE FAIT LA PAIX

Date	Mintage	F	VF	XF	Unc	BU
2005 Proof	50,000	Value: 45.00				

KM# 2020 1-1/2 EURO
22.2000 g., 0.9000 Silver 0.6423 oz. ASW **Subject:** World Cup Soccer **Obv:** Tropny and soccer ball motif **Rev:** Value within map of France

Date	Mintage	F	VF	XF	Unc	BU
2005 Proof	30,000	Value: 45.00				

KM# 2027 1-1/2 EURO
22.2000 g., 0.9000 Silver 0.6423 oz. ASW **Subject:** Frederic Chopin, 195th Anniversary of Birth **Obv:** Profile at left, piano keys at right vertically **Rev:** Monument in Wausau park at left, piano keys at right vertically

Date	Mintage	F	VF	XF	Unc	BU
2005 Proof	Est. 3,000	Value: 300				

KM# 2029 1-1/2 EURO
22.2000 g., 0.9000 Silver 0.6423 oz. ASW **Subject:** Jules Verne, 100th Anniversary of Death **Obv:** Around the World in 80 days

Date	Mintage	F	VF	XF	Unc	BU
2005 Proof	5,000	Value: 100				

KM# 2036 1-1/2 EURO
22.2000 g., 0.9000 Silver 0.6423 oz. ASW **Subject:** Hello Kitty **Rev:** Kitty with umbrella in color flying above Paris skyline

Date	Mintage	F	VF	XF	Unc	BU
2005 Proof	Est. 4,000	Value: 55.00				

KM# 1453 1-1/2 EURO
22.2000 g., 0.9000 Silver 0.6423 oz. ASW, 37 mm. **Subject:** 100th Anniversary - Death of Paul Cézanne **Obv:** Self portrait **Obv. Inscription:** PAUL / CÉZANNE **Rev:** "The Card Players" **Rev. Legend:** LIBERTÉ ÉGALITÉ FRATERNITÉ

Date	Mintage	F	VF	XF	Unc	BU
2006 Proof	5,000	Value: 65.00				

KM# 1455 1-1/2 EURO
22.2000 g., 0.9000 Silver 0.6423 oz. ASW, 37 mm. **Obv:** Map of the Basilica **Rev:** Bust of Pope Benedict XVI with arms outstretched facing 3/4 right at lower left, Basilica in background **Rev. Legend:** 500 ANS de la BASILIQUE SAINT-PIERRE

Date	Mintage	F	VF	XF	Unc	BU
2006 Proof	5,000	Value: 65.00				

KM# 1456 1-1/2 EURO
22.2000 g., 0.9000 Silver 0.6423 oz. ASW, 37 mm. **Rev:** Half of Arc at left, eternal flame above WW I plaque at right **Rev. Legend:** ARC DE TRIOMPHE

Date	Mintage	F	VF	XF	Unc	BU
2006 Proof	10,000	Value: 50.00				

KM# 1458 1-1/2 EURO
22.2000 g., 0.9000 Silver 0.6423 oz. ASW, 37 mm. **Subject:** 300th Anniversary - Completion of the Dome of Les Invalides **Rev:** Dome between Jules-Hardouin Mansart at left, Louis XIV at right **Rev. Legend:** SAINT-LOUIS - DES INVALIDES **Rev. Inscription:** 28/AOÛT - 1706

Date	Mintage	F	VF	XF	Unc	BU
2006 Proof	10,000	Value: 50.00				

KM# 1444 1-1/2 EURO
22.2000 g., 0.9000 Silver 0.6423 oz. ASW, 37 mm. **Subject:** 100th Anniversary - French Grand Prix **Obv:** Steering wheel with early race car in upper segment, two gauges at lower left, R / F at lower right **Obv. Legend:** LE MANS 1906 - CENTENAIRE du 1er GRAND PRIX de l'AUTOMOBILE CLUB de FRANCE **Rev:** Modern racing car's steering wheel **Rev. Legend:** MAGNY-COURS

Date	Mintage	F	VF	XF	Unc	BU
2006 Proof	5,000	Value: 65.00				

KM# 1447 1-1/2 EURO
22.2000 g., 0.9000 Silver 0.6423 oz. ASW, 37 mm. **Obv:** Strogoff on horseback wielding sword, city at left, soldiers at lower left, calvalry at right **Obv. Legend:** MICHEL STROGOFF **Rev:** Head of Verne facing 3/4 right at left center, instruments and anchor in curved band **Rev. Legend:** 1828 JULES VERNE 1905 - LIBERTÉ . ÉGALITÉ . FRATERNITÉ

Date	Mintage	F	VF	XF	Unc	BU
2006 Proof	500	Value: 100				

KM# 1450 1-1/2 EURO
22.2000 g., 0.9000 Silver 0.6423 oz. ASW, 37 mm. **Subject:** Jules Verne **Obv:** Hot air balloon, parrots at left, native masks at lower left, foliage at right, native huts below, map of Africa in background **Obv. Legend:** CINQ SEMAINES EN BAILON **Rev:** Head of Verne facing 3/4 right at left center, instruments and anchor in curved band **Rev. Legend:** 1828 JULES VERNE 1905

Date	Mintage	F	VF	XF	Unc	BU
2006 Proof	5,000	Value: 65.00				

KM# 1452 1-1/2 EURO
22.2000 g., 0.9000 Silver 0.6423 oz. ASW, 37 mm. **Subject:** Formula 1 World Championship **Obv:** Race car outline on checker board background **Obv. Legend:** LIBERTÉ ÉGALITÉ FRATERNITÉ **Rev:** Race car outline in victory sprays with star **Rev. Legend:** RENAULT - CHAMPION DU MONDE FIA 2005 DES CONSTRUCTEURS DE FORMULE 1

Date	Mintage	F	VF	XF	Unc	BU
2006 Proof	10,000	Value: 50.00				

KM# 2037 1-1/2 EURO
22.2000 g., 0.9000 Silver 0.6423 oz. ASW **Subject:** Robert Schuman, 120th Anniversary of Birth

Date	Mintage	F	VF	XF	Unc	BU
2006 Proof	40,000	Value: 35.00				

KM# 2041 1-1/2 EURO
22.2000 g., 0.9000 Silver 0.6423 oz. ASW **Subject:** Bejing Olympics **Obv:** Three fencing foils on globe map pointing at Bejing **Rev:** Two fencers

Date	Mintage	F	VF	XF	Unc	BU
2006 Proof	10,000	Value: 45.00				

KM# 2048 1-1/2 EURO
22.2000 g., 0.9000 Silver 0.6423 oz. ASW **Subject:** Marie Amélie of Orleans and Carlos I of Portugal, 120th Anniversary of Marriage **Obv:** Bust in tiara left **Rev:** Two shields crowned

Date	Mintage	F	VF	XF	Unc	BU
2006 Proof	Est. 3,000	Value: 150				

KM# 2055 1-1/2 EURO
22.2000 g., 0.9000 Silver 0.6423 oz. ASW **Subject:** Abolition of the Death Penalty, 25th Anniversary **Obv:** Sower advancing left **Rev:** Guillotine

Date	Mintage	F	VF	XF	Unc	BU
2006 Proof	Est. 10,000	Value: 45.00				

KM# 2064 1-1/2 EURO
22.2000 g., 0.9000 Silver 0.6423 oz. ASW **Subject:** Jules Verne, 100th Anniversary of Death **Obv:** Voyage to the center of the Earth

Date	Mintage	F	VF	XF	Unc	BU
2006 Proof	2,411	Value: 100				

KM# 1484 1-1/2 EURO
22.2000 g., 0.9000 Silver 0.6423 oz. ASW, 37 mm. **Subject:** 2007 Rugby World Cup **Obv:** Two players and goal **Rev:** Logo and goal

Date	Mintage	F	VF	XF	Unc	BU
2007 Proof	5,000	Value: 50.00				

KM# 1501 1-1/2 EURO
22.2000 g., 0.9000 Silver 0.6423 oz. ASW, 37 mm. **Subject:** Georges Pompendev Center, 30th Anniversary

Date	Mintage	F	VF	XF	Unc	BU
2007 Proof	—	Value: 50.00				

KM# 1462 1-1/2 EURO
22.0000 g., 0.9000 Silver 0.6366 oz. ASW, 37 mm. **Subject:** Sebastien Le Prestre de Vauban, 300th Anniversary of Death

Date	Mintage	F	VF	XF	Unc	BU
2007 Proof	30,000	Value: 40.00				

KM# 1465 1-1/2 EURO
22.2000 g., 0.9000 Silver 0.6423 oz. ASW, 37 mm. **Subject:** Le Petit Prince, 60th Anniversary **Obv:** Prince standing, multicolor

Date	Mintage	F	VF	XF	Unc	BU
2007 Proof	3,000	Value: 55.00				

KM# 1467 1-1/2 EURO
22.2000 g., 0.9000 Silver 0.6423 oz. ASW, 37 mm. **Subject:** Le Petit Prince, 60th Anniversary **Obv:** Prince lying in field, multicolor

Date	Mintage	F	VF	XF	Unc	BU
2007 Proof	3,000	Value: 55.00				

KM# 1469 1-1/2 EURO
22.2000 g., 0.9000 Silver 0.6423 oz. ASW, 37 mm. **Subject:** Le Petite Prince, 60th Anniversary **Obv:** Prince standing with rabbit, multicolor

Date	Mintage	F	VF	XF	Unc	BU
2007 Proof	—	Value: 55.00				

KM# 1473 1-1/2 EURO
22.2000 g., 0.9000 Silver 0.6423 oz. ASW, 37 mm. **Subject:** Paul E. Victor, 100th Birthday **Obv:** International Polar Year Logo **Rev:** Bust at left, Islands

Date	Mintage	F	VF	XF	Unc	BU
2007 Proof	5,000	Value: 55.00				

KM# 1475 1-1/2 EURO
22.2000 g., 0.9000 Silver 0.6423 oz. ASW, 37 mm. **Obv:** Formula 1 race car on checkered background **Rev:** Legend in wreath on checkered background

Date	Mintage	F	VF	XF	Unc	BU
2007//2006 Proof	5,000	Value: 55.00				

KM# 1477 1-1/2 EURO
22.2000 g., 0.9000 Silver 0.6423 oz. ASW, 37 mm. **Subject:** 29th Summer Olympic Games Beijing **Obv:** Rider on horseback, globe map of China **Rev:** Equestrian jump over orienteal fence

Date	Mintage	F	VF	XF	Unc	BU
2007 Proof	10,000	Value: 50.00				

KM# 1479 1-1/2 EURO
22.2000 g., 0.9000 Silver 0.6423 oz. ASW, 37 mm. **Subject:** Airbus A380 **Obv:** Airplane **Rev:** Europa head and flags

Date	Mintage	F	VF	XF	Unc	BU
2007 Proof	5,000	Value: 50.00				

KM# 1488 1-1/2 EURO
22.2000 g., 0.9000 Silver 0.6423 oz. ASW, 37 mm. **Obv:** Christian Dior bust **Rev:** Dior Museum building

Date	Mintage	F	VF	XF	Unc	BU
2007 Proof	3,000	Value: 75.00				

KM# 1505 1-1/2 EURO
22.2000 g., 0.9000 Silver 0.6423 oz. ASW, 37 mm. **Subject:** George Remir Centennial **Obv:** Wand and sparkles **Rev:** Tin Tin and the Professor calculus in multicolor

Date	Mintage	F	VF	XF	Unc	BU
2007 Proof	10,000	Value: 60.00				

KM# 1506 1-1/2 EURO
22.2000 g., 0.9000 Silver 0.6423 oz. ASW, 37 mm. **Subject:** Georges Remi Centennial **Obv:** Wand and sparkles **Rev:** Tin Tin and Captain Haddock in multicolor

Date	Mintage	F	VF	XF	Unc	BU
2007 Proof	10,000	Value: 65.00				

KM# 1507 1-1/2 EURO
22.2000 g., 0.9000 Silver 0.6423 oz. ASW, 37 mm. **Subject:** Georges Remi Centennial **Obv:** Wand and sparkles **Rev:** Tin Tin and Chang in multicolor

Date	Mintage	F	VF	XF	Unc	BU
2007 Proof	10,000	Value: 65.00				

KM# 1511 1-1/2 EURO
22.2000 g., 0.9000 Silver 0.6423 oz. ASW, 37 mm. **Subject:** Aristides de Sousa Mendes, Portuguese diplomat **Obv:** Bust right **Rev:** Plaque

Date	Mintage	F	VF	XF	Unc	BU
2007 Proof	3,000	Value: 55.00				

KM# 1516 1-1/2 EURO
22.2000 g., 0.9000 Silver 0.6423 oz. ASW, 37 mm. **Subject:** Asterix **Rev:** The Banquet

Date	Mintage	F	VF	XF	Unc	BU
2007 Proof	3,000	Value: 55.00				

KM# 1517 1-1/2 EURO
22.2000 g., 0.9000 Silver 0.6423 oz. ASW, 37 mm. **Subject:** Asterix **Rev:** The posion

Date	Mintage	F	VF	XF	Unc	BU
2007 Proof	3,000	Value: 55.00				

KM# 1518 1-1/2 EURO
22.2000 g., 0.9000 Silver 0.6423 oz. ASW, 37 mm. **Subject:** Asterix **Rev:** The Chase

Date	Mintage	F	VF	XF	Unc	BU
2007 Proof	3,000	Value: 55.00				

KM# 1527 1-1/2 EURO
22.2000 g., 0.9000 Silver 0.6423 oz. ASW, 37 mm. **Subject:** French Presidency of European Union **Obv:** Text written stars **Rev:** Europa head and flags

Date	Mintage	F	VF	XF	Unc	BU
2008 Proof	10,000	Value: 50.00				

KM# 1532 1-1/2 EURO
22.2000 g., 0.9000 Silver 0.6423 oz. ASW **Subject:** Eurpean Parliament, 50th Anniversary **Obv:** Map of EU within stars **Rev:** European Parliament Building in Strasboury **Shape:** 37

Date	Mintage	F	VF	XF	Unc	BU
2008 Proof	30,000	Value: 50.00				

KM# 1537 1-1/2 EURO
22.2000 g., 0.9000 Silver 0.6423 oz. ASW, 37 mm. **Subject:** 5th Republic, 50th Anniversasry **Obv:** Sower **Rev:** deGaulle head right

Date	Mintage	F	VF	XF	Unc	BU
2008 Proof	10,000	Value: 50.00				

KM# 1543 1-1/2 EURO
22.2000 g., 0.9000 Silver 0.6423 oz. ASW, 37 mm. **Subject:** 29th Summer Olympic Games - Beijing **Obv:** Swimmer and globe **Rev:** Diver and oriental screen

Date	Mintage	F	VF	XF	Unc	BU
2008 Proof	10,000	Value: 65.00				

KM# 1546 1-1/2 EURO
22.2000 g., 0.9000 Silver 0.6423 oz. ASW, 37 mm. **Subject:** UEFA **Obv:** French soccer team **Rev:** UEFA logo

Date	Mintage	F	VF	XF	Unc	BU
2008 Proof	5,000	Value: 55.00				

KM# 1548 1-1/2 EURO
22.2000 g., 0.9000 Silver 0.6423 oz. ASW, 37 mm. **Subject:** Franco - Japanese Relators, 150th Anniversary **Obv:** Eiffel Tower and Kimono forming logo **Rev:** Delacroix "La Liberte"

Date	Mintage	F	VF	XF	Unc	BU
2008 Proof	5,000	Value: 65.00				

KM# 1549 1-1/2 EURO
22.2000 g., 0.9000 Silver 0.6423 oz. ASW, 37 mm. **Subject:** Franco - Japanese Relators - 150th Anniversary **Obv:** Eillfel Tower and Kimono forming logo **Rev:** Ichikawa Ebizo IV portrait painting

Date	Mintage	F	VF	XF	Unc	BU
2008 Proof	5,000	Value: 65.00				

KM# 1550 1-1/2 EURO
22.2000 g., 0.9000 Silver 0.6423 oz. ASW, 37 mm. **Subject:** Franco - Japanese Relators - 150th Anniversary **Obv:** Eillfel Tower and Kimono forming logo **Rev:** Scenes of Paris and Tokyo - Eillfel Tower and Pagoda Sensoji

Date	Mintage	F	VF	XF	Unc	BU
2008 Proof	5,000	Value: 65.00				

KM# 1551 1-1/2 EURO
22.2000 g., 0.9000 Silver 0.6423 oz. ASW, 37 mm. **Subject:** Franco - Japanese Relators - 150th Anniversary **Obv:** Eiflfel Tower and Kimono forming logo **Rev:** Japanese cash coin of "Kanei Tsuho"

Date	Mintage	F	VF	XF	Unc	BU
2008 Proof	5,000	Value: 65.00				

KM# 1555 1-1/2 EURO
22.2000 g., 0.9000 Silver 0.6423 oz. ASW, 37 mm. **Subject:** André Citronën **Obv:** First front wheel drive auto **Rev:** Bust 1/4 left

Date	Mintage	F	VF	XF	Unc	BU
2008 Proof	5,000	Value: 65.00				

KM# 1558 1-1/2 EURO
22.2000 g., 0.9000 Silver 0.6423 oz. ASW, 37 mm. **Subject:** Rouen Armada **Obv:** Cape Horn, sextant, hour glass **Rev:** Sailing ship

Date	Mintage	F	VF	XF	Unc	BU
2008 Proof	5,000	Value: 65.00				

KM# 1561 1-1/2 EURO
22.2000 g., 0.9000 Silver 0.6423 oz. ASW, 37 mm. **Subject:** Lourdes, 150th Anniversary **Obv:** Church of Notre Dame at Lourdes **Rev:** Cross with Pope John Paul II, Pope Benedict XVI and Bernadette Soubirous in quadrants

Date	Mintage	F	VF	XF	Unc	BU
2008 Proof	15,000	Value: 60.00				

KM# 1574 1-1/2 EURO
22.2000 g., 0.9000 Silver 0.6423 oz. ASW, 37 mm. **Subject:** UNESCO - Grand Canyon **Obv:** Grand Canyon **Rev:** UNESCO logos

Date	Mintage	F	VF	XF	Unc	BU
2008 Proof	5,000	Value: 65.00				

KM# 1576 1-1/2 EURO
22.2000 g., 0.9000 Silver 0.6423 oz. ASW, 37 mm. **Subject:** International Polar Year **Obv:** IPY logo **Rev:** Emperor Penguin and map of Antartica

Date	Mintage	F	VF	XF	Unc	BU
2008 Proof	5,000	Value: 65.00				

KM# 1578 1-1/2 EURO
22.2000 g., 0.9000 Silver 0.6423 oz. ASW, 37 mm. **Subject:** Spirou, 70th Anniversary **Obv:** Character Spirou in thought **Rev:** 70th Anniversary logo

Date	Mintage	F	VF	XF	Unc	BU
2008 Proof	10,000	Value: 60.00				

KM# 1633 1-1/2 EURO
11.0000 g., Aluminum-Bronze, 30 mm. **Obv:** Stadium view, soccer player **Rev:** Shield of Olympique Lyonnais

Date	Mintage	F	VF	XF	Unc	BU
2009	25,000	—	—	—	15.00	20.00

KM# 1723 1-1/2 EURO
11.0000 g., Aluminum-Bronze, 30 mm. **Obv:** Soccer player **Rev:** Girondins de Bordeaux logo

Date	Mintage	F	VF	XF	Unc	BU
2010	25,000	—	—	—	15.00	20.00

KM# 1754 1-1/2 EURO
11.0000 g., Aluminum-Bronze, 30 mm. **Subject:** Olympique de Marseille **Obv:** Soccer player **Rev:** OM logo

Date	Mintage	F	VF	XF	Unc	BU
2011	25,000	—	—	—	—	15.00

KM# 1918 1-1/2 EURO
11.0000 g., Aluminum-Bronze, 30 mm. **Subject:** Paris Saint Germain **Obv:** Stadium and player **Rev:** Team logo

Date	Mintage	F	VF	XF	Unc	BU
2012(a)	25,000	—	—	—	—	15.00

KM# 1289 2 EURO
8.5000 g., Bi-Metallic Nickel-Brass center in Copper-Nickel ring, 25.75 mm. **Obv:** Stylized tree divides RF within circle, date below **Rev:** Denomination and map **Edge:** Reeded with 2's and stars

Date	Mintage	F	VF	XF	Unc	BU
2001	237,950,793	—	—	—	3.75	6.00
2001 Proof	15,000	Value: 20.00				
2002	153,700,000	—	—	—	3.75	6.00
2002 Proof	21,453	Value: 18.00				
2003 In sets only	180,000	—	—	—	—	13.50
2003 Proof	40,000	Value: 20.00				
2004 In sets only	160,000	—	—	—	—	13.50
2004 Proof	20,000	Value: 20.00				
2005 In sets only	120,000	—	—	—	—	13.50
2005 Proof	10,000	Value: 20.00				
2006 In sets only	67,600	—	—	—	—	13.50
2006 Proof	10,000	Value: 20.00				

KM# 1414 2 EURO
8.5000 g., Bi-Metallic Nickel-Brass center in Copper-Nickel ring, 25.75 mm. **Obv:** Stylized tree divides RF within circle, date below **Rev:** Relief map of Western Europe, stars, lines and value **Edge:** Reeded with 2's and stars

Date	Mintage	F	VF	XF	Unc	BU
2007 In sets only	58,000	—	—	—	—	15.00
2007 Proof	7,500	Value: 25.00				
2008 In sets only	57,000	—	—	—	—	6.00
2008 Proof	7,500	Value: 25.00				
2009 In sets only	50,500	—	—	—	—	6.00
2009 Proof	7,500	Value: 25.00				
2010	—	—	—	—	—	6.00
2010 Proof	—	Value: 25.00				
2011	—	—	—	—	—	6.00
2011 Proof	—	Value: 25.00				
2012	—	—	—	—	—	6.00
2012 Proof	—	Value: 25.00				
2013	—	—	—	—	—	6.00
2013 Proof	—	Value: 25.00				

KM# 1460 2 EURO
8.5000 g., Bi-Metallic Nickel-Brass center in Copper-Nickel ring, 25.75 mm. **Subject:** Treaty of Rome 50th Anniversary **Edge:** Reeded with 2's and stars

Date	Mintage	F	VF	XF	Unc	BU
2007	9,600,000	—	—	—	5.50	6.50

KM# 1459 2 EURO
8.5000 g., Bi-Metallic Nickel-Brass center in Copper-Nickel ring, 25.75 mm. **Subject:** European Union Presidency **Obv:** Inscription **Obv. Inscription:** PRÉSIDENCE / FRANÇAISE / UNION / EUROPÉENNE / RF **Rev:** Large value "2" at left, modified map of Europe at right **Edge:** Reeded with 2's and stars

Date	Mintage	F	VF	XF	Unc	BU
2008(a)	20,100,000	—	—	—	5.50	6.50

KM# 1542 2 EURO
8.5000 g., Bi-Metallic Nickel-Brass center in Copper-Nickel ring, 25.75 mm. **Subject:** 5th Republic, 50th Anniversary **Obv:** Text within stars **Rev:** Value at left, relief map of the EU at right **Edge:** Reeded with 2's and stars

Date	Mintage	F	VF	XF	Unc	BU
2008(a)	10,000,000	—	—	—	6.50	7.50
2008(a) Sets only	20,000	—	—	—	—	20.00
2008(a) Proof	10,000	Value: 40.00				

KM# 1590 2 EURO
8.5000 g., Bi-Metallic Nickel-Brass center in Copper-Nickel ring, 25.75 mm. **Subject:** EMU 10th Anniversary **Obv:** Stick figure and E design **Edge:** Reeded with 2's and stars

Date	Mintage	F	VF	XF	Unc	BU
2009	—	—	—	—	8.00	10.00
2009 Proof	10,000	Value: 15.00				

KM# 1676 2 EURO
8.5000 g., Bi-Metallic Nickel-Brass center in Copper-Nickel ring, 25.75 mm. **Subject:** 70th Anniversary, June 18th Appeal **Obv:** General Charles DeGaulle giving BBC speech **Rev:** Value and map **Edge:** Reeded with 2's and stars

Date	Mintage	F	VF	XF	Unc	BU
2010	20,000	—	—	—	8.00	10.00
2010 Proof	10,000	Value: 15.00				

KM# 1789 2 EURO
8.5000 g., Bi-Metallic Nickel-Brass center in Copper-Nickel ring, 25.75 mm. **Subject:** International Music Day, 30th Anniversary **Obv:** Youth jamming **Rev:** Value and map of Western Europe **Edge:** Reeded with 2's and stars

Date	Mintage	F	VF	XF	Unc	BU
2011	10,000,000	—	—	—	5.00	—
2011 Special Unc.	20,000	—	—	—	—	8.00
2011 Proof	10,000	Value: 15.00				

KM# 1847 2 EURO
22.2000 g., 0.9000 Silver 0.6423 oz. ASW, 37 mm. **Obv:** Sailing ship L'Hermione **Rev:** Ship figurehead at right, ship's wheel at bottom

Date	Mintage	F	VF	XF	Unc	BU
2012(a) Proof	10,000	Value: 35.00				

KM# 1846 2 EURO
8.5000 g., Bi-Metallic Nickel-Brass center in Copper-Nickel ring, 25.75 mm. **Subject:** Euro coinage, 10th Anniversary **Obv:** Euro symbol on globe, child-like drawing around

Date	Mintage	F	VF	XF	Unc	BU
2012(a)	10,000,000	—	—	—	6.50	7.50
2012(a) Special Unc.	—	—	—	—	—	10.00
2012(a) Proof	—	Value: 15.00				

KM# 1894 2 EURO
8.5000 g., Bi-Metallic Nickel-Brass center in Copper-Nickel ring, 25.75 mm. **Subject:** abbé Pierre, 100th anniversary of Birth **Obv:** Portrait facing of abbé Pierre, wearing beret

Date	Mintage	F	VF	XF	Unc	BU
2012(a)	1,000,000	—	—	—	6.00	7.00
2012(a) Special Unc.	10,000	—	—	—	—	10.00
2012(a) Proof	10,000	Value: 25.00				

KM# 2094 2 EURO
8.5000 g., Bi-Metallic Nickel-Brass center in Copper-Nickel ring, 25.75 mm. **Subject:** French-German Friendship, 50th Anniversary

Date	Mintage	F	VF	XF	Unc	BU
2013	—	—	—	—	7.00	10.00
2013 Proof	—	Value: 15.00				

KM# 1347 5 EURO
24.9000 g., 0.9000 Bi-Metallic .900 Silver 22.2g planchet with .750 Gold 2.7g insert 0.7205 oz., 37 mm. **Obv:** The Seed Sower on gold insert **Rev:** Denomination and map **Edge:** Plain

Date	Mintage	F	VF	XF	Unc	BU
2002 Proof	10,000	Value: 550				

KM# 1371 5 EURO
24.9000 g., Bi-Metallic .750 Gold 2.7 g insert on .900 Silver 22.2g planchet, 37 mm. **Obv:** The Seed Sower on gold insert **Rev:** French face map and denomination **Edge:** Plain

Date	Mintage	F	VF	XF	Unc	BU
2004 Proof	3,000	Value: 550				

KM# 2010 5 EURO
12.0000 g., 0.9000 Silver 0.3472 oz. ASW, 29 mm. **Obv:** Tree within hexagon **Rev:** Pantheon and large value

Date	Mintage	F	VF	XF	Unc	BU
2004 Proof	—	Value: 25.00				
2005 Proof	—	Value: 25.00				
2006 Proof	—	Value: 25.00				

KM# 1523 5 EURO
22.2000 g., 0.9000 Silver 0.6423 oz. ASW, 37 mm. **Subject:** Euro - 5th Anniversary **Obv:** The Seed Sower

Date	Mintage	F	VF	XF	Unc	BU
2007 Proof	5,000	Value: 55.00				

KM# 1524 5 EURO
163.8000 g., 0.9500 Silver 5.0028 oz. ASW, 50 mm. **Subject:** Euro 5th Anniversary **Obv:** Sower

Date	Mintage	F	VF	XF	Unc	BU
2007 Proof	500	Value: 325				

KM# 1525 5 EURO
1.2400 g., 0.9990 Gold 0.0398 oz. AGW, 14 mm. **Subject:** Euro 5th Anniversary **Obv:** The Seed Sower

Date	Mintage	F	VF	XF	Unc	BU
2007 Proof	20,000	Value: 75.00				

KM# 1526 5 EURO
31.1050 g., 0.9200 Gold 0.9200 oz. AGW, 31 mm. **Subject:** Euro 5th Anniversary **Obv:** The Seed Sower

Date	Mintage	F	VF	XF	Unc	BU
2007 Proof	500	Value: 1,600				

KM# 1534 5 EURO
10.0000 g., 0.5000 Silver 0.1607 oz. ASW, 27 mm. **Obv:** Sower, full length **Rev:** Value within hexagon design

Date	Mintage	F	VF	XF	Unc	BU
2008 Proof	2,000,000	Value: 15.00				

KM# 1538 5 EURO
1.2400 g., 0.9990 Gold 0.0398 oz. AGW, 13.9 mm. **Subject:** 5th Republic, 50th Anniversary **Obv:** Sower **Rev:** de Gaulle head right

Date	Mintage	F	VF	XF	Unc	BU
2008 Proof	20,000	Value: 75.00				

KM# 1566 5 EURO
22.2000 g., 0.9000 Silver 0.6423 oz. ASW, 37 mm. **Subject:** Gabrielle Chanel **Obv:** Bust right in hat **Rev:** Value on "Matelassé" pattern

Date	Mintage	F	VF	XF	Unc	BU
2008 Proof	10,000	Value: 65.00				

KM# 1567 5 EURO
8.4500 g., 0.9200 Gold 0.2499 oz. AGW, 22 mm. **Subject:** Gabrielle Chanel **Obv:** Portrait in hat, right **Rev:** Value on "Matelassé" pattern

Date	Mintage	F	VF	XF	Unc	BU
2008 Proof	500	Value: 475				

KM# 1568 5 EURO
163.8000 g., 0.9500 Silver 5.0028 oz. ASW, 50 mm. **Subject:** Gabrielle Chanel **Obv:** Portrait in hat, right **Rev:** Vlaue on "Matelassé" pattern

Date	Mintage	F	VF	XF	Unc	BU
2008 Proof	500	Value: 350				

KM# 1582 5 EURO
155.5000 g., 0.9990 Gold 4.9942 oz. AGW **Subject:** CoCo Chanel, 125th Anniversary of Birth **Obv:** Profile at left **Rev:** Diamond handbag pattern

Date	Mintage	F	VF	XF	Unc	BU
2008 Proof	Est. 99	Value: 9,500				

KM# 1586 5 EURO
1.2400 g., 0.9990 Gold 0.0398 oz. AGW, 13.9 mm. **Subject:** Court of Human Rights, 50th Anniversary **Obv:** The Seed Sower left **Rev:** Text

Date	Mintage	F	VF	XF	Unc	BU
2009P Proof	10,000	Value: 75.00				

KM# 1625 5 EURO
15.0000 g., 0.9000 Silver 0.4340 oz. ASW, 30 x 21 mm. **Subject:** Monet **Obv:** Le Bassin Aux Nympheas, 1900 painting **Rev:** Multicolor pallet and brushes, portrait **Shape:** Rectangle

Date	Mintage	F	VF	XF	Unc	BU
2009P Proof	20,000	Value: 45.00				

KM# 1627 5 EURO
22.2000 g., 0.9000 Silver 0.6423 oz. ASW, 37 mm. **Subject:** Year of the Ox **Obv:** Oxen within Asia screen garden **Rev:** Portrait of La Fontaine

Date	Mintage	F	VF	XF	Unc	BU
2009P Proof	10,000	Value: 35.00				

KM# 1643 5 EURO
15.0000 g., 0.9000 Silver 0.4340 oz. ASW **Subject:** Pierre Auguste Renoir **Obv:** Boaters Lunch in color **Rev:** Portrait and paint brushes **Shape:** Rectangle

Date	Mintage	F	VF	XF	Unc	BU
2009	20,000	—	—	—	—	40.00

KM# 1674 5 EURO
1.2400 g., 0.9990 Gold 0.0398 oz. AGW, 13.9 mm. **Obv:** The Seed Sower left **Rev:** Wheat and olive branch

Date	Mintage	F	VF	XF	Unc	BU
2010 Proof	10,000	Value: 75.00				

KM# 1680 5 EURO
0.5000 g., 0.9990 Gold 0.0161 oz. AGW, 11 mm. **Subject:** Cluny Abbey, 1100th Anniversary **Obv:** Europa head facing **Rev:** Cluny Abbey

Date	Mintage	F	VF	XF	Unc	BU
2010 Proof	20,000	Value: 45.00				

KM# 1715 5 EURO
22.2000 g., 0.9000 Silver 0.6423 oz. ASW, 37 mm. **Obv:** Tiger within border **Rev:** La Fontaine bust at left, animals at right

Date	Mintage	F	VF	XF	Unc	BU
2010 Proof	10,000	Value: 65.00				

KM# 1785 5 EURO
1.2440 g., 0.9990 Gold 0.0400 oz. AGW, 13.9 mm. **Subject:** Euro Starter Kit, 10th Anniversary **Obv:** Sower **Rev:** Euro starter kit

Date	Mintage	F	VF	XF	Unc	BU
2011 Proof	10,000	Value: 100				

KM# 1791 5 EURO
0.5000 g., 0.9990 Gold 0.0161 oz. AGW, 11 mm. **Subject:** International Music Day, 30th Anniversary **Obv:** Europa **Rev:** Youth jamming

Date	Mintage	F	VF	XF	Unc	BU
2011 Proof	20,000	Value: 100				

KM# 1810 5 EURO
0.5000 g., 0.9990 Gold 0.0161 oz. AGW, 11 mm. **Subject:** UNESCO World Heritage Site - Palace of Versailles

Date	Mintage	F	VF	XF	Unc	BU
2011 Proof	20,000	Value: 100				

KM# 1833 5 EURO
22.2000 g., 0.9000 Silver 0.6423 oz. ASW, 37 mm. **Subject:** Year of the Rabbit **Obv:** Rabbit seated facing right **Rev:** Fontaine and animals

Date	Mintage	F	VF	XF	Unc	BU
2011 Proof	10,000	Value: 50.00				

KM# 1851 5 EURO
0.5000 g., 0.9990 Gold 0.0161 oz. AGW, 11 mm. **Subject:** Eurocorps, 20th Anniversary **Obv:** Mitterrand and Kohl standing clasping hands **Rev:** Europa facing

Date	Mintage	F	VF	XF	Unc	BU
2012(a) Proof	10,000	Value: 65.00				

KM# 1890 5 EURO
0.5000 g., 0.9990 Gold 0.0161 oz. AGW, 11 mm. **Subject:** Euro, 10th Anniversary **Obv:** The Sower advancing left **Rev:** Value on globe with child-like renderings around

Date	Mintage	F	VF	XF	Unc	BU
2012(a) Proof	10,000	Value: 75.00				

KM# 1896 5 EURO
1.2440 g., 0.9990 Gold 0.0400 oz. AGW, 13.9 mm. **Subject:** abbé Pierre, 100th anniversary of Birth **Obv:** Pierre's bust at left, shaddow figure at right **Rev:** Emmaus International logo and quote

Date	Mintage	F	VF	XF	Unc	BU
2012(a) Proof	10,000	Value: 100				

KM# 1907 5 EURO
0.5000 g., 0.9990 Gold 0.0161 oz. AGW, 11 mm. **Subject:** UNESCO - World Heritage Site **Obv:** Abu Simbel temple **Rev:** Sphinx and Pyramids

Date	Mintage	F	VF	XF	Unc	BU
2012(a) Proof	10,000	Value: 75.00				

KM# 2092 5 EURO
0.5000 g., 0.9990 Gold 0.0161 oz. AGW, 11 mm. **Subject:** French - German Friendship **Rev:** Europa head facing at right, banners at left

Date	Mintage	F	VF	XF	Unc	BU
2013 Proof	—	Value: 75.00				

KM# 2099 5 EURO
0.5000 g., 0.9990 Gold 0.0161 oz. AGW, 11 mm. **Subject:** Notre Dame, 850th Anniversary **Obv:** Seal at right, cathedral details **Rev:** Seal at left, cathedral details

Date	Mintage	F	VF	XF	Unc	BU
2013 Proof	15,000	Value: 100				

KM# 1302 10 EURO
8.4500 g., 0.9990 Gold 0.2714 oz. AGW, 22 mm. **Subject:** Europa **Obv:** Eight French euro coin designs **Rev:** Portrait and flags design of 6.55957 francs KM-1265 **Edge:** Reeded

Date	Mintage	F	VF	XF	Unc	BU
2002 Proof	3,000	Value: 525				

KM# 1326 10 EURO
8.4500 g., 0.9200 Gold 0.2499 oz. AGW, 22 mm. **Obv:** Tour de France logo **Rev:** Cyclist going left **Edge:** Reeded

Date	Mintage	F	VF	XF	Unc	BU
2003 (Ht) Proof	5,000	Value: 500				

KM# 1348 10 EURO
8.4500 g., 0.9200 Gold 0.2499 oz. AGW, 22 mm. **Obv:** The seed sower **Rev:** Denomination and map **Edge:** Plain

Date	Mintage	F	VF	XF	Unc	BU
2003 Proof	15,000	Value: 475				

KM# 1352 10 EURO
8.4500 g., 0.9200 Gold 0.2499 oz. AGW, 22 mm. **Obv:** Obverse design of first one franc coin **Rev:** Reverse design of first one franc coin **Edge:** Plain

Date	Mintage	F	VF	XF	Unc	BU
2003 Proof	10,000	Value: 475				

KM# 1362 10 EURO
8.4500 g., 0.9200 Gold 0.2499 oz. AGW, 22 mm. **Obv:** Pierre de Coubertin **Rev:** Olympic runners **Edge:** Plain

Date	Mintage	F	VF	XF	Unc	BU
2003 Proof	15,000	Value: 475				

KM# 1992 10 EURO
8.4500 g., 0.9200 Gold 0.2499 oz. AGW **Obv:** Curved cross with coins **Rev:** Europa head at right, flags at left

Date	Mintage	F	VF	XF	Unc	BU
2003 Proof	Est. 7,000	Value: 550				

KM# 1367 10 EURO
6.4100 g., 0.9000 Gold 0.1855 oz. AGW, 22 mm. **Obv:** Book, denomination and eagle **Rev:** Napoleon and coronation scene **Edge:** Plain

Date	Mintage	F	VF	XF	Unc	BU
2004 Proof	5,000	Value: 400				

KM# 1375 10 EURO
8.4500 g., 0.9200 Gold 0.2499 oz. AGW, 22 mm. **Obv:** Half soccer ball and denomination **Rev:** Eiffel tower and soccer balls **Edge:** Plain

Date	Mintage	F	VF	XF	Unc	BU
2004 Proof	10,000	Value: 475				

KM# 1392 10 EURO
8.4500 g., 0.9200 Gold 0.2499 oz. AGW, 22 mm. **Subject:** European Union Expansion **Obv:** Partial face and flags **Rev:** Puzzle map **Edge:** Reeded

Date	Mintage	F	VF	XF	Unc	BU
2004 Proof	5,000	Value: 500				

KM# 1403 10 EURO
8.4500 g., 0.9200 Gold 0.2499 oz. AGW, 22 mm. **Subject:** Jules Verne **Obv:** Various scenes from Verne's novel "Around The World in 80 Days" **Rev:** Jules Verne's portrait left of value and date

Date	Mintage	F	VF	XF	Unc	BU
2005 Proof	2,000	Value: 575				

KM# 1424 10 EURO
8.4500 g., 0.9200 Gold 0.2499 oz. AGW, 22 mm. **Subject:** Biathlon **Rev:** Skier at right facing 3/4 left, mountain peaks in background **Rev. Inscription:** JEUX D'HIVER

Date	Mintage	F	VF	XF	Unc	BU
2005 Proof	—	Value: 475				

KM# 1426 10 EURO
8.4500 g., 0.9200 Gold 0.2499 oz. AGW, 22 mm. **Series:** Jules Verne **Subject:** From the earth to the moon **Rev:** Crowd observing at lower left, volcano erupting above, moon at upper right, Verne in spaceship at lower right, chimneys belching smoke in backgroud **Rev. Legend:** DE LA TERRE À LA LUNE

Date	Mintage	F	VF	XF	Unc	BU
2005 Proof	2,000	Value: 500				

KM# 1429 10 EURO
8.4500 g., 0.9200 Gold 0.2499 oz. AGW, 22 mm. **Rev:** Kitty at the Spectacle, multicolor **Rev. Legend:** Hello Kitty

Date	Mintage	F	VF	XF	Unc	BU
2005 Proof	1,000	Value: 550				

KM# 1432 10 EURO
6.4100 g., 0.9000 Gold 0.1855 oz. AGW, 21 mm. **Subject:** Bicentennial - Victory at Austerlitz **Rev:** Battle scene **Rev. Legend:** LIBERTÉ ÉGALITÉ FRATERNITÉ

Date	Mintage	F	VF	XF	Unc	BU
2005 Proof	3,000	Value: 400				

KM# 1435 10 EURO
8.4500 g., 0.9200 Gold 0.2499 oz. AGW, 22 mm. **Subject:** 50th Anniversary - Flag of Europe **Rev:** Stars at left, partial flag at center right

Date	Mintage	F	VF	XF	Unc	BU
2005 Proof	3,000	Value: 475				

KM# 1439 10 EURO
8.4500 g., 0.9200 Gold 0.2499 oz. AGW, 22 mm. **Series:** Jules Verne **Subject:** 20,000 Leagues Under the Sea **Rev:** Submarine above plants and divers **Rev. Legend:** VINGT MILLE LIEUES SOUS LES MERS

Date	Mintage	F	VF	XF	Unc	BU
2005 Proof	2,000	Value: 500				

KM# 2021 10 EURO
8.4500 g., 0.9200 Gold 0.2499 oz. AGW **Subject:** World Cup Soccer **Obv:** World Cup Trophy and soccer ball **Rev:** Large value and map of France

Date	Mintage	F	VF	XF	Unc	BU
2005 Proof	Est. 10,000	Value: 550				

KM# 2023 10 EURO
8.4500 g., 0.9200 Gold 0.2499 oz. AGW **Obv:** Globe and map of Europe **Rev:** Doves in flight above globe

Date	Mintage	F	VF	XF	Unc	BU
2005 Proof	3,000	Value: 550				

KM# 2026 10 EURO
8.4500 g., 0.9200 Gold 0.2499 oz. AGW **Subject:** Bordeaux, 150th Anniversary **Obv:** Female holding bounty **Rev:** Stylized fingers and a grape

Date	Mintage	F	VF	XF	Unc	BU
2005 Proof	500	Value: 550				

KM# 1446 10 EURO
8.4500 g., 0.9200 Gold 0.2499 oz. AGW, 22 mm. **Subject:** Marshal Bernadotte under Napoleon **Rev:** Military bust facing 3/4 right at left, building in backgound at right **Rev. Legend:** LIBERTÉ GALITÉ FRATERNITÉ - KARL XIV JOHAN ROI DE SUÉDE

Date	Mintage	F	VF	XF	Unc	BU
2006 Proof	1,000	Value: 500				

KM# 1416 10 EURO
8.4500 g., 0.9200 Gold 0.2499 oz. AGW, 22 mm. **Obv:** Jean de la Fontaine, value, Chinese astrological animals, date, Paris mint privy marks but without national identification **Rev:** Dog in wreath **Edge:** Reeded

Date	Mintage	F	VF	XF	Unc	BU
2006 Proof	500	Value: 525				

KM# 1448 10 EURO
8.4500 g., 0.9200 Gold 0.2499 oz. AGW, 22 mm. **Subject:** 20,000 Leagues Under the Sea **Obv:** Strogoff horseback wielding a sword, city at left, soldiers at lower left, calvary at right - the Tartars, Siberia and the Tsar's Army **Obv. Legend:** MICHEL STROGOFF **Rev:** Head of Verne facing 3/4 right at left center, instruments and anchor in curved band **Rev. Legend:** 1828 JULES VERNE 1905

Date	Mintage	F	VF	XF	Unc	BU
2006 Proof	500	Value: 525				

KM# 1449 10 EURO
8.4500 g., 0.9200 Gold 0.2499 oz. AGW, 22 mm. **Subject:** 20,000 Leagues Under the Sea **Obv:** Hot air balloon, parrots at left, native masks below left, foliage at right, huts below, map of Africa in background. **Obv. Legend:** CINQ SEMAINES EN BALLON **Rev:** Head of Verne facing 3/4 right at left center, instruments and anchor in curved band **Rev. Legend:** 1828 JULES VERNE 1905 - LIBERTÉ . ÉGALITÉ . FRATERNITÉ

Date	Mintage	F	VF	XF	Unc	BU
2006 Proof	500	Value: 525				

KM# 1451 10 EURO
8.4500 g., 0.9200 Gold 0.2499 oz. AGW, 22 mm. **Subject:** 100th Anniversary - French Grand Prix **Obv:** Steering wheel with early race car in upper segment, two gauges at lower left, R / F at lower right **Obv. Legend:** LE MANS 1906 - CENTENAIRE du 1er GRAND PRIX de l'AUTOMOBILE CLUB de FRANCE **Rev. Legend:** MAGNY-COURS

Date	Mintage	F	VF	XF	Unc	BU
2006 Proof	500	Value: 525				

KM# 2038 10 EURO
8.4500 g., 0.9200 Gold 0.2499 oz. AGW **Subject:** Robert Schuman, 120th Anniversary of Birth

Date	Mintage	F	VF	XF	Unc	BU
2006 Proof	—	Value: 550				

KM# 2042 10 EURO
8.4500 g., 0.9200 Gold 0.2499 oz. AGW **Subject:** Bejing Olympics **Obv:** Three fencing foils on globe map pointing toward Bejing **Rev:** Two fencers

Date	Mintage	F	VF	XF	Unc	BU
2006 Proof	1,000	Value: 550				

KM# 2043 10 EURO
8.4500 g., 0.9200 Gold 0.2499 oz. AGW **Subject:** Benjamin Franklin, 300th anniversary of Birth **Obv:** Bust at left, kite in thunderclouds at right **Rev:** French and American flags

Date	Mintage	F	VF	XF	Unc	BU
2006 Proof	1,000	Value: 525				

KM# 2045 10 EURO
8.4500 g., 0.9200 Gold 0.2499 oz. AGW **Subject:** St. Peter's Basilica, 500th Anniversary **Obv:** Floorplan of St. Peter's **Rev:** Façade and Pope Benedict XVI

Date	Mintage	F	VF	XF	Unc	BU
2006 Proof	1,000	Value: 525				

KM# 2049 10 EURO
8.4500 g., 0.9200 Gold 0.2499 oz. AGW **Subject:** Marie Amélie of Orleans and Carlos I of Portugal, 120th Anniversary of Marriage **Obv:** Bust with tiara left **Rev:** Two shields crowned

Date	Mintage	F	VF	XF	Unc	BU
2006 Proof	500	Value: 600				

KM# 2053 10 EURO
8.4500 g., 0.9200 Gold 0.2499 oz. AGW **Obv:** Partial monuments forming map of France **Rev:** Arc de Triomphe and Tomb of Unknown Soldier

Date	Mintage	F	VF	XF	Unc	BU
2006 Proof	500	Value: 525				

KM# 2054 10 EURO
8.4500 g., 0.9200 Gold 0.2499 oz. AGW **Subject:** Church of St. Louis des Invalides **Obv:** Monument fragments forming map of France **Rev:** Church Façade flanked by two men

Date	Mintage	F	VF	XF	Unc	BU
2006 Proof	500	Value: 525				

KM# 2063 10 EURO
8.4500 g., 0.9200 Gold 0.2499 oz. AGW **Subject:** Wolfgang Amadeus Mozart, 250th Anniversary of Birth **Obv:** Youthful bust **Rev:** Hands at piano keys, music above

Date	Mintage	F	VF	XF	Unc	BU
2006 Proof	1,000	Value: 525				

KM# 2068 10 EURO
8.4500 g., 0.9200 Gold 0.2499 oz. AGW **Subject:** Jules Verne, 100th Anniversary of Death **Obv:** Voyage to the center of the Earth

Date	Mintage	F	VF	XF	Unc	BU
2006 Proof	500	Value: 525				

KM# 1420 10 EURO
8.4500 g., 0.9200 Gold 0.2499 oz. AGW, 22 mm. **Obv:** Military bust of Lafayette facing 3/4 left **Obv. Legend:** LA FAYETTE. HÉROS DELA RÉVOLUTION AMÉRICAINE **Obv. Inscription:** 1757/1854 at left, RF monogram at right **Rev:** Sailing ship L' Hermione **Rev. Legend:** LA FAYETTE, HERO OF THE AMERICAN REVOLUTION **Edge:** Plain

Date	Mintage	F	VF	XF	Unc	BU
2007 (a) Proof	500	Value: 525				

KM# 1502 10 EURO
8.4500 g., 0.9200 Gold 0.2499 oz. AGW, 22 mm. **Subject:** Georges Pompidou Center, 30th Anniversary

Date	Mintage	F	VF	XF	Unc	BU
2007 Proof	—	Value: 525				

KM# 1418 10 EURO
8.4500 g., 0.9200 Gold 0.2499 oz. AGW, 22 mm. **Obv:** Jean de la Fontaine, value, Chinese astrological animals, date, Paris mint privy marks but without national identification **Rev:** Pig in wreath **Edge:** Reeded **Note:** anonymous issue

Date	Mintage	F	VF	XF	Unc	BU
2007 Proof	500	Value: 525				

KM# 1463 10 EURO
8.4500 g., 0.9200 Gold 0.2499 oz. AGW, 22 mm. **Subject:** Sebastien Le Prestre de Vauban, 300th Anniversary of Death

Date	Mintage	F	VF	XF	Unc	BU
2007 Proof	3,000	Value: 475				

KM# 1474 10 EURO
8.4500 g., 0.9200 Gold 0.2499 oz. AGW, 22 mm. **Subject:** Paul E. Victor, 100th birthday **Obv:** International polar year logo **Rev:** Bust at left, Islands

Date	Mintage	F	VF	XF	Unc	BU
2007	500	—	—	—	—	500

KM# 1476 10 EURO
8.4500 g., 0.9200 Gold 0.2499 oz. AGW, 22 mm. **Obv:** Formula 1 race car on checkered background **Rev:** Legend in wreath on checkered background

Date	Mintage	F	VF	XF	Unc	BU
2007//2006 Proof	500	Value: 525				

KM# 1478 10 EURO
8.4500 g., 0.9200 Gold 0.2499 oz. AGW, 22 mm. **Subject:** 29th Summer Olympic Games Beijing **Obv:** Rider on horseback, globe map of China **Rev:** Equestrian jump over oriental fence

Date	Mintage	F	VF	XF	Unc	BU
2007 Proof	500	Value: 525				

KM# 1480 10 EURO
8.4500 g., 0.9200 Gold 0.2499 oz. AGW, 22 mm. **Subject:** Airbus A380 **Obv:** Airplane **Rev:** Europa head and flags

Date	Mintage	F	VF	XF	Unc	BU
2007 Proof	1,000	Value: 500				

KM# 1485 10 EURO
8.4500 g., 0.9200 Gold 0.2499 oz. AGW, 22 mm. **Subject:** 2007 Rugby World Cup **Obv:** Two players and goal **Rev:** Logo and goal

Date	Mintage	F	VF	XF	Unc	BU
2007 Proof	500	Value: 525				

KM# 1489 10 EURO
8.4500 g., 0.9200 Gold 0.2499 oz. AGW, 22 mm. **Obv:** Christian Dior **Rev:** Dior Museum building

Date	Mintage	F	VF	XF	Unc	BU
2007 Proof	500	Value: 525				

KM# 1508 10 EURO
8.4500 g., 0.9200 Gold 0.2499 oz. AGW, 22 mm. **Subject:** Georges Remi Centennial **Obv:** Wand and sparkles **Rev:** Tin Tin raising cap

Date	Mintage	F	VF	XF	Unc	BU
2007 Proof	1,000	Value: 500				

KM# 1512 10 EURO
8.4500 g., 0.9200 Gold 0.2499 oz. AGW, 22 mm. **Subject:** Aristides de Sousa Mendes, Portuguese diplomat **Obv:** Bust right **Rev:** Plaque

Date	Mintage	F	VF	XF	Unc	BU
2007 Proof	500	Value: 525				

KM# 1519 10 EURO
8.4500 g., 0.9200 Gold 0.2499 oz. AGW, 22 mm. **Subject:** Asterix **Rev:** Character with torch

Date	Mintage	F	VF	XF	Unc	BU
2007 Proof	500	Value: 525				

KM# 1544 10 EURO
8.4500 g., 0.9200 Gold 0.2499 oz. AGW, 22 mm. **Subject:** 29th Summer Olympic Games - Beijing **Obv:** Swimmer and globe **Rev:** Diver and oriental screen

Date	Mintage	F	VF	XF	Unc	BU
2008 Proof	1,000	Value: 500				

KM# 1528 10 EURO
8.4500 g., 0.9200 Gold 0.2499 oz. AGW, 22 mm. **Subject:** French Presidency of European Union **Obv:** Text within stars **Rev:** Europa head and flags

Date	Mintage	F	VF	XF	Unc	BU
2008 Proof	1,000	Value: 500				

KM# 1533 10 EURO
8.4500 g., 0.9200 Gold 0.2499 oz. AGW, 22 mm. **Subject:** European Parliament, 50th Anniversary **Obv:** Map of EU within stars **Rev:** European Parliament Building in Strasbourg

Date	Mintage	F	VF	XF	Unc	BU
2008 Proof	3,000	Value: 475				

KM# 1539 10 EURO

8.4500 g., 0.9990 Gold 0.2714 oz. AGW, 22 mm. **Subject:** 5th Republic, 50th Anniversary **Obv:** The Seed Sower **Rev:** de Gaulle head right

Date	Mintage	F	VF	XF	Unc	BU
2008 Proof	1,000	Value: 500				

KM# 1547 10 EURO

8.4500 g., 0.9200 Gold 0.2499 oz. AGW, 22 mm. **Subject:** UEFA **Obv:** French soccer team **Rev:** UEFA logo

Date	Mintage	F	VF	XF	Unc	BU
2008 Proof	500	Value: 525				

KM# 1552 10 EURO

8.4500 g., 0.9200 Gold 0.2499 oz. AGW, 22 mm. **Subject:** Franco - Japanese Relators - 150th Anniversary **Obv:** Eiffel Tower and Kimono forming logo **Rev:** Delacroix's "La Liberte"

Date	Mintage	F	VF	XF	Unc	BU
2008 Proof	3,000	Value: 475				

KM# 1553 10 EURO

8.4500 g., 0.9200 Gold 0.2499 oz. AGW, 22 mm. **Subject:** Franco - Japanese Relators - 150th Anniversary **Obv:** Eiffel Tower and Kimono forming logo **Rev:** "Ichikawa Ebizo IV" portrait painting

Date	Mintage	F	VF	XF	Unc	BU
2008 Proof	3,000	Value: 475				

KM# 1554 10 EURO

8.4500 g., 0.9200 Gold 0.2499 oz. AGW, 22 mm. **Subject:** Franco - Japanese Relators - 150th Anniversary **Obv:** Eiffel Tower and Kimono forming logo **Rev:** Japanese cash coin from "Kanci Tsuho"

Date	Mintage	F	VF	XF	Unc	BU
2008 Proof	3,000	Value: 475				

KM# 1556 10 EURO

0.4500 g., 0.9200 Gold 0.0133 oz. AGW, 22 mm. **Subject:** André Citronë **Obv:** First front wheel drive auto **Rev:** Bust 1/4 left

Date	Mintage	F	VF	XF	Unc	BU
2008 Proof	500	Value: 525				

KM# 1559 10 EURO

8.4500 g., 0.9200 Gold 0.2499 oz. AGW, 22 mm. **Subject:** Rouen Armada **Obv:** Cape Hown, sextant, hour glass **Edge:** Sailing ship

Date	Mintage	F	VF	XF	Unc	BU
2008 Proof	500	Value: 525				

KM# 1562 10 EURO

8.4500 g., 0.9200 Gold 0.2499 oz. AGW, 22 mm. **Subject:** Lourdes, 150th Anniversary **Obv:** Church of Notre Dame at Lourdes **Rev:** Cross with Pope John Paul II, Pope Benedict XVI and Bernadette Soubirous in quadrants

Date	Mintage	F	VF	XF	Unc	BU
2008 Proof	1,000	Value: 500				

KM# 1573 10 EURO

8.4500 g., 0.9200 Gold 0.2499 oz. AGW, 22 mm. **Subject:** Lunar New Year - Year of the Rat **Obv:** Bust of Jean de la Fontaine and twelve awards **Rev:** Rat within border

Date	Mintage	F	VF	XF	Unc	BU
2008 Proof	500	Value: 525				

KM# 1575 10 EURO

8.4500 g., 0.9200 Gold 0.2499 oz. AGW, 22 mm. **Subject:** UNESCO - Grand Canyon **Obv:** Grand Canyon **Rev:** UNESCO logos

Date	Mintage	F	VF	XF	Unc	BU
2008 Proof	500	Value: 525				

KM# 1577 10 EURO

8.4500 g., 0.9200 Gold 0.2499 oz. AGW, 22 mm. **Subject:** International Polar Year **Obv:** IPY logo **Rev:** Emperor Penguin and map of Antartica

Date	Mintage	F	VF	XF	Unc	BU
2008 Proof	500	Value: 525				

KM# 1579 10 EURO

8.4500 g., 0.9200 Gold 0.2499 oz. AGW, 22 mm. **Subject:** Spirou, 70th Anniversary **Obv:** Character Spirou in thought **Rev:** 70th Aniversary logo

Date	Mintage	F	VF	XF	Unc	BU
2008 Proof	500	Value: 525				

KM# 1675 10 EURO

22.2000 g., 0.9000 Silver 0.6423 oz. ASW, 37 mm. **Obv:** Sower left **Rev:** Wheat and olive branch

Date	Mintage	F	VF	XF	Unc	BU
2009	—	—	—	—	30.00	—
2010 Proof	10,000	Value: 35.00				

KM# 1591 10 EURO

27.2000 g., 0.9000 Silver 0.7870 oz. ASW, 37 mm. **Subject:** Europa - Fall of Berlin Wall **Obv:** Brandenburg gate and doves in flight **Rev:** Head facing and flags

Date	Mintage	F	VF	XF	Unc	BU
2009P Proof	10,000	Value: 37.50				

KM# 1580 10 EURO

12.0000 g., 0.9000 Silver 0.3472 oz. ASW, 29 mm. **Obv:** Modernistic sower advancing right **Rev:** Wreath and value

Date	Mintage	F	VF	XF	Unc	BU
2009P	2,000,000	—	—	—	—	17.50

KM# 1584 10 EURO

22.2000 g., 0.9000 Silver 0.6423 oz. ASW, 37 mm. **Subject:** Court of Human Rights, 50th Anniversary **Obv:** Sower left **Rev:** Text

Date	Mintage	F	VF	XF	Unc	BU
2009P Proof	10,000	Value: 35.00				

KM# 1596 10 EURO

22.2000 g., 0.9000 Silver 0.6423 oz. ASW, 37 mm. **Subject:** Concorde 40th Anniversary **Obv:** Concorde in flight **Rev:** Tail emblems

Date	Mintage	F	VF	XF	Unc	BU
2009P Proof	3,000	Value: 40.00				

KM# 1601 10 EURO

20.8900 g., 0.9000 Silver 0.6044 oz. ASW, 37 mm. **Obv:** Eiffel Tower Structure **Rev:** Gustave Eiffel at left

Date	Mintage	F	VF	XF	Unc	BU
2009P Proof	10,000	Value: 35.00				

KM# 1606 10 EURO

27.2000 g., 0.9000 Silver 0.7870 oz. ASW, 37 mm. **Subject:** Bugatti 100th Anniversary **Obv:** Ettore Bugatti at left **Rev:** Race car and quilt motif

Date	Mintage	F	VF	XF	Unc	BU
2009P Proof	10,000	Value: 35.00				

KM# 1611 10 EURO

22.2000 g., 0.9000 Silver 0.6423 oz. ASW, 37 mm. **Subject:** Curie Institute, 100th Anniversary

Date	Mintage	F	VF	XF	Unc	BU
2009P Proof	10,000	Value: 35.00				

KM# 1616 10 EURO

27.2000 g., 0.9000 Silver 0.7870 oz. ASW, 37 mm. **Subject:** Unesco site - The Kremlin in Moscow **Obv:** Wall Tower and cathedral

Date	Mintage	F	VF	XF	Unc	BU
2009P Proof	20,000	Value: 37.50				

KM# 1621 10 EURO

22.2000 g., 0.9000 Silver 0.6423 oz. ASW, 37 mm. **Subject:** First Moon Landing, 40th Anniversary **Obv:** Footprint on the moon

Date	Mintage	F	VF	XF	Unc	BU
2009P Proof	10,000	Value: 35.00				

KM# 1629 10 EURO

22.2000 g., 0.9000 Silver 0.6423 oz. ASW, 37 mm. **Subject:** Comic strip heroes **Obv:** Wanted posted **Rev:** Lucky Luke on horseback

Date	Mintage	F	VF	XF	Unc	BU
2009P Proof	5,000	Value: 40.00				

KM# 1631 10 EURO

22.2000 g., 0.9000 Silver 0.6423 oz. ASW, 37 mm. **Obv:** Soccer player **Rev:** Shield of Stade Francais in color

Date	Mintage	F	VF	XF	Unc	BU
2009P Proof	5,000	Value: 40.00				

KM# 1634 10 EURO
27.2000 g., 0.9000 Silver 0.7870 oz. ASW, 37 mm. **Subject:** Alpine skiing **Obv:** Globe and downhill skier **Rev:** Downhill skier on mountainside

Date	Mintage	F	VF	XF	Unc	BU
2009P Proof	10,000	Value: 37.50				

KM# 1636 10 EURO
22.2000 g., 0.9000 Silver 0.6423 oz. ASW, 37 mm. **Subject:** FIFA World Cup, South Africa **Obv:** Soccer player on field **Rev:** Soccerball, map of Africa, Prorea flower

Date	Mintage	F	VF	XF	Unc	BU
2009P Proof	15,000	Value: 35.00				

KM# 1645 10 EURO
12.0000 g., 0.9000 Silver 0.3472 oz. ASW, 29 mm. **Subject:** Aquitaine **Rev:** Value at center, wreath horizontal

Date	Mintage	F	VF	XF	Unc	BU
2010	7,690	—	—	—	—	22.50

KM# 1646 10 EURO
12.0000 g., 0.9000 Silver 0.3472 oz. ASW, 29 mm. **Subject:** Auvergne **Rev:** Value at center, wreath horizontal

Date	Mintage	F	VF	XF	Unc	BU
2010	7,690	—	—	—	—	22.50

KM# 1647 10 EURO
12.0000 g., 0.9000 Silver 0.3472 oz. ASW, 29 mm. **Subject:** Basse - Normandie **Rev:** Value at center, wreath horizontal

Date	Mintage	F	VF	XF	Unc	BU
2010	7,690	—	—	—	—	22.50

KM# 1648 10 EURO
12.0000 g., 0.9000 Silver 0.3472 oz. ASW, 29 mm. **Subject:** Bretagne **Rev:** Value at center, wreath horizontal

Date	Mintage	F	VF	XF	Unc	BU
2010	7,690	—	—	—	—	22.50

KM# 1649 10 EURO
12.0000 g., 0.9000 Silver 0.3472 oz. ASW, 29 mm. **Subject:** Burgundy **Rev:** Value at center, wreath horizontal

Date	Mintage	F	VF	XF	Unc	BU
2010	7,690	—	—	—	—	22.50

KM# 1650 10 EURO
12.0000 g., 0.9000 Silver 0.3472 oz. ASW, 29 mm. **Subject:** Centre **Rev:** Value at center, wreath horizontal

Date	Mintage	F	VF	XF	Unc	BU
2010	7,690	—	—	—	—	22.50

KM# 1651 10 EURO
12.0000 g., 0.9000 Silver 0.3472 oz. ASW, 29 mm. **Subject:** Champagne - Ardenne **Rev:** Value at center, wreath horizontal

Date	Mintage	F	VF	XF	Unc	BU
2010	7,690	—	—	—	—	22.50

KM# 1652 10 EURO
12.0000 g., 0.9000 Silver 0.3472 oz. ASW, 29 mm. **Subject:** Alsace **Rev:** Value at center, wreath horizontal

Date	Mintage	F	VF	XF	Unc	BU
2010	7,690	—	—	—	—	22.50

KM# 1653 10 EURO
12.0000 g., 0.9000 Silver 0.3472 oz. ASW, 29 mm. **Subject:** French - Comte **Rev:** Value at center, wreath horizontal

Date	Mintage	F	VF	XF	Unc	BU
2010	7,690	—	—	—	—	22.50

KM# 1654 10 EURO
12.0000 g., 0.9000 Silver 0.3472 oz. ASW, 29 mm. **Subject:** French Guiana **Rev:** Value at center, wreath horizontal

Date	Mintage	F	VF	XF	Unc	BU
2010	7,690	—	—	—	—	22.50

KM# 1655 10 EURO
12.0000 g., 0.9000 Silver 0.3472 oz. ASW, 29 mm. **Subject:** Guadeloupe **Rev:** Value at center, wreath horizontal

Date	Mintage	F	VF	XF	Unc	BU
2010	7,690	—	—	—	—	22.50

KM# 1656 10 EURO
12.0000 g., 0.9000 Silver 0.3472 oz. ASW, 29 mm. **Subject:** Haute - Normandie **Rev:** Value at center, wreath horizontal

Date	Mintage	F	VF	XF	Unc	BU
2010	7,690	—	—	—	—	22.50

KM# 1657 10 EURO
12.0000 g., 0.9000 Silver 0.3472 oz. ASW, 29 mm. **Subject:** Ile-de-France **Rev:** Value at center, wreath horizontal

Date	Mintage	F	VF	XF	Unc	BU
2010	7,690	—	—	—	—	22.50

KM# 1658 10 EURO
12.0000 g., 0.9000 Silver 0.3472 oz. ASW, 29 mm. **Subject:** Corsica **Rev:** Value at center, wreath horizontal

Date	Mintage	F	VF	XF	Unc	BU
2010	7,690	—	—	—	—	22.50

KM# 1659 10 EURO
12.0000 g., 0.9000 Silver 0.3472 oz. ASW, 29 mm. **Subject:** Languedoc - Roussillon **Rev:** Value at center, wreath horizontal

Date	Mintage	F	VF	XF	Unc	BU
2010	7,690	—	—	—	—	22.50

KM# 1660 10 EURO
12.0000 g., 0.9000 Silver 0.3472 oz. ASW, 29 mm. **Subject:** Limousin **Rev:** Value at center, wreath horizontal

Date	Mintage	F	VF	XF	Unc	BU
2010	7,690	—	—	—	—	22.50

KM# 1661 10 EURO
12.0000 g., 0.9000 Silver 0.3472 oz. ASW, 29 mm. **Subject:** Lorroaine **Rev:** Value at center, wreath horizontal

Date	Mintage	F	VF	XF	Unc	BU
2010	7,690	—	—	—	—	22.50

KM# 1662 10 EURO
12.0000 g., 0.9000 Silver 0.3472 oz. ASW, 29 mm. **Subject:** Martinique **Rev:** Value at center, wreath horizontal

Date	Mintage	F	VF	XF	Unc	BU
2010	7,690	—	—	—	—	22.50

KM# 1663 10 EURO
12.0000 g., 0.9000 Silver 0.3472 oz. ASW, 29 mm. **Subject:** Midi - Pyrenees **Rev:** Value at center, wreath horizontal

Date	Mintage	F	VF	XF	Unc	BU
2010	7,690	—	—	—	—	22.50

KM# 1664 10 EURO
12.0000 g., 0.9000 Silver 0.3472 oz. ASW, 29 mm. **Subject:** Nord - Pas de - Calais **Rev:** Value at center, wreath horizontal

Date	Mintage	F	VF	XF	Unc	BU
2010	7,690	—	—	—	—	22.50

KM# 1665 10 EURO
12.0000 g., 0.9000 Silver 0.3472 oz. ASW, 29 mm. **Subject:** Pays de la Loire **Rev:** Value at center, wreath horizontal

Date	Mintage	F	VF	XF	Unc	BU
2010	7,690	—	—	—	—	22.50

KM# 1666 10 EURO
12.0000 g., 0.9000 Silver 0.3472 oz. ASW, 29 mm. **Subject:** Picardie **Rev:** Value at center, wreath horizontal

Date	Mintage	F	VF	XF	Unc	BU
2010	7,690	—	—	—	—	22.50

KM# 1667 10 EURO
12.0000 g., 0.9000 Silver 0.3472 oz. ASW, 29 mm. **Subject:** Poitou - Charentes **Rev:** Value at center, wreath horizontal

Date	Mintage	F	VF	XF	Unc	BU
2010	7,690	—	—	—	—	22.50

KM# 1668 10 EURO
12.0000 g., 0.9000 Silver 0.3472 oz. ASW, 29 mm. **Subject:** Provence - Alpes - Cote d'Azur **Rev:** Value at center, wreath horizontal

Date	Mintage	F	VF	XF	Unc	BU
2010	7,690	—	—	—	—	22.50

KM# 1669 10 EURO
12.0000 g., 0.9000 Silver 0.3472 oz. ASW, 29 mm. **Subject:** Reunion **Rev:** Value at center, wreath horizontal

Date	Mintage	F	VF	XF	Unc	BU
2010	7,690	—	—	—	—	22.50

KM# 1670 10 EURO
12.0000 g., 0.9000 Silver 0.3472 oz. ASW, 29 mm. **Subject:** Rhone - Alpes **Rev:** Value at center, wreath horizontal

Date	Mintage	F	VF	XF	Unc	BU
2010	7,690	—	—	—	—	22.50

KM# 1681 10 EURO
22.2000 g., 0.9990 Silver 0.7130 oz. ASW, 37 mm. **Subject:** Cluny Abbey, 1100th Anniversary **Obv:** Europa head facing **Rev:** Cluny Abbey

Date	Mintage	F	VF	XF	Unc	BU
2010 Proof	10,000	Value: 50.00				

KM# 1686 10 EURO
22.2000 g., 0.9000 Silver 0.6423 oz. ASW, 37 mm. **Obv:** Georges Pompidou Center design **Rev:** Design detail

Date	Mintage	F	VF	XF	Unc	BU
2010 Proof	30,000	Value: 40.00				

KM# 1691 10 EURO
22.2000 g., Nickel-Copper Aeronotical alloy, 37 mm. **Obv:** Marcel Dassault **Rev:** Mirage III plane

Date	Mintage	F	VF	XF	Unc	BU
2010 Proof	20,000	Value: 45.00				

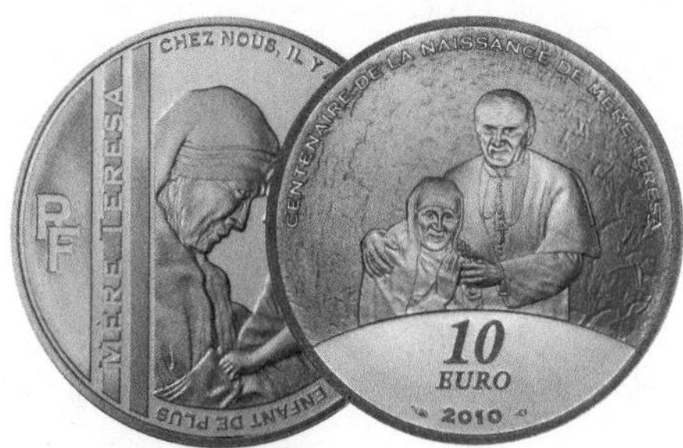

KM# 1695 10 EURO
22.2000 g., 0.9000 Silver 0.6423 oz. ASW, 37 mm. **Obv:** Mother Teresa and child **Rev:** Mother Teresa and Pope John Paul II

Date	Mintage	F	VF	XF	Unc	BU
2010 Proof	20,000	Value: 40.00				

KM# 1700 10 EURO
22.2000 g., 0.9000 Silver 0.6423 oz. ASW, 37 mm. **Obv:** Taj Mahal **Rev:** UNESCO offices

Date	Mintage	F	VF	XF	Unc	BU
2010 Proof	10,000	Value: 55.00				

KM# 1705 10 EURO
22.2000 g., 0.9000 Silver 0.6423 oz. ASW, 37 mm. **Obv:** Lille station and route map **Rev:** Three TGV trains

Date	Mintage	F	VF	XF	Unc	BU
2010 Proof	30,000	Value: 35.00				

KM# 1708 10 EURO
15.0000 g., 0.9000 Silver 0.4340 oz. ASW, 30x21 mm. **Rev:** Georges Braque **Shape:** Rectangle

Date	Mintage	F	VF	XF	Unc	BU
2010 Proof	20,000	Value: 50.00				

KM# 1713 10 EURO
15.0000 g., 0.9000 Silver 0.4340 oz. ASW, 30x21 mm. **Rev:** Picasso **Shape:** Rectangle

Date	Mintage	F	VF	XF	Unc	BU
2010 Proof	20,000	Value: 60.00				

KM# 1717 10 EURO
22.2000 g., 0.9000 Silver 0.6423 oz. ASW, 37 mm. **Obv:** Blake and Mortimer **Rev:** "Secret of the Swordfish" scene, arrest of Col. Olrik.

Date	Mintage	F	VF	XF	Unc	BU
2010 Proof	10,000	Value: 50.00				

KM# 1720 10 EURO
22.2000 g., 0.9000 Silver 0.6423 oz. ASW, 37 mm. **Obv:** Handball player and globe **Rev:** Handball player, net and Big Ben

Date	Mintage	F	VF	XF	Unc	BU
2010 Proof	10,000	Value: 40.00				

KM# 1722 10 EURO
22.2000 g., 0.9000 Silver 0.6423 oz. ASW, 37 mm. **Obv:** Soccer player **Rev:** Stade Toulousain logo, multicolor

Date	Mintage	F	VF	XF	Unc	BU
2010 Proof	5,000	Value: 50.00				

KM# 1726 10 EURO
10.0000 g., 0.5000 Silver 0.1607 oz. ASW, 29 mm. **Subject:** Mayotte **Obv:** Value at center, wreath horizontal

Date	Mintage	F	VF	XF	Unc	BU
2011	50,000	—	—	—	—	20.00

KM# 1727 10 EURO
10.0000 g., 0.5000 Silver 0.1607 oz. ASW, 29 mm. **Subject:** Aquitaine

Date	Mintage	F	VF	XF	Unc	BU
2011	150,000	—	—	—	—	20.00

KM# 1728 10 EURO
10.0000 g., 0.5000 Silver 0.1607 oz. ASW, 29 mm. **Subject:** Auvergne

Date	Mintage	F	VF	XF	Unc	BU
2011	80,000	—	—	—	—	20.00

KM# 1729 10 EURO
10.0000 g., 0.5000 Silver 0.1607 oz. ASW, 29 mm. **Subject:** Basse - Normindie

Date	Mintage	F	VF	XF	Unc	BU
2011	100,000	—	—	—	—	20.00

KM# 1730 10 EURO
10.0000 g., 0.5000 Silver 0.1607 oz. ASW, 29 mm. **Subject:** Bretagne

Date	Mintage	F	VF	XF	Unc	BU
2011	150,000	—	—	—	—	20.00

KM# 1731 10 EURO
10.0000 g., 0.5000 Silver 0.1607 oz. ASW, 29 mm. **Subject:** Burgundy

Date	Mintage	F	VF	XF	Unc	BU
2011	—	—	—	—	—	20.00

KM# 1732 10 EURO
10.0000 g., 0.5000 Silver 0.1607 oz. ASW, 29 mm. **Subject:** Centre

Date	Mintage	F	VF	XF	Unc	BU
2011	80,000	—	—	—	—	20.00

KM# 1733 10 EURO
10.0000 g., 0.5000 Silver 0.1607 oz. ASW, 29 mm. **Subject:** Campagne - Ardenne

Date	Mintage	F	VF	XF	Unc	BU
2011	50,000	—	—	—	—	20.00

KM# 1734 10 EURO
10.0000 g., 0.5000 Silver 0.1607 oz. ASW, 29 mm. **Subject:** Alsace

Date	Mintage	F	VF	XF	Unc	BU
2011	100,000	—	—	—	—	20.00

KM# 1735 10 EURO
10.0000 g., 0.5000 Silver 0.1607 oz. ASW, 29 mm. **Subject:** France - Comte

Date	Mintage	F	VF	XF	Unc	BU
2011	80,000	—	—	—	—	20.00

KM# 1736 10 EURO
10.0000 g., 0.5000 Silver 0.1607 oz. ASW, 29 mm. **Subject:** Guyane

Date	Mintage	F	VF	XF	Unc	BU
2011	50,000	—	—	—	—	20.00

KM# 1737 10 EURO
10.0000 g., 0.5000 Silver 0.1607 oz. ASW, 29 mm. **Subject:** Guadeloupe

Date	Mintage	F	VF	XF	Unc	BU
2011	50,000	—	—	—	—	20.00

KM# 1738 10 EURO
10.0000 g., 0.5000 Silver 0.1607 oz. ASW, 29 mm. **Subject:** Haute - Normandie

Date	Mintage	F	VF	XF	Unc	BU
2011	80,000	—	—	—	—	20.00

KM# 1739 10 EURO
10.0000 g., 0.5000 Silver 0.1607 oz. ASW, 29 mm. **Subject:** Ile de France

Date	Mintage	F	VF	XF	Unc	BU
2011	310,000	—	—	—	—	20.00

KM# 1740 10 EURO
10.0000 g., 0.5000 Silver 0.1607 oz. ASW, 29 mm. **Subject:** Corsica

Date	Mintage	F	VF	XF	Unc	BU
2011	80,000	—	—	—	—	20.00

KM# 1741 10 EURO
10.0000 g., 0.5000 Silver 0.1607 oz. ASW, 29 mm. **Subject:** Lansuedoc - Rossillon

Date	Mintage	F	VF	XF	Unc	BU
2011	120,000	—	—	—	—	20.00

KM# 1742 10 EURO
10.0000 g., 0.5000 Silver 0.1607 oz. ASW, 29 mm. **Subject:** Limousin

Date	Mintage	F	VF	XF	Unc	BU
2011	80,000	—	—	—	—	20.00

KM# 1743 10 EURO
10.0000 g., 0.5000 Silver 0.1607 oz. ASW, 29 mm. **Subject:** Lorroaine

Date	Mintage	F	VF	XF	Unc	BU
2011	100,000	—	—	—	—	20.00

KM# 1744 10 EURO
10.0000 g., 0.5000 Silver 0.1607 oz. ASW, 29 mm. **Subject:** Martinique

Date	Mintage	F	VF	XF	Unc	BU
2011	50,000	—	—	—	—	20.00

KM# 1745 10 EURO
10.0000 g., 0.5000 Silver 0.1607 oz. ASW, 29 mm. **Subject:** Nord Pas de Calais

Date	Mintage	F	VF	XF	Unc	BU
2011	180,000	—	—	—	—	20.00

KM# 1746 10 EURO
10.0000 g., 0.5000 Silver 0.1607 oz. ASW, 29 mm. **Subject:** Pays de la Loire

Date	Mintage	F	VF	XF	Unc	BU
2011	—	—	—	—	—	20.00

KM# 1747 10 EURO
10.0000 g., 0.5000 Silver 0.1607 oz. ASW, 29 mm. **Subject:** Picardie

Date	Mintage	F	VF	XF	Unc	BU
2011	100,000	—	—	—	—	20.00

KM# 1748 10 EURO
10.0000 g., 0.5000 Silver 0.1607 oz. ASW, 29 mm. **Subject:** Poitou - Charentes

Date	Mintage	F	VF	XF	Unc	BU
2011	100,000	—	—	—	—	20.00

KM# 1749 10 EURO
10.0000 g., 0.5000 Silver 0.1607 oz. ASW, 29 mm. **Subject:** Province - Alpes - Cote d'Azur

Date	Mintage	F	VF	XF	Unc	BU
2011	220,000	—	—	—	—	20.00

KM# 1750 10 EURO
10.0000 g., 0.5000 Silver 0.1607 oz. ASW, 29 mm. **Subject:** Reunion

Date	Mintage	F	VF	XF	Unc	BU
2011	70,000	—	—	—	—	20.00

KM# 1751 10 EURO
10.0000 g., 0.5000 Silver 0.1607 oz. ASW, 29 mm. **Subject:** Rhone - Alpes

Date	Mintage	F	VF	XF	Unc	BU
2011	220,000	—	—	—	—	20.00

KM# 1752 10 EURO
10.0000 g., 0.5000 Silver 0.1607 oz. ASW, 29 mm. **Subject:** Midi - Pyreneis

Date	Mintage	F	VF	XF	Unc	BU
2011	120,000	—	—	—	—	20.00

KM# 1784 10 EURO
22.2000 g., 0.9000 Silver 0.6423 oz. ASW, 37 mm. **Subject:** Euro Starter Kit, 10th Anniversary **Obv:** Sower left **Rev:** Euro starter kit

Date	Mintage	F	VF	XF	Unc	BU
2011 Proof	10,000	Value: 40.00				

KM# 1790 10 EURO
22.2000 g., 0.9000 Silver 0.6423 oz. ASW, 37 mm. **Subject:** International Music Day, 30th Anniversary **Obv:** Europa **Rev:** Youth jamming

Date	Mintage	F	VF	XF	Unc	BU
2011 Proof	10,000	Value: 40.00				

KM# 1795 10 EURO
22.2000 g., 0.9000 Silver 0.6423 oz. ASW, 37 mm. **Subject:** Great Explorers - Jacques Cartier **Obv:** The Grand Hermine sailing away **Rev:** Cartier, globe and compass rose

Date	Mintage	F	VF	XF	Unc	BU
2011 Proof	30,000	Value: 50.00				

KM# 1800 10 EURO
22.2000 g., 0.9000 Silver 0.6423 oz. ASW, 37 mm. **Subject:** Colvis, 481-511 **Obv:** Hands over chalice, reign dates at left, value at right **Rev:** Crowned head left

Date	Mintage	F	VF	XF	Unc	BU
2011 Proof	20,000	Value: 50.00				

KM# 1802 10 EURO
22.2000 g., 0.9000 Silver 0.6423 oz. ASW, 37 mm. **Subject:** Charlemagne, 768-814 **Obv:** Cross on orb, reight dates at left, value at right **Rev:** Crowned head left

Date	Mintage	F	VF	XF	Unc	BU
2011 Proof	20,000	Value: 50.00				

KM# 1804 10 EURO
22.2000 g., 0.9000 Silver 0.6423 oz. ASW, 37 mm. **Subject:** Charles II, 840-877 **Obv:** KARLOS monogram **Rev:** Crowned head left

Date	Mintage	F	VF	XF	Unc	BU
2011 Proof	20,000	Value: 50.00				

KM# 1806 10 EURO
22.2000 g., 0.9000 Silver 0.6423 oz. ASW, 37 mm. **Subject:** WWF - Audouin's Gull **Obv:** Gull in flight right **Rev:** Gull standing right, WWF panda logo

Date	Mintage	F	VF	XF	Unc	BU
2011 Proof	20,000	Value: 50.00				

KM# 1809 10 EURO
22.2000 g., 0.9000 Silver 0.6423 oz. ASW, 37 mm. **Subject:** UNESCO World Heritage Site - Palace of Versailles **Obv:** Building and garden plan **Rev:** Top view of UNESCO's Paris headquarters

Date	Mintage	F	VF	XF	Unc	BU
2011 Proof	20,000	Value: 50.00				

KM# 1814 10 EURO
22.2000 g., 0.9000 Silver 0.6423 oz. ASW, 37 mm. **Obv:** Metz railroad station **Rev:** TGV and ICE trains

Date	Mintage	F	VF	XF	Unc	BU
2011 Proof	10,000	Value: 50.00				

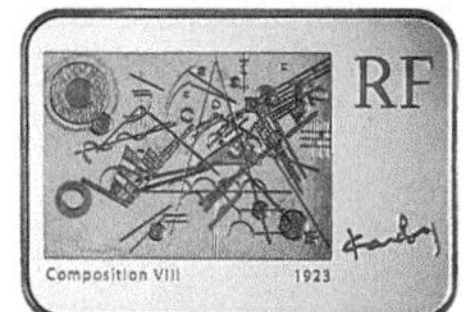

KM# 1819 10 EURO
15.0000 g., 0.9000 Silver 0.4340 oz. ASW, 30x21 mm. **Subject:** Vassily Kandinsky **Shape:** Rectangle

Date	Mintage	F	VF	XF	Unc	BU
2011 Proof	10,000	Value: 60.00				

KM# 1823 10 EURO
15.0000 g., 0.9000 Silver 0.4340 oz. ASW, 31 mm. **Subject:** Andy Warhol **Obv:** Portrait facing **Rev:** Dollar sign in color

Date	Mintage	F	VF	XF	Unc	BU
2011 Proof	10,000	Value: 60.00				

KM# 1827 10 EURO
22.2000 g., 0.9000 Silver 0.6423 oz. ASW, 37 mm. **Obv:** Cosette - Les Miserables **Rev:** Victor Hugo

Date	Mintage	F	VF	XF	Unc	BU
2011 Proof	10,000	Value: 50.00				

KM# 1829 10 EURO
22.2000 g., 0.9000 Silver 0.6423 oz. ASW, 37 mm. **Obv:** Nana **Rev:** Emile Zola

Date	Mintage	F	VF	XF	Unc	BU
2011 Proof	5,000	Value: 50.00				

KM# 1831 10 EURO
22.2000 g., 0.9000 Silver 0.6423 oz. ASW, 37 mm. **Obv:** The Stranger **Rev:** Albert Camus

Date	Mintage	F	VF	XF	Unc	BU
2011 Proof	—	Value: 50.00				

KM# 1835 10 EURO
22.2000 g., 0.9000 Silver 0.6423 oz. ASW, 37 mm. **Subject:** Comic Strip XIII **Obv:** Montage of characters **Rev:** Profile left and large XIII

Date	Mintage	F	VF	XF	Unc	BU
2011 Proof	10,000	Value: 50.00				

KM# 1755 10 EURO
22.2000 g., 0.9000 Silver 0.6423 oz. ASW, 37 mm. **Obv:** Bicycle racer **Rev:** Metro 92 logo

Date	Mintage	F	VF	XF	Unc	BU
2011 Proof	5,000	Value: 50.00				

KM# 1838 10 EURO
22.2000 g., 0.9000 Silver 0.6423 oz. ASW, 37 mm. **Obv:** Female figure skater and globe **Rev:** Figure skating pair

Date	Mintage	F	VF	XF	Unc	BU
2011 Proof	10,000	Value: 50.00				

KM# 1850 10 EURO
22.2000 g., 0.9000 Silver 0.6423 oz. ASW, 27 mm. **Subject:** Eurocorps, 20th Anniversary **Obv:** Mitterrand and Kohl standing clasping hands **Rev:** Europa facing

Date	Mintage	F	VF	XF	Unc	BU
2012(a) Proof	10,000	Value: 35.00				

KM# 1856 10 EURO
22.2000 g., 0.9000 Silver 0.6423 oz. ASW, 37 mm. **Subject:** Hugues Capet **Obv:** Crowned head faicing **Rev:** Right hand raised in benidiction

Date	Mintage	F	VF	XF	Unc	BU
2012(a) Proof	20,000	Value: 35.00				

KM# 1857 10 EURO
22.2000 g., 0.9000 Silver 0.6423 oz. ASW, 37 mm. **Subject:** Saint Louis **Obv:** Crowned head facing **Rev:** Oak tree

Date	Mintage	F	VF	XF	Unc	BU
2012(a) Proof	20,000	Value: 35.00				

KM# 1859 10 EURO
22.2000 g., 0.9000 Silver 0.6423 oz. ASW, 37 mm. **Subject:** The Three Musketeers **Obv:** D'Artagnan, cross emblem and three musketeers standing with swords raised **Rev:** Musketeers motto: "Un pour tours…" at left, Alexandre Dumas portrait at right

Date	Mintage	F	VF	XF	Unc	BU
2012(a) Proof	5,000	Value: 35.00				

KM# 1862 10 EURO
10.0000 g., 0.5000 Silver 0.1607 oz. ASW, 29 mm. **Subject:** Mayotte **Obv:** Value at center, wreath horizontal

Date	Mintage	F	VF	XF	Unc	BU
2012(a)	—	—	—	—	—	20.00

KM# 1863 10 EURO
10.0000 g., 0.5000 Silver 0.1607 oz. ASW, 29 mm. **Subject:** Aquitaine **Obv:** Value at center, wreath horizontal

Date	Mintage	F	VF	XF	Unc	BU
2012(a)	—	—	—	—	—	20.00

KM# 1864 10 EURO
10.0000 g., 0.5000 Silver 0.1607 oz. ASW, 29 mm. **Subject:** Auvergne **Obv:** Value at center, wreath horizontal

Date	Mintage	F	VF	XF	Unc	BU
2012(a)	—	—	—	—	—	20.00

KM# 1865 10 EURO
10.0000 g., 0.5000 Silver 0.1607 oz. ASW, 29 mm. **Subject:** Basse - Normandie **Obv:** Value at center, wreath horizontal

Date	Mintage	F	VF	XF	Unc	BU
2012(a)	—	—	—	—	—	20.00

KM# 1866 10 EURO
10.0000 g., 0.5000 Silver 0.1607 oz. ASW, 29 mm. **Subject:** Bretagne **Obv:** Value at center, wreath horizontal

Date	Mintage	F	VF	XF	Unc	BU
2012(a)	—	—	—	—	—	20.00

KM# 1867 10 EURO
10.0000 g., 0.5000 Silver 0.1607 oz. ASW, 29 mm. **Subject:** Burgundy **Obv:** Value at center, wreath horizontal

Date	Mintage	F	VF	XF	Unc	BU
2012(a)	—	—	—	—	—	20.00

KM# 1868 10 EURO
10.0000 g., 0.5000 Silver 0.1607 oz. ASW, 29 mm. **Subject:** Centre **Obv:** Value at center, wreath horizontal

Date	Mintage	F	VF	XF	Unc	BU
2012(a)	—	—	—	—	—	20.00

KM# 1869 10 EURO
10.0000 g., 0.5000 Silver 0.1607 oz. ASW, 29 mm. **Subject:** Champagne - Ardenne **Obv:** Value at center, wreath horizontal

Date	Mintage	F	VF	XF	Unc	BU
2012(a)	—	—	—	—	—	20.00

KM# 1870 10 EURO
10.0000 g., 0.5000 Silver 0.1607 oz. ASW, 29 mm. **Subject:** Alsace **Obv:** Value at center, wreath horizontal

Date	Mintage	F	VF	XF	Unc	BU
2012(a)	—	—	—	—	—	20.00

KM# 1871 10 EURO
10.0000 g., 0.5000 Silver 0.1607 oz. ASW, 29 mm. **Subject:** France - Comte

Date	Mintage	F	VF	XF	Unc	BU
2012(a)	—	—	—	—	—	20.00

KM# 1872 10 EURO
10.0000 g., 0.5000 Silver 0.1607 oz. ASW, 29 mm. **Subject:** French Guiana **Obv:** Value at center, wreath horizontal

Date	Mintage	F	VF	XF	Unc	BU
2012(a)	—	—	—	—	—	20.00

KM# 1873 10 EURO
10.0000 g., 0.5000 Silver 0.1607 oz. ASW, 29 mm. **Subject:** Guadeloupe **Obv:** Value at center, wreath horizontal

Date	Mintage	F	VF	XF	Unc	BU
2012(a)	—	—	—	—	—	20.00

KM# 1874 10 EURO
10.0000 g., 0.5000 Silver 0.1607 oz. ASW, 29 mm. **Subject:** Haute - Normandie **Obv:** Value at center, wreath horizontal

Date	Mintage	F	VF	XF	Unc	BU
2012(a)	—	—	—	—	—	20.00

KM# 1875 10 EURO
10.0000 g., 0.5000 Silver 0.1607 oz. ASW, 29 mm. **Subject:** Ile de France **Obv:** Value at center, wreath horizontal

Date	Mintage	F	VF	XF	Unc	BU
2012(a)	—	—	—	—	—	20.00

KM# 1876 10 EURO
10.0000 g., 0.5000 Silver 0.1607 oz. ASW, 29 mm. **Subject:** Corsica **Obv:** Value at center, wreath horizontal

Date	Mintage	F	VF	XF	Unc	BU
2012(a)	—	—	—	—	—	20.00

KM# 1877 10 EURO
10.0000 g., 0.5000 Silver 0.1607 oz. ASW, 29 mm. **Subject:** Languedoc - Rossillon **Obv:** Value at center, wreath horizontal

Date	Mintage	F	VF	XF	Unc	BU
2012(a)	—	—	—	—	—	20.00

KM# 1878 10 EURO
10.0000 g., 0.5000 Silver 0.1607 oz. ASW, 29 mm. **Subject:** Limousin **Obv:** Value at center, wreath horizontal

Date	Mintage	F	VF	XF	Unc	BU
2012(a)	—	—	—	—	—	20.00

KM# 1879 10 EURO
10.0000 g., 0.5000 Silver 0.1607 oz. ASW, 29 mm. **Subject:** Martinique **Obv:** Value at center, wreath horizontal

Date	Mintage	F	VF	XF	Unc	BU
2012(a)	—	—	—	—	—	20.00

KM# 1880 10 EURO
10.0000 g., 0.5000 Silver 0.1607 oz. ASW, 29 mm. **Subject:** Nord Pas de Calais **Obv:** Value at center, wreath horizontal

Date	Mintage	F	VF	XF	Unc	BU
2012(a)	—	—	—	—	—	20.00

KM# 1881 10 EURO
10.0000 g., 0.5000 Silver 0.1607 oz. ASW, 29 mm. **Subject:** Pays de la Loire **Obv:** Value at center, wreath horizontal

Date	Mintage	F	VF	XF	Unc	BU
2012(a)	—	—	—	—	—	20.00

KM# 1882 10 EURO
10.0000 g., 0.5000 Silver 0.1607 oz. ASW, 29 mm. **Subject:** Picardie **Obv:** Value at center, wreath horizontal

Date	Mintage	F	VF	XF	Unc	BU
2012(a)	—	—	—	—	—	20.00

KM# 1883 10 EURO
10.0000 g., 0.5000 Silver 0.1607 oz. ASW, 29 mm. **Subject:** Poitou - Charentes **Obv:** Value at center, wreath horizontal

Date	Mintage	F	VF	XF	Unc	BU
2012(a)	—	—	—	—	—	20.00

KM# 1884 10 EURO
10.0000 g., 0.5000 Silver 0.1607 oz. ASW, 29 mm. **Subject:** Province - Alpes - Cote d'Azur **Obv:** Value at center, wreath horizontal

Date	Mintage	F	VF	XF	Unc	BU
2012(a)	—	—	—	—	—	20.00

KM# 1885 10 EURO
10.0000 g., 0.5000 Silver 0.1607 oz. ASW, 29 mm. **Subject:** Reunion **Obv:** Value at center, wreath horizontal

Date	Mintage	F	VF	XF	Unc	BU
2012(a)	—	—	—	—	—	20.00

KM# 1886 10 EURO
10.0000 g., 0.5000 Silver 0.1607 oz. ASW, 29 mm. **Subject:** Rhone - Alpes **Obv:** Value at center, wreath horizontal

Date	Mintage	F	VF	XF	Unc	BU
2012(a)	—	—	—	—	—	20.00

KM# 1887 10 EURO
10.0000 g., 0.5000 Silver 0.1607 oz. ASW, 29 mm. **Subject:** Midi - Pyrenees **Obv:** Value at center, wreath horizontal

Date	Mintage	F	VF	XF	Unc	BU
2012(a)	—	—	—	—	—	20.00

KM# 1888 10 EURO
10.0000 g., 0.5000 Silver 0.1607 oz. ASW, 29 mm. **Subject:** Lorraine **Obv:** Value at center, wreath horizontal

Date	Mintage	F	VF	XF	Unc	BU
2012(a)	—	—	—	—	—	20.00

KM# 1889 10 EURO
22.2000 g., 0.9000 Silver 0.6423 oz. ASW, 37 mm. **Subject:** Euro, 10th Anniversary **Obv:** The Sower advancing left **Rev:** Value at center on globe, child-like drawings around

Date	Mintage	F	VF	XF	Unc	BU
2012(a) Proof	15,000	Value: 35.00				

KM# 1895 10 EURO
22.2000 g., 0.9000 Silver 0.6423 oz. ASW, 37 mm. **Subject:** abbé Pierre, 100th anniversary of Birth **Obv:** Pierre at left, shadow at right **Rev:** Emmaus International logo and quote

Date	Mintage	F	VF	XF	Unc	BU
2012(a) Proof	10,000	Value: 35.00				

KM# 1905 10 EURO
22.2000 g., 0.9000 Silver 0.6423 oz. ASW, 37 mm. **Subject:** UNESCO - World Heritage Site **Obv:** Abu Simbel temple

Date	Mintage	F	VF	XF	Unc	BU
2012(a) Proof	10,000	Value: 35.00				

KM# 1911 10 EURO
22.2000 g., 0.9000 Silver 0.6423 oz. ASW, 37 mm. **Subject:** TGV South-East **Obv:** Lyon Saint-Exupery station **Rev:** Two modern locomotives

Date	Mintage	F	VF	XF	Unc	BU
2012(a) Proof	5,000	Value: 35.00				

KM# 1916 10 EURO
22.2000 g., 0.9000 Silver 0.6423 oz. ASW, 37 mm. **Subject:** Comic strip hero **Obv:** Largo Winch and building **Rev:** Winch riding motorcycle being chased by two cars

Date	Mintage	F	VF	XF	Unc	BU
2012(a) Proof	5,000	Value: 35.00				

KM# 1919 10 EURO
22.2000 g., 0.9000 Silver 0.6423 oz. ASW, 37 mm. **Subject:** Toulonnais Rugby Club **Obv:** Value and Stadium field view **Rev:** Colored shield and portrait Felix Mayol

Date	Mintage	F	VF	XF	Unc	BU
2012(a) Proof	5,000	Value: 45.00				

KM# 1921 10 EURO
22.2000 g., 0.9000 Silver 0.6423 oz. ASW, 37 mm. **Subject:** 2012 Summer Olympics, London **Obv:** Two judo athletes and map of Europe **Rev:** Two judo athletes

Date	Mintage	F	VF	XF	Unc	BU
2012(a) Proof	10,000	Value: 35.00				

KM# 1924 10 EURO
22.2000 g., 0.9000 Silver 0.6423 oz. ASW, 37 mm. **Subject:** Year of the Dragon **Obv:** Dragon **Rev:** La Fontaine and zodiac animals

Date	Mintage	F	VF	XF	Unc	BU
2012(a) Proof	10,000	Value: 45.00				

KM# 2073 10 EURO
10.0000 g., 0.5000 Silver 0.1607 oz. ASW, 29 mm. **Obv:** Horizontal wreath, value within **Rev:** Hercules group standing

Date	Mintage	F	VF	XF	Unc	BU
2012	491,000	—	—	—	—	15.00
2012 Proof	19,000	Value: 35.00				

KM# 2075 10 EURO
22.2000 g., 0.9000 Silver 0.6423 oz. ASW, 37 mm. **Obv:** Palice de Louvre **Rev:** Philipp II August, head facing

Date	Mintage	F	VF	XF	Unc	BU
2012	Est. 20,000	—	—	—	—	65.00

KM# 2078 10 EURO
22.2000 g., 0.9000 Silver 0.6423 oz. ASW, 37 mm. **Obv:** Aircraft Carrier Jean de Arc **Rev:** Anchor chain below convoy of ships

Date	Mintage	F	VF	XF	Unc	BU
2012 Proof	Est. 10,000	Value: 45.00				

KM# 2079 10 EURO
22.2000 g., 0.9000 Silver 0.6423 oz. ASW, 37 mm. **Obv:** Trans-atlantic liner France **Rev:** Two winged smoke-stacks, partial porthole

Date	Mintage	F	VF	XF	Unc	BU
2012 Proof	Est. 10,000	Value: 45.00				

KM# 2081 10 EURO
163.8000 g., 0.9500 Silver 5.0028 oz. ASW, 50 mm. **Obv:** Trans-atlantic liner France **Rev:** Winged smoke stacks, partial porthole

Date	Mintage	F	VF	XF	Unc	BU
2012 Proof	Est. 500	Value: 300				

KM# 2084 10 EURO
22.2000 g., 0.9000 Silver 0.6423 oz. ASW, 37 mm. **Obv:** Roxane on the Balcony **Rev:** Edmond Rostand and quote

Date	Mintage	F	VF	XF	Unc	BU
2012 Proof	Est. 5,000	Value: 35.00				

KM# 2085 10 EURO
22.2000 g., 0.9000 Silver 0.6423 oz. ASW, 37 mm. **Obv:** Puss in boots **Rev:** Charles Perrault and quite

Date	Mintage	F	VF	XF	Unc	BU
2012 Proof	Est. 5,000	Value: 35.00				

KM# 2087 10 EURO
22.2000 g., 0.9000 Silver 0.6423 oz. ASW, 37 mm. **Obv:** Yves Klein, blue hand **Rev:** Klein artwork

Date	Mintage	F	VF	XF	Unc	BU
2012 Proof	—	Value: 35.00				

KM# 2091 10 EURO
22.2000 g., 0.9000 Silver 0.6423 oz. ASW, 37 mm. **Subject:** French-German Friendship, 50th Anniversary **Rev:** Europa head facing at right, banners at left

Date	Mintage	F	VF	XF	Unc	BU
2013 Proof	—	Value: 35.00				

KM# 2095 10 EURO
22.2000 g., 0.9000 Silver 0.6423 oz. ASW, 37 mm. **Subject:** Rudolf Noureev **Obv:** Portrait at right **Rev:** Dancer and National Theater

Date	Mintage	F	VF	XF	Unc	BU
2013 Proof	—	Value: 35.00				

KM# 2097 10 EURO
22.2000 g., 0.9000 Silver 0.6423 oz. ASW, 37 mm. **Subject:** Notre Dame, 850th Anniversary **Obv:** Seal at right, cathedral details, blue highlights **Rev:** Seal at left, cathedral details, blue highlights

Date	Mintage	F	VF	XF	Unc	BU
2013 Proof	—	Value: 50.00				

KM# A1450 15 EURO
31.0000 g., 0.9000 Silver 0.8970 oz. ASW, 31 mm. **Rev:** Pantheon

Date	Mintage	F	VF	XF	Unc	BU
2007 Proof	7,500	Value: 75.00				

KM# 1535 15 EURO
15.0000 g., 0.9000 Silver 0.4340 oz. ASW, 31 mm. **Obv:** Sower, half length advancing right **Rev:** Value within hexagon

Date	Mintage	F	VF	XF	Unc	BU
2008	500,000	—	—	—	—	45.00
2008 Proof	7,500	Value: 55.00				
2009 Proof	7,500	Value: 55.00				
2010 Proof	9,000	Value: 55.00				

KM# 1333 20 EURO
17.0000 g., 0.9200 Gold 0.5028 oz. AGW, 31 mm. **Obv:** Victor Hugo, denomination and map **Rev:** "Gavroche" **Edge:** Plain

Date	Mintage	F	VF	XF	Unc	BU
2002 Proof	2,000	Value: 900				

KM# 1306 20 EURO
17.0000 g., 0.9200 Gold 0.5028 oz. AGW, 31 mm. **Subject:** French Landmarks **Obv:** French map **Rev:** Le Mont St. Michel **Edge:** Plain

Date	Mintage	F	VF	XF	Unc	BU
2002 Proof	1,000	Value: 950				

KM# 1308 20 EURO
17.0000 g., 0.9200 Gold 0.5028 oz. AGW, 31 mm. **Subject:** French Landmarks **Obv:** French map **Rev:** La Butte Montmartre **Edge:** Plain

Date	Mintage	F	VF	XF	Unc	BU
2002 Proof	1,000	Value: 875				

KM# 1982 20 EURO
17.0000 g., 0.9200 Gold 0.5028 oz. AGW **Obv:** French euro coin designs **Rev:** Europa head facing, flags at left

Date	Mintage	F	VF	XF	Unc	BU
2002 Proof	3,000	Value: 1,000				

KM# 1984 20 EURO
17.0000 g., 0.9200 Gold 0.5028 oz. AGW **Subject:** Charles Lindburg's Flight, 75th Anniversary **Obv:** Map of Northern France, portrait of Lindburg **Rev:** Spirit of St. Louis plane and U.S. Coastline

Date	Mintage	F	VF	XF	Unc	BU
2002 Proof	1,000	Value: 1,000				

KM# 1986 20 EURO
163.8000 g., 0.9500 Silver 5.0028 oz. ASW, 50 mm. **Obv:** Victor Hugo bust facing at left **Rev:** Street scene from Les Miserables **Rev. Legend:** GAVROCHE

Date	Mintage	F	VF	XF	Unc	BU
2002 Proof	500	Value: 1,400				

KM# 1987 20 EURO
17.0000 g., 0.9200 Gold 0.5028 oz. AGW **Subject:** Children's stories **Rev:** Cinderilla

Date	Mintage	F	VF	XF	Unc	BU
2002 Proof	926	Value: 1,000				

KM# 1988 20 EURO
17.0000 g., 0.9200 Gold 0.5028 oz. AGW **Subject:** Children's Stories **Rev:** Snow White

Date	Mintage	F	VF	XF	Unc	BU
2002 Proof	950	Value: 1,000				

KM# 1989 20 EURO
17.0000 g., 0.9200 Gold 0.5028 oz. AGW **Subject:** Children's Stories **Rev:** Pinocchio

Date	Mintage	F	VF	XF	Unc	BU
2002 Proof	1,000	Value: 1,000				

KM# 1990 20 EURO
17.0000 g., 0.9200 Gold 0.5028 oz. AGW **Obv:** Sower advancing left **Rev:** Large value and map of Europe

Date	Mintage	F	VF	XF	Unc	BU
2002 Proof	4,182	Value: 1,000				

KM# 1334 20 EURO
17.0000 g., 0.9200 Gold 0.5028 oz. AGW, 31 mm. **Obv:** Tour de France logo **Rev:** Cyclist going left **Edge:** Plain

Date	Mintage	F	VF	XF	Unc	BU
2003 Proof	5,000	Value: 875				

KM# 1337 20 EURO
17.0000 g., 0.9200 Gold 0.5028 oz. AGW, 31 mm. **Obv:** Jefferson and Napoleon with Louisiana Purchase map **Rev:** Jazz musician, mansion and river boat **Edge:** Plain

Date	Mintage	F	VF	XF	Unc	BU
2003 Proof	1,000	Value: 900				

KM# 1339 20 EURO
17.0000 g., 0.9200 Gold 0.5028 oz. AGW, 31 mm. **Obv:** Curved cross design with multiple values **Rev:** Goddess Europa and flags **Edge:** Plain

Date	Mintage	F	VF	XF	Unc	BU
2003 Proof	3,000	Value: 875				

KM# 1342 20 EURO
17.0000 g., 0.9200 Gold 0.5028 oz. AGW, 31 mm. **Obv:** Denomination and compass face **Rev:** SS Normandie and New York City skyline **Edge:** Plain

Date	Mintage	F	VF	XF	Unc	BU
2003 Proof	1,000	Value: 900				

KM# 1344 20 EURO
17.0000 g., 0.9200 Gold 0.5028 oz. AGW, 31 mm. **Obv:** Denomination and compass face **Rev:** Airplane and Tokyo Geisha **Edge:** Plain

Date	Mintage	F	VF	XF	Unc	BU
2003 Proof	1,000	Value: 900				

KM# 1346 20 EURO
17.0000 g., 0.9200 Gold 0.5028 oz. AGW, 31 mm. **Obv:** Paul Gauguin **Rev:** Native woman **Edge:** Plain

Date	Mintage	F	VF	XF	Unc	BU
2003 Proof	2,000	Value: 875				

KM# 1349 20 EURO
17.0000 g., 0.9200 Gold 0.5028 oz. AGW, 31 mm. **Obv:** The Seed Sower **Rev:** Denomination and map **Edge:** Plain

Date	Mintage	F	VF	XF	Unc	BU
2003 Proof	5,000	Value: 875				

KM# 1354 20 EURO
17.0000 g., 0.9200 Gold 0.5028 oz. AGW, 31 mm. **Obv:** Mona Lisa **Rev:** Leonardo da Vinci and denomination **Edge:** Plain

Date	Mintage	F	VF	XF	Unc	BU
2003 Proof	1,000	Value: 900				

KM# 1356 20 EURO
17.0000 g., 0.9200 Gold 0.5028 oz. AGW, 31 mm. **Obv:** Map and denomination **Rev:** Chateau Chambord **Edge:** Plain

Date	Mintage	F	VF	XF	Unc	BU
2003 Proof	1,000	Value: 900				

KM# 1358 20 EURO
17.0000 g., 0.9200 Gold 0.5028 oz. AGW, 31 mm. **Obv:** Denomination in swirling design **Rev:** Hansel and Gretel, witch and house **Edge:** Plain

Date	Mintage	F	VF	XF	Unc	BU
2003 Proof	1,000	Value: 900				

KM# 1360 20 EURO
17.0000 g., 0.9200 Gold 0.5028 oz. AGW, 31 mm. **Obv:** Denomination in swirling design **Rev:** Alice in Wonderland **Edge:** Plain

Date	Mintage	F	VF	XF	Unc	BU
2003 Proof	1,000	Value: 900				

KM# 1363 20 EURO
17.0000 g., 0.9200 Gold 0.5028 oz. AGW, 31 mm. **Obv:** Pierre de Coubertin **Rev:** Olympic runners **Edge:** Plain

Date	Mintage	F	VF	XF	Unc	BU
2003 Proof	3,000	Value: 875				

KM# 1327 20 EURO
8.4500 g., 0.9200 Gold 0.2499 oz. AGW, 31 mm. **Obv:** Tour de France logo **Rev:** Group of cyclists and Arch de Triumph **Edge:** Reeded

Date	Mintage	F	VF	XF	Unc	BU
2003A Proof	5,000	Value: 475				

KM# 1328 20 EURO
8.4500 g., 0.9200 Gold 0.2499 oz. AGW, 31 mm. **Obv:** Tour de France logo **Rev:** Two cyclists and spectators **Edge:** Reeded

Date	Mintage	F	VF	XF	Unc	BU
2003A Proof	5,000	Value: 475				

KM# 1329 20 EURO
8.4500 g., 0.9200 Gold 0.2499 oz. AGW, 31 mm. **Obv:** Tour de France logo **Rev:** Two groups of cyclists **Edge:** Reeded

Date	Mintage	F	VF	XF	Unc	BU
2003A Proof	5,000	Value: 475				

KM# 1330 20 EURO
8.4500 g., 0.9200 Gold 0.2499 oz. AGW, 31 mm. **Obv:** Tour de France logo **Rev:** Cyclist, stop watch and gears **Edge:** Reeded

Date	Mintage	F	VF	XF	Unc	BU
2003A Proof	5,000	Value: 4.75				

KM# 1998 20 EURO
17.0000 g., 0.9200 Gold 0.5028 oz. AGW **Subject:** Athletic World Championships **Obv:** Winner podium before buildings **Rev:** Runner

Date	Mintage	F	VF	XF	Unc	BU
2003 Proof	1,165	Value: 1,000				

KM# 1999 20 EURO
17.0000 g., 0.9200 Gold 0.5028 oz. AGW **Subject:** Athletic World Championships **Obv:** Winner podium before buildgins **Rev:** High jumper

Date	Mintage	F	VF	XF	Unc	BU
2003 Proof	863	Value: 1,000				

KM# 2000 20 EURO
17.0000 g., 0.9200 Gold 0.5028 oz. AGW **Subject:** Athletic World Championships **Obv:** Winner podium before buildings

Date	Mintage	F	VF	XF	Unc	BU
2003 Proof	867	Value: 1,000				

KM# 2004 20 EURO
163.8000 g., 0.9500 Silver 5.0028 oz. ASW, 50 mm. **Obv:** Mona Lisa **Rev:** Leonardo DaVinci bust at left, large value at right

Date	Mintage	F	VF	XF	Unc	BU
2003 Proof	999	Value: 400				

KM# 2007 20 EURO
17.0000 g., 0.9200 Gold 0.5028 oz. AGW **Subject:** Orient Express, Hagia Sophia in Istanbul **Obv:** Compass Rose **Rev:** Steam locomotive

Date	Mintage	F	VF	XF	Unc	BU
2003 Proof	1,000	Value: 1,000				

KM# 2009 20 EURO
17.0000 g., 0.9200 Gold 0.5028 oz. AGW **Subject:** Childhood Fairy Tales **Rev:** Sleeping Beauty

Date	Mintage	F	VF	XF	Unc	BU
2003 Proof	309	Value: 1,250				

KM# 2016 20 EURO
17.0000 g., 0.9200 Gold 0.5028 oz. AGW **Subject:** Childhood stories **Rev:** Peter Pan

Date	Mintage	F	VF	XF	Unc	BU
2004 Proof	362	Value: 1,000				

KM# 1365 20 EURO
17.0000 g., 0.9200 Gold 0.5028 oz. AGW, 31 mm. **Obv:** Map with denomination **Rev:** Avignon Popes Palace **Edge:** Plain

Date	Mintage	F	VF	XF	Unc	BU
2004 Proof	1,000	Value: 900				

KM# 1370 20 EURO
17.0000 g., 0.9200 Gold 0.5028 oz. AGW, 31 mm. **Obv:** Soldiers and Normandy invasion scene **Rev:** "D-DAY" above denomination **Edge:** Plain

Date	Mintage	F	VF	XF	Unc	BU
2004 Proof	2,000	Value: 875				

KM# 1376 20 EURO
17.0000 g., 0.9200 Gold 0.5028 oz. AGW, 31 mm. **Subject:** Centenary Law of Dec. 9, 1905 **Obv:** "Sower" left in ring of stars **Rev:** Denomination and French map face design **Edge:** Plain

Date	Mintage	F	VF	XF	Unc	BU
2004 Proof	3,000	Value: 875				
2006 Proof	1,000	Value: 900				

KM# 1379 20 EURO
17.0000 g., 0.9200 Gold 0.5028 oz. AGW, 31 mm. **Obv:** Compass rose **Rev:** Ocean liner **Edge:** Plain

Date	Mintage	F	VF	XF	Unc	BU
2004 Proof	1,000	Value: 900				

KM# 1381 20 EURO
17.0000 g., 0.9200 Gold 0.5028 oz. AGW, 31 mm. **Obv:** Compass rose **Rev:** Trans-Siberian Railroad **Edge:** Plain

Date	Mintage	F	VF	XF	Unc	BU
2004 Proof	1,000	Value: 900				

KM# 1383 20 EURO
17.0000 g., 0.9200 Gold 0.5028 oz. AGW, 31 mm. **Obv:** Compass rose **Rev:** Half-track vehicle **Edge:** Plain

Date	Mintage	F	VF	XF	Unc	BU
2004 Proof	1,000	Value: 900				

KM# 1385 20 EURO
17.0000 g., 0.9200 Gold 0.5028 oz. AGW, 31 mm. **Obv:** Compass rose **Rev:** Biplane airliner **Edge:** Plain

Date	Mintage	F	VF	XF	Unc	BU
2004 Proof	1,000	Value: 900				

KM# 1387 20 EURO
155.5000 g., 0.9500 Silver 4.7493 oz. ASW, 50 mm. **Obv:** Statue of Liberty **Rev:** F. A. Bartholdi **Edge:** Plain

Date	Mintage	F	VF	XF	Unc	BU
2004 Proof	999	Value: 225				

KM# 1388 20 EURO
17.0000 g., 0.9200 Gold 0.5028 oz. AGW, 31 mm. **Obv:** Statue of Liberty **Rev:** F. A. Bartholdi **Edge:** Plain

Date	Mintage	F	VF	XF	Unc	BU
2004 Proof	2,000	Value: 875				

KM# 1393 20 EURO
17.0000 g., 0.9200 Gold 0.5028 oz. AGW, 31 mm. **Subject:** European Union Expansion **Obv:** Partial face and flags **Rev:** Puzzle map **Edge:** Plain

Date	Mintage	F	VF	XF	Unc	BU
2004 Proof	3,000	Value: 875				

KM# 2011 20 EURO
17.0000 g., 0.9200 Gold 0.5028 oz. AGW **Subject:** French-English Treaty, 100th Anniversary **Obv:** Two busts and treaty document **Rev:** Marianne and Britannia

Date	Mintage	F	VF	XF	Unc	BU
2004 Proof	339	Value: 1,500				

KM# 2015 20 EURO
17.0000 g., 0.9200 Gold 0.5028 oz. AGW **Subject:** Childhood stories **Rev:** Aladdin

Date	Mintage	F	VF	XF	Unc	BU
2004 Proof	316	Value: 1,200				

KM# 1433 20 EURO
17.0000 g., 0.9200 Gold 0.5028 oz. AGW, 31 mm. **Subject:** Bicentennial Victory at Austerlitz **Rev:** Battle scene **Rev. Legend:** LIBERTÉ ÉGALITÉ FRATERNITÉ

Date	Mintage	F	VF	XF	Unc	BU
2005 Proof	5,000	Value: 875				

KM# 1437 20 EURO
17.0000 g., 0.9200 Gold 0.5028 oz. AGW, 31 mm. **Subject:** Centenary - Law of Dec. 9, 1905 **Obv:** "Sower" at left in ring of stars

Date	Mintage	F	VF	XF	Unc	BU
2005 Proof	1,500	Value: 875				

KM# 2022 20 EURO
17.0000 g., 0.9200 Gold 0.5028 oz. AGW **Subject:** World Cup Soccer **Obv:** World Cup trophy and soccer ball **Rev:** Large value and map of France

Date	Mintage	F	VF	XF	Unc	BU
2005 Proof	Est. 3,000	Value: 1,000				

KM# 2025 20 EURO
155.5500 g., 0.9990 Gold 4.9958 oz. AGW **Obv:** Napoleon looking out over land towards Sunrise **Rev:** Napoleon and troops in the field

Date	Mintage	F	VF	XF	Unc	BU
2005 Proof	Est. 99	Value: 10,000				

KM# 2028 20 EURO
17.0000 g., 0.9200 Gold 0.5028 oz. AGW **Subject:** Frederic Chopin, 195th Anniversary of Birth **Obv:** Profile at left, piano keys at right vertically **Rev:** Statue in Wausau park at left, piano keys at right vertically

Date	Mintage	F	VF	XF	Unc	BU
2005 Proof	500	Value: 3,000				

KM# 2030 20 EURO
163.8000 g., 0.9500 Silver 5.0028 oz. ASW, 50 mm. **Subject:** Jules Verne, 100th Anniversary of Death **Obv:** Around the World in 80 days

Date	Mintage	F	VF	XF	Unc	BU
2005 Proof	Est. 500	Value: 300				

KM# 2031 20 EURO
163.5000 g., 0.9500 Silver 4.9936 oz. ASW, 50 mm. **Subject:** Jules Verne, 100th Anniversary of Death **Obv:** 20,000 leagues under the sea

Date	Mintage	F	VF	XF	Unc	BU
2005 Proof	500	Value: 300				

KM# 2032 20 EURO
163.5000 g., 0.9500 Silver 4.9936 oz. ASW, 50 mm. **Subject:** Jules Verne, 100th Anniversary of Death **Rev:** From the earth to the moon

Date	Mintage	F	VF	XF	Unc	BU
2005 Proof	500	Value: 300				

KM# 1454 20 EURO
155.5000 g., 0.9500 Silver 4.7493 oz. ASW, 50 mm. **Subject:** 100th Anniversary - Paul Cézanne's death **Obv:** Self portrait **Rev:** "The Card Players" **Rev. Legend:** LIBERTÉ ÉGALITÉ FRATERNITÉ

Date	Mintage	F	VF	XF	Unc	BU
2006 Proof	500	Value: 225				

KM# 1443 20 EURO
155.5200 g., 0.9500 Silver 4.7499 oz. ASW, 50 mm. **Obv:** Bust of Franklin facing slightly right at left, his diplomatic and technical successes at right **Obv. Legend:** BENJAMIN FRANKLIN 1706-2006 **Obv. Inscription:** AMI DE LA FRANCE

Date	Mintage	F	VF	XF	Unc	BU
2006 Proof	500	Value: 225				

KM# 2050 20 EURO
163.8000 g., 0.9500 Silver 5.0028 oz. ASW, 50 mm. **Subject:** Marie Curie, 100th Anniversary of Sorbonne Professorship **Obv:** Bust and atom **Rev:** Building tower and students

Date	Mintage	F	VF	XF	Unc	BU
2006 Proof	500	Value: 500				

KM# 2051 20 EURO
17.0000 g., 0.9200 Gold 0.5028 oz. AGW **Subject:** Marie Curie, 100th Anniversary of Sorbonne Professorship **Obv:** Bust and atom **Rev:** Building tower and students

Date	Mintage	F	VF	XF	Unc	BU
2006 Proof	500	Value: 1,400				

KM# 2052 20 EURO
163.8000 g., 0.9500 Silver 5.0028 oz. ASW, 50 mm. **Obv:** Monument parts as map of France **Rev:** Arc de Triomphe and tomb of Unknown soldier

Date	Mintage	F	VF	XF	Unc	BU
2006 Proof	500	Value: 250				

Note: Individually numbered

KM# 2056 20 EURO
17.0000 g., 0.9200 Gold 0.5028 oz. AGW **Subject:** Abolition of the Death Penalty, 25th Anniversary **Obv:** Sower advancing left **Rev:** Guillotine

Date	Mintage	F	VF	XF	Unc	BU
2006 Proof	Est. 1,000	Value: 1,000				

KM# 2059 20 EURO
17.0000 g., 0.9200 Gold 0.5028 oz. AGW **Subject:** Paul Cézanne, 100th Anniversary of Death **Obv:** Bust **Rev:** Two men seated at table, wine bottle between them

Date	Mintage	F	VF	XF	Unc	BU
2006 Proof	500	Value: 1,100				

KM# 2062 20 EURO
163.8000 g., 0.9500 Silver 5.0028 oz. ASW **Subject:** Wolfgang Amadeus Mozart, 250th Anniversary of Birth **Obv:** Youthful bust **Rev:** Hands at piano keys, music above

Date	Mintage	F	VF	XF	Unc	BU
2006 Proof	500	Value: 375				

Note: Individually numbered

KM# 2065 20 EURO
163.8000 g., 0.9500 Silver 5.0028 oz. ASW, 50 mm. **Subject:** Jules Verne, 100th Anniversary of Death **Obv:** Voyage to the center of the earth

Date	Mintage	F	VF	XF	Unc	BU
2006 Proof	500	Value: 300				

KM# 2066 20 EURO
165.3000 g., 0.9990 Silver 5.3090 oz. ASW, 50 mm. **Subject:** Jules Verne, 100th Anniversary of Death **Obv:** Michel Strogoff, the curier of the Tsar

Date	Mintage	F	VF	XF	Unc	BU
2006 Proof	500	Value: 300				

KM# 2067 20 EURO
163.8000 g., 0.9990 Silver 5.2608 oz. ASW, 50 mm. **Subject:** Jules Verne, 100th Anniversary of Death **Obv:** Five weeks in a balloon

Date	Mintage	F	VF	XF	Unc	BU
2006 Proof	500	Value: 300				

KM# 1520 20 EURO
155.5000 g., 0.9500 Silver 4.7493 oz. ASW, 50 mm. **Subject:** Asterix **Rev:** Character running downhill

Date	Mintage	F	VF	XF	Unc	BU
2007 Proof	500	Value: 325				

KM# 1422 20 EURO
17.0000 g., 0.9200 Gold 0.5028 oz. AGW, 30x21 mm. **Subject:** Edgar Degas, 90th Anniversary of Seuth **Obv:** Degas painting of dancer **Rev:** Brushes and Degas portrait **Shape:** Rectangle

Date	Mintage	F	VF	XF	Unc	BU
2007 Proof	500	Value: 1,000				

KM# 1468 20 EURO
17.0000 g., 0.9200 Gold 0.5028 oz. AGW, 31 mm. **Subject:** Le Petit Prince, 60th Anniversary **Obv:** Prince lying in field

Date	Mintage	F	VF	XF	Unc	BU
2007 Proof	2,000	Value: 875				

KM# 1471 20 EURO
155.5500 g., 0.9500 Silver 4.7508 oz. ASW, 50 mm. **Obv:** Two dragons in flight **Rev:** Merlin and Excalibur

Date	Mintage	F	VF	XF	Unc	BU
2007 Proof	500	Value: 300				

KM# 1472 20 EURO
17.0000 g., 0.9200 Gold 0.5028 oz. AGW, 31 mm. **Obv:** Two dragons in flight **Rev:** Merlin & Excalibur

Date	Mintage	F	VF	XF	Unc	BU
2007 Proof	500	Value: 900				

KM# 1494 20 EURO
155.5500 g., 0.9500 Silver 4.7508 oz. ASW, 50 mm. **Subject:** Point Neuf - 400th Anniversary **Obv:** Moments of France logo **Rev:** Point Neuf Bridge and Paris Mint Building

Date	Mintage	F	VF	XF	Unc	BU
2007 Proof	500	Value: 300				

KM# 1496 20 EURO
155.5500 g., 0.9500 Silver 4.7508 oz. ASW, 50 mm. **Subject:** Cannes Film Festival, 60th Anniversary **Obv:** Cinema screen and stage, Golden Palm Award

Date	Mintage	F	VF	XF	Unc	BU
2007 Proof	500	Value: 300				

KM# 1509 20 EURO
100.0000 g., 0.9500 Silver 3.0542 oz. ASW, 49 mm. **Subject:** Georges Remi Centennial **Rev:** Tin Tin and Snowy

Date	Mintage	F	VF	XF	Unc	BU
2007 Proof	500	Value: 325				

KM# 1513 20 EURO
155.5000 g., 0.9500 Silver 4.7493 oz. ASW, 50 mm. **Subject:** Stanislas Leszczynski **Obv:** Bust and shield **Rev:** Palace Stanislas - Nancy

Date	Mintage	F	VF	XF	Unc	BU
2007 Proof	500	Value: 325				

KM# 1521 20 EURO
17.0000 g., 0.9200 Gold 0.5028 oz. AGW, 31 mm. **Subject:** Asterix **Rev:** Asterix and Cleopatria

Date	Mintage	F	VF	XF	Unc	BU
2007 Proof	500	Value: 900				

KM# 1529 20 EURO
163.8000 g., 0.9500 Silver 5.0028 oz. ASW, 50 mm. **Subject:** French Presidency of European Union **Obv:** Text within stars **Rev:** Europa head and flags

Date	Mintage	F	VF	XF	Unc	BU
2008 Proof	500	Value: 250				

KM# 1540 20 EURO
163.8000 g., 0.9500 Silver 5.0028 oz. ASW, 50 mm. **Subject:** 5th Republic, 50th Anniversary **Obv:** Sower **Rev:** de Gaulle head right

Date	Mintage	F	VF	XF	Unc	BU
2008 Proof	500	Value: 250				

KM# 1541 20 EURO
17.0000 g., 0.9205 Gold 0.5031 oz. AGW, 31 mm. **Subject:** 5th Republic, 50th Anniversary **Obv:** Sower **Rev:** de Gaulle head right

Date	Mintage	F	VF	XF	Unc	BU
2008 Proof	500	Value: 900				

KM# 1557 20 EURO
163.8000 g., 0.9500 Silver 5.0028 oz. ASW, 50 mm. **Subject:** André Citronë **Obv:** First front wheel drive auto **Rev:** Bust 1/4 left

Date	Mintage	F	VF	XF	Unc	BU
2008 Proof	500	Value: 325				

KM# 1560 20 EURO
163.8000 g., 0.9500 Silver 5.0028 oz. ASW, 50 mm. **Subject:** Rouen Armada **Obv:** Cape Horn, sextant, hour glass **Rev:** Sailing ship

Date	Mintage	F	VF	XF	Unc	BU
2008 Proof	—	Value: 350				

KM# 1563 20 EURO
163.8000 g., 0.9500 Silver 5.0028 oz. ASW, 50 mm. **Subject:** Lourdes, 150th Anniversary **Obv:** Church of Notre Dame at Lourdes **Rev:** Cross with Pope John Paul II, Pope Benedict XVI and Bernadette Soubirous in quadrants

Date	Mintage	F	VF	XF	Unc	BU
2008 Proof	500	Value: 300				

KM# 1571 20 EURO
17.0000 g., 0.9200 Gold 0.5028 oz. AGW, 30x21 mm. **Subject:** Edward Manet **Obv:** Manet's "Olympia" painting **Rev:** Paint brushes and Manet's portrait **Shape:** Rectangle

Date	Mintage	F	VF	XF	Unc	BU
2008 Proof	500	Value: 950				

KM# 1602 20 EURO
44.4000 g., 0.9000 Silver 1.2847 oz. ASW, 37 mm. **Obv:** Eiffel Tower Structure **Rev:** Gustave Eiffel at left

Date	Mintage	F	VF	XF	Unc	BU
2009P Proof	5,000	Value: 100				

KM# 1607 20 EURO
44.4000 g., 0.9000 Silver 1.2847 oz. ASW, 37 mm. **Subject:** Bugatti 100th Anniversary **Obv:** Ettore Bugatti at left **Rev:** Race car and grill motif

Date	Mintage	F	VF	XF	Unc	BU
2009P Proof	5,000	Value: 100				

KM# 1612 20 EURO
44.4000 g., 0.9000 Silver 1.2847 oz. ASW, 37 mm. **Subject:** Curie Institute, 100th Anniversary

Date	Mintage	F	VF	XF	Unc	BU
2009P Proof	5,000	Value: 70.00				

KM# 1617 20 EURO
163.8000 g., 0.9500 Silver 5.0028 oz. ASW, 50 mm. **Subject:** Unesco site - The Kremlin in Moscow **Obv:** Wall Tower and cathedral

Date	Mintage	F	VF	XF	Unc	BU
2009P Proof	500	Value: 250				

KM# 1690 20 EURO
44.4000 g., 0.9000 Silver 1.2847 oz. ASW, 37 mm. **Obv:** Marcel Dassault **Rev:** Mirage III plane

Date	Mintage	F	VF	XF	Unc	BU
2010 Proof	2,000	Value: 75.00				

KM# 1704 20 EURO
44.4000 g., 0.9000 Silver 1.2847 oz. ASW, 37 mm. **Obv:** Lille station and route map **Rev:** Three TGV trains

Date	Mintage	F	VF	XF	Unc	BU
2010 Proof	2,000	Value: 75.00				

KM# 1815 20 EURO
44.4000 g., 0.9000 Silver 1.2847 oz. ASW, 37 mm. **Obv:** Metz railroad station **Rev:** TGV and ICE trains

Date	Mintage	F	VF	XF	Unc	BU
2011 Proof	1,000	Value: 100				

KM# 2070 20 EURO
15.0000 g., 0.9000 Silver 0.4340 oz. ASW, 31 mm. **Subject:** G-20 Meeting in Cannes **Obv:** Sower advancing right **Rev:** Laurel tree and oak tree in the shape of a Euro symbol with value specification in the hexagon as stylization national borders

Date	Mintage	F	VF	XF	Unc	BU
2011	2,000	—	—	—	—	100

KM# 1912 20 EURO
44.4000 g., 0.9000 Silver 1.2847 oz. ASW, 37 mm. **Subject:** TGV South East **Obv:** Lyon Saint-Exupery station **Rev:** Two modern locomotives

Date	Mintage	F	VF	XF	Unc	BU
2012(a) Proof	1,000	Value: 75.00				

KM# 1581 25 EURO
18.0000 g., 0.9000 Silver 0.5208 oz. ASW, 33 mm. **Obv:** Modernistic sower advancing right **Rev:** Value and wreath

Date	Mintage	F	VF	XF	Unc	BU
2009P	250,000	—	—	—	—	35.00

KM# 1303 50 EURO

31.0000 g., 0.9990 Gold 0.9956 oz. AGW, 37 mm. **Subject:** Europa **Obv:** Eight French euro coin designs **Rev:** Portrait and flags design of 6.55957 francs KM-1265 **Edge:** Plain

Date	Mintage	F	VF	XF	Unc	BU
2002 Proof	2,000	Value: 1,800				

KM# 1335 50 EURO

31.1000 g., 0.9990 Gold 0.9988 oz. AGW, 37 mm. **Obv:** Tour de France logo **Rev:** Cyclist going left **Edge:** Plain

Date	Mintage	F	VF	XF	Unc	BU
2003 Proof	5,000	Value: 1,750				

KM# 1340 50 EURO

1000.0000 g., 0.9500 Silver 30.541 oz. ASW, 100 mm. **Obv:** Curved cross design with multiple values **Rev:** Goddess Europa and flags **Edge:** Plain with three line inscription at six o'clock

Date	Mintage	F	VF	XF	Unc	BU
2003 Proof	2,000	Value: 1,150				

KM# 1993 50 EURO

31.1050 g., 0.9990 Gold 0.9990 oz. AGW **Obv:** Curved cross with coins **Rev:** Europa head at right, flags at left

Date	Mintage	F	VF	XF	Unc	BU
2003 Proof	Est. 2,000	Value: 1,850				

KM# 1368 50 EURO

31.1000 g., 0.9990 Gold 0.9988 oz. AGW, 37 mm. **Obv:** Book, denomination and eagle **Rev:** Napoleon and coronation scene **Edge:** Plain

Date	Mintage	F	VF	XF	Unc	BU
2004 Proof	2,000	Value: 1,800				

KM# 1394 50 EURO

31.1040 g., 0.9990 Gold 0.9990 oz. AGW, 37 mm. **Subject:** European Union Expansion **Obv:** Partial face and flags **Rev:** Puzzle map **Edge:** Plain

Date	Mintage	F	VF	XF	Unc	BU
2004 Proof	2,000	Value: 1,800				

KM# 1430 50 EURO

31.1040 g., 0.9990 Gold 0.9990 oz. AGW, 37 mm. **Rev:** Kitty and Daniel in Versailles **Rev. Legend:** Hello Kitty

Date	Mintage	F	VF	XF	Unc	BU
2005 Proof	1,000	Value: 1,850				

KM# 2018 50 EURO

31.1000 g., 0.9990 Gold 0.9988 oz. AGW **Subject:** European Union, 50th Anniversary **Obv:** Flag of the European Union **Rev:** Europa head facing at right, banners at left

Date	Mintage	F	VF	XF	Unc	BU
2005 Proof	500	Value: 1,800				

KM# 2039 50 EURO

31.1000 g., 0.9990 Gold 0.9988 oz. AGW **Subject:** Robert Schuman, 120th Anniversary of Birth **Rev:** Europa head facing at right, with color highlights

Date	Mintage	F	VF	XF	Unc	BU
2006 Proof	500	Value: 1,900				

KM# 2046 50 EURO

31.1050 g., 0.9990 Gold 0.9990 oz. AGW **Subject:** St. Peter's Bascilica, 500th Anniversary **Obv:** St. Peter's floor plan **Rev:** Façade of St. Peter's, Pope Benedict XVI

Date	Mintage	F	VF	XF	Unc	BU
2006 Proof	500	Value: 1,900				

KM# 2057 50 EURO

31.1050 g., 0.9990 Gold 0.9990 oz. AGW **Subject:** Abolishment of the Death Penalty, 25th Anniversary **Obv:** Sower advancing left **Rev:** Guillotine

Date	Mintage	F	VF	XF	Unc	BU
2006 Proof	Est. 500	Value: 1,800				

KM# 1466 50 EURO

31.1050 g., 0.9990 Gold 0.9990 oz. AGW, 37 mm. **Subject:** Le Petit Prince, 60th Anniversary **Obv:** Prince standing

Date	Mintage	F	VF	XF	Unc	BU
2007 Proof	2,000	Value: 1,800				

KM# 1481 50 EURO

31.1000 g., 0.9990 Gold 0.9988 oz. AGW, 37 mm. **Subject:** Airbus A380 **Obv:** Airplane **Rev:** Europa and flags

Date	Mintage	F	VF	XF	Unc	BU
2007 Proof	500	Value: 1,900				

KM# 1487 50 EURO

1000.0000 g., 0.9500 Silver 30.541 oz. ASW **Subject:** 2007 Rugby World Cup **Obv:** Two players and goal **Rev:** Logo and goal **Shape:** Oval

Date	Mintage	F	VF	XF	Unc	BU
2007 Proof	299	Value: 1,250				

KM# 1510 50 EURO

31.1050 g., 0.9990 Gold 0.9990 oz. AGW, 37 mm. **Subject:** Georges Remi Centennial **Obv:** Wand and sparkles **Rev:** Tin Tin and dog Snowy

Date	Mintage	F	VF	XF	Unc	BU
2007 Proof	500	Value: 1,900				

KM# 1522 50 EURO

31.0500 g., 0.9990 Gold 0.9972 oz. AGW, 37 mm. **Subject:** Asterix **Rev:** Asterix and the Butcher of Arverne

Date	Mintage	F	VF	XF	Unc	BU
2007 Proof	500	Value: 1,900				

KM# 1530 50 EURO

31.1040 g., 0.9990 Gold 0.9990 oz. AGW, 37 mm. **Subject:** French Presidency of the Euopean Union **Obv:** Text within stars **Rev:** Europa head within flags

Date	Mintage	F	VF	XF	Unc	BU
2008 Proof	500	Value: 1,900				

KM# 1564 50 EURO

31.1040 g., 0.9990 Gold 0.9990 oz. AGW, 37 mm. **Subject:** Lourdes, 150th Anniversary **Obv:** Church of Notre Dame at Lourdes **Rev:** Cross with Pope John Paul II, Pope Benedict XVI and Bernadette Soubirous in quadrants

Date	Mintage	F	VF	XF	Unc	BU
2008 Proof	500	Value: 1,900				

KM# 1603 50 EURO

163.8000 g., 0.9500 Silver 5.0028 oz. ASW, 50 mm. **Obv:** Eiffel Tower Structure **Rev:** Gustave Eiffel at left

Date	Mintage	F	VF	XF	Unc	BU
2009P Proof	1,000	Value: 250				

KM# 1597 50 EURO

163.8000 g., 0.9500 Silver 5.0028 oz. ASW, 50 mm. **Subject:** Concorde 40th Anniversary **Obv:** Concorde in flight **Rev:** Tail emblems

Date	Mintage	F	VF	XF	Unc	BU
2009P Proof	1,000	Value: 250				

KM# 1585 50 EURO

163.8000 g., 0.9500 Silver 5.0028 oz. ASW, 50 mm. **Subject:** Court of Human Rights, 50th Anniversary **Obv:** Sower left **Rev:** Text

Date	Mintage	F	VF	XF	Unc	BU
2009P Proof	500	Value: 275				

KM# 1592 50 EURO

8.4500 g., 0.9200 Gold 0.2499 oz. AGW, 22 mm. **Subject:** Europa - Fall of Berlin Wall **Obv:** Brandenburg gate and doves in flight **Rev:** Head facing and flags

Date	Mintage	F	VF	XF	Unc	BU
2009P	1,000	Value: 500				

KM# 1598 50 EURO

8.4500 g., 0.9200 Gold 0.2499 oz. AGW, 22 mm. **Subject:** Concorde 40th Anniversary **Obv:** Concorde in flight **Rev:** Tail emblems

Date	Mintage	F	VF	XF	Unc	BU
2009P Proof	3,000	Value: 475				

KM# 1604 50 EURO

8.4500 g., 0.9200 Gold 0.2499 oz. AGW, 22 mm. **Obv:** Eiffel Tower Structure **Rev:** Gustave Eiffel at left

Date	Mintage	F	VF	XF	Unc	BU
2009P Proof	1,000	Value: 500				

KM# 1608 50 EURO

163.8000 g., 0.9500 Silver 5.0028 oz. ASW, 50 mm. **Subject:** Bugatti 100th Anniverary **Obv:** Ettore Bugatti at left **Rev:** Race car and grill motif

Date	Mintage	F	VF	XF	Unc	BU
2009P Proof	500	Value: 325				

KM# 1609 50 EURO

8.4500 g., 0.9200 Gold 0.2499 oz. AGW, 22 mm. **Subject:** Bugatti 100th Anniversary **Obv:** Ettore Bugatti at left **Rev:** Race car and grill motif

Date	Mintage	F	VF	XF	Unc	BU
2009P Proof	1,000	Value: 500				

KM# 1613 50 EURO

163.8000 g., 0.9500 Silver 5.0028 oz. ASW, 50 mm. **Subject:** Curie Institute, 100th Anniversary

Date	Mintage	F	VF	XF	Unc	BU
2009P Proof	500	Value: 275				

KM# 1614 50 EURO
8.4500 g., 0.9200 Gold 0.2499 oz. AGW, 22 mm. **Subject:** Curie Institute, 100th Anniversary

Date	Mintage	F	VF	XF	Unc	BU
2009P Proof	1,000	Value: 500				

KM# 1618 50 EURO
163.8000 g., 0.9500 Silver 5.0028 oz. ASW, 50 mm. **Subject:** UNESCO Site - The Kremlin in Moscow

Date	Mintage	F	VF	XF	Unc	BU
2009 Proof	Est. 1,000	Value: 275				

KM# 1622 50 EURO
163.8000 g., 0.9500 Silver 5.0028 oz. ASW, 50 mm. **Subject:** First Moon Landing, 40th Anniversary **Obv:** Footprint on the moon

Date	Mintage	F	VF	XF	Unc	BU
2009P Proof	500	Value: 275				

KM# 1623 50 EURO
8.4500 g., 0.9200 Gold 0.2499 oz. AGW, 22 mm. **Subject:** First Moon Landing, 40th Anniversary **Obv:** Footprint on the moon

Date	Mintage	F	VF	XF	Unc	BU
2009P Proof	1,000	Value: 475				

KM# 1628 50 EURO
8.4500 g., 0.9200 Gold 0.2499 oz. AGW, 22 mm. **Subject:** Year of the Ox **Obv:** Oxen within Asian screen **Rev:** Portrait of LaFontaine

Date	Mintage	F	VF	XF	Unc	BU
2009P Proof	500	Value: 525				

KM# 1630 50 EURO
8.4500 g., 0.9200 Gold 0.2499 oz. AGW, 22 mm. **Subject:** Comic strip heroes **Obv:** Wanted Poster **Rev:** Lucky Luke on horseback

Date	Mintage	F	VF	XF	Unc	BU
2009P Proof	1,000	Value: 500				

KM# 1632 50 EURO
8.4500 g., 0.9200 Gold 0.2499 oz. AGW, 22 mm. **Obv:** Rugby player **Rev:** State Francais

Date	Mintage	F	VF	XF	Unc	BU
2009P Proof	500	Value: 525				

KM# 1635 50 EURO
8.4500 g., 0.9200 Gold 0.2499 oz. AGW, 22 mm. **Subject:** Alpine skiing **Obv:** Globe and downhill skier **Rev:** Downhill skier on mountainside

Date	Mintage	F	VF	XF	Unc	BU
2009P Proof	1,000	Value: 500				

KM# 1637 50 EURO
163.8000 g., 0.9500 Silver 5.0028 oz. ASW, 50 mm. **Subject:** FIFA World Cup, South Africa 2010 **Obv:** Soccer player on field **Rev:** Soccerball, Map of Africa, Protrea flower

Date	Mintage	F	VF	XF	Unc	BU
2009P Proof	500	Value: 275				

KM# 1638 50 EURO
8.4500 g., 0.9200 Gold 0.2499 oz. AGW, 22 mm. **Subject:** FIFA World Cup, South Africa 2010 **Obv:** Soccer Player on field **Rev:** Soccerball, Map of Africa, Protea flower

Date	Mintage	F	VF	XF	Unc	BU
2009P Proof	7,500	Value: 475				

KM# 1644 50 EURO
36.0000 g., 0.9000 Silver 1.0416 oz. ASW, 36 mm. **Obv:** The Seed Sower advancing right, sun rays from above **Rev:** Value at center, wreath horizontal

Date	Mintage	F	VF	XF	Unc	BU
2010	100,000	—	—	—	—	45.00

KM# 1673 50 EURO
8.4500 g., 0.9200 Gold 0.2499 oz. AGW, 22 mm. **Obv:** The Seed Sower left **Rev:** Wheat and olive branch

Date	Mintage	F	VF	XF	Unc	BU
2010 Proof	500	Value: 525				

KM# 1679 50 EURO
8.4500 g., 0.9250 Gold 0.2513 oz. AGW, 22 mm. **Subject:** Cluny Abbey, 1100th Anniversary **Obv:** Europa head facing **Rev:** Cluney Abbey

Date	Mintage	F	VF	XF	Unc	BU
2010 Proof	1,000	Value: 500				

KM# 1684 50 EURO
8.4500 g., 0.9200 Gold 0.2499 oz. AGW, 22 mm. **Obv:** Georges Pompidou Center design **Rev:** Design detail

Date	Mintage	F	VF	XF	Unc	BU
2010 Proof	3,000	Value: 475				

KM# 1685 50 EURO
163.8000 g., 0.9500 Silver 5.0028 oz. ASW, 50 mm. **Obv:** Georges Pompidou Center design **Rev:** Design detail

Date	Mintage	F	VF	XF	Unc	BU
2010 Proof	1,000	Value: 225				

KM# 1688 50 EURO
8.4500 g., 0.9200 Gold 0.2499 oz. AGW, 22 mm. **Obv:** Marcel Dassault **Rev:** Mirage III plane

Date	Mintage	F	VF	XF	Unc	BU
2010 Proof	1,000	Value: 500				

KM# 1694 50 EURO
8.4500 g., 0.9200 Gold 0.2499 oz. AGW, 22 mm. **Obv:** Mother Teresa and child **Rev:** Mother Teresa and Pope John Paul II

Date	Mintage	F	VF	XF	Unc	BU
2010 Proof	1,000	Value: 500				

KM# 1699 50 EURO
8.4500 g., 0.9200 Gold 0.2499 oz. AGW, 22 mm. **Obv:** Taj Mahal **Rev:** UNESCO offices

Date	Mintage	F	VF	XF	Unc	BU
2010 Proof	1,000	Value: 500				

KM# 1702 50 EURO
8.4500 g., 0.9200 Gold 0.2499 oz. AGW, 22 mm. **Obv:** Lille station and route map **Rev:** Three TGV trains

Date	Mintage	F	VF	XF	Unc	BU
2010 Proof	1,000	Value: 500				

KM# 1703 50 EURO
163.8000 g., 0.9500 Silver 5.0028 oz. ASW, 50 mm. **Obv:** Lille station and route map **Rev:** Three TGV trains

Date	Mintage	F	VF	XF	Unc	BU
2010 Proof	500	Value: 275				

KM# 1714 50 EURO
8.4500 g., 0.9200 Gold 0.2499 oz. AGW, 22 mm. **Obv:** Tiger within border **Rev:** La Fontaine bust at left, animals at right

Date	Mintage	F	VF	XF	Unc	BU
2010 Proof	500	Value: 525				

KM# 1716 50 EURO
8.4500 g., 0.9200 Gold 0.2499 oz. AGW, 22 mm. **Obv:** Blake and Mortimer **Rev:** "Secret of the Swordfish" scene, the arrest of Col. Olrik

Date	Mintage	F	VF	XF	Unc	BU
2010 Proof	500	Value: 525				

KM# 1719 50 EURO
8.4500 g., 0.9200 Gold 0.2499 oz. AGW, 22 mm. **Obv:** Handball player on globe **Rev:** Handball player, net, Big Ben

Date	Mintage	F	VF	XF	Unc	BU
2010 Proof	1,000	Value: 500				

KM# 1721 50 EURO
8.4500 g., 0.9200 Gold 0.2499 oz. AGW, 22 mm. **Obv:** Soccer player **Rev:** Stade Toulousain logo, multicolor

Date	Mintage	F	VF	XF	Unc	BU
2010 Proof	500	Value: 525				

KM# 1786 50 EURO
8.4500 g., 0.9200 Gold 0.2499 oz. AGW, 22 mm. **Subject:** Euro Starter Kit, 10th Anniversary **Obv:** Sower **Rev:** Euro starter kit

Date	Mintage	F	VF	XF	Unc	BU
2011 Proof	3,000	Value: 475				

KM# 1792 50 EURO
8.4500 g., 0.9200 Gold 0.2499 oz. AGW, 22 mm. **Subject:** International Music Day, 30th Anniversary **Obv:** Europa **Rev:** Youth jamming

Date	Mintage	F	VF	XF	Unc	BU
2011 Proof	3,000	Value: 475				

KM# 1796 50 EURO
8.4500 g., 0.9200 Gold 0.2499 oz. AGW, 22 mm. **Subject:** Great Explorers - Jacques Cartier **Obv:** The Grande Hermine sailing away **Rev:** Carter, globe and compass rose

Date	Mintage	F	VF	XF	Unc	BU
2011 Proof	3,000	Value: 475				

KM# 1801 50 EURO
8.4500 g., 0.9200 Gold 0.2499 oz. AGW, 22 mm. **Subject:** Clovis, 481-511 **Obv:** Hands over chalice, reign dates at left, value at right **Rev:** Crowned head left

Date	Mintage	F	VF	XF	Unc	BU
2011 Proof	1,500	Value: 485				

KM# 1803 50 EURO
8.4500 g., 0.9200 Gold 0.2499 oz. AGW, 22 mm. **Subject:** Charlemagne, 768-814 **Obv:** Cross on orb, reight dates at left, value at right **Rev:** Crowned head left

Date	Mintage	F	VF	XF	Unc	BU
2011 Proof	1,500	Value: 485				

KM# 1805 50 EURO
8.4500 g., 0.9200 Gold 0.2499 oz. AGW, 22 mm. **Subject:** Charles II, 840-877 **Obv:** KARLOS monogram **Rev:** Crowned head left

Date	Mintage	F	VF	XF	Unc	BU
2011 Proof	1,500	Value: 485				

KM# 1807 50 EURO
8.4500 g., 0.9200 Gold 0.2499 oz. AGW, 22 mm. **Subject:** WWF - Audouin's Gull **Obv:** Gull in flight right **Rev:** Gull standing right, WWF logo at right

Date	Mintage	F	VF	XF	Unc	BU
2011 Proof	1,000	Value: 500				

KM# 1811 50 EURO
8.4500 g., 0.9200 Gold 0.2499 oz. AGW, 22 mm. **Subject:** UNESCO World Heritage Site - Palace of Versailles

Date	Mintage	F	VF	XF	Unc	BU
2011 Proof	1,000	Value: 500				

KM# 1816 50 EURO
163.8000 g., 0.9500 Silver 5.0028 oz. ASW, 50 mm. **Obv:** Metz railroad station **Rev:** TGV and ICE trains

Date	Mintage	F	VF	XF	Unc	BU
2011 Proof	500	Value: 250				

KM# 1817 50 EURO
8.4500 g., 0.9200 Gold 0.2499 oz. AGW, 22 mm. **Obv:** Metz railroad station **Rev:** TGV and ICE trains

Date	Mintage	F	VF	XF	Unc	BU
2011 Proof	1,000	Value: 500				

KM# 1828 50 EURO

8.4500 g., 0.9200 Gold 0.2499 oz. AGW, 22 mm. **Obv:** Cosette - Les Miserables **Rev:** Victor Hugo

Date	Mintage	F	VF	XF	Unc	BU
2011 Proof	3,000	Value: 475				

KM# 1830 50 EURO

8.4500 g., 0.9200 Gold 0.2499 oz. AGW, 22 mm. **Obv:** Nana **Rev:** Emile Zola

Date	Mintage	F	VF	XF	Unc	BU
2011 Proof	1,000	Value: 500				

KM# 1832 50 EURO

8.4500 g., 0.9200 Gold 0.2499 oz. AGW, 22 mm. **Obv:** The Stranger **Rev:** Albert Camus

Date	Mintage	F	VF	XF	Unc	BU
2011 Proof	—	Value: 500				

KM# 1834 50 EURO

8.4500 g., 0.9200 Gold 0.2499 oz. AGW, 22 mm. **Subject:** Year of the Rabbit **Obv:** Rabbit seated facing right **Rev:** Fontaine and animals

Date	Mintage	F	VF	XF	Unc	BU
2011 Proof	500	Value: 525				

KM# 1837 50 EURO

8.4500 g., 0.9200 Gold 0.2499 oz. AGW, 22 mm. **Obv:** Comic Characters **Rev:** Profile left and large XIII

Date	Mintage	F	VF	XF	Unc	BU
2011 Proof	1,000	Value: 500				

KM# 1839 50 EURO

8.4500 g., 0.9200 Gold 0.2499 oz. AGW, 22 mm. **Obv:** Female figure skater on globe **Rev:** Figure skating pair

Date	Mintage	F	VF	XF	Unc	BU
2011 Proof	1,000	Value: 500				

KM# 1756 50 EURO

8.4500 g., 0.9200 Gold 0.2499 oz. AGW, 22 mm. **Obv:** Bicycle racer **Rev:** Metro 92 logo

Date	Mintage	F	VF	XF	Unc	BU
2011 Proof	500	Value: 500				

KM# 2071 50 EURO

36.0000 g., 0.9000 Silver 1.0416 oz. ASW, 41 mm. **Subject:** G-20 Meeting in Cannes **Obv:** Sower advancing right **Rev:** Laurel tree and oak tree in the shape of a Euro symbol with value specification in the hexagon as stylization national borders

Date	Mintage	F	VF	XF	Unc	BU
2011	200	—	—	—	—	200

KM# 1848 50 EURO

163.8000 g., 0.9250 Silver 4.8711 oz. ASW, 50 mm. **Obv:** Battleship Jeanne de Arc **Rev:** WWII convoy image, anchor chain below

Date	Mintage	F	VF	XF	Unc	BU
2012(a) Proof	500	Value: 275				

KM# 1849 50 EURO

8.4500 g., 0.9200 Gold 0.2499 oz. AGW, 22 mm. **Obv:** SS France waterline view **Rev:** Winged funnels, porthole detail below

Date	Mintage	F	VF	XF	Unc	BU
2012(a) Proof	1,500	Value: 485				

KM# 1852 50 EURO

8.4500 g., 0.9200 Gold 0.2499 oz. AGW, 22 mm. **Subject:** Eurocorps, 20th Anniversary **Obv:** Mitterrand and Kohl standing clasping hands **Rev:** Europa facing

Date	Mintage	F	VF	XF	Unc	BU
2012(a) Proof	1,500	Value: 475				

KM# 1858 50 EURO

8.4500 g., 0.9200 Gold 0.2499 oz. AGW, 22 mm. **Subject:** Philippe II Auguste **Obv:** Crowned head facing **Rev:** The Louvre's original design

Date	Mintage	F	VF	XF	Unc	BU
2012(a) Proof	1,500	Value: 485				

KM# 1860 50 EURO

8.4500 g., 0.9200 Gold 0.2499 oz. AGW, 22 mm. **Subject:** Savinien Cyrano de Bergerac **Obv:** Half-length figure of Cyrano at left, Roxane on balcony at top right **Rev:** Quote at left, Edmond Rostand portrait at right

Date	Mintage	F	VF	XF	Unc	BU
2012(a) Proof	1,000	Value: 500				

KM# 1861 50 EURO

8.4500 g., 0.9200 Gold 0.2499 oz. AGW, 22 mm. **Subject:** Puss in boots **Obv:** Puss in boots standing, castle in background **Rev:** Quote at left, Charles Perrault portrait at right

Date	Mintage	F	VF	XF	Unc	BU
2012(a) Proof	1,000	Value: 500				

KM# 1891 50 EURO

8.4500 g., 0.9200 Gold 0.2499 oz. AGW, 22 mm. **Subject:** Euro, 10th Anniversary **Obv:** The Sower advancing left **Rev:** Value on globe, child-like renderings around

Date	Mintage	F	VF	XF	Unc	BU
2012(a) Proof	1,000	Value: 500				

KM# 1897 50 EURO

8.4500 g., 0.9200 Gold 0.2499 oz. AGW, 22 mm. **Subject:** abbé Pierre, 100th anniversary of Birth **Obv:** Pierre's bust at left, shaddow figure at right **Rev:** Emmaus International logo and quote

Date	Mintage	F	VF	XF	Unc	BU
2012(a) Proof	1,000	Value: 500				

KM# 1906 50 EURO

163.8000 g., 0.9500 Silver 5.0028 oz. ASW, 50 mm. **Subject:** UNESCO - World Heritage Site **Obv:** Abu Simbel temple

Date	Mintage	F	VF	XF	Unc	BU
2012(a) Proof	500	Value: 250				

KM# 1908 50 EURO

8.4500 g., 0.9200 Gold 0.2499 oz. AGW, 22 mm. **Subject:** UNESCO - World Heritage Site **Obv:** Abu Simbel temple

Date	Mintage	F	VF	XF	Unc	BU
2012(a) Proof	1,500	Value: 485				

KM# 1913 50 EURO

163.8000 g., 0.9500 Silver 5.0028 oz. ASW, 50 mm. **Subject:** TGV South-East **Obv:** Lyon Saint-Exupery station **Rev:** Two modern locomotives

Date	Mintage	F	VF	XF	Unc	BU
2012(a) Proof	500	Value: 250				

KM# 1914 50 EURO

8.4500 g., 0.9200 Gold 0.2499 oz. AGW, 22 mm. **Subject:** TGV Sud-East **Obv:** Lyon Saint-Exupery station **Rev:** Two modern locomotives

Date	Mintage	F	VF	XF	Unc	BU
2012(a) Proof	1,000	Value: 500				

KM# 1917 50 EURO

8.4500 g., 0.9200 Gold 0.2499 oz. AGW, 22 mm. **Subject:** Comic strip hero **Obv:** Largo Winch and building **Rev:** Winch riding motocycle being chased by two cars

Date	Mintage	F	VF	XF	Unc	BU
2012(a) Proof	500	Value: 525				

KM# 1920 50 EURO

8.4500 g., 0.9200 Gold 0.2499 oz. AGW, 22 mm. **Subject:** Toulonnais Rugby Club **Obv:** Value and stadium field view **Rev:** Shield and portrait of Felix Mayol

Date	Mintage	F	VF	XF	Unc	BU
2012(a) Proof	500	Value: 525				

KM# 1922 50 EURO

8.4500 g., 0.9200 Gold 0.2499 oz. AGW, 22 mm. **Subject:** 2012 Summer Olympics, London **Obv:** Two judo athletes and map of Europe **Rev:** Two judo athletes

Date	Mintage	F	VF	XF	Unc	BU
2012(a) Proof	1,000	Value: 500				

KM# 1925 50 EURO

8.4500 g., 0.9200 Gold 0.2499 oz. AGW, 22 mm. **Subject:** Year of the Dragon **Obv:** Dragon **Rev:** La Fontaine and zodiac animals

Date	Mintage	F	VF	XF	Unc	BU
2012(a) Proof	1,000	Value: 500				

KM# 2076 50 EURO

8.4500 g., 0.9200 Gold 0.2499 oz. AGW **Obv:** Hand raised in benidiction **Rev:** Hugues Capet head facing

Date	Mintage	F	VF	XF	Unc	BU
2012	Est. 1,500	—	—	—	—	500

KM# 2077 50 EURO

8.4500 g., 0.9200 Gold 0.2499 oz. AGW **Obv:** Oak tree **Rev:** Saint Louis head facing

Date	Mintage	F	VF	XF	Unc	BU
2012	Est. 1,500	—	—	—	—	500

KM# 2080 50 EURO

163.8000 g., 0.9500 Silver 5.0028 oz. ASW, 50 mm. **Obv:** Sailing ship Hermione **Rev:** Ship wheel, sails, figurehead

Date	Mintage	F	VF	XF	Unc	BU
2012 Proof	Est. 500	Value: 300				

KM# 2082 50 EURO

8.4500 g., 0.9200 Gold 0.2499 oz. AGW, 22 mm. **Obv:** Sailing ship Hermione **Rev:** Ship wheel, sails, figurehead

Date	Mintage	F	VF	XF	Unc	BU
2012 Proof	Est. 1,500	Value: 500				

KM# 2083 50 EURO

8.4500 g., 0.9200 Gold 0.2499 oz. AGW, 22 mm. **Obv:** Cruiser Jean d'Arc **Rev:** Anchor chain below convoy of ships

Date	Mintage	F	VF	XF	Unc	BU
2012 Proof	Est. 1,500	Value: 500				

KM# 2086 50 EURO

8.4500 g., 0.9200 Gold 0.2499 oz. AGW **Obv:** d'Artagnan **Rev:** Alexander Dumas and quote

Date	Mintage	F	VF	XF	Unc	BU
2012 Proof	Est. 1,000	Value: 500				

KM# 2088 50 EURO

163.8000 g., 0.9500 Silver 5.0028 oz. ASW, 50 mm. **Obv:** Yves Klein, blue hand **Rev:** Klein artwork

Date	Mintage	F	VF	XF	Unc	BU
2012 Proof	—	Value: 275				

KM# 2090 50 EURO

8.4500 g., 0.9200 Gold 0.2499 oz. AGW, 22 mm. **Obv:** Yves Klein and hand **Rev:** Klein artwork

Date	Mintage	F	VF	XF	Unc	BU
2012 Proof	—	Value: 525				

KM# 2093 50 EURO

8.4500 g., 0.9200 Gold 0.2499 oz. AGW, 22 mm. **Subject:** French-German Friendship, 50th Anniversary **Rev:** Europa head facing at right, banners at left

Date	Mintage	F	VF	XF	Unc	BU
2013 Proof	—	Value: 525				

KM# 2096 50 EURO

8.4500 g., 0.9200 Gold 0.2499 oz. AGW, 22 mm. **Subject:** Rudolf Noureev **Obv:** Portrait at right **Rev:** Dancer and National Theater

Date	Mintage	F	VF	XF	Unc	BU
2013 Proof	—	Value: 525				

KM# 2098 50 EURO

163.8000 g., 0.9500 Silver 5.0028 oz. ASW, 50 mm. **Subject:** Notre Dame, 850th Anniversary **Obv:** Seal at right, cathedral details, blue highlights **Rev:** Seal at left, cathedral details, blue highlights

Date	Mintage	F	VF	XF	Unc	BU
2013 Proof	850	Value: 300				

KM# 2100 50 EURO

8.4500 g., 0.9200 Gold 0.2499 oz. AGW, 22 mm. **Subject:** Notre Dame, 850th Anniversary **Obv:** Seal at right, cathedral details **Rev:** Seal at left, cathedral details

Date	Mintage	F	VF	XF	Unc	BU
2013 Proof	1,000	Value: 600				

KM# 1304 100 EURO
155.5175 g., 0.9990 Gold 4.9948 oz. AGW, 50 mm. **Subject:** Europa **Obv:** Eight French euro coin designs **Rev:** Portrait and flags design of 6.55957 francs KM-1265 **Edge:** Plain

Date	Mintage	F	VF	XF	Unc	BU
2002 Proof	99	Value: 10,000				

KM# 1985 100 EURO
155.5500 g., 0.9990 Gold 4.9958 oz. AGW **Subject:** Charles Lindburg, 75th Anniverversary of Flight **Obv:** Map of Northern France **Rev:** Spirit of St. Louis, U.S. Coastline

Date	Mintage	F	VF	XF	Unc	BU
2002 Proof	99	Value: 12,500				

KM# 2005 100 EURO
155.5500 g., 0.9990 Gold 4.9958 oz. AGW **Obv:** Mona Lisa **Rev:** Leonardo DaVinci head left, large value right

Date	Mintage	F	VF	XF	Unc	BU
2003 Proof	99	Value: 10,000				

KM# 1377 100 EURO
155.5175 g., 0.9990 Gold 4.9948 oz. AGW, 50 mm. **Subject:** D-Day 60th Anniversary **Obv:** Soldiers and Normandy invasion scene **Rev:** "D-Day" inscription above denomination **Edge:** Plain

Date	Mintage	F	VF	XF	Unc	BU
2004 Proof	299	Value: 9,500				

KM# 1389 100 EURO
155.5000 g., 0.9990 Gold 4.9942 oz. AGW, 50 mm. **Obv:** Statue of Liberty **Rev:** F. A. Bartholdi **Edge:** Plain

Date	Mintage	F	VF	XF	Unc	BU
2004 Proof	99	Value: 10,000				

KM# 1395 100 EURO
155.5500 g., 0.9990 Gold 4.9958 oz. AGW, 50 mm. **Subject:** European Union Expansion **Obv:** Partial face and flags **Rev:** Puzzle map **Edge:** Plain

Date	Mintage	F	VF	XF	Unc	BU
2004 Proof	99	Value: 10,000				

KM# 2012 100 EURO
155.5500 g., 0.9990 Gold 4.9958 oz. AGW **Subject:** Napoleon's coronation, 200th Anniversary **Obv:** Napoleon, laureate **Rev:** Notre Dame cathedral façade

Date	Mintage	F	VF	XF	Unc	BU
2004 Proof	99	Value: 10,000				

KM# 2019 100 EURO
155.5500 g., 0.9990 Gold 4.9958 oz. AGW **Subject:** European Union, 50th Anniversary **Obv:** European Union Flag **Rev:** Europa head facing at right, banners at left

Date	Mintage	F	VF	XF	Unc	BU
2005 Proof	99	Value: 10,000				

KM# 2024 100 EURO
155.5500 g., 0.9990 Gold 4.9958 oz. AGW **Obv:** Stars and map of Europe **Rev:** Doves in flight above globe

Date	Mintage	F	VF	XF	Unc	BU
2005 Proof	Est. 99	Value: 10,000				

KM# 2033 100 EURO
155.5500 g., 0.9990 Gold 4.9958 oz. AGW **Subject:** Jules Verne, 100th Anniversary of Death **Obv:** Around the world in 80 days

Date	Mintage	F	VF	XF	Unc	BU
2005 Proof	80	Value: 11,000				

KM# 2034 100 EURO
155.5500 g., 0.9990 Gold 4.9958 oz. AGW **Subject:** Jules Verne, 100th Anniversary of Death **Obv:** 20,000 leagues under the sea

Date	Mintage	F	VF	XF	Unc	BU
2005 Proof	71	Value: 11,000				

KM# 2035 100 EURO
155.5500 g., 0.9990 Gold 4.9958 oz. AGW **Subject:** Jules Verne, 100th Anniversary of Death **Obv:** From the earth to the moon

Date	Mintage	F	VF	XF	Unc	BU
2005 Proof	71	Value: 11,000				

KM# 2040 100 EURO
155.5500 g., 0.9990 Gold 4.9958 oz. AGW **Subject:** Robert Schuman, 120th Anniversary of Birth **Rev:** Europa head facing at right, color highlights

Date	Mintage
	99 Value: 10,000

Note: Individually numbered

KM# 2044 100 EURO
155.5500 g., 0.9990 Gold 4.9958 oz. AGW **Subject:** Benjamin Franklin, 300th Anniversary of Birth **Obv:** Bust at left, kite in thunderclouds at right **Rev:** French and American flags

Date	Mintage	F	VF	XF	Unc	BU
2006 Proof	99	Value: 10,000				

Note: Individually numbered

KM# 2047 100 EURO
155.5500 g., 0.9990 Gold 4.9958 oz. AGW **Subject:** St. Peter's Basilica, 500th Anniversary **Obv:** St. Peter's floor plan **Rev:** Façade of St. Peter's, Pope Benedict XVI

Date	Mintage	F	VF	XF	Unc	BU
2006 Proof	99	Value: 10,000				

Note: Individually numbered

KM# 2058 100 EURO
155.5500 g., 0.9990 Gold 4.9958 oz. AGW **Subject:** Abolishment of the Death Penalty, 25th Anniversary **Obv:** Sower advancing left **Rev:** Guillotine

Date	Mintage	F	VF	XF	Unc	BU
2006 Proof	Est. 99	Value: 10,000				

Note: Individually numbered

KM# 2060 100 EURO
155.5500 g., 0.9990 Gold 4.9958 oz. AGW **Subject:** Paul Cézanne, 100th Anniversary of Death **Obv:** Bust **Rev:** Two men seated at table, wine bottle between them

Date	Mintage	F	VF	XF	Unc	BU
2006 Proof	Est. 99	Value: 10,000				

Note: Individually numbered

KM# 2069 100 EURO
155.5000 g., 0.9990 Gold 4.9942 oz. AGW **Subject:** Jules Verne, 100th Anniversary of Death **Obv:** Voyage to the center of the Earth

Date	Mintage	F	VF	XF	Unc	BU
2006 Proof	92	Value: 10,000				

KM# 1482 100 EURO
155.5500 g., 0.9990 Gold 4.9958 oz. AGW, 50 mm. **Subject:** Airbus A380 **Rev:** Europa head and flags

Date	Mintage	F	VF	XF	Unc	BU
2007 Proof	99	Value: 10,000				

KM# 1497 100 EURO
155.5000 g., 0.9990 Gold 4.9942 oz. AGW, 50 mm. **Subject:** Cannes Film Festival, 60th Anniversary **Obv:** Cinema screen and stage, Golden Palm Award

Date	Mintage	F	VF	XF	Unc	BU
2007 Proof	99	Value: 10,000				

KM# 1536 100 EURO
3.1000 g., 0.9990 Gold 0.0996 oz. AGW, 15 mm. **Obv:** Modernistic sower advancing right **Rev:** Value and wreath

Date	Mintage	F	VF	XF	Unc	BU
2008	50,000	—	—	—	—	180
2009	50,000	—	—	—	—	180
2010	50,000	—	—	—	—	180

KM# 1531 100 EURO
155.5000 g., 0.9990 Gold 4.9942 oz. AGW, 50 mm. **Subject:** French Presidency of the European Union **Obv:** Text within stars **Rev:** Europa head and flags

Date	Mintage	F	VF	XF	Unc	BU
2008 Proof	99	Value: 10,000				

KM# 1545 100 EURO
155.5000 g., 0.9990 Gold 4.9942 oz. AGW, 50 mm. **Subject:** 29th Summer Olympic Games - Beijing **Obv:** Swimmer and globe **Rev:** Diver and oriental screen

Date	Mintage	F	VF	XF	Unc	BU
2008 Proof	99	Value: 10,000				

KM# 1565 100 EURO
155.5000 g., 0.9990 Gold 4.9942 oz. AGW, 50 mm. **Subject:** Lourdes, 150th Anniversary **Obv:** Church of Notre Dame at Lourdes **Rev:** Cross with Pope John Paul II, Pope Benedict XVI and Bernadette Soubirous in quadrants

Date	Mintage	F	VF	XF	Unc	BU
2008 Proof	99	Value: 10,000				

KM# 1588 100 EURO
31.1050 g., 0.9200 Gold 0.9200 oz. AGW, 47 mm. **Subject:** Court of Human Rights, 50th Anniversary **Obv:** The Seed Sower left **Rev:** Text

Date	Mintage	F	VF	XF	Unc	BU
2009P Proof	500	Value: 1,750				

KM# 1626 100 EURO
17.0000 g., 0.9200 Gold 0.5028 oz. AGW, 30 x 21 mm. **Subject:** Renoir **Obv:** Le dejuner des canotiers, 1881 painting **Rev:** Brushes and portrait **Shape:** Rectangle

Date	Mintage	F	VF	XF	Unc	BU
2009P Proof	500	Value: 1,000				

KM# 1641 100 EURO
17.0000 g., 0.9200 Gold 0.5028 oz. AGW **Subject:** Claude Monet **Obv:** Bassin of the Nymphs in color **Rev:** Portrait and paint brushes **Shape:** Rectangle

Date	Mintage	F	VF	XF	Unc	BU
2009 Proof	Est. 500	Value: 950				

KM# 1672 100 EURO
17.0000 g., 0.9200 Gold 0.5028 oz. AGW, 18 mm. **Obv:** The Seed Sower left **Rev:** Wheat and olive branch

Date	Mintage	F	VF	XF	Unc	BU
2010 Proof	500	Value: 925				

KM# 1689 100 EURO
327.6000 g., 0.9500 Silver 10.005 oz. ASW, 65 mm. **Obv:** Marcel Dassault **Rev:** Mirage III plane

Date	Mintage	F	VF	XF	Unc	BU
2010 Proof	500	Value: 400				

KM# 1707 100 EURO
17.0000 g., 0.9200 Gold 0.5028 oz. AGW, 30x21 mm. **Rev:** Georges Braque **Shape:** Rectangle

Date	Mintage	F	VF	XF	Unc	BU
2010 Proof	500	Value: 975				

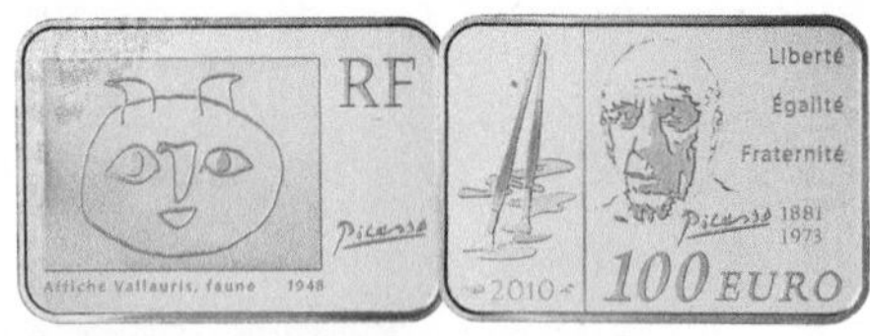

KM# 1711 100 EURO
17.0000 g., 0.9200 Gold 0.5028 oz. AGW, 30x21 mm. **Rev:** Picasso **Shape:** Rectangle

Date	Mintage	F	VF	XF	Unc	BU
2010 Proof	500	Value: 1,000				

KM# 1724 100 EURO
50.0000 g., 0.9000 Silver 1.4467 oz. ASW, 47 mm. **Obv:** Value at center, wreath horizontal **Rev:** Hercules goup

Date	Mintage	F	VF	XF	Unc	BU
2011	50,000	—	—	—	—	150
2012	50,000	—	—	—	—	150

KM# 1787 100 EURO
17.0000 g., 0.9200 Gold 0.5028 oz. AGW, 31 mm. **Subject:** Euro Starter Kit, 10th Anniversary **Obv:** Sower **Rev:** Euro starter kit

Date	Mintage	F	VF	XF	Unc	BU
2011 Proof	500	Value: 925				

KM# 1820 100 EURO
17.0000 g., 0.9200 Gold 0.5028 oz. AGW, 30x21 mm. **Subject:** Vassily Kandinsky **Shape:** Rectangle

Date	Mintage	F	VF	XF	Unc	BU
2011 Proof	500	Value: 975				

KM# 1824 100 EURO
17.0000 g., 0.9200 Gold 0.5028 oz. AGW, 31 mm. **Subject:** Andy Warhol **Obv:** Portrait facing **Rev:** Dollar sign

Date	Mintage	F	VF	XF	Unc	BU
2011 Proof	500	Value: 975				

KM# 1836 100 EURO
327.6000 g., 0.9500 Silver 10.005 oz. ASW, 75 mm. **Obv:** Commic characters **Rev:** Profile left and large XIII

Date	Mintage	F	VF	XF	Unc	BU
2011 Proof	500	Value: 400				

KM# 1892 100 EURO
17.0000 g., 0.9200 Gold 0.5028 oz. AGW, 31 mm. **Subject:** Euro, 10th Anniversary **Obv:** The Sower advancing left **Rev:** Value on globe at center, child-like renderings around

Date	Mintage	F	VF	XF	Unc	BU
2012(a) Proof	500	Value: 950				

KM# 2089 100 EURO
327.6000 g., 0.9500 Silver 10.005 oz. ASW, 75 mm. **Obv:** Yves Klein and blue hand **Rev:** Klein artwork

Date	Mintage	F	VF	XF	Unc	BU
2012 Proof	500	Value: 1,250				

KM# 1589 200 EURO
31.1040 g., 0.9990 Gold 0.9990 oz. AGW, 37 mm. **Subject:** Court of Human Rights - 50th Anniversary **Obv:** The Seed Sower left **Rev:** Text

Date	Mintage	F	VF	XF	Unc	BU
2009P Proof	500	Value: 1,850				

KM# 1593 200 EURO
31.1040 g., 0.9990 Gold 0.9990 oz. AGW, 37 mm. **Subject:** Europa - Fall of Berlin Wall **Obv:** Brandenburg gate and doves in flight **Rev:** Head facing and flags

Date	Mintage	F	VF	XF	Unc	BU
2009P Proof	500	Value: 1,850				

KM# 1624 200 EURO
31.1040 g., 0.9990 Gold 0.9990 oz. AGW, 37 mm. **Subject:** First Moon Landing, 40th Anniversary **Obv:** Footprint on the moon

Date	Mintage	F	VF	XF	Unc	BU
2009P Proof	1,000	Value: 1,850				

KM# 1639 200 EURO
31.1040 g., 0.9990 Gold 0.9990 oz. AGW, 37 mm. **Subject:** FIFA World Cup, South Africa 2010 **Obv:** Soccer player on field **Rev:** Soccerball, Map of Africa, Protea flower

Date	Mintage	F	VF	XF	Unc	BU
2009P Proof	500	Value: 1,850				

KM# 1678 200 EURO
31.1040 g., 0.9990 Gold 0.9990 oz. AGW, 37 mm. **Subject:** Cluny Abbey, 1100th Anniversary **Obv:** Europa head facing **Rev:** Cluny Abbey

Date	Mintage	F	VF	XF	Unc	BU
2010 Proof	500	Value: 1,850				

KM# 1683 200 EURO
31.1040 g., 0.9990 Gold 0.9990 oz. AGW, 37 mm. **Obv:** Georges Pompidou Center design **Rev:** Design detail

Date	Mintage	F	VF	XF	Unc	BU
2010 Proof	500	Value: 1,850				

KM# 1693 200 EURO
31.1040 g., 0.9990 Gold 0.9990 oz. AGW, 37 mm. **Obv:** Mother Teresa and child **Rev:** Mother Teresa and Pope John Paul II

Date	Mintage	F	VF	XF	Unc	BU
2010 Proof	500	Value: 1,850				

KM# 1698 200 EURO
31.1040 g., 0.9990 Gold 0.9990 oz. AGW, 37 mm. **Obv:** Taj Mahal **Rev:** UNESCO offices

Date	Mintage	F	VF	XF	Unc	BU
2010 Proof	1,000	Value: 1,800				

KM# 1701 200 EURO
31.1040 g., 0.9990 Gold 0.9990 oz. AGW, 37 mm. **Obv:** Lille station and route map **Rev:** Three TGV trains

Date	Mintage	F	VF	XF	Unc	BU
2010 Proof	500	Value: 1,850				

KM# 1818 200 EURO
31.1040 g., 0.9990 Gold 0.9990 oz. AGW, 37 mm. **Obv:** Metz railroad station **Rev:** TGV and ICE trains

Date	Mintage	F	VF	XF	Unc	BU
2011 Proof	—	Value: 1,850				

KM# 1757 200 EURO
4.0000 g., 0.9990 Gold 0.1285 oz. AGW, 21 mm. **Obv:** French region names around RF within stylized map of France **Rev:** Value within wreath

Date	Mintage	F	VF	XF	Unc	BU
2011(a) Proof	50,000	—	—	—	—	265

KM# 1793 200 EURO
31.1040 g., 0.9990 Gold 0.9990 oz. AGW, 37 mm. **Subject:** International Music Day, 30th Anniversary **Obv:** Europa **Rev:** Youth jamming

Date	Mintage	F	VF	XF	Unc	BU
2011 Proof	500	Value: 1,900				

KM# 1797 200 EURO
31.1040 g., 0.9990 Gold 0.9990 oz. AGW, 37 mm. **Subject:** Great Explorers - Jacques Cartier **Obv:** The Grande Hermine sailing away **Rev:** Cartier, globe and compass rose

Date	Mintage	F	VF	XF	Unc	BU
2011 Proof	500	Value: 1,850				

KM# 1808 200 EURO
31.1040 g., 0.9990 Gold 0.9990 oz. AGW, 37 mm. **Subject:** WWF - Audouin's Gull **Obv:** Gull in flight right **Rev:** Gull standing right, WWF logo right

Date	Mintage	F	VF	XF	Unc	BU
2011 Proof	500	Value: 1,850				

KM# 2072 200 EURO
4.0000 g., 0.9990 Gold 0.1285 oz. AGW, 21 mm. **Subject:** G-20 Meeting in Cannes **Obv:** Sower advancing right **Rev:** Laurel tree and oak tree in the shape of a Euro symbol with value specification in the hexagon as stylization national borders

Date	Mintage	F	VF	XF	Unc	BU
2011	100	—	—	—	—	400

KM# 1853 200 EURO
31.1040 g., 0.9990 Gold 0.9990 oz. AGW, 37 mm. **Subject:** Eurocorps, 20th Anniversary **Obv:** Mitterrand and Kohl standing clasping hands **Rev:** Europa facing

Date	Mintage	F	VF	XF	Unc	BU
2012(a) Proof	500	Value: 1,850				

KM# 1898 200 EURO
31.1040 g., 0.9990 Gold 0.9990 oz. AGW, 37 mm. **Subject:** abbé Pierre, 100th anniversary of Birth **Obv:** Pierre's bust at left, shaddow figure at right **Rev:** Emmaus International logo, quote below

Date	Mintage	F	VF	XF	Unc	BU
2012(a) Proof	500	Value: 1,850				

KM# 1915 200 EURO
31.1040 g., 0.9990 Gold 0.9990 oz. AGW, 37 mm. **Subject:** TGV South-East **Obv:** Lyon Saint-Exupery station **Rev:** Two modern locomotives

Date	Mintage	F	VF	XF	Unc	BU
2012(a) Proof	500	Value: 1,850				

KM# 1923 200 EURO
31.1040 g., 0.9990 Gold 0.9990 oz. AGW, 37 mm. **Subject:** 2012 Summer Olympics, London **Obv:** Two judo athletes and map of Europe **Rev:** Two judo athletes

Date	Mintage	F	VF	XF	Unc	BU
2012(a) Proof	500	Value: 1,850				

KM# 1926 200 EURO
31.1040 g., 0.9990 Gold 0.9990 oz. AGW, 37 mm. **Subject:** Year of the Dragon **Obv:** Dragon **Rev:** La Fontaine and zodiac animals

Date	Mintage	F	VF	XF	Unc	BU
2012(a) Proof	500	Value: 1,850				

KM# 2074 200 EURO
4.0000 g., 0.9990 Gold 0.1285 oz. AGW, 21 mm. **Obv:** French province names in horizontal lines, RF in center in stylized map of France **Rev:** Laural and oak wreath, value within

Date	Mintage	F	VF	XF	Unc	BU
2012	50,000	—	—	—	—	325

KM# 2101 200 EURO
31.1050 g., 0.9990 Gold 0.9990 oz. AGW, 37 mm. **Subject:** Notre Dame, 850th Anniversary **Obv:** Seal at right, cathedral details **Rev:** Seal at left, cathedral details

Date	Mintage	F	VF	XF	Unc	BU
2013 Proof	500	Value: 2,750				

KM# 1583 250 EURO
8.4500 g., 0.9200 Gold 0.2499 oz. AGW, 22 mm. **Obv:** Modernistic sower advancing right **Rev:** Value and wreath

Date	Mintage	F	VF	XF	Unc	BU
2009P	25,000	—	—	—	—	500

KM# 1671 250 EURO
62.2080 g., 0.9990 Gold 1.9979 oz. AGW, 37 mm. **Obv:** The Seed Sower left **Rev:** Wheat and olive branch

Date	Mintage	F	VF	XF	Unc	BU
2010 Proof	500	Value: 3,550				

KM# 1788 250 EURO
62.2080 g., 0.9990 Gold 1.9979 oz. AGW, 37 mm. **Subject:** Euro Starter Kit, 10th Anniversary **Obv:** Sower **Rev:** Euro starter kit **Note:** Thick planchet.

Date	Mintage	F	VF	XF	Unc	BU
2011 Proof	500	Value: 3,550				

KM# 1893 250 EURO
62.2080 g., 0.9990 Gold 1.9979 oz. AGW, 37 mm. **Subject:** Euro, 10th Anniversary **Obv:** The Sower advancing left **Rev:** Value on globe at center, child-like renderings around

Date	Mintage	F	VF	XF	Unc	BU
2012(a) Proof	500	Value: 3,600				

KM# 1396 500 EURO
1000.0000 g., 0.9990 Gold 32.117 oz. AGW, 85 mm. **Subject:** European Union Expansion **Obv:** Partial face and flags **Rev:** Puzzle map **Edge:** Plain **Note:** Illustration reduced.

Date	Mintage	F	VF	XF	Unc	BU
2004 Proof	20	Value: 60,000				

KM# 1594 500 EURO
155.5000 g., 0.9990 Gold 4.9942 oz. AGW, 50 mm. **Subject:** Europa - Fall of Berlin Wall **Obv:** Brandenburg gate and doves in flight **Rev:** Head facing and flags

Date	Mintage	F	VF	XF	Unc	BU
2009P Proof	99	Value: 9,250				

KM# 1599 500 EURO
155.5000 g., 0.9990 Gold 4.9942 oz. AGW, 50 mm. **Subject:** Concorde 40th Anniversary **Obv:** Concorde in flight **Rev:** Tail emblems

Date	Mintage	F	VF	XF	Unc	BU
2009P Proof	99	Value: 9,250				

KM# 1605 500 EURO
155.5000 g., 0.9990 Gold 4.9942 oz. AGW, 50 mm. **Obv:** Eiffel Tower Structure **Rev:** Gustave Eiffel at left

Date	Mintage	F	VF	XF	Unc	BU
2009P Proof	99	Value: 9,250				

KM# 1610 500 EURO
155.5000 g., 0.9990 Gold 4.9942 oz. AGW, 50 mm. **Subject:** Bugatti 100th Anniversary **Obv:** Ettore Bugatti at left **Rev:** Race car and grill motif

Date	Mintage	F	VF	XF	Unc	BU
2009P Proof	99	Value: 9,975				

KM# 1615 500 EURO
155.5000 g., 0.9990 Gold 4.9942 oz. AGW, 50 mm. **Subject:** Curie Institute, 100th Anniversary

Date	Mintage	F	VF	XF	Unc	BU
2009P Proof	99	Value: 9,250				

KM# 1619 500 EURO
155.5000 g., 0.9990 Gold 4.9942 oz. AGW, 50 mm. **Subject:** Unesco site - The Kremlin in Moscow **Obv:** Wall Tower and cathedral

Date	Mintage	F	VF	XF	Unc	BU
2009P Proof	99	Value: 9,250				

KM# 1640 500 EURO
155.5000 g., 0.9990 Gold 4.9942 oz. AGW, 50 mm. **Subject:** FIFA World Cup, South Africa 2010 **Obv:** Soccer player on field **Rev:** Soccerball, Map of Africa, Protea flower

Date	Mintage	F	VF	XF	Unc	BU
2009P Proof	99	Value: 9,250				

KM# 1642 500 EURO
12.0000 g., 0.9990 Gold 0.3854 oz. AGW, 31 mm. **Obv:** The Seed Sower advancing right, sun rays from below **Rev:** Value in center, wreath horizontal

Date	Mintage	F	VF	XF	Unc	BU
2010	25,000	—	—	—	—	700

KM# 1687 500 EURO
155.5000 g., 0.9990 Gold 4.9942 oz. AGW, 50 mm. **Obv:** Marcel Dassault **Rev:** Mirage III plane

Date	Mintage	F	VF	XF	Unc	BU
2010 Proof	99	Value: 9,250				

KM# 1692 500 EURO
155.5000 g., 0.9990 Gold 4.9942 oz. AGW, 50 mm. **Obv:** Mother Teresa and child **Rev:** Mother Teresa and Pope John Paul II

Date	Mintage	F	VF	XF	Unc	BU
2010 Proof	99	Value: 9,250				

KM# 1697 500 EURO
155.5000 g., 0.9990 Gold 4.9942 oz. AGW, 50 mm. **Obv:** Taj Mahal **Rev:** UNESCO offices

Date	Mintage	F	VF	XF	Unc	BU
2010 Proof	99	Value: 9,250				

KM# 1706 500 EURO
155.5000 g., 0.9990 Gold 4.9942 oz. AGW **Obv:** Doves **Rev:** Georges Baraque **Shape:** 50

Date	Mintage	F	VF	XF	Unc	BU
2010 Proof	99	Value: 9,250				

KM# 1710 500 EURO
155.5000 g., 0.9990 Gold 4.9942 oz. AGW, 50 mm. **Rev:** Picasso

Date	Mintage	F	VF	XF	Unc	BU
2010 Proof	99	Value: 9,250				

KM# 1712 500 EURO
1000.0000 g., 0.9500 Silver 30.541 oz. ASW, 100 mm. **Rev:** Picasso

Date	Mintage	F	VF	XF	Unc	BU
2010 Proof	500	Value: 1,200				

KM# 1718 500 EURO
155.5000 g., 0.9990 Gold 4.9942 oz. AGW, 50 mm. **Obv:** Handball player on globe **Rev:** Handball player, net, Big Ben

Date	Mintage	F	VF	XF	Unc	BU
2010 Proof	99	Value: 9,250				

KM# 1798 500 EURO
155.5000 g., 0.9990 Gold 4.9942 oz. AGW, 50 mm. **Subject:** Great Explorers - Jacques Cartier **Obv:** The Grande Hermine sailing away **Rev:** Cartier, globe and compass rose

Date	Mintage	F	VF	XF	Unc	BU
2011 Proof	99	Value: 9,500				

KM# 1812 500 EURO
155.5000 g., 0.9990 Gold 4.9942 oz. AGW, 50 mm. **Subject:** UNESCO World Heritage Site - Palace of Versailles

Date	Mintage	F	VF	XF	Unc	BU
2011 Proof	99	Value: 9,250				

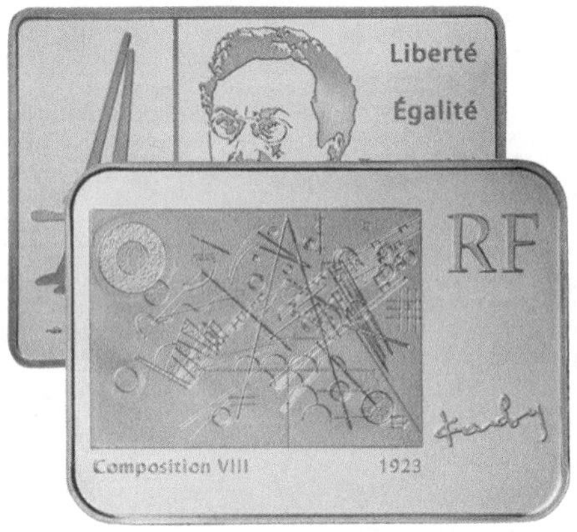

KM# 1821 500 EURO
155.5000 g., 0.9990 Gold 4.9942 oz. AGW, 53x37 mm. **Subject:** Vassily Kandinsky **Shape:** Rectangle

Date	Mintage	F	VF	XF	Unc	BU
2011 Proof	99	Value: 9,975				

KM# 1825 500 EURO
155.5000 g., 0.9990 Gold 4.9942 oz. AGW, 53x37 mm. **Subject:** Andy Warhol **Shape:** Rectangle

Date	Mintage	F	VF	XF	Unc	BU
2011 Proof	99	Value: 9,500				

KM# 1854 500 EURO
155.5900 g., 0.9990 Gold 4.9971 oz. AGW, 50 mm. **Subject:** Eurocorps, 20th Anniversary **Obv:** Mitterrand and Kohl standing clasping hands **Rev:** Europa facing

Date	Mintage	F	VF	XF	Unc	BU
2012(a) Proof	99	Value: 9,250				

KM# 1899 500 EURO
155.5000 g., 0.9990 Gold 4.9942 oz. AGW, 50 mm. **Subject:** abbé Pierre, 100th anniversary of Birth **Obv:** Pierre's bust at left, shadow at right **Rev:** Emmaus International logo, quote below

Date	Mintage	F	VF	XF	Unc	BU
2012(a) Proof	99	Value: 9,250				

KM# 1909 500 EURO
155.5000 g., 0.9990 Gold 4.9942 oz. AGW, 50 mm. **Subject:** UNESCO - World Heritage Site **Obv:** Abu Simbel temple **Rev:** Sphinx and Pyramids

Date	Mintage	F	VF	XF	Unc	BU
2012(a) Proof	99	Value: 9,250				

KM# 1927 500 EURO
155.5000 g., 0.9990 Gold 4.9942 oz. AGW, 50 mm. **Subject:** Year of the Dragon **Obv:** Dragon **Rev:** La Fontaine and zodiac animals

Date	Mintage	F	VF	XF	Unc	BU
2012(a) Proof	99	Value: 9,250				

KM# 1595 1000 EURO
311.0000 g., 0.9990 Gold 9.9885 oz. AGW, 65 mm. **Subject:** Europa - Fall of Berlin Wall **Obv:** Brandenburg gate and doves in flight **Rev:** Head facing and flags

Date	Mintage	F	VF	XF	Unc	BU
2009P Proof	20	Value: 18,500				

KM# 1600 1000 EURO
311.0000 g., 0.9990 Gold 9.9885 oz. AGW, 65 mm. **Subject:** Concorde 40 Anniversary **Obv:** Concorde in flight **Rev:** Tail emblems

Date	Mintage	F	VF	XF	Unc	BU
2009P Proof	20	Value: 18,500				

KM# 1677 1000 EURO
31.1000 g., 0.9990 Gold 0.9988 oz. AGW, 65 mm. **Subject:** Cluny Abbey, 1100th Anniversary **Obv:** Europa head facing **Rev:** Cluny Abby view

Date	Mintage	F	VF	XF	Unc	BU
2010 Proof	39	Value: 18,500				

KM# 1682 1000 EURO
311.0000 g., 0.9990 Gold 9.9885 oz. AGW, 65 mm. **Obv:** Georges Pompidou Center design **Rev:** Design detail

Date	Mintage	F	VF	XF	Unc	BU
2010 Proof	39	Value: 18,500				

KM# 1725 1000 EURO
20.0000 g., 0.9990 Gold 0.6423 oz. AGW, 39 mm. **Obv:** Value at center, wreath horizontal **Rev:** Hercules goup

Date	Mintage	F	VF	XF	Unc	BU
2011	10,000	—	—	—	—	1,250
2012	10,000	—	—	—	—	1,250

KM# 1794 1000 EURO
311.0000 g., 0.9990 Gold 9.9885 oz. AGW, 65 mm. **Subject:** International Music Day, 30th Anniversary **Obv:** Europa **Rev:** Youth jamming

Date	Mintage	F	VF	XF	Unc	BU
2011 Proof	39	Value: 18,500				

KM# 1799 1000 EURO
311.0000 g., 0.9990 Gold 9.9885 oz. AGW, 65 mm. **Subject:** Great Explorers - Jacques Cartier **Obv:** The Grande Hermine sailing away **Rev:** Cartier, globe and compass rose

Date	Mintage	F	VF	XF	Unc	BU
2011 Proof	39	Value: 18,500				

KM# 1855 1000 EURO

311.0000 g., 0.9990 Gold 9.9885 oz. AGW, 65 mm. **Subject:** Eurocorps, 20th Anniversary **Obv:** Mitterrand and Kohl standing clasping hands **Rev:** Europa facing

Date	Mintage	F	VF	XF	Unc	BU
2012(a) Proof	39	Value: 18,500				

KM# 1620 5000 EURO

1000.0000 g., 0.9990 Gold 32.117 oz. AGW, 85 mm. **Subject:** Unesco site - The Kremlin in Moscow **Obv:** Wall Tower and cathedral

Date	Mintage	F	VF	XF	Unc	BU
2009P Proof	39	Value: 60,000				

KM# 1696 5000 EURO

1000.0000 g., 0.9990 Gold 32.117 oz. AGW, 85 mm. **Obv:** Taj Mahal and diamond inserts **Rev:** UNESCO offices

Date	Mintage	F	VF	XF	Unc	BU
2010 Proof	29	Value: 60,000				

KM# 1709 5000 EURO

1000.0000 g., 0.9990 Gold 32.117 oz. AGW, 85 mm. **Rev:** Picasso

Date	Mintage	F	VF	XF	Unc	BU
2010 Proof	29	Value: 60,000				

KM# 1813 5000 EURO

1000.0000 g., 0.9990 Gold 32.117 oz. AGW, 85 mm. **Subject:** UNESCO World Heritage Site - Palace of Versailles

Date	Mintage	F	VF	XF	Unc	BU
2011 Proof	29	Value: 60,000				

KM# 1822 5000 EURO

1000.0000 g., 0.9990 Gold 32.117 oz. AGW, 90x63 mm. **Subject:** Vassily Kandinsky **Shape:** Rectangle

Date	Mintage	F	VF	XF	Unc	BU
2011 Proof	29	Value: 60,000				

KM# 1826 5000 EURO

1000.0000 g., 0.9990 Gold 32.117 oz. AGW, 90x63 mm. **Subject:** Andy Warhol **Shape:** Rectangle

Date	Mintage	F	VF	XF	Unc	BU
2011 Proof	29	Value: 60,000				

KM# 1910 5000 EURO

1000.0000 g., 0.9990 Gold 32.117 oz. AGW, 85 mm. **Subject:** UNESCO - World Heritage Site **Obv:** Abu Simbel temple **Rev:** Sphinx and Pyramids

Date	Mintage	F	VF	XF	Unc	BU
2012(a) Proof	29	Value: 60,000				

KM# 1928 5000 EURO

75.0000 g., 0.9990 Gold 2.4088 oz. AGW, 45 mm. **Obv:** Value at center, wreath horizontal **Rev:** Hercules group

Date	Mintage	F	VF	XF	Unc	BU
2012(a)	2,000	—	—	—	—	4,500

MINT SETS

KM#	Date	Mintage	Identification	Issue Price	Mkt Val
MS20	2001 (2)	10,000	KM#925.1a, 928a	—	590
MS21	2001 (8)	35,000	KM#1282-1289	20.25	20.00
MS22	2002 (8)	35,000	KM#1282-1289	20.25	40.00
MS23	2003 (8)	—	KM#1282-89	—	55.00
MS24	2004 (8)	—	KM#1282-1289	—	45.00
MS25	2005 (8)	—	KM#1282-1289	—	45.00
MS26	2005 (8)	40,000	KM#1282-1289 Moebius set plus token	45.00	55.00
MS27	2005 (8)	10,000	KM1282-1289, French Memories - Bordeaux	45.00	45.00
MS28	2006 (8)	70,000	KM#1282-1289	36.50	42.50
MS29	2006 (8)	500	KM#1282-1289, Denver, Colorado special ANA Coin Convention Set	45.00	70.00
MS30	2006 (8)	500	KM#1282-1289, Berlin Coin Fair set	45.00	55.00
MS31	2006 (8)	500	KM1282-1289, Pierre Curie set	45.00	50.00
MS32	2006 (8)	500	KM#1282-1289, Musee de la Monnaie set	45.00	50.00
MS33	2006 (8)	500	KM#1282-1289, Journees du Patrimoine set	45.00	50.00
MS34	2006 (8)	500	KM#1282-1289, Bourgogne set	45.00	50.00
MS35	2006 (8)	500	KM#1282-1289, "Coree set" (Korea)	45.00	50.00
MS36	2006 (8)	500	KM#1282-1289, Nord Pas-de-Calais set	45.00	50.00
MS37	2006 (8)	500	KM#1282-1289, Jacques Chirac set	45.00	50.00
MS38	2006 (8)	500	KM#1282-1289, Mitterand & Khol	45.00	50.00
MS39	2006 (8)	500	KM#1282-1289, Birthday 1 set	45.00	45.00
MS40	2006 (8)	500	KM#1282-1289, Birthday 2 set	45.00	45.00
MS41	2006 (8)	500	KM#1282-1289, Tokyo set	45.00	50.00
MS42	2006 (8)	500	KM#1282-1289, Viaduc de Millau set	45.00	50.00
MS43	2006 (8)	500	KM#1282-1289, Ile-de-France set	45.00	50.00

PROOF SETS

KM#	Date	Mintage	Identification	Issue Price	Mkt Val
PS21	2001 (8)	15,000	KM#1282-1289	59.00	125
PS22	2002 (8)	40,000	KM#1282-1289	59.00	110
PS23	2003 (5)	150,000	KM#1321, 1322, 1323, 1324, 1325	—	260
PS24	2003 (5)	5,000	KM#1326, 1327, 1328, 1329, 1330	—	1,900
PS25	2003 (8)	—	KM#1282-1289	—	110
PS26	2004 (9)	20,000	KM#1282-1289 plus Pantheon 5 Euro	—	150
PS27	2005 (9)	10,000	KM#1282-1289 plus Pantheon 5 Euro	—	150
PS28	2006 (9)	10,000	KM#1282-1289 plus Pantheon 5 Euro	—	150
PS29	2007 (9)	7,500	KM#1282-84, 1410-1414 plus 15 Euro	—	150
PS30	2008 (10)	7,500	KM#1282-84, 1410-1414, 1535	—	200
PS31	2009 (10)	7,500	KM#1282-84, 1410-1414, 1535	—	200
PS32	2010 (9)	9,000	KM#1282-84, 1410-1414 plus 15 Euro	—	150
PS33	2011 (9)	9,000	KM#1282-84, 1410-1414, 1795	—	200
PS34	2012 (9)	10,000	KM#1282-84, 1410-1414 plus Hercules 10 Euro	—	150

FRENCH POLYNESIA

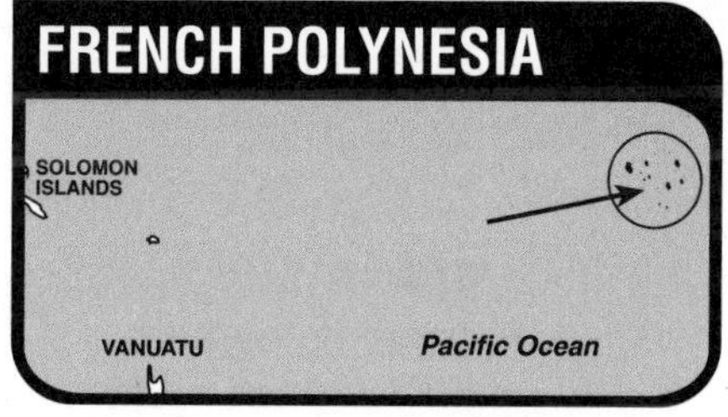

The Territory of French Polynesia (formerly French Oceania) has an area of 1,544 sq. mi. (3,941 sq. km.) and a population of 220,000. It is comprised of the same five archipelagoes that were grouped administratively to form French Oceania.

The colony of French Oceania became the Territory of French Polynesia by act of the French National Assembly in March, 1957. In Sept. of 1958 it voted in favor of the new constitution of the Fifth Republic, thereby electing to remain within the new French Community.

Picturesque, mountainous Tahiti, the setting of many tales of adventure and romance, is one of the most inspiringly beautiful islands in the world. Robert Louis Stevenson called it 'God's sweetest works'. It was there that Paul Gaugin, one of the pioneers of the Impressionist movement, painted the brilliant, exotic pictures that later made him famous. The arid coral atolls of Tuamotu comprise the most economically valuable area of French Polynesia. Pearl oysters thrive in the warm, limpid lagoons, and extensive portions of the atolls are valuable phosphate rock.

RULER

French

MINT MARK

(a) - Paris, privy marks only

MONETARY SYSTEM

100 Centimes = 1 Franc

FRENCH OVERSEAS TERRITORY

DECIMAL COINAGE

KM# 11 FRANC

1.3000 g., Aluminum, 23 mm. **Obv:** Seated Liberty with torch and cornucopia right, date below, legend added flanking figure's feet **Obv. Legend:** I. E. O. M. **Rev:** Legend and island scene divide denomination

Date	Mintage	F	VF	XF	Unc	BU
2001(a)	2,900,000	—	—	—	0.50	1.00
2002(a)	1,600,000	—	—	—	0.50	1.00
2003(a)	4,200,000	—	—	—	0.50	1.00
2004(a)	2,400,000	—	—	—	0.50	1.00
2005(a)	—	—	—	—	0.50	1.00
2006(a)	2,100,000	—	—	—	0.50	1.00
2007(a) Coin rotation	3,400,000	—	—	—	0.50	1.00
2007(a) Medal rotation	Inc. above	—	—	—	—	30.00
2008(a)	4,800,000	—	—	—	0.50	1.00
2009(a)	3,200,000	—	—	—	0.50	1.00
2010(a)	2,100,000	—	—	—	0.50	1.00
2011(a)	—	—	—	—	0.50	1.00

KM# 10 2 FRANCS

2.3000 g., Aluminum, 27 mm. **Obv:** Seated Liberty with torch and cornucopia right, date below, legend added flanking figure's feet **Obv. Legend:** I. E. O. M. **Rev:** Legend and island scene divide denomination

Date	Mintage	F	VF	XF	Unc	BU
2001(a)	2,400,000	—	—	—	0.75	1.50
2002(a)	2,500,000	—	—	—	0.75	1.50
2003(a)	3,200,000	—	—	—	0.75	1.50
2004(a)	3,000,000	—	—	—	0.75	1.50
2005(a)	900,000	—	—	—	0.75	1.50
2006(a)	1,600,000	—	—	—	0.75	1.50
2007(a)	640,000	—	—	—	0.75	1.50
2008(a)	1,900,000	—	—	—	0.75	1.50
2009(a)	1,600,000	—	—	—	0.75	1.50
2010(a)	2,400,000	—	—	—	0.75	1.50
2011(a)	1,600,000	—	—	—	0.75	1.50

KM# 12 5 FRANCS

3.7500 g., Aluminum, 31 mm. **Obv:** Seated Liberty with torch and cornucopia right, date below, legend added flanking figure's feet **Obv. Legend:** I. E. O. M. **Rev:** Legend and island divide denomination

Date	Mintage	F	VF	XF	Unc	BU
2001(a)	1,600,000	—	—	—	1.00	2.00
2002(a)	400,000	—	—	—	1.00	2.00
2003(a)	1,000,000	—	—	—	1.00	2.00
2004(a)	600,000	—	—	—	1.00	2.00
2005(a)	600,000	—	—	—	1.00	2.00
2006(a)	720,000	—	—	—	1.00	2.00
2007(a)	1,000,000	—	—	—	1.00	2.00
2008(a)	1,060,000	—	—	—	1.00	2.00
2009(a)	900,000	—	—	—	1.00	2.00
2010(a)	700,000	—	—	—	1.00	2.00
2011(a)	900,000	—	—	—	1.00	2.00

KM# 8 10 FRANCS

6.0000 g., Nickel, 24 mm. **Obv:** Capped head left, date and legend below **Obv. Legend:** I. E. O. M. **Rev:** Native art, denomination below **Edge:** Reeded

Date	Mintage	F	VF	XF	Unc	BU
2001(a)	500,000	—	—	—	1.25	2.75
2002(a)	600,000	—	—	—	1.25	2.75
2003(a)	1,000,000	—	—	—	1.25	2.75
2004(a)	600,000	—	—	—	1.25	2.75
2005(a)	200,000	—	—	—	1.25	2.75

KM# 8a 10 FRANCS

6.0000 g., Copper-Nickel, 24 mm. **Obv:** Capped head left, date and legend below **Obv. Legend:** I. E. O. M. **Rev:** Native art, denomination below **Edge:** Reeded

Date	Mintage	F	VF	XF	Unc	BU
2006(a)	620,000	—	—	—	1.25	2.75
2007(a)	800,000	—	—	—	1.25	2.75
2008(a)	820,000	—	—	—	1.25	2.75
2009(a)	1,000,000	—	—	—	1.25	2.75
2010(a)	500,000	—	—	—	1.25	2.75
2011(a)	200,000	—	—	—	1.25	2.75

KM# 9 20 FRANCS

10.0000 g., Nickel, 28.3 mm. **Obv:** Capped head left, date and legend below **Obv. Legend:** I. E. O. M. **Rev:** Flowers, vanilla shoots, bread fruit **Edge:** Reeded

Date	Mintage	F	VF	XF	Unc	BU
2001(a)	500,000	—	—	—	1.75	3.25
2002(a)	300,000	—	—	—	1.75	3.25
2003(a)	700,000	—	—	—	1.75	3.00
2004(a)	600,000	—	—	—	1.75	3.00
2005(a)	30,000	—	—	—	20.00	35.00

KM# 9a 20 FRANCS

10.0000 g., Copper-Nickel, 28.3 mm. **Obv:** Capped head left, date and legend below **Obv. Legend:** I. E. O. M. **Rev:** Flowers, vanilla shoots, bread fruit **Edge:** Reeded

Date	Mintage	F	VF	XF	Unc	BU
2006(a)	300,000	—	—	—	1.75	3.00
2007(a)	450,000	—	—	—	1.75	3.00
2008(a)	610,000	—	—	—	1.75	3.00
2009(a)	750,000	—	—	—	1.75	3.00
2010(a)	200,000	—	—	—	1.75	3.00
2011(a)	400,000	—	—	—	1.75	3.00

KM# 13 50 FRANCS

15.0000 g., Nickel, 33 mm. **Obv:** Capped head left, date and legend below **Obv. Legend:** I. E. O. M. **Rev:** Denomination above Moorea Harbor **Edge:** Reeded

Date	Mintage	F	VF	XF	Unc	BU
2001(a)	300,000	—	—	—	2.00	4.00
2002(a)	—	—	—	—	2.00	4.00
2003(a)	240,000	—	—	—	2.00	4.00
2004(a)	100,000	—	—	—	2.00	4.00
2005(a)	100,000	—	—	—	2.00	4.00

KM# 13a 50 FRANCS

15.0000 g., Copper-Nickel, 33 mm. **Obv:** Capped head left, date and legend below **Obv. Legend:** I. E. O. M. **Rev:** Denomination above Moorea Harbor **Edge:** Reeded

Date	Mintage	F	VF	XF	Unc	BU
2006(a)	15,000	—	—	—	3.00	5.00
2007(a)	310,000	—	—	—	2.00	4.00
2008(a)	200,000	—	—	—	2.00	4.00
2009(a)	300,000	—	—	—	2.00	4.00
2010(a)	120,000	—	—	—	2.00	4.00
2011(a)	130,000	—	—	—	2.00	4.00

KM# 14 100 FRANCS

10.0000 g., Nickel-Bronze, 30 mm. **Obv:** Capped head left, date below **Rev:** Denomination above Moorea Harbor **Edge:** Reeded

Date	Mintage	F	VF	XF	Unc	BU
2001(a)	200,000	—	—	—	3.00	5.00
2002(a)	—	—	—	—	3.00	5.00
2003(a)	600,000	—	—	—	2.75	5.00
2004(a)	450,000	—	—	—	2.75	5.00
2005(a)	300,000	—	—	—	2.75	5.00

KM# 14a 100 FRANCS

10.0000 g., Aluminum-Bronze, 30 mm. **Obv:** Capped head left, date below **Obv. Legend:** I. E. O. M. **Rev:** Denomination above Moorea Harbor **Edge:** Reeded

Date	Mintage	F	VF	XF	Unc	BU
2006(a)	200,000	—	—	—	2.75	5.00
2007(a)	650,000	—	—	—	2.75	5.00
2008(a)	690,000	—	—	—	2.75	5.00
2009(a)	—	—	—	—	2.75	5.00
2010(a)	—	—	—	—	2.75	5.00
2011(a)	—	—	—	—	2.75	5.00

MINT SETS

KM#	Date	Mintage	Identification	Issue Price	Mkt Val
MS1	2001 (7)	3,000	KM#8-14	—	22.50
MS2	2002 (7)	5,000	KM#8-14	—	22.50
MS3	2003 (7)	3,000	KM#8-14	—	22.50

GAMBIA

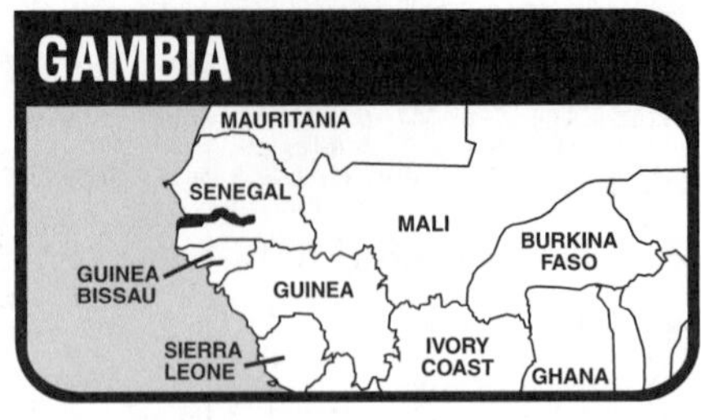

The Republic of The Gambia, occupies a strip of land 7 miles (11km.) to 20 miles (32 km.) wide and 200 miles (322 km.) long encompassing both sides of West Africa's Gambia River, and completely surrounded by Senegal. The republic, one of Africa's smallest countries, has an area of 4,127 sq. mi. (11,300 sq. km.) and a population of 989,273. Capital: Banjul. Agriculture and tourism are the principal industries. Peanuts constitute 95 per cent of export earnings.

The Gambia was once part of the great empires of Ghana and Songhay. When Portuguese gold seekers and slave traders visited The Gambia in the 15th century, it was part of the Kingdom of Mali. In 1588 the territory became, through purchase, the first British colony in Africa. English slavers established Fort James, the first settlement, on a small island a dozen miles up the Gambia River in 1664. After alternate periods of union with Sierra Leone and existence as a separate colony The Gambia became a British colony in 1888. On Feb. 18, 1965, The Gambia achieved independence as a constitutional monarchy within the Commonwealth of Nations, with Elizabeth II as Head of State as Queen of The Gambia. It became a republic on April 24, 1970, remaining a member of the Commonwealth, but with the president as Chief of State and Head of Government.

Together with Senegal, The Gambia formed a confederation on February 1, 1982. This confederation was officially dissolved on September 21, 1989. In July, 1994 a military junta took control of The Gambia and disbanded its elected government.

For earlier coinage see British West Africa.

RULER

British until 1970

REPUBLIC

DECIMAL COINAGE

100 Bututs = 1 Dalasi

KM# 58 50 BUTUTS

Copper-Nickel, 28.8 mm. **Obv:** National arms, date below **Rev:** African domestic ox divides denomination

Date	Mintage	F	VF	XF	Unc	BU
2008	—	—	—	—	1.50	2.00

KM# 72 DALASI

Gold **Subject:** 7th Confrence of the African Union in Banjul

Date	Mintage	F	VF	XF	Unc	BU
2006 Proof	—	—	—	—	—	—

KM# 59 DALASI

8.8100 g., Copper-Nickel, 28 mm. **Obv:** National arms, date below **Rev:** Slender-snouted crocodile, denomination at right **Shape:** 7-sided

Date	Mintage	F	VF	XF	Unc	BU
2008	—	—	—	2.75	6.00	7.50
2011	—	—	—	2.75	6.00	7.50

GEORGIA

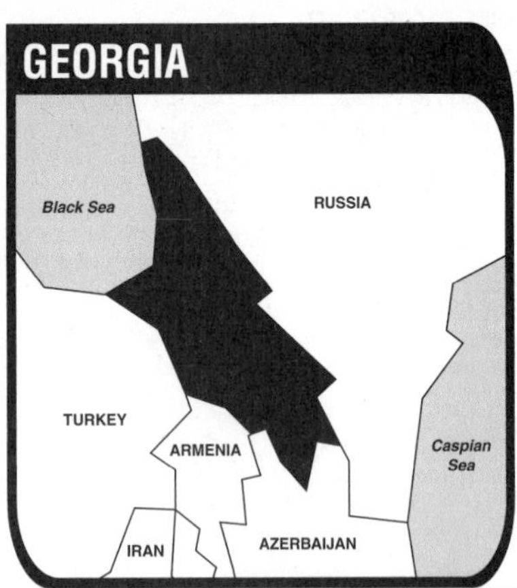

Georgia (formerly the Georgian Social Democratic Republic under the U.S.S.R.), is bounded by the Black Sea to the west and by Turkey, Armenia and Azerbaijan. It occupies the western part of Transcaucasia covering an area of 26,900 sq. mi. (69,700 sq. km.) and a population of 5.7 million. Capitol: Tbilisi. Hydro-electricity, minerals, forestry and agriculture are the chief industries.

Germano-- Georgian treaty was signed on May 28, 1918, followed by a Turko-Georgian peace treaty on June 4. The end of WW I and the collapse of the central powers allowed free The collapse of the U.S.S.R. allowed full transition to independence and on April 9, 1991 a unanimous vote declared the republic an independent state based on its original treaty of independence of May 1918.

MONETARY SYSTEM

100 Thetri = 1 Lari

INDEPENDENT STATE (C.I.S.)

STANDARD COINAGE

100 Thetri = 1 Lari

KM# 89 50 THETRI

6.5000 g., Copper-Nickel, 24 mm. **Obv:** National arms **Rev:** Value **Edge:** Reeded and lettered

Date	Mintage	F	VF	XF	Unc	BU
2006	—	—	—	—	3.00	4.00

KM# 95 LARI

28.2800 g., 0.9990 Silver 0.9083 oz. ASW, 38.61 mm. **Subject:** World Cup Soccer, 2006 Germany **Obv:** Map of Georgia, flag **Rev:** World Cup trophy, two soccer players

Date	Mintage	F	VF	XF	Unc	BU
2004 Proof	50,000	Value: 45.00				

KM# 90 LARI

7.8000 g., Copper-Nickel, 26.2 mm. **Obv:** National arms **Rev:** Value **Edge:** Reeded and lettered

Date	Mintage	F	VF	XF	Unc	BU
2006	—	—	—	—	5.00	6.50

KM# 92 2 LARI

12.9200 g., Copper-Nickel, 31 mm. **Obv:** Trophy cup, value and date **Rev:** UFFA Winners Cup and soccer player **Edge:** Plain

Date	Mintage	F	VF	XF	Unc	BU
2006	10,000	—	—	—	—	18.00

KM# 94 2 LARI
8.0000 g., Bi-Metallic Aluminum-Bronze center in Copper-Nickel ring, 27 mm. **Obv:** National arms **Rev:** Large value **Edge:** Reeded and lettered

Date	Mintage	F	VF	XF	Unc	BU
2006	—	—	—	—	7.50	9.00

KM# 103 2 LARI
28.2800 g., 0.9250 Silver 0.8410 oz. ASW, 38.61 mm. **Obv:** Trophy cup, value and date **Rev:** UEFA Winners Cup and soccer player

Date	Mintage	F	VF	XF	Unc	BU
2006 Proof	6,000	Value: 60.00				

KM# 93 3 LARI
12.8000 g., Copper-Nickel, 31 mm. **Obv:** Three oil wells **Rev:** Map with "Baku-Tbilisi-Ceyhan" route **Edge:** Lettered

Date	Mintage	F	VF	XF	Unc	BU
2006	3,000	—	—	—	—	25.00

KM# 102 3 LARI
28.2800 g., Silver, 38.61 mm. **Obv:** Three oil wells **Rev:** Map with "Baku-Tbilisi-Ceyhan" route

Date	Mintage	F	VF	XF	Unc	BU
2006 Proof	5,000	Value: 60.00				

KM# 106 10 LARI
28.2800 g., 0.9250 Silver 0.8410 oz. ASW, 38.61 mm. **Subject:** St. George's Day **Obv:** Drawing of church by Don Christoforo de Castelli **Rev:** Church of St. george in Ilora

Date	Mintage	F	VF	XF	Unc	BU
2009 Proof	1,500	Value: 75.00				

KM# 104 20 LARI
28.2800 g., 0.9250 Silver 0.8410 oz. ASW, 38.61 mm. **Obv:** Two classical runners **Rev:** Exterior of Bird's Nest Stadium, torch

Date	Mintage	F	VF	XF	Unc	BU
2008 Proof	1,500	Value: 75.00				

KM# 105 20 LARI
8.5000 g., 0.9000 Gold 0.2459 oz. AGW, 25 mm. **Obv:** Two classical runners **Rev:** Exterior of Bird's Nest Stadium, torch

Date	Mintage	F	VF	XF	Unc	BU
2008 Proof	—	Value: 500				

BULLION COINAGE

KM# 96 10 LARI
3.1100 g., 0.9990 Gold 0.0999 oz. AGW, 16 mm. **Obv:** Ancient sailing vessel, trade route **Rev:** Golden Fleece

Date	Mintage	F	VF	XF	Unc	BU
2006	4,000	—	—	—	—	175

KM# 97 25 LARI
7.7800 g., 0.9990 Gold 0.2499 oz. AGW, 22 mm. **Obv:** Ancient sailing ship trade route map **Rev:** Golden Feece

Date	Mintage	F	VF	XF	Unc	BU
2006	—	—	—	—	—	450

KM# 98 50 LARI
28.0000 g., 0.9990 Gold 0.8993 oz. AGW, 28 mm. **Obv:** Ancient sailing ship, trade route map **Rev:** Golden Fleece

Date	Mintage	F	VF	XF	Unc	BU
2006	—	—	—	—	—	1,600

KM# 99 100 LARI
31.1050 g., 0.9990 Gold 0.9990 oz. AGW, 37 mm. **Obv:** Ancient sailing ship, trade route map **Rev:** Golden Fleece

Date	Mintage	F	VF	XF	Unc	BU
2006	—	—	—	—	—	1,750

KM# 100 300 LARI
155.5000 g., 0.9990 Gold 4.9942 oz. AGW, 50 mm. **Obv:** Ancient sailing ship, trade route map **Rev:** Golden Fleece

Date	Mintage	F	VF	XF	Unc	BU
2006	—	—	—	—	—	9,000

KM# 101 1000 LARI
311.0000 g., 0.9990 Gold 9.9885 oz. AGW, 60 mm. **Obv:** Ancient sailing ship, trade route map **Rev:** Golden Fleece

Date	Mintage	F	VF	XF	Unc	BU
2006	—	—	—	—	—	17,500

GERMANY-FEDERAL REPUBLIC

1949-

The Federal Republic of Germany, located in north-central Europe, has an area of 137,744 sq. mi. (356,910sq. km.) and a population of 81.1 million. Capital: Berlin. The economy centers about one of the world's foremost industrial establishments. Machinery, motor vehicles, iron, steel, yarns and fabrics are exported.

MINT MARKS
A - Berlin
D - Munich
F - Stuttgart
G - Karlsruhe
J - Hamburg

MONETARY SYSTEM
100 Pfennig = 1 Deutsche Mark (DM)

FEDERAL REPUBLIC

STANDARD COINAGE

KM# 105 PFENNIG
2.0000 g., Copper Plated Steel, 16.5 mm. **Obv:** Five oak leaves, date below **Obv. Legend:** BUNDESREPUBLIK DEUTSCHLAND **Rev:** Denomination

Date	Mintage	F	VF	XF	Unc	BU
2001A In sets only	130,000	—	—	—	5.00	—
2001A Proof	78,000	Value: 5.00				
2001D In sets only	130,000	—	—	—	5.00	—
2001D Proof	78,000	Value: 5.00				
2001F In sets only	130,000	—	—	—	5.00	—
2001F Proof	78,000	Value: 5.00				
2001G In sets only	130,000	—	—	—	5.00	—
2001G Proof	78,000	Value: 5.00				
2001J In sets only	130,000	—	—	—	5.00	—
2001J Proof	78,000	Value: 5.00				

KM# 106a 2 PFENNIG
2.9000 g., Copper Plated Steel, 19.25 mm. **Obv:** Five oak leaves, date below **Rev:** Denomination

Date	Mintage	F	VF	XF	Unc	BU
2001A In sets only	130,000	—	—	—	5.00	—
2001A Proof	78,000	Value: 5.00				
2001D In sets only	130,000	—	—	—	5.00	—
2001D Proof	78,000	Value: 5.00				
2001F In sets only	130,000	—	—	—	5.00	—
2001F Proof	78,000	Value: 5.00				
2001G In sets only	130,000	—	—	—	5.00	—
2001G Proof	78,000	Value: 5.00				
2001J In sets only	130,000	—	—	—	5.00	—
2001J Proof	78,000	Value: 5.00				

KM# 107 5 PFENNIG
3.0000 g., Brass Clad Steel, 18.5 mm. **Obv:** Five oak leaves, date below **Obv. Legend:** BUNDESREPUBLIK DEUTSCHLAND **Rev:** Denomination

Date	Mintage	F	VF	XF	Unc	BU
2001A In sets only	130,000	—	—	—	5.00	—
2001A Proof	78,000	Value: 5.00				
2001D In sets only	130,000	—	—	—	5.00	—
2001D Proof	78,000	Value: 5.00				
2001F In sets only	130,000	—	—	—	5.00	—
2001F Proof	78,000	Value: 5.00				
2001G In sets only	130,000	—	—	—	5.00	—
2001G Proof	78,000	Value: 5.00				
2001J In sets only	130,000	—	—	—	5.00	—
2001J Proof	78,000	Value: 5.00				

KM# 108 10 PFENNIG
4.0000 g., Brass Clad Steel, 21.5 mm. **Obv:** Five oak leaves, date below **Obv. Legend:** BUNDESREPUBLIK DEUTSCHLAND **Rev:** Denomination **Edge:** Plain

Date	Mintage	F	VF	XF	Unc	BU
2001A In sets only	130,000	—	—	—	5.00	—
2001A Proof	78,000	Value: 5.00				
2001D In sets only	130,000	—	—	—	5.00	—
2001D Proof	78,000	Value: 5.00				
2001F In sets only	130,000	—	—	—	5.00	—
2001F Proof	78,000	Value: 5.00				
2001G In sets only	130,000	—	—	—	5.00	—
2001G Proof	78,000	Value: 5.00				
2001J In sets only	130,000	—	—	—	5.00	—
2001J Proof	78,000	Value: 5.00				

KM# 109.2 50 PFENNIG
3.5000 g., Copper-Nickel, 20 mm. **Obv:** Denomination **Obv. Legend:** BUNDESREPUBLIK DEUTSCHLAND **Rev:** Woman planting an oak seedling **Edge:** Plain

Date	Mintage	F	VF	XF	Unc	BU
2001A In sets only	130,000	—	—	—	10.00	—
2001A Proof	78,000	Value: 10.00				

Date	Mintage	F	VF	XF	Unc	BU
2001D In sets only	130,000	—	—	—	10.00	—
2001D Proof	78,000	Value: 10.00				
2001F In sets only	130,000	—	—	—	10.00	—
2001F Proof	78,000	Value: 10.00				
2001G In sets only	130,000	—	—	—	10.00	—
2001G Proof	78,000	Value: 10.00				
2001J In sets only	130,000	—	—	—	10.00	—
2001J Proof	78,000	Value: 10.00				

KM# 110 MARK

5.5000 g., Copper-Nickel, 23.5 mm. **Obv:** Eagle **Rev:** Denomination flanked by oak leaves, date below

Date	Mintage	F	VF	XF	Unc	BU
2001A In sets only	130,000	—	—	—	15.00	—
2001A Proof	78,000	Value: 15.00				
2001D In sets only	130,000	—	—	—	15.00	—
2001D Proof	78,000	Value: 15.00				
2001F In sets only	130,000	—	—	—	15.00	—
2001F Proof	78,000	Value: 15.00				
2001G In sets only	130,000	—	—	—	15.00	—
2001G Proof	78,000	Value: 15.00				
2001J In sets only	130,000	—	—	—	15.00	—
2001J Proof	78,000	Value: 15.00				

KM# 203 MARK

12.0000 g., 0.9999 Gold 0.3858 oz. AGW, 23.5 mm. **Subject:** Retirement of the Mark Currency **Obv:** Eagle **Rev:** Denomination flanked by oak leaves, date below **Edge:** Arabeskes

Date	Mintage	F	VF	XF	Unc	BU
2001A Proof	200,000	Value: 750				
2001D Proof	200,000	Value: 750				
2001G Proof	200,000	Value: 750				
2001J Proof	200,000	Value: 750				
2001F Proof	200,000	Value: 750				

KM# 170 2 MARK

7.0000 g., Copper-Nickel Clad Nickel, 26.75 mm. **Subject:** Ludwig Erhard **Obv:** Eagle above denomination **Rev:** Head facing divides dates **Edge Lettering:** EINIGKEIT UND RECHT UND FREIHEIT

Date	Mintage	F	VF	XF	Unc	BU
2001A In sets only	130,000	—	—	—	10.00	—
2001A Proof	78,000	Value: 10.00				
2001D In sets only	130,000	—	—	—	10.00	—
2001D Proof	78,000	Value: 10.00				
2001F In sets only	130,000	—	—	—	10.00	—
2001F Proof	78,000	Value: 10.00				
2001G In sets only	130,000	—	—	—	10.00	—
2001G Proof	78,000	Value: 10.00				
2001J In sets only	130,000	—	—	—	10.00	—
2001J Proof	78,000	Value: 10.00				

KM# 175 2 MARK

7.0400 g., Copper-Nickel Clad Nickel, 26.8 mm. **Subject:** Franz Joseph Strauss **Obv:** Eagle above denomination **Rev:** Head left divides dates **Edge Lettering:** EINIGKEIT UND RECHT UND FREIHEIT

Date	Mintage	F	VF	XF	Unc	BU
2001A In sets only	130,000	—	—	—	10.00	—
2001A Proof	78,000	Value: 10.00				

Date	Mintage	F	VF	XF	Unc	BU
2001D In sets only	130,000	—	—	—	10.00	—
2001D Proof	78,000	Value: 10.00				
2001F In sets only	130,000	—	—	—	10.00	—
2001F Proof	78,000	Value: 10.00				
2001G In sets only	130,000	—	—	—	10.00	—
2001G Proof	78,000	Value: 10.00				
2001J In sets only	130,000	—	—	—	10.00	—
2001J Proof	78,000	Value: 10.00				

KM# 183 2 MARK

7.0000 g., Copper-Nickel Clad Nickel, 26.75 mm. **Subject:** Willy Brandt **Obv:** Eagle above denomination **Rev:** Head facing divides dates **Edge Lettering:** EINIGKEIT UND RECHT UND FREIHEIT

Date	Mintage	F	VF	XF	Unc	BU
2001A In sets only	130,000	—	—	—	10.00	—
2001A Proof	78,000	Value: 10.00				
2001D In sets only	130,000	—	—	—	10.00	—
2001D Proof	78,000	Value: 10.00				
2001F In sets only	130,000	—	—	—	10.00	—
2001F Proof	78,000	Value: 10.00				
2001G In sets only	130,000	—	—	—	10.00	—
2001G Proof	78,000	Value: 10.00				
2001J In sets only	130,000	—	—	—	10.00	—
2001J Proof	78,000	Value: 10.00				

KM# 140.1 5 MARK

10.0000 g., Copper-Nickel Clad Nickel, 29 mm. **Obv:** Denomination within rounded square therefore nicknamed "TV-Fives" **Rev:** Eagle above date **Edge Lettering:** EINIGKEIT UND RECHT UND FREIHEIT

Date	Mintage	F	VF	XF	Unc	BU
2001A In sets only	130,000	—	—	—	30.00	—
2001A Proof	78,000	Value: 30.00				
2001D In sets only	130,000	—	—	—	30.00	—
2001D Proof	78,000	Value: 30.00				
2001F In sets only	130,000	—	—	—	30.00	—
2001F Proof	78,000	Value: 30.00				
2001G In sets only	130,000	—	—	—	30.00	—
2001G Proof	78,000	Value: 30.00				
2001J In sets only	130,000	—	—	—	30.00	—
2001J Proof	78,000	Value: 30.00				

COMMEMORATIVE COINAGE

KM# 204 10 MARK

15.5000 g., 0.9250 Silver 0.4609 oz. ASW, 32.5 mm. **Obv:** Imperial eagle above denomination **Rev:** Naval Museum, Stralsund **Edge Lettering:** "OHNE WASSER KEIN LEBEN"

Date	Mintage	F	VF	XF	Unc	BU
2001A	2,500,000	—	—	—	17.50	18.50
2001A Proof	163,000	Value: 22.00				
2001D Proof	163,000	Value: 22.00				
2001F Proof	163,000	Value: 22.00				
2001G Proof	163,000	Value: 22.00				
2001J Proof	163,000	Value: 22.00				

KM# 206 10 MARK

15.5000 g., 0.9250 Silver 0.4609 oz. ASW, 32.5 mm. **Subject:** Federal Court of Constitution: 50th Anniversary **Obv:** Stylized eagle above denomination **Rev:** Justice holding books and scale **Edge:** Lettered **Edge Lettering:** FÜR DAS GESAMTE DEUTSCHE VOLK

Date	Mintage	F	VF	XF	Unc	BU
2001G	2,000,000	—	—	—	17.50	18.50
2001G Proof	151,000	Value: 22.00				
2001A Proof	151,000	Value: 22.00				
2001D Proof	151,000	Value: 22.00				
2001F Proof	151,000	Value: 22.00				
2001J Proof	151,000	Value: 22.00				

KM# 205 10 MARK

15.5000 g., 0.9250 Silver 0.4609 oz. ASW, 32.5 mm. **Subject:** 200th Anniversary - Birth of Albert Gustav Lortzing **Obv:** Stylized eagle above denomination **Rev:** Portrait and music **Edge Lettering:** * WILDSCHUETZ * UNDINE * ZAR UND ZIMMERMANN *

Date	Mintage	F	VF	XF	Unc	BU
2001J	2,500,000	—	—	—	17.50	18.50
2001J Proof	163,000	Value: 22.00				
2001 Proof	163,000	Value: 22.00				
2001 Proof	163,000	Value: 22.00				
2001 Proof	163,000	Value: 22.00				
2001 Proof	163,000	Value: 22.00				

EURO COINAGE

European Union Issues

KM# 207 EURO CENT

2.3000 g., Copper Plated Steel, 16.25 mm. **Obv:** Oak leaves **Rev:** Denomination and globe **Edge:** Plain

Date	Mintage	F	VF	XF	Unc	BU
2002A	800,090,000	—	—	—	0.35	—
2002A Proof	75,000	Value: 1.00				
2002D	840,090,000	—	—	—	0.35	—
2002D Proof	75,000	Value: 1.00				
2002F	960,090,000	—	—	—	0.35	—
2002F Proof	75,000	Value: 1.00				
2002G	560,090,000	—	—	—	0.35	—
2002G Proof	75,000	Value: 1.00				
2002J	840,090,000	—	—	—	0.35	—
2002J Proof	75,000	Value: 1.00				
2003A In sets only	90,000	—	—	—	4.50	—
2003A Proof	75,000	Value: 1.00				
2003D In sets only	90,000	—	—	—	4.50	—
2003D Proof	75,000	Value: 1.00				
2003F In sets only	90,000	—	—	—	4.50	—
2003F Proof	75,000	Value: 1.00				
2003G In sets only	90,000	—	—	—	4.50	—
2003G Proof	75,000	Value: 1.00				
2003J In sets only	90,000	—	—	—	4.50	—
2003J Proof	75,000	Value: 1.00				
2004A	280,090,000	—	—	—	0.35	—
2004A Proof	75,000	Value: 1.00				
2004D	294,090,000	—	—	—	0.35	—
2004D Proof	75,000	Value: 1.00				
2004F	336,090,000	—	—	—	0.35	—
2004F Proof	75,000	Value: 1.00				
2004G	196,090,000	—	—	—	0.35	—
2004G Proof	75,000	Value: 1.00				
2004J	294,090,000	—	—	—	0.35	—
2004J Proof	75,000	Value: 1.00				
2005A	120,090,000	—	—	—	0.35	—
2005A Proof	75,000	Value: 1.00				
2005D	126,090,000	—	—	—	0.35	—

Date	Mintage	F	VF	XF	Unc	BU
2005D Proof	75,000	Value: 1.00				
2005F	144,090,000	—	—	—	0.35	—
2005F Proof	75,000	Value: 1.00				
2005G	84,090,000	—	—	—	0.35	—
2005G Proof	75,000	Value: 1.00				
2005J	126,090,000	—	—	—	0.35	—
2005J Proof	75,000	Value: 1.00				
2006A In sets only	90,000	—	—	—	4.50	—
2006A Proof	75,000	Value: 1.00				
2006D In sets only	90,000	—	—	—	4.50	—
2006D Proof	75,000	Value: 1.00				
2006F In sets only	90,000	—	—	—	4.50	—
2006F Proof	75,000	Value: 1.00				
2006G In sets only	90,000	—	—	—	4.50	—
2006G Proof	75,000	Value: 1.00				
2006J In sets only	90,000	—	—	—	4.50	—
2006J Proof	75,000	Value: 1.00				
2007A	119,490,000	—	—	—	0.35	—
2007A Proof	75,000	Value: 1.00				
2007D	125,460,000	—	—	—	0.35	—
2007D Proof	75,000	Value: 1.00				
2007F	143,370,000	—	—	—	0.35	—
2007F Proof	75,000	Value: 1.00				
2007G	83,670,000	—	—	—	0.35	—
2007G Proof	75,000	Value: 1.00				
2007J	125,460,000	—	—	—	0.35	—
2007J Proof	75,000	Value: 1.00				
2008A	101,280,000	—	—	—	0.35	—
2008A Proof	70,000	Value: 1.00				
2008D	106,340,000	—	—	—	0.35	—
2008D Proof	70,000	Value: 1.00				
2008F	121,520,000	—	—	—	0.35	—
2008F Proof	70,000	Value: 1.00				
2008G	70,920,000	—	—	—	0.35	—
2008G Proof	70,000	Value: 1.00				
2008J	106,340,000	—	—	—	0.35	—
2008J Proof	70,000	Value: 1.00				
2009A	100,060,000	—	—	—	0.35	—
2009A Proof	50,000	Value: 1.00				
2009D	105,060,000	—	—	—	0.35	—
2009D Proof	50,000	Value: 1.00				
2009F	120,060,000	—	—	—	0.35	—
2009F Proof	50,000	Value: 1.00				
2009G	70,060,000	—	—	—	0.35	—
2009G Proof	50,000	Value: 1.00				
2009J	105,060,000	—	—	—	0.35	—
2009J Proof	50,000	Value: 1.00				
2010A	94,454,000	—	—	—	0.35	—
2010A Proof	45,150	Value: 1.00				
2010D	99,167,000	—	—	—	0.35	—
2010D Proof	40,120	Value: 1.00				
2010F	113,327,000	—	—	—	0.35	—
2010F Proof	40,120	Value: 1.00				
2010G	66,127,000	—	—	—	0.35	—
2010G Proof	40,120	Value: 1.00				
2010J	99,167,000	—	—	—	0.35	—
2010J Proof	40,120	Value: 1.00				
2011A	118,448,000	—	—	—	0.35	—
2011A Proof	43,000	Value: 1.25				
2011D	124,364,000	—	—	—	0.35	—
2011D Proof	37,000	Value: 1.25				
2011F	142,124,000	—	—	—	0.35	—
2011F Proof	37,000	Value: 1.25				
2011G	82,924,000	—	—	—	0.35	—
2011G Proof	37,000	Value: 1.25				
2011J	124,364,000	—	—	—	0.35	—
2011J Proof	37,000	Value: 1.25				
2012A	Est. 104,250,000	—	—	—	0.35	—
2012A Proof	Est. 40,000	Value: 1.25				
2012D	Est. 109,460,000	—	—	—	0.35	—
2012D Proof	Est. 40,000	Value: 1.25				
2012F	Est. 125,090,000	—	—	—	0.35	—
2012F Proof	Est. 40,000	Value: 1.25				
2012G	Est. 72,990	—	—	—	0.35	—
2012G Proof	Est. 40,000	Value: 1.25				
2012J	Est. 109,460,000	—	—	—	0.35	—
2012J Proof	Est. 40,000	Value: 1.25				
2013A	—	—	—	—	0.20	—
2013A Proof	Est. 40,000	Value: 1.25				
2013D	—	—	—	—	0.20	—
2013D Proof	Est. 40,000	Value: 1.25				
2013F	—	—	—	—	0.20	—
2013F Proof	Est. 40,000	Value: 1.25				
2013G	—	—	—	—	0.20	—
2013G Proof	Est. 40,000	Value: 1.25				
2013J	—	—	—	—	0.20	—
2013J Proof	Est. 40,000	Value: 1.25				

KM# 208 2 EURO CENT

3.0600 g., Copper Plated Steel, 18.75 mm. **Obv:** Oak leaves **Rev:** Denomination and globe **Edge:** Grooved

Date	Mintage	F	VF	XF	Unc	BU
2002A	360,090,000	—	—	—	0.50	—
2002A Proof	75,000	Value: 1.50				
2002D	483,090,000	—	—	—	0.50	—
2002D Proof	75,000	Value: 1.50				
2002F	507,890,000	—	—	—	0.50	—
2002F Proof	75,000	Value: 1.50				
2002G	311,890,000	—	—	—	0.50	—
2002G Proof	75,000	Value: 1.50				
2002J	419,490,000	—	—	—	0.50	—
2002J Proof	75,000	Value: 1.50				
2003A	200,090,000	—	—	—	0.50	—
2003A Proof	75,000	Value: 1.50				
2003D	105,090,000	—	—	—	0.50	—
2003D Proof	75,000	Value: 1.50				
2003F	164,290,000	—	—	—	0.50	—
2003F Proof	75,000	Value: 1.50				
2003G	80,290,000	—	—	—	0.50	—
2003G Proof	75,000	Value: 1.50				
2003J	168,690,000	—	—	—	0.50	—
2003J Proof	75,000	Value: 1.50				
2004A	127,090,000	—	—	—	0.50	—
2004A Proof	75,000	Value: 1.50				
2004D	133,440,000	—	—	—	0.50	—
2004D Proof	75,000	Value: 1.50				
2004F	152,490,000	—	—	—	0.50	—
2004F Proof	75,000	Value: 1.50				
2004G	88,990,000	—	—	—	0.50	—
2004G Proof	75,000	Value: 1.50				
2004J	133,440,000	—	—	—	0.50	—
2004J Proof	75,000	Value: 1.50				
2005A	73,090,000	—	—	—	0.50	—
2005A Proof	75,000	Value: 1.50				
2005D	76,740,000	—	—	—	0.50	—
2005D Proof	75,000	Value: 1.50				
2005F	87,690,000	—	—	—	0.50	—
2005F Proof	75,000	Value: 1.50				
2005G	51,590,000	—	—	—	0.50	—
2005G Proof	75,000	Value: 1.50				
2005J	76,740,000	—	—	—	0.50	—
2005J Proof	75,000	Value: 1.50				
2006A	108,090,000	—	—	—	0.50	—
2006A Proof	75,000	Value: 1.50				
2006D	113,490,000	—	—	—	0.50	—
2006D Proof	75,000	Value: 1.50				
2006F	129,640,000	—	—	—	0.50	—
2006F Proof	75,000	Value: 1.50				
2006G	75,690,000	—	—	—	0.50	—
2006G Proof	75,000	Value: 1.50				
2006J	148,490,000	—	—	—	0.50	—
2006J Proof	75,000	Value: 1.50				
2007A	100,090,000	—	—	—	0.50	—
2007A Proof	75,000	Value: 1.50				
2007D	105,090,000	—	—	—	0.50	—
2007D Proof	75,000	Value: 1.50				
2007F	120,090,000	—	—	—	0.50	—
2007F Proof	75,000	Value: 1.50				
2007G	70,090,000	—	—	—	0.50	—
2007G Proof	75,000	Value: 1.50				
2007J	105,090,000	—	—	—	0.50	—
2007J Proof	75,000	Value: 1.50				
2008A	80,080,000	—	—	—	0.50	—
2008A Proof	70,000	Value: 1.50				
2008D	84,080,000	—	—	—	0.50	—
2008D Proof	70,000	Value: 1.50				
2008F	96,080,000	—	—	—	0.50	—
2008F Proof	70,000	Value: 1.50				
2008G	56,080,000	—	—	—	0.50	—
2008G Proof	70,000	Value: 1.50				
2008J	84,080,000	—	—	—	0.50	—
2008J Proof	70,000	Value: 1.50				
2009A	59,060,000	—	—	—	0.50	—
2009A Proof	50,000	Value: 1.50				
2009D	62,010,000	—	—	—	0.50	—
2009D Proof	50,000	Value: 1.50				
2009F	70,860,000	—	—	—	0.50	—
2009F Proof	50,000	Value: 1.50				
2009G	41,360,000	—	—	—	0.50	—
2009G Proof	50,000	Value: 1.50				
2009J	62,010,000	—	—	—	0.50	—
2009J Proof	50,000	Value: 1.50				
2010A	72,854,000	—	—	—	0.50	—
2010A Proof	45,150	Value: 1.50				
2010D	76,487,000	—	—	—	0.50	—
2010D Proof	40,120	Value: 1.50				
2010F	87,407,000	—	—	—	0.50	—
2010F Proof	40,120	Value: 1.50				
2010G	51,007,000	—	—	—	0.50	—
2010G Proof	40,120	Value: 1.50				
2010J	76,487,000	—	—	—	0.50	—
2010J Proof	40,120	Value: 1.50				
2011A	100,448,000	—	—	—	0.50	—
2011A Proof	Est. 43,000	Value: 1.50				
2011D	105,464,000	—	—	—	0.50	—
2011D Proof	37,000	Value: 1.50				
2011F	120,524,000	—	—	—	0.50	—
2011F Proof	Est. 37,000	Value: 1.50				
2011G	70,324,000	—	—	—	0.50	—
2011G Proof	37,000	Value: 1.50				
2011G	105,464,000	—	—	—	0.50	—
2011J Proof	Est. 37,000	Value: 1.50				
2012A	Est. 77,490,000	—	—	—	0.50	—
2012A Proof	Est. 40,000	Value: 1.75				
2012D	Est. 81,320,000	—	—	—	0.50	—
2012D Proof	Est. 40,000	Value: 1.75				
2012F	Est. 92,930,000	—	—	—	0.50	—
2012F Proof	Est. 40,000	Value: 1.75				
2012G	Est. 54,230,000	—	—	—	0.50	—
2012G Proof	Est. 40,000	Value: 1.75				
2012J	Est. 81,320,000	—	—	—	0.50	—
2012J Proof	Est. 40,000	Value: 1.75				

KM# 209 5 EURO CENT

3.9200 g., Copper Plated Steel, 21.25 mm. **Obv:** Oak leaves **Rev:** Denomination and globe **Edge:** Plain

Date	Mintage	F	VF	XF	Unc	BU
2002A	480,090,000	—	—	—	0.75	—
2002A Proof	75,000	Value: 2.00				
2002D	504,090,000	—	—	—	0.75	—
2002D Proof	75,000	Value: 2.00				
2002F	576,090,000	—	—	—	0.75	—
2002F Proof	75,000	Value: 2.00				
2002G	336,090,000	—	—	—	0.75	—
2002G Proof	75,000	Value: 2.00				
2002J	504,090,000	—	—	—	0.75	—
2002J Proof	90,000	Value: 2.00				
2003A In sets only	75,000	—	—	—	4.50	—
2003A Proof	90,000	Value: 2.00				
2003D In sets only	75,000	—	—	—	4.50	—
2003D Proof	90,000	Value: 2.00				
2003F In sets only	75,000	—	—	—	4.50	—
2003F Proof	90,000	Value: 2.00				
2003G In sets only	75,000	—	—	—	4.50	—
2003G Proof	90,000	Value: 2.00				
2003J In sets only	90,000	—	—	—	4.50	—
2003J Proof	75,000	Value: 2.00				
2004A	112,090,000	—	—	—	0.75	—
2004A Proof	75,000	Value: 2.00				
2004D	117,690,000	—	—	—	0.75	—
2004D Proof	75,000	Value: 2.00				
2004F	134,490,000	—	—	—	0.75	—
2004F Proof	75,000	Value: 2.00				
2004G	78,490,000	—	—	—	0.75	—
2004G Proof	75,000	Value: 2.00				
2004J	117,690,000	—	—	—	0.75	—
2004J Proof	75,000	Value: 2.00				
2005A	44,090,000	—	—	—	0.75	—
2005A Proof	75,000	Value: 2.00				
2005D	46,290,000	—	—	—	0.75	—
2005D Proof	75,000	Value: 2.00				
2005F	52,890,000	—	—	—	0.75	—
2005F Proof	75,000	Value: 2.00				
2005G	30,890,000	—	—	—	0.75	—
2005G Proof	75,000	Value: 2.00				
2005J	46,290,000	—	—	—	0.75	—
2005J Proof	75,000	Value: 2.00				
2006A	27,090,000	—	—	—	0.75	—
2006A Proof	75,000	Value: 2.00				
2006D	28,440,000	—	—	—	0.75	—
2006D Proof	75,000	Value: 2.00				
2006F	32,490,000	—	—	—	0.75	—
2006F Proof	75,000	Value: 2.00				
2006G	18,990,000	—	—	—	0.75	—
2006G Proof	75,000	Value: 2.00				
2006J	28,440,000	—	—	—	0.75	—
2006J Proof	75,000	Value: 2.00				
2007A	52,490,000	—	—	—	0.75	—
2007A Proof	75,000	Value: 2.00				
2007D	55,110,000	—	—	—	0.75	—
2007D Proof	75,000	Value: 2.00				
2007F	62,970,000	—	—	—	0.75	—
2007F Proof	75,000	Value: 2.00				
2007G	36,770,000	—	—	—	0.75	—
2007G Proof	75,000	Value: 2.00				
2007J	55,110,000	—	—	—	0.75	—
2007J Proof	75,000	Value: 2.00				
2008A	29,280,000	—	—	—	0.75	—
2008A Proof	70,000	Value: 2.00				
2008D	30,740,000	—	—	—	0.75	—
2008D Proof	70,000	Value: 2.00				
2008F	35,120,000	—	—	—	0.75	—
2008F Proof	70,000	Value: 2.00				
2008G	24,520,000	—	—	—	0.75	—
2008G Proof	70,000	Value: 2.00				
2008J	30,740,000	—	—	—	0.75	—
2008J Proof	70,000	Value: 2.00				
2009A	39,660,000	—	—	—	0.75	—
2009A Proof	50,000	Value: 2.00				
2009D	41,640,000	—	—	—	0.75	—
2009D Proof	50,000	Value: 2.00				
2009F	47,580,000	—	—	—	0.75	—
2009F Proof	50,000	Value: 2.00				
2009G	77,780,000	—	—	—	0.75	—
2009G Proof	50,000	Value: 2.00				
2009J	41,640,000	—	—	—	0.75	—
2009J Proof	50,000	Value: 2.00				
2010A	39,854,000	—	—	—	0.75	—
2010A Proof	45,150	Value: 2.00				

Date	Mintage	F	VF	XF	Unc	BU
2010D	41,837,000	—	—	—	0.75	—
2010D Proof	40,120	Value: 2.00				
2010F	47,807,000	—	—	—	0.75	—
2010F Proof	40,120	Value: 2.00				
2010G	20,903,000	—	—	—	0.75	—
2010G Proof	40,120	Value: 2.00				
2010J	41,837,000	—	—	—	0.75	—
2010J Proof	40,120	Value: 2.00				
2011A	59,248,000	—	—	—	0.75	—
2011A Proof	Est. 43,000	Value: 2.25				
2011D	62,204,000	—	—	—	0.75	—
2011D Proof	Est. 37,000	Value: 2.25				
2011F	710,814,000	—	—	—	0.75	—
2011F Proof	Est. 37,000	Value: 2.25				
2011G	41,484,000	—	—	—	0.75	—
2011G Proof	Est. 37,000	Value: 2.25				
2011J	62,240,000	—	—	—	0.75	—
2011J Proof	Est. 37,000	Value: 2.25				
2012A	41,850,000	—	—	—	0.75	—
2012A Proof	Est. 40,940	Value: 2.25				
2012D	43,940,000	—	—	—	0.75	—
2012D Proof	Est. 40,000	Value: 2.25				
2012F	50,210,000	—	—	—	0.75	—
2012F Proof	Est. 40,000	Value: 2.25				
2012G	29,310,000	—	—	—	0.75	—
2012G Proof	Est. 40,000	Value: 2.25				
2012J	43,940,000	—	—	—	0.75	—
2012J Proof	Est. 40,000	Value: 2.25				
2013A	—	—	—	—	0.40	—
2013A Proof	Est. 40,000	Value: 2.25				
2013D	—	—	—	—	0.40	—
2013D Proof	Est. 40,000	Value: 2.25				
2013F	—	—	—	—	0.40	—
2013F Proof	Est. 40,000	Value: 2.25				
2013G	—	—	—	—	0.40	—
2013G Proof	Est. 40,000	Value: 2.25				
2013J	—	—	—	—	0.40	—
2013J Proof	Est. 40,000	Value: 2.50				

KM# 210 10 EURO CENT

4.1000 g., Brass, 19.75 mm. **Obv:** Brandenburg Gate **Rev:** Denomination and map **Edge:** Reeded

Date	Mintage	F	VF	XF	Unc	BU
2002A	696,240,000	—	—	—	0.75	—
2002A Proof	75,000	Value: 2.00				
2002D	722,040,000	—	—	—	0.75	—
2002D Proof	75,000	Value: 2.00				
2002F	838,890,000	—	—	—	0.75	—
2002F Proof	75,000	Value: 2.00				
2002G	494,390,000	—	—	—	0.75	—
2002G Proof	75,000	Value: 2.00				
2002J	758,730,000	—	—	—	0.75	—
2002J Proof	75,000	Value: 2.00				
2003A	50,750,000	—	—	—	1.25	—
2003A Proof	75,000	Value: 2.00				
2003D	50,940,000	—	—	—	1.25	—
2003D Proof	75,000	Value: 2.00				
2003F	6,090,000	—	—	—	2.00	—
2003F Proof	75,000	Value: 2.00				
2003G	13,090,000	—	—	—	1.25	—
2003G Proof	75,000	Value: 2.00				
2003J	25,590,000	—	—	—	1.25	—
2003J Proof	75,000	Value: 2.00				
2004A In sets only	99,000	—	—	—	4.50	—
2004A Proof	75,000	Value: 2.00				
2004D	11,290,000	—	—	—	1.25	—
2004D Proof	75,000	Value: 2.00				
2004F	51,450,000	—	—	—	1.25	—
2004F Proof	75,000	Value: 2.00				
2004G	15,550,000	—	—	—	1.25	—
2004G Proof	75,000	Value: 2.00				
2004J In sets only	90,000	—	—	—	4.50	—
2004J Proof	75,000	Value: 2.00				
2005A In sets only	90,000	—	—	—	4.50	—
2005A Proof	75,000	Value: 2.00				
2005D In sets only	90,000	—	—	—	4.50	—
2005D Proof	75,000	Value: 2.00				
2005F In sets only	90,000	—	—	—	4.50	—
2005F Proof	75,000	Value: 2.00				
2005G In sets only	90,000	—	—	—	4.50	—
2005G Proof	75,000	Value: 2.00				
2005J In sets only	90,000	—	—	—	4.50	—
2005J Proof	75,000	Value: 2.00				
2006A In sets only	90,000	—	—	—	4.50	—
2006A Proof	75,000	Value: 2.00				
2006D In sets only	90,000	—	—	—	4.50	—
2006D Proof	75,000	Value: 2.00				
2006F In sets only	90,000	—	—	—	4.50	—
2006F Proof	75,000	Value: 2.00				
2006G In sets only	90,000	—	—	—	4.50	—
2006G Proof	75,000	Value: 2.00				
2006J In sets only	90,000	—	—	—	4.50	—
2006J Proof	75,000	Value: 2.00				

KM# 254 10 EURO CENT

4.1000 g., Brass, 19.75 mm. **Obv:** Brandenburg Gate **Rev:** Relief map of Western Europe, stars, lines and value **Edge:** Reeded

Date	Mintage	F	VF	XF	Unc	BU
2007A In sets only	90,000	—	—	—	4.50	—
2007A Proof	75,000	Value: 2.00				
2007D In sets only	90,000	—	—	—	4.50	—
2007D Proof	75,000	Value: 2.00				
2007F In sets only	90,000	—	—	—	4.50	—
2007F Proof	75,000	Value: 2.00				
2007G In sets only	90,000	—	—	—	4.50	—
2007G Proof	75,000	Value: 2.00				
2007J In sets only	90,000	—	—	—	4.50	—
2007J Proof	75,000	Value: 2.00				
2008A In sets only	80,000	—	—	—	4.50	—
2008A Proof	70,000	Value: 2.00				
2008D In sets only	80,000	—	—	—	4.50	—
2008D Proof	70,000	Value: 2.00				
2008F In sets only	80,000	—	—	—	4.50	—
2008F Proof	70,000	Value: 2.00				
2008G In sets only	80,000	—	—	—	4.50	—
2008G Proof	70,000	Value: 2.00				
2008J In sets only	80,000	—	—	—	4.50	—
2008J Proof	70,000	Value: 2.00				
2009A In sets only	60,000	—	—	—	4.50	—
2009A Proof	50,000	Value: 2.00				
2009D In sets only	60,000	—	—	—	4.50	—
2009D Proof	50,000	Value: 2.00				
2009F Proof	50,000	Value: 2.00				
2009G In sets only	60,000	—	—	—	4.50	—
2009G Proof	50,000	Value: 2.00				
2009J In sets only	60,000	—	—	—	4.50	—
2009J Proof	50,000	Value: 2.00				
2010A In sets only	53,800	—	—	—	4.00	—
2010A Proof	45,150	Value: 2.00				
2010D In sets only	46,800	—	—	—	4.00	—
2010D Proof	40,120	Value: 2.00				
2010F In sets only	46,800	—	—	—	4.00	—
2010F Proof	40,120	Value: 2.00				
2010G In sets only	46,800	—	—	—	4.00	—
2010G Proof	40,120	Value: 2.00				
2010J In sets only	46,800	—	—	—	4.00	—
2010J Proof	40,120	Value: 2.00				
2011A In sets only	Est. 55,000	—	—	—	4.00	—
2011A Proof	48,000	Value: 2.75				
2011D In sets only	43,000	—	—	—	4.00	—
2011D Proof	37,000	Value: 2.75				
2011F In sets only	44,000	—	—	—	4.00	—
2011F Proof	37,000	Value: 2.75				
2011G In sets only	44,000	—	—	—	4.00	—
2011G Proof	37,000	Value: 2.75				
2011J In sets only	44,000	—	—	—	4.00	—
2011J Proof	37,000	Value: 2.75				
2012A In sets only	Est. 50,000	—	—	—	3.00	—
2012A Proof	Est. 40,000	Value: 2.75				
2012D In sets only	Est. 50,000	—	—	—	3.00	—
2012D Proof	Est. 40,000	Value: 2.75				
2012F In sets only	Est. 50,000	—	—	—	3.00	—
2012F Proof	Est. 40,000	Value: 2.75				
2012G In sets only	Est. 50,000	—	—	—	3.00	—
2012G Proof	Est. 40,000	Value: 2.75				
2012J In sets only	Est. 50,000	—	—	—	3.00	—
2012J Proof	Est. 40,000	Value: 2.75				
2013A	—	—	—	—	—	—
2013A Proof	Est. 40,000	Value: 2.75				
2013D	—	—	—	—	—	—
2013D Proof	Est. 40,000	Value: 2.75				
2013F	—	—	—	—	—	—
2013F Proof	Est. 40,000	Value: 2.75				
2013F	—	—	—	—	—	—
2013G Proof	Est. 40,000	Value: 2.75				
2013J	—	—	—	—	—	—
2013J Proof	Est. 40,000	Value: 2.75				

KM# 211 20 EURO CENT

5.7400 g., Brass, 22.25 mm. **Obv:** Brandenburg Gate **Rev:** Denomination and map **Edge:** Notched

Date	Mintage	F	VF	XF	Unc	BU
2002A	378,240,000	—	—	—	1.00	—
2002A Proof	75,000	Value: 3.00				
2002D	367,090,000	—	—	—	1.00	—
2002D Proof	75,000	Value: 3.00				
2002F	421,690,000	—	—	—	1.00	—
2002F Proof	75,000	Value: 3.00				
2002G	251,990,000	—	—	—	1.00	—
2002G Proof	75,000	Value: 3.00				
2002J	441,090,000	—	—	—	1.00	—
2002J Proof	75,000	Value: 3.00				
2003A	41,950,000	—	—	—	1.00	—
2003A Proof	75,000	Value: 3.00				
2003D	24,190,000	—	—	—	1.00	—
2003D Proof	75,000	Value: 3.00				
2003F	82,490,000	—	—	—	1.00	—
2003F Proof	75,000	Value: 3.00				
2003G	42,190,000	—	—	—	1.00	—
2003G Proof	75,000	Value: 3.00				
2003J In sets only	90,000	—	—	—	4.50	—
2003J Proof	75,000	Value: 3.00				
2004A In sets only	90,000	—	—	—	4.50	—
2004A Proof	75,000	Value: 3.00				
2004D	49,850,000	—	—	—	2.50	—
2004D Proof	75,000	Value: 3.00				
2004F In sets only	90,000	—	—	—	4.50	—
2004F Proof	75,000	Value: 3.00				
2004G In sets only	90,000	—	—	—	4.50	—
2004G Proof	75,000	Value: 3.00				
2004J In sets only	90,000	—	—	—	4.50	—
2004J Proof	75,000	Value: 3.00				
2005A	8,090,000	—	—	—	1.00	—
2005A Proof	75,000	Value: 3.00				
2005D	8,490,000	—	—	—	1.00	—
2005D Proof	75,000	Value: 3.00				
2005F	9,690,000	—	—	—	1.00	—
2005F Proof	75,000	Value: 3.00				
2005G	5,690,000	—	—	—	1.00	—
2005G Proof	75,000	Value: 3.00				
2005J	8,490,000	—	—	—	1.00	—
2005J Proof	75,000	Value: 3.00				
2006A	39,090,000	—	—	—	1.00	—
2006A Proof	75,000	Value: 3.00				
2006D	41,040,000	—	—	—	1.00	—
2006D Proof	75,000	Value: 3.00				
2006F	46,890,000	—	—	—	1.00	—
2006F Proof	75,000	Value: 3.00				
2006G	27,390,000	—	—	—	1.00	—
2006G Proof	75,000	Value: 3.00				
2006J	41,040,000	—	—	—	1.00	—
2006J Proof	75,000	Value: 3.00				
2007F Error die paring	—	—	—	60.00	75.00	—

KM# 255 20 EURO CENT

5.7400 g., Brass, 22.25 mm. **Obv:** Brandenburg Gate **Rev:** Relief map of Western Europe, stars, lines and value **Edge:** Notched

Date	Mintage	F	VF	XF	Unc	BU
2007A	21,690,000	—	—	—	1.00	—
2007A Proof	75,000	Value: 3.00				
2007D	22,770,000	—	—	—	1.00	—
2007D Proof	75,000	Value: 3.00				
2007F	26,010,000	—	—	—	1.00	—
2007F Proof	75,000	Value: 3.00				
2007G	15,210,000	—	—	—	1.00	—
2007G Proof	75,000	Value: 3.00				
2007J	23,020,000	—	—	—	1.00	—
2007J Proof	75,000	Value: 3.00				
2008A	15,880,000	—	—	—	1.00	—
2008A Proof	70,000	Value: 3.00				
2008D	16,670,000	—	—	—	1.00	—
2008D Proof	70,000	Value: 3.00				
2008F	19,040,000	—	—	—	1.00	—
2008F Proof	70,000	Value: 3.00				
2008G	11,140,000	—	—	—	1.00	—
2008G Proof	70,000	Value: 3.00				
2008J	16,420,000	—	—	—	1.00	—
2008J Proof	70,000	Value: 3.00				
2009A	21,660,000	—	—	—	1.00	—
2009A Proof	50,000	Value: 3.00				
2009D	22,740,000	—	—	—	1.00	—
2009D Proof	50,000	Value: 3.00				
2009F	25,980,000	—	—	—	1.00	—
2009F Proof	50,000	Value: 3.00				
2009G	15,180,000	—	—	—	1.00	—
2009G Proof	50,000	Value: 3.00				
2009J	22,740,000	—	—	—	1.00	—
2009J Proof	50,000	Value: 3.00				
2010A	24,454,000	—	—	—	1.00	—
2010A Proof	45,150	Value: 3.00				
2010D	25,667,000	—	—	—	1.00	—
2010D Proof	40,120	Value: 3.00				
2010F	29,327,000	—	—	—	1.00	—
2010F Proof	40,120	Value: 3.00				
2010G	17,127,000	—	—	—	1.00	—
2010G Proof	40,120	Value: 3.00				
2010J	25,667,000	—	—	—	1.00	—
2010J Proof	40,120	Value: 3.00				
2011A	33,048,000	—	—	—	1.00	—
2011A Proof	43,000	Value: 3.00				
2011D	34,694,000	—	—	—	1.00	—
2011D Proof	37,000	Value: 3.00				
2011F	39,644,000	—	—	—	1.00	—
2011F Proof	37,000	Value: 3.00				
2011G	23,144,000	—	—	—	1.00	—
2011F Proof	37,000	Value: 3.00				
2011J	34,694,000	—	—	—	1.00	—
2011J Proof	37,000	Value: 3.00				
2012A	29,250,000	—	—	—	1.00	—
2012A Proof	Est. 40,000	Value: 3.00				

Date	Mintage	F	VF	XF	Unc	BU
2012D	Est. 23,810,000	—	—	—	1.00	—
2012D Proof	Est. 40,000	Value: 3.00				
2012F	Est. 25,490,000	—	—	—	1.00	—
2012F Proof	Est. 40,000	Value: 3.00				
2012G	Est. 14,890,000	—	—	—	1.00	—
2012G Proof	Est. 40,000	Value: 3.00				
2012J	Est. 22,310,000	—	—	—	1.00	—
2012J Proof	Est. 40,000	Value: 3.00				
2013A	—	—	—	—	0.70	—
2013A Proof	Est. 40,000	Value: 3.00				
2013D	—	—	—	—	0.70	—
2013D Proof	Est. 40,000	Value: 3.00				
2013F	—	—	—	—	0.70	—
2013F Proof	Est. 40,000	Value: 3.00				
2013G	—	—	—	—	0.70	—
2013G Proof	Est. 40,000	Value: 3.00				
2013J	—	—	—	—	0.70	—
2013J Proof	Est. 40,000	Value: 3.00				

KM# 212 50 EURO CENT

7.8000 g., Brass, 24.25 mm. **Obv:** Brandenburg Gate **Rev:** Denomination and map **Edge:** Reeded

Date	Mintage	F	VF	XF	Unc	BU
2002A	337,840,000	—	—	—	1.75	—
2002A Proof	75,000	Value: 4.00				
2002D	370,330,000	—	—	—	1.75	—
2002D Proof	75,000	Value: 4.00				
2002F	430,570,000	—	—	—	1.75	—
2002F Proof	75,000	Value: 4.00				
2002G	256,650,000	—	—	—	1.75	—
2002G Proof	75,000	Value: 4.00				
2002J	401,490,000	—	—	—	1.75	—
2002J Proof	75,000	Value: 4.00				
2003A In sets only	90,000	—	—	—	4.50	—
2003A Proof	75,000	Value: 4.00				
2003D	70,710,000	—	—	—	2.00	—
2003D Proof	75,000	Value: 4.00				
2003F In sets only	90,000	—	—	—	4.50	—
2003F Proof	75,000	Value: 4.00				
2003G In sets only	90,000	—	—	—	4.50	—
2003G Proof	75,000	Value: 4.00				
2003J	39,690,000	—	—	—	1.75	—
2003J Proof	75,000	Value: 4.00				
2004A	82,350,000	—	—	—	1.75	—
2004A Proof	75,000	Value: 4.00				
2004D In sets only	90,000	—	—	—	4.50	—
2004D Proof	75,000	Value: 4.00				
2004F	73,610,000	—	—	—	1.75	—
2004F Proof	75,000	Value: 4.00				
2004G	37,530,000	—	—	—	1.75	—
2004G Proof	75,000	Value: 4.00				
2004J In sets only	90,000	—	—	—	4.50	—
2004J Proof	75,000	Value: 4.00				
2005A In sets only	90,000	—	—	—	4.50	—
2005A Proof	75,000	Value: 4.00				
2005D In sets only	90,000	—	—	—	4.50	—
2005D Proof	75,000	Value: 4.00				
2005F In sets only	90,000	—	—	—	4.50	—
2005F Proof	75,000	Value: 4.00				
2005G In sets only	90,000	—	—	—	4.50	—
2005G Proof	75,000	Value: 4.00				
2005J In sets only	90,000	—	—	—	4.50	—
2005J Proof	75,000	Value: 4.00				
2006A In sets only	90,000	—	—	—	4.50	—
2006A Proof	75,000	Value: 4.00				
2006D In sets only	90,000	—	—	—	4.50	—
2006D Proof	75,000	Value: 4.00				
2006F In sets only	90,000	—	—	—	4.50	—
2006F Proof	75,000	Value: 4.00				
2006G In sets only	90,000	—	—	—	4.50	—
2006G Proof	75,000	Value: 4.00				
2006J In sets only	90,000	—	—	—	4.50	—
2006J Proof	75,000	Value: 4.00				

KM# 256 50 EURO CENT

7.8000 g., Brass, 24.25 mm. **Obv:** Brandenburg Gate **Rev:** Relief map of Western Europe, stars, lines and value **Edge:** Reeded

Date	Mintage	F	VF	XF	Unc	BU
2007A In sets only	90,000	—	—	—	4.50	—
2007A Proof	75,000	Value: 4.00				
2007D In sets only	90,000	—	—	—	4.50	—
2007D Proof	75,000	Value: 4.00				
2007F In sets only	90,000	—	—	—	4.50	—
2007F Proof	75,000	Value: 4.00				
2007G In sets only	90,000	—	—	—	4.50	—
2007G Proof	75,000	Value: 4.00				
2007J In sets only	90,000	—	—	—	4.50	—
2007J Proof	75,000	Value: 4.00				
2008A In sets only	80,000	—	—	—	4.50	—
2008A Proof	70,000	Value: 4.00				
2008D In sets only	80,000	—	—	—	4.50	—
2008D Proof	70,000	Value: 4.00				
2008F In sets only	80,000	—	—	—	4.50	—
2008F Proof	70,000	Value: 4.00				
2008G In sets only	80,000	—	—	—	4.50	—
2008G Proof	70,000	Value: 4.00				
2008J In sets only	80,000	—	—	—	4.50	—
2008J Proof	70,000	Value: 4.00				
2009A In sets only	60,000	—	—	—	4.50	—
2009A Proof	50,000	Value: 4.00				
2009D In sets only	60,000	—	—	—	4.50	—
2009D Proof	50,000	Value: 4.00				
2009F In sets only	60,000	—	—	—	4.50	—
2009F Proof	50,000	Value: 4.00				
2009G In sets only	60,000	—	—	—	4.50	—
2009G Proof	50,000	Value: 4.00				
2009J In sets only	60,000	—	—	—	4.50	—
2009J Proof	50,000	Value: 4.00				
2010A In sets only	53,800	—	—	—	4.00	—
2010A Proof	45,150	Value: 4.00				
2010D In sets only	46,800	—	—	—	4.00	—
2010D Proof	40,120	Value: 4.00				
2010F In sets only	46,800	—	—	—	4.00	—
2010F Proof	40,120	Value: 4.00				
2010G In sets only	46,800	—	—	—	4.00	—
2010G Proof	40,120	Value: 4.00				
2010J In sets only	46,800	—	—	—	4.00	—
2010J Proof	40,120	Value: 4.00				
2011A In sets only	Est. 48,000	—	—	—	4.00	—
2011A Proof	Est. 43,000	Value: 4.00				
2011D In sets only	Est. 44,000	—	—	—	4.00	—
2011D Proof	Est. 37,000	Value: 4.00				
2011F In sets only	Est. 44,000	—	—	—	4.00	—
2011F Proof	Est. 37,000	Value: 4.00				
2011G In sets only	Est. 44,000	—	—	—	4.00	—
2011G Proof	Est. 37,000	Value: 4.00				
2011J In sets only	Est. 44,000	—	—	—	4.00	—
2011J Proof	Est. 37,000	Value: 4.00				
2012A In sets only	Est. 50,000	—	—	—	4.00	—
2012A Proof	Est. 40,000	Value: 4.00				
2012D In sets only	Est. 50,000	—	—	—	4.00	—
2012D Proof	Est. 40,000	Value: 4.00				
2012F In sets only	Est. 50,000	—	—	—	4.00	—
2012F Proof	Est. 40,000	Value: 4.00				
2012G In sets only	Est. 50,000	—	—	—	4.00	—
2012G Proof	Est. 40,000	Value: 4.00				
2012J In sets only	Est. 50,000	—	—	—	4.00	—
2012J Proof	Est. 40,000	Value: 4.00				
2013A	—	—	—	—	—	—
2013A Proof	Est. 40,000	Value: 4.00				
2013D	—	—	—	—	—	—
2013D Proof	Est. 40,000	Value: 4.00				
2013F	—	—	—	—	—	—
2013F Proof	Est. 40,000	Value: 4.00				
2013G	—	—	—	—	—	—
2013G Proof	Est. 40,000	Value: 4.00				
2013J	—	—	—	—	—	—
2013J Proof	Est. 40,000	Value: 4.00				

KM# 213 EURO

7.5000 g., Bi-Metallic Copper-Nickel center in Nickel-Brass ring, 23.25 mm. **Obv:** Stylized eagle **Rev:** Denomination over map **Edge:** Segmented reeding

Date	Mintage	F	VF	XF	Unc	BU
2002A	367,990,000	—	—	—	2.50	—
2002A Proof	75,000	Value: 6.50				
2002D	372,690,000	—	—	—	2.50	—
2002D Proof	75,000	Value: 6.50				
2002F	439,890,000	—	—	—	2.50	—
2002F Proof	75,000	Value: 6.50				
2002G	266,440,000	—	—	—	2.50	—
2002G Proof	75,000	Value: 6.50				
2002J	372,400,000	—	—	—	2.50	—
2002J Proof	75,000	Value: 6.50				
2003A	50,340,000	—	—	—	2.50	—
2003A Proof	75,000	Value: 6.50				
2003D In sets only	90,000	—	—	—	5.50	—
2003D Proof	75,000	Value: 6.50				
2003F In sets only	90,000	—	—	—	5.50	—
2003F Proof	75,000	Value: 6.50				
2003G In sets only	90,000	—	—	—	5.50	—
2003G Proof	75,000	Value: 6.50				
2003J	29,940,000	—	—	—	2.50	—
2003J Proof	75,000	Value: 6.50				
2004A	21,950,000	—	—	—	2.50	—
2004A Proof	75,000	Value: 6.50				
2004D	89,350,000	—	—	—	2.50	—
2004D Proof	75,000	Value: 6.50				
2004F	88,290,000	—	—	—	2.50	—
2004F Proof	75,000	Value: 6.50				
2004G	41,740,000	—	—	—	2.50	—
2004G Proof	75,000	Value: 6.50				
2004J In sets only	90,000	—	—	—	5.50	—
2004J Proof	75,000	Value: 6.50				
2005A In sets only	90,000	—	—	—	5.50	—
2005A Proof	75,000	Value: 5.00				
2005D In sets only	90,000	—	—	—	5.50	—
2005D Proof	75,000	Value: 5.00				
2005F In sets only	90,000	—	—	—	5.50	—
2005F Proof	75,000	Value: 5.00				
2005G In sets only	90,000	—	—	—	5.50	—
2005G Proof	75,000	Value: 5.00				
2005J	59,930,000	—	—	—	2.50	—
2005J Proof	75,000	Value: 5.00				
2006A In sets only	90,000	—	—	—	5.50	—
2006A Proof	75,000	Value: 5.00				
2006D In sets only	90,000	—	—	—	5.50	—
2006D Proof	75,000	Value: 5.00				
2006F In sets only	90,000	—	—	—	5.50	—
2006F Proof	75,000	Value: 5.00				
2006G In sets only	90,000	—	—	—	5.50	—
2006G Proof	75,000	Value: 5.00				
2006J In sets only	90,000	—	—	—	5.50	—
2006J Proof	75,000	Value: 5.00				

KM# 257 EURO

7.5000 g., Bi-Metallic Copper-Nickel center in Nickel-Brass ring, 23.25 mm. **Obv:** Stylized eagle **Rev:** Relief map of Western Europe, stars, lines and value **Edge:** Segmented reeding

Date	Mintage	F	VF	XF	Unc	BU
2007A In sets only	90,000	—	—	—	5.50	—
2007A Proof	75,000	Value: 5.00				
2007D In sets only	90,000	—	—	—	5.50	—
2007D Proof	75,000	Value: 5.00				
2007F In sets only	90,000	—	—	—	5.50	—
2007F Proof	75,000	Value: 5.00				
2007G In sets only	90,000	—	—	—	5.50	—
2007G Proof	75,000	Value: 5.00				
2007J In sets only	90,000	—	—	—	5.50	—
2007J Proof	75,000	Value: 5.00				
2008A In sets only	80,000	—	—	—	5.50	—
2008A Proof	70,000	Value: 5.00				
2008D In sets only	80,000	—	—	—	5.50	—
2008D Proof	70,000	Value: 5.00				
2008F In sets only	80,000	—	—	—	5.50	—
2008F Proof	70,000	Value: 5.00				
2008G In sets only	80,000	—	—	—	5.50	—
2008G Proof	70,000	Value: 5.00				
2008J In sets only	80,000	—	—	—	5.50	—
2008J Proof	70,000	Value: 5.00				
2009A In sets only	60,000	—	—	—	5.50	—
2009A Proof	50,000	Value: 5.00				
2009D In sets only	60,000	—	—	—	5.50	—
2009D Proof	50,000	Value: 5.00				
2009F In sets only	60,000	—	—	—	5.50	—
2009F Proof	50,000	Value: 5.00				
2009G In sets only	60,000	—	—	—	5.50	—
2009G Proof	50,000	Value: 5.00				
2009J In sets only	60,000	—	—	—	5.50	—
2009J Proof	50,000	Value: 5.00				
2010A In sets only	53,800	—	—	—	4.00	—
2010A Proof	45,150	Value: 5.00				
2010D In sets only	46,800	—	—	—	4.00	—
2010D Proof	40,120	Value: 5.00				
2010F In sets only	46,800	—	—	—	4.00	—
2010F Proof	40,120	Value: 5.00				
2010G In sets only	46,800	—	—	—	4.00	—
2010G Proof	40,120	Value: 5.00				
2010J In sets only	46,800	—	—	—	4.00	—
2010J Proof	40,120	Value: 5.00				
2011A In sets only	48,000	—	—	—	4.00	—
2011A Proof	43,000	Value: 5.00				
2011D In sets only	44,000	—	—	—	4.00	—
2011D Proof	37,000	Value: 5.00				
2011F In sets only	44,000	—	—	—	4.00	—
2011F Proof	37,000	Value: 5.00				
2011G In sets only	44,000	—	—	—	4.00	—
2011G Proof	37,000	Value: 5.00				
2011J In sets only	44,000	—	—	—	4.00	—
2011J Proof	Est. 50,000	Value: 5.00				
2012A In sets only	Est. 50,000	—	—	—	4.00	—
2012A Proof	Est. 40,000	Value: 5.00				
2012D In sets only	Est. 50,000	—	—	—	4.00	—
2012D Proof	Est. 40,000	Value: 5.00				
2012F In sets only	Est. 50,000	—	—	—	4.00	—
2012F Proof	Est. 40,000	Value: 5.00				
2012G In sets only	Est. 50,000	—	—	—	4.00	—
2012G Proof	Est. 40,000	Value: 5.00				
2012J In sets only	Est. 50,000	—	—	—	4.00	—
2012J Proof	Est. 40,000	Value: 5.00				

KM# 214 2 EURO

8.5000 g., Bi-Metallic Nickel-Brass center in Copper-Nickel ring, 25.75 mm. **Obv:** Stylized eagle **Rev:** Denomination and map **Edge:** Reeded and "EINIGKEIT UND RECHT UND FREIHEIT"

Date	Mintage	F	VF	XF	Unc	BU
2002A	239,010,000	—	—	—	4.50	—
2002A Proof	75,000	Value: 12.50				

Date	Mintage	F	VF	XF	Unc	BU
2002D	231,390,000	—	—	—	4.50	—
2002D Proof	75,000	Value: 12.50				
2002F	281,180,000	—	—	—	4.50	—
2002F Proof	75,000	Value: 12.50				
2002G	181,040,000	—	—	—	4.50	—
2002G Proof	75,000	Value: 12.50				
2002J	257,910,000	—	—	—	4.50	—
2002J Proof	75,000	Value: 12.50				
2003A	20,560,000	—	—	—	4.50	—
2003A Proof	75,000	Value: 12.50				
2003D	22,260,000	—	—	—	4.50	—
2003D Proof	75,000	Value: 12.50				
2003F	24,550,000	—	—	—	4.50	—
2003F Proof	75,000	Value: 12.50				
2003G	29,239,000	—	—	—	4.50	—
2003G Proof	75,000	Value: 12.50				
2003J	19,590,000	—	—	—	4.50	—
2003J Proof	75,000	Value: 12.50				
2004A	31,660,000	—	—	—	4.50	—
2004A Proof	75,000	Value: 12.50				
2004D	19,930,000	—	—	—	4.50	—
2004D Proof	75,000	Value: 12.50				
2004F In sets only	90,000	—	—	—	5.50	—
2004F Proof	75,000	Value: 12.50				
2004G In sets only	90,000	—	—	—	5.50	—
2004G Proof	75,000	Value: 12.50				
2004J	22,600,000	—	—	—	4.50	—
2004J Proof	75,000	Value: 12.50				
2005A In sets only	90,000	—	—	—	5.50	—
2005A Proof	75,000	Value: 10.00				
2005D In sets only	90,000	—	—	—	5.50	—
2005D Proof	75,000	Value: 10.00				
2005F In sets only	90,000	—	—	—	5.50	—
2005F Proof	75,000	Value: 10.00				
2005G In sets only	90,000	—	—	—	5.50	—
2005G Proof	75,000	Value: 10.00				
2005J In sets only	90,000	—	—	—	5.50	—
2005J Proof	75,000	Value: 10.00				
2006A In sets only	90,000	—	—	—	5.50	—
2006A Proof	75,000	Value: 10.00				
2006D In sets only	90,000	—	—	—	5.50	—
2006D Proof	75,000	Value: 10.00				
2006F In sets only	90,000	—	—	—	5.50	—
2006F Proof	75,000	Value: 10.00				
2006G In sets only	90,000	—	—	—	5.50	—
2006G Proof	75,000	Value: 10.00				
2006J In sets only	90,000	—	—	—	5.50	—
2006J Proof	75,000	Value: 10.00				

KM# 253 2 EURO

8.5000 g., Bi-Metallic Nickel-Brass center in Copper-Nickel ring, 25.75 mm. **Obv:** Schleswig Holstein castle **Obv. Legend:** BUNDESREPULIK DEUTSCHLAND **Obv. Inscription:** SCHLESWIG- / HOLSTEIN **Rev:** Denomination over map

Date	Mintage	F	VF	XF	Unc	BU
2006A	6,170,000	—	—	—	5.00	6.00
2006A Proof	145,000	Value: 10.00				
2006D	6,470,000	—	—	—	5.00	6.00
2006D Proof	145,000	Value: 10.00				
2006F	7,370,000	—	—	—	5.00	6.00
2006F Proof	145,000	Value: 10.00				
2006G	4,370,000	—	—	—	5.00	6.00
2006G Proof	145,000	Value: 10.00				
2006J	6,470,000	—	—	—	5.00	6.00
2006J Proof	145,000	Value: 10.00				

KM# 259 2 EURO

8.5000 g., Bi-Metallic Nickel-Brass center in Copper-Nickel ring, 25.75 mm. **Subject:** 50th Anniversary Treaty of Rome **Obv:** Open treaty book **Obv. Legend:** BUNDESREPUBLIK DEUTSCHLAND **Rev:** Large value at left, modified outline of Europe at right **Edge Lettering:** EINIGKEIT UND RECHT UND FREIHEIT

Date	Mintage	F	VF	XF	Unc	BU
2007A	1,090,000	—	—	—	4.00	5.00
2007A Proof	125,000	Value: 10.00				
2007D	14,590,000	—	—	—	4.00	5.50
2007D Proof	125,000	Value: 10.00				
2007F	8,090,000	—	—	—	4.00	5.50
2007F Proof	125,000	Value: 10.00				
2007G	5,090,000	—	—	—	4.00	5.50
2007G Proof	125,000	Value: 10.00				
2007J	1,590,000	—	—	—	4.00	5.50
2007J Proof	125,000	Value: 10.00				

KM# 260 2 EURO

8.5000 g., Bi-Metallic Nickel-Brass center in Copper-Nickel ring, 25.75 mm. **Obv:** City buildings, Mecklenburg's Schwerin Castle **Obv. Legend:** BUNDESREPUBLIK DEUTSCHLAND **Obv. Inscription:** MECKLENBURG- / VORPOMMERN **Rev:** Large value at left, modified map of Europe at right **Edge Lettering:** EINIGKEIT UND RECHT UND FREIHEIT

Date	Mintage	F	VF	XF	Unc	BU
2007A	1,210,000	—	—	—	4.00	5.50
2007A Proof	145,000	Value: 10.00				
2007D	12,010,000	—	—	—	4.00	5.50
2007D Proof	145,000	Value: 10.00				
2007F	12,110,000	—	—	—	4.00	5.50
2007F Proof	145,000	Value: 10.00				
2007G	4,370,000	—	—	—	4.00	5.50
2007G Proof	145,000	Value: 10.00				
2007J	1,240,000	—	—	—	4.00	5.50
2007J Proof	145,000	Value: 10.00				

KM# 258 2 EURO

8.5000 g., Bi-Metallic Nickel-Brass center in Copper-Nickel ring, 25.75 mm. **Obv:** Stylized eagle **Rev:** Relief map of Western Europe, stars, lines and value **Edge Lettering:** EINIGKEIT UND RECHT UND FREIHEIT

Date	Mintage	F	VF	XF	Unc	BU
2008A	11,480,000	—	—	—	4.50	—
2008A Proof	70,000	Value: 10.00				
2008D	12,050,000	—	—	—	4.50	—
2008D Proof	70,000	Value: 10.00				
2008F	13,760,000	—	—	—	4.50	—
2008F Proof	70,000	Value: 10.00				
2008G	8,060,000	—	—	—	4.50	—
2008G Proof	70,000	Value: 10.00				
2008J	12,050,000	—	—	—	4.50	—
2008J Proof	70,000	Value: 10.00				
2010A	19,654,000	—	—	—	4.50	—
2010A Proof	45,150	Value: 10.00				
2010D	20,627,000	—	—	—	4.50	—
2010D Proof	40,120	Value: 10.00				
2010F	23,567,000	—	—	—	4.50	—
2010F Proof	40,120	Value: 10.00				
2010G	13,767,000	—	—	—	4.50	—
2010G Proof	40,120	Value: 10.00				
2010J	20,627,000	—	—	—	4.50	—
2010J Proof	40,120	Value: 10.00				
2011A	22,848,000	—	—	—	4.50	—
2011A Proof	43,000	Value: 10.00				
2011D	23,984,000	—	—	—	4.50	—
2011D Proof	37,000	Value: 10.00				
2011F	27,404,000	—	—	—	4.50	—
2011F Proof	37,000	Value: 10.00				
2011G	16,004,000	—	—	—	4.50	—
2011G Proof	37,000	Value: 10.00				
2011J	23,984,000	—	—	—	4.50	—
2011J Proof	37,000	Value: 10.00				
2012A Proof	—	Value: 10.00				
2012J Proof	—	Value: 10.00				

KM# 261 2 EURO

8.5000 g., Bi-Metallic Nickel-Brass center in Copper-Nickel ring, 25.75 mm. **Obv:** Hamburg Cathedral **Obv. Legend:** BUNDESREPUBLIK DEUTSCHLAND **Obv. Inscription:** HAMBURG **Rev:** Large value at left, modified outline of Europe at right **Edge Lettering:** EINIGKEIT UND RECHT UND FREIHEIT

Date	Mintage	F	VF	XF	Unc	BU
2008A	1,160,000	—	—	—	4.00	5.50
2008A Proof	140,000	Value: 10.00				
2008D	9,060,000	—	—	—	4.00	5.50
2008D Proof	140,000	Value: 10.00				
2008F	9,760,000	—	—	—	4.00	5.50
2008F Proof	140,000	Value: 10.00				
2008G	4,360,000	—	—	—	4.00	5.50
2008G Proof	140,000	Value: 10.00				
2008J	6,460,000	—	—	—	4.00	5.50
2008J Proof	140,000	Value: 10.00				

KM# 261A 2 EURO

8.5000 g., Bi-Metallic Nickel-Brass center in Copper-Nickel ring, 25.75 mm. **Obv:** Hamburg Cathedral **Rev:** Denomination over map **Edge Lettering:** EINIGKEIT UND RECHT UND FREIHEIT **Note:** Mule with old reverse Euro Zone map.

Date	Mintage	F	VF	XF	Unc	BU
2008F	Inc. above	—	—	—	—	30.00

KM# 277 2 EURO

8.5000 g., Bi-Metallic Nickel-Brass center in Copper-Nickel ring, 25.75 mm. **Subject:** EMU, 10th Anniversary **Obv:** Stick figure and E symbol

Date	Mintage	F	VF	XF	Unc	BU
2009A	6,060,000	—	—	—	4.50	5.00
2009A Proof	80,000	Value: 10.00				
2009D	6,360,000	—	—	—	4.50	5.00
2009D Proof	80,000	Value: 10.00				
2009F	7,260,000	—	—	—	4.50	5.00
2009F Proof	80,000	Value: 10.00				
2009G	4,260,000	—	—	—	4.50	5.00
2009G Proof	80,000	Value: 10.00				
2009J	6,360,000	—	—	—	4.50	5.00
2009J Proof	80,000	Value: 10.00				

KM# 276 2 EURO

8.5000 g., Bi-Metallic Nickel-Brass center in Copper-Nickel ring, 25.75 mm. **Obv:** Building in Saarland **Rev:** Value and map

Date	Mintage	F	VF	XF	Unc	BU
2009A	6,110,000	—	—	—	4.50	5.00
2009A Proof	100,000	Value: 10.00				
2009D	6,410,000	—	—	—	4.50	5.00
2009D Proof	100,000	Value: 10.00				
2009F	7,310,000	—	—	—	4.50	5.00
2009F Proof	100,000	Value: 10.00				
2009G	4,310,000	—	—	—	4.50	5.00
2009G Proof	100,000	Value: 10.00				
2009J	6,410,000	—	—	—	4.50	5.00
2009J Proof	100,000	Value: 10.00				

KM# 285 2 EURO

8.5000 g., Bi-Metallic Nickel-Brass center in Copper-Nickel ring, 25.75 mm. **Obv:** Bremen town hall and statue and knight statue **Rev:** Value and map

Date	Mintage	F	VF	XF	Unc	BU
2010A	6,104,000	—	—	—	4.50	5.00
2010A Proof	100,000	Value: 10.00				
2010D	6,397,000	—	—	—	4.50	5.00
2010D Proof	100,000	Value: 10.00				
2010F	7,297,000	—	—	—	4.50	5.00
2010F Proof	100,000	Value: 10.00				
2010G	4,297,000	—	—	—	4.50	5.00
2010G Proof	100,000	Value: 10.00				
2010J	6,397,000	—	—	—	4.50	5.00
2010J Proof	100,000	Value: 10.00				

KM# 293 2 EURO

8.5000 g., Bi-Metallic Nickel-Brass center in Copper-Nickel ring, 25.75 mm. **Obv:** Cologne Cathedral **Obv. Legend:** NORDRHEIN - WESTFALEN

Date	Mintage	F	VF	XF	Unc	BU
2011A	6,102,000	—	—	—	5.00	7.50
2011A Proof	102,000	Value: 10.00				
2011D	6,402,000	—	—	—	5.00	7.50

Date	Mintage	F	VF	XF	Unc	BU
2011D Proof	102,000	Value: 10.00				
2011F	7,302,000	—	—	—	5.00	7.50
2011F Proof	102,000	Value: 10.00				
2011G	4,302,000	—	—	—	5.00	7.50
2011G Proof	102,000	Value: 10.00				
2011J	6,402,000	—	—	—	5.00	7.50
2011J Proof	102,000	Value: 10.00				

KM# 305 2 EURO

8.5000 g., Bi-Metallic Nickel-Brass center in Copper-Nickel ring, 25.75 mm. **Series:** German States **Subject:** Bavaria, Neuschwanstein Castle **Rev:** Relief map of Europe, stars, lines and value **Edge Lettering:** EINIGKEIT UND RECHT UND FREIHEIT

Date	Mintage	F	VF	XF	Unc	BU
2012A	Est. 6,100,000	—	—	—	4.00	5.00
2012A Proof	—	Value: 10.00				
2012D	Est. 6,400,000	—	—	—	4.00	5.00
2012D Proof	—	Value: 10.00				
2012F	Est. 7,300,000	—	—	—	4.00	5.00
2012F Proof	—	Value: 10.00				
2012G	Est. 4,300,000	—	—	—	4.00	5.00
2012G Proof	—	Value: 10.00				
2012J	Est. 6,400,000	—	—	—	4.00	5.00
2012J Proof	—	Value: 10.00				

KM# 306 2 EURO

8.5000 g., Bi-Metallic Nickel-Brass center in Copper-Nickel ring, 25.75 mm. **Subject:** Euro coinage, 10th Anniversary **Obv:** Euro symbol on globe at center, child-like rendering around **Rev:** Reliev map of Europe, stars, lines and value **Edge Lettering:** EINIGKEIT UND RECHT UND FREIHEIT

Date	Mintage	F	VF	XF	Unc	BU
2012A	Est. 6,100,000	—	—	—	4.00	5.00
2012A Proof	—	Value: 10.00				
2012D	Est. 6,400,000	—	—	—	4.00	5.00
2012D Proof	—	Value: 10.00				
2012F	Est. 7,300,000	—	—	—	4.00	5.00
2012F Proof	—	Value: 10.00				
2012G	Est. 4,300,000	—	—	—	4.00	5.00
2012G Proof	—	Value: 10.00				
2012J	Est. 6,400,000	—	—	—	4.00	5.00
2012J Proof	—	Value: 10.00				

KM# 315 2 EURO

8.5000 g., Bi-Metallic Nickel-Brass center in Copper-Nickel ring, 25.75 mm. **Subject:** Fiftieth Anniversary of the Elysée (Paris) Treaty **Obv:** Heads of Konrad Adenauer and Charles de Gaulle **Rev:** Relief map of Europe, stars, lines and value **Rev. Legend:** TRAITÉ DE L' ÉLYSÉE, ÉLYSÉE-VERTAG and 50 ANS JAHRE **Edge Lettering:** EINIGKEIT UND RECHT UND FREIHEIT

Date	Mintage	F	VF	XF	Unc	BU
2013A	Est. 2,300,000	—	—	—	4.00	5.00
2013A Proof	—	Value: 9.00				
2013D	Est. 2,410,000	—	—	—	4.00	5.00
2013D Proof	—	Value: 9.00				
2013F	Est. 2,740,000	—	—	—	4.00	5.00
2013F Proof	—	Value: 9.00				
2013G	Est. 1,640,000	—	—	—	4.00	5.00
2013G Proof	—	Value: 9.00				
2013J	Est. 2,410,000	—	—	—	4.00	5.00
2013J Proof	—	Value: 9.00				

KM# 314 2 EURO

8.5000 g., Bi-Metallic Nickel-Brass center in Copper-Nickel ring, 25.75 mm. **Series:** German States **Subject:** Baden-Wurttenberg, Maulbrunn Cloister **Obv:** Maulbrunn Cloiser **Obv. Legend:** BADEN-WURTTEMBERG **Rev:** Relief map of Europe, stars, lines and value **Edge Lettering:** EINIGKEIT UND RECHT UND FREIHEIT

Date	Mintage	F	VF	XF	Unc	BU
2013A	Est. 6,100,000	—	—	—	4.00	5.00
2013A Proof	—	Value: 9.00				
2013D	Est. 6,400,000	—	—	—	4.00	5.00
2013D Proof	—	Value: 9.00				
2013F	Est. 7,300,000	—	—	—	4.00	5.00
2013F Proof	—	Value: 9.00				
2013G	Est. 4,300,000	—	—	—	4.00	5.00
2013G Proof	—	Value: 9.00				
2013J	Est. 6,400,000	—	—	—	4.00	5.00
2013J Proof	—	Value: 9.00				

KM# 215 10 EURO

18.0000 g., 0.9250 Silver 0.5353 oz. ASW, 32.5 mm. **Subject:** Introduction of the Euro Currency **Obv:** Stylized round eagle **Rev:** Euro symbol and map **Edge Lettering:** IM ZEICHEN DER EINIGUNG EUROPAS

Date	Mintage	F	VF	XF	Unc	BU
2002F	2,000,000	—	—	—	22.00	25.00
2002F Proof	400,000	Value: 30.00				

KM# 216 10 EURO

18.0000 g., 0.9250 Silver 0.5353 oz. ASW, 32.5 mm. **Subject:** Berlin Subway Centennial **Obv:** Stylized squarish eagle **Rev:** Elevated and subterranean train views **Edge Lettering:** HISTORISCH UND ZUKUNFTS WEISEND

Date	Mintage	F	VF	XF	Unc	BU
2002D	2,000,000	—	—	—	22.00	25.00
2002D Proof	400,000	Value: 30.00				

KM# 217 10 EURO

18.0000 g., 0.9250 Silver 0.5353 oz. ASW, 32.5 mm. **Subject:** Documenta Kassel Art Exposition **Obv:** Stylized eagle above inscription **Rev:** Exposition logo **Edge Lettering:** ART (in nine languages)

Date	Mintage	F	VF	XF	Unc	BU
2002J	2,000,000	—	—	—	22.00	25.00
2002J Proof	300,000	Value: 30.00				

KM# 218 10 EURO

18.0000 g., 0.9250 Silver 0.5353 oz. ASW, 32.5 mm. **Subject:** Museum Island, Berlin **Obv:** Stylized eagle **Rev:** Aerial view of museum complex **Edge Lettering:** FREISTÄTTE FÜR KUNST UND WISSENSCHAFT

Date	Mintage	F	VF	XF	Unc	BU
2002A	2,000,000	—	—	—	22.00	25.00
2002A Proof	280,000	Value: 30.00				

KM# 219 10 EURO

18.0000 g., 0.9250 Silver 0.5353 oz. ASW, 32.5 mm. **Subject:** 50 Years - German Television **Obv:** Stylized eagle silhouette **Rev:** Television screen silhouette **Edge Lettering:** BILDUNG UNTERHALTUNG INFORMATION

Date	Mintage	F	VF	XF	Unc	BU
2002G	2,000,000	—	—	—	22.00	25.00
2002G Proof	290,000	Value: 32.00				

KM# 222 10 EURO

18.0000 g., 0.9250 Silver 0.5353 oz. ASW, 32.5 mm. **Subject:** Justus von Liebig **Obv:** Eagle above denomination **Rev:** Liebig's portrait **Edge Lettering:** FORSCHEN • LEHREN • ANWENDEN •

Date	Mintage	F	VF	XF	Unc	BU
2003J	2,050,000	—	—	—	22.00	25.00
2003J Proof	350,000	Value: 30.00				

KM# 227 10 EURO

18.0000 g., 0.9250 Silver 0.5353 oz. ASW, 32.5 mm. **Obv:** Stylized eagle above denomination **Rev:** Gottfried Semper and floor plan **Edge Lettering:** ARCHITEKT • FORSCHER • KOSMOPOLIT • DEMOKRAT•

Date	Mintage	F	VF	XF	Unc	BU
2003G	2,050,000	—	—	—	22.00	25.00
2003G Proof	350,000	Value: 30.00				

KM# 223 10 EURO

18.0000 g., 0.9250 Silver 0.5353 oz. ASW, 32.5 mm. **Subject:** World Cup Soccer **Obv:** Stylized round eagle above denomination **Rev:** German map on soccer ball **Edge Lettering:** DIE WELT ZU GAST BEI FREUNDEN A • D • F • G • J • **Note:** Mint is determined by which letter "E" in the edge inscription has a short center bar. If the first letter "E" has the short center bar the coin is from the Berlin mint. Second "E"= Munich, third "E"=Stuttgart, fourth "E"=Karlsruhe, fifth "E"=Hamburg

Date	Mintage	F	VF	XF	Unc	BU
2003A	710,000	—	—	—	22.00	25.00
2003A Proof	80,000	Value: 32.00				
2003D	710,000	—	—	—	22.00	25.00
2003D Proof	80,000	Value: 32.00				
2003F	710,000	—	—	—	22.00	25.00
2003F Proof	80,000	Value: 32.00				
2003G	710,000	—	—	—	22.00	25.00
2003G Proof	80,000	Value: 32.00				
2003J	710,000	—	—	—	22.00	25.00
2003J Proof	80,000	Value: 32.00				

KM# 224 10 EURO

18.0000 g., 0.9250 Silver 0.5353 oz. ASW, 32.5 mm. **Subject:** Ruhr Industrial District **Obv:** Stylized eagle, denomination below **Rev:** Various city views **Edge Lettering:** RUHRPOTT KULTURLANDSCHAFT

Date	Mintage	F	VF	XF	Unc	BU
2003F	2,050,000	—	—	—	22.00	25.00
2003F Proof	350,000	Value: 30.00				

KM# 226 10 EURO

18.0000 g., 0.9250 Silver 0.5353 oz. ASW, 32.5 mm. **Subject:** 50th Anniversary of the Ill-fated East German Revolution **Obv:** Stylized eagle, denomination at left **Rev:** Tank tracks over slogans **Edge Lettering:** ERINNERUNG AN DEN VOLKSAUFSTAND IN DER DDR

Date	Mintage	F	VF	XF	Unc	BU
2003A	2,050,000	—	—	—	22.00	25.00
2003A Proof	350,000	Value: 30.00				

KM# 225 10 EURO
18.0000 g., 0.9250 Silver 0.5353 oz. ASW, 32.5 mm. **Subject:** German Museum München Centennial **Obv:** Stylized eagle, denomination at left **Rev:** Abstract design **Edge Lettering:** SAMMELN • AUSSTELLEN • FORSCHEN • BILDEN •

Date	Mintage	F	VF	XF	Unc	BU
2003D	2,050,000	—	—	—	22.00	25.00
2003D Proof	350,000	Value: 30.00				

KM# 230 10 EURO
18.0000 g., 0.9250 Silver 0.5353 oz. ASW, 32.5 mm. **Obv:** Stylized eagle, stars and denomination **Rev:** Bauhaus Dessau geometric shapes design **Edge Lettering:** KUNST TECHNIK LEHRE

Date	Mintage	F	VF	XF	Unc	BU
2004A	1,800,000	—	—	—	22.00	25.00
2004A Proof	300,000	Value: 30.00				

KM# 232 10 EURO
18.0000 g., 0.9250 Silver 0.5353 oz. ASW, 32.5 mm. **Obv:** Stylized eagle and denomination **Rev:** Geese flying over Wattenmeer National Park **Edge Lettering:** MEERESGRUND TRIFFT HORIZONT

Date	Mintage	F	VF	XF	Unc	BU
2004J	1,800,000	—	—	—	22.00	25.00
2004J Proof	300,000	Value: 30.00				

KM# 233 10 EURO
18.0000 g., 0.9250 Silver 0.5353 oz. ASW, 32.5 mm. **Obv:** Stylized eagle **Rev:** Eduard Moerike **Edge Lettering:** OHNE DAS SCHÖNE WAS SOLL DER GEWINN

Date	Mintage	F	VF	XF	Unc	BU
2004F	1,800,000	—	—	—	22.00	25.00
2004F Proof	300,000	Value: 30.00				

KM# 234 10 EURO
18.0000 g., 0.9250 Silver 0.5353 oz. ASW, 32.5 mm. **Obv:** Stylized eagle, denomination below **Rev:** Space station above the earth **Edge Lettering:** RAUMFAHRT VERBINDET DIE WELT

Date	Mintage	F	VF	XF	Unc	BU
2004D	1,800,000	—	—	—	22.00	25.00
2004D Proof	300,000	Value: 30.00				

KM# 231 10 EURO
18.0000 g., 0.9250 Silver 0.5353 oz. ASW, 32.5 mm. **Obv:** Stylized eagle above denomination **Rev:** European Union country names and dates **Edge Lettering:** FREUDE SCHÖNER GÖTTERFUNKEN

Date	Mintage	F	VF	XF	Unc	BU
2004G	1,800,000	—	—	—	22.00	25.00
2004G Proof	300,000	Value: 30.00				

KM# 229 10 EURO
18.0000 g., 0.9250 Silver 0.5353 oz. ASW, 32.5 mm. **Obv:** Stylized eagle, denomination below **Rev:** Soccer ball orbiting the earth **Edge Lettering:** DIE WELT ZU GAST BEI FREUNDEN A D F G J **Note:** Soccer Series: Mint determination same as KM-223

Date	Mintage	F	VF	XF	Unc	BU
2004A	800,000	—	—	—	22.00	25.00
2004A Proof	80,000	Value: 30.00				
2004D	800,000	—	—	—	22.00	25.00
2004D Proof	80,000	Value: 30.00				
2004F	800,000	—	—	—	22.00	25.00
2004F Proof	80,000	Value: 30.00				
2004G	800,000	—	—	—	22.00	25.00
2004G Proof	80,000	Value: 30.00				
2004J	800,000	—	—	—	22.00	25.00
2004J Proof	80,000	Value: 30.00				

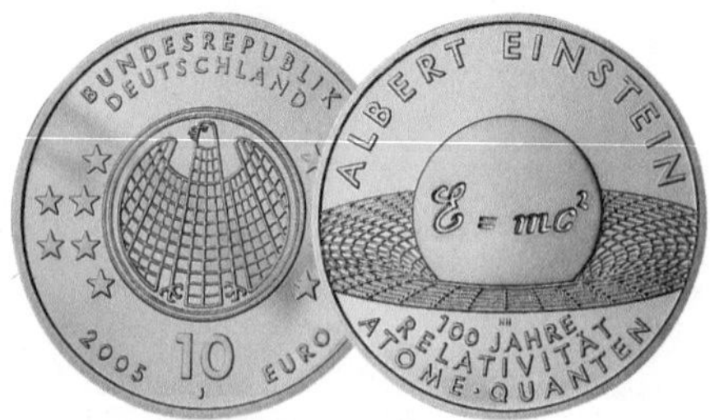

KM# 238 10 EURO
18.0000 g., 0.9250 Silver 0.5353 oz. ASW, 32.5 mm. **Subject:** Albert Einstein **Obv:** Stylized eagle within circle, denomination below **Rev:** E=mc2 on a sphere resting on a net **Edge Lettering:** NICHT AUFHOREN ZU FRAGEN

Date	Mintage	F	VF	XF	Unc	BU
2005J	1,800,000	—	—	—	22.00	25.00
2005J Proof	300,000	Value: 30.00				

KM# 239 10 EURO
18.0000 g., 0.9250 Silver 0.5353 oz. ASW, 32.5 mm. **Subject:** Friedrich von Schiller **Obv:** Stylized eagle **Rev:** Schiller portrait **Edge Lettering:** ERNST IST DAS LEBEN. HEITER IST DIE KUNST

Date	Mintage	F	VF	XF	Unc	BU
2005G	1,800,000	—	—	—	22.00	25.00
2005G Proof	300,000	Value: 30.00				

KM# 240 10 EURO
18.0000 g., 0.9250 Silver 0.5353 oz. ASW, 32.5 mm. **Subject:** Magdeburg **Obv:** Stylized eagle, denomination below **Rev:** Church flanked by landmarks and objects **Edge Lettering:** MAGADOBURG 805 • MAGDEBURG 2005 •

Date	Mintage	F	VF	XF	Unc	BU
2005A	1,800,000	—	—	—	22.00	25.00
2005A Proof	300,000	Value: 30.00				

KM# 241 10 EURO
18.0000 g., 0.9250 Silver 0.5353 oz. ASW, 32.5 mm. **Subject:** Bavarian Forest National Park **Obv:** Stylized eagle **Rev:** Various park scenes **Edge:** Lettered

Date	Mintage	F	VF	XF	Unc	BU
2005D	1,800,000	—	—	—	22.00	25.00
2005D Proof	300,000	Value: 30.00				

KM# 242 10 EURO
18.0000 g., 0.9250 Silver 0.5353 oz. ASW, 32.5 mm. **Subject:** Bertha von Suttner **Obv:** Stylized eagle above stars **Rev:** Suttner's portrait **Edge Lettering:** EIPHNH PAX FRIEDEN twice

Date	Mintage	F	VF	XF	Unc	BU
2005F	1,800,000	—	—	—	22.00	25.00
2005F Proof	300,000	Value: 30.00				

KM# 243 10 EURO
18.0000 g., 0.9250 Silver 0.5353 oz. ASW, 32.5 mm. **Subject:** World Cup Soccer **Obv:** Round stylized eagle **Rev:** Ball and legs seen through a net **Edge Lettering:** DIE WELT ZU GAST BEI FREUNDEN

Date	Mintage	F	VF	XF	Unc	BU
2005A	800,000	—	—	—	22.00	25.00
2005A Proof	80,000	Value: 32.00				
2005D	800,000	—	—	—	22.00	25.00
2005D Proof	80,000	Value: 32.00				
2005F	800,000	—	—	—	22.00	25.00
2005F Proof	80,000	Value: 32.00				
2005G	800,000	—	—	—	22.00	25.00
2005G Proof	80,000	Value: 32.00				
2005J	800,000	—	—	—	22.00	25.00
2005J Proof	80,000	Value: 32.00				

KM# 245 10 EURO
18.0000 g., 0.9250 Silver 0.5353 oz. ASW, 32.5 mm. **Subject:** Karl Friedrich Schinkel **Obv:** Stylized eagle **Rev:** Kneeling brick layer **Edge Lettering:** DER MENSCH BILDE SICH IN ALLEM SCHÖN

Date	Mintage	F	VF	XF	Unc	BU
2006F	1,600,000	—	—	—	22.00	25.00
2006F Proof	300,000	Value: 30.00				

KM# 246 10 EURO
18.0000 g., 0.9250 Silver 0.5353 oz. ASW, 32.5 mm. **Subject:** Dresden **Obv:** Stylized eagle **Rev:** City view and reflection **Edge Lettering:** 1206 1485 1547 1697 1832 1945 1989 2006

Date	Mintage	F	VF	XF	Unc	BU
2006A	1,600,000	—	—	—	22.00	25.00
2006A Proof	300,000	Value: 30.00				

KM# 247 10 EURO
18.0000 g., 0.9250 Silver 0.5353 oz. ASW, 32.5 mm. **Subject:** Hanseatic League **Obv:** Stylized eagle **Rev:** Old sail boat **Edge Lettering:** Wandel durch Handel - von der Hanse nach Europa

Date	Mintage	F	VF	XF	Unc	BU
2006J	1,600,000	—	—	—	22.00	25.00
2006J Proof	300,000	Value: 30.00				

KM# 248 10 EURO
18.0000 g., 0.9250 Silver 0.5353 oz. ASW, 32.5 mm. **Subject:** Mozart **Obv:** Stylized eagle, music and denomination above **Rev:** Bust left, dates above **Edge Lettering:** -- MOZART -- DIE WELT HAT EINEN SINN

Date	Mintage	F	VF	XF	Unc	BU
2006D	1,600,000	—	—	—	22.00	25.00
2006D Proof	300,000	Value: 30.00				

KM# 249 10 EURO
18.0000 g., 0.9250 Silver 0.5353 oz. ASW, 32.5 mm. **Subject:** World Cup Soccer **Obv:** Stylized eagle **Rev:** Brandenburg Gate on ball on globe **Edge Lettering:** DIE WELT ZU GAST BEI FREUNDEN - ADFGJ **Note:** Mint is determined by which letter "E" in the edge inscription has a short center bar. If the first letter "E" has the short center bar the coin is from the Berlin mint. Second "E"= Munich, third "E"=Stuttgart, fourth "E"=Karlsruhe, fifth "E"=Hamburg

Date	Mintage	F	VF	XF	Unc	BU
2006A	800,000	—	—	—	20.00	22.00
2006A Proof	80,000	Value: 25.00				
2006D	800,000	—	—	—	20.00	22.00
2006D Proof	80,000	Value: 25.00				
2006F	800,000	—	—	—	20.00	22.00
2006F Proof	80,000	Value: 25.00				
2006G	800,000	—	—	—	20.00	22.00
2006G Proof	80,000	Value: 25.00				
2006J	800,000	—	—	—	20.00	22.00
2006J Proof	80,000	Value: 25.00				

KM# 263 10 EURO
18.0000 g., 0.9250 Silver 0.5353 oz. ASW, 32.5 mm. **Subject:** Saarland, 50th Anniversary of German control **Obv:** Eagle **Rev:** Modern town view, four stylized heads

Date	Mintage	F	VF	XF	Unc	BU
2007G	1,600,000	—	—	—	22.00	25.00
2007G Proof	300,000	Value: 30.00				

KM# 264 10 EURO
18.0000 g., 0.9250 Silver 0.5353 oz. ASW, 32.5 mm. **Subject:** Treaty of Rome, 50th Anniversary **Obv:** Eagle **Rev:** Map of Central Europe and stars

Date	Mintage	F	VF	XF	Unc	BU
2007F	1,600,000	—	—	—	22.00	25.00
2007F Proof	300,000	Value: 30.00				

KM# 265 10 EURO
18.0000 g., 0.9250 Silver 0.5353 oz. ASW, 32.5 mm. **Subject:** Wilhelm Busch, 175th Anniversary of Birth **Obv:** Eagle within square **Rev:** Portrait of Busch, characters Helene, Max and Moritz flanking

Date	Mintage	F	VF	XF	Unc	BU
2007D	1,600,000	—	—	—	22.00	25.00
2007D Proof	300,000	Value: 30.00				

KM# 266 10 EURO
18.0000 g., 0.9250 Silver 0.5353 oz. ASW, 32.5 mm. **Subject:** Deutsche Bundesbank, 50th Aniversary **Obv:** Eagle on rectangle design **Rev:** Buildings on graph

Date	Mintage	F	VF	XF	Unc	BU
2007J	1,600,000	—	—	—	22.00	25.00
2007J Proof	300,000	Value: 30.00				

KM# 268 10 EURO
18.0000 g., 0.9250 Silver 0.5353 oz. ASW, 32.5 mm. **Subject:** Eagle **Rev:** St. Elisabeth von Thuringen

Date	Mintage	F	VF	XF	Unc	BU
2007A	1,160,000	—	—	—	22.00	25.00
2007A Proof	300,000	Value: 30.00				

KM# 271 10 EURO
18.0000 g., 0.9250 Silver 0.5353 oz. ASW, 32.5 mm. **Subject:** Franz Kafka, 125th Anniversary of Birth **Obv:** Eagle **Rev:** Prague Cathedral, writings & portrait **Edge Lettering:** EIN KÄFIG GING EINEN VOGEL SUCHEN

Date	Mintage	F	VF	XF	Unc	BU
2008G	1,500,000	—	—	—	22.00	25.00
2008G Proof	260,000	Value: 30.00				

KM# 272 10 EURO
18.0000 g., 0.9250 Silver 0.5353 oz. ASW, 32.5 mm. **Subject:** Max Planck, 150th Anniversary of Birth **Obv:** Eagle **Rev:** Graph and portrait **Edge Lettering:** DEM ANWENDEN MUSS DAS + ERKENNEN VORAUSGEHEN

Date	Mintage	F	VF	XF	Unc	BU
2008F	1,500,000	—	—	—	22.00	25.00
2008F Proof	260,000	Value: 30.00				

KM# 273 10 EURO

18.0000 g., 0.9250 Silver 0.5353 oz. ASW **Subject:** Carl Spitzweg - 200th Anniversary of Birth **Obv:** Eagle **Rev:** Spitzweg reclining in bed with books, umbrella above **Edge Lettering:** ACH, DIE VERGANGENHEIT ÌST SCHÖN **Shape:** 32.5

Date	Mintage	F	VF	XF	Unc	BU
2008D	1,500,000	—	—	—	22.00	25.00
2008D Proof	260,000	Value: 30.00				

KM# 274 10 EURO

18.0000 g., 0.9250 Silver 0.5353 oz. ASW, 32.5 mm. **Subject:** Gorch Fock II, 50th Anniversary **Obv:** Eagle **Rev:** Naval training sailing ship Gorch Fock II **Edge Lettering:** SEEFAHRT ÌST NOT

Date	Mintage	F	VF	XF	Unc	BU
2008J	1,500,000	—	—	—	22.00	25.00
2008J Proof	260,000	Value: 30.00				

KM# 294 10 EURO

18.0000 g., 0.9250 Silver 0.5353 oz. ASW, 32.5 mm. **Subject:** Archaology in Germany **Obv:** Eagle, stars flanking **Rev:** Sun, moon and star shield

Date	Mintage	F	VF	XF	Unc	BU
2008A	1,500,000	—	—	—	22.00	25.00
2008A Proof	260,000	Value: 30.00				

KM# 279 10 EURO

18.0000 g., 0.9250 Silver 0.5353 oz. ASW, 32.5 mm. **Subject:** IAAF World Championships - Berlin **Obv:** Eagle and value **Rev:** Female javelin thrower in stadium **Note:** Mint Marks letters are in Morse Code.

Date	Mintage	F	VF	XF	Unc	BU
2009A	362,000	—	—	—	22.00	25.00
2009A Proof	40,000	Value: 30.00				
2009D	362,000	—	—	—	22.00	25.00
2009D Proof	40,000	Value: 30.00				
2009F	362,000	—	—	—	22.00	25.00
2009F Proof	40,000	Value: 30.00				
2009G	362,000	—	—	—	22.00	25.00
2009G Proof	40,000	Value: 30.00				
2009J	362,000	—	—	—	22.00	25.00
2009J Proof	40,000	Value: 30.00				

KM# 280 10 EURO

18.0000 g., 0.9250 Silver 0.5353 oz. ASW, 32.5 mm. **Subject:** Kepler's Laws - 400th Anniversary **Obv:** Eagle above value **Rev:** Portrait and geometric diagram demonstrating planetary orbits

Date	Mintage	F	VF	XF	Unc	BU
2009F	1,643,000	—	—	—	22.00	25.00
2009F Proof	200,000	Value: 30.00				

KM# 281 10 EURO

18.0000 g., 0.9250 Silver 0.5353 oz. ASW, 32.5 mm. **Subject:** International Aerospace Expo, 100th Anniversary **Obv:** Eagle above value **Rev:** Plane landing, montage of plane development

Date	Mintage	F	VF	XF	Unc	BU
2009D	1,650,000	—	—	—	22.00	25.00
2009D Proof	200,000	Value: 30.00				

KM# 282 10 EURO

18.0000 g., 0.9250 Silver 0.5353 oz. ASW, 32.5 mm. **Subject:** Leipzig University - 600th Anniversary **Obv:** Eagle above value **Rev:** University seal, portrait of Gottfried Wilhelm Leibniz

Date	Mintage	F	VF	XF	Unc	BU
2009A	1,613,000	—	—	—	22.00	25.00
2009G Proof	200,000	Value: 30.00				

KM# 284 10 EURO

18.0000 g., 0.9250 Silver 0.5353 oz. ASW, 32.5 mm. **Subject:** Marion Countess Donhoff - 100th Anniversary of Birth **Obv:** Eagle and value **Rev:** Profile right

Date	Mintage	F	VF	XF	Unc	BU
2009J	1,600,000	—	—	—	22.00	25.00
2009J Proof	200,000	Value: 30.00				

KM# 281a 10 EURO

18.0000 g., 0.9250 Silver partially gilt 0.5353 oz. ASW, 32.5 mm. **Subject:** International Air Travel, 100th Anniversary **Obv:** Stylized eagle **Rev:** Airplanes, partially gilt

Date	Mintage	F	VF	XF	Unc	BU
2009D	1,650,000	—	—	—	22.00	25.00
2009D Proof	200,000	Value: 30.00				

KM# 283 10 EURO

18.0000 g., 0.9250 Silver 0.5353 oz. ASW, 32.5 mm. **Subject:** Youth hostels - 100th Anniversary **Obv:** Eagle and value **Rev:** Stylized mountain, Alternal hostel in Westphalia

Date	Mintage	F	VF	XF	Unc	BU
2009G	1,610,000	—	—	—	22.00	25.00
2009G Proof	200,000	Value: 30.00				

KM# 290 10 EURO

18.0000 g., 0.9250 Silver 0.5353 oz. ASW, 32.5 mm. **Subject:** German Unification, 20th Anniversary **Edge Lettering:** EINIGKEIT UND RECHT UND FREIHEIT

Date	Mintage	F	VF	XF	Unc	BU
2010A	2,100,000	—	—	—	20.00	22.00
2010A Proof	184,200	Value: 25.00				

KM# 291 10 EURO

18.0000 g., 0.9250 Silver 0.5353 oz. ASW **Subject:** 175th Anniversary of German Railroads **Edge Lettering:** AUF VEREINTEN GLEISEN 1835-2010

Date	Mintage	F	VF	XF	Unc	BU
2010D	2,041,000	—	—	—	21.00	23.00
2010D Proof	186,000	Value: 30.00				

KM# 287 10 EURO

18.0000 g., 0.9250 Silver 0.5353 oz. ASW, 32.5 mm. **Subject:** Porcelain Production in Germany, 300th Anniversary

Date	Mintage	F	VF	XF	Unc	BU
2010F	1,749,000	—	—	—	20.00	22.00
2010F Proof	182,900	Value: 25.00				

KM# 288 10 EURO

18.0000 g., 0.9250 Silver 0.5353 oz. ASW, 32.5 mm. **Subject:** Robert Schumann - 200th Birth Anniversary

Date	Mintage	F	VF	XF	Unc	BU
2010J	1,700,000	—	—	—	20.00	22.00
2010J Proof	182,900	Value: 25.00				

KM# 289 10 EURO

14.0000 g., 0.9250 Silver 0.4163 oz. ASW, 32.5 mm. **Subject:** Konrad Zuse, 100th Birth Anniversary

Date	Mintage	F	VF	XF	Unc	BU
2010G	1,706,000	—	—	—	20.00	22.00
2010G Proof	182,900	Value: 25.00				

KM# 298 10 EURO

18.0000 g., 0.9250 Silver 0.5353 oz. ASW, 32.5 mm. **Subject:** FIS World Alpine Ski Championships **Edge Lettering:** FESTSPIELE IM SHNEE (Issued in 2010)

Date	Mintage	F	VF	XF	Unc	BU
2011A	400,000	—	—	—	21.00	23.00
2011A	41,400	Value: 30.00				

Date	Mintage	F	VF	XF	Unc	BU
2011D	400,000	—	—	—	21.00	23.00
2011D	41,400	Value: 30.00				
2011F	400,000	—	—	—	21.00	23.00
2011F	41,400	Value: 30.00				
2011G	400,000	—	—	—	21.00	23.00
2011G	41,400	Value: 30.00				
2011J	400,000	—	—	—	21.00	23.00
2011J	41,400	Value: 30.00				

KM# 299 10 EURO

14.0000 g., Copper-Nickel, 32.5 mm. **Subject:** Soccer (Football) Women's World Cup in Germany **Edge Lettering:** DIE ZUKUNFT DES FUSSBALLS IST WEIBLICH

Date	Mintage	F	VF	XF	Unc	BU
2011A	446,000	—	—	—	14.50	15.00
2011D	446,000	—	—	—	14.50	15.00
2011F	446,000	—	—	—	14.50	15.00
2011G	446,000	—	—	—	14.50	15.00
2011J	446,000	—	—	—	14.50	15.00

KM# 299a 10 EURO

16.0000 g., 0.6250 Silver 0.3215 oz. ASW, 32.5 mm. **Subject:** Soccer (Football) Women's World Cup in Germany **Edge Lettering:** DIE ZUKUNFT DES FUSSBALLS IST WEIBLICH

Date	Mintage	F	VF	XF	Unc	BU
2011A Proof	47,000	Value: 30.00				
2011D Proof	47,000	Value: 30.00				
2011F Proof	47,000	Value: 30.00				
2011G Proof	47,000	Value: 30.00				
2011J Proof	47,000	Value: 30.00				

KM# 295 10 EURO

16.0000 g., 0.6250 Silver 0.3215 oz. ASW, 32.5 mm. **Subject:** Franz Liszt, 200th Anniversary of Birth **Edge Lettering:** CGME OBLICE - GENIE VEPPUCHIT

Date	Mintage	F	VF	XF	Unc	BU
2011G	2,187,000	—	—	—	15.00	16.00
2011G Proof	178,000	Value: 30.00				

KM# 296 10 EURO

14.0000 g., 0.6250 Copper-Nickel 0.2813 oz., 32.5 mm. **Subject:** 125th Anniversary of the Automobile **Obv:** Stylized eagle, stars, country name, denomination and date **Obv. Legend:** 125 JAHRE AUTOMOBIL **Rev:** Hand on steering wheel, zig-sag roadway **Edge Lettering:** WAS UNS BEWEGT

Date	Mintage	F	VF	XF	Unc	BU
2011F Proof	223,000	Value: 30.00				

KM# 300 10 EURO

14.0000 g., Copper-Nickel, 32.5 mm. **Subject:** Till Eulenspiegel, 500th Anniversary **Edge Lettering:** SO BIN ICH DOCH HIE GEWESEN

Date	Mintage	F	VF	XF	Unc	BU
2011D	Est. 1,800,000	—	—	—	14.50	15.00

KM# 300a 10 EURO

16.0000 g., 0.6250 Silver 0.3215 oz. ASW, 32.5 mm. **Subject:** Til Eulenspiegel, 500th Anniversary **Edge Lettering:** SO BIN ICH DOCH HIE GEWESEN

Date	Mintage	F	VF	XF	Unc	BU
2011D Proof	223,000	Value: 30.00				

KM# 301 10 EURO

14.0000 g., Copper-Nickel, 32.5 mm. **Subject:** Discovery of the Archaeopteryx, 150th Anniversary **Edge Lettering:** ARCHAEOPTERYX - ZEUGE DER EVOLUTION

Date	Mintage	F	VF	XF	Unc	BU
2011A	Est. 1,800,000	—	—	—	14.50	15.00

KM# 301a 10 EURO

16.0000 g., 0.6250 Silver 0.3215 oz. ASW, 32.5 mm. **Subject:** Discovery of the Archaeopteryx, 150th Anniversary **Edge Lettering:** ARCHAEOPTERYX - ZEUGE DER EVOLUTION

Date	Mintage	F	VF	XF	Unc	BU
2011A Proof	223,000	Value: 30.00				

KM# 302 10 EURO

14.0000 g., Copper-Nickel, 32.5 mm. **Subject:** Elbe Tunnel, Hamburg, 100th Anniversary **Edge Lettering:** VERBINDUNG VON STADT UND HAFEN

Date	Mintage	F	VF	XF	Unc	BU
2011J	—	—	—	—	14.50	15.00

KM# 302a 10 EURO

16.0000 g., 0.6250 Silver 0.3215 oz. ASW, 32.5 mm. **Subject:** Elbe Tunnel, Hamburg, 100th Anniversary **Edge Lettering:** VERBINDUNG VON STADT UND HAFEN

Date	Mintage	F	VF	XF	Unc	BU
2011J Proof	223,000	Value: 30.00				

KM# 308 10 EURO

14.0000 g., 0.9250 Copper-Nickel 0.4163 oz., 32.5 mm. **Subject:** Friedrich der Grosse, 300th Anniversary of Birth **Obv:** Head of Friedrich the Great facing left **Obv. Legend:** 300 GEBURTSTAG FRIEDRICH II 1712-1786 **Rev:** Stylized eagle, stars, country name, denomination and date **Edge Lettering:** MICH MEINEN MITBÜRGERN NÜTZLICH ERWEISEN

Date	Mintage	F	VF	XF	Unc	BU
2012A	Est. 1,700,000	—	—	—	14.50	15.00

KM# 309 10 EURO

14.0000 g., 0.9250 Copper-Nickel 0.4163 oz., 32.5 mm. **Subject:** German Argo Action, 50th Anniversary of **Obv:** Sprouting seedling **Obv. Legend:** 50 JAHRE DEUTSCHE WELTHUNGERHILFE **Rev:** Stylized eagle, stars, country name, denomination and date **Edge Lettering:** HILFE ZUR SELBSTHILFE

Date	Mintage	F	VF	XF	Unc	BU
2012G	Est. 1,750,000	—	—	—	14.50	15.00

KM# 310 10 EURO

14.0000 g., 0.9250 Copper-Nickel 0.4163 oz., 32.5 mm. **Subject:** Brothers Grimm, 200th Anniversary **Obv:** Conjoined heads of Grimm Brothers facing left **Obv. Legend:** 200 JAHRE GRIMMS MARCHEN **Rev:** Stylized eagle, stars, country name, denomination and date **Edge Lettering:** UND WENN SIE NICHT GESTORBEN SIND...

Date	Mintage	F	VF	XF	Unc	BU
2012F	Est. 1,760,000	—	—	—	14.50	15.00

KM# 311 10 EURO

14.0000 g., 0.9250 Copper-Nickel 0.4163 oz., 32.5 mm. **Subject:** German National Library, 100th Anniversary **Obv:** Head facing left, design **Obv. Legend:** DEUTSCHE NATIONAL BIBLIOTECK 100 JAHRE **Rev:** Stylized eagle, country name, denomination and date **Edge Lettering:** BÜCHER SIND DER EINGANG ZUR WELT

Date	Mintage	F	VF	XF	Unc	BU
2012D	1,490,000	—	—	—	14.50	15.00

KM# 312 10 EURO

14.0000 g., 0.9250 Copper-Nickel 0.4163 oz., 32.5 mm. **Subject:** Gerhart Hauptmann, 150th Anniversary of Birth **Obv:** Head of Gerhart Hauptmann **Obv. Legend:** 150 GEBURTSTAG GERHART HAUPTMANN **Rev:** Stylized eagle, stars country name, denomination and date **Edge Lettering:** A JEDER MENSCH HAT HALT 'NE SEHNSUCHT

Date	Mintage	F	VF	XF	Unc	BU
2012J	Est. 1,432,000	—	—	—	14.50	15.00

KM# 318 10 EURO

16.0000 g., 0.9250 Silver 0.4758 oz. ASW, 32.5 mm. **Subject:** Georg Buchner, 200th Anniversary of Birth

Date	Mintage	F	VF	XF	Unc	BU
2012	—	—	—	—	—	25.00
2012 Proof	—	Value: 30.00				

KM# 316 10 EURO

18.0000 g., 0.9250 Silver 0.5353 oz. ASW **Subject:** Richard Wagner, 200th Anniversary of Birth

Date	Mintage	F	VF	XF	Unc	BU
2013	—	—	—	—	—	25.00
2013 Proof	—	Value: 30.00				

KM# 317 10 EURO

18.0000 g., 0.9250 Silver 0.5353 oz. ASW, 32.5 mm. **Subject:** Friedrich III

Date	Mintage	F	VF	XF	Unc	BU
2013	—	—	—	—	—	25.00
2013 Proof	—	Value: 30.00				

KM# 319 10 EURO

16.0000 g., 0.9250 Silver 0.4758 oz. ASW, 32.5 mm. **Subject:** Heinrich Herz, Electric Rays, 125th Anniversary

Date	Mintage	F	VF	XF	Unc	BU
2013	—	—	—	—	—	25.00
2013 Proof	—	Value: 30.00				

KM# 320 10 EURO

16.0000 g., 0.9250 Silver 0.4758 oz. ASW, 32.5 mm. **Subject:** Red Cross, 150th Anniversary

Date	Mintage	F	VF	XF	Unc	BU
2013	—	—	—	—	—	25.00
2013 Proof	—	Value: 30.00				

KM# 321 10 EURO

16.0000 g., 0.9250 Silver 0.4758 oz. ASW **Subject:** German Fairy Tales - Snow White

Date	Mintage	F	VF	XF	Unc	BU
2013	—	—	—	—	—	25.00
2013 Proof	—	Value: 30.00				

KM# 297 20 EURO

3.8900 g., 0.9999 Gold 0.1250 oz. AGW, 17.5 mm. **Series:** German Forest **Subject:** Oak Tree **Obv:** Stylized eagle, stars, legend "BUNDERSREPUBLIK DEUTSCHLAND", date and value **Rev:** Oak leaf and legends "DEUTSCHER WALD" and "EICHE" **Edge:** Reeded

Date	Mintage	F	VF	XF	Unc	BU
2010A	40,000	—	—	—	—	275
2010D	40,000	—	—	—	—	275
2010F	40,000	—	—	—	—	275
2010G	40,000	—	—	—	—	275
2010J	40,000	—	—	—	—	275

KM# 303 20 EURO

3.8900 g., 0.9999 Gold 0.1250 oz. AGW, 17.5 mm. **Series:** German Forest **Subject:** Beech Tree **Obv:** Stylized eagle, stars, legend, date and value **Obv. Legend:** BUNDERSREPUBLIK DEUTSCHLAND **Rev:** Beech leaf and legends **Rev. Legend:** DEUTSCHER WALD / BUCHE **Edge:** Reeded

Date	Mintage	F	VF	XF	Unc	BU
2011A	40,000	—	—	—	—	275
2011D	40,000	—	—	—	—	275
2011F	40,000	—	—	—	—	275
2011G	40,000	—	—	—	—	275
2011J	40,000	—	—	—	—	275

KM# 307 20 EURO

3.8900 g., 0.9999 Gold 0.1250 oz. AGW, 17.5 mm. **Series:** German Forest **Subject:** Spruce Tree **Obv:** Stylized eagle, stars, date and value **Obv. Legend:** BUNDESREPUBLIK DEUTSCHLAND **Rev:** Spruce branch end and legends **Rev. Legend:** DEUTSCHER WALD / FICHTE **Edge:** Reeded

Date	Mintage	F	VF	XF	Unc	BU
2012A	40,000	—	—	—	—	275
2012D	40,000	—	—	—	—	275
2012F	40,000	—	—	—	—	275
2012G	40,000	—	—	—	—	275
2012J	40,000	—	—	—	—	275

KM# 324 20 EURO

3.8900 g., 0.9999 Gold 0.1250 oz. AGW, 17.5 mm. **Series:** German Forest **Subject:** Pine Tree **Obv:** Stylized eagle, stars, country name, date and denomination **Rev:** Pine needles **Rev. Legend:** DEUTSCHER WALD and KIEFER **Edge:** Reeded

Date	Mintage	F	VF	XF	Unc	BU
2013	Est. 40,000	—	—	—	—	275

KM# 220 100 EURO

15.5500 g., 0.9999 Gold 0.4999 oz. AGW, 28 mm. **Subject:** Introduction of the Euro Currency **Obv:** Stylized round eagle **Rev:** Euro symbol and arches **Edge:** Reeded

Date	Mintage	F	VF	XF	Unc	BU
2002A Proof	100,000	Value: 975				
2002D Proof	100,000	Value: 975				
2002F Proof	100,000	Value: 975				
2002G Proof	100,000	Value: 975				
2002J Proof	100,000	Value: 975				

KM# 228 100 EURO

15.5500 g., 0.9999 Gold 0.4999 oz. AGW, 28 mm. **Obv:** Stylized eagle, denomination below **Rev:** Quedlinburg Abbey in monogram **Edge:** Reeded

Date	Mintage	F	VF	XF	Unc	BU
2003A Proof	80,000	Value: 975				
2003D Proof	80,000	Value: 975				
2003F Proof	80,000	Value: 975				
2003G Proof	80,000	Value: 975				
2003J Proof	80,000	Value: 975				

KM# 235 100 EURO

15.5500 g., 0.9999 Gold 0.4999 oz. AGW, 28 mm. **Obv:** Stylized eagle, denomination below **Rev:** Bamberg city view **Edge:** Reeded

Date	Mintage	F	VF	XF	Unc	BU
2004A Proof	80,000	Value: 975				
2004D Proof	80,000	Value: 975				
2004F Proof	80,000	Value: 975				
2004G Proof	80,000	Value: 975				
2004J Proof	80,000	Value: 975				

KM# 236 100 EURO

15.5500 g., 0.9999 Gold 0.4999 oz. AGW **Subject:** UNESCO - Weimar **Obv:** Stylized eagle **Rev:** Historical City of Weimar buildings **Edge:** Reeded

Date	Mintage	F	VF	XF	Unc	BU
2006A Proof	70,000	Value: 975				
2006D Proof	70,000	Value: 975				
2006F Proof	70,000	Value: 975				
2006G Proof	70,000	Value: 975				
2006J Proof	70,000	Value: 975				

KM# 237 100 EURO

15.5500 g., 0.9999 Gold 0.4999 oz. AGW, 28 mm. **Subject:** Soccer - Germany 2006 **Obv:** Round stylized eagle **Rev:** Aerial view of stadium

Date	Mintage	F	VF	XF	Unc	BU
2005A Proof	70,000	Value: 975				
2005D Proof	70,000	Value: 975				
2005F Proof	70,000	Value: 975				
2005G Proof	70,000	Value: 975				
2005J Proof	70,000	Value: 975				

KM# 267 100 EURO

15.5500 g., 0.9999 Gold 0.4999 oz. AGW, 28 mm. **Subject:** Lubeck - UNESCO Heritage site **Obv:** Eagle **Rev:** City view

Date	Mintage	F	VF	XF	Unc	BU
2007A	66,000	Value: 975				
2007D	66,000	Value: 975				
2007F	66,000	Value: 975				
2007G	66,000	Value: 975				
2007J	66,000	Value: 975				

KM# 270 100 EURO

15.5500 g., 0.9999 Gold 0.4999 oz. AGW, 28 mm. **Subject:** Goslar - UNESCO Heritage site **Obv:** Eagle **Edge:** Reeded

Date	Mintage	F	VF	XF	Unc	BU
2008A	64,000	Value: 975				
2008D	64,000	Value: 975				
2008F	64,000	Value: 975				
2008G	64,000	Value: 975				
2008J	64,000	Value: 975				

KM# 278 100 EURO

15.5500 g., 0.9999 Gold 0.4999 oz. AGW, 28 mm. **Subject:** Trier - UNESCO Heritage site **Obv:** Eagle and denomination **Rev:** Riverside montage of buildings **Edge:** Reeded

Date	Mintage	F	VF	XF	Unc	BU
2009A Proof	64,000	Value: 975				
2009D Proof	64,000	Value: 975				
2009F Proof	64,000	Value: 975				
2009G Proof	64,000	Value: 975				
2009J Proof	64,000	Value: 975				

KM# 286 100 EURO

15.5500 g., 0.9999 Gold 0.4999 oz. AGW, 28 mm. **Subject:** Wûrzburg - UNESCO Heritage site **Rev:** Wûrzburg residence and court garden

Date	Mintage	F	VF	XF	Unc	BU
2010A Proof	64,000	Value: 975				
2010D Proof	64,000	Value: 975				
2010F Proof	64,000	Value: 975				
2010G Proof	64,000	Value: 975				
2010J Proof	64,000	Value: 975				

KM# 304 100 EURO

15.5500 g., 0.9999 Gold 0.4999 oz. AGW **Subject:** UNESCO World Heritage Site - Wartburg Castle **Obv:** Stylized eagle, stars, legend date and value **Obv. Legend:** BUNDERSREPUBLIK DEUTSCHLAND **Rev:** Wartburg Castle and legends **Rev. Legend:** UNESCO WELTERE WARTBURG / GEGR 1067 LUDWIG DER SPRINGER HERMANN I... **Edge:** Reeded

Date	Mintage	F	VF	XF	Unc	BU
2011A Proof	60,000	Value: 975				
2011D Proof	60,000	Value: 975				
2011F Proof	60,000	Value: 975				
2011G Proof	60,000	Value: 975				
2011J Proof	60,000	Value: 975				

KM# 313 100 EURO

15.5500 g., 0.9999 Gold 0.4999 oz. AGW, 28 mm. **Subject:** UNESCO - Aachen Cathedral **Obv:** Eagle **Rev:** Side view of Cathedral **Designer:** Erich Ott

Date	Mintage	F	VF	XF	Unc	BU
2012A Proof	54,000	Value: 975				
2012D Proof	54,000	Value: 975				
2012F Proof	54,000	Value: 975				
2012G Proof	54,000	Value: 975				
2012J Proof	54,000	Value: 975				

KM# 322 100 EURO

15.5500 g., 0.9990 Gold 0.4994 oz. AGW, 28 mm. **Subject:** Aachen Cathedral, European Heritage Site.

Date	Mintage	F	VF	XF	Unc	BU
2012A	—	Value: 950				
2012D	—	Value: 950				
2012F	—	Value: 950				
2012G	—	Value: 950				
2012J	—	Value: 950				

KM# 221 200 EURO

31.1000 g., 0.9999 Gold 0.9997 oz. AGW, 32.5 mm. **Subject:** Introduction of the Euro Currency **Obv:** Stylized round eagle **Rev:** Euro symbol and arches **Edge Lettering:** IM ... ZEICHEN ... DER ... EINIGUNG ... EUROPAS

Date	Mintage	F	VF	XF	Unc	BU
2002A Proof	20,000	Value: 1,950				
2002D Proof	20,000	Value: 1,950				
2002F Proof	20,000	Value: 1,950				
2002G Proof	20,000	Value: 1,950				
2002J Proof	20,000	Value: 1,950				

MINT SETS

KM#	Date	Mintage	Identification	Issue Price	Mkt Val
MS119	2001A (10)	130,000	KM105,106a,107-108,109.2,110,140.1,170,175,183	—	40.00
MS120	2001D (10)	130,000	KM105,106a,107-108,109.2,110,140.1,170,175,183	—	40.00
MS121	2001F (10)	130,000	KM105,106a,107-108,109.2,110,140.1,170,175,183	—	40.00
MS122	2001G (10)	130,000	KM105,106a,107-108,109.2,110,140.1,170,175,183	—	40.00
MS123	2001J (10)	130,000	KM105,106a,107-108,109.2,110,140.1,170,175,183	—	40.00
MS124	2002A (8)	90,000	KM#207-214	—	20.00
MS125	2002D (8)	90,000	KM#207-214	—	20.00
MS126	2002F (8)	90,000	KM#207-214	—	20.00
MS127	2002G (8)	90,000	KM#207-214	—	20.00
MS128	2002J (8)	90,000	KM#207-214	—	20.00
MS129	2003A (8)	90,000	KM#207-214	—	25.00
MS130	2003D (8)	90,000	KM#207-214	—	27.50
MS131	2003F (8)	90,000	KM#207-214	—	27.50
MS132	2003G (8)	90,000	KM#207-214	—	27.50
MS133	2003J (8)	90,000	KM#207-214	—	25.00
MS134	2004A (8)	90,000	KM#207-214	—	24.00
MS135	2004D (8)	90,000	KM#207-214	—	22.00
MS136	2004F (8)	90,000	KM#207-214	—	24.00
MS137	2004G (8)	90,000	KM#207-214	—	24.00
MS138	2004J (8)	90,000	KM#207-214	—	28.00
MS139	2005A (8)	90,000	KM#207-214	—	28.00
MS142	2005G (8)	90,000	KM#207-214	—	28.00
MS140	2005D (8)	90,000	KM#207-214	—	28.00
MS141	2005F (8)	90,000	KM#207-214	—	28.00
MS143	2005J (8)	90,000	KM#207-214	—	26.00
MS144	2006A (9)	90,000	KM#207-214, 253	—	35.00
MS149	2006 (5)	80,000	KM#253 (A, D, F, G and J)	—	23.00
MS145	2006D (9)	90,000	KM#207-214, 253	—	35.00
MS146	2006F (9)	90,000	KM#207-214, 253	—	35.00
MS147	2006G (9)	90,000	KM#207-214, 253	—	35.00
MS148	2006J (9)	90,000	KM#207-214, 253	—	35.00
MS150	2007A (9)	90,000	KM#207-209, 254-257, 259, 260	—	27.00
MS151	2007D (9)	90,000	KM#207-209, 254-257, 259, 260	—	27.00
MS152	2007F (9)	90,000	KM#207-209, 254-257, 259, 260	—	27.00
MS153	2007G (9)	90,000	KM#207-209, 254-257, 259, 260	—	27.00
MS154	2007J (9)	90,000	KM#207-209, 254-257, 259, 260	—	27.00
MS155	2007 (5)	80,000	KM#260 (A, D, F, G and J)	—	23.00
MS156	2008A (9)	80,000	KM#207-209, 254-258, 261	—	27.00
MS159	2008G (9)	80,000	KM#207-209, 254-258, 261	—	27.00
MS157	2008D (9)	80,000	KM#207-209, 254-258, 261	—	27.00
MS158	2008F (9)	80,000	KM#207-209, 254-258, 261	—	27.00
MS160	2008J (9)	80,000	KM#207-209, 254-258, 261	—	27.00
MS161	2008 (5)	80,000	KM#261 (A, D, F, G, J)	—	23.00
MS162	2009A (9)	60,000	KM#207-209, 254-257, 276, 277	—	27.00
MS163	2009D (9)	60,000	KM#207-209, 254-257, 276, 277	—	27.00
MS164	2009F (9)	60,000	KM#207-209, 254-257, 276, 277	—	27.00
MS165	2009G (9)	60,000	KM#207-209, 254-257, 276, 277	—	27.00
MS166	2009J (9)	60,000	KM#207-209, 254-257, 276, 277	—	27.00
MS167	2009 (5)	50,000	KM#276 (A, D, F, G, J)	—	23.00
MS168	2010A (9)	53,800	KM#207-209, 254-258, 285	—	20.00
MS169	2010D (9)	46,800	KM#207-209, 254-258, 285	—	20.00
MS170	2010F (9)	46,800	KM#207-209, 254-258, 285	—	20.00
MS171	2010G (9)	46,800	KM#207-209, 254-258, 285	—	20.00
MS172	2010J (9)	46,800	KM#207-209, 254-258, 285	—	20.00
MS173	2010 (5)	45,000	KM#285 (A, D, F, G, J)	—	23.00
MS174	2011A (9)	48,000	KM#207-209, 254-258, 293	—	20.00
MS175	2011D (9)	44,000	KM#207-209, 254-258, 293	—	20.00
MS176	2011F (9)	44,000	KM#207-209, 254-258, 293	—	20.00
MS177	2011G (9)	44,000	KM#207-209, 254-258, 293	—	20.00
MS178	2011J (9)	44,000	KM#207-209, 254-258, 293	—	20.00
MS179	2011 (5)	147,000	KM#293 (A, D, F, G, J)	—	23.00
MS180	2012A (9)	50,000	KM#207-209, 254-257, 305, 306	—	20.00
MS182	2012G (9)	50,000	KM#207-209, 254-257, 305, 306	—	20.00
MS181	2012D (9)	50,000	KM#207-209, 254-257, 305, 306	—	20.00
MS183	2012G (9)	50,000	KM#207-209, 254-257, 305, 306	—	20.00
MS184	2012J (9)	50,000	KM#207-209, 254-257, 305, 306	—	20.00
MS185	2012 (5)	45,000	KM#305 (A, D, F, G and J)	—	24.00
MS186	2012 (6)	45,000	KM#306 (A, D, F, G and J)	—	38.00

PROOF SETS

KM#	Date	Mintage	Identification	Issue Price	Mkt Val
PS150	2001A (10)	78,000	KM105,106a,107-108,109.2,110,140.1,170,175,183	—	50.00
PS151	2001D (10)	78,000	KM105,106a,107-108,109.2,110,140.1,170,175,183	—	50.00
PS152	2001F (10)	78,000	KM105,106a,107-108,110,140.1,170,175,183	—	50.00
PS153	2001G (10)	78,000	KM105,106a,107-108,109.2,110,140.1,170,175,183	—	50.00
PS154	2001J (10)	78,000	KM105,106a,107-108,109.2,110,140.1,170,175,183	—	50.00
PS155	2002A (8)	75,000	KM#207-214	—	20.00
PS156	2002D (8)	75,000	KM#207-214	—	20.00
PS216	2011D (9)	37,000	KM#207-209, 254-258, 293	—	40.00
PS157	2002F (8)	75,000	KM#207-214	—	20.00
PS158	2002G (8)	75,000	KM#207-214	—	20.00
PS159	2002J (8)	75,000	KM#207-214	—	20.00
PS221	2002 (5)	80,000	KM#215-219	—	150
PS222	2003 (6)	80,000	KM#222-227	—	180
PS160	2003A (8)	75,000	KM#207-214	—	20.00
PS161	2003D (8)	75,000	KM#207-214	—	20.00
PS162	2003F (8)	75,000	KM#207-214	—	20.00
PS163	2003G (8)	75,000	KM#207-214	—	20.00
PS164	2003J (8)	75,000	KM#207-214	—	20.00
PS223	2004 (6)	80,000	KM#229-234	—	180
PS165	2004A (8)	75,000	KM#207-214	—	20.00
PS166	2004D (8)	75,000	KM#207-214	—	20.00
PS167	2004F (8)	75,000	KM#207-214	—	20.00
PS168	2004G (8)	75,000	KM#207-214	—	20.00
PS169	2004J (8)	75,000	KM#207-214	—	20.00
PS224	2005 (6)	80,000	KM#238-243	—	2,005
PS170	2005A (8)	75,000	KM#207-214	—	20.00
PS171	2005D (8)	75,000	KM#207-214	—	20.00
PS172	2005F (8)	75,000	KM#207-214	—	20.00
PS173	2005G (8)	75,000	KM#207-214	—	20.00
PS174	2005J (8)	75,000	KM#207-214	—	20.00
PS225	2006 (6)	80,000	KM#245-249	—	150
PS175	2006A (9)	75,000	KM#207-214, 253	—	35.00
PS176	2006D (9)	75,000	KM#207-214, 253	—	35.00
PS177	2006F (9)	75,000	KM#207-214, 253	—	35.00
PS178	2006G (9)	75,000	KM#207-214, 253	—	35.00
PS179	2006J (9)	75,000	KM#207-214, 253	—	35.00
PS180	2006 (5)	70,000	KM#253 (A, D, F, G, J)	—	30.00
PS226	2007 (5)	50,000	KM#259 (A, D, F, G and J)	—	42.00
PS181	2007A (9)	70,000	KM#207-209, 254-257, 259, 260	—	35.00
PS182	2007D (9)	70,000	KM#207-209, 254-257, 259, 260	—	35.00
PS183	2007F (9)	70,000	KM#207-209, 254-257, 259, 260	—	35.00
PS184	2007G (9)	75,000	KM#207-209, 254-257, 259, 260	—	35.00
PS185	2007J (9)	75,000	KM#207-209, 254-257, 259, 260	—	35.00
PS186	2007 (5)	70,000	KM#260 (A, D, F, G, J)	—	40.00
PS227	2007 (5)	80,000	KM#263-266, 268	—	150
PS187	2008A (9)	70,000	KM#207-209, 254-258, 261	—	35.00
PS188	2008D (9)	70,000	KM#207-209, 254-258, 261	—	35.00
PS194	2009D (9)	50,000	KM#207-209, 254-258, 276	—	35.00
PS189	2008F (9)	70,000	KM#207-209, 254-258, 261	—	35.00
PS190	2008G (9)	70,000	KM#207-209, 254-258, 261	—	35.00
PS191	2008J (9)	70,000	KM#207-209, 254-258, 261	—	35.00
PS192	2008 (5)	70,000	KM#261 (A, D, F, G, J)	—	40.00
PS228	228 (5)	80,000	KM#271-274, 294	—	150
PS193	2009A (9)	50,000	KM#207-209, 254-258, 276	—	35.00
PS195	2009F (9)	50,000	KM#207-209, 254-258, 276	—	35.00
PS196	2009G (9)	50,000	KM#207-209, 254-258, 276	—	35.00
PS197	2009J (9)	50,000	KM#207-209, 254-258, 276	—	35.00
PS230	2009 (6)	60,000	KM#279, 281, 281a, 282-284	—	180
PS229	2009 (5)	20,000	KM#277 (A, D, F, G and J)	—	42.00
PS198	2009 (5)	50,000	KM#276 (A, D, F, G, J)	—	40.00
PS231	2010 (5)	57,900	KM#287-291, 298a	—	180
PS199	2010A (9)	45,150	KM#207-209, 254-258, 285	—	40.00
PS200	2010D (9)	40,120	KM#207-209, 254-258, 285	—	40.00
PS201	2010F (9)	40,120	KM#207-209, 254-258, 285	—	40.00
PS202	2010G (9)	40,120	KM#207-209, 254-258, 285	—	40.00
PS203	2010J (9)	40,120	KM#207-209, 254-258, 285	—	40.00
PS204	2010 (5)	45,000	KM#285 (A, D, F, G, J)	—	40.00
PS215	2011A (9)	43,000	KM#207-209, 254-258, 293	—	40.00
PS217	2011F (9)	37,000	KM#207-209, 254-258, 293	—	40.00
PS218	2011G (9)	37,000	KM#207-209, 254-258, 293	—	40.00
PS219	2011J (9)	37,000	KM#207-209, 254-258, 293	—	40.00
PS220	2011 (5)	55,000	KM#293 (A, D, F, G, J)	—	40.00
PS232	2011 (1)	63,000	KM#295, 296a, 299a-302a	—	180
PS233	2012A (10)	40,000	KM#207-209, 254-258, 305, 306	—	30.00
PS237	2012J (10)	40,000	KM#207-209, 254-258, 305, 306	—	30.00
PS236	2012G (9)	40,000	KM#207-209, 254-257, 305, 306	—	30.00
PS234	2012D (9)	40,000	KM#207-209, 254-257, 305, 306	—	30.00
PS235	2012F (9)	40,000	KM#207-209, 254-257, 305, 306	—	30.00
PS238	2012 (5)	52,000	KM#306 (A, D, F, G and J)	—	42.00

GHANA

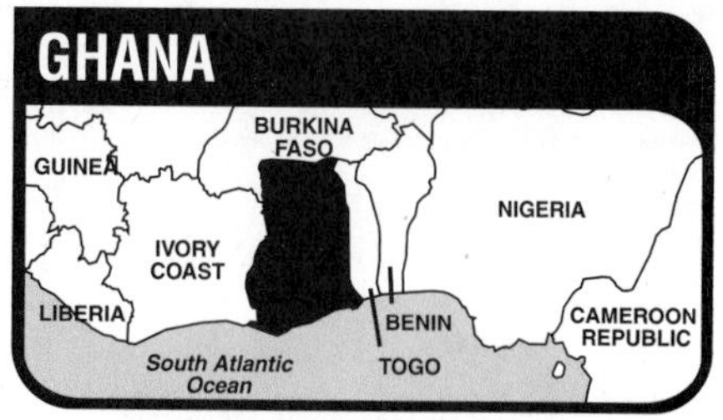

The Republic of Ghana, a member of the Commonwealth of Nations situated on the West Coast of Africa between Ivory Coast and Togo, has an area of 92,100 sq. mi. (238,540 sq. km.) and a population of 14 million, almost entirely African. Capital: Accra. Cocoa (the major crop), coconuts, palm kernels and coffee are exported. Mining, second in importance to agriculture, is concentrated on gold, manganese and industrial diamonds.

MONETARY SYSTEM

1 Cedi = 100 Pesewas, 1965-2007
1 (new) Cedi = 10,000 (old) Cedis, 2007-

REPUBLIC

DECIMAL COINAGE

KM# 36 10 CEDIS

4.4100 g., Copper-Nickel, 22.9 mm. **Obv:** National arms divides date and denomination **Rev:** Gorilla family **Edge:** Plain

Date	Mintage	F	VF	XF	Unc	BU
2003	—	—	—	—	1.50	2.00

REFORM COINAGE

2007-

KM# 37 PESEWA

1.8200 g., Copper Plated Steel, 17 mm. **Obv:** National arms **Obv. Legend:** GHANA **Rev:** Adomi Bridge **Edge:** Plain

Date	Mintage	F	VF	XF	Unc	BU
2007	—	—	—	—	—	0.75

KM# 38 5 PESEWAS

2.5000 g., Nickel Clad Steel, 18 mm. **Obv:** National arms **Obv. Legend:** GHANA **Rev:** Native male blowing horn **Edge:** Plain

Date	Mintage	F	VF	XF	Unc	BU
2007	—	—	—	—	—	1.25

KM# 39 10 PESEWAS

3.2300 g., Nickel Clad Steel, 20.4 mm. **Obv:** National arms **Obv. Legend:** GHANA **Rev:** Open book, pen **Edge:** Reeded

Date	Mintage	F	VF	XF	Unc	BU
2007	—	—	—	—	—	2.50

KM# 40 20 PESEWAS

4.4000 g., Nickel Plated Steel, 23.5 mm. **Obv:** National arms **Obv. Legend:** GHANA **Rev:** Split open cocoa pod **Edge:** Plain

Date	Mintage	F	VF	XF	Unc	BU
2007	—	—	—	—	—	3.50

KM# 41 50 PESEWAS

6.0800 g., Nickel Plated Steel, 26.4 mm. **Obv:** National arms **Obv. Legend:** GHANA **Rev:** 1/2 length figure of market woman facing **Edge:** Reeded

Date	Mintage	F	VF	XF	Unc	BU
2007	—	—	—	—	—	6.00

KM# 42 CEDI

7.4000 g., Bi-Metallic Brass center in Nickel Plated Steel ring, 28 mm. **Obv:** National arms **Obv. Legend:** GHANA **Rev:** Scale of Justice in sprays **Edge:** Segmented reeding

Date	Mintage	F	VF	XF	Unc	BU
2007	—	—	—	—	—	10.00

GIBRALTAR

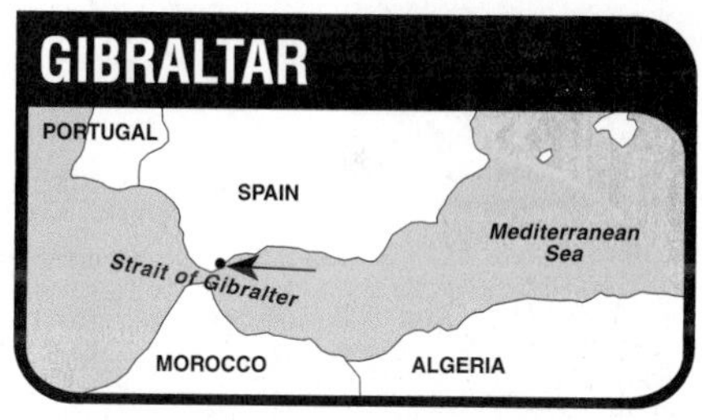

The British Colony of Gibraltar, located at the southernmost point of the Iberian Peninsula, has an area of 2.25 sq. mi. (6.5 sq. km.) and a population of 29,651. Capital (and only town): Gibraltar. Aside from its strategic importance as guardian of the western entrance to the Mediterranean Sea, Gibraltar is also a free port and a British naval base.

RULERS

British

MINT MARKS

PM - Pobjoy Mint
PMM – Pobjoy Mint (only appears on coins dated 2000)

NOTE: ALL coins for 1988 –2003 include the PM mint mark except the 2000 dated circulation pieces which instead have PMM.

MINT PRIVY MARKS

U - Unc finish

MONETARY SYSTEM

100 Pence = 1 Pound

BRITISH COLONY

DECIMAL COINAGE

KM# 773 PENNY

3.5600 g., Copper Plated Steel, 20.32 mm. **Ruler:** Elizabeth II **Obv:** Head with tiara right **Rev:** Barbary partridge left divides denomination

Date	Mintage	F	VF	XF	Unc	BU
2001 AA	—	—	—	—	0.35	0.50
2002 AA	—	—	—	—	0.35	0.50
2003 AA	—	—	—	—	0.35	0.50

KM# 1046 PENNY

3.5600 g., Copper Plated Steel, 20.32 mm. **Ruler:** Elizabeth II **Subject:** 300th Anniversary **Obv:** Crowned bust right **Rev:** Monkey **Edge:** Plain

Date	Mintage	F	VF	XF	Unc	BU
2004	—	—	—	—	0.30	0.50

KM# 1079 PENNY
3.5600 g., Copper Plated Steel, 20.32 mm. **Ruler:** Elizabeth II **Obv:** Bust right **Rev:** Sceptre

Date	Mintage	F	VF	XF	Unc	BU
2005	—	—	—	—	0.35	0.50
2006	—	—	—	—	0.35	0.50
2007	—	—	—	—	0.35	0.50
2008	—	—	—	—	0.35	0.50
2009	—	—	—	—	0.35	0.50
2010	—	—	—	—	0.35	0.50

KM# 1098 PENNY
3.5400 g., Bronze Plated Steel, 20.5 mm. **Ruler:** Elizabeth II **Rev:** Bird left

Date	Mintage	F	VF	XF	Unc	BU
2010	—	—	—	—	0.35	0.50

KM# 774 2 PENCE
7.1200 g., Copper Plated Steel, 25.91 mm. **Ruler:** Elizabeth II **Obv:** Head with tiara right

Date	Mintage	F	VF	XF	Unc	BU
2001 AA	—	—	—	—	0.50	0.85
2001PM AB	—	—	—	—	0.50	0.85
2002	—	—	—	—	0.50	0.85
2003 AA	—	—	—	—	0.50	0.85

KM# 1044 2 PENCE
7.1200 g., Copper Plated Steel, 25.91 mm. **Ruler:** Elizabeth II **Subject:** 300th Anniversary **Obv:** Crowned bust right **Rev:** Four old keys **Edge:** Plain

Date	Mintage	F	VF	XF	Unc	BU
2004	—	—	—	—	0.50	0.65

KM# 1065 2 PENCE
7.1200 g., Copper Plated Steel, 25.91 mm. **Ruler:** Elizabeth II **Subject:** Operation Torch, 1942 **Rev:** Three soldiers

Date	Mintage	F	VF	XF	Unc	BU
2005	—	—	—	—	0.50	0.65
2006	—	—	—	—	0.50	0.65
2007	—	—	—	—	0.50	0.65
2008	—	—	—	—	0.50	0.65
2009	—	—	—	—	0.50	0.65
2010	—	—	—	—	0.50	0.65
2011	—	—	—	—	0.50	0.65

KM# 1080 2 PENCE
7.1200 g., Copper Plated Steel, 25.91 mm. **Ruler:** Elizabeth II **Subject:** Diamond Wedding **Rev:** Conjoined busts of Elizabeth II and Philip

Date	Mintage	F	VF	XF	Unc	BU
2007	—	—	—	—	0.50	0.65

KM# 775 5 PENCE
3.2500 g., Copper-Nickel, 18 mm. **Ruler:** Elizabeth II **Obv:** Head with tiara right **Rev:** Barbary Ape left divides denomination **Edge:** Reeded

Date	Mintage	F	VF	XF	Unc	BU
2001 AB	—	—	—	—	0.60	0.75
2002 AB	—	—	—	—	0.60	0.75
2003 AA	—	—	—	—	0.60	0.75

KM# 1049 5 PENCE
3.2500 g., Copper-Nickel, 18 mm. **Ruler:** Elizabeth II **Subject:** Tercentenary 1704-2004 **Obv:** Elizabeth II **Rev:** British Royal Sceptre **Edge:** Reeded

Date	Mintage	F	VF	XF	Unc	BU
2004	—	—	—	—	—	1.50

KM# 1081 5 PENCE
3.2500 g., Copper-Nickel, 18 mm. **Ruler:** Elizabeth II **Obv:** Bust in diadem right **Rev:** Barbary ape seated **Edge:** Reeded

Date	Mintage	F	VF	XF	Unc	BU
2005	—	—	—	—	0.60	0.75
2006	—	—	—	—	0.60	0.75
2007	—	—	—	—	0.60	0.75
2008	—	—	—	—	0.60	0.75
2009	—	—	—	—	0.60	0.75
2010	—	—	—	—	0.60	0.75
2011	—	—	—	—	0.60	0.75

KM# 776 10 PENCE
6.5000 g., Copper-Nickel, 24.5 mm. **Ruler:** Elizabeth II **Obv:** Head with tiara right, date below **Rev:** Denomination below building **Edge:** Reeded

Date	Mintage	F	VF	XF	Unc	BU
2001 AA	—	—	—	—	1.00	1.25
2001 AB	—	—	—	—	1.00	1.25
2001 AC	—	—	—	—	1.00	1.25
2001 AE	—	—	—	—	1.00	1.25
2002 AC	—	—	—	—	1.00	1.25
2003 AA	—	—	—	—	1.00	1.25

KM# 1047 10 PENCE
6.5000 g., Copper-Nickel, 24.5 mm. **Ruler:** Elizabeth II **Subject:** 300th Anniversary **Obv:** Elizabeth II **Rev:** Three military officers planning Operation Torch 1942 **Edge:** Reeded

Date	Mintage	F	VF	XF	Unc	BU
2004	—	—	—	—	0.75	1.00

KM# 1082 10 PENCE
6.5000 g., Copper-Nickel, 24.5 mm. **Ruler:** Elizabeth II **Subject:** The Great Siege, 1779-1783 **Obv:** Bust in diadem right **Rev:** Cannon left **Edge:** Reeded

Date	Mintage	F	VF	XF	Unc	BU
2005	—	—	—	—	0.75	1.00
2006	—	—	—	—	0.75	1.00
2007	—	—	—	—	0.75	1.00
2008	—	—	—	—	0.75	1.00
2009	—	—	—	—	0.75	1.00
2010	—	—	—	—	0.75	1.00
2011	—	—	—	—	0.75	1.00

KM# 777 20 PENCE
5.0000 g., Copper-Nickel, 21.4 mm. **Ruler:** Elizabeth II **Obv:** Head with tiara right, date below **Rev:** Our Lady of Europa, denomination below and right **Shape:** 7-sided

Date	Mintage	F	VF	XF	Unc	BU
2001 AA	—	—	—	—	1.50	2.00

KM# 1048 20 PENCE
5.0000 g., Copper-Nickel, 21.4 mm. **Ruler:** Elizabeth II **Subject:** 300th Anniversary **Obv:** Crowned buat right **Rev:** Neanderthal skull found in Gibraltar in 1848 **Edge:** Plain **Shape:** 7-sided

Date	Mintage	F	VF	XF	Unc	BU
2004	—	—	—	—	1.00	1.50

KM# 1083 20 PENCE
5.0000 g., Copper-Nickel, 21.4 mm. **Ruler:** Elizabeth II **Obv:** Bust in diadem right **Rev:** Keyring with four keys **Shape:** 7-sided

Date	Mintage	F	VF	XF	Unc	BU
2005	—	—	—	—	1.50	2.00
2006	—	—	—	—	1.50	2.00
2007	—	—	—	—	1.50	2.00
2008	—	—	—	—	1.50	2.00
2009	—	—	—	—	1.50	2.00
2010	—	—	—	—	1.50	2.00
2011	—	—	—	—	1.50	2.00

KM# 971 50 PENCE
8.0000 g., Copper-Nickel, 27.3 mm. **Ruler:** Elizabeth II **Subject:** Christmas **Obv:** Head with tiara right, date below **Rev:** Three wise men **Edge:** Plain **Shape:** 7-sided

Date	Mintage	F	VF	XF	Unc	BU
2001 BB	30,000	—	—	—	10.00	12.00

KM# 971a 50 PENCE
8.0000 g., 0.9250 Silver 0.2379 oz. ASW, 27.3 mm. **Ruler:** Elizabeth II **Obv:** Head with tiara right, date below **Rev:** Three wise men **Edge:** Plain **Shape:** 7-sided

Date	Mintage	F	VF	XF	Unc	BU
2001 Proof	5,000	Value: 35.00				

KM# 971b 50 PENCE
8.0000 g., 0.9167 Gold 0.2358 oz. AGW, 27.3 mm. **Ruler:** Elizabeth II **Obv:** Head with tiara right, date below **Rev:** Three wise men **Edge:** Plain **Shape:** 7-sided

Date	Mintage	F	VF	XF	Unc	BU
2001 Proof	250	Value: 645				

KM# 778 50 PENCE
8.0000 g., Copper-Nickel, 27.3 mm. **Ruler:** Elizabeth II **Obv:** Head with tiara right **Rev:** Dolphins surround denomination **Edge:** Plain **Shape:** 7-sided

Date	Mintage	F	VF	XF	Unc	BU
2001 AA	—	—	—	—	4.50	5.50
2001 AB	—	—	—	—	4.50	5.50
2003 AB	—	—	—	—	4.50	5.50

KM# 1026 50 PENCE

8.0000 g., Copper-Nickel, 27.3 mm. **Ruler:** Elizabeth II **Subject:** Christmas **Obv:** Head with tiara right, date below **Rev:** Shepherds **Edge:** Plain **Shape:** 7-sided

Date	Mintage	F	VF	XF	Unc	BU
2002PM BB	30,000	—	—	—	10.00	12.00

KM# 1026a 50 PENCE

8.0000 g., 0.9250 Silver 0.2379 oz. ASW, 27.3 mm. **Ruler:** Elizabeth II **Subject:** Christmas **Obv:** Head with tiara right, date below **Rev:** Two shepherds **Edge:** Plain **Shape:** 7-sided

Date	Mintage	F	VF	XF	Unc	BU
2002PM Proof	2,002	Value: 35.00				

KM# 1063a 50 PENCE

8.0000 g., 0.9250 Silver 0.2379 oz. ASW, 27.3 mm. **Ruler:** Elizabeth II **Subject:** Christmas **Rev:** Joseph & Mary **Shape:** 7-sided

Date	Mintage	F	VF	XF	Unc	BU
2003PM BB	—	—	—	—	12.00	14.00

KM# 1063 50 PENCE

8.0000 g., Copper-Nickel, 27.3 mm. **Ruler:** Elizabeth II **Series:** Christmas **Obv:** Head with tiara right, date below **Rev:** Joseph & Mary **Shape:** 7-sided

Date	Mintage	F	VF	XF	Unc	BU
2003PM BB	—	—	—	—	10.00	12.00

KM# 1050 50 PENCE

8.0000 g., Copper-Nickel, 27.3 mm. **Ruler:** Elizabeth II **Subject:** Tercentenary 1704-2004 **Obv:** Elizabeth II **Rev:** HMS Victory sailing past Gibraltar **Edge:** Plain **Shape:** 7-sided

Date	Mintage	F	VF	XF	Unc	BU
2004	—	—	—	—	—	3.00

KM# 1066 50 PENCE

8.0000 g., Copper-Nickel, 27.3 mm. **Ruler:** Elizabeth II **Subject:** Christmas **Rev:** Santa Claus walking left with sack over shoulder and waving **Shape:** 7-sided

Date	Mintage	F	VF	XF	Unc	BU
2004	—	—	—	—	10.00	12.00

KM# 1084 50 PENCE

8.0000 g., Copper-Nickel, 27.3 mm. **Ruler:** Elizabeth II **Subject:** Glorious 1st of June, 1794 **Rev:** Marines firing from deck of Naval ship **Shape:** 7-sided

Date	Mintage	F	VF	XF	Unc	BU
2004	—	—	—	—	10.00	12.00

KM# 1085 50 PENCE

8.0000 g., Copper-Nickel, 27.3 mm. **Ruler:** Elizabeth II **Subject:** Siege of Sebastopol, 1854 **Rev:** Troops in the Crimea **Shape:** 7-sided

Date	Mintage	F	VF	XF	Unc	BU
2004	—	—	—	—	10.00	12.00

KM# 1086 50 PENCE

8.0000 g., Copper-Nickel, 27.3 mm. **Ruler:** Elizabeth II **Subject:** World War I **Rev:** Troops advancing right **Shape:** 7-sided

Date	Mintage	F	VF	XF	Unc	BU
2004	—	—	—	—	10.00	12.00

KM# 1087 50 PENCE

8.0000 g., Copper-Nickel, 27.3 mm. **Ruler:** Elizabeth II **Subject:** World War II **Rev:** Troops in fox hole **Shape:** 7-sided

Date	Mintage	F	VF	XF	Unc	BU
2004	—	—	—	—	10.00	12.00

KM# 1088 50 PENCE

8.0000 g., Copper-Nickel, 27.3 mm. **Ruler:** Elizabeth II **Subject:** The Falklands, 1982 **Rev:** Troops advancing forward **Shape:** 7-sided

Date	Mintage	F	VF	XF	Unc	BU
2004	—	—	—	—	10.00	12.00

KM# 1067 50 PENCE

8.0000 g., Copper-Nickel, 27.3 mm. **Ruler:** Elizabeth II **Subject:** Christmas **Rev:** Mary and child **Shape:** 7-sided

Date	Mintage	F	VF	XF	Unc	BU
2005	—	—	—	—	10.00	12.00

KM# 1074 50 PENCE

8.0000 g., Copper-Nickel, 27.3 mm. **Ruler:** Elizabeth II **Subject:** Capture of Gibraltar **Rev:** Naval Battle **Shape:** 7-sided

Date	Mintage	F	VF	XF	Unc	BU
2005	—	—	—	—	7.50	10.00

KM# 1089 50 PENCE

8.0000 g., Copper-Nickel, 27.3 mm. **Ruler:** Elizabeth II **Subject:** Capture of Gibraltar, 1704 **Rev:** Naval Battle **Shape:** 7-sided

Date	Mintage	F	VF	XF	Unc	BU
2006	—	—	—	—	4.50	5.50
2007	—	—	—	—	4.50	5.50
2008	—	—	—	—	4.50	5.50
2009	—	—	—	—	4.50	5.50
2010	—	—	—	—	4.50	5.50

KM# 1068 50 PENCE

8.0000 g., Copper-Nickel, 27.3 mm. **Ruler:** Elizabeth II **Subject:** Christmas **Rev:** Tree **Shape:** 7-sided

Date	Mintage	F	VF	XF	Unc	BU
2006	—	—	—	—	10.00	12.00

KM# 1069 50 PENCE

8.0000 g., Copper-Nickel, 27.3 mm. **Ruler:** Elizabeth II **Subject:** Christmas **Rev:** Santa, large face **Shape:** 7-sided

Date	Mintage	F	VF	XF	Unc	BU
2007	—	—	—	—	10.00	12.00

KM# 1070 50 PENCE

8.0000 g., Copper-Nickel, 27.3 mm. **Ruler:** Elizabeth II **Subject:** Christmas **Shape:** 7-sided

Date	Mintage	F	VF	XF	Unc	BU
2008	—	—	—	—	10.00	12.00

KM# 1090 50 PENCE

8.0000 g., Copper-Nickel, 27.3 mm. **Ruler:** Elizabeth II **Subject:** Our Lady of Europe **Rev:** Madonna and Child seated **Shape:** 7-sided

Date	Mintage	F	VF	XF	Unc	BU
2008	—	—	—	—	7.50	9.00

KM# 1071 50 PENCE

8.0000 g., Copper-Nickel, 27.3 mm. **Ruler:** Elizabeth II **Subject:** Christmas **Shape:** 7-sided

Date	Mintage	F	VF	XF	Unc	BU
2009	—	—	—	—	10.00	12.00

KM# 988 1/25 CROWN

1.2240 g., 0.9990 Gold 0.0393 oz. AGW, 13.92 mm. **Ruler:** Elizabeth II **Subject:** Peter Rabbit Centennial **Obv:** Crowned bust right **Rev:** Peter Rabbit **Edge:** Reeded

Date	Mintage	F	VF	XF	Unc	BU
2002 Proof	5,000	Value: 75.00				

KM# 988a 1/25 CROWN

1.2240 g., 0.9990 Platinum 0.0393 oz. APW, 13.92 mm. **Ruler:** Elizabeth II **Subject:** Peter Rabbit Centennial **Obv:** Crowned bust right **Rev:** Peter Rabbit **Edge:** Reeded

Date	Mintage	F	VF	XF	Unc	BU
2002 Proof	3,000	Value: 85.00				

KM# 1016 1/25 CROWN

1.2441 g., 0.9999 Gold 0.0400 oz. AGW, 13.92 mm. **Ruler:** Elizabeth II **Subject:** Peter Pan **Obv:** Crowned bust right **Rev:** Peter Pan and Tinkerbell flying above city **Edge:** Reeded

Date	Mintage	F	VF	XF	Unc	BU
2002 Proof	10,000	Value: 75.00				

KM# 989 1/10 CROWN

3.1100 g., 0.9990 Gold 0.0999 oz. AGW, 17.95 mm. **Ruler:** Elizabeth II **Subject:** Peter Rabbit Centennial **Obv:** Crowned bust right **Rev:** Peter Rabbit **Edge:** Reeded

Date	Mintage	F	VF	XF	Unc	BU
2002 Proof	5,000	Value: 185				

KM# 989a 1/10 CROWN

3.1100 g., 0.9990 Platinum 0.0999 oz. APW, 17.95 mm. **Ruler:** Elizabeth II **Subject:** Peter Rabbit Centennial **Obv:** Crowned bust right **Rev:** Peter Rabbit **Edge:** Reeded

Date	Mintage	F	VF	XF	Unc	BU
2002 Proof	2,000	Value: 225				

KM# 1017 1/10 CROWN

3.1104 g., 0.9999 Gold 0.1000 oz. AGW, 17.95 mm. **Ruler:** Elizabeth II **Subject:** Peter Pan **Obv:** Crowned bust right **Rev:** Peter Pan and Tinkerbell flying above city **Edge:** Reeded

Date	Mintage	F	VF	XF	Unc	BU
2002 Proof	7,500	Value: 185				

KM# 902 1/5 CROWN

6.2200 g., 0.9999 Gold 0.1999 oz. AGW, 22 mm. **Ruler:** Elizabeth II **Subject:** Queen Mother **Obv:** Bust with tiara right **Rev:** 1953 Coronation scene **Edge:** Reeded

Date	Mintage	F	VF	XF	Unc	BU
2001 Proof	5,000	Value: 375				

KM# 903 1/5 CROWN

6.2200 g., 0.9999 Gold 0.1999 oz. AGW, 22 mm. **Ruler:** Elizabeth II **Obv:** Bust with tiara right **Rev:** Queen Mother and Prince Charles in 1954

Date	Mintage	F	VF	XF	Unc	BU
2001 Proof	5,000	Value: 375				

KM# 909 1/5 CROWN

6.2200 g., 0.9999 Gold 0.1999 oz. AGW, 22 mm. **Ruler:** Elizabeth II **Series:** Victorian Era - Victoria's Coronation 1838 **Obv:** Bust with tiara right **Rev:** 1838 Coronation scene **Edge:** Reeded

Date	Mintage	F	VF	XF	Unc	BU
2001 Proof	5,000	Value: 375				

KM# 909.1 1/5 CROWN

6.2200 g., 0.9999 Gold 0.1999 oz. AGW, 22 mm. **Ruler:** Elizabeth II **Series:** Victorian Era **Obv:** Bust with tiara right **Rev:** 1838 Coronation scene with a tiny emerald set in the field below the 1838 date **Edge:** Reeded

Date	Mintage	F	VF	XF	Unc	BU
2001 Proof	2,001	Value: 375				

KM# 911.1 1/5 CROWN

6.2200 g., 0.9999 Gold 0.1999 oz. AGW, 22 mm. **Ruler:** Elizabeth II **Series:** Victorian Era - Empress of India 1876 **Obv:** Bust with tiara right **Rev:** Crowned portrait of Victoria and two elephants **Edge:** Reeded

Date	Mintage	F	VF	XF	Unc	BU
2001 Proof	5,000	Value: 375				

KM# 911.2 1/5 CROWN

6.2200 g., 0.9999 Gold 0.1999 oz. AGW, 22 mm. **Ruler:** Elizabeth II **Series:** Victorian Era - Empress of India 1876 **Obv:** Bust with tiara right **Rev:** Tiny ruby set in the field behind Victoria's head **Edge:** Reeded

Date	Mintage	F	VF	XF	Unc	BU
2001 Proof	2,001	Value: 375				

KM# 913.1 1/5 CROWN

6.2200 g., 0.9999 Gold 0.1999 oz. AGW, 22 mm. **Ruler:** Elizabeth II **Series:** Victorian Era - Diamond Jubilee 1897 **Obv:** Bust with tiara right **Rev:** Victoria's cameo portrait above naval ships **Edge:** Reeded

Date	Mintage	F	VF	XF	Unc	BU
2001 Proof	5,000	Value: 375				

KM# 913.2 1/5 CROWN

6.2200 g., 0.9999 Gold 0.1999 oz. AGW, 22 mm. **Ruler:** Elizabeth II **Series:** Victorian Era - Diamond Jubilee 1897 **Obv:** Bust with tiara right **Rev:** Tiny diamond set at the top of the fourth mast **Edge:** Reeded

Date	Mintage	F	VF	XF	Unc	BU
2001 Proof	2,001	Value: 375				

KM# 915.1 1/5 CROWN

6.2200 g., 0.9999 Gold 0.1999 oz. AGW, 22 mm. **Ruler:** Elizabeth II **Series:** Victorian Era - Victoria's Death 1901 **Obv:** Bust with tiara right **Rev:** Victoria's cameo portrait and Osborne Manor **Edge:** Reeded

Date	Mintage	F	VF	XF	Unc	BU
2001 Proof	5,000	Value: 375				

KM# 915.2 1/5 CROWN

6.2200 g., 0.9999 Gold 0.1999 oz. AGW, 22 mm. **Ruler:** Elizabeth II **Series:** Victorian Era - Victoria's Death 1901 **Obv:** Bust with tiara right **Rev:** Tiny sapphire set in the field between the towers **Edge:** Reeded

Date	Mintage	F	VF	XF	Unc	BU
2001 Proof	2,001	Value: 375				

KM# 917 1/5 CROWN

6.2200 g., 0.9999 Gold 0.1999 oz. AGW, 22 mm. **Ruler:** Elizabeth II **Series:** Victorian Era - Prince Albert and the Great Exhibition 1851 **Obv:** Bust with tiara right **Rev:** Albert's cameo portrait and the exhibit hall **Edge:** Reeded

Date	Mintage	F	VF	XF	Unc	BU
2001 Proof	5,000	Value: 375				

KM# 919 1/5 CROWN

6.2200 g., 0.9999 Gold 0.1999 oz. AGW, 22 mm. **Ruler:** Elizabeth II **Series:** Victorian Era - Isambard K. Brunel **Obv:** Bust with tiara right **Rev:** Portrait in top hat and railroad bridge **Edge:** Reeded

Date	Mintage	F	VF	XF	Unc	BU
2001 Proof	5,000	Value: 375				

KM# 921 1/5 CROWN

6.2200 g., 0.9999 Gold 0.1999 oz. AGW, 22 mm. **Ruler:** Elizabeth II **Series:** Victorian Era - Charles Dickens **Obv:** Bust with tiara right **Rev:** Portrait and scene from "Oliver Twist" **Edge:** Reeded

Date	Mintage	F	VF	XF	Unc	BU
2001 Proof	5,000	Value: 375				

KM# 923 1/5 CROWN

6.2200 g., 0.9999 Gold 0.1999 oz. AGW, 22 mm. **Ruler:** Elizabeth II **Series:** Victorian Era - Charles Darwin **Obv:** Bust with tiara right **Rev:** Portrait, ship and a squatting aboriginal figure **Edge:** Reeded

Date	Mintage	F	VF	XF	Unc	BU
2001 Proof	5,000	Value: 375				

KM# 925 1/5 CROWN

6.2200 g., 0.9999 Gold 0.1999 oz. AGW, 22 mm. **Ruler:** Elizabeth II **Series:** Mythology of the Solar System **Obv:** Queens portrait **Rev:** Standing goddess with snake basket **Edge:** Reeded

Date	Mintage	F	VF	XF	Unc	BU
2001 Proof	5,000	Value: 375				

KM# 926 1/5 CROWN

Bi-Metallic 0.925 Silver center in 0.999 Gold ring, 32.25 mm. **Ruler:** Elizabeth II **Series:** Mythology of the Solar System **Obv:** Bust with tiara right **Rev:** Standing goddess with snake basket **Edge:** Reeded

Date	Mintage	F	VF	XF	Unc	BU
2001 In Proof sets only	999	Value: 500				

KM# 929.1 1/5 CROWN

6.2200 g., 0.9999 Gold 0.1999 oz. AGW, 22 mm. **Ruler:** Elizabeth II **Series:** Mythology of the Solar System - Sun **Obv:** Bust with tiara right **Rev:** Helios in chariot and the sun **Edge:** Reeded

Date	Mintage	F	VF	XF	Unc	BU
2001 Proof	5,000	Value: 375				

KM# 929.2 1/5 CROWN

6.2200 g., 0.9999 Gold 0.1999 oz. AGW, 22 mm. **Ruler:** Elizabeth II **Series:** Mythology of the Solar System **Obv:** Bust with tiara right **Rev:** Fiery hologram in the sun **Edge:** Reeded

Date	Mintage	F	VF	XF	Unc	BU
2001 In Proof sets only	999	Value: 375				

KM# 931.1 1/5 CROWN

6.2200 g., 0.9999 Gold 0.1999 oz. AGW, 22 mm. **Ruler:** Elizabeth II **Series:** Mythology of the Solar System - Moon **Obv:** Bust with tiara right **Rev:** Goddess Diana and the moon **Edge:** Reeded

Date	Mintage	F	VF	XF	Unc	BU
2001 Proof	5,000	Value: 375				

KM# 931.2 1/5 CROWN

6.2200 g., 0.9999 Gold 0.1999 oz. AGW, 22 mm. **Ruler:** Elizabeth II **Series:** Mythology of the Solar System - Moon **Obv:** Bust with tiara right **Rev:** Small pearl set in the moon **Edge:** Reeded

Date	Mintage	F	VF	XF	Unc	BU
2001 In Proof sets only	999	Value: 375				

KM# 933.1 1/5 CROWN

6.2200 g., 0.9999 Gold 0.1999 oz. AGW, 22 mm. **Ruler:** Elizabeth II **Series:** Mythology of the Solar System - Atlas **Obv:** Bust with tiara right **Rev:** Atlas carrying the earth **Edge:** Reeded

Date	Mintage	F	VF	XF	Unc	BU
2001 Proof	5,000	Value: 375				

KM# 933.2 1/5 CROWN

6.2200 g., 0.9999 Gold 0.1999 oz. AGW, 22 mm. **Ruler:** Elizabeth II **Series:** Mythology of the Solar System - Atlas **Obv:** Bust with tiara right **Rev:** Tiny diamond set in the earth **Edge:** Reeded

Date	Mintage	F	VF	XF	Unc	BU
2001 In Proof sets only	999	Value: 375				

KM# 935 1/5 CROWN

6.2200 g., 0.9999 Gold 0.1999 oz. AGW, 22 mm. **Ruler:** Elizabeth II **Series:** Mythology of the Solar System - Neptune **Obv:** Bust with tiara right **Rev:** Seated god with trident and ringed planet **Edge:** Reeded

Date	Mintage	F	VF	XF	Unc	BU
2001 Proof	5,000	Value: 375				

KM# 937 1/5 CROWN

6.2200 g., 0.9999 Gold 0.1999 oz. AGW, 22 mm. **Ruler:** Elizabeth II **Series:** Mythology of the Solar System - Jupiter **Obv:** Bust with tiara right **Rev:** Seated god with lightning bolts and a planet **Edge:** Reeded

Date	Mintage	F	VF	XF	Unc	BU
2001 Proof	5,000	Value: 375				

KM# 939 1/5 CROWN

6.2200 g., 0.9999 Gold 0.1999 oz. AGW, 22 mm. **Ruler:** Elizabeth II **Series:** Mythology of the Solar System - Mars **Obv:** Bust with tiara right **Rev:** Standing Roman solider and a planet **Edge:** Reeded

Date	Mintage	F	VF	XF	Unc	BU
2001 Proof	5,000	Value: 375				

KM# 941 1/5 CROWN

6.2200 g., 0.9999 Gold 0.1999 oz. AGW, 22 mm. **Ruler:** Elizabeth II **Series:** Mythology of the Solar System - Mercury **Obv:** Bust with tiara right **Rev:** Seated god with caduceus and a planet **Edge:** Reeded

Date	Mintage	F	VF	XF	Unc	BU
2001 Proof	5,000	Value: 375				

KM# 943 1/5 CROWN

6.2200 g., 0.9999 Gold 0.1999 oz. AGW, 22 mm. **Ruler:** Elizabeth II **Series:** Mythology of the Solar System - Uranus **Obv:** Bust with tiara right **Rev:** Seated god with scepter **Edge:** Reeded

Date	Mintage	F	VF	XF	Unc	BU
2001 Proof	5,000	Value: 375				

KM# 945 1/5 CROWN

6.2200 g., 0.9999 Gold 0.1999 oz. AGW, 22 mm. **Ruler:** Elizabeth II **Series:** Mythology of the Solar System - Saturn **Obv:** Bust with tiara right **Rev:** Seated god with long handled sickle and a ringed planet **Edge:** Reeded

Date	Mintage	F	VF	XF	Unc	BU
2001 Proof	5,000	Value: 375				

KM# 947 1/5 CROWN

6.2200 g., 0.9999 Gold 0.1999 oz. AGW, 22 mm. **Ruler:** Elizabeth II **Series:** Mythology of the Solar System - Pluto **Obv:** Bust with tiara right **Rev:** Seated god with dogs and a planet **Edge:** Reeded

Date	Mintage	F	VF	XF	Unc	BU
2001 Proof	5,000	Value: 375				

KM# 949 1/5 CROWN

6.2200 g., 0.9999 Gold 0.1999 oz. AGW, 22 mm. **Ruler:** Elizabeth II **Series:** Mythology of the Solar System - Venus **Obv:** Bust with tiara right **Rev:** Goddess seated on a half shell **Edge:** Reeded

Date	Mintage	F	VF	XF	Unc	BU
2001 Proof	5,000	Value: 375				

KM# 951 1/5 CROWN

6.2200 g., 0.9999 Gold 0.1999 oz. AGW, 22 mm. **Ruler:** Elizabeth II **Subject:** Queen's 76th Birthday **Obv:** Bust with tiara right **Rev:** Queen in Order of the Garter robes with a tiny inset diamond **Edge:** Reeded

Date	Mintage	F	VF	XF	Unc	BU
2001 Proof	2,001	Value: 375				

KM# 954 1/5 CROWN

6.2200 g., 0.9999 Gold 0.1999 oz. AGW, 22 mm. **Ruler:** Elizabeth II **Series:** Victorian Age Part II - Victoria's Accession to the Throne **Obv:** Bust with tiara right **Rev:** Victoria learning of her accession **Edge:** Reeded

Date	Mintage	F	VF	XF	Unc	BU
2001 Proof	5,000	Value: 375				

KM# 956 1/5 CROWN

6.2200 g., 0.9999 Gold 0.1999 oz. AGW, 22 mm. **Ruler:** Elizabeth II **Series:** Victorian Age Part II - Royal Family **Rev:** Victoria and Albert seated with children **Edge:** Reeded

Date	Mintage	F	VF	XF	Unc	BU
2001 Proof	5,000	Value: 375				

KM# 958 1/5 CROWN

6.2200 g., 0.9999 Gold 0.1999 oz. AGW, 22 mm. **Ruler:** Elizabeth II **Series:** Victorian Age Part II - Victoria in Scotland **Obv:** Bust with tiara right **Rev:** Victoria on horse and servant **Edge:** Reeded

Date	Mintage	F	VF	XF	Unc	BU
2001 Proof	5,000	Value: 375				

KM# 960 1/5 CROWN

6.2200 g., 0.9999 Gold 0.1999 oz. AGW, 22 mm. **Ruler:** Elizabeth II **Series:** Victorian Age Part II **Obv:** Bust with tiara right **Rev:** Portraits of Gladstone and Disaraeli **Edge:** Reeded

Date	Mintage	F	VF	XF	Unc	BU
2001 Proof	5,000	Value: 375				

KM# 962 1/5 CROWN

6.2200 g., 0.9999 Gold 0.1999 oz. AGW, 22 mm. **Ruler:** Elizabeth II **Series:** Victorian Age Part II **Obv:** Bust with tiara right **Rev:** Florence Nightingale holding lantern **Edge:** Reeded

Date	Mintage	F	VF	XF	Unc	BU
2001 Proof	5,000	Value: 375				

KM# 964 1/5 CROWN

6.2200 g., 0.9999 Gold 0.1999 oz. AGW, 22 mm. **Ruler:** Elizabeth II **Series:** Victorian Age Part II **Obv:** Bust with tiara right **Rev:** Lord Tennyson with the Light Brigade in background **Edge:** Reeded

Date	Mintage	F	VF	XF	Unc	BU
2001 Proof	5,000	Value: 375				

KM# 966 1/5 CROWN

6.2200 g., 0.9999 Gold 0.1999 oz. AGW, 22 mm. **Ruler:** Elizabeth II **Series:** Victorian Age Part II **Obv:** Bust with tiara right **Rev:** Stanley meeting Dr. Livingstone **Edge:** Reeded

Date	Mintage	F	VF	XF	Unc	BU
2001 Proof	5,000	Value: 375				

KM# 968 1/5 CROWN

6.2200 g., 0.9999 Gold 0.1999 oz. AGW, 22 mm. **Ruler:** Elizabeth II **Series:** Victorian Age Part II **Obv:** Bust with tiara right **Rev:** Bronte sisters **Edge:** Reeded

Date	Mintage	F	VF	XF	Unc	BU
2001 Proof	5,000	Value: 375				

KM# 978 1/5 CROWN

6.2200 g., 0.9990 Gold 0.1998 oz. AGW, 22 mm. **Ruler:** Elizabeth II **Subject:** Queen Mother's Life **Obv:** Bust right **Rev:** Prince William's christening scene **Edge:** Reeded

Date	Mintage	F	VF	XF	Unc	BU
2002 Proof	5,000	Value: 375				

KM# 980 1/5 CROWN

6.2200 g., 0.9999 Gold 0.1999 oz. AGW, 22 mm. **Ruler:** Elizabeth II **Subject:** World Cup Soccer **Obv:** Bust right **Rev:** Two players about to collide **Edge:** Reeded

Date	Mintage	F	VF	XF	Unc	BU
2002 Proof	5,000	Value: 375				

KM# 982 1/5 CROWN

6.2200 g., 0.9999 Gold 0.1999 oz. AGW, 22 mm. **Ruler:** Elizabeth II **Subject:** World Cup Soccer **Obv:** Bust right **Rev:** Two players facing viewer **Edge:** Reeded

Date	Mintage	F	VF	XF	Unc	BU
2002 Proof	5,000	Value: 375				

KM# 984 1/5 CROWN
6.2200 g., 0.9999 Gold 0.1999 oz. AGW, 22 mm. **Ruler:** Elizabeth II **Subject:** World Cup Soccer **Obv:** Bust right **Rev:** Two horizontal players **Edge:** Reeded

Date	Mintage	F	VF	XF	Unc	BU
2002 Proof	5,000	Value: 375				

KM# 986 1/5 CROWN
6.2200 g., 0.9999 Gold 0.1999 oz. AGW, 22 mm. **Ruler:** Elizabeth II **Subject:** World Cup Soccer **Obv:** Bust right **Rev:** Two players moving to the left **Edge:** Reeded

Date	Mintage	F	VF	XF	Unc	BU
2002 Proof	5,000	Value: 375				

KM# 990 1/5 CROWN
6.2200 g., 0.9990 Gold 0.1998 oz. AGW, 22 mm. **Ruler:** Elizabeth II **Subject:** Peter Rabbit Centennial **Obv:** Bust right **Rev:** Peter Rabbit **Edge:** Reeded

Date	Mintage	F	VF	XF	Unc	BU
2002 Proof	3,500	Value: 375				

KM# 990a 1/5 CROWN
6.2200 g., 0.9990 Platinum 0.1998 oz. APW, 22 mm. **Ruler:** Elizabeth II **Subject:** Peter Rabbit Centennial **Obv:** Bust right **Rev:** Peter Rabbit **Edge:** Reeded

Date	Mintage	F	VF	XF	Unc	BU
2002 Proof	1,500	Value: 400				

KM# 993 1/5 CROWN
6.2200 g., 0.3750 Gold 0.0750 oz. AGW, 22 mm. **Ruler:** Elizabeth II **Subject:** Queen's Golden Jubilee **Obv:** Bust with tiara right **Rev:** Royal couple and tree house **Edge:** Reeded

Date	Mintage	F	VF	XF	Unc	BU
2002 Proof	5,000	Value: 140				

KM# 993a 1/5 CROWN
6.2200 g., 0.9999 Gold 0.1999 oz. AGW, 22 mm. **Ruler:** Elizabeth II **Subject:** Queen's Golden Jubilee **Obv:** Bust with tiara right **Rev:** Royal couple and tree house **Edge:** Reeded

Date	Mintage	F	VF	XF	Unc	BU
2002 Proof	2,002	Value: 375				

KM# 995 1/5 CROWN
6.2200 g., 0.3750 Gold 0.0750 oz. AGW, 22 mm. **Ruler:** Elizabeth II **Subject:** Queen's Golden Jubilee **Obv:** Bust with tiara right **Rev:** Royal coach **Edge:** Reeded

Date	Mintage	F	VF	XF	Unc	BU
2002 Proof	5,000	Value: 140				

KM# 995a 1/5 CROWN
6.2200 g., 0.9999 Gold 0.1999 oz. AGW, 22 mm. **Ruler:** Elizabeth II **Subject:** Queen's Golden Jubilee **Obv:** Bust with tiara right **Rev:** Royal coach **Edge:** Reeded

Date	Mintage	F	VF	XF	Unc	BU
2002 Proof	2,002	Value: 375				

KM# 997 1/5 CROWN
6.2200 g., 0.3750 Gold 0.0750 oz. AGW, 22 mm. **Ruler:** Elizabeth II **Subject:** Queen's Golden Jubilee **Obv:** Bust with tiara right **Rev:** Queen holding baby **Edge:** Reeded

Date	Mintage	F	VF	XF	Unc	BU
2002 Proof	5,000	Value: 140				

KM# 997a 1/5 CROWN
6.2200 g., 0.9999 Gold 0.1999 oz. AGW, 22 mm. **Ruler:** Elizabeth II **Subject:** Queen's Golden Jubilee **Obv:** Bust with tiara right **Rev:** Queen holding baby **Edge:** Reeded

Date	Mintage	F	VF	XF	Unc	BU
2002 Proof	2,002	Value: 375				

KM# 999 1/5 CROWN
6.2200 g., 0.3750 Gold 0.0750 oz. AGW, 22 mm. **Ruler:** Elizabeth II **Subject:** Queen's Golden Jubilee **Obv:** Bust with tiara right **Rev:** Yacht under Tower bridge **Edge:** Reeded

Date	Mintage	F	VF	XF	Unc	BU
2002 Proof	5,000	Value: 140				

KM# 999a 1/5 CROWN
6.2200 g., 0.9999 Gold 0.1999 oz. AGW, 22 mm. **Ruler:** Elizabeth II **Subject:** Queen's Golden Jubilee **Obv:** Bust with tiara right **Rev:** Yacht under Tower bridge **Edge:** Reeded

Date	Mintage	F	VF	XF	Unc	BU
2002 Proof	2,002	Value: 375				

KM# 1001 1/5 CROWN
6.2200 g., 0.9999 Gold 0.1999 oz. AGW, 22 mm. **Ruler:** Elizabeth II **Subject:** Queen's Golden Jubilee **Obv:** Bust with tiara right **Rev:** Crown jewels inset with a tiny diamond, ruby, sapphire and emerald **Edge:** Reeded

Date	Mintage	F	VF	XF	Unc	BU
2002 Proof	2,002	Value: 375				

KM# 1003 1/5 CROWN
6.2200 g., Electrum Special alloy of equal parts of gold and silver, 22 mm. **Ruler:** Elizabeth II **Series:** Ancient Coins **Obv:** Bust with tiara right **Rev:** Head of Athena left **Edge:** Reeded **Note:** From a Mysia electrum coin c.520BC.

Date	Mintage	F	VF	XF	Unc	BU
2002 Proof	3,500	Value: 175				

KM# 1005 1/5 CROWN
6.2200 g., Electrum Special alloy of equal parts of gold and silver., 22 mm. **Ruler:** Elizabeth II **Series:** Ancient Coins **Obv:** Bust with tiara right **Rev:** Head of Hercules right **Edge:** Reeded **Note:** From a Lesbos coin c. 480-450 BC.

Date	Mintage	F	VF	XF	Unc	BU
2002 Proof	3,500	Value: 175				

KM# 1007 1/5 CROWN
6.2200 g., 0.9990 Electrum Special alloy of equal parts of gold and silver. 0.1998 oz., 22 mm. **Ruler:** Elizabeth II **Series:** Ancient Coins **Obv:** Bust with tiara right **Rev:** Pegasus **Edge:** Reeded **Note:** From a Lampsakos electrum coin c. 450 BC.

Date	Mintage	F	VF	XF	Unc	BU
2002 Proof	3,500	Value: 175				

KM# 1009 1/5 CROWN
6.2200 g., Electrum Special Alloy of equal parts of gold and silver., 22 mm. **Ruler:** Elizabeth II **Series:** Ancient Coins **Obv:** Bust with tiara right **Rev:** Lion and bull facing **Edge:** Reeded **Note:** From a Kroisos "sic" coin c. 560-546 BC.

Date	Mintage	F	VF	XF	Unc	BU
2002 Proof	3,500	Value: 175				

KM# 1012 1/5 CROWN
6.2200 g., 0.9999 Gold 0.1999 oz. AGW, 22 mm. **Ruler:** Elizabeth II **Subject:** Queen Mother **Obv:** Bust with tiara right **Rev:** Queen Mother trout fishing **Edge:** Reeded

Date	Mintage	F	VF	XF	Unc	BU
2002 Proof	5,000	Value: 375				

KM# 1014 1/5 CROWN
6.2200 g., 0.9999 Gold 0.1999 oz. AGW, 22 mm. **Ruler:** Elizabeth II **Subject:** Princess Diana **Obv:** Bust right **Rev:** Diana's portrait **Edge:** Reeded

Date	Mintage	F	VF	XF	Unc	BU
2002 Proof	5,000	Value: 375				

KM# 1018 1/5 CROWN
6.2200 g., 0.9999 Gold 0.1999 oz. AGW, 22 mm. **Ruler:** Elizabeth II **Subject:** Peter Pan **Obv:** Bust right **Rev:** Peter Pan and Tinkerbell flying above city **Edge:** Reeded

Date	Mintage	F	VF	XF	Unc	BU
2002 Proof	5,000	Value: 375				

KM# 1020 1/5 CROWN
6.2200 g., 0.9999 Gold 0.1999 oz. AGW, 22 mm. **Ruler:** Elizabeth II **Subject:** Grand Masonic Lodge **Obv:** Bust right **Rev:** Masonic seal above Gibraltar **Edge:** Reeded

Date	Mintage	F	VF	XF	Unc	BU
2002 Proof	5,000	Value: 375				

KM# 991 1/2 CROWN
15.5500 g., 0.9990 Gold 0.4994 oz. AGW, 30 mm. **Ruler:** Elizabeth II **Subject:** Peter Rabbit Centennial **Obv:** Bust right **Rev:** Peter Rabbit **Edge:** Reeded

Date	Mintage	F	VF	XF	Unc	BU
2002 Proof	1,000	Value: 900				

KM# 1002 1/2 CROWN
15.5500 g., 0.9999 Gold 0.4999 oz. AGW, 30 mm. **Ruler:** Elizabeth II **Subject:** Queen's Golden Jubilee **Obv:** Bust with tiara right **Rev:** Crown jewels inset with a tiny diamond, ruby, sapphire and emerald **Edge:** Reeded

Date	Mintage	F	VF	XF	Unc	BU
2002 Proof	999	Value: 900				

KM# 1004 1/2 CROWN
15.5500 g., Electrum Special alloy of equal parts of gold and silver., 32.2 mm. **Ruler:** Elizabeth II **Series:** Ancient Coins **Obv:** Bust with tiara right **Rev:** Head of Athena left **Edge:** Reeded **Note:** From a Mysia electrum coin c. 520 BC.

Date	Mintage	F	VF	XF	Unc	BU
2002 Proof	2,000	Value: 300				

KM# 1006 1/2 CROWN
15.5500 g., Electrum Special alloy of equal parts of gold and silver., 32.2 mm. **Ruler:** Elizabeth II **Series:** Ancient Coins **Obv:** Bust with tiara right **Rev:** Head of Hercules right **Edge:** Reeded **Note:** From a Lesbos coin c. 480-450 BC.

Date	Mintage	F	VF	XF	Unc	BU
2002 Proof	2,000	Value: 300				

KM# 1008 1/2 CROWN
15.5500 g., Gold With Silver Special alloy of equal parts of gold and silver., 32.2 mm. **Ruler:** Elizabeth II **Series:** Ancient Coins **Obv:** Bust with tiara right **Rev:** Pegasus **Edge:** Reeded **Note:** From a Lampsakos electrum coin c. 450 BC.

Date	Mintage	F	VF	XF	Unc	BU
2002 Proof	2,000	Value: 300				

KM# 1010 1/2 CROWN
15.5500 g., Electrum Special alloy of equal parts of gold and silver., 32.2 mm. **Ruler:** Elizabeth II **Series:** Ancient Coins **Obv:** Bust with tiara right **Rev:** Lion and bull facing **Edge:** Reeded **Note:** From a Kroisos [sic] coin c. 560-546 BC.

Date	Mintage	F	VF	XF	Unc	BU
2002 Proof	2,000	Value: 300				

KM# 904 CROWN
28.2800 g., Copper-Nickel, 38.6 mm. **Ruler:** Elizabeth II **Subject:** The Life of Queen Elizabeth - The Queen Mother **Obv:** Bust with tiara right **Rev:** 1953 Coronation scene **Edge:** Reeded

Date	Mintage	F	VF	XF	Unc	BU
2001	—	—	—	—	10.00	12.00

KM# 904a CROWN
28.2800 g., 0.9250 Silver 0.8410 oz. ASW, 38.6 mm. **Ruler:** Elizabeth II **Subject:** The Life of Queen Elizabeth - The Queen Mother **Obv:** Bust with tiara right **Rev:** 1953 Coronation scene **Edge:** Reeded

Date	Mintage	F	VF	XF	Unc	BU
2001 Proof	10,000	Value: 47.50				

KM# 905 CROWN
28.2800 g., Copper-Nickel, 38.6 mm. **Ruler:** Elizabeth II **Subject:** The Life of Queen Elizabeth - The Queen Mother **Obv:** Bust with tiara right **Rev:** Queen Mother with Prince Charles in 1954 **Edge:** Reeded

Date	Mintage	F	VF	XF	Unc	BU
2001	—	—	—	—	10.00	12.00

KM# 905a CROWN
28.2800 g., 0.9250 Silver 0.8410 oz. ASW, 38.6 mm. **Ruler:** Elizabeth II **Subject:** The Life of Queen Elizabeth - The Queen Mother **Obv:** Bust with tiara right **Rev:** Queen Mother with Prince Charles in 1954 **Edge:** Reeded

Date	Mintage	F	VF	XF	Unc	BU
2001 Proof	10,000	Value: 47.50				

KM# 906 CROWN
28.2800 g., Copper-Nickel, 38.6 mm. **Ruler:** Elizabeth II **Subject:** 21st Century **Obv:** Crowned bust right, date below **Rev:** Celtic cross, Viking ship and modern technological items **Edge:** Reeded

Date	Mintage	F	VF	XF	Unc	BU
2001	—	—	—	—	10.00	12.00

KM# 906a CROWN
31.1035 g., 0.9990 Silver 0.9990 oz. ASW, 38.6 mm. **Ruler:** Elizabeth II **Subject:** 21st Century **Obv:** Crowned bust right, date below **Rev:** Celtic cross, Viking ship and modern technological items **Edge:** Reeded **Note:** 31.1035 .999 Silver, 1.0000 ASW with a gold plated inner ring and a blackened outer ring.

Date	Mintage	F	VF	XF	Unc	BU
2001 Proof	2,001	Value: 75.00				

KM# 906b CROWN

31.1000 g., Tri-Metallic Center .9995 Platinum 5.2g. Inner Ring .9999 Gold 14.2g. Outer Ring .999 Silver 11.7g **Ruler:** Elizabeth II **Subject:** 21st Century **Obv:** Crowned bust right, date below **Rev:** Celtic cross, Viking ship and modern technological items

Date	Mintage	F	VF	XF	Unc	BU
2001 Proof	999	Value: 750				

KM# 910 CROWN

28.2800 g., Copper-Nickel, 38.6 mm. **Ruler:** Elizabeth II **Series:** The Victorian Age **Obv:** Bust with tiara right **Rev:** 1838 Coronation of Queen Victoria **Edge:** Reeded

Date	Mintage	F	VF	XF	Unc	BU
2001	—	—	—	—	10.00	12.00

KM# 910a CROWN

28.2800 g., 0.9250 Silver 0.8410 oz. ASW, 38.6 mm. **Ruler:** Elizabeth II **Series:** Victorian Era **Obv:** Bust with tiara right **Rev:** 1838 Coronation scene **Edge:** Reeded

Date	Mintage	F	VF	XF	Unc	BU
2001 Proof	10,000	Value: 47.50				

KM# 912 CROWN

Copper-Nickel, 38.6 mm. **Ruler:** Elizabeth II **Series:** Victorian Era - Empress of India 1876 **Obv:** Bust with tiara right **Rev:** Crowned portrait of Victoria and two elephants

Date	Mintage	F	VF	XF	Unc	BU
2001	—	—	—	—	10.00	12.00

KM# 912a CROWN

28.2800 g., 0.9250 Silver 0.8410 oz. ASW **Ruler:** Elizabeth II **Series:** The Victorian Age - Empress of India 1876 **Obv:** Bust with tiara right **Rev:** Crowned portrait of Victoria and two elephants

Date	Mintage	F	VF	XF	Unc	BU
2001 Proof	10,000	Value: 47.50				

KM# 914 CROWN

Copper-Nickel, 38.6 mm. **Ruler:** Elizabeth II **Series:** Victorian Era - Diamond Jubilee **Obv:** Bust with tiara right **Rev:** Victoria's cameo portrait above naval ships

Date	Mintage	F	VF	XF	Unc	BU
2001	—	—	—	—	10.00	12.00

KM# 914a CROWN

28.2800 g., 0.9250 Silver 0.8410 oz. ASW **Ruler:** Elizabeth II **Series:** The Victorian Age - Diamond Jubilee 1897 **Obv:** Bust with tiara right **Rev:** Victoria's cameo above naval ships, Spithead Review

Date	Mintage	F	VF	XF	Unc	BU
2001 Proof	10,000	Value: 47.50				

KM# 916 CROWN

Copper-Nickel, 38.6 mm. **Ruler:** Elizabeth II **Series:** The Victorian Age - Victoria's Death 1901 **Obv:** Bust with tiara right **Rev:** Victoria's cameo portrait and Osborne Manor

Date	Mintage	F	VF	XF	Unc	BU
2001	—	—	—	—	10.00	12.00

KM# 916a CROWN

28.2800 g., 0.9250 Silver 0.8410 oz. ASW, 38.6 mm. **Ruler:** Elizabeth II **Series:** The Victorian Age - Victoria's Death 1901 **Obv:** Bust with tiara right **Rev:** Victoria's cameo portrait and Osborne Manor

Date	Mintage	F	VF	XF	Unc	BU
2001 Proof	10,000	Value: 47.50				

KM# 918 CROWN

Copper-Nickel, 38.6 mm. **Ruler:** Elizabeth II **Series:** The Victorian Age - Prince Albert and the Great Exhibition 1851 **Obv:** Bust with tiara right **Rev:** Albert's cameo portrait and the exhibit hall

Date	Mintage	F	VF	XF	Unc	BU
2001 Proof	5,000	Value: 175				

KM# 918a CROWN

28.2800 g., 0.9250 Silver 0.8410 oz. ASW, 38.6 mm. **Ruler:** Elizabeth II **Series:** The Victorian Age - Prince Albert and the Great Exhibition 1851 **Obv:** Bust with tiara right **Rev:** Albert's cameo portrait and the exhibit hall

Date	Mintage	F	VF	XF	Unc	BU
2001 Proof	10,000	Value: 47.50				

KM# 920 CROWN

Copper-Nickel, 38.6 mm. **Ruler:** Elizabeth II **Series:** The Victorian Age **Obv:** Bust with tiara right **Rev:** 1/2 bust of Isambard K. Brunel half left in front of railroad bridge

Date	Mintage	F	VF	XF	Unc	BU
2001	—	—	—	—	10.00	12.00

KM# 920a CROWN

28.2800 g., 0.9250 Silver 0.8410 oz. ASW, 38.6 mm. **Ruler:** Elizabeth II **Series:** Victorian Era **Obv:** Bust with tiara right **Rev:** 1/2 bust of Isambard K. Brunel half left in front of railroad bridge

Date	Mintage	F	VF	XF	Unc	BU
2001 Proof	10,000	Value: 47.50				

KM# 922 CROWN

Copper-Nickel, 38.6 mm. **Ruler:** Elizabeth II **Series:** The Victorian Age **Obv:** Bust with tiara right **Rev:** 1/2 length bust of Charles Dickens half left, scene from "Oliver Twist" in background

Date	Mintage	F	VF	XF	Unc	BU
2001	—	—	—	—	10.00	12.00

KM# 922a CROWN

28.2800 g., 0.9250 Silver 0.8410 oz. ASW, 38.6 mm. **Series:** The Victorian Age **Obv:** Bust with tiara right **Rev:** 1/2 length bust of Charles Dickens half left, scene from "Oliver Twist" in background

Date	Mintage	F	VF	XF	Unc	BU
2001 Proof	10,000	Value: 47.50				

KM# 924 CROWN

Copper-Nickel, 38.6 mm. **Ruler:** Elizabeth II **Series:** The Victorian Age **Obv:** Bust with tiara right **Rev:** 3/4-length figure of Charles Darwin right, ship and a squatting aboriginal figure

Date	Mintage	F	VF	XF	Unc	BU
2001	—	—	—	—	10.00	12.00

KM# 924a CROWN

28.2800 g., 0.9250 Silver 0.8410 oz. ASW, 38.6 mm. **Ruler:** Elizabeth II **Series:** The Victorian Age **Obv:** Bust with tiara right **Rev:** 3/4-length figure of Charles Darwin right, ship and a squatting aboriginal figure

Date	Mintage	F	VF	XF	Unc	BU
2001 Proof	10,000	Value: 47.50				

KM# 927 CROWN

28.2800 g., Copper-Nickel, 38.6 mm. **Ruler:** Elizabeth II **Series:** Mythology of the Solar System **Obv:** Bust with tiara right **Rev:** Standing goddess with snake basket **Edge:** Reeded

Date	Mintage	F	VF	XF	Unc	BU
2001	—	—	—	—	10.00	12.00

KM# 927a CROWN

28.2800 g., 0.9250 Silver 0.8410 oz. ASW, 38.6 mm. **Ruler:** Elizabeth II **Series:** Mythology of the Solar System **Obv:** Bust with tiara right **Rev:** Standing goddess with snake basket **Edge:** Reeded

Date	Mintage	F	VF	XF	Unc	BU
2001 Proof	10,000	Value: 47.50				

KM# 928 CROWN

Bi-Metallic Titanium center in Silver ring, 32.25 mm. **Ruler:** Elizabeth II **Series:** Mythology of the Solar System **Obv:** Bust with tiara right **Rev:** Standing goddess with snake basket **Edge:** Reeded

Date	Mintage	F	VF	XF	Unc	BU
2001 In Proof sets only	2,001	Value: 150				

KM# 930 CROWN

Copper-Nickel, 38.6 mm. **Ruler:** Elizabeth II **Series:** Mythology of the Solar System - Sun **Obv:** Bust with tiara right **Rev:** Helios in chariot and the sun

Date	Mintage	F	VF	XF	Unc	BU
2001	—	—	—	—	10.00	12.00

KM# 930a CROWN

28.2800 g., 0.9250 Silver 0.8410 oz. ASW, 38.6 mm. **Ruler:** Elizabeth II **Series:** Mythology of the Solar System - Sun **Obv:** Bust with tiara right **Rev:** Helios in chariot and the sun

Date	Mintage	F	VF	XF	Unc	BU
2001 Proof	10,000	Value: 47.50				

KM# 930a.1 CROWN

28.2800 g., 0.9250 Silver 0.8410 oz. ASW **Ruler:** Elizabeth II **Series:** Mythology of the Solar System - Sun **Obv:** Bust with tiara right **Rev:** Fiery hologram in the sun

Date	Mintage	F	VF	XF	Unc	BU
2001 Proof	2,001	Value: 87.50				

KM# 932 CROWN

Copper-Nickel, 38.6 mm. **Ruler:** Elizabeth II **Series:** Mythology of the Solar System - Moon **Obv:** Bust with tiara right **Rev:** Goddess Diana and the moon

Date	Mintage	F	VF	XF	Unc	BU
2001	—	—	—	—	10.00	12.00

KM# 932a CROWN

28.2800 g., 0.9250 Silver 0.8410 oz. ASW, 38.6 mm. **Ruler:** Elizabeth II **Series:** Mythology of the Solar System - Moon **Obv:** Bust with tiara right **Rev:** Goddess Diana and the moon

Date	Mintage	F	VF	XF	Unc	BU
2001 Proof	10,000	Value: 47.50				

KM# 932a.1 CROWN

28.2800 g., 0.9250 Silver 0.8410 oz. ASW, 38.6 mm. **Ruler:** Elizabeth II **Series:** Mythology of the Solar System - Moon **Obv:** Bust with tiara right **Rev:** Small pearl set in the moon

Date	Mintage	F	VF	XF	Unc	BU
2001 Proof	2,001	Value: 87.50				

KM# 934 CROWN

Copper-Nickel **Ruler:** Elizabeth II **Series:** Mythology of the Solar System - Atlas **Obv:** Bust with tiara right **Rev:** Atlas carrying the earth

Date	Mintage	F	VF	XF	Unc	BU
2001	—	—	—	—	10.00	12.00

KM# 934a CROWN

28.2800 g., 0.9250 Silver 0.8410 oz. ASW, 38.6 mm. **Ruler:** Elizabeth II **Series:** Mythology of the Solar System - Atlas **Obv:** Bust with tiara right **Rev:** Atlas carrying the earth

Date	Mintage	F	VF	XF	Unc	BU
2001 Proof	10,000	Value: 47.50				

KM# 934a.1 CROWN

28.2800 g., 0.9250 Silver 0.8410 oz. ASW, 38.6 mm. **Ruler:** Elizabeth II **Series:** Mythology of the Solar System - Atlas **Obv:** Bust with tiara right **Rev:** Fancy diamond set in the earth

Date	Mintage	F	VF	XF	Unc	BU
2001 Proof	2,001	Value: 87.50				

KM# 936 CROWN

Copper-Nickel, 38.6 mm. **Ruler:** Elizabeth II **Series:** Mythology of the Solar System **Obv:** Bust with tiara right **Rev:** Seated Neptune with trident and ringed planet

Date	Mintage	F	VF	XF	Unc	BU
2001	—	—	—	—	10.00	12.00

KM# 936a CROWN

28.2800 g., 0.9250 Silver 0.8410 oz. ASW, 38.6 mm. **Ruler:** Elizabeth II **Series:** Mythology of the Solar System **Obv:** Bust with tiara right **Rev:** Seated Neptune with trident and ringed planet

Date	Mintage	F	VF	XF	Unc	BU
2001 Proof	10,000	Value: 47.50				

KM# 938 CROWN

Copper-Nickel, 38.6 mm. **Ruler:** Elizabeth II **Series:** Mythology of the Solar System **Obv:** Bust with tiara right **Rev:** Seated Jupiter with lightening bolts and a planet

Date	Mintage	F	VF	XF	Unc	BU
2001	—	—	—	—	10.00	12.00

KM# 938a CROWN

28.2800 g., 0.9250 Silver 0.8410 oz. ASW, 38.6 mm. **Ruler:** Elizabeth II **Series:** Mythology of the Solar System **Obv:** Bust with tiara right **Rev:** Seated Jupiter with lightening bolts and a planet

Date	Mintage	F	VF	XF	Unc	BU
2001 Proof	10,000	Value: 47.50				

KM# 940 CROWN

Copper-Nickel, 38.6 mm. **Ruler:** Elizabeth II **Series:** Mythology of the Solar System - Mars **Obv:** Bust with tiara right **Rev:** Standing Roman soldier and a planet

Date	Mintage	F	VF	XF	Unc	BU
2001	—	—	—	—	10.00	12.00

KM# 940a CROWN

28.2800 g., 0.9250 Silver 0.8410 oz. ASW, 38.6 mm. **Ruler:** Elizabeth II **Series:** Mythology of the Solar System - Mars **Obv:** Bust with tiara right **Rev:** Standing Roman soldier and a planet

Date	Mintage	F	VF	XF	Unc	BU
2001 Proof	10,000	Value: 47.50				

KM# 942 CROWN

Copper-Nickel, 38.6 mm. **Ruler:** Elizabeth II **Series:** Mythology of the Solar System **Obv:** Bust with tiara right **Rev:** Seated Mercury with caduceus and a planet

Date	Mintage	F	VF	XF	Unc	BU
2001	—	—	—	—	10.00	12.00

KM# 942a CROWN

28.2800 g., 0.9250 Silver 0.8410 oz. ASW, 38.6 mm. **Ruler:** Elizabeth II **Series:** Mythology of the Solar System **Obv:** Bust with tiara right **Rev:** Seated Mercury with caduceus and a planet

Date	Mintage	F	VF	XF	Unc	BU
2001 Proof	10,000	Value: 47.50				

KM# 944 CROWN

Copper-Nickel, 38.6 mm. **Ruler:** Elizabeth II **Series:** Mythology of the Solar System **Obv:** Bust with tiara right **Rev:** Seated Uranus with scepter

Date	Mintage	F	VF	XF	Unc	BU
2001	—	—	—	—	10.00	12.00

KM# 944a CROWN

28.2800 g., 0.9250 Silver 0.8410 oz. ASW, 38.6 mm. **Ruler:** Elizabeth II **Series:** Mythology of the Solar System **Obv:** Bust with tiara right **Rev:** Seated Uranus with scepter

Date	Mintage	F	VF	XF	Unc	BU
2001 Proof	10,000	Value: 47.50				

KM# 946 CROWN

Copper-Nickel, 38.6 mm. **Ruler:** Elizabeth II **Series:** Mythology of the Solar System **Obv:** Bust with tiara right **Rev:** Seated Saturn with long handled sickle and a ringed planet

Date	Mintage	F	VF	XF	Unc	BU
2001	—	—	—	—	10.00	12.00

KM# 946a CROWN

28.2800 g., 0.9250 Silver 0.8410 oz. ASW, 38.6 mm. **Ruler:** Elizabeth II **Series:** Mythology of the Solar System **Obv:** Bust with tiara right **Rev:** Seated Saturn with long handled sickle and a ringed planet

Date	Mintage	F	VF	XF	Unc	BU
2001 Proof	10,000	Value: 47.50				

KM# 948 CROWN

Copper-Nickel, 38.6 mm. **Ruler:** Elizabeth II **Series:** Mythology of the Solar System **Obv:** Bust with tiara right **Rev:** Seated Pluto with dogs and planet

Date	Mintage	F	VF	XF	Unc	BU
2001	—	—	—	—	10.00	12.00

KM# 948a CROWN

28.2800 g., 0.9250 Silver 0.8410 oz. ASW, 38.6 mm. **Ruler:** Elizabeth II **Series:** Mythology of the Solar System **Obv:** Bust with tiara right **Rev:** Seated Pluto with dogs and planet

Date	Mintage	F	VF	XF	Unc	BU
2001 Proof	10,000	Value: 47.50				

KM# 950 CROWN

Copper-Nickel, 38.6 mm. **Ruler:** Elizabeth II **Series:** Mythology of the Solar System **Obv:** Bust with tiara right **Rev:** Venus seated on a half shell

Date	Mintage	F	VF	XF	Unc	BU
2001	—	—	—	—	10.00	12.00

KM# 950a CROWN

28.2800 g., 0.9250 Silver 0.8410 oz. ASW, 38.6 mm. **Ruler:** Elizabeth II **Series:** Mythology of the Solar System **Obv:** Bust with tiara right **Rev:** Venus seated on a half shell

Date	Mintage	F	VF	XF	Unc	BU
2001 Proof	10,000	Value: 47.50				

KM# 952 CROWN

28.2800 g., Copper-Nickel, 38.6 mm. **Ruler:** Elizabeth II **Subject:** Queen's 75th Birthday **Obv:** Bust with tiara right **Rev:** Queen in Order of Garter robes **Edge:** Reeded

Date	Mintage	F	VF	XF	Unc	BU
2001	—	—	—	—	10.00	12.00

KM# 952a CROWN

28.2800 g., 0.9250 Silver 0.8410 oz. ASW, 38.6 mm. **Ruler:** Elizabeth II **Subject:** Queen's 75th Birthday **Obv:** Bust with tiara right **Rev:** Queen in Order of Garter robes **Edge:** Reeded

Date	Mintage	F	VF	XF	Unc	BU
2001 Proof	10,000	Value: 47.50				

KM# 955 CROWN

28.2800 g., Copper-Nickel, 38.6 mm. **Ruler:** Elizabeth II **Series:** Victorian Age Part II **Obv:** Bust with tiara right **Rev:** Victoria learning of her accession **Edge:** Reeded

Date	Mintage	F	VF	XF	Unc	BU
2001	—	—	—	—	10.00	12.00

KM# 955a CROWN

28.2800 g., 0.9250 Silver 0.8410 oz. ASW, 38.6 mm. **Ruler:** Elizabeth II **Series:** Victorian Age Part II **Obv:** Bust with tiara right **Rev:** Victoria learning of her accession **Edge:** Reeded

Date	Mintage	F	VF	XF	Unc	BU
2001 Proof	10,000	Value: 47.50				

KM# 957 CROWN

Copper-Nickel, 38.6 mm. **Ruler:** Elizabeth II **Series:** Victorian Age Part II - Royal Family **Obv:** Bust with tiara right **Rev:** Victoria and Albert seated with children **Edge:** Reeded

Date	Mintage	F	VF	XF	Unc	BU
2001	—	—	—	—	10.00	12.00

KM# 957a CROWN

28.2800 g., 0.9250 Silver 0.8410 oz. ASW, 38.6 mm. **Ruler:** Elizabeth II **Series:** Victorian Age Part II - Royal Family **Obv:** Bust with tiara right **Rev:** Victoria and Albert seated with children **Edge:** Reeded

Date	Mintage	F	VF	XF	Unc	BU
2001 Proof	10,000	Value: 47.50				

KM# 959 CROWN

Copper-Nickel, 38.6 mm. **Ruler:** Elizabeth II **Series:** Victorian Age Part II - Victoria in Scotland **Obv:** Bust with tiara right **Rev:** Victoria on horse with servant **Edge:** Reeded

Date	Mintage	F	VF	XF	Unc	BU
2001	2,001	—	—	—	10.00	12.00

KM# 959a CROWN

28.2800 g., 0.9250 Silver 0.8410 oz. ASW, 38.6 mm. **Ruler:** Elizabeth II **Series:** Victorian Age Part II - Victoria in Scotland **Obv:** Bust with tiara right **Rev:** Victoria on horse with servant **Edge:** Reeded

Date	Mintage	F	VF	XF	Unc	BU
2001 Proof	10,000	Value: 47.50				

KM# 961 CROWN

Copper-Nickel, 38.6 mm. **Ruler:** Elizabeth II **Series:** Victorian Age Part II - Gladstone and Disraeli **Obv:** Bust with tiara right **Rev:** Portraits of both politicians **Edge:** Reeded

Date	Mintage	F	VF	XF	Unc	BU
2001	—	—	—	—	10.00	12.00

KM# 961a CROWN

28.2800 g., 0.9250 Silver 0.8410 oz. ASW, 38.6 mm. **Ruler:** Elizabeth II **Series:** Victorian Age Part II - Gladstone and Disraeli **Obv:** Bust with tiara right **Rev:** Portraits of both politicians **Edge:** Reeded

Date	Mintage	F	VF	XF	Unc	BU
2001 Proof	10,000	Value: 47.50				

KM# 963 CROWN

Copper-Nickel, 38.6 mm. **Ruler:** Elizabeth II **Series:** Victorian Age Part II **Obv:** Bust with tiara right **Rev:** Florence Nightingale holding lantern **Edge:** Reeded

Date	Mintage	F	VF	XF	Unc	BU
2001	—	—	—	—	10.00	12.00

KM# 963a CROWN

28.2800 g., 0.9250 Silver 0.8410 oz. ASW, 38.6 mm. **Ruler:** Elizabeth II **Series:** Victorian Age Part II **Obv:** Bust with tiara right **Rev:** Florence Nightingale holding lantern **Edge:** Reeded

Date	Mintage	F	VF	XF	Unc	BU
2001 Proof	10,000	Value: 47.50				

KM# 965 CROWN

Copper-Nickel, 38.6 mm. **Ruler:** Elizabeth II **Series:** Victorian Age Part II **Obv:** Bust with tiara right **Rev:** Lord Tennyson with the Light Brigade in background **Edge:** Reeded

Date	Mintage	F	VF	XF	Unc	BU
2001	—	—	—	—	10.00	12.00

KM# 965a CROWN

28.2800 g., 0.9250 Silver 0.8410 oz. ASW, 38.6 mm. **Ruler:** Elizabeth II **Series:** Victorian Age Part II **Obv:** Bust with tiara right **Rev:** Lord Tennyson with the Light Brigade in background **Edge:** Reeded

Date	Mintage	F	VF	XF	Unc	BU
2001 Proof	10,000	Value: 47.50				

KM# 967 CROWN

Copper-Nickel, 38.6 mm. **Ruler:** Elizabeth II **Series:** Victorian Age Part II **Obv:** Bust with tiara right **Rev:** Stanley meeting Dr. Livingstone **Edge:** Reeded

Date	Mintage	F	VF	XF	Unc	BU
2001	—	—	—	—	10.00	12.00

KM# 967a CROWN

28.2800 g., 0.9250 Silver 0.8410 oz. ASW, 38.6 mm. **Ruler:** Elizabeth II **Series:** Victorian Age Part II **Obv:** Bust with tiara right **Rev:** Stanley meeting Dr. Livingstone **Edge:** Reeded

Date	Mintage	F	VF	XF	Unc	BU
2001 Proof	10,000	Value: 47.50				

KM# 969 CROWN

Copper-Nickel, 38.6 mm. **Ruler:** Elizabeth II **Series:** Victorian Age Part II **Obv:** Bust with tiara right **Rev:** Bronte sisters **Edge:** Reeded

Date	Mintage	F	VF	XF	Unc	BU
2001	—	—	—	—	10.00	12.00

KM# 969a CROWN

28.2800 g., 0.9250 Silver 0.8410 oz. ASW, 38.6 mm. **Ruler:** Elizabeth II **Series:** Victorian Age Part II **Obv:** Bust with tiara right **Rev:** Bronte sisters **Edge:** Reeded

Date	Mintage	F	VF	XF	Unc	BU
2001 Proof	10,000	Value: 47.50				

KM# 1061 CROWN

31.1000 g., Electrum Special alloy of equal parts of gold and silver. **Ruler:** Elizabeth II **Series:** Ancient Coins **Obv:** Crowned bust right **Rev:** Lion and bull facing **Note:** From a Kroisos [sic] coin c. 560-546 BC.

Date	Mintage	F	VF	XF	Unc	BU
2002 Proof	—	Value: 700				

KM# 1060 CROWN

31.1000 g., Electrum Special alloy of equal parts of gold and silver. **Ruler:** Elizabeth II **Series:** Ancient Coins. **Obv:** Crowned bust right **Rev:** Lion and bull facing **Note:** From a Lampsakos electrum coin c. 450 BC.

Date	Mintage	F	VF	XF	Unc	BU
2002 Proof	—	Value: 700				

KM# 1059 CROWN

31.1000 g., Electrum Special alloy of equal parts of gold and silver. **Ruler:** Elizabeth II **Series:** Ancient Coins **Obv:** Crowned bust right **Rev:** Head of Hercules right **Note:** From a Lesbos coin c. 480-450

Date	Mintage	F	VF	XF	Unc	BU
2002 Proof	—	Value: 700				

KM# 1058 CROWN

31.1000 g., 1.0000 Electrum Special alloy of equal parts of gold and silver. 0.9998 oz. **Ruler:** Elizabeth II **Series:** Ancient Coins **Obv:** Crowned head right **Rev:** Head of Athena left **Note:** From a Mysia electrum coin c. 520 BC.

Date	Mintage	F	VF	XF	Unc	BU
2002 Proof	—	Value: 700				

KM# 979 CROWN

28.2800 g., Copper-Nickel, 38.6 mm. **Ruler:** Elizabeth II **Subject:** Queen Mother's Life **Obv:** Bust with tiara right **Rev:** Christening of Prince William **Edge:** Reeded

Date	Mintage	F	VF	XF	Unc	BU
2002	—	—	—	—	10.00	12.00

KM# 979a CROWN

28.2800 g., 0.9250 Silver 0.8410 oz. ASW, 38.6 mm. **Ruler:** Elizabeth II **Subject:** Queen Mother's Life **Obv:** Bust with tiara right **Rev:** Prince William's christening **Edge:** Reeded

Date	Mintage	F	VF	XF	Unc	BU
2002 Proof	10,000	Value: 47.50				

KM# 981 CROWN

28.2800 g., Copper-Nickel, 38.6 mm. **Ruler:** Elizabeth II **Subject:** World Cup Soccer **Obv:** Bust with tiara right **Rev:** Two players about to collide **Edge:** Reeded

Date	Mintage	F	VF	XF	Unc	BU
2002	—	—	—	—	10.00	11.50

KM# 981a CROWN

28.2800 g., 0.9250 Silver 0.8410 oz. ASW, 38.6 mm. **Ruler:** Elizabeth II **Subject:** World Cup Soccer **Obv:** Bust with tiara right **Rev:** Two players about to collide **Edge:** Reeded

Date	Mintage	F	VF	XF	Unc	BU
2002 Proof	10,000	Value: 47.50				

KM# 983 CROWN

28.2800 g., Copper-Nickel, 38.6 mm. **Ruler:** Elizabeth II **Subject:** World Cup Soccer **Obv:** Bust with tiara right **Rev:** Two players facing viewer **Edge:** Reeded

Date	Mintage	F	VF	XF	Unc	BU
2002	—	—	—	—	10.00	11.50

KM# 983a CROWN

28.2800 g., 0.9250 Silver 0.8410 oz. ASW, 38.6 mm. **Ruler:** Elizabeth II **Subject:** World Cup Soccer **Obv:** Bust with tiara right **Rev:** Two players facing viewer **Edge:** Reeded

Date	Mintage	F	VF	XF	Unc	BU
2002 Proof	10,000	Value: 47.50				

KM# 985 CROWN

28.2800 g., Copper-Nickel, 38.6 mm. **Ruler:** Elizabeth II **Subject:** World Cup Soccer **Obv:** Bust with tiara right **Rev:** Two horizontal players **Edge:** Reeded

Date	Mintage	F	VF	XF	Unc	BU
2002	—	—	—	—	10.00	11.50

KM# 985a CROWN

28.2800 g., 0.9250 Silver 0.8410 oz. ASW, 38.6 mm. **Ruler:** Elizabeth II **Subject:** World Cup Soccer **Obv:** Bust with tiara right **Rev:** Two horizontal players **Edge:** Reeded

Date	Mintage	F	VF	XF	Unc	BU
2002 Proof	10,000	Value: 47.50				

KM# 987 CROWN

28.2800 g., Copper-Nickel, 38.6 mm. **Ruler:** Elizabeth II **Subject:** World Cup Soccer **Obv:** Bust with tiara right **Rev:** Two players moving to left **Edge:** Reeded

Date	Mintage	F	VF	XF	Unc	BU
2002	—	—	—	—	10.00	11.50

KM# 987a CROWN

28.2800 g., 0.9250 Silver 0.8410 oz. ASW, 38.6 mm. **Ruler:** Elizabeth II **Subject:** World Cup Soccer **Obv:** Bust with tiara right **Rev:** Two players moving to left **Edge:** Reeded

Date	Mintage	F	VF	XF	Unc	BU
2002 Proof	10,000	Value: 47.50				

KM# 992.1 CROWN

28.2800 g., Copper-Nickel, 38.6 mm. **Ruler:** Elizabeth II **Subject:** Peter Rabbit Centennial **Obv:** Bust with tiara right **Rev:** Peter Rabbit **Edge:** Reeded

Date	Mintage	F	VF	XF	Unc	BU
2002	—	—	—	—	10.00	12.00

KM# 992a CROWN

28.2800 g., 0.9250 Silver 0.8410 oz. ASW, 38.6 mm. **Ruler:** Elizabeth II **Subject:** Peter Rabbit Centennial **Obv:** Bust with tiara right **Rev:** Peter Rabbit **Edge:** Reeded

Date	Mintage	F	VF	XF	Unc	BU
2002 Proof	10,000	Value: 47.50				

KM# 992.2 CROWN
Copper-Nickel **Ruler:** Elizabeth II **Obv:** Bust with tiara right **Rev:** Peter Rabbit in multi-color

Date	Mintage	F	VF	XF	Unc	BU
2002	—	—	—	—	10.00	12.00

KM# 994 CROWN
28.2800 g., Copper-Nickel, 38.6 mm. **Ruler:** Elizabeth II **Subject:** Queen's Golden Jubilee **Obv:** Bust with tiara right **Rev:** Royal couple and tree house **Edge:** Reeded

Date	Mintage	F	VF	XF	Unc	BU
2002	—	—	—	—	10.00	12.00

KM# 994a CROWN
Yellow Brass, 38.6 mm. **Ruler:** Elizabeth II **Subject:** Queen's Golden Jubilee **Obv:** Bust with tiara right **Rev:** Royal couple and tree house **Edge:** Reeded

Date	Mintage	F	VF	XF	Unc	BU
2002 Proof	15,000	Value: 20.00				

KM# 994b CROWN
28.2800 g., 0.9250 Gold Clad Silver 0.8410 oz., 38.6 mm. **Ruler:** Elizabeth II **Subject:** Queen's Golden Jubilee **Obv:** Bust with tiara right **Rev:** Royal couple and tree house **Edge:** Reeded

Date	Mintage	F	VF	XF	Unc	BU
2002 Proof	10,000	Value: 55.00				

KM# 996 CROWN
28.2800 g., Copper-Nickel, 38.6 mm. **Ruler:** Elizabeth II **Subject:** Queen's Golden Jubilee **Obv:** Bust with tiara right **Rev:** Royal coach **Edge:** Reeded

Date	Mintage	F	VF	XF	Unc	BU
2002	—	—	—	—	10.00	12.00

KM# 996a CROWN
Yellow Brass, 38.6 mm. **Ruler:** Elizabeth II **Subject:** Queen's Golden Jubilee **Obv:** Bust with tiara right **Rev:** Royal coach **Edge:** Reeded

Date	Mintage	F	VF	XF	Unc	BU
2002 Proof	15,000	Value: 20.00				

KM# 996b CROWN
28.2800 g., 0.9250 Gold Clad Silver 0.8410 oz., 38.6 mm. **Ruler:** Elizabeth II **Subject:** Queen's Golden Jubilee **Obv:** Bust with tiara right **Rev:** Royal coach **Edge:** Reeded

Date	Mintage	F	VF	XF	Unc	BU
2002 Proof	10,000	Value: 55.00				

KM# 998 CROWN
28.2800 g., Copper-Nickel, 38.6 mm. **Ruler:** Elizabeth II **Subject:** Queen's Golden Jubilee **Obv:** Bust with tiara right **Rev:** Royal couple with baby **Edge:** Reeded

Date	Mintage	F	VF	XF	Unc	BU
2002	—	—	—	—	10.00	12.00

KM# 998a CROWN
Yellow Brass, 38.6 mm. **Ruler:** Elizabeth II **Subject:** Queen's Golden Jubilee **Obv:** Bust with tiara right **Rev:** Royal couple with baby **Edge:** Reeded

Date	Mintage	F	VF	XF	Unc	BU
2002 Proof	15,000	Value: 20.00				

KM# 998b CROWN
28.2800 g., 0.9250 Gold Clad Silver 0.8410 oz., 38.6 mm. **Ruler:** Elizabeth II **Subject:** Queen's Golden Jubilee **Obv:** Bust with tiara right **Rev:** Royal couple with baby **Edge:** Reeded

Date	Mintage	F	VF	XF	Unc	BU
2002 Proof	1,000	Value: 55.00				

KM# 1000 CROWN
28.2800 g., Copper-Nickel, 38.6 mm. **Ruler:** Elizabeth II **Subject:** Queen's Golden Jubilee **Obv:** Bust with tiara right **Rev:** Royal yacht under Tower bridge **Edge:** Reeded

Date	Mintage	F	VF	XF	Unc	BU
2002	—	—	—	—	10.00	12.00

KM# 1000a CROWN
Yellow Brass, 38.6 mm. **Ruler:** Elizabeth II **Subject:** Queen's Golden Jubilee **Obv:** Bust with tiara right **Rev:** Royal yacht under Tower bridge **Edge:** Reeded

Date	Mintage	F	VF	XF	Unc	BU
2002 Proof	15,000	Value: 20.00				

KM# 1000b CROWN
28.2800 g., 0.9250 Gold Clad Silver 0.8410 oz., 38.6 mm. **Ruler:** Elizabeth II **Subject:** Queen's Golden Jubilee **Obv:** Bust with tiara right **Rev:** Royal yacht under Tower bridge **Edge:** Reeded

Date	Mintage	F	VF	XF	Unc	BU
2002 Proof	10,000	Value: 55.00				

KM# 1013 CROWN
28.2800 g., Copper-Nickel dark patina, 38.6 mm. **Ruler:** Elizabeth II **Subject:** Death of Queen Mother **Obv:** Bust with tiara right **Rev:** Queen Mother trout fishing **Edge:** Reeded

Date	Mintage	F	VF	XF	Unc	BU
2002	—	—	—	—	10.00	12.00

KM# 1013a CROWN
28.2800 g., 0.9250 Silver 0.8410 oz. ASW, 38.6 mm. **Ruler:** Elizabeth II **Subject:** Queen Mother **Obv:** Bust with tiara right **Rev:** Queen Mother trout fishing **Edge:** Reeded **Note:** Obv. and rev. have blackened legends.

Date	Mintage	F	VF	XF	Unc	BU
2002 Proof	5,000	Value: 175				

KM# 1015 CROWN
28.2800 g., Copper-Nickel, 38.6 mm. **Ruler:** Elizabeth II **Subject:** Princess Diana **Obv:** Bust with tiara right **Rev:** Diana's portrait **Edge:** Reeded

Date	Mintage	F	VF	XF	Unc	BU
2002	—	—	—	—	10.00	12.00

KM# 1015a CROWN
28.2800 g., 0.9250 Silver 0.8410 oz. ASW, 38.6 mm. **Ruler:** Elizabeth II **Subject:** Princess Diana **Obv:** Bust with tiara right **Rev:** Diana's portrait **Edge:** Reeded

Date	Mintage	F	VF	XF	Unc	BU
2002 Proof	10,000	Value: 47.50				

KM# 1019 CROWN
28.2800 g., Copper-Nickel, 38.6 mm. **Ruler:** Elizabeth II **Subject:** Peter Pan **Obv:** Bust with tiara right **Rev:** Peter Pan and Tinkerbell flying above city **Edge:** Reeded

Date	Mintage	F	VF	XF	Unc	BU
2002	—	—	—	—	10.00	12.00

KM# 1019a CROWN
28.2800 g., 0.9250 Silver 0.8410 oz. ASW, 38.6 mm. **Ruler:** Elizabeth II **Subject:** Peter Pan **Obv:** Bust with tiara right **Rev:** Peter Pan and Tinkerbell flying above city **Edge:** Reeded

Date	Mintage	F	VF	XF	Unc	BU
2002 Proof	10,000	Value: 47.50				

KM# 1021 CROWN
28.2800 g., Copper-Nickel, 38.6 mm. **Ruler:** Elizabeth II **Subject:** Grand Masonic Lodge **Obv:** Bust with tiara right **Rev:** Masonic seal above Gibraltar **Edge:** Reeded

Date	Mintage	F	VF	XF	Unc	BU
2002 Proof	5,000	Value: 12.00				

KM# 1021a CROWN
28.2800 g., 0.9250 Silver 0.8410 oz. ASW, 38.6 mm. **Ruler:** Elizabeth II **Subject:** Grand Masonic Lodge **Obv:** Bust with tiara right **Rev:** Masonic seal above Gibraltar **Edge:** Reeded

Date	Mintage	F	VF	XF	Unc	BU
2002 Proof	10,000	Value: 47.50				

KM# 1025 CROWN
28.2800 g., Copper-Nickel, 38.6 mm. **Ruler:** Elizabeth II **Subject:** Calpe Conference **Obv:** Bust with tiara right **Rev:** Crossed flags and arms **Edge:** Reeded

Date	Mintage	F	VF	XF	Unc	BU
2002PM	—	—	—	—	10.00	12.00

KM# 1025a CROWN
28.2800 g., 0.9250 Silver 0.8410 oz. ASW, 38.6 mm. **Ruler:** Elizabeth II **Subject:** Calpe Conference **Obv:** Bust with tiara right **Rev:** Crossed flags and arms **Edge:** Reeded

Date	Mintage	F	VF	XF	Unc	BU
2002PM Proof	10,000	Value: 47.50				

KM# 1052 CROWN
Copper-Nickel **Ruler:** Elizabeth II **Subject:** 2004 Athens Olympics **Rev:** Horse jumping left

Date	Mintage	F	VF	XF	Unc	BU
2003	—	—	—	—	10.00	12.00

KM# 1053 CROWN
Copper-Nickel **Ruler:** Elizabeth II **Subject:** 2004 Athens Olympics **Rev:** Javelin thrower

Date	Mintage	F	VF	XF	Unc	BU
2003	—	—	—	—	10.00	12.00

KM# 1054 CROWN
Copper-Nickel **Ruler:** Elizabeth II **Subject:** 2004 Athens Olympics **Rev:** Field Hockey

Date	Mintage	F	VF	XF	Unc	BU
2003	—	—	—	—	10.00	12.00

KM# 1055 CROWN
Copper-Nickel **Ruler:** Elizabeth II **Subject:** 2004 Athens Olympics **Rev:** Wrestlers

Date	Mintage	F	VF	XF	Unc	BU
2003	—	—	—	—	10.00	12.00

KM# 1035 CROWN
28.2800 g., Nickel-Brass, 38.6 mm. **Ruler:** Elizabeth II **Subject:** 1700th Anniversary - Death of St. George **Obv:** Bust with tiara right **Rev:** St. George and the dragon **Edge:** Reeded

Date	Mintage	F	VF	XF	Unc	BU
2003	—	—	—	—	9.00	10.00

KM# 1035a CROWN
28.2800 g., 0.9250 Silver 0.8410 oz. ASW, 38.6 mm. **Ruler:** Elizabeth II **Subject:** 1700th Anniversary - Death of St. George **Obv:** Bust with tiara right **Rev:** St. George and the dragon **Edge:** Reeded

Date	Mintage	F	VF	XF	Unc	BU
2003 Proof	10,000	Value: 47.50				

KM# 1039 CROWN
28.3000 g., Copper-Nickel, 38.6 mm. **Ruler:** Elizabeth II **Subject:** Peter Rabbit **Obv:** Bust with tiara right **Rev:** Peter Rabbit holding carrot **Edge:** Reeded

Date	Mintage	F	VF	XF	Unc	BU
2003PM	—	—	—	—	9.00	10.00

KM# 1040 CROWN
28.2800 g., Copper-Nickel, 38.6 mm. **Ruler:** Elizabeth II **Subject:** Centennial of Powered Flight **Obv:** Queens portrait **Rev:** Stealth bomber within circles of WWI and WWII planes **Edge:** Reeded

Date	Mintage	F	VF	XF	Unc	BU
2003PM	—	—	—	—	10.00	12.00

KM# 1040a CROWN
31.1000 g., Tri-Metallic .9995 Platinum 5.2g center in .9999 Gold 14.2 g ring within .999 Silver 11.7 g outer ring, 38.6 mm. **Ruler:** Elizabeth II **Subject:** Centennial of Powered Flight **Obv:** Queens portrait **Rev:** Stealth bomber within circles of WWI and WWII planes **Edge:** Reeded

Date	Mintage	F	VF	XF	Unc	BU
2003PM Proof	999	Value: 1,750				

KM# 1041 CROWN
28.2800 g., Copper-Nickel, 38.6 mm. **Ruler:** Elizabeth II **Subject:** 50th Anniversary of Coronation **Obv:** Queens portrait **Rev:** Buckingham Palace **Edge:** Reeded

Date	Mintage	F	VF	XF	Unc	BU
2003PM	—	—	—	—	10.00	12.00

KM# 1094 CROWN
28.2800 g., Copper-Nickel, 38.6 mm. **Ruler:** Elizabeth II **Rev:** Battleship Bismark under fire, colored poppy below

Date	Mintage	F	VF	XF	Unc	BU
2004	—	—	—	—	10.00	12.00

KM# 1075 CROWN
28.2800 g., Copper-Nickel, 38.6 mm. **Ruler:** Elizabeth II **Subject:** Trafalgar - First Shot **Rev:** Naval battle scene

Date	Mintage	F	VF	XF	Unc	BU
2005	—	—	—	—	10.00	12.00

KM# 1076 CROWN
28.2800 g., Copper-Nickel, 38.6 mm. **Ruler:** Elizabeth II **Subject:** Trafalgar - Breaking the line **Rev:** Naval battle

Date	Mintage	F	VF	XF	Unc	BU
2005	—	—	—	—	10.00	12.00

KM# 1077 CROWN
28.2800 g., Copper-Nickel, 38.6 mm. **Ruler:** Elizabeth II **Subject:** Trafalgar - Hardy **Rev:** Bust facing

Date	Mintage	F	VF	XF	Unc	BU
2005	—	—	—	—	10.00	12.00

KM# 1078 CROWN

28.2800 g., Copper-Nickel, 38.6 mm. **Ruler:** Elizabeth II **Subject:** Trafalgar - Nelson **Rev:** Bust facing

Date	Mintage	F	VF	XF	Unc	BU
2005	—	—	—	—	10.00	12.00

KM# 1034 2 CROWN

41.5000 g., Bi-Metallic .999 Silver 11.5g. star shaped center in Copper outer ring, 50 mm. **Ruler:** Elizabeth II **Subject:** Euro's First Anniversary **Obv:** Crowned bust right within star silhouette **Rev:** Europa riding a bull, stars and star silhouette in background **Edge:** Reeded

Date	Mintage	F	VF	XF	Unc	BU
2003PM Proof	3,500	Value: 125				

KM# 1034a 2 CROWN

50.0000 g., Bi-Metallic .9999 Gold 20g star shaped center in Copper outer ring, 50 mm. **Ruler:** Elizabeth II **Subject:** 1st Anniversary - Euro **Obv:** Crowned bust right within star silhouette **Rev:** Europa riding the bull, stars and star silhouette in background **Edge:** Reeded

Date	Mintage	F	VF	XF	Unc	BU
2003PM Proof	2,003	Value: 850				

KM# 1034b 2 CROWN

56.3000 g., Bi-Metallic .9999 Gold 20.8g star shaped center in a .999 Silver 35.5g outer ring, 50 mm. **Ruler:** Elizabeth II **Subject:** 1st Anniversary - Euro **Obv:** Crowned bust right within star silhouette **Rev:** Europa riding the bull, stars and star silhouette in background **Edge:** Reeded

Date	Mintage	F	VF	XF	Unc	BU
2003PM Proof	2,003	Value: 900				

KM# 907 5 CROWN

Tri-Metallic Center .9995 Platinum 26.9g. Inner Ring .9999 Gold 73.41g. Outer Ring .999 Silver 55.19g, 50 mm. **Ruler:** Elizabeth II **Subject:** 21st Century **Obv:** Crowned bust right, date below **Rev:** Celtic cross, Viking ship and modern technological items **Edge:** Reeded

Date	Mintage	F	VF	XF	Unc	BU
2001 Proof	199	Value: 6,500				

KM# 1042 5 CROWN

155.5500 g., 0.9990 Silver 4.9958 oz. ASW, 65 mm. **Ruler:** Elizabeth II **Subject:** 50th Anniversary of Coronation **Obv:** Queens portrait **Rev:** Buckingham Palace with tiny .01ct ruby, diamond and sapphire inserts above the main entrance **Edge:** Reeded

Date	Mintage	F	VF	XF	Unc	BU
2003PM Proof	2,003	Value: 225				

KM# 1045 32 CROWNS

1000.0000 g., 0.9990 Silver 32.117 oz. ASW **Ruler:** Elizabeth II **Subject:** Beatrix Potter's Peter Rabbit **Obv:** Bust with tiara right **Rev:** Multicolor Peter Rabbit holding carrot, with blue coat and red slippers

Date	Mintage	F	VF	XF	Unc	BU
2003 Proof	1,000	Value: 1,150				

KM# 869 POUND

9.5000 g., Nickel-Brass, 22.5 mm. **Ruler:** Elizabeth II **Obv:** Head with tiara right **Rev:** Gibraltar coat of arms - castle and key

Date	Mintage	F	VF	XF	Unc	BU
2001 AA	—	—	—	—	3.50	4.50
2001 AB	—	—	—	—	3.50	4.50
2002 AC	—	—	—	—	3.50	4.50

KM# 1036 POUND

9.5000 g., Nickel-Brass, 22 mm. **Ruler:** Elizabeth II **Subject:** 1700th Anniversary - Death of St. George **Obv:** Bust with tiara right **Rev:** St. George and the dragon **Edge:** Reeded

Date	Mintage	F	VF	XF	Unc	BU
2003	—	—	—	—	9.00	10.00

KM# 1051 POUND

9.5000 g., Nickel-Brass, 22.5 mm. **Ruler:** Elizabeth II **Subject:** Tercentenary 1704-2004 **Obv:** Elizabeth II **Rev:** Old cannon set for a downhill target **Edge:** Reeded

Date	Mintage	F	VF	XF	Unc	BU
2004PM	—	—	—	—	—	4.00

KM# 1091 POUND

9.5000 g., Nickel-Brass, 22.5 mm. **Ruler:** Elizabeth II **Obv:** Bust in diadem right **Rev:** Neanderthal Skull

Date	Mintage	F	VF	XF	Unc	BU
2005	—	—	—	—	3.50	4.50
2006	—	—	—	—	3.50	4.50
2007	—	—	—	—	3.50	4.50
2008	—	—	—	—	3.50	4.50
2009	—	—	—	—	3.50	4.50
2010	—	—	—	—	3.50	4.50
2011	—	—	—	—	3.50	4.50

KM# 970 2 POUNDS

12.0000 g., Bi-Metallic Copper-Nickel center in Nickel-Brass ring, 28.4 mm. **Ruler:** Elizabeth II **Subject:** Bicentennial of the Union Jack **Obv:** Head with tiara right **Rev:** Standing Britannia wearing flag as a cape **Edge:** Reeded

Date	Mintage	F	VF	XF	Unc	BU
2001 AA	—	—	—	—	10.00	12.00

KM# 970a 2 POUNDS

12.0000 g., 0.9990 Bi-Metallic Silver center in Gold plated Silver ring 0.3854 oz., 28.4 mm. **Ruler:** Elizabeth II **Subject:** Bicentennial of the Union Jack **Obv:** Head with tiara right **Rev:** Standing Britannia wearing flag as a cape **Edge:** Reeded

Date	Mintage	F	VF	XF	Unc	BU
2001	7,500	—	—	—	35.00	40.00

KM# 1043 2 POUNDS

12.0000 g., Bi-Metallic Copper-Nickel center in Nickel-Brass ring, 28.4 mm. **Ruler:** Elizabeth II **Obv:** Head with tiara right **Rev:** Old cannon **Edge:** Reeded

Date	Mintage	F	VF	XF	Unc	BU
2003PM	—	—	—	—	10.00	12.00

KM# 1057 2 POUNDS

12.0000 g., Bi-Metallic Copper-Nickel center in Nickel-Brass ring, 28.4 mm. **Ruler:** Elizabeth II **Subject:** Tercentenary 1704-2004 **Obv:** Elizabeth II **Rev:** Naval Battle, capture of Gibraltar **Edge:** Reeded

Date	Mintage	F	VF	XF	Unc	BU
2004PM	—	—	—	—	10.00	12.00

KM# 1072 2 POUNDS

12.0000 g., Bi-Metallic Copper-Nickel center in Nickel-Brass ring, 28.4 mm. **Ruler:** Elizabeth II **Subject:** Capture of Gibraltar **Rev:** Sea Battle

Date	Mintage	F	VF	XF	Unc	BU
2004	—	—	—	—	10.00	12.00

KM# 1092 2 POUNDS

12.0000 g., Bi-Metallic Copper-Nickel center in Nickel-Brass ring, 28.4 mm. **Ruler:** Elizabeth II **Subject:** Battle of Trafalgar **Rev:** Two Naval vessels and rock in backbround

Date	Mintage	F	VF	XF	Unc	BU
2005	—	—	—	—	10.00	12.00
2006	—	—	—	—	10.00	12.00
2007	—	—	—	—	10.00	12.00
2008	—	—	—	—	10.00	12.00
2009	—	—	—	—	10.00	12.00
2010	—	—	—	—	10.00	12.00
2011	—	—	—	—	10.00	12.00

KM# 1073 2 POUNDS

12.0000 g., Bi-Metallic Copper-Nickel center in Nickel-Brass ring, 28.4 mm. **Ruler:** Elizabeth II **Subject:** Battle of Trafalgar **Rev:** Sea Battle

Date	Mintage	F	VF	XF	Unc	BU
2005	—	—	—	—	10.00	12.00

KM# 1093 2 POUNDS
12.0000 g., Bi-Metallic Copper-Nickel center in Nickel-Brass ring, 28.4 mm. **Ruler:** Elizabeth II **Subject:** Diamond Wedding Anniversary **Obv:** Bust in diadem right **Rev:** Conjoined busts of Elizabeth and Philip

Date	Mintage	F	VF	XF	Unc	BU
2007	—	—	—	—	10.00	12.00

KM# 953 5 POUNDS
20.0000 g., Virenium, 36.1 mm. **Ruler:** Elizabeth II **Subject:** Gibraltar Chronicle 200 Years **Obv:** Head with tiara right **Rev:** Naval battle scene with newspaper in background **Edge:** Reeded

Date	Mintage	F	VF	XF	Unc	BU
2001	—	—	—	—	17.00	20.00

KM# 953a 5 POUNDS
23.5000 g., 0.9250 Silver 0.6988 oz. ASW, 36.1 mm. **Ruler:** Elizabeth II **Subject:** Gibraltar Chronicle 200 Years **Obv:** Head with tiara right **Rev:** Naval battle scene with newspaper in background **Edge:** Reeded

Date	Mintage	F	VF	XF	Unc	BU
2001 Proof	10,000	Value: 50.00				

KM# 953b 5 POUNDS
39.8300 g., 0.9167 Gold 1.1738 oz. AGW, 36.1 mm. **Ruler:** Elizabeth II **Subject:** Gibraltar Chronicle 200 Years **Obv:** Head with tiara right **Rev:** Naval battle scene with newspaper in background **Edge:** Reeded

Date	Mintage	F	VF	XF	Unc	BU
2001 Proof	850	Value: 2,100				

KM# 1011 5 POUNDS
20.0000 g., Virenium, 36.1 mm. **Ruler:** Elizabeth II **Subject:** Queen's Golden Jubilee **Obv:** Head with tiara right **Rev:** Coronation scene **Edge:** Reeded

Date	Mintage	F	VF	XF	Unc	BU
2002	—	—	—	—	17.00	20.00

KM# 1011a 5 POUNDS
23.5000 g., 0.9250 Silver 0.6988 oz. ASW, 36.1 mm. **Ruler:** Elizabeth II **Subject:** Queen's Golden Jubilee **Obv:** Head with tiara right **Rev:** Coronation scene **Edge:** Reeded

Date	Mintage	F	VF	XF	Unc	BU
2002 Proof	10,000	Value: 50.00				

KM# 1011b 5 POUNDS
39.8300 g., 0.9166 Gold 1.1737 oz. AGW, 36.1 mm. **Ruler:** Elizabeth II **Subject:** Queen's Golden Jubilee **Obv:** Head with tiara right **Rev:** Coronation scene **Edge:** Reeded

Date	Mintage	F	VF	XF	Unc	BU
2002 Proof	850	Value: 2,100				

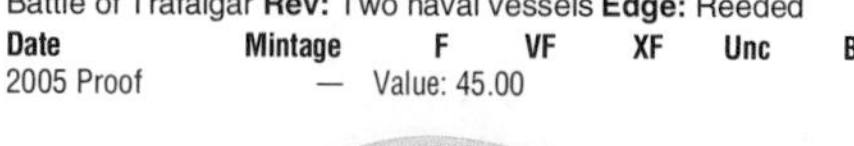

KM# 1064 5 POUNDS
Silver, 38 mm. **Ruler:** Elizabeth II **Subject:** 200th Anniversary, Battle of Trafalgar **Rev:** Two naval vessels **Edge:** Reeded

Date	Mintage	F	VF	XF	Unc	BU
2005 Proof	—	Value: 45.00				

KM# 1095 5 POUNDS
Silver, 38.6 mm. **Ruler:** Elizabeth II **Subject:** History fo the RAF - Flypast **Obv:** Bust in crown right **Rev:** Bomber and two planes in flight

Date	Mintage	F	VF	XF	Unc	BU
2007 Proof	—	Value: 50.00				

KM# 1096 5 POUNDS
Silver, 38.61 mm. **Ruler:** Elizabeth II **Subject:** History of the RAF - Avro Lancaster **Obv:** Bust in crown right **Rev:** Lancaster bomber flying right

Date	Mintage	F	VF	XF	Unc	BU
2007 Proof	—	Value: 50.00				

SOVEREIGN COINAGE

KM# 1037 1/5 SOVEREIGN
1.2200 g., 0.9999 Gold 0.0392 oz. AGW, 13.92 mm. **Ruler:** Elizabeth II **Subject:** Death of St. George **Obv:** Bust with tiara right **Rev:** St. George and the dragon **Edge:** Reeded

Date	Mintage	F	VF	XF	Unc	BU
2003 Proof	10,000	Value: 75.00				

KM# 1038 SOVEREIGN
6.2200 g., 0.9999 Gold 0.1999 oz. AGW, 22 mm. **Ruler:** Elizabeth II **Subject:** Death of St. George **Obv:** Bust with tiara right **Rev:** St. George and the dragon **Edge:** Reeded

Date	Mintage	F	VF	XF	Unc	BU
2003 Proof	5,000	Value: 375				

ROYAL COINAGE

KM# 896 1/25 ROYAL
1.2441 g., 0.9999 Gold 0.0400 oz. AGW, 13.92 mm. **Ruler:** Elizabeth II **Subject:** Bullion **Obv:** Bust with tiara right **Rev:** Two cherubs **Edge:** Reeded

Date	Mintage	F	VF	XF	Unc	BU
2001	—	—	—	—	—	75.00
2001 Proof	1,000	Value: 77.50				

KM# 972 1/25 ROYAL
1.2440 g., 0.9990 Gold 0.0400 oz. AGW, 13.92 mm. **Ruler:** Elizabeth II **Subject:** Cherubs **Obv:** Bust with tiara right **Rev:** Two cherubs shooting arrrows **Edge:** Reeded

Date	Mintage	F	VF	XF	Unc	BU
2002	—	—	—	—	—	75.00
2002 Proof	1,000	Value: 77.50				

KM# 1027 1/25 ROYAL
1.2440 g., 0.9999 Gold 0.0400 oz. AGW, 13.92 mm. **Ruler:** Elizabeth II **Obv:** Bust with tiara right **Rev:** Cherub with crossed arms **Edge:** Reeded

Date	Mintage	F	VF	XF	Unc	BU
2003PM	—	—	—	—	—	75.00
2003PM Proof	—	Value: 77.50				

KM# 897 1/10 ROYAL
3.1100 g., 0.9999 Gold 0.1000 oz. AGW, 18 mm. **Ruler:** Elizabeth II **Subject:** Bullion **Obv:** Bust with tiara right **Rev:** Two cherubs **Edge:** Reeded

Date	Mintage	F	VF	XF	Unc	BU
2001	—	—	—	—	—	175
2001 Proof	1,000	Value: 180				

KM# 973 1/10 ROYAL
3.1100 g., 0.9990 Gold 0.0999 oz. AGW, 17.95 mm. **Ruler:** Elizabeth II **Subject:** Cherubs **Obv:** Bust with tiara right **Rev:** Two cherubs shooting arrows **Edge:** Reeded

Date	Mintage	F	VF	XF	Unc	BU
2002	—	—	—	—	—	175
2002 Proof	1,000	Value: 180				

KM# 1028 1/10 ROYAL
3.1100 g., 0.9999 Gold 0.1000 oz. AGW, 17.95 mm. **Ruler:** Elizabeth II **Obv:** Bust with tiara right **Rev:** Cherub with crossed arms **Edge:** Reeded

Date	Mintage	F	VF	XF	Unc	BU
2003PM	—	—	—	—	—	175
2003PM Proof	—	Value: 180				

KM# 898 1/5 ROYAL
6.2200 g., 0.9990 Gold 0.1998 oz. AGW, 22 mm. **Ruler:** Elizabeth II **Subject:** Bullion **Obv:** Bust with tiara right **Rev:** Two cherubs **Edge:** Reeded

Date	Mintage	F	VF	XF	Unc	BU
2001	—	—	—	—	—	350
2001 Proof	1,000	Value: 355				

KM# 974 1/5 ROYAL
6.2200 g., 0.9990 Gold 0.1998 oz. AGW, 22 mm. **Ruler:** Elizabeth II **Obv:** Bust with tiara right **Rev:** Two cherubs shooting arrows **Edge:** Reeded

Date	Mintage	F	VF	XF	Unc	BU
2002	—	—	—	—	—	350
2002 Proof	1,000	Value: 355				

KM# 1029 1/5 ROYAL
6.2200 g., 0.9999 Gold 0.1999 oz. AGW, 22 mm. **Ruler:** Elizabeth II **Obv:** Bust with tiara right **Rev:** Cherub with crossed arms **Edge:** Reeded

Date	Mintage	F	VF	XF	Unc	BU
2003PM	—	—	—	—	—	350
2003PM Proof	—	Value: 355				

KM# 899 1/2 ROYAL
15.5517 g., 0.9999 Gold 0.4999 oz. AGW, 30 mm. **Ruler:** Elizabeth II **Subject:** Bullion **Obv:** Bust with tiara right **Rev:** Two cherubs **Edge:** Reeded

Date	Mintage	F	VF	XF	Unc	BU
2001	—	—	—	—	—	875
2001 Proof	1,000	Value: 880				

KM# 975 1/2 ROYAL
15.5510 g., 0.9990 Gold 0.4995 oz. AGW, 30 mm. **Ruler:** Elizabeth II **Obv:** Bust with tiara right **Rev:** Two cherubs shooting arrows **Edge:** Reeded

Date	Mintage	F	VF	XF	Unc	BU
2002	—	—	—	—	—	875
2002 Proof	1,000	Value: 880				

KM# 1030 1/2 ROYAL
15.5510 g., 0.9999 Gold 0.4999 oz. AGW, 30 mm. **Ruler:** Elizabeth II **Obv:** Bust with tiara right **Rev:** Cherub with crossed arms **Edge:** Reeded

Date	Mintage	F	VF	XF	Unc	BU
2003PM	—	—	—	—	—	875
2003PM Proof	—	Value: 880				

KM# 900 ROYAL
28.2800 g., Copper-Nickel, 38.6 mm. **Ruler:** Elizabeth II **Obv:** Bust with tiara right **Rev:** Two cherubs **Edge:** Reeded

Date	Mintage	F	VF	XF	Unc	BU
2001	—	—	—	—	10.00	12.00

KM# 900a ROYAL

31.1035 g., 0.9990 Silver 0.9990 oz. ASW **Ruler:** Elizabeth II **Obv:** Bust with tiara right **Rev:** Two cherubs

Date	Mintage	F	VF	XF	Unc	BU
2001 Proof	10,000	Value: 47.50				

KM# 901 ROYAL

31.1035 g., 0.9999 Gold 0.9999 oz. AGW, 32.7 mm. **Ruler:** Elizabeth II **Subject:** Bullion **Obv:** Bust with tiara right **Rev:** Two cherubs **Edge:** Reeded

Date	Mintage	F	VF	XF	Unc	BU
2001	—	—	—	—	—	1,750
2001 Proof	1,000	Value: 1,800				

KM# 976 ROYAL

28.2800 g., Copper-Nickel, 38.6 mm. **Ruler:** Elizabeth II **Obv:** Bust with tiara right **Rev:** Two cherubs shooting arrows **Edge:** Reeded

Date	Mintage	F	VF	XF	Unc	BU
2002	—	—	—	—	10.00	12.00

KM# 976a ROYAL

31.1035 g., 0.9990 Silver 0.9990 oz. ASW **Ruler:** Elizabeth II **Obv:** Bust with tiara right **Rev:** Two cherubs shooting arrows **Edge:** Reeded

Date	Mintage	F	VF	XF	Unc	BU
2002 Proof	1,000	Value: 47.50				

KM# 977 ROYAL

31.1035 g., 0.9990 Gold 0.9990 oz. AGW, 32.7 mm. **Ruler:** Elizabeth II **Obv:** Bust with tiara right **Rev:** Two cherubs shooting arrows **Edge:** Reeded

Date	Mintage	F	VF	XF	Unc	BU
2002	—	—	—	—	—	1,750
2002 Proof	1,000	Value: 1,800				

KM# 1031 ROYAL

28.2800 g., Copper-Nickel, 38.6 mm. **Ruler:** Elizabeth II **Obv:** Bust with tiara right **Rev:** Cherub with crossed arms **Edge:** Reeded

Date	Mintage	F	VF	XF	Unc	BU
2003PM	—	—	—	—	10.00	12.00

KM# 1031a ROYAL

28.2800 g., 0.9990 Silver 0.9083 oz. ASW, 38.6 mm. **Ruler:** Elizabeth II **Obv:** Bust with tiara right **Rev:** Cherub with crossed arms **Edge:** Reeded

Date	Mintage	F	VF	XF	Unc	BU
2003PM Proof	10,000	Value: 47.50				

KM# 1032 ROYAL

31.1035 g., 0.9999 Gold 0.9999 oz. AGW, 32.7 mm. **Ruler:** Elizabeth II **Obv:** Bust with tiara right **Rev:** Cherub with crossed arms **Edge:** Reeded

Date	Mintage	F	VF	XF	Unc	BU
2003PM	—	—	—	—	—	1,750
2003PM Proof	—	Value: 1,800				

PROOF SETS

KM#	Date	Mintage	Identification	Issue Price	Mkt Val
PS29	2001 (5)	1,000	KM#896-899, 901	—	3,300
PS30	2003 (5)	1,000	KM#1027-30, 1032	—	3,300

GREAT BRITAIN

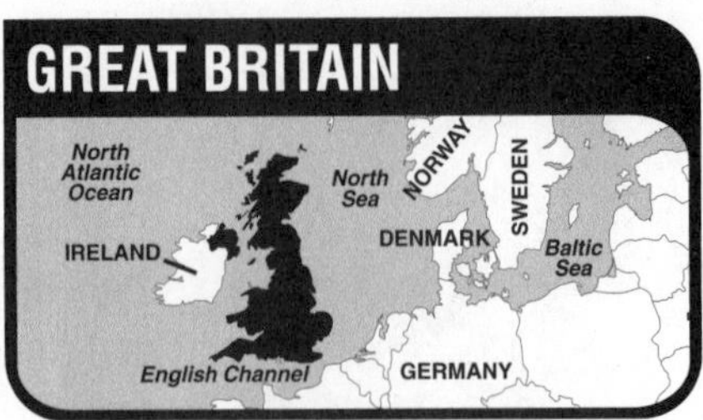

The United Kingdom of Great Britain and Northern Ireland, located off the northwest coast of the European continent, has an area of 94,227 sq. mi. (244,820 sq. km.) and a population of 54 million. Capital: London. The economy is based on industrial activity and trading. Machinery, motor vehicles, chemicals, and textile yarns and fabrics are exported.

By the mid-20th century, most of the territories formerly comprising the British Empire had gained independence, and the empire had evolved into the Commonwealth of Nations, an association of equal and autonomous states, which enjoy special trade interests. The Commonwealth is presently composed of 54 member nations, including the United Kingdom. All recognize the British monarch as head of the Commonwealth. Sixteen continue to recognize the British monarch as Head of State. They are: United Kingdom, Antigua and Barbuda, Australia, Bahamas, Barbados, Belize, Canada, Grenada, Jamaica, New Zealand, Papua New Guinea, St. Christopher & Nevis, Saint Lucia, Saint Vincent and the Grenadines, Solomon Islands, and Tuvalu. Elizabeth II is personally, and separately, the Queen of the sovereign, independent countries just mentioned. There is no other British connection between the several individual, national sovereignties, except that High Commissioners represent them each instead of ambassadors in each other's countries.

RULERS

Elizabeth II, 1952-

MINT MARKS

H - Heaton

KN - King's Norton

KINGDOM

PRE-DECIMAL COINAGE

KM# 898 PENNY

0.4713 g., 0.9250 Silver 0.0140 oz. ASW, 11 mm. **Ruler:** Elizabeth II **Obv:** Laureate bust right **Rev:** Crowned value in sprays divides date within wreath **Edge:** Reeded

Date	Mintage	F	VF	XF	Unc	BU
2001 Prooflike	1,132	—	—	—	50.00	55.00
2002 Prooflike	1,681	—	—	—	50.00	55.00
2003 Prooflike	1,608	—	—	—	55.00	60.00
2004 Prooflike	1,613	—	—	—	55.00	60.00
2005 Prooflike	1,685	—	—	—	55.00	60.00
2006 Prooflike	1,811	—	—	—	55.00	60.00
2006 Proof	6,394	—	—	—	—	—
2007 Prooflike	1,985	—	—	—	55.00	60.00
2008 Prooflike	1,833	—	—	—	55.00	60.00
2009 Prooflike	1,602	—	—	—	55.00	60.00
2010 Prooflike	1,617	—	—	—	55.00	60.00
2011 Prooflike	—	—	—	—	55.00	60.00
2012 Prooflike	—	—	—	—	55.00	60.00

KM# 898a PENNY

0.9167 Gold, 11 mm. **Ruler:** Elizabeth II **Obv:** Laureate bust right **Rev:** Crowned denomination divides date within wreath

Date	Mintage	F	VF	XF	Unc	BU
2002 Proof	2,002	Value: 1,000				

KM# 899 2 PENCE

0.9426 g., 0.9250 Silver 0.0280 oz. ASW, 13 mm. **Ruler:** Elizabeth II **Obv:** Laureate bust right **Obv. Legend:** Without BRITT OMN **Rev:** Crowned value in sprays divides date within wreath **Edge:** Reeded

Date	Mintage	F	VF	XF	Unc	BU
2001 Prooflike	1,132	—	—	—	60.00	70.00
2002 Prooflike	1,681	—	—	—	60.00	70.00
2003 Prooflike	1,608	—	—	—	65.00	75.00
2004 Prooflike	1,613	—	—	—	65.00	75.00
2005 Prooflike	1,685	—	—	—	65.00	75.00
2006 Prooflike	1,811	—	—	—	65.00	75.00
2006 Proof	6,394	—	—	—	—	—
2007 Prooflike	1,822	—	—	—	65.00	75.00
2008 Prooflike	1,999	—	—	—	65.00	75.00
2009 Prooflike	1,602	—	—	—	65.00	75.00
2010 Prooflike	1,617	—	—	—	65.00	75.00
2011 Prooflike	—	—	—	—	65.00	75.00
2012 Prooflike	—	—	—	—	65.00	75.00

KM# 899a 2 PENCE

0.9167 Gold, 13 mm. **Ruler:** Elizabeth II **Series:** Maundy Sets **Obv:** Laureate bust right **Obv. Legend:** Without BRITT OMN **Rev:** Crowned denomination divides date within wreath

Date	Mintage	F	VF	XF	Unc	BU
2002 Proof	2,002	Value: 1,100				

KM# 901 3 PENCE

1.4138 g., 0.9250 Silver 0.0420 oz. ASW, 16 mm. **Ruler:** Elizabeth II **Obv:** Laureate bust right **Obv. Legend:** without BRITT OMN **Rev:** Crowned value in sprays divides date within wreath **Edge:** Reeded

Date	Mintage	F	VF	XF	Unc	BU
2001 Prooflike	1,132	—	—	—	65.00	75.00
2002 Prooflike	1,681	—	—	—	65.00	75.00
2003 Prooflike	1,608	—	—	—	70.00	80.00
2004 Prooflike	1,613	—	—	—	70.00	80.00
2005 Prooflike	1,685	—	—	—	70.00	80.00
2006 Prooflike	1,811	—	—	—	70.00	80.00
2006 Proof	6,394	—	—	—	—	—
2007 Prooflike	1,822	—	—	—	70.00	80.00
2008 Prooflike	1,833	—	—	—	70.00	80.00
2009 Prooflike	1,794	—	—	—	70.00	80.00
2010 Prooflike	1,617	—	—	—	70.00	80.00
2011 Prooflike	—	—	—	—	70.00	80.00
2012 Prooflike	—	—	—	—	70.00	80.00

KM# 901a 3 PENCE

0.9167 Gold, 16 mm. **Ruler:** Elizabeth II **Obv:** Laureate bust right **Obv. Legend:** Without RITT OMN **Rev:** Crowned denomination divides date within wreath

Date	Mintage	F	VF	XF	Unc	BU
2002 Proof	2,002	Value: 1,150				

KM# 902 4 PENCE (Groat)

1.8851 g., 0.9250 Silver 0.0561 oz. ASW, 18 mm. **Ruler:** Elizabeth II **Obv:** Laureate bust right **Obv. Legend:** without BRITT OMN **Rev:** Crowned denomination divides date within wreath **Edge:** Reeded

Date	Mintage	F	VF	XF	Unc	BU
2001 Prooflike	1,132	—	—	—	65.00	75.00
2002 Prooflike	1,681	—	—	—	65.00	75.00
2003 Prooflike	1,608	—	—	—	65.00	75.00
2004 Prooflike	1,613	—	—	—	65.00	75.00
2005 Prooflike	1,685	—	—	—	65.00	75.00
2006 Prooflike	1,811	—	—	—	65.00	75.00
2006 Proof	6,394	—	—	—	—	—
2007 Prooflike	1,822	—	—	—	65.00	75.00
2008 Prooflike	1,833	—	—	—	65.00	75.00
2009 Prooflike	1,602	—	—	—	65.00	75.00
2010 Prooflike	1,787	—	—	—	65.00	75.00
2011 Prooflike	—	—	—	—	65.00	75.00
2012 Prooflike	—	—	—	—	65.00	75.00

KM# 902a 4 PENCE

0.9167 Gold, 18 mm. **Ruler:** Elizabeth II **Obv:** Laureate bust right **Obv. Legend:** Without BRITT OMN **Rev:** Crowned denomination divides date within wreath

Date	Mintage	F	VF	XF	Unc	BU
2002 Proof	2,002	Value: 1,250				

DECIMAL COINAGE

1971-1981: 100 New Pence = 1 Pound;
1982-present: 100 Pence = 1 Pound

KM# 986 PENNY

3.5600 g., Copper Plated Steel, 20.32 mm. **Ruler:** Elizabeth II **Subject:** Badge of Henry VII **Obv:** Head with tiara right **Rev:** Crowned portcullis with chains **Edge:** Plain

Date	Mintage	F	VF	XF	Unc	BU
2001	928,698,000	—	—	0.15	1.75	2.50
2001 Proof	—	Value: 3.25				
2002	601,446,000	—	—	0.15	1.75	2.50
2002 Proof	60,770	Value: 3.25				
2003	539,436,000	—	—	0.15	1.75	2.50
2003 Proof	43,513	Value: 3.25				
2004	739,764,000	—	—	0.15	1.75	2.50
2004 Proof	35,020	Value: 3.25				
2005	536,318,000	—	—	0.15	1.75	2.50
2005 Proof	40,563	Value: 3.25				
2006	524,605,000	—	—	0.15	1.75	2.50
2006 Proof	37,689	Value: 3.25				
2007	548,002,000	—	—	0.15	1.75	2.50
2007 Proof	38,215	Value: 3.25				
2008	180,600,000	—	—	0.25	2.50	3.00
2008 Proof	36,333	Value: 3.25				

KM# 986c PENNY

0.9167 Gold, 20.3 mm. **Ruler:** Elizabeth II **Obv:** Head with tiara right **Rev:** Crowned portcullis

Date	Mintage	F	VF	XF	Unc	BU
2002 Proof	—	Value: 750				
2008 Proof	2,008	Value: 550				

KM# 1107 PENNY

3.5900 g., Copper Plated Steel, 20.3 mm. **Ruler:** Elizabeth II **Obv:** Head with tiara right **Rev:** Section of the Royal Arms - Lion and Harp

Date	Mintage	F	VF	XF	Unc	BU
2008	507,952,000	—	—	—	—	0.20
2008 Proof	—	Value: 3.50				
2009	556,412,000	—	—	—	—	0.20
2009 Proof	—	Value: 3.50				
2010	421,002,000	—	—	—	—	0.20
2010 Proof	—	Value: 3.50				
2011	—	—	—	—	—	0.20
2011 Proof	—	Value: 3.50				
2012	—	—	—	—	—	0.20
2012 Proof	—	Value: 3.50				
2013	—	—	—	—	—	0.20
2013 Proof	—	Value: 3.50				

KM# 1107a PENNY

3.5600 g., 0.9250 Silver 0.1059 oz. ASW, 20.3 mm. **Ruler:** Elizabeth II **Obv:** Head with tiara right **Rev:** Section of the Royal Arms - Lion and Harp

Date	Mintage	F	VF	XF	Unc	BU
2008 Proof	—	Value: 13.50				
2009	—	—	—	—	—	25.00
2009 Proof	—	Value: 25.00				
2010	—	—	—	—	—	25.00
2010 Proof	3,500	Value: 25.00				
2013 Proof	2,013	Value: 25.00				

KM# 986b PENNY

3.5600 g., 0.9250 Silver 0.1059 oz. ASW, 20.3 mm. **Ruler:** Elizabeth II **Obv:** Head with tiara right **Rev:** Crowned portcullis **Edge:** Plain

Date	Mintage	F	VF	XF	Unc	BU
2008 Proof	10,000	Value: 16.50				

KM# 1107b PENNY

0.9167 Gold, 20.3 mm. **Ruler:** Elizabeth II **Obv:** Head with tiara right **Rev:** Section of the Royal Arms - Lion and Harp

Date	Mintage	F	VF	XF	Unc	BU
2008 Proof	—	Value: 350				

KM# 1107c PENNY

Platinum APW, 20.3 mm. **Ruler:** Elizabeth II **Obv:** Head with tiara right **Rev:** Section of the Royal Arms - Lion and Harp

Date	Mintage	F	VF	XF	Unc	BU
2008 Proof	—	Value: 600				

KM# 1107a.1 PENNY

3.5600 g., 0.9250 Silver partially gilt 0.1059 oz. ASW, 20.3 mm. **Ruler:** Elizabeth II **Obv:** Head with tiara right **Rev:** Section of the Royal Arms - Lion and Harp, gilt

Date	Mintage	F	VF	XF	Unc	BU
2012 Proof	—	Value: 25.00				

KM# 987 2 PENCE

7.1400 g., Copper Plated Steel, 25.86 mm. **Ruler:** Elizabeth II **Obv:** Head with tiara right **Rev:** Welsh plumes and crown **Edge:** Plain

Date	Mintage	F	VF	XF	Unc	BU
2001	551,880,000	—	—	0.15	1.75	2.50
2002	168,556,000	—	—	0.15	1.75	2.50
2003	260,225,000	—	—	0.15	1.75	2.50
2003 Proof	43,513	Value: 3.25				
2004	356,396,000	—	—	0.15	1.75	2.50
2004 Proof	35,020	Value: 3.25				
2005	280,396,000	—	—	0.15	1.75	2.50
2005 Proof	40,563	Value: 3.25				
2006	170,637,000	—	—	0.15	1.75	2.50
2006 Proof	37,689	Value: 3.25				
2007	254,500,000	—	—	0.15	1.75	2.50
2007 Proof	38,215	Value: 3.25				
2008	10,600,000	—	—	0.25	3.00	3.50

KM# 987a 2 PENCE

Bronze, 25.91 mm. **Ruler:** Elizabeth II **Obv:** Head with tiara right **Rev:** Welsh plumes and crown

Date	Mintage	F	VF	XF	Unc	BU
2002 Proof	60,770	Value: 2.50				
2003 Proof	43,513	Value: 2.50				
2004 Proof	35,020	Value: 2.50				

KM# 987c 2 PENCE

0.9167 Gold, 25.91 mm. **Ruler:** Elizabeth II **Subject:** Queen's Golden Jubilee - 1952-2002 **Obv:** Head with tiara right **Rev:** Welsh plumes and crown

Date	Mintage	F	VF	XF	Unc	BU
2002 Proof	—	Value: 850				
2008 Proof	2,008	Value: 650				

KM# 1108 2 PENCE

7.1000 g., Copper Plated Steel, 25.86 mm. **Ruler:** Elizabeth II **Obv:** Head with tiara right **Rev:** Section of the Royal Arms - Lion

Date	Mintage	F	VF	XF	Unc	BU
2008	241,679,000	—	—	0.15	2.50	1.75
2008 Proof	36,333	Value: 3.25				
2009	150,400,500	—	—	0.15	2.50	1.75
2009 Proof	40,000	Value: 3.25				
2010	38,000,000	—	—	0.15	2.50	1.75
2010 Proof	40,000	Value: 3.25				
2011	—	—	—	0.15	2.50	1.75
2011 Proof	—	Value: 3.25				
2012	—	—	—	0.15	2.50	1.75
2012 Proof	—	Value: 3.25				
2013	—	—	—	0.15	2.50	1.75
2013 Proof	—	Value: 3.25				

KM# 1108a 2 PENCE

7.1200 g., 0.9250 Silver 0.2117 oz. ASW, 25.86 mm. **Ruler:** Elizabeth II **Obv:** Head in tiara right **Rev:** Section of the Royal Arms - Lion

Date	Mintage	F	VF	XF	Unc	BU
2008 Proof	—	Value: 17.50				
2009 Proof	—	Value: 17.50				
2010 Proof	3,500	Value: 17.50				
2011 Proof	—	Value: 25.00				

Note: Also exists as a Piedfort, P78.

Date	Mintage	F	VF	XF	Unc	BU
2013 Proof	2,013	Value: 25.00				

KM# 987b 2 PENCE

7.1200 g., 0.9250 Silver 0.2117 oz. ASW, 25.9 mm. **Ruler:** Elizabeth II **Obv:** Head with tiara right **Rev:** Welsh plumes and crown **Edge:** Plain

Date	Mintage	F	VF	XF	Unc	BU
2008 Proof	10,000	Value: 18.50				

KM# 1108b 2 PENCE

0.9167 Gold, 25.9 mm. **Ruler:** Elizabeth II **Obv:** Head in tiara right **Rev:** Section of the Royal Arms - Lion

Date	Mintage	F	VF	XF	Unc	BU
2008 Proof	—	Value: 700				

KM# 1108c 2 PENCE

Platinum APW, 25.9 mm. **Ruler:** Elizabeth II **Obv:** Head in tiara right **Rev:** Section of Royal Arms - Lion

Date	Mintage	F	VF	XF	Unc	BU
2008 Proof	—	Value: 1,100				

KM# 1108a.1 2 PENCE

7.1200 g., 0.9250 Silver partially gilt 0.2117 oz. ASW, 25.86 mm. **Ruler:** Elizabeth II **Obv:** Head with tiara right **Rev:** Section of the Royal Arms - Lion

Date	Mintage	F	VF	XF	Unc	BU
2012 Proof	—	Value: 17.50				

KM# 988 5 PENCE

3.2500 g., Copper-Nickel, 18 mm. **Ruler:** Elizabeth II **Obv:** Head with tiara right **Rev:** Crowned thistle

Date	Mintage	F	VF	XF	Unc	BU
2001	337,930,000	—	—	0.25	2.00	2.50
2001 Proof	45,617	Value: 3.00				
2002	219,258,000	—	—	0.25	2.00	2.50
2002 Proof	60,770	Value: 3.00				
2003	333,230,000	—	—	0.25	2.00	2.50
2003 Proof	43,513	Value: 3.00				
2004	271,810,000	—	—	0.25	2.00	2.50
2004 Proof	35,020	Value: 3.00				
2005	236,212,000	—	—	0.25	2.00	2.50
2005 Proof	40,563	Value: 3.00				
2006	317,697,000	—	—	0.25	2.00	2.50
2006 Proof	37,689	Value: 3.00				
2007	246,720,000	—	—	0.25	2.00	2.50
2007 Proof	38,215	Value: 3.00				
2008	92,880,000	—	—	—	4.50	5.00

KM# 988b 5 PENCE

0.9167 Gold, 18 mm. **Ruler:** Elizabeth II **Obv:** Head with tiara right **Rev:** Crowned thistle

Date	Mintage	F	VF	XF	Unc	BU
2002 Proof	—	Value: 450				
2008 Proof	—	Value: 400				

KM# 1109 5 PENCE

3.2500 g., Copper-Nickel, 18 mm. **Ruler:** Elizabeth II **Obv:** Head with tiara right **Rev:** Section of the Royal Arms - Center of shield

Date	Mintage	F	VF	XF	Unc	BU
2008	165,172,000	—	—	0.25	2.00	2.50
2008 Proof	36,333	Value: 3.00				
2009	132,960,300	—	—	0.25	2.00	2.50
2009 Proof	40,000	Value: 3.00				
2010	180,250,500	—	—	0.25	2.00	2.50
2010 Proof	40,000	Value: 3.00				

KM# 1109a 5 PENCE

3.2500 g., 0.9250 Silver 0.0966 oz. ASW, 18 mm. **Ruler:** Elizabeth II **Obv:** Head in tiara right **Rev:** Section of Royal Arms - Center of shield

Date	Mintage	F	VF	XF	Unc	BU
2008 Proof	—	Value: 20.00				
2009 Proof	—	Value: 20.00				
2010 Proof	3,500	Value: 20.00				
2011 Proof	—	Value: 35.00				

Note: Also exists as a Piedfort, P79.

Date	Mintage	F	VF	XF	Unc	BU
2013 Proof	2,013	Value: 35.00				

KM# 988a 5 PENCE

3.2500 g., 0.9250 Silver 0.0966 oz. ASW, 18 mm. **Ruler:** Elizabeth II **Obv:** Head with tiara right **Rev:** Crowned thistle **Edge:** Reeded

Date	Mintage	F	VF	XF	Unc	BU
2008 Proof	10,000	Value: 22.50				

KM# 1109b 5 PENCE

0.9167 Gold, 18 mm. **Ruler:** Elizabeth II **Obv:** Head in tiara right **Rev:** Section of Royal Arms - Center

Date	Mintage	F	VF	XF	Unc	BU
2008 Proof	—	Value: 500				

KM# 1109c 5 PENCE

Platinum APW, 18 mm. **Ruler:** Elizabeth II **Obv:** Head in tiara right **Rev:** Section of Royal Arms - Center

Date	Mintage	F	VF	XF	Unc	BU
2008 Proof	—	Value: 800				

KM# 1109d 5 PENCE

3.2500 g., Nickel Plated Steel, 18 mm. **Ruler:** Elizabeth II **Obv:** Head with tiara right **Rev:** Section of Royal Arms - Center of shield

Date	Mintage	F	VF	XF	Unc	BU
2011	—	—	—	0.25	2.00	2.50
2011 Proof	—	Value: 3.00				

Date	Mintage	F	VF	XF	Unc	BU
2012	—	—	—	0.25	2.00	2.50
2012 Proof	—	Value: 3.00				
2013	—	—	—	0.25	2.00	2.50
2013 Proof	—	Value: 3.00				

KM# 1109a.1 5 PENCE

3.2500 g., 0.9250 Silver with fully gilt reverse 0.0966 oz. ASW, 18 mm. **Ruler:** Elizabeth II **Obv:** Head with tiara right **Rev:** Section of the Royal Arms - Center of shield

Date	Mintage	F	VF	XF	Unc	BU
2012 Proof	—	Value: 20.00				

KM# 989 10 PENCE

6.5000 g., Copper-Nickel, 24.5 mm. **Ruler:** Elizabeth II **Obv:** Head with tiara right **Rev:** Crowned lion passant left

Date	Mintage	F	VF	XF	Unc	BU
2001	129,281,000	—	—	0.50	3.50	4.00
2001 Proof	45,617	Value: 3.50				
2002	80,934,000	—	—	0.50	3.50	4.00
2002 Proof	60,770	Value: 3.50				
2003	88,118,000	—	—	0.50	3.50	4.00
2003 Proof	43,513	Value: 3.50				
2004	99,602,000	—	—	0.50	3.50	4.00
2004 Proof	35,020	Value: 3.50				
2005	69,604,000	—	—	0.50	3.50	4.00
2005 Proof	40,563	Value: 3.50				
2006	118,803,000	—	—	0.50	3.50	4.00
2006 Proof	37,689	Value: 3.50				
2007	72,720,000	—	—	0.50	3.50	4.00
2007 Proof	38,215	Value: 3.50				
2008	9,720,000	—	—	0.50	3.50	4.00

KM# 989b 10 PENCE

0.9167 Gold, 24.5 mm. **Ruler:** Elizabeth II **Obv:** Head with tiara right **Rev:** Crowned lion prancing left

Date	Mintage	F	VF	XF	Unc	BU
2002 Proof	—	Value: 650				
2008 Proof	2,008	Value: 550				

KM# 1110 10 PENCE

6.5000 g., Copper-Nickel, 24.5 mm. **Ruler:** Elizabeth II **Obv:** Head with tiara right **Rev:** Section of the Royal Arms - two lions

Date	Mintage	F	VF	XF	Unc	BU
2008	71,447,000	—	—	0.50	4.00	3.50
2008 Proof	36,333	Value: 3.50				
2009	84,360,000	—	—	0.50	4.00	3.50
2009 Proof	40,000	Value: 3.50				
2010	25,320,500	—	—	0.50	4.00	3.50
2010 Proof	40,000	Value: 3.50				

KM# 1110a 10 PENCE

6.5000 g., 0.9250 Silver 0.1933 oz. ASW, 24.5 mm. **Ruler:** Elizabeth II **Obv:** Head with tiara right **Rev:** Section of the Royal Arms - two lions

Date	Mintage	F	VF	XF	Unc	BU
2008 Proof	—	Value: 25.00				
2009 proof	—	Value: 25.00				
2010 Proof	3,500	Value: 25.00				
2011 Proof	—	Value: 80.00				

Note: Also exists as a Piedfort, P80.

Date	Mintage	F	VF	XF	Unc	BU
2013 Proof	2,013	Value: 80.00				

KM# 989a 10 PENCE

6.5000 g., 0.9250 Silver 0.1933 oz. ASW, 24.5 mm. **Ruler:** Elizabeth II **Obv:** Head with tiara right **Rev:** Crowned lion prancing left **Edge:** Reeded

Date	Mintage	F	VF	XF	Unc	BU
2008 Proof	10,000	Value: 20.00				

KM# 1110b 10 PENCE

0.9167 Gold, 24.5 mm. **Ruler:** Elizabeth II **Obv:** Head in tiara right **Rev:** Section of Royal Arms - two lions

Date	Mintage	F	VF	XF	Unc	BU
2008 Proof	—	Value: 950				

KM# 1110c 10 PENCE

Platinum APW, 24.5 mm. **Ruler:** Elizabeth II **Obv:** Head in tiara right **Rev:** Section of Royal Arms - two lions

Date	Mintage	F	VF	XF	Unc	BU
2008 Proof	—	Value: 1,600				

KM# 1110d 10 PENCE

6.5000 g., Nickel Plated Steel, 24.5 mm. **Ruler:** Elizabeth II **Obv:** Head with tiara right **Rev:** Section of Royal Arms - two lions

Date	Mintage	F	VF	XF	Unc	BU
2011	—	—	—	0.50	3.50	4.00
2011 Proof	—	Value: 3.50				
2012	—	—	—	0.50	3.50	4.00
2012 Proof	—	Value: 3.50				
2013	—	—	—	0.50	3.50	4.00
2013 Proof	—	Value: 3.50				

KM# 1110a.1 10 PENCE

6.5000 g., 0.9250 Silver 0.1933 oz. ASW, 24.5 mm. **Ruler:** Elizabeth II **Obv:** Head with tiara right **Rev:** Section of the Royal Arms - two lions

Date	Mintage	F	VF	XF	Unc	BU
2012 Proof	—	Value: 25.00				

KM# 990 20 PENCE

5.0000 g., Copper-Nickel, 21.4 mm. **Ruler:** Elizabeth II **Obv:** Head with tiara right **Rev:** Crowned double rose **Shape:** 7-sided

Date	Mintage	F	VF	XF	Unc	BU
2001	148,122,500	—	—	0.50	3.50	4.00
2001 Proof	45,617	Value: 4.50				
2002	93,360,000	—	—	0.50	3.50	4.00
2002 Proof	60,770	Value: 4.50				
2003	153,383,750	—	—	0.50	3.50	4.00
2003 Proof	43,513	Value: 4.50				
2004	120,212,500	—	—	0.50	3.50	4.00
2004 Proof	35,020	Value: 4.50				
2005	124,488,750	—	—	0.50	3.50	4.00
2005 Proof	40,563	Value: 4.50				
2006	114,800,000	—	—	0.50	3.50	4.00
2006 Proof	37,689	Value: 4.50				
2007	117,075,000	—	—	0.50	3.50	4.00
2007 Proof	38,215	Value: 4.50				
2008	11,900,000	—	—	0.50	3.50	4.00

KM# 990b 20 PENCE

0.9167 Gold, 21.4 mm. **Ruler:** Elizabeth II **Obv:** Head with tiara right **Rev:** Crowned double rose **Shape:** 7-sided

Date	Mintage	F	VF	XF	Unc	BU
2002 Proof	—	Value: 550				
2008 Proof	2,008	Value: 500				

KM# 1111 20 PENCE

5.0000 g., Copper-Nickel, 21.4 mm. **Ruler:** Elizabeth II **Obv:** Head with tiara right **Rev:** Section of the Royal Arms - lion's tails **Shape:** 7-sided

Date	Mintage	F	VF	XF	Unc	BU
2008	115,022,000	—	—	0.50	3.50	4.00
2008 Proof	36,333	Value: 4.50				
2009	121,625,300	—	—	0.50	3.50	4.00
2009 Proof	40,000	Value: 4.50				
2010	91,700,500	—	—	0.50	3.35	4.00
2010 Proof	40,000	Value: 4.50				
2011	—	—	—	5.00	3.50	4.00
2011 Proof	—	Value: 4.50				
2012	—	—	—	0.50	3.50	4.00
2012 Proof	—	Value: 4.50				
2013	—	—	—	0.50	3.50	4.00
2013 Proof	—	Value: 4.50				

KM# 1111a 20 PENCE

5.0000 g., 0.9250 Silver 0.1487 oz. ASW, 21.4 mm. **Ruler:** Elizabeth II **Obv:** Head in tiara right **Rev:** Section of the Royal Arms - lion's tails **Shape:** 7-sided

Date	Mintage	F	VF	XF	Unc	BU
2008 Proof	—	Value: 35.00				
2009 Proof	—	Value: 35.00				
2010 Proof	3,500	Value: 35.00				
2011 Proof	—	Value: 80.00				

Note: Also exists as a Piedfort, P81.

Date	Mintage	F	VF	XF	Unc	BU
2013 Proof	2,013	Value: 80.00				

KM# 990a 20 PENCE

5.0000 g., 0.9250 Silver 0.1487 oz. ASW, 21.4 mm. **Ruler:** Elizabeth II **Obv:** Head with tiara right **Rev:** Crowned double rose **Edge:** Plain **Shape:** 7-sided

Date	Mintage	F	VF	XF	Unc	BU
2008 Proof	10,000	Value: 22.50				

KM# 1111b 20 PENCE

0.9167 Gold, 21.4 mm. **Ruler:** Elizabeth II **Obv:** Head in tiara right **Rev:** Section of Royal Arms - lion's tails **Shape:** 7-sided

Date	Mintage	F	VF	XF	Unc	BU
2008 Proof	—	Value: 700				

KM# 1111c 20 PENCE

Platinum APW, 21.4 mm. **Ruler:** Elizabeth II **Obv:** Head in tiara right **Rev:** Section of Royal Arms - lion's tails **Shape:** 7-sided

Date	Mintage	F	VF	XF	Unc	BU
2008 Proof	—	Value: 1,200				

KM# 1122 20 PENCE

5.0000 g., Copper-Nickel, 21.4 mm. **Ruler:** Elizabeth II **Obv:** Head right. Obverse of KM#990 **Rev:** Royal Arms part. Reverse of KM#1111 **Note:** Mule.

Date	Mintage	F	VF	XF	Unc	BU
ND(2008)	—	20.00	30.00	40.00	—	—

KM# 1111a.1 20 PENCE

5.0000 g., 0.9250 Silver partially gilt 0.1487 oz. ASW, 21.4 mm. **Ruler:** Elizabeth II **Obv:** Head with tiara right **Rev:** Section of Royal Arms - lion's tails

Date	Mintage	F	VF	XF	Unc	BU
2012 Proof	—	Value: 35.00				

KM# 991 50 PENCE

8.0000 g., Copper-Nickel, 27.3 mm. **Ruler:** Elizabeth II **Obv:** Head with tiara right **Rev:** Britannia seated right with shield, spear and lion **Shape:** 7-sided

Date	Mintage	F	VF	XF	Unc	BU
2001	84,998,500	—	—	1.00	3.50	4.00
2001 Proof	45,617	Value: 4.00				
2002	23,907,500	—	—	1.00	3.50	4.00
2002 Proof	60,770	Value: 4.00				
2003	23,583,000	—	—	1.00	3.50	4.00
2003 Proof	43,513	Value: 4.00				
2004	35,315,500	—	—	1.00	3.50	4.00
2004 Proof	35,020	Value: 4.00				
2005	25,363,500	—	—	1.00	3.50	4.00
2005 Proof	40,563	Value: 4.00				
2006	24,567,000	—	—	1.00	3.50	4.00
2006 Proof	37,689	Value: 4.00				
2007	11,200,000	—	—	1.00	3.50	4.00
2007 Proof	38,215	Value: 4.00				
2008	3,500,000	—	—	1.50	5.00	6.00

KM# 991b 50 PENCE

0.9167 Gold, 27.3 mm. **Ruler:** Elizabeth II **Obv:** Head with tiara right **Rev:** Britannia seated right with shield, spear and lion **Shape:** 7-sided

Date	Mintage	F	VF	XF	Unc	BU
2002 Proof	—	Value: 700				
2008 Proof	—	Value: 650				

KM# 1036 50 PENCE

8.0000 g., Copper-Nickel, 27.3 mm. **Ruler:** Elizabeth II **Subject:** Woman's Social and Political Union, 100th Anniversary **Obv:** Head with tiara right **Rev:** Standing suffragette chained to railings and holding banner **Edge:** Plain **Shape:** 7-sided

Date	Mintage	F	VF	XF	Unc	BU
2003	3,124,030	—	—	1.00	3.50	4.00
2003 Proof	35,513	Value: 9.50				

KM# 1036a 50 PENCE

8.0000 g., 0.9250 Silver 0.2379 oz. ASW, 27.3 mm. **Ruler:** Elizabeth II **Subject:** Woman's Social and Political Union, 100th Anniversary **Obv:** Head with tiara right **Rev:** Standing suffragette chained to railings and holding banner **Edge:** Plain **Shape:** 7-sided

Date	Mintage	F	VF	XF	Unc	BU
2003 Proof	6,267	Value: 45.00				

Note: Also exists as a Piefort, P40.

KM# 1036b 50 PENCE

15.5000 g., 0.9166 Gold 0.4568 oz. AGW, 27.3 mm. **Ruler:** Elizabeth II **Subject:** Woman's Social and Political Union, 100th Anniversary **Obv:** Head with tiara right **Rev:** Standing suffragette chained to railings and holding banner **Edge:** Plain **Shape:** 7-sided

Date	Mintage	F	VF	XF	Unc	BU
2003 Proof	942	Value: 800				

KM# 1047 50 PENCE

8.0000 g., Copper-Nickel, 27.3 mm. **Ruler:** Elizabeth II **Subject:** Roger Bannister, 50th Anniversary of the four minute mile **Obv:** Head with tiara right **Rev:** Running legs, stop watch and value **Edge:** Plain

Date	Mintage	F	VF	XF	Unc	BU
2004	9,032,500	—	—	1.50	5.00	6.00
2004 Proof	35,020	Value: 7.50				

KM# 1047a 50 PENCE

8.0000 g., 0.9250 Silver 0.2379 oz. ASW, 27.3 mm. **Ruler:** Elizabeth II **Subject:** Roger Bannister, 50th Anniversary four minute mile **Obv:** Head with tiara right **Rev:** Running legs, stop watch and value **Shape:** 7-sided

Date	Mintage	F	VF	XF	Unc	BU
2004 Proof	4,924	Value: 50.00				

Note: Also exists as a Piedfort, P43.

KM# 1050 50 PENCE

8.0000 g., Copper-Nickel, 27.3 mm. **Ruler:** Elizabeth II **Subject:** Samuel Johnson's Dictonary of the English Language, 250th Anniversary **Obv:** Head with tiara right **Rev:** Dictonary entries for Fifty and Pence **Edge:** Plain **Shape:** 7-sided

Date	Mintage	F	VF	XF	Unc	BU
2005	17,649,000	—	—	1.00	3.50	4.00
2005 Proof	40,563	Value: 6.00				

KM# 1050a 50 PENCE

8.0000 g., 0.9250 Silver 0.2379 oz. ASW, 27.3 mm. **Ruler:** Elizabeth II **Subject:** Samuel Johnson's Dictonary of the English Language, 250th Anniversary **Obv:** Head with tiara right **Rev:** Dictonary entries for Fifty and Pence **Edge:** Plain **Shape:** 7-sided

Date	Mintage	F	VF	XF	Unc	BU
2005 Proof	4,029	Value: 45.00				

Note: Also exists as a Piedfort, P48.

KM# 1050b 50 PENCE

15.5000 g., 0.9167 Gold 0.4568 oz. AGW, 27.3 mm. **Ruler:** Elizabeth II **Subject:** Samuel Johnson's Dictonary of the English Language, 250th Anniversary **Obv:** Head with tiara right **Rev:** Dictonary entries for Fifty and Pence **Edge:** Plain **Shape:** 7-sided

Date	Mintage	F	VF	XF	Unc	BU
2005 Proof	1,000	Value: 800				

KM# 1057 50 PENCE

8.0000 g., Copper-Nickel, 27.3 mm. **Ruler:** Elizabeth II **Subject:** Victoria Cross, 150th Anniversary **Obv:** Head with tiara right **Rev:** Victoria Cross Medal, obverse and reverse views **Edge:** Plain **Shape:** 7-sided

Date	Mintage	F	VF	XF	Unc	BU
2006	12,087,000	—	—	1.50	5.00	6.00
2006 Proof	Est. 50,000	Value: 7.50				
2007 Proof	—	Value: 7.50				

KM# 1057a 50 PENCE

8.0000 g., 0.9250 Silver 0.2379 oz. ASW **Ruler:** Elizabeth II **Subject:** Victoria Cross, 150th Anniversary **Obv:** Head with tiara right **Rev:** Victoria Cross Medal, obverse and reverse views

Date	Mintage	F	VF	XF	Unc	BU
2006 Proof	7,500	Value: 40.00				

Note: Also exists as a Piedfort, P53.

KM# 1058a 50 PENCE

8.0000 g., 0.9250 Silver 0.2379 oz. ASW, 27.3 mm. **Ruler:** Elizabeth II **Subject:** Victoria Cross, 150th Anniversary **Obv:** Head with tiara right **Rev:** Heroic Act scene of a soldier carring a wounded comrade with outline of the Victoria Cross in the background **Shape:** 7-sided

Date	Mintage	F	VF	XF	Unc	BU
2006 Proof	—	Value: 40.00				

Note: Also exists as a Piedfort, P-54.

KM# 1058 50 PENCE

8.0000 g., Copper-Nickel, 27.3 mm. **Ruler:** Elizabeth II **Subject:** Victoria Cross, 150th Anniversary **Obv:** Head with tiara right **Rev:** Heroic Act scene of a soldier carring a wounded comrade with outline of the Victoria Cross in the background **Edge:** Plain **Shape:** 7-sided

Date	Mintage	F	VF	XF	Unc	BU
2006	10,000,500	—	—	1.50	5.00	6.00
2006 Proof	Est. 50,000	Value: 7.50				

KM# 1073 50 PENCE

8.0000 g., Copper-Nickel, 27.3 mm. **Ruler:** Elizabeth II **Subject:** Scouting Movement, 100th Anniversary **Obv:** Head with tiara right **Rev:** Fleur-de-lis emblem superimposed on globe **Edge:** Plain **Shape:** Seven sided

Date	Mintage	F	VF	XF	Unc	BU
2007	7,710,750	—	—	1.50	5.00	6.00
2007 Proof	Est. 50,000	Value: 7.50				

KM# 1073a 50 PENCE

8.0000 g., 0.9250 Silver 0.2379 oz. ASW, 27.3 mm. **Ruler:** Elizabeth II **Subject:** Scouting Movement, 100th Anniversary **Obv:** Head with tiara right **Rev:** Fleur-de-lis emblem superimposed on globe **Edge:** Plain **Shape:** 7-sided

Date	Mintage	F	VF	XF	Unc	BU
2007 Proof	10,895	Value: 60.00				

Note: Also exists as a Piedfort, P-59.

KM# 1073b 50 PENCE

15.5000 g., 0.9166 Gold 0.4568 oz. AGW, 27.3 mm. **Ruler:** Elizabeth II **Subject:** Scouting Movement, 100th Anniversary **Obv:** Head with tiara right **Rev:** Fleur-de-lis emblem superimposed on globe **Edge:** Plain **Shape:** 7-sided

Date	Mintage	F	VF	XF	Unc	BU
2007 Proof	1,250	Value: 800				

KM# 1112 50 PENCE

8.0000 g., Copper-Nickel, 27.3 mm. **Ruler:** Elizabeth II **Obv:** Head with tiara right **Rev:** Section of the Royal Arms - bottom center **Shape:** 7-sided

Date	Mintage	F	VF	XF	Unc	BU
2008	22,747,000	—	—	1.00	3.50	4.00
2008 Proof	36,333	Value: 7.00				
2009 In sets only	—	—	—	—	3.50	4.00
2009 Proof	40,000	Value: 7.00				
2010 In sets only	—	—	—	—	3.50	4.00
2010 Proof	40,000	Value: 7.00				
2011 In sets only	—	—	—	—	3.50	4.00
2011 Proof	—	Value: 7.00				
2012	—	—	—	1.00	3.50	4.00
2012 Proof	—	Value: 7.00				
2013	—	—	—	1.00	3.50	4.00
2013 Proof	—	Value: 7.00				

KM# 1112a 50 PENCE

8.0000 g., 0.9250 Silver 0.2379 oz. ASW, 27.3 mm. **Ruler:** Elizabeth II **Obv:** Head in tiara right **Rev:** Section of Royal Arms - bottom center **Shape:** 7-sided

Date	Mintage	F	VF	XF	Unc	BU
2008 Proof	—	Value: 50.00				

Note: Also exists as a Piedfort, P-97.

Date	Mintage	F	VF	XF	Unc	BU
2009 Proof	—	Value: 50.00				
2010 Proof	3,500	Value: 50.00				
2011 Proof	—	Value: 50.00				

Note: Also exists as a Piedfort, P-82.

Date	Mintage	F	VF	XF	Unc	BU
2013 Proof	2,013	Value: 50.00				

KM# 1112b 50 PENCE

15.5000 g., 0.9167 Gold 0.4568 oz. AGW, 27.3 mm. **Ruler:** Elizabeth II **Obv:** Head in tiara right **Rev:** Section of Royal Arms - bottom center **Shape:** 7-sided

Date	Mintage	F	VF	XF	Unc	BU
2008 Proof	—	Value: 825				
2009 Proof	—	Value: 825				

KM# 1112c 50 PENCE

Platinum APW, 27.3 mm. **Ruler:** Elizabeth II **Obv:** Head in tiara right **Rev:** Section of Royal Arms - bottom center **Shape:** 7-sided

Date	Mintage	F	VF	XF	Unc	BU
2008 Proof	—	Value: 1,350				

KM# 1150 50 PENCE

8.0000 g., Copper-Nickel, 27.3 mm. **Ruler:** Elizabeth II **Subject:** London Olympics, 2012 - Athletics **Obv:** Head with tiara right **Rev:** Youth's drawing of kid going over vault **Edge:** Plain **Shape:** 7-sided

Date	Mintage	F	VF	XF	Unc	BU
2009	—	—	—	1.00	3.50	4.00
2011	900,000	—	—	—	2.50	3.50

KM# 1114 50 PENCE

8.0000 g., Copper-Nickel, 27.3 mm. **Ruler:** Elizabeth II **Subject:** Royal Botanical Gardens at Kew, 250th Anniversary **Obv:** Head with tiara right **Rev:** Pagoda and vine, 1759-2009 **Edge:** Plain **Shape:** 7-sided

Date	Mintage	F	VF	XF	Unc	BU
2009	10,000	—	—	1.50	6.00	5.00
2009 Proof	—	Value: 7.50				

KM# 1114a 50 PENCE

8.0000 g., 0.9250 Silver 0.2379 oz. ASW, 27.3 mm. **Ruler:** Elizabeth II **Subject:** Royal Botanical Gardens at Kew, 250th Anniversary **Obv:** Head right **Rev:** Pagoda and vine, 1759 2009 **Edge:** Plain **Shape:** 7-sided

Date	Mintage	F	VF	XF	Unc	BU
2009 Proof	7,500	Value: 50.00				

Note: Also exists as a Piedfort, P98

KM# 1114b 50 PENCE
15.5000 g., 0.9160 Gold 0.4565 oz. AGW, 27.3 mm. **Ruler:** Elizabeth II **Subject:** Royal Botanical Gardens at Kew, 250th Anniversary **Obv:** Head right **Rev:** Pagoda and vine, 1759 2009 **Edge:** Plain **Shape:** 7-sided

Date	Mintage	F	VF	XF	Unc	BU
2009 Proof	1,000	Value: 800				

KM# 1150a 50 PENCE
8.0000 g., 0.9250 Silver 0.2379 oz. ASW, 27.3 mm. **Ruler:** Elizabeth II **Subject:** London Olympics, 2012 **Obv:** Head with tiara right **Rev:** Youth drawing of high jumper

Date	Mintage	F	VF	XF	Unc	BU
2009 Proof	—	Value: 50.00				

KM# 1165 50 PENCE
8.0000 g., Copper-Nickel, 27.3 mm. **Ruler:** Elizabeth II **Subject:** Girl Guides, 100th Anniversary **Obv:** Head with tiara right **Rev:** Circle of six trifoils **Edge:** Plain **Shape:** 7-sided

Date	Mintage	F	VF	XF	Unc	BU
2010	510,090	—	—	1.50	4.00	5.00
2010 Proof	—	Value: 10.00				

KM# 1165a 50 PENCE
8.0000 g., 0.9250 Silver 0.2379 oz. ASW, 27.3 mm. **Ruler:** Elizabeth II **Subject:** Girl Guides, 100th Anniversary **Obv:** Head with tiara right **Rev:** Circle of six trifoils **Edge:** Plain **Shape:** 7-sided

Date	Mintage	F	VF	XF	Unc	BU
2010 Proof	—	Value: 50.00				

Note: Also exists as a Piedfort, P99

KM# 1166 50 PENCE
8.0000 g., Copper-Nickel, 27.3 mm. **Ruler:** Elizabeth II **Subject:** 2012 London Olympics - Aquatics **Obv:** Head with tiara right **Edge:** Plain **Shape:** 7-sided

Date	Mintage	F	VF	XF	Unc	BU
2011	1,000,000	—	—	1.50	5.00	6.00

KM# 1167 50 PENCE
8.0000 g., Copper-Nickel, 27.3 mm. **Ruler:** Elizabeth II **Subject:** 2012 London Paralympics - Archery **Obv:** Head with tirara right **Edge:** Plain **Shape:** 7-sided

Date	Mintage	F	VF	XF	Unc	BU
2011	800,000	—	—	1.50	5.00	6.00

KM# 1168 50 PENCE
8.0000 g., Copper-Nickel, 27.3 mm. **Ruler:** Elizabeth II **Subject:** 2012 London Olympics - Canoeing **Obv:** Head with tiara right **Edge:** Plain **Shape:** 7-sided

Date	Mintage	F	VF	XF	Unc	BU
2011	800,000	—	—	1.50	5.00	6.00

KM# 1169 50 PENCE
8.0000 g., Copper-Nickel, 27.3 mm. **Ruler:** Elizabeth II **Subject:** 2012 London Olympics - Cycling **Obv:** Head with tiara right **Rev:** Cycle racing in a Velodrome **Edge:** Plain **Shape:** 7-sided

Date	Mintage	F	VF	XF	Unc	BU
2011	400,000	—	—	1.50	5.00	6.00

KM# 1170 50 PENCE
8.0000 g., Copper-Nickel, 27.3 mm. **Ruler:** Elizabeth II **Subject:** 2012 London Olympics - Gymnastics **Obv:** Head with tiara right **Edge:** Plain **Shape:** 7-sided

Date	Mintage	F	VF	XF	Unc	BU
2011	900,000	—	—	1.50	5.00	6.00

KM# 1171 50 PENCE
8.0000 g., Copper-Nickel, 27.3 mm. **Ruler:** Elizabeth II **Subject:** 2012 London Olympics - Hockey **Obv:** Head with tiara right **Edge:** Plain **Shape:** 7-sided

Date	Mintage	F	VF	XF	Unc	BU
2011	1,000,000	—	—	1.50	5.00	6.00

KM# 1172 50 PENCE
8.0000 g., Copper-Nickel, 27.3 mm. **Ruler:** Elizabeth II **Subject:** 2012 London Olympics - Rowing **Obv:** Head with tiara right **Edge:** Plain **Shape:** 7-sided

Date	Mintage	F	VF	XF	Unc	BU
2011	700,000	—	—	1.50	5.00	6.00

KM# 1173 50 PENCE
8.0000 g., Copper-Nickel, 27.3 mm. **Ruler:** Elizabeth II **Subject:** 2012 London Olympics - Triathlon **Obv:** Head with tiara right **Edge:** Plain **Shape:** 7-sided

Date	Mintage	F	VF	XF	Unc	BU
2011	1,000,000	—	—	1.50	5.00	6.00

KM# 1174 50 PENCE
8.0000 g., Copper-Nickel, 27.3 mm. **Ruler:** Elizabeth II **Subject:** 2012 London Olympics - Badminton **Obv:** Head with tiara right **Edge:** Plain **Shape:** 7-sided

Date	Mintage	F	VF	XF	Unc	BU
2011	900,000	—	—	1.50	5.00	6.00

KM# 1175 50 PENCE
8.0000 g., Copper-Nickel, 27.3 mm. **Ruler:** Elizabeth II **Subject:** 2012 London Olympics - Boxing **Obv:** Head with tiara right **Edge:** Plain **Shape:** 7-sided

Date	Mintage	F	VF	XF	Unc	BU
2011	800,000	—	—	1.50	5.00	6.00

KM# 1176 50 PENCE
8.0000 g., Copper-Nickel, 27.3 mm. **Ruler:** Elizabeth II **Subject:** 2012 London Olympics - Equestrian **Obv:** Head with tiara right **Edge:** Plain **Shape:** 7-sided

Date	Mintage	F	VF	XF	Unc	BU
2011	—	—	—	1.50	5.00	6.00

KM# 1177 50 PENCE
8.0000 g., Copper-Nickel, 27.3 mm. **Ruler:** Elizabeth II **Subject:** 2012 London Olympics - Modern Pentathlon **Obv:** Head with tiara right **Edge:** Plain **Shape:** 7-sided

Date	Mintage	F	VF	XF	Unc	BU
2011	—	—	—	1.50	5.00	6.00

KM# 1179 50 PENCE
8.0000 g., Copper-Nickel, 27.3 mm. **Ruler:** Elizabeth II **Subject:** 2012 London Olympics - Shooting **Obv:** Head with tiara right **Edge:** Plain **Shape:** 7-sided

Date	Mintage	F	VF	XF	Unc	BU
2011	—	—	—	1.50	5.00	6.00

KM# 1180 50 PENCE
8.0000 g., Copper-Nickel, 27.3 mm. **Ruler:** Elizabeth II **Subject:** 2012 London Paralympics - Table Tennis **Obv:** Head with tiara right **Edge:** Plain **Shape:** 7-sided

Date	Mintage	F	VF	XF	Unc	BU
2011	1,000,000	—	—	1.50	5.00	6.00

KM# 1181 50 PENCE
8.0000 g., Copper-Nickel, 27.3 mm. **Ruler:** Elizabeth II **Subject:** 2012 London Olympics - Volleyball **Shape:** 7-sided

Date	Mintage	F	VF	XF	Unc	BU
2011	1,000,000	—	—	1.50	5.00	6.00

KM# 1182 50 PENCE
8.0000 g., Copper-Nickel, 27.3 mm. **Ruler:** Elizabeth II **Subject:** 2012 London Olympics - Canoeing **Shape:** 7-sided

Date	Mintage	F	VF	XF	Unc	BU
2011	800,000	—	—	1.50	5.00	6.00

KM# 1183 50 PENCE

8.0000 g., Copper-Nickel, 27.3 mm. **Ruler:** Elizabeth II **Subject:** 2012 London Paralympics - Goalball **Obv:** Head with tiara right **Edge:** Plain **Shape:** 7-sided

Date	Mintage	F	VF	XF	Unc	BU
2011	900,000	—	—	1.50	5.00	6.00

KM# 1185 50 PENCE

8.0000 g., Copper-Nickel, 27.3 mm. **Ruler:** Elizabeth II **Subject:** 2012 London Olympics - Taekwondo **Obv:** Head with tiara right **Edge:** Plain **Shape:** 7-sided

Date	Mintage	F	VF	XF	Unc	BU
2011	—	—	—	1.50	5.00	6.00

KM# 1186 50 PENCE

8.0000 g., Copper-Nickel, 27.3 mm. **Ruler:** Elizabeth II **Subject:** 2012 London Olympics - Weightlifting **Obv:** Head with tiara right **Edge:** Plain **Shape:** 7-sided

Date	Mintage	F	VF	XF	Unc	BU
2011	—	—	—	1.50	5.00	6.00

KM# 1187 50 PENCE

8.0000 g., Copper-Nickel, 27.3 mm. **Ruler:** Elizabeth II **Subject:** 2012 London Paralympics - Wheelchair Rugby **Obv:** Head with tiara right **Edge:** Plain **Shape:** 7-sided

Date	Mintage	F	VF	XF	Unc	BU
2011	—	—	—	1.50	5.00	6.00

KM# 1188 50 PENCE

8.0000 g., Copper-Nickel, 27.3 mm. **Ruler:** Elizabeth II **Subject:** 2012 Summer Olympics - Wrestling **Obv:** Head with tiara right **Edge:** Plain **Shape:** 7-sided

Date	Mintage	F	VF	XF	Unc	BU
2011	—	—	—	1.50	5.00	6.00

KM# 1189 50 PENCE

8.0000 g., Copper-Nickel, 27.3 mm. **Ruler:** Elizabeth II **Subject:** 2012 London Paralympics - Boccia **Obv:** Head with tiara right **Edge:** Plain **Shape:** 7-sided

Date	Mintage	F	VF	XF	Unc	BU
2011	900,000	—	—	1.50	5.00	6.00

KM# 1190 50 PENCE

8.0000 g., Copper-Nickel, 27.3 mm. **Ruler:** Elizabeth II **Subject:** 2012 London Olympics - Basketball **Obv:** Head with tiara right **Edge:** Plain **Shape:** 7-sided

Date	Mintage	F	VF	XF	Unc	BU
2011	—	—	—	1.50	5.00	6.00

KM# 1191 50 PENCE

8.0000 g., Copper-Nickel, 27.3 mm. **Ruler:** Elizabeth II **Subject:** 2012 London Olympics - Fencing **Obv:** Head with tiara right **Edge:** Plain **Shape:** 7-sided

Date	Mintage	F	VF	XF	Unc	BU
2011	1,000,000	—	—	1.50	5.00	6.00

KM# 1192 50 PENCE

8.0000 g., Copper-Nickel, 27.3 mm. **Ruler:** Elizabeth II **Subject:** 2012 London Olympics - Handball **Obv:** Head with tiara right **Edge:** Plain **Shape:** 7-sided

Date	Mintage	F	VF	XF	Unc	BU
2011	—	—	—	1.50	5.00	6.00

KM# 1193 50 PENCE

8.0000 g., Copper-Nickel, 27.3 mm. **Ruler:** Elizabeth II **Subject:** 2012 London Olympics - Football (Soccer) **Obv:** Head with tiara right **Edge:** Plain **Shape:** 7-sided

Date	Mintage	F	VF	XF	Unc	BU
2011	—	—	—	1.50	5.00	6.00

KM# 1194 50 PENCE

8.0000 g., Copper-Nickel, 27.3 mm. **Ruler:** Elizabeth II **Subject:** 2012 London Olympics - Tennis **Obv:** Head with tiara right **Edge:** Plain **Shape:** 7-sided

Date	Mintage	F	VF	XF	Unc	BU
2011	—	—	—	1.50	5.00	6.00

KM# 1195 50 PENCE

8.0000 g., Copper-Nickel, 27.3 mm. **Ruler:** Elizabeth II **Subject:** London Olympics - Sailing **Obv:** Head with tiara right **Edge:** Plain **Shape:** 7-sided

Date	Mintage	F	VF	XF	Unc	BU
2011	—	—	—	1.00	5.00	6.00

KM# 1196 50 PENCE

8.0000 g., Copper-Nickel, 27.3 mm. **Ruler:** Elizabeth II **Subject:** World Wildlife Fund, 50th Anniversary **Obv:** Head with tiara right **Rev:** Panda in center of animal shaped blocks **Edge:** Plain **Shape:** 7-sided

Date	Mintage	F	VF	XF	Unc	BU
2011	Est. 40,000	—	—	1.50	5.00	6.00
2011 Proof	—	Value: 8.50				

KM# 1196a 50 PENCE

8.0000 g., 0.9250 Silver 0.2379 oz. ASW, 27.3 mm. **Ruler:** Elizabeth II **Subject:** World Wildlife Fund, 50th Anniversary **Obv:** Head with tiara right **Rev:** Panda at center, animal shapes as blocks **Edge:** Plain **Shape:** 7-sided

Date	Mintage	F	VF	XF	Unc	BU
2011 Proof	—	Value: 50.00				

Note: Also exists as a Piedfort, P86

KM# 1184 50 PENCE

8.0000 g., Copper-Nickel, 24.3 mm. **Ruler:** Elizabeth II **Subject:** 2012 London Olympics - Judo **Obv:** Head with tiara right **Edge:** Plain **Shape:** 7-sided

Date	Mintage	F	VF	XF	Unc	BU
2011	—	—	—	1.50	5.00	6.00

KM# 1112a.1 50 PENCE

8.0000 g., 0.9250 Silver partially gilt 0.2379 oz. ASW, 27.3 mm. **Ruler:** Elizabeth II **Obv:** Head with tiara right **Rev:** Section of Royal Arms - bottom center

Date	Mintage	F	VF	XF	Unc	BU
2012 Proof	—	Value: 50.00				

KM# 1178 50 PENCE

8.0000 g., Copper-Nickel, 27.3 mm. **Ruler:** Elizabeth II **Subject:** 2012 London Olympics - Sailing **Obv:** Head with tiara right **Edge:** Plain **Shape:** 7-sided

Date	Mintage	F	VF	XF	Unc	BU
2012	—	—	—	1.50	5.00	6.00

KM# 1246 50 PENCE

8.0000 g., Copper-Nickel, 27.3 mm. **Ruler:** Elizabeth II **Subject:** Christopher Ironside, 100th Anniversary of Birth **Obv:** Head with tiara right **Rev:** Royal Arms **Shape:** 7-sided

Date	Mintage	F	VF	XF	Unc	BU
2013	—	—	—	—	—	15.00
2013 Proof	44,000	Value: 50.00				

KM# 1246a 50 PENCE

8.0000 g., 0.9250 Silver 0.2379 oz. ASW, 27.3 mm. **Ruler:** Elizabeth II **Subject:** Christopher Ironside, 100th Anniversary of Birth **Obv:** Bust with tiara right **Rev:** Royal arms with supporters **Shape:** 7-sided

Date	Mintage	F	VF	XF	Unc	BU
2013 Proof	2,013	Value: 50.00				

KM# 1013 POUND

9.5000 g., Nickel-Brass, 22.5 mm. **Ruler:** Elizabeth II **Subject:** Northern Ireland **Obv:** Head with tiara right **Rev:** Celtic cross with a pimpernel flower at the center **Edge:** Reeded and lettered **Edge Lettering:** DECUS ET TUTAMEN

Date	Mintage	F	VF	XF	Unc	BU
2001	63,968,065	—	—	3.00	6.00	7.50
2001 Proof	45,617	Value: 7.50				

KM# 1013a POUND

9.5000 g., 0.9250 Silver 0.2825 oz. ASW, 22.5 mm. **Ruler:** Elizabeth II **Subject:** Northern Ireland **Obv:** Head with tiara right **Rev:** Celtic cross with a pimpernel flower in the center **Edge:** Reeded and lettered **Edge Lettering:** DECUS ET TUTAMEN

Date	Mintage	F	VF	XF	Unc	BU
2001 Proof	25,000	Value: 45.00				

Note: Also exists as a Piedfort, P101

KM# 1030 POUND

9.5000 g., Nickel-Brass, 22.5 mm. **Ruler:** Elizabeth II **Subject:** England **Obv:** Head with tiara right **Rev:** Three lions passant left **Edge:** Reeded and lettered **Edge Lettering:** DECUS ET TUTAMEN

Date	Mintage	F	VF	XF	Unc	BU
2002	77,818,000	—	—	3.00	6.00	7.00
2002 Proof	60,770	Value: 7.50				

KM# 1030a POUND

9.5000 g., 0.9250 Silver 0.2825 oz. ASW, 22.5 mm. **Ruler:** Elizabeth II **Subject:** England **Obv:** Head with tiara right **Rev:** Three lions passant left **Edge:** Reeded and lettered **Edge Lettering:** DECUS ET TUTAMEN

Date	Mintage	F	VF	XF	Unc	BU
2002 Proof	—	Value: 45.00				

Note: Also exists as a Piedfort, P102

KM# 1030b POUND

0.9167 Gold, 22.5 mm. **Ruler:** Elizabeth II **Subject:** England **Obv:** Head with tiara right **Rev:** Three lions left passant left **Edge:** Reeded and lettered **Edge Lettering:** DECUS ET TUTAMEN

Date	Mintage	F	VF	XF	Unc	BU
2002 Proof	—	Value: 850				

KM# 993 POUND

9.5000 g., Nickel-Brass, 22.5 mm. **Ruler:** Elizabeth II **Subject:** United Kingdom **Obv:** Head with tiara right **Rev:** Royal Arms with supporters **Edge:** Reeded and lettered **Edge Lettering:** DECUS ET TUTAMEN

Date	Mintage	F	VF	XF	Unc	BU
2003	61,596,500	—	—	3.00	6.00	7.50
2003 Proof	43,513	Value: 7.50				

KM# 1048 POUND

9.5000 g., Nickel-Brass, 22.5 mm. **Ruler:** Elizabeth II **Obv:** Head with tiara right **Rev:** Forth Rail Bridge in Scotland **Edge:** Reeded and ornamented

Date	Mintage	F	VF	XF	Unc	BU
2004	39,162,000	—	—	3.50	7.50	9.00
2004 Proof	35,020	Value: 9.00				

KM# 1048a POUND

9.5000 g., 0.9250 Silver 0.2825 oz. ASW, 22.5 mm. **Ruler:** Elizabeth II **Obv:** Head with tiara right **Rev:** Forth Railway Bridge in Scotland **Edge:** Ornamented and reeded

Date	Mintage	F	VF	XF	Unc	BU
2004 Proof	Est. 20,000	Value: 45.00				

Note: Also exists as a Piedfort, P44

KM# 1048b POUND

19.6190 g., 0.9166 Gold 0.5781 oz. AGW, 22.5 mm. **Ruler:** Elizabeth II **Obv:** Head with tiara right **Rev:** Forth Railway Bridge in Scotland **Edge:** Reeded and ornamented

Date	Mintage	F	VF	XF	Unc	BU
2004 Proof	Est. 1,500	Value: 1,100				

KM# 1051 POUND

9.5000 g., Nickel-Brass, 22.5 mm. **Ruler:** Elizabeth II **Obv:** Head with tiara right **Rev:** Menai Bridge to the Isle of Anglesey

Date	Mintage	F	VF	XF	Unc	BU
2005	99,429,500	—	—	3.00	6.00	7.50
2005 Proof	40,563	Value: 10.00				

KM# 1051a POUND

9.5000 g., 0.9250 Silver 0.2825 oz. ASW, 22.5 mm. **Ruler:** Elizabeth II **Obv:** Head with tiara right **Rev:** Menai Bridge to the Isle of Anglesey **Edge:** Reeded and lettered **Edge Lettering:** PLEIDOL WYF I'M GWLAD

Date	Mintage	F	VF	XF	Unc	BU
2005 Proof	Est. 15,000	Value: 45.00				

Note: Also exists as a Piedfort, P50

KM# 1051b POUND

19.6190 g., 0.9167 Gold 0.5782 oz. AGW, 22.5 mm. **Ruler:** Elizabeth II **Obv:** Head with tiara right **Rev:** Menai Bridge to the Isle of Anglesey **Edge:** Reeded and lettered **Edge Lettering:** PLEIDOL WYF I'M GWLAD

Date	Mintage	F	VF	XF	Unc	BU
2005 Proof	Est. 1,500	Value: 1,000				

KM# 1051a.2 POUND

9.5000 g., 0.9250 Silver 0.2825 oz. ASW, 22.5 mm. **Ruler:** Elizabeth II **Obv:** Elizabeth II **Rev:** Menai Bridge to the Isle of Anglesey **Edge:** Reeded and ornamented

Date	Mintage	F	VF	XF	Unc	BU
2005 Proof	Est. 20,000	Value: 45.00				

KM# 1051b.2 POUND

19.6190 g., 0.9166 Gold 0.5781 oz. AGW, 22.5 mm. **Ruler:** Elizabeth II **Obv:** Head with tiara right **Rev:** Menai Bridge to the Isle of Anglesey **Edge:** Reeded and ornamented

Date	Mintage	F	VF	XF	Unc	BU
2005 Proof	Est. 1,500	Value: 1,000				

KM# 1059 POUND

9.6000 g., Nickel-Brass, 22.5 mm. **Ruler:** Elizabeth II **Obv:** Head with tiara right **Rev:** Egyptian Arch Railway Bridge at Newry **Edge:** Reeded and lettered

Date	Mintage	F	VF	XF	Unc	BU
2006	38,938,000	—	—	4.00	8.00	9.00
2006 Proof	37,689	Value: 10.00				
2007 Proof	—	Value: 10.00				

KM# 1059a POUND

9.5000 g., 0.9250 Silver 0.2825 oz. ASW, 22.5 mm. **Ruler:** Elizabeth II **Obv:** Head with tiara right **Rev:** Egyptian Arch Railway Bridge at Newry **Edge:** Reeded and lettered **Edge Lettering:** DECUS ET TUTAMEN

Date	Mintage	F	VF	XF	Unc	BU
2006 Proof	Est. 20,000	Value: 50.00				

Note: Also exists as a Piedfort, P55

KM# 1059a.2 POUND

9.5000 g., 0.9250 Silver 0.2825 oz. ASW, 22.5 mm. **Ruler:** Elizabeth II **Obv:** Head with tiara right **Rev:** Egyptian Arch Railway Bridge at Newry **Edge:** Reeded and ornamented

Date	Mintage	F	VF	XF	Unc	BU
2006 Proof	Est. 20,000	Value: 45.00				

KM# 1059b POUND

19.6190 g., 0.9167 Gold 0.5782 oz. AGW, 22.5 mm. **Ruler:** Elizabeth II **Obv:** Head with tiara right **Rev:** Egyptian Arch Railway Bridge at Newry **Edge:** Reeded and lettered **Edge Lettering:** DECUS ET TUTAMEN

Date	Mintage	F	VF	XF	Unc	BU
2006 Proof	—	Value: 1,000				

KM# 1059b.2 POUND

19.6190 g., 0.9166 Gold 0.5781 oz. AGW, 22.5 mm. **Ruler:** Elizabeth II **Obv:** Head with tiara right **Rev:** Egyptian Arch Railway Bridge at Newry **Edge:** Reeded and ornamented

Date	Mintage	F	VF	XF	Unc	BU
2006 Proof	Est. 1,500	Value: 1,100				

KM# 1074 POUND

9.5000 g., Nickel-Brass, 22.5 mm. **Ruler:** Elizabeth II **Obv:** Head with tiara right **Rev:** Millennium Bridge at Gateshead **Edge:** Reeded and ornamented

Date	Mintage	F	VF	XF	Unc	BU
2007	26,180,160	—	—	4.00	8.00	9.00
2007 Proof	38,215	Value: 10.00				

KM# 1074a POUND

9.5000 g., 0.9250 Silver 0.2825 oz. ASW, 22.5 mm. **Ruler:** Elizabeth II **Obv:** head with tiara right **Rev:** Millennium Bridge at Gateshead **Edge:** Reeded and ornamented

Date	Mintage	F	VF	XF	Unc	BU
2007 Proof	Est. 20,000	Value: 45.00				

Note: Also exists as a Piedfort, P60

KM# 1074b POUND

19.6190 g., 0.9166 Gold 0.5781 oz. AGW, 22.5 mm. **Ruler:** Elizabeth II **Obv:** Head with tiara right **Rev:** Millennium Bridge at Gateshead **Edge:** Reeded and ornamented

Date	Mintage	F	VF	XF	Unc	BU
2007 Proof	Est. 1,500	Value: 1,000				

KM# 993a POUND

9.5000 g., 0.9250 Silver 0.2825 oz. ASW, 22.5 mm. **Ruler:** Elizabeth II **Subject:** United Kingdom **Obv:** Head with tiara right **Rev:** Royal Arms with supporters **Edge:** Reeded and lettered **Edge Lettering:** DECUS ET TUTAMEN

Date	Mintage	F	VF	XF	Unc	BU
2003 Proof	15,830	Value: 45.00				

Note: Also exists as a Piedfort, P41

KM# 993b POUND

19.6000 g., 0.9167 Gold 0.5776 oz. AGW, 22.5 mm. **Ruler:** Elizabeth II **Subject:** United Kingdom **Obv:** Head with tiara right **Rev:** Royal Arms with supporters **Edge:** Reeded and lettered **Edge Lettering:** DECUS ET TUTAMEN

Date	Mintage	F	VF	XF	Unc	BU
2008 Proof	Est. 2,008	Value: 1,100				
2013 Proof	100	Value: 1,200				

KM# 1113 POUND

9.5000 g., Nickel-Brass, 22.5 mm. **Ruler:** Elizabeth II **Obv:** Head with tiara right **Rev:** Shield of the Royal Arms **Edge:** Reeded and lettered **Edge Lettering:** DECUS ET TUTAMEN

Date	Mintage	F	VF	XF	Unc	BU
2008	43,827,300	—	—	3.00	7.50	6.00
2008 Proof	36,333	Value: 7.50				
2009	27,625,600	—	—	4.00	9.00	8.00
2009 Proof	40,000	Value: 9.00				
2010	38,505,000	—	—	3.00	7.50	6.00
2010 Proof	40,000	Value: 7.50				
2011	—	—	—	3.00	7.50	6.00
2011 Proof	—	Value: 7.50				
2012	—	—	—	3.00	7.50	6.00
2012 Proof	—	Value: 7.50				
2013	—	—	—	3.00	7.50	6.00
2013 Proof	—	Value: 7.50				

KM# 1113a POUND

9.5000 g., 0.9250 Silver 0.2825 oz. ASW, 22.5 mm. **Ruler:** Elizabeth II **Obv:** Head in tiara right **Rev:** Shield of the Royal Arms

Date	Mintage	F	VF	XF	Unc	BU
2008 Proof	5,000	Value: 50.00				

Note: Also exists as a Piedfort, P103

Date	Mintage	F	VF	XF	Unc	BU
2009	50,000	—	—	—	—	50.00
2009 Proof	20,000	Value: 60.00				
2010	50,000	—	—	—	—	50.00
2010 Proof	20,000	Value: 60.00				

KM# 1113b POUND

16.6190 g., 0.9167 Gold 0.4898 oz. AGW, 22.5 mm. **Ruler:** Elizabeth II **Obv:** Head in tiara right **Rev:** Shield of the Royal Arms

Date	Mintage	F	VF	XF	Unc	BU
2008 Proof	860	Value: 1,100				
2009 Proof	1,000	Value: 1,050				
2013 Proof	100	Value: 1,200				

KM# 1113c POUND

Platinum APW, 22.5 mm. **Ruler:** Elizabeth II **Obv:** Head in tiara right **Rev:** Shield of the Royal Arms

Date	Mintage	F	VF	XF	Unc	BU
2008 Proof	—	Value: 1,650				

KM# 1158 POUND
9.5000 g., Nickel-Brass, 22.5 mm. **Ruler:** Elizabeth II **Obv:** Head with tiara right **Rev:** City of London arms, three smaller arms below **Edge:** Reeded and lettered **Edge Lettering:** DOMINE DIRIGE NOS

Date	Mintage	F	VF	XF	Unc	BU
2010	—	—	—	3.00	6.00	7.50
2010 Proof	—	Value: 10.00				

KM# 1158a POUND
9.5000 g., 0.9250 Silver 0.2825 oz. ASW, 22.5 mm. **Ruler:** Elizabeth II **Obv:** Head with tiara right **Rev:** City of London arms, three smaller arms below

Date	Mintage	F	VF	XF	Unc	BU
2010 Proof	20,000	Value: 60.00				

Note: Also exists as a Piedfort, P75

KM# 1158b POUND
19.6190 g., 0.9167 Gold 0.5782 oz. AGW, 22.5 mm. **Ruler:** Elizabeth II **Obv:** Head with tiara right **Rev:** City of London arms, three smaller arms below

Date	Mintage	F	VF	XF	Unc	BU
2010 Proof	2,500	Value: 1,100				

KM# 1159 POUND
9.5000 g., Nickel-Brass, 22.5 mm. **Ruler:** Elizabeth II **Obv:** Head with tiara right **Rev:** City of Belfast arms, three smaller arms below **Edge:** Reeded and lettered **Edge Lettering:** PRO TANTO QUID RETRIBUAMUS

Date	Mintage	F	VF	XF	Unc	BU
2010	—	—	—	3.00	6.00	7.50
2010 Proof	—	Value: 10.00				

KM# 1159a POUND
9.5000 g., 0.9250 Silver 0.2825 oz. ASW, 22.5 mm. **Ruler:** Elizabeth II **Obv:** Head with tiara right **Rev:** City of Belfast arms, three smaller arms below

Date	Mintage	F	VF	XF	Unc	BU
2010 Proof	20,000	Value: 60.00				

Note: Also exists as a Piedfort, P76

KM# 1159b POUND
19.6190 g., 0.9167 Gold 0.5782 oz. AGW, 22.5 mm. **Ruler:** Elizabeth II **Obv:** Head with tiara right **Rev:** City of Belfast arms, three smaller arms below

Date	Mintage	F	VF	XF	Unc	BU
2010 Proof	2,500	Value: 1,100				

KM# 1197 POUND
9.5000 g., Nickel-Brass, 22.5 mm. **Ruler:** Elizabeth II **Obv:** Head with tiara right **Rev:** Edinburgh city arms, three smaller arms below **Edge:** Reeded and lettered **Edge Lettering:** NISI DOMINUS FRUSTRA

Date	Mintage	F	VF	XF	Unc	BU
2011	—	—	—	3.00	6.00	7.50
2011 Proof	—	Value: 10.00				

KM# 1197a POUND
9.5000 g., 0.9250 Silver 0.2825 oz. ASW, 22.5 mm. **Ruler:** Elizabeth II **Obv:** Head with tiara right **Rev:** Edinburgh City arms, three smaller arms below

Date	Mintage	F	VF	XF	Unc	BU
2011 Proof	—	Value: 45.00				

Note: Also exists as a Piedfort, P83

KM# 1198 POUND
9.5000 g., Nickel-Brass, 22.5 mm. **Ruler:** Elizabeth II **Obv:** Head with tiara right **Rev:** Cardiff city arms, three smaller arms below **Edge:** Reeded and lettered **Edge Lettering:** DDRAIG GOCH DDYRY CYCHWYN

Date	Mintage	F	VF	XF	Unc	BU
2011	—	—	—	3.00	6.00	7.50
2011 Proof	—	Value: 10.00				

KM# 1198a POUND
9.5000 g., 0.9250 Silver 0.2825 oz. ASW, 22.5 mm. **Ruler:** Elizabeth II **Obv:** Head with tiara right **Rev:** Cardiff city arms, three smaller arms below

Date	Mintage	F	VF	XF	Unc	BU
2011 Proof	—	Value: 45.00				

Note: Also exists as a Piedfort, P84

KM# 1113a.1 POUND
9.5000 g., 0.9250 Silver partially gilt 0.2825 oz. ASW, 22.5 mm. **Ruler:** Elizabeth II **Obv:** Head with tiara right **Rev:** Shield of the Royal Arms

Date	Mintage	F	VF	XF	Unc	BU
2012 Proof	—	Value: 60.00				

KM# 1237 POUND
9.5000 g., Nickel-Brass, 22.5 mm. **Ruler:** Elizabeth II **Obv:** Head with tiara right **Rev:** England flora - Rose and oak

Date	Mintage	F	VF	XF	Unc	BU
2013	—	—	—	3.00	6.00	7.50
2013 Proof	—	Value: 10.00				

KM# 1237a POUND
9.5000 g., 0.9250 Silver 0.2825 oz. ASW, 22.5 mm. **Ruler:** Elizabeth II **Obv:** Bust with tiara right **Rev:** England flora - Rose and oak

Date	Mintage	F	VF	XF	Unc	BU
2013 Proof	12,500	Value: 40.00				

KM# 1237b POUND
19.6100 g., 0.9167 Gold 0.5779 oz. AGW, 22.5 mm. **Ruler:** Elizabeth II **Obv:** Head with tiara right **Rev:** England Flora - oak and rose

Date	Mintage	F	VF	XF	Unc	BU
2013 Proof	560	Value: 1,400				

KM# 1238 POUND
9.5000 g., Nickel-Brass, 22.5 mm. **Ruler:** Elizabeth II **Obv:** Head with tiara right **Rev:** Wales flora - Leek and daffodil

Date	Mintage	F	VF	XF	Unc	BU
2013	—	—	—	3.00	6.00	7.50
2013 Proof	—	Value: 10.00				

KM# 1238a POUND
9.5000 g., 0.9250 Silver 0.2825 oz. ASW, 22.5 mm. **Ruler:** Elizabeth II **Obv:** Head with tiara right **Rev:** Wales flora - leek and daffodil

Date	Mintage	F	VF	XF	Unc	BU
2013 Proof	12,500	Value: 40.00				

KM# 1238b POUND
19.6100 g., 0.9167 Gold 0.5779 oz. AGW, 22.5 mm. **Ruler:** Elizabeth II **Obv:** Head with tiara right **Rev:** Wales flora - leek and daffodil

Date	Mintage	F	VF	XF	Unc	BU
2013 Proof	560	Value: 1,400				

KM# 1245 POUND
16.6190 g., 0.9170 Gold 0.4899 oz. AGW, 22.5 mm. **Ruler:** Elizabeth II **Obv:** Head with tiara right **Rev:** Crowned shield of the United Kingdom **Edge Lettering:** DECUS ET TUTAMEN

Date	Mintage	F	VF	XF	Unc	BU
2013 Proof	100	Value: 1,200				

KM# 994 2 POUNDS
12.0000 g., Bi-Metallic Copper-Nickel center in Nickel-Brass ring, 28.4 mm. **Ruler:** Elizabeth II **Subject:** Technology **Obv:** Head with tiara right **Rev:** Symbolic depiction in concentric circles of technological development from the Iron Age to the Internet **Edge Lettering:** STANDING ON THE SHOULDERS OF GIANTS

Date	Mintage	F	VF	XF	Unc	BU
2001	34,984,750	—	—	5.00	9.50	12.00
2001 Proof	—	Value: 12.00				
2002	13,024,750	—	—	5.00	9.50	12.00
2002 Proof	—	Value: 12.00				
2003	17,531,250	—	—	5.00	9.50	12.00
2003 Proof	43,513	Value: 12.00				
2004	11,981,500	—	—	5.00	9.50	12.00
2004 Proof	35,020	Value: 12.00				
2005	3,837,250	—	—	5.00	9.50	12.00
2005 Proof	40,563	Value: 12.00				
2006	16,715,000	—	—	5.00	9.50	12.00
2006 Proof	—	Value: 12.00				
2007	10,270,000	—	—	5.00	9.50	12.00
2007 Proof	—	Value: 12.00				
2008	30,107,000	—	—	5.00	9.50	12.00
2008 Proof	—	Value: 12.00				
2009	8,775,000	—	—	5.00	9.50	12.00
2009 Proof	—	Value: 12.00				
2010	2,015,000	—	—	5.00	9.50	12.00
2010 Proof	—	Value: 12.00				
2011	—	—	—	5.00	9.50	12.00
2011 Proof	—	Value: 12.00				
2012	—	—	—	5.00	9.50	12.00
2012 Proof	—	Value: 12.00				
2013	—	—	—	5.00	9.50	12.00
2013 Proof	—	Value: 12.00				

KM# 1014 2 POUNDS
11.9700 g., Bi-Metallic Copper-Nickel center in Nickel-Brass ring, 28.35 mm. **Ruler:** Elizabeth II **Subject:** First Transatlantic Radio Transmission **Obv:** Head with tiara right within circle **Rev:** Symbolic design **Edge:** Reeded and inscribed **Edge Lettering:** WIRELESS BRIDGES THE ATLANTIC... MARCONI... 1901

Date	Mintage	F	VF	XF	Unc	BU
2001	4,558,000	—	—	5.00	9.50	12.00
2001 Proof	—	Value: 12.00				

KM# 1014a 2 POUNDS
12.0000 g., 0.9250 Silver with gilt ring 0.3569 oz. ASW, 28.4 mm. **Ruler:** Elizabeth II **Subject:** First Transatlantic Radio Transmission **Obv:** Head with tiara right within circle **Rev:** Symbolic design **Edge Lettering:** WIRELESS BRIDGES THE ATLANTIC...MARCONI 1901...

Date	Mintage	F	VF	XF	Unc	BU
2001 Proof	11,488	Value: 45.00				

Note: Also exists as a Piefort, P106

KM# 1014b 2 POUNDS
15.9700 g., 0.9166 Gold Yellow gold plated Red Gold center in Red Gold ring 0.4706 oz. AGW, 28.4 mm. **Ruler:** Elizabeth II **Subject:** First Transatlantic Radio Transmission **Obv:** Head with tiara right **Rev:** Symbolic design

Date	Mintage	F	VF	XF	Unc	BU
2001 Proof	1,658	Value: 900				

KM# 994c 2 POUNDS
15.9800 g., 0.9167 Gold 0.4710 oz. AGW, 28.35 mm. **Ruler:** Elizabeth II **Subject:** Technology **Obv:** Head with tiara right **Rev:** Symbolic depiction in concentric circles of technological development from the Iron Age to the Internet

Date	Mintage	F	VF	XF	Unc	BU
2002 Proof	—	Value: 900				

KM# 1031 2 POUNDS
12.0000 g., Bi-Metallic Copper-Nickel center in Nickel-Brass ring, 28.4 mm. **Ruler:** Elizabeth II **Subject:** 17th Commonwealth Games - Manchester, England **Obv:** Head with tiara right **Rev:** Runner breaking ribbon at finish line, national flag of England in circle behind athlete **Edge:** Reeded and lettered **Edge Lettering:** SPIRIT OF FRIENDSHIP MANCHESTER 2002

Date	Mintage	F	VF	XF	Unc	BU
2002	650,500	—	—	6.00	12.00	15.00
2002 Proof	—	Value: 15.00				

KM# 1031a 2 POUNDS
12.0000 g., 0.9250 Silver Silver center in Gold plated ring 0.3569 oz. ASW, 28.4 mm. **Ruler:** Elizabeth II **Subject:** Commonwealth Games - England **Obv:** Head with tiara right **Rev:** Runner breaking ribbon at finish line **Edge:** Reeded and lettered

Date	Mintage	F	VF	XF	Unc	BU
2002 Proof	10,000	Value: 45.00				

Note: Also exists as a Piefort, P107

KM# 1031b 2 POUNDS
15.9800 g., 0.9160 Gold Yellow gold center in Red Gold ring 0.4706 oz. AGW, 28.4 mm. **Ruler:** Elizabeth II **Subject:** Commonwealth Games - England **Obv:** Head with tiara right **Rev:** Runner breaking ribbon at finish line **Edge:** Reeded and lettered

Date	Mintage	F	VF	XF	Unc	BU
2002 Proof	500	Value: 950				

KM# 1032 2 POUNDS
12.0000 g., Bi-Metallic Copper-Nickel center in Nickel-Brass ring, 28.4 mm. **Ruler:** Elizabeth II **Subject:** 17th Commonwealth Games - Manchester, England **Obv:** Head with tiara right **Rev:** Runner breaking ribbon at finish line, national flag of Scotland in circle behind athlete **Edge:** Reeded and lettered

Date	Mintage	F	VF	XF	Unc	BU
2002	771,750	—	—	6.00	12.00	15.00
2002 Proof	—	Value: 15.00				

KM# 1032a 2 POUNDS
12.0000 g., 0.9250 Silver Silver center with Gold plated ring 0.3569 oz. ASW, 28.4 mm. **Ruler:** Elizabeth II **Subject:** Commonwealth Games - Scotland **Obv:** Head with tiara right **Rev:** Runner breaking ribbon at finish line **Edge:** Reeded and lettered

Date	Mintage	F	VF	XF	Unc	BU
2002 Proof	10,000	Value: 35.00				

Note: Also exists as a Piefort, P108

KM# 1032b 2 POUNDS
15.9800 g., 0.9160 Gold Yellow gold center in Red Gold ring 0.4706 oz. AGW, 28.4 mm. **Ruler:** Elizabeth II **Subject:** Commonwealth Games - Scotland **Obv:** Head with tiara right **Rev:** Runner breaking ribbon at finish line **Edge:** Reeded and lettered

Date	Mintage	F	VF	XF	Unc	BU
2002 Proof	500	Value: 950				

KM# 1033 2 POUNDS
12.0000 g., Bi-Metallic Copper-Nickel center in Nickel-Brass ring, 28.4 mm. **Ruler:** Elizabeth II **Subject:** 17th Commonwealth Games - Manchester, England **Obv:** Head with tiara right **Rev:** Runner breaking ribbon at finish line, national flag of Wales in circle behind athlete **Edge:** Reeded and lettered **Edge Lettering:** SPIRIT OF FRIENDSHIP MANCHESTER 2002

Date	Mintage	F	VF	XF	Unc	BU
2002	588,500	—	—	6.00	12.00	15.00
2002 Proof	—	Value: 15.00				

KM# 1033a 2 POUNDS
12.0000 g., 0.9250 Silver Silver center in Gold plated ring 0.3569 oz. ASW, 28.4 mm. **Ruler:** Elizabeth II **Subject:** Commonwealth Games - Wales **Obv:** Head with tiara right **Rev:** Runner breaking ribbon at finish line **Edge:** Reeded and lettered

Date	Mintage	F	VF	XF	Unc	BU
2002 Proof	10,000	Value: 35.00				

Note: Also exists as a Piefort, P109

KM# 1033b 2 POUNDS
15.9800 g., 0.9160 Gold Yellow Gold center in Red Gold ring 0.4706 oz. AGW, 28.4 mm. **Ruler:** Elizabeth II **Subject:** Commonwealth Games - Wales **Obv:** Head with tiara right **Rev:** Runner breaking ribbon at finish line **Edge:** Reeded and lettered

Date	Mintage	F	VF	XF	Unc	BU
2002 Proof	500	Value: 950				

KM# 1034 2 POUNDS
12.0000 g., Bi-Metallic Copper-Nickel center in Nickel-Brass ring, 28.4 mm. **Ruler:** Elizabeth II **Subject:** 17th Commonwealth Games - Manchester, England **Obv:** Head with tiara right **Rev:** Runner breaking ribbon at finish line, national flag of Northern Ireland in circle behind athlete **Edge:** Reeded and lettered **Edge Lettering:** SPIRIT OF FRIENDSHIP MANCHESTER 2002

Date	Mintage	F	VF	XF	Unc	BU
2002	485,500	—	—	6.00	12.00	15.00
2002 Proof	—	Value: 15.00				

KM# 1034a 2 POUNDS
12.0000 g., 0.9250 Silver Silver center in Gold plated ring 0.3569 oz. ASW, 28.4 mm. **Ruler:** Elizabeth II **Subject:** Commonwealth Games - Northern Ireland **Obv:** Head with tiara right **Rev:** Runner breaking ribbon at finish line **Edge:** Reeded and lettered

Date	Mintage	F	VF	XF	Unc	BU
2002 Proof	10,000	Value: 35.00				

Note: Also exists as a Piefort, P110

KM# 1034b 2 POUNDS
15.9800 g., 0.9160 Gold Yellow Gold center in Red Gold ring 0.4706 oz. AGW, 28.4 mm. **Ruler:** Elizabeth II **Subject:** Commonwealth Games - Northern Ireland **Obv:** Head with tiara right **Rev:** Runner breaking ribbon at finish line **Edge:** Reeded and lettered

Date	Mintage	F	VF	XF	Unc	BU
2002 Proof	500	Value: 950				

KM# 1037 2 POUNDS
12.0000 g., Bi-Metallic Copper-Nickel center in Nickel-Brass ring, 28.4 mm. **Ruler:** Elizabeth II **Subject:** 50th Anniversary of the Discovery of DNA **Obv:** Head with tiara right **Rev:** DNA Double Helix **Edge:** Reeded and inscribed **Edge Lettering:** DEOXYRIBONUCLEIC ACID

Date	Mintage	F	VF	XF	Unc	BU
ND(2003)	4,299,000	—	—	6.00	12.00	15.00
ND(2003) Proof	43,513	Value: 15.00				

KM# 1037a 2 POUNDS
12.0000 g., 0.9250 Silver Silver center in Gold plated ring 0.3569 oz. ASW, 28.4 mm. **Ruler:** Elizabeth II **Obv:** Head with tiara right **Rev:** DNA Double Helix **Edge:** Reeded and lettered

Date	Mintage	F	VF	XF	Unc	BU
ND(2003) Proof	11,204	Value: 35.00				

Note: Also exists as a Piefort, P42

KM# 1037b 2 POUNDS
15.9800 g., 0.9167 Gold Yellow gold center in Red gold ring 0.4710 oz. AGW, 28.4 mm. **Ruler:** Elizabeth II **Obv:** Head with tiara right **Rev:** DNA Double Helix **Edge:** Reeded and lettered

Date	Mintage	F	VF	XF	Unc	BU
ND2003 Proof	1,500	Value: 900				

KM# 1049 2 POUNDS
12.0000 g., Bi-Metallic Copper-Nickel center in Nickel-Brass ring, 28.4 mm. **Ruler:** Elizabeth II **Subject:** Richard Trevithick, Inventor of the First Steam Locomotive **Obv:** Head with tiara right **Rev:** First steam locomotive **Rev. Legend:** 2004 R. TREVITHICK 1804 INVENTION-INDUSTRY-PROGRESS **Edge:** Incuse railway line motif

Date	Mintage	F	VF	XF	Unc	BU
2004	5,004,500	—	—	6.00	12.00	15.00
2004 Proof	35,020	Value: 15.00				

KM# 1049a 2 POUNDS
12.0000 g., 0.9250 Silver Silver center in Gold plated ring 0.3569 oz. ASW, 28.4 mm. **Ruler:** Elizabeth II **Obv:** Head with tiara right **Rev:** First steam locomotive **Rev. Legend:** 2004 R. TREVITHICK 1804 INVENTION-INDUSTRY-PROGRESS **Edge:** Incuse railway line motif

Date	Mintage	F	VF	XF	Unc	BU
2004	1,923	—	—	—	—	50.00
2004 Proof	19,233	Value: 35.00				

Note: Also exists as a Piefort, P45

KM# 1049b 2 POUNDS
15.9800 g., 0.9166 Gold Yellow Gold center in Red Gold ring 0.4709 oz. AGW, 28.4 mm. **Ruler:** Elizabeth II **Obv:** Head with tiara right **Rev:** First steam locomotive **Rev. Legend:** 2004 R. TREVITHICK 1804 INVENTION-INDUSTRY-PROGRESS **Edge:** Incuse railway line motif

Date	Mintage	F	VF	XF	Unc	BU
2004 Proof	1,500	Value: 900				

KM# 1052 2 POUNDS
12.0000 g., Bi-Metallic Copper-Nickel center in Nickel-Brass ring, 28.4 mm. **Ruler:** Elizabeth II **Subject:** 400th Anniversary - The Gunpowder Plot **Obv:** Head with tiara right **Rev:** Circular design of Royal scepters, swords and crosiers **Edge:** Reeded and lettered **Edge Lettering:** REMEMBER REMEMBER THE FIFTH OF NOVEMBER

Date	Mintage	F	VF	XF	Unc	BU
ND(2005)	5,140,500	—	—	6.00	12.00	15.00
ND(2005) Proof	40,563	Value: 15.00				

Note: Also exists as a Piefort, P46

KM# 1056 2 POUNDS
Bi-Metallic Copper-Nickel center in Nickel-Brass ring, 28.4 mm. **Ruler:** Elizabeth II **Subject:** 60th Anniversary of the End of WW II **Obv:** Head with tiara right **Rev:** St. Paul's Cathedral amid search light beams **Edge:** Reeded and lettered **Edge Lettering:** IN VICTORY MAGNANIMITY IN PEACE GOODWILL

Date	Mintage	F	VF	XF	Unc	BU
ND (2005)	10,191,000	—	—	6.00	12.00	15.00

KM# 1056a 2 POUNDS
12.0000 g., 0.9250 Silver center in Gold-plated ring 0.3569 oz. ASW, 28.4 mm. **Ruler:** Elizabeth II **Subject:** 60th Anniversary of the End of WWII **Obv:** Crowned head right **Rev:** St. Paul's Cathedral amid search light beams **Edge:** Reeded and lettered **Edge Lettering:** IN VICTORY MAGNANIMITY IN PEACE GOODWILL

Date	Mintage	F	VF	XF	Unc	BU
ND(2005) Proof	21,734	Value: 35.00				

Note: Also exists as a Piefort, P49

KM# 1056b 2 POUNDS
15.9700 g., 0.9167 Gold 0.4707 oz. AGW, 28.4 mm. **Ruler:** Elizabeth II **Subject:** 60th Anniversary of the End of WWII **Obv:** Crowned head right **Rev:** St. Paul's Cathedral amid search light beams **Edge:** Reeded and lettered **Edge Lettering:** IN VICTORY MAGNANIMITY IN PEACE GOODWILL

Date	Mintage	F	VF	XF	Unc	BU
ND(2005) Proof	2,924	Value: 900				

KM# 994a 2 POUNDS
12.0000 g., 0.9250 Silver 0.3569 oz. ASW, 28.35 mm. **Ruler:** Elizabeth II **Subject:** Technology **Obv:** Head with tiara right **Rev:** Symbolic depiction in concentric circles of technological development from the Iron Age to the Internet **Note:** Gold plated silver ring, silver center.

Date	Mintage	F	VF	XF	Unc	BU
2006 Proof	—	Value: 45.00				

KM# 1060 2 POUNDS
12.0000 g., Bi-Metallic Copper-Nickel center in Nickel-Brass ring, 28.4 mm. **Ruler:** Elizabeth II **Subject:** 200th Birthday of Engineer Isambard Kingdom Brunel **Obv:** Head with tiara right **Rev:** Isambard Brunel **Edge Lettering:** 1806-1859 ISAMBARD KINGDOM BRUNEL ENGINEER

Date	Mintage	F	VF	XF	Unc	BU
2006	7,925,250	—	—	—	16.00	20.00
2006 Proof	Est. 50,000	Value: 20.00				

KM# 1061 2 POUNDS

12.0000 g., Bi-Metallic Copper-Nickel center in Nickel-Brass ring, 28.4 mm. **Ruler:** Elizabeth II **Subject:** Engineering Achievements of Isambard Kingdom Brunel **Obv:** Head with tiara right **Rev:** Paddington Station structural supports **Edge Lettering:** SO MANY IRONS IN THE FIRE

Date	Mintage	F	VF	XF	Unc	BU
2006	7,452,250	—	—	—	16.00	20.00
2006 Proof	Est. 50,000	Value: 20.00				

KM# 1060a 2 POUNDS

12.0000 g., 0.9250 Silver with gilt ring 0.3569 oz. ASW, 28.4 mm. **Ruler:** Elizabeth II **Subject:** Brunel's 200th Birthday **Obv:** Head with tiara right **Rev:** Brunel and gears

Date	Mintage	F	VF	XF	Unc	BU
2006 Proof	—	Value: 55.00				

Note: Also exists as a Piefort, P56

KM# 1060b 2 POUNDS

15.9800 g., 0.9160 Gold Yellow Gold center in Red Gold ring 0.4706 oz. AGW, 28.4 mm. **Ruler:** Elizabeth II **Subject:** Brunel's 200th Birthday **Obv:** Head with tiara right **Rev:** Brunel and gears

Date	Mintage	F	VF	XF	Unc	BU
2006 Proof	—	Value: 900				

KM# 1061a 2 POUNDS

12.0000 g., 0.9250 Silver center in gilt ring 0.3569 oz. ASW, 28.4 mm. **Ruler:** Elizabeth II **Subject:** Brunel's engineering achievements **Obv:** Head with tiara right **Rev:** Archways

Date	Mintage	F	VF	XF	Unc	BU
2006 Proof	—	Value: 55.00				

Note: Also exists as a Piefort, P57

KM# 1061b 2 POUNDS

15.9800 g., 0.9160 Gold Yellow Gold center in Red Gold ring 0.4706 oz. AGW, 28.4 mm. **Ruler:** Elizabeth II **Subject:** Brunel's engineering achievements **Obv:** Head with tiara right **Rev:** Archways

Date	Mintage	F	VF	XF	Unc	BU
2006 Proof	—	Value: 900				

KM# 1075 2 POUNDS

12.0000 g., Bi-Metallic Copper-Nickel center in Nickel-Brass ring, 28.4 mm. **Ruler:** Elizabeth II **Subject:** 200th Anniversary of the Abolition of the Slave Trade **Obv:** Bust right **Rev:** Chain crossing 1807 date **Edge:** Reeded and lettered **Edge Lettering:** AM I NOT A MAN AND A BROTHER

Date	Mintage	F	VF	XF	Unc	BU
2007	8,445,000	—	—	6.00	12.50	15.00
2007 Proof	Est. 50,000	Value: 15.00				

KM# 1075a 2 POUNDS

12.0000 g., 0.9250 Silver center in Gold plated ring 0.3569 oz. ASW, 28.4 mm. **Ruler:** Elizabeth II **Subject:** Abolition of the Slave Trade **Obv:** Elizabeth II right **Rev:** Zero in 1807 date as a broken chain link **Edge:** Reeded and lettered **Edge Lettering:** AM I NOT A MAN AND A BROTHER

Date	Mintage	F	VF	XF	Unc	BU
2007 Proof	7,095	Value: 55.00				

Note: Also exists as a Piefort, P61

KM# 1075b 2 POUNDS

15.9700 g., 0.9166 Gold Yellow Gold center in Red Gold ring 0.4706 oz. AGW, 28.4 mm. **Ruler:** Elizabeth II **Subject:** Abolition of the Slave Trade **Obv:** Head with tiara right **Rev:** Zero in 1807 date as a broken chain link **Edge:** Reeded and lettered **Edge Lettering:** AM I NOT A MAN AND A BROTHER

Date	Mintage	F	VF	XF	Unc	BU
2007 Proof	1,000	Value: 900				

KM# 1076 2 POUNDS

12.0000 g., Bi-Metallic Copper-Nickel center in Nickel-Brass ring, 28.4 mm. **Ruler:** Elizabeth II **Subject:** 300th Anniversary of the Act of Union of England and Scotland **Obv:** Head with tiara right **Rev:** Combination of British and Scottish arms **Edge:** Reeded and lettered **Edge Lettering:** UNITED INTO ONE KINGDOM

Date	Mintage	F	VF	XF	Unc	BU
2007	7,545,000	—	—	6.00	12.50	15.00
2007 Proof	Est. 50,000	Value: 15.00				

KM# 1076a 2 POUNDS

12.0000 g., 0.9250 Silver center in Gold Plated ring 0.3569 oz. ASW, 28.4 mm. **Ruler:** Elizabeth II **Subject:** 300th Anniv. Union of Scotland and England **Obv:** Head with tiara right **Rev:** Combined English and Scottish arms **Edge:** Reeded and lettered

Date	Mintage	F	VF	XF	Unc	BU
2007 Proof	8,310	Value: 55.00				

Note: Also exists as a Piefort, P62

KM# 1076b 2 POUNDS

15.9800 g., 0.9166 Gold Yellow Gold center in Red Gold ring 0.4709 oz. AGW, 28.4 mm. **Ruler:** Elizabeth II **Subject:** 300th Anniv. Union of Scotland and England **Obv:** Head with tiara right **Rev:** Combined English and Scottish arms **Edge:** Reeded and lettered

Date	Mintage	F	VF	XF	Unc	BU
2007 Proof	750	Value: 900				

KM# 1105 2 POUNDS

12.0000 g., Bi-Metallic Copper-Nickel center in Nickel-Brass ring, 28.4 mm. **Ruler:** Elizabeth II **Subject:** London 1908 - Olympics **Obv:** Head with tiara right **Rev:** Sprint track **Edge:** Lettered and reeded **Edge Lettering:** THE 4TH OLYMPIAD LONDON

Date	Mintage	F	VF	XF	Unc	BU
2008	910,000	—	—	6.00	15.00	12.50
2008 Proof	—	Value: 15.00				

KM# 1106 2 POUNDS

12.0000 g., Bi-Metallic Copper-Nickel center in Nickel-Brass ring, 28.4 mm. **Ruler:** Elizabeth II **Subject:** Beijing - London Olympic Flag handoff **Obv:** Head with tiara right **Rev:** London 2012 Games Flag hand off **Edge Lettering:** I CALL UPON THE YOUTH OF THE WORLD

Date	Mintage	F	VF	XF	Unc	BU
2008	918,000	—	—	—	18.00	22.00
2008 Proof	Est. 250,000	Value: 45.00				

KM# 1106a 2 POUNDS

12.0000 g., 0.9250 Silver Silver center in Gilt ring 0.3569 oz. ASW, 28.4 mm. **Ruler:** Elizabeth II **Obv:** Head with tiara right **Rev:** Handoff of the Olympic Flag

Date	Mintage	F	VF	XF	Unc	BU
2008 Proof	—	Value: 55.00				

Note: Also exists as a Piefort, P65

KM# 1106b 2 POUNDS

15.9800 g., 0.9160 Gold 0.4706 oz. AGW, 28.4 mm. **Ruler:** Elizabeth II **Subject:** Countdown to 2010 London Olympics **Obv:** Head right **Rev:** Handoff of the Olympic flag **Edge Lettering:** I CALL UPON THE YOUTH OF THE WORLD

Date	Mintage	F	VF	XF	Unc	BU
2009 Proof	3,000	Value: 875				

KM# 1115 2 POUNDS

12.0000 g., Bi-Metallic Copper-Nickel center in Nickel-Brass ring., 28.4 mm. **Ruler:** Elizabeth II **Subject:** Charles Darwin, 200th Anniversary of Birth **Obv:** Head with tiara right **Rev:** Darwin and ape heads facing **Edge Lettering:** ON THE ORIGIN OF SPECIES 1859

Date	Mintage	F	VF	XF	Unc	BU
2009	3,903,000	—	—	—	16.00	20.00
2009 Proof	—	Value: 25.00				

KM# 1115a 2 POUNDS

12.0000 g., 0.9250 Silver Silver center in Gilt ring 0.3569 oz. ASW, 28.4 mm. **Ruler:** Elizabeth II **Subject:** Charles Darwin, 200th Anniversary of Brith **Obv:** Head with tiara right **Rev:** Darwin and ape heads facing

Date	Mintage	F	VF	XF	Unc	BU
2009 Proof	—	Value: 55.00				

Note: Also exists as a Piefort, P66

KM# 1115b 2 POUNDS

15.9800 g., 0.9160 Gold Yellow Gold center in Red Gold ring 0.4706 oz. AGW, 28.4 mm. **Ruler:** Elizabeth II **Subject:** Charles Darwin, 200th Anniversary of Birth **Obv:** Head with tiara right **Rev:** Darwin and ape heads facing

Date	Mintage	F	VF	XF	Unc	BU
2009 Proof	—	Value: 900				

KM# 1116 2 POUNDS

12.0000 g., Bi-Metallic Copper-Nickel center in Nickel-Brass ring, 28.4 mm. **Ruler:** Elizabeth II **Subject:** Robert Burns, 250th Anniversary of Birth **Obv:** Head with tiara right **Rev:** Text **Edge:** Reeded and lettered **Edge Lettering:** SHOULD AULD ACQUAINTANCE BE FORGOT

Date	Mintage	F	VF	XF	Unc	BU
2009	3,253,000	—	—	—	16.00	20.00
2009 Proof	—	Value: 25.00				

KM# 1116a 2 POUNDS

12.0000 g., 0.9250 Silver Sivler center in Gilt ring 0.3569 oz. ASW, 28.4 mm. **Ruler:** Elizabeth II **Subject:** Robert Burns, 250th Anniversary of Birth **Obv:** Head with tiara right **Rev:** Text

Date	Mintage	F	VF	XF	Unc	BU
2009 Proof	—	Value: 55.00				

Note: Also exists as a Piefort, P

KM# 1116b 2 POUNDS

15.9700 g., 0.9167 Gold Yellow Gold center in Red Gold ring 0.4707 oz. AGW, 28.4 mm. **Ruler:** Elizabeth II **Subject:** Robert Burns, 250th Anniversary of Birth **Obv:** Head with tiara right **Rev:** Text

Date	Mintage	F	VF	XF	Unc	BU
2009 Proof	1,000	Value: 900				

KM# 1160 2 POUNDS

11.9700 g., Bi-Metallic Copper-Nickel center in Nickel-Brass ring, 28.35 mm. **Ruler:** Elizabeth II **Subject:** Florence Nightengale, 100th Anniversary of Death **Obv:** Head with tiara right **Rev:** Hand taking pulse **Edge Lettering:** 150 YEARS OF NURSING

Date	Mintage	F	VF	XF	Unc	BU
2010	—	—	—	6.00	12.00	15.00
2010 Proof	—	Value: 15.00				

KM# 1199 2 POUNDS

11.9700 g., Bi-Metallic Copper-Nickel center in Nickel-Brass ring, 28.4 mm. **Ruler:** Elizabeth II **Subject:** Mary Rose, 500th Anniversary **Obv:** Head with tiara right **Rev:** H.M.S. Mary Rose under sail **Edge Lettering:** YOUR NOBLEST SHIPPE 1511

Date	Mintage	F	VF	XF	Unc	BU
2011	—	—	—	6.00	12.00	15.00

KM# 1199a 2 POUNDS

12.0000 g., 0.9250 Silver center in Gilt ring 0.3569 oz. ASW, 28.4 mm. **Ruler:** Elizabeth II **Subject:** Mary Rose, 500th Anniversary **Obv:** Head with tiara right **Rev:** H.M.S. Mary Rose under sail **Edge Lettering:** YOUR NOBLEST SHIPPE 1511

Date	Mintage	F	VF	XF	Unc	BU
2011 Proof	—	Value: 55.00				

Note: Also exists as a Piefort, P87

KM# 1199b 2 POUNDS

15.9800 g., 0.9166 Gold Yellow Gold center in Red Gold ring 0.4709 oz. AGW, 28.4 mm. **Ruler:** Elizabeth II **Subject:** Mary Rose, 500th Anniversary **Obv:** Head with tiara right **Rev:** H.M.S. Mary Rose under sail **Edge Lettering:** YOUR NOBLEST SHIPPE 1511

Date	Mintage	F	VF	XF	Unc	BU
2011 Proof	—	Value: 1,600				

KM# 1200 2 POUNDS
11.9700 g., Bi-Metallic Copper-Nickel center in Nickel-Brass ring, 28.4 mm. **Ruler:** Elizabeth II **Subject:** King James Bible, 400th Anniversary **Obv:** Head in tiara right **Rev:** Lead type and printed page of bible text **Edge:** Reeded and lettered **Edge Lettering:** THE AUTHORIZED VERSION

Date	Mintage	F	VF	XF	Unc	BU
2011	—	—	—	6.00	12.00	15.00
2011 Proof	—	Value: 15.00				

KM# 1200a 2 POUNDS
12.0000 g., 0.9250 Silver center in Gilt ring 0.3569 oz. ASW, 28.4 mm. **Ruler:** Elizabeth II **Subject:** King James Bible, 500th Anniversary **Obv:** Head with tiara right **Rev:** Lead type and printed page

Date	Mintage	F	VF	XF	Unc	BU
2011 Proof	—	Value: 55.00				

Note: Also exists as a Piefort, P88

KM# 994a.1 2 POUNDS
12.0000 g., 0.9250 Silver partially gilt 0.3569 oz. ASW, 28.35 mm. **Ruler:** Elizabeth II **Obv:** Head with tiara right **Rev:** Symbolic depictions of technological development

Date	Mintage	F	VF	XF	Unc	BU
2012 Proof	—	Value: 50.00				

KM# 1244 2 POUNDS
12.0000 g., Bi-Metallic Copper-Nickel center in Nickel-Brass ring, 28.4 mm. **Ruler:** Elizabeth II **Subject:** Olympic flag handoff to Brazil - Rio, 2016 **Obv:** Head with tiara right **Rev:** UK and Brazil flags **Edge Lettering:** I CALL UPON THE YOUTH OF THE WORLD

Date	Mintage	F	VF	XF	Unc	BU
2012	—	—	—	6.00	12.50	15.00
2012 Proof	—	Value: 15.00				

KM# 1244a 2 POUNDS
12.0000 g., 0.9250 Bi-Metallic Silver center in Gold plated silver ring 0.3569 oz., 28.4 mm. **Ruler:** Elizabeth II

Date	Mintage	F	VF	XF	Unc	BU
2012 Proof	12,000	Value: 145				

KM# 1244b 2 POUNDS
15.9700 g., 0.9160 Gold 0.4703 oz. AGW, 28.4 mm. **Ruler:** Elizabeth II

Date	Mintage	F	VF	XF	Unc	BU
2012 Proof	1,200	Value: 2,250				

KM# 1239 2 POUNDS
12.0000 g., Bi-Metallic Copper-nickel center in Nickel-Brass ring, 28.4 mm. **Ruler:** Elizabeth II **Subject:** London Subway, 125th Anniversary **Obv:** Head with tiara right **Rev:** London Subway train in tube **Edge:** Linear representation of the Tube map

Date	Mintage	F	VF	XF	Unc	BU
2013	—	—	—	6.00	12.00	15.00
2013 Proof	—	Value: 15.00				

KM# 1239a 2 POUNDS
12.0000 g., 0.9250 Silver center in Gilt ring 0.3569 oz. ASW, 28.4 mm. **Ruler:** Elizabeth II **Obv:** Head with tiara right **Rev:** London Subway in tube **Edge:** Linear representation of the Tube map

Date	Mintage	F	VF	XF	Unc	BU
2013 Proof	12,000	Value: 75.00				

KM# 1239b 2 POUNDS
15.9700 g., 0.9167 Gold - Yellow gold center in Red Gold ring 0.4707 oz. AGW, 28.4 mm. **Ruler:** Elizabeth II **Obv:** Head with tiara right **Rev:** London Subway train in tube **Edge:** Linear representation of the Tube map

Date	Mintage	F	VF	XF	Unc	BU
2013 Proof	960	Value: 1,600				

KM# 1240 2 POUNDS
12.0000 g., Bi-Metallic Copper-Nickel center in Nickel-Brass ring, 28.4 mm. **Ruler:** Elizabeth II **Subject:** London Subway, 125th Anniversary **Obv:** Head with tiara right **Rev:** Underground logo **Edge Lettering:** MIND THE GAP

Date	Mintage	F	VF	XF	Unc	BU
2013	—	—	—	6.00	12.00	15.00
2013 Proof	—	Value: 15.00				

KM# 1240a 2 POUNDS
12.0000 g., 0.9250 Silver center in Gilt ring 0.3569 oz. ASW, 28.4 mm. **Ruler:** Elizabeth II **Obv:** Head with tiara right **Rev:** Underground logo **Edge Lettering:** MIND THE GAP

Date	Mintage	F	VF	XF	Unc	BU
2013 Proof	12,000	Value: 75.00				

KM# 1240b 2 POUNDS
15.9700 g., 0.9167 Gold - Yellow Gold center in Rose Gold ring 0.4707 oz. AGW, 28.4 mm. **Ruler:** Elizabeth II **Obv:** Head with tiara right **Rev:** London Underground logo **Edge Lettering:** MIND THE GAP

Date	Mintage	F	VF	XF	Unc	BU
2013 Proof	960	Value: 1,600				

KM# 1241 2 POUNDS
12.0000 g., Bi-Metallic Copper-Nickel center in Nickel-Brass ring, 28.4 mm. **Ruler:** Elizabeth II **Subject:** Anniversary of the Spade Guinea coinage of George III **Obv:** Head with tiara right **Rev:** Spade shield crowned **Edge Lettering:** WHAT IS A GUINEA? 'TIS A SPLENDID THING

Date	Mintage	F	VF	XF	Unc	BU
2013	—	—	—	6.00	12.00	15.00
2013 Proof	44,000	Value: 15.00				

KM# 1241a 2 POUNDS
12.0000 g., 0.9250 Silver center in Gilt ring 0.3569 oz. ASW, 28.4 mm. **Ruler:** Elizabeth II **Obv:** Head with tiara right **Rev:** Spade shield crowned **Edge Lettering:** WHAT IS A GUINEA? 'TIS A SPLENDID THING

Date	Mintage	F	VF	XF	Unc	BU
2013 Proof	2,013	Value: 55.00				

KM# 1015 5 POUNDS
28.2800 g., Copper-Nickel, 38.6 mm. **Ruler:** Elizabeth II **Subject:** Centennial of Queen Victoria's death **Obv:** Head with tiara right **Rev:** Young portrait from stamp, within industrial "V" **Edge:** Reeded

Date	Mintage	F	VF	XF	Unc	BU
2001	851,491	—	—	—	15.00	18.00
2001 Proof	—	Value: 20.00				

KM# 1015a 5 POUNDS
28.2800 g., 0.9250 Silver 0.8410 oz. ASW, 38.6 mm. **Ruler:** Elizabeth II **Subject:** Centennial of Queen Victoria **Obv:** Head with tiara right **Rev:** Queen Victoria's portrait within "V"

Date	Mintage	F	VF	XF	Unc	BU
2001 Proof	—	Value: 50.00				

KM# 1015b 5 POUNDS
39.9400 g., 0.9167 Gold 1.1771 oz. AGW **Ruler:** Elizabeth II **Subject:** Centennial of Queen Victoria **Obv:** Head with tiara right **Rev:** Queen Victoria's portrait within "V"

Date	Mintage	F	VF	XF	Unc	BU
2001 Proof	1,000	Value: 2,100				

KM# 1024 5 POUNDS
28.2800 g., Copper-Nickel, 38.6 mm. **Ruler:** Elizabeth II **Subject:** Queen's Golden Jubilee of Reign **Obv:** Crowned bust in royal garb right **Rev:** Queen on horse **Edge:** Reeded

Date	Mintage	F	VF	XF	Unc	BU
2002	3,469,243	—	—	—	15.00	18.00

Note: Mintage figure includes KM#1035

Date	Mintage	F	VF	XF	Unc	BU
2002 Proof	—	Value: 20.00				

KM# 1024a 5 POUNDS
28.2800 g., 0.9250 Silver 0.8410 oz. ASW, 38.6 mm. **Ruler:** Elizabeth II **Subject:** Queen's Golden Jubilee of Reign **Obv:** Crowned bust in royal garb right **Rev:** Queen on horse **Edge:** Reeded

Date	Mintage	F	VF	XF	Unc	BU
2002 Proof	—	Value: 50.00				

KM# 1024b 5 POUNDS
39.9400 g., 0.9167 Gold 1.1771 oz. AGW, 38.6 mm. **Ruler:** Elizabeth II **Subject:** Queen's Golden Jubilee of Reign **Obv:** Crowned bust in royal garb right **Rev:** Queen on horse left **Edge:** Reeded

Date	Mintage	F	VF	XF	Unc	BU
2002 Proof	—	Value: 2,100				

KM# 1035 5 POUNDS
28.2800 g., Copper-Nickel, 38.6 mm. **Ruler:** Elizabeth II **Subject:** Queen Mother **Obv:** Head with tiara right **Rev:** Queen Mother's portrait in wreath **Edge:** Reeded

Date	Mintage	F	VF	XF	Unc	BU
ND(2002)	—	—	—	—	15.00	18.00

Note: Mintage included with KM#1024.

Date	Mintage	F	VF	XF	Unc	BU
ND(2002) Proof	—	Value: 20.00				

KM# 1035a 5 POUNDS
28.2800 g., Silver, 38.6 mm. **Ruler:** Elizabeth II **Subject:** Queen Mother **Obv:** Head with tiara right **Rev:** Queen Mother's portrait in wreath **Edge:** Reeded

Date	Mintage	F	VF	XF	Unc	BU
ND(2002) Proof	25,000	Value: 50.00				

KM# 1035b 5 POUNDS
39.9400 g., 0.9167 Gold 1.1771 oz. AGW, 38.6 mm. **Ruler:** Elizabeth II **Subject:** Queen Mother **Obv:** Head with tiara right **Rev:** Queen Mother's portrait in wreath **Edge:** Reeded

Date	Mintage	F	VF	XF	Unc	BU
ND(2002) Proof	3,000	Value: 2,100				

KM# 1038 5 POUNDS
28.2800 g., Copper-Nickel, 38.6 mm. **Ruler:** Elizabeth II **Subject:** Queen's Golden Jubilee **Obv:** Queen's stylized portrait **Rev:** Childlike lettering **Edge:** Reeded **Designer:** Tom Phillips

Date	Mintage	F	VF	XF	Unc	BU
2003	1,307,147	—	—	—	15.00	18.00
2003 Proof	43,513	Value: 20.00				

KM# 1038a 5 POUNDS
28.2800 g., 0.9250 Silver 0.8410 oz. ASW, 38.6 mm. **Ruler:** Elizabeth II **Subject:** Queen's Golden Jubilee **Obv:** Stylized Queens portrait **Rev:** Childlike lettering **Edge:** Reeded **Designer:** Tom Phillips

Date	Mintage	F	VF	XF	Unc	BU
2003 Proof	28,758	Value: 50.00				

KM# 1038b 5 POUNDS
39.9400 g., 0.9166 Gold 1.1770 oz. AGW, 38.6 mm. **Ruler:** Elizabeth II **Subject:** Queen's Golden Jubilee **Obv:** Stylized Queens portrait **Rev:** Childlike lettering **Edge:** Reeded **Designer:** Tom Phillips

Date	Mintage	F	VF	XF	Unc	BU
2003 Proof	1,896	Value: 2,100				

KM# 1055 5 POUNDS
28.2800 g., Copper-Nickel, 38.6 mm. **Ruler:** Elizabeth II **Subject:** Entente Cordiale **Obv:** Head with tiara right **Rev:** Britannia and Marianne **Edge:** Reeded

Date	Mintage	F	VF	XF	Unc	BU
2004	1,205,594	—	—	—	15.00	18.00
2004 Proof	51,527	Value: 20.00				

KM# 1055a 5 POUNDS
28.2800 g., 0.9250 Silver 0.8410 oz. ASW, 38.6 mm. **Ruler:** Elizabeth II **Subject:** Entente Cordiale **Obv:** Head with tiara right **Rev:** Britannia and Marianne **Edge:** Reeded

Date	Mintage	F	VF	XF	Unc	BU
2004 Proof	11,295	Value: 50.00				

Note: Also exists as a Piefort, P47

KM# 1055b 5 POUNDS
39.9400 g., 0.9167 Gold 1.1771 oz. AGW, 38.6 mm. **Ruler:** Elizabeth II **Subject:** Entente Cordiale **Obv:** Head with tiara right **Rev:** Britannia and Marianne **Edge:** Reeded

Date	Mintage	F	VF	XF	Unc	BU
2004 Proof	926	Value: 2,100				

KM# 1055c 5 POUNDS
94.2000 g., 0.9995 Platinum 3.0270 oz. APW, 38.6 mm. **Ruler:** Elizabeth II **Subject:** Entente Cordiale **Obv:** Head with tiara right **Rev:** Britannia and Marianne **Edge:** Reeded

Date	Mintage	F	VF	XF	Unc	BU
2004 Proof	501	Value: 5,700				

KM# 1053 5 POUNDS
28.2800 g., Copper-Nickel, 38.6 mm. **Ruler:** Elizabeth II **Subject:** Battle of Trafalgar **Obv:** Head with tiara right **Obv. Legend:** ELIZABETH • II D • G • REG • F • D **Rev:** HMS Victory and HMS Temeraire at Trafalgar **Rev. Legend:** TRAFALGAR **Edge:** Reeded

Date	Mintage	F	VF	XF	Unc	BU
2005	1,075,516	—	—	—	15.00	18.00
2005 Proof	40,563	Value: 20.00				

KM# 1053a 5 POUNDS
28.2800 g., 0.9250 Silver 0.8410 oz. ASW, 38.6 mm. **Ruler:** Elizabeth II **Subject:** Battle of Trafalgar **Obv:** Head with tiara right **Obv. Legend:** ELIZABETH • II D • G • REG • F • D **Rev:** Ships HMS Victory and Temeraire at Trafalgar **Rev. Legend:** TRAFALGAR **Edge:** Reeded

Date	Mintage	F	VF	XF	Unc	BU
2005 Proof	21,448	Value: 50.00				

Note: Also exists as a Piefort, P51

KM# 1053b 5 POUNDS
39.9400 g., 0.9167 Gold 1.1771 oz. AGW, 38.6 mm. **Ruler:** Elizabeth II **Subject:** Battle of Trafalgar **Obv:** Head with tiara right **Obv. Legend:** ELIZABETH • II D • G • REG • F • D **Rev:** Ships HMS Victory and Temeraire at Trafalgar **Rev. Legend:** TRAFALGAR **Edge:** Reeded

Date	Mintage	F	VF	XF	Unc	BU
2005 Proof	1,805	Value: 2,100				

KM# 1054 5 POUNDS
28.2800 g., Copper-Nickel, 38.6 mm. **Ruler:** Elizabeth II **Obv:** Head with tiara right **Obv. Legend:** ELIZABETH • II D • G • REG • F • D **Rev:** Uniformed facing 1/2 bust of Admiral Horatio Nelson **Rev. Legend:** HORATIO NELSON **Edge:** Reeded

Date	Mintage	F	VF	XF	Unc	BU
2005	—	—	—	—	15.00	18.00

Note: Mintage included with KM#1053b, 2005.

Date	Mintage	F	VF	XF	Unc	BU
2005 Proof	40,563	Value: 20.00				

KM# 1054a 5 POUNDS
28.2800 g., 0.9250 Silver 0.8410 oz. ASW, 38.6 mm. **Ruler:** Elizabeth II **Obv:** Queen's head with tiara right **Obv. Legend:** ELIZABETH • II D • G • REG • F • D **Rev:** Uniformed facing 1/2 bust of Admiral Horatio Nelson **Rev. Legend:** HORATIO NELSON

Date	Mintage	F	VF	XF	Unc	BU
2005 Proof	12,852	Value: 50.00				

Note: Also exists as a Piefort, P52

KM# 1054b 5 POUNDS
39.9400 g., 0.9167 Gold 1.1771 oz. AGW, 38.6 mm. **Ruler:** Elizabeth II **Subject:** Battle of Trafalgar **Obv:** Queen's head with tiara right **Obv. Legend:** ELIZABETH • II D • G • REG • F • D **Rev:** Uniformed facing 1/2 bust of Admiral Horatio Nelson **Rev. Legend:** HORATIO NELSON

Date	Mintage	F	VF	XF	Unc	BU
2005 Proof	1,700	Value: 2,100				

KM# 1062 5 POUNDS
28.2800 g., Copper-Nickel, 38.6 mm. **Ruler:** Elizabeth II **Obv:** Head with tiara right **Rev:** Three bannered trumpets **Edge:** Reeded

Date	Mintage	F	VF	XF	Unc	BU
2006	—	—	—	—	20.00	25.00
2006 Proof	Est. 50,000	Value: 30.00				

KM# 1062a 5 POUNDS
28.2800 g., 0.9250 Silver 0.8410 oz. ASW **Ruler:** Elizabeth II **Subject:** Queen's 80th Birthday Celebration **Obv:** Queens head right **Obv. Legend:** ELIZABETH • II D • G • REG • F • D **Rev:** Three bannered trumpets **Rev. Legend:** VIVAT REGINA **Edge:** Reeded

Date	Mintage	F	VF	XF	Unc	BU
2006 Proof	—	Value: 50.00				

Note: Also exists as a Piefort, P58

KM# 1062b 5 POUNDS
39.9400 g., 0.9167 Gold 1.1771 oz. AGW, 38.6 mm. **Ruler:** Elizabeth II **Subject:** Queen's 80th Birthday Celebration **Obv:** Queen's head with tiara right **Obv. Legend:** ELIZABETH • II D • G • REG • F • D **Rev:** Three bannered trumpets **Rev. Legend:** VIVAT REGINA **Edge:** Reeded

Date	Mintage	F	VF	XF	Unc	BU
2006 Proof	—	Value: 2,100				

KM# 1077 5 POUNDS
28.2800 g., Copper-Nickel, 38.6 mm. **Ruler:** Elizabeth II **Subject:** Queen's 60th Wedding Anniversary **Obv:** Conjoined busts of Queen Elizabeth II and Prince Philip **Rev:** Westminster Abbey's North Rose Window **Edge:** Reeded

Date	Mintage	F	VF	XF	Unc	BU
2007	—	—	—	—	20.00	25.00
2007 Proof	Est. 50,000	Value: 30.00				

KM# 1077a 5 POUNDS
28.2800 g., 0.9250 Silver 0.8410 oz. ASW, 38.6 mm. **Ruler:** Elizabeth II **Subject:** 60th Wedding Anniversary **Obv:** Conjoined busts of Queen Elizabeth II and Prince Philip **Rev:** Westminster Abbey's North Rose Window **Edge Lettering:** MY STRENGTH AND STAY

Date	Mintage	F	VF	XF	Unc	BU
ND (2007) Proof	Est. 35,000	Value: 50.00				

Note: Also exists as a Piefort, P63

KM# 1077b 5 POUNDS
39.9400 g., 0.9167 Gold 1.1771 oz. AGW, 28.4 mm. **Ruler:** Elizabeth II **Subject:** 60th Wedding Anniversary **Obv:** Conjoined busts of Queen Elizabeth II and Prince Philip **Rev:** Westminster Abbey's North Rose Window **Edge Lettering:** MY STRENGTH AND STAY

Date	Mintage	F	VF	XF	Unc	BU
ND (2007) Proof	Est. 2,500	Value: 2,100				

Note: Also exists as a Piefort, P64

KM# 1103 5 POUNDS
28.2800 g., Copper-Nickel, 38.6 mm. **Ruler:** Elizabeth II **Subject:** Charles, Prince of Wales 60th Birthday **Obv:** Head with tiara right **Rev:** Head right of Prince Charles

Date	Mintage	F	VF	XF	Unc	BU
2008	500,000	—	—	—	18.00	15.00
2008 Proof	—	Value: 20.00				

KM# 1104 5 POUNDS

28.2800 g., Copper-Nickel, 38.6 mm. **Ruler:** Elizabeth II **Subject:** Elizabeth I Accession 1558-2008 **Obv:** Head with tiara right **Rev:** Bust of Elizabeth I

Date	Mintage	F	VF	XF	Unc	BU
2008	500,000	—	—	—	15.00	18.00
2008 Proof	—	Value: 20.00				

KM# 1103a 5 POUNDS

28.2800 g., 0.9250 Silver 0.8410 oz. ASW, 38.6 mm. **Ruler:** Elizabeth II **Subject:** Charles, Prince of Wales 60th Birthday **Obv:** Head with tiara right **Rev:** Head right of Prince Charles

Date	Mintage	F	VF	XF	Unc	BU
2008 Proof	10,398	Value: 50.00				

Note: Exists as a Piedfort, P113.

KM# 1104a 5 POUNDS

28.2800 g., 0.9250 Silver 0.8410 oz. ASW, 38.6 mm. **Ruler:** Elizabeth II **Subject:** Elizabeth I Accession 1558-2008 **Obv:** Head with tiara right **Rev:** Bust of Elizabeth I

Date	Mintage	F	VF	XF	Unc	BU
2008 Proof	7,446	Value: 2,100				

Note: Exists as a Piedfort, P67

KM# 1118 5 POUNDS

28.2800 g., Copper-Nickel, 38.6 mm. **Ruler:** Elizabeth II **Obv:** Head with tiara right **Rev:** Henry VIII standing, HR flanking

Date	Mintage	F	VF	XF	Unc	BU
2009 Proof	—	Value: 40.00				

KM# 1118a 5 POUNDS

28.2800 g., 0.9250 Silver 0.8410 oz. ASW, 38.6 mm. **Ruler:** Elizabeth II **Obv:** Head with tiara right **Rev:** Henry VIII standing, HR flanking

Date	Mintage	F	VF	XF	Unc	BU
2009 Proof	20,000	Value: 50.00				

Note: Also exists as a Piedfort, P70

KM# 1121 5 POUNDS

28.2800 g., Copper-Nickel, 38.61 mm. **Ruler:** Elizabeth II **Subject:** Countdown to 2012 London Olympics **Obv:** Bust right **Rev:** Swimmer, stopwatch, 3 in center

Date	Mintage	F	VF	XF	Unc	BU
2009	500,000	—	—	—	20.00	25.00
2009 Proof	—	Value: 30.00				

KM# 1121a 5 POUNDS

28.2800 g., 0.9250 Silver 0.8410 oz. ASW, 38.61 mm. **Ruler:** Elizabeth II **Subject:** Countdown to the 2010 London Olympics **Obv:** Bust right **Rev:** Swimmer, stopwatch, 3 in center

Date	Mintage	F	VF	XF	Unc	BU
2009 Proof	30,000	Value: 50.00				

KM# 1121b 5 POUNDS

39.9400 g., 0.9167 Gold 1.1771 oz. AGW, 38.61 mm. **Ruler:** Elizabeth II **Subject:** Countdown to 2012 London Olympics **Rev:** 3 in large stopwatch, swimmer

Date	Mintage	F	VF	XF	Unc	BU
2009 Proof	—	Value: 2,100				

KM# 1140 5 POUNDS

28.2800 g., 0.9250 Silver 0.8410 oz. ASW, 38.6 mm. **Ruler:** Elizabeth II **Subject:** London Olympics, 2012 **Obv:** Head with tiara right **Rev:** Angel of the North, blue logo

Date	Mintage	F	VF	XF	Unc	BU
2009 Proof	95,000	Value: 50.00				

KM# 1141 5 POUNDS

28.2800 g., 0.9250 Silver 0.8410 oz. ASW, 38.6 mm. **Ruler:** Elizabeth II **Subject:** London Olympics, 2012 **Obv:** Head with tiara right **Rev:** Big Ben, blue logo

Date	Mintage	F	VF	XF	Unc	BU
2009 Proof	95,000	Value: 50.00				

KM# 1141a 5 POUNDS

28.2800 g., Copper-Nickel, 38.6 mm. **Ruler:** Elizabeth II **Subject:** London Olympics, 2012 **Obv:** Head in tiara right **Rev:** Big Ben, blue logo

Date	Mintage	F	VF	XF	Unc	BU
2009 Proof	—	Value: 30.00				

KM# 1142 5 POUNDS

28.2800 g., 0.9250 Silver 0.8410 oz. ASW, 38.6 mm. **Ruler:** Elizabeth II **Subject:** London Olympics, 2012 **Obv:** Head with tiara right **Rev:** Flying Scotsman, blue logo

Date	Mintage	F	VF	XF	Unc	BU
2009 Proof	95,000	Value: 50.00				

KM# 1143 5 POUNDS

28.2800 g., 0.9250 Silver 0.8410 oz. ASW, 38.6 mm. **Ruler:** Elizabeth II **Subject:** London Olympics, 2012 **Obv:** Head with tiara right **Rev:** Globe Theatre, blue logo

Date	Mintage	F	VF	XF	Unc	BU
2009 Proof	95,000	Value: 50.00				

KM# 1144 5 POUNDS

28.2800 g., 0.9250 Silver 0.8410 oz. ASW, 38.6 mm. **Ruler:** Elizabeth II **Subject:** London Olympics, 2012 **Obv:** Head with tiara right **Rev:** Man in leg braces, Issac Newton quote, blue logo

Date	Mintage	F	VF	XF	Unc	BU
2009 Proof	95,000	Value: 50.00				

KM# 1145 5 POUNDS

28.2800 g., 0.9250 Silver 0.8410 oz. ASW, 38.6 mm. **Ruler:** Elizabeth II **Series:** London Olympics, 2012 **Obv:** Head with tiara right **Rev:** Stonehenge, blue logo

Date	Mintage	F	VF	XF	Unc	BU
2009 Proof	95,000	Value: 50.00				

KM# 1139 5 POUNDS

28.2800 g., Copper-Nickel, 38.6 mm. **Ruler:** Elizabeth II **Obv:** Head with tiara right **Rev:** Runners and stopwatch, 2 in center

Date	Mintage	F	VF	XF	Unc	BU
2010	500,000	—	—	—	20.00	25.00
2010 Proof	—	Value: 30.00				

KM# 1139a 5 POUNDS

28.2800 g., 0.9250 Silver 0.8410 oz. ASW, 38.6 mm. **Ruler:** Elizabeth II **Obv:** Head with tiara right **Rev:** Runners and stopwatch, 2 in center

Date	Mintage	F	VF	XF	Unc	BU
2010 Proof	—	Value: 50.00				

KM# 1139b 5 POUNDS

39.9400 g., 0.9167 Gold 1.1771 oz. AGW, 38.61 mm. **Ruler:** Elizabeth II **Subject:** Countdown to the 2012 London Olympics **Obv:** Head with tiara right **Rev:** Runners and stopwatch, 2 in center

Date	Mintage	F	VF	XF	Unc	BU
2010 Proof	—	Value: 2,100				

KM# 1146 5 POUNDS

28.2800 g., 0.9250 Silver 0.8410 oz. ASW, 38.6 mm. **Ruler:** Elizabeth II **Subject:** London Olympics, 2012 **Obv:** Head with tiara right **Rev:** Churchill figure and quote, blue logo

Date	Mintage	F	VF	XF	Unc	BU
2010 Proof	95,000	Value: 50.00				

KM# 1146a 5 POUNDS

28.2800 g., Copper-Nickel, 38.6 mm. **Ruler:** Elizabeth II **Subject:** London Olympics, 2012 **Obv:** Head with tiara right **Rev:** Churchill figure and quote, blue logo

Date	Mintage	F	VF	XF	Unc	BU
2010 Proof	—	Value: 40.00				

KM# 1147 5 POUNDS

28.2800 g., 0.9250 Silver 0.8410 oz. ASW, 38.6 mm. **Ruler:** Elizabeth II **Subject:** London Olympics, 2012 **Obv:** Head with tiara right **Rev:** Unity, flora, blue logo

Date	Mintage	F	VF	XF	Unc	BU
2010 Proof	95,000	Value: 50.00				

KM# 1148 5 POUNDS

28.2800 g., 0.9990 Silver 0.9083 oz. ASW, 38.6 mm. **Ruler:** Elizabeth II **Subject:** London Olympics, 2012 **Obv:** Head with tiara right **Rev:** Buckingham Palace and the Mall, blue logo

Date	Mintage	F	VF	XF	Unc	BU
2010 Proof	95,000	Value: 50.00				

KM# 1148a 5 POUNDS

28.2800 g., Copper-Nickel, 38.6 mm. **Ruler:** Elizabeth II **Subject:** London Olympics, 2012 **Obv:** Head with tiara right **Rev:** Buckingham Palace and the Mall, blue logo

Date	Mintage	F	VF	XF	Unc	BU
2010 Proof	—	Value: 40.00				

KM# 1149 5 POUNDS

28.2800 g., 0.9250 Silver 0.8410 oz. ASW, 38.6 mm. **Ruler:** Elizabeth II **Subject:** London Olympics, 2010 **Obv:** Head with tiara right **Rev:** Musical instruments, blue logo

Date	Mintage	F	VF	XF	Unc	BU
2010 Proof	95,000	Value: 50.00				

KM# 1151 5 POUNDS

28.2800 g., Copper-Nickel, 38.6 mm. **Ruler:** Elizabeth II **Subject:** Restoration of the Monarchy, 1660 **Obv:** Head with tiara right

Date	Mintage	F	VF	XF	Unc	BU
2010	—	—	—	—	20.00	25.00

KM# 1151a 5 POUNDS

28.2800 g., 0.9250 Silver 0.8410 oz. ASW, 38.6 mm. **Ruler:** Elizabeth II **Subject:** Restoration of the Monarchy, 1660 **Obv:** Head with tiara right

Date	Mintage	F	VF	XF	Unc	BU
2010 Proof	—	Value: 50.00				

Note: Also exists as a Piedfort, P114

KM# 1151b 5 POUNDS

39.9400 g., 0.9167 Gold 1.1771 oz. AGW, 38.61 mm. **Ruler:** Elizabeth II **Subject:** Restoration of the Monarchy, 1660 **Obv:** Head with tiara right **Rev:** Crown above wreath

Date	Mintage	F	VF	XF	Unc	BU
2010 Proof	—	Value: 2,100				

KM# 1152 5 POUNDS

28.2800 g., 0.9250 Silver 0.8410 oz. ASW, 38.6 mm. **Ruler:** Elizabeth II **Subject:** London Olympics, 2012 **Obv:** Head with tiara right **Rev:** Giants Causeway, orange logo

Date	Mintage	F	VF	XF	Unc	BU
2010 Proof	95,000	Value: 50.00				

KM# 1153 5 POUNDS

28.2800 g., 0.9250 Silver 0.8410 oz. ASW, 38.6 mm. **Ruler:** Elizabeth II **Subject:** London Olympics, 2012 **Obv:** Head with tiara right **Rev:** Coastline, orange logo

Date	Mintage	F	VF	XF	Unc	BU
2010 Proof	95,000	Value: 50.00				

KM# 1154 5 POUNDS

28.2800 g., 0.9250 Silver 0.8410 oz. ASW, 38.6 mm. **Ruler:** Elizabeth II **Subject:** London Olympics, 2012 **Obv:** Head with tiara right **Rev:** River Thames, orange logo

Date	Mintage	F	VF	XF	Unc	BU
2010 Proof	95,000	Value: 50.00				

KM# 1155 5 POUNDS

28.2800 g., 0.9250 Silver 0.8410 oz. ASW, 38.6 mm. **Ruler:** Elizabeth II **Subject:** London Olympics, 2012 **Obv:** Head with tiara right **Rev:** British flora -oak leaves and acorn, orange logo

Date	Mintage	F	VF	XF	Unc	BU
2010 Proof	95,000	Value: 50.00				

KM# 1156 5 POUNDS

28.2800 g., 0.9250 Silver 0.8410 oz. ASW, 38.6 mm. **Ruler:** Elizabeth II **Subject:** London Olympics, 2012 **Obv:** Head with tiara right **Rev:** Owl, orange logo

Date	Mintage	F	VF	XF	Unc	BU
2010 Proof	95,000	Value: 50.00				

KM# 1157 5 POUNDS

28.2800 g., 0.9250 Silver 0.8410 oz. ASW, 38.6 mm. **Ruler:** Elizabeth II **Subject:** London Olympics, 2012 **Obv:** Head with tiara right **Rev:** Weather vane, orange logo

Date	Mintage	F	VF	XF	Unc	BU
2010 Proof	95,000	Value: 50.00				

KM# 1201 5 POUNDS

28.2800 g., Copper-Nickel, 38.6 mm. **Ruler:** Elizabeth II **Subject:** Prince Philip's 90th Birthday **Obv:** Head with tiara right **Rev:** Large head of Prince Philip in profile right

Date	Mintage	F	VF	XF	Unc	BU
2011	—	—	—	—	20.00	25.00
2011 Proof	—	Value: 30.00				

KM# 1201a 5 POUNDS

28.2800 g., 0.9250 Silver 0.8410 oz. ASW, 38.6 mm. **Ruler:** Elizabeth II **Subject:** Prince Philip, 90th Birthday

Date	Mintage	F	VF	XF	Unc	BU
2011 Proof	—	Value: 50.00				

Note: Also exists as a Piedfort, P89

KM# 1201b 5 POUNDS

39.9400 g., 0.9167 Gold 1.1771 oz. AGW, 38.61 mm. **Ruler:** Elizabeth II **Subject:** Prince Philip's 90th Birthday **Obv:** Head with tiara right **Rev:** Large head of Prince Philip in profile right

Date	Mintage	F	VF	XF	Unc	BU
2011 Proof	—	Value: 2,100				

KM# 1202 5 POUNDS

28.2800 g., Copper-Nickel, 38.6 mm. **Ruler:** Elizabeth II **Subject:** Countdown to London Olympics, 2012 **Obv:** Head with tiara right **Rev:** 1 between wheels of cyclist traveling left

Date	Mintage	F	VF	XF	Unc	BU
2011	—	—	—	—	20.00	25.00
2011 Proof	—	Value: 30.00				

KM# 1202a 5 POUNDS
28.2800 g., 0.9250 Silver 0.8410 oz. ASW, 38.6 mm. **Ruler:** Elizabeth II **Subject:** Countdown to London Olympics, 2012 **Obv:** Head with tiara right **Rev:** 1 between wheels of cyclist traveling left

Date	Mintage	F	VF	XF	Unc	BU
2011 Proof	—	Value: 50.00				

KM# 1203 5 POUNDS
28.2800 g., Copper-Nickel, 38.6 mm. **Ruler:** Elizabeth II **Subject:** Royal Wedding - William and Katherine **Rev:** Heads facing

Date	Mintage	F	VF	XF	Unc	BU
2011	—	—	—	—	20.00	25.00

KM# 1203a 5 POUNDS
28.2800 g., 0.9250 Silver 0.8410 oz. ASW, 38.6 mm. **Ruler:** Elizabeth II **Subject:** Royal Wedding - William and Catherine

Date	Mintage	F	VF	XF	Unc	BU
2011 Proof	—	Value: 50.00				

KM# 1216 5 POUNDS
28.2800 g., Copper-Nickel, 38.61 mm. **Ruler:** Elizabeth II **Subject:** Elizabeth's 60th anniversary of reign **Obv:** Bust with tiara in robes of the Garter, right **Rev:** Young head portrait right

Date	Mintage	F	VF	XF	Unc	BU
2012 Proof	—	Value: 25.00				

KM# 1242 5 POUNDS
28.2800 g., Copper-Nickel, 38.61 mm. **Ruler:** Elizabeth II **Subject:** Elizabeth's coronation, 60th Anniversary **Obv:** Head with tiara right **Rev:** State Crown

Date	Mintage	F	VF	XF	Unc	BU
2013	—	—	—	—	—	25.00
2013 Proof	44,000	Value: 35.00				

KM# 1242a 5 POUNDS
28.2800 g., 0.9250 Silver 0.8410 oz. ASW, 38.61 mm. **Ruler:** Elizabeth II **Subject:** Elizabeth's coronation, 60th Anniversary **Obv:** Head with tiara right **Rev:** State Crown

Date	Mintage	F	VF	XF	Unc	BU
2013 Proof	60,000	Value: 125				

KM# 1242b 5 POUNDS
28.2800 g., 0.9990 Silver gold plated 0.9083 oz. ASW, 38.61 mm. **Ruler:** Elizabeth II **Subject:** Elizabeth's coronation, 60th Anniversary **Obv:** Head with tiara right **Rev:** State Crown

Date	Mintage	F	VF	XF	Unc	BU
2013 Proof	12,500	Value: 150				

KM# 1242c 5 POUNDS
39.9400 g., 0.9167 Gold 1.1771 oz. AGW, 38.61 mm. **Ruler:** Elizabeth II **Subject:** Elizabeth's coronation, 60th Anniversary **Obv:** Head with tiara right **Rev:** State Crown

Date	Mintage	F	VF	XF	Unc	BU
2013 Proof	2,060	Value: 3,500				

KM# 1242d 5 POUNDS
94.2000 g., 0.9995 Platinum 3.0270 oz. APW, 38.61 mm. **Ruler:** Elizabeth II **Subject:** Elizabeth's coronation, 60th Anniversary **Obv:** Head with tiara right **Rev:** State Crown

Date	Mintage	F	VF	XF	Unc	BU
2013 Proof	150	Value: 9,000				

KM# 1247 5 POUNDS
28.2800 g., 0.9250 Silver 0.8410 oz. ASW, 38.61 mm. **Ruler:** Elizabeth II **Obv:** Young Head Portrait **Rev:** Royal Arms

Date	Mintage	F	VF	XF	Unc	BU
2013 Proof	Est. 5,000	Value: 150				

KM# 1247a 5 POUNDS
39.9490 g., 0.9167 Gold 1.1774 oz. AGW, 38.61 mm. **Ruler:** Elizabeth II **Obv:** Young bust right **Rev:** Royal Arms

Date	Mintage	F	VF	XF	Unc	BU
2013 Proof	Est. 500	Value: 3,000				

KM# 1248a 5 POUNDS
39.9490 g., 0.9167 Gold 1.1774 oz. AGW, 38.61 mm. **Ruler:** Elizabeth II **Obv:** Bust with tiara right **Rev:** Royal Arms

Date	Mintage	F	VF	XF	Unc	BU
2013 Proof	Est. 500	Value: 3,000				

KM# 1249 5 POUNDS
28.2800 g., 0.9250 Silver 0.8410 oz. ASW, 38.61 mm. **Ruler:** Elizabeth II **Obv:** Head with crown right **Rev:** Royal Arms

Date	Mintage	F	VF	XF	Unc	BU
2013 Proof	Est. 5,000	Value: 150				

KM# 1249a 5 POUNDS
39.9490 g., 0.9167 Gold 1.1774 oz. AGW, 38.61 mm. **Ruler:** Elizabeth II **Obv:** Head with crown right **Rev:** Royal Arms

Date	Mintage	F	VF	XF	Unc	BU
2013 Proof	Est. 500	Value: 3,000				

KM# 1250 5 POUNDS
28.2800 g., 0.9250 Silver 0.8410 oz. ASW, 38.61 mm. **Ruler:** Elizabeth II **Obv:** Head with tiara right **Rev:** Royal Arms

Date	Mintage	F	VF	XF	Unc	BU
2013 Proof	Est. 5,000	Value: 150				

KM# 1250a 5 POUNDS
39.9400 g., 0.9167 Gold 1.1771 oz. AGW, 38.61 mm. **Ruler:** Elizabeth II **Obv:** Head with tiara right **Rev:** Royal Arms

Date	Mintage	F	VF	XF	Unc	BU
2013 Proof	Est. 500	Value: 3,000				

KM# 1248 5 POUNDS
28.2800 g., 0.9250 Silver 0.8410 oz. ASW, 38.61 mm. **Ruler:** Elizabeth II **Obv:** Bust right by Arnold Machin **Rev:** Royal Arms

Date	Mintage	F	VF	XF	Unc	BU
2013 Proof	Est. 5,000	Value: 150				

KM# 1227 10 POUNDS
155.5000 g., 0.9990 Silver 4.9942 oz. ASW **Ruler:** Elizabeth II **Obv:** Head with tiara right **Rev:** Pegasus right

Date	Mintage	F	VF	XF	Unc	BU
2012 Proof	—	Value: 225				

KM# 1227a 10 POUNDS
155.5000 g., 0.9990 Gold 4.9942 oz. AGW **Ruler:** Elizabeth II **Obv:** Head with tiara right **Rev:** Pegasus right

Date	Mintage	F	VF	XF	Unc	BU
2012 Proof	—	Value: 9,500				

KM# 1163 25 POUNDS
8.5100 g., 0.9167 Gold 0.2508 oz. AGW, 22 mm. **Ruler:** Elizabeth II **Subject:** London Olympics, 2012 **Obv:** Head with tiara right **Rev:** Mercury and cyclists

Date	Mintage	F	VF	XF	Unc	BU
2010 Proof	20,000	Value: 800				

KM# 1164 25 POUNDS
8.5100 g., 0.9167 Gold 0.2508 oz. AGW, 22 mm. **Ruler:** Elizabeth II **Subject:** London Olympics, 2012 **Obv:** Head with tiara right **Rev:** Diana and cyclists

Date	Mintage	F	VF	XF	Unc	BU
2010 Proof	20,000	Value: 800				

KM# 1218 25 POUNDS
8.5100 g., 0.9167 Gold 0.2508 oz. AGW, 22 mm. **Ruler:** Elizabeth II **Subject:** London Olympics, 2012 **Obv:** Head with tiara right **Rev:** Juno

Date	Mintage	F	VF	XF	Unc	BU
2011 Proof	—	Value: 800				

KM# 1219 25 POUNDS
8.5100 g., 0.9167 Gold 0.2508 oz. AGW, 22 mm. **Ruler:** Elizabeth II **Obv:** Head with tiara right **Rev:** Apollo

Date	Mintage	F	VF	XF	Unc	BU
2011 Proof	—	Value: 800				

KM# 1221 25 POUNDS
8.5100 g., 0.9167 Gold 0.2508 oz. AGW, 22 mm. **Ruler:** Elizabeth II **Obv:** Head with tiara right **Rev:** Minervia

Date	Mintage	F	VF	XF	Unc	BU
2012 Proof	—	Value: 800				

KM# 1222 25 POUNDS
8.5100 g., 0.9167 Gold 0.2508 oz. AGW, 22 mm. **Ruler:** Elizabeth II **Obv:** Head with tiara right **Rev:** Vulcan

Date	Mintage	F	VF	XF	Unc	BU
2012 Proof	—	Value: 800				

KM# 1162 100 POUNDS
32.6900 g., 0.9167 Gold 0.9634 oz. AGW, 32.7 mm. **Ruler:** Elizabeth II **Subject:** London Olympics, 2012 **Obv:** Head with tiara right **Rev:** Neptune and sailing

Date	Mintage	F	VF	XF	Unc	BU
2010 Proof	7,500	Value: 1,850				

KM# 1220 100 POUNDS
32.6900 g., 0.9167 Gold 0.9634 oz. AGW, 32.7 mm. **Ruler:** Elizabeth II **Obv:** Head with tiara right **Rev:** Jupiter

Date	Mintage	F	VF	XF	Unc	BU
2011 Proof	—	Value: 1,850				

KM# 1223 100 POUNDS
32.6900 g., 0.9167 Gold 0.9634 oz. AGW, 32.7 mm. **Ruler:** Elizabeth II **Obv:** Head with tiara right **Rev:** Mars

Date	Mintage	F	VF	XF	Unc	BU
2012 Proof	—	Value: 1,850				

KM# 1235 500 POUNDS
1000.0000 g., 0.9999 Silver 32.146 oz. ASW **Ruler:** Elizabeth II **Subject:** London Olympics, 2012 **Rev:** Ring of Penants around central legend

Date	Mintage	F	VF	XF	Unc	BU
2012 Proof	2,012	Value: 1,500				

KM# 1243 500 POUNDS
1000.0000 g., 0.9999 Silver 32.146 oz. ASW **Ruler:** Elizabeth II **Obv:** Bust with tiara and in robes of the Garter right **Rev:** Royal Arms crowned and supported within wreath

Date	Mintage	F	VF	XF	Unc	BU
2012 Proof	—	Value: 1,300				

KM# 1236 1000 POUNDS
1000.0000 g., 0.9990 Gold 32.117 oz. AGW **Ruler:** Elizabeth II **Rev:** Weight bar bell and wreath

Date	Mintage	F	VF	XF	Unc	BU
2012 Proof	60	Value: 58,000				

SOVEREIGN COINAGE

KM# 1117 1/4 SOVEREIGN
2.0000 g., 0.9170 Gold 0.0590 oz. AGW, 13.5 mm. **Ruler:** Elizabeth II **Obv:** Head with tiara right **Rev:** St. George slaying dragon

Date	Mintage	F	VF	XF	Unc	BU
2009	50,000	—	—	—	—	115
2009 Proof	25,000	Value: 135				
2010	250,000	—	—	—	—	115
2010 Proof	25,000	Value: 135				
2011	—	—	—	—	—	115
2011 Proof	15,000	Value: 135				
2013	—	—	—	—	—	115
2013 Proof	5,645	Value: 135				

KM# 1205 1/4 SOVEREIGN
2.0000 g., 0.9170 Gold 0.0590 oz. AGW, 13.5 mm. **Ruler:** Elizabeth II **Obv:** Head with tiara right **Rev:** St. George spearing dragon head

Date	Mintage	F	VF	XF	Unc	BU
2012 Proof	—	Value: 135				

KM# 1001 1/2 SOVEREIGN
3.9900 g., 0.9170 Gold 0.1176 oz. AGW **Ruler:** Elizabeth II **Obv:** Head with tiara right **Rev:** St. George slaying the dragon

Date	Mintage	F	VF	XF	Unc	BU
2001	94,763	—	—	—	—	BV
2001 Proof	10,000	BV+5%				
2002	61,347	—	—	—	—	BV
2003	47,818	—	—	—	—	BV
2003 Proof	14,750	BV+5%				
2004	34,924	—	—	—	—	BV
2006	30,299	—	—	—	—	BV
2006 Proof	8,500	BV+5%				
2007	75,000	—	—	—	—	BV
2007 Proof	7,500	BV+5%				
2008	75,000	—	—	—	—	BV
2008 Proof	7,500	BV+5%				

KM# 1025 1/2 SOVEREIGN
3.9900 g., 0.9167 Gold 0.1176 oz. AGW, 19.3 mm. **Ruler:** Elizabeth II **Subject:** Queen Elizabeth II's Golden Jubilee **Obv:** Head with tiara right **Rev:** Crowned arms within wreath, date below **Edge:** Reeded

Date	Mintage	F	VF	XF	Unc	BU
2002	61,347	—	—	—	—	BV+10%
2002 Proof	10,000	BV+25%				

KM# 1064 1/2 SOVEREIGN
3.9940 g., 0.9167 Gold 0.1177 oz. AGW, 19.3 mm. **Ruler:** Elizabeth II **Obv:** Head with tiara right **Rev:** Knight fighting dragon with sword **Edge:** Reeded

Date	Mintage	F	VF	XF	Unc	BU
2005	30,299	—	—	—	—	BV
2005 Proof	5,011	BV+15%				

KM# 1001.1 1/2 SOVEREIGN
3.9900 g., 0.9170 Gold 0.1176 oz. AGW **Ruler:** Elizabeth II **Obv:** Head with tiara right **Rev:** St. George slaying the dragon

Date	Mintage	F	VF	XF	Unc	BU
2009	50,000	—	—	—	—	BV+5%
2009 Proof	6,000	BV+15%				
2010	250,000	—	—	—	—	BV+5%
2010 Proof	7,000	BV+15%				
2011	—	—	—	—	—	BV+5%
2011 Proof	—	BV+15%				
2013	—	—	—	—	—	BV+5%
2013 Proof	4,795	BV+15%				

KM# 1206 1/2 SOVEREIGN
3.9900 g., 0.9170 Gold 0.1176 oz. AGW, 19.3 mm. **Ruler:** Elizabeth II **Obv:** Head with tiara right **Rev:** St. George spearing dragon head

Date	Mintage	F	VF	XF	Unc	BU
2012 Proof	—	BV+15%				

KM# 1002 SOVEREIGN
7.9881 g., 0.9170 Gold 0.2355 oz. AGW **Ruler:** Elizabeth II **Obv:** Head with tiara right **Rev:** St. George slaying the dragon

Date	Mintage	F	VF	XF	Unc	BU
2001	49,462	—	—	—	—	BV
2001 Proof	15,000	Value: 425				
2002	75,264	—	—	—	—	BV
2003	43,230	—	—	—	—	BV
2003 Proof	19,750	Value: 425				
2004	30,688	—	—	—	—	BV
2006	45,542	—	—	—	—	BV
2006 Proof	16,000	Value: 425				
2007	75,000	—	—	—	—	BV
2007 Proof	12,500	Value: 425				
2008	75,000	—	—	—	—	BV
2008 Proof	12,500	Value: 425				

KM# 1026 SOVEREIGN
7.9800 g., 0.9167 Gold 0.2352 oz. AGW, 22 mm. **Ruler:** Elizabeth II **Subject:** Queen Elizabeth II's Golden Jubilee **Obv:** Head with tiara right **Rev:** Crowned arms within wreath, date below **Edge:** Reeded

Date	Mintage	F	VF	XF	Unc	BU
2002	75,264	—	—	—	—	BV
2002 Proof	20,500	Value: 425				

KM# 1065 SOVEREIGN
7.9880 g., 0.9176 Gold 0.2356 oz. AGW, 22.05 mm. **Ruler:** Elizabeth II **Obv:** Head with tiara right **Rev:** Knight fighting dragon with sword **Edge:** Reeded

Date	Mintage	F	VF	XF	Unc	BU
2005	45,542	—	—	—	—	BV
2005 Proof	17,500	Value: 425				

KM# 1002.1 SOVEREIGN
7.9810 g., 0.9170 Gold 0.2353 oz. AGW **Ruler:** Elizabeth II **Obv:** Head with tiara right **Rev:** St. George slaying the dragon

Date	Mintage	F	VF	XF	Unc	BU
2009	75,000	—	—	—	—	BV+5%
2009 Proof	12,500	Value: 425				
2010	250,000	—	—	—	—	BV+5%
2010 Proof	12,500	Value: 425				
2011	—	—	—	—	—	BV+5%
2011 Proof	12,500	Value: 425				
2013	—	—	—	—	—	BV+5%
2013 Proof	10,295	Value: 425				

KM# 1207 SOVEREIGN
7.9881 g., 0.9170 Gold 0.2355 oz. AGW, 22 mm. **Ruler:** Elizabeth II **Obv:** Head with tiara right **Rev:** St. George spearing dragon head

Date	Mintage	F	VF	XF	Unc	BU
2012 Proof	—	Value: 425				

KM# 1027 2 POUNDS
15.9700 g., 0.9167 Gold 0.4707 oz. AGW, 28.4 mm. **Ruler:** Elizabeth II **Subject:** Queen Elizabeth II's Golden Jubilee **Obv:** Head with tiara right **Rev:** Crowned arms within wreath, date below **Edge:** Reeded

Date	Mintage	F	VF	XF	Unc	BU
2002 Proof	8,000	Value: 850				

KM# 1066 2 POUNDS
15.9760 g., 0.9167 Gold 0.4708 oz. AGW, 28.4 mm. **Ruler:** Elizabeth II **Obv:** Head with tiara right **Rev:** Knight fighting dragon with sword **Edge:** Reeded

Date	Mintage	F	VF	XF	Unc	BU
2005 Proof	5,000	Value: 850				

KM# 1072 2 POUNDS
15.9700 g., 0.9167 Gold 0.4707 oz. AGW, 28.4 mm. **Ruler:** Elizabeth II **Obv:** Head with tiara right **Rev:** St. George slaying the Dragon **Edge:** Reeded

Date	Mintage	F	VF	XF	Unc	BU
2006 Proof	3,500	Value: 850				
2007 Proof	2,500	Value: 875				
2008 Proof	2,500	Value: 875				

KM# 1072.1 2 POUNDS
15.9700 g., 0.9170 Gold 0.4708 oz. AGW **Ruler:** Elizabeth II **Obv:** Head with tiara right **Rev:** St. George slaying the dragon

Date	Mintage	F	VF	XF	Unc	BU
2009 Proof	2,500	Value: 875				
2010 Proof	2,750	Value: 875				
2011 Proof	2,950	Value: 875				
2013 Proof	1,895	Value: 875				

KM# 1208 2 POUNDS
15.9700 g., 0.9167 Gold 0.4707 oz. AGW, 28.4 mm. **Ruler:** Elizabeth II **Obv:** Head with tiara right **Rev:** St. George spearing dragon's head

Date	Mintage	F	VF	XF	Unc	BU
2012 Proof	—	Value: 875				

KM# 1003 5 POUNDS
39.9400 g., 0.9170 Gold 1.1775 oz. AGW, 36 mm. **Ruler:** Elizabeth II **Obv:** Head with tiara right **Rev:** St. George slaying dragon **Edge:** Reeded

Date	Mintage	F	VF	XF	Unc	BU
2001 (u)	1,000	—	—	—	—	2,100
2001 Proof	1,000	Value: 2,250				
2003	812	—	—	—	—	2,100
2003 Proof	2,250	Value: 2,150				
2004	1,000	—	—	—	—	2,100
2004 Proof	1,750	—	—	—	—	—
2006	1,000	—	—	—	—	2,100
2006 Proof	1,750	Value: 2,150				
2007	768	—	—	—	—	2,100
2007 Proof	1,750	Value: 2,150				
2008	750	—	—	—	—	2,100
2008 Proof	1,750	Value: 2,150				

KM# 1028 5 POUNDS
39.9400 g., 0.9167 Gold 1.1771 oz. AGW, 36 mm. **Ruler:** Elizabeth II **Subject:** Queen Elizabeth II's Golden Jubilee **Obv:** Head with tiara right **Rev:** Crowned arms within wreath **Edge:** Reeded

Date	Mintage	F	VF	XF	Unc	BU
2002	1,370	—	—	—	—	2,100
2002 Proof	3,000	Value: 2,150				

KM# 1067 5 POUNDS
39.9400 g., 0.9167 Gold 1.1771 oz. AGW, 36 mm. **Ruler:** Elizabeth II **Obv:** Head with tiara right **Rev:** Knight fighting dragon with sword **Edge:** Reeded

Date	Mintage	F	VF	XF	Unc	BU
2005	936	—	—	—	—	2,100
2005 Proof	2,500	Value: 2,150				

KM# 1003.1 5 POUNDS
39.9400 g., 0.9170 Gold 1.1775 oz. AGW **Ruler:** Elizabeth II **Obv:** Head with tiara right **Rev:** St. George slaying the dragon

Date	Mintage	F	VF	XF	Unc	BU
2009	1,000	—	—	—	—	2,100
2009 Proof	1,750	Value: 2,150				
2010	1,000	—	—	—	—	2,100
2010 Proof	2,000	Value: 2,150				
2011 Proof	—	Value: 2,150				
2013 Proof	1,000	Value: 2,150				

KM# 1209 5 POUNDS
39.9400 g., 0.9167 Gold 1.1771 oz. AGW, 36 mm. **Ruler:** Elizabeth II **Obv:** Head with tiara right **Rev:** St. George spearing dragon's head

Date	Mintage	F	VF	XF	Unc	BU
2012 Proof	—	Value: 2,250				

BULLION COINAGE

Until 1990, .917 Gold was commonly alloyed with copper by the British Royal Mint. Starting in 2013 the bullion coins have been struck at .999 fine.

All proof issues have designers name as P. Nathan. The uncirculated issues use only Nathan.

KM# 1016 20 PENCE
3.2400 g., 0.9584 Silver 0.0998 oz. ASW, 16.5 mm. **Ruler:** Elizabeth II **Subject:** Britannia Bullion **Obv:** Head with tiara right **Rev:** Una and Lion **Edge:** Reeded

Date	Mintage	F	VF	XF	Unc	BU
2001 Proof	15,000	Value: 25.00				

KM# 1079 20 PENCE
3.2400 g., 0.9584 Silver 0.0998 oz. ASW, 16.5 mm. **Ruler:** Elizabeth II **Obv:** Head with tiara right **Rev:** Britannia standing **Edge:** Reeded

Date	Mintage	F	VF	XF	Unc	BU
2002 Proof	—	Value: 25.00				
2004 Proof	—	Value: 25.00				
2006 Proof	—	Value: 25.00				
2012 Proof	—	Value: 25.00				

KM# 1044 20 PENCE
3.2400 g., 0.9584 Silver 0.0998 oz. ASW, 16.5 mm. **Ruler:** Elizabeth II **Obv:** Head with tiara right **Rev:** Britannia portrait behind wavy lines **Edge:** Reeded

Date	Mintage	F	VF	XF	Unc	BU
2003 Proof	5,848	Value: 35.00				

KM# 1085 20 PENCE
3.2400 g., 0.9584 Silver 0.0998 oz. ASW, 16.5 mm. **Ruler:** Elizabeth II **Obv:** Head with tiara right **Rev:** Britannia seated with shield left **Edge:** Reeded

Date	Mintage	F	VF	XF	Unc	BU
2005 Proof	3,273	Value: 25.00				

KM# 1088 20 PENCE
3.2400 g., 0.9584 Silver 0.0998 oz. ASW, 16.5 mm. **Ruler:** Elizabeth II **Obv:** Head with tiara right **Rev:** Britannia seated with reclining lion right **Edge:** Reeded

Date	Mintage	F	VF	XF	Unc	BU
2007 Proof	3,401	Value: 25.00				

KM# 1095 20 PENCE
3.2400 g., 0.9584 Silver 0.0998 oz. ASW, 16.5 mm. **Ruler:** Elizabeth II **Obv:** Head with tiara right **Rev:** Britannia standing facing left with trident, flowing garment, shield **Edge:** Reeded

Date	Mintage	F	VF	XF	Unc	BU
2008 Proof	5,000	Value: 35.00				

KM# 1123 20 PENCE
3.2400 g., 0.9580 Silver 0.0998 oz. ASW, 16.5 mm. **Ruler:** Elizabeth II **Obv:** Head right **Rev:** Britania in chariot right

Date	Mintage	F	VF	XF	Unc	BU
2009 Proof	6,000	Value: 35.00				

KM# 1131 20 PENCE
3.2400 g., 0.9580 Silver 0.0998 oz. ASW, 16.5 mm. **Ruler:** Elizabeth II **Obv:** Head right **Rev:** Britannia bust right

Date	Mintage	F	VF	XF	Unc	BU
2010 Proof	8,000	Value: 35.00				

KM# 1017 50 PENCE
8.1100 g., 0.9584 Silver 0.2499 oz. ASW, 27.3 mm. **Ruler:** Elizabeth II **Subject:** Britannia Bullion **Obv:** Head with tiara right **Rev:** Una and Lion **Edge:** Reeded

Date	Mintage	F	VF	XF	Unc	BU
2001 Proof	5,000	Value: 35.00				

KM# 1080 50 PENCE
8.1100 g., 0.9584 Silver 0.2499 oz. ASW, 22 mm. **Ruler:** Elizabeth II **Obv:** Head with tiara right **Rev:** Britannia standing **Edge:** Reeded

Date	Mintage	F	VF	XF	Unc	BU
2002 Proof	—	Value: 35.00				
2004 Proof	—	Value: 35.00				
2006 Proof	—	Value: 35.00				
2012 Proof	—	Value: 35.00				

KM# 1045 50 PENCE
8.1100 g., 0.9584 Silver 0.2499 oz. ASW, 22 mm. **Ruler:** Elizabeth II **Obv:** Head with tiara right **Rev:** Britannia portrait behind wavy lines **Edge:** Reeded

Date	Mintage	F	VF	XF	Unc	BU
2003 Proof	3,669	Value: 35.00				

KM# 1086 50 PENCE
8.1100 g., 0.9584 Silver 0.2499 oz. ASW, 22 mm. **Ruler:** Elizabeth II **Obv:** Head with tiara right **Rev:** Britannia seated with shield left **Edge:** Reeded

Date	Mintage	F	VF	XF	Unc	BU
2005 Proof	2,360	Value: 35.00				

KM# 1089 50 PENCE
8.1100 g., 0.9584 Silver 0.2499 oz. ASW, 22 mm. **Ruler:** Elizabeth II **Obv:** Head with tiara right **Rev:** Britannia seated with reclining lion right **Edge:** Reeded

Date	Mintage	F	VF	XF	Unc	BU
2007 Proof	2,500	Value: 35.00				

KM# 1096 50 PENCE

8.1100 g., 0.9584 Silver 0.2499 oz. ASW, 22 mm. **Ruler:** Elizabeth II **Obv:** Head with tiara right **Rev:** Britannia standing facing left with trident, flowing garment, shield **Edge:** Reeded

Date	Mintage	F	VF	XF	Unc	BU
2008 Proof	2,500	Value: 45.00				

KM# 1124 50 PENCE

8.1100 g., 0.9580 Silver 0.2498 oz. ASW, 22 mm. **Ruler:** Elizabeth II **Obv:** Head right **Rev:** Britannia in chariot right

Date	Mintage	F	VF	XF	Unc	BU
2009 Proof	2,500	Value: 50.00				

KM# 1132 50 PENCE

8.1100 g., 0.9580 Silver 0.2498 oz. ASW, 22 mm. **Ruler:** Elizabeth II **Obv:** Head right **Rev:** Britannia bust right

Date	Mintage	F	VF	XF	Unc	BU
2010 Proof	3,500	Value: 50.00				

KM# 1228 50 PENCE

8.1100 g., 0.9584 Silver 0.2499 oz. ASW, 22 mm. **Ruler:** Elizabeth II **Obv:** Head with tiara right **Rev:** Britannia seated behind Union Jack veil

Date	Mintage	F	VF	XF	Unc	BU
2011 Proof	—	Value: 50.00				

KM# 1018 POUND

16.2200 g., 0.9584 Silver 0.4998 oz. ASW, 27 mm. **Ruler:** Elizabeth II **Obv:** Head with tiara right **Rev:** Una and Lion **Edge:** Reeded

Date	Mintage	F	VF	XF	Unc	BU
2001 Proof	5,000	Value: 50.00				
2012 Proof	2,012	Value: 115				

KM# 1081 POUND

16.2200 g., 0.9584 Silver 0.4998 oz. ASW, 27 mm. **Ruler:** Elizabeth II **Obv:** Head with tiara right **Rev:** Britannia standing **Edge:** Reeded

Date	Mintage	F	VF	XF	Unc	BU
2002 Proof	—	Value: 50.00				
2004 Proof	—	Value: 50.00				
2006 Proof	—	Value: 50.00				
2012 Proof	2,012	Value: 115				

KM# 1046 POUND

16.2200 g., 0.9584 Silver 0.4998 oz. ASW, 27 mm. **Ruler:** Elizabeth II **Obv:** Head with tiara right **Rev:** Britannia portrait behind wavy lines **Edge:** Reeded

Date	Mintage	F	VF	XF	Unc	BU
2003 Proof	3,669	Value: 50.00				
2012 Proof	2,012	Value: 115				

KM# 1087 POUND

16.2200 g., 0.9584 Silver 0.4998 oz. ASW, 27 mm. **Ruler:** Elizabeth II **Obv:** Head with tiara right **Rev:** Britannia seated with shield left **Edge:** Reeded

Date	Mintage	F	VF	XF	Unc	BU
2005 Proof	2,360	Value: 70.00				
2012 Proof	2,012	Value: 115				

KM# 1090 POUND

16.2200 g., 0.9584 Silver 0.4998 oz. ASW, 27 mm. **Ruler:** Elizabeth II **Obv:** Head with tiara right **Rev:** Britannia seated with reclining lion right **Edge:** Reeded

Date	Mintage	F	VF	XF	Unc	BU
2007 Proof	2,500	Value: 70.00				
2012 Proof	2,012	Value: 115				

KM# 1097 POUND

16.2200 g., 0.9584 Silver 0.4998 oz. ASW, 27 mm. **Ruler:** Elizabeth II **Obv:** Head with tiara right **Rev:** Britannia standing facing left with trident, flowing garment, shield **Edge:** Reeded

Date	Mintage	F	VF	XF	Unc	BU
2008 Proof	2,500	Value: 70.00				
2012 Proof	2,012	Value: 115				

KM# 1125 POUND

16.2200 g., 0.9580 Silver 0.4996 oz. ASW, 27 mm. **Ruler:** Elizabeth II **Obv:** Head right **Rev:** Britannia in chariot right

Date	Mintage	F	VF	XF	Unc	BU
2009 Proof	2,500	Value: 70.00				
2012 Proof	2,012	Value: 115				

KM# 1133 POUND

16.2200 g., 0.9580 Silver 0.4996 oz. ASW, 27 mm. **Ruler:** Elizabeth II **Obv:** Head right **Rev:** Britannia bust right

Date	Mintage	F	VF	XF	Unc	BU
2010 Proof	3,500	Value: 70.00				
2012 Proof	2,012	Value: 115				

KM# 1229 POUND

16.2200 g., 0.9584 Silver 0.4998 oz. ASW, 27 mm. **Ruler:** Elizabeth II **Obv:** Head with tiara right **Rev:** Britannia seated behind Union Jack veil

Date	Mintage	F	VF	XF	Unc	BU
2011 Proof	—	Value: 60.00				
2012 Proof	2,012	Value: 115				

KM# 1019 2 POUNDS

32.4500 g., 0.9584 Silver 0.9998 oz. ASW, 40 mm. **Ruler:** Elizabeth II **Subject:** Britannia Bullion **Obv:** Head with tiara right **Rev:** Una and Lion **Edge:** Reeded

Date	Mintage	F	VF	XF	Unc	BU
2001	44,816	—	—	—	38.00	42.00
2001 Proof	3,047	Value: 65.00				

KM# 1029 2 POUNDS

32.5400 g., 0.9580 Silver 1.0022 oz. ASW, 40 mm. **Ruler:** Elizabeth II **Obv:** Head with tiara right **Rev:** Standing Britannia **Edge:** Reeded

Date	Mintage	F	VF	XF	Unc	BU
2002	36,543	—	—	—	—	38.00
2002 Proof	—	Value: 60.00				
2004	100,000	—	—	—	—	38.00
2004 Proof	2,174	Value: 60.00				
2006	100,000	—	—	—	—	38.00
2006 Proof	2,529	Value: 60.00				
2012	—	—	—	—	—	38.00
2012 Proof	—	Value: 60.00				
2013	—	—	—	—	—	38.00
2013 Proof	—	Value: 60.00				

KM# 1039 2 POUNDS

32.4500 g., 0.9580 Silver 0.9994 oz. ASW, 40 mm. **Ruler:** Elizabeth II **Subject:** Britannia Bullion **Obv:** Head with tiara right **Rev:** Britannia portrait behind wavy puzzle-like lines **Edge:** Reeded

Date	Mintage	F	VF	XF	Unc	BU
2003	73,271	—	—	—	—	38.00
2003 Proof	2,016	Value: 65.00				

KM# 1063 2 POUNDS

32.4500 g., 0.9580 Silver 0.9994 oz. ASW, 40 mm. **Ruler:** Elizabeth II **Obv:** Head with tiara right **Rev:** Seated Britannia **Edge:** Reeded

Date	Mintage	F	VF	XF	Unc	BU
2005	100,000	—	—	—	—	38.00
2005 Proof	1,539	Value: 70.00				

KM# 1039a 2 POUNDS
32.4500 g., 0.9580 Silver partially gilt 0.9994 oz. ASW, 40 mm. **Ruler:** Elizabeth II **Obv:** Head with tiara right **Rev:** Britannia head gilt **Edge:** Reeded

Date	Mintage	F	VF	XF	Unc	BU
2006 Proof	3,000	Value: 100				

KM# 1063a 2 POUNDS
32.4500 g., 0.9580 Silver partially gilt 0.9994 oz. ASW, 40 mm. **Ruler:** Elizabeth II **Obv:** Head with tiara right **Rev:** Britannia seated, gilt **Edge:** Reeded

Date	Mintage	F	VF	XF	Unc	BU
2006 Proof	3,000	Value: 100				

KM# 1000a 2 POUNDS
32.4500 g., 0.9580 Silver partially gilt 0.9994 oz. ASW, 40 mm. **Ruler:** Elizabeth II **Obv:** Head with tiara right **Rev:** Britannia in chariot, gilt **Edge:** Reeded

Date	Mintage	F	VF	XF	Unc	BU
2006 Proof	3,000	Value: 100				

KM# 1019a 2 POUNDS
32.4500 g., 0.9580 Silver 0.9994 oz. ASW, 40 mm. **Ruler:** Elizabeth II **Subject:** Golden Silhouette Britannias **Obv:** Head with tiara right **Rev:** Gold plated Britannia and Lion **Edge:** Reeded

Date	Mintage	F	VF	XF	Unc	BU
2006 Proof	3,000	Value: 100				

KM# 1029a 2 POUNDS
32.4500 g., 0.9580 Silver partially gilt 0.9994 oz. ASW, 40 mm. **Ruler:** Elizabeth II **Obv:** Head with tiara right **Rev:** Britannia standing with shield, gilt **Edge:** Reeded

Date	Mintage	F	VF	XF	Unc	BU
2006 Proof	3,000	Value: 100				

KM# 1078 2 POUNDS
32.4500 g., 0.9580 Silver 0.9994 oz. ASW, 40 mm. **Ruler:** Elizabeth II **Subject:** Britannia series **Obv:** Elizabeth II **Rev:** Seated, bareheaded Britannia with a recumbent lion at her feet **Edge:** Reeded

Date	Mintage	F	VF	XF	Unc	BU
2007	100,000	—	—	—	—	40.00
2007 Proof	2,500	Value: 65.00				

KM# 1098 2 POUNDS
32.4500 g., 0.9584 Silver 0.9998 oz. ASW, 40 mm. **Ruler:** Elizabeth II **Obv:** Head with tiara right **Rev:** Britannia standing facing left with trident, flowing garment, shield **Edge:** Reeded

Date	Mintage	F	VF	XF	Unc	BU
2008	—	—	—	—	—	40.00
2008 Proof	—	Value: 80.00				

KM# 1000 2 POUNDS
32.5400 g., 0.9580 Silver 1.0022 oz. ASW, 40 mm. **Ruler:** Elizabeth II **Obv:** Head with tiara right **Rev:** Britannia in chariot **Edge:** Reeded

Date	Mintage	F	VF	XF	Unc	BU
2009	—	—	—	—	—	40.00
2009 Proof	—	Value: 60.00				

KM# 1134 2 POUNDS
32.4500 g., 0.9580 Silver 0.9994 oz. ASW, 40 mm. **Ruler:** Elizabeth II **Obv:** Head right **Rev:** Britannia bust right

Date	Mintage	F	VF	XF	Unc	BU
2010	—	—	—	—	—	38.00
2010 Proof	8,000	Value: 90.00				

KM# 1230 2 POUNDS
32.5400 g., 0.9580 Silver 1.0022 oz. ASW, 40 mm. **Ruler:** Elizabeth II **Obv:** Head with tiara right **Rev:** Britannia seated behind Union Jack veil

Date	Mintage	F	VF	XF	Unc	BU
2011	—	—	—	—	—	40.00
2011 Proof	—	Value: 80.00				

KM# 1029b 2 POUNDS
31.1050 g., 0.9990 Silver 0.9990 oz. ASW, 40 mm. **Ruler:** Elizabeth II **Obv:** Head with tiara right **Rev:** Standing Britannia **Edge:** Reeded

Date	Mintage	F	VF	XF	Unc	BU
2013	—	—	—	—	—	45.00
2013 Proof	—	Value: 60.00				

KM# 1020 10 POUNDS
3.4100 g., 0.9167 Gold 0.1005 oz. AGW, 16.5 mm. **Ruler:** Elizabeth II **Subject:** Britannia Bullion **Obv:** Head with tiara right **Rev:** Stylized "Britannia and the Lion" **Edge:** Reeded

Date	Mintage	F	VF	XF	Unc	BU
2001	1,100	—	—	—	—	BV+16%
2001 Proof	1,557	Value: 210				

KM# 1008 10 POUNDS
3.4100 g., 0.9167 Gold 0.1005 oz. AGW, 16.5 mm. **Ruler:** Elizabeth II **Obv:** Head with tiara right **Rev:** Britannia standing **Edge:** Reeded

Date	Mintage	F	VF	XF	Unc	BU
2002	—	—	—	—	—	BV+16%
2002 Proof	1,500	Value: 210				
2004 Proof	929	Value: 225				
2006 Proof	700	Value: 225				

KM# 1040 10 POUNDS
3.4100 g., 0.9167 Gold 0.1005 oz. AGW, 16.5 mm. **Ruler:** Elizabeth II **Obv:** Head with tiara right **Rev:** Britannia portrait behind wavy lines **Edge:** Reeded

Date	Mintage	F	VF	XF	Unc	BU
2003	—	—	—	—	—	BV+16%
2003 Proof	4,000	Value: 210				

KM# 1068 10 POUNDS
3.4100 g., 0.9167 Gold 0.1005 oz. AGW, 16.5 mm. **Ruler:** Elizabeth II **Obv:** Head with tiara right **Rev:** Seated Britannia **Edge:** Reeded

Date	Mintage	F	VF	XF	Unc	BU
2005 Proof	1,225	Value: 210				

KM# 1091 10 POUNDS
3.4100 g., 0.9167 Gold 0.1005 oz. AGW, 16.5 mm. **Ruler:** Elizabeth II **Obv:** Head with tiara right **Rev:** Britannia seated with reclining lion right **Edge:** Reeded

Date	Mintage	F	VF	XF	Unc	BU
2007	—	BV+16%				
2007 Proof	893	Value: 225				

KM# 1091a 10 POUNDS
3.1100 g., 0.9999 Platinum 0.1000 oz. APW, 16.5 mm. **Ruler:** Elizabeth II **Obv:** Head with tiara right **Rev:** Britannia seated with reclining lion right **Edge:** Reeded

Date	Mintage	F	VF	XF	Unc	BU
2007 Proof	691	Value: 300				

KM# 1099 10 POUNDS
3.4100 g., 0.9167 Gold 0.1005 oz. AGW, 16.5 mm. **Ruler:** Elizabeth II **Obv:** Head with tiara right **Rev:** Britannia standing facing left with trident, flowing garment, shield **Edge:** Reeded

Date	Mintage	F	VF	XF	Unc	BU
2008 Proof	—	Value: 210				

KM# 1099a 10 POUNDS
3.1100 g., 0.9999 Platinum 0.1000 oz. APW, 16.5 mm. **Ruler:** Elizabeth II **Obv:** Head with tiara right **Rev:** Britannia standing facing left with trident, flowing garment, shield **Edge:** Reeded

Date	Mintage	F	VF	XF	Unc	BU
2008 Proof	—	Value: 300				

KM# 1127 10 POUNDS
3.4100 g., 0.9160 Gold 0.1004 oz. AGW, 16.5 mm. **Ruler:** Elizabeth II **Obv:** Head right **Rev:** Britannia in chariot right

Date	Mintage	F	VF	XF	Unc	BU
2009 Proof	2,000	Value: 210				

KM# 1135 10 POUNDS
3.4100 g., 0.9160 Gold 0.1004 oz. AGW, 16.5 mm. **Ruler:** Elizabeth II **Obv:** Head right **Rev:** Britannia bust right

Date	Mintage	F	VF	XF	Unc	BU
2010 Proof	750	Value: 225				

KM# 1231 10 POUNDS
3.4100 g., 0.9167 Gold 0.1005 oz. AGW, 22 mm. **Ruler:** Elizabeth II **Obv:** Head with tiara right **Rev:** Britannia seated behind Union Jack veil

Date	Mintage	F	VF	XF	Unc	BU
2011 Proof	—	Value: 210				

KM# 1021 25 POUNDS
8.5100 g., 0.9167 Gold 0.2508 oz. AGW, 22 mm. **Ruler:** Elizabeth II **Subject:** Britannia Bullion **Obv:** Head with tiara right **Rev:** Stylized "Britannia and the Lion" **Edge:** Reeded

Date	Mintage	F	VF	XF	Unc	BU
2001	1,100	—	—	—	BV+25%	—
2001 Proof	1,500	Value: 450				
2006 Proof	—	Value: 450				

KM# 1009 25 POUNDS
8.5100 g., 0.9167 Gold 0.2508 oz. AGW, 22 mm. **Ruler:** Elizabeth II **Obv:** Head with tiara right **Rev:** Britannia standing **Edge:** Reeded

Date	Mintage	F	VF	XF	Unc	BU
2002 Proof	750	Value: 465				
2004 Proof	750	Value: 465				
2006 Proof	1,000	Value: 465				

KM# 1041 25 POUNDS
8.5100 g., 0.9167 Gold 0.2508 oz. AGW, 22 mm. **Ruler:** Elizabeth II **Obv:** Head with tiara right **Rev:** Britannia portrait behind wavy lines **Edge:** Reeded

Date	Mintage	F	VF	XF	Unc	BU
2003 Proof	609	Value: 465				
2006 Proof	—	Value: 465				

KM# 1069 25 POUNDS
8.5100 g., 0.9167 Gold 0.2508 oz. AGW, 22 mm. **Ruler:** Elizabeth II **Obv:** Head with tiara right **Rev:** Seated Britannia **Edge:** Reeded

Date	Mintage	F	VF	XF	Unc	BU
2005 Proof	750	Value: 465				
2006 Proof	—	Value: 465				

KM# 1204 25 POUNDS
8.5100 g., 0.9167 Gold 0.2508 oz. AGW **Ruler:** Elizabeth II **Rev:** Standing Britannia in horse drawn chariot

Date	Mintage	F	VF	XF	Unc	BU
2006 Proof	—	Value: 465				
2009 Proof	—	Value: 465				

KM# 1092 25 POUNDS
8.5100 g., 0.9167 Gold 0.2508 oz. AGW, 22 mm. **Ruler:** Elizabeth II **Obv:** Head with tiara right **Rev:** Britannia seated with reclining lion right **Edge:** Reeded

Date	Mintage	F	VF	XF	Unc	BU
2007	—	—	—	—	—	BV+25%
2007 Proof	1,000	Value: 465				

KM# 1092a 25 POUNDS
0.9999 Platinum APW, 22 mm. **Ruler:** Elizabeth II **Obv:** Head with tiara right **Rev:** Britannia seated with reclining lion right **Edge:** Reeded

Date	Mintage	F	VF	XF	Unc	BU
2007 Proof	—	Value: 650				

KM# 1100 25 POUNDS
8.5100 g., 0.9167 Gold 0.2508 oz. AGW, 22 mm. **Ruler:** Elizabeth II **Obv:** Head with tiara right **Rev:** Britannia standing facing left with trident, flowing garment, shield **Edge:** Reeded

Date	Mintage	F	VF	XF	Unc	BU
2008 Proof	1,000	Value: 465				

KM# 1100a 25 POUNDS
0.9999 Platinum APW, 22 mm. **Ruler:** Elizabeth II **Obv:** Head with tiara right **Rev:** Britannia standing facing left with trident, flowing garment, shield **Edge:** Reeded

Date	Mintage	F	VF	XF	Unc	BU
2008 Proof	—	Value: 650				

KM# 1128 25 POUNDS
8.5100 g., 0.9160 Gold 0.2506 oz. AGW, 22 mm. **Ruler:** Elizabeth II **Obv:** Head right **Rev:** Britannia in chariot right

Date	Mintage	F	VF	XF	Unc	BU
2009 Proof	2,250	Value: 450				

KM# 1136 25 POUNDS
8.5100 g., 0.9160 Gold 0.2506 oz. AGW, 22 mm. **Ruler:** Elizabeth II **Obv:** Head right **Rev:** Britannia bust right

Date	Mintage	F	VF	XF	Unc	BU
2010 Proof	3,000	Value: 450				

KM# 1232 25 POUNDS
8.5100 g., 0.9167 Gold 0.2508 oz. AGW, 22 mm. **Ruler:** Elizabeth II **Obv:** Head with tiara right **Rev:** Britannia seated behind Union Jack veil

Date	Mintage	F	VF	XF	Unc	BU
2011 Proof	—	Value: 450				

KM# 1022 50 POUNDS
17.0200 g., 0.9167 Gold 0.5016 oz. AGW, 27 mm. **Ruler:** Elizabeth II **Subject:** Britannia Bullion **Obv:** Head with tiara right **Rev:** Stylized "Britannia and the Lion" **Edge:** Reeded

Date	Mintage	F	VF	XF	Unc	BU
2001	600	—	—	—	BV+25%	—
2001 Proof	1,000	BV+10%				

KM# 1010 50 POUNDS
17.0300 g., 0.9167 Gold 0.5019 oz. AGW, 27 mm. **Ruler:** Elizabeth II **Obv:** Head with tiara right **Rev:** Britannia standing **Edge:** Reeded

Date	Mintage	F	VF	XF	Unc	BU
2002 Proof	1,000	BV+10%				
2004 Proof	—	BV+15%				
2006 Proof	—	BV+15%				

KM# 1042 50 POUNDS
17.0200 g., 0.9167 Gold 0.5016 oz. AGW, 27 mm. **Ruler:** Elizabeth II **Obv:** Head with tiara right **Rev:** Britannia portrait behind wavy lines **Edge:** Reeded

Date	Mintage	F	VF	XF	Unc	BU
2003	—	—	—	—	BV+15%	—
2003 Proof	2,500	BV+5%				

KM# 1070 50 POUNDS
17.0300 g., 0.9167 Gold 0.5019 oz. AGW, 27 mm. **Ruler:** Elizabeth II **Obv:** Head with tiara right **Rev:** Seated Britannia **Edge:** Reeded

Date	Mintage	F	VF	XF	Unc	BU
2005 Proof	2,000	BV+5%				

KM# 1093 50 POUNDS
17.0250 g., 0.9167 Gold 0.5017 oz. AGW, 27 mm. **Ruler:** Elizabeth II **Obv:** Head with tiara right **Rev:** Britannia seated with reclining lion right **Edge:** Reeded

Date	Mintage	F	VF	XF	Unc	BU
2007	—	—	—	—	—	BV+15%
2007 Proof	—	BV+10%				

KM# 1093a 50 POUNDS
0.9999 Platinum APW, 27 mm. **Ruler:** Elizabeth II **Obv:** Head with tiara right **Rev:** Britannia seated with reclining lion right **Edge:** Reeded

Date	Mintage	F	VF	XF	Unc	BU
2007 Proof	—	Value: 1,500				

KM# 1101 50 POUNDS
17.0250 g., 0.9167 Gold 0.5017 oz. AGW, 27 mm. **Ruler:** Elizabeth II **Obv:** Head with tiara right **Rev:** Britannia standing facing left with trident, flowing garment, shield **Edge:** Reeded

Date	Mintage	F	VF	XF	Unc	BU
2008 Proof	—	BV+10%				

KM# 1101a 50 POUNDS
0.9999 Platinum APW, 27 mm. **Ruler:** Elizabeth II **Obv:** Head with tiara right **Rev:** Britannia standing facing left with trident, flowing garment, shield **Edge:** Reeded

Date	Mintage	F	VF	XF	Unc	BU
2008 Proof	—	Value: 1,500				

KM# 1129 50 POUNDS
17.0250 g., 0.9160 Gold 0.5014 oz. AGW, 27 mm. **Ruler:** Elizabeth II **Obv:** Head right **Rev:** Britania in chariot right

Date	Mintage	F	VF	XF	Unc	BU
2009	—	—	—	—	—	BV+15%
2009 Proof	1,250	BV+10%				

KM# 1137 50 POUNDS
17.0200 g., 0.9160 Gold 0.5012 oz. AGW, 27 mm. **Ruler:** Elizabeth II **Obv:** Head right **Rev:** Britannia bust right

Date	Mintage	F	VF	XF	Unc	BU
2010 Proof	1,250	BV+10%				

KM# 1233 50 POUNDS
17.0200 g., 0.9167 Gold 0.5016 oz. AGW, 27 mm. **Ruler:** Elizabeth II

Date	Mintage	F	VF	XF	Unc	BU
2011 Proof	—	Value: 1,500				

KM# 1023 100 POUNDS
34.0500 g., 0.9167 Gold 1.0035 oz. AGW, 32.7 mm. **Ruler:** Elizabeth II **Subject:** Britannia Bullion **Obv:** Head with tiara right **Rev:** Stylized "Britannia and the Lion" **Edge:** Reeded

Date	Mintage	F	VF	XF	Unc	BU
2001	900	—	—	—	BV+15%	—
2001 Proof	1,000	BV+5%				

KM# 1011 100 POUNDS
34.0500 g., 0.9167 Gold 1.0035 oz. AGW, 32.7 mm. **Ruler:** Elizabeth II **Obv:** Head with tiara right **Rev:** Britannia standing **Edge:** Reeded

Date	Mintage	F	VF	XF	Unc	BU
2002 Proof	1,000	BV+5%				
2004	—	—	—	—	—	BV+15%
2004 Proof	—	BV+5%				
2006 Proof	—	BV+5%				
2012 Proof	—	BV+5%				

KM# 1043 100 POUNDS
34.0500 g., 0.9167 Gold 1.0035 oz. AGW, 32.7 mm. **Ruler:** Elizabeth II **Obv:** Head with tiara right **Rev:** Britannia portrait behind wavy lines **Edge:** Reeded

Date	Mintage	F	VF	XF	Unc	BU
2003	—	—	—	—	BV+15%	—
2003 Proof	1,500	BV+5%				

KM# 1071 100 POUNDS
34.0500 g., 0.9167 Gold 1.0035 oz. AGW, 32.7 mm. **Ruler:** Elizabeth II **Obv:** Head with tiara right **Rev:** Seated Britannia **Edge:** Reeded

Date	Mintage	F	VF	XF	Unc	BU
2005 Proof	1,500	BV+5%				

KM# 1094 100 POUNDS
34.0500 g., 0.9167 Gold 1.0035 oz. AGW, 32.7 mm. **Ruler:** Elizabeth II **Obv:** Head with tiara right **Rev:** Britannia seated with reclining lion right **Edge:** Reeded

Date	Mintage	F	VF	XF	Unc	BU
2007	—	—	—	—	BV+15%	—
2007 Proof	—	BV+5%				

KM# 1094a 100 POUNDS
0.9999 Platinum APW, 32.7 mm. **Ruler:** Elizabeth II **Obv:** Head with tiara right **Rev:** Britannia seated with reclining lion right **Edge:** Reeded

Date	Mintage	F	VF	XF	Unc	BU
2007 Proof	—	Value: 2,900				

KM# 1102 100 POUNDS
34.0500 g., 0.9167 Gold 1.0035 oz. AGW, 32.7 mm. **Ruler:** Elizabeth II **Obv:** Head with tiara right **Rev:** Britannia standing facing left with trident, flowing garment, shield **Edge:** Reeded

Date	Mintage	F	VF	XF	Unc	BU
2008	—	—	—	—	BV+15%	—
2008 Proof	—	BV+5%				

KM# 1102a 100 POUNDS

0.9999 Platinum APW, 32.7 mm. **Ruler:** Elizabeth II **Obv:** Head with tiara right **Rev:** Britannia standing facing left with trident, flowing garment, shield **Edge:** Reeded

Date	Mintage	F	VF	XF	Unc	BU
2008 Proof	—	Value: 2,900				

KM# 1130 100 POUNDS

32.6900 g., 0.9160 Gold 0.9627 oz. AGW, 32.6 mm. **Ruler:** Elizabeth II **Obv:** Head right **Rev:** Britannia in chariot right

Date	Mintage	F	VF	XF	Unc	BU
2009	—	—	—	—	—	BV+15%
2009 Proof	1,250	BV+5%				

KM# 1138 100 POUNDS

34.0500 g., 0.9160 Gold 1.0027 oz. AGW, 32.7 mm. **Ruler:** Elizabeth II **Obv:** Head right **Rev:** Britannia bust right

Date	Mintage	F	VF	XF	Unc	BU
2010	—	—	—	—	—	BV+15%
2010 Proof	1,250	BV+5%				

KM# 1234 100 POUNDS

34.0500 g., 0.9167 Gold 1.0035 oz. AGW, 32.7 mm. **Ruler:** Elizabeth II **Obv:** Head with tiara right **Rev:** Britannia seated behind Union Jack veil

Date	Mintage	F	VF	XF	Unc	BU
2011 Proof	—	BV+5%				

KM# 1011a 100 POUNDS

31.1050 g., 0.9990 Gold 0.9990 oz. AGW, 32.7 mm. **Ruler:** Elizabeth II **Obv:** Head with tiara right **Rev:** Britannia standing **Edge:** Reeded

Date	Mintage	F	VF	XF	Unc	BU
2013	—	—	—	—	—	BV+15%
2013 Proof	—	BV+5%				

PIEDFORT

KM#	Date	Mintage	Identification	Issue Price	Mkt Val
P101	2001	8,464	Pound. 0.9250 Silver. 19.0000 g. KM#1013a	—	115
P102	2002	6,599	Pound. 0.9250 Silver. 19.0000 g. KM#1030a	—	115
P106	2001	6,759	2 Pounds. 0.9250 Silver. 24.0000 g. KM#1014a	—	115
P107	2002	—	2 Pounds. 0.9250 Silver. 24.0000 g. KM#1031a	—	125
P108	2002	—	2 Pounds. 0.9250 Silver. 24.0000 g. KM#1032a	—	125
P109	2002	—	2 Pounds. 0.9250 Silver. 24.0000 g. KM#1033a	—	125
P110	2002	—	2 Pounds. 0.9250 Silver. 24.0000 g. Piedfort w/color. KM#1034a.	—	125
P42	ND2003	8,728	2 Pounds. 0.9250 Silver. 24.0000 g. KM#1037a.	—	95.00
P41	2003	9,871	Pound. 0.9250 Silver. 19.0000 g. KM#993a.	—	115
P40	2003	6,795	50 Pence. 0.9250 Silver. 16.0000 g. KM#1036a.	—	110
P43	2004	4,054	50 Pence. 0.9250 Silver. 24.0000 g. KM#1047a.	—	110
P45	2004	5,303	2 Pounds. 0.9250 Silver. 24.0000 g. KM#1049a.	—	125
P47	2004	2,500	5 Pounds. 0.9250 Silver. 56.5600 g. KM#1055a.	—	150
P44	2004	7,013	Pound. 0.9250 Silver. 19.0000 g. KM#1048a.	—	115
P46	ND2005	4,585	2 Pounds. 0.9250 Silver. 24.0000 g. KM#1052a.	—	95.00
P49	ND2005	4,798	2 Pounds. 0.9250 Silver. 24.0000 g. KM#1056a.	—	95.00
P48	2005	3,808	50 Pence. 0.9250 Silver. 16.0000 g. KM#1050a.	—	110
P50	2005	6,007	Pound. 0.9250 Silver. 19.0000 g. KM#1051a.	—	115
P52	2005	—	5 Pounds. 0.9250 Silver. KM#1054a.	—	150
P51	2005	—	5 Pounds. 0.9250 Silver. KM#1053a.	—	150
P54	2006	3,415	50 Pence. 0.9250 Silver. 16.0000 g. KM#1058a.	—	110
P53	2006	3,532	50 Pence. 0.9250 Silver. 16.0000 g. KM#1057a.	—	110
P57	2006	3,018	2 Pounds. 0.9250 Silver. 24.0000 g. KM#1061a.	—	115
P56	2006	3,199	2 Pounds. 0.9250 Silver. 24.0000 g. KM#1060a.	—	115
P55	2006	7,500	Pound. 0.9250 Silver. 19.0000 g. KM#1051a.	—	125
P58	2006	5,000	5 Pounds. 0.9250 Silver. KM#1062a.	—	150
P62	2007	3,990	2 Pounds. 0.9250 Silver. 24.0000 g. KM#1076a.	—	115
P61	2007	4,000	2 Pounds. 0.9250 Silver. 24.0000 g. KM#1075a.	—	115
P63	2007	2,000	5 Pounds. 0.9250 Silver. 56.5600 g. KM#1077a.	—	150
P64	2007	250	5 Pounds. 0.9995 Platinum. 94.2000 g.	—	7,500
P60	2007	5,739	Pound. 0.9250 Silver. 19.0000 g. KM#1074a.	—	95.00
P59	2007	1,555	50 Pence. 0.9250 Silver. 16.0000 g. KM#1073a.	—	135
P65	2008	—	2 Pounds. 0.9250 Silver. 24.0000 g. KM#1106a.	—	115
P97	2008	—	50 Pence. Silver. KM#1112a	—	125
P67	2008	—	5 Pounds. 0.9250 Silver. 56.5600 g. KM#1104.	—	150
P68	2008	—	5 Pounds. 0.9250 Silver. 56.5600 g. KM#1103.	—	150
P113	2008	5,000	5 Pounds. Silver. 56.5600 g. KM#1103a	—	150
P103	2008	8,000	Pound. 0.9250 Silver. 19.0000 g. KM#1113a	—	125
P66	2009	3,500	2 Pounds. 0.9250 Silver. 24.0000 g. KM#1115a.	—	115
P111	2009	3,500	2 Pounds. Silver. 24.0000 g.	—	115
P98	2009	—	50 Pence. Silver. KM#1114a	—	125
P70	2009	4,009	5 Pounds. 0.9250 Silver. 56.5600 g. KM#1118a.	—	180
P75	2010	3,000	Pound. 0.9250 Silver. 19.0000 g. KM#1158a.	—	110
P99	2010	—	50 Pence. Silver. KM#1165a	—	125
P114	2010	—	5 Pounds. Silver. 56.5600 g. KM#1151a	—	160
P76	2010	5,000	Pound. 0.9250 Silver. 19.0000 g.	—	110
P77	2011	—	Penny. 0.9250 Silver. KM#1107a.	—	15.00
P78	2011	—	2 Pence. 0.9250 Silver. KM#1108a.	—	25.00
P79	2011	—	5 Pence. 0.9250 Silver. KM#1109a.	—	35.00
P80	2011	—	10 Pence. 0.9250 Silver. KM#1110a.	—	80.00
P81	2011	—	20 Pence. 0.9250 Silver. KM#1111a.	—	80.00
P85	2011	—	Pound. 0.9250 Silver. 19.0000 g. KM#1198a.	—	115
P87	2011	—	2 Pounds. 0.9250 Silver. 24.0000 g. KM#1199a.	—	115
P88	2011	—	2 Pounds. 0.9250 Silver. 24.0000 g. KM#1200a.	—	115
P82	2011	—	50 Pence. 0.9250 Silver. KM#1112a.	—	125
P86	2011	—	50 Pence. 0.9250 Silver. 24.0000 g. KM#1196a.	—	125
P89	2011	—	5 Pounds. 0.9250 Silver. 56.5600 g. KM#1201a.	—	150
P83	2011	—	Pound. 0.9250 Silver. KM#1113a.	—	115
P84	2011	—	Pound. 0.9250 Silver. 19.0000 g. KM#1197a.	—	115

MAUNDY SETS

KM#	Date	Mintage	Identification	Issue Price	Mkt Val
MDS260	2001 (4)	1,132	KM#898-899, 901-902. Westminster Abbey	—	300
MDS261	2002 (4)	1,681	KM#898-899, 901-902. Canterbury Cathedral	—	300
MDS262	2003 (4)	1,608	KM#898-899, 901-902. Gloucester Cathedral	—	325
MDS263	2004 (4)	1,613	KM#898-899, 901-902. Liverpool Cathedral	—	325
MDS264	2005 (4)	1,685	KM#898-899, 901-902. Wakefield Cathedral	—	325
MDS265	2006 (4)	1,811	KM#898-899, 901-902. Guilford Cathedral	—	325
MDS266	2007 (4)	1,822	KM#898-899, 901-902. Manchester Cathedral	—	325
MDS267	2008 (4)	1,833	KM#898-899, 901-902. St. Patrick's Cathedral	—	325
MDS268	2009 (4)	1,602	KM#898-899, 901-902.	—	325
MDS269	2010 (4)	1,617	KM#898-899, 901-902.	—	325
MDS270	2011 (4)	—	KM#898-899, 901-902.	—	325

MINT SETS

KM#	Date	Mintage	Identification	Issue Price	Mkt Val
MS129	2001 (9)	57,741	KM#986-991, 994, 1013-1015 B.U. set	22.50	25.00
MS130	2001 (9)	—	KM#986-991, 994, 1013-1014 Wedding Collection	27.50	25.00
MS131	2001 (9)	—	KM#986-991, 994, 1013-1014 Baby Gift Set	27.50	25.00
MS132	2002 (8)	60,539	KM#986-991, 994, 1030	22.50	20.00
MS133	2002 (8)	—	KM#986-991, 994, 1030 Wedding Collection	27.50	20.00
MS134	2002 (8)	—	KM#986-991, 994, 1030 Baby Gift Set	27.50	20.00
MS135	2003 (10)	62,741	KM#986-991, 993, 994, 1036-1037 BU Set	22.50	35.00
MS136	2003 (10)	7,130	KM#986-991, 993, 994, 1036-1037 Wedding Collection	27.50	30.00
MS137	2003 (10)	43,128	KM#986-991, 993, 994, 1036-1037 Baby Gift Set	27.50	30.00
MSA135	2004 (10)	46,032	KM#986-991, 994, 1047-1049 BU Set	—	35.00
MSB135	2004 (10)	4,214	KM#986-991, 994, 1047-1049, 1055 Wedding Collection	—	35.00
MSC135	2004 (10)	34,371	KM#986-991, 994, 1047-1049, 1055 Baby Gift Set	—	35.00
MS138	2005 (10)	51,776	KM#986-991, 994, 1050-1052	26.50	30.00
MS139	2005 (10)	29,924	KM#986-991, 994, 1050-1052 Baby Gift Set	36.50	35.00
MS140	2005 (3)	—	KM#1050-1052 New Coinage Set	16.25	17.50
MS141	2005 (2)	—	KM#1053-1054 Trafalgar Set	36.00	35.00
MS142	2006 (10)	74,231	KM#986-990, 1057-1061, BV set	30.00	60.00
MS143	2006 (10)	25,878	KM#986-990, 1057-1061 Baby Gift Set	38.50	60.00
MS144	2007 (6)	—	KM#986-991	—	10.00

PROOF SETS

KM#	Date	Mintage	Identification	Issue Price	Mkt Val
PS118	2001 (4)	5,000	KM#1016-1019	—	175
PS127	2001 (10)	10,000	KM#986-991, 994, 1013-1015 Executive Proof Set in display case	115	80.00
PS128	2001 (10)	30,000	KM#986-991, 994, 1013-1015 Deluxe Proof Set in red leather case	72.50	80.00
PS129	2001 (10)	28,244	KM#986-991, 994, 1013-1015 Standard Proof Set in simple case	50.00	65.00
PS130	2001 (10)	1,351	KM#986-991, 994, 1013-1015 Gift Proof Set with a pack of occasion cards	65.00	65.00
PS131	2002 (9)	5,000	KM#986-991, 994, 1024, 1030 Executive Proof Set	100	60.00
PS119	2001 (4)	1,000	KM#1020-1023	1,595	3,200
PS116	2001 (3)	1,500	KM#1001-1002, 1014a	795	525
PS117	2001 (4)	1,000	KM#1001-1003,1014a	1,645	2,250
PSA119	2001 (3)	1,500	KM#1001, 1002, 1014b	—	525
PSB119	2001 (4)	1,000	KM#1001, 1002, 1014b, 1015b	—	2,700
PS120	2002 (3)	5,000	KM#1025-1027	795	1,275
PS121	2002 (4)	3,000	KM#1025-1028	1,645	3,000
PS126	2002 (4)	1,000	KM#1008-1011	1,600	3,200
PS132	2002 (9)	30,000	KM#986-991, 994, 1024, 1030 Deluxe Proof Set	70.00	55.00
PS133	2002 (9)	30,884	KM#986-991, 994, 1024, 1030 Standard Proof Set	48.00	55.00
PS134	2002 (9)	1,544	KM#986-991, 994, 1024, 1030 Gift Proof Set	62.40	55.00
PS160	2002 (4)	—	KM#1029, 1079-1081	—	175
PSA135	2002 (13)	—	KM#898a, 899a, 901a, 902a, 986c, 987c, 988b, 989b, 990b, 991b, 1030b, 994c, 1024b Queen Elizabeth II - Golden Jubilee 1952-2002, set is struck in gold (including Maundy set), in presentation box	—	11,250
PS122	2002 (4)	3,358	KM#1031-1034; Standard Set	34.95	35.00
PS123	2002 (4)	673	KM#1031-1034; Display Set	44.95	40.00
PS124	2002 (4)	2,553	KM#1031a-1034a; Display Set	120	150
PS125	2002 (4)	315	KM#1031b-1034b; Display Set	1,675	3,000
PS135	2003 (11)	5,000	KM#986-991, 993, 994, 1036-1038 Executive Proof Set	100	85.00
PS136	2003 (11)	14,863	KM#986-991, 993, 994, 1036-1038 Deluxe Proof Set	72.00	80.00
PS137	2003 (11)	23,650	KM#986-991, 993, 994, 1036-1038 Standard Proof Set	50.00	80.00
PS161	2003 (4)	1,250	KM#1040-1043	—	2,800
PSA138	2003 (4)	3,669	KM#1039, 1044-1046	—	180
PS162	2004 (4)	—	KM#1029, 1079-1081	—	175
PS165	2006 (4)	—	KM#1029, 1079-1081	—	175
PSB138	2004 (11)	4,101	KM#986-991, 994, 1047-1049, 1055 Executive Proof Set	—	80.00
PSC138	2004 (11)	12,968	KM#986-991, 994, 1047-1049, 1055 Deluxe Proof Set	—	80.00
PSD138	2004 (11)	17,951	KM#986-991, 994, 1047-1049, 1055 Standard Proof Set	—	80.00
PS163	2004 (4)	973	KM#1008-1011	—	3,000
PS138	2005 (12)	4,290	KM#986-991, 994, 1050-1054 Executive Set	146	95.00
PS139	2005 (12)	14,899	KM#986-991, 994, 1050-1054 Deluxe Proof Set	80.00	95.00
PS140	2005 (12)	21,374	KM#986-991, 994, 1050-1054, Standard Proof Set	60.00	95.00
PS141	2005 (3)	417	KM#1068-1070	850	1,350
PS142	2005 (4)	1,439	KM#1068-1071	1,895	2,850
PS143	2005 (3)	2,500	KM#1064-1066	820	1,100

KM#	Date	Mintage	Identification	Issue Price	Mkt Val
PS144	2005 (4)	2,500	KM#1064-1067	1,925	2,600
PS145	2005 (2)	—	P39, P40	—	175
PS164	2005 (4)	2,360	KM#1063, 1085-1087	—	185
PS149	2006 (5)	3,000	KM#1000a, 1012a, 1018a, 1039, 1063a	475	525
PS150	2006 (3)	1,750	KM#1001, 1002, 1072	1,015	1,150
PS151	2006 (4)	1,750	KM#1001-1003, 1072	2,091	2,650
PS166	2006 (4)	—	KM#1008-1011	—	2,900
PS146	2006 (13)	5,000	KM#986-991, 994, 1057-1062 Executive Proof Set, wooden case	—	140
PS147	2006 (13)	15,000	KM#986-991, 994, 1057-1062 Deluxe Proof Set	82.50	140
PS148	2006 (13)	17,689	KM#986-991, 994, 1057-1062 Standard Proof Set	65.00	140
PS152	2007 (13)	18,215	KM#986-991, 994, 1057-1062	65.00	140
PS153	2007 (4)	1,750	KM#1001-1003, 1072	—	2,850
PS154	2007 (3)	750	KM#1001-1002, 1072	—	1,200
PS156	2007 (5)	3,000	KM#P33, P35-P38	450	500
PS167	2007 (4)	—	KM#1078, 1088-1090	—	185
PS168	2007 (4)	—	KM#1091-1094	—	2,950
PS169	2007 (4)	—	KM#1091a-1094a	—	5,850
PS155	2007 (2)	5,000	KM#1001-1002	—	550
PS170	2008 (4)	—	KM#1095-1098	—	225
PS171	2008 (4)	—	KM#1099-1102	—	3,000
PS172	2008 (4)	—	KM#1099a-1102a	—	5,850

The Hellenic (Greek) Republic is situated in southeastern Europe on the southern tip of the Balkan Peninsula. The republic includes many islands, the most important of which are Crete and the Ionian Islands. Greece (including islands) has an area of 50,944 sq. mi. (131,940 sq. km.) and a population of 10.3 million. Capital: Athens. Greece is still largely agricultural. Tobacco, cotton, fruit and wool are exported.

MONETARY SYSTEM

100 Euro Cent = 1 Euro

REPUBLIC

EURO COINAGE

European Union Issues

The Greek Euro coinage series contains the denomination in Lepta as well.

KM# 181 EURO CENT

2.2700 g., Copper Plated Steel, 16.2 mm. **Obv:** Ancient Athenian trireme **Rev:** Denomination and globe **Edge:** Plain

Date	Mintage	F	VF	XF	Unc	BU
2002	101,000,000	—	—	—	0.35	—
2002 F in star	15,000,000	—	—	—	1.25	—
2003	35,200,000	—	—	—	0.35	—
2004	50,000,000	—	—	—	0.35	—
2005	15,000,000	—	—	—	0.35	—
2006	45,000,000	—	—	—	0.35	—
2007	60,000,000	—	—	—	0.35	—
2008	24,000,000	—	—	—	0.35	—
2009	50,000,000	—	—	—	0.35	—
2010	27,000,000	—	—	—	0.35	—
2011	35,000,000	—	—	—	0.35	—
2011 Proof, In sets only	2,500	Value: 15.00				
2012	48,000,000	—	—	—	0.35	—
2012 Proof, In sets only	2,500	Value: 15.00				

KM# 182 2 EURO CENT

3.0300 g., Copper Plated Steel, 18.7 mm. **Obv:** Corvette sailing ship **Rev:** Denomination and globe **Edge:** Grooved

Date	Mintage	F	VF	XF	Unc	BU
2002	176,000,000	—	—	—	0.50	—
2002 F in star	18,000,000	—	—	—	1.00	—
2003	10,000,000	—	—	—	0.50	—
2004	25,000,000	—	—	—	0.50	—
2005	15,000,000	—	—	—	0.50	—
2006	45,000,000	—	—	—	0.50	—
2007	25,000,103	—	—	—	0.50	—
2008	68,000,000	—	—	—	0.50	—
2009	16,000,000	—	—	—	0.50	—
2010	32,000,000	—	—	—	0.50	—
2011	47,000,000	—	—	—	0.50	—
2011 Proof	2,500	Value: 15.00				
2012	34,000,000	—	—	—	0.50	—
2012 Proof, In sets only	2,500	Value: 15.00				

KM# 183 5 EURO CENT

3.8600 g., Copper Plated Steel, 21.2 mm. **Obv:** Freighter **Rev:** Denomination and globe **Edge:** Plain

Date	Mintage	F	VF	XF	Unc	BU
2002	211,000,000	—	—	—	1.00	—
2002 F in star	90,000,000	—	—	—	1.25	—
2003	750,000	—	—	—	1.00	—
2004	250,000	—	—	—	1.00	—
2005	1,000,000	—	—	—	1.00	—
2006	50,000,000	—	—	—	1.00	—
2007	55,005,598	—	—	—	1.00	—
2008	50,000,000	—	—	—	1.00	—
2009	38,000,000	—	—	—	1.00	—
2010	5,000,000	—	—	—	1.00	—
2011	34,000,000	—	—	—	1.00	—
2011 Proof	2,500	Value: 15.00				
2012	1,000,000	—	—	—	1.00	—
2012 Proof	2,500	Value: 15.00				

KM# 184 10 EURO CENT

4.0700 g., Brass, 19.7 mm. **Obv:** Bust of Rhgas Feriaou's half right **Rev:** Denomination and map **Edge:** Reeded

Date	Mintage	F	VF	XF	Unc	BU
2002	138,000,000	—	—	—	1.25	—
2002 F in star	100,000,000	—	—	—	2.00	—
2003	600,000	—	—	—	1.25	—
2004	10,000,000	—	—	—	1.25	—
2005	25,000,000	—	—	—	1.25	—
2006	45,000,000	—	—	—	1.25	—

KM# 211 10 EURO CENT

4.0700 g., Brass, 19.25 mm. **Obv:** Bust of Rhgas Feriaou's half right **Rev:** Relief map of Western Europe, stars, lines and value **Edge:** Reeded

Date	Mintage	F	VF	XF	Unc	BU
2007	63,000,000	—	—	—	1.25	1.50
2008	40,000,000	—	—	—	1.25	1.50
2009	46,000,000	—	—	—	1.25	1.50
2010	5,000,000	—	—	—	1.25	1.50
2011	36,000,000	—	—	—	1.25	1.50
2011 Proof	2,500	Value: 15.00				
2012	1,000,000	—	—	—	1.25	1.50
2012 Proof	2,500	Value: 15.00				

KM# 185 20 EURO CENT

5.7300 g., Brass, 22.25 mm. **Obv:** Bust of John Kapodistrias half right **Rev:** Denomination and map **Edge:** Notched

Date	Mintage	F	VF	XF	Unc	BU
2002	209,000,000	—	—	—	1.25	—
2002 E in star	120,000,000	—	—	—	2.25	—
2003	800,000	—	—	—	1.25	—
2004	500,000	—	—	—	1.25	—
2005	1,000,000	—	—	—	1.25	—
2006	1,000,000	—	—	—	1.25	—

KM# 212 20 EURO CENT

5.7300 g., Brass, 22.1 mm. **Obv:** Bust of John Kapodistrias' half right **Rev:** Relief map of Western Europe, stars, lines and value **Edge:** Notched

Date	Mintage	F	VF	XF	Unc	BU
2007	1,000,000	—	—	—	1.25	—
2008	20,000,000	—	—	—	1.25	—
2009	24,000,000	—	—	—	1.25	—
2010	12,000,000	—	—	—	1.25	—
2011	965,000	—	—	—	1.25	—
2011 Proof	2,500	Value: 20.00				
2012	1,000,000	—	—	—	1.25	—
2012 Proof	2,500	Value: 20.00				

KM# 186 50 EURO CENT

7.8100 g., Brass, 24.2 mm. **Obv:** Bust of El. Venizelos half left **Rev:** Denomination and map **Edge:** Reeded

Date	Mintage	F	VF	XF	Unc	BU
2002	93,000,000	—	—	—	1.50	—
2002 F in star	70,000,000	—	—	—	2.50	—
2003	700,000	—	—	—	1.50	—
2004	500,000	—	—	—	1.50	—
2005	1,000,000	—	—	—	1.50	—
2006	1,000,000	—	—	—	1.50	—

KM# 213 50 EURO CENT

7.8100 g., Brass, 24.2 mm. **Obv:** Bust of El. Venizelos half left **Rev:** Relief map of Western Europe, stars, lines and value **Edge:** Reeded

Date	Mintage	F	VF	XF	Unc	BU
2007	1,000,000	—	—	—	1.00	1.50
2008	10,000,000	—	—	—	1.00	1.50
2009	7,000,000	—	—	—	1.00	1.50
2010	6,000,000	—	—	—	1.00	1.50
2011	7,000,000	—	—	—	1.00	1.50
2011 Proof	2,500	Value: 25.00				
2012	1,000,000	—	—	—	1.00	1.50
2012 Proof	2,500	Value: 25.00				

KM# 187 EURO

7.5000 g., Bi-Metallic Copper-Nickel center in Nickel-Brass ring, 23.25 mm. **Obv:** Ancient Athenian coin design **Rev:** Denomination and map **Edge:** Segmented reeding

Date	Mintage	F	VF	XF	Unc	BU
2002	61,500,000	—	—	—	4.00	—
2002 S in star	50,000,000	—	—	—	6.00	—
2003	11,000,000	—	—	—	7.50	—
2004	10,000,000	—	—	—	5.00	—
2005	10,000,000	—	—	—	5.00	—
2006	10,000,000	—	—	—	5.00	—

KM# 214 EURO

7.5000 g., Bi-Metallic Copper-Nickel center in Nickel-Brass ring, 23.25 mm. **Obv:** Ancient Athenian coin design **Rev:** Relief map of Western Europe, stars, lines and value **Edge:** Segmented reeding

Date	Mintage	F	VF	XF	Unc	BU
2007	24,000,000	—	—	—	3.00	4.00
2008	4,000,000	—	—	—	3.00	4.00
2009	18,000,000	—	—	—	3.00	4.00

Date	Mintage	F	VF	XF	Unc	BU
2010	11,000,000	—	—	—	3.00	4.00
2011	965,000	—	—	—	3.00	4.00
2011 Proof	2,500	Value: 40.00				
2012	1,000,000	—	—	—	3.00	4.00
2012 Proof	2,500	Value: 40.00				

KM# 188 2 EURO

8.5000 g., Bi-Metallic Nickel-Brass center in Copper-Nickel ring, 25.75 mm. **Obv:** Europa seated on a bull **Rev:** Denomination and map **Edge:** Reeded with Greek legend and stars

Date	Mintage	F	VF	XF	Unc	BU
2002	75,400,000	—	—	—	4.00	—
2002 S in star	70,000,000	—	—	—	6.50	—
2003	550,000	—	—	—	20.00	—
2004 In sets only	30,000	—	—	—	50.00	—
2005	1,000,000	—	—	—	4.00	—
2006	1,000,000	—	—	—	4.00	—

KM# 209 2 EURO

8.5000 g., Bi-Metallic Nickel-Brass center in Copper-Nickel ring., 25.75 mm. **Subject:** 2004 Olympics **Obv:** Discus thrower **Rev:** Denomination and map **Edge:** Reeded with Greek legend and stars

Date	Mintage	F	VF	XF	Unc	BU
2004	49,500,000	—	—	—	4.00	6.00
2004 Prooflike	500,000	—	—	—	—	15.00

KM# 215 2 EURO

8.5000 g., Bi-Metallic Nickel-Brass center in Copper-Nickel ring, 25.75 mm. **Obv:** Europa seated on a bull **Rev:** Relief map of Western Europe, stars, lines and value **Edge:** Reeded with Greek legend and stars

Date	Mintage	F	VF	XF	Unc	BU
2007 In sets only	15,000	—	—	—	—	25.00
2008	2,000,000	—	—	—	3.00	10.00
2009	982,000	—	—	—	3.00	5.00
2010	2,000,000	—	—	—	3.00	5.00
2011	—	—	—	—	3.00	5.00
2011 Proof	2,500	Value: 50.00				
2012	2,000,000	—	—	—	3.00	5.00
2012 Proof	2,500	Value: 50.00				

KM# 216 2 EURO

8.5000 g., Bi-Metallic Nickel-Brass center in Copper-Nickel ring, 25.75 mm. **Subject:** 50th Anniversary - Treaty of Rome **Obv:** Open treaty book **Rev:** Large value at left, modified outline of Europe at right **Edge:** Reeded with Greek legend and stars

Date	Mintage	F	VF	XF	Unc	BU
2007	4,000,000	—	—	—	—	9.00

KM# 227 2 EURO

8.5000 g., Bi-Metallic Nickel-Brass center in Copper-Nickel ring, 25.75 mm. **Subject:** European Monetary Union, 10th Anniversary **Obv:** Stick figure and Euro symbol **Edge:** Reeded with Greek legend and stars

Date	Mintage	F	VF	XF	Unc	BU
2009	4,000,000	—	—	—	—	7.00

KM# 236 2 EURO

8.5000 g., Bi-Metallic Nickel-Brass center in Copper-Nickel ring, 25.75 mm. **Subject:** Battle of Marathon, 2500th Anniversary **Obv:** Ancient Greek Warrior holding javelin running **Edge:** Reeded with Greek legend and stars

Date	Mintage	F	VF	XF	Unc	BU
2010	3,500,000	—	—	—	—	9.00

KM# 239 2 EURO

8.5000 g., Bi-Metallic Nickel-Brass center in Copper-Nickel ring, 25.75 mm. **Subject:** Special Olympics - Athens **Obv:** Figure standing in spiral, laureal weath at left

Date	Mintage	F	VF	XF	Unc	BU
2011	1,000,000	—	—	—	6.00	7.50

KM# 245 2 EURO

8.5000 g., Bi-Metallic Nickel-Brass center in Copper-Nickel ring, 25.75 mm. **Subject:** Euro coinage, 10th Anniversary **Obv:** Euro symbol on globe at center, child-like rendering around

Date	Mintage	F	VF	XF	Unc	BU
2012	1,000,000	—	—	—	6.00	8.00
2012 Special Unc.	5,000	—	—	—	—	15.00
2012 Proof, In sets only	2,500	Value: 50.00				

KM# 190 10 EURO

34.0000 g., 0.9250 Silver 1.0111 oz. ASW, 40 mm. **Subject:** Olympics **Obv:** Olympic rings in wreath above value within circle of stars **Rev:** Ancient and modern runners **Edge:** Plain **Note:** Olympics

Date	Mintage	F	VF	XF	Unc	BU
ND (2003) Proof	68,000	Value: 60.00				

KM# 191 10 EURO

34.0000 g., 0.9250 Silver 1.0111 oz. ASW, 40 mm. **Subject:** Olympics **Obv:** Olympic rings in wreath above value within circle of stars **Rev:** Ancient and modern discus throwers **Edge:** Plain

Date	Mintage	F	VF	XF	Unc	BU
ND(2003) Proof	68,000	Value: 60.00				

KM# 193 10 EURO

34.0000 g., 0.9250 Silver 1.0111 oz. ASW, 40 mm. **Subject:** Olympics **Obv:** Olympic rings in wreath above value within circle of stars **Rev:** Ancient and modern javelin throwers **Edge:** Plain

Date	Mintage	F	VF	XF	Unc	BU
ND(2003) Proof	68,000	Value: 60.00				

KM# 194 10 EURO

34.0000 g., 0.9250 Silver 1.0111 oz. ASW, 40 mm. **Subject:** Olympics **Obv:** Olympic rings in wreath above value within circle of stars **Rev:** Ancient and modern long jumpers **Edge:** Plain

Date	Mintage	F	VF	XF	Unc	BU
ND(2003) Proof	68,000	Value: 60.00				

KM# 196 10 EURO

34.0000 g., 0.9250 Silver 1.0111 oz. ASW, 40 mm. **Subject:** Olympics **Obv:** Olympic rings in wreath above value within circle of stars **Rev:** Ancient and modern relay runners **Edge:** Plain

Date	Mintage	F	VF	XF	Unc	BU
ND(2003) Proof	68,000	Value: 60.00				

KM# 197 10 EURO

34.0000 g., 0.9250 Silver 1.0111 oz. ASW, 40 mm. **Subject:** Olympics **Obv:** Olympic rings in wreath above value within circle of stars **Rev:** Ancient and modern horsemen **Edge:** Plain

Date	Mintage	F	VF	XF	Unc	BU
ND(2003) Proof	68,000	Value: 60.00				

KM# 199 10 EURO

34.0000 g., 0.9250 Silver 1.0111 oz. ASW, 40 mm. **Subject:** Olympics **Obv:** Olympic rings in wreath above value within circle of stars **Rev:** Modern ribbon dancer and two ancient female acrobats **Edge:** Plain

Date	Mintage	F	VF	XF	Unc	BU
ND(2003) Proof	68,000	Value: 60.00				

KM# 200 10 EURO

34.0000 g., 0.9250 Silver 1.0111 oz. ASW, 40 mm. **Subject:** Olympics **Obv:** Olympic rings in wreath above value within a circle of stars **Rev:** Ancient and modern female swimmers **Edge:** Plain

Date	Mintage	F	VF	XF	Unc	BU
ND(2003) Proof	68,000	Value: 60.00				

KM# 208 10 EURO

9.7500 g., 0.9250 Silver 0.2899 oz. ASW, 28.25 mm. **Subject:** Greek Presidency of E. U. **Obv:** National arms in wreath above value **Rev:** Stylized document design **Edge:** Notched

Date	Mintage	F	VF	XF	Unc	BU
2003 Proof	50,000	Value: 80.00				

KM# 202 10 EURO

34.0000 g., 0.9250 Silver 1.0111 oz. ASW, 40 mm. **Subject:** Olympics **Obv:** Olympic rings in wreath above value within circle of stars **Rev:** Ancient and modern weight lifters **Edge:** Plain

Date	Mintage	F	VF	XF	Unc	BU
ND(2004) Proof	68,000	Value: 60.00				

KM# 203 10 EURO

34.0000 g., 0.9250 Silver 1.0111 oz. ASW, 40 mm. **Subject:** Olympics **Obv:** Olympic rings in wreath above value within circle of stars **Rev:** Ancient and modern wrestlers **Edge:** Plain

Date	Mintage	F	VF	XF	Unc	BU
ND(2004) Proof	68,000	Value: 60.00				

KM# 205 10 EURO

34.0000 g., 0.9250 Silver 1.0111 oz. ASW, 40 mm. **Subject:** Olympics **Obv:** Olympic rings in wreath above value within circle of stars **Rev:** Ancient and modern handball players **Edge:** Plain

Date	Mintage	F	VF	XF	Unc	BU
ND(2004) Proof	68,000	Value: 60.00				

KM# 206 10 EURO

34.0000 g., 0.9250 Silver 1.0111 oz. ASW, 40 mm. **Subject:** Olympics **Obv:** Olympic rings in wreath above value within circle of stars **Rev:** Ancient and modern soccer players **Edge:** Plain

Date	Mintage	F	VF	XF	Unc	BU
ND(2004) Proof	68,000	Value: 60.00				

KM# 230 10 EURO

34.0000 g., 0.9250 Silver 1.0111 oz. ASW, 40 mm. **Obv:** Wreath **Rev:** Torch runner and map of Australia

Date	Mintage	F	VF	XF	Unc	BU
2004 Proof	10,000	Value: 110				

KM# 231 10 EURO

34.0000 g., 0.9250 Silver 1.0111 oz. ASW, 40 mm. **Rev:** Torch runner and map of Asia

Date	Mintage	F	VF	XF	Unc	BU
2004 Proof	10,000	Value: 110				

KM# 232 10 EURO

34.0000 g., 0.9250 Silver 1.0111 oz. ASW, 40 mm. **Rev:** Torch runner and map of Africa

Date	Mintage	F	VF	XF	Unc	BU
2004 Proof	10,000	Value: 110				

KM# 233 10 EURO

34.0000 g., 0.9250 Silver 1.0111 oz. ASW, 40 mm. **Rev:** Torch runner and map of North and South America

Date	Mintage	F	VF	XF	Unc	BU
2004 Proof	10,000	Value: 110				

KM# 217 10 EURO

9.7500 g., 0.9250 Silver 0.2899 oz. ASW **Subject:** Olympic National Park **Obv:** National arms above stylized flowers **Rev:** Four Titans above flowers in camp

Date	Mintage	F	VF	XF	Unc	BU
2005 Proof	25,000	Value: 45.00				

KM# 218 10 EURO

9.7500 g., 0.9250 Silver 0.2899 oz. ASW, 28.25 mm. **Subject:** PATRA - European Capitol of Culture - Achaia **Obv:** National arms at upper right, stylized bridge below **Rev:** PATRA logo **Edge:** Plain

Date	Mintage	F	VF	XF	Unc	BU
2006 Proof	—	Value: 50.00				

KM# 219 10 EURO

34.0000 g., 0.9250 Silver 1.0111 oz. ASW, 40 mm. **Obv:** National arms above stylized flowers **Rev:** Outline of Greece at left, statue of Zeus, flowers at right **Edge:** Plain

Date	Mintage	F	VF	XF	Unc	BU
2006 Proof	5,000	Value: 55.00				

KM# 220 10 EURO

34.0000 g., 0.9250 Silver 1.0111 oz. ASW, 40 mm. **Subject:** National Parks - Mount Olympus - International Biosphere Reserve **Obv:** National arms above stylized flowers **Rev:** Archaeological outline of Dion City above landscape **Edge:** Plain

Date	Mintage	F	VF	XF	Unc	BU
2006 Proof	5,000	Value: 55.00				

KM# 221 10 EURO

34.0000 g., 0.9250 Silver 1.0111 oz. ASW, 40 mm. **Subject:** National Parks - Arkoudorema River in Southern Pindos - Valia Kalda **Obv:** National arms on stylized tree **Rev:** Outlined map at upper left, bird perched on stalk, flowers at center right **Edge:** Plain

Date	Mintage	F	VF	XF	Unc	BU
2007 Proof	5,000	Value: 60.00				

KM# 222 10 EURO

34.0000 g., 0.9250 Silver 1.0111 oz. ASW, 40 mm. **Subject:** National Parks - Valia Kalda - Southern Pindos **Obv:** National arms on stylized tree **Rev:** Tree line **Edge:** Plain

Date	Mintage	F	VF	XF	Unc	BU
2007 Proof	5,000	Value: 60.00				

KM# 223 10 EURO

9.7500 g., 0.9250 Silver 0.2899 oz. ASW, 28.25 mm. **Subject:** 30th Anniversary Death of Maria Callas, Operatic Soprano **Obv:** National arms above denomination, facsimile signature below, music scores in background **Rev:** Bust of Maria Callas right **Edge:** Plain **Shape:** Spanish Flower

Date	Mintage	F	VF	XF	Unc	BU
2007 Proof	5,000	Value: 50.00				

KM# 224 10 EURO

9.7500 g., 0.9250 Silver 0.2899 oz. ASW, 28.25 mm. **Subject:** 50th Anniversary death of Nikos Kazantzakis, Author **Obv:** National arms above denomination, facsimile signature below **Rev:** Head of N. Kazantzakis facing 3/4 left **Edge:** Plain **Shape:** Spanish Flower

Date	Mintage	F	VF	XF	Unc	BU
2007 Proof	5,000	Value: 50.00				

KM# 225 10 EURO

9.7500 g., 0.9250 Silver 0.2899 oz. ASW, 28.25 mm. **Subject:** Acropolis Museum **Obv:** Panoramic view of the Acropolis **Rev:** Pediment sculpture

Date	Mintage	F	VF	XF	Unc	BU
2008	10,000	—	—	—	—	50.00

KM# 226 10 EURO

9.7500 g., 0.9250 Silver 0.2899 oz. ASW, 28.25 mm. **Subject:** Yannis Ritsas

Date	Mintage	F	VF	XF	Unc	BU
2009 Proof	—	Value: 50.00				

KM# 228 10 EURO

9.7500 g., 0.9250 Silver 0.2899 oz. ASW, 28.25 mm. **Subject:** International Year of Astronomy

Date	Mintage	F	VF	XF	Unc	BU
2009 Proof	—	Value: 45.00				

KM# 237 10 EURO

34.0000 g., 0.9250 Silver 1.0111 oz. ASW, 40 mm. **Subject:** Sofia Vempo, 100th Anniversary of Birth **Obv:** Sofia Vempo portrait **Rev:** Stave, national emblem and value **Shape:** Spanish flower

Date	Mintage	F	VF	XF	Unc	BU
2010 Proof	5,000	Value: 65.00				

KM# 238 10 EURO

9.7500 g., 0.9250 Silver 0.2899 oz. ASW, 28.25 mm. **Subject:** International Year of Biodiversity **Obv:** Various species of Biodiversity **Rev:** Nature's species, national emblem and value **Shape:** Spanish flower

Date	Mintage	F	VF	XF	Unc	BU
2010 Proof	5,000	Value: 50.00				

KM# 240 10 EURO

9.7500 g., 0.9250 Silver 0.2899 oz. ASW, 28.25 mm. **Subject:** XIII Special Olympics, Special Olympics Founder Declaration **Obv:** Declaration over the Acropolis of Athens, Radiant Sun **Rev:** Special Olympics emblem, National arms below value **Shape:** 5 double edge notches

Date	Mintage	F	VF	XF	Unc	BU
		—	—	—	—	—
2011 Proof, In sets only	7,500	Value: 40.00				

KM# 241 10 EURO

9.7500 g., 0.9250 Silver 0.2899 oz. ASW, 28.25 mm. **Subject:** XIII Special Olympics, Athletes in Union **Obv:** Stylized athletes around a radiant sun and olive branch **Rev:** Panathenaikon Stadium below the National Arms and value **Shape:** 5 double edge notches

Date	Mintage	F	VF	XF	Unc	BU
2011	—	—	—	—	—	—
2011 Proof, in sets only	7,500	Value: 40.00				

KM# 242 10 EURO

34.1000 g., 0.9250 Silver 1.0141 oz. ASW, 40 mm. **Subject:** Special Olympics, Highlight **Obv:** Highlight from an event during the games **Rev:** Stylized elements from the XIII Special Olympics emblem in Athens, National Arms, value below **Designer:** G. Stamatopoulos

Date	Mintage	F	VF	XF	Unc	BU
2011 Proof	2,000	Value: 130				

KM# 243 10 EURO

34.1000 g., 0.9250 Silver 1.0141 oz. ASW, 40 mm. **Subject:** Special Olympics, Torch-bearer **Obv:** Torch-bearer **Rev:** Stylized elements from the XIII Special Olympics emblem in Athens, National Arms, value below **Designer:** G. Stamatopoulos

Date	Mintage	F	VF	XF	Unc	BU
2011 Proof	2,000	Value: 130				

KM# 246 10 EURO

9.7500 g., 0.9250 Silver 0.2899 oz. ASW, 28.25 mm. **Subject:** Dr. George N. Papanicolaou **Obv:** Dr. Papanicolaou and a microscope **Rev:** Shaped human cells around the national emblem and value **Shape:** 5 double edge notches

Date	Mintage	F	VF	XF	Unc	BU
2012 Prooflike, In sets only	10,000	—	—	—	—	60.00

KM# 247 10 EURO

34.1000 g., 0.9250 Silver 1.0141 oz. ASW, 40 mm. **Subject:** "Greek Culture" - Poet: Aeschylus **Obv:** Aeschylus (524-455 B.C.) portrait. **Rev:** Ancient lyrics, national emblem, value and date

Date	Mintage	F	VF	XF	Unc	BU
2012 Proof	5,000	Value: 120				

KM# 248 10 EURO

34.1000 g., 0.9250 Silver 1.0141 oz. ASW **Subject:** "Greek Culture" - Socrates **Obv:** Socrates (469-399 B.C.) portrait facing left **Rev:** Ancient sayings, national emblem, value and date

Date	Mintage	F	VF	XF	Unc	BU
2012 Proof	5,000	Value: 120				

KM# 210 20 EURO

24.0000 g., 0.9250 Silver 0.7137 oz. ASW, 37 mm. **Subject:** Bank of Greece 75th Anniversary **Obv:** Value **Rev:** Flag

Date	Mintage	F	VF	XF	Unc	BU
2003 Proof	15,000	Value: 170				

KM# 251 50 EURO

1.0000 g., 0.9999 Gold 0.0321 oz. AGW, 14 mm. **Subject:** Ancient Pella (Macedonia), Northern Greece. **Obv:** Wave and geometric pattern, ornaments of a stone slab table (Hellenistic era) found in Pella, capital of ancient Macedonia **Rev:** Wave shaped ornament of a stove slab table (Hellensitic era) found in Pella, capital of ancient Macedonia, Pella, and the national arms of Greece, value below

Date	Mintage	F	VF	XF	Unc	BU
2012 Proof	4,000	Value: 95.00				

KM# 192 100 EURO

10.0000 g., 0.9999 Gold 0.3215 oz. AGW, 25 mm. **Subject:** Olympics **Obv:** Olympic rings in wreath above value within circle of stars **Rev:** Knossos Palace **Edge:** Plain

Date	Mintage	F	VF	XF	Unc	BU
ND(2003) Proof	28,000	Value: 600				

KM# 195 100 EURO

10.0000 g., 0.9999 Gold 0.3215 oz. AGW, 25 mm. **Subject:** Olympics **Obv:** Olympic rings in wreath above value within circle of stars **Rev:** Krypte archway **Edge:** Plain

Date	Mintage	F	VF	XF	Unc	BU
ND(2003) Proof	28,000	Value: 600				

KM# 198 100 EURO

10.0000 g., 0.9999 Gold 0.3215 oz. AGW, 25 mm. **Subject:** Olympics **Obv:** Olympic rings in wreath above value within circle of stars **Rev:** Panathenean Stadium **Edge:** Plain

Date	Mintage	F	VF	XF	Unc	BU
ND(2003) Proof	28,000	Value: 600				

KM# 201 100 EURO

10.0000 g., 0.9999 Gold 0.3215 oz. AGW, 25 mm. **Subject:** Olympics **Obv:** Olympic rings in wreath above value within circle of stars **Rev:** Zappeion Mansion **Edge:** Plain

Date	Mintage	F	VF	XF	Unc	BU
ND(2003) Proof	28,000	Value: 600				

KM# 204 100 EURO

10.0000 g., 0.9999 Gold 0.3215 oz. AGW, 25 mm. **Subject:** Olympics **Obv:** Olympic rings in wreath above value within circle of stars **Rev:** Acropolis **Edge:** Plain

Date	Mintage	F	VF	XF	Unc	BU
ND(2004) Proof	28,000	Value: 600				

KM# 207 100 EURO

10.0000 g., 0.9999 Gold 0.3215 oz. AGW, 25 mm. **Subject:** Olympics **Obv:** Olympic rings in wreath above value within circle of stars **Rev:** Academy of Athens **Edge:** Plain

Date	Mintage	F	VF	XF	Unc	BU
ND(2004) Proof	28,000	Value: 600				

KM# 234 100 EURO

10.0000 g., 0.9990 Gold 0.3212 oz. AGW, 25 mm. **Rev:** Classical female handing torch to kneeling runner

Date	Mintage	F	VF	XF	Unc	BU
2004 Proof	10,000	Value: 600				

KM# 235 100 EURO

10.0000 g., 0.9990 Gold 0.3212 oz. AGW, 25 mm. **Rev:** Torch runner and flag

Date	Mintage	F	VF	XF	Unc	BU
2004 Proof	10,000	Value: 600				

KM# 244 100 EURO

7.9881 g., 0.9166 Gold 0.2354 oz. AGW, 22.1 mm. **Subject:** Special Olympics' Athletes in Union **Obv:** Stylized Athletes around a radiant sun and olive branch **Rev:** Panathenaikon Stadium below the National Arms and value **Designer:** G. Stamatopoulos

Date	Mintage	F	VF	XF	Unc	BU
2011 Proof	1,000	Value: 1,300				

KM# 249 100 EURO

7.9881 g., 0.9166 Gold 0.2354 oz. AGW, 22.1 mm. **Subject:** Liberation of Thessaloniki, 100th Anniversary **Obv:** Golden round ornament with rosette (480 B.C.) from an ancient tomb, flag of modern Greece background. **Rev:** The White Tower (symbol of Thewsaloniki) with the National Arms engraved and value, shaped laurels above

Date	Mintage	F	VF	XF	Unc	BU
2012 Proof	1,500	Value: 800				

KM# 250 100 EURO

7.9881 g., 0.9160 Gold 0.2352 oz. AGW, 22.1 mm. **Subject:** Balkan Wars outbreak, 100th Anniversary **Obv:** Admiral Parlos Kountouriotis bust, the flag of Greece on the background **Rev:** The battleship "Averoph", national arms above left and value below

Date	Mintage	F	VF	XF	Unc	BU
2012 Proof	1,500	Value: 800				

KM# 229 200 EURO

31.1050 g., 0.9990 Gold 0.9990 oz. AGW, 37 mm. **Subject:** Bank of Greece, 75th Anniversary

Date	Mintage	F	VF	XF	Unc	BU
2003 Proof	1,000	Value: 3,500				

MINT SETS

KM#	Date	Mintage	Identification	Issue Price	Mkt Val
MS6	2002 (8)	50,000	KM#181-188	—	30.00
MS7	2002F (8)	5,000	KM#181-188 Issued by Ministry of Finance	—	300
MS8	2003 (8)	—	KM#181-188	—	40.00
MS9	2003 (9)	—	KM#181-188, 208	—	80.00
MS11	2004 (8)	20,000	KM#181-188 2004 Discobole commemorating Olympic Games in Athens	—	65.00
MS12	2005 (8)	25,000	KM#181-188	—	35.00
MS13	2005 (9)	25,000	KM#181-188, 220 Mount Olympus as a National Park	—	70.00
MS14	2006 (9)	25,000	KM#181-188 (2005), 220 Aegina - Korinth set	28.00	70.00
MS15	2006 (9)	25,000	KM#181-188, 218 Patras - Cultural Capital of Europe	50.00	70.00
MS16	2007 (8)	15,000	KM#181-183, 211-215 Ancient Coins of the Aegean Sea	—	50.00
MS17	2007 (9)	15,000	KM#181-183, 211-215, 224 Nikos Kazantzakis	50.00	75.00
MS18	2007 (9)	15,000	KM#181-183, 211-215, 223 Maria Callas	50.00	95.00
MS19	2008 (8)	15,000	KM#181-183, 211-215	28.00	40.00
MS20	2008 (9)	10,000	KM#181-183, 211-215, 225	45.00	55.00
MS21	2009 (8)	7,500	KM#181-183, 211-215	28.00	45.00
MS22	2009 (9)	5,000	KM#181-183, 211-215, 226	45.00	55.00
MS23	2009 (9)	5,000	KM#181-183, 211-215, 228	45.00	55.00
MS24	2010 (8)	7,500	KM#181-183, 211-215	28.00	30.00
MS25	2010 (8)	7,500	KM#181-183, 211-214, 236	28.00	30.00
MS26	2010 (9)	5,000	KM#181-183, 211-215, 237 Sofia Vempo 100th Anniversary of Birth	45.00	80.00
MS27	2010 (9)	5,000	KM#181-183, 211-215, 238 International Year of Biodiversity	45.00	75.00
MS28	2011 (8)	15,000	KM#181-183, 211-215	28.00	40.00
MS29	2011 (9)	5,000	KM#181-183, 211-215, 239	28.00	45.00
MS30	2011 (9)	7,500	KM#181-183, 211-215, 240 Special Olympics - Declaration	45.00	70.00
MS31	2011 (9)	7,500	KM#181-183, 211-215, 241 Special Olympics - Unity	45.00	70.00
MS32	2012 (9)	10,000	KM#181-183, 211-215, 246, Dr. George Papanicolaou	45.00	65.00
MS33	2012 (8)	20,000	KM#181-183, 211-215. Santorini, the Island of Lava	28.00	40.00

PROOF SETS

KM#	Date	Mintage	Identification	Issue Price	Mkt Val
PS6	2011 (8)	2,500	KM#181-183, 211-215	115	300
PS7	2012 (9)	2,500	KM#181-183, 211-215, 245	—	250

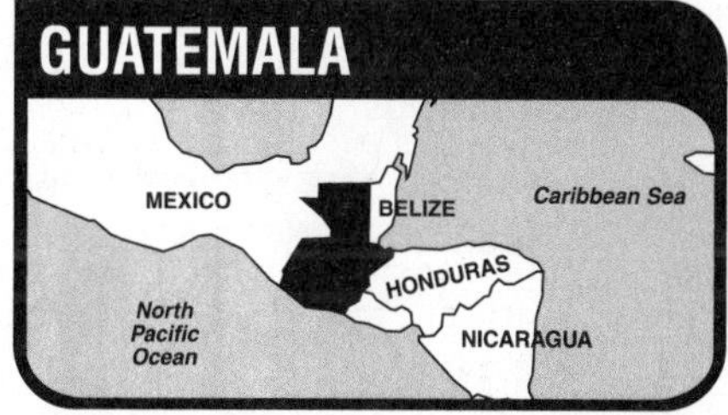

The Republic of Guatemala, the northernmost of the five Central American republics, has an area of 42,042 sq. mi. (108,890 sq. km.) and a population of 10.7 million. Capital: Guatemala City. The economy of Guatemala is heavily dependent on agriculture, however, the country is rich in nickel resources which are being developed. Coffee, cotton and bananas are exported.

Guatemala, once the site of an ancient Mayan civilization, was conquered by Pedro de Alvarado, the resourceful lieutenant of Cortes who undertook the conquest from Mexico. Cruel but strategically skillful, he progressed rapidly along the Pacific coastal lowlands to the highland plain of Quetzaltenango where the decisive battle for Guatemala was fought. After routing the Indian forces, he established the city of Guatemala in 1524. The Spanish Captaincy-General of Guatemala included all Central America but Panama. Guatemala declared its independence of Spain in 1821 and was absorbed into the Mexican empire of Augustin Iturbide (1822-23). From 1823 to 1839 Guatemala was a constituent state of the Central American Republic. Upon dissolution of that confederation, Guatemala proclaimed itself an independent republic. Like El Salvador, Guatemala suffered from internal strife between right-wing, US-backed military government and leftist indigenous peoples from ca. 1954 to ca. 1997.

MINT MARKS

(L) – London, Royal Mint

REPUBLIC

REFORM COINAGE

100 Centavos = 1 Quetzal

KM# 282 CENTAVO (Un)

0.8000 g., Aluminum, 19 mm. **Subject:** Fray Bartolome de las Casas **Obv:** National arms **Rev:** Bust left **Edge:** Plain **Note:** 7-sided interior field

Date	Mintage	F	VF	XF	Unc	BU
2007	—	—	—	0.15	0.25	0.50

KM# 276.6 5 CENTAVOS

1.6000 g., Copper-Nickel, 16 mm. **Obv:** National arms, smaller sized emblem, no dots by date **Obv. Legend:** REPUBLICA DE GUATEMALA 1997 **Rev:** Kapok tree center, value at right, ground below **Edge:** Reeded **Note:** Varieties exist.

Date	Mintage	F	VF	XF	Unc	BU
2006	—	—	—	0.15	0.30	0.50
2008	—	—	—	0.15	0.30	0.50
2009	—	—	—	0.15	0.30	0.50
2010	—	—	—	0.15	0.30	0.50

KM# 277.6 10 CENTAVOS

3.2000 g., Copper-Nickel, 21 mm. **Obv:** National arms, small letters in legend **Obv. Legend:** REPUBLICA DE GUATEMALA **Rev:** Monolith **Note:** Varieties exist.

Date	Mintage	F	VF	XF	Unc	BU
2006	—	—	0.15	0.25	0.75	1.00
2008	—	—	0.15	0.25	0.75	1.00
2009	—	—	0.15	0.25	0.75	1.00

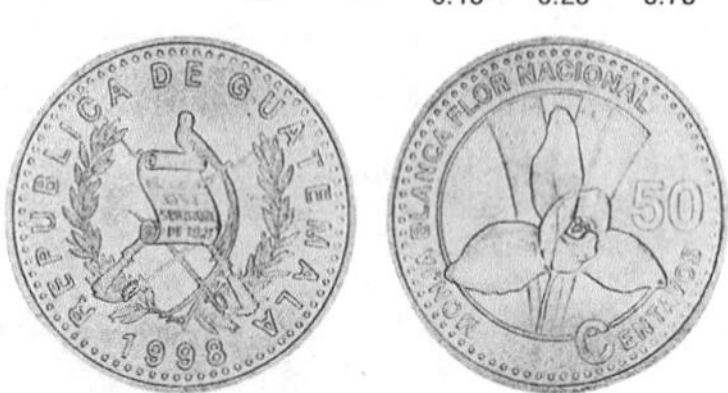

KM# 283 50 CENTAVOS

5.5000 g., Nickel-Brass, 26.5 mm. **Obv:** National arms **Rev:** Whitenun orchid (lycaste skinneri var. alba orchidaceae) **Edge:** Reeded

Date	Mintage	F	VF	XF	Unc	BU
2001	—	—	—	0.50	1.25	1.75
2007	—	—	—	0.50	1.25	1.75

KM# 284 QUETZAL

11.0000 g., Nickel-Brass, 29 mm. **Obv:** National arms **Rev:** PAZ above stylized dove **Edge:** Reeded

Date	Mintage	F	VF	XF	Unc	BU
2001 Small letters	—	—	—	1.00	2.50	3.00
2006	—	—	—	1.00	2.50	3.00
2008	—	—	—	1.00	2.50	3.00
2011	—	—	—	1.00	2.50	3.00

KM# 287 QUETZAL

31.1035 g., 0.9999 Silver 0.9999 oz. ASW, 30 mm. **Subject:** Canonization of Brother Pedro Betancourt **Obv:** National arms **Rev:** Standing monk **Edge:** Plain

Date	Mintage	F	VF	XF	Unc	BU
ND(2002) Proof	6,000	Value: 60.00				

KM# 288 QUETZAL

31.1035 g., 0.9990 Silver 0.9990 oz. ASW **Subject:** Discovery of the Americas **Obv:** Shields around inner circle holding arms with date below **Rev:** Nature with fish in canoe

Date	Mintage	F	VF	XF	Unc	BU
2002 Proof	—	Value: 60.00				

KM# 289 QUETZAL

27.0000 g., 0.9250 Silver 0.8029 oz. ASW, 40 mm. **Obv:** Arms at center surrounded by odler arms **Rev:** Ancient temple

Date	Mintage	F	VF	XF	Unc	BU
2005 Proof	—	Value: 60.00				

KM# 290 QUETZAL

27.0000 g., 0.9250 Silver 0.8029 oz. ASW, 40 mm. **Obv:** Arms surrounded by older arms **Rev:** Female dancer and figures

Date	Mintage	F	VF	XF	Unc	BU
2007 Proof	—	Value: 60.00				

KM# 291 QUETZAL

27.0000 g., 0.9250 Silver 0.8029 oz. ASW, 40 mm. **Subject:** Ibero-American series

Date	Mintage	F	VF	XF	Unc	BU
2010 Proof	—	Value: 60.00				

GUERNSEY

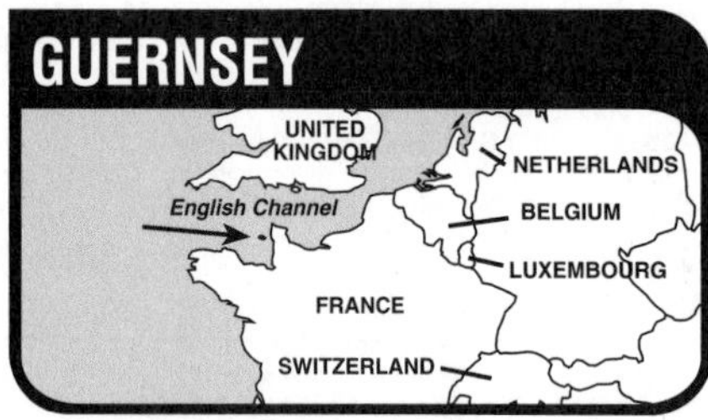

The Bailiwick of Guernsey, a British crown dependency located in the English Channel 30 miles (48 km.) west of Normandy, France, has an area of 30 sq. mi. (194 sq. km.)(including the isles of Alderney, Jethou, Herm, Brechou, and Sark), and a population of 54,000. Capital: St. Peter Port. Agriculture and cattle breeding are the main occupations.

Guernsey is administered by its own laws and customs. Unless the island is mentioned specifically, acts passed by the British Parliament are not applicable to Guernsey. During World War II, German troops occupied the island from June 30, 1940 till May 9,1945.

RULER

British

MONETARY SYSTEM

100 Pence = 1 Pound

BRITISH DEPENDENCY

DECIMAL COINAGE

KM# 89 PENNY

3.5600 g., Copper Plated Steel, 20.32 mm. **Ruler:** Elizabeth II **Obv:** Head with tiara right **Rev:** Edible crab **Edge:** Plain

Date	Mintage	F	VF	XF	Unc	BU
2003	1,302,600	—	—	—	0.35	1.00
2006	1,731,000	—	—	—	0.35	0.75

KM# 96 2 PENCE

7.1200 g., Copper Plated Steel, 25.91 mm. **Ruler:** Elizabeth II **Obv:** Head with tiara, shield at left **Rev:** Guernsey cows **Edge:** Plain

Date	Mintage	F	VF	XF	Unc	BU
2003	662,600	—	—	—	0.50	1.00
2006	1,322,000	—	—	—	0.50	1.00
2011	—	—	—	—	0.50	1.00
2012	—	—	—	—	0.50	1.00

KM# 97 5 PENCE

3.2500 g., Copper-Nickel, 18 mm. **Ruler:** Elizabeth II **Obv:** Head with tiara right **Rev:** Sailboat **Edge:** Reeded

Date	Mintage	F	VF	XF	Unc	BU
2003	292,600	—	—	—	0.45	0.65
2006	1,217,000	—	—	—	0.45	0.65
2010	—	—	—	—	0.45	0.65

KM# 97a 5 PENCE

3.2500 g., Nickel Plated Steel, 18 mm. **Ruler:** Elizabeth II **Obv:** Head with tiara right **Rev:** Sailboat **Edge:** Reeded

Date	Mintage	F	VF	XF	Unc	BU
2012	—	—	—	—	0.45	0.65

KM# 149 10 PENCE

6.5000 g., Copper-Nickel, 24.5 mm. **Ruler:** Elizabeth II **Obv:** Crowned head right **Rev:** Tomato plant **Edge:** Reeded

Date	Mintage	F	VF	XF	Unc	BU
2003	32,600	—	—	—	0.60	0.85
2006	26,000	—	—	—	0.60	0.85

KM# 149a 10 PENCE

6.5000 g., Nickel Plated Steel, 24.5 mm. **Ruler:** Elizabeth II **Obv:** Head with tiara right **Rev:** Tomato plant **Edge:** Reeded

Date	Mintage	F	VF	XF	Unc	BU
2012	—	—	—	—	0.60	0.85

KM# 90 20 PENCE

5.0000 g., Copper-Nickel, 21.4 mm. **Ruler:** Elizabeth II **Obv:** Head with tiara right, small arms at left **Rev:** Island map within cogwheel **Shape:** 7-sided

Date	Mintage	F	VF	XF	Unc	BU
2003	732,600	—	—	—	0.90	1.25
2006	16,250	—	—	—	0.90	1.25
2009	—	—	—	—	0.90	1.25

KM# 145 50 PENCE

8.0000 g., Copper-Nickel, 27.3 mm. **Ruler:** Elizabeth II **Subject:** Coronation Jubilee **Obv:** Head with tiara right **Rev:** Queen on horseback **Edge:** Plain **Shape:** 7-sided

Date	Mintage	F	VF	XF	Unc	BU
2003	—	—	—	—	1.50	2.50

KM# 145a 50 PENCE

8.1000 g., 0.9250 Silver 0.2409 oz. ASW, 27.3 mm. **Ruler:** Elizabeth II **Subject:** Coronation Jubilee **Obv:** Head with tiara right **Rev:** Queen on horseback **Edge:** Plain **Shape:** 7-sided

Date	Mintage	F	VF	XF	Unc	BU
2003 Proof	—	Value: 25.00				

KM# 146 50 PENCE

8.0000 g., Copper-Nickel, 27.3 mm. **Ruler:** Elizabeth II **Subject:** Coronation Jubilee **Obv:** Head with tiara right **Rev:** Queen on throne **Edge:** Plain **Shape:** 7-sided

Date	Mintage	F	VF	XF	Unc	BU
2003	—	—	—	—	1.50	2.50

KM# 146a 50 PENCE

8.1000 g., 0.9250 Silver 0.2409 oz. ASW, 27.3 mm. **Ruler:** Elizabeth II **Subject:** Coronation Jubilee **Obv:** Head with tiara right **Rev:** Queen on throne **Edge:** Plain **Shape:** 7-sided

Date	Mintage	F	VF	XF	Unc	BU
2003 Proof	—	Value: 25.00				

KM# 147 50 PENCE
8.0000 g., Copper-Nickel, 27.3 mm. **Ruler:** Elizabeth II **Subject:** Coronation Jubilee **Obv:** Head with tiara right **Rev:** Crown **Edge:** Plain **Shape:** 7-sided

Date	Mintage	F	VF	XF	Unc	BU
2003	—	—	—	—	1.50	2.50

KM# 147a 50 PENCE
8.1000 g., 0.9250 Silver 0.2409 oz. ASW, 27.3 mm. **Ruler:** Elizabeth II **Subject:** Coronation Jubilee **Obv:** Head with tiara right **Rev:** Crown **Edge:** Plain **Shape:** 7-sided

Date	Mintage	F	VF	XF	Unc	BU
2003 Proof	—	Value: 25.00				

KM# 148 50 PENCE
8.0000 g., Copper-Nickel, 27.3 mm. **Ruler:** Elizabeth II **Subject:** Coronation Jubilee **Obv:** Head with tiara right **Rev:** Crowned ERII monogram **Edge:** Plain **Shape:** 7-sided

Date	Mintage	F	VF	XF	Unc	BU
2003	—	—	—	—	1.50	2.50

KM# 148a 50 PENCE
8.1000 g., 0.9250 Silver 0.2409 oz. ASW, 27.3 mm. **Ruler:** Elizabeth II **Subject:** Coronation Jubilee **Obv:** Head with tiara right **Rev:** Crowned ERII monogram **Edge:** Plain **Shape:** 7-sided

Date	Mintage	F	VF	XF	Unc	BU
2003 Proof	—	Value: 25.00				

KM# 156 50 PENCE
8.0000 g., Copper-Nickel, 27.3 mm. **Ruler:** Elizabeth II **Obv:** Head with tiara right **Rev:** Crossed flowers **Edge:** Plain **Shape:** 7-sided

Date	Mintage	F	VF	XF	Unc	BU
2003	—	—	—	—	1.75	2.75
2006	19,000	—	—	—	1.75	2.75
2008	—	—	—	—	1.75	2.75

KM# 110 POUND
9.5000 g., Nickel-Brass, 22.5 mm. **Ruler:** Elizabeth II **Subject:** Circulation Type **Obv:** Head with tiara right **Rev:** Denomination **Edge:** Reeded

Date	Mintage	F	VF	XF	Unc	BU
2001	175,000	—	—	—	2.50	3.50
2003	46,600	—	—	—	2.50	3.50
2006	11,000	—	—	—	2.50	3.50

KM# 111 POUND
9.5000 g., 0.9250 Silver 0.2825 oz. ASW, 22.5 mm. **Ruler:** Elizabeth II **Subject:** Elizabeth II, 75th Birthday **Obv:** Head with tiara right **Rev:** Queen's portrait in wreath **Edge:** Reeded

Date	Mintage	F	VF	XF	Unc	BU
2001 Proof	50,000	Value: 28.00				

KM# 142 POUND
30.9300 g., 0.9250 Silver 0.9198 oz. ASW, 38.6 mm. **Ruler:** Elizabeth II **Obv:** Head with tiara right **Rev:** 1/2-bust of William, Duke of Normandy holding sword at left **Edge:** Reeded

Date	Mintage	F	VF	XF	Unc	BU
2002	—	—	—	—	40.00	50.00

KM# 83 2 POUNDS
12.0000 g., Bi-Metallic Copper-Nickel center in Nickel-Brass ring, 28.4 mm. **Ruler:** Elizabeth II **Obv:** Head with tiara right **Rev:** Latent image arms on cross **Edge:** BAILIWICK OF GUERNSEY

Date	Mintage	F	VF	XF	Unc	BU
2003	19,600	—	—	—	8.50	10.00
2006	9,500	—	—	—	8.50	10.00

KM# 106 5 POUNDS
28.2800 g., Copper-Nickel, 38.6 mm. **Ruler:** Elizabeth II **Subject:** Queen Victoria Centennial **Obv:** Head with tiara right **Rev:** Bust of Queen Victoria left **Edge:** Reeded

Date	Mintage	F	VF	XF	Unc	BU
2001	12,754	—	—	—	7.50	8.50
2001 Proof	30,000	Value: 20.00				

KM# 106a 5 POUNDS
28.2800 g., 0.9250 Silver 0.8410 oz. ASW, 38.6 mm. **Ruler:** Elizabeth II **Subject:** Queen Victoria 1837-1901 **Obv:** Head with tiara right **Rev:** Bust of Queen Victoria left **Edge:** Reeded

Date	Mintage	F	VF	XF	Unc	BU
2001 Proof	10,000	Value: 50.00				

KM# 108 5 POUNDS
28.2800 g., Copper-Nickel, 38.6 mm. **Ruler:** Elizabeth II **Subject:** Queen Elizabeth's 75th Birthday **Obv:** Head with tiara right **Rev:** Queen's portrait in wreath **Edge:** Reeded

Date	Mintage	F	VF	XF	Unc	BU
2001	14,000	—	—	—	6.00	7.00

KM# 108a 5 POUNDS
28.2800 g., 0.9250 Silver 0.8410 oz. ASW, 38.6 mm. **Ruler:** Elizabeth II **Subject:** Queen's 75th Birthday **Obv:** Head with tiara right **Rev:** Queen's portrait in wreath **Edge:** Reeded

Date	Mintage	F	VF	XF	Unc	BU
2001 Proof	20,000	Value: 55.00				

KM# 114 5 POUNDS
28.2800 g., Copper-Nickel, 38.6 mm. **Ruler:** Elizabeth II **Subject:** 19th Century Monarchy **Obv:** Head with tiara right **Rev:** Four portraits **Edge:** Reeded

Date	Mintage	F	VF	XF	Unc	BU
2001	5,700	—	—	—	11.50	12.50

KM# 114a 5 POUNDS
28.2800 g., 0.9250 Silver 0.8410 oz. ASW, 38.6 mm. **Ruler:** Elizabeth II **Obv:** Head with tiara right **Rev:** Four portraits **Edge:** Reeded

Date	Mintage	F	VF	XF	Unc	BU
2001 Proof	10,000	Value: 55.00				

KM# 106b 5 POUNDS
39.9400 g., 0.9170 Gold 1.1775 oz. AGW, 38.61 mm. **Ruler:** Elizabeth II **Subject:** Queen Victoria 1837-1901 **Obv:** Head with tiara right **Rev:** Queen Victoria's portrait **Edge:** Reeded

Date	Mintage	F	VF	XF	Unc	BU
2001 Proof	300	Value: 2,250				

KM# 108b 5 POUNDS
39.9400 g., 0.9170 Gold 1.1775 oz. AGW, 38.61 mm. **Ruler:** Elizabeth II **Subject:** Queen's 75th Birthday **Obv:** Head with tiara right **Rev:** Queen's portrait in wreath **Edge:** Reeded

Date	Mintage	F	VF	XF	Unc	BU
2001 Proof	250	Value: 2,150				

KM# 114b 5 POUNDS
39.9400 g., 0.9166 Gold 1.1770 oz. AGW, 38.6 mm. **Ruler:** Elizabeth II **Subject:** 19th Century Monarchy **Obv:** Head with tiara right **Rev:** Four royal portraits **Edge:** Reeded

Date	Mintage	F	VF	XF	Unc	BU
2001 Proof	200	Value: 2,200				

KM# 119 5 POUNDS
27.7100 g., Copper-Nickel, 38.6 mm. **Ruler:** Elizabeth II **Subject:** The Golden Jubilee **Obv:** Head with tiara right **Rev:** The queen in her coach **Edge:** Reeded

Date	Mintage	F	VF	XF	Unc	BU
2002	9,250	—	—	—	16.50	18.00

KM# 119a 5 POUNDS
28.2800 g., Base Metal Gilt Gold plated copper-nickel, 38.6 mm. **Ruler:** Elizabeth II **Subject:** Golden Jubilee **Obv:** Head with tiara right **Rev:** Queen in coach **Edge:** Reeded

Date	Mintage	F	VF	XF	Unc	BU
2002	50,000	—	—	—	15.00	16.50

KM# 119b 5 POUNDS
28.2800 g., 0.9250 Silver 0.8410 oz. ASW, 38.6 mm. **Ruler:** Elizabeth II **Subject:** Queen's Golden Jubilee **Obv:** Head with tiara right **Rev:** Queen in her coach **Edge:** Reeded **Note:** Prev. KM#119a.

Date	Mintage	F	VF	XF	Unc	BU
2002 Proof	20,000	Value: 50.00				

KM# 119c 5 POUNDS
39.9400 g., 0.9166 Gold 1.1770 oz. AGW, 38.6 mm. **Ruler:** Elizabeth II **Subject:** Golden Jubilee **Obv:** Head with tiara right **Rev:** Queen in coach **Edge:** Reeded

Date	Mintage	F	VF	XF	Unc	BU
2002 Proof	250	Value: 2,200				

KM# 121 5 POUNDS
27.7100 g., Copper-Nickel, 38.6 mm. **Ruler:** Elizabeth II **Subject:** Queen's Golden Jubilee **Obv:** Head with tiara right **Rev:** Trooping the Colors scene **Edge:** Reeded

Date	Mintage	F	VF	XF	Unc	BU
2002	2,000	—	—	—	17.50	20.00

KM# 121a 5 POUNDS
28.2800 g., 0.9250 Silver 0.8410 oz. ASW, 38.6 mm. **Ruler:** Elizabeth II **Subject:** Queen's Golden Jubilee **Obv:** Head with tiara right **Rev:** Trooping the Colors scene **Edge:** Reeded

Date	Mintage	F	VF	XF	Unc	BU
2002 Proof	20,000	Value: 50.00				

KM# 121b 5 POUNDS
39.9400 g., 0.9166 Gold 1.1770 oz. AGW, 38.6 mm. **Ruler:** Elizabeth II **Subject:** Golden Jubilee **Obv:** Head with tiara right **Rev:** Trooping the Colors scene **Edge:** Reeded

Date	Mintage	F	VF	XF	Unc	BU
2002 Proof	250	Value: 2,200				

KM# 122 5 POUNDS
28.2800 g., Copper-Nickel, 38.6 mm. **Ruler:** Elizabeth II **Subject:** Princess Diana **Obv:** Head with tiara right **Rev:** World and children behind cameo portrait of Diana **Edge:** Reeded

Date	Mintage	F	VF	XF	Unc	BU
2002	4,231	—	—	—	13.50	15.00

KM# 122a 5 POUNDS
28.2800 g., 0.9250 Silver 0.8410 oz. ASW, 38.61 mm. **Ruler:** Elizabeth II **Subject:** Princess Diana **Obv:** Head with tiara right **Rev:** World and children behind Diana's cameo portrait **Edge:** Reeded

Date	Mintage	F	VF	XF	Unc	BU
2002 Proof	20,000	Value: 45.00				

KM# 122b 5 POUNDS
39.9400 g., 0.9167 Gold 1.1771 oz. AGW, 38.61 mm. **Ruler:** Elizabeth II **Subject:** Princess Diana **Obv:** Head with tiara right **Rev:** World and children behind Diana's cameo portrait **Edge:** Reeded

Date	Mintage	F	VF	XF	Unc	BU
2002 Proof	100	Value: 2,250				

KM# 124 5 POUNDS
28.2800 g., Copper-Nickel, 38.6 mm. **Ruler:** Elizabeth II **Subject:** 18th Century British Monarchy **Obv:** Head with tiara right **Rev:** Five royal portraits **Edge:** Reeded

Date	Mintage	F	VF	XF	Unc	BU
2002	1,300	—	—	—	15.00	16.50

KM# 124a 5 POUNDS
28.2800 g., 0.9250 Silver 0.8410 oz. ASW, 38.6 mm. **Ruler:** Elizabeth II **Subject:** 18th Century British Monarchy **Obv:** Head with tiara right **Rev:** Five royal portraits **Edge:** Reeded

Date	Mintage	F	VF	XF	Unc	BU
2002 Proof	10,000	Value: 50.00				

KM# 124b 5 POUNDS
39.9400 g., 0.9166 Gold 1.1770 oz. AGW, 38.6 mm. **Ruler:** Elizabeth II **Subject:** 18th Century British Monarchy **Obv:** Head with tiara right **Rev:** Five royal portraits **Edge:** Reeded

Date	Mintage	F	VF	XF	Unc	BU
2002 Proof	200	Value: 2,200				

KM# 127 5 POUNDS
28.2800 g., Copper-Nickel, 38.6 mm. **Ruler:** Elizabeth II **Subject:** Queen Mother **Obv:** Head with tiara right **Rev:** The late Queen Mother's portrait **Edge:** Reeded

Date	Mintage	F	VF	XF	Unc	BU
2002	1,750	—	—	—	15.00	16.50
2002 Proof	1,680	Value: 20.00				

KM# 127a 5 POUNDS
28.2800 g., 0.9250 Silver 0.8410 oz. ASW, 38.6 mm. **Ruler:** Elizabeth II **Subject:** Queen Mother **Obv:** Head with tiara right **Rev:** The late Queen Mother's portrait **Edge:** Reeded

Date	Mintage	F	VF	XF	Unc	BU
2002 Proof	15,000	Value: 50.00				

KM# 127b 5 POUNDS
39.9400 g., 0.9166 Gold 1.1770 oz. AGW, 38.6 mm. **Ruler:** Elizabeth II **Subject:** Queen Mother **Obv:** Head with tiara right **Rev:** Queen Mother's portrait **Edge:** Reeded

Date	Mintage	F	VF	XF	Unc	BU
2002 Proof	250	Value: 2,200				

KM# 129 5 POUNDS
28.2800 g., Copper-Nickel, 38.6 mm. **Ruler:** Elizabeth II **Subject:** The Duke of Wellington **Obv:** Head with tiara right **Rev:** Portrait with mounted dragoons in background **Edge:** Reeded

Date	Mintage	F	VF	XF	Unc	BU
2002	675	—	—	—	22.50	25.00

KM# 129a 5 POUNDS
28.2800 g., 0.9250 Silver 0.8410 oz. ASW, 38.6 mm. **Ruler:** Elizabeth II **Subject:** The Duke of Wellington **Obv:** Head with tiara right **Rev:** Portrait with multicolor mounted dragoons in background **Edge:** Reeded

Date	Mintage	F	VF	XF	Unc	BU
2002 Proof	15,000	Value: 50.00				

KM# 129b 5 POUNDS
39.9400 g., 0.9166 Gold 1.1770 oz. AGW, 38.6 mm. **Ruler:** Elizabeth II **Subject:** Duke of Wellington **Obv:** Head with tiara right **Rev:** Wellington's portrait with multicolor cavalry scene **Edge:** Reeded

Date	Mintage	F	VF	XF	Unc	BU
2002 Proof	200	Value: 2,200				

KM# 158 5 POUNDS
28.2800 g., Copper-Nickel, 38.7 mm. **Ruler:** Elizabeth II **Subject:** Golden Hind **Obv:** Head with tiara right **Rev:** The Golden Hind ship **Edge:** Reeded

Date	Mintage	F	VF	XF	Unc	BU
2003	300	—	—	—	—	25.00

KM# 159 5 POUNDS
Copper-Nickel **Ruler:** Elizabeth II **Subject:** 17th Century Monarchs **Obv:** Head with tiara right

Date	Mintage	F	VF	XF	Unc	BU
2003	500	—	—	—	—	22.50

KM# 160 5 POUNDS
Copper-Nickel **Ruler:** Elizabeth II **Subject:** Royal Navy - H. Nelson **Obv:** Head with tiara right

Date	Mintage	F	VF	XF	Unc	BU
2003	550	—	—	—	—	22.50

KM# 143 5 POUNDS
28.2800 g., Copper-Nickel, 38.6 mm. **Ruler:** Elizabeth II **Obv:** Head with tiara right **Rev:** Prince William wearing sweater **Edge:** Reeded

Date	Mintage	F	VF	XF	Unc	BU
2003	3,700	—	—	—	17.50	20.00

KM# 143a 5 POUNDS
28.2800 g., 0.9250 Silver 0.8410 oz. ASW, 38.6 mm. **Ruler:** Elizabeth II **Obv:** Head with tiara right **Rev:** Prince William wearing sweater **Edge:** Reeded

Date	Mintage	F	VF	XF	Unc	BU
2003 Proof	5,000	Value: 50.00				

KM# 143b 5 POUNDS
39.9400 g., 0.9166 Gold 1.1770 oz. AGW, 38.6 mm. **Ruler:** Elizabeth II **Obv:** Head with tiara right **Rev:** Prince William wearing sweater **Edge:** Reeded

Date	Mintage	F	VF	XF	Unc	BU
2003 Proof	200	Value: 2,200				

KM# 160a 5 POUNDS
28.3200 g., Nickel-Brass, 38 mm. **Ruler:** Elizabeth II **Subject:** History of the Royal Navy **Rev:** Two naval vessels and Horatio Nelson, flag in color

Date	Mintage	F	VF	XF	Unc	BU
2003 Proof	—	Value: 40.00				

KM# 160b 5 POUNDS
39.9400 g., 0.9170 Gold 1.1775 oz. AGW, 38.61 mm. **Ruler:** Elizabeth II **Subject:** History of the Navy - Horatio Nelson

Date	Mintage	F	VF	XF	Unc	BU
2003 Proof	—	Value: 2,150				

KM# 161 5 POUNDS
Copper-Nickel **Ruler:** Elizabeth II **Subject:** 16th Century Monarchs **Obv:** Head with tiara right

Date	Mintage	F	VF	XF	Unc	BU
2004	500	—	—	—	—	22.50

KM# 162 5 POUNDS
Copper-Nickel **Ruler:** Elizabeth II **Subject:** Mallard Locomotive **Obv:** Head with tiara right

Date	Mintage	F	VF	XF	Unc	BU
2004	2,193	—	—	—	—	17.50

KM# 163 5 POUNDS
Copper-Nickel **Ruler:** Elizabeth II **Subject:** City of Truro Train **Obv:** Head with tiara right

Date	Mintage	F	VF	XF	Unc	BU
2004	500	—	—	—	—	22.50

KM# 164 5 POUNDS
Copper-Nickel **Ruler:** Elizabeth II **Subject:** The Boat Train **Obv:** Head with tiara right

Date	Mintage	F	VF	XF	Unc	BU
2004	250	—	—	—	—	25.00

KM# 165 5 POUNDS
Copper-Nickel **Ruler:** Elizabeth II **Subject:** Train Spotter **Obv:** Head with tiara right

Date	Mintage	F	VF	XF	Unc	BU
2004	300	—	—	—	—	25.00

KM# 166 5 POUNDS
Copper-Nickel **Ruler:** Elizabeth II **Subject:** Royal Navy - Henry VIII **Obv:** Head with tiara right

Date	Mintage	F	VF	XF	Unc	BU
2004	300	—	—	—	—	25.00

KM# 167 5 POUNDS
Copper-Nickel **Ruler:** Elizabeth II **Subject:** Royal Navy - Invincible **Obv:** Head with tiara right

Date	Mintage	F	VF	XF	Unc	BU
2004	300	—	—	—	—	25.00

KM# 150 5 POUNDS
28.2800 g., Copper-Nickel, 38.6 mm. **Ruler:** Elizabeth II **Subject:** D-Day **Obv:** Head with tiara right **Rev:** British troops storming ashore **Edge:** Reeded

Date	Mintage	F	VF	XF	Unc	BU
2004	65,611	—	—	—	15.00	16.50

KM# 154 5 POUNDS
28.2800 g., 0.9250 Silver 0.8410 oz. ASW, 38.6 mm. **Ruler:** Elizabeth II **Subject:** D-Day **Obv:** Head with tiara right **Rev:** British soldier advancing to left **Edge:** Reeded

Date	Mintage	F	VF	XF	Unc	BU
2004 Proof	10,000	Value: 85.00				

KM# 154a 5 POUNDS
39.9400 g., 0.9167 Gold 1.1771 oz. AGW, 38.6 mm. **Ruler:** Elizabeth II **Subject:** D-Day **Obv:** Head with tiara right **Rev:** British soldier advancing to left **Edge:** Reeded

Date	Mintage	F	VF	XF	Unc	BU
2004 Proof	500	Value: 2,100				

KM# 155 5 POUNDS
28.2800 g., Copper-Nickel, 38.6 mm. **Ruler:** Elizabeth II **Subject:** 150th Anniversary of the Crimean War **Obv:** Head with tiara right **Rev:** Sgt. Luke O'Connor , first army Victoria Cross winner, above Battle of Alma scene with multicolor flag **Edge:** Reeded

Date	Mintage	F	VF	XF	Unc	BU
2004 plain	—	—	—	—	25.00	27.50
2004 partial color	1,060	—	—	—	25.00	27.50

KM# 155a 5 POUNDS
28.2800 g., 0.9250 Silver 0.8410 oz. ASW, 38.6 mm. **Ruler:** Elizabeth II **Obv:** Head with tiara right **Rev:** Sgt. Luke O'Conner, first army Victoria Cross winner, above Battle of Alma scene with multicolor flag **Edge:** Reeded

Date	Mintage	F	VF	XF	Unc	BU
2004 Proof	10,000	Value: 85.00				

KM# 155b 5 POUNDS
39.9400 g., 0.9166 Gold 1.1770 oz. AGW, 38.6 mm. **Ruler:** Elizabeth II **Obv:** Head with tiara right **Rev:** Sgt. Luke O'Connor, first army Victoria Cross winner, above Battle of Alma scene with multicolor flag **Edge:** Reeded

Date	Mintage	F	VF	XF	Unc	BU
2004 Proof	500	Value: 2,100				

KM# 176 5 POUNDS
28.3200 g., Silver, 38 mm. **Ruler:** Elizabeth II **Subject:** History of the Royal Navy **Rev:** HMS Invincible, flag in color

Date	Mintage	F	VF	XF	Unc	BU
2004 Proof	—	Value: 50.00				

KM# 130 5 POUNDS
28.2800 g., Copper-Nickel, 38.61 mm. **Ruler:** Elizabeth II **Subject:** Steam Locomotives **Rev:** Tower switchman at leavers

Date	Mintage	F	VF	XF	Unc	BU
2004	—	—	—	—	—	25.00

KM# 130a 5 POUNDS
28.2800 g., 0.9250 Silver 0.8410 oz. ASW, 38.61 mm. **Ruler:** Elizabeth II **Subject:** Steam Locomotives **Rev:** Tower switchman at leavers

Date	Mintage	F	VF	XF	Unc	BU
2004 Proof	Est. 10,000	Value: 60.00				

KM# 133 5 POUNDS
28.2800 g., Copper-Nickel, 38.61 mm. **Ruler:** Elizabeth II **Subject:** Steam Locomotives **Rev:** Two locomotives side-by-side view of tender being refilled with water, and fireman shoveling coal

Date	Mintage	F	VF	XF	Unc	BU
2004	—	—	—	—	—	25.00

KM# 133a 5 POUNDS
28.2800 g., 0.9250 Silver 0.8410 oz. ASW, 38.61 mm. **Ruler:** Elizabeth II **Subject:** Steam Locomotives **Rev:** Two locomotives side-by-side view of tender being refilled with water, and fireman shoveling coal

Date	Mintage	F	VF	XF	Unc	BU
2004 Proof	Est. 10,000	Value: 60.00				

KM# 168a 5 POUNDS
28.2800 g., 0.9250 Silver 0.8410 oz. ASW, 38.6 mm. **Ruler:** Elizabeth II **Subject:** End of WWII **Obv:** Head with tiara right **Rev:** Churchill and George VI **Edge:** Reeded

Date	Mintage	F	VF	XF	Unc	BU
2005 Proof	5,000	Value: 85.00				

KM# 168b 5 POUNDS
39.9400 g., 0.9167 Gold 1.1771 oz. AGW, 38.6 mm. **Ruler:** Elizabeth II **Subject:** End of WWII **Obv:** Head with tiara right **Rev:** Churchill and George VI **Edge:** Reeded

Date	Mintage	F	VF	XF	Unc	BU
2005 Proof	150	Value: 2,250				

KM# 169a 5 POUNDS
39.9400 g., 0.9167 Gold 1.1771 oz. AGW, 38.6 mm. **Ruler:** Elizabeth II **Subject:** WWII Liberation **Obv:** Head with tiara right **Rev:** Soldiers and waving crowd **Edge:** Reeded

Date	Mintage	F	VF	XF	Unc	BU
2005 Proof	150	Value: 2,250				

KM# 186 5 POUNDS
28.2800 g., Copper-Nickel, 38.61 mm. **Ruler:** Elizabeth II **Subject:** Royal Navy - Sir John Jellicoe

Date	Mintage	F	VF	XF	Unc	BU
2005	—	—	—	—	—	17.50

KM# 186a 5 POUNDS
28.2800 g., 0.9250 Silver 0.8410 oz. ASW, 38.61 mm. **Ruler:** Elizabeth II **Subject:** Royal Navy - Sir John Jellicoe **Rev:** Flag in color

Date	Mintage	F	VF	XF	Unc	BU
2005 Proof	Est. 15,000	Value: 60.00				

KM# 187 5 POUNDS
28.2800 g., Copper-Nickel, 38.61 mm. **Ruler:** Elizabeth II **Subject:** Royal Navy **Rev:** H.M.S. Ark Royal

Date	Mintage	F	VF	XF	Unc	BU
2005	—	—	—	—	—	17.50

KM# 187a 5 POUNDS
28.2800 g., 0.9250 Silver 0.8410 oz. ASW, 38.61 mm. **Ruler:** Elizabeth II **Subject:** Royal Navy **Rev:** H.M.S. Ark Royal, flag in color

Date	Mintage	F	VF	XF	Unc	BU
2005 Proof	Est. 15,000	Value: 60.00				

KM# 189 5 POUNDS
28.2800 g., Copper-Nickel, 38.61 mm. **Ruler:** Elizabeth II **Subject:** Battle of Trafalgar, 200th Anniversary **Rev:** H.M.S. Victory

Date	Mintage	F	VF	XF	Unc	BU
2005	—	—	—	—	—	17.50

KM# 189a 5 POUNDS
28.2800 g., 0.9250 Silver 0.8410 oz. ASW, 38.61 mm. **Ruler:** Elizabeth II **Subject:** Battle of Trafalgar, 200th Anniversary **Rev:** H.M.S. Victory

Date	Mintage	F	VF	XF	Unc	BU
2005 Proof	—	Value: 60.00				

KM# 189b 5 POUNDS
39.9400 g., 0.9170 Gold 1.1775 oz. AGW, 38.61 mm. **Ruler:** Elizabeth II **Subject:** Battle of Trafalgar, 200th Anniversary **Rev:** H.M.S. Victory

Date	Mintage	F	VF	XF	Unc	BU
2005 Proof	—	Value: 2,250				

KM# 170 5 POUNDS
28.2800 g., 0.9250 Silver 0.8410 oz. ASW, 38.6 mm. **Ruler:** Elizabeth II **Subject:** Queen's 80th Birthday **Obv:** Head with tiara right - gilt **Obv. Legend:** ELIZABETH II BAILIWICK OF GUERNSEY **Rev:** Bust at left looking upwards, tower and florals at upper right

Date	Mintage	F	VF	XF	Unc	BU
2006 Proof	—	Value: 45.00				

KM# 173 5 POUNDS
28.2800 g., 0.9250 Silver 0.8410 oz. ASW, 22 mm. **Ruler:** Elizabeth II **Subject:** FIFA - XVIII World Football Championship - Germany 2006 **Rev:** Wembley Stadium

Date	Mintage	F	VF	XF	Unc	BU
2006 Proof	50,000	Value: 65.00				

KM# 130b 5 POUNDS
28.2800 g., 0.9250 Silver selectively gilt 0.8410 oz. ASW, 38.61 mm. **Ruler:** Elizabeth II **Subject:** Steam Locomotives **Rev:** Tower Switchmen at leavers

Date	Mintage	F	VF	XF	Unc	BU
2006 Proof	25,000	Value: 60.00				

KM# 133b 5 POUNDS
28.2800 g., 0.9250 Silver partially gilt 0.8410 oz. ASW, 38.61 mm. **Ruler:** Elizabeth II **Subject:** Steam Locomotives **Rev:** Two locomotives side-by-side view of tender being refilled with water, and fireman shoveling coal

Date	Mintage	F	VF	XF	Unc	BU
2006 Proof	Est. 25,000	Value: 60.00				

KM# 191 5 POUNDS
28.2800 g., Copper-Nickel, 38.61 mm. **Ruler:** Elizabeth II **Rev:** Horatio Nelson

Date	Mintage	F	VF	XF	Unc	BU
2006	—	—	—	—	—	15.00

KM# 191a 5 POUNDS
28.2800 g., 0.9250 Silver 0.8410 oz. ASW, 38.61 mm. **Ruler:** Elizabeth II **Rev:** Horatio Nelson

Date	Mintage	F	VF	XF	Unc	BU
2006 Proof	25,000	Value: 60.00				

KM# 192 5 POUNDS
28.2800 g., Copper-Nickel, 38.61 mm. **Ruler:** Elizabeth II **Rev:** Isambard Kingdom Brunel

Date	Mintage	F	VF	XF	Unc	BU
2006	—	—	—	—	—	15.00

KM# 192a 5 POUNDS
28.2800 g., 0.9250 Silver 0.8410 oz. ASW, 38.61 mm. **Ruler:** Elizabeth II **Rev:** Isambard Kingdom Brunel

Date	Mintage	F	VF	XF	Unc	BU
2006 Proof	25,000	Value: 60.00				

KM# 193 5 POUNDS
28.2800 g., 0.9250 Silver 0.8410 oz. ASW, 38.61 mm. **Ruler:** Elizabeth II **Rev:** Robert Falcon Scott

Date	Mintage	F	VF	XF	Unc	BU
2006 Proof	25,000	Value: 60.00				

KM# 194 5 POUNDS
28.2800 g., 0.9250 Silver 0.8410 oz. ASW, 38.61 mm. **Ruler:** Elizabeth II **Rev:** Queen Victoria

Date	Mintage	F	VF	XF	Unc	BU
2006 Proof	25,000	Value: 60.00				

KM# 195 5 POUNDS
28.2800 g., Copper-Nickel, 38.61 mm. **Ruler:** Elizabeth II **Subject:** Elizabeth II, 80th Birthday **Rev:** Elizabeth II and Queen Mother

Date	Mintage	F	VF	XF	Unc	BU
2006	—	—	—	—	—	15.00

KM# 195a 5 POUNDS
28.2800 g., 0.9250 Silver partially gilt 0.8410 oz. ASW, 38.61 mm. **Ruler:** Elizabeth II **Subject:** Elizabeth II, 80th Birthday **Rev:** Elizabeth II and Queen Mother, gilt

Date	Mintage	F	VF	XF	Unc	BU
2006 Proof	25,000	Value: 60.00				

KM# 196 5 POUNDS
28.2800 g., 0.9250 Silver 0.8410 oz. ASW, 38.61 mm. **Ruler:** Elizabeth II **Subject:** Elizabeth II, 80th Birthday **Rev:** Elizabeth II portrait by Mary Gillick

Date	Mintage	F	VF	XF	Unc	BU
2006 Proof	—	Value: 60.00				

KM# 196a 5 POUNDS
39.9400 g., 0.9170 Gold 1.1775 oz. AGW, 8.61 mm. **Ruler:** Elizabeth II **Subject:** Elizabeth II, 80th Birthday **Rev:** Elizabeth II portrait by Mary Gillick

Date	Mintage	F	VF	XF	Unc	BU
2006 Proof	—	Value: 2,250				

KM# 197 5 POUNDS
28.2800 g., Copper-Nickel, 38.61 mm. **Ruler:** Elizabeth II **Subject:** Victoria Cross, 150th Anniversary **Rev:** Herbert Wallace le Patourel

Date	Mintage	F	VF	XF	Unc	BU
2006	—	—	—	—	—	15.00

KM# 197a 5 POUNDS
28.2800 g., 0.9250 Silver 0.8410 oz. ASW, 38.61 mm. **Ruler:** Elizabeth II **Subject:** Victoria Cross, 150th Anniversary **Rev:** Herbert Wallace le Patourel

Date	Mintage	F	VF	XF	Unc	BU
2006 Proof	Est. 30,000	Value: 60.00				

KM# 198 5 POUNDS
28.2800 g., 0.9250 Silver 0.8410 oz. ASW, 38.61 mm. **Ruler:** Elizabeth II **Subject:** Victoria Cross, 150th Anniversary **Rev:** Victor Buller Turner

Date	Mintage	F	VF	XF	Unc	BU
2006 Proof	Est. 30,000	Value: 60.00				

KM# 199 5 POUNDS
28.2800 g., 0.9250 Silver 0.8410 oz. ASW, 38.61 mm. **Ruler:** Elizabeth II **Subject:** Victoria Cross, 150th Anniversary **Rev:** William Leefe Robinson

Date	Mintage	F	VF	XF	Unc	BU
2006 Proof	30,000	Value: 60.00				

KM# 200 5 POUNDS
28.2800 g., 0.9250 Silver 0.8410 oz. ASW, 38.61 mm. **Ruler:** Elizabeth II **Subject:** Victoria Cross, 150th Anniversary **Rev:** Gerard Roope

Date	Mintage	F	VF	XF	Unc	BU
2006 Proof	Est. 30,000	Value: 60.00				

KM# 201 5 POUNDS
28.2800 g., 0.9250 Silver 0.8410 oz. ASW, 38.61 mm. **Ruler:** Elizabeth II **Subject:** Victoria Cross, 150th Anniversary **Rev:** Robert Henry Cain

Date	Mintage	F	VF	XF	Unc	BU
2006 Proof	Est. 30,000	Value: 60.00				

KM# 202 5 POUNDS
28.2800 g., 0.9250 Silver 0.8410 oz. ASW, 38.61 mm. **Ruler:** Elizabeth II **Subject:** Victoria Cross, 150th Anniversary **Rev:** Eugene Esmonde

Date	Mintage	F	VF	XF	Unc	BU
2006 Proof	Est. 30,000	Value: 60.00				

KM# 203 5 POUNDS
28.2800 g., 0.9250 Silver 0.8410 oz. ASW, 38.61 mm. **Ruler:** Elizabeth II **Rev:** Sir Alexander Fleming

Date	Mintage	F	VF	XF	Unc	BU
2007 Proof	25,000	Value: 55.00				

KM# 204 5 POUNDS
28.2800 g., 0.9250 Silver 0.8410 oz. ASW, 38.61 mm. **Ruler:** Elizabeth II **Rev:** Montgomery

Date	Mintage	F	VF	XF	Unc	BU
2007 Proof	Est. 25,000	Value: 55.00				

KM# 205 5 POUNDS
28.2800 g., 0.9250 Silver 0.8410 oz. ASW, 38.61 mm. **Ruler:** Elizabeth II **Rev:** Oliver Cromwell

Date	Mintage	F	VF	XF	Unc	BU
2007 Proof	Est. 25,000	Value: 55.00				

KM# 206 5 POUNDS
28.2800 g., 0.9250 Silver 0.8410 oz. ASW, 38.61 mm. **Ruler:** Elizabeth II **Rev:** Alexander Graham Bell

Date	Mintage	F	VF	XF	Unc	BU
2007 Proof	Est. 25,000	Value: 55.00				

KM# 207 5 POUNDS
28.2800 g., Copper-Nickel, 38.61 mm. **Ruler:** Elizabeth II **Subject:** Elizabeth II and Prince Philip, 60th Wedding Anniversary **Rev:** Busts

Date	Mintage	F	VF	XF	Unc	BU
2007	—	—	—	—	—	15.00

KM# 207a 5 POUNDS
28.2800 g., 0.9250 Silver 0.8410 oz. ASW, 38.61 mm. **Ruler:** Elizabeth II **Subject:** Elizabeth II and Prince Philip, 60th Wedding Anniversary **Rev:** Busts

Date	Mintage	F	VF	XF	Unc	BU
2007 Proof	—	Value: 55.00				

KM# 208 5 POUNDS
28.2800 g., Copper-Nickel, 38.61 mm. **Ruler:** Elizabeth II **Subject:** Elizabeth II and Prince Philip, 60th Wedding Anniversary **Rev:** Honeymoon

Date	Mintage	F	VF	XF	Unc	BU
2007	—	—	—	—	—	15.00

KM# 208a 5 POUNDS
28.2800 g., 0.9250 Silver 0.8410 oz. ASW, 38.61 mm. **Ruler:** Elizabeth II **Subject:** Elizabeth II and Prince Philip, 60th Wedding Anniversary **Rev:** Honeymoon

Date	Mintage	F	VF	XF	Unc	BU
2007 Proof	—	Value: 55.00				

KM# 209 5 POUNDS
28.2800 g., Copper-Nickel, 38.61 mm. **Ruler:** Elizabeth II **Subject:** Elizabeth II and Prince Philip, 60th Wedding Anniversary **Rev:** Bouquet

Date	Mintage	F	VF	XF	Unc	BU
2007	—	—	—	—	—	15.00

KM# 209a 5 POUNDS
28.2800 g., 0.9250 Silver 0.8410 oz. ASW, 38.61 mm. **Ruler:** Elizabeth II **Subject:** Elizabeth II and Prince Philip, 60th Wedding Anniversary **Rev:** Bouquet

Date	Mintage	F	VF	XF	Unc	BU
2007 Proof	—	Value: 55.00				

KM# 210 5 POUNDS
28.2800 g., 0.9250 Copper-Nickel 0.8410 oz., 38.61 mm. **Ruler:** Elizabeth II **Subject:** Elizabeth II and Prince Philip, 60th Wedding Anniversary **Rev:** Wedding scene

Date	Mintage	F	VF	XF	Unc	BU
2007	—	—	—	—	—	15.00

KM# 210a 5 POUNDS
28.2800 g., 0.9250 Silver 0.8410 oz. ASW, 38.61 mm. **Ruler:** Elizabeth II **Subject:** Elizabeth II and Prince Philip, 60th Wedding Anniversary **Rev:** Wedding scene

Date	Mintage	F	VF	XF	Unc	BU
2007 Proof	—	Value: 55.00				

KM# 217 5 POUNDS
28.2800 g., 0.9250 Silver 0.8410 oz. ASW, 38.61 mm. **Ruler:** Elizabeth II **Subject:** Royal Air Force, 90th Anniversary **Rev:** Gulf War

Date	Mintage	F	VF	XF	Unc	BU
2008 Proof	Est. 25,000	Value: 55.00				

KM# 179 5 POUNDS
28.2800 g., Copper-Nickel, 38.61 mm. **Ruler:** Elizabeth II **Subject:** Royal Air Force, 90th Anniversary **Obv:** Head with tiara right **Rev:** Air battle

Date	Mintage	F	VF	XF	Unc	BU
2008	—	—	—	—	—	15.00

KM# 179a 5 POUNDS
28.2800 g., 0.9250 Silver 0.8410 oz. ASW, 38.61 mm. **Ruler:** Elizabeth II **Subject:** Royal Air Force, 90th Anniversary **Rev:** Air battle

Date	Mintage	F	VF	XF	Unc	BU
2008 Proof	Est. 25,000	Value: 55.00				

KM# 211 5 POUNDS
28.2800 g., Copper-Nickel, 38.61 mm. **Ruler:** Elizabeth II **Subject:** Royal Air Force, 90th Anniversary **Rev:** Lancaster bomber

Date	Mintage	F	VF	XF	Unc	BU
2008	—	—	—	—	—	15.00

KM# 211a 5 POUNDS
28.2800 g., 0.9250 Silver 0.8410 oz. ASW, 38.61 mm. **Ruler:** Elizabeth II **Subject:** Royal Air Force, 90th Anniversary **Rev:** Lancaster bomber

Date	Mintage	F	VF	XF	Unc	BU
2008 Proof	Est. 25,000	Value: 55.00				

KM# 212 5 POUNDS
28.2800 g., 0.9250 Silver 0.8410 oz. ASW, 38.61 mm. **Ruler:** Elizabeth II **Subject:** Royal Air Force, 90th Anniversary **Rev:** Founding of the Air Force, 1918

Date	Mintage	F	VF	XF	Unc	BU
2008 Proof	Est. 25,000	Value: 55.00				

KM# 213 5 POUNDS
28.2800 g., 0.9250 Silver 0.8410 oz. ASW, 38.61 mm. **Ruler:** Elizabeth II **Subject:** Royal Air Force, 90th Anniversary **Rev:** Berlin Airlift, 1949

Date	Mintage	F	VF	XF	Unc	BU
2008 Proof	Est. 25,000	Value: 55.00				

KM# 214 5 POUNDS
28.2800 g., 0.9250 Silver 0.8410 oz. ASW, 38.61 mm. **Ruler:** Elizabeth II **Subject:** Royal Air Force, 90th Anniversary **Rev:** Monarchy

Date	Mintage	F	VF	XF	Unc	BU
2008 Proof	Est. 25,000	Value: 55.00				

KM# 215 5 POUNDS
28.2800 g., 0.9250 Silver 0.8410 oz. ASW, 38.61 mm. **Ruler:** Elizabeth II **Subject:** Royal Air Force, 90th Anniversary **Rev:** Schneider Trophy

Date	Mintage	F	VF	XF	Unc	BU
2008 Proof	Est. 25,000	Value: 55.00				

KM# 216 5 POUNDS
28.2800 g., 0.9250 Silver 0.8410 oz. ASW, 38.61 mm. **Ruler:** Elizabeth II **Subject:** Royal Air Force, 90th Anniversary **Rev:** Falkland Islands War, 1982

Date	Mintage	F	VF	XF	Unc	BU
2008 Proof	Est. 25,000	Value: 55.00				

KM# 219 5 POUNDS
28.2800 g., Copper-Nickel, 38.61 mm. **Ruler:** Elizabeth II **Subject:** British Warships **Rev:** H.M.S. Daring, drestoyer

Date	Mintage	F	VF	XF	Unc	BU
2009	—	—	—	—	—	15.00

KM# 219a 5 POUNDS
28.2800 g., 0.9250 Silver 0.8410 oz. ASW, 38.61 mm. **Ruler:** Elizabeth II **Subject:** British Warships **Rev:** H.M.S. Daring, destroyer

Date	Mintage	F	VF	XF	Unc	BU
2009 Proof	Est. 25,000	Value: 55.00				

KM# 220 5 POUNDS
28.2800 g., Copper-Nickel, 38.61 mm. **Ruler:** Elizabeth II **Subject:** British Warships **Rev:** H.M.S. Mary Rose, 1511

Date	Mintage	F	VF	XF	Unc	BU
2009	—	—	—	—	—	15.00

KM# 220a 5 POUNDS
28.2800 g., 0.9250 Silver 0.8410 oz. ASW, 38.61 mm. **Ruler:** Elizabeth II **Subject:** British Warships **Rev:** H.M.S. Mary Rose, 1511

Date	Mintage	F	VF	XF	Unc	BU
2009 Proof	25,000	Value: 55.00				

KM# 222 5 POUNDS
28.2800 g., Copper-Nickel, 38.61 mm. **Ruler:** Elizabeth II **Subject:** British Aircraft carriers, 100th Anniversary **Rev:** H.M.S. Ark Royal IV with combat aircraft

Date	Mintage	F	VF	XF	Unc	BU
2009	—	—	—	—	—	15.00

KM# 222a 5 POUNDS
28.2800 g., 0.9250 Silver 0.8410 oz. ASW, 38.61 mm. **Ruler:** Elizabeth II **Subject:** British Aircraft Carrier, 100th Anniversary **Rev:** H.M.S. Royal Ark VI and fighter aircraft

Date	Mintage	F	VF	XF	Unc	BU
2009 Proof	—	Value: 55.00				

KM# 223 5 POUNDS
28.2800 g., 0.9250 Copper-Nickel 0.8410 oz., 38.61 mm. **Ruler:** Elizabeth II **Subject:** Apollo 11 moon landing, 40th Anniversary **Rev:** Lunar Module Eagle and moon in color

Date	Mintage	F	VF	XF	Unc	BU
2009	—	—	—	—	—	15.00

KM# 223a 5 POUNDS
28.2800 g., 0.9250 Silver 0.8410 oz. ASW, 38.61 mm. **Ruler:** Elizabeth II **Subject:** Apollo 11 moon landing, 40th Anniversary **Rev:** Lunar module Eagle and moon

Date	Mintage	F	VF	XF	Unc	BU
2009 Proof	—	Value: 55.00				

KM# 225 5 POUNDS
28.2800 g., Copper-Nickel, 38.61 mm. **Ruler:** Elizabeth II **Subject:** Decimialization, 40th Anniversary **Rev:** Coins in color

Date	Mintage	F	VF	XF	Unc	BU
2011 Proof	—	Value: 17.50				

KM# 226 5 POUNDS
28.2800 g., Copper-Nickel, 38.61 mm. **Ruler:** Elizabeth II **Subject:** Royal Wedding **Rev:** Prince William and Catherine Middleton

Date	Mintage	F	VF	XF	Unc	BU
2011	—	—	—	—	—	15.00

KM# 226a 5 POUNDS
28.2800 g., 0.9250 Silver 0.8410 oz. ASW, 38.61 mm. **Ruler:** Elizabeth II **Subject:** Royal Wedding **Rev:** Prince William and Catherine Middleton

Date	Mintage	F	VF	XF	Unc	BU
2011 Proof	—	Value: 55.00				

KM# 227 5 POUNDS
28.2800 g., Copper-Nickel, 38.61 mm. **Ruler:** Elizabeth II **Subject:** Prince Philip, 90th Birthday

Date	Mintage	F	VF	XF	Unc	BU
2011	—	—	—	—	—	20.00

KM# 228 5 POUNDS
28.2800 g., Brass gilt, 38.61 mm. **Ruler:** Elizabeth II **Subject:** Royal British Legion, 90th Anniversary **Rev:** Poppies in color on the battlefield of the Somme

Date	Mintage	F	VF	XF	Unc	BU
2011	Est. 19,500	—	—	—	—	35.00

KM# 116 10 POUNDS
141.7500 g., 0.9990 Silver 4.5526 oz. ASW, 65 mm. **Ruler:** Elizabeth II **Subject:** 19th Century Monarchy **Obv:** Head with tiara right **Rev:** Four portraits **Edge:** Reeded

Date	Mintage	F	VF	XF	Unc	BU
2001 Proof	950	Value: 225				

KM# 126 10 POUNDS
155.5175 g., 0.9990 Silver 4.9948 oz. ASW, 65 mm. **Ruler:** Elizabeth II **Subject:** British Monarchy 18th Century **Obv:** Head with tiara right **Rev:** Five royal portraits **Edge:** Reeded

Date	Mintage	F	VF	XF	Unc	BU
2002 Proof	950	Value: 225				

KM# 125 10 POUNDS
155.5000 g., 0.9250 Silver 4.6243 oz. ASW, 65 mm. **Ruler:** Elizabeth II **Subject:** British Monarchs, 1700 years

Date	Mintage	F	VF	XF	Unc	BU
2003 Proof	Est. 950	Value: 275				

KM# 151 10 POUNDS
155.5170 g., 0.9250 Silver 4.6248 oz. ASW, 65 mm. **Ruler:** Elizabeth II **Subject:** D-Day **Obv:** Head with tiara right **Rev:** British troops storming ashore **Edge:** Reeded

Date	Mintage	F	VF	XF	Unc	BU
2004 Proof	1,944	Value: 400				

KM# 175 10 POUNDS
155.5000 g., 0.9250 Silver 4.6243 oz. ASW, 65 mm. **Ruler:** Elizabeth II **Subject:** British monarch of the 1500s **Rev:** Five portraits

Date	Mintage	F	VF	XF	Unc	BU
2004 Proof	Est. 950	Value: 275				

KM# 180 10 POUNDS
155.5000 g., 0.9170 Gold 4.5843 oz. AGW, 65 mm. **Ruler:** Elizabeth II **Subject:** Crimea, 150th Anniversary

Date	Mintage	F	VF	XF	Unc	BU
2004 Proof	—	Value: 11,000				

KM# 182 10 POUNDS
155.5000 g., 0.9250 Silver 4.6243 oz. ASW, 65 mm. **Ruler:** Elizabeth II **Subject:** End of WWII, 60th Anniversary

Date	Mintage	F	VF	XF	Unc	BU
2005 Proof	—	Value: 280				

KM# 182a 10 POUNDS
155.5000 g., 0.9170 Gold 4.5843 oz. AGW, 65 mm. **Ruler:** Elizabeth II **Subject:** End of WWII, 60th Anniversary

Date	Mintage	F	VF	XF	Unc	BU
2005 Proof	—	Value: 11,000				

KM# 182b 10 POUNDS
155.5000 g., 0.9995 Platinum 4.9967 oz. APW, 65 mm. **Ruler:** Elizabeth II **Subject:** End of WWII, 60th Anniversary

Date	Mintage	F	VF	XF	Unc	BU
2005 Proof	—	Value: 11,000				

KM# 184 10 POUNDS
155.5000 g., 0.9250 Silver 4.6243 oz. ASW, 65 mm. **Ruler:** Elizabeth II **Subject:** Return of the Islanders

Date	Mintage	F	VF	XF	Unc	BU
2005 Proof	—	Value: 300				

KM# 184a 10 POUNDS
155.5000 g., 0.9170 Gold 4.5843 oz. AGW, 65 mm. **Ruler:** Elizabeth II **Subject:** Return of the Islanders

Date	Mintage	F	VF	XF	Unc	BU
2005 Proof	—	Value: 11,000				

KM# 190 10 POUNDS
155.5000 g., 0.9170 Gold 4.5843 oz. AGW, 65 mm. **Ruler:** Elizabeth II **Subject:** Battle of Trafalgar, 200th Anniversary **Rev:** H.M.S. Victory

Date	Mintage	F	VF	XF	Unc	BU
2005 Proof	—	Value: 9,500				

KM# 224 10 POUNDS
155.5000 g., 0.9990 Silver 4.9942 oz. ASW, 65 mm. **Ruler:** Elizabeth II **Subject:** Apollo 11 moon landing, 40th Anniversary **Rev:** Lunar module Eagle and moon

Date	Mintage	F	VF	XF	Unc	BU
2009 Proof	—	Value: 275				

KM# 224a 10 POUNDS
155.5000 g., 0.9170 Gold 4.5843 oz. AGW, 65 mm. **Ruler:** Elizabeth II **Subject:** Apollo 11 moon landing, 40th Anniversary **Rev:** Lunar module Eagle and moon scape

Date	Mintage	F	VF	XF	Unc	BU
2009 Proof	—	Value: 9,000				

KM# 107 25 POUNDS
7.8100 g., 0.9170 Gold 0.2302 oz. AGW, 22 mm. **Ruler:** Elizabeth II **Subject:** Queen Victoria Centennial **Obv:** Head with tiara right **Rev:** Queen Victoria's portrait **Edge:** Reeded

Date	Mintage	F	VF	XF	Unc	BU
2001 Proof	2,500	Value: 450				

KM# 112 25 POUNDS
7.8100 g., 0.9170 Gold 0.2302 oz. AGW, 22 mm. **Ruler:** Elizabeth II **Subject:** Queen's 75th Birthday **Obv:** Head with tiara right **Rev:** Queen's portrait in wreath **Edge:** Reeded

Date	Mintage	F	VF	XF	Unc	BU
2001 Proof	5,000	Value: 425				

KM# 123 25 POUNDS
7.9800 g., 0.9167 Gold 0.2352 oz. AGW, 22.05 mm. **Ruler:** Elizabeth II **Subject:** Princess Diana **Obv:** Head with tiara right **Rev:** Diana's cameo portrait in wreath **Edge:** Reeded

Date	Mintage	F	VF	XF	Unc	BU
2002 Proof	2,500	Value: 450				

KM# 131 25 POUNDS
7.8100 g., 0.9166 Gold 0.2301 oz. AGW, 22 mm. **Ruler:** Elizabeth II **Subject:** The Duke of Wellington **Obv:** Head with tiara right **Rev:** Portrait with mounted dragoons in the background **Edge:** Reeded

Date	Mintage	F	VF	XF	Unc	BU
2002 Proof	2,500	Value: 425				

KM# 139 25 POUNDS
7.9800 g., 0.9166 Gold 0.2352 oz. AGW, 22 mm. **Ruler:** Elizabeth II **Subject:** Golden Jubilee **Obv:** Head with tiara right **Rev:** Queen in coach **Edge:** Reeded

Date	Mintage	F	VF	XF	Unc	BU
2002 Proof	5,000	Value: 445				

KM# 140 25 POUNDS
7.9800 g., 0.9166 Gold 0.2352 oz. AGW, 22 mm. **Ruler:** Elizabeth II **Subject:** Queen Mother **Obv:** Head with tiara right **Rev:** Queen Mother's portrait **Edge:** Reeded

Date	Mintage	F	VF	XF	Unc	BU
2002 Proof	2,500	Value: 450				

KM# 141 25 POUNDS
7.9800 g., 0.9166 Gold 0.2352 oz. AGW, 22 mm. **Ruler:** Elizabeth II **Subject:** Golden Jubilee **Obv:** Head with tiara right **Rev:** Trooping the Colors scene **Edge:** Reeded

Date	Mintage	F	VF	XF	Unc	BU
2003 Proof	5,000	Value: 445				

KM# 128 25 POUNDS
7.9800 g., 0.9170 Gold 0.2353 oz. AGW, 22 mm. **Ruler:** Elizabeth II **Subject:** Royal Navy - Golden Hind and Sir Francis Drake

Date	Mintage	F	VF	XF	Unc	BU
2003 Proof	—	Value: 525				

KM# 152 25 POUNDS
7.9800 g., 0.9167 Gold 0.2352 oz. AGW, 22 mm. **Ruler:** Elizabeth II **Subject:** D-Day **Obv:** Head with tiara right **Rev:** Advancing British soldier **Edge:** Reeded

Date	Mintage	F	VF	XF	Unc	BU
2004 Proof	500	Value: 475				

KM# 144 25 POUNDS
7.9800 g., 0.9170 Gold 0.2353 oz. AGW, 22 mm. **Ruler:** Elizabeth II **Subject:** Steam Locomotives **Rev:** Mallard Locomotive

Date	Mintage	F	VF	XF	Unc	BU
2004 Proof	Est. 2,500	Value: 525				

KM# 172 25 POUNDS
7.9800 g., 0.9170 Gold 0.2353 oz. AGW, 22 mm. **Ruler:** Elizabeth II **Subject:** Steam Locomotives **Rev:** City of Truro locomotive

Date	Mintage	F	VF	XF	Unc	BU
2004 Proof	Est. 2,500	Value: 525				

KM# 181 25 POUNDS
7.9800 g., 0.9170 Gold 0.2353 oz. AGW, 22 mm. **Ruler:** Elizabeth II **Subject:** Crimea, 150th Anniversary

Date	Mintage	F	VF	XF	Unc	BU
2004 Proof	—	Value: 525				

KM# 183 25 POUNDS
7.9800 g., 0.9170 Gold 0.2353 oz. AGW, 22 mm. **Ruler:** Elizabeth II **Subject:** End of WWII, 60th Anniversary

Date	Mintage	F	VF	XF	Unc	BU
2005 Proof	—	Value: 525				

KM# 185 25 POUNDS
7.9800 g., 0.9170 Gold 0.2353 oz. AGW, 22 mm. **Ruler:** Elizabeth II **Rev:** Return of the Islanders

Date	Mintage	F	VF	XF	Unc	BU
2005 Proof	—	Value: 525				

KM# 188 25 POUNDS
7.9800 g., 0.9170 Gold 0.2353 oz. AGW, 22 mm. **Ruler:** Elizabeth II **Subject:** Royal Navy **Rev:** H.M.S. Ark Royal

Date	Mintage	F	VF	XF	Unc	BU
2005 Proof	—	Value: 525				

KM# 174 25 POUNDS
7.9800 g., 0.9166 Gold 0.2352 oz. AGW, 22 mm. **Ruler:** Elizabeth II **Subject:** FIFA - XVIII World Football Championship - Germany 2006 **Rev:** Wembley Stadium

Date	Mintage	F	VF	XF	Unc	BU
2006 Proof	2,500	Value: 445				

KM# 218 25 POUNDS
7.9800 g., 0.9170 Gold 0.2353 oz. AGW, 22 mm. **Ruler:** Elizabeth II **Subject:** Royal Air Force, 90th Anniversary **Rev:** Lancaster

Date	Mintage	F	VF	XF	Unc	BU
2008 Proof	—	Value: 475				

KM# 221 25 POUNDS
7.9800 g., 0.9170 Gold 0.2353 oz. AGW, 22 mm. **Ruler:** Elizabeth II **Subject:** British Warships **Rev:** H.M.S. Mary Rose, 1511

Date	Mintage	F	VF	XF	Unc	BU
2009 Proof	Est. 995	Value: 475				

KM# 177 50 POUNDS
1000.0000 g., 0.9160 Silver 29.448 oz. ASW, 100 mm. **Ruler:** Elizabeth II **Subject:** Coronation, 50th Anniversary **Rev:** Buckingham Palace

Date	Mintage	F	VF	XF	Unc	BU
2003 Proof	Est. 999	Value: 1,100				

KM# 153 50 POUNDS
1000.0000 g., 0.9250 Silver 29.738 oz. ASW, 100 mm. **Ruler:** Elizabeth II **Subject:** D-Day **Obv:** Head with tiara right **Rev:** British troops storming ashore **Edge:** Reeded

Date	Mintage	F	VF	XF	Unc	BU
2004 Proof	600	Value: 1,300				

KM# 178 50 POUNDS
7.9800 g., 0.9160 Gold 0.2350 oz. AGW, 22.05 mm. **Ruler:** Elizabeth II **Subject:** Royal Air Force, 90th Anniversary **Rev:** Pilots scrambling to planes, some in the sky **Edge:** Reeded

Date	Mintage	F	VF	XF	Unc	BU
2008 Proof	—	Value: 475				

MINT SETS

KM#	Date	Mintage	Identification	Issue Price	Mkt Val
MS10	2003 (8)	—	KM#83, 89-90, 96-97, 110, 148-49	—	22.50
MS11	2004 (1)	—	Guernsey KM#155, Alderney KM#43, Jersey KM#126, 150th Anniversary of the Crimean War	—	80.00

GUINEA

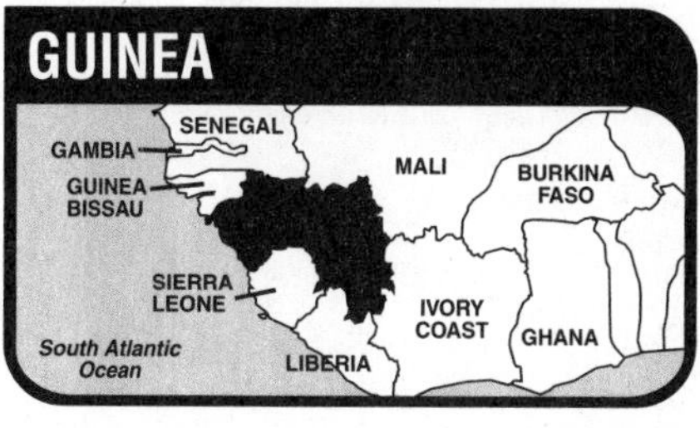

The Republic of Guinea, situated on the Atlantic Coast of Africa between Sierra Leone and Guinea-Bissau, has an area of 94,964 sq. mi. (245,860 sq. km.) and a population of 6.4 million. Capital: Conakry. Although Guinea contains one-third of the world's reserves of bauxite and significant deposits of iron ore, gold and diamonds, the economy is still dependent on agriculture, aluminum, bananas, copra and coffee are exported.

The coast of Guinea was known to Portuguese navigators of the 15th century but was seldom visited by European traders of the 16th-18th centuries because of its dangerous coastal waters. French penetration of the area began in the mid-19th century with the entering into of protectorate treaties with several of the coastal chiefs. After a long struggle with Guinea's native leader Samory Toure, France secured the area and until 1890 administered it as a part of Senegal. In 1895 the colony (Guinee Francais) became an autonomous part of the federation of French West Africa. The inhabitants were extended French citizenship in 1946 when the colony became an overseas territory of the French Union. Guinea became an independent republic on Oct. 2, 1958, when it declined to enter the new French Community.

MONETARY SYSTEM
100 Centimes = 1 Franc

REPUBLIC

REFORM COINAGE

KM# 65 2000 FRANCS
22.2000 g., 0.9000 Silver 0.6423 oz. ASW, 37 mm. **Obv:** National Arms **Rev:** Map and female figure

Date	Mintage	F	VF	XF	Unc	BU
2002 Proof	500	Value: 120				

GUYANA

The Cooperative Republic of Guyana, is situated on the northeast coast of South America, has an area of 83,000 sq. mi. (214,970 sq. km.) and a population of 729,000. Capital: Georgetown. The economy is basically agrarian. Sugar, rice and bauxite are exported.

The original area of Essequibo and Demerary, which included present-day Suriname, French Guiana, and parts of Brazil and Venezuela was sighted by Columbus in 1498. Guyana became a republic on Feb. 23, 1970. It is a member of the Commonwealth of Nations. The president is the Chief of State. The prime minister is the Head of Government. Guyana is a member of the Caribbean Community and Common Market (CARICOM).

REPUBLIC

DECIMAL COINAGE

KM# 50 DOLLAR

2.4000 g., Copper Plated Steel, 17 mm. **Obv:** Helmeted and supported arms **Rev:** Hand gathering rice **Edge:** Reeded

Date	Mintage	F	VF	XF	Unc	BU
2001	—	—	—	—	0.50	0.65
2002	—	—	—	—	0.50	0.65
2005	—	—	—	—	0.50	0.65
2008	—	—	—	—	0.50	0.65
2011	—	—	—	—	0.50	0.65

KM# 51 5 DOLLARS

3.7800 g., Copper Plated Steel, 20.5 mm. **Obv:** Helmeted and supported arms **Rev:** Sugar cane **Edge:** Reeded

Date	Mintage	F	VF	XF	Unc	BU
2002	—	—	—	0.35	0.75	1.00
2005	—	—	—	0.35	0.75	1.00
2008	—	—	—	0.35	0.75	1.00
2009	—	—	—	0.35	0.75	1.00

KM# 52 10 DOLLARS

5.0000 g., Nickel Plated Steel, 23 mm. **Obv:** Helmeted and supported arms **Rev:** Gold mining scene **Edge:** Reeded **Shape:** 7-sided **Note:** Slightly different die for each date.

Date	Mintage	F	VF	XF	Unc	BU
2007	—	—	—	0.75	1.25	1.50
2009	—	—	—	0.75	1.25	1.50

KM# 54 1000 DOLLARS

28.2800 g., 0.9250 Silver partially gilt 0.8410 oz. ASW, 38.6 mm. **Subject:** Bank of Guyana, 40th Anniversary **Obv:** Arms **Rev:** Bank building, partially gilt

Date	Mintage	F	VF	XF	Unc	BU
2005 Proof	1,000	Value: 85.00				

KM# 54a 1000 DOLLARS

28.2800 g., Copper-Nickel, 38.61 mm. **Subject:** Central Bank, 40th Anniversary **Obv:** Supported arms **Rev:** Building

Date	Mintage	F	VF	XF	Unc	BU
2005	—	—	—	—	—	50.00

KM# 55 2000 DOLLARS

28.2800 g., 0.9250 Silver 0.8410 oz. ASW, 38.61 mm. **Obv:** National Arms **Rev:** National soccer stadium

Date	Mintage	F	VF	XF	Unc	BU
2007 Proof	Est. 4,000	Value: 90.00				

KM# 56 2000 DOLLARS

25.0000 g., Copper-Nickel, 39 mm. **Obv:** National Arms **Rev:** Face design

Date	Mintage	F	VF	XF	Unc	BU
2008	—	—	—	—	—	75.00

HAITI

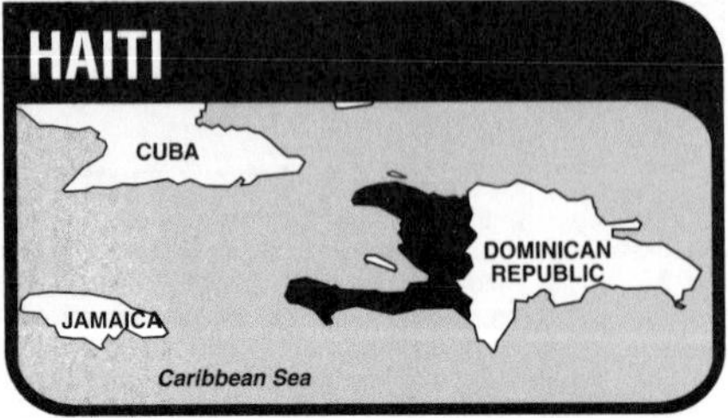

The Republic of Haiti, which occupies the western one-third of the island of Hispaniola in the Caribbean Sea between Puerto Rico and Cuba, has an area of 10,714 sq. mi. (27,750 sq. km.) and a population of 6.5 million. Capital: Port-au-Prince. The economy is based on agriculture; but light manufacturing and tourism are increasingly important. Coffee, bauxite, sugar, essential oils and handicrafts are exported.

The French language is used on Haitian coins although it is spoken by only about 10% of the populace. A form of Creole is the language of the Haitians.

MINT MARKS

A - Paris

(a) - Paris, privy marks only

R - Rome

MONETARY SYSTEM

100 Centimes = 1 Gourde

REPUBLIC

DECIMAL COINAGE

KM# 155 GOURDE

6.3000 g., Brass Plated Steel, 23 mm. **Obv:** Citadelle de Roi Christophe **Shape:** 7-sided

Date	Mintage	F	VF	XF	Unc	BU
2003	—	—	—	—	1.75	2.00
2009	—	—	—	—	1.75	2.00

KM# 156 5 GOURDES

9.2000 g., Brass Plated Steel, 28 mm. **Obv:** Four portraits in circle of Haitian statesmen top: Gen. Tonsaint Louverture, Left: Henri Christophe, Right: Jean Jacques Dessalines, Bottom: Alexandre Petion, date below **Rev:** National arms **Shape:** 7-sided

Date	Mintage	F	VF	XF	Unc	BU
2007	—	—	—	—	2.75	3.00

HONDURAS

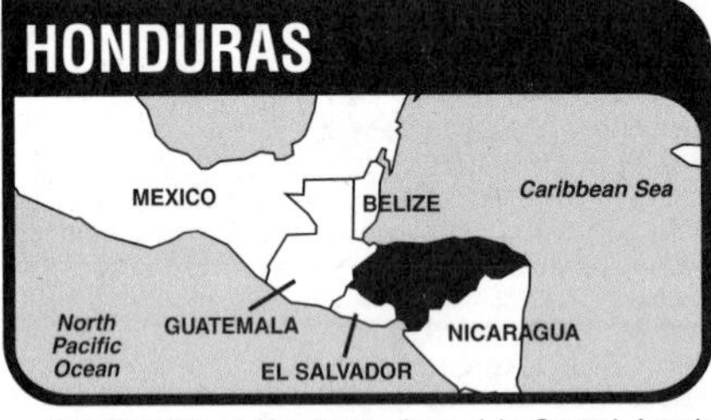

The Republic of Honduras, situated in Central America alongside El Salvador, between Nicaragua and Guatemala, has an area of 43,277 sq. mi. (112,090 sq. km.) and a population of 5.6 million. Capital: Tegucigalpa. Agriculture, mining (gold and silver), and logging are the major economic activities, with increasing tourism and emerging petroleum resource discoveries. Precious metals, bananas, timber and coffee are exported.

From 1933 to 1940 General Tiburcio Carias Andino was dictator president of the Republic. Since 1990 democratic practices have become more consistent.

MINT MARKS

T.G. - Yoro

T.L. – Comayagua

MONETARY SYSTEM

100 Centavos = 1 Lempira

REPUBLIC

REFORM COINAGE

KM# 72.4 5 CENTAVOS

3.2000 g., Brass, 21 mm. **Obv:** National arms **Rev:** Value in circle within sprays **Edge:** Plain

Date	Mintage	F	VF	XF	Unc	BU
2002	—	—	—	0.10	0.25	0.35
2003	—	—	—	0.10	0.25	0.35
2005	—	—	—	0.10	0.25	0.35
2006	—	—	—	0.10	0.25	0.35
2007	—	—	—	0.10	0.25	0.35

KM# 76.3 10 CENTAVOS

6.0000 g., Brass, 26 mm. **Obv:** National arms, without clouds behind pyramid **Rev:** Denomination within circle, wreath surrounds **Edge:** Plain

Date	Mintage	F	VF	XF	Unc	BU
2002	—	—	—	0.20	0.45	0.65
2003	—	—	—	0.20	0.45	0.65
2005	—	—	—	0.20	0.45	0.65
2006	—	—	—	0.20	0.45	0.65
2007	—	—	—	0.20	0.45	0.65

KM# 76.4 10 CENTAVOS

6.0000 g., Brass, 26 mm. **Obv:** National arms, slightly larger legend, large date **Rev:** Value in circle within wreath **Edge:** Plain

Date	Mintage	F	VF	XF	Unc	BU
2006	—	—	—	0.15	0.35	0.45
2007	—	—	—	0.15	0.35	0.45
2010	—	—	—	0.15	0.35	0.45

KM# 83a.2 20 CENTAVOS

2.0000 g., Nickel Plated Steel, 18 mm. **Obv:** National arms, without clouds **Rev:** Chief Lempira head left within circle **Edge:** Reeded

Date	Mintage	F	VF	XF	Unc	BU
2007	—	—	—	0.20	0.60	1.00
2010	—	—	—	0.20	0.60	1.00

KM# 84a.2 50 CENTAVOS

5.0000 g., Nickel Plated Steel, 24 mm. **Obv:** National arms above date **Rev:** Chief Lempira head left within circle **Edge:** Reeded

Date	Mintage	F	VF	XF	Unc	BU
2005	—	—	0.15	0.35	0.90	1.25
2007	—	—	0.15	0.35	0.90	1.25

KM# 91 10 LEMPIRAS

27.0000 g., 0.9250 Silver 0.8029 oz. ASW, 40 mm. **Obv:** State arms **Rev:** Bust of Jose Trinidad Cabanas Fiallos, president 1852-1855

Date	Mintage	F	VF	XF	Unc	BU
2005 Proof	Est. 500	Value: 120				

HONG KONG

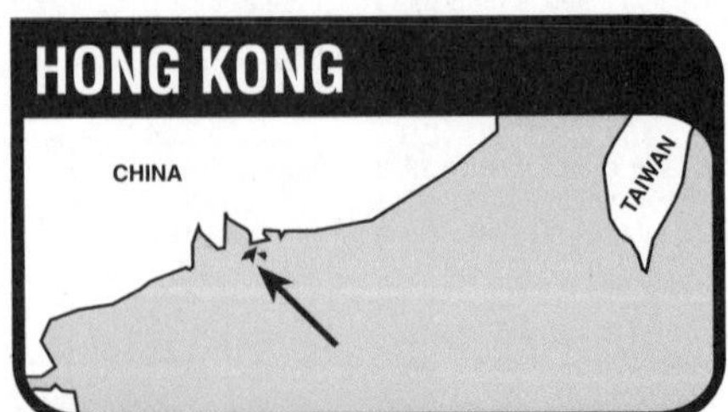

Hong Kong, a former British colony, reverted to control of the People's Republic of China on July 1, 1997 as a Special Administrative Region. It is situated at the mouth of the Canton or Pearl River 90 miles (145 km.) southeast of Canton, has an area of 403 sq. mi. (1,040 sq. km.) and an estimated population of 6.3 million. Capital: Victoria. The free port of Hong Kong, the commercial center of the Far East, is a trans-shipment point for goods destined for China and the countries of the Pacific Rim. Light manufacturing and tourism are important components of the economy.

SPECIAL ADMINISTRATION REGION (S.A.R.)

DECIMAL COINAGE

KM# 80 50 DOLLARS

35.4300 g., 0.9250 Silver Gold plated center 1.0536 oz. ASW, 40 mm. **Series:** Five Blessings **Obv:** Bauhinia flower **Rev:** Jade Ju-I

Date	Mintage	F	VF	XF	Unc	BU
2002 Proof	60,000	Value: 85.00				

KM# 81 50 DOLLARS

35.4300 g., 0.9250 Silver Gold plated center 1.0536 oz. ASW, 40 mm. **Series:** Five Blessings **Obv:** Bauhinia flower **Rev:** Fish

Date	Mintage	F	VF	XF	Unc	BU
2002 Proof	60,000	Value: 85.00				

KM# 82 50 DOLLARS

35.2500 g., 0.9250 Silver Gold plated center 1.0483 oz. ASW, 40 mm. **Series:** Five Blessings **Obv:** Bauhinia flower **Rev:** Horses

Date	Mintage	F	VF	XF	Unc	BU
2002 Proof	60,000	Value: 85.00				

KM# 83 50 DOLLARS

35.3400 g., 0.9250 Silver Gold plated center 1.0509 oz. ASW, 40 mm. **Series:** Five Blessings **Obv:** Bauhinia flower **Rev:** Peony flower

Date	Mintage	F	VF	XF	Unc	BU
2002 Proof	60,000	Value: 85.00				

KM# 84 50 DOLLARS

35.1400 g., 0.9250 Silver Gold plated center 1.0450 oz. ASW, 40 mm. **Series:** Five Blessings **Obv:** Bauhinia flower **Rev:** Windmills

Date	Mintage	F	VF	XF	Unc	BU
2002 Proof	60,000	Value: 85.00				

PROOF SETS

KM#	Date	Mintage	Identification	Issue Price	Mkt Val
PS8	2002 (5)	60,000	KM#80-84 plus 7.8g, .9999, AGW .2508, 25mm gold medal	370	850

HUNGARY

Hungary, located in central Europe, has an area of 35,929 sq. mi. (93,030 sq. km.) and a population of 10.7 million. Capital: Budapest. The economy is based on agriculture, bauxite and a rapidly expanding industrial sector. Machinery, chemicals, iron and steel, and fruits and vegetables are exported.

MINT MARKS

BP - Budapest

MONETARY SYSTEM

Commencing 1946

100 Filler = 1 Forint

SECOND REPUBLIC

DECIMAL COINAGE

KM# 692 FORINT

2.0500 g., Nickel-Brass, 16.5 mm. **Obv:** Crowned shield **Rev:** Denomination

Date	Mintage	F	VF	XF	Unc	BU
2001BP	—	—	—	—	0.10	0.25
2001BP Proof	3,000	Value: 3.75				
2002BP	—	—	—	—	0.10	0.25
2002BP Proof	3,000	Value: 3.75				
2003BP	—	—	—	—	0.10	0.25
2003BP Proof	7,000	Value: 3.50				
2004BP	—	—	—	—	0.10	0.25
2004BP Proof	7,000	Value: 3.50				
2005BP	—	—	—	—	0.10	0.25
2005BP Proof	—	Value: 3.50				
2006BP	—	—	—	—	0.10	0.25
2006BP Proof	—	Value: 3.50				
2007BP	—	—	—	—	0.10	0.25
2007BP Proof	—	Value: 3.50				
2008BP Proof, in sets only	9,010	Value: 3.50				

KM# 693 2 FORINT

3.1000 g., Copper-Nickel, 19.2 mm. **Obv:** Native flower: Colchicum Hungaricum **Rev:** Denomination **Edge:** Reeded

Date	Mintage	F	VF	XF	Unc	BU
2001BP	—	—	—	—	0.20	0.35
2001BP Proof	3,000	Value: 4.25				
2002BP	—	—	—	—	0.20	0.35
2002BP Proof	3,000	Value: 4.25				
2003BP	—	—	—	—	0.20	0.35
2003BP Proof	7,000	Value: 4.00				
2004BP	—	—	—	—	0.20	0.35
2004BP Proof	7,000	Value: 4.00				
2005BP	—	—	—	—	0.20	0.35
2005BP Proof	—	Value: 4.00				
2006BP	—	—	—	—	0.20	0.35
2006BP Proof	—	Value: 4.00				
2007	—	—	—	—	0.20	0.35
2007 Proof	—	Value: 4.00				
2008BP Proof, in sets only	9,010	Value: 4.00				

KM# 694 5 FORINT

4.2000 g., Nickel-Brass, 21.2 mm. **Obv:** Great White Egret **Rev:** Denomination

Date	Mintage	F	VF	XF	Unc	BU
2001BP	—	—	—	—	1.00	1.50
2001BP Proof	3,000	Value: 5.00				
2002BP	—	—	—	—	1.00	1.50
2002BP Proof	3,000	Value: 5.00				
2003BP	—	—	—	—	1.00	1.50
2003BP Proof	7,000	Value: 4.50				
2004BP	—	—	—	—	1.00	1.50
2004BP Proof	7,000	Value: 4.50				
2005BP	—	—	—	—	1.00	1.50
2005BP Proof	—	Value: 4.50				
2006BP	—	—	—	—	1.00	1.50
2006BP Proof	—	Value: 4.50				
2007BP	—	—	—	—	1.00	1.50
2007BP Proof	—	Value: 4.50				
2008BP	—	—	—	—	1.00	1.50
2008BP Proof	—	Value: 4.50				
2009BP	—	—	—	—	1.00	1.50
2009BP Proof	—	Value: 4.50				
2010BP	—	—	—	—	1.00	1.50
2010BP Proof	—	Value: 4.50				
2011BP	—	—	—	—	1.00	1.50
2011BP Proof	—	Value: 4.50				

KM# 847 5 FORINT

4.2000 g., Nickel-Brass, 21.2 mm. **Obv:** Great White Egret **Obv. Legend:** MAGYARORSZAG **Rev:** Denomination

Date	Mintage	F	VF	XF	Unc	BU
2012BP	10,000,000	—	—	—	1.00	1.50
2012BP Proof	4,000	Value: 2.50				

KM# 695 10 FORINT

6.1000 g., Copper-Nickel, 24.8 mm. **Obv:** Crowned shield **Rev:** Denomination **Edge:** Segmented reeding

Date	Mintage	F	VF	XF	Unc	BU
2001BP	—	—	—	—	1.00	2.50
2001BP Proof	3,000	Value: 5.50				
2002BP	—	—	—	—	1.00	2.50
2002BP Proof	3,000	Value: 5.50				

Date	Mintage	F	VF	XF	Unc	BU
2003BP	—	—	—	—	1.00	2.50
2003BP Proof	7,000	Value: 5.00				
2004BP	—	—	—	—	1.00	2.50
2004BP Proof	7,000	Value: 5.00				
2005BP	—	—	—	—	1.00	2.50
2005BP Proof	—	Value: 5.00				
2006BP	—	—	—	—	1.00	2.50
2006BP Proof	—	Value: 5.00				
2007	—	—	—	—	1.00	2.50
2007 Proof	—	Value: 5.00				
2008	—	—	—	—	1.00	2.50
2008 Proof	—	Value: 5.00				
2009	—	—	—	—	1.00	2.50
2009 Proof	—	Value: 5.00				
2010	—	—	—	—	1.00	2.50
2010 Proof	—	Value: 5.00				
2011	—	—	—	—	1.00	2.50
2011 Proof	—	Value: 5.00				

KM# 779 10 FORINT

6.1000 g., Copper-Nickel, 24.8 mm. **Obv:** Attila Jozsef **Rev:** Value **Edge:** Segmented reeding

Date	Mintage	F	VF	XF	Unc	BU
2005BP	20,000	—	—	—	2.50	3.00
2005BP Proof	7,000	Value: 3.50				

KM# 848 10 FORINT

6.1000 g., Copper-Nickel, 24.8 mm. **Obv:** Crowned shield **Obv. Legend:** MAGYARORSZAG **Rev:** Denomination **Edge:** Segmented reeding

Date	Mintage	F	VF	XF	Unc	BU
2012BP	10,000,000	—	—	—	1.00	2.50
2012BP Proof	4,000	Value: 5.00				

KM# 696 20 FORINT

6.9000 g., Nickel-Brass, 26.3 mm. **Obv:** Hungarian Iris **Rev:** Denomination **Edge:** Reeded

Date	Mintage	F	VF	XF	Unc	BU
2001BP	—	—	—	—	1.50	2.00
2001BP Proof	3,000	Value: 4.50				
2002BP	—	—	—	—	1.50	2.00
2002BP Proof	3,000	Value: 4.50				
2003BP	—	—	—	—	1.50	2.00
2003BP Proof	7,000	Value: 4.00				
2004BP	—	—	—	—	1.50	2.00
2004BP Proof	7,000	Value: 4.00				
2005BP	—	—	—	—	1.50	2.00
2005BP Proof	—	Value: 4.00				
2006BP	—	—	—	—	1.50	2.00
2006BP Proof	—	Value: 4.00				
2007BP	—	—	—	—	1.50	2.00
2007BP Proof	—	Value: 4.00				
2008BP	—	—	—	—	1.50	2.00
2008BP Proof	—	Value: 4.00				
2009BP	—	—	—	—	1.50	2.00
2009BP Proof	—	Value: 4.00				
2010BP	—	—	—	—	1.50	2.00
2010BP Proof	—	Value: 4.00				
2011BP	—	—	—	—	1.50	2.00
2011BP Proof	—	Value: 4.00				

KM# 768 20 FORINT

6.9000 g., Nickel-Brass, 26.3 mm. **Obv:** Ferenc Deak **Rev:** Denomination **Edge:** Reeded

Date	Mintage	F	VF	XF	Unc	BU
2003BP	993,000	—	—	—	1.50	2.00
2003BP Proof	7,000	Value: 4.00				

KM# 849 20 FORINT

6.9000 g., Nickel-Brass, 26.3 mm. **Obv:** Hungarian Iris **Obv. Legend:** MAGYARORSZAG **Rev:** Denomination **Edge:** Reeded

Date	Mintage	F	VF	XF	Unc	BU
2012BP	10,000,000	—	—	—	1.50	2.50
2012BP Proof	4,000	Value: 5.00				

KM# 697 50 FORINT

7.6000 g., Copper-Nickel, 27.5 mm. **Obv:** Saker falcon **Rev:** Denomination

Date	Mintage	F	VF	XF	Unc	BU
2001BP	—	—	—	—	3.00	4.00
2001BP Proof	3,000	Value: 6.00				
2002BP	—	—	—	—	3.00	3.50
2002BP Proof	3,000	Value: 5.50				
2003BP	—	—	—	—	3.00	3.50
2003BP Proof	7,000	Value: 5.00				
2004BP	—	—	—	—	3.00	3.50
2004BP Proof	7,000	Value: 5.00				
2005BP	—	—	—	—	3.00	3.50
2005BP Proof	—	Value: 5.00				
2006BP	—	—	—	—	3.00	3.50
2006BP Proof	—	Value: 5.00				
2007BP	—	—	—	—	3.00	3.50
2007BP Proof	—	Value: 5.00				
2008BP	—	—	—	—	3.00	3.50
2008BP Proof	—	Value: 5.00				
2009BP	—	—	—	—	3.00	3.50
2009BP Proof	—	Value: 5.00				
2010BP	—	—	—	—	3.00	3.50
2010BP Proof	—	Value: 5.00				
2011BP	—	—	—	—	3.00	3.50
2011BP Proof	—	Value: 5.00				

KM# 773 50 FORINT

7.7000 g., Copper-Nickel, 27.5 mm. **Obv:** National arms above Euro Union star circle **Rev:** Denomination **Edge:** Plain

Date	Mintage	F	VF	XF	Unc	BU
2004BP	993,000	—	—	—	3.00	3.50
2004BP Proof	7,000	Value: 6.00				

KM# 780 50 FORINT

7.7000 g., Copper-Nickel, 27.4 mm. **Subject:** International Childrens Safety Service **Obv:** Stylized crying child **Rev:** Denomination **Edge:** Plain

Date	Mintage	F	VF	XF	Unc	BU
2005BP	2,000,000	—	—	—	3.00	3.50

KM# 788 50 FORINT

7.7000 g., Copper-Nickel, 27.4 mm. **Obv:** Hungarian Red Cross 125th Anniversary seal above date and country name **Rev:** Value **Edge:** Plain

Date	Mintage	F	VF	XF	Unc	BU
2006BP	2,000,000	—	—	—	3.00	3.50

KM# 789 50 FORINT

7.7000 g., Copper-Nickel, 27.4 mm. **Subject:** 1956 Revolution **Obv:** Holed flag with Parliament building in background **Rev:** Value **Edge:** Plain

Date	Mintage	F	VF	XF	Unc	BU
2006BP	2,000,000	—	—	—	3.00	3.50

KM# 805 50 FORINT

7.7000 g., Copper-Nickel, 27.4 mm. **Subject:** Celebrating 50 years of the Treaty of Rome **Obv:** Book logo **Rev:** Value

Date	Mintage	F	VF	XF	Unc	BU
2007	2,000,000	—	—	—	1.50	2.00
2007 Proof	5,000	Value: 3.50				

KM# 850 50 FORINT

7.6000 g., Copper-Nickel, 27.5 mm. **Obv:** Saker falcon **Obv. Legend:** MAGYARORSZAG **Rev:** Denomination

Date	Mintage	F	VF	XF	Unc	BU
2012BP	—	—	—	—	3.00	3.50
2012BP Proof	4,000	Value: 7.00				

KM# 721 100 FORINT

8.0000 g., Bi-Metallic Brass Plated Steel center in Stainless Steel ring, 23.8 mm. **Obv:** Crowned shield **Rev:** Denomination **Edge:** Reeded

Date	Mintage	F	VF	XF	Unc	BU
2001BP	—	—	—	—	3.50	5.00
2001BP Proof	3,000	Value: 8.00				
2002BP	—	—	—	—	3.50	5.00
2002BP Proof	3,000	Value: 8.00				
2003BP	—	—	—	—	3.50	5.00
2003BP Proof	7,000	Value: 7.50				
2004BP	—	—	—	—	3.50	5.00
2004BP Proof	7,000	Value: 7.50				
2005BP	—	—	—	—	3.50	5.00
2005BP Proof	—	Value: 7.50				
2006BP	—	—	—	—	3.50	5.00
2006BP Proof	—	Value: 7.50				
2007BP	—	—	—	—	3.50	5.00
2007BP Proof	—	Value: 7.50				
2008BP	—	—	—	—	3.50	5.00
2008BP Proof	—	Value: 7.50				
2009BP	—	—	—	—	3.50	5.00
2009BP Proof	—	Value: 7.50				
2010BP	—	—	—	—	3.50	5.00
2010BP Proof	—	Value: 7.50				
2011BP	—	—	—	—	3.50	5.00
2011BP Proof	—	Value: 7.50				

KM# 760 100 FORINT

8.0000 g., Bi-Metallic Brass Plated Steel center in Stainless Steel ring, 23.8 mm. **Subject:** Lajos Kossuth **Obv:** Head right within circle **Rev:** Denomination within circle **Edge:** Reeded

Date	Mintage	F	VF	XF	Unc	BU
2002BP	997,000	—	—	—	2.00	2.50
2002BP Proof	3,000	Value: 5.00				

KM# 851 100 FORINT

8.0000 g., Bi-Metallic Brass Plated Steel center in Stainless Steel ring, 23.6 mm. **Obv:** Crowned shield **Obv. Legend:** MAGYARORZAG **Rev:** Denomination

Date	Mintage	F	VF	XF	Unc	BU
2012BP	—	—	—	—	3.50	5.00
2012BP Proof	4,000	Value: 10.00				

KM# 844 100 FORINT

10.0000 g., Copper-Nickel, 30 mm. **Subject:** Hungarian Scout Association, 100th Anniversary **Obv:** Hungarian Scout emblem at right **Rev:** Scout in uniform blowing bugle towards left **Shape:** 12-sided **Designer:** Zoltan Toth

Date	Mintage	F	VF	XF	Unc	BU
2012BP	5,000	—	—	—	—	20.00
2012BP Proof	10,000	Value: 25.00				

KM# 754 200 FORINT

9.4000 g., Brass, 29.2 mm. **Subject:** Childrens Literature: Ludas Matyi **Obv:** Denomination **Rev:** Man holding a goose **Edge:** Plain

Date	Mintage	F	VF	XF	Unc	BU
2001BP	12,000	—	—	—	7.50	9.50
2001BP Proof	5,000	Value: 15.00				

KM# 755 200 FORINT

Brass, 29.2 mm. **Subject:** Childrens Literature: Janos Vitez **Obv:** Denomination **Rev:** Soldier riding a flying bird **Edge:** Plain

Date	Mintage	F	VF	XF	Unc	BU
2001BP	12,000	—	—	—	7.50	9.50
2001BP Proof	5,000	Value: 15.00				

KM# 756 200 FORINT

Brass, 29.2 mm. **Subject:** Childrens Literature: Toldi **Obv:** Denomination **Rev:** Knight kicking a boat off the shore **Edge:** Plain

Date	Mintage	F	VF	XF	Unc	BU
2001BP	12,000	—	—	—	7.50	9.50
2001BP Proof	5,000	Value: 15.00				

KM# 757 200 FORINT

Brass, 29.2 mm. **Subject:** Childrens Literature: A Pal Utcai Fiuk **Obv:** Denomination **Rev:** Two men and cordwood **Edge:** Plain

Date	Mintage	F	VF	XF	Unc	BU
2001	12,000	—	—	—	7.50	9.50
2001 Proof	5,000	Value: 15.00				

KM# 826 200 FORINT

9.0000 g., Bi-Metallic Copper-Nickel center in Nickel-Brass ring, 28.3 mm. **Obv:** Suspension Bridge over the Danube **Rev:** Value **Edge:** Segmented reeding

Date	Mintage	F	VF	XF	Unc	BU
2009BP	—	—	—	—	4.00	5.00
2009BP Proof	—	—	—	—	—	—
2010BP	—	—	—	—	4.00	5.00
2010BP Proof	—	—	—	—	—	—
2011BP	—	—	—	—	4.00	5.00
2011BP Proof	—	—	—	—	—	—

KM# 852 200 FORINT

9.0000 g., Bi-Metallic Copper-Nickel center in Nickel-Brass ring, 28.3 mm. **Obv:** Suspension Bridge over the Danube **Obv. Legend:** MAGYARORSZAG **Rev:** Denomination **Edge:** Segmented reeding

Date	Mintage	F	VF	XF	Unc	BU
2012BP	—	—	—	—	4.00	5.00
2012BP Proof	4,000	Value: 10.00				

KM# 764 500 FORINT

13.9000 g., Copper-Nickel **Subject:** Farkas Kempelen's Chess Machine **Obv:** Denomination, letters A-H and numbers 1-8 repeated along edges **Rev:** Robotic human form chess playing machine built in 1769 **Edge:** Plain **Shape:** Square, 28.43 x 28.43 mm

Date	Mintage	F	VF	XF	Unc	BU
2002BP	5,000	—	—	—	20.00	24.00
2002BP Proof	5,000	Value: 35.00				

KM# 765 500 FORINT

13.8000 g., Copper-Nickel **Subject:** Rubik's Cube **Obv:** Inscription on Rubik's Cube design **Rev:** Rubik's Cube with inscription **Edge:** Plain **Shape:** Square, 28.43 x 28.43 mm

Date	Mintage	F	VF	XF	Unc	BU
2002BP	5,000	—	—	—	18.00	22.00
2002BP Proof	5,000	Value: 32.00				

KM# 781 500 FORINT

14.0000 g., Copper-Nickel **Obv:** Old wheel **Rev:** First Hungarian Post Office motor vehicle **Edge:** Plain **Shape:** Square **Note:** 28.43 x 28.43mm

Date	Mintage	F	VF	XF	Unc	BU
2005BP	5,000	—	—	—	17.00	22.00
2005BP Proof	10,000	Value: 32.00				

KM# 766 1000 FORINT

19.5000 g., Bronze Hollow coin unscrews to open **Obv:** Denomination and satellite dish **Rev:** Mercury

Date	Mintage	F	VF	XF	Unc	BU
2002BP	15,000	—	—	—	15.00	16.50

KM# 787 1000 FORINT

13.8100 g., Copper-Nickel, 28.3 mm. **Obv:** Value and partial front view of antique automobile **Rev:** Model T Ford **Edge:** Plain **Shape:** Square

Date	Mintage	F	VF	XF	Unc	BU
2006BP	10,000	—	—	—	17.00	20.00
2006BP Proof	10,000	Value: 28.00				

KM# 797 1000 FORINT

14.0000 g., Copper-Nickel, 28.43 x 28.43 mm. **Subject:** 125th Anniversary - Birth of János Adorján **Obv:** Early two cylinder aircraft motor with propeller **Obv. Legend:** MAGYAR / KOZTARSASAG **Rev:** Early monoplane **Rev. Legend:** ADORJAN JANOS / AZ ELSO SIKERES MAGYAR / REPULOGEP TERVEZOJE **Edge:** Plain **Shape:** Square

Date	Mintage	F	VF	XF	Unc	BU
2007BP	10,000	—	—	—	17.00	20.00
2007BP Proof	10,000	Value: 27.00				

KM# 809 1000 FORINT

14.0000 g., Copper-Nickel, 28.43 x 28.43 mm. **Subject:** Telephone Herald **Edge:** Plain **Shape:** Square **Designer:** Áron Bohus

Date	Mintage	F	VF	XF	Unc	BU
2008	10,000	—	—	—	17.00	20.00
2008 Proof	15,000	Value: 27.00				

KM# 813 1000 FORINT

14.0000 g., Copper-Nickel, 28.4 x 28.4 mm. **Subject:** Donat Banki, 150th Anniversary of Birth **Obv:** Denomination view of crossflow turbine **Rev:** Portrait facing in suit **Shape:** Square

Date	Mintage	F	VF	XF	Unc	BU
2009BP	10,000	—	—	—	16.00	18.00
2009BP Proof	10,000	Value: 25.00				

KM# 818 1000 FORINT

14.0000 g., Copper-Nickel, 28.4 x 28.4 mm. **Subject:** Laszlo Jozsef Biro, Inventor of the ball point pen **Obv:** Ball point pen schematic **Rev:** Bust facing **Shape:** Square

Date	Mintage	F	VF	XF	Unc	BU
2010BP	10,000	—	—	—	16.00	18.00
2010BP Proof	10,000	Value: 25.00				

KM# 829 1000 FORINT

14.0000 g., Copper-Nickel, 28.43x28.43 mm. **Subject:** Anyos Jedlik, principals of the dynamo, 1861 **Obv:** Dynamo **Rev:** Jedlik portrait

Date	Mintage	F	VF	XF	Unc	BU
2011BP	10,000	—	—	—	—	15.00
2011BP Proof	10,000	Value: 20.00				

KM# 840 1000 FORINT

14.0000 g., Copper-Nickel, 28.43x28.43 mm. **Subject:** Masat-1 satellite launch **Obv:** Land-based antenna **Rev:** Satellite above Eastern Europe map, Hungary highlighted **Designer:** Aron Huf

Date	Mintage	F	VF	XF	Unc	BU
2012BP	5,000	—	—	—	—	25.00
2012BP Proof	5,000	Value: 25.00				

KM# 752 3000 FORINT

31.4600 g., 0.9250 Silver 0.9356 oz. ASW, 38.5 mm. **Subject:** Hungarian Silver Coinage Millennium **Obv:** Denomination in ornamental frame **Rev:** Thaler design circa 1500 portraying Ladislaus I (1077-95) with the title of saint **Edge:** Reeding over "1001-2001" **Edge Lettering:** BP • NX • KB • HX • GY • F • AF • MM • C +

Date	Mintage	F	VF	XF	Unc	BU
2001BP	5,000	—	—	—	40.00	45.00
2001BP Proof	5,000	Value: 50.00				

KM# 759 3000 FORINT

31.8000 g., 0.9250 Silver 0.9457 oz. ASW, 38.7 mm. **Subject:** Centennial of First Hungarian Film "The Dance" **Obv:** Denomination **Rev:** Two dancers on film **Edge:** Reeded

Date	Mintage	F	VF	XF	Unc	BU
2001BP	3,500	—	—	—	42.00	47.50
2001BP Proof	3,500	Value: 55.00				

KM# 761 3000 FORINT

31.3300 g., 0.9250 Silver 0.9317 oz. ASW, 38.6 mm. **Subject:** Hortobagy National Park **Obv:** Landscape, denomination **Rev:** Hungarian Grey Longhorn bull **Edge:** Reeded

Date	Mintage	F	VF	XF	Unc	BU
2002BP	5,000	—	—	—	37.50	50.00
2002BP Proof	5,000	Value: 65.00				

KM# 767 3000 FORINT

31.4600 g., 0.9250 Silver 0.9356 oz. ASW **Subject:** 100th Anniversary - Birth of Kovacs Margit (1902-1977) **Obv:** Denomination **Rev:** The "Trumpet of Judgement Day"

Date	Mintage	F	VF	XF	Unc	BU
2002	4,000	—	—	—	40.00	45.00
2002 Proof	4,000	Value: 55.00				

KM# 762 3000 FORINT

31.4600 g., 0.9250 Silver 0.9356 oz. ASW, 38.5 mm. **Subject:** 200th Anniversary - National Library **Obv:** Small coat of arms in ornate frame **Rev:** Interior view of library **Edge:** Reeded

Date	Mintage	F	VF	XF	Unc	BU
2002BP	3,000	—	—	—	40.00	45.00
2002BP Proof	3,000	Value: 50.00				

KM# 763 3000 FORINT

31.4600 g., 0.9250 Silver 0.9356 oz. ASW, 38.5 mm. **Subject:** Janos Bolyai's publication of his "Appendix" **Obv:** Circular graph **Rev:** Signature above 7-line inscription, name and dates **Edge:** Reeded

Date	Mintage	F	VF	XF	Unc	BU
2002BP	3,000	—	—	—	40.00	45.00
2002BP Proof	3,000	Value: 50.00				

KM# 817 3000 FORINT

10.0000 g., 0.9250 Silver 0.2974 oz. ASW **Subject:** Ferenc Kazinczy, 250th Anniversary of Birth **Obv:** Quill pen and rolled document **Rev:** Bust facing

Date	Mintage	F	VF	XF	Unc	BU
2009	5,000	—	—	—	17.00	20.00
2009 Proof	5,000	Value: 30.00				

KM# 828 3000 FORINT
10.0000 g., 0.9250 Silver 0.2974 oz. ASW, 30 mm. **Subject:** Hungary's EU Council Presidency, 2011 **Obv:** Crowned shield within grometric design **Rev:** Skyline view below EU star circle **Designer:** Attila Ronay

Date	Mintage	F	VF	XF	Unc	BU
2011BP	3,000	—	—	—	—	30.00
2011BP Proof	5,000	Value: 45.00				

KM# 842 3000 FORINT
24.0000 g., 0.9250 Silver 0.7137 oz. ASW, 30 mm. **Subject:** XXX Summer Olympics, London **Obv:** Two kayak paddles **Rev:** Three kayakers advancing right **Designer:** Balazs Bito

Date	Mintage	F	VF	XF	Unc	BU
2012BP	3,000	—	—	—	—	45.00
2012BP Proof	5,000	Value: 50.00				

KM# 845 3000 FORINT
10.0000 g., 0.9250 Silver 0.2974 oz. ASW, 30x25 mm. **Subject:** Albert Szent-Gyorgyi, Nobel prize winner **Obv:** Paprika, value at upper right **Rev:** Szent-Gyorgyi bust at left **Shape:** Horizontal oval **Designer:** Fanni Vekony

Date	Mintage	F	VF	XF	Unc	BU
2012BP	2,000	—	—	—	—	45.00
2012BP Proof	5,000	Value: 50.00				

KM# 846 3000 FORINT
20.0000 g., 0.9250 Silver 0.5948 oz. ASW, 34 mm. **Subject:** Sandor Popovics, 150th Anniversary of Birth **Obv:** Architectural statuary group **Rev:** Popovics bust **Designer:** Marta Csikai

Date	Mintage	F	VF	XF	Unc	BU
2012BP	2,000	—	—	—	—	45.00
2012BP Proof	4,000	Value: 50.00				

KM# 837 3000 FORINT
20.0000 g., 0.9250 Silver 0.5948 oz. ASW, 34 mm. **Subject:** Imre Madach's The Tragedy of Man, 150th Anniversary **Obv:** Bust at left, large value **Rev:** Two figures standing on hilltop, guardian in background **Designer:** Eniko Szollossy

Date	Mintage	F	VF	XF	Unc	BU
2012BP	2,000	—	—	—	—	45.00
2012BP Proof	4,000	Value: 50.00				

KM# 751 4000 FORINT
31.4600 g., 0.9250 Silver 0.9356 oz. ASW, 26.4 x 39.6 mm. **Subject:** Godollo Artist Colony Centennial **Obv:** Denomination **Rev:** "Sisters" stained glass window design **Edge:** Plain **Shape:** Vertical rectangle

Date	Mintage	F	VF	XF	Unc	BU
2001BP	4,000	—	—	—	40.00	45.00
2001BP Proof	4,000	Value: 50.00				

KM# 769 5000 FORINT
31.4600 g., 0.9250 Silver 0.9356 oz. ASW, 38.6 mm. **Subject:** Budapest Philharmonic Orchestra **Obv:** Crowned arms in wreath **Rev:** Four coin-like portraits of Erkel, Dohnanyi, Bartók and Kodaly **Edge:** Reeded

Date	Mintage	F	VF	XF	Unc	BU
2003BP	4,000	—	—	—	37.50	42.50
2003BP Proof	4,000	Value: 50.00				

KM# 770 5000 FORINT
31.4600 g., 0.9250 Silver 0.9356 oz. ASW, 38.6 mm. **Subject:** Janos Neumann, 100th Anniversary of Birth **Obv:** Denomination and binary number date **Rev:** Portrait and building **Edge:** Reeded

Date	Mintage	F	VF	XF	Unc	BU
2003BP	3,000	—	—	—	40.00	45.00
2003BP Proof	3,000	Value: 55.00				

KM# 771 5000 FORINT
31.4600 g., 0.9250 Silver 0.9356 oz. ASW, 38.6 mm. **Subject:** Rakoczi's War of Liberation **Obv:** Transylvanian ducat design above country name, value and date **Rev:** Kuruc cavalryman with sword and trumpet **Edge:** Reeded

Date	Mintage	F	VF	XF	Unc	BU
2003BP	3,000	—	—	—	45.00	50.00
2003BP Proof	3,000	Value: 60.00				

KM# 772 5000 FORINT
31.4600 g., 0.9250 Silver 0.9356 oz. ASW, 38.6 mm. **Subject:** World Heritage in Hungary - Holloko **Obv:** Holloko castle ruins above country name, value and date **Rev:** Village view behind woman in folk costume **Edge:** Reeded

Date	Mintage	F	VF	XF	Unc	BU
2003BP	5,000	—	—	—	42.50	45.00
2003BP Proof	5,000	Value: 50.00				

KM# 774 5000 FORINT
31.4600 g., 0.9250 Silver 0.9356 oz. ASW, 38.6 mm. **Obv:** Value **Rev:** Two Olympic boxers **Edge:** Reeded

Date	Mintage	F	VF	XF	Unc	BU
2004BP	3,000	—	—	—	45.00	47.50
2004BP Proof	9,000	Value: 50.00				

KM# 775 5000 FORINT

31.4600 g., 0.9250 Silver 0.9356 oz. ASW, 38.6 mm. **Obv:** "Solomon Tower" above value **Rev:** Visegrad Castle with the Solomon Tower **Edge:** Reeded

Date	Mintage	F	VF	XF	Unc	BU
2004BP	4,000	—	—	—	45.00	50.00
2004BP Proof	4,000	Value: 60.00				

KM# 776 5000 FORINT

31.4600 g., 0.9250 Silver 0.9356 oz. ASW, 38.6 mm. **Obv:** Value and country name above Euro Union stars **Rev:** Mythical stag seen through an ornate window **Edge:** Reeded

Date	Mintage	F	VF	XF	Unc	BU
2004BP Proof	10,000	Value: 50.00				

KM# 778 5000 FORINT

31.4600 g., 0.9250 Silver 0.9356 oz. ASW, 38.6 mm. **Subject:** Ancient Christian Necropolis at Pecs **Obv:** Value and ancient artifact **Rev:** Interior view of tomb **Edge:** Reeded

Date	Mintage	F	VF	XF	Unc	BU
2004BP	5,000	—	—	—	40.00	45.00
2004BP Proof	5,000	Value: 50.00				

KM# 782 5000 FORINT

31.4600 g., 0.9250 Silver 0.9356 oz. ASW, 38.6 mm. **Obv:** Bat flying above value **Rev:** Interior cave view **Edge:** Reeded

Date	Mintage	F	VF	XF	Unc	BU
2005BP	5,000	—	—	—	45.00	50.00
2005BP Proof	5,000	Value: 55.00				

KM# 783 5000 FORINT

31.4600 g., 0.9250 Silver 0.9356 oz. ASW, 38.6 mm. **Obv:** Hungarian National Bank building **Rev:** Ignac Alpar and life dates **Edge:** Reeded

Date	Mintage	F	VF	XF	Unc	BU
ND (2005)BP	3,000	—	—	—	45.00	50.00
ND (2005)BP Proof	3,000	Value: 60.00				

KM# 784 5000 FORINT

31.4600 g., 0.9250 Silver 0.9356 oz. ASW, 38.6 mm. **Obv:** Knight on horse with lance **Rev:** Diosgyor Castle **Edge:** Reeded

Date	Mintage	F	VF	XF	Unc	BU
2005BP	4,000	—	—	—	45.00	50.00
2005BP Proof	4,000	Value: 60.00				

KM# 785 5000 FORINT

31.4600 g., 0.9250 Silver 0.9356 oz. ASW, 38.6 mm. **Obv:** Large building above value **Rev:** Karoli Gaspar Reformed (Calvinist) University seal **Edge:** Reeded

Date	Mintage	F	VF	XF	Unc	BU
2005BP	3,000	—	—	—	45.00	50.00
2005BP Proof	3,000	Value: 60.00				

KM# 786 5000 FORINT

31.4600 g., 0.9250 Silver 0.9356 oz. ASW, 38.6 mm. **Obv:** Coin design of a Transylvanian KM-10 thaler reverse dated 1605 **Rev:** Stephan Bocskai (1557-1606) **Edge:** Reeded

Date	Mintage	F	VF	XF	Unc	BU
2005BP	3,000	—	—	—	45.00	50.00
2005BP Proof	3,000	Value: 55.00				

KM# 790 5000 FORINT

31.4600 g., 0.9250 Silver 0.9356 oz. ASW, 38.61 mm. **Series:** Masterpieces of Ecclesiastical Architecture **Obv:** View of interior of dome **Obv. Legend:** MAGYAR KÖZTÁRSASÁG **Rev:** Basilica facade **Rev. Legend:** ESZTERGOMI BAZILIKA

Date	Mintage	F	VF	XF	Unc	BU
2006BP	2,500	—	—	—	50.00	55.00
2006BP Proof	3,500	Value: 65.00				

KM# 791 5000 FORINT

31.4600 g., 0.9250 Silver 0.9356 oz. ASW, 38.61 mm. **Subject:** 125th Anniversary - Birth of Béla Bartók **Obv:** Transylvanian woodcarving **Obv. Legend:** MAGYAR KÖZTÁRSASÁG **Rev:** Bust of Bartók right, Euro star behind **Edge:** Reeded and lettered **Edge Lettering:** Bartók Béla repeated three times

Date	Mintage	F	VF	XF	Unc	BU
2006BP Proof	25,000	Value: 45.00				

KM# 792 5000 FORINT

31.4600 g., 0.9250 Silver 0.9356 oz. ASW, 38.61 mm. **Series:** Heritage Sites **Obv:** Great White Egret in flight **Obv. Legend:** MAGYAR - KÖZTÁRSASÁG **Rev:** Landscape, Schneeberg Mountain above Esterházy palace facade

Date	Mintage	F	VF	XF	Unc	BU
2006BP	5,000	—	—	—	42.50	47.50
2006BP Proof	5,000	Value: 55.00				

KM# 793 5000 FORINT

31.4600 g., 0.9250 Silver 0.9356 oz. ASW, 38.61 mm. **Series:** Hungarian Castles **Subject:** Hungarian Castles **Obv:** Portrait of Ilona Zrinyi **Obv. Legend:** MAGYAR KÖZTÁRSASÁG **Rev:** Munkács Castle

Date	Mintage	F	VF	XF	Unc	BU
2006BP	4,000	—	—	—	42.50	47.50
2006BP Proof	4,000	Value: 55.00				

KM# 794 5000 FORINT

31.4600 g., 0.9250 Silver 0.9356 oz. ASW, 38.61 mm. **Subject:** 500th Anniversary - Victory in Nándorfehévár **Obv:** Decorative sword hilt **Obv. Legend:** MAGYAR KÖZTÁRSASÁG **Rev:** János Hunyadi in armor at left, John Capistrano in monk's garb at right **Rev. Inscription:** NÁNDORFEHÉRVÁRI / DIADAL

Date	Mintage	F	VF	XF	Unc	BU
2006BP	2,500	—	—	—	45.00	50.00
2006BP Proof	3,500	Value: 60.00				

KM# 795 5000 FORINT

31.4600 g., 0.9250 Silver 0.9356 oz. ASW, 38.61 mm. **Subject:** 50th Anniversary - Hungarian Revolution **Obv:** 1956 repeated in stone blocks at right **Obv. Legend:** MAGYAR KÖZTÁRSASÁG **Rev:** 1956 repeated in stone blocks at left, freedom fighter's flag at center **Rev. Legend:** MAGYAR FORRADALOM ÉS SZABADSÁGHARC

Date	Mintage	F	VF	XF	Unc	BU
2006BP	5,000	—	—	—	42.50	47.50
2006BP Proof	5,000	Value: 55.00				

KM# 798 5000 FORINT

31.4600 g., 0.9250 Silver 0.9356 oz. ASW, 38.61 mm. **Series:** Hungarian Castles **Obv:** Walled tower **Obv. Inscription:** MAGYAR / KÖZTÁRSASÁG **Rev:** Gyula castle **Rev. Inscription:** GYULAI / VÁR

Date	Mintage	F	VF	XF	Unc	BU
2007BP	4,000	—	—	—	55.00	60.00
2007BP Proof	4,000	Value: 70.00				

KM# 799 5000 FORINT

31.4600 g., 0.9250 Silver 0.9356 oz. ASW, 38.61 mm. **Subject:** 200th Anniversary - Birth of Count Lajos Batthyány **Obv:** Seal dated 1848 with crowned arms above Batthyány's autograph **Obv. Legend:** MAGYAR KÖZTÁRASÁG **Rev:** 1/2 length figure of Batthyány facing **Rev. Legend:** BATTHYÁNY LAJOS

Date	Mintage	F	VF	XF	Unc	BU
2007BP Proof	20,000	Value: 45.00				

KM# 800 5000 FORINT

31.4600 g., 0.9250 Silver 0.9356 oz. ASW, 38.61 mm. **Subject:** 125th Anniversary - Birth of Zoltán Kodály **Obv:** Gramaphone **Obv. Legend:** MAGYAR KÖZTÁRSASÁG **Rev:** Bust of Kodály facing 3/4 right

Date	Mintage	F	VF	XF	Unc	BU
2007BP	4,000	—	—	—	42.50	47.50
2007BP Proof	6,000	Value: 50.00				

KM# 802 5000 FORINT

31.4600 g., 0.9250 Silver 0.9356 oz. ASW, 38.61 mm. **Subject:** 8ooth Anniversary - Birth of St. Elizabeth **Obv:** Stylized image of St. Elizabeth feeding the hungry **Obv. Inscription:** Magyar / Köztárszág **Rev:** 3/4 length figure of St. Elizabeth seated facing holding roses and bread rolls in her lap

Date	Mintage	F	VF	XF	Unc	BU
2007BP	4,000	—	—	—	52.50	55.00
2007BP Proof	4,000	Value: 65.00				

KM# 804 5000 FORINT

31.4600 g., 0.9250 Silver 0.9356 oz. ASW, 38.61 mm. **Subject:** Great Reformed Church - Debrecen **Obv:** Church interior **Obv. Legend:** MAGYAR KOZTARSASAG **Rev:** Church facade **Rev. Legend:** DEBRECENI REFORMATUS NAGYTEMPLOM **Edge:** Plain **Shape:** 12-sided **Designer:** SZ.EGYED Emma

Date	Mintage	F	VF	XF	Unc	BU
2007BP	4,000	—	—	—	42.50	47.50
2007BP Proof	6,000	Value: 50.00				

KM# 811 5000 FORINT

31.4600 g., 0.9250 Silver 0.9356 oz. ASW, 38.6 mm. **Subject:** Europa heritage site Tokaj Wine Region **Obv:** Value within grape wreath **Rev:** Tokaj Hill and TV tower **Edge:** Reeded

Date	Mintage	F	VF	XF	Unc	BU
2008BP	5,000	—	—	—	—	48.00
2008BP Proof	15,000	Value: 55.00				

KM# 806 5000 FORINT

31.4600 g., 0.9250 Silver 0.9356 oz. ASW, 38.61 mm. **Obv:** Grape wreath rim with denomination, legend & mintmark inside **Rev:** Tokaj hill, TV tower, grapefield with a village & church **Edge:** Milled **Designer:** Gáti Gábor

Date	Mintage	F	VF	XF	Unc	BU
2008	5,000	—	—	—	—	48.00
2008 Proof	15,000	Value: 55.00				

KM# 807 5000 FORINT

31.4600 g., 0.9250 Silver 0.9356 oz. ASW, 38.61 mm. **Subject:** Castle of the Siklós **Obv:** Castle, tower, Franciscan monastery & church **Rev:** Castle of the Siklós **Designer:** Szöllössy Enikö

Date	Mintage	F	VF	XF	Unc	BU
2008	4,000	—	—	—	—	45.00
2008 Proof	6,000	Value: 50.00				

KM# 808 5000 FORINT

31.4600 g., 0.9250 Silver 0.9356 oz. ASW, 38.61 mm. **Subject:** 29th Summer Olympics **Obv:** Coat of arms over water **Rev:** Water polo player **Edge:** Milled

Date	Mintage	F	VF	XF	Unc	BU
2008	4,000	—	—	—	—	40.00
2008 Proof	14,000	Value: 45.00				

KM# 810 5000 FORINT

31.4600 g., 0.9250 Silver 0.9356 oz. ASW, 38.61 mm. **Subject:** Centenery birth of Ede Teller **Obv:** Diagram of Deuterium-tritium fusion reaction **Rev:** Portrait Ede Teller **Designer:** Mihály Fritz

Date	Mintage	F	VF	XF	Unc	BU
2008	4,000	—	—	—	—	45.00
2008 Proof	6,000	Value: 50.00				

KM# 812 5000 FORINT

31.4600 g., 0.9250 Silver 0.9356 oz. ASW **Subject:** Miklós Badnóti, 100th Anniversary of Birth **Obv:** Value **Rev:** Bust in suit facing

Date	Mintage	F	VF	XF	Unc	BU
2009	4,000	—	—	—	—	50.00
2009 Proof	4,000	Value: 55.00				

KM# 814 5000 FORINT

31.4600 g., 0.9250 Silver 0.9356 oz. ASW, 38.6 mm. **Subject:** Dohany Street Synagogue, 150th Anniversary **Obv:** Stained glass window **Rev:** Synagogue facade **Shape:** 12-sided

Date	Mintage	F	VF	XF	Unc	BU
2009BP	4,000	—	—	—	—	50.00
2009BP Proof	4,000	Value: 65.00				

KM# 815 5000 FORINT

31.4600 g., 0.9250 Silver 0.9356 oz. ASW, 38.61 mm. **Subject:** Budapest - World Heritage Site **Obv:** Street scene **Rev:** Panoramic view of Danube and Parliament

Date	Mintage	F	VF	XF	Unc	BU
2009	5,000	—	—	—	—	50.00
2009 Proof	5,000	Value: 60.00				

KM# 827 5000 FORINT

31.4600 g., 0.9250 Silver 0.9356 oz. ASW, 38.6 mm. **Subject:** John Calvin, 500th Anniversary

Date	Mintage	F	VF	XF	Unc	BU
2009BP Proof	—	Value: 65.00				

KM# 819 5000 FORINT

31.4600 g., 0.9250 Silver 0.9356 oz. ASW, 38.61 mm. **Subject:** Kosztolanyi Dezso, 125th Anniversary of Birth **Obv:** Architectural element of stone **Rev:** Portrait

Date	Mintage	F	VF	XF	Unc	BU
2010BP	3,000	—	—	—	40.00	45.00
2010BP Proof	5,000	Value: 50.00				

KM# 820 5000 FORINT

31.4600 g., 0.9250 Silver 0.9356 oz. ASW, 39.6x26.4 mm. **Subject:** Orseg National Park **Obv:** Butterfly **Rev:** Traditional rural buildings **Shape:** Rectangle

Date	Mintage	F	VF	XF	Unc	BU
2010BP	3,000	—	—	—	40.00	45.00
2010BP Proof	5,000	Value: 50.00				

KM# 821 5000 FORINT

31.4600 g., 0.9250 Silver 0.9356 oz. ASW, 38.61 mm. **Subject:** European Watersports Championships **Obv:** Value and waves **Rev:** Swimmer with butterfly stroke

Date	Mintage	F	VF	XF	Unc	BU
2010BP	4,000	—	—	—	40.00	45.00
2010BP Proof	6,000	Value: 50.00				

KM# 822 5000 FORINT

0.5000 g., 0.9990 Gold 0.0161 oz. AGW, 11 mm. **Subject:** Ferenc Erkel - 200th Anniversary of Birth **Obv:** Denomination **Rev:** Large bust facing

Date	Mintage	F	VF	XF	Unc	BU
2010BP Proof	10,000	Value: 50.00				

KM# 823 5000 FORINT

31.4600 g., 0.9250 Silver 0.9356 oz. ASW, 38.61 mm. **Subject:** Ferenc Erkel, 200th Anniversary of Birth **Obv:** House **Rev:** Bust facing, signature below

Date	Mintage	F	VF	XF	Unc	BU
2010BP Proof	5,000	Value: 55.00				

KM# 830 5000 FORINT

31.4600 g., 0.9250 Silver 0.9356 oz. ASW, 38.61 mm. **Subject:** Busojaras Carnival in Mohacs **Obv:** Standing figure in carnival costume **Rev:** Horned demon face **Designer:** Gabor Gati

Date	Mintage	F	VF	XF	Unc	BU
2011BP	3,000	—	—	—	—	45.00
2011BP Proof	5,000	Value: 55.00				

KM# 831 5000 FORINT

31.4600 g., 0.9250 Silver 0.9356 oz. ASW, 38.61 mm. **Subject:** Árpád Tóth, 125th Anniversary of Birth **Obv:** Handwritten poem at center **Rev:** Tóth bust **Designer:** Marta Csikai

Date	Mintage	F	VF	XF	Unc	BU
2011BP	2,000	—	—	—	—	45.00
2011BP Proof	4,000	Value: 50.00				

KM# 832 5000 FORINT

31.4600 g., 0.9250 Silver 0.9356 oz. ASW, 39.6x26.4 mm. **Subject:** Duna-Drava National Park **Obv:** Riverside scene **Rev:** Bird in flight **Designer:** Marta Csikai

Date	Mintage	F	VF	XF	Unc	BU
2011BP	3,000	—	—	—	—	45.00
2011BP Proof	5,000	Value: 50.00				

KM# 833 5000 FORINT

31.4600 g., 0.9250 Silver 0.9356 oz. ASW, 38.61 mm. **Subject:** Deak-Ter Evangelistic Church, Budapest **Obv:** Altar detail **Rev:** Church exterior **Shape:** Scalloped **Designer:** Gabor Keresztury

Date	Mintage	F	VF	XF	Unc	BU
2011BP	3,000	—	—	—	—	45.00
2011BP Proof	5,000	Value: 50.00				

KM# 834 5000 FORINT

31.4600 g., 0.9250 Silver 0.9356 oz. ASW, 38.61 mm. **Subject:** István Bibó, 100 Anniversary of Birth **Obv:** Value and legend **Rev:** Bibó seated, writing at table

Date	Mintage	F	VF	XF	Unc	BU
2011BP Proof	6,000	Value: 55.00				

KM# 835 5000 FORINT

0.5000 g., 0.9990 Gold 0.0161 oz. AGW, 11 mm. **Subject:** Adam Clark, 200th Anniversary of Birth **Obv:** Large value **Rev:** Large portrait **Designer:** Laszlo Szlavics Jr.

Date	Mintage	F	VF	XF	Unc	BU
2011BP Prooflike	10,000	—	—	—	—	75.00

KM# 843 5000 FORINT

0.5000 g., 0.9990 Gold 0.0161 oz. AGW, 11 mm. **Subject:** XXX Summer Olympics, London **Obv:** Paddle in water **Rev:** Canoeist advancing front **Designer:** Andrea Horvath

Date	Mintage	F	VF	XF	Unc	BU
2012BP Prooflike	10,000	—	—	—	—	75.00

KM# 838 5000 FORINT

31.4600 g., 0.9250 Silver 0.9356 oz. ASW, 38.61 mm. **Subject:** Jozsef Remenyi, 125th Anniversary of Birth **Obv:** Kneeling nude female with vase on shoulder **Rev:** Remenyi profile left **Designer:** Mihaly Fritz

Date	Mintage	F	VF	XF	Unc	BU
2012BP Proof	6,000	Value: 50.00				

KM# 839 5000 FORINT

31.4600 g., 0.9250 Silver 0.9356 oz. ASW, 38.61 mm. **Subject:** István Örkény, 100th Anniversary of Birth **Obv:** Text forming rectangle at center **Rev:** Large portrait **Designer:** Vilmos Kiraly

Date	Mintage	F	VF	XF	Unc	BU
2012BP	2,000	—	—	—	—	45.00
2012BP Proof	4,000	Value: 50.00				

KM# 841 10000 FORINT (Tizezer)

13.9640 g., 0.9860 Gold 0.4426 oz. AGW, 20 mm. **Subject:** Charles I florin **Obv:** Old coin: Fleur-dis-lis at center **Rev:** Old coin: St. John standing **Designer:** Tamas Soltra

Date	Mintage	F	VF	XF	Unc	BU
2012BP Proof	5,000	Value: 800				

Note: A piefort of this type exists with edge lettering

KM# 753 20000 FORINT

6.9820 g., 0.9860 Gold 0.2213 oz. AGW, 22 mm. **Subject:** Hungarian Coinage Millennium **Obv:** Denomination **Rev:** Hammered coinage minting scene above old coin design **Edge:** Plain

Date	Mintage	F	VF	XF	Unc	BU
2001BP Proof	3,000	Value: 425				

KM# 777 50000 FORINT
13.9640 g., 0.9860 Gold 0.4426 oz. AGW, 25 mm. **Obv:** Value and country name above Euro Union stars **Rev:** Mythical stag seen through ornate window **Edge:** Reeded

Date	Mintage	F	VF	XF	Unc	BU
2004BP Proof	7,000	Value: 800				

KM# 803 50000 FORINT
10.0000 g., 0.9860 Gold 0.3170 oz. AGW, 25 mm. **Subject:** 550th Anniversary - Enthronement of Matthias Hunyadi **Obv:** Raven holding a ring in its beak **Rev:** Portrait of Mátyás Hunyadi based on a marble relief **Edge:** Smooth **Designer:** László Szlávics, Jr.

Date	Mintage	F	VF	XF	Unc	BU
2008 Proof	5,000	Value: 600				

KM# 816 50000 FORINT
10.0000 g., 0.9860 Gold 0.3170 oz. AGW, 25 mm. **Subject:** Ferenc Kazinczy, 250th Anniversary of Birth **Obv:** Value and classical facade **Rev:** Bust at left

Date	Mintage	F	VF	XF	Unc	BU
2009 Proof	5,000	Value: 600				

KM# 825 50000 FORINT
6.9820 g., 0.9860 Gold 0.2213 oz. AGW, 22 mm. **Subject:** St. Stephen and St. Emeric **Obv:** Medieval document **Rev:** St. Stephen and prince standing

Date	Mintage	F	VF	XF	Unc	BU
2010BP Proof	5,000	Value: 425				

KM# 836 50000 FORINT
6.9820 g., 0.9860 Gold 0.2213 oz. AGW, 22 mm. **Subject:** Franz Liszt, 200th Anniversary of Birth **Obv:** Open piano case above musical score **Rev:** Bust right **Edge:** Plain **Designer:** Tamas Soltra

Date	Mintage	F	VF	XF	Unc	BU
2011BP Proof	5,000	Value: 450				

Note: A piefort exists with edge lettering

KM# 758 100000 FORINT
31.1040 g., 0.9860 Gold 0.9860 oz. AGW, 37 mm. **Subject:** Saint Stephen **Obv:** Angels crowning coat of arms **Rev:** King seated on throne **Edge:** Reeded

Date	Mintage	F	VF	XF	Unc	BU
2001BP Proof	3,000	Value: 1,750				

KM# 796 100000 FORINT
20.9460 g., 0.9860 Gold 0.6640 oz. AGW, 38.61 mm. **Subject:** 50th Anniversary - Hungarian Revolution **Obv:** 1956 repeated in cut out stone **Rev:** 1956 repeated in cut out stone with two freedom fighter's flags

Date	Mintage	F	VF	XF	Unc	BU
2006BP Proof	5,000	Value: 1,250				

KM# 824 500,000 FORINT
62.8380 g., 0.9860 Gold 1.9919 oz. AGW, 46 mm. **Subject:** St. Stephan and St. Emeric **Obv:** Medieval document **Rev:** King and prince standing **Note:** 18 Ducats

Date	Mintage	F	VF	XF	Unc	BU
2010BP Proof	500	Value: 3,750				

PIEDFORT

KM#	Date	Mintage	Identification	Mkt Val
P27	2011BP	1,500	50000 Forint. 0.9860 Gold. 13.9640 g. 22 mm. Lettered edge. KM#836.	800
P28	2012BP	1,500	10000 Forint. 0.9860 Gold. 13.9640 g. 20 mm. Lettered edge. KM#341	900

MINT SETS

KM#	Date	Mintage	Identification	Issue Price	Mkt Val
MS32	2001 (7)	—	KM#692-697, 721	—	16.50
MS33	2002 (8)	—	KM#692, 693, 694, 695, 696, 697, 721, 760	—	18.00
MS34	2003 (8)	—	KM#692, 693, 694, 695, 696, 697, 721, 768	—	17.50
MS35	2004 (8)	—	KM#692, 693, 694, 695, 696, 697, 721, 773	—	19.00
MS36	2005 (8)	—	KM#692-697, 721, 779 Magyarorszag Penzemei	—	20.00
MS37	2006 (7)	—	KM#692-697, 721, plus silver 1946 KM532	—	17.50
MS38	2009 (6)	—	KM#694-697, 721, 826	—	20.00
MS39	2010 (6)	—	KM#694-697, 721, 826	—	20.00
MS40	2011 (6)	—	KM#694-697, 721, 826	—	20.00
MS41	2012 (6)	—	KM#847-852	—	20.00

PROOF SETS

KM#	Date	Mintage	Identification	Issue Price	Mkt Val
PS28	2001 (7)	—	KM#692-697, 721	35.00	37.50
PS29	2002 (8)	—	KM#692-697, 721, 760	—	42.50
PS30	2003 (8)	—	KM#692-697, 721, 768	—	40.00
PS31	2004 (8)	—	KM#692-697, 721, 773	—	40.00
PS32	2005 (8)	7,000	KM#692-697, 721, 779	—	37.50
PS33	2006 (7)	—	KM#692-697, 721	—	35.00
PS34	2007 (8)	—	KM#692-697, 721, 805	—	40.00
PS35	2008 (7)	—	KM#692-697, 721	—	35.00
PS37	2009 (6)	—	KM#694-697, 721, 826	—	28.00
PS38	2010 (6)	—	KM#694-697, 721, 826	—	28.00
PS39	2011 (6)	—	KM#694-697, 721, 826	—	28.00
PS36	2012 (6)	4,000	KM#847-852	—	40.00
PS40	2012 (6)	—	KM#847-852	—	40.00

ICELAND

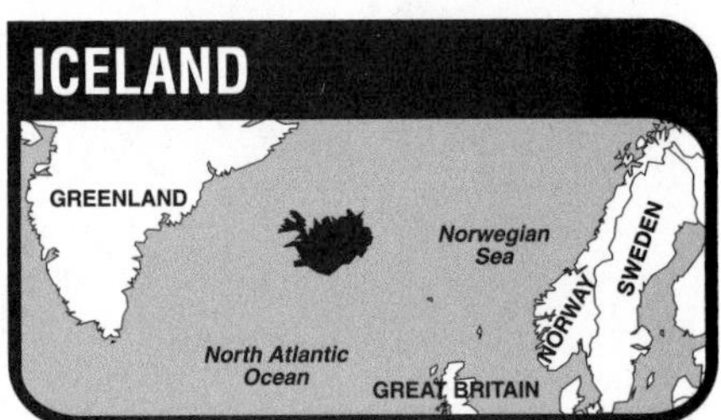

Iceland, an island of recent volcanic origin in the North Atlantic east of Greenland and immediately south of the Arctic Circle, has an area of 39,768 sq. mi. (103,000 sq. km.) and a population of just over 300,000. Capital: Reykjavik. Fishing is the chief industry and accounts for a little less than 60 percent of the exports.

REPUBLIC

REFORM COINAGE

100 Old Kronur = 1 New Krona

KM# 27a KRONA
4.0000 g., Nickel Plated Steel, 21.5 mm. **Obv:** Giant facing **Rev:** Cod **Edge:** Reeded

Date	Mintage	F	VF	XF	Unc	BU
2003	5,144,000	—	—	—	0.85	1.70
2005	5,000,000	—	—	—	0.85	1.70
2006	10,000,000	—	—	—	0.85	1.70
2007	10,000,000	—	—	—	0.85	1.70
2011	—	—	—	—	0.85	1.70

KM# 28a 5 KRONUR
5.6000 g., Nickel Plated Steel, 24.5 mm. **Obv:** Quartered design of Eagle, dragon, bull and giant **Rev:** Two dolphins leaping left **Edge:** Reeded

Date	Mintage	F	VF	XF	Unc	BU
2005	2,000,000	—	—	—	2.25	3.25
2007	10,000,000	—	—	—	2.25	3.25
2008	—	—	—	—	2.25	3.25

KM# 29.1a 10 KRONUR
7.0000 g., Nickel Plated Steel, 27.5 mm. **Obv:** Quartered design of Eagle, dragon, bull and giant **Rev:** Four capelins left **Edge:** Reeded

Date	Mintage	F	VF	XF	Unc	BU
2004	2,000,000	—	—	—	1.85	2.75
2005	4,505,000	—	—	—	1.85	2.75
2006	7,800,000	—	—	—	1.85	2.75
2008	—	—	—	—	1.85	2.75

KM# 31 50 KRONUR
8.2500 g., Nickel-Brass, 23 mm. **Obv:** Quartered design of eagle, dragon, bull and giant **Rev:** Crab **Edge:** Reeded **Designer:** Throstur Magnusson

Date	Mintage	F	VF	XF	Unc	BU
2001	2,000,000	—	—	—	4.25	5.00
2005	2,000,000	—	—	—	4.25	5.00

KM# 35 100 KRONUR
8.5000 g., Nickel-Brass, 25.5 mm. **Obv:** Quartered design of Eagle, dragon, bull and giant **Rev:** Lumpfish left **Edge:** Reeded **Designer:** Throstur Magnusson

Date	Mintage	F	VF	XF	Unc	BU
2001	2,140,000	—	—	—	6.50	7.75
2004	2,400,000	—	—	—	6.50	7.75
2006	2,000,000	—	—	—	6.50	7.75
2007	3,000,000	—	—	—	6.50	7.75
2011	—	—	—	—	6.50	7.75

INDIA - REPUBLIC

The Republic of India, a subcontinent jutting southward from the mainland of Asia, has an area of 1,269,346 sq. mi. (3,287,590 sq. km.) and a population of over 900 million, second only to that of the People's Republic of China. Capital: New Delhi. India's economy is based on agriculture and industrial activity. Engineering goods, cotton apparel and fabrics, handicrafts, tea, iron and steel are exported.

The Republic of India is a member of the Common-wealth of Nations. The president is the Chief of State. The prime minister is the Head of Government.

MINT MARKS

(Mint marks usually appear directly below the date.)

B - Mumbai (Bombay), proof issues only
(B) - Mumbai (Bombay), diamond
(C) - Calcutta, no mint mark
(H) - Hyderabad, star (1963--)
M - Mumbai (Bombay), proof only after 1996
(N) - Noida, dot
(T) - Taegu (Korea), star below first or last date digit

REPUBLIC

DECIMAL COINAGE

KM# 54 25 PAISE
2.8200 g., Stainless Steel, 19 mm. **Obv:** Small Lion capitol of Ashoka Pillar above value **Rev:** Rhinoceros left **Edge:** Plain **Note:** Varieties of date size exist.

Date	Mintage	F	VF	XF	Unc	BU
2001(B)	—	—	1.00	3.00	4.00	7.00
2001(C)	—	—	1.00	3.00	4.00	7.00
2001(H)	—	—	1.00	3.00	4.00	7.00
2002(B)	—	—	1.00	3.00	4.00	7.00
2002(C)	—	—	1.00	3.00	4.00	7.00
2002(H)	—	—	1.00	3.00	4.00	7.00

KM# 69 50 PAISE
3.8000 g., Stainless Steel, 22 mm. **Subject:** Parliament Building in New Delhi **Obv:** Denomination **Rev:** Building

Date	Mintage	F	VF	XF	Unc	BU
2001(B)	—	—	1.00	1.50	2.00	4.00
2001(C)	—	—	1.00	1.50	2.00	4.00
2001(H)	—	—	1.00	1.50	2.00	4.00
2001(N)	—	—	1.00	1.50	2.00	4.00
2002(B)	—	—	1.00	1.50	2.00	4.00
2002(C)	—	—	1.00	1.50	2.00	4.00
2002(H)	—	—	1.00	1.50	2.00	4.00
2002(N)	—	—	1.00	1.50	2.00	4.00
2003(B)	—	—	4.00	5.00	6.00	10.00
2007(C)	—	—	6.00	7.00	8.00	10.00
2007(N)	—	—	6.00	7.00	8.00	10.00

KM# 374 50 PAISE
3.8000 g., Stainless Steel, 23 mm. **Obv:** Lion capitol of Ashoka Pillar **Rev:** Clenched fist and value

Date	Mintage	F	VF	XF	Unc	BU
2008(B)	—	—	0.30	0.60	1.00	1.50
2008(C)	—	—	0.30	0.60	1.00	1.50
2008(H)	—	—	0.30	0.60	1.00	1.50
2008(N)	—	—	0.30	0.60	1.00	1.50
2009(B)	—	—	0.30	0.60	1.00	1.50
2009(C)	—	—	0.30	0.60	1.00	1.50
2010(C)	—	—	1.00	1.50	2.00	3.00

KM# 398 50 PAISE
Stainless Steel, 19 mm. **Obv:** Lion capitol of Ashoka Pillar **Rev:** Value flanked by flora **Edge:** Reeded

Date	Mintage	F	VF	XF	Unc	BU
2011(B)	—	—	—	1.00	3.00	—
2011(H)	—	—	—	0.50	1.50	—

KM# 92.2 RUPEE
4.9000 g., Stainless Steel, 25 mm. **Obv:** Lion capitol of Ashoka Pillar **Rev:** Denomination and date, grain ears flank **Edge:** Plain **Note:** Mint mark varieties exist.

Date	Mintage	F	VF	XF	Unc	BU
2001(B)	—	—	0.50	1.00	1.50	—
2001(C)	—	—	0.50	1.00	1.50	—
2001(K)	—	—	0.50	1.00	1.50	—
2001(N)	—	—	0.50	1.00	1.50	—
2001(H)	—	—	0.50	1.00	1.50	—
Note: Small and large mint mark exist, doubled left or right of wheat stalks						
2002(B)	—	—	0.50	1.00	1.50	—
2002(N)	—	—	0.50	1.00	1.50	—
2002(C)	—	—	0.50	1.00	1.50	—
2002(H)	—	—	0.50	1.00	1.50	—
2003(B)	—	—	0.50	1.00	1.50	—
2003(C)	—	—	0.50	1.00	1.50	—
2003(H)	—	—	0.50	1.00	1.50	—
2004(B)	—	—	1.50	2.00	3.00	—
2004(C)	—	—	1.50	2.00	3.00	—
2004(H)	—	—	1.50	2.00	3.00	—
2004(N)	—	—	1.50	2.00	3.00	—

KM# 313 RUPEE
4.9500 g., Stainless Steel, 25 mm. **Subject:** 100th Anniversary - Birth of Jaya Prakash Narayan **Obv:** Lion capitol of Ashoka Pillar **Rev:** Bust of Jaya Prakash Narayan slightly left **Edge:** Plain

Date	Mintage	F	VF	XF	Unc	BU
2002	—	—	30.00	40.00	50.00	—
Note: B without mint mark						
2002(B)	—	—	4.00	5.00	6.00	—
2002(B) Proof	—	Value: 40.00				
2002(H)	—	—	2.00	3.00	4.00	—

KM# 314 RUPEE
4.9500 g., Stainless Steel, 25 mm. **Subject:** Maharana Pratap **Obv:** Lion capitol of Ashoka Pillar **Rev:** Bust left in national costume **Edge:** Plain

Date	Mintage	F	VF	XF	Unc	BU
2003(B)	—	—	4.00	7.00	10.00	—
2003(B) Proof	—	Value: 60.00				
2003(H)	—	—	2.00	3.00	7.00	—

KM# 316 RUPEE
4.8500 g., Stainless Steel, 25 mm. **Obv:** Lion capitol of Ashoka Pillar **Rev:** 3/4 length military figure Veer Durgadass with spear left **Edge:** Plain **Note:** Weak strike typical for 2003(H)

Date	Mintage	F	VF	XF	Unc	BU
2003(B) Proof	—	Value: 40.00				
2003(H)	—	—	1.00	2.00	6.00	—

KM# 322 RUPEE
4.9500 g., Stainless Steel, 24.8 mm. **Obv:** Lion capitol of Ashoka Pillar at left, value at right **Rev:** Cross dividing four dots **Edge:** Plain

Date	Mintage	F	VF	XF	Unc	BU
2004(B)	—	—	10.00	20.00	30.00	—
2005(C)	—	—	0.50	2.00	3.00	—
2005(B)	—	—	0.50	1.00	1.50	—
2005(H)	—	—	0.50	1.00	1.50	—
2005(N)	—	—	0.50	1.00	1.50	—
2006(N)	—	—	4.00	6.00	10.00	—

KM# 321 RUPEE
5.0000 g., Stainless Steel, 24.9 mm. **Subject:** 150th Anniversary of the Indian Postal Service **Obv:** Lion capitol of Ashoka Pillar above value **Rev:** Partial postage stamp design **Edge:** Grooved

Date	Mintage	F	VF	XF	Unc	BU
2004(C)	—	—	6.00	8.00	10.00	—
2004(C) Proof	—	Value: 50.00				
2004(C) Proof, restrike	—	Value: 40.00				

KM# 331 RUPEE
4.9000 g., Stainless Steel, 25 mm. **Subject:** Bharata Natyam Dance Expressions **Obv:** Lion capitol of Ashoka Pillar **Rev:** Gesture of hand with thumb up **Edge:** Plain

Date	Mintage	F	VF	XF	Unc	BU
2007(C)	—	—	0.50	1.00	1.50	—
2007(H)	—	—	0.50	1.00	1.50	—
2007(N)	—	—	0.50	1.00	1.50	—
2008(B)	—	—	0.50	1.00	1.50	—
2008(C)	—	—	0.50	1.00	1.50	—

Date	Mintage	F	VF	XF	Unc	BU
2008(Hy)	—	—	0.50	1.00	1.50	—
2008(N)	—	—	0.50	1.00	1.50	—
2009(B)	—	—	0.50	1.00	1.50	—
2009(C)	—	—	0.50	1.00	1.50	—
2009(Hy)	—	—	0.50	1.00	1.50	—
2009(N)	—	—	0.50	1.00	1.50	—
2010(B)	—	—	0.50	1.00	1.50	—
2010(C)	—	—	0.50	1.00	1.50	—
2010(H)	—	—	0.50	1.00	1.50	—
2010(N)	—	—	0.50	1.00	1.50	—
2011(C)	—	—	1.00	1.50	2.00	—
2011(H)	—	—	1.00	1.50	2.00	—
2011(N)	—	—	1.00	1.50	2.00	—

KM# 385 RUPEE

4.9500 g., Stainless Steel, 24.8 mm. **Subject:** Reserve Bank of India, 75th Anniversary **Obv:** Lion capitol of Ashoka Pillar above value **Rev:** Lion advancing left, palm tree in background

Date	Mintage	F	VF	XF	Unc	BU
2010(B) Proof	—	Value: 20.00				
2010(H)	—	—	1.00	1.50	2.00	—

KM# 394 RUPEE

4.9500 g., Stainless Steel, 22 mm. **Obv:** Lion capitol of Ashoka Pillar **Rev:** New Rupee symbol above value

Date	Mintage	F	VF	XF	Unc	BU
2011(B)	—	—	—	—	0.40	—
2011(C)	—	—	—	—	0.40	—
2011(H)	—	—	—	—	0.40	—
2011(N)	—	—	—	—	0.40	—
2012(B)	—	—	—	—	0.40	—
2012(C)	—	—	—	—	0.40	—
2012(H)	—	—	—	—	0.40	—
2012(N)	—	—	—	—	0.40	—

KM# 121.5 2 RUPEES

6.0600 g., Copper-Nickel, 26 mm. **Subject:** National Integration **Obv:** Type C Lion capitol of Ashoka Pillar **Rev:** Flag on map **Edge:** Plain **Note:** 11-sided

Date	Mintage	F	VF	XF	Unc	BU
2001(B)	—	—	0.60	0.80	1.20	—
2001(C)	—	—	0.60	0.80	1.20	—
2001(H)	—	—	0.60	0.80	1.20	—
2002(B)	—	—	0.60	0.80	1.20	—
2002(C)	—	—	0.60	0.80	1.20	—
2002(H)	—	—	0.60	0.80	1.20	—
2002(N)	—	—	0.60	0.80	1.20	—
2003(B)	—	—	0.60	0.80	1.20	—
2003(C)	—	—	0.60	0.80	1.20	—
2003(H)	—	—	0.60	0.80	1.20	—
2004(B)	—	—	1.00	1.50	2.00	—
2004(C)	—	—	4.00	20.00	40.00	—
2004(H)	—	—	2.00	3.00	4.00	—

KM# 121.3 2 RUPEES

6.0000 g., Copper-Nickel, 26 mm. **Subject:** National Integration **Obv:** Type A Lion capitol of Ashoka Pillar **Rev:** Flag on map **Edge:** Plain **Shape:** 11-sided **Note:** Reduced size, non magnetic.

Date	Mintage	F	VF	XF	Unc	BU
2001(B)	—	—	1.00	1.50	2.00	—
2001(C)	—	—	1.00	1.50	2.00	—

Date	Mintage	F	VF	XF	Unc	BU
2002(C)	—	—	1.00	1.50	2.00	—
2003(C)	—	—	1.00	1.50	2.00	—
2003(H)	—	—	1.00	1.50	2.00	—

KM# 303 2 RUPEES

6.2400 g., Copper-Nickel, 25.7 mm. **Subject:** 100th Anniversary - Birth of Dr. Syama P. Mookerjee **Obv:** Type B Lion capitol of Ashoka Pillar above denomination **Rev:** Bust of Dr. Mookerjeeright **Edge:** Plain

Date	Mintage	F	VF	XF	Unc	BU
2001(C)	—	—	5.00	8.00	10.00	—
2001(C) Proof	—	Value: 40.00				
2001(H)	—	—	1.00	1.50	2.00	—
2001(N)	—	—	1.00	1.50	2.00	—

KM# 305 2 RUPEES

6.1000 g., Copper-Nickel, 25.7 mm. **Subject:** Sant Tukaram **Obv:** Lion capitol of Ashoka Pillar above value **Rev:** Seated musician **Shape:** 11-sided

Date	Mintage	F	VF	XF	Unc	BU
2002(B)	—	—	1.00	2.50	4.00	—
2002(C)	—	—	4.00	5.00	6.00	—
2002(C) Proof	—	Value: 60.00				
2002(H)	—	—	1.00	1.50	2.00	—
2002(N)	—	—	4.00	7.00	10.00	—

KM# 307 2 RUPEES

6.0500 g., Copper-Nickel **Subject:** 150th Anniversary - Indian Railways **Obv:** Lion capitol of Ashoka Pillar above value **Rev:** Cartoon elephant holding railroad lantern **Edge:** Plain **Shape:** 11-sided **Note:** Generally poor strike quality.

Date	Mintage	F	VF	XF	Unc	BU
2003(B)	—	—	1.50	2.50	4.00	—
2003(C)	—	—	1.50	2.50	4.00	—
2003(C) Proof	—	Value: 40.00				
2003(C) Proof, restrike	—	Value: 30.00				
2003(H)	—	—	1.00	1.50	2.00	—
2003(N)	—	—	4.00	7.00	10.00	—

KM# 334 2 RUPEES

6.0000 g., Copper-Nickel, 26 mm. **Subject:** 150th Anniversary - Telecommunications **Obv:** Lion capitol of Ashoka Pillar **Rev:** Cartoon bird standing holding cell phone **Edge:** Plain **Shape:** 11-sided

Date	Mintage	F	VF	XF	Unc	BU
2004(C) Proof	—	Value: 60.00				
Note: Issued only as part of a set.						
2004(C) Proof, restrike	—	Value: 50.00				

KM# 326 2 RUPEES

5.8000 g., Stainless Steel **Obv:** Lion capitol of Ashoka Pillar at left and value at right **Rev:** Cross with U-shaped arms and dots **Edge:** Plain **Note:** Size varies 26.75 - 27.07 mm

Date	Mintage	F	VF	XF	Unc	BU
2005(B)	—	—	0.40	0.60	1.00	—
2005(C)	—	—	0.40	0.60	1.00	—

Date	Mintage	F	VF	XF	Unc	BU
2005(C) Reverse same as 2007 Calcutta	—	—	10.00	20.00	30.00	—
2005(H)	—	—	0.40	0.60	1.00	—
2005(N)	—	—	0.40	0.60	1.00	—
2006(B) small date	—	—	0.40	0.60	1.00	—
2006(B) large date	—	—	0.40	0.60	1.00	—
2006(H)	—	—	0.40	0.60	1.00	—
2006(N)	—	—	0.40	0.60	1.00	—
2007(B)	—	—	0.40	0.60	1.00	—
2007(C)	—	—	0.40	0.60	1.00	—
2007(C) Reverse same as 2005 Calcutta	—	—	6.00	12.00	20.00	—
2007(H)	—	—	0.40	0.60	1.00	—
2007(N)	—	—	1.00	1.50	2.00	—

KM# 327 2 RUPEES

5.8000 g., Stainless Steel, 27 mm. **Obv:** Lion capitol of Ashoka Pillar at center **Obv. Inscription:** INDIA in Hindi and English **Rev:** Hasta Mudra - hand gesture from the dance Bharata Natyam **Edge:** Plain

Date	Mintage	F	VF	XF	Unc	BU
2007(B)	—	—	0.40	0.60	1.00	—
2007(C)	—	—	0.40	0.60	1.00	—
2007(H)	—	—	0.40	0.60	1.00	—
2007(N)	—	—	0.40	0.60	1.00	—
2008(B)	—	—	0.40	0.60	1.00	—
2008(C)	—	—	0.40	0.60	1.00	—
2008(H)	—	—	0.40	0.60	1.00	—
2008(N)	—	—	0.40	0.60	1.00	—
2009(B)	—	—	0.40	0.60	1.00	—
2009(C)	—	—	0.40	0.60	1.00	—
2009(H)	—	—	0.40	0.60	1.00	—
2009(N)	—	—	0.40	0.60	1.00	—
2010(B)	—	—	0.40	0.60	1.00	—
2010(C)	—	—	0.40	0.60	1.00	—
2010(H)	—	—	0.40	0.60	1.00	—
2010(N)	—	—	0.40	0.60	1.00	—
2011(H)	—	—	0.40	0.60	1.00	—
2011(N)	—	—	0.40	0.60	1.00	—

KM# 350 2 RUPEES

6.0000 g., Stainless Steel, 26.9 mm. **Subject:** 75th Anniversary Indian Air Force **Obv:** Lion capitol of Ashoka Pillar at left and value at right **Rev:** Planes in flight **Edge:** Plain **Shape:** 11-sided

Date	Mintage	F	VF	XF	Unc	BU
2007(C)	—	—	—	6.00	8.00	10.00
2007(C) Proof	—	Value: 40.00				

KM# 362 2 RUPEES

5.7000 g., Stainless Steel, 27 mm. **Subject:** Khadi & Village Industries Commission, 50th Anniversary

Date	Mintage	F	VF	XF	Unc	BU
2007	—	—	—	—	8.00	10.00
2007 Proof	—	Value: 5.00				

KM# 375 2 RUPEES

5.8000 g., Stainless Steel, 27 mm. **Subject:** Natya Mudra **Obv:** Lion capitol of Ashoka Pillar **Rev:** Hasta Mudra - hand gesture from the dance Bharata Natyam **Note:** Issued in Mule only

Date	Mintage	F	VF	XF	Unc	BU
2008(C)	—	—	200	350	500	—

KM# 368 2 RUPEES

5.8000 g., Stainless Steel, 27 mm. **Subject:** Louis Braille, 200th Anniversary of Birth **Obv:** Lion capitol of Ashoka Pillar **Rev:** Facing portrait above Braille text

Date	Mintage	F	VF	XF	Unc	BU
2009(B)	—	—	1.00	1.50	2.00	—
2009(C)	—	—	1.00	1.50	2.00	—
2009(C) Packaged	—	—	—	—	—	5.00
2009(C) Proof	—	Value: 20.00				
2009(C) Proof, packaged	—	Value: 7.00				
2009(Hy) Packaged	—	—	—	—	—	5.00

KM# 386 2 RUPEES

5.8000 g., Stainless Steel, 27 mm. **Subject:** Reserve Bank of India, 75th Anniversary **Obv:** Lion capitol of Ashoka Pillar **Rev:** Lion advancing left, palm tree in background

Date	Mintage	F	VF	XF	Unc	BU
2010(B) Proof	—	Value: 20.00				
2010(C)	—	—	1.00	1.50	3.50	—

KM# 401 2 RUPEES

5.7500 g., Stainless Steel, 25 mm. **Subject:** 19th Commonwealth Games

Date	Mintage	F	VF	XF	Unc	BU
2010(B)	—	—	—	—	3.00	—
2010(C)	—	—	—	—	1.25	—
2010(C) Proof	—	Value: 5.00				
2010(Hy)	—	—	—	—	3.00	—
2010(Hy) Packaged	—	—	—	—	—	4.00
2010(N)	—	—	—	—	1.25	—

KM# 395 2 RUPEES

4.8500 g., Stainless Steel, 25 mm. **Obv:** Lion capitol of Ashoka Pillar **Rev:** New Rupee symbol above value **Edge:** Reeded **Note:** The spacing in the reeding is different at some mints.

Date	Mintage	F	VF	XF	Unc	BU
2011(B)	—	—	0.40	0.60	1.00	—
2011(C)	—	—	0.40	0.60	1.00	—
2011(H)	—	—	0.40	0.60	1.00	—
2011(N)	—	—	0.40	0.60	1.00	—
2012(B)	—	—	0.40	0.60	1.00	—
2012(H)	—	—	0.40	0.60	1.00	—

KM# 154.2 5 RUPEES

8.9100 g., Copper-Nickel, 23 mm. **Obv:** Lion capitol of Ashoka Pillar **Rev:** Denomination flanked by flowers **Edge:** Reeded

Date	Mintage	F	VF	XF	Unc	BU
2001(C)	—	—	10.00	19.00	20.00	—
2002(C)	—	—	10.00	19.00	20.00	—
2003(C)	—	—	10.00	19.00	20.00	—

KM# 154.4 5 RUPEES

9.3000 g., Copper-Nickel, 23.4 mm. **Obv:** Lion capitol of Ashoka Pillar, Type II, Small Lion **Rev:** Denomination flanked by flowers **Edge:** Security

Date	Mintage	F	VF	XF	Unc	BU
2001(B)	—	—	1.00	1.50	2.00	—
2002(B)	—	—	1.00	1.50	2.00	—
2003(B)	—	—	1.00	1.50	2.00	—
2004(B)	—	—	1.00	1.50	2.00	—

KM# 154.1 5 RUPEES

9.3000 g., Copper-Nickel, 23.4 mm. **Obv:** Lion capitol of Ashoka Pillar. Type I **Rev:** Denomination flanked by flowers **Edge:** Security **Note:** (C) - Calcutta mint has issued 2 distinctly different security edge varieties every year 1992-2003 with large dots and thick center line, w/small dots and narrow center line.

Date	Mintage	F	VF	XF	Unc	BU
2001(N)	—	—	1.00	1.50	2.00	—
2001(C) Plain 1	—	—	1.00	1.50	2.00	—
2001(C) Serif 1	—	—	1.00	1.50	2.00	—
2001(H)	—	—	1.00	1.50	2.00	—
2002(C)	—	—	1.00	1.50	2.00	—
2002(H)	—	—	1.00	1.50	2.00	—
2002(N)	—	—	1.00	1.50	2.00	—
2003(C)	—	—	1.00	1.50	2.00	—
2003(H)	—	—	1.00	1.50	2.00	—
2003(N)	—	—	1.00	1.50	2.00	—
2004(C)	—	—	10.00	15.00	20.00	—
2004(H)	—	—	2.00	3.00	4.00	—
2004(N)	—	—	1.00	1.50	2.00	—

KM# 304 5 RUPEES

9.0700 g., Copper-Nickel, 23.19 mm. **Subject:** 2600th Anniversary Birth of Bhagwan Mahavir **Obv:** Lion capitol of Ashoka Pillar above denomination **Rev:** Swastika above hand in irregular frame **Edge:** Security

Date	Mintage	F	VF	XF	Unc	BU
2001(B)	—	—	2.00	6.00	10.00	—
2001(B) Proof	—	Value: 70.00				
2001(N)	—	—	2.00	6.00	10.00	—

KM# 308 5 RUPEES

8.9200 g., Copper-Nickel, 23.1 mm. **Subject:** Dadabhai Naroji **Obv:** Lion capitol of Ashoka Pillar above value **Rev:** Bust of Naroji 3/4 right **Edge:** Security

Date	Mintage	F	VF	XF	Unc	BU
ND(2003)(B)	—	—	2.50	4.50	6.50	—
ND(2003)(C)	—	—	2.00	4.00	6.00	—
ND(2003)(H)	—	—	2.00	4.00	6.00	—

KM# A308 5 RUPEES

Copper-Nickel, 23.1 mm. **Subject:** Dadabhai Naroji **Obv:** Lion capital of Ashoka Pillar above denomination **Rev:** Bust of Naroji 3/4 right **Edge:** Security

Date	Mintage	F	VF	XF	Unc	BU
ND(2003)(C)	—	—	10.00	15.00	20.00	—
ND(2003)(C) Reeded Edge	—	—	10.00	18.00	30.00	—

KM# 317.1 5 RUPEES

8.8000 g., Copper-Nickel, 23.1 mm. **Obv:** Lion capitol of Ashoka Pillar **Rev:** K. Kamaraj bust 3/4 left, dates below **Edge:** Security

Date	Mintage	F	VF	XF	Unc	BU
ND(2003)(B)	—	—	2.00	7.00	11.00	—
ND(2003)(B) Proof	—	Value: 40.00				
ND(2003)(B) Proof, restrike	—	Value: 30.00				
ND(2003)(H)	—	—	2.00	4.00	6.00	—

KM# 317.2 5 RUPEES

8.8000 g., Copper-Nickel, 23.1 mm. **Obv:** Lion capitol of Ashoka Pillar **Rev:** K. Kamaraj 3/4 left, dates below **Edge:** Reeded

Date	Mintage	F	VF	XF	Unc	BU
ND (2003)(H)	—	—	10.00	15.00	20.00	—

KM# 329 5 RUPEES

9.0700 g., Copper-Nickel, 23.1 mm. **Obv:** Lion capitol of Ashoka Pillar, value below **Rev:** Shastri bust 3/4 left **Rev. Legend:** LALBAHADUR SHASTRI BIRTH CENTENARY **Edge:** Security

Date	Mintage	F	VF	XF	Unc	BU
ND(2004)(C)	—	—	4.00	10.00	20.00	—
ND(2004)(C) Proof	—	Value: 40.00				

KM# 329a 5 RUPEES

6.0300 g., Stainless Steel, 23 mm. **Obv:** Lion capital of Ashoka Pillar, value below **Rev:** Shastri bust 3/4 left **Rev. Legend:** LALBAHADUR SHASTRI BIRTH CENTENARY **Edge:** Security

Date	Mintage	F	VF	XF	Unc	BU
2004(C)	—	—	6.00	12.00	20.00	—

KM# 325 5 RUPEES

8.8500 g., Copper-Nickel, 23 mm. **Subject:** 75th Anniversary Dandi March **Obv:** Lion capitol of Ashoka Pillar **Rev:** Ghandi leading marchers **Edge:** Security type

Date	Mintage	F	VF	XF	Unc	BU
ND(2005)(B)	—	—	50.00	75.00	100	—
ND(2005)(B) Proof	—	Value: 125				
ND(2005)(B) Proof, restrike	—	Value: 100				

KM# 325a 5 RUPEES

6.0300 g., Stainless Steel, 23 mm. **Subject:** 75th Anniversary Dandi March **Obv:** Lion capital of Ashoka Pillar **Rev:** Ghandi leading marchers **Edge:** Security

Date	Mintage	F	VF	XF	Unc	BU
ND(2005)(B)	—	—	2.00	3.00	4.00	—

KM# A365 5 RUPEES

6.0300 g., Stainless Steel, 23 mm. **Subject:** Dandi March, 75th Anniversary **Note:** New design

Date	Mintage	F	VF	XF	Unc	BU
2005(B)	—	—	1.00	1.50	2.00	—

KM# 324 5 RUPEES

8.8500 g., Copper-Nickel, 23 mm. **Obv:** Lion capitol of Ashoka Pillar **Rev:** Mahatma Basaveshwara bust 3/4 left **Edge:** Security

Date	Mintage	F	VF	XF	Unc	BU
ND(2006)(B)	—	—	4.00	6.00	10.00	—
ND(2006)(B) Proof	—	Value: 15.00				
ND(2006)(B) Proof, packaged	—	Value: 10.00				

KM# 324a 5 RUPEES

6.0000 g., Stainless Steel **Subject:** Mahatma Basveshwara

Date	Mintage	F	VF	XF	Unc	BU
ND(2006)(B)	—	—	—	—	4.00	—

KM# A324 5 RUPEES

6.0300 g., Stainless Steel, 23 mm. **Obv:** Lion capital of Ashoka Pillar **Rev:** Mahatma Basaveshwara bust 3/4 left **Edge:** Security

Date	Mintage	F	VF	XF	Unc	BU
ND(2006)(B)	—	—	6.00	8.00	10.00	—

KM# 354 5 RUPEES
6.0300 g., Stainless Steel, 22.8 mm. **Subject:** O.N.G.C., 50th Anniversary **Obv:** Lion capitol of Ashoka Pillar, value below

Date	Mintage	F	VF	XF	Unc	BU
ND(2006)(C)	—	—	—	—	2.00	—
ND(2006)(C) Proof	—	Value: 20.00				
ND(2006)(H)	—	—	—	—	2.00	—

KM# 355 5 RUPEES
9.5000 g., Copper-Nickel, 23.1 mm. **Subject:** Jagathguru Sree Narayana Guruden **Obv:** Lion capitol of Ashoka Pillar **Rev:** Bust facing

Date	Mintage	F	VF	XF	Unc	BU
ND(2006)(B)	—	—	4.00	6.00	10.00	—
ND(2006)(B) Proof	—	Value: 40.00				

KM# 355a 5 RUPEES
6.0300 g., Stainless Steel, 22.9 mm. **Subject:** Jagadguru Shree Narayan Guru **Obv:** Lion capitol of Ashoka Pilar **Rev:** Bust facing

Date	Mintage	F	VF	XF	Unc	BU
ND(2006)(B)	—	—	—	—	6.00	—

KM# 357 5 RUPEES
6.0300 g., Stainless Steel, 22.9 mm. **Subject:** State Bank of India, 200th Anniversary **Obv:** Lion capitol of Ashoka Pillar, value below **Edge:** Security

Date	Mintage	F	VF	XF	Unc	BU
ND(2006)(C)	—	—	—	—	2.00	—
ND(2006)(C) Proof	—	Value: 10.00				
ND(2006)(C) Proof, restrike	—	Value: 7.50				
ND(2006)(H)	—	—	—	—	2.00	—

KM# 330 5 RUPEES
6.0300 g., Stainless Steel, 23 mm. **Subject:** Information Technology **Obv:** Lion capitol of Ashoka Pillar **Rev:** Waves below value **Edge:** Security

Date	Mintage	F	VF	XF	Unc	BU
2007(B)	—	—	—	1.00	4.00	—
2007(C)	—	—	—	1.00	4.00	—
2007(H)	—	—	—	1.00	4.00	—
2008(B)	—	—	—	1.00	4.00	—
2008(C)	—	—	—	1.00	4.00	—
2008(H)	—	—	—	1.00	4.00	—

KM# 409 5 RUPEES
Nickel-Brass, 23 mm. **Subject:** Kuka Movement, 150th Anniversary **Note:** Issued in 2013.

Date	Mintage	F	VF	XF	Unc	BU
1857-2007	—	—	—	—	1.00	3.00

KM# A330 5 RUPEES
6.0300 g., Stainless Steel, 23 mm. **Subject:** Information Technology **Obv:** Lion capitol of Ashoka Pillar **Rev:** Waves below value **Edge:** Security **Note:** Mule, Obv of 50 Paisa

Date	Mintage	F	VF	XF	Unc	BU
2007(B)	—	—	60.00	80.00	100	—

KM# 356 5 RUPEES
6.0300 g., Copper-Nickel, 22.9 mm. **Subject:** Lokmanya Bal Gangadhar Tilak, 150th Anniversary

Date	Mintage	F	VF	XF	Unc	BU
2007(B) Proof	—	Value: 20.00				
2007(N)	—	—	—	—	100	—

Note: Withdrawn.

KM# 359 5 RUPEES
6.0300 g., Stainless Steel, 22.9 mm. **Subject:** First War of Independence **Obv:** Lion capitol of Ashoka Pillar, value below

Date	Mintage	F	VF	XF	Unc	BU
ND(2007)(B)	—	—	—	—	4.00	—
ND(2007)(B) Proof	—	Value: 20.00				
ND(2007)(B) Proof, restrike	—	Value: 10.00				

KM# 360.1 5 RUPEES
6.0300 g., Stainless Steel, 23 mm. **Subject:** Khadi and Village Industries Commission, 50th Anniversary **Rev:** Ghandi seated facing

Date	Mintage	F	VF	XF	Unc	BU
2007(B)	—	—	—	—	10.00	—

KM# 360.1a 5 RUPEES
9.5000 g., Copper-Nickel, 23 mm. **Rev:** Ghandi seated facing

Date	Mintage	F	VF	XF	Unc	BU
2007(B)	—	—	—	—	100	—
2007(B) Proof	—	Value: 60.00				

KM# 360.2 5 RUPEES
6.0300 g., Stainless Steel, 23 mm. **Rev:** Ghandi seated facing **Note:** Mint mark "M" in between 2007

Date	Mintage	F	VF	XF	Unc	BU
2007(B)	—	—	—	—	12.00	—

KM# 390 5 RUPEES
6.0300 g., Stainless Steel, 22.9 mm. **Obv:** Lion capitol of Ashoka Pillar **Rev:** Cross

Date	Mintage	F	VF	XF	Unc	BU
2007(C)	—	—	—	—	20.00	—

KM# 403.2 5 RUPEES
Nickel-Brass, 23 mm. **Subject:** Comptroller & Auditgeneral of India, 150th Anniversary **Obv:** Lion capital of Ashoka Pillar **Rev:** Logo **Note:** The date on coin is 2007 but issued in 2012

Date	Mintage	F	VF	XF	Unc	BU
2007(C) Proof	—	Value: 40.00				
2007(H)	—	—	—	—	1.00	—

KM# 406 5 RUPEES
6.0000 g., Stainless Steel, 23 mm. **Subject:** Shaheed Bhagat Singh, 100th Anniversary of Birth **Obv:** Lion capital of Ashoka Pillar **Rev:** Bust facing wearing hat **Note:** Dated 2007, but released in 2012.

Date	Mintage	F	VF	XF	Unc	BU
1907-2007(C)	—	—	—	2.00	6.50	—
1907-2007(C) Proof	—	Value: 40.00				
1907-2007(H)	—	—	—	2.00	6.50	—
1907-2007(Hy) Packaged	—	—	—	—	—	6.00

KM# 373 5 RUPEES
6.0000 g., Nickel-Brass, 23 mm. **Obv:** Lion capitol of Ashoka Pillar **Rev:** Value flanked by flowers

Date	Mintage	F	VF	XF	Unc	BU
2009(B)	—	—	—	—	1.00	—
2009(C)	—	—	—	—	1.00	—
2009(H)	—	—	—	—	1.00	—
2010(B)	—	—	—	—	1.00	—
2010(C)	—	—	—	—	1.00	—
2010(H)	—	—	—	—	1.00	—
2010(N)	—	—	—	—	2.00	—

KM# 365 5 RUPEES
6.0300 g., Nickel-Brass, 23 mm. **Subject:** St. Alphonsa, 100th Anniversary **Obv:** Lion capitol of Ashoka Pillar **Rev:** Bust facing in habit

Date	Mintage	F	VF	XF	Unc	BU
2009(B)	—	—	—	—	3.00	—
2009(B) Packaged	—	—	—	—	—	6.00
2009(B) Proof	—	Value: 40.00				
2009(C)	—	—	—	—	4.00	—
2009(H)	—	—	—	—	4.50	—

KM# 367 5 RUPEES
6.0300 g., Nickel-Brass, 23 mm. **Subject:** C. N. Annadurai, 100th Anniversary of Birth **Obv:** Lion capitol of Ashoka Pillar **Rev:** Portrait, signature below

Date	Mintage	F	VF	XF	Unc	BU
2009(B)	—	—	—	—	3.00	—
2009(C)	—	—	—	—	2.00	—
2009(C) Proof	—	Value: 30.00				
2009(H)	—	—	—	—	6.00	—

KM# 376 5 RUPEES
6.0300 g., Nickel-Brass, 23 mm. **Subject:** 60th Anniversary of Commonwealth **Obv:** Lion capitol of Ashoka Pillar **Rev:** Building

Date	Mintage	F	VF	XF	Unc	BU
2009(B)	—	—	—	—	3.00	—
2009(B) Proof	—	Value: 30.00				
2009(C)	—	—	—	—	2.00	—
2009(H)	—	—	—	—	4.00	—

KM# 392 5 RUPEES
6.0300 g., Nickel-Brass, 23 mm. **Subject:** Dr. Rajendra Prasad **Obv:** Lion capitol of Ashoka Pillar

Date	Mintage	F	VF	XF	Unc	BU
2009(B)	—	—	—	2.50	4.00	—
2009(C)	—	—	—	—	2.00	—
2009(C) Proof	—	Value: 30.00				
2009(Hy)	—	—	—	—	2.00	—
2009(Hy) Packaged	—	—	—	—	—	5.00
2009(N)	—	—	—	—	2.00	—

KM# 413 5 RUPEES
6.0000 g., Nickel-Brass, 23 mm. **Subject:** Perarignar Anna, 100th Anniversary of Birth

Date	Mintage	F	VF	XF	Unc	BU
2009	—	—	—	—	—	50.00
2009 Proof	—	Value: 75.00				

KM# 379 5 RUPEES
6.0000 g., Nickel-Brass, 23 mm. **Subject:** Income Tax, 150th Anniversary **Obv:** Lion capitol of Ashoka Pillar **Rev:** Chanakya portrait at right **Edge:** Reeded

Date	Mintage	F	VF	XF	Unc	BU
2010(B)	—	—	—	1.00	4.00	—
2010(C)	—	—	—	1.00	4.00	—
2010(C) Proof	—	Value: 20.00				
2010(Hy)	—	—	—	1.00	4.00	—
2010(Hy) Packaged	—	—	—	—	—	5.50
2011(C)	—	—	—	1.00	4.00	—
2011(N)	—	—	—	1.00	4.00	—

KM# 377 5 RUPEES
6.0000 g., Nickel-Brass, 23 mm. **Obv:** Lion capitol of Ashoka Pillar **Rev:** C. Subramaniam facing **Edge:** Reeded

Date	Mintage	F	VF	XF	Unc	BU
2010	—	—	—	—	3.00	—
Note: (B)without mint mark						
2010(B) Proof	—	Value: 30.00				
2010(C)	—	—	—	—	3.00	—
2010(Hy)	—	—	—	—	1.00	—
2010(Hy) Packaged	—	—	—	—	—	5.50
2010(N)	—	—	—	—	1.00	—

KM# 378 5 RUPEES
6.0000 g., Nickel-Brass, 23 mm. **Subject:** Brihadeeswarar Temple, 1000th Anniversary **Obv:** Lion capitol of Ashoka Pillar **Rev:** Statue of King Raja Rajan I before temple **Edge:** Reeded

Date	Mintage	F	VF	XF	Unc	BU
2010(B)	—	—	—	—	1.00	—
2010(B) Proof	—	Value: 30.00				
2010(C)	—	—	—	—	2.00	—
2010(Hy)	—	—	—	—	1.00	—
2010(Hy) Packaged	—	—	—	—	—	5.50
2010(N)	—	—	—	—	1.00	—

KM# 381 5 RUPEES
6.0300 g., Nickel-Brass, 23 mm. **Subject:** Mother Theresa, 100th Anniversary of Birth **Obv:** Lion capitol of Ashoka Pillar **Rev:** Bust facing

Date	Mintage	F	VF	XF	Unc	BU
2010	—	—	—	—	3.00	—
Note: (B) without mint mark						
2010(C)	—	—	—	—	1.00	—
2010(C) Proof	—	Value: 30.00				
2010(Hy)	—	—	—	—	1.00	—
2010(Hy) Packaged	—	—	—	—	—	5.50
2010(N)	—	—	—	—	1.00	—

KM# 387 5 RUPEES
6.0300 g., Nickel-Brass, 23 mm. **Subject:** Reserve Bank of India, 75th Anniversary **Obv:** Lion capitol of Ashoka Pillar **Rev:** Lion advancing left, palm tree in background

Date	Mintage	F	VF	XF	Unc	BU
2010(B)	—	—	0.75	1.00	2.00	—
2010(B) Proof	—	Value: 30.00				

KM# 391 5 RUPEES
6.0000 g., Nickel-Brass, 23 mm. **Subject:** 19th Commonwealth Games Delhi 2010 **Obv:** Lion capital of Ashoka Pillar **Rev:** Logo of commonwealth

Date	Mintage	F	VF	XF	Unc	BU
2010(B)	—	—	—	—	3.00	—
2010(C)	—	—	—	—	1.00	—
2010(C) Proof	—	Value: 30.00				
2010(Hy)	—	—	—	—	1.00	—
2010(Hy) Packaged	—	—	—	—	—	5.50
2010(N)	—	—	—	—	1.00	—

KM# A391 5 RUPEES
6.0000 g., Nickel-Brass **Subject:** XIX Commonwealth Game Delhi 2010 **Obv:** Lion capital of Ashoka Pillar, KM#399.1 **Rev:** Logo of Commonwealth Games **Note:** Mule, without Denomination

Date	Mintage	F	VF	XF	Unc	BU
2010(C)	—	—	50.00	100	200	—

KM# 403.1 5 RUPEES
Nickel-Brass, 23 mm. **Subject:** Comptroller & Auditgeneral of India, 150th Anniversary **Obv:** Lion capital of Ashoka Pillar **Rev:** Logo

Date	Mintage	F	VF	XF	Unc	BU
2010(B)	—	—	—	2.50	4.00	—
2010(C)	—	—	—	2.50	4.00	—
2010(C) Proof	—	Value: 30.00				
2010(H)	—	—	—	2.50	4.00	—
2010(N)	—	—	—	2.50	4.00	—

KM# 399.3 5 RUPEES
Nickel-Brass, 23 mm. **Obv:** Lion capitol of Ashoka Pillar **Rev:** New rupee value flanked by flora **Edge:** Reeded

Date	Mintage	F	VF	XF	Unc	BU
2011(C)	—	—	—	—	10.00	—
2012(C)	—	—	—	—	10.00	—

KM# 399.1 5 RUPEES
6.0000 g., Nickel-Brass, 23 mm. **Obv:** Lion capitol of Ashoka Pillar **Rev:** New rupee value flanked by flora **Edge:** Reeded **Note:** Type I

Date	Mintage	F	VF	XF	Unc	BU
2011(C)	—	—	—	—	1.00	—
2011(H)	—	—	—	—	1.00	—
2011(N)	—	—	—	—	1.00	—
2012(B)	—	—	—	—	1.00	—
2012(C)	—	—	—	—	1.00	—
2012(H)	—	—	—	—	1.00	—
2012(N)	—	—	—	—	1.00	—

KM# 393 5 RUPEES
6.0000 g., Nickel-Brass, 23 mm. **Subject:** Rabindranath Tagore, 150th Anniversary of Birth **Obv:** Lion capitol of Ashoka Pillar **Rev:** Bust facing **Edge:** Reeded

Date	Mintage	F	VF	XF	Unc	BU
2011(B)	—	—	—	—	3.00	—
2011(C)	—	—	—	—	2.00	—
2011(C) Proof	—	Value: 40.00				
2011(C) Proof, packaged	—	Value: 4.00				
2011(Hy)	—	—	—	—	2.00	—
2011(Hy) Packaged	—	—	—	—	—	5.50
2011(N)	—	—	—	—	1.00	—

KM# 396 5 RUPEES
6.0000 g., Nickel-Brass, 23 mm. **Subject:** Indian Council of Medical Research, 100th Anniversary **Obv:** Lion capitol of Ashoka Pillar **Rev:** Anniversary Logo

Date	Mintage	F	VF	XF	Unc	BU
2011(B)	—	—	—	1.00	4.00	—
2011(B) Proof	—	Value: 30.00				
2011(C)	—	—	—	1.00	4.00	—
2011(H)	—	—	—	1.00	4.00	—
2011(N)	—	—	—	1.00	4.00	—

KM# 397 5 RUPEES
Nickel-Brass, 23 mm. **Subject:** Civil Aviation, 100th Anniversary **Obv:** Lion capitol of Ashoka Pillar **Rev:** Aircraft above 100

Date	Mintage	F	VF	XF	Unc	BU
2011(B)	—	—	—	1.00	4.00	—
2011(B) Proof	—	Value: 40.00				
2011(C)	—	—	—	1.00	4.00	—
2011(H)	—	—	—	1.00	4.00	—
2011(N)	—	—	—	1.00	4.00	—

KM# 399.2 5 RUPEES
Nickel-Brass, 23 mm. **Obv:** Lion capital of Ashoka Pillar **Rev:** New rupee value flanked by flora **Edge:** Reeded **Note:** Type 2

Date	Mintage	F	VF	XF	Unc	BU
2011(B)	—	—	—	—	10.00	—

KM# 405 5 RUPEES
6.0000 g., Nickel-Brass, 23 mm. **Subject:** Madan Mohan Malaviya, 150th Anniversary of Birth **Obv:** Lion capital of Ashoka Pillar **Rev:** Bust facing **Note:** Released in 2013.

Date	Mintage	F	VF	XF	Unc	BU
2011(B)	—	—	—	—	4.00	5.00

KM# 404 5 RUPEES
6.0000 g., Nickel-Brass, 23 mm. **Subject:** Indian Parliament, 60th Anniversary **Obv:** Lion capital of Ashoka Pillar **Rev:** Building at center

Date	Mintage	F	VF	XF	Unc	BU
2012(B)	—	—	0.50	2.00	4.00	—
2012(H)	—	—	0.50	2.00	4.00	—

KM# 309 10 RUPEES
12.5000 g., Copper-Nickel, 31 mm. **Subject:** 100th Anniversary Birth of Dr. Syama P. Mookerjee **Obv:** Lion capitol of Ashoka Pillar **Rev:** Bust of Dr. Mookerjee 1/2 right **Edge:** Reeded

Date	Mintage	F	VF	XF	Unc	BU
2001(C)	—	—	—	200	250	—
2001(C) Proof	—	Value: 350				

KM# 344 10 RUPEES
12.5000 g., Copper-Nickel, 31 mm. **Subject:** 100th Anniversary Birth of Jaya Prakash Narayan **Obv:** Lion capitol of Ashoka Pillar **Rev:** Bust of Jaya Prakash Narayan slightly left **Edge:** Reeded

Date	Mintage	F	VF	XF	Unc	BU
2002(B)	—	—	—	80.00	110	—
2002(B) Proof	—	Value: 175				

KM# 347 10 RUPEES

12.5000 g., Copper-Nickel, 31 mm. **Subject:** Sant Tukaram **Obv:** Lion capitol of Ashoka Pillar **Edge:** Reeded

Date	Mintage	F	VF	XF	Unc	BU
2002(C)	—	—	—	250	350	—
2002(C) Proof	—	Value: 500				

KM# 319 10 RUPEES

12.5000 g., Copper-Nickel, 31 mm. **Obv:** Lion capitol of Ashoka Pillar **Rev:** Bust of Maharana Pratap left

Date	Mintage	F	VF	XF	Unc	BU
2003(B)	—	—	—	80.00	100	—
2003(B) Proof	—	Value: 150				

KM# 332 10 RUPEES

12.5000 g., Copper-Nickel, 31 mm. **Obv:** Lion capitol of Ashoka Pillar **Rev:** 3/4 length military figure Veer Durgadass with spear left **Edge:** Reeded

Date	Mintage	F	VF	XF	Unc	BU
2003(B)	—	—	—	50.00	70.00	—
2003(B) Proof	—	Value: 100				

KM# 353 10 RUPEES

7.7000 g., Bi-Metallic Copper-Nickel center in Brass ring., 27 mm. **Subject:** Unity in Diversity **Obv:** Asoka Pillar **Rev:** Four heads sharing a common body

Date	Mintage	F	VF	XF	Unc	BU
2005(N)	—	—	—	—	9.00	—
2006(N)	—	—	—	—	4.00	—
2007(N)	—	—	—	—	6.00	—

Note: Poor strike quality

KM# 363 10 RUPEES

7.7000 g., Bi-Metallic Copper-Nickel center in Brass ring, 27 mm. **Subject:** Connectivity and Information Technology **Obv:** Lion capitol of Ashoka Pillar **Rev:** Large 10, wide rays above

Date	Mintage	F	VF	XF	Unc	BU
2008(N)	—	—	—	—	2.00	—
2009(N)	—	—	—	—	4.00	—
2010(B)	—	—	—	—	16.50	—
2010(N)	—	—	—	—	2.00	—

KM# 371 10 RUPEES

7.7000 g., Bi-Metallic Copper-Nickel center in Brass ring, 27 mm. **Subject:** Tercentenary of Gurta-Gaddi of Shri Guru Granth Sahibji **Obv:** Lion capitol of Ashoka Pillar and value

Date	Mintage	F	VF	XF	Unc	BU
2008(Hy) Packaged	—	—	—	—	—	7.00
2008(M) Packaged	—	—	—	—	—	7.00
2008(M) Proof	—	Value: 20.00				

KM# 372 10 RUPEES

7.7000 g., Bi-Metallic Copper-Nickel center in Brass ring, 27 mm. **Subject:** Dr. Homi Bhabha - 100th Anniversary of Birth **Obv:** Lion capitol of Ashoka Pillar and value **Rev:** Portrait

Date	Mintage	F	VF	XF	Unc	BU
2009(B)	—	—	—	—	9.00	—
2009(B) Proof	—	Value: 20.00				
2009(N)	—	—	—	—	2.00	—

KM# 388 10 RUPEES

8.0000 g., Bi-Metallic Copper-Nickel center in Aluminum-Bronze ring, 27 mm. **Subject:** Reserve Bank of India, 75th Anniversary **Obv:** Lion capitol of Ashoka Pillar **Rev:** Lion advancing left, palm tree in background

Date	Mintage	F	VF	XF	Unc	BU
2010(B)	—	—	—	2.00	6.00	—
2010(B) Proof	—	Value: 20.00				
2010(N)	—	—	—	4.00	7.00	—

KM# 400 10 RUPEES

Bi-Metallic Copper-Nickel center in Aluminum-Bronze ring, 27 mm. **Obv:** Lion capitol of Ashoka Pillar **Rev:** New rupee symbol above value

Date	Mintage	F	VF	XF	Unc	BU
2011(B)	—	—	—	—	6.00	—
2011(C)	—	—	—	—	6.00	—
2011(H)	—	—	—	—	6.00	—
2011(N)	—	—	—	—	6.00	—
2012(B)	—	—	—	—	4.00	—
2012(C)	—	—	—	—	3.00	—
2012(H)	—	—	—	—	3.00	—
2012(N)	—	—	—	—	2.00	—

KM# 407 10 RUPEES

8.0000 g., Bi-Metallic Copper-Nickel center in Aluminum-Bronze ring, 27 mm. **Subject:** Indian Parliament, 60th Anniversary **Obv:** Lion capital of Ashoka Pillar, value below **Rev:** Parliament Building

Date	Mintage	F	VF	XF	Unc	BU
2012(B)	—	—	—	4.00	6.00	—
2012(N)	—	—	—	4.00	6.00	—

KM# 310 50 RUPEES

30.0000 g., Copper-Nickel, 39 mm. **Subject:** 100th Anniversary Birth of Dr. Syama P. Mookerjee **Obv:** Lion capitol of Ashoka Pillar **Rev:** Bust of Dr. Mookerjee 1/2 right **Edge:** Reeded

Date	Mintage	F	VF	XF	Unc	BU
2001(C)	—	—	—	300	340	—
2001(C) Proof	—	Value: 450				

KM# 348 50 RUPEES

30.0000 g., Copper-Nickel, 39 mm. **Subject:** Sant Tukaram **Obv:** Lion capitol of Ashoka Pillar **Edge:** Reeded

Date	Mintage	F	VF	XF	Unc	BU
2002(C)	—	—	—	300	340	—
2002(C) Proof	—	Value: 450				

KM# 352 50 RUPEES

30.0000 g., Copper-Nickel, 39 mm. **Subject:** O.N.G.C., 50th Anniversary

Date	Mintage	F	VF	XF	Unc	BU
2006	—	—	—	—	20.00	30.00
2006 Proof	—	Value: 50.00				

KM# 408 60 RUPEES

Silver **Subject:** 60th Anniversary of Indian Parliament **Obv:** Lion capital of Ashoka Pillar

Date	Mintage	F	VF	XF	Unc	BU
2012 Proof	—	Value: 50.00				

KM# 389 75 RUPEES

35.0000 g., 0.5000 Silver 0.5626 oz. ASW, 42 mm. **Subject:** Reserve Bank of India, 75th Anniversary **Obv:** Lion capitol of Ashoka Pillar **Rev:** Lion advancing left, palm tree in background

Date	Mintage	F	VF	XF	Unc	BU
2010(B)	—	—	—	—	50.00	55.00
2010B Proof	—	Value: 85.00				
2010(C)	—	—	—	—	50.00	55.00
2010(N)	—	—	—	—	50.00	55.00

KM# 311 100 RUPEES

35.0000 g., 0.5000 Silver 0.5626 oz. ASW, 44 mm. **Subject:** 10th Anniversary Dr, Syama P. Mookerjee **Obv:** Lion capitol of Ashoka Pillar **Rev:** Bust of Dr. Mookerjee 1/2 right **Edge:** Reeded

Date	Mintage	F	VF	XF	Unc	BU
2001(C)	—	—	—	325	400	—
2001(C) Proof	—	Value: 500				

KM# 312 100 RUPEES

35.0000 g., 0.5000 Silver 0.5626 oz. ASW, 44 mm. **Subject:** 2600th Anniversary Birth of Bhagwan Mahavir **Obv:** Lion capitol of Ashoka Pillar **Rev:** Swastika above hand in irregular frame **Edge:** Reeded

Date	Mintage	F	VF	XF	Unc	BU
2001(B)	—	—	—	350	400	—
2001(B) Proof	—	Value: 500				

KM# 345 100 RUPEES

35.0000 g., 0.5000 Silver 0.5626 oz. ASW, 44 mm. **Subject:** 100th Anniversary Birth of Jaya Prakash Narayan **Obv:** Lion capitol of Ashoka Pillar **Rev:** Bust of Jaya Prakash Narayan slightly left **Edge:** Reeded

Date	Mintage	F	VF	XF	Unc	BU
2002(B)	—	—	—	200	—	250
2002(B) Proof	—	Value: 325				

KM# 349 100 RUPEES

35.0000 g., 0.5000 Silver 0.5626 oz. ASW, 44 mm. **Subject:** Sant Tukaram **Obv:** Lion capitol of Ashoka Pillar **Edge:** Reeded

Date	Mintage	F	VF	XF	Unc	BU
2002(C)	—	—	—	400	—	450
2002(C) Proof	—	Value: 60.00				

KM# 318 100 RUPEES

35.0000 g., 0.5000 Silver 0.5626 oz. ASW, 44 mm. **Obv:** Lion capitol of Ashoka Pillar **Rev:** K. Kamaraj above life dates **Edge:** Reeded

Date	Mintage	F	VF	XF	Unc	BU
ND(2003)(B)	—	—	—	80.00	120	—
ND(2003)(B) Proof	—	Value: 150				
ND(2003)(B) Proof, restrike	—	Value: 80.00				

KM# 320 100 RUPEES

35.0000 g., 0.5000 Silver 0.5626 oz. ASW, 44 mm. **Obv:** Lion capitol of Ashoka Pillar **Rev:** Bust of Maharana Pratap left **Edge:** Reeded

Date	Mintage	F	VF	XF	Unc	BU
2003(B)	—	—	—	120	140	—
2003(B) Proof	—	Value: 225				

KM# 333 100 RUPEES

35.0000 g., 0.5000 Silver 0.5626 oz. ASW, 44 mm. **Obv:** Lion capitol of Ashoka Pillar **Rev:** 3/4 length military figure Veer Durgadass with spear left **Edge:** Reeded

Date	Mintage	F	VF	XF	Unc	BU
2003(B)	—	—	—	60.00	80.00	—
2003(B) Proof	—	Value: 120				

KM# 340 100 RUPEES

35.0000 g., 0.5000 Silver 0.5626 oz. ASW, 44 mm. **Subject:** 150th Anniversary Indian Railways **Obv:** Lion capitol of Ashoka Pillar **Rev:** Cartoon elephant holding railroad lantern **Edge:** Reeded

Date	Mintage	F	VF	XF	Unc	BU
2003(C)	—	—	—	60.00	80.00	—
2003(C) Proof	—	Value: 120				
2003(C) Proof, restrike	—	Value: 80.00				

KM# 335 100 RUPEES

35.0000 g., 0.5000 Silver 0.5626 oz. ASW, 44 mm. **Subject:** 150th Anniversary Telecommunications **Obv:** Lion capitol of Ashoka Pillar **Rev:** Cartoon bird standing holding cell phone **Edge:** Reeded

Date	Mintage	F	VF	XF	Unc	BU
2004(B)	—	—	—	60.00	100	—
2004(B) Proof	—	Value: 120				
2004(B) Proof, restrike	—	Value: 80.00				

KM# 337 100 RUPEES

35.0000 g., 0.5000 Silver 0.5626 oz. ASW, 44 mm. **Subject:** 100th Anniversary Birth of Lal Bahadur Shasti **Obv:** Lion capitol of Ashoka Pillar **Rev:** Bust of Lal Bahadur Shastri 3/4 left **Edge:** Reeded

Date	Mintage	F	VF	XF	Unc	BU
ND(2004)(C)	—	—	—	60.00	80.00	—
ND(2004)(C) Proof	—	Value: 120				

KM# 343 100 RUPEES

35.0000 g., 0.5000 Silver 0.5626 oz. ASW, 44 mm. **Subject:** Indian Postal Service, 150th Anniversary **Obv:** Lion capitol of Ashoka Pillar **Rev:** Perforation corner of a postage stamp **Edge:** Reeded

Date	Mintage	F	VF	XF	Unc	BU
2004(C)	—	—	—	60.00	80.00	—
2004(C) Proof	—	Value: 120				
2004(C) Proof, restrike	—	Value: 80.00				

KM# 338 100 RUPEES

35.0000 g., 0.5000 Silver 0.5626 oz. ASW, 44 mm. **Subject:** 75th Anniversary Dandi March **Obv:** Lion capitol of Ashoka Pillar **Rev:** Ghandi leading marchers **Edge:** Reeded

Date	Mintage	F	VF	XF	Unc	BU
ND(2005)(B)	—	—	—	50.00	60.00	—
ND(2005)(B) Proof	—	Value: 80.00				
ND(2005)(B) Proof, restrike	—	Value: 75.00				

KM# 339 100 RUPEES

35.0000 g., 0.5000 Silver 0.5626 oz. ASW, 44 mm. **Obv:** Lion capitol of Ashoka Pillar **Rev:** Bust of Mahatma Basaveshwara slightly left **Edge:** Reeded

Date	Mintage	F	VF	XF	Unc	BU
ND(2006)B	—	—	—	50.00	60.00	—
ND(2006)B Proof	—	Value: 80.00				

KM# 358 100 RUPEES

35.0000 g., 0.5000 Silver 0.5626 oz. ASW, 44 mm. **Subject:** State Bank of India, 200th Anniversary

Date	Mintage	F	VF	XF	Unc	BU
2006	—	—	—	—	—	65.00
2006(C) Proof	—	Value: 90.00				
2006(C) Proof, restrike	—	Value: 75.00				

KM# 364 100 RUPEES

35.0000 g., 0.5000 Silver 0.5626 oz. ASW, 44 mm. **Subject:** Jagatguru Shree Narayan Gurudev

Date	Mintage	F	VF	XF	Unc	BU
2006	—	—	—	—	40.00	50.00
2006 Proof	—	Value: 100				

KM# 410 100 RUPEES

35.0000 g., 0.5000 Silver 0.5626 oz. ASW, 44 mm. **Subject:** Kuka Movement, 150th Anniversary **Note:** Issued in 2012.

Date	Mintage	F	VF	XF	Unc	BU
1857-2007 Proof	—	Value: 55.00				

KM# 351 100 RUPEES

35.0000 g., 0.5000 Silver 0.5626 oz. ASW, 44 mm. **Subject:** 75th Anniversary Indian Air Force **Obv:** Lion capitol of Ashoka Pillar **Edge:** Reeded

Date	Mintage	F	VF	XF	Unc	BU
2007(C)	—	—	—	50.00	60.00	—
2007(C) Proof	—	Value: 80.00				

KM# 366 100 RUPEES

35.0000 g., 0.5000 Silver 0.5626 oz. ASW, 44 mm. **Subject:** Lokmanya Bal Gangadhar Tilak, 150th Anniversary

Date	Mintage	F	VF	XF	Unc	BU
2007	—	—	—	—	—	50.00
2007 Proof	—	Value: 100				

KM# 384 100 RUPEES

35.0000 g., 0.5000 Silver 0.5626 oz. ASW, 44 mm. **Subject:** First War of Independence, 150th Anniversary

Date	Mintage	F	VF	XF	Unc	BU
2007	—	—	—	—	—	50.00
2007 Proof	—	Value: 90.00				
2007 Proof, restrike	—	Value: 70.00				

KM# 370 100 RUPEES

35.0000 g., 0.5000 Silver 0.5626 oz. ASW, 44 mm. **Subject:** Gur-Ta Gaddi, 300th Anniversary

Date	Mintage	F	VF	XF	Unc	BU
2008	—	—	—	—	—	75.00
2008 Proof	—	Value: 100				

KM# 369 100 RUPEES

35.0000 g., 0.5000 Silver 0.5626 oz. ASW, 44 mm. **Subject:** Louis Braille, 200th Anniversary of Birth **Obv:** Lion capitol of Ashoka Pillar

Date	Mintage	F	VF	XF	Unc	BU
2009	—	—	—	50.00	60.00	—
2009 Proof	—	Value: 80.00				

KM# 383 100 RUPEES

35.0000 g., 0.5000 Silver 0.5626 oz. ASW, 44 mm. **Subject:** Homi Bhamba **Obv:** Lion capitol of Ashoka Pillar

Date	Mintage	F	VF	XF	Unc	BU
2009	—	—	—	50.00	60.00	—
2009 Proof	—	Value: 80.00				

KM# 411 100 RUPEES

35.0000 g., 0.5000 Silver 0.5626 oz. ASW, 44 mm. **Subject:** Saint Alphanso, 100th Anniversary of Birth

Date	Mintage	F	VF	XF	Unc	BU
2009	—	—	—	—	—	50.00
2009 Proof	—	Value: 75.00				

KM# 412 100 RUPEES

35.0000 g., 0.5000 Silver 0.5626 oz. ASW, 44 mm. **Subject:** Perarignar Anna, 100th Anniversary

Date	Mintage	F	VF	XF	Unc	BU
2009	—	—	—	—	—	50.00
2009 Proof	—	Value: 75.00				

KM# 414 100 RUPEES

35.0000 g., 0.5000 Silver 0.5626 oz. ASW, 44 mm. **Subject:** Commonwealth, 60th Anniversary

Date	Mintage	F	VF	XF	Unc	BU
2009	—	—	—	—	—	50.00
2009 Proof	—	Value: 75.00				

KM# 382 100 RUPEES

35.0000 g., 0.5000 Silver 0.5626 oz. ASW, 44 mm. **Subject:** Mother Theresa, 100th Anniversary of birth **Obv:** Lion capitol of Ashoka Pillar **Rev:** Bust facing

Date	Mintage	F	VF	XF	Unc	BU
2010	—	—	—	50.00	60.00	—
2010 Proof	—	Value: 80.00				

KM# 415 100 RUPEES

35.0000 g., 0.5000 Silver 0.5626 oz. ASW, 44 mm. **Subject:** Dr. Rajendra Prasad, 125th Anniversary of Birth

Date	Mintage	F	VF	XF	Unc	BU
2010	—	—	—	—	—	50.00
2010 Proof	—	Value: 75.00				

KM# 417 100 RUPEES

35.0000 g., 0.5000 Silver 0.5626 oz. ASW, 44 mm. **Subject:** 19th Commonwealth Games, Delhi

Date	Mintage	F	VF	XF	Unc	BU
2010	—	—	—	—	—	50.00
2010 Proof	—	Value: 75.00				

KM# 418 100 RUPEES

35.0000 g., 0.5000 Silver 0.5626 oz. ASW, 44 mm. **Subject:** C. Subramaniam, 100th Anniversary of Birth

Date	Mintage	F	VF	XF	Unc	BU
2010	—	—	—	—	—	40.00
2010 Proof	—	Value: 70.00				

KM# 420 100 RUPEES

35.0000 g., 0.5000 Silver 0.5626 oz. ASW, 44 mm. **Subject:** Civil Aviation, 100th Anniversary

Date	Mintage	F	VF	XF	Unc	BU
2011	—	—	—	—	—	50.00
2011 Proof	—	Value: 70.00				

KM# 421 100 RUPEES

35.0000 g., 0.5000 Silver 0.5626 oz. ASW, 44 mm. **Subject:** Council of Medical Research, 100th Anniversary

Date	Mintage	F	VF	XF	Unc	BU
2011	—	—	—	—	—	50.00
2011 Proof	—	Value: 70.00				

KM# 380 150 RUPEES

35.0000 g., 0.5000 Silver 0.5626 oz. ASW, 44 mm. **Subject:** Income Tax, 150th Anniversary **Obv:** Lion capitol of Ashoka Pillar **Rev:** Chanakya portrait at right

Date	Mintage	F	VF	XF	Unc	BU
2010(C)	—	—	—	50.00	60.00	—
2010(C) Proof	—	Value: 80.00				

KM# 416 150 RUPEES

35.0000 g., 0.5000 Silver 0.5626 oz. ASW, 44 mm. **Subject:** Rabindranth Tagore, 150th Anniversary of Birth

Date	Mintage	F	VF	XF	Unc	BU
2010	—	—	—	—	—	50.00
2010 Proof	—	Value: 80.00				

KM# 419 150 RUPEES

35.0000 g., 0.5000 Silver 0.5626 oz. ASW, 44 mm. **Subject:** Comptroller & Auditor General, 150th Anniversary

Date	Mintage	F	VF	XF	Unc	BU
2011	—	—	—	—	—	40.00
2011 Proof	—	Value: 75.00				

KM# 361 1000 RUPEES

35.0000 g., 0.5000 Silver 0.5626 oz. ASW, 44 mm. **Subject:** Khadi & Village Industries Commission, 50th Anniversary

Date	Mintage	F	VF	XF	Unc	BU
2007	—	—	—	—	—	50.00
2007 Proof	—	Value: 100				

KM# 422 1000 RUPEES

35.0000 g., 0.5000 Silver 0.5626 oz. ASW, 44 mm. **Subject:** Brihadeeswarar Temple, 1000th Anniversary

Date	Mintage	F	VF	XF	Unc	BU
2010	—	—	—	—	—	75.00
2010 Proof	—	Value: 90.00				

MINT SETS

KM#	Date	Mintage	Identification	Issue Price	Mkt Val
MS61	2001 (3)	—	KM#309, 310, 311. Shyama Prasad Mookherji.	—	750
MS62	2001 (2)	—	KM#304, 312 Bhagwan Mahavir.	—	325
MS63	2002 (3)	—	KM#313, 344, 345 Kok Nayak Jaiparakash Narayan.	—	275
MS60	2002 (3)	—	KM#347, 348, 349 Saint Tukaram.	—	780
MS66	2003 (2)	—	KM#316, 332, 333 Veer Durgadas.	—	150
MS66A	2003 (2)	—	KM#307, 340 Railways, restrike 2010.	—	80.00
MS64	2003 (3)	—	KM#314, 319, 320 Maharana Pratap.	—	200
MS68	2003 (2)	—	KM#317.1, 318 Bharat Ratna Shri K. Kamraj.	—	130
MS68A	2003 (2)	—	KM#317.1, 318 Bharat Ratna K. Kamraj, reminted 2012.	—	125
MS67	2004 (2)	—	KM#321, 343 India Post.	—	110
MS67A	2004 (2)	—	KM#321, 343 India Post, restrike 2010.	—	80.00
MS71	2005 (2)	—	KM#329, 337 Lal Bahadur Shastri.	—	120
MS69	2004 (2)	—	KM#334, 335 Telecommunications.	—	110
MS69A	2004 (2)	—	KM#334, 335 Telecommunication, reminted 2010.	—	100
MS70	2005 (2)	—	KM#325, 338 Dandi march.	—	150
MS70A	2005 (2)	—	KM#325, 338 Dandi march, reminted 2012.	—	125
MS73	2006 (2)	—	KM#324, 339 Mahatma Basveshwar.	—	120
MS74	2006 (2)	—	KM#352, 354 O.N.G.C.	—	30.00

KM#	Date	Mintage	Identification	Issue Price	Mkt Val
MS75	2006 (2)	—	KM#355, 364 Jagatguru Shree Narayan Gurudev	—	120
MS72	2006 (2)	—	KM#357, 358 State Bank of India.	—	90.00
MS72A	2006 (2)	—	KM#357, 358 State Bank of India, restrike 2010.	—	80.00
MS77	2007 (2)	—	KM#350, 351 Indian Air Force	—	85.00
MS76	2007 (2)	—	KM#356, 366 Lokmanya Bal Gangadhar Tilak	—	120
MS79	2007 (2)	—	KM#359, 384 First War of Independence	—	120
MS79A	2007 (2)	—	KM#359, 384 First War of Independence, restruck 2012	—	100
MS78	2007 (2)	—	KM#361, 362 Khadi & Village Industies	—	120
MS80	2007 (2)	—	MK#402, 406 Shaheed Bhagat Singh	—	100
MS80A	2007 (2)	—	KM#402, 406 Shaheed Shagat Singh	—	110
MS81	2008 (2)	—	KM#370, 371 Gaddi, front cover big gurudwara	—	100
MS81A	2008 (2)	—	KM#370, 371 Gaddi, front cover small gurudwara	—	100
MS85	2009 (2)	—	KM#372, 383 Homi Bhabha	—	100
MS82	2009 (2)	—	KM#368, 369 Louis Braille	—	70.00
MS83	2009 (2)	—	KM#365, 411 Saint Alphanso	—	100
MS86	2009 (2)	—	KM#376, 414 Commonwealth	—	100
MS87	2010 (2)	—	KM#392, 415 Dr. Rajendra Prasad	—	100
MS84	2009 (2)	—	KM#412, 413 Perarignar Anna	—	100
MS92	2010 (2)	—	KM#377, 418 Subramanian, 5 Rupee Z type	—	70.00
MS92A	2010 (2)	—	KM#377, 418 Subramanian, 5 Rupee round type	—	90.00
MS98	2010 (2)	—	KM#378, 422, released 2011 Brihadeeswrar Temple	—	90.00
MS94	2011 (2)	—	KM#379, 380 Income Tax	—	100
MS91	2010 (2)	—	KM#381, 382 Teresa, back cover coin design	—	70.00
MS91A	2010 (2)	—	KM#381, 382 Teresa, back cover mother with child	—	70.00
MS89	2010 (5)	—	KM#385-389 Reserve Bank of India	—	100
MS90	2010 (3)	—	KM#391, 401, 417 XIX Commonwealth Games	—	90.00
MS95	2011 (2)	—	KM#403.1, 419 Comptroller & Auditor General	—	90.00
MS88	2010 (2)	—	MS#393, 416 Rabindranath Tagore	—	100
MS93	2011 (5)	—	KM#394, 395, 398, 399.1, 400 New Rupee Logo	—	11.00
MS97	2011 (2)	—	KM#396, 421 Council of Medical Research	—	100
MS96	2011 (2)	—	KM#397, 420 Civil Aviation of India	—	100

PROOF SETS

KM#	Date	Mintage	Identification	Issue Price	Mkt Val
PS70	2001 (4)	—	KM#303, 309, 310, 311 Dr. Syhama Prasad Mookherji.	—	1,200
PS71	2001 (2)	—	KM#304, 312 Bhagwam Mahavir 2600th Janm Kalyanak.	—	480
PS72	2002B (3)	—	KM#313, 344, 345 Lok Nayak Jaiprakash Narayan.	—	400
PS69	2002(C) (4)	—	KM#346-349	—	1,200
PS75	2003(C) (2)	—	KM#307, 340 Railways.	—	180
PS76	2003 (2)	—	KM#307, 340 Railways, 2010 restrike.	—	120
PS73	2003 (3)	—	KM#314, 319, 320 Maharana Pratap.	—	320
PS74	2003B (3)	—	KM#316, 332, 333 Veer Durgdas.	—	210
PS79	ND(2003) (2)	—	KM#317.1, 318 Bharat Ratna Shri K. Kamraj.	—	150
PS80	2004 (2)	—	KM#317.1, 318 Bharat Ratna Shri K. Kamraj, 2012 restrike.	—	150
PS81	2004 (2)	—	KM#317.1, 318 Bharat Ratna Shri K. Kamraj, Executive restrike.	—	170
PS77	2004 (2)	—	KM#321, 343 India Post.	—	140
PS78	2004 (2)	—	KM#324, 343 India Post, 2010 restrike.	—	80.00
PS82	2004B (2)	—	KM#334, 335 Telecommunications.	—	150
PS83	2005 (2)	—	KM#3334, 335 Telecommunications, restrike.	—	140
PS87	2004(C) (2)	—	KM#336, 337 Lal Bahadur Shastri.	—	160
PS84	2005B (2)	—	KM#325, 338 Dandi march.	—	150
PS85	2005 (2)	—	KM#325, 338 Dandi march, restrike.	—	140
PS86	2005 (2)	—	KM#325, 338 Dandi march, Executive restrike.	—	175
PS90	2006B (2)	—	KM#324, 339 Mahatma Basveshwara.	—	150
PS91	2006 (2)	—	KM#352, 354 O.N.G.C.	—	352
PS92	2006 (2)	—	KM#355, 364 Jagatguru Shree Narayan Gurudev.	—	150
PS88	2006 (2)	—	KM#357, 358 State Bank	—	110
PS89	2006 (2)	—	KM#357, 358 State Bank, 2010 restrike.	—	90.00
PS94	2007 (2)	—	KM#350, 351 Indian Air Force.	—	100
PS93	2007 (2)	—	KM#356, 366 Lokmanya Bal Gangadhar Tilak.	—	150
PS96	2007 (2)	—	KM#359, 384 First War of Independence.	—	150
PS97	2007 (2)	—	KM#359, 384 First War of Independence. 2012 Restrike.	—	140
PS95	2007 (2)	—	KM#361, 362 Khadi & Village Industries Commission.	—	150
PS98	2007 (2)	—	KM#402, 406 Shaheed Bhagat Singh.	—	135
PS99	2007 (2)	—	KM#402, 406 Spelled as Shagat Singh.	—	140
PS100	2008 (2)	—	KM#370, 371 Gur-Ta Gaddi, large image of Gurudwara (temple) on front cover.	—	150
PS101	2008 (2)	—	KM#370, 371 Gur-Ta Gaddi, small image of Gurudwara (temple) on front cover.	—	140
PS105	2009 (2)	—	KM#372, 383 Homi Bhabha.	—	150
PS102	2009 (2)	—	KM#368, 369 Louis Braille.	—	140
PS103	2009 (2)	—	KM#365, 411 Saint Alphanso.	—	150
PS106	2009 (2)	—	KM#376, 414 Commonwealth.	—	150
PS107	2010 (2)	—	KM#392, 415 Dr. Rajendra Prasad.	—	135
PS104	2009 (2)	—	KM#412, 413 Perarignar Anna	—	140
PS109	2010 (5)	—	KM#385, 386, 387, 388, 389 Reserve Bank of India.	—	140
PS114	2010 (2)	—	KM#377, 418 C. Subramaniam.	—	140
PS115	2010 (2)	—	KM#377, 418 C. Subramaniam, executive package.	—	155
PS120	2010 (2)	—	KM#378, 422 Brihadeeswarar Temple.	—	110
PS121	2010 (2)	—	KM#378, 422 Brihadeeswarar Temple, executive set.	—	150
PS122	2010 (2)	—	KM#378, 422 Brihadeeswarar Temple, VIP set.	—	180
PS116	2011 (2)	—	KM#379, 380 Income tax.	—	140
PS111	2010 (2)	—	KM#381, 382 Mother Teresa, Error Hindi "tursa" on package.	—	110
PS112	2010 (2)	—	KM#381, 382 Mother Teresa.	—	80.00
PS113	2010 (2)	—	KM#381, 382 Mother Teresa. Back cover Mother with child.	—	80.00
PS110	2010 (3)	—	KM#391, 401, 417 19th Commonwealth Games.	—	135
PS117	2011 (2)	—	KM#403.1, 419 Comptroller & Auditor General.	—	135
PS108	2010 (2)	—	KM#393, 416 Rabindranth Tagore.	—	150
PS119	2011 (2)	—	KM#396, 421 Council of Medical Research.	—	135
PS118	2011 (2)	—	KM#397, 420 Civil Aviation.	—	135

The Republic of Indonesia, the world's largest archipelago, extends for more than 3,000 miles (4,827 km.) along the equator from the mainland of southeast Asia to Australia. The 17,508 islands comprising the archipelago have a combined area of 788,425 sq. mi. (1,919,440 sq. km.) and a population of 205 million, including East Timor. On August 30, 1999, the Timorese majority voted for independence. The Inter FET (International Forces for East Timor) is now in charge of controlling the chaotic situation. Capitol: Jakarta. Petroleum, timber, rubber, and coffee are exported.

Modern coinage issued by the Republic of Indonesia includes separate series for West Irian and for the Riau Archipelago, an area of small islands between Singapore and Sumatra.

MONETARY SYSTEM

100 Sen = 1 Rupiah

REPUBLIC

STANDARD COINAGE

KM# 60 50 RUPIAH

1.3500 g., Aluminum, 19.95 mm. **Obv:** National emblem **Rev:** Black-naped Oriole **Edge:** Plain

Date	Mintage	F	VF	XF	Unc	BU
2001	—	—	—	—	0.30	1.00
2002	—	—	—	—	0.30	1.00

KM# 61 100 RUPIAH

1.7900 g., Aluminum, 23 mm. **Obv:** National emblem **Rev:** Palm Cockatoo **Edge:** Plain

Date	Mintage	F	VF	XF	Unc	BU
2001	—	—	—	—	0.75	1.25
2002	—	—	—	—	0.75	1.25
2003	—	—	—	—	0.75	1.25
2004	—	—	—	—	0.75	1.25
2005	—	—	—	—	0.75	1.25
2008	—	—	—	—	0.75	1.25

KM# 66 200 RUPIAH

2.4000 g., Aluminum, 25 mm. **Obv:** National arms **Rev:** Balinese starling bird above value **Edge:** Plain

Date	Mintage	F	VF	XF	Unc	BU
2003	—	—	—	—	1.00	1.50
2008	—	—	—	—	1.00	1.50

KM# 59 500 RUPIAH

5.3500 g., Aluminum-Bronze, 24 mm. **Obv:** National emblem **Rev:** Jasmine above denomination

Date	Mintage	F	VF	XF	Unc	BU
2001	—	—	—	—	1.75	2.25
2002	—	—	—	—	1.75	2.25
2003	—	—	—	—	1.75	2.25

KM# 67 500 RUPIAH

3.0500 g., Aluminum, 27.2 mm. **Obv:** National arms **Rev:** Jasmine flower above value **Edge:** Segmented reeding

Date	Mintage	F	VF	XF	Unc	BU
2003	—	—	—	—	2.00	2.50
2008	—	—	—	—	2.00	2.50

KM# 70 1000 RUPIAH
4.5000 g., Nickel Plated Steel, 24 mm. **Obv:** National arms above value **Rev:** Angklung - a traditional bamboo musical instrument; West Java Provincial's Governor office in Bandung in background **Rev. Legend:** ANGKLUNG / date

Date	Mintage	F	VF	XF	Unc	BU
2010	—	—	—	—	0.75	1.00

KM# 64 25000 RUPIAH
28.2800 g., 0.9250 Silver 0.8410 oz. ASW, 38.6 mm. **Subject:** Centennial of Sukarno's Birth **Obv:** National arms **Rev:** Uniformed bust of Sukarno **Edge:** Reeded

Date	Mintage	F	VF	XF	Unc	BU
2001 Proof	500	Value: 120				

KM# 68 25000 RUPIAH
28.2800 g., 0.9250 Silver 0.8410 oz. ASW, 38.61 mm. **Subject:** Mohammas Hatta, vice-president (1945-1956) **Obv:** National Arms **Rev:** Bust facing

Date	Mintage	F	VF	XF	Unc	BU
2002 Proof	2,000	Value: 120				

KM# 65 500,000 RUPIAH
15.0000 g., 0.9990 Gold 0.4818 oz. AGW, 28.2 mm. **Subject:** Centennial of Sukarno's Birth **Obv:** National arms **Rev:** Head left **Edge:** Reeded

Date	Mintage	F	VF	XF	Unc	BU
2001 Proof	500	Value: 1,050				

KM# 69 500,000 RUPIAH
15.0000 g., 0.9990 Gold 0.4818 oz. AGW, 28.2 mm. **Subject:** Mohammad Hatta, vice-president (1945-1956) **Obv:** National Arms **Rev:** Bust facing

Date	Mintage	F	VF	XF	Unc	BU
2002 Proof	2,000	Value: 875				

IRAN

The Islamic Republic of Iran, located between the Caspian Sea and the Persian Gulf in southwestern Asia, has an area of 636,296 sq. mi. (1,648,000 sq. km.) and a population of 59.7 million. Capital: Tehran. Although predominantly an agricultural state, Iran depends heavily on oil for foreign exchange. Crude oil, carpets and agricultural products are exported.

In 1931 the Kingdom of Persia became known as the Kingdom of Iran. In 1979 the monarchy was toppled and an Islamic Republic proclaimed.

TITLES

دار الخلافة

Dar al-Khilafat

RULERS
Islamic Republic, SH1358-/1979-AD

MINT NAME

طهران

Tehran

تفليس

Tiflis

MINT MARKS
H - Heaton (Birmingham)
L - Leningrad (St. Petersburg)

COIN DATING
Iranian coins were dated according to the Moslem lunar calendar until March 21, 1925 (AD), when dating was switched to a new calendar based on the solar year, indicated by the notation SH. The monarchial calendar system was adopted in 1976 = MS2535 and was abandoned in 1978 = MS2537. The previously used solar year calendar was restored at that time.

MONETARY SYSTEM
20 Shahis = 1 Rial (100 Dinars)

ISLAMIC REPUBLIC

MILLED COINAGE

KM# 1260 50 RIALS
Copper-Nickel, 26 mm. **Subject:** Shrine of Hazrat Masumah **Obv:** Value and date **Rev:** Shrine within beaded circle **Edge:** Reeded

Date	Mintage	F	VF	XF	Unc	BU
SH1380 (2001)	—	—	2.50	3.50	5.00	—
SH1382 (2003)	—	—	2.50	3.50	5.00	—

KM# 1266 50 RIALS
3.5100 g., Aluminum-Bronze, 20.1 mm. **Obv:** Value and date **Rev:** Hazrat Masumah Shrine **Edge:** Reeded **Mint:** Tehran

Date	Mintage	F	VF	XF	Unc	BU
SH1382(2003)	—	—	—	—	50.00	—
SH1383(2004)	—	—	—	—	2.50	—
SH1384(2005)	—	—	—	—	2.50	—
SH1385(2006)	—	—	—	—	2.50	—

KM# 1261.2 100 RIALS
Copper-Nickel, 29 mm. **Obv:** Value and date **Rev:** Shrine within designed border **Note:** Thick denomination and numerals

Date	Mintage	F	VF	XF	Unc	BU
SH1380 (2001)	—	—	—	—	6.50	—
SH1382 (2003)	—	—	—	—	6.50	—

KM# 1267 100 RIALS
4.6200 g., Aluminum-Bronze, 22.9 mm. **Obv:** Value, date divides wreath below **Rev:** Imam Reza Shrine **Edge:** Reeded **Mint:** Tehran

Date	Mintage	F	VF	XF	Unc	BU
SH1382(2003)	—	—	—	—	50.00	—
SH1383(2004)	—	—	—	—	3.50	—
SH1384(2005)	—	—	—	—	3.50	—
SH1385(2006)	—	—	—	—	3.50	—

KM# 1262 250 RIALS
10.7000 g., Bi-Metallic Copper-Nickel center in Brass ring, 28.3 mm. **Obv:** Value within circle, inscription and date divide wreath **Rev:** Stylized flower within circle and wreath

Date	Mintage	F	VF	XF	Unc	BU
SH1381 (2002)	—	—	—	—	7.50	—
SH1382 (2003)	—	—	—	—	7.50	—

KM# 1268 250 RIALS
5.5000 g., Copper-Nickel, 24.6 mm. **Obv:** Value, date below divides sprays **Rev:** Stylized flower within sprays **Edge:** Plain **Mint:** Tehran

Date	Mintage	F	VF	XF	Unc	BU
SH1382(2003)	—	—	—	—	50.00	—
SH1383(2004)	—	—	—	—	4.50	—
SH1384(2005)	—	—	—	—	4.50	—
SH1385(2006)	—	—	—	—	4.50	—

KM# 1282 250 RIALS
5.0000 g., Aluminum-Bronze, 24 mm. **Obv:** Value, date below divides sprays **Rev:** Stylized flower within sprays **Mint:** Tehran

Date	Mintage	F	VF	XF	Unc	BU
SH1386(2007)	—	—	—	—	0.75	1.75

KM# 1269 500 RIALS
8.9100 g., Bi-Metallic Aluminum-Bronze center in Copper-Nickel ring, 27.1 mm. **Obv:** Value **Rev:** Bird and flowers **Edge:** Reeded **Mint:** Tehran

Date	Mintage	F	VF	XF	Unc	BU
SH1382(2003)	—	—	—	—	50.00	—
SH1383(2004)	—	—	—	—	6.00	—
SH1384(2005)	—	—	—	—	6.00	—
SH1385(2006)	—	—	—	—	6.00	—

KM# 1283 500 RIALS
6.3500 g., Aluminum-Bronze, 25.5 mm. **Obv:** Value in ornamental circle **Rev:** Bird and flowers **Mint:** Tehran

Date	Mintage	F	VF	XF	Unc	BU
SH1386(2007)	—	—	—	—	1.50	3.00

REFORM COINAGE

KM# 1270 250 RIALS
2.8000 g., Copper-Nickel, 18.5 mm. **Rev:** Feyziyeh School

Date	Mintage	F	VF	XF	Unc	BU
AH1387 (2008)	—	—	—	—	—	5.00
SH1388 (2009)	—	—	—	—	—	5.00

KM# 1271 500 RIALS
3.9000 g., Copper-Nickel, 20.6 mm. **Rev:** Saadi Tomb

Date	Mintage	F	VF	XF	Unc	BU
SH1388 (2009)	—	—	—	—	—	6.00

KM# 1281 500 RIALS
3.9000 g., Copper-Nickel, 20.6 mm. **Subject:** Freedom of Khorramshahr **Obv:** Value in wreath **Rev:** Stylized flower

Date	Mintage	F	VF	XF	Unc	BU
SH1390 (2011)	—	—	—	—	2.00	5.00

KM# 1285 500 RIALS
3.5000 g., Aluminum-Bronze, 20.3 mm. **Obv:** Vlaue **Rev:** Dove shaped tulip **Mint:** Tehran

Date	Mintage	F	VF	XF	Unc	BU
AH1390 (2011)	50,000,000	—	—	—	1.50	3.00

KM# 1272 1000 RIALS
5.8000 g., Copper-Nickel, 23.7 mm. **Rev:** Khajou Bridge in Isfahan

Date	Mintage	F	VF	XF	Unc	BU
SH1388 (2009)	—	—	—	—	—	12.00

KM# 1274 1000 RIALS
5.8000 g., Copper-Nickel, 23.7 mm. **Rev:** Ali in star

Date	Mintage	F	VF	XF	Unc	BU
SH1389(2010)	—	—	—	—	—	12.00

KM# 1275 1000 RIALS
5.8000 g., Copper-Nickel, 23.7 mm. **Rev:** Kaaba Cubus

Date	Mintage	F	VF	XF	Unc	BU
SH1389(2010)	—	—	—	—	—	12.00

KM# 1284 1000 RIALS
5.8000 g., Aluminum-Bronze, 23.7 mm. **Subject:** National Statistical Office, 75th Anniversary **Obv:** Mountain above value **Rev:** Tile motif **Mint:** Tehran

Date	Mintage	F	VF	XF	Unc	BU
AH1389 (2010)	—	—	—	—	2.25	4.50

KM# 1286 1000 RIALS
4.6000 g., Aluminum-Bronze, 23 mm. **Obv:** Value **Rev:** Dafoldills **Mint:** Tehran

Date	Mintage	F	VF	XF	Unc	BU
AH1390 (2011)	60,000,000	—	—	—	2.25	4.50

KM# 1276 2000 RIALS
6.8000 g., Copper-Nickel, 23.7 mm. **Subject:** Central Bank of the Islamic Republic of Iran, 50th Anniversary

Date	Mintage	F	VF	XF	Unc	BU
SH1389(2010)	—	—	—	—	—	25.00

KM# 1278 2000 RIALS
Copper-Nickel **Obv:** Value **Rev:** Mosque

Date	Mintage	F	VF	XF	Unc	BU
SH1389 (2010)	—	—	—	—	—	—

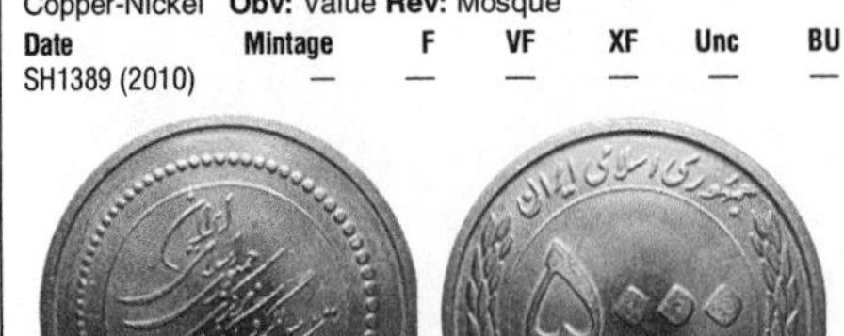

KM# 1277 5000 RIALS
Copper-Nickel

Date	Mintage	F	VF	XF	Unc	BU
SH1389(2010)	—	—	—	—	—	—

KM# 1279 5000 RIALS
Copper-Nickel **Obv:** Value

Date	Mintage	F	VF	XF	Unc	BU
SH1389 (2010)	—	—	—	—	—	—

KM# 1280 5000 RIALS
Copper-Nickel **Obv:** Value **Rev:** Two roses

Date	Mintage	F	VF	XF	Unc	BU
SH1389 (2010)	—	—	—	—	—	—

BULLION COINAGE

Issued by the National Bank of Iran

KM# 1250.2 1/2 AZADI
4.0680 g., 0.9000 Gold 0.1177 oz. AGW **Obv:** Legend larger **Obv. Legend:** "Spring of Freedom"

Date	Mintage	F	VF	XF	Unc	BU
SH1381 (2002)	—	—	—	—	215	—
SH1383 (2004)	—	—	—	—	215	—

IRAQ

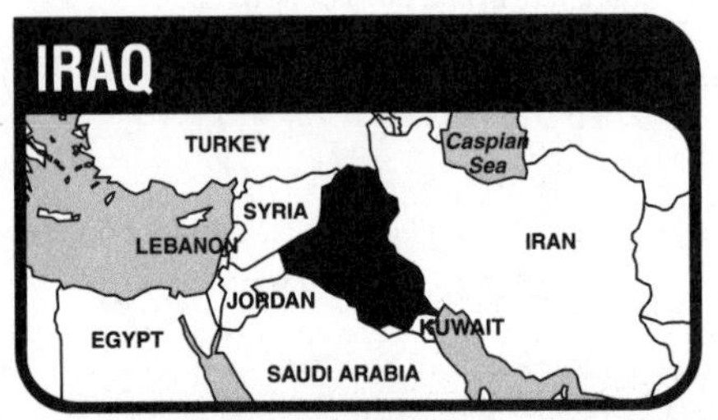

The Republic of Iraq, historically known as Mesopotamia, is located in the Near East and is bordered by Kuwait, Iran, Turkey, Syria, Jordan and Saudi Arabia. It has an area of 167,925 sq. mi. (434,920 sq. km.) and a population of 19 million. Capital: Baghdad. The economy of Iraq is based on agriculture and petroleum. Crude oil accounted for 94 percent of the exports before the war with Iran began in 1980.

Mesopotamia was the site of a number of flourishing civilizations of antiquity - Sumeria, Assyria, Babylonia, Parthia, Persia and the Biblical cities of Ur, Ninevehand and Babylon. Desired because of its favored location, which embraced the fertile alluvial plains of the Tigris and Euphrates Rivers, Mesopotamia - 'land between the rivers'- was conquered by Cyrus the Great of Persia, Alexander of Macedonia and by Arabs who made the legendary city of Baghdad the capital of the ruling caliphate. Suleiman the Magnificent conquered Mesopotamia for Turkey in1534, and it formed part of the Ottoman Empire until 1623, and from 1638 to 1917. Great Britain, given a League of Nations mandate over the territory in 1920, recognized Iraq as a kingdom in 1922. Iraq became an independent constitutional monarchy presided over by the Hashemite family, direct descendants of the prophet Mohammed, in 1932. In 1958, the army-led revolution of July 14 overthrew the monarchy and proclaimed a republic.

MONETARY SYSTEM

Falus, Fulus — Fals, Fils — Falsan

50 Fils = 1 Dirham
200 Fils = 1 Riyal
1000 Fils = 1 Dinar (Pound)

REPUBLIC

DECIMAL COINAGE

KM# 175 25 DINARS
2.5000 g., Copper Plated Steel, 17.4 mm. **Obv:** Value **Rev:** Map **Edge:** Plain

Date	Mintage	F	VF	XF	Unc	BU
AH1425-2004	—	—	—	0.30	0.75	1.00

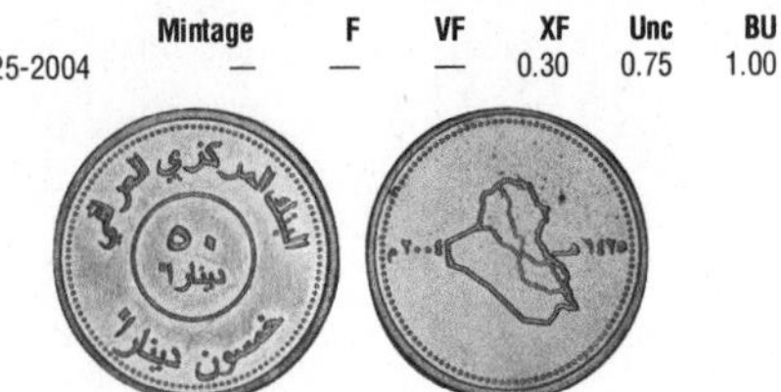

KM# 176 50 DINARS
4.3400 g., Brass Plated Steel, 22 mm. **Obv:** Value and legend **Rev:** Map **Edge:** Plain

Date	Mintage	F	VF	XF	Unc	BU
AH1425-2004	—	—	—	0.50	1.20	1.60

KM# 177 100 DINARS
4.3000 g., Stainless Steel, 22 mm. **Obv:** Value **Rev:** Map **Edge:** Reeded

Date	Mintage	F	VF	XF	Unc	BU
AH1425-2004	—	—	—	0.80	2.00	2.50

IRELAND REPUBLIC

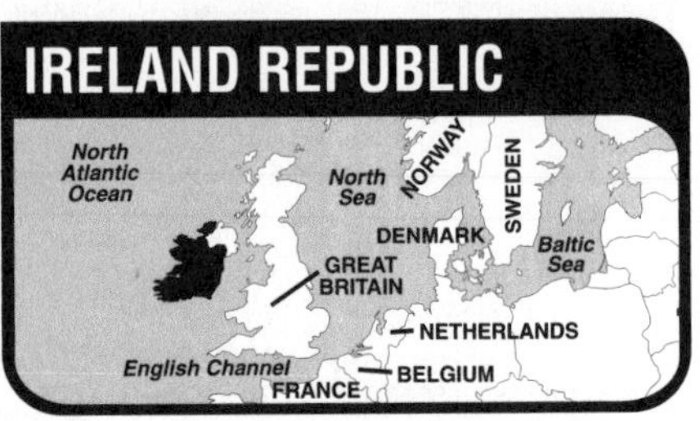

Ireland, which occupies five-sixths of the island of Ireland located in the Atlantic Ocean west of Great Britain, has an area of 27,136 sq. mi. (70,280 sq. km.) and a population of 4.3 million. Capital: Dublin. Agriculture and dairy farming are the principal industries. Meat, livestock, dairy products and textiles are exported.

REPUBLIC

EURO COINAGE

European Union Issues

KM# 32 EURO CENT
2.2700 g., Copper Plated Steel, 16.25 mm. **Obv:** Harp **Rev:** Denomination and globe **Edge:** Plain

Date	Mintage	F	VF	XF	Unc	BU
2002	404,339,788	—	—	—	0.35	—
2003	67,902,182	—	—	—	0.35	—
2004	174,833,634	—	—	—	0.35	—
2005	126,964,391	—	—	—	0.35	—
2006	105,413,273	—	—	—	0.35	—
2006 Proof	5,000	Value: 15.00				
2007	18,515,843	—	—	—	0.35	—
2007 Proof	10,000	Value: 12.00				
2008	59,002,134	—	—	—	0.35	—
2009	42,109,347	—	—	—	0.35	—
2009 Proof	5,000	Value: 12.00				
2010	4,946,711	—	—	—	0.35	—
2010 Proof	5,000	Value: 12.00				
2011	—	—	—	—	0.35	—
2011 Proof	5,000	Value: 12.00				
2012	—	—	—	—	0.35	—
2012 Proof	—	Value: 12.00				
2013	—	—	—	—	0.35	—
2013 Proof	—	Value: 12.00				

KM# 33 2 EURO CENT
3.0000 g., Copper Plated Steel, 18.75 mm. **Obv:** Harp **Rev:** Denomination and globe **Edge:** Plain with groove

Date	Mintage	F	VF	XF	Unc	BU
2002	354,643,386	—	—	—	0.50	—
2003	177,290,034	—	—	—	0.50	—
2004	143,004,694	—	—	—	0.50	—

Date	Mintage	F	VF	XF	Unc	BU
2005	72,544,884	—	—	—	0.50	—
2006	26,568,597	—	—	—	0.50	—
2006 Proof	5,000	Value: 15.00				
2007	84,291,248	—	—	—	0.50	—
2007 Proof	10,000	Value: 12.00				
2008	42,116,152	—	—	—	0.50	—
2009	7,284,499	—	—	—	0.50	—
2009 Proof	5,000	Value: 12.00				
2010	3,496,511	—	—	—	0.50	—
2010 Proof	5,000	Value: 12.00				
2011	—	—	—	—	0.50	—
2011 Proof	5,000	Value: 12.00				
2012	—	—	—	—	0.50	—
2012 Proof	—	Value: 12.00				
2013	—	—	—	—	0.50	—
2013 Proof	—	Value: 12.00				

KM# 34 5 EURO CENT

4.0000 g., Copper Plated Steel, 19.60 mm. **Obv:** Harp **Rev:** Denomination and globe **Edge:** Plain

Date	Mintage	F	VF	XF	Unc	BU
2002	456,270,848	—	—	—	0.75	—
2003	48,352,370	—	—	—	0.75	—
2004	80,354,322	—	—	—	0.75	—
2005	56,454,380	—	—	—	0.75	—
2006	88,003,370	—	—	—	0.75	—
2006 Proof	5,000	Value: 18.00				
2007	36,225,742	—	—	—	0.75	—
2007 Proof	10,000	Value: 15.00				
2008	61,844,008	—	—	—	0.75	—
2009	10,333,341	—	—	—	0.75	—
2009 Proof	5,000	Value: 15.00				
2010	1,023,881	—	—	—	0.75	—
2010 Proof	5,000	Value: 15.00				
2011	—	—	—	—	0.75	—
2011 Proof	5,000	Value: 15.00				
2012	—	—	—	—	0.75	—
2012 Proof	—	Value: 15.00				
2013	—	—	—	—	0.75	—
2013 Proof	—	Value: 15.00				

KM# 35 10 EURO CENT

4.0700 g., Brass, 19.75 mm. **Obv:** Harp **Rev:** Denomination and map **Edge:** Reeded

Date	Mintage	F	VF	XF	Unc	BU
2002	275,913,000	—	—	—	1.00	—
2003	133,815,907	—	—	—	1.00	—
2004	36,732,778	—	—	—	1.00	—
2005	4,652,786	—	—	—	1.00	—
2006	9,208,411	—	—	—	1.00	—
2006 Proof	5,000	Value: 18.00				

KM# 47 10 EURO CENT

4.0700 g., Brass, 19.75 mm. **Obv:** Harp **Rev:** Relief map of Western Europe, stars, lines and value **Edge:** Reeded

Date	Mintage	F	VF	XF	Unc	BU
2007	54,434,307	—	—	—	1.00	—
2007 Proof	10,000	Value: 15.00				
2008	53,997,990	—	—	—	1.00	—
2009	10,850,328	—	—	—	1.00	—
2009 Proof	5,000	Value: 15.00				
2010	1,078,313	—	—	—	1.00	—
2010 Proof	5,000	Value: 15.00				
2011	—	—	—	—	1.00	—
2011 Proof	5,000	Value: 15.00				
2012	—	—	—	—	1.00	—
2012 Proof	—	Value: 15.00				
2013	—	—	—	—	1.00	—
2013 Proof	—	Value: 15.00				

KM# 36 20 EURO CENT

5.7300 g., Brass, 22.25 mm. **Obv:** Harp **Rev:** Denomination and map **Edge:** Notched

Date	Mintage	F	VF	XF	Unc	BU
2002	234,575,562	—	—	—	1.25	—
2003	57,142,221	—	—	—	1.25	—
2004	32,421,447	—	—	—	1.25	—
2005	40,439,062	—	—	—	1.25	—
2006	10,357,229	—	—	—	1.25	—
2006 Proof	5,000	Value: 20.00				

KM# 48 20 EURO CENT

5.7300 g., Brass, 22.25 mm. **Obv:** Harp **Rev:** Relief map of Western Europe, stars, lines and value **Edge:** Notched

Date	Mintage	F	VF	XF	Unc	BU
2007	12,953,789	—	—	—	1.25	—
2007 Proof	10,000	Value: 18.00				
2008	45,990,533	—	—	—	1.25	—
2009	4,279,307	—	—	—	1.25	—
2009 Proof	5,000	Value: 18.00				
2010	1,027,059	—	—	—	1.25	—
2010 Proof	5,000	Value: 18.00				
2011	—	—	—	—	1.25	—
2011 Proof	5,000	Value: 18.00				
2012	—	—	—	—	1.25	—
2012 Proof	—	Value: 18.00				
2013	—	—	—	—	1.25	—
2013 Proof	—	Value: 18.00				

KM# 37 50 EURO CENT

7.8100 g., Brass, 24.25 mm. **Obv:** Harp **Rev:** Denomination and map **Edge:** Reeded

Date	Mintage	F	VF	XF	Unc	BU
2002	144,144,592	—	—	—	1.50	—
2003	11,811,926	—	—	—	1.50	—
2004	6,748,912	—	—	—	1.50	—
2005	17,253,568	—	—	—	1.50	—
2006	966,138	—	—	—	1.50	—
2006 Proof	5,000	—	—	—	—	—

KM# 49 50 EURO CENT

7.8100 g., Brass, 24.25 mm. **Obv:** Harp **Rev:** Relief map of Western Europe, stars, lines and value **Edge:** Reeded

Date	Mintage	F	VF	XF	Unc	BU
2007	4,991,002	—	—	—	1.50	—
2007 Proof	10,000	Value: 20.00				
2008	1,122,371	—	—	—	1.50	—
2009	1,876,011	—	—	—	1.50	—
2009 Proof	5,000	Value: 20.00				
2010	1,173,242	—	—	—	1.50	—
2010 Proof	5,000	Value: 20.00				
2011	—	—	—	—	1.50	—
2011 Proof	5,000	Value: 20.00				
2012	—	—	—	—	1.50	—
2012 Proof	—	Value: 20.00				
2013	—	—	—	—	1.50	—
2013 Proof	—	Value: 20.00				

KM# 38 EURO

7.5000 g., Bi-Metallic Copper-Nickel center in Brass ring, 23.25 mm. **Obv:** Harp **Rev:** Denomination and map **Edge:** Reeded and plain sections

Date	Mintage	F	VF	XF	Unc	BU
2002	135,139,737	—	—	—	2.75	—
2003	2,520,000	—	—	—	2.75	—
2004	1,632,990	—	—	—	2.75	—
2005	6,769,777	—	—	—	2.75	—
2006	4,023,722	—	—	—	2.75	—
2006 Proof	5,000	Value: 25.00				

KM# 50 EURO

7.5000 g., Bi-Metallic Copper-Nickel center in Brass ring, 23.25 mm. **Obv:** Harp **Rev:** Relief map of Western Europe, stars, lines and value **Edge:** Reeded and plain sections

Date	Mintage	F	VF	XF	Unc	BU
2007	1,850,049	—	—	—	2.75	—
2007 Proof	10,000	Value: 22.00				
2008	2,609,757	—	—	—	2.75	—
2009	3,314,828	—	—	—	2.75	—
2009 Proof	5,000	Value: 22.00				
2010	1,082,716	—	—	—	2.75	—
2010 Proof	5,000	Value: 22.00				
2011	—	—	—	—	2.75	—
2011 Proof	5,000	Value: 22.00				
2012	—	—	—	—	2.75	—
2012 Proof	—	Value: 22.00				
2013	—	—	—	—	2.75	—
2013 Proof	—	Value: 22.00				

KM# 39 2 EURO

8.5200 g., Bi-Metallic Nickel-Brass center in Copper-Nickel ring, 25.7 mm. **Obv:** Harp **Rev:** Denomination and map **Edge:** Reeded with 2's and stars

Date	Mintage	F	VF	XF	Unc	BU
2002	90,548,166	—	—	—	4.00	—
2003	2,631,076	—	—	—	4.00	—
2004	3,738,186	—	—	—	4.00	—
2005	11,982,981	—	—	—	4.00	—
2006	3,860,519	—	—	—	4.00	—
2006 Proof	5,000	Value: 28.00				

KM# 51 2 EURO

8.5200 g., Bi-Metallic Nickel-Brass center in Copper-Nickel ring, 25.7 mm. **Obv:** Harp **Rev:** Relief map of Western Europe, stars, lines and value **Edge:** Reeded with 2's and stars

Date	Mintage	F	VF	XF	Unc	BU
2007	7,595,260	—	—	—	4.00	—
2007 Proof	10,000	Value: 25.00				
2008	5,792,003	—	—	—	4.00	—
2009	30,063	—	—	—	4.00	—
2009 Proof	5,000	Value: 25.00				
2010	1,448,746	—	—	—	4.00	—
2010 Proof	5,000	Value: 25.00				
2011	—	—	—	—	4.00	—
2011 Proof	5,000	Value: 25.00				
2012	—	—	—	—	4.00	—
2012 Proof	—	Value: 25.00				
2013	—	—	—	—	4.00	—
2013 Proof	—	Value: 25.00				

KM# 53 2 EURO
8.4500 g., Bi-Metallic Nickel-Brass center in Copper-Nickel ring, 25.72 mm. **Subject:** 50th Anniversary Treaty of Rome **Obv:** Open treaty book **Rev:** Large value at left, modified outline of Europe at right **Edge:** Reeded with stars and 2's

Date	Mintage	F	VF	XF	Unc	BU
2007	4,605,112	—	—	—	5.00	10.00
2007 Special Unc.	35,000	—	—	—	—	20.00
2007 Proof	10,000	Value: 25.00				

KM# 62 2 EURO
8.5200 g., Bi-Metallic Nickel-Brass center in Copper-Nickel ring, 25.72 mm. **Subject:** EMU, 10th Anniversary

Date	Mintage	F	VF	XF	Unc	BU
2009	5,000,000	—	—	—	8.00	10.00
2009 Proof	7,000	Value: 115				

KM# 71 2 EURO
8.5000 g., Bi-Metallic Nickel-Brass center in Copper-Nickel ring, 25.75 mm. **Subject:** Euro Coinage, 10th Anniversary **Obv:** Euro symbol on globe at center, child-like rendering around **Designer:** Helmut Andexlinger

Date	Mintage	F	VF	XF	Unc	BU
2012	3,000,000	—	—	—	6.00	8.00
2012 Proof	—	Value: 25.00				

KM# 40 5 EURO
14.1900 g., Copper-Nickel, 28.4 mm. **Subject:** Special Olympics **Obv:** Harp **Rev:** Multicolor games logo **Edge:** Reeded

Date	Mintage	F	VF	XF	Unc	BU
2003	35,000	—	—	—	15.00	18.00
2003 Proof	25,000	Value: 25.00				

KM# 56 5 EURO
8.5200 g., 0.9250 Silver 0.2534 oz. ASW, 28 mm. **Subject:** International Polar Year **Obv:** Harp within wreath **Rev:** Ernest Shackleton, Tom Crean and The Endurance in distance **Edge:** Reeded

Date	Mintage	F	VF	XF	Unc	BU
2008 Proof	5,000	Value: 90.00				

KM# 41 10 EURO
28.2800 g., 0.9250 Silver 0.8410 oz. ASW, 38.61 mm. **Subject:** Special Olympics **Obv:** Gold highlighted harp, 2003, Eire **Rev:** Gold highlighted games logo **Edge:** Reeded

Date	Mintage	F	VF	XF	Unc	BU
2003 Proof	30,000	Value: 50.00				

KM# 42 10 EURO
28.2800 g., 0.9250 Silver 0.8410 oz. ASW, 38.61 mm. **Subject:** EU Presidency **Obv:** 2004, Eire, Harp **Rev:** Stylized Celtic swan **Edge:** Reeded

Date	Mintage	F	VF	XF	Unc	BU
2004 Proof	50,000	Value: 45.00				

KM# 44 10 EURO
28.2800 g., 0.9250 Silver 0.8410 oz. ASW, 38.6 mm. **Subject:** Sir William R. Hamilton **Obv:** Eire, 2005, Harp **Rev:** Triangle in circle of Greek letters used as math symbols **Edge:** Reeded

Date	Mintage	F	VF	XF	Unc	BU
2005 Proof	30,000	Value: 55.00				

KM# 45 10 EURO
28.2800 g., 0.9250 Silver 0.8410 oz. ASW, 38.61 mm. **Subject:** Samuel Beckett 1906-1989 **Obv:** 2006, Eire, Harp **Rev:** Face, value and play scene **Edge:** Reeded **Designer:** Emmet Mullins

Date	Mintage	F	VF	XF	Unc	BU
2006 Proof	35,000	Value: 50.00				

KM# 58 10 EURO
28.2800 g., 0.9250 Silver 0.8410 oz. ASW, 38.6 mm. **Subject:** European Culture - Ireland **Obv:** Irish Harp **Rev:** Celtic design

Date	Mintage	F	VF	XF	Unc	BU
2007 Proof	35,000	Value: 55.00				

KM# 54 10 EURO
28.2800 g., 0.9250 Silver 0.8410 oz. ASW, 38.61 mm. **Subject:** Skellig Michael Island **Rev:** Birds and 12 stars above island **Rev. Legend:** SCEILIG MHICHIL

Date	Mintage	F	VF	XF	Unc	BU
2008 Proof	25,000	Value: 65.00				

KM# 60 10 EURO
28.2800 g., 0.9250 Silver 0.8410 oz. ASW, 38.61 mm. **Subject:** First currency, 80th Anniversary **Obv:** Irish harp **Rev:** Ploughman design

Date	Mintage	F	VF	XF	Unc	BU
2009 Proof	15,000	Value: 55.00				

KM# 65 10 EURO
28.2800 g., 0.9250 Silver 0.8410 oz. ASW, 38.61 mm. **Subject:** The President's Award - Gaisce **Designer:** Michael Guilfoyle

Date	Mintage	F	VF	XF	Unc	BU
2010 Proof	8,000	Value: 60.00				

KM# 67 10 EURO
28.2800 g., 0.9250 Silver 0.8410 oz. ASW, 38.61 mm. **Subject:** St. Brendan the Navigator **Rev:** Medieval ship **Designer:** Michael Guilfoyle

Date	Mintage	F	VF	XF	Unc	BU
2011 Proof	15,000	Value: 60.00				

KM# 70 10 EURO
28.2800 g., 0.9250 Silver 0.8410 oz. ASW, 38.61 mm. **Subject:** Jack B. Yates **Designer:** Michael Guilfoyle

Date	Mintage	F	VF	XF	Unc	BU
2012 Proof	12,000	Value: 60.00				

KM# 75 10 EURO
28.2800 g., 0.9250 Silver 0.8410 oz. ASW, 38.61 mm. **Subject:** Micahel Collins **Rev:** Bust facing

Date	Mintage	F	VF	XF	Unc	BU
2012 Proof	14,000	Value: 80.00				

KM# 52 15 EURO
28.2800 g., 0.9250 Silver 0.8410 oz. ASW, 37 mm. **Obv:** Stylized clover with date and harp **Rev:** Ivan Mestroviae's Seated Woman with Harp design **Edge:** Plain **Note:** Illustration reduced.

Date	Mintage	F	VF	XF	Unc	BU
2007 Proof	10,000	Value: 85.00				

Note: 8,000 were sold in a single coin case. 1,000 were sold in a two coin set with the corresponding Croatian coin, as an Ireland set. An additional 1,000 were sold with the corresponding Croatian coin as a Croatia set. coins in both sets were the same but the packaging was different.

KM# 63 15 EURO
28.2800 g., 0.9250 Silver 0.8410 oz. ASW, 38.61 mm. **Subject:** Gaelic Athletics, 125 years **Designer:** Michael Guilfoyle

Date	Mintage	F	VF	XF	Unc	BU
2009 Proof	10,000	Value: 75.00				

KM# 64 15 EURO
28.2800 g., 0.9250 Silver 0.8410 oz. ASW, 38.61 mm. **Rev:** Foal and mare

Date	Mintage	F	VF	XF	Unc	BU
2010 Proof	15,000	Value: 75.00				

KM# 68 15 EURO
28.2800 g., 0.9250 Silver 0.8410 oz. ASW, 38.61 mm. **Rev:** Salmon

Date	Mintage	F	VF	XF	Unc	BU
2011 Proof	12,000	Value: 75.00				

KM# 72 15 EURO
28.2800 g., 0.9250 Silver 0.8410 oz. ASW, 38.61 mm. **Rev:** Wolfhounds

Date	Mintage	F	VF	XF	Unc	BU
2012 Proof	8,000	Value: 75.00				

KM# 46 20 EURO
1.2400 g., 0.9990 Gold 0.0398 oz. AGW, 14 mm. **Subject:** Samuel Beckett 1906-1989 **Obv:** 2006, Eire, Harp **Rev:** Face, value and play **Edge:** Reeded **Designer:** Emmet Mullins

Date	Mintage	F	VF	XF	Unc	BU
2006 Proof	20,000	Value: 85.00				

KM# 59 20 EURO
1.2440 g., 0.9990 Gold 0.0400 oz. AGW, 14 mm. **Subject:** European Culture - Ireland **Obv:** Map **Rev:** Celtic design **Designer:** Mary Gregorly

Date	Mintage	F	VF	XF	Unc	BU
2007 Proof	25,000	Value: 95.00				

KM# 55 20 EURO
1.2440 g., 0.9990 Gold 0.0400 oz. AGW, 14 mm. **Subject:** Skellig Michael Island **Rev:** Birds and 12 stars above island **Rev. Legend:** SCEILIG MHICHIL **Designer:** Michael Guilfoyle

Date	Mintage	F	VF	XF	Unc	BU
2008 Proof	15,000	Value: 100				

KM# 61 20 EURO
1.2440 g., 0.9990 Gold 0.0400 oz. AGW, 14 mm. **Subject:** First currency, 80th Anniversary

Date	Mintage	F	VF	XF	Unc	BU
2009 Proof	15,000	Value: 90.00				

KM# 66 20 EURO
1.2400 g., 0.9990 Gold 0.0398 oz. AGW, 14 mm. **Subject:** The President's Award - Gaisce **Designer:** Michael Guilfoyle

Date	Mintage	F	VF	XF	Unc	BU
2010 Proof	6,000	Value: 90.00				

KM# 69 20 EURO
0.5000 g., 0.9990 Gold 0.0161 oz. AGW, 11 mm. **Rev:** Celtic Cross **Designer:** Thomas Ryan

Date	Mintage	F	VF	XF	Unc	BU
2011 Proof	12,000	Value: 50.00				

KM# 73 20 EURO
0.5000 g., 0.9990 Gold 0.0161 oz. AGW, 11 mm. **Obv:** Irish Monastic Art **Rev:** Book of Kells

Date	Mintage	F	VF	XF	Unc	BU
2012 Proof	12,000	Value: 75.00				

KM# 74 20 EURO
0.5000 g., 0.9990 Gold 0.0161 oz. AGW **Rev:** Michael Collins

Date	Mintage	F	VF	XF	Unc	BU
2012 Proof	18,000	Value: 75.00				

KM# 57 100 EURO
15.5500 g., 0.9990 Gold 0.4994 oz. AGW, 28 mm. **Subject:** International Polar Year **Obv:** Harp within wreath **Rev:** Ernest Shackleton, Tom Crean and The Endurance in distance **Edge:** Reeded

Date	Mintage	F	VF	XF	Unc	BU
2008 Proof	2,000	Value: 950				

MINT SETS

KM#	Date	Mintage	Identification	Issue Price	Mkt Val
MS10	2002 (8)	20,000	KM#32-39	16.00	200
MS11	2003 (8)	30,000	KM#32-39	20.00	65.00
MS12	2003 (9)	35,000	KM#32-40 Special Olympics	25.00	90.00
MS13	2004 (8)	40,000	KM#32-39	25.00	45.00
MS14	2005 (8)	50,000	KM#32-39 Heywood Gardens	29.00	40.00
MS15	2006 (8)	40,000	KM#32-39 Glenveagh National Park and Castle	26.00	40.00
MS16	2006 (8)	—	KM#32-39 Boy Baby Set	35.00	42.50
MS17	2006 (8)	—	KM#32-39 Girl Baby Set	35.00	42.50
MS18	2007 (8)	20,000	KM#32-34, 47-51 Aran Islands	29.00	30.00
MS19	2007 (8)	—	KM#32-34, 47-51 Boy Baby Set	—	30.00
MS20	2007 (8)	—	KM#32-34, 47-51 Girl Baby Set	—	30.00
MS21	2007 (9)	20,000	KM#32-34, 47-51, 53	—	30.00
MS22	2008 (8)	30,000	KM#32-34, 47-51 Newgrange	—	30.00
MS23	2008 (8)	—	KM#32-34, 47-51 Boy Baby Set	—	30.00
MS24	2008 (8)	—	KM#32-34, 47-51 Girl Baby Set	—	30.00
MS25	2009 (8)	25,000	KM#32-34, 47-51 GAA 125th Anniversary	—	30.00
MS26	2009 (8)	—	KM#32-34, 47-51 Boy Baby Set	—	30.00
MS27	2009 (8)	—	KM#32-34, 47-51 Girl Baby Set	—	30.00
MS28	2010 (8)	20,000	KM#32-34, 47-51 Horse	45.00	45.00
MS29	2010 (8)	—	KM#32-34, 47-51 Baby Set	45.00	45.00
MS30	2011 (8)	20,000	KM#32-34, 47-51	—	45.00
MS31	2012 (8)	—	KM#32-34, 47-51	—	45.00

PROOF SETS

KM#	Date	Mintage	Identification	Issue Price	Mkt Val
PS6	2006 (8)	5,000	KM#32-39	125	165
PS7	2006 (2)	—	KM#45, 46	—	135
PS8	2007 (9)	10,000	KM#32-34, 47-51, 53	—	165
PS9	2007 (2)	—	KM#58-59	—	150
PS10	2008 (2)	—	KM#54-55	—	165
PS11	2008 (2)	—	KM#56-57	—	950
PS12	2009 (9)	—	KM#32-34, 47-51, 58 GAA 125th Anniversary	—	200
PS13	2009 (9)	5,000	KM#32-34, 47-51, 61.	—	225
PS14	2009 (2)	5,000	KM#60, 61. Ploughman Bank Note	—	160
PS15	2010 (2)	—	KM#65-66	—	150
PS16	2010 (8)	5,000	KM#32-34, 47-51	—	200
PS17	2011 (8)	5,000	KM#32-34, 47-51	—	200
PS18	2012 (9)	5,000	KM#32-34, 47-51, 71	—	125
PS19	2012 (4)	6,000	KM#74, 75	—	150

ISLE OF MAN

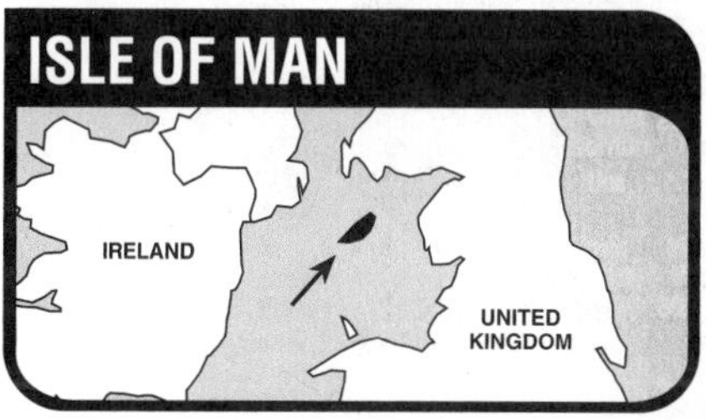

The Isle of Man, a dependency of the British Crown located in the Irish Sea equidistant from Ireland, Scotland and England, has an area of 227 sq. mi. (588 sq. km.) and a population of 68,000. Capital: Douglas. Agriculture, dairy farming, fishing and tourism are the chief industries.

MINT MARK
PM - Pobjoy Mint

BRITISH DEPENDENCY

DECIMAL COINAGE

100 Pence = 1 Pound

KM# 1036 PENNY
3.5600 g., Copper Plated Steel, 20.32 mm. **Ruler:** Elizabeth II **Obv:** Head with tiara right with small triskeles dividing legend **Rev:** Ruins **Edge:** Plain

Date	Mintage	F	VF	XF	Unc	BU
2001PM AA	—	—	—	—	0.25	0.45
2001PM AC	—	—	—	—	0.25	0.45
2002PM AA	—	—	—	—	0.25	0.45
2002PM AE	—	—	—	—	0.25	0.45

Date	Mintage	F	VF	XF	Unc	BU
2003PM AA	—	—	—	—	0.25	0.45
2003PM AE	—	—	—	—	0.25	0.45

KM# 1253 PENNY

3.5600 g., Copper Plated Steel, 20.3 mm. **Ruler:** Elizabeth II **Obv:** Head with tiara right **Rev:** Santon War Memorial

Date	Mintage	F	VF	XF	Unc	BU
2004PM AA	—	—	—	—	0.25	0.45
2004PM AB	—	—	—	—	0.25	0.45
2005PM AA	—	—	—	—	0.25	0.45
2005PM AB	—	—	—	—	0.25	0.45
2006PM AA	—	—	—	—	0.25	0.45
2006PM AB	—	—	—	—	0.25	0.45
2007PM AA	—	—	—	—	0.25	0.45
2007PM AB	—	—	—	—	0.25	0.45
2007PM BA	—	—	—	—	0.25	0.45
2008PM AA	—	—	—	—	0.25	0.45
2009PM AA	—	—	—	—	0.25	0.45
2010PM AA	—	—	—	—	0.25	0.45
2011PM AA	—	—	—	—	0.25	0.45
2012PM AA	—	—	—	—	0.25	0.45

KM# 1037 2 PENCE

7.1200 g., Copper Plated Steel, 25.9 mm. **Ruler:** Elizabeth II **Obv:** Head with tiara right **Rev:** Sailboat **Edge:** Plain

Date	Mintage	F	VF	XF	Unc	BU
2001PM AA	—	—	—	—	0.40	0.60
2001PM AB	—	—	—	—	0.40	0.60
2001PM AC	—	—	—	—	0.40	0.60
2002PM AA	—	—	—	—	0.40	0.60
2002PM AB	—	—	—	—	0.40	0.60
2002PM AC	—	—	—	—	0.40	0.60
2002PM AF	—	—	—	—	0.40	0.60
2003PM AA	—	—	—	—	0.40	0.60
2003PM AF	—	—	—	—	0.40	0.60

KM# 1254 2 PENCE

7.1200 g., Copper Plated Steel, 25.9 mm. **Ruler:** Elizabeth II **Obv:** Head with tiara right **Rev:** Albert Tower

Date	Mintage	F	VF	XF	Unc	BU
2004PM AA	—	—	—	—	0.40	0.60
2004PM AB	—	—	—	—	0.40	0.60
2005PM AA	—	—	—	—	0.40	0.60
2005PM AB	—	—	—	—	0.40	0.60
2006PM AA	—	—	—	—	0.40	0.60
2006PM AB	—	—	—	—	0.40	0.60
2007PM AA	—	—	—	—	0.40	0.60
2007PM AB	—	—	—	—	0.40	0.60
2007PM BA	—	—	—	—	0.40	0.60
2008PM AA	—	—	—	—	0.40	0.60
2009PM AA	—	—	—	—	0.40	0.60
2010PM AA	—	—	—	—	0.40	0.60
2011PM AA	—	—	—	—	0.40	0.60
2012PM AA	—	—	—	—	0.40	0.60

KM# 1038 5 PENCE

3.2500 g., Copper-Nickel, 18 mm. **Ruler:** Elizabeth II **Obv:** Head with tiara right **Rev:** Gaut's Cross **Edge:** Reeded

Date	Mintage	F	VF	XF	Unc	BU
2001PM AA	—	—	—	—	0.75	1.00
2002PM AA	—	—	—	—	0.75	1.00
2002PM AC	—	—	—	—	0.75	1.00
2002PM AD	—	—	—	—	0.75	1.00
2002PM AE	—	—	—	—	0.75	1.00

Date	Mintage	F	VF	XF	Unc	BU
2003PM AA	—	—	—	—	0.75	1.00
2003PM AB	—	—	—	—	0.75	1.00
2003PM AD	—	—	—	—	0.75	1.00

KM# 1255 5 PENCE

3.2500 g., Copper-Nickel, 18 mm. **Ruler:** Elizabeth II **Obv:** Head with tiara right **Rev:** Tower of Refuge **Edge:** Reeded

Date	Mintage	F	VF	XF	Unc	BU
2004PM AA	—	—	—	—	0.75	1.00
2004PM AB	—	—	—	—	0.75	1.00
2005PM AA	—	—	—	—	0.75	1.00
2005PM AB	—	—	—	—	0.75	1.00
2006PM AA	—	—	—	—	0.75	1.00
2006PM AB	—	—	—	—	0.75	1.00
2007PM AA	—	—	—	—	0.75	1.00
2007PM AB	—	—	—	—	0.75	1.00
2008PM AA	—	—	—	—	0.75	1.00
2009PM AA	—	—	—	—	0.75	1.00
2010PM AA	—	—	—	—	0.75	1.00
2011PM AA	—	—	—	—	0.75	1.00
2012PM AA	—	—	—	—	0.75	1.00

KM# 1039 10 PENCE

6.5000 g., Copper-Nickel, 24.5 mm. **Ruler:** Elizabeth II **Obv:** Head with tiara right **Rev:** Cathedral **Edge:** Reeded

Date	Mintage	F	VF	XF	Unc	BU
2001PM AA	—	—	—	—	1.00	1.50
2002PM AA	—	—	—	—	1.00	1.50
2003PM AA	—	—	—	—	1.00	1.50

KM# 1256 10 PENCE

6.5000 g., Copper-Nickel, 24.5 mm. **Ruler:** Elizabeth II **Obv:** Head with tiara right **Rev:** Chicken Rock Lighthouse **Edge:** Reeded

Date	Mintage	F	VF	XF	Unc	BU
2004PM AA	—	—	—	—	1.00	1.50
2004PM AB	—	—	—	—	1.00	1.50
2005PM AA	—	—	—	—	1.00	1.50
2005PM AB	—	—	—	—	1.00	1.50
2006PM AA	—	—	—	—	1.00	1.50
2006PM AB	—	—	—	—	1.00	1.50
2007PM AA	—	—	—	—	1.00	1.50
2007PM AB	—	—	—	—	1.00	1.50
2008PM AA	—	—	—	—	1.00	1.50
2009PM AA	—	—	—	—	1.00	1.50
2010PM AA	—	—	—	—	1.00	1.50
2011PM AA	—	—	—	—	1.00	1.50
2012PM AA	—	—	—	—	1.00	1.50

KM# 1040 20 PENCE

5.0000 g., Copper-Nickel, 21.4 mm. **Ruler:** Elizabeth II **Subject:** Rushen Abbey **Obv:** Head with tiara right **Rev:** Monk writing **Edge:** Plain **Shape:** 7-sided

Date	Mintage	F	VF	XF	Unc	BU
2001PM AA	—	—	—	—	1.50	2.00
2001PM AB	—	—	—	—	1.50	2.00
2002PM AA	—	—	—	—	1.50	2.00
2002PM AB	—	—	—	—	1.50	2.00
2002PM AC	—	—	—	—	1.50	2.00
2003PM AA	—	—	—	—	1.50	2.00
2003PM BA	—	—	—	—	1.50	2.00

KM# 1257 20 PENCE

5.0000 g., Copper-Nickel, 21.4 mm. **Ruler:** Elizabeth II **Obv:** Head with tiara right **Rev:** Castle Rushen Clock **Edge:** Plain **Shape:** 7-sided

Date	Mintage	F	VF	XF	Unc	BU
2004PM AA	—	—	—	—	1.50	2.00
2004PM AB	—	—	—	—	1.50	2.00
2005PM AA	—	—	—	—	1.50	2.00
2005PM AB	—	—	—	—	1.50	2.00
2006PM AA	—	—	—	—	1.50	2.00
2006PM AB	—	—	—	—	1.50	2.00
2007PM AA	—	—	—	—	1.50	2.00
2007PM AB	—	—	—	—	1.50	2.00
2008PM AA	—	—	—	—	1.50	2.00
2009PM AA	—	—	—	—	1.50	2.00
2010PM AA	—	—	—	—	1.50	2.00
2011PM AA	—	—	—	—	1.50	2.00
2012PM AA	—	—	—	—	1.50	2.00

KM# 1041 50 PENCE

8.0000 g., Copper-Nickel, 27.3 mm. **Ruler:** Elizabeth II **Obv:** Head with tiara right **Rev:** Stylized crucifix **Edge:** Plain **Shape:** 7-sided

Date	Mintage	F	VF	XF	Unc	BU
2001PM AA	—	—	—	—	2.25	2.75
2002PM AA	—	—	—	—	2.25	2.75
2003PM AA	—	—	—	—	2.25	2.75

KM# 1105 50 PENCE

8.0000 g., Copper-Nickel, 27.3 mm. **Ruler:** Elizabeth II **Subject:** Christmas **Obv:** Head with tiara right **Rev:** Postman and children **Edge:** Plain **Shape:** 7-sided

Date	Mintage	F	VF	XF	Unc	BU
2001PM BB	30,000	—	—	—	4.50	6.00

KM# 1105a 50 PENCE

8.0000 g., 0.9250 Silver 0.2379 oz. ASW, 27.3 mm. **Ruler:** Elizabeth II **Obv:** Head with tiara right **Rev:** Postman and children **Edge:** Plain **Shape:** 7-sided

Date	Mintage	F	VF	XF	Unc	BU
2001PM Proof	5,000	Value: 35.00				

KM# 1105b 50 PENCE

8.0000 g., 0.9167 Gold 0.2358 oz. AGW, 27.3 mm. **Ruler:** Elizabeth II **Obv:** Head with tiara right **Rev:** Postman and children **Edge:** Plain **Shape:** 7-sided

Date	Mintage	F	VF	XF	Unc	BU
2001PM Proof	250	Value: 450				

KM# 1160 50 PENCE

8.0000 g., Copper-Nickel, 27.3 mm. **Ruler:** Elizabeth II **Subject:** Christmas **Obv:** Head with tiara right **Rev:** Scrooge in bed **Edge:** Plain **Shape:** 7-sided

Date	Mintage	F	VF	XF	Unc	BU
2002BB PM	30,000	—	—	—	4.50	6.00

KM# 1160a 50 PENCE

8.0000 g., 0.9250 Silver 0.2379 oz. ASW, 27.3 mm. **Ruler:** Elizabeth II **Subject:** Christmas **Obv:** Head with tiara right **Rev:** Scrooge in bed **Edge:** Plain **Shape:** 7-sided

Date	Mintage	F	VF	XF	Unc	BU
2002PM Proof	5,000	Value: 35.00				

KM# 1160b 50 PENCE
8.0000 g., 0.9167 Gold 0.2358 oz. AGW, 27.3 mm. **Ruler:** Elizabeth II **Subject:** Christmas **Obv:** Head with tiara right **Rev:** Scrooge in bed **Edge:** Plain **Shape:** 7-sided

Date	Mintage	F	VF	XF	Unc	BU
2002PM Proof	250	Value: 450				

KM# 1183 50 PENCE
8.0000 g., Copper-Nickel, 27.3 mm. **Ruler:** Elizabeth II **Obv:** Head with tiara right **Rev:** "The Snowman and James" **Edge:** Plain **Shape:** 7-sided

Date	Mintage	F	VF	XF	Unc	BU
2003PM BB	10,000	—	—	—	6.50	8.00
2008PM	—	—	—	—	6.50	8.00

KM# 1183a 50 PENCE
8.0000 g., 0.9250 Silver 0.2379 oz. ASW, 27.3 mm. **Ruler:** Elizabeth II **Subject:** Christmas **Obv:** Head with tiara right **Rev:** "The Snowman and James" **Edge:** Plain **Shape:** 7-sided

Date	Mintage	F	VF	XF	Unc	BU
2003PM Proof	3,000	Value: 35.00				

KM# 1183b 50 PENCE
8.0000 g., 0.9167 Gold 0.2358 oz. AGW, 27.3 mm. **Ruler:** Elizabeth II **Obv:** Head with tiara right **Rev:** "The Snowman and James" **Edge:** Plain **Shape:** 7-sided

Date	Mintage	F	VF	XF	Unc	BU
2003PM Proof	100	Value: 475				

KM# 1258 50 PENCE
8.0000 g., Copper-Nickel, 27.3 mm. **Ruler:** Elizabeth II **Obv:** Head with tiara right **Rev:** Milner's Tower **Edge:** Plain **Shape:** 7-sided

Date	Mintage	F	VF	XF	Unc	BU
2004PM AA	—	—	—	—	2.25	2.75
2004PM AB	—	—	—	—	2.25	2.75
2005PM AA	—	—	—	—	2.25	2.75
2005PM AB	—	—	—	—	2.25	2.75
2006PM AA	—	—	—	—	2.25	2.75
2006PM AB	—	—	—	—	2.25	2.75
2007PM AA	—	—	—	—	2.25	2.75
2007PM AB	—	—	—	—	2.25	2.75
2008PM AA	—	—	—	—	2.25	2.75
2009PM AA	—	—	—	—	2.25	2.75
2010PM AA	—	—	—	—	2.25	2.75
2011PM AA	—	—	—	—	2.25	2.75
2012PM AA	—	—	—	—	2.25	2.75

KM# 1293 50 PENCE
8.0000 g., Copper-Nickel, 27.3 mm. **Ruler:** Elizabeth II **Obv:** Queen's new portrait **Rev:** Tourist Trophy Races **Shape:** 7-sided

Date	Mintage	F	VF	XF	Unc	BU
2004PM AA	—	—	—	—	6.00	7.00
2007PM AA	—	—	—	—	6.00	7.00

KM# 1262 50 PENCE
8.0000 g., Copper-Nickel, 27.3 mm. **Ruler:** Elizabeth II **Subject:** Christmas **Obv:** Head with tiara right **Rev:** Laxey Wheel **Edge:** Plain **Shape:** 7-sided

Date	Mintage	F	VF	XF	Unc	BU
2004PM AA	—	—	—	—	6.00	7.00
2004PM BA	30,000	—	—	—	6.00	7.00

KM# 1262a 50 PENCE
9.1852 g., 0.9250 Silver 0.2732 oz. ASW, 27.3 mm. **Ruler:** Elizabeth II **Subject:** Christmas **Obv:** Head with tiara right **Rev:** Laxey Wheel **Edge:** Plain **Shape:** 7-sided

Date	Mintage	F	VF	XF	Unc	BU
2004PM Proof	5,000	Value: 35.00				

KM# 1262b 50 PENCE
15.4074 g., 0.9167 Gold 0.4541 oz. AGW, 27.3 mm. **Ruler:** Elizabeth II **Subject:** Christmas **Obv:** Head with tiara right **Rev:** Laxey Wheel **Edge:** Plain **Shape:** 7-sided

Date	Mintage	F	VF	XF	Unc	BU
2004PM Proof	250	Value: 850				

KM# 1294 50 PENCE
8.0000 g., Copper-Nickel, 27.3 mm. **Ruler:** Elizabeth II **Obv:** Queen's new portrait **Rev:** Partridge in a pear tree **Shape:** 7-sided

Date	Mintage	F	VF	XF	Unc	BU
2005	—	—	—	—	6.50	8.00

KM# 1320.1 50 PENCE
8.0000 g., Copper-Nickel, 27.3 mm. **Ruler:** Elizabeth II **Series:** 12 Days of Christmas **Obv:** Head with tiara right **Obv. Legend:** ISLE OF MAN - ELIZABETH II **Rev:** Partridge in a Pear Tree **Rev. Legend:** CHRISTMAS **Edge:** Plain **Shape:** 7-sided

Date	Mintage	F	VF	XF	Unc	BU
2005PM AA	30,000	—	—	—	—	16.00

KM# 1320.2 50 PENCE
8.0000 g., Copper-Nickel, 27.3 mm. **Ruler:** Elizabeth II **Series:** 12 Days of Christmas **Obv:** Head with tiara right **Obv. Legend:** ISLE OF MAN - ELIZABETH II **Rev:** Partidge in a Pear Tree multicolor **Rev. Legend:** CHRISTMAS **Edge:** Plain **Shape:** 7-sided

Date	Mintage	F	VF	XF	Unc	BU
2005PM	Inc. above	—	—	—	—	20.00

KM# 1320.1a 50 PENCE
9.1825 g., 0.9250 Silver 0.2731 oz. ASW, 27.3 mm. **Ruler:** Elizabeth II **Series:** 12 Days of Christmas **Obv:** Head with tiara right **Obv. Legend:** ISLE OF MAN - ELIZABETH II **Rev:** Partridge in a Pear Tree **Rev. Legend:** CHRISTMAS **Edge:** Plain **Shape:** 7-sided

Date	Mintage	F	VF	XF	Unc	BU
2005PM Proof	—	Value: 35.00				

KM# 1320.2a 50 PENCE
8.0000 g., 0.9250 Silver 0.2379 oz. ASW, 27.3 mm. **Ruler:** Elizabeth II **Series:** 12 Days of Christmas **Obv:** Head with tiara right **Obv. Legend:** ISLE OF MAN - ELIZABETH II **Rev:** Partridge in a Pear Tree multicolor **Rev. Legend:** CHRISTMAS **Edge:** Plain **Shape:** 7-sided

Date	Mintage	F	VF	XF	Unc	BU
2005PM Proof	—	Value: 35.00				

KM# 1320b 50 PENCE
0.9167 Gold, 27.3 mm. **Ruler:** Elizabeth II **Series:** 12 Days of Christmas **Obv:** Head with tiara right **Obv. Legend:** ISLE OF MAN - ELIZABETH II **Rev:** Partridge in a Pear Tree **Rev. Legend:** CHRISTMAS **Edge:** Plain **Shape:** 7-sided

Date	Mintage	F	VF	XF	Unc	BU
2005PM Proof	—	Value: 850				

KM# 1321.1 50 PENCE
8.0000 g., Copper-Nickel, 27.3 mm. **Ruler:** Elizabeth II **Series:** 12 Days of Christmas **Obv:** Head with tiara right **Obv. Legend:** ISLE OF MAN - ELIZABETH II **Rev:** Two Turtle Doves **Rev. Legend:** CHRISTMAS **Edge:** Plain **Shape:** 7-sided

Date	Mintage	F	VF	XF	Unc	BU
2006PM AA	—	—	—	—	6.00	7.00

KM# 1321.2 50 PENCE
8.0000 g., Copper-Nickel, 27.3 mm. **Ruler:** Elizabeth II **Series:** 12 Days of Christmas **Obv:** Head with tiara right **Obv. Legend:** ISLE OF MAN - ELIZABETH II **Rev:** 2 Turtle Doves multicolor **Rev. Legend:** CHRISTMAS **Edge:** Plain **Shape:** 7-sided

Date	Mintage	F	VF	XF	Unc	BU
2006PM	—	—	—	—	8.00	10.00

KM# 1321.1a 50 PENCE
0.9250 Silver, 27.3 mm. **Ruler:** Elizabeth II **Series:** 12 Days of Christmas **Obv:** Head with tiara right **Obv. Legend:** ISLE OF MAN - ELIZABETH II **Rev:** Two Turtle Doves **Rev. Legend:** CHRISTMAS **Edge:** Plain **Shape:** 7-sided

Date	Mintage	F	VF	XF	Unc	BU
2006PM Proof	—	Value: 35.00				

KM# 1321.2a 50 PENCE
0.9250 Silver, 27.3 mm. **Ruler:** Elizabeth II **Series:** 12 Days of Christmas **Obv:** Head with tiara right **Obv. Legend:** ISLE OF MAN - ELIZABETH II **Rev:** 2 Turtle Doves multicolor **Rev. Legend:** CHRISTMAS **Edge:** Plain **Shape:** 7-sided

Date	Mintage	F	VF	XF	Unc	BU
2006PM Proof	—	Value: 40.00				

KM# 1321b 50 PENCE
0.9167 Gold, 27.3 mm. **Ruler:** Elizabeth II **Series:** 12 Days of Christmas **Obv:** Head with tiara right **Obv. Legend:** ISLE OF MAN - ELIZABETH II **Rev:** 2 Turtle Doves **Rev. Legend:** CHRISTMAS **Edge:** Plain **Shape:** 7-sided

Date	Mintage	F	VF	XF	Unc	BU
2006PM Proof	—	Value: 850				

KM# 1322.1 50 PENCE
8.0000 g., Copper-Nickel, 27.3 mm. **Ruler:** Elizabeth II **Series:** 12 Days of Christmas **Obv:** Head with tiara right **Obv. Legend:** ISLE OF MAN - ELIZABETH II **Rev:** 3 French Hens **Rev. Legend:** CHRISTMAS **Edge:** Plain **Shape:** 7-sided

Date	Mintage	F	VF	XF	Unc	BU
2007PM AA	—	—	—	—	6.00	7.00

KM# 1322.2 50 PENCE
8.0000 g., Copper-Nickel, 27.3 mm. **Ruler:** Elizabeth II **Series:** 12 Days of Christmas **Obv:** Head with tiara right **Obv. Legend:** ISLE OF MAN - ELIZABETH II **Rev:** 3 French Hens multicolor **Rev. Legend:** CHRISTMAS **Edge:** Plain **Shape:** 7-sided

Date	Mintage	F	VF	XF	Unc	BU
2007PM	—	—	—	—	8.00	10.00

KM# 1322.1a 50 PENCE
0.9250 Silver, 27.3 mm. **Ruler:** Elizabeth II **Series:** 12 Days of Christmas **Obv:** Head with tiara right **Obv. Legend:** ISLE OF MAN - ELIZABETH II **Rev:** 3 French Hens **Rev. Legend:** CHRISTMAS **Edge:** Plain **Shape:** 7-sided

Date	Mintage	F	VF	XF	Unc	BU
2007PM Proof	—	Value: 35.00				

KM# 1322.2a 50 PENCE
0.9250 Silver, 27.3 mm. **Ruler:** Elizabeth II **Series:** 12 Days of Christmas **Obv:** Head with tiara right **Obv. Legend:** ISLE OF MAN - ELIZABETH II **Rev:** 3 French Hens multicolor **Rev. Legend:** CHRISTMAS **Edge:** Plain **Shape:** 7-sided

Date	Mintage	F	VF	XF	Unc	BU
2007PM Proof	—	Value: 40.00				

KM# 1322b 50 PENCE
0.9167 Gold, 27.3 mm. **Ruler:** Elizabeth II **Series:** 12 Days of Christmas **Obv:** Head with tiara right **Obv. Legend:** ISLE OF MAN - ELIZABETH II **Rev:** 3 French Hens **Rev. Legend:** CHRISTMAS **Edge:** Plain **Shape:** 7-sided

Date	Mintage	F	VF	XF	Unc	BU
2007PM Proof	250	Value: 850				

KM# 1425 50 PENCE
8.0000 g., Copper-Nickel, 27.3 mm. **Ruler:** Elizabeth II **Subject:** TT Centennial **Obv:** Head with tiara right **Rev:** Two motorcyclists within wreath **Shape:** 7-sided

Date	Mintage	F	VF	XF	Unc	BU
2007PM	—	—	—	—	8.00	10.00

KM# 1393.1 50 PENCE
8.0000 g., Copper-Nickel, 27.3 mm. **Ruler:** Elizabeth II **Subject:** Christmas **Rev:** Snowman **Shape:** 7-sided

Date	Mintage	F	VF	XF	Unc	BU
2008PM	—	—	—	—	10.00	12.00

KM# 1393.2 50 PENCE
8.0000 g., Copper-Nickel, 27.3 mm. **Ruler:** Elizabeth II **Subject:** Christmas **Rev:** Snowman, multicolored **Shape:** 7-sided

Date	Mintage	F	VF	XF	Unc	BU
2008PM	—	—	—	—	10.00	12.00

KM# 1487 50 PENCE
8.0000 g., Copper-Nickel, 27.3 mm. **Ruler:** Elizabeth II **Subject:** Christmas **Rev:** 4 Calling Birds **Shape:** 7-sided

Date	Mintage	F	VF	XF	Unc	BU
2008PM	—	—	—	—	—	9.00

KM# 1487a 50 PENCE
8.0000 g., 0.9250 Silver 0.2379 oz. ASW, 27.3 mm. **Ruler:** Elizabeth II **Subject:** Christmas **Rev:** 4 Calling birds **Shape:** 7-sided

Date	Mintage	F	VF	XF	Unc	BU
2008PM Proof	—	Value: 25.00				

KM# 1487b 50 PENCE
8.0000 g., 0.9167 Gold 0.2358 oz. AGW, 27.3 mm. **Ruler:** Elizabeth II **Subject:** Christmas **Rev:** 4 Calling birds **Shape:** 7-sided

Date	Mintage	F	VF	XF	Unc	BU
2008PM Proof	—	Value: 500				

KM# 1372 50 PENCE
8.0000 g., Copper-Nickel, 27.3 mm. **Ruler:** Elizabeth II **Subject:** Honda, 50th Anniversary TT **Shape:** 7-sided

Date	Mintage	F	VF	XF	Unc	BU
2009PM AA	—	—	—	—	—	9.00

KM# 1431 50 PENCE
8.0000 g., Copper-Nickel, 27.3 mm. **Ruler:** Elizabeth II **Subject:** Fifth day of Christmas **Rev:** Five rings **Shape:** 7-sided

Date	Mintage	F	VF	XF	Unc	BU
2009PM	30,000	—	—	—	—	10.00

KM# 1431a 50 PENCE
8.0000 g., 0.9250 Silver 0.2379 oz. ASW, 27.3 mm. **Ruler:** Elizabeth II **Subject:** Fifth day of Christmas **Rev:** Five golden rings **Shape:** 7-sided

Date	Mintage	F	VF	XF	Unc	BU
2009PM Proof	5,000	Value: 20.00				

KM# 1431b 50 PENCE
8.0000 g., 0.9167 Gold 0.2358 oz. AGW, 27.3 mm. **Ruler:** Elizabeth II **Subject:** Fifth day of Christmas **Rev:** Five golden rings **Shape:** 7-sided

Date	Mintage	F	VF	XF	Unc	BU
2009PM Proof	250	Value: 500				

KM# 1433.1a 50 PENCE
8.0000 g., 0.9250 Silver 0.2379 oz. ASW, 27.3 mm. **Ruler:** Elizabeth II **Subject:** Christmas **Rev:** Six geese a laying **Shape:** 7-sided

Date	Mintage	F	VF	XF	Unc	BU
2009PM Proof	5,000	Value: 15.00				

KM# 1433.1 50 PENCE
8.0000 g., Copper-Nickel, 27.3 mm. **Ruler:** Elizabeth II **Rev:** Six Geese a laying **Shape:** 7-sided

Date	Mintage	F	VF	XF	Unc	BU
2010PM	30,000	—	—	—	—	10.00

KM# 1433.1b 50 PENCE
8.0000 g., 0.9167 Gold 0.2358 oz. AGW, 27.3 mm. **Ruler:** Elizabeth II **Subject:** Christmas **Rev:** Six geese a laying **Shape:** 7-sided

Date	Mintage	F	VF	XF	Unc	BU
2010PM Proof	—	Value: 500				

KM# 1433.2 50 PENCE
8.0000 g., Copper-Nickel, 27.3 mm. **Ruler:** Elizabeth II **Subject:** Christmas **Rev:** Six geese a laying in color **Shape:** 7-sided

Date	Mintage	F	VF	XF	Unc	BU
2010PM	—	—	—	—	—	12.00

KM# 1469 50 PENCE
8.0000 g., Copper-Nickel, 27.3 mm. **Ruler:** Elizabeth II **Subject:** Isle of Man TT race **Rev:** Suzuki driver right **Shape:** 7-sided

Date	Mintage	F	VF	XF	Unc	BU
2010PM	—	—	—	—	—	9.00

KM# 1453.1 50 PENCE
8.0000 g., Copper-Nickel, 27.3 mm. **Ruler:** Elizabeth II **Subject:** Christmas **Rev:** Santa Claus **Shape:** 7-sided

Date	Mintage	F	VF	XF	Unc	BU
2011PM	30,000	—	—	—	—	10.00

KM# 1453.1a 50 PENCE
8.0000 g., 0.9250 Silver 0.2379 oz. ASW, 27.3 mm. **Ruler:** Elizabeth II **Subject:** Christmas **Rev:** Santa Claus **Shape:** 7-sided

Date	Mintage	F	VF	XF	Unc	BU
2011PM Proof	5,000	Value: 25.00				

KM# 1453.2 50 PENCE
8.0000 g., Copper-Nickel, 27.3 mm. **Ruler:** Elizabeth II **Subject:** Christmas **Rev:** Santa Claus in color **Shape:** 7-sided

Date	Mintage	F	VF	XF	Unc	BU
2011PM	—	—	—	—	—	12.00

KM# 1453.1b 50 PENCE
8.0000 g., 0.9167 Gold 0.2358 oz. AGW, 27.3 mm. **Ruler:** Elizabeth II **Subject:** Christmas **Rev:** Santa Claus **Shape:** 7-sided

Date	Mintage	F	VF	XF	Unc	BU
2011PM proof	250	Value: 500				

KM# 1454 50 PENCE
8.0000 g., Copper-Nickel, 27.3 mm. **Ruler:** Elizabeth II **Subject:** Isle of Man Tourist Trophy race **Rev:** Yamaha motorcycle and racer **Shape:** 7-sided

Date	Mintage	F	VF	XF	Unc	BU
2011PM	—	—	—	—	—	10.00

KM# 1454a 50 PENCE
8.0000 g., 0.9250 Silver 0.2379 oz. ASW, 27.3 mm. **Ruler:** Elizabeth II **Subject:** Isle of Man Tourist Trophy race **Rev:** Yamaha motorcycle and racer **Shape:** 7-sided

Date	Mintage	F	VF	XF	Unc	BU
2011PM Proof	5,000	Value: 25.00				

KM# 1488 50 PENCE
8.0000 g., Copper-Nickel, 27.3 mm. **Ruler:** Elizabeth II **Subject:** Diamond Jubilee

Date	Mintage	F	VF	XF	Unc	BU
2012PM	—	—	—	—	—	6.50

KM# 1128 60 PENCE
Bi-Metallic Bronze finished base metal with a silver finished rotator on reverse., 38.6 mm. **Ruler:** Elizabeth II **Subject:** Euro Currency Converter **Obv:** Head with tiara right **Rev:** Rotating map with cut out arrow revealing the Euro equivalent of the country's currency to which the arrow is pointed **Edge:** Reeded

Date	Mintage	F	VF	XF	Unc	BU
2002	15,000	—	—	—	20.00	22.50

KM# 1042 POUND
9.5000 g., Nickel-Brass, 22.5 mm. **Ruler:** Elizabeth II **Subject:** Millennium Bells **Obv:** Head with tiara right **Rev:** Triskeles and three bells **Edge:** Segmented reeding

Date	Mintage	F	VF	XF	Unc	BU
2001PM AA	—	—	—	—	4.00	5.00
2002PM AA	—	—	—	—	4.00	5.00
2003PM AA	—	—	—	—	4.00	5.00
2003PM BA	—	—	—	—	4.00	5.00

KM# 1259 POUND
9.5000 g., Nickel-Brass, 22.5 mm. **Ruler:** Elizabeth II **Obv:** Head with tiara right **Rev:** St. John's Chapel **Edge:** Segmented reeding

Date	Mintage	F	VF	XF	Unc	BU
2004PM	—	—	—	—	4.00	5.00
2004PM AA	—	—	—	—	4.00	5.00
2004PM AB	—	—	—	—	4.00	5.00
2004PM AC	—	—	—	—	4.00	5.00
2005PM AA	—	—	—	—	4.00	5.00
2005PM AB	—	—	—	—	4.00	5.00
2006PM AA	—	—	—	—	4.00	5.00
2006PM AB	—	—	—	—	4.00	5.00
2007PM AA	—	—	—	—	4.00	5.00
2007PM BA	—	—	—	—	4.00	5.00
2007PM AB	—	—	—	—	4.00	5.00
2008PM AA	—	—	—	—	4.00	5.00
2008PM BA	—	—	—	—	4.00	5.00
2009PM AA	—	—	—	—	4.00	5.00
2010PM AA	—	—	—	—	4.00	5.00
2011PM AA	—	—	—	—	4.00	5.00
2012PM AA	—	—	—	—	4.00	5.00

KM# 1043 2 POUNDS
12.0000 g., Bi-Metallic Copper-Nickel center in Nickel-Brass ring, 28.4 mm. **Ruler:** Elizabeth II **Subject:** Thorwald's Cross **Obv:** Head with tiara right within beaded circle **Rev:** Ancient drawing within circle **Edge:** Reeded

Date	Mintage	F	VF	XF	Unc	BU
2001PM AA	—	—	—	—	6.50	7.50
2002PM AA	—	—	—	—	6.50	7.50
2003PM AA	—	—	—	—	6.50	7.50
2003PM AB	—	—	—	—	6.50	7.50

KM# 1260 2 POUNDS
12.0000 g., Bi-Metallic Copper-Nickel center in Nickel-Brass ring, 28.4 mm. **Ruler:** Elizabeth II **Obv:** Head with tiara right **Rev:** Round Tower of Peel Castle **Edge:** Reeded

Date	Mintage	F	VF	XF	Unc	BU
2004PM AA	—	—	—	—	6.50	7.50
2005PM AA	—	—	—	—	6.50	7.50
2006PM AA	—	—	—	—	6.50	7.50
2007PM AA	—	—	—	—	6.50	7.50
2007PM AB	—	—	—	—	6.50	7.50
2008PM AA	—	—	—	—	6.50	7.50
2009PM AA	—	—	—	—	6.50	7.50
2010PM AA	—	—	—	—	6.50	7.50
2011PM AA	—	—	—	—	6.50	7.50
2012PM AA	—	—	—	—	6.50	7.50

KM# 1476 2 POUNDS
12.0000 g., Bi-Metallic Copper-Nickel center in Nickel-Brass ring, 28.4 mm. **Ruler:** Elizabeth II **Obv:** Head with tiara right **Rev:** Tosha the cat, games mascot and games logo

Date	Mintage	F	VF	XF	Unc	BU
2011PM	—	—	—	—	6.00	7.50

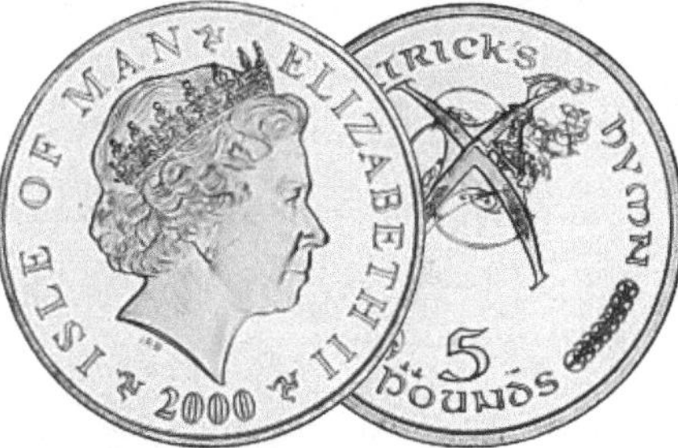

KM# 1044 5 POUNDS
20.1000 g., Virenium, 36.5 mm. **Ruler:** Elizabeth II **Subject:** St. Patrick's Hymn **Obv:** Head with tiara right **Rev:** Stylized cross design **Edge:** Segmented reeding

Date	Mintage	F	VF	XF	Unc	BU
2001PM AA	—	—	—	—	15.00	16.50
2002PM AA	—	—	—	—	15.00	16.50
2003PM AA	—	—	—	—	15.00	16.50

KM# 1261 5 POUNDS
20.1000 g., Virenium, 36 mm. **Ruler:** Elizabeth II **Obv:** Head with tiara right **Rev:** Laxey Wheel **Edge:** Reeded

Date	Mintage	F	VF	XF	Unc	BU
2004PM AA	—	—	—	—	15.00	16.50
2005PM AA	—	—	—	—	15.00	16.50
2006PM AA	—	—	—	—	15.00	16.50
2007PM AA	—	—	—	—	15.00	16.50
2007PM AB	—	—	—	—	15.00	16.50
2008PM AA	—	—	—	—	15.00	16.50
2009PM AA	—	—	—	—	15.00	16.50
2010PM AA	—	—	—	—	15.00	16.50
2011PM AA	—	—	—	—	15.00	16.50
2012PM AA	—	—	—	—	15.00	16.50

CROWN SERIES

(M) MATTE - Normal circulation strike

(U) SPECIAL UNCIRCULATED - Polished or prooflike in appearance, slightly frosted features.

(P) PROOF - The highest quality obtainable having mirror-like fields and frosted features.

KM# 1472 1/64 CROWN
0.4860 g., 0.9999 Gold 0.0156 oz. AGW **Ruler:** Elizabeth II **Obv:** Bust in tiara right **Rev:** Buckingham Palace

Date	Mintage	F	VF	XF	Unc	BU
2010PM Proof	—	Value: 50.00				

KM# 1129 1/32 CROWN
1.0000 g., 0.9720 Gold 0.0312 oz. AGW, 9.8 mm. **Ruler:** Elizabeth II **Subject:** Queen's Golden Jubilee **Obv:** Head with tiara right **Rev:** Seated crowned Queen holding sceptre at her coronation **Edge:** Plain

Date	Mintage	F	VF	XF	Unc	BU
2002 Prooflike	—	—	—	—	—	60.00

KM# 1058 1/25 CROWN
1.2440 g., 0.9999 Gold 0.0400 oz. AGW, 13.92 mm. **Ruler:** Elizabeth II **Subject:** Year of the Snake **Obv:** Bust with tiara right **Rev:** Snake **Edge:** Reeded

Date	Mintage	F	VF	XF	Unc	BU
2001 Proof	20,000	Value: 75.00				

KM# 1067 1/25 CROWN
1.2440 g., 0.9999 Gold 0.0400 oz. AGW, 13.9 mm. **Ruler:** Elizabeth II **Subject:** Somali Kittens **Obv:** Head with tiara right **Rev:** Two kittens **Edge:** Reeded

Date	Mintage	F	VF	XF	Unc	BU
2001	—	—	—	—	—	72.50
2001 Proof	1,000	Value: 75.00				

KM# 1067a 1/25 CROWN
1.2441 g., 0.9995 Platinum 0.0400 oz. APW, 13.9 mm. **Ruler:** Elizabeth II **Subject:** Somali Kittens **Obv:** Head with tiara right **Rev:** Two kittens **Edge:** Reeded

Date	Mintage	F	VF	XF	Unc	BU
2001	—	—	—	—	—	80.00

KM# 1086 1/25 CROWN
1.2441 g., 0.9999 Gold 0.0400 oz. AGW, 13.9 mm. **Ruler:** Elizabeth II **Subject:** Harry Potter **Obv:** Bust with tiara right **Rev:** Boy with magic wand **Edge:** Reeded

Date	Mintage	F	VF	XF	Unc	BU
2001 Proof	10,000	Value: 75.00				

KM# 1088 1/25 CROWN
1.2441 g., 0.9999 Gold 0.0400 oz. AGW, 13.9 mm. **Ruler:** Elizabeth II **Series:** Harry Potter **Subject:** Journey to Hogwarts School **Obv:** Bust with tiara right **Rev:** Boat full of children going to Hogwarts School **Edge:** Reeded

Date	Mintage	F	VF	XF	Unc	BU
2001 Proof	10,000	Value: 75.00				

KM# 1090 1/25 CROWN
1.2441 g., 0.9999 Gold 0.0400 oz. AGW, 13.9 mm. **Ruler:** Elizabeth II **Series:** Harry Potter **Subject:** First Quidditch Match **Obv:** Bust with tiara right **Rev:** Harry flying a broom **Edge:** Reeded

Date	Mintage	F	VF	XF	Unc	BU
2001 Proof	10,000	Value: 75.00				

KM# 1092 1/25 CROWN
1.2441 g., 0.9999 Gold 0.0400 oz. AGW, 13.9 mm. **Ruler:** Elizabeth II **Series:** Harry Potter **Subject:** Birth of Norbert **Obv:** Bust with tiara right **Edge:** Reeded

Date	Mintage	F	VF	XF	Unc	BU
2001 Proof	10,000	Value: 75.00				

KM# 1094 1/25 CROWN
1.2441 g., 0.9999 Gold 0.0400 oz. AGW, 13.9 mm. **Ruler:** Elizabeth II **Series:** Harry Potter **Subject:** School **Obv:** Bust with tiara right **Rev:** Harry in Potions class **Edge:** Reeded

Date	Mintage	F	VF	XF	Unc	BU
2001 Proof	10,000	Value: 75.00				

KM# 1096 1/25 CROWN
1.2441 g., 0.9999 Gold 0.0400 oz. AGW, 13.9 mm. **Ruler:** Elizabeth II **Series:** Harry Potter **Subject:** Keys **Obv:** Bust with tiara right **Rev:** Harry chasing the golden snitch **Edge:** Reeded

Date	Mintage	F	VF	XF	Unc	BU
2001 Proof	10,000	Value: 75.00				

KM# 1098 1/25 CROWN
1.2441 g., 0.9999 Gold 0.0400 oz. AGW, 13.9 mm. **Ruler:** Elizabeth II **Subject:** Year of the Horse **Obv:** Bust with tiara right **Rev:** Two horses **Edge:** Reeded

Date	Mintage	F	VF	XF	Unc	BU
2002 Proof	20,000	Value: 75.00				

KM# 1107 1/25 CROWN
1.2440 g., 0.9990 Gold 0.0400 oz. AGW, 13.92 mm. **Ruler:** Elizabeth II **Subject:** Bengal Cat **Obv:** Head with tiara right **Rev:** Cat and kitten **Edge:** Reeded

Date	Mintage	F	VF	XF	Unc	BU
2002	—	—	—	—	—	80.00
2002 Proof	1,000	Value: 85.00				

KM# 1107a 1/25 CROWN
1.2440 g., 0.9990 Platinum 0.0400 oz. APW, 13.92 mm. **Ruler:** Elizabeth II **Subject:** Bengal Cat **Obv:** Head with tiara right **Rev:** Cat and kitten **Edge:** Reeded

Date	Mintage	F	VF	XF	Unc	BU
2002 Proof	—	Value: 90.00				

KM# 1145 1/25 CROWN
1.2440 g., 0.9999 Gold 0.0400 oz. AGW, 13.92 mm. **Ruler:** Elizabeth II **Subject:** Harry Potter Series **Obv:** Bust with tiara right **Rev:** Harry and friends making Polyjuice potion **Edge:** Reeded

Date	Mintage	F	VF	XF	Unc	BU
2002PM Proof	10,000	Value: 75.00				

KM# 1143 1/25 CROWN
1.2440 g., 0.9999 Gold 0.0400 oz. AGW, 13.92 mm. **Ruler:** Elizabeth II **Subject:** Harry Potter **Obv:** Bust with tiara right **Rev:** Tom Riddle twirling Harry's magic wand **Edge:** Reeded

Date	Mintage	F	VF	XF	Unc	BU
2002PM Proof	10,000	Value: 75.00				

KM# 1147 1/25 CROWN
1.2440 g., 0.9999 Gold 0.0400 oz. AGW, 13.92 mm. **Ruler:** Elizabeth II **Subject:** Harry Potter **Obv:** Bust with tiara right **Rev:** Harry arrives at the Burrow in a flying car **Edge:** Reeded

Date	Mintage	F	VF	XF	Unc	BU
2002PM Proof	10,000	Value: 75.00				

KM# 1149 1/25 CROWN
1.2440 g., 0.9999 Gold 0.0400 oz. AGW, 13.92 mm. **Ruler:** Elizabeth II **Subject:** Harry Potter Series **Obv:** Bust with tiara right **Rev:** Harry retrieves Gryffindor sword from snake **Edge:** Reeded

Date	Mintage	F	VF	XF	Unc	BU
2002PM Proof	10,000	Value: 75.00				

KM# 1151 1/25 CROWN
1.2240 g., 0.9999 Gold 0.0393 oz. AGW, 13.92 mm. **Ruler:** Elizabeth II **Series:** Harry Potter **Obv:** Bust with tiara right **Rev:** Harry and Ron encounter the spider Aragog **Edge:** Reeded

Date	Mintage	F	VF	XF	Unc	BU
2002PM Proof	10,000	Value: 75.00				

KM# 1153 1/25 CROWN
1.2440 g., 0.9999 Gold 0.0400 oz. AGW, 13.92 mm. **Ruler:** Elizabeth II **Series:** Harry Potter **Obv:** Bust with tiara right **Rev:** Harry in hospital **Edge:** Reeded

Date	Mintage	F	VF	XF	Unc	BU
2002PM Proof	10,000	Value: 75.00				

KM# 1186 1/25 CROWN
1.2440 g., 0.9999 Gold 0.0400 oz. AGW, 13.9 mm. **Ruler:** Elizabeth II **Subject:** Lord of the Rings **Obv:** Bust with tiara right **Rev:** Frodo Baggins with short sword **Edge:** Reeded

Date	Mintage	F	VF	XF	Unc	BU
2003PM Proof	6,000	Value: 75.00				

KM# 1161 1/25 CROWN
1.2440 g., 0.9999 Gold 0.0400 oz. AGW, 13.92 mm. **Ruler:** Elizabeth II **Subject:** Cat **Obv:** Head with tiara right **Rev:** Two Balinese kittens **Edge:** Reeded

Date	Mintage	F	VF	XF	Unc	BU
2003PM	—	—	—	—	—	72.50
2003PM Proof	—	Value: 75.00				

KM# 1161a 1/25 CROWN
1.2440 g., 0.9995 Platinum 0.0400 oz. APW, 13.92 mm. **Ruler:** Elizabeth II **Subject:** Cat **Obv:** Head with tiara right **Rev:** Two Balinese kittens **Edge:** Reeded

Date	Mintage	F	VF	XF	Unc	BU
2003PM Proof	—	Value: 85.00				

KM# 1167 1/25 CROWN
1.2441 g., 0.9999 Gold 0.0400 oz. AGW, 13.9 mm. **Ruler:** Elizabeth II **Subject:** Year of the Goat **Obv:** Head with tiara right **Rev:** Three goats **Edge:** Reeded

Date	Mintage	F	VF	XF	Unc	BU
2003PM Proof	20,000	Value: 75.00				

KM# 1203 1/25 CROWN
1.2440 g., 0.9999 Gold 0.0400 oz. AGW, 14 mm. **Ruler:** Elizabeth II **Obv:** Bust with tiara right **Rev:** Harry Potter and patron fighting off a spectre **Edge:** Reeded

Date	Mintage	F	VF	XF	Unc	BU
2004PM Proof	2,500	Value: 75.00				

KM# 1205 1/25 CROWN
1.2440 g., 0.9999 Gold 0.0400 oz. AGW, 14 mm. **Ruler:** Elizabeth II **Obv:** Bust with tiara right **Rev:** Harry Potter in the shrieking shack **Edge:** Reeded

Date	Mintage	F	VF	XF	Unc	BU
2004PM Proof	2,500	Value: 75.00				

KM# 1207 1/25 CROWN
1.2440 g., 0.9999 Gold 0.0400 oz. AGW, 14 mm. **Ruler:** Elizabeth II **Obv:** Bust with tiara right **Rev:** Harry Potter and Professor Dumbledore **Edge:** Reeded

Date	Mintage	F	VF	XF	Unc	BU
2004PM Proof	2,500	Value: 75.00				

KM# 1209 1/25 CROWN
1.2440 g., 0.9999 Gold 0.0400 oz. AGW, 14 mm. **Ruler:** Elizabeth II **Obv:** Bust with tiara right **Rev:** Sirius Black on flying griffin **Edge:** Reeded

Date	Mintage	F	VF	XF	Unc	BU
2004PM Proof	2,500	Value: 75.00				

KM# 1211 1/25 CROWN
1.2440 g., 0.9999 Gold 0.0400 oz. AGW, 14 mm. **Ruler:** Elizabeth II **Obv:** Head with tiara right **Rev:** Three Olympic Swimmers **Edge:** Reeded

Date	Mintage	F	VF	XF	Unc	BU
2004PM Proof	5,000	Value: 75.00				

KM# 1213 1/25 CROWN
1.2440 g., 0.9999 Gold 0.0400 oz. AGW, 14 mm. **Ruler:** Elizabeth II **Obv:** Head with tiara right **Rev:** Three Olympic Cyclists **Edge:** Reeded

Date	Mintage	F	VF	XF	Unc	BU
2004PM Proof	5,000	Value: 75.00				

KM# 1215 1/25 CROWN
1.2440 g., 0.9999 Gold 0.0400 oz. AGW, 14 mm. **Ruler:** Elizabeth II **Obv:** Head with tiara right **Rev:** Three Olympic Runners **Edge:** Reeded

Date	Mintage	F	VF	XF	Unc	BU
2004PM Proof	5,000	Value: 75.00				

KM# 1217 1/25 CROWN
1.2440 g., 0.9999 Gold 0.0400 oz. AGW, 14 mm. **Ruler:** Elizabeth II **Obv:** Head with tiara right **Rev:** Three Olympic Sail Boarders **Edge:** Reeded

Date	Mintage	F	VF	XF	Unc	BU
2004PM Proof	5,000	Value: 75.00				

KM# 1240 1/25 CROWN
1.2440 g., 0.9999 Gold 0.0400 oz. AGW, 14 mm. **Ruler:** Elizabeth II **Obv:** Head with tiara right **Rev:** Monkey **Edge:** Reeded

Date	Mintage	F	VF	XF	Unc	BU
2004PM Proof	20,000	Value: 75.00				

KM# 1247 1/25 CROWN
1.2440 g., 0.9999 Gold 0.0400 oz. AGW, 14 mm. **Ruler:** Elizabeth II **Obv:** Head with tiara right **Rev:** Two Tonkinese cats **Edge:** Reeded

Date	Mintage	F	VF	XF	Unc	BU
2004PM	—	—	—	—	—	80.00
2004PM Proof	1,000	Value: 85.00				

KM# 1269 1/25 CROWN
1.2440 g., 0.9999 Gold 0.0400 oz. AGW, 13.92 mm. **Ruler:** Elizabeth II **Obv:** Bust with tiara right **Rev:** Himalayan cat and two kittens **Edge:** Reeded

Date	Mintage	F	VF	XF	Unc	BU
2005PM Proof	—	Value: 75.00				

KM# 1269a 1/25 CROWN
1.2440 g., 0.9950 Platinum 0.0398 oz. APW, 13.92 mm. **Ruler:** Elizabeth II **Obv:** Bust with tiara right **Rev:** Himalayan cat and two kittens **Edge:** Reeded

Date	Mintage	F	VF	XF	Unc	BU
2005PM Proof	—	Value: 85.00				

KM# 1340 1/25 CROWN
1.2441 g., 0.9999 Gold 0.0400 oz. AGW, 13.92 mm. **Ruler:** Elizabeth II **Obv:** Bust with tiara right **Rev:** Three Exotic Shorthair cats sitting facing **Edge:** Reeded

Date	Mintage	F	VF	XF	Unc	BU
2006PM	—	—	—	—	—	80.00

KM# 1343 1/25 CROWN
1.2441 g., 0.9999 Gold 0.0400 oz. AGW, 13.92 mm. **Ruler:** Elizabeth II **Obv:** Bust with tiara right **Obv. Legend:** ELIZABETH II - ISLE OF MAN **Rev:** Ragdoll cat with two kittens sitting facing **Edge:** Reeded

Date	Mintage	F	VF	XF	Unc	BU
2007PM	—	—	—	—	—	80.00

KM# 1349 1/25 CROWN
1.2440 g., 0.9999 Gold 0.0400 oz. AGW, 13.92 mm. **Ruler:** Elizabeth II **Subject:** The Tale of Peter Rabbit **Obv:** Bust with tiara right **Obv. Legend:** ELIZABETH II - ISLE OF MAN **Rev:** Peter walking with friends **Edge:** Reeded

Date	Mintage	F	VF	XF	Unc	BU
2007PM	—	—	—	—	—	72.50

KM# 1308 1/25 CROWN
1.2441 g., 0.9999 Gold 0.0400 oz. AGW, 13.92 mm. **Ruler:** Elizabeth II **Subject:** 100th Anniversary of Scouting **Obv:** Bust with tiara right **Obv. Legend:** ELIZABETH II - ISLE OF MAN **Rev:** 3/4 length figure of Robert Baden-Powell standing facing 3/4 left, Fleur-de-lys below, images of scouting at left and right **Rev. Legend:** CENTENARY OF SCOUTING **Edge:** Reeded

Date	Mintage	F	VF	XF	Unc	BU
2007PM Proof	—	Value: 75.00				

KM# 1314 1/25 CROWN
1.2400 g., 0.9999 Gold 0.0399 oz. AGW, 13.92 mm. **Ruler:** Elizabeth II **Obv:** Bust with tiara right **Obv. Legend:** ELIZABETH II - ISLE OF MAN **Rev:** Two swans facing **Edge:** Reeded

Date	Mintage	F	VF	XF	Unc	BU
2007 Proof	10,000	Value: 75.00				

KM# 1383 1/25 CROWN
1.2400 g., 0.9999 Gold 0.0399 oz. AGW, 13.92 mm. **Ruler:** Elizabeth II **Obv:** Bust right **Rev:** Chinchilla cat and kitten

Date	Mintage	F	VF	XF	Unc	BU
2009	—	—	—	—	—	80.00
2009 Proof	1,000	Value: 85.00				

KM# 1387 1/25 CROWN
1.2400 g., 0.9950 Platinum 0.0397 oz. APW, 13.92 mm. **Ruler:** Elizabeth II **Obv:** Bust right **Rev:** Chinchilla cat and kitten

Date	Mintage	F	VF	XF	Unc	BU
2009	—	—	—	—	—	85.00

KM# 1473 1/25 CROWN
1.2400 g., 0.9990 Gold 0.0398 oz. AGW, 13.92 mm. **Ruler:** Elizabeth II **Subject:** George F. Handel, 325th Anniversary of Birth **Obv:** Bust in tiara right **Rev:** Handel bust, music score in background

Date	Mintage	F	VF	XF	Unc	BU
2010PM Proof	—	Value: 100				

KM# 1435 1/25 CROWN
1.2400 g., 0.9999 Gold 0.0399 oz. AGW, 13.92 mm. **Ruler:** Elizabeth II **Subject:** Turkish Angora cat

Date	Mintage	F	VF	XF	Unc	BU
2011PM	—	—	—	—	—	100
2011PM Proof	1,000	Value: 115				

KM# 1059 1/10 CROWN
3.1100 g., 0.9999 Gold 0.1000 oz. AGW, 17.95 mm. **Ruler:** Elizabeth II **Subject:** Year of the Snake **Obv:** Bust with tiara right **Rev:** Snake **Edge:** Reeded

Date	Mintage	F	VF	XF	Unc	BU
2001 Proof	15,000	Value: 180				

KM# 1068 1/10 CROWN
3.1100 g., 0.9999 Gold 0.1000 oz. AGW, 18 mm. **Ruler:** Elizabeth II **Obv:** Head with tiara right **Rev:** Somali kittens **Edge:** Reeded

Date	Mintage	F	VF	XF	Unc	BU
2001	—	—	—	—	—	175
2001 Proof	1,000	Value: 180				

KM# 1068a 1/10 CROWN
3.1100 g., 0.9995 Platinum 0.0999 oz. APW, 18 mm. **Ruler:** Elizabeth II **Obv:** Head with tiara right **Rev:** Somali kittens **Edge:** Reeded

Date	Mintage	F	VF	XF	Unc	BU
2001 Proof	—	Value: 200				

KM# 1328 1/10 CROWN
3.1100 g., 0.9990 Gold 0.0999 oz. AGW, 18 mm. **Ruler:** Elizabeth II **Subject:** Harry Potter **Obv:** Bust right **Rev:** Boy with magic wand **Edge:** Reeded

Date	Mintage	F	VF	XF	Unc	BU
2001 Proof	7,500	Value: 180				

KM# 1329 1/10 CROWN
3.1100 g., 0.9990 Gold 0.0999 oz. AGW, 18 mm. **Ruler:** Elizabeth II **Subject:** Harry Potter - Journey to Hogwarts **Obv:** Bust right **Rev:** Boat full of children going to Hogwarts School **Edge:** Reeded

Date	Mintage	F	VF	XF	Unc	BU
2001 Proof	7,500	Value: 180				

KM# 1330 1/10 CROWN
3.1100 g., 0.9990 Gold 0.0999 oz. AGW, 18 mm. **Ruler:** Elizabeth II **Subject:** Harry Potter **Obv:** Bust right **Rev:** Harry flying on a broomstick **Edge:** Reeded

Date	Mintage	F	VF	XF	Unc	BU
2001 Proof	7,500	Value: 180				

KM# 1331 1/10 CROWN
3.1100 g., 0.9990 Gold 0.0999 oz. AGW, 18 mm. **Ruler:** Elizabeth II **Subject:** Harry Potter **Obv:** Bust right **Rev:** Birth of Norbert the dragon **Edge:** Reeded

Date	Mintage	F	VF	XF	Unc	BU
2001 Proof	7,500	Value: 180				

KM# 1332 1/10 CROWN
3.1100 g., 0.9990 Gold 0.0999 oz. AGW, 18 mm. **Ruler:** Elizabeth II **Subject:** Harry Potter **Obv:** Bust right **Rev:** Harry in Potions class **Edge:** Reeded

Date	Mintage	F	VF	XF	Unc	BU
2001 Proof	7,500	Value: 180				

KM# 1333 1/10 CROWN
3.1100 g., 0.9990 Gold 0.0999 oz. AGW, 18 mm. **Ruler:** Elizabeth II **Subject:** Harry Potter **Obv:** Bust right **Rev:** Harry chasing a snitch **Edge:** Reeded

Date	Mintage	F	VF	XF	Unc	BU
2001 Proof	7,500	Value: 180				

KM# 1099 1/10 CROWN
3.1100 g., 0.9999 Gold 0.1000 oz. AGW, 17.95 mm. **Ruler:** Elizabeth II **Subject:** Year of the Horse **Obv:** Bust with tiara right **Rev:** Two horses **Edge:** Reeded

Date	Mintage	F	VF	XF	Unc	BU
2002 Proof	15,000	Value: 180				

KM# 1155 1/10 CROWN
3.1100 g., 0.9990 Gold 0.0999 oz. AGW, 17.95 mm. **Ruler:** Elizabeth II **Subject:** Queen's Golden Jubilee **Obv:** Queen's portrait **Rev:** Queen on horse **Edge:** Reeded

Date	Mintage	F	VF	XF	Unc	BU
2002PM Proof	500	Value: 180				

KM# 1108 1/10 CROWN
3.1100 g., 0.9990 Gold 0.0999 oz. AGW, 17.95 mm. **Ruler:** Elizabeth II **Subject:** Bengal Cat **Obv:** Head with tiara right **Rev:** Cat and kitten **Edge:** Reeded

Date	Mintage	VG	F	VF	XF	Unc
2002	—	—	—	—	—	185
2002 Proof	—	Value: 190				

KM# 1108a 1/10 CROWN
3.1100 g., 0.9990 Platinum 0.0999 oz. APW, 17.95 mm. **Ruler:** Elizabeth II **Subject:** Bengal Cat **Obv:** Head with tiara right **Rev:** Cat and kitten **Edge:** Reeded

Date	Mintage	F	VF	XF	Unc	BU
2002	—	—	—	—	—	195

KM# 1162 1/10 CROWN
3.1100 g., 0.9999 Gold 0.1000 oz. AGW, 17.95 mm. **Ruler:** Elizabeth II **Subject:** Cat **Obv:** Head with tiara right **Rev:** Two Balinese kittens **Edge:** Reeded

Date	Mintage	F	VF	XF	Unc	BU
2003PM	—	—	—	—	—	175
2003PM Proof	—	Value: 180				

KM# 1162a 1/10 CROWN
3.1100 g., 0.9995 Platinum 0.0999 oz. APW, 17.95 mm. **Ruler:** Elizabeth II **Subject:** Cat **Obv:** Head with tiara right **Rev:** Two Balinese kittens **Edge:** Reeded

Date	Mintage	F	VF	XF	Unc	BU
2003PM	—	—	—	—	—	190

KM# 1168 1/10 CROWN
3.1100 g., 0.9999 Gold 0.1000 oz. AGW, 17.95 mm. **Ruler:** Elizabeth II **Subject:** Year of the Goat **Obv:** Bust with tiara right **Rev:** Three goats **Edge:** Reeded

Date	Mintage	F	VF	XF	Unc	BU
2003PM Proof	—	Value: 180				

KM# 1187 1/10 CROWN
3.1100 g., 0.9999 Gold 0.1000 oz. AGW, 18 mm. **Ruler:** Elizabeth II **Subject:** Lord of the Rings **Obv:** Bust with tiara right **Rev:** Aragorn with broad sword **Edge:** Reeded

Date	Mintage	F	VF	XF	Unc	BU
2003PM Proof	4,500	Value: 180				

KM# 1241 1/10 CROWN
3.1100 g., 0.9999 Gold 0.1000 oz. AGW, 18 mm. **Ruler:** Elizabeth II **Obv:** Head with tiara right **Rev:** Monkey **Edge:** Reeded

Date	Mintage	F	VF	XF	Unc	BU
2004PM Proof	15,000	Value: 180				

KM# 1248 1/10 CROWN
3.1100 g., 0.9999 Gold 0.1000 oz. AGW, 18 mm. **Ruler:** Elizabeth II **Obv:** Head with tiara right **Rev:** Two Tonkinese cats **Edge:** Reeded

Date	Mintage	F	VF	XF	Unc	BU
2004PM	—	—	—	—	—	185
2004PM Proof	1,000	Value: 190				

KM# 1270 1/10 CROWN
3.1100 g., 0.9999 Gold 0.1000 oz. AGW, 18 mm. **Ruler:** Elizabeth II **Obv:** Bust with tiara right **Rev:** Himalayan cat and two kittens **Edge:** Reeded

Date	Mintage	F	VF	XF	Unc	BU
2005PM Proof	—	Value: 190				

KM# 1270a 1/10 CROWN
3.1100 g., 0.9950 Platinum 0.0995 oz. APW, 18 mm. **Ruler:** Elizabeth II **Obv:** Queen Elizabeth II **Rev:** Himalayan cat and two kittens **Edge:** Reeded

Date	Mintage	F	VF	XF	Unc	BU
2005PM Proof	—	Value: 200				

KM# 1341 1/10 CROWN
3.1100 g., 0.9999 Gold 0.1000 oz. AGW, 18 mm. **Ruler:** Elizabeth II **Obv:** Bust with tiara right **Rev:** Three Exotic Shorthair cats sitting facing **Edge:** Reeded

Date	Mintage	F	VF	XF	Unc	BU
2006PM	—	—	—	—	—	180

KM# 1350 1/10 CROWN
3.1100 g., 0.9999 Gold 0.1000 oz. AGW, 18 mm. **Ruler:** Elizabeth II **Subject:** The Tale of Peter Rabbit **Obv:** Bust with tiara right **Obv. Legend:** ELIZABETH II - ISLE OF MAN **Rev:** Peter walking with friends **Edge:** Reeded

Date	Mintage	F	VF	XF	Unc	BU
2007PM	—	—	—	—	—	175

KM# 1344 1/10 CROWN
3.1100 g., 0.9999 Gold 0.1000 oz. AGW, 18 mm. **Ruler:** Elizabeth II **Obv:** Bust with tiara right **Obv. Legend:** ELIZABETH II - ISLE OF MAN **Rev:** Ragdoll cat with two kittens sitting facing **Edge:** Reeded

Date	Mintage	F	VF	XF	Unc	BU
2007PM	—	—	—	—	—	185

KM# 1382 1/10 CROWN
3.1100 g., 0.9999 Gold 0.1000 oz. AGW, 18 mm. **Ruler:** Elizabeth II **Obv:** Bust right **Rev:** Chinchilla cat and kitten

Date	Mintage	F	VF	XF	Unc	BU
2009	—	—	—	—	—	185
2009 Proof	1,000	Value: 190				

KM# 1386 1/10 CROWN
3.1100 g., 0.9950 Platinum 0.0995 oz. APW, 18 mm. **Ruler:** Elizabeth II **Obv:** Bust right **Rev:** Chinchilla cat and kitten

Date	Mintage	F	VF	XF	Unc	BU
2009	—	—	—	—	—	190

KM# 1436 1/10 CROWN
3.1100 g., 0.9999 Gold 0.1000 oz. AGW, 18 mm. **Ruler:** Elizabeth II **Subject:** Turkish Angora Cat

Date	Mintage	F	VF	XF	Unc	BU
2011PM	—	—	—	—	—	225
2011PM Proof	1,000	Value: 240				

KM# 1060 1/5 CROWN

6.2200 g., 0.9999 Gold 0.1999 oz. AGW, 22 mm. **Ruler:** Elizabeth II **Subject:** Year of the Snake **Obv:** Bust with tiara right **Rev:** Snake **Edge:** Reeded

Date	Mintage	F	VF	XF	Unc	BU
2001 Proof	12,000	Value: 355				

KM# 1069 1/5 CROWN

6.2200 g., 0.9999 Gold 0.1999 oz. AGW, 22 mm. **Ruler:** Elizabeth II **Obv:** Head with tiara right **Rev:** Two Somali kittens **Edge:** Reeded

Date	Mintage	F	VF	XF	Unc	BU
2001	—	—	—	—	—	350
2001 Proof	1,000	Value: 355				

KM# 1069a 1/5 CROWN

6.2200 g., 0.9995 Platinum 0.1999 oz. APW, 22 mm. **Ruler:** Elizabeth II **Obv:** Head with tiara right **Rev:** Somali kittens **Edge:** Reeded

Date	Mintage	F	VF	XF	Unc	BU
2001	—	—	—	—	—	400

KM# 1074 1/5 CROWN

6.2200 g., 0.9999 Gold 0.1999 oz. AGW, 22 mm. **Ruler:** Elizabeth II **Subject:** Queen Mother **Obv:** Head with tiara right **Rev:** 1948 Silver wedding anniversary **Edge:** Reeded

Date	Mintage	F	VF	XF	Unc	BU
2001 Proof	5,000	Value: 355				

KM# 1075 1/5 CROWN

6.2200 g., 0.9999 Gold 0.1999 oz. AGW, 22 mm. **Ruler:** Elizabeth II **Subject:** Queen Mother **Obv:** Head with tiara right **Rev:** 1948 holding baby Prince Charles **Edge:** Reeded

Date	Mintage	F	VF	XF	Unc	BU
2001 Proof	5,000	Value: 355				

KM# 1078 1/5 CROWN

6.2200 g., 0.9999 Gold 0.1999 oz. AGW, 22 mm. **Ruler:** Elizabeth II **Subject:** Martin Frobisher **Obv:** Head with tiara right **Rev:** Portrait, ship and map **Edge:** Reeded

Date	Mintage	F	VF	XF	Unc	BU
2001 Proof	5,000	Value: 355				

KM# 1079 1/5 CROWN

6.2200 g., 0.9999 Gold 0.1999 oz. AGW, 22 mm. **Ruler:** Elizabeth II **Subject:** Ronald Amundsen **Obv:** Head with tiara right **Rev:** Portrait, ship and dirigible **Edge:** Reeded

Date	Mintage	F	VF	XF	Unc	BU
2001 Proof	5,000	Value: 355				

KM# 1082 1/5 CROWN

6.2200 g., 0.9999 Gold 0.1999 oz. AGW, 22 mm. **Ruler:** Elizabeth II **Subject:** Queen's 75th Birthday **Obv:** Head with tiara right **Rev:** Flower bouquet with a tiny diamond mounted on the bow of the ribbon **Edge:** Reeded

Date	Mintage	F	VF	XF	Unc	BU
2001 Proof	2,000	Value: 355				

KM# 1339 1/5 CROWN

6.1500 g., 0.9990 Gold 0.1975 oz. AGW, 22 mm. **Ruler:** Elizabeth II **Subject:** Harry Potter **Obv:** Bust right **Rev:** Harry chasing a jeweled snitch **Edge:** Reeded

Date	Mintage	F	VF	XF	Unc	BU
2001 Proof	5,000	Value: 355				

KM# 1334 1/5 CROWN

6.1500 g., 0.9990 Gold 0.1975 oz. AGW, 22 mm. **Ruler:** Elizabeth II **Subject:** Harry Potter **Obv:** Bust right **Rev:** Harry with magic wand **Edge:** Reeded

Date	Mintage	F	VF	XF	Unc	BU
2001 Proof	5,000	Value: 355				

KM# 1335 1/5 CROWN

6.1500 g., 0.9990 Gold 0.1975 oz. AGW, 22 mm. **Ruler:** Elizabeth II **Subject:** Harry Potter - Journey to Hogwarts School **Obv:** Bust right **Rev:** Boat full of children going to Hogwarts School **Edge:** Reeded

Date	Mintage	F	VF	XF	Unc	BU
2001 Proof	5,000	Value: 355				

KM# 1336 1/5 CROWN

6.1500 g., 0.9990 Gold 0.1975 oz. AGW, 22 mm. **Ruler:** Elizabeth II **Subject:** Harry Potter - First Quidditch Match **Obv:** Bust right **Rev:** Harry flying a broom in a quidditch match **Edge:** Reeded

Date	Mintage	F	VF	XF	Unc	BU
2001 Proof	5,000	Value: 355				

KM# 1337 1/5 CROWN

6.1500 g., 0.9990 Gold 0.1975 oz. AGW, 22 mm. **Ruler:** Elizabeth II **Subject:** Harry Potter **Obv:** Bust right **Rev:** Birth of Norbert, the dragon **Edge:** Reeded

Date	Mintage	F	VF	XF	Unc	BU
2001 Proof	5,000	Value: 355				

KM# 1338 1/5 CROWN

6.1500 g., 0.9990 Gold 0.1975 oz. AGW, 22 mm. **Ruler:** Elizabeth II **Subject:** Harry Potter **Obv:** Bust right **Rev:** Harry in Potions class **Edge:** Reeded

Date	Mintage	F	VF	XF	Unc	BU
2001 Proof	5,000	Value: 355				

KM# 1156 1/5 CROWN

6.2200 g., 0.9990 Gold 0.1998 oz. AGW, 22 mm. **Ruler:** Elizabeth II **Subject:** Queen's Golden Jubilee **Obv:** Queen's portrait **Rev:** Queen on horse **Edge:** Reeded

Date	Mintage	F	VF	XF	Unc	BU
2002PM Proof	500	Value: 355				

KM# 1117 1/5 CROWN

6.2200 g., 0.9990 Gold 0.1998 oz. AGW, 22 mm. **Ruler:** Elizabeth II **Subject:** Queen Mother's Love of Horses **Obv:** Bust with tiara right **Rev:** Queen Mother and horse **Edge:** Reeded

Date	Mintage	F	VF	XF	Unc	BU
2002 Proof	5,000	Value: 355				

KM# 1109 1/5 CROWN

6.2200 g., 0.9990 Gold 0.1998 oz. AGW, 22 mm. **Ruler:** Elizabeth II **Subject:** Bengal Cat **Obv:** Head with tiara right **Rev:** Cat and kitten **Edge:** Reeded

Date	Mintage	VG	F	VF	XF	Unc
2002	—	—	—	—	—	—
2002 Proof	1,000	Value: 400				

KM# 1109a 1/5 CROWN

6.2200 g., 0.9990 Platinum 0.1998 oz. APW, 22 mm. **Ruler:** Elizabeth II **Subject:** Bengal Cat **Obv:** Head with tiara right **Rev:** Cat and kitten **Edge:** Reeded

Date	Mintage	F	VF	XF	Unc	BU
2002	—	—	—	—	—	400

KM# 1100 1/5 CROWN

6.2200 g., 0.9999 Gold 0.1999 oz. AGW, 22 mm. **Ruler:** Elizabeth II **Subject:** Year of the Horse **Obv:** Bust with tiara right **Rev:** Two horses **Edge:** Reeded

Date	Mintage	F	VF	XF	Unc	BU
2002 Proof	12,000	Value: 355				

KM# 1113 1/5 CROWN

6.2200 g., 0.9990 Gold 0.1998 oz. AGW, 22 mm. **Ruler:** Elizabeth II **Subject:** Olympics - Salt Lake City **Obv:** Bust with tiara right **Rev:** Skier, torch and flag **Edge:** Reeded

Date	Mintage	F	VF	XF	Unc	BU
2002 Proof	5,000	Value: 355				

KM# 1114 1/5 CROWN

6.2200 g., 0.9990 Gold 0.1998 oz. AGW, 22 mm. **Ruler:** Elizabeth II **Subject:** Olympics - Salt Lake City **Obv:** Bust with tiara right **Rev:** Bobsled, torch and stadium **Edge:** Reeded

Date	Mintage	F	VF	XF	Unc	BU
2002 Proof	5,000	Value: 355				

KM# 1120 1/5 CROWN

6.2200 g., 0.9990 Gold 0.1998 oz. AGW, 22 mm. **Ruler:** Elizabeth II **Subject:** World Cup 2002 Japan - Korea **Obv:** Bust with tiara right **Rev:** Player running right **Edge:** Reeded

Date	Mintage	F	VF	XF	Unc	BU
2002 Proof	5,000	Value: 355				

KM# 1122 1/5 CROWN

6.2200 g., 0.9990 Gold 0.1998 oz. AGW, 22 mm. **Ruler:** Elizabeth II **Subject:** World Cup 2002 Japan - Korea **Obv:** Bust with tiara right **Rev:** Player kicking to right **Edge:** Reeded

Date	Mintage	F	VF	XF	Unc	BU
2002 Proof	5,000	Value: 355				

KM# 1124 1/5 CROWN

6.2200 g., 0.9990 Gold 0.1998 oz. AGW, 22 mm. **Ruler:** Elizabeth II **Subject:** World Cup 2002 Japan - Korea **Obv:** Head with tiara right **Rev:** Player kicking to left **Edge:** Reeded

Date	Mintage	F	VF	XF	Unc	BU
2002 Proof	5,000	Value: 355				

KM# 1126 1/5 CROWN

6.2200 g., 0.9990 Gold 0.1998 oz. AGW, 22 mm. **Ruler:** Elizabeth II **Subject:** World Cup 2002 Japan - Korea **Obv:** Head with tiara right **Rev:** Player running to left **Edge:** Reeded

Date	Mintage	F	VF	XF	Unc	BU
2002 Proof	5,000	Value: 355				

KM# 1130 1/5 CROWN

6.2200 g., 0.3750 Gold 0.0750 oz. AGW, 22 mm. **Ruler:** Elizabeth II **Subject:** Elizabeth II's Golden Jubilee **Obv:** Bust with tiara right **Rev:** Seated crowned Queen holding scepter at her coronation **Edge:** Reeded

Date	Mintage	F	VF	XF	Unc	BU
2002 Proof	2,002	Value: 140				

KM# 1132 1/5 CROWN

6.2200 g., 0.3750 Gold 0.0750 oz. AGW, 22 mm. **Ruler:** Elizabeth II **Subject:** Elizabeth II's Golden Jubilee **Obv:** Bust with tiara right **Rev:** Queen on horse **Edge:** Reeded

Date	Mintage	F	VF	XF	Unc	BU
2002 Proof	2,002	Value: 140				

KM# 1134 1/5 CROWN

6.2200 g., 0.3750 Gold 0.0750 oz. AGW, 22 mm. **Ruler:** Elizabeth II **Subject:** Elizabeth II's Golden Jubilee **Obv:** Head with tiara right **Rev:** Queen with dog **Edge:** Reeded

Date	Mintage	F	VF	XF	Unc	BU
2002 Proof	2,002	Value: 140				

KM# 1136 1/5 CROWN

6.2200 g., 0.3750 Gold 0.0750 oz. AGW, 22 mm. **Ruler:** Elizabeth II **Subject:** Elizabeth II's Golden Jubilee **Obv:** Bust with tiara right **Rev:** Queen at war memorial **Edge:** Reeded

Date	Mintage	F	VF	XF	Unc	BU
2002 Proof	2,002	Value: 140				

KM# 1138 1/5 CROWN

6.2200 g., 0.9990 Gold 0.1998 oz. AGW, 22 mm. **Ruler:** Elizabeth II **Subject:** Queen Mother **Obv:** Bust with tiara right **Rev:** Queen Mother and Castle May **Edge:** Reeded

Date	Mintage	F	VF	XF	Unc	BU
2002 Proof	5,000	Value: 355				

KM# 1140 1/5 CROWN

6.2200 g., 0.9999 Gold 0.1999 oz. AGW, 22 mm. **Ruler:** Elizabeth II **Subject:** Princess Diana **Obv:** Bust with tiara right **Rev:** Diana's portrait **Edge:** Reeded

Date	Mintage	F	VF	XF	Unc	BU
2002 Proof	5,000	Value: 355				

KM# 1163 1/5 CROWN

6.2200 g., 0.9999 Gold 0.1999 oz. AGW, 22 mm. **Ruler:** Elizabeth II **Subject:** Cat **Obv:** Head with tiara right **Rev:** Two Balinese kittens **Edge:** Reeded

Date	Mintage	F	VF	XF	Unc	BU
2003PM	—	—	—	—	—	350
2003PM Proof	—	Value: 355				

KM# 1163a 1/5 CROWN

6.2200 g., 0.9995 Platinum 0.1999 oz. APW, 22 mm. **Ruler:** Elizabeth II **Subject:** Cat **Obv:** Head with tiara right **Rev:** Two Balinese kittens **Edge:** Reeded

Date	Mintage	F	VF	XF	Unc	BU
2003PM	—	—	—	—	—	385

KM# 1169 1/5 CROWN

6.2200 g., 0.9999 Gold 0.1999 oz. AGW, 22 mm. **Ruler:** Elizabeth II **Subject:** Year of the Goat **Obv:** Bust with tiara right **Rev:** Three goats **Edge:** Reeded

Date	Mintage	F	VF	XF	Unc	BU
2003PM Proof	—	Value: 355				

KM# 1175 1/5 CROWN

6.2200 g., 0.9999 Gold 0.1999 oz. AGW, 22 mm. **Ruler:** Elizabeth II **Subject:** Olympics **Obv:** Bust with tiara right **Rev:** Swimmers **Edge:** Reeded

Date	Mintage	F	VF	XF	Unc	BU
2003PM Proof	5,000	Value: 355				

KM# 1177 1/5 CROWN

6.2200 g., 0.9999 Gold 0.1999 oz. AGW, 22 mm. **Ruler:** Elizabeth II **Subject:** Olympics **Obv:** Bust with tiara right **Rev:** Runners **Edge:** Reeded

Date	Mintage	F	VF	XF	Unc	BU
2003PM Proof	5,000	Value: 355				

KM# 1179 1/5 CROWN

6.2200 g., 0.9999 Gold 0.1999 oz. AGW, 22 mm. **Ruler:** Elizabeth II **Subject:** Olympics **Obv:** Bust with tiara right **Rev:** Bicyclists **Edge:** Reeded

Date	Mintage	F	VF	XF	Unc	BU
2003PM Proof	5,000	Value: 355				

KM# 1181 1/5 CROWN

6.2200 g., 0.9999 Gold 0.1999 oz. AGW, 22 mm. **Ruler:** Elizabeth II **Subject:** Olympics **Obv:** Head with tiara right **Rev:** Sail Boarders **Edge:** Reeded

Date	Mintage	F	VF	XF	Unc	BU
2003PM Proof	—	Value: 355				

KM# 1188 1/5 CROWN

6.2200 g., 0.9999 Gold 0.1999 oz. AGW, 22 mm. **Ruler:** Elizabeth II **Subject:** Lord of the Rings **Obv:** Bust with tiara right **Rev:** Legolas with bow and arrow **Edge:** Reeded

Date	Mintage	F	VF	XF	Unc	BU
2003PM Proof	3,500	Value: 355				

KM# 1223 1/5 CROWN

6.2200 g., 0.9999 Gold 0.1999 oz. AGW, 22 mm. **Ruler:** Elizabeth II **Obv:** Bust with tiara right **Rev:** D-Day Invasion Plan Map **Edge:** Reeded

Date	Mintage	F	VF	XF	Unc	BU
2004PM Proof	5,000	Value: 355				

KM# 1225 1/5 CROWN

6.2200 g., 0.9999 Gold 0.1999 oz. AGW, 22 mm. **Ruler:** Elizabeth II **Obv:** Bust with tiara right **Rev:** Victoria Cross and battle scene **Edge:** Reeded

Date	Mintage	F	VF	XF	Unc	BU
2004PM Proof	5,000	Value: 355				

KM# 1227 1/5 CROWN

6.2200 g., 0.9999 Gold 0.1999 oz. AGW, 22 mm. **Ruler:** Elizabeth II **Obv:** Bust with tiara right **Rev:** Silver Star and battle scene **Edge:** Reeded

Date	Mintage	F	VF	XF	Unc	BU
2004PM Proof	5,000	Value: 355				

KM# 1229 1/5 CROWN

6.2200 g., 0.9999 Gold 0.1999 oz. AGW, 22 mm. **Ruler:** Elizabeth II **Obv:** Bust with tiara right **Rev:** George Cross and rescue scene **Edge:** Reeded

Date	Mintage	F	VF	XF	Unc	BU
2004PM Proof	5,000	Value: 355				

KM# 1231 1/5 CROWN

6.2200 g., 0.9999 Gold 0.1999 oz. AGW, 22 mm. **Ruler:** Elizabeth II **Obv:** Bust with tiara right **Rev:** White Rose of Finland Medal and battle scene **Edge:** Reeded

Date	Mintage	F	VF	XF	Unc	BU
2004PM Proof	5,000	Value: 355				

KM# 1233 1/5 CROWN

6.2200 g., 0.9999 Gold 0.1999 oz. AGW, 22 mm. **Ruler:** Elizabeth II **Obv:** Bust with tiara right **Rev:** The Norwegian War Medal and naval battle scene **Edge:** Reeded

Date	Mintage	F	VF	XF	Unc	BU
2004PM Proof	5,000	Value: 355				

KM# 1235 1/5 CROWN

6.2200 g., 0.9999 Gold 0.1999 oz. AGW, 22 mm. **Ruler:** Elizabeth II **Obv:** Bust with tiara right **Rev:** French Croix de Guerre and Partisan battle scene **Edge:** Reeded

Date	Mintage	F	VF	XF	Unc	BU
2004PM Proof	5,000	Value: 355				

KM# 1249.1 1/5 CROWN

6.2200 g., 0.9999 Gold 0.1999 oz. AGW, 22 mm. **Ruler:** Elizabeth II **Obv:** Head with tiara right **Rev:** Two Tonkinese cats **Edge:** Reeded

Date	Mintage	F	VF	XF	Unc	BU
2004PM	—	—	—	—	—	370
2004PM Proof	1,000	Value: 375				

KM# 1249.2 1/5 CROWN

6.2200 g., 0.9999 Gold 0.1999 oz. AGW, 22 mm. **Ruler:** Elizabeth II **Obv:** Head with tiara right **Rev:** Two multicolor Tonkinese cats **Edge:** Reeded

Date	Mintage	F	VF	XF	Unc	BU
2004PM Proof	—	Value: 375				

KM# 1198 1/5 CROWN

6.2200 g., 0.9990 Palladium 0.1998 oz., 22 mm. **Ruler:** Elizabeth II **Subject:** Palladium Bicentennial **Obv:** Head with tiara right **Rev:** Athena **Edge:** Reeded

Date	Mintage	F	VF	XF	Unc	BU
2004PM Proof	999	Value: 175				

KM# 1271 1/5 CROWN

6.2200 g., 0.9999 Gold 0.1999 oz. AGW, 22 mm. **Ruler:** Elizabeth II **Obv:** Bust with tiara right **Rev:** Himalayan cat and two kittens **Edge:** Reeded

Date	Mintage	F	VF	XF	Unc	BU
2005PM Proof	—	Value: 375				

KM# 1271a 1/5 CROWN

6.2200 g., 0.9950 Platinum 0.1990 oz. APW, 22 mm. **Ruler:** Elizabeth II **Obv:** Bust with tiara right **Rev:** Himalayan cat and two kittens **Edge:** Reeded

Date	Mintage	F	VF	XF	Unc	BU
2005PM Proof	—	Value: 390				

KM# 1295 1/5 CROWN

6.2200 g., 0.9999 Gold 0.1999 oz. AGW, 22 mm. **Ruler:** Elizabeth II **Subject:** Battles that Changed the World **Obv:** Elizabeth II **Rev:** Trojan War scene **Edge:** Reeded

Date	Mintage	F	VF	XF	Unc	BU
2006PM Proof	5,000	Value: 355				

KM# 1297 1/5 CROWN

6.2200 g., 0.9999 Gold 0.1999 oz. AGW, 22 mm. **Ruler:** Elizabeth II **Subject:** Battles that Changed the World **Obv:** Elizabeth II **Rev:** Battle of Arbela scene **Edge:** Reeded

Date	Mintage	F	VF	XF	Unc	BU
2006PM Proof	5,000	Value: 355				

KM# 1299 1/5 CROWN

6.2200 g., 0.9999 Gold 0.1999 oz. AGW, 22 mm. **Ruler:** Elizabeth II **Subject:** Battles that Changed the World **Obv:** Elizabeth II **Rev:** Battle of Thapsus scene **Edge:** Reeded

Date	Mintage	F	VF	XF	Unc	BU
2006PM Proof	5,000	Value: 355				

KM# 1301 1/5 CROWN

6.2200 g., 0.9999 Gold 0.1999 oz. AGW, 22 mm. **Ruler:** Elizabeth II **Subject:** Battles that Changed the World **Obv:** Elizabeth II **Rev:** Battle of Cologne scene **Edge:** Reeded

Date	Mintage	F	VF	XF	Unc	BU
2006PM Proof	5,000	Value: 355				

KM# 1303 1/5 CROWN

6.2200 g., 0.9999 Gold 0.1999 oz. AGW, 22 mm. **Ruler:** Elizabeth II **Subject:** Battles that Changed the World **Obv:** Elizabeth II **Rev:** Siege of Valencia scene **Edge:** Reeded

Date	Mintage	F	VF	XF	Unc	BU
2006PM Proof	5,000	Value: 355				

KM# 1305 1/5 CROWN

6.2200 g., 0.9999 Gold 0.1999 oz. AGW, 22 mm. **Ruler:** Elizabeth II **Subject:** Battles that Changed the World **Obv:** Elizabeth II **Rev:** Battle of Agincourt scene **Edge:** Reeded

Date	Mintage	F	VF	XF	Unc	BU
2006PM Proof	5,000	Value: 355				

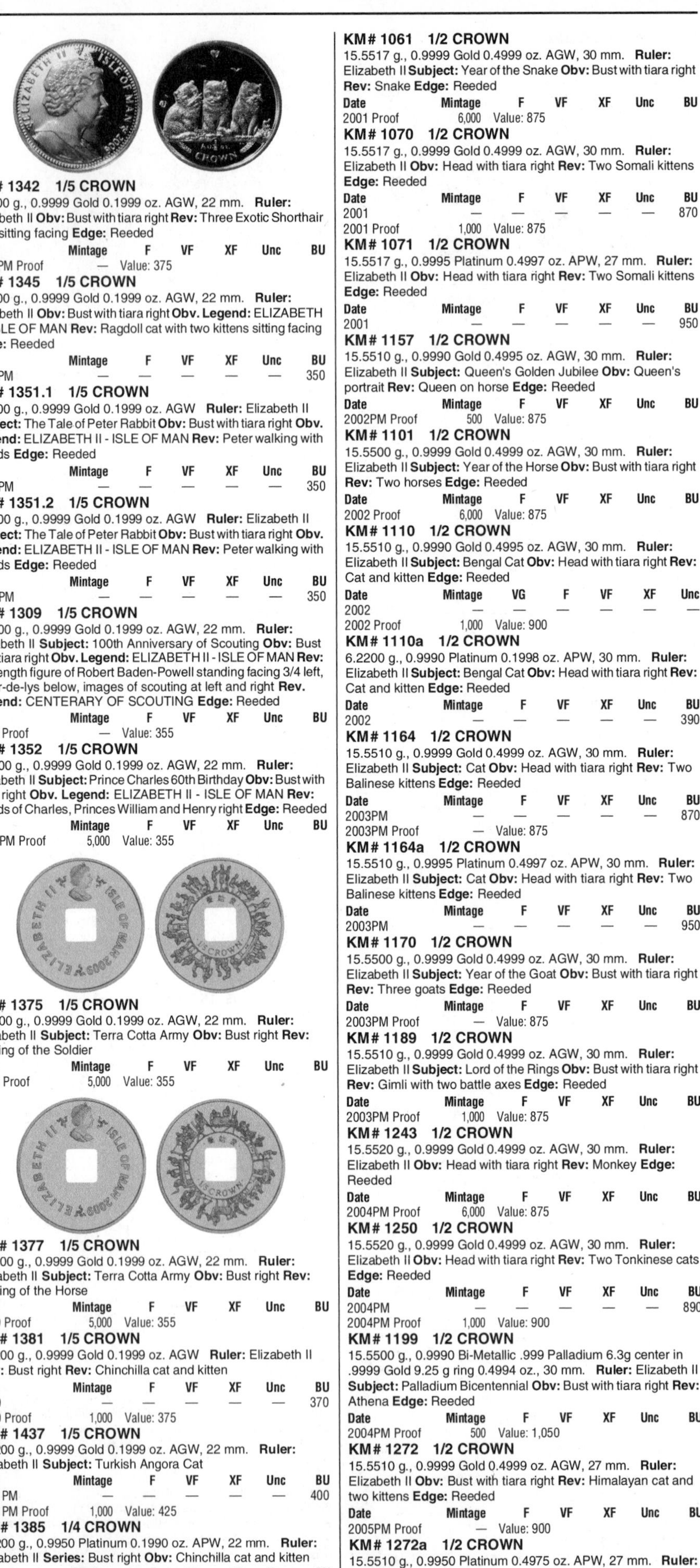

KM# 1342 1/5 CROWN

6.2200 g., 0.9999 Gold 0.1999 oz. AGW, 22 mm. **Ruler:** Elizabeth II **Obv:** Bust with tiara right **Rev:** Three Exotic Shorthair cats sitting facing **Edge:** Reeded

Date	Mintage	F	VF	XF	Unc	BU
2006PM Proof	—	Value: 375				

KM# 1345 1/5 CROWN

6.2200 g., 0.9999 Gold 0.1999 oz. AGW, 22 mm. **Ruler:** Elizabeth II **Obv:** Bust with tiara right **Obv. Legend:** ELIZABETH II - ISLE OF MAN **Rev:** Ragdoll cat with two kittens sitting facing **Edge:** Reeded

Date	Mintage	F	VF	XF	Unc	BU
2007PM	—	—	—	—	—	350

KM# 1351.1 1/5 CROWN

6.2200 g., 0.9999 Gold 0.1999 oz. AGW **Ruler:** Elizabeth II **Subject:** The Tale of Peter Rabbit **Obv:** Bust with tiara right **Obv. Legend:** ELIZABETH II - ISLE OF MAN **Rev:** Peter walking with friends **Edge:** Reeded

Date	Mintage	F	VF	XF	Unc	BU
2007PM	—	—	—	—	—	350

KM# 1351.2 1/5 CROWN

6.2200 g., 0.9999 Gold 0.1999 oz. AGW **Ruler:** Elizabeth II **Subject:** The Tale of Peter Rabbit **Obv:** Bust with tiara right **Obv. Legend:** ELIZABETH II - ISLE OF MAN **Rev:** Peter walking with friends **Edge:** Reeded

Date	Mintage	F	VF	XF	Unc	BU
2007PM	—	—	—	—	—	350

KM# 1309 1/5 CROWN

6.2200 g., 0.9999 Gold 0.1999 oz. AGW, 22 mm. **Ruler:** Elizabeth II **Subject:** 100th Anniversary of Scouting **Obv:** Bust with tiara right **Obv. Legend:** ELIZABETH II - ISLE OF MAN **Rev:** 3/4 length figure of Robert Baden-Powell standing facing 3/4 left, Fleur-de-lys below, images of scouting at left and right **Rev. Legend:** CENTERARY OF SCOUTING **Edge:** Reeded

Date	Mintage	F	VF	XF	Unc	BU
2007 Proof	—	Value: 355				

KM# 1352 1/5 CROWN

6.2200 g., 0.9999 Gold 0.1999 oz. AGW, 22 mm. **Ruler:** Elizabeth II **Subject:** Prince Charles 60th Birthday **Obv:** Bust with tiara right **Obv. Legend:** ELIZABETH II - ISLE OF MAN **Rev:** Heads of Charles, Princes William and Henry right **Edge:** Reeded

Date	Mintage	F	VF	XF	Unc	BU
2008PM Proof	5,000	Value: 355				

KM# 1375 1/5 CROWN

6.2200 g., 0.9999 Gold 0.1999 oz. AGW, 22 mm. **Ruler:** Elizabeth II **Subject:** Terra Cotta Army **Obv:** Bust right **Rev:** Making of the Soldier

Date	Mintage	F	VF	XF	Unc	BU
2009 Proof	5,000	Value: 355				

KM# 1377 1/5 CROWN

6.2200 g., 0.9999 Gold 0.1999 oz. AGW, 22 mm. **Ruler:** Elizabeth II **Subject:** Terra Cotta Army **Obv:** Bust right **Rev:** Making of the Horse

Date	Mintage	F	VF	XF	Unc	BU
2009 Proof	5,000	Value: 355				

KM# 1381 1/5 CROWN

6.2200 g., 0.9999 Gold 0.1999 oz. AGW **Ruler:** Elizabeth II **Obv:** Bust right **Rev:** Chinchilla cat and kitten

Date	Mintage	F	VF	XF	Unc	BU
2009	—	—	—	—	—	370
2009 Proof	1,000	Value: 375				

KM# 1437 1/5 CROWN

6.2200 g., 0.9999 Gold 0.1999 oz. AGW, 22 mm. **Ruler:** Elizabeth II **Subject:** Turkish Angora Cat

Date	Mintage	F	VF	XF	Unc	BU
2011PM	—	—	—	—	—	400
2011PM Proof	1,000	Value: 425				

KM# 1385 1/4 CROWN

6.2200 g., 0.9950 Platinum 0.1990 oz. APW, 22 mm. **Ruler:** Elizabeth II **Series:** Bust right **Obv:** Chinchilla cat and kitten

Date	Mintage	F	VF	XF	Unc	BU
2009	—	—	—	—	—	385

KM# 1061 1/2 CROWN

15.5517 g., 0.9999 Gold 0.4999 oz. AGW, 30 mm. **Ruler:** Elizabeth II **Subject:** Year of the Snake **Obv:** Bust with tiara right **Rev:** Snake **Edge:** Reeded

Date	Mintage	F	VF	XF	Unc	BU
2001 Proof	6,000	Value: 875				

KM# 1070 1/2 CROWN

15.5517 g., 0.9999 Gold 0.4999 oz. AGW, 30 mm. **Ruler:** Elizabeth II **Obv:** Head with tiara right **Rev:** Two Somali kittens **Edge:** Reeded

Date	Mintage	F	VF	XF	Unc	BU
2001	—	—	—	—	—	870
2001 Proof	1,000	Value: 875				

KM# 1071 1/2 CROWN

15.5517 g., 0.9995 Platinum 0.4997 oz. APW, 27 mm. **Ruler:** Elizabeth II **Obv:** Head with tiara right **Rev:** Two Somali kittens **Edge:** Reeded

Date	Mintage	F	VF	XF	Unc	BU
2001	—	—	—	—	—	950

KM# 1157 1/2 CROWN

15.5510 g., 0.9990 Gold 0.4995 oz. AGW, 30 mm. **Ruler:** Elizabeth II **Subject:** Queen's Golden Jubilee **Obv:** Queen's portrait **Rev:** Queen on horse **Edge:** Reeded

Date	Mintage	F	VF	XF	Unc	BU
2002PM Proof	500	Value: 875				

KM# 1101 1/2 CROWN

15.5500 g., 0.9999 Gold 0.4999 oz. AGW, 30 mm. **Ruler:** Elizabeth II **Subject:** Year of the Horse **Obv:** Bust with tiara right **Rev:** Two horses **Edge:** Reeded

Date	Mintage	F	VF	XF	Unc	BU
2002 Proof	6,000	Value: 875				

KM# 1110 1/2 CROWN

15.5510 g., 0.9990 Gold 0.4995 oz. AGW, 30 mm. **Ruler:** Elizabeth II **Subject:** Bengal Cat **Obv:** Head with tiara right **Rev:** Cat and kitten **Edge:** Reeded

Date	Mintage	VG	F	VF	XF	Unc
2002	—	—	—	—	—	—
2002 Proof	1,000	Value: 900				

KM# 1110a 1/2 CROWN

6.2200 g., 0.9990 Platinum 0.1998 oz. APW, 30 mm. **Ruler:** Elizabeth II **Subject:** Bengal Cat **Obv:** Head with tiara right **Rev:** Cat and kitten **Edge:** Reeded

Date	Mintage	F	VF	XF	Unc	BU
2002	—	—	—	—	—	390

KM# 1164 1/2 CROWN

15.5510 g., 0.9999 Gold 0.4999 oz. AGW, 30 mm. **Ruler:** Elizabeth II **Subject:** Cat **Obv:** Head with tiara right **Rev:** Two Balinese kittens **Edge:** Reeded

Date	Mintage	F	VF	XF	Unc	BU
2003PM	—	—	—	—	—	870
2003PM Proof	—	Value: 875				

KM# 1164a 1/2 CROWN

15.5510 g., 0.9995 Platinum 0.4997 oz. APW, 30 mm. **Ruler:** Elizabeth II **Subject:** Cat **Obv:** Head with tiara right **Rev:** Two Balinese kittens **Edge:** Reeded

Date	Mintage	F	VF	XF	Unc	BU
2003PM	—	—	—	—	—	950

KM# 1170 1/2 CROWN

15.5500 g., 0.9999 Gold 0.4999 oz. AGW, 30 mm. **Ruler:** Elizabeth II **Subject:** Year of the Goat **Obv:** Bust with tiara right **Rev:** Three goats **Edge:** Reeded

Date	Mintage	F	VF	XF	Unc	BU
2003PM Proof	—	Value: 875				

KM# 1189 1/2 CROWN

15.5510 g., 0.9999 Gold 0.4999 oz. AGW, 30 mm. **Ruler:** Elizabeth II **Subject:** Lord of the Rings **Obv:** Bust with tiara right **Rev:** Gimli with two battle axes **Edge:** Reeded

Date	Mintage	F	VF	XF	Unc	BU
2003PM Proof	1,000	Value: 875				

KM# 1243 1/2 CROWN

15.5520 g., 0.9999 Gold 0.4999 oz. AGW, 30 mm. **Ruler:** Elizabeth II **Obv:** Head with tiara right **Rev:** Monkey **Edge:** Reeded

Date	Mintage	F	VF	XF	Unc	BU
2004PM Proof	6,000	Value: 875				

KM# 1250 1/2 CROWN

15.5520 g., 0.9999 Gold 0.4999 oz. AGW, 30 mm. **Ruler:** Elizabeth II **Obv:** Head with tiara right **Rev:** Two Tonkinese cats **Edge:** Reeded

Date	Mintage	F	VF	XF	Unc	BU
2004PM	—	—	—	—	—	890
2004PM Proof	1,000	Value: 900				

KM# 1199 1/2 CROWN

15.5500 g., 0.9990 Bi-Metallic .999 Palladium 6.3g center in .9999 Gold 9.25 g ring 0.4994 oz., 30 mm. **Ruler:** Elizabeth II **Subject:** Palladium Bicentennial **Obv:** Bust with tiara right **Rev:** Athena **Edge:** Reeded

Date	Mintage	F	VF	XF	Unc	BU
2004PM Proof	500	Value: 1,050				

KM# 1272 1/2 CROWN

15.5510 g., 0.9999 Gold 0.4999 oz. AGW, 27 mm. **Ruler:** Elizabeth II **Obv:** Bust with tiara right **Rev:** Himalayan cat and two kittens **Edge:** Reeded

Date	Mintage	F	VF	XF	Unc	BU
2005PM Proof	—	Value: 900				

KM# 1272a 1/2 CROWN

15.5510 g., 0.9950 Platinum 0.4975 oz. APW, 27 mm. **Ruler:** Elizabeth II **Obv:** Bust with tiara right **Rev:** Himalayan cat and two kittens **Edge:** Reeded

Date	Mintage	F	VF	XF	Unc	BU
2005PM	—	—	—	—	—	950
2005PM Proof	—	Value: 960				

KM# 1346 1/2 CROWN

15.5500 g., 0.9999 Gold 0.4999 oz. AGW **Ruler:** Elizabeth II **Obv:** Bust with tiara right **Obv. Legend:** ELIZABETH II - ISLE OF MAN **Rev:** Ragdoll cat with two kittens sitting facing **Edge:** Reeded

Date	Mintage	F	VF	XF	Unc	BU
2007PM	—	—	—	—	—	900

KM# 1396 1/2 CROWN

6.2200 g., 0.9999 Gold 0.1999 oz. AGW, 30x20 mm. **Ruler:** Elizabeth II **Rev:** Tut's golden mask

Date	Mintage	F	VF	XF	Unc	BU
2008PM	—	—	—	—	—	355

KM# 1399 1/2 CROWN

6.2200 g., 0.9999 Gold 0.1999 oz. AGW **Ruler:** Elizabeth II **Obv:** Bust with tiara right in Egyptian motif **Rev:** Statue standing **Shape:** Triangle

Date	Mintage	F	VF	XF	Unc	BU
2008PM Proof	—	Value: 355				

KM# 1400 1/2 CROWN

6.2200 g., 0.9999 Gold 0.1999 oz. AGW **Ruler:** Elizabeth II **Obv:** Bust with tiara right in Egyptian motif **Rev:** Statue standing, vile of sand above **Shape:** Triangle

Date	Mintage	F	VF	XF	Unc	BU
2008PM Proof	—	Value: 355				

KM# 1380 1/2 CROWN

15.5500 g., 0.9999 Gold 0.4999 oz. AGW, 30 mm. **Ruler:** Elizabeth II **Obv:** Bust right **Rev:** Chinchilla cat and kitten

Date	Mintage	F	VF	XF	Unc	BU
2009	—	—	—	—	—	890
2009 Proof	1,000	Value: 900				

KM# 1384 1/2 CROWN

15.5500 g., 0.9950 Platinum 0.4974 oz. APW, 27 mm. **Ruler:** Elizabeth II **Obv:** Bust right **Rev:** Chinchilla cat and kitten

Date	Mintage	F	VF	XF	Unc	BU
2009	—	—	—	—	—	950

KM# 1474 1/2 CROWN

Titanium **Ruler:** Elizabeth II **Subject:** George F. Handel, 325th Anniversary of Birth **Obv:** Bust in tiara right **Rev:** Fireworks above river barges **Note:** Blue in color.

Date	Mintage	F	VF	XF	Unc	BU
2010PM Proof	—	Value: 125				

KM# 1438 1/2 CROWN

15.5500 g., 0.9999 Gold 0.4999 oz. AGW, 30 mm. **Ruler:** Elizabeth II **Subject:** Turkish Angora Cat

Date	Mintage	F	VF	XF	Unc	BU
2011PM	—	—	—	—	—	950
2011PM Proof	1,000	Value: 975				

KM# 1447 1/2 CROWN

12.0000 g., 0.9990 Silver 0.3854 oz. ASW, 38.6 mm. **Ruler:** Elizabeth II **Subject:** Olympics, London **Rev:** Horse jumper

Date	Mintage	F	VF	XF	Unc	BU
2012PM Proof	10,000	Value: 25.00				

KM# 1448 1/2 CROWN

12.0000 g., 0.9990 Silver 0.3854 oz. ASW, 38.6 mm. **Ruler:** Elizabeth II **Subject:** Olympics, London **Rev:** Track Cyclist, road cyclist in background

Date	Mintage	F	VF	XF	Unc	BU
2012PM Proof	10,000	Value: 25.00				

KM# 1449 1/2 CROWN

12.0000 g., 0.9990 Silver 0.3854 oz. ASW, 38.6 mm. **Ruler:** Elizabeth II **Subject:** Olympics, London **Rev:** Swimmer, two divers in background

Date	Mintage	F	VF	XF	Unc	BU
2012PM Proof	10,000	Value: 25.00				

KM# 1450 1/2 CROWN

12.0000 g., 0.9990 Silver 0.3854 oz. ASW, 38.6 mm. **Ruler:** Elizabeth II **Subject:** Olympics, London **Rev:** Canoeist, two rowers in background

Date	Mintage	F	VF	XF	Unc	BU
2012PM Proof	10,000	Value: 25.00				

KM# 1451 1/2 CROWN

12.0000 g., 0.9990 Silver 0.3854 oz. ASW, 38.6 mm. **Ruler:** Elizabeth II **Subject:** Olympics, London **Rev:** Judo players, two boxers in background

Date	Mintage	F	VF	XF	Unc	BU
2012PM Proof	10,000	Value: 25.00				

KM# 1452 1/2 CROWN

12.0000 g., 0.9990 Silver 0.3854 oz. ASW, 38.6 mm. **Ruler:** Elizabeth II **Subject:** Olympics, London **Rev:** Table tennis, Lawn tennis in background

Date	Mintage	F	VF	XF	Unc	BU
2012PM Proof	10,000	Value: 25.00				

KM# 1457 1/2 CROWN

12.0000 g., 0.9990 Silver 0.3854 oz. ASW, 38.6 mm. **Ruler:** Elizabeth II **Subject:** European Football Championships 2012 **Rev:** Player heading a football, Statue of Liberty in Lviv and Neptune's fountain in Gdansk

Date	Mintage	F	VF	XF	Unc	BU
2012PM Proof	10,000	Value: 25.00				

KM# 1458 1/2 CROWN

12.0000 g., 0.9990 Silver 0.3854 oz. ASW, 38.6 mm. **Ruler:** Elizabeth II **Subject:** European Football Championships 2012 **Rev:** Player passing the ball, Motherland statue in Kiev and King Sigismund's statue in Warsaw in background

Date	Mintage	F	VF	XF	Unc	BU
2012PM Proof	10,000	Value: 25.00				

KM# 1459 1/2 CROWN

12.0000 g., 0.9990 Silver 0.3854 oz. ASW, 38.6 mm. **Ruler:** Elizabeth II **Subject:** European Football Championships 2012 **Rev:** Footballer shooting, Cathedral of the Transfiguration in Donetsk and the Raclawice Panorama in Wroclaw in background

Date	Mintage	F	VF	XF	Unc	BU
2012PM Proof	10,000	Value: 25.00				

KM# 1460 1/2 CROWN

12.0000 g., 0.9990 Silver 0.3854 oz. ASW, 38.6 mm. **Ruler:** Elizabeth II **Subject:** European Football Championships 2012 **Rev:** Two footballers tackling, Cathedral of the Annunciation in Kharkiv and the Cathedral in Poznan in background

Date	Mintage	F	VF	XF	Unc	BU
2012PM Proof	10,000	Value: 25.00				

KM# 1073 CROWN

31.1035 g., 0.9999 Gold 0.9999 oz. AGW, 32.7 mm. **Ruler:** Elizabeth II **Subject:** Somali Kittens **Obv:** Bust with tiara right **Rev:** Two kittens **Edge:** Reeded

Date	Mintage	F	VF	XF	Unc	BU
2001	—	—	—	—	—	1,825
2001 Proof	1,000	Value: 1,850				

KM# 1076 CROWN

28.2800 g., Copper-Nickel, 38.6 mm. **Ruler:** Elizabeth II **Subject:** Queen Mother **Obv:** Bust with tiara right **Rev:** 1948 Silver wedding anniversary **Edge:** Reeded

Date	Mintage	F	VF	XF	Unc	BU
2001	—	—	—	—	10.00	12.00

KM# 1076a CROWN

28.2800 g., 0.9250 Silver 0.8410 oz. ASW, 38.6 mm. **Ruler:** Elizabeth II **Subject:** Queen Mother **Obv:** Bust with tiara right **Rev:** 1948 Silver wedding anniversary **Edge:** Reeded

Date	Mintage	F	VF	XF	Unc	BU
2001 Proof	10,000	Value: 47.50				

KM# 1077 CROWN

Copper-Nickel, 38.6 mm. **Ruler:** Elizabeth II **Subject:** Queen Mother **Obv:** Bust with tiara right **Rev:** 1948 holding baby Prince Charles **Edge:** Reeded

Date	Mintage	F	VF	XF	Unc	BU
2001	—	—	—	—	10.00	12.00

KM# 1077a CROWN

28.2800 g., 0.9250 Silver 0.8410 oz. ASW, 38.6 mm. **Ruler:** Elizabeth II **Subject:** Queen Mother **Obv:** Head with tiara right **Rev:** 1948 holding baby Prince Charles **Edge:** Reeded

Date	Mintage	F	VF	XF	Unc	BU
2001 Proof	10,000	Value: 47.50				

KM# 1080 CROWN

Copper-Nickel, 38.6 mm. **Ruler:** Elizabeth II **Subject:** Martin Frobisher **Obv:** Bust with tiara right **Rev:** Bust at left, ship at right and map below **Edge:** Reeded

Date	Mintage	F	VF	XF	Unc	BU
2001	—	—	—	—	10.00	12.00

KM# 1080a CROWN

28.2800 g., 0.9250 Silver 0.8410 oz. ASW, 38.6 mm. **Ruler:** Elizabeth II **Subject:** Martin Frobisher **Obv:** Bust of Queen Elizabeth II right **Edge:** Reeded

Date	Mintage	F	VF	XF	Unc	BU
2001 Proof	10,000	Value: 47.50				

KM# 1081 CROWN

Copper-Nickel, 38.6 mm. **Ruler:** Elizabeth II **Subject:** Roald Amundsen **Obv:** Bust with tiara right **Rev:** Bust at right, ship at center, dirigible above at left **Edge:** Reeded

Date	Mintage	F	VF	XF	Unc	BU
2001	—	—	—	—	10.00	12.00

KM# 1081a CROWN

28.2800 g., 0.9250 Silver 0.8410 oz. ASW, 38.6 mm. **Ruler:** Elizabeth II **Subject:** Roald Amundsen **Obv:** Bust with tiara right **Rev:** Bust at right, ship at center, dirigible at upper left **Edge:** Reeded

Date	Mintage	F	VF	XF	Unc	BU
2001 Proof	10,000	Value: 47.50				

KM# 1085 CROWN

28.2800 g., Copper-Nickel, 38.6 mm. **Ruler:** Elizabeth II **Subject:** Joey Dunlop (1952-2000) **Obv:** Bust with tiara right **Rev:** Motorcycle racer **Edge:** Reeded

Date	Mintage	F	VF	XF	Unc	BU
2001 Black finish	—	—	—	—	10.00	12.00

KM# 1085a CROWN

28.2800 g., 0.9250 Silver 0.8410 oz. ASW, 38.6 mm. **Ruler:** Elizabeth II **Subject:** Joey Dunlop (1952-2000) **Obv:** Bust with tiara right **Rev:** Motorcycle racer **Edge:** Reeded

Date	Mintage	F	VF	XF	Unc	BU
2001 Proof	10,000	Value: 47.50				

KM# 1083 CROWN

28.2800 g., Copper-Nickel, 38.6 mm. **Ruler:** Elizabeth II **Subject:** Queen's 75th Birthday **Obv:** Bust with tiara right **Rev:** Flower bouquet **Edge:** Reeded

Date	Mintage	F	VF	XF	Unc	BU
2001	—	—	—	—	14.00	16.00

KM# 1083a CROWN

28.2800 g., 0.9250 Silver 0.8410 oz. ASW, 38.6 mm. **Ruler:** Elizabeth II **Subject:** Queen's 75th Birthday **Obv:** Bust with tiara right **Rev:** Flower bouquet **Edge:** Reeded

Date	Mintage	F	VF	XF	Unc	BU
2001 Proof	10,000	Value: 50.00				

KM# 1087 CROWN

28.2800 g., Copper-Nickel, 38.6 mm. **Ruler:** Elizabeth II **Series:** Harry Potter **Obv:** Bust with tiara right **Rev:** Harry with magic wand **Edge:** Reeded

Date	Mintage	F	VF	XF	Unc	BU
2001	—	—	—	—	10.00	12.00

KM# 1087a CROWN

28.2800 g., 0.9250 Silver 0.8410 oz. ASW, 38.6 mm. **Ruler:** Elizabeth II **Series:** Harry Potter **Obv:** Bust with tiara right **Rev:** Harry with magic wand **Edge:** Reeded

Date	Mintage	F	VF	XF	Unc	BU
2001 Proof	15,000	Value: 47.50				

KM# 1089 CROWN

28.2800 g., Copper-Nickel, 38.6 mm. **Ruler:** Elizabeth II **Series:** Harry Potter **Subject:** Journey to Hogwart's **Obv:** Bust with tiara right **Rev:** Boat full of children going to Hogwart's **Edge:** Reeded

Date	Mintage	F	VF	XF	Unc	BU
2001	—	—	—	—	10.00	12.00

KM# 1089a CROWN

28.2800 g., 0.9250 Silver 0.8410 oz. ASW, 38.6 mm. **Ruler:** Elizabeth II **Series:** Harry Potter **Obv:** Bust with tiara right **Rev:** Boat full of children going to Hogwart's **Edge:** Reeded

Date	Mintage	F	VF	XF	Unc	BU
2001 Proof	15,000	Value: 47.50				

KM# 1091 CROWN

Copper-Nickel **Ruler:** Elizabeth II **Series:** Harry Potter **Subject:** First Quidditch Match **Obv:** Bust with tiara right **Rev:** Harry flying his Nimbus 2000

Date	Mintage	F	VF	XF	Unc	BU
2001	—	—	—	—	10.00	12.00

KM# 1091a CROWN

28.2800 g., 0.9250 Silver 0.8410 oz. ASW **Ruler:** Elizabeth II **Series:** Harry Potter **Subject:** First Quidditch Match **Obv:** Bust with tiara right **Rev:** Harry flying his Nimbus 2000

Date	Mintage	F	VF	XF	Unc	BU
2001 Proof	15,000	Value: 47.50				

KM# 1093 CROWN

Copper-Nickel **Ruler:** Elizabeth II **Series:** Harry Potter **Subject:** Birth of Norbert **Obv:** Bust with tiara right **Rev:** Hagrid and children watching Norbert hatch

Date	Mintage	F	VF	XF	Unc	BU
2001	—	—	—	—	10.00	14.00

KM# 1093a CROWN

28.2800 g., 0.9250 Silver 0.8410 oz. ASW **Ruler:** Elizabeth II **Series:** Harry Potter **Subject:** Birth of Norbert **Obv:** Bust with tiara right **Rev:** Hagrid and children watching Norbert hatch

Date	Mintage	F	VF	XF	Unc	BU
2001 Proof	15,000	Value: 47.50				

KM# 1095 CROWN

Copper-Nickel **Ruler:** Elizabeth II **Series:** Harry Potter **Subject:** School **Obv:** Bust with tiara right **Rev:** Harry in Potions class

Date	Mintage	F	VF	XF	Unc	BU
2001	—	—	—	—	10.00	12.00

KM# 1095a CROWN

28.2800 g., 0.9250 Silver 0.8410 oz. ASW **Ruler:** Elizabeth II **Series:** Harry Potter **Subject:** School **Obv:** Bust with tiara right **Rev:** Harry in Potions class

Date	Mintage	F	VF	XF	Unc	BU
2001 Proof	15,000	Value: 47.50				

KM# 1097 CROWN

Copper-Nickel, 38.72 mm. **Ruler:** Elizabeth II **Series:** Harry Potter **Obv:** Bust with tiara right **Rev:** Harry catching the golden snitch **Edge:** Reeded

Date	Mintage	F	VF	XF	Unc	BU
2001	—	—	—	—	10.00	12.00

KM# 1097a CROWN

28.2800 g., 0.9250 Silver 0.8410 oz. ASW, 38.71 mm. **Ruler:** Elizabeth II **Series:** Harry Potter **Obv:** Bust with tiara right **Rev:** Harry catching the golden snitch **Edge:** Reeded

Date	Mintage	F	VF	XF	Unc	BU
2001 Proof	15,000	Value: 47.50				

KM# 1062 CROWN
28.2800 g., Copper-Nickel, 38.6 mm. **Ruler:** Elizabeth II **Subject:** Year of the Snake **Obv:** Bust with tiara right **Rev:** Snake **Edge:** Reeded

Date	Mintage	F	VF	XF	Unc	BU
2001	—	—	—	—	10.00	15.00

KM# 1062a CROWN
28.2800 g., 0.9250 Silver 0.8410 oz. ASW, 38.6 mm. **Ruler:** Elizabeth II **Subject:** Year of the Snake **Obv:** Head with tiara right **Rev:** Snake **Edge:** Reeded

Date	Mintage	F	VF	XF	Unc	BU
2001 Proof	30,000	Value: 47.50				

KM# 1063 CROWN
31.1035 g., 0.9999 Gold 0.9999 oz. AGW, 32.7 mm. **Ruler:** Elizabeth II **Subject:** Year of the Snake **Obv:** Bust with tiara right **Rev:** Snake **Edge:** Reeded

Date	Mintage	F	VF	XF	Unc	BU
2001	—	—	—	—	—	1,800
2001 Proof	2,000	Value: 1,825				

KM# 1072 CROWN
28.2800 g., Copper-Nickel, 38.6 mm. **Ruler:** Elizabeth II **Subject:** Somali Kittens **Obv:** Bust with tiara right **Rev:** Two kittens **Edge:** Reeded

Date	Mintage	F	VF	XF	Unc	BU
2001	—	—	—	—	11.00	15.00

KM# 1072a CROWN
31.1035 g., 0.9990 Silver 0.9990 oz. ASW, 38.6 mm. **Ruler:** Elizabeth II **Subject:** Somali Kittens **Obv:** Bust with tiara right **Rev:** Two kittens **Edge:** Reeded

Date	Mintage	F	VF	XF	Unc	BU
2001 Proof	50,000	Value: 47.50				

KM# 1102 CROWN
28.2800 g., Copper-Nickel, 38.6 mm. **Ruler:** Elizabeth II **Subject:** Year of the Horse **Obv:** Bust with tiara right **Rev:** Two horses **Edge:** Reeded

Date	Mintage	F	VF	XF	Unc	BU
2002	—	—	—	—	12.00	15.00

KM# 1102a CROWN
28.2800 g., 0.9250 Silver 0.8410 oz. ASW, 38.6 mm. **Ruler:** Elizabeth II **Subject:** Year of the Horse **Obv:** Bust with tiara right **Rev:** Two horses **Edge:** Reeded

Date	Mintage	F	VF	XF	Unc	BU
2002 Proof	30,000	Value: 47.50				

KM# 1103 CROWN
31.1000 g., 0.9999 Gold 0.9997 oz. AGW **Ruler:** Elizabeth II **Subject:** Year of the Horse **Obv:** Bust with tiara right

Date	Mintage	F	VF	XF	Unc	BU
2002 Proof	2,000	Value: 1,800				

KM# 1111 CROWN
28.2800 g., Copper-Nickel, 38.6 mm. **Ruler:** Elizabeth II **Subject:** Bengal Cat **Obv:** Bust with tiara right **Rev:** Cat and kitten **Edge:** Reeded

Date	Mintage	F	VF	XF	Unc	BU
2002	—	—	—	—	12.50	14.00

KM# 1111a CROWN
31.1035 g., 0.9990 Silver 0.9990 oz. ASW, 38.6 mm. **Ruler:** Elizabeth II **Subject:** Bengal Cat **Obv:** Bust with tiara right **Rev:** Cat and kitten **Edge:** Reeded

Date	Mintage	F	VF	XF	Unc	BU
2002 Proof	10,000	Value: 70.00				

KM# 1112 CROWN
31.1035 g., 0.9990 Gold 0.9990 oz. AGW, 33 mm. **Ruler:** Elizabeth II **Subject:** Bengal Cat **Obv:** Bust with tiara right **Rev:** Cat and kitten **Edge:** Reeded

Date	Mintage	F	VF	XF	Unc	BU
2002	—	—	—	—	—	1,800
2002 Proof	1,000	Value: 1,825				

KM# 1115 CROWN
28.2800 g., Copper-Nickel, 38.6 mm. **Ruler:** Elizabeth II **Subject:** Olympics - Salt Lake City **Obv:** Bust with tiara right **Rev:** Skier, torch and flag **Edge:** Reeded

Date	Mintage	F	VF	XF	Unc	BU
2002	—	—	—	—	10.00	12.00

KM# 1115a CROWN
28.2800 g., 0.9250 Silver 0.8410 oz. ASW, 38.6 mm. **Ruler:** Elizabeth II **Subject:** Olympics - Salt Lake City **Obv:** Bust with tiara right **Rev:** Skier, torch and flag **Edge:** Reeded

Date	Mintage	F	VF	XF	Unc	BU
2002 Proof	10,000	Value: 47.50				

KM# 1116 CROWN
28.2800 g., Copper-Nickel, 38.6 mm. **Ruler:** Elizabeth II **Subject:** Olympics - Salt Lake City **Obv:** Bust with tiara right **Rev:** Bobsled, torch and stadium **Edge:** Reeded

Date	Mintage	F	VF	XF	Unc	BU
2002	—	—	—	—	10.00	12.00

KM# 1116a CROWN
28.2800 g., 0.9250 Silver 0.8410 oz. ASW, 38.6 mm. **Ruler:** Elizabeth II **Subject:** Olympics - Salt Lake City **Obv:** Bust with tiara right **Rev:** Bobsled, torch and stadium **Edge:** Reeded

Date	Mintage	F	VF	XF	Unc	BU
2002 Proof	10,000	Value: 47.50				

KM# 1118 CROWN
28.2800 g., Copper-Nickel, 38.6 mm. **Ruler:** Elizabeth II **Subject:** Queen Mother's Love of Horses **Obv:** Bust with tiara right **Rev:** Queen Mother and horse **Edge:** Reeded

Date	Mintage	F	VF	XF	Unc	BU
2002	—	—	—	—	10.00	12.00

KM# 1118a CROWN
28.2800 g., 0.9250 Silver 0.8410 oz. ASW, 38.6 mm. **Ruler:** Elizabeth II **Subject:** Queen Mother's Love of Horses **Obv:** Bust with tiara right **Rev:** Queen Mother and horse **Edge:** Reeded

Date	Mintage	F	VF	XF	Unc	BU
2002 Proof	10,000	Value: 47.50				

KM# 1119 CROWN
35.0000 g., 0.7500 Gold 0.8439 oz. AGW, 38.6 mm. **Ruler:** Elizabeth II **Subject:** Golden Jubilee **Obv:** Bust with tiara right **Rev:** Queen Elizabeth II's young laureate bust right **Edge:** Reeded **Note:** Red Gold center in a White Gold inner ring within a Yellow Gold outer ring.

Date	Mintage	F	VF	XF	Unc	BU
2002 Proof	999	Value: 1,550				

KM# 1121 CROWN

28.2800 g., Copper-Nickel, 38.6 mm. **Ruler:** Elizabeth II **Subject:** World Cup 2002 Japan - Korea **Obv:** Bust with tiara right **Rev:** Player running right **Edge:** Reeded

Date	Mintage	F	VF	XF	Unc	BU
2002	—	—	—	—	10.00	12.00

KM# 1121a CROWN

28.2800 g., 0.9250 Silver 0.8410 oz. ASW, 38.6 mm. **Ruler:** Elizabeth II **Subject:** World Cup 2002 Japan - Korea **Obv:** Bust with tiara right **Rev:** Player running right **Edge:** Reeded

Date	Mintage	F	VF	XF	Unc	BU
2002 Proof	10,000	Value: 47.50				

KM# 1123 CROWN

28.2800 g., Copper-Nickel, 38.6 mm. **Ruler:** Elizabeth II **Subject:** World Cup 2002 Japan - Korea **Obv:** Bust with tiara right **Rev:** Player kicking to right **Edge:** Reeded

Date	Mintage	F	VF	XF	Unc	BU
2002	—	—	—	—	10.00	12.00

KM# 1123a CROWN

28.2800 g., 0.9250 Silver 0.8410 oz. ASW, 38.6 mm. **Ruler:** Elizabeth II **Subject:** World Cup 2002 Japan - Korea **Obv:** Bust with tiara right **Rev:** Player kicking to right **Edge:** Reeded

Date	Mintage	F	VF	XF	Unc	BU
2002 Proof	10,000	Value: 47.50				

KM# 1125 CROWN

28.2800 g., Copper-Nickel, 38.6 mm. **Ruler:** Elizabeth II **Subject:** World Cup 2002 Japan - Korea **Obv:** Bust with tiara right **Rev:** Player kicking to left **Edge:** Reeded

Date	Mintage	F	VF	XF	Unc	BU
2002	—	—	—	—	10.00	12.00

KM# 1125a CROWN

28.2800 g., 0.9250 Silver 0.8410 oz. ASW, 38.6 mm. **Ruler:** Elizabeth II **Subject:** World Cup 2002 Japan - Korea **Obv:** Bust with tiara right **Rev:** Player kicking to left **Edge:** Reeded

Date	Mintage	F	VF	XF	Unc	BU
2002 Proof	10,000	Value: 47.50				

KM# 1127 CROWN

28.2800 g., Copper-Nickel, 38.6 mm. **Ruler:** Elizabeth II **Subject:** World Cup 2002 Japan - Korea **Obv:** Bust with tiara right **Rev:** Player running to left **Edge:** Reeded

Date	Mintage	F	VF	XF	Unc	BU
2002	—	—	—	—	10.00	12.00

KM# 1127a CROWN

28.2800 g., 0.9250 Silver 0.8410 oz. ASW, 38.6 mm. **Ruler:** Elizabeth II **Subject:** World Cup 2002 Japan - Korea **Obv:** Bust with tiara right **Rev:** Player running to left **Edge:** Reeded

Date	Mintage	F	VF	XF	Unc	BU
2002 Proof	10,000	Value: 47.50				

KM# 1131 CROWN

28.2800 g., Copper-Nickel, 38.6 mm. **Ruler:** Elizabeth II **Subject:** Queen Elizabeth II's Golden Jubilee **Obv:** Bust with tiara right **Rev:** Seated crowned Queen holding scepter at her coronation **Edge:** Reeded

Date	Mintage	F	VF	XF	Unc	BU
2002	—	—	—	—	10.00	12.00

KM# 1131a CROWN

28.2800 g., Gold Color Base Metal, 38.6 mm. **Ruler:** Elizabeth II **Subject:** Queen Elizabeth II's Golden Jubilee **Obv:** Bust with tiara right **Rev:** Seated crowned Queen holding scepter at her coronation **Edge:** Reeded

Date	Mintage	F	VF	XF	Unc	BU
2002	15,000	—	—	—	10.00	12.00

KM# 1131b CROWN

28.2800 g., 0.9250 Gold Clad Silver 0.8410 oz., 38.6 mm. **Ruler:** Elizabeth II **Subject:** Queen Elizabeth II's Golden Jubilee **Obv:** Bust with tiara right **Rev:** Seated crowned Queen holding scepter at her coronation **Edge:** Reeded

Date	Mintage	F	VF	XF	Unc	BU
2002 Proof	10,000	Value: 47.50				

KM# 1133 CROWN

28.2800 g., Copper-Nickel, 38.6 mm. **Ruler:** Elizabeth II **Subject:** Queen Elizabeth II's Golden Jubilee **Obv:** Bust with tiara right **Rev:** Queen on horse **Edge:** Reeded

Date	Mintage	F	VF	XF	Unc	BU
2002	—	—	—	—	10.00	12.00

KM# 1133a CROWN

28.2800 g., Gold Color Base Metal, 38.6 mm. **Ruler:** Elizabeth II **Subject:** Queen Elizabeth II's Golden Jubilee **Obv:** Bust with tiara right **Rev:** Queen on horse **Edge:** Reeded

Date	Mintage	F	VF	XF	Unc	BU
2002	15,000	—	—	—	10.00	12.00

KM# 1133b CROWN

28.2800 g., 0.9250 Gold Clad Silver 0.8410 oz., 38.6 mm. **Ruler:** Elizabeth II **Subject:** Queen Elizabeth II's Golden Jubilee **Obv:** Bust with tiara right **Rev:** Queen on horse half left **Edge:** Reeded

Date	Mintage	F	VF	XF	Unc	BU
2002 Proof	10,000	Value: 47.50				

KM# 1135 CROWN

28.2800 g., Copper-Nickel, 38.6 mm. **Ruler:** Elizabeth II **Subject:** Queen Elizabeth II's Golden Jubilee **Obv:** Bust with tiara right **Rev:** Queen with her pet Corgi **Edge:** Reeded

Date	Mintage	F	VF	XF	Unc	BU
2002	—	—	—	—	10.00	12.00

KM# 1135a CROWN

28.2800 g., Gold Color Base Metal, 38.6 mm. **Ruler:** Elizabeth II **Subject:** Queen Elizabeth II's Golden Jubilee **Obv:** Bust with tiara right **Rev:** Seated Queen with her pet Corgi **Edge:** Reeded

Date	Mintage	F	VF	XF	Unc	BU
2002	15,000	—	—	—	10.00	12.00

KM# 1135b CROWN

28.2800 g., 0.9250 Gold Clad Silver 0.8410 oz., 38.6 mm. **Ruler:** Elizabeth II **Subject:** Queen Elizabeth II's Golden Jubilee **Obv:** Bust with tiara right **Rev:** Queen with her pet Corgi **Edge:** Reeded

Date	Mintage	F	VF	XF	Unc	BU
2002 Proof	10,000	Value: 47.50				

KM# 1137 CROWN

28.2800 g., Copper-Nickel, 38.6 mm. **Ruler:** Elizabeth II **Subject:** Queen Elizabeth II's Golden Jubilee **Obv:** Bust with tiara right **Rev:** Queen at war memorial **Edge:** Reeded

Date	Mintage	F	VF	XF	Unc	BU
2002	—	—	—	—	10.00	12.00

KM# 1137a CROWN

28.2800 g., Gold Color Base Metal, 38.6 mm. **Ruler:** Elizabeth II **Subject:** Queen Elizabeth II's Golden Jubilee **Obv:** Bust with tiara right **Rev:** Queen at war memorial **Edge:** Reeded

Date	Mintage	F	VF	XF	Unc	BU
2002	15,000	—	—	—	10.00	12.00

KM# 1137b CROWN

28.2800 g., Gold Clad Silver, 38.6 mm. **Ruler:** Elizabeth II **Subject:** Queen Elizabeth II's Golden Jubilee **Obv:** Bust with tiara right **Rev:** Queen at war memorial **Edge:** Reeded

Date	Mintage	F	VF	XF	Unc	BU
2002 Proof	10,000	Value: 47.50				

KM# 1139 CROWN

Copper-Nickel dark patina, 38.6 mm. **Ruler:** Elizabeth II **Subject:** Queen Mother **Obv:** Bust with tiara right **Rev:** Queen Mother and Castle May **Edge:** Reeded

Date	Mintage	F	VF	XF	Unc	BU
2002	—	—	—	—	10.00	12.00

KM# 1139a CROWN
28.2800 g., 0.9250 Silver 0.8410 oz. ASW, 38.6 mm. **Ruler:** Elizabeth II **Obv:** Head with tiara right with blackened legends **Rev:** Queen Mother standing at left in front of Castle May with blackened legends

Date	Mintage	F	VF	XF	Unc	BU
2002 Proof	10,000	Value: 47.50				

KM# 1141 CROWN
28.2800 g., Copper-Nickel, 38.6 mm. **Ruler:** Elizabeth II **Subject:** Princess Diana **Obv:** Bust with tiara right **Rev:** Diana's bust facing **Edge:** Reeded

Date	Mintage	F	VF	XF	Unc	BU
2002	—	—	—	—	10.00	12.00

KM# 1141a CROWN
28.2800 g., 0.9250 Silver 0.8410 oz. ASW, 38.6 mm. **Ruler:** Elizabeth II **Subject:** Princess Diana **Obv:** Bust with tiara right **Rev:** Diana facing **Edge:** Reeded

Date	Mintage	F	VF	XF	Unc	BU
2002 Proof	10,000	Value: 47.50				

KM# 1144 CROWN
28.2800 g., Copper-Nickel, 38.6 mm. **Ruler:** Elizabeth II **Series:** Harry Potter **Obv:** Bust with tiara right **Rev:** Tom Riddle twirling Harry's magic wand **Edge:** Reeded

Date	Mintage	F	VF	XF	Unc	BU
2002PM	—	—	—	—	10.00	12.00

KM# 1144a CROWN
28.2800 g., 0.9250 Silver 0.8410 oz. ASW, 28.6 mm. **Ruler:** Elizabeth II **Series:** Harry Potter **Obv:** Bust with tiara right **Rev:** Tom Riddle twirling Harry's magic wand **Edge:** Reeded

Date	Mintage	F	VF	XF	Unc	BU
2002PM Proof	15,000	Value: 50.00				

KM# 1146 CROWN
28.2800 g., Copper-Nickel, 38.6 mm. **Ruler:** Elizabeth II **Series:** Harry Potter **Obv:** Bust with tiara right **Rev:** Harry and friends making Polyjuice potion **Edge:** Reeded

Date	Mintage	F	VF	XF	Unc	BU
2002PM	—	—	—	—	10.00	12.00

KM# 1146a CROWN
28.2800 g., 0.9250 Silver 0.8410 oz. ASW, 38.6 mm. **Ruler:** Elizabeth II **Series:** Harry Potter **Obv:** Bust with tiara right **Rev:** Harry Potter and friends making Polyjuice potion **Edge:** Reeded

Date	Mintage	F	VF	XF	Unc	BU
2002PM Proof	15,000	Value: 50.00				

KM# 1148 CROWN
28.2800 g., Copper-Nickel, 38.6 mm. **Ruler:** Elizabeth II **Series:** Harry Potter **Obv:** Bust with tiara right **Rev:** Harry arrives at the Burrow in a flying car **Edge:** Reeded

Date	Mintage	F	VF	XF	Unc	BU
2002PM	—	—	—	—	10.00	12.00

KM# 1148a CROWN
28.2800 g., 0.9250 Silver 0.8410 oz. ASW, 38.6 mm. **Ruler:** Elizabeth II **Series:** Harry Potter **Obv:** Bust with tiara right **Rev:** Harry arrives at the Burrow in a flying car **Edge:** Reeded

Date	Mintage	F	VF	XF	Unc	BU
2002PM Proof	15,000	Value: 50.00				

KM# 1150 CROWN
28.2800 g., Copper-Nickel, 38.6 mm. **Ruler:** Elizabeth II **Series:** Harry Potter **Obv:** Bust with tiara right **Rev:** Harry retrieves Gryffindor sword from sorting hat **Edge:** Reeded

Date	Mintage	F	VF	XF	Unc	BU
2002PM	—	—	—	—	10.00	12.00

KM# 1150a CROWN
28.2800 g., 0.9250 Silver 0.8410 oz. ASW, 38.6 mm. **Ruler:** Elizabeth II **Series:** Harry Potter **Obv:** Bust with tiara right **Rev:** Harry retrieves Gryffindor sword from sorting hat **Edge:** Reeded

Date	Mintage	F	VF	XF	Unc	BU
2002PM Proof	15,000	Value: 50.00				

KM# 1152 CROWN
28.2800 g., Copper-Nickel, 38.6 mm. **Ruler:** Elizabeth II **Series:** Harry Potter **Obv:** Bust with tiara right **Rev:** Harry and Ron encounter the spider Aragog **Edge:** Reeded

Date	Mintage	F	VF	XF	Unc	BU
2002PM	—	—	—	—	10.00	12.00

KM# 1152a CROWN
28.2800 g., 0.9250 Silver 0.8410 oz. ASW, 38.6 mm. **Ruler:** Elizabeth II **Series:** Harry Potter **Obv:** Bust with tiara right **Rev:** Harry and Ron encounter the spider Aragog **Edge:** Reeded

Date	Mintage	F	VF	XF	Unc	BU
2002PM Proof	15,000	Value: 50.00				

KM# 1154 CROWN
28.2800 g., Copper-Nickel, 38.6 mm. **Ruler:** Elizabeth II **Series:** Harry Potter **Obv:** Bust with tiara right **Rev:** Harry in hospital with Dobby **Edge:** Reeded

Date	Mintage	F	VF	XF	Unc	BU
2002PM	—	—	—	—	10.00	12.00

KM# 1154a CROWN
28.2800 g., 0.9250 Silver 0.8410 oz. ASW, 38.6 mm. **Ruler:** Elizabeth II **Series:** Harry Potter **Obv:** Bust with tiara right **Rev:** Harry in hospital with Dobby **Edge:** Reeded

Date	Mintage	F	VF	XF	Unc	BU
2002PM Proof	15,000	Value: 50.00				

KM# 1185 CROWN
28.2800 g., Copper-Nickel, 38.6 mm. **Ruler:** Elizabeth II **Obv:** Bust with tiara right **Rev:** Lord of the Rings characters **Edge:** Reeded

Date	Mintage	F	VF	XF	Unc	BU
2003PM	100,000	—	—	—	12.50	14.50

KM# 1185a CROWN
28.2800 g., 0.9250 Silver 0.8410 oz. ASW, 38.6 mm. **Ruler:** Elizabeth II **Obv:** Bust with tiara right **Rev:** Lord of the Rings characters **Edge:** Reeded

Date	Mintage	F	VF	XF	Unc	BU
2003PM Proof	10,000	Value: 50.00				

KM# 1190 CROWN
31.1035 g., 0.9999 Gold 0.9999 oz. AGW, 32.7 mm. **Ruler:** Elizabeth II **Subject:** Lord of the Rings **Obv:** Bust with tiara right **Rev:** Man on horse **Edge:** Reeded

Date	Mintage	F	VF	XF	Unc	BU
2003PM Proof	1,000	Value: 1,825				

KM# 1191 CROWN
28.2800 g., 0.9250 Silver 0.8410 oz. ASW, 38.6 mm. **Ruler:** Elizabeth II **Subject:** Lord of the Rings **Obv:** Bust with tiara right **Rev:** Man with short sword **Edge:** Reeded

Date	Mintage	F	VF	XF	Unc	BU
2003PM Proof	5,000	Value: 47.50				

KM# 1192 CROWN
28.2800 g., 0.9250 Silver 0.8410 oz. ASW, 38.6 mm. **Ruler:** Elizabeth II **Subject:** Lord of the Rings **Obv:** Bust with tiara right **Rev:** Aragorn with broadsword **Edge:** Reeded

Date	Mintage	F	VF	XF	Unc	BU
2003PM Proof	5,000	Value: 47.50				

KM# 1193 CROWN
28.2800 g., 0.9250 Silver 0.8410 oz. ASW, 38.6 mm. **Ruler:** Elizabeth II **Subject:** Lord of the Rings **Obv:** Bust with tiara right **Rev:** Legolas **Edge:** Reeded

Date	Mintage	F	VF	XF	Unc	BU
2003PM Proof	5,000	Value: 47.50				

KM# 1194 CROWN
28.2800 g., 0.9250 Silver 0.8410 oz. ASW, 38.6 mm. **Ruler:** Elizabeth II **Subject:** Lord of the Rings **Obv:** Bust with tiara right **Rev:** Gimli with two battle axes **Edge:** Reeded

Date	Mintage	F	VF	XF	Unc	BU
2003PM Proof	5,000	Value: 47.50				

KM# 1195 CROWN

28.2800 g., 0.9250 Silver 0.8410 oz. ASW, 38.6 mm. **Ruler:** Elizabeth II **Subject:** Lord of the Rings **Obv:** Bust with tiara right **Rev:** Man on horse **Edge:** Reeded

Date	Mintage	F	VF	XF	Unc	BU
2003PM Proof	5,000	Value: 47.50				

KM# 1165 CROWN

28.2800 g., Copper-Nickel, 38.6 mm. **Ruler:** Elizabeth II **Subject:** Cat **Obv:** Bust with tiara right **Rev:** Two Balinese kittens **Edge:** Reeded

Date	Mintage	F	VF	XF	Unc	BU
2003PM	—	—	—	—	12.00	14.00

KM# 1165a CROWN

31.1035 g., 0.9990 Silver 0.9990 oz. ASW, 38.6 mm. **Ruler:** Elizabeth II **Subject:** Cat **Obv:** Head with tiara right **Rev:** Two Balinese kittens **Edge:** Reeded

Date	Mintage	F	VF	XF	Unc	BU
2003PM Proof	50,000	Value: 70.00				

KM# 1166 CROWN

31.1035 g., 0.9999 Gold 0.9999 oz. AGW, 32.7 mm. **Ruler:** Elizabeth II **Subject:** Cat **Obv:** Head with tiara right **Rev:** Two Balinese kittens **Edge:** Reeded

Date	Mintage	F	VF	XF	Unc	BU
2003PM	—	—	—	—	—	1,800
2003PM Proof	—	Value: 1,825				

KM# 1171 CROWN

28.2800 g., Copper-Nickel, 38.6 mm. **Ruler:** Elizabeth II **Subject:** Year of the Goat **Obv:** Bust with tiara right **Rev:** Three goats **Edge:** Reeded

Date	Mintage	F	VF	XF	Unc	BU
2003PM	—	—	—	—	12.00	14.00

KM# 1171a CROWN

28.2800 g., 0.9250 Silver 0.8410 oz. ASW, 38.6 mm. **Ruler:** Elizabeth II **Subject:** Year of the Goat **Obv:** Bust with tiara right **Rev:** Three goats **Edge:** Reeded

Date	Mintage	F	VF	XF	Unc	BU
2003PM Proof	30,000	Value: 47.50				

KM# 1172 CROWN

31.1035 g., 0.9999 Gold 0.9999 oz. AGW, 32.7 mm. **Ruler:** Elizabeth II **Subject:** Year of the Goat **Obv:** Bust with tiara right **Rev:** Three goats **Edge:** Reeded

Date	Mintage	F	VF	XF	Unc	BU
2003PM Proof	2,000	Value: 1,825				

KM# 1174 CROWN

28.5300 g., Copper-Nickel, 38.6 mm. **Ruler:** Elizabeth II **Obv:** Bust with tiara right **Rev:** The Star of India sailing ship **Edge:** Reeded

Date	Mintage	F	VF	XF	Unc	BU
2003PM	—	—	—	—	10.00	12.00

KM# 1176 CROWN

28.2800 g., Copper-Nickel, 38.6 mm. **Ruler:** Elizabeth II **Subject:** Olympics **Obv:** Bust with tiara right **Rev:** Swimmers **Edge:** Reeded

Date	Mintage	F	VF	XF	Unc	BU
2003PM	—	—	—	—	10.00	12.00

KM# 1176a CROWN

28.2800 g., 0.9250 Silver 0.8410 oz. ASW, 38.6 mm. **Ruler:** Elizabeth II **Subject:** Olympics **Obv:** Bust with tiara right **Rev:** Swimmers **Edge:** Reeded

Date	Mintage	F	VF	XF	Unc	BU
2003PM Proof	10,000	Value: 47.50				

KM# 1178 CROWN

28.2800 g., Copper-Nickel, 38.6 mm. **Ruler:** Elizabeth II **Subject:** Olympics **Obv:** Bust with tiara right **Rev:** Runners **Edge:** Reeded

Date	Mintage	F	VF	XF	Unc	BU
2003PM	—	—	—	—	10.00	12.00

KM# 1178a CROWN

28.2800 g., 0.9250 Silver 0.8410 oz. ASW, 38.6 mm. **Ruler:** Elizabeth II **Subject:** Olympics **Obv:** Bust with tiara right **Rev:** Runners **Edge:** Reeded

Date	Mintage	F	VF	XF	Unc	BU
2003PM Proof	10,000	Value: 47.50				

KM# 1180 CROWN

28.2800 g., Copper-Nickel, 38.6 mm. **Ruler:** Elizabeth II **Subject:** Olympics **Obv:** Bust with tiara right **Rev:** Bicyclists **Edge:** Reeded

Date	Mintage	F	VF	XF	Unc	BU
2003PM	—	—	—	—	10.00	12.00

KM# 1180a CROWN

28.2800 g., 0.9250 Silver 0.8410 oz. ASW, 38.6 mm. **Ruler:** Elizabeth II **Subject:** Olympics **Obv:** Bust with tiara right **Rev:** Bicyclists **Edge:** Reeded

Date	Mintage	F	VF	XF	Unc	BU
2003PM Proof	10,000	Value: 47.50				

KM# 1182 CROWN

28.2800 g., Copper-Nickel, 38.6 mm. **Ruler:** Elizabeth II **Subject:** Olympics **Obv:** Bust with tiara right **Rev:** Sail Boarders **Edge:** Reeded

Date	Mintage	F	VF	XF	Unc	BU
2003PM	—	—	—	—	10.00	12.00

KM# 1182a CROWN

28.2800 g., 0.9250 Silver 0.8410 oz. ASW, 38.6 mm. **Ruler:** Elizabeth II **Subject:** Olympics **Obv:** Bust with tiara right **Rev:** Sail Boarders **Edge:** Reeded

Date	Mintage	F	VF	XF	Unc	BU
2003PM Proof	10,000	Value: 47.50				

KM# 1196 CROWN

28.4400 g., Copper-Nickel, 38.6 mm. **Ruler:** Elizabeth II **Obv:** Bust with tiara right **Rev:** Four pre-1918 airplanes **Edge:** Reeded

Date	Mintage	F	VF	XF	Unc	BU
2003PM	—	—	—	—	10.00	12.00

KM# 1197 CROWN

28.4400 g., Copper-Nickel, 38.6 mm. **Obv:** Bust with tiara right **Rev:** Propeller plain, Zeppelin and two jet airliners **Edge:** Reeded

Date	Mintage	F	VF	XF	Unc	BU
2003PM	—	—	—	—	10.00	12.00

KM# 1201 CROWN

28.2800 g., Copper-Nickel, 38.6 mm. **Ruler:** Elizabeth II **Obv:** Bust with tiara right **Rev:** European Union map within hand held rope circle **Edge:** Reeded

Date	Mintage	F	VF	XF	Unc	BU
2004PM	—	—	—	—	10.00	12.00

KM# 1201a CROWN

28.2800 g., 0.9250 Silver 0.8410 oz. ASW, 38.6 mm. **Ruler:** Elizabeth II **Obv:** Bust with tiara right **Rev:** European Union map within a hand held rope circle **Edge:** Reeded

Date	Mintage	F	VF	XF	Unc	BU
2004PM Proof	10,000	Value: 50.00				

KM# 1202 CROWN

28.2800 g., Copper-Nickel, 38.6 mm. **Ruler:** Elizabeth II **Obv:** Bust with tiara right **Rev:** Harry Potter and patron fighting off a Deventer **Edge:** Reeded

Date	Mintage	F	VF	XF	Unc	BU
2004PM	—	—	—	—	15.00	17.00

KM# 1202a CROWN
28.2800 g., 0.9250 Silver 0.8410 oz. ASW, 38.6 mm. **Ruler:** Elizabeth II **Obv:** Bust with tiara right **Rev:** Harry Potter and patron fighting off a Deventer **Edge:** Reeded

Date	Mintage	F	VF	XF	Unc	BU
2004PM Proof	10,000	Value: 50.00				

KM# 1204 CROWN
28.2800 g., Copper-Nickel, 38.6 mm. **Ruler:** Elizabeth II **Obv:** Bust with tiara right **Rev:** Harry Potter in the shrieking shed **Edge:** Reeded

Date	Mintage	F	VF	XF	Unc	BU
2004PM	—	—	—	—	15.00	17.00

KM# 1204a CROWN
28.2800 g., 0.9250 Silver 0.8410 oz. ASW, 38.6 mm. **Ruler:** Elizabeth II **Obv:** Bust with tiara right **Rev:** Harry Potter in the shrieking shack **Edge:** Reeded

Date	Mintage	F	VF	XF	Unc	BU
2004PM Proof	10,000	Value: 50.00				

KM# 1206 CROWN
28.2800 g., Copper-Nickel, 38.6 mm. **Ruler:** Elizabeth II **Obv:** Bust with tiara right **Rev:** Harry Potter and Professor Dumbledore **Edge:** Reeded

Date	Mintage	F	VF	XF	Unc	BU
2004PM	—	—	—	—	15.00	17.00

KM# 1206a CROWN
28.2800 g., 0.9250 Silver 0.8410 oz. ASW, 38.6 mm. **Ruler:** Elizabeth II **Obv:** Bust with tiara right **Rev:** Harry Potter and Professor Dumbledore **Edge:** Reeded

Date	Mintage	F	VF	XF	Unc	BU
2004PM Proof	10,000	Value: 50.00				

KM# 1208 CROWN
28.2800 g., Copper-Nickel, 38.6 mm. **Ruler:** Elizabeth II **Obv:** Bust with tiara right **Rev:** Sirius Black on flying griffin **Edge:** Reeded

Date	Mintage	F	VF	XF	Unc	BU
2004PM	—	—	—	—	15.00	17.00

KM# 1208a CROWN
28.2800 g., 0.9250 Silver 0.8410 oz. ASW, 38.6 mm. **Ruler:** Elizabeth II **Obv:** Bust with tiara right **Rev:** Sirius Black on flying griffin **Edge:** Reeded

Date	Mintage	F	VF	XF	Unc	BU
2004PM Proof	10,000	Value: 50.00				

KM# 1210 CROWN
28.2800 g., Copper-Nickel, 38.6 mm. **Ruler:** Elizabeth II **Obv:** Bust with tiara right **Rev:** Three Olympic Swimmers **Edge:** Reeded

Date	Mintage	F	VF	XF	Unc	BU
2004PM	—	—	—	—	10.00	12.00

KM# 1210a CROWN
28.2800 g., 0.9250 Silver 0.8410 oz. ASW, 38.6 mm. **Ruler:** Elizabeth II **Obv:** Bust with tiara right **Rev:** Three Olympic Swimmers **Edge:** Reeded

Date	Mintage	F	VF	XF	Unc	BU
2004PM Proof	10,000	Value: 50.00				

KM# 1212 CROWN
28.2800 g., Copper-Nickel, 38.6 mm. **Ruler:** Elizabeth II **Obv:** Bust with tiara right **Rev:** Three Olympic Cyclists **Edge:** Reeded

Date	Mintage	F	VF	XF	Unc	BU
2004PM	—	—	—	—	10.00	12.00

KM# 1212a CROWN
28.2800 g., 0.9250 Silver 0.8410 oz. ASW, 38.6 mm. **Ruler:** Elizabeth II **Obv:** Bust with tiara right **Rev:** Three Olympic Cyclists **Edge:** Reeded

Date	Mintage	F	VF	XF	Unc	BU
2004PM Proof	10,000	Value: 50.00				

KM# 1214 CROWN
28.2800 g., Copper-Nickel, 38.6 mm. **Ruler:** Elizabeth II **Obv:** Bust with tiara right **Rev:** Three Olympic Runners **Edge:** Reeded

Date	Mintage	F	VF	XF	Unc	BU
2004PM	—	—	—	—	10.00	12.00

KM# 1214a CROWN
28.2800 g., 0.9250 Silver 0.8410 oz. ASW, 38.6 mm. **Ruler:** Elizabeth II **Obv:** Bust with tiara right **Rev:** Three Olympic Runners **Edge:** Reeded

Date	Mintage	F	VF	XF	Unc	BU
2004PM Proof	10,000	Value: 50.00				

KM# 1216 CROWN
28.2800 g., Copper-Nickel, 38.6 mm. **Ruler:** Elizabeth II **Obv:** Bust with tiara right **Rev:** Three Olympic Sail Boarders **Edge:** Reeded

Date	Mintage	F	VF	XF	Unc	BU
2004PM	—	—	—	—	10.00	12.00

KM# 1216a CROWN
28.2800 g., 0.9250 Silver 0.8410 oz. ASW, 38.6 mm. **Ruler:** Elizabeth II **Obv:** Bust with tiara right **Rev:** Three Olympic Sail Boarders **Edge:** Reeded

Date	Mintage	F	VF	XF	Unc	BU
2004PM Proof	10,000	Value: 50.00				

KM# 1218 CROWN
28.2800 g., Copper-Nickel, 38.6 mm. **Ruler:** Elizabeth II **Obv:** Bust with tiara right **Rev:** Ocean Liner Queen Mary 2 **Edge:** Reeded

Date	Mintage	F	VF	XF	Unc	BU
2004PM	—	—	—	—	15.00	17.00

KM# 1220 CROWN
28.2800 g., Copper-Nickel, 38.6 mm. **Ruler:** Elizabeth II **Obv:** Bust with tiara right **Rev:** Lt. Quillan portrait above Battle of Trafalgar scene **Edge:** Reeded

Date	Mintage	F	VF	XF	Unc	BU
2004PM	—	—	—	—	15.00	17.00

KM# 1220a CROWN
28.2800 g., 0.9250 Silver 0.8410 oz. ASW, 38.6 mm. **Ruler:** Elizabeth II **Obv:** Bust with tiara right **Rev:** Lt. Quillan portrait above Battle of Trafalgar scene **Edge:** Reeded

Date	Mintage	F	VF	XF	Unc	BU
2004PM Proof	10,000	Value: 50.00				

KM# 1221 CROWN
28.2800 g., Copper-Nickel, 38.6 mm. **Ruler:** Elizabeth II **Obv:** Bust with tiara right **Rev:** Napoleon and Nelson portraits above Battle of Trafalgar scene **Edge:** Reeded

Date	Mintage	F	VF	XF	Unc	BU
2004PM	—	—	—	—	15.00	17.00

KM# 1221a CROWN
28.2800 g., 0.9990 Silver 0.9083 oz. ASW, 38.6 mm. **Ruler:** Elizabeth II **Obv:** Bust with tiara right **Rev:** Napoleon and Nelson portraits above Battle of Trafalgar scene **Edge:** Reeded

Date	Mintage	F	VF	XF	Unc	BU
2004PM Proof	10,000	Value: 50.00				

KM# 1222 CROWN
28.2800 g., Copper-Nickel, 38.6 mm. **Ruler:** Elizabeth II **Obv:** Bust with tiara right **Rev:** D-Day Invasion Plan Map **Edge:** Reeded

Date	Mintage	F	VF	XF	Unc	BU
2004PM	—	—	—	—	15.00	17.00

KM# 1222a CROWN
28.2800 g., 0.9250 Silver 0.8410 oz. ASW, 38.6 mm. **Ruler:** Elizabeth II **Obv:** Bust with tiara right **Rev:** D-Day Invasion Plan Map **Edge:** Reeded

Date	Mintage	F	VF	XF	Unc	BU
2004PM Proof	10,000	Value: 50.00				

KM# 1224 CROWN
28.2800 g., Copper-Nickel, 38.6 mm. **Ruler:** Elizabeth II **Obv:** Bust with tiara right **Rev:** Victoria Cross and battle scene **Edge:** Reeded

Date	Mintage	F	VF	XF	Unc	BU
2004PM	—	—	—	—	15.00	17.00

KM# 1224a CROWN
28.2800 g., 0.9250 Silver 0.8410 oz. ASW, 38.6 mm. **Ruler:** Elizabeth II **Obv:** Bust with tiara right **Rev:** Victoria Cross and battle scene **Edge:** Reeded

Date	Mintage	F	VF	XF	Unc	BU
2004PM Proof	10,000	Value: 50.00				

KM# 1226 CROWN
28.2800 g., Copper-Nickel, 38.6 mm. **Ruler:** Elizabeth II **Obv:** Bust with tiara right **Rev:** Silver Star and battle scene **Edge:** Reeded

Date	Mintage	F	VF	XF	Unc	BU
2004PM	—	—	—	—	15.00	17.00

KM# 1226a CROWN
28.2800 g., 0.9250 Silver 0.8410 oz. ASW, 38.6 mm. **Ruler:** Elizabeth II **Obv:** Bust with tiara right **Rev:** Silver Star and battle scene **Edge:** Reeded

Date	Mintage	F	VF	XF	Unc	BU
2004PM Proof	10,000	Value: 50.00				

KM# 1228 CROWN
28.2800 g., Copper-Nickel, 38.6 mm. **Ruler:** Elizabeth II **Obv:** Bust with tiara right **Rev:** George Cross and rescue scene **Edge:** Reeded

Date	Mintage	F	VF	XF	Unc	BU
2004PM	—	—	—	—	15.00	17.00

KM# 1228a CROWN
28.2800 g., 0.9250 Silver 0.8410 oz. ASW, 38.6 mm. **Ruler:** Elizabeth II **Obv:** Bust with tiara right **Rev:** George Cross and rescue scene **Edge:** Reeded

Date	Mintage	F	VF	XF	Unc	BU
2004PM Proof	10,000	Value: 50.00				

KM# 1230 CROWN
28.2800 g., Copper-Nickel, 38.6 mm. **Ruler:** Elizabeth II **Obv:** Bust with tiara right **Rev:** White Rose of Finland Medal and battle scene **Edge:** Reeded

Date	Mintage	F	VF	XF	Unc	BU
2004PM	—	—	—	—	15.00	17.00

KM# 1230a CROWN
28.2800 g., 0.9250 Silver 0.8410 oz. ASW, 38.6 mm. **Ruler:** Elizabeth II **Obv:** Bust with tiara right **Rev:** White Rose of Finland Medal and battle scene **Edge:** Reeded

Date	Mintage	F	VF	XF	Unc	BU
2004PM Proof	10,000	Value: 50.00				

KM# 1232 CROWN
28.2800 g., Copper-Nickel, 38.6 mm. **Ruler:** Elizabeth II **Obv:** Bust with tiara right **Rev:** The Norwegian War Medal and naval battle scene **Edge:** Reeded

Date	Mintage	F	VF	XF	Unc	BU
2004PM	—	—	—	—	15.00	17.00

KM# 1232a CROWN
28.2800 g., 0.9250 Silver 0.8410 oz. ASW, 38.6 mm. **Ruler:** Elizabeth II **Obv:** Bust with tiara right **Rev:** The Norwegian War Medal and a naval battle scene **Edge:** Reeded

Date	Mintage	F	VF	XF	Unc	BU
2004PM Proof	10,000	Value: 50.00				

KM# 1234 CROWN
28.2800 g., Copper-Nickel, 38.6 mm. **Ruler:** Elizabeth II **Obv:** Bust with tiara right **Rev:** French Croix de Guerre and partisan battle scene **Edge:** Reeded

Date	Mintage	F	VF	XF	Unc	BU
2004PM	—	—	—	—	15.00	17.00

KM# 1234a CROWN
28.2800 g., 0.9250 Silver 0.8410 oz. ASW, 38.6 mm. **Ruler:** Elizabeth II **Obv:** Bust with tiara right **Rev:** French Croix de Guerre and partisan battle scene **Edge:** Reeded

Date	Mintage	F	VF	XF	Unc	BU
2004PM Proof	10,000	Value: 50.00				

KM# 1236 CROWN
28.2800 g., Copper-Nickel, 38.6 mm. **Ruler:** Elizabeth II **Obv:** Bust with tiara right **Rev:** Multicolor cartoon soccer player **Edge:** Reeded

Date	Mintage	F	VF	XF	Unc	BU
2004PM	—	—	—	—	10.00	12.00

KM# 1236a CROWN
28.2800 g., 0.9250 Silver 0.8410 oz. ASW, 38.6 mm. **Ruler:** Elizabeth II **Obv:** Bust with tiara right **Rev:** Multicolor cartoon soccer player **Edge:** Reeded

Date	Mintage	F	VF	XF	Unc	BU
2004PM Proof	7,500	Value: 50.00				

KM# 1237 CROWN
28.2800 g., Copper-Nickel, 38.6 mm. **Ruler:** Elizabeth II **Obv:** Bust with tiara right **Rev:** Soccer ball in flight **Edge:** Reeded

Date	Mintage	F	VF	XF	Unc	BU
2004PM	—	—	—	—	10.00	12.00

KM# 1237a CROWN
28.2800 g., 0.9250 Silver 0.8410 oz. ASW, 38.6 mm. **Ruler:** Elizabeth II **Obv:** Bust with tiara right **Rev:** Soccer ball in flight **Edge:** Reeded

Date	Mintage	F	VF	XF	Unc	BU
2004PM Proof	7,500	Value: 50.00				

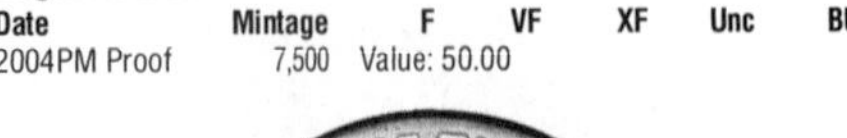

KM# 1238 CROWN
28.2800 g., Copper-Nickel, 38.6 mm. **Ruler:** Elizabeth II **Obv:** Bust with tiara right **Rev:** Gibbon monkey **Edge:** Reeded

Date	Mintage	F	VF	XF	Unc	BU
2004PM	—	—	—	—	10.00	15.00

KM# 1238a CROWN
28.2800 g., 0.9250 Silver 0.8410 oz. ASW, 38.6 mm. **Ruler:** Elizabeth II **Obv:** Bust with tiara right **Rev:** Monkey **Edge:** Reeded

Date	Mintage	F	VF	XF	Unc	BU
2004PM Proof	30,000	Value: 50.00				

KM# 1239 CROWN
31.1035 g., 0.9999 Gold 0.9999 oz. AGW, 32.7 mm. **Ruler:** Elizabeth II **Obv:** Bust with tiara right **Rev:** Monkey **Edge:** Reeded

Date	Mintage	F	VF	XF	Unc	BU
2004PM Proof	2,000	Value: 1,825				

KM# 1242 CROWN
6.2200 g., 0.9999 Gold 0.1999 oz. AGW, 22 mm. **Ruler:** Elizabeth II **Obv:** Bust with tiara right **Rev:** Monkey **Edge:** Reeded

Date	Mintage	F	VF	XF	Unc	BU
2004PM Proof	12,000	Value: 375				

KM# 1245 CROWN
28.2800 g., Copper-Nickel, 38.6 mm. **Ruler:** Elizabeth II **Subject:** Lord of the Rings **Obv:** Bust with tiara right **Rev:** Nine characters **Edge:** Reeded

Date	Mintage	F	VF	XF	Unc	BU
2004PM	100,000	—	—	—	15.00	17.00

KM# 1245a CROWN
28.2800 g., 0.9250 Silver 0.8410 oz. ASW, 38.6 mm. **Ruler:** Elizabeth II **Subject:** Lord of the Rings **Obv:** Bust with tiara right **Rev:** Nine characters **Edge:** Reeded

Date	Mintage	F	VF	XF	Unc	BU
2004PM Proof	10,000	Value: 50.00				

KM# 1246.1 CROWN
28.2800 g., Copper-Nickel, 38.6 mm. **Ruler:** Elizabeth II **Obv:** Head with tiara right **Rev:** Pair of Tonkinese cats **Edge:** Reeded

Date	Mintage	F	VF	XF	Unc	BU
2004PM	—	—	—	—	14.00	16.00

KM# 1246a.1 CROWN
31.1035 g., 0.9990 Silver 0.9990 oz. ASW, 38.6 mm. **Ruler:** Elizabeth II **Obv:** Head with tiara right **Rev:** Two Tonkinese cats **Edge:** Reeded

Date	Mintage	F	VF	XF	Unc	BU
2004PM Proof	50,000	Value: 70.00				

KM# 1246a.2 CROWN
31.1035 g., 0.9990 Silver 0.9990 oz. ASW, 38.6 mm. **Ruler:** Elizabeth II **Obv:** Head with tiara right **Rev:** Two multicolor Tonkinese cats **Edge:** Reeded

Date	Mintage	F	VF	XF	Unc	BU
2004PM Proof	—	Value: 75.00				

KM# 1251 CROWN
31.1035 g., 0.9999 Gold 0.9999 oz. AGW, 32.7 mm. **Ruler:** Elizabeth II **Obv:** Head with tiara right **Rev:** Two Tonkinese cats **Edge:** Reeded

Date	Mintage	F	VF	XF	Unc	BU
2004PM	—	—	—	—	—	1,800
2004PM Proof	1,000	Value: 1,825				

KM# 1246.2 CROWN
28.2800 g., Copper-Nickel **Ruler:** Elizabeth II **Obv:** Head with tiara right **Rev:** Two multicolor Tonkinese cats **Edge:** Reeded

Date	Mintage	F	VF	XF	Unc	BU
2004PM	—	—	—	—	14.00	16.00

KM# 1266 CROWN
28.3300 g., Copper-Nickel, 38.7 mm. **Ruler:** Elizabeth II **Obv:** Bust with tiara right **Rev:** Himalayan cat with two kittens **Edge:** Reeded

Date	Mintage	F	VF	XF	Unc	BU
2005PM	—	—	—	—	12.00	14.00

KM# 1266a CROWN
31.1030 g., 0.9990 Silver 0.9989 oz. ASW, 38.6 mm. **Ruler:** Elizabeth II **Obv:** Bust with tiara right **Rev:** Himalayan cat and two kittens **Edge:** Reeded

Date	Mintage	F	VF	XF	Unc	BU
2005PM Proof	50,000	Value: 70.00				

KM# 1268 CROWN
31.1030 g., 0.9999 Gold 0.9998 oz. AGW, 32.7 mm. **Ruler:** Elizabeth II **Obv:** Bust with tiara right **Rev:** Himalayan cat and two kittens **Edge:** Reeded

Date	Mintage	F	VF	XF	Unc	BU
2005PM Proof	—	Value: 1,825				

KM# 1273 CROWN
28.2800 g., Copper-Nickel, 38.6 mm. **Ruler:** Elizabeth II **Obv:** Bust with tiara right **Rev:** Harry Potter and the Hungarian Horn Tail, Tri-Wizard Tournament feat **Edge:** Reeded

Date	Mintage	F	VF	XF	Unc	BU
2005PM	—	—	—	—	15.00	17.00

KM# 1274 CROWN
28.2800 g., Copper-Nickel, 38.6 mm. **Ruler:** Elizabeth II **Subject:** 60th Anniversary - End of WW II **Obv:** Bust with tiara right **Rev:** Sir Winston Churchill

Date	Mintage	F	VF	XF	Unc	BU
2005	—	—	—	—	10.00	12.00

KM# 1275 CROWN

28.2800 g., Copper-Nickel, 38.6 mm. **Ruler:** Elizabeth II **Subject:** 400th Anniversary - Gunpowder plot **Obv:** Bust with tiara right **Rev:** Tower of London, Beefeaters

Date	Mintage	F	VF	XF	Unc	BU
2005	—	—	—	—	10.00	12.00

KM# 1276 CROWN

28.2800 g., Copper-Nickel, 38.6 mm. **Ruler:** Elizabeth II **Obv:** Bust with tiara right **Rev:** Harry Potter and Tri-Wizard Tournament feat - Underwater retrieval

Date	Mintage	F	VF	XF	Unc	BU
2005	—	—	—	—	10.00	12.00

KM# 1277 CROWN

28.2800 g., Copper-Nickel, 38.6 mm. **Ruler:** Elizabeth II **Obv:** Bust with tiara right **Rev:** Harry Potter and pensive

Date	Mintage	F	VF	XF	Unc	BU
2005	—	—	—	—	10.00	12.00

KM# 1278 CROWN

28.2800 g., Copper-Nickel, 38.6 mm. **Ruler:** Elizabeth II **Obv:** Bust with tiara right **Rev:** Harry Potter and portkey

Date	Mintage	F	VF	XF	Unc	BU
2005	—	—	—	—	10.00	12.00

KM# 1291 CROWN

28.2800 g., Copper-Nickel, 38.6 mm. **Ruler:** Elizabeth II **Subject:** Trafalgar - 200th Anniversary **Obv:** Bust with tiara right **Rev:** Nelson at Battle of Copenhagen

Date	Mintage	F	VF	XF	Unc	BU
2005	—	—	—	—	10.00	12.00

KM# 1279 CROWN

28.2800 g., Copper-Nickel, 38.6 mm. **Ruler:** Elizabeth II **Subject:** The Battle of Cape St. Vincent **Obv:** Bust with tiara right **Rev:** Naval battle scene

Date	Mintage	F	VF	XF	Unc	BU
2005	—	—	—	—	10.00	12.00

KM# 1280 CROWN

28.2800 g., Copper-Nickel, 38.6 mm. **Ruler:** Elizabeth II **Subject:** Nelson Funeral Procession **Obv:** Bust with tiara right **Rev:** Thames and Greenwich view

Date	Mintage	F	VF	XF	Unc	BU
2005	—	—	—	—	10.00	12.00

KM# 1281 CROWN

Copper-Nickel **Ruler:** Elizabeth II **Subject:** Battle of the Nile **Obv:** Bust with tiara right **Rev:** Naval battle

Date	Mintage	F	VF	XF	Unc	BU
2005	—	—	—	—	10.00	12.00

KM# 1282 CROWN

28.2800 g., Copper-Nickel, 38.6 mm. **Ruler:** Elizabeth II **Subject:** Norway Independence **Obv:** Bust with tiara right **Rev:** Three swords

Date	Mintage	F	VF	XF	Unc	BU
2005	—	—	—	—	10.00	12.00

KM# 1283 CROWN

28.2800 g., Copper-Nickel, 38.6 mm. **Ruler:** Elizabeth II **Subject:** Nelson - Trafalgar 200th Anniversary **Rev:** Nelson portrait

Date	Mintage	F	VF	XF	Unc	BU
2005	—	—	—	—	10.00	12.00

KM# 1284 CROWN

28.2800 g., Copper-Nickel, 38.6 mm. **Ruler:** Elizabeth II **Subject:** Battle of Trafalgar **Rev:** Naval battle scene

Date	Mintage	F	VF	XF	Unc	BU
2005	—	—	—	—	10.00	12.00

KM# 1285 CROWN

28.2800 g., Copper-Nickel, 38.6 mm. **Ruler:** Elizabeth II **Subject:** Steam Packet - King Orry III **Obv:** Bust with tiara right **Rev:** Ship view

Date	Mintage	F	VF	XF	Unc	BU
2005	—	—	—	—	10.00	12.00

KM# 1286 CROWN

28.2800 g., Copper-Nickel, 38.6 mm. **Ruler:** Elizabeth II **Subject:** Isle of Man Steam Packet Company - 175th Anniversary **Obv:** Bust with tiara right **Rev:** Modern and early ferry

Date	Mintage	F	VF	XF	Unc	BU
2005	—	—	—	—	10.00	12.00

KM# 1287 CROWN

28.2800 g., Copper-Nickel, 38.6 mm. **Ruler:** Elizabeth II **Rev:** Motorcycle right

Date	Mintage	F	VF	XF	Unc	BU
2005	—	—	—	—	10.00	12.00

KM# 1288 CROWN

28.2800 g., Copper-Nickel, 38.6 mm. **Ruler:** Elizabeth II **Rev:** Motorcycle forward

Date	Mintage	F	VF	XF	Unc	BU
2005	—	—	—	—	10.00	12.00

KM# 1289 CROWN

28.2800 g., Copper-Nickel, 38.6 mm. **Ruler:** Elizabeth II **Subject:** Ugly Duckling story **Obv:** Bust with tiara right **Rev:** Farm animals

Date	Mintage	F	VF	XF	Unc	BU
2005	—	—	—	—	12.00	14.00

KM# 1428 CROWN

28.2800 g., Copper-Nickel, 38.6 mm. **Ruler:** Elizabeth II **Subject:** Traflagar, 200th Anniversary **Rev:** Quillian portrait above naval battle scene

Date	Mintage	F	VF	XF	Unc	BU
2005PM	—	—	—	—	10.00	12.00

KM# 1429 CROWN

28.2800 g., Copper-Nickel, 38.6 mm. **Ruler:** Elizabeth II **Subject:** Trafalgar, 200th Anniversary **Rev:** Napoleon and Nelson portraits above Naval battle scene

Date	Mintage	F	VF	XF	Unc	BU
2005PM	—	—	—	—	10.00	12.00

KM# 1323.1 CROWN

28.2800 g., Copper-Nickel, 38.60 mm. **Ruler:** Elizabeth II **Subject:** Hans Christian Anderson's Fairy Tales **Obv:** Bust with tiarra right **Obv. Legend:** ELIZABETH II - ISLE OF MAN **Rev:** Three bears startling Goldilocks in bed **Rev. Legend:** Goldilocks and the Three Bears **Edge:** Reeded

Date	Mintage	F	VF	XF	Unc	BU
2006PM	—	—	—	—	—	35.00

KM# 1296 CROWN

28.2800 g., Copper-Nickel, 38.6 mm. **Ruler:** Elizabeth II **Subject:** Battles that Changed the World **Obv:** Elizabeth II **Rev:** Trojan War scene **Edge:** Reeded

Date	Mintage	F	VF	XF	Unc	BU
2006PM	—	—	—	—	10.00	12.00

KM# 1296a CROWN

28.2800 g., 0.9250 Silver 0.8410 oz. ASW, 38.6 mm. **Ruler:** Elizabeth II **Subject:** Battles that Changed the World **Obv:** Elizabeth II **Rev:** Trojan War scene **Edge:** Reeded

Date	Mintage	F	VF	XF	Unc	BU
2006PM Proof	10,000	Value: 47.50				

KM# 1298 CROWN

28.2800 g., Copper-Nickel, 38.6 mm. **Ruler:** Elizabeth II **Subject:** Battles that Changed the World **Obv:** Elizabeth II **Rev:** Battle of Arbela scene **Edge:** Reeded

Date	Mintage	F	VF	XF	Unc	BU
2006PM	—	—	—	—	10.00	12.00

KM# 1298a CROWN

28.2800 g., 0.9250 Silver 0.8410 oz. ASW, 38.6 mm. **Ruler:** Elizabeth II **Subject:** Battles that Changed the World **Obv:** Elizabeth II **Rev:** Battle of Arbela scene **Edge:** Reeded

Date	Mintage	F	VF	XF	Unc	BU
2006PM Proof	10,000	Value: 47.50				

KM# 1300 CROWN

28.2800 g., Copper-Nickel, 38.6 mm. **Ruler:** Elizabeth II **Subject:** Battles that Changed the World **Obv:** Elizabeth II **Rev:** Battle of Thapsus scene **Edge:** Reeded

Date	Mintage	F	VF	XF	Unc	BU
2006PM	—	—	—	—	10.00	12.00

KM# 1300a CROWN

28.2800 g., 0.9250 Silver 0.8410 oz. ASW, 38.6 mm. **Ruler:** Elizabeth II **Subject:** Battles that Changed the World **Obv:** Elizabeth II **Rev:** Battle of Thapsus scene **Edge:** Reeded

Date	Mintage	F	VF	XF	Unc	BU
2006PM Proof	10,000	Value: 47.50				

KM# 1302 CROWN

28.2800 g., Copper-Nickel, 38.6 mm. **Ruler:** Elizabeth II **Subject:** Battles that Changed the World **Obv:** Elizabeth II **Rev:** Battle of Cologne scene **Edge:** Reeded

Date	Mintage	F	VF	XF	Unc	BU
2006PM	—	—	—	—	10.00	12.00

KM# 1302a CROWN

28.2800 g., 0.9250 Silver 0.8410 oz. ASW, 38.6 mm. **Ruler:** Elizabeth II **Subject:** Battles that Changed the World **Obv:** Elizabeth II **Rev:** Battle of Cologne scene **Edge:** Reeded

Date	Mintage	F	VF	XF	Unc	BU
2006PM Proof	10,000	Value: 47.50				

KM# 1304 CROWN
28.2800 g., Copper-Nickel, 38.6 mm. **Ruler:** Elizabeth II **Subject:** Battles that Changed the World **Obv:** Elizabeth II **Rev:** Siege of Valencia scene **Edge:** Reeded

Date	Mintage	F	VF	XF	Unc	BU
2006PM	—	—	—	—	10.00	12.00

KM# 1304a CROWN
28.2800 g., 0.9250 Silver 0.8410 oz. ASW, 38.6 mm. **Ruler:** Elizabeth II **Subject:** Battles that Changed the World **Obv:** Elizabeth II **Rev:** Siege of Valencia scene **Edge:** Reeded

Date	Mintage	F	VF	XF	Unc	BU
2006PM Proof	10,000	Value: 47.50				

KM# 1306 CROWN
28.2800 g., Copper-Nickel, 38.6 mm. **Ruler:** Elizabeth II **Subject:** Battles that Changed the World **Obv:** Elizabeth II **Rev:** Battle of Agincourt scene **Edge:** Reeded

Date	Mintage	F	VF	XF	Unc	BU
2006PM	—	—	—	—	10.00	12.00

KM# 1306a CROWN
28.2800 g., 0.9250 Silver 0.8410 oz. ASW, 38.6 mm. **Ruler:** Elizabeth II **Subject:** Battles that Changed the World **Obv:** Elizabeth II **Rev:** Battle of Agincourt scene **Edge:** Reeded

Date	Mintage	F	VF	XF	Unc	BU
2006PM Proof	10,000	Value: 47.50				

KM# 1323.2 CROWN
28.2800 g., Copper-Nickel, 38.60 mm. **Ruler:** Elizabeth II **Subject:** Hans Christian Anderson's Fairy Tales **Obv:** Bust with tiara right **Obv. Legend:** ELIZABETH II - ISLE OF MAN **Rev:** Three bears startling Goldilocks in bed multicolor **Rev. Legend:** Goldilocks and the Three Bears **Edge:** Reeded

Date	Mintage	F	VF	XF	Unc	BU
2006PM	—	—	—	—	—	40.00

KM# 1323.1a CROWN
28.2800 g., 0.9250 Silver 0.8410 oz. ASW, 38.60 mm. **Ruler:** Elizabeth II **Subject:** Hans Christian Anderson's Fairy Tales **Obv:** Bust with tiara right **Obv. Legend:** ELIZABETH II - ISLE OF MAN **Rev:** Three bears startling Goldilocks in bed **Rev. Legend:** Goldilocks and the Three Bears **Edge:** Reeded

Date	Mintage	F	VF	XF	Unc	BU
2006PM Proof	—	Value: 80.00				

KM# 1323.2a CROWN
28.2800 g., 0.9250 Silver 0.8410 oz. ASW, 38.60 mm. **Ruler:** Elizabeth II **Subject:** Hans Christian Anderson's Fairy Tales **Obv:** Bust with tiara right **Obv. Legend:** ELIZABETH II - ISLE OF MAN **Rev:** Three bears startling Goldilocks in bed multicolor **Rev. Legend:** Goldilocks and the Three Bears **Edge:** Reeded

Date	Mintage	F	VF	XF	Unc	BU
2006PM Proof	—	Value: 100				

KM# 1290a CROWN
28.2800 g., Copper-Nickel, 38.6 mm. **Ruler:** Elizabeth II **Obv:** Bust with tiara right **Rev:** Three Exotic Shorthair cats sitting facing **Edge:** Reeded

Date	Mintage	F	VF	XF	Unc	BU
2006PM	—	—	—	—	12.00	14.00

KM# 1290b CROWN
28.2800 g., 0.9250 Silver 0.8410 oz. ASW, 38.6 mm. **Ruler:** Elizabeth II **Obv:** Bust with tiara right **Rev:** Three Exotic Shorthair cats sitting facing **Edge:** Reeded

Date	Mintage	F	VF	XF	Unc	BU
2006PM	—	—	—	—	—	70.00

KM# 1290c CROWN
31.1030 g., 0.9999 Gold 0.9998 oz. AGW **Ruler:** Elizabeth II **Obv:** Bust with tiara right **Rev:** Three Exotic Shorthair cats sitting facing, multicolor **Edge:** Reeded

Date	Mintage	F	VF	XF	Unc	BU
2006PM	—	—	—	—	—	1,825

KM# 1423.1 CROWN
28.2800 g., Copper-Nickel, 38.6 mm. **Ruler:** Elizabeth II **Subject:** Concord, 30th Anniversary of transatlantic service **Obv:** Bust with tiara right **Rev:** Concord in flight, buildings below

Date	Mintage	F	VF	XF	Unc	BU
2006PM Proof	—	Value: 30.00				

KM# 1423.2 CROWN
28.2800 g., Copper-Nickel, 38.6 mm. **Ruler:** Elizabeth II **Subject:** Concorde, 30th Anniversary of transatlantic service **Obv:** Bust with tiara right **Rev:** Concorde in flight, multicolor

Date	Mintage	F	VF	XF	Unc	BU
2006PM Proof	—	Value: 50.00				

KM# 1347 CROWN
31.1030 g., 0.9999 Gold 0.9998 oz. AGW **Ruler:** Elizabeth II **Obv:** Bust with tiara right **Obv. Legend:** ELIZABETH II - ISLE OF MAN **Rev:** Ragdoll cat with two kittens sitting facing **Edge:** Reeded

Date	Mintage	F	VF	XF	Unc	BU
2007PM	—	—	—	—	—	1,825

KM# 1348.1 CROWN
Copper-Nickel **Ruler:** Elizabeth II **Subject:** The Tale of Peter Rabbit **Obv:** Bust with tiara right **Obv. Legend:** ELIZABETH II - ISLE OF MAN **Rev:** Peter walking with friends **Edge:** Reeded

Date	Mintage	F	VF	XF	Unc	BU
2007PM	—	—	—	—	—	30.00

KM# 1348.2 CROWN
Copper-Nickel **Ruler:** Elizabeth II **Subject:** The Tale of Peter Rabbit **Obv:** Bust with tiara right **Obv. Legend:** ELIZABETH II - ISLE OF MAN **Rev:** Peter walking with friends, multicolor **Edge:** Reeded

Date	Mintage	F	VF	XF	Unc	BU
2007PM	—	—	—	—	—	35.00

KM# 1348.1a CROWN
0.9250 Silver **Ruler:** Elizabeth II **Subject:** The Tale of Peter Rabbit **Obv:** Bust with tiara right **Obv. Legend:** ELIZABETH II - ISLE OF MAN **Rev:** Peter walking with friends **Edge:** Reeded

Date	Mintage	F	VF	XF	Unc	BU
2007PM Proof	—	Value: 50.00				

KM# 1348.2a CROWN
0.9250 Silver **Ruler:** Elizabeth II **Subject:** The Tale of Peter Rabbit **Obv:** Bust with tiara right **Obv. Legend:** ELIZABETH II - ISLE OF MAN **Rev:** Peter walking with friends, multicolor **Edge:** Reeded

Date	Mintage	F	VF	XF	Unc	BU
2007PM Proof	—	Value: 75.00				

KM# 1310 CROWN
28.2800 g., Copper-Nickel, 38.6 mm. **Ruler:** Elizabeth II **Subject:** 100th Anniversary of Scouting **Obv:** Bust with tiara right **Obv. Legend:** ELIZABETH II - ISLE OF MAN **Rev:** 3/4 length figure of Robert Baden-Powell standing facing 3/4 left, Fleur-de-lys below, images of scouting at left and right **Rev. Legend:** CENTENARY OF SCOUTING **Edge:** Reeded

Date	Mintage	F	VF	XF	Unc	BU
2007	—	—	—	—	17.00	20.00

KM# 1311 CROWN
28.2800 g., 0.9167 Silver 0.8334 oz. ASW **Ruler:** Elizabeth II **Subject:** 100th Anniversary of Scouting **Obv:** Bust with tiara right **Obv. Legend:** ELIZABETH II - ISLE OF MAN **Rev:** 3/4 length figure of Robert Baden-Powell standing facing 3/4 left, Fleur-de-lys below, images of scouting at left and right **Rev. Legend:** CENTENARY OF SCOUTING **Edge:** Reeded

Date	Mintage	F	VF	XF	Unc	BU
2007 Proof	—	Value: 50.00				

KM# 1312 CROWN
0.7500 Gold Yellow, white and red Gold **Ruler:** Elizabeth II **Subject:** Diamond Wedding Anniversary **Obv:** Bust with tiara right **Obv. Legend:** ELIZABETH II - ISLE OF MAN **Rev:** Crowned pair of doves surrounded by a leek, thistle, rose and shamrock **Edge:** Reeded

Date	Mintage	F	VF	XF	Unc	BU
2007 Proof	—	Value: 2,000				

KM# 1313 CROWN
28.2800 g., Copper-Nickel, 38.60 mm. **Ruler:** Elizabeth II **Obv:** Bust with tiara right **Obv. Legend:** ELIZABETH II - ISLE OF MAN **Rev:** Two swans facing **Edge:** Reeded

Date	Mintage	F	VF	XF	Unc	BU
2007	—	—	—	—	15.00	18.00

KM# 1315 CROWN
28.2800 g., 0.9167 Silver 0.8334 oz. ASW, 38.60 mm. **Ruler:** Elizabeth II **Obv:** Bust with tiara right **Obv. Legend:** ELIZABETH II - ISLE OF MAN **Rev:** Two swans facing **Edge:** Reeded

Date	Mintage	F	VF	XF	Unc	BU
2007 Proof	10,000	Value: 50.00				

KM# 1316 CROWN
28.2800 g., Copper-Nickel, 38.6 mm. **Ruler:** Elizabeth II **Subject:** Diamond Wedding Anniversary **Obv:** Conjoined busts with Philip right **Obv. Legend:** ELIZABETH II - ISLE OF MAN **Rev:** Bridal bouquet of white orchids **Rev. Legend:** Diamond Wedding of H.M. Queen Elizabeth II & H.R.H. Prince Philip **Edge:** Reeded

Date	Mintage	F	VF	XF	Unc	BU
2007	—	—	—	—	15.00	18.00

KM# 1316a CROWN
28.2800 g., 0.9167 Silver 0.8334 oz. ASW **Ruler:** Elizabeth II **Subject:** Diamond Wedding Anniversary **Obv:** Conjoined busts with Philip right **Obv. Legend:** ELIZABETH II - ISLE OF MAN **Rev:** Bridal bouquet of white orchids **Rev. Legend:** Diamond Wedding of H.M. Queen Elizabeth II & H.R.H. Prince Philip **Edge:** Reeded

Date	Mintage	F	VF	XF	Unc	BU
2007 Proof	—	Value: 50.00				

KM# 1317 CROWN
28.2800 g., Copper-Nickel **Ruler:** Elizabeth II **Subject:** Diamond Wedding Anniversary **Obv:** Conjoined busts with Philip right **Obv. Legend:** ELIZABETH II - ISLE OF MAN **Rev:** Westminster Abbey **Rev. Legend:** Diamond Wedding of H.M. Queen Elizabeth II & H.R.H. Prince Philip **Edge:** Reeded

Date	Mintage	F	VF	XF	Unc	BU
2007	—	—	—	—	15.00	18.00

KM# 1317a CROWN
28.2800 g., 0.9167 Silver 0.8334 oz. ASW **Ruler:** Elizabeth II **Subject:** Diamond Wedding Anniversary **Obv:** Conjoined busts with Philip right **Obv. Legend:** ELIZABETH II - ISLE OF MAN **Rev:** Westminster Abbey **Rev. Legend:** Diamond Wedding of H.M. Queen Elizabeth II & H.R.H. Prince Philip **Edge:** Reeded

Date	Mintage	F	VF	XF	Unc	BU
2007 Proof	—	Value: 50.00				

KM# 1318 CROWN
28.2800 g., Copper-Nickel, 38.6 mm. **Ruler:** Elizabeth II **Subject:** Diamond Wedding Anniversary **Obv:** Conjoined busts with Philip right **Obv. Legend:** ELIZABETH II - ISLE OF MAN **Rev:** Royal Family of five standing facing **Rev. Legend:** Diamond Wedding of H.M. Queen Elizabeth II & H.R.H. Prince Philip **Edge:** Reeded

Date	Mintage	F	VF	XF	Unc	BU
2007	—	—	—	—	15.00	18.00

KM# 1318a CROWN
28.2800 g., 0.9167 Silver 0.8334 oz. ASW, 38.6 mm. **Ruler:** Elizabeth II **Subject:** Diamond Wedding Anniversary **Obv:** Conjoined busts with Philip right **Obv. Legend:** ELIZABETH II - ISLE OF MAN **Rev:** Royal Family of five standing facing **Rev. Legend:** Diamond Wedding of H.M. Queen Elizabeth II & H.R.H. Prince Philip **Edge:** Reeded

Date	Mintage	F	VF	XF	Unc	BU
2007 Proof	—	Value: 50.00				

KM# 1319 CROWN
28.2800 g., Copper-Nickel, 38.6 mm. **Ruler:** Elizabeth II **Subject:** Diamond Wedding Anniversary **Obv:** Conjoined busts with Philip right **Obv. Legend:** ELIZABETH II - ISLE OF MAN **Rev:** Bride and groom standing facing **Rev. Legend:** Diamond Wedding of H.M. Queen Elizabeth II & H.R.H. Prince Philip **Edge:** Reeded

Date	Mintage	F	VF	XF	Unc	BU
2007	—	—	—	—	15.00	18.00

KM# 1319a CROWN
28.2800 g., 0.9167 Silver 0.8334 oz. ASW, 38.6 mm. **Ruler:** Elizabeth II **Subject:** Diamond Wedding Anniversary **Obv:** Conjoined busts with Philip right **Obv. Legend:** ELIZABETH II - ISLE OF MAN **Rev:** Bride and groom standing facing **Rev. Legend:** Diamond Wedding of H.M. Queen Elizabeth II & H.R.H. Prince Philip **Edge:** Reeded

Date	Mintage	F	VF	XF	Unc	BU
2007 Proof	—	Value: 50.00				

KM# 1325.1 CROWN
28.2800 g., Copper-Nickel, 38.60 mm. **Ruler:** Elizabeth II **Subject:** Hans Christian Anderson's Fairy Tales **Obv:** Bust with tiara right **Obv. Legend:** ELIZABETH II - ISLE OF MAN **Rev:** Wolf at right trying to blow pig's house down, two pigs fleeing above in background **Rev. Legend:** Three Little Pigs **Edge:** Reeded

Date	Mintage	F	VF	XF	Unc	BU
2007PM	—	—	—	—	—	35.00

KM# 1325.2 CROWN
28.2800 g., Copper-Nickel, 38.60 mm. **Ruler:** Elizabeth II **Subject:** Hans Christian Anderson's Fairy Tales **Obv:** Bust with tiara right **Obv. Legend:** ELIZABETH II - ISLE OF MAN **Rev:** Wolf at right trying to blow pig's house down, two pigs fleeing above in backgound multicolor **Rev. Legend:** Three Little Pigs **Edge:** Reeded

Date	Mintage	F	VF	XF	Unc	BU
2007PM	—	—	—	—	—	40.00

KM# 1325.1a CROWN
28.2800 g., 0.9250 Silver 0.8410 oz. ASW, 38.60 mm. **Ruler:** Elizabeth II **Subject:** Hans Christian Anderson's Fairy Tales **Obv:** Bust with tiara right **Obv. Legend:** ELIZABETH II - ISLE OF MAN **Rev:** Wolf at right trying to blow pig's house down, two pigs fleeing above in background **Rev. Legend:** Three Little Pigs **Edge:** Reeded

Date	Mintage	F	VF	XF	Unc	BU
2007PM Proof	—	Value: 50.00				

KM# 1325.2a CROWN
28.2800 g., 0.9250 Silver 0.8410 oz. ASW, 38.60 mm. **Ruler:** Elizabeth II **Subject:** Hans Christian Anderson's Fairy Tales **Obv:** Bust with tiara right **Obv. Legend:** ELIZABETH II - ISLE OF MAN **Rev:** Wolf at right trying to blow pig's house down, two pigs fleeing above in background multicolor **Rev. Legend:** Three Little Pigs **Edge:** Reeded

Date	Mintage	F	VF	XF	Unc	BU
2007PM Proof	—	Value: 75.00				

KM# 1307.1 CROWN
28.2800 g., Copper-Nickel, 38.6 mm. **Ruler:** Elizabeth II **Rev:** Ragdoll cat and kittens

Date	Mintage	F	VF	XF	Unc	BU
2007	—	—	—	—	15.00	18.00

KM# 1307.2 CROWN
28.2800 g., Copper-Nickel, 38.6 mm. **Ruler:** Elizabeth II **Rev:** Three cats, multicolor

Date	Mintage	F	VF	XF	Unc	BU
2007PM	—	—	—	—	—	25.00

KM# 1324.1 CROWN
28.2800 g., Copper-Nickel, 38.60 mm. **Ruler:** Elizabeth II **Subject:** Hans Christian Anderson's Fairy Tales **Obv:** Bust with tiara right **Obv. Legend:** ELIZABETH II - ISLE OF MAN **Rev:** Prince awakening Sleeping Beauty, castle in background **Rev. Legend:** Sleeping Beauty **Edge:** Reeded

Date	Mintage	F	VF	XF	Unc	BU
2007PM	—	—	—	—	—	25.00

KM# 1324.1a CROWN
28.2800 g., 0.9250 Silver 0.8410 oz. ASW, 38.60 mm. **Ruler:** Elizabeth II **Subject:** Hans Christian Anderson's Fairy Tales **Obv:** Bust with tiara right **Obv. Legend:** ELIZABETH II - ISLE OF MAN **Rev:** Prince wakening Sleeping Beauty, castle in background **Rev. Legend:** Sleeping Beauty **Edge:** Reeded

Date	Mintage	F	VF	XF	Unc	BU
2007PM Proof	—	Value: 50.00				

KM# 1324.2 CROWN
28.2800 g., Copper-Nickel, 38.60 mm. **Ruler:** Elizabeth II **Subject:** Hans Christian Anderson's Fairy Tales **Obv:** Bust with tiara right **Obv. Legend:** ELIZABET II - ISLE OF MAN **Rev:** Prince awakening Sleeping Beauty, castle in backgound multicolor **Rev. Legend:** Sleeping Beauty **Edge:** Reeded

Date	Mintage	F	VF	XF	Unc	BU
2007PM	—	—	—	—	—	25.00

KM# 1324.2a CROWN
28.2800 g., 0.9250 Silver 0.8410 oz. ASW, 38.60 mm. **Ruler:** Elizabeth II **Subject:** Hans Christian Anderson's Fairy Tales **Obv:** Bust with tiara right **Obv. Legend:** ELIZABETH II - ISLE OF MAN **Rev:** Prince awakening Sleeping Beauty, castle in background multicolor **Rev. Legend:** Sleeping Beauty **Edge:** Reeded

Date	Mintage	F	VF	XF	Unc	BU
2007PM Proof	—	Value: 50.00				

KM# 1418 CROWN
28.2800 g., Copper-Nickel, 38.6 mm. **Ruler:** Elizabeth II **Subject:** TT Centennial **Obv:** Bust with tiara right **Rev:** Motorcyclist left

Date	Mintage	F	VF	XF	Unc	BU
2007PM	—	—	—	—	15.00	17.00

KM# 1419 CROWN
28.2800 g., Copper-Nickel, 38.6 mm. **Ruler:** Elizabeth II **Subject:** TT Centennial **Obv:** Bust with tiara right **Rev:** Motorcyclists Dunlop

Date	Mintage	F	VF	XF	Unc	BU
2007PM	—	—	—	—	15.00	17.00

KM# 1420 CROWN
28.2800 g., Copper-Nickel, 38.6 mm. **Ruler:** Elizabeth II **Subject:** TT Centennial **Obv:** Bust with tiara right **Rev:** Motorcyclists Woods

Date	Mintage	F	VF	XF	Unc	BU
2007PM	—	—	—	—	15.00	17.00

KM# 1421 CROWN
28.2800 g., Copper-Nickel, 38.6 mm. **Ruler:** Elizabeth II **Subject:** TT Centennial **Obv:** Bust with tiara right **Rev:** Motorcyclists Haliwood

Date	Mintage	F	VF	XF	Unc	BU
2007PM	—	—	—	—	15.00	17.00

KM# 1422 CROWN
28.2800 g., Copper-Nickel, 38.6 mm. **Ruler:** Elizabeth II **Subject:** TT Centennial **Obv:** Bust with tiara right **Rev:** Motorcyclists Colier

Date	Mintage	F	VF	XF	Unc	BU
2007PM	—	—	—	—	15.00	17.00

KM# 1394 CROWN
28.2800 g., Copper-Nickel, 38.6 mm. **Ruler:** Elizabeth II **Rev:** Snowman and James

Date	Mintage	F	VF	XF	Unc	BU
2008PM AA	—	—	—	—	—	20.00

KM# 1397 CROWN
0.9250 Silver, 56.2x40 mm. **Ruler:** Elizabeth II **Obv:** Bust with tiara right within Egyptian motif **Rev:** Seated figure and attendant **Shape:** Triangle

Date	Mintage	F	VF	XF	Unc	BU
2008PM Proof	2,500	Value: 75.00				

KM# 1398 CROWN
0.9250 Silver, 56.2x40 mm. **Ruler:** Elizabeth II **Obv:** Bust right in Tiaria within Egyptian motif **Rev:** Statue standing **Shape:** Triangle

Date	Mintage	F	VF	XF	Unc	BU
2008PM Proof	2,500	Value: 75.00				

KM# 1401 CROWN
28.2800 g., 0.9250 Silver 0.8410 oz. ASW, 38.6 mm. **Ruler:** Elizabeth II **Obv:** Bust with tiara right, multicolor band around **Rev:** Seated figures, multicolor band

Date	Mintage	F	VF	XF	Unc	BU
2008PM Proof	—	Value: 65.00				

KM# 1403 CROWN
28.2800 g., Copper-Nickel, 38.6 mm. **Ruler:** Elizabeth II **Subject:** Bejing Olympics **Obv:** Bust with tiara right **Rev:** Torch runner and Great Wall of China

Date	Mintage	F	VF	XF	Unc	BU
2008PM Proof	—	Value: 25.00				

KM# 1404 CROWN
28.2800 g., Copper-Nickel, 38.6 mm. **Ruler:** Elizabeth II **Obv:** Bust wiht tiara right **Rev:** Paddington Bear

Date	Mintage	F	VF	XF	Unc	BU
2008PM Proof	—	Value: 25.00				

KM# 1405 CROWN
31.1030 g., 0.9990 Silver 0.9989 oz. ASW, 56.2x40.7 mm. **Ruler:** Elizabeth II **Obv:** Bust with tiara right **Rev:** Three figures standing, vile of sand above **Shape:** Triangle

Date	Mintage	F	VF	XF	Unc	BU
2008PM Proof	3,000	Value: 75.00				

KM# 1353 CROWN
28.2800 g., Copper-Nickel, 38.6 mm. **Ruler:** Elizabeth II **Subject:** Prince Charles 60th Birthday **Obv:** Bust with tiara right **Obv. Legend:** ELIZABETH II - ISLE OF MAN **Rev:** Heads of Charles, Princes William and Henry right **Edge:** Reeded

Date	Mintage	F	VF	XF	Unc	BU
2008PM	—	—	—	—	10.00	12.00

KM# 1353a CROWN
28.2800 g., 0.9250 Silver 0.8410 oz. ASW, 38.6 mm. **Ruler:** Elizabeth II **Subject:** Prince Charles 60th Birthday **Obv:** Bust with tiara right **Obv. Legend:** ELIZABETH II - ISLE OF MAN **Rev:** Heads of Charles, Princes William and Henry right **Edge:** Reeded

Date	Mintage	F	VF	XF	Unc	BU
2008PM Proof	10,000	Value: 50.00				

KM# 1424 CROWN
28.2800 g., Copper-Nickel, 38.6 mm. **Ruler:** Elizabeth II **Obv:** Bust with tiara right **Rev:** Two cats seated

Date	Mintage	F	VF	XF	Unc	BU
2008PM	—	—	—	—	15.00	17.00

KM# 1424a CROWN
31.1050 g., 0.9990 Silver 0.9990 oz. ASW, 38.6 mm. **Ruler:** Elizabeth II **Obv:** Bust with tiara right **Rev:** Two cats seated

Date	Mintage	F	VF	XF	Unc	BU
2008PM Proof	—	Value: 70.00				

KM# 1373 CROWN
28.2800 g., Copper-Nickel, 38.6 mm. **Ruler:** Elizabeth II **Rev:** Berlin Wall and Brandenburg Gate statue group

Date	Mintage	F	VF	XF	Unc	BU
2009	—	—	—	—	15.00	18.00

KM# 1373a CROWN
28.2800 g., 0.9250 Silver 0.8410 oz. ASW, 38.6 mm. **Ruler:** Elizabeth II **Rev:** Berlin Wall and Brandenberg Gate

Date	Mintage	F	VF	XF	Unc	BU
2009 Proof	10,000	Value: 40.00				

KM# 1374 CROWN
28.2800 g., Copper-Nickel, 38.6 mm. **Ruler:** Elizabeth II **Subject:** Terra Cotta Army **Obv:** Bust right **Rev:** Making of the Soldier

Date	Mintage	F	VF	XF	Unc	BU
2009	—	—	—	—	12.00	15.00

KM# 1374a CROWN
28.2800 g., 0.9250 Silver 0.8410 oz. ASW, 38.6 mm. **Ruler:** Elizabeth II **Subject:** Terra Cotta Army **Obv:** Bust right **Rev:** Making of the Soldier

Date	Mintage	F	VF	XF	Unc	BU
2009 Proof	10,000	Value: 40.00				

KM# 1376 CROWN
28.2800 g., 0.9250 Copper-Nickel 0.8410 oz., 38.6 mm. **Ruler:** Elizabeth II **Subject:** Terra Cotta Army **Obv:** Bust right **Rev:** Making of the Horse

Date	Mintage	F	VF	XF	Unc	BU
2009	—	—	—	—	12.00	15.00

KM# 1376a CROWN
28.2800 g., 0.9250 Silver 0.8410 oz. ASW, 38.6 mm. **Ruler:** Elizabeth II **Subject:** Terra Cotta Army **Obv:** Bust right **Rev:** Making of the Horse

Date	Mintage	F	VF	XF	Unc	BU
2009 Proof	10,000	Value: 40.00				

KM# 1379 CROWN
31.1050 g., 0.9999 Gold 0.9999 oz. AGW, 32.7 mm. **Ruler:** Elizabeth II **Obv:** Bust right **Rev:** Chinchilla cat and kitten

Date	Mintage	F	VF	XF	Unc	BU
2009	—	—	—	—	—	1,800
2009 Proof	1,000	Value: 1,825				

KM# 1388 CROWN
31.1050 g., 0.9999 Gold 0.9999 oz. AGW, 45x31.1 mm. **Ruler:** Elizabeth II **Subject:** Howard Carter, 70th Anniversary of Death **Obv:** Bust right **Rev:** Pharoah and Anubis carving, encased with sand **Shape:** Triangle

Date	Mintage	F	VF	XF	Unc	BU
2009 Proof	250	Value: 1,850				

KM# 1389 CROWN
31.1030 g., 0.9990 Silver 0.9989 oz. ASW, 56.2x40.7 mm. **Ruler:** Elizabeth II **Subject:** Howard Carter, 70th Anniversary of death **Obv:** Bust right **Rev:** Pharoah and Anubis, encased with sand **Shape:** Triangle

Date	Mintage	F	VF	XF	Unc	BU
2009 Proof	3,000	Value: 125				

KM# 1391 CROWN
28.2800 g., Copper-Nickel, 38.6 mm. **Ruler:** Elizabeth II **Obv:** Bust right **Rev:** Henry VIII and portraits of wives

Date	Mintage	F	VF	XF	Unc	BU
2009	—	—	—	—	15.00	18.00

KM# 1391a CROWN
28.2800 g., 0.9250 Silver 0.8410 oz. ASW, 38.6 mm. **Ruler:** Elizabeth II **Obv:** Bust right **Rev:** Henry VIII

Date	Mintage	F	VF	XF	Unc	BU
2009 Proof	10,000	Value: 40.00				

KM# 1392 CROWN
28.2800 g., Copper-Nickel, 38.6 mm. **Ruler:** Elizabeth II **Subject:** FIFA World Cup - South Africa **Obv:** Bust right **Rev:** Two soccer players

Date	Mintage	F	VF	XF	Unc	BU
2009	—	—	—	—	15.00	18.00

KM# 1392a CROWN
28.2800 g., 0.9250 Silver 0.8410 oz. ASW, 38.6 mm. **Ruler:** Elizabeth II **Subject:** FIFA World Cup - South Africa **Obv:** Bust right

Date	Mintage	F	VF	XF	Unc	BU
2009 Proof	10,000	Value: 40.00				

KM# 1378.1 CROWN
28.2800 g., Copper-Nickel, 38.6 mm. **Ruler:** Elizabeth II **Obv:** Bust right **Rev:** Chinchilla cat and kitten

Date	Mintage	F	VF	XF	Unc	BU
2009	—	—	—	—	15.00	18.00

KM# 1378.1a CROWN
31.1050 g., 0.9990 Silver 0.9990 oz. ASW, 38.6 mm. **Ruler:** Elizabeth II **Obv:** Bust with tiara right **Rev:** Two cats

Date	Mintage	F	VF	XF	Unc	BU
2009PM Proof	—	Value: 70.00				

KM# 1378.2 CROWN
28.2800 g., Copper-Nickel, 38.6 mm. **Ruler:** Elizabeth II **Obv:** Bust right **Rev:** Multicolor chinchilla cat and kitten

Date	Mintage	F	VF	XF	Unc	BU
2009	—	—	—	—	—	25.00

KM# 1378.2a CROWN
31.1050 g., 0.9990 Silver 0.9990 oz. ASW, 38.6 mm. **Ruler:** Elizabeth II **Obv:** Bust with tiara right **Rev:** Two cats, multicolor

Date	Mintage	F	VF	XF	Unc	BU
2009PM Proof	—	Value: 80.00				

KM# 1390.1 CROWN
28.2800 g., Copper-Nickel, 38.6 mm. **Ruler:** Elizabeth II **Subject:** Concorde test flight, 40th Anniversary **Obv:** Bust right **Rev:** Concorde and five world landmarks

Date	Mintage	F	VF	XF	Unc	BU
2009	—	—	—	—	15.00	18.00

KM# 1390.1a CROWN
28.2800 g., 0.9250 Silver 0.8410 oz. ASW, 38.6 mm. **Ruler:** Elizabeth II **Subject:** Corcorde test flight, 40th Anniversary **Obv:** Bust right **Rev:** Concorde and five world landmarks

Date	Mintage	F	VF	XF	Unc	BU
2009 Proof	10,000	Value: 40.00				

KM# 1390.2 CROWN
28.2800 g., Copper-Nickel, 38.6 mm. **Ruler:** Elizabeth II **Subject:** 40th Anniversary of test flight **Rev:** Concorde in color

Date	Mintage	F	VF	XF	Unc	BU
2009PM	—	—	—	—	—	25.00

KM# 1406 CROWN
28.2800 g., Copper-Nickel, 38.6 mm. **Ruler:** Elizabeth II **Series:** London Olympics 2012 **Obv:** Bust wiht tiara right **Rev:** Three cyclists before Buckingham Palace

Date	Mintage	F	VF	XF	Unc	BU
2009PM Proof	—	Value: 25.00				

KM# 1406a CROWN
28.2800 g., 0.9250 Silver 0.8410 oz. ASW, 38.6 mm. **Ruler:** Elizabeth II **Series:** Olympics, London **Rev:** Three cyclists speeding past Buckingham Palace

Date	Mintage	F	VF	XF	Unc	BU
2009PM Proof	10,000	Value: 50.00				

KM# 1407 CROWN
28.2800 g., Copper-Nickel, 38.6 mm. **Ruler:** Elizabeth II **Subject:** London Olympics, 2012 **Obv:** Bust with tiara right **Rev:** Rowers before Big Ben and Parliament

Date	Mintage	F	VF	XF	Unc	BU
2009PM Proof	—	Value: 25.00				

KM# 1407a CROWN
28.2800 g., 0.9250 Silver 0.8410 oz. ASW, 38.6 mm. **Ruler:** Elizabeth II **Subject:** Olympics, London **Rev:** Skull of 4 rowers on Thames

Date	Mintage	F	VF	XF	Unc	BU
2009PM Proof	10,000	Value: 50.00				

KM# 1408 CROWN
28.2800 g., Copper-Nickel, 38.6 mm. **Ruler:** Elizabeth II **Subject:** London Olympics, 2012 **Obv:** Bust with tiara right **Rev:** Swimmer before Tower of London

Date	Mintage	F	VF	XF	Unc	BU
2009PM Proof	—	Value: 25.00				

KM# 1408a CROWN
28.2800 g., 0.9250 Silver 0.8410 oz. ASW, 38.6 mm. **Ruler:** Elizabeth II **Subject:** Olympics, London **Rev:** Swimmer in the Thames, Tower of London in background

Date	Mintage	F	VF	XF	Unc	BU
2009PM Proof	10,000	Value: 50.00				

KM# 1409 CROWN
28.2800 g., Copper-Nickel, 38.6 mm. **Ruler:** Elizabeth II **Subject:** London Olympics, 2012 **Obv:** Bust with tiara right **Rev:** Two runners before St. Paul's Cathedral

Date	Mintage	F	VF	XF	Unc	BU
2009PM Proof	—	Value: 25.00				

KM# 1409a CROWN
28.2800 g., 0.9250 Silver 0.8410 oz. ASW, 38.6 mm. **Ruler:** Elizabeth II **Subject:** Olympics, London **Rev:** Two female runners by St. Paul's Cathedral

Date	Mintage	F	VF	XF	Unc	BU
2009PM Proof	10,000	Value: 50.00				

KM# 1410 CROWN
28.2800 g., Copper-Nickel, 38.6 mm. **Ruler:** Elizabeth II **Subject:** London Olympics, 2012 **Obv:** Bust with tiara right **Rev:** Two sailboats before Tower Bridge

Date	Mintage	F	VF	XF	Unc	BU
2009PM Proof	—	Value: 25.00				

KM# 1410a CROWN
28.2800 g., 0.9250 Silver 0.8410 oz. ASW, 38.6 mm. **Ruler:** Elizabeth II **Subject:** Olympics, London **Rev:** Sailing on the Thames, Tower Bridge in background

Date	Mintage	F	VF	XF	Unc	BU
2009PM Proof	10,000	Value: 50.00				

KM# 1411 CROWN
28.2800 g., Copper-Nickel, 38.6 mm. **Ruler:** Elizabeth II **Subject:** London Olympics, 2012 **Obv:** Bust with tiara right **Rev:** Two boxers before London Wheel and skyline

Date	Mintage	F	VF	XF	Unc	BU
2009PM Proof	—	Value: 25.00				

KM# 1411a CROWN
28.2800 g., 0.9250 Silver 0.8410 oz. ASW, 38.6 mm. **Ruler:** Elizabeth II **Subject:** Olympics, London **Rev:** Boxers with London architecture in background

Date	Mintage	F	VF	XF	Unc	BU
2009PM Proof	10,000	Value: 50.00				

KM# 1412 CROWN
28.2800 g., Copper-Nickel, 38.6 mm. **Ruler:** Elizabeth II **Subject:** Vancouver Olympics, 2010 **Obv:** Bust with tiara right **Rev:** Torch at center of four sports, hockey, sled, figure skating and bobsled

Date	Mintage	F	VF	XF	Unc	BU
2009PM Proof	—	Value: 25.00				

KM# 1413 CROWN
28.2800 g., Copper-Nickel, 38.6 mm. **Ruler:** Elizabeth II **Subject:** Vancouver Olympics, 2010 **Obv:** Bust with tiara right **Rev:** Torch at center of four sports, ski jump, snoboardiong, biathlon and Salom

Date	Mintage	F	VF	XF	Unc	BU
2009PM Proof	—	Value: 25.00				

KM# 1414 CROWN
28.2800 g., Copper-Nickel, 38.6 mm. **Ruler:** Elizabeth II **Subject:** Bee Gee's 50th Anniversary **Obv:** Bust with tiara right **Rev:** Band name at center

Date	Mintage	F	VF	XF	Unc	BU
2009PM Proof	—	Value: 25.00				

KM# 1415 CROWN
28.2800 g., Copper-Nickel, 38.6 mm. **Ruler:** Elizabeth II **Subject:** First man on the Moon, 40th Anniversary **Obv:** Bust with tiara right **Rev:** Man in space suit with American Flag on moon

Date	Mintage	F	VF	XF	Unc	BU
2009PM Proof	—	Value: 25.00				

KM# 1465 CROWN
31.1030 g., 0.9999 Gold with sand insert 0.9998 oz. AGW, 45x32.1 mm. **Ruler:** Elizabeth II **Subject:** Howard Carter, 70th Anniversary of Death **Shape:** Triangle

Date	Mintage	F	VF	XF	Unc	BU
2009PM Proof	250	Value: 1,850				

KM# 1417 CROWN
0.9990 Silver **Ruler:** Elizabeth II **Obv:** Bust with tiara right within ornimentation **Rev:** Kubla Kahn standing **Shape:** Vertical rectangle

Date	Mintage	F	VF	XF	Unc	BU
2010PM Proof	—	Value: 50.00				

KM# 1426 CROWN
28.2800 g., Copper-Nickel, 38.6 mm. **Ruler:** Elizabeth II **Obv:** Bust with tiara right **Rev:** Abyssinian Cat standing right over kitten **Edge:** Reeded

Date	Mintage	F	VF	XF	Unc	BU
2010PM	—	—	—	—	15.00	17.00

KM# 1426a CROWN
31.1050 g., 0.9990 Silver 0.9990 oz. ASW, 38.6 mm. **Ruler:** Elizabeth II **Obv:** Bust with tiara right **Rev:** Cat standing right

Date	Mintage	F	VF	XF	Unc	BU
2010PM Proof	—	Value: 70.00				

KM# 1471 CROWN
28.2800 g., Copper-Nickel, 38.6 mm. **Ruler:** Elizabeth II **Obv:** Bust in tiara right **Rev:** Buckingham Palace

Date	Mintage	F	VF	XF	Unc	BU
2010PM	—	—	—	—	—	10.00

KM# 1471a CROWN
28.2800 g., 0.9250 Silver 0.8410 oz. ASW, 38.6 mm. **Ruler:** Elizabeth II **Obv:** Bust in tiara right **Rev:** Buckingham Palace

Date	Mintage	F	VF	XF	Unc	BU
2010PM	—	Value: 50.00				
2010PM	—	Value: 55.00				

Note: Script WK privy mark for engagement

KM# 1439 CROWN
31.1050 g., 0.9999 Gold 0.9999 oz. AGW, 32.7 mm. **Ruler:** Elizabeth II **Subject:** Turkish Angora Cat

Date	Mintage	F	VF	XF	Unc	BU
2011PM	—	—	—	—	—	1,850
2011PM Proof	1,000	Value: 1,875				

KM# 1440 CROWN
28.2800 g., Copper-Nickel, 38.6 mm. **Ruler:** Elizabeth II **Subject:** Turkish Angora Cat

Date	Mintage	F	VF	XF	Unc	BU
2011PM	—	—	—	—	—	10.00

KM# 1440a.1 CROWN
31.1050 g., 0.9990 Silver 0.9990 oz. ASW, 38.6 mm. **Ruler:** Elizabeth II **Subject:** Turkish Angora Cat

Date	Mintage	F	VF	XF	Unc	BU
2011PM Proof	10,000	Value: 70.00				

KM# 1440a.2 CROWN
31.1050 g., 0.9990 Silver 0.9990 oz. ASW, 38.6 mm. **Ruler:** Elizabeth II **Rev:** Two cats in color

Date	Mintage	F	VF	XF	Unc	BU
2011PM	—	—	—	—	—	75.00

KM# 1455 CROWN
28.2800 g., Copper-Nickel, 38.6 mm. **Ruler:** Elizabeth II **Subject:** Isle of Man Tourist Trophy race **Rev:** Two racers and outline map of the Isle of Man

Date	Mintage	F	VF	XF	Unc	BU
2011PM	—	—	—	—	—	10.00

KM# 1455a CROWN
28.2800 g., 0.9250 Silver 0.8410 oz. ASW, 38.6 mm. **Ruler:** Elizabeth II **Subject:** Isle of Man Tourist Trophy race **Rev:** Two racers and map of the Isle of Man

Date	Mintage	F	VF	XF	Unc	BU
2011PM Proof	10,000	Value: 50.00				

KM# 1456 CROWN
31.1030 g., 0.9999 Gold 0.9998 oz. AGW, 32.7 mm. **Ruler:** Elizabeth II **Subject:** Donatello's Chellini Madonna **Rev:** Mary and child in very high relief

Date	Mintage	F	VF	XF	Unc	BU
2011PM Proof	999	Value: 1,850				

KM# 1477 CROWN
28.2800 g., Copper-Nickel, 38.6 mm. **Ruler:** Elizabeth II **Rev:** Busts right of Elizabeth II and Prince Philip, flags flanking, royal shield below

Date	Mintage	F	VF	XF	Unc	BU
2011PM	—	—	—	—	—	10.00

KM# 1477a CROWN

28.2800 g., 0.9250 Silver 0.8410 oz. ASW, 38.6 mm. **Ruler:** Elizabeth II **Rev:** Busts right of Elizabeth II and Prince Philip, flags flanking, royal shield below

Date	Mintage	F	VF	XF	Unc	BU
2011PM Proof	10,000	Value: 50.00				

KM# 1478 CROWN

28.2800 g., Copper-Nickel, 38.6 mm. **Ruler:** Elizabeth II **Subject:** Royal Wedding **Rev:** Busts left of Catherine Middleton in large hat and Prince William

Date	Mintage	F	VF	XF	Unc	BU
2011PM	—	—	—	—	—	10.00

KM# 1478a CROWN

28.2800 g., 0.9250 Silver 0.8410 oz. ASW, 38.6 mm. **Ruler:** Elizabeth II **Subject:** Royal Wedding **Rev:** Busts left of Catherine Middleton in large hat and Prince William

Date	Mintage	F	VF	XF	Unc	BU
2011PM Proof	10,000	Value: 50.00				

KM# 1485 CROWN

28.2800 g., Copper-Nickel, 38.6 mm. **Ruler:** Elizabeth II **Subject:** Year of the Rabbit **Rev:** Image of Beatrix Potter's Peter Rabbit

Date	Mintage	F	VF	XF	Unc	BU
2011PM	—	—	—	—	—	10.00

KM# 1485a CROWN

28.2800 g., 0.9250 Silver 0.8410 oz. ASW, 38.6 mm. **Ruler:** Elizabeth II **Subject:** Year of the Rabbit **Rev:** Beatrix Potter's Peter Rabbit

Date	Mintage	F	VF	XF	Unc	BU
2011PM Proof	10,000	Value: 50.00				

KM# 1442 CROWN

28.2800 g., Copper-Nickel, 38.6 mm. **Ruler:** Elizabeth II **Subject:** Olympics, London **Rev:** Track cyclist

Date	Mintage	F	VF	XF	Unc	BU
2012PM	—	—	—	—	—	10.00

KM# 1441 CROWN

28.2800 g., Copper-Nickel, 38.6 mm. **Ruler:** Elizabeth II **Subject:** Olympics, London **Rev:** Horse Jumping

Date	Mintage	F	VF	XF	Unc	BU
2012PM	—	—	—	—	—	10.00

KM# 1441a CROWN

28.2800 g., 0.9250 Silver 0.8410 oz. ASW, 38.6 mm. **Ruler:** Elizabeth II **Subject:** Olympics, London **Rev:** Horse jumping

Date	Mintage	F	VF	XF	Unc	BU
2012PM Proof	10,000	Value: 50.00				

KM# 1442a CROWN

28.2800 g., 0.9250 Silver 0.8410 oz. ASW, 38.6 mm. **Ruler:** Elizabeth II **Subject:** Olympics, London **Rev:** Track Cyclist

Date	Mintage	F	VF	XF	Unc	BU
2012PM Proof	10,000	Value: 50.00				

KM# 1443 CROWN

28.2800 g., Copper-Nickel, 38.6 mm. **Ruler:** Elizabeth II **Subject:** Olympics, London **Rev:** Swimmer with divers in background

Date	Mintage	F	VF	XF	Unc	BU
2012PM	—	—	—	—	—	10.00

KM# 1443a CROWN

28.2800 g., 0.9250 Silver 0.8410 oz. ASW, 38.6 mm. **Ruler:** Elizabeth II **Subject:** Olympics, London **Rev:** Swimmer, divers in background

Date	Mintage	F	VF	XF	Unc	BU
2012PM Proof	10,000	Value: 50.00				

KM# 1444 CROWN

28.2800 g., Copper-Nickel, 38.6 mm. **Ruler:** Elizabeth II **Subject:** Olympics, London **Rev:** Canoeist, two rowers in background

Date	Mintage	F	VF	XF	Unc	BU
2012PM	—	—	—	—	—	10.00

KM# 1444a CROWN

28.2800 g., 0.9250 Silver 0.8410 oz. ASW, 38.6 mm. **Ruler:** Elizabeth II **Subject:** Olympics, London **Rev:** Canoeist, two rowers in background

Date	Mintage	F	VF	XF	Unc	BU
2012PM Proof	10,000	Value: 50.00				

KM# 1445 CROWN

28.2800 g., Copper-Nickel, 38.6 mm. **Ruler:** Elizabeth II **Subject:** Olympics, London **Rev:** Judo players, two boxers in background

Date	Mintage	F	VF	XF	Unc	BU
2012PM	—	—	—	—	—	10.00

KM# 1445a CROWN

28.2800 g., 0.9250 Silver 0.8410 oz. ASW, 38.6 mm. **Ruler:** Elizabeth II **Subject:** Olympics, London **Rev:** Judo players, two boxers in background

Date	Mintage	F	VF	XF	Unc	BU
2012PM Proof	10,000	Value: 50.00				

KM# 1446 CROWN

28.2800 g., Copper-Nickel, 38.6 mm. **Ruler:** Elizabeth II **Subject:** Olympics, London **Rev:** Table tennis players, Lawn Tennis players in background

Date	Mintage	F	VF	XF	Unc	BU
2012PM	—	—	—	—	—	10.00

KM# 1446a CROWN

28.2800 g., 0.9250 Silver 0.8410 oz. ASW, 38.6 mm. **Ruler:** Elizabeth II **Subject:** Olympics, London **Rev:** Table tennis players, Lawn tennis players in background

Date	Mintage	F	VF	XF	Unc	BU
2012PM Proof	10,000	Value: 50.00				

KM# 1461 CROWN

28.2800 g., Copper-Nickel, 38.6 mm. **Ruler:** Elizabeth II **Subject:** European Football Championships 2012 **Obv:** Player heading a football, Sitting Statue of Liberty in Lviv and Neptune's fountain in Gdansk in background

Date	Mintage	F	VF	XF	Unc	BU
2012PM	—	—	—	—	—	10.00

KM# 1461a CROWN

28.2800 g., 0.9250 Silver 0.8410 oz. ASW, 38.6 mm. **Ruler:** Elizabeth II **Subject:** European Football Championships 2012 **Rev:** Footballer heading ball, Sitting Statue of Liberty in Lviv and Neptune's fountain in Gdansk in background

Date	Mintage	F	VF	XF	Unc	BU
2012PM Proof	10,000	Value: 50.00				

KM# 1462 CROWN

28.2800 g., Copper-Nickel, 38.6 mm. **Ruler:** Elizabeth II **Subject:** European Football Championships 2012 **Rev:** Player passing ball, Motherland Statue in Kiev and King Sigismund's statue in Warsaw

Date	Mintage	F	VF	XF	Unc	BU
2012PM	—	—	—	—	—	10.00

KM# 1462a CROWN

28.2800 g., 0.9250 Silver 0.8410 oz. ASW, 38.6 mm. **Ruler:** Elizabeth II **Subject:** European Football Championships 2012 **Rev:** Player passing the ball, Motherland Statue in Kiev and King Sigismund's statue in Warsaw in background

Date	Mintage	F	VF	XF	Unc	BU
2012PM Proof	10,000	Value: 50.00				

KM# 1463 CROWN

28.2800 g., Copper-Nickel, 38.6 mm. **Ruler:** Elizabeth II **Subject:** European Football Championships 2012 **Rev:** Footballer shooting, Cathedral of the Transfiguration in Donetsk and the Raclawice Panorama in Wroclaw in background

Date	Mintage	F	VF	XF	Unc	BU
2012PM	—	—	—	—	—	10.00

KM# 1463a CROWN

28.2800 g., 0.9250 Silver 0.8410 oz. ASW, 38.6 mm. **Ruler:** Elizabeth II **Subject:** European Football Championships 2012 **Rev:** Footballer shooting, Cathedral of the Transfiguration in Donetsk and the Raclawice Panorama in Wroclaw in background

Date	Mintage	F	VF	XF	Unc	BU
2012PM Proof	10,000	Value: 50.00				

KM# 1464 CROWN

28.2800 g., Copper-Nickel, 38.6 mm. **Ruler:** Elizabeth II **Subject:** European Football Championships 2012 **Rev:** Two footballers tackling, Cathedral of the Annunciation in Kharkiv and the Cathedral in Poznan in background

Date	Mintage	F	VF	XF	Unc	BU
2012PM	—	—	—	—	—	10.00

KM# 1464a CROWN

28.2800 g., 0.9250 Silver 0.8410 oz. ASW, 38.6 mm. **Ruler:** Elizabeth II **Subject:** European Football Championships 2012 **Rev:** Two footballers tackling, Catheral of the annunciation in Kharkiv and the Cathedral in Poznan in background

Date	Mintage	F	VF	XF	Unc	BU
2012PM Proof	10,000	Value: 50.00				

KM# 1480 CROWN

28.2800 g., Copper-Nickel, 38.6 mm. **Ruler:** Elizabeth II **Obv:** Conjoined busts right **Rev:** Elizabeth II at coronation with scepter, orb and state crown

Date	Mintage	F	VF	XF	Unc	BU
2012PM	—	—	—	—	—	10.00

KM# 1480a CROWN

28.2800 g., 0.9250 Silver 0.8410 oz. ASW, 38.6 mm. **Ruler:** Elizabeth II **Obv:** Conjoined busts right **Rev:** Elizabeth II at coronation with sceptre, orb and state crown

Date	Mintage	F	VF	XF	Unc	BU
2012PM Proof	10,000	Value: 50.00				

KM# 1481 CROWN

28.2800 g., Copper-Nickel, 38.6 mm. **Ruler:** Elizabeth II **Obv:** Conjoined busts right **Rev:** Elizabeth II during 2010 visit to Canada

Date	Mintage	F	VF	XF	Unc	BU
2012PM	—	—	—	—	—	10.00

KM# 1481a CROWN

28.2800 g., 0.9250 Silver 0.8410 oz. ASW, 38.6 mm. **Ruler:** Elizabeth II **Obv:** Conjoined busts right **Rev:** Elizabeth, the Queen Mother

Date	Mintage	F	VF	XF	Unc	BU
2012PM Proof	10,000	Value: 50.00				

KM# 1482 CROWN

28.2800 g., Copper-Nickel, 38.6 mm. **Ruler:** Elizabeth II **Obv:** Conjoined busts right **Rev:** Passengers boarding Titanic

Date	Mintage	F	VF	XF	Unc	BU
2012PM	—	—	—	—	—	10.00

KM# 1482a CROWN

28.2800 g., 0.9250 Silver 0.8410 oz. ASW, 38.6 mm. **Ruler:** Elizabeth II **Obv:** Conjoined busts right **Rev:** Passengers boarding Titanic

Date	Mintage	F	VF	XF	Unc	BU
2012PM Proof	10,000	Value: 55.00				

KM# 1483 CROWN

28.2800 g., Copper-Nickel, 38.6 mm. **Ruler:** Elizabeth II **Obv:** Conjoined busts right **Rev:** Titanic sailing into icefield

Date	Mintage	F	VF	XF	Unc	BU
2012PM	—	—	—	—	—	10.00

KM# 1483a CROWN

28.2800 g., 0.9250 Silver 0.8410 oz. ASW, 38.6 mm. **Ruler:** Elizabeth II **Obv:** Conjoined busts right **Rev:** Titanic sailing into icefield

Date	Mintage	F	VF	XF	Unc	BU
2012PM Proof	10,000	Value: 50.00				

KM# 1200 2 CROWNS

62.2000 g., 0.9990 Palladium 1.9977 oz., 40 mm. **Ruler:** Elizabeth II **Subject:** Discovery of Palladium Bicentennial **Obv:** Bust with tiara right **Rev:** Pallas Athena left **Edge:** Reeded

Date	Mintage	F	VF	XF	Unc	BU
2004PM Proof	300	Value: 1,650				

KM# 1402 2 CROWNS

0.9250 Silver, 40 mm. **Ruler:** Elizabeth II **Obv:** Bust with tiara right **Rev:** Seven Wonders of the World, multicolor central item

Date	Mintage	F	VF	XF	Unc	BU
2008PM Proof	—	Value: 100				

KM# 1064 5 CROWN

155.5175 g., 0.9999 Gold 4.9993 oz. AGW, 65 mm. **Ruler:** Elizabeth II **Subject:** Year of the Snake **Obv:** Bust with tiara right **Rev:** Snake **Edge:** Reeded

Date	Mintage	F	VF	XF	Unc	BU
2001 Proof	250	Value: 9,500				

KM# 1104 5 CROWN

155.5100 g., 0.9999 Gold 4.9991 oz. AGW, 65 mm. **Ruler:** Elizabeth II **Subject:** Year of the Horse **Obv:** Bust with tiara right **Rev:** Two horses **Edge:** Reeded

Date	Mintage	F	VF	XF	Unc	BU
2002 Proof	250	Value: 9,500				

KM# 1173 5 CROWN

155.5100 g., 0.9999 Gold 4.9991 oz. AGW, 65 mm. **Ruler:** Elizabeth II **Subject:** Year of the Goat **Obv:** Bust with tiara right **Rev:** Three goats **Edge:** Reeded

Date	Mintage	F	VF	XF	Unc	BU
2003PM Proof	250	Value: 9,500				

KM# 1244 5 CROWN

155.5175 g., 0.9999 Gold 4.9993 oz. AGW, 65 mm. **Ruler:** Elizabeth II **Obv:** Bust with tiara right **Rev:** Monkey **Edge:** Reeded

Date	Mintage	F	VF	XF	Unc	BU
2004PM Proof	250	Value: 9,500				

KM# 1219 64 CROWNS

2000.0000 g., 0.9990 Silver 64.234 oz. ASW, 140 mm. **Ruler:** Elizabeth II **Obv:** Bust with tiara right **Rev:** Ocean Liner Queen Mary 2 **Edge:** Reeded

Date	Mintage	F	VF	XF	Unc	BU
2004PM Proof	500	Value: 2,350				

KM# 1142 100 CROWNS

3000.0000 g., 0.9999 Silver 96.438 oz. ASW, 130 mm. **Ruler:** Elizabeth II **Subject:** Queen's Golden Jubilee **Obv:** Bust with tiara right **Rev:** Queen on horse **Edge:** Reeded **Note:** Illustration reduced.

Date	Mintage	F	VF	XF	Unc	BU
2002 Proof	500	Value: 3,500				

KM# 1184 130 CROWNS
4000.0000 g., 0.9990 Silver 128.46 oz. ASW, 130 mm. **Ruler:** Elizabeth II **Obv:** Bust with tiara right **Rev:** Gold clad cameo portrait of Elizabeth I with a .035ct ruby inset on her forehead all within a circle of portraits **Edge:** Reeded

Date	Mintage	F	VF	XF	Unc	BU
2003PM Proof	500	Value: 4,700				

SILVER BULLION COINAGE
Angel Series

KM# 1475 ANGEL
31.1050 g., 0.9990 Silver 0.9990 oz. ASW **Ruler:** Elizabeth II **Subject:** 15th Anniversary of the Angel **Obv:** Bust in tiara right **Rev:** St. Michael slaying dragon

Date	Mintage	F	VF	XF	Unc	BU
2010PM Proof	—	Value: 50.00				

Note: Privy mark: 15

SILVER BULLION COINAGE
Nobel Series

KM# 1484 NOBLE
31.1050 g., 0.9999 Silver 0.9999 oz. ASW, 38.6 mm. **Ruler:** Elizabeth II **Obv:** Bust with tiara right **Rev:** Viking ship

Date	Mintage	F	VF	XF	Unc	BU
2011PM Prooflike	—	—	—	—	—	50.00

GOLD BULLION COINAGE
Angel Issues

KM# 1479 1/64 ANGEL
0.4860 g., 0.9999 Gold 0.0156 oz. AGW **Ruler:** Elizabeth II **Rev:** St. Michael slaying dragon

Date	Mintage	F	VF	XF	Unc	BU
2011PM Proof	—	Value: 50.00				

Note: Privy mark: Wedding bells and date

KM# 1106 1/20 ANGEL
1.5552 g., 0.9999 Gold 0.0500 oz. AGW, 18 mm. **Ruler:** Elizabeth II **Obv:** Bust with tiara right **Rev:** St. Michael slaying dragon, three crown privy mark at right **Edge:** Reeded

Date	Mintage	F	VF	XF	Unc	BU
2001 (3c) Proof	1,000	Value: 95.00				
2002 Proof	—	Value: 95.00				

Note: With candy cane privy mark

KM# 393 1/20 ANGEL
1.5551 g., 0.9999 Gold 0.0500 oz. AGW, 18 mm. **Ruler:** Elizabeth II **Obv:** Crowned bust right **Rev:** Archangel Michael slaying dragon right

Date	Mintage	F	VF	XF	Unc	BU
2001	—	—	—	—	—	90.00
2001 Proof	—	Value: 90.00				
2001 Proof	—	Value: 95.00				

Note: Privy mark: 3 Kings

Date	Mintage	F	VF	XF	Unc	BU
2002	—	—	—	—	—	90.00
2002 Proof	—	Value: 90.00				
2002 Proof	—	Value: 95.00				

Note: Privy mark: Candy cane

Date	Mintage	F	VF	XF	Unc	BU
2003	—	—	—	—	—	90.00
2003 Proof	—	Value: 90.00				
2003 Proof	—	Value: 95.00				

Note: Privy mark: Candy

Date	Mintage	F	VF	XF	Unc	BU
2004	—	—	—	—	—	90.00
2004 Proof	—	Value: 90.00				
2004 Proof	—	Value: 95.00				

Note: Privy mark: Partridge in a Pear Tree

Date	Mintage	F	VF	XF	Unc	BU
2005	—	—	—	—	—	90.00
2005 Proof	—	Value: 90.00				
2005 Proof	—	Value: 95.00				

Note: Privy mark: 2 Turtle doves

Date	Mintage	F	VF	XF	Unc	BU
2006	—	—	—	—	—	90.00
2006 Proof	—	Value: 90.00				
2006 Proof	—	Value: 95.00				

Note: Privy mark: 3 French hens

Date	Mintage	F	VF	XF	Unc	BU
2007	—	—	—	—	—	90.00
2007 Proof	—	Value: 90.00				
2007 Proof	—	Value: 95.00				

Note: Privy mark: 4 Calling birds

KM# 1252 1/20 ANGEL
1.5550 g., 0.9999 Gold 0.0500 oz. AGW, 18 mm. **Ruler:** Elizabeth II **Obv:** Bust with tiara right **Rev:** St. Michael and Christmas privy mark **Edge:** Reeded

Date	Mintage	F	VF	XF	Unc	BU
2004PM Proof	1,000	Value: 95.00				

KM# 1430 1/20 ANGEL
1.5500 g., 0.9999 Gold 0.0498 oz. AGW, 18 mm. **Ruler:** Elizabeth II **Rev:** St. Michael slaying the dragon

Date	Mintage	F	VF	XF	Unc	BU
2009PM Six Geese a laying privy mark Proof	1,000	Value: 125				
2010PM Seven swans a swimming privy mark Proof	1,000	Value: 125				
2011PM Eight maids a milking privy mark Proof	1,000	Value: 125				

KM# 394 1/10 ANGEL
3.1103 g., 0.9999 Gold 0.1000 oz. AGW, 23 mm. **Ruler:** Elizabeth II **Obv:** Crowned bust right **Rev:** Archangel Michael

Date	Mintage	F	VF	XF	Unc	BU
2001	—	—	—	—	—	175
2001 Proof	—	Value: 180				
2002	—	—	—	—	—	175
2002 Proof	—	Value: 180				
2003	—	—	—	—	—	175
2003 Proof	—	Value: 180				
2004	—	—	—	—	—	175
2004 Proof	—	Value: 180				
2005	—	—	—	—	—	175
2005 Proof	—	Value: 180				

KM# 395 1/4 ANGEL
7.7758 g., 0.9999 Gold 0.2500 oz. AGW **Ruler:** Elizabeth II **Obv:** Crowned bust right **Rev:** Archangel Michael slaying dragon

Date	Mintage	F	VF	XF	Unc	BU
2001	—	—	—	—	—	450
2001 Proof	—	Value: 455				
2002	—	—	—	—	—	450
2002 Proof	—	Value: 455				
2003	—	—	—	—	—	450
2003 Proof	—	Value: 455				
2004	—	—	—	—	—	450
2004 Proof	—	Value: 455				
2005	—	—	—	—	—	450
2005 Proof	—	Value: 455				

KM# 397 ANGEL
31.1035 g., 0.9999 Gold 0.9999 oz. AGW **Ruler:** Elizabeth II **Obv:** Crowned bust right **Rev:** Archangel Michael slaying dragon right

Date	Mintage	F	VF	XF	Unc	BU
2001	—	—	—	—	—	1,725
2001 Proof	—	Value: 1,750				
2002	—	—	—	—	—	1,725
2002 Proof	—	Value: 1,750				
2003	—	—	—	—	—	1,725
2003 Proof	—	Value: 1,750				
2004	—	—	—	—	—	1,725
2004 Proof	—	Value: 1,750				
2005	—	—	—	—	—	1,725
2005 Proof	—	Value: 1,750				
2006	—	—	—	—	—	1,725
2006 Proof	500	Value: 1,750				
2007	—	—	—	—	—	1,725
2007 Proof	—	Value: 1,750				

KM# 397.1 ANGEL
31.1035 g., 0.9990 Gold 0.9990 oz. AGW **Ruler:** Elizabeth II **Obv:** Crowned bust right **Rev:** Archangel Michael slaying dragon right

Date	Mintage	F	VF	XF	Unc	BU
2006 Proof, High Relief	Est. 1,000	Value: 1,725				
2007 Proof, High Relief	Est. 1,000	Value: 1,725				

KM# 1466 ANGEL
31.1050 g., 0.9999 Gold 0.9999 oz. AGW, 33 mm. **Ruler:** Elizabeth II **Obv:** Bust in tiara right **Rev:** St. Michael slaying dragon

Date	Mintage	F	VF	XF	Unc	BU
2008PM	—	—	—	—	—	1,850
2008PM Proof	—	Value: 1,875				

KM# 1467 ANGEL
31.1050 g., 0.9999 Gold 0.9999 oz. AGW, 33 mm. **Ruler:** Elizabeth II **Obv:** Bust with tiara right **Rev:** St. Michael lunging right with spear

Date	Mintage	F	VF	XF	Unc	BU
2009PM Proof	—	Value: 1,875				

KM# 1468 ANGEL
31.1050 g., 0.9999 Gold 0.9999 oz. AGW, 33 mm. **Ruler:** Elizabeth II **Obv:** Bust with tiara right **Rev:** Dragon receiving spear wound

Date	Mintage	F	VF	XF	Unc	BU
2009PM Proof	—	Value: 1,875				

BI-METALLIC BULLION COINAGE

KM# 1486 NOBLE

39.1000 g., Bi-Metallic 31.105 .999 Gold center in 9.39 .999 Silver ring, 36.7 mm. **Ruler:** Elizabeth II **Rev:** Viking ship, 15 in left field

Date	Mintage	F	VF	XF	Unc	BU
2009PM Proof	3,000	Value: 1,900				

MINT SETS

KM#	Date	Mintage	Identification	Issue Price	Mkt Val
MS30	2001 (8)	—	KM#1036-1043	—	22.50
MS31	2001 (9)	—	KM#1036-1044	—	40.00
MS32	2002 (8)	—	KM#1036-1043	—	22.50
MS33	2002 (9)	—	KM#1036-1044	—	40.00
MS34	2003 (8)	—	KM#1036-1043	—	22.50
MS35	2003 (9)	—	KM#1036-1044	—	40.00
MS36	2004 (8)	—	KM#1253-1260	—	25.00
MS37	2004 (9)	—	KM#1253-1261	—	40.00
MS38	2005 (8)	—	KM#1253-1260	—	22.50
MS39	2005 (9)	—	KM#1253-1261	—	40.00
MS40	2006 (8)	—	MS#1253-1260	35.00	25.00
MS41	2006 (9)	—	KM1253-1261	42.50	40.00
MS42	2007 (8)	—	KM#1253-1260	35.00	22.50
MS43	2007 (9)	—	KM1253-1261	42.50	40.00

PROOF SETS

KM#	Date	Mintage	Identification	Issue Price	Mkt Val
PS59	2001 (5)	1,000	KM#1067-1070, 1073	—	3,350
PS60	2003 (3)	—	KM#1186, 1187, 1188	—	650
PS61	2003 (5)	—	KM#1186, 1187, 1188, 1189, 1190 w/gold ring	—	3,300
PS62	2003 (5)	—	KM#1191-1195 w/gold-plated silver ring	—	245
PS63	2004 (5)	1,000	KM#1247, 1248, 1249.1, 1250, 1251	—	3,375

ISRAEL

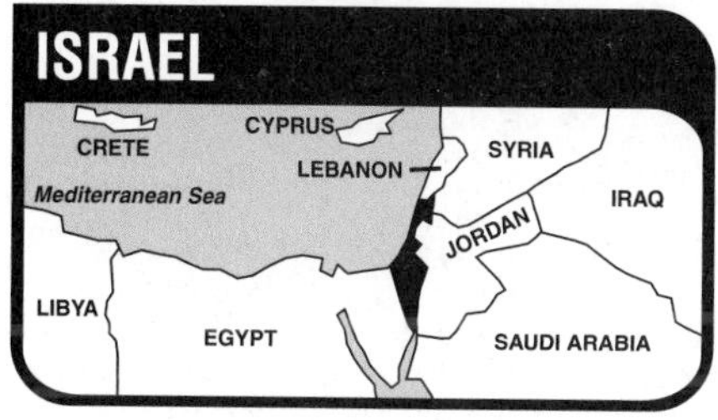

The state of Israel, a Middle Eastern republic at the eastern end of the Mediterranean Sea, bounded by Lebanon on the north, Syria on the northeast, Jordan on the east, and Egypt on the southwest, has an area of 9,000sq. mi. (20,770 sq. km.) and a population of 6 million. Capital: Jerusalem. Finished diamonds, chemicals, citrus, textiles, minerals, electronic and transportation equipment are exported.

HEBREW COIN DATING

Israeli coins are dated according to the Christian year (AD). The JE New Year falls in September or during the first few days of October. In the case of dual-dated coins, with some exceptions, the JE date is 3,760 years greater than the AD date. Thus, for example, JE5735 is equivalent to AD1975. Exceptions are almost all of the Hanukka (Festival of Lights) commemorative coins because Hanukka falls early in the JE year and late in the AD year (late November or December) and certain other commemorative coins issued early in the JE year. In the case of the dual-dated Hanukka coins (other than the JE5720 coin) and certain others, the difference is 3,761 years. However, for ease of reference, except in the case of such dual-dated coins, the AD date given is always 3,760 years greater than the JE date (including the Hanukka coins bearing only a JE date). In the case of Hanukka mint sets, however, where the packaging gives an AD date that differs from the JE date by 3,761 years, the AD date on the packaging is indicated by the issued date in brackets.

Israel's coins carry Hebrew dating formed from a combination of the 22 consonant letters of the Hebrew alphabet and read from right to left. The Jewish calendar dates back more than 5700 years; but five millenniums are assumed in the dating of coins (until 1981). Thus, the year 5735 (1975AD) appears as 735, with the first two characters from the right indicating the number of years in hundreds; tav (400), plus shin (300). The next is lamedh (30), followed by a separation mark which has the appearance of double quotation marks, then heh (5).

The separation mark - generally similar to a single quotation mark through 5718 (1958 AD), and like a double quotation mark thereafter - serves the purpose of indicating that the letters form a number, not a word, and on some issues can be confused with the character yodh (10), which in a stylized rendering can appear similar, although slightly larger and thicker. The separation mark does not appear in either form on a few commemorative issues.

The Star of David is not a mintmark. It appears only on some coins sold by the Israel Government Coins and Medals Corporation Ltd., which is owned by the Israel government, and is a division of the Prime Minister's office and sole distributor to collectors. The Star of David was first used in 1971 on the science coin to signify that it was minted in Jerusalem, but was later used by different mint facilities.

AD Date		Jewish Era
2001	התשס"א	5761
2002	התשס"ב	5762
2003	התשס"ג	5763
2004	התשס"ד	5764
2005	התשס"ה	5765
2006	התשס"ו	5766
2007	התשס"ז	5767
2008	התשס"ח	5768
2009	התשס"ט	5769
2010	התש"ע	5770
2011	התשע"א	5771
2012	התשע"ב	5772
2013	התשע"ג	5773
2014	התשע"ד	5774
2015	התשע"ה	5775

MINT MARKS

(a) -	Athens
(b) -	Berne (Swiss mint)
(bp) -	Budapest
(c) -	Canberra (Royal Australian mint)
(d) -	Munich
(dg) -	Daejeon (Korea; KOMSCO)
(f) -	Stuttgart
H, (ht) -	Heaton (Birmingham)
(h) -	Kongsberg (Norway)
(hn) -	Holon (location of machine shop in which Israel's first coins were minted)
(i) -	Imperial Chemical Industries (Great Britain)
(ig) -	Israel Government Coins and Medals Corp.
(j) -	Jerusalem
(k) -	Kretschmer (private mint in Jerusalem)
(ld)	Tower Mint, England
(m) -	Madrid
(o) -	Ottawa
(p) -	Paris
(r) -	Rome
(s) -	San Francisco
(sa) -	Pretoria (South African mint)
(sg) -	Singapore
(sl) -	Seoul
(so) -	Santiago
(t) -	Tel Aviv
(u) -	Utrecht (Netherlands)
(v) -	Vantaa (Finland)
(va) -	Vienna
(w) -	Warsaw
(wg) -	Winnipeg

NOTE:

All proof commemoratives with the exception of the 1 and 5 Lirot issues of 1958 are distinguished from the uncirculated editions by the presence fo the Hebrew letter "mem".

REPUBLIC

REFORM COINAGE

100 Agorot = 1 New Sheqel
1,000 Sheqalim = 1 New Sheqel; September 4, 1985-present

KM# 157 5 AGOROT

3.0000 g., Aluminum-Bronze, 19.5 mm. **Obv:** Ancient coin **Rev:** Value within lined square **Edge:** Plain

Date	Mintage	F	VF	XF	Unc	BU
JE5761 (2001)(dj)	6,144,000	—	—	—	0.15	—
JE5762 (2002)(dj)	6,144,000	—	—	—	0.15	—
JE5764 (2004)	—	—	—	—	0.15	—
JE5765 (2005)	—	—	—	—	0.15	—
JE5766 (2006)	—	—	—	—	0.15	—
JE5767 (2007)	—	—	—	—	0.15	—

KM# 172 5 AGOROT

3.0000 g., Aluminum-Bronze, 19.5 mm. **Subject:** Hanukka **Obv:** Ancient coin **Rev:** Value within lined square **Note:** JE5754-5768 coins contain the Star of David mint mark; the JE5747-5753 coins do not.

Date	Mintage	F	VF	XF	Unc	BU
JE5761 (2001)(u) In sets only	4,000	—	—	—	2.50	—
JE5762 (2002)(u) In sets only	4,000	—	—	—	2.50	—
JE5763 (2003)(u) In sets only	3,000	—	—	—	3.00	—
JE5764 (2004)(u) In sets only	3,000	—	—	—	3.00	—
JE5765 (2005)(u) In sets only	2,500	—	—	—	3.00	—
JE5766 (2006)(u) In sets only	3,000	—	—	—	3.00	—
JE5767 (2007)(u) In sets only	3,000	—	—	—	3.00	—
JE5768 (2008)(u) In sets only	3,000	—	—	—	3.00	—

KM# 158 10 AGOROT

4.0000 g., Aluminum-Bronze, 22 mm. **Obv:** Menorah **Rev:** Value within lined square **Edge:** Plain

Date	Mintage	F	VF	XF	Unc	BU
JE5761 (2001)(dj)	46,140,000	—	—	—	0.20	—
Note: Sides of central part of zero are rounded.						
JE5761 (2001)(so)	32,256,000	—	—	—	0.20	—
Note: Sides of central part of zero are straight.						
JE5762 (2002)(w)	4,608,000	—	—	—	0.20	—
JE5763 (2003)(dj)	22,980,000	—	—	—	0.20	—
JE5764 (2004)	—	—	—	—	0.20	—
JE5765 (2005)	—	—	—	—	0.20	—
JE5766 (2006)	—	—	—	—	0.20	—
JE5767 (2007)(dj)	—	—	—	—	0.20	—
JE5768 (2008)(dj)	—	—	—	—	0.20	—
JE5769 (2009)(dj)	—	—	—	—	0.20	—
JE5770 (2010)(dj)	—	—	—	—	0.20	—
JE5771 (2011)(dj)	—	—	—	—	0.20	—
JE5772 (2012)(dj)	—	—	—	—	0.20	—

KM# 173 10 AGOROT

4.0000 g., Aluminum-Bronze, 22 mm. **Subject:** Hanukka **Obv:** Menorah **Rev:** Value within lined square **Edge:** Plain **Note:** JE5754-5770 have the Star of David mint mark, JE5747-5753 coins do not.

Date	Mintage	F	VF	XF	Unc	BU
JE5761 (2001)(u) In sets only	4,000	—	—	—	3.00	—
JE5762 (2002)(u) In sets only	4,000	—	—	—	3.00	—
JE5763 (2003)(u) In sets only	3,000	—	—	—	3.00	—
JE5764 (2004)(u) In sets only	3,000	—	—	—	3.00	—
JE5765 (2005)(u) In sets only	2,500	—	—	—	3.00	—
JE5766 (2006)(u) In sets only	3,000	—	—	—	3.00	—
JE5767 (2007)(u) In sets only	3,000	—	—	—	3.00	—
JE5768 (2008)(u) In sets only	3,000	—	—	—	3.00	—
JE5769 (2009)(u) In sets only	1,800	—	—	—	3.50	—
JE5770 (2010)(u) In sets only	1,800	—	—	—	3.50	—

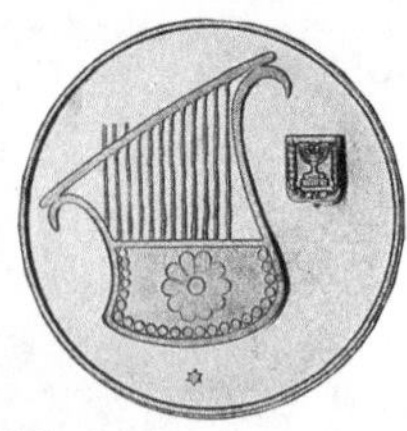

KM# 174 1/2 NEW SHEQEL

6.5000 g., Aluminum-Bronze, 26 mm. **Subject:** Hanukka **Obv:** Value **Rev:** Lyre **Note:** Coins dated JE5754-5770 have the Star of David mint mark; the coins dated JE5747-5753 do not.

Date	Mintage	F	VF	XF	Unc	BU
JE5761 (2001)(u)	4,000	—	—	—	3.50	—
In sets only						
JE5762 (2002)(u)	4,000	—	—	—	3.50	—
In sets only						
JE5763 (2003)(u)	3,000	—	—	—	3.50	—
In sets only						
JE5764 (2004)(u)	3,000	—	—	—	3.50	—
In sets only						
JE5765 (2005)(u)	2,500	—	—	—	3.50	—
In sets only						
JE5766 (2006)(u)	3,000	—	—	—	3.50	—
In sets only						
JE5767 (2007)(u)	3,000	—	—	—	3.50	—
In sets only						
JE5768 (2008)(u)	3,000	—	—	—	3.50	—
In sets only						
JE5769 (2009)(u)	1,800	—	—	—	3.50	—
In sets only						
JE5770 (2010)(u)	1,800	—	—	—	3.50	—
In sets only						

KM# 354 1/2 NEW SHEQEL

6.5000 g., Aluminum-Bronze, 26 mm. **Subject:** Hanukka **Obv:** Denomination **Rev:** Curacao Hanukka lamp **Edge:** Plain **Shape:** 12-sided **Note:** Struck for sets only

Date	Mintage	F	VF	XF	Unc	BU
JE5761 (2001)(u)	4,000	—	—	—	11.00	—

KM# 159 1/2 NEW SHEQEL

6.5000 g., Aluminum-Bronze, 26 mm. **Obv:** Value **Rev:** Lyre **Edge:** Plain

Date	Mintage	F	VF	XF	Unc	BU
JE5762 (2002)(so)	2,880,000	—	—	—	0.75	—
JE5762 (2002)(v)	5,760,000	—	—	—	0.75	—
Note: Length of fraction line is 4 or 4.5 mm. but which mint produced which coin is not known.						
JE5763 (2003)	—	—	—	—	0.75	—
JE5764 (2004)(so)	2,640,000	—	—	—	0.75	—
JE5765 (2005)	—	—	—	—	0.75	—
JE5766 (2006)	—	—	—	—	0.75	—
JE5767 (2007)	—	—	—	—	0.75	—
JE5768 (2008)(dj)	—	—	—	—	0.75	—
JE5769 (2009)(dj)	—	—	—	—	0.60	—
JE5770 (2010)(dj)	—	—	—	—	0.60	—
JE5771 (2011)(v)	—	—	—	—	0.60	—
JE5772(dj)	—	—	—	—	0.50	—

KM# 355 1/2 NEW SHEQEL

6.5000 g., Aluminum-Bronze, 26 mm. **Obv:** Value **Rev:** Yemenite Hanukka Lamp **Edge:** Twelve plain sections **Note:** Struck for sets only

Date	Mintage	F	VF	XF	Unc	BU
JE5762 (2002)(u)	4,000	—	—	—	11.00	—

KM# 389 1/2 NEW SHEQEL

6.5000 g., Aluminum-Bronze, 26 mm. **Obv:** Value **Rev:** Polish Hanukka Lamp **Edge:** Plain **Shape:** 12-sided **Note:** Struck for sets only

Date	Mintage	F	VF	XF	Unc	BU
JE5763 (2003)(u)	3,000	—	—	—	12.00	—
Note: Even though not a proof, the coin has a mem						

KM# 390 1/2 NEW SHEQEL

6.5000 g., Aluminum-Bronze, 26 mm. **Obv:** Value **Rev:** Iraqi Hanukka Lamp **Edge:** Plain **Shape:** 12-sided **Note:** Struck for sets only

Date	Mintage	F	VF	XF	Unc	BU
JE5764 (2004)(u)	3,000	—	—	—	12.00	—

KM# 391 1/2 NEW SHEQEL

6.5000 g., Aluminum-Bronze, 26 mm. **Obv:** Value **Rev:** Syrian Hanukka Lamp **Edge:** Plain **Shape:** 12-sided **Note:** Struck for sets only

Date	Mintage	F	VF	XF	Unc	BU
JE5765 (2005)(u)	2,500	—	—	—	12.00	—

KM# 415 1/2 NEW SHEQEL

6.5000 g., Aluminum-Bronze, 26 mm. **Obv:** Value and mini-Hanukka Lamp **Rev:** Dutch Hanukka Lamp **Edge:** Plain **Shape:** 12-sided **Note:** Struck for sets only

Date	Mintage	F	VF	XF	Unc	BU
JE5766 (2006)(u)	3,000	—	—	—	12.00	—

KM# 422 1/2 NEW SHEQEL

6.5000 g., Aluminum-Bronze, 26 mm. **Obv:** Value and mini-Hanukka Lamp **Rev:** Corfu (Greek) Hanukka Lamp **Edge:** Plain **Shape:** 12-sided **Note:** Struck for sets only

Date	Mintage	F	VF	XF	Unc	BU
JE5767 (2007)(u)	3,000	—	—	—	12.00	—

KM# 434 1/2 NEW SHEQEL

6.5000 g., Aluminum-Bronze, 26 mm. **Subject:** Hanukka **Obv:** Value, date, inscriptions and menorah **Rev:** Egyptian Hanukka lamp **Shape:** 12-sided **Note:** Struck for sets only

Date	Mintage	F	VF	XF	Unc	BU
JE5768 (2008)(u)	3,000	—	—	—	12.00	—

KM# 436 1/2 NEW SHEQEL

6.5000 g., Aluminum-Bronze, 26 mm. **Subject:** Hanukka **Obv:** Value, date, inscriptions and menorah **Rev:** Prague Hanukka Lamp **Shape:** 12-sided **Note:** Struck for sets only

Date	Mintage	F	VF	XF	Unc	BU
JE5769 (2009)(u)	1,800	—	—	—	12.00	—

KM# 466 1/2 NEW SHEQEL

6.5000 g., Aluminum-Bronze, 26 mm. **Subject:** Hanukka **Obv:** Value, date, inscriptions and menorah **Rev:** Algerian Hanukka Lamp **Edge:** Plain **Note:** Struck for sets only

Date	Mintage	F	VF	XF	Unc	BU
JE5770 (2010)(u)	1,800	—	—	—	12.00	—

KM# 160a NEW SHEQEL

3.4500 g., Nickel Plated Steel, 17.97 mm. **Obv:** Value **Rev:** Lily, state emblem and ancient Hebrew inscription **Edge:** Plain

Date	Mintage	F	VF	XF	Unc	BU
JE5761 (2001)(h)	9,648,000	—	—	—	1.00	—
JE5762 (2002)(h)	18,816,000	—	—	—	1.00	—
JE5763 (2003)(v)	10,198,500	—	—	—	1.00	—
JE5765 (2005)	—	—	—	—	1.00	—
JE5766 (2006)	—	—	—	—	1.00	—
Note: Coin alignment error exists. Value: $100 in Unc, $50 in XF.						
JE5767 (2007)	—	—	—	—	1.00	—
JE5769 (2009)	—	—	—	—	1.00	—
JE5771 (2011)	—	—	—	—	0.75	—
JE5772 (2012)	—	—	—	—	0.75	—

KM# 344 NEW SHEQEL

14.4000 g., 0.9250 Silver 0.4282 oz. ASW, 30 mm. **Series:** Independence Day **Subject:** Education **Obv:** Denomination **Rev:** Pomegranate full of symbols - Hebrew 'ABC-123', etc. **Edge:** Plain

Date	Mintage	F	VF	XF	Unc	BU
JE5761-2001(u) Prooflike	1,653	—	—	—	—	32.00

KM# 351 NEW SHEQEL

14.4000 g., 0.9250 Silver 0.4282 oz. ASW, 30 mm. **Series:** Art and Culture in Israel **Subject:** Music **Obv:** National arms and denomination **Rev:** Musical instruments **Edge:** Plain

Date	Mintage	F	VF	XF	Unc	BU
JE5761-2001(u) Prooflike	1,182	—	—	—	—	35.00

KM# 163b NEW SHEQEL

3.5000 g., Nickel Bonded Steel, 18 mm. **Subject:** Hanukka **Obv:** Value, small menorah, country name in Hebrew, English and Arabic and inscription "HANUKKA" in Hebrew and English **Rev:** Lily, state emblem, ancient Hebrew inscription and Star of David mintmark **Edge:** Plain

Date	Mintage	F	VF	XF	Unc	BU
JE5761 (2001)(u)	4,000	—	—	—	4.00	—
Note: In sets only						
JE5762 (2002)(u)	4,000	—	—	—	4.00	—
Note: In sets only						
JE5763 (2003)(u)	3,000	—	—	—	4.00	—
Note: In sets only						
JE5764 (2004)(u)	3,000	—	—	—	4.00	—
Note: In sets only						
JE5765 (2005)(u)	2,500	—	—	—	4.00	—
Note: In sets only						
JE5766 (2006)(u)	3,000	—	—	—	4.00	—
Note: In sets only						
JE5767 (2007)(u)	3,000	—	—	—	4.00	—
Note: In sets only						
JE5769 (2009)(u)	1,800	—	—	—	4.00	—
Note: In sets only						
JE5770 (2010)(u)	1,800	—	—	—	4.00	—
Note: In sets only						

KM# 163 NEW SHEQEL

4.0000 g., Copper-Nickel, 18 mm. **Subject:** Hanukka **Obv:** Value **Rev:** Lily, state emblem and ancient Hebrew inscription. **Note:** Coins dated JE5754-5769 have the Star of David mint mark; the JE5746-5753 coins do not.

Date	Mintage	F	VF	XF	Unc	BU
JE5761 (2001)(u)	4,000	—	—	—	4.00	—
Note: In sets only						
JE5770 (2010)	1,800	—	—	—	4.00	—
JE5762 (2002)(u)	4,000	—	—	—	4.00	—
Note: In sets only						
JE5763 (2003)(u)	3,000	—	—	—	4.00	—
Note: In sets only						
JE5764 (2004)(u)	3,000	—	—	—	4.00	—
Note: In sets only						
JE5765 (2005)(u)	2,500	—	—	—	4.00	—
Note: In sets only						
JE5766 (2006)(u)	3,000	—	—	—	4.00	—
Note: In sets only						
JE5767 (2007)(u)	3,000	—	—	—	4.00	—
Note: In sets only						
JE5769 (2009)(u)	1,800	—	—	—	4.00	—
Note: In sets only						
JE5770 (2010)(u)	—	—	—	—	4.00	—
Note: In sets only						

KM# 356 NEW SHEQEL

14.4000 g., 0.9250 Silver 0.4282 oz. ASW, 30 mm. **Series:** Independence Day **Subject:** Volunteering **Obv:** Denomination **Rev:** Heart in hands **Edge:** Plain

Date	Mintage	F	VF	XF	Unc	BU
JE5762-2002(o) Prooflike	1,364	—	—	—	—	30.00

KM# 359 NEW SHEQEL

14.4000 g., 0.9250 Silver 0.4282 oz. ASW, 30 mm. **Series:** Biblical Art **Subject:** Tower of Babel **Obv:** National arms in spiral inscription **Rev:** Tower of Hebrew verses **Edge:** Plain

Date	Mintage	F	VF	XF	Unc	BU
JE5762 (2002)(o) Prooflike	1,312	—	—	—	—	55.00

KM# 371 NEW SHEQEL

14.4000 g., 0.9250 Silver 0.4282 oz. ASW, 30 mm. **Series:** Independence Day **Subject:** Space Exploration **Obv:** "Ofeq" satellite in orbit **Rev:** "Shavit" rocket **Edge Lettering:** Hebrew: "In memory of Ilan Ramon and his colleagues in the Columbia"

Date	Mintage	F	VF	XF	Unc	BU
JE5763-2003(v) Prooflike	1,233	—	—	—	—	40.00

KM# 374 NEW SHEQEL

14.4000 g., 0.9250 Silver 0.4282 oz. ASW, 30 mm. **Series:** Biblical Art **Subject:** Jacob and Rachel **Obv:** Value **Rev:** Jacob and Rachel floating in air **Edge:** Plain

Date	Mintage	F	VF	XF	Unc	BU
JE5763-2003(u) Prooflike	1,661	—	—	—	—	55.00

KM# 380 NEW SHEQEL
14.4000 g., 0.9250 Silver 0.4282 oz. ASW, 30 mm. **Series:** Independence Day **Subject:** Children of Israel **Obv:** Value **Rev:** Parent and child **Edge:** Plain

Date	Mintage	F	VF	XF	Unc	BU
JE5764-2004(u) Prooflike	1,446	—	—	—	—	35.00

KM# 383 NEW SHEQEL
14.4000 g., 0.9250 Silver 0.4282 oz. ASW, 30 mm. **Subject:** 2004 Summer Olympics **Obv:** Four windsurfers, value and national arms **Rev:** Eight windsurfers **Edge:** Plain

Date	Mintage	F	VF	XF	Unc	BU
JE5764-2004(v) Prooflike	2,800	—	—	—	—	40.00

KM# 386 NEW SHEQEL
14.4000 g., 0.9250 Silver 0.4282 oz. ASW, 30 mm. **Series:** Biblical Art **Subject:** Burning Bush **Obv:** Burning twig and value **Rev:** Burning Bush **Edge:** Plain

Date	Mintage	F	VF	XF	Unc	BU
JE5764-2004(v)	1,274	—	—	—	—	55.00

KM# 405.1 NEW SHEQEL
1.2440 g., 0.9990 Gold 0.0400 oz. AGW, 13.92 mm. **Series:** Biblical Art **Subject:** Jacob and Rachel **Obv:** Value **Rev:** Jacob and Rachel floating in air **Edge:** Reeded

Date	Mintage	F	VF	XF	Unc	BU
JE5764 (2004)(u) Proof	6,057	Value: 100				

KM# 405.2 NEW SHEQEL
1.2440 g., 0.9990 Gold 0.0400 oz. AGW, 13.92 mm. **Series:** Biblical Art **Subject:** Jacob and Rachel **Obv:** Value **Rev:** Jacob and Rachel floating in air. Arabic legend Israel is mispelled **Edge:** Reeded

Date	Mintage	F	VF	XF	Unc	BU
JE5764 (2004)(u) Proof	682	Value: 150				

KM# 406 NEW SHEQEL
14.4000 g., 0.9250 Silver 0.4282 oz. ASW, 30 mm. **Subject:** FIFA 2006 World Cup **Obv:** Value and soccer ball **Rev:** Map and soccer ball **Edge:** Plain

Date	Mintage	F	VF	XF	Unc	BU
JE5764-2004(u) Prooflike	Est. 2,800	—	—	—	—	40.00

Note: Issued in 2006

KM# 377 NEW SHEQEL
14.4000 g., 0.9250 Silver 0.4282 oz. ASW, 30 mm. **Series:** Art and Culture in Israel **Subject:** Architecture and design **Obv:** Value **Rev:** Architecture and design **Edge:** Plain **Note:** With enamel.

Date	Mintage	F	VF	XF	Unc	BU
JE5764-2004(u)	930	—	—	—	—	35.00

KM# 412 NEW SHEQEL
14.4000 g., 0.9250 Silver 0.4282 oz. ASW, 30 mm. **Series:** Art and Culture in Israel **Subject:** Naomi Shemer **Obv:** Value **Rev:** Portrait of Naomi Shemer **Edge:** Plain

Date	Mintage	F	VF	XF	Unc	BU
JE5765-2005(u) Prooflike	1,100	—	—	—	—	35.00

KM# 396 NEW SHEQEL
14.4000 g., 0.9250 Silver 0.4282 oz. ASW, 30 mm. **Subject:** Einstein's Relativity Theory **Obv:** Concentric circles above equation **Rev:** Value above signature

Date	Mintage	F	VF	XF	Unc	BU
JE5765-2005(v) Prooflike	1,100	—	—	—	—	48.00

KM# 399 NEW SHEQEL
14.4000 g., 0.9250 Silver 0.4282 oz. ASW, 30 mm. **Series:** Biblical Art **Subject:** Moses and the Ten Commandments **Obv:** Ten Commandments and value **Rev:** Moses and the Ten Commandments

Date	Mintage	F	VF	XF	Unc	BU
JE5765-2005(u) Prooflike	1,400	—	—	—	—	55.00

KM# 402 NEW SHEQEL
14.4000 g., 0.9250 Silver 0.4282 oz. ASW, 30 mm. **Series:** Independence Day **Subject:** Israel 57th Anniversary The Golden Years **Obv:** Value and olive branch **Rev:** Twisted olive tree

Date	Mintage	F	VF	XF	Unc	BU
JE5765-2005(u) Prooflike	1,100	—	—	—	—	35.00

KM# 409 NEW SHEQEL
14.4000 g., 0.9250 Silver 0.4282 oz. ASW, 30 mm. **Series:** Biblical Art **Subject:** Abraham and the Three Angels **Obv:** Value and stars **Rev:** Abraham and the three angels **Edge:** Reeded

Date	Mintage	F	VF	XF	Unc	BU
JE5766-2006(ig)	1,075	—	—	—	—	55.00

KM# 416 NEW SHEQEL
14.4000 g., 0.9250 Silver 0.4282 oz. ASW, 30 mm. **Series:** Independence Day **Subject:** Higher Education in Israel **Obv:** Value and design **Rev:** Symbols of Science, Humanities, Technology and Mathematics **Edge:** Plain

Date	Mintage	F	VF	XF	Unc	BU
JE5766-2006(ig)	737	—	—	—	—	45.00

KM# 419 NEW SHEQEL
14.4000 g., 0.9250 Silver 0.4282 oz. ASW, 30 mm. **Series:** UNESCO World Heritage Sites in Israel **Subject:** White City of Tel Aviv **Obv:** Value and Bauhaus building **Rev:** Fall of Bauhaus style building and UNESCO symbol **Edge:** Plain

Date	Mintage	F	VF	XF	Unc	BU
JE5766-2006(ig) Prooflike	844	—	—	—	—	50.00

KM# 423 NEW SHEQEL
14.4000 g., 0.9250 Silver 0.4282 oz. ASW, 30 mm. **Series:** Independence Day **Subject:** Performing Arts in Israel **Obv:** Value, state emblem and inscriptions **Rev:** Stylized actor, dancer and musician and inscription in Hebrew, English and Arabic, Performing Arts in Israel **Edge:** Plain

Date	Mintage	F	VF	XF	Unc	BU
JE5767-2007(ig) Prooflike	765	—	—	—	—	50.00

KM# 426 NEW SHEQEL
14.4000 g., 0.9250 Silver 0.4282 oz. ASW, 30 mm. **Subject:** 2008 Olympics - Judo **Obv:** Value, state emblem, judo belt and inscriptions **Rev:** 2 judo athletes and inscriptions in Hebrew, English and Arabic **Edge:** Plain

Date	Mintage	F	VF	XF	Unc	BU
JE5767-2007(u) Prooflike	1,160	—	—	—	—	50.00

KM# 429 NEW SHEQEL
14.4000 g., 0.9250 Silver 0.4282 oz. ASW, 30 mm. **Series:** Biblical Art **Subject:** Isaiah, Wolf with the Lamb **Obv:** Value, state emblem and inscriptions in Hebrew, English and Arabic **Obv. Inscription:** And the Wolf shall dwell with the Lamb **Rev:** Wolf and lamb lying together under a tree **Edge:** Plain

Date	Mintage	F	VF	XF	Unc	BU
JE5767-2007(v) Prooflike	1,363	—	—	—	—	55.00

KM# 437 NEW SHEQEL
1.2440 g., 0.9990 Gold 0.0400 oz. AGW, 13.92 mm. **Series:** Biblical Art **Subject:** Abraham and the Angels **Obv:** Value, state emblem and Moses in Hebrew, English and Arabic **Rev:** Abraham greeting three angels **Edge:** Reeded

Date	Mintage	F	VF	XF	Unc	BU
JE5767-2007(v) Proof	1,500	Value: 120				

KM# 438 NEW SHEQEL
1.2440 g., 0.9990 Gold 0.0400 oz. AGW, 13.92 mm. **Series:** Biblical Art **Subject:** Moses and the Ten Commandments **Obv:** Value, state emblem and Moses in Hebrew **Rev:** Moses holding the Ten Commandments **Edge:** Reeded

Date	Mintage	F	VF	XF	Unc	BU
JE5767-2007 Proof	2,467	Value: 120				

KM# 163a NEW SHEQEL
4.0000 g., Copper-Nickel, 18 mm. **Subject:** Hanukka **Obv:** Value, small menorah, country name in Hebrew, English and Arabic and inscription "HANUKKA" in Hebrew and English **Rev:** Lily, state emblem, ancient Hebrew inscription and Star of David mintmark **Note:** Non-magnetic.

Date	Mintage	F	VF	XF	Unc	BU
JE5768 (2008)(u)	3,000	—	—	—	4.00	—

Note: In sets only.

KM# 439 NEW SHEQEL
14.4000 g., 0.9250 Silver 0.4282 oz. ASW, 30 mm. **Series:** Israeli Nobel Prize Laureates **Subject:** Shmuel Yosef Agnon **Obv:** Value, state emblem, outline of Agnon **Rev:** Portrait of Agnon **Edge:** Plain

Date	Mintage	F	VF	XF	Unc	BU
JE5768-2008(ig) Prooflike	666	—	—	—	—	60.00

KM# 440 NEW SHEQEL

1.2440 g., 0.9990 Gold 0.0400 oz. AGW, 13.92 mm. **Series:** Biblical Art **Subject:** Isaiah, Wolf with the Lamb **Obv:** Value, state emblem, and inscriptions **Rev:** Wolf and lamb lying under tree **Edge:** Reeded

Date	Mintage	F	VF	XF	Unc	BU
JE5768-2008(v) Proof	3,302	Value: 120				

KM# 441 NEW SHEQEL

14.4000 g., 0.9250 Silver 0.4282 oz. ASW, 30 mm. **Series:** Independence Day **Subject:** Israel's Sixtieth Anniversary **Obv:** Value, state emblem and inscriptions including "Independence Day" **Rev:** "60" the zero is shaped like a pomegranite and a dove

Date	Mintage	F	VF	XF	Unc	BU
JE5768-2008(v) Prooflike	1,800	—	—	—	—	60.00

KM# 442 NEW SHEQEL

14.4000 g., 0.9250 Silver 0.4282 oz. ASW, 30 mm. **Subject:** Israel Defense Forces Reserves **Obv:** Triangle, state emblem and inscription **Rev:** Teddy bear pendant over soldier's ID tag

Date	Mintage	F	VF	XF	Unc	BU
JE5768-2008(ig) Prooflike	492	—	—	—	—	60.00

KM# 444 NEW SHEQEL

14.4000 g., 0.9250 Silver 0.4282 oz. ASW, 30 mm. **Series:** Biblical Art **Subject:** Parting of the Red Sea **Obv:** Value, state emblem and inscriptions **Rev:** Israelites passing through the Red Sea

Date	Mintage	F	VF	XF	Unc	BU
JE5769-2008(v) Prooflike	Est. 1,800	—	—	—	—	60.00

KM# 453 NEW SHEQEL

14.4000 g., 0.9250 Silver 0.4282 oz. ASW, 30 mm. **Series:** UNESCO World Heritage Sites in Israel **Subject:** Masada **Obv:** Value, state emblem, image of Masada **Rev:** View of Masada, UNESCO emblem, World Heritage Site emblem **Edge:** Plain

Date	Mintage	F	VF	XF	Unc	BU
JE5769 (2009)(u) Prooflike	Est. 1,800	—	—	—	—	60.00

KM# 456 NEW SHEQEL

14.4000 g., 0.9250 Silver 0.4282 oz. ASW, 30 mm. **Series:** Independence Day **Subject:** Israel's Sixty-first Anniversary Birds of Israel **Obv:** Value, state emblem, finch **Rev:** Three birds, hoopoe, warbler and finch **Edge:** Plain

Date	Mintage	F	VF	XF	Unc	BU
JE5769 (2009)(u) Prooflike	1,800	—	—	—	—	60.00

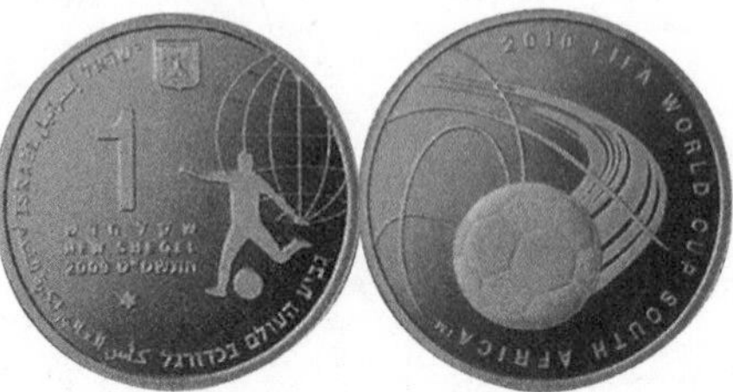

KM# 459 NEW SHEQEL

14.4000 g., 0.9250 Silver 0.4282 oz. ASW, 30 mm. **Subject:** 2010 FIFA World Cup South Africa **Obv:** Soccer Player, ball, outline of globe, value, state emblem **Rev:** Soccer ball with design **Edge:** Plain

Date	Mintage	F	VF	XF	Unc	BU
JE5769 (2009)(u) Prooflike	Est. 1,800	—	—	—	—	60.00

KM# 462 NEW SHEQEL

1.2440 g., 0.9990 Gold 0.0400 oz. AGW, 13.92 mm. **Series:** Biblical Art **Subject:** Samson and the Lion **Obv:** Small stylized palm tree, value, state emblem **Rev:** Stylized Samson wrestling a lion and small stylized palm tree **Edge:** Reeded

Date	Mintage	F	VF	XF	Unc	BU
JE5769 (2009)(u) Proof	Est. 5,000	Value: 120				

KM# 463 NEW SHEQEL

14.4000 g., 0.9250 Silver 0.4282 oz. ASW, 30 mm. **Series:** Biblical Art **Subject:** Samson and the Lion **Obv:** Small stylized palm tree, value, state emblem **Rev:** Stylized Samson wrestling a lion and small stylized palm tree **Edge:** Plain

Date	Mintage	F	VF	XF	Unc	BU
JE5769 (2009)(u) Prooflike	Est. 1,800	—	—	—	—	60.00

KM# 468 NEW SHEQEL

14.4000 g., 0.9250 Silver 0.4282 oz. ASW, 30 mm. **Series:** UNESCO World Heritage Sites in Israel **Subject:** Old Akko (Acre) **Obv:** Fortress of Akko as seen agains backdrop of Mediterranean Sea, state emblem, value UNESCO logo **Rev:** Ancient fortress walls, Khan-el-Undan caravanseraie and its clock tower, underground Crussader Knights' hall, White Mosque and other buildings **Edge:** Plain

Date	Mintage	F	VF	XF	Unc	BU
JE5770 (2010)(h) Prooflike	Est. 1,800	—	—	—	—	60.00

KM# 471 NEW SHEQEL

14.4000 g., 0.9250 Silver 0.4282 oz. ASW, 30 mm. **Series:** Independence Day **Subject:** Israeli National Trail 62nd Anniversary **Obv:** Trail forming stylized 62, state emblem **Rev:** Map of Isreal highlighting trail, boot, flowers **Edge:** Plain

Date	Mintage	F	VF	XF	Unc	BU
JE5770-2010(h) Prooflike	Est. 1,800	—	—	—	—	60.00

KM# 474 NEW SHEQEL

1.2440 g., 0.9990 Gold 0.0400 oz. AGW, 13.92 mm. **Series:** Biblical Art **Subject:** Jonah in the Whale **Obv:** Small image of Jonah, value, state emblem **Rev:** Stylized Jonah in belly of whale **Edge:** Reeded

Date	Mintage	F	VF	XF	Unc	BU
JE5770-2010(v) Proof	Est. 5,000	Value: 140				

KM# 475 NEW SHEQEL

14.4000 g., 0.9250 Silver 0.4282 oz. ASW, 30 mm. **Series:** Biblical Art **Subject:** Jonah in the Whale **Obv:** Small image of Jonah, value, state emblem **Rev:** Stylized Jonah in belly of whale **Edge:** Plain

Date	Mintage	F	VF	XF	Unc	BU
JE5770-2010(v) Prooflike	Est. 1,800	—	—	—	—	70.00

KM# 478 NEW SHEQEL

14.4000 g., 0.9250 Silver 0.4282 oz. ASW, 30 mm. **Series:** Israeli Nobel Prize Laureates **Subject:** Menachem Begin **Obv:** Menachem Begin, Jimmy Carter and Anwar Sadat in triple handshake on White House lawn **Rev:** Portrait of Begin **Edge:** Plain

Date	Mintage	F	VF	XF	Unc	BU
JE5771-2010(u) Prooflike	Est. 2,800	—	—	—	—	65.00

KM# 481 NEW SHEQEL

14.4000 g., 0.9250 Silver 0.4282 oz. ASW, 30 mm. **Series:** Independence Day **Subject:** Israel's sixty-third anniversary, Dead Sea **Obv:** Image of Dead Sea region, ibex and legend "DEAD SEA" in Hebrew, English and Arabic **Rev:** Value, mirror image of value, state emblem, dates, country name in Hebrew, English and Arabic and legend "INDEPENDENCE DAY" in Hebrew and English

Date	Mintage	F	VF	XF	Unc	BU
JE5771-2011(u) Prooflike	Est. 1,800	—	—	—	—	75.00

KM# 484 NEW SHEQEL

14.4000 g., 0.9250 Silver 0.4282 oz. ASW, 30 mm. **Subject:** 2012 London Olympics, Gymnastics **Obv:** Stlyized gymnast holding a ribbon in the shape of the Star of David and legends "THE OLYMPIC DELEGATION OF ISRAEL 2012" and "gymnastics" in Hebrew, English and Arabic **Rev:** Ribbon representation of Israeli flag, statem emblem, value, dates, country name in Hebrew, English and Arabic and inscription

Date	Mintage	F	VF	XF	Unc	BU
JE5771-2011(u) Prooflike	Est. 2,800	Value: 75.00				

KM# 487 NEW SHEQEL

14.4000 g., 0.9250 Silver 0.4282 oz. ASW, 30 mm. **Series:** Biblical Art **Subject:** Elijah in the Whirlwind **Obv:** State emblem, dates, country name in Hebrew, English and Arabic and inscription "ELIJAH WENT UP BY A WHIRLWIND INTO HEAVEN" in Hebrew, English and Arabic **Rev:** Stylized Elijah ascending to heaven in a horse-drawn chariot of fire in a whirlwind with Elisha below

Date	Mintage	F	VF	XF	Unc	BU
JE5771-2011(v) Prooflike	Est. 1,800	—	—	—	—	75.00

KM# 488 NEW SHEQEL

1.2440 g., 0.9990 Gold 0.0400 oz. AGW, 13.92 mm. **Series:** Biblical Art **Subject:** Elijah in the Whirlwind

Date	Mintage	F	VF	XF	Unc	BU
JE5771-2011(v) Proof	5,000	Value: 125				

KM# 492 NEW SHEQEL

14.4000 g., 0.9250 Silver 0.4282 oz. ASW, 30 mm. **Subject:** Tel Megiddo, UNESCO Heritage site

Date	Mintage	F	VF	XF	Unc	BU
JE5772-2012 Proof	—	Value: 80.00				

KM# 495 NEW SHEQEL

14.4000 g., 0.9250 Silver 0.4282 oz. ASW, 30 mm. **Subject:** Yitzhak Rabin **Rev:** Bust left

Date	Mintage	F	VF	XF	Unc	BU
JE5772-2012 Proof	—	Value: 80.00				

KM# 352 2 NEW SHEQALIM

28.8000 g., 0.9250 Silver 0.8565 oz. ASW, 38.7 mm. **Series:** Art and Culture in Israel **Subject:** Music **Obv:** National arms and denomination **Rev:** Musical instruments **Edge:** Reeded

Date	Mintage	F	VF	XF	Unc	BU
JE5761-2001(u) Proof	1,747	Value: 55.00				

KM# 349 2 NEW SHEQALIM

28.8000 g., 0.9250 Silver 0.8565 oz. ASW, 38.7 mm. **Series:** Wildlife **Subject:** Wild goat and acacia tree **Obv:** Acacia tree **Rev:** Ibex **Edge:** Reeded

Date	Mintage	F	VF	XF	Unc	BU
JE5761-2000(u) Proof	2,000	Value: 60.00				

KM# 345 2 NEW SHEQALIM

28.8000 g., 0.9250 Silver 0.8565 oz. ASW, 38.7 mm. **Series:** Independence Day **Subject:** Education **Obv:** Denomination **Rev:** Pomegranate full of symbols **Edge:** Reeded **Designer:** Asher Kalderon

Date	Mintage	F	VF	XF	Unc	BU
JE5761-2001(u) Proof	1,847	Value: 70.00				

KM# 357 2 NEW SHEQALIM

28.8000 g., 0.9250 Silver 0.8565 oz. ASW, 38.7 mm. **Series:** Independence Day **Subject:** Volunteering **Obv:** Denomination **Rev:** Heart in hands **Edge:** Reeded

Date	Mintage	F	VF	XF	Unc	BU
JE5762-2002(o) Proof	1,426	Value: 48.00				

KM# 360 2 NEW SHEQALIM

28.8000 g., 0.9250 Silver 0.8565 oz. ASW, 38.7 mm. **Series:** Biblical Art **Subject:** Tower of Babel **Obv:** National arms in spiral inscription **Rev:** Tower of Hebrew verses **Edge:** Reeded

Date	Mintage	F	VF	XF	Unc	BU
JE5762-2002(o) Proof	1,295	Value: 100				

KM# 372 2 NEW SHEQALIM

28.8000 g., 0.9250 Silver 0.8565 oz. ASW, 38.7 mm. **Subject:** Space Exploration **Obv:** "Amos" satellite in orbit **Rev:** "Shavit" rocket **Edge Lettering:** Hebrew: "In memory of Ilan Ramon and his colleagues in the Columbia"

Date	Mintage	F	VF	XF	Unc	BU
JE5763-2003(v) Proof	1,249	Value: 60.00				

KM# 375 2 NEW SHEQALIM

28.8000 g., 0.9250 Silver 0.8565 oz. ASW, 38.7 mm. **Series:** Biblical Art **Subject:** Jacob and Rachel **Obv:** Value **Rev:** Figures floating in air above flower and sheep **Edge:** Reeded

Date	Mintage	F	VF	XF	Unc	BU
JE5763-2003(u) Proof	1,377	Value: 100				

KM# 378 2 NEW SHEQALIM

28.8000 g., 0.9250 Silver 0.8565 oz. ASW, 38.7 mm. **Series:** Art and Culture in Israel **Subject:** Architecture and design **Obv:** Value and enameled shapes **Rev:** Architectural design **Edge:** Reeded

Date	Mintage	F	VF	XF	Unc	BU
JE5764-2004(u) Proof	1,084	Value: 60.00				

KM# 381 2 NEW SHEQALIM

28.8000 g., 0.9250 Silver 0.8565 oz. ASW, 38.7 mm. **Series:** Independence Day **Subject:** Children of Israel **Obv:** Value and stylized human shapes **Rev:** Stylized parent and child **Edge:** Reeded

Date	Mintage	F	VF	XF	Unc	BU
JE5764-2004(u) Proof	1,182	Value: 50.00				

KM# 384 2 NEW SHEQALIM
28.8000 g., 0.9250 Silver 0.8565 oz. ASW, 38.7 mm. **Subject:** 2004 Summer Olympics **Obv:** Four windsurfers, value and national arms **Rev:** Eight windsurfers **Edge:** Reeded

Date	Mintage	F	VF	XF	Unc	BU
JE5764-2004(v) Proof	2,800	Value: 60.00				

KM# 387 2 NEW SHEQALIM
28.8000 g., 0.9250 Silver 0.8565 oz. ASW, 38.7 mm. **Series:** Biblical Art **Subject:** Burning Bush **Obv:** Burning twig and value **Rev:** Burning Bush **Edge:** Reeded

Date	Mintage	F	VF	XF	Unc	BU
JE5764-2004(v) Proof	1,354	Value: 100				

KM# 407 2 NEW SHEQALIM
28.8000 g., 0.9250 Silver 0.8565 oz. ASW, 38.7 mm. **Subject:** FIFA 2006 World Cup **Obv:** Value and soccer ball **Rev:** Map and soccer ball **Edge:** Reeded

Date	Mintage	F	VF	XF	Unc	BU
JE5764-2004(u) Proof	Est. 5,000	Value: 60.00				

Note: Issued in 2006

KM# 413 2 NEW SHEQALIM
28.8000 g., 0.9250 Silver 0.8565 oz. ASW, 38.7 mm. **Series:** Art and Culture in Israel **Subject:** Naomi Shemer **Obv:** Value **Rev:** Portrait of Naomi Shemer **Edge:** Reeded

Date	Mintage	F	VF	XF	Unc	BU
JE5765-2005(u) Proof	1,100	Value: 60.00				

KM# 397 2 NEW SHEQALIM
28.8000 g., 0.9250 Silver 0.8565 oz. ASW, 38.7 mm. **Subject:** Einstein's Relativity Theory **Obv:** Concentric circles above equation **Rev:** Value above signature

Date	Mintage	F	VF	XF	Unc	BU
JE5765-2005(v) Proof	1,600	Value: 85.00				

KM# 400 2 NEW SHEQALIM
28.8000 g., 0.9250 Silver 0.8565 oz. ASW, 38.7 mm. **Series:** Biblical Art **Subject:** Moses and the Ten Commandments **Obv:** Ten Commandments and value **Rev:** Moses and Ten Commandments

Date	Mintage	F	VF	XF	Unc	BU
JE5765-2005(u) Proof	1,400	Value: 100				

KM# 403 2 NEW SHEQALIM
28.8000 g., 0.9250 Silver 0.8565 oz. ASW, 38.7 mm. **Series:** Independence Day **Subject:** Israel 57th Anniversary - The Golden Years **Obv:** Value and olive branch **Rev:** Twisted olive tree **Edge:** Reeded

Date	Mintage	F	VF	XF	Unc	BU
JE5765-2005(u) Proof	1,100	Value: 50.00				

KM# 417 2 NEW SHEQALIM
28.8000 g., 0.9250 Silver 0.8565 oz. ASW, 38.7 mm. **Series:** Independence Day **Subject:** Higher Education in Israel **Obv:** Value and design **Rev:** Symbols of Science, Humanities, Technology and Mathematics **Edge:** Reeded

Date	Mintage	F	VF	XF	Unc	BU
JE5766-2006(ig) Proof	846	Value: 60.00				

KM# 410 2 NEW SHEQALIM
28.8000 g., 0.9250 Silver 0.8565 oz. ASW, 38.7 mm. **Series:** Biblical Art **Subject:** Abraham and the Three Angels **Obv:** Value and stars **Rev:** Abraham and the three angels **Edge:** Reeded

Date	Mintage	F	VF	XF	Unc	BU
JE5766-2006(ig) Proof	967	Value: 110				

KM# 420 2 NEW SHEQALIM
28.8000 g., 0.9250 Silver 0.8565 oz. ASW, 38.7 mm. **Series:** UNESCO World Heritage Sites in Israel **Subject:** White City of Tel Aviv **Obv:** Value and Bauhaus building **Rev:** Fall of Bauhaus building and UNESCO symbol **Edge:** Reeded

Date	Mintage	F	VF	XF	Unc	BU
JE5766-2006(ig) Proof	837	Value: 75.00				

KM# 424 2 NEW SHEQALIM
28.8000 g., 0.9250 Silver 0.8565 oz. ASW, 38.7 mm. **Series:** Independence Day **Subject:** Performing Arts in Israel **Obv:** Value, state emblem and inscriptions **Rev:** Stylized actor, dancer and musician and inscription in Hebrew, English and Arabiv **Edge:** Reeded

Date	Mintage	F	VF	XF	Unc	BU
JE5767-2007(ig) Proof	756	Value: 75.00				

KM# 427 2 NEW SHEQALIM
28.8000 g., 0.9250 Silver 0.8565 oz. ASW, 38.7 mm. **Subject:** 2008 Olympics - Judo **Obv:** Value, state emblem, judo belt and inscriptions **Rev:** 2 judo athletes and inscriptions **Edge:** Reeded

Date	Mintage	F	VF	XF	Unc	BU
JE5767-2007(u) Proof	5,211	Value: 75.00				

KM# 430 2 NEW SHEQALIM
28.8000 g., 0.9250 Silver 0.8565 oz. ASW, 38.7 mm. **Series:** Biblical Art **Subject:** Isaiah, Wolf with the Lamb **Obv:** Value, state emblem and inscriptions in Hebrew, English and Arabic **Obv. Inscription:** And the Wolf shall dwell with the Lamb **Rev:** Wolf and lamb lying together under a tree **Edge:** Reeded

Date	Mintage	F	VF	XF	Unc	BU
JE5767-2007(v) Proof	1,734	Value: 100				

KM# 432 2 NEW SHEQALIM
5.7000 g., Nickel Plated Steel, 21.6 mm. **Subject:** Hanukka **Obv:** Value, date, inscriptions and menorah **Rev:** Double cornucopiae (horns of plenty) draped in ribbons and filled with fruit and grain including a pomegranate **Edge:** Plain with 4 notches

Date	Mintage	F	VF	XF	Unc	BU
JE5768 (2008)(u)	3,000	—	—	—	5.00	—
Note: In sets only						
JE5769 (2009)(u)	1,800	—	—	—	5.00	—
Note: In sets only						
JE5770 (2010)(u)	1,800	—	—	—	5.00	—
Note: In sets only						

KM# 433 2 NEW SHEQALIM
5.7000 g., Nickel Plated Steel, 21.6 mm. **Obv:** Value, date and inscriptions **Rev:** Double cornucopiae (horns of plenty) draped in ribbons and filled with fruit and grain including a pomegranate **Edge:** Plain with 4 notches

Date	Mintage	F	VF	XF	Unc	BU
JE5768 (2008)(u)	Est. 26,000,000	—	—	—	1.00	—
JE5769 (2009)(u)	—	—	—	—	1.00	—
JE5770 (2010)(u)	—	—	—	—	1.00	—
JE5771 (2011)(v)	—	—	—	—	1.00	—

KM# 445 2 NEW SHEQALIM
28.8000 g., 0.9250 Silver 0.8565 oz. ASW, 38.7 mm. **Series:** Israeli Nobel Prize Laureates **Subject:** Shmuel Yosef Agnon **Obv:** Value, state emblem and outline of Agnon **Rev:** Portrait of Agnon **Edge:** Reeded

Date	Mintage	F	VF	XF	Unc	BU
JE5768-2008(ig) Proof	666	Value: 90.00				

KM# 446 2 NEW SHEQALIM
28.8000 g., 0.9250 Silver 0.8565 oz. ASW, 38.7 mm. **Series:** Independence Day **Subject:** Israel's 60th Anniversary **Obv:** Value, state emblem and inscription "Independence Day" **Rev:** "60" the zero is shaped like a pomegranate and a dove

Date	Mintage	F	VF	XF	Unc	BU
JE5768-2008(v) Proof	1,800	Value: 110				

KM# 447 2 NEW SHEQALIM
28.8000 g., 0.9250 Silver 0.8565 oz. ASW, 38.7 mm. **Subject:** Israel Defense Forces Reserves **Obv:** Triangle, state emblem and inscription **Rev:** Teddy bear pendant over a soldier's ID tag

Date	Mintage	F	VF	XF	Unc	BU
JE5768-2008(ig) Proof	481	Value: 95.00				

KM# 443 2 NEW SHEQALIM
1.2440 g., 0.9990 Gold 0.0400 oz. AGW, 13.92 mm. **Series:** Biblical Art **Subject:** Parting of the Red Sea **Obv:** Value, state emblem and inscriptions **Rev:** Israelites passing through the Red Sea **Edge:** Reeded

Date	Mintage	F	VF	XF	Unc	BU
JE5769-2008(v) Proof	Est. 5,000	Value: 120				

KM# 448 2 NEW SHEQALIM
28.8000 g., 0.9250 Silver 0.8565 oz. ASW, 38.7 mm. **Series:** Biblical Art **Subject:** Parting of the Red Sea **Obv:** Value, state emblem and inscriptions **Rev:** Israelites passing through the Red Sea **Edge:** Reeded

Date	Mintage	F	VF	XF	Unc	BU
JE5769-2008(v) Proof	1,800	Value: 100				

KM# 454 2 NEW SHEQALIM
28.8000 g., 0.9250 Silver 0.8565 oz. ASW, 38.7 mm. **Series:** UNESCO World Heritage Sites in Israel **Subject:** Masada **Obv:** Value, state emblem, image of Masada **Rev:** View of Masada, UNESCO emblem, World Heritage Site emblem **Edge:** Reeded

Date	Mintage	F	VF	XF	Unc	BU
JE5769 (2009)(u) Proof	Est. 1,800	Value: 90.00				

KM# 457 2 NEW SHEQALIM
28.8000 g., 0.9250 Silver 0.8565 oz. ASW, 38.7 mm. **Series:** Independence Day **Subject:** Israel's Sixty-first Anniversary-Birds of Israel **Obv:** Value, state emblem, hoopoe **Rev:** Three birds, hoopoe, warbler and finch **Edge:** Reeded

Date	Mintage	F	VF	XF	Unc	BU
JE5769 (2009)(u) Proof	2,800	Value: 100				

KM# 460 2 NEW SHEQALIM
28.8000 g., 0.9250 Silver 0.8565 oz. ASW, 38.7 mm. **Subject:** 2010 FIFA World Cup South Africa **Obv:** Soccer Player, ball, outline of globe **Rev:** Soccer player with design **Edge:** Reeded

Date	Mintage	F	VF	XF	Unc	BU
JE5769 (2009)(u) Proof	Est. 5,000	Value: 90.00				

KM# 464 2 NEW SHEQALIM
28.8000 g., 0.9250 Silver 0.8565 oz. ASW, 38.7 mm. **Series:** Biblical Art **Subject:** Samson and the Lion **Obv:** Small stylized palm tree, value, state emblem **Rev:** Stylized Samson wrestling with a lion and small stylized palm tree **Edge:** Reeded

Date	Mintage	F	VF	XF	Unc	BU
JE5769 (2009)(u) Proof	Est. 2,800	Value: 100				

KM# 469 2 NEW SHEQALIM
28.8000 g., 0.9250 Silver 0.8565 oz. ASW, 38.7 mm. **Series:** UNESCO World Heritage Sites in Israel **Subject:** Old Akko (Acre) **Obv:** Fortress of Akko as seen against backdrop of Mediterranean Sea, state emblem, value **Rev:** Ancient fortress walls, Khan-el-Umdan caravanseraie and its clock tower, underground Crusader Knights' Hall, White Mosque and other buildings **Edge:** Reeded

Date	Mintage	F	VF	XF	Unc	BU
JE5770 (2010)(h) Proof	Est. 2,800	Value: 90.00				

KM# 472 2 NEW SHEQALIM
28.8000 g., 0.9250 Silver 0.8565 oz. ASW, 38.7 mm. **Series:** Independence Day **Subject:** Israel National Trail **Obv:** Trail forming stylized 62, state emblem **Rev:** Map of Israel highlighting national trail, boot, flowers **Edge:** Reeded

Date	Mintage	F	VF	XF	Unc	BU
JE5770-2010(h) Proof	Est. 1,800	Value: 90.00				

KM# 476 2 NEW SHEQALIM
28.8000 g., 0.9250 Silver 0.8565 oz. ASW, 38.7 mm. **Series:** Biblical Art **Subject:** Jonah in the Whale **Obv:** Small image of Jonah, value, state emblem **Rev:** Stylized Jonah in belly of whale **Edge:** Reeded

Date	Mintage	F	VF	XF	Unc	BU
JE5770-2010(v) Proof	Est. 2,800	Value: 120				

KM# 479 2 NEW SHEQALIM
28.8000 g., 0.9250 Silver 0.8565 oz. ASW, 38.7 mm. **Series:** Israeli Nobel Pize Laureates **Subject:** Menachem Begin **Obv:** Menachem Begin, Jimmy Carter and Anwar Sadat in triple handshake on White House lawn, state emblem **Rev:** Portrait of Menachem Begin **Edge:** Reeded

Date	Mintage	F	VF	XF	Unc	BU
JE5771-2010(u) Proof	Est. 2,800	Value: 120				

KM# 482 2 NEW SHEQALIM
28.8000 g., 0.9250 Silver 0.8565 oz. ASW, 38.7 mm. **Series:** Independence Day **Subject:** Israel's sixty-third anniversary, Dead Sea **Obv:** Image of Dead Sea region, ibex and legend "DEAD SEA" in Hebrew, English and Arabic **Rev:** Value, mirror image of value, state emblem, dates, country name in Hebrew, English and Arabic and legend "INDEPENDENCE DAY" in Hebrew and English **Edge:** Reeded

Date	Mintage	F	VF	XF	Unc	BU
JE5771-2011 Proof	Est. 5,000	Value: 120				

KM# 485 2 NEW SHEQALIM
28.8000 g., 0.9250 Silver 0.8565 oz. ASW, 38.7 mm. **Subject:** 2012 London Olympics, Gymnastics **Obv:** Stylized gymnast holding a ribbon in the shape of the Star of David and legends "THE OLYMPIC DELEGATION OF ISRAEL 2012" and "gymnastics" in Hebrew, English and Arabic **Rev:** Ribbon representation of Israeli flag, state emblem, value, dates, country name in Hebrew, English and Arabic and inscription **Edge:** Reeded

Date	Mintage	F	VF	XF	Unc	BU
JE5771-2011(u) Proof	Est. 5,000	Value: 120				

KM# 489 2 NEW SHEQALIM
28.8000 g., 0.9250 Silver 0.8565 oz. ASW, 38.7 mm. **Series:** Biblical Art **Subject:** Elijah caught up in the firestorm **Obv:** State emblem, dates, country name in Hebrew, English and Arabic and inscription "ELIJAH WENT UP BY A WHIRLWIND INTO HEAVEN" in Hebrew, English and Arabic **Rev:** Stylized Elijah ascending to heaven in a horse-drawn chariot of fire in a whirlwind with Elisha below **Edge:** Reeded

Date	Mintage	F	VF	XF	Unc	BU
JE5771-2011(v) Proof	Est. 2,800	Value: 120				

KM# 493 2 NEW SHEQALIM
28.8000 g., 0.9250 Silver 0.8565 oz. ASW, 38.7 mm. **Subject:** Tel Megiddo, UNESCO Heritage site

Date	Mintage	F	VF	XF	Unc	BU
JE5772-2012 Proof	—	Value: 120				

KM# 496 2 NEW SHEQALIM
28.2800 g., 0.9250 Silver 0.8410 oz. ASW, 38.7 mm. **Subject:** Yitzhak Rabin **Rev:** Bust left

Date	Mintage	F	VF	XF	Unc	BU
JE5772-2012 Proof	—	Value: 120				

KM# 207 5 NEW SHEQALIM
8.2000 g., Copper-Nickel, 24 mm. **Obv:** Value **Rev:** Ancient column capitol **Edge:** Plain **Shape:** 12-sided

Date	Mintage	F	VF	XF	Unc	BU
JE5762 (2002)(wg)	4,464,000	—	—	—	3.75	—
Note: The JE5762 coins are practically round.						
JE5765 (2005)	—	—	—	—	3.00	—
JE5766 (2006)	—	—	—	—	3.00	—
JE5768 (2008)(dj)	—	—	—	—	3.00	—
JE5769 (2009)(dj)	—	—	—	—	3.00	—
JE5771 (2011)(dj)	—	—	—	—	3.00	—
JE5772 (2012)(dj)	—	—	—	—	2.50	—

KM# 217 5 NEW SHEQALIM
8.2000 g., Copper-Nickel, 24 mm. **Obv:** Value, small menorah and inscription Hanukka **Rev:** Ancient column capitol **Edge:** Plain **Shape:** 12-sided **Note:** Coins dated JE5754-5770 have the Star of David mint mark; the JE5751-5753 coins do not.

Date	Mintage	F	VF	XF	Unc	BU
JE5762 (2002)(u)	4,000	—	—	—	7.00	—
Note: In sets only						
JE5763 (2003)(u)	3,000	—	—	—	8.00	—
Note: In sets only						
JE5764 (2004)(u)	3,000	—	—	—	8.00	—
Note: In sets only						
JE5765 (2005)(u)	2,500	—	—	—	8.00	—
Note: In sets only						
JE5766 (2006)(u)	3,000	—	—	—	8.00	—
Note: In sets only						
JE5767 (2007)(u)	3,000	—	—	—	8.00	—
Note: In sets only						
JE5768 (2008)(u)	3,000	—	—	—	8.00	—
Note: In sets only						
JE5769 (2009)(u)	1,800	—	—	—	8.00	—
Note: In sets only						
JE5770 (2010)(u)	1,800	—	—	—	8.00	—
Note: In sets only						

KM# 408 5 NEW SHEQALIM
7.7770 g., 0.9990 Gold 0.2498 oz. AGW, 27 mm. **Subject:** FIFA 2006 World Cup **Obv:** Value and soccer ball **Rev:** Map and soccer ball **Edge:** Reeded **Note:** Issued in 2006

Date	Mintage	F	VF	XF	Unc	BU
JE5764-2004(u) Proof	Est. 655	Value: 550				

KM# 461 5 NEW SHEQALIM
7.7700 g., 0.9990 Gold 0.2496 oz. AGW, 27 mm. **Subject:** 2010 FIFA World Cup South Africa **Obv:** Soccer Player, ball, outline of globe **Rev:** Soccer ball with design **Edge:** Reeded

Date	Mintage	F	VF	XF	Unc	BU
JE5769 (2009)(u) Proof	Est. 888	Value: 550				

KM# 315 10 NEW SHEQALIM
7.0000 g., Bi-Metallic Aureate Bonded Bronze center in Nickel Bonded Steel ring, 23 mm. **Subject:** Hanukka **Obv:** Value, text and menorah within circle and vertical lines **Rev:** Palm tree and baskets within half beaded circle **Edge:** Reeded

Date	Mintage	F	VF	XF	Unc	BU
JE5761 (2001)(u)	4,000	—	—	—	9.00	—
Note: In sets only						
JE5762 (2002)(u)	4,000	—	—	—	9.00	—
Note: In sets only						
JE5763 (2003)(u)	3,000	—	—	—	10.00	—
Note: In sets only						
JE5764 (2004)(u)	3,000	—	—	—	10.00	—
Note: In sets only						
JE5765 (2005)(u)	2,500	—	—	—	10.00	—
Note: In sets only						
JE5766 (2006)(u)	3,000	—	—	—	10.00	—
Note: In sets only						
JE5767 (2007)(u)	3,000	—	—	—	10.00	—
Note: In sets only						
JE5768 (2008)(u)	3,000	—	—	—	10.00	—
Note: In sets only						
JE5769 (2009)(u)	1,800	—	—	—	10.00	—
Note: In sets only						
JE5770 (2010)(u)	1,800	—	—	—	10.00	—
Note: In sets only						

KM# 346 10 NEW SHEQALIM
16.9600 g., 0.9170 Gold 0.5000 oz. AGW, 30 mm. **Series:** Independence Day **Subject:** Education **Obv:** Value **Rev:** Pomegranate full of symbols - Hebrew for 'ABC - 123', etc. **Edge:** Reeded **Designer:** Asher Kalderon

Date	Mintage	F	VF	XF	Unc	BU
JE5761-2001(u) Proof	660	Value: 1,100				

KM# 353 10 NEW SHEQALIM
16.9600 g., 0.9170 Gold 0.5000 oz. AGW, 30 mm. **Series:** Art and Culture in Israel **Subject:** Music **Obv:** National arms and value **Rev:** Musical instruments **Edge:** Reeded

Date	Mintage	F	VF	XF	Unc	BU
JE5761-2001(u) Proof	766	Value: 1,100				

KM# 358 10 NEW SHEQALIM
16.9600 g., 0.9166 Gold 0.4998 oz. AGW, 30 mm. **Series:** Independence Day **Subject:** Volunteering **Obv:** Value **Rev:** Heart in hands **Edge:** Reeded

Date	Mintage	F	VF	XF	Unc	BU
JE5762-2002(o) Proof	617	Value: 1,100				

KM# 361 10 NEW SHEQALIM
16.9600 g., 0.9170 Gold 0.5000 oz. AGW, 30 mm. **Series:** Biblical Art **Subject:** Tower of Babel **Obv:** National arms in spiral inscription **Rev:** Tower of Hebrew verses **Edge:** Reeded

Date	Mintage	F	VF	XF	Unc	BU
JE5762-2002(o) Proof	750	Value: 1,200				

KM# 270 10 NEW SHEQALIM
7.0000 g., Bi-Metallic Aureate Bonded Bronze center in Nickel Bonded Steel ring, 23 mm. **Obv:** Value, vertical lines and text within circle **Rev:** Palm tree and baskets within half beaded circle **Edge:** Reeded

Date	Mintage	F	VF	XF	Unc	BU
JE5762 (2002)(h)	4,749,000	—	—	—	5.00	—
JE5765 (2005)	—	—	—	—	5.00	—
Note: Coin alignment error exists. Value: $200 in Unc, $100 in XF.						
JE5766 (2006)	—	—	—	—	5.00	—
JE5769 (2009)	—	—	—	—	5.00	—
JE5770 (2010)	—	—	—	—	5.00	—
JE5771 (2011)(h)	—	—	—	—	5.00	—
JE5772 (2012)(v)	—	—	—	—	4.00	—

KM# 373 10 NEW SHEQALIM
16.9600 g., 0.9170 Gold 0.5000 oz. AGW, 30 mm. **Series:** Independence Day **Subject:** Space Exploration **Obv:** "Eros" satellite in orbit **Rev:** "Shavit" rocket **Edge Lettering:** Hebrew: In memory of Ilan Ramon and his colleagues in the Columbia"

Date	Mintage	F	VF	XF	Unc	BU
JE5763-2003(v) Proof	573	Value: 1,125				

KM# 376 10 NEW SHEQALIM
16.9600 g., 0.9170 Gold 0.5000 oz. AGW, 30 mm. **Series:** Biblical Art **Subject:** Jacob and Rachel **Obv:** Value **Rev:** Jacob and Rachel floating in air above tree and sheep **Edge:** Reeded

Date	Mintage	F	VF	XF	Unc	BU
JE5763-2003(u) Proof	686	Value: 1,200				

KM# 379 10 NEW SHEQALIM
16.9600 g., 0.9170 Gold 0.5000 oz. AGW, 30 mm. **Series:** Art and Culture in Israel **Subject:** Architecture and Design **Obv:** Value **Rev:** Architectural design **Edge:** Reeded

Date	Mintage	F	VF	XF	Unc	BU
JE5764-2004(u) Proof	555	Value: 1,100				

KM# 382 10 NEW SHEQALIM
16.9600 g., 0.9170 Gold 0.5000 oz. AGW, 30 mm. **Series:** Independence Day **Subject:** Children of Israel **Obv:** Value **Rev:** Stylized parent and child **Edge:** Reeded

Date	Mintage	F	VF	XF	Unc	BU
JE5764-2004(u) Proof	539	Value: 1,100				

KM# 385 10 NEW SHEQALIM
16.9600 g., 0.9170 Gold 0.5000 oz. AGW, 30 mm. **Subject:** 2004 Summer Olympics **Obv:** Four windsurfers, value and national arms **Rev:** Eight windsurfers **Edge:** Reeded

Date	Mintage	F	VF	XF	Unc	BU
JE5764-2004(v) Proof	540	Value: 1,100				

KM# 388 10 NEW SHEQALIM
16.9600 g., 0.9170 Gold 0.5000 oz. AGW, 30 mm. **Series:** Biblical Art **Subject:** Burning Bush **Obv:** Burning twig and value **Rev:** Burning Bush **Edge:** Reeded

Date	Mintage	F	VF	XF	Unc	BU
JE5764-2004(v) Proof	555	Value: 1,200				

KM# 398 10 NEW SHEQALIM
16.9600 g., 0.9166 Gold 0.4998 oz. AGW, 30 mm. **Subject:** Einstein's Relativity Theory **Obv:** Concentric circles above equation **Rev:** Value above signature **Edge:** Reeded

Date	Mintage	F	VF	XF	Unc	BU
JE5765-2005(v) Proof	555	Value: 1,200				

KM# 401 10 NEW SHEQALIM
16.9600 g., 0.9166 Gold 0.4998 oz. AGW, 30 mm. **Series:** Biblical Art **Subject:** Moses and the Ten Commandments **Obv:** The Ten Commandments and value **Rev:** Moses and the Ten Commandments **Edge:** Reeded

Date	Mintage	F	VF	XF	Unc	BU
JE5765-2005(u) Proof	555	Value: 1,200				

KM# 404 10 NEW SHEQALIM
16.9600 g., 0.9166 Gold 0.4998 oz. AGW, 30 mm. **Series:** Independence Day **Subject:** Israel 57th Anniversary - Golden years **Obv:** Value and olive branch **Rev:** Twisted olive tree **Edge:** Reeded

Date	Mintage	F	VF	XF	Unc	BU
JE5765-2005(u) Proof	485	Value: 1,100				

KM# 414 10 NEW SHEQALIM
16.9600 g., 0.9170 Gold 0.5000 oz. AGW, 30 mm. **Series:** Art and Culture in Israel **Subject:** Naomi Shemer **Obv:** Value **Rev:** Portrait of Naomi Shemer **Edge:** Reeded

Date	Mintage	F	VF	XF	Unc	BU
JE5765-2005(u) Proof	455	Value: 1,150				

KM# 418 10 NEW SHEQALIM
16.9600 g., 0.9170 Gold 0.5000 oz. AGW, 30 mm. **Series:** Independence Day **Subject:** Higher Education in Israel **Obv:** Value and design **Rev:** Symbols of Science, Humanities, Technology and Mathematics **Edge:** Reeded

Date	Mintage	F	VF	XF	Unc	BU
JE5766-2006(ig) Proof	444	Value: 1,100				

KM# 411 10 NEW SHEQALIM
16.9600 g., 0.9170 Gold 0.5000 oz. AGW, 30 mm. **Series:** Biblical Art **Subject:** Abraham and the Three Angels **Obv:** Value and stars **Rev:** Abraham and the three angels **Edge:** Reeded

Date	Mintage	F	VF	XF	Unc	BU
JE5766-2006(ig) Proof	555	Value: 1,200				

KM# 421 10 NEW SHEQALIM
16.9600 g., 0.9170 Gold 0.5000 oz. AGW, 30 mm. **Series:** UNESCO World Heritage Sites in Israel **Subject:** White City of Tel Aviv **Obv:** Value and Bauhaus building **Rev:** Face of Bauhaus building and UNESCO symbol **Edge:** Reeded

Date	Mintage	F	VF	XF	Unc	BU
JE5766-2006(ig) Proof	383	Value: 1,150				

KM# 425 10 NEW SHEQALIM
16.9600 g., 0.9170 Gold 0.5000 oz. AGW, 30 mm. **Series:** Independence Day **Subject:** Performing Arts in Israel **Obv:** Value, state emblem and inscriptions **Rev:** Stylized actor, dancer and musician and inscription in Hebrew, English and Arabic, "Performing Arts in Israel" **Edge:** Reeded

Date	Mintage	F	VF	XF	Unc	BU
JE5767-2007(ig) Proof	332	Value: 1,200				

KM# 428 10 NEW SHEQALIM
16.9600 g., 0.9170 Gold 0.5000 oz. AGW, 30 mm. **Subject:** 2008 Olympics - Judo **Obv:** Value, state emblem, judo belt and inscriptions **Rev:** 2 judo athletes and inscriptions in Hebrew, English and Arabic **Edge:** Reeded

Date	Mintage	F	VF	XF	Unc	BU
JE5767 (2007)(u) Proof	548	Value: 1,125				

KM# 431 10 NEW SHEQALIM
16.9600 g., 0.9170 Gold 0.5000 oz. AGW, 30 mm. **Series:** Biblical Art **Subject:** Isaiah, Wolf with the Lamb **Obv:** Value, state emblem and inscriptions in Hebrew, English and Arabic **Obv. Inscription:** And the Wolf shall dwell with the Lamb **Rev:** Wolf and lamb lying together under a tree **Edge:** Reeded

Date	Mintage	F	VF	XF	Unc	BU
JE5767-2007(v) Proof	553	Value: 1,200				

KM# 452 10 NEW SHEQALIM
16.9600 g., 0.9170 Gold 0.5000 oz. AGW, 30 mm. **Series:** Biblical Art **Subject:** Parting of the Red Sea **Obv:** Value, state emblem and inscriptions **Rev:** Israelites passing through the Red Sea **Edge:** Reeded

Date	Mintage	F	VF	XF	Unc	BU
JE5769-2008(v) Proof	Est. 555	Value: 1,175				

KM# 449 10 NEW SHEQALIM
16.9600 g., 0.9170 Gold 0.5000 oz. AGW, 30 mm. **Series:** Israeli Nobel Prize Laureates **Subject:** Shmuel Yosef Agnon **Obv:** Value, state emblem and outline of Agnon **Rev:** Portrait of Agnon **Edge:** Reeded

Date	Mintage	F	VF	XF	Unc	BU
JE5768-2008(ig) Proof	322	Value: 1,150				

KM# 450 10 NEW SHEQALIM
16.9600 g., 0.9170 Gold 0.5000 oz. AGW, 30 mm. **Series:** Independence Day **Subject:** Israel's 60th Anniversary **Obv:** Value, state emblem and inscription "Independence Day" **Rev:** "60" the zero is shaped like a pomegranite and a dove **Edge:** Reeded

Date	Mintage	F	VF	XF	Unc	BU
JE5768-2008(v) Proof	444	Value: 1,100				

KM# 451 10 NEW SHEQALIM
16.9600 g., 0.9170 Gold 0.5000 oz. AGW, 30 mm. **Subject:** Israel Defense Force Reserves **Obv:** Value over a triangle, state emblem and inscriptions **Rev:** Teddy bear pendant over a soldier's ID tag **Edge:** Reeded

Date	Mintage	F	VF	XF	Unc	BU
JE5768-2008 Proof	262	Value: 1,200				

KM# 455 10 NEW SHEQALIM
16.9600 g., 0.9170 Gold 0.5000 oz. AGW, 30 mm. **Series:** UNESCO World Heritage Sites in Israel **Subject:** Masada **Obv:** Value, state emblem, image of Masada **Rev:** View of Masada, UNESCO emblem, World Heritage Site Emblem **Edge:** Reeded

Date	Mintage	F	VF	XF	Unc	BU
JE5679 (2009)(u) Proof	Est. 555	Value: 1,150				

KM# 458 10 NEW SHEQALIM
16.9600 g., 0.9170 Gold 0.5000 oz. AGW, 30 mm. **Series:** Independence Day **Subject:** Israel's Sixty-first Anniversary Birds of Israel **Obv:** Value, state emblem, warbler **Rev:** Three birds, hoopoe, warbler and finch **Edge:** Reeded

Date	Mintage	F	VF	XF	Unc	BU
JE5769 (2009)(u) Proof	Est. 650	Value: 1,150				

KM# 465 10 NEW SHEQALIM
16.9600 g., 0.9170 Gold 0.5000 oz. AGW, 30 mm. **Series:** Biblical Art **Subject:** Samson and the Lion **Obv:** Small stylized palm tree, value, state emblem **Rev:** Stylized Samson wrestling a lion, stylized palm tree **Edge:** Reeded

Date	Mintage	F	VF	XF	Unc	BU
JE5769 (2009)(u) Proof	Est. 555	Value: 1,175				

KM# 470 10 NEW SHEQALIM

16.9600 g., 0.9170 Gold 0.5000 oz. AGW, 30 mm. **Series:** UNESCO World Heritage Sites in Israel **Subject:** Old Akko (Acre) **Obv:** Fortress of Akko as seen against backdrop of Mediterranean Sea, state emblem, value **Rev:** Ancient fortress walls, Khan-el-Umdan caravanseraie and its clock tower, underground Crusader Knights' hall, White Mosque and other buildings **Edge:** Reeded

Date	Mintage	F	VF	XF	Unc	BU
JE5770 (2010)(h) Proof	Est. 555	Value: 1,175				

KM# 473 10 NEW SHEQALIM

16.9500 g., 0.9170 Gold 0.4997 oz. AGW, 30 mm. **Series:** Independence Day **Subject:** Israel National Trail **Obv:** Trail forming stylized 62, state emblem **Rev:** Map of Israel highlighting trail, boot, flowers **Edge:** Reeded

Date	Mintage	F	VF	XF	Unc	BU
JE5770-2010(h) Proof	Est. 555	Value: 1,150				

KM# 477 10 NEW SHEQALIM

16.9600 g., 0.9170 Gold 0.5000 oz. AGW, 30 mm. **Series:** Biblical Art **Subject:** Jonah in the Whale **Obv:** Small image of Jonah, value, state emblem **Rev:** Stylized Jonah in belly of whale **Edge:** Reeded

Date	Mintage	F	VF	XF	Unc	BU
JE5770-2010 Proof	Est. 555	Value: 1,200				

KM# 480 10 NEW SHEQALIM

16.9600 g., 0.9170 Gold 0.5000 oz. AGW, 30 mm. **Series:** Israeli Nobel Prize Laureates **Subject:** Menachem Begin **Obv:** Menachem Begin, Jimmy Carter and Anwar Sadat in triple handshake on White House lawn, state emblem **Rev:** Portrait of Menachem Begin **Edge:** Reeded

Date	Mintage	F	VF	XF	Unc	BU
JE5771-2010(u) Proof	Est. 888	Value: 1,200				

KM# 483 10 NEW SHEQALIM

16.9600 g., 0.9170 Gold 0.5000 oz. AGW, 30 mm. **Series:** Independence Day **Subject:** Israel's sixty-third anniversary, Dead Sea **Obv:** Image of Dead Sea region, ibex and legend "DEAD SEA" in Hebrew, English and Arabic **Rev:** Western wall of the Temple, dates and legends "JERUSALEM" in Hebrew, English and Arabic and "1 OZ FINE GOLD .999" in English and Hebrew

Date	Mintage	F	VF	XF	Unc	BU
JE5771-2011(u) Proof	Est. 555	Value: 1,200				

KM# 486 10 NEW SHEQALIM

16.9600 g., 0.9170 Gold 0.5000 oz. AGW, 30 mm. **Subject:** 2012 London Olympics, Gymnastics **Obv:** Stylized gymnast holding a ribbon in the shape of the Star of David and legends "THE OLYMPIC DELEGATION OF ISRAEL 2012" and "gymnastics" in Hebrew, English and Arabic **Rev:** Ribbon represenatation of Israeli flag, state emblem, value, dates, country name in Hebrew, English and Arabic and inscription **Edge:** Reeded

Date	Mintage	F	VF	XF	Unc	BU
JE5771-2011(u) Proof	Est. 555	Value: 1,200				

KM# 490 10 NEW SHEQALIM

16.9600 g., 0.9170 Gold 0.5000 oz. AGW, 30 mm. **Series:** Biblical Art **Subject:** Elijah in the Whirlwind **Obv:** State emblem, dates, country name in Hebrew, English and Arabic and inscription "ELIJAH WENT UP BY A WHIRLWIND INTO HEAVEN" in Hebrew, English and Arabic **Rev:** Stylized Elijah ascending to heaven in a horse-drawn chariot of fire in a whirlwind with Elisha below **Edge:** Reeded

Date	Mintage	F	VF	XF	Unc	BU
JE5771-2011 Proof	Est. 555	Value: 1,200				

KM# 494 10 NEW SHEQALIM

16.9600 g., 0.9170 Gold 0.5000 oz. AGW, 30 mm. **Subject:** Tel Megiddo, UNESCO Heritage site

Date	Mintage	F	VF	XF	Unc	BU
JE5772-2012 Proof	—	Value: 1,100				

KM# 497 10 NEW SHEQALIM

16.9000 g., 0.9170 Gold 0.4982 oz. AGW, 30 mm. **Subject:** Yitzhak Rabin **Rev:** Bust left

Date	Mintage	F	VF	XF	Unc	BU
JE5772-2012 Proof	—	Value: 1,100				

BULLION COINAGE

KM# 467 20 NEW SHEQALIM

31.1000 g., 0.9990 Gold 0.9988 oz. AGW, 32 mm. **Series:** Jerusalem of Gold **Subject:** Tower of David **Obv:** State emblem above lion of Megiddo and country name in Hebrew, English and Arabic **Rev:** Tower of David near the Jaffa Gate in Jerusalem **Edge:** Plain

Date	Mintage	F	VF	XF	Unc	BU
JE5770 (2010)(u)	3,600	—	—	—	—	BV+20%

KM# 491 20 NEW SHEQALIM

31.1000 g., 0.9990 Gold 0.9988 oz. AGW, 32 mm. **Series:** Jerusalem of Gold **Subject:** Western Wall of the Temple **Obv:** State emblem above lion of Megiddo **Rev:** Sestern wall of the Temple, dates and legends "JERUSALEM" in Hebrew, English and Arabic and "1 OZ FINE GOLD .9999" in English and Hebrew

Date	Mintage	F	VF	XF	Unc	BU
JE5771 (2011)(u)	Est. 3,600	—	—	—	—	BV+20%

MINT SETS

KM#	Date	Mintage	Identification	Issue Price	Mkt Val
MS86	JE5761 (2001) (7)	4,000	KM#163b, 172-174, 217, 315, 354 (plastic case) 350th Anniversary of the Jewish Community of Curacao	24.00	37.00
MS89	JE5761-5762 (2001-2002) (9)	3,000	KM#157, 158, 160a (JE5761), 157-159, 160a, 207, 270 (JE5762) plus Twin Towers medal (folder) Israel - New York	—	30.00
MS94	JE5761-5763 (2001-2003) (6)	3,000	KM#157-159, 160a, 207, 270 (various dates) (folder) Bank of Israel Jubilee; (given or sold to Bank of Israel employees and VIP guests, not to the general public; issued 2004)	—	45.00
MS88	JE5762 (2002) (7)	4,000	KM#163b, 172-174, 217, 315, 355 (plastic case) Yemenite Jewry (issued 2001)	27.00	40.00
MS91	JE5763 (2003) (7)	3,000	KM#163b, 172-174, 217, 315, 389 (plastic case) The March of the Living into Poland (issued 2002)	30.00	42.00
MS93	JE5764 (2004) (7)	3,000	KM#163b, 172-174, 217, 315, 390 (plastic case) Iraqi Jewry (issued 2003)	—	40.00
MS97	JE5764-5765 (2004-2005) (6)	3,000	KM#158, 159 (JE5764), 157, 160a, 207, 270 (JE5765) (folder) Israel Today	37.00	35.00
MS96	JE5765 (2005) (7)	2,500	KM#163b, 172-174, 217, 315, 391 (plastic case) Syrian Jewry (issued 2004)	—	42.00
MS100	JE5766 (2006) (6)	2,000	KM#157-159, 160a, 207, 270 (folder) To the North With Love	37.00	35.00
MS103	JE5767-5768 (2007-2008) (8)	1,000	KM#157-159, 160a (JE5767), 158, 159, 207, 433 (JE5768) (folder) The Negev Shall Blossom	37.00	46.00
MS98	JE5766 (2006) (7)	2,700	KM#163b, 172-174, 217, 315, 415 (folder) Dutch Jewry (issued 2005)	45.00	45.00
MS99	JE5766 (2006) (7)	300	KM#163b, 172-174, 217, 315, 415 (plastic case) Dutch Jewry (issued 2005)	—	45.00
MS101	JE5767 (2007) (7)	3,000	KM#163b, 172-174, 217, 315, 422 (folder) Greek Jewry (issued 2006)	43.00	42.00
MS102	JE5768 (2008) (8)	3,000	KM#163a, 172-174, 217, 315, 432, 434 (folder) Egyptian Jewry (issued 2007)	43.00	45.00
MS104	JE5769 (2009) (7)	1,800	KM#163b, 173, 174, 217, 315, 432, 436 (folder) Glorious Prague (issued 2008)	43.00	45.00
MS107	JE5769-5770 (2009-10) (6)	—	KM#160a, 207, 433 (JE5769), 158, 159, 270 (JE5770) (folder) 2010 coin set, Type II	29.95	30.00
MS105	JE5770 (2010) (7)	1,800	KM#163b, 173, 174, 217, 315, 432, 466 (folder) Jews of Algeria	43.00	45.00
MS108	JE5770-5771 (2010-2011) (5)	—	KM#433 (JE5770), 158, 159, 160a, 207, 270 (JE5771) The Western Wall, 2011 Uncirculated Coin Set	36.00	36.00

MINT SETS NON-STANDARD METALS

KM#	Date	Mintage	Identification	Issue Price	Mkt Val
MS85	JE5761 (2001) (7)	4,000	KM#163b, 172-174, 217, 315, 354 (folder) 350th Anniversary of the Jewish Community of Curacao (issued 2000)	32.00	38.00
MS87	JE5762 (2002) (7)	4,000	KM#163b, 172-174, 217, 315, 355 (folder) Yemenite Jewry (issued 2001)	32.00	40.00
MS90	JE5763 (2003) (7)	3,000	KM#163b, 172-174, 217, 315, 389 (folder) The March of the Living into Poland (issued 2002)	33.00	39.00
MS92	JE5764 (2004) (7)	3,000	KM#163b, 172-174, 217, 315, 390 (folder) Iraqi Jewry (issued 2003)	39.00	40.00
MS95	JE5765 (2005) (7)	2,500	KM#163b, 172-174, 217, 315, 391 (folder) Syrian Jewry (issued 2004)	39.00	40.00

The Italian Republic, a 700-mile-long peninsula extending into the heart of the Mediterranean Sea, has an area of 116,304 sq. mi. (301,230 sq. km.) and a population of 60 million. Capital: Rome. The economy centers around agriculture, manufacturing, forestry and fishing. Machinery, textiles, clothing and motor vehicles are exported.

MINT

R - Rome

REPUBLIC

DECIMAL COINAGE

KM# 91 LIRA

0.6200 g., Aluminum, 17 mm. **Obv:** Balance scales **Rev:** Cornucopia, value and date **Designer:** Giuseppe Romagnoli **Note:** The 1968-1969 and 1982-2001 dates were issued in sets only.

Date	Mintage	F	VF	XF	Unc	BU
2001R	100,000	—	—	—	20.00	—
2001R Proof	10,000	Value: 40.00				

KM# 219 LIRA

11.0000 g., 0.8350 Silver 0.2953 oz. ASW, 29 mm. **Subject:** History of the Lira - Lira of 1946 (KM#87) **Obv:** Head with laureate left within circle **Rev:** Apple on branch within circle flanked by sprigs **Edge:** Reeded **Note:** This is a Lira Series reproducing an old coin design in the center of each coin.

Date	Mintage	F	VF	XF	Unc	BU
2001R	50,000	—	—	—	50.00	—
2001R Proof	6,100	Value: 100				

KM# 220 LIRA

6.0000 g., 0.8350 Silver 0.1611 oz. ASW, 24 mm. **Subject:** History of the Lira - Lira of 1951 (KM#91) **Obv:** Balance scale within circle **Rev:** Value and cornucopia within circle **Edge:** Reeded **Note:** This is a Lira Series reproducing an old coin design in the center of each coin.

Date	Mintage	F	VF	XF	Unc	BU
2001R	50,000	—	—	—	50.00	—
2001R Proof	6,100	Value: 100				

KM# 87a LIRA

8.0000 g., 0.9000 Gold 0.2315 oz. AGW, 21.6 mm. **Obv:** Ceres **Rev:** Orange on branch **Edge:** Plain **Note:** Official Restrike

Date	Mintage	F	VF	XF	Unc	BU
1946 (2006)R Proof	1,999	Value: 750				

KM# 91a LIRA

4.0000 g., 0.9000 Gold 0.1157 oz. AGW, 17.2 mm. **Obv:** Balance scale **Rev:** Cornucopia, date and value **Edge:** Plain **Note:** Official Restrike

Date	Mintage	F	VF	XF	Unc	BU
1951 (2006)R Proof	1,999	Value: 400				

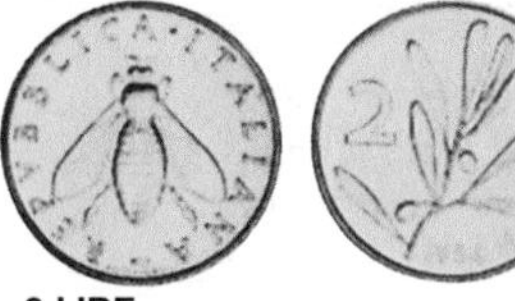

KM# 94 2 LIRE

0.8000 g., Aluminum, 18 mm. **Obv:** Honey bee **Rev:** Olive branch and value **Edge:** Reeded **Designer:** G. Romagnoli **Note:** The 1968-1969 and 1982-2001 dates were issued in sets only.

Date	Mintage	F	VF	XF	Unc	BU
2001R	100,000	—	—	—	10.00	—
2001R Proof	10,000	Value: 40.00				

KM# 88a 2 LIRE

11.0000 g., 0.9000 Gold 0.3183 oz. AGW, 24.1 mm. **Obv:** Farmer plowing field **Rev:** Wheat ear **Edge:** Plain **Note:** Official Restrike

Date	Mintage	F	VF	XF	Unc	BU
1946 (2006)R Proof	1,999	Value: 900				

KM# 94a 2 LIRE

5.0000 g., 0.9000 Gold 0.1447 oz. AGW, 18.3 mm. **Obv:** Honey bee **Rev:** Olive branch **Edge:** Reeded **Note:** Official Restrike

Date	Mintage	F	VF	XF	Unc	BU
1953 (2006)R Proof	1,999	Value: 550				

KM# 92 5 LIRE

1.0350 g., Aluminum, 20.12 mm. **Obv:** Rudder **Rev:** Dolphin and value **Edge:** Plain **Designer:** Giuseppe Romagnoli

Date	Mintage	F	VF	XF	Unc	BU
2001R	100,000	—	—	—	12.00	—
2001R Proof	10,000	Value: 20.00				

KM# 89a 5 LIRE

16.0000 g., 0.9000 Gold 0.4630 oz. AGW, 26.7 mm. **Obv:** Italia with torch **Rev:** Bunch of grapes **Edge:** Reeded **Note:** Official Restrike

Date	Mintage	F	VF	XF	Unc	BU
1946 (2006)R Proof	1,999	Value: 1,200				

KM# 92a 5 LIRE

6.0000 g., 0.9000 Gold 0.1736 oz. AGW, 20.2 mm. **Obv:** Rudder **Rev:** Dolphin and value **Edge:** Plain **Note:** Official Restrike

Date	Mintage	F	VF	XF	Unc	BU
1951 (2006)R Proof	1,999	Value: 650				

KM# 93 10 LIRE

1.6000 g., Aluminum, 23.25 mm. **Obv:** Plow **Rev:** Value within wheat ears **Edge:** Plain **Designer:** Giuseppe Romagnoli

Date	Mintage	F	VF	XF	Unc	BU
2001R	100,000	—	—	—	12.00	—
2001R Proof	10,000	Value: 35.00				

KM# 90a 10 LIRE

19.0000 g., 0.9000 Gold 0.5498 oz. AGW, 29 mm. **Obv:** Pegasus **Rev:** Olive branch **Edge:** Lettered **Edge Lettering:** REPVBBLICA ITALIANA **Note:** Official Restrike

Date	Mintage	F	VF	XF	Unc	BU
1946 (2006)R Proof	1,999	Value: 1,400				

KM# 93a 10 LIRE

10.0000 g., 0.9000 Gold 0.2893 oz. AGW, 23.3 mm. **Obv:** Plow **Rev:** Value within wheat ears **Edge:** Plain **Note:** Official Restrike

Date	Mintage	F	VF	XF	Unc	BU
1951 (2006)R Proof	1,999	Value: 800				

KM# 97.2 20 LIRE

3.6000 g., Aluminum-Bronze, 21.25 mm. **Obv:** Wheat sprigs within head left **Rev:** Oak leaves divide value and date **Edge:** Plain **Designer:** Pietro Giampaoli

Date	Mintage	F	VF	XF	Unc	BU
2001R	100,000	—	—	—	12.00	—
2001R Proof	10,000	Value: 35.00				

KM# 97.1a 20 LIRE

8.0000 g., 0.9000 Gold 0.2315 oz. AGW, 21.3 mm. **Obv:** Head laureate left **Rev:** Oak leaves divides date and value **Edge:** Reeded **Note:** Official Restrike

Date	Mintage	F	VF	XF	Unc	BU
1957 (2006)R Proof	1,999	Value: 800				

KM# 183 50 LIRE

4.5000 g., Copper-Nickel, 19 mm. **Obv:** Turreted head left **Rev:** Large value within wreath of produce **Designer:** L. Cretara

Date	Mintage	F	VF	XF	Unc	BU
2001R	100,000	—	—	—	10.00	—
2001R Proof	10,000	Value: 18.00				

KM# 95.1a 50 LIRE

14.0000 g., 0.9000 Gold 0.4051 oz. AGW, 24.8 mm. **Obv:** Italia **Rev:** Vulcan **Edge:** Reeded **Note:** Official Restrike

Date	Mintage	F	VF	XF	Unc	BU
1954 (2006)R Proof	1,999	Value: 1,000				

KM# 183a 50 LIRE

9.0000 g., 0.9000 Gold 0.2604 oz. AGW, 19.2 mm. **Obv:** Roma **Rev:** Value within wreath **Edge:** Plain **Note:** Official Restrike

Date	Mintage	F	VF	XF	Unc	BU
1996 (2006)R Proof	1,999	Value: 700				

KM# 159 100 LIRE

4.5000 g., Copper-Nickel, 22 mm. **Obv:** Turreted head left **Rev:** Large value within circle flanked by sprigs **Edge:** Segmented reeding **Designer:** Laura Cretara

Date	Mintage	F	VF	XF	Unc	BU
2001R	100,000	—	—	—	12.00	—
2001R Proof	10,000	Value: 35.00				

KM# 96.1a 100 LIRE

18.0000 g., 0.9000 Gold 0.5208 oz. AGW, 27.8 mm. **Obv:** Ancient athlete **Rev:** Minerva standing **Edge:** Reeded **Note:** Official Restrike

Date	Mintage	F	VF	XF	Unc	BU
1955 (2006)R Proof	1,999	Value: 1,300				

KM# 159a 100 LIRE

9.0000 g., 0.9000 Gold 0.2604 oz. AGW, 22 mm. **Obv:** Turreted head left **Rev:** Large value within circle flanked by sprigs **Edge:** Segmented reeding **Note:** Official Restrike

Date	Mintage	F	VF	XF	Unc	BU
1993 (2006)R Proof	1,999	Value: 650				

KM# 105 200 LIRE

5.0000 g., Aluminum-Bronze, 24 mm. **Obv:** Head right **Rev:** Value within gear **Edge:** Reeded **Designer:** M. Vallucci

Date	Mintage	F	VF	XF	Unc	BU
2001R	100,000	—	—	—	12.00	—
2001R Proof	10,000	Value: 40.00				

KM# 105a 200 LIRE

11.0000 g., 0.9000 Gold 0.3183 oz. AGW, 24 mm. **Obv:** Head right **Rev:** Value within gear **Edge:** Reeded **Note:** Official Restrike

Date	Mintage	F	VF	XF	Unc	BU
1977 (2006)R Proof	1,999	Value: 900				

KM# 98 500 LIRE

11.0000 g., 0.8350 Silver 0.2953 oz. ASW, 29.3 mm. **Obv:** Columbus' ships **Rev:** Bust left within wreath **Edge:** Dates in raised lettering

Date	Mintage	F	VF	XF	Unc	BU
2001R	100,000	—	—	—	45.00	—
2001R Proof	10,000	Value: 215				

KM# 111 500 LIRE
6.8000 g., Bi-Metallic Aluminum-Bronze center in Stainless Steel ring, 25.8 mm. **Obv:** Head left within circle **Rev:** Plaza within circle flanked by sprigs **Edge:** Segmented reeding **Designer:** Cretara

Date	Mintage	F	VF	XF	Unc	BU
2001R	100,000	—	—	—	12.00	—
2001R Proof	10,000	Value: 35.00				

KM# 98a 500 LIRE
18.0000 g., 0.9000 Gold 0.5208 oz. AGW, 29 mm. **Obv:** Columbus' ships **Rev:** Bust left within wreath **Edge:** Lettered **Edge Lettering:** REPVBBLICA ITALIANA *** 1958*** **Note:** Official Restrike

Date	Mintage	F	VF	XF	Unc	BU
1958 (2006)R Proof	1,999	Value: 1,300				

KM# 99a 500 LIRE
18.0000 g., 0.9000 Gold 0.5208 oz. AGW, 29 mm. **Obv:** Seated Italia **Rev:** Lady **Edge:** Lettered **Edge Lettering:** "1 CENTENARIO VNITA'D'ITALIA * 1861-1961* " **Note:** Official Restrike

Date	Mintage	F	VF	XF	Unc	BU
1961 (2006)R Proof	1,999	Value: 1,300				

KM# 100a 500 LIRE
18.0000 g., 0.9000 Gold 0.5208 oz. AGW, 29 mm. **Obv:** Dante **Rev:** Hell **Edge:** Lettered **Edge Lettering:** "7 CENTENARIO DELLA NASCITA DI DANTE" **Note:** Official Restrike

Date	Mintage	F	VF	XF	Unc	BU
1965 (2006)R Proof	1,999	Value: 1,300				

KM# 111a 500 LIRE
14.0000 g., Bi-Metallic .750 Gold center in .900 Gold ring, 25.8 mm. **Obv:** Head left within circle **Rev:** Plaza within circle flanked by sprigs **Edge:** Segmented reeding **Note:** Official Restrike

Date	Mintage	F	VF	XF	Unc	BU
1982 (2006)R Proof	1,999	Value: 650				

KM# 194 1000 LIRE
8.8000 g., Bi-Metallic Copper-Nickel center in Aluminum-Bronze ring, 27 mm. **Subject:** European Union **Obv:** Head left within circle **Rev:** Corrected map with United Germany within globe design **Edge:** Segmented reeding

Date	Mintage	F	VF	XF	Unc	BU
2001R	100,000	—	—	—	10.00	—
2001R Proof	10,000	Value: 35.00				

KM# 236 1000 LIRE
14.6000 g., 0.8350 Silver 0.3919 oz. ASW, 31.4 mm. **Obv:** Giuseppe Verdi **Rev:** Building **Designer:** E. L. Frapiccini

Date	Mintage	F	VF	XF	Unc	BU
2001R	115,000	—	—	—	50.00	—
2001R Proof	10,000	Value: 100				

KM# 190a 1000 LIRE
17.0000 g., 0.9000 Gold 0.4919 oz. AGW, 27 mm. **Obv:** Roma **Rev:** European map **Edge:** Segmented reeding **Note:** Official Restrike

Date	Mintage	F	VF	XF	Unc	BU
1997 (2006)R Proof	1,999	Value: 1,250				

KM# 101a 1000 LIRE
24.0000 g., 0.9000 Gold 0.6944 oz. AGW, 31.2 mm. **Obv:** Concordia **Rev:** Geometric shape above value **Edge Lettering:** REPVBBLICA ITALIANA **Note:** Official restrike.

Date	Mintage	F	VF	XF	Unc	BU
1970 (2006)R Proof	1,999	Value: 1,500				

KM# 234 50000 LIRE
7.5000 g., 0.9000 Gold 0.2170 oz. AGW, 20 mm. **Subject:** 250th Anniversary - Palace of Caserta **Obv:** Front view of palace **Rev:** Fountain, date and denomination **Designer:** L. De Simoni

Date	Mintage	F	VF	XF	Unc	BU
2001R Proof	6,200	Value: 650				

KM# 233 100000 LIRE
15.0000 g., 0.9000 Gold 0.4340 oz. AGW, 25 mm. **Subject:** 700th Anniversary - Pulpit at the Church of St. Andrea a Pistoia **Obv:** Full pulpit **Rev:** Enlarged detail of the pulpit **Designer:** C. Momoni

Date	Mintage	F	VF	XF	Unc	BU
2001R Proof	4,500	Value: 1,350				

EURO COINAGE

European Union Issues

KM# 210 EURO CENT
2.3000 g., Copper Plated Steel, 16.25 mm. **Obv:** Castle del Monte **Rev:** Value and globe **Edge:** Plain

Date	Mintage	F	VF	XF	Unc	BU
2002R	1,348,899,500	—	—	—	0.25	—
2003R	9,629,000	—	—	—	0.35	—
2003R Proof	12,000	Value: 10.00				
2004R	100,000,000	—	—	—	0.25	—
2004R Proof	12,000	Value: 7.00				
2005R	180,000,000	—	—	—	0.35	—
2005R Proof	12,000	Value: 5.00				
2006R	159,000,000	—	—	—	0.25	—
2006R Proof	12,000	Value: 5.00				
2007R	215,000,000	—	—	—	0.25	—
2007R Proof	12,000	Value: 5.00				
2008R	180,000,000	—	—	—	0.25	—
2008R Proof	5,000	Value: 5.00				
2009R	174,951,500	—	—	—	0.25	—
2009R Proof	5,500	Value: 5.00				
2010R	42,000,000	—	—	—	0.25	—
2010R Proof	5,000	Value: 5.00				
2011R	134,000,000	—	—	—	0.25	—
2011R Proof	5,000	Value: 5.00				
2012R	—	—	—	—	0.25	—
2012R Proof	—	Value: 5.00				
2013R	—	—	—	—	0.25	—
2013R Proof	—	Value: 5.00				

KM# 211 2 EURO CENT
3.0600 g., Copper Plated Steel, 18.75 mm. **Obv:** Observation tower in Turin **Rev:** Value and globe **Edge:** Grooved

Date	Mintage	F	VF	XF	Unc	BU
2002R	1,099,166,250	—	—	—	0.25	—
2003R	21,817,000	—	—	—	0.25	—
2003R Proof	12,000	Value: 10.00				
2004R	120,000,000	—	—	—	0.25	—
2004R Proof	12,000	Value: 7.00				
2005R	120,000,000	—	—	—	0.25	—
2005R Proof	12,000	Value: 5.00				
2006R	196,000,000	—	—	—	0.25	—
2006R Proof	12,000	Value: 5.00				
2007R	140,000,000	—	—	—	0.25	—
2007R Proof	12,000	Value: 5.00				
2008R	135,000,000	—	—	—	0.25	—
2008R Proof	5,000	Value: 5.00				
2009R	184,951,500	—	—	—	0.25	—
2009R Proof	5,500	Value: 5.00				
2010R	115,000,000	—	—	—	0.25	—
2010R Proof	5,000	Value: 5.00				
2011R	109,000,000	—	—	—	0.25	—
2011R Proof	5,000	Value: 5.00				
2012R	—	—	—	—	0.25	—
2012R Proof	—	Value: 5.00				
2013R	—	—	—	—	0.25	—
2013R Proof	—	Value: 5.00				

KM# 212 5 EURO CENT
3.9200 g., Copper Plated Steel, 21.25 mm. **Obv:** Colosseum **Rev:** Value and globe **Edge:** Plain

Date	Mintage	F	VF	XF	Unc	BU
2002R	1,341,742,204	—	—	—	0.25	—
2003R	1,960,000	—	—	—	10.00	—
2003R Proof	12,000	Value: 20.00				
2004R	10,000,000	—	—	—	0.25	—
2004R Proof	12,000	Value: 8.00				
2005R	70,000,000	—	—	—	0.25	—
2005R Proof	12,000	Value: 6.00				
2006R	119,000,000	—	—	—	0.25	—
2006R Proof	12,000	Value: 6.00				
2007R	85,000,000	—	—	—	0.25	—
2007R Proof	12,000	Value: 6.00				
2008R	90,000,000	—	—	—	0.25	—
2008R Proof	5,000	Value: 6.00				
2009R	84,955,000	—	—	—	0.25	—
2009R Proof	5,500	Value: 6.00				
2010R	32,000,000	—	—	—	0.25	—
2010R Proof	5,000	Value: 6.00				

Date	Mintage	F	VF	XF	Unc	BU
2011R	37,000,000	—	—	—	0.25	—
2011R Proof	5,000	Value: 6.00				
2012R	—	—	—	—	0.25	—
2012R Proof	—	Value: 6.00				
2013R	—	—	—	—	0.25	—
2013R Proof	—	Value: 6.00				

KM# 213 10 EURO CENT
4.1000 g., Brass, 19.75 mm. **Obv:** Venus by Botticelli **Rev:** Value and map **Edge:** Reeded

Date	Mintage	F	VF	XF	Unc	BU
2002R	1,142,383,000	—	—	—	0.25	—
Note: Three varieties in size of the obverse designer's name						
2003R	29,976,000	—	—	—	0.30	—
2003R Proof	12,000	Value: 15.00				
2004R	5,000,000	—	—	—	5.00	—
2004R Proof	12,000	Value: 10.00				
2005R	100,000,000	—	—	—	0.30	—
2005R Proof	12,000	Value: 7.00				
2006R	180,000,000	—	—	—	0.30	—
2006R Proof	12,000	Value: 7.00				
2007R	105,000,000	—	—	—	0.30	—
2007R Proof	12,000	Value: 7.00				

KM# 247 10 EURO CENT
4.1000 g., Brass, 19.75 mm. **Obv:** Venus by Botticelli **Rev:** Relief Map of Western Europe, stars, lines and value **Edge:** Reeded

Date	Mintage	F	VF	XF	Unc	BU
2008R	104,955,000	—	—	—	0.25	0.35
2008R Proof	5,000	Value: 7.00				
2009R	105,951,500	—	—	—	0.25	—
2009R Proof	5,500	Value: 7.00				
2010R	57,000,000	—	—	—	0.25	—
2010R Proof	5,000	Value: 7.00				
2011R	76,000,000	—	—	—	0.25	—
2011R Proof	5,000	Value: 7.00				
2012R	—	—	—	—	0.25	—
2012R Proof	—	Value: 7.00				
2013R	—	—	—	—	0.25	—
2013R Proof	—	Value: 7.00				

KM# 214 20 EURO CENT
5.7400 g., Brass, 22.25 mm. **Obv:** Futuristic sculpture by Boccioni **Rev:** Value and map **Edge:** Notched

Date	Mintage	F	VF	XF	Unc	BU
2002R	1,411,836,000	—	—	—	0.30	—
2003R	26,155,000	—	—	—	0.30	—
2003R Proof	12,000	Value: 16.00				
2004R	5,000,000	—	—	—	0.30	—
2004R Proof	12,000	Value: 14.00				
2005R	5,000,000	—	—	—	0.30	—
2005R Proof	12,000	Value: 8.00				
2006R	5,000,000	—	—	—	0.30	—
2006R Proof	12,000	Value: 8.00				
2007R	5,000,000	—	—	—	0.30	—
2007R Proof	12,000	Value: 8.00				

KM# 248 20 EURO CENT
5.7400 g., Brass, 22.25 mm. **Obv:** Futuristic sculpture **Rev:** Relief map of Western Europe, stars, lines and value **Edge:** Notched

Date	Mintage	F	VF	XF	Unc	BU
2008R	4,955,000	—	—	—	0.30	—
2008R Proof	5,000	Value: 8.00				
2009R	59,951,500	—	—	—	0.30	—
2009R Proof	5,500	Value: 8.00				
2010R	23,000,000	—	—	—	0.30	—
2010R Proof	5,000	Value: 8.00				

Date	Mintage	F	VF	XF	Unc	BU
2011R	67,000,000	—	—	—	0.30	—
2011R Proof	5,000	Value: 8.00				
2012R	—	—	—	—	0.30	—
2012R Proof	—	Value: 8.00				
2013R	—	—	—	—	0.30	—
2013R Proof	—	Value: 8.00				

KM# 215 50 EURO CENT

7.8000 g., Brass, 24.25 mm. **Obv:** Sculpture of Marcus Aurelius on horseback **Rev:** Value and map **Edge:** Reeded

Date	Mintage	F	VF	XF	Unc	BU
2002R	1,136,718,000	—	—	—	0.80	—
2003R	44,825,000	—	—	—	1.00	—
2003R Proof	12,000	Value: 18.00				
2004R	5,000,000	—	—	—	1.00	—
2004R Proof	12,000	Value: 16.00				
2005R	5,000,000	—	—	—	1.00	—
2005R Proof	12,000	Value: 10.00				
2006R	5,000,000	—	—	—	1.00	—
2006R Proof	12,000	Value: 10.00				
2007R	5,000,000	—	—	—	1.00	—
2007R Proof	12,000	Value: 10.00				

KM# 249 50 EURO CENT

7.8000 g., Brass, 24.25 mm. **Obv:** Sculpture of Marcus Aurelius on horseback **Rev:** Relief map of Western Europe, stars, lines and value **Edge:** Reeded

Date	Mintage	F	VF	XF	Unc	BU
2008R	4,955,000	—	—	—	1.00	—
2008R Proof	5,000	Value: 10.00				
2009R	2,451,500	—	—	—	1.00	—
2009R Proof	5,500	Value: 10.00				
2010R	9,000,000	—	—	—	1.00	—
2010R Proof	5,000	Value: 10.00				
2011R	5,000,000	—	—	—	1.00	—
2011R Proof	5,000	Value: 10.00				
2012R	—	—	—	—	1.00	—
2012R Proof	—	Value: 10.00				
2013R	—	—	—	—	1.00	—
2013R Proof	—	Value: 10.00				

KM# 216 EURO

7.5000 g., Bi-Metallic Copper-Nickel center in Nickel-Brass ring, 23.25 mm. **Obv:** Male figure drawing by Leonardo da Vinci within circle of stars **Rev:** Value and map within circle **Edge:** Segmented reeding

Date	Mintage	F	VF	XF	Unc	BU
2002R	966,025,300	—	—	—	1.50	—
Note: A variety exists which lacks the artist's signature						
2003R	66,474,000	—	—	—	1.50	—
2003R Proof	12,000	Value: 20.00				
2004R	5,000,000	—	—	—	1.50	—
2004R Proof	12,000	Value: 18.00				
2005R	5,000,000	—	—	—	1.50	—
2005R Proof	12,000	Value: 15.00				
2006R	108,000,000	—	—	—	1.50	—
2006R Proof	12,000	Value: 15.00				
2007R	135,000,000	—	—	—	1.50	—
2007R Proof	12,000	Value: 15.00				

KM# 250 EURO

7.5000 g., Bi-Metallic Copper-Nickel center in Nickel-Brass ring, 23.25 mm. **Obv:** Male figure drawing by Leonardo da Vinci **Rev:** Relief map of Western Europe, stars, lines and value **Edge:** Segmented reeding

Date	Mintage	F	VF	XF	Unc	BU
2008R	134,955,000	—	—	—	1.50	—
2008R Proof	5,000	Value: 15.00				
2009R	144,951,500	—	—	—	1.50	—
2009R Proof	5,500	Value: 15.00				
2010R	50,000,000	—	—	—	1.50	—
2010R Proof	5,000	Value: 15.00				

Date	Mintage	F	VF	XF	Unc	BU
2011R	88,000,000	—	—	—	1.50	—
2011R Proof	5,000	Value: 15.00				
2012R	—	—	—	—	1.50	—
2012R Proof	—	Value: 15.00				
2013R	—	—	—	—	1.50	—
2013R Proof	—	Value: 15.00				

KM# 217 2 EURO

8.5000 g., Bi-Metallic Nickel-Brass center in Copper-Nickel ring, 25.75 mm. **Obv:** Bust of Dante Aligheri left **Rev:** Value and map within circle **Edge:** Reeded **Edge Lettering:** 2's and stars

Date	Mintage	F	VF	XF	Unc	BU
2002R	463,702,000	—	—	—	4.00	—
2003R	36,160,000	—	—	—	4.00	—
2003R Proof	12,000	Value: 25.00				
2004R	7,000,000	—	—	—	5.00	—
2004R Proof	12,000	Value: 22.00				
2005R	62,000,000	—	—	—	4.00	—
2005R Proof	12,000	Value: 20.00				
2006R	10,000,000	—	—	—	4.00	—
2006R Proof	12,000	Value: 20.00				
2007R	5,000,000	—	—	—	5.00	—
2007R Proof	12,000	Value: 20.00				

KM# 237 2 EURO

8.5000 g., Bi-Metallic Nickel-Brass center in Copper-Nickel ring, 25.75 mm. **Obv:** World Food Program globe within circle **Rev:** Value and map within circle **Edge:** Reeded and lettered **Edge Lettering:** 2's and stars

Date	Mintage	F	VF	XF	Unc	BU
2004R	16,000,000	—	—	—	4.00	—

KM# 245 2 EURO

8.5000 g., Bi-Metallic Nickel-Brass center in Copper-Nickel ring, 25.75 mm. **Subject:** European Constitution **Obv:** Europa holding an open book while sitting on a bull within circle **Rev:** Value and map within circle **Edge:** Reeding over stars and 2's

Date	Mintage	F	VF	XF	Unc	BU
2005R	18,000,000	—	—	—	4.00	—

KM# 246 2 EURO

8.5000 g., Bi-Metallic Nickel-Brass center in Copper-Nickel ring, 25.75 mm. **Subject:** Torino Winter Olympics **Obv:** Skier and other designs within circle **Rev:** Value and map within circle **Edge:** Reeded with stars and 2's

Date	Mintage	F	VF	XF	Unc	BU
2006R	40,000,000	—	—	—	4.00	—

KM# 280 2 EURO

8.5000 g., Bi-Metallic Nickel-Brass center in Copper-Nickel ring, 25.75 mm. **Subject:** Turin Olympics **Obv:** Skier and town view **Rev:** Value and map within circle

Date	Mintage	F	VF	XF	Unc	BU
2006R	40,000,000	—	—	—	—	4.00

KM# 311 2 EURO

8.5000 g., Bi-Metallic Nickel-Brass center in Copper-Nickel ring, 25.75 mm. **Subject:** Treaty of Rome, 50th Anniversary **Obv:** Open treaty

Date	Mintage	F	VF	XF	Unc	BU
2007R	5,000,000	—	—	—	4.00	—

KM# 251 2 EURO

8.5000 g., Bi-Metallic Nickel-Brass center in Copper-Nickel ring, 25.75 mm. **Obv:** Bust of Dante Aligheri **Rev:** Relief map of Western Europe, stars, lines and value **Edge:** Reeded **Edge Lettering:** 2's and stars

Date	Mintage	F	VF	XF	Unc	BU
2008R	2,455,000	—	—	—	4.00	—
2008R Proof	5,000	Value: 10.00				
2009R	1,951,500	—	—	—	4.00	—
2009R Proof	5,500	Value: 10.00				
2010R	6,000,000	—	—	—	4.00	—
2010R Proof	5,000	Value: 10.00				
2011R	20,000,000	—	—	—	4.00	—
2011R Proof	5,000	Value: 10.00				
2012R	—	—	—	—	4.00	—
2012R Proof	—	Value: 10.00				
2013R	—	—	—	—	4.00	—
2013R Proof	—	Value: 10.00				

KM# 301 2 EURO

8.5000 g., Bi-Metallic Nickel-Brass center in Copper-Nickel ring, 25.75 mm. **Subject:** Declaration of Rights **Obv:** Nude male and female figures

Date	Mintage	F	VF	XF	Unc	BU
2008R	5,000,000	—	—	—	5.00	—

KM# 310 2 EURO

8.5000 g., Bi-Metallic Nickel-Brass center in Copper-Nickel ring, 25.75 mm. **Subject:** Louis Braille **Obv:** Hand reading book in braille font

Date	Mintage	F	VF	XF	Unc	BU
2009R	2,000,000	—	—	—	5.00	—

KM# 312 2 EURO

8.5000 g., Bi-Metallic Nickel-Brass center in Copper-Nickel ring, 25.75 mm. **Subject:** European Monetrary Union, 10th Anniversary **Obv:** Stick figure and Euro symbol

Date	Mintage	F	VF	XF	Unc	BU
2009R	2,000,000	—	—	—	5.00	—
2009R Proof	5,500	Value: 25.00				

KM# 328 2 EURO

8.5000 g., Bi-Metallic Nickel-Brass center in Copper-Nickel ring., 25.75 mm. **Subject:** Camillo Benso Count of Cavour **Obv:** Bust 3/4 right

Date	Mintage	F	VF	XF	Unc	BU
2010R	4,000,000	—	—	—	5.00	—
2010R Special Unc.	16,000	—	—	—	—	8.00
2010R Proof	5,000	Value: 25.00				

KM# 338 2 EURO

8.5000 g., Bi-Metallic Nickel-Brass center in Copper-Nickel ring, 25.75 mm. **Subject:** Italian Unification, 150th Anniversary **Obv:** Three banners

Date	Mintage	F	VF	XF	Unc	BU
2011R	10,000,000	—	—	—	6.00	—
2011R Special Unc.	20,000	—	—	—	—	15.00
2011R Proof	5,000	Value: 25.00				

KM# 350 2 EURO

8.5000 g., Bi-Metallic Nickel-Brass center in Copper-Nickel ring, 25.75 mm. **Subject:** Eurocoinage, 10th Anniversary **Obv:** Euro symbol on globe at center, child-like drawings around

Date	Mintage	F	VF	XF	Unc	BU
2012R	15,000,000	—	—	—	5.00	—

KM# 355 2 EURO
8.5000 g., Bi-Metallic Nickel-Brass plated Nickel center in Copper-Nickel ring, 25.75 mm. **Subject:** Giovanni Pascoli, 100th Anniversary of Death **Obv:** Giovanni Pascoli bust **Edge:** Reeded with 2's and stars

Date	Mintage	F	VF	XF	Unc	BU
2012R	15,000,000	—	—	—	5.00	—

KM# 302 5 EURO
18.0000 g., 0.9250 Silver 0.5353 oz. ASW, 32 mm. **Subject:** Antonia Meucci - 200th Birthday

Date	Mintage	F	VF	XF	Unc	BU
2003R	—	—	—	—	—	40.00

KM# 252 5 EURO
18.0000 g., 0.9250 Silver 0.5353 oz. ASW, 32 mm. **Subject:** People in Europe

Date	Mintage	F	VF	XF	Unc	BU
2003R	25,000	Value: 40.00				
2003R Proof	8,000	Value: 65.00				

KM# 253 5 EURO
18.0000 g., 0.9250 Silver 0.5353 oz. ASW, 32 mm. **Subject:** Work in Europe

Date	Mintage	F	VF	XF	Unc	BU
2003R	50,000	—	—	—	35.00	—
2003R Proof	12,000	Value: 65.00				

KM# 238 5 EURO
18.0000 g., 0.9250 Silver 0.5353 oz. ASW, 32 mm. **Subject:** World Cup Soccer - Germany 2006 **Obv:** Santa Croce Square in Florence **Rev:** Soccer ball and world globe design

Date	Mintage	F	VF	XF	Unc	BU
2004R Proof	35,000	Value: 100				

KM# 239 5 EURO
18.0000 g., 0.9250 Silver 0.5353 oz. ASW, 32 mm. **Subject:** Madam Butterfly **Obv:** La Scala Opera House, where Madam Butterfly was first performed there in 1904 **Rev:** Geisha

Date	Mintage	F	VF	XF	Unc	BU
2004R	30,000	—	—	—	30.00	40.00
2004R Proof	12,000	Value: 40.00				

KM# 254 5 EURO
18.0000 g., 0.9250 Silver 0.5353 oz. ASW, 32 mm. **Subject:** 50th Anniversary of Italian Television

Date	Mintage	F	VF	XF	Unc	BU
2004R	40,000	—	—	—	35.00	—
2004R Proof	15,000	Value: 65.00				

KM# 255 5 EURO
18.0000 g., 0.9250 Silver 0.5353 oz. ASW, 32 mm. **Subject:** 85th Birthday of Federico Fellini

Date	Mintage	F	VF	XF	Unc	BU
2005R	35,000	—	—	—	30.00	—
2005R Proof	22,000	Value: 60.00				

KM# 256 5 EURO
18.0000 g., 0.9250 Silver 0.5353 oz. ASW, 32 mm. **Subject:** 2006 Olympic Winter Games Torino Ski Jump

Date	Mintage	F	VF	XF	Unc	BU
2005R	35,000	—	—	—	30.00	—
2005R Proof	40,000	Value: 60.00				

KM# 257 5 EURO
18.0000 g., 0.9250 Silver 0.5353 oz. ASW, 32 mm. **Subject:** 2006 Olympic Winter Games Cross Country Skiing

Date	Mintage	F	VF	XF	Unc	BU
2005R	35,000	—	—	—	30.00	—
2005R Proof	40,000	Value: 50.00				

KM# 266 5 EURO
18.0000 g., 0.9250 Silver 0.5353 oz. ASW, 32 mm. **Subject:** 2006 Olympic Games Torino Figure Skating

Date	Mintage	F	VF	XF	Unc	BU
2005	40,000	—	—	—	30.00	—
2005 Proof	—	Value: 50.00				

KM# 282 5 EURO
18.0000 g., 0.9250 Silver 0.5353 oz. ASW, 32 mm. **Subject:** FIFA World Cup 12

Date	Mintage	F	VF	XF	Unc	BU
2006R Proof	—	Value: 65.00				

KM# 294 5 EURO
18.0000 g., 0.9250 Silver 0.5353 oz. ASW, 32 mm. **Subject:** Arturo Toscani - 50th Aniversary Death

Date	Mintage	F	VF	XF	Unc	BU
2007R	7,000	—	—	—	50.00	—

KM# 291 5 EURO
18.0000 g., 0.9250 Silver 0.5353 oz. ASW, 32 mm. **Subject:** Kyoto Agreement - 5th Anniversary **Obv:** Allegorical representation of nature rebelling against pollution **Rev:** Allegorical representation of clear air with a spiral of vital energy

Date	Mintage	F	VF	XF	Unc	BU
2007R Special Unc	20,000	—	—	—	40.00	—
2007R Proof	7,000	Value: 100				

KM# 292 5 EURO
18.0000 g., 0.9250 Silver 0.5353 oz. ASW, 32 mm. **Subject:** Giuseppe Garibaldi - 200th Anniversary Birth **Obv:** Portrait facing **Rev:** Harbor Lympia in Nice

Date	Mintage	F	VF	XF	Unc	BU
2007R Special Unc.	8,000	—	—	—	40.00	—

KM# 293 5 EURO
18.0000 g., 0.9250 Silver 0.5353 oz. ASW, 32 mm. **Subject:** Aitero Spinelini 100th Birthday **Obv:** Bust 3/4 facing **Rev:** Representation of Ventotene island and Parliament hemicycle

Date	Mintage	F	VF	XF	Unc	BU
2007R Special Unc.	7,000	—	—	—	50.00	—

KM# 323 5 EURO
18.0000 g., 0.9250 Silver 0.5353 oz. ASW, 32 mm. **Subject:** Arturo Toscanini. 50th Death Anniversary **Obv:** Profile left **Rev:** Hand with baton, and musical instruments

Date	Mintage	F	VF	XF	Unc	BU
2007R Special Unc.	7,000	—	—	—	40.00	—

KM# 303 5 EURO
18.0000 g., 0.9250 Silver 0.5353 oz. ASW, 32 mm. **Subject:** Anna Magnani - 100th Birthday

Date	Mintage	F	VF	XF	Unc	BU
2008R	9,000	—	—	—	—	62.00
2008R Proof	—	Value: 65.00				

KM# 281 5 EURO
18.0000 g., 0.9250 Silver 0.5353 oz. ASW, 32 mm. **Subject:** Italian Republic - 60th Anniversary

Date	Mintage	F	VF	XF	Unc	BU
2008R	9,000	—	—	—	55.00	—
2008R Proof	—	Value: 65.00				

KM# 325 5 EURO
18.0000 g., 0.9250 Silver 0.5353 oz. ASW, 32 mm. **Series:** IFAD, 30th Anniversary

Date	Mintage	F	VF	XF	Unc	BU
2008R	20,000	—	—	—	35.00	—
2008R Proof	5,000	Value: 75.00				

KM# 326 5 EURO
18.0000 g., 0.9250 Silver 0.5353 oz. ASW, 32 mm. **Subject:** Antonio Meucci **Obv:** Bust 3/4 facing right

Date	Mintage	F	VF	XF	Unc	BU
2008R Proof	9,000	Value: 45.00				

KM# 313 5 EURO
18.0000 g., 0.9250 Silver 0.5353 oz. ASW, 32 mm. **Subject:** Giro d'Italy - Cycling Race Centennial **Obv:** Two cyclists **Rev:** Bicycle and map of Italy **Designer:** V. De Seta

Date	Mintage	F	VF	XF	Unc	BU
2009R Special Unc.	14,000	—	—	—	45.00	—

KM# 315 5 EURO
18.0000 g., 0.9250 Silver 0.5353 oz. ASW, 32 mm. **Subject:** Herculaneum Discovery, 300th Anniversary **Obv:** Four dogs nipping at horse **Rev:** Marble relief of nymph drawing water with a horn **Designer:** M. C. Colaneri

Date	Mintage	F	VF	XF	Unc	BU
2009R	9,000	—	—	—	35.00	—

KM# 327 5 EURO

18.0000 g., 0.9250 Silver 0.5353 oz. ASW, 32 mm. **Subject:** FINA, 13th Anniversary **Obv:** Sculpture Allegory of the Tiber River **Rev:** Swimmer Mosaics decorating the Foro Italico **Designer:** Roberto Mauri

Date	Mintage	F	VF	XF	Unc	BU
2009R	21,000	—	—	—	35.00	—
2009R Proof	5,500	Value: 65.00				

KM# 329 5 EURO

18.0000 g., 0.9250 Silver 0.5353 oz. ASW, 32 mm. **Subject:** Alfa Romeo 100th Anniversary **Obv:** Two Automobiles: 24HP in back, new Giulietta in front **Rev:** Company logo **Designer:** V. De Seta

Date	Mintage	F	VF	XF	Unc	BU
2010R	17,000	—	—	—	35.00	—
2010R Proof	5,500	Value: 60.00				

KM# 330 5 EURO

18.0000 g., 0.9250 Silver 0.5353 oz. ASW, 32 mm. **Subject:** Confindustria 100th Anniversary **Obv:** Female head left, mechanical gears within spiral at right **Rev:** Linear eagle and 100 logo **Designer:** L. De Simani

Date	Mintage	F	VF	XF	Unc	BU
2010R	7,500	—	—	—	45.00	—

KM# 331 5 EURO

18.0000 g., 0.9250 Silver 0.5353 oz. ASW, 32 mm. **Subject:** Santa Chiara in Naples **Obv:** Church facade **Rev:** Cloister interior

Date	Mintage	F	VF	XF	Unc	BU
2010R Proof	7,500	Value: 50.00				

KM# 341 5 EURO

18.0000 g., 0.9250 Silver 0.5353 oz. ASW, 32 mm. **Subject:** Italian unification, 150th Anniversary

Date	Mintage	F	VF	XF	Unc	BU
2011R Proof	—	Value: 50.00				

KM# 343 5 EURO

18.0000 g., 0.9250 Silver 0.5353 oz. ASW, 32 mm. **Subject:** Italian Council of State, 180th Anniversary

Date	Mintage	F	VF	XF	Unc	BU
2011R Proof	7,000	Value: 50.00				

KM# 344 5 EURO

18.0000 g., 0.9250 Silver 0.5353 oz. ASW, 32 mm. **Subject:** Historical Building of the Italian Mint, 100th Anniversary

Date	Mintage	F	VF	XF	Unc	BU
2011R Proof	7,000	Value: 50.00				

KM# 345 5 EURO

18.0000 g., 0.9250 Silver 0.5353 oz. ASW, 32 mm. **Subject:** Art in Italy - Anagini

Date	Mintage	F	VF	XF	Unc	BU
2011R Proof	7,000	Value: 50.00				

KM# 353 5 EURO

18.0000 g., 0.9250 Silver 0.5353 oz. ASW, 32 mm. **Subject:** Italian Monetary Unification, 150th Anniversary **Obv:** Italia head in vertical oval **Rev:** Alegory and fruits

Date	Mintage	F	VF	XF	Unc	BU
2012R Proof	—	Value: 50.00				

KM# 258 10 EURO

22.0000 g., 0.9250 Silver 0.6542 oz. ASW, 34 mm. **Subject:** People In Europe

Date	Mintage	F	VF	XF	Unc	BU
2003	25,000	—	—	—	70.00	75.00
2003R Proof	8,000	Value: 120				

KM# 259 10 EURO

22.0000 g., 0.9250 Silver 0.6542 oz. ASW, 34 mm. **Subject:** Italian Presidency of E.U.

Date	Mintage	F	VF	XF	Unc	BU
2003R	40,000	—	—	—	45.00	—
2003R Proof	8,000	Value: 100				

KM# 240 10 EURO

22.0000 g., 0.9250 Silver 0.6542 oz. ASW, 34 mm. **Subject:** City of Genoa **Obv:** Sculpture and art works **Rev:** Tower and harbor map

Date	Mintage	F	VF	XF	Unc	BU
2004R	20,000	—	—	—	68.00	—
2004R Proof	10,500	Value: 70.00				

KM# 241 10 EURO

22.0000 g., 0.9250 Silver 0.6542 oz. ASW, 34 mm. **Subject:** Giacomo Puccini **Obv:** Puccini wearing hat **Rev:** Stage, music and quill

Date	Mintage	F	VF	XF	Unc	BU
2004R	13,500	—	—	—	60.00	—
2004R Proof	8,000	Value: 70.00				

KM# 260 10 EURO

22.0000 g., 0.9250 Silver 0.6542 oz. ASW, 34 mm. **Subject:** 2006 Olympic Winter Games Torino Alpine Skiing

Date	Mintage	F	VF	XF	Unc	BU
2005R Proof	40,000	Value: 85.00				

KM# 261 10 EURO

22.0000 g., 0.9250 Silver 0.6542 oz. ASW, 34 mm. **Subject:** 2006 Olympic Winter Games Torino Ice Hockey

Date	Mintage	F	VF	XF	Unc	BU
2005R Proof	35,000	Value: 85.00				

KM# 262 10 EURO

22.0000 g., 0.9250 Silver 0.6542 oz. ASW, 34 mm. **Subject:** 2006 Olympic Winter Games Torino Speed Skating

Date	Mintage	F	VF	XF	Unc	BU
2005R Proof	35,000	Value: 85.00				

KM# 268 10 EURO

22.0000 g., 0.9250 Silver 0.6542 oz. ASW, 34 mm. **Subject:** 60th Anniversary UN "ONU"

Date	Mintage	F	VF	XF	Unc	BU
2005	25,000	—	—	—	50.00	—

KM# 271 10 EURO

22.0000 g., 0.9250 Silver 0.6542 oz. ASW, 34 mm. **Subject:** Peace and Freedom In Europe

Date	Mintage	F	VF	XF	Unc	BU
2005 Proof	22,000	Value: 60.00				

KM# 283 10 EURO

22.0000 g., 0.9250 Silver 0.6542 oz. ASW, 34 mm. **Subject:** FIFA World Cup - Germany

Date	Mintage	F	VF	XF	Unc	BU
2006R Proof	20,000	Value: 85.00				

KM# 284 10 EURO

22.0000 g., 0.9250 Silver 0.6542 oz. ASW **Subject:** Andre Martenga - 500th Anniversary

Date	Mintage	F	VF	XF	Unc	BU
2006R Proof	8,000	Value: 75.00				

KM# 285 10 EURO

22.0000 g., 0.9250 Silver 0.6542 oz. ASW, 34 mm. **Subject:** Leonardo da Vinci

Date	Mintage	F	VF	XF	Unc	BU
2006R Proof	25,000	Value: 75.00				

KM# 286 10 EURO

22.0000 g., 0.9250 Silver 0.6542 oz. ASW, 34 mm. **Subject:** UNICEF 60th Anniversary

Date	Mintage	F	VF	XF	Unc	BU
2006R Proof	15,000	Value: 75.00				

KM# 295 10 EURO

22.0000 g., 0.9250 Silver 0.6542 oz. ASW, 34 mm. **Subject:** Treaty of Rome, 50th Anniversary

Date	Mintage	F	VF	XF	Unc	BU
2007R Proof	20,504	Value: 75.00				

KM# 296 10 EURO

22.0000 g., 0.9250 Silver 0.6542 oz. ASW, 34 mm. **Subject:** Antonia Canova - 250th Anniversary Birth **Obv:** Portrait facing **Rev:** Sculpture Eros and Psyche

Date	Mintage	F	VF	XF	Unc	BU
2007R Proof	8,000	Value: 65.00				

KM# 297 10 EURO

22.0000 g., 0.9250 Silver 0.6542 oz. ASW, 34 mm. **Subject:** Mint of Rome's School of Medallic Art - 100th Anniversary **Obv:** Sculptor designing medal, from a medal by Giuseppe Romagnoli **Rev:** School logo

Date	Mintage	F	VF	XF	Unc	BU
2007R Proof	8,000	Value: 65.00				

KM# 324 10 EURO

22.0000 g., 0.9250 Silver 0.6542 oz. ASW, 34 mm. **Subject:** Treaty of Rome, 50th Anniversary **Obv:** Pavement pattern from Capitol Square in Rome **Rev:** Steps leading up to Capitol

Date	Mintage	F	VF	XF	Unc	BU
2007R Proof	22,000	Value: 65.00				

KM# 305 10 EURO

22.0000 g., 0.9250 Silver 0.6542 oz. ASW, 34 mm. **Subject:** Andrea Palladio - 500th Birthday

Date	Mintage	F	VF	XF	Unc	BU
2008 Proof	16,000	Value: 75.00				

KM# 306 10 EURO
22.0000 g., 0.9250 Silver 0.6542 oz. ASW, 34 mm. **Subject:** University of Perugia - 700th Anniversary

Date	Mintage	F	VF	XF	Unc	BU
2008 Proof	9,000	Value: 75.00				

KM# 316 10 EURO
22.0000 g., 0.9250 Silver 0.6542 oz. ASW, 34 mm. **Subject:** International Year of Astronomy **Obv:** Head right, astrolabe at left **Rev:** Galilei's telescope, details of an astrolabe and sky **Designer:** L. De Simoni

Date	Mintage	F	VF	XF	Unc	BU
2009R Proof	9,000	Value: 75.00				

KM# 317 10 EURO
22.0000 g., 0.9250 Silver 0.6542 oz. ASW, 34 mm. **Subject:** Guglielmo Maroni's Nobel Prize in Physics **Obv:** Bust and yacht Elettra **Rev:** Radio receiver and antenna and radio waves **Designer:** U. Pemazza

Date	Mintage	F	VF	XF	Unc	BU
2009R Proof	18,000	Value: 75.00				

KM# 318 10 EURO
22.0000 g., 0.9250 Silver 0.6542 oz. ASW, 34 mm. **Subject:** Annibale Carracci, 400th Anniversary **Obv:** 1/2 length figure standing **Rev:** Historical cart **Designer:** U. Pemazza

Date	Mintage	F	VF	XF	Unc	BU
2009R Proof	9,000	Value: 75.00				

KM# 319 10 EURO
22.0000 g., 0.9250 Silver 0.6542 oz. ASW, 34 mm. **Subject:** Futurist movement, 100th Anniversary **Obv:** Building design **Rev:** Round sculpture **Designer:** Momoni

Date	Mintage	F	VF	XF	Unc	BU
2009R Proof	9,000	Value: 75.00				

KM# 337 10 EURO
22.0000 g., 0.9250 Silver 0.6542 oz. ASW, 34 mm. **Subject:** L'Aquila Earthquake, reconstruction

Date	Mintage	F	VF	XF	Unc	BU
2009R Proof	—	Value: 75.00				

KM# 332 10 EURO
22.0000 g., 0.9250 Silver 0.6542 oz. ASW, 34 mm. **Subject:** Caravaggio 400th Death Anniversary **Obv:** Bust 3/4 facing left, basket of fruit below **Rev:** Medussa head painting detail **Designer:** U. Pemazza

Date	Mintage	F	VF	XF	Unc	BU
2010R Proof	7,500	Value: 70.00				

KM# 333 10 EURO
22.0000 g., 0.9250 Silver 0.6542 oz. ASW, 34 mm. **Subject:** Giorgione, 500th Death Anniverdary **Obv:** Bust 3/4 left **Rev:** Detail from the painting "La Tempesta"

Date	Mintage	F	VF	XF	Unc	BU
2010R Proof	7,500	Value: 70.00				

KM# 334 10 EURO
22.0000 g., 0.9250 Silver 0.6542 oz. ASW, 34 mm. **Subject:** Arts of Italy, Aquileia **Obv:** Basilica and architechtural floorplan **Rev:** Interpertation from the "Tabula Peuntigeriana" **Designer:** R. Mauri

Date	Mintage	F	VF	XF	Unc	BU
2010R Proof	7,500	Value: 70.00				

KM# 339 10 EURO
22.0000 g., 0.9250 Silver 0.6542 oz. ASW, 34 mm. **Subject:** Amerigo Vespucci

Date	Mintage	F	VF	XF	Unc	BU
2011R Proof	7,000	Value: 70.00				

KM# 340 10 EURO
22.0000 g., 0.9250 Silver 0.6542 oz. ASW, 34 mm. **Subject:** Alcide de Gasperi, 130th Anniversary of Birth

Date	Mintage	F	VF	XF	Unc	BU
2011R Proof	7,000	Value: 70.00				

KM# 342 10 EURO
22.0000 g., 0.9250 Silver 0.6542 oz. ASW, 34 mm. **Subject:** Giorgio Vasari, 500th Anniversary of Birth

Date	Mintage	F	VF	XF	Unc	BU
2011R Proof	7,000	Value: 70.00				

KM# 346 10 EURO
22.0000 g., 0.9250 Silver 0.6542 oz. ASW, 34 mm. **Subject:** Art in Italy - Torino

Date	Mintage	F	VF	XF	Unc	BU
2011R Proof	7,000	Value: 70.00				

KM# 349 10 EURO
22.0000 g., 0.9250 Silver 0.6542 oz. ASW, 34 mm. **Subject:** Bari **Obv:** St. Nicolas Church

Date	Mintage	F	VF	XF	Unc	BU
2011R Proof	7,000	Value: 70.00				

KM# 354 10 EURO
22.0000 g., 0.9250 Silver 0.6542 oz. ASW, 34 mm. **Subject:** Francesco Guardi, 300th anniversary of Birth **Obv:** Venice from the lagoon **Rev:** Guardi bust

Date	Mintage	F	VF	XF	Unc	BU
2012R Proof	—	Value: 70.00				

KM# 356 10 EURO
22.0000 g., 0.9250 Silver 0.6542 oz. ASW, 34 mm. **Obv:** Bust right, signature below **Rev:** David statue and Holy Year Door

Date	Mintage	F	VF	XF	Unc	BU
2012R Proof	—	Value: 75.00				

KM# 263 20 EURO
6.4500 g., 0.9000 Gold 0.1866 oz. AGW, 21 mm. **Subject:** Arts in Europe - Italy

Date	Mintage	F	VF	XF	Unc	BU
2003R Proof	6,000	Value: 500				

KM# 242 20 EURO
6.4500 g., 0.9000 Gold 0.1866 oz. AGW, 21 mm. **Obv:** Arts In Europe: Belgium **Rev:** Flying bird obscuring a man's face

Date	Mintage	F	VF	XF	Unc	BU
2004R Proof	6,000	Value: 500				

KM# 243 20 EURO
6.4500 g., 0.9000 Gold 0.1866 oz. AGW, 21 mm. **Subject:** World Cup Soccer - Germany 2006 **Obv:** Mascot **Rev:** Soccer ball and world globe

Date	Mintage	F	VF	XF	Unc	BU
2004R Proof	7,500	Value: 500				

KM# 265 20 EURO
6.4500 g., 0.9000 Gold 0.1866 oz. AGW, 21 mm. **Subject:** 2006 Olympic Winter Games Torino Porte Palatine Gate

Date	Mintage	F	VF	XF	Unc	BU
2005R Proof	10,000	Value: 650				

KM# 267 20 EURO
6.4500 g., 0.9000 Gold 0.1866 oz. AGW, 21 mm. **Subject:** 2006 Olympic Games Torino Madama Palace

Date	Mintage	F	VF	XF	Unc	BU
2005R Proof	10,000	Value: 500				

KM# 269 20 EURO
6.4500 g., 0.9000 Gold 0.1866 oz. AGW, 21 mm. **Subject:** 2006 Olympic Games Torino Stupinigi Palace

Date	Mintage	F	VF	XF	Unc	BU
2005R Proof	10,000	Value: 500				

KM# 272 20 EURO
6.4500 g., 0.9000 Gold 0.1866 oz. AGW, 21 mm. **Subject:** Art In Europe - Finland **Obv:** Sailing ship

Date	Mintage	F	VF	XF	Unc	BU
2005R Proof	5,000	Value: 500				

KM# 287 20 EURO
6.4500 g., 0.9000 Gold 0.1866 oz. AGW, 21 mm. **Subject:** FIFA World Cup

Date	Mintage	F	VF	XF	Unc	BU
2006R Proof	4,350	Value: 500				

KM# 288 20 EURO
6.4500 g., 0.9000 Gold 0.1866 oz. AGW, 21 mm. **Subject:** European Arts - Germany

Date	Mintage	F	VF	XF	Unc	BU
2006R Proof	3,100	Value: 500				

KM# 298 20 EURO
6.4500 g., 0.9000 Gold 0.1866 oz. AGW, 21 mm. **Subject:** Treaty of Rome - 50th Anniversary **Obv:** Pavement pattern in Capital Square in Rome **Rev:** Steps leading to Capital Building

Date	Mintage	F	VF	XF	Unc	BU
2007R Proof	4,000	Value: 500				

KM# 299 20 EURO
6.4500 g., 0.9000 Gold 0.1866 oz. AGW, 21 mm. **Subject:** European Art - Ireland **Obv:** Sailing ship **Rev:** Tara Brooch

Date	Mintage	F	VF	XF	Unc	BU
2007R Proof	3,500	Value: 500				

KM# 307 20 EURO
6.4500 g., 0.9000 Gold 0.1866 oz. AGW, 21 mm. **Subject:** Andrea Palladio - 500th Birthday **Obv:** Head left **Rev:** Building façade and floorplans

Date	Mintage	F	VF	XF	Unc	BU
2008R Proof	5,500	Value: 450				

KM# 308 20 EURO
6.4500 g., 0.9000 Gold 0.1866 oz. AGW, 21 mm. **Subject:** Arts in Europe - Netherlands **Obv:** Sailing ship

Date	Mintage	F	VF	XF	Unc	BU
2008R Proof	2,011	Value: 550				

KM# 320 20 EURO
6.4500 g., 0.9000 Gold 0.1866 oz. AGW, 21 mm. **Subject:** Guglielmo Marconi, 100th Anniversary of Nobel in Physics **Obv:** Bust and yacht Elettra **Rev:** Radio receiver with antenna and radio waves **Designer:** U. Pemazza

Date	Mintage	F	VF	XF	Unc	BU
2009R Proof	5,000	Value: 500				

KM# 321 20 EURO
6.4500 g., 0.9000 Gold 0.1866 oz. AGW, 21 mm. **Subject:** Arts in Europe - Great Britain **Obv:** Sailing ship **Rev:** Venus by Edward B. Jones **Designer:** E. L. Frapiccini

Date	Mintage	F	VF	XF	Unc	BU
2009R Proof	3,000	Value: 500				

KM# 335 20 EURO
6.4500 g., 0.9000 Gold 0.1866 oz. AGW, 21 mm. **Subject:** Arts of Europe - Sweden **Obv:** Sailing ship **Rev:** Viking Helmet **Designer:** E. L. Frapiccini

Date	Mintage	F	VF	XF	Unc	BU
2010R Proof	2,000	Value: 550				

KM# 347 20 EURO
6.4500 g., 0.9000 Gold 0.1866 oz. AGW, 21 mm. **Subject:** Flora in art

Date	Mintage	F	VF	XF	Unc	BU
2011R Proof	1,500	Value: 550				

KM# 352 20 EURO
6.4510 g., 0.9000 Gold 0.1867 oz. AGW, 21 mm. **Subject:** Fauna in Art - Middle ages **Obv:** Face at center of triskles **Rev:** Two peacocks face-to-face

Date	Mintage	F	VF	XF	Unc	BU
2012R Proof	—	Value: 500				

KM# 264 50 EURO
16.1300 g., 0.9000 Gold 0.4667 oz. AGW, 28 mm. **Subject:** Arts in Europe - Austria

Date	Mintage	F	VF	XF	Unc	BU
2003R Proof	6,000	Value: 1,200				

KM# 244 50 EURO
16.1300 g., 0.9000 Gold 0.4667 oz. AGW, 28 mm. **Obv:** Arts In Europe: Denmark **Rev:** Angel carrying away two children

Date	Mintage	F	VF	XF	Unc	BU
2004R Proof	6,000	Value: 1,200				

KM# 270 50 EURO
16.1300 g., 0.9000 Gold 0.4667 oz. AGW, 28 mm. **Subject:** 2006 Olympic Games Torino Emanuele Filiberto

Date	Mintage	F	VF	XF	Unc	BU
2005R Proof	6,000	Value: 1,200				

KM# 273 50 EURO
16.1300 g., 0.9000 Gold 0.4667 oz. AGW, 28 mm. **Subject:** Art In Europe - France

Date	Mintage	F	VF	XF	Unc	BU
2005R Proof	5,000	Value: 1,200				

KM# 274 50 EURO
16.1300 g., 0.9000 Gold 0.4667 oz. AGW, 28 mm. **Subject:** 2006 Olympic Games Torino Olympic Torch

Date	Mintage	F	VF	XF	Unc	BU
2006R Proof	5,000	Value: 1,200				

KM# 289 50 EURO
16.1300 g., 0.9000 Gold 0.4667 oz. AGW, 28 mm. **Subject:** European Arts - Greece

Date	Mintage	F	VF	XF	Unc	BU
2006R Proof	1,792	Value: 1,300				

KM# 300 50 EURO
16.1300 g., 0.9000 Gold 0.4667 oz. AGW, 28 mm. **Subject:** European Art - Norway **Obv:** Sailing ship **Rev:** Painting "The Scream" by Edvard Munch

Date	Mintage	F	VF	XF	Unc	BU
2007R Proof	2,000	Value: 1,250				

KM# 309 50 EURO
16.1300 g., 0.9000 Gold 0.4667 oz. AGW, 28 mm. **Subject:** Arts in Europe - Portugal

Date	Mintage	F	VF	XF	Unc	BU
2008R Proof	2,000	Value: 1,250				

KM# 322 50 EURO
16.1300 g., 0.9000 Gold 0.4667 oz. AGW, 28 mm. **Subject:** Arts in Europe - Spain **Obv:** Sailing ship **Rev:** Sagrada Familia of Antoni Gaudí **Designer:** E. L. Frapiccini

Date	Mintage	F	VF	XF	Unc	BU
2009R Proof	2,000	Value: 1,250				

KM# 336 50 EURO
16.1300 g., 0.9000 Gold 0.4667 oz. AGW, 28 mm. **Subject:** Arts of Europe - Hungary **Obv:** Sailing ship **Rev:** Detail of painting "Rozsi Szinyei Merse" by Pal Szinyel Merse **Designer:** E. L. Frapiccini

Date	Mintage	F	VF	XF	Unc	BU
2010R Proof	1,500	Value: 1,300				

KM# 348 50 EURO
16.1300 g., 0.9000 Gold 0.4667 oz. AGW, 28 mm. **Subject:** Flora in art

Date	Mintage	F	VF	XF	Unc	BU
2011R Proof	1,000	Value: 1,300				

KM# 351 50 EURO
16.1290 g., 0.9000 Gold 0.4667 oz. AGW, 28 mm. **Subject:** Flora in Art - Middle ages **Obv:** Stylized animal's head facing **Rev:** Statue of lions confronted

Date	Mintage	F	VF	XF	Unc	BU
2012R Proof	—	Value: 1,200				

MINT SETS

KM#	Date	Mintage	Identification	Issue Price	Mkt Val
MS39	2001 (12)	125,200	KM#91-94, 97.2, 98, 105, 111, 159, 183, 194, 236	—	110
MS40	2002 (8)	50,000	KM#210-217	—	25.00
MS41	2003 (8)	50,000	KM#210-217	—	50.00
MS42	2003 (9)	50,000	KM#210-217, 253	—	60.00
MS43	2004 (8)	40,000	KM#210-217	—	35.00
MS44	2004 (9)	40,000	KM#210-217, 254	—	75.00
MS45	2005 (8)	35,000	KM#210-217	—	35.00
MS46	2005 (9)	35,000	KM#210-217, 255	—	75.00
MS47	2006 (8)	25,000	KM#210-217	—	30.00
MS48	2007 (8)	20,000	KM#210-217	—	30.00
MS49	2008 (8)	20,000	KM#210-216, 301	—	45.00
MS50	2008 (9)	5,000	KM#210-217, 281	—	125
MS51	2009 (8)	—	KM#210-212; 247-251	—	25.00
MS52	2010 (8)	—	KM#210-212; 247-251	—	25.00

PROOF SETS

KM#	Date	Mintage	Identification	Issue Price	Mkt Val
PS25	2001 (12)	10,000	KM#91-94, 97.2, 98, 105, 111, 159, 183, 194, 236	—	500
PS26	2003 (9)	12,000	KM#210-217, 253	—	160
PS27	2004 (9)	15,000	KM#210-217, 254	—	100
PS28	2005 (9)	12,000	KM#210-217, 255	—	100
PS29	2006 (8)	10,000	KM#210-217	—	100
PS30	2007 (8)	7,000	KM#210-217	—	100
PS31	2008 (9)	5,000	KM#210-212, 247-251, 325	—	160
PS32	2009 (10)	5,500	KM#210-212, 247-251, 312, 327	—	120
PS33	2010 (10)	5,000	KM#210-212, 247-251, 328, 329	—	130
PS34	2011 (10)	5,000	KM#210-212, 247-251, 338, 341	—	130

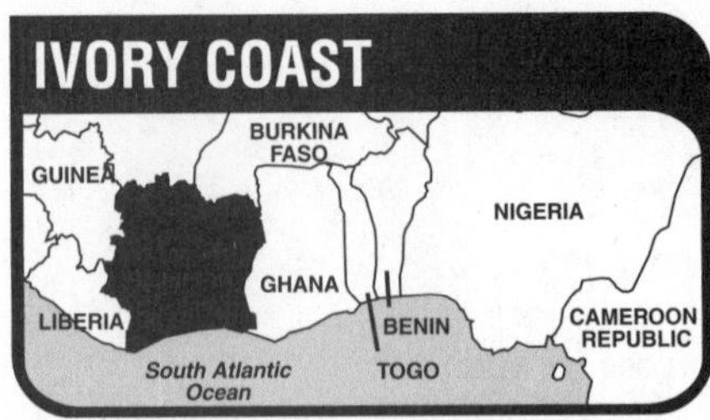

The Republic of the Ivory Coast, (Cote d'Ivoire), a former French Overseas territory located on the south side of the African bulge between Liberia and Ghana, has an area of 124,504 sq. mi. (322,463 sq. km.) and a population of 11.8 million. Capital: Yamoussoukro. The predominantly agricultural economy is one of Africa's most prosperous. Coffee, tropical woods, cocoa, and bananas are exported.

REPUBLIC

DECIMAL COINAGE

KM# 6 1000 FRANCS

25.0000 g., 0.9250 Silver 0.7435 oz. ASW, 38.6 mm. **Obv:** National arms **Rev:** Mamouth and embedded tooth fragment

Date	Mintage	F	VF	XF	Unc	BU
2010 Proof	2,500	Value: 75.00				

KM# 8 1000 FRANCS

25.0000 g., 0.9250 Silver 0.7435 oz. ASW, 38.61 mm. **Obv:** National arms **Rev:** Map of Africa with montage of animals, blue field

Date	Mintage	F	VF	XF	Unc	BU
2010 Proof	2,500	Value: 75.00				

KM# 7 1500 FRANCS

273.0000 g., 0.9250 Silver 8.1185 oz. ASW, 50 mm. **Subject:** Qibia Compass **Obv:** National arms **Rev:** Legend and design around center disc for compass spoon

Date	Mintage	F	VF	XF	Unc	BU
2010 Antique patina	—	—	—	—	500	—

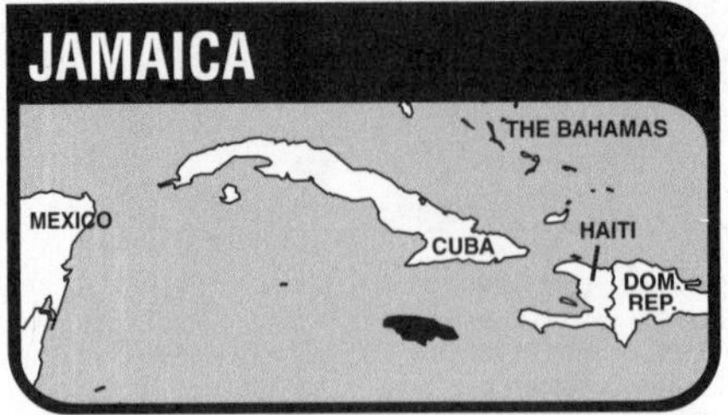

Jamaica is situated in the Caribbean Sea 90 miles south of Cuba, has an area of 4,244 sq. mi. (10,990 sq. km.) and a population of 2.1 million. Capital: Kingston. The economy is founded chiefly on mining, tourism and agriculture. Aluminum, bauxite, sugar, rum and molasses are exported.

Jamaica is a member of the Commonwealth of Nations. Elizabeth II is the Head of State, as Queen of Jamaica.

MONETARY SYSTEM
100 Cents = 1 Dollar

COMMONWEALTH

DECIMAL COINAGE

The Franklin Mint and Royal Mint had both struck 1 Cent through 1 Dollar coinage. In 1970 both mints used similar dies without mintmark. The Royal Mint issues have JAMAICA extending beyond the native headdress feathers. The Franklin Mint issues from 1971-84 have JAMAICA within the headdress feathers.

KM# 64 CENT

1.2200 g., Aluminum, 21.08 mm. **Ruler:** Elizabeth II **Series:** F.A.O. **Obv:** National arms, country named spaced beyond supporters **Obv. Legend:** JAMAICA **Rev:** Ackee fruit above value **Edge:** Plain **Shape:** 12-sided **Designer:** Christopher Ironside

Date	Mintage	F	VF	XF	Unc	BU
2002	—	—	—	0.25	0.50	0.75
2002 Proof	500	Value: 1.00				

KM# 146.2 10 CENTS

2.4000 g., Copper Plated Steel, 17 mm. **Ruler:** Elizabeth II **Series:** National Heroes **Subject:** Paul Bogle **Obv:** National arms **Obv. Legend:** JAMAICA **Rev:** Bust facing **Edge:** Plain **Note:** Reduced size.

Date	Mintage	F	VF	XF	Unc	BU
2002	—	—	—	0.25	0.50	0.75
2002 Proof	500	Value: 2.00				
2003	—	—	—	0.25	0.50	0.75
2008	—	—	—	0.25	0.50	0.75

KM# 167 25 CENTS

3.6000 g., Copper Plated Steel, 20 mm. **Ruler:** Elizabeth II **Series:** National Heroes **Subject:** Marcus Garvey **Obv:** National arms **Obv. Legend:** JAMAICA **Rev:** Head 1/4 right **Edge:** Plain

Date	Mintage	F	VF	XF	Unc	BU
2002	—	—	—	0.25	0.50	0.75
2002 Proof	500	Value: 3.00				
2003	—	—	—	0.25	0.50	0.75

KM# 164 DOLLAR

2.9100 g., Nickel Plated Steel, 18.5 mm. **Ruler:** Elizabeth II **Series:** National Heroes **Subject:** Sir Alexander Bustamante **Obv:** National arms **Obv. Legend:** JAMAICA **Rev:** Bust facing **Edge:** Plain **Shape:** 7-sided

Date	Mintage	F	VF	XF	Unc	BU
2002	—	—	—	0.40	1.00	1.50
2002 Proof	500	Value: 4.00				
2003	—	—	—	0.40	1.00	1.50
2005	—	—	—	0.40	1.00	1.50
2006	—	—	—	0.40	1.00	1.50
2008	—	—	—	0.40	1.00	1.50

KM# 189 DOLLAR

2.9000 g., Nickel Plated Steel, 18.5 mm. **Ruler:** Elizabeth II **Rev:** Sir Alexander Bustamante

Date	Mintage	F	VF	XF	Unc	BU
2008	—	—	—	—	1.00	1.50
2009	—	—	—	—	1.00	1.50

KM# 163 5 DOLLARS

4.3000 g., Nickel Plated Steel, 21.5 mm. **Ruler:** Elizabeth II **Series:** National Heroes **Subject:** Norman Manley **Obv:** National arms **Obv. Legend:** JAMAICA **Rev:** Head left **Edge:** Reeded

Date	Mintage	F	VF	XF	Unc	BU
2002	—	—	—	1.50	2.50	3.50
2002 Proof	500	Value: 5.00				
2006	—	—	—	1.50	2.50	3.50

KM# 197 10 DOLLARS

28.2800 g., 0.9250 Silver 0.8410 oz. ASW, 38.61 mm. **Ruler:** Elizabeth II **Subject:** UNICEF, 55th Anniversary

Date	Mintage	F	VF	XF	Unc	BU
2001 Proof	Est. 500	Value: 125				

KM# 181 10 DOLLARS

5.9400 g., Nickel Plated Steel **Ruler:** Elizabeth II **Series:** National Heroes **Subject:** George William Gordon **Obv:** National arms **Obv. Legend:** JAMAICA / TEN DOLLARS - (date) **Rev:** Bust facing **Edge:** Plain **Shape:** Scalloped **Note:** Diameter varies: 24-24.6.

Date	Mintage	F	VF	XF	Unc	BU
2002	—	—	—	1.50	3.00	4.00
2002 Proof	500	Value: 9.00				
2005	—	—	—	1.50	3.00	4.00

KM# 190 10 DOLLARS

6.0000 g., Nickel Plated Steel, 24.5 mm. **Ruler:** Elizabeth II **Obv:** Arms **Obv. Legend:** JAMAICA / TEN DOLLARS (date) **Rev:** George William Gordon

Date	Mintage	F	VF	XF	Unc	BU
2008	—	—	—	—	6.00	7.50
2009	—	—	—	—	6.00	7.50

KM# 182 20 DOLLARS

7.8000 g., Bi-Metallic Copper-Nickel center in Nickel-Brass ring, 23 mm. **Ruler:** Elizabeth II **Series:** National Heroes **Subject:** Marcus Garvey **Obv:** Value above national arms within circle **Obv. Legend:** JAMAICA **Rev:** Head 1/4 right within circle **Edge:** Segmented reeding

Date	Mintage	F	VF	XF	Unc	BU
2001	—	—	—	1.50	3.00	4.00
2002	—	—	—	1.50	3.00	4.00
2002 Proof	500	Value: 15.00				

KM# 186 25 DOLLARS

28.2800 g., 0.9250 Silver 0.8410 oz. ASW, 38.6 mm. **Ruler:** Elizabeth II **Subject:** UNICEF **Obv:** Arms with supporters **Rev:** Two boys above "Pals" **Edge:** Reeded

Date	Mintage	F	VF	XF	Unc	BU
2001 Proof	—	Value: 65.00				

KM# 185 25 DOLLARS

28.2800 g., 0.9250 Silver 0.8410 oz. ASW, 38.6 mm. **Ruler:** Elizabeth II **Subject:** IAAF World Junior Championships **Obv:** Arms with supporters and value **Rev:** Female runner **Edge:** Reeded

Date	Mintage	F	VF	XF	Unc	BU
2002 Proof	5,500	Value: 70.00				

KM# 184 50 DOLLARS

28.4500 g., 0.9250 Silver 0.8461 oz. ASW, 38.6 mm. **Ruler:** Elizabeth II **Subject:** Millennium **Obv:** Arms with supporters **Rev:** Family within radiant sun **Edge:** Reeded

Date	Mintage	F	VF	XF	Unc	BU
ND(2002) Proof	5,000	Value: 65.00				

PROOF SETS

KM#	Date	Mintage	Identification	Issue Price	Mkt Val
PS33	2002 (8)	500	KM#64, 146.2, 163, 164, 167, 181, 182, 185	99.00	110

JAPAN

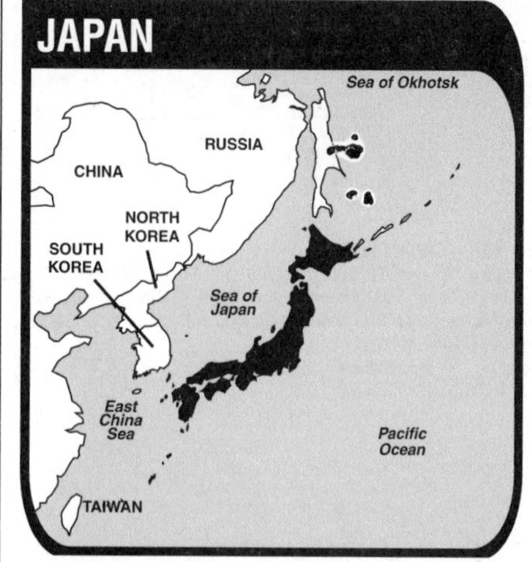

Japan, a constitutional monarchy situated off the east coast of Asia, has an area of 145,809 sq. mi. (377,835 sq. km.) and a population of 123.2 million. Capital: Tokyo. Japan, one of the major industrial nations of the world, exports machinery, motor vehicles, electronics and chemicals.

Japanese coinage of concern to this catalog includes those issued for the Ryukyu Islands (also called Liuchu), a chain of islands extending southwest from Japan toward Taiwan (Formosa), before the Japanese government converted the islands into a prefecture under the name Okinawa. Many of the provinces of Japan issued their own definitive coinage under the Shogunate.

RULERS

Emperors

Akihito (Heisei), 1989-

Years 1 – 昭和

NOTE: The personal name of the emperor is followed by the name that he chose for his regnal era.

MONETARY UNITS

Yen 円 or 圓 or 圓

EMPIRE

REFORM COINAGE

Y# 95.2 YEN

1.0000 g., Aluminum, 20 mm. **Ruler:** Akihito **Obv:** Sprouting branch divides authority and value **Rev:** Value within circles above date **Edge:** Plain

Date	Mintage	F	VF	XF	Unc	BU
Yr,13(2001)	7,786,000	—	—	0.70	1.25	1.50
Yr.13(2001) Proof	238,000	Value: 3.00				
Yr.14(2002)	9,428,000	—	—	0.70	1.25	1.50
Yr.14(2002) Proof	239,000	Value: 5.00				
Yr.15(2003)	117,131,000	—	—	—	—	0.50
Yr.15(2003) Proof	275,000	Value: 3.00				
Yr.16(2004)	52,629,000	—	—	—	—	0.50
Yr.16(2004) Proof	283,000	Value: 3.00				
Yr.17(2005)	29,771,000	—	—	—	—	0.50
Yr.17(2005) Proof	258,000	Value: 3.00				
Yr.18(2006)	129,347,000	—	—	—	—	0.25
Yr.18(2006) Proof	247,000	Value: 3.00				
Yr.19(2007)	223,702,200	—	—	—	—	0.25
Yr.19(2007) Proof	201,800	Value: 3.00				
Yr.20(2008)	134,642,800	—	—	—	—	0.25
Yr.20(2008) Proof	168,200	Value: 3.00				
Yr.21(2009)	47,871,000	—	—	—	—	0.25
Yr.21(2009) Proof	132,000	Value: 3.00				
Yr.22(2010)	7,775,000	—	—	—	—	0.25
Yr.22(2010) Proof	—	Value: 3.00				
Yr.23(2011)	348,000	—	—	—	0.75	1.00
Yr.23(2011) Proof	108,000	Value: 3.00				
Yr.24 (2012)	—	—	—	—	3.50	5.00
Yr.24 (2012) Proof	—	Value: 3.00				

Y# 96.2 5 YEN

3.7500 g., Brass, 22 mm. **Ruler:** Akihito **Obv:** Hole in center flanked by a seed leaf with authority on top and date below **Rev:** Gear design around center hole with bending rice stalk above value in horizontal lines below

Date	Mintage	F	VF	XF	Unc	BU
Yr.13(2001)	77,787,000	—	—	—	—	0.35
Yr.13(2001) Proof	238,000	Value: 1.75				
Yr.14(2002)	143,423,000	—	—	—	—	0.35
Yr.14(2002) Proof	239,000	Value: 1.75				
Yr.15(2003)	102,031,000	—	—	—	—	0.35
Yr.15(2003) Proof	275,000	Value: 1.75				
Yr.16(2004)	70,620,000	—	—	—	—	0.35
Yr.16(2004) Proof	283,000	Value: 1.75				
Yr.17(2005)	15,771,000	—	—	0.50	0.75	1.00
Yr.17(2005) Proof	258,000	Value: 3.00				
Yr.18(2006)	9,347,000	—	—	0.75	1.25	1.50
Yr.18(2006) Proof	247,000	Value: 4.00				
Yr.19(2007)	9,702,200	—	—	0.75	1.25	1.50
Yr.19(2007) Proof	201,800	Value: 4.00				
Yr.20(2008)	9,642,800	—	—	0.75	1.25	1.50
Yr.20(2008) Proof	168,200	Value: 4.00				
Yr.21(2009)	3,871,000	—	—	0.50	1.25	1.50
Yr.21(2009) Proof	132,000	Value: 4.00				
Yr.22(2010)	380,000	—	—	3.00	4.00	6.00
Yr.22(2010) Proof	—	Value: 4.00				
Yr.23(2011)	348,000	—	—	3.00	4.00	6.00
Yr.23(2011) Proof	108,000	Value: 4.00				
Yr.24 (2012)	—	—	—	1.25	1.75	2.00
Yr.24 (2012) Proof	—	Value: 4.00				

Y# 97.2 10 YEN

4.5000 g., Bronze, 23.5 mm. **Ruler:** Akihito **Obv:** Temple divides authority and value **Rev:** Value within wreath

Date	Mintage	F	VF	XF	Unc	BU
Yr.13(2001)	541,786,000	—	—	—	—	0.45
Yr.13(2001) Proof	238,000	Value: 1.75				
Yr.14(2002)	445,428,000	—	—	—	—	0.45
Yr.14(2002) Proof	239,000	Value: 1.75				
Yr.15(2003)	551,131,000	—	—	—	—	0.45
Yr.15(2003) Proof	275,000	Value: 1.75				
Yr.16(2004)	592,620,000	—	—	—	—	0.45
Yr.16(2004) Proof	283,000	Value: 1.75				
Yr.17(2005)	503,771,000	—	—	—	—	0.45
Yr.17(2005) Proof	258,000	Value: 1.75				
Yr.18(2006)	440,347,000	—	—	—	—	0.45
Yr.18(2006) Proof	247,000	Value: 1.75				
Yr.19(2007)	388,702,200	—	—	—	—	0.45
Yr.19(2007) Proof	201,800	Value: 1.75				
Yr.20(2008)	362,642,800	—	—	—	—	0.45
Yr.20(2008) Proof	168,200	Value: 1.75				
Yr.21(2009)	337,871,000	—	—	—	—	0.45
Yr.21(2009) Proof	132,000	Value: 1.75				
Yr.22(2010)	—	—	—	—	—	0.45
Yr.22(2010) Proof	—	Value: 1.75				
Yr.23(2011)	255,828,000	—	—	—	—	0.45
Yr.23(2011) Proof	108,000	Value: 1.75				
Yr.24(2012)	—	—	—	—	—	0.45
Yr.24(2012) Proof	—	Value: 1.75				

Y# 101.2 50 YEN

4.0000 g., Copper-Nickel, 21 mm. **Ruler:** Akihito **Obv:** Center hole flanked by chrysanthemums, authority at top and value below **Rev:** Value above hole in center **Edge:** Reeded

Date	Mintage	F	VF	XF	Unc	BU
Yr.13(2001)	7,786,000	—	—	—	—	3.00
Yr.13(2001) Proof	238,000	Value: 4.00				
Yr.14(2002)	11,428,000	—	—	—	—	3.00
Yr.14(2002) Proof	239,000	Value: 7.00				
Yr.15(2003)	10,131,000	—	—	—	—	3.00
Yr.15(2003) Proof	275,000	Value: 7.00				
Yr.16(2004)	9,620,000	—	—	—	—	3.00
Yr.16(2004) Proof	283,000	Value: 7.00				

Date	Mintage	F	VF	XF	Unc	BU
Yr.17(2005)	9,771,000	—	—	—	—	3.00
Yr.17(2005) Proof	258,000	Value: 7.00				
Yr.18(2006)	10,347,000	—	—	—	—	3.00
Yr.18(2006) Proof	247,000	Value: 7.00				
Yr.19(2007)	9,702,200	—	—	—	—	3.00
Yr.19(2007) Proof	201,800	Value: 7.00				
Yr.20(2008)	8,642,800	—	—	—	—	3.00
Yr.20(2008) Proof	168,200	Value: 7.00				
Yr.21(2009)	4,871,000	—	—	—	—	4.00
Yr.21(2009) Proof	132,000	Value: 7.00				
Yr.22(2010)	—	—	—	5.50	—	7.00
Yr.22(2010) Proof	—	Value: 7.00				
Yr.23(2011)	348,000	—	—	5.50	—	7.00
Yr.23(2011) Proof	108,000	Value: 7.00				
Yr.24(2012)	—	—	—	—	—	4.00
Yr.24(2012) Proof	—	Value: 7.00				

Y# 98.2 100 YEN

4.8000 g., Copper-Nickel, 22.6 mm. **Ruler:** Akihito **Obv:** Cherry blossoms **Rev:** Large numeral 100, date in western numerals **Edge:** Reeded

Date	Mintage	F	VF	XF	Unc	BU
Yr.13(2001)	7,786,000	—	—	—	—	7.50
Yr.13(2001) Proof	238,000	Value: 10.00				
Yr.14(2002)	10,428,000	—	—	—	—	5.00
Yr.14(2002) Proof	239,000	Value: 8.00				
Yr.15(2003)	98,131,000	—	—	—	—	2.50
Yr.15(2003) Proof	275,000	Value: 5.00				
Yr.16(2004)	204,620,000	—	—	—	—	2.50
Yr.16(2004) Proof	283,000	Value: 5.00				
Yr.17(2005)	299,771,000	—	—	—	—	2.50
Yr.17(2005) Proof	258,000	Value: 5.00				
Yr.18(2006)	216,347,000	—	—	—	—	2.00
Yr.18(2006) Proof	247,000	Value: 5.00				
Yr.19(2007)	129,702,200	—	—	—	—	2.00
Yr.19(2007) Proof	201,800	Value: 5.00				
Yr.20(2008)	93,642,800	—	—	—	—	2.00
Yr.20(2008) Proof	168,200	Value: 5.00				
Yr.21(2009)	114,871,000	—	—	—	—	2.00
Yr.21(2009) Proof	132,000	Value: 5.00				
Yr.22(2010)	—	—	—	—	—	2.00
Yr.22(2010) Proof	—	Value: 5.00				
Yr.23(2011)	178,828,000	—	—	—	—	2.00
Yr.23(2011) Proof	108,000	Value: 5.00				
Yr.24(2012)	—	—	—	—	—	2.00
Yr.24(2012) Proof	—	Value: 5.00				

Y# 125 500 YEN

7.0000 g., Nickel-Brass, 26.5 mm. **Ruler:** Akihito **Obv:** Pawlownia flower and highlighted legends **Rev:** Value with latent zeros **Edge:** Slanted reeding

Date	Mintage	F	VF	XF	Unc	BU
Yr.13(2001)	607,813,000	—	—	—	—	9.00
Yr.13(2001) Proof	238,000	Value: 15.00				
Yr.14(2002)	504,422,000	—	—	—	—	9.00
Yr.14(2002) Proof	239,000	Value: 15.00				
Yr.15(2003)	438,130,000	—	—	—	—	9.00
Yr.15(2003) Proof	275,000	Value: 15.00				
Yr.16(2004)	356,620,000	—	—	—	—	9.00
Yr.16(2004) Proof	283,000	Value: 15.00				
Yr.17(2005)	344,772,000	—	—	—	—	9.00
Yr.17(2005) Proof	258,000	Value: 15.00				
Yr.18(2006)	381,346,000	—	—	—	—	9.00
Yr.18(2006) Proof	247,000	Value: 15.00				
Yr.19(2007)	409,701,200	—	—	—	—	9.00
Yr.19(2007) Proof	201,800	Value: 15.00				
Yr.20(2008)	432,642,800	—	—	—	—	9.00
Yr.20(2008) Proof	168,200	Value: 15.00				
Yr.21(2009)	342,871,000	—	—	—	—	9.00
Yr.21(2009) Proof	132,000	Value: 15.00				
Yr.22(2010)	—	—	—	—	—	9.00
Yr.22(2010) Proof	—	Value: 15.00				
Yr.23(2011)	301,828,000	—	—	—	—	9.00
Yr.23(2011) Proof	108,000	Value: 15.00				
Yr.24(2012)	—	—	—	—	—	9.00
Yr.24(2012) Proof	—	Value: 15.00				

Y# 126 500 YEN

7.0000 g., Copper-Nickel-Zinc, 26.5 mm. **Ruler:** Akihito **Subject:** World Cup Soccer - Europe & Africa **Obv:** Four players and map background **Rev:** Games logo within shooting star wreath **Edge:** Reeded

Date	Mintage	VG	F	VF	XF	BU
Yr.14(2002)	10,000,000	—	—	—	—	10.00

Y# 127 500 YEN

7.0000 g., Copper-Nickel-Zinc, 26.5 mm. **Ruler:** Akihito **Subject:** World Cup Soccer - Asia & Oceania **Obv:** Three players and map background **Rev:** Games logo within shooting star wreath **Edge:** Reeded

Date	Mintage	VG	F	VF	XF	BU
Yr. 14(2002)	10,000,000	—	—	—	—	10.00

Y# 128 500 YEN

7.0000 g., Copper-Nickel-Zinc, 26.5 mm. **Ruler:** Akihito **Subject:** World Cup Soccer - North & South America **Obv:** Four players and map background **Rev:** Games logo **Edge:** Reeded

Date	Mintage	VG	F	VF	XF	BU
Yr. 14 (2002)	10,000,000	—	—	—	—	10.00

Y# 133 500 YEN

7.0000 g., Copper-Nickel-Zinc, 26.5 mm. **Ruler:** Akihito **Subject:** Expo 2005 - Aichi, Japan **Obv:** Pacific map an globe **Rev:** Circular Expo logo

Date	Mintage	VG	F	VF	XF	BU
Yr. 17(2005)	8,241,000	—	—	—	—	10.00

Y# 134 500 YEN

15.6000 g., 0.9990 Silver 0.5010 oz. ASW, 28 mm. **Ruler:** Akihito **Subject:** Chubu International Airport **Obv:** Aircraft wing in flight over airport **Rev:** Aircraft silhouettes over maps

Date	Mintage	F	VF	XF	Unc	BU
Yr. 17(2005) Proof	50,000	Value: 85.00				

Y# 137 500 YEN

7.0000 g., Copper-Nickel-Zinc, 26.5 mm. **Ruler:** Akihito **Subject:** 50th Anniversary of Japanese Antarctic Research **Obv:** Ship and two dogs **Rev:** Map of Antarctica **Edge:** Helical ridges

Date	Mintage	F	VF	XF	Unc	BU
Yr.19(2007)	6,600,000	—	—	—	—	12.00

Y# 139 500 YEN

7.0000 g., Copper-Nickel-Zinc, 26.5 mm. **Ruler:** Akihito **Subject:** Centenary of Japanese immigration to Brazil/Japan-Brazil year of exchange **Obv:** Ship **Rev:** Crossed sprigs of cherry and coffee **Note:** Prev. #Y143.

Date	Mintage	F	VF	XF	Unc	BU
Yr. 20 (2008)	4,800,000	—	—	—	—	15.00

Y# 145 500 YEN

7.1000 g., Bi-Metallic Copper-Nickel center in Nickel-Brass ring, 26.5 mm. **Ruler:** Akihito **Subject:** Local Autonomy - Shimane Prefecture **Obv:** Bell shaped bronze vessel, artifact from Kamoiwakura **Rev:** Cash coin

Date	Mintage	F	VF	XF	Unc	BU
Yr.20(2008)	1,940,000	—	—	—	15.00	17.50
Yr.20(2008) Proof	30,000	Value: 50.00				

Y# 141 500 YEN

7.1000 g., Bi-Metallic Copper-Nickel center in Nickel-Brass ring, 26.5 mm. **Ruler:** Akihito **Subject:** Local Autonomy - Hokkaido Prefecture **Obv:** Lake Toya and the former Hokkaido Government Building

Date	Mintage	F	VF	XF	Unc	BU
Yr.20(2008)	2,070,000	—	—	—	15.00	17.50
Yr.20(2008) Proof	30,000	Value: 50.00				

Y# 143 500 YEN

7.1000 g., Bi-Metallic Copper-Nickel center in Nickel-Brass ring, 26.5 mm. **Ruler:** Akihito **Subject:** Local Autonomy - Kyoto Prefecture **Obv:** Scene from an antique illustrated version of the Tale of Genji **Rev:** Cash coin

Date	Mintage	F	VF	XF	Unc	BU
Yr.20(2008)	2,020,000	—	—	—	15.00	17.50
Yr20(2008) Proof	30,000	Value: 50.00				

Y# 147 500 YEN

7.1000 g., Bi-Metallic Copper-Nickel center in Nickel-Brass ring, 26.5 mm. **Ruler:** Akihito **Subject:** Local Autonomy - Nagano Prefecture **Obv:** Zenkoji Temple and ox

Date	Mintage	F	VF	XF	Unc	BU
Yr.21(2009)	1,800,000	—	—	—	15.00	17.50
Yr.21(2009) Proof	30,000	Value: 50.00				

Y# 149 500 YEN

7.1000 g., Bi-Metallic Copper-Nickel center in Nickel-Brass ring, 26.5 mm. **Ruler:** Akihito **Subject:** Local Autonomy - Niigata Prefecture **Obv:** Two Japanese crested ibises and rice terrace

Date	Mintage	F	VF	XF	Unc	BU
Yr.21(2009)	1,800,000	—	—	—	15.00	17.50
Yr.21(2009) Proof	30,000	Value: 50.00				

Y# 153 500 YEN

7.1000 g., Bi-Metallic Copper-Nickel center in Nickel-Brass ring, 26.5 mm. **Ruler:** Akihito **Subject:** Local Autonomy - Ibaraki Prefecture **Obv:** Kairakuen Garden and plum tree **Rev:** Cast Japanese coin

Date	Mintage	F	VF	XF	Unc	BU
Yr.21(2009)	1,840,000	—	—	—	15.00	17.50
Yr.21(2009) Proof	30,000	Value: 50.00				

Y# 155 500 YEN

7.1000 g., Bi-Metallic Copper-Nickel center in Nickel-Brass ring, 26.5 mm. **Ruler:** Akihito **Subject:** Local Autonomy - Nara Prefecture **Obv:** Kentoshi-sen, ship of the Japanese envoy to China in Tang Dynasty **Rev:** Cast Japanese coin

Date	Mintage	F	VF	XF	Unc	BU
Yr.21(2009)	1,770,000	—	—	—	15.00	17.50
Yr.21(2009) Proof	30,000	Value: 50.00				

Y# 157 500 YEN

7.0000 g., Nickel-Brass, 26.5 mm. **Ruler:** Akihito **Subject:** 20th Anniversary of Emperor's Enthronement **Obv:** Imperial chrysthantem crest **Rev:** Chrysthantem blosums

Date	Mintage	F	VF	XF	Unc	BU
Yr.21(2009)	9,950,000	—	—	—	—	12.50
Yr.21(2009) Proof	50,000	Value: 30.00				

Y# 159 500 YEN

7.1000 g., Bi-Metallic Copper-Nickel center in Nickel-Brass ring, 26.5 mm. **Ruler:** Akihito **Subject:** Local Autonomy commemorative - Kochi Prefecture **Obv:** SAKAMOTO Ryoma **Rev:** Legend for 47 prefectures coin program, and ancient coin design reading "local autonomy"

Date	Mintage	F	VF	XF	Unc	BU
Yr.22(2010)	1,930,000	—	—	—	15.00	17.50
Yr.22(2010) Proof	30,000	Value: 50.00				

Y# 161 500 YEN

7.1000 g., Bi-Metallic Copper-Nickel center in Nickel-Brass ring, 26.5 mm. **Ruler:** Akihito **Subject:** Local Autonomy commemorative - Gifu Prefecture **Obv:** Shirakawa village and Chinese milk vetch **Rev:** Legend for 47 prefectures coin program, and ancient coin design reading "local autonomy"

Date	Mintage	F	VF	XF	Unc	BU
Yr.22(2010)	1,830,000	—	—	—	15.00	17.50
Yr.22(2010) Proof	30,000	Value: 50.00				

Y# 163 500 YEN

7.1000 g., Bi-Metallic Copper-Nickel center in Nickel-Brass ring, 26.5 mm. **Ruler:** Akihito **Subject:** Local Autonomy commemorative - Fukui Prefecture **Obv:** Fukuiraptor (foreground) and Fukuisaurus **Rev:** Legend for 47 prefectures coin program, and ancient coin design reading "local autonomy"

Date	Mintage	F	VF	XF	Unc	BU
Yr.22(2010)	1,800,000	—	—	—	15.00	17.50
Yr.22(2010) Proof	30,000	Value: 50.00				

Y# 165 500 YEN

7.1000 g., Bi-Metallic Copper-Nickel center in Nickel-Brass ring, 26.5 mm. **Ruler:** Akihito **Subject:** Local Autonomy commemorative - Aichi Prefecture **Obv:** Prefectural capitol building and rabbit-ear iris **Rev:** Legend for 47 prefectures coin program, and ancient coin design reading "local autonomy"

Date	Mintage	F	VF	XF	Unc	BU
Yr.22 (2010)	1,920,000	—	—	—	15.00	17.50
Yr.22 (2010) Proof	30,000	Value: 50.00				

Y# 167 500 YEN

7.1000 g., Bi-Metallic Copper-Nickel center in Nickel-Brass ring, 26.5 mm. **Ruler:** Akihito **Subject:** Local Autonomy commemorative - Aomori Prefecture **Obv:** Jomon period structure and figurines **Rev:** Legend for 47 prefectures coin program and ancient coin design reading "local autonomy"

Date	Mintage	F	VF	XF	Unc	BU
Yr.22 (2010)	1,870,000	—	—	—	15.00	17.50
Yr.22 (2010) Proof	30,000	Value: 50.00				

Y# 169 500 YEN

7.1000 g., Bi-Metallic Copper-Nickel center in Nickel-Brass ring, 26.5 mm. **Ruler:** Akihito **Subject:** Local Autonomy commemorative - Saga Prefecture **Obv:** OKUMA Shigenobu and Saga Nishiki fabric **Rev:** Legend for 47 prefectures coin program, and ancient coin design reading "local autonomy"

Date	Mintage	F	VF	XF	Unc	BU
Yr.22 (2010)	1,880,000	—	—	—	15.00	17.50
Yr.22 (2010) Proof	30,000	Value: 50.00				

Y# 171 500 YEN

7.1000 g., Bi-Metallic Copper-Nickel center in Nickel-Brass ring, 26.5 mm. **Ruler:** Akihito **Subject:** Local Autonomy commemorative - Toyama Prefecture **Obv:** Owara Kaze-no-bon Festival dancers **Rev:** Legend for 47 prefectures coin program and ancient coin design reading "local autonomy"

Date	Mintage	F	VF	XF	Unc	BU
Yr. 23 (2011)	1,770,000	—	—	—	15.00	17.50
Yr. 23 (2011) Proof	30,000	Value: 50.00				

Y# 173 500 YEN

7.1000 g., Bi-Metallic Copper-Nickel center in Nickel-Brass ring, 26.5 mm. **Ruler:** Akihito **Subject:** Local Autonomy commemorative - Tottori Prefecture **Obv:** Nageiredo Hall at Mitokusan Sanbutsuji Temple **Rev:** Legend for 47 prefectures coin program and ancient coin design reading "local autonomy"

Date	Mintage	F	VF	XF	Unc	BU
Yr. 23 (2011)	1,740,000	—	—	—	15.00	17.50
Yr. 23 (2011) Proof	30,000	Value: 50.00				

Y# 175 500 YEN

7.1000 g., Bi-Metallic Copper-Nickel center in Nickel-Brass ring, 26.5 mm. **Ruler:** Akihito **Subject:** Local Autonomy commemorative - Kumamoto Prefecture **Obv:** Kumamoto Castle **Rev:** Legend for 47 prefectures con program and ancient coin design reading "local autonomy"

Date	Mintage	F	VF	XF	Unc	BU
Yr. 23 (2011)	1,840,000	—	—	—	15.00	17.50
Yr. 23 (2011) Proof	30,000	Value: 50.00				

Y# 177 500 YEN

7.1000 g., Bi-Metallic Copper-Nickel center in Nickel-Brass ring, 26.5 mm. **Ruler:** Akihito **Subject:** Local Autonomy - Shiga Prefecture **Obv:** Biwa catfish and Round Crucian carp

Date	Mintage	F	VF	XF	Unc	BU
Yr. 23 (2011)	1,740,000	—	—	—	15.00	17.50
Yr. 23 (2011) Proof	30,000	Value: 50.00				

Y# 179 500 YEN

7.1000 g., Bi-Metallic Copper-Nickel center in Nickel-Brass ring, 26.5 mm. **Ruler:** Akihito **Subject:** Local Autonomy - Iwate Prefecture **Obv:** Water Poetry Party at Môtsû-ji

Date	Mintage	F	VF	XF	Unc	BU
Yr. 23 (2011)	1,760,000	—	—	—	15.00	17.50
Yr. 23 (2011) Proof	30,000	Value: 50.00				

Y# 181 500 YEN

7.1000 g., Bi-Metallic Copper-Nickel center in Nickel-Brass ring, 26.5 mm. **Ruler:** Akihito **Subject:** Local Autonomy - Akita Prefecture **Obv:** Nobu Shirase (explorer) and Kanto festival

Date	Mintage	F	VF	XF	Unc	BU
Yr. 23 (2011)	1,710,000	—	—	—	15.00	17.50
Yr. 23 (2011) Proof	30,000	Value: 50.00				

Y# 183 500 YEN

7.1000 g., Bi-Metallic Copper-Nickel center in Nickel-Brass ring, 26.5 mm. **Ruler:** Akihito **Subject:** Local Autonomy - Okinawa Prefecture **Rev:** Naha Giant Tug-of-war and Eisa folk dance

Date	Mintage	F	VF	XF	Unc	BU
Yr.24(2012)	—	—	—	—	15.00	17.50
Yr.24(2012) Proof	—	Value: 50.00				

Y# 185 500 YEN

7.1000 g., Bi-Metallic Copper-Nickel center in Nickel-Brass ring, 26.5 mm. **Ruler:** Akihito **Subject:** Local Autonomy - Kanagawa Prefecture **Rev:** Great Buddah of Kamakura

Date	Mintage	F	VF	XF	Unc	BU
Yr.24(2012)	—	—	—	—	15.00	17.50
Yr.24(2012) Proof	Est. 30,000	Value: 50.00				

Y# 187 500 YEN

7.1000 g., Bi-Metallic Copper-Nickel center in Nickel-Brass ring, 26.5 mm. **Ruler:** Akihito **Subject:** Local Autonomy - Miyazaki Prefecture **Rev:** Miyazaki Prefectural Government Building

Date	Mintage	F	VF	XF	Unc	BU
Yr.24(2012)	—	—	—	—	15.00	17.50
Yr.24(2012) Proof	Est. 30,000	Value: 50.00				

Y# 189 500 YEN

7.1000 g., Bi-Metallic Copper-Nickel center in Nickel-Brass ring, 26.5 mm. **Ruler:** Akihito **Subject:** Local Autonomy - Tochigi **Obv:** Sleeping cat in flora **Rev:** Ancient cash

Date	Mintage	F	VF	XF	Unc	BU
Yr. 24 (2012)	—	—	—	—	15.00	17.50
Yr. 24 (2012) Proof	—	Value: 50.00				

Y# 191 500 YEN

7.1000 g., Bi-Metallic Copper-Nickel center in Nickel-Brass ring, 26.5 mm. **Ruler:** Akihito **Subject:** Hyogo **Obv:** Two black beak storks **Rev:** Ancient cast coin

Date	Mintage	F	VF	XF	Unc	BU
Yr. 24 (2012)	—	—	—	—	15.00	17.50
Yr.24 (2012) Proof	—	Value: 50.00				

Y# 193 500 YEN

7.1000 g., Bi-Metallic Copper-Nickel center in Nickel-Brass ring, 26.5 mm. **Ruler:** Akihito **Subject:** Oita **Obv:** Buddha statue **Rev:** Ancient cash coin

Date	Mintage	F	VF	XF	Unc	BU
Yr.24 (2012)	—	—	—	—	15.00	17.50
Yr.24 (2012) Proof	—	Value: 50.00				

Y# 196 500 YEN

Bi-Metallic, 26.5 mm. **Ruler:** Akihito **Subject:** Miyagi Prefecture **Obv:** Tassles in the wind **Rev:** Historical coin design

Date	Mintage	F	VF	XF	Unc	BU
yr.25 (2013)	—	—	—	—	15.00	17.50
yr.25 (2013) Proof	—	Value: 50.00				

Y# 198 500 YEN

Bi-Metallic, 26.5 mm. **Ruler:** Akihito **Subject:** Hiroshima Prefecture

Date	Mintage	F	VF	XF	Unc	BU
yr.25 (2013)	—	—	—	—	15.00	17.50
yr.25 (2013) Proof	—	Value: 50.00				

Y# 200 500 YEN

Bi-Metallic, 26.5 mm. **Ruler:** Akihito **Subject:** Gunma Prefecture

Date	Mintage	F	VF	XF	Unc	BU
yr. 25 (2013)	—	—	—	—	15.00	17.50
yr. 25 (2013) Proof	—	Value: 50.00				

Y# 202 500 YEN

Bi-Metallic, 26.5 mm. **Ruler:** Akihito **Subject:** Yamanashi Prefecture

Date	Mintage	F	VF	XF	Unc	BU
yr. 25 (2013)	—	—	—	—	15.00	17.50
yr. 25 (2013) Proof	—	Value: 50.00				

Y# 204 500 YEN

Bi-Metallic, 26.5 mm. **Ruler:** Akihito **Subject:** Shizuoka Prefecture

Date	Mintage	F	VF	XF	Unc	BU
yr. 25 (2013)	—	—	—	—	15.00	17.50
yr. 25 (2013) Proof	—	Value: 50.00				

Y# 206 500 YEN

Bi-Metallic, 26.5 mm. **Ruler:** Akihito **Subject:** Okayama Prefecture

Date	Mintage	F	VF	XF	Unc	BU
yr. 25 (2013)	—	—	—	—	15.00	17.50
yr. 25 (2013) Proof	—	Value: 50.00				

Y# 208 500 YEN

Bi-Metallic, 26.5 mm. **Ruler:** Akihito **Subject:** Kagoshima Prefecture

Date	Mintage	F	VF	XF	Unc	BU
yr. 25 (2013)	—	—	—	—	15.00	17.50
yr. 25 (2013) Proof	—	Value: 50.00				

Y# 129 1000 YEN

31.1000 g., 0.9990 Silver 0.9988 oz. ASW, 40 mm. **Ruler:** Akihito **Subject:** World Cup Soccer **Obv:** Trophy within flower sprigs **Rev:** Games logo flanked by players **Edge:** Reeded

Date	Mintage	F	VF	XF	Unc	BU
Yr. 14 (2002) Proof	100,000	Value: 200				

Y# 132 1000 YEN

31.1000 g., 0.9990 Silver 0.9988 oz. ASW, 40 mm. **Ruler:** Akihito **Subject:** 50th Anniversary of the reversion of the Amami Islands **Obv:** Lily and bird in multicolor enamel **Rev:** Map of the Amami-shoto

Date	Mintage	F	VF	XF	Unc	BU
Yr. 15 (2003) Proof	50,000	Value: 220				

Y# 131 1000 YEN

31.1000 g., 0.9990 Silver 0.9988 oz. ASW, 40 mm. **Ruler:** Akihito **Subject:** 5th Winter Asian Games, Aomori **Obv:** Skier and skater **Rev:** Three red apples and multicolor games logo

Date	Mintage	VG	F	VF	XF	BU
Yr.15 (2003) Proof	50,000	Value: 625				

Y# 135 1000 YEN

31.1000 g., 0.9990 Silver 0.9988 oz. ASW, 40 mm. **Ruler:** Akihito **Subject:** Expo 2005 **Obv:** Blue and white enamel Pacific map in wreath **Rev:** Expo logo

Date	Mintage	F	VF	XF	Unc	BU
Yr. 16(2004) Proof	70,000	Value: 165				

Y# 138 1000 YEN

31.1000 g., 1.0000 Silver 0.9998 oz. ASW, 40 mm. **Ruler:** Akihito **Subject:** 50th Anniversary of Japan's Entry into the United Nations **Obv:** Globe and plum blossom wreath (enameled blue, pink and green) **Rev:** UN emblem

Date	Mintage	F	VF	XF	Unc	BU
Yr.18(2006) Proof	70,000	Value: 165				

Y# 140 1000 YEN

31.1000 g., 0.9990 Silver 0.9988 oz. ASW, 40 mm. **Ruler:** Akihito **Obv:** Dual multicolor rainbows **Obv. Inscription:** SKILLS / 2007 **Rev:** Mount Fuji **Rev. Legend:** International Skills Festival for All, Japan **Edge:** Helical ridges **Note:** Prev. #Y142.

Date	Mintage	F	VF	XF	Unc	BU
Yr.19(2007) Proof	80,000	Value: 75.00				

Y# 142 1000 YEN

31.1000 g., 0.9990 Silver 0.9988 oz. ASW, 40 mm. **Ruler:** Akihito **Subject:** Local Autonomy - Hokkaido Prefecture **Obv:** Lake Toya and two multicolor red-crowned cranes in flight **Rev:** Snowflakes, cherry blossoms and crescent

Date	Mintage	F	VF	XF	Unc	BU
Yr.20(2008) Proof	100,000	Value: 135				

Y# 144 1000 YEN

31.1000 g., 0.9990 Silver 0.9988 oz. ASW, 40 mm. **Ruler:** Akihito **Subject:** Local Autonomy - Kyoto Prefecture **Obv:** Multicolor scene from an antique illustrated version of the Tale of Genji **Rev:** Snowflakes, cherry blossoms and crescent **Edge:** Reeded

Date	Mintage	F	VF	XF	Unc	BU
Yr.20(2008) Proof	100,000	Value: 120				

Y# 146 1000 YEN

31.1000 g., 0.9990 Silver 0.9988 oz. ASW, 40 mm. **Ruler:** Akihito **Subject:** Local Autonomy - Shimane Prefecture **Obv:** Multicolor peony flowers and Otoriosame chogin coin **Rev:** Snowflakes, cherry blossoms and crescent **Edge:** Reeded

Date	Mintage	F	VF	XF	Unc	BU
Yr.20(2008) Proof	100,000	Value: 115				

Y# 154 1000 YEN

31.1000 g., 0.9990 Silver 0.9988 oz. ASW **Ruler:** Akihito **Subject:** Local Autonomy - Ibaraki Prefecture **Obv:** Multicolor H-II launch vehicle and Mt. Tsukuba **Rev:** Snowflakes, cherry blossoms and crescent **Edge:** Reeded

Date	Mintage	F	VF	XF	Unc	BU
Yr.21(2008) Proof	100,000	Value: 100				

Y# 156 1000 YEN

31.1000 g., 0.9990 Silver 0.9988 oz. ASW **Ruler:** Akihito **Subject:** Local Autonomy - Nara Prefecture **Obv:** Daigokuden Audience Hall in multicolor, cherry blossoms and Kemari (ancient ball players) **Rev:** Snowflakes, cherry blossoms and crescent **Edge:** Reeded

Date	Mintage	F	VF	XF	Unc	BU
Yr.21(2008) Proof	100,000	Value: 115				

Y# 148 1000 YEN

31.1000 g., 0.9990 Silver 0.9988 oz. ASW, 40 mm. **Ruler:** Akihito **Subject:** Local Autonomy - Nagano Prefecture **Obv:** Multicolor Japan Alps and Kamikochi **Rev:** Snowflakes, cherry blossoms and crescent **Edge:** Reeded

Date	Mintage	F	VF	XF	Unc	BU
Yr.21(2009) Proof	100,000	Value: 115				

Y# 150 1000 YEN

31.1000 g., 0.9990 Silver 0.9988 oz. ASW, 40 mm. **Ruler:** Akihito **Subject:** Local Autonomy - Niigata Prefecture **Obv:** Two Japanese crested ibis and Sado Island **Rev:** Snowflakes, cherry blossoms and crescent **Edge:** Reeded

Date	Mintage	F	VF	XF	Unc	BU
Yr.21(2009) Proof	100,000	Value: 100				

Y# 160 1000 YEN

31.1000 g., 0.9990 Silver 0.9988 oz. ASW, 40 mm. **Ruler:** Akihito **Subject:** Local Autonomy commemorative - Kochi Prefecture **Obv:** SAKAMOTO Ryoma and Katsurahama Beach **Rev:** Snowflakes, cherry blossoms and crescent **Rev. Legend:** Local Autonomy 60 Years **Edge:** Reeded

Date	Mintage	F	VF	XF	Unc	BU
Yr.22(2010) Proof; colorized	100,000	Value: 130				

Y# 162 1000 YEN

31.1000 g., 0.9990 Silver 0.9988 oz. ASW, 40 mm. **Ruler:** Akihito **Subject:** Local Autonomy commemorative - Gifu Prefecture **Obv:** Cormorant fishing on the Nagara River **Rev:** Snowflakes, cherry blossoms, and crescent moon with legend **Rev. Legend:** Local Autonomy 60 Years **Edge:** Reeded

Date	Mintage	F	VF	XF	Unc	BU
Yr.22(2010) Proof; colorized	100,000	Value: 130				

Y# 164 1000 YEN

31.1000 g., 0.9990 Silver 0.9988 oz. ASW, 40 mm. **Ruler:** Akihito **Subject:** Local Autonomy commemorative - Fukui Prefecture **Obv:** Fukuiraptor and Tojinbo Cliffs **Rev:** Snowflakes, cherry blossoms, and crescent moon with legend **Rev. Legend:** Local Autonomy 60 Years **Edge:** Reeded

Date	Mintage	F	VF	XF	Unc	BU
Yr.22(2010) Proof; colorized	100,000	Value: 130				

Y# 166 1000 YEN

31.1000 g., 1.0000 Silver 0.9998 oz. ASW, 40 mm. **Ruler:** Akihito **Subject:** Local Autonomy commemorative - Aichi Prefecture **Obv:** Golden dolphin, rabbit-ear iris and the Atsumi Peninsula **Rev:** Snowflakes, cherry blossoms and crescent moon with legend reading "local autonomy 60 years" **Edge:** Reeded

Date	Mintage	F	VF	XF	Unc	BU
Yr.22 (2010) Proof	100,000	Value: 130				

Y# 168 1000 YEN

31.1000 g., 1.0000 Silver 0.9998 oz. ASW, 40 mm. **Ruler:** Akihito **Subject:** Local Autonomy commemorative - Aomori Prefecture **Obv:** Traditional parade floats and apples **Rev:** Snowflakes, cherry blossoms and crescent moon with legend reading "local autonomy 60 years" **Edge:** Reeded

Date	Mintage	F	VF	XF	Unc	BU
Yr.22 (2010) Proof	100,000	Value: 130				

Y# 170 1000 YEN

31.1000 g., 1.0000 Silver 0.9998 oz. ASW, 40 mm. **Ruler:** Akihito **Subject:** Local Autonomy commemorative - Saga Prefecture **Obv:** OKUMA Shigenobu and Imari - Arita ware **Rev:** Snowflakes, cherry blossoms and crescent moon with legend reading "local autonomy 60 years" **Edge:** Reeded

Date	Mintage	F	VF	XF	Unc	BU
Yr.22 (2010) Proof	100,000	Value: 130				

Y# 172 1000 YEN

31.1050 g., 1.0000 Silver 1.0000 oz. ASW, 40 mm. **Ruler:** Akihito **Subject:** Local Autonomy commemorative - Toyama Prefecture **Obv:** Tateyama mountain range rising from the sea **Rev:** Snowflakes, cherry blossoms and crescent moon with legend reading "local autonomy 60 years" **Edge:** Reeded

Date	Mintage	F	VF	XF	Unc	BU
Yr. 23 (2011) Proof	100,000	Value: 130				

Y# 174 1000 YEN

31.1000 g., 1.0000 Silver 0.9998 oz. ASW, 40 mm. **Ruler:** Akihito **Subject:** Local Autonomy commemorative - Tottori Prefecture **Obv:** Tottori Sand Dunes and San'in Kaigan Coast **Rev:** Snowflakes, cherry blossoms and crescent moon with legend reading "local autonomy 60 years" **Edge:** Reeded

Date	Mintage	F	VF	XF	Unc	BU
Yr. 23 (2011) Proof	100,000	Value: 130				

Y# 176 1000 YEN

31.1000 g., 1.0000 Silver 0.9998 oz. ASW, 40 mm. **Ruler:** Akihito **Subject:** Local Autonomy commemorative - Kumamoto Prefecture **Obv:** Mount Aso **Rev:** Snowflakes, cherry blossoms and crescent moon with legend reading "local autonomy 60 years" **Edge:** Reeded

Date	Mintage	F	VF	XF	Unc	BU
Yr. 23 (2011) Proof	100,000	Value: 130				

Y# 178 1000 YEN

31.1050 g., 0.9990 Silver 0.9990 oz. ASW, 40 mm. **Ruler:** Akihito **Subject:** Local Autonomy - Shiga Prefecture **Obv:** Lake Biwa, family of little grebe birds and Ukimido temple **Edge:** Reeded

Date	Mintage	F	VF	XF	Unc	BU
Yr. 23 (2011) Proof	100,000	Value: 115				

Y# 180 1000 YEN

31.1050 g., 0.9990 Silver 0.9990 oz. ASW, 40 mm. **Ruler:** Akihito **Subject:** Local Autonomy - Iwate Prefecture **Obv:** Konjiko-do, the golden hall of Chuson-ji Temple, lotus and Pure Land Garden of Motsu-ji temple **Edge:** Reeded

Date	Mintage	F	VF	XF	Unc	BU
Yr. 23 (2011) Proof	100,000	Value: 110				

Y# 182 1000 YEN

31.1050 g., 0.9990 Silver 0.9990 oz. ASW, 40 mm. **Ruler:** Akihito **Subject:** Local Autonomy - Akita Prefecture **Obv:** Nobu Shirase, Antartic explorer, Namahage folk ritual **Edge:** Reeded

Date	Mintage	F	VF	XF	Unc	BU
Yr. 23 (2011) Proof	100,000	Value: 110				

Y# 184 1000 YEN

31.1000 g., 0.9990 Silver 0.9988 oz. ASW, 40 mm. **Ruler:** Akihito **Subject:** Local Autonomy - Okinawa Prefecture **Obv:** State Hall in Suri and Kumidori dancer **Edge:** Reeded

Date	Mintage	F	VF	XF	Unc	BU
Yr.24(2012) Proof	100,000	Value: 100				

Y# 186 1000 YEN

31.1000 g., 0.9990 Silver 0.9988 oz. ASW, 40 mm. **Ruler:** Akihito **Subject:** Local Autonomy - Kanagawa Prefecture **Obv:** Tsurugaoka Hachimangu Shrine and horseback archery - Yabusame **Edge:** Reeded

Date	Mintage	F	VF	XF	Unc	BU
Yr.24(2012) Proof	100,000	Value: 100				

Y# 188 1000 YEN

31.1000 g., 0.9990 Silver 0.9988 oz. ASW, 40 mm. **Ruler:** Akihito **Subject:** Local Autonomy - Miyazaki Prefecture **Obv:** Miyazaki Prefectural Government Building and Takachiho Yokagura dancer **Edge:** Reeded

Date	Mintage	F	VF	XF	Unc	BU
Yr.24(2012) Proof	100,000	Value: 100				

Y# 190 1000 YEN

31.1300 g., 0.9990 Silver 0.9998 oz. ASW, 40 mm. **Ruler:** Akihito **Subject:** Tochigi **Obv:** Tokugawa Ieyasu Mausoleum in Nikko in color **Rev:** Crescent moon, flora and snowflake

Date	Mintage	F	VF	XF	Unc	BU
Yr.24 (2012) Proof	—	Value: 95.00				

Y# 192 1000 YEN

31.1300 g., 0.9990 Silver 0.9998 oz. ASW, 40 mm. **Ruler:** Akihito **Subject:** Hyogo **Obv:** Black beaked stork in flight over Himeji temple **Rev:** Crescent moon, flora and snowflake

Date	Mintage	F	VF	XF	Unc	BU
Yr. 24 (2012) Proof	100,000	Value: 95.00				

Y# 194 1000 YEN

31.1300 g., 0.9990 Silver 0.9998 oz. ASW, 40 mm. **Ruler:** Akihito **Subject:** Oita **Obv:** Sumo wreestler Akiyoski Sadaji, and Usa shrine **Rev:** Crescent moon, flora and snowflake

Date	Mintage	F	VF	XF	Unc	BU
Yr.24 (2012) Proof	100,000	Value: 95.00				

Y# 195 1000 YEN

31.1300 g., 0.9990 Silver 0.9998 oz. ASW, 40 mm. **Ruler:** Akihito **Subject:** International Monatary Fund Meeting, Toyko **Obv:** Mt. Fuji and traditional pesants in color **Rev:** Pan-Pacific map

Date	Mintage	F	VF	XF	Unc	BU
Yr.24 (2012) Proof	—	Value: 95.00				

Y# 199 1000 YEN

Silver, 40 mm. **Ruler:** Akihito **Subject:** Hiroshima Prefecture

Date	Mintage	F	VF	XF	Unc	BU
yr. 25 (2013) Proof	—	Value: 100				

Y# 201 1000 YEN

Silver, 40 mm. **Ruler:** Akihito **Subject:** Gunma Prefecture

Date	Mintage	F	VF	XF	Unc	BU
yr. 25 (2013) Proof	—	Value: 100				

Y# 203 1000 YEN

Silver, 40 mm. **Ruler:** Akihito **Subject:** Yamanashi Prefecture

Date	Mintage	F	VF	XF	Unc	BU
yr. 25 (2013) Proof	—	Value: 100				

Y# 205 1000 YEN

Silver, 40 mm. **Ruler:** Akihito **Subject:** Shizuoka Prefecture

Date	Mintage	F	VF	XF	Unc	BU
yr. 25 (2013) Proof	—	Value: 100				

Y# 207 1000 YEN

Silver, 40 mm. **Ruler:** Akihito **Subject:** Okayama Prefecture

Date	Mintage	F	VF	XF	Unc	BU
yr. 25 (2013) Proof	—	Value: 100				

Y# 209 1000 YEN

Silver, 40 mm. **Ruler:** Akihito **Subject:** Kagoshima Prefecture

Date	Mintage	F	VF	XF	Unc	BU
yr. 25 (2013) Proof	—	Value: 100				

Y# 130 10000 YEN

15.6000 g., 0.9990 Gold 0.5010 oz. AGW, 26 mm. **Ruler:** Akihito **Subject:** World Cup Soccer **Obv:** Two soccer players **Rev:** Games logo **Edge:** Reeded

Date	Mintage	F	VF	XF	Unc	BU
Yr.14(2002) Proof	100,000	Value: 1,000				

Y# 136 10000 YEN

15.6000 g., 0.9990 Gold 0.5010 oz. AGW, 26 mm. **Ruler:** Akihito **Subject:** Expo 2005 **Obv:** Two owls on globe **Rev:** Expo logo

Date	Mintage	F	VF	XF	Unc	BU
Yr. 16(2004) Proof	70,000	Value: 1,000				

Y# 158 10000 YEN

20.0000 g., 0.9990 Gold 0.6423 oz. AGW, 28 mm. **Ruler:** Akihito **Subject:** 20th Anniversary of Emperor's enthronment **Obv:** Imperial christaniumn crest **Rev:** Phoenix, an auspicious cloud, Niju-bashi bridge

Date	Mintage	F	VF	XF	Unc	BU
Yr.21(2009) Proof	100,000	Value: 1,200				

MINT SETS

KM#	Date	Mintage	Identification	Issue Price	Mkt Val
MS125	2001 (6)	8,000	Y#95.2-98.2, 101.2, 125 Mint exhibition in Fukuoka	16.00	30.00
MS126	2001 (6)	85,000	Y#95.2-98.2, 101.2, 125 Osaka cherry blossoms box	17.00	30.00
MS127	2001 (6)	10,000	Y#95.2-98.2, 101.2, 125 Hiroshima cherry blossoms box	17.00	33.00
MS128	2001 (6)	10,000	Y#95.2-98.2, 101.2, 125 12th Tokyo International Coin Convention	17.00	30.00
MS129	2001 (6)	5,000	Y#95.2-98.2, 101.2, 125 Beautiful Future Exposition	17.00	30.00
MS130	2001 (6)	8,000	Y#95.2-98.2, 101.2, 125 Kagoshima Coin and Stamp Show	17.00	30.00
MS131	2001 (6)	5,000	Y#95.2-98.2, 101.2, 125 Tokyo Mint Fair	17.00	33.00
MS132	2001 (6)	5,000	Y#95.2-98.2, 101.2, 125 Yamaguchi Exposition	17.00	40.00
MS133	2001 (6)	193,600	Y#95.2-98.2, 101.2, 125 21st Century Commemorative Respect for the Aged	17.00	27.00
MS134	2001 (6)	190,300	Y#95.2-98.2, 101.2, 125 Ryukyu World Cultural Sites	17.00	27.00
MS135	2001 (6)	8,300	Y#95.2-98.2, 101.2, 125 "Anniversary" folder	18.00	33.00
MS136	2001 (1)	4,000	Y#125 Mint Visit Commemorative	8.00	10.00
MS137	2001 (6)	224,000	Y#95.2-98.2, 101.2, 125 Mint Bureau Box	15.00	27.00
MS138	2001 (6)	7,300	Y#95.2-98.2, 101.2, 125 "Japan Coins"	17.00	30.00
MS139	2001 (2)	5,000	Y#96.2, 125 "Japan Coins" (short set)	8.50	13.00

KM#	Date	Mintage	Identification	Issue Price	Mkt Val
MS140	2001 (6)	128,700	Y#95.2-98.2, 101.2, 125 World Intangible Heritage - Nogaku	17.00	27.00
MS141	2002 (1)	3,000	Y#125 Mint Visit Commemorative	7.50	10.00
MS142	2002 (6)	7,000	Y#95.2-98.2, 102.2, 125 "Anniversary" folder	18.00	27.00
MS143	2002 (2)	4,000	Y#96.2, 125. "Japan Coins" (short set)	8.50	13.00
MS144	2002 (6)	6,000	Y#95.2-98.2, 101.2, 125 "Japan Coins"	17.00	23.00
MS145	2002 (6)	4,000	Y#95.2-98.2, 101.2, 125 Mint exhibition in Takamatsu	16.00	33.00
MS146	2002 (6)	80,000	Y#95.2-98.2, 101.2, 125 Osaka cherry blossoms	16.00	20.00
MS147	2002 (6)	10,000	Y#95.2-98.2, 101.2, 125 Hiroshima cherry blossoms	16.00	23.00
MS148	2002 (6)	10,000	Y#95.2-98.2, 101.2, 125 13th Tokyo Int'l Coin Convention	16.00	20.00
MS149	2002 (6)	6,000	Y#95.2-98.2, 101.2, 125 Mint exhibition in Sendai	16.00	23.00
MS150	2002 (6)	194,000	Y#95.2-98.2, 101.2, 125 Respect for the Aged	19.00	20.00
MS151	2002 (6)	6,000	Y#95.2-98.2, 101.2, 125 Matsuyama Coin and Stamp Show	16.00	23.00
MS152	2002 (6)	3,000	Y395.2-98.2, 101.2, 125 Tokyo Mint Fair	16.00	120
MS153	2002 (6)	2,000	Y#95.2-98.2, 101,2, 125 Birthday folder (with sound recording function)	25.00	40.00
MS154	2002 (6)	214,800	Y395.2-98.2, 101.2, 125 Mint Bureau box	15.00	20.00
MSA141	2002 (3)	50,000	Y#126-128 World Cup soccer	26.00	35.00
MS155	2003 (6)	8,000	Y#95.2-98.2, 101,2, 125 "Japan Coins"	17.00	20.00
MS156	2003 (6)	7,000	Y#95.2-98.2, 101.2, 125 "Anniversary" folder	18.00	20.00
MS157	2003 (6)	3,000	Y#95.2-98.2, 101.2, 125 "Anniversary" folder (with sound recording function)	25.00	27.00
MS158	2003 (6)	6,000	Y#95.2-98.2, 101.2, 125 Mint exhibition in Okayama	16.00	30.00
MS159	2003 (6)	80,000	Y#95.2-98.2, 101.2, 125 Osaka cherry blossoms	16.00	20.00
MS160	2003 (6)	10,000	Y#95.2-98.2, 101.2, 125 Hiroshima cherry blossoms	16.00	20.00
MS161	2003 (6)	10,000	Y#95.2-98.2, 101.2, 125 14th Tokyo Int'l Coin Convention	16.00	20.00
MS162	2003 (6)	6,000	Y#95.2-98.2, 101.2, 125 First Osaka Coin Show	16.00	20.00
MS163	2003 (6)	235,000	Y#95.2-98.2, 101.2, 125 Birth of Astro Boy	19.00	20.00
MS164	2003 (6)	130,000	Y#95.2-98.2, 101.2, 125 Respect for the Aged	19.00	17.00
MS165	2003 (6)	5,000	Y#95.2-98.2, 101.2, 125 Tokyo Mint Fair - Mint Collection in Omote-sando	17.00	30.00
MS166	2003 (6)	5,000	Y#95.2-98.2, 101.2, 125 Mint exhibition in Sapporo	17.00	27.00
MS167	2003 (6)	5,000	Y#95.2-98.2, 101.2, 125 Yonago Coin and Stamp Show	17.00	23.00
MS168	2003 (6)	205,000	Y#95.2-98.2, 101.2, 125 Mint Bureau box	17.00	16.00
MS169	2003 (6)	100,000	Y#95.2-98.2, 101.2, 125 2003 Central League Champions - Hanshin Tigers	22.00	27.00
MS170	2003 (6)	100,000	Y#95.2-98.2, 101.2, 125 2003 Pacific league Champions - Fukuoka Daiei Hawks	22.00	16.00
MS171	2003 (6)	5,000	Y#95.2-98.2, 101.2, 126 400th Anniversary of the Establishment of Government in Edo	22.00	200
MS172	2004 (6)	8,000	Y#95.2-98.2, 101.2, 125 "Japan Coin Set"	19.00	20.00
MS173	2004 (6)	5,000	Y#95.2-98.2, 101.2, 125 "Anniversary" folder	20.00	22.00
MS174	2004 (6)	5,000	Y#95.2-98.2, 101.2, 125 Anniversary folder (with sound recording function)	28.50	27.00
MS175	2004 (6)	4,000	Y#95.2-98.2, 101.2, 125 Mint exhibition in Fukui	18.00	53.00
MS176	2004 (6)	70,000	Y#95.2-98.2, 101.2, 125 Osaka cherry blossoms	18.00	20.00
MS177	2004 (6)	10,000	Y#95.2-98.2, 101.2, 125 Hiroshima cherry blossoms	18.00	20.00
MS178	2004 (6)	10,000	Y#95.2-98.2, 101.2, 125 15th Tokyo Int'l Coin Convention	18.00	20.00
MS179	2004 (6)	6,000	Y#95.2-98.2, 101.2, 125 Second Osaka Coin Show	18.00	20.00
MS180	2004 (6)	100,000	Y#95.2-98.2, 101.2, 125 World Intangible Heritage series: Bunraku puppets	19.00	20.00
MS181	2004 (6)	122,500	Y#95.2-98.2, 101.2, 125 Respect for the Aged	20.00	20.00
MS182	2004 (6)	5,000	Y#95.2-98.2, 101.2, 125 Mint exhibition in Tosu	18.00	23.00
MS183	2004 (6)	189,000	Y#95.2-98.2, 101.2, 125 Mint Bureau box	16.00	17.00
MS184	2004 (6)	5,000	Y#95.2-98.2, 101.2, 125 Gifu Coin and Stamp Show	17.00	23.00
MS185	2004 (6)	226,000	Y#95.2-98.2, 101.2, 125 30th Birthday of Hello Kitty (cartoon character)	22.00	23.00
MS186	2004 (6)	5,000	Y#95.2-98.2, 101.2, 125 Tokyo Mint Fair - 40th Anniversary - Issue of Commemorative Coins	17.00	33.00
MS187	2004 (6)	44,000	Y#95.2-98.2, 101.2, 125 2004 Central League Champions - Chunichi Dragons	21.00	17.00
MS188	2004 (6)	38,500	Y#95.2-98.2, 101.2, 125 2004 Pacific League Champions - Seibu Lions	21.00	17.00
MS189	2005 (6)	200,000	Y#95.2-98.2, 101.2, 133 Expo 2005, Aichi	22.00	23.00
MS190	2005 (6)	8,000	Y#95.2-98.2, 101.2, 125 "Japan Coin Set"	17.00	16.00
MS191	2005 (6)	5,000	Y#95.2-98.2, 101.2, 125 "Anniversary" folder	19.00	20.00
MS192	2005 (6)	2,000	Y#95.2-98.2, 101.2, 125 Anniversary folder (with sound recording function)	27.50	27.00
MS193	2005 (6)	5,000	Y#95.2-98.2, 101.2, 125 Mint exhibition in Shizuoka	17.00	33.00
MS194	2005 (6)	60,000	Y#95.2-98.2, 101.2, 125 Osaka cherry blossoms	17.00	23.00
MS195	2005 (6)	10,000	Y#95.2-98.2, 101.2, 125 Hiroshima Flower Tour	17.00	20.00
MS196	2005 (6)	10,000	Y#95.2-98.2, 101.2, 125 16th Tokyo International Coin Convention	17.00	20.00
MS197	2005 (6)	5,000	Y#95.2-98.2, 101.2, 125 Third Osaka Coin Show	17.00	20.00
MS198	2005 (6)	126,500	Y#95.2-98.2, 101.2, 125 World Cultural Heritage Series: Kii Hills Sacred Places and Pilgrimage Trails	18.00	20.00
MS199	2005 (6)	104,500	Y#95.2-98.2, 101.2, 125 Respect for the Aged	19.00	20.00
MS200	2005 (6)	5,000	Y#95.2-98.2, 101.2, 125 Mint Exhibition in Morioka	18.00	23.00
MS201	2005 (6)	5,000	Y#95.2-98.2, 101.2, 125 Koriyama Coin and Stamp Show	17.00	23.00
MS202	2005 (6)	182,000	Y#95.2-98.2, 101.2, 125 35th Anniversary of Doraemon (cartoon character)	17.00	30.00
MS203	2005 (6)	141,000	Y#95.2-98.2, 101.2, 125 Mint Bureau Box	16.00	18.00
MS204	2005 (6)	75,800	Y#95.2-98.2, 101.2, 125 World Natural Heritage	18.00	20.00
MS205	2005 (6)	5,000	Y#95.2-98.2, 101.2, 125 Mint Bureau Tokyo Fair / 50th Anniversary of One-Yen Aluminum Coin	17.00	40.00
MS206	2005 (6)	83,600	Y#95.2-98.2, 101.2, 125 2005 Central League Champions - Hanshin Tigers	21.00	20.00
MS207	2005 (6)	56,600	Y#95.2-98.2, 101.2, 125 2005 Pacific League Champions - Chiba Lotte Marines	21.00	20.00
MSA189	2005 (6)	1,000	Y#95.2-98.2, 101.2, 125 34th International Coin Convention, Basel	—	—
MS208	2006 (6)	5,000	Y#95.2-98.2, 101.2, 125 Mint exhibition in Oita	17.00	17.50
MS209	2006 (6)	9,000	Y#95.2-98.2, 101.2, 125 "Japan Coin Set"	18.00	18.00
MS210	2006 (6)	5,000	Y#95.2-98.2, 101.2, 125 "Anniversary" Folder	19.00	20.00
MS211	2006 (6)	189,400	Y#95.2-98.2, 101.2, 125 Mint Bureau box	16.00	17.00
MS212	2006 (6)	66,000	Y#95.2-98.2, 101.2, 125 World Intangible Heritage Series: Kabuki Theater	18.00	18.00
MS213	2006 (6)	60,000	Y#95.2-98.2, 101.2, 125 Osaka Cherry Blossoms	17.00	17.50
MS214	2006 (6)	8,000	Y#95.2-98.2, 101.2, 125 Hiroshima Flower Tour	17.00	17.50
MS215	2006 (6)	8,000	Y#95.2-98.2, 101.2, 125 17th Tokyo International Coin Convention	17.00	18.50
MS216	2006 (6)	85,500	Y#95.2-98.2, 101.2, 125 Respect for the Aged	19.00	20.00
MS217	2006 (6)	4,000	Y#95.2-98.2, 101.2, 125 Third Osaka Coin Show	17.00	18.50
MS218	2006 (6)	4,000	Y#95.2-98.2, 101.2, 125 Mint Exhibition in Kofu	17.00	17.50
MS219	2006 (6)	105,200	Y#95.2-98.2, 101.2, 125 80th Anniversary of Pooh-Bear	22.00	22.50
MS220	2006 (6)	3,500	Y#95.2-98.2, 101.2, 125 Nagasaki Coin and Stamp Show	17.00	17.50
MS221	2006 (6)	4,000	Y#95.2-98.2, 101.2, 125 Mint Bureau Tokyo Fair/"The Dawn of Modern Japan"	17.00	50.00
MS222	2006 (6)	49,600	Y#95.2-98.2, 101.2, 125 2006 Central League Champions - Chunichi Dragons	21.00	27.00
MS223	2006 (6)	56,600	Y#95.2-98.2, 101.2, 125 2006 Pacific League Champions - Japan Hamfighters	21.00	27.00
MS224	2007 (6)	180,000	Y#95.2-98.2, 101.2, 137 50th Anniversary of Japanese Antarctic Research	23.00	30.00
MS225	2007 (6)	4,000	Y#95.2-98.2, 101.2, 125 Mint exhibition in Tsukuba	17.00	18.00
MS226	2007 (6)	8,000	Y#95.2-98.2, 101.2, 125 "Japan Coin Set"	18.00	20.00
MS227	2007 (6)	5,700	Y#95.2-98.2, 101.2, 125 "Anniversary" folder	19.00	20.00
MS228	2007 (6)	150,000	Y#95.2-98.2, 101.2, 125 Mint Bureau box	16.00	18.00
MS229	2007 (6)	82,200	Y#95.2-98.2, 101.2, 125 "Gongitsune" 75th Anniversary of Publication	22.00	25.00
MS230	2007 (6)	7,000	Y#95.2-98.2, 101.2, 125 Hiroshima Flower Tour	18.00	20.00
MS231	2007 (6)	60,000	Y#95.2-98.2, 101.2, 125 Osaka cherry blossoms	17.00	18.00
MS232	2007 (6)	6,000	Y#95.2-98.2, 101.2, 125 18th Tokyo International Coin Convention	17.00	18.00
MS233	2007 (6)	4,000	Y#95.2-98.2, 101.2, 125 Fifth Osaka Coin Show	17.00	18.00
MS234	2007 (6)	76,500	Y#95.2-98.2, 101.2, 125 Rose of Versailles, Lady Oscar	22.00	25.00
MS235	2007 (6)	2,720	Y#95.2-98.2, 101.2, 125 Mint exhibition in Matsue	17.00	18.00
MS236	2007 (6)	4,000	Y#95.2-98.2, 101.2, 125 Nagoya Coin and Stamp Show	17.00	18.00
MS237	2007 (6)	69,000	Y#95.2-98.2, 101.2, 125 Respect for the Aged	19.00	20.00
MS238	2007 (6)	4,000	Y#95.2-98.2, 101.2, 125 Mint Bureau Tokyo Fair/50th anniversary of introduction of the 100-yen coin	17.00	18.00
MS239	2007 (6)	45,200	Y#95.2-98.2, 101.2, 125 2007 Central League Champions - Yomiuri Giants	21.00	22.00
MS240	2007 (6)	36,500	Y#95.2-98.2, 101.2, 125 2007 Pacific League Champions - Japan Hamfighters	21.00	22.00
MS241	2007 (6)	74,500	Y#95.2-98.2, 101.2, 125 World Cultural Heritage Series: Iwami Silver Mines Ruins and Cultural Landscape	18.00	20.00
MS242	2008 (6)	4,000	Y#95.2-98.2, 101.2, 125, Mint exhibition in Miyazaki	18.00	20.00
MS243	2008 (6)	15,100	Y95.2-98.2, 101.2, 125, "Japan Coin Set"	19.00	20.00
MS244	2008 (6)	7,500	Y95.2-98.2, 101.2, 125, "Anniversary" folder	20.00	20.00
MS245	2008 (6)	154,022	Y95.2-98.2, 101.2, 125, Mint Bureau Box	17.00	20.00
MS246	2008 (6)	4,500	Y95.2-98.2, 101.2, 125, Hiroshima Flower Tour	18.00	20.00
MS247	2008 (6)	60,000	Y95.2-98.2, 101.2, 125, Osaka cherry blossoms	18.00	20.00
MS248	2008 (6)	5,500	Y95.2-98.2, 101.2, 125, 19th Tokyo International Coin Convention	18.00	20.00
MS249	2008 (6)	4,000	Y25.2-98.2, 101.2, 125, G8 Finance Ministers' meeting, Osaka	18.00	18.00
MS250	2008 (6)	3,500	Y95.2-98.2, 101.2, 125, Sixth Osaka Coin Show.	18.00	20.00
MS251	2008 (6)	4,000	Y95.2-98.2, 101.2, 125, Kobe Coin and Stamp Exposition.	18.00	18.00
MS252	2008 (6)	142,000	Y95.2-98.2, 101.2, 125, Japan-Brazil Year of Exchange and Centenary of Japanese Immigration to Brazil	24.00	25.00
MS253	2008 (6)	100,000	Y95.2-98.2, 101.2, 125, Children's song coin set, Red Dragonfly.	23.00	25.00
MS254	2008 (6)	4,000	Y95.2-98.2, 101.2, 125 Mint Bureau Tokyo Fair/"Japan's Attractions"	20.00	20.00

KM#	Date	Mintage	Identification	Issue Price	Mkt Val
MS255	2009 (6)	3,950	Y95.2-Y98.2, 101.2, 125 32nd World Money Festival, Nagoya	20.00	21.00
MS256	2009 (6)	11,500	Y95.2-Y98.2, 101.2, 125 Japan Coin Set	21.00	22.00
MS257	2009 (6)	7,650	Y95.2-Y98.2, 101.2, 125 Anniversary folder	22.00	22.00
MS258	2009 (6)	4,500	Y95.2-Y98.2, 101.2, 125 Hiroshima Flower Tour	20.00	20.00
MS259	2009 (6)	60,000	Y95.2-Y98.2, 101.2, 125 Osaka cherry blossoms	20.00	20.00
MS260	2009 (6)	5,500	Y95.2-Y98.2, 101.2, 125 20th Toyko International Coin Convention	20.00	20.00
MS261	2009 (6)	152,637	Y95.2-Y98.2, 101.2, 125 Mint Bureau box	19.00	20.00
MS262	2009 (6)	4,850	Y95.2-Y98.2, 101.2, 125 Mint exhibition in Niigata	20.00	20.00
MS263	2009 (6)	4,000	Y95.2-Y98.2, 101.2, 125 Seventh Osaka Coin Show	20.00	20.00
MS264	2009 (6)	5,300	Y95.2-Y98.2, 101.2, 125 Aqua Metropolis Osaka 2009	20.00	20.00
MS265	2009 (6)	4,000	Y95.2-Y98.2, 101.2, 125 Yamagata Coin and Stamp Exibition	20.00	20.00
MS266	2009 (6)	7,413	Y95.2-98.2, 101.2, 125 2009 Niigata Sports Festival	19.00	20.00
MS267	2009 (6)	70,000	Y95.2-98.2, 101.2, 125 Music box set, "My Home Town"	25.00	25.00
MS268	2009 (6)	4,000	Y95.2-98.2, 101.2, 125 Mint Future Fair, "Hallmark" case	20.00	20.00
MS270	2010 (6)	7,900	Y95.2-98.2, 101.2, 125 33rd World Money Festival	20.00	20.00
MS276	2010 (6)	6,000	Y95.2-98.2, 101.2, 125 21st Tokyo International Coin Convention	20.00	20.00
MS269	2010 (6)	152,500	Y95.2-98.2, 101.2, 125 "Mint Set 2010"	19.00	25.00
MS271	2010 (6)	10,500	Y95.2-98.2, 101.2, 125 "Japan Coin Set"	20.00	21.00
MS272	2010 (6)	4,748	Y95.2-98.2, 101.2, 125 "Anniversary" folder	22.00	22.00
MS273	2010 (6)	4,748	Y95.2-98.2, 101.2, 125 Toshima Monozukuri set	20.00	20.00
MS274	2010 (6)	5,000	Y95.2-98.2, 101.2, 125 Hiroshima Flower Tour	20.00	20.00
MS275	2010 (6)	60,000	Y95.2-98.2, 101.2, 125 Osaka cherry blossoms	20.00	20.00
MS277	2010 (6)	4,000	Y95.2-98.2, 101.2, 125 Mint Exhibition in Gifu	20.00	20.00
MS278	2010 (6)	4,572	Y95.2-98.2, 101.2, 125 Eighth Osaka Coin Show	20.00	20.00
MS279	2010 (6)	4,267	Y95.2-98.2, 101.2, 125 Kumamoto Coin and Stamp Exhibition	20.00	20.00
MS280	2010 (6)	42,300	Y95.2-98.2, 101.2, 125 Intangible Cultural Heritage (2009 enrollments)	22.00	22.00
MS281	2010 (6)	8,012	Y95.2-98.2, 101.2, 125 2010 Chiba Sports Festival	20.00	20.00
MS282	2010 (6)	58,001	Y95.2-98.2, 101.2, 125 Music box set, "Snow"	26.00	28.00

PIEFORT PROOF SETS (PPS)

KM#	Date	Mintage	Identification	Issue Price	Mkt Val
PS85	2010 (6)	20,000	Y95.2-98.2, 101.2, 125 120 years of Japan-Turkey Amity (with 50 lira Turkish coin on same subject included)	144	150

PROOF SETS

KM#	Date	Mintage	Identification	Issue Price	Mkt Val
PS32	2001 (6)	138,000	Y#95.2-98.2, 101.2, 125 Mint Bureau Box	62.50	47.00
PS33	2001 (6)	100,000	Y#95.2-98.2, 101.2, 125 Old Type Coin Series (Trade dollar medallet)	62.50	53.00
PS38	2002 (2)	50,000	Y#129, 130 World Cup	385	550
PS34	2002 (6)	144,000	Y#95.2-98.2, 101.2, 125 Mint Bureau box	62.50	53.00
PS35	2002 (6)	3,000	Y#95.2-98.2, 101.2, 125 15th Anniversary of Proof Sets	62.50	100
PS36	2002 (6)	95,000	Y#95.2-98.2, 101.2, 125 Techno medal set	62.50	53.00
PS39	2003 (6)	98,400	Y#95.2-98.2, 101.2, 125 Mint Bureau box, with date plaquette	67.50	53.00
PS40	2003 (6)	90,000	Y#95.2-98.2, 101.2, 125 Astro Boy	115	100
PS41	2003 (6)	5,000	Y#95.2-98.2, 101.2, 125 Tokyo Mint Fair - Mint Collection in Omote-Sando	67.50	100
PS42	2003 (6)	70,000	Y#95.2-98.2, 101.2, 125 Mickey Mouse	125	120
PS43	2003 (6)	5,000	Y#95.2-98.2, 101.2, 125 400th Anniversary - Establishment of Government in Edo	67.50	165
PS50	2004 (2)	35,000	Y#135-136 Expo 2005, Aichi	425	500
PS44	2004 (6)	94,900	Y#95.2-98.2, 101.2, 125 Mint Bureau box with date plaquette	71.00	60.00
PS45	2004 (6)	13,100	Y#95.2-98.2, 101.2, 125 Mint Bureau box without date plaquette	70.00	100
PS46	2004 (6)	60,000	Y#95.2-98.2, 101.2, 125 70h Anniversary - Pro Baseball	120	145
PS47	2004 (6)	60,000	Y#95.2-98.2, 101.2, 125 Techno Medal Series 2	71.00	60.00
PS48	2004 (6)	50,000	Y#95.2-98.2, 101.2, 125 30th Birthday of Hello Kitty (cartoon character)	120	150
PS49	2004 (6)	5,000	Y#95.2-98.2, 101.2, 125 Tokyo Mint Fair - 40th Anniversary - Issue of Commemorative Coins	71.00	100
PSA40	2003 (6)	6,600	Y#95.2-98.2, 101.2, 125 Mint Bureau Box without Date Plaquette	66.00	100
PS51	2005 (6)	76,700	Y#95.2-98.2, 101.2, 125 Mint Bureau Box with date plaquette	71.00	65.00
PS52	2005 (6)	10,000	Y#95.2-98.2, 101.2, 125 Mint Bureau Box without date plaquette	70.00	100
PS53	2005 (6)	60,000	Y#95.2-98.2, 101.2, 125 35th Anniversary of Doraemon (cartoon character)	125	170
PS54	2005 (6)	34,000	Y#95.2-98.2, 101.2, 125 50th Anniversary of One-Yen Aluminum Coin	125	170
PS55	2005 (6)	30,000	Y#95.2-98.2, 101.2, 125 50th Anniversary of the Pencil Rocket	125	100
PS56	2005 (6)	47,300	Y#95.2-98.2, 101.2, 125 Techno Medal Series #3	71.00	65.00
PS62	2006 (6)	4,000	Y#95.2-98.2, 101.2, 125 Mint Bureau Tokyo Fair/"The Dawn of Modern Japan"	71.00	150
PS57	2006 (6)	63,420	Y#95.2-98.2, 101.2, 125 Mint Bureau box with date plaquette	71.00	65.00
PS58	2006 (6)	8,700	Y#95.2-98.2, 101.2, 125 Mint Bureau Box without date plaquette	70.00	65.00
PS59	2006 (6)	35,000	Y#95.2-98.2, 101.2, 125 120th Anniversary of Cherry Blossom Viewing at the Mint	125	125
PS60	2006 (6)	46,000	Y#95.2-98.2, 101.2, 125 Australia-Japan Year of Exchange; includes Australian 1oz Silver coin KM#838	128	145
PS61	2006 (6)	49,900	Y#95.2-98.2, 101.2, 125 50th Anniversary of Debut of Ishihara Yujiro (film actor)	125	120
PS63	2007 (6)	40,000	Y#95.2-98.2, 101.2, 125 20-yen Gold Coin Memorial	125	150
PS64	2007 (6)	53,200	Y#95.2-98.2, 101.2, 125 Mint Bureau box, with date plaquette	71.00	75.00
PS65	2007 (6)	7,000	Y#95.2-98.2, 101.2, 125 Mint Bureau box, without date plaquette	70.00	75.00
PS66	2007 (6)	35,000	Y#95.2-98.2, 101.2, 125 60th Anniversary of Resumption of Cherry Blossom Viewing (at the Mint)	125	125
PS67	2007 (6)	40,100	Y#95.2-98.2, 101.2, 125 Sakamoto Ryohma (pre-Meiji loyalist, assassinated 1867)	125	125
PS68	2007 (6)	33,500	Y#95.2-98.2, 101.2, 125 11th IAAF World Championships in Athletics, Osaka (plus silver medal)	125	125
PS69	2007 (6)	3,000	Y#95.2-98.2, 101.2, 125 Mint Bureau Tokyo Fair/50th anniversary of introduction of the 100-yen coin	71.00	75.00
PS70	2007 (6)	30,000	Y#95.2-98.2, 101.2, 125 Japan-New Zealand Friendship (with NZ KM#232 coin)	125	125
PSA39	2003 (6)	7,000	Y#95.2-98.2, 101.2, 125 Mint Bureau box, without date plaquette	66.00	100
PS71	2008 (6)	55,200	Y95.2-95.2, 101.2, 125 Mint Bureau box with date plaquette	75.00	75.00
PS72	2008 (6)	6,000	Y95.2-98.2, 101.2, 125 Mint Bureau box without date plaquette	73.50	75.00
PS73	2008 (6)	27,000	Y95.2-98.2, 101.2, 125 Cherry blossom viewing (at the mint)	130	130
PS74	2008 (6)	44,000	Y95.2-Y98.2, 101.2, 125 150th Anniversary of Japanese-French relations (with French 1.5 euro coin KM1550.)	130	130
PS75	2008 (6)	33,000	Y95.2-98.2, 101.2, 125 1300th Anniversary of the Wado Kaichin coin (with a silver replica)	100	100
PS76	2008 (6)	3,000	Y95.2-Y98.2, 101.2, 125 Mint Bureau Tokyo Fair - Japan Attractions	79.00	75.00
PS77	2009 (6)	48,400	Y95.2-Y98.2, 101.2, 125 Mint Bureau box with date plaquette	79.00	70.00
PS78	2009 (6)	5,600	Y95.2-Y98.2, 101.2, 125 Mint Bureau box without date plaquette	77.50	80.00
PS79	2009 (6)	25,000	Y95.2-Y98.2, 101.2, 125 Cherry blossom viewing (at the mint)	136	135
PS80	2009 (6)	25,000	Y95.2-Y98.2, 101.2, 125 80 years of Japan/Canada Amity (with $5 Canadian coin KM#1036 included)	136	135
PS81	2009 (6)	30,000	Y95.2-Y98.2, 101.2, 125 400 years of Japan/Dutch Commerce (with Dutch 5 coin, KM287 included)	136	135
PS82	2009 (6)	3,000	Y95.2-98.2, 101.2, 125 Mint Bureau Tokyo Fair/"Hallmark 80 years"	83.00	85.00
PS83	2010 (6)	41,687	Y95.2-98.2, 101.2, 125 Mint Bureau box, with date plaquette	83.00	80.00
PS84	2010 (6)	20,000	Y95.2-98.2, 101.2, 125 Cherry blossom viewing (at the Mint)	144	150
PS86	2010 (6)	20,000	Y95.2-98.2, 101.2, 125 Techno set, with medal included showing iridescent features (new mint technology)	111	115
PS87	2010 (6)	20,000	Y95.2-98.2, 101.2, 125 "A Dog of Flanders" set, with Belgian 20 KM#305 proof coin included	144	150

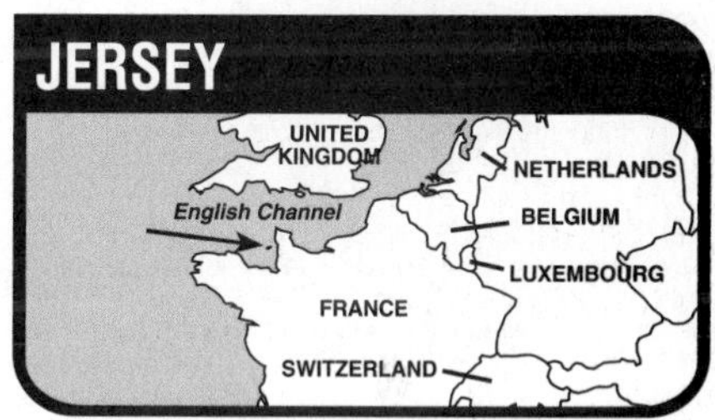

The Bailiwick of Jersey, a British Crown dependency located in the English Channel 12 miles (19 km.) west of Normandy, France, has an area of 45 sq. mi. (117 sq. km.) and a population of 74,000. Capital: St. Helier. The economy is based on agriculture and cattle breeding – the importation of cattle is prohibited to protect the purity of the island's world-famous strain of milk cows.

The island together with the Bailiwick of Guernsey, is the only part of the Dutchy of Normandy belonging to the British Crown, has been a possession of Britain since the Norman conquest of 1066. Jersey is administered by its own laws and customs. Unless the island is mentioned specifically, acts passed by the British Parliament are not applicable to Jersey. During WW II, German troops occupied the island from 1940 to 1945.

RULER

British

MINT MARK

H - Heaton, Birmingham

BRITISH DEPENDENCY

DECIMAL COINAGE

100 New Pence = 1 Pound

KM# 103 PENNY

3.5600 g., Copper Plated Steel, 20.3 mm. **Ruler:** Elizabeth II **Obv:** Crowned head right **Rev:** Le Hoeq Watchtower, St. Clement **Edge:** Plain

Date	Mintage	F	VF	XF	Unc	BU
2002	1,520,000	—	—	0.15	0.65	—
2003	1,575,000	—	—	0.15	0.65	—
2005	—	—	—	0.15	0.65	—

Date	Mintage	F	VF	XF	Unc	BU
2006	585,000	—	—	0.15	0.65	—
2008	4,800,000	—	—	0.15	0.65	—
2012	—	—	—	—	—	—

KM# 104 2 PENCE
7.1200 g., Copper Plated Steel, 25.91 mm. **Ruler:** Elizabeth II **Obv:** Head with tiara right **Rev:** L'Hermitage, St. Helier **Edge:** Plain

Date	Mintage	F	VF	XF	Unc	BU
2002	1,259,000	—	—	0.20	0.65	—
2003	10,000	—	—	0.20	0.65	—
2005	400,000	—	—	0.20	0.65	—
2006	1,200,000	—	—	0.20	0.65	—
2008	2,459,000	—	—	0.20	0.65	—

KM# 105 5 PENCE
3.2500 g., Copper-Nickel, 18 mm. **Ruler:** Elizabeth II **Obv:** Head with tiara right **Rev:** Seymour Tower, Grouville, L'Avathigon **Edge:** Reeded

Date	Mintage	F	VF	XF	Unc	BU
2002	1,200,000	—	—	0.20	0.65	—
2003	1,005,000	—	—	0.20	0.65	—
2006	1,200,000	—	—	0.20	0.65	—
2008	3,600,000	—	—	0.20	0.65	—

KM# 106 10 PENCE
6.5000 g., Copper-Nickel, 24.5 mm. **Ruler:** Elizabeth II **Obv:** Head with tiara right **Rev:** La Hougne Bie, Faldouet, St. Martin

Date	Mintage	F	VF	XF	Unc	BU
2002	500,000	—	—	—	1.25	1.50
2003	10,000	—	—	—	1.25	1.50
2005	—	—	—	—	1.25	1.50
2006	—	—	—	—	1.25	1.50
2007	630,000	—	—	—	1.25	1.50
2010	—	—	—	—	1.25	1.50

KM# 107 20 PENCE
5.0000 g., Copper-Nickel, 21.4 mm. **Ruler:** Elizabeth II **Obv:** Head with tiara right

Date	Mintage	F	VF	XF	Unc	BU
2002	975,500	—	—	—	1.00	1.25
2003	10,000	—	—	—	1.00	1.25
2005	500,000	—	—	—	1.00	1.25
2006	500,000	—	—	—	1.00	1.25
2007	780,000	—	—	—	1.00	1.25
2009	1,500,000	—	—	—	1.00	1.25

KM# 108 50 PENCE
8.0000 g., Copper-Nickel, 27.3 mm. **Ruler:** Elizabeth II **Obv:** Crowned bust right **Rev:** Gothic gate arch **Edge:** Plain **Shape:** 7-sided

Date	Mintage	F	VF	XF	Unc	BU
2003	10,000	—	—	1.00	2.50	3.00
2005	200,000	—	—	1.00	2.50	3.00
2006	300,000	—	—	1.00	2.50	3.00
2009	480,000	—	—	1.00	2.50	3.00

KM# 123a 50 PENCE
8.0000 g., 0.9250 Silver 0.2379 oz. ASW, 27.3 mm. **Ruler:** Elizabeth II **Subject:** Coronation, 50th Anniversary **Obv:** Crowned head right **Rev:** Archbishop crowning Queen **Edge:** Plain **Shape:** 7-sided

Date	Mintage	F	VF	XF	Unc	BU
2003 Proof	15,000	Value: 25.00				

KM# 123 50 PENCE
8.0000 g., Copper-Nickel, 27.3 mm. **Ruler:** Elizabeth II **Subject:** Coronation, 50th Anniversary **Obv:** Crowned head right **Rev:** Archbishop crowning Queen **Edge:** Plain **Shape:** 7-sided

Date	Mintage	F	VF	XF	Unc	BU
2003	10,000	—	—	—	2.50	3.00

KM# 148 50 PENCE
8.0000 g., Copper-Nickel, 27.3 mm. **Ruler:** Elizabeth II **Subject:** Coronation, 50th Anniversary **Rev:** Regalia in quatrilobe **Shape:** 7-sided

Date	Mintage	F	VF	XF	Unc	BU
2003	—	—	—	—	2.50	3.50

KM# 148a 50 PENCE
8.0000 g., 0.9250 Silver 0.2379 oz. ASW, 27.3 mm. **Ruler:** Elizabeth II **Subject:** Coronation, 50th Anniversary **Rev:** Regalia in quatrilobe **Shape:** 7-sided

Date	Mintage	F	VF	XF	Unc	BU
2003 Proof	15,000	Value: 25.00				

KM# 149 50 PENCE
8.0000 g., Copper-Nickel, 27.3 mm. **Ruler:** Elizabeth II **Subject:** Coronation, 50th Anniversary **Rev:** Queen facing, seated on throne **Shape:** 7-sided

Date	Mintage	F	VF	XF	Unc	BU
2003	10,000	—	—	—	2.50	3.50

KM# 149a 50 PENCE
8.0000 g., 0.9250 Silver 0.2379 oz. ASW, 27.3 mm. **Ruler:** Elizabeth II **Subject:** Coronation, 50th Anniversary **Rev:** Queen facing, seated on throne **Shape:** 7-sided

Date	Mintage	F	VF	XF	Unc	BU
2003 Proof	15,000	Value: 25.00				

KM# 150 50 PENCE
8.0000 g., Copper-Nickel, 27.3 mm. **Ruler:** Elizabeth II **Subject:** Coronation, 50th Anniversary **Rev:** Crown, scepter and shield **Shape:** 7-sided

Date	Mintage	F	VF	XF	Unc	BU
2003	10,000	—	—	—	2.50	3.50

KM# 150a 50 PENCE
8.0000 g., 0.9250 Silver 0.2379 oz. ASW, 27.3 mm. **Ruler:** Elizabeth II **Subject:** Coronation, 50th Anniversary **Rev:** Crown, sceptre and shield **Shape:** 7-sided

Date	Mintage	F	VF	XF	Unc	BU
2003 Proof	15,000	Value: 25.00				

KM# 101 POUND
9.5000 g., Nickel-Brass, 22.5 mm. **Ruler:** Elizabeth II **Obv:** Head with tiara right **Rev:** Schooner, Resolute **Edge Lettering:** CAESAREA INSULA

Date	Mintage	F	VF	XF	Unc	BU
2003	10,000	—	—	—	4.00	4.50
2005	200,000	—	—	—	4.00	4.50
2006	93,000	—	—	—	4.00	4.50

KM# 160 POUND
1.2400 g., 0.9990 Gold 0.0398 oz. AGW, 13.92 mm. **Ruler:** Elizabeth II **Subject:** Trafalgar, 200th Anniversary

Date	Mintage	F	VF	XF	Unc	BU
2005 Proof	—	Value: 100				

KM# 173 POUND
1.2400 g., 0.9990 Gold 0.0398 oz. AGW, 13.92 mm. **Ruler:** Elizabeth II **Subject:** Princess Diana

Date	Mintage	F	VF	XF	Unc	BU
2007 Proof	—	Value: 100				

KM# 102 2 POUNDS
12.0000 g., Bi-Metallic Copper-Nickel center in Nickel-Brass ring, 28.4 mm. **Ruler:** Elizabeth II **Obv:** Head with tiara right **Rev:** Latent image value within circle of assorted shields **Edge Lettering:** CAESAREA INSULA

Date	Mintage	F	VF	XF	Unc	BU
2003	10,000	—	—	—	10.00	12.00
2006	3,500	—	—	—	10.00	12.00

KM# 111 5 POUNDS
28.2800 g., Copper-Nickel, 38.6 mm. **Ruler:** Elizabeth II **Subject:** Princess Diana **Obv:** Crowned head right **Rev:** Diana's cameo above people **Edge:** Reeded

Date	Mintage	F	VF	XF	Unc	BU
2002	—	—	—	—	13.50	15.00

KM# 111a 5 POUNDS
28.2800 g., 0.9250 Silver 0.8410 oz. ASW, 38.6 mm. **Ruler:** Elizabeth II **Subject:** Princess Diana **Obv:** Crowned head right **Rev:** Diana's cameo above people **Edge:** Reeded

Date	Mintage	F	VF	XF	Unc	BU
2002 Proof	20,000	Value: 45.00				

KM# 111b 5 POUNDS
39.9400 g., 0.9167 Gold 1.1771 oz. AGW, 38.6 mm. **Ruler:** Elizabeth II **Subject:** Princess Diana **Obv:** Crowned head right **Rev:** Diana's cameo above people **Edge:** Reeded

Date	Mintage	F	VF	XF	Unc	BU
2002 Proof	100	Value: 2,150				

KM# 113 5 POUNDS
28.2800 g., Copper-Nickel, 38.6 mm. **Ruler:** Elizabeth II **Subject:** Queen Mother **Obv:** Crowned head right **Rev:** Queen Mother's bust right (circa 1918) **Rev. Legend:** HER MAJESTY QUEEN ELIZABETH THE QUEEN MOTHER **Edge:** Reeded

Date	Mintage	F	VF	XF	Unc	BU
2002	—	—	—	—	13.50	15.00

KM# 113a 5 POUNDS

28.2800 g., 0.9250 Silver 0.8410 oz. ASW, 38.6 mm. **Ruler:** Elizabeth II **Subject:** Queen Mother **Obv:** Crowned head right **Rev:** Queen Mother's bust right, (circa 1918) **Rev. Legend:** HER MAJESTY QUEEN ELIZABETH THE QUEEN MOTHER **Edge:** Reeded

Date	Mintage	F	VF	XF	Unc	BU
2002 Proof	15,000	Value: 50.00				

KM# 113b 5 POUNDS

39.9400 g., 0.9166 Gold 1.1770 oz. AGW, 38.6 mm. **Ruler:** Elizabeth II **Subject:** Queen Mother **Obv:** Crowned head right **Rev:** Queen Mother's bust right, (circa 1918) **Rev. Legend:** HER MAJESTY QUEEN ELIZABETH THE QUEEN MOTHER **Edge:** Reeded

Date	Mintage	F	VF	XF	Unc	BU
2002 Proof	250	Value: 2,100				

KM# 115 5 POUNDS

28.2800 g., Copper-Nickel, 38.6 mm. **Ruler:** Elizabeth II **Subject:** Golden Jubilee **Obv:** Crowned head right **Rev:** Abbey procession scene **Edge:** Reeded

Date	Mintage	F	VF	XF	Unc	BU
2002	—	—	—	—	13.50	15.00

KM# 115a 5 POUNDS

28.2800 g., 0.9250 Silver 0.8410 oz. ASW, 38.6 mm. **Ruler:** Elizabeth II **Subject:** Golden Jubilee **Obv:** Crowned head right **Rev:** Abbey procession scene **Edge:** Reeded

Date	Mintage	F	VF	XF	Unc	BU
2002 Proof	20,000	Value: 50.00				

KM# 115b 5 POUNDS

39.9400 g., 0.9166 Gold 1.1770 oz. AGW, 38.6 mm. **Ruler:** Elizabeth II **Subject:** Golden Jubilee **Obv:** Crowned head right **Rev:** Abbey procession scene **Edge:** Reeded

Date	Mintage	F	VF	XF	Unc	BU
2002 Proof	100	Value: 2,150				

KM# 117 5 POUNDS

28.2800 g., Copper-Nickel, 38.6 mm. **Ruler:** Elizabeth II **Subject:** Duke of Wellington **Obv:** Crowned head right **Rev:** Wellington's portrait with multicolor infantry scene **Edge:** Reeded

Date	Mintage	F	VF	XF	Unc	BU
2002	—	—	—	—	13.50	15.00

KM# 117a 5 POUNDS

28.2800 g., 0.9250 Silver 0.8410 oz. ASW, 38.6 mm. **Ruler:** Elizabeth II **Subject:** Duke of Wellington **Obv:** Crowned head right **Rev:** Wellington's portrait with multicolor infantry scene **Edge:** Reeded

Date	Mintage	F	VF	XF	Unc	BU
2002 Proof	15,000	Value: 50.00				

KM# 117b 5 POUNDS

39.9400 g., 0.9166 Gold 1.1770 oz. AGW, 38.6 mm. **Ruler:** Elizabeth II **Subject:** Duke of Wellington **Obv:** Crowned head right **Rev:** Wellington's portrait with multicolor infantry scene **Edge:** Reeded

Date	Mintage	F	VF	XF	Unc	BU
2002 Proof	200	Value: 2,100				

KM# 119 5 POUNDS

28.2800 g., Copper-Nickel, 38.6 mm. **Ruler:** Elizabeth II **Subject:** Golden Jubilee **Obv:** Crowned head right **Rev:** Honor guard and memorial **Edge:** Reeded

Date	Mintage	F	VF	XF	Unc	BU
2003	—	—	—	—	13.50	15.00

KM# 119a 5 POUNDS

28.2800 g., 0.9250 Silver 0.8410 oz. ASW, 38.6 mm. **Ruler:** Elizabeth II **Subject:** Golden Jubilee **Obv:** Crowned head right **Rev:** Honor guard and monument **Edge:** Reeded

Date	Mintage	F	VF	XF	Unc	BU
2003 Proof	20,000	Value: 50.00				

KM# 119b 5 POUNDS

39.9400 g., 0.9166 Gold 1.1770 oz. AGW, 38.6 mm. **Ruler:** Elizabeth II **Subject:** Golden Jubilee **Obv:** Crowned head right **Rev:** Honor guard and monument **Edge:** Reeded

Date	Mintage	F	VF	XF	Unc	BU
2003 Proof	250	Value: 2,100				

KM# 121 5 POUNDS

28.2800 g., Copper-Nickel, 38.6 mm. **Ruler:** Elizabeth II **Obv:** Crowned head right **Rev:** Bust of Prince William facing and crowned arms with supporters **Edge:** Reeded

Date	Mintage	F	VF	XF	Unc	BU
2003	—	—	—	—	16.50	18.00

KM# 121a 5 POUNDS

28.2800 g., 0.9250 Silver 0.8410 oz. ASW, 38.6 mm. **Ruler:** Elizabeth II **Obv:** Crowned head right **Rev:** Bust of Prince William facing and crowned arms with supporters **Edge:** Reeded

Date	Mintage	F	VF	XF	Unc	BU
2003 Proof	5,000	Value: 47.50				

KM# 121b 5 POUNDS

39.9400 g., 0.9166 Gold 1.1770 oz. AGW, 38.6 mm. **Ruler:** Elizabeth II **Obv:** Crowned head right **Rev:** Bust of Prince William facing and crowned arms with supporters **Edge:** Reeded

Date	Mintage	F	VF	XF	Unc	BU
2003 Proof	200	Value: 2,100				

KM# 130 5 POUNDS

28.2800 g., Copper-Nickel, 38.6 mm. **Ruler:** Elizabeth II **Subject:** Sir Francis Drake **Obv:** Crowned head right

Date	Mintage	F	VF	XF	Unc	BU
2003	—	—	—	—	—	15.00

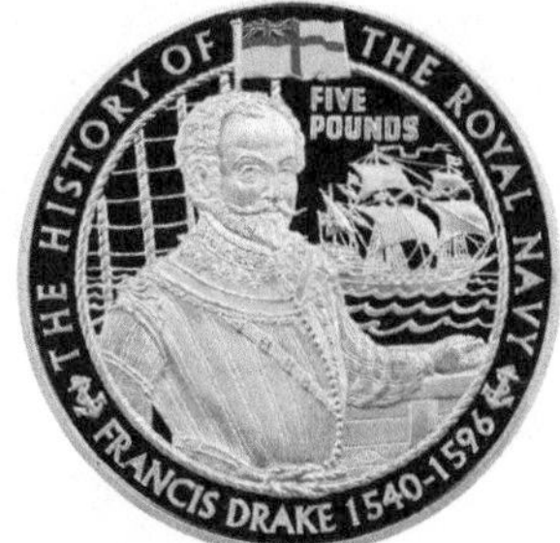

KM# 130a 5 POUNDS

28.2800 g., 0.9250 Silver 0.8410 oz. ASW, 38.6 mm. **Ruler:** Elizabeth II **Subject:** Drake **Obv:** Crowned head right **Rev:** Naval leader Sir Francis Drake

Date	Mintage	F	VF	XF	Unc	BU
2003 Proof	—	Value: 75.00				

KM# 131 5 POUNDS

28.2800 g., Copper-Nickel, 38.6 mm. **Ruler:** Elizabeth II **Subject:** Sovereign of the Seas **Obv:** Crowned head right **Rev:** Sailing ship

Date	Mintage	F	VF	XF	Unc	BU
2003	—	—	—	—	—	15.00

KM# 131a 5 POUNDS

28.2800 g., 0.9250 Silver 0.8410 oz. ASW, 38.6 mm. **Ruler:** Elizabeth II **Subject:** Sovereign Of The Seas **Obv:** Crowned head right **Rev:** The Sovereign of the Seas ship

Date	Mintage	F	VF	XF	Unc	BU
2003 Proof	—	Value: 75.00				

KM# 132 5 POUNDS

28.2800 g., Copper-Nickel, 38.6 mm. **Ruler:** Elizabeth II **Obv:** Crowned head right **Rev:** WWI naval leader Sir John Fisher

Date	Mintage	F	VF	XF	Unc	BU
2003	—	—	—	—	—	15.00

KM# 132a 5 POUNDS

28.2800 g., 0.9250 Silver 0.8410 oz. ASW, 38.6 mm. **Ruler:** Elizabeth II **Subject:** John Fisher **Obv:** Crowned head right **Rev:** WWI Naval leader Sir John Fisher

Date	Mintage	F	VF	XF	Unc	BU
2003 Proof	—	Value: 75.00				

KM# 133 5 POUNDS

28.2800 g., Copper-Nickel, 38.6 mm. **Ruler:** Elizabeth II **Subject:** HMS Victory **Obv:** Crowned head right **Rev:** Nelson's flagship HMS Victory

Date	Mintage	F	VF	XF	Unc	BU
2003	—	—	—	—	—	15.00

KM# 133a 5 POUNDS

28.2800 g., 0.9250 Silver 0.8410 oz. ASW, 38.6 mm. **Ruler:** Elizabeth II **Subject:** HMS Victory **Obv:** Crowned head right **Rev:** Nelson's flag ship HMS Victory, multicolor flag at top

Date	Mintage	F	VF	XF	Unc	BU
2004 Proof	—	Value: 75.00				

KM# 134a 5 POUNDS

28.2800 g., 0.9250 Silver 0.8410 oz. ASW, 38.6 mm. **Ruler:** Elizabeth II **Subject:** Cunningham **Obv:** Crowned head right **Rev:** WWII Admiral Andrew B. Cunningham

Date	Mintage	F	VF	XF	Unc	BU
2003 Proof	—	Value: 75.00				

KM# 134 5 POUNDS

28.2800 g., Copper-Nickel, 38.6 mm. **Ruler:** Elizabeth II **Obv:** Crowned head right **Rev:** WWII Admiral Andrew B. Cunningham

Date	Mintage	F	VF	XF	Unc	BU
2003	—	—	—	—	—	15.00

KM# 135 5 POUNDS

28.2800 g., Copper-Nickel, 38.6 mm. **Ruler:** Elizabeth II **Subject:** HMS Conqueror **Obv:** Crowned head right **Rev:** Submarine HMS Conqueror

Date	Mintage	F	VF	XF	Unc	BU
2003	—	—	—	—	—	15.00

KM# 135a 5 POUNDS

28.2800 g., 0.9250 Silver 0.8410 oz. ASW, 38.6 mm. **Ruler:** Elizabeth II **Subject:** Conqueror **Obv:** Crowned head right **Rev:** Submarine HMS Conqueror

Date	Mintage	F	VF	XF	Unc	BU
2003 Proof	—	Value: 75.00				

KM# 144 5 POUNDS

28.2800 g., Copper-Nickel, 38.6 mm. **Ruler:** Elizabeth II **Subject:** History of the Royal Navy **Rev:** Five heads, four ships and a sub

Date	Mintage	F	VF	XF	Unc	BU
2003	—	—	—	—	—	15.00

KM# 144a 5 POUNDS

28.2800 g., 0.9250 Silver 0.8410 oz. ASW, 38.61 mm. **Ruler:** Elizabeth II **Subject:** History of the Royal Navy **Obv:** Head left with tiarra **Obv. Legend:** ELIZABETH II BALIWICK - OF JERSEY **Rev:** Five heads of King Alfred the Great, Sir Francis Drake, Admirals Horatio Nelson, John Fisher and John Woodward at five ships, colored flag at top **Edge:** Reeded

Date	Mintage	F	VF	XF	Unc	BU
2003 Proof	—	Value: 75.00				

KM# 139a 5 POUNDS

28.2800 g., 0.9250 Silver 0.8410 oz. ASW, 38.6 mm. **Ruler:** Elizabeth II **Subject:** Driver and Fireman **Obv:** Crowned head right **Rev:** Familiar image from the Golden Age of Steam: the driver and fireman

Date	Mintage	F	VF	XF	Unc	BU
2004 Proof	—	Value: 75.00				

KM# 124 5 POUNDS

28.2800 g., Copper-Nickel, 38.6 mm. **Ruler:** Elizabeth II **Obv:** Crowned head right **Rev:** British Horsa gliders in flight **Edge:** Reeded **Note:** D-Day

Date	Mintage	F	VF	XF	Unc	BU
2004	—	—	—	—	15.00	17.00

KM# 124a 5 POUNDS

28.2800 g., 0.9250 Silver 0.8410 oz. ASW, 38.6 mm. **Ruler:** Elizabeth II **Obv:** Crowned head right **Rev:** British Horsa gliders in flight

Date	Mintage	F	VF	XF	Unc	BU
2004 Proof	10,000	Value: 85.00				

KM# 124b 5 POUNDS

39.9400 g., 0.9167 Gold 1.1771 oz. AGW, 38.6 mm. **Ruler:** Elizabeth II **Obv:** Crowned head right **Rev:** British Horsa gliders in flight

Date	Mintage	F	VF	XF	Unc	BU
2004 Proof	500	Value: 2,100				

KM# 126 5 POUNDS

28.2800 g., Copper-Nickel, 38.6 mm. **Ruler:** Elizabeth II **Subject:** 150th Anniversary of the Crimean War **Obv:** Crowned head right **Rev:** Charge of the Light Brigade scene with one blue uniform behind the Earl of Cardigan **Edge:** Reeded

Date	Mintage	F	VF	XF	Unc	BU
2004 plain	—	—	—	—	25.00	27.50

KM# 126a 5 POUNDS

28.2800 g., 0.9250 Silver 0.8410 oz. ASW, 38.6 mm. **Ruler:** Elizabeth II **Obv:** Crowned head right **Rev:** Charge of the Light Brigade scene with one blue uniform behind the Earl of Cardigan **Edge:** Reeded

Date	Mintage	F	VF	XF	Unc	BU
2004 Proof	10,000	Value: 85.00				

KM# 126b 5 POUNDS

39.9400 g., 0.9166 Gold 1.1770 oz. AGW, 38.6 mm. **Ruler:** Elizabeth II **Obv:** Crowned head right **Rev:** Charge of the Light Brigade scene with one blue uniform behind the Earl of Cardigan **Edge:** Reeded

Date	Mintage	F	VF	XF	Unc	BU
2004 Proof	500	Value: 2,100				

KM# 136 5 POUNDS

28.2800 g., Copper-Nickel, 38.6 mm. **Ruler:** Elizabeth II **Subject:** Steam Locomotive - Coronation **Obv:** Crowned head right **Rev:** The Pacific class (4-6-2) Coronation

Date	Mintage	F	VF	XF	Unc	BU
2004	—	—	—	—	—	15.00

KM# 136a 5 POUNDS

28.2800 g., 0.9250 Silver 0.8410 oz. ASW, 38.6 mm. **Ruler:** Elizabeth II **Subject:** Coronation **Obv:** Crowned head right **Rev:** The Pacific Class Coronation

Date	Mintage	F	VF	XF	Unc	BU
2004 Proof	—	Value: 75.00				

KM# 137 5 POUNDS

28.2800 g., Copper-Nickel, 38.6 mm. **Ruler:** Elizabeth II **Subject:** Steam Locomotive - Flying Scotsman **Obv:** Crowned head right **Rev:** Sir Nigel Gresley's Flying Scotsman

Date	Mintage	F	VF	XF	Unc	BU
2004	—	—	—	—	—	15.00

KM# 137a 5 POUNDS

28.2800 g., 0.9250 Silver 0.8410 oz. ASW, 38.6 mm. **Ruler:** Elizabeth II **Subject:** Flying Scotsman **Obv:** Crowned head right **Rev:** Famous Flying Scotsman Locomotive, designed by Sir Nigel Gresley

Date	Mintage	F	VF	XF	Unc	BU
2004 Proof	—	Value: 75.00				

KM# 138 5 POUNDS

28.2800 g., Copper-Nickel, 38.6 mm. **Ruler:** Elizabeth II **Subject:** Steam Locomotive - The Golden Arrow **Obv:** Crowned head right **Rev:** The Golden Arrow, London-Dover to Paris service

Date	Mintage	F	VF	XF	Unc	BU
2004	—	—	—	—	—	15.00

KM# 138a 5 POUNDS

28.2800 g., 0.9250 Silver 0.8410 oz. ASW, 38.6 mm. **Ruler:** Elizabeth II **Subject:** Golden Arrow **Obv:** Crowned head right **Rev:** The Golden Arrow, which ran from London to Dover en route to Paris

Date	Mintage	F	VF	XF	Unc	BU
2004 Proof	—	Value: 75.00				

KM# 139 5 POUNDS

28.2800 g., Copper-Nickel, 38.6 mm. **Ruler:** Elizabeth II **Subject:** Steam Locomotive driver and fireman **Obv:** Crowned head right **Rev:** Driver and Fireman

Date	Mintage	F	VF	XF	Unc	BU
2004	—	—	—	—	—	15.00

KM# 140 5 POUNDS

28.2800 g., Copper-Nickel, 38.6 mm. **Ruler:** Elizabeth II **Subject:** Tunnel **Obv:** Crowned head right **Rev:** Steam locomotive exiting tunnel

Date	Mintage	F	VF	XF	Unc	BU
2004	—	—	—	—	—	15.00

KM# 140a 5 POUNDS

28.2800 g., 0.9250 Silver 0.8410 oz. ASW, 38.6 mm. **Ruler:** Elizabeth II **Subject:** Tunnel **Obv:** Crowned head right **Rev:** Steam locomotive exiting from tunnel

Date	Mintage	F	VF	XF	Unc	BU
2004	—	Value: 75.00				

KM# 141 5 POUNDS

28.2800 g., Copper-Nickel, 38.6 mm. **Ruler:** Elizabeth II **Subject:** The Evening Star **Obv:** Crowned head right **Rev:** The Evening Star, representing the last British Steam Locomotive

Date	Mintage	F	VF	XF	Unc	BU
2004	—	—	—	—	—	15.00

KM# 141a 5 POUNDS

28.2800 g., 0.9250 Silver 0.8410 oz. ASW, 38.6 mm. **Ruler:** Elizabeth II **Subject:** Evening Star **Obv:** Crowned head right **Rev:** The Evening Star - representing the last British Rail Steam Locomotive

Date	Mintage	F	VF	XF	Unc	BU
2004 Proof	—	Value: 75.00				

KM# 127 5 POUNDS

28.2800 g., Copper-Nickel, 38.61 mm. **Ruler:** Elizabeth II **Subject:** Battle of Trafalgar **Obv:** Crowned head right

Date	Mintage	F	VF	XF	Unc	BU
2005	—	—	—	—	7.50	10.00

KM# 127a 5 POUNDS

28.2800 g., 0.9250 Silver 0.8410 oz. ASW, 38.6 mm. **Ruler:** Elizabeth II **Subject:** Nelson Trafalger **Obv:** Crowned head right **Rev:** 200th Anniversary of the Battle of Trafalgar, image of Nelson with a gilded ship in the background

Date	Mintage	F	VF	XF	Unc	BU
2005 Proof	—	Value: 75.00				

KM# 128 5 POUNDS

28.2800 g., Copper-Nickel, 38.61 mm. **Ruler:** Elizabeth II **Subject:** 60th Anniversary - End of WW II **Obv:** Crowned head right **Rev:** Big Ben Tower

Date	Mintage	F	VF	XF	Unc	BU
2005	—	—	—	—	7.50	10.00

KM# 128a 5 POUNDS

28.2800 g., 0.9250 Silver 0.8410 oz. ASW, 38.6 mm. **Ruler:** Elizabeth II **Subject:** WWII Liberation **Obv:** Crowned head right **Rev:** Big Ben Tower **Edge:** Reeded

Date	Mintage	F	VF	XF	Unc	BU
2005 Proof	5,000	Value: 85.00				

KM# 128b 5 POUNDS

39.9400 g., 0.9167 Gold 1.1771 oz. AGW, 38.6 mm. **Ruler:** Elizabeth II **Subject:** WWII Liberation **Obv:** Crowned head right **Rev:** Big Ben Tower **Edge:** Reeded

Date	Mintage	F	VF	XF	Unc	BU
2005 Proof	150	Value: 2,150				

KM# 129 5 POUNDS

28.2800 g., Copper-Nickel, 38.61 mm. **Ruler:** Elizabeth II **Subject:** WW II Liberation **Obv:** Crowned head right **Rev:** Returning evacuees **Edge:** Reeded

Date	Mintage	F	VF	XF	Unc	BU
2005	—	—	—	—	7.50	10.00

KM# 129a 5 POUNDS

39.9400 g., 0.9167 Gold 1.1771 oz. AGW, 38.6 mm. **Ruler:** Elizabeth II **Subject:** WWII Liberation **Obv:** Crowned head right **Rev:** Returning evacuees **Edge:** Reeded

Date	Mintage	F	VF	XF	Unc	BU
2005 Proof	150	Value: 2,150				

KM# 164 5 POUNDS

28.2800 g., 0.9250 Silver 0.8410 oz. ASW, 38.61 mm. **Ruler:** Elizabeth II **Subject:** Charles Robert Darwin

Date	Mintage	F	VF	XF	Unc	BU
2005 Proof	Est. 25,000	Value: 60.00				

KM# 142 5 POUNDS

28.2800 g., 0.9250 Silver 0.8410 oz. ASW, 38.6 mm. **Ruler:** Elizabeth II **Subject:** Queen's 80th Birthday **Obv:** Head with tiara right - gilt **Obv. Legend:** ELIZABETH II BAILIWICK - OF JERSEY **Rev:** Queen horseback facing

Date	Mintage	F	VF	XF	Unc	BU
2006 Proof	—	Value: 45.00				

KM# 142a 5 POUNDS

28.2800 g., 0.9250 Silver partially gilt 0.8410 oz. ASW, 38.6 mm. **Ruler:** Elizabeth II **Subject:** Elizabeth II's 80th Birthday **Obv:** Head with tiara right **Obv. Legend:** ELIZABETH II BAILIWICK - OF JERSEY **Rev:** Queen on horseback **Edge:** Reeded

Date	Mintage	F	VF	XF	Unc	BU
2006 Proof	—	Value: 45.00				

KM# 145 5 POUNDS

28.2800 g., Copper-Nickel, 38.61 mm. **Ruler:** Elizabeth II **Subject:** Elizabeth II's 80th Birthday **Rev:** Bobby Moore and Wembley's Royal Box

Date	Mintage	F	VF	XF	Unc	BU
2006	—	—	—	—	—	15.00

KM# 145a 5 POUNDS

28.2800 g., 0.9250 Silver 0.8410 oz. ASW, 38.61 mm. **Ruler:** Elizabeth II **Subject:** Elizabeth II, 80th Birthday **Rev:** Bobby Moor and Wembley's Royal Box

Date	Mintage	F	VF	XF	Unc	BU
2006 Proof	—	Value: 60.00				

KM# 163 5 POUNDS

28.2800 g., 0.9250 Silver 0.8410 oz. ASW **Ruler:** Elizabeth II **Subject:** Sir Winston Churchill

Date	Mintage	F	VF	XF	Unc	BU
2006 Proof	Est. 25,000	Value: 60.00				

KM# 165 5 POUNDS

28.2800 g., 0.9250 Silver 0.8410 oz. ASW, 38.61 mm. **Ruler:** Elizabeth II **Subject:** Robert (Bobby) Moore, soccerplayer

Date	Mintage	F	VF	XF	Unc	BU
2006 Proof	Est. 25,000	Value: 60.00				

KM# 166 5 POUNDS

28.2800 g., 0.9250 Silver 0.8410 oz. ASW, 38.61 mm. **Ruler:** Elizabeth II **Subject:** Florence Nightingale

Date	Mintage	F	VF	XF	Unc	BU
2006 Proof	25,000	Value: 60.00				

KM# 167 5 POUNDS

28.2800 g., Copper-Nickel, 38.61 mm. **Ruler:** Elizabeth II **Subject:** Guy Penrose Gibson, Victoria Cross

Date	Mintage	F	VF	XF	Unc	BU
2006	—	—	—	—	—	15.00

KM# 167a 5 POUNDS

28.2800 g., 0.9250 Silver 0.8410 oz. ASW, 38.61 mm. **Ruler:** Elizabeth II **Subject:** Guy Penrose Gibson, Victoria Cross

Date	Mintage	F	VF	XF	Unc	BU
2006 Proof	Est. 30,000	Value: 50.00				

KM# 168 5 POUNDS

28.2800 g., 0.9250 Silver 0.8410 oz. ASW, 38.61 mm. **Ruler:** Elizabeth II **Subject:** Nicholson

Date	Mintage	F	VF	XF	Unc	BU
2006 Proof	—	Value: 50.00				

KM# 169 5 POUNDS

28.2800 g., 0.9250 Silver 0.8410 oz. ASW, 38.61 mm. **Ruler:** Elizabeth II **Subject:** Hook, Char and Bro

Date	Mintage	F	VF	XF	Unc	BU
2006 Proof	—	Value: 50.00				

KM# 170 5 POUNDS

28.2800 g., 0.9250 Silver 0.8410 oz. ASW, 38.61 mm. **Ruler:** Elizabeth II **Subject:** First Lanc Fusiliers

Date	Mintage	F	VF	XF	Unc	BU
2006 Proof	—	Value: 50.00				

KM# 171 5 POUNDS

28.2800 g., 0.9250 Silver 0.8410 oz. ASW, 38.61 mm. **Ruler:** Elizabeth II **Subject:** Noel Godfrey Chavasse

Date	Mintage	F	VF	XF	Unc	BU
2006 Proof	—	Value: 50.00				

KM# 172 5 POUNDS

28.2800 g., 0.9250 Silver 0.8410 oz. ASW, 38.61 mm. **Ruler:** Elizabeth II **Subject:** David MacKay

Date	Mintage	F	VF	XF	Unc	BU
2006 Proof	—	Value: 50.00				

KM# 174 5 POUNDS

28.2800 g., 0.9250 Silver 0.8410 oz. ASW, 38.61 mm. **Ruler:** Elizabeth II **Subject:** Elizabeth, the Queen Mother

Date	Mintage	F	VF	XF	Unc	BU
2007 Proof	Est. 2,500	Value: 60.00				

KM# 175 5 POUNDS

28.2800 g., 0.9250 Silver 0.8410 oz. ASW, 38.61 mm. **Ruler:** Elizabeth II **Subject:** Henry VIII

Date	Mintage	F	VF	XF	Unc	BU
2007 Proof	Est. 25,000	Value: 60.00				

KM# 176 5 POUNDS

28.2800 g., 0.9250 Silver 0.8410 oz. ASW, 38.61 mm. **Ruler:** Elizabeth II **Subject:** Diana, Princess of Wales

Date	Mintage	F	VF	XF	Unc	BU
2007 Proof	Est. 25,000	Value: 60.00				

KM# 177 5 POUNDS

28.2800 g., 0.9250 Silver 0.8410 oz. ASW, 38.61 mm. **Ruler:** Elizabeth II **Subject:** Christopher Wren

Date	Mintage	F	VF	XF	Unc	BU
2007 Proof	Est. 25,000	Value: 60.00				

KM# 178 5 POUNDS

28.2800 g., Copper-Nickel, 38.61 mm. **Ruler:** Elizabeth II **Subject:** Elizabeth II and Prince Philip, 60th Wedding Anniversary **Rev:** Elizabeth and Philip, 1947

Date	Mintage	F	VF	XF	Unc	BU
2007	—	—	—	—	—	15.00

KM# 178a 5 POUNDS

28.2800 g., 0.9250 Silver 0.8410 oz. ASW, 38.61 mm. **Ruler:** Elizabeth II **Subject:** Elizabeth II and Prince Philip, 60th Wedding Anniversary **Rev:** Elizabeth and Philip, 1947

Date	Mintage	F	VF	XF	Unc	BU
2007 Proof	—	Value: 60.00				

KM# 179 5 POUNDS

28.2800 g., Copper-Nickel, 38.61 mm. **Ruler:** Elizabeth II **Subject:** Elizabeth II and Prince Philip, 60th Wedding Anniversary **Rev:** Westminster Abbey

Date	Mintage	F	VF	XF	Unc	BU
2007	—	—	—	—	—	15.00

KM# 179a 5 POUNDS

28.2800 g., 0.9250 Silver 0.8410 oz. ASW, 38.61 mm. **Ruler:** Elizabeth II **Subject:** Elizabeth II and Prince Philip, 60th Wedding Anniversary **Rev:** Westminster Abbey

Date	Mintage	F	VF	XF	Unc	BU
2007 Proof	—	Value: 60.00				

KM# 180 5 POUNDS

28.2800 g., Copper-Nickel, 38.61 mm. **Ruler:** Elizabeth II **Subject:** Elizabeth II and Prince Philip, 60th Wedding Anniversary **Rev:** Wedding cake

Date	Mintage	F	VF	XF	Unc	BU
2007	—	—	—	—	—	15.00

KM# 180a 5 POUNDS

28.2800 g., 0.9250 Silver 0.8410 oz. ASW, 38.61 mm. **Ruler:** Elizabeth II **Subject:** Elizabeth II and Prince Philip, 60th Wedding Anniversary **Rev:** Wedding cake

Date	Mintage	F	VF	XF	Unc	BU
2007 Proof	—	Value: 60.00				

KM# 181 5 POUNDS

28.2800 g., Copper-Nickel, 38.61 mm. **Ruler:** Elizabeth II **Subject:** Elizabeth II and Prince Philip, 60th Wedding Anniversary **Rev:** Elizabeth and Prince Philip, 2007

Date	Mintage	F	VF	XF	Unc	BU
2007	—	—	—	—	—	15.00

KM# 181a 5 POUNDS

28.2800 g., 0.9250 Silver 0.8410 oz. ASW, 38.61 mm. **Ruler:** Elizabeth II **Subject:** Elizabeth II and Prince Philip, 60th Wedding Anniversary **Rev:** Elizabeth and Philip, 2007

Date	Mintage	F	VF	XF	Unc	BU
2007 Proof	—	Value: 60.00				

KM# 182 5 POUNDS

28.2800 g., Copper-Nickel, 38.61 mm. **Ruler:** Elizabeth II **Subject:** Royal Air Force **Rev:** Barnes Wallis, Roy Chadwick, Guy Penrose Gibson

Date	Mintage	F	VF	XF	Unc	BU
2008	—	—	—	—	—	15.00

KM# 182a 5 POUNDS

26.0000 g., Brass, 38.61 mm. **Ruler:** Elizabeth II **Subject:** Royal Air Force **Rev:** Barnes Wallis, Roy Chadwick, Guy Penrose Gibson

Date	Mintage	F	VF	XF	Unc	BU
2008 Proof	Est. 25,000	Value: 30.00				

KM# 182b 5 POUNDS

28.2800 g., 0.9250 Silver 0.8410 oz. ASW, 38.61 mm. **Ruler:** Elizabeth II **Subject:** Royal Air Force **Rev:** Barnes Wallis, Roy Chadwick, Guy Penrose Gibson

Date	Mintage	F	VF	XF	Unc	BU
2008 Proof	Est. 25,000	Value: 60.00				

KM# 183 5 POUNDS

28.2800 g., Copper-Nickel, 38.61 mm. **Ruler:** Elizabeth II **Subject:** Royal Air Force **Rev:** Reginald Joseph MItchell, Spitfire

Date	Mintage	F	VF	XF	Unc	BU
2008	—	—	—	—	—	15.00

KM# 183a 5 POUNDS

28.2800 g., 0.9250 Silver 0.8410 oz. ASW, 38.61 mm. **Ruler:** Elizabeth II **Subject:** Royal Air Force **Rev:** Reginald Joseph MItchell, Spitfire

Date	Mintage	F	VF	XF	Unc	BU
2008 Proof	—	Value: 60.00				

KM# 184 5 POUNDS

28.2800 g., Copper-Nickel, 38.61 mm. **Ruler:** Elizabeth II **Subject:** Royal Air Force **Rev:** Battle of Britain

Date	Mintage	F	VF	XF	Unc	BU
2008	—	—	—	—	—	15.00

KM# 185 5 POUNDS

28.2800 g., Copper-Nickel, 38.61 mm. **Ruler:** Elizabeth II **Subject:** Royal Air Force **Rev:** Frank Whittle

Date	Mintage	F	VF	XF	Unc	BU
2008	—	—	—	—	—	15.00

KM# 186 5 POUNDS

28.2800 g., Copper-Nickel, 38.61 mm. **Ruler:** Elizabeth II **Subject:** Royal Air Force **Rev:** Hugh Trenchard, founder of the British Air Force

Date	Mintage	F	VF	XF	Unc	BU
2008	—	—	—	—	—	15.00

KM# 186a 5 POUNDS

28.2800 g., 0.9250 Silver 0.8410 oz. ASW, 38.61 mm. **Ruler:** Elizabeth II **Subject:** Royal Air Force **Rev:** Hugh Trenchard, founder of the British Air Force

Date	Mintage	F	VF	XF	Unc	BU
2008 Proof	—	Value: 60.00				

KM# 187 5 POUNDS

28.2800 g., Copper-Nickel, 38.61 mm. **Ruler:** Elizabeth II **Subject:** British Air Force

Date	Mintage	F	VF	XF	Unc	BU
2008	—	—	—	—	—	15.00

KM# 188 5 POUNDS

28.2800 g., Copper-Nickel, 38.61 mm. **Ruler:** Elizabeth II **Subject:** Royal Air Force

Date	Mintage	F	VF	XF	Unc	BU
2008	—	—	—	—	—	15.00

KM# 189 5 POUNDS

28.2800 g., Copper-Nickel, 38.61 mm. **Ruler:** Elizabeth II **Subject:** Royal Air Force

Date	Mintage	F	VF	XF	Unc	BU
2008	—	—	—	—	—	15.00

KM# 190 5 POUNDS

28.2800 g., Copper-Nickel, 38.61 mm. **Ruler:** Elizabeth II **Subject:** Royal Air Force

Date	Mintage	F	VF	XF	Unc	BU
2008	—	—	—	—	—	15.00

KM# 191 5 POUNDS

28.2800 g., Copper-Nickel, 38.61 mm. **Ruler:** Elizabeth II **Subject:** Royal Air Force

Date	Mintage	F	VF	XF	Unc	BU
2008	—	—	—	—	—	15.00

KM# 193.1 5 POUNDS

Copper-Nickel, 38.61 mm. **Ruler:** Elizabeth II **Subject:** End of World War I **Obv:** Head in tiara right **Rev:** Sundial motif **Shape:** Number 8

Date	Mintage	F	VF	XF	Unc	BU
2008	—	—	—	—	—	18.00

KM# 193.2 5 POUNDS

Copper-Nickel, 38.61 mm. **Ruler:** Elizabeth II **Subject:** End of World War I **Obv:** Head in tiara right **Rev:** Sundial motif in color **Shape:** Number 8

Date	Mintage	F	VF	XF	Unc	BU
2008	—	—	—	—	—	25.00

KM# 193a 5 POUNDS

28.0000 g., 0.9250 Silver 0.8327 oz. ASW, 38.61 mm. **Ruler:** Elizabeth II **Subject:** End of World War I **Obv:** Head with tiara right **Rev:** Sundial motif **Shape:** Number 8

Date	Mintage	F	VF	XF	Unc	BU
2008 Proof	9,500	Value: 60.00				

KM# 193b 5 POUNDS

28.0000 g., 0.9160 Gold 0.8246 oz. AGW, 38.61 mm. **Ruler:** Elizabeth II **Subject:** End of World War I **Obv:** Head with tiara right **Rev:** Sundial motif **Shape:** Numeral 8

Date	Mintage	F	VF	XF	Unc	BU
2008 Proof	Est. 450	Value: 1,500				

KM# 194 5 POUNDS

Silver **Ruler:** Elizabeth II **Rev:** St. George slaying the dragon

Date	Mintage	F	VF	XF	Unc	BU
2008	—	—	—	—	—	—

KM# 146 5 POUNDS

28.2800 g., 0.9250 Silver 0.8410 oz. ASW, 38.6 mm. **Ruler:** Elizabeth II **Subject:** Battle of Agincourt, 1415 **Obv:** Head right **Rev:** Archers and horsemen

Date	Mintage	F	VF	XF	Unc	BU
2009 Proof	2,500	Value: 55.00				

KM# 147 5 POUNDS

155.5000 g., 0.9250 Silver partially gilt 4.6243 oz. ASW, 65 mm. **Ruler:** Elizabeth II **Obv:** Head right **Rev:** St. George slaying dragon, partially gilt

Date	Mintage	F	VF	XF	Unc	BU
2009 Proof	450	Value: 350				

KM# 195 5 POUNDS

28.2800 g., Copper-Nickel, 38.61 mm. **Ruler:** Elizabeth II **Subject:** Henry VIII, 500th Anniversary of reign

Date	Mintage	F	VF	XF	Unc	BU
2009	—	—	—	—	—	15.00

KM# 195a 5 POUNDS

28.2800 g., 0.9250 Silver 0.8410 oz. ASW, 38.61 mm. **Ruler:** Elizabeth II **Subject:** Henry VIII, 500th Anniversary of reign

Date	Mintage	F	VF	XF	Unc	BU
2009 Proof	—	Value: 60.00				

KM# 195b 5 POUNDS

39.9400 g., 0.9160 Gold 1.1762 oz. AGW, 38.91 mm. **Ruler:** Elizabeth II **Subject:** Henry VIII, 500th Anniversary of reign

Date	Mintage	F	VF	XF	Unc	BU
2009 Proof	—	Value: 2,150				

KM# 197 5 POUNDS

28.2800 g., 0.9250 Silver 0.8410 oz. ASW, 38.61 mm. **Ruler:** Elizabeth II **Subject:** British Battles - Agincourt

Date	Mintage	F	VF	XF	Unc	BU
2009 Proof	25,000	Value: 60.00				

KM# 198 5 POUNDS

28.2800 g., 0.9250 Silver 0.8410 oz. ASW, 38.61 mm. **Ruler:** Elizabeth II **Subject:** British Battles - Somme

Date	Mintage	F	VF	XF	Unc	BU
2009 Proof	Est. 25,000	Value: 60.00				

KM# 199 5 POUNDS

28.2800 g., 0.9250 Silver 0.8410 oz. ASW, 38.61 mm. **Ruler:** Elizabeth II **Subject:** British Battles - Normandie

Date	Mintage	F	VF	XF	Unc	BU
2009 Proof	Est. 25,000	Value: 60.00				

KM# 200 5 POUNDS

28.2800 g., 0.9250 Silver 0.8410 oz. ASW, 38.61 mm. **Ruler:** Elizabeth II **Subject:** British Battles - El Alamein

Date	Mintage	F	VF	XF	Unc	BU
2009 Proof	Est. 25,000	Value: 60.00				

KM# 201 5 POUNDS

28.2800 g., 0.9250 Silver 0.8410 oz. ASW, 38.61 mm. **Ruler:** Elizabeth II **Subject:** British Battles - Hastings

Date	Mintage	F	VF	XF	Unc	BU
2009 Proof	Est. 25,000	Value: 60.00				

KM# 202 5 POUNDS

28.2800 g., 0.9250 Silver 0.8410 oz. ASW, 38.61 mm. **Ruler:** Elizabeth II **Subject:** British Battles - Bosworth

Date	Mintage	F	VF	XF	Unc	BU
2009 Proof	Est. 25,000	Value: 60.00				

KM# 203 5 POUNDS

28.2800 g., 0.9250 Silver 0.8410 oz. ASW, 38.61 mm. **Ruler:** Elizabeth II **Subject:** British Battles - Naseby

Date	Mintage	F	VF	XF	Unc	BU
2009 Proof	Est. 25,000	Value: 60.00				

KM# 204 5 POUNDS

28.2800 g., 0.9250 Silver 0.8410 oz. ASW, 38.61 mm. **Ruler:** Elizabeth II **Subject:** British Battles - Culloden

Date	Mintage	F	VF	XF	Unc	BU
2009 Proof	Est. 25,000	Value: 60.00				

KM# 205 5 POUNDS

28.2800 g., 0.9250 Silver 0.8410 oz. ASW, 38.61 mm. **Ruler:** Elizabeth II **Subject:** British Battles - Waterloo

Date	Mintage	F	VF	XF	Unc	BU
2009 Proof	Est. 25,000	Value: 60.00				

KM# 206 5 POUNDS

28.2800 g., 0.9250 Silver 0.8410 oz. ASW, 38.61 mm. **Ruler:** Elizabeth II **Subject:** British Battles - Alma

Date	Mintage	F	VF	XF	Unc	BU
2009 Proof	Est. 25,000	Value: 60.00				

KM# 207 5 POUNDS

28.2800 g., 0.9250 Silver 0.8410 oz. ASW, 38.61 mm. **Ruler:** Elizabeth II **Subject:** British Battles - Rorkes Drift

Date	Mintage	F	VF	XF	Unc	BU
2009 Proof	Est. 25,000	Value: 60.00				

KM# 208 5 POUNDS

28.2800 g., 0.9250 Silver 0.8410 oz. ASW, 38.61 mm. **Ruler:** Elizabeth II **Subject:** British Battles - Mafeking

Date	Mintage	F	VF	XF	Unc	BU
2009 Proof	Est. 25,000	Value: 60.00				

KM# 211a 5 POUNDS

28.2800 g., 0.9250 Silver 0.8410 oz. ASW, 38.61 mm. **Ruler:** Elizabeth II **Subject:** James Cook

Date	Mintage	F	VF	XF	Unc	BU
2009 Proof	—	Value: 60.00				

KM# 212 5 POUNDS

28.2800 g., Copper-Nickel, 38.61 mm. **Ruler:** Elizabeth II **Subject:** Robert F. Scott

Date	Mintage	F	VF	XF	Unc	BU
2009	—	—	—	—	—	15.00

KM# 211 5 POUNDS

28.2800 g., Copper-Nickel, 38.61 mm. **Ruler:** Elizabeth II **Subject:** James Cook

Date	Mintage	F	VF	XF	Unc	BU
2009	—	—	—	—	—	15.00

KM# 212a 5 POUNDS

28.2800 g., 0.9250 Silver 0.8410 oz. ASW, 38.61 mm. **Ruler:** Elizabeth II **Subject:** Robert F. Scott

Date	Mintage	F	VF	XF	Unc	BU
2009 Proof	—	Value: 60.00				

KM# 213 5 POUNDS

28.2800 g., Copper-Nickel, 38.61 mm. **Ruler:** Elizabeth II **Subject:** Naval Airforce

Date	Mintage	F	VF	XF	Unc	BU
2009	—	—	—	—	—	15.00

KM# 213a 5 POUNDS

28.2800 g., 0.9250 Silver 0.8410 oz. ASW, 38.61 mm. **Ruler:** Elizabeth II **Subject:** Naval Airforce

Date	Mintage	F	VF	XF	Unc	BU
2009 Proof	—	Value: 60.00				

KM# 214 5 POUNDS

28.2800 g., Copper-Nickel, 38.61 mm. **Ruler:** Elizabeth II **Subject:** Falkland War

Date	Mintage	F	VF	XF	Unc	BU
2009	—	—	—	—	—	15.00

KM# 214a 5 POUNDS

28.2800 g., 0.9250 Copper-Nickel 0.8410 oz., 38.61 mm. **Ruler:** Elizabeth II **Subject:** Falkland War

Date	Mintage	F	VF	XF	Unc	BU
2009 Proof	—	Value: 60.00				

KM# 215 5 POUNDS

28.2800 g., Copper-Nickel, 38.61 mm. **Ruler:** Elizabeth II **Subject:** H.M.S. Ark Royal

Date	Mintage	F	VF	XF	Unc	BU
2009	—	—	—	—	—	15.00

KM# 216 5 POUNDS

28.2800 g., 0.9250 Silver 0.8410 oz. ASW, 38.61 mm. **Ruler:** Elizabeth II **Subject:** H.M.S. Ark Royal

Date	Mintage	F	VF	XF	Unc	BU
2009 Proof	—	Value: 60.00				

KM# 217 5 POUNDS

28.2800 g., 0.9250 Silver 0.8410 oz. ASW, 38.6 mm. **Ruler:** Elizabeth II **Obv:** Head with tiara right **Rev:** Katherine Middleton and Prince WIlliam facing

Date	Mintage	F	VF	XF	Unc	BU
2011 Proof	—	Value: 85.00				

KM# 143 10 POUNDS

155.5000 g., 0.9250 Silver partially gilt 4.6243 oz. ASW, 65 mm. **Ruler:** Elizabeth II **Subject:** 50th Anniversary of Coronation **Obv:** Queens silver portrait on gold plated fields **Rev:** Crown and scepter above arms, gold plated

Date	Mintage	F	VF	XF	Unc	BU
2003	2,000	—	—	—	135	150

KM# 154 10 POUNDS

155.5000 g., 0.9160 Gold 4.5793 oz. AGW, 65 mm. **Ruler:** Elizabeth II **Subject:** Crimean War, 150th anniversary **Rev:** Light Brigade, Earl of Cardigan

Date	Mintage	F	VF	XF	Unc	BU
2004 Proof	—	Value: 8,500				

KM# 159 10 POUNDS

155.5000 g., 0.9250 Silver 4.6243 oz. ASW, 65 mm. **Ruler:** Elizabeth II **Subject:** End of World War II, 60th Anniversary **Rev:** Parlament buildings

Date	Mintage	F	VF	XF	Unc	BU
2005 Proof	—	Value: 200				

KM# 161 10 POUNDS

155.5000 g., 0.9160 Gold 4.5793 oz. AGW, 65 mm. **Ruler:** Elizabeth II **Subject:** Trafalgar, 200th Anniversary

Date	Mintage	F	VF	XF	Unc	BU
2005 Proof	—	Value: 8,500				

KM# 192 10 POUNDS

155.5000 g., 0.9250 Silver 4.6243 oz. ASW, 65 mm. **Ruler:** Elizabeth II **Subject:** Royal Air Force **Rev:** Reginald Joseph Mitchell, founder of the Royal Air Force

Date	Mintage	F	VF	XF	Unc	BU
2008 Proof	Est. 1,943	Value: 200				

KM# 112 25 POUNDS

7.9800 g., 0.9167 Gold 0.2352 oz. AGW, 22.05 mm. **Ruler:** Elizabeth II **Subject:** Princess Diana **Obv:** Crowned head right **Rev:** Diana's portrait **Edge:** Reeded

Date	Mintage	F	VF	XF	Unc	BU
2002 Proof	2,500	Value: 450				

KM# 114 25 POUNDS

7.9800 g., 0.9166 Gold 0.2352 oz. AGW, 22 mm. **Ruler:** Elizabeth II **Subject:** Queen Mother **Obv:** Crowned head right **Rev:** Queen Mother's portrait circa 1918 **Edge:** Reeded

Date	Mintage	F	VF	XF	Unc	BU
2002 Proof	2,500	Value: 450				

KM# 116 25 POUNDS

7.9800 g., 0.9166 Gold 0.2352 oz. AGW, 22 mm. **Ruler:** Elizabeth II **Subject:** Golden Jubilee **Obv:** Crowned head right **Rev:** Abbey procession scene **Edge:** Reeded

Date	Mintage	F	VF	XF	Unc	BU
2002 Proof	2,500	Value: 450				

KM# 118 25 POUNDS

7.9800 g., 0.9166 Gold 0.2352 oz. AGW, 22 mm. **Ruler:** Elizabeth II **Subject:** Duke of Wellington **Obv:** Crowned head right **Rev:** Wellington's portrait with infantry scene **Edge:** Reeded

Date	Mintage	F	VF	XF	Unc	BU
2002 Proof	2,500	Value: 450				

KM# 151 25 POUNDS

7.9800 g., 0.9160 Gold 0.2350 oz. AGW, 22.05 mm. **Ruler:** Elizabeth II **Rev:** Multipe portraits of Alfred, Drake, Nelson, Fisher and Woodward and the Mary Rose, Visctory, Warspite, Ark Royal and Conqueror

Date	Mintage	F	VF	XF	Unc	BU
2003 Proof	—	Value: 450				

KM# 120 25 POUNDS

7.9800 g., 0.9166 Gold 0.2352 oz. AGW, 22 mm. **Ruler:** Elizabeth II **Subject:** Golden Jubilee **Obv:** Crowned head right **Rev:** Honor guard and monument **Edge:** Reeded

Date	Mintage	F	VF	XF	Unc	BU
2003 Proof	5,000	Value: 450				

KM# 155 25 POUNDS

7.9800 g., 0.9160 Gold 0.2350 oz. AGW, 22.05 mm. **Ruler:** Elizabeth II **Subject:** Crimean War, 150th anniversary **Rev:** Light Brigade, Earl of Cardigan

Date	Mintage	F	VF	XF	Unc	BU
2004 Proof	—	Value: 450				

KM# 125 25 POUNDS

7.9800 g., 0.9167 Gold 0.2352 oz. AGW, 22 mm. **Ruler:** Elizabeth II **Subject:** D-Day **Obv:** Crowned head right **Rev:** British Horsa gliders in flight **Edge:** Reeded

Date	Mintage	F	VF	XF	Unc	BU
2004 Proof	500	Value: 450				

KM# 152 25 POUNDS

7.9800 g., 0.9160 Gold 0.2350 oz. AGW, 22.05 mm. **Ruler:** Elizabeth II **Rev:** Locomotive 6220 Coronation, and LMSR Pacific

Date	Mintage	F	VF	XF	Unc	BU
2004 Proof	Est. 2,500	Value: 450				

KM# 153 25 POUNDS

7.9800 g., 0.9160 Gold 0.2350 oz. AGW, 22.05 mm. **Ruler:** Elizabeth II **Rev:** British Railway's locomotive 92229 Evening Star

Date	Mintage	F	VF	XF	Unc	BU
2004 Proof	Est. 2,500	Value: 450				

KM# 156 25 POUNDS

7.9800 g., 0.9160 Gold 0.2350 oz. AGW, 22.05 mm. **Ruler:** Elizabeth II **Subject:** Royal Navy **Rev:** H.M.S. Vicotry

Date	Mintage	F	VF	XF	Unc	BU
2004 Proof	—	Value: 450				

KM# 157 25 POUNDS

7.9800 g., 0.9160 Gold 0.2350 oz. AGW, 22.05 mm. **Ruler:** Elizabeth II **Subject:** Royal Navy **Rev:** Admiral Andrew B. Cunningham

Date	Mintage	F	VF	XF	Unc	BU
2004 Proof	—	Value: 450				

KM# 158 25 POUNDS

7.9800 g., 0.9160 Gold 0.2350 oz. AGW, 22.05 mm. **Ruler:** Elizabeth II **Subject:** Royal Navy **Rev:** Submarine H.M.S. Conqueror

Date	Mintage	F	VF	XF	Unc	BU
2004 Proof	—	Value: 450				

KM# 162 25 POUNDS

7.9800 g., 0.9160 Gold 0.2350 oz. AGW, 22.05 mm. **Ruler:** Elizabeth II **Subject:** Trafalgar, 200th Anniversary

Date	Mintage	F	VF	XF	Unc	BU
2005 Proof	—	Value: 450				

KM# 196 25 POUNDS

7.9800 g., 0.9160 Gold 0.2350 oz. AGW, 22.05 mm. **Ruler:** Elizabeth II **Subject:** Henry VIII, 500th Anniversary of reign

Date	Mintage	F	VF	XF	Unc	BU
2009 Proof	Est. 995	Value: 450				

KM# 209 25 POUNDS

7.9800 g., 0.9160 Gold 0.2350 oz. AGW, 22.05 mm. **Ruler:** Elizabeth II **Subject:** British Battles - Agincourt

Date	Mintage	F	VF	XF	Unc	BU
2009 Proof	Est. 995	Value: 450				

KM# 210 25 POUNDS

7.9800 g., 0.9160 Gold 0.2350 oz. AGW, 22.05 mm. **Ruler:** Elizabeth II **Subject:** British Battles - Somme

Date	Mintage	F	VF	XF	Unc	BU
2009 Proof	Est. 995	Value: 450				

KM# 122 50 POUNDS

1000.0000 g., 0.9250 Silver 29.738 oz. ASW, 100 mm. **Ruler:** Elizabeth II **Obv:** Crowned head right **Rev:** Bust facing and crowned arms with supporters **Edge:** Reeded

Date	Mintage	F	VF	XF	Unc	BU
2003 Proof	500	Value: 1,150				

PIEDFORT

KM#	Date	Mintage	Identification	Mkt Val
P3	2002	100	5 Pounds. 0.9166 Gold. 56.5600 g. 38.6 mm. Queen's portrait. Abbey procession scene. Reeded edge. Underweight piefort	1,900

MINT SETS

KM#	Date	Mintage	Identification	Issue Price	Mkt Val
MS7	2004 (1)	—	Jersey KM#126, Guernsey KM#155, Alderney KM#43, 150th Anniversary of the Crimean War	—	100

JORDAN

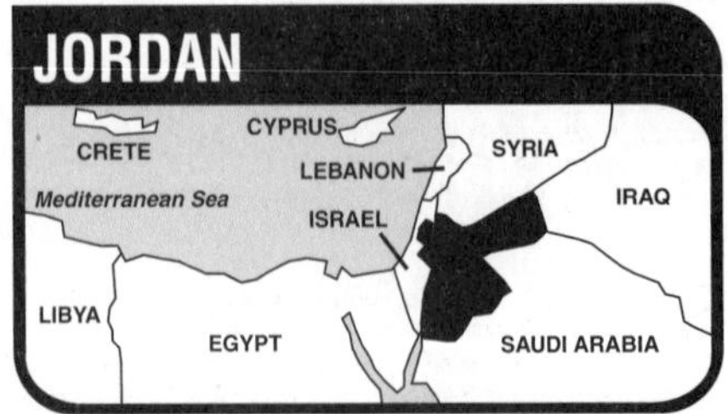

The Hashemite Kingdom of Jordan, a constitutional monarchy in southwest Asia, has an area of 37,738 sq. mi.(91,880 sq. km.) and a population of 3.5 million. Capital: Amman. Agriculture and tourism comprise Jordan's economic base. Chief exports are phosphates, tomatoes and oranges.

RULER

Abdullah Ibn Al-Hussein, 1999-

MONETARY SYSTEM

100 Piastres = 1 Dinar

KINGDOM

DECIMAL COINAGE

KM# 78.1 QIRSH (Piastre)

5.4700 g., Copper Plated Steel, 25 mm. **Ruler:** Abdullah II **Obv:** King Abdullah II **Rev:** Christian date left, Islamic date right **Edge:** Plain

Date	Mintage	F	VF	XF	Unc	BU
AH1430-2009	—	—	—	—	1.00	1.50
AH1432-2011	—	—	—	—	1.00	1.50

KM# 78.2 QIRSH (Piastre)

5.4700 g., Copper Plated Steel, 24.9 mm. **Ruler:** Abdullah **Obv:** King Abdullah II **Rev:** Islamic date left, Christian date right **Edge:** Plain

Date	Mintage	F	VF	XF	Unc	BU
AH1430-2009	—	—	—	—	7.50	10.00

KM# 73 5 PIASTRES

5.0000 g., Nickel Plated Steel, 25.8 mm. **Ruler:** Abdullah II **Obv:** Bust right **Rev:** Value to left within lines below date with written value at lower right **Edge:** Milled

Date	Mintage	F	VF	XF	Unc	BU
AH1427-2006	—	—	—	—	1.50	2.00
AH1429-2008	—	—	—	—	1.50	2.00
AH1430-2009	—	—	—	—	1.50	2.00

KM# 74 10 PIASTRES

8.0000 g., Nickel Plated Steel, 28 mm. **Ruler:** Abdullah II **Obv:** Bust right **Rev:** Value at left within lines below date with written value at lower right **Edge:** Milled

Date	Mintage	F	VF	XF	Unc	BU
AH1425-2004	—	—	—	—	1.75	3.50
AH1427-2006	—	—	—	—	1.75	3.50
AH1429-2008	—	—	—	—	1.75	3.50
AH1430-2009	—	—	—	—	1.75	3.50

KM# 83 1/4 DINAR

7.4000 g., Nickel-Brass, 26.5 mm. **Ruler:** Abdullah II **Obv:** Bust right **Edge:** Plain **Shape:** 7-sided

Date	Mintage	F	VF	XF	Unc	BU
AH1425-2004	—	—	—	—	2.00	3.00
AH1427-2006	—	—	—	—	2.00	3.00
AH1429-2008	—	—	—	—	2.00	3.00
AH1430-2009	—	—	—	—	2.00	3.00

KM# 79 1/2 DINAR

9.6700 g., Bi-Metallic Copper-Nickel center in Brass ring, 29 mm. **Ruler:** Abdullah II **Obv:** Bust right within circle **Rev:** Value in center of circled wreath **Edge:** Plain **Shape:** 7-sided

Date	Mintage	F	VF	XF	Unc	BU
AH1427-2006	—	—	—	—	3.00	4.00
AH1429-2008	—	—	—	—	3.00	4.00
AH1430-2009	—	—	—	—	3.00	4.00

KM# 75 3 DINARS
28.5000 g., Brass, 40 mm. **Ruler:** Abdullah II **Subject:** Amman: Arabic Culture Capital **Obv:** Bust right **Rev:** Building **Edge:** Milled

Date	Mintage	F	VF	XF	Unc	BU
AH1423//2002	2,000	—	—	—	120	—

Note: Only 500 sold to collectors. Rest were taken by Amman municipality as official gifts

KM# 86 5 DINARS
120.0000 g., Bronze, 60 mm. **Ruler:** Abdullah **Subject:** Selection of Petra as one of the new Seven Wonders of the World **Obv:** King Abdullah II and Queen Rania **Rev:** Petra **Edge:** Milled

Date	Mintage	F	VF	XF	Unc	BU
AH1428-2008 Proof	500	Value: 160				

KM# 84 10 DINARS
120.0000 g., 0.9990 Silver 3.8541 oz. ASW, 60 mm. **Ruler:** Abdullah **Subject:** 60th Anniversary of Jordan's Independence **Obv:** King Abdullah I and Independence speech **Rev:** The National Assembly building **Edge:** Milled

Date	Mintage	F	VF	XF	Unc	BU
2006 Proof	250	Value: 250				

Note: Issued primarily for use as official state gifts

KM# 88 10 DINARS
31.1050 g., 0.9990 Silver 0.9990 oz. ASW, 40 mm. **Ruler:** Abdullah II **Subject:** Accession, 10th Anniversary **Obv:** Bust facing **Rev:** Crowned and mantled shield

Date	Mintage	F	VF	XF	Unc	BU
2009 Proof	2,250	Value: 150				

KM# 87 20 DINARS
120.0000 g., 0.9990 Silver 3.8541 oz. ASW, 60 mm. **Ruler:** Abdullah **Subject:** Selection of Petra as one of the new Seven Wonders of the World **Obv:** King Abdullah II and Queen Rania **Rev:** Petra **Edge:** Milled

Date	Mintage	F	VF	XF	Unc	BU
AH1428-2008 Proof	500	Value: 260				

KM# 89 50 DINARS
16.9600 g., 0.9990 Gold 0.5447 oz. AGW, 30 mm. **Ruler:** Abdullah II **Subject:** Accession, 10th Anniversary **Obv:** Bust **Rev:** Arms

Date	Mintage	F	VF	XF	Unc	BU
2009 Proof	1,750	Value: 975				

KM# 85 60 DINARS
72.7500 g., 0.9170 Gold 2.1447 oz. AGW, 40 mm. **Ruler:** Abdullah **Subject:** 60th Anniversary of Jordan's Independence **Obv:** King Abdullah II **Rev:** Treasury in Petra **Edge:** Milled

Date	Mintage	F	VF	XF	Unc	BU
2006 Proof	250	Value: 3,750				

Note: Issued primarily for use as official state gifts

MINT SETS

KM#	Date	Mintage	Identification	Issue Price	Mkt Val
MS4	2000-2004 (5)	—	KM#73-74, 78.1, 79, 83, mixed dates	—	20.00

PROOF SETS

KM#	Date	Mintage	Identification	Issue Price	Mkt Val
PS14	2006 (2)	250	KM#84-85	—	3,500
PS15	2008 (2)	—	KM#86-87	—	425

KAZAKHSTAN

The Republic of Kazakhstan (formerly Kazakhstan S.S.R.) is bordered to the west by the Caspian Sea and Russia, to the north by Russia, in the east by the Peoples Republic of China and in the south by Uzbekistan and Kirghizia. It has an area of 1,049,155 sq. mi. (2,717,300 sq. km.) and a population of 16.7 million. Capital: Astana. Rich in mineral resources including coal, tungsten, copper, lead, zinc and manganese with huge oil and natural gas reserves. Agriculture is very important, (it previously represented 20 percent of the total arable acreage of the combined U.S.S.R.) Non-ferrous metallurgy, heavy engineering and chemical industries are leaders in its economy.

MONETARY SYSTEM
100 Tyin = 1 Tenge

REPUBLIC

DECIMAL COINAGE

KM# 23 TENGE
1.6000 g., Nickel-Brass, 15 mm. **Obv:** National emblem **Rev:** Value flanked by designs **Edge:** Plain

Date	Mintage	F	VF	XF	Unc	BU
2002	—	—	—	—	0.50	0.85
2004	—	—	—	—	0.50	0.85
2005	—	—	—	—	0.50	0.85
2011	—	—	—	—	0.50	0.85
2012	—	—	—	—	0.50	0.85

KM# 64 2 TENGE
1.8200 g., Nickel-Brass, 16 mm. **Obv:** National emblem **Rev:** Value flanked by designs **Edge:** Plain

Date	Mintage	F	VF	XF	Unc	BU
2005	—	—	—	—	0.65	1.20
2006	—	—	—	—	0.65	1.20

KM# 24 5 TENGE
2.2000 g., Nickel-Brass, 17.3 mm. **Obv:** National emblem **Rev:** Value flanked by designs

Date	Mintage	F	VF	XF	Unc	BU
2002	—	—	—	—	0.50	0.85
2004	—	—	—	—	0.50	0.85
2005	—	—	—	—	0.50	0.85
2006	—	—	—	—	0.50	0.85
2010	—	—	—	—	0.50	0.85
2011	—	—	—	—	0.50	0.85
2012	—	—	—	—	0.50	0.85

KM# 25 10 TENGE
2.8000 g., Nickel-Brass, 19.6 mm. **Obv:** National emblem **Rev:** Value above design

Date	Mintage	F	VF	XF	Unc	BU
2002	—	—	—	—	0.75	1.25
2004	—	—	—	—	0.75	1.25
2005	—	—	—	—	0.75	1.25
2006	—	—	—	—	0.75	1.25
2010	—	—	—	—	0.75	1.25
2011	—	—	—	—	0.75	1.25
2012	—	—	—	—	0.75	1.25

KM# 26 20 TENGE
2.9000 g., Copper-Nickel-Zinc, 18.3 mm. **Obv:** National emblem **Rev:** Value above design **Edge:** Segmented reeding **Edge Lettering:** * CTO TENGE * Y 3 TENGE

Date	Mintage	F	VF	XF	Unc	BU
2002	—	—	—	—	1.00	1.75
2004	—	—	—	—	1.00	1.75
2006	—	—	—	—	1.00	1.75
2010	—	—	—	—	1.00	1.75
2011	—	—	—	—	1.00	1.75
2012	—	—	—	—	1.00	1.75

KM# 40 50 TENGE
11.5000 g., Copper-Nickel, 31 mm. **Obv:** Eagle superimposed on ornate 10 **Edge:** Reeded and plain sections

Date	Mintage	F	VF	XF	Unc	BU
2001	—	—	—	—	4.00	6.50

KM# 41 50 TENGE
11.2000 g., Copper-Nickel, 31.1 mm. **Subject:** Gabiden Mustafin **Obv:** National emblem above value **Rev:** Bust 1/4 left **Edge:** Segmented reeding

Date	Mintage	F	VF	XF	Unc	BU
ND(2002)	—	—	—	—	4.00	6.50

KM# 69 50 TENGE
Copper-Nickel, 31 mm. **Subject:** Gabit Mosrepov **Obv:** Symbol and value **Rev:** Bust facing

Date	Mintage	F	VF	XF	Unc	BU
2002	—	—	—	—	4.00	6.50

KM# 27 50 TENGE
4.7000 g., Copper-Nickel-Zinc, 23 mm. **Obv:** National emblem **Rev:** Value above design

Date	Mintage	F	VF	XF	Unc	BU
2002	—	—	—	—	2.00	3.50

KM# 70 50 TENGE
Copper-Nickel, 31 mm. **Subject:** 200th Anniversary of Makhambet Utemisov **Obv:** Symbol and value

Date	Mintage	F	VF	XF	Unc	BU
2003	—	—	—	—	7.00	10.00

KM# 54 50 TENGE
11.5000 g., Copper-Nickel, 31.1 mm. **Obv:** National emblem above value **Rev:** Painter Abylichan Kasteev (1904-1973) **Edge:** Reeded and plain sections

Date	Mintage	F	VF	XF	Unc	BU
2004	—	—	—	—	7.00	10.00

KM# 65 50 TENGE
11.5000 g., Copper-Nickel, 31.1 mm. **Subject:** Alken Margulan **Obv:** National emblem above value **Rev:** Bust facing **Edge:** Segmented reeding

Date	Mintage	F	VF	XF	Unc	BU
2004	—	—	—	—	7.00	10.00

KM# 58 50 TENGE
11.5000 g., Copper-Nickel, 31.1 mm. **Subject:** 10th Anniversary of the Constitution **Obv:** National emblem above value **Rev:** National emblem within circle above book **Edge:** Segmented reeding

Date	Mintage	F	VF	XF	Unc	BU
2005	—	—	—	—	7.00	10.00

KM# 71 50 TENGE
10.9500 g., Copper-Nickel, 31 mm. **Subject:** 60 Years Victory WWII **Obv:** Symbol and value

Date	Mintage	F	VF	XF	Unc	BU
2005	—	—	—	—	7.00	10.00

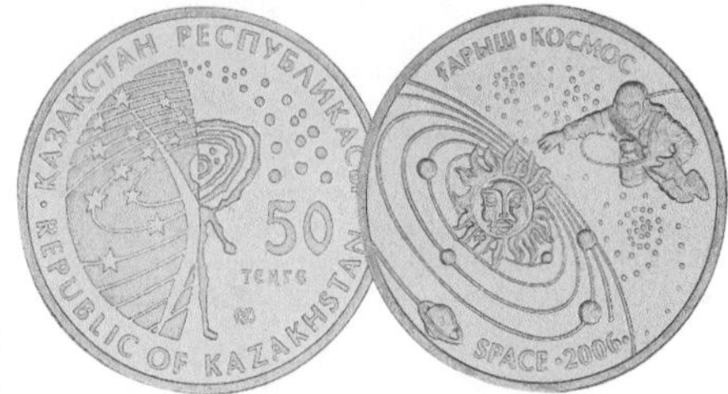

KM# 73 50 TENGE
11.3700 g., Copper-Nickel, 31 mm. **Obv:** Human figure and solar system **Rev:** Astronaut and solar system **Edge:** Segmented reeding

Date	Mintage	F	VF	XF	Unc	BU
2006	50,000	—	—	—	7.00	10.00

KM# 74 50 TENGE
11.3700 g., Copper-Nickel, 31 mm. **Obv:** National arms on tapestry **Rev:** Woman with baby in cradle **Edge:** Segmented reeding

Date	Mintage	F	VF	XF	Unc	BU
2006	—	—	—	—	7.00	10.00

KM# 75 50 TENGE
11.3700 g., Copper-Nickel, 31 mm. **Obv:** National arms **Rev:** Altai Snowcock **Edge:** Segmented reeding

Date	Mintage	F	VF	XF	Unc	BU
2006	50,000	—	—	—	7.00	10.00

KM# 77 50 TENGE
11.3700 g., Copper-Nickel, 31 mm. **Obv:** National arms **Rev:** Altyn Kyran Order Breast Star **Edge:** Segmented reeding

Date	Mintage	F	VF	XF	Unc	BU
2006	50,000	—	—	—	7.00	10.00

KM# 78 50 TENGE
11.3700 g., Copper-Nickel, 31 mm. **Obv:** National arms **Rev:** Zhubanov bust and music score **Edge:** Segmented reeding

Date	Mintage	F	VF	XF	Unc	BU
2006	50,000	—	—	—	7.00	10.00

KM# 79 50 TENGE
11.2200 g., Copper-Nickel, 31 mm. **Subject:** 20th Anniversary **Obv:** National arms above value **Rev:** Happy woman **Edge:** Segmented reeding

Date	Mintage	F	VF	XF	Unc	BU
1986-2006	—	—	—	—	7.00	10.00

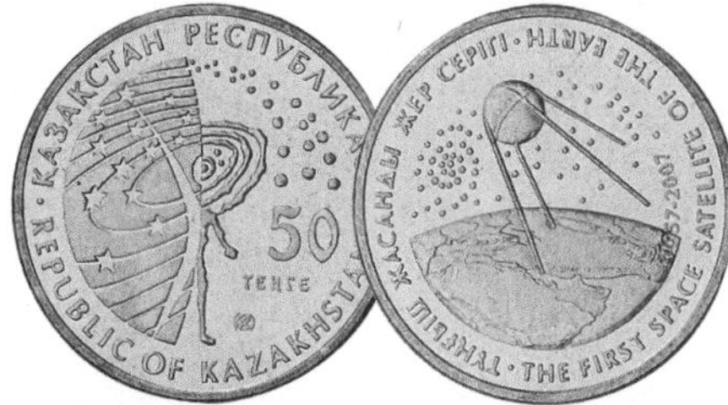

KM# 80 50 TENGE
10.8900 g., Copper-Nickel, 31.10 mm. **Subject:** 50th Anniversary Launch of Sputnik I **Obv:** Stylized view of solar system **Obv. Legend:** REPUBLIC OF KAZAKHSTAN **Rev:** Sputnik I in space, earth in background **Rev. Legend:** THE FIRST SPACE SATELLITE OF THE EARTH **Edge:** Segmented reeding

Date	Mintage	F	VF	XF	Unc	BU
1957-2007	—	—	—	—	7.00	10.00

KM# 81 50 TENGE
11.1100 g., Copper-Nickel, 31 mm. **Obv:** National arms, value below **Obv. Legend:** КАЗАКСТАН.... **Rev:** Eurasian Spoonbill standing left **Rev. Legend:** ... • PLATALEA LEUCORODIA **Edge:** Segmented reeding

Date	Mintage	F	VF	XF	Unc	BU
2007	—	—	—	—	7.00	10.00

KM# 164 50 TENGE
11.3700 g., Copper-Nickel, 31 mm. **Obv:** National arms on tapestry **Rev:** Child and two men

Date	Mintage	F	VF	XF	Unc	BU
2007	—	—	—	—	7.00	10.00

KM# 165 50 TENGE
11.3700 g., Copper-Nickel, 31 mm. **Obv:** National arms above value **Rev:** Otan badge

Date	Mintage	F	VF	XF	Unc	BU
2007	—	—	—	—	7.00	10.00

KM# 86 50 TENGE
Copper-Nickel, 31 mm. **Obv:** National Arms

Date	Mintage	F	VF	XF	Unc	BU
2008 Prooflike	—	—	—	—	—	12.00

KM# 169 50 TENGE
11.3700 g., Copper-Nickel, 31 mm. **Obv:** National arms on tapersry background **Rev:** Two horsemen

Date	Mintage	F	VF	XF	Unc	BU
2008	—	—	—	—	7.00	10.00

KM# 170 50 TENGE
11.3700 g., Copper-Nickel, 31 mm. **Obv:** National arms above vlaue **Rev:** Dank Order Star

Date	Mintage	F	VF	XF	Unc	BU
2008	—	—	—	—	7.00	10.00

KM# 171 50 TENGE
11.3700 g., Copper-Nickel, 31 mm. **Obv:** National arms **Rev:** Aibyn Order Star

Date	Mintage	F	VF	XF	Unc	BU
2008	—	—	—	—	7.00	10.00

KM# 172 50 TENGE
11.3700 g., Copper-Nickel, 31 mm. **Subject:** Astana capital, 10th Anniversary **Obv:** National arms **Rev:** Architecture

Date	Mintage	F	VF	XF	Unc	BU
2008	—	—	—	—	7.00	10.00

KM# 201 50 TENGE
11.3700 g., Copper-Nickel, 31 mm. **Obv:** National emblem **Rev:** Building views

Date	Mintage	F	VF	XF	Unc	BU
2008	50,000	—	—	—	7.00	10.00

KM# 202 50 TENGE
11.3700 g., Copper-Nickel, 31 mm. **Obv:** Human figure and solar system **Rev:** Spaceship Vostok

Date	Mintage	F	VF	XF	Unc	BU
2008	50,000	—	—	—	7.00	10.00

KM# 132 50 TENGE
Copper-Nickel, 31 mm. **Subject:** Betashar **Obv:** Arms **Rev:** Two figures standing

Date	Mintage	F	VF	XF	Unc	BU
2009	50,000	—	—	—	7.00	10.00

KM# 135 50 TENGE
0.5000 g., 0.9990 Gold 0.0161 oz. AGW, 11 mm. **Obv:** Value **Rev:** Cat head sculpture

Date	Mintage	F	VF	XF	Unc	BU
2009 Proof	14,000	—	—	—	—	50.00

KM# 140 50 TENGE
Copper-Nickel, 31 mm. **Obv:** Arms **Rev:** Parassat medal insignia

Date	Mintage	F	VF	XF	Unc	BU
2009	50,000	—	—	—	7.00	10.00

KM# 141 50 TENGE
Copper-Nickel **Obv:** Arms **Rev:** Porcupine advancing right **Shape:** 31

Date	Mintage	F	VF	XF	Unc	BU
2009	50,000	—	—	—	7.00	15.00

KM# 144 50 TENGE

Copper-Nickel, 31 mm. **Obv:** Man standing in solar system **Rev:** Apollo-Soyoz space craft

Date	Mintage	F	VF	XF	Unc	BU
2009	50,000	—	—	—	7.00	10.00

KM# 145 50 TENGE

Copper-Nickel, 31 mm. **Obv:** Arms **Rev:** Star of the Order of Dostyk

Date	Mintage	F	VF	XF	Unc	BU
2009	50,000	—	—	—	7.00	10.00

KM# 146 50 TENGE

Copper-Nickel, 31 mm. **Subject:** T. Bassenov, 100th Anniversary of Birth **Obv:** Arms **Rev:** Bust at right, architectural column

Date	Mintage	F	VF	XF	Unc	BU
2009	50,000	—	—	—	7.00	10.00

KM# 152 50 TENGE

0.5000 g., 0.9990 Gold 0.0161 oz. AGW, 11 mm. **Subject:** Ahalavlinky Treasure **Obv:** Value **Rev:** Historical jewlery design

Date	Mintage	F	VF	XF	Unc	BU
2009 Proof	14,000	Value: 45.00				

KM# 174 50 TENGE

Copper-Nickel, 31 mm. **Subject:** Moon Exploration, 40th Anniversary **Obv:** Figure standing within solar system design **Rev:** Lunar Rover vehicle

Date	Mintage	F	VF	XF	Unc	BU
2010	—	—	—	—	7.00	10.00

KM# 175 50 TENGE

Copper-Nickel, 31 mm. **Subject:** Great Victory, 65th Anniversary **Obv:** National Emblem, value below **Rev:** Order star, 1945 above

Date	Mintage	F	VF	XF	Unc	BU
2010	—	—	—	—	7.00	10.00

KM# 224 50 TENGE

Copper-Nickel, 31 mm. **Obv:** Arms **Rev:** Star of the Order of Kormet

Date	Mintage	F	VF	XF	Unc	BU
2010	—	—	—	—	—	10.00

KM# 206 50 TENGE

Copper-Nickel, 31 mm. **Subject:** Aktobe **Rev:** Griffin seal

Date	Mintage	F	VF	XF	Unc	BU
2011	—	—	—	—	2.25	7.50

KM# 207 50 TENGE

Copper-Nickel **Subject:** Aitys **Obv:** National arms **Rev:** Celebration **Shape:** 31

Date	Mintage	F	VF	XF	Unc	BU
2011	—	—	—	—	2.25	7.50

KM# 208 50 TENGE

Copper-Nickel, 31 mm. **Subject:** Ust Kamenogorsk **Obv:** Shield **Rev:** Value

Date	Mintage	F	VF	XF	Unc	BU
2011	—	—	—	—	2.25	7.50

KM# 209 50 TENGE

Copper-Nickel **Subject:** Karaganda **Obv:** Shield **Rev:** Value

Date	Mintage	F	VF	XF	Unc	BU
2011	—	—	—	—	2.25	7.50

KM# 210 50 TENGE

Copper-Nickel, 31 mm. **Subject:** Independence, 20th Anniversary **Obv:** Arms **Rev:** Anniversary logo

Date	Mintage	F	VF	XF	Unc	BU
2011	—	—	—	—	5.00	10.00

KM# 39 100 TENGE

6.2300 g., Bi-Metallic Copper-Nickel-Zinc center in Nickel-Brass ring, 24.4 mm. **Obv:** National emblem **Rev:** Value within lined circle flanked by designs **Edge:** Reeding over incuse value

Date	Mintage	F	VF	XF	Unc	BU
2002	—	—	—	—	3.50	5.50
2004	—	—	—	—	3.50	5.50
2005	—	—	—	—	3.50	5.50
2006	—	—	—	—	3.50	5.50
2007	—	—	—	—	3.50	5.50

KM# 49 100 TENGE

6.4000 g., Bi-Metallic Copper-Nickel-Zinc center in Nickel-Brass ring, 24.5 mm. **Obv:** Stylized chicken **Rev:** Value within lined circle flanked by designs **Edge:** Reeded and lettered

Date	Mintage	F	VF	XF	Unc	BU
2003	100,000	—	—	—	4.00	6.50

KM# 50 100 TENGE

6.4000 g., Bi-Metallic Copper-Nickel-Zinc center in Nickel-Brass ring, 24.5 mm. **Obv:** Stylized panther **Rev:** Value within lined circle flanked by designs **Edge:** Reeded and lettered

Date	Mintage	F	VF	XF	Unc	BU
2003	100,000	—	—	—	4.00	6.50

KM# 51 100 TENGE

6.4000 g., Bi-Metallic Copper-Nickel-Zinc center in Nickel-Brass ring, 24.5 mm. **Obv:** Stylized wolf's head **Rev:** Value within lined circle flanked by designs **Edge:** Reeded and lettered

Date	Mintage	F	VF	XF	Unc	BU
2003	100,000	—	—	—	4.00	6.50

KM# 52 100 TENGE

6.4000 g., Bi-Metallic Copper-Nickel-Zinc center in Nickel-Brass ring, 24.5 mm. **Obv:** Stylized sheep's head **Rev:** Value within lined circle flanked by designs **Edge:** Reeded and lettered

Date	Mintage	F	VF	XF	Unc	BU
2003	100,000	—	—	—	4.00	6.50

KM# 116 100 TENGE
31.1000 g., 0.9250 Silver 0.9249 oz. ASW, 37 mm. **Subject:** Olympics **Obv:** Arms and stylized stadium **Rev:** Two cyclists

Date	Mintage	F	VF	XF	Unc	BU
2004 Proof	—	Value: 55.00				

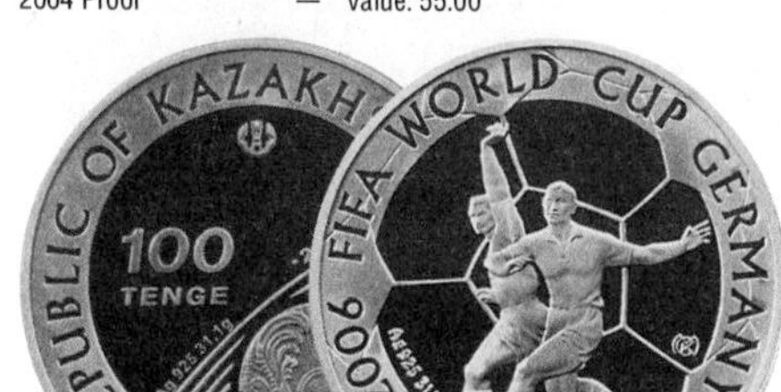

KM# 119 100 TENGE
31.1000 g., 0.9250 Silver 0.9249 oz. ASW, 37 mm. **Subject:** FIFA World Cup, Germany **Obv:** Arms and stylized stadium **Rev:** Two soccer players and large ball

Date	Mintage	F	VF	XF	Unc	BU
2004 Proof	—	Value: 55.00				

KM# 120 100 TENGE
1.2400 g., 0.9990 Gold 0.0398 oz. AGW, 13.92 mm. **Subject:** King Kroisos **Obv:** Arms **Rev:** Head left, coin, temple

Date	Mintage	F	VF	XF	Unc	BU
2004 Proof	—	Value: 85.00				

KM# 121 100 TENGE
1.2400 g., 0.9990 Gold 0.0398 oz. AGW, 13.92 mm. **Subject:** King Midas **Rev:** King Midas reclining on bench

Date	Mintage	F	VF	XF	Unc	BU
2004 Proof	—	Value: 85.00				

KM# 122 100 TENGE
1.2400 g., 0.9990 Gold 0.0398 oz. AGW, 13.92 mm. **Subject:** Ancient Turkestan **Obv:** Arms **Rev:** Camel caravan and building

Date	Mintage	F	VF	XF	Unc	BU
2004 Proof	—	Value: 85.00				

KM# 188 100 TENGE
1.2400 g., 0.9990 Gold 0.0398 oz. AGW, 13.92 mm. **Rev:** Marco Polo

Date	Mintage	F	VF	XF	Unc	BU
2004 Proof	15,000	Value: 100				

KM# 57 100 TENGE
6.4000 g., Bi-Metallic Copper-Nickel-Zinc center in Nickel-Brass ring, 24.5 mm. **Subject:** 60th Anniversary of the UN **Obv:** UN logo as part of the number 60 **Rev:** Value within lined circle flanked by designs **Edge:** Reeded and lettered

Date	Mintage	F	VF	XF	Unc	BU
2005	—	—	—	—	5.00	7.50

KM# 191 100 TENGE
31.1050 g., 0.9250 Silver 0.9250 oz. ASW, 38.61 mm. **Subject:** Torino Winter Olympics **Rev:** Three stone cross-country skiers

Date	Mintage	F	VF	XF	Unc	BU
2005 Proof	10,000	Value: 60.00				

KM# 95 100 TENGE
31.1050 g., 0.9250 Silver 0.9250 oz. ASW, 38.61 mm. **Subject:** Baiturramman Mosque **Rev:** Mosque and reflecting pool

Date	Mintage	F	VF	XF	Unc	BU
2006 (2008) Proof	6,000	Value: 80.00				

KM# 98 100 TENGE
31.1050 g., 0.9250 Silver 0.9250 oz. ASW, 38.61 mm. **Subject:** Zahir Mosque **Rev:** Mosque

Date	Mintage	F	VF	XF	Unc	BU
2006 Proof	6,000	Value: 80.00				

KM# 195 100 TENGE
31.1050 g., 0.9250 Silver 0.9250 oz. ASW, 38.61 mm. **Subject:** Olympics 2008 **Obv:** National emblem in stadium **Rev:** Boxers

Date	Mintage	F	VF	XF	Unc	BU
2006 Proof	4,000	Value: 75.00				

KM# 200 100 TENGE
1.2400 g., 0.9990 Gold 0.0398 oz. AGW, 13.92 mm. **Obv:** National emblem **Rev:** Decoration

Date	Mintage	F	VF	XF	Unc	BU
2006 Proof	18,000	Value: 100				

KM# 166 100 TENGE
31.1000 g., 0.9250 Silver 0.9249 oz. ASW, 37 mm. **Subject:** Olympics - Pentathlon **Obv:** National arms and stylized stadium **Rev:** Five sports

Date	Mintage	F	VF	XF	Unc	BU
2007 Proof	—	Value: 55.00				

KM# 96 100 TENGE
31.1050 g., 0.9250 Silver 0.9250 oz. ASW, 38.61 mm. **Subject:** Faisal Mosque, Islamabad **Rev:** Mosque

Date	Mintage	F	VF	XF	Unc	BU
2006 (2008) Proof	6,000	Value: 80.00				

KM# 97 100 TENGE
31.1050 g., 0.9250 Silver 0.9250 oz. ASW, 38.61 mm. **Subject:** Hodja Akhmed Yassavi Mausoleum Turkestan **Rev:** Mausoleum

Date	Mintage	F	VF	XF	Unc	BU
2006 (2008) Proof	6,000	Value: 80.00				

KM# 110 100 TENGE
31.1050 g., 0.9250 Silver 0.9250 oz. ASW, 38.61 mm. **Subject:** Chingis Khan **Rev:** Khan on horseback facing

Date	Mintage	F	VF	XF	Unc	BU
2008 Proof	13,000	Value: 65.00				

KM# 125 100 TENGE
31.1050 g., 0.9250 Silver 0.9250 oz. ASW, 38.61 mm. **Subject:** Attila the Hun **Rev:** Medallic Profile right

Date	Mintage	F	VF	XF	Unc	BU
2009 Proof	13,000	Value: 75.00				

KM# 126 100 TENGE
31.1050 g., 0.9250 Silver 0.9250 oz. ASW, 38.61 mm. **Subject:** 2010 Olympics **Rev:** Ski jumper over Vancouver skyline

Date	Mintage	F	VF	XF	Unc	BU
2009 Proof	12,000	Value: 55.00				

KM# 134 100 TENGE
31.1000 g., 0.9990 Silver partially gilt 0.9988 oz. ASW **Subject:** Caracal **Obv:** Arms **Rev:** Caracal cat head facing, partially gilt

Date	Mintage	F	VF	XF	Unc	BU
2009 Proof	13,000	Value: 55.00				

KM# 136 100 TENGE
1.2400 g., 0.9990 Gold 0.0398 oz. AGW, 13.92 mm. **Obv:** Value **Rev:** Cat head sculpture

Date	Mintage	F	VF	XF	Unc	BU
2009 Proof	9,500	Value: 85.00				

KM# 147 100 TENGE
31.1000 g., 0.9250 Silver 0.9249 oz. ASW, 38.6 mm. **Obv:** Arms **Rev:** Tiger advancing right

Date	Mintage	F	VF	XF	Unc	BU
2009 Proof	13,000	Value: 65.00				

KM# 151 100 TENGE
31.1000 g., 0.9990 Silver 0.9988 oz. ASW, 38.61 mm. **Subject:** World Cup, South Africa **Obv:** Arms and stadium **Rev:** Soccer Player, gilt ball

Date	Mintage	F	VF	XF	Unc	BU
2009 Proof	—	Value: 50.00				

KM# 153 100 TENGE
1.2400 g., 0.9990 Gold 0.0398 oz. AGW, 13.92 mm. **Subject:** Zhalavlinky Treasure **Obv:** Arms **Rev:** Historic jewelery design

Date	Mintage	F	VF	XF	Unc	BU
2009 Proof	9,500	Value: 85.00				

KM# 220 100 TENGE
1.2400 g., 0.9990 Gold 0.0398 oz. AGW, 13.92 mm. **Rev:** Two lions on rock

Date	Mintage	F	VF	XF	Unc	BU
2009 Proof	—	Value: 125				

KM# 176 100 TENGE
31.1000 g., 0.9250 Silver 0.9249 oz. ASW, 38.61 mm. **Obv:** State Emblem, gilt horsemen at right **Rev:** Queen Tomris

Date	Mintage	F	VF	XF	Unc	BU
2010 Proof	—	Value: 70.00				

KM# 211 100 TENGE
31.1050 g., 0.9250 Silver 0.9250 oz. ASW, 38.61 mm. **Subject:** Olympics, 2014 **Rev:** Speed Skating

Date	Mintage	F	VF	XF	Unc	BU
2011 Proof	—	Value: 75.00				

KM# 66 500 TENGE
24.0000 g., 0.9250 Silver 0.7137 oz. ASW, 37 mm. **Obv:** Man seated under tree playing stringed instrument **Rev:** Stringed instrument, musical notes

Date	Mintage	F	VF	XF	Unc	BU
2001 Proof	—	Value: 50.00				

KM# 37 500 TENGE
23.9000 g., 0.9250 Silver 0.7107 oz. ASW, 37 mm. **Subject:** Wildlife **Obv:** Value **Rev:** Female Saiga with two calves **Edge:** Plain

Date	Mintage	F	VF	XF	Unc	BU
2001 Proof	3,000	Value: 90.00				

KM# 38 500 TENGE
23.8100 g., 0.9250 Silver 0.7081 oz. ASW, 36.9 mm. **Subject:** 10 Years of Independence **Obv:** Monument and flag **Rev:** National emblem within design above value **Edge:** Plain

Date	Mintage	F	VF	XF	Unc	BU
2001 Proof	3,000	Value: 125				

KM# 55 500 TENGE
24.0000 g., 0.9250 Silver 0.7137 oz. ASW, 37 mm. **Obv:** Value **Rev:** Altai Mountain petroglyph **Edge:** Plain

Date	Mintage	F	VF	XF	Unc	BU
2001 Proof	3,000	Value: 175				

KM# 112 500 TENGE
24.0000 g., 0.9250 Silver 0.7137 oz. ASW **Subject:** Applied art, stringed instrument **Obv:** Man seated under tree **Rev:** Stringed instrument and notes

Date	Mintage	F	VF	XF	Unc	BU
2001 Proof	—	Value: 42.00				

KM# 42 500 TENGE
23.9000 g., 0.9250 Silver 0.7107 oz. ASW, 37 mm. **Subject:** Music **Obv:** Musician and value divided by tree **Rev:** Musical instruments **Edge:** Plain

Date	Mintage	F	VF	XF	Unc	BU
2002 Proof	—	Value: 165				

KM# 43 500 TENGE
23.9000 g., 0.9250 Silver 0.7107 oz. ASW, 37 mm. **Subject:** Prehistoric Art **Obv:** Value **Rev:** Prehistoric cave art **Edge:** Plain

Date	Mintage	F	VF	XF	Unc	BU
2002 Proof	3,000	Value: 140				

KM# 44 500 TENGE
23.9000 g., 0.9250 Silver 0.7107 oz. ASW, 37 mm. **Subject:** Bighorn Sheep **Obv:** Value **Rev:** Kazakhstan Argali Ram **Edge:** Plain

Date	Mintage	F	VF	XF	Unc	BU
2002 Proof	3,000	Value: 120				

KM# 113 500 TENGE
24.0000 g., 0.9250 Silver 0.7137 oz. ASW, 37 mm. **Subject:** Petroglyph **Obv:** Value on traditional weave pattern **Rev:** Horse petroglyph

Date	Mintage	F	VF	XF	Unc	BU
2002 Proof	—	Value: 60.00				

KM# 183 500 TENGE
24.0000 g., 0.9250 Silver 0.7137 oz. ASW, 36. mm. **Obv:** Large value within brick arch design **Rev:** Byzantine church and floor plan

Date	Mintage	F	VF	XF	Unc	BU
2002 Proof	3,000	Value: 75.00				

KM# 53 500 TENGE
24.0000 g., 0.9250 Silver 0.7137 oz. ASW, 37 mm. **Obv:** Value **Rev:** Great Bustard bird standing on ground **Edge:** Plain

Date	Mintage	F	VF	XF	Unc	BU
2003 Proof	3,000	Value: 75.00				

KM# 56 500 TENGE
24.0000 g., 0.9250 Silver 0.7137 oz. ASW, 37 mm. **Subject:** Applied Arts **Obv:** Folk Dancer **Rev:** Cultural artifacts **Edge:** Plain

Date	Mintage	F	VF	XF	Unc	BU
2003 Proof	3,000	Value: 80.00				

KM# 184 500 TENGE
24.0000 g., 0.9250 Silver 0.7137 oz. ASW **Rev:** Warriors in a cave

Date	Mintage	F	VF	XF	Unc	BU
2003 Proof	3,000	Value: 75.00				

KM# 185 500 TENGE
24.0000 g., 0.9250 Silver 0.7137 oz. ASW, 36 mm. **Obv:** Intricate tile design **Rev:** View of Kecensci Mausoleum

Date	Mintage	F	VF	XF	Unc	BU
2003 Proof	3,000	Value: 75.00				

KM# 59 500 TENGE
31.1000 g., 0.9250 Bi-Metallic Blackend silver center in proof silver ring 0.9249 oz., 38.6 mm. **Subject:** "Denga" **Obv:** Black square holed coin design above value **Rev:** Black square holed coin design and metal content statement **Edge:** Reeded

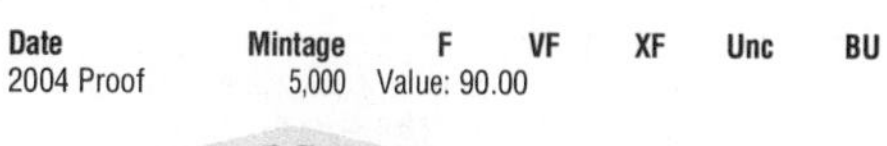

Date	Mintage	F	VF	XF	Unc	BU
2004 Proof	5,000	Value: 90.00				

KM# 117 500 TENGE
31.1000 g., 0.9250 Silver partially gilt 0.9249 oz. ASW, 38.6 mm. **Obv:** Three riders **Rev:** Golden deer ornament **Shape:** 12-sided

Date	Mintage	F	VF	XF	Unc	BU
2004 Proof	—	Value: 100				

KM# 186 500 TENGE
24.0000 g., 0.9250 Silver 0.7137 oz. ASW **Rev:** Saker Falcon

Date	Mintage	F	VF	XF	Unc	BU
2004 Proof	3,000	Value: 75.00				

KM# 187 500 TENGE
24.0000 g., 0.9250 Silver 0.7137 oz. ASW, 37 mm. **Rev:** Cave painting of a Shaman in Tamgaly

Date	Mintage	F	VF	XF	Unc	BU
2004 Proof	3,000	Value: 75.00				

KM# 189 500 TENGE
24.0000 g., 0.9250 Silver 0.7137 oz. ASW, 36 mm. **Obv:** Tree of Life **Rev:** Three stone figures

Date	Mintage	F	VF	XF	Unc	BU
2004 Proof	3,000	Value: 75.00				

KM# 190 500 TENGE
24.0000 g., 0.9250 Silver 0.7137 oz. ASW, 36 mm. **Obv:** Woman in national costume playing the zither **Rev:** Zither and musical notes

Date	Mintage	F	VF	XF	Unc	BU
2004 Proof	3,000	Value: 75.00				

KM# 60 500 TENGE
24.0000 g., 0.9250 Silver 0.7137 oz. ASW, 37 mm. **Obv:** Value **Rev:** Prehistoric art horseman **Edge:** Plain

Date	Mintage	F	VF	XF	Unc	BU
2005 Proof	3,000	Value: 70.00				

KM# 61 500 TENGE
24.0000 g., 0.9250 Silver 0.7137 oz. ASW, 37 mm. **Obv:** Value **Rev:** Two Goitered Gazelles **Edge:** Plain

Date	Mintage	F	VF	XF	Unc	BU
2005 Proof	3,000	Value: 70.00				

KM# 62 500 TENGE
31.1000 g., 0.9250 Silver 0.9249 oz. ASW, 38.6 mm. **Obv:** Horse race and value **Rev:** Gold plated tiger **Edge:** Plain **Shape:** 12-sided

Date	Mintage	F	VF	XF	Unc	BU
2005 Proof	5,000	Value: 120				

KM# 63 500 TENGE
31.1000 g., 0.9250 Bi-Metallic Blackened Silver center in proof Silver ring 0.9249 oz., 38.6 mm. **Subject:** "Drakhma" coin **Obv:** Old coin design **Rev:** Old coin design **Edge:** Reeded

Date	Mintage	F	VF	XF	Unc	BU
2005 Proof	5,000	Value: 65.00				

KM# 72 500 TENGE
31.1000 g., 0.9250 Silver 0.9249 oz. ASW, 38.6 mm. **Obv:** Horse race and value **Rev:** Gold plated rider **Edge:** Plain

Date	Mintage	F	VF	XF	Unc	BU
2005 Proof	5,000	Value: 100				

KM# 124 500 TENGE
24.0000 g., 0.9250 Silver 0.7137 oz. ASW, 37 mm. **Subject:** Zhoshi Khan Mausoleum **Rev:** 3/4 view of building facade

Date	Mintage	F	VF	XF	Unc	BU
2005 Proof	—	Value: 50.00				

KM# 192 500 TENGE
24.0000 g., 0.9250 Silver 0.7137 oz. ASW, 36 mm. **Obv:** Man seated with stringed musical instrument **Rev:** two string musical instruments, musical notes at right

Date	Mintage	F	VF	XF	Unc	BU
2005 Proof	3,000	Value: 75.00				

KM# 193 500 TENGE
7.7800 g., 0.9990 Gold 0.2499 oz. AGW, 25 mm. **Obv:** State shield **Rev:** head of a dhole

Date	Mintage	F	VF	XF	Unc	BU
2005 Proof	—	Value: 750				

KM# 162 500 TENGE
0.9990 Gold **Obv:** Archway **Rev:** Al-Baram Mosque in Mecca

Date	Mintage	F	VF	XF	Unc	BU
2006 Proof	—	Value: 500				

KM# 163 500 TENGE
0.9990 Gold **Obv:** Archway **Rev:** Al-Nabawi Mosque in Medina

Date	Mintage	F	VF	XF	Unc	BU
2006 Proof	—	Value: 500				

KM# 76 500 TENGE
31.1000 g., 0.9250 Silver 0.9249 oz. ASW **Series:** Flora **Rev:** Tulopa Regeli in multicolor

Date	Mintage	F	VF	XF	Unc	BU
2006 Proof	—	Value: 150				

KM# 83 500 TENGE
24.0000 g., 0.9250 Silver 0.7137 oz. ASW, 38.7 mm. **Obv:** Value at center **Rev:** Tetraogallus Altalcus, Altai Snowcock

Date	Mintage	F	VF	XF	Unc	BU
2006 Proof	3,000	Value: 100				

KM# 84 500 TENGE
31.1000 g., 0.9250 Bi-Metallic Blackened Silver center in proof Silver ring. 0.9249 oz., 38.6 mm. **Subject:** "Dirkhem" coin **Obv:** Old coin design **Rev:** Old coin design **Edge:** Reeded

Date	Mintage	F	VF	XF	Unc	BU
2006 Proof	5,000	Value: 65.00				

KM# 194 500 TENGE
24.0000 g., 0.9250 Silver 0.7137 oz. ASW **Rev:** Triumph cars

Date	Mintage	F	VF	XF	Unc	BU
2006 Proof	3,000	Value: 75.00				

KM# 196 500 TENGE
31.1050 g., 0.9250 Silver 0.9250 oz. ASW, 38.61 mm. **Obv:** National emblem **Rev:** Figure seated at loom

Date	Mintage	F	VF	XF	Unc	BU
2006 Proof	4,000	Value: 75.00				

KM# 197 500 TENGE
31.1050 g., 0.9250 Silver 0.9250 oz. ASW, 38.61 mm. **Obv:** State emblem **Rev:** Central Mosque in Almati

Date	Mintage	F	VF	XF	Unc	BU
2006 Proof	4,000	Value: 75.00				

KM# 198 500 TENGE
31.1050 g., 0.9250 Silver 0.9250 oz. ASW, 38.61 mm. **Rev:** female with apples, a drawing by Sidorkin

Date	Mintage	F	VF	XF	Unc	BU
2006 Proof	4,000	Value: 75.00				

KM# 199 500 TENGE
41.0000 g., Bi-Metallic Silver and Tantalium, 38.61 mm. **Obv:** Figure standing within solar system **Rev:** Spaceman and orbits of planets

Date	Mintage	F	VF	XF	Unc	BU
2006 Proof	4,000	Value: 135				

KM# 168 500 TENGE
7.7700 g., 0.9990 Gold 0.2496 oz. AGW, 25 mm. **Obv:** Arms **Rev:** Lynx, crystal eyes **Rev. Legend:** FELIS LYNX

Date	Mintage	F	VF	XF	Unc	BU
2007 Proof	—	Value: 475				

KM# 82 500 TENGE
41.4000 g., Bi-Metallic Tantalum center in .925 Silver ring., 38.61 mm. **Subject:** 50th Anniversary Launch of Sputnik I **Obv:** Stylized view of our solar system, multicolor **Obv. Legend:** REPUBLIC OF KAZAKHSTAN **Rev:** Sputnik I in space, earth in background, multicolor **Rev. Legend:** THE FIRST SPACE SATELLITE OF THE EARTH **Edge:** Reeded

Date	Mintage	F	VF	XF	Unc	BU
ND(2007) Proof	4,000	Value: 100				

KM# 85 500 TENGE
31.1000 g., 0.9250 Bi-Metallic Blackened Silver center in proof Silver ring. 0.9249 oz., 38.6 mm. **Subject:** "Otyrar" coin **Obv:** Old coin design **Rev:** Old coin design **Edge:** Reeded

Date	Mintage	F	VF	XF	Unc	BU
2007 Proof	4,000	Value: 75.00				

KM# 87 500 TENGE
24.0000 g., 0.9250 Silver 0.7137 oz. ASW, 38.6 mm. **Obv:** Value **Rev:** Terekin Valley - noble deer petraglyph

Date	Mintage	F	VF	XF	Unc	BU
2007 Proof	3,000	Value: 90.00				

KM# 88 500 TENGE
31.1000 g., 0.9250 Silver 0.9249 oz. ASW **Subject:** Movement series - myth **Obv:** Value within square **Rev:** Design

Date	Mintage	F	VF	XF	Unc	BU
2007 Proof	4,000	Value: 80.00				

KM# 89 500 TENGE
31.1000 g., 0.9250 Silver 0.9249 oz. ASW, 38.6 mm. **Subject:** Gold of the Romans **Obv:** Four horseman **Rev:** Gilt Roman seal ring **Shape:** 12-sided

Date	Mintage	F	VF	XF	Unc	BU
2007 Proof	5,000	Value: 100				

KM# 90 500 TENGE
31.1000 g., 0.9250 Silver 0.9249 oz. ASW, 38.6 mm. **Obv:** State emblem **Rev:** Church

Date	Mintage	F	VF	XF	Unc	BU
2007 Proof	4,000	Value: 75.00				

KM# 91 500 TENGE
31.1000 g., 0.9250 Silver 0.9249 oz. ASW, 38.6 mm. **Obv:** State emblem **Rev:** Traditional family

Date	Mintage	F	VF	XF	Unc	BU
2007 Proof	4,000	Value: 70.00				

KM# 92 500 TENGE
31.1000 g., 0.9250 Silver 0.9249 oz. ASW, 38.6 mm. **Obv:** Leaves **Rev:** Tree growth rings, multicolor seeds

Date	Mintage	F	VF	XF	Unc	BU
2007 Proof	4,000	Value: 75.00				

KM# 93 500 TENGE
24.0000 g., 0.9250 Silver 0.7137 oz. ASW, 38.6 mm. **Subject:** Spoon billed duck **Obv:** Value **Rev:** Duck in reeds

Date	Mintage	F	VF	XF	Unc	BU
2007 Proof	3,000	Value: 85.00				

KM# 167 500 TENGE
7.7800 g., 0.9990 Gold 0.2499 oz. AGW, 25 mm. **Subject:** Olympics, high jump **Obv:** Arms and stylized stadium **Rev:** Female high jump

Date	Mintage	F	VF	XF	Unc	BU
2007 Proof	—	Value: 460				

KM# 94 500 TENGE
31.1050 g., 0.9250 Silver 0.9250 oz. ASW, 38.6 mm. **Subject:** National currency, 15th Anniversary **Obv:** Three coin designs

Date	Mintage	F	VF	XF	Unc	BU
2008 Proof	5,000	Value: 75.00				

KM# 99 500 TENGE
31.1050 g., 0.9250 Silver 0.9250 oz. ASW, 38.61 mm. **Subject:** Eurasic Capitals - Astana **Rev:** Skyline montage

Date	Mintage	F	VF	XF	Unc	BU
2008 Proof	5,000	Value: 75.00				

KM# 100 500 TENGE
24.0000 g., 0.9250 Silver 0.7137 oz. ASW, 38.61 mm. **Subject:** Tien Shan - Brown Bear **Rev:** Bear seated

Date	Mintage	F	VF	XF	Unc	BU
2008 Proof	3,000	Value: 85.00				

KM# 101 500 TENGE
31.1050 g., 0.9250 Silver 0.9250 oz. ASW, 38.61 mm. **Subject:** Nomad Gold **Rev:** Diadem fragment **Shape:** 12-sided

Date	Mintage	F	VF	XF	Unc	BU
2008 Proof	5,000	Value: 115				

KM# 102 500 TENGE
31.1050 g., 0.9250 Silver 0.9250 oz. ASW, 38.61 mm. **Subject:** Kalmykov **Rev:** Fantasy scene

Date	Mintage	F	VF	XF	Unc	BU
2008 Proof	4,000	Value: 80.00				

KM# 103 500 TENGE
31.1050 g., 0.9250 Silver 0.9250 oz. ASW, 38.61 mm. **Subject:** Kyz Kuu **Rev:** Two horseback riders

Date	Mintage	F	VF	XF	Unc	BU
2008 Proof	4,000	Value: 80.00				

KM# 104 500 TENGE
31.1050 g., 0.9250 Silver 0.9250 oz. ASW, 38.61 mm. **Subject:** Linum Olgae **Rev:** Flowers

Date	Mintage	F	VF	XF	Unc	BU
2008 Proof	4,000	Value: 100				

KM# 106 500 TENGE
24.0000 g., 0.9250 Silver 0.7137 oz. ASW, 38.6x28.8 mm. **Subject:** Papilio Alexanor **Rev:** Two butterflies **Shape:** oval

Date	Mintage	F	VF	XF	Unc	BU
2008 Proof	4,000	Value: 115				

KM# 107 500 TENGE
31.1050 g., 0.9250 Silver 0.9250 oz. ASW, 38.61 mm. **Subject:** Saraichik Coin **Rev:** Coin of the 14th Century

Date	Mintage	F	VF	XF	Unc	BU
2008 Proof	5,000	Value: 75.00				

KM# 108 500 TENGE
41.4000 g., Bi-Metallic Tantalum center in .925 Silver ring., 38.61 mm. **Subject:** Vostok **Rev:** Space ship

Date	Mintage	F	VF	XF	Unc	BU
2008 Proof	4,000	Value: 110				

KM# 109 500 TENGE
31.1050 g., 0.9250 Silver 0.9250 oz. ASW, 38.61 mm. **Subject:** Zharkent Mosque **Rev:** Mosque

Date	Mintage	F	VF	XF	Unc	BU
2008 Proof	400	Value: 75.00				

KM# 118 500 TENGE
24.0000 g., 0.9250 Silver 0.7137 oz. ASW, 37 mm. **Subject:** Kazakhstan Railroads, 100th Anniversary **Obv:** Arms **Rev:** Modern train and Steam locomotive, country route map in background

Date	Mintage	F	VF	XF	Unc	BU
2008 Proof	—	Value: 55.00				

KM# 131 500 TENGE
31.1050 g., 0.9250 Silver 0.9250 oz. ASW, 38.61 mm. **Subject:** Almaty Aport **Rev:** Apple tree branch and flower

Date	Mintage	F	VF	XF	Unc	BU
2009 Proof	4,000	Value: 80.00				

KM# 149 500 TENGE
31.1050 g., 0.9250 Silver 0.9250 oz. ASW, 38.61 mm. **Subject:** Balkhash Tiger **Rev:** Tiger on the hunt

Date	Mintage	F	VF	XF	Unc	BU
2009 Proof	5,000	Value: 75.00				

KM# 133 500 TENGE
31.1050 g., 0.9990 Silver 0.9990 oz. ASW, 38.61 mm. **Subject:** Betashar **Rev:** Two figures standing

Date	Mintage	F	VF	XF	Unc	BU
2009 Proof	4,000	Value: 75.00				

KM# 139 500 TENGE
31.1050 g., 0.9250 Silver 0.9250 oz. ASW, 38.6 mm. **Subject:** Nur-Astana Mosque **Rev:** Mosque

Date	Mintage	F	VF	XF	Unc	BU
2009 Proof	4,000	Value: 75.00				

KM# 142 500 TENGE
24.0000 g., 0.9250 Silver 0.7137 oz. ASW, 38.61 mm. **Rev:** Porcupine left with quills raised

Date	Mintage	F	VF	XF	Unc	BU
2009 Proof	3,000	Value: 90.00				

KM# 143 500 TENGE
31.1050 g., 0.9990 Silver 0.9990 oz. ASW, 38.61 mm. **Rev:** Satir head facing **Shape:** 12-sided

Date	Mintage	F	VF	XF	Unc	BU
2009 Proof	5,000	Value: 100				

KM# 130 500 TENGE
41.4000 g., Bi-Metallic Tantalum center in .925 Silver ring., 38.61 mm. **Subject:** Apollo - Soyoz Missions **Rev:** Spacecraft docked in orbit above the earth

Date	Mintage	F	VF	XF	Unc	BU
2009 Proof	4,000	Value: 115				

KM# 137 500 TENGE
31.1050 g., 0.9250 Silver 0.9250 oz. ASW, 38.61 mm. **Subject:** Coin of Almaty **Rev:** 13th Century coin

Date	Mintage	F	VF	XF	Unc	BU
2009 Proof	4,000	Value: 100				

KM# 127 500 TENGE
7.7800 g., 0.9990 Gold 0.2499 oz. AGW, 25 mm. **Subject:** Olympics - Biathlon **Obv:** Arms and stylized stadium **Rev:** Biathlon, 2 cross country skiers and shooter

Date	Mintage	F	VF	XF	Unc	BU
2009 Proof	5,000	Value: 445				

KM# 128 500 TENGE
31.1000 g., 0.9990 Silver 0.9988 oz. ASW, 38.6 mm. **Subject:** Almaty Aport **Obv:** Value and leaves **Rev:** Apples and flower

Date	Mintage	F	VF	XF	Unc	BU
2009 Proof	4,000	Value: 65.00				

KM# 129 500 TENGE
31.1000 g., 0.9250 Silver 0.9249 oz. ASW, 36.6 mm. **Subject:** Alpamys Batyr **Obv:** Arms **Rev:** Historical figure

Date	Mintage	F	VF	XF	Unc	BU
2009 Proof	5,000	Value: 55.00				

KM# 138 500 TENGE
24.0000 g., 0.9250 Silver 0.7137 oz. ASW, 28.61x28.81 mm. **Subject:** Flamingo **Obv:** Partial butterfly **Rev:** Pair of flamings standing in holographic water **Shape:** Vertical oval

Date	Mintage	F	VF	XF	Unc	BU
2009 Proof	4,000	Value: 80.00				

KM# 148 500 TENGE
7.7800 g., 0.9990 Gold 0.2499 oz. AGW, 21.87 mm. **Rev:** Tiger walking right

Date	Mintage	F	VF	XF	Unc	BU
2009 Proof	3,000	Value: 450				

KM# 150 500 TENGE
7.7800 g., 0.9990 Gold 0.2499 oz. AGW, 25 mm. **Subject:** Uncia **Obv:** Arms **Rev:** Snow Leopard head left

Date	Mintage	F	VF	XF	Unc	BU
2009 Proof	5,000	Value: 445				

KM# 179 500 TENGE
31.1000 g., 0.9250 Silver 0.9249 oz. ASW, 38.6 mm. **Obv:** Three horsemen **Rev:** Buckle, gilt pair of seated raindeer **Shape:** 12-sided

Date	Mintage	F	VF	XF	Unc	BU
2010 Proof	5,000	Value: 85.00				

KM# 177 500 TENGE
31.1000 g., 0.9250 Silver 0.9249 oz. ASW **Obv:** Outline of three pelicans **Rev:** Pelecanus Crispus, pelican standing

Date	Mintage	F	VF	XF	Unc	BU
2010 Proof	5,000	Value: 75.00				

KM# 178 500 TENGE
31.1000 g., 0.9250 Silver 0.9249 oz. ASW, 38.6 mm. **Subject:** Otau Koteru **Obv:** National Emblem **Rev:** Horseman and large ceremonial umbrella

Date	Mintage	F	VF	XF	Unc	BU
2010 Proof	5,000	Value: 90.00				

KM# 180 500 TENGE
31.1000 g., 0.9250 Silver 0.9249 oz. ASW **Subject:** Flora **Rev:** Papaver Pavoninum in color

Date	Mintage	F	VF	XF	Unc	BU
2010 Proof	4,000	Value: 90.00				

KM# 181 500 TENGE
3.1100 g., 0.9990 Gold 0.0999 oz. AGW, 16 mm. **Obv:** Archway **Rev:** Dome of the Rock, Jerusalem

Date	Mintage	F	VF	XF	Unc	BU
2010 Proof	—	Value: 200				

KM# 182 500 TENGE
31.1000 g., 0.9250 Silver 0.9249 oz. ASW **Rev:** Musical instrument

Date	Mintage	F	VF	XF	Unc	BU
2010 Proof	—	Value: 75.00				

KM# 205 500 TENGE
24.0000 g., 0.9250 Silver 0.7137 oz. ASW, 38.61 mm. **Obv:** Stylized owl at right **Rev:** Owl on branch

Date	Mintage	F	VF	XF	Unc	BU
2011 Proof	—	Value: 85.00				

KM# 212 500 TENGE
31.1050 g., 0.9250 Silver partially gilt 0.9250 oz. ASW, 38.61 mm. **Subject:** Independence, 20th Anniversary **Obv:** Map **Rev:** Architecture

Date	Mintage	F	VF	XF	Unc	BU
2011 Proof	—	Value: 75.00				

KM# 213 500 TENGE
31.1050 g., 0.9250 Silver 0.9250 oz. ASW, 38.61 mm. **Subject:** Issyk Chieftain **Rev:** Standing figure, gilt **Shape:** 8-sided

Date	Mintage	F	VF	XF	Unc	BU
2011 Proof	—	Value: 100				

KM# 214 500 TENGE
24.0000 g., 0.9250 Silver partially gilt 0.7137 oz. ASW, 38.61x28.8 mm. **Subject:** Sturgen **Shape:** Oval

Date	Mintage	F	VF	XF	Unc	BU
2011 Proof	5,000	Value: 75.00				

KM# 215 500 TENGE
31.1000 g., 0.9250 Silver 0.9249 oz. ASW, 38.61 mm. **Subject:** Aldar Rose **Obv:** Arms **Rev:** Figure riding donkey

Date	Mintage	F	VF	XF	Unc	BU
2011 Proof	—	Value: 75.00				

KM# 217 500 TENGE
31.1050 g., 0.9250 Silver partially gilt 0.9250 oz. ASW, 38.61 mm. **Subject:** Gold of the Nomads - Elk's head **Rev:** Artistic elk's head gilt **Shape:** 12-sided

Date	Mintage	F	VF	XF	Unc	BU
2011 Proof	—	Value: 100				

KM# 218 500 TENGE
40.7000 g., Bi-Metallic .925 Silver center in Tantalum ring, 38.61 mm. **Obv:** Stylized view of solar system, man standing at center **Rev:** First astronaut at right, spacecraft at left

Date	Mintage	F	VF	XF	Unc	BU
2011 Proof	—	Value: 100				

KM# 219 500 TENGE
31.1050 g., 0.9250 Silver 0.9250 oz. ASW, 38.61 mm. **Subject:** Year of the Rabbit **Obv:** Zodiac constelations of the Milky Way **Rev:** Rabbit in center of 12-year sysle of animals **Shape:** 12-sided

Date	Mintage	F	VF	XF	Unc	BU
2011 Proof	—	Value: 100				

KM# 221 500 TENGE
7.7700 g., 0.9990 Gold 0.2496 oz. AGW, 25 mm. **Rev:** Eagle owl head, crystal eye

Date	Mintage	F	VF	XF	Unc	BU
2011 Proof	—	Value: 475				

KM# 222 500 TENGE
31.1000 g., 0.9990 Silver 0.9988 oz. ASW, 38.6 mm. **Subject:** Kolobuk **Rev:** Fairy tale characters

Date	Mintage	F	VF	XF	Unc	BU
2012 Proof	—	Value: 75.00				

KM# 223 500 TENGE
0.9250 g., 31.1050 Silver 0.9250 oz. ASW, 38.61 mm. **Obv:** Soviet and Kazakhstan arms **Rev:** Portrait of D. Kunaev facing **Shape:** 8-sided

Date	Mintage	F	VF	XF	Unc	BU
2012 Proof	—	Value: 75.00				

KM# 68 1000 TENGE
7.7800 g., 0.9990 Gold 0.2499 oz. AGW, 20 mm. **Obv:** Two winged ibexes **Rev:** Ancient warrior **Edge:** Reeded

Date	Mintage	F	VF	XF	Unc	BU
2001 Proof	—	Value: 445				

KM# 114 1000 TENGE
67.2500 g., 0.9250 Silver 1.9999 oz. ASW, 50 mm. **Subject:** National Currency, 10th Anniversary **Obv:** Flag, multicolor **Rev:** Coin and bank note designs

Date	Mintage	F	VF	XF	Unc	BU
2003 Proof	—	Value: 150				

KM# 115 1000 TENGE
67.2500 g., 0.9250 Silver 1.9999 oz. ASW, 50 mm. **Subject:** National Currency, 10th Anniversary **Obv:** Arms, gilt and blue enamel **Rev:** Coin montage

Date	Mintage	F	VF	XF	Unc	BU
2003 Proof	—	Value: 170				

KM# 67 5000 TENGE
1000.0000 g., 0.9250 Silver 29.738 oz. ASW, 100 mm. **Subject:** 10th Anniversary of Independence **Obv:** National arms above value **Rev:** Monument statue

Date	Mintage	F	VF	XF	Unc	BU
2001 Proof	—	Value: 1,150				

KM# 173 5000 TENGE
1000.0000 g., 0.9250 Silver 29.738 oz. ASW, 100 mm. **Subject:** Astana capitol, 10th anniversary **Obv:** National arms **Rev:** Architectural elements

Date	Mintage	F	VF	XF	Unc	BU
2008 Proof	—	Value: 1,250				

KM# 105 50000 TENGE
1000.0000 g., 0.9999 Gold 32.146 oz. AGW, 100 mm. **Subject:** National Currency, 15th Anniversary **Rev:** Coin and bank note montage

Date	Mintage	F	VF	XF	Unc	BU
2008 Proof	100	Value: 60,000				

KM# 216 50000 TENGE
1000.0000 g., 0.9990 Gold 32.117 oz. AGW, 100 mm. **Subject:** Independence, 20th Anniversary **Obv:** Map and national arms **Rev:** Architecture montage

Date	Mintage	F	VF	XF	Unc	BU
2011 Proof	—	Value: 60,000				

BULLION COINAGE

KM# 161 TENGE
31.1050 g., 0.9990 Silver 0.9990 oz. ASW, 38.61 mm. **Obv:** Arms **Rev:** Snow Leopard standing right on rock

Date	Mintage	F	VF	XF	Unc	BU
2009	—	—	—	—	—	65.00

KM# 160 2 TENGE
64.2100 g., 0.9990 Silver 2.0622 oz. ASW, 50 mm. **Obv:** Arms **Rev:** Snow Leopard standing right on rock

Date	Mintage	F	VF	XF	Unc	BU
2009	—	—	—	—	—	125

KM# 159 5 TENGE
155.0000 g., 0.9990 Silver 4.9782 oz. ASW, 65 mm. **Obv:** Arms **Rev:** Snow Leopard standing right on rock

Date	Mintage	F	VF	XF	Unc	BU
2009	—	—	—	—	—	250

KM# 157 10 TENGE
3.1100 g., 0.9990 Gold 0.0999 oz. AGW **Obv:** Arms **Rev:** Snow Leopard standing right on rock

Date	Mintage	F	VF	XF	Unc	BU
2009	—	—	—	—	—	225

KM# 158 10 TENGE
311.0500 g., 0.9990 Silver 9.9901 oz. ASW **Obv:** Arms **Rev:** Snow Leopard standing right on rock

Date	Mintage	F	VF	XF	Unc	BU
2009	—	—	—	—	—	550

KM# 156 20 TENGE
7.7800 g., 0.9990 Gold 0.2499 oz. AGW **Obv:** Arms **Rev:** Snow Leopard standing right on rock

Date	Mintage	F	VF	XF	Unc	BU
2009	—	—	—	—	—	450

KM# 155 50 TENGE
15.5500 g., 0.9990 Gold 0.4994 oz. A6.6GW, 25 mm. **Obv:** Arms **Rev:** Snow Leopard standing right on rock

Date	Mintage	F	VF	XF	Unc	BU
2009	—	—	—	—	—	900

KM# 154 100 TENGE
31.1050 g., 0.9990 Gold 0.9990 oz. AGW, 32 mm. **Obv:** Arms **Rev:** Snow Leopard standing right on rock

Date	Mintage	F	VF	XF	Unc	BU
2009	—	—	—	—	—	1,750

KENYA

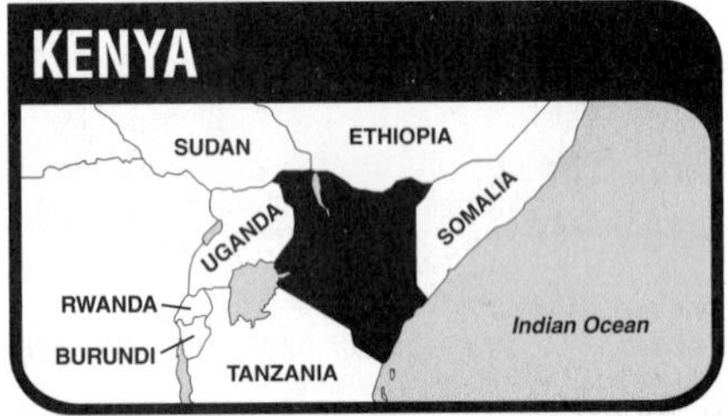

The Republic of Kenya, located on the east coast of Central Africa, has an area of 224,961 sq. mi (582,650 sq. km.) and a population of 20.1 million. Capital: Nairobi. The predominantly agricultural country exports coffee, tea and petroleum products.

Independence was attained on Dec. 12, 1963. Kenya became a republic in 1964. It is a member of the Commonwealth of Nations. The president is Chief of State and Head of Government.

MONETARY SYSTEM
100 Cents = 1 Shilling

REPUBLIC

STANDARD COINAGE

KM# 39 5 CENTS
Copper Clad Steel **Subject:** First President **Obv:** National arms **Rev:** Bust of Mzee Jomo Kenyatta left **Note:** Initially a planned issue, abandoned prior to release for circulation.

Date	Mintage	F	VF	XF	Unc	BU
2005	—	—	—	—	—	—

KM# 40 10 CENTS
Copper Clad Steel **Subject:** First President **Obv:** National arms **Rev:** Bust of Mzee Jomo Kenyatta left **Note:** Initially a planned issue, abandoned prior to release for circulation.

Date	Mintage	F	VF	XF	Unc	BU
2005	—	—	—	—	—	—

KM# 41 50 CENTS
4.5000 g., Nickel Plated Steel, 21.9 mm. **Subject:** First President **Obv:** National arms, value **Rev:** Bust of Mwee Jomo Kenyatta left

Date	Mintage	F	VF	XF	Unc	BU
2005	—	—	—	—	0.60	0.80
2009	—	—	—	—	0.60	0.80

KM# 34 SHILLING
5.4600 g., Nickel Plated Steel, 23.9 mm. **Subject:** First President **Obv:** Value above national arms **Rev:** Bust of President Mzee Jomo Kenyatta left **Edge:** Segmented reeding

Date	Mintage	F	VF	XF	Unc	BU
2005	—	—	—	—	0.80	1.20
2009	—	—	—	—	0.80	1.20
2010	—	—	—	—	0.80	1.20

KM# 37.1 5 SHILLINGS
3.7500 g., Bi-Metallic Aluminum-Bronze center in Copper-Nickel ring, 19.5 mm. **Subject:** First President **Obv:** Value above national arms **Obv. Legend:** REPUBLIC OF KENYA **Rev:** Bust of President Mzee Jomo Kenyatta left **Edge:** Reeded

Date	Mintage	F	VF	XF	Unc	BU
2005	—	—	—	0.60	1.50	2.00
2009	—	—	—	0.60	1.50	2.00

KM# 37.2 5 SHILLINGS
3.7500 g., Bi-Metallic Aluminum-Bronze center in Copper-Nickel ring, 19.5 mm. **Obv:** Value above national arms **Rev:** Bust of President Mzee Jomo Kenyatta **Edge:** Reeded **Note:** Larger numeral and smaller shield.

Date	Mintage	F	VF	XF	Unc	BU
2010	—	—	—	0.60	1.00	2.00

KM# 35.1 10 SHILLINGS
5.0000 g., Bi-Metallic Copper-Nickel center in Aluminum-Bronze ring, 23 mm. **Subject:** First President **Obv:** Value above national arms **Obv. Legend:** REPUBLIC OF KENYA **Rev:** Bust of President Mzee Jomo Kenyatta left **Edge:** Reeded

Date	Mintage	F	VF	XF	Unc	BU
2005	—	—	—	0.90	2.25	3.00
2009	—	—	—	0.90	2.25	3.00

KM# 35.2 10 SHILLINGS
5.0000 g., Bi-Metallic Copper-Nickel center in Aluminum-Bronze ring, 23 mm. **Obv:** Value above national arms **Rev:** Bust of President Mzee Jomo Kenyatta left **Edge:** Reeded **Note:** Larger value and smaller shield.

Date	Mintage	F	VF	XF	Unc	BU
2010	—	—	—	0.90	2.25	3.00

KM# 36 20 SHILLINGS
9.0000 g., Bi-Metallic Aluminum-Bronze center in Copper-Nickel ring, 26 mm. **Subject:** First President **Obv:** Large value above national arms **Obv. Legend:** REPUBLIC OF KENYA **Rev:** Bust of President Mzee Jomo Kenyatta left **Edge:** Segmented reeding

Date	Mintage	F	VF	XF	Unc	BU
2005	—	—	—	1.20	3.00	4.00
2009	—	—	—	1.20	3.00	4.00

KM# 33 40 SHILLINGS
11.0000 g., Bi-Metallic Copper-Nickel center in Nickel-Brass ring, 27.5 mm. **Obv:** Bust of H. E. Mwai Kibaki facing **Rev:** National arms, value below **Edge:** Reeded and lettered **Edge Lettering:** 40 YEARS OF INDEPENDENCE **Note:** Issued December 11, 2003.

Date	Mintage	F	VF	XF	Unc	BU
ND(2003)	—	—	—	—	6.00	7.50

KM# 38 1000 SHILLINGS
28.2800 g., 0.9250 Silver 0.8410 oz. ASW, 38.61 mm. **Subject:** 40th Anniversary Independence **Obv:** National arms **Rev:** Bust of President H. E. Mwai Kibaki facing

Date	Mintage	F	VF	XF	Unc	BU
1963-2003 Proof	—	Value: 65.00				

KM# 43 5000 SHILLINGS
39.9400 g., 0.9167 Gold 1.1771 oz. AGW, 27.5 mm. **Obv:** National arms **Rev:** H.E. Mwai Kibaki, 3rd president **Edge:** Reeded

Date	Mintage	F	VF	XF	Unc	BU
1963-2003 Proof	—	Value: 2,200				

KIRIBATI

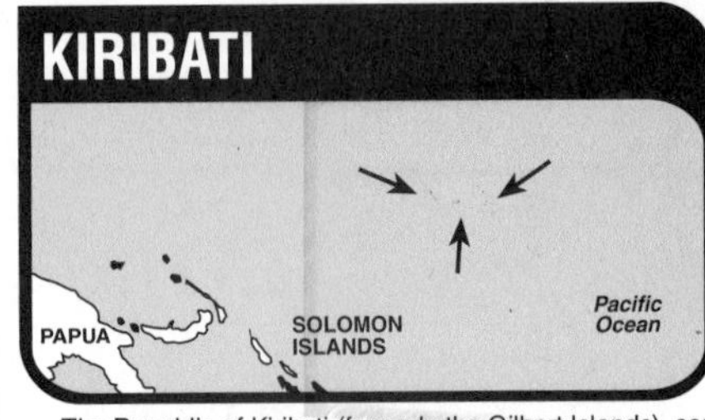

The Republic of Kiribati (formerly the Gilbert Islands), consists of 30 coral atolls and islands spread over more than one million sq. mi. (2,590,000 sq. km.) of the southwest Pacific Ocean, has an area of 332 sq. mi. (717 sq. km.) and a population of 64,200. Capital: Bairiki, on Tarawa. In addition to the Gilbert Islands proper, Kiribati includes Ocean Island, the Central and Southern Line Islands, and the Phoenix Islands, though possession of Canton and Enderbury of the Phoenix Islands is disputed with the United States. Most families engage in subsistence fishing. Copra and phosphates are exported, mostly to Australia and New Zealand.

Kiribati is a member of the Commonwealth of Nations. The President is the Head of State and Head of Government.

MONETARY SYSTEM
100 Cents = 1 Dollar

REPUBLIC

DECIMAL COINAGE

KM# 40 5 CENTS
4.2400 g., Brass, 22.9 mm. **Obv:** National arms **Rev:** Gorilla **Edge:** Reeded

Date	Mintage	F	VF	XF	Unc	BU
2003	—	—	—	—	1.00	1.50

KM# 60 DOLLAR

26.0000 g., Silver Plated Copper, 38.61 mm. **Subject:** London Olympics, 2012 **Obv:** Shield **Rev:** Weightlifter and sunrise

Date	Mintage	F	VF	XF	Unc	BU
2011 Proof	Est. 10,000	Value: 20.00				

KM# 62 DOLLAR

0.5000 g., 0.9990 Gold 0.0161 oz. AGW, 11 mm. **Obv:** Shield **Rev:** Mary, Child Jesus and Joseph, in manger with cattle

Date	Mintage	F	VF	XF	Unc	BU
2011 Proof	Est. 5,000	Value: 55.00				

KM# 54 10 DOLLARS

1.2500 g., 0.9990 Gold 0.0401 oz. AGW, 13.92 mm. **Obv:** Shield **Rev:** Angel with horn

Date	Mintage	F	VF	XF	Unc	BU
2005 Proof	Est. 15,000	Value: 85.00				

KM# 55 10 DOLLARS

1.2400 g., 0.9990 Gold 0.0398 oz. AGW, 13.92 mm. **Obv:** Shield **Rev:** Angel

Date	Mintage	F	VF	XF	Unc	BU
2006 Proof	Est. 15,000	Value: 85.00				

KM# 58 10 DOLLARS

31.1050 g., 0.9990 Silver 0.9990 oz. ASW, 38.61 mm. **Obv:** Shield **Rev:** The Magi

Date	Mintage	F	VF	XF	Unc	BU
2011 Proof	10,000	Value: 50.00				

KM# 59 10 DOLLARS

28.2800 g., 0.9250 Silver 0.8410 oz. ASW, 38.61 mm. **Subject:** London Olympics, 2012 **Obv:** Shield **Rev:** Weightlifting and sunrise

Date	Mintage	F	VF	XF	Unc	BU
2011 Proof	Est. 10,000	Value: 40.00				

KM# 61 10 DOLLARS

28.2800 g., 0.9250 Silver 0.8410 oz. ASW, 38.61 mm. **Subject:** Ships and explorers **Obv:** Shield **Rev:** Mayflower, 1620

Date	Mintage	F	VF	XF	Unc	BU
2011 Proof	Est. 5,000	Value: 45.00				

KM# 63 10 DOLLARS

28.2800 g., 0.9250 Silver 0.8410 oz. ASW, 38.61 mm. **Subject:** Elizabeth II 60th Anniversary of reign, 90th Birthday of Prince Philip **Obv:** Shield **Rev:** Prince Philip at right, Philip and Elizabeth at right

Date	Mintage	F	VF	XF	Unc	BU
2011 Proof	10,000	Value: 40.00				

KM# 65 10 DOLLARS

1.2400 g., 0.9990 Gold 0.0398 oz. AGW, 13.92 mm. **Obv:** Shield **Rev:** Joseph, Jesus and Mary, in manger, with cattle

Date	Mintage	F	VF	XF	Unc	BU
2011 Proof	Est. 7,500	Value: 85.00				

KM# 53 50 DOLLARS

3.1100 g., 0.9990 Gold 0.0999 oz. AGW, 18.5 mm. **Obv:** Shield **Rev:** Jesus and Mary riding donkey, Joseph walking beside

Date	Mintage	F	VF	XF	Unc	BU
2005 Proof	1,500	Value: 185				

KM# 56 50 DOLLARS

3.1100 g., 0.9990 Gold 0.0999 oz. AGW, 18.5 mm. **Obv:** Shield **Rev:** Holy family in manger

Date	Mintage	F	VF	XF	Unc	BU
2006 Proof	1,500	Value: 185				

KM# 64 50 DOLLARS

7.7700 g., 0.9990 Gold 0.2496 oz. AGW, 25 mm. **Obv:** Shield **Rev:** Angel, facing hands in prayer

Date	Mintage	F	VF	XF	Unc	BU
2011 Proof	Est. 1,500	Value: 475				

KM# 52 200 DOLLARS

31.1050 g., 0.9990 Gold 0.9990 oz. AGW, 40 mm. **Obv:** Shield **Rev:** The Holy Family - Joseph, Mary and Jesus

Date	Mintage	F	VF	XF	Unc	BU
2005 Proof	500	Value: 1,800				

KM# 57 200 DOLLARS

31.1050 g., 0.9990 Gold 0.9990 oz. AGW, 40 mm. **Obv:** Shield **Rev:** Holy Family and shepards in manger

Date	Mintage	F	VF	XF	Unc	BU
2006 Proof	500	Value: 1,800				

The Democratic Peoples Republic of Korea, situated in northeastern Asia on the northern half of the Korean peninsula between the Peoples Republic of China and the Republic of Korea, has an area of 46,540 sq. mi. (120,540 sq. km.) and a population of 20 million. Capital: Pyongyang. The economy is based on heavy industry and agriculture. Metals, minerals and farm produce are exported.

MONETARY SYSTEM

100 Chon = 1 Won

MINT

Pyongyang

DATING

In the year 2001 the North Korean adopted the "Juche" dating system which is based on the birth year of Kim Il Sung, founder of North Korea. He was born in 1911. "Quel" refers to month and "Quil" refers to day. 9 Quel 3 Quil refers to September 3rd. The western dates on these coins follow the "Juche" date in parenthesis.

PEOPLES REPUBLIC

DECIMAL COINAGE

KM# 183 1/2 CHON

2.1600 g., Aluminum, 27.02 mm. **Obv:** State arms **Rev:** Horse **Edge:** Plain

Date	Mintage	F	VF	XF	Unc	BU
2002	—	—	—	—	1.25	1.50

KM# 184 1/2 CHON

2.1600 g., Aluminum, 27.02 mm. **Obv:** State arms **Rev:** Orangutan **Edge:** Plain

Date	Mintage	F	VF	XF	Unc	BU
2002	—	—	—	—	1.25	1.50

KM# 185 1/2 CHON

2.1600 g., Aluminum, 27.02 mm. **Obv:** State arms **Rev:** Leopard **Edge:** Plain

Date	Mintage	F	VF	XF	Unc	BU
2002	—	—	—	—	1.25	1.50

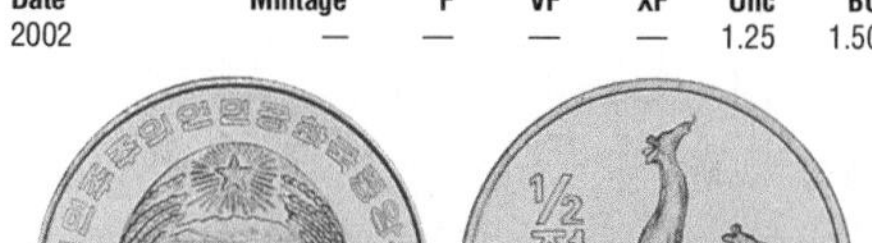

KM# 186 1/2 CHON

2.1600 g., Aluminum, 27.02 mm. **Obv:** State arms **Rev:** Two giraffes **Edge:** Plain

Date	Mintage	F	VF	XF	Unc	BU
2002	—	—	—	—	1.25	1.50

KM# 187 1/2 CHON

2.1600 g., Aluminum, 27.02 mm. **Obv:** State arms **Rev:** Helmeted guineafowl **Edge:** Plain

Date	Mintage	F	VF	XF	Unc	BU
2002	—	—	—	—	1.25	1.50

KM# 188 1/2 CHON

2.1600 g., Aluminum, 27.02 mm. **Obv:** State arms **Rev:** Mamushi pit viper **Edge:** Plain

Date	Mintage	F	VF	XF	Unc	BU
2002	—	—	—	—	1.25	1.50

KM# 189 1/2 CHON

2.1600 g., Aluminum, 27.02 mm. **Obv:** State arms **Rev:** Bighorn sheep **Edge:** Plain

Date	Mintage	F	VF	XF	Unc	BU
2002	—	—	—	—	1.25	1.50

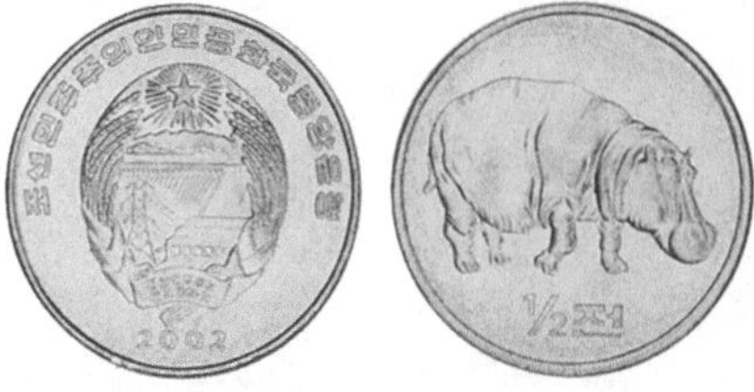

KM# 190 1/2 CHON

2.1600 g., Aluminum, 27.02 mm. **Obv:** State arms **Rev:** Hippopotamus **Edge:** Plain

Date	Mintage	F	VF	XF	Unc	BU
2002	—	—	—	—	1.25	1.50

KM# 191 1/2 CHON

2.1600 g., Aluminum, 27.02 mm. **Subject:** FAO **Obv:** State arms **Rev:** Ancient ship **Edge:** Plain

Date	Mintage	F	VF	XF	Unc	BU
2002	—	—	—	—	1.25	1.50

KM# 192 1/2 CHON

2.1600 g., Aluminum, 27.02 mm. **Subject:** FAO **Obv:** State arms **Rev:** Archaic ship **Edge:** Plain

Date	Mintage	F	VF	XF	Unc	BU
2002	—	—	—	—	1.25	1.50

KM# 193 1/2 CHON

2.1600 g., Aluminum, 27.02 mm. **Subject:** FAO **Obv:** State arms **Rev:** Modern train **Edge:** Plain

Date	Mintage	F	VF	XF	Unc	BU
2002	—	—	—	—	1.25	1.50

KM# 194 1/2 CHON

2.1600 g., Aluminum, 27.02 mm. **Subject:** FAO **Obv:** State arms **Rev:** Jet airliner **Edge:** Plain

Date	Mintage	F	VF	XF	Unc	BU
2002	—	—	—	—	1.25	1.50

KM# 195 CHON

4.6300 g., Brass, 21.7 mm. **Subject:** FAO **Obv:** State arms **Rev:** Antique steam locomotive **Edge:** Plain

Date	Mintage	F	VF	XF	Unc	BU
2002	—	—	—	—	1.50	1.75

KM# 196 CHON

4.6300 g., Brass, 21.7 mm. **Subject:** FAO **Obv:** State arms **Rev:** Antique automobile **Edge:** Plain

Date	Mintage	F	VF	XF	Unc	BU
2002	—	—	—	—	1.50	1.75

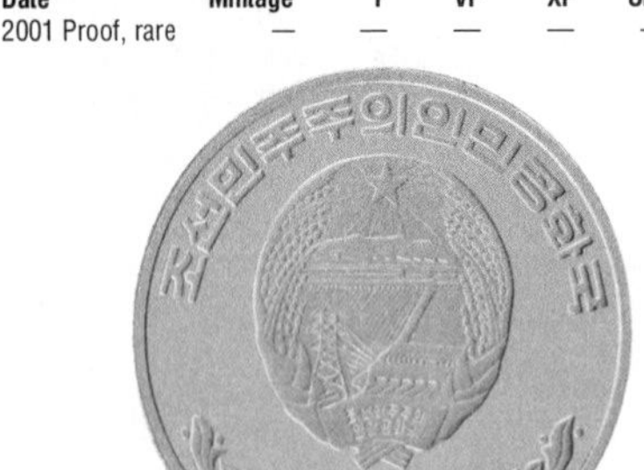

KM# 197 2 CHON

6.0400 g., Copper-Nickel, 24.2 mm. **Subject:** FAO **Obv:** State arms **Rev:** Antique touring car **Edge:** Plain

Date	Mintage	F	VF	XF	Unc	BU
2002	—	—	—	—	2.00	2.50

KM# 499 50 CHON

Aluminum, 27 mm. **Rev:** Two bicyclists

Date	Mintage	F	VF	XF	Unc	BU
2001 Proof, rare	—	—	—	—	—	—

KM# 162.2 WON

7.0000 g., Aluminum, 40 mm. **Obv:** State arms, date above value **Rev:** Radiant Korean map and landmarks **Edge:** Plain

Date	Mintage	F	VF	XF	Unc	BU
2001 Proof	—	Value: 15.00				

KM# 351 WON

7.0000 g., Aluminum, 40 mm. **Obv:** State arms, date and value below **Rev:** North Korean Arch of Triumph **Edge:** Plain

Date	Mintage	F	VF	XF	Unc	BU
2001 Proof	—	Value: 12.00				

KM# 352 WON

28.6000 g., Brass, 40.1 mm. **Obv:** State arms, value below **Rev:** North Korean Arch of Triumph **Edge:** Plain

Date	Mintage	F	VF	XF	Unc	BU
2001 Proof	—	Value: 15.00				

KM# 353 WON

6.4500 g., Aluminum, 40 mm. **Obv:** State arms, value below **Rev:** N. Korean landmarks and tourists above ship **Edge:** Plain

Date	Mintage	F	VF	XF	Unc	BU
2001 Proof	—	Value: 12.00				

KM# 354 WON

27.6300 g., Brass, 40 mm. **Obv:** State arms, date and value below **Rev:** N. Korean landmarks and tourists above ship **Edge:** Plain

Date	Mintage	F	VF	XF	Unc	BU
2001 Proof	—	Value: 15.00				

KM# 355 WON

6.7500 g., Aluminum, 40 mm. **Obv:** State arms, value below **Rev:** Temple of Heaven above Hong Kong city view below **Edge:** Plain

Date	Mintage	F	VF	XF	Unc	BU
ND Proof	—	Value: 12.00				

KM# 356 WON

28.1000 g., Brass, 40 mm. **Obv:** State arms, date and value below **Rev:** Temple of Heaven above, Hong Kong city view below **Edge:** Plain

Date	Mintage	F	VF	XF	Unc	BU
2001 Proof	—	Value: 15.00				

KM# 294a WON

6.7500 g., Aluminum, 40 mm. **Obv:** State arms **Rev:** Antique ceramics **Edge:** Plain

Date	Mintage	F	VF	XF	Unc	BU
2001 Proof	—	Value: 15.00				

KM# 358 WON

6.7500 g., Aluminum, 40 mm. **Obv:** State arms **Rev:** Old fort **Edge:** Plain

Date	Mintage	F	VF	XF	Unc	BU
2001 Proof	—	Value: 12.00				

KM# 358a WON

28.1000 g., Brass, 40 mm. **Obv:** State arms **Rev:** Old fort **Edge:** Plain

Date	Mintage	F	VF	XF	Unc	BU
2001 Proof	—	Value: 15.00				

KM# 359 WON

7.0000 g., Aluminum, 40.1 mm. **Obv:** State arms **Rev:** Old couple above dates1945-2000 **Edge:** Plain

Date	Mintage	F	VF	XF	Unc	BU
2001 Proof	—	Value: 12.00				

KM# 359a WON

27.8000 g., Brass, 40.1 mm. **Obv:** State arms **Rev:** Old couple above dates 1945-2000 **Edge:** Plain

Date	Mintage	F	VF	XF	Unc	BU
2001 Proof	—	Value: 15.00				

KM# 360 WON

27.8000 g., Brass, 40.1 mm. **Obv:** State arms **Rev:** Blue Dragon **Edge:** Plain

Date	Mintage	F	VF	XF	Unc	BU
2001 Proof	—	Value: 20.00				

KM# 361 WON

7.0000 g., Aluminum, 40.1 mm. **Obv:** State arms **Rev:** Head of Deng Zio Ping 3/4 left, 1904-1997 flanking, sprigs below **Edge:** Plain

Date	Mintage	F	VF	XF	Unc	BU
2001 Proof	—	Value: 12.00				

KM# 361a WON

27.8000 g., Brass, 40.1 mm. **Obv:** State arms **Rev:** Head 3/4 left divides dates(1904-1997) flanked by sprigs **Edge:** Plain

Date	Mintage	F	VF	XF	Unc	BU
2001 Proof	—	Value: 15.00				

KM# 362 WON

7.0000 g., Aluminum, 40.1 mm. **Obv:** State arms **Rev:** Children flying a kite **Edge:** Plain

Date	Mintage	F	VF	XF	Unc	BU
2001 Proof	—	Value: 15.00				

KM# 362a WON

27.8000 g., Brass, 40.1 mm. **Obv:** State arms **Rev:** Children flying a kite **Edge:** Plain

Date	Mintage	F	VF	XF	Unc	BU
2001 Proof	—	Value: 17.50				

KM# 363 WON

7.0000 g., Aluminum, 40.1 mm. **Obv:** State arms **Rev:** Children on seesaw **Edge:** Plain

Date	Mintage	F	VF	XF	Unc	BU
2001 Proof	—	Value: 15.00				

KM# 363a WON

27.8000 g., Brass, 40.1 mm. **Obv:** State arms **Rev:** Children on seesaw **Edge:** Plain

Date	Mintage	F	VF	XF	Unc	BU
2001 Proof	—	Value: 17.50				

KM# 364 WON

7.0000 g., Aluminum, 40.1 mm. **Obv:** State arms **Rev:** Children wrestling **Edge:** Plain

Date	Mintage	F	VF	XF	Unc	BU
2001 Proof	—	Value: 15.00				

KM# 364a WON

27.8000 g., Brass, 40.1 mm. **Obv:** State arms **Rev:** Children wrestling **Edge:** Plain

Date	Mintage	F	VF	XF	Unc	BU
2001 Proof	—	Value: 17.50				

KM# 365 WON

7.0000 g., Aluminum, 40.1 mm. **Obv:** State arms **Rev:** Girl on swing **Edge:** Plain

Date	Mintage	F	VF	XF	Unc	BU
2001 Proof	—	Value: 15.00				

KM# 365a WON

27.8000 g., Brass, 40.1 mm. **Obv:** State arms **Rev:** Girl on swing **Edge:** Plain

Date	Mintage	F	VF	XF	Unc	BU
2001 Proof	—	Value: 17.50				

KM# 366 WON

7.0000 g., Aluminum, 40.1 mm. **Obv:** State arms **Rev:** Girls jumping rope **Edge:** Plain

Date	Mintage	F	VF	XF	Unc	BU
2001 Proof	—	Value: 15.00				

KM# 366a WON

27.8000 g., Brass, 40.1 mm. **Obv:** State arms **Rev:** Girls jumping rope **Edge:** Plain

Date	Mintage	F	VF	XF	Unc	BU
2001 Proof	—	Value: 17.50				

KM# 367 WON

8.7000 g., Aluminum, 40.4 mm. **Obv:** State arms **Rev:** "Kumdang-2 Injection" in center square on leaves **Edge:** Plain

Date	Mintage	F	VF	XF	Unc	BU
2001 Proof	—	Value: 15.00				

KM# 367a WON

26.5400 g., Brass, 40.2 mm. **Obv:** State arms **Rev:** "Kumdang-2 Injection" in center square on leaves **Edge:** Plain

Date	Mintage	F	VF	XF	Unc	BU
2001 Proof	—	Value: 17.50				

KM# 368 WON

27.6100 g., Brass, 40.2 mm. **Obv:** State arms **Rev:** Bust of Kim Il-Sung, 1912-1994 flanking, sprigs below **Edge:** Plain

Date	Mintage	F	VF	XF	Unc	BU
JU90-2001 Proof	—	Value: 17.50				

KM# 369 WON

6.5500 g., Aluminum, 40.4 mm. **Obv:** State arms **Rev:** Train at left, couple below jet plane at right **Edge:** Plain

Date	Mintage	F	VF	XF	Unc	BU
2001 Proof	—	Value: 15.00				

KM# 370 WON

27.5600 g., Brass, 40.1 mm. **Obv:** State arms **Rev:** Train at left, couple below jet plane at right **Edge:** Plain

Date	Mintage	F	VF	XF	Unc	BU
2001 Proof	—	Value: 17.50				

KM# 371 WON

5.0500 g., Aluminum, 35 mm. **Obv:** State arms **Rev:** Hong Kong city view **Edge:** Plain

Date	Mintage	F	VF	XF	Unc	BU
2001 Proof	—	Value: 10.00				

KM# 372 WON

6.4000 g., Aluminum, 40 mm. **Obv:** State arms **Rev:** Bust with beard facing flanked by text **Edge:** Plain

Date	Mintage	F	VF	XF	Unc	BU
2001 Proof	—	Value: 12.00				

KM# 372a WON

27.7000 g., Brass, 40 mm. **Obv:** State arms **Rev:** Bust with beard facing flanked by text **Edge:** Plain

Date	Mintage	F	VF	XF	Unc	BU
2001 Proof	—	Value: 15.00				

KM# 373 WON

6.9000 g., Aluminum, 40 mm. **Subject:** 1996 Olympics **Obv:** State arms **Rev:** Two green gymnasts and multicolor flame **Edge:** Plain

Date	Mintage	F	VF	XF	Unc	BU
2001 Proof	—	Value: 15.00				

KM# 374 WON

7.0000 g., Aluminum, 40 mm. **Obv:** State arms **Rev:** Taedong Gatehouse **Edge:** Plain

Date	Mintage	F	VF	XF	Unc	BU
2001 Proof	—	Value: 15.00				

KM# 375 WON

8.5000 g., Aluminum, 40.2 mm. **Obv:** State arms **Rev:** Logo above Baektn Mountain volcano crater **Edge:** Plain

Date	Mintage	F	VF	XF	Unc	BU
JU90-2001 Proof	—	Value: 10.00				

KM# 238a WON

7.1400 g., Aluminum, 40.1 mm. **Obv:** State arms **Rev:** Tiger and cub **Edge:** Plain

Date	Mintage	F	VF	XF	Unc	BU
2001 Proof	—	Value: 17.00				

KM# 376 WON

7.1000 g., Aluminum, 40.1 mm. **Subject:** 1996 Olympics **Obv:** State arms **Rev:** Horse jumping **Edge:** Plain

Date	Mintage	F	VF	XF	Unc	BU
2001 Proof	—	Value: 15.00				

KM# 377 WON

7.0000 g., Aluminum, 40.1 mm. **Subject:** 1996 Olympics **Obv:** State arms **Rev:** Four runners **Edge:** Plain

Date	Mintage	F	VF	XF	Unc	BU
2001 Proof	—	Value: 15.00				

KM# 378 WON

6.8400 g., Aluminum, 40.1 mm. **Obv:** State arms **Rev:** Monument flanked by multicolor flags and flowers **Edge:** Plain

Date	Mintage	F	VF	XF	Unc	BU
2001 Proof	—	Value: 12.00				

KM# 379 WON

6.6000 g., Aluminum, 40.1 mm. **Obv:** State arms **Rev:** Olympic diver **Edge:** Plain

Date	Mintage	F	VF	XF	Unc	BU
2001 Proof	—	Value: 15.00				

KM# 380 WON

6.9100 g., Aluminum, 40.1 mm. **Obv:** State arms **Rev:** Olympic handball player **Edge:** Plain

Date	Mintage	F	VF	XF	Unc	BU
2001 Proof	—	Value: 15.00				

KM# 381 WON

7.1100 g., Aluminum, 40.2 mm. **Obv:** State arms **Rev:** Olympic high bar gymnast **Edge:** Plain

Date	Mintage	F	VF	XF	Unc	BU
2001 Proof	—	Value: 15.00				

KM# 381a WON

28.8200 g., Brass, 40.1 mm. **Obv:** State arms **Rev:** Olympic high bar gymnast **Edge:** Plain

Date	Mintage	F	VF	XF	Unc	BU
2001 Proof	—	Value: 17.50				

KM# 382 WON

6.5000 g., Aluminum, 40.1 mm. **Obv:** State arms **Rev:** Olympic archer **Edge:** Plain

Date	Mintage	F	VF	XF	Unc	BU
2001 Proof	—	Value: 15.00				

KM# 382a WON

27.4100 g., Brass, 40.2 mm. **Obv:** State arms **Rev:** Olympic archer **Edge:** Plain

Date	Mintage	F	VF	XF	Unc	BU
2001 Proof	—	Value: 17.50				

KM# 383 WON

7.1000 g., Aluminum, 40.1 mm. **Obv:** State arms **Rev:** Olympic hurdler **Edge:** Plain

Date	Mintage	F	VF	XF	Unc	BU
2001 Proof	—	Value: 15.00				

KM# 383a WON

28.0000 g., Brass, 40.1 mm. **Obv:** State arms **Rev:** Olympic hurdler **Edge:** Plain

Date	Mintage	F	VF	XF	Unc	BU
2001 Proof	—	Value: 17.50				

KM# 384 WON

7.1500 g., Aluminum, 40.1 mm. **Obv:** State arms **Rev:** Kim Il Sung's birthplace side view **Edge:** Plain

Date	Mintage	F	VF	XF	Unc	BU
JU90-2001 Proof	—	Value: 15.00				

KM# 385 WON

7.0000 g., Aluminum, 40.1 mm. **Obv:** State arms **Rev:** Mt. Kumgang Fairy playing flute **Edge:** Plain

Date	Mintage	F	VF	XF	Unc	BU
2001 Proof	—	Value: 12.00				

KM# 385a WON

28.1600 g., Brass, 40.2 mm. **Obv:** State arms **Rev:** Mt. Kumgang Fairy playing flute **Edge:** Plain

Date	Mintage	F	VF	XF	Unc	BU
2001 Proof	—	Value: 15.00				

KM# 452 WON

27.4400 g., Brass, 40 mm. **Obv:** State arms **Rev:** Early sailing ship **Rev. Legend:** • HISTORY OF SEAFARING • MERCHANTMAN - THE DPR KOREA . KORYO PERIOD . 918-1392 **Edge:** Plain

Date	Mintage	F	VF	XF	Unc	BU
2001 Proof	—	Value: 9.00				

KM# 505 WON

28.0000 g., Brass **Obv:** National arms **Rev:** Rainbow lori

Date	Mintage	F	VF	XF	Unc	BU
2001 Proof	—	Value: 8.50				

KM# 157 WON

6.7000 g., Aluminum, 40 mm. **Subject:** Seafaring Ships **Obv:** State arms **Rev:** Cruise ship below stylized head left profile **Edge:** Plain

Date	Mintage	F	VF	XF	Unc	BU
JU90-2001 Proof	—	Value: 10.00				

KM# 157a WON

29.0500 g., Brass, 40.2 mm. **Obv:** State arms **Rev:** Cruise ship below stylized head profile left **Edge:** Plain

Date	Mintage	F	VF	XF	Unc	BU
2001 Proof	—	Value: 17.50				

KM# 458 WON

5.0000 g., Aluminum, 35 mm. **Obv:** National arms, Country name **Rev:** Krugenstern

Date	Mintage	F	VF	XF	Unc	BU
2001 Proof	—	Value: 7.00				

KM# 158 WON

17.0000 g., Copper-Nickel, 35 mm. **Subject:** First Nobel Prize Winner in Literature - Sully Prudhomme **Obv:** State arms **Rev:** Half length seated bust left flanked by shelves and books **Edge:** Plain

Date	Mintage	F	VF	XF	Unc	BU
ND(2001) Proof	2,000	Value: 100				

KM# 158a WON

5.0000 g., Aluminum, 35 mm. **Subject:** Nobel prize in literature, Sully Prudhomme

Date	Mintage	F	VF	XF	Unc	BU
2001 Proof	—	Value: 6.00				

KM# 158b WON

16.2000 g., Brass, 35 mm. **Subject:** First Nobel Prize Winner in Literature - Sully Prudhomme **Obv:** State arms **Rev:** Half length seated bust left flanked by shelves and books **Edge:** Plain

Date	Mintage	F	VF	XF	Unc	BU
ND(2001) Proof	—	Value: 10.00				

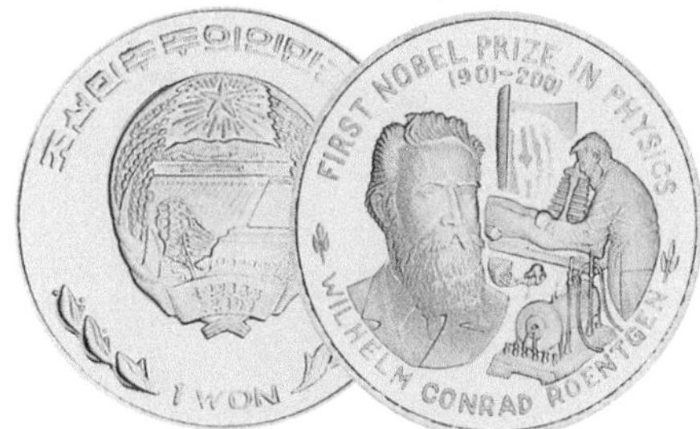

KM# 159 WON

17.0000 g., Copper-Nickel, 35 mm. **Subject:** First Nobel Prize Winner in Physics - Wilhelm C. Roentgen **Obv:** State arms **Rev:** Bust 3/4 right at left with same person seated in lab at right **Edge:** Plain

Date	Mintage	F	VF	XF	Unc	BU
ND(2001) Proof	2,000	Value: 100				

KM# 159a WON

5.0000 g., Aluminum, 35 mm. **Subject:** Nobel in Physics, Wilhelm C. Rontgen

Date	Mintage	F	VF	XF	Unc	BU
2001 Proof	—	Value: 6.00				

KM# 159b WON

16.2000 g., Brass, 35 mm. **Subject:** First Nobel Prize in Physics - Wiliam C. Rontgen **Obv:** State arms **Rev:** Bust 3/4 right at left with same person seated in lab at right **Edge:** Plain

Date	Mintage	F	VF	XF	Unc	BU
ND(2001) Proof	—	Value: 10.00				

KM# 160 WON

16.2000 g., Brass, 35 mm. **Subject:** Nipponia Nippon **Obv:** State arms **Rev:** Two nest building Japanese ibis **Edge:** Plain

Date	Mintage	F	VF	XF	Unc	BU
JU90-2001 Proof	—	Value: 15.00				

KM# 160a WON

17.0000 g., Copper-Nickel, 35 mm. **Subject:** Wildlife **Obv:** State arms **Rev:** Two nesting Japanese Ibis birds **Edge:** Plain

Date	Mintage	F	VF	XF	Unc	BU
JU2001 Proof	200	Value: 100				

KM# 160b WON

5.3500 g., Aluminum, 35.1 mm. **Obv:** State arms **Rev:** Two nest building Japanese Ibis birds **Edge:** Plain

Date	Mintage	F	VF	XF	Unc	BU
JU90-2001 Proof	—	Value: 15.00				

KM# 202 WON

17.0000 g., Copper-Nickel, 35 mm. **Subject:** School Ships **Obv:** State arms **Rev:** SS Krusenstern **Edge:** Plain

Date	Mintage	F	VF	XF	Unc	BU
ND(2001) Proof	200	Value: 100				

KM# 204 WON

17.0000 g., Copper-Nickel, 35 mm. **Subject:** Wildlife **Obv:** State arms **Rev:** Two standing Japanese Ibis birds **Edge:** Plain

Date	Mintage	F	VF	XF	Unc	BU
JU90-2001 Proof	100	Value: 150				

KM# 207 WON

17.0000 g., Copper-Nickel, 35 mm. **Subject:** Wildlife **Obv:** State arms **Rev:** Two Korean Longtail Gorals **Edge:** Plain

Date	Mintage	F	VF	XF	Unc	BU
JU90-2001 Proof	200	Value: 100				

KM# 207a WON

16.0500 g., Brass, 35 mm. **Obv:** State arms **Rev:** Two Longtail Gorals **Edge:** Plain

Date	Mintage	F	VF	XF	Unc	BU
JU90-2001 Proof	—	Value: 12.50				

KM# 207b WON

5.3500 g., Aluminum, 35.1 mm. **Obv:** State arms **Rev:** Two Longtail Gorals **Edge:** Plain

Date	Mintage	F	VF	XF	Unc	BU
JU90-2001 Proof	—	Value: 10.00				

KM# 209 WON

17.0000 g., Copper-Nickel, 35 mm. **Subject:** First Nobel Prize Winner in Medicine - Emil A. von Behring **Obv:** State arms **Rev:** Lab beaker divides half length figures facing each other **Edge:** Plain

Date	Mintage	F	VF	XF	Unc	BU
ND(2001) Proof	2,000	Value: 100				

KM# 209b WON

16.0000 g., Brass, 35 mm. **Subject:** Nobel prize in Medicine, Emil von Behring

Date	Mintage	F	VF	XF	Unc	BU
2001 Proof	—	Value: 7.00				

KM# 209a WON

5.0000 g., Aluminum, 35 mm. **Subject:** Nobel prize in Medicine, Emil von Behring

Date	Mintage	F	VF	XF	Unc	BU
2001 Proof	—	Value: 6.00				

KM# 210 WON

17.0000 g., Copper-Nickel, 35 mm. **Subject:** First Nobel Prize Winner in Peace - Henri Dunant **Obv:** State arms **Rev:** Bust facing at left, war wounded at right **Edge:** Plain

Date	Mintage	F	VF	XF	Unc	BU
ND(2001) Proof	2,000	Value: 100				

KM# 210a WON

5.0000 g., Aluminum, 35 mm. **Subject:** Nobel Peace Prize, Jean H. Dunant

Date	Mintage	F	VF	XF	Unc	BU
2001 Proof	—	Value: 6.00				

KM# 210b WON

5.0000 g., Aluminum, 35 mm. **Subject:** Nobel Peace prize, Jean H. Dunant

Date	Mintage	F	VF	XF	Unc	BU
2001 Proof	—	Value: 7.00				

KM# 211 WON

17.0000 g., Copper-Nickel, 35 mm. **Subject:** First Nobel Prize Winner in Chemistry - Jacobus Van't Hoff **Obv:** State arms **Rev:** Standing figures in lab scene **Edge:** Plain

Date	Mintage	F	VF	XF	Unc	BU
ND(2001) Proof	2,000	Value: 100				

KM# 211a WON

5.0000 g., Aluminum, 35 mm. **Subject:** Nobel in Chemistry, Jacob van't Hoff

Date	Mintage	F	VF	XF	Unc	BU
2001 Proof	—	Value: 6.00				

KM# 211b WON

16.0000 g., Brass, 35 mm. **Subject:** Nobel prize in Chemistry, Jabob van't Hoff

Date	Mintage	F	VF	XF	Unc	BU
2001 Proof	—	Value: 7.00				

KM# 212 WON

17.0000 g., Copper-Nickel, 35 mm. **Subject:** First Nobel Prize Winner in Peace - Frederic Passy **Obv:** State arms **Rev:** Head left at right with allegorical scene at left **Edge:** Plain

Date	Mintage	F	VF	XF	Unc	BU
ND(2001) Proof	2,000	Value: 100				

KM# 212a WON

5.0000 g., Aluminum, 35 mm. **Subject:** Nobel Peace Prize, Frederic Passy

Date	Mintage	F	VF	XF	Unc	BU
2001 Proof	—	Value: 6.00				

KM# 212b WON

16.0000 g., Brass, 35 mm. **Subject:** Nobel Peace Prize, Frederic Passy

Date	Mintage	F	VF	XF	Unc	BU
2001 Proof	—	Value: 7.00				

KM# 232 WON

28.1100 g., Brass, 40 mm. **Obv:** State arms **Rev:** White-bellied woodpecker **Edge:** Plain

Date	Mintage	F	VF	XF	Unc	BU
2001 Proof	—	Value: 27.50				

KM# 233 WON

28.1100 g., Brass, 40 mm. **Obv:** State arms **Rev:** Black grouse **Edge:** Plain

Date	Mintage	F	VF	XF	Unc	BU
2001 Proof	—	Value: 27.50				

KM# 234 WON

28.1100 g., Brass, 40 mm. **Obv:** State arms **Rev:** Sand grouse **Edge:** Plain

Date	Mintage	F	VF	XF	Unc	BU
2001 Proof	—	Value: 27.50				

KM# 235 WON

28.1100 g., Brass, 40 mm. **Obv:** State arms **Rev:** Fairy Pitta bird **Edge:** Plain

Date	Mintage	F	VF	XF	Unc	BU
2001 Proof	—	Value: 27.50				

KM# 236 WON

28.1100 g., Brass, 40 mm. **Obv:** State arms **Rev:** Mythical "Hyonmu" **Edge:** Plain

Date	Mintage	F	VF	XF	Unc	BU
2001 Proof	—	Value: 27.50				

KM# 236a WON

7.0000 g., Aluminum, 40 mm. **Obv:** State arms **Rev:** "Hyonmu" **Edge:** Plain

Date	Mintage	F	VF	XF	Unc	BU
2001 Proof	—	Value: 17.50				

KM# 237 WON

28.1100 g., Brass, 40 mm. **Obv:** State arms **Rev:** Blue Dragon **Edge:** Plain

Date	Mintage	F	VF	XF	Unc	BU
2001 Proof	—	Value: 27.50				

KM# 238 WON

28.1100 g., Brass, 40 mm. **Obv:** State arms **Rev:** Two tigers **Edge:** Plain

Date	Mintage	F	VF	XF	Unc	BU
2001 Proof	—	Value: 27.50				

KM# 239 WON

28.1100 g., Brass, 40 mm. **Obv:** State arms **Rev:** Brontosaurus **Edge:** Plain

Date	Mintage	F	VF	XF	Unc	BU
2001 Proof	—	Value: 27.50				

KM# 247 WON

26.9500 g., Brass, 40 mm. **Obv:** State arms **Rev:** Soldier watching an air raid on a Yalu River bridge **Edge:** Plain

Date	Mintage	F	VF	XF	Unc	BU
2001 Proof	—	Value: 20.00				

KM# 248 WON

7.0000 g., Aluminum, 40 mm. **Obv:** State arms **Rev:** Multicolor rabbit and hearts **Edge:** Plain **Note:** Year of the Rabbit

Date	Mintage	F	VF	XF	Unc	BU
2001 Proof	—	Value: 20.00				

KM# 290 WON

28.2000 g., Brass, 40.1 mm. **Obv:** State arms **Rev:** Bust of Kim Johg-Il facing above flower sprigs **Edge:** Plain

Date	Mintage	F	VF	XF	Unc	BU
JU90-2001 Proof	—	Value: 20.00				

KM# 291 WON

28.2000 g., Brass, 40.1 mm. **Obv:** State arms **Rev:** Bust of Kim Jung-Suk facing, 1917-1949 flanking, flower sprigs below **Edge:** Plain

Date	Mintage	F	VF	XF	Unc	BU
JU90-2001 Proof	—	Value: 20.00				

KM# 293 WON

28.2000 g., Brass, 40.2 mm. **Obv:** State arms **Rev:** Olympic runners **Edge:** Crude reeding

Date	Mintage	F	VF	XF	Unc	BU
2001 Proof	—	Value: 20.00				

KM# 294 WON

28.2000 g., Brass, 40.2 mm. **Obv:** State arms **Rev:** Antique porcelain objects **Edge:** Plain

Date	Mintage	F	VF	XF	Unc	BU
2001 Proof	—	Value: 20.00				

KM# 310 WON

Aluminum **Obv:** State arms **Rev:** Tomb of King Tongmyong

Date	Mintage	F	VF	XF	Unc	BU
2001 Proof	—	Value: 12.00				

KM# 458a WON

16.0000 g., Brass, 35 mm. **Subject:** Tall ships **Obv:** Arms **Rev:** Krugenstern

Date	Mintage	F	VF	XF	Unc	BU
2001 Proof	—	Value: 8.00				

KM# 459 WON

Brass, 35 mm. **Subject:** Return of Hong Kong **Obv:** Arms **Rev:** Architecture

Date	Mintage	F	VF	XF	Unc	BU
2001 Proof	—	Value: 6.50				

KM# 460 WON

Brass, 35 mm. **Subject:** Return of Hong Kong **Obv:** Skyline **Rev:** Dragon boat

Date	Mintage	F	VF	XF	Unc	BU
2001 Proof	—	Value: 12.00				

KM# 461 WON

6.0000 g., Aluminum, 38 mm. **Obv:** National arms, Central Bank name **Rev:** Speed skater

Date	Mintage	F	VF	XF	Unc	BU
2001 Proof	—	—	—	—	—	—

KM# 461a WON

25.0000 g., Brass **Subject:** 2002 Olympics **Obv:** Arms **Rev:** Speedskater

Date	Mintage	F	VF	XF	Unc	BU
2001 Proof	—	Value: 10.00				

KM# 462 WON

Aluminum, 40 mm. **Subject:** Tae Kwon do **Obv:** Arms **Rev:** Two sportsmen

Date	Mintage	F	VF	XF	Unc	BU
2001 Proof	—	Value: 8.00				

KM# 462a WON

28.0000 g., Brass, 40 mm. **Obv:** National arms, Country name **Rev:** Two Taekwondo players

Date	Mintage	F	VF	XF	Unc	BU
2001 Proof	—	Value: 7.00				

KM# 463 WON

Aluminum, 40 mm. **Obv:** Arms **Rev:** Multicolor flowers

Date	Mintage	F	VF	XF	Unc	BU
2001 Proof	—	Value: 8.00				

KM# 464 WON

Aluminum, 40 mm. **Obv:** Arms **Rev:** Woodpecker on branch (Dryocopus Javensis)

Date	Mintage	F	VF	XF	Unc	BU
2001 Proof	—	Value: 8.00				

KM# 465 WON

Aluminum, 35 mm. **Obv:** Arms **Rev:** Zhou Enlai portrait facing

Date	Mintage	F	VF	XF	Unc	BU
2001 Proof	—	Value: 8.00				

KM# 466 WON

Aluminum, 40 mm. **Obv:** Arms **Rev:** Buddha seated, facing

Date	Mintage	F	VF	XF	Unc	BU
2001 Proof	—	Value: 7.00				

KM# 467 WON

Brass **Obv:** Arms **Rev:** Buddha seated, facing

Date	Mintage	F	VF	XF	Unc	BU
2001 Proof	—	Value: 10.00				

KM# 468 WON

Brass **Obv:** Arms **Rev:** Couple embracing, 1945-2000

Date	Mintage	F	VF	XF	Unc	BU
ND(2001) Proof	—	Value: 10.00				

KM# 504 WON

7.0000 g., Aluminum, 40 mm. **Obv:** National arms **Rev:** Rainbow lori in color

Date	Mintage	F	VF	XF	Unc	BU
2001 Proof	—	Value: 8.50				

KM# 506 WON

7.0000 g., Aluminum **Rev:** Mandarian Ducks in color

Date	Mintage	F	VF	XF	Unc	BU
2001	—	Value: 8.50				

KM# 507 WON

Brass **Rev:** Mandarin Ducks

Date	Mintage	F	VF	XF	Unc	BU
2001 Proof	—	Value: 9.00				

KM# 535 WON

7.0000 g., Aluminum, 40 mm. **Obv:** National arms **Rev:** Power in teh frowing area of Kaeseong in color

Date	Mintage	F	VF	XF	Unc	BU
2001 Proof	—	—	—	—	—	—

KM# 539 WON

7.0000 g., Aluminum, 40 mm. **Obv:** National arms **Rev:** Panda seated in color, eating

Date	Mintage	F	VF	XF	Unc	BU
2001 Proof	—	Value: 7.50				

KM# 541 WON

7.0000 g., Aluminum, 40 mm. **Obv:** National arms **Rev:** Two pandas in color

Date	Mintage	F	VF	XF	Unc	BU
2001 Proof	—	Value: 7.50				

KM# 542 WON

28.0000 g., Brass **Obv:** National arms, name of the Central Bank **Rev:** Two pandas

Date	Mintage	F	VF	XF	Unc	BU
2001 Proof	—	Value: 8.00				

KM# 548 WON

7.0000 g., Aluminum, 40 mm. **Obv:** National arms, name of the Central Bank **Rev:** Rainbow lori in color

Date	Mintage	F	VF	XF	Unc	BU
2001 Proof	—	Value: 7.50				

KM# 549 WON

7.0000 g., Aluminum, 40 mm. **Obv:** National arms, name of the Central Bank **Rev:** Manderin duck in color

Date	Mintage	F	VF	XF	Unc	BU
2001 Proof	—	Value: 7.50				

KM# 556 WON

Brass **Rev:** Show jumper

Date	Mintage	F	VF	XF	Unc	BU
2001 Proof	—	Value: 8.00				

KM# 557 WON

7.0000 g., Aluminum, 40 mm. **Obv:** National arms, name of the Central Bank **Rev:** Rythem dancers and logo in color

Date	Mintage	F	VF	XF	Unc	BU
2001 Proof	—	Value: 7.50				

KM# 558 WON

7.0000 g., Aluminum, 40 mm. **Obv:** National arms, name of the Central Bank **Rev:** Chinese Peony

Date	Mintage	F	VF	XF	Unc	BU
2001 Proof	—	Value: 7.50				

KM# 559 WON

7.0000 g., Aluminum, 40 mm. **Obv:** National arms, name of the Central Bank **Rev:** Panda seated in color eating

Date	Mintage	F	VF	XF	Unc	BU
2001 Proof	—	Value: 7.50				

KM# 560 WON

Brass, 28 mm. **Obv:** National arms, name of the Central Bank **Rev:** Panda seated eating

Date	Mintage	F	VF	XF	Unc	BU
2001 Proof	—	Value: 8.00				

KM# 561 WON

28.0000 g., Brass, 40 mm. **Obv:** National arms, name of the Central Bank **Rev:** Soldiers attack bridge over the Yalu river at Dandong (1951)

Date	Mintage	F	VF	XF	Unc	BU
2001 Proof	—	Value: 7.50				

KM# 562 WON

28.0000 g., Brass, 40 mm. **Obv:** National arms **Rev:** Soldiers attack bridge over the Yalu river at Dandong (1951)

Date	Mintage	F	VF	XF	Unc	BU
2001 Proof	—	Value: 7.50				

KM# 563 WON

28.0000 g., Brass, 40 mm. **Obv:** National arms, name of the Central Bank **Rev:** Tower of Friendship in Pyeongyang with North Korean and P.R.C. flags

Date	Mintage	F	VF	XF	Unc	BU
2001 Proof	—	Value: 8.00				

KM# 568 WON

7.0000 g., Aluminum, 40 mm. **Obv:** National arms **Rev:** Rocket and satelite

Date	Mintage	F	VF	XF	Unc	BU
2001 Proof	—	Value: 6.50				

KM# 568a WON

28.0000 g., Brass, 40 mm. **Obv:** National arms **Rev:** Rocket and satellite

Date	Mintage	F	VF	XF	Unc	BU
2001	—	Value: 7.50				

KM# 572 WON

28.0000 g., Brass, 40 mm. **Obv:** National arms, country name **Rev:** Dragon rising

Date	Mintage	F	VF	XF	Unc	BU
2001 Proof	—	Value: 7.50				

KM# 573 WON

28.0000 g., Brass, 40 mm. **Obv:** National arms, name of the Central Bank **Rev:** Dragon rising

Date	Mintage	F	VF	XF	Unc	BU
2001 Proof	—	Value: 7.50				

KM# 574 WON

Brass **Obv:** National arms, country name **Rev:** Two girls on the seasaw

Date	Mintage	F	VF	XF	Unc	BU
2001 Proof	—	Value: 7.50				

KM# 575 WON

Brass **Obv:** National arms, Central Bank name **Rev:** Two girls on the seasaw

Date	Mintage	F	VF	XF	Unc	BU
2001 Proof	—	Value: 7.50				

KM# 576 WON

Brass **Obv:** National arms, country name **Rev:** Korean struggle

Date	Mintage	F	VF	XF	Unc	BU
2001 Proof	—	Value: 7.50				

KM# 577 WON

Brass **Obv:** National arms, Central Bank name **Rev:** Korean struggle

Date	Mintage	F	VF	XF	Unc	BU
2001 Proof	—	Value: 7.50				

KM# 578 WON

Brass **Obv:** National arms, country name **Rev:** Child on swing

Date	Mintage	F	VF	XF	Unc	BU
2001 Proof	—	Value: 7.50				

KM# 579 WON

Brass **Obv:** National arms, Central Bank name **Rev:** Child on swing

Date	Mintage	F	VF	XF	Unc	BU
2001 Proof	—	Value: 7.50				

KM# 580 WON

Brass **Obv:** National arms, country name **Rev:** Children skipping

Date	Mintage	F	VF	XF	Unc	BU
2001 Proof	—	Value: 7.50				

KM# 581 WON

28.0000 g., Brass, 40 mm. **Obv:** National arms, Central Bank name **Rev:** Children skipping

Date	Mintage	F	VF	XF	Unc	BU
2001 Proof	—	Value: 7.50				

KM# 608 WON

7.0000 g., Aluminum, 40 mm. **Obv:** National arms, Central Bank name **Rev:** Rabbit in color

Date	Mintage	F	VF	XF	Unc	BU
2001 Proof	—	Value: 7.50				

KM# 609 WON

28.0000 g., Brass, 40 mm. **Obv:** National arms, country name **Rev:** Rabbit

Date	Mintage	F	VF	XF	Unc	BU
2001 Proof	—	Value: 7.50				

KM# 616 WON

7.0000 g., Aluminum, 40 mm. **Obv:** National arms, Central Bank name **Rev:** White bellied woodpecker

Date	Mintage	F	VF	XF	Unc	BU
2001 Proof	—	Value: 6.00				

KM# 617 WON

7.0000 g., Aluminum, 40 mm. **Obv:** National arms, Country name **Rev:** Black grouse

Date	Mintage	F	VF	XF	Unc	BU
2001 Proof	—	Value: 6.00				

KM# 618 WON

7.0000 g., Aluminum, 40 mm. **Obv:** National arms, Country name **Rev:** Sand grouse

Date	Mintage	F	VF	XF	Unc	BU
2001 Proof	—	Value: 6.00				

KM# 619 WON

7.0000 g., Aluminum, 40 mm. **Obv:** National arms, Country name **Rev:** Indian Pitta bird

Date	Mintage	F	VF	XF	Unc	BU
2001 Proof	—	Value: 6.00				

KM# 636 WON

28.0000 g., Brass, 40 mm. **Obv:** National arms, Country name **Rev:** Two siberian tigers

Date	Mintage	F	VF	XF	Unc	BU
2001 Proof	—	Value: 7.00				

KM# 641 WON

7.0000 g., Aluminum, 40 mm. **Obv:** National arms, Country name **Rev:** Gojumong, first king

Date	Mintage	F	VF	XF	Unc	BU
2001 Proof	—	Value: 6.00				

KM# 642 WON
28.0000 g., Brass, 40 mm. **Obv:** National arms, Country name **Rev:** Gojumong, 1st king

Date	Mintage	F	VF	XF	Unc	BU
2001 Proof	—	Value: 7.00				

KM# 643 WON
28.0000 g., Brass, 40 mm. **Obv:** National arms, Central Bank name **Rev:** Gojumong, 1st king

Date	Mintage	F	VF	XF	Unc	BU
2001 Proof	—	Value: 7.00				

KM# 644 WON
7.0000 g., Aluminum, 40 mm. **Obv:** National arms, Country name **Rev:** Buddha figure as Myogilsand as rock relief in inner diamond mountain

Date	Mintage	F	VF	XF	Unc	BU
2001 Proof	—	Value: 6.00				

KM# 645 WON
28.0000 g., Brass, 40 mm. **Obv:** National arms, Country name **Rev:** Buddha figure Myogilsang as rock relief in inner diamond mountain

Date	Mintage	F	VF	XF	Unc	BU
2001 Proof	—	Value: 7.00				

KM# 646 WON
Aluminum **Obv:** Dragon and country name **Rev:** King Gojoseon

Date	Mintage	F	VF	XF	Unc	BU
2001 Proof	—	Value: 6.00				

KM# 647 WON
28.0000 g., Brass, 40 mm. **Obv:** Dragon and country name **Rev:** King Gojoseon

Date	Mintage	F	VF	XF	Unc	BU
2001 Proof	—	Value: 7.00				

KM# 648 WON
28.0000 g., Brass, 40 mm. **Obv:** Dragon, Central Bank name **Rev:** King Gojoseon

Date	Mintage	F	VF	XF	Unc	BU
2001 Proof	—	Value: 7.00				

KM# 663 WON
7.0000 g., Aluminum, 40 mm. **Obv:** National arms, Central Bank name **Rev:** Map of Korea in circle

Date	Mintage	F	VF	XF	Unc	BU
2001 Proof	—	Value: 6.00				

KM# 664 WON
28.0000 g., Brass, 40 mm. **Obv:** National arms, Country name **Rev:** Map of Korea in circle

Date	Mintage	F	VF	XF	Unc	BU
2001 Proof	—	Value: 7.00				

KM# 666 WON
28.0000 g., Brass, 40 mm. **Obv:** National arms, Country name **Rev:** First married couple to see again after the 1945 seperation

Date	Mintage	F	VF	XF	Unc	BU
2001 Proof	—	Value: 7.00				

KM# 670 WON
28.0000 g., Brass, 40 mm. **Obv:** National arms, Central Bank name **Rev:** Kim Jeongil and Kim Daejung embrace

Date	Mintage	F	VF	XF	Unc	BU
2001 Proof	—	Value: 7.00				

KM# 671 WON
28.0000 g., Brass, 40 mm. **Obv:** National arms, Central bank name **Rev:** Picture pose of Kim Jeongil and Kim Daejung

Date	Mintage	F	VF	XF	Unc	BU
2001 Proof	—	Value: 7.00				

KM# 672 WON
28.0000 g., Brass, 40 mm. **Obv:** National arms, Central Bank name **Rev:** Kim Jeongil and Kim Daejung sign joint agreement

Date	Mintage	F	VF	XF	Unc	BU
2001 Proof	—	Value: 7.00				

KM# 674 WON
28.0000 g., Brass, 40 mm. **Subject:** Sydney Olympics, 2000 **Obv:** National arms, Country name **Rev:** Archer

Date	Mintage	F	VF	XF	Unc	BU
2001 Proof	—	Value: 7.00				

KM# 675 WON
28.0000 g., Brass, 40 mm. **Obv:** National arms, Country name **Rev:** Handball player

Date	Mintage	F	VF	XF	Unc	BU
2001 Proof	—	Value: 7.00				

KM# 676 WON
7.0000 g., Aluminum, 40 mm. **Obv:** National arms, Country name **Rev:** Korean ringer

Date	Mintage	F	VF	XF	Unc	BU
2001 Proof	—	Value: 6.00				

KM# 677 WON
28.0000 g., Brass, 40 mm. **Subject:** Sydney Olympics **Obv:** National arms, Country name **Rev:** Korean ringer

Date	Mintage	F	VF	XF	Unc	BU
2001 Proof	—	Value: 7.00				

KM# 691 WON
28.0000 g., Brass, 40 mm. **Subject:** Kim Ilseong's 90th birthday **Obv:** National arms, Central Bank name **Rev:** Kim Ilseong

Date	Mintage	F	VF	XF	Unc	BU
2001 Proof	—	Value: 7.00				

KM# 692 WON
28.0000 g., Brass, 40 mm. **Obv:** National arms, Central Bank name **Rev:** Kim Jeongil

Date	Mintage	F	VF	XF	Unc	BU
2001 Proof	—	Value: 7.00				

KM# 693 WON
28.0000 g., Brass, 40 mm. **Obv:** National arms, Central Bank name **Rev:** Kim Jeongsuk

Date	Mintage	F	VF	XF	Unc	BU
2001 Proof	—	Value: 7.00				

KM# 698 WON
7.0000 g., Aluminum, 40 mm. **Obv:** National arms, Country name **Rev:** House where Kim Ilseong was born

Date	Mintage	F	VF	XF	Unc	BU
2001 Proof	—	Value: 6.00				

KM# 699 WON
28.0000 g., Brass, 40 mm. **Obv:** National arms, Country name **Rev:** House were Kim Ilseong was born

Date	Mintage	F	VF	XF	Unc	BU
2001 Proof	—	Value: 7.00				

KM# 700 WON
28.0000 g., Brass, 40 mm. **Obv:** National arms, Central Bank name **Rev:** House where Kim Ilseong was born

Date	Mintage	F	VF	XF	Unc	BU
2001 Proof	—	Value: 7.00				

KM# 701 WON
28.0000 g., Brass, 40 mm. **Obv:** National arms **Rev:** Mountain hut

Date	Mintage	F	VF	XF	Unc	BU
2001 Proof	—	—	—	—	—	—

KM# 702 WON
7.0000 g., Aluminum, 40 mm. **Obv:** National arms **Rev:** House where Kim Jeongsuk was born

Date	Mintage	F	VF	XF	Unc	BU
2001 Proof	—	—	—	—	—	—

KM# 703 WON
28.0000 g., Brass, 40 mm. **Obv:** National arms **Rev:** House where Kim Jeongsuk was born

Date	Mintage	F	VF	XF	Unc	BU
2001 Proof	—	—	—	—	—	—

KM# 706 WON
7.0000 g., Aluminum, 40 mm. **Obv:** National arms, Country name **Rev:** East gate of Pyeongyang

Date	Mintage	F	VF	XF	Unc	BU
2001 Proof	—	Value: 6.00				

KM# 707 WON
28.0000 g., Brass, 40 mm. **Obv:** National arms, Country name **Rev:** East gate of Pyeongyang

Date	Mintage	F	VF	XF	Unc	BU
2001 Proof	—	Value: 7.00				

KM# 708 WON
28.0000 g., Brass, 40 mm. **Obv:** National arms, Central Bank name **Rev:** East gate of Pyeongyang

Date	Mintage	F	VF	XF	Unc	BU
2001 Proof	—	Value: 7.00				

KM# 709 WON
7.0000 g., Aluminum, 40 mm. **Obv:** National arms, Country name **Rev:** North gate of Pyeongyang reconstructed

Date	Mintage	F	VF	XF	Unc	BU
2001 Proof	—	Value: 6.00				

KM# 710 WON
28.0000 g., Brass, 40 mm. **Obv:** National arms, Country name **Rev:** North gate of Pyeongyang reconstructed

Date	Mintage	F	VF	XF	Unc	BU
2001 Proof	—	Value: 7.00				

KM# 711 WON
28.0000 g., Brass, 40 mm. **Obv:** National arms, Central Bank name **Rev:** North gate of Pyeongyang reconstructed

Date	Mintage	F	VF	XF	Unc	BU
2001 Proof	—	Value: 7.00				

KM# 712 WON
28.0000 g., Brass, 40 mm. **Obv:** National arms, Country name with date **Rev:** Celadon pottery

Date	Mintage	F	VF	XF	Unc	BU
2001 Proof	—	Value: 7.00				

KM# 713 WON
28.0000 g., Brass, 40 mm. **Obv:** National arms, Country name **Rev:** Celadon pottery

Date	Mintage	F	VF	XF	Unc	BU
2001 Proof	—	Value: 7.00				

KM# 714 WON
28.0000 g., Brass, 40 mm. **Obv:** National arms, Central bank name **Rev:** Celadon pottery

Date	Mintage	F	VF	XF	Unc	BU
2001 Proof	—	Value: 7.00				

KM# 719 WON
28.0000 g., Brass, 40 mm. **Obv:** National arms, Central Bank name **Rev:** Ginsing plant

Date	Mintage	F	VF	XF	Unc	BU
2001 Proof	—	Value: 7.00				

KM# 721 WON
7.0000 g., Aluminum, 40 mm. **Obv:** National arms, Central Bank name **Rev:** Fairwell to the steam railway, 1945 and again in 2001

Date	Mintage	F	VF	XF	Unc	BU
2001 Proof	—	Value: 6.00				

KM# 722 WON
28.0000 g., Brass, 40 mm. **Obv:** National arms, Central Bank name **Rev:** Fairwell to the steam train, 1945, and then again, 2001

Date	Mintage	F	VF	XF	Unc	BU
2001 Proof	—	Value: 7.00				

KM# 724 WON
7.0000 g., Aluminum, 40 mm. **Obv:** National arms. Central Bank name **Rev:** Married couple in front of Pyongyang attractions with national flag and ferryboat

Date	Mintage	F	VF	XF	Unc	BU
2001 Proof	—	Value: 6.00				

KM# 725 WON
28.0000 g., Brass, 40 mm. **Obv:** National arms, Country name **Rev:** Married couple in front of Pyongyang attractions with national flag and ferryboat

Date	Mintage	F	VF	XF	Unc	BU
2001 Proof	—	Value: 7.00				

KM# 726 WON
7.0000 g., Aluminum, 40 mm. **Obv:** National arms, Central Bank name **Rev:** Ferryboat from Koreans in Japan on the route from Niigata to Wonsan

Date	Mintage	F	VF	XF	Unc	BU
2001 Proof	—	Value: 6.00				

KM# 727 WON
28.0000 g., Brass, 40 mm. **Obv:** National arms, Central Bank name **Rev:** Ferryboat from Koreans in Japan on the route from Niigata to Wonsan

Date	Mintage	F	VF	XF	Unc	BU
2001 Proof	—	Value: 7.00				

KM# 728 WON
7.0000 g., Aluminum, 40 mm. **Obv:** National arms, Country name **Rev:** Arch of Triumph on Moranbong in Pyeongyang

Date	Mintage	F	VF	XF	Unc	BU
2001 Proof	—	Value: 6.00				

KM# 729 WON
28.0000 g., Brass, 40 mm. **Obv:** National arms, Central Bank name **Rev:** Arch of Triumph on Moranbong in Pyeongyang

Date	Mintage	F	VF	XF	Unc	BU
2001 Proof	—	Value: 7.00				

KM# 730 WON
7.0000 g., Aluminum, 40 mm. **Obv:** National arms, Central Bank name **Rev:** Chonji crater on the Paektusan

Date	Mintage	F	VF	XF	Unc	BU
2001 Proof	—	Value: 6.00				

KM# 731 WON
28.0000 g., Brass, 40 mm. **Obv:** National arms, Central Bank name **Rev:** Chonji crater on the Paektusan

Date	Mintage	F	VF	XF	Unc	BU
2001 Proof	—	Value: 7.00				

KM# 746 WON
28.0000 g., Brass, 40 mm. **Obv:** National arms **Rev:** Kim Jeongill in Pudong industrial area of Shanghai

Date	Mintage	F	VF	XF	Unc	BU
2001 Proof	—	—	—	—	—	—

KM# 718 WON
Aluminum, 40 mm. **Obv:** National arms, Central Bank name **Rev:** Ginsing plant

Date	Mintage	F	VF	XF	Unc	BU
2001 Proof	—	Value: 7.00				

KM# 749 WON
28.0000 g., Brass, 40 mm. **Obv:** National arms, Central Bank name **Rev:** Deng Xiaoping between peonies

Date	Mintage	F	VF	XF	Unc	BU
2001 Proof	—	Value: 7.00				

KM# 750 WON
17.0000 g., Copper-Nickel, 35 mm. **Obv:** National arms **Rev:** Orca before tourist boat

Date	Mintage	F	VF	XF	Unc	BU
2001 Proof	—	Value: 14.00				

KM# 751 WON
5.0000 g., Aluminum, 35 mm. **Obv:** National arms, Central Bank name **Rev:** Orca before tourist boat

Date	Mintage	F	VF	XF	Unc	BU
2001 Proof	—	Value: 6.00				

KM# 751a WON
16.0000 g., Brass, 35 mm. **Obv:** National arms, Central Bank name **Rev:** Orca before tourist boat

Date	Mintage	F	VF	XF	Unc	BU
2001 Proof	—	Value: 7.00				

KM# 752 WON
17.0000 g., Copper-Nickel, 35 mm. **Obv:** National arms, Country name **Rev:** Humpback whale

Date	Mintage	F	VF	XF	Unc	BU
2001 Proof	—	Value: 14.00				

KM# 753 WON
5.0000 g., Aluminum, 35 mm. **Obv:** National arms, Central Bank name **Rev:** Humpback whale

Date	Mintage	F	VF	XF	Unc	BU
2001 Proof	—	Value: 6.00				

KM# 753a WON
16.0000 g., Brass, 35 mm. **Obv:** National arms, Central Bank name **Rev:** Humpback whale

Date	Mintage	F	VF	XF	Unc	BU
2001 Proof	—	Value: 7.00				

KM# 754 WON
17.0000 g., Copper-Nickel, 35 mm. **Obv:** National arms, Country name **Rev:** Sperm whale

Date	Mintage	F	VF	XF	Unc	BU
2001 Proof	—	Value: 14.00				

KM# 755 WON
5.0000 g., Aluminum, 35 mm. **Obv:** National arms, Central Bank name **Rev:** Sperm whale

Date	Mintage	F	VF	XF	Unc	BU
2001 Proof	—	Value: 6.00				

KM# 755a WON
16.0000 g., Brass, 35 mm. **Obv:** National arms, Central Bank name **Rev:** Sperm whale

Date	Mintage	F	VF	XF	Unc	BU
2001 Proof	—	Value: 7.00				

KM# 756 WON
17.0000 g., Copper-Nickel, 35 mm. **Obv:** National arms, Country name **Rev:** Pilot whale

Date	Mintage	F	VF	XF	Unc	BU
2001 Proof	—	Value: 14.00				

KM# 757 WON
5.0000 g., Aluminum, 35 mm. **Obv:** National arms, Central Bank name **Rev:** Pilot whale

Date	Mintage	F	VF	XF	Unc	BU
2001 Proof	—	Value: 6.00				

KM# 757a WON
16.0000 g., Brass, 35 mm. **Obv:** National arms, Central Bank name **Rev:** Pilot whale

Date	Mintage	F	VF	XF	Unc	BU
2001 Proof	—	Value: 7.00				

KM# 758 WON
17.0000 g., Copper-Nickel, 35 mm. **Obv:** National arms, Country name **Rev:** Northern Right Whale

Date	Mintage	F	VF	XF	Unc	BU
2001 Proof	—	Value: 14.00				

KM# 759 WON
5.0000 g., Aluminum, 35 mm. **Obv:** National arms, Central Bank name **Rev:** Northern Right Whale

Date	Mintage	F	VF	XF	Unc	BU
2001 Proof	—	Value: 14.00				

KM# 759a WON
16.0000 g., Brass, 35 mm. **Obv:** National arms, Central Bank name **Rev:** Northern Right Whale

Date	Mintage	F	VF	XF	Unc	BU
2001 Proof	—	Value: 10.00				

KM# 760 WON
17.0000 g., Copper-Nickel, 35 mm. **Obv:** National arms, Country name **Rev:** Blue whale

Date	Mintage	F	VF	XF	Unc	BU
2001 Proof	—	Value: 14.00				

KM# 761 WON
5.0000 g., Aluminum, 35 mm. **Obv:** National arms, Central Bank name **Rev:** Blue Whale

Date	Mintage	F	VF	XF	Unc	BU
2001 Proof	—	Value: 6.00				

KM# 761a WON
16.0000 g., Brass, 35 mm. **Obv:** National arms, Central Bank name **Rev:** Blue whale

Date	Mintage	F	VF	XF	Unc	BU
2001 Proof	—	Value: 7.00				

KM# 762 WON
17.0000 g., Copper-Nickel, 35 mm. **Obv:** National arms, Country name **Rev:** Bowhead whale

Date	Mintage	F	VF	XF	Unc	BU
2001 Proof	—	Value: 14.00				

KM# 763 WON
5.0000 g., Aluminum, 35 mm. **Obv:** National arms, Central Bank name **Rev:** Bowhead whale

Date	Mintage	F	VF	XF	Unc	BU
2001 Proof	—	Value: 6.00				

KM# 763a WON
16.0000 g., Brass, 35 mm. **Obv:** National arms, Central Bank name **Rev:** Bowhead whale

Date	Mintage	F	VF	XF	Unc	BU
2001 Proof	—	Value: 7.00				

KM# 764 WON
17.0000 g., Copper-Nickel, 35 mm. **Obv:** National arms, Country name **Rev:** Killer whale off the coast

Date	Mintage	F	VF	XF	Unc	BU
2001 Proof	—	Value: 14.00				

KM# 765 WON
5.0000 g., Aluminum, 35 mm. **Obv:** Naitonal arms, Central Bank name **Rev:** Killer whale off the coast

Date	Mintage	F	VF	XF	Unc	BU
2001 Proof	—	Value: 6.00				

KM# 765a WON
16.0000 g., Brass, 35 mm. **Obv:** National arms, Central Bank name **Rev:** Killer whale off the coast

Date	Mintage	F	VF	XF	Unc	BU
2001 Proof	—	Value: 7.00				

KM# 766 WON
15.0000 g., 0.9990 Silver 0.4818 oz. ASW, 35 mm. **Obv:** National arms, Country name **Rev:** Northern Right Whale

Date	Mintage	F	VF	XF	Unc	BU
2001 Proof	—	Value: 35.00				

KM# 767 WON
5.0000 g., Aluminum, 35 mm. **Obv:** National arms, Country name **Rev:** Chinese dragon boat

Date	Mintage	F	VF	XF	Unc	BU
2001 Proof	—	Value: 6.00				

KM# 767a WON
Brass, 35 mm. **Obv:** National arms, Country name **Rev:** Chinese dragon boat

Date	Mintage	F	VF	XF	Unc	BU
2001 Proof	—	Value: 7.00				

KM# 769 WON
16.0000 g., Brass, 35 mm. **Obv:** East gate of Pyeongyang **Rev:** Krusenstern

Date	Mintage	F	VF	XF	Unc	BU
2001 Proof	—	Value: 7.00				

KM# 771 WON
6.0000 g., Aluminum, 38 mm. **Obv:** National arms, Central Bank name **Rev:** White-tailed sea eagle

Date	Mintage	F	VF	XF	Unc	BU
2001 Proof	—	Value: 8.00				

KM# 771a WON
25.0000 g., Brass, 38 mm. **Obv:** National arms, Central Bank name **Rev:** White-tailed sea eagle

Date	Mintage	F	VF	XF	Unc	BU
2001 Proof	—	—	—	—	—	—

KM# 772 WON
7.0000 g., Aluminum, 40 mm. **Obv:** National arms, Country name **Rev:** Taekwondo kicker

Date	Mintage	F	VF	XF	Unc	BU
2001 Proof	—	Value: 6.00				

KM# 772a WON
28.0000 g., Brass, 40 mm. **Obv:** National arms, Country name **Rev:** Taekwondo kicker

Date	Mintage	F	VF	XF	Unc	BU
2001 Proof	—	Value: 7.00				

KM# 773 WON
7.0000 g., Aluminum, 40 mm. **Obv:** National arms, Country name **Rev:** Taekwondo kicker

Date	Mintage	F	VF	XF	Unc	BU
2001 Proof	—	—	—	—	—	—

KM# 774 WON
Aluminum, 40 mm. **Obv:** National arms, Central Bank name **Rev:** Two taekwondo players

Date	Mintage	F	VF	XF	Unc	BU
2001 Proof	—	Value: 6.00				

KM# 470 WON
Brass, 35 mm. **Subject:** 2004 Olympics **Obv:** Arms **Rev:** Three Karate Sportsmen

Date	Mintage	F	VF	XF	Unc	BU
2002 Proof	—	Value: 6.50				

KM# 471 WON
Brass **Obv:** Arms **Rev:** Bridge

Date	Mintage	F	VF	XF	Unc	BU
2002 (91) Proof	—	Value: 7.50				

KM# 305 WON
7.0000 g., Aluminum, 40 mm. **Obv:** Arms **Rev:** Tomb of King Kong Min

Date	Mintage	F	VF	XF	Unc	BU
2002 Proof	—	Value: 7.50				

KM# 474 WON
Brass **Obv:** Arms **Rev:** Family about to hug

Date	Mintage	F	VF	XF	Unc	BU
2002 Proof	—	Value: 10.00				

KM# 475 WON
Brass, 40 mm. **Obv:** Arms **Rev:** Three people in group hug

Date	Mintage	F	VF	XF	Unc	BU
2002 Proof	—	Value: 10.00				

KM# 476 WON
Brass **Obv:** Arms **Rev:** Four dragons around map of North Korea

Date	Mintage	F	VF	XF	Unc	BU
2002 Proof	—	Value: 10.00				

KM# 305a WON
28.2000 g., Brass, 40.2 mm. **Obv:** State arms **Rev:** Tomb of King Kong Min **Edge:** Plain

Date	Mintage	F	VF	XF	Unc	BU
JU91-2002 Proof	—	Value: 20.00				

KM# 306 WON
7.1000 g., Aluminum, 40 mm. **Obv:** State arms **Rev:** Two horses within circle of Asian zodiac animals **Edge:** Plain **Note:** Prev. KM#398.

Date	Mintage	F	VF	XF	Unc	BU
2002 Proof	—	Value: 20.00				

KM# 306a WON
28.2000 g., Brass, 40.2 mm. **Obv:** State arms **Rev:** Two horses within circle of Asian zodiac animals **Edge:** Plain

Date	Mintage	F	VF	XF	Unc	BU
2002 Proof	—	Value: 20.00				

KM# 308 WON
6.9000 g., Aluminum, 40 mm. **Obv:** State arms **Rev:** Arirang dancer with cranes flying above **Edge:** Plain **Note:** Prev. KM#390.

Date	Mintage	F	VF	XF	Unc	BU
JU91-(2002) Proof	—	Value: 15.00				

KM# 308a WON
28.2000 g., Brass, 40.2 mm. **Subject:** Arirang **Obv:** State arms **Rev:** Performers and flying cranes **Edge:** Plain

Date	Mintage	F	VF	XF	Unc	BU
JU91-(2002) Proof	—	Value: 20.00				

KM# 313 WON
6.7000 g., Aluminum, 40 mm. **Obv:** State arms **Rev:** Arirang dancer **Edge:** Plain **Note:** Prev. KM#389.

Date	Mintage	F	VF	XF	Unc	BU
JU91-(2002) Proof	—	Value: 15.00				

KM# 313a WON
28.2000 g., Brass, 40.2 mm. **Subject:** Arirang **Obv:** State arms **Rev:** Dancer with upheld arms **Edge:** Plain

Date	Mintage	F	VF	XF	Unc	BU
JU91-(2002) Proof	—	Value: 20.00				

KM# 388 WON
7.1000 g., Aluminum, 40 mm. **Obv:** State arms **Rev:** Arirang dancer Silhouette **Edge:** Plain

Date	Mintage	F	VF	XF	Unc	BU
2002 Proof	—	Value: 15.00				

KM# 391 WON

7.1000 g., Aluminum, 40 mm. **Obv:** State arms **Rev:** Arirang ribbon dancer **Edge:** Plain

Date	Mintage	F	VF	XF	Unc	BU
JU91-2002 Proof	—	Value: 15.00				

KM# 392 WON

7.0000 g., Aluminum, 40 mm. **Obv:** State arms **Rev:** May Day Stadium **Edge:** Plain

Date	Mintage	F	VF	XF	Unc	BU
JU91-2002 Proof	—	Value: 12.00				

KM# 392a WON

28.5000 g., Brass, 40.1 mm. **Obv:** State arms **Rev:** May Day Stadium **Edge:** Plain

Date	Mintage	F	VF	XF	Unc	BU
JU91-2002 Proof	—	Value: 15.00				

KM# 393 WON

7.1000 g., Aluminum, 40 mm. **Obv:** State arms **Rev:** Woman floating above stadium **Edge:** Plain

Date	Mintage	F	VF	XF	Unc	BU
JU91-2002 Proof	—	Value: 15.00				

KM# 393a WON

28.2000 g., Brass, 40 mm. **Obv:** State arms **Rev:** Woman floating above stadium **Edge:** Plain

Date	Mintage	F	VF	XF	Unc	BU
JU91-2002 Proof	—	Value: 17.50				

KM# 394 WON

27.5000 g., Brass, 40 mm. **Obv:** State arms **Rev:** Ribbon dancer with Korea shaped ribbon **Edge:** Plain

Date	Mintage	F	VF	XF	Unc	BU
JU91-2002 Proof	—	Value: 17.50				

KM# 395 WON

27.5000 g., Brass, 40 mm. **Obv:** State arms **Rev:** Dancer in the shape of Korea **Edge:** Plain

Date	Mintage	F	VF	XF	Unc	BU
JU91-2002 Proof	—	Value: 17.50				

KM# 396 WON

7.0000 g., Aluminum, 40 mm. **Obv:** State arms **Rev:** Bust with hat facing divides dates(1337-1392) above building foundation **Edge:** Plain

Date	Mintage	F	VF	XF	Unc	BU
JU91-2002 Proof	—	Value: 15.00				

KM# 397 WON

7.0000 g., Aluminum, 40 mm. **Obv:** State arms **Rev:** Victorious athletes hugging **Edge:** Plain

Date	Mintage	F	VF	XF	Unc	BU
JU91-(2002) Proof	—	Value: 10.00				

KM# 397a WON

28.2400 g., Brass, 40 mm. **Obv:** State arms **Rev:** Victorious athletes hugging **Edge:** Plain

Date	Mintage	F	VF	XF	Unc	BU
JU91-(2002) Proof	—	Value: 12.50				

KM# 399 WON

4.8600 g., Aluminum, 35 mm. **Obv:** State arms **Rev:** Cantering horse **Edge:** Plain

Date	Mintage	F	VF	XF	Unc	BU
JU91-(2002) Proof	—	Value: 15.00				

KM# 399a WON

16.9300 g., Brass, 35 mm. **Obv:** State arms **Rev:** Cantering horse **Edge:** Plain

Date	Mintage	F	VF	XF	Unc	BU
JU91-(2002) Proof	—	Value: 15.00				

KM# 400 WON

5.1000 g., Aluminum, 35 mm. **Obv:** State arms **Rev:** Two wrestlers **Edge:** Plain

Date	Mintage	F	VF	XF	Unc	BU
JU91-(2002) Proof	—	Value: 12.50				

KM# 400a WON

16.5000 g., Brass, 35 mm. **Obv:** State arms **Rev:** Two wrestlers **Edge:** Plain

Date	Mintage	F	VF	XF	Unc	BU
JU91-(2002) Proof	—	Value: 15.00				

KM# 310a WON

28.2000 g., Brass, 40.2 mm. **Obv:** State arms **Rev:** Tomb of King Tongmyong **Edge:** Plain

Date	Mintage	F	VF	XF	Unc	BU
JU91-2002 Proof	—	Value: 15.00				

KM# 786 WON
5.0000 g., Aluminum, 35 mm. **Subject:** Year of the Horse **Obv:** National arms, Country name **Rev:** Horse head

Date	Mintage	F	VF	XF	Unc	BU
2002 Proof	—	Value: 6.00				

KM# 786a WON
16.0000 g., Brass, 35 mm. **Obv:** National arms, Country name **Rev:** Horse head

Date	Mintage	F	VF	XF	Unc	BU
2002 Proof	—	Value: 7.00				

KM# 794 WON
7.0000 g., Aluminum, 40 mm. **Obv:** National arms **Rev:** Reconstruction of the Mausoleums for King Dangun

Date	Mintage	F	VF	XF	Unc	BU
2002 Proof	—	Value: 6.00				

KM# 795 WON
28.0000 g., Brass, 40 mm. **Obv:** Naitonal arms, Country name **Rev:** Reconstruction of the mausoleum for King Dangun

Date	Mintage	F	VF	XF	Unc	BU
2002 Proof	—	Value: 7.00				

KM# 796 WON
7.0000 g., Aluminum, 40 mm. **Obv:** National arms **Rev:** Dongmyeong, 1st King of Goguryeo

Date	Mintage	F	VF	XF	Unc	BU
2002 Proof	—	Value: 6.00				

KM# 797 WON
28.0000 g., Brass, 40 mm. **Obv:** National arms **Rev:** Dongmyeong, 1st King of Goguryeo

Date	Mintage	F	VF	XF	Unc	BU
2002 Proof	—	Value: 7.00				

KM# 798 WON
7.0000 g., Aluminum, 40 mm. **Obv:** National arms, Central Bank name **Rev:** Wanggeon, 1st King of Goryeo dynasty

Date	Mintage	F	VF	XF	Unc	BU
2002 Proof	—	Value: 6.00				

KM# 799 WON
28.0000 g., Brass, 40 mm. **Obv:** National arms, Central Bank name **Rev:** Wanggeon, 1st King of Goryeo dynasty

Date	Mintage	F	VF	XF	Unc	BU
2002 Proof	—	Value: 7.00				

KM# 800 WON
7.0000 g., Aluminum, 40 mm. **Obv:** National arms **Rev:** Jeon Bongjun

Date	Mintage	F	VF	XF	Unc	BU
2002 Proof	—	Value: 6.00				

KM# 801 WON
28.0000 g., Brass, 40 mm. **Obv:** National arms, Central Bank name **Rev:** Jeon Bongjun

Date	Mintage	F	VF	XF	Unc	BU
2002 Proof	—	Value: 7.00				

KM# 821 WON
7.0000 g., Aluminum, 40 mm. **Obv:** National arms **Rev:** Prince Hodong and Princess Nakrang on horseback

Date	Mintage	F	VF	XF	Unc	BU
2002 Proof	—	Value: 6.00				

KM# 821a WON
28.0000 g., Brass, 40 mm. **Obv:** National arms **Rev:** Prince Hodong and Princess Nakrang on horseback

Date	Mintage	F	VF	XF	Unc	BU
2002 Proof	—	Value: 7.00				

KM# 822 WON
7.0000 g., Aluminum, 40 mm. **Obv:** National arms **Rev:** Half-length figures of Prince Hodong and Princess Nakrang

Date	Mintage	F	VF	XF	Unc	BU
2002 Proof	—	Value: 6.00				

KM# 822a WON
28.0000 g., Brass, 40 mm. **Obv:** National arms **Rev:** Half-length figures of Prince Hodong and Princess Nakrang

Date	Mintage	F	VF	XF	Unc	BU
2002 Proof	—	Value: 8.00				

KM# 836 WON
4.0000 g., Aluminum, 35 mm. **Obv:** National arms, Central Bank and Country name **Rev:** Ariang inscription

Date	Mintage	F	VF	XF	Unc	BU
2002 Proof	Est. 1,000	Value: 6.00				

KM# 837 WON
4.0000 g., Aluminum, 35 mm. **Obv:** National arms, Central Bank and Country name **Rev:** Three soldiers

Date	Mintage	F	VF	XF	Unc	BU
2002 Proof	—	Value: 7.00				

KM# 838 WON
4.0000 g., Aluminum, 35 mm. **Obv:** Naitonal arms, Central Bank and Country name **Rev:** Princess fairy paying flute

Date	Mintage	F	VF	XF	Unc	BU
2002 Proof	—	Value: 7.00				

KM# 839 WON
4.0000 g., Aluminum, 35 mm. **Obv:** National arms, Central Bank and Country name **Rev:** Bronze statue

Date	Mintage	F	VF	XF	Unc	BU
2002 Proof	—	Value: 6.00				

KM# 840 WON
4.0000 g., Aluminum, 35 mm. **Obv:** National arms, Central Bank and Country name **Rev:** Women in the worship of the Sun

Date	Mintage	F	VF	XF	Unc	BU
2002	—	Value: 6.00				

KM# 841 WON
4.0000 g., Aluminum, 35 mm. **Obv:** National arms, Central Bank and Country name **Rev:** Three principals of unification

Date	Mintage	F	VF	XF	Unc	BU
2002 Proof	—	Value: 6.00				

KM# 842 WON
4.0000 g., Aluminum, 35 mm. **Obv:** National arms, Central Bank and Country name **Rev:** Dancing children

Date	Mintage	F	VF	XF	Unc	BU
2002 Proof	—	Value: 6.00				

KM# 843 WON
31.1050 g., 0.9990 Gold 0.9990 oz. AGW, 35 mm. **Obv:** National arms, Central Bank and Country name **Rev:** Arirang inscription

Date	Mintage	F	VF	XF	Unc	BU
2002 Proof	—	Value: 1,800				

KM# 882 WON
Copper-Nickel, 38 mm. **Obv:** National arms, Central Bank name **Rev:** World cup tophy, player and Brandenburg gate

Date	Mintage	F	VF	XF	Unc	BU
2002 Proof	—	Value: 14.00				

KM# 882b WON
25.0000 g., Brass, 38 mm. **Obv:** National arms, Central Bank name **Rev:** World cup, player and Brandenberg Gate

Date	Mintage	F	VF	XF	Unc	BU
2002 Proof	—	Value: 7.00				

KM# 882a WON
6.0000 g., Aluminum, 38 mm. **Obv:** National arms, Central Bank name **Rev:** World cup, player and Brandenburg Gate

Date	Mintage	F	VF	XF	Unc	BU
2002 Proof	—	Value: 6.00				

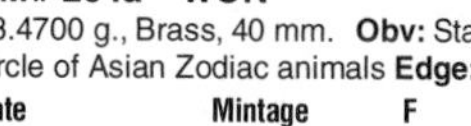

KM# 264a WON
28.4700 g., Brass, 40 mm. **Obv:** State arms **Rev:** Sheep within circle of Asian Zodiac animals **Edge:** Plain

Date	Mintage	F	VF	XF	Unc	BU
2003 Proof	—	Value: 22.00				

KM# 264 WON
7.0000 g., Aluminum, 40 mm. **Obv:** National arms **Rev:** Sheep in center of Asian Zodiac animals

Date	Mintage	F	VF	XF	Unc	BU
2003 Proof	—	Value: 6.00				

KM# 319 WON
9.6200 g., Aluminum, 40 mm. **Obv:** State arms **Rev:** Helmeted head with two antenna-like horns on the helmet **Edge:** Plain

Date	Mintage	F	VF	XF	Unc	BU
JU92-2003 Proof	—	Value: 15.00				

KM# 319a WON
28.2000 g., Brass, 40.2 mm. **Obv:** State arms **Rev:** Helmeted head with two antenna-like horns on helmet **Edge:** Plain

Date	Mintage	F	VF	XF	Unc	BU
JU92-2003 Proof	—	Value: 17.50				

KM# 323 WON
6.9400 g., Aluminum, 40 mm. **Obv:** State arms **Rev:** Turtle shaped armoured ship of 1592 **Edge:** Plain

Date	Mintage	F	VF	XF	Unc	BU
JU92-2003 Proof	—	Value: 15.00				

KM# 323a WON
28.1000 g., Brass, 40.2 mm. **Obv:** State arms **Rev:** Turtle-shaped armoured ship of 1592 **Edge:** Plain

Date	Mintage	F	VF	XF	Unc	BU
JU92-2003 Proof	—	Value: 20.00				

KM# 403 WON
7.0000 g., Aluminum, 40 mm. **Obv:** National arms, Central Bank name **Rev:** Kang Kam-cheo bust facing

Date	Mintage	F	VF	XF	Unc	BU
2003 Proof	—	Value: 7.00				

KM# 403a WON
22.1000 g., Brass, 40 mm. **Obv:** State arms **Rev:** Kang Kam-cheo bust facing **Edge:** Plain

Date	Mintage	F	VF	XF	Unc	BU
JU92-2003 Proof	—	Value: 17.50				

KM# 404 WON
9.6300 g., Aluminum, 40 mm. **Obv:** State arms **Rev:** Armored bust wearing a horned helmet **Edge:** Plain

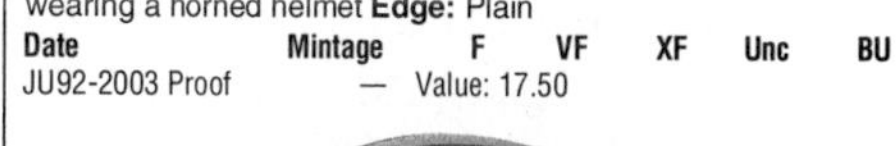

Date	Mintage	F	VF	XF	Unc	BU
JU92-2003 Proof	—	Value: 15.00				

KM# 404a WON
22.2500 g., Brass, 40 mm. **Obv:** State arms **Rev:** Armored bust wearing a horned helmet **Edge:** Plain

Date	Mintage	F	VF	XF	Unc	BU
JU92-2003 Proof	—	Value: 17.50				

KM# 405 WON
7.0000 g., Aluminum, 40 mm. **Obv:** State arms **Rev:** Ram within circle of Asian Zodiac animals **Edge:** Plain

Date	Mintage	F	VF	XF	Unc	BU
2003 Proof	—	Value: 15.00				

KM# 405a WON

28.4400 g., Brass, 40 mm. **Obv:** State arms **Rev:** Ram within circle of Asian Zodiac animals **Edge:** Plain

Date	Mintage	F	VF	XF	Unc	BU
2003 Proof	—	Value: 17.50				

KM# 406 WON

10.1500 g., Aluminum, 40 mm. **Obv:** State arms **Rev:** Children kicking a shuttlecock **Edge:** Plain

Date	Mintage	F	VF	XF	Unc	BU
JU92-2003 Proof	—	Value: 15.00				

KM# 406a WON

24.6300 g., Brass, 40 mm. **Obv:** State arms **Rev:** Children kicking a shuttlecock **Edge:** Plain

Date	Mintage	F	VF	XF	Unc	BU
JU92-2003 Proof	—	Value: 17.50				

KM# 407a WON

23.1000 g., Brass, 40 mm. **Obv:** State arms **Rev:** Children playing jacks **Edge:** Plain

Date	Mintage	F	VF	XF	Unc	BU
JU92-2003 Proof	—	Value: 17.50				

KM# 408a WON

24.5600 g., Brass, 40 mm. **Obv:** State arms **Rev:** Children spinning tops **Edge:** Plain

Date	Mintage	F	VF	XF	Unc	BU
JU92-2003 Proof	—	Value: 17.50				

KM# 410a WON

24.6400 g., Brass, 40 mm. **Obv:** State arms **Rev:** Large dome building **Edge:** Plain

Date	Mintage	F	VF	XF	Unc	BU
JU92-2003 Proof	—	Value: 17.50				

KM# 904 WON

31.1050 g., 0.9990 Silver 0.9990 oz. ASW, 40 mm. **Subject:** Athens olympics **Obv:** National arms, Central Bank name **Rev:** Wrestlers

Date	Mintage	F	VF	XF	Unc	BU
2003 Proof	Est. 1,000	Value: 45.00				

KM# 918 WON

25.0000 g., Brass, 38 mm. **Obv:** National arms, Central Bank name **Rev:** Steamship Princess Charlotte of Prussia

Date	Mintage	F	VF	XF	Unc	BU
2003 Proof	Est. 500	Value: 45.00				

KM# 919 WON

25.0000 g., Brass, 35 mm. **Obv:** National arms, Central Bank name **Rev:** Ship Queen Maria

Date	Mintage	F	VF	XF	Unc	BU
2003 Proof	—	Value: 45.00				

KM# 920 WON

25.0000 g., Brass, 38 mm. **Obv:** National arms **Rev:** Trans-atlantic sail steamship Helena Sloman

Date	Mintage	F	VF	XF	Unc	BU
2003 Proof	—	Value: 45.00				

KM# 924 WON

25.0000 g., Brass, 38 mm. **Obv:** National arms, Central Bank name **Rev:** Alder, 1835 steam locomotive

Date	Mintage	F	VF	XF	Unc	BU
2003 Proof	Est. 500	Value: 45.00				

KM# 925 WON

25.0000 g., Silver, 38 mm. **Obv:** National arms, Central Bank name **Rev:** Saxonia, 1838 steam locomotive

Date	Mintage	F	VF	XF	Unc	BU
2003 Proof	—	Value: 45.00				

KM# 926 WON

25.0000 g., Brass, 38 mm. **Obv:** National arms, Central Bank name **Rev:** Rheingold, 1928 Steam locomotive

Date	Mintage	F	VF	XF	Unc	BU
2003 Proof	—	Value: 45.00				

KM# 930 WON

25.0000 g., Brass, 38 mm. **Obv:** National arms, Central Bank name **Rev:** Gorch Fock 1 sailing ship

Date	Mintage	F	VF	XF	Unc	BU
2003 Proof	—	Value: 45.00				

KM# 265 WON

17.7000 g., Brass, 23.2 x 40.1 mm. **Obv:** State arms **Rev:** White-tufted-ear Marmoset **Edge:** Plain

Date	Mintage	F	VF	XF	Unc	BU
2004	—	Value: 27.50				

KM# 266 WON

17.7000 g., Brass, 23.2 x 40.1 mm. **Obv:** State arms **Rev:** Cercopjthecus Mitis monkey **Edge:** Plain

Date	Mintage	F	VF	XF	Unc	BU
2004 Proof	—	Value: 27.50				

KM# 267 WON

17.7000 g., Brass, 23.2 x 40.1 mm. **Obv:** State arms **Rev:** Two Saguinus Midas monkeys **Edge:** Plain

Date	Mintage	F	VF	XF	Unc	BU
2004 Proof	—	Value: 27.50				

KM# 330 WON

9.9200 g., Aluminum, 45 mm. **Obv:** State arms **Rev:** Mountain cabin **Edge:** Plain **Note:** Prev. KM#411.

Date	Mintage	F	VF	XF	Unc	BU
JU93-2004 Proof	—	Value: 15.00				

KM# 330a WON

26.4500 g., Brass, 45 mm. **Obv:** State arms **Rev:** Mountain cabin **Edge:** Plain

Date	Mintage	F	VF	XF	Unc	BU
JU93-2004 Proof	—	Value: 20.00				

KM# 331 WON

10.0000 g., Aluminum, 45 mm. **Obv:** State arms **Rev:** Kim Il Sung's birthplace, front view **Edge:** Plain **Note:** Prev. KM#412.

Date	Mintage	F	VF	XF	Unc	BU
JU93-2004 Proof	—	Value: 15.00				

KM# 331a WON

26.4500 g., Brass, 45 mm. **Obv:** State arms **Rev:** Sung's birth place, front view **Edge:** Plain

Date	Mintage	F	VF	XF	Unc	BU
JU93-2004 Proof	—	Value: 20.00				

KM# 332 WON

10.0000 g., Aluminum, 45 mm. **Obv:** State arms **Rev:** Kim Il Sung's birthplace, side view **Edge:** Plain **Note:** Prev. KM#413.

Date	Mintage	F	VF	XF	Unc	BU
JU93-2004 Proof	—	Value: 15.00				

KM# 332a WON

26.4500 g., Brass, 45 mm. **Obv:** State arms **Rev:** Sung's birthplace, side view **Edge:** Plain

Date	Mintage	F	VF	XF	Unc	BU
JU93-2004 Proof	—	Value: 20.00				

KM# 333 WON

10.0000 g., Aluminum, 45 mm. **Obv:** Naitonal arms, Central Bank name **Rev:** Kim Jeongsuk

Date	Mintage	F	VF	XF	Unc	BU
2004 Proof	—	Value: 8.00				

KM# 333a WON

26.4500 g., Brass, 45 mm. **Obv:** State arms **Rev:** Kim Jung Sook facing **Edge:** Plain

Date	Mintage	F	VF	XF	Unc	BU
JU93-2004 Proof	—	Value: 22.50				

KM# 334 WON

10.0000 g., Aluminum, 45 mm. **Obv:** National arms, Central Bank name **Rev:** Kim Jeong-il bust facing

Date	Mintage	F	VF	XF	Unc	BU
2004 Proof	—	Value: 8.00				

KM# 334a WON

26.4500 g., Brass, 45 mm. **Obv:** State arms **Rev:** Kim Jong-il bust facing **Edge:** Plain

Date	Mintage	F	VF	XF	Unc	BU
JU93-2004 Proof	—	Value: 22.50				

KM# 335 WON

10.0000 g., Aluminum, 45 mm. **Obv:** National arms, Central Bank name **Rev:** Kim Il-seong bust facing

Date	Mintage	F	VF	XF	Unc	BU
2004 Proof	—	Value: 8.00				

KM# 335a WON

26.4500 g., Brass, 45 mm. **Obv:** State arms **Rev:** Kim Il-seong bust facing **Edge:** Plain

Date	Mintage	F	VF	XF	Unc	BU
JU93-2004 Proof	—	Value: 22.50				

KM# 336 WON

10.1000 g., Aluminum, 45 mm. **Obv:** State arms **Rev:** Kim Il-sung flower, orchid **Edge:** Plain **Note:** Prev. KM#414.

Date	Mintage	F	VF	XF	Unc	BU
JU93-2004 Proof	—	Value: 15.00				

KM# 336a WON

26.4500 g., Brass, 45 mm. **Obv:** State arms **Rev:** Kim Il-sung flower, orchid **Edge:** Plain

Date	Mintage	F	VF	XF	Unc	BU
JU93-2004 Proof	—	Value: 20.00				

KM# 337 WON

10.1000 g., Aluminum, 45 mm. **Obv:** State arms **Rev:** Kim Jong-Il flower, peony **Edge:** Plain **Note:** Prev. KM#415.

Date	Mintage	F	VF	XF	Unc	BU
JU93-2004 Proof	—	Value: 15.00				

KM# 337a WON

26.4500 g., Brass, 45 mm. **Obv:** State arms **Rev:** Kim Jong-Il flower, peony **Edge:** Plain

Date	Mintage	F	VF	XF	Unc	BU
JU93-2004 Proof	—	Value: 20.00				

KM# 338 WON

9.9300 g., Aluminum, 45 mm. **Obv:** State arms **Rev:** Jin Dal Lae flower, Rose of Sharon **Edge:** Plain **Note:** Prev. KM#416.

Date	Mintage	F	VF	XF	Unc	BU
JU93-2004 Proof	—	Value: 15.00				

KM# 338a WON

26.4500 g., Brass, 45 mm. **Obv:** State arms **Rev:** Rose of Sharon flowers **Edge:** Plain

Date	Mintage	F	VF	XF	Unc	BU
JU93-2004 Proof	—	Value: 20.00				

KM# 410 WON

20.0000 g., Aluminum, 40 mm. **Obv:** National arms, Central bank name **Rev:** Sports hall in Pyeongyang

Date	Mintage	F	VF	XF	Unc	BU
2004 Proof	—	Value: 16.00				

KM# 939 WON

7.0000 g., Aluminum, 40 mm. **Obv:** National arms, Central Bank arms **Rev:** Monkey in the center of the Zodiac

Date	Mintage	F	VF	XF	Unc	BU
2004 Proof	—	Value: 10.00				

KM# 939a WON

28.0000 g., Brass, 35 mm. **Obv:** National arms, Central Bank name **Rev:** Monkey in center of Zodiac

Date	Mintage	F	VF	XF	Unc	BU
2004 Proof	—	Value: 30.00				

KM# 994 WON

25.0000 g., Brass, 38 mm. **Obv:** National arms, Central Bank name **Rev:** Statsraad Lehmkuhl sailing ship

Date	Mintage	F	VF	XF	Unc	BU
2004 Proof	—	Value: 45.00				

KM# 995 WON

25.0000 g., Brass, 38 mm. **Obv:** Naitonal arms, Central Bank name **Rev:** Henry Hudson's Halve Maen

Date	Mintage	F	VF	XF	Unc	BU
2004 Proof	—	Value: 45.00				

KM# 1016 WON

7.0000 g., Aluminum, 40 mm. **Obv:** National arms, Central Bank name **Rev:** Rooster within Zodiac circle

Date	Mintage	F	VF	XF	Unc	BU
2005 Proof	—	Value: 17.50				

KM# 1016a WON

28.0000 g., Brass, 40 mm. **Obv:** National arms, Central Bank name **Rev:** Rooster in Zodiac circle

Date	Mintage	F	VF	XF	Unc	BU
2005 Proof	—	Value: 20.00				

KM# 1019 WON

28.0000 g., 0.9990 Brass 0.8993 oz., 40 mm. **Obv:** National arms, Central Bank name **Rev:** Timber and tap in color

Date	Mintage	F	VF	XF	Unc	BU
2005 Proof	—	—	—	—	—	30.00

KM# 1020 WON

7.0000 g., Aluminum, 40 mm. **Obv:** National arms, Central Bank name **Rev:** Hae Mosu in the sky with the five dragons

Date	Mintage	F	VF	XF	Unc	BU
2005 Proof	—	Value: 17.50				

KM# 1020a WON

28.0000 g., Brass, 40 mm. **Obv:** National arms, Central Bank name **Rev:** Hae Mosu in flight with the five dragons

Date	Mintage	F	VF	XF	Unc	BU
2005 Proof	—	Value: 20.00				

KM# 1024 WON

7.0000 g., Aluminum, 40 mm. **Obv:** National arms, Central Bank name **Rev:** Admiral Yi Sunsin and turtle boat

Date	Mintage	F	VF	XF	Unc	BU
2005 Proof	—	Value: 10.00				

KM# 1024a WON

28.0000 g., Brass, 40 mm. **Obv:** National arms, Central Bank name **Rev:** Admiral Yi Sunsin and turtle boat

Date	Mintage	F	VF	XF	Unc	BU
2005 Proof	—	Value: 15.00				

KM# 1025 WON

7.0000 g., Aluminum, 40 mm. **Obv:** National arms, Central Bank name **Rev:** General Hong Beomdo

Date	Mintage	F	VF	XF	Unc	BU
2005 Proof	—	Value: 14.00				

KM# 1025a WON

28.0000 g., Brass, 40 mm. **Obv:** National arms, Central Bank name **Rev:** General Hong Beomdo

Date	Mintage	F	VF	XF	Unc	BU
2005 Proof	—	Value: 20.00				

KM# 1034 WON

25.0000 g., Brass, 40 mm. **Obv:** National arms, Central Bank name **Rev:** Rally in front of the monument ot the three principals of reunification

Date	Mintage	F	VF	XF	Unc	BU
2005 Proof	—	Value: 20.00				

KM# 1035 WON

28.0000 g., Brass, 40 mm. **Obv:** National arms, Central Bank name **Rev:** Demonstration on the crater lake

Date	Mintage	F	VF	XF	Unc	BU
2005 Proof	—	Value: 20.00				

KM# 1036 WON

28.0000 g., Brass, 40 mm. **Obv:** National arms, Central Bank name **Rev:** Three drum dance

Date	Mintage	F	VF	XF	Unc	BU
2005 Proof	—	Value: 20.00				

KM# 1040 WON

28.0000 g., Brass, 40 mm. **Obv:** National arms, Central Bank name **Rev:** Map of Korea, pair of peace doves, rainbow

Date	Mintage	F	VF	XF	Unc	BU
2005 Proof	—	Value: 10.00				

KM# 1043 WON

28.0000 g., Brass **Obv:** National arms, Central Bank name **Rev:** Tomb of the Unknown Soldier in Moscow, Russian legend **Edge Lettering:** 40

Date	Mintage	F	VF	XF	Unc	BU
2005 Proof	—	Value: 14.00				

KM# 1044 WON

28.0000 g., Brass, 40 mm. **Obv:** National arms, Central Bank name **Rev:** Memorial to mothers in St. Petersburg, Russian legend

Date	Mintage	F	VF	XF	Unc	BU
2005 Proof	—	Value: 14.00				

KM# 1074 WON

6.0000 g., Aluminum, 38 mm. **Subject:** Torino Winter Olympics, 2006 **Obv:** National arms, Central Bank name **Rev:** Bobsled

Date	Mintage	F	VF	XF	Unc	BU
2005 Proof	—	Value: 12.00				

KM# 1074a WON
25.0000 g., Brass, 38 mm. **Subject:** Torino Winter Olympics, 2006 **Obv:** National arms, Central Bank name **Rev:** Bobsled

Date	Mintage	F	VF	XF	Unc	BU
2005 Proof	—	Value: 30.00				

KM# 1088 WON
28.0000 g., Brass, 40 mm. **Obv:** National arms, Central Bank name **Rev:** Dog in color

Date	Mintage	F	VF	XF	Unc	BU
2006 Proof	—	Value: 30.00				

KM# 1089 WON
7.0000 g., Aluminum, 40 mm. **Obv:** National arms, Central Bank name **Rev:** Ryuhwa, Mother of King Dongmyeong

Date	Mintage	F	VF	XF	Unc	BU
2006 Proof	—	Value: 10.00				

KM# 1089a WON
28.0000 g., Brass, 40 mm. **Obv:** National arms, Central Bank name **Rev:** Ryuhwa, Mother of King Dongmyeong

Date	Mintage	F	VF	XF	Unc	BU
2006 Proof	—	Value: 14.00				

KM# 1109 WON
28.0000 g., Brass, 40 mm. **Obv:** National arms, Central Bank name **Rev:** Pig in color

Date	Mintage	F	VF	XF	Unc	BU
2007 Proof	—	Value: 30.00				

KM# 483 WON
Copper-Nickel **Subject:** Uzgn Monument **Obv:** Arms **Rev:** Map and building

Date	Mintage	F	VF	XF	Unc	BU
2008 Proof	—	Value: 15.00				

KM# 781 2 WON
7.0000 g., 0.9990 Silver 0.2248 oz. ASW, 30 mm. **Obv:** National arms, Central Bank name **Rev:** Panda in color

Date	Mintage	F	VF	XF	Unc	BU
2001 Proof	Est. 5,000	Value: 30.00				

KM# 892 2 WON
7.0000 g., 0.9990 Silver 0.2248 oz. ASW, 30 mm. **Obv:** National arms, Central Bank name **Rev:** Two panda in color

Date	Mintage	F	VF	XF	Unc	BU
2002 Proof	Est. 5,000	Value: 30.00				

KM# 249 2 WON
7.0000 g., 0.9990 Silver 0.2248 oz. ASW, 30 mm. **Obv:** State arms **Rev:** Two multicolor pandas **Edge:** Plain

Date	Mintage	F	VF	XF	Unc	BU
2003 Proof	—	Value: 30.00				

KM# 933 2 WON
7.0000 g., 0.9990 Silver 0.2248 oz. ASW, 30 mm. **Obv:** National arms, Central Bank name **Rev:** High speed train in Aichi

Date	Mintage	F	VF	XF	Unc	BU
2003 Proof	—	Value: 30.00				

KM# 934 2 WON
7.0000 g., 0.9990 Silver 0.2248 oz. ASW, 30 mm. **Obv:** National Arms, Central Bank name **Rev:** Two soccer players in color

Date	Mintage	F	VF	XF	Unc	BU
2003 Proof	—	Value: 30.00				

KM# 417 2 WON
24.6600 g., Brass, 31.6x45.75 mm. **Obv:** State arms **Rev:** Half length uniformed figure standing in land rover saluting below dates 1904-2004 **Edge:** Plain **Shape:** Rectangle

Date	Mintage	F	VF	XF	Unc	BU
ND(2004) Proof	—	Value: 25.00				

KM# 969 2 WON
25.0000 g., Brass, 40 mm. **Obv:** Dokdo, rocky islands, Central Bank name **Rev:** Map of the Island group

Date	Mintage	F	VF	XF	Unc	BU
2004 Proof	—	Value: 25.00				

KM# 970 2 WON
25.0000 g., Brass, 40 mm. **Obv:** Dokdo, rocky islands, Central Bank name **Rev:** Fisher Ahn Yongbok

Date	Mintage	F	VF	XF	Unc	BU
2004 Proof	—	Value: 25.00				

KM# 971 2 WON
25.0000 g., Brass, 40 mm. **Obv:** Dokdo, rocky islands, Central Bank name **Rev:** Seodo, western island

Date	Mintage	F	VF	XF	Unc	BU
2004 Proof	2,004	Value: 25.00				

KM# 972 2 WON
25.0000 g., Brass, 40 mm. **Obv:** Dokdo, rocky islands, Central Bank name **Rev:** Eastern island, Dongdo

Date	Mintage	F	VF	XF	Unc	BU
2004 Proof	—	Value: 25.00				

KM# 973 2 WON
25.0000 g., Brass, 40 mm. **Obv:** Dokdo, rocky islands, Central Bank name **Rev:** Three brother islands

Date	Mintage	F	VF	XF	Unc	BU
2004 Proof	—	Value: 25.00				

KM# 974 2 WON
25.0000 g., Brass, 40 mm. **Obv:** Dokdo, rocky islands, Central Bank name **Rev:** Chicken island

Date	Mintage	F	VF	XF	Unc	BU
2004 Proof	—	Value: 25.00				

KM# 975 2 WON
25.0000 g., Brass, 40 mm. **Obv:** Dokdo, rocky islands, Central Bank name **Rev:** Candle island

Date	Mintage	F	VF	XF	Unc	BU
2004 Proof	—	Value: 25.00				

KM# 976 2 WON
25.0000 g., Brass, 40 mm. **Obv:** Dokdo, rocky islands, Central Bank name **Rev:** Dome island

Date	Mintage	F	VF	XF	Unc	BU
2004 Proof	—	Value: 25.00				

KM# 1008 2 WON
7.0000 g., 0.9990 Silver 0.2248 oz. ASW, 30 mm. **Obv:** National arms, Central Bank name **Rev:** Three pandas in color

Date	Mintage	F	VF	XF	Unc	BU
2004 Proof	Est. 5,000	Value: 30.00				

KM# 1078 2 WON
7.0000 g., Silver, 30 mm. **Obv:** National arms, Central Bank name **Rev:** Panda in color

Date	Mintage	F	VF	XF	Unc	BU
2005 Proof	Est. 5,000	Value: 30.00				

KM# 1079 2 WON
7.0000 g., 0.9990 Silver partially gilt 0.2248 oz. ASW, 30 mm. **Subject:** Battle of Trafalgar, 200th Anniversary **Obv:** National arms, Central Bank name **Rev:** Horatio Nelson and the H.M.S. Victory, partially gilt

Date	Mintage	F	VF	XF	Unc	BU
2005 Proof	Est. 5,000	Value: 30.00				

KM# 1101 2 WON
7.0000 g., 0.9990 Silver 0.2248 oz. ASW, 30 mm. **Obv:** National arms, Central Bank name **Rev:** Two pandas in color

Date	Mintage	F	VF	XF	Unc	BU
2006 Proof	Est. 5,000	Value: 30.00				

KM# 1124 2 WON
7.0000 g., 0.9990 Silver 0.2248 oz. ASW, 30 mm. **Obv:** National arms, Central Bank name **Rev:** Panda in color

Date	Mintage	F	VF	XF	Unc	BU
2007 Proof	Est. 5,000	Value: 30.00				

KM# 339 3 WON
12.5500 g., Aluminum, 50.1 mm. **Obv:** Korean map **Rev:** Huh Jun Chosun doctor at left, books at right **Edge:** Plain

Date	Mintage	F	VF	XF	Unc	BU
JU93-2004 Proof	—	Value: 20.00				

KM# 339a 3 WON
40.5300 g., Brass, 50.2 mm. **Obv:** Korean map **Rev:** Huh Jun Chosun doctor at left, books at right **Edge:** Plain

Date	Mintage	F	VF	XF	Unc	BU
JU93-2004 Proof	—	Value: 25.00				

KM# 203 5 WON
15.0000 g., 0.9990 Silver 0.4818 oz. ASW, 35 mm. **Subject:** School Ships **Obv:** State arms **Rev:** SS Krusenstern **Edge:** Plain

Date	Mintage	F	VF	XF	Unc	BU
ND(2001) Proof	500	Value: 75.00				

KM# 205 5 WON
15.0000 g., 0.9990 Silver 0.4818 oz. ASW, 35 mm. **Subject:** Wildlife **Obv:** State arms **Rev:** Two standing Japanese Ibis birds **Edge:** Plain

Date	Mintage	F	VF	XF	Unc	BU
JU90-2001 Proof	100	Value: 200				

KM# 206 5 WON
15.0000 g., 0.9990 Silver 0.4818 oz. ASW, 35 mm. **Subject:** Wildlife **Obv:** State arms **Rev:** Two nesting Japanese Ibis birds **Edge:** Plain

Date	Mintage	F	VF	XF	Unc	BU
JU90-2001 Proof	3,000	Value: 50.00				

KM# 208 5 WON
15.0000 g., 0.9990 Silver 0.4818 oz. ASW, 35 mm. **Subject:** Wildlife **Obv:** State arms **Rev:** Two Korean Longtail Gorals **Edge:** Plain

Date	Mintage	F	VF	XF	Unc	BU
JU90-2001 Proof	3,000	Value: 50.00				

KM# 219 5 WON
14.9600 g., 0.9990 Silver 0.4805 oz. ASW, 35 mm. **Obv:** State arms **Rev:** Dragon ship **Edge:** Plain

Date	Mintage	F	VF	XF	Unc	BU
2001 Proof	5,000	Value: 35.00				

KM# 226 5 WON
20.0000 g., 0.9990 Silver 0.6423 oz. ASW, 33.8 mm. **Subject:** Olympics **Obv:** State arms **Rev:** Hurdler **Edge:** Reeded

Date	Mintage	F	VF	XF	Unc	BU
2001 Proof	—	Value: 35.00				

KM# 240 5 WON
14.9400 g., 0.9990 Silver 0.4798 oz. ASW, 35 mm. **Obv:** State arms **Rev:** "Orca" (Killer Whale) **Edge:** Plain

Date	Mintage	F	VF	XF	Unc	BU
2001 Proof	—	Value: 60.00				

KM# 241 5 WON
14.9200 g., 0.9990 Silver 0.4792 oz. ASW, 35 mm. **Obv:** State arms **Rev:** Orca and Eco-Tourists in boat **Edge:** Plain

Date	Mintage	F	VF	XF	Unc	BU
2001 Proof	—	Value: 60.00				

KM# 242 5 WON
14.8700 g., 0.9990 Silver 0.4776 oz. ASW, 35 mm. **Obv:** State arms **Rev:** "Pottwal" (Sperm Whale) **Edge:** Plain

Date	Mintage	F	VF	XF	Unc	BU
2001 Proof	—	Value: 60.00				

KM# 243 5 WON
14.9500 g., 0.9990 Silver 0.4802 oz. ASW, 35 mm. **Obv:** State arms **Rev:** "Buckelwal" (Humpback Whale) **Edge:** Plain

Date	Mintage	F	VF	XF	Unc	BU
2001 Proof	—	Value: 60.00				

KM# 244 5 WON
14.9300 g., 0.9990 Silver 0.4795 oz. ASW, 35 mm. **Obv:** State arms **Rev:** "Groenlandwal" (Greenland Right Whale) **Edge:** Plain

Date	Mintage	F	VF	XF	Unc	BU
2001 Proof	—	Value: 60.00				

KM# 245 5 WON
14.9500 g., 0.9990 Silver 0.4802 oz. ASW, 35 mm. **Obv:** State arms **Rev:** "Blauwal" (Blue Whale) **Edge:** Plain

Date	Mintage	F	VF	XF	Unc	BU
2001 Proof	—	Value: 60.00				

KM# 246 5 WON
14.9600 g., 0.9990 Silver 0.4805 oz. ASW, 35 mm. **Obv:** State arms **Rev:** "Grindwal" (Pilot Whale) **Edge:** Plain

Date	Mintage	F	VF	XF	Unc	BU
2001 Proof	—	Value: 60.00				

KM# 250 5 WON
14.9600 g., 0.9990 Silver 0.4805 oz. ASW, 35 mm. **Subject:** Return of Hong Kong to China **Obv:** State arms **Rev:** City view **Edge:** Plain

Date	Mintage	F	VF	XF	Unc	BU
2001 Proof	—	Value: 20.00				

KM# 694 5 WON
27.0000 g., 0.9990 Silver 0.8672 oz. ASW, 40 mm. **Obv:** National arms, Country name **Rev:** Kim Ilseong

Date	Mintage	F	VF	XF	Unc	BU
2001 Proof	—	Value: 70.00				

KM# 695 5 WON
Silver, 40 mm. **Obv:** National arms, Country name **Rev:** Kim Jeongil

Date	Mintage	F	VF	XF	Unc	BU
2001 Proof	—	Value: 75.00				

KM# 696 5 WON
27.0000 g., 0.9990 Silver 0.8672 oz. ASW, 40 mm. **Obv:** National arms, Central Bank name **Rev:** Kim Jeongsuk

Date	Mintage	F	VF	XF	Unc	BU
2001 Proof	—	Value: 75.00				

KM# 747 5 WON
27.0000 g., Silver, 40 mm. **Obv:** National arms, Country name **Rev:** Confucius

Date	Mintage	F	VF	XF	Unc	BU
2001 Proof	—	Value: 135				

KM# 770 5 WON
15.0000 g., 0.9990 Silver 0.4818 oz. ASW, 35 mm. **Obv:** National arms, Central Bank name **Rev:** Krusenstern

Date	Mintage	F	VF	XF	Unc	BU
2001 Proof	—	Value: 32.00				

KM# 782 5 WON
15.0000 g., Silver, 35 mm. **Obv:** National arms, Central Bank name **Rev:** Two pandas

Date	Mintage	F	VF	XF	Unc	BU
2001 Proof	Est. 5,000	Value: 32.00				

KM# 783 5 WON
15.0000 g., 0.9990 Silver 0.4818 oz. ASW, 35 mm. **Obv:** National arms, Central Bank name **Rev:** Titanic

Date	Mintage	F	VF	XF	Unc	BU
2001 Proof	Est. 5,000	Value: 32.00				

KM# 784 5 WON
Silver **Obv:** National arms, Central Bank name **Rev:** Five masted ship, Royal Clipper

Date	Mintage	F	VF	XF	Unc	BU
2001 Proof	—	Value: 32.00				

KM# 785 5 WON
15.0000 g., 0.9990 Silver 0.4818 oz. ASW, 35 mm. **Subject:** 2002 Soccer - Korea and Japan **Obv:** National arms, Central Bank name **Rev:** Player and stadium

Date	Mintage	F	VF	XF	Unc	BU
2001 Proof	Est. 5,000	Value: 32.00				

KM# 251 5 WON
14.9000 g., 0.9990 Silver 0.4785 oz. ASW, 35 mm. **Subject:** Year of the Horse **Obv:** State arms **Rev:** Cantering horse **Edge:** Plain

Date	Mintage	F	VF	XF	Unc	BU
2002 Proof	—	Value: 30.00				

KM# 252 5 WON
14.9200 g., 0.9990 Silver 0.4792 oz. ASW, 35 mm. **Subject:** Korean Games **Obv:** State arms **Rev:** Two wrestlers **Edge:** Plain

Date	Mintage	F	VF	XF	Unc	BU
JU91-2002 Proof	—	Value: 20.00				

KM# 303 5 WON
15.0000 g., 0.9990 Silver 0.4818 oz. ASW, 35 mm. **Obv:** State arms **Rev:** Janggo dancer **Edge:** Segmented reeding

Date	Mintage	F	VF	XF	Unc	BU
JU91-2002 Proof	—	Value: 30.00				

KM# 304 5 WON
15.0000 g., 0.9990 Silver 0.4818 oz. ASW, 35 mm. **Obv:** State arms **Rev:** Armored Knight **Edge:** Segmented reeding

Date	Mintage	F	VF	XF	Unc	BU
JU91-2002 Proof	—	Value: 30.00				

KM# 790 5 WON
15.0000 g., 0.9990 Silver 0.4818 oz. ASW **Obv:** National arms, Country name **Rev:** Horse head **Shape:** 35

Date	Mintage	F	VF	XF	Unc	BU
2002 Proof	—	Value: 35.00				

KM# 877 5 WON
15.0000 g., 0.9990 Silver 0.4818 oz. ASW, 35 mm. **Obv:** National arms, Central Bank name **Rev:** Map of Korea

Date	Mintage	F	VF	XF	Unc	BU
2002 Proof	—	Value: 45.00				

KM# 878 5 WON
15.0000 g., 0.9990 Silver 0.4818 oz. ASW, 35 mm. **Obv:** National arms, Central Bank name **Rev:** Traditional Korean wedding

Date	Mintage	F	VF	XF	Unc	BU
2002 Proof	—	Value: 35.00				

KM# 879 5 WON
15.0000 g., 0.9990 Silver 0.4818 oz. ASW, 35 mm. **Obv:** National arms, Central Bank name **Rev:** Trasitional wedding procession

Date	Mintage	F	VF	XF	Unc	BU
2002 Proof	—	Value: 35.00				

KM# 893 5 WON
20.0000 g., 0.9990 Silver 0.6423 oz. ASW, 38 mm. **Obv:** Naitonal arms, Central Bank name **Rev:** Asian wild ox

Date	Mintage	F	VF	XF	Unc	BU
2002 Proof	—	Value: 60.00				

KM# 894 5 WON
20.0000 g., 0.9990 Silver 0.6423 oz. ASW, 38 mm. **Obv:** National arms, Central Bank name **Rev:** Two scocer players with flag

Date	Mintage	F	VF	XF	Unc	BU
2002 Proof	Est. 5,000	Value: 35.00				

KM# 895 5 WON
20.0000 g., 0.9990 Silver 0.6423 oz. ASW, 38 mm. **Obv:** National arms, Central Bank name **Rev:** Celebrating player in Yokohama stadium

Date	Mintage	F	VF	XF	Unc	BU
2002 Proof	—	Value: 60.00				

KM# 327 5 WON
20.0000 g., 0.9990 Silver 0.6423 oz. ASW, 35 mm. **Obv:** State arms **Rev:** "Turtle Boat " of 1592 **Edge:** Segmented reeding

Date	Mintage	F	VF	XF	Unc	BU
JU92-2003 Proof	—	Value: 35.00				

KM# 328 5 WON
20.0000 g., 0.9990 Silver 0.6423 oz. ASW, 35 mm. **Obv:** State arms **Rev:** Olympic fencers **Edge:** Segmented reeding

Date	Mintage	F	VF	XF	Unc	BU
JU92-2003 Proof	—	Value: 35.00				

KM# 329 5 WON
20.0000 g., 0.9990 Silver 0.6423 oz. ASW, 35 mm. **Obv:** State arms **Rev:** Three wild horses **Edge:** Segmented reeding

Date	Mintage	F	VF	XF	Unc	BU
JU92-2003 Proof	—	Value: 35.00				

KM# 900 5 WON
20.0000 g., 0.9990 Silver 0.6423 oz. ASW, 35 mm. **Obv:** National arms, Central Bank name **Rev:** Swan

Date	Mintage	F	VF	XF	Unc	BU
2003 Proof	Est. 1,000	Value: 45.00				

KM# 901 5 WON
20.0000 g., 0.9990 Silver 0.6423 oz. ASW, 35 mm. **Obv:** National arms, Central Bank name **Rev:** Pelican

Date	Mintage	F	VF	XF	Unc	BU
2003 Proof	—	Value: 45.00				

KM# 902 5 WON
20.0000 g., 0.9990 Silver 0.6423 oz. ASW, 35 mm. **Obv:** National arms, **Rev:** Stone eagle

Date	Mintage	F	VF	XF	Unc	BU
2003 Proof	—	Value: 45.00				

KM# 903 5 WON
31.1050 g., 0.9990 Silver 0.9990 oz. ASW, 40 mm. **Obv:** National arms, Central Bank name **Rev:** Chinese pangolin and young

Date	Mintage	F	VF	XF	Unc	BU
2003 Proof	Est. 1,000	Value: 60.00				

KM# 935 5 WON
15.0000 g., 0.9990 Silver 0.4818 oz. ASW, 30 mm. **Subject:** Franz Schubert, 175th anniversary of death **Obv:** National arms, Central Bank name **Rev:** Franz Schubert

Date	Mintage	F	VF	XF	Unc	BU
2003 Proof	—	Value: 45.00				

KM# 936 5 WON
20.0000 g., 0.9990 Silver 0.6423 oz. ASW, 38 mm. **Obv:** National arms, Central Bank name **Rev:** Horatio Nelson and H.M.S. Victory

Date	Mintage	F	VF	XF	Unc	BU
2003 Proof	—	Value: 45.00				

KM# 937 5 WON
20.0000 g., 0.9990 Silver 0.6423 oz. ASW, 38 mm. **Obv:** National arms, Central Bank name **Rev:** Leopard

Date	Mintage	F	VF	XF	Unc	BU
2003 Proof	Est. 5,000	Value: 40.00				

KM# 1009 5 WON
15.0000 g., 0.9990 Silver 0.4818 oz. ASW, 35 mm. **Obv:** National arms, Central Bank name **Rev:** Red deer in forest glade in color

Date	Mintage	F	VF	XF	Unc	BU
2004 Proof	—	Value: 60.00				

KM# 1010 5 WON
15.0000 g., 0.9990 Silver 0.4818 oz. ASW, 35 mm. **Obv:** National arms, Central Bank name **Rev:** Kingfisher in color

Date	Mintage	F	VF	XF	Unc	BU
2004 Proof	—	Value: 60.00				

KM# 1011 5 WON
31.1050 g., 0.9990 Silver 0.9990 oz. ASW, 35 mm. **Obv:** National arms, Central Bank name **Rev:** Bewick's swan in flight in color

Date	Mintage	F	VF	XF	Unc	BU
2004 Proof	—	Value: 60.00				

KM# 1012 5 WON
15.0000 g., 0.9990 Silver 0.4818 oz. ASW, 35 mm. **Obv:** National arms, Central Bank name **Rev:** Two blue whales and iceberg in color

Date	Mintage	F	VF	XF	Unc	BU
2004 Proof	—	Value: 60.00				

KM# 1013 5 WON
15.0000 g., 0.9990 Silver 0.4818 oz. ASW, 35 mm. **Obv:** National arms, Central Bank name **Rev:** Lion in color

Date	Mintage	F	VF	XF	Unc	BU
2004 Proof	—	Value: 60.00				

KM# 1014 5 WON
20.0000 g., 0.9990 Silver 0.6423 oz. ASW, 38 mm. **Obv:** National arms, Central Bank name **Rev:** Leopard

Date	Mintage	F	VF	XF	Unc	BU
2004 Proof	—	Value: 45.00				

KM# 1015 5 WON
1.1500 g., Aluminum, 21 mm. **Obv:** National arms, Central Bank name **Rev:** Large numeral 5

Date	Mintage	F	VF	XF	Unc	BU
2005	—	—	—	—	3.00	5.00

KM# 1080 5 WON
15.0000 g., 0.9990 Silver 0.4818 oz. ASW, 35 mm. **Subject:** Tschaikowsky, 165 Birthday **Obv:** National arms, Central Bank name **Rev:** Peter Tschaikowsky

Date	Mintage	F	VF	XF	Unc	BU
2005 Proof	—	Value: 45.00				

KM# 1081 5 WON
15.0000 g., 0.9990 Silver 0.4818 oz. ASW, 35 mm. **Obv:** National arms, Central Bank name **Rev:** Squirel in color

Date	Mintage	F	VF	XF	Unc	BU
2005 Proof	—	Value: 30.00				

KM# 1082 5 WON
15.0000 g., 0.9990 Silver 0.4818 oz. ASW, 35 mm. **Obv:** National arms, Central Bank name **Rev:** Firefox in color

Date	Mintage	F	VF	XF	Unc	BU
2005 Proof	—	Value: 30.00				

KM# 1083 5 WON
20.0000 g., 0.9990 Silver 0.6423 oz. ASW, 38 mm. **Obv:** National arms, Central Bank name **Rev:** Saiga antelope

Date	Mintage	F	VF	XF	Unc	BU
2005 Proof	—	Value: 45.00				

KM# 1084 5 WON
20.0000 g., 0.9990 Silver 0.6423 oz. ASW, 38 mm. **Obv:** National arms, Central Bank name **Rev:** Malayian Tapir and young

Date	Mintage	F	VF	XF	Unc	BU
2005 Proof	Est. 5,000	Value: 45.00				

KM# 1085 5 WON
20.0000 g., 0.9990 Silver 0.6423 oz. ASW, 38 mm. **Obv:** National arms, Central Bank name **Rev:** Sedov sailing ship

Date	Mintage	F	VF	XF	Unc	BU
2005 Proof	Est. 5,000	Value: 45.00				

KM# 1102 5 WON
15.0000 g., 0.9990 Silver 0.4818 oz. ASW, 35 mm. **Obv:** National arms, Central Bank name **Rev:** Orca whale in color

Date	Mintage	F	VF	XF	Unc	BU
2006 Proof	—	Value: 60.00				

KM# 1103 5 WON
15.0000 g., 0.9990 Silver 0.4818 oz. ASW, 35 mm. **Obv:** National arms, Central Bank name **Rev:** javanese flying frog in color

Date	Mintage	F	VF	XF	Unc	BU
2006 Proof	—	Value: 60.00				

KM# 1104 5 WON
15.0000 g., 0.9990 Silver 0.4818 oz. ASW, 35 mm. **Obv:** National arms, Central Bank name **Rev:** Hymalayian Pheasant in color

Date	Mintage	F	VF	XF	Unc	BU
2006 Proof	—	Value: 60.00				

KM# 1105 5 WON
15.0000 g., 0.9990 Silver 0.4818 oz. ASW, 35 mm. **Obv:** National arms, Central Bank name **Rev:** Karl Marx bust left

Date	Mintage	F	VF	XF	Unc	BU
2006 Proof	—	Value: 45.00				

KM# 1106 5 WON
20.0000 g., 0.9990 Silver 0.6423 oz. ASW, 38 mm. **Obv:** National arms, Central Bank name **Rev:** Mir sailing ship

Date	Mintage	F	VF	XF	Unc	BU
2006 Proof	Est. 5,000	Value: 45.00				

KM# 1107 5 WON

20.0000 g., 0.9990 Silver 0.6423 oz. ASW, 38 mm. **Subject:** Bejing Summer Olympics, 2008 **Obv:** National arms, Central Bank name **Rev:** Handball player making shot

Date	Mintage	F	VF	XF	Unc	BU
2006 Proof	Est. 5,000	Value: 35.00				

KM# 1108 5 WON

20.0000 g., 0.9990 Silver 0.6423 oz. ASW, 38 mm. **Subject:** Bejing Summer Olympics, 2008 **Obv:** National arms, Central Bank name **Rev:** Archer before target

Date	Mintage	F	VF	XF	Unc	BU
2006 Proof	Est. 5,000	Value: 35.00				

KM# 1125 5 WON

15.0000 g., 0.9990 Silver 0.4818 oz. ASW, 35 mm. **Obv:** National arms, Central Bank name **Rev:** Japanese snow money in color

Date	Mintage	F	VF	XF	Unc	BU
2007 Proof	—	Value: 60.00				

KM# 1126 5 WON

20.0000 g., 0.9990 Silver 0.6423 oz. ASW, 38 mm. **Obv:** National arms, Central Bank name **Rev:** Siberian musk deer

Date	Mintage	F	VF	XF	Unc	BU
2007 Proof	Est. 5,000	Value: 60.00				

KM# 1127 5 WON

20.0000 g., 0.9990 Silver 0.6423 oz. ASW, 38 mm. **Obv:** National arms, Central Bank name **Rev:** Ming treasure ship

Date	Mintage	F	VF	XF	Unc	BU
2007 Proof	Est. 5,000	Value: 45.00				

KM# 220 7 WON

20.0000 g., 0.9990 Silver 0.6423 oz. ASW, 38 mm. **Subject:** 2002 Olympics **Obv:** State arms **Rev:** Two speed skaters **Edge:** Plain

Date	Mintage	F	VF	XF	Unc	BU
2001 Proof	10,000	Value: 40.00				

KM# 221 7 WON

20.0000 g., 0.9990 Silver 0.6423 oz. ASW, 38 mm. **Subject:** Endangered Wildlife **Obv:** State arms **Rev:** White-tailed sea Eagle **Edge:** Plain

Date	Mintage	F	VF	XF	Unc	BU
2001 Proof	10,000	Value: 35.00				

KM# 881 7 WON

20.0000 g., 0.9990 Silver 0.6423 oz. ASW **Obv:** Naitonal arms, Central Bank name **Rev:** Taekwondo **Shape:** 38

Date	Mintage	F	VF	XF	Unc	BU
2002 Proof	—	Value: 35.00				

KM# 883 7 WON

20.0000 g., 0.9990 Silver 0.6423 oz. ASW, 38 mm. **Obv:** National arms, Central Bank name **Rev:** World Cup, player and Brandenburg Gate

Date	Mintage	F	VF	XF	Unc	BU
2002 Proof	—	Value: 30.00				

KM# 921 7 WON

20.0000 g., 0.9990 Silver 0.6423 oz. ASW, 38 mm. **Obv:** National arms, Central Bank name **Rev:** Steamer Princess Charlotte of Prussia

Date	Mintage	F	VF	XF	Unc	BU
2003 Proof	Est. 500	Value: 70.00				

KM# 922 7 WON

20.0000 g., 0.9990 Silver 0.6423 oz. ASW, 35 mm. **Obv:** National arms, Central Bank name **Rev:** Steamship Queen Maria

Date	Mintage	F	VF	XF	Unc	BU
2003 Proof	—	Value: 75.00				

KM# 923 7 WON

20.0000 g., 0.9990 Silver 0.6423 oz. ASW, 38 mm. **Obv:** National arms, Central Bank name **Rev:** Transatlantic sail steamship Helena Sloman

Date	Mintage	F	VF	XF	Unc	BU
2003 Proof	Est. 500	Value: 75.00				

KM# 927 7 WON

20.0000 g., 0.9990 Silver 0.6423 oz. ASW, 38 mm. **Obv:** National arms, Central Bank name **Rev:** Adler, 1835 steam locomotive

Date	Mintage	F	VF	XF	Unc	BU
2003 Proof	—	Value: 60.00				

KM# 928 7 WON

20.0000 g., 0.9990 Silver 0.6423 oz. ASW, 38 mm. **Obv:** National arms, Central Bank name **Rev:** Saxonia, 1838 steam locomotive

Date	Mintage	F	VF	XF	Unc	BU
2003 Proof	—	Value: 60.00				

KM# 929 7 WON

20.0000 g., 0.9990 Silver 0.6423 oz. ASW, 38 mm. **Obv:** National arms, Central Bank name **Rev:** Rheingold, 1928 steam locomotive

Date	Mintage	F	VF	XF	Unc	BU
2003 Proof	—	Value: 60.00				

KM# 931 7 WON

20.0000 g., 0.9990 Silver 0.6423 oz. ASW, 38 mm. **Obv:** National arms, Central Bank name **Rev:** Gorch Fock I, sailing ship

Date	Mintage	F	VF	XF	Unc	BU
2003 Proof	—	Value: 60.00				

KM# 932 7 WON

20.0000 g., 0.9990 Silver 0.6423 oz. ASW, 38 mm. **Obv:** National arms, Central Bank name **Rev:** Skier

Date	Mintage	F	VF	XF	Unc	BU
2003 Proof	Est. 5,000	Value: 40.00				

KM# 477 7 WON

20.0000 g., Bi-Metallic Silver center in Brass ring. **Obv:** Arms **Rev:** Stadium along river

Date	Mintage	F	VF	XF	Unc	BU
2004 Proof	—	Value: 55.00				

KM# 945 7 WON

20.0000 g., Silver, 23x40 mm. **Obv:** East gate of Pyeongyang **Rev:** Mormoset **Shape:** Rectangle

Date	Mintage	F	VF	XF	Unc	BU
2004 Proof	—	Value: 35.00				

KM# 946 7 WON

20.0000 g., 0.9990 Silver 0.6423 oz. ASW, 23x40 mm. **Obv:** East gate of Pyeongyang **Rev:** Blue monkey **Shape:** Rectangle

Date	Mintage	F	VF	XF	Unc	BU
2004 Proof	—	Value: 35.00				

KM# 947 7 WON

20.0000 g., Silver, 23x40 mm. **Obv:** East gate of Pyeongyang **Rev:** Monkies **Shape:** Rectangle

Date	Mintage	F	VF	XF	Unc	BU
2004 Proof	—	Value: 35.00				

KM# 996 7 WON

20.0000 g., 0.9990 Silver 0.6423 oz. ASW, 38 mm. **Obv:** National arms, Central Bank name **Rev:** Statsraad Lehmkuhl sailing ship

Date	Mintage	F	VF	XF	Unc	BU
2004 Proof	Est. 3,000	Value: 60.00				

KM# 997 7 WON

20.0000 g., 0.9990 Silver 0.6423 oz. ASW, 38 mm. **Obv:** National arms, Central Bank name **Rev:** Henry Hudson's Halve Maen

Date	Mintage	F	VF	XF	Unc	BU
2004 Proof	Est. 3,000	Value: 60.00				

KM# 998 7 WON

20.0000 g., 0.9990 Silver 0.6423 oz. ASW, 38 mm. **Subject:** 1980 Lake PLacid Olympics **Obv:** National arms, Central Bank name **Rev:** Speed skater

Date	Mintage	F	VF	XF	Unc	BU
2004 Proof	Est. 5,000	Value: 35.00				

KM# 1071 7 WON

20.0000 g., 0.9990 Silver 0.6423 oz. ASW, 38 mm. **Subject:** Squaw Valley 1960 Winter Olympics **Obv:** National arms, Central Bank name **Rev:** Ice Dancing

Date	Mintage	F	VF	XF	Unc	BU
2005 Proof	Est. 5,000	Value: 45.00				

KM# 1072 7 WON

20.0000 g., 0.9990 Silver 0.6423 oz. ASW, 38 mm. **Subject:** Calgary Winter Olympics, 1988 **Obv:** National arms, Central Bank name

Date	Mintage	F	VF	XF	Unc	BU
2005 Proof	Est. 5,000	Value: 45.00				

KM# 1073 7 WON

20.0000 g., 0.9990 Silver 0.6423 oz. ASW, 38 mm. **Subject:** Nagano Winter Olympics, 1998 **Obv:** National arms, Central Bank name **Rev:** Snowboarder

Date	Mintage	F	VF	XF	Unc	BU
2005 Proof	—	Value: 45.00				

KM# 1075 7 WON

20.0000 g., 0.9990 Silver 0.6423 oz. ASW, 38 mm. **Subject:** Torino Winter Olympics, 2006 **Obv:** National arms, Central Bank name **Rev:** bobsled

Date	Mintage	F	VF	XF	Unc	BU
2005 Proof	—	Value: 45.00				

KM# 1076 7 WON

20.0000 g., 0.9990 Silver 0.6423 oz. ASW, 38 mm. **Obv:** National arms, Central Bank name **Rev:** Black faced spoonbill

Date	Mintage	F	VF	XF	Unc	BU
2005 Proof	Est. 5,000	Value: 60.00				

KM# 1077 7 WON

20.0000 g., 0.9990 Silver 0.6423 oz. ASW, 38 mm. **Obv:** National arms, Central Bank name **Rev:** Flying dog

Date	Mintage	F	VF	XF	Unc	BU
2005 Proof	Est. 5,000	Value: 60.00				

KM# 292 10 WON

31.0000 g., 0.9990 Silver 0.9956 oz. ASW, 40.2 mm. **Obv:** State arms **Rev:** Kim Il-Seung bust facing, 1912-1994 flanking, sprigs below **Edge:** Plain

Date	Mintage	F	VF	XF	Unc	BU
JU90-2001 Proof	—	Value: 45.00				

KM# 295 10 WON

31.0000 g., 0.9990 Silver 0.9956 oz. ASW, 40.2 mm. **Obv:** State arms **Rev:** Mountain cabin **Edge:** Plain

Date	Mintage	F	VF	XF	Unc	BU
JU90-2001 Proof	—	Value: 45.00				

KM# 296 10 WON

31.0000 g., 0.9990 Silver 0.9956 oz. ASW, 40.2 mm. **Obv:** State arms **Rev:** "KUMDANG - 2 INJECTION" in center of leaves **Edge:** Plain

Date	Mintage	F	VF	XF	Unc	BU
2001 Proof	—	Value: 50.00				

KM# 297 10 WON

31.0000 g., 0.9990 Silver 0.9956 oz. ASW, 40.2 mm. **Obv:** State arms **Rev:** Train scene and a couple below a jet liner **Rev. Legend:** ...1945 - 2001... **Edge:** Plain

Date	Mintage	F	VF	XF	Unc	BU
ND(2001) Proof	—	Value: 45.00				

KM# 298 10 WON

31.0000 g., 0.9990 Silver 0.9956 oz. ASW, 40.2 mm. **Obv:** State arms **Rev:** Cruise ship below stylized head left profile **Edge:** Plain

Date	Mintage	F	VF	XF	Unc	BU
JU90-2001 Proof	—	Value: 50.00				

KM# 299 10 WON
31.0000 g., 0.9990 Silver 0.9956 oz. ASW, 40.2 mm. **Obv:** State arms **Rev:** Old fortress **Edge:** Plain

Date	Mintage	F	VF	XF	Unc	BU
JU90-2001 Proof	—	Value: 47.50				

KM# 300 10 WON
31.0000 g., 0.9990 Silver 0.9956 oz. ASW, 40.2 mm. **Obv:** State arms **Rev:** Landmarks, flag and tourist couple above cruise ship **Edge:** Plain

Date	Mintage	F	VF	XF	Unc	BU
JU90-2001 Proof	—	Value: 45.00				

KM# 301 10 WON
31.0000 g., 0.9990 Silver 0.9956 oz. ASW, 40.2 mm. **Obv:** State arms **Rev:** 2 facing half length men shaking hands **Edge:** Plain

Date	Mintage	F	VF	XF	Unc	BU
JU90-2001 Proof	—	Value: 45.00				

KM# 302 10 WON
31.0000 g., 0.9990 Silver 0.9956 oz. ASW, 40.1 mm. **Obv:** State arms **Rev:** Great East Gate **Edge:** Plain

Date	Mintage	F	VF	XF	Unc	BU
JU90-2001 Proof	—	Value: 47.50				

KM# 357 10 WON
31.0000 g., 0.9990 Silver 0.9956 oz. ASW, 40.2 mm. **Obv:** State arms **Rev:** Antique ceramic items **Edge:** Plain

Date	Mintage	F	VF	XF	Unc	BU
2001 Proof	—	Value: 45.00				

KM# 386 10 WON
30.7600 g., 0.9990 Silver 0.9879 oz. ASW, 40.1 mm. **Obv:** State arms **Rev:** Kim Jung Sook facing flanked by dates (1917-1949) above flower sprigs **Edge:** Plain

Date	Mintage	F	VF	XF	Unc	BU
JU90-2001 Proof	—	Value: 47.50				

KM# 387 10 WON
30.7600 g., 0.9990 Silver 0.9879 oz. ASW, 40.1 mm. **Obv:** State arms **Rev:** Kim Jung-Il bust facing, sprigs below **Edge:** Plain

Date	Mintage	F	VF	XF	Unc	BU
JU90-2001 Proof	—	Value: 47.50				

KM# 152 10 WON
31.0000 g., 0.9990 Silver 0.9956 oz. ASW, 39.8 mm. **Subject:** Asian Money Fair **Obv:** State arms **Rev:** Two snakes **Edge:** Reeded and plain sections

Date	Mintage	F	VF	XF	Unc	BU
2001 Proof	—	Value: 60.00				

KM# 153 10 WON
31.0000 g., 0.9990 Silver 0.9956 oz. ASW, 39.8 mm. **Subject:** Tortoise-Serpent **Obv:** State arms **Rev:** Mythical creature **Edge:** Reeded and plain sections

Date	Mintage	F	VF	XF	Unc	BU
2001 Proof	—	Value: 55.00				

KM# 227 10 WON
31.0600 g., 0.9250 Silver 0.9237 oz. ASW, 39.9 mm. **Subject:** General Ri Sun Sin **Obv:** State arms **Rev:** Helmeted head 1/4 left **Edge:** Reeded

Date	Mintage	F	VF	XF	Unc	BU
2001 Proof	—	Value: 47.50				

KM# 253 10 WON
31.1100 g., 0.9990 Silver 0.9992 oz. ASW, 40.2 mm. **Obv:** State arms **Rev:** Deng Xio Ping head 3/4 left, 1904-1997 flanking, sprigs below **Edge:** Plain

Date	Mintage	F	VF	XF	Unc	BU
2001	—	Value: 45.00				

KM# 697 10 WON
27.0000 g., 0.9990 Silver 0.8672 oz. ASW, 40 mm. **Obv:** National arms, value in English **Rev:** Kim Jeongsuk

Date	Mintage	F	VF	XF	Unc	BU
2001 Proof	—	Value: 60.00				

KM# 704 10 WON
31.1050 g., Silver, 40 mm. **Obv:** National arms, Country name **Rev:** House where Kim Ilseong was born

Date	Mintage	F	VF	XF	Unc	BU
2001 Proof	—	Value: 75.00				

KM# 705 10 WON
31.1050 g., 0.9990 Silver 0.9990 oz. ASW, 40 mm. **Obv:** National arms, Country name **Rev:** House where Kim Jeongsuk was born

Date	Mintage	F	VF	XF	Unc	BU
2001 Proof	—	Value: 75.00				

KM# 732 10 WON
7.0000 g., Aluminum, 40 mm. **Obv:** East gate of Pyeongyang **Rev:** Married couple before flag and ferryboat

Date	Mintage	F	VF	XF	Unc	BU
2001 Proof	—	Value: 15.00				

KM# 733 10 WON
7.0000 g., Aluminum, 40 mm. **Obv:** East gate of Pyeongyang **Rev:** Ferryboat between Korea and Japan

Date	Mintage	F	VF	XF	Unc	BU
2001 Proof	—	Value: 15.00				

KM# 734 10 WON
7.0000 g., Aluminum, 40 mm. **Obv:** East gate of Pyeongyang **Rev:** Triumphial arch of Moranbong in Pyeongyang

Date	Mintage	F	VF	XF	Unc	BU
2001 Proof	—	Value: 15.00				

KM# 735 10 WON
Aluminum, 40 mm. **Obv:** East gate of Pyeongyang **Rev:** Chonji crater in Paektusan

Date	Mintage	F	VF	XF	Unc	BU
2001 Proof	—	Value: 15.00				

KM# 740 10 WON
Silver, 40 mm. **Obv:** National arms, Country name **Rev:** Triumphial arch of Moranbong in Pyeongyang

Date	Mintage	F	VF	XF	Unc	BU
2001 Proof	—	Value: 15.00				

KM# 741 10 WON
Silver, 40 mm. **Obv:** National arms, Country name **Rev:** Chonji crater in Paektusan

Date	Mintage	F	VF	XF	Unc	BU
2001 Proof	—	Value: 15.00				

KM# 775 10 WON
7.0000 g., Aluminum, 40 mm. **Obv:** East gate in Pyeongyang **Rev:** Taekwondo player

Date	Mintage	F	VF	XF	Unc	BU
2001 Proof	—	Value: 6.00				

KM# 776 10 WON
7.0000 g., Aluminum, 40 mm. **Obv:** National arms, Country name **Rev:** Two taekwondo players

Date	Mintage	F	VF	XF	Unc	BU
2001 Proof	—	Value: 6.00				
2007 Proof	—	Value: 6.00				

KM# 779 10 WON
31.1050 g., 0.9990 Silver 0.9990 oz. ASW, 40 mm. **Obv:** National arms, Central Bank name **Rev:** Taewankdo kicker

Date	Mintage	F	VF	XF	Unc	BU
2001 Proof	—	Value: 60.00				

KM# 780 10 WON
31.1050 g., 0.9990 Silver 0.9990 oz. ASW, 40 mm. **Obv:** National arms, Central Bank name **Rev:** Two taekwondo players

Date	Mintage	F	VF	XF	Unc	BU
2001 Proof	—	Value: 60.00				

KM# 401 10 WON
31.0000 g., 0.9990 Silver 0.9956 oz. ASW, 40.1 mm. **Obv:** State arms **Rev:** Arirang dancer **Edge:** Plain

Date	Mintage	F	VF	XF	Unc	BU
JU91-2002 Proof	—	Value: 45.00				

KM# 402 10 WON
31.0000 g., 0.9990 Silver 0.9956 oz. ASW, 40.1 mm. **Obv:** State arms **Rev:** Arirang ribbon dancer **Edge:** Plain

Date	Mintage	F	VF	XF	Unc	BU
JU91-2002 Proof	—	Value: 45.00				

KM# 307 10 WON
31.0000 g., 0.9990 Silver 0.9956 oz. ASW, 40.1 mm. **Obv:** State arms **Rev:** Two horses within a circle of Asian Zodiac animals **Edge:** Plain

Date	Mintage	F	VF	XF	Unc	BU
2002 Proof	—	Value: 45.00				

KM# 309 10 WON
31.0000 g., 0.9990 Silver 0.9956 oz. ASW, 40.2 mm. **Subject:** Arirang **Obv:** State arms **Rev:** Performers and flying cranes **Edge:** Plain

Date	Mintage	F	VF	XF	Unc	BU
JU91-2002 Proof	—	Value: 45.00				

KM# 311 10 WON
31.0000 g., 0.9990 Silver 0.9956 oz. ASW, 40.2 mm. **Obv:** State arms **Rev:** Tomb of King Tongmyong **Edge:** Plain

Date	Mintage	F	VF	XF	Unc	BU
JU91-2002 Proof	—	Value: 45.00				

KM# 312 10 WON
31.0000 g., 0.9990 Silver 0.9956 oz. ASW, 40.2 mm. **Obv:** State arms **Rev:** Tomb of King Kong Min **Edge:** Plain

Date	Mintage	F	VF	XF	Unc	BU
JU91-2002 Proof	—	Value: 45.00				

KM# 314 10 WON
31.0000 g., 0.9990 Silver 0.9956 oz. ASW, 40.2 mm. **Subject:** Arirang **Obv:** State arms **Rev:** Stylized dancer **Edge:** Plain

Date	Mintage	F	VF	XF	Unc	BU
2002 Proof	—	Value: 45.00				

KM# 315 10 WON
31.0000 g., 0.9990 Silver 0.9956 oz. ASW, 40.2 mm. **Obv:** State arms **Rev:** Korean map shaped dancer **Edge:** Plain

Date	Mintage	F	VF	XF	Unc	BU
JU91-2002 Proof	—	Value: 47.50				

KM# 316 10 WON
31.0000 g., 0.9990 Silver 0.9956 oz. ASW, 40.2 mm. **Obv:** State arms **Rev:** Korean map shaped ribbon dancer **Edge:** Plain

Date	Mintage	F	VF	XF	Unc	BU
JU91-2002 Proof	—	Value: 47.50				

KM# 317 10 WON
31.0000 g., 0.9990 Silver 0.9956 oz. ASW, 40.2 mm. **Obv:** State arms **Rev:** Victorious athletes hugging **Edge:** Plain

Date	Mintage	F	VF	XF	Unc	BU
JU91-2002 Proof	—	Value: 45.00				

KM# 318 10 WON

31.0000 g., 0.9990 Silver 0.9956 oz. ASW, 40.2 mm. **Obv:** State arms **Rev:** Woman floating above arena **Edge:** Plain

Date	Mintage	F	VF	XF	Unc	BU
JU91-2002 Proof	—	Value: 45.00				

KM# 254 10 WON

30.7700 g., 0.9990 Silver 0.9882 oz. ASW, 40.15 mm. **Obv:** State arms **Rev:** Tangun bust facing and his tomb **Edge:** Plain

Date	Mintage	F	VF	XF	Unc	BU
JU91-2002 Proof	—	Value: 42.50				

KM# 255 10 WON

30.9400 g., 0.9990 Silver 0.9937 oz. ASW, 40.2 mm. **Subject:** Jongmongju and Sonjukgyo **Obv:** State arms **Rev:** Head with hat facing above building foundation **Edge:** Plain

Date	Mintage	F	VF	XF	Unc	BU
JU91-2002 Proof	—	Value: 42.50				

KM# 231 10 WON

31.0000 g., 0.9990 Silver 0.9956 oz. ASW, 39.9 mm. **Subject:** Kim Il Sung **Obv:** State arms **Rev:** Bust facing **Edge:** Segmented reeding

Date	Mintage	F	VF	XF	Unc	BU
JU91-2002 Proof	—	Value: 50.00				

KM# 812 10 WON

31.1050 g., 0.9990 Silver 0.9990 oz. ASW, 40 mm. **Obv:** National arms, Central Bank name **Rev:** Dongmyeong, 1st King of Goguryeo

Date	Mintage	F	VF	XF	Unc	BU
2002 Proof	—	Value: 60.00				

KM# 813 10 WON

31.1050 g., 0.9990 Silver 0.9990 oz. ASW, 40 mm. **Obv:** National arms, Central Bank name **Rev:** Wanggeon, 1st King of Goryeo dynasty

Date	Mintage	F	VF	XF	Unc	BU
2002 Proof	—	Value: 60.00				

KM# 814 10 WON

31.1050 g., 0.9990 Silver 0.9990 oz. ASW, 40 mm. **Obv:** National arms, Central Bank name **Rev:** Jeon Bongjun

Date	Mintage	F	VF	XF	Unc	BU
2002 Proof	—	Value: 60.00				

KM# 823 10 WON

31.1050 g., 0.9990 Silver 0.9990 oz. ASW, 40 mm. **Obv:** National arms **Rev:** Prince Hodong and Princess Nakrang on horseback

Date	Mintage	F	VF	XF	Unc	BU
2002 Proof	—	Value: 60.00				

KM# 824 10 WON

31.1050 g., 0.9990 Silver 0.9990 oz. ASW, 40 mm. **Obv:** National arms **Rev:** Half-length figures of Prince Hodong and Princess Nakrang

Date	Mintage	F	VF	XF	Unc	BU
2002 Proof	—	Value: 60.00				

KM# 827 10 WON

7.0000 g., Aluminum, 40 mm. **Obv:** East gate of Pyeongyang **Rev:** Reconstruction of the Mausoleum of King Dongmyeong

Date	Mintage	F	VF	XF	Unc	BU
2002 Proof	—	Value: 7.00				

KM# 828 10 WON

7.0000 g., Aluminum, 40 mm. **Obv:** East gate in Pyeongyang **Rev:** Mausoleum for Gongmin

Date	Mintage	F	VF	XF	Unc	BU
2002 Proof	—	Value: 7.00				

KM# 829 10 WON

7.0000 g., Aluminum, 40 mm. **Obv:** East gate in Pyeongyang **Rev:** Stadium

Date	Mintage	F	VF	XF	Unc	BU
2002 Proof	—	Value: 7.00				

KM# 860 10 WON

7.0000 g., Aluminum, 40 mm. **Obv:** East gate of Pyeongyang **Rev:** The family

Date	Mintage	F	VF	XF	Unc	BU
2002 Proof	—	Value: 7.00				

KM# 861 10 WON

7.0000 g., Aluminum, 40 mm. **Obv:** East gate of Pyeongyang **Rev:** Map of Korea with the four cardinal compass points

Date	Mintage	F	VF	XF	Unc	BU
2002 Proof	—	Value: 7.00				

KM# 862 10 WON

7.0000 g., Aluminum, 40 mm. **Obv:** East gate of Pyeongyang **Rev:** Ryhmathic dancing and map of Korea

Date	Mintage	F	VF	XF	Unc	BU
2002 Proof	—	Value: 7.00				

KM# 863 10 WON

7.0000 g., Aluminum, 40 mm. **Obv:** East gate of Pyeongyang **Rev:** Drum dancer in form of the map of Korea

Date	Mintage	F	VF	XF	Unc	BU
2002 Proof	—	Value: 7.00				

KM# 864 10 WON

7.0000 g., Aluminum, 40 mm. **Obv:** East gate of Pyeongyang **Rev:** Victory celebration of Korean Teammates

Date	Mintage	F	VF	XF	Unc	BU
2002 Proof	—	Value: 7.00				

KM# 865 10 WON

28.0000 g., Brass, 40 mm. **Obv:** East gate of Pyeongyang **Rev:** Family

Date	Mintage	F	VF	XF	Unc	BU
2002 Proof	—	Value: 7.00				

KM# 870 10 WON

31.1050 g., 0.9990 Silver 0.9990 oz. ASW, 40 mm. **Obv:** National arms, Central Bank name **Rev:** Family

Date	Mintage	F	VF	XF	Unc	BU
2002 Proof	—	Value: 60.00				

KM# 871 10 WON

31.1050 g., 0.9990 Silver 0.9990 oz. ASW, 40 mm. **Obv:** National arms, Central Bank name **Rev:** Map of Korea with the four cardinal points

Date	Mintage	F	VF	XF	Unc	BU
2002 Proof	—	Value: 60.00				

KM# 833 10 WON

31.1050 g., 0.9990 Silver 0.9990 oz. ASW, 40 mm. **Obv:** National arms, Central Bank name **Rev:** Stadium

Date	Mintage	F	VF	XF	Unc	BU
2002 Proof	—	Value: 60.00				

KM# 884 10 WON

31.1050 g., 0.9990 Silver 0.9990 oz. ASW, 40 mm. **Subject:** Final issue of the German Mark **Obv:** National arms, Central Bank name **Rev:** Mark coin and Brandenburg Gate in color

Date	Mintage	F	VF	XF	Unc	BU
2002 Proof	Est. 2,001	Value: 85.00				

KM# 885 10 WON

31.1050 g., 0.9990 Silver 0.9990 oz. ASW, 40 mm. **Subject:** Final issue of the Belgian franc **Obv:** National arms, Central Bank name **Rev:** Franc and Axon in Brussels

Date	Mintage	F	VF	XF	Unc	BU
2002 Proof	Est. 2,001	Value: 85.00				

KM# 886 10 WON

31.1050 g., 0.9990 Silver 0.9990 oz. ASW, 40 mm. **Subject:** Final issue of the Greek Drachma **Obv:** National arms, Central Bank name **Rev:** Drachma and Acropolis in color

Date	Mintage	F	VF	XF	Unc	BU
2002 Proof	Est. 2,001	Value: 85.00				

KM# 887 10 WON

31.1050 g., 0.9990 Silver 0.9990 oz. ASW, 40 mm. **Subject:** Final issue of the Austrian schilling **Obv:** National arms, Central bank name **Rev:** Schilling and St. Stephen's in Vienna in color

Date	Mintage	F	VF	XF	Unc	BU
2002 Proof	Est. 2,001	Value: 85.00				

KM# 888 10 WON

31.1050 g., 0.9990 Silver 0.9990 oz. ASW, 40 mm. **Subject:** Final issue of the Netherland Gulden **Obv:** National arms, Central Bank name **Rev:** Gulden and Windmill in color

Date	Mintage	F	VF	XF	Unc	BU
2002 Proof	Est. 2,001	Value: 85.00				

KM# 889 10 WON

31.1050 g., 0.9990 Silver 0.9990 oz. ASW, 40 mm. **Subject:** Final issue of the San Marino Lira **Obv:** National arms, Central Bank name **Rev:** Lira and Mount Titano in color

Date	Mintage	F	VF	XF	Unc	BU
2002 Proof	Est. 2,001	Value: 85.00				

KM# 890 10 WON

31.1050 g., 0.9990 Silver 0.9990 oz. ASW, 40 mm. **Subject:** Final Vatican Lira **Obv:** National arms, Central Bank name **Rev:** Lira coin and St. Peter's in color

Date	Mintage	F	VF	XF	Unc	BU
2002 Proof	Est. 2,001	Value: 85.00				

KM# 409 10 WON

30.9400 g., 0.9990 Silver 0.9937 oz. ASW, 40 mm. **Obv:** State arms **Rev:** Children spinning tops **Edge:** Plain

Date	Mintage	F	VF	XF	Unc	BU
JU92-2003 Proof	—	Value: 45.00				

KM# 320 10 WON

31.0000 g., 0.9990 Silver 0.9956 oz. ASW, 40.2 mm. **Obv:** State arms **Rev:** Helmeted head with two antenna-like horns on helmet **Edge:** Plain

Date	Mintage	F	VF	XF	Unc	BU
JU92-2003 Proof	—	Value: 47.50				

KM# 321 10 WON

31.0000 g., 0.9990 Silver 0.9956 oz. ASW, 40.2 mm. **Obv:** State arms **Rev:** Helmeted head with horns **Edge:** Plain

Date	Mintage	F	VF	XF	Unc	BU
JU92-2003 Proof	—	Value: 47.50				

KM# 322 10 WON

31.0000 g., 0.9990 Silver 0.9956 oz. ASW, 40.2 mm. **Obv:** State arms **Rev:** Armored bust of Kang Kam-cheon facing (948-1031) wearing winged helmet **Edge:** Plain

Date	Mintage	F	VF	XF	Unc	BU
JU92-2003 Proof	—	Value: 47.50				

KM# 324 10 WON

31.0000 g., 0.9990 Silver 0.9956 oz. ASW, 40.2 mm. **Obv:** State arms **Rev:** Turtle-shaped armored ship of 1592 **Edge:** Plain

Date	Mintage	F	VF	XF	Unc	BU
JU92-2003 Proof	—	Value: 45.00				

KM# 325 10 WON

31.0000 g., 0.9990 Silver 0.9956 oz. ASW, 40.2 mm. **Obv:** State arms **Rev:** Children playing jacks **Edge:** Plain

Date	Mintage	F	VF	XF	Unc	BU
JU92-2003 Proof	—	Value: 45.00				

KM# 326 10 WON

31.0000 g., 0.9990 Silver 0.9956 oz. ASW, 40.2 mm. **Obv:** State arms **Rev:** Children kicking a shuttlecock **Edge:** Plain

Date	Mintage	F	VF	XF	Unc	BU
JU92-2003 Proof	—	Value: 45.00				

KM# 453 10 WON

31.0000 g., 0.9990 Silver 0.9956 oz. ASW **Subject:** FIFA World Championship - Germany 2006 **Obv:** National arms **Rev:** Two hands holding up cup in rays at lower right, two smallplayers at left. **Rev. Legend:** WORLD CUP **Rev. Inscription:** FIFA

Date	Mintage	F	VF	XF	Unc	BU
JU92-2003 Proof	—	Value: 60.00				

KM# 896 10 WON

7.0000 g., Aluminum, 40 mm. **Obv:** East gate of Pyeongand **Rev:** Sheep in center of Zodac

Date	Mintage	F	VF	XF	Unc	BU
2003 Proof	—	Value: 7.00				

KM# 898 10 WON

31.1050 g., 0.9990 Silver 0.9990 oz. ASW, 40 mm. **Obv:** Naitonal arms **Rev:** Sheep at center of Zodiac

Date	Mintage	F	VF	XF	Unc	BU
2003 Proof	—	Value: 60.00				

KM# 905 10 WON

31.1050 g., 0.9990 Silver 0.9990 oz. ASW, 40 mm. **Obv:** National arms, Central Bank name **Rev:** Highway and vehicles, train

Date	Mintage	F	VF	XF	Unc	BU
2003 Proof	Est. 1,000	Value: 70.00				

KM# 906 10 WON

7.0000 g., Aluminum, 40 mm. **Obv:** East gate of Pyeongyang **Rev:** Eulji Mundeok

Date	Mintage	F	VF	XF	Unc	BU
2003 Proof	—	Value: 7.00				

KM# 907 10 WON

7.0000 g., Aluminum, 40 mm. **Obv:** East gate of Pyrongyang **Rev:** Yeon Gaesomun

Date	Mintage	F	VF	XF	Unc	BU
2003 Proof	—	Value: 7.00				

KM# 908 10 WON

7.0000 g., Aluminum, 40 mm. **Obv:** East gate of Pyeongyang **Rev:** Gang Gaesomun

Date	Mintage	F	VF	XF	Unc	BU
2003 Proof	—	Value: 7.00				

KM# 911 10 WON

28.0000 g., Brass, 40 mm. **Obv:** East gate of Pyeongyang **Rev:** Gang Camchan

Date	Mintage	F	VF	XF	Unc	BU
2003 Proof	—	Value: 7.00				

KM# 915 10 WON

7.0000 g., Aluminum, 40 mm. **Obv:** East gate of Pyeongyang **Rev:** Turtle boat

Date	Mintage	F	VF	XF	Unc	BU
2003 Proof	—	Value: 7.00				

KM# 342 10 WON

31.0000 g., 0.9990 Silver 0.9956 oz. ASW, 40 mm. **Obv:** State arms **Rev:** Domed building **Edge:** Plain

Date	Mintage	F	VF	XF	Unc	BU
JU93-2004 Proof	—	Value: 47.50				

KM# 343 10 WON

31.0000 g., 0.9990 Silver 0.9956 oz. ASW, 40 mm. **Obv:** State arms **Rev:** Pigeon on branch **Edge:** Segmented reeding

Date	Mintage	F	VF	XF	Unc	BU
JU93-2004 Proof	—	Value: 45.00				

KM# 344 10 WON

31.0000 g., 0.9990 Silver 0.9956 oz. ASW, 40 mm. **Obv:** State arms **Rev:** Two Leiothrix birds **Edge:** Segmented reeding

Date	Mintage	F	VF	XF	Unc	BU
JU93-2004 Proof	—	Value: 45.00				

KM# 345 10 WON

31.0000 g., 0.9990 Silver 0.9956 oz. ASW, 40 mm. **Obv:** State arms **Rev:** Two cranes standing in water **Edge:** Segmented reeding

Date	Mintage	F	VF	XF	Unc	BU
JU93-2004 Proof	—	Value: 47.50				

KM# 346 10 WON

31.0000 g., 0.9990 Silver 0.9956 oz. ASW, 40 mm. **Obv:** State arms **Rev:** Curlew bird **Edge:** Segmented reeding

Date	Mintage	F	VF	XF	Unc	BU
JU93-2004 Proof	—	Value: 45.00				

KM# 347 10 WON

31.0000 g., 0.9990 Silver 0.9956 oz. ASW, 40 mm. **Obv:** State arms **Rev:** Goshawk on branch **Edge:** Segmented reeding

Date	Mintage	F	VF	XF	Unc	BU
JU93-2004 Proof	—	Value: 45.00				

KM# 418 10 WON

31.0000 g., 0.9990 Silver 0.9956 oz. ASW, 39.7 mm. **Obv:** State arms **Rev:** Ibis standing in water **Edge:** Segmented reeding

Date	Mintage	F	VF	XF	Unc	BU
JU93-2004 Proof	—	Value: 50.00				

KM# 938 10 WON

31.1050 g., 0.9990 Silver 0.9990 oz. ASW, 40 mm. **Obv:** National arms, Central Bank name **Rev:** Monkey King Sun Wukong from Journey to the West

Date	Mintage	F	VF	XF	Unc	BU
2004 Proof	—	Value: 70.00				

KM# 940 10 WON

31.1050 g., 0.9990 Silver 0.9990 oz. ASW, 40 mm. **Obv:** National arms, Central Bank name **Rev:** Monkey in center of Zodiac

Date	Mintage	F	VF	XF	Unc	BU
2004 Proof	—	Value: 60.00				

KM# 948 10 WON

Silver, 32x46 mm. **Subject:** Deng Xiaoping, 100th Birth Anniversary **Obv:** National arms **Rev:** Deng Xiaoping saluting **Shape:** Vertical rectangle

Date	Mintage	F	VF	XF	Unc	BU
2004 Proof	—	Value: 60.00				

KM# 951 10 WON

31.1050 g., 0.9990 Silver 0.9990 oz. ASW, 40 mm. **Obv:** Naitonal arms, Central Bank name **Rev:** Broad throaded bird

Date	Mintage	F	VF	XF	Unc	BU
2004 Proof	—	Value: 45.00				

KM# 952 10 WON

31.1050 g., 0.9990 Silver 0.9990 oz. ASW, 40 mm. **Obv:** Naitonal arms, Central Bank name **Rev:** Imperial eagle

Date	Mintage	F	VF	XF	Unc	BU
2004 Proof	—	Value: 45.00				

KM# 953 10 WON

31.1050 g., 0.9990 Silver 0.9990 oz. ASW, 40 mm. **Obv:** National arms, Central Bank name **Rev:** Bittern

Date	Mintage	F	VF	XF	Unc	BU
2004 Proof	—	Value: 45.00				

KM# 954 10 WON

31.1050 g., 0.9990 Silver 0.9990 oz. ASW, 40 mm. **Obv:** National arms, Central Bank name **Rev:** Pheasant

Date	Mintage	F	VF	XF	Unc	BU
2004 Proof	—	Value: 45.00				

KM# 999 10 WON

31.1050 g., 0.9990 Silver 0.9990 oz. ASW, 40 mm. **Obv:** National arms, Central Bank name **Rev:** Tallinn castle in color, Estonian Krone

Date	Mintage	F	VF	XF	Unc	BU
2004 Proof	Est. 2,004	Value: 85.00				

KM# 1000 10 WON

31.1050 g., 0.9990 Silver 0.9990 oz. ASW, 40 mm. **Obv:** National arms, Central Bank name **Rev:** Malta's lira and Fort St. Angelo in color

Date	Mintage	F	VF	XF	Unc	BU
2004 Proof	Est. 2,004	Value: 85.00				

KM# 1001 10 WON

31.1050 g., 0.9990 Silver 0.9990 oz. ASW, 40 mm. **Obv:** National arms, Central Bank name **Rev:** Polish zloty and Danzig Grain Tower in color

Date	Mintage	F	VF	XF	Unc	BU
2004 Proof	—	Value: 85.00				

KM# 1002 10 WON

31.1050 g., 0.9990 Silver 0.9990 oz. ASW, 40 mm. **Obv:** National arms, Central Bank name **Rev:** Slovakian Korun and Bratislava castle in color

Date	Mintage	F	VF	XF	Unc	BU
2004 Proof	Est. 2,004	Value: 85.00				

KM# 1003 10 WON

31.1050 g., 0.9990 Silver 0.9990 oz. ASW, 40 mm. **Obv:** National arms, Central Bank name **Rev:** Czech Korun and Prague castle in color

Date	Mintage	F	VF	XF	Unc	BU
2004 Proof	Est. 2,004	Value: 85.00				

KM# 1004 10 WON

31.1050 g., 0.9990 Silver 0.9990 oz. ASW, 40 mm. **Obv:** National arms, Central Bank name **Rev:** Hungarian Forint and St. Stephan statue in Budapest castle in color

Date	Mintage	F	VF	XF	Unc	BU
2004 Proof	Est. 2,004	Value: 85.00				

KM# 1005 10 WON

31.1050 g., 0.9990 Silver 0.9990 oz. ASW, 40 mm. **Obv:** National arms, Central Bank name **Rev:** Cypriot Pound and Temple of Apollo

Date	Mintage	F	VF	XF	Unc	BU
2004 Proof	Est. 2,004	Value: 85.00				

KM# 1006 10 WON

31.1050 g., 0.9990 Silver 0.9990 oz. ASW, 40 mm. **Subject:** Athens olympics **Obv:** National arms, Central Bank name **Rev:** Discus thrower in color

Date	Mintage	F	VF	XF	Unc	BU
2004 Proof	—	Value: 115				

KM# 1007 10 WON

31.1050 g., 0.9990 Silver 0.9990 oz. ASW, 40 mm. **Obv:** National arms, Central Bank name **Rev:** Gorch Fock II sailing ship in color

Date	Mintage	F	VF	XF	Unc	BU
2004 Proof	Est. 2,004	Value: 115				

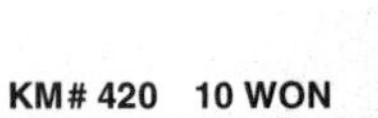

KM# 420 10 WON

30.9100 g., 0.9990 Silver 0.9927 oz. ASW, 40 mm. **Subject:** End of WWII 60th Anniversary **Obv:** State arms **Rev:** Multicolor radiant map, doves, rainbow and inscription **Edge:** Plain

Date	Mintage	F	VF	XF	Unc	BU
JU94-2005 Proof	—	Value: 45.00				

KM# 425 10 WON

1.6700 g., Aluminum, 23 mm. **Obv:** State arms **Rev:** Value

Date	Mintage	F	VF	XF	Unc	BU
JU94(2005)	—	—	—	—	1.00	1.25

KM# 1017 10 WON

31.1050 g., 0.9990 Silver 0.9990 oz. ASW, 40 mm. **Obv:** National arms, Central Bank name **Rev:** Rooster within Zodiac circle

Date	Mintage	F	VF	XF	Unc	BU
2005 Proof	—	Value: 50.00				

KM# 1021 10 WON

7.0000 g., Aluminum, 40 mm. **Obv:** East gate in Pyeongyang **Rev:** Hae Mosu in flight with the five dragons

Date	Mintage	F	VF	XF	Unc	BU
2005 Proof	—	Value: 20.00				

KM# 1023 10 WON

31.1050 g., 0.9990 Silver 0.9990 oz. ASW, 40 mm. **Obv:** National arms, Central Bank name **Rev:** Hae Mosu in flight with the five dragons

Date	Mintage	F	VF	XF	Unc	BU
2005 Proof	—	Value: 50.00				

KM# 1026 10 WON

7.0000 g., Aluminum, 40 mm. **Obv:** East gate of Pyeongyang **Rev:** Admiral Yi Sunsin and turtle boat

Date	Mintage	F	VF	XF	Unc	BU
2005 Proof	—	Value: 20.00				

KM# 1027 10 WON

7.0000 g., Aluminum, 40 mm. **Obv:** East gate of Pyeongyang **Rev:** General Hong Beomdo

Date	Mintage	F	VF	XF	Unc	BU
2005 Proof	—	Value: 20.00				

KM# 1030 10 WON

31.1050 g., 0.9990 Silver 0.9990 oz. ASW, 40 mm. **Obv:** National arms, Central Bank name **Rev:** Admiral Yi Sunsin and turtle boat

Date	Mintage	F	VF	XF	Unc	BU
2005 Proof	—	Value: 50.00				

KM# 1031 10 WON

31.1050 g., 0.9990 Silver 0.9990 oz. ASW, 40 mm. **Obv:** National arms, Central Bank name **Rev:** General Hong Beomdo

Date	Mintage	F	VF	XF	Unc	BU
2005 Proof	—	Value: 85.00				

KM# 1037 10 WON

31.1050 g., 0.9990 Silver 0.9990 oz. ASW, 40 mm. **Obv:** National arms, Central Bank name **Rev:** March before the monument of the three principals of reunification

Date	Mintage	F	VF	XF	Unc	BU
2005 Proof	—	Value: 50.00				

KM# 1038 10 WON

31.1050 g., 0.9990 Silver 0.9990 oz. ASW, 40 mm. **Obv:** National arms, Central Bank name **Rev:** Demonstrations before crater lake

Date	Mintage	F	VF	XF	Unc	BU
2005 Proof	—	Value: 50.00				

KM# 1039 10 WON

31.1050 g., 0.9990 Silver 0.9990 oz. ASW, 40 mm. **Obv:** National arms, Central Bank name **Rev:** Three drum dance

Date	Mintage	F	VF	XF	Unc	BU
2005 Proof	—	Value: 50.00				

KM# 1045 10 WON

31.1050 g., 0.9990 Silver 0.9990 oz. ASW, 40 mm. **Obv:** National arms, Central Bank name **Rev:** Tomb of the unknown solder in Moscow

Date	Mintage	F	VF	XF	Unc	BU
2005 Proof	—	Value: 85.00				

KM# 1046 10 WON

31.1050 g., 0.9990 Silver 0.9990 oz. ASW, 40 mm. **Obv:** National arms, Central Bank name **Rev:** Monument to mothers in St. Petersburg, Russian legend

Date	Mintage	F	VF	XF	Unc	BU
2005 Proof	—	Value: 85.00				

KM# 1090 10 WON

7.0000 g., Aluminum, 40 mm. **Obv:** East gate of Pyeongyang **Rev:** Ryuhwa, mother of King Dongmyeong

Date	Mintage	F	VF	XF	Unc	BU
2006 Proof	—	Value: 15.00				

KM# 1091 10 WON

31.1050 g., 0.9990 Silver 0.9990 oz. ASW, 40 mm. **Obv:** National arms, Central Bank name **Rev:** Ryuhwa, mother of King Dongmyeong

Date	Mintage	F	VF	XF	Unc	BU
2006 proof	—	Value: 50.00				

KM# 496 10 WON

7.0000 g., Aluminum, 40 mm. **Rev:** Eastern City Gate in Pyeongyang

Date	Mintage	F	VF	XF	Unc	BU
2007 Proof	—	Value: 7.50				

KM# 501 10 WON

7.0000 g., Aluminum, 40 mm. **Obv:** Eastern city gate in Pyeongyang **Rev:** Brontosaurus

Date	Mintage	F	VF	XF	Unc	BU
2007 Proof	—	Value: 6.50				

KM# 508 10 WON

7.0000 g., Aluminum, 40 mm. **Obv:** Eastern gate in Pyeongyang **Rev:** Rainbow lori in color

Date	Mintage	F	VF	XF	Unc	BU
2007 Proof	—	Value: 8.50				

KM# 509 10 WON

7.0000 g., Aluminum **Obv:** Eastern Gate in Pyeongyang **Rev:** Manderian Duck in color

Date	Mintage	F	VF	XF	Unc	BU
2007 Proof	—	Value: 8.50				

KM# 514 10 WON

7.0000 g., Aluminum, 40 mm. **Obv:** East gate in Pyeoongyang **Rev:** Sports gym and emblem in color

Date	Mintage	F	VF	XF	Unc	BU
2007 Proof	—	Value: 8.50				

KM# 536 10 WON

7.0000 g., Aluminum, 40 mm. **Obv:** Eastern gate in Pyeongyang **Rev:** Growth in the Kaeseong area

Date	Mintage	F	VF	XF	Unc	BU
2007 Proof	—	Value: 7.50				

KM# 538 10 WON

7.0000 g., Aluminum, 40 mm. **Obv:** Eastern gate in Pyeongyang **Rev:** Chinese Peony

Date	Mintage	F	VF	XF	Unc	BU
	—	Value: 7.50				

KM# 540 10 WON

7.0000 g., Aluminum, 40 mm. **Obv:** Eastern gate of Pyeongyang **Rev:** Panda seated eating

Date	Mintage	F	VF	XF	Unc	BU
2007 Proof	—	Value: 7.50				

KM# 543 10 WON

7.0000 g., Aluminum, 40 mm. **Obv:** Eastern gate in Pyeongyang **Rev:** Two pandas

Date	Mintage	F	VF	XF	Unc	BU
2007 Proof	—	Value: 7.50				

KM# 569 10 WON

7.0000 g., Aluminum, 40 mm. **Obv:** Eastern gate in Pyeongyang **Rev:** Rocket and satellite

Date	Mintage	F	VF	XF	Unc	BU
2007 Proof	—	Value: 6.50				

KM# 582 10 WON

7.0000 g., Aluminum, 40 mm. **Obv:** Eastern gate in Pyeongyang **Rev:** Dragon rising

Date	Mintage	F	VF	XF	Unc	BU
2007 Proof	—	Value: 6.00				

KM# 583 10 WON

7.0000 g., Aluminum, 40 mm. **Obv:** Eastern gate in Pyeongyang **Rev:** Two girls on seasaw

Date	Mintage	F	VF	XF	Unc	BU
2007 Proof	—	Value: 6.00				

KM# 584 10 WON

7.0000 g., Aluminum, 40 mm. **Obv:** Eastern gate in Pyeongyang **Rev:** Korean struggle

Date	Mintage	F	VF	XF	Unc	BU
2007 Proof	—	Value: 6.00				

KM# 585 10 WON

7.0000 g., Aluminum, 40 mm. **Obv:** Eastern gate in Pyeongyang **Rev:** Girl on swing

Date	Mintage	F	VF	XF	Unc	BU
2007 Proof	—	Value: 6.00				

KM# 586 10 WON

7.0000 g., Aluminum, 40 mm. **Obv:** Eastern gate in Pyeongyang **Rev:** Girls skipping

Date	Mintage	F	VF	XF	Unc	BU
2007 Proof	—	Value: 6.00				

KM# 610 10 WON

7.0000 g., Aluminum, 40 mm. **Obv:** Eastern gate in Pyeongyang **Rev:** Rabbit

Date	Mintage	F	VF	XF	Unc	BU
2007 Proof	—	Value: 7.50				

KM# 620 10 WON

7.0000 g., Aluminum, 40 mm. **Obv:** Eastern gate in Pyeongyang **Rev:** White bellied woodpecker

Date	Mintage	F	VF	XF	Unc	BU
2007 Proof	—	Value: 6.00				

KM# 621 10 WON

7.0000 g., Aluminum, 40 mm. **Obv:** Eastern gate in Pyeongyang **Rev:** Black grouse

Date	Mintage	F	VF	XF	Unc	BU
2007 Proof	—	Value: 6.00				

KM# 622 10 WON

7.0000 g., Aluminum, 40 mm. **Obv:** Eastern gate in Pyeongyang **Rev:** Sand Grouse

Date	Mintage	F	VF	XF	Unc	BU
2007 Proof	—	Value: 6.00				

KM# 623 10 WON

7.0000 g., Aluminum, 40 mm. **Obv:** Eastern gate in Pyeongyang **Rev:** Indian Pitta bird

Date	Mintage	F	VF	XF	Unc	BU
2007 Proof	—	Value: 6.00				

KM# 632 10 WON
7.0000 g., Aluminum, 40 mm. **Obv:** Eastern gate in Pyeongyang **Rev:** Blue dragon right

Date	Mintage	F	VF	XF	Unc	BU
2007 Proof	—	Value: 15.00				

KM# 637 10 WON
7.0000 g., Aluminum, 40 mm. **Obv:** Eastern gate in Pyeongyang **Rev:** Two siberian tigers

Date	Mintage	F	VF	XF	Unc	BU
2007 Proof	—	Value: 6.00				

KM# 649 10 WON
Aluminum, 40 mm. **Obv:** Eastern gate in Pyeongyang **Rev:** King Goguryeo

Date	Mintage	F	VF	XF	Unc	BU
2007 Proof	—	Value: 15.00				

KM# 650 10 WON
Aluminum, 40 mm. **Obv:** Eastern gate in Pyeongyang **Rev:** Buddha figure

Date	Mintage	F	VF	XF	Unc	BU
2007 Proof	—	Value: 15.00				

KM# 651 10 WON
Aluminum, 40 mm. **Obv:** Eastern gate in Pyeongyang **Rev:** King Gojoseon

Date	Mintage	F	VF	XF	Unc	BU
2007 Proof	—	Value: 6.00				

KM# 667 10 WON
7.0000 g., Aluminum, 40 mm. **Obv:** Eastern gate in Pyeongyang **Rev:** First married couple to see again since the 1945 division

Date	Mintage	F	VF	XF	Unc	BU
2007 Proof	—	Value: 15.00				

KM# 715 10 WON
7.0000 g., Aluminum, 40 mm. **Obv:** East gate of Pyeongyang **Rev:** Celadon pottery

Date	Mintage	F	VF	XF	Unc	BU
2007 Proof	—	Value: 6.00				

KM# 802 10 WON
7.0000 g., Aluminum, 40 mm. **Obv:** East gate in Pyeongyang **Rev:** Reconstruction of the mausoleum for King Dangun

Date	Mintage	F	VF	XF	Unc	BU
2007 Proof	—	Value: 10.00				

KM# 803 10 WON
7.0000 g., Aluminum, 40 mm. **Obv:** East gatet in Pyeongyang **Rev:** Dongmyeong, 1st King of Goguryeb

Date	Mintage	F	VF	XF	Unc	BU
2007 Proof	—	Value: 10.00				

KM# 804 10 WON
7.0000 g., Aluminum, 40 mm. **Obv:** East gate in Pyeongyang **Rev:** Wanggeon, 1st king of Goryeo dynasty

Date	Mintage	F	VF	XF	Unc	BU
2007 Proof	—	Value: 10.00				

KM# 805 10 WON
7.0000 g., Aluminum, 40 mm. **Obv:** East gate in Pyeongyang **Rev:** Jeong Mongju

Date	Mintage	F	VF	XF	Unc	BU
2007 Proof	—	Value: 10.00				

KM# 806 10 WON
7.0000 g., Aluminum, 40 mm. **Obv:** East gate in Pyeongyang **Rev:** Jeon Bongjun

Date	Mintage	F	VF	XF	Unc	BU
2007 Proof	—	Value: 10.00				

KM# 850 10 WON
7.0000 g., Aluminum, 40 mm. **Obv:** East gate of Pyeongyang **Rev:** Dancer

Date	Mintage	F	VF	XF	Unc	BU
2007 Proof	—	Value: 6.00				

KM# 851 10 WON
7.0000 g., Aluminum, 40 mm. **Obv:** East gate of Pyeongyang **Rev:** Dancer

Date	Mintage	F	VF	XF	Unc	BU
2007 Proof	—	Value: 7.00				

KM# 852 10 WON
7.0000 g., Aluminum, 40 mm. **Obv:** National arms, Central Bank name **Rev:** Female in national costume

Date	Mintage	F	VF	XF	Unc	BU
2007 Proof	—	Value: 7.00				

KM# 853 10 WON
7.0000 g., Aluminum, 40 mm. **Obv:** National arms, Central Bank name **Rev:** Crane dancer

Date	Mintage	F	VF	XF	Unc	BU
2007 Proof	—	Value: 7.00				

KM# 854 10 WON
7.0000 g., Aluminum, 40 mm. **Obv:** National arms, Central Bank name **Rev:** Fairy princess

Date	Mintage	F	VF	XF	Unc	BU
2007 Proof	—	Value: 7.00				

KM# 880 10 WON
6.0000 g., 0.9990 Aluminum 0.1927 oz., 38 mm. **Obv:** East gate of Pyeongyang **Rev:** Taekwando

Date	Mintage	F	VF	XF	Unc	BU
2007 Proof	—	Value: 6.00				

KM# 736 20 WON
28.0000 g., Brass, 40 mm. **Obv:** East gate of Pyeongyang **Rev:** Married couple before Korean flag and ferryboat

Date	Mintage	F	VF	XF	Unc	BU
2001 Proof	—	Value: 20.00				

KM# 737 20 WON
28.0000 g., Brass, 40 mm. **Obv:** East gate of Pyeongyang **Rev:** Ferryboat between Korea and Japan

Date	Mintage	F	VF	XF	Unc	BU
2001 Proof	—	Value: 7.00				

KM# 738 20 WON
28.0000 g., Brass, 40 mm. **Obv:** East gate in Pyeongyang **Rev:** Triumphial arch of Moranbong in Pyeongyang

Date	Mintage	F	VF	XF	Unc	BU
2001 Proof	—	Value: 20.00				

KM# 739 20 WON
28.0000 g., Brass, 40 mm. **Obv:** East gate in Pyeongyang **Rev:** Chonji crater in Paektusan

Date	Mintage	F	VF	XF	Unc	BU
2001 Proof	—	Value: 20.00				

KM# 768 20 WON
16.0000 g., Brass, 35 mm. **Obv:** East gate of Pyeongyang **Rev:** Chinese Dragon boat

Date	Mintage	F	VF	XF	Unc	BU
2001 Proof	—	Value: 7.00				

KM# 777 20 WON
28.0000 g., Brass, 40 mm. **Obv:** East gate of Pyeongyang **Rev:** Taekwondo kicker

Date	Mintage	F	VF	XF	Unc	BU
2001 Proof	—	Value: 7.00				

KM# 778 20 WON
28.0000 g., Brass, 40 mm. **Obv:** East gate of Pyeongyang **Rev:** Two taekwondo players

Date	Mintage	F	VF	XF	Unc	BU
2001 Proof	—	Value: 7.00				

KM# 787 20 WON
16.0000 g., Brass, 35 mm. **Obv:** East gate of Pyeongyang **Rev:** Horse head

Date	Mintage	F	VF	XF	Unc	BU
2002 Proof	—	Value: 7.00				

KM# 788 20 WON
16.0000 g., Brass, 35 mm. **Obv:** East gate of Pyeongyang **Rev:** Horse right

Date	Mintage	F	VF	XF	Unc	BU
2002 Proof	—	Value: 20.00				

KM# 789 20 WON
28.0000 g., Brass, 40 mm. **Obv:** East gate of Pyeongyang **Rev:** Two horses

Date	Mintage	F	VF	XF	Unc	BU
2002 Proof	—	Value: 7.00				

KM# 809 20 WON
28.0000 g., Brass, 40 mm. **Obv:** East gate of Pyeongyang **Rev:** Wanggeon, 1st King of Goryeo dynasty

Date	Mintage	F	VF	XF	Unc	BU
2002 Proof	—	Value: 7.00				

KM# 810 20 WON
28.0000 g., Brass, 40 mm. **Obv:** East gate of Pyeongyang **Rev:** Jeong Mongju

Date	Mintage	F	VF	XF	Unc	BU
2002 Proof	—	Value: 7.00				

KM# 830 20 WON
28.0000 g., Brass, 40 mm. **Obv:** East gate of Pyeongyang **Rev:** Resconstruction of the Mausoleums of King Dongmyeong

Date	Mintage	F	VF	XF	Unc	BU
2002 Proof	—	Value: 7.00				

KM# 831 20 WON
28.0000 g., Brass, 40 mm. **Obv:** East gate of Pyeongyang **Rev:** Mausoleum of King Gongmin

Date	Mintage	F	VF	XF	Unc	BU
2002 Proof	—	Value: 7.00				

KM# 832 20 WON
28.0000 g., Brass, 40 mm. **Obv:** East gate of Pyeongyang **Rev:** Stadium

Date	Mintage	F	VF	XF	Unc	BU
2002 Proof	—	Value: 7.00				

KM# 866 20 WON
28.0000 g., Brass, 40 mm. **Obv:** East gate of Pyeongyang **Rev:** Map of Korea with the four cardinal directions

Date	Mintage	F	VF	XF	Unc	BU
2002 Proof	—	Value: 7.00				

KM# 867 20 WON
28.0000 g., Brass, 40 mm. **Obv:** East gate of Pyeongyang **Rev:** Rythem dancers and map of Korea

Date	Mintage	F	VF	XF	Unc	BU
2002 Proof	—	Value: 7.00				

KM# 897 20 WON
28.0000 g., Brass, 40 mm. **Obv:** East gate of Pyeongyang **Rev:** Sheep in center of Zodiac

Date	Mintage	F	VF	XF	Unc	BU
2003 Proof	—	Value: 7.00				

KM# 909 20 WON
28.0000 g., Brass, 40 mm. **Obv:** East gate of Pyeongyang **Rev:** Eulji Mundeok

Date	Mintage	F	VF	XF	Unc	BU
2003 Proof	—	Value: 7.00				

KM# 910 20 WON
28.0000 g., Brass, 40 mm. **Obv:** East gate in Pyeongyang **Rev:** Yeon Gaesomun

Date	Mintage	F	VF	XF	Unc	BU
2003 Proof	—	Value: 7.00				

KM# 916 20 WON
28.0000 g., Brass, 40 mm. **Obv:** East gate of Pyeongyang **Rev:** Turtle boat

Date	Mintage	F	VF	XF	Unc	BU
2003 Proof	—	Value: 7.00				

KM# 256 20 WON
42.0600 g., 0.9990 Silver 1.3509 oz. ASW, 45.1 mm. **Obv:** State arms **Rev:** Rose of sharon flower **Edge:** Plain

Date	Mintage	F	VF	XF	Unc	BU
JU93-2004 Proof	—	Value: 65.00				

KM# 257 20 WON
42.2160 g., 0.9990 Silver 1.3559 oz. ASW, 45.1 mm. **Obv:** State arms **Rev:** Kim Jong-Il, Peony flower **Edge:** Plain

Date	Mintage	F	VF	XF	Unc	BU
JU93-2004 Proof	—	Value: 65.00				

KM# 258 20 WON
41.9200 g., 0.9990 Silver 1.3464 oz. ASW, 45.1 mm. **Obv:** State arms **Rev:** Kim Il-seung, Orchid flowers **Edge:** Plain

Date	Mintage	F	VF	XF	Unc	BU
JU93-2004 Proof	—	Value: 65.00				

KM# 259 20 WON

42.0000 g., 0.9990 Silver 1.3489 oz. ASW, 45.1 mm. **Obv:** State arms **Rev:** Kim Il Sung's birth place, side view **Edge:** Plain

Date	Mintage	F	VF	XF	Unc	BU
JU93-2004 Proof	—	Value: 65.00				

KM# 260 20 WON

41.6200 g., 0.9990 Silver 1.3367 oz. ASW, 45.1 mm. **Obv:** State arms **Rev:** Mountain cabin **Edge:** Plain

Date	Mintage	F	VF	XF	Unc	BU
JU93-2004 Proof	—	Value: 65.00				

KM# 261 20 WON

41.9100 g., 0.9990 Silver 1.3460 oz. ASW, 45.1 mm. **Obv:** State arms **Rev:** Kim Il Sung's birth place, front view **Edge:** Plain

Date	Mintage	F	VF	XF	Unc	BU
JU93-2004 Proof	—	Value: 65.00				

KM# 340 20 WON

31.0000 g., 0.9990 Silver 0.9956 oz. ASW, 39.8 mm. **Obv:** State arms **Rev:** Kim Jong-Il and Vladimir Putin clasping hands **Edge:** Segmented reeding

Date	Mintage	F	VF	XF	Unc	BU
2004 Proof	—	Value: 50.00				

KM# 341 20 WON

31.0000 g., 0.9990 Silver 0.9956 oz. ASW, 39.8 mm. **Obv:** State arms **Rev:** Bust facing **Edge:** Segmented reeding

Date	Mintage	F	VF	XF	Unc	BU
2004 Proof	—	Value: 50.00				

KM# 419 20 WON

31.0000 g., 0.9990 Silver 0.9956 oz. ASW, 39.75 mm. **Subject:** Historic Pyongyang Meeting **Obv:** State arms **Rev:** Kim Jong-Il and Kim Dae-Jung clasping hands, English legend **Edge:** Segmented reeding

Date	Mintage	F	VF	XF	Unc	BU
2004 Proof	—	Value: 50.00				

KM# 942 20 WON

19.0000 g., Copper, 23x40 mm. **Obv:** East gate of Pyeongyang **Rev:** Marmoset **Shape:** Rectangle

Date	Mintage	F	VF	XF	Unc	BU
2004 Proof	—	Value: 8.00				

KM# 943 20 WON

19.0000 g., Copper, 23x40 mm. **Obv:** East gate of Pyeongyang **Rev:** Blue monkey

Date	Mintage	F	VF	XF	Unc	BU
2004 Proof	—	Value: 8.00				

KM# 944 20 WON

19.0000 g., Copper, 23x40 mm. **Obv:** East gate of Pyeongyang **Rev:** two monkies

Date	Mintage	F	VF	XF	Unc	BU
2004 Proof	—	Value: 8.00				

KM# 949 20 WON

Brass, 40 mm. **Obv:** East gate of Pyeongyang **Rev:** Sports hall in Pyeongyang

Date	Mintage	F	VF	XF	Unc	BU
2004 Proof	—	Value: 14.00				

KM# 955 20 WON

42.2160 g., 0.9990 Silver 1.3559 oz. ASW, 45 mm. **Obv:** National arms, Central Bank name **Rev:** Kim Ilseong

Date	Mintage	F	VF	XF	Unc	BU
2004 Proof	—	Value: 70.00				

KM# 956 20 WON

42.2160 g., 0.9990 Silver 1.3559 oz. ASW, 45 mm. **Obv:** National arms, Central Bank name **Rev:** Kim Jeongil

Date	Mintage	F	VF	XF	Unc	BU
2004 Proof	—	Value: 70.00				

KM# 957 20 WON

42.2160 g., 0.9990 Silver 1.3559 oz. ASW, 45 mm. **Obv:** Naitonal arms, Central Bank name **Rev:** Kim Jeongsuk

Date	Mintage	F	VF	XF	Unc	BU
2004 Proof	—	Value: 70.00				

KM# 966 20 WON

31.1050 g., 0.9990 Silver 0.9990 oz. ASW, 40 mm. **Obv:** National arms, Central Bank name **Rev:** Kim Jeongil and Hu Jintao

Date	Mintage	F	VF	XF	Unc	BU
2004 Proof	—	Value: 60.00				

KM# 977 20 WON

31.1050 g., 0.9990 Silver 0.9990 oz. ASW, 40 mm. **Obv:** Dokdo, rocky islands, Central Bank name **Rev:** Map of the island group

Date	Mintage	F	VF	XF	Unc	BU
2004 Proof	—	Value: 70.00				

KM# 978 20 WON

31.1050 g., 0.9990 Silver 0.9990 oz. ASW, 40 mm. **Obv:** Dokdo, rocky islands, Central Bank name **Rev:** Fisher Ahn Yongbok

Date	Mintage	F	VF	XF	Unc	BU
2004 Proof	—	Value: 70.00				

KM# 979 20 WON

31.1050 g., 0.9990 Silver 0.9990 oz. ASW, 40 mm. **Obv:** Dokdo, rocky islands, Central Bank name **Rev:** West island

Date	Mintage	F	VF	XF	Unc	BU
2004 Proof	—	Value: 70.00				

KM# 980 20 WON

31.1050 g., 0.9990 Silver 0.9990 oz. ASW, 40 mm. **Obv:** Dokdo, rocky islands, Central Bank name **Rev:** East island

Date	Mintage	F	VF	XF	Unc	BU
2004 Proof	—	Value: 70.00				

KM# 981 20 WON

31.1050 g., 0.9990 Silver 0.9990 oz. ASW, 40 mm. **Obv:** Dokdo, rocky islands, Central Bank name **Rev:** Three brother island

Date	Mintage	F	VF	XF	Unc	BU
2004 Proof	—	Value: 70.00				

KM# 982 20 WON

31.1050 g., 0.9990 Silver 0.9990 oz. ASW, 40 mm. **Obv:** Dokdo, rocky islands, Central Bank name **Rev:** Chicken island

Date	Mintage	F	VF	XF	Unc	BU
2004 Proof	—	Value: 70.00				

KM# 983 20 WON

31.1050 g., 0.9990 Silver 0.9990 oz. ASW, 40 mm. **Obv:** Dokdo, rocky islands, Central Bank name **Rev:** Candle island

Date	Mintage	F	VF	XF	Unc	BU
2004 Proof	—	Value: 70.00				

KM# 984 20 WON

31.1050 g., 0.9990 Silver 0.9990 oz. ASW, 40 mm. **Obv:** Dokdo, rocky islands, Central Bank name **Rev:** Dome island

Date	Mintage	F	VF	XF	Unc	BU
2004 Proof	—	Value: 70.00				

KM# 478 20 WON

27.3000 g., Brass, 40 mm. **Obv:** Temple **Rev:** Multicolor rooster right

Date	Mintage	F	VF	XF	Unc	BU
2005 Proof	—	Value: 10.00				

KM# 479 20 WON

31.1050 g., 0.9990 Silver 0.9990 oz. ASW **Obv:** Arms **Rev:** A puppy, dog's head facing

Date	Mintage	F	VF	XF	Unc	BU
2005 Proof	—	Value: 45.00				

KM# 1022 20 WON

28.0000 g., Brass, 40 mm. **Obv:** East gate of Pyeongyang **Rev:** Hae Mosu in flight with the five dragons

Date	Mintage	F	VF	XF	Unc	BU
2005 Proof	—	Value: 20.00				

KM# 1028 20 WON

28.0000 g., Brass, 40 mm. **Obv:** East gate of Pyeongyang **Rev:** Admiral Yi Sunsin and turtle boat

Date	Mintage	F	VF	XF	Unc	BU
2005 Proof	—	Value: 12.50				

KM# 1029 20 WON

28.0000 g., Brass, 40 mm. **Obv:** East gate of Pyeongyong **Rev:** General Hong Beomdo

Date	Mintage	F	VF	XF	Unc	BU
2005 Proof	—	Value: 12.50				

KM# 1041 20 WON

28.0000 g., Brass, 40 mm. **Obv:** East gate of Pyeongyang **Rev:** Map of Korea, pair of peace doves, rainbow

Date	Mintage	F	VF	XF	Unc	BU
2005 Proof	—	Value: 12.50				

KM# 1049 20 WON

31.1050 g., 0.9990 Silver 0.9990 oz. ASW, 40 mm. **Obv:** National arms, Central Bank name **Rev:** Dongmyeong, 1st king of Goguryeo

Date	Mintage	F	VF	XF	Unc	BU
2005 Proof	—	Value: 65.00				

KM# 1050 20 WON

31.1050 g., 0.9990 Silver 0.9990 oz. ASW, 40 mm. **Obv:** National arms, Central Bank name **Rev:** Blue dragon, Cheongryong, of the East

Date	Mintage	F	VF	XF	Unc	BU
2005 Proof	—	Value: 45.00				

KM# 1051 20 WON

31.1050 g., 0.9990 Silver 0.9990 oz. ASW, 40 mm. **Obv:** National arms, Central Bank name **Rev:** Red bird, Jujak, of the South

Date	Mintage	F	VF	XF	Unc	BU
2005 Proof	—	Value: 45.00				

KM# 1052 20 WON

31.1050 g., 0.9990 Silver 0.9990 oz. ASW, 40 mm. **Obv:** National arms, Central Bank name **Rev:** White tiger, Baekho, of the West

Date	Mintage	F	VF	XF	Unc	BU
2005 Proof	—	Value: 45.00				

KM# 1053 20 WON

31.1050 g., 0.9990 Silver 0.9990 oz. ASW, 40 mm. **Obv:** National arms, Central Bank name **Rev:** Black snake, Hyeonmu, of the North

Date	Mintage	F	VF	XF	Unc	BU
2005 Proof	—	Value: 45.00				

KM# 1054 20 WON

31.1050 g., 0.9990 Silver 0.9990 oz. ASW, 40 mm. **Obv:** National arms, Central Bank name **Rev:** Horse and rider

Date	Mintage	F	VF	XF	Unc	BU
2005 Proof	—	Value: 45.00				

KM# 1055 20 WON

31.1050 g., 0.9990 Silver 0.9990 oz. ASW, 40 mm. **Obv:** National arms, Central Bank name **Rev:** Horse drummers

Date	Mintage	F	VF	XF	Unc	BU
2005 Proof	—	Value: 45.00				

KM# 1056 20 WON
31.1050 g., 0.9990 Silver 0.9990 oz. ASW, 40 mm. **Obv:** National arms, Central Bank name **Rev:** Bugler to horse

Date	Mintage	F	VF	XF	Unc	BU
2005 Proof	—	Value: 45.00				

KM# 1057 20 WON
31.1050 g., 0.9990 Silver 0.9990 oz. ASW, 40 mm. **Obv:** National arms, Central Bank name **Rev:** Horseback hunter

Date	Mintage	F	VF	XF	Unc	BU
2005 Proof	—	Value: 45.00				

KM# 1058 20 WON
31.1050 g., 0.9990 Silver 0.9990 oz. ASW, 40 mm. **Obv:** National arms, Central Bank name **Rev:** Crane and bamboo image by Yi Kyeongyun

Date	Mintage	F	VF	XF	Unc	BU
2005 Proof	—	Value: 65.00				

KM# 1059 20 WON
31.1050 g., 0.9990 Silver 0.9990 oz. ASW, 40 mm. **Obv:** National arms, Central Bank name **Rev:** Ibis, image by Kim Sik

Date	Mintage	F	VF	XF	Unc	BU
2005 Proof	—	Value: 65.00				

KM# 1060 20 WON
31.1050 g., 0.9990 Silver 0.9990 oz. ASW, 40 mm. **Obv:** National arms, Central Bank name **Rev:** Pheasant by Jang Seungeop

Date	Mintage	F	VF	XF	Unc	BU
2005 Proof	—	Value: 65.00				

KM# 1061 20 WON
31.1050 g., 0.9990 Silver 0.9990 oz. ASW, 40 mm. **Obv:** National arms, Central Bank name **Rev:** Fairy princess of the diamond mountain

Date	Mintage	F	VF	XF	Unc	BU
2005 Proof	—	Value: 65.00				

KM# 1062 20 WON
31.1050 g., 0.9990 Silver 0.9990 oz. ASW, 40 mm. **Obv:** National arms, Central Bank name **Rev:** Big stone in the diamond mountain

Date	Mintage	F	VF	XF	Unc	BU
2005 Proof	—	Value: 65.00				

KM# 1063 20 WON
31.1050 g., 0.9990 Silver 0.9990 oz. ASW, 40 mm. **Obv:** National arms, Central Bank name **Rev:** Two rabbits

Date	Mintage	F	VF	XF	Unc	BU
2005 Proof	Est. 2,000	Value: 45.00				

KM# 1064 20 WON
31.1050 g., 0.9990 Silver 0.9990 oz. ASW, 40 mm. **Obv:** National arms, Central Bank name **Rev:** Cat

Date	Mintage	F	VF	XF	Unc	BU
2005 Proof	Est. 2,000	Value: 45.00				

KM# 1065 20 WON
31.1050 g., 0.9990 Silver 0.9990 oz. ASW, 40 mm. **Subject:** North-South Railway connection **Obv:** National arms, Central Bank name **Rev:** Map of Korea and railway line

Date	Mintage	F	VF	XF	Unc	BU
2005 Proof	—	Value: 65.00				

KM# 1066 20 WON
31.1050 g., 0.9990 Silver 0.9990 oz. ASW, 40 mm. **Obv:** National arms, Central Bank name **Rev:** FIFA World Cup trophy

Date	Mintage	F	VF	XF	Unc	BU
2005 Proof	—	Value: 45.00				

KM# 480 20 WON
23.7000 g., Brass, 40 mm. **Obv:** Temple **Rev:** Multicolor German shepard

Date	Mintage	F	VF	XF	Unc	BU
2006 Proof	—	Value: 10.00				

KM# 481 20 WON
Brass **Obv:** Arms **Rev:** Bejeweled female head

Date	Mintage	F	VF	XF	Unc	BU
2006 Proof	—	Value: 10.00				

KM# 482 20 WON
27.3000 g., Brass, 40 mm. **Obv:** Temple **Rev:** Multicolor pig and pigletts

Date	Mintage	F	VF	XF	Unc	BU
2007 Proof	—	Value: 10.00				

KM# 497 20 WON
28.0000 g., Brass, 40 mm. **Rev:** Eastern city gate of Pyeongyang

Date	Mintage	F	VF	XF	Unc	BU
2007 Proof	—	Value: 8.50				

KM# 502 20 WON
28.0000 g., Brass, 40 mm. **Obv:** Eastern city gate of Pyeongyang **Rev:** Brontosaurus

Date	Mintage	F	VF	XF	Unc	BU
2007 Proof	—	Value: 8.50				

KM# 570 20 WON
28.0000 g., Brass, 40 mm. **Obv:** Eastern gate in Pyeongyang **Rev:** Rocket and satellite

Date	Mintage	F	VF	XF	Unc	BU
2007 Proof	—	Value: 7.50				

KM# 587 20 WON
28.0000 g., Brass, 40 mm. **Obv:** Eastern gate in Pyeongyang **Rev:** Dragon rising

Date	Mintage	F	VF	XF	Unc	BU
2007 Proof	—	Value: 7.50				

KM# 588 20 WON
28.0000 g., Brass, 40 mm. **Obv:** Eastern gate in Pyeongyang **Rev:** Two girls on seasaw

Date	Mintage	F	VF	XF	Unc	BU
2007 Proof	—	Value: 7.50				

KM# 589 20 WON
28.0000 g., Brass, 40 mm. **Obv:** Eastern gate in Pyeongyang **Rev:** Korean struggle

Date	Mintage	F	VF	XF	Unc	BU
2007 Proof	—	Value: 7.50				

KM# 590 20 WON
28.0000 g., Brass, 40 mm. **Obv:** Eastern gate in Pyeongyang **Rev:** Girl on swing

Date	Mintage	F	VF	XF	Unc	BU
2007 Proof	—	Value: 7.50				

KM# 591 20 WON
28.0000 g., Brass, 40 mm. **Obv:** Eastern gate in Pyeongyang **Rev:** Children Skipping

Date	Mintage	F	VF	XF	Unc	BU
2007 Proof	—	Value: 7.50				

KM# 624 20 WON
28.0000 g., Brass, 40 mm. **Obv:** Eastern gate in Pyeongyang **Rev:** White bellied woodpecker

Date	Mintage	F	VF	XF	Unc	BU
2007 Proof	—	Value: 7.00				

KM# 625 20 WON
28.0000 g., Brass, 40 mm. **Obv:** Eastern gate in Pyeongyang **Rev:** Black grouse

Date	Mintage	F	VF	XF	Unc	BU
2007 Proof	—	Value: 7.00				

KM# 626 20 WON
28.0000 g., Brass, 40 mm. **Obv:** Eastern gate in Pyeongyang **Rev:** Sand Grouse

Date	Mintage	F	VF	XF	Unc	BU
2007 Proof	—	Value: 7.00				

KM# 627 20 WON
28.0000 g., Brass, 40 mm. **Obv:** Eastern gate in Pyeongyang **Rev:** Indian Pitta bird

Date	Mintage	F	VF	XF	Unc	BU
2007 Proof	—	Value: 7.00				

KM# 633 20 WON
28.0000 g., Brass, 40 mm. **Obv:** Eastern gate in Pyeongyang **Rev:** Blue dragon right

Date	Mintage	F	VF	XF	Unc	BU
2007 Proof	—	Value: 7.00				

KM# 638 20 WON
28.0000 g., Brass, 40 mm. **Obv:** Eastern gate in Pyeongyang **Rev:** Two siberian tigers

Date	Mintage	F	VF	XF	Unc	BU
2007 Proof	—	Value: 7.00				

KM# 652 20 WON
28.0000 g., Brass, 40 mm. **Obv:** Eastern gate in Pyeongyang **Rev:** Dongmyeong, King of Goguryeo

Date	Mintage	F	VF	XF	Unc	BU
2007 Proof	—	Value: 7.00				

KM# 653 20 WON
28.0000 g., Brass, 40 mm. **Obv:** Eastern gate in Pyeongyang **Rev:** Buddha figure

Date	Mintage	F	VF	XF	Unc	BU
2007 Proof	—	Value: 7.00				

KM# 654 20 WON
28.0000 g., Brass, 40 mm. **Obv:** Eastern gate in Pyeongyang **Rev:** Dangun, King of Gojoseon

Date	Mintage	F	VF	XF	Unc	BU
2007 Proof	—	Value: 7.00				

KM# 668 20 WON
28.0000 g., Brass, 40 mm. **Obv:** Eastern gate in Pyeongyang **Rev:** First married couple to meet again after the 1945 division

Date	Mintage	F	VF	XF	Unc	BU
2007 Proof	—	Value: 7.00				

KM# 690 20 WON
28.0000 g., Brass, 40 mm. **Obv:** East gate of Pyeongyang **Rev:** Hyonmu

Date	Mintage	F	VF	XF	Unc	BU
2007 Proof	—	Value: 7.00				

KM# 716 20 WON
28.0000 g., Brass, 40 mm. **Obv:** East gate of Pyeongyang **Rev:** Celadon pottery

Date	Mintage	F	VF	XF	Unc	BU
2007 Proof	—	Value: 7.00				

KM# 807 20 WON
28.0000 g., Brass, 40 mm. **Obv:** East gate in Pyeongyang **Rev:** Reconstruction of the mausoleum of King Dangun

Date	Mintage	F	VF	XF	Unc	BU
2007 Proof	—	Value: 7.00				

KM# 808 20 WON
28.0000 g., Brass, 40 mm. **Obv:** East gate of Pyeongyang **Rev:** Dongmyeong, 1st King of Goguryeo

Date	Mintage	F	VF	XF	Unc	BU
2007 Proof	—	Value: 7.00				

KM# 811 20 WON
28.0000 g., Brass, 40 mm. **Obv:** East gate of Pyeongyang **Rev:** Jeon Bongjun

Date	Mintage	F	VF	XF	Unc	BU
2007 Proof	—	Value: 7.00				

KM# 855 20 WON
28.0000 g., Brass, 40 mm. **Obv:** East gate of Pyeongyang **Rev:** Dancer

Date	Mintage	F	VF	XF	Unc	BU
2007 Proof	—	Value: 7.00				

KM# 856 20 WON
28.0000 g., Brass, 40 mm. **Obv:** East gate of Pyeongyang **Rev:** Dancer

Date	Mintage	F	VF	XF	Unc	BU
2007 Proof	—	Value: 7.00				

KM# 857 20 WON
28.0000 g., Brass, 40 mm. **Obv:** East gate of Pyeongyang **Rev:** Woman in national costume

Date	Mintage	F	VF	XF	Unc	BU
2007 Proof	—	Value: 7.00				

KM# 858 20 WON
28.0000 g., Brass, 40 mm. **Obv:** East gate of Pyeongyang **Rev:** Crane dancer

Date	Mintage	F	VF	XF	Unc	BU
2007 Proof	—	Value: 7.00				

KM# 859 20 WON
28.0000 g., Brass, 40 mm. **Obv:** East gate of Pyeongyang **Rev:** Fairy princess

Date	Mintage	F	VF	XF	Unc	BU
2007 Proof	—	Value: 7.00				

KM# 868 20 WON
28.0000 g., Brass, 40 mm. **Obv:** East gate of Pyeongyang **Rev:** Drum dancers in shape of Korean map

Date	Mintage	F	VF	XF	Unc	BU
2007 Proof	—	Value: 7.00				

KM# 869 20 WON
28.0000 g., Brass, 40 mm. **Obv:** East gate of Pyeongyang **Rev:** Korean team victory celebration

Date	Mintage	F	VF	XF	Unc	BU
2007 Proof	—	Value: 7.00				

KM# 1128 20 WON
28.0000 g., Brass, 40 mm. **Obv:** National arms, Central Bank name **Rev:** Hoopoe

Date	Mintage	F	VF	XF	Unc	BU
2007 Proof	Est. 2,000	Value: 17.50				

KM# 1129 20 WON
28.0000 g., Brass, 40 mm. **Obv:** National arms, Central Bank name **Rev:** Ural owl

Date	Mintage	F	VF	XF	Unc	BU
2007 Proof	Est. 2,000	Value: 17.50				

KM# 1130 20 WON
28.0000 g., Brass, 40 mm. **Obv:** National arms, Central Bank name **Rev:** Eagle

Date	Mintage	F	VF	XF	Unc	BU
2007 Proof	Est. 2,000	Value: 17.50				

KM# 1131 20 WON
28.0000 g., Brass, 40 mm. **Obv:** National arms, Central Bank name **Rev:** White rhino

Date	Mintage	F	VF	XF	Unc	BU
2007 Proof	Est. 2,000	Value: 17.50				

KM# 1132 20 WON
28.0000 g., Brass, 40 mm. **Obv:** National arms, Central Bank name **Rev:** African elephant family

Date	Mintage	F	VF	XF	Unc	BU
2007 Proof	Est. 2,000	Value: 17.50				

KM# 1133 20 WON
28.0000 g., Brass, 40 mm. **Obv:** National arms, Central Bank name **Rev:** Lion family

Date	Mintage	F	VF	XF	Unc	BU
2007 Proof	Est. 2,000	Value: 17.50				

KM# 1134 20 WON
28.0000 g., Brass, 40 mm. **Obv:** National arms, Central Bank name **Rev:** Cape Buffalo

Date	Mintage	F	VF	XF	Unc	BU
2007 Proof	Est. 2,000	Value: 17.50				

KM# 1135 20 WON
28.0000 g., Brass **Obv:** National arms, Central Bank name **Rev:** Marine turtle

Date	Mintage	F	VF	XF	Unc	BU
2007 Proof	Est. 2,000	Value: 17.50				

KM# 1136 20 WON
28.0000 g., Brass, 40 mm. **Obv:** National arms, Central Bank name **Rev:** Penguin

Date	Mintage	F	VF	XF	Unc	BU
2007 Proof	Est. 2,000	Value: 17.50				

KM# 1137 20 WON
28.0000 g., Brass, 40 mm. **Obv:** National arms, Central Bank name **Rev:** Emu

Date	Mintage	F	VF	XF	Unc	BU
2007 Proof	—	Value: 17.50				

KM# 1138 20 WON
28.0000 g., Brass, 40 mm. **Obv:** National arms, Central Bank name **Rev:** Eagle owl

Date	Mintage	F	VF	XF	Unc	BU
2007 Proof	Est. 2,000	Value: 17.50				

KM# 1139 20 WON
28.0000 g., Brass, 40 mm. **Obv:** National arms, Central Bank name **Rev:** Lemur

Date	Mintage	F	VF	XF	Unc	BU
2007 Proof	Est. 2,000	Value: 17.50				

KM# 1140 20 WON
28.0000 g., Brass, 40 mm. **Obv:** National arms, Central Bank name **Rev:** Lion

Date	Mintage	F	VF	XF	Unc	BU
2007 Proof	Est. 2,000	Value: 17.50				

KM# 1141 20 WON
28.0000 g., Brass, 40 mm. **Obv:** National arms, Central Bank name **Rev:** Two Arfican elephants

Date	Mintage	F	VF	XF	Unc	BU
2007 Proof	Est. 2,000	Value: 17.50				

KM# 484 20 WON
27.3000 g., Brass, 40 mm. **Obv:** Temple **Rev:** Multicolor goat left

Date	Mintage	F	VF	XF	Unc	BU
2008 Proof	—	Value: 10.00				

KM# 485 20 WON
27.3000 g., Brass, 40 mm. **Obv:** Temple **Rev:** Multicolor snake and flowers

Date	Mintage	F	VF	XF	Unc	BU
2008 Proof	—	Value: 10.00				

KM# 486 20 WON
27.3000 g., Brass, 40 mm. **Obv:** Temple **Rev:** Multicolor, two rabbits

Date	Mintage	F	VF	XF	Unc	BU
2008 Proof	—	Value: 10.00				

KM# 487 20 WON
27.3000 g., Brass, 40 mm. **Obv:** Temple **Rev:** Multicolor two white rats

Date	Mintage	F	VF	XF	Unc	BU
2008 Proof	—	Value: 10.00				

KM# 488 20 WON
27.3000 g., Brass, 40 mm. **Obv:** Temple **Rev:** Multicolor monkey seated on branch

Date	Mintage	F	VF	XF	Unc	BU
2008 Proof	—	Value: 10.00				

KM# 489 20 WON
27.3000 g., Brass, 40 mm. **Obv:** Temple **Rev:** Multicolor tiger

Date	Mintage	F	VF	XF	Unc	BU
2008 Proof	—	Value: 10.00				

KM# 490 20 WON
27.3000 g., Brass, 40 mm. **Obv:** Temple **Rev:** Multicolor horse prancing right

Date	Mintage	F	VF	XF	Unc	BU
2008 Proof	—	Value: 10.00				

KM# 491 20 WON
27.3000 g., Brass, 40 mm. **Obv:** Temple **Rev:** Multicolor two oxen

Date	Mintage	F	VF	XF	Unc	BU
2009 Proof	—	Value: 10.00				

KM# 495 20 WON
Aluminum, 45 mm. **Obv:** Raised Pagoda in ornamental loop **Rev:** Tiger with color inlay **Edge:** Plain

Date	Mintage	F	VF	XF	Unc	BU
2010	—	—	—	—	—	20.00

KM# 891 50 WON
155.0000 g., 0.9990 Silver 4.9782 oz. ASW, 65 mm. **Obv:** National arms, Central Bank name **Rev:** Orca whale

Date	Mintage	F	VF	XF	Unc	BU
2002 Proof	Est. 500	Value: 400				

KM# 815 50 WON
1.2400 g., 0.9990 Gold 0.0398 oz. AGW, 14 mm. **Obv:** Naitonal arms, Central Bank name **Rev:** Wanggeon, 1st King of Goryeo Dynasty

Date	Mintage	F	VF	XF	Unc	BU
2003 Proof	Est. 20,000	Value: 90.00				

KM# 262 50 WON
70.0000 g., 0.9990 Silver 2.2482 oz. ASW, 50 mm. **Obv:** Korean map **Rev:** Huh Jun Chosun doctor at left, books at right **Edge:** Plain

Date	Mintage	F	VF	XF	Unc	BU
JU93-2004 Proof	—	Value: 100				

KM# 426 50 WON
2.0100 g., Aluminum, 25 mm. **Obv:** State arms **Rev:** Value

Date	Mintage	F	VF	XF	Unc	BU
JU94-2005	—	—	—	—	1.20	1.50

KM# 427 100 WON
2.2700 g., Aluminum, 27 mm. **Obv:** State arms **Rev:** Value

Date	Mintage	F	VF	XF	Unc	BU
JU94-2005	—	—	—	—	1.35	1.75

KM# 445 200 WON
5.1900 g., 0.9990 Silver 0.1667 oz. ASW, 30.00 mm. **Series:** Endangered Wildlife **Obv:** Fortress Gate **Rev:** Polar Bear standing facing **Rev. Legend:** URSUS MARITIMUS **Edge:** Plain

Date	Mintage	F	VF	XF	Unc	BU
2007 Proof	5,000	Value: 15.00				

KM# 1110 200 WON
25.0000 g., Brass, 38 mm. **Subject:** Railways in Russia, 170th Anniversary **Obv:** East gate of Pyeongyang **Rev:** Steam train

Date	Mintage	F	VF	XF	Unc	BU
2007 Proof	Est. 200	Value: 70.00				

KM# 1111 200 WON
25.0000 g., Brass, 35 mm. **Obv:** East gate of Pyeongyang **Rev:** Constantine Eduardovic and Sputnik

Date	Mintage	F	VF	XF	Unc	BU
2007 Proof	—	Value: 25.00				

KM# 1086 250 WON
26.9600 g., 0.9000 Silver 0.7801 oz. ASW **Obv:** Old coins and Central Bank name

Date	Mintage	F	VF	XF	Unc	BU
2005	Est. 1,000	—	—	—	—	25.00

KM# 835 400 WON
20.0000 g., 0.9990 Gold 0.6423 oz. AGW, 35 mm. **Obv:** National arms, Central Bank name **Rev:** Korean folk games, wrestling

Date	Mintage	F	VF	XF	Unc	BU
2002 Proof	—	Value: 1,200				

KM# 441 500 WON
12.0000 g., 0.9990 Silver 0.3854 oz. ASW, 38.00 mm. **Subject:** 170th Anniversary First Public Railway St. Petersburg - Zarskoje Selo **Obv:** Fortress Gate **Rev:** First train arriving **Edge:** Plain

Date	Mintage	F	VF	XF	Unc	BU
ND(2007) Proof	5,000	Value: 70.00				

KM# 447 500 WON
12.0000 g., 0.9990 Silver 0.3854 oz. ASW, 38.00 mm. **Subject:** 150th Anniversary Birth of Ziolkowski and 50th Anniversary Launch of Sputnik I **Obv:** Fortress Gate **Rev:** Bust of Ziolkowski facing 3/4 right at lower left, Sputnik circling earth at upper right **Edge:** Plain

Date	Mintage	F	VF	XF	Unc	BU
ND(2007) Proof	5,000	Value: 65.00				

KM# 1112 500 WON
12.0000 g., Silver, 38 mm. **Obv:** East gate of Pyeongyong **Rev:** Great Wall and Temple of Heaven in Bejing

Date	Mintage	F	VF	XF	Unc	BU
2007 Proof	Est. 5,000	Value: 35.00				

KM# 1113 500 WON
12.0000 g., 0.9990 Silver 0.3854 oz. ASW, 38 mm. **Subject:** Bejing Olympics, 2008 **Obv:** East gate of Pyeongyong **Rev:** Fencing

Date	Mintage	F	VF	XF	Unc	BU
2007 Proof	Est. 5,000	Value: 35.00				

KM# 1114 500 WON
12.0000 g., 0.9990 Silver 0.3854 oz. ASW, 38 mm. **Subject:** Bejing Olympics, 2008 **Obv:** East gate of Pyeongyong **Rev:** Boxing

Date	Mintage	F	VF	XF	Unc	BU
2007 Proof	—	Value: 35.00				

KM# 1115 500 WON
12.0000 g., 0.9990 Silver 0.3854 oz. ASW, 38 mm. **Subject:** Bejing Olympics, 2008 **Obv:** East gate of Pyeongyong **Rev:** Swimming

Date	Mintage	F	VF	XF	Unc	BU
2007 Proof	Est. 5,000	Value: 35.00				

KM# 1116 500 WON
12.0000 g., 0.9990 Silver 0.3854 oz. ASW, 38 mm. **Subject:** Bejing Olympics, 2008 **Obv:** East gate of Pyeongyong **Rev:** Weightlifting

Date	Mintage	F	VF	XF	Unc	BU
2007 Proof	Est. 5,000	Value: 35.00				

KM# 1117 500 WON
12.0000 g., 0.9990 Silver 0.3854 oz. ASW, 38 mm. **Subject:** Bejing Olympics, 2008 **Obv:** East gate of Pyeongyong **Rev:** Baseball

Date	Mintage	F	VF	XF	Unc	BU
2007 Proof	Est. 5,000	Value: 35.00				

KM# 1118 500 WON
12.0000 g., 0.9990 Silver 0.3854 oz. ASW, 38 mm. **Subject:** Bejing Olympics, 2008 **Obv:** East gate of Pyeongyong **Rev:** Wrestlers

Date	Mintage	F	VF	XF	Unc	BU
2007 Proof	—	Value: 35.00				

KM# 1119 500 WON
12.0000 g., 0.9990 Silver 0.3854 oz. ASW, 38 mm. **Subject:** Bejing Olympics, 2008 **Obv:** East gate of Pyeongyong **Rev:** Gymnast

Date	Mintage	F	VF	XF	Unc	BU
2007 Proof	—	Value: 35.00				

KM# 1120 500 WON
12.0000 g., 0.9990 Silver 0.3854 oz. ASW, 28 mm. **Subject:** Bejing Olympics, 2008 **Obv:** East gate of Pyeongyong **Rev:** Kayakers

Date	Mintage	F	VF	XF	Unc	BU
2007 Proof	Est. 5,000	Value: 35.00				

KM# 1121 500 WON
12.0000 g., 0.9990 Silver 0.3854 oz. ASW, 38 mm. **Subject:** Bejing Olympics, 2008 **Obv:** East gate of Pyeongyong **Rev:** Hurdler

Date	Mintage	F	VF	XF	Unc	BU
2007 Proof	Est. 5,000	Value: 35.00				

KM# 1122 500 WON
12.0000 g., 0.9990 Silver 0.3854 oz. ASW, 38 mm. **Subject:** Bejing Olympics, 2008 **Obv:** East gate of Pyeongyong **Rev:** Taekwondo

Date	Mintage	F	VF	XF	Unc	BU
2007 Proof	Est. 5,000	Value: 35.00				

KM# 1123 500 WON
12.0000 g., 0.9990 Silver 0.3854 oz. ASW, 38 mm. **Subject:** Bejing Olympics, 2008 **Obv:** East gate of Pyeongyong **Rev:** Olympic Sport

Date	Mintage	F	VF	XF	Unc	BU
2007 Proof	Est. 5,000	Value: 35.00				

KM# 443 500 WON
12.0000 g., 0.9990 Silver 0.3854 oz. ASW, 38.00 mm. **Subject:** Lunar Year of the Rat **Obv:** Fortress Gate **Rev:** Two rats within circle of Lunar figures **Edge:** Plain

Date	Mintage	F	VF	XF	Unc	BU
2008	—	—	—	—	—	50.00
2008 Proof	5,000	Value: 70.00				

KM# 1178 500 WON
12.0000 g., 0.9990 Silver 0.3854 oz. ASW, 38 mm. **Subject:** Bejing Summer Olympics, 2008 **Obv:** East gate of Pyeongyang **Rev:** Great Wall, Temple of Heaven and Soccer player

Date	Mintage	F	VF	XF	Unc	BU
2008 Proof	Est. 5,000	Value: 35.00				

KM# 1179 500 WON
12.0000 g., 0.9990 Silver 0.3854 oz. ASW, 38 mm. **Subject:** Bejing Summer Olympics, 2008 **Obv:** East gate of Pyeongyang **Rev:** Hockey player

Date	Mintage	F	VF	XF	Unc	BU
2008 Proof	Est. 5,000	Value: 35.00				

KM# 1180 500 WON
12.0000 g., 0.9990 Silver 0.3854 oz. ASW, 38 mm. **Subject:** Bejing Summer Olympics, 2008 **Obv:** East gate of Pyeongyang **Rev:** Basketball player

Date	Mintage	F	VF	XF	Unc	BU
2008 Proof	Est. 5,000	Value: 35.00				

KM# 1181 500 WON
12.0000 g., 0.9990 Silver 0.3854 oz. ASW, 38 mm. **Subject:** Bejing Summer Olympics, 2008 **Obv:** East gate of Pyeongyang **Rev:** Archer

Date	Mintage	F	VF	XF	Unc	BU
2008 Proof	Est. 5,000	Value: 35.00				

KM# 1182 500 WON
12.0000 g., 0.9990 Silver 0.3854 oz. ASW, 38 mm. **Subject:** Bejing Summer Olympics, 2008 **Obv:** East gate of Pyeongyang **Rev:** Volleyball

Date	Mintage	F	VF	XF	Unc	BU
2008 Proof	Est. 5,000	Value: 35.00				

KM# 1183 500 WON
12.0000 g., 0.9990 Silver 0.3854 oz. ASW, 38 mm. **Subject:** Bejing Summer Olympics, 2008 **Obv:** East gate of Pyeongyang **Rev:** Table tennis

Date	Mintage	F	VF	XF	Unc	BU
2008 Proof	Est. 5,000	Value: 35.00				

KM# 1184 500 WON
12.0000 g., 0.9990 Silver 0.3854 oz. ASW, 38 mm. **Subject:** Bejing Summer Olympics, 2008 **Obv:** East gate of Pyeongyang **Rev:** Rowers

Date	Mintage	F	VF	XF	Unc	BU
2008 Proof	Est. 5,000	Value: 35.00				

KM# 717 700 WON
31.1050 g., 0.9990 Gold 0.9990 oz. AGW **Obv:** National arms **Rev:** Caledon pottery

Date	Mintage	F	VF	XF	Unc	BU
2001 Proof	—	Value: 1,800				

KM# 720 700 WON
31.1050 g., 0.9990 Gold 0.9990 oz. AGW, 40 mm. **Obv:** National arms, Central Bank name **Rev:** Ginsing plant

Date	Mintage	F	VF	XF	Unc	BU
2001 Proof	—	Value: 1,800				

KM# 723 700 WON
31.1050 g., 0.9990 Gold 0.9990 oz. AGW, 40 mm. **Obv:** National arms **Rev:** End of the steam train in 1945 and again in 2001

Date	Mintage	F	VF	XF	Unc	BU
2001 Proof	—	Value: 1,800				

KM# 742 700 WON
31.1050 g., 0.9990 Gold 0.9990 oz. AGW, 40 mm. **Obv:** National arms, Central Bank name **Rev:** Ferryboat, married couple and flag

Date	Mintage	F	VF	XF	Unc	BU
2001 Proof	—	Value: 1,800				

KM# 743 700 WON
31.1050 g., 0.9999 Gold 0.9999 oz. AGW, 40 mm. **Obv:** National arms, Central Bank name **Rev:** Ferryboat between Korea and Japan

Date	Mintage	F	VF	XF	Unc	BU
2001 Proof	—	Value: 1,800				

KM# 744 700 WON
31.1050 g., 0.9990 Gold 0.9990 oz. AGW, 40 mm. **Obv:** National arms, Central Bank name **Rev:** Triumphial arch of Moranbong in Pyeongyang

Date	Mintage	F	VF	XF	Unc	BU
2001 Proof	—	Value: 1,800				

KM# 745 700 WON
31.1050 g., 0.9990 Gold 0.9990 oz. AGW, 40 mm. **Obv:** National arms, Central Bank name **Rev:** Chonji crater in Paektusan

Date	Mintage	F	VF	XF	Unc	BU
2001 Proof	—	Value: 1,800				

KM# 748 700 WON
31.1050 g., 0.9990 Gold 0.9990 oz. AGW, 40 mm. **Obv:** National arms, Central Bank name **Rev:** Kim Jeongil and Jiang Zemin clasping hands

Date	Mintage	F	VF	XF	Unc	BU
2001 Proof	—	Value: 1,800				

KM# 503 700 WON
31.1050 g., 0.9990 Gold 0.9990 oz. AGW, 40 mm. **Obv:** National arms **Rev:** Brontosaurus

Date	Mintage	F	VF	XF	Unc	BU
2002 Proof	—	Value: 1,800				

KM# 537 700 WON
31.1050 g., 0.9990 Gold 0.9990 oz. AGW **Obv:** National arms **Rev:** Zhou Enlai, president of the P.R.C.

Date	Mintage	F	VF	XF	Unc	BU
2002 Proof	—	Value: 1,800				

KM# 612 700 WON
31.1050 g., 0.9990 Gold 0.9990 oz. AGW **Obv:** National arms **Rev:** Chinese Junk at sail

Date	Mintage	F	VF	XF	Unc	BU
2002 Proof	—	Value: 1,800				

KM# 634 700 WON
31.1050 g., 0.9990 Gold 0.9990 oz. AGW **Obv:** National arms, Central Bank name **Rev:** Blue dragon right

Date	Mintage	F	VF	XF	Unc	BU
2002 Proof	—	Value: 1,800				

KM# 640 700 WON
31.1050 g., 0.9990 Gold 0.9990 oz. AGW **Obv:** National arms, Country name **Rev:** Two siberian tigers

Date	Mintage	F	VF	XF	Unc	BU
2002 Proof	—	Value: 1,800				

KM# 655 700 WON
31.1050 g., 0.9990 Gold 0.9990 oz. AGW, 40 mm. **Obv:** National arms, Central Bank name **Rev:** Dongmyeong, King of Goguryeo

Date	Mintage	F	VF	XF	Unc	BU
2002 Proof	—	Value: 1,800				

KM# 656 700 WON
31.1050 g., 0.9990 Gold 0.9990 oz. AGW, 40 mm. **Obv:** National arms, Central Bank name **Rev:** Buddha figure

Date	Mintage	F	VF	XF	Unc	BU
2002 Proof	—	Value: 1,800				

KM# 657 700 WON
31.1050 g., 0.9990 Gold 0.9990 oz. AGW, 40 mm. **Obv:** National arms, Central Bank name **Rev:** Dangun, King of Gojoseon

Date	Mintage	F	VF	XF	Unc	BU
2002 Proof	—	Value: 1,800				

KM# 791 700 WON
31.1050 g., 0.9990 Gold 0.9990 oz. AGW, 35 mm. **Obv:** National arms **Rev:** Horse head

Date	Mintage	F	VF	XF	Unc	BU
2002 Proof	—	Value: 1,800				

KM# 792 700 WON
31.1050 g., 0.9990 Gold 0.9990 oz. AGW, 35 mm. **Obv:** National arms **Rev:** Horse to the right

Date	Mintage	F	VF	XF	Unc	BU
2002 Proof	—	Value: 1,800				

KM# 793 700 WON
31.1050 g., 0.9990 Gold 0.9990 oz. AGW, 35 mm. **Obv:** National arms **Rev:** Two horses in center of the Zodiac

Date	Mintage	F	VF	XF	Unc	BU
2002 Proof	—	Value: 1,800				

KM# 816 700 WON
31.1050 g., 0.9990 Gold 0.9990 oz. AGW, 40 mm. **Obv:** National arms, Central Bank name **Rev:** Reconstruction of the Mousoleum for King Dangun

Date	Mintage	F	VF	XF	Unc	BU
2002 Proof	—	Value: 1,800				

KM# 817 700 WON
31.1050 g., 0.9990 Gold 0.9990 oz. AGW, 40 mm. **Obv:** National arms, Central Bank name **Rev:** Dongmyeong, 1st King of Goguryeo

Date	Mintage	F	VF	XF	Unc	BU
2002 Proof	—	Value: 1,800				

KM# 818 700 WON
31.1050 g., 0.9990 Gold 0.9990 oz. AGW, 40 mm. **Obv:** National arms, Central Bank name **Rev:** Wanggeon, 1st King of Boryeo Dynasty

Date	Mintage	F	VF	XF	Unc	BU
2002 Proof	—	Value: 1,800				

KM# 819 700 WON
31.1050 g., 0.9990 Gold 0.9990 oz. AGW, 40 mm. **Obv:** National arms, Central Bank name **Rev:** Jeong Mongju

Date	Mintage	F	VF	XF	Unc	BU
2002 Proof	—	Value: 1,800				

KM# 820 700 WON
31.1050 g., 0.9990 Gold 0.9990 oz. AGW, 40 mm. **Obv:** National arms, Central Bank name **Rev:** Jeon Bongjun

Date	Mintage	F	VF	XF	Unc	BU
2002 Proof	—	Value: 1,800				

KM# 825 700 WON
31.1050 g., 0.9990 Gold 0.9990 oz. AGW, 40 mm. **Obv:** National arms **Rev:** Prince Hodong and Princess Nakrang on horseback

Date	Mintage	F	VF	XF	Unc	BU
2002 Proof	—	Value: 1,800				

KM# 826 700 WON
31.1050 g., 0.9990 Gold 0.9990 oz. AGW, 40 mm. **Obv:** National arms **Rev:** Half-length figures of Prince Hodong and Princess Nakrang

Date	Mintage	F	VF	XF	Unc	BU
2002 Proof	—	Value: 1,800				

KM# 834 700 WON
31.1050 g., 0.9990 Gold 0.9990 oz. AGW, 35 mm. **Obv:** National Arms, Central Bank name **Rev:** Bust of Kim Ilseong

Date	Mintage	F	VF	XF	Unc	BU
2002 Proof	—	Value: 1,800				

KM# 844 700 WON
31.1050 g., 0.9990 Gold 0.9990 oz. AGW, 35 mm. **Obv:** National arms, Central Bank and Country name **Rev:** The soldiers

Date	Mintage	F	VF	XF	Unc	BU
2002 Proof	—	Value: 1,800				

KM# 845 700 WON
31.1050 g., 0.9990 Gold 0.9990 oz. AGW, 35 mm. **Obv:** National arms, Central Bank and Country name **Rev:** Fairy princess

Date	Mintage	F	VF	XF	Unc	BU
2002 Proof	—	Value: 1,800				

KM# 846 700 WON
31.1050 g., 0.9990 Gold 0.9990 oz. AGW, 35 mm. **Obv:** National arms, Central Bank and Country name **Rev:** Bronze statue

Date	Mintage	F	VF	XF	Unc	BU
2002 Proof	—	Value: 1,800				

KM# 847 700 WON
31.1050 g., 0.9990 Gold 0.9990 oz. AGW, 35 mm. **Obv:** National arms, Central Bank and Country name **Rev:** Female worshipers of the sun

Date	Mintage	F	VF	XF	Unc	BU
2002 Proof	—	Value: 1,800				

KM# 848 700 WON
31.1050 g., 0.9990 Gold 0.9990 oz. AGW, 35 mm. **Obv:** National arms, Central Bank and Country name **Rev:** Trhee prinicpals of re-unification

Date	Mintage	F	VF	XF	Unc	BU
2002 Proof	—	Value: 1,800				

KM# 849 700 WON
31.1050 g., 0.9990 Gold 0.9990 oz. AGW, 35 mm. **Obv:** National arms, Central Bank and Country name **Rev:** Dancing children

Date	Mintage	F	VF	XF	Unc	BU
2002 Proof	—	Value: 1,800				

KM# 872 700 WON
31.1050 g., 0.9990 Gold 0.9990 oz. AGW, 40 mm. **Obv:** National arms, Central bank name **Rev:** Family

Date	Mintage	F	VF	XF	Unc	BU
2002 Proof	—	Value: 1,800				

KM# 873 700 WON
31.1050 g., 0.9990 Gold 0.9990 oz. AGW, 40 mm. **Obv:** National arms, Central Bank name **Rev:** Map of Korea with four cardinal compass points

Date	Mintage	F	VF	XF	Unc	BU
2002 Proof	—	Value: 1,800				

KM# 874 700 WON
31.1050 g., 0.9990 Gold 0.9990 oz. AGW, 40 mm. **Obv:** Naitonal arms, Central Bank name **Rev:** Rythem dancer and map of Korea

Date	Mintage	F	VF	XF	Unc	BU
2002 Proof	—	Value: 1,800				

KM# 875 700 WON
31.1050 g., 0.9990 Gold 0.9990 oz. AGW, 40 mm. **Obv:** National arms, Central Bank name **Rev:** Drum dancers and map of Korea

Date	Mintage	F	VF	XF	Unc	BU
2002 Proof	—	Value: 1,800				

KM# 876 700 WON
31.1050 g., 0.9990 Gold 0.9990 oz. AGW, 40 mm. **Obv:** National arms, Central Bank name **Rev:** Korean team victory celebration

Date	Mintage	F	VF	XF	Unc	BU
2002 Proof	—	Value: 1,800				

KM# 899 700 WON
31.1050 g., 0.9990 Gold 0.9990 oz. AGW, 40 mm. **Obv:** East gate of Pyeongyang **Rev:** Sheep at center of Zodiac

Date	Mintage	F	VF	XF	Unc	BU
2003 Proof	—	Value: 1,800				

KM# 912 700 WON
31.1050 g., 0.9990 Gold 0.9990 oz. AGW, 40 mm. **Obv:** National arms, Central Bank name **Rev:** Eulji Mundeok

Date	Mintage	F	VF	XF	Unc	BU
2003 Proof	—	Value: 1,800				

KM# 913 700 WON
31.1050 g., 0.9990 Gold 0.9990 oz. AGW, 40 mm. **Obv:** National arms, Central Bank name **Rev:** Yeon Gaesomun

Date	Mintage	F	VF	XF	Unc	BU
2003 Proof	—	Value: 1,800				

KM# 914 700 WON
31.1050 g., 0.9990 Gold 0.9990 oz. AGW, 40 mm. **Obv:** National arms, Central Bank name **Rev:** Gang Camchan

Date	Mintage	F	VF	XF	Unc	BU
2003 Proof	—	Value: 1,800				

KM# 917 700 WON
31.1050 g., 0.9990 Gold 0.9990 oz. AGW, 40 mm. **Obv:** National arms, Central Bank name **Rev:** Turtle boat

Date	Mintage	F	VF	XF	Unc	BU
2003 Proof	—	Value: 1,800				

KM# 941 700 WON
31.1050 g., 0.9990 Gold 0.9990 oz. AGW, 40 mm. **Obv:** Naitonal arms, Central Bank name **Rev:** Monkey at center of Zodiac

Date	Mintage	F	VF	XF	Unc	BU
2004 Proof	—	Value: 1,800				

KM# 1018 700 WON
31.1050 g., 0.9990 Gold 0.9990 oz. AGW, 40 mm. **Obv:** National arms, Central Bank name **Rev:** Rooster within Zodiac circle

Date	Mintage	F	VF	XF	Unc	BU
2005 Proof	—	Value: 1,800				

KM# 1032 700 WON
31.1050 g., 0.9990 Gold 0.9990 oz. AGW, 40 mm. **Obv:** National arms, Central Bank name **Rev:** Admiral Yi Sunsin and turtle boat

Date	Mintage	F	VF	XF	Unc	BU
2005 Proof	—	Value: 1,800				

KM# 1033 700 WON
31.1050 g., 0.9990 Gold 0.9990 oz. AGW, 40 mm. **Obv:** National arms, Central Bank name **Rev:** General Hong Beomdo

Date	Mintage	F	VF	XF	Unc	BU
2005 Proof	—	Value: 1,800				

KM# 1042 700 WON
31.1050 g., 0.9990 Gold 0.9990 oz. AGW, 40 mm. **Obv:** National arms, Central Bank name **Rev:** Map of Korea, two peace doves, rainbow

Date	Mintage	F	VF	XF	Unc	BU
2005 Proof	—	Value: 1,800				

KM# 1047 700 WON

31.1050 g., 0.9990 Gold 0.9990 oz. AGW, 40 mm. **Obv:** National arms, Central Bank name **Rev:** Tomb of the unknown soldier in Moscow, Russian legend

Date	Mintage	F	VF	XF	Unc	BU
2005 Proof	—	Value: 1,800				

KM# 1048 700 WON

31.1050 g., 0.9990 Gold 0.9990 oz. AGW, 40 mm. **Obv:** National arms, Central Bank name **Rev:** Memorial to mothers in St. Petersburg

Date	Mintage	F	VF	XF	Unc	BU
2005 Proof	—	Value: 1,800				

KM# 428 700 WON

[illegible] **Series:** [illegible] **Obv:** [illegible] **Rev:** [illegible] **Edge:** [illegible]

Date	Mintage	F	VF	XF	Unc	BU
2006 Proof	3,000	Value: 70.00				

KM# 429 700 WON

15.5500 g., 0.9990 Silver 0.4994 oz. ASW, 30.00 mm. **Series:** European Union Euro Commemoratives **Obv:** National arms **Rev:** Vatican in relief in tiger's-eye **Edge:** Plain

Date	Mintage	F	VF	XF	Unc	BU
2006 Proof	3,000	Value: 70.00				

KM# 430 700 WON

15.5500 g., 0.9990 Silver 0.4994 oz. ASW, 30.00 mm. **Series:** European Union Euro Commemoratives **Obv:** National arms **Rev:** Male Olympic statue - discus - Athens in relief in tiger's-eye **Edge:** Plain

Date	Mintage	F	VF	XF	Unc	BU
2006 Proof	3,000	Value: 70.00				

KM# 431 700 WON

15.5500 g., 0.9990 Silver 0.4994 oz. ASW, 30.00 mm. **Series:** European Union Euro Commemoratives **Obv:** National arms **Rev:** 50th Anniversary Austrian States Treaty in relief in tiger's-eye **Edge:** Plain

Date	Mintage	F	VF	XF	Unc	BU
2006 Proof	3,000	Value: 70.00				

KM# 432 700 WON

15.5500 g., 0.9990 Silver 0.4994 oz. ASW, 30.00 mm. **Series:** European Union Euro Commemoratives **Obv:** National arms **Rev:** Don Quixote in relief in tiger's-eye **Edge:** Plain

Date	Mintage	F	VF	XF	Unc	BU
2006 Proof	3,000	Value: 70.00				

KM# 433 700 WON

15.5500 g., 0.9990 Silver 0.4994 oz. ASW, 30.00 mm. **Series:** European Union Euro Commemoratives **Obv:** National arms **Rev:** Head of Henri, Grand Duke of Luxembourg at left facing right, crowned H at right in relief in tiger's-eye **Edge:** Plain

Date	Mintage	F	VF	XF	Unc	BU
2006 Proof	3,000	Value: 70.00				

KM# 434 700 WON

15.5500 g., 0.9990 Silver 0.4994 oz. ASW, 30 mm. **Series:** European Union Euro Commemoratives **Obv:** National arms **Rev:** Italian FAO logo in relief in tiger's-eye **Edge:** Plain

Date	Mintage	F	VF	XF	Unc	BU
2006 Proof	3,000	Value: 70.00				

KM# 435 700 WON

15.5500 g., 0.9990 Silver 0.4994 oz. ASW, 30 mm. **Series:** European Union Euro Commemoratives **Obv:** National arms **Rev:** Finland - stylized flower in relief in tiger's-eye **Edge:** Plain

Date	Mintage	F	VF	XF	Unc	BU
2006 Proof	3,000	Value: 70.00				

KM# 436 700 WON

15.5500 g., 0.9990 Silver 0.4994 oz. ASW, 30 mm. **Series:** European Union Euro Commemoratives **Obv:** National arms **Rev:** Conjoined heads of Grand Duke Henri of Luxembourg and King Albert of Belgium left in relief in tiger's-eye **Edge:** Plain

Date	Mintage	F	VF	XF	Unc	BU
2006 Proof	3,000	Value: 70.00				

KM# 437 700 WON

15.5500 g., 0.9990 Silver 0.4994 oz. ASW, 30 mm. **Series:** European Union Euro Commemoratives **Obv:** National arms **Rev:** San Marino - bust of Bartolomeo Borghesi slightly right in relief in tiger's-eye **Edge:** Plain

Date	Mintage	F	VF	XF	Unc	BU
2006 Proof	3,000	Value: 70.00				

KM# 438 700 WON

15.5500 g., 0.9990 Silver tigereye colored center 0.4994 oz. ASW, 30 mm. **Series:** European Union Euro Commemoratives **Obv:** National arms **Rev:** Vatican - World Youth Day in Cologne **Edge:** Plain

Date	Mintage	F	VF	XF	Unc	BU
2006 Proof	3,000	Value: 70.00				

KM# 439 700 WON

15.5500 g., 0.9990 Silver 0.4994 oz. ASW, 30 mm. **Series:** European Union Euro Commemoratives **Obv:** National arms **Rev:** San Marino - Year of Physics design in relief in tiger's-eye **Edge:** Plain

Date	Mintage	F	VF	XF	Unc	BU
2006 Proof	3,000	Value: 70.00				

KM# 958 1000 WON

42.2160 g., 0.9990 Gold 1.3559 oz. AGW, 45 mm. **Obv:** National arms, Central Bank name **Rev:** Kim Ilseong

Date	Mintage	F	VF	XF	Unc	BU
2004 Proof	—	Value: 2,450				

KM# 959 1000 WON

42.2160 g., 0.9990 Gold 1.3559 oz. AGW, 45 mm. **Obv:** National arms, Central Bank name **Rev:** Kim Jeongil

Date	Mintage	F	VF	XF	Unc	BU
2004 Proof	—	Value: 2,500				

KM# 960 1000 WON

42.2160 g., 0.9990 Gold 1.3559 oz. AGW, 45 mm. **Obv:** National arms, Central Bank name **Rev:** Kim Jeongsuk

Date	Mintage	F	VF	XF	Unc	BU
2004 Proof	—	Value: 2,500				

KM# 961 1000 WON

42.2160 g., 0.9990 Gold 1.3559 oz. AGW, 45 mm. **Obv:** National arms, Central Bank name **Rev:** Kim Ilseong's birthplace

Date	Mintage	F	VF	XF	Unc	BU
2004 Proof	—	Value: 2,500				

KM# 962 1000 WON

42.2160 g., 0.9990 Gold 1.3559 oz. AGW, 45 mm. **Obv:** National arms, Central Bank name **Rev:** Mountain cottage of Kim Jeongil

Date	Mintage	F	VF	XF	Unc	BU
2004 Proof	—	Value: 2,500				

KM# 963 1000 WON

42.2160 g., 0.9990 Gold 1.3559 oz. AGW, 45 mm. **Obv:** National arms, Central Bank name **Rev:** House where Kim Jeongsuk was born

Date	Mintage	F	VF	XF	Unc	BU
2004 Proof	—	Value: 2,500				

KM# 1097 1000 WON

20.0000 g., 0.9990 Silver 0.6423 oz. ASW, 38 mm. **Subject:** Lake Placid Winter Olympics, 1936 **Obv:** National arms, Central Bank name **Rev:** Bobsled

Date	Mintage	F	VF	XF	Unc	BU
2006 Proof	Est. 5,000	Value: 45.00				

KM# 1098 1000 WON

20.0000 g., 0.9990 Silver 0.6423 oz. ASW, 38 mm. **Subject:** Sarajevo Winter Olympics, 1984 **Obv:** National arms, Central Bank name **Rev:** Ice Hockey player

Date	Mintage	F	VF	XF	Unc	BU
2006 Proof	Est. 5,000	Value: 45.00				

KM# 1099 1000 WON

20.0000 g., 0.9990 Silver 0.6423 oz. ASW, 38 mm. **Obv:** National arms, Central Bank name **Rev:** Soccer player and Brazil flag and map

Date	Mintage	F	VF	XF	Unc	BU
2006 Proof	Est. 5,000	Value: 45.00				

KM# 1100 1000 WON

20.0000 g., 0.9990 Silver 0.6423 oz. ASW, 38 mm. **Subject:** Bejing Summer Olympics, 2008 **Obv:** National arms, Central Bank name **Rev:** Gymnast on pommel horse

Date	Mintage	F	VF	XF	Unc	BU
2006 Proof	—	Value: 35.00				

KM# 440 1000 WON

20.0000 g., 0.9990 Silver 0.6423 oz. ASW, 38 mm. **Obv:** National arms **Rev:** Arctic animals with map of North Pole in background **Rev. Legend:** INTERNATIONAL POLAR YEAR / ARCTIC ANIMALS **Edge:** Plain

Date	Mintage	F	VF	XF	Unc	BU
ND(2007) Proof	—	Value: 85.00				

KM# 446 1000 WON
20.0000 g., 0.9990 Silver 0.6423 oz. ASW, 38 mm. **Series:** Endangered Wildlife **Obv:** Fortress Gate **Rev:** Polar Bear standing facing **Rev. Legend:** URSUS MAITIMUS **Edge:** Plain

Date	Mintage	F	VF	XF	Unc	BU
2007 Proof	5,000	Value: 70.00				

KM# 1186 1000 WON
20.0000 g., 0.9990 Silver 0.6423 oz. ASW, 38 mm. **Subject:** Vancouver Winter Olympics, 2010 **Obv:** East gate of Pyeongyang **Rev:** Nordic Combine and triumphial arch

Date	Mintage	F	VF	XF	Unc	BU
2008 Proof	—	Value: 45.00				

KM# 1187 1000 WON
20.0000 g., 0.9990 Silver 0.6423 oz. ASW, 38 mm. **Subject:** Wold Cup Soccer, South Africa, 2010 **Obv:** East gate of Pyeongyang **Rev:** Soccer foul play

Date	Mintage	F	VF	XF	Unc	BU
2008 Proof	Est. 5,000	Value: 35.00				

KM# 993 1500 WON
70.0000 g., 0.9990 Gold 2.2482 oz. AGW, 50 mm. **Obv:** Map of Korea, Central Bank name **Rev:** Court physician Heo Jun

Date	Mintage	F	VF	XF	Unc	BU
2004 Proof	—	Value: 4,000				

KM# 1067 1500 WON
31.1050 g., 0.9990 Silver 0.9990 oz. ASW, 40 mm. **Obv:** Trumpeter, Central Bank name **Rev:** Triumphial arch in Pyeongyang

Date	Mintage	F	VF	XF	Unc	BU
2005 Proof	—	Value: 115				

KM# 1069 1500 WON
31.1050 g., 0.9990 Silver 0.9990 oz. ASW, 40 mm. **Subject:** Worker's Party, 60th Anniversary **Obv:** National arms, Central Bank name **Rev:** Party emblem

Date	Mintage	F	VF	XF	Unc	BU
2005 Proof	—	Value: 115				

KM# 1070 1500 WON
31.1050 g., 0.9990 Gold 0.9990 oz. AGW, 40 mm. **Subject:** Worker's Party,60th Anniversary **Obv:** National arms, Central Bank name **Rev:** Party emblem

Date	Mintage	F	VF	XF	Unc	BU
2005 Proof	—	Value: 1,800				

KM# 1092 1500 WON
31.1050 g., 0.9990 Silver 0.9990 oz. ASW, 40 mm. **Obv:** National arms, Central Bank name **Rev:** Two dogs

Date	Mintage	F	VF	XF	Unc	BU
2006 Proof	Est. 2,000	Value: 60.00				

KM# 1093 1500 WON
31.1050 g., 0.9990 Silver 0.9990 oz. ASW, 40 mm. **Obv:** National arms, Central Bank name **Rev:** Bronze staue of flying horse

Date	Mintage	F	VF	XF	Unc	BU
2006 Proof	—	Value: 115				

KM# 1094 1500 WON
31.1050 g., 0.9990 Silver 0.9990 oz. ASW, 40 mm. **Obv:** National arms, Central Bank name **Rev:** Triumphial arch

Date	Mintage	F	VF	XF	Unc	BU
2006 Proof	—	Value: 115				

KM# 1142 1500 WON
31.1050 g., 0.9990 Silver 0.9990 oz. ASW, 40 mm. **Obv:** National arms, Central Bank name **Rev:** Hoopoe

Date	Mintage	F	VF	XF	Unc	BU
2007 Proof	Est. 500	Value: 60.00				

KM# 1143 1500 WON
31.1050 g., 0.9990 Silver 0.9990 oz. ASW, 40 mm. **Obv:** National arms, Central Bank name **Rev:** Ural owl

Date	Mintage	F	VF	XF	Unc	BU
2007 Proof	Est. 500	Value: 100				

KM# 1144 1500 WON
31.1050 g., 0.9990 Silver 0.9990 oz. ASW, 40 mm. **Obv:** National arms, Central Bank name **Rev:** Eagle

Date	Mintage	F	VF	XF	Unc	BU
2007 Proof	—	Value: 60.00				

KM# 1145 1500 WON
31.1050 g., 0.9990 Silver 0.9990 oz. ASW, 40 mm. **Obv:** National arms, Central Bank name **Rev:** White Rhino

Date	Mintage	F	VF	XF	Unc	BU
2007 Proof	Est. 500	Value: 60.00				

KM# 1146 1500 WON
31.1050 g., 0.9990 Silver 0.9990 oz. ASW, 40 mm. **Obv:** National arms, Central Bank name **Rev:** African elephant family

Date	Mintage	F	VF	XF	Unc	BU
2007 Proof	Est. 500	Value: 60.00				

KM# 1147 1500 WON
31.1050 g., 0.9990 Silver 0.9990 oz. ASW, 40 mm. **Obv:** National arms, Central Bank name **Rev:** Lion family

Date	Mintage	F	VF	XF	Unc	BU
2007 Proof	Est. 500	Value: 60.00				

KM# 1148 1500 WON
31.1050 g., 0.9990 Silver 0.9990 oz. ASW, 40 mm. **Obv:** National arms, Central Bank name **Rev:** Cape buffalo

Date	Mintage	F	VF	XF	Unc	BU
2007 Proof	Est. 500	Value: 60.00				

KM# 1149 1500 WON
31.1050 g., 0.9990 Silver 0.9990 oz. ASW, 40 mm. **Obv:** National arms, Central Bank name **Rev:** Marine turtle

Date	Mintage	F	VF	XF	Unc	BU
2007 Proof	Est. 500	Value: 60.00				

KM# 1150 1500 WON
31.1050 g., 0.9990 Silver 0.9990 oz. ASW, 40 mm. **Obv:** National arms, Central Bank name **Rev:** Penguin

Date	Mintage	F	VF	XF	Unc	BU
2007 Proof	Est. 500	Value: 60.00				

KM# 1151 1500 WON
31.1050 g., 0.9990 Silver 0.9990 oz. ASW, 40 mm. **Obv:** National arms, Central Bank name **Rev:** Emu

Date	Mintage	F	VF	XF	Unc	BU
2007 Proof	Est. 500	Value: 60.00				

KM# 1152 1500 WON
31.1050 g., 0.9990 Silver 0.9990 oz. ASW, 40 mm. **Obv:** National arms, Central Bank name **Rev:** Eagle owl

Date	Mintage	F	VF	XF	Unc	BU
2007 Proof	Est. 500	Value: 60.00				

KM# 1153 1500 WON
31.1050 g., 0.9990 Silver 0.9990 oz. ASW, 40 mm. **Obv:** National arms, Central Bank name **Rev:** Lemur

Date	Mintage	F	VF	XF	Unc	BU
2007 Proof	Est. 500	Value: 60.00				

KM# 1154 1500 WON
31.1050 g., 0.9990 Silver 0.9990 oz. ASW, 40 mm. **Obv:** National arms, Central Bank name **Rev:** Lion

Date	Mintage	F	VF	XF	Unc	BU
2007 Proof	Est. 500	Value: 60.00				

KM# 1155 1500 WON
31.1050 g., 0.9990 Silver 0.9990 oz. ASW, 40 mm. **Obv:** National arms, Central Bank name **Rev:** Two African elephants

Date	Mintage	F	VF	XF	Unc	BU
2007 Proof	Est. 500	Value: 60.00				

KM# 1176 1500 WON
31.1050 g., 0.9990 Silver 0.9990 oz. ASW, 40 mm. **Subject:** Nationhood, 60th Anniversary **Obv:** National arms, Central Bank name **Rev:** National flag, star above

Date	Mintage	F	VF	XF	Unc	BU
2008 Proof	—	Value: 115				

KM# 1185 1500 WON
31.1050 g., 0.9990 Silver 0.9990 oz. ASW, 40 mm. **Subject:** Bejing Summer Olympics, 2008 **Obv:** East gate of Pyeongyang **Rev:** Ancient ring gymnast

Date	Mintage	F	VF	XF	Unc	BU
2008 Proof	Est. 5,000	Value: 60.00				

KM# 950 2000 WON
31.1050 g., 0.9990 Bi-Metallic Gold center in Silver ring 0.9990 oz., 40 mm. **Obv:** National arms, Central Bank name **Rev:** Sports hall in Pyeongyang

Date	Mintage	F	VF	XF	Unc	BU
2004 Proof	—	Value: 2,200				

KM# 964 2000 WON
31.1050 g., 0.9990 Gold 0.9990 oz. AGW, 35 mm. **Subject:** 10th Anniversary of the takeover **Obv:** National arms, Central Bank name **Rev:** Kim Jeongil

Date	Mintage	F	VF	XF	Unc	BU
2004 Proof	—	Value: 2,100				

KM# 965 2000 WON
31.1050 g., 0.9990 Gold 0.9990 oz. AGW, 35 mm. **Obv:** National arms, Central Bank name **Rev:** Kim Jeongil and Kim Daejung

Date	Mintage	F	VF	XF	Unc	BU
2004 Proof	—	Value: 2,000				

KM# 967 2000 WON
31.1050 g., 0.9990 Gold 0.9990 oz. AGW, 35 mm. **Obv:** National arms, Central Bank name **Rev:** Kim Jeongil and Hu Jintao

Date	Mintage	F	VF	XF	Unc	BU
2004 Proof	—	Value: 2,000				

KM# 968 2000 WON
31.1050 g., 0.9990 Gold 0.9990 oz. AGW, 35 mm. **Obv:** National arms, Central Bank name **Rev:** Kim Jeongil and Vladimir Putin

Date	Mintage	F	VF	XF	Unc	BU
2004 Proof	—	Value: 2,100				

KM# 985 2000 WON
31.1050 g., 0.9990 Gold 0.9990 oz. AGW, 40 mm. **Obv:** Dokdo, rocky islands, Central Bank name **Rev:** Island group map

Date	Mintage	F	VF	XF	Unc	BU
2004 Proof	—	Value: 2,000				

KM# 986 2000 WON
31.1050 g., 0.9990 Gold 0.9990 oz. AGW, 40 mm. **Obv:** Dokdo, rocky islands, Central Bank name **Rev:** Fisher Ahn Yongbok

Date	Mintage	F	VF	XF	Unc	BU
2004 Proof	—	Value: 2,100				

KM# 987 2000 WON
31.1050 g., 0.9990 Gold 0.9990 oz. AGW, 40 mm. **Obv:** Dokdo, rocky islands, Central Bank name **Rev:** West Island

Date	Mintage	F	VF	XF	Unc	BU
2004 Proof	—	Value: 2,100				

KM# 988 2000 WON
31.1050 g., 0.9990 Gold 0.9990 oz. AGW, 40 mm. **Obv:** Dokdo, rocky islands, Central Bank name **Rev:** East island

Date	Mintage	F	VF	XF	Unc	BU
2004 Proof	—	Value: 2,100				

KM# 989 2000 WON
31.1050 g., 0.9990 Gold 0.9990 oz. AGW, 40 mm. **Obv:** Dokdo, rocky islands, Central Bank name **Rev:** Three brothers islands

Date	Mintage	F	VF	XF	Unc	BU
2004 Proof	—	Value: 2,100				

KM# 990 2000 WON
31.1050 g., 0.9990 Gold 0.9990 oz. AGW, 40 mm. **Obv:** Dokdo, rocky islands, Central Bank name **Rev:** Chicken island

Date	Mintage	F	VF	XF	Unc	BU
2004 Proof	—	Value: 2,100				

KM# 991 2000 WON
31.1050 g., 0.9990 Gold 0.9990 oz. AGW, 40 mm. **Obv:** Dokdo, rocky islands, Central Bank name **Rev:** Candle island

Date	Mintage	F	VF	XF	Unc	BU
2004 Proof	—	Value: 2,100				

KM# 1087 2500 WON
33.3300 g., 0.9000 Gold 0.9644 oz. AGW **Obv:** Old coins and Central Bank name

Date	Mintage	F	VF	XF	Unc	BU
2005	Est. 200	—	—	—	—	2,050

KM# 442 15000 WON
7.7800 g., 0.9990 Gold 0.2499 oz. AGW, 26 mm. **Subject:** 170th Anniversary First Public Railway St. Petersburg - Zarskoje Selo **Obv:** Fortress Gate **Rev:** First train arriving **Edge:** Plain

Date	Mintage	F	VF	XF	Unc	BU
ND(2007) Proof	2,000	Value: 550				

KM# 448 15000 WON
7.7800 g., 0.9990 Gold 0.2499 oz. AGW, 26 mm. **Subject:** 150th Anniversary Birth of Ziolkowski and 50th Anniversary Launch of Sputnik I **Obv:** Fortress Gate **Rev:** Bust of Ziolkowski facing 3/4 right at lower left, Sputnik circling earth at top right **Edge:** Plain

Date	Mintage	F	VF	XF	Unc	BU
ND(2007) Proof	2,000	Value: 550				

KM# 444 15000 WON
7.7800 g., 0.9990 Gold 0.2499 oz. AGW, 26 mm. **Subject:** Lunar Year of the Rat **Obv:** Fortress Gate **Rev:** Two rats within circle of Lunar figures **Edge:** Plain

Date	Mintage	F	VF	XF	Unc	BU
2008 Proof	2,000	Value: 550				

KM# 1068 60000 WON
31.1050 g., 0.9990 Gold 0.9990 oz. AGW, 35 mm. **Obv:** Trumpeter, Central Bank name **Rev:** Triumphia arch in Pyeongyang

Date	Mintage	F	VF	XF	Unc	BU
2005 Proof	—	Value: 1,800				

KM# 1095 60000 WON
31.1050 g., 0.9990 Gold 0.9990 oz. AGW, 35 mm. **Obv:** National arms, Central Bank name **Rev:** Bronze statue of flying horse

Date	Mintage	F	VF	XF	Unc	BU
2006 Proof	—	Value: 2,100				

KM# 1096 60000 WON
31.1050 g., 0.9990 Gold 0.9990 oz. AGW, 35 mm. **Obv:** National arms, Central Bank name **Rev:** Triumphial arch

Date	Mintage	F	VF	XF	Unc	BU
2006 Proof	—	Value: 2,100				

KM# 1156 60000 WON
31.1050 g., 0.9990 Gold 0.9990 oz. AGW, 35 mm. **Obv:** National arms, Central Bank name **Rev:** Hoopoe

Date	Mintage	F	VF	XF	Unc	BU
2007 Proof	Est. 500	Value: 2,100				

KM# 1157 60000 WON
31.1050 g., 0.9990 Gold 0.9990 oz. AGW, 35 mm. **Obv:** National arms, Central Bank name **Rev:** Ural owl

Date	Mintage	F	VF	XF	Unc	BU
2007 Proof	Est. 500	Value: 2,100				

KM# 1158 60000 WON
31.1050 g., 0.9990 Gold 0.9990 oz. AGW, 35 mm. **Obv:** National arms, Central Bank name **Rev:** Eagle

Date	Mintage	F	VF	XF	Unc	BU
2007 Proof	Est. 500	Value: 2,100				

KM# 1159 60000 WON
31.1050 g., 0.9990 Gold 0.9990 oz. AGW, 35 mm. **Obv:** National arms, Central Bank name **Rev:** White rhino

Date	Mintage	F	VF	XF	Unc	BU
2007 Proof	Est. 500	Value: 2,100				

KM# 1160 60000 WON
31.1050 g., 0.9990 Gold 0.9990 oz. AGW, 35 mm. **Obv:** National arms, Central Bank name **Rev:** African elephant family

Date	Mintage	F	VF	XF	Unc	BU
2007 Proof	Est. 500	Value: 2,100				

KM# 1161 60000 WON
31.1050 g., 0.9990 Gold 0.9990 oz. AGW, 35 mm. **Obv:** National arms, Central Bank name **Rev:** Lion family

Date	Mintage	F	VF	XF	Unc	BU
2007 Proof	Est. 500	Value: 2,100				

KM# 1162 60000 WON
31.1050 g., 0.9990 Gold 0.9990 oz. AGW, 35 mm. **Obv:** National arms, Central Bank name **Rev:** Cape buffalo

Date	Mintage	F	VF	XF	Unc	BU
2007 Proof	Est. 500	Value: 2,100				

KM# 1163 60000 WON
31.1050 g., 0.9990 Gold 0.9990 oz. AGW, 35 mm. **Obv:** National arms, Central Bank name **Rev:** Marine turtle

Date	Mintage	F	VF	XF	Unc	BU
2007 Proof	Est. 500	Value: 2,100				

KM# 1164 60000 WON
31.1050 g., 0.9990 Gold 0.9990 oz. AGW, 35 mm. **Obv:** National arms, Central Bank name **Rev:** Penguin

Date	Mintage	F	VF	XF	Unc	BU
2007 Proof	Est. 500	Value: 2,100				

KM# 1165 60000 WON

31.1050 g., 0.9990 Gold 0.9990 oz. AGW, 35 mm. **Obv:** National arms, Central Bank name **Rev:** Emu

Date	Mintage	F	VF	XF	Unc	BU
2007 Proof	Est. 500	Value: 2,100				

KM# 1166 60000 WON

31.1050 g., 0.9990 Gold 0.9990 oz. AGW, 35 mm. **Obv:** National arms, Central Bank name **Rev:** Eagle owl

Date	Mintage	F	VF	XF	Unc	BU
2007 Proof	Est. 500	Value: 2,100				

KM# 1167 60000 WON

31.1050 g., 0.9990 Gold 0.9990 oz. AGW, 35 mm. **Obv:** National arms, Central Bank name **Rev:** Lemur

Date	Mintage	F	VF	XF	Unc	BU
2007 Proof	Est. 500	Value: 2,100				

KM# 1168 60000 WON

31.1050 g., 0.9990 Gold 0.9990 oz. AGW, 35 mm. **Obv:** National arms, Central Bank name **Rev:** Lion

Date	Mintage	F	VF	XF	Unc	BU
2007 Proof	Est. 500	Value: 2,100				

KM# 1169 60000 WON

31.1050 g., 0.9990 Gold 0.9990 oz. AGW, 35 mm. **Obv:** National arms, Central Bank name **Rev:** Two African elephants

Date	Mintage	F	VF	XF	Unc	BU
2007 Proof	Est. 500	Value: 2,100				

KM# 1177 60000 WON

31.1050 g., 0.9990 Gold 0.9990 oz. AGW, 35 mm. **Subject:** Nationhood, 60th Anniversary **Obv:** National arms, Central Bank name **Rev:** National flag, star above

Date	Mintage	F	VF	XF	Unc	BU
2008 Proof	—	Value: 2,100				

REFORM COINAGE

100 (Old) Won = 1 (new) Won

KM# 1170 CHON

Aluminum, 18 mm. **Obv:** National arms, Central Bank name

Date	Mintage	F	VF	XF	Unc	BU
2008	—	—	—	—	3.00	5.00

KM# 1171 5 CHON

Aluminum, 19 mm. **Obv:** National arms, Central Bank name **Rev:** Magnolia

Date	Mintage	F	VF	XF	Unc	BU
2008	—	—	—	—	3.00	5.00

KM# 1172 10 CHON

1.0000 g., Aluminum, 20 mm. **Obv:** National arms, Central Bank name **Rev:** Rhododendron

Date	Mintage	F	VF	XF	Unc	BU
2002	—	—	—	—	1.00	1.75

KM# 1173 50 CHON

1.5000 g., Aluminum, 22 mm. **Obv:** National arms, Central Bank name **Rev:** Begonia

Date	Mintage	F	VF	XF	Unc	BU
2002	—	—	—	—	1.00	2.00

KM# 1174 WON

1.8000 g., Aluminum, 24 mm. **Obv:** National arms, Central Bank name **Rev:** Beognia

Date	Mintage	F	VF	XF	Unc	BU
2002	—	—	—	—	1.50	2.50

KM# 1188 2 WON

7.0000 g., 0.9990 Silver 0.2248 oz. ASW, 30 mm. **Obv:** National arms, Central Bank name **Rev:** Panda in color

Date	Mintage	F	VF	XF	Unc	BU
2008 Proof	Est. 5,000	Value: 30.00				

KM# 1217 2 WON

7.0000 g., 0.9990 Silver 0.2248 oz. ASW, 30 mm. **Obv:** National arms, Central Bank name **Rev:** Panda in color

Date	Mintage	F	VF	XF	Unc	BU
2009 Proof	Est. 5,000	Value: 30.00				

KM# 1220 2 WON

7.0000 g., 0.9990 Silver 0.2248 oz. ASW, 30 mm. **Obv:** National arms, Central Bank name **Rev:** Corwn gate of the Dresden Zwingers

Date	Mintage	F	VF	XF	Unc	BU
2009 Proof	—	Value: 30.00				

KM# 1221 2 WON

7.0000 g., 0.9990 Silver 0.2248 oz. ASW, 30 mm. **Obv:** National arms, Central Bank name **Rev:** Acropolis in Athens

Date	Mintage	F	VF	XF	Unc	BU
2009 Proof	—	Value: 30.00				

KM# 1222 2 WON

7.0000 g., 0.9990 Silver 0.2248 oz. ASW, 30 mm. **Obv:** National arms, Central Bank name **Rev:** Sydney Opera House

Date	Mintage	F	VF	XF	Unc	BU
2009 Proof	—	Value: 30.00				

KM# 1223 2 WON

7.0000 g., 0.9990 Silver 0.2248 oz. ASW, 30 mm. **Obv:** National arms, Central Bank name **Rev:** Angkor Wat temple complex

Date	Mintage	F	VF	XF	Unc	BU
2009 Proof	—	Value: 30.00				

KM# 1224 2 WON

7.0000 g., 0.9990 Silver 0.2248 oz. ASW, 30 mm. **Obv:** National arms, Central Bank name **Rev:** Minakshi and Sundareshwara temples in Madurai

Date	Mintage	F	VF	XF	Unc	BU
2009 Proof	—	Value: 30.00				

KM# 1225 2 WON

7.0000 g., 0.9990 Silver 0.2248 oz. ASW, 30 mm. **Obv:** National arms, Central Bank name **Rev:** Kremlin in Moscow

Date	Mintage	F	VF	XF	Unc	BU
2009 Proof	—	Value: 30.00				

KM# 1226 2 WON

7.0000 g., 0.9990 Silver 0.2248 oz. ASW, 30 mm. **Obv:** National arms, Central Bank name **Rev:** Abu Simbel

Date	Mintage	F	VF	XF	Unc	BU
2009 Proof	—	Value: 30.00				

KM# 1227 2 WON

7.0000 g., 0.9990 Silver 0.2248 oz. ASW, 30 mm. **Obv:** National arms, Central Bank name **Rev:** Eiffel Tower in Paris

Date	Mintage	F	VF	XF	Unc	BU
2009 Proof	—	Value: 30.00				

KM# 1228 2 WON

7.0000 g., 0.9990 Silver 0.2248 oz. ASW, 30 mm. **Obv:** National arms, Central Bank name **Rev:** Dalai Lama's Palace in Lhasa

Date	Mintage	F	VF	XF	Unc	BU
2009 Proof	—	Value: 30.00				

KM# 1229 2 WON

7.0000 g., 0.9990 Silver 0.2248 oz. ASW, 30 mm. **Obv:** National arms, Central Bank name **Rev:** Terracotta warriors of King Qin Shihuangdi in China

Date	Mintage	F	VF	XF	Unc	BU
2009 Proof	—	Value: 30.00				

KM# 1230 2 WON

7.0000 g., 0.9990 Silver 0.2248 oz. ASW, 30 mm. **Obv:** National arms, Central Bank name **Rev:** Palace at Versailles

Date	Mintage	F	VF	XF	Unc	BU
2009 Proof	—	Value: 30.00				

KM# 1231 2 WON

7.0000 g., 0.9990 Silver 0.2248 oz. ASW, 30 mm. **Obv:** National arms, Central Bank name **Rev:** Aachen Cathedral

Date	Mintage	F	VF	XF	Unc	BU
2010 Proof	—	Value: 30.00				

KM# 1232 2 WON

7.0000 g., 0.9990 Silver 0.2248 oz. ASW, 30 mm. **Obv:** National arms, Central Bank name **Rev:** Leaning Tower of Pisa

Date	Mintage	F	VF	XF	Unc	BU
2010 Proof	—	Value: 30.00				

KM# 1233 2 WON

7.0000 g., 0.9990 Silver 0.2248 oz. ASW, 30 mm. **Obv:** National arms, Central Bank name **Rev:** Chapel in Luzern

Date	Mintage	F	VF	XF	Unc	BU
2010 Proof	—	Value: 30.00				

KM# 1272 2 WON

7.0000 g., 0.9990 Silver 0.2248 oz. ASW, 30 mm. **Obv:** National arms, Central Bank name **Rev:** Three pandas in color

Date	Mintage	F	VF	XF	Unc	BU
2010 Proof	Est. 5,000	Value: 30.00				

KM# 1276 2 WON

7.0000 g., 0.9990 Silver 0.2248 oz. ASW, 30 mm. **Obv:** National arms, Central Bank name **Rev:** Great Mosque of Cordoba

Date	Mintage	F	VF	XF	Unc	BU
2010 Proof	—	Value: 30.00				

KM# 1277 2 WON

7.0000 g., 0.9990 Silver 0.2248 oz. ASW, 30 mm. **Obv:** National arms, Central Bank name **Rev:** Cathedral of Santiago de Compostela

Date	Mintage	F	VF	XF	Unc	BU
2010 Proof	—	Value: 30.00				

KM# 1278 2 WON

7.0000 g., 0.9990 Silver 0.2248 oz. ASW, 30 mm. **Obv:** National arms, Central Bank name **Rev:** Timbuktu

Date	Mintage	F	VF	XF	Unc	BU
2010 Proof	—	Value: 30.00				

KM# 1279 2 WON

7.0000 g., 0.9990 Silver 0.2248 oz. ASW, 30 mm. **Obv:** National arms, Central Bank name **Rev:** London's Big Ben clock tower

Date	Mintage	F	VF	XF	Unc	BU
2010 Proof	—	Value: 30.00				

KM# 1280 2 WON

7.0000 g., 0.9990 Silver 0.2248 oz. ASW, 30 mm. **Obv:** National arms, Central Bank name **Rev:** Prague castle

Date	Mintage	F	VF	XF	Unc	BU
2010 Proof	—	Value: 30.00				

KM# 1281 2 WON

7.0000 g., 0.9990 Silver 0.2248 oz. ASW, 30 mm. **Obv:** National arms, Central Bank name **Rev:** Teoihuacan pyramid

Date	Mintage	F	VF	XF	Unc	BU
2010 Proof	—	Value: 30.00				

KM# 1282 2 WON

7.0000 g., 0.9990 Silver 0.2248 oz. ASW, 30 mm. **Obv:** National arms, Central Bank name **Rev:** Forbidden city

Date	Mintage	F	VF	XF	Unc	BU
2010 Proof	—	Value: 30.00				

KM# 1189 5 WON

20.0000 g., 0.9990 Silver 0.6423 oz. ASW, 38 mm. **Obv:** National arms, Central Bank name **Rev:** Sailing ship Grand Duchess Elizabeth

Date	Mintage	F	VF	XF	Unc	BU
2008 Proof	Est. 5,000	Value: 45.00				

KM# 1191 5 WON

20.0000 g., 0.9990 Silver 0.6423 oz. ASW, 38 mm. **Obv:** National arms, Central Bank name **Rev:** Four-masted schooner Elizabeth Bandi and three-masted bark Seute Deern

Date	Mintage	F	VF	XF	Unc	BU
2008 Proof	Est. 5,000	Value: 45.00				

KM# 1219 5 WON

20.0000 g., 0.9990 Silver 0.6423 oz. ASW, 38 mm. **Obv:** National arms, Central Bank name **Rev:** U.S.C.G. Barque Eagle

Date	Mintage	F	VF	XF	Unc	BU
2008 Proof	—	Value: 45.00				

KM# 1190 5 WON

20.0000 g., 0.9990 Silver 0.6423 oz. ASW, 38 mm. **Obv:** National arms, Central Bank name **Rev:** Three-masted sailing ship Passat

Date	Mintage	F	VF	XF	Unc	BU
2009 Proof	Est. 5,000	Value: 45.00				

KM# 1192 5 WON

20.0000 g., 0.9990 Silver 0.6423 oz. ASW, 38 mm. **Obv:** National arms, Central Bank name **Rev:** Sail training ship Deutschland

Date	Mintage	F	VF	XF	Unc	BU
2009 Proof	Est. 5,000	Value: 45.00				

KM# 1193 5 WON

20.0000 g., 0.9990 Silver 0.6423 oz. ASW, 38 mm. **Obv:** National arms, Central Bank name **Rev:** Three-masted sailing ship Gorch Fock II

Date	Mintage	F	VF	XF	Unc	BU
2009 Proof	Est. 5,000	Value: 45.00				

KM# 1218 5 WON

20.0000 g., 0.9990 Silver 0.6423 oz. ASW, 38 mm. **Obv:** National arms, Central Bank name **Rev:** Sailing ship Dar Mlodziezy

Date	Mintage	F	VF	XF	Unc	BU
2009 Proof	—	Value: 45.00				

KM# 1273 5 WON

20.0000 g., 0.9990 Silver 0.6423 oz. ASW, 38 mm. **Obv:** National arms, Central Bank name **Rev:** Philippine hood eagle

Date	Mintage	F	VF	XF	Unc	BU
2010 Proof	—	Value: 60.00				

KM# 1274 5 WON

20.0000 g., 0.9990 Silver 0.6423 oz. ASW, 38 mm. **Obv:** National arms, Central Bank name **Rev:** Tibetian ox

Date	Mintage	F	VF	XF	Unc	BU
2010 Proof	—	Value: 60.00				

KM# 1194 10 WON

1.0000 g., 0.9160 Gold 0.0294 oz. AGW, 16 mm. **Obv:** National arms, Central Bank name **Rev:** Rickmer Rickmers

Date	Mintage	F	VF	XF	Unc	BU
2008	7,500	—	—	—	—	75.00

KM# 1195 10 WON

1.0000 g., 0.9160 Gold 0.0294 oz. AGW, 16 mm. **Obv:** National arms, Central Bank name **Rev:** Prussen

Date	Mintage	F	VF	XF	Unc	BU
2008	Est. 7,500	—	—	—	—	75.00

KM# 1196.1 10 WON

1.0000 g., 0.9160 Gold 0.0294 oz. AGW, 16 mm. **Obv:** National arms, Central Bank name **Rev:** Alexander von Humboldt **Rev. Legend:** ...Humoldt **Note:** Error spelling of ship's name

Date	Mintage	F	VF	XF	Unc	BU
2008	401	—	—	—	—	90.00

KM# 1196.2 10 WON

1.0000 g., 0.9160 Gold 0.0294 oz. AGW, 16 mm. **Obv:** National arms, Central Bank name **Rev:** Alexander von Humbolt **Rev. Legend:** ...Humboldt **Note:** Ship's name corrected.

Date	Mintage	F	VF	XF	Unc	BU
2008	7,100	—	—	—	—	75.00

KM# 1197 10 WON

1.0000 g., 0.9160 Gold 0.0294 oz. AGW, 16 mm. **Obv:** National arms, Central Bank name **Rev:** Grand Duchess Elizabeth

Date	Mintage	F	VF	XF	Unc	BU
2008	Est. 7,500	—	—	—	—	75.00

KM# 1198 10 WON

1.0000 g., 0.9160 Gold 0.0294 oz. AGW, 16 mm. **Obv:** National arms, Central Bank name **Rev:** Three masted training ship Passat

Date	Mintage	F	VF	XF	Unc	BU
2008	7,500	—	—	—	—	75.00

KM# 1199 10 WON

1.0000 g., 0.9160 Gold 0.0294 oz. AGW, 16 mm. **Obv:** National arms, Central Bank name **Rev:** Four-masted schoner Elizabeth Bandi and three-masted bark Seute Deern

Date	Mintage	F	VF	XF	Unc	BU
2008 Proof	—	—	—	—	—	75.00

KM# 1200 10 WON

1.0000 g., 0.9160 Gold 0.0294 oz. AGW, 16 mm. **Obv:** National arms, Central Bank name **Rev:** Sail training ship Deutschland

Date	Mintage	F	VF	XF	Unc	BU
2008	Est. 7,500	—	—	—	—	75.00

KM# 1201 10 WON

1.0000 g., 0.9160 Gold 0.0294 oz. AGW, 16 mm. **Obv:** National arms, Central Bank name **Rev:** Three-masted barque Gorch Fock II

Date	Mintage	F	VF	XF	Unc	BU
2008	Est. 7,500	—	—	—	—	75.00

KM# 1235 10 WON

0.5000 g., 0.9990 Gold 0.0161 oz. AGW, 11 mm. **Obv:** National arms, Central Bank name **Rev:** Alhambra in Granada

Date	Mintage	F	VF	XF	Unc	BU
2009 Proof	—	Value: 45.00				

KM# 1234 10 WON

0.5000 g., 0.9990 Gold 0.0161 oz. AGW, 11 mm. **Obv:** National arms, Central Bank name **Rev:** Cathedral of the Holy Family in Barcelona

Date	Mintage	F	VF	XF	Unc	BU
2009 Proof	—	Value: 45.00				

KM# 1236 10 WON

1.0000 g., 0.9990 Gold 0.0321 oz. AGW, 14 mm. **Obv:** National arms, Central Bank name **Rev:** Crown tower in Dresden Zwigers

Date	Mintage	F	VF	XF	Unc	BU
2009 Proof	—	Value: 75.00				

KM# 1237 10 WON

1.0000 g., 0.9990 Gold 0.0321 oz. AGW, 14 mm. **Obv:** National arms, Central Bank name **Rev:** Acropolis in Athens

Date	Mintage	F	VF	XF	Unc	BU
2009 Proof	—	Value: 75.00				

KM# 1238 10 WON

1.0000 g., 0.9990 Silver 0.0321 oz. ASW, 14 mm. **Obv:** National arms, Central Bank name **Rev:** Sydney Opera House

Date	Mintage	F	VF	XF	Unc	BU
2009 Proof	—	Value: 75.00				

KM# 1239 10 WON

1.0000 g., 0.9990 Gold 0.0321 oz. AGW, 14 mm. **Obv:** National arms, Central Bank name **Rev:** Angkor Wat temple complex

Date	Mintage	F	VF	XF	Unc	BU
2009 Proof	—	Value: 75.00				

KM# 1240 10 WON

1.0000 g., 0.9990 Gold 0.0321 oz. AGW, 14 mm. **Obv:** National arms, Central Bank name **Rev:** Minaksji and Sundareshwara Temples in Madurai

Date	Mintage	F	VF	XF	Unc	BU
2009 Proof	—	Value: 75.00				

KM# 1241 10 WON

1.0000 g., 0.9990 Gold 0.0321 oz. AGW, 14 mm. **Obv:** National arms, Central Bank name **Rev:** Kremlin in Moscow

Date	Mintage	F	VF	XF	Unc	BU
2009 Proof	—	Value: 75.00				

KM# 1242 10 WON

1.0000 g., 0.9990 Gold 0.0321 oz. AGW, 14 mm. **Obv:** National arms, Central Bank name **Rev:** Abu Simbel

Date	Mintage	F	VF	XF	Unc	BU
2009 Proof	—	Value: 75.00				

KM# 1243 10 WON

1.0000 g., 0.9990 Gold 0.0321 oz. AGW, 14 mm. **Obv:** National arms, Central Bank name **Rev:** Eiffel Tower in Paris

Date	Mintage	F	VF	XF	Unc	BU
2009 Proof	—	Value: 75.00				

KM# 1244 10 WON

1.0000 g., 0.9990 Gold 0.0321 oz. AGW, 14 mm. **Obv:** National arms, Central Bank name **Rev:** Dali Lama's Palace in Lhasa

Date	Mintage	F	VF	XF	Unc	BU
2009 Proof	—	Value: 75.00				

KM# 1245 10 WON

1.0000 g., 0.9990 Gold 0.0321 oz. AGW, 14 mm. **Obv:** National arms, Central Bank name **Rev:** Terra Cotta Warriors

Date	Mintage	F	VF	XF	Unc	BU
2009 Proof	—	Value: 75.00				

KM# 1246 10 WON

1.0000 g., 0.9990 Gold 0.0321 oz. AGW, 14 mm. **Obv:** National arms, Central Bank name **Rev:** Palace in Versalles

Date	Mintage	F	VF	XF	Unc	BU
2009 Proof	—	Value: 75.00				

KM# 1247 10 WON

1.0000 g., 0.9990 Gold 0.0321 oz. AGW, 14 mm. **Obv:** National arms, Central Bank name **Rev:** Aachen Cathedral

Date	Mintage	F	VF	XF	Unc	BU
2009 Proof	—	Value: 75.00				

KM# 1248 10 WON

1.0000 g., 0.9990 Gold 0.0321 oz. AGW, 14 mm. **Obv:** National arms, Central Bank name **Rev:** Leaning tower of Pisa

Date	Mintage	F	VF	XF	Unc	BU
2009 Proof	—	Value: 75.00				

KM# 1249 10 WON

1.0000 g., 0.9990 Gold 0.0321 oz. AGW, 14 mm. **Obv:** National arms, Central Bank name **Rev:** Chapel in Luzern

Date	Mintage	F	VF	XF	Unc	BU
2009 Proof	—	Value: 75.00				

KM# 1262 10 WON

Brass, 40 mm. **Obv:** National arms, Central Bank name **Rev:** South tower in Kaeseong

Date	Mintage	F	VF	XF	Unc	BU
2010 Proof	—	Value: 7.00				

KM# 1263 10 WON

Brass, 40 mm. **Obv:** National arms, Central Bank name **Rev:** Mausoleum of King Wanggeon

Date	Mintage	F	VF	XF	Unc	BU
2010 Proof	—	Value: 7.00				

KM# 1264 10 WON

Brass, 40 mm. **Obv:** National arms, Central Bank name **Rev:** Birthplace of Pyochung

Date	Mintage	F	VF	XF	Unc	BU
2010 Proof	—	Value: 7.00				

KM# 1265 10 WON

Brass, 40 mm. **Obv:** National arms, Central Bank name **Rev:** Stone pagoda of Hyunhwa in Seongkyunkwan

Date	Mintage	F	VF	XF	Unc	BU
2010 Proof	—	Value: 7.00				

KM# 1266 10 WON

Brass, 40 mm. **Obv:** National arms, Central Bank name **Rev:** Seongkyunkwan

Date	Mintage	F	VF	XF	Unc	BU
2010 Proof	—	Value: 7.00				

KM# 1267 10 WON

Brass, 40 mm. **Obv:** National arms, Central Bank name **Rev:** Anhwa Temple

Date	Mintage	F	VF	XF	Unc	BU
2010 Proof	—	Value: 7.00				

KM# 1268 10 WON

Brass, 40 mm. **Obv:** National arms, Central Bank name **Rev:** Nahanjun in Anhwa Temple

Date	Mintage	F	VF	XF	Unc	BU
2010 Proof	—	Value: 7.00				

KM# 1269 10 WON

Brass, 40 mm. **Obv:** National arms, Central Bank name **Rev:** Turned wheel in Yungtong Temple

Date	Mintage	F	VF	XF	Unc	BU
2010 Proof	—	Value: 7.00				

KM# 1270 10 WON

Brass, 40 mm. **Obv:** National arms, Central Bank name **Rev:** Shrine in Sungyang Sowon

Date	Mintage	F	VF	XF	Unc	BU
2010 Proof	—	Value: 7.00				

KM# 1271 10 WON

Brass, 40 mm. **Obv:** National arms, Central Bank name **Rev:** Waterfall in Pakyeon

Date	Mintage	F	VF	XF	Unc	BU
2010 Proof	—	Value: 7.00				

KM# 1275 10 WON

0.5000 g., 0.9990 Gold 0.0161 oz. AGW, 11 mm. **Obv:** National arms, Central Bank name **Rev:** Ernesto "Che" Guevara

Date	Mintage	F	VF	XF	Unc	BU
2010 Proof	—	Value: 50.00				

KM# 1283 10 WON

1.0000 g., 0.9990 Gold 0.0321 oz. AGW, 14 mm. **Obv:** National arms, Central Bank name **Rev:** Grand Mosque in Cordoba

Date	Mintage	F	VF	XF	Unc	BU
2010 Proof	—	Value: 75.00				

KM# 1284 10 WON

1.0000 g., 0.9990 Gold 0.0321 oz. AGW, 14 mm. **Obv:** National arms, Central Bank name **Rev:** Cathedral of Santiago de Compostela

Date	Mintage	F	VF	XF	Unc	BU
2010 Proof	—	Value: 75.00				

KM# 1285 10 WON

1.0000 g., 0.9990 Gold 0.0321 oz. AGW, 14 mm. **Obv:** National arms, Central Bank name **Rev:** Timbuktu

Date	Mintage	F	VF	XF	Unc	BU
2010 Proof	—	Value: 75.00				

KM# 1286 10 WON

1.0000 g., 0.9990 Gold 0.0321 oz. AGW, 14 mm. **Obv:** National arms, Central Bank name **Rev:** London's Big Ben tower

Date	Mintage	F	VF	XF	Unc	BU
2010 Proof	—	Value: 75.00				

KM# 1287 10 WON

1.0000 g., 0.9990 Gold 0.0321 oz. AGW, 14 mm. **Obv:** National arms, Central Bank name **Rev:** Prague castle

Date	Mintage	F	VF	XF	Unc	BU
2010 Proof	—	Value: 75.00				

KM# 1288 10 WON

1.0000 g., 0.9990 Gold 0.0321 oz. AGW, 14 mm. **Obv:** National arms, Central Bank name **Rev:** Teotihuacan pyramid

Date	Mintage	F	VF	XF	Unc	BU
2010 Proof	—	Value: 75.00				

KM# 1289 10 WON

1.0000 g., 0.9990 Gold 0.0321 oz. AGW, 14 mm. **Obv:** National arms, Central Bank name **Rev:** Forbidden City

Date	Mintage	F	VF	XF	Unc	BU
2010 Proof	—	Value: 75.00				

KM# 1175 20 WON

28.0000 g., Brass, 40 mm. **Obv:** East gate of Pyeongyang **Rev:** Dragon in color

Date	Mintage	F	VF	XF	Unc	BU
2008 Proof	—	Value: 7.50				

KM# 1202 20 WON

Brass, 30 mm. **Obv:** East gate of Pyeongyang **Rev:** Rat in color

Date	Mintage	F	VF	XF	Unc	BU
2009 Proof	—	Value: 6.00				

KM# 1203 20 WON

Brass, 30 mm. **Obv:** East gate of Pyeongyang **Rev:** Ox in color

Date	Mintage	F	VF	XF	Unc	BU
2009 Proof	—	Value: 6.00				

KM# 1204 20 WON

Brass, 30 mm. **Obv:** East gate of Pyeongyang **Rev:** Tiger in color

Date	Mintage	F	VF	XF	Unc	BU
2009 Proof	—	Value: 6.00				

KM# 1205 20 WON

Brass, 30 mm. **Obv:** East gate of Pyeongyang **Rev:** Rabbit in color

Date	Mintage	F	VF	XF	Unc	BU
2009 Proof	—	Value: 6.00				

KM# 1206 20 WON

Brass, 30 mm. **Obv:** East gate of Pyeongyang **Rev:** Dragon in color

Date	Mintage	F	VF	XF	Unc	BU
2009 Proof	—	Value: 6.00				

KM# 1207 20 WON

Brass, 30 mm. **Obv:** East gate of Pyeongyang **Rev:** Snake in color

Date	Mintage	F	VF	XF	Unc	BU
2009 Proof	—	Value: 6.00				

KM# 1208 20 WON

Brass, 30 mm. **Obv:** East gate of Pyeongyang **Rev:** Horse in color

Date	Mintage	F	VF	XF	Unc	BU
2009 Proof	—	Value: 6.00				

KM# 1209 20 WON

Brass, 30 mm. **Obv:** East gate of Pyeongyang **Rev:** Goat in color

Date	Mintage	F	VF	XF	Unc	BU
2009 Proof	—	Value: 6.00				

KM# 1210 20 WON

Brass, 30 mm. **Obv:** East gate of Pyeongyang **Rev:** Monkey in color

Date	Mintage	F	VF	XF	Unc	BU
2009 Proof	—	Value: 6.00				

KM# 1211 20 WON

Brass, 30 mm. **Obv:** East gate of Pyeongyang **Rev:** Rooster in color

Date	Mintage	F	VF	XF	Unc	BU
2009 Proof	—	Value: 6.00				

KM# 1212 20 WON

Brass, 30 mm. **Obv:** East gate of Pyeongyang **Rev:** Dog in color

Date	Mintage	F	VF	XF	Unc	BU
2009 Proof	—	Value: 6.00				

KM# 1213 20 WON
Brass, 30 mm. **Obv:** East gate of Pyeongyang **Rev:** Pin in color

Date	Mintage	F	VF	XF	Unc	BU
2009 Proof	—	Value: 6.00				

KM# 492 20 WON
Aluminum, 45 mm. **Obv:** Raised Pagoda in ornamental loop **Rev:** Hippopotamus with color inlay **Rev. Legend:** Hippopotamus amphibius **Edge:** Plain

Date	Mintage	F	VF	XF	Unc	BU
2010	—	—	—	—	—	20.00

KM# 493 20 WON
Aluminum, 45 mm. **Obv:** Raised Pagoda with ornamental loop **Rev:** Rabbit with color inlay **Edge:** Plain

Date	Mintage	F	VF	XF	Unc	BU
2010	—	—	—	—	—	20.00

KM# 494 20 WON
Aluminum, 45 mm. **Obv:** Raised Pagoda in ornamental loop **Rev:** Deer with color inlay **Edge:** Plain

Date	Mintage	F	VF	XF	Unc	BU
2010	—	—	—	—	—	20.00

KM# 1250 20 WON
Brass, 45 mm. **Obv:** East gate in Pyeongyang **Rev:** Rat in center of Zodiac

Date	Mintage	F	VF	XF	Unc	BU
2010 Proof	—	—	—	—	—	7.00

KM# 1251 20 WON
Brass, 45 mm. **Obv:** East gate in Pyeongyang **Rev:** Buffalo at center of Zodiac

Date	Mintage	F	VF	XF	Unc	BU
2010 Proof	—	Value: 7.00				

KM# 1252 20 WON
Brass, 45 mm. **Obv:** East gate in Pyeongyang **Rev:** Tiger at center of Zodiac

Date	Mintage	F	VF	XF	Unc	BU
2010 Proof	—	Value: 7.00				

KM# 1253 20 WON
Brass, 45 mm. **Obv:** East gate in Pyeongyang **Rev:** Rabbit in center of Zodiac

Date	Mintage	F	VF	XF	Unc	BU
2010 Proof	—	Value: 7.00				

KM# 1254 20 WON
Brass, 45 mm. **Obv:** East gate in Pyeongyang **Rev:** Dragon at center of Zodiac

Date	Mintage	F	VF	XF	Unc	BU
2010 Proof	—	Value: 7.00				

KM# 1255 20 WON
Brass, 45 mm. **Obv:** East gate in Pyeongyang **Rev:** Snake in center of Zodiac

Date	Mintage	F	VF	XF	Unc	BU
2010 Proof	—	Value: 7.00				

KM# 1256 20 WON
Brass, 45 mm. **Obv:** East gate in Pyeongyang **Rev:** Horse in center of Zodiac

Date	Mintage	F	VF	XF	Unc	BU
2010 Proof	—	Value: 7.00				

KM# 1257 20 WON
Brass, 45 mm. **Obv:** East gate in Pyeongyang **Rev:** Goat in center of Zodiac

Date	Mintage	F	VF	XF	Unc	BU
2010 Proof	—	Value: 7.00				

KM# 1258 20 WON
Brass, 45 mm. **Obv:** East gate in Pyeongyang **Rev:** Monkey in center of Zodiac

Date	Mintage	F	VF	XF	Unc	BU
2010 Proof	—	Value: 7.00				

KM# 1259 20 WON
Brass, 45 mm. **Obv:** East gate in Pyeongyang **Rev:** Rooster in center of Zodiac

Date	Mintage	F	VF	XF	Unc	BU
2010 Proof	—	Value: 7.00				

KM# 1260 20 WON
Brass, 45 mm. **Obv:** East gate in Pyeongyang **Rev:** Dog in center of Zodiac

Date	Mintage	F	VF	XF	Unc	BU
2010 Proof	—	Value: 7.00				

KM# 1261 20 WON
Brass, 45 mm. **Obv:** East gate in Pyeongyang **Rev:** Pig in center of Zodiac

Date	Mintage	F	VF	XF	Unc	BU
2010 Proof	—	Value: 7.00				

KM# 1214 350 WON
6.2000 g., 0.9990 Silver 0.1991 oz. ASW, 35 mm. **Obv:** East gate of Pyeongyang **Rev:** Chinese Junk, Marco Polo

Date	Mintage	F	VF	XF	Unc	BU
2009 Proof	Est. 5,000	Value: 25.00				

KM# 1215 350 WON
6.2000 g., 0.9990 Silver 0.1991 oz. ASW, 35 mm. **Obv:** East gate of Pyeongyang **Rev:** Viking ship and map of the Atlantic, Leif Eriksson

Date	Mintage	F	VF	XF	Unc	BU
2009 Proof	Est. 5,000	Value: 25.00				

KM# 1216 1000 WON
20.0000 g., 0.9990 Silver 0.6423 oz. ASW, 38 mm. **Subject:** World Cup Soccer, South Africa, 2010 **Obv:** East gate of Pyeongyang **Rev:** Two soccer players

Date	Mintage	F	VF	XF	Unc	BU
2009 Proof	Est. 10,000	Value: 35.00				

SOUTH KOREA

The Republic of Korea, situated in northeastern Asia on the southern half of the Korean peninsula between North Korea and the Korean Strait, has an area of 38,025 sq. mi. (98,480 sq. km.) and a population of 42.5 million. Capital: Seoul. The economy is based on agriculture and light and medium industry. Some of the world's largest oil tankers are built here. Automobiles, plywood, electronics, and textile products are exported.

NOTE: For earlier coinage see Korea.

MINT

KOMSCO - Korea Minting and Security Printing Corporation

REPUBLIC

REFORM COINAGE

10 Hwan = 1 Won

KM# 31 WON
0.7290 g., Aluminum, 17.2 mm. **Obv:** Rose of Sharon **Rev:** Value and date

Date	Mintage	F	VF	XF	Unc	BU
2001	130,000	—	—	—	0.15	0.25
2002	122,000	—	—	—	0.15	0.25
2003	20,000	—	—	—	0.15	0.25
2004	25,500	—	—	—	0.15	0.25
2005	38,000	—	—	—	0.15	0.25
2006	53,000	—	—	—	0.15	0.25
2007	53,000	—	—	—	0.15	0.25
2008	—	—	—	—	0.15	0.25
2009	—	—	—	—	0.15	0.25
2010	—	—	—	—	0.15	0.25
2011	—	—	—	—	0.15	0.25
2012	—	—	—	—	0.15	0.25

KM# 32 5 WON
2.9500 g., Brass, 20.4 mm. **Obv:** Iron-clad turtle boat **Rev:** Value and date **Edge:** Plain

Date	Mintage	F	VF	XF	Unc	BU
2001	130,000	—	—	0.10	0.20	0.30
2002	120,000	—	—	0.10	0.20	0.30
2003	20,000	—	—	0.10	0.20	0.30
2004	25,500	—	—	0.10	0.20	0.30
2005	38,000	—	—	0.10	0.20	0.30
2006	53,000	—	—	0.10	0.20	0.30
2007	53,000	—	—	0.10	0.20	0.30
2008	—	—	—	0.10	0.20	0.30
2009	—	—	—	0.10	0.20	0.30
2010	—	—	—	0.10	0.20	0.30
2011	—	—	—	0.10	0.20	0.30
2012	—	—	—	0.10	0.20	0.30

KM# 33.2 10 WON
4.0600 g., Brass **Obv:** Pagoda at Pul Guk Temple **Rev:** Thicker value below date

Date	Mintage	F	VF	XF	Unc	BU
2001	345,000,000	—	—	—	0.35	0.50
2002	100,000,000	—	—	—	0.35	0.50
2003	128,000,000	—	—	—	0.35	0.50
2004	135,000,000	—	—	—	0.35	0.50
2005	250,000,000	—	—	—	0.35	0.50

KM# 33.2a 10 WON
1.2200 g., Aluminum-Bronze, 18 mm. **Obv:** Pagoda at Pul Guk Temple **Rev:** Value below date

Date	Mintage	F	VF	XF	Unc	BU
2006	109,200,000	—	—	—	0.10	0.35
2007	—	—	—	—	0.10	0.35
2008	—	—	—	—	0.10	0.35
2009	—	—	—	—	0.10	0.35

KM# 103 10 WON
1.2200 g., Copper Clad Aluminum, 18 mm. **Obv:** Pagoda at Pul Guk Temple **Rev:** Value below date **Edge:** Plain **Mint:** KOMSCO **Note:** Prev. KM #106.

Date	Mintage	F	VF	XF	Unc	BU
2006	40,800,000	—	—	0.10	0.20	0.25
2007	210,000,000	—	—	0.10	0.20	0.25
2008	—	—	—	0.10	0.20	0.25
2009	—	—	—	0.10	0.20	0.25
2010	—	—	—	0.10	0.20	0.25
2011	—	—	—	0.10	0.20	0.25
2012	—	—	—	0.10	0.20	0.25

KM# 34 50 WON
4.1600 g., Copper-Nickel-Zinc, 21.6 mm. **Series:** F.A.O. **Obv:** Text below sagging oat sprig **Rev:** Value and date **Edge:** Reeded **Note:** Die varieties exist.

Date	Mintage	F	VF	XF	Unc	BU
2001	102,000,000	—	—	0.10	0.35	1.00
2002	100,000,000	—	—	0.10	0.35	0.50
2003	169,000,000	—	—	0.10	0.35	0.50
2004	100,000,000	—	—	0.10	0.45	1.00
2005	90,000,000	—	—	0.10	0.35	0.50
2006	120,000,000	—	—	0.10	0.35	0.50
2007	50,000,000	—	—	0.10	0.35	0.50
2008	—	—	—	0.10	0.35	0.50
2009	—	—	—	0.10	0.35	0.50
2010	—	—	—	0.10	0.35	0.50
2011	—	—	—	0.10	0.35	0.50
2012	—	—	—	0.10	0.35	0.50

KM# 35.2 100 WON
5.4200 g., Copper-Nickel, 24 mm. **Obv:** Admiral Yi-Sun-Sin, large bust with hat facing **Rev:** Value and date **Edge:** Reeded

Date	Mintage	F	VF	XF	Unc	BU
2001	470,000,000	—	0.25	0.50	1.00	3.00
2002	490,000,000	—	0.15	0.25	0.55	1.00
2003	415,000,000	—	0.15	0.25	0.55	1.00
2004	250,000,000	—	0.15	0.25	0.55	1.00
2005	205,000,000	—	0.15	0.25	0.55	1.00
2006	310,000,000	—	0.15	0.25	0.55	0.75
2007	240,000,000	—	0.15	0.25	0.55	0.75
2008	—	—	0.15	0.25	0.55	0.75
2009	—	—	0.15	0.25	0.55	0.75
2010	—	—	0.15	0.25	0.55	0.75
2011	—	—	0.15	0.25	0.55	0.75
2012	—	—	0.15	0.25	0.55	0.75

KM# 27 500 WON
7.7000 g., Copper-Nickel, 26.5 mm. **Obv:** Manchurian crane **Rev:** Value and date **Edge:** Reeded

Date	Mintage	F	VF	XF	Unc	BU
2001	113,000,000	—	—	1.00	2.50	5.00
2002	110,000,000	—	—	1.00	2.50	5.00
2003	122,000,000	—	—	1.00	2.50	5.00
2004	45,000,000	—	—	1.00	2.50	5.00
2005	105,000,000	—	—	1.00	2.50	5.00
2006	170,000,000	—	—	1.00	2.50	5.00
2007	70,000,000	—	—	1.00	2.50	5.00
2008	—	—	—	1.00	2.50	5.00
2009	—	—	—	1.00	2.50	5.00
2010	—	—	—	1.00	2.50	5.00
2011	—	—	—	1.00	2.50	5.00
2012	—	—	—	1.00	2.50	5.00

KM# 89 1000 WON
12.0000 g., Brass, 32 mm. **Series:** World Cup Soccer **Obv:** FIFA World Cup logo **Rev:** Mascot soccer player **Edge:** Reeded **Mint:** Seoul

Date	Mintage	F	VF	XF	Unc	BU
2001	102,000	—	—	—	10.00	12.00

KM# 112 1000 WON
12.0000 g., Aluminum-Bronze, 32 mm. **Rev:** Soccer player **Mint:** KOMSCO

Date	Mintage	F	VF	XF	Unc	BU
2002	102,002	—	—	—	—	12.50

KM# 127 1000 WON
10.1000 g., Tri-Metallic Copper center in Copper-Nickel inner ring in Copper-Nickel-Zinc outer ring, 28.2 mm. **Subject:** Expo 2012 **Obv:** Mascots Yeony and Suny **Rev:** Expo logo **Mint:** KOMSCO

Date	Mintage	F	VF	XF	Unc	BU
2012	137,512	—	—	—	—	20.00

KM# 115 2000 WON
26.0000 g., Copper, 40 mm. **Subject:** 14th Asian Games, Busan **Rev:** Bird sanctuary **Mint:** KOMSCO

Date	Mintage	F	VF	XF	Unc	BU
2002 Proof	—	Value: 20.00				

KM# 116 2000 WON
26.0000 g., Copper-Nickel, 40 mm. **Rev:** Torch and sport images **Mint:** KOMSCO

Date	Mintage	F	VF	XF	Unc	BU
2002 Proof	—	Value: 30.00				

KM# 124 5000 WON
15.5000 g., 0.9990 Silver 0.4978 oz. ASW, 32 mm. **Subject:** Expo 2012 **Obv:** Korean Pavilion with latent image **Rev:** Expo logo in color **Mint:** KOMSCO

Date	Mintage	F	VF	XF	Unc	BU
2012 Proof	20,000	Value: 45.00				

KM# 125 5000 WON
15.5000 g., 0.9990 Silver 0.4978 oz. ASW, 32 mm. **Subject:** Expo 2012 **Obv:** Theme Pavilion and latent image **Rev:** Expo logo in color **Mint:** KOMSCO

Date	Mintage	F	VF	XF	Unc	BU
2012 Proof	20,000	Value: 40.00				

KM# 90 10000 WON
31.1035 g., 0.9990 Silver 0.9990 oz. ASW, 35 mm. **Series:** World Cup Soccer **Subject:** Gwangju Stadium **Obv:** Multicolor soccer logo **Rev:** Player heading the ball **Edge:** Reeded **Mint:** Seoul

Date	Mintage	F	VF	XF	Unc	BU
2001 Proof	37,000	Value: 50.00				

KM# 91 10000 WON
31.1035 g., 0.9990 Silver 0.9990 oz. ASW, 35 mm. **Series:** World Sup Soccer **Subject:** Busan Stadium **Obv:** Multicolor soccer logo **Rev:** Player kicking the ball **Edge:** Reeded **Mint:** Seoul

Date	Mintage	F	VF	XF	Unc	BU
2001 Proof	37,000	Value: 50.00				

KM# 92 10000 WON
31.1035 g., 0.9990 Silver 0.9990 oz. ASW, 35 mm. **Series:** World Cup Soccer **Subject:** Daegu Stadium **Obv:** Multicolor soccer logo **Rev:** Player controlling the ball **Edge:** Reeded **Mint:** Seoul

Date	Mintage	F	VF	XF	Unc	BU
2001 Proof	37,000	Value: 50.00				

KM# 93 10000 WON
31.1035 g., 0.9990 Silver 0.9990 oz. ASW, 35 mm. **Series:** World Cup Soccer **Subject:** Suwon Stadium **Obv:** Multicolor soccer logo **Rev:** Player kicking the ball **Edge:** Reeded **Mint:** Seoul

Date	Mintage	F	VF	XF	Unc	BU
2001 Proof	37,000	Value: 50.00				

KM# 98 10000 WON
31.1035 g., 0.9990 Silver 0.9990 oz. ASW, 35 mm. **Obv:** Multicolor FIFA World Cup logo **Rev:** Player "Heading" ball **Edge:** Reeded **Mint:** Seoul

Date	Mintage	F	VF	XF	Unc	BU
2002 Proof	—	Value: 50.00				

KM# 99 10000 WON

31.1035 g., 0.9990 Silver 0.9990 oz. ASW, 35 mm. **Obv:** Multi-color FIFA World Cup logo **Rev:** Goalie catching ball **Edge:** Reeded **Mint:** Seoul

Date	Mintage	F	VF	XF	Unc	BU
2002 Proof	—	Value: 50.00				

KM# 100 10000 WON

31.1035 g., 0.9990 Silver 0.9990 oz. ASW, 35 mm. **Obv:** Multi-color FIFA World Cup logo **Rev:** Player's leg kicking ball **Edge:** Reeded **Mint:** Seoul

Date	Mintage	F	VF	XF	Unc	BU
2002 Proof	—	Value: 50.00				

KM# 101 10000 WON

31.1035 g., 0.9990 Silver 0.9990 oz. ASW, 35 mm. **Obv:** Multi-color FIFA World Cup logo **Rev:** Two players' legs and ball **Edge:** Reeded **Mint:** Seoul

Date	Mintage	F	VF	XF	Unc	BU
2002 Proof	—	Value: 50.00				

KM# 118 10000 WON

Silver, 38.61 mm. **Subject:** 14th Asian Games, Busan **Obv:** Multicolor games logo **Rev:** Two dancers **Mint:** KOMSCO

Date	Mintage	F	VF	XF	Unc	BU
2002 Proof	—	Value: 90.00				

KM# 117 10000 WON

31.1050 g., 0.9990 Silver 0.9990 oz. ASW, 40 mm. **Rev:** Stadium, mascott at top **Mint:** KOMSCO

Date	Mintage	F	VF	XF	Unc	BU
2005 Proof	—	Value: 90.00				

KM# 126 10000 WON

31.1050 g., 0.9990 Silver 0.9990 oz. ASW, 40 mm. **Subject:** Expo 2012 **Obv:** Exposition's Sky Tower and sea image **Rev:** Expo logo in color **Mint:** KOMSCO

Date	Mintage	F	VF	XF	Unc	BU
2012 Proof	20,000	Value: 60.00				

KM# 128 15000 WON

7.7700 g., 0.9990 Gold 0.2496 oz. AGW, 22 mm. **Subject:** Expo 2012 **Obv:** The Big-O maine stage **Rev:** Expo logo **Mint:** KOMSCO

Date	Mintage	F	VF	XF	Unc	BU
2012 Proof	10,000	Value: 500				

KM# 94 20000 WON

15.5518 g., 0.9990 Gold 0.4995 oz. AGW, 28 mm. **Series:** World Cup Soccer **Obv:** Soccer logo **Rev:** World Cup soccer trophy **Edge:** Reeded **Mint:** Seoul

Date	Mintage	F	VF	XF	Unc	BU
2001 Proof	20,000	Value: 900				

KM# 113 20000 WON

15.5500 g., 0.9990 Gold 0.4994 oz. AGW, 28 mm. **Rev:** World Cup venues on map **Mint:** KOMSCO

Date	Mintage	F	VF	XF	Unc	BU
2002 Proof	19,502	Value: 925				

KM# 119 20000 WON

15.5500 g., 0.9990 Gold 0.4994 oz. AGW **Subject:** 14th Asian Games, Busan **Obv:** Games logo **Rev:** Crown **Mint:** KOMSCO

Date	Mintage	F	VF	XF	Unc	BU
2002 Proof	—	Value: 925				

KM# 102 20000 WON

20.7000 g., 0.9990 Silver 0.6648 oz. ASW **Subject:** 60th Anniversary of Independence **Obv:** Adult hand reaching out towards child's hand **Mint:** KOMSCO **Note:** Prev. KM #103.

Date	Mintage	F	VF	XF	Unc	BU
2005 Proof	10,000	Value: 65.00				

KM# 97 20000 WON

20.7000 g., Silver, 35 mm. **Obv:** Blue circle with APEC, 2005 Korea at bottom at upper center, Vista Pacific Economic Cooperation and value below **Rev:** APEC on World map at upper center, building below with Korean words below it

Date	Mintage	F	VF	XF	Unc	BU
2005 Proof	10,000	Value: 65.00				

KM# 104 20000 WON

19.0000 g., 0.9990 Silver 0.6102 oz. ASW **Subject:** 560th Year of Hangeul - Alphabet **Obv:** Early alphabet characters **Obv. Legend:** THE BANK OF KOREA **Rev:** Modern alphabet characters **Shape:** Round with square center hole **Mint:** KOMSCO

Date	Mintage	F	VF	XF	Unc	BU
2006 Proof	—	Value: 75.00				

KM# 105 20000 WON

19.0000 g., 0.9990 Silver 0.6102 oz. ASW, 33.00 mm. **Series:** Traditional Folk Dance **Subject:** Talchum - Mask Dances **Obv:** Mask at center surrounded by 6 other masks **Obv. Legend:** THE BANK OF KOREA **Rev:** Mask dancer at left center **Edge:** Plain **Shape:** 12-sided **Mint:** KOMSCO **Note:** Prev. KM #102.

Date	Mintage	F	VF	XF	Unc	BU
2007 Proof	50,000	Value: 75.00				

KM# 106 20000 WON

19.0000 g., 0.9990 Silver 0.6102 oz. ASW, 33 mm. **Subject:** Mask dance **Rev:** Ganggangsullae ("Circle dance") **Shape:** 12-sided **Mint:** KOMSCO

Date	Mintage	F	VF	XF	Unc	BU
2008 Proof	50,000	Value: 75.00				

KM# 108 20000 WON

19.0000 g., 0.9000 Silver 0.5498 oz. ASW, 33 mm. **Subject:** Mask dance **Rev:** Youngsan Juldarigi (Tug of War) **Mint:** KOMSCO

Date	Mintage	F	VF	XF	Unc	BU
2009 Proof	50,000	Value: 75.00				

KM# 109 20000 WON

19.0000 g., 0.9990 Silver 0.6102 oz. ASW, 33 mm. **Subject:** Traditional Folk Games - Yeongsan Juldarigi (Tug of war) **Mint:** KOMSCO

Date	Mintage	F	VF	XF	Unc	BU
2009 Proof	50,000	Value: 55.00				

KM# 129 20000 WON

15.5500 g., 0.9990 Gold 0.4994 oz. AGW, 28 mm. **Subject:** Expo 2012 **Obv:** International Pavilion **Rev:** Expo logo **Mint:** KOMSCO

Date	Mintage	F	VF	XF	Unc	BU
2012 Proof	6,000	Value: 950				

KM# 95 30000 WON

31.1035 g., 0.9990 Gold 0.9990 oz. AGW, 35 mm. **Series:** World Cup Soccer **Obv:** Soccer logo **Rev:** Nude soccer player flanked by other players **Edge:** Reeded **Mint:** Seoul

Date	Mintage	F	VF	XF	Unc	BU
2001 Proof	12,000	Value: 1,775				

KM# 114 30000 WON

31.1050 g., 0.9990 Gold 0.9990 oz. AGW, 35 mm. **Obv:** World Cup soccer trophy **Rev:** Stadium, fireworks, soccer ball **Mint:** KOMSCO

Date	Mintage	F	VF	XF	Unc	BU
2002 Proof	12,002	Value: 1,800				

KM# 120 30000 WON

31.1050 g., 0.9990 Gold 0.9990 oz. AGW, 35 mm. **Subject:** 14th Asian Games, Busan **Obv:** Games logo **Rev:** Many hands reaching upwards **Mint:** KOMSCO

Date	Mintage	F	VF	XF	Unc	BU
2002 Proof	—	Value: 1,850				

KM# 107 30000 WON

Silver **Subject:** Flag, 60th Anniversary **Obv:** Flag **Rev:** Multicolor 60 logo **Mint:** KOMSCO

Date	Mintage	F	VF	XF	Unc	BU
2008 Proof	—	Value: 75.00				

KM# 110 30000 WON

19.0000 g., 0.9990 Silver 0.6102 oz. ASW, 33 mm. **Subject:** UNESCO World Heritage Site - Jongmyo Shrine **Obv:** Main Hall of the Jongmyo Shrine **Rev:** Scene of the Royal Ancestral Ritual in the shrine **Edge:** Reeded **Mint:** KOMSCO

Date	Mintage	F	VF	XF	Unc	BU
2010 Proof	50,000	Value: 60.00				

KM# 111 30000 WON

19.0000 g., 0.9990 Silver 0.6102 oz. ASW, 33 mm. **Subject:** G-20 Summit in Seoul **Obv:** Gwang-Hwa-Mun restored on Independence Day **Rev:** Multicolor lantern in national colors **Edge:** Reeded **Mint:** KOMSCO

Date	Mintage	F	VF	XF	Unc	BU
2010 Proof	50,000	Value: 55.00				

KM# 121 50000 WON
19.0000 g., 0.9990 Silver 0.6102 oz. ASW, 33 mm. **Subject:** Jeju Volcanic Island and Lava Tubes - UNESCO World Heritage Site **Obv:** Volcano Crater **Rev:** Lava tubes **Mint:** KOMSCO

Date	Mintage	F	VF	XF	Unc	BU
2011 Proof	30,000	Value: 55.00				

KM# 122 50000 WON
19.0000 g., 0.9990 Silver 0.6102 oz. ASW, 33 mm. **Subject:** International Association of Athletics Federations Championships **Obv:** High Jumping athlete **Rev:** Athlete running thru finish line tape in color **Mint:** KOMSCO

Date	Mintage	F	VF	XF	Unc	BU
2011 Proof	30,000	Value: 100				

KM# 123 50000 WON
19.0000 g., 0.9990 Silver 0.6102 oz. ASW, 33 mm. **Subject:** Nuclear Security Summit **Obv:** Five hands raising up globe **Rev:** Summit logo in color **Mint:** KOMSCO

Date	Mintage	F	VF	XF	Unc	BU
2012 Proof	20,000	Value: 40.00				

KM# 130 50000 WON
19.0000 g., 0.9990 Silver 0.6102 oz. ASW, 33 mm. **Subject:** UNESCO World Heritage Site - Seokguram Grotto and Bulguksa Temple **Mint:** KOMSCO

Date	Mintage	F	VF	XF	Unc	BU
2012 Proof	—	Value: 50.00				

MINT SETS

KM#	Date	Mintage	Identification	Issue Price	Mkt Val
MS8	2001 (7)	—	KM#27, 31, 32, 33.2, 34, 35.2, 89	10.00	22.50

PROOF SETS

KM#	Date	Mintage	Identification	Issue Price	Mkt Val
PS10	2001 (6)	2,002	KM#90-95	—	2,500

KUWAIT

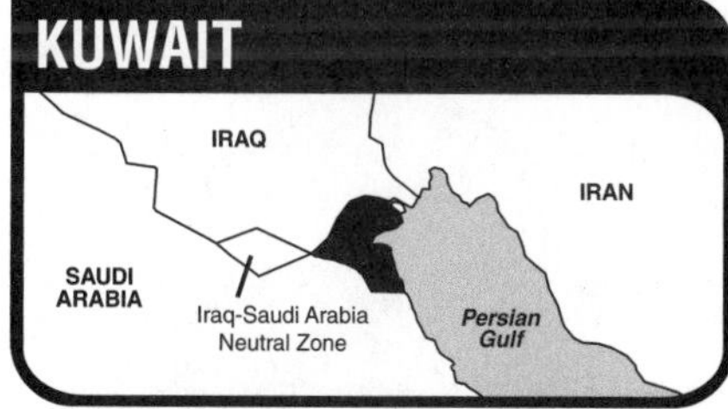

The State of Kuwait, a constitutional monarchy located on the Arabian Peninsula at the northwestern corner of the Persian Gulf, has an area of 6,880 sq. mi. (17,820 sq. km.) and a population of 1.7 million. Capital: Kuwait. Petroleum, the basis of the economy, provides 95 percent of the exports.

RULERS

Al Sabah Dynasty

Jabir Ibn Ahmad, 1977-2006
Sabah Al Ahmad Al Sabah, 2006-

MONETARY SYSTEM

1000 Fils = 1 Dinar

SOVEREIGN EMIRATE

MODERN COINAGE

KM# 9a FILS
2.4100 g., 0.9250 Silver 0.0717 oz. ASW, 17 mm. **Ruler:** Jabir Ibn Ahmad **Obv:** Value within circle **Rev:** Ship with sails

Date	Mintage	F	VF	XF	Unc	BU
AH1429-2008 Proof	—	Value: 65.00				

KM# 9c FILS
2.4100 g., 0.9250 Silver Gilt 0.0717 oz. ASW, 17 mm. **Obv:** Value within circle **Rev:** Dhow, dates below

Date	Mintage	F	VF	XF	Unc	BU
AH1429-2008 Proof	—	Value: 75.00				

KM# 10 5 FILS
2.5000 g., Nickel-Brass, 19.5 mm. **Ruler:** Jabir Ibn Ahmad **Obv:** Value within circle **Rev:** Dhow, dates below

Date	Mintage	F	VF	XF	Unc	BU
AH1422-2001	—	—	0.10	0.20	0.40	—
AH1424-2003	—	—	0.10	0.20	0.40	—
AH1426-2005	—	—	0.10	0.20	0.40	—
AH1427-2006	—	—	0.10	0.20	0.40	—
AH1427-2007	—	—	0.10	0.20	0.40	—
AH1428-2008	—	—	0.10	0.20	0.40	—
AH1429-2008	—	—	0.10	0.20	0.40	—
AH1430-2009	—	—	0.10	0.20	0.40	—
AH1431-2010	—	—	0.10	0.20	0.40	—

KM# 10a 5 FILS
3.0100 g., 0.9250 Silver 0.0895 oz. ASW, 19.5 mm. **Ruler:** Jabir Ibn Ahmad **Obv:** Value within circle **Rev:** Ship with sails

Date	Mintage	F	VF	XF	Unc	BU
AH1429-2008 Proof	—	Value: 70.00				

KM# 10c 5 FILS
3.0100 g., 0.9250 Silver Gilt 0.0895 oz. ASW, 19.5 mm. **Obv:** Value in circle **Rev:** Dhow, dates below

Date	Mintage	F	VF	XF	Unc	BU
AH1429-2008 Proof	—	Value: 80.00				

KM# 11 10 FILS
3.7500 g., Nickel-Brass, 21 mm. **Ruler:** Jabir Ibn Ahmad **Obv:** Value within circle **Rev:** Dhow, dates below

Date	Mintage	F	VF	XF	Unc	BU
AH1422-2001	—	—	—	0.25	0.75	—
AH1424-2003	—	—	—	0.25	0.75	—
AH1426-2005	—	—	—	0.25	0.75	—
AH1427-2006	—	—	—	0.25	0.75	—
AH1428-2007	—	—	—	0.25	0.75	—
AH1429-2008	—	—	—	0.25	0.75	—
AH1430-2009	—	—	—	0.25	0.75	—
AH1431-2010	—	—	—	0.25	0.75	—

KM# 11a 10 FILS
4.3500 g., 0.9250 Silver 0.1294 oz. ASW, 21 mm. **Ruler:** Jabir Ibn Ahmad **Obv:** Value within circle **Rev:** Ship with sails

Date	Mintage	F	VF	XF	Unc	BU
AH1429-2008 Proof	—	Value: 75.00				

KM# 11c 10 FILS
4.3500 g., 0.9250 Silver Gilt 0.1294 oz. ASW, 21 mm. **Obv:** Value within circle **Rev:** Dhow, dates below

Date	Mintage	F	VF	XF	Unc	BU
AH1429-2008 Proof	—	Value: 85.00				

KM# 12c 20 FILS
Stainless Steel, 20 mm. **Ruler:** Jabir Ibn Ahmad **Obv:** Value **Rev:** Dhow, dates below

Date	Mintage	F	VF	XF	Unc	BU
AH1422-2001	—	—	0.20	0.35	1.00	—
AH1424-2003	—	—	0.20	0.35	1.00	—
AH1426-2005	—	—	0.20	0.35	1.00	—

KM# 12 20 FILS
3.0000 g., Copper-Nickel, 20 mm. **Ruler:** Jabir Ibn Ahmad **Obv:** Value within circle **Rev:** Dhow, dates below **Edge:** Reeded **Note:** Varieties exist.

Date	Mintage	F	VF	XF	Unc	BU
AH1422-2001	—	—	0.20	0.45	2.00	—
AH1423-2002	—	—	0.20	0.45	2.00	—
AH1424-2002	—	—	0.20	0.45	2.00	—
AH1424-2003	—	—	0.20	0.45	2.00	—
AH1426-2005	—	—	0.20	0.45	2.00	—
AH1427-2006	—	—	0.20	0.45	2.00	—
AH1428-2007	—	—	0.20	0.45	2.00	—
AH1429-2008	—	—	0.20	0.45	2.00	—
AH1430-2009	—	—	0.20	0.45	2.00	—

KM# 12a 20 FILS
3.3700 g., 0.9250 Silver 0.1002 oz. ASW, 20 mm. **Ruler:** Jabir Ibn Ahmad **Obv:** Value within circle **Rev:** Dhow, dates below

Date	Mintage	F	VF	XF	Unc	BU
AH1429-2008 Proof	—	Value: 80.00				

KM# 12d 20 FILS
3.3700 g., 0.9250 Silver Gilt 0.1002 oz. ASW, 20 mm. **Obv:** Value within cricle **Rev:** Dhow, dates below

Date	Mintage	F	VF	XF	Unc	BU
1429-2008 Proof	—	Value: 90.00				

KM# 13 50 FILS
4.5000 g., Copper-Nickel, 23 mm. **Ruler:** Jabir Ibn Ahmad **Obv:** Value within circle **Rev:** Dhow, dates below **Edge:** Reeded

Date	Mintage	F	VF	XF	Unc	BU
AH1422-2001	—	—	0.25	0.35	1.25	—
AH1424-2003	—	—	0.25	0.35	1.00	—
AH1426-2005	—	—	0.25	0.35	1.00	—
AH1427-2006	—	—	0.25	0.35	1.00	—
AH1428-2007	—	—	0.25	0.35	1.00	—
AH1429-2008	—	—	0.25	0.35	1.00	—
AH1430-2009	—	—	0.25	0.35	1.00	—
AH1431-2010	—	—	0.25	0.35	1.00	—
AH1432-2011	—	—	0.25	0.35	1.00	—

KM# 13a 50 FILS
5.0700 g., 0.9250 Silver 0.1508 oz. ASW, 23 mm. **Ruler:** Jabir Ibn Ahmad **Obv:** Value within circle **Rev:** Ship with sails

Date	Mintage	F	VF	XF	Unc	BU
AH1429-2008 Proof	—	Value: 85.00				

KM# 13c 50 FILS
5.0700 g., 0.9250 Silver Gilt 0.1508 oz. ASW, 23 mm. **Obv:** Value within circle **Rev:** Dhow, dates below

Date	Mintage	F	VF	XF	Unc	BU
1429-2008 Proof	—	Value: 100				

KM# 14 100 FILS
6.5000 g., Copper-Nickel, 26 mm. **Ruler:** Jabir Ibn Ahmad **Obv:** Value within circle **Rev:** Dhow, dates below **Edge:** Reeded

Date	Mintage	F	VF	XF	Unc	BU
AH1424-2003	—	—	0.50	0.75	1.50	—
AH1426-2005	—	—	0.50	0.75	1.50	—
AH1427-2006	—	—	0.50	0.75	1.50	—
AH1428-2007	—	—	0.50	0.75	1.50	—
AH1429-2008	—	—	0.50	0.75	1.50	—
AH1430-2009	—	—	0.50	0.75	1.50	—
AH1431-2010	—	—	0.50	0.75	1.50	—

KM# 14a 100 FILS
7.3400 g., 0.9250 Silver 0.2183 oz. ASW, 26 mm. **Ruler:** Jabir Ibn Ahmad **Obv:** Value within circle **Rev:** Ship with sails

Date	Mintage	F	VF	XF	Unc	BU
AH1429-2008 Proof	—	Value: 90.00				

KM# 14c 100 FILS
7.3400 g., 0.9250 Silver Gilt 0.2183 oz. ASW, 26 mm. **Obv:** Value within circle **Rev:** Dhow, dates below

Date	Mintage	F	VF	XF	Unc	BU
1429-2008 Proof	—	Value: 110				

PROOF SETS

KM#	Date	Mintage	Identification	Issue Price	Mkt Val
PS5	2008 (6)	—	KM#9a-14a	—	475
PS6	2008 (6)	—	KM#9c-11c, 12d, 13c-14c	—	500

KYRGYZSTAN

The Kyrgyz Republic, (formerly Kirghiz S.S.R., a Union Republic of the U.S.S.R.), is an independent state since Aug. 31, 1991, a member of the United Nations and of the C.I.S. It was the last state of the Union Republics to declare its sovereignty. Capital: Bishkek (formerly Frunze).

MONETARY SYSTEM

100 Tiyin = 1 Som

REPUBLIC

STANDARD COINAGE

KM# 11 TIYIN

1.0000 g., Aluminum-Bronze, 13.98 mm. **Obv:** National arms **Rev:** Flower at left of value **Edge:** Reeded **Note:** Prev. KM #8.

Date	Mintage	F	VF	XF	Unc	BU
2008 In sets only	95,000	—	—	—	0.65	1.00

KM# 12 10 TIYIN

1.3000 g., Brass Plated Steel, 15 mm. **Obv:** National arms **Rev:** Flower at left of value **Edge:** Plain **Note:** Prev. KM #9.

Date	Mintage	F	VF	XF	Unc	BU
2008	—	—	—	—	0.85	1.50

KM# 13 50 TIYIN

1.8000 g., Brass Plated Steel, 17 mm. **Obv:** National arms **Rev:** Flower at left of value **Edge:** Plain **Note:** Prev. KM #10.

Date	Mintage	F	VF	XF	Unc	BU
2008	—	—	—	—	1.25	2.00

KM# 19 SOM

12.0000 g., Copper-Nickel, 30 mm. **Series:** Great Silk Road **Subject:** Tashrabat **Obv:** Arms **Rev:** Fortress

Date	Mintage	F	VF	XF	Unc	BU
2008 Prooflike	5,000	—	—	—	10.00	15.00

KM# 14 SOM

2.5000 g., Nickel Plated Steel, 19 mm. **Obv:** National arms **Rev:** Symbol at left of denomination **Edge:** Reeded **Note:** Prev. KM #11.

Date	Mintage	F	VF	XF	Unc	BU
2008	—	—	—	—	1.50	2.25

KM# 21 SOM

12.0000 g., Copper-Nickel, 30 mm. **Subject:** Uzgen Architectural Complex **Obv:** Arms **Rev:** Tower and building - map above

Date	Mintage	F	VF	XF	Unc	BU
2008 Prooflike	5,000	—	—	—	10.00	15.00

KM# 35 SOM

12.0000 g., Copper-Nickel, 30 mm. **Series:** Great Silk Road **Subject:** Burana Tower **Rev:** Tower and map

Date	Mintage	F	VF	XF	Unc	BU
2008 Prooflike	5,000	—	—	—	10.00	15.00

KM# 31 SOM

12.0000 g., Copper-Nickel, 30 mm. **Series:** Great Silk Road **Subject:** Suilaman Mountain

Date	Mintage	F	VF	XF	Unc	BU
2009 Prooflike	5,000	—	—	—	10.00	15.00

KM# 33 SOM

12.0000 g., Copper-Nickel, 30 mm. **Series:** Great Silk Road **Subject:** Lake Issykkul

Date	Mintage	F	VF	XF	Unc	BU
2009 Prooflike	5,000	—	—	—	10.00	15.00

KM# 45 SOM

12.0000 g., Copper-Nickel, 30 mm. **Subject:** Pobeda Peak **Obv:** National arms above stylized peaks **Rev:** Mountian range

Date	Mintage	F	VF	XF	Unc	BU
2011	5,000	—	—	—	—	25.00

KM# 47 SOM

12.0000 g., Copper-Nickel, 30 mm. **Obv:** National arms **Rev:** Khan-Tengri Peak

Date	Mintage	F	VF	XF	Unc	BU
2011	5,000	—	—	—	—	25.00

KM# 15 3 SOM

3.2000 g., Nickel Plated Steel, 21 mm. **Obv:** National arms **Rev:** Symbol above right of denomination **Edge:** Reeded **Note:** Prev. KM #12.

Date	Mintage	F	VF	XF	Unc	BU
2008	—	—	—	—	1.25	2.00

KM# 16 5 SOM

4.2000 g., Nickel Plated Steel, 23 mm. **Obv:** National arms **Rev:** Symbol at right of value **Edge:** Reeded **Note:** Prev. KM #13.

Date	Mintage	F	VF	XF	Unc	BU
2008	—	—	—	—	1.50	2.50

KM# 4 10 SOM

28.2800 g., 0.9250 Silver 0.8410 oz. ASW, 38.6 mm. **Subject:** Tenth Anniversary of Republic **Obv:** National arms within circle **Rev:** Value and Khan Tengri mountain **Edge:** Reeded **Note:** Prev. KM #3.

Date	Mintage	F	VF	XF	Unc	BU
2001 Proof	1,000	Value: 175				

KM# 5 10 SOM

28.2800 g., 0.9250 Silver 0.8410 oz. ASW, 38.6 mm. **Subject:** International Year of the mountains **Obv:** National arms **Rev:** Edelweiss flower and mountain **Edge:** Reeded **Note:** Prev. KM #4.

Date	Mintage	F	VF	XF	Unc	BU
2002 Proof	1,000	Value: 125				

KM# 6 10 SOM
28.2800 g., 0.9250 Silver 0.8410 oz. ASW, 38.6 mm. **Subject:** International Year of the Mountains **Obv:** National arms **Rev:** Argali Ram head and mountain **Edge:** Reeded **Note:** Prev. KM #5.

Date	Mintage	F	VF	XF	Unc	BU
2002 Proof	1,000	Value: 125				

KM# 36 10 SOM
28.2800 g., 0.9250 Silver partially gilt 0.8410 oz. ASW, 38.6 mm. **Subject:** Som, 10th Anniversary **Obv:** National arms **Rev:** Som coin designs, some gilt

Date	Mintage	F	VF	XF	Unc	BU
2003 Proof	—	Value: 150				

KM# 7 10 SOM
28.2800 g., 0.9250 Silver partially gilt 0.8410 oz. ASW, 38.6 mm. **Subject:** Genesis of the Kyrgyz Statehood **Obv:** Arms **Rev:** Classical designs

Date	Mintage	F	VF	XF	Unc	BU
2003 Proof	1,000	Value: 250				

KM# 8 10 SOM
28.2800 g., 0.9250 Silver 0.8410 oz. ASW, 38.6 mm. **Subject:** 60 Years of Great Victory **Rev:** Figure of a mother, eternal light, Victory Memorial complex **Note:** Prev. KM #6.

Date	Mintage	F	VF	XF	Unc	BU
2005 Proof	1,000	Value: 110				

KM# 9 10 SOM
28.2800 g., 0.8250 Silver partially gilt 0.7501 oz. ASW, 38.6 mm. **Series:** Great Silk Road **Subject:** Tashrabat **Note:** Prev. KM #7.

Date	Mintage	F	VF	XF	Unc	BU
2005 Proof	1,500	Value: 100				

KM# 10 10 SOM
28.2800 g., 0.9250 Silver 0.8410 oz. ASW, 38.6 mm. **Subject:** Shanghai Cooperation **Obv:** Arms **Rev:** Multicolor logo of the Shanghai Cooperation Organization

Date	Mintage	F	VF	XF	Unc	BU
2007 Proof	1,000	Value: 180				

KM# 22 10 SOM
28.2800 g., 0.9250 Silver partially gilt 0.8410 oz. ASW, 38.6 mm. **Series:** Great Silk Road **Subject:** Uzgen Architectural Complex

Date	Mintage	F	VF	XF	Unc	BU
2007 Proof	1,500	Value: 120				

KM# 18 10 SOM
28.2800 g., 0.9250 Silver partially gilt 0.8410 oz. ASW, 38.6 mm. **Series:** Great Silk Road **Subject:** Burana Tower **Rev:** Buildings with partial gilting

Date	Mintage	F	VF	XF	Unc	BU
2008 Proof	1,500	Value: 110				

KM# 23 10 SOM
28.2800 g., 0.9250 Silver 0.8410 oz. ASW, 38.6 mm. **Series:** Capitals of the Eurasia Economic Community **Subject:** City of Bishkek **Obv:** National emblem **Rev:** Horseman statue, multicolor logo

Date	Mintage	F	VF	XF	Unc	BU
2008 Proof	2,500	Value: 90.00				

KM# 24 10 SOM
28.2800 g., 0.9250 Silver 0.8410 oz. ASW, 38.6 mm. **Rev:** Chynqyz Aytmatov

Date	Mintage	F	VF	XF	Unc	BU
2009 Proof	2,000	Value: 75.00				

KM# 25 10 SOM
28.2800 g., 0.9250 Silver 0.8410 oz. ASW, 38.6 mm. **Series:** Chinqiz Aitmatov's work's **Rev:** Jamila

Date	Mintage	F	VF	XF	Unc	BU
2009 Proof	3,000	Value: 75.00				

KM# 26 10 SOM
28.2800 g., 0.9250 Silver 0.8410 oz. ASW, 38.6 mm. **Series:** Chinqiz Aitmatov's works **Rev:** Duishen

Date	Mintage	F	VF	XF	Unc	BU
2009 Proof	3,000	Value: 75.00				

KM# 27 10 SOM
28.2800 g., 0.9250 Silver 0.8410 oz. ASW, 38.6 mm. **Series:** Chinqiz Aitmatov's works **Rev:** Mother field

Date	Mintage	F	VF	XF	Unc	BU
2009 Proof	3,000	Value: 75.00				

KM# 28 10 SOM
28.2800 g., 0.9250 Silver 0.8410 oz. ASW, 38.5 mm. **Series:** Chinqiz Aitmatov's works **Rev:** Farewell, Gulsary!

Date	Mintage	F	VF	XF	Unc	BU
2009 Proof	3,000	Value: 75.00				

KM# 29 10 SOM
28.2800 g., 0.9250 Silver 0.8410 oz. ASW, 38.5 mm. **Series:** Chinqiz Aitmatov's works **Rev:** The white ship

Date	Mintage	F	VF	XF	Unc	BU
2009 Proof	3,000	Value: 75.00				

KM# 32 10 SOM
28.2800 g., 0.9250 Silver Partially gilt 0.8410 oz. ASW, 38.6 mm. **Series:** Great Silk Road **Subject:** Suliman Mountain

Date	Mintage	F	VF	XF	Unc	BU
2009 Proof	1,500	Value: 110				

KM# 34 10 SOM
28.2800 g., 0.9250 Silver partially gilt 0.8410 oz. ASW, 38.6 mm. **Series:** Great Silk Road **Subject:** Lake Issykkul

Date	Mintage	F	VF	XF	Unc	BU
2009 Proof	1,500	Value: 110				

KM# 38 10 SOM
31.1000 g., 0.9250 Silver 0.9249 oz. ASW, 38.6 mm. **Obv:** National arms at top of repeating motif **Rev:** Eagle in flight right, multicolor logo below

Date	Mintage	F	VF	XF	Unc	BU
2009 Proof	3,000	Value: 90.00				

KM# 41 10 SOM
31.1000 g., 0.9250 Silver 0.9249 oz. ASW, 38.6 mm. **Obv:** National emblem and linear design **Rev:** Two people riding deer, as in a cave painting; multicolor logo below

Date	Mintage	F	VF	XF	Unc	BU
2009 Proof	3,000	Value: 95.00				

KM# 43 10 SOM
5.4000 g., Nickel Plated Steel, 24.5 mm. **Obv:** National Arms **Rev:** Symbol above value

Date	Mintage	F	VF	XF	Unc	BU
2009	—	—	—	—	4.50	6.00

KM# 39 10 SOM
31.1000 g., 0.9250 Silver 0.9249 oz. ASW, 38.6 mm. **Obv:** National Arms, multicolor design **Rev:** Frame construction of a Yurta

Date	Mintage	F	VF	XF	Unc	BU
2010 Proof	3,000	Value: 75.00				

KM# 40 10 SOM
31.1000 g., 0.9250 Silver 0.9249 oz. ASW, 38.6 mm. **Subject:** EurAsEC 10th Anniversary **Obv:** National arms and globe **Rev:** Five world sites, multicolor logo at center

Date	Mintage	F	VF	XF	Unc	BU
2010 Proof	2,000	Value: 75.00				

KM# 44 10 SOM
28.2800 g., Silver partially gilt, 38.6 mm. **Obv:** National arms **Rev:** Colored flag above map with Manas on horseback right **Edge:** Reeded

Date	Mintage	F	VF	XF	Unc	BU
2011 Proof	Est. 2,000	Value: 75.00				

KM# 46 10 SOM

28.2800 g., 0.9250 Silver 0.8410 oz. ASW, 38.6 mm. **Subject:** Pobeda Peak **Obv:** National arms above stylized mountains **Rev:** Mountian range **Edge:** Reeded

Date	Mintage	F	VF	XF	Unc	BU
2011 Proof	3,000	Value: 75.00				

KM# 48 10 SOM

31.1000 g., 0.9250 Silver partially gilt 0.9249 oz. ASW, 38.6 mm. **Subject:** Great Silk Road **Obv:** National arms above caravan riding right **Rev:** Skyline views and Silk Road map of Eurasia, color logo at top **Edge:** Reeded

Date	Mintage	F	VF	XF	Unc	BU
2011 Proof	Est. 2,000	Value: 75.00				

KM# 49 10 SOM

33.9400 g., 0.9250 Silver 1.0093 oz. ASW, 38.6 mm. **Subject:** World of our Children **Obv:** National arms and six flowers **Rev:** Child's drawing in color of sun, girl and medow **Edge:** Reeded

Date	Mintage	F	VF	XF	Unc	BU
2011 Proof	Est. 3,000	Value: 75.00				

KM# 50 10 SOM

28.2800 g., 0.9250 Silver 0.8410 oz. ASW, 38.6 mm. **Subject:** Kumranjan Datka, 200th Anniversary **Obv:** Arms, horseman below **Rev:** Turbaned head facing

Date	Mintage	F	VF	XF	Unc	BU
2012 Proof	—	Value: 110				

KM# 37 100 SOM

6.2200 g., 0.9990 Gold 0.1998 oz. AGW, 22 mm. **Rev:** Two horsemen

Date	Mintage	F	VF	XF	Unc	BU
2008 Proof	—	Value: 375				

KM# 42 100 SOM

31.1000 g., 0.9250 Silver 0.9249 oz. ASW, 38.61 mm. **Rev:** Panthera Tigris, gilt tiger

Date	Mintage	F	VF	XF	Unc	BU
2009 Proof	13,000	Value: 100				

MINT SETS

KM#	Date	Mintage	Identification	Issue Price	Mkt Val
MS1	2008 (6)	—	KM#11-16	—	30.00

LAO

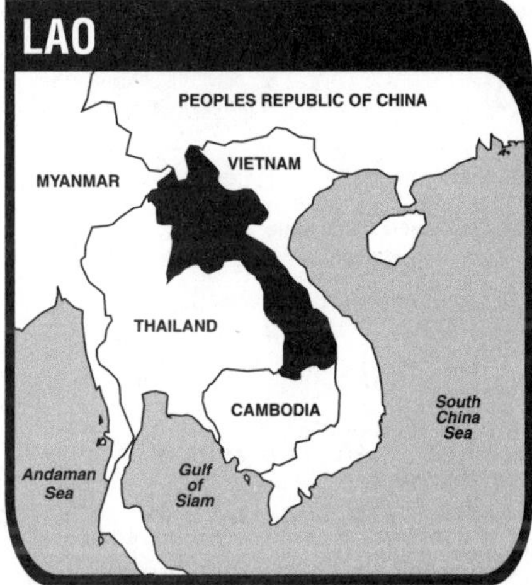

The Lao Peoples Democratic Republic, located on the Indo-Chinese Peninsula between the Socialist Republic of Vietnam and the Kingdom of Thailand, has an area of 91,428 sq. mi. (236,800 km.) and a population of 3.6 million. Capital Vientiane. Agriculture employs 95 per cent of the people. Tin, lumber and coffee are exported.

MONETARY SYSTEM

100 Att = 1 Kip

PEOPLES DEMOCRATIC REPUBLIC

STANDARD COINAGE

KM# 159 500 KIP

0.5000 g., 0.9990 Gold 0.0161 oz. AGW, 11 mm. **Obv:** National emblem **Rev:** Peacock

Date	Mintage	F	VF	XF	Unc	BU
2008 Proof	15,000	Value: 60.00				

KM# 160 500 KIP

0.5000 g., 0.9990 Gold 0.0161 oz. AGW, 11 mm. **Obv:** National emblem **Rev:** Victory Gate, Patouxai

Date	Mintage	F	VF	XF	Unc	BU
2008 Proof	10,000	Value: 60.00				

KM# 151 500 KIP

0.5000 g., 0.9990 Gold 0.0161 oz. AGW, 11 mm. **Rev:** Lion's head

Date	Mintage	F	VF	XF	Unc	BU
2009 Proof	—	Value: 50.00				

KM# 152 500 KIP

0.5000 g., 0.9990 Gold 0.0161 oz. AGW, 11 mm. **Subject:** Year of the Tiger **Rev:** Tiger

Date	Mintage	F	VF	XF	Unc	BU
2010 Proof	Est. 5,000	Value: 50.00				

KM# 162 500 KIP

0.5000 g., 0.9990 Gold 0.0161 oz. AGW, 11 mm. **Obv:** National emblem **Rev:** Buddha seated in archway

Date	Mintage	F	VF	XF	Unc	BU
2010 Proof	Est. 5,000	Value: 60.00				

KM# 165 500 KIP

0.5000 g., 0.9990 Gold 0.0161 oz. AGW, 11 mm. **Subject:** Year of the Rabbit **Obv:** National emblem **Rev:** Rabbit seated upright right, head looking left

Date	Mintage	F	VF	XF	Unc	BU
2011 Proof	Est. 5,000	Value: 50.00				

KM# 85 1000 KIP

31.5000 g., 0.9990 Silver 1.0117 oz. ASW, 38.5 mm. **Subject:** Olympics **Obv:** State emblem **Rev:** Freestyle skier **Edge:** Reeded

Date	Mintage	F	VF	XF	Unc	BU
2001 Proof	—	Value: 50.00				

KM# 96 1000 KIP

31.4500 g., 0.9990 Silver 1.0101 oz. ASW, 38.5 mm. **Obv:** State emblem **Rev:** Soccer player **Edge:** Reeded

Date	Mintage	F	VF	XF	Unc	BU
2001 Proof	—	Value: 50.00				

KM# 122 1000 KIP

1.2400 g., 0.9990 Gold 0.0398 oz. AGW, 13.92 mm. **Rev:** Tiger head

Date	Mintage	F	VF	XF	Unc	BU
2003 Proof	Est. 15,000	Value: 90.00				

KM# 126 1000 KIP
Silver **Subject:** Beijing olympics, 2008 **Rev:** Torch relay between Parthenon in Athens and Temple of Heaven in Beijing

Date	Mintage	F	VF	XF	Unc	BU
2004	—	Value: 35.00				

KM# 136 1000 KIP
1.2400 g., 0.9990 Gold 0.0398 oz. AGW, 13.92 mm. **Rev:** Wat Phu Champasak

Date	Mintage	F	VF	XF	Unc	BU
2005 Proof	—	Value: 90.00				

KM# 161 1000 KIP
1.2400 g., 0.9990 Gold 0.0398 oz. AGW, 13.92 mm. **Subject:** Rennes le Chateau **Obv:** National emblem **Rev:** Town gate and menorah

Date	Mintage	F	VF	XF	Unc	BU
2007 Proof	Est. 15,000	Value: 85.00				

KM# 150 1000 KIP
28.2800 g., 0.9250 Silver 0.8410 oz. ASW, 38.61 mm. **Subject:** Qinghai - Tibet Railway **Obv:** National emblem **Rev:** Train and map of the railroad from Zining to Lhasa

Date	Mintage	F	VF	XF	Unc	BU
2008 Proof	—	Value: 75.00				

KM# 157 1000 KIP
28.2800 g., 0.9250 Silver 0.8410 oz. ASW, 38.61 mm. **Subject:** Beijing to London Olympic transfer **Obv:** National emblem **Rev:** Temple of Heaven, Tower Bridge and athlete

Date	Mintage	F	VF	XF	Unc	BU
2008 Proof	Est. 10,000	Value: 75.00				

KM# 104 1000 KIP
36.4700 g., 0.9250 Silver 1.0846 oz. ASW, 38.6 mm. **Subject:** Terra Cotta Warriors **Obv:** Arms **Rev:** Gilt warrior standing, background warriors face right **Note:** Central gilt warrior is detachable and stands upright.

Date	Mintage	F	VF	XF	Unc	BU
2009 Proof	5,000	Value: 100				

KM# 105 1000 KIP
36.4700 g., 0.9250 Silver 1.0846 oz. ASW, 38.61 mm. **Subject:** Terra Cotta Warrior **Obv:** Arms **Rev:** Gilt standing warrior, warriors in background facing **Note:** Central gilt warrior is detachable and stands upright.

Date	Mintage	F	VF	XF	Unc	BU
2009 Proof	5,000	Value: 100				

KM# 106 1000 KIP
36.4700 g., 0.9250 Silver 1.0846 oz. ASW, 38.6 mm. **Subject:** Terra Cotta Warrior **Obv:** Arms **Rev:** Archer kneeling **Note:** Central gilt warrior is detachable and stands upright.

Date	Mintage	F	VF	XF	Unc	BU
2009 Proof	1,000	Value: 100				

KM# 107 1000 KIP
36.4700 g., 0.9250 Silver 1.0846 oz. ASW **Subject:** Terra Cotta Warrior **Obv:** Arms **Rev:** Gilt horse **Note:** Central gilt warrior is detachable and stands upright.

Date	Mintage	F	VF	XF	Unc	BU
2009 Proof	1,000	Value: 100				

KM# 153 1000 KIP
28.2800 g., 0.9250 Silver 0.8410 oz. ASW, 38.61 mm. **Subject:** World Cup 2010 in South Africa **Rev:** Sculpture of soccer players

Date	Mintage	F	VF	XF	Unc	BU
2010 Proof	—	Value: 60.00				

KM# 163 1000 KIP
1.0000 g., 0.9990 Gold 0.0321 oz. AGW, 13.92 mm. **Obv:** National emblem **Rev:** Buddha Park, stone staute head

Date	Mintage	F	VF	XF	Unc	BU
2010 Proof	Est. 10,000	Value: 75.00				

KM# 164 2000 KIP
62.2100 g., 0.9990 Silver selective gilt and with jade inlay 1.9980 oz. ASW, 55 mm. **Subject:** Year of the Rabbit **Obv:** Naitonal emblem **Rev:** Rabbit and jade inlay

Date	Mintage	F	VF	XF	Unc	BU
2011 Proof	Est. 2,888	Value: 200				

KM# 155 2000 KIP
62.2000 g., 0.9990 Silver 1.9977 oz. ASW, 55 mm. **Subject:** Year of the Dragon **Obv:** National arms **Rev:** Dragon with jade ring

Date	Mintage	F	VF	XF	Unc	BU
2012 Proof	2,888	Value: 140				

KM# 119 5000 KIP
0.3000 g., 0.9990 Gold 0.0096 oz. AGW, 7 mm. **Rev:** Cichlasoma fish

Date	Mintage	F	VF	XF	Unc	BU
2003	—	—	—	—	—	50.00

KM# 124 5000 KIP
0.3000 g., 0.9990 Gold 0.0096 oz. AGW, 7 mm. **Rev:** Rhino

Date	Mintage	F	VF	XF	Unc	BU
2004	—	—	—	—	—	50.00

KM# 127 5000 KIP
37.0000 g., Gold Plated Bronze, 45 mm. **Rev:** Majextic rooster as a laser engraving

Date	Mintage	F	VF	XF	Unc	BU
2005	Est. 28,000	—	—	—	—	35.00

KM# 129 5000 KIP
0.3000 g., 0.9990 Gold 0.0096 oz. AGW, 7 mm. **Rev:** Majestic rooster in pose

Date	Mintage	F	VF	XF	Unc	BU
2005 Proof	—	Value: 50.00				

KM# 139 5000 KIP
0.3000 g., 0.9990 Gold 0.0096 oz. AGW, 7 mm. **Subject:** Year of the Dog **Rev:** Dog with kinegram background

Date	Mintage	F	VF	XF	Unc	BU
2006	—	—	—	—	—	50.00

KM# 158 5000 KIP
7.7700 g., 0.5830 Gold 0.1456 oz. AGW, 25 mm. **Subject:** Beijing to London Olympic transfer **Obv:** National emblem **Rev:** Temple of Heaven, Tower Bridge and athlete

Date	Mintage	F	VF	XF	Unc	BU
2008 Proof	Est. 1,000	Value: 450				

KM# 113 10000 KIP
1.2400 g., 0.9990 Gold 0.0398 oz. AGW, 13.92 mm. **Rev:** Two redshank dress apes

Date	Mintage	F	VF	XF	Unc	BU
2001 Proof	—	Value: 90.00				

KM# 114 10000 KIP
1.2400 g., 0.9990 Gold 0.0398 oz. AGW, 13.92 mm. **Rev:** Horse drawing in color by Xu Beihong

Date	Mintage	F	VF	XF	Unc	BU
2002	—	—	—	—	—	90.00

KM# 120 10000 KIP
1.2400 g., 0.9990 Gold 0.0398 oz. AGW, 13.92 mm. **Rev:** Cichlasoma fish

Date	Mintage	F	VF	XF	Unc	BU
2003	—	—	—	—	—	90.00

KM# 125 10000 KIP
1.2400 g., 0.9990 Gold 0.0398 oz. AGW, 13.92 mm. **Rev:** Black crested gibbon

Date	Mintage	F	VF	XF	Unc	BU
2004	—	—	—	—	—	90.00

KM# 130 10000 KIP
1.2400 g., 0.9990 Gold 0.0398 oz. AGW, 13.92 mm. **Obv:** National Arms **Rev:** Majestic rooster right

Date	Mintage	F	VF	XF	Unc	BU
2005	—	—	—	—	—	80.00

KM# 133 10000 KIP
1.2400 g., 0.9990 Gold 0.0398 oz. AGW, 13.92 mm. **Obv:** National arms **Rev:** Mazu seated, waves in background

Date	Mintage	F	VF	XF	Unc	BU
2005	Est. 6,888	Value: 90.00				

KM# 140 10000 KIP
1.2400 g., 0.9990 Gold 0.0398 oz. AGW, 13.92 mm. **Subject:** Year of the Dog **Rev:** Don seated

Date	Mintage	F	VF	XF	Unc	BU
2006	—	—	—	—	—	90.00

KM# 142 10000 KIP
1.2400 g., 0.9990 Gold 0.0398 oz. AGW, 13.92 mm. **Rev:** Mazu standing

Date	Mintage	F	VF	XF	Unc	BU
2006	—	—	—	—	—	90.00

KM# 146 10000 KIP
1.2400 g., 0.9990 Gold 0.0398 oz. AGW **Rev:** Buddha in meditation **Shape:** 13.92

Date	Mintage	F	VF	XF	Unc	BU
2006	Est. 6,888	—	—	—	—	90.00

KM# 149 10000 KIP
1.2400 g., 0.9990 Gold 0.0398 oz. AGW, 13.92 mm. **Subject:** Year of the Pig **Obv:** National arms **Rev:** Pig

Date	Mintage	F	VF	XF	Unc	BU
2007	—	—	—	—	—	90.00

KM# 154 10000 KIP
1.0000 g., 0.9990 Gold 0.0321 oz. AGW, 13.92 mm. **Subject:** World Cup Soccer, South Africa **Rev:** Sculpture of soccer players

Date	Mintage	F	VF	XF	Unc	BU
2010 Proof	—	Value: 90.00				

KM# 86 15000 KIP
20.0000 g., 0.9250 Silver 0.5948 oz. ASW, 38.7 mm. **Subject:** Year of the Horse **Obv:** State emblem **Rev:** Multicolor horse **Edge:** Reeded

Date	Mintage	F	VF	XF	Unc	BU
2002 Proof	9,500	Value: 50.00				

KM# 87 15000 KIP
20.0000 g., 0.9250 Silver 0.5948 oz. ASW, 38.7 mm. **Subject:** Year of the Horse **Obv:** State emblem **Rev:** Horse with multicolor holographic background **Edge:** Reeded

Date	Mintage	F	VF	XF	Unc	BU
2002 Proof	9,500	Value: 55.00				

KM# 116 15000 KIP
20.0000 g., 0.9250 Silver 0.5948 oz. ASW **Obv:** National arms **Rev:** Shoulder-spot cichlid in color

Date	Mintage	F	VF	XF	Unc	BU
2003 Proof	Est. 2,300	Value: 60.00				

KM# 117 15000 KIP
20.0000 g., 0.9250 Silver 0.5948 oz. ASW, 38 mm. **Rev:** Chilasoma flower horn fish swimming left

Date	Mintage	F	VF	XF	Unc	BU
2003 Proof	—	Value: 60.00				

KM# 118 15000 KIP
20.0000 g., 0.9250 Silver 0.5948 oz. ASW, 38 mm. **Rev:** Fish in color kinegram

Date	Mintage	F	VF	XF	Unc	BU
2003 Proof	—	Value: 60.00				

KM# 123 15000 KIP
20.0000 g., 0.9990 Silver 0.6423 oz. ASW **Rev:** Black crested gibbon

Date	Mintage	F	VF	XF	Unc	BU
2004 Proof	Est. 3,800	Value: 60.00				

KM# 94 15000 KIP
20.0000 g., 0.9990 Silver 0.6423 oz. ASW, 38.7 mm. **Obv:** State emblem **Rev:** Multicolor Golden Monkey **Edge:** Reeded

Date	Mintage	F	VF	XF	Unc	BU
2004 Proof	2,300	Value: 55.00				

KM# 128 15000 KIP
20.0000 g., 0.9990 Silver 0.6423 oz. ASW **Rev:** Majestic Rooster with kinegram background

Date	Mintage	F	VF	XF	Unc	BU
2005 Proof	Est. 3,800	Value: 60.00				

KM# 132 15000 KIP
20.0000 g., 0.9250 Silver 0.5948 oz. ASW, 38 mm. **Obv:** National arms **Rev:** Mazu seated, waves in background

Date	Mintage	F	VF	XF	Unc	BU
2005 Proof	Est. 6,888	Value: 60.00				

KM# 98 15000 KIP
Silver, 38.7 mm. **Issuer:** Bank of Lao PDR **Obv:** National arms **Obv. Legend:** THE LAO PEOPLE'S DEMOCRATIC REPUBLIC **Rev:** Statue of Mazu with stylized Phoenix at left and right **Rev. Legend:** GODDESS OF THE SEA **Edge:** Reeded

Date	Mintage	F	VF	XF	Unc	BU
2006 Proof	6,888	Value: 65.00				

KM# 137 15000 KIP
20.0000 g., 0.9990 Silver 0.6423 oz. ASW, 38 mm. **Subject:** Year of the Dog **Rev:** Three dogs

Date	Mintage	F	VF	XF	Unc	BU
2006 Proof	—	Value: 60.00				

KM# 138 15000 KIP
Silver **Subject:** Year of the Dog **Rev:** Dog with kinegram background

Date	Mintage	F	VF	XF	Unc	BU
2006 Proof	—	Value: 60.00				

KM# 145 15000 KIP
20.0000 g., 0.9250 Silver 0.5948 oz. ASW, 38 mm. **Rev:** Buddha head facing

Date	Mintage	F	VF	XF	Unc	BU
2006 Proof	Est. 6,888	Value: 60.00				

KM# 148 15000 KIP
20.0000 g., 0.9990 Silver 0.6423 oz. ASW, 38 mm. **Subject:** Year of the Pig **Obv:** National arms **Rev:** Pig with kinegram background

Date	Mintage	F	VF	XF	Unc	BU
2007 Proof	—	Value: 60.00				

KM# 115 50000 KIP
7.7800 g., 0.9990 Gold 0.2499 oz. AGW, 22 mm. **Obv:** National arms **Rev:** Horse advancing right

Date	Mintage	F	VF	XF	Unc	BU
2002	—	—	—	—	—	475

KM# 88 60000 KIP
155.5175 g., 0.9250 Silver 4.6248 oz. ASW, 65 mm. **Subject:** Year of the Horse **Obv:** State emblem **Rev:** Multicolor horse **Edge:** Reeded

Date	Mintage	F	VF	XF	Unc	BU
2002 Proof	1,000	Value: 225				

KM# 89 100000 KIP
15.5518 g., 0.9999 Gold 0.4999 oz. AGW, 27 mm. **Subject:** Year of the Horse **Obv:** State emblem **Rev:** Horse **Edge:** Reeded

Date	Mintage	F	VF	XF	Unc	BU
2002	2,000	Value: 925				

KM# 121 100000 KIP
15.5500 g., 0.9990 Gold 0.4994 oz. AGW, 27 mm. **Rev:** Cichlasoma fish left

Date	Mintage	F	VF	XF	Unc	BU
2003 Proof	Est. 888	Value: 950				

KM# 95 100000 KIP
15.5518 g., 0.9990 Gold 0.4995 oz. AGW, 27 mm. **Obv:** State emblem **Rev:** Black Gibbon on holographic background **Edge:** Reeded

Date	Mintage	F	VF	XF	Unc	BU
2004 Proof	888	Value: 950				

KM# 131 100000 KIP
15.5500 g., 0.9990 Gold 0.4994 oz. AGW, 27 mm. **Rev:** Majestic rooster right , kinegram background

Date	Mintage	F	VF	XF	Unc	BU
2005 Proof	Est. 888	Value: 950				

KM# 134 100000 KIP
15.5500 g., 0.9990 Gold 0.4994 oz. AGW **Rev:** Mazu seated, waves in background

Date	Mintage	F	VF	XF	Unc	BU
2005 Proof	688	Value: 950				

KM# 141 100000 KIP
15.5500 g., 0.9990 Gold 0.4994 oz. AGW **Subject:** Year of the Dog

Date	Mintage	F	VF	XF	Unc	BU
2006 Proof	Est. 888	Value: 950				

KM# 143 100000 KIP
15.5500 g., 0.9990 Gold 0.4994 oz. AGW, 27 mm. **Rev:** Mazu half lenght left

Date	Mintage	F	VF	XF	Unc	BU
2006 Proof	Est. 688	Value: 950				

KM# 147 100000 KIP
15.5500 g., 0.9990 Gold 0.4994 oz. AGW, 27 mm. **Rev:** Buddha in meditation

Date	Mintage	F	VF	XF	Unc	BU
2006 Proof	Est. 688	Value: 950				

KM# 103 100000 KIP
7.7750 g., 0.9990 Gold 0.2497 oz. AGW, 27 mm. **Subject:** President Print Souphanouvong, 100th Anniversary of Birth **Obv:** Bust facing **Rev:** Presidential Palace

Date	Mintage	F	VF	XF	Unc	BU
ND (2009) Proof	1,000	Value: 475				

KM# 102 100000 KIP
38.5000 g., 0.9250 Silver 1.1449 oz. ASW, 36.5 mm. **Subject:** President Print Souphanouvong, 100th Anniversary of Birth **Obv:** Bust facing **Rev:** Presidential Palace

Date	Mintage	F	VF	XF	Unc	BU
ND (2009) Proof	1,000	Value: 100				

KM# 90 1000000 KIP
155.5175 g., 0.9999 Gold 4.9993 oz. AGW, 55 mm. **Subject:** Year of the Horse **Obv:** State emblem **Rev:** Horse with multicolor holographic background **Edge:** Reeded

Date	Mintage	F	VF	XF	Unc	BU
2002 Proof	500	Value: 9,250				

KM# 135 1000000 KIP
155.5000 g., 0.9990 Gold 4.9942 oz. AGW **Rev:** Mazu seated, waves in background

Date	Mintage	F	VF	XF	Unc	BU
2005 Proof	99	Value: 9,750				

KM# 99 1000000 KIP
155.5150 g., 0.9999 Gold 4.9992 oz. AGW, 55.0 mm. **Issuer:** Bank of Lao PDR **Obv:** National arms **Obv. Legend:** THE LAO PEOPLE'S DEMOCRATIC REPUBLIC **Rev:** Multi-latent color bust of Lord Buddha "Fo Guang Pu Zhao" facing with diamond insert in forehead **Edge:** Reeded

Date	Mintage	F	VF	XF	Unc	BU
2006 Proof	99	Value: 9,750				

KM# 144 1000000 KIP
155.5000 g., 0.9990 Gold 4.9942 oz. AGW **Rev:** Mazu standing

Date	Mintage	F	VF	XF	Unc	BU
2006 Proof	Est. 99	Value: 9,750				

PROOF SETS

KM#	Date	Mintage	Identification	Issue Price	Mkt Val
PS7	2000-2001 (3)	3,500	KM#74-76	138	200
PS8	2000-2001 (3)	500	KM#74-76	214	300
PS9	2000-2001 (2)	800	KM#78, 83	—	1,100

LATVIA

The Republic of Latvia, the central Baltic state in east Europe, has an area of 24,749 sq. mi. (43,601 sq. km.) and a population of *2.6 million. Capital: Riga. Livestock raising and manufacturing are the chief industries. Butter, bacon, fertilizers and telephone equipment are exported.

MONETARY SYSTEM
100 Santimu = 1 Lats

MODERN REPUBLIC
1991-present
STANDARD COINAGE

KM# 15 SANTIMS
1.6000 g., Copper Clad Steel, 15.65 mm. **Obv:** National arms **Rev:** Value flanked by diamonds below lined arch **Edge:** Plain **Designer:** Gunars Lusis and Janis Strupulis

Date	Mintage	F	VF	XF	Unc	BU
2003	30,000,000	—	—	0.10	0.30	0.40
2005	20,000,000	—	—	0.10	0.30	0.40
2007	25,000,000	—	—	0.10	0.30	0.40
2008	75,000,000	—	—	0.10	0.30	0.40

KM# 21 2 SANTIMI
1.9000 g., Copper Clad Steel, 17 mm. **Obv:** National arms **Rev:** Lined arch above value flanked by diamonds **Edge:** Plain **Designer:** Gunars Lusis and Janis Strupulis

Date	Mintage	F	VF	XF	Unc	BU
2006	18,000,000	—	—	0.20	0.45	0.60
2007	30,000,000	—	—	0.20	0.45	0.60
2009	50,000,000	—	—	0.20	0.45	0.60

KM# 16 5 SANTIMI
2.5000 g., Nickel-Brass, 18.5 mm. **Obv:** National arms **Obv. Legend:** LATVIJAS REPUBLIKA **Rev:** Lined arch above value flanked by diamonds **Edge:** Plain **Designer:** Gunars Lusis and Janis Strupulis

Date	Mintage	F	VF	XF	Unc	BU
2006	8,000,000	—	—	0.30	0.75	1.00
2007	15,000,000	—	—	0.30	0.75	1.00
2009	10,000,000	—	—	0.30	0.75	1.00

KM# 17 10 SANTIMU
3.2500 g., Nickel-Brass, 19.9 mm. **Obv:** National arms **Rev:** Lined arch above value flanked by diamonds **Edge:** Plain **Designer:** Gunars Lusis and Janis Strupulis

Date	Mintage	F	VF	XF	Unc	BU
2008	15,000,000	—	—	0.50	1.00	1.50

KM# 22.1 20 SANTIMU
4.0000 g., Nickel-Brass, 21.5 mm. **Obv:** National arms **Rev:** Lined arch above value flanked by diamonds **Edge:** Plain **Designer:** Gunars Lusis and Janis Strupulis **Note:** 1.5mm thick.

Date	Mintage	F	VF	XF	Unc	BU
2007	7,000,000	—	—	0.50	1.00	2.00
2009	10,000,000	—	—	0.50	1.00	2.00

KM# 13 50 SANTIMU
3.5000 g., Copper-Nickel, 18.8 mm. **Obv:** National arms **Rev:** Triple sprig above value **Edge:** Reeded **Designer:** Gunars Lusis and Janis Strupulis

Date	Mintage	F	VF	XF	Unc	BU
2007	4,000,000	—	—	2.00	3.00	4.00
2009	5,000,000	—	—	2.00	3.00	4.00

KM# 70 100 SANTIMU
31.4700 g., 0.9250 Silver 0.9359 oz. ASW, 38.6 mm. **Obv:** Baron von Muenchausen with chain of birds around a dog with a lantern hanging from its tail. **Rev:** Baron von Muenchausen and dog hunting a circle of animals **Edge Lettering:** LATVIJAS BANKA LATVIJAS REPUBLIKA **Designer:** Arvids Priedite and Janis Strupulis

Date	Mintage	F	VF	XF	Unc	BU
2005 Proof	Est. 5,000	Value: 65.00				

KM# 49 LATS
31.4700 g., 0.9250 Silver 0.9359 oz. ASW, 38.6 mm. **Subject:** Hanseatic City of Cesis **Obv:** City arms **Rev:** Sailing ship above, inverted walled city view below **Edge Lettering:** LATVIJAS REPUBLIKA • LATVIJAS BANKA **Designer:** Gunars Krollis and Janis Strupulis

Date	Mintage	F	VF	XF	Unc	BU
2001 Proof	Est. 15,000	Value: 75.00				

KM# 50 LATS
31.4700 g., 0.9250 Silver 0.9359 oz. ASW **Series:** Ice Hockey **Obv:** Arms with supporters **Rev:** Hockey player **Designer:** Andris Varpa

Date	Mintage	F	VF	XF	Unc	BU
2001 Proof	Est. 15,000	Value: 90.00				

KM# 51 LATS

31.4700 g., 0.9250 Silver 0.9359 oz. ASW, 38.6 mm. **Subject:** Heaven **Obv:** Stylized design **Rev:** Stylized woman holding sun **Edge:** Plain **Designer:** Juris Petraskevics and Ligita Franckevica

Date	Mintage	F	VF	XF	Unc	BU
2001 Proof	Est. 5,000	Value: 55.00				

KM# 54 LATS

4.8000 g., Copper-Nickel, 21.75 mm. **Obv:** Arms with supporters **Rev:** Nesting stork above value **Edge Lettering:** LATVIJAS BANKA • LATVIJAS BANKA

Date	Mintage	F	VF	XF	Unc	BU
2001	250,000	—	—	7.00	12.00	15.00

KM# 55 LATS

31.4700 g., 0.9250 Silver 0.9359 oz. ASW, 38.6 mm. **Subject:** National Library **Obv:** Country name and diamonds pattern **Rev:** Library building sketch and diamonds design **Edge Lettering:** GAISMU SAUCA • GAISMA AUSA **Designer:** Arnis Kleinberg and Janis Strupulis

Date	Mintage	F	VF	XF	Unc	BU
2002 Proof	Est. 5,000	Value: 80.00				

KM# 56 LATS

15.0000 g., 0.9250 Silver with gilt obverse 0.4461 oz. ASW, 28 mm. **Subject:** Coin of Fortune **Obv:** Totally gold plated sun above country name **Rev:** Waning moon, date and value **Edge:** Plain **Designer:** Ilmars Blumbergs and Janis Ronis

Date	Mintage	F	VF	XF	Unc	BU
2002 Proof	Est. 5,000	Value: 250				

KM# 52 LATS

31.4700 g., 0.9250 Silver 0.9359 oz. ASW, 38.6 mm. **Subject:** Destiny **Obv:** Stylized design **Rev:** Apple tree and landscape **Edge:** Plain **Designer:** Juris Petraskevics and Ligita Franckevica

Date	Mintage	F	VF	XF	Unc	BU
2002 Proof	Est. 5,000	Value: 85.00				

KM# 53 LATS

31.4700 g., 0.9250 Silver 0.9359 oz. ASW, 38.6 mm. **Subject:** Hanseatic City of Kuldiga **Obv:** City arms **Rev:** City view and ships **Edge:** Lettered **Designer:** Gunars Krollis and Janis Strupulis

Date	Mintage	F	VF	XF	Unc	BU
2002 Proof	Est. 15,000	Value: 80.00				

KM# 57 LATS

31.4700 g., 0.9250 Silver 0.9359 oz. ASW, 38.6 mm. **Subject:** Olympics 2004 **Obv:** Arms with supporters **Rev:** Ancient wrestlers **Edge Lettering:** LATVIJAS BANKA • LATVIJAS BANKA **Designer:** Dainis Pundurs and Ligita Franckevica

Date	Mintage	F	VF	XF	Unc	BU
2002 Proof	Est. 26,000	Value: 70.00				

KM# 60 LATS

31.4700 g., 0.9250 Silver 0.9359 oz. ASW, 38.6 mm. **Subject:** Courland **Obv:** Crowned arms above partially built ship **Rev:** Hemp weighing scene with Iron foundry and brick wall in background **Edge Lettering:** LATVIJAS REPUBLIKA • LATVIJAS BANKA **Designer:** Arvids Priedite and Ligita Franckevica

Date	Mintage	F	VF	XF	Unc	BU
2003 Proof	Est. 5,000	Value: 80.00				

KM# 71 LATS

31.4700 g., 0.9250 Silver 0.9359 oz. ASW, 38.6 mm. **Subject:** Vidzeme **Obv:** Crowned arms above horse drawn wagon **Rev:** Two men sawing wood **Edge Lettering:** LATVIJAS BANKA • LATVIJAS REPUBLIKA **Designer:** Arvids Priedite and Ligita Franckevica

Date	Mintage	F	VF	XF	Unc	BU
ND (2003) Proof	—	Value: 65.00				
2004 Proof	Est. 5,000	Value: 65.00				

KM# 72 LATS

31.4700 g., 0.9250 Silver 0.9359 oz. ASW, 38.6 mm. **Subject:** Latgale **Obv:** Madonna and Child above landscape **Rev:** Man sowing seeds and an angel **Edge Lettering:** LATVIJAS BANKA • LATVIJAS REPUBLIKA **Designer:** Arvids Priedite and Ligita Franckevica

Date	Mintage	F	VF	XF	Unc	BU
ND (2003) Proof	—	Value: 60.00				
2004 Proof	Est. 5,000	Value: 60.00				

KM# 75 LATS
31.4700 g., 0.9250 Silver 0.9359 oz. ASW, 38.61 mm. **Subject:** Hanseatic City of Valmiera **Obv:** Coat of arms **Rev:** St. Simanis Church with VALMIERA and reflection of sailing ship **Edge:** LATVIJAS REPUBLIKA • LATVIJAS BANKA **Designer:** Gunars Krollis and Janis Strupulis

Date	Mintage	F	VF	XF	Unc	BU
2003 Proof	Est. 15,000	Value: 55.00				

KM# 58 LATS
4.8000 g., Copper-Nickel, 21.75 mm. **Obv:** Arms with supporters **Rev:** Ant above value **Edge Lettering:** LATVIJAS BANKA • LATVIJAS BANKA

Date	Mintage	F	VF	XF	Unc	BU
2003	250,000	—	—	5.00	6.50	8.00

KM# 64 LATS
31.4700 g., 0.9250 Silver 0.9359 oz. ASW, 38.6 mm. **Subject:** Latvian European Union Membership **Obv:** Arms with supporters **Rev:** P.S. LATVIJA-ES 2004 above value **Edge Lettering:** LATVIJAS BANKA • LATVIJAS BANKA **Designer:** Sandra Belsone and Janis Strupulis

Date	Mintage	F	VF	XF	Unc	BU
2004 Proof	Est. 15,000	Value: 65.00				

KM# 61 LATS
4.8000 g., Copper-Nickel, 21.75 mm. **Obv:** Arms with supporters **Rev:** Spriditis with shovel above value **Edge Lettering:** LATVIJAS BANKA • LATVIJAS BANKA

Date	Mintage	F	VF	XF	Unc	BU
2004	500,000	—	—	3.00	4.00	6.00

KM# 62 LATS
17.1500 g., Bi-Metallic Dark Blue Niobium 7.15g center in .900 Silver 10g ring, 34 mm. **Subject:** Coin of Time **Obv:** Heraldic Rose **Rev:** Clock dial in center, rings of hours, minutes, months and days around **Edge:** Plain **Designer:** Laimonis Senberg and Janis Strupulis

Date	Mintage	F	VF	XF	Unc	BU
2004	Est. 5,000	—	—	—	75.00	85.00

KM# 63 LATS
31.4700 g., 0.9250 Silver 0.9359 oz. ASW, 38.6 mm. **Obv:** Arms with supporters **Rev:** World Cup Soccer player **Edge Lettering:** LATVIJA three times **Designer:** Henrihs Vorkals and Ligita Franckevica

Date	Mintage	F	VF	XF	Unc	BU
2004 Proof	Est. 50,000	Value: 70.00				

KM# 67 LATS
4.8000 g., Copper-Nickel, 21.75 mm. **Obv:** National arms **Obv. Legend:** LATVIJAS REPUBLIKA **Rev:** Mushroom above value **Edge Lettering:** LATVIJAS BANKA • LATVIJAS BANKA **Designer:** Guntars Sietins and Janis Strupulis

Date	Mintage	F	VF	XF	Unc	BU
2004	500,000	—	—	3.00	4.00	5.00

KM# 68 LATS
31.4700 g., 0.9250 Silver 0.9359 oz. ASW, 38.6 mm. **Subject:** Janis Plieksans "Rainis" **Obv:** Mountains and value **Rev:** Laser picture of Rainis the mountain climbing poet, dramatist and patriot. **Edge Lettering:** LATVIJAS BANKA • LATVIJAS REPUBLIKA **Designer:** Arta Ozola-Jaunaraja and Ligita Franckevica

Date	Mintage	F	VF	XF	Unc	BU
2005 Proof	Est. 5,000	Value: 45.00				

KM# 69 LATS
31.4700 g., 0.9250 Silver 0.9359 oz. ASW, 38.6 mm. **Obv:** National arms **Rev:** Bobsled **Edge Lettering:** LATVIJA (three times) **Designer:** Henrihs Vorkals and Janis Strupulis

Date	Mintage	F	VF	XF	Unc	BU
2005 Proof	Est. 15,000	Value: 50.00				

KM# 65 LATS
4.8000 g., Copper-Nickel, 21.75 mm. **Obv:** Arms with supporters **Rev:** Weathercock (from the spire of Riga's St. Peter Church) above value **Edge Lettering:** LATVIJAS BANKA • LATVIJAS BANKA

Date	Mintage	F	VF	XF	Unc	BU
2005	500,000	—	—	3.00	6.00	7.00

KM# 76 LATS
31.4700 g., 0.9250 Silver 0.9359 oz. ASW, 38.61 mm. **Subject:** Ice Hockey World Championship **Obv:** Large coat of arms, date below **Rev:** Two hockey players viewed from above, RIGA 2006 on either side with hockey puck in center **Edge Lettering:** LATVIJA (three times)

Date	Mintage	F	VF	XF	Unc	BU
2005 Proof	Est. 5,000	Value: 55.00				

KM# 77 LATS
31.4700 g., 0.9250 Silver 0.9359 oz. ASW, 38.61 mm. **Subject:** Hanseatic City of Koknese **Obv:** Coat of arms **Rev:** Koknese castle on top with moon and sun on sides, reflection of Hanseatic Castle and ship on bottom **Edge Lettering:** LATVIJAS REPUBLIKA • LATVIJAS BANKA **Designer:** Gunars Krollis and Janis Strupulis

Date	Mintage	F	VF	XF	Unc	BU
2005 Proof	Est. 15,000	Value: 50.00				

KM# 81 LATS
1.2442 g., 0.9999 Gold 0.0400 oz. AGW, 13.92 mm. **Subject:** Art Nouveau **Obv:** Ribbon design **Obv. Legend:** RIGAS / LATVIJAS REPUBLIKA **Rev:** Stone face **Edge:** Reeded **Designer:** Guntars Sietins and Ligita Franckevica

Date	Mintage	F	VF	XF	Unc	BU
2005 Proof	Est. 20,000	Value: 100				

KM# 66 LATS

4.8000 g., Copper-Nickel, 21.75 mm. **Obv:** National arms **Obv. Legend:** LATVIJAS REPUBLIKA **Rev:** Pretzel above value **Edge Lettering:** LATVIJAS BANKA • LATVIJAS BANKA

Date	Mintage	F	VF	XF	Unc	BU
2005	500,000	—	—	3.00	4.00	6.00

KM# 73 LATS

4.8000 g., Copper-Nickel, 21.75 mm. **Subject:** Summer Solstice **Obv:** National arms **Rev:** Head wearing Ligo wreath above value **Edge Lettering:** LATVIJAS BANKA • LATVIJAS BANKA

Date	Mintage	F	VF	XF	Unc	BU
2006	500,000	—	—	3.00	4.00	6.00

KM# 74 LATS

4.8000 g., Copper-Nickel, 21.75 mm. **Obv:** National arms **Rev:** Pine cone above value **Edge Lettering:** LATVIJAS BANKA • LATVIJAS BANKA **Designer:** Guntars Sietins and Janis Strupulis

Date	Mintage	F	VF	XF	Unc	BU
2006	1,000,000	—	—	3.00	5.00	6.00

KM# 78 LATS

31.4700 g., 0.9250 Silver 0.9359 oz. ASW, 38.61 mm. **Subject:** The Barricades of January 1991 **Obv:** Stylized bonfire flames **Obv. Legend:** janvāris 1991 **Rev:** Latvian mythological hero with raised sword against the background of concrete block barricades, rising sun behind **Edge Lettering:** LATVIJAS BANKA (twice) **Designer:** Juris Petraskevics and Andris Varpa

Date	Mintage	F	VF	XF	Unc	BU
2006 Proof	Est. 5,000	Value: 65.00				

KM# 79 LATS

31.4700 g., 0.9250 Silver 0.9359 oz. ASW, 38.61 mm. **Subject:** Krisjanis Barons **Obv:** Starry sky on left with value on right side **Rev:** Portrait of Barons on right side and starry sky on left **Edge Lettering:** LATVIJAS BANKA • LATVIJAS REPUBLIKA **Designer:** Arta Ozola-Jaunaraja and Ligita Franckevica

Date	Mintage	F	VF	XF	Unc	BU
2006 Proof	Est. 5,000	Value: 65.00				

KM# 80 LATS

31.4700 g., 0.9250 Silver 0.9359 oz. ASW, 38.61 mm. **Subject:** Krishjanis Valdemars **Obv:** Seagul flying above water on left, value on right **Rev:** Portrait of Valdemars on right with sea on left **Edge Lettering:** LATVIJAS BANKA • LATVIJAS REPUBLIKA **Designer:** Arta Ozola-Jaunaraja and Ligita Franckevica

Date	Mintage	F	VF	XF	Unc	BU
2006 Proof	Est. 5,000	Value: 65.00				

KM# 82 LATS

31.4700 g., 0.9250 Silver 0.9359 oz. ASW, 38.61 mm. **Subject:** Fight for Freedom **Obv:** Outline of Latvia with three stars above **Obv. Inscription:** LATVIJAS REPUBLIKA **Rev:** Two crossed swords outlined against the sun **Rev. Inscription:** NO ZOBENA SAULE LECA **Edge:** Plain **Designer:** Ivo Grundulis and Ligita Franckevica

Date	Mintage	F	VF	XF	Unc	BU
2006 Proof	Est. 5,000	Value: 65.00				

KM# 83 LATS

31.4700 g., 0.9250 Silver 0.9359 oz. ASW, 38.61 mm. **Subject:** Hanseatic City of Straupe **Obv:** Coat of arms, date and value below **Obv. Inscription:** ROOP / 1 LATS **Rev:** Lielstraupe castle church top, reflection of Hanseatic ship with trees on both sides on bottom **Edge Lettering:** LATVIJAS REPUBLIKA • LATVIJAS BANKA **Designer:** Gunars Krollis and Janis Strupulis

Date	Mintage	F	VF	XF	Unc	BU
2006 Proof	Est. 15,000	Value: 55.00				

KM# 84 LATS

27.0000 g., 0.9990 Silver 0.8672 oz. ASW, 38.61 mm. **Subject:** Coin of Digits **Obv:** Arabic O in center of haptagon against an oriental background **Rev:** Roman I in center of heptagon **Shape:** 7-sided **Designer:** Ilmars Blumbergs and Janis Struplis

Date	Mintage	F	VF	XF	Unc	BU
2006 Proof	2,007	Value: 400				

KM# 12 LATS

4.8000 g., Copper-Nickel, 21.75 mm. **Obv:** Arms with supporters **Rev:** Salmon above value **Edge Lettering:** LATVIJAS BANKA • LATVIJAS BANKA

Date	Mintage	F	VF	XF	Unc	BU
2007	7,000,000	—	—	2.00	4.00	7.00
2008	25,000,000	—	—	2.00	4.00	7.00

KM# 85 LATS

4.8000 g., Copper-Nickel, 21.75 mm. **Obv:** National arms **Obv. Legend:** LATVIJAS REPUBLIKA **Rev:** Snowman **Edge Lettering:** LATVIJAS BANKA • LATVIJAS BANKA **Designer:** Daina Lapina and Ligita Franckevica

Date	Mintage	F	VF	XF	Unc	BU
2007	1,000,000	—	—	3.00	4.00	6.00

KM# 86 LATS

4.8000 g., Copper-Nickel, 21.75 mm. **Obv:** National arms **Obv. Legend:** LATVIJAS REPUBLIKA **Rev:** Medieval owl figurine **Edge Lettering:** LATVIJAS BANKA • LATVIJAS BANKA

Date	Mintage	F	VF	XF	Unc	BU
2007	1,000,000	—	—	2.00	4.00	6.00

KM# 87 LATS

31.4700 g., 0.9250 Silver 0.9359 oz. ASW, 38.6 mm. **Subject:** Foreign Rulers **Obv:** Fragment of a large coat of arms **Rev:** Large coat of arms broken into fragments **Edge:** Plain **Designer:** Ivo Grundulis and Ligita Franckevica

Date	Mintage	F	VF	XF	Unc	BU
2007 Proof	—	Value: 65.00				

KM# 88 LATS

31.4700 g., 0.9250 Silver 0.9359 oz. ASW, 38.6 mm. **Subject:** Rebirth of the State **Obv:** Large coat of arms **Rev:** Sun with its rays forming the red-white-red flag of the Republic **Edge:** Plain **Designer:** Ivo Grundulis and Ligita Franckevica

Date	Mintage	F	VF	XF	Unc	BU
2007 Proof	Est. 5,000	Value: 65.00				

KM# 89 LATS

31.4700 g., 0.9250 Silver 0.9359 oz. ASW, 38.6 mm. **Subject:** Sigulda **Obv:** Horse and sword within pendant **Rev:** Gauja Valley with the Turaida Castle and Sigulda Castle **Edge Lettering:** LATVIJAS REPUBLIKA • LATVIJAS BANKA **Designer:** Arvids Priedite and Janis Strupulis

Date	Mintage	F	VF	XF	Unc	BU
2007 Proof	Est. 5,000	Value: 65.00				

KM# 90 LATS

17.1500 g., Bi-Metallic Dark Purple, 34 mm. **Subject:** Coin of Time II **Obv:** Heraldic rose at center **Rev:** Outer ring signs of the zodiac, inner circle different evolutionary stages of the plant world **Edge:** Plain **Designer:** Laimonis Senbergs and Janis Strupulis

Date	Mintage	F	VF	XF	Unc	BU
2007	7,000	—	—	—	75.00	85.00

KM# 91 LATS

1.2442 g., 0.9990 Gold 0.0400 oz. AGW, 13.92 mm. **Obv:** Small coat of arms **Rev:** Logo of the publishing house Zelta abele **Edge:** Reeded **Designer:** Laimonis Senbergs and Janis Strupulis

Date	Mintage	F	VF	XF	Unc	BU
2007 Proof	Est. 15,000	Value: 80.00				

KM# 97 LATS
31.4700 g., 0.9250 Silver 0.9359 oz. ASW, 38.6 mm. **Subject:** Coin of life **Obv:** Mother holding gilt wrapped child **Rev:** Golden heart-shaped leaves **Edge:** Plain **Designer:** Ilmars Blumbergs and Ligita Franckevica

Date	Mintage	F	VF	XF	Unc	BU
2007 Proof	5,000	Value: 85.00				

KM# 98 LATS
22.0000 g., 0.9250 Silver 0.6542 oz. ASW, 35 mm. **Subject:** Lucky Coin **Obv:** Cat pearched on rooftop peak **Rev:** Chimney-sweep with ladder and rope coil with bruch and weight. **Edge Lettering:** LATVIJAS BANKA • LATVIJAS BANKA **Designer:** Arvids Priedite and Janis Strupulis

Date	Mintage	F	VF	XF	Unc	BU
2008 Proof	5,000	Value: 65.00				

KM# 99 LATS
31.4700 g., 0.9250 Silver 0.9359 oz. ASW, 38.6 mm. **Subject:** 90th Anniversary of Statehood **Obv:** First Arms of the Republic **Rev:** Two children holding multicolor flag **Edge Lettering:** LATVIJAS BANKA (twice) **Designer:** Aigars Bikse

Date	Mintage	F	VF	XF	Unc	BU
2008 Proof	5,000	Value: 85.00				

KM# 92 LATS
4.8000 g., Copper-Nickel, 21.75 mm. **Obv:** National arms **Obv. Legend:** LATVIJAS REPUBLIKA **Rev:** Water Lily **Edge Lettering:** LATVIJAS BANKA • LATVIJAS BANKA

Date	Mintage	F	VF	XF	Unc	BU
2008	1,000,000	—	—	3.00	4.00	6.00

KM# 93 LATS
12.4000 g., Copper-Nickel, 30 mm. **Obv:** Woman walking holding flowers **Rev:** Man walking holding wreath **Edge Lettering:** DZIESMAI SODIEN LIELA DIENA **Designer:** Arvids Priedite and Ligita Franckevica

Date	Mintage	F	VF	XF	Unc	BU
2008	30,000	—	—	—	7.00	9.00

KM# 93a LATS
31.4700 g., 0.9250 Silver 0.9359 oz. ASW, 38.61 mm. **Obv:** Woman walking holding flowers **Rev:** Man walking holding wreath **Edge Lettering:** DZIESMAI SODIEN LIELA DIENA **Designer:** Arvids Priedite and Ligita Franckevica

Date	Mintage	F	VF	XF	Unc	BU
2008 Proof	10,000	Value: 65.00				

KM# 94 LATS
31.4700 g., 0.9250 Silver 0.9359 oz. ASW, 38.61 mm. **Subject:** Hanseatic City of Limbazi **Obv:** Hanseatic city seal with coat of arms **Rev:** Limbazi Castle ruins and St. Johns Church with reflection of Hanseatic Ship on lower half **Edge Lettering:** LATVIJAS REPUBLIKA • LATVIJAS BANKA **Designer:** Gunars Krollis and Janis Strupulis

Date	Mintage	F	VF	XF	Unc	BU
2008 Proof	15,000	Value: 65.00				

KM# 95 LATS
31.4700 g., 0.9250 Silver 0.9359 oz. ASW, 38.6 mm. **Subject:** Basketball **Obv:** Three stars and stylized basket ball design **Rev:** Two basketball players and a jump shot **Edge Lettering:** LATVIJAS BANKA • LATVIJAS REPUBLIKA **Designer:** Franceska Kirke and Ligita Franckevica

Date	Mintage	F	VF	XF	Unc	BU
2008 Proof	5,000	Value: 70.00				

KM# 107 LATS
4.8000 g., Copper-Nickel, 21.75 mm. **Obv:** National arms **Rev:** Chimney sweep standing with brush and ladder **Edge Lettering:** LATVIJAS BANKA • LATVIJAS BANKA

Date	Mintage	F	VF	XF	Unc	BU
2008	1,000,000	—	—	—	4.00	6.00

KM# 101 LATS
4.8000 g., Copper-Nickel, 21.75 mm. **Obv:** National Arms **Rev:** Namejs ring **Edge Lettering:** LATVIJAS BANKA • LATVIJAS BANKA

Date	Mintage	F	VF	XF	Unc	BU
2009	1,000,000	—	—	2.00	4.00	6.00

KM# 100 LATS
20.0000 g., 0.9250 Silver 0.5948 oz. ASW, 34 mm. **Subject:** Children's drawing contest - My Dream Coin **Obv:** State Arms **Rev:** Piglet right **Edge Lettering:** LATVIJAS BANKA • LATVIJAS BANKA

Date	Mintage	F	VF	XF	Unc	BU
2009 Proof	5,000	Value: 60.00				

KM# 102 LATS
31.4700 g., 0.9250 Silver 0.9359 oz. ASW, 38.6 mm. **Subject:** Time of the Land-Surveyors, Novel's 130th Anniversary **Obv:** Brali Kaudzites standing **Rev:** Six figures form novel, forming spokes of wheel **Edge Lettering:** LATVIJAS REPUBLICA • LATVIJAS BANKA **Designer:** Laimonis Senbergs and Ligita Franckevica

Date	Mintage	F	VF	XF	Unc	BU
2009 Proof	7,000	Value: 60.00				

KM# 103 LATS
31.4700 g., 0.9250 Silver 0.9359 oz. ASW, 38.6 mm. **Subject:** University of Latvia **Obv:** Oak tree within wreath, partially minted photo image **Rev:** Owl standing on open book, University building in background **Edge Lettering:** VIVAT • CRESCAT • FLOREAT **Designer:** Guntars Sietins and Janis Strupulis

Date	Mintage	F	VF	XF	Unc	BU
2009 Proof	7,000	Value: 65.00				

KM# 104 LATS
26.0000 g., 0.9250 Silver 0.7732 oz. ASW, 32x32 mm. **Subject:** Coin of Water **Obv:** Water droplets **Rev:** Snowflake crystal **Edge:** Plain **Shape:** Square **Designer:** Ilmars Blumbergs and Janis Strupulis

Date	Mintage	F	VF	XF	Unc	BU
2009 Proof	7,000	Value: 70.00				

KM# 105 LATS
22.0000 g., 0.9250 Silver 0.6542 oz. ASW, 35 mm. **Subject:** Christmas Tree, 500th Anniversary **Obv:** Three children in folktale costumes **Rev:** Man walking with cut tree in moonlight, squirrel jumping from tree **Edge Lettering:** LATVIJAS BANKA • LATVIJAS REPUBLIKA **Designer:** Edgars Folks and Janis Strupulis

Date	Mintage	F	VF	XF	Unc	BU
2009 Proof	20,000	Value: 60.00				

KM# 106 LATS
4.8000 g., Copper-Nickel, 21.75 mm. **Obv:** National Arms **Rev:** Christmas tree, heart as ornament **Edge Lettering:** LATVIJAS BANKA • LATVIJAS BANKA

Date	Mintage	F	VF	XF	Unc	BU
2009	1,000,000	—	—	—	4.00	6.00

KM# 108 LATS
4.8000 g., Copper-Nickel, 21.75 mm. **Obv:** National arms **Rev:** Toad **Edge Lettering:** LATVIJAS BANKA • LATVIJAS BANKA

Date	Mintage	F	VF	XF	Unc	BU
2010	1,000,000	—	—	—	4.00	5.00

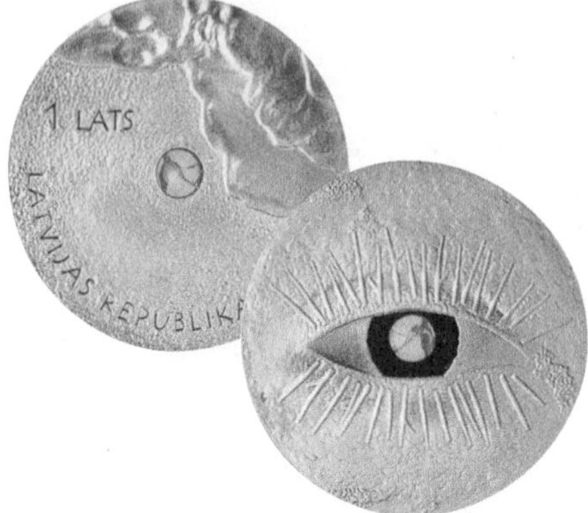

KM# 109 LATS
20.7000 g., 0.9250 Silver with amber insert 0.6156 oz. ASW, 35 mm. **Subject:** Amber Coin **Obv:** Amber stone on seashore **Rev:** Eye with amber as pupil **Edge:** Plain **Designer:** Aigars Bikse

Date	Mintage	F	VF	XF	Unc	BU
2010 Proof	7,000	Value: 65.00				

KM# 110 LATS
12.4000 g., Copper-Nickel, 30 mm. **Subject:** The Latvian ABC Book **Obv:** Cock **Rev:** Teacher with students **Edge Lettering:** LATVIJAS BANKA • LATVIJAS REPUBLIKA **Designer:** Arvids Priedite and Ligita Franckevica

Date	Mintage	F	VF	XF	Unc	BU
2010	10,000	—	—	—	—	10.00

KM# 111 LATS
31.4700 g., 0.9250 Silver 0.9359 oz. ASW, 38.61 mm. **Subject:** Latvian ABC Book **Obv:** Cock **Rev:** Teacher and students **Edge Lettering:** LATVIJAS BANKA • LATVIJAS REPUBLIKA **Designer:** Arvids Priedite and Ligita Franckevica

Date	Mintage	F	VF	XF	Unc	BU
2010 Proof	5,000	Value: 75.00				

KM# 112 LATS
31.4700 g., 0.9250 Silver 0.9359 oz. ASW, 38.61 mm. **Subject:** Duke Jacob, 400th Anniversary of birth **Obv:** Bust right, value at bottom **Rev:** Arms **Edge Lettering:** LATVIJAS REPUBLIKA • LATVIJAS BANKA **Designer:** Ilze Libiete and Ligita Franckevica

Date	Mintage	F	VF	XF	Unc	BU
2010 Proof	5,000	Value: 75.00				

KM# 113 LATS
31.4700 g., 0.9250 Silver 0.9359 oz. ASW, 38.61 mm. **Subject:** Declaration of Independence, 20th Anniversary **Obv:** Three small buds, red in color **Rev:** Elderly female with yoke of oppression **Edge Lettering:** LATVIJAS BANKA (twice) **Designer:** Ilmars Blumbergs and Ligita Franckevica

Date	Mintage	F	VF	XF	Unc	BU
2010 Proof	7,000	Value: 65.00				

KM# 114 LATS
17.1500 g., Bi-Metallic Niobium center within 10g of .900 Silver ring, 34 mm. **Subject:** Coin of Time III **Obv:** Heraldic Rose **Rev:** Forests, fields, rocks and water in center, eight lunar phases around **Edge:** Plain **Designer:** Laimonis Senbergs and Janis Strupulis

Date	Mintage	F	VF	XF	Unc	BU
2010	7,000	—	—	—	65.00	75.00

KM# 117 LATS
4.8000 g., Copper-Nickel, 21.75 mm. **Obv:** National arms **Rev:** Horseshoe with open end upwards **Edge Lettering:** LATVIJAS BANKA • LATVIJAS BANKA **Designer:** Franceska Kirke and Laura Medne

Date	Mintage	F	VF	XF	Unc	BU
2010	500,000	—	—	—	4.00	6.00

KM# 118 LATS
4.8000 g., Copper-Nickel, 21.75 mm. **Obv:** Naitonal arms **Rev:** Horseshoe with open end downwards **Edge Lettering:** LATVIJAS BANKA • LATVIJAS BANKA **Designer:** Franceska Kirke and Laura Medne

Date	Mintage	F	VF	XF	Unc	BU
2010	500,000	—	—	—	4.00	6.00

KM# 119 LATS
4.8000 g., Copper-Nickel, 21.75 mm. **Obv:** National arms **Rev:** Beer stein **Edge Lettering:** LATVIJAS BANKA • LATVIJAS BANKA **Designer:** Juris Dimiters and Andris Varpa

Date	Mintage	F	VF	XF	Unc	BU
2011	1,000,000	—	—	—	4.00	6.00

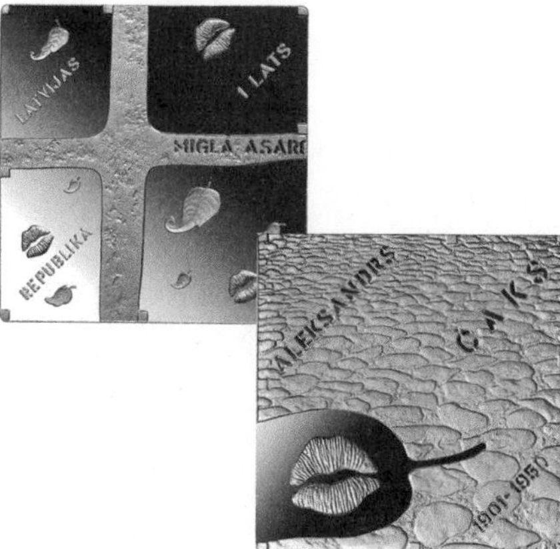

KM# 120 LATS
26.0000 g., 0.9250 Silver 0.7732 oz. ASW, 32x32 mm. **Subject:** Aleksandris Caks **Obv:** Window, glass with imprints of lips and leaves **Rev:** Cobble-stone paving, leave with lips imprint **Designer:** Ilmars Blumbergs and Ligita Franckevica

Date	Mintage	F	VF	XF	Unc	BU
2011 Proof	7,000	Value: 70.00				

KM# 121 LATS
31.4700 g., 0.9250 Silver 0.9359 oz. ASW, 38.61 mm. **Subject:** Rundale Palace **Obv:** Arms of Earl Ernst Johann von Biron **Rev:** Ariel view of the palace and gardens

Date	Mintage	F	VF	XF	Unc	BU
2011 Proof	5,000	Value: 65.00				

KM# 122 LATS
31.4700 g., 0.9250 Silver 0.9359 oz. ASW, 38.61 mm. **Subject:** Hansa Cities - Riga **Obv:** Riga arms, gothic ornaments flanking **Rev:** Riga city view at top, Hanseatic ship inverted below **Designer:** Gunars Krollis and Janis Strupulis

Date	Mintage	F	VF	XF	Unc	BU
2011 Proof	15,000	Value: 65.00				

KM# 123 LATS
22.0000 g., 0.9250 Silver 0.6542 oz. ASW, 35 mm. **Subject:** Riga Cathedral **Obv:** Angel at left **Rev:** Cross at left, cathedral exterior at right **Designer:** Kristaps Gelzis and Ligita Franckevica

Date	Mintage	F	VF	XF	Unc	BU
2011 Proof	5,000	Value: 60.00				

KM# 124 LATS
12.5000 g., 0.9250 Silver 0.3717 oz. ASW, 28 mm. **Subject:** Riga coinage, 800th Anniversary **Obv:** Pfennig of Bishop Albert (1198-1229) - Bishop in mitre **Rev:** Pfennig of Bishop Albert on frosted surface **Designer:** Inta Sarkane and Janis Strupulis

Date	Mintage	F	VF	XF	Unc	BU
2011 Proof	5,000	Value: 65.00				

KM# 125 LATS
22.0000 g., 0.9250 Silver 0.6542 oz. ASW, 35 mm. **Subject:** Railways in Latvia, 50th Anniversary **Obv:** Steam locomotive's drive wheel **Rev:** Steam locomotive profile **Designer:** Aigars Ozolins and Ligita Franckevica

Date	Mintage	F	VF	XF	Unc	BU
2011 Proof	5,000	Value: 65.00				

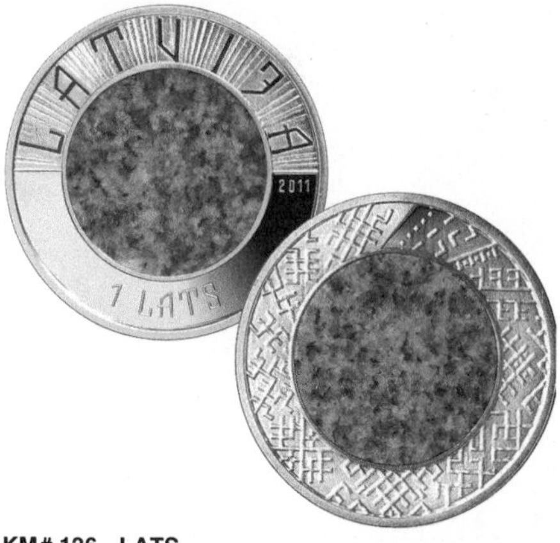

KM# 126 LATS
Bi-Metallic Granite center in .925 Silver ring, 35 mm. **Subject:** Granite Stone **Obv:** Country name at top, denomination at bottom **Rev:** National folk ornamentation **Designer:** Laqimonis Senbergs and Janis Strupulis

Date	Mintage	F	VF	XF	Unc	BU
2011 Proof	7,000	Value: 80.00				

KM# 127 LATS
4.8000 g., Copper-Nickel, 21.75 mm. **Obv:** National arms with supporters **Rev:** Gingerbread heart **Edge Lettering:** LATVIJAS BANKA • LATVIJAS BANKA **Designer:** Ruta Briede and Laura Medne

Date	Mintage	F	VF	XF	Unc	BU
2011	1,000,000	—	—	—	4.00	5.00

KM# 128 LATS
22.0000 g., 0.9250 Silver 0.6542 oz. ASW, 35 mm. **Subject:** Latvia's participation in the 2012 London Olympics **Obv:** Three Latvian runners right **Rev:** Three ancient Greek runners right **Designer:** Aigars Bikse

Date	Mintage	F	VF	XF	Unc	BU
2012 Proof	5,000	Value: 60.00				

KM# 129 LATS
22.0000 g., 0.9250 Silver 0.6542 oz. ASW, 35 mm. **Subject:** Riga Zoo, 100th Anniversary **Obv:** Zoo entrance gate and exotic animals **Rev:** Seven animal figures **Edge Lettering:** LATVIJAS BANKA • LATVIJAS REPUBLIKA • 2012 **Designer:** Ivars Mailitis and Ligita Franckevica

Date	Mintage	F	VF	XF	Unc	BU
2012 Proof	5,000	Value: 65.00				

KM# 131 LATS
26.0000 g., 0.9250 Silver 0.7732 oz. ASW, 32x32 mm. **Subject:** Riga Technical University, 150th Anniversary **Obv:** Curved guage and mm scale **Rev:** Town view, gilt dividers and drafting triangle **Designer:** Kristaps Gelzis **Note:** Two-part.

Date	Mintage	F	VF	XF	Unc	BU
2012 Proof	3,000	Value: 70.00				

KM# 132 LATS
22.0000 g., 0.9250 Silver 0.6542 oz. ASW, 35 mm. **Subject:** K. Zale **Obv:** Head left **Rev:** Sculpture: Dying Horseman I **Edge Lettering:** LATVIJAS BANKA • LATVIJAS REPUBLIKA • 2012

Date	Mintage	F	VF	XF	Unc	BU
2012 Proof	7,000	Value: 60.00				

KM# 133 LATS
22.0000 g., 0.9250 Silver 0.6542 oz. ASW, 35 mm. **Subject:** Latvian National Traditions

Date	Mintage	F	VF	XF	Unc	BU
2012 Proof	5,000	Value: 65.00				

KM# 134 LATS
22.0000 g., 0.9250 Silver 0.6542 oz. ASW, 35 mm. **Subject:** K. Blaumanis

Date	Mintage	F	VF	XF	Unc	BU
2012 Proof	3,000	Value: 70.00				

KM# 135 LATS
4.8000 g., Copper-Nickel, 21.75 mm. **Subject:** Hedgehog **Obv:** National arms **Rev:** Hedgehog **Edge Lettering:** LATVIJAS BANKA • LATVIJAS BANKA **Designer:** Andris Vitolins and Laura Medne

Date	Mintage	F	VF	XF	Unc	BU
2012	1,000,000	—	—	—	—	3.00

KM# 136 LATS
4.8000 g., Copper-Nickel, 21.75 mm. **Subject:** Christmas Bells **Obv:** National arms **Rev:** Christmas bells **Edge Lettering:** LATVIJAS BANKA • LATVIJAS BANKA **Designer:** Holgers Elers and Laura Medne

Date	Mintage	F	VF	XF	Unc	BU
2012	1,000,000	—	—	—	—	3.00

KM# 38 2 LATI
9.5000 g., Bi-Metallic Nickel-Brass center in Copper-Nickel ring, 26.3 mm. **Obv:** Arms with supporters within circle **Rev:** Cow above value within circle **Edge Lettering:** LATVIJAS BANKA

Date	Mintage	F	VF	XF	Unc	BU
2003 In sets only	30,000	—	—	—	—	12.00
2009	2,000,000	—	—	7.00	8.00	9.00

KM# 59 5 LATI
1.2442 g., 0.9999 Gold 0.0400 oz. AGW, 13.92 mm. **Obv:** Bust right **Rev:** Arms with supporters above value **Edge:** Reeded **Note:** Remake of the popular KM-9 design

Date	Mintage	F	VF	XF	Unc	BU
2003 Proof	Est. 20,000	Value: 125				

KM# 130 5 LATI
25.0000 g., 0.9250 Silver 0.7435 oz. ASW, 37 mm. **Subject:** Bank of Latvia and national currency, 90th Anniversary **Obv:** Female head in national costume right **Rev:** National arms **Edge Lettering:** DIEVS SVETI LATVIJS **Designer:** Rihards Zarins

Date	Mintage	F	VF	XF	Unc	BU
2012 Proof	Est. 10,000	Value: 65.00				

KM# 96 20 LATI
10.0000 g., 0.9990 Gold 0.3212 oz. AGW, 22 mm. **Obv:** Woman's head covered with scarf **Rev:** Vessel with a milk bottle, apple, jug of milk, bread & knife on table **Designer:** Tedors Zalkalns and Ligita Franckevica

Date	Mintage	F	VF	XF	Unc	BU
2008	5,000	—	—	—	—	675

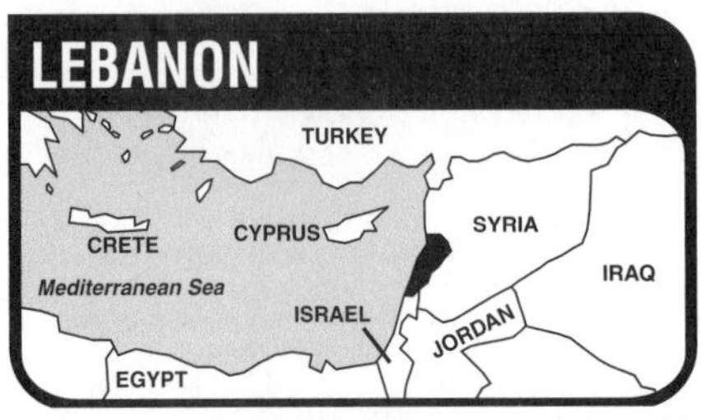

The Lebanese Republic, situated on the eastern shore of the Mediterranean Sea between Syria and Israel, has an area of 4,015 sq. mi. (10,400 sq. km.) and a population of 3.5 million. Capital: Beirut. The economy is based on agriculture, trade and tourism. Fruit, other foodstuffs and textiles are exported.

MONETARY SYSTEM
100 Piastres = 1 Livre (Pound)

REPUBLIC
STANDARD COINAGE

KM# 40 25 LIVRES
2.8200 g., Nickel Plated Steel, 20.5 mm. **Obv:** Large value on cedar tree **Rev:** Value within square design **Rev. Legend:** BANQUE DU LIBAN **Edge:** Plain

Date	Mintage	F	VF	XF	Unc	BU
2002(c)	—	—	—	0.30	0.80	1.20
2009(v)	—	—	—	0.30	0.80	1.20

KM# 37a 50 LIVRES
Nickel, 18.35 mm. **Obv:** Cedar tree with Arabic value superimposed. Arabic legend above, date below. **Rev:** Value in center.

Date	Mintage	F	VF	XF	Unc	BU
2006	—	—	—	0.50	1.20	1.80

KM# 38a 100 LIVRES
4.0500 g., Stainless Steel, 22.48 mm. **Obv:** Arabic legend above large value on cedar tree **Rev:** Stylized flag above large value "100" **Rev. Legend:** BANQUE DU LIBAN **Edge:** Plain

Date	Mintage	F	VF	XF	Unc	BU
2003(c)	—	—	—	0.60	1.50	2.00

KM# 38b 100 LIVRES
4.0700 g., Copper Plated Steel, 22.49 mm. **Obv:** Arabic legend above large value on cedar tree **Rev:** Stylized flag above large value "100" **Rev. Legend:** BANQUE DU LIBAN **Edge:** Plain

Date	Mintage	F	VF	XF	Unc	BU
2006	—	—	—	0.60	1.50	2.00
2009	—	—	—	0.60	1.50	2.00

KM# 38 100 LIVRES
4.0000 g., Brass, 22.5 mm. **Obv:** Arabic legend above large value on cedar tree **Rev:** Stylized flag above large value "100" **Rev. Legend:** BANQUE DU LIBAN **Edge:** Plain

Date	Mintage	F	VF	XF	Unc	BU
2006(c)	—	—	—	0.65	1.50	2.00

KM# 36 250 LIVRES
5.0000 g., Aluminum-Bronze, 23.5 mm. **Obv:** Arabic legend above large value on cedar tree **Rev:** Large 250 within elliptical border design **Edge:** Reeded

Date	Mintage	F	VF	XF	Unc	BU
2003(c)	—	—	—	0.75	1.85	2.50
2006(a)	—	—	—	0.75	1.85	2.50
2009(v)	—	—	—	0.75	1.85	2.50
2012	—	—	—	0.75	1.85	2.50

KM# 39 500 LIVRES
6.0600 g., Nickel Plated Steel, 24.5 mm. **Obv:** Arabic legend above large value on cedar tree **Rev:** Large value "500", thick segmented circular border **Rev. Legend:** BANQUE DU LIBAN **Edge:** Plain

Date	Mintage	F	VF	XF	Unc	BU
2003(c)	—	—	—	0.90	2.25	3.00
2006(a)	—	—	—	0.90	2.25	3.00
2009(v)	—	—	—	0.90	2.25	3.00

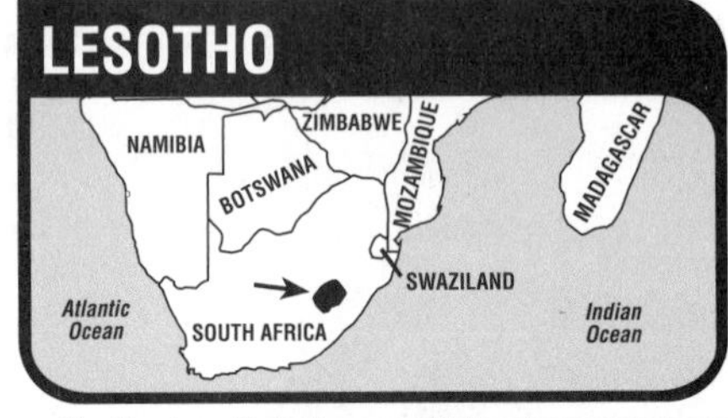

The Kingdom of Lesotho, a constitutional monarchy located within the east-central part of the Republic of South Africa, has an area of 11,720 sq. mi. (30,350 sq. km.) and a population of 1.5 million. Capital: Maseru. The economy is based on subsistence agriculture and livestock raising. Wool, mohair, and cattle are exported.

Lesotho (formerly Basutoland) was sparsely populated until the end of the 16th century. Between the 16th and 19th centuries an influx of refugees from tribal wars led to the development of a distinct Basotho group. During the reign of tribal chief Mashoeshoe I (1823-70), a series of wars with the Orange Free State resulted in the loss of large areas of territory to South Africa. Mashoeshoe appealed to the British for help, and Basutoland was constituted a native state under British protection. In 1871 it was annexed to Cape Colony, but was restored to direct control by the Crown in 1884. From 1884 to 1959 legislative and executive authority was vested in a British High Commissioner. The constitution of 1959 recognized the expressed wish of the people for independence, which was attained on Oct.4, 1966.

Lesotho is a member of the Commonwealth of Nations. The king is Head of State.

RULERS
Moshoeshoe II, 1995-

MONETARY SYSTEM
100 Licente/Lisente = 1 Maloti/Loti

KINGDOM

STANDARD COINAGE

100 Licente / Lisente = 1 Maloti / Loti

KM# 62 5 LICENTE (Lisente)
1.6400 g., Brass Plated Steel, 15 mm. **Ruler:** Letsie III **Obv:** Arms with supporters **Rev:** Two pine trees among grass, hills and value

Date	Mintage	F	VF	XF	Unc	BU
2006	—	—	—	0.35	0.75	1.00

KM# 63 10 LICENTE (Lisente)
1.9600 g., Brass Plated Steel, 16 mm. **Ruler:** Moshoeshoe II **Obv:** Arms with supporters **Rev:** Angora goat

Date	Mintage	F	VF	XF	Unc	BU
2010	—	—	—	—	1.00	1.50

KM# 66 LOTI
3.8800 g., Nickel Plated Steel, 21 mm. **Ruler:** Letsie III **Obv:** Native seated right **Rev:** Value at left of arms with supporters

Date	Mintage	F	VF	XF	Unc	BU
2010	—	—	—	—	1.50	2.00

KM# 59 5 MALOTI
6.3700 g., Nickel Plated Steel, 25 mm. **Ruler:** Moshoeshoe II **Obv:** Arms with supporters **Rev:** Wheat sprigs and value

Date	Mintage	F	VF	XF	Unc	BU
2010	—	—	—	—	4.50	5.00

KM# 73 25 MALOTI
Silver **Ruler:** Moshoeshoe II **Subject:** Central Bank, 25th Anniversary

Date	Mintage	F	VF	XF	Unc	BU
2005 Proof	—	Value: 75.00				

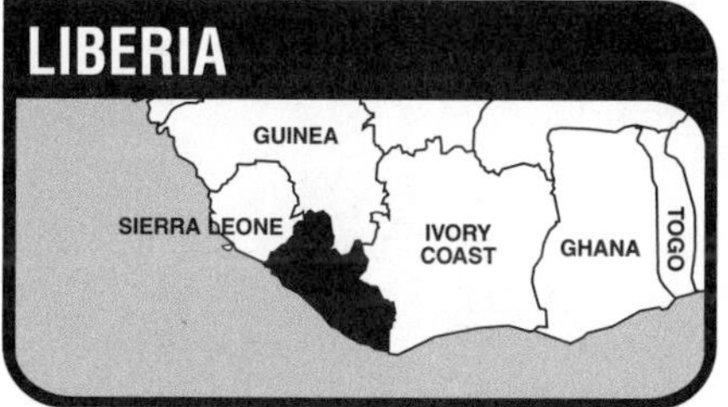

The Republic of Liberia, located on the southern side of the West African bulge between Sierra Leone and Ivory Coast, has an area of 38,250 sq. mi. (111,370 sq. km) and a population of 2.2 million. Capital: Monrovia. The major industries are agriculture, mining and lumbering. Iron ore, diamonds, rubber, coffee and coca are exported.

MINT MARKS
PM - Pobjoy Mint

MONETARY SYSTEM
100 Cents = 1 Dollar

REPUBLIC

STANDARD COINAGE

KM# 618 5 CENTS
5.0200 g., Copper-Nickel, 23.8 mm. **Obv:** National arms **Rev:** Chimpanzee family **Edge:** Plain

Date	Mintage	F	VF	XF	Unc	BU
2003	—	—	—	—	1.50	2.00

KM# 1003 2 DOLLARS
15.5500 g., 0.9990 Silver 0.4994 oz. ASW, 38.6 mm. **Obv:** National arms **Rev:** Santa in sleigh in color

Date	Mintage	F	VF	XF	Unc	BU
2011 Proof	—	Value: 45.00				

KM# 1004 2 DOLLARS
15.5500 g., 0.9990 Silver 0.4994 oz. ASW, 38.6 mm. **Obv:** National arms **Rev:** Christmas toys in color

Date	Mintage	F	VF	XF	Unc	BU
2011 Proof	—	Value: 45.00				

KM# 1005 2 DOLLARS
15.5500 g., 0.9990 Silver 0.4994 oz. ASW, 38.6 mm. **Obv:** National arms **Rev:** Christmas Angel in color

Date	Mintage	F	VF	XF	Unc	BU
2011 Proof	—	Value: 45.00				

KM# 1006 2 DOLLARS
15.5500 g., 0.9990 Silver 0.4994 oz. ASW, 38.6 mm. **Obv:** National arms **Rev:** Christmas - Drummer in color

Date	Mintage	F	VF	XF	Unc	BU
2011 Proof	—	Value: 45.00				

KM# 1007 2 DOLLARS
15.5500 g., 0.9990 Silver 0.4994 oz. ASW, 38.6 mm. **Obv:** National arms **Rev:** Christmas - bells in color

Date	Mintage	F	VF	XF	Unc	BU
2011 Proof	—	Value: 45.00				

KM# 1008 2 DOLLARS
15.5500 g., 0.9990 Silver 0.4994 oz. ASW, 38.6 mm. **Obv:** National arms **Rev:** Christmas Nutcracker in color

Date	Mintage	F	VF	XF	Unc	BU
2011 Proof	—	Value: 45.00				

KM# 651 5 DOLLARS
14.5600 g., Copper-Nickel, 38 mm. **Obv:** National arms **Rev:** Japanese "Zero" flying over Pearl Harbor **Edge:** Reeded

Date	Mintage	F	VF	XF	Unc	BU
2001	—	—	—	—	10.00	12.00

KM# 568 5 DOLLARS
14.6300 g., Copper-Nickel, 33.1 mm. **Subject:** Battle of Gettysburg **Obv:** National arms **Rev:** Cannon and crossed flags divides busts facing **Edge:** Reeded **Note:** This also exists in an obverse denominated type for $2,000. Also see KM828.

Date	Mintage	F	VF	XF	Unc	BU
2001B	—	—	—	—	12.00	14.00

KM# 494 5 DOLLARS
8.5000 g., 0.9999 Silver 0.2732 oz. ASW, 30 mm. **Subject:** Soccer **Obv:** National arms **Rev:** Soccer player divides circle **Edge:** Reeded

Date	Mintage	F	VF	XF	Unc	BU
2002 Proof	3,000	Value: 30.00				

KM# 829 5 DOLLARS
14.9400 g., Copper-Nickel, 32.9 mm. **Subject:** 12th Anniversary Columbia Space Shuttle **Obv:** National arms **Rev:** Astronaut, space shuttle **Edge:** Reeded

Date	Mintage	F	VF	XF	Unc	BU
2003	—	—	—	—	8.00	10.00

KM# 831 5 DOLLARS
15.5500 g., 0.9990 Niobium 0.4994 oz., 38 mm. **Series:** From ancient to Modern Sports **Obv:** National arms **Rev:** Discus throwers **Edge:** Plain

Date	Mintage	F	VF	XF	Unc	BU
2004	2,004	—	—	—	—	30.00

KM# 832 5 DOLLARS
15.5500 g., 0.9990 Niobium 0.4994 oz., 38 mm. **Series:** From Ancient to Modern Sports **Obv:** National arms **Rev:** Javelin throwers **Edge:** Plain

Date	Mintage	F	VF	XF	Unc	BU
2004	2,004	—	—	—	—	30.00

KM# 833 5 DOLLARS
15.5500 g., 0.9990 Niobium 0.4994 oz., 38 mm. **Series:** From ancient to Modern Sports **Obv:** National arms **Rev:** Broad jumpers **Edge:** Plain

Date	Mintage	F	VF	XF	Unc	BU
2004	2,004	—	—	—	—	30.00

KM# 834 5 DOLLARS
15.5500 g., 0.9990 Niobium 0.4994 oz., 38 mm. **Series:** From Ancient to Modern Sports **Obv:** National arms **Rev:** Runners **Edge:** Plain

Date	Mintage	F	VF	XF	Unc	BU
2004	2,004	—	—	—	—	30.00

KM# 835 5 DOLLARS
15.5500 g., 0.9990 Niobium 0.4994 oz., 38 mm. **Series:** From Ancient to Modern Sports **Obv:** National arms **Rev:** Wrestlers **Edge:** Plain

Date	Mintage	F	VF	XF	Unc	BU
2004	2,004	—	—	—	—	30.00

KM# 664 5 DOLLARS
6.4000 g., Bi-Metallic Brass center in Copper-Nickel ring, 25.7 mm. **Obv:** National arms **Rev:** Pope and cathedral within circle **Edge:** Reeded

Date	Mintage	F	VF	XF	Unc	BU
2005	—	—	—	—	12.00	14.00

KM# 809 5 DOLLARS
25.9500 g., Silver, 39.97 mm. **Subject:** Papal visits to Africa **Obv:** National arms **Rev:** !/2 length multicolor figure of Pope John Paul II at center left, outlined map of Africa at center right in background **Edge:** Reeded

Date	Mintage	F	VF	XF	Unc	BU
2005 Proof	—	Value: 35.00				

KM# 810 5 DOLLARS
25.7200 g., Silver, 39.92 mm. **Obv:** National arms **Rev:** St. Peter's square in background, multicolor bust of Pope Benedict XVI in oval frame at upper right **Edge:** Reeded

Date	Mintage	F	VF	XF	Unc	BU
2005 Proof	—	Value: 40.00				

KM# 865 5 DOLLARS
7.7800 g., Niobium partially gilt, 35 mm. **Subject:** 10th Anniversary of the Euro - San Marino **Rev:** Castle

Date	Mintage	F	VF	XF	Unc	BU
2006 Proof	10,000	Value: 50.00				

KM# 866 5 DOLLARS
7.7800 g., Niobium partially gilt, 35 mm. **Subject:** 10th Anniversary of the Euro - Slovakia **Rev:** Bratislava Castle

Date	Mintage	F	VF	XF	Unc	BU
2006 Proof	10,000	Value: 50.00				

KM# 867 5 DOLLARS
7.7800 g., Niobium partially gilt, 35 mm. **Subject:** 10th Anniversary of the Euro - Latvia **Rev:** Old Buildings

Date	Mintage	F	VF	XF	Unc	BU
2006 Proof	10,000	Value: 50.00				

KM# 868 5 DOLLARS
7.7800 g., Niobium partially gilt, 35 mm. **Subject:** 10th Anniversary of the Euro - Monaco **Rev:** Ariel view of Principality

Date	Mintage	F	VF	XF	Unc	BU
2006 Proof	10,000	Value: 50.00				

KM# 869 5 DOLLARS
7.7800 g., Niobium partially gilt, 35 mm. **Subject:** 10th Anniversary of the Euro - Slovenia **Rev:** Hill-top buildings

Date	Mintage	F	VF	XF	Unc	BU
2006 Proof	10,000	Value: 50.00				

KM# 724 5 DOLLARS
26.3000 g., Silver Plated Bronze, 38.6 mm. **Obv:** National arms **Rev:** Multicolor Pope John Paul II with cross **Edge:** Reeded

Date	Mintage	F	VF	XF	Unc	BU
2007 Proof	—	Value: 30.00				

KM# 733 5 DOLLARS
27.0000 g., Copper-Nickel Silvered and Gilt, 38.61 mm. **Subject:** The Black Madonna of Czestochowa **Obv:** Arms **Obv. Legend:** REPUBLIC OF LIBERIA **Rev:** 1/2 length figure of Madonna facing with child

Date	Mintage	F	VF	XF	Unc	BU
2007 Proof	1,000	Value: 40.00				

KM# 1022 5 DOLLARS
28.2800 g., 0.9990 Silver 0.9083 oz. ASW, 38.6 mm. **Obv:** National arms **Rev:** Christ at center, apostles in 12 segments around

Date	Mintage	F	VF	XF	Unc	BU
2008 Proof	—	Value: 35.00				

KM# 1024 5 DOLLARS
28.2800 g., 0.9990 Silver 0.9083 oz. ASW, 38.6 mm. **Subject:** Tanks of WWII **Obv:** National arms **Rev:** T-34 in color applique

Date	Mintage	F	VF	XF	Unc	BU
2008 Proof	—	Value: 32.00				

KM# 1025 5 DOLLARS
28.2800 g., 0.9990 Silver 0.9083 oz. ASW, 38.6 mm. **Subject:** Tanks of WWII **Obv:** National arms **Rev:** Mark IV Churchill

Date	Mintage	F	VF	XF	Unc	BU
2008 Proof	—	Value: 32.00				

KM# 1026 5 DOLLARS
28.2800 g., 0.9990 Silver 0.9083 oz. ASW, 38.6 mm. **Subject:** Tanks of WWII **Obv:** National arms **Rev:** M4 Sherman

Date	Mintage	F	VF	XF	Unc	BU
2008 Proof	—	Value: 32.00				

KM# 1027 5 DOLLARS
28.2800 g., 0.9990 Silver 0.9083 oz. ASW, 38.6 mm. **Subject:** Tanks of WWII **Obv:** National arms **Rev:** VI Tiger

Date	Mintage	F	VF	XF	Unc	BU
2008 Proof	—	Value: 32.00				

KM# 1028 5 DOLLARS
28.2800 g., 0.9990 Silver 0.9083 oz. ASW, 38.6 mm. **Subject:** Tanks of WWII **Obv:** National arms **Rev:** Type 95

Date	Mintage	F	VF	XF	Unc	BU
2008 Proof	—	Value: 32.00				

KM# 958 5 DOLLARS
31.1050 g., Copper-Nickel Silver plated **Rev:** Martin van Buren multicolor applique

Date	Mintage	F	VF	XF	Unc	BU
2009	—	—	—	—	—	5.00

KM# 951 5 DOLLARS
31.1050 g., Copper-Nickel Silver plated **Rev:** George Washington multicolor applique

Date	Mintage	F	VF	XF	Unc	BU
2009	—	—	—	—	—	5.00

KM# 952 5 DOLLARS
31.1050 g., Copper-Nickel Silver plated **Rev:** John Adams multicolor applique

Date	Mintage	F	VF	XF	Unc	BU
2009	—	—	—	—	—	5.00

KM# 953 5 DOLLARS
31.1050 g., Copper-Nickel Silver plated **Rev:** Thomas Jefferson multicolor applique

Date	Mintage	F	VF	XF	Unc	BU
2009	—	—	—	—	—	5.00

KM# 954 5 DOLLARS
31.1050 g., Copper-Nickel Silver plated **Rev:** James Madison multicolor applique

Date	Mintage	F	VF	XF	Unc	BU
2009	—	—	—	—	—	5.00

KM# 955 5 DOLLARS
31.1050 g., Copper-Nickel Silver plated **Rev:** James Monroe multicolor applique

Date	Mintage	F	VF	XF	Unc	BU
2009	—	—	—	—	—	5.00

KM# 956 5 DOLLARS
31.1050 g., Copper-Nickel Silver plated **Rev:** John Quincey Adams multicolor applique

Date	Mintage	F	VF	XF	Unc	BU
2009	—	—	—	—	—	5.00

KM# 957 5 DOLLARS
31.1050 g., Copper-Nickel Silver plated **Rev:** Andrew Jackson multicolor applique

Date	Mintage	F	VF	XF	Unc	BU
2009	—	—	—	—	—	5.00

KM# 959 5 DOLLARS
31.1050 g., Copper-Nickel Silver plated **Rev:** William Henry Harrison multicolor applique

Date	Mintage	F	VF	XF	Unc	BU
2009	—	—	—	—	—	5.00

KM# 960 5 DOLLARS
31.1050 g., Copper-Nickel Silver plated **Rev:** John Tyler multicolor applique

Date	Mintage	F	VF	XF	Unc	BU
2009	—	—	—	—	—	5.00

KM# 961 5 DOLLARS
31.1050 g., Copper-Nickel Silver plated **Rev:** James K. Polk multicolor applique

Date	Mintage	F	VF	XF	Unc	BU
2009	—	—	—	—	—	5.00

KM# 962 5 DOLLARS
31.1050 g., Copper-Nickel Silver plated **Rev:** Zachary Taylor multicolor applique

Date	Mintage	F	VF	XF	Unc	BU
2009	—	—	—	—	—	5.00

KM# 963 5 DOLLARS
31.1050 g., Copper-Nickel Silver plated **Rev:** Millard Filmore multicolor applique

Date	Mintage	F	VF	XF	Unc	BU
2009	—	—	—	—	—	5.00

KM# 964 5 DOLLARS
31.1050 g., Copper-Nickel Silver plated **Rev:** Franklin Pierce multicolor applique

Date	Mintage	F	VF	XF	Unc	BU
2009	—	—	—	—	—	5.00

KM# 965 5 DOLLARS
31.1050 g., Copper-Nickel Silver plated **Rev:** James Buchanan multicolor applique

Date	Mintage	F	VF	XF	Unc	BU
2009	—	—	—	—	—	5.00

KM# 966 5 DOLLARS
31.1050 g., Copper-Nickel Silver plated **Rev:** Abraham Lincoln multicolor applique

Date	Mintage	F	VF	XF	Unc	BU
2009	—	—	—	—	—	5.00

KM# 967 5 DOLLARS
31.1050 g., Copper-Nickel Silver plated **Rev:** Andrew Johnson multicolor applique

Date	Mintage	F	VF	XF	Unc	BU
2009	—	—	—	—	—	5.00

KM# 968 5 DOLLARS
31.1050 g., Copper-Nickel Silver plated **Rev:** Ulysses S. Grant multicolor applique

Date	Mintage	F	VF	XF	Unc	BU
2009	—	—	—	—	—	5.00

KM# 969 5 DOLLARS
31.1050 g., Copper-Nickel Silver plated **Rev:** Rutherford B. Hayes multicolor applique

Date	Mintage	F	VF	XF	Unc	BU
2009	—	—	—	—	—	5.00

KM# 970 5 DOLLARS
31.1050 g., Copper-Nickel Silver plated **Rev:** James A. Garfield multicolor applique

Date	Mintage	F	VF	XF	Unc	BU
2009	—	—	—	—	—	5.00

KM# 971 5 DOLLARS
31.1050 g., Copper-Nickel Silver plated **Rev:** Chester Arthur multicolor underprint

Date	Mintage	F	VF	XF	Unc	BU
2009	—	—	—	—	—	5.00

KM# 972 5 DOLLARS
31.1050 g., Copper-Nickel Silver plated **Rev:** Grover Cleveland multicolor applique

Date	Mintage	F	VF	XF	Unc	BU
2009	—	—	—	—	—	5.00

KM# 973 5 DOLLARS
31.1050 g., Copper-Nickel Silver plated **Rev:** Benjamin Harrison multicolor applique

Date	Mintage	F	VF	XF	Unc	BU
2009	—	—	—	—	—	5.00

KM# 974 5 DOLLARS
31.1050 g., Copper-Nickel Silver plated **Rev:** William McKinley multicolor applique

Date	Mintage	F	VF	XF	Unc	BU
2009	—	—	—	—	—	5.00

KM# 975 5 DOLLARS
31.1050 g., Copper-Nickel Silver plated **Rev:** Theodore Roosevelt multicolor applique

Date	Mintage	F	VF	XF	Unc	BU
2009	—	—	—	—	—	5.00

KM# 976 5 DOLLARS
31.1050 g., Copper-Nickel Silver plated **Rev:** William Howard Taft multicolor applique

Date	Mintage	F	VF	XF	Unc	BU
2009	—	—	—	—	—	5.00

KM# 977 5 DOLLARS
31.1050 g., Copper-Nickel Silver plated **Rev:** Woodrow Wilson multicolor applique

Date	Mintage	F	VF	XF	Unc	BU
2009	—	—	—	—	—	5.00

KM# 978 5 DOLLARS
31.1050 g., Copper-Nickel Silver plated **Rev:** Warren G. Harding multicolor applique

Date	Mintage	F	VF	XF	Unc	BU
2009	—	—	—	—	—	5.00

KM# 979 5 DOLLARS
31.1050 g., Copper-Nickel Silver plated **Rev:** Calvin Collidge multicolor applique

Date	Mintage	F	VF	XF	Unc	BU
2009	—	—	—	—	—	5.00

KM# 980 5 DOLLARS
31.1050 g., Copper-Nickel Silver plated **Rev:** Herbert Hoover multicolor applique

Date	Mintage	F	VF	XF	Unc	BU
2009	—	—	—	—	—	5.00

KM# 981 5 DOLLARS
31.1050 g., Copper-Nickel Silver plated **Rev:** Franklin D. Roosevelt multicolor applique

Date	Mintage	F	VF	XF	Unc	BU
2009	—	—	—	—	—	5.00

KM# 982 5 DOLLARS
31.1050 g., Copper-Nickel Silver plated **Rev:** Harry S Truman multicolor applique

Date	Mintage	F	VF	XF	Unc	BU
2009	—	—	—	—	—	5.00

KM# 983 5 DOLLARS
31.1050 g., Copper-Nickel Silver plated **Rev:** Swight D. Eisenhower multicolor applique

Date	Mintage	F	VF	XF	Unc	BU
2009	—	—	—	—	—	5.00

KM# 984 5 DOLLARS
31.1050 g., Copper-Nickel Silver plated **Rev:** John F. Kennedy multicolor applique

Date	Mintage	F	VF	XF	Unc	BU
2009	—	—	—	—	—	5.00

KM# 985 5 DOLLARS
31.1050 g., Copper-Nickel Silver plated **Rev:** Lyndon B. Johnson multicolor applique

Date	Mintage	F	VF	XF	Unc	BU
2009	—	—	—	—	—	5.00

KM# 986 5 DOLLARS
31.1050 g., Copper-Nickel Silver plated **Rev:** Richard M. Nixon multicolor applique

Date	Mintage	F	VF	XF	Unc	BU
2009	—	—	—	—	—	5.00

KM# 987 5 DOLLARS
31.1050 g., Copper-Nickel Silver plated **Rev:** Gerald R. Ford multicolor applique

Date	Mintage	F	VF	XF	Unc	BU
2009	—	—	—	—	—	5.00

KM# 988 5 DOLLARS
31.1050 g., Copper-Nickel Silver plated **Rev:** Jimmy Carter multicolor applique

Date	Mintage	F	VF	XF	Unc	BU
2009	—	—	—	—	—	5.00

KM# 989 5 DOLLARS
31.1050 g., Copper-Nickel Silver plated **Rev:** Ronald Reagan multicolor applique

Date	Mintage	F	VF	XF	Unc	BU
2009	—	—	—	—	—	5.00

KM# 990 5 DOLLARS
31.1050 g., Copper-Nickel Silver plated **Rev:** George H. W. Bush multicolor applique

Date	Mintage	F	VF	XF	Unc	BU
2009	—	—	—	—	—	5.00

KM# 991 5 DOLLARS
31.1050 g., Copper-Nickel Silver plated **Rev:** Bill Clinton multicolor applique

Date	Mintage	F	VF	XF	Unc	BU
2009	—	—	—	—	—	5.00

KM# 992 5 DOLLARS
31.1050 g., Copper-Nickel Silver plated **Rev:** George W. Bush multicolor applique

Date	Mintage	F	VF	XF	Unc	BU
2009	—	—	—	—	—	5.00

KM# 993 5 DOLLARS
31.1050 g., Copper-Nickel Silver plated **Rev:** Barack Obama multicolor applique

Date	Mintage	F	VF	XF	Unc	BU
2009	—	—	—	—	—	5.00

KM# 1023 5 DOLLARS
28.2800 g., 0.9990 Silver 0.9083 oz. ASW, 38.6 mm. **Obv:** National arms **Rev:** Saint standing at center, 12 segments of artibutes around

Date	Mintage	F	VF	XF	Unc	BU
2009 Proof	—	Value: 35.00				

KM# 997 5 DOLLARS
28.2800 g., 0.9990 Silver 0.9083 oz. ASW, 38.6 mm. **Obv:** National arms **Rev:** Kremlin - Tsar Canon, gilt shield

Date	Mintage	F	VF	XF	Unc	BU
2011 Proof	—	Value: 90.00				

KM# 998 5 DOLLARS
28.2800 g., 0.9990 Silver 0.9083 oz. ASW, 38.6 mm. **Obv:** National arms **Rev:** Kremlin - Tsar bell, gilt shield

Date	Mintage	F	VF	XF	Unc	BU
2011 Proof	—	Value: 90.00				

KM# 999 5 DOLLARS
28.2800 g., 0.9990 Silver 0.9083 oz. ASW, 38.6 mm. **Obv:** National arms **Rev:** Kremlin - Golden Cap, gilt shield

Date	Mintage	F	VF	XF	Unc	BU
2011 Proof	—	Value: 90.00				

KM# 1000 5 DOLLARS
28.2800 g., 0.9990 Silver 0.9083 oz. ASW, 38.6 mm. **Obv:** National arms **Rev:** Kremlin - Palace, gilt shield

Date	Mintage	F	VF	XF	Unc	BU
2011 Proof	—	Value: 90.00				

KM# 1001 5 DOLLARS
28.2800 g., 0.9990 Silver 0.9083 oz. ASW, 38.6 mm. **Obv:** National arms **Rev:** Kremlin - Uspenski Cathedral, gilt shield

Date	Mintage	F	VF	XF	Unc	BU
2011 Proof	—	Value: 90.00				

KM# 1002 5 DOLLARS
28.2800 g., 0.9990 Silver 0.9083 oz. ASW, 38.6 mm. **Obv:** National arms **Rev:** Kremlin - Spasski tower, gilt shield

Date	Mintage	F	VF	XF	Unc	BU
2011 Proof	—	Value: 90.00				

KM# 1010 5 DOLLARS
20.0000 g., 0.9990 Silver 0.6423 oz. ASW, 38.6 mm. **Subject:** Trains **Obv:** National arms **Rev:** Adler in color

Date	Mintage	F	VF	XF	Unc	BU
2011 Proof	—	Value: 70.00				

KM# 1011 5 DOLLARS
20.0000 g., 0.9990 Silver 0.6423 oz. ASW, 38.6 mm. **Subject:** Trains **Obv:** National arms **Rev:** KKSTB 310.23

Date	Mintage	F	VF	XF	Unc	BU
2011 Proof	—	Value: 70.00				

KM# 1012 5 DOLLARS
20.0000 g., 0.9990 Silver 0.6423 oz. ASW, 38.6 mm. **Subject:** Trains **Obv:** National arms **Rev:** Mallard locomotive in color

Date	Mintage	F	VF	XF	Unc	BU
2011 Proof	—	Value: 70.00				

KM# 1013 5 DOLLARS
20.0000 g., 0.9990 Silver 0.6423 oz. ASW, 38.6 mm. **Subject:** Trains **Obv:** National arms **Rev:** Flying Scottsman locomotive in color

Date	Mintage	F	VF	XF	Unc	BU
2011 Proof	—	Value: 70.00				

KM# 1014 5 DOLLARS
20.0000 g., 0.9990 Silver 0.6423 oz. ASW, 38.6 mm. **Subject:** Trains **Obv:** National arms **Rev:** Trans-Siberian Express in color

Date	Mintage	F	VF	XF	Unc	BU
2011 Proof	—	Value: 70.00				

KM# 1015 5 DOLLARS
20.0000 g., 0.9990 Silver 0.6423 oz. ASW, 38.6 mm. **Subject:** Trains **Obv:** National arms **Rev:** Blue Train in color

Date	Mintage	F	VF	XF	Unc	BU
2011 Proof	—	Value: 70.00				

KM# 513 10 DOLLARS
28.5000 g., Copper-Nickel, 38.6 mm. **Series:** Moments of Freedom **Subject:** Hungarian Revolution of 1848 **Obv:** National arms **Rev:** Multicolor heroic scene **Edge:** Reeded

Date	Mintage	F	VF	XF	Unc	BU
2001 Proof	9,999	Value: 12.00				

KM# 491 10 DOLLARS
25.2500 g., 0.9250 Silver 0.7509 oz. ASW, 36.8 mm. **Subject:** Illusion **Obv:** National arms **Rev:** Styilized head with glasses facing **Edge:** Plain **Shape:** 10-sided

Date	Mintage	F	VF	XF	Unc	BU
2001 Proof	5,000	Value: 37.50				

KM# 777 10 DOLLARS
14.5500 g., Copper-Nickel, 32 mm. **Subject:** 43rd President of USA **Obv:** National arms **Obv. Legend:** REPUBLIC OF LIBERIA **Rev:** George W. Bush, flag in background

Date	Mintage	F	VF	XF	Unc	BU
2001 Proof	—	Value: 12.00				

KM# 822 10 DOLLARS
1.2400 g., Gold, 13.68 mm. **Obv:** National arms **Rev:** Bust of Marlene Dietrich facing **Edge:** Reeded

Date	Mintage	F	VF	XF	Unc	BU
2001 Proof	—	Value: 75.00				

KM# 493 10 DOLLARS
770.0000 g., Copper, 100 mm. **Subject:** Wreck of the Princess Louisa **Obv:** National arms **Rev:** Sailing ship **Edge:** Reeded **Note:** Illustration reduced. With an encased glass shard recovered from the wreck site of the Princess Louisa.

Date	Mintage	F	VF	XF	Unc	BU
2001	2,000	—	—	—	225	—

KM# 510 10 DOLLARS
33.2400 g., Copper Gilt, 40.1 mm. **Obv:** National arms **Rev:** Multicolor holographic bald eagle **Edge:** Reeded

Date	Mintage	F	VF	XF	Unc	BU
2001	20,000	—	—	—	—	35.00

KM# 537 10 DOLLARS
28.5000 g., Copper-Nickel, 38.6 mm. **Subject:** Moments of Freedom **Obv:** National arms **Rev:** Multicolor Buddha, spelled "Budha" on the coin **Edge:** Reeded

Date	Mintage	F	VF	XF	Unc	BU
2001 Proof	9,999	Value: 12.00				

KM# 538 10 DOLLARS
28.5000 g., Copper-Nickel, 38.6 mm. **Subject:** Moments of Freedom **Obv:** National arms **Rev:** Multicolor Battle of Marathon scene **Edge:** Reeded

Date	Mintage	F	VF	XF	Unc	BU
2001 Proof	9,999	Value: 12.00				

KM# 539 10 DOLLARS
28.5000 g., Copper-Nickel, 38.6 mm. **Series:** Moments of Freedom **Obv:** National arms **Rev:** Multicolor founding of Liberia design **Edge:** Reeded

Date	Mintage	F	VF	XF	Unc	BU
2001 Proof	9,999	Value: 12.00				

KM# 540 10 DOLLARS
28.5000 g., Copper-Nickel, 38.6 mm. **Series:** Moments of Freedom **Obv:** National arms **Rev:** Multicolor portrait of Constantine I **Edge:** Reeded

Date	Mintage	F	VF	XF	Unc	BU
2001 Proof	9,999	Value: 12.00				

KM# 541 10 DOLLARS
28.5000 g., Copper-Nickel, 38.6 mm. **Series:** Moments of Freedom **Obv:** National arms **Rev:** Multicolor William Tell statue **Edge:** Reeded

Date	Mintage	F	VF	XF	Unc	BU
2001 Proof	9,999	Value: 12.00				

KM# 542 10 DOLLARS
28.5000 g., Copper-Nickel, 38.6 mm. **Series:** Moments of Freedom **Obv:** National arms **Rev:** Multicolor bust facing **Edge:** Reeded

Date	Mintage	F	VF	XF	Unc	BU
2001 Proof	9,999	Value: 12.00				

KM# 543 10 DOLLARS
28.5000 g., Copper-Nickel, 38.6 mm. **Series:** Moments of Freedom **Obv:** National arms **Rev:** Multicolor head with headdress and battle scene **Edge:** Reeded

Date	Mintage	F	VF	XF	Unc	BU
2001 Proof	9,999	Value: 12.00				

KM# 544 10 DOLLARS
28.5000 g., Copper-Nickel, 38.6 mm. **Series:** Moments of Freedom **Obv:** National arms **Rev:** Multicolor Brandenburg Gate scene **Edge:** Reeded

Date	Mintage	F	VF	XF	Unc	BU
2001 Proof	9,999	Value: 12.00				

KM# 545 10 DOLLARS
28.5000 g., Copper-Nickel, 38.6 mm. **Series:** Moments of Freedom **Obv:** National arms **Rev:** Multicolor half length figure facing **Edge:** Reeded

Date	Mintage	F	VF	XF	Unc	BU
2001 Proof	9,999	Value: 12.00				

KM# 546 10 DOLLARS
28.5000 g., Copper-Nickel, 38.6 mm. **Series:** Moments of Freedom **Obv:** National arms **Rev:** Multicolor Sitting Bull portrait **Edge:** Reeded

Date	Mintage	F	VF	XF	Unc	BU
2001 Proof	9,999	Value: 12.00				

KM# 547 10 DOLLARS
28.5000 g., Copper-Nickel, 38.6 mm. **Series:** Moments of Freedom **Obv:** National arms **Rev:** Multicolor Declaration of Independence scene **Edge:** Reeded

Date	Mintage	F	VF	XF	Unc	BU
2001 Proof	9,999	Value: 12.00				

KM# 548 10 DOLLARS
28.5000 g., Copper-Nickel, 38.6 mm. **Series:** Moments of Freedom **Obv:** National arms **Rev:** Multicolor allegorical woman **Edge:** Reeded

Date	Mintage	F	VF	XF	Unc	BU
2001 Proof	9,999	Value: 12.00				

KM# 549 10 DOLLARS
28.5000 g., Copper-Nickel, 38.6 mm. **Series:** Moments of Freedom **Obv:** National arms **Rev:** Multicolor bust of Gandhi looking down **Edge:** Reeded

Date	Mintage	F	VF	XF	Unc	BU
2001 Proof	9,999	Value: 12.00				

KM# 550 10 DOLLARS
28.5000 g., Copper-Nickel, 38.6 mm. **Series:** Moments of Freedom **Obv:** National arms **Rev:** Multicolor picture of a soldier at the moment he is shot in battle **Edge:** Reeded

Date	Mintage	F	VF	XF	Unc	BU
2001 Proof	9,999	Value: 12.00				

KM# 551 10 DOLLARS
28.5000 g., Copper-Nickel, 38.6 mm. **Series:** Moments of Freedom **Obv:** National arms **Rev:** Multicolor inmates behind wire fence scene **Edge:** Reeded

Date	Mintage	F	VF	XF	Unc	BU
2001 Proof	9,999	Value: 12.00				

KM# 552 10 DOLLARS
28.5000 g., Copper-Nickel, 38.6 mm. **Series:** Moments of Freedom **Obv:** National arms **Rev:** Multicolor Iwo Jima flag raising scene **Edge:** Reeded

Date	Mintage	F	VF	XF	Unc	BU
2001 Proof	9,999	Value: 12.00				

KM# 553 10 DOLLARS
28.5000 g., Copper-Nickel, 38.6 mm. **Series:** Moments of Freedom **Obv:** National arms **Rev:** Multicolor UN logo and dove **Edge:** Reeded

Date	Mintage	F	VF	XF	Unc	BU
2001 Proof	9,999	Value: 12.00				

KM# 554 10 DOLLARS
28.5000 g., Copper-Nickel, 38.6 mm. **Series:** Moments of Freedom **Obv:** National arms **Rev:** Multicolor Solzhenitsyn portrait **Edge:** Reeded

Date	Mintage	F	VF	XF	Unc	BU
2001 Proof	9,999	Value: 12.00				

KM# 555 10 DOLLARS
28.5000 g., Copper-Nickel, 38.6 mm. **Series:** Moments of Freedom **Obv:** National arms **Rev:** Multicolor Spartacus and troops **Edge:** Reeded

Date	Mintage	F	VF	XF	Unc	BU
2001 Proof	9,999	Value: 12.00				

KM# 556 10 DOLLARS
28.5000 g., Copper-Nickel, 38.6 mm. **Series:** Moments of Freedom **Obv:** National arms **Rev:** Multicolor Soviet tank in Prague **Edge:** Reeded

Date	Mintage	F	VF	XF	Unc	BU
2001 Proof	9,999	Value: 12.00				

KM# 557 10 DOLLARS
28.5000 g., Copper-Nickel, 38.6 mm. **Series:** Moments of Freedom **Obv:** National arms **Rev:** Multicolor Bastille scene **Edge:** Reeded

Date	Mintage	F	VF	XF	Unc	BU
2001 Proof	9,999	Value: 12.00				

KM# 558 10 DOLLARS
28.5000 g., Copper-Nickel, 38.6 mm. **Series:** Moments of Freedom **Obv:** National arms **Rev:** Multicolor Nelson Mandela and fist **Edge:** Reeded

Date	Mintage	F	VF	XF	Unc	BU
2001 Proof	9,999	Value: 12.00				

KM# 559 10 DOLLARS
28.5000 g., Copper-Nickel, 38.6 mm. **Series:** Moments of Freedom **Obv:** National arms **Rev:** Multicolor circuit board and world globe **Edge:** Reeded

Date	Mintage	F	VF	XF	Unc	BU
2001 Proof	9,999	Value: 12.00				

KM# 994 10 DOLLARS
0.9990 Gold, 12 mm. **Obv:** National Arms **Rev:** Franklin, Jefferson, Adams and Declaration of Independence

Date	Mintage	F	VF	XF	Unc	BU
2001 Proof	—	Value: 70.00				

KM# 654 10 DOLLARS
15.3300 g., Copper-Nickel, 33.2 mm. **Obv:** National arms **Rev:** "GEORGE W. BUSH..." No value at bottom **Edge:** Reeded

Date	Mintage	F	VF	XF	Unc	BU
2002	—	—	—	—	—	10.00

KM# 705 10 DOLLARS
31.1035 g., 0.9990 Silver 0.9990 oz. ASW, 38.6 mm. **Subject:** 2002 World Football Championship - Japan - South Korea **Obv:** National arms **Rev:** Pagoda superimposed on a soccer ball, legend around **Edge:** Reeded

Date	Mintage	F	VF	XF	Unc	BU
2002 Proof	—	Value: 45.00				

KM# 806 10 DOLLARS
14.3000 g., Copper-Nickel, 33.11 mm. **Obv:** National arms **Rev:** Bust of President Bush facing at left, soldier standing at right facing, flag in background **Rev. Legend:** America's Fight For Freedom **Edge:** Reeded

Date	Mintage	F	VF	XF	Unc	BU
2002	—	—	—	—	10.00	12.00

KM# 1016 10 DOLLARS
Copper-Nickel **Obv:** National arms **Rev:** San Francisco cablecar hologram

Date	Mintage	F	VF	XF	Unc	BU
2002 Proof	—	Value: 35.00				

KM# 602 10 DOLLARS
25.0000 g., 0.9250 Silver 0.7435 oz. ASW, 38.6 mm. **Obv:** National arms **Rev:** Icarus and Daedalus in flight **Edge:** Reeded

Date	Mintage	F	VF	XF	Unc	BU
2003 Proof	—	Value: 35.00				

KM# 603 10 DOLLARS
25.0000 g., 0.9250 Silver 0.7435 oz. ASW, 38.6 mm. **Obv:** National arms **Rev:** First parachute **Edge:** Reeded

Date	Mintage	F	VF	XF	Unc	BU
2003 Proof	—	Value: 35.00				

KM# 604 10 DOLLARS
25.0000 g., 0.9250 Silver 0.7435 oz. ASW, 38.6 mm. **Obv:** National arms **Rev:** Montgolfier ballon **Edge:** Reeded

Date	Mintage	F	VF	XF	Unc	BU
2003 Proof	—	Value: 35.00				

KM# 605 10 DOLLARS
25.0000 g., 0.9250 Silver 0.7435 oz. ASW, 38.6 mm. **Obv:** National arms **Rev:** Otto v. Lillenthal **Edge:** Reeded

Date	Mintage	F	VF	XF	Unc	BU
2003 Proof	—	Value: 35.00				

KM# 606 10 DOLLARS
25.0000 g., 0.9250 Silver 0.7435 oz. ASW, 38.6 mm. **Obv:** National arms **Rev:** Wright Brothers **Edge:** Reeded

Date	Mintage	F	VF	XF	Unc	BU
2003 Proof	—	Value: 35.00				

KM# 607 10 DOLLARS
25.0000 g., 0.9250 Silver 0.7435 oz. ASW, 38.6 mm. **Obv:** National arms **Rev:** Mach 1- Bell X **Edge:** Reeded

Date	Mintage	F	VF	XF	Unc	BU
2003 Proof	—	Value: 35.00				

KM# 608 10 DOLLARS
25.0000 g., 0.9250 Silver 0.7435 oz. ASW, 38.6 mm. **Obv:** National arms **Rev:** The Concorde **Edge:** Reeded

Date	Mintage	F	VF	XF	Unc	BU
2003 Proof	—	Value: 35.00				

KM# 807 10 DOLLARS
26.3000 g., Copper-Nickel, 40.36 mm. **Subject:** America's First Ladies **Obv:** National arms **Rev:** Bust of Jacqueline Kennedy facing, small oval portrait of President John F. Kennedy at right **Edge:** Reeded

Date	Mintage	F	VF	XF	Unc	BU
2003 Proof	—	Value: 15.00				

KM# 824 10 DOLLARS
14.6000 g., Copper-Nickel, 33 mm. **Subject:** Abraham Lincoln **Obv:** National arms **Rev:** Bust facing at left, Lincoln Memorial in background **Edge:** Reeded

Date	Mintage	F	VF	XF	Unc	BU
2003 Proof	20,000	Value: 12.00				

KM# 708 10 DOLLARS
25.1000 g., 0.9250 Silver 0.7464 oz. ASW, 38.6 mm. **Obv:** National arms **Rev:** Clipper ship "Flying Cloud" **Edge:** Reeded

Date	Mintage	F	VF	XF	Unc	BU
2003 Proof	—	Value: 35.00				

KM# 1030 10 DOLLARS
Silver **Subject:** Hapag 1848 Deutschland **Rev:** Sailing ship left

Date	Mintage	F	VF	XF	Unc	BU
2003 Proof	—	Value: 50.00				

KM# 823 10 DOLLARS
1.2300 g., Gold, 13.88 mm. **Subject:** 2006 World Football championship Germany **Obv:** National arms **Rev:** Football at lower left, stadium at center **Rev. Legend:** DEUTSCHLAND 2006 **Edge:** Reeded

Date	Mintage	F	VF	XF	Unc	BU
2004 Proof	—	Value: 75.00				

KM# 611 10 DOLLARS
62.2070 g., 0.9990 Silver 1.9979 oz. ASW, 50 mm. **Obv:** National arms left of window design with Tiffany Glass inlay **Rev:** Window design with Tiffany Glass inlay **Edge:** Plain

Date	Mintage	F	VF	XF	Unc	BU
2004	999	—	—	—	—	200

KM# 740 10 DOLLARS

20.0000 g., 0.9990 Silver partially gilt 0.6423 oz. ASW, 38.00 mm. **Series:** Endangered Wildlife **Obv:** National arms **Obv. Legend:** REPUBLIC OF LIBERIA **Rev:** Gilt Siberian Tiger with diamonds inset in eyes **Rev. Legend:** RUSSIA **Edge:** Plain

Date	Mintage	F	VF	XF	Unc	BU
2004 Proof	5,000	Value: 175				

KM# 741 10 DOLLARS

20.0000 g., 0.9990 Silver partially gilt 0.6423 oz. ASW, 38.00 mm. **Series:** Endangered Wildlife **Obv:** National arms **Obv. Legend:** REPUBLIC OF LIBERIA **Rev:** Two gilt Hyacinth Macaws perched on branch with diamond insets in eyes **Rev. Legend:** BRAZIL **Edge:** Plain

Date	Mintage	F	VF	XF	Unc	BU
2004 Proof	5,000	Value: 175				

KM# 742 10 DOLLARS

20.0000 g., 0.9990 Silver partially gilt 0.6423 oz. ASW, 38.00 mm. **Series:** Endangered Wildlife **Obv:** National arms **Obv. Legend:** REPUBLIC OF LIBERIA **Rev:** Gilt young Giant Panda seated eating bamboo shoots **Rev. Legend:** CHINA **Edge:** Plain

Date	Mintage	F	VF	XF	Unc	BU
2004 Proof	5,000	Value: 175				

KM# 743 10 DOLLARS

20.0000 g., 0.9990 Silver partially gilt 0.6423 oz. ASW, 38.00 mm. **Subject:** Endangered Wildlife **Obv:** National arms **Obv. Legend:** REPUBLIC OF LIBERIA **Rev:** Two gilt Bald Eagles. one perched at left, one alighting at center right **Rev. Legend:** USA **Edge:** Plain

Date	Mintage	F	VF	XF	Unc	BU
2004 Proof	5,000	Value: 175				

KM# 744 10 DOLLARS

20.0000 g., 0.9990 Silver partially gilt 0.6423 oz. ASW, 38 mm. **Series:** Endangered Wildlife **Obv:** National arms **Obv. Legend:** REPUBLIC OF LIBERIA **Rev:** Gilt Puma standing with diamonds inset in eyes **Rev. Legend:** MEXICO **Edge:** Plain

Date	Mintage	F	VF	XF	Unc	BU
2004 Proof	5,000	Value: 175				

KM# 745 10 DOLLARS

20.0000 g., 0.9990 Silver partially gilt 0.6423 oz. ASW, 38 mm. **Series:** Endangered Wildlife **Obv:** National arms **Obv. Legend:** REPUBLIC OF LIBERIA **Rev:** Gilt Red-ruffed Lemur on branch with diamonds inset in eyes **Rev. Legend:** MADAGASCAR **Edge:** Plain

Date	Mintage	F	VF	XF	Unc	BU
2004 Proof	5,000	Value: 175				

KM# 746 10 DOLLARS

20.0000 g., 0.9990 Silver partially gilt 0.6423 oz. ASW, 38 mm. **Series:** Endangered Wildlife **Obv:** National arms **Obv. Legend:** REPUBLIC OF LIBERIA **Rev:** Two gilt Andean Condors, one lifting off at center, one perched at right **Rev. Legend:** CHILE **Edge:** Plain

Date	Mintage	F	VF	XF	Unc	BU
2004 Proof	5,000	Value: 175				

KM# 747 10 DOLLARS

20.0000 g., 0.9990 Silver partially gilt 0.6423 oz. ASW, 38 mm. **Series:** Endangered Wildlife **Obv:** National arms **Obv. Legend:** REPUBLIC OF LIBERIA **Rev:** Two gilt Yellow-eyed Penguins standing facing with diamonds inset in eyes **Rev. Legend:** NEW ZEALAND **Edge:** Plain

Date	Mintage	F	VF	XF	Unc	BU
2004 Proof	5,000	Value: 175				

KM# 748 10 DOLLARS

20.0000 g., 0.9990 Silver partially gilt 0.6423 oz. ASW, 38 mm. **Series:** Endangered Wildlife **Obv:** National arms **Obv. Legend:** REPUBLIC OF LIBERIA **Rev:** Gilt African lion standing facing with diamonds inset in eyes **Rev. Legend:** SOUTH AFRICA **Edge:** Plain

Date	Mintage	F	VF	XF	Unc	BU
2004 Proof	5,000	Value: 175				

KM# 749 10 DOLLARS

20.0000 g., 0.9990 Silver partially gilt 0.6423 oz. ASW, 38 mm. **Series:** Endangered Wildlife **Obv:** National arms **Obv. Legend:** REPUBLIC OF LIBERIA **Rev:** Two gilt perched Kookaburras with diamonds inset in eyes **Rev. Legend:** AUSTRALIA **Edge:** Plain

Date	Mintage	F	VF	XF	Unc	BU
2004 Proof	5,000	Value: 175				

KM# 750 10 DOLLARS

20.0000 g., 0.9990 Silver partially gilt 0.6423 oz. ASW, 38 mm. **Series:** Endangered Wildlife **Obv:** National arms **Obv. Legend:** REPUBLIC OF LIBERIA **Rev:** Gilt Polar Bear standing facing with diamonds inset in eyes **Rev. Legend:** CANADA **Edge:** Plain

Date	Mintage	F	VF	XF	Unc	BU
2004 Proof	5,000	Value: 175				

KM# 751 10 DOLLARS

20.0000 g., 0.9990 Silver partially gilt 0.6423 oz. ASW **Series:** Endangered Wildlife **Obv:** National arms **Obv. Legend:** REPUBLIC OF LIBERIA **Rev:** Gilt perched Blakiston's Fish-owl with diamonds inset in eyes **Rev. Legend:** JAPAN

Date	Mintage	F	VF	XF	Unc	BU
2004 Proof	5,000	Value: 175				

KM# 808 10 DOLLARS
14.5800 g., Copper-Nickel, 32.98 mm. **Obv:** National arms **Rev:** Bust of President Ronald Reagon facing, flag in background **Edge:** Reeded

Date	Mintage	F	VF	XF	Unc	BU
2004	—	—	—	—	8.00	10.00

KM# 830 10 DOLLARS
15.6200 g., Copper-Nickel, 33.3 mm. **Obv:** National arms **Rev:** Flag at left, bust of 43rd President George W. Bush facing at right **Edge:** Reeded

Date	Mintage	F	VF	XF	Unc	BU
2004	—	—	—	—	10.00	12.00

KM# 738 10 DOLLARS
27.1900 g., Copper-Nickel, 43 mm. **Subject:** Death of Pope John-Paul II **Edge:** Reeded

Date	Mintage	F	VF	XF	Unc	BU
2005	—	—	—	—	12.00	14.00

KM# 739.1 10 DOLLARS
25.0000 g., 0.9250 Silver 0.7435 oz. ASW **Subject:** Death of Pope John-Paul II **Rev:** Silhouette of John-Paul gilt, backgound in Ruthenium

Date	Mintage	F	VF	XF	Unc	BU
2005	7,500	—	—	—	—	60.00

KM# 739.2 10 DOLLARS
25.0000 g., 0.9250 Silver 0.7435 oz. ASW **Subject:** Death of Pope John-Paul II **Rev:** Silhouette of John-Paul gilt, blackened background

Date	Mintage	F	VF	XF	Unc	BU
2005	7,500	—	—	—	—	47.50

KM# 752 10 DOLLARS
20.0000 g., 0.9990 Silver partially gilt 0.6423 oz. ASW, 38 mm. **Series:** Endangered Wildlife **Obv:** National arms **Obv. Legend:** REPUBLIC OF LIBERIA **Rev:** Gilt Koala perched on branch with diamonds inset in eyes **Rev. Legend:** AUSTRALIA **Edge:** Plain

Date	Mintage	F	VF	XF	Unc	BU
2005 Proof	5,000	Value: 150				

KM# 753 10 DOLLARS
20.0000 g., 0.9990 Silver partially gilt 0.6423 oz. ASW, 38 mm. **Series:** Endangered Wildlife **Obv:** National arms **Obv. Legend:** REPUBLIC OF LIBERIA **Rev:** Two perched gilt Yellow-eared Conures with diamonds inset in eyes **Rev. Legend:** COLOMBIA **Edge:** Plain

Date	Mintage	F	VF	XF	Unc	BU
2005 Proof	5,000	Value: 150				

KM# 754 10 DOLLARS
20.0000 g., 0.9990 Silver partially gilt 0.6423 oz. ASW, 38 mm. **Series:** Endangered Wildlife **Obv:** National arms **Obv. Legend:** REPUBLIC OF LIBERIA **Rev:** Gilt Iberian Lynx standing facing with diamonds inset in eyes **Rev. Legend:** SPAIN **Edge:** Plain

Date	Mintage	F	VF	XF	Unc	BU
2005 Proof	5,000	Value: 150				

KM# 755 10 DOLLARS
20.0000 g., 0.9990 Silver partially gilt 0.6423 oz. ASW, 38 mm. **Series:** Endangered Wildlife **Obv:** National arms **Obv. Legend:** REPUBLIC OF LIBERIA **Rev:** Two perched gilt Yellow-crested Cockatoos **Rev. Legend:** INDONESIA **Edge:** Plain

Date	Mintage	F	VF	XF	Unc	BU
2005 Proof	5,000	Value: 150				

KM# 756 10 DOLLARS
20.0000 g., 0.9990 Silver partially gilt 0.6423 oz. ASW, 38 mm. **Series:** Endangered Wildlife **Obv:** National arms **Obv. Legend:** REPUBLIC OF LIBERIA **Rev:** Gilt Jaguar resting on branch with diamonds inset in eyes **Rev. Legend:** BELIZE **Edge:** Plain

Date	Mintage	F	VF	XF	Unc	BU
2005 Proof	5,000	Value: 150				

KM# 757 10 DOLLARS
20.0000 g., 0.9990 Silver partially gilt 0.6423 oz. ASW, 38 mm. **Series:** Endangered Wildlife **Obv:** National arms **Obv. Legend:** REPUBLIC OF LIBERIA **Rev:** Two perched gilt Plate-billed Mountain Toucans with diamonds inset in eyes **Rev. Legend:** ECUADOR **Edge:** Plain

Date	Mintage	F	VF	XF	Unc	BU
2005 Proof	5,000	Value: 150				

KM# 758 10 DOLLARS
20.0000 g., 0.9990 Silver partially gilt 0.6423 oz. ASW, 38 mm. **Series:** Endangered Wildlife **Obv:** National arms **Obv. Legend:** REPUBLIC OF LIBERIA **Rev:** Gilt Red Panda resting facing with diamonds inset in eyes **Rev. Legend:** INDIA **Edge:** Plain

Date	Mintage	F	VF	XF	Unc	BU
2005 Proof	5,000	Value: 150				

KM# 759 10 DOLLARS
20.0000 g., 0.9990 Silver partially gilt 0.6423 oz. ASW, 38 mm. **Series:** Endangered Wildlife **Obv:** National arms **Obv. Legend:** REPUBLIC OF LIBERIA **Rev:** Two perched gilt Resplendent Quetzals with diamonds inset in eyes **Rev. Legend:** GUATEMALA **Edge:** Plain

Date	Mintage	F	VF	XF	Unc	BU
2005 Proof	5,000	Value: 150				

KM# 760 10 DOLLARS
20.0000 g., 0.9990 Silver partially gilt 0.6423 oz. ASW, 38 mm. **Series:** Endangered Wildlife **Obv:** National arms **Obv. Legend:** REPUBLIC OF LIBERIA **Rev:** Gilt Snow Leopard standing left looking back with diamonds inset in eyes **Rev. Legend:** NEPAL **Edge:** Plain

Date	Mintage	F	VF	XF	Unc	BU
2005 Proof	5,000	Value: 150				

KM# 761 10 DOLLARS
20.0000 g., 0.9990 Silver partially gilt 0.6423 oz. ASW, 38 mm. **Series:** Endangered Wildlife **Obv:** National arms **Obv. Legend:** REPUBLIC OF LIBERIA **Rev:** Gilt Fossa standing right on branch facing with diamonds inset in eyes **Rev. Legend:** MADAGASCAR **Edge:** Plain

Date	Mintage	F	VF	XF	Unc	BU
2005 Proof	5,000	Value: 150				

KM# 762 10 DOLLARS
20.0000 g., 0.9990 Silver partially gilt 0.6423 oz. ASW, 38 mm. **Series:** Endangered Wildlife **Obv:** National arms **Obv. Legend:** REPUBLIC OF LIBERIA **Rev:** Two gilt Chilean Flamingos standing left with diamonds inset in eyes **Rev. Legend:** ARGENTINA **Edge:** Plain

Date	Mintage	F	VF	XF	Unc	BU
2005 Proof	5,000	Value: 150				

KM# 763 10 DOLLARS
20.0000 g., 0.9990 Silver partially gilt 0.6423 oz. ASW, 38 mm. **Series:** Endangered Wildlife **Obv:** National arms **Obv. Legend:** REPUBLIC OF LIBERIA **Rev:** Two gilt White-winged ducks, one standing, one swimming right with diamonds inset in eyes **Rev. Legend:** THAILAND **Edge:** Plain

Date	Mintage	F	VF	XF	Unc	BU
2005 Proof	5,000	Value: 150				

KM# 860 10 DOLLARS
25.0000 g., 0.9250 Silver 0.7435 oz. ASW, 38.6 mm. **Subject:** Poison frogs **Rev:** Green Frog, multicolor

Date	Mintage	F	VF	XF	Unc	BU
2005 Proof	2,500	Value: 50.00				

KM# 861 10 DOLLARS
25.0000 g., 0.9250 Silver 0.7435 oz. ASW, 38.6 mm. **Subject:** Poison frogs **Rev:** Red frog, multicolor

Date	Mintage	F	VF	XF	Unc	BU
2005 Proof	2,500	Value: 50.00				

KM# 862 10 DOLLARS
25.0000 g., 0.9250 Silver 0.7435 oz. ASW, 38.6 mm. **Subject:** Poison frogs **Rev:** Blue frog, multicolor

Date	Mintage	F	VF	XF	Unc	BU
2005 Proof	2,500	Value: 50.00				

KM# 864 10 DOLLARS
0.5000 g., 0.5850 Gold 0.0094 oz. AGW, 11 mm. **Subject:** 25th Anniversary of the Krugerrand **Obv:** Shield **Rev:** Paul Krueger bust left

Date	Mintage	F	VF	XF	Unc	BU
2005 Proof	—	Value: 35.00				

KM# 996 10 DOLLARS
62.2000 g., 0.9990 Silver 1.9977 oz. ASW, 50 mm. **Subject:** Romanesque Architecture **Rev:** Facade, Tiffany Glass insert

Date	Mintage	F	VF	XF	Unc	BU
2005 Antique finish	999	—	—	—	125	—

KM# 1017 10 DOLLARS
Silver **Subject:** Election of Pope Benedict XVI **Rev:** Pope with outstretched arms, St. Peter's in background

Date	Mintage	F	VF	XF	Unc	BU
2005 Proof	—	Value: 35.00				

KM# 1018 10 DOLLARS
Silver **Subject:** Moric Benovsky **Obv:** Naitonal arms **Rev:** Sailing ship right

Date	Mintage	F	VF	XF	Unc	BU
2005	—	Value: 35.00				

KM# 1019 10 DOLLARS
Silver, oval mm. **Obv:** National arms **Rev:** Titanic with recovered coal insert

Date	Mintage	F	VF	XF	Unc	BU
2005 Proof	—	Value: 35.00				

KM# 843 10 DOLLARS
0.7300 g., 0.9990 Gold 0.0234 oz. AGW, 11 mm. **Obv:** Arms **Rev:** John F. Kennedy head left

Date	Mintage	F	VF	XF	Unc	BU
2006 Proof	20,000	Value: 60.00				

KM# 764 10 DOLLARS
20.0000 g., 0.9990 Silver partially gilt 0.6423 oz. ASW, 38 mm. **Series:** Endangered Wildlife **Obv:** National arms **Obv. Legend:** REPUBLIC OF LIBERIA **Rev:** Gilt Crested Genet on branch facing with diamonds inset in eyes **Rev. Legend:** CAMEROON **Edge:** Plain

Date	Mintage	F	VF	XF	Unc	BU
2006 Proof	5,000	Value: 150				

KM# 765 10 DOLLARS
20.0000 g., 0.9990 Silver partially gilt 0.6423 oz. ASW, 38 mm. **Series:** Endangered Wildlife **Obv:** National arms **Obv. Legend:** REPUBLIC OF LIBERIA **Rev:** Two gilt Dalmatian Pelicans, one swimming, one standing with diamonds inset in eyes **Rev. Legend:** MONTENEGRO **Edge:** Plain

Date	Mintage	F	VF	XF	Unc	BU
2006 Proof	5,000	Value: 150				

KM# 766 10 DOLLARS
20.0000 g., 0.9990 Silver partially gilt 0.6423 oz. ASW, 38 mm. **Series:** Endangered Wildlife **Obv:** National arms **Obv. Legend:** REPUBLIC OF LIBERIA **Rev:** Gilt Hairy-bared Dwarf Lemue standing on branch with diamonds inset in eyes **Rev. Legend:** MADAGASCAR **Edge:** Plain

Date	Mintage	F	VF	XF	Unc	BU
2006 Proof	5,000	Value: 150				

KM# 767 10 DOLLARS
20.0000 g., 0.9990 Silver partially gilt 0.6423 oz. ASW, 38 mm. **Series:** Endangered Wildlife **Obv:** National arms **Obv. Legend:** REPUBLIC OF LIBERIA **Rev:** Two gilt Visayan Tarictics perched on branches with diamonds inset in eyes **Rev. Legend:** Philippines **Edge:** Plain

Date	Mintage	F	VF	XF	Unc	BU
2006 Proof	5,000	Value: 150				

KM# 768 10 DOLLARS
20.0000 g., 0.9990 Silver partially gilt 0.6423 oz. ASW, 38 mm. **Series:** Endangered Wildlife **Obv:** National arms **Obv. Legend:** REPUBLIC OF LIBERIA **Rev:** Two gilt Ethiopian Wolves, one seated, one laying with diamonds inset in eyes **Rev. Legend:** ETHIOPIA **Edge:** Plain

Date	Mintage	F	VF	XF	Unc	BU
2006 Proof	5,000	Value: 150				

KM# 769 10 DOLLARS
20.0000 g., 0.9990 Silver partially gilt 0.6423 oz. ASW, 38 mm. **Series:** Endangered Wildlife **Obv:** National arms **Obv. Legend:** REPUBLIC OF LIBERIA **Rev:** Two gilt Kakapos perched on a branch with diamonds inset in eyes **Rev. Legend:** NEW ZEALAND **Edge:** Plain

Date	Mintage	F	VF	XF	Unc	BU
2006 Proof	5,000	Value: 150				

KM# 770 10 DOLLARS
20.0000 g., 0.9990 Silver partially gilt 0.6423 oz. ASW, 38 mm. **Series:** Endangered Wildlife **Obv:** National arms **Obv. Legend:** REPUBLIC OF LIBERIA **Rev:** Gilt Spectacled Bear standing with diamonds inset in eyes **Rev. Legend:** BOLIVIA **Edge:** Plain

Date	Mintage	F	VF	XF	Unc	BU
2006 Proof	5,000	Value: 150				

KM# 771 10 DOLLARS
20.0000 g., 0.9990 Silver partially gilt 0.6423 oz. ASW, 38 mm. **Series:** Endangered Wildlife **Obv:** National arms **Obv. Legend:** REPUBLIC OF LIBERIA **Rev:** Two gilt Mauritius Kestrels perched on branch with diamonds inset in eyes **Rev. Legend:** MAURITIUS **Edge:** Plain

Date	Mintage	F	VF	XF	Unc	BU
2006 Proof	5,000	Value: 150				

KM# 772 10 DOLLARS
20.0000 g., 0.9990 Silver Partially gilt 0.6423 oz. ASW, 38 mm. **Series:** Endangered Wildlife **Obv:** National arms **Obv. Legend:** REPUBLIC OF LIBERIA **Rev:** Two gilt Mhorr Gazelles, one standing, one resting with diamonds inset in eyes **Rev. Legend:** MALI **Edge:** Plain

Date	Mintage	F	VF	XF	Unc	BU
2006 Proof	5,000	Value: 150				

KM# 773 10 DOLLARS
20.0000 g., 0.9990 Silver partially gilt 0.6423 oz. ASW, 38 mm. **Series:** Endangered Wildlife **Obv:** National arms **Obv. Legend:** REPUBLIC OF LIBERIA **Rev:** Two gilt Blue Lorikeets perched on branches with diamonds inset in eyes **Rev. Legend:** FRENCH POLYNESIA **Edge:** Plain

Date	Mintage	F	VF	XF	Unc	BU
2006 Proof	5,000	Value: 150				

KM# 774 10 DOLLARS
20.0000 g., 0.9990 Silver partially gilt 0.6423 oz. ASW, 38 mm. **Series:** Endangered Wildlife **Obv:** National arms **Obv. Legend:** REPUBLIC OF LIBERIA **Rev:** Gilt resting Arabian Leopard with diamonds inset in eyes **Rev. Legend:** SAUDI ARABIA **Edge:** Plain

Date	Mintage	F	VF	XF	Unc	BU
2006 Proof	5,000	Value: 150				

KM# 775 10 DOLLARS
20.0000 g., 0.9990 Silver partially gilt 0.6423 oz. ASW, 38 mm. **Series:** Endangered Wildlife **Obv:** National arms **Obv. Legend:** REPUBLIC OF LIBERIA **Rev:** Two gilt Hawaiian Geese standing with diamonds inset in eyes **Rev. Legend:** USA **Edge:** Plain

Date	Mintage	F	VF	XF	Unc	BU
2006 Proof	5,000	Value: 150				

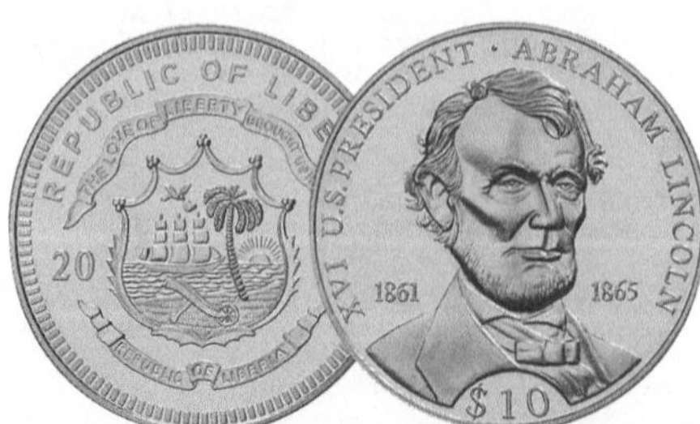

KM# 827 10 DOLLARS
14.6000 g., Copper-Nickel, 33 mm. **Subject:** Abraham Lincoln **Obv:** National arms **Rev:** Bust facing 3/4 right **Edge:** Reeded

Date	Mintage	F	VF	XF	Unc	BU
2006 Proof	50,000	Value: 10.00				

KM# 725 10 DOLLARS
3.1100 g., 0.9990 Gold 0.0999 oz. AGW, 16 mm. **Obv:** National arms **Rev:** Leopard head **Edge:** Reeded

Date	Mintage	F	VF	XF	Unc	BU
2007 Proof	120	Value: 200				

KM# 734 10 DOLLARS
25.0000 g., 0.9250 Silver 0.7435 oz. ASW, 38.61 mm. **Subject:** The Black Madonna of Czestochowa **Obv:** Arms **Obv. Legend:** REPUBLIC OF LIBERIA **Rev:** 1/2 length figure of Madonna facing with child

Date	Mintage	F	VF	XF	Unc	BU
2007 Proof	1,000	Value: 70.00				

KM# 1009 10 DOLLARS
62.2100 g., 0.9990 Silver 1.9980 oz. ASW **Obv:** National arms **Rev:** Christmas tree in color

Date	Mintage	F	VF	XF	Unc	BU
2010 Proof	—	Value: 150				

KM# 1029 12 DOLLARS
0.6220 g., 0.9990 Gold 0.0200 oz. AGW, 10 mm. **Rev:** Christ at center, apostles in 12 segments around

Date	Mintage	F	VF	XF	Unc	BU
2007 Proof	—	Value: 70.00				

KM# 643 20 DOLLARS
15.5500 g., 0.9990 Silver 0.4994 oz. ASW, 30.4 mm. **Obv:** St. Peter's Basilica **Rev:** Bust of Pope facing **Edge:** Reeded

Date	Mintage	F	VF	XF	Unc	BU
2001S Proof	—	Value: 28.00				

KM# 650 20 DOLLARS
19.9100 g., 0.9990 Silver 0.6395 oz. ASW, 40 mm. **Obv:** National arms **Rev:** Bust of Charles Lindbergh facing and Spirit of St. Louis in background **Edge:** Reeded

Date	Mintage	F	VF	XF	Unc	BU
2001 Proof	—	Value: 40.00				

KM# 715 20 DOLLARS
20.0000 g., 0.9990 Silver 0.6423 oz. ASW, 40.3 mm. **Series:** American History **Obv:** National arms **Rev:** First Continental Congress in prayer **Edge:** Reeded

Date	Mintage	F	VF	XF	Unc	BU
2001 Proof	20,000	Value: 32.00				

KM# 716 20 DOLLARS
20.0000 g., 0.9990 Silver 0.6423 oz. ASW, 40.3 mm. **Series:** American History **Obv:** National arms **Rev:** U.S. Constitution Ratification, text in stars of folded flag **Edge:** Reeded

Date	Mintage	F	VF	XF	Unc	BU
2001 Proof	20,000	Value: 32.00				

KM# 717 20 DOLLARS
20.0000 g., 0.9990 Silver 0.6423 oz. ASW, 40.3 mm. **Series:** American History **Obv:** National arms **Rev:** Washington's Inauguration scene **Edge:** Reeded

Date	Mintage	F	VF	XF	Unc	BU
2001 Proof	20,000	Value: 32.00				

KM# 718 20 DOLLARS
20.0000 g., 0.9990 Silver 0.6423 oz. ASW, 40.3 mm. **Series:** American History **Obv:** National arms **Rev:** Appomattox Courthouse surrender scene with Lee and Grant **Edge:** Reeded

Date	Mintage	F	VF	XF	Unc	BU
2001 Proof	20,000	Value: 32.00				

KM# 719 20 DOLLARS
20.0000 g., 0.9990 Silver 0.6423 oz. ASW, 40.3 mm. **Series:** American History **Obv:** National arms **Rev:** Prohibition, hatchet, barrels and bottles destruction **Edge:** Reeded

Date	Mintage	F	VF	XF	Unc	BU
2001 Proof	20,000	Value: 32.00				

KM# 720 20 DOLLARS
20.0000 g., 0.9990 Silver 0.6423 oz. ASW, 40.3 mm. **Series:** American History **Obv:** National arms **Rev:** Cuban Missile Crisis, Castro, Khrushchev, Kennedy, missiles and map **Edge:** Reeded

Date	Mintage	F	VF	XF	Unc	BU
2001 Proof	20,000	Value: 32.00				

KM# 721 20 DOLLARS
20.0000 g., 0.9990 Silver 0.6423 oz. ASW, 40.3 mm. **Series:** American History **Obv:** National arms **Rev:** First Man on Moon, Armstrong and Lander **Edge:** Reeded

Date	Mintage	F	VF	XF	Unc	BU
2001 Proof	20,000	Value: 32.00				

KM# 722 20 DOLLARS
20.0000 g., 0.9990 Silver 0.6423 oz. ASW, 40.3 mm. **Series:** American History **Obv:** National arms **Rev:** Desert Storm, soldier, helicopter, rocket launcher etc. **Edge:** Reeded

Date	Mintage	F	VF	XF	Unc	BU
2001 Proof	20,000	Value: 32.00				

KM# 514 20 DOLLARS
31.1035 g., 0.9990 Silver 0.9990 oz. ASW, 38.2 mm. **Subject:** Bush-Cheney Inauguration **Obv:** White House **Rev:** Conjoined busts right **Edge:** Reeded

Date	Mintage	F	VF	XF	Unc	BU
2001 Proof	—	Value: 45.00				

KM# 616 20 DOLLARS
31.2000 g., 0.9990 Silver gilt 1.0021 oz. ASW, 38.7 mm. **Obv:** National arms **Rev:** Diamond studded scorpion (Scorpio) **Edge:** Reeded

Date	Mintage	F	VF	XF	Unc	BU
2002 Proof	—	Value: 60.00				

KM# 617 20 DOLLARS
31.2000 g., 0.9990 Silver gilt 1.0021 oz. ASW, 38.7 mm. **Obv:** National arms **Rev:** Diamond studded archer (Sagittarius) **Edge:** Reeded

Date	Mintage	F	VF	XF	Unc	BU
2002 Proof	—	Value: 60.00				

KM# 825 20 DOLLARS
20.0000 g., Silver, 40 mm. **Series:** America's First Ladies **Subject:** Mary Todd Lincoln **Obv:** National arms **Rev:** Bust facing slightly left at center left, oval portrait of Abraham Lincoln at right **Edge:** Reeded

Date	Mintage	F	VF	XF	Unc	BU
2003 Proof	20,000	Value: 32.50				

KM# 826 20 DOLLARS
20.0000 g., Silver, 40 mm. **Series:** History of America **Subject:** Emancipation Proclamation **Obv:** National arms **Rev:** Lincoln seated with seven politicians gathered **Edge:** Reeded

Date	Mintage	F	VF	XF	Unc	BU
2004 Proof	20,000	Value: 37.50				

KM# 1020 20 DOLLARS
Silver **Subject:** U.S. Constitution

Date	Mintage	F	VF	XF	Unc	BU
2006 Proof	—	Value: 35.00				

KM# 1021 20 DOLLARS
1.2500 g., 0.9990 Gold 0.0401 oz. AGW, 14 mm. **Subject:** World Cup Soccer, Germany **Obv:** National arms **Rev:** Soccer player heading ball

Date	Mintage	F	VF	XF	Unc	BU
2006 Proof	—	Value: 80.00				

KM# 634 25 DOLLARS
0.7300 g., 0.9990 Gold 0.0234 oz. AGW, 11.1 mm. **Obv:** National arms **Rev:** Joan of Arc **Edge:** Reeded

Date	Mintage	F	VF	XF	Unc	BU
2001 Proof	—	Value: 60.00				

KM# 666 25 DOLLARS
1.5200 g., Gold, 13.68 mm. **Subject:** Abraham Lincoln **Obv:** National arms **Rev:** Statue of Lincoln seated **Edge:** Reeded

Date	Mintage	F	VF	XF	Unc	BU
2001 Proof	—	Value: 95.00				

KM# 667 25 DOLLARS
0.7300 g., 0.9990 Gold 0.0234 oz. AGW, 11 mm. **Obv:** National arms **Rev:** Mount Rushmore **Edge:** Reeded

Date	Mintage	F	VF	XF	Unc	BU
2001 Proof	20,000	Value: 65.00				

KM# 995 25 DOLLARS
0.7300 g., 0.9990 Gold 0.0234 oz. AGW, 11 mm. **Obv:** National Arms **Rev:** Martin Luther King and Washington Monument

Date	Mintage	F	VF	XF	Unc	BU
2001 Proof	—	Value: 70.00				

KM# 669 25 DOLLARS
0.7300 g., 0.9990 Gold 0.0234 oz. AGW, 11 mm. **Subject:** Abraham Lincoln **Obv:** National arms **Rev:** Bust facing at right, Lincoln Memorial in background **Edge:** Reeded

Date	Mintage	F	VF	XF	Unc	BU
2002 Proof	20,000	Value: 65.00				

KM# 730 25 DOLLARS
0.0234 g., 0.9990 Gold 0.0008 oz. AGW **Obv:** Shield **Rev:** Map of Germany and stars

Date	Mintage	F	VF	XF	Unc	BU
2003B Proof	—	Value: 35.00				

KM# 804 25 DOLLARS
1.2500 g., 0.9990 Gold 0.0401 oz. AGW, 14.5 x 9 mm. **Subject:** R. M. S. Titanic - Expedition 2000 **Obv:** National arms **Obv. Legend:** REPUBLIC OF LIBERIA **Rev:** Titanic with small piece of recovered coal embedded in hull. **Edge:** Reeded **Shape:** Oval

Date	Mintage	F	VF	XF	Unc	BU
2005 Proof	—	Value: 80.00				

KM# 731 50 DOLLARS
222.0800 g., 0.9990 Silver 7.1326 oz. ASW, 80.04 mm. **Subject:** Japanese Attack on Pearl Harbor **Obv:** National arms **Obv. Legend:** REPUBLIC OF LIBERIA **Rev:** USA flag hologram at upper left, bust of Franklin D. Roosevelt facing above Japanese aircraft attacking ship in harbor **Rev. Legend:** REMEMBERING PEARL HARBOR - DECEMBER 7, 1941

Date	Mintage	F	VF	XF	Unc	BU
2001 Proof	—	Value: 275				

KM# 495 50 DOLLARS
907.0000 g., 0.9990 Silver 29.130 oz. ASW, 100 mm. **Subject:** Wreck of the Princess Louisa **Obv:** National arms and value **Rev:** Ship under sail **Edge:** Reeded **Note:** Each coin has a cob coin recovered from the wreck site encased in a hole with clear resin. Illustration reduced.

Date	Mintage	F	VF	XF	Unc	BU
2001	500	—	—	—	1,150	—

KM# 776 50 DOLLARS
93.3000 g., 0.9990 Silver partially gilt 2.9965 oz. ASW, 65.00 mm. **Series:** Endangered Wildlife **Obv:** National arms **Obv. Legend:** REPUBLIC OF LIBERIA **Rev:** Two gilt Cheetahs, one sitting, one resting with diamonds inset in eyes **Rev. Legend:** TANZANIA **Edge:** Plain

Date	Mintage	F	VF	XF	Unc	BU
2005 Proof	999	Value: 450				

KM# 726 50 DOLLARS
62.2070 g., 0.9990 Silver 1.9979 oz. ASW, 50 mm. **Obv:** National arms **Rev:** Leopard lying across a map of Africa **Edge:** Reeded

Date	Mintage	F	VF	XF	Unc	BU
2007 Proof	500	Value: 125				

KM# 844 100 DOLLARS
1000.0000 g., 0.9990 Silver 32.117 oz. ASW **Subject:** Tanks of World War II - T-34

Date	Mintage	F	VF	XF	Unc	BU
2008 Proof	1,000	Value: 1,500				

KM# 845 100 DOLLARS
1000.0000 g., 0.9990 Silver 32.117 oz. ASW **Subject:** Tanks of World War II - VI-Tiger

Date	Mintage	F	VF	XF	Unc	BU
2008 Proof	1,000	Value: 1,500				

KM# 846 100 DOLLARS
1000.0000 g., 0.9990 Silver 32.117 oz. ASW, 120 mm. **Obv:** Arms **Rev:** St. Paul standing, events of his life around

Date	Mintage	F	VF	XF	Unc	BU
2008 Proof	1,000	Value: 2,000				

KM# 727 2500 DOLLARS
155.5175 g., 0.9990 Gold 4.9948 oz. AGW, 60 mm. **Obv:** National arms **Rev:** Leopard lying across a map of Africa **Edge:** Reeded

Date	Mintage	F	VF	XF	Unc	BU
2007 Proof	48	Value: 9,500				

PATTERNS

Including off metal strikes

KM#	Date	Mintage	Identification	Mkt Val
Pn58	2001	—	10 Dollars. Copper-Nickel. 29.2500 g. 38.2 mm. National arms. "9-11" Flag raising scene. Plain edge.	250
Pn59	2001	—	20 Dollars. Silver Plated Base Metal. 5.3100 g. 20 mm. National arms. "9-11" Flag raising scene. Plain edge.	150
Pn60	2001	—	100 Dollars. Base Metal Gilt. 3.4200 g. 16 mm. National arms. "9-11" Flag raising scene. Plain edge.	125

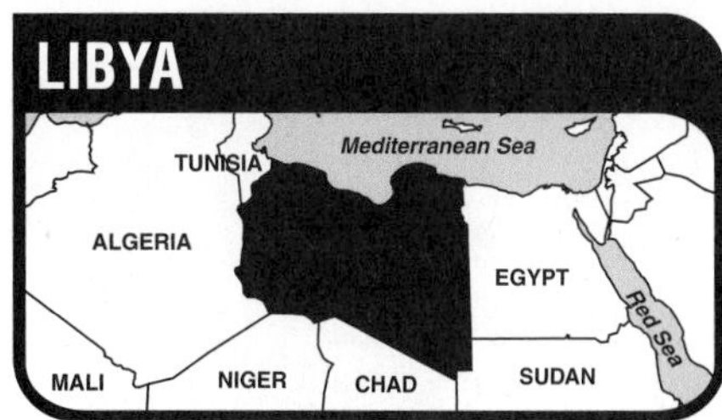

The Socialist People's Libyan Arab Jamahariya, located on the north-central coast of Africa between Tunisia and Egypt, has an area of 679,358 sq. mi. (1,759,540 sq. km.) and a population of 3.9 million. Capital: Tripoli. Crude oil, which accounts for 90 per cent of the export earnings, is the mainstay of the economy.

TITLES

المملكة الليبية

al-Mamlaka(t) al-Libiya(t)

al-Jomhuriya(t) al-Arabiya(t) al-Libiya(t)

MONETARY SYSTEM
10 Milliemes = 1 Piastre
100 Piastres = 1 Pound

GREAT SOCIALIST PEOPLE'S LIBYAN ARAB JAMAHIRIYA

STANDARD COINAGE

1000 Dirhams = 1 Dinar

KM# 28 50 DIRHAMS
6.2500 g., Copper-Nickel, 25 mm. **Obv:** Armored equestrian **Rev:** Value at center **Shape:** Scalloped

Date	Mintage	F	VF	XF	Unc	BU
MD1377-2009	—	—	—	2.50	6.00	—

KM# 29 100 DIRHAMS
Copper-Nickel, 27 mm. **Obv:** Armored Equestrian **Rev:** Value at center

Date	Mintage	F	VF	XF	Unc	BU
MD1377-2009	—	—	—	4.50	9.00	—

KM# 26 1/4 DINAR
11.1500 g., Nickel-Brass, 28 mm. **Obv:** Libyan knight on horse with gun 1/2 left surrounded by name of Libyan Arab Jamahiriya, ornamental legend with date **Rev:** Value in Arabic script above wheat ears in ornamented frame **Edge:** Ten alternating reeded and plain flat sections **Shape:** 10-sided

Date	Mintage	F	VF	XF	Unc	BU
MD1369	—	—	—	5.00	8.00	10.00

Note: Restruck in 2001-2002

KM# 30 1/4 DINAR
11.5000 g., Nickel-Brass, 28 mm. **Obv:** Armored horseman **Rev:** Value at center **Shape:** 10-sided

Date	Mintage	F	VF	XF	Unc	BU
MD1377-2009	—	—	—	9.00	12.50	—

KM# 27 1/2 DINAR
11.5000 g., Bi-Metallic Aluminumn bronze center in Copper-Nickel ring., 30 mm. **Obv:** Man on horse with gun 1/2 left, ornamental legend with date **Rev:** Value in Arabic script above wheat ears in ornamented frame **Edge:** Reeded

Date	Mintage	F	VF	XF	Unc	BU
MD1372	—	—	—	—	10.00	12.00

KM# 31 1/2 DINAR
11.5000 g., Bi-Metallic Aluminum-Bronze center in Copper-Nickel ring, 30 mm. **Obv:** Armored horseman **Rev:** Value at center **Edge:** Reeded

Date	Mintage	F	VF	XF	Unc	BU
MD1377-2009	—	—	—	12.50	15.00	—

The Principality of Liechtenstein, located in central Europe on the east bank of the Rhine between Austria and Switzerland, has an area of 62 sq. mi. (160 sq. km.) and a population of 27,200. Capital: Vaduz. The economy is based on agriculture and light manufacturing. Canned goods, textiles, ceramics and precision instruments are exported.

RULERS
Prince Hans Adam II, 1990-

MINT MARKS
B - Bern

PRINCIPALITY

REFORM COINAGE

100 Rappen = 1 Frank

Y# 24 10 FRANKEN
29.9500 g., 0.9000 Silver 0.8666 oz. ASW, 37.3 mm. **Ruler:** Prince Hans Adam II **Subject:** 200 Years of Sovereignty **Obv:** Vertical inscription between crowned arms and value **Rev:** Johann I (1760-1836) **Edge:** Reeded

Date	Mintage	F	VF	XF	Unc	BU
ND (2006)B Proof	—	Value: 55.00				

Y# 25 50 FRANKEN
8.8800 g., 0.9990 Gold 0.2852 oz. AGW **Ruler:** Prince Hans Adam II **Subject:** 200th Anniversary of Sovereignty

Date	Mintage	F	VF	XF	Unc	BU
ND (2006)B Proof	—	Value: 535				

The Republic of Lithuania, southernmost of the Baltic states in east Europe, has an area of 25,174 sq. mi.(65,201 sq. km.) and a population of *3.6 million. Capital: Vilnius. The economy is based on livestock raising and manufacturing. Hogs, cattle, hides and electric motors are exported.

Lithuania declared its independence March 11, 1990 and it was recognized by the United States on Sept. 2, 1991, followed by the Soviet government in Moscow on Sept. 6. They were seated in the UN General Assembly on Sept. 17, 1991.

MODERN REPUBLIC

1991-present

REFORM COINAGE

100 Centas = 1 Litas

KM# 106 10 CENTU
2.6000 g., Nickel-Brass, 17 mm. **Obv:** National arms **Rev:** Value **Edge:** Reeded

Date	Mintage	F	VF	XF	Unc	BU
2003 Prooflike	10,000	—	—	—	—	4.00
2006	—	—	—	—	—	0.40
2006 Proof	2,000	Value: 45.00				
2007	—	—	—	—	—	0.40
2008	—	—	—	—	—	0.40
2008 Prooflike	200	—	—	—	—	5.00
2009	—	—	—	—	—	0.40
2009 Prooflike	500	—	—	—	—	20.00
2010	—	—	—	—	—	0.40
2011 In sets only	4,500	—	—	—	—	0.75
2012 In sets only	4,000	—	—	—	—	0.75
2013 In sets only	7,000	—	—	—	—	0.75

KM# 107 20 CENTU
4.8000 g., Nickel-Brass, 20.5 mm. **Obv:** National arms **Rev:** Value **Edge:** Reeded

Date	Mintage	F	VF	XF	Unc	BU
2003 In sets only	—	—	—	—	—	1.50
2003 Proof	10,000	Value: 2.00				
2007	—	—	—	—	—	1.00
2008	—	—	—	—	—	1.00
2008 Prooflike	200	—	—	—	—	5.00
2009	—	—	—	—	—	1.00
2009 Prooflike	500	—	—	—	—	3.00
2010	—	—	—	—	—	1.00
2011 In sets only	4,500	—	—	—	—	2.00
2012 In sets only	4,000	—	—	—	—	2.00
2013 In sets only	7,500	—	—	—	—	2.00

KM# 108 50 CENTU
6.0000 g., Nickel-Brass, 23 mm. **Obv:** National arms **Rev:** Value within designed circle **Edge:** Reeded

Date	Mintage	F	VF	XF	Unc	BU
2003 In sets only	—	—	—	—	—	4.00
2003 Proof	10,000	Value: 2.00				
2008	—	—	—	—	0.50	1.50
2008 Prooflike	200	—	—	—	—	30.00
2009 In sets only	5,000	—	—	—	—	10.00
2009 Prooflike	500	—	—	—	—	4.00
2010 In sets only	3,500	—	—	—	—	10.00
2011 In sets only	4,500	—	—	—	—	4.00
2012 In sets only	4,000	—	—	—	—	4.00
2013 In sets only	7,500	—	—	—	—	4.00

KM# 111 LITAS
6.2500 g., Copper-Nickel, 22.3 mm. **Obv:** National arms **Rev:** Value within circle above lined designs **Edge:** Reeded

Date	Mintage	F	VF	XF	Unc	BU
2001	—	—	—	—	1.50	2.00
2002	—	—	—	—	1.50	2.00
2003 In sets only	—	—	—	—	—	5.00
2003 Proof	10,000	Value: 8.00				
2008	—	—	—	—	1.50	2.00
2008 Prooflike	200	—	—	—	—	6.00
2009	—	—	—	—	1.50	2.00
2009 Prooflike	500	—	—	—	—	4.00
2010	—	—	—	—	1.50	2.00
2011 In sets only	4,500	—	—	—	—	3.00
2012 In sets only	4,000	—	—	—	—	3.00
2013 In sets only	7,500	—	—	—	—	3.00

KM# 137 LITAS
6.2500 g., Copper-Nickel, 22.3 mm. **Subject:** 425th Anniversary - University of Vilnius **Obv:** Knight on horse within rope wreath **Rev:** Building within court yard **Edge:** Segmented reeding

Date	Mintage	F	VF	XF	Unc	BU
2004	200,000	—	—	—	3.00	5.00

KM# 142 LITAS
6.2500 g., Copper-Nickel, 22.3 mm. **Obv:** Knight on horse within circle **Rev:** Palace **Edge:** Segmented reeding

Date	Mintage	F	VF	XF	Unc	BU
2005	1,000,000	—	—	—	1.75	2.50

KM# 162 LITAS
6.2500 g., Copper-Nickel, 22.3 mm. **Subject:** Vilnius - European Culture Capital **Obv:** National Arms **Rev:** Female figure standing at easel **Edge:** Segmented reeding

Date	Mintage	F	VF	XF	Unc	BU
2009	1,000,000	—	—	—	2.00	3.00

KM# 172 LITAS
6.2500 g., Copper-Nickel, 22.3 mm. **Subject:** Battle of Grunwald, 600th Anniversary **Obv:** National arms **Rev:** Long spears attacking each other **Edge:** Segmented reeding

Date	Mintage	F	VF	XF	Unc	BU
2010	1,000,000	—	—	—	2.00	3.00

KM# 177 LITAS
6.2500 g., Copper-Nickel, 22.3 mm. **Subject:** European Basketball Championship **Obv:** National arms **Rev:** Basketball **Edge:** Reeded

Date	Mintage	F	VF	XF	Unc	BU
2011	1,000,000	—	—	—	3.00	7.00

KM# 112 2 LITAI
7.5000 g., Bi-Metallic Copper-Nickel center in Aluminum-Bronze ring, 25 mm. **Obv:** National arms within circle **Rev:** Value within circle **Edge:** Segmented reeding

Date	Mintage	F	VF	XF	Unc	BU
2001	—	—	—	—	3.00	5.00
2002	—	—	—	—	3.00	5.00
2003 Proof	10,000	Value: 3.50				
2008	—	—	—	—	2.25	3.00
2008 Prooflike	200	—	—	—	—	30.00
2009	—	—	—	—	3.00	5.00
2009 Prooflike	500	—	—	—	—	25.00
2010	—	—	—	—	3.00	5.00
2011 In sets only	4,500	—	—	—	—	5.00
2012 In sets only	4,000	—	—	—	—	5.00
2013 In sets only	7,500	—	—	—	—	5.00

KM# 132 5 LITAI
28.2800 g., 0.9250 Silver 0.8410 oz. ASW, 38.6 mm. **Series:** Endangered Wildlife **Obv:** Knight on horse **Rev:** Barn owl in flight **Edge Lettering:** LIETUVOS BANKAS

Date	Mintage	F	VF	XF	Unc	BU
2002 Proof	3,000	Value: 150				

KM# 113 5 LITAI
10.1000 g., Bi-Metallic Aluminum-Bronze center in Copper-Nickel ring, 27.5 mm. **Obv:** National arms within circle **Rev:** Value within circle **Edge Lettering:** PENKI LITAI

Date	Mintage	F	VF	XF	Unc	BU
2003 In sets only	—	—	—	—	—	14.00
2003 Proof	10,000	Value: 15.00				
2008 In sets only	3,800	—	—	—	—	15.00
2008 Prooflike	200	—	—	—	—	30.00
2009	—	—	—	—	4.00	6.00
2009 Prooflike	500	—	—	—	—	20.00
2010 In sets only	3,500	—	—	—	—	15.00
2011 In sets only	4,500	—	—	—	—	10.00
2012 In sets only	4,000	—	—	—	—	10.00
2013 In sets only	7,500	—	—	—	—	10.00

KM# 131 10 LITU
13.1500 g., Copper-Nickel, 28.7 mm. **Obv:** Knight on horse on shield within aerial harbor view **Rev:** Shield within city view **Edge Lettering:** KLAIPEDAI - 75 (twice)

Date	Mintage	F	VF	XF	Unc	BU
2002 Proof	5,000	Value: 25.00				

KM# 160 10 LITU
1.2400 g., 0.9990 Gold 0.0398 oz. AGW, 13.92 mm. **Obv:** Castle gate **Rev:** Geometric design

Date	Mintage	F	VF	XF	Unc	BU
2007LMK Proof	7,000	Value: 120				

KM# 169 10 LITU
11.4000 g., 0.9250 Silver 0.3390 oz. ASW, 28.7 mm. **Subject:** Lithuanian Culture - Music **Obv:** Vilnus **Rev:** Two chello and musical notations

Date	Mintage	F	VF	XF	Unc	BU
2010 Proof	10,000	Value: 50.00				

KM# 175 10 LITU
12.4400 g., 0.9250 Silver 0.3699 oz. ASW, 28.7 mm. **Subject:** Lithuanian Culture - Theatre **Obv:** State emblem **Rev:** Theatre motif, two half faces **Edge Lettering:** LIETUVOS KULTURA * TEATRAS (twice) **Designer:** Giedrius Paulauskis

Date	Mintage	F	VF	XF	Unc	BU
2011 Proof	10,000	Value: 50.00				

KM# 129 50 LITU
28.2800 g., 0.9250 Silver 0.8410 oz. ASW, 38.61 mm. **Subject:** Motiejus Valancius' 200th Birthday **Obv:** Knight on horse within shield above church and landscape **Rev:** Bust facing **Edge Lettering:** LIETUVISKAS ZODIS RASTAS IR TIKEJMAS TAUTOS GYVASTIS

Date	Mintage	F	VF	XF	Unc	BU
2001 Proof	2,000	Value: 200				

KM# 130 50 LITU
28.2800 g., 0.9250 Silver 0.8410 oz. ASW, 38.61 mm. **Subject:** Jonas Basanavicius (1851-1927) **Obv:** Knight on horse **Rev:** Jonas Basanavlcius **Edge Lettering:** KAD AUSRAI AUSTANT PRAVISTU IR LIETUVOS DVASIA

Date	Mintage	F	VF	XF	Unc	BU
2001 Proof	2,000	Value: 200				

KM# 133 50 LITU
28.2800 g., 0.9250 Silver 0.8410 oz. ASW, 38.61 mm. **Series:** Historical Architecture **Obv:** Republic of Lithuania coat of arms **Rev:** Trakai Island Castle **Edge Lettering:** ISTORIJOS IR ARCHITEKTUROS PAMINKLAI

Date	Mintage	F	VF	XF	Unc	BU
2002 Proof	1,500	Value: 200				

KM# 134 50 LITU
28.2800 g., 0.9250 Silver 0.8410 oz. ASW, 38.6 mm. **Obv:** Knight on horse above value **Rev:** Vilnius Cathedral **Edge Lettering:** ISTORIJOS IR ARCHITEKTUROS PAMINKLAI

Date	Mintage	F	VF	XF	Unc	BU
2003 Proof	1,500	Value: 175				

KM# 135 50 LITU
28.2800 g., 0.9250 Silver 0.8410 oz. ASW, 38.6 mm. **Subject:** Olympics **Obv:** Knight on horse above value **Rev:** Stylized cyclists **Edge Lettering:** XXVIII OLIMPIADOS ZAIDYNEMS

Date	Mintage	F	VF	XF	Unc	BU
2003 Proof	2,000	Value: 150				

KM# 138 50 LITU
28.2800 g., 0.9250 Silver 0.8410 oz. ASW, 38.6 mm. **Series:** Historical Architecture **Subject:** 425th Anniversary - University of Vilnius **Obv:** Knight on horse **Rev:** Old university buildings **Edge:** Lettered **Edge Lettering:** ISTORIJOS IR ARCHITEKTUROS PAMINKLAI

Date	Mintage	F	VF	XF	Unc	BU
2004 Proof	2,000	Value: 150				

KM# 139 50 LITU
28.2800 g., 0.9250 Silver 0.8410 oz. ASW, 38.6 mm. **Obv:** Knight on horse **Rev:** Pazaislis Monastery **Edge:** Lettered **Edge Lettering:** ISTORIJOS IR ARCHITEKTUROS PAMINKLAI

Date	Mintage	F	VF	XF	Unc	BU
2004 Proof	1,500	Value: 150				

KM# 140 50 LITU
28.2800 g., 0.9250 Silver 0.8410 oz. ASW, 38.6 mm. **Subject:** First Lithuanian Statute of 1529 **Obv:** Knight on horse **Rev:** Seated and kneeling figures **Edge:** Lettered **Edge Lettering:** "BUKIME TEISES VERGAI, KAD GALETUME NAUDOTIS LAISVEMIS"

Date	Mintage	F	VF	XF	Unc	BU
2004 Proof	1,000	Value: 200				

KM# 141 50 LITU
28.2800 g., 0.9250 Silver 0.8410 oz. ASW, 38.6 mm. **Subject:** Curonian Spit **Obv:** Knight on horse **Rev:** Shifting sand dunes design **Edge:** Ornamented pattern from Neringa emblem

Date	Mintage	F	VF	XF	Unc	BU
2004 Proof	2,000	Value: 175				

KM# 143 50 LITU
28.2800 g., 0.9250 Silver 0.8410 oz. ASW, 38.61 mm. **Series:** Historical Architecture **Obv:** Denar coin with Knight on horse **Rev:** Kernavé hill fort **Edge Lettering:** ISTORIJOS IR ARCHITEKTUROS PAMINKLAI

Date	Mintage	F	VF	XF	Unc	BU
2005 Proof	2,000	Value: 150				

KM# 147 50 LITU
28.2800 g., 0.9250 Silver 0.8410 oz. ASW, 38.6 mm. **Subject:** 1905 Lithuanian Congress **Obv:** Knight on horse **Rev:** Legend and inscription **Edge:** Ornamented

Date	Mintage	F	VF	XF	Unc	BU
2005 Proof	1,500	Value: 225				

KM# 144 50 LITU
28.2800 g., 0.9250 Silver 0.8410 oz. ASW, 38.6 mm. **Subject:** 150th Anniversary - National Museum **Obv:** Trio of ancient Lithuanian coins **Rev:** Man blowing horn **Edge Lettering:** PRO PUBLICO BONO

Date	Mintage	F	VF	XF	Unc	BU
2005 Proof	1,500	Value: 325				

KM# 145 50 LITU
28.2800 g., 0.9250 Silver 0.8410 oz. ASW, 38.6 mm. **Subject:** Knight on horse and cross **Rev:** Cardinal Vincentas Sladkevicius **Edge Lettering:** LET OUR LIFE BE BUILT ON GOODNESS AND HOPE

Date	Mintage	F	VF	XF	Unc	BU
2005 Proof	2,000	Value: 175				

KM# 148 50 LITU
28.2800 g., 0.9250 Silver 0.8410 oz. ASW, 38.6 mm. **Obv:** National arms on forest background **Rev:** Lynx prowling **Edge:** Stylized lynx paw prints

Date	Mintage	F	VF	XF	Unc	BU
2006 Proof	3,000	Value: 175				

KM# 149 50 LITU
28.2800 g., 0.9250 Silver 0.8410 oz. ASW, 38.6 mm. **Obv:** National arms against castle wall background **Rev:** Medininkai Castle **Edge Lettering:** ISTORIJOS IR ARCHITEKTUROS PAMINKLAI

Date	Mintage	F	VF	XF	Unc	BU
2006 Proof	2,500	Value: 200				

KM# 151 50 LITU
28.2800 g., 0.9250 Silver 0.8410 oz. ASW, 38.61 mm. **Subject:** 1831 Uprising **Obv:** Small national arms above battle scene **Obv. Legend:** LIETUVA **Rev:** Bust of Pliaterytè facing **Rev. Legend:** EMILIJA PLIATERYTÈ **Edge Lettering:** 1831 * SUKILIMAS **Designer:** Giedrius Paulauskis

Date	Mintage	F	VF	XF	Unc	BU
2006 Proof	2,500	Value: 200				

KM# 152 50 LITU
28.2800 g., 0.9250 Silver 0.8410 oz. ASW, 38.6 mm. **Subject:** XXIX Olympics 2008 - Beijing **Obv:** National arms **Obv. Legend:** LIETUVA **Rev:** Stylized swimmer right **Rev. Legend:** PEKINAS

Date	Mintage	F	VF	XF	Unc	BU
2007 Proof	5,000	Value: 150				

KM# 161 50 LITU
28.2800 g., 0.9250 Silver 0.8410 oz. ASW, 38.6 mm. **Subject:** Panemune Castle **Obv:** Shield and fortress detail **Rev:** Castle towers

Date	Mintage	F	VF	XF	Unc	BU
2007LMK Proof	5,000	Value: 150				

KM# 153 50 LITU
28.2800 g., 0.9250 Silver 0.8410 oz. ASW, 38.6 mm. **Series:** European Cultural Heritage **Obv:** National arms surrounded by seven archaic crosses **Obv. Legend:** LIETUVA **Rev:** Circular latent image surrounded by seven archaic crosses

Date	Mintage	F	VF	XF	Unc	BU
2008 Proof	10,000	Value: 150				

KM# 155 50 LITU
28.2800 g., 0.9250 Silver 0.8410 oz. ASW, 38.6 mm. **Obv:** National arms **Obv. Legend:** LIETUVA **Rev:** Partial castle wall, towers **Rev. Legend:** KAUNO PILIS

Date	Mintage	F	VF	XF	Unc	BU
2008 Proof	10,000	Value: 150				

KM# 154 50 LITU

28.2800 g., 0.9250 Silver 0.8410 oz. ASW, 38.6 mm. **Subject:** 550th Anniversary Birth of St. Casimer **Obv:** National arms on shield **Obv. Legend:** LIETUVA **Rev:** St. Casimer standing holding flowers **Rev. Legend:** SV. KAZIMIERAS

Date	Mintage	F	VF	XF	Unc	BU
2008 Proof	5,000	Value: 250				

KM# 159 50 LITU

28.2800 g., 0.9250 Silver 0.8410 oz. ASW, 38.6 mm. **Subject:** Lithuania Nature **Obv:** National Arms **Rev:** Bee

Date	Mintage	F	VF	XF	Unc	BU
2008 Proof	10,000	Value: 200				

KM# 163 50 LITU

28.2800 g., 0.9250 Silver 0.8410 oz. ASW, 38.6 mm. **Subject:** Vilnius - European Culture Capital **Obv:** National Arms **Rev:** Female figure standing at easle

Date	Mintage	F	VF	XF	Unc	BU
2009 Proof	10,000	Value: 200				

KM# 164 50 LITU

28.2800 g., 0.9250 Silver 0.8410 oz. ASW, 38.6 mm. **Subject:** Tytuvenai **Obv:** National Arms in Shield **Rev:** Tytuvenai Church facade at left

Date	Mintage	F	VF	XF	Unc	BU
2009 Proof	10,000	Value: 200				

KM# 165 50 LITU

28.2800 g., 0.9250 Silver 0.8410 oz. ASW, 38.6 mm. **Subject:** Nature, Naktiziede **Obv:** Knight on horseback left **Rev:** Flowers

Date	Mintage	F	VF	XF	Unc	BU
2009LMK Proof	—	Value: 175				

KM# 170 50 LITU

28.2800 g., 0.9250 Silver 0.8410 oz. ASW, 38.61 mm. **Subject:** Biržai Castle **Obv:** Viltus in shield **Rev:** Castle view and ariel plan

Date	Mintage	F	VF	XF	Unc	BU
2010 Proof	10,000	Value: 100				

KM# 171 50 LITU

28.2800 g., 0.9250 Silver 0.8410 oz. ASW, 38.61 mm. **Obv:** Vilnus **Rev:** Misgurnus Fossilis - European Weather Loach **Edge Lettering:** LIETUVOS GAMTA

Date	Mintage	F	VF	XF	Unc	BU
2010 Proof	10,000	Value: 100				

KM# 176 50 LITU

3.1000 g., 0.9999 Gold 0.0997 oz. AGW, 16.25 mm. **Subject:** European Basketball Championship **Obv:** State emblem **Rev:** Basketball **Edge:** Reeded

Date	Mintage	F	VF	XF	Unc	BU
2011 Proof	5,000	Value: 650				

KM# 174 50 LITU

28.2800 g., 0.9250 Silver 0.8410 oz. ASW, 38.61 mm. **Subject:** Gabriele Petkevicaite-Bite, 150th Anniversary of Birth **Obv:** State emblem **Rev:** Portrait **Edge Lettering:** AD ASTRA (repeated 3 times)

Date	Mintage	F	VF	XF	Unc	BU
2011 Proof	10,000	Value: 100				

KM# 158 100 LITU

7.7800 g., 0.9990 Gold 0.2499 oz. AGW, 22.3 mm. **Subject:** Use of the Name Lithuania Millenium **Obv:** Linear National Arms **Rev:** Circular Legend

Date	Mintage	F	VF	XF	Unc	BU
2007 Proof	5,000	Value: 600				

KM# 156 100 LITU

7.7800 g., 0.9999 Gold 0.2501 oz. AGW, 22.3 mm. **Subject:** Millennium of name "Lithuania" **Obv:** Stylized national arms **Obv. Legend:** LIETUVA **Rev:** Partial parchment **Rev. Legend:** LIETUVOS DIDZIOJI KUNIGAIKSTYSTS

Date	Mintage	F	VF	XF	Unc	BU
2008 Proof	10,000	Value: 550				

KM# 166 100 LITU
7.7800 g., 0.9990 Gold 0.2499 oz. AGW, 22.3 mm. **Subject:** 1000th Anniversary of Name Lithuania **Obv:** Linear knight **Rev:** Timeline

Date	Mintage	F	VF	XF	Unc	BU
2009LMK Proof	10,000	Value: 550				

KM# 136 200 LITU
15.0000 g., Bi-Metallic .900 Gold 7.9g. center in a .925 Silver 7.1g. ring, 27 mm. **Subject:** 750th Anniversary - King Mindaugas **Obv:** Knight on horse **Obv. Legend:** LIETUVA **Rev:** Seated King **Rev. Legend:** MINDAUGO KARUNAVIMAS **Edge Lettering:** LIETUVOS KARALYSTE 1253

Date	Mintage	F	VF	XF	Unc	BU
2003 Proof	2,000	Value: 1,250				

KM# 146 500 LITU
31.1000 g., 0.9999 Gold 0.9997 oz. AGW, 32.5 mm. **Obv:** Knight on horse **Rev:** Palace **Edge:** Plain

Date	Mintage	F	VF	XF	Unc	BU
2005 Proof	1,000	Value: 2,000				

KM# 173 500 LITU
31.1000 g., 0.9990 Gold 0.9988 oz. AGW, 32.5 mm. **Subject:** Battle of Grunwald **Obv:** Shield around seated king **Rev:** Knights on horseback, warriors on foot

Date	Mintage	F	VF	XF	Unc	BU
2010 Proof	1,000	Value: 1,950				

MINT SETS

KM#	Date	Mintage	Identification	Issue Price	Mkt Val
MS4	2003 (6)	10,000	KM#106-108, 111-113	7.50	35.00
MS5	2008 (9)	4,000	KM#85-87 (dated 1991), 106-108, 111-113	30.00	30.00
MS6	2009 (9)	5,000	KM#85-87, 106-108, 111-113	—	30.00
MS7	2010 (7)	3,500	KM#106-108, 111-113 plus medal	—	35.00
MS8	2011 (7)	4,500	KM#106-108, 111-113 plus medal	—	25.00
MS9	2012 (7)	4,000	KM#106-108, 111-113 plus medal	—	25.00
MS10	2013 (7)	3,500	KM#106-108, 111-113 plus medal. Victorious battles of the Grand Duchy of Lithuania.	—	25.00
MS11	2013 (7)	3,500	KM#106-108, 111-113 plus medal. Transatlantic flight anniversary.	—	25.00

PROOF-LIKE SETS (PL)

KM#	Date	Mintage	Identification	Issue Price	Mkt Val
PL1	2008 (6)	200	KM#106-108, 111-113	—	115
PL2	2009 (6)	500	KM#106-108, 111-113	—	75.00

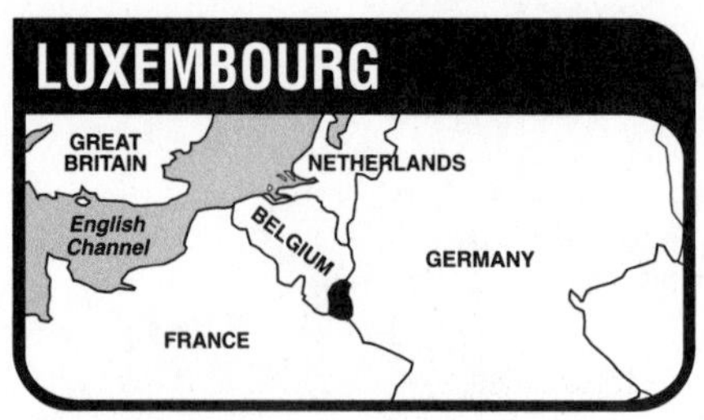

The Grand Duchy of Luxembourg is located in western Europe between Belgium, Germany and France, has an area of 1,103 sq. mi. (2,586 sq. km.) and a population of 377,100. Capital: Luxembourg. The economy is based on steel.

RULER
Henri, 2000-

MINT MARKS
A - Paris
(b) - Brussels, privy marks only
H – Gunzburg
(n) – lion - Namur
(u) - Utrecht, privy marks only

GRAND DUCHY

EURO COINAGE

European Economic Community Issues

KM# 75 EURO CENT
2.3000 g., Copper Plated Steel, 16.25 mm. **Ruler:** Henri **Obv:** Head right **Rev:** Value and globe **Edge:** Plain

Date	Mintage	F	VF	XF	Unc	BU
2002(u)	34,557,500	—	—	—	0.35	0.50
2002(u) Proof	1,500	Value: 3.00				
2003(u)	1,500,000	—	—	—	0.50	0.75
2003(u) Proof	1,500	Value: 3.00				
2004(u)	21,001,000	—	—	—	0.35	0.50
2004(u) Proof	1,500	Value: 3.00				
2005(u)	7,000,000	—	—	—	0.35	0.50
2005(u) Proof	1,500	Value: 3.00				
2006(u)	4,000,000	—	—	—	0.35	0.50
2006(u) Proof	2,000	Value: 4.00				
2007(a)	6,000,000	—	—	—	0.35	0.50
2007(a) Proof	2,500	Value: 4.00				
2008(a)	10,000,000	—	—	—	0.35	0.50
2008(a) Proof	2,500	Value: 4.00				
2009(u)	4,000,000	—	—	—	0.35	0.50
2009(u) Proof	2,500	Value: 4.00				
2010(u)	6,000,000	—	—	—	0.35	0.50
2010(u) Proof	1,500	Value: 4.00				
2011(u)	—	—	—	—	0.35	0.50
2011(u) Proof	1,500	Value: 4.00				
2012(u)	—	—	—	—	0.35	0.50
2012(u) Proof	—	Value: 4.00				

KM# 76 2 EURO CENT
3.0600 g., Copper Plated Steel, 18.75 mm. **Ruler:** Henri **Obv:** Head right **Rev:** Value and globe **Edge:** Grooved

Date	Mintage	F	VF	XF	Unc	BU
2002(u)	35,917,500	—	—	—	0.50	0.75
2002(u) Proof	1,500	Value: 5.00				
2003(u)	1,500,000	—	—	—	0.65	0.85
2003(u) Proof	1,500	Value: 5.00				
2004(u)	20,001,000	—	—	—	0.50	0.75
2004(u) Proof	1,500	Value: 5.00				
2005(u)	13,000,000	—	—	—	0.50	0.75
2005(u) Proof	1,500	Value: 5.00				
2006(u)	4,000,000	—	—	—	0.50	0.75
2006(u) Proof	2,000	Value: 6.00				
2007(a)	8,000,000	—	—	—	0.50	0.75
2007(a) Proof	2,500	Value: 6.00				
2008(a)	12,000,000	—	—	—	0.50	0.75
2008(a) Proof	2,500	Value: 6.00				
2009(u)	3,000,000	—	—	—	0.50	0.75
2009(u) Proof	2,500	Value: 6.00				
2010(u)	8,000,000	—	—	—	0.50	0.75
2010(u) Proof	1,500	Value: 6.00				
2011(u)	—	—	—	—	0.50	0.75
2011(u) Proof	1,500	Value: 6.00				
2012(u)	—	—	—	—	0.50	0.75
2012(u) Proof	—	Value: 6.00				

KM# 77 5 EURO CENT
3.9200 g., Copper Plated Steel, 21.25 mm. **Ruler:** Henri **Obv:** Head right **Rev:** Value and globe **Edge:** Plain

Date	Mintage	F	VF	XF	Unc	BU
2002(u)	28,917,500	—	—	—	0.75	1.00
2002(u) Proof	1,500	Value: 7.00				
2003(u)	4,500,000	—	—	—	1.00	1.25
2003(u) Proof	1,500	Value: 7.00				
2004(u)	16,001,000	—	—	—	0.75	1.00
2004(u) Proof	1,500	Value: 7.00				
2005(u)	6,000,000	—	—	—	0.75	1.00
2005(u) Proof	1,500	Value: 7.00				
2006(u)	5,000,000	—	—	—	0.75	1.00
2006(u) Proof	2,000	Value: 8.00				
2007(a)	5,000,000	—	—	—	0.75	1.00
2007(a) Proof	2,500	Value: 9.00				
2008(a)	9,000,000	—	—	—	0.75	1.00
2008(a) Proof	2,500	Value: 9.00				
2009(u)	6,000,000	—	—	—	0.75	1.00
2009(u) Proof	2,500	Value: 9.00				
2010(u)	6,000,000	—	—	—	0.75	1.00
2010(u) Proof	1,500	Value: 9.00				
2011(u)	—	—	—	—	0.75	1.00
2011(u) Proof	1,500	Value: 9.00				
2012(u)	—	—	—	—	0.75	1.00
2012(u) Proof	—	Value: 9.00				

KM# 78 10 EURO CENT
4.1000 g., Brass, 19.75 mm. **Ruler:** Henri **Obv:** Grand Duke's portrait **Rev:** Value and map **Edge:** Reeded

Date	Mintage	F	VF	XF	Unc	BU
2002(u)	25,117,500	—	—	—	0.75	—
2002(u) Proof	1,500	Value: 14.00				
2003(u)	1,500,000	—	—	—	1.00	—
2003(u) Proof	1,500	Value: 14.00				
2004(u)	12,001,000	—	—	—	0.75	—
2004(u) Proof	1,500	Value: 14.00				
2005(u)	2,000,000	—	—	—	0.75	—
2005(u) Proof	1,500	Value: 14.00				
2006(u)	4,000,000	—	—	—	0.75	—
2006(u) Proof	2,000	Value: 14.00				

KM# 89 10 EURO CENT
4.1000 g., Brass, 19.75 mm. **Ruler:** Henri **Obv:** Prince's portrait **Rev:** Relief map of Western Europe, stars, lines and value **Edge:** Reeded

Date	Mintage	F	VF	XF	Unc	BU
2007(a)	5,000,000	—	—	—	0.75	1.00
2007(a) Proof	2,500	Value: 14.00				
2008(a)	5,000,000	—	—	—	0.75	1.00
2008(a) Proof	2,500	Value: 14.00				
2009(u)	4,000,000	—	—	—	0.75	1.00
2009(u) Proof	2,500	Value: 14.00				
2010(u)	4,000,000	—	—	—	0.75	1.00
2010(u) Proof	1,500	Value: 14.00				
2011(u)	—	—	—	—	0.75	1.00
2011(u) Proof	1,500	Value: 14.00				
2012(u)	—	—	—	—	0.75	1.00
2012(u) Proof	—	Value: 14.00				

KM# 79 20 EURO CENT
5.7400 g., Brass, 22.25 mm. **Ruler:** Henri **Obv:** Grand Duke's portrait **Rev:** Value and map **Edge:** Notched

Date	Mintage	F	VF	XF	Unc	BU
2002(u)	25,717,500	—	—	—	1.00	—
2002(u) Proof	1,500	Value: 16.00				

Date	Mintage	F	VF	XF	Unc	BU
2003(u)	1,500,000	—	—	—	1.25	—
2003(u) Proof	1,500	Value: 16.00				
2004(u)	14,001,000	—	—	—	1.00	—
2004(u) Proof	1,500	Value: 16.00				
2005(u)	6,000,000	—	—	—	1.00	—
2005(u) Proof	1,500	Value: 16.00				
2006(u)	7,000,000	—	—	—	1.00	—
2006(u) Proof	2,000	Value: 16.00				

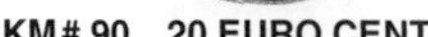

KM# 90 20 EURO CENT

5.7400 g., Brass, 22.25 mm. **Ruler:** Henri **Obv:** Prince's portrait **Rev:** Relief map of Western Europe, stars, lines and value **Edge:** Notched

Date	Mintage	F	VF	XF	Unc	BU
2007(a)	8,000,000	—	—	—	1.00	1.25
2007(a) Proof	2,500	Value: 16.00				
2008(a)	6,000,000	—	—	—	1.00	1.25
2008(a) Proof	2,500	Value: 16.00				
2009(u)	5,000,000	—	—	—	1.00	1.25
2009(u) Proof	2,500	Value: 16.00				
2010(u)	8,000,000	—	—	—	1.00	1.25
2010(u) Proof	1,500	Value: 16.00				
2011(u)	—	—	—	—	1.00	1.25
2011(u) Proof	1,500	Value: 16.00				
2012(u)	—	—	—	—	1.00	1.25
2012(u) Proof	—	Value: 16.00				

KM# 80 50 EURO CENT

7.8000 g., Brass, 24.25 mm. **Ruler:** Henri **Obv:** Grand Duke's portrait **Rev:** Value and map **Edge:** Reeded

Date	Mintage	F	VF	XF	Unc	BU
2002(u)	21,917,500	—	—	—	1.25	—
2002(u) Proof	1,500	Value: 18.00				
2003(u)	2,500,000	—	—	—	1.50	—
2003(u) Proof	1,500	Value: 18.00				
2004(u)	10,001,000	—	—	—	1.25	—
2004(u) Proof	1,500	Value: 18.00				
2005(u)	3,000,000	—	—	—	1.25	—
2005(u) Proof	1,500	Value: 18.00				
2006(u)	3,000,000	—	—	—	1.25	—
2006(u) Proof	2,000	Value: 18.00				

KM# 91 50 EURO CENT

7.8000 g., Brass, 24.25 mm. **Ruler:** Henri **Obv:** Prince's portrait **Rev:** Relief map of Western Europe, stars, lines and value **Edge:** Reeded

Date	Mintage	F	VF	XF	Unc	BU
2007(a)	4,000,000	—	—	—	1.25	1.50
2007(a) Proof	2,500	Value: 18.00				
2008(a)	4,000,000	—	—	—	1.25	1.50
2008(a) Proof	2,500	Value: 18.00				
2009(u)	2,000,000	—	—	—	1.25	1.50
2009(u) Proof	2,500	Value: 18.00				
2010(u)	5,000,000	—	—	—	1.25	1.50
2010(u) Proof	1,500	Value: 18.00				
2011(u)	—	—	—	—	1.25	1.50
2011(u) Proof	1,500	Value: 18.00				
2012(u)	—	—	—	—	1.25	1.50
2012(u) Proof	—	Value: 18.00				

KM# 81 EURO

7.5000 g., Bi-Metallic Copper-Nickel center in Nickel-Brass ring, 23.25 mm. **Ruler:** Henri **Obv:** Grand Duke's portrait **Rev:** Value and map within divided circle **Edge:** Segmented reeding

Date	Mintage	F	VF	XF	Unc	BU
2002(u)	21,318,525	—	—	—	2.50	—
2002(u) Proof	1,500	Value: 18.00				
2003(u)	1,500,000	—	—	—	2.75	—
2003(u) Proof	1,500	Value: 18.00				
2004(u)	9,001,000	—	—	—	2.50	—
2004(u) Proof	1,500	Value: 18.00				
2005(u)	2,000,000	—	—	—	2.50	—
2005(u) Proof	1,500	Value: 18.00				
2006(u)	1,000,000	—	—	—	2.50	—
2006(u) Proof	2,000	Value: 18.00				

KM# 92 EURO

7.5000 g., Bi-Metallic Copper-Nickel center in Nickel-Brass ring, 23.25 mm. **Ruler:** Henri **Obv:** Prince's portrait **Rev:** Relief map of Western Europe, stars, lines and value **Edge:** Segmented reeding

Date	Mintage	F	VF	XF	Unc	BU
2007(a)	480,000	—	—	—	2.25	2.75
2007(a) Proof	2,500	Value: 24.00				
2008(a)	480,000	—	—	—	2.25	2.75
2008(a) Proof	2,500	Value: 24.00				
2009(u)	240,000	—	—	—	2.25	2.75
2009(u) Proof	2,500	Value: 24.00				
2010(u)	1,000,000	—	—	—	2.25	2.75
2010(u) Proof	1,500	Value: 24.00				
2011(u)	—	—	—	—	2.25	2.75
2011(u) Proof	1,500	Value: 24.00				
2012(u)	—	—	—	—	2.25	2.75
2012(u) Proof	—	Value: 24.00				

KM# 82 2 EURO

8.5000 g., Bi-Metallic Nickel-Brass center in Copper-Nickel ring, 25.75 mm. **Ruler:** Henri **Obv:** Grand Duke's portrait **Rev:** Value and map within divided circle **Edge:** Reeded with 2's and stars

Date	Mintage	F	VF	XF	Unc	BU
2002(u)	18,517,500	—	—	—	3.75	—
2002(u) Proof	1,500	Value: 28.00				
2003(u)	3,500,000	—	—	—	4.50	—
2003(u) Proof	1,500	Value: 28.00				
2004(u)	7,553,200	—	—	—	4.00	—
2004(u) Proof	1,500	Value: 28.00				
2005(u)	3,500,000	—	—	—	4.00	—
2005(u) Proof	1,500	Value: 28.00				
2006(u)	2,000,000	—	—	—	4.00	—
2006(u) Proof	2,000	Value: 28.00				

KM# 85 2 EURO

8.5000 g., Bi-Metallic Nickel-Brass center in Copper-Nickel ring, 25.75 mm. **Ruler:** Henri **Obv:** Head right and crowned monogram within 1/2 star circle **Rev:** Value and map within divided circle **Edge:** Reeded with 2's and stars

Date	Mintage	F	VF	XF	Unc	BU
2004(u)	2,447,800	—	—	—	7.00	9.00
2004(u) Special Unc.	10,000	—	—	—	—	50.00
2004(u) Proof	4,000	Value: 50.00				

KM# 87 2 EURO

8.5000 g., Bi-Metallic Nickel-Brass center in Copper-Nickel ring, 25.75 mm. **Ruler:** Henri **Obv:** Conjoined heads right within circle **Rev:** Value and map within divided circle **Edge:** Reeded with 2's and stars

Date	Mintage	F	VF	XF	Unc	BU
2005	2,720,000	—	—	—	7.00	9.00
2005 Special Unc.	10,000	—	—	—	—	75.00
2005 Proof	4,000	Value: 50.00				

KM# 88 2 EURO

8.5000 g., Bi-Metallic Nickel-Brass center in Copper-Nickel ring, 25.75 mm. **Ruler:** Henri **Obv:** Conjoined heads right within circle and star border **Rev:** Value and map within divided circle **Edge:** Reeded with 2's and stars

Date	Mintage	F	VF	XF	Unc	BU
2006	1,030,000	—	—	—	7.00	9.00
2006 Special Unc.	15,000	—	—	—	—	32.00
2006 Proof	4,500	Value: 50.00				

KM# 93 2 EURO

8.5000 g., Bi-Metallic Nickel-Brass center in Copper-Nickel ring, 25.75 mm. **Ruler:** Henri **Obv:** Prince's portrait **Rev:** Relief map of Western Europe, stars, lines and value **Edge:** Reeded with 2's and stars

Date	Mintage	F	VF	XF	Unc	BU
2007(a)	4,000,000	—	—	—	4.00	5.00
2007(a) Proof	2,500	Value: 28.00				
2008(a)	6,000,000	—	—	—	4.00	5.00
2008(a) Proof	2,500	Value: 28.00				
2009(u)	240,000	—	—	—	6.00	7.50
2009(u) Proof	2,500	Value: 30.00				
2010(u)	3,500,000	—	—	—	4.00	5.00
2010(u) Proof	1,500	Value: 30.00				
2011(u)	—	—	—	—	4.00	5.00
2011(u) Proof	1,500	Value: 30.00				
2012(u)	—	—	—	—	4.00	5.00
2012(u) Proof	—	Value: 30.00				

KM# 94 2 EURO

8.5000 g., Bi-Metallic Nickel-Brass center in Copper-Nickel ring, 25.75 mm. **Ruler:** Henri **Subject:** 50th Anniversary Treaty of Rome **Obv:** Open treaty book with latent image on left hand page **Obv. Legend:** LËTZEBUERG **Rev:** Large value at left, modified outline of Europe at right **Edge:** Reeded with 2's and stars

Date	Mintage	F	VF	XF	Unc	BU
2007(a)	2,026,000	—	—	—	6.50	9.00
2007(a) Special Unc.	15,000	—	—	—	—	25.00
2007(a) Proof	5,000	Value: 30.00				

KM# 95 2 EURO

8.5000 g., Bi-Metallic Nickel-Brass center in Copper-Nickel ring, 25.75 mm. **Ruler:** Henri **Obv:** Palace in background at left, head 3/4 left at right **Obv. Legend:** LETZEBUERG **Rev:** Large value at left, modified outline of Europe at right **Edge:** Reeded with 2's and stars

Date	Mintage	F	VF	XF	Unc	BU
2007(a)	1,011,000	—	—	—	6.50	9.00
2007(a) Special Unc.	15,000	—	—	—	—	25.00
2007(a) Proof	5,000	Value: 40.00				

KM# 96 2 EURO
8.5000 g., Bi-Metallic Nickel-Brass center in Copper-Nickel ring, 25.75 mm. **Ruler:** Henri **Obv:** Head at left, Chateau de Berg at right **Obv. Legend:** LETZEBUERG **Rev:** Large value at left, modified outline of Europe at right **Edge:** Reeded with 2's and stars

Date	Mintage	F	VF	XF	Unc	BU
2008(a)	1,000,000	—	—	4.00	5.00	6.25
2008(a) Proof	5,000	Value: 15.00				
2008(a) Special Unc.	15,000	—	—	—	—	30.00

KM# 106 2 EURO
8.5000 g., Bi-Metallic Nickel-Brass center in Copper-Nickel ring, 25.75 mm. **Ruler:** Henri **Subject:** 90th Anniversary of Grand Duchess Charlotte **Obv:** Conjoined busts of Charlotte and Henri **Edge:** Reeded with 2's and stars

Date	Mintage	F	VF	XF	Unc	BU
2009	822,500	—	—	—	7.00	9.00
2009 Special Unc.	10,000	—	—	—	—	30.00
2009 Proof	2,500	Value: 15.00				

KM# 107 2 EURO
8.5000 g., Bi-Metallic Nickel-Brass center in Copper-Nickel ring, 25.75 mm. **Ruler:** Henri **Subject:** European Monetary Union - 10th Anniversary **Obv:** Alternating stick figure with Euro emblem design or Head of Grand-Duke **Edge:** Reeded with 2's and stars

Date	Mintage	F	VF	XF	Unc	BU
2009	812,500	—	—	—	5.00	6.00
2009 Special Unc.	10,000	—	—	—	—	30.00
2009 Proof	2,500	Value: 15.00				

KM# 115 2 EURO
8.5000 g., Bi-Metallic Nickel-Brass center in Copper-Nickel ring, 25.75 mm. **Ruler:** Henri **Obv:** Henry head facing, crowned shield **Rev:** Large value at left, modified outline mape of Europe at right **Edge:** Reeded with 2's and stars

Date	Mintage	F	VF	XF	Unc	BU
2010(a)	500,000	—	—	—	6.50	9.00
2010(a) Special Unc.	7,500	—	—	—	—	30.00
2010(a) Proof	1,500	Value: 20.00				

KM# 116 2 EURO
8.5000 g., Bi-Metallic Nickel-Brass center in Copper-Nickel ring, 25.75 mm. **Ruler:** Henri **Subject:** Jean of Luxembourg - Nassau, 50th Anniversary of his appointment as Grand Duke **Obv:** Conjoined head left of Charlotte, Jean and Henri **Edge:** Reeded with 2's and stars

Date	Mintage	F	VF	XF	Unc	BU
2011	707,500	—	—	—	7.00	9.00
2011 Special Unc.	7,500	—	—	—	—	30.00
2011 Proof	1,500	Value: 15.00				

KM# 119 2 EURO
8.5000 g., Bi-Metallic Nickel-Brass center in Copper-Nickel ring, 25.75 mm. **Ruler:** Henri **Subject:** Euro coinage, 10th Anniversary **Obv:** Euro symbol on globe, child-like rendering around

Date	Mintage	F	VF	XF	Unc	BU
2012	1,400,000	—	—	—	6.00	8.00

KM# 84 5 EURO
6.2200 g., 0.9990 Gold 0.1998 oz. AGW, 20 mm. **Ruler:** Henri **Subject:** European Central Bank **Obv:** Grand Duke Henri **Rev:** Building

Date	Mintage	F	VF	XF	Unc	BU
2003(u) Proof	20,000	Value: 375				

KM# 108 5 EURO
16.6000 g., Bi-Metallic Niobium center in .925 Silver ring, 34 mm. **Ruler:** Henri **Subject:** Vianden Castle **Obv:** Head right **Rev:** Castle view

Date	Mintage	F	VF	XF	Unc	BU
2009	7,500	—	—	—	—	150

KM# 109 5 EURO
Bi-Metallic Nordic Gold center in .925 Silver ring, 34 mm. **Ruler:** Henri **Subject:** Common Kestrel **Obv:** Head right **Rev:** Bird

Date	Mintage	F	VF	XF	Unc	BU
2009 Proof	3,000	Value: 60.00				

KM# 111 5 EURO
16.6000 g., Bi-Metallic Niobium center in .925 Silver ring, 34 mm. **Ruler:** Henri **Subject:** Chateau d'Esch-Sur-Sûre **Obv:** Head right **Rev:** Chateau view

Date	Mintage	F	VF	XF	Unc	BU
2010 Prooflike	3,000	—	—	—	—	100

KM# 112 5 EURO
Bi-Metallic Nordic Gold center in .925 Silver ring, 34 mm. **Ruler:** Henri **Subject:** Flora and Fauna - Arnica Montana **Obv:** Head right **Rev:** Flowers

Date	Mintage	F	VF	XF	Unc	BU
2010 Proof	3,000	Value: 50.00				

KM# 117 5 EURO
16.6000 g., Bi-Metallic Niobium center in .925 Silver ring, 34 mm. **Ruler:** Henri **Subject:** Mersch Castle **Obv:** Head right **Rev:** Castle vie

Date	Mintage	F	VF	XF	Unc	BU
2011 Prooflike	3,000	—	—	—	—	100

KM# 113 700 EURO CENTS
20.0000 g., 0.9250 Silver 0.5948 oz. ASW, 34 mm. **Ruler:** Henri **Subject:** 700th Anniversary - Marriage of John of Luxembourg

Date	Mintage	F	VF	XF	Unc	BU
2010 Proof	3,000	Value: 75.00				

KM# 97 10 EURO
3.1100 g., 0.9990 Gold 0.0999 oz. AGW, 25.71 mm. **Ruler:** Henri **Subject:** Culture **Obv:** Head right **Rev:** Hellenic sculpture head

Date	Mintage	F	VF	XF	Unc	BU
2004 Proof	5,000	Value: 200				

KM# 99 10 EURO
8.0000 g., Bi-Metallic Titanium center in .925 Silver ring, 26 mm. **Ruler:** Henri **Subject:** State Bank 150th Anniversary **Obv:** Head right **Rev:** Bank Plaza

Date	Mintage	F	VF	XF	Unc	BU
2006	7,500	—	—	—	—	150

KM# 101 10 EURO
3.1100 g., 0.9990 Gold 0.0999 oz. AGW, 16 mm. **Ruler:** Henri **Obv:** Head right **Rev:** Wild pig of Titelberg

Date	Mintage	F	VF	XF	Unc	BU
2006 Proof	5,000	Value: 200				

KM# 104 10 EURO
10.3700 g., 0.9990 Gold 0.3331 oz. AGW, 23 mm. **Ruler:** Henri **Subject:** Banque Central - 10th Anniversary **Obv:** Head right **Rev:** Old and new bank buildings

Date	Mintage	F	VF	XF	Unc	BU
2008 Proof	1,250	Value: 600				

KM# 110 10 EURO
3.1100 g., 0.9990 Gold 0.0999 oz. AGW, 16 mm. **Ruler:** Henri **Subject:** Deer of Orval's Refuge **Obv:** Head right **Rev:** Stag seated, flower in background

Date	Mintage	F	VF	XF	Unc	BU
2009 Proof	3,000	Value: 200				

KM# 114 10 EURO
13.5000 g., Bi-Metallic Titanium center in .925 Silver ring, 34 mm. **Ruler:** Henri **Subject:** Schengen Accord, 25th Anniversary **Obv:** Head right **Rev:** Building

Date	Mintage	F	VF	XF	Unc	BU
2010 Prooflike	3,000	—	—	—	—	125

KM# 118 10 EURO
16.1500 g., Bi-Metallic Nordic Gold center in .925 Silver ring, 34 mm. **Ruler:** Henri **Subject:** Flora and Fauna - Otter

Date	Mintage	F	VF	XF	Unc	BU
2011 Proof	3,000	Value: 50.00				

KM# 102 20 EURO
13.5000 g., Bi-Metallic Titanium center in .925 Silver ring, 34 mm. **Ruler:** Henri **Obv:** Three heads facing **Rev:** Council D'Etat building

Date	Mintage	F	VF	XF	Unc	BU
2006	4,000	—	—	—	—	120

KM# 83 25 EURO
22.8500 g., 0.9250 Silver 0.6795 oz. ASW, 37 mm. **Ruler:** Henri **Subject:** European Court System **Obv:** Grand Duke Henri **Rev:** Sword scale on law book

Date	Mintage	F	VF	XF	Unc	BU
2002(u) Proof	20,000	Value: 100				

KM# 86 25 EURO
22.8500 g., 0.9250 Silver 0.6795 oz. ASW, 37 mm. **Ruler:** Henri **Subject:** European Parliament **Obv:** Grand Duke Henri **Rev:** Parliament

Date	Mintage	F	VF	XF	Unc	BU
2004(u) Proof	20,000	Value: 100				

KM# 98 25 EURO
22.8000 g., 0.9250 Silver 0.6780 oz. ASW, 37 mm. **Ruler:** Henri **Subject:** EU Presidency **Obv:** Head right **Rev:** Conseil de l'Union building in Brussels

Date	Mintage	F	VF	XF	Unc	BU
2005 Proof	10,000	Value: 100				

KM# 100 25 EURO
22.8000 g., 0.9250 Silver 0.6780 oz. ASW, 37 mm. **Ruler:** Henri **Obv:** Head right **Rev:** European Commission building "Berlaymont" in Brussels

Date	Mintage	F	VF	XF	Unc	BU
2006 Proof	5,000	Value: 110				

KM# 103 25 EURO
22.8500 g., 0.9250 Silver 0.6795 oz. ASW, 37 mm. **Ruler:** Henri **Subject:** European Court of Auditors 30th Anniversary

Date	Mintage	F	VF	XF	Unc	BU
2007 Proof	3,000	Value: 80.00				

KM# 105 25 EURO
22.8500 g., 0.9250 Silver 0.6795 oz. ASW, 37 mm. **Ruler:** Henri **Subject:** European Investment Bank

Date	Mintage	F	VF	XF	Unc	BU
2008 Proof	4,000	Value: 275				

MINT SETS

KM#	Date	Mintage	Identification	Issue Price	Mkt Val
MS7	2002 (8)	35,000	KM#75-82	—	20.00
MS8	2002 (8)	—	KM#75-82	—	20.00
MS9	2003 (8)	50,000	KM#75-82, Adolph Brucke	—	30.00
MS10	2003 (8)	3,500	KM#75-82 plus stamps	—	75.00
MS11	2004 (8)	40,000	KM#75-82	—	50.00
MS12	2004 (8)	6,400	KM#75-82 plus stamps	—	50.00
MS13	2004 (8)	500	KM#75-82, Grand Duke	—	—
MS14	2004 (8)	500	KM#75-82, Ducal Palace	—	—
MS15	2005 (9)	20,000	KM#75-82, 87	40.00	65.00
MS16	2005 (8)	6,500	KM#75-82 plus stamps	—	55.00
MS17	2005 (8)	2,000	KM#75-82, Women and Myth, signed by Gastauer	—	75.00
MS18	2006 (9)	15,000	KM#75-82, 88	40.00	65.00
MS19	2006 (8)	2,000	KM#75-82 plus stamps	—	75.00
MS20	2007 (9)	11,000	KM#75-78, 89-93, 94	37.50	50.00
MS21	2008 (9)	10,000	KM#75-77, 89-93, 96	37.50	40.00
MS22	2009 (9)	10,000	KM#75-77, 89-93, 106	37.50	40.00
MS23	2010 (9)	7,500	KM#75-77, 89-93, 115	37.50	40.00
MS24	2011 (9)	7,500	KM#75-77, 89-93, 116	37.50	40.00

PROOF SETS

KM#	Date	Mintage	Identification	Issue Price	Mkt Val
PS2	2002 (8)	1,500	KM#75-82	100	300
PS3	2003 (8)	1,500	KM#75-82	100	300
PS4	2004 (9)	1,500	KM#75-82, 85	105	300
PS5	2005 (9)	1,500	KM#75-82, 87	105	250
PS6	2006 (9)	2,000	KM#75-82, 88	120	200
PS7	2007 (10)	2,500	KM#75-77, 89-95	125	200
PS8	2008 (9)	2,500	KM#75-77, 89-93, 96	125	250
PS9	2004-2008 (6)	2,500	KM#85, 87, 88, 94, 95, 96	105	200
PS10	2009 (10)	2,000	KM#75-77, 89-93, 106, 107	125	250
PS11	2010 (9)	2,500	KM#75-77, 89-93, 115	125	250
PS12	2011 (9)	1,500	KM#75-77, 89-93, 116	125	200

MACAU

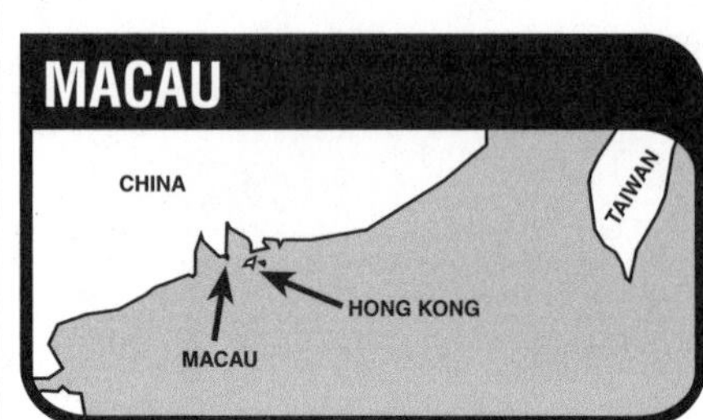

The Province of Macau, a Portuguese overseas province located in the South China Sea 40 miles southwest of Hong Kong, consists of the peninsula of Macau and the islands of Taipa and Coloane. It has an area of 6.2 sq. mi.(16 sq. km.) and a population of 500,000. Capital: Macau. Macau's economy is based on light industry, commerce, tourism, fishing, and gold trading - Macau is one of the entirely free markets for gold in the world. Cement, textiles, fireworks, vegetable oils, and metal products are exported.

In 1987, Portugal and China agreed that Macau would become a Chinese Territory in 1999. In December of 1999, Macau became a special administrative zone of China.

MINT MARKS
(p) - Pobjoy Mint
(s) - Singapore Mint

Pobjoy Mint

Singapore Mint

MONETARY SYSTEM
100 Avos = 1 Pataca

SPECIAL ADMINISTRATIVE REGION (S.A.R.)

STANDARD COINAGE

100 Avos = 1 Pataca

KM# 70 10 AVOS
1.3800 g., Brass, 17 mm. **Obv:** MACAU written at center with date below **Rev:** Crowned lion dance scene above value flanked by mint marks **Designer:** Justino Lei

Date	Mintage	F	VF	XF	Unc	BU
2005	—	—	—	—	0.75	1.25
2007	—	—	—	—	0.75	1.25

KM# 72 50 AVOS
4.5900 g., Brass, 23 mm. **Obv:** MACAU written across center of globe with date below **Rev:** The dragon dance led by a man **Designer:** Justino Lei

Date	Mintage	F	VF	XF	Unc	BU
2003	—	—	—	—	1.50	2.50
2005	—	—	—	—	1.50	2.50

KM# 57 PATACA
9.1800 g., Copper-Nickel, 25.98 mm. **Obv:** MACAU written across center of globe with date below **Rev:** Guia Fortress and Chapel of Our Lady of Guia **Edge:** Reeded **Designer:** Justino Lei

Date	Mintage	F	VF	XF	Unc	BU
2003	—	—	—	0.60	1.50	2.00
2005	—	—	—	0.60	1.50	2.00
2007	—	—	—	—	1.50	2.00

KM# 56 5 PATACAS
10.1000 g., Copper-Nickel **Obv:** MACAU written across center of globe with date below **Rev:** Chinese junk, ruins of St. Paul's Cathedral in background **Edge:** Plain **Shape:** 12-sided **Designer:** Justino Lei

Date	Mintage	F	VF	XF	Unc	BU
2003	—	—	—	—	6.50	10.00
2005	—	—	—	—	6.50	10.00
2007	—	—	—	—	6.50	10.00

KM# 153 10 PATACAS
0.3000 g., 0.9990 Gold 0.0096 oz. AGW, 7 mm. **Obv:** A Ma statue **Rev:** Lotus flower

Date	Mintage	F	VF	XF	Unc	BU
2009 Proof	Est. 5,000	Value: 25.00				

KM# 142 20 PATACAS
31.1050 g., 0.9990 Silver 0.9990 oz. ASW, 40.7 mm. **Subject:** Year of the Rat **Obv:** A Ma Temple **Rev:** Rat, multicolor flowers at right

Date	Mintage	F	VF	XF	Unc	BU
2008 Proof	6,000	Value: 130				

KM# 145 20 PATACAS
31.1050 g., 0.9990 Silver 0.9990 oz. ASW, 40.7 mm. **Subject:** Year of the Ox **Obv:** Moorish Barracks **Rev:** Ox, multicolor flowers at right

Date	Mintage	F	VF	XF	Unc	BU
2009 Proof	—	Value: 60.00				

KM# 151 20 PATACAS
31.1050 g., 0.9990 Silver 0.9990 oz. ASW, 40.7 mm. **Obv:** A Ma statue **Rev:** Lotus flower

Date	Mintage	F	VF	XF	Unc	BU
2009 Proof	Est. 5,600	Value: 75.00				

KM# 156 20 PATACAS
31.1050 g., 0.9990 Silver 0.9990 oz. ASW, 40.7 mm. **Subject:** Year of the Tiger **Rev:** Tiger in color

Date	Mintage	F	VF	XF	Unc	BU
2010 Proof	Est. 6,000	Value: 75.00				

KM# 159 20 PATACAS
31.1050 g., 0.9990 Silver 0.9990 oz. ASW, 40.7 mm. **Obv:** Rabbit in color **Rev:** Dom Pedro V theater

Date	Mintage	F	VF	XF	Unc	BU
2011 Proof	Est. 6,000	Value: 75.00				

KM# 162 20 PATACAS
28.2800 g., 0.9250 Silver 0.8410 oz. ASW, 40.7 mm. **Subject:** Year of the Dragon **Obv:** Dragon in color

Date	Mintage	F	VF	XF	Unc	BU
2012 Proof	—	Value: 150				

KM# 128 50 PATACAS
28.2800 g., 0.9250 Silver partially gilt 0.8410 oz. ASW **Subject:** 1st World Championship Grand Prix **Rev:** Two race cars - gilt

Date	Mintage	F	VF	XF	Unc	BU
2003 Proof	5,000	Value: 75.00				

KM# 154 50 PATACAS
1.2400 g., 0.9990 Gold 0.0398 oz. AGW, 13.92 mm. **Obv:** A Ma statue **Rev:** Lotus flower

Date	Mintage	F	VF	XF	Unc	BU
2009 Proof	Est. 5,000	Value: 90.00				

KM# 102 100 PATACAS
28.2800 g., 0.9250 Silver 0.8410 oz. ASW **Subject:** Year of the Snake **Obv:** Church façade **Rev:** Snake

Date	Mintage	F	VF	XF	Unc	BU
2001 Proof	4,000	Value: 55.00				

KM# 107 100 PATACAS
28.2800 g., 0.9250 Silver 0.8410 oz. ASW, 38.6 mm. **Subject:** Year of the Horse **Obv:** Church façade flanked by stars **Rev:** Horse above value **Edge:** Reeded

Date	Mintage	F	VF	XF	Unc	BU
2002 Proof	4,000	Value: 45.00				

KM# 122 100 PATACAS
28.2800 g., 0.9250 Silver 0.8410 oz. ASW **Subject:** 5th Anniversary Return of Macao to China

Date	Mintage	F	VF	XF	Unc	BU
2004 Proof	10,000	Value: 60.00				

KM# 130 100 PATACAS
28.2800 g., 0.9250 Silver 0.8410 oz. ASW **Series:** Lunar **Subject:** Year of the Monkey

Date	Mintage	F	VF	XF	Unc	BU
2004	1,000	—	—	—	—	60.00
2004 Proof	4,000	Value: 75.00				

KM# 134 100 PATACAS
28.2800 g., 0.9250 Silver 0.8410 oz. ASW **Series:** Lunar **Subject:** Year of the Rooster **Rev:** Stylized rooster walking left

Date	Mintage	F	VF	XF	Unc	BU
2005 Proof	—	Value: 90.00				

KM# 137 100 PATACAS
28.2800 g., 0.9250 Silver 0.8410 oz. ASW **Subject:** IV East Asian Games - FRIENDSHIP

Date	Mintage	F	VF	XF	Unc	BU
2005 Proof	6,000	Value: 75.00				

KM# 139 100 PATACAS
28.2800 g., 0.9250 Silver 0.8410 oz. ASW **Series:** Lunar **Subject:** Year of the Dog **Rev:** Stylized dog standing left

Date	Mintage	F	VF	XF	Unc	BU
2006 Proof	—	Value: 90.00				

KM# 148 100 PATACAS
31.1050 g., 0.9250 Silver 0.9250 oz. ASW, 40 mm. **Subject:** Year of the Pig **Rev:** Pig in color

Date	Mintage	F	VF	XF	Unc	BU
2007 Proof	Est. 15,000	Value: 90.00				

KM# 143 100 PATACAS
155.5000 g., 0.9990 Silver 4.9942 oz. ASW, 65 mm. **Subject:** Year of the Rat **Obv:** A Ma Temple **Rev:** Rat, multicolor flowers at right **Note:** Illustration reduced.

Date	Mintage	F	VF	XF	Unc	BU
2008 Proof	500	Value: 250				

KM# 146 100 PATACAS
155.5000 g., 0.9990 Silver 4.9942 oz. ASW, 65 mm. **Subject:** Year of the Ox **Obv:** Moorish Barracks **Rev:** Ox, multicolor flowers at right **Note:** Illustration reduced.

Date	Mintage	F	VF	XF	Unc	BU
2009 Proof	500	Value: 250				

KM# 152 100 PATACAS
155.5000 g., 0.9990 Silver 4.9942 oz. ASW, 65 mm. **Obv:** A Ma statue **Rev:** Lotus flower

Date	Mintage	F	VF	XF	Unc	BU
2009 Proof	Est. 1,000	Value: 275				

KM# 157 100 PATACAS
155.5000 g., 0.9990 Silver 4.9942 oz. ASW, 65 mm. **Subject:** Year of the Tiger **Rev:** Tiger in color

Date	Mintage	F	VF	XF	Unc	BU
2010 Proof	Est. 500	Value: 450				

KM# 160 100 PATACAS
155.5000 g., 0.9990 Silver 4.9942 oz. ASW, 65 mm. **Subject:** Year of the Rabbit **Obv:** Rabbit in color **Rev:** Dom Pedro V theater

Date	Mintage	F	VF	XF	Unc	BU
2011 Proof	500	Value: 400				

KM# 163 100 PATACAS
155.5000 g., 0.9990 Silver 4.9942 oz. ASW, 65 mm. **Subject:** Year of the Dragon **Obv:** Dragon in color

Date	Mintage	F	VF	XF	Unc	BU
2012 Proof	—	Value: 750				

KM# 123 200 PATACAS
28.2800 g., 0.9250 Silver partially gilt. 0.8410 oz. ASW **Subject:** 5th Anniversary Return of Macao to China

Date	Mintage	F	VF	XF	Unc	BU
2004 Proof	10,000	Value: 75.00				

KM# 138 200 PATACAS
28.2800 g., 0.9250 Silver partially gilt 0.8410 oz. ASW **Subject:** IV East Asian Games **Rev:** U-N-I-T-Y in blocks at left - bottom. logo at upper right

Date	Mintage	F	VF	XF	Unc	BU
2005 Proof	6,000	Value: 120				

KM# 103 250 PATACAS
3.9900 g., 0.9167 Gold 0.1176 oz. AGW **Subject:** Year of the Snake **Obv:** Church façade **Rev:** Snake

Date	Mintage	F	VF	XF	Unc	BU
2001 Proof	2,500	Value: 240				

KM# 108 250 PATACAS
3.9900 g., 0.9167 Gold 0.1176 oz. AGW, 19.3 mm. **Subject:** Year of the Horse **Obv:** Church of St. Paul façade **Rev:** Horse above value **Edge:** Reeded

Date	Mintage	F	VF	XF	Unc	BU
2002 Proof	2,500	Value: 240				

KM# 119 250 PATACAS
3.9900 g., 0.9167 Gold 0.1176 oz. AGW, 19.3 mm. **Subject:** Year of the Goat **Obv:** Church façade **Rev:** Goat above value **Edge:** Reeded

Date	Mintage	F	VF	XF	Unc	BU
2003 Proof	2,500	Value: 240				

KM# 131 250 PATACAS
3.9900 g., 0.9167 Gold 0.1176 oz. AGW **Series:** Lunar **Subject:** Year of the Monkey

Date	Mintage	F	VF	XF	Unc	BU
2004 Proof	2,500	Value: 280				

KM# 135 250 PATACAS
2.8300 g., 0.9990 Gold 0.0909 oz. AGW **Series:** Lunar **Subject:** Year of the Rooster **Rev:** Stylized rooster walking left

Date	Mintage	F	VF	XF	Unc	BU
2005 Proof	—	Value: 280				

KM# 140 250 PATACAS
3.1100 g., 0.9990 Gold 0.0999 oz. AGW **Series:** Lunar **Subject:** Year of the Dog **Rev:** Stylized dog standing left - multicolor

Date	Mintage	F	VF	XF	Unc	BU
2006 Proof	—	Value: 280				

KM# 149 250 PATACAS
3.1100 g., 0.9990 Gold 0.0999 oz. AGW, 18 mm. **Subject:** Year of the Pig **Rev:** Pig in color

Date	Mintage	F	VF	XF	Unc	BU
2007 Proof	Est. 7,000	Value: 220				

KM# 144 250 PATACAS
7.7900 g., 0.9990 Gold 0.2502 oz. AGW **Subject:** Year of the Rat **Obv:** Temple **Rev:** Rat and multicolor flowers at right

Date	Mintage	F	VF	XF	Unc	BU
2008 Proof	—	Value: 525				

KM# 147 250 PATACAS
7.7700 g., 0.9990 Gold 0.2496 oz. AGW **Subject:** Year of the Ox **Obv:** Moorish Barracks **Rev:** Ox, multicolor flowers at right

Date	Mintage	F	VF	XF	Unc	BU
2009 Proof	—	Value: 550				

KM# 155 250 PATACAS
7.7800 g., 0.9990 Gold 0.2499 oz. AGW, 22 mm. **Obv:** A Ma statue **Rev:** Lotus flower

Date	Mintage	F	VF	XF	Unc	BU
2009 Proof	Est. 1,600	Value: 550				

KM# 158 250 PATACAS
7.7800 g., 0.9990 Gold 0.2499 oz. AGW, 22 mm. **Subject:** Year of the Tiger **Rev:** Tiger in color

Date	Mintage	F	VF	XF	Unc	BU
2010 Proof	Est. 3,000	Value: 700				

KM# 161 250 PATACAS
7.7800 g., 0.9990 Gold 0.2499 oz. AGW, 22 mm. **Subject:** Year of the Rabbit **Obv:** Rabbit in color **Rev:** Dom Pedro V theater

Date	Mintage	F	VF	XF	Unc	BU
2011(s) Proof	Est. 3,000	Value: 700				

KM# 104 500 PATACAS
7.9900 g., 0.9167 Gold 0.2355 oz. AGW **Subject:** Year of the Snake **Obv:** Church façade **Rev:** Snake

Date	Mintage	F	VF	XF	Unc	BU
2001 Proof	2,500	Value: 550				

KM# 109 500 PATACAS
7.9800 g., 0.9167 Gold 0.2352 oz. AGW, 22.05 mm. **Subject:** Year of the Horse **Obv:** Church façade **Rev:** Horse above value **Edge:** Reeded

Date	Mintage	F	VF	XF	Unc	BU
2002 Proof	2,500	Value: 550				

KM# 120 500 PATACAS
7.9800 g., 0.9167 Gold 0.2352 oz. AGW, 22 mm. **Subject:** Year of the Goat **Obv:** Church façade **Rev:** Goat above value **Edge:** Reeded

Date	Mintage	F	VF	XF	Unc	BU
2003 Proof	2,500	Value: 550				

KM# 129 500 PATACAS
7.9600 g., 0.9167 Gold 0.2346 oz. AGW **Subject:** 1st World Championship Grand Prix **Rev:** Two race cars

Date	Mintage	F	VF	XF	Unc	BU
2003 Proof	2,000	Value: 550				

KM# 124 500 PATACAS
62.2060 g., 0.9990 Silver partially gilt 1.9979 oz. ASW **Subject:** 5th Anniversary Return of Macao to China

Date	Mintage	F	VF	XF	Unc	BU
2004 Proof	1,000	Value: 120				

KM# 132 500 PATACAS
7.9800 g., 0.9167 Gold 0.2352 oz. AGW **Series:** Lunar **Subject:** Year of the Monkey

Date	Mintage	F	VF	XF	Unc	BU
2004 Proof	2,500	Value: 525				

KM# 136 500 PATACAS
7.9600 g., 0.9990 Gold 0.2557 oz. AGW **Series:** Lunar **Subject:** Year of the Rooster **Rev:** Stylized rooster walking left

Date	Mintage	F	VF	XF	Unc	BU
2005 Proof	—	Value: 550				

KM# 141 500 PATACAS
7.9600 g., 0.9990 Gold 0.2557 oz. AGW **Series:** Lunar **Subject:** Year of the Dog **Rev:** Stylized dog standing left

Date	Mintage	F	VF	XF	Unc	BU
2006 Proof	—	Value: 550				

KM# 150 500 PATACAS
7.9600 g., 0.9990 Gold 0.2557 oz. AGW, 22 mm. **Subject:** Year of the Pig **Rev:** Pig in color

Date	Mintage	F	VF	XF	Unc	BU
2007 Proof	Est. 4,000	Value: 600				

KM# 164 500 PATACAS
7.7800 g., 0.9990 Gold 0.2499 oz. AGW, 22 mm. **Subject:** Year of the Dragon **Obv:** Dragon in color

Date	Mintage	F	VF	XF	Unc	BU
2012 Proof	—	Value: 950				

KM# 105 1000 PATACAS
16.9760 g., 0.9167 Gold 0.5003 oz. AGW **Subject:** Year of the Snake **Obv:** Church façade flanked by stars **Rev:** Snake

Date	Mintage	F	VF	XF	Unc	BU
2001 Proof	4,000	Value: 1,000				

KM# 110 1000 PATACAS
15.9700 g., 0.9167 Gold 0.4707 oz. AGW, 28.4 mm. **Subject:** Year of the Horse **Obv:** Church façade **Rev:** Horse above value **Edge:** Reeded

Date	Mintage	F	VF	XF	Unc	BU
2002 Proof	4,000	Value: 1,000				

KM# 118 1000 PATACAS
28.2800 g., 0.9250 Silver 0.8410 oz. ASW, 38.6 mm. **Subject:** Year of the Goat **Obv:** Church façade **Rev:** Goat above value **Edge:** Reeded

Date	Mintage	F	VF	XF	Unc	BU
2003 Proof	4,000	Value: 45.00				

KM# 121 1000 PATACAS
15.9760 g., 0.9170 Gold 0.4710 oz. AGW **Subject:** Year of the Goat **Obv:** Church façade flanked by stars **Rev:** Goat above value **Edge:** Reeded

Date	Mintage	F	VF	XF	Unc	BU
2003 Proof	4,000	Value: 1,000				

KM# 125 1000 PATACAS
155.5150 g., 0.9990 Silver 4.9947 oz. ASW **Subject:** 5th Anniversary Return of Macao to China

Date	Mintage	F	VF	XF	Unc	BU
2004 Proof	3,000	Value: 310				

KM# 133 1000 PATACAS
15.9800 g., 0.9167 Gold 0.4710 oz. AGW **Series:** Lunar **Subject:** Year of the Monkey

Date	Mintage	F	VF	XF	Unc	BU
2004	500	—	—	—	950	—
2004 Proof	4,000	Value: 1,000				

KM# 126 2000 PATACAS
155.5150 g., 0.9990 Silver partially gilt 4.9947 oz. ASW **Subject:** 5th Anniversary Return of Macao to China

Date	Mintage	F	VF	XF	Unc	BU
2004 Proof	1,500	Value: 300				

PROOF SETS

KM#	Date	Mintage	Identification	Issue Price	Mkt Val
PS16	2001 (3)	2,500	KM#103-105	849	1,800
PS17	2002 (3)	4,000	KM#108-110	849	1,800
PS18	2003 (3)	2,500	KM#119-121	849	1,800
PS19	2004 (4)	—	KM#130-133	—	2,000
PS20	2005 (3)	—	KM#134-136	—	925
PS21	2006 (3)	—	KM#139-141	—	925
PS22	2007 (3)	—	KM#148-150	—	925
PS23	2008 (3)	—	KM#142-144	—	925
PS24	2009 (3)	—	KM#145-147	—	875
PS25	2010 (3)	—	KM#156-158	—	1,225
PS26	2011 (3)	—	KM#159-161	—	1,175
PS27	2012 (3)	—	KM#162-164	—	1,850

The Republic of Macedonia is land-locked, and is bordered in the north by Yugoslavia, to the east by Bulgaria, in the south by Greece and to the west by Albania and has an area of 9,781 sq. mi. (25,713 sq. km.) and a population at the 1991 census was 2,038,847, of which the predominating ethnic groups were Macedonians. The capital is Skopje.

On Nov. 20, 1991 parliament promulgated a new constitution, and declared its independence on Nov.20, 1992, but failed to secure EC and US recognition owing to Greek objections to use of the name *Macedonia.* On Dec. 11, 1992, the UN Security Council authorized the expedition of a small peacekeeping force to prevent hostilities spreading into Macedonia.

There is a 120-member single-chamber National Assembly.

REPUBLIC

STANDARD COINAGE

KM# 2 DENAR

5.1500 g., Brass, 23.7 mm. **Obv:** Macedonian sheepdog **Obv. Legend:** РЕПУБЛИКА МАКЕДОНИЈА **Rev:** Radiant value **Edge:** Plain

Date	Mintage	F	VF	XF	Unc	BU
2001	12,874,000	—	0.20	0.35	1.50	4.00
2006	—	—	—	—	1.25	3.75
2008	—	—	—	—	1.25	3.75

KM# 3 2 DENARI

5.1500 g., Brass, 23.7 mm. **Obv:** Trout above water **Obv. Legend:** РЕПУБЛИКА МАКЕДОНИЈА **Rev:** Radiant value **Edge:** Plain

Date	Mintage	F	VF	XF	Unc	BU
2001	11,672,000	—	—	0.50	1.25	3.00
2006	—	—	—	0.50	1.00	2.50
2008	—	—	—	—	1.00	2.50

KM# 4 5 DENARI

7.2500 g., Brass, 27.5 mm. **Obv:** European lynx **Obv. Legend:** РЕПУБЛИКА МАКЕДОНИЈА **Rev:** Radiant value **Edge:** Plain

Date	Mintage	F	VF	XF	Unc	BU
2001	6,921,000	—	0.35	0.75	1.75	3.50
2006	—	—	—	—	1.50	3.00
2008	—	—	—	—	1.50	3.00

KM# 13 10 DENARI

10.0000 g., 0.9160 Gold 0.2945 oz. AGW, 27 mm. **Subject:** 10th Anniversary of Independence **Obv:** Value in circle within radiant map **Rev:** Grape vine

Date	Mintage	F	VF	XF	Unc	BU
2001	1,000	—	—	—	550	575

KM# 31 10 DENARI

6.6000 g., Copper-Nickel-Zinc, 24.5 mm. **Obv:** Peacock **Rev:** Value within rays

Date	Mintage	F	VF	XF	Unc	BU
2008	—	—	—	—	—	2.00

KM# 32 50 DENARI

7.7000 g., Brass, 26.5 mm. **Obv:** Classical female bust right **Rev:** Value within rays

Date	Mintage	F	VF	XF	Unc	BU
2008	—	—	—	—	—	2.00

KM# 22 60 DENARI

6.0000 g., 0.9160 Gold 0.1767 oz. AGW, 23.8 mm. **Subject:** 100th Anniversary - Statehood **Obv:** Monument above value within circle **Rev:** Djorce Petrov

Date	Mintage	F	VF	XF	Unc	BU
2003	500	—	—	—	375	400

KM# 23 60 DENARI

6.0000 g., 0.9160 Gold 0.1767 oz. AGW, 23.8 mm. **Subject:** 100th Anniversary - Statehood **Obv:** Monument above value within circle **Rev:** Krste Petkov-Misirkov

Date	Mintage	F	VF	XF	Unc	BU
2003	500	—	—	—	375	400

KM# 24 60 DENARI

6.0000 g., 0.9160 Gold 0.1767 oz. AGW, 23.8 mm. **Subject:** 100th Anniversary - Statehood **Obv:** Monument above value within circle **Rev:** Metodije Andonov

Date	Mintage	F	VF	XF	Unc	BU
2003	500	—	—	—	375	400

KM# 25 60 DENARI

6.0000 g., 0.9160 Gold 0.1767 oz. AGW, 23.8 mm. **Subject:** 100th Anniversary - Statehood **Obv:** Monument above value within circle **Rev:** Mihailo Apostolski

Date	Mintage	F	VF	XF	Unc	BU
2003	500	—	—	—	375	400

KM# 26 60 DENARI

6.0000 g., 0.9160 Gold 0.1767 oz. AGW, 23.8 mm. **Subject:** 100th Anniversary - Statehood **Obv:** Monument above value within circle **Rev:** Blaze Koneski

Date	Mintage	F	VF	XF	Unc	BU
2003	500	—	—	—	375	400

KM# 21 60 DENARI

8.0000 g., 0.9160 Gold 0.2356 oz. AGW, 23.8 mm. **Subject:** 50th Anniversary of separation from Greece **Obv:** The Monifest **Rev:** Monastery

Date	Mintage	F	VF	XF	Unc	BU
2004	500	—	—	—	425	450

KM# 14 100 DENARI

6.0000 g., 0.9160 Gold 0.1767 oz. AGW, 23.8 mm. **Subject:** 100th Anniversary of Statehood **Obv:** Monument above value within circle **Rev:** Cherry tree cannon divides circle

Date	Mintage	F	VF	XF	Unc	BU
2003 Proof	500	Value: 400				

KM# 15 100 DENARI

6.0000 g., 0.9160 Gold 0.1767 oz. AGW, 23.8 mm. **Subject:** 100th Anniversary of Statehood - Goce Delcev **Obv:** Monument above value within circle **Rev:** Bust facing within circle

Date	Mintage	F	VF	XF	Unc	BU
2003 Proof	500	Value: 400				

KM# 16 100 DENARI

6.0000 g., 0.9160 Gold 0.1767 oz. AGW, 23.8 mm. **Subject:** 100th Anniversary of Statehood - Pitu Guli **Obv:** Monument above value within circle **Rev:** Head with hat facing within circle

Date	Mintage	F	VF	XF	Unc	BU
2003 Proof	500	Value: 400				

KM# 17 100 DENARI

6.0000 g., 0.9160 Gold 0.1767 oz. AGW, 23.8 mm. **Subject:** 100th Anniversary of Statehood - Jane Sandanski **Obv:** Monument above value within circle **Rev:** Head facing within circle

Date	Mintage	F	VF	XF	Unc	BU
2003 Proof	500	Value: 400				

KM# 18 100 DENARI

6.0000 g., 0.9160 Gold 0.1767 oz. AGW, 23.8 mm. **Subject:** 100th Anniversary of Statehood - Dame Gruev **Obv:** Monument above value within circle **Rev:** Bust left within circle

Date	Mintage	F	VF	XF	Unc	BU
2003 Proof	500	Value: 400				

KM# 19 100 DENARI

6.0000 g., 0.9160 Gold 0.1767 oz. AGW, 23.8 mm. **Subject:** 100th Anniversary of Statehood - Nikola Karev **Obv:** Monument above value within circle **Rev:** Bust right within circle

Date	Mintage	F	VF	XF	Unc	BU
2003 Proof	500	Value: 400				

KM# 28 100 DENARI

6.0000 g., 0.9160 Gold 0.1767 oz. AGW **Subject:** 100th Anniversary of Statehood - Djorce Petrov **Obv:** Monument **Rev:** Bust facing

Date	Mintage	F	VF	XF	Unc	BU
2003 Proof	500	Value: 400				

KM# 29 100 DENARI

6.0000 g., 0.9160 Gold 0.1767 oz. AGW **Subject:** 100th Anniversary of Statehood - Krste Petkov-Misirkov **Obv:** Monument **Rev:** Bust facing

Date	Mintage	F	VF	XF	Unc	BU
2003 Proof	500	Value: 400				

KM# 30 100 DENARI

6.0000 g., 0.9160 Gold 0.1767 oz. AGW **Subject:** 100th Anniversary of statehood - Metodije Adamov-Cengo **Obv:** Monument **Rev:** Bust facing

Date	Mintage	F	VF	XF	Unc	BU
2003 Proof	500	Value: 400				

KM# 33 100 DENARI

6.0000 g., 0.9160 Gold 0.1767 oz. AGW, 23.8 mm. **Subject:** 100th Anniversary of Statehood - Mihailo Apostolski **Obv:** Monument **Rev:** Bust facing in field cap

Date	Mintage	F	VF	XF	Unc	BU
2003 Proof	500	Value: 400				

KM# 34 100 DENARI

6.0000 g., 0.9160 Gold 0.1767 oz. AGW, 23.8 mm. **Subject:** 100th Anniversary of Statehood - Blaze Koneski **Obv:** Monument **Rev:** Bust facing, wearing glasses

Date	Mintage	F	VF	XF	Unc	BU
2003 Proof	500	Value: 400				

PATTERNS

(Including off-metal strikes)

KM#	Date	Mintage	Identification	Mkt Val
Pn1	2003	50	100 Denari. 0.9250 Silver. 7.0000 g. KM#14	150
Pn2	2003	50	100 Denari. 0.9260 Silver. 7.0000 g. KM#15.	150
Pn3	2003	50	100 Denari. 0.9250 Silver. 7.0000 g. KM#16.	150
Pn4	2003	50	100 Denari. 0.9250 Silver. 7.0000 g. KM#17.	150
Pn5	2003	50	100 Denari. 0.9250 Silver. 7.0000 g. KM#18.	150
Pn6	2003	50	100 Denari. 0.9250 Silver. 7.0000 g. KM#19.	150
Pn7	2003	50	100 Denari. 0.9250 Silver. 7.0000 g.	150
Pn8	2003	50	100 Denari. 0.9250 Silver. 7.0000 g. KM#29.	150
Pn9	2003	50	100 Denari. 0.9250 Silver. 7.0000 g. KM#30.	150
Pn10	2003	50	100 Denari. 0.9250 Silver. 7.0000 g. KM#33.	150
Pn11	2003	50	100 Denari. 0.9250 Silver. 7.0000 g.	100

MADAGASCAR

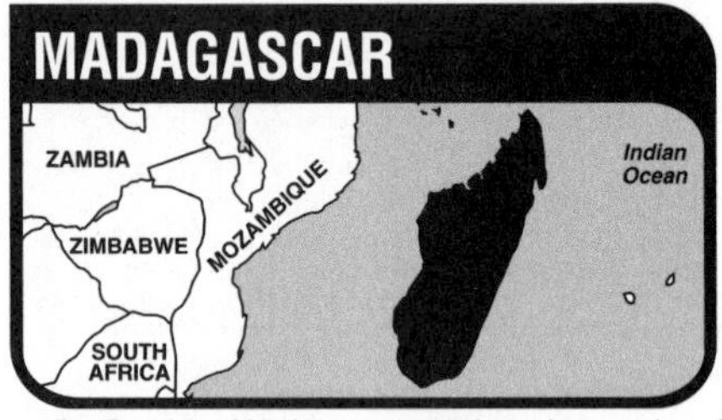

The Republic of Madagascar, an independent member of the French Community located in the Indian Ocean 250 miles (402 km.) off the southeast coast of Africa, has an area of 226,656 sq. mi. (587,040 sq. km.) and a population of 10 million. Capital: Antananarivo. The economy is primarily agricultural; large bauxite deposits are being developed. Coffee, vanilla, graphite, and rice are exported.

MONETARY SYSTEM

100 Centimes = 1 Franc

MINT MARKS

(a) - Paris, privy marks only

SA - Pretoria

MALAGASY REPUBLIC

STANDARD COINAGE

1 Ariary = 100 Iraimbilanja

KM# 8 FRANC

2.4000 g., Stainless Steel **Obv:** Poinsettia **Rev:** Value within horns of ox head above sprigs

Date	Mintage	F	VF	XF	Unc	BU
2002(a)	—	0.15	0.20	0.40	1.45	—

MADAGASIKARA REPUBLIC

STANDARD COINAGE

1 Ariary = 100 Iraimbilanja

KM# 28 10 FRANCS (2 Ariary)

4.3400 g., Bronze (Red To Yellow), 21.9 mm. **Obv:** Monkey **Obv. Legend:** BANKY FOIBEN'I MADAGASIKARA **Rev:** Value within steer horns flanked by sprigs **Edge:** Plain

Date	Mintage	F	VF	XF	Unc	BU
2003	—	—	—	1.00	2.50	3.50

KM# 29 ARIARY

4.9300 g., Stainless Steel, 22 mm. **Obv:** Flower **Obv. Legend:** BANKY FOIBEN'I MADAGASIKARA **Rev:** Value within steer horns above sprigs **Edge:** Plain

Date	Mintage	F	VF	XF	Unc	BU
2004(a)	—	—	—	0.90	2.25	3.00

KM# 30 2 ARIARY

3.2300 g., Copper Plated Steel, 21 mm. **Obv:** Plant **Obv. Legend:** BANKY FOIBEN'I MADAGASIKARA **Rev:** Value within steer horns flanked by sprigs **Edge:** Reeded

Date	Mintage	F	VF	XF	Unc	BU
2003	—	—	—	0.90	2.25	3.00

KM# 25.2 50 ARIARY

10.1500 g., Stainless Steel, 30 mm. **Obv:** Star above value within sprays **Rev:** Avenue of the Baobabs **Rev. Inscription:** Motto C **Edge:** Plain **Shape:** 11-sided

Date	Mintage	F	VF	XF	Unc	BU
2005	—	—	—	2.40	6.00	—

MALAWI

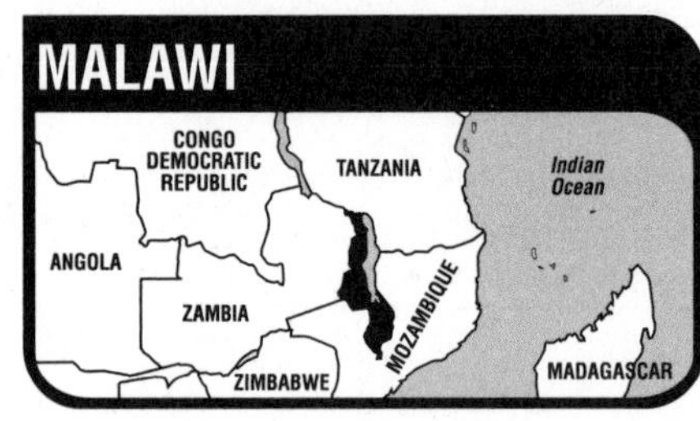

The Republic of Malawi (formerly Nyasaland), located in southeastern Africa to the west of Lake Malawi (Nyasa), has an area of 45,745 sq. mi. (118,480 sq. km.) and a population of 7 million. Capital: Lilongwe. The economy is predominantly agricultural. Tobacco, tea, peanuts and cotton are exported.

REPUBLIC

DECIMAL COINAGE

100 Tambala = 1 Kwacha

KM# 33a TAMBALA

Copper Plated Steel, 17.3 mm. **Obv:** Arms with supporters **Rev:** 2 Talapia fish **Edge:** Plain

Date	Mintage	F	VF	XF	Unc	BU
2003	—	—	—	—	1.00	1.50

KM# 34a 2 TAMBALA

Copper Plated Steel, 20.3 mm. **Obv:** Arms with supporters **Rev:** Paradise whydah bird divides date and value, designer's initials "P.V." **Edge:** Plain

Date	Mintage	F	VF	XF	Unc	BU
2003	—	—	—	—	1.00	1.50

KM# 32.2 5 TAMBALA

Nickel Plated Steel, 19.35 mm. **Obv:** Arms with supporters **Rev:** Purple heron, value, designer's initials "P.V."

Date	Mintage	F	VF	XF	Unc	BU
2003	—	—	—	—	2.50	3.00

KM# 27 10 TAMBALA

5.6200 g., Nickel Plated Steel, 23.6 mm. **Obv:** Bust right **Rev:** Bundled corn cobs divide date and value

Date	Mintage	F	VF	XF	Unc	BU
2003	—	—	—	—	2.25	3.00

KM# 29 20 TAMBALA

7.5200 g., Nickel Clad Steel, 26.5 mm. **Obv:** Bust right **Rev:** Elephants

Date	Mintage	F	VF	XF	Unc	BU
2003	—	—	—	—	3.75	4.50

KM# 30 50 TAMBALA

4.4000 g., Brass Plated Steel, 22 mm. **Obv:** Bust right **Rev:** Arms with supporters **Shape:** 7-sided

Date	Mintage	F	VF	XF	Unc	BU
2003	—	—	—	—	4.50	5.00
2004	—	—	—	—	4.50	5.00

KM# 66 50 TAMBALA

4.4000 g., Brass Plated Steel, 22 mm. **Obv:** State arms and supporters with country name below **Rev:** Zebras with date above and value below **Shape:** 7-sided

Date	Mintage	F	VF	XF	Unc	BU
2004	—	—	—	—	4.50	5.00

KM# 28 KWACHA

9.0000 g., Brass Plated Steel, 26 mm. **Obv:** Bust right **Rev:** Fish eagle

Date	Mintage	F	VF	XF	Unc	BU
2003	—	—	—	—	7.00	10.00

KM# 65 KWACHA

Brass Plated Steel, 26 mm. **Obv:** State arms, country name **Rev:** Fish eagle, date

Date	Mintage	F	VF	XF	Unc	BU
2004	—	—	—	—	2.50	3.50

KM# 201 KWACHA

31.1050 g., 0.9990 Silver 0.9990 oz. ASW, 47x27 mm. **Rev:** Impalla

Date	Mintage	F	VF	XF	Unc	BU
2009 Proof	100	—	—	—	—	—

Note: Individually numbered

KM# 202 KWACHA

0.6200 g., 0.9990 Gold 0.0199 oz. AGW, 11 mm. **Rev:** Impalla

Date	Mintage	F	VF	XF	Unc	BU
2009 Proof	100	Value: 50.00				

KM# 203 KWACHA

3.1100 g., 0.9990 Gold 0.0999 oz. AGW, 18 mm. **Rev:** Impalla

Date	Mintage	F	VF	XF	Unc	BU
2009 Proof	100	Value: 250				

KM# 204 KWACHA

7.7800 g., 0.9990 Gold 0.2499 oz. AGW, 25 mm. **Rev:** Impalla

Date	Mintage	F	VF	XF	Unc	BU
2009 Proof	100	Value: 550				

KM# 205 KWACHA

15.5500 g., 0.9990 Gold 0.4994 oz. AGW, 30 mm. **Rev:** Impalla

Date	Mintage	F	VF	XF	Unc	BU
2009 Proof	100	Value: 1,150				

KM# 59 5 KWACHA
Brass, 45x27.5 mm. **Obv:** National arms, date and value **Rev:** USS Coral Sea aircraft carrier **Edge:** Plain

Date	Mintage	F	VF	XF	Unc	BU
2005 Proof	—	Value: 22.50				

KM# 62 5 KWACHA
Brass, 45x27.5 mm. **Obv:** National arms,date and value **Rev:** Ship USSR Molotov **Edge:** Plain

Date	Mintage	F	VF	XF	Unc	BU
2005 Proof	—	Value: 22.50				

KM# 63 5 KWACHA
Brass, 45x27.5 mm. **Obv:** National arms,date and value **Rev:** Ship USS Missouri **Edge:** Plain

Date	Mintage	F	VF	XF	Unc	BU
2005 Proof	—	Value: 22.50				

KM# 64 5 KWACHA
Brass, 45x27.5 mm. **Obv:** National arms,date and value **Rev:** Ship HMS Hood **Edge:** Plain

Date	Mintage	F	VF	XF	Unc	BU
2005 Proof	—	Value: 22.50				

KM# 98 5 KWACHA
29.1000 g., Copper-Nickel, 38.7 mm. **Obv:** Arms **Rev:** Pope John Paul II holding child

Date	Mintage	F	VF	XF	Unc	BU
2005 Proof	—	Value: 25.00				

KM# 44 5 KWACHA
22.0000 g., Silver Plated Copper-Nickel, 40 mm. **Subject:** Asian Zodiac Animals **Obv:** Queen Elizabeth II above Zambian arms **Rev:** Multicolor stylized rat **Edge:** Reeded

Date	Mintage	F	VF	XF	Unc	BU
2005 Prooflike	835	—	—	—	—	17.50

KM# 45 5 KWACHA
22.0000 g., Silver Plated Copper-Nickel, 40 mm. **Subject:** Asian Zodiac Animals **Obv:** Queen Elizabeth II above Zambian arms **Rev:** Multicolor stylized ox **Edge:** Reeded

Date	Mintage	F	VF	XF	Unc	BU
2005 Prooflike	835	—	—	—	—	17.50

KM# 46 5 KWACHA
22.0000 g., Silver Plated Copper-Nickel, 40 mm. **Subject:** Asian Zodiac Animals **Obv:** Queen Elizabeth II above Zambian arms **Rev:** Multicolor stylized tiger **Edge:** Reeded

Date	Mintage	F	VF	XF	Unc	BU
2005 Prooflike	835	—	—	—	—	17.50

KM# 47 5 KWACHA
22.0000 g., Silver Plated Copper-Nickel, 40 mm. **Subject:** Asian Zodiac Animals **Obv:** Queen Elizabeth II above Zambian arms **Rev:** Multicolor stylized rabbit **Edge:** Reeded

Date	Mintage	F	VF	XF	Unc	BU
2005 Prooflike	835	—	—	—	—	17.50

KM# 48 5 KWACHA
22.0000 g., Silver Plated Copper-Nickel, 40 mm. **Subject:** Asian Zodiac Animals **Obv:** Queen Elizabeth II above Zambian arms **Rev:** Multicolor stylized dragon **Edge:** Reeded

Date	Mintage	F	VF	XF	Unc	BU
2005 Prooflike	835	—	—	—	—	17.50

KM# 49 5 KWACHA
22.0000 g., Silver Plated Copper-Nickel, 40 mm. **Subject:** Asian Zodiac Animals **Obv:** Queen Elizabeth II above Zambian arms **Rev:** Multicolor stylized snake **Edge:** Reeded

Date	Mintage	F	VF	XF	Unc	BU
2005 Prooflike	835	—	—	—	—	17.50

KM# 50 5 KWACHA
22.0000 g., Silver Plated Copper-Nickel, 40 mm. **Subject:** Asian Zodiac Animals **Obv:** Queen Elizabeth II above Zambian arms **Rev:** Multicolor stylized horse **Edge:** Reeded

Date	Mintage	F	VF	XF	Unc	BU
2005 Prooflike	835	—	—	—	—	17.50

KM# 51 5 KWACHA
22.0000 g., Silver Plated Copper-Nickel, 40 mm. **Subject:** Asian Zodiac Animals **Obv:** Queen Elizabeth II above Zambian arms **Rev:** Multicolor stylized goat **Edge:** Reeded

Date	Mintage	F	VF	XF	Unc	BU
2005 Prooflike	835	—	—	—	—	17.50

KM# 52 5 KWACHA
22.0000 g., Silver Plated Copper-Nickel, 40 mm. **Subject:** Asian Zodiac Animals **Obv:** Queen Elizabeth II above Zambian arms **Rev:** Multicolor stylized monkey **Edge:** Reeded

Date	Mintage	F	VF	XF	Unc	BU
2005 Proolike	835	—	—	—	—	17.50

KM# 53 5 KWACHA
22.0000 g., Silver Plated Copper-Nickel, 40 mm. **Subject:** Asian Zodiac Animals **Obv:** Queen Elizabeth II above Zambian arms **Rev:** Multicolor stylized rooster **Edge:** Reeded

Date	Mintage	F	VF	XF	Unc	BU
2005 Prooflike	835	—	—	—	—	17.50

KM# 54 5 KWACHA
22.0000 g., Silver Plated Copper-Nickel, 40 mm. **Subject:** Asian Zodiac Animals **Obv:** Queen Elizabeth II above Zambian arms **Rev:** Multicolor stylized dog **Edge:** Reeded

Date	Mintage	F	VF	XF	Unc	BU
2005 Prooflike	835	—	—	—	—	17.50

KM# 55 5 KWACHA
22.0000 g., Silver Plated Copper-Nickel, 40 mm. **Subject:** Asian Zodiac Animals **Obv:** Queen Elizabeth II above Zambian arms **Rev:** Multicolor stylized pig **Edge:** Reeded

Date	Mintage	F	VF	XF	Unc	BU
2005 Prooflike	835	—	—	—	—	17.50

KM# 57 5 KWACHA
10.2500 g., Bi-Metallic Copper-Nickel ring and Nickel-Brass center, 27 mm. **Obv:** State arms and supporters with country name below **Obv. Legend:** MALAWI **Rev:** Fisherman at work with date above and value below **Edge:** Reeded

Date	Mintage	F	VF	XF	Unc	BU
2006	—	—	—	—	3.50	5.00

KM# 159 5 KWACHA
28.2800 g., 0.9250 Silver 0.8410 oz. ASW, 38.61 mm. **Subject:** Journey through Africa **Obv:** National arms **Rev:** Lion

Date	Mintage	F	VF	XF	Unc	BU
2006 Proof	Est. 15,000	Value: 60.00				

KM# 160 5 KWACHA
28.2800 g., 0.9250 Silver 0.8410 oz. ASW, 38.61 mm. **Subject:** Journey through Africa **Obv:** National arms **Rev:** African elephant

Date	Mintage	F	VF	XF	Unc	BU
2006 Proof	Est. 15,000	Value: 60.00				

KM# 161 5 KWACHA
28.2800 g., 0.9250 Silver 0.8410 oz. ASW, 38.61 mm. **Subject:** Journey through Africa **Obv:** National Arms **Rev:** Lake Malawi

Date	Mintage	F	VF	XF	Unc	BU
2006 Proof	Est. 15,000	Value: 60.00				

KM# 162 5 KWACHA
28.2800 g., 0.9250 Silver 0.8410 oz. ASW, 38.61 mm. **Subject:** Journey through Africa **Obv:** National arms **Rev:** Sahara lizard

Date	Mintage	F	VF	XF	Unc	BU
2006 Proof	Est. 15,000	Value: 60.00				

KM# 163 5 KWACHA
28.2800 g., 0.9250 Silver 0.8410 oz. ASW, 38.61 mm. **Subject:** Journey through Afica **Obv:** National arms **Rev:** Mt. Kilimanjaro

Date	Mintage	F	VF	XF	Unc	BU
2006 Proof	Est. 15,000	Value: 60.00				

KM# 164 5 KWACHA
28.2800 g., 0.9250 Silver 0.8410 oz. ASW, 38.61 mm. **Subject:** Journey through Africa **Obv:** National arms **Rev:** Tribal life

Date	Mintage	F	VF	XF	Unc	BU
2006 Proof	Est. 15,000	Value: 60.00				

KM# 165 5 KWACHA
28.2800 g., 0.9250 Silver 0.8410 oz. ASW, 38.61 mm. **Rev:** Safari in color

Date	Mintage	F	VF	XF	Unc	BU
2006 Proof	Est. 15,000	Value: 60.00				

KM# 166 5 KWACHA
31.1050 g., 0.9250 Silver 0.9250 oz. ASW, 38.61 mm. **Rev:** Victoria Falls in color

Date	Mintage	F	VF	XF	Unc	BU
2006 Proof	Est. 15,000	Value: 60.00				

KM# 167 5 KWACHA
28.2800 g., 0.9250 Silver 0.8410 oz. ASW, 38.61 mm. **Rev:** Table top mountain in Cape town

Date	Mintage	F	VF	XF	Unc	BU
2006 Proof	Est. 15,000	Value: 60.00				

KM# 168 5 KWACHA
28.2800 g., 0.9250 Silver 0.8410 oz. ASW, 38.61 mm. **Rev:** Nile in color

Date	Mintage	F	VF	XF	Unc	BU
2006 Proof	Est. 15,000	Value: 60.00				

KM# 169 5 KWACHA
28.2800 g., 0.9250 Silver 0.8410 oz. ASW, 38.61 mm. **Rev:** Pyramids in color

Date	Mintage	F	VF	XF	Unc	BU
2006 Proof	Est. 15,000	Value: 60.00				

KM# 170 5 KWACHA
28.2800 g., 0.9250 Silver 0.8410 oz. ASW, 38.61 mm. **Rev:** Great Sphinx in color

Date	Mintage	F	VF	XF	Unc	BU
2006 Proof	Est. 15,000	Value: 60.00				

KM# 196 5 KWACHA
27.0000 g., Copper-Nickel, 40 mm. **Subject:** 2000th Anniversary of the ambush in the forest against the legions of Varus **Rev:** Centopah of Marcus Caelius and the 18th Legion

Date	Mintage	F	VF	XF	Unc	BU
2009	Est. 5,000	—	—	—	—	20.00

KM# 197 5 KWACHA
20.0000 g., Silver Plated Copper, 40 mm. **Rev:** Battleship Bismarck in color

Date	Mintage	F	VF	XF	Unc	BU
2009	Est. 5,000	—	—	—	—	30.00

KM# 198 5 KWACHA
20.0000 g., Silver Plated Copper, 40 mm. **Rev:** Ship Tirpitz in color

Date	Mintage	F	VF	XF	Unc	BU
2009	Est. 5,000	—	—	—	—	30.00

KM# 199 5 KWACHA
20.0000 g., Silver Plated Copper, 40 mm. **Rev:** Ship Gneisenau in color

Date	Mintage	F	VF	XF	Unc	BU
2009	Est. 5,000	—	—	—	—	30.00

KM# 200 5 KWACHA
20.0000 g., Silver Plated Copper, 40 mm. **Rev:** Ship Scharnhorst in color

Date	Mintage	F	VF	XF	Unc	BU
2009	Est. 5,000	—	—	—	—	30.00

KM# 195 5 KWACHA
27.0000 g., Copper-Nickel, 40 mm. **Subject:** 2000th Anniversary of the ambush in the forest against the legions of Varus **Rev:** Arminius

Date	Mintage	F	VF	XF	Unc	BU
2009	Est. 5,000	—	—	—	—	20.00

KM# 207 5 KWACHA
30.7000 g., Silver, 38.6 mm. **Subject:** John Paul II, 10th Anniversary of visits to Kazakistan and Armenia **Obv:** National arms **Rev:** John Paul II

Date	Mintage	F	VF	XF	Unc	BU
2011 Proof	1,000	Value: 75.00				

KM# 39 10 KWACHA
29.1000 g., Copper-Nickel, 38.7 mm. **Subject:** Soccer World Championship **Obv:** Arms with supporters **Rev:** Soccer players **Edge:** Reeded

Date	Mintage	F	VF	XF	Unc	BU
2002 Proof	—	Value: 50.00				

KM# 117 10 KWACHA
Silver **Rev:** U.S.S. Nimitz

Date	Mintage	F	VF	XF	Unc	BU
2002 Proof	—	Value: 40.00				

KM# 80 10 KWACHA
24.0000 g., 0.9990 Silver 0.7708 oz. ASW, 38.5 mm. **Obv:** Arms **Rev:** Pope John Paul II in mitre and vestments

Date	Mintage	F	VF	XF	Unc	BU
2003 Proof	—	Value: 30.00				

KM# 42 10 KWACHA
19.7400 g., 0.9990 Silver 0.6340 oz. ASW, 29.9 mm. **Subject:** XXVII Olympic Games - Athens 2004 **Obv:** Arms with supporters divides date **Obv. Legend:** REPUBLIC OF MALAWI **Rev:** Two rowers within circle flanked by sprigs **Edge:** Reeded

Date	Mintage	F	VF	XF	Unc	BU
2003 Proof	—	Value: 40.00				

KM# 102 10 KWACHA
19.3000 g., Silver, 38 mm. **Subject:** Antelopes of Africa **Obv:** National arms **Rev:** Eland

Date	Mintage	F	VF	XF	Unc	BU
2003 Proof	—	Value: 25.00				

KM# 103 10 KWACHA
19.3000 g., Silver, 38 mm. **Subject:** Antelopes of Africa **Obv:** National Arms **Rev:** Nyala

Date	Mintage	F	VF	XF	Unc	BU
2003 Proof	—	Value: 25.00				

KM# 104 10 KWACHA
19.3000 g., Silver, 38 mm. **Subject:** Antelopes of Africa **Obv:** National Arms **Rev:** Springbok

Date	Mintage	F	VF	XF	Unc	BU
2003 Proof	—	Value: 25.00				

KM# 105 10 KWACHA
19.3000 g., Silver, 38 mm. **Subject:** Antelopes of Africa **Obv:** National Arms **Rev:** Kudu

Date	Mintage	F	VF	XF	Unc	BU
2003 Proof	—	Value: 25.00				

KM# 106 10 KWACHA
19.3000 g., Silver, 38 mm. **Subject:** Antelopes of Africa **Obv:** National Arms **Rev:** Sable pair

Date	Mintage	F	VF	XF	Unc	BU
2003 Proof	—	Value: 25.00				

KM# 107 10 KWACHA
Bronze gilt **Obv:** National Arms **Rev:** John Paul II in mitre and vestments

Date	Mintage	F	VF	XF	Unc	BU
2003 Proof	—	Value: 7.50				

KM# 118 10 KWACHA
Silver **Subject:** Elizabeth, the Queen Mother, First anniversary of death

Date	Mintage	F	VF	XF	Unc	BU
2003 Proof	—	Value: 30.00				

KM# 119 10 KWACHA
0.9250 Silver, 38.6 mm. **Rev:** Trans-Siberian Railway

Date	Mintage	F	VF	XF	Unc	BU
2003 Proof	—	Value: 45.00				

KM# 120 10 KWACHA
Silver **Subject:** Los Angeles Olympics, 1984 **Rev:** Ribbon dancer

Date	Mintage	F	VF	XF	Unc	BU
2003 Proof	—	Value: 45.00				

KM# 61 10 KWACHA
29.1500 g., Copper-Nickel silver plated, 38.7 mm. **Subject:** Endangered Wildlife **Obv:** National arms **Rev:** Multicolor Leopard with cub **Edge:** Reeded

Date	Mintage	F	VF	XF	Unc	BU
2004 Proof	—	Value: 17.00				

KM# 86 10 KWACHA
29.1500 g., Copper-Nickel silver plated, 38.7 mm. **Subject:** Endangered Wildlife **Obv:** National arms **Rev:** Multicolor Lion and cub **Edge:** Reeded

Date	Mintage	F	VF	XF	Unc	BU
2004 Proof	—	Value: 17.00				

KM# 60 10 KWACHA
29.1500 g., Copper-Nickel silver plated, 38.7 mm. **Subject:** Endangered Wildlife **Obv:** National arms **Rev:** Multicolor Zebra and colt **Edge:** Reeded

Date	Mintage	F	VF	XF	Unc	BU
2004 Proof	—	Value: 17.00				

KM# 84 10 KWACHA
29.1400 g., Copper-Nickel, 38.7 mm. **Obv:** National arms **Rev:** Multicolor elephant and calf **Edge:** Reeded

Date	Mintage	F	VF	XF	Unc	BU
2004 Proof	—	Value: 17.00				

KM# 89 10 KWACHA
29.1500 g., Copper-Nickel silver plated, 38.7 mm. **Obv:** National arms **Rev:** Multicolor Deer and fawn **Edge:** Reeded

Date	Mintage	F	VF	XF	Unc	BU
2004 Proof	—	Value: 17.00				

KM# 90 10 KWACHA
29.1500 g., Copper-Nickel silver plated, 38.7 mm. **Obv:** National arms **Rev:** Multicolor Giraffe and her calf **Edge:** Reeded

Date	Mintage	F	VF	XF	Unc	BU
2004 Proof	—	Value: 17.00				

KM# 81 10 KWACHA
Copper-Nickel silver plated **Obv:** Arms **Rev:** Chevrotain advancing left

Date	Mintage	F	VF	XF	Unc	BU
2005 Proof	—	Value: 17.00				

KM# 82 10 KWACHA
Copper-Nickel silver plated **Obv:** Arms **Rev:** Lemur on branch

Date	Mintage	F	VF	XF	Unc	BU
2005 Proof	—	Value: 17.00				

KM# 83 10 KWACHA
Copper-Nickel silver plated **Obv:** Arms **Rev:** Pigmy Hippo

Date	Mintage	F	VF	XF	Unc	BU
2005 Proof	—	Value: 17.00				

KM# 88 10 KWACHA
Copper-Nickel **Obv:** Arms **Rev:** Oryx in photo insert

Date	Mintage	F	VF	XF	Unc	BU
2005	—	—	—	—	—	20.00

KM# 71 10 KWACHA
23.5000 g., Silver Plated Copper-Nickel, 39 mm. **Subject:** Endangered wildlife **Obv:** National arms **Rev:** Tree pangolin (Manis Tricuspis)

Date	Mintage	F	VF	XF	Unc	BU
2005 Proof	—	Value: 17.00				

KM# 87 10 KWACHA
Copper-Nickel **Obv:** Arms **Rev:** Monkies in photo insert

Date	Mintage	F	VF	XF	Unc	BU
2005 Proof	—	Value: 17.50				

KM# 130 10 KWACHA
24.5000 g., Silver Plated Brass, 38.6 mm. **Obv:** State shield **Rev:** Crocodile

Date	Mintage	F	VF	XF	Unc	BU
2005 Proof	Est. 1,000	Value: 15.00				

KM# 131 10 KWACHA
24.5000 g., Silver Plated Brass, 38.6 mm. **Rev:** Pygmy Chimpanzie

Date	Mintage	F	VF	XF	Unc	BU
2005 Proof	—	Value: 15.00				

KM# 132 10 KWACHA
24.5000 g., Silver Plated Brass, 38.6 mm. **Rev:** Corner

Date	Mintage	F	VF	XF	Unc	BU
2005 Proof	1,000	Value: 15.00				

KM# 58 10 KWACHA
15.1000 g., Bi-Metallic Copper-Nickel center with Nickel-Brass ring, 28 mm. **Obv:** State arms and supporters with country name below **Obv. Legend:** MALAWI **Rev:** Farm worker harvesting **Edge:** Coarse reeding

Date	Mintage	F	VF	XF	Unc	BU
2006	—	—	—	—	4.50	6.00

KM# 157 10 KWACHA
Silver Plated **Subject:** World Cup Soccer 2006 **Obv:** National arms **Rev:** Soccer player in the stadium

Date	Mintage	F	VF	XF	Unc	BU
2006 Proof	—	Value: 15.00				

KM# 158 10 KWACHA
28.2800 g., 0.9250 Silver 0.8410 oz. ASW, 38.6 mm. **Subject:** Elizabeth II, 80th Birthday **Obv:** National arms **Rev:** Elizabeth II

Date	Mintage	F	VF	XF	Unc	BU
2006 Proof	—	Value: 37.50				

KM# 99 10 KWACHA
0.9990 Silver, 20x40 mm. **Obv:** Arms **Rev:** deRutter painting of ships

Date	Mintage	F	VF	XF	Unc	BU
2007 Proof	—	Value: 45.00				

KM# 100 10 KWACHA
Silver, 38.6 mm. **Obv:** Arms **Rev:** Puccini colorized

Date	Mintage	F	VF	XF	Unc	BU
2007 Proof	—	Value: 40.00				

KM# 185 10 KWACHA
Silver Plated Copper-Nickel, 45x30 mm. **Obv:** State arms **Rev:** Treaty of Rome anniversary in color

Date	Mintage	F	VF	XF	Unc	BU
2007 Proof	—	Value: 15.00				

KM# 186 10 KWACHA
Silver Plated Copper-Nickel, 45x30 mm. **Rev:** Mother Theresa in color

Date	Mintage	F	VF	XF	Unc	BU
2007 Proof	—	Value: 15.00				

KM# 187 10 KWACHA
Silver Plated Copper-Nickel, 45x30 mm. **Rev:** Verdespaleis Centennial

Date	Mintage	F	VF	XF	Unc	BU
2007 Proof	—	Value: 15.00				

KM# 188 10 KWACHA
Silver Plated Copper-Nickel, 45x30 mm. **Rev:** Ship painting of Michiel de Ruyter

Date	Mintage	F	VF	XF	Unc	BU
2007 Proof	—	Value: 15.00				

KM# 189 10 KWACHA
Silver Plated Copper-Nickel, 45x30 mm. **Rev:** Tulips in color

Date	Mintage	F	VF	XF	Unc	BU
2007 Proof	—	Value: 15.00				

KM# 190 10 KWACHA
Silver Plated Copper-Nickel **Rev:** 60th Anniversary, treaty of Rome, color

Date	Mintage	F	VF	XF	Unc	BU
2007 Proof	—	Value: 15.00				

KM# 191 10 KWACHA
Silver Plated Copper-Nickel **Rev:** Love and Psyche, in color

Date	Mintage	F	VF	XF	Unc	BU
2007 Proof	—	Value: 15.00				

KM# 192 10 KWACHA
Silver Plated Copper-Nickel **Rev:** Giuseppe Garibaldi in color

Date	Mintage	F	VF	XF	Unc	BU
2007 Proof	—	Value: 15.00				

KM# 110 10 KWACHA
62.2000 g., 0.9990 Silver 1.9977 oz. ASW, 42x42 mm. **Rev:** Lion with two crystal eyes

Date	Mintage	F	VF	XF	Unc	BU
2009 Proof	2,500	Value: 135				

KM# 91 10 KWACHA
23.5000 g., Silver Plated Copper-Nickel, 39 mm. **Subject:** Endangered Frogs - Blue Poison Arrowfrog **Rev:** Multicolor blue frog right

Date	Mintage	F	VF	XF	Unc	BU
2010 Proof	—	Value: 24.00				

KM# 92 10 KWACHA
23.5000 g., Silver Plated Copper-Nickel, 39 mm. **Subject:** Endangered Frogs - Dyeing Poison Arrow frog **Rev:** Multicolor blue frog left

Date	Mintage	F	VF	XF	Unc	BU
2010 Proof	—	Value: 24.00				

KM# 93 10 KWACHA
23.5000 g., Silver Plated Copper-Nickel, 39 mm. **Subject:** Endangered Frogs - Darwin Frog **Rev:** Multicolor green frog right

Date	Mintage	F	VF	XF	Unc	BU
2010 Proof	—	Value: 24.00				

KM# 94 10 KWACHA
23.5000 g., Silver Plated Copper-Nickel, 39 mm. **Subject:** Endangered Frogs - Panamanian Spotted frog **Rev:** Multicolor orange and black frog

Date	Mintage	F	VF	XF	Unc	BU
2010 Proof	—	Value: 24.00				

KM# 95 10 KWACHA
23.5000 g., Silver Plated Copper-Nickel, 39 mm. **Subject:** Endangered Frogs - Purple frog **Rev:** Multicolor purple frog left

Date	Mintage	F	VF	XF	Unc	BU
2010 Proof	—	Value: 24.00				

KM# 96 10 KWACHA
23.5000 g., Silver Plated Copper-Nickel, 39 mm. **Subject:** Endangered Frogs - Carnileri Harlequin **Rev:** Multicolor red frog left

Date	Mintage	F	VF	XF	Unc	BU
2010 Proof	—	Value: 24.00				

KM# 97 10 KWACHA
23.5000 g., Silver Plated Copper-Nickel, 39 mm. **Subject:** Endangered Frogs - Tree frog **Rev:** Multicolor tree frog

Date	Mintage	F	VF	XF	Unc	BU
2010 Proof	—	Value: 24.00				

KM# 184 15 KWACHA
20.0000 g., 0.9990 Silver 0.6423 oz. ASW, 38 mm. **Rev:** Brandenburg gate in color, map of Germany

Date	Mintage	F	VF	XF	Unc	BU
2006 Proof	Est. 1,000	Value: 90.00				

KM# 56 20 KWACHA
31.1000 g., 0.9990 Silver 0.9988 oz. ASW, 38.6 mm. **Series:** The Big Five **Obv:** National arms **Rev:** Two water buffalo on green malachite center insert **Edge:** Plain

Date	Mintage	F	VF	XF	Unc	BU
2004 Proof	3,000	Value: 55.00				

KM# 67 20 KWACHA
31.1000 g., 0.9990 Silver 0.9988 oz. ASW, 38.6 mm. **Series:** The Big Five **Obv:** National arms **Rev:** Elephant family on Haematite (blood stone) center insert **Edge:** Plain

Date	Mintage	F	VF	XF	Unc	BU
2004 Proof	3,000	Value: 55.00				

KM# 68 20 KWACHA
31.1000 g., 0.9990 Silver 0.9988 oz. ASW, 38.6 mm. **Series:** The Big Five **Obv:** National arms **Rev:** Leopard family on hawk or falcon-eye center insert **Edge:** Plain

Date	Mintage	F	VF	XF	Unc	BU
2004 Proof	3,000	Value: 55.00				

KM# 69 20 KWACHA
31.1000 g., 0.9990 Silver 0.9988 oz. ASW, 38.6 mm. **Series:** The Big Five **Obv:** National arms **Rev:** Lion family on tiger-eye center insert **Edge:** Plain

Date	Mintage	F	VF	XF	Unc	BU
2004 Proof	3,000	Value: 55.00				

KM# 70 20 KWACHA
31.1000 g., 0.9990 Silver 0.9988 oz. ASW, 38.6 mm. **Series:** The Big Five **Obv:** National arms **Rev:** Rhinoceros family on heliotrope center insert **Edge:** Plain

Date	Mintage	F	VF	XF	Unc	BU
2004 Proof	3,000	Value: 55.00				

KM# 133 20 KWACHA
Acrylic, 65 mm. **Subject:** Year of the Dog

Date	Mintage	F	VF	XF	Unc	BU
2006	Est. 2,000	—	—	—	—	75.00

KM# 134 20 KWACHA
31.1050 g., 0.9990 Silver 0.9990 oz. ASW, 31x25 mm. **Subject:** Year of the Rat **Obv:** Temple of Heaven

Date	Mintage	F	VF	XF	Unc	BU
2006 Proof	Est. 2,000	Value: 75.00				

KM# 135 20 KWACHA
31.1050 g., 0.9990 Silver 0.9990 oz. ASW, 31x25 mm. **Subject:** Year of the Ox **Obv:** Temple of Heaven

Date	Mintage	F	VF	XF	Unc	BU
2006 Proof	Est. 2,000	Value: 75.00				

KM# 136 20 KWACHA
31.1050 g., 0.9990 Silver 0.9990 oz. ASW, 31x25 mm. **Subject:** Year of the Tiger **Obv:** Temple of Heaven

Date	Mintage	F	VF	XF	Unc	BU
2006 Proof	Est. 2,000	Value: 75.00				

KM# 137 20 KWACHA
31.1050 g., 0.9990 Silver 0.9990 oz. ASW, 31x25 mm. **Subject:** Year of the Hare **Obv:** Temple of Heaven

Date	Mintage	F	VF	XF	Unc	BU
2006 Proof	Est. 2,000	Value: 75.00				

KM# 138 20 KWACHA
31.1050 g., 0.9990 Silver 0.9990 oz. ASW, 31x25 mm. **Subject:** Year of the dragon **Obv:** Temple of Heaven

Date	Mintage	F	VF	XF	Unc	BU
2006 Proof	Est. 2,000	Value: 75.00				

KM# 139 20 KWACHA
31.1050 g., 0.9990 Silver 0.9990 oz. ASW, 31x25 mm. **Subject:** Year of the Snake **Obv:** Temple of Heaven

Date	Mintage	F	VF	XF	Unc	BU
2006 Proof	Est. 2,000	Value: 75.00				

KM# 140 20 KWACHA
31.1050 g., 0.9990 Silver 0.9990 oz. ASW, 31x25 mm. **Subject:** Year of the Horse **Obv:** Temple of Heaven

Date	Mintage	F	VF	XF	Unc	BU
2006 Proof	Est. 2,000	Value: 75.00				

KM# 141 20 KWACHA
31.1050 g., 0.9990 Silver 0.9990 oz. ASW, 31x25 mm. **Subject:** Year of the goat **Obv:** Temple of Heaven

Date	Mintage	F	VF	XF	Unc	BU
2006 Proof	Est. 2,000	Value: 75.00				

KM# 142 20 KWACHA
31.1050 g., 0.9990 Silver 0.9990 oz. ASW, 31x25 mm. **Subject:** Year of the monkey **Obv:** Temple of Heaven

Date	Mintage	F	VF	XF	Unc	BU
2006 Proof	Est. 2,000	Value: 75.00				

KM# 143 20 KWACHA
31.1050 g., 0.9990 Silver 0.9990 oz. ASW, 31x25 mm. **Subject:** Year of the Rooster **Obv:** Temple of Heaven

Date	Mintage	F	VF	XF	Unc	BU
2006 Proof	Est. 2,000	Value: 75.00				

KM# 144 20 KWACHA
31.1050 g., 0.9990 Silver 0.9990 oz. ASW, 31x25 mm. **Subject:** Year of the Dog **Obv:** Temple of Heaven

Date	Mintage	F	VF	XF	Unc	BU
2006 Proof	Est. 2,000	Value: 75.00				

KM# 145 20 KWACHA
31.1050 g., 0.9990 Silver 0.9990 oz. ASW, 31x25 mm. **Subject:** Year of the pig **Obv:** Temple of Heaven

Date	Mintage	F	VF	XF	Unc	BU
2006 Proof	Est. 2,000	Value: 75.00				

KM# 147 20 KWACHA
31.1050 g., 0.9990 Silver 0.9990 oz. ASW **Rev:** Sitting panda, city view of Moscow and flag in color

Date	Mintage	F	VF	XF	Unc	BU
2006 Proof	Est. 5,000	Value: 60.00				

KM# 148 20 KWACHA
31.1050 g., 0.9990 Silver 0.9990 oz. ASW **Rev:** Sitting panda, city view of Osaka and flag in color

Date	Mintage	F	VF	XF	Unc	BU
2006 Proof	Est. 5,000	Value: 60.00				

KM# 149 20 KWACHA
31.1050 g., 0.9990 Silver 0.9990 oz. ASW **Rev:** Sitting panda, city view of Paris and flag in color

Date	Mintage	F	VF	XF	Unc	BU
2006 Proof	Est. 5,000	Value: 60.00				

KM# 150 20 KWACHA
31.1050 g., 0.9990 Silver 0.9990 oz. ASW **Rev:** Sitting panda, city view of Mexico City and flag in color

Date	Mintage	F	VF	XF	Unc	BU
2006 Proof	Est. 5,000	Value: 60.00				

KM# 151 20 KWACHA
31.1050 g., 0.9990 Silver 0.9990 oz. ASW **Rev:** Sitting panda, city view of Madrid and flag in color

Date	Mintage	F	VF	XF	Unc	BU
2006 Proof	Est. 5,000	Value: 60.00				

KM# 152 20 KWACHA
31.1050 g., 0.9990 Silver 0.9990 oz. ASW **Rev:** Panda on rock, city view of Pyeongyang and flag in color

Date	Mintage	F	VF	XF	Unc	BU
2006 Proof	5,000	Value: 60.00				

KM# 153 20 KWACHA
31.1050 g., 0.9990 Silver 0.9990 oz. ASW

Date	Mintage	F	VF	XF	Unc	BU
2006 Proof	Est. 5,000	Value: 60.00				

KM# 154 20 KWACHA
31.1050 g., 0.9990 Silver 0.9990 oz. ASW **Rev:** Panda on rock, city view of Berlin and flag in color

Date	Mintage	F	VF	XF	Unc	BU
2006 Proof	Est. 3,000	Value: 60.00				

KM# 155 20 KWACHA
31.1050 g., 0.9990 Silver 0.9990 oz. ASW **Rev:** Panda on rock, city view of London and flag in color

Date	Mintage	F	VF	XF	Unc	BU
2006 Proof	5,000	Value: 60.00				

KM# 156 20 KWACHA
31.1050 g., 0.9990 Silver 0.9990 oz. ASW **Rev:** Panda on rock, city view of Hong Kong and flag in color

Date	Mintage	F	VF	XF	Unc	BU
2006 Proof	Est. 5,000	Value: 60.00				

KM# 74 20 KWACHA
0.5000 g., 0.9990 Gold 0.0161 oz. AGW **Subject:** Springbnok, 40 years, first design

Date	Mintage	F	VF	XF	Unc	BU
2007 Proof	—	Value: 70.00				

KM# 75 20 KWACHA
0.5000 g., 0.9990 Gold 0.0161 oz. AGW **Subject:** Springbok, 40th Anniversary, second desgin

Date	Mintage	F	VF	XF	Unc	BU
2007 Proof	—	Value: 70.00				

KM# 76 20 KWACHA
0.5000 g., 0.9990 Gold 0.0161 oz. AGW **Subject:** Springbok, 40th Anniversary, third design

Date	Mintage	F	VF	XF	Unc	BU
2007 Proof	—	Value: 70.00				

KM# 111 20 KWACHA
28.2800 g., 0.9250 Silver 0.8410 oz. ASW, 38.61 mm. **Subject:** Biosphere Reserves **Obv:** National Arms **Rev:** Goat on hillside, multicolor flower

Date	Mintage	F	VF	XF	Unc	BU
2010 Proof	8,000	Value: 60.00				

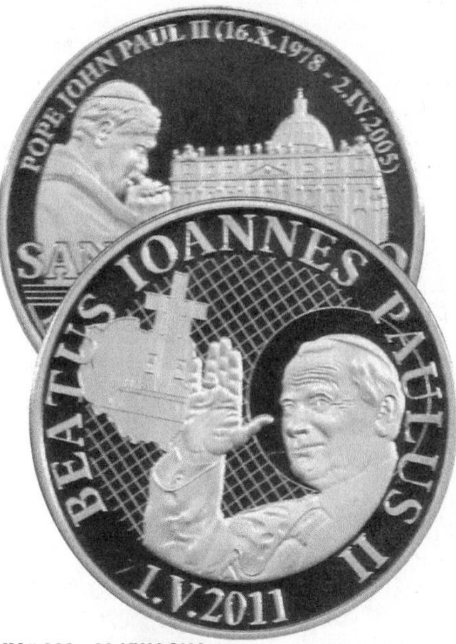

KM# 208 20 KWACHA
50.0000 g., Silver Plated Base Metal, 65 mm. **Obv:** John Paul II and St. Peter's **Rev:** John Paul II hand raised in benidiction

Date	Mintage	F	VF	XF	Unc	BU
2011 Proof	2,000	Value: 100				

KM# 209 20 KWACHA
28.2800 g., 0.9250 Silver 0.8410 oz. ASW, 38.61 mm. **Obv:** National arms **Rev:** Bison Zubr and grass in color

Date	Mintage	F	VF	XF	Unc	BU
2011 Proof	5,000	Value: 150				

KM# 210 20 KWACHA
28.2800 g., 0.9250 Silver 0.8410 oz. ASW, 28x40 mm. **Rev:** Elephant hunt in color **Shape:** Vertical rectangle

Date	Mintage	F	VF	XF	Unc	BU
2011 Proof	3,000	Value: 150				

KM# 211 20 KWACHA
28.2800 g., 0.9250 Silver 0.8410 oz. ASW, 28x40 mm. **Rev:** Duck hunt in color **Shape:** Vertical rectangle

Date	Mintage	F	VF	XF	Unc	BU
2011 Proof	—	Value: 150				

KM# 77 40 KWACHA

1.0000 g., 0.9990 Gold 0.0321 oz. AGW **Rev:** Springbok

Date	Mintage	F	VF	XF	Unc	BU
2008 Proof	—	Value: 100				

KM# 78 40 KWACHA

1.0000 g., 0.9990 Palladium 0.0321 oz. **Rev:** Springbok

Date	Mintage	F	VF	XF	Unc	BU
2008 Proof	—	Value: 75.00				

KM# 79 40 KWACHA

1.0000 g., 0.9990 Platinum 0.0321 oz. APW **Rev:** Springbok

Date	Mintage	F	VF	XF	Unc	BU
2008 Proof	—	Value: 125				

KM# 43 50 KWACHA

141.2100 g., Bronze with Gold Plated center and Silver Plated ring, 65 mm. **Subject:** Republic of China **Obv:** Large building above value within circle **Rev:** Conjoined busts facing within circle **Edge:** Reeded **Note:** Illustration reduced.

Date	Mintage	F	VF	XF	Unc	BU
2004 Proof	1,000	Value: 85.00				

KM# 108 50 KWACHA

Silver **Obv:** National Arms **Rev:** Soccer ball in flight from Germany to South Africa

Date	Mintage	F	VF	XF	Unc	BU
2006 Proof	—	Value: 45.00				

KM# 109 50 KWACHA

Silver **Obv:** National Arms **Rev:** Two female hurdlers

Date	Mintage	F	VF	XF	Unc	BU
2008 Proof	—	Value: 45.00				

KM# 193 50 KWACHA

27.0000 g., Silver Plated Brass with sterling silver inlay, 38.6 mm. **Rev:** Springbock

Date	Mintage	F	VF	XF	Unc	BU
2008	Est. 4,444	—	—	—	—	70.00

KM# 194 50 KWACHA

1.0000 g., 0.9990 Silver 0.0321 oz. ASW, 8.5x15 mm. **Rev:** Springbock

Date	Mintage	F	VF	XF	Unc	BU
2008 Proof	Est. 5,000	Value: 14.00				

KM# 85 50 KWACHA

62.2100 g., 0.9990 Silver 1.9980 oz. ASW, 42x42 mm. **Obv:** Arms **Rev:** White lion with crystal inserts in eyes **Shape:** Square

Date	Mintage	F	VF	XF	Unc	BU
2009 Proof	2,500	Value: 175				

KM# 146 75 KWACHA

4.0000 g., 0.9990 Gold 0.1285 oz. AGW, 20 mm. **Obv:** Temple of Mazu **Rev:** Mazu, goddess of protection

Date	Mintage	F	VF	XF	Unc	BU
2006 Proof	Est. 3,000	Value: 275				

KM# 171 100 KWACHA

Gold **Subject:** 2008 Bejing Olympics **Rev:** Two hurdlers

Date	Mintage	F	VF	XF	Unc	BU
2006 Proof	—	—	—	—	—	—

PATTERNS

Including off metal strikes

KM#	Date	Mintage	Identification	Mkt Val
Pn2	2002	—	10 Kwacha. Copper-Nickel. 29.0200 g. 38.7 mm. National arms. Alexander the Great. Reeded edge.	—
Pn3	2002	—	10 Kwacha. Copper-Nickel. 29.0200 g. 38.7 mm. National arms. Olympic torch under two world globes. Reeded edge.	—
Pn4	2002	—	10 Kwacha. Copper-Nickel. 29.0200 g. 38.7 mm. National arms. "MILLENNIUM" above Mona Lisa like portrait. Reeded edge.	—
Pn5	2003	—	10 Kwacha. Silver Plated. 29.4500 g. 38.7 mm. National arms. Trans-Siberian Express train. Reeded edge.	—
Pn6	2003	—	10 Kwacha. Silver Plated. 29.4500 g. 38.7 mm. National arms. Blesbok antelope. Reeded edge.	—
Pn7	2003	—	10 Kwacha. Copper-Nickel. 29.0200 g. 38.7 mm. National arms. Eland antelope. Reeded edge.	—
Pn8	2003	—	10 Kwacha. Copper-Nickel. 29.0200 g. 38.7 mm. National arms. Kudu antelope. Reeded edge.	—
Pn9	2003	—	10 Kwacha. Silver Plated. 29.4500 g. 38 mm. Nyala antelope.	—
Pn15	ND (2004)	—	10 Kwacha. Silver Plated. 29.2200 g. 38.7 mm. National arms. Multicolor pair of birds with chick. Reeded edge.	15.00

MALAYSIA

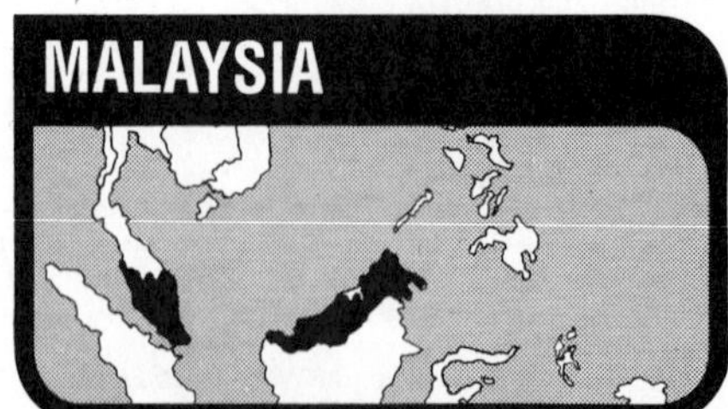

The independent limited constitutional monarchy of Malaysia, which occupies the southern part of the Malay Peninsula in Southeast Asia and the northern part of the island of Borneo, has an area of 127,316 sq. mi. (329,750 sq. km.) and a population of 15.4 million. Capital: Kuala Lumpur. The economy is based on agriculture, mining and forestry. Rubber, tin, timber and palm oil are exported.

Malaysia came into being on Sept. 16, 1963, as a federation of Malaya (Johore, Kelantan, Kedah, Perlis, Trengganu, Negri-Sembilan, Pahang, Perak, Selangor, Penang, Malacca), Singapore, Sabah (British North Borneo) and Sarawak. Following two serious racial riots involving Malays and Chinese, Singapore withdrew from the federation on Aug. 9, 1965. Malaysia is a member of the Commonwealth of Nations.

MINT MARK

FM - Franklin Mint, U.S.A.

CONSTITUTIONAL MONARCHY

STANDARD COINAGE

100 Sen = 1 Ringgit (Dollar)

KM# 49 SEN

1.8000 g., Bronze Clad Steel, 17.66 mm. **Obv:** Value divides date below flower blossom **Obv. Legend:** BANK NEGARA MALAYSIA **Rev:** Drum **Edge:** Plain

Date	Mintage	F	VF	XF	Unc	BU
2001	213,645,000	—	—	—	0.15	0.25
2002	185,220,000	—	—	—	0.15	0.25
2003	235,350,000	—	—	—	0.15	0.25
2004	227,700,000	—	—	—	0.15	0.25
2005	437,400,000	—	—	—	0.15	0.25
2006	328,050,000	—	—	—	0.15	0.25
2007	—	—	—	—	0.15	0.25

KM# 50 5 SEN

1.4000 g., Copper-Nickel, 16.25 mm. **Obv:** Value divides date below flower blossom **Obv. Legend:** BANK NEGARA MALAYSIA **Rev:** Top with string **Edge:** Reeded

Date	Mintage	F	VF	XF	Unc	BU
2001	94,617,472	—	—	—	0.15	0.25
2002	85,316,000	—	—	—	0.15	0.25
2003	75,690,000	—	—	—	0.15	0.25
2004	11,520,000	—	—	—	0.15	0.25
2005	119,520,000	—	—	—	0.15	0.25
2006	87,120,000	—	—	—	0.15	0.25
2007	97,200,338	—	—	—	0.15	0.25
2008	91,440,000	—	—	—	0.15	0.25
2009	125,172,842	—	—	—	0.15	0.25
2010	—	—	—	—	0.15	0.25
2011	—	—	—	—	0.15	0.25

KM# 201 5 SEN

1.7200 g., Stainless Steel, 17.78 mm. **Obv:** Flower, date and value **Obv. Legend:** BANK NEGARA MALAYSIA **Rev:** Geometric pattern

Date	Mintage	F	VF	XF	Unc	BU
2011	—	—	—	—	0.15	0.25
2012	—	—	—	—	0.15	0.25

KM# 51 10 SEN

2.8200 g., Copper-Nickel, 19.4 mm. **Obv:** Value divides date below flower blossom **Obv. Legend:** BANK NEGARA MALAYSIA **Rev:** Ceremonial table **Edge:** Reeded

Date	Mintage	F	VF	XF	Unc	BU
2001	313,422,000	—	—	—	0.25	0.40
2002	290,451,948	—	—	—	0.25	0.40
2003	8,640,000	—	—	—	0.25	0.40
2004	170,640,000	—	—	—	0.25	0.40
2005	316,800,000	—	—	—	0.25	0.40
2006	304,560,000	—	—	—	0.25	0.40
2007	237,967,970	—	—	—	0.25	0.40
2008	241,560,000	—	—	—	0.25	0.40
2009	336,150,800	—	—	—	0.25	0.40
2010	—	—	—	—	0.25	0.40
2011	—	—	—	—	0.25	0.40

KM# 202 10 SEN

2.9800 g., Stainless Steel, 18.8 mm. **Obv:** Flower, date and value **Obv. Legend:** BANK NEGARA MALAYSIA **Rev:** Star-like geometric pattern **Edge:** Reeded

Date	Mintage	F	VF	XF	Unc	BU
2011	—	—	—	—	0.25	0.40
2012	—	—	—	—	0.25	0.40

KM# 52 20 SEN

5.6600 g., Copper-Nickel, 23.6 mm. **Obv:** Value divides date below flower blossom **Obv. Legend:** BANK NEGARA MALAYSIA **Rev:** Basket with food and utensils **Edge:** Reeded

Date	Mintage	F	VF	XF	Unc	BU
2001	278,802,000	—	—	—	0.35	0.50
2002	131,279,881	—	—	—	0.35	0.50
2003	—	—	—	—	0.35	0.50
2004	96,840,000	—	—	—	0.35	0.50
2005	209,700,000	—	—	—	0.35	0.50
2006	155,880,000	—	—	—	0.35	0.50
2007	212,897,236	—	—	—	0.35	0.50
2008	19,764,000	—	—	—	0.35	0.50
2009	—	—	—	—	0.35	0.50
2010	—	—	—	—	0.35	0.50
2011	—	—	—	—	0.35	0.50

KM# 203 20 SEN

4.1800 g., Nickel-Brass, 20.6 mm. **Obv:** Flower, date and value **Obv. Legend:** BANK NEGARA MALAYSIA **Rev:** flowers on patterned background

Date	Mintage	F	VF	XF	Unc	BU
2011	—	—	—	—	0.35	0.50
2012	—	—	—	—	0.35	0.50

KM# 77 25 SEN

9.1400 g., Brass, 30 mm. **Series:** Endangered Species **Obv:** Logo left, value right **Rev:** Sumatran Rhinoceros **Edge:** Reeded

Date	Mintage	F	VF	XF	Unc	BU
2003	100,000	—	—	—	—	5.00

KM# 78 25 SEN

9.1400 g., Brass, 30 mm. **Series:** Endangered Species **Obv:** Logo left, value right **Rev:** Elephant **Edge:** Reeded

Date	Mintage	F	VF	XF	Unc	BU
2003	100,000	—	—	—	—	8.00

KM# 79 25 SEN

9.1400 g., Brass, 30 mm. **Series:** Endangered Species **Obv:** Logo left, value right **Rev:** Orangutan **Edge:** Reeded

Date	Mintage	F	VF	XF	Unc	BU
2003	100,000	—	—	—	—	5.00

KM# 80 25 SEN

9.1400 g., Brass, 30 mm. **Series:** Endangered Species **Obv:** Logo left, value right **Rev:** Sumatran Tiger **Edge:** Reeded

Date	Mintage	F	VF	XF	Unc	BU
2003	100,000	—	—	—	—	5.00

KM# 81 25 SEN

9.1400 g., Brass, 30 mm. **Series:** Endangered Species **Obv:** Logo left, value right **Rev:** Slow Loris on branch **Edge:** Reeded

Date	Mintage	F	VF	XF	Unc	BU
2003	100,000	—	—	—	—	5.00

KM# 82 25 SEN

9.1400 g., Brass, 30 mm. **Series:** Endangered Species **Obv:** Logo left, value right **Rev:** Barking Deer **Edge:** Reeded

Date	Mintage	F	VF	XF	Unc	BU
2003	100,000	—	—	—	—	5.00

KM# 83 25 SEN

9.1400 g., Brass, 30 mm. **Series:** Endangered Species **Obv:** Logo left, value right **Rev:** Malayan Tapir **Edge:** Reeded

Date	Mintage	F	VF	XF	Unc	BU
2003	100,000	—	—	—	—	5.00

KM# 84 25 SEN

9.1400 g., Brass, 30 mm. **Series:** Endangered Species **Obv:** Logo left, value right **Rev:** Serow **Edge:** Reeded

Date	Mintage	F	VF	XF	Unc	BU
2003	100,000	—	—	—	—	5.00

KM# 85 25 SEN

9.1400 g., Brass, 30 mm. **Series:** Endangered Species **Obv:** Logo left, value right **Rev:** Sambar Deer **Edge:** Reeded

Date	Mintage	F	VF	XF	Unc	BU
2003	100,000	—	—	—	—	5.00

KM# 86 25 SEN

9.1400 g., Brass, 30 mm. **Series:** Endangered Species **Obv:** Logo left, value right **Rev:** Seated Proboscis Monkey flanked by sprigs **Edge:** Reeded

Date	Mintage	F	VF	XF	Unc	BU
2003	100,000	—	—	—	—	5.00

KM# 87 25 SEN

9.1400 g., Brass, 30 mm. **Series:** Endangered Species **Obv:** Logo left, value right **Rev:** Gaur **Edge:** Reeded

Date	Mintage	F	VF	XF	Unc	BU
2003	100,000	—	—	—	—	5.00

KM# 88 25 SEN

9.1400 g., Brass, 30 mm. **Series:** Endangered Species **Obv:** Logo left, value right **Rev:** Clouded Leopard **Edge:** Reeded

Date	Mintage	F	VF	XF	Unc	BU
2003	100,000	—	—	—	—	5.00

KM# 89 25 SEN

9.1400 g., Brass, 30 mm. **Series:** Endangered Species **Obv:** Logo left, value right **Obv. Legend:** BANK NEGARA MALAYSIA - SIRI HAIWAN TERANCAM **Rev:** Straw-headed Bulbul bird (Barau-Barau) **Edge:** Reeded

Date	Mintage	F	VF	XF	Unc	BU
2005	—	—	—	—	—	5.00

KM# 90 25 SEN

9.1400 g., Brass, 30 mm. **Series:** Endangered Species **Obv:** Logo left, value right **Obv. Legend:** BANK NEGARA MALAYSIA - SIRI HAIWAN TERANCAM **Rev:** Great Argus Pheasant (Kuang Raya) **Edge:** Reeded

Date	Mintage	F	VF	XF	Unc	BU
2005	40,000	—	—	—	—	5.00

KM# 91 25 SEN

9.1400 g., Brass, 30 mm. **Series:** Endangered Species **Obv:** Logo left, value right **Obv. Legend:** BANK NEGARA MALAYSIA - SIRI HAIWAN TERANCAM **Rev:** White-collared Kingfisher (Pekaka Sungai) **Edge:** Reeded

Date	Mintage	F	VF	XF	Unc	BU
2005	40,000	—	—	—	—	5.00

KM# 92 25 SEN

9.1400 g., Brass, 30 mm. **Series:** Endangered Species **Obv:** Logo left, value right **Obv. Legend:** BANK NEGARA MALAYSIA - SIRI HAIWAN TERANCAM **Rev:** White-bellied Sea Eagle (Lang Siput) perched on branch **Edge:** Reeded

Date	Mintage	F	VF	XF	Unc	BU
2005	40,000	—	—	—	—	5.00

KM# 93 25 SEN

9.1600 g., Brass, 30 mm. **Series:** Endangered Species **Obv:** Logo left, value right **Obv. Legend:** BANK NEGARA MALAYSIA - SIRI HAIWAN TERANCAM **Rev:** Asian Fairy Bluebird (Dendang Gajah) **Edge:** Reeded

Date	Mintage	F	VF	XF	Unc	BU
2005	40,000	—	—	—	—	5.00

KM# 94 25 SEN

9.1600 g., Brass, 30 mm. **Series:** Endangered Species **Obv:** Logo left, value right **Obv. Legend:** BANK NEGARA MALAYSIA - SIRI HAIWAN TERANCAM **Rev:** Rhinoceros Hornbill bird (Enggang Badak) **Edge:** Reeded

Date	Mintage	F	VF	XF	Unc	BU
2005	40,000	—	—	—	—	5.00

KM# 95 25 SEN

9.1600 g., Brass, 30 mm. **Series:** Endangered Species **Obv:** Logo left, value right **Obv. Legend:** BANK NEGARA MALAYSIA - SIRI HAIWAN TERANCAM **Rev:** Nicobar Pigeon (Merpati Emas) **Edge:** Reeded

Date	Mintage	F	VF	XF	Unc	BU
2005	40,000	—	—	—	—	5.00

KM# 96 25 SEN

9.1600 g., Brass, 30 mm. **Series:** Endangered Species **Obv:** Logo left, value right **Obv. Legend:** BANK NEGARA MALAYSIA - SIRI HAIWAN TERANCAM **Rev:** Two Crested Wood Partridges (Siul Berjambul) **Edge:** Reeded

Date	Mintage	F	VF	XF	Unc	BU
2005	40,000	—	—	—	—	5.00

KM# 97 25 SEN

9.1600 g., Brass, 30 mm. **Series:** Endangered Species **Obv:** Logo left, value right **Obv. Legend:** BANK NEGARA MALAYSIA - SIRI HAIWAN TERANCAM **Rev:** Black and Red Broadbill bird (Takau Rakit) **Edge:** Reeded

Date	Mintage	F	VF	XF	Unc	BU
2005	40,000	—	—	—	—	5.00

KM# 98 25 SEN

9.1600 g., Brass, 30 mm. **Series:** Endangered Species **Obv:** Logo left, value right **Obv. Legend:** BANK NEGARA MALAYSIA - SIRI HAIWAN TERANCAM **Rev:** Green Imperial Pigeon (Pergam Besar) on branch **Edge:** Reeded

Date	Mintage	F	VF	XF	Unc	BU
2005	40,000	—	—	—	—	5.00

KM# 99 25 SEN

9.1600 g., Brass, 30 mm. **Series:** Endangered Species **Obv:** Logo left, value right **Obv. Legend:** BANK NEGARA MALAYSIA - SIRI HAIWAN TERANCAM **Rev:** Great Egret (Bangau Besar) **Edge:** Reeded

Date	Mintage	F	VF	XF	Unc	BU
2005	40,000	—	—	—	—	5.00

KM# 100 25 SEN

9.1600 g., Brass, 30 mm. **Series:** Endangered Species **Obv:** Logo left, value right **Obv. Legend:** BANK NEGARA MALAYSIA - SIRI HAIWAN TERANCAM **Rev:** Brown Shrike (Tirjup Tanah) on branch **Edge:** Reeded

Date	Mintage	F	VF	XF	Unc	BU
2005	40,000	—	—	—	—	5.00

KM# 104 25 SEN
Brass, 34 mm. **Series:** Endangered Species **Obv:** Logo and value **Obv. Legend:** BANK NEGARA MALAYSIA - SIRI HAIWAN TERANCAM **Rev:** Hawksbill turtle (Penyu Karah)

Date	Mintage	F	VF	XF	Unc	BU
2006	40,000	—	—	—	—	5.00

KM# 103 25 SEN
Brass, 34 mm. **Series:** Endangered Species **Obv:** Logo and value **Obv. Legend:** BANK NEGARA MALAYSIA - SIRI HAIWAN TERANCAM **Rev:** Green turtle (Penyu Agar)

Date	Mintage	F	VF	XF	Unc	BU
2006	40,000	—	—	—	—	5.00

KM# 102 25 SEN
Brass, 34 mm. **Series:** Endangered Species **Obv:** Logo and value **Obv. Legend:** BANK NEGARA MALAYSIA - SIRI HAIWAN TERANCAM **Rev:** Leatherback turtle (Penyu Belimbing)

Date	Mintage	F	VF	XF	Unc	BU
2006	40,000	—	—	—	—	5.00

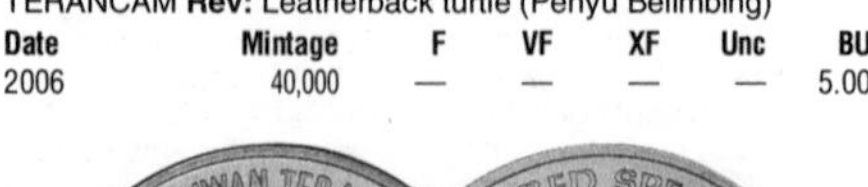

KM# 101 25 SEN
Brass, 34 mm. **Series:** Endangered Species **Obv:** Logo and value **Obv. Legend:** BANK NEGARA MALAYSIA - SIRI HAIWAN TERANCAM **Rev:** Olive Ridley Turtle (Pengu Lipas)

Date	Mintage	F	VF	XF	Unc	BU
2006	40,000	—	—	—	—	5.00

KM# 105 25 SEN
15.5000 g., Brass, 34 mm. **Series:** Endangered Species **Obv:** Logo and value **Obv. Legend:** BANK NEGARA MALAYSIA - SIRI HAIWAN TERANCAM **Rev:** Dugong **Edge:** Reeded

Date	Mintage	F	VF	XF	Unc	BU
2006	40,000	—	—	—	—	8.00

KM# 106 25 SEN
15.5000 g., Brass, 34 mm. **Series:** Endangered Species **Obv:** Logo and value **Obv. Legend:** BANK NEGARA MALAYSIA - SIRI HAIWAN TERANCAM **Rev:** Whale Shark (Jerung Paus) **Edge:** Reeded

Date	Mintage	F	VF	XF	Unc	BU
2006	40,000	—	—	—	—	5.00

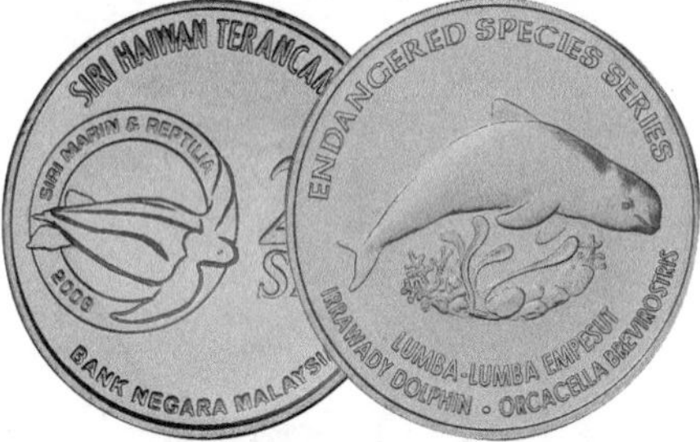

KM# 107 25 SEN
15.5000 g., Brass, 34 mm. **Series:** Endangered Species **Obv:** Logo and value **Obv. Legend:** BANK NEGARA MALAYSIA - SIRI HAIWAN TERANCAM **Rev:** Irraddy Dolphin (Lumba-Lumba Empesut) **Edge:** Reeded

Date	Mintage	F	VF	XF	Unc	BU
2006	40,000	—	—	—	—	5.00

KM# 108 25 SEN
15.5000 g., Brass, 34 mm. **Series:** Endangered Species **Obv:** Logo and value **Obv. Legend:** BANK NEGARA MALAYSIA - SIRI HAIWAN TERANCAM **Rev:** Bottlenose Dolphin (Lumba Lumba) **Edge:** Reeded

Date	Mintage	F	VF	XF	Unc	BU
2006	40,000	—	—	—	—	5.00

KM# 109 25 SEN
15.5000 g., Brass, 34 mm. **Series:** Endangered Species **Obv:** Logo and value **Obv. Legend:** BANK NEGARA MALAYSIA - SIRI HAIWAN TERANCAM **Rev:** Siamese Crocodile (Buaya Siam) **Edge:** Reeded

Date	Mintage	F	VF	XF	Unc	BU
2006	40,000	—	—	—	—	5.00

KM# 110 25 SEN
15.5000 g., Brass, 34 mm. **Series:** Endangered Species **Obv:** Logo and value **Obv. Legend:** BANK NEGARA MALAYSIA - SIRI HAIWAN TERANCAM **Rev:** Indopacific Crocodile (Buaya Tembaga) **Edge:** Reeded

Date	Mintage	F	VF	XF	Unc	BU
2006	40,000	—	—	—	—	5.00

KM# 111 25 SEN
15.5000 g., Brass, 34 mm. **Series:** Endangered Species **Obv:** Logo and value **Obv. Legend:** BANK NEGARA MALAYSIA - SIRI HAIWAN TERANCAM **Rev:** Malayan Gharial (Buaya Julong) **Edge:** Reeded

Date	Mintage	F	VF	XF	Unc	BU
2006	40,000	—	—	—	—	5.00

KM# 112 25 SEN
15.5000 g., Brass, 34 mm. **Series:** Endangered Species **Obv:** Logo and value **Obv. Legend:** BANK NEGARA MALAYSIA - SIRI HAIWAN TERANCAM **Rev:** Painted Terrapin turtle (Tuntung Laut) **Edge:** Reeded

Date	Mintage	F	VF	XF	Unc	BU
2006	40,000	—	—	—	—	5.00

KM# 53 50 SEN

9.3300 g., Copper-Nickel, 27.75 mm. **Obv:** Value divides date below flower blossom **Obv. Legend:** BANK NEGARA MALAYSIA **Rev:** Ceremonial kite **Edge Lettering:** BANK NEGARA MALAYSIA (twice)

Date	Mintage	F	VF	XF	Unc	BU
2001	67,371,000	—	—	—	0.65	0.85
2002	61,928,000	—	—	—	0.65	0.85
2003	32,580,000	—	—	—	0.65	0.85
2004	37,890,000	—	—	—	0.65	0.85
2005	691,680,006	—	—	—	0.65	0.85
2006	19,480,006	—	—	—	0.65	0.85
2007	—	—	—	—	0.65	0.85
2008	61,380,000	—	—	—	0.65	0.85
2009	94,691,783	—	—	—	0.65	0.85
2010	—	—	—	—	0.65	0.85
2011	—	—	—	—	0.65	0.85

KM# 204 50 SEN

5.6600 g., Nickel-Brass Plated Copper, 22.65 mm. **Obv:** Flower, date and value **Obv. Legend:** BANK NEGARA MALAYSIA **Rev:** Vine on patterned circle **Edge:** Notched

Date	Mintage	F	VF	XF	Unc	BU
2011	—	—	—	—	0.65	0.85
2012	—	—	—	—	0.65	0.85

KM# 71 RINGGIT

16.8000 g., Copper-Nickel, 33.7 mm. **Subject:** XXI SEA Games **Obv:** Games logo **Rev:** Cartoon mascot **Edge:** Reeded

Date	Mintage	F	VF	XF	Unc	BU
2001	200,000	—	—	—	5.00	6.00

KM# 165 RINGGIT

10.4000 g., Copper Plated Zinc, 26 mm. **Subject:** 10th Men's Hockey World Cup **Obv:** Logo **Obv. Legend:** BANK NEGARA MALAYSIA **Rev:** 2 stylized players **Rev. Legend:** KEJOHANAN HOKI LELAKI PIALA DUNIA **Edge:** Reeded

Date	Mintage	F	VF	XF	Unc	BU
2002	100,000	—	—	—	—	12.00

KM# 168 RINGGIT

Brass **Subject:** 45th National Day **Obv:** Buildings, tower, metro liner **Obv. Legend:** BANK NEGARA MALAYSIA **Rev:** Stylized waving flag **Rev. Legend:** 45 TAHUN MERDEKA

Date	Mintage	F	VF	XF	Unc	BU
2002	10,000	—	—	—	—	10.00

KM# 74 RINGGIT

16.8000 g., Copper-Nickel, 33.7 mm. **Subject:** Coronation of Agong XII **Obv:** Head with headdress facing **Rev:** Arms with supporters within sprigs **Edge:** Reeded **Note:** Prev. KM#72.

Date	Mintage	F	VF	XF	Unc	BU
ND(2002)	100,000	—	—	—	6.00	7.00

KM# 171 RINGGIT

Brass **Subject:** XIII NAM Summit **Obv:** Modern building, plaza **Obv. Legend:** MALAYSIA - BANK NEGARA MALAYSIA **Rev:** Stylized dove in rays **Rev. Legend:** XIII CONFERENCE OF HEADS OF STATE OR GOVERNMENT OF THE NON-ALIGNED MOVEMENT

Date	Mintage	F	VF	XF	Unc	BU
2003 Proof	9,400	Value: 10.00				

KM# 174 RINGGIT

Brass **Subject:** LIMA - 7th Bi-annual Langkawi Island Trade Fair **Obv:** Jet fighter plane above naval missile corvette **Obv. Legend:** BANK NEGARA MALAYSIA **Rev:** Logo **Rev. Legend:** LANGKAWI INTERNATIONAL MARITIME & AEROSPACE

Date	Mintage	F	VF	XF	Unc	BU
2003	25,000	—	—	—	—	10.00

KM# 177 RINGGIT

Brass **Subject:** 10th Session Islamic Summit Conference **Obv:** Circular Arabic text **Obv. Legend:** BANK NEGARA MALAYSIA **Rev:** Symmetrical design **Rev. Legend:** PERSIDANGAN KETUA-KETUA NEGARASLAM

Date	Mintage	F	VF	XF	Unc	BU
2003	25,000	—	—	—	—	10.00

KM# 200 RINGGIT

8.1500 g., Bi-Metallic Copper-Nickel center in Nickel-Brass ring, 26.5 mm. **Subject:** 46th Anniversary of Independence **Rev:** Group of four people

Date	Mintage	F	VF	XF	Unc	BU
2003	—	—	—	—	—	6.00

KM# 114 RINGGIT

Copper-Nickel **Subject:** Century of Tunku Abdul Rahman **Obv:** National arms **Obv. Legend:** BANK NEGARA MALAYSIA - BAPA KEMERDEKAAN **Rev:** 3/4 length figure of Tunku Abdul Rahman left with right hand raised **Rev. Legend:** Y. T. M. TUNKU ABDUL RAHMAN PUTRA AL-HAJ

Date	Mintage	F	VF	XF	Unc	BU
2005	25,000	—	—	—	—	10.00

KM# 132 RINGGIT

Brass **Subject:** 30th Annual Meeting Islamic Development Bank **Obv:** Circular Arabic text **Obv. Legend:** BANK NEGARA MALYSIA - MESYUARAT TAHUNAN BANK PEMBANCUNAN ISLAM KE - 30 **Rev:** Logo

Date	Mintage	F	VF	XF	Unc	BU
2005	20,000	—	—	—	—	10.00

KM# 135 RINGGIT

Copper-Nickel **Subject:** 11th ASEAN Summit **Obv:** Twin towers center right **Obv. Legend:** BANK NEGARA MALAYSIA - SIDANG KEMUNCAK ASEAN KE-11 **Rev:** Logo

Date	Mintage	F	VF	XF	Unc	BU
2005	20,000	—	—	—	—	8.00

KM# 138 RINGGIT

Bi-Metallic **Subject:** Songket - The Regal Heritage **Obv:** Stylized flower - Bunga Ketola **Obv. Legend:** BANK NEGARA MALAYSIA **Rev:** Floral pattern below inscription

Date	Mintage	F	VF	XF	Unc	BU
2005	20,000	—	—	—	—	8.00

KM# 141 RINGGIT

Brass **Subject:** 50th Anniversary Mara Technology University **Obv:** Large "50" with horizontal lines in background **Obv. Legend:** BANK NEGARA MALAYSIA - JUBLI EMAS UITM **Rev:** Logo **Rev. Legend:** Universiti Teknologi Mara

Date	Mintage	F	VF	XF	Unc	BU
ND(2006)	12,050	—	—	—	—	8.00

KM# 144 RINGGIT

Brass **Subject:** 50th Anniversary P. Felda **Obv:** 1/2 length figure of Felda 3/4 right **Obv. Legend:** BANK NEGARA MALYSIA **Rev:** Two opposed hands holding symbol **Rev. Legend:** MENEMPA KEJAYAAN

Date	Mintage	F	VF	XF	Unc	BU
2006	10,000	—	—	—	—	8.00

KM# 147 RINGGIT

Brass **Subject:** 9th Malaysian Plan **Obv:** Bust 3/4 right **Obv. Legend:** BANK NEGARA MALAYSIA - CEMERLANG GEMILANG TERBILANg **Rev:** Globe logo **Rev. Legend:** RANCANGAN MALAYSIA KE SEMBILAN

Date	Mintage	F	VF	XF	Unc	BU
2006	10,000	—	—	—	—	8.00

KM# 162 RINGGIT

Brass **Subject:** 200th Anniversary Malaysian Police Force **Obv:** Police badge **Obv. Legend:** BANK NEGARA MALAYSIA **Rev:** Two hands clasped in sprays

Date	Mintage	F	VF	XF	Unc	BU
2007	20,000	—	—	—	—	7.00

KM# 182 RINGGIT

8.8000 g., Aluminum-Bronze, 30 mm. **Subject:** Installation of Agong XIII **Obv:** National arms within wreath **Rev:** Facing portrait

Date	Mintage	F	VF	XF	Unc	BU
2007	10,000	—	—	—	—	7.00
2007 Proof	600	—	—	—	—	—

KM# 185 RINGGIT

8.8000 g., Aluminum-Bronze, 30 mm. **Subject:** Independence, 50th Anniversary **Obv:** National Arms **Rev:** 50 above city skyline

Date	Mintage	F	VF	XF	Unc	BU
2007	10,000	—	—	—	—	7.00
2007 Proof	2,000	—	—	—	—	—

KM# 188 RINGGIT

8.8000 g., Aluminum-Bronze, 30 mm. **Subject:** Royal Malaysian Air Force, 50th Anniversary **Obv:** Air Force insignia **Rev:** Old and modern plane

Date	Mintage	F	VF	XF	Unc	BU
2008	10,000	—	—	—	—	7.00
2008 Proof	350	—	—	—	—	—

KM# 191 RINGGIT

8.8000 g., Aluminum-Bronze, 30 mm. **Subject:** St. John's Ambulance, 100th Anniversary **Obv:** St. John's insignia in wreath above valye **Rev:** Cliernt being loaded into ambulance

Date	Mintage	F	VF	XF	Unc	BU
2008	10,000	—	—	—	—	7.00
2008 Proof	350	—	—	—	—	—

KM# 155 RINGGIT

8.8000 g., Brass, 30 mm. **Subject:** Bank Negara Malaysia, 50th Anniversary **Obv:** Bank logo **Rev:** 14-pointed star

Date	Mintage	F	VF	XF	Unc	BU
2009	13,700	—	—	—	—	7.00
2009 Proof	3,300	—	—	—	—	—

KM# 159 RINGGIT

8.0000 g., Brass, 30 mm. **Subject:** Parliament, 50th Anniversary **Obv:** National Arms and 2 maces **Rev:** Parliament Building

Date	Mintage	F	VF	XF	Unc	BU
2009	10,000	—	—	—	—	7.00
2009 Proof	450	—	—	—	—	—

KM# 194 RINGGIT

8.8000 g., Aluminum-Bronze, 30 mm. **Subject:** International Year of Astronomy **Obv:** Adult and Child looking to the heavens **Rev:** Langkawi National Observatory

Date	Mintage	F	VF	XF	Unc	BU
2009	10,000	—	—	—	—	6.00
2009 Proof	350	—	—	—	—	—

KM# 197 RINGGIT

8.8000 g., Aluminum-Bronze, 30 mm. **Subject:** Royal Malaysian Navy, 75th Anniversary **Obv:** Submarine **Rev:** Navy insignia

Date	Mintage	F	VF	XF	Unc	BU
2009	10,000	—	—	—	—	6.00
2009 Proof	450	—	—	—	—	—

KM# 72 10 RINGGIT

21.7000 g., 0.9250 Silver 0.6453 oz. ASW, 35.7 mm. **Subject:** XXI SEA Games **Obv:** Games logo **Rev:** Cartoon mascot **Edge:** Reeded

Date	Mintage	F	VF	XF	Unc	BU
2001 Proof	3,000	Value: 70.00				

KM# 75 10 RINGGIT

21.7000 g., 0.9250 Silver 0.6453 oz. ASW, 35.7 mm. **Subject:** Coronation of Agong XII **Obv:** Head with headdress facing **Rev:** Arms with supporters within sprigs **Edge:** Reeded

Date	Mintage	F	VF	XF	Unc	BU
ND(2002) Proof	10,000	Value: 120				

KM# 166 10 RINGGIT

16.8000 g., 0.9250 Silver 0.4996 oz. ASW, 32 mm. **Subject:** 10th Men's Hockey World Cup **Obv:** Official logo of the World Cup games **Obv. Legend:** BANK NEGARA MALAYSIA **Rev:** 2 stylized players in front of the Kuala Lumpur skyline **Rev. Legend:** KEJOHANAN HOKI LELAKI PIALA

Date	Mintage	F	VF	XF	Unc	BU
2002 Proof	3,000	Value: 160				

KM# 169 10 RINGGIT

0.9250 Silver **Subject:** 45th National Day **Obv:** Buildings, tower, metro liner **Obv. Legend:** BANK NEGARA MALAYSIA **Rev:** Stylized waving flag **Rev. Legend:** 45 TAHUN MERDEKA

Date	Mintage	F	VF	XF	Unc	BU
2002 Proof	1,800	Value: 120				

KM# 172 10 RINGGIT

0.9250 Silver **Subject:** XIII NAM Summit **Obv:** Modern building, plaza **Obv. Legend:** MALAYSIA - BANK NEGARA MALAYSIA **Rev:** Stylized dove in rays **Rev. Legend:** XIII CONFERENCE OF HEADS OF STATE OR GOVERNMENT OF THE NON-ALIGNED MOVEMENT

Date	Mintage	F	VF	XF	Unc	BU
2003 Proof	2,400	Value: 120				

KM# 175 10 RINGGIT

0.9250 Silver **Subject:** LIMA - 7th bi-annual Langkawi Island Trade Fair **Obv:** Jet fighter plane above naval missile corvette **Obv. Legend:** BANK NEGARA MALAYSIA **Rev:** Logo **Rev. Legend:** LANGKAWI INTERNATIONAL MARITIME & SPACE

Date	Mintage	F	VF	XF	Unc	BU
2003 Proof	—	Value: 120				

KM# 178 10 RINGGIT

0.9250 Silver **Subject:** 10th Session Islamic Summit Conference **Obv:** Circular Arabic Text **Obv. Legend:** BANK NEGARA MALAYSIA **Rev:** Symmetrical pattern **Rev. Legend:** PERSIDANGAN KETUA - KETUA NEGARA ISLAM

Date	Mintage	F	VF	XF	Unc	BU
2003 Proof	300	Value: 120				

KM# 115 10 RINGGIT

0.9250 Silver **Subject:** Century of Tunku Abdul Rahman **Obv:** National arms **Obv. Legend:** BANK NEGARA MALAYSIA - BAPA KEMERDEKAAN **Rev:** 3/4 length figure of Tunku Abdul Rahman left with right hand raised **Rev. Legend:** Y. T. M. TUNKU ABDUL RAHMAN PUTRA AL-HAJ

Date	Mintage	F	VF	XF	Unc	BU
2005 Proof	200	Value: 120				

KM# 136 10 RINGGIT

21.7000 g., Silver, 35.7 mm. **Subject:** 11th ASEAN Summit **Obv:** Twin towers center right **Obv. Legend:** BANK NEGARA MALAYSIA - SIDANG KEMUNCAK ASEAN KE-11 **Rev:** Logo

Date	Mintage	F	VF	XF	Unc	BU
2005 Proof	250	Value: 120				

KM# 139 10 RINGGIT

21.7000 g., Silver, 35.7 mm. **Subject:** Songket - The Regal Heritage **Obv:** Uniform pattern - Bunga Bintang **Obv. Legend:** BANK NEGARA MALAYSIA **Rev:** Floral pattern below inscription

Date	Mintage	F	VF	XF	Unc	BU
2005 Proof	250	Value: 120				

KM# 142 10 RINGGIT

21.7000 g., Silver, 35.7 mm. **Subject:** 50th Anniversary Mara Technology Universit **Obv:** Large "50" with horizontal lines in background **Obv. Legend:** BANK NEGARA MALAYSIA - JUBLI EMAS UITM **Rev:** Logo **Rev. Legend:** Universiti Teknologi Mara

Date	Mintage	F	VF	XF	Unc	BU
ND(2006) Proof	500	Value: 110				

KM# 145 10 RINGGIT
31.1100 g., Silver, 40 mm. **Subject:** 50th Anniversary P. Felda **Obv:** Outlined map of South East Asia above logo **Obv. Legend:** BANK NEGARA MALAYSIA **Rev:** Monument at left, Felda with 4 others at right **Rev. Legend:** MENEMPA KEJAYAAN

Date	Mintage	F	VF	XF	Unc	BU
2006 Proof	300	Value: 110				

KM# 148 10 RINGGIT
21.0000 g., Silver, 35.7 mm. **Subject:** 9th Malaysian Plan **Obv:** Bust 3/4 right **Obv. Legend:** BANK NEGARA MALAYSIA - CEMERLANG GEMILANG TERBILANG **Rev:** Globe logo **Rev. Legend:** RANCANGAN MALAYSIA KE SEMBILAN

Date	Mintage	F	VF	XF	Unc	BU
2006 Proof	300	Value: 110				

KM# 163 10 RINGGIT
21.0000 g., Silver, 35.70 mm. **Subject:** 200th Anniversary Malaysian Police Force **Obv:** Police badge **Obv. Legend:** BANK NEGARA MALAYSIA **Rev:** Two hands clasped in sprays

Date	Mintage	F	VF	XF	Unc	BU
2007 Proof	500	Value: 110				

KM# 183 10 RINGGIT
21.0000 g., 0.9250 Silver 0.6245 oz. ASW, 35.7 mm. **Subject:** Installation of Agong XIII **Obv:** National arms in wreath **Rev:** Portrait facing

Date	Mintage	F	VF	XF	Unc	BU
2007 Proof	200	Value: 100				

KM# 186 10 RINGGIT
21.0000 g., 0.9250 Silver 0.6245 oz. ASW, 35.7 mm. **Subject:** Independence, 50th Anniversary **Obv:** National Arms **Rev:** 50 above city skyline

Date	Mintage	F	VF	XF	Unc	BU
2007 Proof	200	Value: 110				

KM# 189 10 RINGGIT
21.0000 g., 0.9250 Silver 0.6245 oz. ASW, 35.7 mm. **Subject:** Royal Malaysian Air Force, 50th Anniversary **Obv:** Air Force insignia **Rev:** Old and new plane

Date	Mintage	F	VF	XF	Unc	BU
2008 Proof	350	Value: 100				

KM# 192 10 RINGGIT
21.0000 g., 0.9250 Silver 0.6245 oz. ASW, 35.7 mm. **Subject:** St. John's Ambulance **Obv:** St. John's emblem in wreath above vlaue **Rev:** Client being loaded into ambulance

Date	Mintage	F	VF	XF	Unc	BU
2008 Proof	350	Value: 100				

KM# 156 10 RINGGIT
21.0000 g., 0.9250 Silver 0.6245 oz. ASW, 35.7 mm. **Subject:** Bank Negara Malaysia, 50th Anniversary **Obv:** Bank logo **Rev:** 14-pointed star

Date	Mintage	F	VF	XF	Unc	BU
2009 Proof	400	Value: 100				

KM# 160 10 RINGGIT
21.0000 g., 0.9250 Silver 0.6245 oz. ASW, 35.7 mm. **Subject:** Parliament, 50th Anniversary **Obv:** National Arms and 2 maces **Rev:** Parliament Building

Date	Mintage	F	VF	XF	Unc	BU
2009 Proof	300	Value: 120				

KM# 195 10 RINGGIT
21.0000 g., 0.9250 Silver 0.6245 oz. ASW, 35.7 mm. **Subject:** International Year of Astronomy **Obv:** Adult and child looking to the heavens **Rev:** Langkawi Naitonal Observatory

Date	Mintage	F	VF	XF	Unc	BU
2009 Proof	350	Value: 120				

KM# 198 10 RINGGIT
21.0000 g., 0.9250 Silver 0.6245 oz. ASW, 35.7 mm. **Subject:** Royal Malaysian navy, 75th Anniversary **Obv:** Submarine **Rev:** Navy insignia

Date	Mintage	F	VF	XF	Unc	BU
2009 Proof	300	Value: 120				

KM# 206 10 RINGGIT
Silver **Rev:** Belia flower

Date	Mintage	F	VF	XF	Unc	BU
2011 Proof	—	Value: 125				

KM# 207 10 RINGGIT
0.9990 Silver **Rev:** Wanita flower

Date	Mintage	F	VF	XF	Unc	BU
2011 Proof	—	Value: 125				

KM# 133 20 RINGGIT
31.1000 g., Silver, 40 mm. **Subject:** 30th Annual Meeting Islamic Development Bank **Obv:** Mosque **Obv. Legend:** BANK NEGARA MALAYSIA **Rev:** Logo

Date	Mintage	F	VF	XF	Unc	BU
2005 Proof	1,000	Value: 100				

KM# 157 50 RINGGIT
10.0700 g., 0.9990 Gold 0.3234 oz. AGW, 25 mm. **Subject:** Bank Negara Malaysia, 50th Anniversary **Obv:** Bank logo **Rev:** 14-pointed star

Date	Mintage	F	VF	XF	Unc	BU
2009 Proof	300	Value: 1,000				

KM# 73 100 RINGGIT
8.6000 g., 0.9160 Gold 0.2533 oz. AGW, 22 mm. **Subject:** XXI SEA Games **Obv:** Games logo **Rev:** Cartoon mascot **Edge:** Reeded

Date	Mintage	F	VF	XF	Unc	BU
2001 Proof	500	Value: 800				

KM# 76 100 RINGGIT
8.6000 g., 0.9160 Gold 0.2533 oz. AGW, 22 mm. **Subject:** Coronation of Agong XII **Obv:** Head with headdress facing **Rev:** Arms with supporters within sprigs **Edge:** Reeded

Date	Mintage	F	VF	XF	Unc	BU
ND(2002) Proof	300	Value: 900				

KM# 167 100 RINGGIT
9.0000 g., 0.9000 Gold 0.2604 oz. AGW, 22 mm. **Subject:** 10th Men's Hockey World Cup **Obv:** Logo **Obv. Legend:** BANK NEGARA MALAYSIA **Rev:** 2 stylized players in front of Kuala Lumpur skyline **Rev. Legend:** KEJOHANAN HOKI LELAKI PIALA

Date	Mintage	F	VF	XF	Unc	BU
2002 Proof	1,000	Value: 700				

KM# 170 100 RINGGIT
8.6000 g., 0.9999 Gold 0.2765 oz. AGW **Subject:** 45th National Day **Obv:** Buildings, tower, metro liner **Obv. Legend:** BANK NEGARA MALAYSIA **Rev:** Stylized waving flag **Rev. Legend:** 45 TAHUN MERDEKA

Date	Mintage	F	VF	XF	Unc	BU
2002 Proof	300	Value: 900				

KM# 173 100 RINGGIT
8.6000 g., 0.9999 Gold 0.2765 oz. AGW, 22 mm. **Subject:** XIII NAM Summit **Obv:** Modern building, plaza **Obv. Legend:** MALAYSIA - BANK NEGARA MALAYSIA **Rev:** Stylized dove in rays **Rev. Legend:** XIII CONFERENCE OF HEADS OF STATE OR GOVERNMENT OF THE NON-ALIGNED MOVEMENT

Date	Mintage	F	VF	XF	Unc	BU
2003 Proof	300	Value: 900				

KM# 176 100 RINGGIT
8.6000 g., 0.9999 Gold 0.2765 oz. AGW, 22 mm. **Subject:** LIMA - 7th bi-annual Langkawi Island Trade Fair **Obv:** Jet fighter plane above naval missile corvette **Obv. Legend:** BANK NEGARA MALAYSIA **Rev:** Logo **Rev. Legend:** LANGKAWI INTERNATIONAL MARITIME & AEROSPACE

Date	Mintage	F	VF	XF	Unc	BU
2003 Proof	50	Value: 1,400				

KM# 179 100 RINGGIT
8.6000 g., 0.9999 Gold 0.2765 oz. AGW, 22 mm. **Obv:** Circular Arabic text **Obv. Legend:** BANK NEGARA MALAYSIA **Rev:** Symmetrical design **Rev. Legend:** PERSIDANGAN KETUA - KETUA NEGARA ISLAM

Date	Mintage	F	VF	XF	Unc	BU
2003 Proof	200	Value: 900				

KM# 116 100 RINGGIT
0.9999 Gold **Subject:** Century of Tunku Abdul Rahman **Obv:** National arms **Obv. Legend:** BANK NEGARA MALAYSIA - BAPA KEMERDEKAAN **Rev:** 3/4 length figure of Tunku Abdul Rahman left with right hand raised **Rev. Legend:** Y. T. M. TUNKU ABDUL RAHMAN PUTRA AL-HAJ

Date	Mintage	F	VF	XF	Unc	BU
2005 Proof	100	Value: 900				

KM# 137 100 RINGGIT
8.6000 g., Gold, 22 mm. **Subject:** 11th ASEAN Summit **Obv:** Twin towers center right **Obv. Legend:** BANK NEGARA MALAYSIA - SIDANG KEMUNCAK ASEAN KE-11 **Rev:** Logo

Date	Mintage	F	VF	XF	Unc	BU
2005 Proof	200	Value: 900				

KM# 140 100 RINGGIT
8.6000 g., Gold, 22 mm. **Subject:** Songket - The Regal Heritage **Obv:** Uniform pattern - Tampur Kesemak **Obv. Legend:** BANK NEGARA MALAYSIA **Rev:** Floral pattern below inscription

Date	Mintage	F	VF	XF	Unc	BU
2005 Proof	150	Value: 900				

KM# 143 100 RINGGIT
8.6000 g., Gold, 22 mm. **Subject:** 50th Anniversary Mara Technology University **Obv:** Large "50" with horizontal lines in background **Obv. Legend:** BANK NEGARA MALAYSIA - JUBLI EMAS UITM **Rev:** Logo **Rev. Legend:** Universiti Teknologi Mara

Date	Mintage	F	VF	XF	Unc	BU
ND(2006) Proof	300	Value: 900				

KM# 146 100 RINGGIT
9.0000 g., Gold, 22 mm. **Subject:** 50th Anniversary P. Felda **Obv:** 1/2 length figure of Felda 3/4 right **Obv. Legend:** BANK NEGARA MALAYSIA **Rev:** Stylized palm tree at left, rubber tree trunk at right **Rev. Legend:** MENEMPA KEJAYAAN

Date	Mintage	F	VF	XF	Unc	BU
2006 Proof	200	Value: 900				

KM# 149 100 RINGGIT
7.9600 g., Gold, 22 mm. **Subject:** 9th Malaysian Plan **Obv:** Bust 3/4 right **Obv. Legend:** BANK NEGARA MALAYSIA - CEMERLANG GEMILANG TERBILANG **Rev:** Globe logo **Rev. Legend:** RANCANGAN MALAYSIA KE SEMBILAN

Date	Mintage	F	VF	XF	Unc	BU
2006 Proof	500	Value: 900				

KM# 164 100 RINGGIT
7.9600 g., Gold, 22 mm. **Subject:** 200th Anniversary Malaysian Police Force **Obv:** Police badge **Obv. Legend:** BANK NEGARA MALAYSIA **Rev:** Two hands clasped in sprays

Date	Mintage	F	VF	XF	Unc	BU
2007 Proof	500	Value: 900				

KM# 184 100 RINGGIT
7.9600 g., 0.9999 Gold 0.2559 oz. AGW, 22 mm. **Subject:** Installation of the King **Obv:** National Arms within wreath **Rev:** Facing portrait

Date	Mintage	F	VF	XF	Unc	BU
2007 Proof	100	Value: 900				

KM# 187 100 RINGGIT
7.9600 g., 0.9999 Gold 0.2559 oz. AGW, 22 mm. **Subject:** Independence, 50th Anniversary **Obv:** National Arms **Rev:** 50 above city skyline

Date	Mintage	F	VF	XF	Unc	BU
2007 Proof	100	Value: 900				

KM# 190 100 RINGGIT
7.9600 g., 0.9999 Gold 0.2559 oz. AGW, 22 mm. **Subject:** Royal Malaysian Air Force, 50th Anniversary **Obv:** Royal Airforce insignia **Rev:** Old and new plane

Date	Mintage	F	VF	XF	Unc	BU
2008 Proof	100	Value: 900				

KM# 193 100 RINGGIT
7.9600 g., 0.9999 Gold 0.2559 oz. AGW, 22 mm. **Subject:** St. John's Ambulance, 100th Anniversary **Obv:** St. John's insignia in wreath above value **Rev:** Client being loaded into ambulance

Date	Mintage	F	VF	XF	Unc	BU
2008 Proof	100	Value: 900				

KM# 158 100 RINGGIT
7.9600 g., 0.9990 Gold 0.2557 oz. AGW, 22 mm. **Subject:** Bank Negara Malaysia, 50th Anniversary **Obv:** Bank logo **Rev:** 14-pointed star

Date	Mintage	F	VF	XF	Unc	BU
2009 Proof	300	Value: 1,000				

KM# 180 100 RINGGIT
7.9600 g., 0.9999 Gold 0.2559 oz. AGW, 22 mm. **Subject:** Parliament, 50th Anniversary **Obv:** National arms above mace and sceptre **Rev:** Parliament buildings, sunburst

Date	Mintage	F	VF	XF	Unc	BU
2009 Proof	100	Value: 800				

KM# 196 100 RINGGIT
7.9600 g., 0.9999 Gold 0.2559 oz. AGW, 22 mm. **Subject:** International Year of Astronomy **Obv:** Adult and child looking to the ehavens **Rev:** Langkawi National Observatory

Date	Mintage	F	VF	XF	Unc	BU
2009 Proof	100	Value: 900				

KM# 199 100 RINGGIT
7.9600 g., 0.9999 Gold 0.2559 oz. AGW, 22 mm. **Subject:** Royal Malaysian Navy, 75th Anniversary **Obv:** Submarine **Rev:** Navy insignia

Date	Mintage	F	VF	XF	Unc	BU
2009 Proof	100	Value: 900				

KM# 134 200 RINGGIT
15.5500 g., Gold, 28 mm. **Subject:** 30th Annual Meeting Islamic Development Bank **Obv:** Mosque in rays **Obv. Legend:** BANK NEGARA MALAYSIA **Rev:** Logo

Date	Mintage	F	VF	XF	Unc	BU
2005 Proof	500	Value: 1,100				

PROOF SETS

KM#	Date	Mintage	Identification	Issue Price	Mkt Val
PS20	2003 (3)	300	KM#171-173	—	1,200
PS21	2003 (2)	300	KM#174, 175	—	200
PS22	2003 (3)	100	KM#174-176	—	1,800
PS23	2003 (2)	500	KM#177, 178	—	150
PS24	2003 (3)	250	KM#177-179	—	1,100
PS25	2005 (2)	300	KM#114, 115	—	150
PS26	2005 (3)	100	KM#114-116	—	1,400
PS27	2005 (2)	1,000	KM#132, 133	—	150
PS28	2005 (3)	500	KM#132-134	—	1,200
PS29	2005 (2)	200	KM#135, 136	—	150
PS30	2005 (3)	150	KM#135-137	—	1,200
PS31	2006 (2)	150	KM#138, 139	—	150
PS32	2005 (3)	150	KM#138-140	—	1,200
PS33	2006 (2)	300	KM#141, 142	—	150
PS34	2006 (3)	300	KM#141-143	—	1,200
PS35	2006 (2)	500	KM#144, 145	—	150
PS36	2006 (3)	500	KM#144-146	—	1,100
PS37	2006 (2)	300	KM#147, 148	—	150
PS38	2006 (3)	500	KM#147-149	—	1,000
PS39	2007 (2)	200	KM#162, 163	—	150
PS40	2007 (3)	200	KM#162-164	—	1,000

MALDIVE ISLANDS

INDIA
SRI LANKA
Indian Ocean

The Republic of Maldives, an archipelago of 2,000 coral islets in the northern Indian Ocean 417 miles (671 km.) west of Ceylon, has an area of 116 sq. mi. (298 sq. km.)and a population of 189,000. Capital: Male. Fishing employs 95% of the male work force. Dried fish, copra and coir yarn are exported.

The Maldive Islands were visited by Arab traders and converted to Islam in 1153. After being harassed in the16th and 17th centuries by Mopla pirates of the Malabar coast and Portuguese raiders, the Maldivians voluntarily placed themselves under the suzerainty of Ceylon. In 1887 the islands became an internally self-governing British protectorate and a nominal dependency of Ceylon. Traditionally a sultanate, the Maldives became a republic in 1953 but restored the sultanate in 1954. The Sultanate of the Maldive Islands attained complete internal and external autonomy on July 26, 1965, and on Nov. 11, 1968, again became a republic. The Maldives is a member of the Commonwealth of Nations.

MONETARY SYSTEM
100 Lari = 1 Rupee (Rufiyaa)

2ND REPUBLIC

STANDARD COINAGE

100 Laari = 1 Rufiyaa

KM# 68 LAARI

0.4600 g., Aluminum, 15 mm. **Obv:** Value **Rev:** Palm tree within circle **Edge:** Plain

Date	Mintage	F	VF	XF	Unc	BU
AH1423-2002	—	—	—	0.10	0.15	0.20
AH1433-2012	—	—	—	0.10	0.15	0.20

KM# 70 10 LAARI

1.9500 g., Aluminum, 23.11 mm. **Obv:** Value **Rev:** Maldivian sailing ship - Odi **Shape:** Scalloped

Date	Mintage	F	VF	XF	Unc	BU
AH1422-2001	—	—	—	0.10	0.20	0.30

KM# 71a 25 LAARI

Brass Plated Steel, 20.2 mm. **Obv:** Value **Rev:** Mosque and minaret at Male

Date	Mintage	F	VF	XF	Unc	BU
AH1429-2008	—	—	—	—	0.15	0.45

KM# 72a 50 LAARI

Brass Plated Steel, 23.6 mm. **Obv:** Value **Rev:** Loggerhead sea turtle

Date	Mintage	F	VF	XF	Unc	BU
AH1429-2008	—	—	—	—	1.50	2.50

KM# 73b RUFIYAA

6.5400 g., Nickel Plated Steel, 25.8 mm. **Obv:** Value **Obv. Legend:** REPUBLIC OF MALDIVES **Rev:** National arms **Edge:** Reeded

Date	Mintage	F	VF	XF	Unc	BU
AH1428-2007	—	—	—	0.50	2.00	3.00

KM# 105 RUFIYAA

26.0000 g., Silver Plated Copper, 38.61 mm. **Subject:** London Olympics **Obv:** National emblem **Rev:** Soccer

Date	Mintage	F	VF	XF	Unc	BU
2011 Proof	Est. 10,000	Value: 25.00				

KM# 88 2 RUFIYAA

11.7000 g., Nickel-Brass, 25.5 mm. **Obv:** Value **Rev:** Pacific triton sea shell **Edge:** Reeded and lettered **Edge Lettering:** REPUBLIC OF MALDIVES

Date	Mintage	F	VF	XF	Unc	BU
AH1428-2007	—	—	—	2.25	5.50	7.50

KM# 103 10 RUFIYAA

6.2200 g., 0.9990 Gold 0.1998 oz. AGW, 35 mm. **Subject:** Ships and Explorers **Obv:** National emblem **Rev:** Cutty Sark and map

Date	Mintage	F	VF	XF	Unc	BU
2011 Proof	Est. 5,000	Value: 550				

KM# 104 20 RUFIYAA

28.2800 g., 0.9250 Silver 0.8410 oz. ASW, 38.61 mm. **Subject:** London Olympics **Obv:** National emblem **Rev:** Soccer

Date	Mintage	F	VF	XF	Unc	BU
2011 Proof	Est. 7,500	Value: 45.00				

KM# 107 20 RUFIYAA

0.5000 g., 0.9990 Gold 0.0161 oz. AGW, 11 mm. **Obv:** National emblem **Rev:** Two Anemonefish left

Date	Mintage	F	VF	XF	Unc	BU
2011 Proof	Est. 5,000	Value: 55.00				

KM# 109 20 RUFIYAA

28.2800 g., 0.9250 Silver 0.8410 oz. ASW, 38.61 mm. **Subject:** Elizabeth II, 60th Anniversary of reign **Obv:** National emblem **Rev:** Windsor castle

Date	Mintage	F	VF	XF	Unc	BU
2011 Proof	10,000	Value: 45.00				

KM# 110 20 RUFIYAA

20.0000 g., 0.9250 Silver 0.5948 oz. ASW, 38.61 mm. **Subject:** 2014 FIFA World Cup, Brazil **Obv:** National emblem **Rev:** Soccer field and ball in color

Date	Mintage	F	VF	XF	Unc	BU
2012 Proof	Est. 10,000	Value: 45.00				

KM# 111 20 RUFIYAA

0.5000 g., 0.5850 Gold with 24kt plating 0.0094 oz. AGW, 11 mm. **Obv:** National emblem **Rev:** Picasso Triggerfish

Date	Mintage	F	VF	XF	Unc	BU
2012 Proof	Est. 5,000	Value: 35.00				

KM# 108 50 RUFIYAA

1.2400 g., 0.9990 Gold 0.0398 oz. AGW, 13.92 mm. **Obv:** National emblem **Rev:** Two anemonefish left

Date	Mintage	F	VF	XF	Unc	BU
2011 Proof	Est. 5,000	Value: 85.00				

KM# 106 500 RUFIYAA

7.7800 g., 0.5850 Gold plated with 24Kt. 0.1463 oz. AGW, 25 mm. **Subject:** London Olympics **Obv:** National emblem **Rev:** Soccer plauers

Date	Mintage	F	VF	XF	Unc	BU
2011 Proof	Est. 1,000	Value: 300				

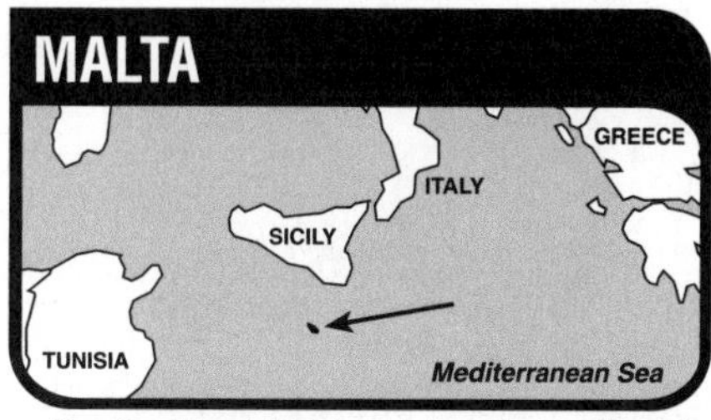

The Republic of Malta, an independent parliamentary democracy, is situated in the Mediterranean Sea between Sicily and North Africa. With the islands of Gozo and Comino, Malta has an area of 124 sq. mi. (320 sq. km.) and a population of 386,000.Capital: Valletta. Malta has no proven mineral resources, agriculture insufficient to its needs, and a small, but expanding, manufacturing facility. Clothing, textile yarns and fabrics, and knitted wear are exported.

Malta became a republic on Dec. 13, 1974, but remained a member of the Commonwealth of Nations. The president is Chief of State. The prime minister is the Head of Government. Malta is also a member of the European Union since May 2004.

REPUBLIC

DECIMAL COINAGE

10 Mils = 1 Cent; 100 Cents = 1 Pound

KM# 5 2 MILS

0.9500 g., Aluminum, 20.3 mm. **Obv:** Maltese cross **Rev:** Value within 3/4 wreath **Shape:** Scalloped **Designer:** Envin Cremona

Date	Mintage	F	VF	XF	Unc	BU
2005 In sets only	—	—	—	—	—	4.00
2006 In sets only	—	—	—	—	—	4.00
2007 In sets only	—	—	—	—	—	4.00

REFORM COINAGE

1982 - Present;
10 Mils = 1 Cent; 100 Cents = 1 Lira

KM# 93 CENT

2.8100 g., Nickel-Brass, 18.51 mm. **Obv:** Crowned shield within sprigs **Rev:** Common Weasel (ballottra) below value **Edge:** Plain

Date	Mintage	F	VF	XF	Unc	BU
2001	—	—	0.40	0.50	1.00	—
2002 In sets only	—	—	—	—	1.00	—
2004	—	—	0.40	0.50	0.75	—
2005 In sets only	—	—	—	—	1.00	—
2006 In sets only	—	—	—	—	1.00	—
2007 In sets only	—	—	—	—	1.00	—

KM# 94 2 CENTS

2.2600 g., Copper-Nickel, 17.78 mm. **Obv:** Crowned shield within sprigs **Rev:** Zebbuga branch and value **Edge:** Reeded

Date	Mintage	F	VF	XF	Unc	BU
2002	—	—	0.75	1.00	1.25	—
2004	—	—	0.75	1.00	1.25	—
2005	—	—	—	—	1.25	—
2006 In sets only	—	—	—	—	1.25	—
2007 In sets only	—	—	—	—	1.25	—

KM# 95 5 CENTS

3.5100 g., Copper-Nickel, 19.78 mm. **Obv:** Crowned shield within sprigs **Rev:** Freshwater Crab (il-Qobru) and value **Edge:** Reeded

Date	Mintage	F	VF	XF	Unc	BU
2001	—	—	0.75	1.00	1.25	2.00
2005 In sets only	—	—	—	—	—	2.00
2006 In sets only	—	—	—	—	—	2.00
2007 In sets only	—	—	—	—	—	2.00

KM# 96 10 CENTS

5.0100 g., Copper-Nickel, 21.78 mm. **Obv:** Crowned shield within sprigs **Rev:** Lampuka and value **Edge:** Reeded

Date	Mintage	F	VF	XF	Unc	BU
2005	—	—	1.25	1.50	2.00	—
2006 In sets only	—	—	—	—	2.00	—
2007 In sets only	—	—	—	—	2.00	—

KM# 97 25 CENTS

6.1900 g., Copper-Nickel, 24.95 mm. **Obv:** Crowned shield within sprigs **Rev:** Ghirlanda flower and value

Date	Mintage	F	VF	XF	Unc	BU
2001	—	—	2.25	2.50	3.00	—
2005	—	—	2.25	2.50	3.00	—
2006 In sets only	—	—	—	—	3.00	—
2007 In sets only	—	—	—	—	3.00	—

KM# 98 50 CENTS

8.0000 g., Copper-Nickel, 27 mm. **Obv:** Crowned shield within sprigs **Rev:** Tulliera plant and value **Edge Lettering:** BANK CENTRALI TA' MALTA

Date	Mintage	F	VF	XF	Unc	BU
2001	—	—	2.50	5.00	10.00	—
2005 In sets only	—	—	—	—	10.00	—
2006 In sets only	—	—	—	—	10.00	—
2007 In sets only	—	—	—	—	10.00	—

KM# 99 LIRA

13.0000 g., Nickel, 29.82 mm. **Obv:** Crowned shield within sprigs **Rev:** Merill bird and value **Edge Lettering:** BANK CENTRALI TA' MALTA

Date	Mintage	F	VF	XF	Unc	BU
2005	—	—	—	4.50	6.50	12.00
2006 In sets only	—	—	—	—	—	12.00
2007 In sets only	—	—	—	—	—	12.00

KM# 117 5 LIRI

28.2800 g., 0.9250 Silver 0.8410 oz. ASW, 38.6 mm. **Obv:** Crowned shield within sprigs **Rev:** Enrico Mizzi right **Edge:** Reeded

Date	Mintage	F	VF	XF	Unc	BU
2001 Proof	2,000	Value: 80.00				

KM# 118 5 LIRI

28.2800 g., 0.9250 Silver 0.8410 oz. ASW, 38.6 mm. **Obv:** Crowned shield within sprigs **Rev:** Nicolo Isouard left **Edge:** Reeded

Date	Mintage	F	VF	XF	Unc	BU
2002 Proof	2,000	Value: 80.00				

KM# 120 5 LIRI
28.2800 g., 0.9250 Silver 0.8410 oz. ASW, 38.6 mm. **Obv:** Crowned shield within sprigs **Rev:** Sir Adriano Dingli as Grand Commander of the St. Michael and George Order **Edge:** Reeded

Date	Mintage	F	VF	XF	Unc	BU
2003 Proof	2,000	Value: 80.00				

KM# 121 5 LIRI
28.2800 g., 0.9250 Silver 0.8410 oz. ASW, 38.6 mm. **Obv:** Crowned shield within sprigs **Rev:** Painter Giuseppe Cali with palette **Edge:** Reeded

Date	Mintage	F	VF	XF	Unc	BU
2004 Proof	2,000	Value: 120				

KM# 138 5 LIRI
Silver, 39 mm. **Subject:** Zammit **Edge:** Reeded

Date	Mintage	F	VF	XF	Unc	BU
2006 Proof	—	Value: 75.00				

KM# 123 5 LIRI
28.2800 g., 0.9250 Silver 0.8410 oz. ASW, 38.61 mm. **Subject:** 450th Anniversary of Jean de la Valette appointed Grand master **Rev:** de la Vallete standing facing left, city of Valletta map at lower left

Date	Mintage	F	VF	XF	Unc	BU
ND(2007) Proof	25,000	Value: 75.00				

KM# 119 10 LIRI
1.2400 g., 0.9990 Gold 0.0398 oz. AGW, 13.92 mm. **Obv:** Crowned shield within sprigs **Rev:** Xprunara sailboat **Edge:** Reeded

Date	Mintage	F	VF	XF	Unc	BU
2002 Prooflike	Est. 25,000	—	—	—	—	130

KM# 122 25 LIRI
3.9940 g., 0.9167 Gold 0.1177 oz. AGW, 19.3 mm. **Subject:** Accession to the European Union **Obv:** Crowned shield within sprigs **Rev:** Maltese flag under European Union star circle **Edge:** Reeded

Date	Mintage	F	VF	XF	Unc	BU
2004 Proof	6,000	Value: 290				

KM# 124 25 LIRI
6.5000 g., 0.9200 Gold 0.1923 oz. AGW, 21 mm. **Subject:** 450th Anniversary Jean de la Valette Appointed as Grand Master **Rev:** de la Valette standing facing left, city of Valletta map at lower left

Date	Mintage	F	VF	XF	Unc	BU
ND(2007) Proof	2,500	Value: 375				

EURO COINAGE

KM# 125 EURO CENT
2.3000 g., Copper Plated Steel, 16.25 mm. **Obv:** Doorway **Rev:** Denomination and globe **Edge:** Plain

Date	Mintage	F	VF	XF	Unc	BU
2008	—	—	—	—	—	1.00
2008 Proof	40,000	Value: 5.00				
2009 In sets only	40,000	—	—	—	—	1.50
2010 In sets only	30,000	—	—	—	—	1.50
2011 In sets only	50,000	—	—	—	—	1.50
2012 In sets only	50,000	—	—	—	—	1.50

KM# 126 2 EURO CENT
3.0600 g., Copper Plated Steel, 18.75 mm. **Obv:** Doorway **Rev:** Denomination and globe **Edge:** Grooved

Date	Mintage	F	VF	XF	Unc	BU
2008	—	—	—	—	—	0.70
2008 Proof	40,000	Value: 5.00				
2009 In sets only	40,000	—	—	—	—	2.00
2010 In sets only	30,000	—	—	—	—	2.00
2011 In sets only	50,000	—	—	—	—	2.00
2012 In sets only	50,000	—	—	—	—	2.00

KM# 127 5 EURO CENT
3.9200 g., Copper Plated Steel, 21.25 mm. **Obv:** Doorway **Rev:** Denomination and globe

Date	Mintage	F	VF	XF	Unc	BU
2008	—	—	—	—	—	0.70
2008 Proof	40,000	Value: 5.00				
2009 In sets only	40,000	—	—	—	—	2.50
2010 In sets only	30,000	—	—	—	—	2.50
2011 In sets only	50,000	—	—	—	—	2.50
2012 In sets only	50,000	—	—	—	—	2.50

KM# 128 10 EURO CENT
4.1000 g., Brass, 19.75 mm. **Obv:** Crowned shield within wreath **Rev:** Value and relief map of Europe **Edge:** Notched

Date	Mintage	F	VF	XF	Unc	BU
2008	—	—	—	—	—	1.00
2008 Proof	40,000	Value: 7.50				
2009 In sets only	40,000	—	—	—	—	3.00
2010 In sets only	30,000	—	—	—	—	3.00
2011 In sets only	50,000	—	—	—	—	3.00
2012 In sets only	50,000	—	—	—	—	3.00

KM# 129 20 EURO CENT
5.7500 g., Brass, 22.25 mm. **Obv:** Crowned shield within wreath **Rev:** Denomination and Map of Western Europe **Edge:** Notched

Date	Mintage	F	VF	XF	Unc	BU
2008	—	—	—	—	—	1.50
2008 Proof	40,000	Value: 7.50				
2009 In sets only	40,000	—	—	—	—	4.00
2010 In sets only	30,000	—	—	—	—	4.00
2011 In sets only	50,000	—	—	—	—	4.00
2012 In sets only	50,000	—	—	—	—	4.00

KM# 130 50 EURO CENT
7.8000 g., Brass, 24.25 mm. **Obv:** Crowned shield within wreath **Rev:** Relief map of Western Europe **Edge:** Reeded

Date	Mintage	F	VF	XF	Unc	BU
2008	—	—	—	—	—	2.00
2008 Proof	40,000	Value: 7.50				
2009 In sets only	40,000	—	—	—	—	5.00
2010 In sets only	30,000	—	—	—	—	5.00
2011 In sets only	50,000	—	—	—	—	5.00
2012 In sets only	50,000	—	—	—	—	5.00

KM# 131 EURO
7.5000 g., Bi-Metallic Copper-Nickel center in Nickel-Brass ring, 23.25 mm. **Obv:** Maltese Cross **Rev:** Value and relief map of Europe **Edge:** Segmented reeding

Date	Mintage	F	VF	XF	Unc	BU
2008	—	—	—	—	—	4.00
2008 Proof	40,000	Value: 15.00				
2009 In sets only	—	—	—	—	—	5.00
2010 In sets only	—	—	—	—	—	5.00
2011 In sets only	—	—	—	—	—	5.00
2012 In sets only	50,000	—	—	—	—	5.00

KM# 132 2 EURO
8.5000 g., Bi-Metallic Nickel-Brass center in Copper-Nickel ring, 25.75 mm. **Obv:** Maltese Cross **Rev:** Value and Relief Map of Western Europe **Edge:** Reeded with 2s and Maltese Crosses

Date	Mintage	F	VF	XF	Unc	BU
2008	—	—	—	—	—	6.00
2008 Proof	40,000	Value: 25.00				
2009 In sets only	—	—	—	—	—	8.00
2010 In sets only	—	—	—	—	—	8.00
2011 In sets only	—	—	—	—	—	8.00
2012 In sets only	50,000	—	—	—	—	8.00

KM# 134 2 EURO
8.5000 g., Bi-Metallic Nickel-Brass center in Copper-Nickel ring, 25.75 mm. **Subject:** E.M.U., 10th Anniversary **Obv:** Stick figure and large E symbol **Rev:** Value and relief map of Western Europe **Edge:** Segmented reeding

Date	Mintage	F	VF	XF	Unc	BU
2009	7,000,000	—	—	—	—	6.00

KM# 144 2 EURO
8.5000 g., Bi-Metallic Nickel-Brass center in Copper-Nickel ring, 25.75 mm. **Subject:** First Elected Representatives of 1849 **Obv:** Hand placing ballot in slot

Date	Mintage	F	VF	XF	Unc	BU
2011	375,000	—	—	—	6.00	8.00
2011 Special Unc.	50,000	—	—	—	—	15.00
2011 Proof	5,000	Value: 25.00				

KM# 139 2 EURO
8.5000 g., Bi-Metallic Nickel-Brass center in Copper-Nickel ring, 25.75 mm. **Subject:** Euro Coinage, 10th Anniversary **Obv:** Euro symbol on globe, child-like rendering around

Date	Mintage	F	VF	XF	Unc	BU
2012	7,000,000	—	—	—	6.00	8.00
2012 Proof	—	Value: 25.00				

KM# 145 2 EURO
8.5000 g., Bi-Metallic Nickel-Brass center in Copper-Nickel ring, 25.75 mm. **Subject:** Majority representation **Obv:** Jubilee crowd at Governor's Palace in Valletta

Date	Mintage	F	VF	XF	Unc	BU
2012	430,000	—	—	—	—	15.00

KM# 136 10 EURO
28.2800 g., 0.9250 Silver 0.8410 oz. ASW, 38.6 mm. **Subject:** Auberge de Castille **Rev:** Building tower

Date	Mintage	F	VF	XF	Unc	BU
2008 Proof	18,000	Value: 60.00				

KM# 133 10 EURO
28.2800 g., 0.9250 Silver 0.8410 oz. ASW, 38.6 mm. **Rev:** La Castellania, Merchant's Street, Valletta

Date	Mintage	F	VF	XF	Unc	BU
2009 Proof	15,000	Value: 60.00				

KM# 140 10 EURO
28.2800 g., 0.9250 Silver 0.8410 oz. ASW, 38.61 mm. **Subject:** Valetta - Auberge d'Italie **Obv:** Crowned shield **Rev:** Archetectural detail

Date	Mintage	F	VF	XF	Unc	BU
2010 Proof	12,500	Value: 65.00				

KM# 142 10 EURO
28.2800 g., 0.9250 Silver 0.8410 oz. ASW, 38.61 mm. **Subject:** Phoenicians in Malta **Obv:** Crowned shield **Rev:** Ancient Phoenician boat

Date	Mintage	F	VF	XF	Unc	BU
2011 Proof	10,000	Value: 75.00				

KM# 137 50 EURO
6.5000 g., 0.9160 Gold 0.1914 oz. AGW, 21 mm. **Subject:** Auberge de Castille **Rev:** Building tower

Date	Mintage	F	VF	XF	Unc	BU
2008 Proof	3,000	Value: 375				

KM# 135 50 EURO
6.5000 g., 0.9160 Gold 0.1914 oz. AGW, 21 mm. **Rev:** La Castellania, Merchant's Street, Valletta

Date	Mintage	F	VF	XF	Unc	BU
2009 Proof	3,000	Value: 375				

KM# 141 50 EURO
6.5000 g., 0.9160 Gold 0.1914 oz. AGW, 21 mm. **Subject:** Valetta - Auberge d'Italie **Obv:** Crowned shield **Rev:** Archetectural detail

Date	Mintage	F	VF	XF	Unc	BU
2010 Proof	3,000	Value: 400				

KM# 143 50 EURO
6.5000 g., 0.9160 Gold 0.1914 oz. AGW, 21 mm. **Subject:** Phoenicians in Malta **Obv:** Crowned shield **Rev:** Ancient Phoenician boat

Date	Mintage	F	VF	XF	Unc	BU
2011 Proof	2,000	Value: 385				

MINT SETS

KM#	Date	Mintage	Identification	Issue Price	Mkt Val
MS26	2005 (8)	—	KM#5, 93-99	—	35.00
MS27	2006 (8)	—	KM#5, 93-99	—	37.50
MS28	2007 (8)	—	KM#5, 93-99	—	45.00
MS29	2008 (8)	40,000	KM#125-132, wooden box	—	70.00
MS30	2008 (8)	30,000	KM#125-132, Malta Post and Lombard Bank card	—	45.00

PROOF SETS

KM#	Date	Mintage	Identification	Issue Price	Mkt Val
PS12	2008 (9)	40,000	KM#125-132, plus ingot	—	80.00

MAURITANIA

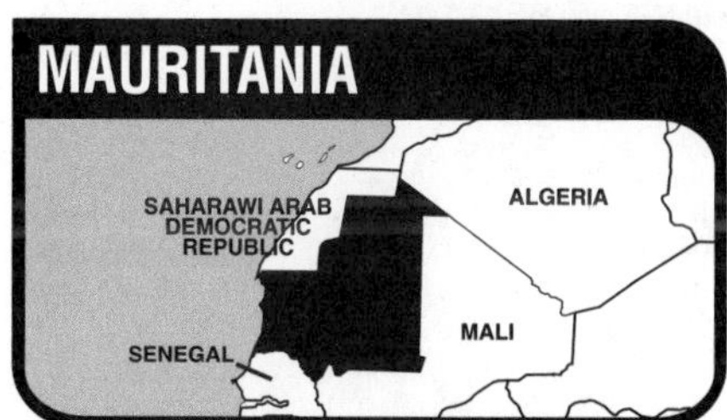

The Islamic Republic of Mauritania, located in northwest Africa bounded by Western Sahara, Mali, Algeria, Senegal and the Atlantic Ocean, has an area of 397,955 sq. mi.(1,030,700 sq. km.) and a population of 1.9 million. Capital: Nouakchott. The economy centers on herding, agriculture, fishing and mining. Iron ore, copper concentrates and fish products are exported.

On June 28, 1973, in a move designed to emphasize its non-alignment with France, Mauritania converted its currency from the old French-supported C.F.A. franc unit to a new unit called the Ouguiya.

MONETARY SYSTEM
5 Khoums = 1 Ouguiya

REPUBLIC

STANDARD COINAGE

KM# 6 OUGUIYA
3.6000 g., Aluminum-Bronze, 21 mm. **Obv:** National emblem divides date above value **Obv. Legend:** BANQUE CENTRALE DE MAURITANIE **Rev:** Star and crescent divide sprigs with legend below value, all within circle **Edge:** Reeded

Date	Mintage	F	VF	XF	Unc	BU
AH1423//2003	—	—	—	0.50	1.25	2.00

KM# 3 5 OUGUIYA
5.8800 g., Aluminum-Bronze, 25 mm. **Obv:** National emblem divides date above value **Obv. Legend:** BANQUE CENTRALE DE MAURITANIE **Rev:** Star and crescent divide sprigs below value within circle **Edge:** Plain

Date	Mintage	F	VF	XF	Unc	BU
AH1423//2003	—	—	—	1.75	3.50	5.00
AH1425//2004	—	—	—	1.75	3.50	5.00

KM# 3a 5 OUGUIYA
6.0000 g., Copper Plated Steel, 25 mm. **Obv:** National emblem divides date above value **Obv. Legend:** BANQUE CENTRALE DE MAURITANIE **Rev:** Star and crescent divides sprigs below value within circle **Edge:** Plain

Date	Mintage	F	VF	XF	Unc	BU
AH1425//2004	—	—	—	1.00	2.00	3.00
AH1426//2005	—	—	—	1.00	2.00	3.00
AH1430//2009	—	—	—	1.00	2.00	3.00

KM# 4 10 OUGUIYA
6.0000 g., Copper-Nickel, 25 mm. **Obv:** National emblem divides date above value **Obv. Legend:** BANQUE CENTRALE DE MAURITANIE **Rev:** Crescent and star divide sprigs below value within circle **Edge:** Reeded

Date	Mintage	F	VF	XF	Unc	BU
AH1423//2003	—	—	—	2.00	4.00	5.50
AH1425//2004	—	—	—	2.00	4.00	5.50

KM# 4a 10 OUGUIYA
5.8000 g., Nickel Plated Steel, 24.5 mm. **Obv:** National emblem divides date above value **Obv. Legend:** BANQUE CENTRALE DE MAURITANIE **Rev:** Crescent and star divides sprigs below value within circle **Edge:** Reeded

Date	Mintage	F	VF	XF	Unc	BU
AH1425//2004	—	—	—	1.25	3.00	4.50
AH1426//2005	—	—	—	1.25	3.00	4.50

KM# 5 20 OUGUIYA
8.0000 g., Copper-Nickel, 28 mm. **Obv:** National emblem divides date above value **Obv. Legend:** BANQUE CENTRALE DE MAURITANIE **Rev:** Star and crescent divide sprigs below value within circle **Edge:** Reeded

Date	Mintage	F	VF	XF	Unc	BU
AH1423//2003	—	—	—	3.00	6.00	8.00
AH1425//2004	—	—	—	3.00	6.00	8.00

KM# 5a 20 OUGUIYA
7.8000 g., Nickel Plated Steel, 28 mm. **Obv:** National emblem divides date above value **Obv. Legend:** BANQUE CENTRALE DE MAURITANIE **Rev:** Star and crescent divide sprigs below value within circle **Edge:** Reeded

Date	Mintage	F	VF	XF	Unc	BU
AH1425//2004	—	—	—	2.00	4.00	6.00
AH1426//2005	—	—	—	2.00	4.00	6.00
AH1430//2009	—	—	—	2.00	4.00	6.00

KM# 8 20 OUGUIYA
Bi-Metallic Copper-Nickel center in Brass ring **Obv:** Value within wreath **Rev:** National arms above value

Date	Mintage	F	VF	XF	Unc	BU
2009	—	—	—	—	6.00	7.50
2010	—	—	—	—	6.00	7.50

KM# 9 50 OUGUIYA
Bi-Metallic Nickel-Brass center in Copper-Nickel ring **Obv:** Value above wreath **Rev:** National arms above value

Date	Mintage	F	VF	XF	Unc	BU
2010	—	—	—	—	5.00	7.50

MAURITIUS

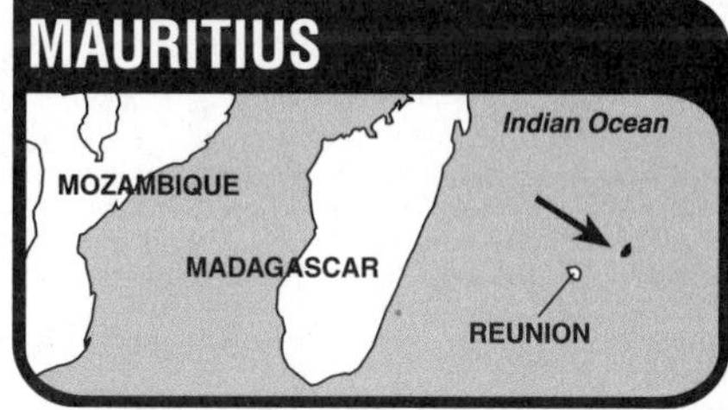

The Republic of Mauritius, is located in the Indian Ocean 500 miles (805 km.) east of Madagascar, has an area of 790 sq. mi. (1,860 sq. km.) and a population of 1 million. Capital: Port Louis. Sugar provides 90 percent of the export revenue.

Mauritius became independent on March 12, 1968. It is a member of the Commonwealth of Nations.

MONETARY SYSTEM
100 Cents = 1 Rupee

REPUBLIC

STANDARD COINAGE

KM# 52 5 CENTS
3.0000 g., Copper Plated Steel **Obv:** Value within beaded circle **Rev:** Bust of Sir Seewoosagur Ramgoolam 3/4 right

Date	Mintage	F	VF	XF	Unc	BU
2003	—	—	—	0.10	0.35	0.50
2004	—	—	—	0.10	0.35	0.50
2005	—	—	—	0.10	0.35	0.50
2007	—	—	—	0.10	0.35	0.50
2010	—	—	—	0.10	0.35	0.50
2012	—	—	—	0.10	0.35	0.50

KM# 53 20 CENTS
3.0000 g., Nickel Plated Steel, 19 mm. **Obv:** Value within beaded circle **Rev:** Bust of Sir Seewoosagur Ramgoolam 3/4 right

Date	Mintage	F	VF	XF	Unc	BU
2001	—	—	—	0.20	0.50	0.75
2003	—	—	—	0.20	0.50	0.75
2004	—	—	—	0.20	0.50	0.75
2005	—	—	—	0.20	0.50	0.75
2007	—	—	—	0.20	0.50	0.75
2010	—	—	—	0.20	0.50	0.75
2012	—	—	—	0.20	0.50	0.75

KM# 54 1/2 RUPEE
5.9000 g., Nickel Plated Steel, 23.6 mm. **Obv:** Stag left **Rev:** Bust of Sir Seewoosagur Ramgoolam 3/4 right

Date	Mintage	F	VF	XF	Unc	BU
2002	—	—	—	0.60	1.50	2.00
2003	—	—	—	0.60	1.50	2.00
2004	—	—	—	0.60	1.50	2.00
2005	—	—	—	0.60	1.50	2.00
2007	—	—	—	0.60	1.50	2.00
2009	—	—	—	0.60	1.50	2.00
2010	—	—	—	0.60	1.50	2.00

KM# 55 RUPEE
7.5000 g., Copper-Nickel, 26.6 mm. **Obv:** Shield divides date above value **Rev:** Bust of Sir Seewoosagur Ramgoolam 3/4 right **Edge:** Reeded

Date	Mintage	F	VF	XF	Unc	BU
2002	—	—	—	0.65	1.65	2.75
2004	—	—	—	0.65	1.65	2.75
2005	—	—	—	0.65	1.65	2.75
2007	—	—	—	0.65	1.65	2.75
2008	—	—	—	0.65	1.65	2.75
2009	—	—	—	0.65	1.65	2.75
2010	—	—	—	0.65	1.65	2.75

KM# 55a RUPEE
Nickel Plated Steel, 26.6 mm. **Obv:** Shield **Rev:** Sir Seewoosagur Ramgoolam 3/4 right

Date	Mintage	F	VF	XF	Unc	BU
2012	—	—	—	—	1.65	2.75

KM# 56 5 RUPEES
12.4000 g., Copper-Nickel, 31 mm. **Obv:** Value within palm trees **Rev:** Bust of Sir Seewoosagur Ramgoolam 3/4 right

Date	Mintage	F	VF	XF	Unc	BU
2009	—	—	—	—	3.00	5.00
2010	—	—	—	—	3.00	5.00
2012	—	—	—	—	3.00	5.00

KM# 66 20 RUPEES
10.1000 g., Bi-Metallic Copper-Nickel center in Aluminum-Bronze ring, 27.96 mm. **Obv:** Modern tower **Rev:** Bust of Sir Seewoosagur Ramgoolam KT 3/4 right **Edge:** Reeded

Date	Mintage	F	VF	XF	Unc	BU
2007	—	—	—	2.00	5.00	7.00

KM# 65 100 RUPEES
36.5700 g., 0.9250 Silver 1.0875 oz. ASW, 43.9 mm. **Obv:** National arms, date below **Obv. Legend:** MAURITIUS ONE HUNDRED RUPEES **Rev:** Bust of Gandhi 3/4 right **Rev. Legend:** MAHATMA GANDHI CENTENARY OF ARRIVAL IN MAURITIUS **Edge:** Reeded

Date	Mintage	F	VF	XF	Unc	BU
2001 Proof	—	Value: 125				

KM# 67 1500 RUPEES
7.7800 g., 0.9990 Platinum 0.2499 oz. APW, 25 mm. **Subject:** Sir Seewoosagur Ramgoolan **Obv:** Portrait **Rev:** State House **Edge:** Plain

Date	Mintage	F	VF	XF	Unc	BU
2009 Proof	—	Value: 500				

MEXICO

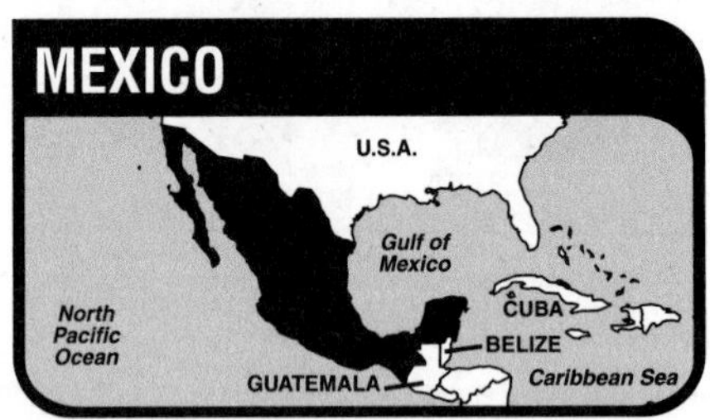

The United Mexican States, located immediately south of the United States has an area of 759,529 sq. mi. (1,967,183 sq. km.) and an estimated population of 100 million. Capital: Mexico City. The economy is based on agriculture, manufacturing and mining. Oil, cotton, silver, coffee, and shrimp are exported.

UNITED STATES

REFORM COINAGE

1 New Peso = 1000 Old Pesos; 100 centavos = 1 New Peso; 100 Centavos = 1 Peso

KM# 546 5 CENTAVOS
1.5800 g., Stainless Steel, 15.5 mm. **Obv:** National arms **Rev:** Large value **Edge:** Plain

Date	Mintage	F	VF	XF	Unc	BU
2001Mo	34,811,000	—	—	0.15	0.20	0.50
2002Mo	14,901,000	—	—	0.20	0.75	1.00

KM# 547 10 CENTAVOS
2.0800 g., Stainless Steel, 17 mm. **Obv:** National arms, eagle left **Rev:** Large value

Date	Mintage	F	VF	XF	Unc	BU
2001Mo	618,061,000	—	—	0.20	0.25	0.30
2002Mo	463,968,000	—	—	0.20	0.25	0.30
2003Mo	378,938,000	—	—	0.20	0.25	0.30
2004Mo	393,705,000	—	—	0.20	0.25	0.30
2005Mo	488,594,000	—	—	0.20	0.25	0.30
2006Mo	473,261,000	—	—	0.20	0.25	0.30
2007Mo	498,735,000	—	—	0.20	0.25	0.30
2008Mo	433,951,000	—	—	0.20	0.25	0.30
2009Mo	90,968,000	—	—	0.20	0.25	0.30

KM# 934 10 CENTAVOS
1.7500 g., Stainless Steel, 14 mm. **Obv:** National arms **Rev:** Large value **Edge:** Grooved

Date	Mintage	F	VF	XF	Unc	BU
2009Mo	343,772,000	—	—	—	0.10	0.25
2010Mo	453,849,000	—	—	—	0.10	0.25
2011Mo	463,960,000	—	—	—	0.10	0.25
2012Mo	—	—	—	—	0.10	0.25

KM# 548 20 CENTAVOS
3.0400 g., Aluminum-Bronze, 19.5 mm. **Obv:** National arms, eagle left **Rev:** Value and date within 3/4 wreath **Shape:** 12-sided

Date	Mintage	F	VF	XF	Unc	BU
2001Mo	234,360,000	—	—	0.25	0.35	0.40
2002Mo	229,256,000	—	—	0.25	0.35	0.40
2003Mo	149,518,000	—	—	0.25	0.35	0.40
2004Mo	174,351,000	—	—	0.25	0.35	0.40
2005Mo	204,426,000	—	—	0.25	0.35	0.40
2006Mo	234,263,000	—	—	0.25	0.35	0.40
2007Mo	234,301,000	—	—	0.25	0.35	0.40
2008Mo	214,313,000	—	—	0.25	0.35	0.40
2009Mo	41,167,000	—	—	0.25	0.35	0.40

KM# 935 20 CENTAVOS
2.2580 g., Stainless Steel, 15.3 mm. **Obv:** National arms **Rev:** Value and date within wreath **Edge:** Segmented reeding

Date	Mintage	F	VF	XF	Unc	BU
2009Mo	164,362,000	—	—	—	0.25	0.35
2010Mo	224,359,000	—	—	—	0.25	0.35
2011Mo	239,362,000	—	—	—	0.25	0.35
2012Mo	—	—	—	—	0.25	0.35

KM# 549 50 CENTAVOS
4.3900 g., Aluminum-Bronze, 22 mm. **Obv:** National arms, eagle left **Rev:** Value and date within 1/2 designed wreath **Shape:** 12-sided

Date	Mintage	F	VF	XF	Unc	BU
2001Mo	199,006,000	—	—	0.45	0.75	1.00
2002Mo	94,552,000	—	—	0.45	0.75	1.00
2003Mo	124,522,000	—	—	0.45	0.75	1.00
2004Mo	154,434,000	—	—	0.45	0.75	1.00
2005Mo	179,296,000	—	—	0.45	0.75	1.00
2006Mo	234,142,000	—	—	0.45	0.75	1.00
2007Mo	253,634,000	—	—	0.45	0.75	1.00
2008Mo	249,279,000	—	—	0.45	0.75	1.00
2009Mo	90,602,000	—	—	0.45	0.75	1.00

KM# 936 50 CENTAVOS
3.1030 g., Stainless Steel, 17 mm. **Obv:** National arms **Rev:** Value and date within wreath **Edge:** Reeded

Date	Mintage	F	VF	XF	Unc	BU
2009Mo	19,910,000	—	—	—	0.75	1.00
2010Mo	114,567,000	—	—	—	0.75	1.00
2011Mo	194,480,000	—	—	—	0.75	1.00
2012Mo	—	—	—	—	0.60	0.75

KM# 603 PESO
3.9500 g., Bi-Metallic Aluminum-Bronze center in Stainless Steel ring, 21 mm. **Obv:** National arms, eagle left within circle **Rev:** Value and date within circle **Note:** Similar to KM#550 but without N.

Date	Mintage	F	VF	XF	Unc	BU
2001Mo	208,576,000	—	—	—	1.25	2.75
2002Mo	119,514,000	—	—	—	1.25	2.75
2003Mo	169,320,000	—	—	—	1.25	2.75
2004Mo	208,611,000	—	—	—	1.25	2.75
2005Mo	253,923,000	—	—	—	1.25	2.75
2006Mo	289,834,000	—	—	—	1.25	2.75

Date	Mintage	F	VF	XF	Unc	BU
2007Mo	368,408,000	—	—	—	1.25	2.75
2008Mo	363,878,000	—	—	—	1.25	2.75
2009Mo	239,229,000	—	—	—	1.25	2.75
2010Mo	209,313,000	—	—	—	0.75	1.25
2011Mo	199,283,000	—	—	—	0.75	1.00
2012Mo	—	—	—	—	0.75	1.00

KM# 604 2 PESOS

5.1900 g., Bi-Metallic Aluminum-Bronze center in Stainless Steel ring, 23 mm. **Obv:** National arms, eagle left within circle **Rev:** Value and date within center circle of assorted emblems **Note:** Similar to KM#551, but denomination without N.

Date	Mintage	F	VF	XF	Unc	BU
2001Mo	74,563,000	—	—	—	2.35	4.00
2002Mo	74,547,000	—	—	—	2.35	4.00
2003Mo	39,814,000	—	—	—	2.35	4.00
2004Mo	89,496,000	—	—	—	2.35	4.00
2005Mo	94,532,000	—	—	—	2.35	4.00
2006Mo	144,123,000	—	—	—	2.35	4.00
2007Mo	129,422,000	—	—	—	2.35	4.00
2008Mo	134,235,000	—	—	—	2.35	4.00
2009Mo	64,650,000	—	—	—	2.35	4.00
2010Mo	34,878,000	—	—	—	1.00	1.50
2011Mo	114,522,000	—	—	—	1.00	1.50
2012Mo	—	—	—	—	1.00	1.25

KM# 651 5 PESOS

31.1710 g., 0.9990 Silver 1.0011 oz. ASW, 40 mm. **Series:** Endangered Wildlife - Nanatee **Obv:** National arms in center of past and present arms **Rev:** Manatee, value and date **Edge:** Reeded

Date	Mintage	F	VF	XF	Unc	BU
2001Mo	30,000	—	—	—	40.00	50.00

KM# 653 5 PESOS

31.1710 g., 0.9990 Silver 1.0011 oz. ASW, 40 mm. **Series:** Endangered Wildlife **Subject:** Harpy Eagle (Aguila Arpia) **Obv:** National arms in center of past and present arms **Rev:** Crowned Harpy Eagle perched on branch, value and date

Date	Mintage	F	VF	XF	Unc	BU
2001Mo	30,000	—	—	—	40.00	50.00

KM# 654 5 PESOS

31.1710 g., 0.9990 Silver 1.0011 oz. ASW, 40 mm. **Series:** Endangered Wildlife **Subject:** Black Bear (Oso Negro) **Obv:** National arms in center of past and present arms **Rev:** Black bear, value and date

Date	Mintage	F	VF	XF	Unc	BU
2001Mo	30,000	—	—	—	40.00	50.00

KM# 658 5 PESOS

31.1710 g., 0.9990 Silver 1.0011 oz. ASW, 40 mm. **Series:** Endangered Wildlife - Jaguar **Obv:** National arms in center of past and present arms **Rev:** Jaguar, value and date

Date	Mintage	F	VF	XF	Unc	BU
2001Mo	30,000	—	—	—	40.00	50.00

KM# 659 5 PESOS

31.1710 g., 0.9990 Silver 1.0011 oz. ASW, 40 mm. **Series:** Endangered Wildlife - Prairie Dog **Obv:** National arms in center of past and present arms **Rev:** Prairie dog, value and date

Date	Mintage	F	VF	XF	Unc	BU
2001Mo	30,000	—	—	—	40.00	50.00

KM# 660 5 PESOS

31.1710 g., 0.9990 Silver 1.0011 oz. ASW, 40 mm. **Series:** Endangered Wildlife - Volcano Rabbit **Obv:** National arms in center of past and present arms **Rev:** Volcano rabbit, value and date

Date	Mintage	F	VF	XF	Unc	BU
2001Mo	30,000	—	—	—	40.00	50.00

KM# 605 5 PESOS

7.0700 g., Bi-Metallic Aluminum-Bronze center in Stainless Steel ring, 25.5 mm. **Obv:** National arms, eagle left within circle **Rev:** Value within circle **Note:** Similar to KM#552 but denomination without N.

Date	Mintage	F	VF	XF	Unc	BU
2001Mo	79,169,000	—	—	2.00	3.50	8.00
2002Mo	34,754,000	—	—	2.00	3.50	6.00
2003Mo	54,676,000	—	—	2.00	3.50	6.00
2004Mo	89,518,000	—	—	2.00	3.50	6.00
2005Mo	94,482,000	—	—	2.00	3.50	6.00
2006Mo	89,447,000	—	—	2.00	3.50	6.00
2007Mo	123,382,000	—	—	2.00	3.50	6.00
2008Mo	9,939,000	—	—	2.50	4.00	6.00
2009Mo	9,898,000	—	—	2.50	4.00	6.00
2010Mo	6,929,000	—	—	2.50	3.00	3.50

Date	Mintage	F	VF	XF	Unc	BU
2011Mo	209,214,000	—	—	1.00	2.00	2.50
2012Mo	—	—	—	1.00	2.00	2.50

KM# 678 5 PESOS

27.0000 g., 0.9250 Silver 0.8029 oz. ASW, 40 mm. **Series:** Ibero-America **Subject:** Acapulco Galleon **Obv:** National arms in center of past and present arms **Rev:** Spanish galleon with Pacific Ocean background and trading scene in foreground **Edge:** Reeded

Date	Mintage	F	VF	XF	Unc	BU
2003Mo Proof	17,015	Value: 90.00				

KM# 765 5 PESOS

31.1035 g., 0.9250 Silver 0.9250 oz. ASW, 40 mm. **Series:** Ibero-America **Subject:** Palacio de Bellas Artes **Obv:** Mexican Eagle and Snake **Rev:** Palace of Fine Arts **Edge:** Reeded

Date	Mintage	F	VF	XF	Unc	BU
2005Mo Proof	8,005	Value: 90.00				

KM# 769 5 PESOS

15.5518 g., 0.9990 Silver 0.4995 oz. ASW, 33 mm. **Subject:** Monetary Reform of 1905 **Obv:** Mexican Eagle and Snake **Rev:** Cap and rays coin design

Date	Mintage	F	VF	XF	Unc	BU
2005Mo Proof	1,505	Value: 60.00				

KM# 770 5 PESOS

31.1035 g., 0.9990 Silver 0.9990 oz. ASW, 40 mm. **Subject:** World Cup Soccer **Obv:** Mexican Eagle and Snake **Rev:** Mayan Pelota player and soccer ball

Date	Mintage	F	VF	XF	Unc	BU
2006Mo Proof	40,005	Value: 90.00				

KM# 805 5 PESOS

31.1050 g., 0.9250 Silver 0.9250 oz. ASW, 40 mm. **Series:** Ibero-America **Obv:** Eagle on cactus within shields **Rev:** Mayan ball game

Date	Mintage	F	VF	XF	Unc	BU
2008Mo Proof	8,013	Value: 75.00				

KM# 900.2 5 PESOS

7.0700 g., 0.9990 Bi-Metallic Aluminum-Bronze center in Stainless Steel ring 0.2271 oz., 25.5 mm. **Series:** Mexican Independence 200th Anniversary **Subject:** Francisco Primode Verdad y Ramos **Obv:** National arms - Eagle left **Rev:** Francisco Primode Verdad y Ramos bust right **Note:** No pellets at 4 and 7 o'clock in legend.

Date	Mintage	F	VF	XF	Unc	BU
2008Mo	Inc. above	—	—	—	—	—

KM# 894 5 PESOS

7.0700 g., Bi-Metallic Aluminum-bronze center in stainless steel ring, 25.5 mm. **Series:** Mexican Independence, 200th Anniversary **Subject:** Ignacio Rayon **Obv:** National Arms - Eagle left **Rev:** Ignacio Rayon bust left

Date	Mintage	F	VF	XF	Unc	BU
2008Mo	9,934,397	—	—	0.75	1.50	—
2008Mo Prooflike	4,267	—	—	—	—	7.50

KM# 895 5 PESOS

7.0700 g., Bi-Metallic Aluminum-bronze center in stainless steel ring, 25.5 mm. **Series:** Mexican Revolution 100th Anniversary **Subject:** Alvaro Obregon **Obv:** National Arms - Eagle left **Rev:** Alvaro Obregon bust 3/4 facing left

Date	Mintage	F	VF	XF	Unc	BU
2008Mo	9,948,722	—	—	0.75	1.50	—
2008Mo Prooflike	4,727	—	—	—	—	7.50

KM# 896 5 PESOS

7.0700 g., Bi-Metallic Aluninum-bronze center in stainless steel ring, 25.5 mm. **Series:** Mexican Independence 200th Anniversary **Subject:** Carlos Maria de Bustamante **Obv:** National Arms - Eagle left **Rev:** Carlos Maria de Bustamante bust left

Date	Mintage	F	VF	XF	Unc	BU
2008Mo	9,941,302	—	—	0.75	1.50	—
2008Mo Prooflike	4,852	—	—	—	—	7.50

KM# 897 5 PESOS

7.0700 g., Bi-Metallic Aluminum-bronze center in stainless steel ring, 25.5 mm. **Series:** Mexican Revolution 100th Anniversary **Subject:** Jose Vasconcelos **Obv:** National Arms - Eagle left **Rev:** Jose Vasconcelos bust left

Date	Mintage	F	VF	XF	Unc	BU
2008Mo	9,939,839	—	—	0.75	1.50	—
2008Mo Prooflike	4,767	—	—	—	—	7.50

KM# 898 5 PESOS

7.0700 g., Bi-Metallic Aluminum-bronze center in stainless steel ring, 25.5 mm. **Series:** Mexican Independence 200th Anniversary **Subject:** Francisco Xavier Mina **Obv:** National Arms - Eagle left **Rev:** Francisco Mina bust 3/4 facing left

Date	Mintage	F	VF	XF	Unc	BU
2008Mo	9,914,938	—	—	0.75	1.50	—
2008Mo Prooflike	4,523	—	—	—	—	7.50

KM# 899 5 PESOS

7.0700 g., Bi-Metallic Aluminum-bronze center in stainless steel ring, 25.5 mm. **Series:** Mexican Revolution 100th Anniversary **Subject:** Francisco Villa **Obv:** National Arms - Eagle left **Rev:** Francisco Villa on horseback left

Date	Mintage	F	VF	XF	Unc	BU
2008Mo	9,917,084	—	—	0.75	1.50	—
2008Mo Prooflike	4,866	—	—	—	—	7.50

KM# 900.1 5 PESOS

7.0700 g., Bi-Metallic Aluminum-Bronze center in Stainless Steel ring, 25.5 mm. **Series:** Mexican Independence 200th Anniversary **Subject:** Francisco Primo de Verdad y Ramos **Obv:** National Arms - Eagle left **Rev:** Francisco Primode Verdad y Ramos bust right **Note:** Pellets at 4 and 7 o'clock in legend.

Date	Mintage	F	VF	XF	Unc	BU
2008Mo	9,937,000	—	—	0.75	1.50	—
2008Mo Prooflike	4,279	—	—	—	—	7.50

KM# 901 5 PESOS

7.0700 g., Bi-Metallic Aluminum-Bronze center in Stainless Steel ring, 25.5 mm. **Series:** Mexican Revolution 100th Anniversary **Subject:** Heriberto Jara **Obv:** National Arms - Eagle left **Rev:** Heriberto Jara bust 3/4 left

Date	Mintage	F	VF	XF	Unc	BU
2008Mo	9,936,333	—	—	0.75	1.50	—
2008Mo Prooflike	4,870	—	—	—	—	7.50

KM# 902 5 PESOS

7.0700 g., Bi-Metallic Aluminum-Bronze center in Stainless Steel ring, 25.5 mm. **Series:** Mexican Independence 200th Anniversary **Subject:** Mariano Matamoros **Obv:** National Arms - Eagle left **Rev:** Mariano Matamoros bust 3/4 facing right

Date	Mintage	F	VF	XF	Unc	BU
2008Mo	9,947,802	—	—	0.75	1.50	—
2008Mo Prooflike	4,820	—	—	—	—	7.50

KM# 903 5 PESOS

7.0700 g., Bi-Metallic Aluminum-Bronze center in Stainless Steel ring, 25.5 mm. **Series:** Mexican Revolution 100th Anniversary **Subject:** Ricardo Magon **Obv:** National Arms - Eagle left **Rev:** Ricardo Magon bust right

Date	Mintage	F	VF	XF	Unc	BU
2008Mo	9,940,278	—	—	0.75	1.50	—
2008Mo Prooflike	4,690	—	—	—	—	7.50

KM# 904 5 PESOS

7.0700 g., Bi-Metallic Aluminum-Bronze center in Stainless Steel ring, 25.5 mm. **Series:** Mexican Independence 200th Anniversary **Subject:** Miguel Ramos Arizpe **Obv:** National Arms - Eagle left **Rev:** Miguel Ramos Arizpe bust right

Date	Mintage	F	VF	XF	Unc	BU
2008Mo	9,927,433	—	—	0.75	1.50	—
2008Mo Prooflike	4,863	—	—	—	—	7.50

KM# 905 5 PESOS

7.0700 g., Bi-Metallic Aluminum-Bronze center in Stainless Steel ring, 25.5 mm. **Series:** Mexican Revolution 100th Anniversary **Subject:** Francisco J. Mugica **Obv:** National arms, eagle left **Rev:** Francisco J. Mugica bust 3/4 facing left

Date	Mintage	F	VF	XF	Unc	BU
2008Mo	9,926,537	—	—	0.75	1.50	—
2008Mo Prooflike	4,588	—	—	—	—	7.50

KM# 906 5 PESOS

7.0700 g., Bi-Metallic Aluminum-Bronze center in Stainless Steel ring, 25.5 mm. **Series:** Mexican Independence 200th Anniversary **Subject:** Hermenegildo Galeana **Obv:** National Arms, eagle left **Rev:** Hermenegildo Galeana bust 3/4 facing left

Date	Mintage	F	VF	XF	Unc	BU
2008Mo	9,935,901	—	—	0.75	1.50	—
2008Mo Prooflike	4,966	—	—	—	—	7.50

KM# 907 5 PESOS

7.0700 g., Bi-Metallic Aluminum-Bronze center in Stainless Steel ring, 25.5 mm. **Series:** Mexican Revolution, 100th Anniversary **Subject:** Filomeno Mata **Obv:** National arms, eagle left **Rev:** Filomeno Mata bust facing left.

Date	Mintage	F	VF	XF	Unc	BU
2009Mo	9,935,689	—	—	0.75	1.50	—
2009Mo Prooflike	4,920	—	—	—	—	7.50

KM# 908 5 PESOS

7.0700 g., Bi-Metallic Aluminum-Bronze cetner in Stainless Steel ring, 25.5 mm. **Series:** Mexican Independence 200th Anniversary **Subject:** Jose Maria Cos **Obv:** National arms, eagle left. **Rev:** Jose Maria Cos bust right

Date	Mintage	F	VF	XF	Unc	BU
2009Mo	9,935,040	—	—	0.75	1.50	—
2009Mo Prooflike	4,950	—	—	—	—	7.50

KM# 909 5 PESOS

7.0700 g., Bi-Metallic Aluminum-Bronze center in Stainless Steel ring, 25.5 mm. **Series:** Mexican Revolution 100th Anniversary **Subject:** Carmen Serdan **Obv:** National Amrs, Eagle left **Rev:** Carmen Serdan bust facing slightly right

Date	Mintage	F	VF	XF	Unc	BU
2009Mo	7,160,841	—	—	0.75	1.50	—
2009Mo Prooflike	4,787	—	—	—	—	7.50

KM# 910 5 PESOS

7.0700 g., Bi-Metallic Aluminum-Bronze center in Stainless Steel ring, 25.5 mm. **Series:** Mexican Independence, 200th Anniversary **Subject:** Pedro Moreno **Obv:** National arms, eagle left **Rev:** Pedro Moreno bust 3/4 right

Date	Mintage	F	VF	XF	Unc	BU
2009Mo	6,942,480	—	—	0.75	1.50	—
2009Mo Prooflike	4,940	—	—	—	—	7.50

KM# 911 5 PESOS

7.0700 g., Bi-Metallic Aluminum-Bronze center in Stainless Steel ring, 25.5 mm. **Series:** Mexican Revolution 100th Anniversary **Subject:** Andres Molina Enriquez **Obv:** National arms, eagle left **Rev:** Andres Molina Enriquez, bust 3/4 right

Date	Mintage	F	VF	XF	Unc	BU
2009Mo	6,942,763	—	—	0.75	1.50	—
2009Mo Prooflike	4,666	—	—	—	—	7.50

KM# 912 5 PESOS

7.0700 g., Bi-Metallic Aluminum-Bronze center in Stainless Steel ring, 25.5 mm. **Series:** Mexican Independence, 200th Anniversary **Subject:** Agustin de Iturbide **Obv:** National arms, eagle left **Rev:** Agustin de Iturbide bust left

Date	Mintage	F	VF	XF	Unc	BU
2009Mo	6,944,222	—	—	0.75	1.50	—
2009Mo Prooflike	4,838	—	—	—	—	7.50

KM# 913 5 PESOS

7.0700 g., Bi-Metallic Aluminumn-Bronze center in Stainless Steel ring, 25.5 mm. **Series:** Mexican Revolution 100th Anniversary **Subject:** Luis Cabrera **Obv:** National Arms, eagle left **Rev:** Luis Cabrera bust 3/4 facing left

Date	Mintage	F	VF	XF	Unc	BU
2009Mo	6,902,593	—	—	0.75	1.50	—
2009Mo Prooflike	4,656	—	—	—	—	7.50

KM# 914 5 PESOS

7.0700 g., Bi-Metallic Aluminum-Bronze center Stainless Steel ring, 25.5 mm. **Series:** Mexican Independence 200th Anniversary **Subject:** Nicolas Bravo **Obv:** National Arms, Eagle left **Rev:** Nicolas Bravo bust 3/4 facing left

Date	Mintage	F	VF	XF	Unc	BU
2009Mo	6,930,174	—	—	0.75	0.50	—
2009Mo Prooflike	4,780	—	—	—	—	7.50

KM# 915 5 PESOS

7.0700 g., Bi-Metallic Aluminum-bronze center in Stainless steel ring, 25.5 mm. **Series:** Mexican Revolution 100th Anniversary **Subject:** Eulalio Gutierrez **Obv:** National Arms, eagle left **Rev:** Eulalio Gutierrez bust 3/4 right

Date	Mintage	F	VF	XF	Unc	BU
2009Mo	6,908,760	—	—	0.75	1.50	—
2009Mo Prooflike	4,862	—	—	—	—	7.50

KM# 916 5 PESOS

7.0700 g., Bi-Metallic Aluminum-Bronze center in Stainless Steel ring, 25.5 mm. **Series:** Mexican Independence 200th Anniversary **Subject:** Servando Teresa de Mier **Obv:** National Arms, eagle left **Rev:** Servando Teresa de Mier bust left

Date	Mintage	F	VF	XF	Unc	BU
2009Mo	6,937,421	—	—	0.75	1.50	—
2009Mo Prooflike	4,675	—	—	—	—	7.50

KM# 917 5 PESOS

7.0700 g., Bi-Metallic Aluminum-Bronze center in Stainless Steel ring, 25.5 mm. **Series:** Mexican Revolution 100th Anniversary **Subject:** Otilio Montano **Obv:** National Arms, eagle left **Rev:** Otilio Montano bust left

Date	Mintage	F	VF	XF	Unc	BU
2009Mo	6,890,052	—	—	0.75	1.50	—
2009Mo Prooflike	4,923	—	—	—	—	7.50

KM# 918 5 PESOS

7.0700 g., Bi-Metallic Aluminum-Bronze center in Stainless Steel ring, 25.5 mm. **Series:** Mexican Revolution 100th Anniversary **Subject:** Belisario Domingez **Obv:** National Arms, eagle left **Rev:** Belisario Dominguez bust 3/4 left

Date	Mintage	F	VF	XF	Unc	BU
2009Mo	6,926,606	—	—	0.75	1.50	—
2009Mo Prooflike	4,773	—	—	—	—	7.50

KM# 919 5 PESOS

7.0700 g., Bi-Metallic Aluminum-Bronze center in Stainless Steel ring, 25.5 mm. **Series:** Mexican Independence 200th Anniversary **Subject:** Leona Vicario **Obv:** National Arms, eagle left **Rev:** Leona Vicario bust left

Date	Mintage	F	VF	XF	Unc	BU
2009Mo	6,937,872	—	—	0.75	1.50	—
2009Mo Prooflike	4,730	—	—	—	—	7.50

KM# 937 5 PESOS

62.2000 g., 0.9990 Silver 1.9977 oz. ASW, 48 mm. **Series:** Mexican Revolution 100th Anniversary **Subject:** Revolutionary woman **Obv:** National arms (eagle and snake facing left) and legend **Obv. Legend:** ESTRADOS UNIDOS MEXICANOS **Rev:** Adelita on a railroad car, denomination and legend **Rev. Legend:** REVOLUCION MEXICANA

Date	Mintage	F	VF	XF	Unc	BU
2010Mo Proof	20,000	Value: 100				

KM# 944 5 PESOS

27.0050 g., 0.9250 Silver 0.8031 oz. ASW, 40 mm. **Series:** Ibero-America **Subject:** Ibero-American Historical Coins **Obv:** National arms (eagle and snake facing left), legend **Obv. Legend:** ESTADOS UNIDOS MEXICANOS **Rev:** Mexican Cabilito Peso, legend **Rev. Legend:** MONEDAS HISTORICAS IBEROAMERICANAS

Date	Mintage	F	VF	XF	Unc	BU
2010Mo Proof	8,000	Value: 80.00				

KM# 920 5 PESOS

7.0700 g., Bi-Metallic Aluminumn-Bronze center in Stainless Steel ring, 25.5 mm. **Series:** Mexican Independence 200th Anniversary **Subject:** Miguel Hidalgo y Costilla **Obv:** National Arms, eagle left **Rev:** Miguel Hidalgo y Costilla bust

Date	Mintage	F	VF	XF	Unc	BU
2010Mo	6,932,486	—	—	0.75	1.50	—
2010Mo Prooflike	4,763	—	—	—	—	7.50

KM# 922 5 PESOS

7.0700 g., Bi-Metallic Aluminum-Bronze center in Stainless Steel ring, 25.5 mm. **Series:** Mexican Revolution 100th Anniversary **Subject:** Francisco I. Madero **Rev:** Francisco I. Madero head facing 1/4 left

Date	Mintage	F	VF	XF	Unc	BU
2010Mo	6,930,998	—	—	0.75	1.50	—
2010Mo Prooflike	4,750	—	—	—	—	7.50

KM# 923 5 PESOS

7.0700 g., Bi-Metallic Aluminum-Bronze center in Stainless Steel ring, 25.5 mm. **Series:** Mexican Independence 200th Anniversary **Subject:** Jose Maria Morelos y Pavon **Rev:** Jose Maria Morelos y Pavon head facing 1/2 right

Date	Mintage	F	VF	XF	Unc	BU
2010Mo	6,927,961	—	—	0.75	1.50	—
2010Mo Prooflike	4,725	—	—	—	—	7.50

KM# 924 5 PESOS

7.0700 g., Bi-Metallic Aluminum-Bronze center in Stainless Steel ring, 25.5 mm. **Series:** Mexican Revolution 100th Anniversary **Subject:** Emiliano Zapata **Rev:** Emiliano Zapata head 1/4 facing left

Date	Mintage	F	VF	XF	Unc	BU
2010Mo	6,921,306	—	—	0.75	1.50	—
2010Mo Prooflike	4,810	—	—	—	—	7.50

KM# 925 5 PESOS

7.0700 g., Bi-Metallic Aluminum-Bronze center in Stainless Steel ring, 25.5 mm. **Series:** Mexican Independence 200th Anniversary **Subject:** Vicente Guerrero **Rev:** Vicente Guerrero head facing 1/4 left

Date	Mintage	F	VF	XF	Unc	BU
2010Mo	6,929,709	—	—	0.75	1.50	—
2010Mo Prooflike	4,716	—	—	—	—	7.50

KM# 926 5 PESOS

7.0700 g., Bi-Metallic Aluminum-Bronze center in Stainless Steel ring, 25.5 mm. **Series:** Mexican Revolution 100th Anniversary **Subject:** Venustiano Carranza **Rev:** Venustiano Carranza head 1/4 facing left

Date	Mintage	F	VF	XF	Unc	BU
2010Mo	6,936,993	—	—	0.75	1.50	—
2010Mo Prooflike	4,837	—	—	—	—	7.50

KM# 927 5 PESOS

7.0700 g., Bi-Metallic Aluminum-Bronze center in Stainless Steel ring, 25.5 mm. **Series:** Mexican Independence 200th Anniversary **Subject:** Ignacio Allende **Rev:** Ignacio Allende head facing 1/2 left

Date	Mintage	F	VF	XF	Unc	BU
2010Mo	6,939,957	—	—	0.75	1.50	—
2010Mo Prooflike	4,752	—	—	—	—	7.50

KM# 928 5 PESOS

7.0700 g., Bi-Metallic Aluminum-Bronze center in Stainless Steel ring, 25.5 mm. **Series:** Mexican Revolution 100th Anniversary **Subject:** La Soldadera **Rev:** Female soldier's head facing 1/4 left

Date	Mintage	F	VF	XF	Unc	BU
2010Mo	6,936,336	—	—	0.75	1.50	—
2010Mo Prooflike	4,730	—	—	—	—	7.50

KM# 929 5 PESOS

7.0700 g., Bi-Metallic Aluminum-Bronze center in Stainless Steel ring, 25.5 mm. **Series:** Mexican Indpendence 200th Anniversary **Subject:** Guadalupe Victoria **Rev:** Guadalupe Victoria head 1/4 facing left

Date	Mintage	F	VF	XF	Unc	BU
2010Mo	6,934,638	—	—	0.75	1.50	—
2010Mo Prooflike	4,767	—	—	—	—	7.50

KM# 930 5 PESOS

7.0700 g., Bi-Metallic Aluminum-Bronze center in Stainless Steel ring, 25.5 mm. **Series:** Mexican Revolution 100th Anniversary **Subject:** Jose Mario Pino Suarez **Rev:** Jose Mario Pino Suarez head

Date	Mintage	F	VF	XF	Unc	BU
2010Mo	6,930,255	—	—	0.75	1.50	—
2010Mo Prooflike	4,752	—	—	—	—	7.50

KM# 931 5 PESOS

7.0700 g., Bi-Metallic Aluminum-Bronze center in Stainless Steel ring, 25.5 mm. **Series:** Mexican Independence 200th Anniversary **Subject:** Josefa Ortiz de Dominguez **Rev:** Josefa Ortiz de Dominguez head right

Date	Mintage	F	VF	XF	Unc	BU
2010Mo	6,936,400	—	—	0.75	1.50	—
2010Mo Prooflike	4,743	—	—	—	—	7.50

KM# 945 5 PESOS

31.1000 g., 0.9990 Silver 0.9988 oz. ASW, 40 mm. **Subject:** Chichen Itza, the Nunnery **Obv:** National arms (eagle and snake facing left), legend **Obv. Legend:** ESTADOS UNIDOS MEXICANOS **Rev:** Nunnery of Chichen Itza, legend

Date	Mintage	F	VF	XF	Unc	BU
ND(2011)Mo Proof	10,000	Value: 90.00				

KM# 946 5 PESOS

31.1000 g., 0.9990 Silver 0.9988 oz. ASW, 40 mm. **Subject:** Chichen Itza, the Observatory **Obv:** National arms (eagle and snake facing left) legend **Obv. Legend:** ESTADOS UNIDOS MEXICANOS **Rev:** Observatory of Chichen Itza, legend **Rev. Legend:** OBSRVATORIO

Date	Mintage	F	VF	XF	Unc	BU
ND(2011) Proof	10,000	Value: 90.00				

KM# 947 5 PESOS

31.1000 g., 0.9990 Silver 0.9988 oz. ASW, 40 mm. **Subject:** Chichen Itza, the Observatory **Obv:** National Arms (eagle and snake facing left) legend **Obv. Legend:** ESTADOS UNIDOS MEXICANOS **Rev:** Observatory of Chichen Itza, legend **Rev. Legend:** CHICHEN ITZA, OBSRVATORIO

Date	Mintage	F	VF	XF	Unc	BU
ND(2011)Mo Proof	3,000	Value: 90.00				

KM# 636 10 PESOS

10.3300 g., Bi-Metallic Copper-Nickel-Zinc center in Aluminum-Bronze ring, 28 mm. **Series:** Millennium **Obv:** National arms **Obv. Legend:** ESTADOS UNIDOS MEXICANOS **Rev:** Aztec carving **Edge Lettering:** ANO (year) repeated 3 times

Date	Mintage	F	VF	XF	Unc	BU
2001Mo	44,768,000	—	—	3.00	4.00	8.00

KM# 616 10 PESOS

10.3300 g., Bi-Metallic Copper-Nickel-Zinc center in Aluminum-Bronze ring, 28 mm. **Obv:** National arms **Obv. Legend:** ESTADOS UNIDOS MEXICANOS **Rev:** Aztec design of Tonatiuh with the Fire Mask

Date	Mintage	F	VF	XF	Unc	BU
2002Mo	44,721,000	—	—	2.50	4.00	8.00
2004Mo	74,739,000	—	—	2.50	4.00	8.00
2005Mo	64,616,000	—	—	2.50	4.00	8.00
2006Mo	84,575,000	—	—	2.50	4.00	8.00
2007Mo	89,678,000	—	—	2.50	4.00	8.00
2008Mo	64,744,000	—	—	2.50	4.00	8.00
2009Mo	54,812,000	—	—	2.00	3.00	6.00
2010Mo	54,822,000	—	—	2.00	3.00	6.00
2011Mo	69,731,000	—	—	—	3.00	6.00
2012Mo	—	—	—	—	3.00	6.00

KM# 679 10 PESOS

31.1040 g., 0.9990 Silver 0.9990 oz. ASW, 39.9 mm. **Series:** First **Subject:** 180th Anniversary of Federation **Obv:** National arms **Obv. Legend:** ESTADOS UNIDOS MEXICANOS **Rev:** State Arms **Rev. Legend:** ESTADO DE ZACATECAS **Edge:** Reeded

Date	Mintage	F	VF	XF	Unc	BU
2003Mo Proof	10,000	Value: 70.00				

KM# 680 10 PESOS

31.1040 g., 0.9990 Silver 0.9990 oz. ASW, 39.9 mm. **Series:** First **Subject:** 180th Anniversary of Federation **Obv:** National arms **Obv. Legend:** ESTADO UNIDOS MEXICANOS **Rev:** State arms **Rev. Legend:** ESTADO DE YUCATÁN **Edge:** Reeded

Date	Mintage	F	VF	XF	Unc	BU
2003Mo Proof	10,000	Value: 70.00				

KM# 681 10 PESOS

31.1040 g., 0.9990 Silver 0.9990 oz. ASW, 39.9 mm. **Series:** First **Subject:** 180th Anniversary of Federation **Obv:** National arms **Obv. Legend:** ESTADOS UNIDOS MEXICANOS **Rev:** State arms **Rev. Legend:** ESTADO DE VERACRUZ-LLAVE **Edge:** Reeded

Date	Mintage	F	VF	XF	Unc	BU
2003Mo Proof	10,000	Value: 70.00				

KM# 682 10 PESOS

31.1040 g., 0.9990 Silver 0.9990 oz. ASW, 39.9 mm. **Series:** First **Subject:** 180th Anniversary of Frederation **Obv:** National arms **Obv. Legend:** ESTADOS UNIDOS MEXICANOS **Rev:** State arms **Rev. Legend:** ESTADO DE TLAXCALA **Edge:** Reeded

Date	Mintage	F	VF	XF	Unc	BU
2003Mo Proof	10,000	Value: 70.00				

KM# 683 10 PESOS

31.1040 g., 0.9990 Silver 0.9990 oz. ASW, 39.9 mm. **Series:** First **Subject:** 180th Anniversary of Federation **Obv:** National arms **Obv. Legend:** ESTADOS UNIDOS MEXICANOS **Rev:** State arms **Rev. Legend:** ESTADO DE TAMAULIPAS **Edge:** Reeded

Date	Mintage	F	VF	XF	Unc	BU
2004Mo Proof	10,000	Value: 70.00				

KM# 684 10 PESOS

31.1040 g., 0.9990 Silver 0.9990 oz. ASW, 39.9 mm. **Series:** First **Subject:** 180th Anniversary of Federation **Obv:** National arms **Obv. Legend:** ESTADOS UNIDOS DE MEXICANOS **Rev:** State arms **Rev. Legend:** ESTADO DE TABASCO **Edge:** Reeded

Date	Mintage	F	VF	XF	Unc	BU
2004Mo Proof	10,000	Value: 70.00				

KM# 685 10 PESOS

31.1040 g., 0.9990 Silver 0.9990 oz. ASW, 39.9 mm. **Series:** First **Subject:** 180th Anniversary of Federation **Obv:** National arms **Obv. Legend:** ESTADOS UNIDOS MEXICANOS **Rev:** State arms **Rev. Legend:** ESTADO DE SONORA **Edge:** Reeded **Note:** Mexican States: Sonora

Date	Mintage	F	VF	XF	Unc	BU
2004Mo Proof	10,000	Value: 70.00				

KM# 686 10 PESOS

31.1040 g., 0.9990 Silver 0.9990 oz. ASW, 39.9 mm. **Series:** First **Subject:** 180th Anniversary of Federation **Obv:** National arms **Obv. Legend:** ESTADOS UNIDOS DE MEXICANOS **Rev:** State arms **Rev. Legend:** ESTADO DE SINALOA **Edge:** Reeded **Note:** Mexican States: Sinaloa

Date	Mintage	F	VF	XF	Unc	BU
2004Mo Proof	10,000	Value: 70.00				

KM# 687 10 PESOS

31.1040 g., 0.9990 Silver 0.9990 oz. ASW, 39.9 mm. **Series:** First **Subject:** 180th Anniversary of Federation **Obv:** National arms **Obv. Legend:** ESTADOS UNIDOS MEXICANOS **Rev:** State arms **Rev. Legend:** ESTADO DE SAN LUIS POTOSÍ **Edge:** Reeded

Date	Mintage	F	VF	XF	Unc	BU
2004Mo Proof	10,000	Value: 70.00				

KM# 735 10 PESOS

31.1040 g., 0.9990 Silver 0.9990 oz. ASW, 39.9 mm. **Series:** First **Subject:** 180th Anniversary of Federation **Obv:** National arms **Obv. Legend:** ESTADOS UNIDOS MEXICANOS **Rev:** State arms **Rev. Legend:** ESTADO DE QUINTANA ROO

Date	Mintage	F	VF	XF	Unc	BU
2004Mo Proof	10,000	Value: 70.00				

KM# 733 10 PESOS
31.1040 g., 0.9990 Silver 0.9990 oz. ASW, 39.9 mm. **Series:** First **Subject:** 180th Anniversary of Federation **Obv:** National arms **Obv. Legend:** ESTADOS UNIDOS MEXICANOS **Rev:** State arms **Rev. Legend:** ESTADO DE QUERÉTARO ARTEAGA **Edge:** Reeded

Date	Mintage	F	VF	XF	Unc	BU
2004Mo Proof	10,000	Value: 70.00				

KM# 737 10 PESOS
31.1040 g., 0.9990 Silver 0.9990 oz. ASW, 39.9 mm. **Series:** First **Subject:** 180th Anniversary of Federation **Obv:** National arms **Obv. Legend:** ESTADOS UNIDOS MEXICANOS **Rev:** State arms **Rev. Legend:** ESTADO DE PUEBLA **Edge:** Reeded

Date	Mintage	F	VF	XF	Unc	BU
2004Mo Proof	10,000	Value: 70.00				

KM# 739 10 PESOS
31.1040 g., 0.9990 Bi-Metallic 0.9990 oz., 39.9 mm. **Series:** First **Subject:** 180th Anniversary of Federation **Obv:** National arms **Obv. Legend:** ESTADOS UNIDOS MEXICANOS **Rev:** State arms **Rev. Legend:** ESTADO DE OAXACA **Edge:** Reeded

Date	Mintage	F	VF	XF	Unc	BU
2004Mo Proof	10,000	Value: 70.00				

KM# 741 10 PESOS
31.1040 g., 0.9990 Silver 0.9990 oz. ASW, 39.9 mm. **Series:** First **Subject:** 180th Anniversary of Federation **Obv:** National arms **Obv. Legend:** ESTADOS UNIDOS MEXICANOS **Rev:** State arms **Rev. Legend:** ESTADO DE NUEVO LEÓN **Edge:** Reeded

Date	Mintage	F	VF	XF	Unc	BU
2004Mo Proof	10,000	Value: 70.00				

KM# 743 10 PESOS
31.1040 g., 0.9990 Silver 0.9990 oz. ASW, 39.9 mm. **Series:** First **Subject:** 180th Anniversary of Federation **Obv:** National arms **Obv. Legend:** ESTADOS UNIDOS MEXICANOS **Rev:** State arms **Rev. Legend:** ESTADO DE NAYARIT **Edge:** Reeded

Date	Mintage	F	VF	XF	Unc	BU
2004Mo Proof	10,000	Value: 70.00				

KM# 745 10 PESOS
31.1040 g., 0.9990 Silver 0.9990 oz. ASW, 39.9 mm. **Series:** First **Subject:** 180th Anniversary of Federation **Obv:** National arms **Obv. Legend:** ESTADOS UNIDOS MEXICANOS **Rev:** State arms **Rev. Legend:** ESTADO DE MORELOS **Edge:** Reeded

Date	Mintage	F	VF	XF	Unc	BU
2004Mo Proof	10,000	Value: 70.00				

KM# 796 10 PESOS
31.1040 g., 0.9990 Silver 0.9990 oz. ASW, 39.9 mm. **Series:** First **Subject:** 180th Anniversary of Federation **Obv:** National arms **Obv. Legend:** ESTADOS UNIDOS MEXICANOS **Rev:** State arms **Rev. Legend:** ESTADO DE MICHOACÁN DE OCAMPO **Edge:** Reeded

Date	Mintage	F	VF	XF	Unc	BU
2004Mo Proof	10,000	Value: 70.00				

KM# 747 10 PESOS
31.1040 g., 0.9990 Silver 0.9990 oz. ASW, 39.9 mm. **Series:** First **Subject:** 180th Anniversary of Federation **Obv:** National arms **Obv. Legend:** ESTADOS UNIDOS MEXICANOS **Rev:** State arms **Rev. Legend:** ESTADO DE MÉXICO **Edge:** Reeded

Date	Mintage	F	VF	XF	Unc	BU
2004Mo Proof	10,000	Value: 70.00				

KM# 749 10 PESOS
31.1040 g., 0.9990 Silver 0.9990 oz. ASW, 39.9 mm. **Series:** First **Subject:** 180th Anniversary of Federation **Obv:** National arms **Obv. Legend:** ESTADOS UNIDOS MEXICANOS **Rev:** State arms **Rev. Legend:** ESTADO DE JALISCO **Edge:** Reeded

Date	Mintage	F	VF	XF	Unc	BU
2004Mo Proof	10,000	Value: 70.00				

KM# 766 10 PESOS
31.1035 g., 0.9990 Silver 0.9990 oz. ASW, 40 mm. **Subject:** Cervantes Festival **Obv:** Mexican Eagle and Snake **Rev:** Don Quixote **Edge:** Reeded

Date	Mintage	F	VF	XF	Unc	BU
2005Mo Proof	1,205	Value: 75.00				

KM# 768 10 PESOS
31.1035 g., 0.9990 Silver 0.9990 oz. ASW, 40 mm. **Subject:** 470th Anniversary - Mexico City Mint **Obv:** Mexican Eagle and Snake **Rev:** Antique coin press

Date	Mintage	F	VF	XF	Unc	BU
2005Mo Proof	2,005	Value: 65.00				

KM# 711 10 PESOS
31.1040 g., 0.9990 Silver 0.9990 oz. ASW, 39.9 mm. **Series:** First **Subject:** 180th Anniversary of Federation **Obv:** National arms **Obv. Legend:** ESTADOS UNIDOS MEXICANOS **Rev:** State arms **Rev. Legend:** ESTADO DE HIDALGO **Edge:** Reeded

Date	Mintage	F	VF	XF	Unc	BU
2005Mo Proof	10,000	Value: 70.00				

KM# 710 10 PESOS
31.1040 g., 0.9990 Silver 0.9990 oz. ASW, 39.9 mm. **Series:** First **Subject:** 180th Anniversary of Federation **Obv:** National arms **Obv. Legend:** ESTADOS UNIDOS MEXICANOS **Rev:** State arms **Rev. Legend:** ESTADO DE GUERRERO **Edge:** Reeded

Date	Mintage	F	VF	XF	Unc	BU
2005Mo Proof	10,000	Value: 70.00				

KM# 709 10 PESOS
31.1040 g., 0.9990 Silver 0.9990 oz. ASW, 39.9 mm. **Series:** First **Subject:** 180th Anniversary of Federation **Obv:** National arms **Obv. Legend:** ESTADOS UNIDOS MEXICANOS **Rev:** State arms **Rev. Legend:** ESTADO DE GUANAJUATO **Edge:** Reeded

Date	Mintage	F	VF	XF	Unc	BU
2005Mo Proof	10,000	Value: 70.00				

KM# 708 10 PESOS
31.1040 g., 0.9990 Silver 0.9990 oz. ASW, 39.9 mm. **Series:** First **Subject:** 180th Anniversary of Federation **Obv:** National arms **Obv. Legend:** ESTADOS UNIDOS MEXICANOS **Rev:** State arms **Rev. Legend:** ESTADO DE DURANGO **Edge:** Reeded

Date	Mintage	F	VF	XF	Unc	BU
2005Mo Proof	10,000	Value: 70.00				

KM# 707 10 PESOS
31.1040 g., 0.9990 Silver 0.9990 oz. ASW, 39.9 mm. **Series:** First **Subject:** 180th Anniversary of Federation **Obv:** National arms **Obv. Legend:** ESTADOS UNIDOS MEXICANOS **Rev:** Federal District arms **Rev. Legend:** DISTRITO FEDERAL **Edge:** Reeded

Date	Mintage	F	VF	XF	Unc	BU
2005Mo Proof	10,000	Value: 70.00				

KM# 753 10 PESOS
31.1040 g., 0.9990 Silver 0.9990 oz. ASW, 39.9 mm. **Series:** First **Subject:** 180th Anniversary of Federation **Obv:** National arms **Obv. Legend:** ESTADOS UNIDOS MEXICANOS **Rev:** State arms **Rev. Legend:** ESTADO DE CHIHUAHUA **Edge:** Reeded

Date	Mintage	F	VF	XF	Unc	BU
2005Mo Proof	10,000	Value: 70.00				

KM# 706 10 PESOS
31.1040 g., 0.9990 Silver 0.9990 oz. ASW, 39.9 mm. **Series:** First **Subject:** 180th Anniversary of Federation **Obv:** National arms **Obv. Legend:** ESTADOS UNIDOS MEXICANOS **Rev:** State arms **Rev. Legend:** ESTADO DE CHIAPAS **Edge:** Reeded

Date	Mintage	F	VF	XF	Unc	BU
2005Mo Proof	10,000	Value: 70.00				

KM# 728 10 PESOS
31.1040 g., 0.9990 Silver 0.9990 oz. ASW, 39.9 mm. **Series:** First **Subject:** 180th Anniversary of Federation **Obv:** National arms **Obv. Legend:** ESTADOS UNIDOS MEXICANOS **Rev:** State arms **Rev. Legend:** ESTADO DE COLIMA **Edge:** Reeded

Date	Mintage	F	VF	XF	Unc	BU
2005Mo Proof	10,000	Value: 70.00				

KM# 751 10 PESOS
31.1040 g., 0.9990 Silver 0.9990 oz. ASW, 39.9 mm. **Series:** First **Subject:** 180th Anniversary of Federation **Obv:** National arms **Obv. Legend:** ESTADOS UNIDOS MEXICANOS **Rev:** State arms **Rev. Legend:** ESTADO DE COAHUILA DE ZARAGOZA **Edge:** Reeded

Date	Mintage	F	VF	XF	Unc	BU
2005Mo Proof	10,000	Value: 70.00				

KM# 726 10 PESOS
31.1040 g., 0.9990 Silver 0.9990 oz. ASW, 39.9 mm. **Series:** First **Subject:** 180th Anniversary of Federation **Obv:** National arms **Obv. Legend:** ESTADOS UNIDOS MEXICANOS **Rev:** State arms **Rev. Legend:** ESTADO DE CAMPECHE **Edge:** Reeded

Date	Mintage	F	VF	XF	Unc	BU
2005Mo Proof	10,000	Value: 70.00				

KM# 724 10 PESOS
31.1040 g., 0.9990 Silver 0.9990 oz. ASW, 39.9 mm. **Series:** First **Subject:** 180th Anniversary of Federation **Obv:** National arms **Obv. Legend:** ESTADOS UNIDOS MEXICANOS **Rev:** State arms **Rev. Legend:** ESTADO DE BAJA CALIFORNIA SUR **Edge:** Reeded

Date	Mintage	F	VF	XF	Unc	BU
2005Mo Proof	10,000	Value: 70.00				

KM# 722 10 PESOS
31.1040 g., 0.9990 Silver 0.9990 oz. ASW, 39.9 mm. **Series:** First **Subject:** 180th Anniversary of Federation **Obv:** National arms **Obv. Legend:** ESTADOS UNIDOS MEXICANOS **Rev:** State arms **Rev. Legend:** ESTADO DE BAJA CALIFORNIA **Edge:** Reeded

Date	Mintage	F	VF	XF	Unc	BU
2005Mo Proof	10,000	Value: 70.00				

KM# 720 10 PESOS
31.1040 g., 0.9990 Silver 0.9990 oz. ASW, 39.9 mm. **Series:** First **Subject:** 180th Anniversary of Federation **Obv:** National arms **Obv. Legend:** ESTADOS UNIDOS MEXICANOS **Rev:** State arms **Rev. Legend:** ESTADO DE AGUASCALIENTES **Edge:** Reeded

Date	Mintage	F	VF	XF	Unc	BU
2005Mo Proof	10,000	Value: 70.00				

KM# 718 10 PESOS
31.1040 g., 0.9990 Silver 0.9990 oz. ASW, 40 mm. **Series:** Second **Obv:** National arms **Obv. Legend:** ESTADOS UNIDOS MEXICANOS **Rev:** Facade of the San Marcos garden above sculpture of national emblem at left, San Antonio Temple at right **Rev. Legend:** AGUASCALIENTES **Edge:** Reeded

Date	Mintage	F	VF	XF	Unc	BU
2005Mo Proof	6,000	Value: 65.00				

KM# 757 10 PESOS

31.1040 g., 0.9990 Silver 0.9990 oz. ASW, 40 mm. **Series:** Second **Obv:** National arms **Obv. Legend:** ESTADOS UNIDOS MEXICANOS **Rev:** Rams head, mountain outline in background **Rev. Legend:** BAJA CALIFORNIA - GOBIERNO DEL ESTADO **Edge:** Reeded

Date	Mintage	F	VF	XF	Unc	BU
2005Mo Proof	6,000	Value: 65.00				

KM# 755 10 PESOS

31.1040 g., 0.9990 Silver 0.9990 oz. ASW, 40 mm. **Obv:** National arms **Rev:** Baja California del Norte arms

Date	Mintage	F	VF	XF	Unc	BU
2005Mo Proof	—	Value: 75.00				

KM# 763 10 PESOS

31.1040 g., 0.9990 Silver 0.9990 oz. ASW, 40 mm. **Obv:** National arms **Rev:** Benito Juarez **Edge:** Reeded

Date	Mintage	F	VF	XF	Unc	BU
2006Mo Proof	—	Value: 75.00				

KM# 761 10 PESOS

31.1040 g., 0.9990 Silver 0.9990 oz. ASW, 40 mm. **Series:** Second **Obv:** National arms **Obv. Legend:** ESTADOS UNIDOS MEXICANOS **Rev:** Outlined map of peninsula at center, cave painting of deer behind, cactus at right **Rev. Legend:** ESTADO DE BAJA CALIFORNIA SUR **Edge:** Reeded

Date	Mintage	F	VF	XF	Unc	BU
2006Mo Proof	6,000	Value: 65.00				

KM# 759 10 PESOS

31.1040 g., 0.9990 Silver 0.9990 oz. ASW, 40 mm. **Series:** Second **Obv:** National arms **Obv. Legend:** ESTADOS UNIDOS MEXICANOS **Rev:** Jade mask - Calakmul, Campeche **Rev. Legend:** ESTADO DE CAMPECHE **Edge:** Reeded

Date	Mintage	F	VF	XF	Unc	BU
2006Mo Proof	6,000	Value: 65.00				

KM# 780 10 PESOS

31.1040 g., 0.9990 Silver 0.9990 oz. ASW, 40 mm. **Series:** Second **Obv:** National arms **Obv. Legend:** ESTADOS UNIDOS MEXICANOS **Rev:** Outlined map with turtle, mine cart above grapes at center, Friendship dam above Christ of the Nodas at left, chimneys above crucibles and bell tower of Santiago's cathedral at right **Rev. Inscription:** COAHUILA DE ZARAGOZA **Edge:** Reeded

Date	Mintage	F	VF	XF	Unc	BU
2006Mo Proof	6,000	Value: 65.00				

KM# 776 10 PESOS

31.1040 g., 0.9990 Silver 0.9990 oz. ASW, 40 mm. **Series:** Second **Obv:** National arms **Obv. Legend:** ESTADOS UNIDOS MEXICANOS **Rev:** State arms at lower center, Nevado de Colima and Volcan de Fuego volcanos in background **Rev. Legend:** *Colima* **Rev. Inscription:** GENEROSO **Edge:** Reeded

Date	Mintage	F	VF	XF	Unc	BU
2006Mo Proof	6,000	Value: 65.00				

KM# 772 10 PESOS

31.1040 g., 0.9990 Silver 0.9990 oz. ASW, 40 mm. **Series:** Second **Obv:** National arms **Obv. Legend:** ESTADOS UNIDOS MEXICANOS **Rev:** Head of Pakal, ancient Mayan king, Palenque **Rev. Legend:** ESTADO DE CHIAPAS - CABEZA MAYA DEL REY PAKAL, PALENQUE **Edge:** Reeded

Date	Mintage	F	VF	XF	Unc	BU
2006Mo Proof	6,000	Value: 65.00				

KM# 774 10 PESOS

31.1040 g., 0.9990 Silver 0.9990 oz. ASW, 40 mm. **Series:** Second **Obv:** National arms **Obv. Legend:** ESTADOS UNIDOS MEXICANOS **Rev:** Angel of Liberty **Rev. Legend:** MÉXICO - ANGEL DE LA LIBERTAD, CHIHUAHUA **Edge:** Reeded

Date	Mintage	F	VF	XF	Unc	BU
2006Mo Proof	6,000	Value: 65.00				

KM# 778 10 PESOS

31.1040 g., 0.9990 Silver 0.9990 oz. ASW, 40 mm. **Series:** Second **Obv:** National arms **Obv. Legend:** ESTADOS UNIDOS MEXICANOS **Rev:** National Palace **Rev. Legend:** DISTRITO FEDERAL - ANTIGUO AYUNTAMIENTO **Edge:** Reeded

Date	Mintage	F	VF	XF	Unc	BU
2006Mo Proof	6,000	Value: 65.00				

KM# 786 10 PESOS

31.1040 g., 0.9990 Silver 0.9990 oz. ASW, 40 mm. **Series:** Second **Obv:** National arms **Obv. Legend:** ESTADOS UNIDOS MEXICANOS **Rev:** Tree **Rev. Legend:** PRIMERA RESERVA NACIONAL FORESTAL - DURANGO **Edge:** Reeded

Date	Mintage	F	VF	XF	Unc	BU
2006Mo Proof	6,000	Value: 65.00				

KM# 788 10 PESOS

31.1040 g., 0.9990 Silver 0.9990 oz. ASW, 40 mm. **Series:** Second **Obv:** National arms **Obv. Legend:** ESTADOS UNIDOS MEXICANOS **Rev:** State arms at center, statue of Miguel Hidalgo at left, monument to Pípila at lower right **Rev. Inscription:** *Guanajuato* **Edge:** Reeded

Date	Mintage	F	VF	XF	Unc	BU
2006Mo Proof	6,000	Value: 65.00				

KM# 790 10 PESOS
31.1040 g., 0.9990 Silver 0.9990 oz. ASW, 40 mm. **Series:** Second **Obv:** National arms **Obv. Legend:** ESTADOS UNIDOS MEXICANOS **Rev:** Stylized portrait of Vicente Guerrero at left, church of Taxco at upper center, Acapulco's la Quebrada with diver above Christmas Eve flower and mask **Rev. Legend:** GUERRERO **Edge:** Reeded

Date	Mintage	F	VF	XF	Unc	BU
2006Mo Proof	6,000	Value: 65.00				

KM# 792 10 PESOS
31.1040 g., 0.9990 Silver 0.9990 oz. ASW, 40 mm. **Series:** Second **Obv:** National arms **Obv. Legend:** ESTADOS UNIDOS MEXICANOS **Rev:** Monument of Pachuca Hidalgo **Rev. Inscription:** *RELOJ / MONUMENTAL / DE / PACHUCA / HIDALGO - La / Bella / Airosa* **Edge:** Reeded

Date	Mintage	F	VF	XF	Unc	BU
2006Mo Proof	6,000	Value: 65.00				

KM# 794 10 PESOS
31.1040 g., 0.9990 Silver 0.9990 oz. ASW, 40 mm. **Series:** Second **Obv:** National arms **Obv. Legend:** ESTADOS UNIDOS MEXICANOS **Rev:** Hospicio Cabañas orphanage **Rev. Legend:** ESTADO DE JALISCCO **Edge:** Reeded

Date	Mintage	F	VF	XF	Unc	BU
2006Mo Proof	6,000	Value: 65.00				

KM# 830 10 PESOS
31.1040 g., 0.9990 Silver 0.9990 oz. ASW, 40 mm. **Series:** Second **Obv:** National arms **Obv. Legend:** ESTADOS UNIDOS MEXICANOS **Rev:** Pyramid de la Loona (Moon) **Rev. Legend:** ESTADO DE MÉXICO **Edge:** Reeded

Date	Mintage	F	VF	XF	Unc	BU
2006Mo Proof	6,000	Value: 65.00				

KM# 831 10 PESOS
31.1040 g., 0.9990 Silver 0.9990 oz. ASW, 40 mm. **Series:** Second **Obv:** National arms **Obv. Legend:** ESTADOS UNIDOS MEXICANOS **Rev:** Four Monarch butterflies **Rev. Legend:** ESTADO DE MICHOACÁN **Edge:** Reeded

Date	Mintage	F	VF	XF	Unc	BU
2006Mo Proof	6,000	Value: 65.00				

KM# 832 10 PESOS
31.1040 g., 0.9990 Silver 0.9990 oz. ASW, 40 mm. **Series:** Second **Obv:** National arms **Obv. Legend:** ESTADOS UNIDOS MEXICANOS **Rev:** 1/2 length figure of Chinelo (local dancer) at right, Palacio de Cortes in background **Rev. Inscription:** ESTADO DE / MORELOS **Edge:** Reeded

Date	Mintage	F	VF	XF	Unc	BU
2006Mo Proof	6,000	Value: 65.00				

KM# 833 10 PESOS
31.1040 g., 0.9990 Silver 0.9990 oz. ASW, 40 mm. **Series:** Second **Obv:** National arms **Obv. Legend:** ESTADOS UNIDOS MEXICANOS **Rev:** Isle de Mexcaltitlán **Rev. Legend:** ESTADO DE NAYARIT **Edge:** Reeded

Date	Mintage	F	VF	XF	Unc	BU
2007Mo Proof	6,000	Value: 65.00				

KM# 834 10 PESOS
31.1040 g., 0.9990 Silver 0.9990 oz. ASW, 40 mm. **Series:** Second **Obv:** National arms **Obv. Legend:** ESTADOS UNIDOS MEXICANOS **Rev:** Old foundry in Pargue Fundidora (public park) at right, Cerro de la Silla (Saddle Hill) in background **Rev. Legend:** ESTADO DE NUEVO LEÓN **Edge:** Reeded

Date	Mintage	F	VF	XF	Unc	BU
2007Mo Proof	6,000	Value: 65.00				

KM# 835 10 PESOS
31.1040 g., 0.9990 Silver 0.9990 oz. ASW, 40 mm. **Series:** Second **Obv:** National arms **Obv. Legend:** ESTADOS UNIDOS MEXICANOS **Rev:** Teatro Macedonio Alcala (theater) **Rev. Legend:** OAXACA **Edge:** Reeded

Date	Mintage	F	VF	XF	Unc	BU
2007Mo Proof	6,000	Value: 65.00				

KM# 836 10 PESOS
31.1040 g., 0.9990 Silver 0.9990 oz. ASW, 40 mm. **Series:** Second **Obv:** National arms **Obv. Legend:** ESTADOS UNIDOS MEXICANOS **Rev:** Talavera porcelain dish **Rev. Legend:** ESTADO DE PUEBLA **Edge:** Reeded

Date	Mintage	F	VF	XF	Unc	BU
2007Mo Proof	6,000	Value: 65.00				

KM# 837 10 PESOS
31.1040 g., 0.9990 Silver 0.9990 oz. ASW, 40 mm. **Series:** Second **Obv:** National arms **Obv. Legend:** ESTADOS UNIDOS MEXICANOS **Rev:** Mask at left, rays above state arms at center, Mayan ruins at right **Rev. Legend:** QUINTANA ROO **Edge:** Reeded

Date	Mintage	F	VF	XF	Unc	BU
2007Mo Proof	6,000	Value: 65.00				

KM# 838 10 PESOS
31.1040 g., 0.9990 Silver 0.9990 oz. ASW, 40 mm. **Series:** Second **Obv:** National arms **Obv. Legend:** ESTADOS UNIDOS MEXICANOS **Rev:** Acqueduct of Querétaro at left, church of Santa Rosa de Viterbo at right **Rev. Legend:** ESTADO DE QUERÉTARO ARTEAGA **Edge:** Reeded

Date	Mintage	F	VF	XF	Unc	BU
2007Mo Proof	6,000	Value: 65.00				

KM# 839 10 PESOS

31.1040 g., Silver, 40 mm. **Series:** Second **Obv:** National arms **Obv. Legend:** ESTADOS UNIDOS MEXICANOS **Rev:** Facade of Caja Real **Rev. Legend:** • SAN LUIS POTOSÍ • **Edge:** Reeded

Date	Mintage	F	VF	XF	Unc	BU
2007Mo Proof	6,000	Value: 65.00				

KM# 840 10 PESOS

31.1040 g., 0.9990 Silver 0.9990 oz. ASW, 40 mm. **Series:** Second **Obv:** National arms **Obv. Legend:** ESTADOS UNIDOS MEXICANOS **Rev:** Shield on pile of cactus fruits **Rev. Legend:** ESTADO DE SINALOA - LUGAR DE PITAHAYAS **Edge:** Reeded

Date	Mintage	F	VF	XF	Unc	BU
2007Mo Proof	6,000	Value: 65.00				

KM# 841 10 PESOS

31.1040 g., 0.9990 Silver 0.9990 oz. ASW, 40 mm. **Series:** Second **Obv:** National arms **Obv. Legend:** ESTADOS UNIDOS MEXICANOS **Rev:** Local in Dance of the Deer at left, cactus at right, mountains in background **Rev. Legend:** ESTADO DE SONORA **Edge:** Reeded

Date	Mintage	F	VF	XF	Unc	BU
2007Mo Proof	6,000	Value: 65.00				

KM# 842 10 PESOS

31.1040 g., 0.9990 Silver 0.9990 oz. ASW, 40 mm. **Series:** Second **Obv:** National arms **Obv. Legend:** ESTADOS UNIDOS MEXICANOS **Rev:** Fuente de los Pescadores (fisherman fountain) at lower left, giant head from the Olmec-pre-Hispanic culture at right, Planetario Tabasco in background **Rev. Legend:** TABASCO **Edge:** Reeded

Date	Mintage	F	VF	XF	Unc	BU
2007Mo Proof	6,000	Value: 65.00				

KM# 843 10 PESOS

31.1040 g., 0.9990 Silver 0.9990 oz. ASW, 40 mm. **Series:** Second **Obv:** National arms **Obv. Legend:** ESTADOS UNIDOS MEXICANOS **Rev:** Ridge - Cerro Del Bernal, Gonzáles **Rev. Legend:** TAMAULIPAS **Edge:** Reeded

Date	Mintage	F	VF	XF	Unc	BU
2007Mo Proof	6,000	Value: 65.00				

KM# 844 10 PESOS

31.1040 g., 0.9990 Silver 0.9990 oz. ASW, 40 mm. **Series:** Second **Obv:** National arms **Obv. Legend:** ESTADOS UNIDOS MEXICANOS **Rev:** Basilica de Ocotlán at left, state arms above Capilla Abierta, Plaza de Toros Ranchero Aguilar below, Exconvento de San Francisco at right **Rev. Legend:** ESTADO DE TLAXCALA **Edge:** Reeded

Date	Mintage	F	VF	XF	Unc	BU
2007Mo Proof	6,000	Value: 65.00				

KM# 845 10 PESOS

31.1040 g., 0.9990 Silver 0.9990 oz. ASW, 40 mm. **Series:** Second **Obv:** National arms **Obv. Legend:** ESTADOS UNIDOS MEXICANOS **Rev:** Pyramid of El Tajín **Rev. Legend:** • VERACRUZ • - • DE IGNACIO DE LA LLAVE • **Edge:** Reeded

Date	Mintage	F	VF	XF	Unc	BU
2007Mo Proof	6,000	Value: 65.00				

KM# 846 10 PESOS

31.1030 g., 0.9990 Silver 0.9989 oz. ASW, 40 mm. **Series:** Second **Obv:** National arms **Obv. Legend:** ESTADOS UNIDOS MEXICANOS **Rev:** Stylized pyramid of Chichén-Itzá **Rev. Legend:** Castillo de Chichén Itzá **Rev. Inscription:** YUCATÁN **Edge:** Reeded

Date	Mintage	F	VF	XF	Unc	BU
2007Mo Proof	6,000	Value: 65.00				

KM# 847 10 PESOS

31.1040 g., 0.9990 Silver 0.9990 oz. ASW, 40 mm. **Series:** Second **Obv:** National arms **Obv. Legend:** ESTADOS UNIDOS MEXICANOS **Rev:** Cable car above Monumento al Minero at left, Cathedral de Zacatecas at center right **Rev. Legend:** Zacatecas **Edge:** Reeded

Date	Mintage	F	VF	XF	Unc	BU
2007Mo Proof	6,000	Value: 65.00				

KM# 938 10 PESOS

62.2000 g., 0.9990 Silver 1.9977 oz. ASW, 48 mm. **Series:** Mexican Revolution 100th Anniversary **Subject:** Railroad **Obv:** National arms (eagle and snake facing left) and legend **Obv. Legend:** ESTADOS UNIDOS MEXICANOS **Rev:** Four seated armed revolutionaries on locomotive **Rev. Legend:** REVOLUCION MEXICANA

Date	Mintage	F	VF	XF	Unc	BU
2010Mo Proof	20,000	Value: 100				

KM# 942 10 PESOS

31.1000 g., 0.9990 Silver 0.9988 oz. ASW, 40 mm. **Subject:** 100th Anniversary of the National Autonomous University of Mexico **Obv:** National arms (eagle and snake facing left) and legend **Obv. Legend:** ESTADOS UNIDOS MEXICANOS **Rev:** University buildings, sculpture and legend **Rev. Legend:** UNIVERSIDAD NACIONAL AUTONOMIA DE MEXICO

Date	Mintage	F	VF	XF	Unc	BU
2010Mo Prooflike	5,000	—	—	—	—	60.00

KM# 948 10 PESOS

62.2000 g., 0.9990 Silver 1.9977 oz. ASW, 65 mm. **Subject:** Chichen Itza, Temple of Warriors **Obv:** National arms (eagle and snake facing left), legend **Obv. Legend:** ESTADOS UNIDOS MEXICANOS **Rev:** Temple of Warriors of Chichen Itza **Rev. Legend:** CHICHEN ITZA, TEMPLO DE LOS GUERROS

Date	Mintage	F	VF	XF	Unc	BU
ND(2011)Mo Proof	3,000	Value: 150				

KM# 956 10 PESOS

10.3300 g., Bi-Metallic Copper-nickel-zinc center in aluminum-bronze ring, 28 mm. **Subject:** Battle of Pueble 150th Anniversary **Obv:** National arms (eagle and snake facing left) and legend **Obv. Legend:** ESTADOS UNIDOS MEXICANOS **Rev:** Head of General Zaragoza facing left, legends **Rev. Legend:** 150 ANNIVERSARIO DE LA BATALLA DE PUEBLA, 5 DE MAYO **Edge:** Reeded

Date	Mintage	F	VF	XF	Unc	BU
2012Mo	—	—	—	—	—	1.00

KM# 637 20 PESOS

Bi-Metallic Copper-Nickel center within Brass ring, 32 mm. **Subject:** Xiuhtecuhtli **Obv:** National arms, eagle left within circle **Rev:** Aztec with torch within spiked circle

Date	Mintage	F	VF	XF	Unc	BU
2001Mo	2,478,000	—	2.50	3.50	16.00	18.00

KM# 638 20 PESOS
Bi-Metallic Copper-Nickel center within Brass ring, 32 mm. **Subject:** Octavio Paz **Obv:** National arms, eagle left within circle **Rev:** Head 1/4 right within circle

Date	Mintage	F	VF	XF	Unc	BU
2001Mo	2,515,000	—	2.50	3.50	16.00	18.50

KM# 704 20 PESOS
62.4000 g., 0.9990 Silver 2.0041 oz. ASW, 48.1 mm. **Subject:** 400th Anniversary of Don Quijote de la Manchia **Obv:** National arms **Rev:** Skeletal figure horseback with spear galloping right **Edge:** Plain

Date	Mintage	F	VF	XF	Unc	BU
ND(2005)Mo Proof	3,605	Value: 85.00				

KM# 767 20 PESOS
62.4000 g., 0.9990 Silver 2.0041 oz. ASW, 48 mm. **Subject:** 80th Anniversary - Bank of Mexico **Obv:** National arms **Rev:** 100 Peso banknote design of 1925

Date	Mintage	F	VF	XF	Unc	BU
2005Mo	—	—	—	—	—	80.00
2005Mo Proof	3,005	Value: 90.00				

KM# 939 20 PESOS
62.2000 g., 0.9990 Silver 1.9977 oz. ASW, 48 mm. **Series:** Mexican Independence 200th Anniversary **Subject:** Dolores Parrish Church **Obv:** National arms (eagle and snake facing left) and legend **Obv. Legend:** ESTADOS UNIDOS MEXICANOS **Rev:** Dolores Parrish church, Independence Bell **Rev. Legend:** Bicentenario de la Independencia de Mexico

Date	Mintage	F	VF	XF	Unc	BU
2010Mo Proof	15,000	Value: 100				

KM# 940 20 PESOS
62.2000 g., 0.9990 Silver 1.9977 oz. ASW, 48 mm. **Series:** Mexican Independence 200th Anniversary **Subject:** Miguel Hidalgo y Costilla and Jose maria Morelos y Pavon **Obv:** National arms (eagle and snake facing left) and legend **Obv. Legend:** ESTADDOS UNIDOS MEXICANOS **Rev:** Miguel Hidalgo y Costilla and Jose Maria Morelos y Pavon, denomination and legend **Rev. Legend:** BICENTENARIO DE LA INDEPENDENCIA

Date	Mintage	F	VF	XF	Unc	BU
2010Mo Proof	15,000	Value: 100				

KM# 943 20 PESOS
15.9450 g., Bi-Metallic Cupro-nickel center in aluminum-bronze ring, 32 mm. **Subject:** 20th Anniversary of Octavio Paz **Obv:** National arms (eagle and snake facing left) and legend **Obv. Legend:** ESTADOS UNIDOS MEXICANOS **Rev:** Bust of Octavio Paz facing right and Legend **Rev. Legend:** Premio Nobel de Lieteratura **Edge:** Segmented reeding

Date	Mintage	F	VF	XF	Unc	BU
2010Mo	4,954,000	—	—	—	—	2.50

KM# 949 20 PESOS
155.5000 g., 0.9990 Silver 4.9942 oz. ASW, 40 mm. **Subject:** Chichen Itza, Pyramid of Kukulcan Church **Obv:** National arms (eagle and snake facing left), legend **Obv. Legend:** ESTADOS UNIDOS MEXICANOS **Rev:** Pyramid of Kukulcan of Chichen Itza, legends **Rev. Legend:** CHICHEN ITZA, PIRAMID DE KUKULCAN

Date	Mintage	F	VF	XF	Unc	BU
ND(2011)Mo Proof	3,000	Value: 300				

KM# 688 100 PESOS
33.9400 g., Bi-Metallic .925 Silver 16.812g center in Aluminum-Bronze ring, 39.04 mm. **Series:** First **Subject:** 180th Anniversary of Federation **Obv:** National arms **Obv. Legend:** ESTADOS UNIDOS MEXICANOS **Rev:** State arms **Rev. Legend:** ESTADO DE ZACATECAS **Edge:** Segmented reeding

Date	Mintage	F	VF	XF	Unc	BU
2003Mo	244,900	—	—	—	40.00	50.00

KM# 696 100 PESOS
29.1690 g., Bi-Metallic .999 Gold 17.154g center in .999 Silver 12.015g ring, 34.5 mm. **Series:** First **Subject:** 180th Anniversary of Federation **Obv:** National arms **Obv. Legend:** ESTADOS UNIDOS MEXICANOS **Rev:** State arms **Rev. Legend:** ESTADO DE ZACATECAS **Edge:** Segmented reeding

Date	Mintage	F	VF	XF	Unc	BU
2003Mo Proof	1,000	Value: 1,200				

KM# 689 100 PESOS
33.9400 g., Bi-Metallic .925 Silver 16.812g center in Aluminum-Bronze ring, 39.04 mm. **Series:** First **Subject:** 180th Anniversary of Federation **Obv:** National arms **Obv. Legend:** ESTADOS UNIDOS MEXICANOS **Rev:** State arms **Rev. Legend:** ESTADO DE YUCATÁN **Edge:** Segmented reeding

Date	Mintage	F	VF	XF	Unc	BU
2003Mo	235,763	—	—	—	40.00	50.00

KM# 697 100 PESOS
29.1690 g., Bi-Metallic .999 Gold 17.154g center in .999 Silver 12.015g ring, 34.5 mm. **Series:** First **Subject:** 180th Anniversary of Federation **Obv:** National arms **Obv. Legend:** ESTADOS UNIDOS MEXICANOS **Rev:** State arms **Rev. Legend:** ESTADO DE YUCATÁN **Edge:** Segmented reeding

Date	Mintage	F	VF	XF	Unc	BU
2003Mo Proof	1,000	Value: 1,200				

KM# 690 100 PESOS
33.9400 g., Bi-Metallic .925 Silver 16.812g center in Aluminum-Bronze ring, 39.04 mm. **Series:** First **Subject:** 180th Anniversary of Federation **Obv:** National arms **Obv. Legend:** ESTADOS UNIDOS MEXICANOS **Rev:** State arms **Rev. Legend:** ESTADO DE VERACRUZ-LLAVE **Edge:** Segmented reeding

Date	Mintage	F	VF	XF	Unc	BU
2003Mo	248,810	—	—	—	40.00	50.00

KM# 698 100 PESOS
29.1690 g., Bi-Metallic .999 Gold 17.154g center in .999 Silver 12.015g ring, 34.5 mm. **Series:** First **Subject:** 180th Anniversary of Federation **Obv:** National arms **Obv. Legend:** ESTADOS UNIDOS MEXICANOS **Rev:** State arms **Rev. Legend:** ESTADO DE VERACRUZ-LLAVE **Edge:** Segmented reeding

Date	Mintage	F	VF	XF	Unc	BU
2003Mo Proof	1,000	Value: 1,200				

KM# 691 100 PESOS
33.9400 g., Bi-Metallic .925 Silver 16.812g center in Aluminum-Bronze ring, 39.9 mm. **Series:** First **Subject:** 180th Anniversary of Federation **Obv:** National arms **Obv. Legend:** ESTADOS UNIDOS MEXICANOS **Rev:** State arms **Rev. Legend:** ESTADO DE TLAXCALA **Edge:** Segmented reeding

Date	Mintage	F	VF	XF	Unc	BU
2003Mo	248,976	—	—	—	35.00	40.00

KM# 699 100 PESOS
29.1690 g., Bi-Metallic .999 Gold 17.154g center in .999 Silver 12.015g ring, 34.5 mm. **Series:** First **Subject:** 180th Anniversary of Federation **Obv:** National arms **Obv. Legend:** ESTADOS UNIDOS MEXICANOS **Rev:** State arms **Rev. Legend:** ESTADO DE TLAXCALA **Edge:** Segmented reeding

Date	Mintage	F	VF	XF	Unc	BU
2003Mo Proof	1,000	Value: 1,200				

KM# 692 100 PESOS
33.9400 g., Bi-Metallic .925 Silver 16.812g center in Aluminum-Bronze ring, 39.04 mm. **Series:** First **Subject:** 180th Anniversay of Federation **Obv:** National arms **Obv. Legend:** ESTADOS UNIDOS MEXICANOS **Rev:** State arms **Rev. Legend:** ESTADO DE TAMAULIPAS **Edge:** Segmented reeding

Date	Mintage	F	VF	XF	Unc	BU
2004Mo	249,398	—	—	—	35.00	40.00

KM# 700 100 PESOS
29.1690 g., Bi-Metallic .999 Gold 17.154g center in .999 Silver 12.015g ring, 34.5 mm. **Series:** First **Subject:** 180th Anniversary of Federation **Obv:** National arms **Obv. Legend:** ESTADOS UNIDOS MEXICANOS **Rev:** State arms **Rev. Legend:** ESTADO DE TAMAULIPAS **Edge:** Segmented reeding

Date	Mintage	F	VF	XF	Unc	BU
2004Mo Proof	1,000	Value: 1,200				

KM# 693 100 PESOS
33.9400 g., Bi-Metallic .925 Silver 16.812g center in Aluminum-Bronze ring, 39.04 mm. **Series:** First **Subject:** 180th Anniversary of Federation **Obv:** National arms **Obv. Legend:** ESTADOS UNIDOS MEXICANOS **Rev:** State arms **Rev. Legend:** ESTADO DE TABASCO **Edge:** Segmented reeding

Date	Mintage	F	VF	XF	Unc	BU
2004Mo	249,318	—	—	—	35.00	40.00

KM# 701 100 PESOS
29.1690 g., Bi-Metallic .999 Gold 17.154g center in .999 Silver 12.015g ring, 34.5 mm. **Series:** First **Subject:** 180th Anniversary of Federation **Obv:** National arms **Obv. Legend:** ESTADOS UNIDOS MEXICANOS **Rev:** State arms **Rev. Legend:** ESTADO DE TABASCO **Edge:** Segmented reeding

Date	Mintage	F	VF	XF	Unc	BU
2004Mo Proof	1,000	Value: 1,200				

KM# 694 100 PESOS
33.9400 g., Bi-Metallic .925 Silver 16.812g center in Aluminum-Bronze ring, 39.04 mm. **Series:** First **Subject:** 180th Anniversary of Federation **Obv:** National arms **Obv. Legend:** ESTADOS UNIDOS MEXICANOS **Rev:** State arms **Rev. Legend:** ESTADO DE SONORA **Edge:** Segmented reeding

Date	Mintage	F	VF	XF	Unc	BU
2004Mo	249,300	—	—	—	35.00	40.00

KM# 702 100 PESOS
29.1690 g., Bi-Metallic .999 Gold 17.154g center in .999 Silver 12.015g ring, 34.5 mm. **Series:** First **Subject:** 180th Anniversary of Federation **Obv:** National arms **Obv. Legend:** ESTADOS UNIDOS MEXICANOS **Rev:** State arms **Rev. Legend:** ESTADO DE SONORA **Edge:** Segmented reeding

Date	Mintage	F	VF	XF	Unc	BU
2004Mo Proof	1,000	Value: 1,200				

KM# 695 100 PESOS
33.9400 g., Bi-Metallic .925 Silver 16.812g center in Aluminum-Bronze ring, 39.04 mm. **Series:** First **Subject:** 180th Anniversary of Federation **Obv:** National arms **Obv. Legend:** ESTADOS UNIDOS MEXICANOS **Rev:** State arms **Rev. Legend:** ESTADO DE SINALOA **Edge:** Segmented reeding

Date	Mintage	F	VF	XF	Unc	BU
2004Mo	244,722	—	—	—	35.00	40.00

KM# 703 100 PESOS
29.1690 g., Bi-Metallic .999 Gold 17.154g center in .999 Silver 12.015g ring, 34.5 mm. **Series:** First **Subject:** 180th Anniversary of Federation **Obv:** National arms **Obv. Legend:** ESTADOS UNIDOS MEXICANOS **Rev:** State arms **Rev. Legend:** ESTADO DE SINALOA **Edge:** Segmented reeding

Date	Mintage	F	VF	XF	Unc	BU
2004Mo Proof	1,000	Value: 1,200				

KM# 803 100 PESOS
33.9400 g., Bi-Metallic .925 Silver 16.812g center in Aluminum-Bronze ring, 39.04 mm. **Series:** First **Subject:** 180th Anniversary of Federation **Obv:** National arms **Obv. Legend:** ESTADOS UNIDOS MEXICANOS **Rev:** State arms **Rev. Legend:** ESTADO DE SAN LUIS POTOSÍ **Edge:** Segmented reeding

Date	Mintage	F	VF	XF	Unc	BU
2004Mo	249,662	—	—	—	35.00	40.00

KM# 806 100 PESOS
29.1690 g., Bi-Metallic .999 Gold 17.154g center in .999 silver 12.015 ring, 34.5 mm. **Series:** First **Subject:** 180th Anniversary of Federation **Obv:** National arms **Obv. Legend:** ESTADOS UNIDOS MEXICANOS **Rev:** State arms **Rev. Legend:** ESTADO DE SAN LUIS POTOSÍ **Edge:** Segmented reeding

Date	Mintage	F	VF	XF	Unc	BU
2004Mo Proof	1,000	Value: 1,200				

KM# 736 100 PESOS
33.9400 g., Bi-Metallic .925 Silver 16.812g center in Aluminum-Bronze ring, 39.04 mm. **Series:** First **Subject:** 180th Anniversary of Federation **Obv:** National arms **Obv. Legend:** ESTADOS UNIDOS MEXICANOS **Rev:** State arms **Rev. Legend:** ESTADO DE QUINTANA ROO **Edge:** Segmented reeding

Date	Mintage	F	VF	XF	Unc	BU
2004Mo	249,134	—	—	—	35.00	40.00

KM# 807 100 PESOS
29.1690 g., Bi-Metallic .999 Gold 17.154g center in .999 Silver 12.015g ring, 34.5 mm. **Series:** First **Subject:** 180th Anniversary of Federation **Obv:** National arms **Obv. Legend:** ESTADOS UNIDOS MEXICANOS **Rev:** State arms **Rev. Legend:** ESTADO DE QUINTANA ROO **Edge:** Segmented reeding

Date	Mintage	F	VF	XF	Unc	BU
2004Mo Proof	1,000	Value: 1,200				

KM# 734 100 PESOS
33.9400 g., Bi-Metallic .925 Silver 16.812g center in Aluminum-Bronze ring, 39.04 mm. **Series:** First **Subject:** 180th Anniversary of Federation **Obv:** National arms **Obv. Legend:** ESTADOS UNIDOS MEXICANOS **Rev:** State arms **Rev. Legend:** ESTADO DE QUERÉTARO ARTEAGA **Edge:** Segmented reeding

Date	Mintage	F	VF	XF	Unc	BU
2004Mo	249,263	—	—	—	35.00	40.00

KM# 808 100 PESOS
29.1690 g., Bi-Metallic .999 Gold 17.154g center in .999 Silver 12.015g ring, 34.5 mm. **Series:** First **Subject:** 180th Anniversary of Federation **Obv:** National arms **Obv. Legend:** ESTADOS UNIDOS MEXICANOS **Rev:** State arms **Rev. Legend:** ESTADO DE QUERÉTARO ARTEAGA **Edge:** Segmented reeding

Date	Mintage	F	VF	XF	Unc	BU
2004Mo Proof	1,000	Value: 1,200				

KM# 738 100 PESOS
33.9400 g., Bi-Metallic .925 Silver 16.812g center in Aluminum-Bronze ring, 39.04 mm. **Series:** First **Subject:** 180th Anniversary of Federation **Obv:** National arms **Obv. Legend:** ESTADOS UNIDOS MEXICANOS **Rev:** State arms **Rev. Legend:** ESTADO DE PUEBLA **Edge:** Segmented reeding

Date	Mintage	F	VF	XF	Unc	BU
2004Mo	248,850	—	—	—	35.00	40.00

KM# 809 100 PESOS
Bi-Metallic .999 Gold 17.154g center in .999 Silver 12.015g ring, 34.5 mm. **Series:** First **Subject:** 180th Anniversary of Federation **Obv:** National arms **Obv. Legend:** ESTADOS UNIDOS MEXICANOS **Rev:** State arms **Rev. Legend:** ESTADO DE PUEBLA **Edge:** Segmented reeding

Date	Mintage	F	VF	XF	Unc	BU
2004Mo Proof	1,000	Value: 1,200				

KM# 740 100 PESOS
33.9400 g., Bi-Metallic .925 Silver 16.812g center in Aluminum-Bronze ring, 39.04 mm. **Series:** First **Subject:** 180th Anniversary of Federation **Obv:** National arms **Obv. Legend:** ESTADOS UNIDOS MEXICANOS **Rev:** State arms **Rev. Legend:** ESTADO DE OAXACA **Edge:** Segmented reeding

Date	Mintage	F	VF	XF	Unc	BU
2004Mo	249,589	—	—	—	35.00	40.00

KM# 810 100 PESOS
29.1690 g., Bi-Metallic .999 Gold 17.154g center in .999 Silver 12.015g ring, 34.5 mm. **Series:** First **Subject:** 180th Anniversary of Federation **Obv:** National arms **Obv. Legend:** ESTADOS UNIDOS MEXICANOS **Rev:** State arms **Rev. Legend:** ESTADO DE OAXACA **Edge:** Segmented reeding

Date	Mintage	F	VF	XF	Unc	BU
2004Mo Proof	1,000	Value: 1,200				

KM# 742 100 PESOS
33.9400 g., Bi-Metallic .925 Silver 16.812g center in Aluminum-Bronze ring, 39.04 mm. **Series:** First **Subject:** 180th Anniversary of Federation **Obv:** National arms **Obv. Legend:** ESTADOS UNIDOS MEXICANOS **Rev:** State arms **Rev. Legend:** ESTADO DE NUEVO LEÓN **Edge:** Segmented reeding

Date	Mintage	F	VF	XF	Unc	BU
2004Mo	249,199	—	—	—	35.00	40.00

KM# 811 100 PESOS
29.1690 g., Bi-Metallic .999 Gold 17.154g center in .999 Silver 12.015g ring, 34.5 mm. **Series:** First **Subject:** 180th Anniversary of Federation **Obv:** National arms **Obv. Legend:** ESTADOS UNIDOS MEXICANOS **Rev:** State arms **Rev. Legend:** ESTADO DE NUEVO LEÓN **Edge:** Segmented reeding

Date	Mintage	F	VF	XF	Unc	BU
2004Mo Proof	1,000	Value: 1,200				

KM# 744 100 PESOS
33.9400 g., Bi-Metallic .925 Silver 16.812g center in Aluminum-Bronze ring, 39.04 mm. **Series:** First **Subject:** 180th Anniversary of Federation **Obv:** National arms **Obv. Legend:** ESTADOS UNIDOS MEXICANOS **Rev:** State arms **Rev. Legend:** ESTADO DE NAYARIT **Edge:** Segmented reeding

Date	Mintage	F	VF	XF	Unc	BU
2004Mo	248,305	—	—	—	35.00	40.00

KM# 812 100 PESOS

29.1690 g., Bi-Metallic .999 Gold 17.154g center in .999 Silver 12.015g ring, 34.5 mm. **Series:** First **Subject:** 180th Anniversary of Federation **Obv:** National arms **Obv. Legend:** ESTADOS UNIDOS MEXICANOS **Rev:** State arms **Rev. Legend:** ESTADO DE NAYARIT **Edge:** Segmented reeding

Date	Mintage	F	VF	XF	Unc	BU
2004Mo Proof	1,000	Value: 1,200				

KM# 746 100 PESOS

33.9400 g., Bi-Metallic .925 Silver 16.812g center in Aluminum-Bronze ring, 39.04 mm. **Series:** First **Subject:** 180th Anniversary of Federation **Obv:** National arms **Obv. Legend:** ESTADOS UNIDOS MEXICANOS **Rev:** State arms **Rev. Legend:** ESTADO DE MORELOS **Edge:** Segmented reeding

Date	Mintage	F	VF	XF	Unc	BU
2004Mo	249,260	—	—	—	35.00	40.00

KM# 813 100 PESOS

29.1690 g., Bi-Metallic .999 Gold 17.154g center in .999 Silver 12.015g ring, 34.5 mm. **Series:** First **Subject:** 180th Anniversary of Federation **Obv:** National arms **Obv. Legend:** ESTADOS UNIDOS MEXICANOS **Rev:** State arms **Rev. Legend:** ESTADO DE MORELOS **Edge:** Segmented reeding

Date	Mintage	F	VF	XF	Unc	BU
2004Mo Proof	1,000	Value: 1,200				

KM# 804 100 PESOS

33.9400 g., Bi-Metallic .925 Silver 16.812g center in Aluminum-Bronze ring, 39.04 mm. **Series:** First **Subject:** 180th Anniversary of Federation **Obv:** National arms **Obv. Legend:** ESTADOS UNIDOS MEXICANOS **Rev:** State arms **Rev. Legend:** ESTADO DE MICHOACÁN DE OCAMPO **Edge:** Segmented reeding

Date	Mintage	F	VF	XF	Unc	BU
2004Mo	249,492	—	—	—	35.00	40.00

KM# 814 100 PESOS

29.1690 g., Bi-Metallic .999 Gold 17.154g center in .999 12.015g ring, 34.5 mm. **Series:** First **Subject:** 180th Anniversary of Federation **Obv:** National arms **Obv. Legend:** ESTADOS UNIDOS MEXICANOS **Rev:** State arms **Rev. Legend:** ESTADO DE MICHOACÁN DE OCAMPO **Edge:** Segmented reeding

Date	Mintage	F	VF	XF	Unc	BU
2004Mo Proof	1,000	Value: 1,200				

KM# 748 100 PESOS

33.9400 g., Bi-Metallic .925 Silver 16.812g center in Aluminum-Bronze ring, 39.04 mm. **Series:** First **Subject:** 180th Anniversary of Federation **Obv:** National arms **Obv. Legend:** ESTADOS UNIDOS MEXICANOS **Rev:** State arms **Rev. Legend:** ESTADO DE MÉXICO **Edge:** Segmented reeding

Date	Mintage	F	VF	XF	Unc	BU
2004Mo	249,800	—	—	—	35.00	40.00

KM# 815 100 PESOS

29.1690 g., Bi-Metallic .999 Gold 17.154 center in .999 Silver 12.015 ring, 34.5 mm. **Series:** First **Subject:** 180th Anniversary of Federation **Obv:** National arms **Obv. Legend:** ESTADOS UNIDOS MEXICANOS **Rev:** State arms **Rev. Legend:** ESTADO DE MÉXICO **Edge:** Segmented reeding

Date	Mintage	F	VF	XF	Unc	BU
2004Mo Proof	1,000	Value: 1,200				

KM# 750 100 PESOS

33.9400 g., Bi-Metallic .925 Silver 16.812g center in Aluminum-Bronze ring, 39.04 mm. **Series:** First **Subject:** 180th Anniversary of Federation **Obv:** National arms **Obv. Legend:** ESTADOS UNIDOS MEXICANOS **Rev:** State arms **Rev. Legend:** ESTADO DE JALISCO **Edge:** Segmented reeding

Date	Mintage	F	VF	XF	Unc	BU
2004Mo	249,115	—	—	—	35.00	40.00

KM# 816 100 PESOS

29.1690 g., Bi-Metallic .999 Gold 17.154g center in .999 Silver 12.015g ring, 34.5 mm. **Series:** First **Subject:** 180th Anniversary of Federation **Obv:** National arms **Obv. Legend:** ESTADOS UNIDOS MEXICANOS **Rev:** State arms **Rev. Legend:** ESTADO DE JALISCO **Edge:** Segmented reeding

Date	Mintage	F	VF	XF	Unc	BU
2004Mo Proof	1,000	Value: 1,200				

KM# 705 100 PESOS

33.7400 g., Bi-Metallic .925 16.812g Silver center in Aluminum-Bronze ring, 39 mm. **Subject:** 400th Anniversary of Don Quijote de la Manchia **Obv:** National arms **Obv. Legend:** ESTADOS UNIDOS MEXICANOS **Rev:** Skeletal figure on horseback with spear galloping right **Edge:** Segmented reeding

Date	Mintage	F	VF	XF	Unc	BU
2005Mo	726,833	—	—	—	25.00	32.00
2005Mo Prooflike	3,761	—	—	—	—	75.00
2006Mo Proof	5,201	Value: 60.00				

KM# 730 100 PESOS

33.8250 g., Bi-Metallic .925 Silver 16.812g center in Aluminum-Bronze ring, 39.9 mm. **Subject:** Monetary Reform Centennial **Obv:** National arms **Rev:** Radiant Liberty Cap divides date above value within circle **Edge:** Segmented reeding

Date	Mintage	F	VF	XF	Unc	BU
2005Mo	49,716	—	—	—	40.00	45.00
2005Mo Proof	—	Value: 75.00				

KM# 731 100 PESOS

33.8250 g., Bi-Metallic .925 Silver 16.812g center in Aluminum-Bronze ring, 39.9 mm. **Subject:** Mexico City Mint's 470th Anniversary **Obv:** National arms **Rev:** Screw press, value and date within circle **Edge:** Segmented reeding

Date	Mintage	F	VF	XF	Unc	BU
2005Mo	49,895	—	—	—	40.00	45.00
2005Mo Proof	—	Value: 95.00				

KM# 732 100 PESOS

33.8250 g., Bi-Metallic .925 Silver 16.812g center in Aluminum-Bronze ring, 39.9 mm. **Subject:** Bank of Mexico's 80th Anniversary **Obv:** National arms **Rev:** Back design of the 1925 hundred peso note **Edge:** Segmented reeding

Date	Mintage	F	VF	XF	Unc	BU
2005Mo	49,712	—	—	—	40.00	45.00
2005Mo Proof	—	Value: 95.00				

KM# 717 100 PESOS

33.9400 g., Bi-Metallic .925 Silver 16.812g center in Brass ring, 39.04 mm. **Series:** First **Subject:** 180th Anniversary of Federation **Obv:** National arms **Obv. Legend:** ESTADOS UNIDOS MEXICANOS **Rev:** State arms **Rev. Legend:** ESTADO DE HIDALGO **Edge:** Segmented reeding

Date	Mintage	F	VF	XF	Unc	BU
2005Mo	249,820	—	—	—	35.00	40.00

KM# 817 100 PESOS

29.1690 g., Bi-Metallic .999 Gold 17.154g center in .999 Silver 12.015g ring, 34.5 mm. **Series:** First **Subject:** 180th Anniversary of Federation **Obv:** National arms **Obv. Legend:** ESTADOS UNIDOS MEXICANOS **Rev:** State arms **Rev. Legend:** ESTADO DE HIDALGO **Edge:** Segmented reeding

Date	Mintage	F	VF	XF	Unc	BU
2005Mo Proof	1,000	Value: 1,200				

KM# 716 100 PESOS

33.9400 g., Bi-Metallic .925 Silver 16.812g center in Brass ring, 39.04 mm. **Series:** First **Subject:** 180th Anniversary of Federation **Obv:** National arms **Obv. Legend:** ESTADOS UNIDOS MEXICANOS **Rev:** State arms **Rev. Legend:** ESTADO DE GUERRERO **Edge:** Segmented reeding

Date	Mintage	F	VF	XF	Unc	BU
2005Mo	248,850	—	—	—	35.00	40.00

KM# 818 100 PESOS

29.1690 g., Bi-Metallic .999 Gold 17.154g center in .999 Silver 12.015 ring, 34.5 mm. **Series:** First **Subject:** 180th Anniversary of Federation **Obv:** National arms **Obv. Legend:** ESTADOS UNIDOS MEXICANOS **Rev:** State arms **Rev. Legend:** ESTADO DE GUERRERO **Edge:** Segmented reeding

Date	Mintage	F	VF	XF	Unc	BU
2005Mo Proof	1,000	Value: 1,200				

KM# 715 100 PESOS

33.9400 g., Bi-Metallic .925 Silver 16.812g center in Brass ring, 39.04 mm. **Series:** First **Subject:** 180th Anniversary of Federation **Obv:** National arms **Obv. Legend:** ESTADOS UNIDOS MEXICANOS **Rev:** State arms **Rev. Legend:** ESTADO DE GUANAJUATO **Edge:** Segmented reeding

Date	Mintage	F	VF	XF	Unc	BU
2005Mo	249,489	—	—	—	35.00	40.00

KM# 819 100 PESOS

29.1690 g., Bi-Metallic .999 Gold 17.154g center in .999 Silver 12.015g ring, 34.5 mm. **Series:** First **Subject:** 180th Anniversary of Federation **Obv:** National arms **Obv. Legend:** ESTADOS UNIDOS MEXICANOS **Rev:** State arms **Rev. Legend:** ESTADO DE GUANAJUATO **Edge:** Segmented reeding

Date	Mintage	F	VF	XF	Unc	BU
2005Mo Proof	1,000	Value: 1,200				

KM# 714 100 PESOS

33.9400 g., Bi-Metallic .925 Silver 16.812g center in Brass ring, 39.04 mm. **Series:** First **Subject:** 180th Anniversary of Federation **Obv:** National arms **Obv. Legend:** ESTADOS UNIDOS MEXICANOS **Rev:** State arms **Rev. Legend:** ESTADO DE DURANGO **Edge:** Segmented reeding

Date	Mintage	F	VF	XF	Unc	BU
2005Mo	249,774	—	—	—	35.00	40.00

KM# 820 100 PESOS

29.1690 g., Bi-Metallic .999 Gold 17.154g center in .999 silver 12.015g ring, 34.5 mm. **Series:** First **Subject:** 180th Anniversary of Federation **Obv:** National arms **Obv. Legend:** ESTADOS UNIDOS MEXICANOS **Rev:** State arms **Rev. Legend:** ESTADO DE DURANGO **Edge:** Segmented reeding

Date	Mintage	F	VF	XF	Unc	BU
2005Mo Proof	1,000	Value: 1,200				

KM# 713 100 PESOS

33.9400 g., Bi-Metallic .925 Silver 16.812g center in Brass ring, 39.04 mm. **Series:** First **Subject:** 180th Anniversary of Federation **Obv:** National arms **Obv. Legend:** ESTADOS UNIDOS MEXICANOS **Rev:** Federal District arms **Rev. Legend:** DISTRITO FEDERAL **Edge:** Segmented reeding

Date	Mintage	F	VF	XF	Unc	BU
2005Mo	249,461	—	—	—	35.00	40.00

KM# 821 100 PESOS

29.1690 g., Bi-Metallic .999 Gold 17.154g center in .999 Silver 12.015g ring, 34.5 mm. **Series:** First **Subject:** 180th Anniversary of Federation **Obv:** National arms **Obv. Legend:** ESTADOS UNIDOS MEXICANOS **Rev:** Federal District arms **Rev. Legend:** DISTRITO FEDERAL **Edge:** Segmented reeding

Date	Mintage	F	VF	XF	Unc	BU
2005Mo Proof	1,000	Value: 1,200				

KM# 754 100 PESOS

33.9400 g., Bi-Metallic .925 Silver 16.812g center in Aluminum-Bronze ring, 39.04 mm. **Series:** First **Subject:** 180th Anniversary of Federation **Obv:** National arms **Obv. Legend:** ESTADOS UNIDOS MEXICANOS **Rev:** State arms **Rev. Legend:** ESTADO DE CHIHUAHUA **Edge:** Segmented reeding

Date	Mintage	F	VF	XF	Unc	BU
2005Mo	249,102	—	—	—	35.00	40.00

KM# 822 100 PESOS

29.1690 g., Bi-Metallic .999 Gold 17.154g center in .999 Silver 12.015g ring, 34.5 mm. **Series:** First **Subject:** 180th Anniversary of Federation **Obv:** National arms **Obv. Legend:** ESTADOS UNIDOS MEXICANOS **Rev:** State arms **Rev. Legend:** ESTADO DE CHIHUAHUA **Edge:** Segmented reeding

Date	Mintage	F	VF	XF	Unc	BU
2005Mo Proof	1,000	Value: 1,200				

KM# 712 100 PESOS

33.9400 g., Bi-Metallic .925 Silver 16.812g center in Brass ring, 39.04 mm. **Series:** First **Subject:** 180th Anniversary of Federation **Obv:** National arms **Obv. Legend:** ESTADOS UNIDOS MEXICANOS **Rev:** State arms **Rev. Legend:** ESTADO DE CHIAPAS **Edge:** Segmented reeding

Date	Mintage	F	VF	XF	Unc	BU
2005Mo	249,417	—	—	—	35.00	40.00

KM# 823 100 PESOS

29.1690 g., Bi-Metallic .999 Gold 17.154g center in .999 Silver 12.015g ring, 34.5 mm. **Series:** First **Subject:** 180th Anniversary of Federation **Obv:** National arms **Obv. Legend:** ESTADOS UNIDOS MEXICANOS **Rev:** State arms **Rev. Legend:** ESTADO DE CHIAPAS **Edge:** Segmented reeding

Date	Mintage	F	VF	XF	Unc	BU
2005Mo Proof	1,000	Value: 1,200				

KM# 729 100 PESOS

33.8250 g., Bi-Metallic .925 Silver 16.812g center in Aluminum-Bronze ring, 39.04 mm. **Series:** First **Subject:** 180th Anniversary of Federation **Obv:** National arms **Obv. Legend:** ESTADOS UNIDOS MEXICANOS **Rev:** State arms **Rev. Legend:** ESTADO DE COLIMA **Edge:** Segmented reeding

Date	Mintage	F	VF	XF	Unc	BU
2005Mo	248,850	—	—	—	35.00	40.00

KM# 824 100 PESOS

29.1690 g., Bi-Metallic .999 Gold 17.154g center in .999 Silver 12.015g ring, 34.5 mm. **Series:** First **Subject:** 180th Anniversary of Federation **Obv:** National arms **Obv. Legend:** ESTADOS UNIDOS MEXICANOS **Rev:** State arms **Rev. Legend:** ESTADO DE COLIMA **Edge:** Segmented reeding

Date	Mintage	F	VF	XF	Unc	BU
2005Mo Proof	1,000	Value: 1,200				

KM# 752 100 PESOS

33.9400 g., Bi-Metallic .925 Silver 16.812g center in Aluminum-Bronze ring, 39.04 mm. **Series:** First **Subject:** 180th Anniversary of Federation **Obv:** National arms **Obv. Legend:** ESTADOS UNIDOS MEXICANOS **Rev:** State arms **Rev. Legend:** ESTADO DE COAHUILA DE ZARAGOZA **Edge:** Segmented reeding

Date	Mintage	F	VF	XF	Unc	BU
2005Mo	247,991	—	—	—	35.00	40.00

KM# 825 100 PESOS

29.1690 g., Bi-Metallic .999 Gold 17.154g center in .999 Silver 12.015g ring, 34.5 mm. **Series:** First **Subject:** 180th Anniversary of Federation **Obv:** National arms **Obv. Legend:** ESTADOS UNIDOS MEXICANOS **Rev:** State arms **Rev. Legend:** ESTADO DE COAHUILA DE ZARAGOZA **Edge:** Segmented reeding

Date	Mintage	F	VF	XF	Unc	BU
2005Mo Proof	1,000	Value: 1,200				

KM# 727 100 PESOS

33.9400 g., Bi-Metallic .925 Silver 16.812g center in Aluminum-Bronze ring, 39.04 mm. **Series:** First **Subject:** 180th Anniversary of Federation **Obv:** National arms **Obv. Legend:** ESTADOS UNIDOS MEXICANOS **Rev:** State arms **Rev. Legend:** ESTADO DE CAMPECHE **Edge:** Segmented reeding

Date	Mintage	F	VF	XF	Unc	BU
2005Mo	249,040	—	—	—	35.00	40.00

KM# 826 100 PESOS

29.1690 g., Bi-Metallic .999 Gold 17.154g center in .999 Silver 12.015g ring, 34.5 mm. **Series:** First **Subject:** 180th Anniversary of Federation **Obv:** National arms **Obv. Legend:** ESTADOS UNIDOS MEXICANOS **Rev:** State arms **Rev. Legend:** ESTADO DE CAMPECHE **Edge:** Segmented reeding

Date	Mintage	F	VF	XF	Unc	BU
2005Mo Proof	1,000	Value: 1,200				

KM# 725 100 PESOS

33.9400 g., Bi-Metallic .925 Silver 16.812g center in Aluminum-Bronze ring, 39.04 mm. **Series:** First **Subject:** 180th Anniversary of Federation **Obv:** National arms **Obv. Legend:** ESTADOS UNIDOS MEXICANOS **Rev:** State arms **Rev. Legend:** ESTADO DE BAJA CALIFORNIA SUR **Edge:** Segmented reeding

Date	Mintage	F	VF	XF	Unc	BU
2005Mo	249,585	—	—	—	35.00	40.00

KM# 827 100 PESOS

29.1690 g., Bi-Metallic .999 Gold 17.154g center in .999 Silver 12.015g ring, 34.5 mm. **Series:** First **Subject:** 180th Anniversary of Federation **Obv:** National arms **Obv. Legend:** ESTADOS UNIDOS MEXICANOS **Rev:** State arms **Rev. Legend:** ESTADO DE BAJA CALIFORNIA SUR **Edge:** Segmented reeding

Date	Mintage	F	VF	XF	Unc	BU
2005Mo Proof	1,000	Value: 1,200				

KM# 723 100 PESOS

33.9400 g., Bi-Metallic .925 Silver 16.812g center in Aluminum-Bronze ring, 39.04 mm. **Series:** First **Subject:** 180th Anniversary of Federation **Obv:** National arms **Obv. Legend:** ESTADOS UNIDOS MEXICANOS **Rev:** State arms **Rev. Legend:** ESTADO DE BAJA CALIFORNIA **Edge:** Segmented reeding

Date	Mintage	F	VF	XF	Unc	BU
2005Mo	249,263	—	—	—	35.00	40.00

KM# 828 100 PESOS

29.1690 g., Bi-Metallic .999 Gold 17.154g center in .999 Silver 12.015g ring, 34.5 mm. **Series:** First **Subject:** 180th Anniversary of Federation **Obv:** National arms **Obv. Legend:** ESTADOS UNIDOS MEXICANOS **Rev:** State arms **Rev. Legend:** ESTADO DE BAJA CALIFORNIA **Edge:** Segmented reeding

Date	Mintage	F	VF	XF	Unc	BU
2005Mo Proof	1,000	Value: 1,200				

KM# 721 100 PESOS

33.9400 g., Bi-Metallic .925 Silver 16.812g center in Aluminum-Bronze ring, 39.04 mm. **Series:** First **Subject:** 180th Anniversary of Federation **Obv:** National arms **Obv. Legend:** ESTADOS UNIDOS MEXICANOS **Rev:** Estados de Aguascalientes state arms **Rev. Legend:** ESTADO DE AGUASCALIENTES **Edge:** Segmented reeding

Date	Mintage	F	VF	XF	Unc	BU
2005Mo	248,410	—	—	—	35.00	40.00

KM# 829 100 PESOS

29.1690 g., Bi-Metallic .999 Gold 17.154g center in .999 Silver 12.015g ring, 34.5 mm. **Series:** First **Subject:** 180th Anniversary of Federation **Obv:** National arms **Obv. Legend:** ESTADOS UNIDOS MEXICANOS **Rev:** State arms **Rev. Legend:** ESTADO DE AGUASCALIENTES **Edge:** Segmented reeding

Date	Mintage	F	VF	XF	Unc	BU
2005Mo Proof	1,000	Value: 1,200				

KM# 719 100 PESOS

33.8250 g., Bi-Metallic .925 Silver 16.812g center in Aluminum-Bronze ring, 39.04 mm. **Series:** Second **Obv:** National arms **Obv. Legend:** ESTADOS UNIDOS MEXICANOS **Rev:** Facade of the San Marcos garden above sculpture of national emblem at left, San Antonio Temple at right **Rev. Legend:** AGUASCALIENTES **Edge:** Segmented reeding

Date	Mintage	F	VF	XF	Unc	BU
2005Mo	149,705	—	—	—	25.00	30.00

KM# 862 100 PESOS

29.1690 g., Bi-Metallic .999 Gold 17.154g center in .999 Silver 12.015g ring, 34.5 mm. **Series:** Second **Obv:** National arms **Obv. Legend:** ESTADOS UNIDOS MEXICANOS **Rev:** Facade of the San Marcos garden above sculpture of national emblem at left, San Antonio temple at right **Rev. Legend:** AGUASCALIENTES **Edge:** Segmented reeding

Date	Mintage	F	VF	XF	Unc	BU
2005Mo Proof	600	Value: 1,200				

KM# 758 100 PESOS

33.9400 g., Bi-Metallic .925 Silver 16.812g center in Aluminum-Bronze ring, 39.04 mm. **Series:** Second **Obv:** National arms **Obv. Legend:** ESTADOS UNIDOS MEXICANOS **Rev:** Ram's head and value within circle **Rev. Legend:** BAJA CALIFORNIA - GOBIERNO DEL ESTADO **Edge:** Segmented reeding

Date	Mintage	F	VF	XF	Unc	BU
2005Mo	149,771	—	—	—	25.00	30.00

KM# 863 100 PESOS

29.1690 g., Bi-Metallic .999 Gold 17.154g center in .999 Silver 12.015g ring, 34.5 mm. **Series:** Second **Obv:** National arms **Obv. Legend:** ESTTADOS UNIDOS MEXICANOS **Rev:** Ram's head, mountain outline in background **Rev. Legend:** BAJA CALIFORNIA - GOBIERNO DEL ESTADO **Edge:** Segmented reeding

Date	Mintage	F	VF	XF	Unc	BU
2005Mo Proof	600	Value: 1,200				

KM# 762 100 PESOS

33.9400 g., Bi-Metallic .925 Silver 16.812g center in Aluminum-Bronze ring, 39.04 mm. **Series:** Second **Obv:** National arms **Obv. Legend:** ESTADOS UNIDOS MEXICANOS **Rev:** Outlined map of peninsula at center, cave painting of deer behind, cactus at right **Rev. Legend:** ESTADO DE BAJA CALIFORNIA SUR **Edge:** Segmented reeding

Date	Mintage	F	VF	XF	Unc	BU
2005Mo	149,152	—	—	—	25.00	30.00

KM# 764 100 PESOS

33.7000 g., Bi-Metallic .925 Silver 16.812g center in Aluminum-Bronze ring **Subject:** 200th Anniversary Birth of Benito Juarez Garcia **Obv:** National arms **Rev:** Bust 1/4 left within circle

Date	Mintage	F	VF	XF	Unc	BU
2006Mo	49,913	—	—	—	40.00	45.00

KM# 864 100 PESOS

29.1690 g., Bi-Metallic .999 Gold 17.154g center in .999 Silver 12.015g ring, 34.5 mm. **Series:** Second **Obv:** National arms **Obv. Legend:** ESTADOS UNIDOS MEXICANOS **Rev:** Outlined map of peninsula at center, cave painting of deer behind, cactus at right **Rev. Legend:** ESTADO DE BAJA CALIFORNIA SUR **Edge:** Segmented reeding

Date	Mintage	F	VF	XF	Unc	BU
2006Mo Proof	600	Value: 1,200				

KM# 760 100 PESOS

33.9400 g., Bi-Metallic .925 Silver 16.812g center in Aluminum-Bronze ring, 39.04 mm. **Series:** Second **Subject:** Estado de Campeche **Obv:** National arms **Obv. Legend:** ESTADOS UNIDOS MEXICANOS **Rev:** Jade mask - Calakmul, Campeche **Rev. Legend:** ESTADO DE CAMPECHE **Edge:** Segmented reeding

Date	Mintage	F	VF	XF	Unc	BU
2006Mo	149,803	—	—	—	25.00	30.00

KM# 865 100 PESOS

29.1690 g., Bi-Metallic .999 Gold 17.154g center in .999 Silver 12.015g ring, 34.5 mm. **Series:** Second **Obv:** National arms **Obv. Legend:** ESTADOS UNIDOS MEXICANOS **Rev:** Jade mask - Calakmul, Campeche **Rev. Legend:** ESTADO DE CAMPECHE **Edge:** Segmented reeding

Date	Mintage	F	VF	XF	Unc	BU
2006Mo Proof	600	Value: 1,200				

KM# 781 100 PESOS

33.7000 g., Bi-Metallic .925 Silver 16.812g center in Aluminum-Bronze ring, 39.04 mm. **Series:** Second **Obv:** National arms **Obv. Legend:** ESTADOS UNIDOS MEXICANOS **Rev:** Outlined map with turtle, mine cart above grapes at center, Friendship Dam above Christ of the Nodas at left, chimneys above crucibles and bell tower of Santiago's cathedral at right **Rev. Legend:** COAHUILA DE ZARAGOZA **Edge:** Segmented reeding

Date	Mintage	F	VF	XF	Unc	BU
2006Mo	149,560	—	—	—	25.00	30.00

KM# 866 100 PESOS

29.1690 g., Bi-Metallic .999 Gold 17.154g center in .999 Silver 12.015g ring, 34.5 mm. **Series:** Second **Obv:** National arms **Obv. Legend:** ESTADOS UNIDOS MEXICANOS **Rev:** Outlined map with turtle, mine cart above grapes at center, Friendship dam above Christ of the Nodas at left, chimneys above crucibles and bell tower of Santiago's cathedral at right **Rev. Inscription:** COAHUILA DE ZARAGOZA **Edge:** Segmented reeding

Date	Mintage	F	VF	XF	Unc	BU
2006Mo Proof	600	Value: 1,200				

KM# 777 100 PESOS
33.9400 g., Bi-Metallic .925 Silver 16.812g center in Aluminum-Bronze ring, 39.04 mm. **Series:** Second **Obv:** National arms **Obv. Legend:** ESTADOS UNIDOS MEXICANOS **Rev:** State arms at lower center, Nevado de Colima and Volcan de Fuego volcanos in background **Rev. Legend:** *Colima* **Rev. Inscription:** GENEROSO **Edge:** Segmented reeding

Date	Mintage	F	VF	XF	Unc	BU
2006Mo	149,041	—	—	—	25.00	30.00

KM# 867 100 PESOS
29.1690 g., Bi-Metallic .999 Gold 17.154g center in .999 Silver 12.015 ring, 34.5 mm. **Series:** Second **Obv:** National arms **Obv. Legend:** ESTADOS UNIDOS MEXICANOS **Rev:** State arms at lower center, Nevado de Colima and Volcan de Fuego volcanos in background **Rev. Legend:** *Colima* **Rev. Inscription:** GENEROSO **Edge:** Segmented reeding

Date	Mintage	F	VF	XF	Unc	BU
2006Mo Proof	600	Value: 1,200				

KM# 773 100 PESOS
33.9400 g., Bi-Metallic .925 Silver 16.812g center in Aluminum-Bronze ring, 39.04 mm. **Series:** Second **Obv:** National arms **Obv. Legend:** ESTADOS UNIDOS MEXICANOS **Rev:** Head of Pakal, ancient Mayan king, Palenque **Rev. Legend:** ESTADO DE CHIAPAS - CABEZA MAYA DEL REY PAKAL, PALENQUE **Edge:** Segmented reeding

Date	Mintage	F	VF	XF	Unc	BU
2006Mo	149,491	—	—	—	25.00	30.00

KM# 868 100 PESOS
29.1690 g., Bi-Metallic .999 Gold 17.154g center in .999 Silver 12.015g ring, 34.5 mm. **Series:** Second **Obv:** National arms **Obv. Legend:** ESTADOS UNIDOS MEXICANOS **Rev:** Head of Pakal, ancient Mayan king, Palenque **Rev. Legend:** ESTADO DE CHIAPAS - CABEZA MAYA DEL REY PAKAL, PALENQUE **Edge:** Segmented reeding

Date	Mintage	F	VF	XF	Unc	BU
2006Mo Proof	600	Value: 1,200				

KM# 775 100 PESOS
33.9400 g., Bi-Metallic .925 Silver 16.812g center in Aluminum-Bronze ring, 39.04 mm. **Series:** Second **Obv:** National arms **Obv. Legend:** ESTADOS UNIDOS MEXICANOS **Rev:** Angel of Liberty **Rev. Legend:** MÉXICO - ANGEL DE LA LIBERTAD, CHIHUAHUA **Edge:** Segmented reeding

Date	Mintage	F	VF	XF	Unc	BU
2006Mo	149,557	—	—	—	25.00	30.00

KM# 869 100 PESOS
29.1690 g., Bi-Metallic .999 Gold 17.154g center in .999 Silver 12.015g ring, 34.5 mm. **Series:** Second **Obv:** National arms **Obv. Legend:** ESTADOS UNIDOS MEXICANOS **Rev:** Angel of Liberty **Rev. Legend:** MÉXICO - ANGEL DE LA LIBERTAD, CHIHUAHUA **Edge:** Segmented reeding

Date	Mintage	F	VF	XF	Unc	BU
2006Mo Proof	600	Value: 1,200				

KM# 779 100 PESOS
33.9400 g., Bi-Metallic .925 Silver 16.812g center in Aluminum-Bronze ring, 39.04 mm. **Series:** Second **Obv:** National arms **Obv. Legend:** ESTADOS UNIDOS MEXICANOS **Rev:** National Palace **Rev. Legend:** DISTRITO FEDERAL - ANTIGUO AYUNTAMIENTO **Edge:** Segmented reeding

Date	Mintage	F	VF	XF	Unc	BU
2006Mo	149,525	—	—	—	25.00	30.00

KM# 870 100 PESOS
29.1690 g., Bi-Metallic .999 Gold 17.154g center in .999 Silver 12.015g ring, 34.5 mm. **Series:** Second **Obv:** National arms **Obv. Legend:** ESTADOS UNIDOS MEXICANOS **Rev:** National palace **Rev. Legend:** DISTRITO FEDERAL - ANTIGUO AYUNTAMIENTO **Edge:** Segmented reeding

Date	Mintage	F	VF	XF	Unc	BU
2006Mo Proof	600	Value: 1,200				

KM# 787 100 PESOS
33.9400 g., Bi-Metallic .925 Silver 16.812g center in Brass ring, 39.04 mm. **Series:** Second **Obv:** National arms **Obv. Legend:** ESTADOS UNIDOS MEXICANOS **Rev:** Tree **Rev. Legend:** PRIMERA RESERVA NACIONAL FORESTAL - DURANGO **Edge:** Segmented reeding

Date	Mintage	F	VF	XF	Unc	BU
2006Mo	149,034	—	—	—	25.00	30.00

KM# 871 100 PESOS
29.1690 g., Bi-Metallic .999 Gold 17.154g center in .999 Silver 12.015g ring, 34.5 mm. **Series:** Second **Obv:** National arms **Obv. Legend:** ESYADOS UNIDOS MEXICANOS **Rev:** Tree **Rev. Legend:** PRIMERA RESERVA NACIONAL RORESTAL - DURANGO **Edge:** Segmented reeding

Date	Mintage	F	VF	XF	Unc	BU
2006Mo Proof	600	Value: 1,200				

KM# 789 100 PESOS
33.9400 g., Bi-Metallic .925 Silver 16.812g center in Brass ring, 39.04 mm. **Series:** Second **Obv:** National arms **Obv. Legend:** ESTADOS UNIDOS MEXICANOS **Rev:** State arms at center, statue of Miguel Hidalgo at left, monument to Pipla at lower right **Rev. Inscription:** *Guanajuato* **Edge:** Segmented reeding

Date	Mintage	F	VF	XF	Unc	BU
2006Mo	149,921	—	—	—	25.00	30.00

KM# 872 100 PESOS
29.1690 g., Bi-Metallic .999 Gold 17.154g center in .999 Silver 12.015g ring, 34.50 mm. **Series:** Second **Obv:** National arms **Obv. Legend:** ESTADOS UNIDOS MEXICANOS **Rev:** State arms at lower center, statue of Miguel Hidalgo at left, monument to Pipila at lower right **Rev. Inscription:** *Guanajauto* **Edge:** Segmented reeding

Date	Mintage	F	VF	XF	Unc	BU
2006Mo Proof	600	Value: 1,200				

KM# 791 100 PESOS
33.9400 g., Bi-Metallic .925 Silver 16.812g center in Brass ring, 39.04 mm. **Series:** Second **Obv:** National arms **Obv. Legend:** ESTADOS UNIDOS MEXICANOS **Rev:** Stylized portrait of Vicente Guerrero at left, church of Taxco at upper center, Acapulco's la Quebrada with diver above Christmas Eve flower and mask **Rev. Legend:** GUERRERO **Edge:** Segmented reeding

Date	Mintage	F	VF	XF	Unc	BU
2006Mo	149,675	—	—	—	25.00	30.00

KM# 873 100 PESOS
29.1690 g., Bi-Metallic .999 Gold 17.154g center in .999 Silver 12.015g ring, 34.5 mm. **Series:** Second **Obv:** National arms **Obv. Legend:** ESTADOS UNIDOS MEXICANOS **Rev:** Stylized portrait of Vicente Guerrero at left, church of Taxco at upper center, Acapulco's la Quebrada with diver over Christmas Eve flower and mask **Rev. Legend:** GUERRERO **Edge:** Segmented reeding

Date	Mintage	F	VF	XF	Unc	BU
2006Mo Proof	600	Value: 1,200				

KM# 793 100 PESOS
33.9400 g., Bi-Metallic .925 Silver 16.812g center in Aluminum-Bronze ring, 39.04 mm. **Series:** Second **Obv:** National arms **Obv. Legend:** ESTADOS UNIDOS MEXICANOS **Rev:** Monument of Pachuca Hidalgo **Rev. Inscription:** *RELOJ / MONUMENTAL / DE / PACHUCA / HIDALGO - La / Bella / Airosa* **Edge:** Segmented reeding

Date	Mintage	F	VF	XF	Unc	BU
2006Mo	149,273	—	—	—	25.00	30.00

KM# 874 100 PESOS
29.1690 g., Bi-Metallic .999 Gold 17.154g center in .999 Silver 12.015g ring, 34.5 mm. **Series:** Second **Obv:** National arms **Obv. Legend:** ESTADOS UNIDOS MEXICANOS **Rev:** Monument of Pachuca Hidalgo **Rev. Inscription:** *RELOJ / MONUMENTAL / DE / PACHUCA / HIDALGO* **Edge:** Segmented reeding

Date	Mintage	F	VF	XF	Unc	BU
2006Mo Proof	600	Value: 1,200				

KM# 795 100 PESOS
33.9400 g., Bi-Metallic .925 Silver 16.812g center in Brass ring, 39.04 mm. **Series:** Second **Obv:** National arms **Obv. Legend:** ESTADOS UNIDOS MEXICANOS **Rev:** Hospicio Cabañas orphanage **Rev. Legend:** ESTADO DE JALISCO **Edge:** Segmented reeding

Date	Mintage	F	VF	XF	Unc	BU
2006Mo	149,750	—	—	—	25.00	30.00

KM# 875 100 PESOS

29.1690 g., Bi-Metallic .999 Gold 17.154g center in .999 Silver 12.015g ring, 34.5 mm. **Series:** Second **Obv:** National arms **Obv. Legend:** ESTADOS UNIDOS MEXICANOS **Rev:** Hospicio Cabañas orphanage **Rev. Legend:** ESTADO DE JALISCO **Edge:** Segmented reeding

Date	Mintage	F	VF	XF	Unc	BU
2006Mo Proof	600	Value: 1,200				

KM# 802 100 PESOS

33.9400 g., Bi-Metallic .925 Silver 16.812g center in Aluminum-Bronze ring, 39.04 mm. **Series:** Second **Obv:** National arms **Obv. Legend:** ESTADOS UNIDOS MEXICANOS **Rev:** Pyramid de la Loona (moon) **Rev. Legend:** ESTADO DE MÉXICO **Edge:** Segmented reeding

Date	Mintage	F	VF	XF	Unc	BU
2006Mo	149,377	—	—	—	25.00	30.00

KM# 876 100 PESOS

29.1690 g., Bi-Metallic .999 Gold 17.154g center in .999 Silver 12.015g ring, 34.5 mm. **Series:** Second **Obv:** National arms **Obv. Legend:** ESTADOS UNIDOS MEXICANOS **Rev:** Pyramid de la Looona (moon) **Rev. Legend:** ESTADO DE MÉXICO **Edge:** Segmented reeding

Date	Mintage	F	VF	XF	Unc	BU
2006Mo Proof	600	Value: 1,200				

KM# 785 100 PESOS

33.9400 g., Bi-Metallic .925 Silver 16.812g center in Aluminum-Bronze ring, 39.04 mm. **Series:** Second **Obv:** National arms **Obv. Legend:** ESTADOS UNIDOS MEXICANOS **Rev:** Four Monarch butterflies **Rev. Legend:** ESTADO DE MICHOACÁN **Edge:** Segmented reeding

Date	Mintage	F	VF	XF	Unc	BU
2006Mo	149,730	—	—	—	25.00	30.00

KM# 877 100 PESOS

29.1690 g., Bi-Metallic .999 Gold 17.154g center in .999 Silver 12.015g ring, 34.5 mm. **Series:** Second **Obv:** National arms **Obv. Legend:** ESTADOS UNIDOS MEXICANOS **Rev:** Four Monarch butterflies **Rev. Legend:** ESTADO DE MICHOACÁN **Edge:** Segmented reeding

Date	Mintage	F	VF	XF	Unc	BU
2006Mo Proof	600	Value: 1,200				

KM# 800 100 PESOS

33.9400 g., Bi-Metallic .925 Silver 16.812g center in Aluminum-Bronze ring, 39.04 mm. **Series:** Second **Obv:** National arms **Obv. Legend:** ESTADOS UNIDOS MEXICANOS **Rev:** 1/2 length figure of Chinelo (local dancer) at right, Palacio de Cortes in background **Rev. Inscription:** ESTADO DE / MORELOS **Edge:** Segmented reeding

Date	Mintage	F	VF	XF	Unc	BU
2006Mo	149,648	—	—	—	25.00	30.00

KM# 878 100 PESOS

29.1690 g., Bi-Metallic .999 Gold 17.154g center in .999 Silver 12.015g ring, 34.5 mm. **Series:** Second **Obv:** National arms **Obv. Legend:** ESTADOS UNIDOS MEXICANOS **Rev:** 1/2 length figure of Chinelo (local dancer) at right, Palacio de Cortes in background **Rev. Inscription:** ESTADO DE / MORELOS **Edge:** Segmented reeding

Date	Mintage	F	VF	XF	Unc	BU
2006Mo Proof	600	Value: 1,200				

KM# 798 100 PESOS

33.9400 g., 33.8250 Bi-Metallic .925 Silver 16.812g center in Aluminum-Bronze ring 36.908 oz., 39.04 mm. **Series:** Second **Obv:** National arms **Obv. Legend:** ESTADOS UNIDOS MEXICANOS **Rev:** Isle de Mexcaltitlán **Rev. Legend:** ESTADO DE NAYARIT **Edge:** Segmented reeding

Date	Mintage	F	VF	XF	Unc	BU
2007Mo	149,560	—	—	—	25.00	30.00

KM# 879 100 PESOS

29.1690 g., Bi-Metallic .999 Gold 17.154g center in .999 12.015g ring, 34.5 mm. **Series:** Second **Obv:** National arms **Obv. Legend:** ESTADOS UNIDOS MEXICANOS **Rev:** Isle de Mexcaltitlán **Rev. Legend:** ESTADO DE NAYARIT **Edge:** Segmented reeding

Date	Mintage	F	VF	XF	Unc	BU
2007Mo Proof	600	Value: 1,200				

KM# 848 100 PESOS

33.9400 g., Bi-Metallic .925 Silver 20.1753 center in Aluminum-Bronze ring, 39.04 mm. **Series:** Second **Obv:** National arms **Obv. Legend:** ESTADOS UNIDOS MEXICANOE **Rev:** Old foundry in Parque Fundidora (public park) at right, Cerro de la Silla (Saddle Hill) in background **Rev. Legend:** ESTADO DE NUEVO LÉON **Edge:** Segmented reeding

Date	Mintage	F	VF	XF	Unc	BU
2007Mo	149,425	—	—	—	25.00	30.00

KM# 880 100 PESOS

29.1690 g., Bi-Metallic .999 Gold 17.154g center in .999 Silver 12.015g ring, 34.5 mm. **Series:** Second **Obv:** National arms **Obv. Legend:** ESTADOS UNIDOS MEXICANOS **Rev:** Old foundry in Parque Fundidora (public park) at right, Cerro de la Silla (Saddle hill) in background **Rev. Legend:** ESTADO DE NUEVO LEÓN **Edge:** Segmented reeding

Date	Mintage	F	VF	XF	Unc	BU
2007Mo Proof	600	Value: 1,200				

KM# 849 100 PESOS

33.9400 g., Bi-Metallic .925 Silver 20.1753g center in Aluminum-Bronze ring, 39.04 mm. **Series:** Second **Obv:** National arms **Obv. Legend:** ESTADOS UNIDOS MEXICANOS **Rev:** Teatro Macedonio Alcala (theater) **Rev. Legend:** OAXACA **Edge:** Segmented reeding

Date	Mintage	F	VF	XF	Unc	BU
2007Mo	149,892	—	—	—	25.00	30.00

KM# 881 100 PESOS

29.1690 g., Bi-Metallic .999 Gold 17.154g center in .999 Silver 12.015g ring, 34.50 mm. **Series:** Second **Obv:** National arms **Obv. Legend:** ESTADOS UNIDOS MEXICANOS **Rev:** Teatro Macedonio Alcala (theater) **Rev. Legend:** OAXACA **Edge:** Segmented reeding

Date	Mintage	F	VF	XF	Unc	BU
2007Mo Proof	600	Value: 1,200				

KM# 850 100 PESOS

33.9400 g., Bi-Metallic .925 Silver 20.1753g center in Aluminum-Bronze ring, 39.04 mm. **Series:** Second **Obv:** National arms **Obv. Legend:** ESTADOS UNIDOS MEXICANOS **Rev:** Talavera porcelain dish **Rev. Legend:** ESTADO DE PUEBLA **Edge:** Segmented reeding

Date	Mintage	F	VF	XF	Unc	BU
2007Mo	149,474	—	—	—	25.00	30.00

KM# 882 100 PESOS

29.1690 g., Bi-Metallic .999 Gold 17.154g center in .999 Silver 12.015g ring, 34.5 mm. **Series:** Second **Obv:** National arms **Obv. Legend:** ESTADOS UNIDOS MEXICANOS **Rev:** Talavera porcelain dish **Rev. Legend:** ESTADO DE PUEBLA **Edge:** Segmented reeding

Date	Mintage	F	VF	XF	Unc	BU
2007Mo Proof	600	Value: 1,200				

KM# 851 100 PESOS

33.9400 g., Bi-Metallic .925 Silver 20.1753g center in Aluminum-Bronze ring, 39.04 mm. **Series:** Second **Obv:** National arms **Obv. Legend:** ESTADOS UNIDOS MEXICANOS **Rev:** Mask at left, rays above state arms at center, Mayan ruins at right **Rev. Legend:** QUINTANA ROO **Edge:** Segmented reeding

Date	Mintage	F	VF	XF	Unc	BU
2007Mo	149,582	—	—	—	25.00	30.00

KM# 883 100 PESOS

29.1690 g., Bi-Metallic .999 Gold 17.154g center in .999 Silver 12.015g ring, 34.5 mm. **Series:** Second **Obv:** National arms **Obv. Legend:** ESTADOS UNIDOS MEXICANOS **Rev:** Mask at left, rays above state arms at center, Mayan ruins at right **Rev. Legend:** QUINTANA ROO **Edge:** Segmented reeding

Date	Mintage	F	VF	XF	Unc	BU
2007Mo Proof	600	Value: 1,200				

KM# 852 100 PESOS

33.9400 g., Bi-Metallic .925 Silver 20.1753 center in Aluminum-Bronze ring, 39.04 mm. **Series:** Second **Obv:** National arms **Obv. Legend:** ESTADOS UNIDOS MEXICANOS **Rev:** Aqueduct of Querétaro at left, church of Santa Rosa de Viterbo at right **Rev. Legend:** ESTADO DE QUERÉTARO ARTEAGA **Edge:** Segmented reeding

Date	Mintage	F	VF	XF	Unc	BU
2007Mo	149,127	—	—	—	25.00	30.00

KM# 884 100 PESOS

29.1690 g., Bi-Metallic .999 Gold 17.154g center in .999 Silver 12.015g ring, 34.5 mm. **Series:** Second **Obv:** National arms **Obv. Legend:** ESTADOS UNIDOS MEXICANOS **Rev:** Aqueduct of Querétaro at left, church of Santa Rosa de Viterbo at right **Rev. Legend:** ESTADO DE QUERÉTARO ARTEAGA **Edge:** Segmented reeding

Date	Mintage	F	VF	XF	Unc	BU
2007Mo Proof	600	Value: 1,200				

KM# 853 100 PESOS

33.9400 g., Bi-Metallic .925 Silver 20.1753g center in Aluminum-Bronze ring, 39.04 mm. **Series:** Second **Obv:** National arms **Obv. Legend:** ESTADOS UNIDOS MEXICANOS **Rev:** Facade of Caja Real **Rev. Legend:** • SAN LUIS POTOSÍ • **Edge:** Segmented reeding

Date	Mintage	F	VF	XF	Unc	BU
2007Mo	148,750	—	—	—	25.00	30.00

KM# 885 100 PESOS

29.1690 g., Bi-Metallic .999 Gold 17.154g center in .999 Silver 12.015 ring, 34.5 mm. **Series:** Second **Obv:** National arms **Obv. Legend:** ESTADOS UNIDOS MEXICANOS **Rev:** Facade of Caja Real **Rev. Legend:** • SAN LUIS POTOSÍ • **Edge:** Segmented reeding

Date	Mintage	F	VF	XF	Unc	BU
2007Mo Proof	600	Value: 1,200				

KM# 854 100 PESOS

33.9400 g., Bi-Metallic .925 Silver 20.1753g center in Aluminum-Bronze ring, 39.04 mm. **Series:** Second **Obv:** National arms **Obv. Legend:** ESTADOS UNIDOS MEXICANOS **Rev:** Shield on pile of cactus fruits **Rev. Legend:** ESTADO DE SINALOA - LUGAR DE PITAHAYAS **Edge:** Segmented reeding

Date	Mintage	F	VF	XF	Unc	BU
2007Mo	149,032	—	—	—	25.00	30.00

KM# 886 100 PESOS

29.1690 g., Bi-Metallic .999 Gold 17.154 center in .999 Silver 12.015g ring, 34.5 mm. **Series:** Second **Obv:** National arms **Obv. Legend:** ESTADOS UNIDOS MEXICANOS **Rev:** Shield on pile of cactus fruits **Rev. Legend:** ESTADO DE SINALOA - LUGAR DE PITAHAYES **Edge:** Segmented reeding

Date	Mintage	F	VF	XF	Unc	BU
2007Mo Proof	600	Value: 1,200				

KM# 855 100 PESOS

33.9400 g., Bi-Metallic .925 Silver 20.1753g center in Aluminum-Bronze ring, 39.04 mm. **Series:** Second **Obv:** National arms **Obv. Legend:** ESTADOS UNIDOS MEXICANOS **Rev:** Local in Dance of the Deer at left, cactus at right, mountains in background **Rev. Legend:** ESTADO DE SONORA **Edge:** Segmented reeding

Date	Mintage	F	VF	XF	Unc	BU
2007Mo	149,891	—	—	—	25.00	30.00

KM# 887 100 PESOS

29.1690 g., Bi-Metallic .999 Gold 17.154g center in .999 Silver 12.015g ring, 34.5 mm. **Series:** Second **Obv:** National arms **Obv. Legend:** ESTADOS UNIDOS MEXICANOS **Rev:** Local in Dance of the Deer at left, cactus at right, mountains in background **Rev. Legend:** ESTADO DE SONORA **Edge:** Segmented reeding

Date	Mintage	F	VF	XF	Unc	BU
2007Mo Proof	600	Value: 1,200				

KM# 856 100 PESOS

33.9400 g., Bi-Metallic .925 Silver 20.1753 center in Aluminum-Bronze ring, 39.04 mm. **Series:** Second **Obv:** National arms **Obv. Legend:** ESTADOS UNIDOS MEXICANOS **Rev:** Fuente de los Pescadores (fisherman fountain) at lower left, giant head from the Olmec-pre-Hispanic culture at right, Planetario Tabasco in background **Rev. Legend:** TABASCO **Edge:** Segmented reeding

Date	Mintage	F	VF	XF	Unc	BU
2007Mo	149,715	—	—	—	25.00	30.00

KM# 888 100 PESOS

29.1690 g., Bi-Metallic .999 Gold 17.154g center in .999 Silver 12.015g ring, 34.5 mm. **Series:** Second **Obv:** National arms **Obv. Legend:** ESTADOS UNIDOS MEXICANOS **Rev:** Fuente de los Pescadores (fisherman fountain) at lower left, giant head from the Olmec-pre-Hispanic culture at right, Planetario Tabasco in background **Rev. Legend:** TABASCO **Edge:** Segmented reeding

Date	Mintage	F	VF	XF	Unc	BU
2007Mo Proof	600	Value: 1,200				

KM# 857 100 PESOS

33.9400 g., Bi-Metallic .925 Silver 20.1753g center in Aluminum-Bronze ring, 39.04 mm. **Series:** Second **Obv:** National arms **Obv. Legend:** ESTADOS UNIDOS MEXICANOS **Rev:** Ridge - Cerro Del Bermal, Gonzáles **Rev. Legend:** TAMAULIPAS **Edge:** Segmented reeding

Date	Mintage	F	VF	XF	Unc	BU
2007Mo	149,776	—	—	—	25.00	30.00

KM# 889 100 PESOS

29.1690 g., Bi-Metallic .999 Gold 17.154g center in .999 Silver 12.015g ring, 34.5 mm. **Series:** Second **Obv:** National arms **Obv. Legend:** ESTADOS DE MEXICANOS **Rev:** Ridge - Cerro Del Bemal, Gonzáles **Rev. Legend:** TAMAULIPAS **Edge:** Segmented reeding

Date	Mintage	F	VF	XF	Unc	BU
2007Mo Proof	600	Value: 1,200				

KM# 858 100 PESOS

33.9400 g., Bi-Metallic .925 Silver 20.1753g center in Aluminum-Bronze ring, 39.04 mm. **Series:** Second **Obv:** National arms **Obv. Legend:** ESTADOS UNIDOS MEXICANOS **Rev:** Basilica de Ocotlán at left, state arms above Capilla Abierta, Plaza de Toros Ranchero Aguilar below, Exconvento de San Francisco at right **Rev. Legend:** ESTADO DE TLAXCALA **Edge:** Segmented reeding

Date	Mintage	F	VF	XF	Unc	BU
2007Mo	149,465	—	—	—	25.00	30.00

KM# 890 100 PESOS

29.1690 g., Bi-Metallic .999 Gold 17.154g center in .999 Silver 12.015g ring, 34.5 mm. **Series:** Second **Obv:** National arms **Obv. Legend:** ESTADOS UNIDOS MEXICANOS **Rev:** Basilica de Ocotlán at left, state arms above Capilla Abierta, Plaza de Toros Ranchero Aguilar below, Exconvento de San Francisco at right **Rev. Legend:** ESTADO DE TLAXCALA **Edge:** Segmented reeding

Date	Mintage	F	VF	XF	Unc	BU
2007Mo Proof	600	Value: 1,200				

KM# 859 100 PESOS

33.9400 g., Bi-Metallic .912 Silver 20.1753g center in Aluminum-Bronze ring, 39.04 mm. **Series:** Second **Obv:** National arms **Obv. Legend:** ESTADOS UNIDOS MEXICANOS **Rev:** Pyramid of El Tajín **Rev. Legend:** • VERACRUZ • - • DE IGNACIO DE LA LLAVE • **Edge:** Segmented reeding

Date	Mintage	F	VF	XF	Unc	BU
2007Mo	149,703	—	—	—	25.00	30.00

KM# 891 100 PESOS

29.1690 g., Bi-Metallic .999 Gold 17.154g center in .999 Silver 12.015g ring, 34.5 mm. **Series:** Second **Obv:** National arms **Obv. Legend:** ESTADOS UNIDOS MEXICANOS **Rev:** Pyramid of El Tajin **Rev. Legend:** • VERACRUZ • - • DE IGNACIO DE LA LLAVE • **Edge:** Segmented reeding

Date	Mintage	F	VF	XF	Unc	BU
2007Mo Proof	600	Value: 1,200				

KM# 860 100 PESOS

33.9400 g., Bi-Metallic .925 Silver 20.1753 center in Aluminum-Bronze ring, 39.04 mm. **Series:** Second **Obv:** National arms **Obv. Legend:** ESTADOS UNIDOS MEXICANOS **Rev:** Stylized pyramid of Chichén Itzá **Rev. Legend:** Castillo de Chichén Itzá **Edge:** Segmented reeding

Date	Mintage	F	VF	XF	Unc	BU
2007Mo	149,579	—	—	—	25.00	30.00

KM# 892 100 PESOS

29.1690 g., Bi-Metallic .999 Gold 17.154g center in .999 Silver 12.015g ring, 34.5 mm. **Series:** Second **Obv:** National arms **Obv. Legend:** ESTADOS UNIDOS MEXICANOS **Rev:** Stylized pyramid of Chichén-Itzá **Rev. Inscription:** YUCATÁN **Edge:** Segmented reeding

Date	Mintage	F	VF	XF	Unc	BU
2007Mo Proof	600	Value: 1,200				

KM# 861 100 PESOS

33.9400 g., Bi-Metallic .925 Silver 20.1753g center in Aluminum-Bronze ring, 39.04 mm. **Series:** Second **Obv:** National arms **Obv. Legend:** ESTADOS UNIDOS MEXICANOS **Rev:** Cable car above Monumento al Minero at left, Cathedral de Zacatecas at center right **Rev. Legend:** ZACATECAS **Edge:** Segmented reeding

Date	Mintage	F	VF	XF	Unc	BU
2007Mo	148,833	—	—	—	25.00	30.00

KM# 893 100 PESOS
29.1690 g., Bi-Metallic .999 Gold 17.154g center in .999 Silver 12.015g ring, 34.5 mm. **Series:** Second **Obv:** National arms **Obv. Legend:** ESTADOS UNIDOS MEXICANOS **Rev:** Cable car above Monumento al Minero at left, Cathedral de Zacatecas at center right **Rev. Legend:** Zacatecas **Edge:** Segmented reeding

Date	Mintage	F	VF	XF	Unc	BU
2007Mo Proof	600	Value: 1,200				

KM# 950 100 PESOS
16.8120 g., 0.9250 Bi-Metallic Silver center in aluminum-bronze ring 0.5000 oz., 39 mm. **Series:** Numismatic Heritage of Mexico **Subject:** 1732 Pillar Dollar **Obv:** National arms (eagle and snake facing left) and legend **Obv. Legend:** ESTADOS UNIDOS MEXICANOS **Rev:** Obverse of 1732 Pillar Dollar, legend **Rev. Legend:** HERENCIA NUMISMATICA DE MEXICO

Date	Mintage	F	VF	XF	Unc	BU
2011Mo Proof	—	Value: 40.00				

KM# 951 100 PESOS
33.9670 g., 0.9250 Bi-Metallic Silver center in aluminum-bronze ring 1.0101 oz., 39 mm. **Series:** Numismatic Heritage of Mexico **Subject:** 1783 Coin with bust of Carlos III **Obv:** National arms (eagle and snake facing left), legend **Obv. Legend:** ESTADOS UNIDOS MEXICANOS **Rev:** Obverse of 1783 coin with bust of Carlos III **Rev. Legend:** HERENCIA NUMISMATICA DE MEXICO

Date	Mintage	F	VF	XF	Unc	BU
2011Mo Proof	—	Value: 40.00				

KM# 952 100 PESOS
16.8120 g., 0.9250 Bi-Metallic Silver center in aluminum-bronze ring 0.5000 oz., 39 mm. **Series:** Numismatic heritage of Mexico **Subject:** SUD 8 Reales **Obv:** National arms (eagle and snake facing left), legend **Obv. Legend:** ESTADOS UNIDOS MEXICANOS **Rev:** Obverse of SUD 8 Rales, legend **Rev. Legend:** HERENCIA NUMISMATICA DE MEXICO

Date	Mintage	F	VF	XF	Unc	BU
2011Mo Proof	—	Value: 40.00				

KM# 953 100 PESOS
33.9670 g., 0.9250 Bi-Metallic Silver center in aluminum-bronze ring 1.0101 oz., 39 mm. **Series:** Numismatic Heritage of Mexico **Subject:** 1824DO 8 Reales **Obv:** National arms (eagle and snake facing left), legend **Obv. Legend:** ESTADOS UNIDOS MEXICANOS **Rev:** Reverse of 1824Do * reales, legend **Rev. Legend:** HERENCIA NUMISMATICA DE MEXICO

Date	Mintage	F	VF	XF	Unc	BU
2011Mo Proof	—	Value: 40.00				

KM# 954 100 PESOS
33.9670 g., 0.9250 Bi-Metallic Silver center in aluminum-bronze ring 1.0101 oz., 39 mm. **Series:** Numismatic Heritage of Mexico **Subject:** 1913 Parral Bolita Peso **Obv:** National arms (eagle and snake facing left) and legend **Obv. Legend:** ESTADOS UNIDOS MEXICANOS **Rev:** Obverse of 1913 Parral Bolita Peso, legend **Rev. Legend:** HERENCIA NUMISMATICA DE MEXICO

Date	Mintage	F	VF	XF	Unc	BU
2011Mo Proof	—	Value: 40.00				

KM# 955 100 PESOS
33.9670 g., 0.9250 Bi-Metallic Silver center in bluminum-bronze ring 1.0101 oz., 39 mm. **Series:** Numismatic Heritage of Mexico **Subject:** 1910 Caballito Peso **Obv:** National arms (eagle and snake facing left) and legend **Obv. Legend:** ESTADOS UNIDOS MEXICANOS **Rev:** Reverse of 1910 Caballito Peso, legend **Rev. Legend:** HERENCIA NUMISMATICA DE MEXICO

Date	Mintage	F	VF	XF	Unc	BU
2011Mo Proof	—	Value: 40.00				

KM# 941 200 PESOS
1000.0000 g., 0.9990 Gold 32.117 oz. AGW, 90 mm. **Series:** Mexican Independence 200th Anniversary **Subject:** Winged Victory **Obv:** National arms (eagle and snake facing left), legend **Obv. Legend:** ESTADOS UNIDOS MEXICANOS **Rev:** Winged Victory, legend **Rev. Legend:** BICENTENARIO **Edge Lettering:** Independencia y Libertad

Date	Mintage	F	VF	XF	Unc	BU
2010Mo Proof	200	Value: 60,000				

KM# 932 200 PESOS
41.6666 g., 0.9000 Gold 1.2056 oz. AGW, 37 mm. **Series:** Mexico Independence 200th Anniversary **Subject:** Winged Victory **Obv:** National Arms **Obv. Legend:** Bicentenario **Rev:** Winged Victory **Edge Lettering:** Independence y Liberted

Date	Mintage	F	VF	XF	Unc	BU
2010Mo	50,000	—	—	—	—	2,800
2010Mo Proof	4,998	Value: 2,500				

KM# 771 50000 PESOS
7.7700 g., 0.9990 Gold 0.2496 oz. AGW, 23 mm. **Subject:** World Cup Soccer **Obv:** Mexican Eagle and Snake **Rev:** Kneeling Mayan Pelota player and soccer ball

Date	Mintage	F	VF	XF	Unc	BU
2006Mo Proof	9,505	Value: 600				

SILVER BULLION COINAGE

Libertad Series

KM# 921 100 PESOS
1000.0000 g., 0.9990 Silver 32.117 oz. ASW **Obv:** National arms in center of past and present arms **Rev:** Aztec Calendar **Edge:** Plain

Date	Mintage	F	VF	XF	Unc	BU
2007Mo Prooflike	303	—	—	—	—	2,200
2008Mo Prooflike	1,000	—	—	—	—	2,000
2009Mo Prooflike	1,500	—	—	—	—	2,000
2010Mo Prooflike	1,500	—	—	—	—	2,000
2011Mo Prooflike	1,500	—	—	—	—	2,000
2012Mo	—	—	—	—	—	1,600

KM# 609 1/20 ONZA (1/20 Troy Ounce of Silver)
1.5551 g., 0.9990 Silver 0.0499 oz. ASW, 16 mm. **Obv:** National arms, eagle left **Rev:** Winged Victory

Date	Mintage	F	VF	XF	Unc	BU
2001Mo	4,500	—	—	—	—	25.00
2001Mo Proof	1,500	Value: 30.00				
2002Mo	50,000	—	—	—	—	16.00
2002Mo Proof	2,800	Value: 25.00				
2003Mo	30,000	—	—	—	—	16.00
2003Mo Proof	4,400	Value: 25.00				
2004Mo	30,000	—	—	—	—	16.00
2004Mo Proof	2,700	Value: 25.00				
2005Mo	15,000	—	—	—	—	16.00
2005Mo Proof	2,600	Value: 25.00				
2006Mo	20,000	—	—	—	—	16.00
2006Mo Proof	3,300	Value: 25.00				
2007Mo	3,500	—	—	—	—	16.00
2007Mo Proof	4,000	Value: 25.00				
2008Mo	7,000	—	—	—	—	16.00
2008Mo Proof	3,300	Value: 25.00				
2009Mo	10,000	—	—	—	—	16.00
2009Mo Proof	5,000	Value: 25.00				
2010Mo	12,000	—	—	—	—	16.00
2010Mo Proof	10,000	Value: 25.00				
2011Mo	15,000	—	—	—	—	16.00
2011Mo Proof	10,000	Value: 25.00				
2012Mo	—	—	—	—	—	16.00
2012Mo Proof	—	Value: 25.00				
2013Mo	—	—	—	—	—	16.00
2013Mo Proof	—	Value: 25.00				

KM# 610 1/10 ONZA (1/10 Troy Ounce of Silver)
3.1103 g., 0.9990 Silver 0.0999 oz. ASW, 20 mm. **Obv:** National arms, eagle left **Rev:** Winged Victory

Date	Mintage	F	VF	XF	Unc	BU
2001Mo	25,000	—	—	—	—	27.50
2001Mo Proof	1,500	Value: 36.00				
2002Mo	35,000	—	—	—	—	20.00
2002Mo Proof	2,800	Value: 30.00				
2003Mo	20,000	—	—	—	—	20.00
2003Mo Proof	4,900	Value: 30.00				
2004Mo	15,000	—	—	—	—	20.00
2004Mo Proof	2,500	Value: 30.00				
2005Mo	9,277	—	—	—	—	20.00
2005Mo Proof	3,000	Value: 27.50				
2006Mo	15,000	—	—	—	—	20.00
2006Mo Proof	3,000	Value: 27.50				
2007Mo	3,500	—	—	—	—	20.00
2007Mo Proof	4,000	Value: 27.50				
2008Mo	10,000	—	—	—	—	20.00
2008Mo Proof	5,000	Value: 27.50				
2009Mo	10,000	—	—	—	—	20.00
2009Mo Proof	5,000	Value: 27.50				
2010Mo	12,000	—	—	—	—	20.00
2010Mo Proof	10,000	Value: 27.50				
2011Mo	15,000	—	—	—	—	20.00
2011Mo Proof	10,000	Value: 27.50				
2012Mo	—	—	—	—	—	20.00
2012Mo Proof	—	Value: 27.50				
2013Mo	—	—	—	—	—	20.00
2013Mo Proof	—	Value: 27.50				

KM# 611 1/4 ONZA (1/4 Troy Ounce of Silver)
7.7758 g., 0.9990 Silver 0.2497 oz. ASW, 27 mm. **Obv:** National arms, eagle left **Rev:** Winged Victory

Date	Mintage	F	VF	XF	Unc	BU
2001Mo	25,000	—	—	—	—	36.00
2001Mo Proof	1,000	Value: 44.00				
2002Mo	35,000	—	—	—	—	27.50
2002Mo Proof	2,800	Value: 40.00				
2003Mo	22,000	—	—	—	—	27.50
2003Mo Proof	3,900	Value: 40.00				
2004Mo	15,000	—	—	—	—	27.50
2004Mo Proof	2,500	Value: 40.00				
2005Mo	15,000	—	—	—	—	27.50
2005Mo Proof	2,400	Value: 37.00				

Date	Mintage	F	VF	XF	Unc	BU
2006Mo	15,000	—	—	—	—	25.00
2006Mo Proof	2,900	Value: 37.00				
2007Mo	3,500	—	—	—	—	25.00
2007Mo Proof	3,000	Value: 37.00				
2008Mo	9,000	—	—	—	—	25.00
2008Mo Proof	2,900	Value: 37.00				
2009Mo	10,000	—	—	—	—	25.00
2009Mo Proof	3,000	Value: 37.00				
2010Mo	15,500	—	—	—	—	25.00
2010Mo Proof	5,000	Value: 37.00				
2011Mo	15,500	—	—	—	—	25.00
2011Mo Proof	5,000	Value: 37.00				
2012Mo	—	—	—	—	—	25.00
2012Mo Proof	—	Value: 37.00				
2013Mo	—	—	—	—	—	25.00
2013Mo Proof	—	Value: 37.00				

KM# 612 1/2 ONZA (1/2 Troy Ounce of Silver)
15.5517 g., 0.9990 Silver 0.4995 oz. ASW, 30 mm. **Obv:** National arms, eagle left **Rev:** Winged Victory

Date	Mintage	F	VF	XF	Unc	BU
2001Mo	20,000	—	—	—	—	45.00
2001Mo Proof	1,000	Value: 60.00				
2002Mo	35,000	—	—	—	—	37.00
2002Mo Proof	2,800	Value: 50.00				
2003Mo	28,000	—	—	—	—	37.00
2003Mo Proof	3,400	Value: 50.00				
2004Mo	20,000	—	—	—	—	37.00
2004Mo Proof	2,500	Value: 50.00				
2005Mo	10,000	—	—	—	—	37.00
2005Mo Proof	2,800	Value: 45.00				
2006Mo	15,000	—	—	—	—	37.00
2006Mo Proof	2,900	Value: 45.00				
2007Mo	3,500	—	—	—	—	37.00
2007Mo Proof	1,500	Value: 45.00				
2008Mo	9,000	—	—	—	—	37.00
2008Mo Proof	2,500	Value: 45.00				
2009Mo	10,000	—	—	—	—	37.00
2009Mo Proof	3,000	Value: 45.00				
2010Mo	20,000	—	—	—	—	37.00
2010Mo Proof	5,000	Value: 45.00				
2011Mo	30,000	—	—	—	—	37.00
2011Mo Proof	5,000	Value: 45.00				
2012Mo	—	—	—	—	—	37.00
2012Mo Proof	—	Value: 45.00				
2013Mo	—	—	—	—	—	37.00
2013Mo Proof	—	Value: 45.00				

KM# 639 ONZA (Troy Ounce of Silver)
31.1000 g., 0.9990 Silver 0.9988 oz. ASW, 40 mm. **Subject:** Libertad **Obv:** National arms, eagle left within center of past and present arms **Rev:** Winged Victory **Edge:** Reeded

Date	Mintage	F	VF	XF	Unc	BU
2001Mo	725,000	—	—	—	—	60.00
2001Mo Proof	2,000	Value: 140				
2002Mo	854,000	—	—	—	—	55.00
2002Mo Proof	3,800	Value: 150				
2003Mo	805,000	—	—	—	—	55.00
2003Mo Proof	5,400	Value: 130				
2004Mo	450,000	—	—	—	—	75.00
2004Mo Proof	3,000	Value: 130				
2005Mo	698,281	—	—	—	—	90.00
2005Mo Proof	3,300	Value: 150				
2006Mo	300,000	—	—	—	—	55.00
2006Mo Proof	4,000	Value: 140				
2007Mo	200,000	—	—	—	—	95.00
2007Mo Proof	5,800	Value: 150				
2008Mo	950,000	—	—	—	—	65.00
2008Mo Proof	11,000	Value: 150				
2009Mo	1,650,000	—	—	—	—	50.00
2009Mo Proof	10,000	Value: 150				
2010Mo	1,000,000	—	—	—	—	50.00

Date	Mintage	F	VF	XF	Unc	BU
2010Mo Proof	10,000	Value: 140				
2011Mo	1,200,000	—	—	—	—	50.00
2011Mo Proof	10,000	Value: 140				
2012Mo	—	—	—	—	—	50.00
2012Mo Proof	—	Value: 140				
2013Mo	—	—	—	—	—	50.00

KM# 614 2 ONZAS (2 Troy Ounces of Silver)
62.2070 g., 0.9990 Silver 1.9979 oz. ASW, 48 mm. **Subject:** Libertad **Obv:** National arms, eagle left within center of past and present arms **Rev:** Winged Victory **Edge:** Reeded

Date	Mintage	F	VF	XF	Unc	BU
2001Mo	6,700	—	—	—	—	120
2001Mo Proof	500	Value: 300				
2002Mo	8,700	—	—	—	—	110
2002Mo Proof	1,000	Value: 225				
2003Mo	9,500	—	—	—	—	110
2003Mo Proof	800	Value: 225				
2004Mo	8,000	—	—	—	—	100
2004Mo Proof	1,000	Value: 175				
2005Mo	3,549	—	—	—	—	100
2005Mo Proof	600	Value: 500				
2006Mo	5,800	—	—	—	—	100
2006Mo Proof	1,100	Value: 175				
2007Mo	8,000	—	—	—	—	100
2007Mo Proof	500	Value: 250				
2008Mo	17,000	—	—	—	—	110
2008Mo Proof	1,000	Value: 170				
2009Mo	46,000	—	—	—	—	110
2009Mo Proof	6,200	Value: 150				
2010Mo	14,000	—	—	—	—	110
2010Mo Proof	1,300	Value: 190				
2011Mo	14,000	—	—	—	—	110
2011Mo Proof	1,000	Value: 190				
2012Mo	—	—	—	—	—	110
2012Mo Proof	—	Value: 190				
2013Mo	—	—	—	—	—	110
2013Mo Proof	—	Value: 190				

KM# 615 5 ONZAS (5 Troy Ounces of Silver)
155.5175 g., 0.9990 Silver 4.9948 oz. ASW, 65 mm. **Subject:** Libertad **Obv:** National arms, eagle left within center of past and present arms **Rev:** Winged Victory **Edge:** Reeded **Note:** Illustration reduced.

Date	Mintage	F	VF	XF	Unc	BU
2001Mo	4,000	—	—	—	—	190
2001Mo Proof	600	Value: 325				
2002Mo	5,200	—	—	—	—	190
2002Mo Proof	1,000	Value: 325				
2003Mo	6,000	—	—	—	—	180
2003Mo Proof	1,500	Value: 250				
2004Mo	3,923	—	—	—	—	180
2004Mo Proof	800	Value: 225				
2005Mo	2,401	—	—	—	—	205
2005Mo Proof	1,000	Value: 225				
2006Mo	3,000	—	—	—	—	180
2006Mo Proof	700	Value: 265				
2007Mo	3,000	—	—	—	—	180
2007Mo Proof	500	Value: 205				
2008Mo	9,000	—	—	—	—	205
2008Mo Proof	900	Value: 270				
2009Mo	21,000	—	—	—	—	225
2009Mo Proof	5,000	Value: 270				
2010Mo	9,500	—	—	—	—	250
2010Mo Proof	2,000	Value: 270				
2011Mo	10,000	—	—	—	—	250
2011Mo Proof	2,000	Value: 270				
2012Mo	—	—	—	—	—	250
2012Mo Proof	—	Value: 270				
2013Mo	—	—	—	—	—	250
2013Mo Proof	—	Value: 270				

KM# 677 KILO (32.15 Troy Ounces of Silver)
999.9775 g., 0.9990 Silver 32.116 oz. ASW, 110 mm. **Subject:** Collector Bullion **Obv:** National arms in center of past and present arms **Rev:** Winged Victory **Edge:** Reeded

Date	Mintage	F	VF	XF	Unc	BU
2001Mo Prooflike	—	—	—	—	—	2,200
2002Mo Prooflike	1,820	—	—	—	—	1,750
2003Mo Prooflike	1,514	—	—	—	—	1,650
2004Mo Prooflike	1,501	—	—	—	—	1,800
2005Mo Prooflike	500	—	—	—	—	1,750
2006Mo Prooflike	874	—	—	—	—	1,650
2007Mo Prooflike	700	—	—	—	—	1,650
2008Mo	2,003	—	—	—	—	1,400
2008Mo Prooflike	1,700	—	—	—	—	1,650
2009Mo	4,000	—	—	—	—	—
2009Mo Prooflike	1,700	—	—	—	—	1,650
2010Mo	4,000	—	—	—	—	1,400
2010Mo Prooflike	1,500	—	—	—	—	1,650
2011Mo	6,000	—	—	—	—	1,400
2011Mo Prooflike	1,000	—	—	—	—	1,650
2012Mo Prooflike	—	—	—	—	—	1,650

GOLD BULLION COINAGE

KM# 957 1.25 GRAMS
1.6667 g., 0.0402 Gold 0.0022 oz. AGW, 13 mm. **Series:** Cultural Fusion **Subject:** Architecture **Obv:** National arms (eagle and snake facing left) and legend **Obv. Legend:** ESTADOS UNIDOS MEXICANOS **Rev:** Heads in profile, mail, woman with a plume **Rev. Legend:** FUSIÓN CULTURAL and 1.25 g DE ORO PURO LEY 0.750

Date	Mintage	F	VF	XF	Unc	BU
2011Mo Proof	2,000	Value: 110				

KM# 958 1.25 GRAMS
1.6667 g., 0.7500 Gold 0.0402 oz. AGW, 13 mm. **Series:** Cultural fusion **Subject:** Architecture **Obv:** Natioan arms (eagle and snake facing left) and legend **Obv. Legend:** ESTADOS UNIDOS MEXICANOS **Rev:** Pyramid, aquedect, church dome and cacao fruit **Rev. Legend:** FUSIÓN CULTURAL and 1.25 g DE ORO PURO LEY 0.750

Date	Mintage	F	VF	XF	Unc	BU
2011Mo Proof	—	Value: 110				

KM# 959 1.25 GRAMS
1.6667 g., 0.7500 Gold 0.0402 oz. AGW, 13 mm. **Series:** Cultural Fusion **Subject:** Cacao **Obv:** National arms (eagle and snake facing left) and legend **Obv. Legend:** ESTADOS UNIDOS MEXICANOS **Rev:** Aztec scuplture of a man carrying a cacao husk, legend **Rev. Legend:** XOCOLATL PARA EL MUNDS, EL CACAO and 1.25 g DE ORO PURO LEY

Date	Mintage	F	VF	XF	Unc	BU
2011Mo 2000	—	Value: 110				

KM# 960 1.25 GRAMS
1.6667 g., 0.7500 Gold 0.0402 oz. AGW, 13 mm. **Series:** Cultural Fusion **Subject:** Merchandise **Obv:** National arms (eagle and snake facing left) and legend **Obv. Legend:** ESTADOS UNIDOS MEXICANOS **Rev:** Allegory of Mesoamerican and Spanish cultural fusion. **Rev. Legend:** FUSIÒN CULTURAL and 1.25 g DE ORO PURO LEY

Date	Mintage	F	VF	XF	Unc	BU
2011Mo Proof	—	Value: 110				

KM# 671 1/20 ONZA (1/20 Ounce of Pure Gold)
1.5551 g., 0.9990 Gold 0.0499 oz. AGW, 13 mm. **Obv:** National arms, eagle left **Rev:** Winged Victory **Edge:** Reeded **Note:** Design similar to KM#609. Value estimates do not include the high taxes and surcharges added to the issue prices by the Mexican Government.

Date	Mintage	F	VF	XF	Unc	BU
2002Mo	5,000	—	—	—	—	BV+30%
2003Mo	800	—	—	—	—	BV+32%
2004Mo	4,000	—	—	—	—	BV+30%
2005Mo	3,200	—	—	—	—	BV+30%
2005Mo Proof	400	BV+35%				
2006Mo	3,000	—	—	—	—	BV+30%
2006Mo Proof	520	BV+35%				
2007Mo	1,200	—	—	—	—	BV+30%
2007Mo Proof	500	BV+35%				
2008Mo	800	—	—	—	—	BV+30%
2008Mo Proof	500	BV+35%				
2009Mo	2,000	—	—	—	—	BV+30%
2009Mo Proof	600	BV+35%				
2010Mo	1,500	—	—	—	—	BV+30%
2010Mo Proof	600	BV+35%				
2011Mo	2,500	—	—	—	—	BV+30%
2011Mo Proof	1,100	BV+35%				

KM# 672 1/10 ONZA (1/10 Ounce of Pure Gold)
3.1103 g., 0.9990 Gold 0.0999 oz. AGW, 16 mm. **Obv:** National arms, eagle left **Rev:** Winged Victory **Edge:** Reeded **Note:** Design similar to KM#610. Value estimates do not include the high taxes and surcharges added to the issue prices by the Mexican Government.

Date	Mintage	F	VF	XF	Unc	BU
2002Mo	5,000	—	—	—	—	BV+20%
2003Mo	300	—	—	—	—	BV+22%
2004Mo	2,000	—	—	—	—	BV+20%
2005Mo	500	—	—	—	—	BV+20%
2005Mo Proof	400	BV+22%				
2006Mo	2,500	—	—	—	—	BV+20%
2006Mo Proof	520	BV+22%				
2007Mo	1,200	—	—	—	—	BV+20%
2007Mo Proof	500	BV+22%				
2008Mo	2,500	—	—	—	—	BV+20%
2008Mo Proof	500	BV+22%				
2009Mo	9,000	—	—	—	—	BV+20%
2009Mo Proof	600	BV+22%				
2010Mo	4,500	—	—	—	—	BV+20%
2010Mo Proof	600	BV+22%				
2011Mo	6,500	—	—	—	—	BV+20%
2011Mo Proof	1,100	BV+22%				

KM# 673 1/4 ONZA (1/4 Ounce of Pure Gold)
7.7758 g., 0.9990 Gold 0.2497 oz. AGW, 23 mm. **Obv:** National arms, eagle left **Rev:** Winged Victory **Edge:** Reeded **Note:** Design similar to KM#611. Value estimates do not include the high taxes and surcharges added to the issue prices by the Mexican Government.

Date	Mintage	F	VF	XF	Unc	BU
2002Mo	5,000	—	—	—	—	BV+12%
2003Mo	300	—	—	—	—	BV+14%
2004Mo	1,500	—	—	—	—	BV+12%
2004Mo Proof	1,000	BV+15%				
2005Mo	500	—	—	—	—	BV+14%
2005Mo Proof	2,600	BV+15%				
2006Mo	1,500	—	—	—	—	BV+12%
2006Mo Proof	2,120	BV+15%				
2007Mo	500	—	—	—	—	BV+14%
2007Mo Proof	1,500	BV+15%				
2008Mo	800	—	—	—	—	BV+14%
2008Mo Proof	800	BV+15%				
2009Mo	3,000	—	—	—	—	BV+12%
2009Mo Proof	1,700	BV+15%				
2010Mo	1,500	—	—	—	—	BV+12%
2010Mo Proof	1,000	BV+15%				
2011Mo	1,500	—	—	—	—	BV+12%
2011Mo Proof	2,000	BV+15%				

KM# 674 1/2 ONZA (1/2 Ounce of Pure Gold)
15.5517 g., 0.9990 Gold 0.4995 oz. AGW, 29 mm. **Obv:** National arms, eagle left **Rev:** Winged Victory **Edge:** Reeded **Note:** Design similar to KM#612. Value estimates do not include the high taxes and surcharges added to the issue prices by the Mexican Government.

Date	Mintage	F	VF	XF	Unc	BU
2002Mo	5,000	—	—	—	—	BV+8%
2003Mo	300	—	—	—	—	BV+10%
2004Mo	500	—	—	—	—	BV+8%
2005Mo	500	—	—	—	—	BV+10%
2005Mo Proof	400	BV+12%				
2006Mo	500	—	—	—	—	BV+10%
2006Mo Proof	520	BV+12%				
2007Mo	500	—	—	—	—	BV+10%
2007Mo Proof	500	BV+12%				
2008Mo	300	—	—	—	—	BV+10%
2008Mo Proof	500	BV+12%				
2009Mo	3,000	—	—	—	—	BV+8%
2009Mo Proof	600	BV+12%				
2010Mo	1,500	—	—	—	—	BV+8%
2010Mo Proof	600	BV+12%				
2011Mo	1,500	—	—	—	—	BV+8%
2011Mo Proof	1,100	BV+12%				

KM# 675 ONZA (Ounce of Pure Gold)
31.1035 g., 0.9990 Gold 0.9990 oz. AGW, 34.5 mm. **Obv:** National arms, eagle left **Rev:** Winged Victory **Edge:** Reeded **Note:** Design similar to KM#639. Value estimates do not include the high taxes and surcharges added to the issue prices by the Mexican Government.

Date	Mintage	F	VF	XF	Unc	BU
2002Mo	15,000	—	—	—	—	BV+3%
2003Mo	500	—	—	—	—	BV+4%
2004Mo	3,000	—	—	—	—	BV+3%
2005Mo	3,000	—	—	—	—	BV+3%
2005Mo Proof	250	BV+5%				
2006Mo	4,000	—	—	—	—	BV+3%
2006Mo Proof	520	BV+5%				
2007Mo	2,500	—	—	—	—	BV+3%
2007Mo Proof	500	BV+5%				
2008Mo	800	—	—	—	—	BV+3%
2008Mo Proof	500	BV+5%				
2009Mo	6,200	—	—	—	—	BV+3%
2009Mo Proof	600	BV+5%				
2010Mo	4,000	—	—	—	—	BV+3%
2010Mo Proof	600	BV+5%				
2011Mo	3,000	—	—	—	—	BV+3%
2011Mo Proof	1,100	BV+5%				
2012Mo	—	—	—	—	—	BV+3%

BANK SETS

Hard Case Sets unless otherwise noted.

KM#	Date	Mintage	Identification	Issue Price	Mkt Val
BS38	2001 (10)	—	KM#546-549, 603-605, 636-638 Set in folder	—	65.00
BS39	2002 (8)	—	KM#546-549, 603-605, 616 Set in folder	—	30.00
BS40	2003 (6)	—	KM#547-549, 603-605 Set in folder	—	30.00

The Republic of Moldova (formerly the Moldavian S.S.R.) is bordered in the north, east and south by the Ukraine and on the west by Romania. It has an area of 13,000 sq.mi. (33,700 sq.km.) and a population of 4.4 million. The capital is Chisinau. Agricultural products are mainly cereals, grapes, tobacco, sugar beets and fruits. Food processing, clothing, building materials and agricultural machinery manufacturing dominate industry.

MONETARY SYSTEM

100 Bani = 1 Leu

REPUBLIC

DECIMAL COINAGE

KM# 1 BAN

0.6700 g., Aluminum, 14.5 mm. **Obv:** National arms **Rev:** Value divides date above monogram **Edge:** Plain

Date	Mintage	F	VF	XF	Unc	BU
2004	—	—	—	—	0.25	0.50
2006	—	—	—	—	0.25	0.50

KM# 2 5 BANI

0.7500 g., Aluminum, 16 mm. **Obv:** National arms **Rev:** Monogram divides sprigs below value and date **Edge:** Plain

Date	Mintage	F	VF	XF	Unc	BU
2001	—	—	—	—	0.35	0.50
2002	—	—	—	—	0.35	0.50
2003	—	—	—	—	0.35	0.50
2004	—	—	—	—	0.35	0.50
2005	—	—	—	—	0.35	0.50
2006	—	—	—	—	0.35	0.50
2008	—	—	—	—	0.35	0.50
2010	—	—	—	—	0.35	0.50
2012	—	—	—	—	0.35	0.50

KM# 7 10 BANI

0.8500 g., Aluminum, 16.6 mm. **Obv:** National arms **Rev:** Value, date and monogram **Edge:** Plain

Date	Mintage	F	VF	XF	Unc	BU
2001	—	—	—	—	0.40	0.60
2002	—	—	—	—	0.40	0.60
2003	—	—	—	—	0.40	0.60
2004	—	—	—	—	0.40	0.60
2005	—	—	—	—	0.40	0.60
2006	—	—	—	—	0.40	0.60
2008	—	—	—	—	0.40	0.60
2010	—	—	—	—	0.40	0.60
2011	—	—	—	—	0.40	0.60

KM# 3 25 BANI

0.9500 g., Aluminum, 17.5 mm. **Obv:** National arms **Rev:** Monogram divides sprigs below value and date **Edge:** Plain

Date	Mintage	F	VF	XF	Unc	BU
2001	—	—	—	0.20	0.50	0.75
2002	—	—	—	0.20	0.50	0.75
2003	—	—	—	0.20	0.50	0.75
2004	—	—	—	0.20	0.50	0.75
2005	—	—	—	0.20	0.50	0.75
2006	—	—	—	0.20	0.50	0.75
2008	—	—	—	0.20	0.50	0.75
2010	—	—	—	0.20	0.50	0.75
2011	—	—	—	0.20	0.50	0.75
2012	—	—	—	0.20	0.50	0.75

KM# 10 50 BANI

3.1000 g., Brass Clad Steel, 19 mm. **Obv:** National arms **Rev:** Value and date within grapevine **Edge:** Reeded

Date	Mintage	F	VF	XF	Unc	BU
2003	—	—	—	—	1.50	2.00
2005	—	—	—	—	1.50	2.00
2008	—	—	—	—	1.50	2.00

KM# 12 10 LEI

13.5000 g., 0.9250 Silver 0.4015 oz. ASW, 24.5 mm. **Obv:** National arms above value **Rev:** European wildcat within circle **Edge:** Plain

Date	Mintage	F	VF	XF	Unc	BU
2001 Proof	1,000	Value: 65.00				

KM# 13 10 LEI

13.5000 g., 0.9250 Silver 0.4015 oz. ASW, 24.5 mm. **Obv:** National arms above value **Rev:** Green Woodpecker on tree within circle **Edge:** Plain

Date	Mintage	F	VF	XF	Unc	BU
2001 Proof	1,000	Value: 60.00				

KM# 19 10 LEI

13.4500 g., 0.9250 Silver 0.4000 oz. ASW, 24.5 mm. **Obv:** National arms above value **Rev:** European Mink within circle **Edge:** Plain

Date	Mintage	F	VF	XF	Unc	BU
2003 Proof	500	Value: 65.00				

KM# 20 10 LEI

13.4500 g., 0.9250 Silver 0.4000 oz. ASW, 24.5 mm. **Obv:** National arms above value **Rev:** Black Storks within circle **Edge:** Plain

Date	Mintage	F	VF	XF	Unc	BU
2003 Proof	500	Value: 65.00				

KM# 25 10 LEI

25.0000 g., Nickel Plated Brass, 30 mm. **Subject:** Wine Holiday **Obv:** National arms above value **Rev:** Wine grapes, goblet and flask **Edge:** Plain

Date	Mintage	F	VF	XF	Unc	BU
2003 Proof	—	Value: 12.50				

KM# 22 10 LEI

13.5000 g., 0.9250 Silver 0.4015 oz. ASW, 24.5 mm. **Obv:** National arms above value **Rev:** Pine Marten within circle **Edge:** Plain

Date	Mintage	F	VF	XF	Unc	BU
2004 Proof	500	Value: 65.00				

KM# 29 10 LEI

25.0000 g., Nickel Plated Brass, 30 mm. **Subject:** European Women's Chess Championship **Obv:** Arms, date at top, value at bottom **Obv. Legend:** REPUBLICA - 2005 - MOLDOVA **Rev:** 2 chess figures on board at left, map at right **Rev. Inscription:** 2005 CHISINAU **Edge:** Plain

Date	Mintage	F	VF	XF	Unc	BU
2005 Proof	—	Value: 12.50				

KM# 30 10 LEI

13.5000 g., 0.9250 Silver 0.4015 oz. ASW, 24.5 mm. **Obv:** Arms, value below **Obv. Legend:** REPUBLICA MOLDOVA **Rev:** Imperial eagle on branch, legend follows the coin circumference **Edge:** Plain

Date	Mintage	F	VF	XF	Unc	BU
2005 Proof	500	Value: 65.00				

KM# 33 10 LEI

13.5000 g., 0.9250 Silver 0.4015 oz. ASW, 24.5 mm. **Obv:** Arms, value below **Obv. Legend:** REPUBLICA - 2006 - MOLDOVA **Rev:** Bird in grass, legend around circumference using Latin name **Edge:** Plain

Date	Mintage	F	VF	XF	Unc	BU
2006 Proof	500	Value: 65.00				

KM# 38 10 LEI

13.5000 g., 0.9250 Silver 0.4015 oz. ASW, 24.5 mm. **Rev:** Common ground squirrel

Date	Mintage	F	VF	XF	Unc	BU
2006 Proof	500	Value: 65.00				

KM# 43 10 LEI

13.5000 g., 0.9250 Silver 0.4015 oz. ASW, 24.5 mm. **Rev:** White water lilly

Date	Mintage	F	VF	XF	Unc	BU
2008 Proof	500	Value: 60.00				

KM# 47 20 LEI

13.5000 g., 0.9250 Silver 0.4015 oz. ASW, 22 mm. **Subject:** Assumption of the Virgin Mary

Date	Mintage	F	VF	XF	Unc	BU
2009 Proof	1,000	Value: 40.00				

KM# 36 50 LEI

16.5000 g., 0.9250 Silver 0.4907 oz. ASW, 30 mm. **Subject:** Vazile Alecsandri, 180th Anniversary **Obv:** Arms **Rev:** Bust and landscape

Date	Mintage	F	VF	XF	Unc	BU
2001 Proof	1,000	Value: 45.00				

KM# 17 50 LEI

16.5000 g., 0.9250 Silver 0.4907 oz. ASW, 30 mm. **Obv:** National arms above value **Rev:** Constantin Brancusi and building **Edge:** Plain

Date	Mintage	F	VF	XF	Unc	BU
2001 Proof	1,000	Value: 65.00				

KM# 18 50 LEI

16.5000 g., 0.9250 Silver 0.4907 oz. ASW, 30 mm. **Obv:** National arms above value **Rev:** Vasile Alecsandri with book and landscape **Edge:** Plain

Date	Mintage	F	VF	XF	Unc	BU
2001 Proof	1,000	Value: 65.00				

KM# 21 50 LEI

16.5000 g., 0.9250 Silver 0.4907 oz. ASW, 29.8 mm. **Subject:** Effigy of Dimitrie Cantemir **Obv:** National arms above value **Rev:** Bust facing flanked by dates and scroll **Edge:** Plain

Date	Mintage	F	VF	XF	Unc	BU
2003 Proof	500	Value: 165				

KM# 14 50 LEI

16.5500 g., 0.9250 Silver 0.4922 oz. ASW, 29.9 mm. **Subject:** Effigy of Miron Costin **Obv:** National arms above value **Rev:** Bust with hat 1/4 right flanked by dates and books **Edge:** Plain

Date	Mintage	F	VF	XF	Unc	BU
2003 Proof	500	Value: 165				

KM# 23 50 LEI

16.5000 g., 0.9250 Silver 0.4907 oz. ASW, 30 mm. **Obv:** National arms above value **Rev:** Bust of Bishop facing holding scepter **Edge:** Plain

Date	Mintage	F	VF	XF	Unc	BU
2004 Proof	500	Value: 90.00				

KM# 31 50 LEI

16.5000 g., 0.9250 Silver 0.4907 oz. ASW, 30 mm. **Subject:** 415th Anniversary - Birth of Grigore Ureche **Obv:** Arms, date divides legend at top, value below, **Obv. Legend:** REPUBLICA MOLDOVA **Rev:** Bust faces right, scroll with feather pen at right, inscription on scroll **Rev. Legend:** GRIGORE URECHE **Rev. Inscription:** Letopisetul Tarii Moldovei **Edge:** Plain

Date	Mintage	F	VF	XF	Unc	BU
2005 Proof	—	Value: 120				

KM# 34 50 LEI

16.5000 g., 0.9250 Silver 0.4907 oz. ASW, 30 mm. **Subject:** 200th Anniversary - Birth of Alexandru Donici **Obv:** Arms, date divides legend above, value below **Obv. Legend:** REPUBLICA MOLDOVA **Rev:** Bust of Donici facing, life dates on ribbon below **Rev. Legend:** ALEXANDRU DONICI

Date	Mintage	F	VF	XF	Unc	BU
2006 Proof	—	Value: 120				

KM# 40 50 LEI

16.5000 g., 0.9250 Silver 0.4907 oz. ASW, 30 mm. **Subject:** Metropolitian Varilaam **Rev:** Bust 3/4 right

Date	Mintage	F	VF	XF	Unc	BU
2007 Proof	500	Value: 120				

KM# 41 50 LEI

16.5000 g., 0.9250 Silver 0.4907 oz. ASW, 30 mm. **Subject:** Pottery Tradition **Rev:** Hand modeling clay vessel on pottery wheel

Date	Mintage	F	VF	XF	Unc	BU
2007 Proof	500	Value: 60.00				

KM# 44 50 LEI

16.5000 g., 0.9250 Silver 0.4907 oz. ASW, 30 mm. **Subject:** Oak tree in Stefan **Rev:** Oak tree

Date	Mintage	F	VF	XF	Unc	BU
2008 Proof	500	Value: 75.00				

KM# 45 50 LEI

16.5000 g., 0.9250 Silver 0.4907 oz. ASW, 30 mm. **Subject:** Cooper Trade **Rev:** Barrell maker

Date	Mintage	F	VF	XF	Unc	BU
2008 Proof	500	Value: 55.00				

KM# 48 50 LEI

16.5000 g., 0.9250 Silver 0.4907 oz. ASW, 30 mm. **Subject:** Geodezic arc of Struve **Rev:** Map

Date	Mintage	F	VF	XF	Unc	BU
2009 Proof	500	Value: 75.00				

KM# 49 50 LEI

16.5000 g., 0.9250 Silver 0.4907 oz. ASW, 30 mm. **Subject:** Rule of Vasile Lupu **Rev:** Open book and coat-of-arms

Date	Mintage	F	VF	XF	Unc	BU
2009 Proof	500	Value: 75.00				

KM# 50 50 LEI

16.5000 g., 0.9250 Silver 0.4907 oz. ASW, 30 mm. **Subject:** Traditional weaving **Rev:** Woman seated at weaving frame

Date	Mintage	F	VF	XF	Unc	BU
2009 Proof	500	Value: 70.00				

KM# 53 50 LEI

16.5000 g., 0.9990 Silver 0.5299 oz. ASW, 30 mm. **Subject:** Traditional Musical Instruments **Obv:** National arms **Rev:** Violin, bagpipe, pan pipe and flute

Date	Mintage	F	VF	XF	Unc	BU
2010 Proof	500	Value: 40.00				

KM# 54 50 LEI

16.5000 g., 0.9990 Silver 0.5299 oz. ASW, 30 mm. **Obv:** National arms **Rev:** Archeological complex of Old Orhei

Date	Mintage	F	VF	XF	Unc	BU
2010 Proof	500	Value: 45.00				

KM# 55 50 LEI

13.0000 g., 0.9990 Silver 0.4175 oz. ASW, 28 mm. **Subject:** Maria Cebotari, 100th Anniversary of Birth **Obv:** National arms **Rev:** Cebotari bust left

Date	Mintage	F	VF	XF	Unc	BU
2010 Proof	500	Value: 45.00				

KM# 56 50 LEI

13.0000 g., 0.9990 Silver 0.4175 oz. ASW, 28 mm. **Subject:** Doina and Ion Aldea-Teodorovici **Obv:** National arms **Rev:** Conjoined busts right

Date	Mintage	F	VF	XF	Unc	BU
2010 Proof	500	Value: 45.00				

KM# 58 50 LEI

16.5000 g., 0.9990 Silver 0.5299 oz. ASW, 30 mm. **Subject:** Moldovan Football, 100th Anniversary **Obv:** National Arms **Rev:** Soccer player

Date	Mintage	F	VF	XF	Unc	BU
2010 Proof	300	Value: 45.00				

KM# 59 50 LEI

16.5000 g., 0.9990 Silver 0.5299 oz. ASW, 30 mm. **Subject:** Annunciation Church in Chisinau, 200th Anniversary **Obv:** National Arms **Rev:** Church façade

Date	Mintage	F	VF	XF	Unc	BU
2010 Proof	500	Value: 45.00				

KM# 60 50 LEI

13.0000 g., 0.9990 Silver 0.4175 oz. ASW, 28 mm. **Subject:** Grigore Vieru **Obv:** National Arms **Rev:** Profile bust right

Date	Mintage	F	VF	XF	Unc	BU
2010 Proof	500	Value: 45.00				

KM# 65 50 LEI

13.0000 g., 0.9990 Silver 0.4175 oz. ASW, 28 mm. **Subject:** Bogdan Petriceicu Hasdeu **Obv:** National arms **Rev:** Bust **Edge:** Reeded

Date	Mintage	F	VF	XF	Unc	BU
2011 Proof	500	Value: 50.00				

KM# 67 50 LEI

13.0000 g., 0.9990 Silver 0.4175 oz. ASW, 28 mm. **Subject:** Alexandru Bernardazzi, 180th Anniversary of Birth **Obv:** National arms **Rev:** Portrait **Edge:** Reeded

Date	Mintage	F	VF	XF	Unc	BU
2011 Proof	500	Value: 50.00				

KM# 68 50 LEI

16.5000 g., 0.9990 Silver 0.5299 oz. ASW, 30 mm. **Obv:** National arms **Rev:** Spoonbill standing left, oval background **Edge:** Reeded

Date	Mintage	F	VF	XF	Unc	BU
2011 Proof	500	Value: 50.00				

KM# 69 50 LEI

16.5000 g., 0.9990 Silver 0.5299 oz. ASW, 30 mm. **Subject:** Holiday Traditions **Obv:** National arms **Rev:** Carolers **Edge:** Reeded

Date	Mintage	F	VF	XF	Unc	BU
2011 Proof	1,000	Value: 50.00				

KM# 70 50 LEI

16.5000 g., 0.9990 Silver 0.5299 oz. ASW, 30 mm. **Subject:** Stefan Cel Mare, 555th Anniversary of Accession **Rev:** Half-length bust facing right

Date	Mintage	F	VF	XF	Unc	BU
2012 Proof	—	Value: 50.00				

KM# 71 50 LEI

16.5000 g., 0.9990 Silver 0.5299 oz. ASW, 30 mm. **Subject:** London Olympics **Rev:** Runner breaking tape at finish line

Date	Mintage	F	VF	XF	Unc	BU
2012 Proof	—	Value: 50.00				

KM# 72 50 LEI

16.5000 g., 0.9990 Silver 0.5299 oz. ASW, 30 mm. **Subject:** Ivo Creanga, 175th Anniversary of Birth

Date	Mintage	F	VF	XF	Unc	BU
2012 Proof	—	Value: 50.00				

KM# 73 50 LEI

16.5000 g., 0.9990 Silver 0.5299 oz. ASW, 30 mm. **Subject:** Soroka Fortress

Date	Mintage	F	VF	XF	Unc	BU
2012 Proof	—	Value: 50.00				

KM# 74 50 LEI

16.5000 g., 0.9990 Silver 0.5299 oz. ASW, 30 mm. **Subject:** Mid-Summer's Day **Obv:** Arms **Rev:** Female head with wheat wreath

Date	Mintage	F	VF	XF	Unc	BU
2012 Proof	—	Value: 50.00				

KM# 16 100 LEI

31.1000 g., 0.9250 Silver 0.9249 oz. ASW, 37 mm. **Subject:** 10th Anniversary of Independence **Obv:** National arms above value **Rev:** Arch monument within circle above value and sprigs **Edge:** Plain

Date	Mintage	F	VF	XF	Unc	BU
2001 Proof	1,000	Value: 220				

KM# 26 100 LEI

7.8000 g., 0.9999 Gold 0.2507 oz. AGW, 24 mm. **Obv:** National arms above value **Rev:** King Stephan the Great (1456-1504) **Edge:** Plain

Date	Mintage	F	VF	XF	Unc	BU
2004 Proof	—	Value: 450				

KM# 32 100 LEI

31.1000 g., 0.9250 Silver 0.9249 oz. ASW, 37 mm. **Subject:** Burebista - King of Dacians **Obv:** Arms, date divides legend at top, value below **Obv. Legend:** REPUBLICA MOLDOVA **Rev:** Bust of Burebista at left, battle scene of Geto-Dacians with Romans at right **Rev. Legend:** BUREBISTA REGELE DACILOR **Edge:** Plain

Date	Mintage	F	VF	XF	Unc	BU
2005 Proof	500	Value: 300				

KM# 35 100 LEI

31.1000 g., 0.9250 Silver 0.9249 oz. ASW, 37 mm. **Subject:** 15th Anniversary - Independence Proclamation of the Republic of Moldova **Obv:** Arms, date divides legend above, value below **Obv. Legend:** REPUBLICA MOLDOVA **Rev:** Map of Moldova within stars in inner circle, legend around **Rev. Legend:** PROCLAMAREA INDEPENDENTEI / 1991-2006 **Edge:** Plain

Date	Mintage	F	VF	XF	Unc	BU
2006 Proof	500	Value: 500				

KM# 39 100 LEI

31.1050 g., 0.9250 Silver 0.9250 oz. ASW, 37 mm. **Subject:** National Bank, 15th Anniversary **Rev:** Bank building

Date	Mintage	F	VF	XF	Unc	BU
2006 Proof	500	Value: 140				

KM# 42 100 LEI
31.1050 g., 0.9250 Silver 0.9250 oz. ASW, 37 mm. **Subject:** Petru Rares **Rev:** Bust 3/4 right

Date	Mintage	F	VF	XF	Unc	BU
2007 Proof	500	Value: 450				

KM# 37 100 LEI
7.7800 g., 0.9990 Gold 0.2499 oz. AGW, 24 mm. **Subject:** Dimitrie Cantemir

Date	Mintage	F	VF	XF	Unc	BU
2008 Proof	Est. 1,000	Value: 600				

KM# 46 100 LEI
31.1000 g., 0.9250 Silver 0.9249 oz. ASW, 37 mm. **Subject:** Antioh Cantemir **Rev:** Half-length figure standing 3/4 left

Date	Mintage	F	VF	XF	Unc	BU
2008 Proof	1,000	Value: 100				

KM# 52 100 LEI
15.5000 g., 0.9990 Gold 0.4978 oz. AGW, 28 mm. **Subject:** Dimitrie Cantemir **Obv:** National Arms **Rev:** Cantemir seated at desk

Date	Mintage	F	VF	XF	Unc	BU
2008 Proof	300	Value: 950				

KM# 51 100 LEI
22.5000 g., 0.9250 Silver 0.6691 oz. ASW, 34 mm. **Subject:** Moldovan Chronicals, 15-18 Centuries **Rev:** Man seated writing

Date	Mintage	F	VF	XF	Unc	BU
2009 Proof	1,000	Value: 90.00				

KM# 57 100 LEI
15.5000 g., 0.9990 Gold 0.4978 oz. AGW, 28 mm. **Subject:** Doina and Ion Aldea-Teodorovici **Obv:** National arms **Rev:** Conjoined busts right

Date	Mintage	F	VF	XF	Unc	BU
2010 Proof	300	Value: 950				

KM# 61 100 LEI
15.5000 g., 0.9990 Gold 0.4978 oz. AGW, 28 mm. **Subject:** Grigore Vieru **Obv:** National Arms **Rev:** Profile bust left

Date	Mintage	F	VF	XF	Unc	BU
2010 Proof	300	Value: 950				

KM# 62 100 LEI
31.1000 g., 0.9990 Silver 0.9988 oz. ASW, 37 mm. **Subject:** National Bank of Moldova, 20th Anniversary **Obv:** National arms **Rev:** National Bank logo **Edge:** Reeded

Date	Mintage	F	VF	XF	Unc	BU
2011 Proof	500	Value: 80.00				

KM# 63 100 LEI
31.1000 g., 0.9990 Silver 0.9988 oz. ASW, 37 mm. **Subject:** Independence, 20th Anniversary **Obv:** National arms **Rev:** Father and son holding Moldovian flag **Edge:** Reeded

Date	Mintage	F	VF	XF	Unc	BU
2011 Proof	1,000	Value: 75.00				

KM# 64 100 LEI
31.1000 g., 0.9990 Silver 0.9988 oz. ASW, 37 mm. **Subject:** Chisinau, 575th Anniversary of Founding of the City **Obv:** National arms **Rev:** Mazarachi Hill **Edge:** Reeded

Date	Mintage	F	VF	XF	Unc	BU
2011 Proof	1,000	Value: 75.00				

KM# 66 100 LEI
7.8000 g., 0.9990 Gold 0.2505 oz. AGW, 24 mm. **Subject:** Bogdan Petriceicu Hasdeu **Obv:** National arms **Rev:** Bust **Edge:** Reeded

Date	Mintage	F	VF	XF	Unc	BU
2011 Proof	300	Value: 475				

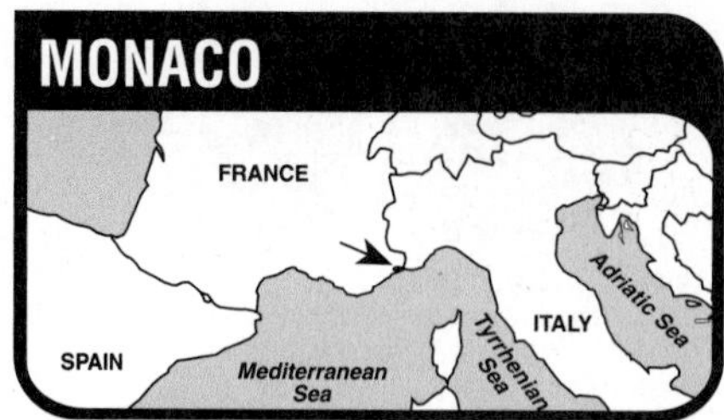

The Principality of Monaco, located on the Mediterranean coast nine miles from Nice, has an area of 0.58 sq. mi. (1.9 sq. km.) and a population of 26,000. Capital: Monaco-Ville. The economy is based on tourism and the manufacture of cosmetics, gourmet foods and highly specialized electronics. Monaco also derives its revenue from a tobacco monopoly and the sale of postage stamps for philatelic purpose. Gambling in Monte Carlo accounts for only a small fraction of the country's revenue.

RULERS
Rainier III, 1949-2005
Albert II, 2005-

MINT PRIVY MARKS
(a) - Paris (privy marks only)
Horseshoe - 2001 and 2002
Heart – 2002-2003
French Horn with starfish in water – 2003-
(p) - Thunderbolt - Poissy

MONETARY SYSTEM
100 Euro Cents = 1 Euro

PRINCIPALITY

EURO COINAGE

KM# 167 EURO CENT
2.3000 g., Copper Plated Steel, 16.25 mm. **Ruler:** Rainier III **Obv:** Crowned arms **Rev:** Value and globe **Edge:** Plain

Date	Mintage	F	VF	XF	Unc	BU
2001(a)	327,200	—	—	—	20.00	35.00
2001(a) Proof	3,500	Value: 75.00				
2002(a) In sets only	40,000	—	—	—	—	75.00
2003(a)	—	—	—	—	—	10.00
2004(a) Proof	14,999	Value: 25.00				
2005(a) Proof	35,000	Value: 50.00				

KM# 188 EURO CENT
2.3000 g., Copper Plated Steel, 16.25 mm. **Ruler:** Albert II **Obv:** Crowned arms within circle of stars **Rev:** Value and globe

Date	Mintage	F	VF	XF	Unc	BU
2006 Proof	11,180	Value: 30.00				
2007	—	—	—	—	—	30.00
2009 In sets only	8,020	—	—	—	—	30.00

KM# 168 2 EURO CENT
3.0600 g., Copper Plated Steel, 18.75 mm. **Ruler:** Rainier III **Obv:** Crowned arms **Rev:** Value and globe **Edge:** Grooved

Date	Mintage	F	VF	XF	Unc	BU
2001(a)	393,400	—	—	—	15.00	30.00
2001(a) Proof	3,500	Value: 85.00				
2002(a) In sets only	40,000	—	—	—	—	85.00
2003(a)	—	—	—	—	—	10.00
2004(a) Proof	14,999	Value: 35.00				
2005(a) Proof	35,000	Value: 50.00				

KM# 189 2 EURO CENT
3.0600 g., Copper Plated Steel, 18.75 mm. **Ruler:** Albert II **Obv:** Crowned arms within circle of stars **Rev:** Value and globe **Edge:** Grooved

Date	Mintage	F	VF	XF	Unc	BU
2006 Proof	11,260	Value: 25.00				
2007	—	—	—	—	—	25.00
2009 In sets only	8,020	—	—	—	—	25.00

KM# 169 5 EURO CENT

3.9200 g., Copper Plated Steel, 21.25 mm. **Ruler:** Rainier III **Obv:** Crowned arms **Rev:** Value and globe **Edge:** Plain

Date	Mintage	F	VF	XF	Unc	BU
2001(a)	320,000	—	—	—	20.00	35.00
2001(a) Proof	3,500	Value: 95.00				
2002(a) In sets only	40,000	—	—	—	—	85.00
2003(a)	—	—	—	—	—	15.00
2004(a) Proof	14,999	Value: 45.00				
2005(a) Proof	35,000	Value: 55.00				

KM# 190 5 EURO CENT

3.9200 g., Copper Plated Steel, 21.25 mm. **Ruler:** Albert II **Obv:** Crowned arms within circle of stars **Rev:** Value and globe

Date	Mintage	F	VF	XF	Unc	BU
2006 Proof	11,180	Value: 30.00				
2007	—	—	—	—	—	30.00
2009 In sets only	8,020	—	—	—	—	30.00
2011 In sets only	7,000	—	—	—	—	30.00

KM# 170 10 EURO CENT

4.1000 g., Brass, 19.75 mm. **Ruler:** Rainier III **Obv:** Knight on horse **Rev:** Value and map **Edge:** Reeded

Date	Mintage	F	VF	XF	Unc	BU
2001(a)	320,000	—	—	—	15.00	25.00
2001(a) Proof	3,500	Value: 110				
2002(a)	407,200	—	—	—	8.00	12.00
2003(a)	100,800	—	—	—	12.00	16.00
2004(a) Proof	14,999	Value: 50.00				

KM# 181 10 EURO CENT

4.1000 g., Brass, 19.75 mm. **Ruler:** Albert II **Obv:** Crowned AA monogram **Rev:** Relief map of Western Europe, stars, lines and value **Edge:** Reeded

Date	Mintage	F	VF	XF	Unc	BU
2006(a) Proof	11,180	Value: 50.00				

KM# 191 10 EURO CENT

4.1000 g., Brass, 19.75 mm. **Ruler:** Albert II **Obv:** Crowned AA monogram **Rev:** Relief map of western Europe, stars, lines and value **Edge:** Reeded

Date	Mintage	F	VF	XF	Unc	BU
2007(a)	—	—	—	—	—	30.00
2009(a) In sets only	8,020	—	—	—	—	30.00
2011(a) In sets only	7,000	—	—	—	—	30.00

KM# 171 20 EURO CENT

5.7400 g., Brass, 22.25 mm. **Ruler:** Rainier III **Obv:** Knight on horse **Rev:** Value and map **Edge:** Notched **Designer:** R. Baron

Date	Mintage	F	VF	XF	Unc	BU
2001(a)	386,400	—	—	—	15.00	20.00
2001(a) Proof	3,500	Value: 120				
2002(a)	376,000	—	—	—	12.00	16.00
2003(a)	100,000	—	—	—	12.00	16.00
2004(a) Proof	14,999	Value: 60.00				

KM# 182 20 EURO CENT

5.7400 g., Brass, 22.25 mm. **Ruler:** Albert II **Obv:** Crowned AA monogram **Rev:** Relief map of Western Europe, stars, lines and value **Edge:** Notched

Date	Mintage	F	VF	XF	Unc	BU
2006(a) Proof	11,180	Value: 60.00				

KM# 192 20 EURO CENT

5.7400 g., Brass, 22.25 mm. **Ruler:** Albert II **Obv:** Crowned AA monogram **Rev:** Relief map of western Europe, stars, lines and value **Edge:** Notched

Date	Mintage	F	VF	XF	Unc	BU
2007(a)	—	—	—	—	—	30.00
2009(a) In sets only	8,020	—	—	—	—	30.00
2011(a) In sets only	7,000	—	—	—	—	30.00

KM# 172 50 EURO CENT

7.8000 g., Brass, 24.25 mm. **Ruler:** Rainier III **Obv:** Knight on horse **Rev:** Value and map **Edge:** Reeded

Date	Mintage	F	VF	XF	Unc	BU
2001 (a)	320,000	—	—	—	15.00	30.00
2001 (a) Proof	3,500	Value: 130				
2002 (a)	364,000	—	—	—	8.00	12.00
2003 (a)	100,000	—	—	—	12.00	16.00
2004 (a) Proof	14,999	Value: 65.00				

KM# 183 50 EURO CENT

7.8000 g., Brass, 24.25 mm. **Ruler:** Albert II **Obv:** Crowned AA monogram **Rev:** Relief map of Western Europe, stars, lines and value **Edge:** Reeded

Date	Mintage	F	VF	XF	Unc	BU
2006(a) Proof	11,180	Value: 65.00				

KM# 193 50 EURO CENT

7.8000 g., Brass, 24.25 mm. **Ruler:** Albert II **Obv:** Crowned AA monogram **Rev:** Relief map of western Europe, stars, lines and values **Edge:** Reeded

Date	Mintage	F	VF	XF	Unc	BU
2007(a)	—	—	—	—	—	30.00
2009(a) In sets only	8,020	—	—	—	—	30.00
2011(a) In sets only	7,000	—	—	—	—	30.00

KM# 173 EURO

7.5000 g., Bi-Metallic Copper-Nickel center in Nickel-Brass ring, 23.25 mm. **Ruler:** Rainier III **Obv:** Conjoined heads of Prince Ranier and Crown Prince Albert right within circle **Rev:** Value and map **Edge:** Segmented reeding

Date	Mintage	F	VF	XF	Unc	BU
2001(a)	991,100	—	—	—	10.00	12.00
2001(a) Proof	3,500	Value: 145				
2002(a)	512,500	—	—	—	11.00	14.00
2003(a)	135,000	—	—	—	13.50	18.50
2004(a) Proof	14,999	Value: 75.00				

KM# 184 EURO

7.5000 g., Bi-Metallic Copper-Nickel center in Nickel-Brass ring, 23.25 mm. **Ruler:** Albert II **Obv:** Head right of Prince Albert **Rev:** Relief map of Western Europe, stars, lines and value **Edge:** Segmented reeding

Date	Mintage	F	VF	XF	Unc	BU
2006(a) Proof	11,180	Value: 75.00				

KM# 194 EURO

7.5000 g., Bi-Metallic Copper-Nickel center in Nickel-Brass ring, 23.25 mm. **Ruler:** Albert II **Obv:** Head right **Rev:** Relief map of western Europe, stars, lines and value **Edge:** Segmented reeding

Date	Mintage	F	VF	XF	Unc	BU
2007(a)	100,000	—	—	—	—	18.00
2009(a) In sets only	8,020	—	—	—	—	30.00
2011(a) In sets only	7,000	—	—	—	—	30.00

KM# 174 2 EURO

8.5000 g., Bi-Metallic Nickel-Brass center in Copper-Nickel ring, 25.75 mm. **Ruler:** Rainier III **Obv:** Head right within circle flanked by stars **Rev:** Value and map **Edge:** Reeded with 2s and stars

Date	Mintage	F	VF	XF	Unc	BU
2001(a)	919,800	—	—	—	14.00	25.00
2001(a) Proof	3,500	Value: 165				
2002(a)	496,000	—	—	—	15.00	18.00
2003(a)	228,000	—	—	—	17.50	22.50
2004(a) Proof	14,999	Value: 100				

KM# 185 2 EURO

8.5000 g., Bi-Metallic Nickel-Brass center in Copper-Nickel ring, 25.75 mm. **Ruler:** Albert II **Obv:** Prince Albert's head right **Rev:** Relief map of Western Europe, stars, lines and value **Edge:** Reeded with 2's and stars

Date	Mintage	F	VF	XF	Unc	BU
2006(a) Proof	11,180	Value: 130				

KM# 186 2 EURO

8.5000 g., Bi-Metallic Nickel-Brass center in Copper-Nickel ring., 25.75 mm. **Ruler:** Albert II **Subject:** Princess Grace, 25th Anniversary of Death **Obv:** Head of Princess Grace left **Rev:** Relief map of Western Europe, stars, lines and value **Edge:** Reeded with 2s and stars

Date	Mintage	F	VF	XF	Unc	BU
2007(a)	20,000	—	—	—	850	1,250

KM# 195 2 EURO

8.5000 g., Bi-Metallic Nickel-Brass center in Copper-Nickel ring, 25.75 mm. **Ruler:** Albert II **Obv:** Head right **Rev:** Relief map of western Europe, stars, lines and values **Edge:** Reeded with 2's and stars

Date	Mintage	F	VF	XF	Unc	BU
2007(a)	—	—	—	—	65.00	—
2009(a)	250,000	—	—	—	35.00	—
2009(a) In sets only	8,000	—	—	—	—	150
2010(a) Proof	25,000	Value: 300				
2011(a)	1,039,052	—	—	—	35.00	150
2012(a)	—	—	—	—	35.00	150

KM# 196 2 EURO

8.5000 g., Bi-Metallic Nickel-Brass center in Copper-Nickel ring, 25.75 mm. **Ruler:** Albert II **Subject:** Royal Wedding of Prince Albert II and Princess Charlène **Obv:** Conjoined heads left

Date	Mintage	F	VF	XF	Unc	BU
2011A	147,877	—	—	—	—	75.00

KM# 199 2 EURO

8.5000 g., Bi-Metallic Nickel-Brass center in Copper-Nickel ring **Ruler:** Albert II **Subject:** 500th Anniversary **Obv:** Lucien I bust left

Date	Mintage	F	VF	XF	Unc	BU
2012(a)	100,000	—	—	—	—	75.00

KM# 180 5 EURO

12.0000 g., 0.9000 Silver 0.3472 oz. ASW, 29 mm. **Ruler:** Rainier III **Obv:** Bust right **Rev:** Saint standing

Date	Mintage	F	VF	XF	Unc	BU
2004 (a) Proof	14,999	Value: 150				

KM# 197 5 EURO

12.0000 g., 0.9000 Silver 0.3472 oz. ASW, 29 mm. **Ruler:** Albert II **Subject:** Prince Albert II, 50th Birthday **Obv:** Bust right **Rev:** Crowned and mantled arms

Date	Mintage	F	VF	XF	Unc	BU
2008(a) Prooflike	9,000	—	—	—	—	185

KM# 178 10 EURO

25.0000 g., 0.9250 Silver 0.7435 oz. ASW, 37 mm. **Ruler:** Rainier III **Obv:** Conjoined busts of Prince Ranier and Crown Prince Albert right **Rev:** Arms

Date	Mintage	F	VF	XF	Unc	BU
2003(a) Proof	4,000	Value: 465				

KM# 187 10 EURO

3.2200 g., 0.9000 Gold 0.0932 oz. AGW **Ruler:** Albert II **Subject:** Death of Rainier III **Obv:** Principality arms **Rev:** Head of Rainier III right

Date	Mintage	F	VF	XF	Unc	BU
2005(a) Proof	3,313	Value: 550				

KM# 177 20 EURO

18.0000 g., 0.9250 Gold 0.5353 oz. AGW, 32 mm. **Ruler:** Rainier III **Obv:** Bust right **Rev:** Arms

Date	Mintage	F	VF	XF	Unc	BU
2002(a) Proof	10,000	Value: 1,100				

KM# 198 20 EURO

6.4500 g., 0.9000 Gold 0.1866 oz. AGW, 21 mm. **Ruler:** Albert II **Subject:** Prince Albert II, 50th Birthday **Obv:** Bust right **Rev:** Crowned and mantled arms

Date	Mintage	F	VF	XF	Unc	BU
2008(a) Proof	3,000	Value: 600				

KM# 179 100 EURO

29.0000 g., 0.9000 Gold 0.8391 oz. AGW **Ruler:** Rainier III **Obv:** Bust right **Rev:** Knight on horse

Date	Mintage	F	VF	XF	Unc	BU
2003(a) Proof	1,000	Value: 3,250				

MINT SETS

KM#	Date	Mintage	Identification	Issue Price	Mkt Val
MS1	2001 (8)	20,000	KM#167-174, exercise caution, privately packaged and deceptively false sets exist	35.00	225
MS2	2002 (8)	40,000	KM#167-174, exercise caution, privately packaged and deceptively false sets exist	35.00	325
MS3	2009 (8)	8,000	KM#188-195	—	600

PROOF SETS

KM#	Date	Mintage	Identification	Issue Price	Mkt Val
PS1	2001 (8)	3,500	KM#167-174	—	1,000
PS2	2004 (9)	14,999	KM#167-174, 180	—	700
PS3	2005 (3)	35,000	KM#167-169	—	160
PS4	2006 (8)	11,180	KM#181-185, 188-190	—	475

MONGOLIA

Mongolia, (formerly the Mongolian Peoples Republic) a landlocked country in central Asia between Russia and the People's Republic of China, has an area of 604,250 sq. mi. (1,565,000 sq. km.) and a population of 2.26 million. Capital: Ulaan Baator. Animal herds and flocks are the chief economic asset. Wool, cattle, butter, meat and hides are exported.

For earlier issues see Russia - Tannu Tuva.

MONETARY SYSTEM

100 Mongo = 1 Tugrik

STATE

DECIMAL COINAGE

KM# 302 100 TUGRIK

Silver **Subject:** XXVI Summer Olympics, Atlanta **Obv:** Arms **Rev:** 1904 St. Louis World's Fair Program Cover

Date	Mintage	F	VF	XF	Unc	BU
2002 Proof	—	Value: 25.00				

KM# 254 100 TUGRIK

25.0000 g., 0.9250 Silver 0.7435 oz. ASW **Obv:** Arms **Rev:** Yin-Yang symbol

Date	Mintage	F	VF	XF	Unc	BU
2007 Proof	—	Value: 30.00				

KM# 306 100 TUGRIK

26.0000 g., 0.9250 Silver 0.7732 oz. ASW, 38.5 mm. **Subject:** Wonders of the World **Obv:** National emblem **Rev:** Rome's Colosseum

Date	Mintage	F	VF	XF	Unc	BU
2008 Prooflike	—	—	—	—	—	35.00

KM# 307 100 TUGRIK

26.4000 g., 0.9250 Silver 0.7851 oz. ASW, 38.5 mm. **Subject:** Wonders of the World **Obv:** National Emblem **Rev:** Chichen Itza pyramid

Date	Mintage	F	VF	XF	Unc	BU
2008 Prooflike	—	—	—	—	—	35.00

KM# 308 100 TUGRIK

25.0000 g., 0.9250 Silver 0.7435 oz. ASW **Obv:** National emblem **Rev:** Treasury at Petra

Date	Mintage	F	VF	XF	Unc	BU
2008 Proof	—	Value: 75.00				

KM# 317 100 TUGRIK

25.0000 g., 0.9250 Silver 0.7435 oz. ASW, 38.6 mm. **Subject:** Machu Picchu

Date	Mintage	F	VF	XF	Unc	BU
2008 Proof	—	Value: 50.00				

KM# 321 100 TUGRIK

26.4000 g., 0.9250 Silver 0.7851 oz. ASW, 38.6 mm. **Subject:** Taj Mahal

Date	Mintage	F	VF	XF	Unc	BU
2008 Proof	—	Value: 50.00				

KM# 282 250 TUGRIK

15.5000 g., 0.9250 Silver 0.4609 oz. ASW, 33 mm. **Subject:** Zodiac - Capricorn **Rev:** Seated goat left, partially gilt

Date	Mintage	F	VF	XF	Unc	BU
2007	7,000	—	—	—	—	25.00

KM# 283 250 TUGRIK

15.5000 g., 0.9250 Silver 0.4609 oz. ASW, 33 mm. **Subject:** Zodiac - Aquarius **Rev:** Man pouring water, partially gilt

Date	Mintage	F	VF	XF	Unc	BU
2007	7,000	—	—	—	—	25.00

KM# 284 250 TUGRIK

15.5000 g., 0.9250 Silver 0.4609 oz. ASW, 33 mm. **Subject:** Zodiac - Piceis **Rev:** Two fish partially gilt

Date	Mintage	F	VF	XF	Unc	BU
2007	7,000	—	—	—	—	25.00

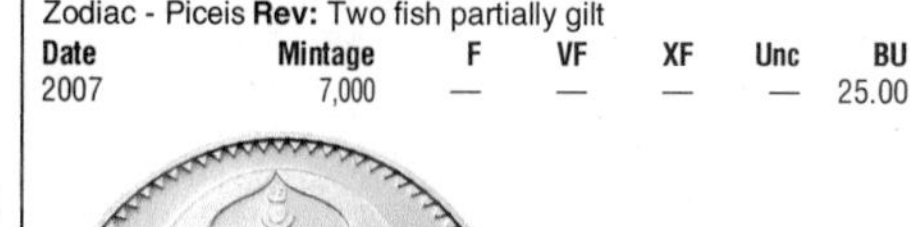

KM# 285 250 TUGRIK

15.5000 g., 0.9250 Silver 0.4609 oz. ASW, 33 mm. **Subject:** Zodiac - Aries **Rev:** Ram seated partially gilt

Date	Mintage	F	VF	XF	Unc	BU
2007	7,000	—	—	—	—	25.00

KM# 286 250 TUGRIK
15.5000 g., 0.9250 Silver 0.4609 oz. ASW, 33 mm. **Subject:** Zodiac - Taurus **Rev:** Bull, partially gilt

Date	Mintage	F	VF	XF	Unc	BU
2007	7,000	—	—	—	—	25.00

KM# 287 250 TUGRIK
15.5000 g., 0.9250 Silver 0.4609 oz. ASW, 33 mm. **Subject:** Zodiac - Gemini **Rev:** Twins, partially gilt

Date	Mintage	F	VF	XF	Unc	BU
2007	7,000	—	—	—	—	25.00

KM# 288 250 TUGRIK
15.5000 g., 0.9250 Silver 0.4609 oz. ASW, 33 mm. **Subject:** Zodiac - Cancer **Rev:** Crab - partially gilt

Date	Mintage	F	VF	XF	Unc	BU
2007	7,000	—	—	—	—	25.00

KM# 289 250 TUGRIK
15.5000 g., 0.9250 Silver 0.4609 oz. ASW, 33 mm. **Subject:** Zodiac - Leo **Rev:** Lion walking left, partially gilt

Date	Mintage	F	VF	XF	Unc	BU
2007	7,000	—	—	—	—	25.00

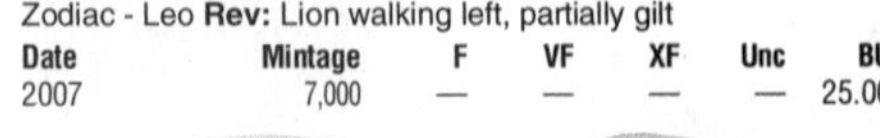

KM# 290 250 TUGRIK
15.5000 g., 0.9250 Silver 0.4609 oz. ASW, 33 mm. **Subject:** Zodiac - Virgo **Rev:** Female, partially gilt

Date	Mintage	F	VF	XF	Unc	BU
2007	7,000	—	—	—	—	25.00

KM# 291 250 TUGRIK
15.5000 g., 0.9250 Silver 0.4609 oz. ASW, 33 mm. **Subject:** Zodiac - Libra **Rev:** Scales, partially gilt

Date	Mintage	F	VF	XF	Unc	BU
2007	7,000	—	—	—	—	25.00

KM# 292 250 TUGRIK
15.5000 g., 0.9250 Silver 0.4609 oz. ASW, 33 mm. **Subject:** Zodiac - Scorpio **Rev:** Scorpion, partially gilt

Date	Mintage	F	VF	XF	Unc	BU
2007	7,000	—	—	—	—	25.00

KM# 293 250 TUGRIK
15.5000 g., 0.9250 Silver 0.4609 oz. ASW, 33 mm. **Subject:** Zodiac - Sagittarius **Rev:** Centar, partailly gilt

Date	Mintage	F	VF	XF	Unc	BU
2007	7,000	—	—	—	—	25.00

KM# 300 250 TUGRIK
15.5000 g., 0.9990 Silver 0.4978 oz. ASW, 33 mm. **Subject:** Moscow Waterworks **Rev:** Building in multicolor, aqueduct in background

Date	Mintage	F	VF	XF	Unc	BU
2007	1,000	—	—	—	—	45.00

KM# 301 250 TUGRIK
15.5000 g., 0.9990 Silver 0.4978 oz. ASW, 33 mm. **Subject:** Moscow Metro **Rev:** Subway train, multicolor

Date	Mintage	F	VF	XF	Unc	BU
2007	1,000	—	—	—	—	45.00

KM# 270 250 TUGRIK
15.5500 g., 0.9250 Silver 0.4624 oz. ASW, 37 mm. **Subject:** Baby Boy **Obv:** Arms **Rev:** Baby seated on flower, multicolor **Shape:** Heart

Date	Mintage	F	VF	XF	Unc	BU
2008 Proof	2,500	Value: 40.00				

KM# 271 250 TUGRIK
15.5500 g., 0.9250 Silver 0.4624 oz. ASW, 37 mm. **Subject:** Baby Girl **Obv:** Arms **Rev:** Baby Girl on flower **Shape:** Heart

Date	Mintage	F	VF	XF	Unc	BU
2008 Proof	2,500	Value: 40.00				

KM# 189 500 TUGRIK
25.0000 g., 0.9250 Silver 0.7435 oz. ASW, 38.7 mm. **Obv:** National emblem above value **Rev:** Protoceratops Andrewsi **Edge:** Reeded

Date	Mintage	F	VF	XF	Unc	BU
2001 Proof	2,500	Value: 45.00				

KM# 190 500 TUGRIK
25.0000 g., 0.9250 Silver 0.7435 oz. ASW **Obv:** National emblem above value **Rev:** Velociraptor Mongoliensis

Date	Mintage	F	VF	XF	Unc	BU
2001 Proof	2,500	Value: 45.00				

KM# 191 500 TUGRIK
25.0000 g., 0.9250 Silver 0.7435 oz. ASW **Series:** Olympics **Obv:** National emblem above value **Rev:** Speed skater

Date	Mintage	F	VF	XF	Unc	BU
2001 Proof	15,000	Value: 35.00				

KM# 192 500 TUGRIK
25.0000 g., 0.9250 Silver 0.7435 oz. ASW **Series:** Olympics **Obv:** National emblem above value **Rev:** Cross-country skiers

Date	Mintage	F	VF	XF	Unc	BU
2001 Proof	20,000	Value: 32.00				

KM# 195 500 TUGRIK
Copper-Nickel, 22.1 mm. **Subject:** Sukhe-Bataar **Obv:** National emblem and value **Rev:** Crowned head facing **Edge:** Plain

Date	Mintage	F	VF	XF	Unc	BU
2001	—	—	—	—	2.50	3.00

KM# 238 500 TUGRIK
20.0000 g., 0.9250 Silver 0.5948 oz. ASW **Subject:** Gobi Desert Brown Bear **Obv:** Arms **Rev:** Bear standing on rock in stream

Date	Mintage	F	VF	XF	Unc	BU
2001 Proof	—	Value: 28.00				

KM# 239 500 TUGRIK
31.1050 g., 0.9990 Silver 0.9990 oz. ASW, 38.5 mm. **Subject:** Year of the Snake **Rev:** Snake

Date	Mintage	F	VF	XF	Unc	BU
2001 Proof	—	Value: 65.00				

KM# 239a 500 TUGRIK
31.1050 g., 0.9990 Silver partially gilt 0.9990 oz. ASW **Subject:** Year of the Snake **Obv:** Arms **Rev:** Snake, gilt

Date	Mintage	F	VF	XF	Unc	BU
2001 Proof	—	Value: 75.00				

KM# 241 500 TUGRIK
31.1050 g., 0.9990 Silver 0.9990 oz. ASW, 38.5 mm. **Subject:** Year of the Horse **Obv:** Arms **Rev:** Horse

Date	Mintage	F	VF	XF	Unc	BU
2002 Proof	—	Value: 65.00				

KM# 241a 500 TUGRIK
31.1050 g., 0.9990 Silver partially gilt 0.9990 oz. ASW, 38.5 mm. **Subject:** Year of the Horse **Rev:** Horse, gilt

Date	Mintage	F	VF	XF	Unc	BU
2002 Proof	—	Value: 75.00				

KM# 200 500 TUGRIK
25.5700 g., 0.9250 Silver 0.7604 oz. ASW, 38.5 mm. **Subject:** Marco Polo, Homeward **Obv:** National emblem above value **Rev:** Five-masted sailing junk **Edge:** Reeded

Date	Mintage	F	VF	XF	Unc	BU
2003 Proof	5,000	Value: 45.00				

KM# 205 500 TUGRIK
25.0000 g., 0.9250 Silver 0.7435 oz. ASW, 38.6 mm. **Obv:** National emblem above value **Rev:** Medallion divides busts **Edge:** Reeded

Date	Mintage	F	VF	XF	Unc	BU
2003 Proof	5,000	Value: 65.00				

KM# 206 500 TUGRIK
1.2440 g., 0.9999 Gold 0.0400 oz. AGW, 13.92 mm. **Obv:** National emblem above value **Rev:** Five masted sailing junk **Edge:** Reeded

Date	Mintage	F	VF	XF	Unc	BU
2003 Proof	25,000	Value: 85.00				

KM# 207 500 TUGRIK
1.2440 g., 0.9999 Gold 0.0400 oz. AGW, 13.92 mm. **Obv:** National emblem above value **Rev:** Medallion divides busts **Edge:** Reeded

Date	Mintage	F	VF	XF	Unc	BU
2003 Proof	25,000	Value: 85.00				

KM# 204 500 TUGRIK
25.0000 g., 0.9250 Silver 0.7435 oz. ASW, 38 mm. **Obv:** National emblem above value **Rev:** Wolf within full moon **Edge:** Reeded

Date	Mintage	F	VF	XF	Unc	BU
2003 Proof	10,000	Value: 90.00				

KM# 229 500 TUGRIK
31.1050 g., 0.9990 Silver 0.9990 oz. ASW **Obv:** Arms above legend **Rev:** Ram standing left

Date	Mintage	F	VF	XF	Unc	BU
2003	—	—	—	—	—	65.00

KM# 229a 500 TUGRIK
31.1050 g., 0.9990 Silver partialy gilt 0.9990 oz. ASW, 38.5 mm. **Subject:** Year of the Ram **Obv:** Arms **Rev:** Ram standing left, gilt

Date	Mintage	F	VF	XF	Unc	BU
2003 Proof	—	Value: 75.00				

KM# 208 500 TUGRIK
25.0000 g., 0.9250 Silver 0.7435 oz. ASW, 38 mm. **Obv:** National emblem above value **Rev:** Holographic Osprey catching fish **Edge:** Reeded

Date	Mintage	F	VF	XF	Unc	BU
2004 Proof	5,000	Value: 45.00				

KM# 219 500 TUGRIK
1.2400 g., 0.9999 Gold 0.0399 oz. AGW **Series:** Chinese Lunar **Subject:** Year of the Monkey **Obv:** National emblem **Rev:** Monkey seated on branch

Date	Mintage	F	VF	XF	Unc	BU
ND(2004) Proof	—	Value: 75.00				

KM# 244 500 TUGRIK
31.1050 g., 0.9990 Silver 0.9990 oz. ASW, 38.5 mm. **Subject:** Year of the Monkey **Obv:** Arms **Rev:** Monkey

Date	Mintage	F	VF	XF	Unc	BU
2004 Proof	—	Value: 65.00				

KM# 244a 500 TUGRIK
31.1050 g., 0.9990 Silver partially gilt 0.9990 oz. ASW, 38.5 mm. **Subject:** Year of the Monkey **Obv:** Arms **Rev:** Monkey, gilt

Date	Mintage	F	VF	XF	Unc	BU
2004 Proof	—	Value: 75.00				

KM# 318 500 TUGRIK
25.0000 g., 0.9250 Silver 0.7435 oz. ASW, 38.6 mm. **Subject:** Osprey

Date	Mintage	F	VF	XF	Unc	BU
2004 Proof	Est. 5,000	Value: 45.00				

KM# 304 500 TUGRIK
31.1000 g., 0.9990 Silver 0.9988 oz. ASW, 38.5 mm. **Obv:** National emblem **Rev:** Sumo Wrestler Yokozuna Ounomatsu in color

Date	Mintage	F	VF	XF	Unc	BU
2005 Proof	—	Value: 125				

KM# 209 500 TUGRIK
24.9300 g., 0.9250 Bi-Metallic with .925 Silver oval in center 0.7414 oz., 30 mm. **Obv:** National emblem above value, niobium leopard in oval center **Rev:** Snow Leopard **Edge:** Reeded **Shape:** Oval

Date	Mintage	F	VF	XF	Unc	BU
2005 Proof	5,000	Value: 95.00				

KM# 210 500 TUGRIK
31.1035 g., 0.9990 Silver 0.9990 oz. ASW, 35x35 mm. **Obv:** Bronze plated horse and rider on antiqued silver with national emblem and value **Rev:** Bronze plated horse and rider on antiqued silver above date **Edge:** Reeded **Shape:** Square

Date	Mintage	F	VF	XF	Unc	BU
2005	2,500	—	—	—	70.00	75.00

KM# 210a 500 TUGRIK
31.1035 g., 0.9990 Silver 0.9990 oz. ASW, 35x35 mm. **Obv:** Gold plated horse and rider with national emblem and value **Rev:** Gold plated horse and rider above date **Edge:** Reeded

Date	Mintage	F	VF	XF	Unc	BU
2005 Proof	2,500	Value: 85.00				

KM# 246 500 TUGRIK
31.1050 g., 0.9990 Silver 0.9990 oz. ASW, 38.5 mm. **Subject:** Year of the Rooster **Obv:** Arms **Rev:** Rooster standing right

Date	Mintage	F	VF	XF	Unc	BU
2005 Proof	—	Value: 70.00				

KM# 246a 500 TUGRIK
31.1050 g., 0.9990 Silver 0.9990 oz. ASW, 38.5 mm. **Subject:** Year of the Rooster **Obv:** Arms **Rev:** Rooster, gilt

Date	Mintage	F	VF	XF	Unc	BU
2005 Proof	—	Value: 80.00				

KM# 319 500 TUGRIK
25.0000 g., 0.9250 Silver 0.7435 oz. ASW, 38.6 mm. **Subject:** Shiranui **Rev:** Classical wrestler in color

Date	Mintage	F	VF	XF	Unc	BU
2005 Proof	—	Value: 100				

KM# 320 500 TUGRIK
25.0000 g., 0.9250 Silver 0.7435 oz. ASW, 38.6 mm. **Subject:** Tanikaze **Rev:** Classical wrestler in color

Date	Mintage	F	VF	XF	Unc	BU
2005 Proof	—	Value: 100				

KM# 230 500 TUGRIK
25.0000 g., 0.9250 Silver 0.7435 oz. ASW **Rev:** Swan with crystal insert

Date	Mintage	F	VF	XF	Unc	BU
2006 Proof	—	Value: 95.00				

KM# 231 500 TUGRIK
25.0000 g., 0.9250 Silver 0.7435 oz. ASW **Rev:** Gobi bear head with crystal inserts

Date	Mintage	F	VF	XF	Unc	BU
2006 Proof	—	Value: 150				

KM# 248 500 TUGRIK
25.0000 g., 0.9250 Silver 0.7435 oz. ASW **Subject:** Long Eared Jerboa **Obv:** Arms **Rev:** Long eared jerboa, crystal eyes **Shape:** 38.6

Date	Mintage	F	VF	XF	Unc	BU
2006 Proof	2,500	Value: 145				

KM# 249 500 TUGRIK
25.0000 g., 0.9250 Silver 0.7435 oz. ASW, 38.6 mm. **Obv:** Arms **Rev:** Scorpion, crystal tail point

Date	Mintage	F	VF	XF	Unc	BU
2006 Proof	2,500	Value: 185				

KM# 250 500 TUGRIK
25.0000 g., 0.9250 Silver 0.7435 oz. ASW, 38.6 mm. **Rev:** Tiger, head facing, crystal eyes

Date	Mintage	F	VF	XF	Unc	BU
2006 Proof	2,500	Value: 135				

KM# 251 500 TUGRIK
31.1050 g., 0.9990 Silver 0.9990 oz. ASW, 38.5 mm. **Subject:** Year of the Dog **Obv:** Arms **Rev:** Dog standing

Date	Mintage	F	VF	XF	Unc	BU
2006 Proof	—	Value: 60.00				

KM# 251a 500 TUGRIK
31.1050 g., 0.9990 Silver 0.9990 oz. ASW, 38.5 mm. **Subject:** Year of the Dog **Obv:** Arms **Rev:** Dog standing, gilt

Date	Mintage	F	VF	XF	Unc	BU
2006 Proof	—	Value: 70.00				

KM# 260 500 TUGRIK
25.0000 g., 0.9250 Silver 0.7435 oz. ASW, 38.6 mm. **Subject:** Great Mongolian State, 800th Anniversary **Obv:** Arms **Rev:** Chinggis Khan and black pennant

Date	Mintage	F	VF	XF	Unc	BU
2006 Proof	2,500	Value: 75.00				

KM# 261 500 TUGRIK
25.0000 g., 0.9250 Silver 0.7435 oz. ASW, 38.61 mm. **Subject:** Great Mongolian State, 800th Anniversary **Obv:** Arms **Rev:** Nine white pennants

Date	Mintage	F	VF	XF	Unc	BU
2006 Proof	2,500	Value: 75.00				

KM# 316 500 TUGRIK
25.0000 g., 0.9250 Silver 0.7435 oz. ASW, 38.5 mm. **Subject:** Ice skating

Date	Mintage	F	VF	XF	Unc	BU
2006 Proof	—	Value: 50.00				

KM# 322 500 TUGRIK
31.1050 g., 0.9990 Silver 0.9990 oz. ASW, 38.6 mm. **Subject:** Year of the Pig

Date	Mintage	F	VF	XF	Unc	BU
2007 Proof	—	Value: 80.00				

KM# 212 500 TUGRIK
31.1050 g., 0.9990 Silver 0.9990 oz. ASW, 38 mm. **Obv:** Arms and value **Rev:** Wolverine head facing with diamonds in eyes **Rev. Inscription:** WILDLIFE PROTECTION GULO GULO

Date	Mintage	F	VF	XF	Unc	BU
2007	—	—	—	—	—	1,350

KM# 265 500 TUGRIK
31.1050 g., 0.9990 Silver 0.9990 oz. ASW, 38.61 mm. **Subject:** Society Space exploration **Obv:** Arms **Rev:** Sputnik, rocket, three figures

Date	Mintage	F	VF	XF	Unc	BU
2007 Proof	1,000	Value: 75.00				

KM# 266 500 TUGRIK
31.1050 g., 0.9990 Silver 0.9990 oz. ASW, 38.61 mm. **Subject:** Soviet Space Exploration **Rev:** Laika, first dog in space

Date	Mintage	F	VF	XF	Unc	BU
2007 Proof	500	Value: 85.00				

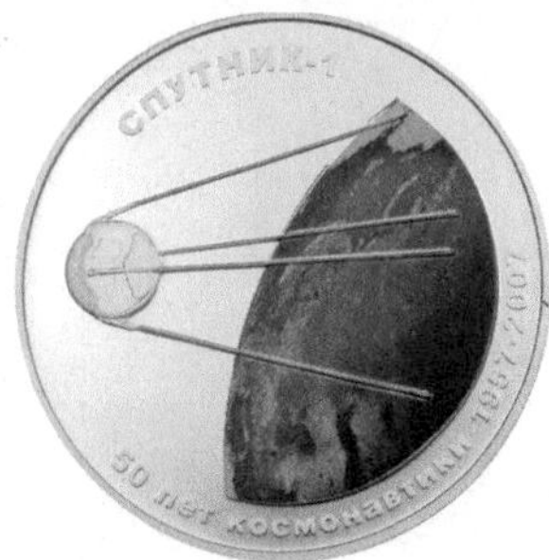

KM# 267 500 TUGRIK
31.1050 g., 0.9990 Silver 0.9990 oz. ASW, 38.61 mm. **Subject:** Soviet Space Exploration **Obv:** Arms **Rev:** Sputnik

Date	Mintage	F	VF	XF	Unc	BU
2007 Proof	500	Value: 85.00				

KM# 268 500 TUGRIK
31.1050 g., 0.9990 Silver 0.9990 oz. ASW, 38.61 mm. **Subject:** Soviet Space Exploration **Obv:** Arms **Rev:** Yuri Gagarian

Date	Mintage	F	VF	XF	Unc	BU
2007 Proof	500	Value: 85.00				

KM# 269 500 TUGRIK
31.1050 g., 0.9990 Silver 0.9990 oz. ASW, 38.61 mm. **Subject:** Soviet Space Exploration **Obv:** Arms **Rev:** Mir space station

Date	Mintage	F	VF	XF	Unc	BU
2007 Proof	1,000	Value: 85.00				

KM# 322a 500 TUGRIK
31.1050 g., 0.9990 Silver partially gilt 0.9990 oz. ASW, 38.6 mm. **Subject:** Year of the Pig

Date	Mintage	F	VF	XF	Unc	BU
2007 Proof	—	Value: 100				

KM# 325 500 TUGRIK
25.0000 g., 0.9250 Silver 0.7435 oz. ASW, 38.6 mm. **Rev:** John F. Kennedy at microphone

Date	Mintage	F	VF	XF	Unc	BU
2007 Proof	—	Value: 125				

KM# 222 500 TUGRIK
25.0000 g., 0.9250 Silver 0.7435 oz. ASW, 38.61 mm. **Subject:** Wonders of the World **Obv:** Arms **Rev:** Multicolor Chichen Itza

Date	Mintage	F	VF	XF	Unc	BU
2008	2,500	—	—	—	—	75.00

KM# 223 500 TUGRIK
25.0000 g., 0.9250 Silver 0.7435 oz. ASW, 38.6 mm. **Subject:** Wonders of the World **Obv:** Arms **Rev:** Multicolor Treasury at Petra

Date	Mintage	F	VF	XF	Unc	BU
2008	2,500	—	—	—	—	95.00

KM# 224 500 TUGRIK

25.0000 g., 0.9250 Silver 0.7435 oz. ASW, 38.61 mm. **Subject:** Wonders of the World **Obv:** Arms **Rev:** Multicolor Taj Mahal

Date	Mintage	F	VF	XF	Unc	BU
2008	2,500	—	—	—	—	75.00

KM# 225 500 TUGRIK

25.0000 g., 0.9250 Silver 0.7435 oz. ASW, 38.61 mm. **Subject:** Wonders of the World **Obv:** Arms **Rev:** Multicolor Machu Picchu

Date	Mintage	F	VF	XF	Unc	BU
2008	2,500	—	—	—	—	85.00

KM# 226 500 TUGRIK

25.0000 g., 0.9250 Silver 0.7435 oz. ASW, 38.61 mm. **Subject:** Wonders of the World **Obv:** Arms **Rev:** Multicolor Great Wall of China

Date	Mintage	F	VF	XF	Unc	BU
2008	2,500	—	—	—	—	85.00

KM# 227 500 TUGRIK

25.0000 g., 0.9250 Silver 0.7435 oz. ASW, 38.61 mm. **Subject:** Wonders of the World **Obv:** Arms **Rev:** Multicolor Colosseum in Rome

Date	Mintage	F	VF	XF	Unc	BU
2008	2,500	—	—	—	—	75.00

KM# 228 500 TUGRIK

25.0000 g., 0.9250 Silver 0.7435 oz. ASW, 38.61 mm. **Subject:** Wonders of the World **Obv:** Arms **Rev:** Multicolor Christ the Redeemer statue in Rio

Date	Mintage	F	VF	XF	Unc	BU
2008	2,500	—	—	—	—	65.00

KM# 213 500 TUGRIK

31.1000 g., 0.9990 Silver 0.9988 oz. ASW, 39mm mm. **Subject:** Year of the Rat **Obv:** National emblem, value below **Rev:** Three rats in grass **Edge:** Reeded

Date	Mintage	F	VF	XF	Unc	BU
2008	20,000	—	—	—	—	45.00

KM# 213a 500 TUGRIK

31.1000 g., 0.9990 Silver 0.9988 oz. ASW, 39.0 mm. **Subject:** Year of the Rat **Obv:** National emblem, value below **Rev:** Three gilt rats in grass **Edge:** Reeded

Date	Mintage	F	VF	XF	Unc	BU
2008 Proof	5,000	Value: 50.00				

KM# 255 500 TUGRIK

25.0000 g., 0.9250 Silver 0.7435 oz. ASW, 38.6 mm. **Subject:** Frederic Chopin **Obv:** Arms **Rev:** Bust right, color keyboard vertical in center

Date	Mintage	F	VF	XF	Unc	BU
2008 Proof	1,000	Value: 90.00				

KM# 256 500 TUGRIK

31.1050 g., 0.9990 Silver 0.9990 oz. ASW, 38.6 mm. **Subject:** Year of the Rat **Obv:** Arms **Rev:** Two mice

Date	Mintage	F	VF	XF	Unc	BU
2008 Proof	—	Value: 55.00				

KM# 256a 500 TUGRIK

31.1050 g., 0.9990 Silver partially gilt 0.9990 oz. ASW, 38.6 mm. **Subject:** Year of the Rat **Obv:** Arms **Rev:** Two mice, gilt

Date	Mintage	F	VF	XF	Unc	BU
2008 Proof	—	Value: 65.00				

KM# 272 500 TUGRIK

25.0000 g., 0.9250 Silver 0.7435 oz. ASW, 38.6 mm. **Series:** Mongolian Olympians, Baatarjav **Obv:** Arms

Date	Mintage	F	VF	XF	Unc	BU
2008 Proof	2,500	Value: 45.00				

KM# 273 500 TUGRIK

25.0000 g., 0.9250 Silver 0.7435 oz. ASW, 38.61 mm. **Subject:** Mongolian Olympians - Badar-Uugan

Date	Mintage	F	VF	XF	Unc	BU
2008 Proof	2,500	Value: 45.00				

KM# 274 500 TUGRIK

25.0000 g., 0.9990 Silver 0.8029 oz. ASW, 38.61 mm. **Subject:** Mongolian Olympians - Serdamba

Date	Mintage	F	VF	XF	Unc	BU
2008 Proof	2,500	Value: 45.00				

KM# 275 500 TUGRIK

25.0000 g., 0.9250 Silver 0.7435 oz. ASW, 38.61 mm. **Subject:** Mongolian Olympians - Tuvshinbayar

Date	Mintage	F	VF	XF	Unc	BU
2008 Proof	2,500	Value: 45.00				

KM# 276 500 TUGRIK
25.0000 g., 0.9250 Silver 0.7435 oz. ASW, 38.61 mm. **Subject:** Mongolian Olympians - Gundegmaa

Date	Mintage	F	VF	XF	Unc	BU
2008 Proof	2,500	Value: 45.00				

KM# 279 500 TUGRIK
0.5000 g., 0.9990 Gold 0.0161 oz. AGW, 11 mm. **Subject:** Mongolian Olympic Sports - Archery

Date	Mintage	F	VF	XF	Unc	BU
2008 Proof	15,000	—	—	—	—	50.00

KM# 280 500 TUGRIK
25.0000 g., 0.9250 Silver 0.7435 oz. ASW, 38.61 mm. **Obv:** Arms **Rev:** Two snow leopards, multicolor

Date	Mintage	F	VF	XF	Unc	BU
2008 Proof	2,500	Value: 75.00				

KM# 281 500 TUGRIK
25.0000 g., 0.9250 Silver 0.7435 oz. ASW, 38.61 mm. **Obv:** Arms **Rev:** The Almas, multicolor changing insert

Date	Mintage	F	VF	XF	Unc	BU
2008 Proof	2,500	Value: 55.00				

KM# 305 500 TUGRIK
25.0000 g., 0.9250 Silver 0.7435 oz. ASW, 38.61 mm. **Subject:** Frederic Chopin **Obv:** National emblem **Rev:** Piano keys in color, bust at right

Date	Mintage	F	VF	XF	Unc	BU
2008 Proof	—	Value: 75.00				

KM# 312 500 TUGRIK
31.1050 g., 0.9990 Silver 0.9990 oz. ASW, 38.61 mm. **Subject:** Year of the Rat **Rev:** Mouse in multicolor

Date	Mintage	F	VF	XF	Unc	BU
2008 Proof	—	Value: 65.00				

KM# 258 500 TUGRIK
31.1050 g., 0.9990 Silver 0.9990 oz. ASW, 38.6 mm. **Subject:** Year of the Ox **Obv:** Arms **Rev:** Ox

Date	Mintage	F	VF	XF	Unc	BU
2009 Proof	—	Value: 60.00				

KM# 258a 500 TUGRIK
31.1050 g., 0.9990 Silver partially gilt 0.9990 oz. ASW, 38.6 mm. **Subject:** Year of the Ox **Obv:** Arms **Rev:** Ox, gilt

Date	Mintage	F	VF	XF	Unc	BU
2009 Proof	—	Value: 70.00				

KM# 309 500 TUGRIK
31.1000 g., 0.9250 Silver 0.9249 oz. ASW, 38.6 mm. **Subject:** Endangered Wildlife **Obv:** National Emblem **Rev:** Owl's head facing (Strix Uralensis) crystal insert eyes

Date	Mintage	F	VF	XF	Unc	BU
2011 Antique finish	2,500	—	—	—	—	650

KM# 310 500 TUGRIK
0.5000 g., 0.9990 Gold 0.0161 oz. AGW, 11 mm. **Subject:** Endangered Wildlife **Obv:** National emblem **Rev:** Ural Owl (Strix Uralersis) standing left

Date	Mintage	F	VF	XF	Unc	BU
2011 Proof	15,000	—	—	—	—	75.00

KM# 314 500 TUGRIK
25.0000 g., 0.9250 Silver 0.7435 oz. ASW, 38.61 mm. **Subject:** Joint Societ - mongolian space flight, 30th Anniversary

Date	Mintage	F	VF	XF	Unc	BU
2011 Proof	—	Value: 70.00				

KM# 315 500 TUGRIK
25.0000 g., 0.9250 Silver 0.7435 oz. ASW, 38.61 mm. **Rev:** Saiga Tatarica in color

Date	Mintage	F	VF	XF	Unc	BU
2011 Proof	2,500	Value: 70.00				

KM# 324 500 TUGRIK
31.1050 g., 0.9990 Silver 0.9990 oz. ASW, 38.61 mm. **Rev:** Baby hedgehog with crystal eyes

Date	Mintage	F	VF	XF	Unc	BU
2012 Antique patina	—	—	—	—	—	450

KM# 199 1000 TUGRIK
31.1100 g., 0.9250 Silver 0.9252 oz. ASW, 38.6 mm. **Obv:** National emblem above value **Obv. Inscription:** Denomination spelled "TOGROG" **Rev:** Head facing **Edge:** Reeded

Date	Mintage	F	VF	XF	Unc	BU
2002	17,000	—	—	—	42.00	45.00

KM# 303 1000 TUGRIK
Copper-Nickel, 38 mm. **Obv:** National emblem **Rev:** Two soccer players

Date	Mintage	F	VF	XF	Unc	BU
2003 Prooflike	2,000	—	—	—	—	10.00

KM# 233 1000 TUGRIK
Gold **Rev:** Snow leopard

Date	Mintage	F	VF	XF	Unc	BU
2005 Proof	—	Value: 95.00				

KM# 253 1000 TUGRIK
1.2400 g., 0.9990 Gold 0.0398 oz. AGW **Subject:** Mozart **Obv:** Arms **Rev:** Portrait and profile heads above building

Date	Mintage	F	VF	XF	Unc	BU
2006 Proof	—	Value: 80.00				

KM# 262 1000 TUGRIK

1.2400 g., 0.9990 Gold 0.0398 oz. AGW, 13.92 mm. **Obv:** Arms **Rev:** Scorpion

Date	Mintage	F	VF	XF	Unc	BU
2006 Proof	25,000	Value: 95.00				

KM# 263 1000 TUGRIK

1.2400 g., 0.9990 Silver 0.0398 oz. ASW, 13.9 mm. **Obv:** Arms **Rev:** Long-eared Jerboa

Date	Mintage	F	VF	XF	Unc	BU
2006 Proof	—	Value: 95.00				

KM# 264 1000 TUGRIK

1.2400 g., 0.9990 Gold 0.0398 oz. AGW, 13.9 mm. **Obv:** Arms **Rev:** Gobi Bear

Date	Mintage	F	VF	XF	Unc	BU
2006 Proof	25,000	Value: 95.00				

KM# 294 1000 TUGRIK

62.2000 g., 0.9990 Silver 1.9977 oz. ASW, 50 mm. **Rev:** Tsarina Catherina multicolor

Date	Mintage	F	VF	XF	Unc	BU
2007 Proof	500	Value: 165				

KM# 295 1000 TUGRIK

62.2000 g., 0.9990 Silver 1.9977 oz. ASW, 50 mm. **Rev:** Tsar Nicholas I, multicolor

Date	Mintage	F	VF	XF	Unc	BU
2007 Proof	500	Value: 165				

KM# 296 1000 TUGRIK

62.2000 g., 0.9990 Silver 1.9977 oz. ASW, 50 mm. **Rev:** Tsar Nicholas II

Date	Mintage	F	VF	XF	Unc	BU
2007 Proof	500	Value: 165				

KM# 297 1000 TUGRIK

62.2000 g., 0.9990 Silver 1.9977 oz. ASW, 50 mm. **Rev:** Tsar Ivan IV, multicolor

Date	Mintage	F	VF	XF	Unc	BU
2007 Proof	500	Value: 165				

KM# 298 1000 TUGRIK

62.2000 g., 0.9990 Silver 1.9977 oz. ASW, 50 mm. **Rev:** Tsar Peter I, multicolor

Date	Mintage	F	VF	XF	Unc	BU
2007 Proof	500	Value: 165				

KM# 299 1000 TUGRIK

62.2000 g., 0.9990 Silver 1.9977 oz. ASW, 50 mm. **Rev:** Tsar Yuri

Date	Mintage	F	VF	XF	Unc	BU
2007 Proof	500	Value: 165				

KM# 214 1000 TUGRIK

1.2400 g., 0.9990 Gold 0.0398 oz. AGW, 14.0 mm. **Subject:** Year of the Rat **Obv:** National emblem, value below **Edge:** Reeded

Date	Mintage	F	VF	XF	Unc	BU
2008 Proof	10,000	Value: 75.00				

KM# 277 1000 TUGRIK

1.2400 g., 0.9990 Gold 0.0398 oz. AGW, 13.92 mm. **Subject:** Mongolian Olympic Sports - Boxing **Rev:** Two fighters in the ring

Date	Mintage	F	VF	XF	Unc	BU
2008 Proof	15,000	Value: 85.00				

KM# 278 1000 TUGRIK

1.2400 g., 0.9990 Gold 0.0398 oz. AGW, 13.92 mm. **Subject:** Mongolian Olympic Sports - Judo **Rev:** Judo athlete getting fliped

Date	Mintage	F	VF	XF	Unc	BU
2008 Proof	15,000	Value: 85.00				

KM# 311 1000 TUGRIK

1.2400 g., 0.9990 Gold 0.0398 oz. AGW, 13.92 mm. **Subject:** Frederic Chopin **Obv:** National Emblem **Rev:** Piano keyboard vertical at left, bust at right

Date	Mintage	F	VF	XF	Unc	BU
2011 Proof	—	Value: 100				

KM# 240 2500 TUGRIK

7.7700 g., 0.9990 Gold 0.2496 oz. AGW **Subject:** Year of the Snake **Obv:** Arms **Rev:** Snake

Date	Mintage	F	VF	XF	Unc	BU
2001 Proof	2,000	Value: 500				

KM# 242 2500 TUGRIK

7.7000 g., 0.9990 Gold 0.2473 oz. AGW **Subject:** Year of the Horse **Obv:** Arms **Rev:** Year of the Horse

Date	Mintage	F	VF	XF	Unc	BU
2002 Proof	—	Value: 500				

KM# 243 2500 TUGRIK

155.5000 g., 0.9990 Silver partially gilt 4.9942 oz. ASW, 65 mm. **Subject:** Year of the Ram **Obv:** Arms **Rev:** Ram standing left, gilt

Date	Mintage	F	VF	XF	Unc	BU
2003 Proof	4,000	Value: 325				

KM# 245 2500 TUGRIK

155.5000 g., 0.9990 Silver partially gilt 4.9942 oz. ASW, 65 mm. **Subject:** Year of the Monkey **Obv:** Arms **Rev:** Monkey, gilt

Date	Mintage	F	VF	XF	Unc	BU
2004 Proof	4,000	Value: 325				

KM# 220 2500 TUGRIK

7.7800 g., 0.9999 Gold 0.2501 oz. AGW **Series:** Chinese Lunar **Subject:** Year of the Monkey **Obv:** National emblem **Rev:** Monkey seated on branch **Edge:** Reeded

Date	Mintage	F	VF	XF	Unc	BU
ND(2004) Proof	2,000	Value: 525				

KM# 247 2500 TUGRIK

155.5000 g., 0.9990 Silver partially gilt 4.9942 oz. ASW, 65 mm. **Subject:** Year of the Rooster **Obv:** Arms **Rev:** Rooster, gilt

Date	Mintage	F	VF	XF	Unc	BU
2005 Proof	4,000	Value: 325				

KM# 252 2500 TUGRIK

155.5000 g., 0.9990 Silver partially gilt 4.9942 oz. ASW, 65 mm. **Subject:** Year of the Dog **Obv:** Arms **Rev:** Dog standing, gilt

Date	Mintage	F	VF	XF	Unc	BU
2006 Proof	—	Value: 325				

KM# 257 2500 TUGRIK

155.5000 g., 0.9990 Silver partially gilt 4.9942 oz. ASW, 65 mm. **Subject:** Year of the Rat **Obv:** Arms **Rev:** Two mice, gilt

Date	Mintage	F	VF	XF	Unc	BU
2008 Proof	—	Value: 325				

KM# 259 2500 TUGRIK

155.5000 g., 0.9990 Silver partially gilt 4.9942 oz. ASW, 65 mm. **Subject:** Year of the Ox **Obv:** Arms **Rev:** Ox, gilt

Date	Mintage	F	VF	XF	Unc	BU
2009 Proof	—	Value: 325				

KM# 198 5000 TUGRIK
155.5000 g., 0.9990 Silver 4.9942 oz. ASW, 40x90 mm. **Subject:** Year of the Horse **Obv:** National emblem above value to left of Palace Museum **Rev:** Five multicolor running horses **Edge:** Plain **Note:** Round-cornered rectangle. Photo reduced.

Date	Mintage	F	VF	XF	Unc	BU
2002 Proof	—	Value: 350				

KM# 232 5000 TUGRIK
155.5000 g., 0.9990 Silver 4.9942 oz. ASW, 40x90 mm. **Rev:** Three sumo wrestlers, multicolor **Shape:** Rectangle **Note:** Illustration reduced.

Date	Mintage	F	VF	XF	Unc	BU
2005 Proof	—	Value: 400				

KM# 221 100000 TUGRIK
3000.0000 g., 0.9990 Silver 96.351 oz. ASW **Series:** Chinese Lunar **Subject:** Year of the Monkey **Obv:** National emblem **Rev:** Monkey seated on branch

Date	Mintage	F	VF	XF	Unc	BU
ND(2004) Proof	—	Value: 3,750				

KM# 215 100000 TUGRIK
3000.0000 g., 0.9990 Silver 96.351 oz. ASW, 130.0 mm. **Subject:** Year of the Rat **Obv:** National emblem, value below **Rev:** Three rats in grass **Edge:** Reeded **Note:** Serial number on edge.

Date	Mintage	F	VF	XF	Unc	BU
2008 Proof	500	Value: 3,750				

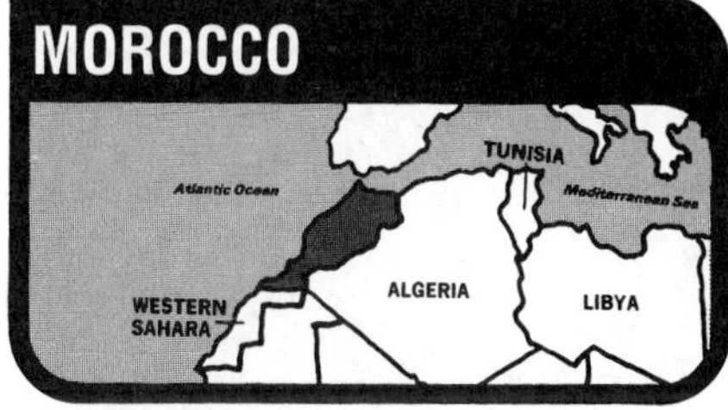

The Kingdom of Morocco, situated on the northwest corner of Africa, has an area of 432,620 sq. mi. (710,850 sq. km.) and a population of 36 million. Capital: Rabat. The economy is essentially agricultural. Phosphates, fresh and preserved vegetables, canned fish, and raw materials are exported.

KINGDOM

Mohammed VI

AH1420/1999AD

REFORM COINAGE

100 Santimat = 1 Dirham

Y# 112 5 SANTIMAT
2.0000 g., Aluminum-Bronze, 17.5 mm. **Obv:** Crowned arms with supporters **Rev:** Value, flower and dates **Edge:** Plain

Date	Mintage	F	VF	XF	Unc	BU
AH1423-2002	—	—	—	—	0.50	1.00

Y# 114 10 SANTIMAT
3.0000 g., Aluminum-Bronze, 20 mm. **Obv:** Crowned arms with supporters **Rev:** Value, design of "sport and solidarity" **Edge:** Reeded

Date	Mintage	F	VF	XF	Unc	BU
AH1423-2002	—	—	—	—	1.00	2.00

Y# 136 10 SANTIMAT
3.0000 g., Brass Plated Steel, 20 mm.

Date	Mintage	F	VF	XF	Unc	BU
AH1432-2011	—	—	—	—	1.00	2.00
AH1433-2012	—	—	—	—	1.00	3.00

Y# 115 20 SANTIMAT
4.0000 g., Aluminum-Bronze, 23 mm. **Obv:** Crowned arms with supporters **Rev:** Value, design of "tourist and craftsmen trade" **Edge:** Reeded

Date	Mintage	F	VF	XF	Unc	BU
AH1423-2002	—	—	—	—	1.50	3.00

Y# 137 20 SANTIMAT
4.0000 g., Brass Plated Steel, 23 mm. **Edge:** Reeded

Date	Mintage	F	VF	XF	Unc	BU
AH1432-2011	—	—	—	—	1.50	3.00
AH1433-2012	—	—	—	—	1.50	3.00

Y# 116 1/2 DIRHAM
4.0000 g., Copper-Nickel, 21 mm. **Obv:** Crowned arms with supporters **Rev:** Value, design theme "telecommunications and new technologies" **Edge:** Reeded

Date	Mintage	F	VF	XF	Unc	BU
AH1423-2002	—	—	—	—	2.00	3.00

Y# 138 1/2 DIRHAM
4.0000 g., Nickel Plated Steel, 21 mm. **Obv:** Crowned national arms with supporters **Rev:** Two fish and large value **Edge:** Reeded

Date	Mintage	F	VF	XF	Unc	BU
AH1432-2011	—	—	—	—	3.00	5.00
AH1433-2012	—	—	—	—	3.00	5.00

Y# 117 DIRHAM
6.0000 g., Copper-Nickel, 24 mm. **Obv:** Head 3/4 left **Rev:** Crowned arms with supporters above value **Edge:** Reeded

Date	Mintage	F	VF	XF	Unc	BU
AH1423-2002	—	—	—	—	3.00	5.00

Y# 139 DIRHAM
6.0000 g., Nickel Plated Steel, 24 mm. **Obv:** Head left **Rev:** Crowned national arms with supporters, value below **Edge:** Reeded

Date	Mintage	F	VF	XF	Unc	BU
AH1432-2011	—	—	—	—	3.50	5.00
AH1433-2012	—	—	—	—	3.50	5.00

Y# 118 2 DIRHAMS
7.0000 g., Copper-Nickel, 26 mm. **Obv:** Head 3/4 left within octagon shape **Rev:** Crowned arms with supporters above value within octagon shape **Edge:** Reeded

Date	Mintage	F	VF	XF	Unc	BU
AH1423-2002	—	—	—	—	4.00	6.00

Y# 109 5 DIRHAMS
7.5000 g., Bi-Metallic Nickel-Brass center in Copper-Nickel ring, 25 mm. **Obv:** Head 3/4 left **Rev:** Crowned arms with supporters above value **Edge:** Segmented reeding

Date	Mintage	F	VF	XF	Unc	BU
AH1423-2002	—	—	—	—	6.00	9.00

Y# 140 5 DIRHAMS
7.5000 g., Bi-Metallic Nordic Gold center in Copper-Nickel ring, 25 mm. **Obv:** Head left **Rev:** Mosque **Edge:** Segmented reeding

Date	Mintage	F	VF	XF	Unc	BU
AH1432-2011	—	—	—	—	6.00	9.00

Y# 110 10 DIRHAMS
9.0000 g., Bi-Metallic Copper-Nickel center in Brass ring, 26.9 mm. **Obv:** Head 3/4 left **Rev:** Crowned arms with supporters above value **Edge:** Reeded

Date	Mintage	F	VF	XF	Unc	BU
AH1423-2002	—	—	—	—	10.00	15.00

Y# 141 10 DIRHAMS
9.0000 g., Bi-Metallic Copper-Nickel center in Nordic Gold ring, 27 mm. **Obv:** Head left **Rev:** Building and palm tree at left, large value at right

Date	Mintage	F	VF	XF	Unc	BU
AH1432-2011	—	—	—	—	10.00	15.00

Y# 107 250 DIRHAMS
25.0000 g., 0.9250 Silver 0.7435 oz. ASW, 37 mm. **Subject:** Inauguration of Mohammed VI 2nd Anniversary **Obv:** Head 3/4 left **Rev:** Crowned arms with supporters above value **Edge:** Reeded

Date	Mintage	F	VF	XF	Unc	BU
AH1422-2001	—	—	—	—	55.00	70.00

Y# 95 250 DIRHAMS
25.0000 g., 0.9250 Silver 0.7435 oz. ASW, 37 mm. **Subject:** World Children's Day **Obv:** Head 3/4 left **Rev:** Children standing on open book within globe **Edge:** Reeded

Date	Mintage	F	VF	XF	Unc	BU
AH1422-2001	—	—	—	—	60.00	80.00
AH1422-2001 Proof	—	Value: 100				

Y# 95a 250 DIRHAMS
25.0000 g., 0.9999 Gold 0.8037 oz. AGW, 37 mm. **Subject:** World Children's Day **Obv:** Head 3/4 left **Rev:** Two children standing on an open book within globe **Edge:** Reeded **Note:** Prev. Y#95.

Date	Mintage	F	VF	XF	Unc	BU
AH1422-2001 Proof	2,800	Value: 1,500				

Y# 108 250 DIRHAMS
25.0000 g., 0.9250 Silver 0.7435 oz. ASW, 37 mm. **Subject:** Mohammed VI's Inauguration 3rd Anniversary **Obv:** Head 3/4 left **Rev:** Crowned arms with supporters above value **Edge:** Reeded **Note:** Slightly different legend of Y-107

Date	Mintage	F	VF	XF	Unc	BU
AH1423-2002	—	—	—	—	60.00	80.00
AH1423-2002 Proof	—	Value: 100				

Y# 113 250 DIRHAMS
25.0000 g., 0.9250 Silver 0.7435 oz. ASW, 37 mm. **Subject:** Marriage of King Mohammed VI, July 12, 2002 **Obv:** Head 3/4 left **Rev:** Crown above radiant flowers **Edge:** Reeded

Date	Mintage	F	VF	XF	Unc	BU
ND (2002) Proof	—	Value: 100				

Y# 119 250 DIRHAMS
25.0000 g., 0.9250 Silver 0.7435 oz. ASW, 37 mm. **Subject:** Birth of Crown Prince Moulay Al Hassan **Obv:** Head 3/4 left **Rev:** Crowned arms with supporters above value

Date	Mintage	F	VF	XF	Unc	BU
ND(2003) Proof	—	Value: 100				

Y# 120 250 DIRHAMS
25.0000 g., 0.9250 Silver 0.7435 oz. ASW, 37 mm. **Subject:** 50th Anniversary - Kingdom **Obv:** Conjoined heads right **Rev:** Crowned arms with supporters above value

Date	Mintage	F	VF	XF	Unc	BU
AH1424-2003	—	—	—	—	60.00	80.00
AH1424-2003 Proof	—	Value: 100				

Y# 111 250 DIRHAMS
25.0000 g., 0.9250 Silver 0.7435 oz. ASW, 37 mm. **Subject:** Mohammed VI's Inauguration 4th Anniversary **Obv:** Head 3/4 left **Rev:** Crowned arms with supporters above value **Edge:** Reeded **Note:** Virtually identical to Y-107 and Y-108.

Date	Mintage	F	VF	XF	Unc	BU
AH1424-2003	—	—	—	—	60.00	80.00

Y# 122 250 DIRHAMS
25.0000 g., 0.9250 Silver 0.7435 oz. ASW, 37 mm. **Subject:** 5th Anniversary of Mohammed VI's Reign **Obv:** Head 3/4 left, national arms **Rev:** Crowned arms with supporters above value **Edge:** Reeded **Note:** Vitually identical to Y-107, 108 and 111.

Date	Mintage	F	VF	XF	Unc	BU
AH1425-2004	—	—	—	—	60.00	80.00

Y# 121 250 DIRHAMS
25.0000 g., 0.9250 Silver 0.7435 oz. ASW, 37 mm. **Subject:** Year of Handicapped Persons **Obv:** Head 3/4 left **Rev:** Stylized figures

Date	Mintage	F	VF	XF	Unc	BU
AH1425-2004	—	—	—	—	60.00	80.00

Y# 123 250 DIRHAMS
25.0000 g., 0.9250 Silver 0.7435 oz. ASW, 37 mm. **Subject:** 30th Anniversary - Green March **Obv:** Head 3/4 left **Rev:** Men marching left with flags aloft

Date	Mintage	F	VF	XF	Unc	BU
AH1426-2005	—	—	—	—	60.00	80.00

Y# 124 250 DIRHAMS
25.0000 g., 0.9250 Silver 0.7435 oz. ASW, 37 mm. **Subject:** 6th Anniversary of Mohammed VI's Reign **Obv:** Head 3/4 left **Rev:** Crowned arms with supporters above value **Edge:** Reeded **Note:** Virtually identical to Y-107, 108, 111 and 122

Date	Mintage	F	VF	XF	Unc	BU
AH1426-2005	—	—	—	—	60.00	80.00

Y# 125 250 DIRHAMS
25.0000 g., 0.9250 Silver 0.7435 oz. ASW, 37 mm. **Subject:** 6th Anniversary of Mohammed VI's Reign **Obv:** Head 3/4 left **Rev:** Crowned arms with supporters above value **Edge:** Reeded **Note:** Virtually identical to Y-107, 108, 111 and 122

Date	Mintage	F	VF	XF	Unc	BU
AH1427-2006	—	—	—	—	60.00	80.00

Y# 126 250 DIRHAMS
25.0000 g., 0.9250 Silver 0.7435 oz. ASW, 37 mm. **Subject:** 8th Anniversary of Mohammed VI's reign **Obv:** Head 3/4 left **Rev:** Corwned arms with supporters, value below **Edge:** Reeded

Date	Mintage	F	VF	XF	Unc	BU
AH1428/2007	—	—	—	—	60.00	80.00

Y# 127 250 DIRHAMS
25.0000 g., 0.9250 Silver 0.7435 oz. ASW, 37 mm. **Subject:** 9th Anniversary of Mohammed VI's reign **Obv:** Head 3/4 left **Rev:** Crowned arms with supporters above value **Edge:** Reeded

Date	Mintage	F	VF	XF	Unc	BU
AH1429-2008 Proof	1,000	Value: 125				

Y# 128 250 DIRHAMS
25.0000 g., 0.9250 Silver 0.7435 oz. ASW, 37 mm. **Subject:** 12 Centuries of Monarchy

Date	Mintage	F	VF	XF	Unc	BU
AH1429-2008 Proof	5,000	Value: 80.00				

Y# 133 250 DIRHAMS
6.4500 g., 0.9000 Gold 0.1866 oz. AGW, 21 mm. **Subject:** 12 Centuries of Monarchy

Date	Mintage	F	VF	XF	Unc	BU
AH1429-2008	3,000	Value: 350				

Y# 129 250 DIRHAMS
25.0000 g., 0.9250 Silver 0.7435 oz. ASW, 37 mm. **Subject:** 10th Anniversary of Mohammed VI's reign **Obv:** Head 3/4 left **Rev:** Crowned arms with supporters above value **Edge:** Reeded

Date	Mintage	F	VF	XF	Unc	BU
AH1430-2009 Proof	1,500	Value: 100				

Y# 130 250 DIRHAMS
25.0000 g., 0.9250 Silver 0.7435 oz. ASW, 37 mm. **Subject:** Bank al Maghrib, 50th Anniversary **Obv:** Head 3/4 left

Date	Mintage	F	VF	XF	Unc	BU
AH1430-2009 Proof	—	Value: 120				

Y# 131 250 DIRHAMS
25.0000 g., 0.9250 Silver 0.7435 oz. ASW, 37 mm. **Subject:** 11th Anniversary of Mohammed VI's reign **Obv:** Head 3/4 left **Rev:** Crowned arms with supporters above value **Edge:** Reeded

Date	Mintage	F	VF	XF	Unc	BU
AH1431-2010 Proof	1,500	Value: 100				

Y# 132 250 DIRHAMS
25.0000 g., 0.9250 Silver 0.7435 oz. ASW, 37 mm. **Subject:** Green March, 35th Anniversary **Edge:** Reeded

Date	Mintage	F	VF	XF	Unc	BU
AH1431-2010 Proof	1,000	Value: 125				

Y# 135 500 DIRHAMS
Bi-Metallic **Obv:** Head left **Rev:** Building **Note:** Silver and gold similar to Y#130.

Date	Mintage	F	VF	XF	Unc	BU
AH1430-2009 Proof	—	Value: 1,650				

MOZAMBIQUE

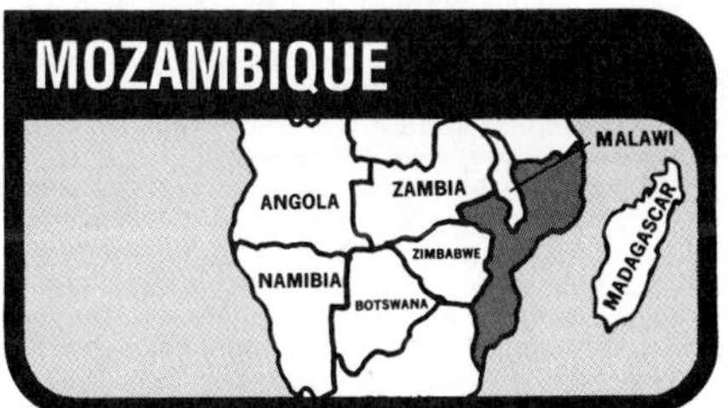

The Republic of Mozambique, a former overseas province of Portugal, stretches for 1,430 miles (2,301 km.) along the southeast coast of Africa, has an area of 302,330 sq. mi. (801,590 sq. km.) and a population of 14.1 million, 99 % of whom are native Africans of the Bantu tribes. Capital: Maputo. Agriculture is the chief industry. Cashew nuts, cotton, sugar, copra and tea are exported.

Mozambique became a member of the Commonwealth of Nations in November 1995. The President is Head of State; the Prime Minister is Head of Government.

REPUBLIC

REFORM COINAGE

100 Centavos = 1 Metical; 1994

KM# 130 1000 METICAIS
25.7100 g., 0.9800 Silver 0.8100 oz. ASW, 38.5 mm. **Subject:** Pedro De Covilha, 1498 **Obv:** National arms within circle **Rev:** Sailing ship within circle **Edge:** Reeded

Date	Mintage	F	VF	XF	Unc	BU
2003 Proof	—	Value: 45.00				

KM# 131 10000 METICAIS
8.0400 g., Bi-Metallic Stainless Steel center in Brass ring, 26.6 mm. **Obv:** National arms within circle **Rev:** Rhino within circle **Edge:** Segmented reeding

Date	Mintage	F	VF	XF	Unc	BU
2003	—	—	3.50	5.00	7.50	12.00

REFORM COINAGE

(New) Metical = 1,000 Meticals; 2005

KM# 132 CENTAVO
2.0000 g., Copper Plated Steel, 15 mm. **Obv:** Bank logo, date **Obv. Legend:** BANCO DE MOÇAMBIQUE **Rev:** Rhinoceros standing left, value **Edge:** Plain

Date	Mintage	F	VF	XF	Unc	BU
2006	—	—	—	—	0.15	0.25

KM# 133 5 CENTAVOS
2.3000 g., Copper Plated Steel, 19 mm. **Obv:** Bank logo, date **Obv. Legend:** BANCO DE MOÇAMBIQUE **Rev:** Cheetah standing left, value **Edge:** Reeded

Date	Mintage	F	VF	XF	Unc	BU
2006	—	—	—	0.10	0.25	0.35

KM# 134 10 CENTAVOS
3.0600 g., Brass Plated Steel, 17 mm. **Obv:** Bank logo, date **Obv. Legend:** BANCO DE MOÇAMBIQUE **Rev:** Farmer cultivating with tractor, value **Edge:** Reeded

Date	Mintage	F	VF	XF	Unc	BU
2006	—	—	—	0.15	0.35	0.50

KM# 135 20 CENTAVOS
4.1000 g., Brass Plated Steel, 20 mm. **Obv:** Bank logo, date **Obv. Legend:** BANCO DE MOÇAMBIQUE **Rev:** Cotton plant, value **Edge:** Reeded

Date	Mintage	F	VF	XF	Unc	BU
2006	—	—	—	0.20	0.50	0.75

KM# 136 50 CENTAVOS
5.7400 g., Brass Plated Steel, 23 mm. **Obv:** Bank logo, date **Obv. Legend:** BANCO DE MOÇAMBIQUE **Rev:** Giant Kingfisher perched on branch, value **Edge:** Reeded

Date	Mintage	F	VF	XF	Unc	BU
2006	—	—	—	0.50	1.25	1.75

KM# 137 METICAL
5.3000 g., Nickel Plated Steel, 21 mm. **Obv:** Bank logo, date **Obv. Legend:** BANCO DE MOÇAMBIQUE **Rev:** Young woman seated left writing, value **Edge:** Plain **Shape:** 7-sided

Date	Mintage	F	VF	XF	Unc	BU
2006	—	—	—	0.45	1.10	1.50

KM# 138 2 METICAIS
6.0000 g., Nickel Plated Steel, 24 mm. **Obv:** Bank logo, date **Obv. Legend:** BANCO DE MOÇAMBIQUE **Rev:** Coelacanth fish, value **Edge:** Segmented reeding

Date	Mintage	F	VF	XF	Unc	BU
2006	—	—	—	0.75	1.80	2.50

KM# 139 5 METICAIS
6.5000 g., Nickel Plated Steel, 27 mm. **Obv:** Bank logo, date **Obv. Legend:** BANCO DE MOÇAMBIQUE **Rev:** Timbila (similar to a xylophone), value **Edge:** Reeded

Date	Mintage	F	VF	XF	Unc	BU
2006	—	—	—	1.20	3.00	4.00

KM# 140 10 METICAIS
7.5000 g., Bi-Metallic Nickel Clad Steel center in Brass ring., 25 mm. **Obv:** Bank logo **Obv. Legend:** BANCO•DE•MOCAMBIQUE **Rev:** Modern bank building, value below **Edge:** Reeded

Date	Mintage	F	VF	XF	Unc	BU
2006	—	—	—	1.50	3.75	5.00

NAGORNO-KARABAKH

Nagorno-Karabakh, an ethnically Armenian enclave inside Azerbaijan (pop., 1991 est.: 193,000), SW region. It occupies an area of 1,700 sq mi (4,400 square km) on the NE flank of the Kara-bakh Mountain Range, with the capital city of Stepanakert.

Russia annexed the area from Persia in 1813, and in 1923 it was established as an autonomous province of the Azerbaijan S.S.R. In 1988 the region's ethnic Armenian majority demonstrated against Azerbaijani rule, and in 1991, after the breakup of the U.S.S.R. brought independence to Armenia and Azerbaijan, war broke out between the two ethnic groups. On January 8, 1992 the leaders of Nagorno-Karabakh declared independence as the Republic of Mountainous Karabakh (RMK). Since 1994, following a cease-fire, ethnic Armenians have held Karabakh, though officially it remains part of Azerbaijan. Karabakh remains sovereign, but the political and military condition is volatile and tensions frequently flare into skirmishes.

Its marvelous nature and geographic situation, have all facilitated Karabakh to be a center of science, poetry and, especially, of the musical culture of Azerbaijan.

MONETARY SYSTEM
100 Luma = 1 Dram

REPUBLIC

STANDARD COINAGE

KM# 6 50 LUMA
0.9500 g., Aluminum, 19.8 mm. **Obv:** National arms **Rev:** Horse cantering left **Edge:** Plain

Date	Mintage	F	VF	XF	Unc	BU
2004	—	—	—	—	1.00	1.25

KM# 7 50 LUMA
0.9500 g., Aluminum, 19.8 mm. **Obv:** National arms **Rev:** Gazelle **Edge:** Plain

Date	Mintage	F	VF	XF	Unc	BU
2004	—	—	—	—	1.00	1.25

KM# 8 DRAM
1.1300 g., Aluminum, 21.7 mm. **Obv:** National arms **Rev:** Pheasant **Edge:** Plain

Date	Mintage	F	VF	XF	Unc	BU
2004	—	—	—	—	1.00	1.25

KM# 9 DRAM
1.1200 g., Aluminum, 21.7 mm. **Obv:** National arms **Rev:** 1/2-length Saint facing **Edge:** Plain

Date	Mintage	F	VF	XF	Unc	BU
2004	—	—	—	—	1.25	1.50

KM# 10 DRAM
1.1300 g., Aluminum, 21.7 mm. **Obv:** National arms **Rev:** Cheetah facing **Edge:** Plain

Date	Mintage	F	VF	XF	Unc	BU
2004	—	—	—	—	1.00	1.25

KM# 11 5 DRAMS
4.4000 g., Brass, 21.8 mm. **Obv:** National arms **Rev:** Church **Edge:** Plain

Date	Mintage	F	VF	XF	Unc	BU
2004	—	—	—	—	1.25	1.50

KM# 12 5 DRAMS
4.5000 g., Brass, 21.8 mm. **Obv:** National arms **Rev:** Monument faces **Edge:** Plain

Date	Mintage	F	VF	XF	Unc	BU
2004	—	—	—	—	1.00	1.25

KM# 23 1000 DRAMS
31.4300 g., 0.9990 Silver 1.0094 oz. ASW, 38.9 mm. **Obv:** National arms **Rev:** Archer **Edge:** Plain

Date	Mintage	F	VF	XF	Unc	BU
2003 Proof	—	Value: 75.00				

KM# 24 1000 DRAMS
31.3300 g., 0.9990 Silver 1.0062 oz. ASW, 38.39 mm. **Series:** Armenian architectural sculpture **Obv:** National arms **Rev:** Church of the Holy Cross at Aghthamar, Turkey **Edge:** Plain

Date	Mintage	F	VF	XF	Unc	BU
2003 Proof	—	Value: 75.00				

KM# 25 1000 DRAMS
31.3000 g., 0.9990 Silver 1.0053 oz. ASW, 38.92 mm. **Obv:** National arms **Rev:** Bust of Kevork Chavoush 3/4 left **Edge:** Plain

Date	Mintage	F	VF	XF	Unc	BU
2004 Proof	—	Value: 75.00				

KM# 19 1000 DRAMS
31.3700 g., 0.9990 Silver 1.0075 oz. ASW, 38.9 mm. **Obv:** National arms **Rev:** Leopard head facing **Edge:** Plain

Date	Mintage	F	VF	XF	Unc	BU
2004 Proof	—	Value: 75.00				

KM# 19a 1000 DRAMS
31.3700 g., 0.9990 Silver Gilt 1.0075 oz. ASW, 38.9 mm. **Obv:** National arms **Rev:** Leopard head facing **Edge:** Plain

Date	Mintage	F	VF	XF	Unc	BU
2004 Proof	—	Value: 75.00				

KM# 20 1000 DRAMS
31.3700 g., 0.9990 Silver 1.0075 oz. ASW, 38.9 mm. **Obv:** National arms **Rev:** Standing Brown Bear **Edge:** Plain

Date	Mintage	F	VF	XF	Unc	BU
2004 Proof	—	Value: 75.00				

KM# 20a 1000 DRAMS
31.3700 g., 0.9990 Silver Gilt 1.0075 oz. ASW, 38.9 mm. **Obv:** National arms **Rev:** Standing Brown Bear **Edge:** Plain

Date	Mintage	F	VF	XF	Unc	BU
2004 Proof	—	Value: 85.00				

KM# 21 1000 DRAMS
31.3700 g., 0.9990 Silver 1.0075 oz. ASW, 38.9 mm. **Obv:** National arms **Rev:** Eagle head within circle **Edge:** Plain

Date	Mintage	F	VF	XF	Unc	BU
2004 Proof	—	Value: 75.00				

KM# 21a 1000 DRAMS
31.3700 g., 0.9990 Silver Gilt 1.0075 oz. ASW, 38.9 mm. **Obv:** National arms **Rev:** Eagle head within circle **Edge:** Plain

Date	Mintage	F	VF	XF	Unc	BU
2004 Proof	—	Value: 85.00				

KM# 22 1000 DRAMS
31.1200 g., 0.9990 Silver 0.9995 oz. ASW, 38.9 mm. **Obv:** National arms **Rev:** 1918 Genocide Victims Monument **Edge:** Plain

Date	Mintage	F	VF	XF	Unc	BU
2004 Proof	—	Value: 65.00				

NAMIBIA

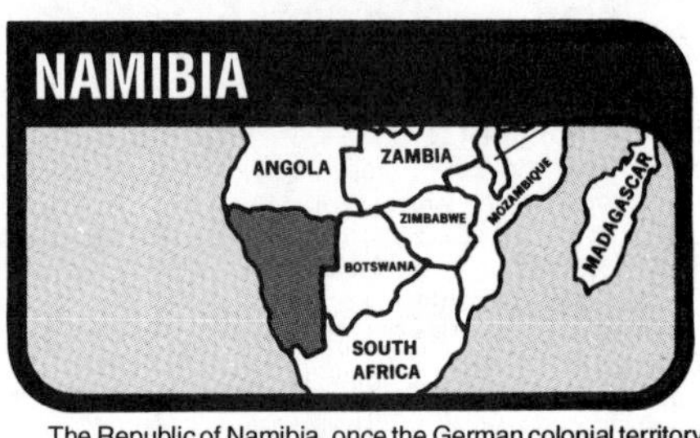

The Republic of Namibia, once the German colonial territory of German South West Africa, and later South West Africa, is situated on the Atlantic coast of southern Africa, bounded on the north by Angola, on the east by Botswana, and on the south by South Africa. It has an area of 318,261 sq. mi. (824,290 sq. km.) and a population of *1.4 million. Capital: Windhoek. Diamonds, copper, lead, zinc, and cattle are exported.

On June 17, 1985 the Transitional Government of National Unity was installed. Negotiations were held in 1988 between Angola, Cuba, and South Africa reaching a peaceful settlement on Aug. 5, 1988. By April 1989 Cuban troops were to withdraw from Angola and South African troops from Namibia. The Transitional Government resigned on Feb. 28, 1988 for the upcoming elections of the constituent assembly in Nov. 1989. Independence was finally achieved on March 12, 1990 within the Commonwealth of Nations. The President is the Head of State; the Prime Minister is Head of Government.

MONETARY SYSTEM
100 Cents = 1 Namibia Dollar

REPUBLIC

DECIMAL COINAGE

KM# 1 5 CENTS
2.2000 g., Nickel Plated Steel, 17 mm. **Obv:** National arms **Rev:** Value left, aloe plant within 3/4 sun design

Date	Mintage	F	VF	XF	Unc	BU
2002	—	—	—	0.20	0.50	0.75
2007	—	—	—	0.20	0.50	0.75
2009	—	—	—	0.20	0.50	0.75

KM# 2 10 CENTS
3.4000 g., Nickel Plated Steel, 21.5 mm. **Obv:** National arms **Rev:** Camelthorn tree right, partial sun design left, value below

Date	Mintage	F	VF	XF	Unc	BU
2002	—	—	—	0.35	1.00	1.25
2009	—	—	—	0.35	1.00	1.25

KM# 3 50 CENTS
4.4300 g., Nickel Plated Steel, 24 mm. **Obv:** National arms **Rev:** Quiver tree right, partial sun design upper left, value below

Date	Mintage	F	VF	XF	Unc	BU
2008	—	—	—	—	1.75	2.00
2010	—	—	—	—	1.75	2.00

KM# 4 DOLLAR
5.0000 g., Brass, 22.4 mm. **Obv:** National arms **Rev:** Value divides Bateleur eagle at right, partial sun design at left

Date	Mintage	F	VF	XF	Unc	BU
2002	—	—	—	1.25	3.50	6.00
2006	—	—	—	1.25	3.50	6.00
2008	—	—	—	1.25	3.50	6.00
2010	—	—	—	1.25	3.50	6.00

KM# 21 10 DOLLARS
Bi-Metallic Aluminum-Bronze center in Copper-Nickel ring, 30 mm. **Subject:** Bank of Namibia, 20th Anniversary **Obv:** National arms **Rev:** Dr. Sam Nujoma bust facing **Edge:** Segmented reeding

Date	Mintage	F	VF	XF	Unc	BU
2010	—	—	—	—	—	7.50

NAURU

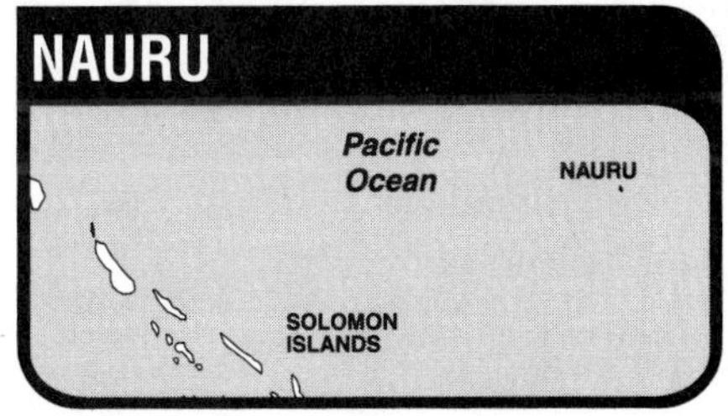

The Republic of Nauru, formerly Pleasant Island, is an island republic in the western Pacific Ocean west of the Gilbert Islands. It has an area of 8-1/2 sq. mi. and a population of 7,254. It is known for its phosphate deposits. Nauru is a special member of the Commonwealth of Nations.

RULER
British, until 1968

MONETARY SYSTEM
100 Cents = 1 (Australian) Dollar

REPUBLIC

DECIMAL COINAGE

KM# 38 DOLLAR
27.0000 g., Silver Plated Copper, 38.6 mm. **Subject:** Guardian Angel **Obv:** Arms **Rev:** Angel standing, swarovski crystals in hair

Date	Mintage	F	VF	XF	Unc	BU
2009 Proof	10,000	Value: 60.00				

KM# 45 5 DOLLARS
Silver, 39 mm. **Subject:** Elizabeth II and Prince Philip, 60th Wedding Anniversary **Obv:** National arms **Rev:** Wedding portraits

Date	Mintage	F	VF	XF	Unc	BU
2007 Proof	—	Value: 40.00				

KM# 46 5 DOLLARS
Silver, 39 mm. **Subject:** Elizabeth II and Prince Philip, 60th Wedding anniversary **Obv:** National arms **Rev:** Engagement photo

Date	Mintage	F	VF	XF	Unc	BU
2007 Proof	—	Value: 40.00				

KM# 36 5 DOLLARS
0.5000 g., 0.9990 Gold 0.0161 oz. AGW, 11 mm. **Subject:** Kaiser Wilhelm **Obv:** Arms **Rev:** Bust right

Date	Mintage	F	VF	XF	Unc	BU
2008 Proof	—	Value: 65.00				

KM# 37 5 DOLLARS
0.5000 g., 0.9990 Gold 0.0161 oz. AGW, 11 mm. **Subject:** Christmas **Obv:** Arms **Rev:** Bells ringing

Date	Mintage	F	VF	XF	Unc	BU
2008 Proof	—	Value: 65.00				

KM# 80 5 DOLLARS
28.2800 g., 0.9250 Silver 0.8410 oz. ASW, 38.61 mm. **Subject:** Royal Air Force, 90th Anniversary **Rev:** De Havilland Tiger Moth and Avro Anson

Date	Mintage	F	VF	XF	Unc	BU
2008 Proof	—	Value: 60.00				

KM# 39 5 DOLLARS
0.5000 g., 0.9990 Gold 0.0161 oz. AGW **Issuer:** 11 **Subject:** Christmas **Obv:** Arms **Rev:** Teddy bear seated

Date	Mintage	F	VF	XF	Unc	BU
2009 Proof	—	Value: 60.00				

KM# 84 5 DOLLARS
0.5000 g., 0.9990 Gold 0.0161 oz. AGW, 11 mm. **Subject:** Investor coins of the World - Vreneli

Date	Mintage	F	VF	XF	Unc	BU
2010 Proof	Est. 10,000	Value: 35.00				

KM# 85 5 DOLLARS
0.5000 g., 0.9990 Gold 0.0161 oz. AGW, 11 mm. **Subject:** Investor gold coins of the world - Franz Joseph I

Date	Mintage	F	VF	XF	Unc	BU
2010 Proof	Est. 10,000	Value: 35.00				

KM# 86 5 DOLLARS
0.5000 g., 0.9990 Gold 0.0161 oz. AGW, 11 mm. **Subject:** Investor coins of the World - French rooster

Date	Mintage	F	VF	XF	Unc	BU
2010 Proof	Est. 5,000	Value: 35.00				

KM# 18 10 DOLLARS
31.1000 g., 0.9990 Silver 0.9988 oz. ASW **Subject:** Discontinuation of the German Mark **Obv:** National arms **Obv. Legend:** BANK OF NAURU

Date	Mintage	F	VF	XF	Unc	BU
2001 Proof	—	Value: 150				

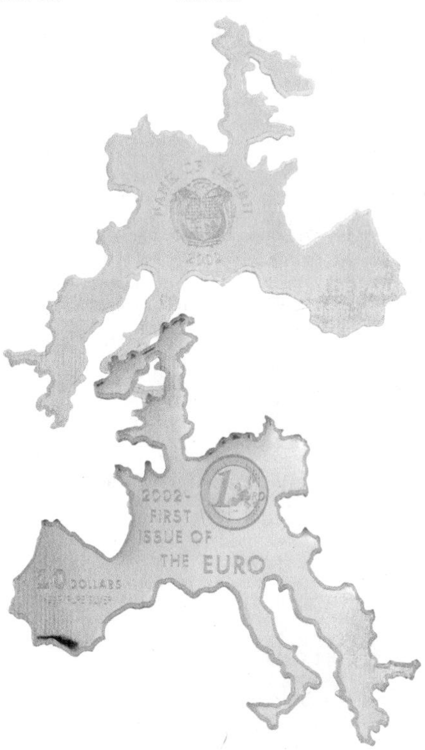

KM# 13 10 DOLLARS
31.2500 g., 0.9990 Silver 71.5 x 72 1.0037 oz. ASW, 72 mm. **Subject:** First Euro Coinage **Obv:** National arms, matte finish **Rev:** Denomination, inscription and partially gold-plated 1 Euro reverse coin design, Proof finish **Edge:** Plain **Shape:** Like a map

Date	Mintage	F	VF	XF	Unc	BU
2002 Proof	—	Value: 150				

KM# 15 10 DOLLARS
31.1000 g., 0.9990 Silver 0.9988 oz. ASW, 40 mm. **Series:** Save the Whales **Obv:** National arms **Obv. Legend:** BANK OF NAURU **Rev:** Blue Whale on mother-of-pearl insert **Edge:** Plain

Date	Mintage	F	VF	XF	Unc	BU
2002 Proof	2,000	Value: 95.00				

KM# 14 10 DOLLARS
34.6000 g., 0.9250 Silver with gold plated or gold attachment 1.0289 oz. ASW, 38.5 mm. **Subject:** Brandenburg Gate **Obv:** National arms **Rev:** Brandenburg Gate **Edge:** Plain **Note:** Gold color 1mm thick

Date	Mintage	F	VF	XF	Unc	BU
2002 Proof/Matte	—	Value: 150				

KM# 50 10 DOLLARS
31.1050 g., 0.9990 Silver 0.9990 oz. ASW, 40 mm. **Rev:** Coloseum in color

Date	Mintage	F	VF	XF	Unc	BU
2002 Proof	2,001	Value: 80.00				

KM# 51 10 DOLLARS
22.2200 g., 0.9990 Silver 0.7136 oz. ASW, 35x45 mm. **Subject:** Indroduction of Euro **Shape:** Irregular

Date	Mintage	F	VF	XF	Unc	BU
2002 Proof	2,500	Value: 55.00				

KM# 19 10 DOLLARS
31.1000 g., 0.9990 Silver 0.9988 oz. ASW **Subject:** European Union - Mark and Euro **Obv:** National arms **Obv. Legend:** BANK OF NAURU

Date	Mintage	F	VF	XF	Unc	BU
2003 Proof	5,000	Value: 100				

KM# 20 10 DOLLARS
1.2400 g., 0.9990 Gold 0.0398 oz. AGW, 13.92 mm. **Subject:** First Anniversary of the Euro **Obv:** National arms **Obv. Legend:** BANK OF NAURU **Rev:** Euro symbol **Edge:** Reeded

Date	Mintage	F	VF	XF	Unc	BU
2003 Proof	—	Value: 85.00				

KM# 21 10 DOLLARS
1.2400 g., 0.9990 Gold 0.0398 oz. AGW **Subject:** Treasure of Priamos in Troja **Obv:** National arms **Obv. Legend:** BANK OF NAURU

Date	Mintage	F	VF	XF	Unc	BU
2003 Proof	—	Value: 95.00				

KM# 22 10 DOLLARS
1.2400 g., 0.9990 Gold 0.0398 oz. AGW **Subject:** Treasure of Nibelungen **Obv:** National arms **Obv. Legend:** BANK OF NAURU

Date	Mintage	F	VF	XF	Unc	BU
2003 Proof	—	Value: 95.00				

KM# 23 10 DOLLARS
30.9500 g., Silver With removable gold or gilt 2.6g Reichstag building attachment with 2004/ NAURU 0077 on reverse **Subject:** European Monuments **Obv:** National arms **Obv. Legend:** BANK OF NAURU **Rev. Legend:** GERMANY - DEUTSCHER REICHSTAG **Edge:** Plain

Date	Mintage	F	VF	XF	Unc	BU
2003 Proof/Matte	—	Value: 150				

KM# 52 10 DOLLARS
31.1000 g., 0.9250 Silver 0.9249 oz. ASW, 38.61 mm. **Subject:** Euro, 1st Anniversary **Rev:** Euro currency symbol

Date	Mintage	F	VF	XF	Unc	BU
2003	5,000	Value: 70.00				

KM# 53 10 DOLLARS
31.1000 g., 0.9250 Silver 0.9249 oz. ASW, 38.61 mm. **Rev:** St. Peter's Basilica

Date	Mintage	F	VF	XF	Unc	BU
2003	Est. 7,500	—	—	—	—	80.00

KM# 54 10 DOLLARS
31.1000 g., 0.9250 Silver 0.9249 oz. ASW, 38.61 mm. **Rev:** Church in Dresden

Date	Mintage	F	VF	XF	Unc	BU
2004	—	—	—	—	—	80.00

KM# 55 10 DOLLARS
31.1000 g., 0.9990 Silver 0.9988 oz. ASW, 38.61 mm. **Rev:** Colesum in Rome

Date	Mintage	F	VF	XF	Unc	BU
2004	7,500	—	—	—	—	80.00

KM# 56 10 DOLLARS
31.1000 g., 0.9250 Silver 0.9249 oz. ASW, 38.61 mm. **Rev:** Royal Palace in Monaco

Date	Mintage	F	VF	XF	Unc	BU
2004	7,500	—	—	—	—	80.00

KM# 24 10 DOLLARS
Silver With removable gold or gilt attachment **Series:** European Monuments **Subject:** Palazzo Pubblico in San Marino **Obv:** National arms **Obv. Legend:** BANK OF NAURU **Edge:** Plain

Date	Mintage	F	VF	XF	Unc	BU
2005 Proof/Matte	—	Value: 150				

KM# 25 10 DOLLARS
1.2400 g., 0.9990 Gold 0.0398 oz. AGW **Subject:** East Gothic stylized eagle broach from Domagnano, Italy in National Museum in Nuremburg **Obv:** National arms **Obv. Legend:** BANK OF NAURU

Date	Mintage	F	VF	XF	Unc	BU
2005 Proof	25,000	Value: 95.00				

KM# 35 10 DOLLARS
31.1050 g., 0.9990 Silver 0.9990 oz. ASW **Subject:** German Railways, 150th Anniversary **Obv:** National Arms **Rev:** Baureihi "01"

Date	Mintage	F	VF	XF	Unc	BU
2005 Proof	—	Value: 60.00				

KM# 40 10 DOLLARS
1.2400 g., 0.9990 Gold 0.0398 oz. AGW, 13.92 mm. **Obv:** National Arms **Rev:** Ludwig Erhard

Date	Mintage	F	VF	XF	Unc	BU
2005 Proof	—	Value: 95.00				

KM# 26 10 DOLLARS
1.2400 g., 0.9990 Gold 0.0398 oz. AGW **Subject:** Angela Dorothea Merkel, Chancellor of Germany **Obv:** National arms **Obv. Legend:** BANK OF NAURU

Date	Mintage	F	VF	XF	Unc	BU
2005 Proof	—	Value: 95.00				

KM# 41 10 DOLLARS
31.1000 g., 0.9990 Silver 0.9988 oz. ASW, 38.61 mm. **Rev:** Tower Bridge, gilt

Date	Mintage	F	VF	XF	Unc	BU
2005	2,000	Value: 200				

KM# 43 10 DOLLARS
31.1050 g., 0.9990 Silver 0.9990 oz. ASW, 38.6 mm. **Rev:** St. Stephens Church, Vienna partially gilt

Date	Mintage	F	VF	XF	Unc	BU
2005 Proof	2,000	Value: 50.00				

KM# 57 10 DOLLARS
31.1000 g., 0.9250 Silver 0.9249 oz. ASW, 38.61 mm. **Rev:** St. Basil's Cathedral, Moscow

Date	Mintage	F	VF	XF	Unc	BU
2005 Proof	7,500	—	—	—	—	80.00

KM# 58 10 DOLLARS
1.2400 g., 0.9990 Gold 0.0398 oz. AGW, 13.92 mm. **Subject:** Konrad Adenauer

Date	Mintage	F	VF	XF	Unc	BU
2005 Proof	—	Value: 90.00				

KM# 59 10 DOLLARS
1.2400 g., 0.9990 Gold 0.0398 oz. AGW, 13.92 mm. **Subject:** Kurt Georg Kiesinger

Date	Mintage	F	VF	XF	Unc	BU
2005 Proof	—	Value: 90.00				

KM# 60 10 DOLLARS
1.2400 g., 0.9990 Gold 0.0398 oz. AGW, 13.92 mm. **Subject:** Willy Brandt

Date	Mintage	F	VF	XF	Unc	BU
2005 Proof	—	Value: 90.00				

KM# 61 10 DOLLARS
1.2400 g., 0.9990 Gold 0.0398 oz. AGW, 13.92 mm. **Subject:** Helmut Schmidt

Date	Mintage	F	VF	XF	Unc	BU
2005 Proof	—	Value: 90.00				

KM# 62 10 DOLLARS
1.2400 g., 0.9990 Gold 0.0398 oz. AGW, 13.92 mm. **Subject:** Helmut Kohl

Date	Mintage	F	VF	XF	Unc	BU
2005 Proof	—	Value: 90.00				

KM# 63 10 DOLLARS
1.2400 g., 0.9990 Gold 0.0398 oz. AGW, 13.92 mm. **Subject:** Gerhard Schröder

Date	Mintage	F	VF	XF	Unc	BU
2005 Proof	—	Value: 90.00				

KM# 27 10 DOLLARS
1.2400 g., 0.9990 Gold 0.0398 oz. AGW **Subject:** Konrad Adenauer at 1949 demonstration **Obv:** National arms **Obv. Legend:** BANK OF NAURU

Date	Mintage	F	VF	XF	Unc	BU
2006 Proof	15,000	Value: 95.00				

KM# 28 10 DOLLARS
1.2400 g., 0.9990 Gold 0.0398 oz. AGW **Subject:** Volkswagen **Obv:** National arms **Obv. Legend:** BANK OF NAURU

Date	Mintage	F	VF	XF	Unc	BU
2006 Proof	—	Value: 95.00				

KM# 29 10 DOLLARS
1.2400 g., 0.9990 Gold 0.0398 oz. AGW **Subject:** Conrad Schumann in Berlin 1961 **Obv:** National arms **Obv. Legend:** BANK OF NAURU

Date	Mintage	F	VF	XF	Unc	BU
2006 Proof	—	Value: 95.00				

KM# 30 10 DOLLARS
1.2400 g., 0.9990 Gold 0.0398 oz. AGW **Subject:** Olympic Stadium in Munich 1972 **Obv:** National arms **Obv. Legend:** BANK OF NAURU

Date	Mintage	F	VF	XF	Unc	BU
2006 Proof	—	Value: 95.00				

KM# 31 10 DOLLARS
1.2400 g., 0.9990 Gold 0.0398 oz. AGW **Subject:** Independent Activists 1980 **Obv:** National arms **Obv. Legend:** BANK OF NAURU

Date	Mintage	F	VF	XF	Unc	BU
2006 Proof	—	Value: 95.00				

KM# 32 10 DOLLARS
1.2400 g., 0.9990 Gold 0.0398 oz. AGW **Subject:** Brandenburg Gate in Berlin 1990 **Obv. Legend:** BANK OF NAURU

Date	Mintage	F	VF	XF	Unc	BU
2006 Proof	—	Value: 95.00				

KM# 33 10 DOLLARS
1.2400 g., 0.9990 Gold 0.0398 oz. AGW **Subject:** European Union 2002 **Obv:** National arms **Obv. Legend:** BANK OF NAURU

Date	Mintage	F	VF	XF	Unc	BU
2006 Proof	—	Value: 95.00				

KM# 34 10 DOLLARS
1.2400 g., 0.9990 Gold 0.0398 oz. AGW **Subject:** Johannes Rau, German President, 1999-2004 **Obv:** National arms **Obv. Legend:** BANK OF NAURU

Date	Mintage	F	VF	XF	Unc	BU
2006 Proof	—	Value: 95.00				

KM# 42 10 DOLLARS
31.1000 g., 0.9990 Silver 0.9988 oz. ASW, 38.61 mm. **Rev:** Tower of Pisa, gilt

Date	Mintage	F	VF	XF	Unc	BU
2006 Proof	2,000	Value: 200				

KM# 64 10 DOLLARS
1.2400 g., 0.9990 Gold 0.0398 oz. AGW, 13.92 mm. **Subject:** Theodor Heuss

Date	Mintage	F	VF	XF	Unc	BU
2006 Proof	Est. 10,000	Value: 90.00				

KM# 65 10 DOLLARS
1.2400 g., 0.9990 Gold 0.0398 oz. AGW, 13.92 mm. **Subject:** Heinrich Lübke

Date	Mintage	F	VF	XF	Unc	BU
2006 Proof	Est. 10,000	Value: 90.00				

KM# 66 10 DOLLARS
1.2400 g., 0.9990 Gold 0.0398 oz. AGW, 13.92 mm. **Subject:** Gustav Heinemann

Date	Mintage	F	VF	XF	Unc	BU
2006 Proof	Est. 10,000	Value: 90.00				

KM# 67 10 DOLLARS
1.2400 g., 0.9990 Gold 0.0398 oz. AGW, 13.92 mm. **Subject:** Walter Scheel

Date	Mintage	F	VF	XF	Unc	BU
2006 Proof	2,006	Value: 90.00				

KM# 68 10 DOLLARS
1.2400 g., 0.9990 Gold 0.0398 oz. AGW, 13.92 mm. **Subject:** Karl Carstens

Date	Mintage	F	VF	XF	Unc	BU
2006 Proof	Est. 10,000	Value: 90.00				

KM# 69 10 DOLLARS
1.2400 g., 0.9990 Gold 0.0398 oz. AGW, 13.92 mm. **Subject:** Richard Freiherr von Weizsäcker

Date	Mintage	F	VF	XF	Unc	BU
2006 Proof	Est. 10,000	Value: 90.00				

KM# 70 10 DOLLARS
1.2400 g., 0.9990 Gold 0.0398 oz. AGW, 13.92 mm. **Subject:** Roman Herzog

Date	Mintage	F	VF	XF	Unc	BU
2006 Proof	Est. 10,000	Value: 90.00				

KM# 71 10 DOLLARS
1.2400 g., 0.9990 Gold 0.0398 oz. AGW, 13.92 mm. **Subject:** Horst Köhler

Date	Mintage	F	VF	XF	Unc	BU
2006 Proof	Est. 10,000	Value: 90.00				

KM# 72 10 DOLLARS
31.1050 g., 0.9250 Silver 0.9250 oz. ASW, 38.61 mm. **Rev:** Cathedral Santiago de Compostela

Date	Mintage	F	VF	XF	Unc	BU
2006	Est. 5,000	—	—	—	—	70.00

KM# 73 10 DOLLARS
31.1050 g., 0.9250 Silver 0.9250 oz. ASW, 38.61 mm. **Rev:** Mt. St. Michel

Date	Mintage	F	VF	XF	Unc	BU
2006	Est. 5,000	—	—	—	—	70.00

KM# 74 10 DOLLARS
31.1050 g., 0.9250 Silver 0.9250 oz. ASW, 38.61 mm. **Rev:** Axon in Brussels

Date	Mintage	F	VF	XF	Unc	BU
2006	Est. 5,000	—	—	—	—	70.00

KM# 75 10 DOLLARS
28.2800 g., 0.9250 Silver 0.8410 oz. ASW, 38.61 mm. **Subject:** World Cup Football **Rev:** Brandenburg Gate

Date	Mintage	F	VF	XF	Unc	BU
2007 Proof	—	Value: 55.00				

KM# 76 10 DOLLARS
1.2400 g., 0.9990 Gold 0.0398 oz. AGW, 13.92 mm. **Rev:** Micronesia

Date	Mintage	F	VF	XF	Unc	BU
2007 Proof	—	Value: 80.00				

KM# 77 10 DOLLARS
28.2800 g., 0.9250 Silver 0.8410 oz. ASW, 38.61 mm. **Subject:** Sylt to Hamburg Steam Train

Date	Mintage	F	VF	XF	Unc	BU
2007 Proof	Est. 5,000	Value: 70.00				

KM# 79 10 DOLLARS
28.2800 g., 0.9250 Silver 0.8410 oz. ASW, 38.61 mm. **Rev:** Suspended subway

Date	Mintage	F	VF	XF	Unc	BU
2008 Proof	—	Value: 70.00				

KM# 81 10 DOLLARS
31.1000 g., 0.9990 Silver 0.9988 oz. ASW, 38.61 mm. **Rev:** Santa Claus in color

Date	Mintage	F	VF	XF	Unc	BU
2008	Est. 15,000	—	—	—	—	70.00

KM# 82 10 DOLLARS
0.9250 Silver **Subject:** Worldcup Soccer in South Africa

Date	Mintage	F	VF	XF	Unc	BU
2009 Proof	Est. 10,000	Value: 60.00				

KM# 83 10 DOLLARS
1.0000 g., 0.9990 Gold 0.0321 oz. AGW, 13.92 mm. **Subject:** World Cup Soccer in South Africa **Rev:** Mascott leopard Zakumi

Date	Mintage	F	VF	XF	Unc	BU
2009 Proof	Est. 5,000	Value: 70.00				

KM# 87 10 DOLLARS
28.2800 g., 0.9250 Silver 0.8410 oz. ASW, 38.61 mm. **Rev:** German Railways Locomotive 18201

Date	Mintage	F	VF	XF	Unc	BU
2010 Proof	Est. 5,000	Value: 70.00				

KM# 88 10 DOLLARS
0.9250 Silver, 34 mm. **Rev:** Leipzig-Dresden Railway's locomotive Saxonia

Date	Mintage	F	VF	XF	Unc	BU
2010 Proof	Est. 10,000	Value: 40.00				

KM# 47 10 DOLLARS
Silver, 39 mm. **Subject:** WWII AZNAC troops **Obv:** Head in tiaria right, National arms at right **Rev:** Flag and Bugler

Date	Mintage	F	VF	XF	Unc	BU
2011 Proof	—	Value: 40.00				

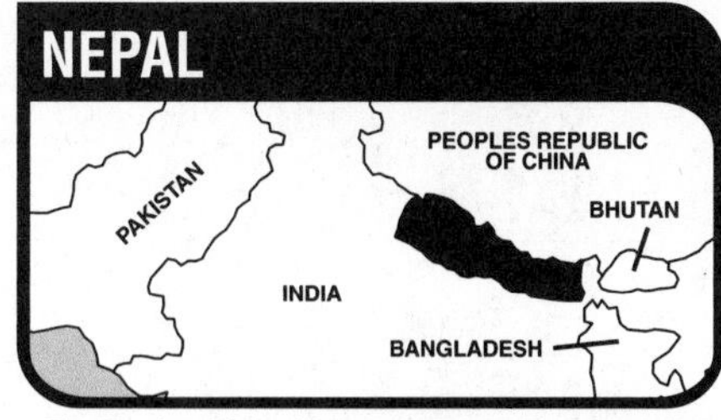

The Kingdom of Nepal, the world's only surviving Hindu kingdom, is a landlocked country occupying the southern slopes of the Himalayas. It has an area of 56,136 sq. mi. (140,800 sq. km.) and a population of 18 million. Capital: Kathmandu. Nepal has deposits of coal, copper, iron and cobalt, but they are largely unexploited. Agriculture is the principal economic activity. Rice, timber and jute are exported, with tourism being the other major foreign exchange earner.

On June 2, 2001 tragedy struck the royal family when Crown Prince Dipendra used an assault rifle to kill his father, mother and other members of the royal family as the result of a dispute over his current lady friend. He died 48 hours later, as King, from self inflicted gunshot wounds. Gyanendra began his second reign as King (his first was a short time as a toddler, 1950-51).

DATING

Bikram Samvat Era (VS)

From 1888AD most copper coins were dated in the Bikram Samvat (VS) era. To convert take VS date - 57 =AD date. Coins with this era have VS before the year in the listing. Tthis era is used for all coins struck in Nepal since 1911AD.

RULER

SHAH DYNASTY

ज्ञानेन्द्र वीर विक्रम

Gyanendra Bir Bikram
VS2058-/2001-AD

NUMERALS

Nepal has used more variations of numerals on their coins than any other nation. The most common are illustrated in the numeral chart in the introduction. The chart below illustrates some variations encompassing the last four centuries.

1	2	3	4	5	6	7	8	9	0
१	२	३	४	५	६	७	८	९	०

NUMERICS

One	एक
Two	दुइ
Ten	दस
Twenty-five	पचीस
Fifty	पचास
Hundred	सय

DENOMINATIONS

Rupee	रुपैयाँ

Legend on reverse

श्री श्री श्री गोरषनाथ

Shri Shri Shri Gorakhanatha in 8 petals

KINGDOM

Gyanendra Bir Bikram

VS2058-2064 / 2001- 2007AD

DECIMAL COINAGE

100 Paisa = 1 Rupee

KM# 1173 10 PAISA
Aluminum, 17 mm. **Obv:** Royal crown **Edge:** Plain

Date	Mintage	F	VF	XF	Unc	BU
VS2058 (2001)	—	—	—	—	1.00	1.50

KM# 1148 25 PAISA
Aluminum, 20 mm. **Obv:** Royal crown **Edge:** Plain

Date	Mintage	F	VF	XF	Unc	BU
VS2058 (2001)	—	—	—	—	0.50	0.75
VS2059 (2002)	—	—	—	—	0.50	0.75
VS2060 (2003)	—	—	—	—	0.50	0.75

KM# 1149 50 PAISA
Aluminum, 22.5 mm. **Obv:** Royal crown **Rev:** Swayambhunath **Edge:** Plain

Date	Mintage	F	VF	XF	Unc	BU
VS2058 (2001)	—	—	—	—	0.50	0.75
VS2059 (2002)	—	—	—	—	0.50	0.75

KM# 1179 50 PAISA
1.4100 g., Aluminum, 22.5 mm. **Obv:** Crown above crossed flags **Rev:** Swayambhunath **Edge:** Plain

Date	Mintage	F	VF	XF	Unc	BU
VS2060 (2003)	—	—	—	—	0.40	0.50
VS2061 (2004)	—	—	—	—	0.40	0.50

KM# 1150.2 RUPEE
Brass Plated Steel **Obv:** Traditional design **Rev:** Small (7mm high) temple, small (4mm) "1" **Edge:** Plain **Note:** Magnetic.

Date	Mintage	F	VF	XF	Unc	BU
VS2058 (2001)	—	—	—	—	1.00	1.50
VS2059 (2002)	—	—	—	—	1.00	1.50
VS2060 (2003)	—	—	—	—	1.00	1.50

KM# 1150.1 RUPEE
Brass Plated Steel **Rev:** Large (8.5mm) temple, medium '1' (4.5mm) **Edge:** Reeded **Note:** Non-magnetic.

Date	Mintage	F	VF	XF	Unc	BU
VS2058 (2001)	—	—	—	—	1.00	1.50

KM# 1150.3 RUPEE
3.9600 g., Brass, 20 mm. **Obv:** Traditional design **Rev:** Small (6.5mm high) temple, small (4mm) "1" **Edge:** Plain

Date	Mintage	F	VF	XF	Unc	BU
VS2058 (2001)	—	—	—	—	0.50	0.75

KM# 1150.4 RUPEE
3.9600 g., Brass Plated Steel, 20 mm. **Obv:** Traditional design **Rev:** Small (7mm high) temple, large (4.5mm) "1" **Note:** Magnetic.

Date	Mintage	F	VF	XF	Unc	BU
VS2059 (2002)	—	—	—	—	1.00	1.50
VS2060 (2003)	—	—	—	—	1.00	1.50

KM# 1180 RUPEE
3.9600 g., Brass Plated Steel, 20 mm. **Obv:** Traditional design **Rev:** Wagheshwari Temple **Edge:** Plain **Note:** "1" in denomination of a different style.

Date	Mintage	F	VF	XF	Unc	BU
VS2061 (2004)	—	—	—	—	0.75	1.00

KM# 1181 RUPEE
3.9400 g., Brass Plated Steel, 19.95 mm. **Obv:** Traditional design **Rev:** Sri Talbarahi Temple with outline mountain scene behind **Edge:** Plain

Date	Mintage	F	VF	XF	Unc	BU
VS2062(2005)	—	—	—	0.50	1.20	1.60

KM# 1170 2 RUPEES
4.9400 g., Brass, 25 mm. **Obv:** Traditional square design **Rev:** People with flag celebrating 50 Years of Democracy **Edge:** Plain

Date	Mintage	F	VF	XF	Unc	BU
VS2058(2001)	—	—	—	—	0.50	0.75

KM# 1151.2 2 RUPEES
Brass, 25 mm. **Obv:** Traditional design **Rev:** Three domed building **Edge:** Plain

Date	Mintage	F	VF	XF	Unc	BU
VS2058 (2001)	—	—	—	—	1.50	2.00
VS2059 (2002)	—	—	—	—	1.50	2.00
VS2060 (2003)	—	—	—	—	1.50	2.00

KM# 1151.1 2 RUPEES
5.0700 g., Brass Plated Steel, 25 mm. **Obv:** Traditional design **Rev:** Three domed building **Edge:** Plain **Note:** Edge varieties exist. Prev. KM#1151. Magnetic.

Date	Mintage	F	VF	XF	Unc	BU
VS2060 (2003)	—	—	—	—	1.50	2.00

KM# 1151.1a 2 RUPEES
6.7000 g., Silver, 25 mm. **Obv:** Traditional design **Rev:** Three domed building **Edge:** Plain

Date	Mintage	F	VF	XF	Unc	BU
VS2060(2003)	—	—	—	—	100	—

KM# 1159 25 RUPEE
8.3600 g., Copper-Nickel, 29.1 mm. **Obv:** Crowned bust right **Rev:** Traditional design **Edge:** Plain

Date	Mintage	F	VF	XF	Unc	BU
VS2058 (2001)	—	—	—	—	4.00	5.00
VS2059 (2002)	—	—	—	—	4.00	5.00

KM# 1164 25 RUPEE
8.6000 g., Copper-Nickel, 29.1 mm. **Subject:** Silver Jubilee **Obv:** Traditional design **Rev:** Stylized face design **Edge:** Plain

Date	Mintage	F	VF	XF	Unc	BU
VS2060 (2003)	—	—	—	—	4.00	5.00

KM# 1183 25 RUPEE
8.5500 g., Copper-Nickel, 29.1 mm. **Subject:** World Hindu Federation **Obv:** Traditional design **Edge:** Plain

Date	Mintage	F	VF	XF	Unc	BU
VS2062 (2005)	—	—	—	—	4.00	5.00

KM# 1160 50 RUPEE
20.1000 g., Brass, 37.7 mm. **Subject:** 50th Anniversary of Scouting in Nepal **Obv:** Traditional design **Rev:** Scouting emblem within beaded wreath **Edge:** Plain

Date	Mintage	F	VF	XF	Unc	BU
VS2058 (2001)	—	—	—	—	9.00	10.00

KM# 1182 50 RUPEE
8.6000 g., Copper-Nickel, 29 mm. **Subject:** Golden Jubilee of Supreme Court **Obv:** Traditional design **Rev:** Supreme Court building **Edge:** Plain

Date	Mintage	F	VF	XF	Unc	BU
VS2063 (2006)	—	—	—	—	6.00	9.00

KM# 1157 100 RUPEE
20.0000 g., Brass, 38.7 mm. **Subject:** Buddha **Obv:** Traditional design **Rev:** Seated Buddha teaching five seated monks **Edge:** Reeded

Date	Mintage	F	VF	XF	Unc	BU
VS2058 (2001)	30,000	—	—	—	10.00	12.00

KM# 1161 200 RUPEE
18.1000 g., 0.5000 Silver 0.2910 oz. ASW, 29.6 mm. **Subject:** 50th Anniversary of the Nepal Chamber of Commerce **Obv:** Traditional design **Rev:** Swastika within rotary gear **Edge:** Plain

Date	Mintage	F	VF	XF	Unc	BU
VS2059 (2002)	—	—	—	—	20.00	25.00

KM# 1162 200 RUPEE
18.1000 g., 0.5000 Silver 0.2910 oz. ASW, 29.6 mm. **Subject:** 50th Anniversary of Civil Service **Obv:** Traditional design **Rev:** Crown above flags and value **Edge:** Plain

Date	Mintage	F	VF	XF	Unc	BU
VS2059 (2002)	—	—	—	—	20.00	25.00

KM# 1171 250 RUPEE
18.0000 g., 0.5000 Silver 0.2893 oz. ASW, 29 mm. **Subject:** 2600th Anniversary of Bhagawan Mahavir **Obv:** Traditional design **Rev:** Haloed head above value **Edge:** Plain

Date	Mintage	F	VF	XF	Unc	BU
VS2058 (2001)	—	—	—	—	25.00	30.00

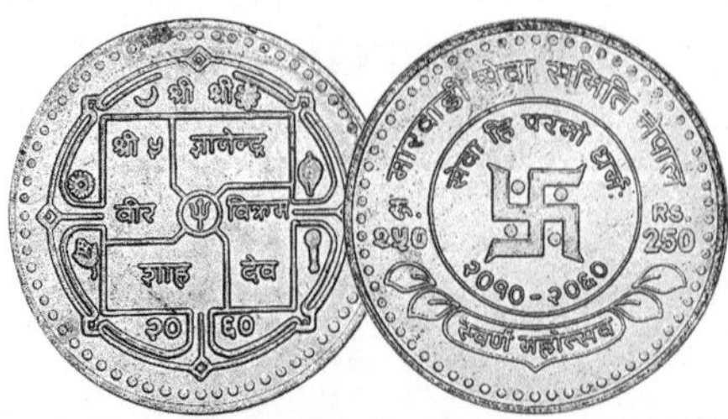

KM# 1176 250 RUPEE
17.8300 g., 0.5000 Silver 0.2866 oz. ASW, 31.6 mm. **Subject:** Marwadi, non-profit making organization **Obv:** Traditional design **Rev:** Swastika within circle **Edge:** Reeded

Date	Mintage	F	VF	XF	Unc	BU
VS2060 (2003)	—	—	—	—	25.00	30.00

KM# 1184 250 RUPEE
18.0000 g., Silver, 32 mm. **Subject:** 400th Anniversary of Guru Granth Sahib **Obv:** Traditional design **Rev:** Holy Book of Sikhs **Edge:** Reeded

Date	Mintage	F	VF	XF	Unc	BU
VS2061 (2004)	—	—	—	—	25.00	30.00

KM# 1174 300 RUPEE
22.5000 g., 0.5000 Silver 0.3617 oz. ASW, 31.8 mm. **Subject:** Economic Growth Through Export **Obv:** Traditional design **Rev:** Two joined hands in front of globe **Edge:** Reeded

Date	Mintage	F	VF	XF	Unc	BU
VS2060 (2003)	—	—	—	—	22.00	28.00

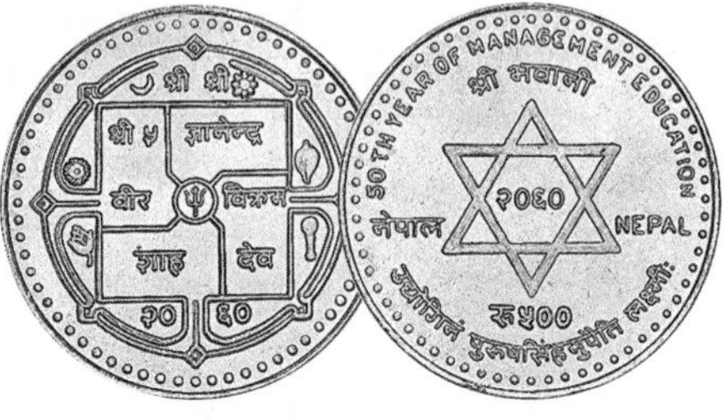

KM# 1177 500 RUPEE
23.0000 g., 0.9000 Silver 0.6655 oz. ASW, 31.7 mm. **Subject:** Management Education 50th Anniversary **Obv:** Traditional design **Rev:** Six point star outline **Edge:** Reeded

Date	Mintage	F	VF	XF	Unc	BU
VS2060 (2003)	—	—	—	—	30.00	35.00

KM# 1163 500 RUPEE
23.3400 g., 0.9000 Silver 0.6753 oz. ASW, 32 mm. **Subject:** 50th Anniversary of the Conquest of Mt. Everest **Obv:** Traditional design **Rev:** Mountain and map above value **Edge:** Reeded

Date	Mintage	F	VF	XF	Unc	BU
VS2060 (2003)	—	—	—	—	30.00	35.00

KM# 1185 500 RUPEE
20.1000 g., Silver, 32 mm. **Subject:** 50th Anniversary of Nepal-United Nations **Obv:** Traditional design **Rev:** Head of the late King Mahendra Bir Birkam **Edge:** Reeded

Date	Mintage	F	VF	XF	Unc	BU
VS2062	—	—	—	—	25.00	30.00

KM# 1175 1000 RUPEE
35.0000 g., Silver, 40 mm. **Subject:** 100 Years - Rotary Club **Edge:** Reeded

Date	Mintage	F	VF	XF	Unc	BU
VS2062 (2005)	—	—	—	—	45.00	50.00

KM# 1178 1000 RUPEE
35.2000 g., 0.5000 Silver 0.5658 oz. ASW, 40 mm. **Subject:** Rastriya Bank 50th Anniversary **Obv:** Traditional square design **Rev:** Bank seal above value **Edge:** Reeded

Date	Mintage	F	VF	XF	Unc	BU
VS2062 (2005)	—	—	—	—	27.00	32.00

KM# 1158 1500 RUPEE
20.0000 g., 0.9250 Silver 0.5948 oz. ASW, 38.7 mm. **Subject:** Buddha **Obv:** Traditional design **Rev:** Seated Buddha teaching five seated monks **Edge:** Reeded

Date	Mintage	F	VF	XF	Unc	BU
VS2058 (2001) Proof	15,000	Value: 35.00				

KM# 1172 2000 RUPEE
31.2000 g., 0.7200 Silver 0.7222 oz. ASW, 40 mm. **Subject:** Gyanendra's Accession to the Throne **Obv:** Crowned bust right **Rev:** Upright sword above value in circular design **Edge:** Reeded

Date	Mintage	F	VF	XF	Unc	BU
VS2058 (2001)	—	—	—	—	40.00	45.00

KM# 1201 2000 RUPEE
31.1050 g., 0.9990 Silver 0.9990 oz. ASW, 40 mm. **Subject:** Conquest of Mt. Everest 50th Anniversary **Rev:** Sir Edmond Hillary and Tenzing Norgay at Summit

Date	Mintage	F	VF	XF	Unc	BU
VS2060 (2003) Proof	8,000	Value: 80.00				

KM# 1191 2000 RUPEE
31.2000 g., 0.9250 Silver 0.9278 oz. ASW, 38.61 mm. **Subject:** 2006 FIFA World Cup - Germany **Obv:** Traditional design

Date	Mintage	F	VF	XF	Unc	BU
VS2063 (2006) (2006)	—	—	—	—	45.00	50.00

ASARFI GOLD COINAGE

(Asarphi)

Fractional designations are approximate for this series. Actual Gold Weight (AGW) is used to identify each type.

KM# 1200 ASARPHI
7.7700 g., 0.9999 Gold 0.2498 oz. AGW, 22 mm. **Subject:** Conquest of Mt. Everest **Rev:** Sir Edward Hillary and Tenzing Norgay at Summit

Date	Mintage	F	VF	XF	Unc	BU
VS2060 (2003)	2,000	—	—	—	800	—

KM# 1153 0.3G ASARPHI
0.3000 g., 0.9999 Gold 0.0096 oz. AGW, 7 mm. **Subject:** Buddha **Obv:** Traditional design **Rev:** Seated Buddha **Edge:** Plain

Date	Mintage	VG	F	VF	XF	BU
VS2058 (2001)	30,000	—	—	—	—	25.00

KM# 1154 1/25-OZ. ASARFI
1.2441 g., 0.9999 Gold 0.0400 oz. AGW, 13.92 mm. **Subject:** Buddha **Obv:** Traditional design **Rev:** Seated Buddha **Edge:** Reeded

Date	Mintage	VG	F	VF	XF	BU
VS2058 (2001)	25,000	—	—	—	—	75.00

KM# 1155 1/10-OZ. ASARFI
3.1104 g., 0.9999 Gold 0.1000 oz. AGW, 17.95 mm. **Subject:** Buddha **Obv:** Traditional design **Rev:** Seated Buddha **Edge:** Reeded

Date	Mintage	VG	F	VF	XF	BU
VS2058 (2001)	15,000	—	—	—	—	185

KM# 1156 1/2-OZ. ASARFI
15.5518 g., 0.9999 Gold 0.4999 oz. AGW, 27 mm. **Subject:** Buddha **Obv:** Traditional design **Rev:** Seated Buddha **Edge:** Reeded

Date	Mintage	VG	F	VF	XF	BU
VS2058 (2001) Proof	2,500	Value: 900				

SECULAR STATE

DECIMAL COINAGE

100 Paisa = 1 Rupee

KM# 1186 25 RUPEE
8.5000 g., Copper-Nickel, 29 mm. **Subject:** 125th Anniversary - First Nepal Postal Stamp Issue **Obv:** Features image of legendary 1 Anna stamp **Rev:** Traditional mailman on the reverse

Date	Mintage	F	VF	XF	Unc	BU
VS2063 (2006)	—	—	—	—	7.00	9.00
VS2064 (2006)	—	—	—	—	7.00	9.00

DEMOCRATIC REPUBLIC

DECIMAL COINAGE

100 Paisa = 1 Rupee

KM# 1204 RUPEE
Brass Plated Steel, 19 mm. **Obv:** Mt. Everest within square **Rev:** Map of Nepal

Date	Mintage	F	VF	XF	Unc	BU
VS2064	—	—	—	—	2.00	3.50

KM# 1188 2 RUPEES
5.0000 g., Brass Plated Steel, 24.93 mm. **Obv:** Mount Everest within square **Rev:** Farmer plowing with water buffalos **Edge:** Plain

Date	Mintage	F	VF	XF	Unc	BU
VS2063(2006)	—	—	—	1.50	2.75	3.50

KM# 1189 50 RUPEE
8.6000 g., Copper-Nickel, 29 mm. **Subject:** 250th Anniversary Hindu festival "Kimari Jatra" **Obv:** Kumari Temple at Durbar Square in Kathmandu **Rev:** Bust of Goddess Kumari facing **Edge:** Plain

Date	Mintage	F	VF	XF	Unc	BU
VS2064 (2006)	—	—	—	—	8.00	10.00

KM# 1190 500 RUPEE
14.1900 g., 0.5000 Silver 0.2281 oz. ASW, 32 mm. **Subject:** 250th Anniversary Hindu festival "Kimari Jatra" **Obv:** Kumari Temple at Durbar Square in Kathmandu **Rev:** Bust of Goddess Kumari facing **Edge:** Reeded

Date	Mintage	F	VF	XF	Unc	BU
VS2064 (2007)	—	—	—	—	25.00	30.00

MINT SETS

KM#	Date	Mintage	Identification	Issue Price	Mkt Val
MSA19	1996, 1995, 2011 (3)	—	KM#709.2 (1996); 711 (1995); 737 (2011)	—	8.00

NETHERLANDS

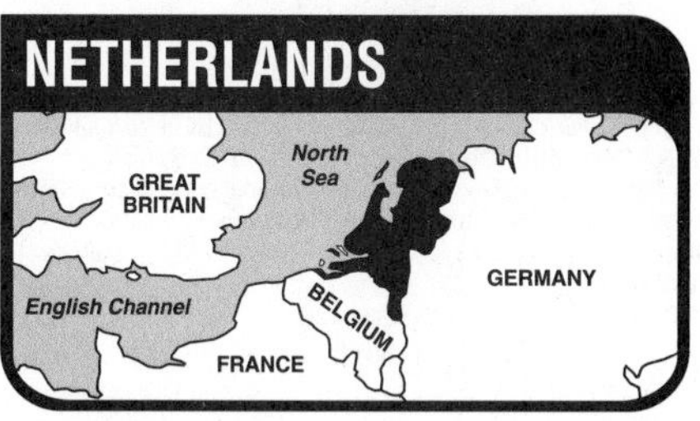

The Kingdom of the Netherlands, a country of Western Europe fronting on the North Sea and bordered by Belgium and Germany, has an area of 15,770 sq. mi. (41,500 sq. km.) and a population of 16.4 million. Capital: Amsterdam, but the seat of government is at The Hague. The economy is based on dairy farming and a variety of industrial activities. Chemicals, yarns and fabrics, and meat products are exported.

NOTE: Excepting the World War II issues struck at U.S. mints, all of the modern coins were struck at the Utrecht Mint (or at the annex in the Birmingham Mint, 1980-2000) and bear the caduceus mint mark of that facility. They also bear the mint-masters' marks.

The BES-islands (Bonaire, St. Eustatius and Saba) have been added to the Netherlands as special municipalities on Oct. 10, 2010. On these islands the U.S. dollar has been the official currency.

RULERS

KINGDOM OF THE NETHERLANDS

Beatrix, 1980-2013
Willam-Alexander 2013-

MINT PRIVY MARKS

Utrecht

Date	Privy Mark
1806-present	Caduceus

MINTMASTERS' PRIVY MARKS

Utrecht Mint

Date	Privy Mark
2001	Wine tendril w/grapes
2002	Wine tendril w/grapes and star
2003	Sails of a clipper

NOTE: A star adjoining the privy mark indicates that the piece was struck at the beginning of the term of office of a successor. (The star was used only if the successor had not chosen his own mark yet.)

NOTE: Since October 1999, the Dutch Mint has taken the title of Royal Dutch Mint.

MONETARY SYSTEM

Until January 29, 2002
100 Cents = 1 Gulden
Since January 1, 2002
100 Euro Cents = 1 Euro

KINGDOM

DECIMAL COINAGE

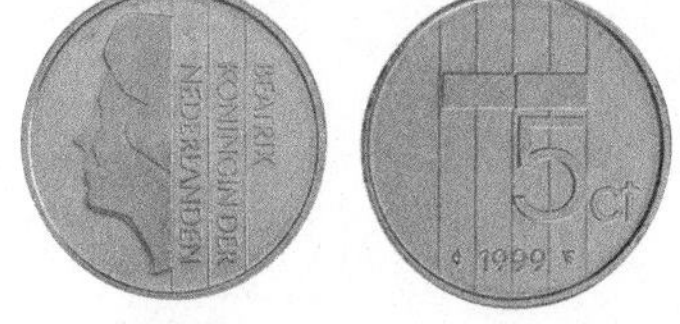

KM# 202 5 CENTS
3.5000 g., Bronze, 21 mm. **Ruler:** Beatrix **Obv:** Head left with vertical inscription **Rev:** Value within vertical lines **Edge:** Plain **Designer:** Bruno Ninaber Van Eyben

Date	Mintage	F	VF	XF	Unc	BU
2001	15,815,000	—	—	—	—	0.70
2001 Proof	17,000	Value: 4.00				

KM# 203 10 CENTS
1.5000 g., Nickel, 15 mm. **Ruler:** Beatrix **Obv:** Head left with vertical inscription **Rev:** Value and vertical lines **Edge:** Reeded **Designer:** Bruno Ninaber Van Eyben

Date	Mintage	F	VF	XF	Unc	BU
2001	25,600,000	—	—	—	0.45	0.75
2001 Proof	17,000	Value: 4.00				

KM# 204 25 CENTS
3.0000 g., Nickel, 19 mm. **Ruler:** Beatrix **Obv:** Head left with vertical inscription **Obv. Inscription:** Beatrix/Konincin Der/Nederlanden **Rev:** Value within vertical and horizontal lines **Edge:** Reeded **Designer:** Bruno Ninaber van Eyben

Date	Mintage	F	VF	XF	Unc	BU
2001	11,515,000	—	—	—	0.30	1.00
2001 Proof	17,000	Value: 5.00				

KM# 205 GULDEN
6.0000 g., Nickel, 25 mm. **Ruler:** Beatrix **Obv:** Head left with vertical inscription **Rev:** Value within vertical and horizontal lines **Edge Lettering:** GOD * ZIJ * MET * ONS * **Designer:** Bruno Ninaber von Eyben

Date	Mintage	F	VF	XF	Unc	BU
2001	6,414,500	—	—	—	—	1.25
2001 Proof	17,000	Value: 5.00				

KM# 233 GULDEN
6.0000 g., Nickel, 25 mm. **Ruler:** Beatrix **Obv:** Head left within inscription **Rev:** Child art design **Edge Lettering:** GOD * ZIJ * MET * ONS *

Date	Mintage	F	VF	XF	Unc	BU
2001B	16,009,000	—	—	—	—	4.00
2001B Prooflike	32,000	—	—	—	—	6.00

KM# 233a GULDEN
7.1000 g., 0.9250 Silver 0.2111 oz. ASW, 25 mm. **Ruler:** Beatrix **Obv:** Head left within inscription **Rev:** Child art design **Edge Lettering:** GOD * ZIJ * MET * ONS *

Date	Mintage	F	VF	XF	Unc	BU
2001B Prooflike	360	—	—	—	—	2,500

Note: Given as gifts to workers at the mint

KM# 233b GULDEN
13.2000 g., 0.9990 Gold 0.4239 oz. AGW, 25 mm. **Ruler:** Beatrix **Obv:** Head left within inscription **Rev:** Child art design **Note:** 98 of 100 pieces melted down, with 2 known in museum collections.

Date	Mintage	F	VF	XF	Unc	BU
2001B Prooflike; Rare	100	—	—	—	—	—

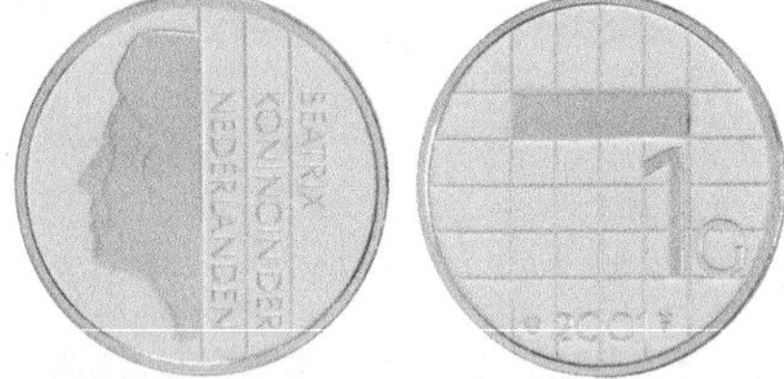

KM# 205a GULDEN
7.1000 g., 0.9250 Silver 0.2111 oz. ASW **Ruler:** Beatrix **Obv:** Head left with vertical inscription **Rev:** Value within vertical and horizontal lines **Edge Lettering:** GOD*ZIJ*MET*OMS*

Date	Mintage	F	VF	XF	Unc	BU
2001B Prooflike	200,000	—	—	—	—	15.00

KM# 205b GULDEN
13.2000 g., 0.9990 Gold 0.4239 oz. AGW **Ruler:** Beatrix **Obv:** Head left with vertical inscription **Rev:** Value within vertical and horizontal lines **Edge Lettering:** GOD*ZIJ*MET*ONS* **Note:** Prev. KM#205a.

Date	Mintage	F	VF	XF	Unc	BU
2001 Prooflike	25,500	—	—	—	—	800

Note: Mintage includes KM#205c.

KM# 205c GULDEN
13.2000 g., 0.9990 Gold 0.4239 oz. AGW **Ruler:** Beatrix **Obv:** Head left with vertical inscription **Rev:** Value within vertical and horizontal lines **Edge:** Plain, missing lettering

Date	Mintage	F	VF	XF	Unc	BU
2001 Prooflike	Est. 500	—	—	—	—	1,000

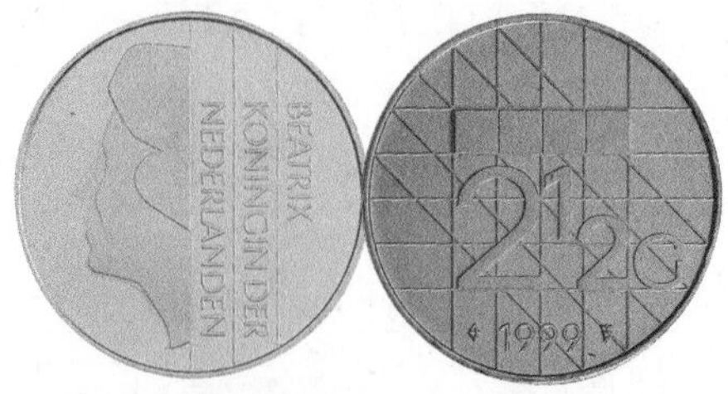

KM# 206 2-1/2 GULDEN
10.0000 g., Nickel, 29 mm. **Ruler:** Beatrix **Obv:** Head left with vertical inscription **Rev:** Value within horizontal, vertical and diagonal lines **Edge Lettering:** GOD * ZIJ * MET * ONS * **Designer:** Bruno Ninaber van Eyben

Date	Mintage	F	VF	XF	Unc	BU
2001	315,000	—	—	—	4.00	6.00
2001 Proof	17,000	Value: 7.50				

KM# 210 5 GULDEN
9.2500 g., Bronze Clad Nickel, 23.5 mm. **Ruler:** Beatrix **Obv:** Head left with vertical inscription **Rev:** Value within horizontal, vertical and diagonal lines **Edge:** GOD * ZIJ * MET * ONS * **Designer:** Bruno Ninaber van Eyben

Date	Mintage	F	VF	XF	Unc	BU
2001	115,000	—	—	—	5.00	10.00
2001 Proof	17,000	Value: 7.00				

EURO COINAGE

European Union Issues

KM# 234 EURO CENT
2.3000 g., Copper Plated Steel, 16.2 mm. **Ruler:** Beatrix **Obv:** Head left among stars **Rev:** Value and globe **Edge:** Plain

Date	Mintage	F	VF	XF	Unc	BU
2001B	179,800,000	—	—	—	0.35	0.50
2001B Proof	16,500	—	—	—	—	—
2002B	600,000	—	—	—	3.00	1.25
2002B Proof	16,500	Value: 5.00				
2003B	5,866,000	—	—	—	0.50	0.75
2003B Proof	13,000	Value: 4.00				
2004B	11,396,000	—	—	—	0.50	0.75
2004B Proof	5,000	Value: 4.00				
2005B	545,000	—	—	—	1.50	2.00
2005B Proof	5,000	Value: 4.00				
2006B	378,000	—	—	—	1.50	2.00
2006B Proof	3,500	Value: 4.00				
2007B	332,000	—	—	—	1.50	2.00
2007B Proof	10,000	Value: 3.50				
2008B	413,000	—	—	—	1.50	2.00
2008B Proof	10,000	Value: 3.50				
2009B	335,000	—	—	—	1.50	2.00
2009B Proof	75,000	Value: 3.50				
2010B	235,000	—	—	—	1.50	2.00
2010B Proof	5,000	Value: 3.50				
2011B	—	—	—	—	1.50	2.00
2011B Proof	5,000	Value: 3.50				
2012B	—	—	—	—	1.50	2.00
2012B Proof	5,000	Value: 3.50				
2013B	—	—	—	—	1.50	2.00
2013B Proof	5,000	Value: 3.50				

KM# 235 2 EURO CENT
3.0600 g., Copper Plated Steel, 18.7 mm. **Ruler:** Beatrix **Obv:** Head left among stars **Rev:** Value and globe **Edge:** Grooved

Date	Mintage	F	VF	XF	Unc	BU
2001B	142,100,000	—	—	—	0.50	0.75
2001B Proof	16,500	—	—	—	—	—
2002B	52,224,000	—	—	—	0.75	1.00
2002B Proof	16,500	—	—	—	—	—
2003B	150,750,000	—	—	—	0.50	0.75
2003B Proof	13,000	—	—	—	—	—
2004B	115,622,000	—	—	—	0.50	0.75
2004B Proof	5,000	Value: 4.00				
2005B	595,000	—	—	—	1.50	2.00
2005B Proof	5,000	Value: 4.00				
2006B	378,000	—	—	—	1.50	2.00
2006B Proof	3,500	Value: 4.00				
2007B	338,000	—	—	—	1.50	2.00
2007B Proof	10,000	Value: 3.50				
2008B	413,000	—	—	—	1.50	2.00
2008B Proof	10,000	Value: 3.50				
2009B	335,000	—	—	—	1.50	2.00
2009B Proof	75,000	Value: 3.50				
2010B	235,000	—	—	—	1.50	2.00
2010B Proof	5,000	Value: 3.50				
2011B	—	—	—	—	1.50	2.00
2011B Proof	5,000	Value: 3.50				
2012B	—	—	—	—	1.50	2.00
2012B Proof	5,000	Value: 3.50				
2013B	—	—	—	—	1.50	2.00
2013B Proof	5,000	Value: 3.50				

KM# 236 5 EURO CENT
3.9200 g., Copper Plated Steel, 21.25 mm. **Ruler:** Beatrix **Obv:** Head left among stars **Rev:** Value and globe **Edge:** Plain

Date	Mintage	F	VF	XF	Unc	BU
2001B	206,400,000	—	—	—	0.50	0.75
2001B Proof	16,500	—	—	—	—	—
2002B	700,000	—	—	—	1.75	3.50
2002B Proof	16,500	—	—	—	—	—
2003B	874,000	—	—	—	1.50	5.00
2003B Proof	13,000	—	—	—	—	—
2004B	306,000	—	—	—	2.00	2.50
2004B Proof	5,000	Value: 4.00				
2005B	80,605,000	—	—	—	1.00	1.25
2005B Proof	5,000	Value: 4.00				
2006B	60,318,000	—	—	—	1.00	1.25
2006B Proof	3,500	Value: 4.00				
2007B	75,764,000	—	—	—	1.00	1.25
2007B Proof	10,000	Value: 3.50				
2008B	50,413,000	—	—	—	1.00	1.25
2008B Proof	10,000	Value: 3.50				
2009B	70,335,000	—	—	—	1.00	1.25
2009B Proof	75,000	Value: 3.50				
2010B	70,235,000	—	—	—	1.00	1.25
2010B Proof	5,000	Value: 3.50				
2011B	40,100,000	—	—	—	1.00	1.25
2011B Proof	5,000	Value: 3.50				
2012B	—	—	—	—	1.00	1.25
2012B Proof	5,000	Value: 3.50				
2013B	—	—	—	—	1.00	1.25
2013B Proof	5,000	Value: 3.50				

KM# 237 10 EURO CENT
4.1000 g., Brass, 19.7 mm. **Ruler:** Beatrix **Obv:** Head left among stars **Rev:** Value and map

Date	Mintage	F	VF	XF	Unc	BU
2001B	194,200,000	—	—	—	0.75	1.00
2001B Proof	16,500	—	—	—	—	—
2002B	600,000	—	—	—	1.50	5.00
2002B Proof	16,500	—	—	—	—	—
2003B	818,000	—	—	—	1.50	2.00
2003B Proof	13,000	—	—	—	—	—
2004B	262,000	—	—	—	2.00	2.50
2004B Proof	5,000	Value: 6.00				
2005B	510,000	—	—	—	1.75	2.00
2005B Proof	5,000	Value: 6.00				
2006B	393,000	—	—	—	1.75	2.50
2006B Proof	3,500	Value: 6.00				

KM# 268 10 EURO CENT
4.1000 g., Brass, 19.7 mm. **Ruler:** Beatrix **Obv:** Head of Queen Beatrix left **Rev:** Relief map of Western Europe, stars, lines and value

Date	Mintage	F	VF	XF	Unc	BU
2006B	—	—	—	—	—	2.50
2007B	292,000	—	—	—	1.75	2.50
2007B Proof	10,000	Value: 5.00				
2008B	363,000	—	—	—	1.75	2.75
2008B Proof	10,000	Value: 5.00				
2009B	285,000	—	—	—	1.75	2.50
2009B Proof	7,500	Value: 5.00				
2010B	202,000	—	—	—	1.75	2.50
2010B Proof	5,000	Value: 5.00				
2011B	—	—	—	—	1.75	2.50
2011B Proof	5,000	Value: 5.00				
2012B	—	—	—	—	1.75	2.50
2012B Proof	5,000	Value: 5.00				
2013B	—	—	—	—	1.75	2.50
2013B Proof	5,000	Value: 5.00				

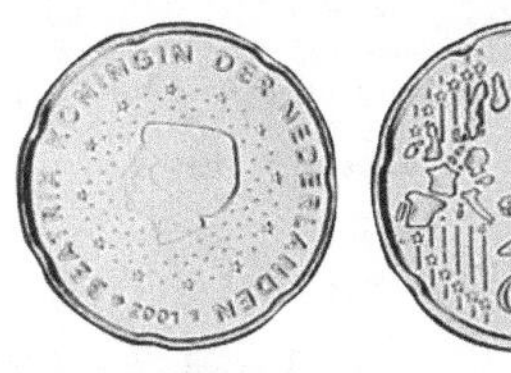

KM# 238 20 EURO CENT

5.7400 g., Brass, 22.2 mm. **Ruler:** Beatrix **Obv:** Head left among stars **Rev:** Value and map **Edge:** Notched

Date	Mintage	F	VF	XF	Unc	BU
2001B	92,300,000	—	—	—	1.00	1.25
2001B Proof	16,500	—	—	—	—	—
2002B	50,691,000	—	—	—	1.00	1.25
2002B Proof	16,500	—	—	—	—	—
2003B	57,821,000	—	—	—	1.00	1.25
2003B Proof	13,000	—	—	—	—	—
2004B	20,430,000	—	—	—	1.00	1.50
2004B Proof	5,000	Value: 8.00				
2005B	510,000	—	—	—	2.00	3.00
2005B Proof	5,000	Value: 8.00				
2006B	393,000	—	—	—	2.00	3.00
2006B Proof	3,500	Value: 8.00				

KM# 269 20 EURO CENT

5.7000 g., Brass, 22.2 mm. **Ruler:** Beatrix **Obv:** Head of Queen Beatrix left **Rev:** Relief map of Western Europe, stars, lines and value **Edge:** Notched

Date	Mintage	F	VF	XF	Unc	BU
2006B	—	—	—	—	—	3.00
2007B	510,000	—	—	—	2.00	3.00
2007B Proof	10,000	Value: 7.00				
2008B	293,000	—	—	—	2.50	3.00
2008B Proof	10,000	Value: 7.00				
2009B	363,000	—	—	—	2.00	3.00
2009B Proof	7,500	Value: 7.00				
2010B	285,000	—	—	—	2.50	3.00
2010B Proof	5,000	Value: 7.00				
2011B	202,000	—	—	—	2.50	3.00
2011B Proof	5,000	Value: 7.00				
2012B	—	—	—	—	2.50	3.00
2012B Proof	5,000	Value: 7.00				
2013B	—	—	—	—	2.50	3.00
2013B Proof	5,000	Value: 7.00				

KM# 239 50 EURO CENT

7.8000 g., Brass, 24.2 mm. **Ruler:** Beatrix **Obv:** Head left among stars **Rev:** Value and map **Edge:** Notched

Date	Mintage	F	VF	XF	Unc	BU
2001B	87,000,000	—	—	—	1.25	1.50
2001B Proof	16,500	—	—	—	—	—
2002B	80,160,000	—	—	—	1.25	1.50
2002B Proof	16,500	—	—	—	—	—
2003B	810,000	—	—	—	2.00	2.50
2003B Proof	13,000	—	—	—	—	—
2004B	269,000	—	—	—	2.25	3.00
2004B Proof	5,000	Value: 10.00				
2005B	510,000	—	—	—	2.00	2.50
2005B Proof	5,964	Value: 10.00				
2006B	363,000	—	—	—	2.00	2.50
2006B Proof	3,500	Value: 10.00				

KM# 270 50 EURO CENT

7.8000 g., Brass, 24.2 mm. **Ruler:** Beatrix **Obv:** Head of Quen Beatrix left **Rev:** Relief map of Western Europe, stars, lines and value **Edge:** Notched

Date	Mintage	F	VF	XF	Unc	BU
2006B	—	—	—	—	—	2.75
2007B	293,000	—	—	—	2.00	2.75
2007B Proof	10,000	Value: 9.00				
2008B	263,000	—	—	—	2.00	2.75
2008B Proof	10,000	Value: 9.00				
2009B	285,000	—	—	—	2.00	2.75
2009B Proof	7,500	Value: 9.00				
2010B	202,000	—	—	—	2.00	2.75
2010B Proof	5,000	Value: 9.00				
2011B	—	—	—	—	2.00	2.75
2011B Proof	5,000	Value: 9.00				
2012B	—	—	—	—	2.00	2.75
2012B Proof	5,000	Value: 9.00				
2013B	—	—	—	—	2.00	2.75
2013B Proof	5,000	Value: 9.00				

KM# 240 EURO

7.5000 g., Bi-Metallic Copper-Nickel center in Brass ring, 23.2 mm. **Ruler:** Beatrix **Obv:** Half head left within 1/2 circle and star border, name within vertical lines **Rev:** Value and map within circle **Edge:** Segmented reeding

Date	Mintage	F	VF	XF	Unc	BU
2001B	67,200,000	—	—	—	2.50	3.00
2001B Proof	16,500	—	—	—	—	—
2002B	22,560,000	—	—	—	2.50	3.00
2002B Proof	16,500	—	—	—	—	—
2003B	950,000	—	—	—	3.50	4.00
2003B Proof	13,000	—	—	—	—	—
2004B	235,000	—	—	—	5.00	6.00
2004B Proof	5,000	Value: 15.00				
2005B	332,000	—	—	—	4.00	5.00
2005B Proof	5,964	Value: 15.00				
2006B	393,000	—	—	—	4.00	5.00
2006B Proof	3,500	Value: 15.00				

KM# 271 EURO

7.5000 g., Bi-Metallic Copper-Nickel center in Nickel-Brass ring, 23.25 mm. **Ruler:** Beatrix **Obv:** Queen's profile left **Rev:** Relief map of Western Europe, stars, lines and value **Edge:** Segmented reeding

Date	Mintage	F	VF	XF	Unc	BU
2006B	—	—	—	—	—	4.00
2007B	224,000	—	—	—	3.50	4.00
2007B Proof	10,000	Value: 14.50				
2008B	288,000	—	—	—	3.50	4.00
2008B Proof	10,000	Value: 14.50				
2009B	185,000	—	—	—	3.50	4.00
2009B Proof	7,500	Value: 14.50				
2010B	166,000	—	—	—	3.50	4.00
2010B Proof	5,000	Value: 14.50				
2011B	—	—	—	—	3.50	4.00
2011B Proof	5,000	Value: 14.50				
2012B	—	—	—	—	3.50	4.00
2012B Proof	5,000	Value: 14.50				
2013B	—	—	—	—	3.50	4.00
2013B Proof	5,000	Value: 14.50				

KM# 241 2 EURO

8.5000 g., Bi-Metallic Nickel-Brass center in Copper-Nickel ring, 25.75 mm. **Ruler:** Beatrix **Obv:** Profile left within 1/2 circle and star border, name within vertical lines **Rev:** Value and map within circle **Edge Lettering:** GOD * ZIJ * MET * ONS *

Date	Mintage	F	VF	XF	Unc	BU
2001B	116,400,000	—	—	—	4.00	4.50
2001B Proof	16,500	—	—	—	—	—
2002B	36,432,000	—	—	—	4.50	12.00
2002B Proof	16,500	—	—	—	—	—
2003B	749,000	—	—	—	5.50	8.00
2003B Proof	13,000	—	—	—	—	—
2004B	245,000	—	—	—	7.00	12.00
2004B Proof	5,000	Value: 18.00				
2005B	332,000	—	—	—	6.00	8.00
2005B Proof	5,964	Value: 18.00				
2006B	341,000	—	—	—	6.00	10.00
2006B Proof	3,500	Value: 18.00				

KM# 272 2 EURO

8.5000 g., Bi-Metallic Nickel-Brass center in Copper-Nickel ring, 25.75 mm. **Ruler:** Beatrix **Obv:** Queen's profile left **Rev:** Relief map of Western Europe, stars, lines and value **Edge Lettering:** GOD * ZIJ * MET * ONS *

Date	Mintage	F	VF	XF	Unc	BU
2006B	—	—	—	—	6.00	—
2007B	345,000	—	—	—	6.00	8.00
2007B Proof	10,000	Value: 17.50				
2008B	288,000	—	—	—	6.00	8.00
2008B Proof	10,000	Value: 17.50				
2009B	225,000	—	—	—	6.00	8.00
2009B Proof	7,500	Value: 17.50				
2010B	166,000	—	—	—	6.00	8.00
2010B Proof	5,000	Value: 17.50				
2011B	—	—	—	—	6.00	8.00
2011B Proof	5,000	Value: 17.50				
2012B	—	—	—	—	6.00	8.00
2012B Proof	5,000	Value: 17.50				
2013B	—	—	—	—	6.00	8.00
2013B Proof	5,000	Value: 17.50				

KM# 273 2 EURO

8.5000 g., Bi-Metallic Nickel-Brass center in Copper-Nickel ring, 25.75 mm. **Ruler:** Beatrix **Subject:** 50th Anniversary Treaty of Rome **Obv:** Open treaty book **Rev:** Large value at left, modified outline of Europe at right **Edge Lettering:** GOD * ZU * MET * ONS * **Note:** 15,000 BU coins are in a Benelux set

Date	Mintage	F	VF	XF	Unc	BU
2007B	6,333,000	—	—	—	6.00	15.00
2007B Proof	10,000	Value: 22.00				

KM# 281 2 EURO

8.5000 g., Bi-Metallic Nickel-Brass center in Copper-Nickel ring, 25.75 mm. **Ruler:** Beatrix **Subject:** European Monetary Union, 10th Anniversary **Rev:** Stick figure and euro symbol **Edge Lettering:** *GOD *ZIJ *MET *ONS

Date	Mintage	F	VF	XF	Unc	BU
2009	5,300,000	—	—	—	4.50	15.00
2009 Proof from set	7,500	Value: 60.00				
2009 Proof in box	2,000	Value: 160				

KM# 298 2 EURO

8.5000 g., Bi-Metallic Nickel-Brass center in Copper-Nickel ring, 25.75 mm. **Ruler:** Beatrix **Obv:** Beatrix at left, Erasmus writing at right

Date	Mintage	F	VF	XF	Unc	BU
2011	4,003,000	—	—	—	4.50	30.00
2011 Proof from set	5,000	Value: 50.00				
2011 Proof in box	2,000	Value: 140				

KM# 308 2 EURO

Bi-Metallic Nickel-Brass center in Copper-Nickel ring, 25.75 mm. **Ruler:** Beatrix **Subject:** 10 years of euro-coins **Obv:** Euro symbol on globe, child-like images around

Date	Mintage	F	VF	XF	Unc	BU
2012	3,500,000	—	—	—	4.50	—
2012 Proof	—	Value: 25.00				
2012 Special Unc.	15,000	—	—	—	—	15.00

KM# 245 5 EURO
11.9000 g., 0.9250 Silver 0.3539 oz. ASW, 29 mm. **Ruler:** Beatrix **Subject:** Vincent Van Gogh **Obv:** Head facing **Rev:** Tilted head facing **Edge Lettering:** GOD * ZIJ * MET * ONS * **Designer:** K. Martens

Date	Mintage	F	VF	XF	Unc	BU
ND(2003)B	1,000,000	—	—	—	BV	15.00
ND(2003)B Prooflike	100,000	—	—	—	—	30.00

KM# 252 5 EURO
11.9000 g., 0.9250 Silver 0.3539 oz. ASW **Ruler:** Beatrix **Subject:** New EEC member countries **Obv:** Head left **Rev:** Names of old and new member countries **Edge Lettering:** GOD * ZIJ * MET * ONS *

Date	Mintage	F	VF	XF	Unc	BU
2004	600,000	—	—	—	BV	17.50
2004 Proof	55,000	Value: 90.00				

KM# 253 5 EURO
11.9000 g., 0.9250 Silver 0.3539 oz. ASW **Ruler:** Beatrix **Subject:** 50th Anniversary - End of colonization of Netherlands Antilles **Obv:** Head left **Rev:** Fruit and date within beaded circle **Edge Lettering:** GOD * ZIJ * MET * ONS *

Date	Mintage	F	VF	XF	Unc	BU
2004	650,000	—	—	—	BV	17.50
2004 Proof	26,900	Value: 45.00				

KM# 254 5 EURO
11.9100 g., 0.9250 Silver 0.3542 oz. ASW, 29 mm. **Ruler:** Beatrix **Subject:** 60th Anniversary of Liberation **Obv:** Queen's image **Rev:** Value and dots **Edge Lettering:** GOD * ZIJ * MET * ONS * **Designer:** Suzan Drummen

Date	Mintage	F	VF	XF	Unc	BU
2005B	630,000	—	—	—	BV	17.50
2005B Proof	40,000	Value: 40.00				

KM# 255 5 EURO
11.9000 g., 0.9250 Silver 0.3539 oz. ASW, 29 mm. **Ruler:** Beatrix **Obv:** Queen's silhouette centered on a world globe **Rev:** Value above Australia on a world globe **Edge Lettering:** GOD * ZIJ * MET * ONS * **Designer:** Irma Boom

Date	Mintage	F	VF	XF	Unc	BU
2006B	500,000	—	—	—	BV	17.50
2006B Proof	22,500	Value: 45.00				

KM# 266 5 EURO
11.9000 g., 0.9250 Silver 0.3539 oz. ASW, 28.9 mm. **Ruler:** Beatrix **Obv:** Queen Beatrix **Rev:** Rembrandt **Edge Lettering:** GOD * Z IJ * MET * ONS * **Designer:** Berend Strik

Date	Mintage	F	VF	XF	Unc	BU
ND(2006)B	655,000	—	—	—	BV	17.50
ND(2006)B Proof	35,000	Value: 35.00				

KM# 267 5 EURO
11.9000 g., 0.9250 Silver 0.3539 oz. ASW, 29 mm. **Ruler:** Beatrix **Subject:** Tax Service, 200th Anniversary **Obv:** Queen's portrait **Rev:** Circles with dates 1806-2006 **Edge Lettering:** GOD * ZIJ * MET * ONS * **Designer:** Hennie Bouwe

Date	Mintage	F	VF	XF	Unc	BU
2006	359,189	—	—	—	BV	17.50
2006 Prooflike	40,000	—	—	—	—	25.00
2006 Proof	15,000	Value: 60.00				

KM# 277 5 EURO
11.9000 g., 0.9250 Silver 0.3539 oz. ASW, 29 mm. **Ruler:** Beatrix **Subject:** Admiral M.A. de Ruyter, 400th Anniversary of Birth **Obv:** Queen's head 1/4 left **Rev:** deRuyter's head 1/4 right **Edge Lettering:** GOD * ZIJ * MET * ONS *

Date	Mintage	F	VF	XF	Unc	BU
2007	520,500	—	—	—	BV	17.50
2007 Proof	17,500	Value: 40.00				

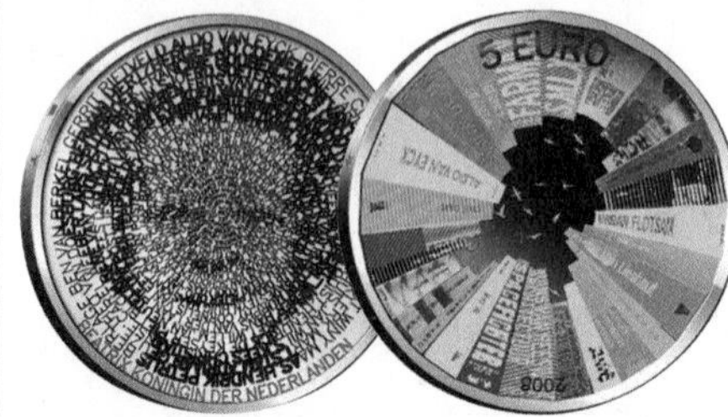

KM# 279 5 EURO
15.5000 g., 0.9250 Silver 0.4609 oz. ASW, 33 mm. **Ruler:** Beatrix **Subject:** Architecture **Obv:** Portrait facing in names of famous architects **Rev:** Books around map of the Netherlands **Edge Lettering:** GOD * ZIJ * MET * ONS * **Designer:** Stani Michiels

Date	Mintage	F	VF	XF	Unc	BU
2008 Proof	24,505	Value: 40.00				

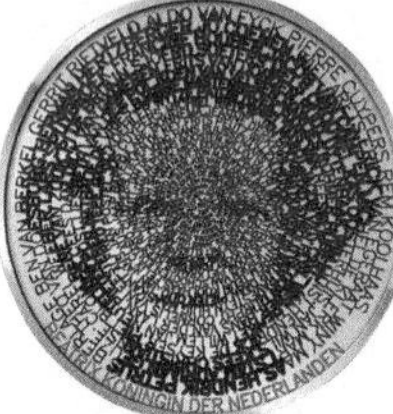

KM# 279a 5 EURO
10.5000 g., Silver Plated Copper, 29 mm. **Ruler:** Beatrix **Subject:** Architecture **Obv:** Portrait facing in names of famous Architects **Rev:** Architecture books around map of the Netherlands

Date	Mintage	F	VF	XF	Unc	BU
2008	350,000	—	—	—	10.00	15.00

KM# 282 5 EURO
15.5000 g., 0.9250 Silver 0.4609 oz. ASW, 33 mm. **Ruler:** Beatrix **Subject:** Manhattan 400th Anniversary **Obv:** Bottom tip of Manhattan Island today **Rev:** Bottom tip of Manhattan Island in 1609 **Edge Lettering:** GOD * ZIJ * MET * ONS * **Designer:** Ronald van Tienhoven

Date	Mintage	F	VF	XF	Unc	BU
2009 Proof	20,000	Value: 55.00				

KM# 282a 5 EURO
10.5000 g., Silver Plated Copper, 29 mm. **Ruler:** Beatrix **Subject:** Manhattan 400th Anniversary **Obv:** Tip of Manhattan Island today **Rev:** Tip of Manhattan Island in 1609 **Designer:** Ronald van Tienhoven

Date	Mintage	F	VF	XF	Unc	BU
2009	303,209	—	—	—	10.00	15.00

KM# 287 5 EURO
15.5000 g., 0.9250 Silver 0.4609 oz. ASW, 33 mm. **Ruler:** Beatrix **Subject:** Netherlands-Japanese Friendship **Obv:** Guilder design of 1982 with Queen **Rev:** Value and date **Edge Lettering:** GOD * ZIJ * MET * ONS * **Designer:** Richard Niessen and Esther de Uries

Date	Mintage	F	VF	XF	Unc	BU
2009 Proof	45,000	Value: 40.00				

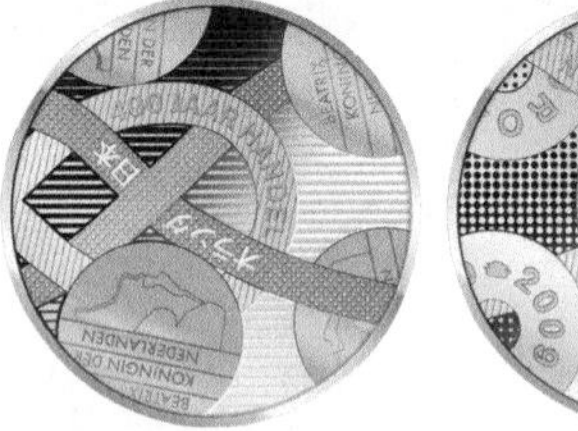
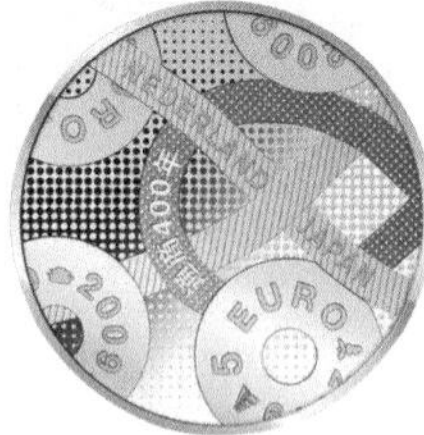

KM# 287a 5 EURO
10.5000 g., Silver Plated Copper, 29 mm. **Ruler:** Beatrix **Subject:** Netherlands-Japanese Friendship **Obv:** Guilder design of 1982 with Queen **Rev:** Value and date

Date	Mintage	F	VF	XF	Unc	BU
2009	343,859	—	—	—	8.00	10.00

KM# 294 5 EURO
11.9000 g., 0.9250 Silver 0.3539 oz. ASW, 33 mm. **Ruler:** Beatrix **Subject:** Max Havelaar, 150th Anniversary **Obv:** Queen **Rev:** Ink pen, words in spiral, figures walking around edge **Edge Lettering:** GOD * ZIJ * MET * ONS * **Designer:** Eelco Brand

Date	Mintage	F	VF	XF	Unc	BU
2010B Proof	15,000	Value: 50.00				

KM# 294a 5 EURO
10.5000 g., Silver Plated Copper, 29 mm. **Ruler:** Beatrix **Subject:** Max Havelaar, 150th Anniversary of Birth **Obv:** Queen **Rev:** Ink pen, words in spiral, figures walking around edge **Edge Lettering:** GOD * ZIJ * MET * ONS * **Designer:** Eelco Brand

Date	Mintage	F	VF	XF	Unc	BU
2010B	275,010	—	—	—	9.00	12.00

KM# 296 5 EURO
15.5000 g., 0.9250 Silver 0.4609 oz. ASW, 33 mm. **Ruler:** Beatrix **Subject:** Waterland **Obv:** Queen's bust facing, and reflected in water **Rev:** Map of the Netherlands, partly below sea level

Date	Mintage	F	VF	XF	Unc	BU
2010	17,500	Value: 45.00				

KM# 296a 5 EURO
10.5000 g., Silver Plated Copper, 29 mm. **Ruler:** Beatrix **Subject:** Waterland **Obv:** Queens bust facing and reflected in water **Rev:** Map of the Netherlands, partly below sea level

Date	Mintage	F	VF	XF	Unc	BU
2010	227,500	—	—	—	—	10.00

KM# 304a 5 EURO
Silver Plated Copper, 29 mm. **Ruler:** Beatrix **Subject:** Painting **Obv:** Queen looking at city view painting **Rev:** Window **Edge Lettering:** GOD * ZIJ * MET * ONS *

Date	Mintage	F	VF	XF	Unc	BU
2011	250,000	—	—	—	—	12.00

KM# 299 5 EURO
15.5000 g., 0.9250 Silver 0.4609 oz. ASW, 33 mm. **Ruler:** Beatrix **Subject:** World Wildlife Fund, 50th Anniversary **Obv:** Profile left at center of tree leaves **Rev:** Value at center of root system **Edge Lettering:** GOD * ZIJ * MET * ONS *

Date	Mintage	F	VF	XF	Unc	BU
2011B Proof	17,500	Value: 40.00				

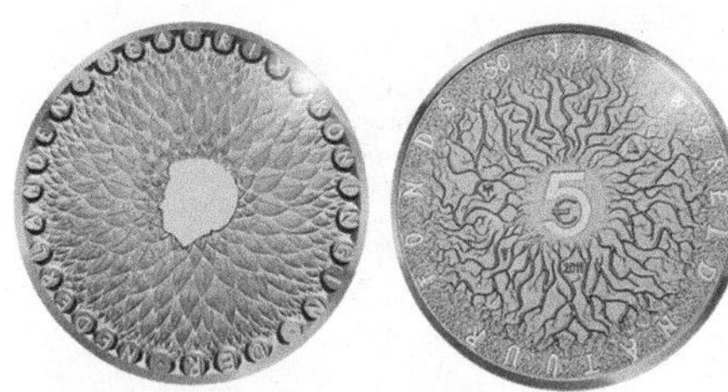

KM# 301 5 EURO
10.5000 g., Silver Plated Copper, 29 mm. **Ruler:** Beatrix **Subject:** World Wildlife Fund, 50th Anniversary **Obv:** Profile head at center of tree leaves **Rev:** Value at center of root system **Edge Lettering:** GOD * ZIJ * MET * ONS *

Date	Mintage	F	VF	XF	Unc	BU
2011B Proof	250,000	Value: 10.00				

KM# 302 5 EURO
15.5000 g., 0.9250 Silver 0.4609 oz. ASW, 33 mm. **Ruler:** Beatrix **Subject:** Mint building, 100th Anniversary. **Obv:** Bust facing **Rev:** Screw press and a QR-code which is to scan with a mobile telephone **Edge Lettering:** GOD * ZIJ * MET * ONS * **Designer:** Juan José Sánchez Castaño

Date	Mintage	F	VF	XF	Unc	BU
2011B Proof	17,500	Value: 40.00				

KM# 302a 5 EURO
10.5000 g., Silver Plated Copper, 29 mm. **Ruler:** Beatrix **Subject:** Mint building, 100th Anniversary. **Obv:** Bust facing **Rev:** Screw press and a QR-code which is to scan with a **Edge Lettering:** GOD * ZIJ * MET * ONS * **Designer:** Juan José Sánchez Castaño

Date	Mintage	F	VF	XF	Unc	BU
2011	71,618	—	—	—	—	15.00

KM# 302b 5 EURO
Gold, 33 mm. **Ruler:** Beatrix **Subject:** Mint building, 100th Anniversary **Obv:** Bust facing **Rev:** Screw press and a QR-code whcih is to be scanned with a mobile telephone **Edge Lettering:** GOD * ZIJ * MET * ONS * **Designer:** Juan José Sánchez Castaño **Note:** Off-metal strike made as presentation item to designer Juan José Sánchez Castaño by the mint director, as the coin won the Coin-of-the-Year award.

Date	Mintage	F	VF	XF	Unc	BU
2011 Proof	1	—	—	—	—	—

KM# 304 5 EURO
15.5000 g., 0.9250 Silver 0.4609 oz. ASW, 33 mm. **Ruler:** Beatrix **Subject:** Painting **Obv:** Queen looking at city view painting **Rev:** Window **Edge Lettering:** GOD * ZIJ * MET * ONS *

Date	Mintage	F	VF	XF	Unc	BU
2011B	250,000	—	—	—	—	30.00
2011B Proof	12,500	Value: 40.00				

KM# 309 5 EURO
15.5000 g., 0.9250 Silver 0.4609 oz. ASW, 33 mm. **Ruler:** Beatrix **Subject:** 400 years of diplomatic relations Netherlands-Turkey **Edge Lettering:** GOD * ZIJ * MET * ONS *

Date	Mintage	F	VF	XF	Unc	BU
2012 Proof	12,500	Value: 45.00				

KM# 309a 5 EURO
10.5000 g., Silver Plated Copper, 29 mm. **Ruler:** Beatrix **Subject:** 400 years of diplomatic relations Netherlands-Turkey **Edge Lettering:** GOD * ZIJ * MET * ONS *

Date	Mintage	F	VF	XF	Unc	BU
2012	250,000	—	—	—	10.00	15.00

KM# 243 10 EURO
17.8000 g., 0.9250 Silver 0.5293 oz. ASW, 33 mm. **Ruler:** Beatrix **Subject:** Wedding of Willem-Alexander and Maxima **Obv:** Queen's head left **Rev:** Conjoined busts left **Edge Lettering:** GOD * ZIJ * MET * ONS * **Designer:** H. van Houwelingen

Date	Mintage	F	VF	XF	Unc	BU
2002B	990,800	—	—	—	BV	40.00
2002B Proof	80,000	Value: 55.00				

KM# 244 10 EURO
6.7200 g., 0.9000 Gold 0.1944 oz. AGW, 22.5 mm. **Ruler:** Beatrix **Subject:** Crown Prince's Wedding **Obv:** Head left **Rev:** Two facing silhouettes **Edge:** Reeded **Designer:** J. van Houwelingen

Date	Mintage	F	VF	XF	Unc	BU
2002B Prooflike	33,000	—	—	—	—	400

KM# 246 10 EURO
6.7200 g., 0.9000 Gold 0.1944 oz. AGW, 22.5 mm. **Ruler:** Beatrix **Subject:** Vincent Van Gogh **Obv:** Head facing **Rev:** Tilted head facing **Edge:** Reeded **Designer:** K. Martens

Date	Mintage	F	VF	XF	Unc	BU
ND(2003)B Prooflike	20,000	—	—	—	—	400

KM# 248 10 EURO
17.8000 g., 0.9250 Silver 0.5293 oz. ASW, 33 mm. **Ruler:** Beatrix **Obv:** Head left **Rev:** Multi-views of Prince Willem-Alexander, Princess Catherina-Amalia and Princess Maxima **Edge Lettering:** GOD * ZIJ * MET * ONS *

Date	Mintage	F	VF	XF	Unc	BU
2004	1,000,000	—	—	—	BV	25.00
2004 Proof	50,000	Value: 40.00				

KM# 247 10 EURO
6.7200 g., 0.9000 Gold 0.1944 oz. AGW, 22.5 mm. **Ruler:** Beatrix **Subject:** New EEC members **Obv:** Head left **Rev:** Value and legend **Edge:** Reeded **Designer:** M. Mieras and H. Mieras

Date	Mintage	F	VF	XF	Unc	BU
2004 Proof	6,000	Value: 700				

KM# 251 10 EURO
6.7200 g., 0.9000 Gold 0.1944 oz. AGW, 22.5 mm. **Ruler:** Beatrix **Subject:** 50 Years of Domestic Autonomy, 1954-2004 (for Netherlands Antilles) **Obv:** Small head left **Rev:** Fruit and date within beaded circle **Edge:** Reeded **Designer:** Rudy Luijters

Date	Mintage	F	VF	XF	Unc	BU
2004 Proof	3,800	Value: 600				

KM# 261 10 EURO
17.8000 g., 0.9250 Silver 0.5293 oz. ASW, 33 mm. **Ruler:** Beatrix **Subject:** Silver Jubilee of Reign **Obv:** Queen's photo **Rev:** Queen taking oath photo **Edge Lettering:** GOD * ZIJ * MET * ONS * **Designer:** Germaine Kruip

Date	Mintage	F	VF	XF	Unc	BU
2005B	1,000,000	—	—	—	BV	25.00
2005B Proof	59,754	Value: 40.00				

KM# 264 10 EURO
6.7200 g., 0.9000 Gold 0.1944 oz. AGW, 22.5 mm. **Ruler:** Beatrix **Subject:** 60th Anniversary of Liberation **Obv:** Queen and dots **Rev:** Value and dots **Edge:** Reeded **Designer:** Suzan Drummen

Date	Mintage	F	VF	XF	Unc	BU
2005B Proof	6,000	Value: 600				

KM# 289 10 EURO
6.7200 g., 0.9000 Gold 0.1944 oz. AGW, 22.5 mm. **Ruler:** Beatrix **Series:** Tax Services, 200th Anniversary **Obv:** Queen's portrait **Rev:** Florin of 1807 **Edge:** Reeded

Date	Mintage	F	VF	XF	Unc	BU
2006 Proof	5,500	Value: 600				

KM# 290 10 EURO
6.7200 g., 0.9000 Gold 0.1944 oz. AGW, 22.5 mm. **Ruler:** Beatrix **Subject:** Netherlands-Australian Friendship, 400th Anniversary **Obv:** Queens portrait within lines of a globe **Rev:** Australia, value and dates **Edge:** Reeded

Date	Mintage	F	VF	XF	Unc	BU
2006 Proof	3,500	Value: 800				

KM# 291 10 EURO
6.7200 g., 0.9000 Gold 0.1944 oz. AGW, 22.5 mm. **Ruler:** Beatrix **Subject:** Rembrandt, 400th Anniversary of Birth **Obv:** Queen's portrait **Rev:** Self-portrait **Edge:** Reeded

Date	Mintage	F	VF	XF	Unc	BU
2006 Proof	8,500	Value: 400				

KM# 278 10 EURO
6.7200 g., 0.9000 Gold 0.1944 oz. AGW, 22.5 mm. **Ruler:** Beatrix **Subject:** Admiral M.A. de Ruyter, 400th Birthday **Obv:** Head 1/4 left **Rev:** Head 1/4 right **Edge:** Reeded **Designer:** Martyn Engelbregt

Date	Mintage	F	VF	XF	Unc	BU
2007 Proof	7,000	Value: 400				

KM# 280 10 EURO
6.7200 g., 0.9000 Gold 0.1944 oz. AGW, 22.5 mm. **Ruler:** Beatrix **Subject:** Architecture **Obv:** Portrait facing in names of famous architects **Rev:** Architecture books around map of the Netherlands **Edge:** Reeded **Designer:** Stani Michiels

Date	Mintage	F	VF	XF	Unc	BU
2008 Proof	8,000	Value: 400				

KM# 283 10 EURO
6.7200 g., 0.9000 Gold 0.1944 oz. AGW, 22.5 mm. **Ruler:** Beatrix **Subject:** Dutch settlement of Manhattan, NY 400th Anniversary **Obv:** Bottom tip of Manhattan Island today **Rev:** Bottom tip of Manhattan Island in 1609 **Edge:** Reeded **Designer:** Ronald van Tienhoven

Date	Mintage	F	VF	XF	Unc	BU
2009 Proof	6,500	Value: 400				

KM# 288 10 EURO
6.7200 g., 0.9000 Gold 0.1944 oz. AGW, 22.5 mm. **Ruler:** Beatrix **Subject:** Netherlands-Japanese Friendship **Obv:** Guilder design of 1982 with Queen **Rev:** Value and date **Edge:** Reeded

Date	Mintage	F	VF	XF	Unc	BU
2009 Proof	5,418	Value: 400				

KM# 295 10 EURO
6.7200 g., 0.9000 Gold 0.1944 oz. AGW, 22.5 mm. **Ruler:** Beatrix **Subject:** Max Havelaar, 150th Anniversary of Birth **Rev:** Ink pen, words in spiral, firgures walking around edge **Edge:** Reeded

Date	Mintage	F	VF	XF	Unc	BU
2010B Proof	4,699	Value: 400				

KM# 297 10 EURO
6.7200 g., 0.9000 Gold 0.1944 oz. AGW, 22.5 mm. **Ruler:** Beatrix **Subject:** Waterland **Obv:** Bust of Queen facing and reflected in water **Rev:** Map of the Netherlands, partly under sea level

Date	Mintage	F	VF	XF	Unc	BU
2010 Proof	4,500	Value: 400				

KM# 300 10 EURO
6.7200 g., 0.9000 Gold 0.1944 oz. AGW, 22.5 mm. **Ruler:** Beatrix **Subject:** World Wildlife Fund, 50th Anniversary **Obv:** Profile left at center of tree leaves **Rev:** Value at center of root system **Edge:** Reeded

Date	Mintage	F	VF	XF	Unc	BU
2011B Proof	4,000	Value: 400				

KM# 303 10 EURO
6.7500 g., 0.9000 Gold 0.1953 oz. AGW, 22.5 mm. **Ruler:** Beatrix **Obv:** Head facing **Rev:** Screw press and a QR-code which is to scan with a mobile telephone **Edge:** Reeded

Date	Mintage	F	VF	XF	Unc	BU
2011B Proof	4,000	Value: 400				

KM# 305 10 EURO
6.7200 g., 0.9000 Gold 0.1944 oz. AGW, 22.5 mm. **Ruler:** Beatrix **Subject:** Painting **Obv:** Queen looking at city view painting **Rev:** Window **Edge:** Reeded

Date	Mintage	F	VF	XF	Unc	BU
2011B Proof	3,500	Value: 400				

KM# 310 10 EURO
6.7200 g., 0.9000 Gold 0.1944 oz. AGW, 22.5 mm. **Ruler:** Beatrix **Subject:** 400 years of diplomatic relations Netherlands-Turkey **Edge:** Reeded

Date	Mintage	F	VF	XF	Unc	BU
2012 Proof	—	Value: 400				

KM# 249 20 EURO
8.5000 g., 0.9000 Gold 0.2459 oz. AGW, 25 mm. **Ruler:** Beatrix **Subject:** Birth of Crown-Princess - Catharina-Amalia - July 12, 2003 **Obv:** Bust left **Rev:** Holographic images: left, Princess Maxima; front, Princess Catharina-Amalia; right, Prince Willem-Alexander **Edge:** Reeded

Date	Mintage	F	VF	XF	Unc	BU
2004 Proof	5,345	Value: 530				

KM# 262 20 EURO
8.5000 g., 0.9000 Gold 0.2459 oz. AGW, 25 mm. **Ruler:** Beatrix **Subject:** Silver Jubilee of Reign **Obv:** Queen's photo **Rev:** Queen taking oath photo **Edge:** Reeded **Designer:** Germaine Kruip

Date	Mintage	F	VF	XF	Unc	BU
2005B Proof	5,001	Value: 530				

KM# 250 50 EURO
13.4400 g., 0.9000 Gold 0.3889 oz. AGW, 27 mm. **Ruler:** Beatrix **Subject:** Birth of Crown-Princess - Catharina-Amalia - July 12, 2003 **Obv:** Bust left **Rev:** Holographic images: left, Princess Maxima; front, Princess Catharina-Amalia; right, Prince Willem-Alexander **Edge:** Reeded

Date	Mintage	F	VF	XF	Unc	BU
2004 Proof	3,500	Value: 775				

KM# 263 50 EURO
13.4400 g., 0.9000 Gold 0.3889 oz. AGW, 27 mm. **Ruler:** Beatrix **Subject:** Silver Jubilee of Reign **Obv:** Queen's photo **Rev:** Queen taking oath photo **Edge:** Reeded **Designer:** Germaine Kruip

Date	Mintage	F	VF	XF	Unc	BU
2005B Proof	3,500	Value: 775				

TRADE COINAGE

KM# 190.2 DUCAT
3.4940 g., 0.9830 Gold 0.1104 oz. AGW **Ruler:** Beatrix **Obv:** Knight divides date with larger letters in legend **Rev:** Inscription within decorated square

Date	Mintage	F	VF	XF	Unc	BU
2001 Proof	7,500	Value: 250				
2002 Proof	3,400	Value: 250				
2003 Proof	3,800	Value: 250				
2004 Proof	2,120	Value: 450				
2005 Proof	2,243	Value: 200				
2006 Proof	2,097	Value: 300				
2007 Proof	2,250	Value: 250				
2008 Proof	3,260	Value: 250				
2009 Proof	2,750	Value: 250				
2010 Proof	1,870	Value: 250				
2011 Proof	—	Value: 250				
2012 Proof	—	Value: 250				

KM# 211 2 DUCAT
6.9880 g., 0.9830 Gold 0.2208 oz. AGW, 26 mm. **Ruler:** Beatrix **Obv:** Knight divides date within beaded circle **Rev:** Inscription within decorated square

Date	Mintage	F	VF	XF	Unc	BU
2002B Proof	6,650	Value: 475				
2003B Proof	4,500	Value: 475				
2004B Proof	2,015	Value: 475				
2005B Proof	3,500	Value: 475				
2006B Proof	1,800	Value: 550				
2007B Proof	2,000	Value: 475				
2008B Proof	2,100	Value: 475				
2009B Proof	2,000	Value: 475				
2010B Proof	2,000	Value: 475				
2011B Proof	1,640	Value: 500				
2012B Proof	—	Value: 500				

SILVER BULLION COINAGE

KM# 242 SILVER DUCAT
28.2500 g., 0.8730 Silver 0.7929 oz. ASW, 40 mm. **Ruler:** Beatrix **Obv:** Crowned shield **Rev:** Armored knight with sword divides date and circle, shield in front **Edge:** Reeded **Note:** Utrecht coin design circa 1659 based on KM#48.

Date	Mintage	F	VF	XF	Unc	BU
2001B Proof	9,000	Value: 40.00				

KM# 256 SILVER DUCAT
28.2500 g., 0.8730 Silver 0.7929 oz. ASW, 40 mm. **Ruler:** Beatrix **Obv:** Crowned shield **Rev:** Armored knight with Gelderland arms **Edge:** Reeded

Date	Mintage	F	VF	XF	Unc	BU
2002B Proof	9,400	Value: 40.00				

KM# 257 SILVER DUCAT
28.2500 g., 0.8730 Silver 0.7929 oz. ASW, 40 mm. **Ruler:** Beatrix **Obv:** Crowned shield **Rev:** Armored knight with sword holding arms of Holland **Edge:** Reeded

Date	Mintage	F	VF	XF	Unc	BU
2003B Proof	4,100	Value: 50.00				

KM# 258 SILVER DUCAT
28.2500 g., 0.8730 Silver 0.7929 oz. ASW, 40 mm. **Ruler:** Beatrix **Obv:** Crowned shield **Rev:** Armored knight holding sword with Zeeland arms **Edge:** Reeded

Date	Mintage	F	VF	XF	Unc	BU
2004B Proof	4,109	Value: 50.00				

KM# 259 SILVER DUCAT
28.2500 g., 0.8730 Silver 0.7929 oz. ASW, 40 mm. **Ruler:** Beatrix **Obv:** Crowned shield **Rev:** Armored knight holding sword with Friesland arms **Edge:** Reeded

Date	Mintage	F	VF	XF	Unc	BU
2005B Proof	4,000	Value: 50.00				

KM# 260 SILVER DUCAT
28.2500 g., 0.8730 Silver 0.7929 oz. ASW, 40 mm. **Ruler:** Beatrix **Obv:** Crowned shield **Rev:** Armored knight holding sword with Groningen arms **Edge:** Reeded

Date	Mintage	F	VF	XF	Unc	BU
2006B Proof	4,000	Value: 50.00				

KM# 275 SILVER DUCAT
28.2500 g., 0.8730 Silver 0.7929 oz. ASW, 40 mm. **Ruler:** Beatrix **Obv:** Crowned shield **Rev:** Armored knight holding sword with Overyssel arms **Edge:** Reeded

Date	Mintage	F	VF	XF	Unc	BU
2007 Proof	3,500	Value: 45.00				

KM# 292 SILVER DUCAT
28.2500 g., 0.8730 Silver 0.7929 oz. ASW, 40 mm. **Ruler:** Beatrix **Subject:** Northern Brabant **Obv:** Crowned shield **Rev:** John I, Count of Brabant standing with shield **Edge:** Reeded

Date	Mintage	F	VF	XF	Unc	BU
2008 Proof	3,000	Value: 50.00				

KM# 284 SILVER DUCAT
28.2500 g., 0.8730 Silver 0.7929 oz. ASW, 40 mm. **Ruler:** Beatrix **Rev:** Jan I standing with sword and Gelderland arms

Date	Mintage	F	VF	XF	Unc	BU
2009 Proof	3,000	Value: 50.00				

KM# 293 SILVER DUCAT
28.2500 g., 0.8730 Silver 0.7929 oz. ASW, 40 mm. **Ruler:** Beatrix **Subject:** Limburg **Obv:** Crowned shield **Rev:** Philip II of Montmorency, Count of Horne, standing **Edge:** Reeded

Date	Mintage	F	VF	XF	Unc	BU
2009 Proof	3,500	Value: 50.00				

KM# 285 SILVER DUCAT
28.2500 g., 0.8750 Silver 0.7947 oz. ASW, 40 mm. **Ruler:** Beatrix **Obv:** William of Orange standing with Zuid-Holland arms **Edge:** Reeded

Date	Mintage	F	VF	XF	Unc	BU
2010 Proof	2,850	Value: 50.00				

KM# 286 SILVER DUCAT
28.2500 g., 0.8750 Silver 0.7947 oz. ASW, 40 mm. **Ruler:** Beatrix **Obv:** Frederik Hendrik standing with Gelderland arms **Edge:** Reeded

Date	Mintage	F	VF	XF	Unc	BU
2010 Proof	3,100	Value: 50.00				

KM# 306 SILVER DUCAT
28.2500 g., 0.8730 Silver 0.7929 oz. ASW, 40 mm. **Ruler:** Beatrix **Obv:** Crowned shield **Rev:** Floris V **Edge:** Reeded

Date	Mintage	F	VF	XF	Unc	BU
2011 Proof	—	Value: 50.00				

KM# 307 SILVER DUCAT
28.2500 g., 0.8750 Silver 0.7947 oz. ASW, 40 mm. **Ruler:** Beatrix **Subject:** Zeeland **Obv:** Crowned shield **Rev:** Michiel de Ruyter with shield of Zeeland **Edge:** Reeded

Date	Mintage	F	VF	XF	Unc	BU
2011 Proof	—	Value: 50.00				

KM# 311 SILVER DUCAT
28.2500 g., 0.8750 Silver 0.7947 oz. ASW, 40 mm. **Ruler:** Beatrix **Subject:** Utrecht **Obv:** Crowned shield **Rev:** Stadtholder Willem III with shield of Utrecht **Edge:** Reeded

Date	Mintage	F	VF	XF	Unc	BU
2012 Proof	—	Value: 60.00				

KM# 312 SILVER DUCAT
28.2500 g., 0.8750 Silver 0.7947 oz. ASW, 40 mm. **Ruler:** Beatrix **Subject:** Friesland **Obv:** Crowned shield **Rev:** Willem Lodewijk van Nassau - Dillenbrug with shield of Friesland **Edge:** Reeded

Date	Mintage	F	VF	XF	Unc	BU
2012 Proof	—	Value: 60.00				

PATTERNS

Including off metal strikes

KM#	Date	Mintage	Identification	Mkt Val
Pn164	2001	—	Gulden. Nickel. Medal rotation	—
Pn165	2001	—	2 Euro Cent. Nickel.	100
Pn166	2001	—	Euro. Brass. KM240	150

MINT SETS

KM#	Date	Mintage	Identification	Issue Price	Mkt Val
MS4	2001 (6)	85,000	KM#202-206, 210	12.00	25.00
MS5	2001 (8)	68,000	KM#234-241 Charity set, Disabled Sports	15.00	15.00
MS6	2002 (8)	105,000	KM#234-241 Charity set, Blind Escort Dogs Fund	15.00	30.00
MS7	2002 (8)	59,500	KM#234-241 Last FDC set	15.00	30.00
MS8	2002 (8)	25,000	KM#234-241 plus bear medal Baby set	15.50	30.00
MS9	2002 (8)	10,000	KM#234-241 plus medal Wedding Set	15.50	35.00
MS10	2002 (8)	3,500	KM#234-241 plus medal Queen Beatrix set	20.00	110
MS11	2002 (8)	2,002	KM#234-241 plus medal 10th Day of the Mint	22.00	150
MS12	2002 (8)	10,000	KM#234-241 plus medal VOC set I	22.00	30.00
MS13	2002 (8)	10,000	KM#234-241 plus medal VOC set II	22.00	30.00
MS14	2002 (9)	10,000	KM#234-241 plus medal VOC set III	22.00	30.00
MS15	2002 (8)	10,000	KM#234-241 plus medal VOC set IV	22.00	30.00
MS16	2002 (8)	3,000	KM#234-241 plus medal BVC	30.00	40.00
MS17A	2002 (8)	2,500	KM#234-241 VVV - Irisgiftset	20.00	40.00
MS17	2002 (1)	9,200	KM#243 plus stamp	30.00	55.00
MS18	2002 (8)	1,000	KM#234-241 plus medal Theo Peters (Christmas)	99.00	60.00
MS19	2003 (8)	75,000	KM#234-241 Charity set, Epilepsy fund	15.50	25.00
MS20	2003 (8)	15,000	KM#234-241 Information set Denmark	20.00	40.00
MS21	2003 (9)	10,000	KM#234-241 VVV - Irisgiftset	15.50	25.00
MS22	2003 (8)	10,000	KM#234-241 plus medal VOC set V	22.00	25.00
MS23	2003 (8)	10,000	KM#234-241 plus medal VOC set VI	42.00	45.00
MS24	2003 (7)	2,003	KM#234-241 plus medal Day of the Mint	25.00	100
MS25	2003 (8)	1,000	KM#234-241 plus bi-color medal Theo Peters Jubilee set	—	25.00
MS26	2003 (7)	100	KM#234-241 plus silver medal Theo Peters Jubilee set	70.00	50.00
MS27	2003 (8)	25	KM#234-241 plus golden medal Theo Peters Jubilee set	400	250
MS28	2003 (8)	25,000	KM#234-241 plus bear medal Baby set	20.00	25.00
MS29	2003 (8)	15,000	KM#234-241 plus medal Wedding set	20.00	25.00
MS30	2003 (8)	1,000	KM#234-241 Theo Peters Christmas set + bi-colour medal	—	25.00
MS31	2003 (8)	150	KM#234-241 plus silver medal Theo Peters Christmas set	70.00	50.00
MS32	2003 (8)	50	KM#234-241 plus golden medal Theo Peters Christmas set	400	275
MS33	2003 (8)	3,500	KM#234-241 plus medal Mintmasters I	20.00	60.00
MS34	2003 (8)	1,000	KM#234-241 World Money Fair	20.00	100
MS35	2003 (8)	15,000	KM234-241 Farewell to Wim Duisenberg	—	35.00
MS36	2003 (8)	20,000	KM#234-241 plus silver medal Royal Birth of Princess Catharina-Amalia	22.00	25.00
MS37	2003 (16)	10,000	KM#234-241 and Luxembourg KM#75-81, 40 Benelux Set	40.00	45.00
MS38	2003 (40)	10,000	KM#224-231 plus Germany KM#207-214 plus Spain KM#1040-1047 plus Belgium KM#224-231 and Austria KM#3082-3089 Charles V Set	85.00	85.00
MS39	2004 (8)	3,500	KM#234-241 plus medal Mintmasters II	20.00	60.00
MS40	2004 (8)	10,000	KM#234-241 Wedding set plus medal	18.00	30.00
MS41	2004 (9)	20,000	KM#234-241 Baby set plus bear medal	20.00	30.00
MS42	2004 (8)	1,000	KM#234-241 Basel World Money Fair	20.00	110
MS43	2004 (24)	35,000	KM#234-241 and Luxembourg KM#75-81 plus Belgium KM#224-231 Benelux set with silver medal	60.00	60.00
MS44	2004 (10)	10,000	KM#234-241 Queen Juliana set plus silver guilder, KM#184 and 30mm silver medal	25.00	30.00
MS45	2004 (9)	1,500	KM#234-241 Theo Peters Christmas set plus bi-color medal	30.00	30.00
MS46	2004 (8)	3,500	KM#234-241 VVV - Iris gift set	20.00	30.00
MS47	2004 (9)	150	KM#234-241 Theo Peters Christmas set plus silver medal	100	100
MS48	2004 (9)	50	KM#234-241 Theo Peters Christmas set plus golden medal	500	500
MS49	2004 (8)	50,000	KM#234-241 Fire - Burn Centre Charity set	18.00	30.00
MS50	2004 (9)	—	KM#234-241 Day of the Mint plus medal	25.00	150
MS51	2005 (9)	3,500	KM#234-241 Mintmasters III plus medal	20.00	60.00
MS52	2005 (9)	—	KM#234-241 Day of the Mint plus medal	25.00	150
MS53	2005 (9)	10,000	KM#234-241 Wedding set plus medal	18.00	27.50
MS54	2005 (9)	20,000	KM#234-241 Baby set plus bear medal	20.00	27.50
MS55	2005 (9)	20,000	KM#234-241 Nijntje set (Dick Bruna) plus medal	18.00	27.50
MS56	2005 (8)	55,000	KM#234-241 Charity set: Princess Beatrix Fonds	18.00	25.00
MS57	2005 (24)	20,000	KM#234-241, Belgium 224-231, Luxembourg 75-81 Benelux set: Belgium, Netherlands plus Luxembourg with silver medal	60.00	60.00
MS58	2005 (8)	1,000	KM#234-241 World Money Fair, Basel	25.00	110
MS59	2005 (8)	15,000	KM#234-241 60th Anniversary Liberation plus Canadian 25 cent	35.00	35.00
MS60	2005 (9)	1,000	KM#234-241 Theo Peters Christmas set plus bi-color medal	30.00	30.00
MS61	2005 (9)	100	KM#234-241 Theo Peters Christmas set plus silver medal	120	80.00
MS62	2005 (9)	25	KM#234-241 Theo Peters Christmas set plus golden medal	550	300
MS63	2006 (10)	3,500	KM#234-241 Mintmasters IV plus medal	20.00	40.00
MS64	2006 (10)	4,000	KM#234-241 5 sets plus a Rembrandt silver medal and 1 set with a Rembrandt 5 Euro coin (6x8)	250	210
MS65	2006 (10)	500	KM#234-241 5 sets with Rembrandt silver medal and one set with Rembrandt 10 euro coin (6x8)	900	900
MS66	2006 (8)	45,000	KM#234-241 Charity set: Kika	18.00	30.00
MS67	2006 (9)	2,750	KM#231-241 Baby set boy plus bear medal	20.00	30.00
MS68	2006 (9)	100	KM#234-241 Baby set boy plus silver medal	—	95.00
MS69	2006 (8)	25	KM#234-241 Baby set boy plus gold medal	—	500
MS70	2006 (9)	2,750	KM#234-241 Baby set girl plus bear medal	20.00	30.00
MS71	2006 (8)	100	KM#234-241 Baby set girl plus silver medal	—	95.00
MS72	2006 (9)	25	KM#234-241 Baby set girl, plus gold medal	—	500
MS73	2006 (9)	15,000	KM#234-241 Benelux set: Belgium, 224-231, Luxembourg 75-81 plus Netherlands	65.00	65.00
MS74	2006 (9)	1,050	KM#234-241 Wedding set plus medal	22.00	30.00
MS75	2006 (8)	1,500	KM#234-241 Royal Dutch Mint Christmas set	30.00	30.00
MS76	2006 (9)	600	KM#234-241 Theo Peters Christmas set plus bi-color medal	35.00	40.00
MS77	2006 (9)	100	KM#234-241 Christmas set plus silver medal	150	100
MS78	2006 (9)	25	KM#234-241 Christmas set plus golden medal	650	400
MS79	2006 (8)	1,000	KM#234-241 Berlin Coin Fair	25.00	45.00
MS80	2006 (9)	—	KM#234-241 Day of the Mint set plus medal	25.00	120
MS81	2006 (8)	10,000	KM#234-241 200 Years of Coins in Kingdom of Holland	25.00	30.00
MS82	2007 (9)	3,500	KM#234-236, 268-272 Mintmasters V plus medal	20.00	40.00
MS83	2007 (9)	100	KM#234-236, 268-272 Mintmasters V plus silver medal	—	500
MS84	2007 (8)	3,500	KM#234-236, 268-272 Michiel de Ruyter sets, 1 plus silver medal and 1 set with Ruyter's 5 euro coin	—	250
MS85	2007 (8)	500	KM#234-236, 268-272 Michiel de Ruyter sets, 1 set with silver medal and 1 set with Ruyter's 10 euro coin	900	900
MS86	2007 (8)	40,000	KM#234-236, 268-272 National set	18.00	27.50
MS87	2007 (9)	3,000	KM#234-236, 268-272 Baby set boy plus bear medal	20.00	27.50
MS88	2007 (9)	100	KM#234-236, 268-272 Baby set boy plus silver medal	—	95.00
MS89	2007 (9)	3,000	KM#234-236, 268-272 Baby set girl plus bear medal	20.00	27.50
MS90	2007 (9)	100	KM#234-236, 268-272 Baby set girl plus silver medal	—	95.00
MS92	2007 (9)	1,050	KM#234-236, 268-272 Wedding set plus medal	22.00	27.50
MS93	2007 (9)	1,000	KM#234-236, 268-272 Christmas set plus bi-color medal	35.00	40.00
MS94	2007 (9)	100	KM#234-236, 268-272 Christmas set plus silver medal	150	150
MS95	2007 (9)	25	KM#234-236, 268-272 Christmas set plus golden medal	650	650
MS96	2007 (8)	1,000	KM#234-236, 268-272 Berlin Coin Fair	25.00	75.00
MS97	2007 (9)	—	KM#234-236, 268-272 Day of the Mint plus medal	25.00	100
MS98	2007 (8)	5,000	KM#234-236, 268-272 200 Years of Royal Predicate	25.00	28.00
MS109	2001 (6)	120,000	KM#202-206, 210 Introduction Euro-coins, no medal	15.00	25.00
MS112	2001 (6)	1,000	KM#202-206, 210 BOLEGO-VOK	—	60.00
MS113	2001 (6)	1,000	KM#202-206, 210 De Akerendam II, with a silver 2 stuiver coin from the wreck	125	145
MS114	2001 (6)	1,000	KM#202-206, 210 United Seven Provinces Groningen	40.00	40.00

KM#	Date	Mintage	Identification	Issue Price	Mkt Val
MS115	2001 (6)	1,000	KM#202-206, 210 United Seven Provinces Utrecht	40.00	40.00
MS116	2001 (6)	21,000	KM#202-206, 210 Baby set + bear medal	15.50	25.00
MS117	2001 (6)	1,015	KM#202-206, 210 Onderlinge "s-Grdevenhage"	—	70.00
MS121	2001 (8)	68,000	KM#234-241 Charity set, disabled sport	15.00	17.00
MS122	2002 (8)	105,000	KM#234-241 Charity set, blind escort dogs fund	15.00	30.00
MS123	2002 (8)	59,500	KM#234-241 Last FDS-set	15.00	30.00
MS124	2002 (8)	25,000	KM#234-241 Baby set + bear medal	15.50	30.00
MS125	2002 (8)	10,000	KM#234-241 Wedding-set + medal	15.50	35.00
MS126	2002 (8)	3,500	KM#234-241 Queen Beatrix + medal	20.00	110
MS127	2002 (8)	2,002	KM#234-241 10th day of the Mint + medal	22.00	175
MS128	2002 (8)	10,000	KM#234-241 VOC set I + medal	22.00	35.00
MS129	2002 (8)	10,000	KM#234-241 VOC set II + medal	22.00	30.00
MS130	2002 (8)	10,000	KM#234-241 VOC set III + medal	22.00	30.00
MS131	2002 (8)	10,000	KM#234-241 VOC set IV + medal	22.00	30.00
MS132	2002 (8)	3,000	KM#234-241 BVC + medal	30.00	40.00
MS133	2002 (8)	9,200	KM#234-241 10 Euro + poststamp	30.00	30.00
MS134	2002 (8)	2,500	KM#234-241VVV-Iris gift set	20.00	40.00
MS135	2002 (8)	1,000	KM#234-241 Theo Peters (Christmas) + medal	99.00	90.00
MS136	2003 (8)	75,000	KM#234-241 Charity set, epilepsy fund	15.50	25.00
MS137	2003 (8)	15,000	KM#234-241 Information set Denmark	20.00	40.00
MS138	2003 (8)	10,000	KM#234-241 VVV-Iris gift set	20.00	25.00
MS139	2003 (8)	10,000	KM#234-241 VOC set V + medal	22.00	25.00
MS140	2003 (8)	10,000	KM#234-241 VOC set VI + medal	42.00	45.00
MS141	2003 (8)	2,003	KM#234-241 Day of the mint + medal	25.00	140
MS142	2003 (8)	1,000	KM#234-241 Theo Peters jubilee set + bi-colour medal	—	30.00
MS143	2003 (8)	100	KM#234-241 Theo Peters jubilee set + silver medal	70.00	70.00
MS144	2003 (8)	25	KM#234-241 Theo Peters jubilee set + golden medal	400	410
MS145	2003 (8)	25,000	KM#234-241 Baby set + bear medal	20.00	25.00
MS146	2003 (8)	15,000	KM#234-241 Wedding-set + medal	20.00	25.00
MS147	2003 (8)	1,000	KM#234-241 Theo Peters Christmas set + bi-colour medal	—	30.00
MS148	2003 (8)	150	KM#234-241 Theo Peters Christmas set + silver medal	70.00	70.00
MS149	2003 (8)	50	KM#234-241 Theo Peters Christmas set + golden medal	400	1,000
MS150	2003 (8)	3,500	KM#234-241 Mint masters I + medal	20.00	60.00
MS151	2003 (8)	1,000	KM#234-241 World Money Fair Basel	20.00	130
MS152	2003 (8)	15,000	KM#234-241 Information set Hungaria	20.00	40.00
MS153	2003 (8)	20,000	KM#234-241 Royal birthset of Princess Catharina-Amalia December 7 + silver medal	22.00	25.00
MS154	2003 (8)	10,000	KM#234-241 Benelux set, with Belgium (8) KM#224-231 and Luxembourg (8) KM#75-81	40.00	45.00
MS155	2003 (8)	10,000	KM#234-241 Charles V set + medal, with Germany (8) KM#207-214, Spain (8) KM#1040-1047, Belgium (8) KM#224-231, and Austria (8) KM#3082-3089	85.00	85.00
MS156	2004 (8)	3,500	KM#234-241 Mintmasters II + medal	20.00	60.00
MS157	2004 (8)	10,000	KM#234-241 Wedding-set + medal	18.00	30.00
MS158	2004 (8)	20,000	KM#234-241 Baby set + bear medal	20.00	30.00
MS159	2004 (8)	1,000	KM#234-241 World Money Fair Basel	20.00	110
MS160	2004 (8)	35,000	KM#234-241 Benelux: Belgium, Netherlands + Luxembourg. With silver medal	60.00	60.00
MS161	2004 (8)	10,000	KM#234-241 Queen Juliana-set + silver guilder KM#184 and 30mm silver medal	25.00	30.00
MS162	2004 (8)	1,500	KM#234-241 Theo Peters Christmas set + bi-colour medal	30.00	30.00
MS163	2004 (8)	3,500	KME234-241 VVV-Iris gift set	30.00	25.00
MS164	2004 (8)	150	KM#234-241 Theo Peters Christmas set + silver medal	100	100
MS165	2004 (8)	50	KM#234-241 Theo Peters Christmas set + golden medal	500	500
MS166	2004 (8)	50,000	KM#234-241 Charity set, Fire-burn Centre	18.00	30.00
MS167	2004 (8)	2,004	KM#234-241 Day of the Mint + medal	25.00	150
MS170	2005 (8)	10,000	KM#234-241 Wedding-set + medal	18.00	27.50
MS168	2005 (8)	3,500	KM#234-241 Mintmasters III + medal	20.00	60.00
MS169	2005 (8)	2,005	KM#234-241 Day of the Mint + medal	25.00	150
MS171	2005 (8)	20,000	KM#234-241 Baby set + bear medal	20.00	27.50
MS172	2005 (8)	20,000	KM#234-241 Nijntje-set (Dick Bruna) + medal	18.00	27.50
MS173	2005 (8)	55,000	KM#234-241 Charity set: Princess Beatrix Fonds	18.00	27.50
MS174	2005 (8)	20,000	KM#234-241 Beneluz: Belgium, Netherlands + Luxembourg. With silver medal	60.00	60.00
MS175	2005 (8)	1,000	KM#234-241 World Money Fair Basel	25.00	110
MS176	2005 (8)	15,000	KM#234-241 60th Anniversary Liberation + Canadian 25 ct	35.00	35.00
MS177	2005 (8)	1,000	KM#234-241 Theo Peters Christmas set + bi-colour medal	30.00	30.00
MS178	2005 (8)	100	KM#234-241 Theo Peters Christmas set + silver medal	120	120
MS179	2005 (8)	25	KM#234-241 Theo Peters Christmas set + golden medal	550	550
MS180	2006 (8)	3,500	KM#234-241 Mintmasters IV + medal	20.00	40.00
MS181	2006 (8)	4,000	KM#234-241 5 sets with a Rembrandt silver medal and one set with the Rembrandt 5 euro coin	250	250
MS182	2006 (8)	500	KM#234-241 5 sets with a Rembrandt silver medal and one set with the Rembrandt 10 euro coin	900	900
MS183	2006 (8)	45,000	KM#234-241 Charity set: (Kika)	18.00	30.00
MS184	2006 (8)	2,750	KM#234-241 Baby set boy + bear medal	20.00	30.00
MS185	2006 (8)	100	KM#234-241 Baby set boy + silver medal	—	95.00
MS186	2006 (8)	25	KM#234-241 Baby set boy + gold medal	—	500
MS187	2006 (8)	2,750	KM#234-241 Baby set girl + bear medal	20.00	30.00
MS188	2006 (8)	100	KM#234-241 Baby set girl + silver medal	—	95.00
MS189	2006 (8)	25	KM#234-241 Baby set girl + gold medal	—	500
MS190	2006 (8)	15,000	KM#234-241 Beneluz: Belgium, Netherlands + Luxembourg. With silver medal	65.00	65.00
MS192	2006 (8)	1,050	KM#234-241 Wedding-set + medal	22.00	30.00
MS193	2006 (8)	1,500	KM#234-241 Christmas set Royal Dutch Mint	30.00	30.00
MS194	2006 (8)	600	KM#234-241 Theo Peters Christmas set + bi-colour medal	35.00	40.00
MS195	2006 (8)	100	KM#234-241 Christmas set + silver medal	150	150
MS196	2006 (8)	25	KM#234-241 Christmas set + golden medal	650	650
MS197	2006 (8)	1,000	KM#234-241 Berlin Coin Fair	25.00	45.00
MS198	2006 (8)	2,006	KM#234-241 Day of the Mint + medal	25.00	120
MS199	2006 (8)	10,000	KM#234-241 200 years coins in Kingdom Holland	25.00	30.00
MS200	2006 (8)	3,500	KM#234-236, 268-272 Mintmasters V + medal	20.00	40.00
MS201	2007 (8)	100	KM#234-236, 268-272 Mintmasters V + silver medal	—	600
MS202	2007 (8)	3,500	KM#234-236, 268-272 5 sets Michiel de Ruyter + silver medal and one set with the Michiel de Ruyter 5 euro coin BU	250	250
MS203	2007 (8)	500	KM#234-236, 268-272 5 sets Michiel de Ruyter + silver medal and one set with the Michiel de Ruyter 10 euro coin	900	900
MS204	2007 (8)	40,000	KM#234-236, 268-272 Charity set	18.00	27.50
MS205	2007 (8)	3,000	KM#234-236, 268-272 Baby set boy + bear medal	20.00	27.50
MS206	2007 (8)	100	KM#234-236, 268-272 Baby set boy + silver medal	—	95.00
MS207	2007 (8)	3,000	KM#234-236, 268-272 Baby set girl + bear medal	20.00	27.50
MS208	2007 (8)	100	KM#234-236, 268-272 Baby set girl + silver medal	—	95.00
MS209	2007 (8)	15,000	KM#234-236, 268-272 Benelux: Belgium, Netherlands + Luxembourg. With silver medal + 3x 2 Euro Rome Treaty	75.00	75.00
MS210	2007 (8)	1,050	KM#234-236, 268-272 Wedding-set + medal	22.00	27.50
MS211	2007 (8)	1,000	KM#234-236, 268-272 Christmas set + bi-colour medal	35.00	40.00
MS212	2007 (8)	100	KM#234-236, 268-272 Christmas set + silver medal	150	150
MS213	2007 (8)	25	KM#234-236, 268-272 Christmas set + golden medal	650	650
MS214	2007 (8)	500	KM#234-236, 268-272 Berlin Coin Fair	25.00	90.00
MS215	2007 (8)	2,007	KM#234-236, 268-272 Day of the Mint + medal	25.00	100
MS216	2007 (8)	5,000	KM#234-236, 268-272 200 years of Royal predicate	25.00	28.00
MS224	2008 (8)	12,500	KM#234-236, 268-272 Benelux: Belgium, Netherlands + Luxembourg. With silver medal	75.00	75.00
MS217	2008 (8)	3,500	KM#234-236, 268-272 Mintmasters VI + medal	20.00	40.00
MS218	2008 (8)	100	KM#234-236, 268-272 Mintmasters VI + silver medal	20.00	500
MS219	2008 (8)	40,000	KM#234-236, 268-272 National set	20.00	27.50
MS220	2008 (8)	2,500	KM#234-236, 268-272 Baby set boy + bear medal	25.00	27.50
MS221	2008 (8)	100	KM#234-236, 268-272 Baby set boy + silver medal	65.00	65.00
MS222	2008 (8)	2,500	KM#234-236, 268-272 Baby set girl + bear medal	25.00	27.50
MS223	2008 (8)	100	KM#234-236, 268-272 Baby set girl + silver medal	65.00	65.00
MS225	2008 (8)	1,250	KM#234-236, 268-272 Wedding-set + medal	22.00	27.50
MS226	2008 (8)	500	KM#234-236, 268-272 Christmas set + bi-colour medal	35.00	40.00
MS227	2008 (8)	50	KM#234-236, 268-272 Christmas set + silver medal	130	135
MS228	2008 (8)	25	KM#234-236, 268-272 Christmas set + golden medal	850	850
MS229	2008 (8)	500	KM#234-236, 268-272 Berlin Coin Fair	25.00	75.00
MS230	2008 (8)	2,008	KM#234-236, 268-272 Day of the Mint + medal	25.00	80.00
MS231	2008 (8)	5,000	KM#234-236, 268-272 150 year Queen Emma + silver medal	32.00	35.00
MS232	2008 (8)	500	KM#234-236, 268-272 Theo Peters Jubilation set + bi-colour medal	35.00	40.00
MS233	2008 (8)	50	KM#234-236, 268-272 Theo Peters Jubilation set + silver medal	130	135
MS234	2008 (8)	25	KM#234-236, 268-272 Theo Peters Jubilation set + golden medal	850	850
MS235	2008 (8)	500	KM#234-236, 268-272 5 sets "2 centuries Amsterdam capitol of the Netherlands" + gold plated silver medals and one set with the golden Arctecture 10 euro coin	900	1,000
MS236	2009 (8)	3,500	KM#234-236, 268-272 Mintmasters VII + medal	22.00	40.00
MS238	2009 (8)	35,000	KM#234-236, 268-272 National set	20.00	27.50
MS239	2009 (8)	2,500	KM#234-236, 268-272 Baby set boy + bear medal	25.00	27.50
MS240	2009 (8)	250	KM#234-236, 268-272 Baby set boy + silver medal	65.00	65.00
MS241	2009 (8)	2,500	KM#234-236, 268-272 Baby set girl + bear medal	25.00	27.50
MS242	2009 (8)	250	KM#234-236, 268-272 Baby set girl + silver medal	65.00	65.00
MS243	2009 (8)	12,500	KM#234-236, 268-272 Benelux: Belgium, Netherlands + Luxembourg. With silver medal	75.00	75.00
MS244	2009 (8)	1,250	KM#234-236, 268-272 Wedding-set + medal	22.00	27.50
MS245	2009 (8)	500	KM#234-236, 268-272 Christmas set + bi-colour medal	35.00	40.00
MS246	2009 (8)	500	KM#234-236, 268-272 Berlin Coin Fair	25.00	95.00
MS247	2009 (8)	2,009	KM#234-236, 268-272	25.00	80.00
MS248	2009 (8)	5,000	KM#234-236, 268-272 100 year anniv. Queen Juliana + silver medal	32.00	35.00
MS249	2009 (8)	1,000	KM#234-236, 268-272 Mercedes jubileum (2010)	—	65.00
MS250	2009 (8)	500	KM#234-236, 268-272 Tokyo Coin Fair	—	375
MS251	2010 (8)	3,500	KM#234-236, 268-272 Museum coin treasures 1 + medal	22.00	40.00
MS252	2010 (8)	100	KM#234-236, 268-272 Museum coin treasures 1 + silver medal	22.00	500
MS253	2010 (8)	25,000	KM#234-236, 268-272 National set	20.00	27.50
MS254	2010 (8)	2,000	KM#234-236, 268-272 Baby set boy + bear medal	30.00	30.00

KM#	Date	Mintage	Identification	Issue Price	Mkt Val
MS255	2010 (8)	250	KM#234-236, 268-272 Baby set boy + silver medal	75.00	75.00
MS256	2010 (8)	2,000	KM#234-236, 268-272 Baby set girl + bear medal	30.00	30.00
MS257	2010 (8)	250	KM#234-236, 268-272 Baby set girl + silver medal	75.00	75.00
MS258	2010 (8)	12,500	KM#234-236, 268-262 Benelux: Belgium, Netherlands + Luxembourg. With silver medal	75.00	75.00
MS259	2010 (8)	1,000	KM#234-236, 268-272 Wedding-set + medal	22.00	27.50
MS260	2010 (8)	500	KM#234-236, 268-272 Christmas set + bi-colour medal	40.00	40.00
MS261	2010 (8)	500	KM#234-236, 268-272 Berlin Coin Fair	25.00	95.00
MS262	2010 (8)	2,010	KM#234-236, 268-272 Day of the Mint + medal	25.00	80.00
MS263	2010 (8)	5,000	KM#234-236, 268-272 30th anniv. Reign Queen Beatrix + silver medal	40.00	40.00
MS264	2011 (8)	3,500	KM#234-236, 268-272 Museum coin treasures 2 + medal	30.00	40.00
MS265	2011 (8)	100	KM#234-236, 268-272 Museum coin treasures 2 + silver medal	30.00	500
MS266	2011 (8)	25,000	KM#234-236, 268-272 National set	30.00	30.00
MS267	2011 (8)	5,000	KM#234-236, 268-272 Birth set + bear medal	30.00	30.00
MS268	2011 (8)	1,250	KM#234-236, 268-272 Baby set boy + bear medal	30.00	30.00
MS269	2011 (8)	100	KM#234-236, 268-272 Baby set boy + silver medal	80.00	80.00
MS270	2011 (8)	2,000	KM#234-236, 268-272 Baby set girl + bear medal	30.00	30.00
MS271	2011 (8)	100	KM#234-236, 268-272 Baby set girl + silver medal	80.00	80.00
MS272	2011 (8)	10,000	KM#234-236, 268-272 Beneluz: Belgium, Netherlands + Luxembourg. With silver medal	75.00	75.00
MS273	2011 (8)	750	KM#234-236, 268-272 Wedding set + medal	30.00	30.00
MS274	2011 (8)	400	KM#234-236, 268-272 Christmas set + bi-colour medal	45.00	45.00
MS275	2011 (9)	400	KM#234-236, 268-272, 298 Christmas set + bi-colour medal	65.00	65.00
MS276	2011 (8)	500	KM#234-236, 268-272 Berlin Coin Fair	25.00	95.00
MS277	2011 (8)	2,011	KM#234-236, 268-272 100th anniv. Bith Prince Bernhard + silver medal	25.00	80.00
MS278	2011 (8)	5,000	KM#234-236, 268-272 100th anniv. Bith Prince Bernhard + silver medal	45.00	45.00
MS279	2012 (8)	—	KM#234-236, 268-272 Museum coin treasures 2 + medal	30.00	40.00
MS280	2012 (8)	—	KM#234-236, 268-272 Museum coin treasures 2 + silver medal	30.00	500
MS281	2012 (8)	—	KM#234-236, 268-272 National set	30.00	30.00
MS282	2012 (8)	—	KM#234-236, 268-272 Birth set + bear medal	30.00	30.00
MS283	2012 (8)	—	KM#234-236, 268-272 Baby set boy + bear medal	30.00	30.00
MS284	2012 (8)	—	KM#234-236, 268-272 Baby set boy + silver medal	80.00	80.00
MS285	2012 (8)	—	KM#234-236, 268-272 Baby set girl + bear medal	30.00	30.00
MS286	2012 (8)	—	KM#234-236, 268-272 Baby set girl + silver medal	80.00	80.00
MS287	2012 (8)	—	KM#234-236, 268-272 Benelux: Belgium Netherlands + Luxembourg. With silver medal	75.00	75.00
MS288	2012 (8)	—	KM#234-236, 268-272 Berlin Coin Fair	25.00	95.00

PROOF SETS

KM#	Date	Mintage	Identification	Issue Price	Mkt Val
PS54	2001 (6)	17,000	KM#202-206, 210 Booklet 5 Guilder	50.00	45.00
PS55	2001 (2)	500	KM#190.2, 242 Gold and Silver Ducat	50.00	220
PS56	2002 (2)	—	KM#190.2, 211 Golden Ducats	—	650
PS58	2003 (2)	—	KM#190.2, 211 Golden ducats in wooden box	230	650
PS59	2003 (8)	2,000	KM#234-241 Frigate "The Netherland" and silver medal and numbered ingot	85.00	125
PS63	2001 (7)	17,000	KM#202-207, 210 Booklet 5 guilder	50.00	110
PS64	2001 (2)	500	KM#190.2, 242 Gold + silver ducat	—	220
PS65	2002 (2)	—	KM#190.2, 211 Golden ducats	—	650
PS66	2002 (3)	—	KM#190.2, 211, 256 Golden ducats + silver ducat	—	665
PS67	2003 (2)	—	KM#190.2, 211 Golden ducats in wooden box	230	650
PS68	2004 (8)	5,000	KM#234-241 Proofset in wooden box	60.00	90.00
PS69	2005 (8)	5,000	KM#234-241 Proofset in wooden box	60.00	90.00
PS70	2005 (2)	2,500	KM#254, 264 60 years of freedom	—	550
PS71	2006 (8)	3,500	KM#234-241, Proofset in wooden box	—	90.00
PS72	2006 (1)	—	5 Euro KM#255, Australian $5	90.00	110
PS73	2006 (1)	—	5 Euro KM#255, 10 Euro, Australian $5 and $10	—	650
PS74	2007 (9)	10,000	KM#234-236, 268-272, 273	—	90.00
PS75	2008 (8)	10,000	KM#234-236, 268-272	—	65.00
PS76	2003 (8)	2,000	KM#234-241 Frigateship "The Netherland" + silver medal and numbered ingot. "Mintmaster Set" in wooden box	125	125
PS77	2004 (8)	1,000	KM#234-241 Value transport over sea during the eighty year of war + silver medal and numbered ingot. "Mintmaster Set" in wooden box	125	125
PS78	2005 (8)	1,000	KM#234-241 Value transport over sea 1650-1750 + silver medal and numbered ingot. "Mintmaster Set" in wooden box	125	125
PS79	2006 (8)	1,500	KM#234-241 Plus silver medal and numbered ingot. "Mintmaster Set" in wooden box	125	125
PS80	2009 (1)	2,000	KM281 EMU	25.00	150
PS81	2009 (9)	7,500	KM234-236, 268-272, 281	—	70.00
PS82	2010 (8)	5,000	KM234-236, 268-272	—	60.00
PS83	2011 (1)	1,500	KM298 Erasmus	30.00	140
PS84	2011 (9)	5,000	KM234-236, 268-272, 298	—	100
PS85	2009 (9)	7,500	KM234-236, 268-272, 281	—	65.00
PS86	2010 (8)	5,000	KM234-236, 268-272	—	60.00
PS87	2011 (9)	5,000	KM234-236, 268-272, 298	—	90.00
PS88	2004 (8)	10,000	KM#234-241	—	70.00
PS89	2005 (8)	10,000	KM#234-241	—	70.00
PS237	2009 (8)	100	KM#234-236, 268-272 Mintmasters VII + silver medal	22.00	500

PROOF-LIKE SETS (PL)

KM#	Date	Mintage	Identification	Issue Price	Mkt Val
PL3	2001 (8)	16,500	KM#234-241	50.00	40.00
PL4	2002 (2)	—	KM#243, 244 Wedding set (10 Euro in silver and gold) in plastic box	145	400
PL5	2002 (2)	—	KM#243, 244 Wedding set in wooden box	145	400
PL6	2002 (8)	15,500	KM#234-241	50.00	40.00
PL7	2003 (8)	10,000	KM#234-241	50.00	40.00
PL12	2001 (8)	16,500	KM#234-241	50.00	40.00
PL13	2002 (2)	—	KM#243-244 Wedding set (10 Euro silver and gold) in plastic box	145	400
PL14	2002 (2)	—	KM#243-244 Wedding set in wooden box	145	400
PL15	2002 (8)	16,500	KM#234-241	50.00	40.00
PL16	2003 (8)	16,500	KM#234-241	50.00	40.00

SELECT SETS (FLEUR DE COIN)

KM#	Date	Mintage	Identification	Issue Price	Mkt Val
SS90	2001 (6)	120,000	KM#202-206, 210 Introduction to Euro Coins	15.00	25.00
SS91	2001 (6)	3,400	KM#202-206, 210 Queen Julianna Medal	17.50	30.00
SS92	2001 (6)	100	KM#202-206, 210 Queen Julianna Medal; some coins dated 2000 in error	17.50	150
SS93	2001 (6)	1,000	KM#202-206, 210 BOLEGO - VOK	—	120
SS94	2001 (6)	1,000	KM#202-206, 210, 2 Stuiver coin from the wreck of the De Akerendam II	125	120
SS95	2001 (6)	1,000	KM#202-206, 210 United Provinces, Groningen Medal	40.00	20.00
SS96	2001 (6)	21,000	KM#202-206, 210 Baby set plus bear medal	15.50	25.00
SS97	2001 (6)	1,015	KM#202-206, 210 Onderlinge "'s-Gravenhage"	70.00	250

SPECIMEN FDC SETS (FLEUR DE COIN)

KM#	Date	Mintage	Identification	Issue Price	Mkt Val
SS95A	2001 (6)	1,000	KM202-206, 210 United Provinces, Utrecht Medal	40.00	40.00

NETHERLANDS ANTILLES

The Netherlands Antilles, comprises two groups of islands in the West Indies: Aruba (until 1986), Bonaire and Curacao and their dependencies near the Venezuelan coast and St. Eustatius, Saba, and the southern part of St. Martin (*St. Maarten*) southeast of Puerto Rico. The island group has an area of 371 sq. mi. (960 sq. km.) and a population of 225,000. Capital: Willemstad. Chief industries are the refining of crude oil and tourism. Petroleum products and phosphates are exported.

RULERS

Beatrix, 1980-

MINT MARKS

Y – York Mint

Utrecht Mint
(privy marks only)

Date	Privy Mark
2001	Wine tendril with grapes
2002	Wine tendril with grapes and star
2003	Sails of a clipper

MONETARY SYSTEM

100 Cents = 1 Gulden

DUTCH ADMINISTRATION

DECIMAL COINAGE

KM# 32 CENT

0.7000 g., Aluminum, 14 mm. **Ruler:** Beatrix **Obv:** Orange blossom within circle **Rev:** Value within circle of geometric designed border **Edge:** Reeded

Date	Mintage	F	VF	XF	Unc	BU
2001(u)	12,806,500	—	—	0.10	0.20	0.50
2002(u) In sets only	6,000	—	—	—	—	2.00
2003(u)	19,604,000	—	—	0.10	0.20	1.50
2004(u) In sets only	7,100	—	—	—	0.60	1.50
2005(u)	—	—	—	0.10	0.60	1.50
2006(u)	—	—	—	0.10	0.60	1.50
2007(u)	—	—	—	0.10	0.60	1.50
2008(u)	—	—	—	0.10	0.60	1.50
2009(u)	—	—	—	0.10	0.60	1.50
2010(u)	—	—	—	0.10	0.60	1.50
2011(u)	—	—	—	0.10	0.60	1.50
2012(u)	—	—	—	0.10	0.60	1.50

KM# 33 5 CENTS

1.1600 g., Aluminum, 16 mm. **Ruler:** Beatrix **Obv:** Orange blossom within circle **Rev:** Value within circle, geometric designed border **Edge:** Reeded

Date	Mintage	F	VF	XF	Unc	BU
2001	2,006,500	—	—	0.20	0.60	1.25
2002 In sets only	6,000	—	—	—	—	2.50
2003	3,104,000	—	—	0.30	0.60	1.25
2004	2,402,100	—	—	0.30	0.50	1.25
2005	—	—	—	0.30	0.50	1.50
2006	—	—	—	0.30	0.50	1.50
2007	—	—	—	0.30	0.50	1.50
2008	—	—	—	0.30	0.50	1.50
2009	—	—	—	0.30	0.50	1.50
2010	—	—	—	0.30	0.50	1.50
2011	—	—	—	0.30	0.50	1.50
2012	—	—	—	0.30	0.50	1.50

KM# 34 10 CENTS

3.0000 g., Nickel Bonded Steel, 18 mm. **Ruler:** Beatrix **Obv:** Orange blossom within circle **Rev:** Value within circle, geometric designed border **Edge:** Reeded

Date	Mintage	F	VF	XF	Unc	BU
2001 In sets only	11,500	—	—	—	—	3.00
2002 In sets only	6,000	—	—	—	—	3.00

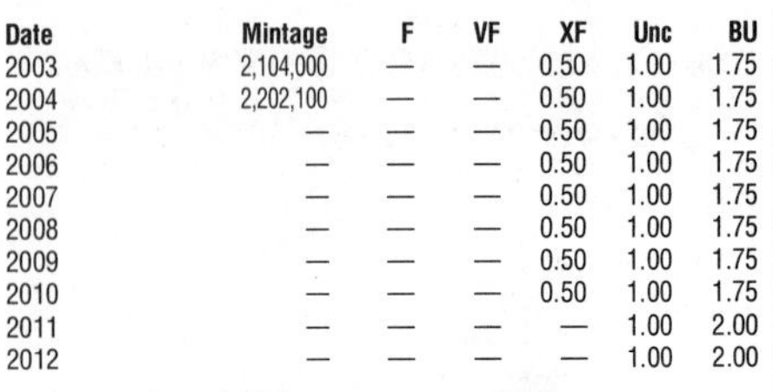

Date	Mintage	F	VF	XF	Unc	BU
2003	2,104,000	—	—	0.50	1.00	1.75
2004	2,202,100	—	—	0.50	1.00	1.75
2005	—	—	—	0.50	1.00	1.75
2006	—	—	—	0.50	1.00	1.75
2007	—	—	—	0.50	1.00	1.75
2008	—	—	—	0.50	1.00	1.75
2009	—	—	—	0.50	1.00	1.75
2010	—	—	—	0.50	1.00	1.75
2011	—	—	—	—	1.00	2.00
2012	—	—	—	—	1.00	2.00

KM# 35 25 CENTS

3.5000 g., Nickel Bonded Steel, 20.2 mm. **Ruler:** Beatrix **Obv:** Orange blossom within circle **Rev:** Value within circle, geometric designed border **Edge:** Reeded

Date	Mintage	F	VF	XF	Unc	BU
2001 In sets only	11,500	—	—	—	—	3.00
2002 In sets only	6,000	—	—	—	—	3.00
2003	1,404,000	—	—	0.50	1.25	1.50
2004	1,502,100	—	—	0.50	1.25	1.50
2005	—	—	—	0.50	1.25	1.50
2006	—	—	—	0.50	1.25	1.50
2007	—	—	—	0.50	1.25	1.50
2008	—	—	—	0.50	1.25	1.50
2009	—	—	—	0.50	1.25	1.50
2010	—	—	—	0.50	1.25	1.50
2011	—	—	—	—	1.25	2.00
2012	—	—	—	—	1.25	2.00

KM# 36 50 CENTS

5.0000 g., Aureate Steel, 24 mm. **Ruler:** Beatrix **Obv:** Orange blossom within circle, designed border **Rev:** Value within circle of pearls and shell border **Edge:** Plain **Shape:** 4-sided

Date	Mintage	F	VF	XF	Unc	BU
2001 In sets only	11,500	—	—	—	—	4.00
2002 In sets only	6,000	—	—	—	—	6.00
2003 In sets only	9,000	—	—	—	—	4.00
2004 In sets only	7,100	—	—	—	—	4.00
2005	—	—	—	0.75	3.00	4.00
2006	—	—	—	0.75	3.00	4.00
2007	—	—	—	0.75	3.00	4.00
2008	—	—	—	0.75	3.00	4.00
2009	—	—	—	0.75	3.00	4.00
2010	—	—	—	0.75	3.00	4.00
2011	—	—	—	—	3.00	5.00
2012	—	—	—	—	3.00	5.00

KM# 37 GULDEN

6.0000 g., Aureate Steel, 24 mm. **Ruler:** Beatrix **Obv:** Head left **Rev:** Crowned shield divides value above date and ribbon **Edge Lettering:** GOD * ZIJ * MET * ONS *

Date	Mintage	F	VF	XF	Unc	BU
2001 In sets only	11,500	—	—	—	—	4.00
2002 In sets only	6,000	—	—	—	—	6.00
2003	504,000	—	—	0.75	3.00	5.00
2004 In sets only	7,100	—	—	—	—	6.00
2005	—	—	—	0.75	3.00	5.00
2006	—	—	—	0.75	3.00	5.00
2007	—	—	—	0.75	3.00	5.00
2008	—	—	—	0.75	3.00	5.00
2009	—	—	—	0.75	3.00	5.00
2010	—	—	—	0.75	3.00	5.00
2011	—	—	—	—	3.00	7.00
2012	—	—	—	—	3.00	7.00

KM# 38 2-1/2 GULDEN

9.0000 g., Aureate Steel, 28 mm. **Ruler:** Beatrix **Obv:** Head left **Rev:** Crowned shield divides value above date and ribbon **Edge Lettering:** GOD * ZIJ * MET * ONS *

Date	Mintage	F	VF	XF	Unc	BU
2001 In sets only	11,500	—	—	—	—	6.00
2002 In sets only	6,000	—	—	—	—	10.00
2003 In sets only	9,000	—	—	—	—	10.00
2004 In sets only	7,100	—	—	—	—	10.00
2005	—	—	—	1.00	5.00	10.00
2006	—	—	—	1.00	5.00	10.00
2007	—	—	—	1.00	5.00	10.00
2008	—	—	—	1.00	5.00	10.00
2009	—	—	—	1.00	5.00	10.00
2010	—	—	—	1.00	5.00	10.00
2011	—	—	—	—	5.00	10.00
2012	—	—	—	—	5.00	10.00

KM# 43 5 GULDEN

14.0000 g., Aureate Bonded Steel, 26 mm. **Ruler:** Beatrix **Obv:** Head left **Rev:** Crowned shield divides value above date and ribbon **Edge Lettering:** GOD * ZIJ * MET * ONS *

Date	Mintage	F	VF	XF	Unc	BU
2001 In sets only	9,500	—	—	—	—	7.50
2002 In sets only	6,000	—	—	—	—	7.50
2003 In sets only	7,000	—	—	—	—	7.50
2004	102,100	—	—	2.00	4.00	8.00
2005	—	—	—	2.00	5.00	10.00
2006	—	—	—	2.00	5.00	10.00
2007	—	—	—	2.00	5.00	10.00
2008	—	—	—	2.00	5.00	10.00
2009	—	—	—	2.00	5.00	10.00
2010	—	—	—	2.00	5.00	10.00
2011	—	—	—	—	5.00	10.00
2012	—	—	—	—	5.00	10.00

KM# 74 5 GULDEN

11.9000 g., 0.9250 Silver 0.3539 oz. ASW, 29 mm. **Ruler:** Beatrix **Subject:** 50th Anniversary - Charter for the Kingdom of Netherlands including Aruba as third party **Obv:** Head left **Rev:** Triangular design with hands writing signatures around value **Edge Lettering:** GOD * ZIJ * MET * ONS * **Designer:** Ans Mezas-Hummelink

Date	Mintage	F	VF	XF	Unc	BU
2004(u) Proof	4,000	Value: 35.00				

KM# 74.1 5 GULDEN

11.0000 g., Aureate Bonded Steel, 26 mm. **Ruler:** Beatrix **Subject:** 50th Anniversary - End To Dutch Colonial Rule **Obv:** Head left **Rev:** Triangular signatures around value **Edge Lettering:** GOD * ZIJ * MET * ONS *

Date	Mintage	F	VF	XF	Unc	BU
2004	10,000	—	—	7.00	15.00	20.00

KM# 76 5 GULDEN

11.9000 g., 0.9250 Silver 0.3539 oz. ASW, 29 mm. **Ruler:** Beatrix **Subject:** Queen's Silver Jubilee **Obv:** Head left **Rev:** Child art and value **Edge Lettering:** GOD * ZIJ * MET * ONS * **Designer:** T. Martha

Date	Mintage	F	VF	XF	Unc	BU
2005(u) Proof	4,000	Value: 35.00				

KM# 76.1 5 GULDEN

11.0000 g., Aureate Bonded Steel, 26 mm. **Ruler:** Beatrix **Subject:** Queen's Silver Jubilee **Obv:** Head left **Rev:** Child art and value **Edge Lettering:** GOD * ZIJ * MET * ONS *

Date	Mintage	F	VF	XF	Unc	BU
2005	10,000	—	—	7.00	15.00	20.00

KM# 80 5 GULDEN

11.9000 g., 0.9250 Silver 0.3539 oz. ASW, 29 mm. **Ruler:** Beatrix **Subject:** 50 Years Brishopric Willemstad **Obv:** Logo Brishopric **Rev:** Cathedral **Edge Lettering:** GOD * Z'J * MET * ONS * **Designer:** Tirzo Martha

Date	Mintage	F	VF	XF	Unc	BU
2008 Proof	—	Value: 35.00				

KM# 79 5 GULDEN

11.9000 g., 0.9250 Silver 0.3539 oz. ASW, 29 mm. **Ruler:** Beatrix **Obv:** Antoine Maduro **Rev:** Crowned shield divides value **Edge Lettering:** GOD * ZIJ * MET * ONS *

Date	Mintage	F	VF	XF	Unc	BU
2009 Proof	1,250	Value: 35.00				

KM# 49 10 GULDEN

31.1035 g., 0.9250 Silver 0.9250 oz. ASW, 40 mm. **Ruler:** Beatrix **Subject:** Gold Trade Coins: Sulla Aureus **Obv:** Crowned shield divides value above date and ribbon **Rev:** Bust facing with two gold coins at lower left **Edge:** Plain

Date	Mintage	F	VF	XF	Unc	BU
2001(u) Proof	589	Value: 80.00				

KM# 50 10 GULDEN

31.1035 g., 0.9250 Silver 0.9250 oz. ASW, 40 mm. **Ruler:** Beatrix **Subject:** Gold Trade Coins: Constantin I Solidus **Obv:** Crowned shield divides value above date and ribbon **Rev:** Bust facing with two gold coins at lower right **Edge:** Plain

Date	Mintage	F	VF	XF	Unc	BU
2001(u) Proof	578	Value: 80.00				

KM# 51 10 GULDEN

31.1035 g., 0.9250 Silver 0.9250 oz. ASW, 40 mm. **Ruler:** Beatrix **Subject:** Gold Trade Coins: Clovis I Tremissis fiorino d'oro **Obv:** Crowned shield divides value above date and ribbon **Rev:** Bust facing with two gold coins **Edge:** Plain

Date	Mintage	F	VF	XF	Unc	BU
2001(u) Proof	566	Value: 80.00				

KM# 52 10 GULDEN

31.1035 g., 0.9250 Silver 0.9250 oz. ASW, 40 mm. **Ruler:** Beatrix **Subject:** Gold Trade Coins: Cosimo de'Medici Fiorino d'oro **Obv:** Crowned shield divides value above date and ribbon **Rev:** Bust facing with two gold coins **Edge:** Plain

Date	Mintage	F	VF	XF	Unc	BU
2001(u) Proof	575	Value: 80.00				

KM# 53 10 GULDEN

31.1035 g., 0.9250 Silver 0.9250 oz. ASW, 40 mm. **Ruler:** Beatrix **Subject:** Gold Trade Coins: Dandolo Ducato d'Oro **Obv:** Crowned shield divides value above date and ribbon **Rev:** Bust facing with two gold coins **Edge:** Plain

Date	Mintage	F	VF	XF	Unc	BU
2001(u) Proof	490	Value: 80.00				

KM# 54 10 GULDEN

31.1035 g., 0.9250 Silver 0.9250 oz. ASW, 40 mm. **Ruler:** Beatrix **Subject:** Gold Trade Coins: Philips IV Ecu d'or la chaise **Obv:** Crowned shield divides value above date and ribbon **Rev:** Bust facing with two gold coins **Edge:** Plain

Date	Mintage	F	VF	XF	Unc	BU
2001(u) Proof	460	Value: 80.00				

KM# 55 10 GULDEN

31.1035 g., 0.9250 Silver 0.9250 oz. ASW, 40 mm. **Ruler:** Beatrix **Subject:** Gold Trade Coins: Edward III Nobel **Obv:** Crowned shield divides value above date and ribbon **Rev:** Crowned bust facing with two gold coins **Edge:** Plain

Date	Mintage	F	VF	XF	Unc	BU
2001(u) Proof	575	Value: 80.00				

KM# 56 10 GULDEN
31.1035 g., 0.9250 Silver 0.9250 oz. ASW, 40 mm. **Ruler:** Beatrix **Subject:** Gold Trade Coins: Carolus IV Rhine Gold Guilder **Obv:** Crowned shield divides value above date and ribbon **Rev:** Bust facing with two gold coins **Edge:** Plain

Date	Mintage	F	VF	XF	Unc	BU
2001(u) Proof	430	Value: 80.00				

KM# 57 10 GULDEN
31.1035 g., 0.9250 Silver 0.9250 oz. ASW, 40 mm. **Ruler:** Beatrix **Subject:** Gold Trade Coins: John II Franc d'or a cheval **Obv:** Crowned shield divides value above date and ribbon **Rev:** Bust facing with two gold coins **Edge:** Plain

Date	Mintage	F	VF	XF	Unc	BU
2001(u) Proof	464	Value: 80.00				

KM# 58 10 GULDEN
31.1035 g., 0.9250 Silver 0.9250 oz. ASW, 40 mm. **Ruler:** Beatrix **Subject:** Gold Trade Coins: Philip the Good Adriesguilder **Obv:** Crowned shield divides value above date and ribbon **Rev:** Bust facing with two gold coins **Edge:** Plain

Date	Mintage	F	VF	XF	Unc	BU
2001(u) Proof	250	Value: 120				

KM# 59 10 GULDEN
31.1035 g., 0.9250 Silver 0.9250 oz. ASW, 40 mm. **Ruler:** Beatrix **Subject:** Gold Trade Coins: Louis XI Ecu d'or au soleil **Obv:** Crowned shield divides value above date and ribbon **Rev:** Bust facing with two gold coins **Edge:** Plain

Date	Mintage	F	VF	XF	Unc	BU
2001(u) Proof	450	Value: 80.00				

KM# 60 10 GULDEN
31.1035 g., 0.9250 Silver 0.9250 oz. ASW, 40 mm. **Ruler:** Beatrix **Subject:** Gold Trade Coins: Elisabeth I Sovereign **Obv:** Crowned shield divides value above date and ribbon **Rev:** Bust facing with two gold coins **Edge:** Plain

Date	Mintage	F	VF	XF	Unc	BU
2001(u) Proof	450	Value: 80.00				

KM# 61 10 GULDEN
31.1035 g., 0.9250 Silver 0.9250 oz. ASW, 40 mm. **Ruler:** Beatrix **Subject:** Gold Trade Coins: Carolus V Carolus Guilder **Obv:** Crowned shield divides value above date and ribbon **Rev:** Bust facing with two gold coins **Edge:** Plain

Date	Mintage	F	VF	XF	Unc	BU
2001(u) Proof	440	Value: 80.00				

KM# 62 10 GULDEN
31.1035 g., 0.9250 Silver 0.9250 oz. ASW, 40 mm. **Ruler:** Beatrix **Subject:** Gold Trade Coins: Philips II Real **Obv:** Crowned shield divides value above date and ribbon **Rev:** Bust facing with two gold coins **Edge:** Plain

Date	Mintage	F	VF	XF	Unc	BU
2001(u) Proof	440	Value: 80.00				

KM# 63 10 GULDEN
31.1035 g., 0.9250 Silver 0.9250 oz. ASW, 40 mm. **Ruler:** Beatrix **Subject:** Gold Trade Coins: Maurits Ducat **Obv:** Crowned shield divides value above date and ribbon **Rev:** Bust facing with two gold coins **Edge:** Plain

Date	Mintage	F	VF	XF	Unc	BU
2001(u) Proof	443	Value: 80.00				

KM# 64 10 GULDEN
31.1035 g., 0.9250 Silver 0.9250 oz. ASW, 40 mm. **Ruler:** Beatrix **Subject:** Gold Trade Coins: Isabella and Albrecht Double Albertin **Obv:** Crowned shield divides value above date and ribbon **Rev:** Conjoined busts facing with two gold coins **Edge:** Plain

Date	Mintage	F	VF	XF	Unc	BU
2001(u) Proof	490	Value: 80.00				

KM# 65 10 GULDEN
31.1035 g., 0.9250 Silver 0.9250 oz. ASW, 40 mm. **Ruler:** Beatrix **Subject:** Gold Trade Coins: William III Golden Rider **Obv:** Crowned shield divides value above date and ribbon **Rev:** Bust facing with two gold coins **Edge:** Plain

Date	Mintage	F	VF	XF	Unc	BU
2001(u) Proof	440	Value: 80.00				

KM# 66 10 GULDEN
31.1035 g., 0.9250 Silver 0.9250 oz. ASW, 40 mm. **Ruler:** Beatrix **Subject:** Gold Trade Coins: Louis XIII Louis d'or **Obv:** Crowned shield divides value above date and ribbon **Rev:** Bust facing with two gold coins **Edge:** Plain

Date	Mintage	F	VF	XF	Unc	BU
2001(u) Proof	440	Value: 80.00				

KM# 67 10 GULDEN
31.1035 g., 0.9250 Silver 0.9250 oz. ASW, 40 mm. **Ruler:** Beatrix **Subject:** Gold Trade Coins: Catharina the Great Rubel **Obv:** Crowned shield divides value above date and ribbon **Rev:** Crowned laureate bust facing with two gold coins **Edge:** Plain

Date	Mintage	F	VF	XF	Unc	BU
2001(u) Proof	560	Value: 100				

KM# 68 10 GULDEN
31.1035 g., 0.9250 Silver 0.9250 oz. ASW, 40 mm. **Ruler:** Beatrix **Subject:** Gold Trade Coins: Maria Theresia Double Sovereign **Obv:** Crowned shield divides value above date and ribbon **Rev:** Bust facing with two gold coins **Edge:** Plain

Date	Mintage	F	VF	XF	Unc	BU
2001(u) Proof	440	Value: 80.00				

KM# 69 10 GULDEN
31.1035 g., 0.9250 Silver 0.9250 oz. ASW, 40 mm. **Ruler:** Beatrix **Subject:** Gold Trade Coins: Napolean Bonaparte 20 Franc **Obv:** Crowned shield divides value above date and ribbon **Rev:** Bust facing with two gold coins **Edge:** Plain

Date	Mintage	F	VF	XF	Unc	BU
2001(u) Proof	555	Value: 80.00				

KM# 70 10 GULDEN
31.1035 g., 0.9250 Silver 0.9250 oz. ASW, 40 mm. **Ruler:** Beatrix **Series:** Gold Trade Coins: Wilhelmina Golden 10 Guilder **Obv:** Crowned shield divides value above date and ribbon **Rev:** Bust facing with two gold coins **Edge:** Plain

Date	Mintage	F	VF	XF	Unc	BU
2001(u) Proof	440	Value: 80.00				

KM# 71 10 GULDEN
31.1035 g., 0.9250 Silver 0.9250 oz. ASW, 40 mm. **Ruler:** Beatrix **Subject:** Gold Trade Coins: George III Sovereign **Obv:** Crowned shield divides value above date and ribbon **Rev:** Bust facing with two gold coins **Edge:** Plain

Date	Mintage	F	VF	XF	Unc	BU
2001(u) Proof	440	Value: 80.00				

KM# 72 10 GULDEN
31.1035 g., 0.9250 Silver 0.9250 oz. ASW, 40 mm. **Ruler:** Beatrix **Subject:** Gold Trade Coins: Albert I Belgium 20 Franc **Obv:** Crowned shield divides value above date and ribbon **Rev:** Bust facing with two gold coins **Edge:** Plain

Date	Mintage	F	VF	XF	Unc	BU
2001(u) Proof	490	Value: 80.00				

KM# 84 10 GULDEN
17.0000 g., 0.9250 Silver 0.5055 oz. ASW, 33 mm. **Ruler:** Beatrix **Subject:** Mariage of Willem-Alexander and Maxima **Obv:** Queen's head left **Rev:** Conjoined busts left **Edge Lettering:** GOD * ZIJ * MET * ONS * **Designer:** G. Colley

Date	Mintage	F	VF	XF	Unc	BU
2002(u) Proof	1,500	Value: 45.00				

KM# 75 10 GULDEN
6.7200 g., 0.9000 Gold 0.1944 oz. AGW **Ruler:** Beatrix **Subject:** 50th Anniversary - End to Dutch Colonial Rule **Obv:** Head left **Rev:** Triangular signatures around value **Edge:** Reeded **Designer:** Ans Mezas-Hummelink

Date	Mintage	F	VF	XF	Unc	BU
2004 Proof	1,000	Value: 400				

KM# 77 10 GULDEN
6.7200 g., 0.9000 Gold 0.1944 oz. AGW, 22.5 mm. **Ruler:** Beatrix **Subject:** Queen's Silver Jubilee **Obv:** Head left **Rev:** Child art and value **Edge:** Reeded

Date	Mintage	F	VF	XF	Unc	BU
2005(u) Proof	1,500	Value: 400				

KM# 78 10 GULDEN
1.2442 g., 0.9990 Gold 0.0400 oz. AGW, 13.92 mm. **Ruler:** Beatrix **Subject:** Year of the dolphin **Obv:** Head left **Obv. Legend:** BEATRIX KONINGIN DER NEDERLANDEN **Rev:** Stylized outlines of birds above dolphins at sunset **Rev. Legend:** NEDERLANDSE ANTILLEN - JAAR VAN DE DOLFIJN **Edge:** Reeded

Date	Mintage	F	VF	XF	Unc	BU
2007(u) Proof	5,000	Value: 90.00				

KM# 81 10 GULDEN
17.8000 g., 0.9250 Silver 0.5293 oz. ASW, 33 mm. **Ruler:** Beatrix **Subject:** Farewell to the Netherlands Antilles **Obv:** Autonomy monument with five birds **Rev:** Crowned shield divided value **Edge Lettering:** GOD * ZIJ * MET * ONS * **Designer:** Susan Wolters

Date	Mintage	F	VF	XF	Unc	BU
2010(u) Proof	5,000	Value: 45.00				

KM# 82 25 GULDEN
25.0000 g., 0.9250 Silver 0.7435 oz. ASW, 38 mm. **Ruler:** Beatrix **Obv:** 175 year Bank of the Netherlands Antilles **Rev:** Sailing ship

Date	Mintage	F	VF	XF	Unc	BU
2003 Prooflike	1,500	—	—	—	—	50.00

KM# 83 25 GULDEN
25.0000 g., 0.9250 Silver 0.7435 oz. ASW, 38 mm. **Ruler:** Beatrix **Obv:** 50 years of monument care **Rev:** Folker FXVIII plane over route map **Edge Lettering:** GOD * ZIJ * MET * ONS *

Date	Mintage	F	VF	XF	Unc	BU
2004 Proof	5,000	Value: 45.00				

MINT SETS

KM#	Date	Mintage	Identification	Issue Price	Mkt Val
MS22	2001 (8)	6,500	KM#32-38, 43	15.00	20.00
MS23	2002 (8)	6,000	KM#32-38, 43	15.00	25.00
MS24	2003 (8)	4,000	KM#32-38, 43	15.00	25.00
MS25	2004 (8)	2,100	KM32-38, 43	15.00	30.00
MS26	2005 (8)	3,500	KM32-38, 43	17.00	25.00
MS27	2006 (8)	2,000	KM#32-38, 43	20.00	30.00
MS28	2007 (8)	2,000	KM#32-38, 43	20.00	25.00
MS29	2008 (8)	2,000	KM#32-38, 43	21.00	25.00
MS30	2009 (8)	2,000	KM#32-38, 43	27.00	27.00
MS31	2010 (8)	2,000	KM#32-38, 43	28.00	28.00
MS32	2011 (8)	2,000	KM#32-38, 43	28.00	30.00
MS33	2012 (8)	2,000	KM#32-38, 43	28.00	30.00

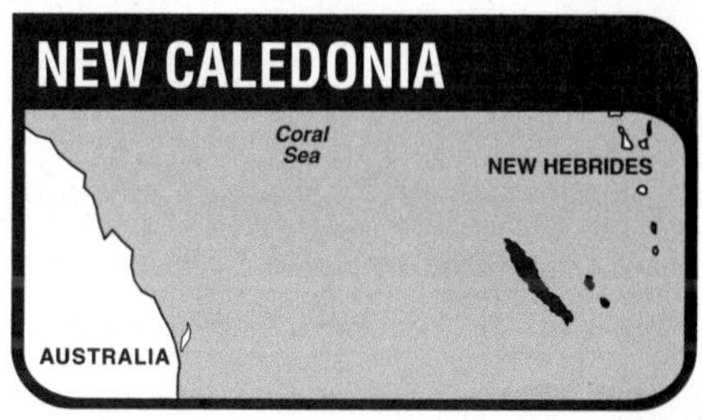

The French Associated State of New Caledonia is a group of about 25 islands in the South Pacific. They are situated about 750 miles (1,207 km.) east of Australia. The territory, which includes the dependencies of Isle des Pins, Loyalty Islands, Isle Huon, Isles Belep, Isles Chesterfield, Isle Walpole, Wallis and Futuna Islands and has a total land area of 7,358 sq. mi.(19,060 sq. km.) and a population of *156,000. Capital: Noumea. The islands are rich in minerals; New Caledonia has some of the world's largest known deposit of nickel. Nickel, nickel castings, coffee and copra are exported.

MINT MARK
Paris, privy marks only

MONETARY SYSTEM
100 Centimes = 1 Franc

FRENCH OVERSEAS TERRITORY

DECIMAL COINAGE

KM# 10 FRANC
1.3000 g., Aluminum, 23 mm. **Obv:** Seated figure holding torch, legend added **Obv. Legend:** I. E. O. M. **Rev:** Kagu bird within sprigs below value **Designer:** G.B.L. Bazor

Date	Mintage	F	VF	XF	Unc	BU
2001(a)	100,000	—	—	—	0.50	1.25
2002(a)	1,200,000	—	—	—	0.50	1.25
2003(a)	2,000,000	—	—	—	0.50	1.25
2004(a)	1,200,000	—	—	—	0.50	1.25
2005(a)	700,000	—	—	—	0.50	1.25
2006(a)	1,600,000	—	—	—	0.50	1.25
2007(a)	2,000,000	—	—	—	0.50	1.25
2008(a)	2,800,000	—	—	—	0.50	1.25
2009(a)	—	—	—	—	0.50	1.25
2010(a)	—	—	—	—	0.50	1.25
2011(a)	—	—	—	—	0.50	1.25
2012(a)	—	—	—	—	0.50	1.25

KM# 14 2 FRANCS

2.2000 g., Aluminum, 27 mm. **Obv:** Seated figure holding torch, legend added **Obv. Legend:** I. E. O. M. **Rev:** Kagu bird and value within sprigs

Date	Mintage	F	VF	XF	Unc	BU
2001(a)	800,000	—	—	0.25	0.75	1.50
2002(a)	1,200,000	—	—	0.25	0.75	1.50
2003(a)	2,400,000	—	—	0.20	0.65	1.50
2004(a)	200,000	—	—	0.20	0.65	1.50
2005(a)	530,000	—	—	0.20	0.65	1.50
2006(a)	1,200,000	—	—	0.20	0.65	1.50
2007(a)	600,000	—	—	0.20	0.65	1.50
2008(a)	2,400,000	—	—	0.20	0.65	1.50
2009(a)	—	—	—	0.20	0.65	1.50
2011(a)	—	—	—	0.20	0.65	1.50

KM# 16 5 FRANCS

3.7500 g., Aluminum, 31 mm. **Obv:** Seated figure holding torch, legend added **Obv. Legend:** I. E. O. M. **Rev:** Kagu bird and value within sprigs **Designer:** G.B.L. Bazor

Date	Mintage	F	VF	XF	Unc	BU
2001(a)	600,000	—	—	0.50	1.00	2.00
2002(a)	480,000	—	—	0.50	1.00	2.00
2003(a)	700,000	—	—	0.40	1.00	2.00
2004(a)	1,000,000	—	—	0.40	1.00	2.00
2005(a)	360,000	—	—	0.40	1.00	2.00
2006(a)	480,000	—	—	0.40	1.00	2.00
2007(a)	960,000	—	—	0.40	1.00	2.00
2008(a)	1,700,000	—	—	0.40	1.00	2.00
2009(a)	—	—	—	0.40	1.00	2.00
2010(a)	—	—	—	0.40	1.00	2.00
2011(a)	—	—	—	0.40	1.00	2.00

KM# 11 10 FRANCS

6.0000 g., Nickel, 24 mm. **Obv:** Liberty head left **Obv. Legend:** I. E. O. M. **Rev:** Sailboat above value **Designer:** R. Joly

Date	Mintage	F	VF	XF	Unc	BU
2001(a)	100,000	—	—	0.65	1.25	2.75
2002(a)	200,000	—	—	0.65	1.25	2.75
2003(a)	800,000	—	—	0.65	1.25	2.75
2004(a)	600,000	—	—	0.65	1.25	2.75
2005(a)	64,000	—	—	0.65	1.25	2.75

KM# 12 20 FRANCS

10.0000 g., Nickel, 28.5 mm. **Obv:** Liberty head left **Obv. Legend:** I. O. E. M. **Rev:** Three ox heads above value **Designer:** R. Joly

Date	Mintage	F	VF	XF	Unc	BU
2001(a)	150,000	—	—	1.00	1.75	3.25
2002(a)	250,000	—	—	1.00	1.75	3.25
2003(a)	250,000	—	—	1.00	1.75	3.25
2004(a)	500,000	—	—	1.00	1.75	3.25
2005(a)	300,000	—	—	1.00	1.75	3.25

KM# 13 50 FRANCS

15.0000 g., Nickel, 33 mm. **Obv:** Liberty head left **Obv. Legend:** I. E. O. M. **Rev:** Hut above value in center of palm and pine trees **Designer:** R. Joly

Date	Mintage	F	VF	XF	Unc	BU
2001(a)	100,000	—	—	1.25	2.00	4.00
2002(a)	—	—	—	1.25	2.00	4.00
2003(a)	75,000	—	—	1.25	2.00	4.00
2004(a)	150,000	—	—	1.25	2.00	4.00
2005(a)	54,000	—	—	1.25	2.00	4.00

KM# 15 100 FRANCS

10.0000 g., Nickel-Bronze, 30 mm. **Obv:** Liberty head left **Rev:** Hut above value in center of palm and pine trees **Designer:** R. Joly

Date	Mintage	F	VF	XF	Unc	BU
2001(a)	100,000	—	—	1.50	3.00	5.00
2002(a)	620,000	—	—	1.50	3.00	6.00
2003(a)	500,000	—	—	1.50	3.00	5.00
2004(a)	500,000	—	—	1.50	3.00	5.00
2005(a)	180,000	—	—	1.50	3.00	5.00

FRENCH ASSOCIATED STATE

DECIMAL COINAGE

KM# 11a 10 FRANCS

6.0000 g., Copper-Nickel, 24 mm. **Obv:** Liberty head left **Rev:** Sailboat above value **Edge:** Reeded

Date	Mintage	F	VF	XF	Unc	BU
2006(a)	60,000	—	—	0.65	1.25	2.75
2007(a)	1,000,000	—	—	0.65	1.25	2.75
2008(a)	1,200,000	—	—	0.65	1.25	2.75
2009(a)	—	—	—	0.65	1.25	2.75
2010(a)	—	—	—	0.65	1.25	2.75
2011(a)	—	—	—	0.65	1.25	2.75

KM# 12a 20 FRANCS

10.0000 g., Copper-Nickel, 28.5 mm. **Obv:** Liberty head left **Rev:** Three ox heads above value **Edge:** Reeded

Date	Mintage	F	VF	XF	Unc	BU
2006(a)	300,000	—	—	1.00	1.75	3.25
2007(a)	800,000	—	—	1.25	1.75	3.25
2008(a)	800,000	—	—	1.25	1.75	3.25
2009(a)	—	—	—	1.25	1.75	3.25
2010(a)	—	—	—	1.25	1.75	3.25
2011(a)	—	—	—	1.25	1.75	3.25

KM# 13a 50 FRANCS

15.0000 g., Copper-Nickel **Obv:** Liberty head left **Rev:** Hut in center of palm and pine trees, value below **Edge:** Reeded

Date	Mintage	F	VF	XF	Unc	BU
2006(a)	75,000	—	—	1.25	2.00	4.00
2007(a)	225,000	—	—	1.25	2.00	4.00
2008(a)	375,000	—	—	1.25	2.00	4.00
2009(a)	—	—	—	1.25	2.00	4.00

KM# 15a 100 FRANCS

10.0000 g., Aluminum-Bronze, 30 mm. **Obv:** Liberty head left **Rev:** Hut above value in center of palm and pine trees **Edge:** Reeded **Designer:** R. Joly

Date	Mintage	F	VF	XF	Unc	BU
2006(a)	300,000	—	—	1.50	3.00	5.00
2007(a)	800,000	—	—	1.50	3.00	5.00
2008(a)	1,100,000	—	—	1.50	3.00	5.00
2009(a)	—	—	—	1.50	3.00	5.00
2010(a)	—	—	—	1.50	3.00	5.00

MINT SETS

KM#	Date	Mintage	Identification	Issue Price	Mkt Val
MS1	2001 (7)	3,000	KM#10-16	—	25.00
MS2	2002 (7)	5,000	KM#10-16	—	25.00
MS3	2004 (7)	3,000	KM#10-16	—	25.00

NEW ZEALAND

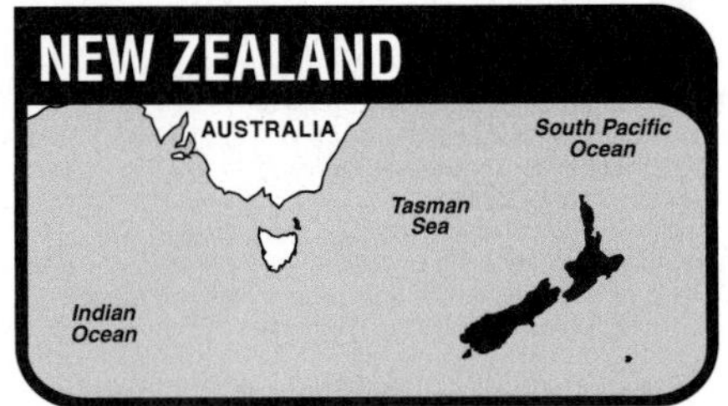

New Zealand, a parliamentary state located in the Southwest Pacific 1,250 miles (2,011 km.) east of Australia, has an area of 103,883 sq. mi. (268,680 sq. km.) and a population of *3.4 million. Capital: Wellington. Wool, meat, dairy products and some manufactured items are exported.

Decimal Currency was introduced in 1967 with special sets commemorating the last issues of pound sterling (1965) and the first of the decimal issues. Since then dollars and sets of coins have been issued nearly every year.

New Zealand is a founding member of the Commonwealth of Nations. Elizabeth II is the Head of State as the Queen of New Zealand; the Prime Minister is the Head of Government.

RULER
British

STATE

DECIMAL COINAGE

100 Cents = 1 Dollar

KM# 116 5 CENTS

2.8300 g., Copper-Nickel, 19.43 mm. **Ruler:** Elizabeth II **Obv:** Head with tiara right **Rev:** Value below tuatara **Edge:** Reeded **Note:** Many recalled and melted in 2006.

Date	Mintage	F	VF	XF	Unc	BU
2001(l)	20,000,000	—	—	0.10	0.50	1.00
2001(c) In sets only	2,910	—	—	—	4.00	5.00
2001(c) Proof	1,364	Value: 3.00				
2002(l)	40,500,000	—	—	0.10	0.50	1.00
2002(c) In sets only	3,000	—	—	—	5.00	6.00
2002(c) Proof	1,500	Value: 3.00				
2003(l)	30,000,000	—	—	—	0.50	1.00
2003(c) In sets only	1,496	—	—	—	5.00	6.00
2003 Proof	3,000	Value: 3.00				
2004(l)	15,000,000	—	—	—	2.00	3.00
Note: All but 48,000 melted. Many of these survivors have recently come onto the NZ market in bulk.						
2004(c) In sets only	2,800	—	—	—	20.00	30.00
2004(c) Proof	1,750	Value: 3.00				
2005(c) In sets only	3,000	—	—	—	8.00	12.00
2005(c) Proof	2,250	Value: 3.00				
2006(c) In sets only	—	—	—	—	8.00	12.00
2006(c) Proof	—	Value: 3.00				

KM# 117 10 CENTS

5.6600 g., Copper-Nickel, 23.62 mm. **Ruler:** Elizabeth II **Obv:** Head with tiara right **Rev:** Value above koruru **Edge:** Reeded **Note:** Many recalled and melted in 2006.

Date	Mintage	F	VF	XF	Unc	BU
2001(l)	10,000,000	—	—	0.10	0.30	0.50
2001(c) In sets only	2,910	—	—	—	6.00	8.00
2001(c) Proof	1,364	Value: 4.00				
2002(l)	10,000,000	—	—	0.10	0.30	0.50
2002(c) In sets only	3,000	—	—	—	3.00	5.00
2002(c) Proof	1,500	Value: 4.00				
2003(l)	13,000,000	—	—	0.10	0.30	0.50
2003(c) In sets only	3,000	—	—	—	5.00	8.00
2003(l) Proof	1,496	Value: 4.00				
2004(l)	6,500,000	—	—	—	0.30	0.50
2004(c) In sets only	—	—	—	—	5.00	8.00
2004(c) Proof	1,750	Value: 4.00				
2005	2,000,000	—	—	—	30.00	40.00
Note: All but 28,000 melted						
2005(c) In sets only	3,000	—	—	—	20.00	30.00
2005(c) Proof	2,250	Value: 4.00				
2006(c) In sets only	3,000	—	—	—	10.00	15.00
2006(c) Proof	2,100	Value: 4.00				

KM# 117a 10 CENTS
3.3100 g., Copper Plated Steel, 20.5 mm. **Ruler:** Elizabeth II **Obv:** Head with tiara right **Rev:** Value above koruru **Edge:** Plain

Date	Mintage	F	VF	XF	Unc	BU
2006(o)	140,200,000	—	—	—	0.20	0.40
2007(o)	15,000,000	—	—	—	—	—
2007(c) In sets only	5,000	—	—	—	—	5.00
2007(c) Proof	3,500	Value: 4.00				
2008(l) In sets only	4,000	—	—	—	—	5.00
2008(l) Proof	3,000	Value: 4.00				
2009(o)	30,000,000	—	—	—	0.20	0.40
2009(w) In sets only	2,000	—	—	—	—	5.00
2009(w) Proof	1,500	Value: 4.00				
2011(o)	10,400,000	—	—	—	2.00	0.40

KM# 234 10 CENTS
3.3100 g., Copper Plated Steel, 20.5 mm. **Ruler:** Elizabeth II **Obv:** Head with tiara right **Rev:** Tuatara right **Edge:** Plain

Date	Mintage	F	VF	XF	Unc	BU
2007(c) In sets only	15,000	—	—	—	0.50	5.00

KM# 117b 10 CENTS
3.7300 g., Copper, 20.5 mm. **Ruler:** Elizabeth II **Obv:** Head with tiara right **Rev:** Value above koruru

Date	Mintage	F	VF	XF	Unc	BU
2010(u)	2,000	—	—	—	—	4.00
2010(u) Proof	1,500	Value: 5.00				
2011(u)	2,000	—	—	—	—	4.00
2011(u) Proof	1,500	Value: 5.00				
2012(u)	2,000	—	—	—	—	4.00
2012(u) Proof	1,500	Value: 5.00				

KM# 117c 10 CENTS
4.3700 g., Silver, 20.5 mm. **Ruler:** Elizabeth II **Obv:** Head with tiara right **Rev:** Value above koruru **Edge:** Plain

Date	Mintage	F	VF	XF	Unc	BU
2011(u) Proof	1,200	Value: 25.00				

KM# 117d 10 CENTS
4.3700 g., Silver selectively gold plated, 20.5 mm. **Ruler:** Elizabeth II **Obv:** Head with tiara right **Rev:** Value above koruru **Edge:** Plain

Date	Mintage	F	VF	XF	Unc	BU
2012(u) Proof	1,000	Value: 25.00				

KM# 118 20 CENTS
11.3100 g., Copper-Nickel, 28.58 mm. **Ruler:** Elizabeth II **Obv:** Head with tiara right **Rev:** Value below Pukaki **Edge:** Reeded **Note:** Many recalled and melted in 2006.

Date	Mintage	F	VF	XF	Unc	BU
2001(c) In sets only	2,910	—	—	—	—	10.00
2001(c) Proof	1,364	Value: 10.00				
2002(l)	7,000,000	—	—	—	0.50	—
2002(c) In sets only	3,000	—	—	—	—	8.00
2002(c) Proof	1,500	Value: 10.00				
2003(c) In sets only	3,000	—	—	—	—	8.00
2003(c) Proof	3,000	Value: 10.00				
2004(l)	8,500,000	—	—	—	0.50	—
2004(c) In sets only	2,800	—	—	—	—	10.00
2004(c) Proof	1,750	Value: 10.00				
2005(l)	4,000,000	—	—	—	—	15.00
Note: All but 178,000 melted						
2005(c) In sets only	3,000	—	—	—	—	8.00
2005(c) Proof	2,250	Value: 10.00				
2006(c) In sets only	3,000	—	—	—	—	8.00
2006(c) Proof	2,100	Value: 10.00				

KM# 118a 20 CENTS
4.0000 g., Nickel Plated Steel, 21.75 mm. **Ruler:** Elizabeth II **Obv:** Head with tiara right **Rev:** Value below Pukaki **Shape:** Scalloped

Date	Mintage	F	VF	XF	Unc	BU
2006(o)	116,600,000	—	—	—	0.40	0.65
2007(c) In sets only	5,000	—	—	—	—	7.00
2007(c) Proof	4,000	Value: 8.00				
2008(o)	80,000,000	—	—	—	0.40	0.65
2008(l) In sets only	4,000	—	—	—	—	7.00
2008(l) Proof	3,000	Value: 8.00				
2009(w) In sets only	2,000	—	—	—	—	7.00
2009(w) Proof	1,500	Value: 8.00				

KM# 118b 20 CENTS
4.4500 g., Copper-Nickel, 21.75 mm. **Ruler:** Elizabeth II **Obv:** Head with tiara right **Rev:** Value below Pukaki **Edge:** Scalloped

Date	Mintage	F	VF	XF	Unc	BU
2010(u)	2,000	—	—	—	—	7.00
2010(u) Proof	1,500	Value: 8.00				
2011(u)	2,000	—	—	—	—	7.00
2011(u) Proof	1,500	Value: 8.00				
2012(u)	2,000	—	—	—	—	7.00
2012(u) Proof	1,500	Value: 8.00				

KM# 118c 20 CENTS
5.3000 g., 0.9990 Silver 0.1702 oz. ASW, 21.75 mm. **Ruler:** Elizabeth II **Obv:** Head with tiara right **Rev:** Value below Pukaki **Edge:** Plain

Date	Mintage	F	VF	XF	Unc	BU
2011(u) Proof	1,200	Value: 30.00				
2012(u) Proof	1,000	Value: 30.00				

KM# 119 50 CENTS
13.6100 g., Copper-Nickel, 31.75 mm. **Ruler:** Elizabeth II **Obv:** Head with tiara right **Rev:** H.M.S. Endeavour and value **Edge:** Segmented reeding **Note:** Many recalled and melted in 2006.

Date	Mintage	F	VF	XF	Unc	BU
2001(l)	5,000,000	—	—	—	1.00	—
2001(c) In sets only	2,910	—	—	—	—	10.00
2001(c) Proof	1,364	Value: 10.00				
2002(l)	3,000,000	—	—	0.50	1.00	—
2002(c) In sets only	3,000	—	—	—	—	8.00
2002(c) Proof	1,500	Value: 10.00				
2003(l)	2,500,000	—	—	0.50	1.00	—
2003(c) In sets only	3,000	—	—	—	—	8.00
2003(c) Proof	1,496	Value: 10.00				
2004(l)	2,000,000	—	—	—	1.00	—
2004(c) In sets only	2,800	—	—	—	—	10.00
2004(c) Proof	1,750	Value: 10.00				
2005(l)	1,000,000	—	—	—	7.50	—
Note: All but 503,800 melted						
2005(c) In sets only	3,000	—	—	—	—	8.00
2005(c) Proof	2,250	Value: 10.00				
2006(c) In sets only	3,000	—	—	—	—	8.00
2006(c) Proof	2,100	Value: 10.00				

KM# 135 50 CENTS
13.6100 g., Copper-Nickel, 31.75 mm. **Ruler:** Elizabeth II **Subject:** Lord of the Rings **Obv:** Head with tiara right **Rev:** Frodo's head facing to left of vine and value **Edge:** Reeded

Date	Mintage	F	VF	XF	Unc	BU
2003(l)	41,221	—	—	—	—	15.00

KM# 136 50 CENTS
13.6100 g., Copper-Nickel, 31.75 mm. **Ruler:** Elizabeth II **Subject:** Lord of the Rings **Obv:** Head with tiara right **Rev:** Head of Gandalf with hat facing and value **Edge:** Reeded

Date	Mintage	F	VF	XF	Unc	BU
2003(l)	41,221	—	—	—	—	15.00

KM# 137 50 CENTS
13.6100 g., Copper-Nickel, 31.75 mm. **Ruler:** Elizabeth II **Subject:** Lord of the Rings **Obv:** Head with tiara right **Rev:** Head of Aragorn facing and value **Edge:** Reeded

Date	Mintage	F	VF	XF	Unc	BU
2003(l)	41,221	—	—	—	—	15.00

KM# 138 50 CENTS
13.6100 g., Copper-Nickel, 31.75 mm. **Ruler:** Elizabeth II **Subject:** Lord of the Rings **Obv:** Head with tiara right **Rev:** Head of Gollum facing and value **Edge:** Reeded

Date	Mintage	F	VF	XF	Unc	BU
2003(l)	38,400	—	—	—	—	15.00

KM# 139 50 CENTS
13.6100 g., Copper-Nickel, 31.75 mm. **Ruler:** Elizabeth II **Subject:** Lord of the Rings **Obv:** Head with tiara right **Rev:** Saruman, value **Edge:** Reeded

Date	Mintage	F	VF	XF	Unc	BU
2003(l)	38,400	—	—	—	—	15.00

KM# 140 50 CENTS
13.6100 g., Copper-Nickel, 31.75 mm. **Ruler:** Elizabeth II **Subject:** Lord of the Rings **Obv:** Head with tiara right **Rev:** Head of Sauron left and value **Edge:** Reeded

Date	Mintage	F	VF	XF	Unc	BU
2003(l)	38,400	—	—	—	—	15.00

KM# 235 50 CENTS

13.6100 g., Copper-Nickel, 31.75 mm. **Ruler:** Elizabeth II **Subject:** Lord of the Rings **Obv:** Head with tiara right **Rev:** Boromir

Date	Mintage	F	VF	XF	Unc	BU
2003(l)	6,889	—	—	—	—	18.00

KM# 236 50 CENTS

13.6100 g., Copper-Nickel, 31.75 mm. **Ruler:** Elizabeth II **Subject:** Lord of the Rings **Obv:** Head with tiara right **Rev:** Gimli

Date	Mintage	F	VF	XF	Unc	BU
2003(l)	6,889	—	—	—	—	18.00

KM# 237 50 CENTS

13.6100 g., Copper-Nickel, 31.75 mm. **Ruler:** Elizabeth II **Subject:** Lord of the Rings **Obv:** Head with tiara right **Rev:** Legolas

Date	Mintage	F	VF	XF	Unc	BU
2003(l)	6,889	—	—	—	—	18.00

KM# 238 50 CENTS

13.6100 g., Copper-Nickel, 31.75 mm. **Ruler:** Elizabeth II **Subject:** Lord of the Rings **Obv:** Head with tiara right **Rev:** Merry

Date	Mintage	F	VF	XF	Unc	BU
2003(l)	6,889	—	—	—	—	18.00

KM# 239 50 CENTS

13.6100 g., Copper-Nickel, 31.75 mm. **Ruler:** Elizabeth II **Subject:** Lord of the Rings **Obv:** Head with tiara right **Rev:** Pippin

Date	Mintage	F	VF	XF	Unc	BU
2003(l)	6,889	—	—	—	—	18.00

KM# 240 50 CENTS

13.6100 g., Copper-Nickel, 31.75 mm. **Ruler:** Elizabeth II **Subject:** Lord of the Rings **Obv:** Head with tiara right **Rev:** Sam

Date	Mintage	F	VF	XF	Unc	BU
2003(l)	6,889	—	—	—	—	18.00

KM# 241 50 CENTS

13.6100 g., Copper-Nickel, 31.75 mm. **Ruler:** Elizabeth II **Subject:** Lord of the Rings **Obv:** Head with tiara right **Rev:** Arwen

Date	Mintage	F	VF	XF	Unc	BU
2003(l)	4,068	—	—	—	—	20.00

KM# 242 50 CENTS

13.6100 g., Copper-Nickel, 31.75 mm. **Ruler:** Elizabeth II **Subject:** Lord of the Rings **Obv:** Head with tiara right **Rev:** Elrond

Date	Mintage	F	VF	XF	Unc	BU
2003(l)	4,068	—	—	—	—	20.00

KM# 243 50 CENTS

13.6100 g., Copper-Nickel, 31.75 mm. **Ruler:** Elizabeth II **Subject:** Lord of the Rings **Obv:** Head with tiara right **Rev:** Eowyn

Date	Mintage	F	VF	XF	Unc	BU
2003(l)	4,068	—	—	—	—	20.00

KM# 244 50 CENTS

13.6100 g., Copper-Nickel, 31.75 mm. **Ruler:** Elizabeth II **Subject:** Lord of the Rings **Obv:** Head with tiara right **Rev:** Galadriel

Date	Mintage	F	VF	XF	Unc	BU
2003(l)	4,068	—	—	—	—	20.00

KM# 245 50 CENTS

13.6100 g., Copper-Nickel, 31.75 mm. **Ruler:** Elizabeth II **Subject:** Lord of the Rings **Obv:** Head with tiara right **Rev:** An Orc

Date	Mintage	F	VF	XF	Unc	BU
2003(l)	4,068	—	—	—	—	20.00

KM# 246 50 CENTS

13.6100 g., Copper-Nickel, 31.75 mm. **Ruler:** Elizabeth II **Subject:** Lord of the Rings **Obv:** Head with tiara right **Rev:** Treebeard

Date	Mintage	F	VF	XF	Unc	BU
2003(l)	4,068	—	—	—	—	20.00

KM# 119a 50 CENTS

5.0000 g., Nickel Plated Steel, 24.75 mm. **Ruler:** Elizabeth II **Obv:** Head with tiara right **Rev:** Ship, H.M.S. Endeavour

Date	Mintage	F	VF	XF	Unc	BU
2006(o)	70,200,000	—	—	—	0.75	1.00
2007(c) In sets only	5,000	—	—	—	—	8.00
2007(c) Proof	3,500	Value: 10.00				
2008(l) In sets only	4,000	—	—	—	—	8.00
2008(l) Proof	3,000	Value: 10.00				
2009(o)	20,000,000	—	—	—	0.75	1.00
2009(w) In sets only	2,000	—	—	—	—	8.00
2009(w) Proof	1,500	Value: 10.00				

KM# 279 50 CENTS

Aluminum-Bronze, 38.74 mm. **Ruler:** Elizabeth II **Subject:** Narnia **Obv:** Head with tiara right **Rev:** Peter

Date	Mintage	F	VF	XF	Unc	BU
2006(c)	20,000	—	—	—	—	6.00

KM# 280 50 CENTS

Aluminum-Bronze, 38.74 mm. **Ruler:** Elizabeth II **Subject:** Narnia **Obv:** Head with tiara right **Rev:** Susan

Date	Mintage	F	VF	XF	Unc	BU
2006(c)	20,000	—	—	—	—	6.00

KM# 281 50 CENTS

Aluminum-Bronze, 38.74 mm. **Ruler:** Elizabeth II **Subject:** Narnia **Obv:** Head with tiara right **Rev:** Edmund

Date	Mintage	F	VF	XF	Unc	BU
2006(c)	20,000	—	—	—	—	6.00

KM# 282 50 CENTS

Aluminum-Bronze, 38.74 mm. **Ruler:** Elizabeth II **Subject:** Narnia **Obv:** Head with tiara right **Rev:** Lucy

Date	Mintage	F	VF	XF	Unc	BU
2006(c)	20,000	—	—	—	—	6.00

KM# 283 50 CENTS

Aluminum-Bronze, 38.74 mm. **Ruler:** Elizabeth II **Subject:** Narnia **Obv:** Head with tiara right **Rev:** Mr. Tumnus

Date	Mintage	F	VF	XF	Unc	BU
2006(c)	20,000	—	—	—	—	6.00

KM# 284 50 CENTS

Aluminum-Bronze, 38.74 mm. **Ruler:** Elizabeth II **Subject:** Narnia **Obv:** Head with tiara right **Rev:** Ginarrbrik

Date	Mintage	F	VF	XF	Unc	BU
2006(c)	20,000	—	—	—	—	6.00

KM# 119b 50 CENTS

5.6000 g., Copper-Nickel, 24.75 mm. **Ruler:** Elizabeth II **Obv:** Head with tiara right **Rev:** Ship, H.M.S. Endeavour

Date	Mintage	F	VF	XF	Unc	BU
2010(u)	2,000	—	—	—	—	8.00
2010(u) Proof	1,500	Value: 10.00				
2011(u)	2,000	—	—	—	—	8.00
2011(u) Proof	1,500	Value: 10.00				
2012(u)	2,000	—	—	—	—	8.00
2012(u) Proof	1,500	Value: 10.00				

KM# 119c 50 CENTS

6.5900 g., 0.9990 Silver 0.2117 oz. ASW, 24.75 mm. **Ruler:** Elizabeth II **Obv:** Head with tiara right **Rev:** Ship, H.M.S. Endeavor **Edge:** Plain

Date	Mintage	F	VF	XF	Unc	BU
2011(u) Proof	1,200	Value: 45.00				
2012(u) Proof	1,000	Value: 45.00				

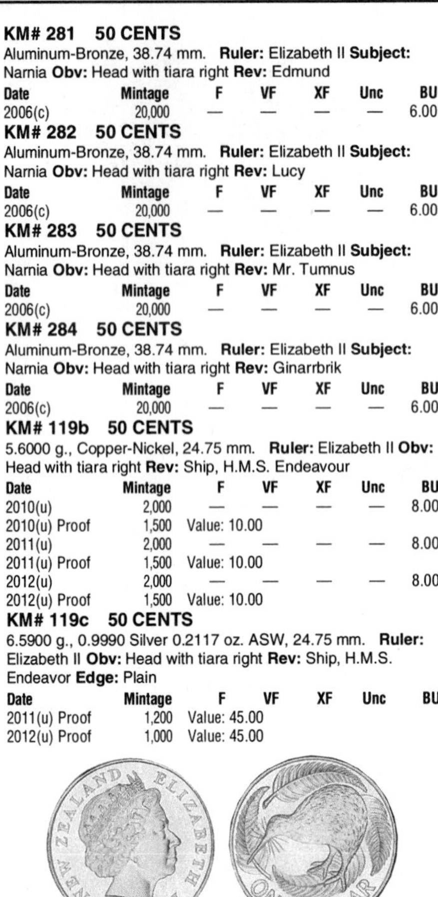

KM# 120 DOLLAR

8.0000 g., Aluminum-Bronze, 23 mm. **Ruler:** Elizabeth II **Obv:** Head with tiara right **Rev:** Kiwi bird within sprigs, value below **Edge:** Segmented reeding

Date	Mintage	F	VF	XF	Unc	BU
2001(c) In sets only	2,910	—	—	—	—	4.00
2001(c) Proof	1,364	Value: 5.00				
2002(l)	8,000,000	—	—	—	1.00	2.50
2002(c) In sets only	4,000	—	—	—	—	4.00
2002(c) Proof	1,500	Value: 5.00				
2003(l)	4,000,000	—	—	—	1.00	2.50
2003(c) In sets only	5,000	—	—	—	—	4.00
2003(c) Proof	1,750	Value: 5.00				
2004(l)	2,700,000	—	—	—	1.00	2.50
2004(c) In sets only	3,500	—	—	—	—	4.00
2004(c) Proof	2,250	Value: 5.00				
2005(l)	2,000,000	—	—	—	1.00	2.50
2005(c) In sets only	4,000	—	—	—	—	4.00
2005(c) Proof	2,250	Value: 5.00				
2006(c) In sets only	3,000	—	—	—	—	4.00
2006(c) Proof	2,100	Value: 5.00				
2007(c)	5,000	—	—	—	—	4.00
2007(c) Proof	3,500	Value: 5.00				
2008(l)	6,000,000	—	—	—	1.00	2.50
2008(l) In sets only	4,000	—	—	—	—	4.00
2008(l) Proof	3,000	Value: 5.00				
2009(w) In sets only	2,000	—	—	—	—	4.00
2009(w) Proof	1,500	Value: 5.00				
2010(l)	10,000,000	—	—	—	1.00	2.50

KM# 141 DOLLAR

28.2800 g., Aluminum-Bronze, 38.61 mm. **Ruler:** Elizabeth II **Subject:** Lord of the Rings **Obv:** Head with tiara right **Rev:** Inscribed ring around value **Edge:** Reeded

Date	Mintage	F	VF	XF	Unc	BU
2003(l)	30,081	—	—	—	—	15.00

Note: Mintage includes 10,454 in sets.

KM# 141a DOLLAR

28.2800 g., 0.9250 Silver selective gold plating 0.8410 oz. ASW, 38.61 mm. **Ruler:** Elizabeth II **Obv:** Head with tiara right **Rev:** Gold-plated ring and edge **Edge:** Reeded

Date	Mintage	F	VF	XF	Unc	BU
2003(l) Proof	39,244	Value: 70.00				

KM# 142 DOLLAR

28.2800 g., Aluminum-Bronze, 38.61 mm. **Ruler:** Elizabeth II **Subject:** Lord of the Rings **Obv:** Head with tiara right **Rev:** Head of Frodo looking down above inscription **Edge:** Reeded

Date	Mintage	F	VF	XF	Unc	BU
2003(l)	10,454	—	—	—	—	10.00

KM# 143 DOLLAR

28.2800 g., Aluminum-Bronze, 38.61 mm. **Ruler:** Elizabeth II **Subject:** Lord of the Rings **Obv:** Head with tiara right **Rev:** View of Sauron, value **Edge:** Reeded

Date	Mintage	F	VF	XF	Unc	BU
2003(l)	10,454	—	—	—	—	10.00

KM# 247 DOLLAR

28.2800 g., 0.9250 Silver 0.8410 oz. ASW, 38.61 mm. **Ruler:** Elizabeth II **Subject:** Lord of the Rings **Obv:** Head with tiara right **Rev:** Aragorn's Coronation

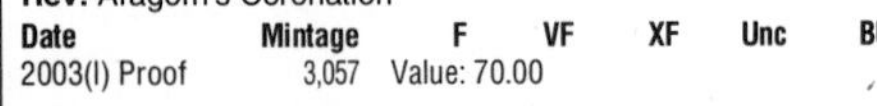

Date	Mintage	F	VF	XF	Unc	BU
2003(l) Proof	3,057	Value: 70.00				

KM# 248 DOLLAR
28.2800 g., 0.9250 Silver 0.8410 oz. ASW, 38.61 mm. **Ruler:** Elizabeth II **Subject:** Lord of the Rings **Obv:** Head with tiara right **Rev:** King Theoden

Date	Mintage	F	VF	XF	Unc	BU
2003(I) Proof	2,022	Value: 70.00				

KM# 249 DOLLAR
28.2800 g., 0.9250 Silver 0.8410 oz. ASW, 38.61 mm. **Ruler:** Elizabeth II **Subject:** Lord of the Rings **Obv:** Head with tiara right **Rev:** Flight to the Ford

Date	Mintage	F	VF	XF	Unc	BU
2003(I) Proof	2,020	Value: 70.00				

KM# 250 DOLLAR
28.2800 g., 0.9250 Silver 0.8410 oz. ASW, 38.61 mm. **Ruler:** Elizabeth II **Subject:** Lord of the Rings **Obv:** Head with tiara right **Rev:** Mirror of Galadriel

Date	Mintage	F	VF	XF	Unc	BU
2003(I) Proof	2,036	Value: 70.00				

KM# 251 DOLLAR
28.2800 g., 0.9250 Silver 0.8410 oz. ASW, 38.61 mm. **Ruler:** Elizabeth II **Subject:** Lord of the Rings **Obv:** Head with tiara right **Rev:** Frodo offering ring to Nazgul

Date	Mintage	F	VF	XF	Unc	BU
2003(I) Proof	1,784	Value: 70.00				

KM# 252 DOLLAR
28.2800 g., 0.9250 Silver 0.8410 oz. ASW, 38.61 mm. **Ruler:** Elizabeth II **Subject:** Lord of the Rings **Obv:** Head with tiara right **Rev:** Bridge of Kazad-Dum

Date	Mintage	F	VF	XF	Unc	BU
2003(I) Proof	952	Value: 70.00				

KM# 253 DOLLAR
28.2800 g., 0.9250 Silver 0.8410 oz. ASW, 38.61 mm. **Ruler:** Elizabeth II **Subject:** Lord of the Rings **Obv:** Head with tiara right **Rev:** Shelob's Lair

Date	Mintage	F	VF	XF	Unc	BU
2003(I) Proof	917	Value: 70.00				

KM# 254 DOLLAR
28.2800 g., 0.9250 Silver 0.8410 oz. ASW, 38.61 mm. **Ruler:** Elizabeth II **Subject:** Lord of the Rings **Obv:** Head with tiara right **Rev:** Taming of Smeagol

Date	Mintage	F	VF	XF	Unc	BU
2003(I) Proof	1,017	Value: 70.00				

KM# 255 DOLLAR
28.2800 g., 0.9250 Silver 0.8410 oz. ASW, 38.61 mm. **Ruler:** Elizabeth II **Subject:** Lord of the Rings **Obv:** Head with tiara right **Rev:** Dark Lord's Tower and the Eye

Date	Mintage	F	VF	XF	Unc	BU
2003(I) Proof	1,002	Value: 70.00				

KM# 256 DOLLAR
28.2800 g., 0.9250 Silver 0.8410 oz. ASW, 38.61 mm. **Ruler:** Elizabeth II **Subject:** Lord of the Rings **Obv:** Head with tiara right **Rev:** Knife in the Dark

Date	Mintage	F	VF	XF	Unc	BU
2003(I) Proof	967	Value: 70.00				

KM# 257 DOLLAR
28.2800 g., 0.9250 Silver 0.8410 oz. ASW, 38.61 mm. **Ruler:** Elizabeth II **Subject:** Lord of the Rings **Obv:** Head with tiara right **Rev:** Gandalf and Saruman

Date	Mintage	F	VF	XF	Unc	BU
2003(I) Proof	867	Value: 70.00				

KM# 258 DOLLAR
28.2800 g., 0.9250 Silver 0.8410 oz. ASW, 38.61 mm. **Ruler:** Elizabeth II **Subject:** Lord of the Rings **Obv:** Head with tiara right **Rev:** Council of Elrond

Date	Mintage	F	VF	XF	Unc	BU
2003(I) Proof	1,204	Value: 70.00				

KM# 259 DOLLAR
28.2800 g., 0.9250 Silver 0.8410 oz. ASW, 38.61 mm. **Ruler:** Elizabeth II **Subject:** Lord of the Rings **Obv:** Head with tiara right **Rev:** Helm's Deep

Date	Mintage	F	VF	XF	Unc	BU
2003(I) Proof	967	Value: 70.00				

KM# 260 DOLLAR
28.2800 g., 0.9250 Silver 0.8410 oz. ASW, 38.61 mm. **Ruler:** Elizabeth II **Subject:** Lord of the Rings **Obv:** Head with tiara right **Rev:** Frodo & Co. at Mt. Doom

Date	Mintage	F	VF	XF	Unc	BU
2003(l) Proof	917	Value: 70.00				

KM# 261 DOLLAR
28.2800 g., 0.9250 Silver 0.8410 oz. ASW, 38.61 mm. **Ruler:** Elizabeth II **Subject:** Lord of the Rings **Obv:** Head with tiara right **Rev:** Departure of Boromir

Date	Mintage	F	VF	XF	Unc	BU
2003(l) Proof	917	Value: 70.00				

KM# 262 DOLLAR
28.2800 g., 0.9250 Silver 0.8410 oz. ASW, 38.61 mm. **Ruler:** Elizabeth II **Subject:** Lord of the Rings **Obv:** Head with tiara right **Rev:** Meeting of Treebeard

Date	Mintage	F	VF	XF	Unc	BU
2003(l) Proof	867	Value: 70.00				

KM# 263 DOLLAR
28.2800 g., 0.9250 Silver 0.8410 oz. ASW, 38.61 mm. **Ruler:** Elizabeth II **Subject:** Lord of the Rings **Obv:** Head with tiara right **Rev:** Battle of Minas Tirith / Pelenor Fields

Date	Mintage	F	VF	XF	Unc	BU
2003(l) Proof	867	Value: 70.00				

KM# 264 DOLLAR
28.2800 g., 0.9250 Silver 0.8410 oz. ASW, 38.61 mm. **Ruler:** Elizabeth II **Subject:** Lord of the Rings **Obv:** Head with tiara right **Rev:** Gandalf Reappears

Date	Mintage	F	VF	XF	Unc	BU
2003(l) Proof	967	Value: 70.00				

KM# 265 DOLLAR
28.2800 g., 0.9250 Silver 0.8410 oz. ASW, 38.61 mm. **Ruler:** Elizabeth II **Subject:** Lord of the Rings **Obv:** Head with tiara right **Rev:** Army of the Dead

Date	Mintage	F	VF	XF	Unc	BU
2003(l) Proof	917	Value: 70.00				

KM# 266 DOLLAR
28.2800 g., 0.9250 Silver 0.8410 oz. ASW, 38.61 mm. **Ruler:** Elizabeth II **Subject:** Lord of the Rings **Obv:** Head with tiara right **Rev:** Travel to the Undying Lands

Date	Mintage	F	VF	XF	Unc	BU
2003(l) Proof	867	Value: 70.00				

KM# 267 DOLLAR
28.2800 g., 0.9250 Silver 0.8410 oz. ASW, 38.61 mm. **Ruler:** Elizabeth II **Subject:** Lord of the Rings **Obv:** Head with tiara right **Rev:** Great River

Date	Mintage	F	VF	XF	Unc	BU
2003(l) Proof	867	Value: 70.00				

KM# 268 DOLLAR
28.2800 g., 0.9250 Silver 0.8410 oz. ASW, 38.61 mm. **Ruler:** Elizabeth II **Subject:** Lord of the Rings **Obv:** Head with tiara right **Rev:** Death of the Witch King

Date	Mintage	F	VF	XF	Unc	BU
2003(l) Proof	867	Value: 70.00				

KM# 269 DOLLAR
28.2800 g., 0.9250 Silver 0.8410 oz. ASW, 38.61 mm. **Ruler:** Elizabeth II **Subject:** Lord of the Rings **Obv:** Head with tiara right **Rev:** March of the Oliphants

Date	Mintage	F	VF	XF	Unc	BU
2003(l) Proof	867	Value: 70.00				

KM# 152 DOLLAR
28.2800 g., Copper-Nickel, 38.6 mm. **Ruler:** Elizabeth II **Obv:** Crowned head right **Rev:** Little spotted kiwi **Edge:** Reeded

Date	Mintage	F	VF	XF	Unc	BU
2004(c)	2,500	—	—	—	—	45.00

KM# 152a DOLLAR
31.1350 g., 0.9990 Silver 1.0000 oz. ASW, 40 mm. **Ruler:** Elizabeth II **Obv:** Crowned head right **Rev:** Little spotted kiwi **Edge:** Reeded

Date	Mintage	F	VF	XF	Unc	BU
2004(c) Proof	2,000	Value: 50.00				

Note: Includes 500 struck in 2008 for sets.

KM# 153 DOLLAR
31.6350 g., 0.9990 Silver 1.0160 oz. ASW, 40 mm. **Ruler:** Elizabeth II **Obv:** Crowned head right **Rev:** Rowi Kiwi **Edge:** Reeded

Date	Mintage	F	VF	XF	Unc	BU
2005(w)	4,000	—	—	—	—	45.00

KM# 153a DOLLAR
31.6350 g., 0.9990 Silver 1.0160 oz. ASW, 38.74 mm. **Ruler:** Elizabeth II **Rev:** Rowi Kiwi

Date	Mintage	F	VF	XF	Unc	BU
2005(w) Proof	2,700	Value: 80.00				

Note: Mintage includes 500 struck in 2008 for sets.

KM# 154 DOLLAR
31.1350 g., 0.9990 Silver 1.0000 oz. ASW, 40 mm. **Ruler:** Elizabeth II **Subject:** ANZAC **Obv:** Crowned head right **Rev:** Soldiers seated, multicolor flag in background **Edge:** Reeded

Date	Mintage	F	VF	XF	Unc	BU
2005(w) P Proof	15,000	Value: 110				

KM# 156 DOLLAR
28.2800 g., Aluminum-Bronze, 38.61 mm. **Ruler:** Elizabeth II **Subject:** Lions Rugby Tour **Obv:** Crowned head right **Rev:** Rugby player, Lions crest and New Zealand map

Date	Mintage	F	VF	XF	Unc	BU
2005(l)	15,000	—	—	—	—	20.00

KM# 156a DOLLAR
28.2800 g., 0.9250 Silver 0.8410 oz. ASW, 38.61 mm. **Ruler:** Elizabeth II **Series:** Rugby player, Lions crest & New Zealand map **Subject:** Lions Rugby Tour **Obv:** Crowned head right **Edge:** Reeded

Date	Mintage	F	VF	XF	Unc	BU
2005(l) Proof	5,000	Value: 50.00				

KM# 157 DOLLAR
Aluminum-Bronze, 38.74 mm. **Ruler:** Elizabeth II **Subject:** ANZAC **Obv:** Crowned head right **Rev:** Soldiers from Chunuk Bair battle with rifles and bayonets **Edge:** Reeded

Date	Mintage	F	VF	XF	Unc	BU
2005 Proof	15,000	Value: 25.00				

KM# 159 DOLLAR
20.0000 g., Aluminum-Bronze, 38.74 mm. **Ruler:** Elizabeth II **Subject:** King Kong **Obv:** Crowned head right **Rev:** King Kong **Edge:** Reeded

Date	Mintage	F	VF	XF	Unc	BU
2005(w)	7,000	—	—	—	—	20.00

KM# 160 DOLLAR
20.0000 g., Aluminum-Bronze, 38.74 mm. **Ruler:** Elizabeth II **Subject:** King Kong **Obv:** Crowned head right **Rev:** Multicolored King Kong **Edge:** Reeded

Date	Mintage	F	VF	XF	Unc	BU
2005(w)	4,000	—	—	—	—	35.00

KM# 161 DOLLAR
20.0000 g., Aluminum-Bronze, 38.74 mm. **Ruler:** Elizabeth II **Subject:** King Kong **Obv:** Crowned head right **Rev:** Carl Denham and camera in multicolor **Edge:** Reeded

Date	Mintage	F	VF	XF	Unc	BU
2005	4,000	—	—	—	—	35.00

KM# 162 DOLLAR
20.0000 g., Aluminum-Bronze, 38.74 mm. **Ruler:** Elizabeth II **Subject:** King Kong **Obv:** Crowned head right **Rev:** Ann Darrow and Jack Driscoll multicolored **Edge:** Reeded

Date	Mintage	F	VF	XF	Unc	BU
2005	4,000	—	—	—	—	35.00

KM# 164 DOLLAR
31.1350 g., 0.9990 Silver partially gold plated 1.0000 oz. ASW, 40.6 mm. **Ruler:** Elizabeth II **Obv:** Crowned head right **Rev:** King Kong partially gold plated

Date	Mintage	F	VF	XF	Unc	BU
2005(w) Proof	3,000	Value: 70.00				

KM# 276 DOLLAR
20.0000 g., Aluminum-Bronze, 38.74 mm. **Ruler:** Elizabeth II **Subject:** Emblem **Obv:** Head with tiara right **Rev:** Rowi and chick inside patterned ring **Note:** Part of a pair issued with Australia.

Date	Mintage	F	VF	XF	Unc	BU
2005(w)	20,000	—	—	—	—	25.00

KM# 158 DOLLAR
28.2800 g., 0.9990 Silver 0.9083 oz. ASW, 38.61 mm. **Ruler:** Elizabeth II **Subject:** FIFA **Obv:** Crowned head right **Rev:** Soccer player, silver fern and map

Date	Mintage	F	VF	XF	Unc	BU
2006(v) Proof	7,500	Value: 50.00				

KM# 285 DOLLAR
31.1000 g., 0.9990 Silver with gold highlights 0.9988 oz. ASW, 40 mm. **Ruler:** Elizabeth II **Subject:** Narnia **Obv:** Head with tiara right **Rev:** White Witch

Date	Mintage	F	VF	XF	Unc	BU
2006(c) Proof	2,000	Value: 70.00				

KM# 286 DOLLAR
20.0000 g., Aluminum-Bronze, 38.74 mm. **Ruler:** Elizabeth II **Subject:** Narnia **Obv:** Head with tiara right **Rev:** Asian, lion standing right

Date	Mintage	F	VF	XF	Unc	BU
2006(c)	8,000	—	—	—	—	20.00

KM# 287 DOLLAR
31.1350 g., 0.9990 Silver With Gold highlights 1.0000 oz. ASW, 40 mm. **Ruler:** Elizabeth II **Subject:** Narnia **Obv:** Head with tiara right **Rev:** Asian

Date	Mintage	F	VF	XF	Unc	BU
2006(c) Proof	4,320	Value: 70.00				

KM# 288 DOLLAR
31.1350 g., 0.9990 Silver 1.0000 oz. ASW, 40 mm. **Ruler:** Elizabeth II **Subject:** Narnia **Obv:** Head with tiara right **Rev:** Wardrobe from the Lion, Witch and Wardrobe series

Date	Mintage	F	VF	XF	Unc	BU
2006(c) Proof	1,000	Value: 70.00				

KM# 289 DOLLAR
20.0000 g., Aluminum-Bronze, 38.74 mm. **Ruler:** Elizabeth II **Subject:** Queen's 80th birthday **Obv:** Head with tiara right **Rev:** Heraldic arms

Date	Mintage	F	VF	XF	Unc	BU
2006	2,000	—	—	—	—	30.00

KM# 290 DOLLAR
31.1350 g., 0.9990 Silver 1.0000 oz. ASW, 38.74 mm. **Ruler:** Elizabeth II **Subject:** Queen's 80th birthday **Obv:** Head with tiara right **Rev:** Heraldic arms

Date	Mintage	F	VF	XF	Unc	BU
2006 Proof	1,500	Value: 85.00				

KM# 291 DOLLAR
31.1350 g., 0.9990 Silver 1.0000 oz. ASW, 40 mm. **Ruler:** Elizabeth II **Obv:** Head with tiara right **Rev:** North Island Brown Kiwi **Edge:** Reeded

Date	Mintage	F	VF	XF	Unc	BU
2006(w)	3,000	—	—	—	—	50.00

KM# 291a DOLLAR
31.1350 g., 0.9990 Silver 1.0000 oz. ASW, 40 mm. **Ruler:** Elizabeth II **Obv:** Head with tiara right **Rev:** North Island Brown Kiwi **Edge:** Reeded

Date	Mintage	F	VF	XF	Unc	BU
2006(w) Proof	2,000	Value: 80.00				

Note: Mintage includes 500 struck in 2008 for sets.

KM# 293 DOLLAR
20.0000 g., Aluminum-Bronze, 38.74 mm. **Ruler:** Elizabeth II **Subject:** NZ Gold Rushes - West Coast **Obv:** Head with tiara right **Rev:** 1860s miners

Date	Mintage	F	VF	XF	Unc	BU
2006(w)	1,500	—	—	—	—	35.00

KM# 294 DOLLAR
31.1350 g., 0.9990 Silver with gold highlights 1.0000 oz. ASW, 40.60 mm. **Ruler:** Elizabeth II **Subject:** NZ Gold Rushes - Thames/Coromandel **Obv:** Head with tiara right **Rev:** Gold panning

Date	Mintage	F	VF	XF	Unc	BU
2006(w) Proof	1,200	Value: 110				

KM# 232 DOLLAR
31.1350 g., 0.9990 Silver 1.0000 oz. ASW, 40 mm. **Ruler:** Elizabeth II **Subject:** Aoraki - Mount Cook, Japanese Friendship **Obv:** Head with tiara right **Obv. Legend:** NEW ZEALAND - ELIZABETH II **Rev:** Flowers in bloom, Mount Cook in background multicolor **Note:** Also released in a Japanese proof set.

Date	Mintage	F	VF	XF	Unc	BU
2007(j) Proof	70,000	Value: 90.00				

KM# 296 DOLLAR
1.2440 g., 0.9990 Gold 0.0400 oz. AGW, 13.92 mm. **Ruler:** Elizabeth II **Subject:** 50th anniversary of Scott Base **Obv:** Head with tiara right **Rev:** Scott Base, Antarctica and International Polar Year logo

Date	Mintage	F	VF	XF	Unc	BU
2007(m) Proof	10,000	Value: 100				

KM# 297 DOLLAR
31.1350 g., 0.9990 Silver 1.0000 oz. ASW, 40 mm. **Ruler:** Elizabeth II **Subject:** 50th anniversary of Scott Base **Obv:** Head with tiara right **Rev:** Scott Base, Antarctica and International Polar Year logo

Date	Mintage	F	VF	XF	Unc	BU
2007(m) Proof	10,000	Value: 80.00				

KM# 298 DOLLAR
28.2800 g., Copper-Nickel, 38.61 mm. **Ruler:** Elizabeth II **Subject:** Scouting centenary **Obv:** Head with tiara right

Date	Mintage	F	VF	XF	Unc	BU
2007(l)	1,900	—	—	—	—	50.00

KM# 298a DOLLAR

28.2800 g., 0.9250 Silver 0.8410 oz. ASW, 38.61 mm. **Ruler:** Elizabeth II **Subject:** Scouting centenary **Obv:** Head with tiara right

Date	Mintage	F	VF	XF	Unc	BU
2007(l) Proof	1,500	Value: 85.00				

KM# 300 DOLLAR

31.1350 g., 0.9990 Silver 1.0000 oz. ASW, 40 mm. **Ruler:** Elizabeth II **Obv:** Head with tiara right **Rev:** Great Spotted Kiwi **Edge:** Reeded

Date	Mintage	F	VF	XF	Unc	BU
2007(m)	4,000	—	—	—	—	50.00

KM# 300a DOLLAR

31.1350 g., 0.9990 Silver 1.0000 oz. ASW, 40 mm. **Ruler:** Elizabeth II **Obv:** Head with tiara right **Rev:** Great Spotted Kiwi **Edge:** Reeded

Date	Mintage	F	VF	XF	Unc	BU
2007(m) Proof	3,000	Value: 100				

Note: Mintage includes 500 struck in 2008 for sets.

KM# 302 DOLLAR

31.1350 g., Copper-Nickel, 40 mm. **Ruler:** Elizabeth II **Subject:** Elizabeth & Philip Diamond Wedding **Obv:** Head with tiara right **Rev:** Royal crests **Edge:** Reeded

Date	Mintage	F	VF	XF	Unc	BU
2007(m)	1,600	—	—	—	—	32.00

KM# 302a DOLLAR

31.1050 g., 0.9990 Silver 0.9990 oz. ASW, 40 mm. **Ruler:** Elizabeth II **Subject:** Elizabeth & Philip Diamond Wedding **Obv:** Head with tiara right **Rev:** Royal crests **Edge:** Reeded

Date	Mintage	F	VF	XF	Unc	BU
2007(m) Proof	1,500	Value: 85.00				

KM# 321 DOLLAR

30.8000 g., Brass, 30 mm. **Ruler:** Elizabeth II **Rev:** Sir Edmond Hillary with Mt. Everest **Edge:** Reeded **Note:** Sold in a PNC cover only

Date	Mintage	F	VF	XF	Unc	BU
2008(w)	4,000	—	—	—	—	20.00

KM# 309 DOLLAR

31.1350 g., 0.9990 Silver 1.0000 oz. ASW, 40 mm. **Ruler:** Elizabeth II **Obv:** Head with tiara right **Rev:** Haast Tokoeka Kiwi

Date	Mintage	F	VF	XF	Unc	BU
2008(w)	8,000	—	—	—	—	60.00

KM# 309a DOLLAR

31.1350 g., 0.9990 Silver 1.0000 oz. ASW, 40 mm. **Ruler:** Elizabeth II **Obv:** Head with tiara right **Rev:** Haast Tokoeka Kiwi

Date	Mintage	F	VF	XF	Unc	BU
2008(w) Proof	5,000	Value: 85.00				

Note: Includes 500 for 2004-2008 sets.

KM# 311 DOLLAR

31.1350 g., 0.9990 Silver 1.0000 oz. ASW, 40.6 mm. **Ruler:** Elizabeth II **Subject:** Sir Edmund Hillary **Obv:** Head with tiara right **Rev:** Hillary with Mt. Everest in background

Date	Mintage	F	VF	XF	Unc	BU
2008(w) Proof	10,000	Value: 90.00				

KM# 323 DOLLAR

31.1350 g., 0.9990 Silver 1.0000 oz. ASW, 40 mm. **Ruler:** Elizabeth II **Obv:** Bust right **Rev:** Southern Right Whale **Edge:** Reeded

Date	Mintage	F	VF	XF	Unc	BU
2009(m) Prooflike	11,500	—	—	—	—	70.00

KM# 324 DOLLAR

31.1350 g., 0.9990 Silver 1.0000 oz. ASW, 40 mm. **Ruler:** Elizabeth II **Rev:** Haast's Eagle

Date	Mintage	F	VF	XF	Unc	BU
2009(m) Prooflike	11,500	—	—	—	—	80.00

KM# 325 DOLLAR

31.1350 g., 0.9990 Silver 1.0000 oz. ASW, 40 mm. **Ruler:** Elizabeth II **Rev:** Giant Moa

Date	Mintage	F	VF	XF	Unc	BU
2009(m) Prooflike	1,500	—	—	—	—	85.00

KM# 326 DOLLAR

31.1350 g., 0.9990 Silver 1.0000 oz. ASW, 40 mm. **Ruler:** Elizabeth II **Rev:** Colossal squid **Edge:** Reeded

Date	Mintage	F	VF	XF	Unc	BU
2009(m) Prooflike	1,500	—	—	—	—	85.00

KM# 327 DOLLAR

31.1350 g., 0.9990 Silver 1.0000 oz. ASW, 40 mm. **Ruler:** Elizabeth II **Rev:** Giant Weta **Edge:** Reeded

Date	Mintage	F	VF	XF	Unc	BU
2009(m) Prooflike	1,500	—	—	—	—	85.00

KM# 328 DOLLAR

26.4500 g., Copper-Nickel-Zinc, 39.19 mm. **Ruler:** Elizabeth II **Subject:** Reserve Bank of New Zealand, 75th Anniversary **Rev:** Tui and Kowhai as on 1940-65 bronze penny

Date	Mintage	F	VF	XF	Unc	BU
2009(o)	2,000	—	—	—	—	30.00

KM# 322 DOLLAR

28.2800 g., Copper-Nickel, 40 mm. **Ruler:** Elizabeth II **Obv:** Head with tiara right **Rev:** Kiwi with map of New Zealand **Edge:** Reeded

Date	Mintage	F	VF	XF	Unc	BU
2009(m)	10,000	—	—	—	—	50.00

KM# 322a DOLLAR

31.1350 g., 0.9990 Silver 1.0000 oz. ASW, 40 mm. **Ruler:** Elizabeth II **Subject:** Icons of New Zealand **Rev:** Kiwi with map of New Zealand **Edge:** Reeded

Date	Mintage	F	VF	XF	Unc	BU
2009(m) Proof	7,500	Value: 80.00				

KM# 120a DOLLAR

8.6000 g., Brass **Ruler:** Elizabeth II **Obv:** Head with tiara right **Rev:** Kiwi bird within sprigs, value below **Edge:** Segmented reeding

Date	Mintage	F	VF	XF	Unc	BU
2010(u)	2,000	—	—	—	—	4.00
2010(u) Proof	1,500	Value: 5.00				
2011(u)	2,000	—	—	—	—	4.00
2011(u) Proof	1,500	Value: 5.00				
2012(u)	2,000	—	—	—	—	4.00
2012(u) Proof	1,500	Value: 5.00				

KM# 331 DOLLAR

31.1350 g., 0.9990 Silver 1.0000 oz. ASW, 40 mm. **Ruler:** Elizabeth II **Subject:** Icons of New Zealand **Rev:** Kiwi and Southern Cross **Edge:** Reeded

Date	Mintage	F	VF	XF	Unc	BU
2010(m)	Est. 12,500	—	—	—	—	60.00

KM# 331a DOLLAR

31.1350 g., 0.9990 Silver 1.0000 oz. ASW, 40 mm. **Ruler:** Elizabeth II **Rev:** Kiwi and Southern Cross **Edge:** Reeded

Date	Mintage	F	VF	XF	Unc	BU
2010(m) Proof	Est. 8,500	Value: 90.00				

KM# 333 DOLLAR

31.1350 g., 0.9990 Silver 1.0000 oz. ASW, 40 mm. **Ruler:** Elizabeth II **Subject:** 2010 FIFA World Cup **Rev:** Soccer player with stylized NZ koru **Edge:** Reeded

Date	Mintage	F	VF	XF	Unc	BU
2010(m)	10,000	—	—	—	—	100

Note: Mintage includes 1500 in NZ Post packaging.

KM# 336 DOLLAR

31.1050 g., 0.9990 Silver 0.9990 oz. ASW, 40 mm. **Ruler:** Elizabeth II **Obv:** Head with tiara right **Rev:** Allosaurus

Date	Mintage	F	VF	XF	Unc	BU
2010(m) Prooflike	1,500	—	—	—	—	90.00

KM# 337 DOLLAR

31.1050 g., 0.9990 Silver 0.9990 oz. ASW, 40 mm. **Ruler:** Elizabeth II **Obv:** Head with tiara right **Rev:** Anhanguera

Date	Mintage	F	VF	XF	Unc	BU
2010(m) Prooflike	1,500	—	—	—	—	90.00

KM# 338 DOLLAR

31.1050 g., 0.9990 Silver 0.9990 oz. ASW, 40 mm. **Ruler:** Elizabeth II **Obv:** Head with tiara right **Rev:** Mauisaurus

Date	Mintage	F	VF	XF	Unc	BU
2010(m) Prooflike	1,500	—	—	—	—	90.00

KM# 339 DOLLAR

31.1050 g., 0.9990 Silver 0.9990 oz. ASW, 40 mm. **Ruler:** Elizabeth II **Obv:** Head with tiara right **Rev:** Moanasaurus

Date	Mintage	F	VF	XF	Unc	BU
2010(m) Prooflike	1,500	—	—	—	—	90.00

KM# 340 DOLLAR

31.1050 g., 0.9990 Silver 0.9990 oz. ASW, 40 mm. **Ruler:** Elizabeth II **Obv:** Head with tiara right **Rev:** Titanosaurus

Date	Mintage	F	VF	XF	Unc	BU
2010(m) Prooflike	1,500	—	—	—	—	90.00

KM# 341 DOLLAR

31.1050 g., 0.9990 Silver 0.9990 oz. ASW, 40 mm. **Ruler:** Elizabeth II **Obv:** Head with tiara right **Rev:** Multicolor tiki with huia feathers

Date	Mintage	F	VF	XF	Unc	BU
2010(m) Proof	4,000	Value: 130				

KM# 344 DOLLAR

31.1050 g., 0.9990 Silver 0.9990 oz. ASW, 40 mm. **Ruler:** Elizabeth II **Obv:** Head with tiara right **Rev:** Black field with repeating fern pattern **Edge:** Reeded

Date	Mintage	F	VF	XF	Unc	BU
2010(m) Proof	10,000	Value: 100				

KM# 120b DOLLAR

10.7300 g., 0.9990 Silver 0.3446 oz. ASW, 23 mm. **Ruler:** Elizabeth II **Obv:** Head with tiara right **Rev:** Kiwi bird within sprigs, value below **Edge:** Segmented reeding

Date	Mintage	F	VF	XF	Unc	BU
2011(u) Proof	1,200	Value: 50.00				
2012(u) Proof	1,000	Value: 50.00				

KM# 335 DOLLAR

31.1350 g., 0.9990 Silver 1.0000 oz. ASW, 40 mm. **Ruler:** Elizabeth II **Obv:** Head with tiara right **Rev:** Kiwi and silver fern **Edge:** Reeded

Date	Mintage	F	VF	XF	Unc	BU
2011(m) Prooflike	10,000	—	—	—	—	65.00

KM# 335a DOLLAR

31.1050 g., 0.9990 Silver 0.9990 oz. ASW, 40 mm. **Ruler:** Elizabeth II **Obv:** Head in tiara right **Rev:** Kiwi and fern

Date	Mintage	F	VF	XF	Unc	BU
2011 Proof	7,000	Value: 75.00				

KM# 343 DOLLAR

Copper-Nickel, 30 mm. **Ruler:** Elizabeth II **Obv:** Head with tiara right **Rev:** All Black logo with repeating fern pattern in background **Edge:** Reeded

Date	Mintage	F	VF	XF	Unc	BU
2011(m)	10,000	—	—	—	—	30.00

KM# 345 DOLLAR

31.1050 g., 0.9990 Silver 0.9990 oz. ASW, 40 mm. **Ruler:** Elizabeth II **Obv:** Head with tiara right **Rev:** All Blacks performing the Haka before a rugby match **Edge Lettering:** KA MATE, KA MATE! KA ORA, KA ORA!

Date	Mintage	F	VF	XF	Unc	BU
2011(m) Proof	3,000	Value: 140				

KM# 346 DOLLAR

31.1050 g., 0.9990 Silver selective gold plating 0.9990 oz. ASW, 40 mm. **Ruler:** Elizabeth II **Obv:** Head with tiara right **Rev:** Webb Ellis Cup selectively gold palted **Edge:** Reeded

Date	Mintage	F	VF	XF	Unc	BU
2011(m) Proof	15,000	Value: 130				

KM# 347 DOLLAR

31.1350 g., 0.9990 Silver 1.0000 oz. ASW, 38.85 mm. **Ruler:** Elizabeth II **Subject:** 1987 Champions **Obv:** Head with tiara right **Rev:** 1987 All Black player fending off opponent **Edge:** Reeded

Date	Mintage	F	VF	XF	Unc	BU
2011(w) Proof	2,011	Value: 150				

KM# 350 DOLLAR

31.1050 g., 0.9990 Silver 0.9990 oz. ASW, 40 mm. **Ruler:** Elizabeth II **Obv:** Head with tiara right **Rev:** Kiwi and kowhai flowers **Edge:** Reeded

Date	Mintage	F	VF	XF	Unc	BU
2012(m) Prooflike	13,500	—	—	—	—	80.00
2012(m) Proof	5,000	Value: 130				

KM# 351 DOLLAR

31.1050 g., 0.9990 Silver 0.9990 oz. ASW, 38.6 mm. **Ruler:** Elizabeth II **Subject:** Maori Art **Obv:** Head with tiara right **Rev:** Hei matau (neck pendant) **Edge:** Notched

Date	Mintage	F	VF	XF	Unc	BU
2012(u) Proof	3,000	Value: 140				

KM# 354 DOLLAR

31.1050 g., 0.9990 Silver 0.9990 oz. ASW, 40 mm. **Ruler:** Elizabeth II **Subject:** 50th years of firendship - New Zealand and Samoa **Rev:** New Zealand and Samoa designs, color background

Date	Mintage	F	VF	XF	Unc	BU
2012 Proof	1,000	Value: 75.00				

KM# 356 DOLLAR

Silver, 40 mm. **Ruler:** Elizabeth II **Subject:** Elizabeth II, 60th Anniversary of reign **Rev:** Elizabeth II delivering Christmas Message, color flora

Date	Mintage	F	VF	XF	Unc	BU
2012 proof	—	Value: 75.00				

KM# 357 DOLLAR
Silver, 40 mm. **Ruler:** Elizabeth II **Subject:** New Zealand Air Force, 75th Anniversary **Rev:** Pilot and Skyhawk aircraft, "missing man" formation

Date	Mintage	F	VF	XF	Unc	BU
2012 Proof	—	Value: 75.00				

KM# 358 DOLLAR
31.1050 g., 0.9990 Silver 0.9990 oz. ASW, 40 mm. **Ruler:** Elizabeth II **Subject:** Bilbo Baggins

Date	Mintage	F	VF	XF	Unc	BU
2012 Proof	1,000	Value: 150				

KM# 359 DOLLAR
31.1050 g., 0.9990 Silver 0.9990 oz. ASW, 40 mm. **Ruler:** Elizabeth II **Subject:** Radagast

Date	Mintage	F	VF	XF	Unc	BU
2012 Proof	1,000	Value: 150				

KM# 360 DOLLAR
31.1050 g., 0.9990 Silver 0.9990 oz. ASW, 40 mm. **Ruler:** Elizabeth II **Subject:** Elrond

Date	Mintage	F	VF	XF	Unc	BU
2012 Proof	1,000	Value: 150				

KM# 361 DOLLAR
31.1050 g., 0.9990 Silver 0.9990 oz. ASW, 40 mm. **Ruler:** Elizabeth II **Subject:** Thorin Oakenshield

Date	Mintage	F	VF	XF	Unc	BU
2012 Proof	1,000	Value: 150				

KM# 362 DOLLAR
31.1050 g., 0.9990 Silver 0.9990 oz. ASW, 40 mm. **Ruler:** Elizabeth II **Subject:** Gandalf

Date	Mintage	F	VF	XF	Unc	BU
2012 Proof	1,000	Value: 150				

KM# 363 DOLLAR
31.1050 g., 0.9990 Silver 0.9990 oz. ASW, 40 mm. **Ruler:** Elizabeth II **Subject:** Gollum

Date	Mintage	F	VF	XF	Unc	BU
2012 Proof	1,000	Value: 150				

KM# 364 DOLLAR
Aluminum-Bronze **Ruler:** Elizabeth II **Rev:** Bilbo Baggins examining contract with Dwarves

Date	Mintage	F	VF	XF	Unc	BU
2012 Proof	—	Value: 15.00				

KM# 365 DOLLAR
Aluminum-Bronze **Ruler:** Elizabeth II **Subject:** Thorin Oakenshield

Date	Mintage	F	VF	XF	Unc	BU
2012 Proof	—	Value: 15.00				

KM# 366 DOLLAR
Aluminum-Bronze **Ruler:** Elizabeth II **Subject:** Gandalf and Radagast

Date	Mintage	F	VF	XF	Unc	BU
2012 Proof	—	Value: 15.00				

KM# 367 DOLLAR
Aluminum-Bronze **Ruler:** Elizabeth II **Subject:** Three Dwarves

Date	Mintage	F	VF	XF	Unc	BU
2012 Proof	—	Value: 15.00				

KM# 372 DOLLAR
31.1050 g., 0.9990 Silver gilt ring 0.9990 oz. ASW, 40 mm. **Ruler:** Elizabeth II **Rev:** Bilbo Baggins, staff in right hand

Date	Mintage	F	VF	XF	Unc	BU
2012 Proof	20,000	Value: 150				

KM# 121 2 DOLLARS
10.0000 g., Aluminum-Bronze, 26.5 mm. **Ruler:** Elizabeth II **Obv:** Head with tiara right **Rev:** White heron (kotuku) above value **Edge:** Reeded with security groove

Date	Mintage	F	VF	XF	Unc	BU
2001(l)	3,000,000	—	—	—	2.50	5.00
2001(c) In sets only	2,910	—	—	—	—	6.00
2001(c) Proof	2,000	Value: 7.50				
2002(l)	6,000,000	—	—	—	2.50	5.00
2002(c) In sets only	3,000	—	—	—	—	6.00
2002(c) Proof	2,000	Value: 7.50				
2003(l)	6,000,000	—	—	—	2.50	5.00
2003(c) In sets only	3,000	—	—	—	—	6.00
2003(c) Proof	3,000	Value: 7.50				
2004(c) In sets only	2,800	—	—	—	—	5.00
2004 Proof	3,500	Value: 7.50				
2005(l)	5,000,000	—	—	—	2.50	5.00
2005(c) In sets only	3,000	—	—	—	—	6.00
2005(c) Proof	3,000	Value: 7.50				
2006(c) In sets only	3,000	—	—	—	—	6.00
2006(c) Proof	2,100	Value: 7.50				
2007(c)	5,000	—	—	—	—	6.00
2007(c) Proof	4,000	Value: 7.50				
2008(l) In sets only	4,000	—	—	—	—	6.00
2008(l) Proof	3,000	Value: 7.50				
2009(w) In sets only	2,000	—	—	—	—	6.00
2009(w) Proof	1,500	Value: 7.50				
2011(l)	8,000,000	—	—	—	2.50	5.00

KM# 121a 2 DOLLARS
11.2500 g., Brass, 26.5 mm. **Ruler:** Elizabeth II **Obv:** Head with tiara right **Rev:** White heron (kotuku) above value **Edge:** Reeded with security groove

Date	Mintage	F	VF	XF	Unc	BU
2010(u)	2,000	—	—	—	—	6.00
2010(u) Proof	1,500	Value: 7.50				
2011(u)	2,000	—	—	—	—	6.00
2011(u) Proof	1,500	Value: 7.50				
2012(u)	2,000	—	—	—	—	6.00
2012(u) Proof	1,500	Value: 7.50				

KM# 121b 2 DOLLARS
14.1200 g., 0.9990 Silver 0.4535 oz. ASW, 26.5 mm. **Ruler:** Elizabeth II **Obv:** Head with tiara right **Rev:** White heron (kotuku) above value **Edge:** Reeded with security groove

Date	Mintage	F	VF	XF	Unc	BU
2011(u) Proof	1,200	Value: 75.00				
2012(u) Proof	1,000	Value: 75.00				

KM# 128 5 DOLLARS
28.2800 g., Copper-Nickel, 38.6 mm. **Ruler:** Elizabeth II **Subject:** Kereru Bird **Obv:** Head with tiara right **Rev:** Wood Pigeon on branch **Edge:** Reeded

Date	Mintage	F	VF	XF	Unc	BU
2001(l)	1,500	—	—	—	25.00	—

KM# 128a 5 DOLLARS
28.2800 g., 0.9990 Silver 0.9083 oz. ASW **Ruler:** Elizabeth II **Obv:** Head with tiara right **Rev:** Pigeon on branch

Date	Mintage	F	VF	XF	Unc	BU
2001 Proof	1,000	Value: 85.00				

KM# 149 5 DOLLARS
28.2800 g., 0.9250 Silver 0.8410 oz. ASW, 38.6 mm. **Ruler:** Elizabeth II **Subject:** Royal Visit (canceled after coin issue) **Obv:** Head with tiara right **Rev:** Queen with flowers and two girls **Edge:** Reeded

Date	Mintage	F	VF	XF	Unc	BU
2001 Proof	2,000	Value: 100				

Note: 200 issued in stamp cover

KM# 131 5 DOLLARS
28.2800 g., Copper-Nickel, 38.6 mm. **Ruler:** Elizabeth II **Subject:** Architectural Heritage **Obv:** Head with tiara right **Rev:** Auckland Sky Tower **Edge:** Reeded

Date	Mintage	F	VF	XF	Unc	BU
2002(l)	3,000	—	—	—	12.50	—

Note: 500 pieces were housed in a stamp cover

KM# 131a 5 DOLLARS
28.2800 g., 0.9250 Silver 0.8410 oz. ASW, 38.6 mm. **Ruler:** Elizabeth II **Subject:** Architectural Heritage **Obv:** Head with tiara right **Rev:** Auckland Sky Tower **Edge:** Reeded

Date	Mintage	F	VF	XF	Unc	BU
2002(l)	2,000	Value: 80.00				

Note: 500 pieces were housed in a stamp cover

KM# 145 5 DOLLARS
27.2200 g., Copper-Nickel, 38.74 mm. **Ruler:** Elizabeth II **Obv:** Head with tiara right **Rev:** Hector's Dolphins jumping out of the water **Edge:** Reeded

Date	Mintage	F	VF	XF	Unc	BU
2002(c)	4,000	—	—	—	35.00	—

Note: 500 pieces were housed in a stamp covers

KM# 145a 5 DOLLARS
27.2220 g., 0.9990 Silver 0.8743 oz. ASW **Ruler:** Elizabeth II **Obv:** Head with tiara right **Rev:** Two Hector's Dolphins jumping out of the water **Edge:** Reeded

Date	Mintage	F	VF	XF	Unc	BU
2002(c)	Est. 2,000	—	—	—	—	100

Note: 500 in stamp covers

KM# 151 5 DOLLARS
28.2800 g., 0.9250 Silver Gilt 0.8410 oz. ASW, 38.61 mm. **Ruler:** Elizabeth II **Subject:** Queen's Jubilee **Obv:** Gilt head with tiara right **Rev:** Scepter with "Great Star of Africa' at left of vertical band with crowns and shields **Edge:** Reeded

Date	Mintage	F	VF	XF	Unc	BU
2002(l) Proof	25,000	Value: 80.00				

Note: 100 pieces were housed in a stamp cover, value $85

KM# 272 5 DOLLARS
28.2800 g., Copper-Nickel, 38.61 mm. **Ruler:** Elizabeth II **Subject:** America's cup

Date	Mintage	F	VF	XF	Unc	BU
2002(l)	6,000	—	—	—	—	20.00

KM# 272a 5 DOLLARS
28.2800 g., 0.9250 Silver 0.8410 oz. ASW, 38.61 mm. **Ruler:** Elizabeth II **Subject:** America's Cup **Obv:** Head with tiara right **Rev:** Yachts

Date	Mintage	F	VF	XF	Unc	BU
2002(l) Proof	4,000	Value: 60.00				

Note: Includes 500 in stamp cover, value $60.

KM# 132 5 DOLLARS
26.7000 g., Copper-Nickel, 38.6 mm. **Ruler:** Elizabeth II **Obv:** Head with tiara right **Rev:** Giant Kokopu fish divides circle **Edge:** Reeded **Designer:** Michael McHalick

Date	Mintage	F	VF	XF	Unc	BU
2003(c)	2,400	—	—	—	14.00	27.50

Note: Includes 400 issued in a stamp cover.

KM# 132a 5 DOLLARS
28.2800 g., 0.9990 Silver Gold plated 0.9083 oz. ASW, 38.6 mm. **Ruler:** Elizabeth II **Obv:** Head with tiara right **Rev:** Giant Kokopu fish **Edge:** Reeded

Date	Mintage	F	VF	XF	Unc	BU
2003(c) Proof	1,700	Value: 75.00				

Note: Includes 200 issued in a stamp cover

KM# 133 5 DOLLARS
26.7200 g., Copper-Nickel, 38.6 mm. **Ruler:** Elizabeth II **Subject:** Chatham Island Taiko **Obv:** Head with tiara right **Rev:** Magenta Petrel **Edge:** Reeded

Date	Mintage	F	VF	XF	Unc	BU
2004(2003)	1,350	—	—	—	—	35.00

KM# 147 5 DOLLARS
28.2300 g., 0.9250 Silver 0.8395 oz. ASW, 38.6 mm. **Ruler:** Elizabeth II **Subject:** 50th Anniversary of Coronation **Obv:** Gold plated crowned head right **Rev:** Crown above fern and flowers **Edge:** Reeded

Date	Mintage	F	VF	XF	Unc	BU
2003 Proof	25,000	Value: 80.00				

Note: Includes 100 issued in a stamp cover

KM# 133a 5 DOLLARS
28.2800 g., 0.9990 Silver 0.9083 oz. ASW, 38.74 mm. **Ruler:** Elizabeth II **Obv:** Head with tiara right **Rev:** Chatham Island Taiko

Date	Mintage	F	VF	XF	Unc	BU
2004 Proof	1,300	Value: 70.00				

KM# 146 5 DOLLARS
27.2200 g., Copper-Nickel, 38.74 mm. **Ruler:** Elizabeth II **Obv:** Head with tiara right **Rev:** Fiordland Crested Penguin **Edge:** Reeded

Date	Mintage	F	VF	XF	Unc	BU
2005(2004)	4,000	—	—	—	25.00	30.00

KM# 146a 5 DOLLARS
27.2200 g., 0.9990 Silver 0.8742 oz. ASW, 38.74 mm. **Ruler:** Elizabeth II **Obv:** Head with tiara right **Rev:** Fiordland Crested Penguin **Edge:** Reeded

Date	Mintage	F	VF	XF	Unc	BU
2005	3,500	—	—	—	—	60.00

KM# 148 5 DOLLARS
27.2200 g., Copper-Nickel, 38.74 mm. **Ruler:** Elizabeth II **Obv:** Head with tiara right **Rev:** Falcon on tree stump **Edge:** Reeded

Date	Mintage	F	VF	XF	Unc	BU
2006	4,000	—	—	—	25.00	30.00

KM# 148a 5 DOLLARS
28.2800 g., 0.9990 Silver 0.9083 oz. ASW, 38.74 mm. **Ruler:** Elizabeth II **Obv:** Head with tiara right **Rev:** New Zealand Falcon on tree stump **Edge:** Reeded

Date	Mintage	F	VF	XF	Unc	BU
2006 Proof	2,500	Value: 60.00				

KM# 150 5 DOLLARS
27.2200 g., Copper-Nickel, 38.74 mm. **Ruler:** Elizabeth II **Subject:** Tuatara **Obv:** Head with tiara right **Rev:** Tuatara (Sphenodon punctatus), a lizard-like reptile **Edge:** Reeded

Date	Mintage	F	VF	XF	Unc	BU
2007(c)	2,200	—	—	—	25.00	30.00

KM# 150a 5 DOLLARS
28.2800 g., 0.9990 Silver 0.9083 oz. ASW, 38.74 mm. **Ruler:** Elizabeth II **Subject:** Tuatara **Obv:** Head with tiara right **Rev:** Tuatara right **Edge:** Reeded

Date	Mintage	F	VF	XF	Unc	BU
2007(c) Proof	2,700	Value: 80.00				

KM# 233 5 DOLLARS
28.2800 g., Copper-Nickel, 38.6 mm. **Ruler:** Elizabeth II **Subject:** Hamilton's frog **Obv:** Head with tiara right **Obv. Legend:** NEW ZEALAND - ELIZABETH II **Rev:** Frog perched on branch at left center

Date	Mintage	F	VF	XF	Unc	BU
2008(l)	4,000	—	—	—	35.00	40.00

KM# 233a 5 DOLLARS
28.2800 g., 0.9990 Silver 0.9083 oz. ASW, 38.61 mm. **Ruler:** Elizabeth II **Rev:** Hamilton's frog **Edge:** Reeded

Date	Mintage	F	VF	XF	Unc	BU
2008(l) Proof	4,000	Value: 90.00				

Note: Mintage includes 1500 struck in 2009

KM# 329 5 DOLLARS
22.0000 g., Copper-Nickel, 38.60 mm. **Ruler:** Elizabeth II **Rev:** Kakapo **Edge:** Reeded

Date	Mintage	F	VF	XF	Unc	BU
2009(w)	2,000	—	—	—	25.00	30.00

KM# 329a 5 DOLLARS
31.1350 g., 0.9990 Silver 1.0000 oz. ASW, 38.61 mm. **Ruler:** Elizabeth II **Rev:** Kakapo

Date	Mintage	F	VF	XF	Unc	BU
2009(w) Proof	4,000	Value: 90.00				

KM# 334 5 DOLLARS
31.1000 g., Copper-Nickel, 38.7 mm. **Ruler:** Elizabeth II **Series:** Maui's Dolphin, subspecies of the Hector Dolphin **Rev:** Dolphin jumping right **Edge:** Reeded

Date	Mintage	F	VF	XF	Unc	BU
2010	2,000	—	—	—	—	35.00

KM# 334a 5 DOLLARS
31.1050 g., 0.9990 Silver 0.9990 oz. ASW, 38.7 mm. **Ruler:** Elizabeth II **Obv:** Head with tiara right **Rev:** Maui's Dolphin **Edge:** Reeded

Date	Mintage	F	VF	XF	Unc	BU
2010(u) Proof	4,000	Value: 89.00				

KM# 348 5 DOLLARS
31.1050 g., Copper-Nickel, 38.7 mm. **Ruler:** Elizabeth II **Obv:** Head with tiara right **Rev:** Yellow-eyed Penguin **Edge:** Reeded

Date	Mintage	F	VF	XF	Unc	BU
2011(u)	2,000	—	—	—	—	35.00

KM# 348a 5 DOLLARS
31.1050 g., 0.9990 Silver 0.9990 oz. ASW, 38.7 mm. **Ruler:** Elizabeth II **Obv:** Head with tiara right **Rev:** Yellow-eyed Penguin **Edge:** Reeded

Date	Mintage	F	VF	XF	Unc	BU
2011(u) Proof	4,000	Value: 100				

KM# 355 5 DOLLARS
Silver, 40 mm. **Ruler:** Elizabeth II **Rev:** Fairy Tern in flight

Date	Mintage	F	VF	XF	Unc	BU
2012 Proof	—	Value: 65.00				

KM# 129 10 DOLLARS
3.8879 g., 0.9990 Gold 0.1249 oz. AGW, 18 mm. **Ruler:** Elizabeth II **Obv:** Head with tiara right **Rev:** Salvage ship above value **Edge:** Reeded

Date	Mintage	F	VF	XF	Unc	BU
2001 Proof	600	Value: 275				

KM# 130 10 DOLLARS
7.7759 g., 0.9990 Gold 0.2497 oz. AGW, 22 mm. **Ruler:** Elizabeth II **Obv:** Head with tiara right **Rev:** Ship above value **Edge:** Reeded

Date	Mintage	F	VF	XF	Unc	BU
2001 Proof	600	Value: 525				

KM# 273 10 DOLLARS
Nickel-Brass gold plated, 28.4 mm. **Ruler:** Elizabeth II **Subject:** America's Cup **Obv:** Head with tiara right **Rev:** Map, cup and yachts

Date	Mintage	F	VF	XF	Unc	BU
2002(l)	5,000	—	—	—	—	45.00

KM# 274 10 DOLLARS
15.5520 g., 0.9990 Gold 0.4995 oz. AGW, 28.4 mm. **Ruler:** Elizabeth II **Subject:** America's Cup **Obv:** Head with tiara right **Rev:** Map, cup and yachts

Date	Mintage	F	VF	XF	Unc	BU
2002(l) Proof	900	Value: 950				

KM# 144 10 DOLLARS
39.9400 g., 0.9170 Gold 1.1775 oz. AGW, 38.61 mm. **Ruler:** Elizabeth II **Subject:** Lord of the Rings **Obv:** Head with tiara right **Rev:** The One Ring **Edge:** Reeded

Date	Mintage	F	VF	XF	Unc	BU
2003(l) Proof	1,198	Value: 2,300				

KM# 270 10 DOLLARS
39.9400 g., 0.9170 Gold 1.1775 oz. AGW, 38.61 mm. **Ruler:** Elizabeth II **Subject:** Lord of the Rings **Obv:** Head with tiara right **Rev:** Frodo **Edge:** Reeded

Date	Mintage	F	VF	XF	Unc	BU
2003(l) Proof	142	Value: 2,300				

KM# 271 10 DOLLARS

39.9400 g., 0.9170 Gold 1.1775 oz. AGW, 38.61 mm. **Ruler:** Elizabeth II **Subject:** Lord of the Rings **Obv:** Head with tiara right **Rev:** Sauron **Edge:** Reeded

Date	Mintage	F	VF	XF	Unc	BU
2003(l) Proof	142	Value: 2,300				

KM# 275 10 DOLLARS

38.5000 g., 0.9170 Gold 1.1350 oz. AGW, 38.61 mm. **Ruler:** Elizabeth II **Subject:** Pukaki **Obv:** Head with tiara right **Rev:** Statue of Pukaki **Edge:** Reeded

Date	Mintage	F	VF	XF	Unc	BU
2004(l) Proof	300	Value: 5,000				
2004(l) NW RB Proof	2	—	—	—	—	—

Note: Initials added for presention to Ngati Whakaue (Maori tribe) and the Reserve Bank.

KM# 165 10 DOLLARS

7.9880 g., 0.9170 Gold 0.2355 oz. AGW, 22.05 mm. **Ruler:** Elizabeth II **Subject:** Lions Rugby Tour **Obv:** Crowned head right **Edge:** Reeded

Date	Mintage	F	VF	XF	Unc	BU
2005(l) Proof	1,000	Value: 475				

KM# 155 10 DOLLARS

7.7770 g., 0.9990 Gold 0.2498 oz. AGW, 20.1 mm. **Ruler:** Elizabeth II **Subject:** ANZAC **Obv:** Crowned head right **Rev:** New Zealand soldier playing bugle in front of War Memorial **Edge:** Reeded

Date	Mintage	F	VF	XF	Unc	BU
2005(w)	1,000	—	—	—	—	500

KM# 295 10 DOLLARS

31.1350 g., 0.9990 Gold 1.0000 oz. AGW, 34 mm. **Ruler:** Elizabeth II **Subject:** Narnia **Obv:** Head with tiara right **Rev:** Asian

Date	Mintage	F	VF	XF	Unc	BU
2006 Proof	365	Value: 2,100				

KM# 307 10 DOLLARS

7.7770 g., 0.9990 Gold 0.2498 oz. AGW, 20 mm. **Ruler:** Elizabeth II **Subject:** Queen's 80th birthday **Obv:** Head with tiara right **Rev:** Heraldic arms

Date	Mintage	F	VF	XF	Unc	BU
2006 Proof	500	Value: 550				

KM# 308 10 DOLLARS

15.5540 g., 0.9990 Gold 0.4996 oz. AGW, 25.10 mm. **Ruler:** Elizabeth II **Subject:** Gold Rushes - Otago **Obv:** Head with tiara right **Rev:** Picks, shovels and nuggets

Date	Mintage	F	VF	XF	Unc	BU
2006(w) Proof	300	Value: 1,000				

KM# 304 10 DOLLARS

7.7750 g., 0.9990 Gold 0.2497 oz. AGW, 26 mm. **Ruler:** Elizabeth II **Subject:** Elizabeth & Philip Diamond Wedding Anniversary **Obv:** Head with tiara right **Rev:** Royal crests

Date	Mintage	F	VF	XF	Unc	BU
2007(m) Proof	300	Value: 550				

KM# 305 10 DOLLARS

31.1350 g., 0.9170 Gold 0.9179 oz. AGW, 38.61 mm. **Ruler:** Elizabeth II **Subject:** Scouting centenary **Obv:** Head with tiara right

Date	Mintage	F	VF	XF	Unc	BU
2007(l) Proof	150	Value: 1,850				

KM# 306 10 DOLLARS

7.7855 g., 0.9990 Gold 0.2500 oz. AGW, 20.6 mm. **Ruler:** Elizabeth II **Subject:** Sir Edmund Hilary **Obv:** Head with tiara right **Rev:** Ed Hilary with Mt. Everest in background

Date	Mintage	F	VF	XF	Unc	BU
2008(w) Proof	1,953	Value: 525				

KM# 330 10 DOLLARS

7.7750 g., 0.9990 Gold 0.2497 oz. AGW, 26 mm. **Ruler:** Elizabeth II **Subject:** Icons of New Zealand **Rev:** Kiwi and map of New Zealand **Edge:** Reeded

Date	Mintage	F	VF	XF	Unc	BU
2009(m) Proof	1,500	Value: 575				

KM# 332 10 DOLLARS

7.7750 g., 0.9990 Gold 0.2497 oz. AGW, 26. mm. **Ruler:** Elizabeth II **Subject:** Icons of New Zealand **Rev:** Kiwi and Southern Cross **Edge:** Reeded

Date	Mintage	F	VF	XF	Unc	BU
2010(m) Proof	1,800	Value: 575				

KM# 342 10 DOLLARS

31.1050 g., 0.9990 Gold 0.9990 oz. AGW, 40 mm. **Ruler:** Elizabeth II **Subject:** Maori Art **Obv:** Head with tiara right **Rev:** Tiki with huia feathers

Date	Mintage	F	VF	XF	Unc	BU
2010(m) Proof	500	Value: 2,650				

KM# 349 10 DOLLARS

7.7700 g., 0.9990 Gold 0.2496 oz. AGW, 26 mm. **Ruler:** Elizabeth II **Obv:** Head with tiara right **Rev:** Kiwi and silver fern **Edge:** Reeded

Date	Mintage	F	VF	XF	Unc	BU
2011(m) Proof	995	Value: 775				

KM# 352 10 DOLLARS

7.7700 g., 0.9990 Gold 0.2496 oz. AGW, 26 mm. **Ruler:** Elizabeth II **Obv:** Head with tiara right **Rev:** Kiwi and kowhai flowers **Edge:** Reeded

Date	Mintage	F	VF	XF	Unc	BU
2012(m) Proof	950	Value: 900				

KM# 353 10 DOLLARS

31.1050 g., 0.9990 Gold with insert 0.9990 oz. AGW, 38.6 mm. **Ruler:** Elizabeth II **Subject:** Maori Art **Obv:** Head with tiara right **Rev:** Hei Matau (neck pendant) **Edge:** Notched

Date	Mintage	F	VF	XF	Unc	BU
2012(u) Proof	250	Value: 3,950				

KM# 368 10 DOLLARS

31.1050 g., 0.9990 Gold 0.9990 oz. AGW, 39 mm. **Ruler:** Elizabeth II **Rev:** Bilbo Baggins, staff in right hand

Date	Mintage	F	VF	XF	Unc	BU
2012 Proof	250	Value: 3,700				

KM# 369 10 DOLLARS

31.1050 g., 0.9990 Gold 0.9990 oz. AGW, 39 mm. **Ruler:** Elizabeth II **Subject:** Gandalf

Date	Mintage	F	VF	XF	Unc	BU
2012 Proof	250	Value: 3,500				

KM# 370 10 DOLLARS

31.1050 g., 0.9990 Gold 0.9990 oz. AGW, 39 mm. **Ruler:** Elizabeth II **Subject:** Thorin Oakenshield

Date	Mintage	F	VF	XF	Unc	BU
2012 Proof	250	Value: 3,500				

KM# 371 10 DOLLARS

31.1050 g., 0.9990 Gold 0.9990 oz. AGW, 39 mm. **Ruler:** Elizabeth II **Rev:** Bilbo Baggins, staff in right hand

Date	Mintage	F	VF	XF	Unc	BU
2012 Proof	1,000	Value: 3,500				

MINT SETS

KM#	Date	Mintage	Identification	Issue Price	Mkt Val
MS50	2001 (7)	2,910	KM#116-121, 128	18.50	60.00
MS51	2002 (7)	3,000	KM#116-121, 145. Hector's dolphin.	18.00	60.00
MS52	2003 (7)	3,000	KM#116-121, 132. Giant Kokopu.	18.00	100
MS53	2003 (6)	34,332	KM#135-140. Lord of the Rings, Light vs. Dark set.	19.95	100
MS54	2003 (9)	2,821	KM#135-137; 235-240. Fellowship of the Ring.	—	175
MS55	2003 (18)	4,068	KM#135-140; 235-246. Lord of the Rings. Character collection.	—	325
MS56	2003 (3)	10,454	KM#141, 142, 143. Lord of the Rings. Battle for the Ring set.	29.95	35.00
MS57	2004 (7)	2,800	KM#116-121, 133. Taiko.	33.00	150
MS60	2003-5-6 (7)	5,000	Mixed Set for Change over to smaller size coins. KM#116 (2003); 117-119 (2005); KM#117a-119a (2006).	7.50	70.00
MS58	2005 (7)	3,000	KM#116-121; 146. Crested Penguin.	33.00	120
MS59	2006 (7)	3,000	KM#116-121; 148. Falcon.	33.00	120
MS61	2007 (6)	5,000	KM#117a-119a; 120-121; 150. Tuatara.	33.00	50.00
MS62	2008 (6)	4,000	KM#117a-119a; 120-121; 233. Hamilton's frog.	37.50	50.00
MS63	2009 (6)	2,000	KM#117a-119a; 120-121; 329. Kakapo.	—	55.00
MS64	2009 (5)	1,500	KM#323-327. Giants of New Zealand.	—	400
MS65	2010 (6)	2,000	KM#117b, 118b, 119b, 120a, 121a, 334. Maui's dolphin.	59.00	65.00
MS66	2010 (5)	1,500	KM#336-340. Ancient Reptiles of New Zealand.	—	450
MS67	2011 (6)	2,000	KM#117b, 118b, 119b, 120a, 121a, 348. Yellow-eyed Penguin.	—	65.00

PROOF SETS

KM#	Date	Mintage	Identification	Issue Price	Mkt Val
PS45	2001 (7)	1,364	KM#116-121, 128a	49.25	170
PS46	2001 (2)	600	KM#129-130	400	800
PS47	2002 (7)	1,500	KM#116-121, 145a	60.00	140
PS48	2003 (6)	810	KM#141a and 5 others.	—	350
PS49	2003	—	Five coins as per PS48, less 141a	—	—
PS50	2003 (3)	133	KM#144; 270; 271. Lord of the Rings. Gold set.	—	6,900
PS51	2003 (2)	9	KM#270; 271. Lord of the Rings.	—	4,600
PS52	2003 (7)	1,496	KM#116-121, 132a.	60.00	125
PS53	2004 (7)	1,750	KM#116-121, 133a. Chatham Islands Taiko	—	200
PS54	2005 (7)	2,250	KM#116-121; 146a. Crested Penguin.	88.00	165
PS55	2006 (7)	2,100	KM#116-121; 148a. Falcon.	90.00	145
PS56	2006 (3)	1,000	KM#285; 287; 288.	—	225
PS57	2007 (6)	2,200	KM#117a-119a; 120-121; 150a. Tuatara.	88.00	115
PS58	2007 (7)	69,000	KM#232, NZ Aoraki dollar and Japan 95.2; 96.2; 97.2; 98.2; 101.2; 125.	115	110
PS59	2008 (6)	1,441	KM#117a-119a; 120-121; 233a. Hamilton's frog.	94.00	125
PS60	2004-08 (4)	500	KM#152; 153a; 291a; 300a; 309a. Kiwi.	375	450
PS61	2009 (6)	1,041	KM#117a-119a; 120-121; 329a. Kakapo.	—	125
PS62	2010 (6)	1,500	KM#117b, 118b, 119b, 120a, 121a, 334a. Maui's dolphin.	149	125
PS63	2011 (6)	500	KM#117b, 118b, 119b, 120a, 121a, 348a. Yellow-eyed Penguin.	—	135
PS64	2011 (5)	2,011	KM346, 347, plus Australian, British and South African coins.	695	700
PS65	2011 (5)	1,200	KM#117c, 118c, 119c, 120b, 121b.	275	225
PS66	2012 (5)	1,000	KM#117d, 118c, 119c, 120b, 121b.	275	225

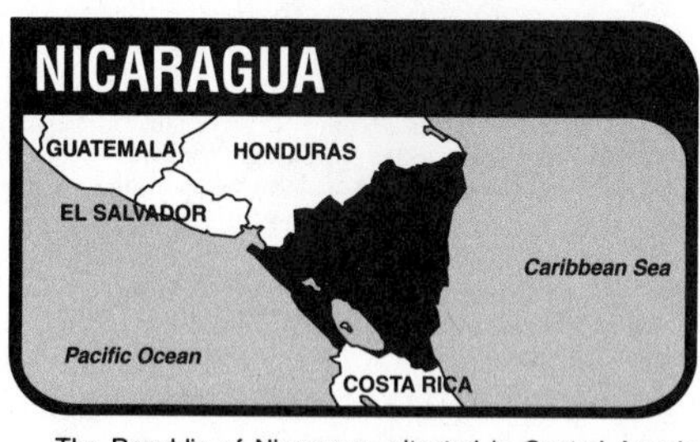

The Republic of Nicaragua, situated in Central America between Honduras and Costa Rica, has an area of 50,193 sq. mi. (129,494 sq. km.) and a population of *3.7 million. Capital: Managua. Agriculture, mining (gold and silver) and hardwood logging are the principal industries. Cotton, meat, coffee and sugar are exported.

MONETARY SYSTEM

100 Centavos = 1 Cordoba

REPUBLIC

DECIMAL COINAGE

KM# 97 5 CENTAVOS

3.0000 g., Copper Plated Steel, 18.5 mm. **Obv:** National arms **Rev:** Value within circle **Edge:** Plain

Date	Mintage	F	VF	XF	Unc	BU
2002	—	—	—	—	0.25	0.50

KM# 98 10 CENTAVOS

4.0000 g., Brass Plated Steel, 20.5 mm. **Obv:** National arms **Rev:** Value within circle **Edge:** Reeded and plain sections

Date	Mintage	F	VF	XF	Unc	BU
2002	—	—	—	—	0.45	0.85

KM# 105 10 CENTAVOS

Aluminum, 20.5 mm. **Obv:** National arms **Rev:** Value at center

Date	Mintage	F	VF	XF	Unc	BU
2007	—	—	—	—	0.45	0.85

KM# 99 25 CENTAVOS

5.0000 g., Brass Plated Steel, 23.25 mm. **Obv:** National arms **Rev:** Value within circle **Edge:** Segmented reeding

Date	Mintage	F	VF	XF	Unc	BU
2002	—	—	—	—	0.65	1.25
2003	—	—	—	—	0.65	1.25
2007	—	—	—	—	0.65	1.25

KM# 104 25 CENTAVOS

Brass **Obv:** Arms **Rev:** Value at center **Rev. Legend:** EN DIOS CONFIAMOS

Date	Mintage	F	VF	XF	Unc	BU
2007	—	—	—	—	1.50	2.50

KM# 89 CORDOBA
6.2000 g., Nickel Clad Steel, 25 mm. **Obv:** National emblem **Rev:** Value above sprigs within circle **Edge:** Reeded

Date	Mintage	F	VF	XF	Unc	BU
2002	—	—	—	—	2.50	3.00

KM# 101 CORDOBA
6.2500 g., Nickel Clad Steel, 25 mm. **Obv:** National arms **Rev:** Large value "1" **Rev. Legend:** EN DIOS CONFIAMOS **Edge:** Reeded

Date	Mintage	F	VF	XF	Unc	BU
2002	—	—	0.35	0.90	2.25	3.00
2007	—	—	0.35	0.90	2.25	3.00
2008	—	—	0.35	0.90	2.25	3.00
2009	—	—	0.35	0.90	2.25	3.00
2010	—	—	0.35	0.90	2.25	3.00

KM# 100 10 CORDOBAS
27.1200 g., 0.9250 Silver 0.8065 oz. ASW, 40 mm. **Subject:** Ibero-America **Obv:** National arms in circle of arms **Rev:** Sail boat **Edge:** Reeded

Date	Mintage	F	VF	XF	Unc	BU
2002 Proof	—	Value: 50.00				

KM# 102 10 CORDOBAS
8.4700 g., Brass Plated Steel, 26.5 mm. **Obv:** National arms **Rev:** Value at upper left, circular latent image BCN below, statue of Andrés Castro at right **Edge Lettering:** B C N repeated 4 times

Date	Mintage	F	VF	XF	Unc	BU
2007	—	—	—	—	—	4.00

NIGER

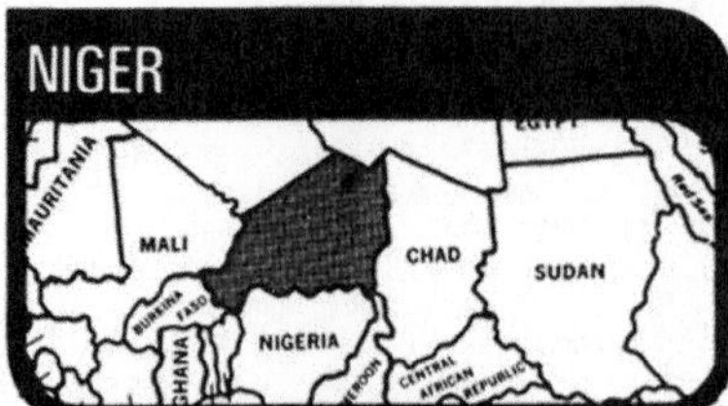

The Republic of Niger, located in West Africa's Sahara region 1,000 miles (1,609 km.) from the Mediterranean shore, has an area of 489,191 sq. mi. (1,267,000 sq. km.) and a population of *7.4 million. Capital: Niamey. The economy is based on subsistence agriculture and raising livestock. Peanuts, peanut oil, and livestock are exported.

REPUBLIC

DECIMAL COINAGE

KM# 17 1000 FRANCS
20.0000 g., 0.9250 Silver 0.5948 oz. ASW, 38.61 mm. **Obv:** Shield and flags **Rev:** Mecca pointer and amethyst crystal

Date	Mintage	F	VF	XF	Unc	BU
2012 Proof	1,000	Value: 100				

KM# 18 1000 FRANCS
20.0000 g., 0.9250 Silver 0.5948 oz. ASW, 38.61 mm. **Subject:** African Hippo **Rev:** Hippo in eater with mouth wide open

Date	Mintage	F	VF	XF	Unc	BU
2012 Proof	500	Value: 125				

KM# 19 1000 FRANCS
20.0000 g., 0.9250 Silver 0.5948 oz. ASW, 38.61 mm. **Obv:** Shield and crossed flags **Rev:** Stripped Jackel (Canis adustus) in color

Date	Mintage	F	VF	XF	Unc	BU
2012 Proof	1,000	Value: 125				

NIGERIA

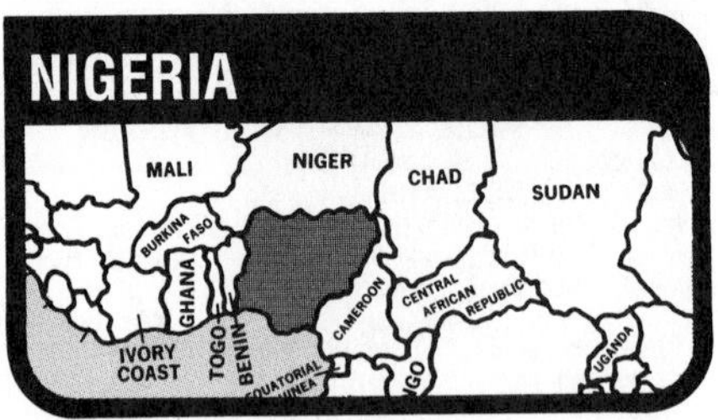

The Federal Republic of Nigeria, situated on the Atlantic coast of West Africa has an area of 356,669 sq. mi. (923,770 sq. km.). Nigeria is a member of the Commonwealth of Nations. The President is the Head of State and the Head of Government.

FEDERAL REPUBLIC

DECIMAL COINAGE

100 Kobo = 1 Naira

KM# 17 KOBO
4.6700 g., Brass, 23.2 mm. **Obv:** Arms with supporters **Rev:** Monkey musicians below value **Edge:** Reeded

Date	Mintage	F	VF	XF	Unc	BU
2003	—	—	—	—	15.00	20.00

KM# 13.3 50 KOBO
3.5000 g., Nickel Clad Steel, 19.44 mm. **Obv:** Arms with supporters **Obv. Legend:** FEDERAL REPUBLIC of NIGERIA **Rev:** Value at left, corn cob and stalk at right **Edge:** Plain **Note:** Reduced size.

Date	Mintage	F	VF	XF	Unc	BU
2006	—	—	—	—	1.00	1.35

KM# 18 NAIRA
5.4300 g., Bi-Metallic Brass center in Stainless Steel ring, 21.48 mm. **Obv:** National arms **Obv. Legend:** FEDERAL REPUBLIC OF NIGERIA **Rev:** Small bust of Herbert Macaulay above value **Edge:** Plain

Date	Mintage	F	VF	XF	Unc	BU
2006	—	—	—	—	2.00	3.00

KM# 19 2 NAIRA
7.4800 g., Bi-Metallic Stainless Steel center in Copper-Brass ring, 25.99 mm. **Obv:** National arms **Obv. Legend:** FEDERAL REPUBLIC OF NIGERIA **Rev:** Large value, National Assembly in background **Edge:** Coarse reeding

Date	Mintage	F	VF	XF	Unc	BU
2006	—	—	—	—	3.00	4.00

PROOF SETS

KM#	Date	Mintage	Identification	Issue Price	Mkt Val
PS1	1959 (6)	1,031	KM1-5, red case, originals	—	125
PS2	1959 (6)	5,000	KM1-5, blue case, restrikes	—	110
PS3	1973 (5)	102,000	KM7, 8.1-10.1,11	14.70	50.00

Niue, or Savage Island, a dependent state of New Zealand, ruled by the Queen of England, is located in the Pacific Ocean east of Tonga and southeast of Samoa. The size is 100 sq. mi. (260 sq. km.) with a population of approx. 1,500. Chief village and port is Alofi. Vanilla, noni and taro are exported.

MINT MARK

PM - Pobjoy Mint

NEW ZEALAND DEPENDENT STATE

DECIMAL COINAGE

KM# 193 5 CENTS

4.3000 g., Copper Plated Bronze, 19 mm. **Ruler:** Elizabeth II **Obv:** Head right **Rev:** Two whales

Date	Mintage	F	VF	XF	Unc	BU
2009	—	—	—	—	1.00	2.00
2010	—	—	—	—	1.00	2.00

KM# 194 10 CENTS

5.8000 g., Copper Plated Bronze, 22 mm. **Ruler:** Elizabeth II **Obv:** Head right **Rev:** Coconut crab **Edge:** Reeded

Date	Mintage	F	VF	XF	Unc	BU
2009	—	—	—	—	1.50	2.00
2010	—	—	—	—	1.50	2.00

KM# 195 20 CENTS

7.3000 g., Nickel Plated Bronze, 25 mm. **Ruler:** Elizabeth II **Obv:** Head right **Rev:** Two scuba divers and coral

Date	Mintage	F	VF	XF	Unc	BU
2009	—	—	—	—	2.00	4.00
2010	—	—	—	—	2.00	4.00

KM# 606 50 CENTS

15.5500 g., 0.9990 Silver 0.4994 oz. ASW, 35 mm. **Ruler:** Elizabeth II **Subject:** Olympics **Rev:** Boxers, ancient and modern

Date	Mintage	F	VF	XF	Unc	BU
2004-2008 Proof	—	Value: 40.00				

KM# 607 50 CENTS

15.5000 g., 0.9990 Silver 0.4978 oz. ASW, 35 mm. **Ruler:** Elizabeth II **Subject:** Olympics **Rev:** Long Jumpers - ancient and modern

Date	Mintage	F	VF	XF	Unc	BU
2004-2008 Proof	—	Value: 40.00				

KM# 608 50 CENTS

15.5000 g., 0.9990 Silver 0.4978 oz. ASW, 35 mm. **Ruler:** Elizabeth II **Subject:** Olympics **Rev:** Shot Put, ancient and modern

Date	Mintage	F	VF	XF	Unc	BU
2004-2008 Proof	—	Value: 40.00				

KM# 609 50 CENTS

15.5000 g., 0.9990 Silver 0.4978 oz. ASW, 35 mm. **Ruler:** Elizabeth II **Subject:** Olympics **Rev:** Archer, ancient and modern

Date	Mintage	F	VF	XF	Unc	BU
2004-2008 Proof	—	Value: 40.00				

KM# 610 50 CENTS

15.5000 g., 0.9990 Silver 0.4978 oz. ASW, 35 mm. **Ruler:** Elizabeth II **Subject:** Olympics **Rev:** Equestrian - ancient and modern views

Date	Mintage	F	VF	XF	Unc	BU
2004-2008 Proof	—	Value: 40.00				

KM# 611 50 CENTS

15.5000 g., 0.9990 Silver 0.4978 oz. ASW, 35 mm. **Ruler:** Elizabeth II **Subject:** Olympics **Rev:** Discus - ancient and modern views

Date	Mintage	F	VF	XF	Unc	BU
2004-2008 Proof	—	Value: 40.00				

KM# 612 50 CENTS

15.5000 g., 0.9990 Silver 0.4978 oz. ASW, 35 mm. **Ruler:** Elizabeth II **Subject:** Olympics **Rev:** Track - ancient and modern views

Date	Mintage	F	VF	XF	Unc	BU
2004-2008 Proof	—	Value: 40.00				

KM# 613 50 CENTS

15.5000 g., 0.9990 Silver 0.4978 oz. ASW, 35 mm. **Ruler:** Elizabeth II **Subject:** Olympics **Rev:** Wrestlers - ancient and modern views

Date	Mintage	F	VF	XF	Unc	BU
2004-2008 Proof	—	Value: 40.00				

KM# 614 50 CENTS

15.5000 g., 0.9990 Silver 0.4978 oz. ASW, 35 mm. **Ruler:** Elizabeth II **Subject:** Olympics **Rev:** Javelin thrower - ancient and modern views

Date	Mintage	F	VF	XF	Unc	BU
2004-2008 Proof	—	Value: 40.00				

KM# 615 50 CENTS

15.5000 g., 0.9990 Silver 0.4978 oz. ASW, 35 mm. **Ruler:** Elizabeth II **Subject:** Olympics **Rev:** Soccer - ancient and modern view

Date	Mintage	F	VF	XF	Unc	BU
2004-2008 Proof	—	Value: 40.00				

KM# 616 50 CENTS

15.5000 g., 0.9990 Silver 0.4978 oz. ASW, 35 mm. **Ruler:** Elizabeth II **Subject:** Olympics **Rev:** Field Hockey - ancient and modern views

Date	Mintage	F	VF	XF	Unc	BU
2004-2008 Proof	—	Value: 40.00				

KM# 263 50 CENTS

15.5500 g., 0.9990 Silver 0.4994 oz. ASW, 35 mm. **Ruler:** Elizabeth II **Series:** Year of the Rooster **Rev:** Multicolor rooster standing right, sunrise

Date	Mintage	F	VF	XF	Unc	BU
2005	—	Value: 30.00				

KM# 292 50 CENTS

15.5500 g., 0.9990 Silver 0.4994 oz. ASW, 35 mm. **Ruler:** Elizabeth II **Subject:** Year of the Dog **Rev:** Multicolor dog

Date	Mintage	F	VF	XF	Unc	BU
2005 Proof	—	Value: 35.00				

KM# 189 50 CENTS

15.5000 g., 0.9990 Silver 0.4978 oz. ASW, 28 mm. **Ruler:** Elizabeth II **Subject:** Year of the Pig **Obv:** Head right **Rev:** Multicolor pig

Date	Mintage	F	VF	XF	Unc	BU
2007 Proof	—	Value: 50.00				

KM# 196 50 CENTS

9.3000 g., Nickel Plated Bronze, 28 mm. **Ruler:** Elizabeth II **Obv:** Head right **Rev:** Outrigger canoe **Edge:** Segmented reeding

Date	Mintage	F	VF	XF	Unc	BU
2009	—	—	—	—	5.00	7.50
2010	—	—	—	—	5.00	7.50

KM# 786 2012 CENTS

31.1000 g., 0.9990 Silver 0.9988 oz. ASW, 30.5x5.5 mm. **Ruler:** Elizabeth II **Obv:** Queen's head at left, Titanic sailing left **Rev:** Ship's bell and other items **Shape:** oval

Date	Mintage	F	VF	XF	Unc	BU
2012 Proof	Est. 200	Value: 100				

KM# 786a 2012 CENTS

31.1000 g., 0.9990 Silver 0.9988 oz. ASW, 31.5x5.5 mm. **Ruler:** Elizabeth II **Obv:** Queen's head at left, Titanic sailing left, sky in color **Rev:** Ship's bell and other items **Shape:** oval

Date	Mintage	F	VF	XF	Unc	BU
2012 Proof	Est. 200	Value: 100				

KM# 462 1/33 DOLLAR

42.5000 g., 0.9990 Silver 1.3650 oz. ASW, 41.7x40 mm. **Ruler:** Elizabeth II **Rev:** Sistine Chapel Corner featuring Haman's punishment

Date	Mintage	F	VF	XF	Unc	BU
2010 Proof	500	Value: 75.00				

KM# 463 1/33 DOLLAR

42.5000 g., 0.9990 Silver 1.3650 oz. ASW, 41.7x40 mm. **Ruler:** Elizabeth II **Rev:** Sistine Chapel Arch featuring the Prophet Jonah

Date	Mintage	F	VF	XF	Unc	BU
2010 Proof	500	Value: 75.00				

KM# 464 1/33 DOLLAR

42.5000 g., 0.9990 Silver 1.3650 oz. ASW, 41.7x40 mm. **Ruler:** Elizabeth II **Rev:** Sistine Chapel Corner Spandrel featuring the Brazen Serpent

Date	Mintage	F	VF	XF	Unc	BU
2010 Proof	500	Value: 75.00				

KM# 465 1/33 DOLLAR

26.8000 g., 0.9990 Silver 0.8607 oz. ASW, 29x36.1 mm. **Ruler:** Elizabeth II **Rev:** Sistine Chapel Arch featuring the Prophet Jeremiah

Date	Mintage	F	VF	XF	Unc	BU
2010 Proof	500	Value: 60.00				

KM# 466 1/33 DOLLAR

26.8000 g., 0.9990 Silver 0.8607 oz. ASW, 29x36.1 mm. **Ruler:** Elizabeth II **Rev:** Sistine Chapel Arch with Salmon

Date	Mintage	F	VF	XF	Unc	BU
2010 Proof	500	Value: 60.00				

KM# 467 1/33 DOLLAR

26.8000 g., 0.9990 Silver 0.8607 oz. ASW, 29x36.1 mm. **Ruler:** Elizabeth II **Rev:** Sistine Chapel Arch with Persian Sibyl

Date	Mintage	F	VF	XF	Unc	BU
2010 Proof	500	Value: 60.00				

KM# 468 1/33 DOLLAR

21.0000 g., 0.9990 Silver 0.6745 oz. ASW, 23x36.1 mm. **Ruler:** Elizabeth II **Rev:** Sistine Chapel Arch with Roboam

Date	Mintage	F	VF	XF	Unc	BU
2010 Proof	500	Value: 45.00				

KM# 469 1/33 DOLLAR

26.8000 g., 0.9990 Silver 0.8607 oz. ASW, 29x36.1 mm. **Ruler:** Elizabeth II **Rev:** Sistine Chapel Arch with Prophet Ezekiel

Date	Mintage	F	VF	XF	Unc	BU
2010 Proof	500	Value: 60.00				

KM# 470 1/33 DOLLAR

26.8000 g., 0.9990 Silver 0.8607 oz. ASW, 29x36.1 mm. **Ruler:** Elizabeth II **Rev:** Sistine Chapel Arch with Ozias

Date	Mintage	F	VF	XF	Unc	BU
2010 Proof	500	Value: 60.00				

KM# 471 1/33 DOLLAR

21.0000 g., 0.9990 Silver 0.6745 oz. ASW, 23x36.1 mm. **Ruler:** Elizabeth II **Rev:** Sistine Chapel Arch with Erythraean Sibyl

Date	Mintage	F	VF	XF	Unc	BU
2010 Proof	500	Value: 45.00				

KM# 472 1/33 DOLLAR

26.8000 g., 0.9990 Silver 0.8607 oz. ASW, 29x36.1 mm. **Ruler:** Elizabeth II **Rev:** Sistine Chapel Arch with Zorobabel

Date	Mintage	F	VF	XF	Unc	BU
2010 Proof	500	Value: 55.00				

KM# 473 1/33 DOLLAR

21.0000 g., 0.9990 Silver 0.6745 oz. ASW, 23x36.1 mm. **Ruler:** Elizabeth II **Rev:** Sistine Chapel Arch with Prophel Joel

Date	Mintage	F	VF	XF	Unc	BU
2010 Proof	500	Value: 45.00				

KM# 474 1/33 DOLLAR

35.5000 g., 0.9990 Silver 1.1402 oz. ASW, 29x47.8 mm. **Ruler:** Elizabeth II **Rev:** Sistine Chapel vault depicting Genesis creation story of Separation of Light from Darkness

Date	Mintage	F	VF	XF	Unc	BU
2010 Proof	500	Value: 75.00				

KM# 475 1/33 DOLLAR

35.5000 g., 0.9990 Silver 1.1402 oz. ASW, 29x47.8 mm. **Ruler:** Elizabeth II **Rev:** Sistine Chapel vault depecting Genesis story of Creation of Sun and Moon

Date	Mintage	F	VF	XF	Unc	BU
2010 Proof	500	Value: 75.00				

KM# 476 1/33 DOLLAR

35.5000 g., 0.9990 Silver 1.1402 oz. ASW, 29x47.8 mm. **Ruler:** Elizabeth II **Rev:** Sistine Chapel vault depicting Genesis creation story of the Separation of Land and Water

Date	Mintage	F	VF	XF	Unc	BU
2010 Proof	500	Value: 75.00				

KM# 477 1/33 DOLLAR

28.0000 g., 0.9990 Silver 0.8993 oz. ASW, 23x47.8 mm. **Ruler:** Elizabeth II **Rev:** Sistine Chapel vault depicting Genesis story of the Creation of Adam

Date	Mintage	F	VF	XF	Unc	BU
2010 Proof	500	Value: 60.00				

KM# 478 1/33 DOLLAR

35.5000 g., 0.9990 Silver 1.1402 oz. ASW, 29x47.8 mm. **Ruler:** Elizabeth II **Rev:** Sistine Chapel vault depicting the story of the Creation of Eve

Date	Mintage	F	VF	XF	Unc	BU
2010 Proof	500	Value: 75.00				

KM# 479 1/33 DOLLAR

28.0000 g., 0.9990 Silver 0.8993 oz. ASW, 23x47.8 mm. **Ruler:** Elizabeth II **Rev:** Sistine Chapel vault depicting the Genesis story of Original Sin

Date	Mintage	F	VF	XF	Unc	BU
2010 Proof	500	Value: 60.00				

KM# 480 1/33 DOLLAR

35.5000 g., 0.9990 Silver 1.1402 oz. ASW, 29x47.7 mm. **Ruler:** Elizabeth II **Rev:** Sistine Chapel vault depicting the Genesis story of the Sacrifice of Noah

Date	Mintage	F	VF	XF	Unc	BU
2010 Proof	500	Value: 75.00				

KM# 481 1/33 DOLLAR

28.0000 g., 0.9990 Silver 0.8993 oz. ASW, 23x47.8 mm. **Ruler:** Elizabeth II **Rev:** Sistine Chapel vault depicting the Genesis story of the Flood

Date	Mintage	F	VF	XF	Unc	BU
2010 Proof	500	Value: 60.00				

KM# 482 1/33 DOLLAR

35.5000 g., 0.9990 Silver 1.1402 oz. ASW, 29x47.8 mm. **Ruler:** Elizabeth II **Rev:** Sistine Chapel vault depicting the Genesis story of the Drunkenness of Noah

Date	Mintage	F	VF	XF	Unc	BU
2010 Proof	500	Value: 75.00				

KM# 483 1/33 DOLLAR

26.8000 g., 0.9990 Silver 0.8607 oz. ASW, 29x36.1 mm. **Ruler:** Elizabeth II **Rev:** Sistine Chapel Arch depicting the Libyan Sibyl

Date	Mintage	F	VF	XF	Unc	BU
2010 Proof	500	Value: 60.00				

KM# 484 1/33 DOLLAR

26.8000 g., 0.9990 Silver 0.8607 oz. ASW, 29x36.1 mm. **Ruler:** Elizabeth II **Rev:** Sistine Chapel Arch depicting Jesse

Date	Mintage	F	VF	XF	Unc	BU
2010 Proof	500	Value: 60.00				

KM# 485 1/33 DOLLAR

26.8000 g., 0.9990 Silver 0.8607 oz. ASW, 29x36.1 mm. **Ruler:** Elizabeth II **Rev:** Sistine Chapel Arch depicting the Prophet Daniel

Date	Mintage	F	VF	XF	Unc	BU
2010 Proof	500	Value: 60.00				

KM# 486 1/33 DOLLAR

21.0000 g., 0.9990 Silver 0.6745 oz. ASW, 23x36.1 mm. **Ruler:** Elizabeth II **Rev:** Sistine Chapel Arch depicting Asa

Date	Mintage	F	VF	XF	Unc	BU
2010 Proof	500	Value: 45.00				

KM# 487 1/33 DOLLAR

26.8000 g., 0.9990 Silver 0.8607 oz. ASW, 29x36.1 mm. **Ruler:** Elizabeth II **Rev:** Sistine Chapel Arch depicting the Cumaean Sibyl

Date	Mintage	F	VF	XF	Unc	BU
2010 Proof	500	Value: 60.00				

KM# 488 1/33 DOLLAR

21.0000 g., 0.9990 Silver 0.6745 oz. ASW, 23x36.1 mm. **Ruler:** Elizabeth II **Rev:** Sistine Chapel Arch depicting Ezzekias

Date	Mintage	F	VF	XF	Unc	BU
2010 Proof	500	Value: 45.00				

KM# 489 1/33 DOLLAR

26.8000 g., 0.9990 Silver 0.8607 oz. ASW, 29x.36.1 mm. **Ruler:** Elizabeth II **Rev:** Sistine Chapel Arch depicting the Prophet Isiah

Date	Mintage	F	VF	XF	Unc	BU
2010 Proof	500	Value: 60.00				

KM# 490 1/33 DOLLAR

26.8000 g., 0.9990 Silver 0.8607 oz. ASW, 29x36.1 mm. **Ruler:** Elizabeth II **Rev:** Sistine Chapel Arch depicting Josias

Date	Mintage	F	VF	XF	Unc	BU
2010 Proof	500	Value: 60.00				

KM# 491 1/33 DOLLAR

21.0000 g., 0.9990 Silver 0.6745 oz. ASW, 23x36.1 mm. **Ruler:** Elizabeth II **Rev:** Sistine Chapel Arch depicting the Delphic Sibyl

Date	Mintage	F	VF	XF	Unc	BU
2010 Proof	500	Value: 45.00				

KM# 492 1/33 DOLLAR

42.5000 g., 0.9990 Silver 1.3650 oz. ASW, 41.7x40 mm. **Ruler:** Elizabeth II **Rev:** Sistine Chapel corner spandrel depicting David & Goliath

Date	Mintage	F	VF	XF	Unc	BU
2010 Proof	500	Value: 75.00				

KM# 493 1/33 DOLLAR

42.5000 g., 0.9990 Silver 1.3650 oz. ASW, 41.7x40 mm. **Ruler:** Elizabeth II **Rev:** Sistine Chapel Arch vault depicting the Prophet Zechariah

Date	Mintage	F	VF	XF	Unc	BU
2010 Proof	500	Value: 75.00				

KM# 494 1/33 DOLLAR

42.5000 g., 0.9990 Silver 1.3650 oz. ASW, 41.7x40 mm. **Ruler:** Elizabeth II **Rev:** Sistine Chapel corner spandrel depicting Judith & Holofornes

Date	Mintage	F	VF	XF	Unc	BU
2010 Proof	500	Value: 75.00				

KM# 526 1/24 DOLLAR

42.5000 g., 0.9990 Silver 1.3650 oz. ASW, 41.7x40 mm. **Ruler:** Elizabeth II **Obv:** Head with tiara right **Rev:** Partial DaVinci drawing

Date	Mintage	F	VF	XF	Unc	BU
2011 Proof	500	Value: 75.00				

KM# 527 1/24 DOLLAR

42.5000 g., 0.9990 Silver 1.3650 oz. ASW, 41.7x40 mm. **Ruler:** Elizabeth II **Obv:** Head with tiara right **Rev:** Partial DaVinci drawing

Date	Mintage	F	VF	XF	Unc	BU
2011 Proof	500	Value: 75.00				

KM# 528 1/24 DOLLAR

42.5000 g., 0.9990 Silver 1.3650 oz. ASW, 41.7x40 mm. **Ruler:** Elizabeth II **Obv:** Head with tiara right **Rev:** Partial DaVinci drawing

Date	Mintage	F	VF	XF	Unc	BU
2011 Proof	500	Value: 75.00				

KM# 529 1/24 DOLLAR

42.5000 g., 0.9990 Silver 1.3650 oz. ASW, 41.7x40 mm. **Ruler:** Elizabeth II **Obv:** Head with tiara right **Rev:** Partial DaVinci drawing

Date	Mintage	F	VF	XF	Unc	BU
2011 Proof	500	Value: 75.00				

KM# 530 1/24 DOLLAR

42.5000 g., 0.9990 Silver 1.3650 oz. ASW, 41.7x40 mm. **Ruler:** Elizabeth II **Obv:** Head with tiara right **Rev:** Partial DaVinci drawing

Date	Mintage	F	VF	XF	Unc	BU
2011 Proof	500	Value: 75.00				

KM# 531 1/24 DOLLAR

42.5000 g., 0.9990 Silver 1.3650 oz. ASW, 41.7x40 mm. **Ruler:** Elizabeth II **Obv:** Head with tiara right **Rev:** Partial DaVinci drawing

Date	Mintage	F	VF	XF	Unc	BU
2011 Proof	500	Value: 75.00				

KM# 534 1/24 DOLLAR

42.5000 g., 0.9990 Silver 1.3650 oz. ASW, 41.7x40 mm. **Ruler:** Elizabeth II **Obv:** Head with tiara right **Rev:** Partial DaVinci drawing

Date	Mintage	F	VF	XF	Unc	BU
2011 Proof	500	Value: 75.00				

KM# 532 1/24 DOLLAR

42.5000 g., 0.9990 Silver 1.3650 oz. ASW, 41.7x40 mm. **Ruler:** Elizabeth II **Obv:** Head with tiara right **Rev:** Partial DaVinci drawing

Date	Mintage	F	VF	XF	Unc	BU
2011 Proof	500	Value: 75.00				

KM# 533 1/24 DOLLAR

42.5000 g., 0.9990 Silver 1.3650 oz. ASW **Ruler:** Elizabeth II **Obv:** Head in tiara right **Rev:** Partial DaVinci drawing

Date	Mintage	F	VF	XF	Unc	BU
2011 Proof	500	Value: 75.00				

KM# 535 1/24 DOLLAR

42.5000 g., 0.9990 Silver 1.3650 oz. ASW, 41.7x40 mm. **Ruler:** Elizabeth II **Obv:** Head with tiara right **Rev:** Partial DaVinci drawing

Date	Mintage	F	VF	XF	Unc	BU
2011 Proof	500	Value: 75.00				

KM# 536 1/24 DOLLAR

42.5000 g., 0.9990 Silver 1.3650 oz. ASW, 41.7x40 mm. **Ruler:** Elizabeth II **Obv:** Head in tiara right **Rev:** Partial DaVinci drawing

Date	Mintage	F	VF	XF	Unc	BU
2011 Proof	500	Value: 75.00				

KM# 537 1/24 DOLLAR

42.5000 g., 0.9990 Silver 1.3650 oz. ASW, 41.7x40 mm. **Ruler:** Elizabeth II **Obv:** Head with tiara right **Rev:** Partial DaVinci drawing

Date	Mintage	F	VF	XF	Unc	BU
2011 Proof	500	Value: 75.00				

KM# 538 1/24 DOLLAR

42.5000 g., 0.9990 Silver 1.3650 oz. ASW, 41.7x40 mm. **Ruler:** Elizabeth II **Obv:** Head with tiara right **Rev:** Partial DaVinci drawing

Date	Mintage	F	VF	XF	Unc	BU
2011 Proof	500	Value: 75.00				

KM# 539 1/24 DOLLAR

42.5000 g., 0.9990 Silver 1.3650 oz. ASW, 41.7x40 mm. **Ruler:** Elizabeth II **Obv:** Head with tiara right **Rev:** Partial DaVinci drawing

Date	Mintage	F	VF	XF	Unc	BU
2011 Proof	500	Value: 75.00				

KM# 540 1/24 DOLLAR

42.5000 g., 0.9990 Silver 1.3650 oz. ASW, 41.7x40 mm. **Ruler:** Elizabeth II **Obv:** Head with tiara right **Rev:** Partial DaVinci drawing

Date	Mintage	F	VF	XF	Unc	BU
2011 Proof	500	Value: 75.00				

KM# 541 1/24 DOLLAR

42.5000 g., 0.9990 Silver 1.3650 oz. ASW, 41.7x40 mm. **Ruler:** Elizabeth II **Obv:** Head with tiara right **Rev:** Partial DaVinci drawing

Date	Mintage	F	VF	XF	Unc	BU
2011 Proof	500	Value: 75.00				

KM# 542 1/24 DOLLAR

42.5000 g., 0.9990 Silver 1.3650 oz. ASW, 41.7x40 mm. **Ruler:** Elizabeth II **Obv:** Head with tiara right **Rev:** Partial DaVinci drawing

Date	Mintage	F	VF	XF	Unc	BU
2011 Proof	500	Value: 75.00				

KM# 543 1/24 DOLLAR

42.5000 g., 0.9990 Silver 1.3650 oz. ASW, 41.7x40 mm. **Ruler:** Elizabeth II **Obv:** Head with tiara right **Rev:** Partial DaVinci drawing

Date	Mintage	F	VF	XF	Unc	BU
2011 Proof	500	Value: 75.00				

KM# 544 1/24 DOLLAR

42.5000 g., 0.9990 Silver 1.3650 oz. ASW, 41.7x40 mm. **Ruler:** Elizabeth II **Obv:** Head with tiara right **Rev:** Partial DaVinci drawing

Date	Mintage	F	VF	XF	Unc	BU
2011 Proof	500	Value: 75.00				

KM# 545 1/24 DOLLAR

42.5000 g., 0.9990 Silver 1.3650 oz. ASW, 41.7x40 mm. **Ruler:** Elizabeth II **Obv:** Head with tiara right **Rev:** Partial DaVinci drawing

Date	Mintage	F	VF	XF	Unc	BU
2011 Proof	500	Value: 75.00				

KM# 546 1/24 DOLLAR

42.5000 g., 0.9990 Silver 1.3650 oz. ASW, 41.7x40 mm. **Ruler:** Elizabeth II **Obv:** Head with tiara right **Rev:** Partial DaVinci drawing

Date	Mintage	F	VF	XF	Unc	BU
2011 Proof	500	Value: 75.00				

KM# 547 1/24 DOLLAR

42.5000 g., 0.9990 Silver 1.3650 oz. ASW, 41.7x40 mm. **Ruler:** Elizabeth II **Obv:** Head with tiara right **Rev:** Partial DaVinci drawing

Date	Mintage	F	VF	XF	Unc	BU
2011 Proof	500	Value: 75.00				

KM# 548 1/24 DOLLAR

42.5000 g., 0.9990 Silver 1.3650 oz. ASW, 41.7x40 mm. **Ruler:** Elizabeth II **Obv:** Head with tiara right **Rev:** Partial DaVinci drawing

Date	Mintage	F	VF	XF	Unc	BU
2011 Proof	500	Value: 75.00				

KM# 549 1/24 DOLLAR

42.5000 g., 0.9990 Silver 1.3650 oz. ASW, 41.7x40 mm. **Ruler:** Elizabeth II **Obv:** Head with tiara right **Rev:** Partial DaVinci drawing

Date	Mintage	F	VF	XF	Unc	BU
2011 Proof	500	Value: 75.00				

KM# 624 1/14 DOLLAR

15.0000 g., 0.9990 Silver 0.4818 oz. ASW, 29x48 mm. **Ruler:** Elizabeth II **Obv:** Head with tiara right **Rev:** Two scenes from the Passion of Christ **Shape:** Vertical rectangle

Date	Mintage	F	VF	XF	Unc	BU
2001 Proof	250	Value: 45.00				

KM# 625 1/14 DOLLAR

15.0000 g., 0.9990 Silver 0.4818 oz. ASW, 29x48 mm. **Ruler:** Elizabeth II **Obv:** Head with tiara right **Rev:** Two scenes from the Passion of Christ **Shape:** Vertical rectangle

Date	Mintage	F	VF	XF	Unc	BU
2011 Proof	250	Value: 45.00				

KM# 626 1/14 DOLLAR

15.0000 g., 0.9990 Silver 0.4818 oz. ASW, 29x48 mm. **Ruler:** Elizabeth II **Obv:** Head in tiara right **Rev:** Two scenes from the Passion of Christ **Shape:** Vertical rectangle

Date	Mintage	F	VF	XF	Unc	BU
2011 Proof	250	Value: 45.00				

KM# 627 1/14 DOLLAR

15.0000 g., 0.9990 Silver 0.4818 oz. ASW, 36x48 mm. **Ruler:** Elizabeth II **Obv:** Head in tiara right **Rev:** The Cruxifixion of Christ **Shape:** Vertical rectangle

Date	Mintage	F	VF	XF	Unc	BU
2011 Proof	250	Value: 50.00				

KM# 628 1/14 DOLLAR

15.0000 g., 0.9990 Silver 0.4818 oz. ASW, 29x48 mm. **Ruler:** Elizabeth II **Obv:** Head with tiara right **Rev:** Two scenes form the Passion of Christ **Shape:** Vertical rectangle

Date	Mintage	F	VF	XF	Unc	BU
2011 Proof	250	Value: 45.00				

KM# 629 1/14 DOLLAR

15.0000 g., 0.9990 Silver 0.4818 oz. ASW, 29x48 mm. **Ruler:** Elizabeth II **Obv:** Head with tiara right **Rev:** Two scenes from the Passion of Christ **Shape:** Vertical rectangle

Date	Mintage	F	VF	XF	Unc	BU
2011 Proof	250	Value: 40.00				

KM# 630 1/14 DOLLAR

15.0000 g., 0.9990 Silver 0.4818 oz. ASW, 29x48 mm. **Ruler:** Elizabeth II **Obv:** Head with tiara right **Rev:** Two scenes from the Passion of Christ **Shape:** Vertical rectangle

Date	Mintage	F	VF	XF	Unc	BU
2011 Proof	250	Value: 45.00				

KM# 631 1/14 DOLLAR

15.0000 g., 0.9990 Silver 0.4818 oz. ASW, 29x48 mm. **Ruler:** Elizabeth II **Obv:** Head with tiara right **Rev:** Two scenes from the Passion of Christ **Shape:** Vertical rectangle

Date	Mintage	F	VF	XF	Unc	BU
2011 Proof	250	Value: 45.00				

KM# 632 1/14 DOLLAR

15.0000 g., 0.9990 Silver 0.4818 oz. ASW, 29x48 mm. **Ruler:** Elizabeth II **Obv:** Head with tiara right **Rev:** Two scenes from the Passion of Christ **Shape:** Vertical rectangle

Date	Mintage	F	VF	XF	Unc	BU
2011 Proof	250	Value: 45.00				

KM# 633 1/14 DOLLAR

15.0000 g., 0.9990 Silver 0.4818 oz. ASW, 29x48 mm. **Ruler:** Elizabeth II **Obv:** Head with tiara right **Rev:** Two scenes from the Passion of Christ **Shape:** Vertical rectangle

Date	Mintage	F	VF	XF	Unc	BU
2011 Proof	250	Value: 45.00				

KM# 634 1/14 DOLLAR

15.0000 g., 0.9990 Silver 0.4818 oz. ASW, 36x48 mm. **Ruler:** Elizabeth II **Obv:** Head with tiara right **Rev:** Two scenes from the Passion of Christ **Shape:** Vertical rectangle

Date	Mintage	F	VF	XF	Unc	BU
2011 Proof	250	Value: 50.00				

KM# 635 1/14 DOLLAR

15.0000 g., 0.9990 Silver 0.4818 oz. ASW, 29x48 mm. **Ruler:** Elizabeth II **Obv:** Head with tiara right **Rev:** Two scenes from the Passion of Christ **Shape:** Vertical rectangle

Date	Mintage	F	VF	XF	Unc	BU
2011 Proof	250	Value: 45.00				

KM# 636 1/14 DOLLAR

15.0000 g., 0.9990 Silver 0.4818 oz. ASW, 29x48 mm. **Ruler:** Elizabeth II **Obv:** Head with tiara right **Rev:** Two scenes from the Passion of Christ **Shape:** Vertical rectangle

Date	Mintage	F	VF	XF	Unc	BU
2011 Proof	250	Value: 45.00				

KM# 637 1/14 DOLLAR

15.0000 g., 0.9990 Silver 0.4818 oz. ASW, 29x48 mm. **Ruler:** Elizabeth II **Obv:** Head with tiara right **Rev:** Two scenes from the Passion of Christ **Shape:** Vertical rectangle

Date	Mintage	F	VF	XF	Unc	BU
2011 Proof	250	Value: 45.00				

KM# 574 1/9 DOLLAR
25.4000 g., 0.9990 Silver 0.8158 oz. ASW, 24x41 mm. **Ruler:** Elizabeth II **Subject:** Fragment of Villa of Mysteries fresco **Shape:** Vertical rectangle **NOTE:** Shown smaller than actual size.

Date	Mintage	F	VF	XF	Unc	BU
2011 Proof	250	Value: 60.00				

KM# 575 1/9 DOLLAR
25.4000 g., 0.9990 Silver 0.8158 oz. ASW, 24x41 mm. **Ruler:** Elizabeth II **Subject:** Villa of Mysteries Fresco

Date	Mintage	F	VF	XF	Unc	BU
2011 Proof	250	Value: 60.00				

KM# 576 1/9 DOLLAR
33.8000 g., 0.9990 Silver 1.0856 oz. ASW, 32x41 mm. **Ruler:** Elizabeth II **Subject:** Villa of Mysteries fresco

Date	Mintage	F	VF	XF	Unc	BU
2011 Proof	250	Value: 60.00				

KM# 577 1/9 DOLLAR
33.8000 g., 0.9990 Silver 1.0856 oz. ASW, 32.41 mm. **Ruler:** Elizabeth II **Subject:** Villa of Mysteries fresco

Date	Mintage	F	VF	XF	Unc	BU
2011 Proof	250	Value: 60.00				

KM# 578 1/9 DOLLAR
50.7000 g., 0.9990 Silver 1.6283 oz. ASW, 48x41 mm. **Ruler:** Elizabeth II **Subject:** Villa of Mysteries fresco

Date	Mintage	F	VF	XF	Unc	BU
2011 Proof	250	Value: 85.00				

KM# 579 1/9 DOLLAR
50.7000 g., 0.9990 Silver 1.6283 oz. ASW, 48x41 mm. **Ruler:** Elizabeth II **Subject:** Villa of Mysteries fresco

Date	Mintage	F	VF	XF	Unc	BU
2011 Proof	250	Value: 85.00				

KM# 580 1/9 DOLLAR
33.8000 g., 0.9990 Silver 1.0856 oz. ASW, 32x41 mm. **Ruler:** Elizabeth II **Subject:** Villa of Mysteries fresco

Date	Mintage	F	VF	XF	Unc	BU
2011 Proof	250	Value: 60.00				

KM# 581 1/9 DOLLAR
50.7000 g., 0.9990 Silver 1.6283 oz. ASW, 48x41 mm. **Ruler:** Elizabeth II **Subject:** Villa of Mysteries fresco

Date	Mintage	F	VF	XF	Unc	BU
2011 Proof	250	Value: 85.00				

KM# 582 1/9 DOLLAR
50.7000 g., 0.9990 Silver 1.6283 oz. ASW, 48x41 mm. **Ruler:** Elizabeth II **Subject:** Villa of Mysteries fresco

Date	Mintage	F	VF	XF	Unc	BU
2011 Proof	250	Value: 85.00				

KM# 123 DOLLAR
28.2800 g., Copper-Nickel, 38.6 mm. **Ruler:** Elizabeth II **Subject:** Snoopy as an Ace **Obv:** Crowned head right **Rev:** Snoopy flying his dog house **Edge:** Reeded

Date	Mintage	F	VF	XF	Unc	BU
2001	100,000	—	—	—	3.00	4.50

KM# 128 DOLLAR
28.2800 g., Copper-Nickel, 38.6 mm. **Ruler:** Elizabeth II **Series:** Pokemon **Obv:** Crowned shield within sprigs **Rev:** Bulbasaur **Edge:** Reeded

Date	Mintage	F	VF	XF	Unc	BU
2001	100,000	—	—	—	12.00	14.00

KM# 129 DOLLAR
7.7700 g., 0.9990 Silver 0.2496 oz. ASW, 22 mm. **Ruler:** Elizabeth II **Series:** Pokemon **Obv:** Crowned shield within sprigs **Rev:** Bulbasaur **Edge:** Reeded

Date	Mintage	F	VF	XF	Unc	BU
2001 Proof	20,000	Value: 18.00				

KM# 131 DOLLAR
28.2800 g., Copper-Nickel, 38.6 mm. **Ruler:** Elizabeth II **Series:** Pokemon **Obv:** Crowned shield within sprigs **Rev:** Charmander **Edge:** Reeded

Date	Mintage	F	VF	XF	Unc	BU
2001	100,000	—	—	—	12.00	14.00

KM# 132 DOLLAR
7.7700 g., 0.9990 Silver 0.2496 oz. ASW, 22 mm. **Ruler:** Elizabeth II **Series:** Pokemon **Obv:** Crowned shield within sprigs **Rev:** Charmander **Edge:** Reeded

Date	Mintage	F	VF	XF	Unc	BU
2001 Proof	20,000	Value: 18.00				

KM# 134 DOLLAR
28.2800 g., Copper-Nickel, 38.6 mm. **Ruler:** Elizabeth II **Series:** Pokemon **Obv:** Crowned shield within sprigs **Rev:** Meowth **Edge:** Reeded

Date	Mintage	F	VF	XF	Unc	BU
2001	100,000	—	—	—	12.00	14.00

KM# 135 DOLLAR
7.7700 g., 0.9990 Silver 0.2496 oz. ASW, 22 mm. **Ruler:** Elizabeth II **Series:** Pokemon **Obv:** Crowned shield within sprigs **Rev:** Meowth **Edge:** Reeded

Date	Mintage	F	VF	XF	Unc	BU
2001 Proof	20,000	Value: 18.00				

KM# 137 DOLLAR
28.2800 g., Copper-Nickel, 38.6 mm. **Ruler:** Elizabeth II **Series:** Pokemon **Obv:** Crowned shield within sprigs **Rev:** Pikachu **Edge:** Reeded

Date	Mintage	F	VF	XF	Unc	BU
2001	100,000	—	—	—	12.00	14.00

KM# 138 DOLLAR
7.7700 g., 0.9990 Silver 0.2496 oz. ASW, 22 mm. **Ruler:** Elizabeth II **Series:** Pokemon **Obv:** Crowned shield within sprigs **Rev:** Pikachu **Edge:** Reeded

Date	Mintage	F	VF	XF	Unc	BU
2001 Proof	20,000	Value: 18.00				

KM# 140 DOLLAR
28.2800 g., Copper-Nickel, 38.6 mm. **Ruler:** Elizabeth II **Series:** Pokemon **Obv:** Crowned shield within sprigs **Rev:** Squirtle **Edge:** Reeded

Date	Mintage	F	VF	XF	Unc	BU
2001	100,000	—	—	—	12.00	14.00

KM# 141 DOLLAR
7.7700 g., 0.9990 Silver 0.2496 oz. ASW, 22 mm. **Ruler:** Elizabeth II **Series:** Pokemon **Obv:** Crowned shield within sprigs **Rev:** Squirtle **Edge:** Reeded

Date	Mintage	F	VF	XF	Unc	BU
2001 Proof	20,000	Value: 18.00				

KM# 146 DOLLAR
28.2800 g., Copper-Nickel, 38.6 mm. **Ruler:** Elizabeth II **Subject:** Pokemon Series **Obv:** Crowned shield within sprigs **Rev:** Pikachu **Edge:** Reeded

Date	Mintage	F	VF	XF	Unc	BU
2002PM	100,000	—	—	—	3.00	4.50

KM# 151 DOLLAR
28.2800 g., Copper-Nickel, 38.6 mm. **Ruler:** Elizabeth II **Subject:** Pokemon Series **Obv:** Crowned shield within sprigs **Rev:** Pichu **Edge:** Reeded

Date	Mintage	F	VF	XF	Unc	BU
2002PM	100,000	—	—	—	3.00	4.50

KM# 156 DOLLAR
28.2800 g., Copper-Nickel, 38.6 mm. **Ruler:** Elizabeth II **Subject:** Pokemon Series **Obv:** Crowned shield within sprigs **Rev:** Mewtwo **Edge:** Reeded

Date	Mintage	F	VF	XF	Unc	BU
2002PM	100,000	—	—	—	3.00	4.50

KM# 161 DOLLAR
28.2800 g., Copper-Nickel, 38.6 mm. **Ruler:** Elizabeth II **Subject:** Pokemon Series **Obv:** Crowned shield within sprigs **Rev:** Entei **Edge:** Reeded

Date	Mintage	F	VF	XF	Unc	BU
2002PM	100,000	—	—	—	3.00	4.50

KM# 166 DOLLAR
28.2800 g., Copper-Nickel, 38.6 mm. **Ruler:** Elizabeth II **Subject:** Pokemon Series **Obv:** Crowned shield within sprigs **Rev:** Celebi **Edge:** Reeded

Date	Mintage	F	VF	XF	Unc	BU
2002PM	100,000	—	—	—	3.00	4.50

KM# 186 DOLLAR
31.1050 g., 0.9990 Silver 0.9990 oz. ASW **Ruler:** Elizabeth II **Subject:** Marshalls of China's Army, 50th Anniversary **Obv:** Head right **Rev:** Multicolor scene of military men

Date	Mintage	F	VF	XF	Unc	BU
2005	1,000	—	—	—	—	70.00

KM# 187 DOLLAR
31.1050 g., 0.9990 Silver 0.9990 oz. ASW **Ruler:** Elizabeth II **Subject:** World War II, 60th Anniversary **Obv:** Bust right **Rev:** Multicolor badge

Date	Mintage	F	VF	XF	Unc	BU
2005	1,000	—	—	—	—	70.00

KM# 188 DOLLAR
31.1050 g., 0.9990 Silver 0.9990 oz. ASW **Ruler:** Elizabeth II **Series:** Bust right **Obv:** Multicolor image of two astronauts, rocket and map of China

Date	Mintage	F	VF	XF	Unc	BU
2005 Proof	—	Value: 75.00				

KM# 293 DOLLAR
31.1050 g., 0.9990 Silver 0.9990 oz. ASW, 45 mm. **Ruler:** Elizabeth II **Subject:** Year of the Dog **Rev:** Multicolor dog

Date	Mintage	F	VF	XF	Unc	BU
2005 Proof	—	Value: 60.00				

KM# 264 DOLLAR
31.1000 g., 0.9990 Silver 0.9988 oz. ASW, 45 mm. **Ruler:** Elizabeth II **Subject:** Year of the Rooster **Rev:** Multicolor rooster standing right, sunrise

Date	Mintage	F	VF	XF	Unc	BU
2005 Proof	—	Value: 55.00				

KM# 262 DOLLAR
Bronze partially silvered, 38.61 mm. **Ruler:** Elizabeth II **Subject:** Thomas Alva Edison **Rev:** Lightbulb

Date	Mintage	F	VF	XF	Unc	BU
2005	—	—	—	—	—	30.00

KM# 262a DOLLAR
31.1050 g., 0.9990 Silver partially gilt 0.9990 oz. ASW **Ruler:** Elizabeth II **Subject:** Thomas Alva Edison **Rev:** Lightbulb, partially gilt

Date	Mintage	F	VF	XF	Unc	BU
2005 Proof	Est. 2,500	Value: 100				

KM# 275 DOLLAR
31.1050 g., 0.9990 Silver 0.9990 oz. ASW **Ruler:** Elizabeth II **Subject:** 60th Anniversary, China

Date	Mintage	F	VF	XF	Unc	BU
2005 Proof	Est. 1,000	Value: 120				

KM# 276 DOLLAR
31.1050 g., 0.9990 Silver 0.9990 oz. ASW **Ruler:** Elizabeth II **Subject:** Mao Zedong and the Red Army in Beijing

Date	Mintage	F	VF	XF	Unc	BU
2005 Proof	—	Value: 100				

KM# 277 DOLLAR
31.1050 g., 0.9990 Silver 0.9990 oz. ASW, 45 mm. **Ruler:** Elizabeth II **Subject:** Chinese space achievements **Rev:** Multicolor rocket, flag, map

Date	Mintage	F	VF	XF	Unc	BU
2005 Proof	Est. 5,000	Value: 75.00				

KM# 300 DOLLAR
31.1050 g., 0.9990 Silver 0.9990 oz. ASW, 45 mm. **Ruler:** Elizabeth II **Subject:** Dogs of the World **Rev:** Multicolor Bichon standing before the Louvre

Date	Mintage	F	VF	XF	Unc	BU
2006 Proof	Est. 3,000	Value: 60.00				

KM# 301 DOLLAR
31.1050 g., 0.9990 Silver 0.9990 oz. ASW, 45 mm. **Ruler:** Elizabeth II **Subject:** Dogs of the World **Rev:** Multicolor Welsh Corgi before Buckingham Palace

Date	Mintage	F	VF	XF	Unc	BU
2006 Proof	Est. 3,000	Value: 60.00				

KM# 302 DOLLAR
31.1050 g., 0.9990 Silver 0.9990 oz. ASW, 45 mm. **Ruler:** Elizabeth II **Subject:** Dogs of the World **Rev:** Poodle before the Palace at Versailles

Date	Mintage	F	VF	XF	Unc	BU
2006 Proof	Est. 3,000	Value: 60.00				

KM# 303 DOLLAR
31.1050 g., 0.9990 Silver 0.9990 oz. ASW, 45 mm. **Ruler:** Elizabeth II **Subject:** Dogs of the World **Rev:** Bare dog before the Potala Plast

Date	Mintage	F	VF	XF	Unc	BU
2006 Proof	Est. 3,000	Value: 60.00				

KM# 304 DOLLAR
31.1050 g., 0.9990 Silver 0.9990 oz. ASW, 45 mm. **Ruler:** Elizabeth II **Subject:** Dogs of the World **Rev:** Pekineese before the Palastmuseum

Date	Mintage	F	VF	XF	Unc	BU
2006 Proof	Est. 3,000	Value: 60.00				

KM# 305 DOLLAR
31.1050 g., 0.9990 Silver 0.9990 oz. ASW, 45 mm. **Ruler:** Elizabeth II **Subject:** Dogs of the World **Rev:** Malteser before the Schonbrunn

Date	Mintage	F	VF	XF	Unc	BU
2006 Proof	Est. 3,000	Value: 60.00				

KM# 306 DOLLAR
31.1050 g., 0.9990 Silver 0.9990 oz. ASW, 45 mm. **Ruler:** Elizabeth II **Subject:** Dogs of the World **Rev:** Japanese Chin before Emperor's palace in Kyoto

Date	Mintage	F	VF	XF	Unc	BU
2006 Proof	Est. 3,000	Value: 60.00				

KM# 307 DOLLAR
31.1050 g., 0.9990 Silver 0.9990 oz. ASW, 45 mm. **Ruler:** Elizabeth II **Subject:** Dogs of the World **Rev:** King Charles Spaniel before Westminster Abbey

Date	Mintage	F	VF	XF	Unc	BU
2006 Proof	Est. 3,000	Value: 60.00				

KM# 308 DOLLAR
31.1050 g., 0.9990 Silver 0.9990 oz. ASW, 45 mm. **Ruler:** Elizabeth II **Subject:** Dogs of the World **Rev:** Butterfly dog before the Kings Palace in Madrid

Date	Mintage	F	VF	XF	Unc	BU
2006 Proof	Est. 3,000	Value: 60.00				

KM# 309 DOLLAR
31.1050 g., 0.9990 Silver 0.9990 oz. ASW, 45 mm. **Ruler:** Elizabeth II **Subject:** Olympics **Rev:** Discus thrower

Date	Mintage	F	VF	XF	Unc	BU
ND Proof	Est. 2,008	Value: 70.00				

KM# 310 DOLLAR
31.1050 g., 0.9990 Silver 0.9990 oz. ASW, 45 mm. **Ruler:** Elizabeth II **Subject:** Olympics **Rev:** Sprinter

Date	Mintage	F	VF	XF	Unc	BU
ND Proof	Est. 2,008	Value: 70.00				

KM# 311 DOLLAR
31.1050 g., 0.9990 Silver 0.9990 oz. ASW, 45 mm. **Ruler:** Elizabeth II **Subject:** Olympics **Rev:** Long Jump

Date	Mintage	F	VF	XF	Unc	BU
ND Proof	Est. 2,008	Value: 70.00				

KM# 312 DOLLAR
31.1050 g., 0.9990 Silver 0.9990 oz. ASW, 45 mm. **Ruler:** Elizabeth II **Subject:** Olympics **Rev:** Javelin Thrower

Date	Mintage	F	VF	XF	Unc	BU
ND Proof	Est. 2,008	Value: 70.00				

KM# 313 DOLLAR
31.1050 g., 0.9990 Silver 0.9990 oz. ASW, 45 mm. **Ruler:** Elizabeth II **Subject:** Olympics **Rev:** Weightlifter

Date	Mintage	F	VF	XF	Unc	BU
ND Proof	Est. 2,008	Value: 70.00				

KM# 314 DOLLAR
31.1050 g., 0.9990 Silver 0.9990 oz. ASW, 45 mm. **Ruler:** Elizabeth II **Subject:** Olympics **Rev:** Hammer Throw

Date	Mintage	F	VF	XF	Unc	BU
ND Proof	Est. 2,008	Value: 70.00				

KM# 315 DOLLAR
31.1050 g., 0.9990 Silver 0.9990 oz. ASW, 45 mm. **Ruler:** Elizabeth II **Subject:** Olympics **Rev:** Archery

Date	Mintage	F	VF	XF	Unc	BU
ND Proof	Est. 2,008	Value: 70.00				

KM# 316 DOLLAR
31.1050 g., 0.9990 Silver 0.9990 oz. ASW, 45 mm. **Ruler:** Elizabeth II **Subject:** Olympics **Rev:** Lacrosse player

Date	Mintage	F	VF	XF	Unc	BU
ND Proof	Est. 2,008	Value: 70.00				

KM# 317 DOLLAR
31.1050 g., 0.9990 Silver 0.9990 oz. ASW, 45 mm. **Ruler:** Elizabeth II **Subject:** Olympics **Rev:** Soccer player

Date	Mintage	F	VF	XF	Unc	BU
ND Proof	Est. 2,008	Value: 70.00				

KM# 318 DOLLAR
31.1050 g., 0.9990 Silver 0.9990 oz. ASW, 45 mm. **Ruler:** Elizabeth II **Subject:** Olympics **Rev:** Boxer

Date	Mintage	F	VF	XF	Unc	BU
ND Proof	Est. 2,008	Value: 70.00				

KM# 319 DOLLAR
31.1050 g., 0.9990 Silver 0.9990 oz. ASW, 45 mm. **Ruler:** Elizabeth II **Subject:** Olympics **Rev:** Equestrian

Date	Mintage	F	VF	XF	Unc	BU
ND Proof	Est. 2,008	Value: 70.00				

KM# 320 DOLLAR
31.1050 g., 0.9990 Silver 0.9990 oz. ASW, 45 mm. **Ruler:** Elizabeth II **Subject:** Olympics **Rev:** Wrestler

Date	Mintage	F	VF	XF	Unc	BU
ND Proof	Est. 2,008	Value: 70.00				

KM# 321 DOLLAR
31.1050 g., 0.9990 Silver 0.9990 oz. ASW, 35x46 mm. **Ruler:** Elizabeth II **Subject:** Life of Christ **Rev:** Radiant Mary **Shape:** Vertical rectangle

Date	Mintage	F	VF	XF	Unc	BU
2006 Proof	Est. 1,000	Value: 100				

KM# 322 DOLLAR
31.1050 g., 0.9990 Silver 0.9990 oz. ASW, 35x46 mm. **Ruler:** Elizabeth II **Subject:** Life of Christ **Rev:** Mary and Child (1483) **Shape:** Vertical rectangle

Date	Mintage	F	VF	XF	Unc	BU
2006 Proof	Est. 1,000	Value: 100				

KM# 323 DOLLAR
31.1050 g., 0.9990 Silver 0.9990 oz. ASW, 35x46 mm. **Ruler:** Elizabeth II **Subject:** Life of Christ **Rev:** Christ in the Jrodan (1478) **Shape:** Vertical rectangle

Date	Mintage	F	VF	XF	Unc	BU
2006 Proof	Est. 1,000	Value: 100				

KM# 324 DOLLAR
31.1050 g., 0.9990 Silver 0.9990 oz. ASW, 35x46 mm. **Ruler:** Elizabeth II **Subject:** Life of Christ **Rev:** Jesus Christ (1481) **Shape:** Vertical rectangle

Date	Mintage	F	VF	XF	Unc	BU
2006 Proof	Est. 1,000	Value: 100				

KM# 325 DOLLAR
31.1050 g., 0.9990 Silver 0.9990 oz. ASW, 35x46 mm. **Ruler:** Elizabeth II **Subject:** Life of Christ **Rev:** betrayal of Judas (1303) **Shape:** Vertical rectangle

Date	Mintage	F	VF	XF	Unc	BU
2006 Proof	Est. 1,000	Value: 100				

KM# 326 DOLLAR
31.1050 g., 0.9990 Silver 0.9990 oz. ASW, 35x46 mm. **Ruler:** Elizabeth II **Subject:** Life of Christ **Rev:** Stations of the Cross (1517) **Shape:** Vertical rectangle

Date	Mintage	F	VF	XF	Unc	BU
2006 Proof	Est. 1,000	Value: 100				

KM# 327 DOLLAR
31.1050 g., 0.9990 Silver 0.9990 oz. ASW, 35x46 mm. **Ruler:** Elizabeth II **Subject:** Life of Christ **Rev:** Jesus on the Cross (1558) **Shape:** Vertical rectangle

Date	Mintage	F	VF	XF	Unc	BU
2006 Proof	Est. 1,000	Value: 100				

KM# 329 DOLLAR
31.1050 g., 0.9990 Silver 0.9990 oz. ASW, 35x45 mm. **Ruler:** Elizabeth II **Subject:** Life of Christ **Rev:** Heaven **Shape:** Vertical rectangle

Date	Mintage	F	VF	XF	Unc	BU
2006 Proof	Est. 1,000	Value: 100				

KM# 331 DOLLAR
28.2800 g., 0.9250 Silver 0.8410 oz. ASW, 38.61 mm. **Ruler:** Elizabeth II **Subject:** Year of the Pig **Rev:** Pig grazing

Date	Mintage	F	VF	XF	Unc	BU
2006	Est. 5,000	—	—	—	—	55.00

KM# 328 DOLLAR

31.1050 g., 0.9990 Silver 0.9990 oz. ASW, 35x46 mm. **Ruler:** Elizabeth II **Subject:** Life of Christ **Rev:** Ascension (1520) **Shape:** Vertical rectangle

Date	Mintage	F	VF	XF	Unc	BU
2006 Proof	Est. 1,000	Value: 100				

KM# 176 DOLLAR

28.2800 g., 0.9250 Silver 0.8410 oz. ASW **Ruler:** Elizabeth II **Obv:** Tiarra head of Elizabeth II right at left, multicolor Van Gogh's painting "Starry Night" with 3 zircon crystals as stars at center right. **Obv. Inscription:** ELIZABETH II - NIUE ISLAND **Rev:** Van Gogh's painting "Vase with Twelve Sunflowers" at left, self portrait of artist with brush at upper right **Rev. Inscription:** VAN GOGH / Vincent **Edge:** Plain **Shape:** Rectangular, 39.94 x 27.97 mm

Date	Mintage	F	VF	XF	Unc	BU
2007 Proof	10,000	Value: 85.00				

KM# 332 DOLLAR

28.2800 g., 0.9250 Silver 0.8410 oz. ASW **Ruler:** Elizabeth II **Subject:** Year of the Pig **Rev:** Three little pigs dancing, brick house, wolf

Date	Mintage	F	VF	XF	Unc	BU
2007	—	—	—	—	—	55.00

KM# 334 DOLLAR

28.2800 g., 0.9250 Silver 0.8410 oz. ASW, 38.61 mm. **Ruler:** Elizabeth II **Rev:** Female advancing left with long dress **Rev. Legend:** Change Flies to the Moon

Date	Mintage	F	VF	XF	Unc	BU
2007	Est. 5,000	—	—	—	—	55.00

KM# 335 DOLLAR

28.2800 g., 0.9250 Silver 0.8410 oz. ASW, 38.61 mm. **Ruler:** Elizabeth II **Rev:** Man weiding axe against tree **Rev. Legend:** Wu Gang cuts the sweet-scented osmanthus tree

Date	Mintage	F	VF	XF	Unc	BU
2007	Est. 5,000	—	—	—	—	55.00

KM# 336 DOLLAR

28.2800 g., 0.9250 Silver 0.8410 oz. ASW, 38.61 mm. **Ruler:** Elizabeth II **Rev:** Group visiting palace **Rev. Legend:** Emperor Mint of Tang Dynasty visit the Moon Palace at Night

Date	Mintage	F	VF	XF	Unc	BU
2007	Est. 5,000	—	—	—	—	65.00

KM# 337 DOLLAR

28.2800 g., 0.9250 Silver 0.8410 oz. ASW, 38.61 mm. **Ruler:** Elizabeth II **Rev:** Rabbit with mortar and pestile in house yard **Rev. Legend:** The jade rabbit pounds the medicine of immortality

Date	Mintage	F	VF	XF	Unc	BU
2007 Proof	Est. 5,000	—	—	—	—	55.00

KM# 212 DOLLAR

Silver **Ruler:** Elizabeth II **Rev:** Ox seated multicolor lotus flower

Date	Mintage	F	VF	XF	Unc	BU
2008 Antique finish	—	—	—	—	—	55.00

KM# 192 DOLLAR

31.1050 g., 0.9990 Silver 0.9990 oz. ASW **Ruler:** Elizabeth II **Subject:** Year of the Ox **Obv:** Head right **Rev:** Multicolor ox

Date	Mintage	F	VF	XF	Unc	BU
2008//2009 Proof	10,000	Value: 75.00				

KM# 201 DOLLAR

28.2800 g., 0.9250 Silver 0.8410 oz. ASW, 38.61 mm. **Ruler:** Elizabeth II **Subject:** Amber Road **Obv:** Roman cart and map, Elizabeth II head at lower left **Rev:** Church, goblet, ancient coin, amber insert **Rev. Legend:** ELBLAG SZLAK BURSZTYNOWY

Date	Mintage	F	VF	XF	Unc	BU
2008 Antique finish	10,000	—	—	—	—	100

KM# 202 DOLLAR

28.2800 g., 0.9250 Silver 0.8410 oz. ASW, 38.61 mm. **Ruler:** Elizabeth II **Subject:** Amber Road **Obv:** Roman cart, map, Elizabeth II head at lower left **Rev:** Antonius Pius coins, Nepture statue, mine shaft, amber insert **Rev. Legend:** GDANSK SZLAK BURSZTYNOWY

Date	Mintage	F	VF	XF	Unc	BU
2008 Antique finish	10,000	—	—	—	—	90.00

KM# 203 DOLLAR

28.2800 g., 0.9250 Silver 0.8410 oz. ASW, 38.61 mm. **Ruler:** Elizabeth II **Subject:** Amber Road **Obv:** Roman cart, map, Elizabeth II head at lower left **Rev:** Building, statue, amber insert **Rev. Legend:** WROCLAW SZLAK BURSZTYNOWY

Date	Mintage	F	VF	XF	Unc	BU
2008 Antique finish	10,000	—	—	—	—	100

KM# 204 DOLLAR

28.2800 g., 0.9990 Silver 0.9083 oz. ASW, 38.61 mm. **Ruler:** Elizabeth II **Subject:** Amber Road **Rev:** Castle, sword, amber insert **Rev. Legend:** SZLAK BURSZTYNOWY KALININGRAD

Date	Mintage	F	VF	XF	Unc	BU
2008 Antique finish	10,000	—	—	—	—	100

KM# 211 DOLLAR

28.2800 g., 0.9250 Silver 0.8410 oz. ASW, 28x40 mm. **Ruler:** Elizabeth II **Obv:** Head of Elizabeth II at lower left, Portrait of Lautrec at top right **Rev:** Toulouse-Lautrec and can-can girl

Date	Mintage	F	VF	XF	Unc	BU
2008 Proof	15,000	Value: 100				

KM# 338 DOLLAR

31.1050 g., 0.9990 Silver 0.9990 oz. ASW, 45 mm. **Ruler:** Elizabeth II **Subject:** Year of the Rat **Rev:** Rat in field, sun rays above

Date	Mintage	F	VF	XF	Unc	BU
2008	Est. 8,000	—	—	—	—	65.00

KM# 339 DOLLAR

31.1050 g., 0.9990 Silver 0.9990 oz. ASW, 45 mm. **Ruler:** Elizabeth II **Subject:** Year of the Rat **Rev:** Rat left before house

Date	Mintage	F	VF	XF	Unc	BU
2008	Est. 8,000	—	—	—	—	65.00

KM# 340 DOLLAR

31.1050 g., 0.9990 Silver 0.9990 oz. ASW, 45 mm. **Ruler:** Elizabeth II **Subject:** Year of the Rat **Rev:** Rat standing on hind legs sniffing flora

Date	Mintage	F	VF	XF	Unc	BU
2008	Est. 8,000	—	—	—	—	70.00

KM# 341 DOLLAR

31.1050 g., 0.9990 Silver 0.9990 oz. ASW, 45 mm. **Ruler:** Elizabeth II **Rev:** Multicolor Happy mouse

Date	Mintage	F	VF	XF	Unc	BU
2008 Proof	—	Value: 60.00				

KM# 342 DOLLAR

31.1050 g., 0.9990 Silver 0.9990 oz. ASW, 45 mm. **Ruler:** Elizabeth II **Rev:** Multicolor wealthy rat

Date	Mintage	F	VF	XF	Unc	BU
2008 Proof	—	Value: 60.00				

KM# 343 DOLLAR

31.1050 g., 0.9990 Silver 0.9990 oz. ASW, 45 mm. **Ruler:** Elizabeth II **Rev:** Multicolor happy rat

Date	Mintage	F	VF	XF	Unc	BU
2008 Proof	—	Value: 60.00				

KM# 344 DOLLAR
31.1050 g., 0.9990 Silver 0.9990 oz. ASW, 45 mm. **Ruler:** Elizabeth II **Rev:** Multicolor successful rat

Date	Mintage	F	VF	XF	Unc	BU
2008 Proof	—	Value: 60.00				

KM# 345 DOLLAR
31.1050 g., 0.9990 Silver 0.9990 oz. ASW, 45 mm. **Ruler:** Elizabeth II **Rev:** Multicolor rat holding charm

Date	Mintage	F	VF	XF	Unc	BU
2008 Proof	Est. 10,000	Value: 60.00				

KM# 346 DOLLAR
3.1100 g., 0.9990 Gold 0.0999 oz. AGW, 18 mm. **Ruler:** Elizabeth II **Rev:** Rat in garden

Date	Mintage	F	VF	XF	Unc	BU
2008 Proof	Est. 10,000	Value: 185				

KM# 347 DOLLAR
28.2800 g., 0.9250 Silver 0.8410 oz. ASW, 38.61 mm. **Ruler:** Elizabeth II **Rev:** Rat standing infront of multicolor cut cheese wheel

Date	Mintage	F	VF	XF	Unc	BU
2008 Proof	Est. 10,000	Value: 50.00				

KM# 348 DOLLAR
28.2800 g., 0.9250 Silver 0.8410 oz. ASW, 38.61 mm. **Ruler:** Elizabeth II **Rev:** Multicolor dancing mice in garland

Date	Mintage	F	VF	XF	Unc	BU
2008 Proof	—	Value: 50.00				

KM# 197 DOLLAR
17.3000 g., Aluminum-Brass, 32 mm. **Ruler:** Elizabeth II **Obv:** Head right **Rev:** Swordfish **Edge:** Reeded

Date	Mintage	F	VF	XF	Unc	BU
2009	—	—	—	—	7.50	12.50

KM# 231 DOLLAR
31.1030 g., 0.9990 Silver 0.9989 oz. ASW, 38.6 mm. **Ruler:** Elizabeth II **Subject:** Year of the Tiger **Rev:** Tiger cub in basket playing with ball

Date	Mintage	F	VF	XF	Unc	BU
2009 Proof	6,000	Value: 80.00				

KM# 232 DOLLAR
31.1030 g., 0.9990 Silver 0.9989 oz. ASW, 38.6 mm. **Ruler:** Elizabeth II **Subject:** Year of the Tiger **Rev:** Tiger advancing left

Date	Mintage	F	VF	XF	Unc	BU
2009 Proof	6,000	Value: 80.00				

KM# 551 DOLLAR
28.2800 g., 0.9250 Silver 0.8410 oz. ASW, 38.61 mm. **Ruler:** Elizabeth II **Subject:** Father Frost **Rev:** Father and Mrs. Frost standing, multicolor

Date	Mintage	F	VF	XF	Unc	BU
2009 Proof	Est. 6,000	Value: 65.00				

KM# 198 DOLLAR
17.3000 g., Copper Plated Bronze, 32 mm. **Ruler:** Elizabeth II **Obv:** Head right **Rev:** Taro leaves **Edge:** Reeded

Date	Mintage	F	VF	XF	Unc	BU
2010	—	—	—	—	7.50	12.50

KM# 234 DOLLAR
28.2800 g., 0.9250 Silver 0.8410 oz. ASW, 40x40 mm. **Ruler:** Elizabeth II **Obv:** Head right, footprints in field **Rev:** Antilocapra Americana, two antelope running right **Shape:** Square

Date	Mintage	F	VF	XF	Unc	BU
2010 Proof	9,000	Value: 80.00				

KM# 235 DOLLAR
28.2800 g., 0.9250 Silver 0.8410 oz. ASW, 38.6 mm. **Ruler:** Elizabeth II **Obv:** Head right **Rev:** Lycaena Virgavreae multicolor butterfly

Date	Mintage	F	VF	XF	Unc	BU
2010 Proof	8,000	Value: 80.00				

KM# 236 DOLLAR
14.1400 g., 0.9250 Silver 0.4205 oz. ASW, 25x28 mm. **Ruler:** Elizabeth II **Obv:** Head right on musical score **Rev:** Chopin bust at left, score **Shape:** Square

Date	Mintage	F	VF	XF	Unc	BU
2010 Proof	6,000	Value: 80.00				

KM# 238 DOLLAR
28.2800 g., 0.9250 Silver 0.8410 oz. ASW, 36.81 mm. **Ruler:** Elizabeth II **Subject:** Fire **Obv:** Head right, images of early man **Rev:** Volcano and men around fire in multicolor

Date	Mintage	F	VF	XF	Unc	BU
2010 Proof	6,000	Value: 100				

KM# 239 DOLLAR
28.2800 g., 0.9250 Silver 0.8410 oz. ASW, 40x28 mm. **Ruler:** Elizabeth II **Obv:** Head right, aircraft propeller, wing schematic **Rev:** Greek warrior shield and multicolor Icarus in flight **Shape:** Rectangle

Date	Mintage	F	VF	XF	Unc	BU
2010 Proof	6,000	Value: 100				

KM# 240 DOLLAR
28.2800 g., 0.9250 Silver 0.8410 oz. ASW, 28x40 mm. **Ruler:** Elizabeth II **Obv:** Head right, propeller, wing schematic **Rev:** Montgolfier brothers and balloon **Shape:** Rectangle

Date	Mintage	F	VF	XF	Unc	BU
2010 Proof	6,000	Value: 75.00				

KM# 241 DOLLAR
28.2800 g., 0.9250 Silver 0.8410 oz. ASW, 40x28 mm. **Ruler:** Elizabeth II **Obv:** Head right, Monet painting **Rev:** Claude Monet portrait and painting **Shape:** Verticle rectangle

Date	Mintage	F	VF	XF	Unc	BU
2010 Proof	15,000	Value: 120				

KM# 242 DOLLAR
28.2800 g., 0.9250 Silver 0.8410 oz. ASW, 38.61 mm. **Ruler:** Elizabeth II **Obv:** Elizabeth II head at top left, building **Rev:** Napoleon at left, troops in color at right

Date	Mintage	F	VF	XF	Unc	BU
2010 Proof	10,000	Value: 90.00				

KM# 243 DOLLAR
28.2800 g., 0.9250 Silver 0.8410 oz. ASW, 38.6 mm. **Ruler:** Elizabeth II **Subject:** 65th Anniversary - End of World War II **Obv:** Head right at top, three Soviet medals below **Rev:** Soviet flat, rose and eternal light

Date	Mintage	F	VF	XF	Unc	BU
2010 Proof	7,000	Value: 95.00				

KM# 244 DOLLAR
28.2800 g., 0.9250 Silver 0.8410 oz. ASW, 38.6 mm. **Ruler:** Elizabeth II **Obv:** Head at left, ship, coins, artifacts **Rev:** Stupsk

Date	Mintage	F	VF	XF	Unc	BU
2010 Proof	8,000	Value: 90.00				

KM# 251 DOLLAR
31.1050 g., 0.9990 Silver 0.9990 oz. ASW, 38.6 mm. **Ruler:** Elizabeth II **Subject:** Peanuts 60th Anniversary **Rev:** Snoopy as conductor with flowers, Woodstock with red ribbon

Date	Mintage	F	VF	XF	Unc	BU
2010 Prooflike	3,000	—	—	—	—	80.00

KM# 365 DOLLAR
28.2800 g., 0.9250 Silver 0.8410 oz. ASW, 38.61 mm. **Ruler:** Elizabeth II **Subject:** WWII, 65th Anniversary **Obv:** Elizabeth II head, WWI medal and two stars below **Rev:** Russian flag and medal ribbon

Date	Mintage	F	VF	XF	Unc	BU
2010 Proof	7,000	Value: 60.00				

KM# 366 DOLLAR
28.2800 g., 0.9250 Silver 0.8410 oz. ASW, 38.61 mm. **Ruler:** Elizabeth II **Obv:** Enlarged butterfly wing **Rev:** Butterfly - Parnassius Apollo

Date	Mintage	F	VF	XF	Unc	BU
2010 Proof	8,000	Value: 65.00				

KM# 367 DOLLAR
28.2800 g., 0.9250 Silver 0.8410 oz. ASW, 38.61 mm. **Ruler:** Elizabeth II **Subject:** Amber Route - Stare Hradisko **Rev:** Amber insert, old celtic style coin

Date	Mintage	F	VF	XF	Unc	BU
2010 Antique finish	10,000	—	—	—	—	85.00

KM# 369 DOLLAR
14.1400 g., 0.9250 Silver 0.4205 oz. ASW, 32 mm. **Ruler:** Elizabeth II **Subject:** Cartoon Characters - Mis Uszatek **Obv:** Elizabeth II head left, movie film **Rev:** Image of rabbits and bear

Date	Mintage	F	VF	XF	Unc	BU
2010 Proof	8,000	Value: 40.00				

KM# 370 DOLLAR
28.2800 g., 0.9250 Silver 0.8410 oz. ASW **Ruler:** Elizabeth II **Obv:** Elizabeth II head right, Cupid **Rev:** Romeo and Juliet about to kiss

Date	Mintage	F	VF	XF	Unc	BU
2010 Proof	9,000	Value: 60.00				

KM# 392 DOLLAR
14.1400 g., 0.9250 Silver 0.4205 oz. ASW, 32 mm. **Ruler:** Elizabeth II **Subject:** Cartoon Characters - Wolf and the HareH **Rev:** Wolf and hare characters in multicolor

Date	Mintage	F	VF	XF	Unc	BU
2010 Proof	8,000	Value: 50.00				

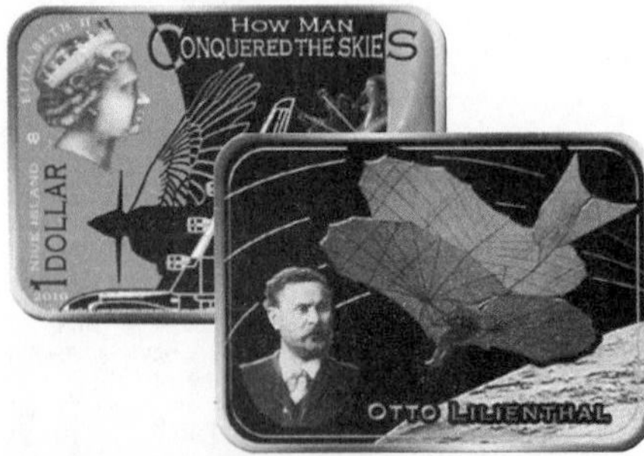

KM# 393 DOLLAR
28.2800 g., 0.9250 Silver 0.8410 oz. ASW, 40x28 mm. **Ruler:** Elizabeth II **Obv:** Queen's head at top left, three airplane views **Rev:** Otto Lilienthal and the glider **Shape:** Rectangle

Date	Mintage	F	VF	XF	Unc	BU
2010 Proof	6,000	Value: 70.00				

KM# 394 DOLLAR
28.2800 g., 0.9250 Silver 0.8410 oz. ASW, 38.8 mm. **Ruler:** Elizabeth II **Obv:** Queen's head right within star pattern **Rev:** Two portraits of Sitting Bull in multicolor

Date	Mintage	F	VF	XF	Unc	BU
2010 Proof	6,000	Value: 75.00				

KM# 395 DOLLAR
28.2800 g., 0.9250 Silver 0.8410 oz. ASW, 40x40 mm. **Ruler:** Elizabeth II **Obv:** Head in tiara right within diamond, footprints in background **Rev:** Platypus (Ornithorhynchus anatinus) **Shape:** Square

Date	Mintage	F	VF	XF	Unc	BU
2010 Proof	9,000	Value: 65.00				

KM# 396 DOLLAR
28.2800 g., 0.9250 Silver with amber insert 0.8410 oz. ASW, 38.61 mm. **Ruler:** Elizabeth II **Subject:** Amber Route - Carnuntum **Rev:** Arches, ancient coin and statue

Date	Mintage	F	VF	XF	Unc	BU
2010 Antique patina	10,000	Value: 85.00				

KM# 398 DOLLAR
28.2800 g., 0.9250 Silver with amber insert 0.8410 oz. ASW, 38.61 mm. **Ruler:** Elizabeth II **Subject:** Amber Route - Szombathely **Rev:** Cathedral, ancient coin

Date	Mintage	F	VF	XF	Unc	BU
2010 Antique patina	10,000	Value: 85.00				

KM# 400 DOLLAR
28.2800 g., 0.9250 Silver 0.8410 oz. ASW, 27x45 mm. **Ruler:** Elizabeth II **Subject:** Milan Cathedral **Obv:** Cathedral's flying buttresses, stained glass colored inset **Rev:** Front facade of cathedral, stained glass colored inset **Shape:** Vertical oval

Date	Mintage	F	VF	XF	Unc	BU
2010 Proof	5,000	Value: 70.00				

KM# 401 DOLLAR
28.2800 g., 0.9250 Silver 0.8410 oz. ASW, 27x45 mm. **Ruler:** Elizabeth II **Subject:** Cologne Cathedral **Obv:** Cathedral side exterior, stained glass colored inset **Rev:** Cathedral floor plan and facade, stained glass colored inset **Shape:** Vertical oval

Date	Mintage	F	VF	XF	Unc	BU
2010 Proof	5,000	Value: 70.00				

KM# 402 DOLLAR
28.2800 g., 0.9250 Silver 0.8410 oz. ASW, 27x45 mm. **Ruler:** Elizabeth II **Subject:** Notre Dame Cathedral **Obv:** Cathedral side view, stained glass colored inset **Rev:** Linear cathedral interior view, cathedral facade, stained glass colored inset **Shape:** Vertical oval

Date	Mintage	F	VF	XF	Unc	BU
2010 Proof	5,000	Value: 70.00				

KM# 403 DOLLAR
28.2800 g., 0.9250 Silver 0.8410 oz. ASW, 28x40 mm. **Ruler:** Elizabeth II **Subject:** Alfons Mucha, 150th Anniversary of Birth **Obv:** Standing Female in multicolor **Rev:** Female portrait and Mucha portrait in multicolor **Shape:** Vertical Rectangle

Date	Mintage	F	VF	XF	Unc	BU
2010 Proof	5,000	Value: 80.00				

KM# 404 DOLLAR
28.2800 g., 0.9250 Silver 0.8410 oz. ASW, 28x40 mm. **Ruler:** Elizabeth II **Subject:** Carl Brullov **Obv:** Female on horseback in color **Rev:** Two females with grape wreath above, Brullov portrait, Three nuns singing below; all in color **Shape:** Vertical Rectangle

Date	Mintage	F	VF	XF	Unc	BU
2010 Proof	5,000	Value: 75.00				

KM# 406 DOLLAR
28.2800 g., 0.9250 Silver 0.8410 oz. ASW, 40x40 mm. **Ruler:** Elizabeth II **Obv:** Head with tiara right, in diamond, footprints in background **Rev:** Venus Flytrap in color **Shape:** Square

Date	Mintage	F	VF	XF	Unc	BU
2010 Proof	9,000	Value: 75.00				

KM# 407 DOLLAR
28.2800 g., 0.9250 Silver 0.8410 oz. ASW, 41 mm. **Ruler:** Elizabeth II **Subject:** Good Luck **Obv:** Head with tiara right, horseshoes below **Rev:** Horseshoes and clover

Date	Mintage	F	VF	XF	Unc	BU
2010 Proof	10,000	Value: 70.00				

KM# 412 DOLLAR
28.2800 g., 0.9250 Silver 0.8410 oz. ASW, 38.61 mm. **Ruler:** Elizabeth II **Subject:** Siberia **Obv:** Head with tiara right **Rev:** Khanty-Mansiysk

Date	Mintage	F	VF	XF	Unc	BU
2010 Proof-like	4,000	—	—	—	—	70.00

KM# 413 DOLLAR
28.2800 g., 0.9250 Silver 0.8410 oz. ASW, 38.61 mm, **Ruler:** Elizabeth II **Subject:** Siberia **Obv:** Head with tiara right **Rev:** Uray

Date	Mintage	F	VF	XF	Unc	BU
2010 Proof-like	4,000	—	—	—	—	70.00

KM# 414 DOLLAR
28.2800 g., 0.9250 Silver 0.8410 oz. ASW, 38.61 mm. **Ruler:** Elizabeth II **Subject:** Siberia **Obv:** Head with tiara right **Rev:** Surgut

Date	Mintage	F	VF	XF	Unc	BU
2010 Proof-like	4,000	—	—	—	—	70.00

KM# 415 DOLLAR
28.2800 g., 0.9250 Silver 0.8410 oz. ASW, 38.61 mm. **Ruler:** Elizabeth II **Subject:** Siberia **Obv:** Head with tiara right **Rev:** Nizhnevartovsk

Date	Mintage	F	VF	XF	Unc	BU
2010 Proof-like	4,000	—	—	—	—	70.00

KM# 417 DOLLAR
28.2800 g., 0.9250 Silver 0.8410 oz. ASW, 38.61 mm. **Ruler:** Elizabeth II **Subject:** Famous Love Stories - Samson and Delilah **Obv:** Head with tiara right, Cupid below **Rev:** Portraits of Samson and Delilah

Date	Mintage	F	VF	XF	Unc	BU
2010 Proof	9,000	Value: 70.00				

KM# 418 DOLLAR
31.1000 g., 0.9990 Silver 0.9988 oz. ASW, 40 mm. **Ruler:** Elizabeth II **Subject:** Jaroslawl, 100th Anniversary **Obv:** Head with tiara right **Rev:** Banner in color

Date	Mintage	F	VF	XF	Unc	BU
2010 Proof	2,000	Value: 75.00				

KM# 419 DOLLAR
31.1000 g., 0.9990 Silver 0.9988 oz. ASW, 40 mm. **Ruler:** Elizabeth II **Subject:** Jaroslawl, 1000th Anniversary **Obv:** Head with tiara right **Rev:** Three church towers in color

Date	Mintage	F	VF	XF	Unc	BU
2010 Proof	9,000	Value: 75.00				

KM# 420 DOLLAR
31.1000 g., 0.9990 Silver 0.9988 oz. ASW, 40 mm. **Ruler:** Elizabeth II **Subject:** Jaroslawl, 1000th Anniversary **Obv:** Head in tiara right **Rev:** Town square in color

Date	Mintage	F	VF	XF	Unc	BU
2010 Proof	9,000	Value: 75.00				

KM# 421 DOLLAR
28.2800 g., 0.9250 Silver 0.8410 oz. ASW, 36.81 mm. **Ruler:** Elizabeth II **Subject:** Cultural Achievements **Obv:** Head with tiara at center **Rev:** Bow and arrows, Bow and firestarting kit

Date	Mintage	F	VF	XF	Unc	BU
2010 Proof	6,000	Value: 80.00				

KM# 422 DOLLAR
28.2800 g., 0.9250 Silver 0.8410 oz. ASW, 44 mm. **Ruler:** Elizabeth II **Subject:** Christmas star **Obv:** Head with tiara right, snowflakes around **Rev:** Children before christmas tree in color **Shape:** 7-pointed star

Date	Mintage	F	VF	XF	Unc	BU
2010 Proof	15,000	Value: 95.00				

KM# 426 DOLLAR
28.2800 g., 0.9250 Silver 0.8410 oz. ASW, 41 mm. **Ruler:** Elizabeth II **Subject:** Four Leaf Clover **Obv:** Head with titara right, clovers **Rev:** four clovers and ripple background

Date	Mintage	F	VF	XF	Unc	BU
2010 Proof	10,000	Value: 70.00				

KM# 427 DOLLAR
28.2800 g., 0.9250 Silver 0.8410 oz. ASW, 38.61 mm. **Ruler:** Elizabeth II **Subject:** Veliky Novgorod **Obv:** Head with tiara right, montage of ship and coins at right **Rev:** Market scene, Church; city arms below

Date	Mintage	F	VF	XF	Unc	BU
2010 Proof	8,000	Value: 75.00				

KM# 428 DOLLAR
28.2800 g., 0.9250 Silver 0.8410 oz. ASW, 38.61 mm. **Ruler:** Elizabeth II **Subject:** Year of the Rabbit **Obv:** Head with tiara right **Rev:** Rabbit seated in field

Date	Mintage	F	VF	XF	Unc	BU
2010 Proof	3,000	Value: 75.00				

KM# 429 DOLLAR
28.2800 g., 0.9250 Silver 0.8410 oz. ASW, 38.61 mm. **Ruler:** Elizabeth II **Subject:** Year of the Rabbit **Obv:** Head with tiara right **Rev:** Two rabbits holding heart at center

Date	Mintage	F	VF	XF	Unc	BU
2010 Proof	3,000	Value: 75.00				

KM# 432 DOLLAR
28.2800 g., 0.9250 Silver 0.8410 oz. ASW, 40x28 mm. **Ruler:** Elizabeth II **Subject:** Francisco Goya **Obv:** Head with tiara right at left, painting of man and woman at right **Rev:** Goya and Clothed female reclining **Shape:** Rectangle

Date	Mintage	F	VF	XF	Unc	BU
2010 Proof	10,000	Value: 70.00				

KM# 433 DOLLAR
28.2800 g., 0.9250 Silver 0.8410 oz. ASW, 38.61 mm. **Ruler:** Elizabeth II **Subject:** Peter the Great **Obv:** Head with tiara right above ship and city view **Rev:** Half-length figure holding coins, map in background

Date	Mintage	F	VF	XF	Unc	BU
2010 Proof	4,000	Value: 75.00				

KM# 434 DOLLAR
28.2800 g., 0.9250 Silver 0.8410 oz. ASW, 38.61 mm. **Ruler:** Elizabeth II **Subject:** Sea of Love **Obv:** Head in tiara right above sunset at sea with heart at center **Rev:** Two white doves in flight over sea, within heart

Date	Mintage	F	VF	XF	Unc	BU
2010 Proof	7,000	Value: 80.00				

KM# 435 DOLLAR
15.5500 g., 0.9250 Silver 0.4624 oz. ASW, 35 mm. **Ruler:** Elizabeth II **Subject:** Prehistoric art - Chauvet cave **Rev:** Two figures of cats

Date	Mintage	F	VF	XF	Unc	BU
2010 Proof	1,000	Value: 65.00				

KM# 436 DOLLAR
15.5500 g., 0.9250 Silver 0.4624 oz. ASW, 35 mm. **Ruler:** Elizabeth II **Subject:** Prehistoric art - Altamira cave **Rev:** Bison artwork

Date	Mintage	F	VF	XF	Unc	BU
2010 Proof	1,000	Value: 65.00				

KM# 437 DOLLAR
15.5500 g., 0.9250 Silver 0.4624 oz. ASW, 35 mm. **Ruler:** Elizabeth II **Subject:** Prehistoric art - Lascaux cave **Rev:** Horse art

Date	Mintage	F	VF	XF	Unc	BU
2010 Proof	1,000	Value: 65.00				

KM# 438 DOLLAR
15.5500 g., 0.9250 Silver 0.4624 oz. ASW, 35 mm. **Ruler:** Elizabeth II **Subject:** Prehistoric art - Jabbaren cave **Rev:** Male figure with bow

Date	Mintage	F	VF	XF	Unc	BU
2010 Proof	1,000	Value: 65.00				

KM# 439 DOLLAR
15.5500 g., 0.9250 Silver 0.4624 oz. ASW, 35 mm. **Ruler:** Elizabeth II **Subject:** Prehistoric art - Tadrart cave **Rev:** Elephant art

Date	Mintage	F	VF	XF	Unc	BU
2010 Proof	1,000	Value: 65.00				

KM# 440 DOLLAR
28.2800 g., Copper-Nickel, 38.61 mm. **Ruler:** Elizabeth II **Subject:** Lifetime of Service **Obv:** Head in tiara right **Rev:** Conjoined busts of Elizabeth II and Prince Philip

Date	Mintage	F	VF	XF	Unc	BU
2010	—	—	—	—	—	20.00

KM# 440a DOLLAR
28.2800 g., 0.9250 Silver 0.8410 oz. ASW, 38.61 mm. **Ruler:** Elizabeth II **Subject:** Lifetime of Service **Obv:** Head with tiara right **Rev:** Conjoined busts of Elizabeth II and Prince Philip

Date	Mintage	F	VF	XF	Unc	BU
2010 Proof	19,500	Value: 50.00				

KM# 441 DOLLAR
31.1000 g., 0.9990 Silver 0.9988 oz. ASW, 38.61 mm. **Ruler:** Elizabeth II **Subject:** Slovic mythology - Perun **Rev:** Two warriors, tree in background

Date	Mintage	F	VF	XF	Unc	BU
2010 Proof	1,000	Value: 65.00				

KM# 454 DOLLAR
Silver **Ruler:** Elizabeth II **Subject:** Polish Stadiums **Rev:** Michail Ktzov stadium

Date	Mintage	F	VF	XF	Unc	BU
2010 Proof	—	Value: 75.00				

KM# 455 DOLLAR
Silver **Ruler:** Elizabeth II **Subject:** Polish Stadiums **Rev:** Gdansk

Date	Mintage	F	VF	XF	Unc	BU
2010 Proof	—	Value: 75.00				

KM# 456 DOLLAR
31.1030 g., 0.9990 Silver 0.9989 oz. ASW, 40 mm. **Ruler:** Elizabeth II **Subject:** Giah Thong - safe conduct pass **Obv:** Head with tiara right **Rev:** Two soldiers below Viet Nam flag

Date	Mintage	F	VF	XF	Unc	BU
2010 Prooflike	—	—	—	—	—	50.00

KM# 495 DOLLAR
28.2800 g., 0.9250 Silver 0.8410 oz. ASW, 38.61 mm. **Ruler:** Elizabeth II **Subject:** Zodiac Mucha Paintings **Rev:** Aries

Date	Mintage	F	VF	XF	Unc	BU
2010 Proof	10,000	Value: 65.00				

KM# 496 DOLLAR
28.2800 g., 0.9250 Silver 0.8410 oz. ASW, 38.61 mm. **Ruler:** Elizabeth II **Subject:** Zodiac Mucha Paintings **Rev:** Taurus

Date	Mintage	F	VF	XF	Unc	BU
2010 Proof	10,000	Value: 65.00				

KM# 497 DOLLAR
28.2800 g., 0.9250 Silver 0.8410 oz. ASW, 38.61 mm. **Ruler:** Elizabeth II **Subject:** Zodiac Mucha Paintings **Rev:** Gemini

Date	Mintage	F	VF	XF	Unc	BU
2010 Proof	10,000	Value: 65.00				

KM# 498 DOLLAR
28.2800 g., 0.9250 Silver 0.8410 oz. ASW, 38.61 mm. **Ruler:** Elizabeth II **Subject:** Zodiac Mucha Paintings **Rev:** Cancer

Date	Mintage	F	VF	XF	Unc	BU
2010 Proof	10,000	Value: 65.00				

KM# 499 DOLLAR
28.2800 g., 0.9250 Silver 0.8410 oz. ASW **Ruler:** Elizabeth II **Subject:** Zodiac Mucha Paintings **Rev:** Leo

Date	Mintage	F	VF	XF	Unc	BU
2010 Proof	10,000	Value: 65.00				

KM# 500 DOLLAR
28.2500 g., 0.9250 Silver 0.8401 oz. ASW, 38.61 mm. **Ruler:** Elizabeth II **Subject:** Zodiac Mucha Paintings **Rev:** Virgo

Date	Mintage	F	VF	XF	Unc	BU
2010 Proof	10,000	Value: 65.00				

KM# 501 DOLLAR
28.2800 g., 0.9250 Silver 0.8410 oz. ASW, 38.61 mm. **Ruler:** Elizabeth II **Subject:** Zodiac Mucha Paintings **Rev:** Libra

Date	Mintage	F	VF	XF	Unc	BU
2010 Proof	10,000	Value: 65.00				

KM# 502 DOLLAR

28.2800 g., 0.9250 Silver 0.8410 oz. ASW, 38.61 mm. **Ruler:** Elizabeth II **Subject:** Zodiac Mucha Paintings **Rev:** Scorpio

Date	Mintage	F	VF	XF	Unc	BU
2010 Proof	10,000	Value: 65.00				

KM# 503 DOLLAR

28.2800 g., 0.9250 Silver 0.8410 oz. ASW, 38.61 mm. **Ruler:** Elizabeth II **Subject:** Zodiac Mucha Paintings **Rev:** Sagittarius

Date	Mintage	F	VF	XF	Unc	BU
2010 Proof	10,000	Value: 65.00				

KM# 557 DOLLAR

28.2800 g., 0.9250 Silver 0.8410 oz. ASW, 30x50 mm. **Ruler:** Elizabeth II **Subject:** Westminister Abbey **Obv:** Head with tiara at left, interior view of end windows **Rev:** Exterior view with rose window detail **Shape:** vertical oval

Date	Mintage	F	VF	XF	Unc	BU
2010 Proof	5,000	Value: 100				

KM# 558 DOLLAR

28.2800 g., 0.9250 Silver 0.8410 oz. ASW, 30x50 mm. **Ruler:** Elizabeth II **Subject:** Stephansdom, Wein **Obv:** Head in tiara at left, view of organ screen and statue detail **Rev:** Exterior rendering and detail **Shape:** Vertical oval

Date	Mintage	F	VF	XF	Unc	BU
2010 Proof	5,000	Value: 100				

KM# 504 DOLLAR

28.2800 g., 0.9250 Silver 0.8410 oz. ASW, 38.61 mm. **Ruler:** Elizabeth II **Subject:** Zodiac Mucha Paintings **Rev:** Capricorn

Date	Mintage	F	VF	XF	Unc	BU
2011 Proof	10,000	Value: 65.00				

KM# 505 DOLLAR

28.2800 g., 0.9250 Silver 0.8410 oz. ASW, 38.61 mm. **Ruler:** Elizabeth II **Subject:** Zodiac Mucha Painting **Rev:** Aquarius

Date	Mintage	F	VF	XF	Unc	BU
2011 Proof	10,000	Value: 65.00				

KM# 506 DOLLAR

28.2800 g., 0.9250 Silver 0.8410 oz. ASW, 38.61 mm. **Ruler:** Elizabeth II **Subject:** Zodiac Mucha Paintings **Rev:** Pisces

Date	Mintage	F	VF	XF	Unc	BU
2011 Proof	10,000	Value: 65.00				

KM# 508 DOLLAR

Silver **Ruler:** Elizabeth II **Subject:** Russian Cartoons

Date	Mintage	F	VF	XF	Unc	BU
2011 Proof	—	Value: 70.00				

KM# 509 DOLLAR

Silver **Ruler:** Elizabeth II **Subject:** Russian Cartoons

Date	Mintage	F	VF	XF	Unc	BU
2011 Proof	—	Value: 70.00				

KM# 510 DOLLAR

28.2800 g., 0.9250 Silver 0.8410 oz. ASW, 55.6x41.6 mm. **Ruler:** Elizabeth II **Subject:** Year of the Rabbit **Rev:** Rabbit in the snow **Shape:** Horizontal oval

Date	Mintage	F	VF	XF	Unc	BU
2011 Proof	5,000	Value: 55.00				

KM# 514 DOLLAR

31.1050 g., Silver Plated Copper-Nickel, 40 mm. **Ruler:** Elizabeth II **Subject:** Royal Engagement **Obv:** Head with tiara right **Rev:** Prince William and Catherine Middleton facing

Date	Mintage	F	VF	XF	Unc	BU
2011 Proof	10,000	Value: 25.00				

KM# 515 DOLLAR

31.1000 g., Silver Plated Copper, 40 mm. **Ruler:** Elizabeth II **Subject:** Diana - A wife, Princess, Mother, Legend

Date	Mintage	F	VF	XF	Unc	BU
2011 Proof	10,000	Value: 20.00				

KM# 516 DOLLAR

31.1000 g., Silver Plated Copper, 40 mm. **Ruler:** Elizabeth II **Subject:** Diana - Wedding to Charles

Date	Mintage	F	VF	XF	Unc	BU
2011 Proof	10,000	Value: 20.00				

KM# 517 DOLLAR

31.1000 g., Silver Plated Copper, 40 mm. **Ruler:** Elizabeth II **Subject:** Diana - Engagement to Prince Charles

Date	Mintage	F	VF	XF	Unc	BU
2011 Proof	10,000	Value: 20.00				

KM# 518 DOLLAR

31.1000 g., Silver Plated Copper, 40 mm. **Ruler:** Elizabeth II **Subject:** Diana - Quote

Date	Mintage	F	VF	XF	Unc	BU
2011 Proof	10,000	Value: 20.00				

KM# 519 DOLLAR

31.1000 g., Silver Plated Copper, 40 mm. **Ruler:** Elizabeth II **Subject:** Diana - Mother Teresa

Date	Mintage	F	VF	XF	Unc	BU
2011 Proof	10,000	Value: 20.00				

KM# 520 DOLLAR
31.1000 g., Silver Plated Copper, 40 mm. **Ruler:** Elizabeth II **Subject:** Diana - We will always remember

Date	Mintage	F	VF	XF	Unc	BU
2011 Proof	10,000	Value: 20.00				

KM# 554 DOLLAR
28.2800 g., 0.9250 Silver 0.8410 oz. ASW, 41 mm. **Ruler:** Elizabeth II **Obv:** Head with tiara right, three elephants and hologram **Rev:** Hologram elephant and two elephants under tree

Date	Mintage	F	VF	XF	Unc	BU
2011 Proof	Est. 10,000	Value: 75.00				

KM# 555 DOLLAR
28.2800 g., 0.9250 Silver 0.8410 oz. ASW, 38.61 mm. **Ruler:** Elizabeth II **Subject:** Hanseatic Towns - Szezecin **Obv:** Head with tiara right at left, map and ship **Rev:** Churches and ship at dock, town shield

Date	Mintage	F	VF	XF	Unc	BU
2011 Proof	Est. 3,000	Value: 75.00				

KM# 556 DOLLAR
28.2800 g., 0.9250 Silver 0.8410 oz. ASW, 38.61 mm. **Ruler:** Elizabeth II **Subject:** Yunona and Avos **Obv:** Head with tiara right, ornate frame in background **Rev:** Couple facing, seascape in background

Date	Mintage	F	VF	XF	Unc	BU
2011 Proof	Est. 5,000	Value: 75.00				

KM# 559 DOLLAR
28.2800 g., 0.9250 Silver 0.8410 oz. ASW, 38.61 mm. **Ruler:** Elizabeth II **Subject:** Russian municipalities - Krasnoyarsk **Obv:** Head with tiara right **Rev:** Town view

Date	Mintage	F	VF	XF	Unc	BU
2011 Proof	2,000	Value: 85.00				

KM# 560 DOLLAR
28.2800 g., 0.9250 Silver 0.8410 oz. ASW, 38.61 mm. **Ruler:** Elizabeth II **Subject:** Russian municipalities - Norilsk **Obv:** Head with tiara right **Rev:** Town view, shield above

Date	Mintage	F	VF	XF	Unc	BU
2011 Proof	2,000	Value: 85.00				

KM# 561 DOLLAR
28.2800 g., 0.9250 Silver 0.8410 oz. ASW, 38.61 mm. **Ruler:** Elizabeth II **Subject:** Russian municipalities - Belgorod **Obv:** Head with tiara right **Rev:** Statue at center, shield at left, tower at right

Date	Mintage	F	VF	XF	Unc	BU
2011 Proof	2,000	Value: 85.00				

KM# 562 DOLLAR
28.2800 g., 0.9250 Silver 0.8410 oz. ASW, 30x50 mm. **Ruler:** Elizabeth II **Subject:** Russian municipalities - Irkutsk **Obv:** Head with tiara right **Rev:** Town view **Shape:** Vertical oval

Date	Mintage	F	VF	XF	Unc	BU
2011 Proof	2,000	Value: 85.00				

KM# 571 DOLLAR
28.2800 g., 0.9250 Silver 0.8410 oz. ASW, 40x40 mm. **Ruler:** Elizabeth II **Obv:** Head with diadem right, tracks in background **Rev:** Flying frog, Rhacophorus reinwardti **Shape:** Square

Date	Mintage	F	VF	XF	Unc	BU
2011 Proof	5,000	Value: 75.00				

KM# 583 DOLLAR
14.1400 g., 0.9250 Silver 0.4205 oz. ASW, 32 mm. **Ruler:** Elizabeth II **Subject:** Russian comics - Bolek i Lolek **Rev:** Two western children on horseback

Date	Mintage	F	VF	XF	Unc	BU
2011 Proof	Est. 4,000	Value: 55.00				

KM# 585 DOLLAR
28.2800 g., 0.9250 Silver 0.8410 oz. ASW, 40x28 mm. **Ruler:** Elizabeth II **Obv:** Head with tiara right, five girls in painting **Rev:** Diego Velazquez and painting of female nude

Date	Mintage	F	VF	XF	Unc	BU
2011 Proof	Est. 5,000	Value: 95.00				

KM# 586 DOLLAR
28.2800 g., 0.9250 Silver 0.8410 oz. ASW, 38.61 mm. **Ruler:** Elizabeth II **Subject:** Amber Route - Aquileia **Rev:** Statue of Romulus and Remus and wolf, amber insert

Date	Mintage	F	VF	XF	Unc	BU
2011 Antique finish	Est. 10,000	—	—	—	—	85.00

KM# 617 DOLLAR
28.2800 g., 0.9250 Silver 0.8410 oz. ASW, 38.61 mm. **Ruler:** Elizabeth II **Obv:** Bust with tiara right before sailing ship in ornate frame **Rev:** Yunona and Avos facing each other in color, ship below

Date	Mintage	F	VF	XF	Unc	BU
2011 Proof	Est. 5,000	Value: 75.00				

KM# 618 DOLLAR
28.2800 g., 0.9250 Silver 0.8410 oz. ASW, 38.61 mm. **Ruler:** Elizabeth II **Obv:** Head with tiara at left, map and sailing ship at right, HANSA on ribbon above **Rev:** Town view of the port of Szczecin

Date	Mintage	F	VF	XF	Unc	BU
2011 Proof	Est. 3,000	Value: 75.00				

KM# 619 DOLLAR
28.2800 g., 0.9250 Silver 0.8410 oz. ASW, 41 mm. **Ruler:** Elizabeth II **Obv:** Head in tiara at left, elephant in designs **Rev:** Two elephants at tree, elephant in hologram

Date	Mintage	F	VF	XF	Unc	BU
2011 Proof	Est. 10,000	Value: 75.00				

KM# 621 DOLLAR
16.8100 g., 0.9250 Silver 0.4999 oz. ASW, 36.81 mm. **Ruler:** Elizabeth II **Obv:** Head with tiara right **Rev:** Chinese dragon prancing right with ball

Date	Mintage	F	VF	XF	Unc	BU
2011 Proof	Est. 6,000	Value: 75.00				

KM# 622 DOLLAR
16.8100 g., 0.9250 Silver 0.4999 oz. ASW, 36.81 mm. **Ruler:** Elizabeth II **Obv:** Head with tiara right **Rev:** Child's fantasy dragon, knight and castle

Date	Mintage	F	VF	XF	Unc	BU
2011 Proof	Est. 6,000	Value: 75.00				

KM# 641 DOLLAR
28.2800 g., 0.9250 Silver 0.8410 oz. ASW, 40x28 mm. **Ruler:** Elizabeth II **Obv:** Portrait at left, painting **Rev:** Portrait at left, painting **Shape:** Horizontal rectangle

Date	Mintage	F	VF	XF	Unc	BU
2011 Proof	5,000	Value: 100				

KM# 647 DOLLAR
31.1050 g., 0.9990 Silver 0.9990 oz. ASW, 38.61 mm. **Ruler:** Elizabeth II **Subject:** First European to cross the Simpson Desert **Obv:** Head with tiara right **Rev:** Simpson Desert and Ted Colson in 3-D color **Edge:** Reeded

Date	Mintage	F	VF	XF	Unc	BU
2011 Proof	2,000	Value: 75.00				

KM# 652 DOLLAR
28.2800 g., 0.9250 Silver 0.8410 oz. ASW, 38.61 mm. **Ruler:** Elizabeth II **Subject:** Papilio Machaon **Obv:** Head in tiara right, butterfly wing in background **Rev:** Butterfly in color

Date	Mintage	F	VF	XF	Unc	BU
2011 Proof	Est. 5,000	Value: 65.00				

KM# 653 DOLLAR
Silver Plated Copper, 40 mm. **Ruler:** Elizabeth II **Subject:** Star Wars - Obi-Wan Kenobi

Date	Mintage	F	VF	XF	Unc	BU
2011	Est. 50,000	—	—	—	—	25.00

KM# 654 DOLLAR
Silver Plated Copper, 40 mm. **Ruler:** Elizabeth II **Subject:** Star Wars - Yoda

Date	Mintage	F	VF	XF	Unc	BU
2011	Est. 50,000	—	—	—	—	25.00

KM# 655 DOLLAR
Silver Plated Copper, 40 mm. **Ruler:** Elizabeth II **Subject:** Star Wars - Princess Leia

Date	Mintage	F	VF	XF	Unc	BU
2011	Est. 50,000	—	—	—	—	25.00

KM# 656 DOLLAR
Silver Plated Copper, 40 mm. **Ruler:** Elizabeth II **Subject:** Star Wars - Luke Skywalker

Date	Mintage	F	VF	XF	Unc	BU
2011	Est. 50,000	—	—	—	—	25.00

KM# 657 DOLLAR
Silver Plated Copper, 40 mm. **Ruler:** Elizabeth II **Subject:** Star Wars - C3PO

Date	Mintage	F	VF	XF	Unc	BU
2011	Est. 50,000	—	—	—	—	25.00

KM# 658 DOLLAR
Silver Plated Copper, 40 mm. **Ruler:** Elizabeth II **Subject:** Star Wars - R2-D2

Date	Mintage	F	VF	XF	Unc	BU
2011	Est. 50,000	—	—	—	—	25.00

KM# 659 DOLLAR
Silver Plated Copper, 40 mm. **Ruler:** Elizabeth II **Subject:** Star Wars - Darth Vader

Date	Mintage	F	VF	XF	Unc	BU
2011	Est. 50,000	—	—	—	—	25.00

KM# 660 DOLLAR
Silver Plated Copper, 40 mm. **Ruler:** Elizabeth II **Subject:** Star Wars - Emperor Palpatine

Date	Mintage	F	VF	XF	Unc	BU
2011	Est. 50,000	—	—	—	—	25.00

KM# 661 DOLLAR
Silver Plated Copper, 40 mm. **Ruler:** Elizabeth II **Subject:** Star Wars - Han Solo

Date	Mintage	F	VF	XF	Unc	BU
2011	Est. 50,000	—	—	—	—	25.00

KM# 662 DOLLAR
Silver Plated Copper, 40 mm. **Ruler:** Elizabeth II **Subject:** Star Wars - Chewbacca

Date	Mintage	F	VF	XF	Unc	BU
2011	Est. 50,000	—	—	—	—	25.00

KM# 674 DOLLAR
28.2800 g., 0.9250 Silver 0.8410 oz. ASW, 40x28 mm. **Ruler:** Elizabeth II **Rev:** Orville and Wilbur Wright **Shape:** Rectangle

Date	Mintage	F	VF	XF	Unc	BU
2011 Proof	Est. 6,000	Value: 75.00				

KM# 688 DOLLAR
16.8100 g., 0.9250 Silver gilt 0.4999 oz. ASW, 38.61 mm. **Ruler:** Elizabeth II **Subject:** Amber Route **Rev:** Map of European cities

Date	Mintage	F	VF	XF	Unc	BU
2011 Proof	Est. 15,000	Value: 85.00				

KM# 690 DOLLAR
28.2800 g., 0.9250 Silver 0.8410 oz. ASW, 40.7 mm. **Ruler:** Elizabeth II **Subject:** Lucky-coin - Ladybug **Obv:** Head with tiara right, ladybug and flowers **Rev:** Ladybug and flowers

Date	Mintage	F	VF	XF	Unc	BU
2011 Proof	Est. 10,000	Value: 80.00				

KM# 703 DOLLAR
10.0000 g., 0.9250 Silver 0.2974 oz. ASW, 13x30 mm. **Ruler:** Elizabeth II **Rev:** Amber insert in gilt floral motif **Shape:** Vertical rectangle

Date	Mintage	F	VF	XF	Unc	BU
2011	Est. 12,000	—	—	—	—	50.00

KM# 704 DOLLAR
28.2800 g., 0.9250 Silver 0.8410 oz. ASW, 30x50 mm. **Ruler:** Elizabeth II **Subject:** Barcerlona Cathedral **Obv:** Cross and interior cathedral view **Rev:** Exterior cathedral view **Shape:** Oval

Date	Mintage	F	VF	XF	Unc	BU
2011 Proof	5,000	Value: 100				

KM# 705 DOLLAR
28.2800 g., 0.9250 Silver 0.8410 oz. ASW, 30x50 mm. **Ruler:** Elizabeth II **Subject:** Prague's St. Wenceslas Cathedral **Obv:** Cathedral window at top, side exterior view below **Rev:** Cathedral window and ceiling motif **Shape:** Vertical Oval

Date	Mintage	F	VF	XF	Unc	BU
2011 Proof	5,000	Value: 100				

KM# 706 DOLLAR
28.2800 g., 0.9250 Silver 0.8410 oz. ASW, 30x50 mm. **Ruler:** Elizabeth II **Subject:** Cracow's St. Mary Cathedral **Obv:** Cathedral window and sculpture scene **Rev:** Cathedral Window, exterior view and ceiling rendering **Shape:** Vertical oval

Date	Mintage	F	VF	XF	Unc	BU
2011 Proof	1,500	Value: 100				

KM# 707 DOLLAR
28.2800 g., 0.9250 Silver 0.8410 oz. ASW, 35x45 mm. **Ruler:** Elizabeth II **Subject:** Love Love Love **Obv:** Queens head within open egg design **Rev:** Two cherubs and heart **Shape:** Vertical oval

Date	Mintage	F	VF	XF	Unc	BU
2011 Proof	7,000	Value: 100				

KM# 709 DOLLAR
16.8100 g., 0.9250 Silver 0.4999 oz. ASW, 38.61 mm. **Ruler:** Elizabeth II **Obv:** Ancient horsecart **Obv. Legend:** SZLAK BURSZTYNOWY **Rev:** Neptune statue, ancient coin, mine building, amber insert **Rev. Legend:** GDANSK

Date	Mintage	F	VF	XF	Unc	BU
2011 Proof	Est. 12,000	Value: 90.00				

KM# 711 DOLLAR
14.1400 g., 0.9250 Silver 0.4205 oz. ASW, 32 mm. **Ruler:** Elizabeth II **Subject:** Russian Cartoon - Reksio **Rev:** Dog, cat and rooster in color

Date	Mintage	F	VF	XF	Unc	BU
2011 Proof	Est. 6,000	Value: 100				

KM# 741 DOLLAR
28.2800 g., 0.9250 Silver 0.8410 oz. ASW **Ruler:** Elizabeth II **Obv:** Head crowned at top, key **Rev:** Cat walking through open door **Shape:** Irregular

Date	Mintage	F	VF	XF	Unc	BU
2011 Proof	7,000	Value: 75.00				

KM# 735 DOLLAR
28.2800 g., 0.9250 Silver 0.8410 oz. ASW, 38.61 mm. **Ruler:** Elizabeth II **Subject:** Hannibal Barkas **Obv:** Two elephant heads facing each other **Rev:** Hannibal's head left above three war elephants

Date	Mintage	F	VF	XF	Unc	BU
2012 Proof	Est. 5,000	Value: 120				

KM# 644 DOLLAR
28.2800 g., 0.9250 Silver 0.8410 oz. ASW, 35.1x45.1 mm. **Ruler:** Elizabeth II **Subject:** Year of the Dragon **Obv:** Head with crown right **Rev:** Multicolor dragon **Shape:** Vertical oval

Date	Mintage	F	VF	XF	Unc	BU
2012 Proof	5,000	Value: 100				

KM# 645 DOLLAR
28.2800 g., 0.9250 Silver 0.8410 oz. ASW, 35.1x45.1 mm. **Ruler:** Elizabeth II **Subject:** Year of the Dragon **Obv:** Head with crown right **Rev:** Multicolor juvenile dragon **Shape:** Vertical oval

Date	Mintage	F	VF	XF	Unc	BU
2012 Proof	5,000	Value: 100				

KM# 646 DOLLAR
28.2800 g., 0.9250 Silver 0.8410 oz. ASW, 45.1x35.1 mm. **Ruler:** Elizabeth II **Subject:** Year of the Dragon **Obv:** Head with crown right **Rev:** Multicolor Love dragon forming heart **Shape:** Horizontal oval

Date	Mintage	F	VF	XF	Unc	BU
2012 Proof	5,000	Value: 100				

KM# 687 DOLLAR
31.1050 g., 0.9250 Silver 0.9250 oz. ASW, 39 mm. **Ruler:** Elizabeth II **Rev:** Crowned fantasy fish **Shape:** 12-sided

Date	Mintage	F	VF	XF	Unc	BU
2012 Proof	2,000	Value: 80.00				

KM# 725 DOLLAR
Nickel Plated Copper, 40.7 mm. **Ruler:** Elizabeth II **Subject:** Star Wars - Tusken Raider

Date	Mintage	F	VF	XF	Unc	BU
2012	50,000	—	—	—	—	25.00

KM# 726 DOLLAR
Nickel Plated Copper, 40.7 mm. **Ruler:** Elizabeth II **Subject:** Star Wars - Ewok Wicket

Date	Mintage	F	VF	XF	Unc	BU
2012	50,000	—	—	—	—	25.00

KM# 727 DOLLAR
Silver, 40.7 mm. **Ruler:** Elizabeth II **Subject:** Star Wars - Nien Nunb

Date	Mintage	F	VF	XF	Unc	BU
2012	50,000	—	—	—	—	25.00

KM# 728 DOLLAR
Nickel Plated Copper, 40.7 mm. **Ruler:** Elizabeth II **Subject:** Star Wars - Lando Calrissian

Date	Mintage	F	VF	XF	Unc	BU
2012	50,000	—	—	—	—	25.00

KM# 729 DOLLAR
Nickel Plated Copper, 40.7 mm. **Ruler:** Elizabeth II **Subject:** Star Wars - Grand Moff Tarkin

Date	Mintage	F	VF	XF	Unc	BU
2012	50,000	—	—	—	—	25.00

KM# 730 DOLLAR

Nickel Plated Copper, 40.7 mm. **Ruler:** Elizabeth II **Subject:** Star Wars - Stormtrooper

Date	Mintage	F	VF	XF	Unc	BU
2012	50,000	—	—	—	—	25.00

KM# 731 DOLLAR

Nickel Plated Copper, 40.7 mm. **Ruler:** Elizabeth II **Subject:** Star Wars - Jabba the Hutt

Date	Mintage	F	VF	XF	Unc	BU
2012	50,000	—	—	—	—	25.00

KM# 732 DOLLAR

Nickel Plated Copper, 40.7 mm. **Ruler:** Elizabeth II **Subject:** Star Wars - Admiral Ackbar

Date	Mintage	F	VF	XF	Unc	BU
2012	50,000	—	—	—	—	25.00

KM# 733 DOLLAR

Nickel Plated Copper, 40.7 mm. **Ruler:** Elizabeth II **Subject:** Star Wars - Jawa

Date	Mintage	F	VF	XF	Unc	BU
2012	50,000	—	—	—	—	25.00

KM# 734 DOLLAR

Nickel Plated Copper, 40.7 mm. **Ruler:** Elizabeth II **Subject:** Star Wars - Boba Fett

Date	Mintage	F	VF	XF	Unc	BU
2012	50,000	—	—	—	—	25.00

KM# 739 DOLLAR

15.5500 g., 0.9990 Silver 0.4994 oz. ASW, 36 mm. **Ruler:** Elizabeth II **Subject:** Viet Nam War, 50th Anniversary of Australia's involvement **Rev:** Two soldiers on patrol, on close, helicopter above

Date	Mintage	F	VF	XF	Unc	BU
2012 Proof	2,500	Value: 50.00				

KM# 757 DOLLAR

25.0000 g., 0.9250 Silver 0.7435 oz. ASW, 40 mm. **Ruler:** Elizabeth II **Subject:** Battle for Australia - Bombing of Darwin **Rev:** Soldier with machine gun post and Japanese plane in sky, ship in distance

Date	Mintage	F	VF	XF	Unc	BU
2012 Proof	Est. 1,942	Value: 75.00				

KM# 758 DOLLAR

25.0000 g., 0.9250 Silver 0.7435 oz. ASW, 40 mm. **Ruler:** Elizabeth II **Subject:** Battle for Australia - Sydney Harbor **Rev:** Sub, ship and pontoon plane with Sydney Harbor bridge

Date	Mintage	F	VF	XF	Unc	BU
2012 Proof	Est. 1,942	Value: 100				

KM# 759 DOLLAR

25.0000 g., 0.9250 Silver 0.7435 oz. ASW, 40 mm. **Ruler:** Elizabeth II **Subject:** Battle for Australia - Kokoda Track **Rev:** Two injured soldiers being protected by third

Date	Mintage	F	VF	XF	Unc	BU
2012 Proof	Est. 1,942	Value: 100				

KM# 760 DOLLAR

25.0000 g., 0.9250 Silver 0.7435 oz. ASW, 40 mm. **Ruler:** Elizabeth II **Subject:** Battle for Australia - Coral Sea **Rev:** Battle ship and planes

Date	Mintage	F	VF	XF	Unc	BU
2012 Proof	Est. 1,942	Value: 100				

KM# 761 DOLLAR

25.0000 g., 0.9250 Silver 0.7435 oz. ASW, 40 mm. **Ruler:** Elizabeth II **Subject:** First car to cross Australia - The Brush **Obv:** Head with crown right **Rev:** Early automobile, color landscape below

Date	Mintage	F	VF	XF	Unc	BU
2012 Proof	Est. 2,500	Value: 100				

KM# 763 DOLLAR

28.2800 g., 0.9250 Silver 0.8410 oz. ASW, 30x50 mm. **Ruler:** Elizabeth II **Rev:** Fisherman and nice trout **Rev. Legend:** BEGINNER'S LUCK **Shape:** Vertical oval

Date	Mintage	F	VF	XF	Unc	BU
2012 Proof	Est. 7,000	Value: 120				

KM# 764 DOLLAR

28.2800 g., 0.9250 Silver 0.8410 oz. ASW, 28x40 mm. **Ruler:** Elizabeth II **Subject:** Ksenia of Petersburg **Rev:** Female saint with cane, church at lower left **Shape:** Vertical rectangle

Date	Mintage	F	VF	XF	Unc	BU
2012 Proof	Est. 7,000	Value: 100				

KM# 765 DOLLAR
28.2800 g., 0.9250 Silver 0.8410 oz. ASW, 38.61 mm. **Ruler:** Elizabeth II **Subject:** Russian Cities - Kuzbas **Rev:** Statue of Worker, gear in background

Date	Mintage	F	VF	XF	Unc	BU
2012 Proof	Est. 4,000	Value: 100				

KM# 766 DOLLAR
28.2800 g., 0.9250 Silver 0.8410 oz. ASW, 38.61 mm. **Ruler:** Elizabeth II **Subject:** Russian Cities - Novosibirsk **Rev:** Church tower, bridge in distance

Date	Mintage	F	VF	XF	Unc	BU
2012 Proof	Est. 2,000	Value: 100				

KM# 767 DOLLAR
28.2800 g., 0.9250 Silver 0.8410 oz. ASW, 38.61 mm. **Ruler:** Elizabeth II **Subject:** Stars Flight **Rev:** International Space Station and Russian stamp

Date	Mintage	F	VF	XF	Unc	BU
2012 Proof	Est. 5,000	Value: 100				

KM# 768 DOLLAR
28.2800 g., 0.9250 Silver 0.8410 oz. ASW, 38.61 mm. **Ruler:** Elizabeth II **Subject:** War of 1812 - Artillery **Rev:** Soldier standing beside cannon

Date	Mintage	F	VF	XF	Unc	BU
2012 Proof	Est. 5,000	Value: 100				

KM# 769 DOLLAR
28.2800 g., 0.9250 Silver 0.8410 oz. ASW, 38.61 mm. **Ruler:** Elizabeth II **Subject:** War of 1812 - Cavalry **Rev:** Horseman with sword

Date	Mintage	F	VF	XF	Unc	BU
2012 Proof	Est. 5,000	Value: 100				

KM# 770 DOLLAR
28.2800 g., 0.9250 Silver 0.8410 oz. ASW, 38.61 mm. **Ruler:** Elizabeth II **Subject:** War of 1812 - Infantry **Rev:** Soldier with rifle

Date	Mintage	F	VF	XF	Unc	BU
2012 Proof	Est. 5,000	Value: 100				

KM# 771 DOLLAR
28.2800 g., 0.9250 Silver 0.8410 oz. ASW, 38.61 mm. **Ruler:** Elizabeth II **Subject:** War of 1812 - Generals

Date	Mintage	F	VF	XF	Unc	BU
2012 Proof	Est. 5,000	Value: 100				

KM# 772 DOLLAR
27.5000 g., Silver Plated Copper-Nickel, 40 mm. **Ruler:** Elizabeth II **Subject:** Benedict XVI's visit to Brazil, 5th Anniversary **Rev:** Statue of Nossa Senhora, image of Benedict

Date	Mintage	F	VF	XF	Unc	BU
2012 Proof	Est. 1,000	Value: 25.00				

KM# 773 DOLLAR
16.8100 g., 0.9250 Silver 0.4999 oz. ASW, 38.61 mm. **Ruler:** Elizabeth II **Subject:** Stare Hradisko **Obv:** Queen's head at left, two horse cart at right **Rev:** Celtic coin image and art, amber insert

Date	Mintage	F	VF	XF	Unc	BU
2012	Est. 12,000	Value: 65.00				

KM# 775 DOLLAR
16.8100 g., 0.9250 Silver 0.4999 oz. ASW, 29x39 mm. **Ruler:** Elizabeth II **Subject:** Imperial Faberge Eggs - Coronation egg **Rev:** Egg and state coach

Date	Mintage	F	VF	XF	Unc	BU
2012 Proof	Est. 9,999	Value: 95.00				

KM# 779 DOLLAR
16.8100 g., 0.9250 Silver 0.4999 oz. ASW, 38.61 mm. **Ruler:** Elizabeth II **Subject:** Silk Route - Wroclaw **Obv:** Queen's head at left, two horse cart at right **Rev:** Old building at left, statue at right

Date	Mintage	F	VF	XF	Unc	BU
2012 Proof	Est. 12,000	Value: 85.00				

KM# 781 DOLLAR
28.2800 g., 0.9250 Silver 0.8410 oz. ASW, 38.61 mm. **Ruler:** Elizabeth II **Subject:** March 8th, International Woman's Day **Obv:** Head with tiara right **Rev:** Flowers, date in Russian

Date	Mintage	F	VF	XF	Unc	BU
2012 Proof	Est. 2,000	Value: 75.00				

KM# 787 DOLLAR
0.3000 g., 0.9990 Gold 0.0096 oz. AGW, 11 mm. **Ruler:** Elizabeth II **Obv:** Head with tiara right **Rev:** Princess Grace of Monaco (Grace Kelly) head left

Date	Mintage	F	VF	XF	Unc	BU
2012 Proof	Est. 5,000	Value: 75.00				

KM# 790 DOLLAR
28.2800 g., 0.9250 Silver 0.8410 oz. ASW, 28x40 mm. **Ruler:** Elizabeth II **Subject:** Art of Hunting, Fox Hunt **Obv:** Pointer, left **Rev:** Fox, hounds and riders **Shape:** Vertical rectangle

Date	Mintage	F	VF	XF	Unc	BU
2012 Proof	4,000	Value: 120				

KM# 792 DOLLAR
14.1400 g., 0.9250 Silver 0.4205 oz. ASW, 49.9x32.8x9.15 mm. **Ruler:** Elizabeth II **Subject:** Swallow's Nest **Obv:** Island view **Rev:** Castle atop cliff **Shape:** Irregular

Date	Mintage	F	VF	XF	Unc	BU
2012 Proof	Est. 3,000	Value: 100				

KM# 794 DOLLAR
16.8100 g., 0.9250 Silver 0.4999 oz. ASW, 38.61 mm. **Ruler:** Elizabeth II **Subject:** Szlak Bursztynowy - Szombathely **Rev:** Old coin, building, amber insert

Date	Mintage	F	VF	XF	Unc	BU
2012 Proof	Est. 12,000	Value: 75.00				

KM# 800 DOLLAR
28.2800 g., 0.9250 Silver 0.8410 oz. ASW, 38.61 mm. **Ruler:** Elizabeth II **Rev:** Goliath Birdwing butterfly **Rev. Legend:** ORNITHOPTERA GOLIATH

Date	Mintage	F	VF	XF	Unc	BU
2012 Proof	Est. 8,000	Value: 100				

KM# 804 DOLLAR
14.1400 g., 0.9250 Silver 0.4205 oz. ASW, 37x30 mm. **Ruler:** Elizabeth II **Subject:** Me **Obv:** Queen's head with tiara right, four baloon hearts **Rev:** Bird facing left **Shape:** Irregular

Date	Mintage	F	VF	XF	Unc	BU
2012 Proof	Est. 10,000	Value: 75.00				

KM# 805 DOLLAR
14.1400 g., 0.9250 Silver 0.4205 oz. ASW, 37x30 mm. **Ruler:** Elizabeth II **Subject:** You **Obv:** Queen's head in tiara at right, three heart baloons **Rev:** Bird facing right **Shape:** Irregular

Date	Mintage	F	VF	XF	Unc	BU
2012 Proof	Est. 10,000	Value: 75.00				

KM# 828 DOLLAR
28.2800 g., 0.9250 Silver 0.8410 oz. ASW, 36.61 mm. **Ruler:** Elizabeth II **Obv:** Crowned ehad right within soccer ball motif **Rev:** Pozan stadium

Date	Mintage	F	VF	XF	Unc	BU
2012 Proof	1,000	Value: 90.00				

KM# 829 DOLLAR
28.2800 g., 0.9250 Silver 0.8410 oz. ASW, 38.61 mm. **Ruler:** Elizabeth II **Obv:** Head in tiara right within soccer ball motif **Rev:** Wroclaw stadium

Date	Mintage	F	VF	XF	Unc	BU
2012 Proof	1,000	Value: 90.00				

KM# 830 DOLLAR
28.2800 g., 0.9250 Silver 0.8410 oz. ASW, 38.61 mm. **Ruler:** Elizabeth II **Obv:** Head with tiara right within soccer ball motif **Rev:** Lviv stadium

Date	Mintage	F	VF	XF	Unc	BU
2012 Proof	1,000	Value: 90.00				

KM# 831 DOLLAR
28.2800 g., 0.9250 Silver 0.8410 oz. ASW, 38.61 mm. **Ruler:** Elizabeth II **Obv:** Head with tiara right within soccer ball motif **Rev:** Kiev stadium

Date	Mintage	F	VF	XF	Unc	BU
2012 Proof	1,000	Value: 90.00				

KM# 832 DOLLAR
28.2800 g., 0.9250 Silver 0.8410 oz. ASW, 38.61 mm. **Ruler:** Elizabeth II **Obv:** Head with tiara right within soccer ball motif **Rev:** Donetsk stadium

Date	Mintage	F	VF	XF	Unc	BU
2012 Proof	1,000	Value: 90.00				

KM# 833 DOLLAR
28.2800 g., 0.9250 Silver 0.8410 oz. ASW, 38.61 mm. **Ruler:** Elizabeth II **Obv:** Head with tiara right within soccer ball motif **Rev:** Kharkiv stadium

Date	Mintage	F	VF	XF	Unc	BU
2012 Proof	1,000	Value: 90.00				

KM# 841 DOLLAR
16.8100 g., 0.9250 Silver 0.4999 oz. ASW, 38.61 mm. **Ruler:** Elizabeth II **Subject:** Amber Route **Obv:** Head with tiara at left, cart, map **Rev:** Ruins, statue, coin and amber insert **Rev. Legend:** CARNUNTUM

Date	Mintage	F	VF	XF	Unc	BU
2012 Proof	12,000	Value: 65.00				

KM# 843 DOLLAR
16.8100 g., 0.9250 Silver 0.4999 oz. ASW, 38.61 mm. **Ruler:** Elizabeth II **Subject:** Amber Route **Obv:** Head with tiara at left, cart, map **Rev:** She-wolf statue, mosaic, coin and amber insert **Rev. Legend:** AQUILEIA

Date	Mintage	F	VF	XF	Unc	BU
2012 Proof	12,000	Value: 65.00				

KM# 847 DOLLAR
0.9990 Silver **Ruler:** Elizabeth II **Obv:** Crowned head right **Rev:** Statue of Amore and Psyche **Shape:** Irregular

Date	Mintage	F	VF	XF	Unc	BU
2012	1,000	Value: 50.00				

KM# 848 DOLLAR
0.9990 Silver **Ruler:** Elizabeth II **Obv:** Crowned head at left **Rev:** Cut out of Amor and Psyche statue **Shape:** 38.61

Date	Mintage	F	VF	XF	Unc	BU
2012 Proof	1,000	Value: 50.00				

KM# 852 DOLLAR
28.2800 g., 0.9250 Silver 0.8410 oz. ASW, 38.61 mm. **Ruler:** Elizabeth II **Subject:** Russian Municipalties - Tyra **Obv:** Crowned head right **Rev:** Ancient carving

Date	Mintage	F	VF	XF	Unc	BU
2012 Proof	2,000	Value: 100				

KM# 853 DOLLAR
20.0000 g., 0.9990 Silver 0.6423 oz. ASW, 40 mm. **Ruler:** Elizabeth II **Obv:** Crowned head right **Rev:** Vysotsky head at right

Date	Mintage	F	VF	XF	Unc	BU
2012 Proof	5,000	Value: 100				

KM# 854 DOLLAR
28.2800 g., 0.9250 Silver 0.8410 oz. ASW, 38.61 mm. **Ruler:** Elizabeth II **Obv:** Crowned head right **Rev:** Alexander Nevski at right, warriors on horseback at left.

Date	Mintage	F	VF	XF	Unc	BU
2012 Proof	5,000	Value: 100				

KM# 855 DOLLAR
16.8100 g., 0.9250 Silver 0.4999 oz. ASW, 29x39 mm. **Ruler:** Elizabeth II **Obv:** Head with tiara right above open egg **Rev:** Imperial Faberge Egg - Cockerel Egg

Date	Mintage	F	VF	XF	Unc	BU
2012 Proof	Est. 9,999	Value: 95.00				

KM# 877 DOLLAR
28.2800 g., 0.9250 Silver 0.8410 oz. ASW, 41 mm. **Ruler:** Elizabeth II **Obv:** Head with tiara right above snake insert **Rev:** Two snakes forming heart shape, snake insert below

Date	Mintage	F	VF	XF	Unc	BU
2012//2013 Proof	Est. 10,000	Value: 85.00				

KM# 878 DOLLAR
16.8100 g., 0.9250 Silver 0.4999 oz. ASW, 38.61 mm. **Ruler:** Elizabeth II **Obv:** Head with tiara right **Rev:** Snake coiled around itself

Date	Mintage	F	VF	XF	Unc	BU
2012//2013 Proof	Est. 10,000	Value: 50.00				

KM# 879 DOLLAR
28.2800 g., 0.9250 Silver 0.8410 oz. ASW, 38.61 mm. **Ruler:** Elizabeth II **Obv:** Head with tiara right **Rev:** Two rabbits holding heart

Date	Mintage	F	VF	XF	Unc	BU
2012 Proof	Est. 15,000	Value: 100				

KM# 849 DOLLAR

20.5000 g., 0.9990 Silver 0.6584 oz. ASW, 38.61 mm. **Ruler:** Elizabeth II **Obv:** Crowned head at left, coiled snake at center **Rev:** Coiled snake at center, cobra below

Date	Mintage	F	VF	XF	Unc	BU
2013 Proof	4,000	Value: 75.00				

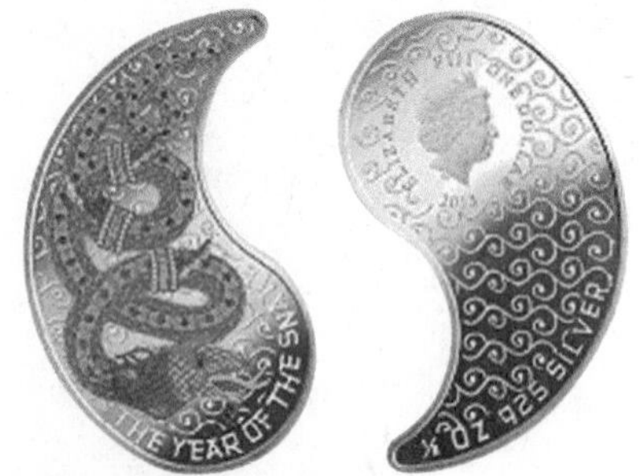

KM# 850 DOLLAR

15.5000 g., 0.9990 Silver 0.4978 oz. ASW, 50 mm. **Ruler:** Elizabeth II **Obv:** Head in tiara right, curles in background **Rev:** Colored snake **Shape:** Ying-Yang

Date	Mintage	F	VF	XF	Unc	BU
2013 Proof	5,000	Value: 55.00				

KM# 851 DOLLAR

15.5000 g., 0.9250 Silver 0.4609 oz. ASW, 50 mm. **Ruler:** Elizabeth II **Obv:** Crowned head right and waves in background **Rev:** Colored snake **Shape:** Ying-Yang

Date	Mintage	F	VF	XF	Unc	BU
2013 Proof	5,000	Value: 55.00				

KM# 861 DOLLAR

7.7700 g., 0.9990 Silver 0.2496 oz. ASW, 22.1x22.1 mm. **Ruler:** Elizabeth II **Obv:** Crowned head right **Rev:** Monopoly board corner square - Go **Shape:** Square

Date	Mintage	F	VF	XF	Unc	BU
2013 Proof	5,000	Value: 40.00				

KM# 862 DOLLAR

7.7700 g., 0.9990 Silver 0.2496 oz. ASW, 22.1x22.1 mm. **Ruler:** Elizabeth II **Obv:** Crowned head right **Rev:** Monopoly board corner square - Free Parking **Shape:** Square

Date	Mintage	F	VF	XF	Unc	BU
2013 Proof	5,000	Value: 40.00				

KM# 863 DOLLAR

7.7700 g., 0.9990 Silver 0.2496 oz. ASW, 22.1x22.1 mm. **Ruler:** Elizabeth II **Obv:** Crowned head right **Rev:** Monopoly board corner square - Go to Jail **Shape:** Square

Date	Mintage	F	VF	XF	Unc	BU
2013 Proof	5,000	Value: 40.00				

KM# 864 DOLLAR

7.7700 g., 0.9990 Silver 0.2496 oz. ASW, 22.1x22.1 mm. **Ruler:** Elizabeth II **Obv:** Crowned head right **Rev:** Monopoly board corner square - Jail **Shape:** Square

Date	Mintage	F	VF	XF	Unc	BU
2013 Proof	5,000	Value: 40.00				

KM# 868 DOLLAR

15.5500 g., 0.9990 Silver 0.4994 oz. ASW, 36 mm. **Ruler:** Elizabeth II **Obv:** Crowned head right **Rev:** Coral Snake, chinese characters above

Date	Mintage	F	VF	XF	Unc	BU
2013 Proof	8,000	Value: 50.00				

KM# 873 DOLLAR

20.0000 g., Silver Plated Copper, 38.61 mm. **Ruler:** Elizabeth II **Obv:** Crowned head right **Rev:** Snake head facing ready to bite

Date	Mintage	F	VF	XF	Unc	BU
2013 Proof-like	1,500	—	—	—	—	25.00

KM# 874 DOLLAR

28.2800 g., 0.9250 Silver 0.8410 oz. ASW, 35x45 mm. **Ruler:** Elizabeth II **Obv:** Crowned head right **Rev:** Snake in color, coiled and raised up **Shape:** Vertical oval

Date	Mintage	F	VF	XF	Unc	BU
2013 Proof	3,000	Value: 100				

KM# 875 DOLLAR

28.2800 g., 0.9250 Silver 0.8410 oz. ASW, 35x45 mm. **Ruler:** Elizabeth II **Obv:** Crowned head right **Rev:** Humorous baby snale in color **Shape:** Vertical oval

Date	Mintage	F	VF	XF	Unc	BU
2013 Proof	7,000	Value: 100				

KM# 876 DOLLAR

28.2800 g., 0.9250 Silver 0.8410 oz. ASW, 35x45 mm. **Ruler:** Elizabeth II **Obv:** Crowned head right **Rev:** Love snake, coiled up as heart **Shape:** Vertical oval

Date	Mintage	F	VF	XF	Unc	BU
2013 Proof	7,000	Value: 100				

KM# 265 2 DOLLARS

62.2100 g., 0.9990 Silver 1.9980 oz. ASW, 55 mm. **Ruler:** Elizabeth II **Subject:** Year of the Rooster **Rev:** Multicolor rooster standing right, sunrise

Date	Mintage	F	VF	XF	Unc	BU
2005 Proof	—	Value: 85.00				

KM# 294 2 DOLLARS

62.2000 g., 0.9990 Silver 1.9977 oz. ASW, 55 mm. **Ruler:** Elizabeth II **Subject:** Year of the Dog **Rev:** Multicolor dog

Date	Mintage	F	VF	XF	Unc	BU
2005 Proof	—	Value: 95.00				

KM# 269 2 DOLLARS

1.2400 g., 0.9990 Gold 0.0398 oz. AGW, 14 mm. **Ruler:** Elizabeth II **Subject:** Year of the Rooster

Date	Mintage	F	VF	XF	Unc	BU
2005 Proof	—	Value: 80.00				

KM# 270 2 DOLLARS

1.5600 g., 0.9990 Gold 0.0501 oz. AGW, 18 mm. **Ruler:** Elizabeth II **Subject:** Year of the Rooster

Date	Mintage	F	VF	XF	Unc	BU
2005 Proof	—	Value: 110				

KM# 271 2 DOLLARS

3.1100 g., 0.9990 Gold 0.0999 oz. AGW, 18 mm. **Ruler:** Elizabeth II **Subject:** Year of the Rooster

Date	Mintage	F	VF	XF	Unc	BU
2005 Proof	—	Value: 185				

KM# 278 2 DOLLARS

3.1100 g., 0.9990 Gold 0.0999 oz. AGW, 18 mm. **Ruler:** Elizabeth II **Subject:** Chinese space achievements **Rev:** Multicolor rocket, flag, map

Date	Mintage	F	VF	XF	Unc	BU
2005 Proof	Est. 3,000	Value: 195				

KM# 279 2 DOLLARS

31.1050 g., 0.9990 Silver 0.9990 oz. ASW, 35x46 mm. **Ruler:** Elizabeth II **Subject:** Impressionist paintings **Rev:** Multicolor painting of a bridge **Shape:** Vertical rectangle

Date	Mintage	F	VF	XF	Unc	BU
2005 Proof	Est. 2,005	Value: 65.00				

KM# 280 2 DOLLARS

31.1050 g., 0.9990 Silver 0.9990 oz. ASW, 35x46 mm. **Ruler:** Elizabeth II **Subject:** Impressionist paintings **Rev:** Multicolor painting of a female **Shape:** Vertical rectangle

Date	Mintage	F	VF	XF	Unc	BU
2005 Proof	Est. 2,005	Value: 65.00				

KM# 281 2 DOLLARS

31.1050 g., 0.9990 Silver 0.9990 oz. ASW, 35x46 mm. **Ruler:** Elizabeth II **Subject:** Impressionists paintings **Rev:** Multicolor painting of a village **Shape:** Vertical rectangle

Date	Mintage	F	VF	XF	Unc	BU
2005 Proof	Est. 2,005	Value: 65.00				

KM# 282 2 DOLLARS

31.1050 g., 0.9990 Silver 0.9990 oz. ASW, 35x46 mm. **Ruler:** Elizabeth II **Subject:** Impressionists paintings **Rev:** Multicolor painting of a seaside **Shape:** Vertical rectangle

Date	Mintage	F	VF	XF	Unc	BU
2005 Proof	Est. 2,005	Value: 65.00				

KM# 283 2 DOLLARS

31.1050 g., 0.9990 Silver 0.9990 oz. ASW, 35x46 mm. **Ruler:** Elizabeth II **Subject:** Impressionists paintings **Rev:** Multicolor painting of Paris **Shape:** Vertical rectangle

Date	Mintage	F	VF	XF	Unc	BU
2005 Proof	Est. 2,005	Value: 65.00				

KM# 284 2 DOLLARS

31.1050 g., 0.9990 Silver 0.9990 oz. ASW, 35x46 mm. **Ruler:** Elizabeth II **Subject:** Impressionists paintings **Rev:** Multicolor painting of female **Shape:** Vertical rectangle

Date	Mintage	F	VF	XF	Unc	BU
2005 Proof	Est. 2,005	Value: 65.00				

KM# 285 2 DOLLARS

31.1050 g., 0.9990 Silver 0.9990 oz. ASW, 35x46 mm. **Ruler:** Elizabeth II **Subject:** Impressionist paintings **Rev:** Multicolor painting of dancers **Shape:** Vertical rectangle

Date	Mintage	F	VF	XF	Unc	BU
2005 Proof	Est. 2,005	Value: 65.00				

KM# 286 2 DOLLARS

31.1050 g., 0.9990 Silver 0.9990 oz. ASW, 35x46 mm. **Ruler:** Elizabeth II **Subject:** Impressionists paintings **Rev:** Multicolor painting of Fifer **Shape:** Vertical rectangle

Date	Mintage	F	VF	XF	Unc	BU
2005 Proof	Est. 2,005	Value: 65.00				

KM# 287 2 DOLLARS

31.1050 g., 0.9990 Silver 0.9990 oz. ASW, 35x46 mm. **Ruler:** Elizabeth II **Subject:** Impressionists paintings **Rev:** Multicolor painting of boats **Shape:** Vertical rectangle

Date	Mintage	F	VF	XF	Unc	BU
2005 Proof	Est. 2,005	Value: 65.00				

KM# 288 2 DOLLARS

31.1050 g., 0.9990 Silver 0.9990 oz. ASW, 35x46 mm. **Ruler:** Elizabeth II **Subject:** Impressionists paintings **Obv:** Multicolor painting of Paris scene **Shape:** Vertical rectangle

Date	Mintage	F	VF	XF	Unc	BU
2005 Proof	Est. 2,005	Value: 65.00				

KM# 289 2 DOLLARS

31.1050 g., 0.9990 Silver 0.9990 oz. ASW, 35x46 mm. **Ruler:** Elizabeth II **Subject:** Impressionists paintings **Rev:** Multicolor painting of a maiden **Shape:** Vertical rectangle

Date	Mintage	F	VF	XF	Unc	BU
2005 Proof	Est. 2,005	Value: 65.00				

KM# 290 2 DOLLARS

31.1050 g., 0.9990 Silver 0.9990 oz. ASW, 35x46 mm. **Ruler:** Elizabeth II **Subject:** Impresionists paintings **Rev:** Multicolor painting of an artist **Shape:** Vertical rectangle

Date	Mintage	F	VF	XF	Unc	BU
2005 Proof	Est. 2,005	Value: 65.00				

KM# 291 2 DOLLARS

31.1050 g., 0.9990 Silver 0.9990 oz. ASW, 35x46 mm. **Ruler:** Elizabeth II **Subject:** Impressionists paintings **Rev:** Multicolor painting of Canada **Shape:** Vertical rectangle

Date	Mintage	F	VF	XF	Unc	BU
2005 Proof	Est. 2,005	Value: 65.00				

KM# 298 2 DOLLARS

1.5600 g., 0.9990 Gold 0.0501 oz. AGW, 16 mm. **Ruler:** Elizabeth II **Subject:** Year of the Dog **Rev:** Multicolor dog

Date	Mintage	F	VF	XF	Unc	BU
2005 Proof	—	Value: 95.00				

KM# 299 2 DOLLARS
3.1100 g., 0.9990 Gold 0.0999 oz. AGW, 18 mm. **Ruler:** Elizabeth II **Subject:** Year of the Dog **Rev:** Multicolor dog

Date	Mintage	F	VF	XF	Unc	BU
2005 Proof	—	Value: 185				

KM# 330 2 DOLLARS
62.2000 g., 0.9990 Silver 1.9977 oz. ASW, 30x70 mm. **Ruler:** Elizabeth II **Subject:** Life of Christ **Rev:** Last Supper (1495) **Shape:** Vertical rectangle

Date	Mintage	F	VF	XF	Unc	BU
2006 Proof	Est. 1,000	Value: 175				

KM# 190 2 DOLLARS
1.5000 g., 0.9990 Gold 0.0482 oz. AGW **Ruler:** Elizabeth II **Subject:** Year of the Pig **Obv:** Head right **Rev:** Multicolor pig

Date	Mintage	F	VF	XF	Unc	BU
2007 Proof	—	Value: 95.00				

KM# 205 2 DOLLARS
31.1050 g., 0.9990 Silver 0.9990 oz. ASW, 40.7 mm. **Ruler:** Elizabeth II **Subject:** Peoples Republic of China, 60th Anniversary **Rev:** Dragon and scenes of China in multicolor

Date	Mintage	F	VF	XF	Unc	BU
2008 Proof	6,888	Value: 150				

KM# 214 2 DOLLARS
62.2100 g., 0.9990 Silver 1.9980 oz. ASW, 63x27 mm. **Ruler:** Elizabeth II **Subject:** Feng Shui **Rev:** Multicolor blossoming peonies **Shape:** Vertical rectangle

Date	Mintage	F	VF	XF	Unc	BU
2009 Prooflike	16,888	—	—	—	—	200

KM# 185 2 DOLLARS
31.1050 g., 0.9990 Silver Partially gilt 0.9990 oz. ASW, 40 mm. **Ruler:** Elizabeth II **Subject:** Year of the Ox **Rev:** Gilt ox advancing left

Date	Mintage	F	VF	XF	Unc	BU
2009 Proof	20,000	Value: 185				

KM# 199 2 DOLLARS
25.0000 g., 0.9250 Silver 0.7435 oz. ASW, 38.6 mm. **Ruler:** Elizabeth II **Rev:** Two spinner dolphins leaping, swarovski crystal chip in eye

Date	Mintage	F	VF	XF	Unc	BU
2009 Proof	2,500	Value: 50.00				

KM# 200 2 DOLLARS
0.5000 g., 0.9990 Gold 0.0161 oz. AGW, 11 mm. **Ruler:** Elizabeth II **Rev:** Two spinner dolphins leaping out of the water

Date	Mintage	F	VF	XF	Unc	BU
2009 Proof	10,000	Value: 50.00				

KM# 209 2 DOLLARS
1.0000 g., 0.9000 Gold 0.0289 oz. AGW **Ruler:** Elizabeth II **Subject:** Frederic Chopin **Obv:** Elizabeth II head right **Rev:** Chopin bust and autograph

Date	Mintage	F	VF	XF	Unc	BU
2009 Proof	10,000	Value: 100				

KM# 210 2 DOLLARS
31.1050 g., 0.9990 Silver 0.9990 oz. ASW, 40.7 mm. **Ruler:** Elizabeth II **Obv:** Head right **Rev:** Two black swans, multicolor

Date	Mintage	F	VF	XF	Unc	BU
2009 Proof	10,000	Value: 80.00				

KM# 215 2 DOLLARS
31.1050 g., 0.9990 Silver 0.9990 oz. ASW, 40 mm. **Ruler:** Elizabeth II **Subject:** Russian Ballet **Rev:** Anna Pavlova in multicolor

Date	Mintage	F	VF	XF	Unc	BU
2009 Prooflike	5,000	—	—	—	—	120

KM# 216 2 DOLLARS
31.1030 g., 0.9990 Silver 0.9989 oz. ASW, 40.7 mm. **Ruler:** Elizabeth II **Subject:** Russian Ballet **Rev:** Matilda Kshesinskaya in multicolor

Date	Mintage	F	VF	XF	Unc	BU
2009 Prooflike	10,000	—	—	—	—	100

KM# 217 2 DOLLARS
31.1050 g., 0.9990 Silver 0.9990 oz. ASW, 40.7 mm. **Ruler:** Elizabeth II **Subject:** Russian Ballet **Rev:** Sergey Lefar in multicolor

Date	Mintage	F	VF	XF	Unc	BU
2009 Prooflike	10,000	—	—	—	—	100

KM# 218 2 DOLLARS
31.1050 g., 0.9990 Silver 0.9990 oz. ASW, 40.7 mm. **Ruler:** Elizabeth II **Subject:** Russian Ballet **Rev:** Sergi Daighilev in multicolor

Date	Mintage	F	VF	XF	Unc	BU
2009 Prooflike	10,000	—	—	—	—	100

KM# 219 2 DOLLARS
31.1030 g., 0.9990 Silver 0.9989 oz. ASW, 40.7 mm. **Ruler:** Elizabeth II **Subject:** Russian Ballet **Rev:** Vaslav Fomich Nijinsky

Date	Mintage	F	VF	XF	Unc	BU
2009 Prooflike	10,000	—	—	—	—	100

KM# 220 2 DOLLARS
31.1050 g., 0.9990 Silver 0.9990 oz. ASW, 40.7 mm. **Ruler:** Elizabeth II **Subject:** Panagyurishte Treasure **Rev:** Vessel in the shape of a female head right

Date	Mintage	F	VF	XF	Unc	BU
2009	5,000	—	—	—	—	120

KM# 221 2 DOLLARS
31.1050 g., 0.9990 Silver 0.9990 oz. ASW, 40.7 mm. **Ruler:** Elizabeth II **Subject:** Panagyurishte Treasure **Rev:** Vessel in shape of female head left

Date	Mintage	F	VF	XF	Unc	BU
2009	5,000	—	—	—	—	120

KM# 222 2 DOLLARS
31.1050 g., 0.9990 Silver 0.9990 oz. ASW, 40.7 mm. **Ruler:** Elizabeth II **Subject:** Panagyurishte Treasure **Rev:** Vessel in shape of ram's head

Date	Mintage	F	VF	XF	Unc	BU
2009	5,000	—	—	—	—	120

KM# 223 2 DOLLARS
31.1050 g., 0.9990 Silver 0.9990 oz. ASW, 40 mm. **Ruler:** Elizabeth II **Subject:** Peoples Republic of China, 60th Anniversary **Rev:** Multicolor background, astronaut, olympic flame and dragon motifs

Date	Mintage	F	VF	XF	Unc	BU
2009 Prooflike	6,888	—	—	—	—	95.00

KM# 224 2 DOLLARS
31.1050 g., 0.9990 Silver 0.9990 oz. ASW, 40.7 mm. **Ruler:** Elizabeth II **Series:** Soviet Automobiles **Rev:** GAZ 12 ZIM in multicolor

Date	Mintage	F	VF	XF	Unc	BU
2009 Prooflike	15,000	—	—	—	—	80.00

KM# 225 2 DOLLARS
31.1050 g., 0.9990 Silver 0.9990 oz. ASW, 40.7 mm. **Ruler:** Elizabeth II **Subject:** Soviet Automobiles **Rev:** GAZ M290 Pobeda in multicolor

Date	Mintage	F	VF	XF	Unc	BU
2009 Prooflike	15,000	—	—	—	—	80.00

KM# 226 2 DOLLARS
31.1050 g., 0.9990 Silver 0.9990 oz. ASW, 40.7 mm. **Ruler:** Elizabeth II **Subject:** Soviet Automobiles **Rev:** GAZ M21 Volga

Date	Mintage	F	VF	XF	Unc	BU
2009 Prooflike	15,000	—	—	—	—	80.00

KM# 227 2 DOLLARS

31.1050 g., 0.9990 Silver 0.9990 oz. ASW, 40.7 mm. **Ruler:** Elizabeth II **Subject:** Soviet Automobiles **Rev:** Moskvich 400

Date	Mintage	F	VF	XF	Unc	BU
2009 Prooflike	15,000	—	—	—	—	80.00

KM# 229 2 DOLLARS

31.1050 g., 0.9990 Silver partially gilt 0.9990 oz. ASW, 40 mm. **Ruler:** Elizabeth II **Subject:** Year of the Ox **Rev:** Ox, partially gilt

Date	Mintage	F	VF	XF	Unc	BU
2009 Proof	2,000	Value: 100				

KM# 350 2 DOLLARS

25.0000 g., 0.9990 Silver 0.8029 oz. ASW, 38.61 mm. **Ruler:** Elizabeth II **Rev:** Partridge in a pear tree

Date	Mintage	F	VF	XF	Unc	BU
2009	1,500	Value: 70.00				

KM# 351 2 DOLLARS

25.0000 g., 0.9990 Silver 0.8029 oz. ASW, 38.61 mm. **Ruler:** Elizabeth II **Rev:** Two turtle doves

Date	Mintage	F	VF	XF	Unc	BU
2009 Proof	1,500	Value: 70.00				

KM# 352 2 DOLLARS

25.0000 g., 0.9990 Silver 0.8029 oz. ASW, 38.61 mm. **Ruler:** Elizabeth II **Rev:** Three French hens

Date	Mintage	F	VF	XF	Unc	BU
2009 Proof	1,500	Value: 70.00				

KM# 353 2 DOLLARS

25.0000 g., 0.9990 Silver 0.8029 oz. ASW, 38.61 mm. **Ruler:** Elizabeth II **Rev:** Four calling birds

Date	Mintage	F	VF	XF	Unc	BU
2009 Proof	1,500	Value: 70.00				

KM# 354 2 DOLLARS

25.0000 g., 0.9990 Silver 0.8029 oz. ASW, 38.61 mm. **Ruler:** Elizabeth II **Rev:** Five golden rings

Date	Mintage	F	VF	XF	Unc	BU
2009 Proof	1,500	Value: 70.00				

KM# 355 2 DOLLARS

25.0000 g., 0.9990 Silver 0.8029 oz. ASW, 38.61 mm. **Ruler:** Elizabeth II **Rev:** Six Geese a-laying

Date	Mintage	F	VF	XF	Unc	BU
2009 Proof	1,500	Value: 70.00				

KM# 356 2 DOLLARS

25.0000 g., 0.9990 Silver 0.8029 oz. ASW, 38.61 mm. **Ruler:** Elizabeth II **Rev:** Seven swans a-swimming

Date	Mintage	F	VF	XF	Unc	BU
2009 Proof	1,500	Value: 70.00				

KM# 357 2 DOLLARS

25.0000 g., 0.9990 Silver 0.8029 oz. ASW, 38.61 mm. **Ruler:** Elizabeth II **Rev:** Eight maids a-milking

Date	Mintage	F	VF	XF	Unc	BU
2009 Proof	1,500	Value: 70.00				

KM# 358 2 DOLLARS

25.0000 g., 0.9990 Silver 0.8029 oz. ASW, 38.61 mm. **Ruler:** Elizabeth II **Rev:** Nine ladies dancing

Date	Mintage	F	VF	XF	Unc	BU
2009 Proof	1,500	Value: 70.00				

KM# 359 2 DOLLARS

25.0000 g., 0.9990 Silver 0.8029 oz. ASW, 38.61 mm. **Ruler:** Elizabeth II **Rev:** Ten Lords a-leaping

Date	Mintage	F	VF	XF	Unc	BU
2009 Proof	1,500	Value: 70.00				

KM# 360 2 DOLLARS

25.0000 g., 0.9990 Silver 0.8029 oz. ASW, 38.61 mm. **Ruler:** Elizabeth II **Rev:** Eleven Pipers Piping

Date	Mintage	F	VF	XF	Unc	BU
2009 Proof	1,500	Value: 70.00				

KM# 361 2 DOLLARS

25.0000 g., 0.9990 Silver 0.8029 oz. ASW, 38.61 mm. **Ruler:** Elizabeth II **Rev:** Twelve drummers drumming

Date	Mintage	F	VF	XF	Unc	BU
2009 Proof	1,500	Value: 70.00				

KM# 362 2 DOLLARS

62.2000 g., 0.9990 Silver 1.9977 oz. ASW, 63x27 mm. **Ruler:** Elizabeth II **Rev:** Flowers **Shape:** Vertical rectangle

Date	Mintage	F	VF	XF	Unc	BU
2009 Proof	16,888	Value: 110				

KM# 363 2 DOLLARS

1.0000 g., 0.9990 Gold 0.0321 oz. AGW, 12 mm. **Ruler:** Elizabeth II **Rev:** Chopin bust

Date	Mintage	F	VF	XF	Unc	BU
2009 Proof	10,000	Value: 80.00				

KM# 552 2 DOLLARS

Silver **Ruler:** Elizabeth II **Subject:** Russian Cartoons

Date	Mintage	F	VF	XF	Unc	BU
2009 Proof	—	Value: 75.00				

KM# 553 2 DOLLARS

Silver **Ruler:** Elizabeth II **Subject:** Russian Cartoons

Date	Mintage	F	VF	XF	Unc	BU
2009 Proof	—	Value: 75.00				

KM# 206 2 DOLLARS

31.1050 g., 0.9990 Silver 0.9990 oz. ASW, 40.7 mm. **Ruler:** Elizabeth II **Rev:** Two white swans, red heart in background

Date	Mintage	F	VF	XF	Unc	BU
2010 Proof	20,000	Value: 65.00				

KM# 213 2 DOLLARS

56.6000 g., 0.9250 Silver 1.6832 oz. ASW, 55.6x41.6 mm. **Ruler:** Elizabeth II **Subject:** Coronation Egg **Obv:** Open egg - Queen Elizabeth head right **Rev:** Faberge Egg and coach **Shape:** Vertical oval

Date	Mintage	F	VF	XF	Unc	BU
2010	5,000	—	—	—	—	100

KM# 228 2 DOLLARS

31.1050 g., 0.9990 Silver 0.9990 oz. ASW, 40 mm. **Ruler:** Elizabeth II **Subject:** Gai Thong Hanh, Safe Conduct Pass **Rev:** Viet Nam flag and soldiers, partially gilt

Date	Mintage	F	VF	XF	Unc	BU
2010 Proof	5,000	Value: 140				

KM# 233 2 DOLLARS

62.2100 g., 0.9990 Silver partially gilt 1.9980 oz. ASW, 40 mm. **Ruler:** Elizabeth II **Subject:** Year of the Tiger **Rev:** Tiger partially gilt

Date	Mintage	F	VF	XF	Unc	BU
2010 Proof	20,000	Value: 120				

KM# 237 2 DOLLARS

1.0000 g., 0.9000 Gold 0.0289 oz. AGW, 12 mm. **Ruler:** Elizabeth II **Obv:** Head right **Rev:** Copernicus bust 3/4 left

Date	Mintage	F	VF	XF	Unc	BU
2010 Proof	5,000	Value: 75.00				

KM# 245 2 DOLLARS

31.1030 g., 0.9990 Silver 0.9989 oz. ASW, 40.7 mm. **Ruler:** Elizabeth II **Subject:** Famous express trains - Trans Siberian Express **Rev:** Steam train traveling left, multicolor

Date	Mintage	F	VF	XF	Unc	BU
2010 Proof	15,000	Value: 80.00				

KM# 246 2 DOLLARS
31.1030 g., 0.9990 Silver 0.9989 oz. ASW, 40.7 mm. **Ruler:** Elizabeth II **Subject:** Famous express trains **Rev:** British Railways Flying Scotsman locomotive right, multicolor

Date	Mintage	F	VF	XF	Unc	BU
2010 Proof	15,000	Value: 80.00				

KM# 247 2 DOLLARS
31.1030 g., 0.9990 Silver 0.9989 oz. ASW, 40.7 mm. **Ruler:** Elizabeth II **Subject:** Famous express trains - Orient Express **Rev:** Steam train right, multicolor

Date	Mintage	F	VF	XF	Unc	BU
2010 Proof	15,000	Value: 80.00				

KM# 248 2 DOLLARS
31.1030 g., 0.9990 Silver 0.9989 oz. ASW, 40.7 mm. **Ruler:** Elizabeth II **Subject:** Famous Express trains - 20th Century Limited **Rev:** Streamlined steam train left, multicolored

Date	Mintage	F	VF	XF	Unc	BU
2010 Proof	15,000	Value: 80.00				

KM# 249 2 DOLLARS
31.1050 g., 0.9990 Silver 0.9990 oz. ASW, 40.7 mm. **Ruler:** Elizabeth II **Subject:** Love is precious **Rev:** Two white swans and red floral heart

Date	Mintage	F	VF	XF	Unc	BU
2010 Proof	20,000	Value: 90.00				

KM# 252 2 DOLLARS
31.1050 g., 0.9990 Silver 0.9990 oz. ASW, 38.6 mm. **Ruler:** Elizabeth II **Subject:** Peanuts 60th Anniversary **Rev:** Charlie Brown with Snoopy and birthday cake

Date	Mintage	F	VF	XF	Unc	BU
2010 Prooflike	3,000	—	—	—	—	80.00

KM# 253 2 DOLLARS
31.1050 g., 0.9990 Silver 0.9990 oz. ASW, 38.6 mm. **Ruler:** Elizabeth II **Subject:** Peanuts 60th Anniversary **Rev:** Schroeder and Lucy by piano

Date	Mintage	F	VF	XF	Unc	BU
2010 Prooflike	3,000	—	—	—	—	80.00

KM# 371 2 DOLLARS
56.5600 g., 0.9250 Silver 1.6820 oz. ASW, 55.6x41.6 mm. **Ruler:** Elizabeth II **Subject:** Faberge egg - Lily of the Valley **Obv:** Elizabeth II head right, open egg **Rev:** Egg on stand **Shape:** Vertical oval

Date	Mintage	F	VF	XF	Unc	BU
2010 Proof	7,000	Value: 100				

KM# 373 2 DOLLARS
31.1050 g., 0.9990 Silver 0.9990 oz. ASW, 37.1x31.9 mm. **Ruler:** Elizabeth II **Subject:** Kiki Lala **Shape:** Heart with ribbon

Date	Mintage	F	VF	XF	Unc	BU
2010 Proof	Est. 3,000	Value: 60.00				

KM# 374 2 DOLLARS
31.1050 g., 0.9990 Silver 0.9990 oz. ASW, 37.1x31.9 mm. **Ruler:** Elizabeth II **Subject:** My Melo **Shape:** Heart with ribbon

Date	Mintage	F	VF	XF	Unc	BU
2010 Proof	Est. 3,000	Value: 60.00				

KM# 381 2 DOLLARS
31.1050 g., 0.9990 Silver 0.9990 oz. ASW, 40.2 mm. **Ruler:** Elizabeth II **Subject:** Russian Musicians **Rev:** Viktor Tsoy at lower right in multicolor

Date	Mintage	F	VF	XF	Unc	BU
2010 Proof	2,000	Value: 65.00				

KM# 382 2 DOLLARS
31.1050 g., 0.9990 Silver 0.9990 oz. ASW, 40.2 mm. **Ruler:** Elizabeth II **Subject:** Russian Musicians **Rev:** Vladimir Vysotsky at lower right in multicolor

Date	Mintage	F	VF	XF	Unc	BU
2010 Proof	2,000	Value: 65.00				

KM# 383 2 DOLLARS
31.1050 g., 0.9990 Silver 0.9990 oz. ASW **Ruler:** Elizabeth II **Rev:** Portrait in multicolor

Date	Mintage	F	VF	XF	Unc	BU
2010 Proof	Est. 2,000	Value: 65.00				

KM# 384 2 DOLLARS
31.1050 g., 0.9990 Silver 0.9990 oz. ASW, 38.61 mm. **Ruler:** Elizabeth II **Subject:** Miffy with friends

Date	Mintage	F	VF	XF	Unc	BU
2010 Proof	Est. 3,000	Value: 60.00				

KM# 385 2 DOLLARS
31.1050 g., 0.9990 Silver 0.9990 oz. ASW, 38.61 mm. **Ruler:** Elizabeth II **Subject:** Miffy on turtle

Date	Mintage	F	VF	XF	Unc	BU
2010 Proof	Est. 3,000	Value: 60.00				

KM# 386 2 DOLLARS
31.1050 g., 0.9990 Silver 0.9990 oz. ASW, 38.61 mm. **Ruler:** Elizabeth II **Subject:** Miffy celebration

Date	Mintage	F	VF	XF	Unc	BU
2010 Proof	Est. 3,000	Value: 60.00				

KM# 390 2 DOLLARS
31.1030 g., 0.9990 Silver 0.9989 oz. ASW, 40.7 mm. **Ruler:** Elizabeth II **Subject:** Yamal **Rev:** Child wearing fur coat in multicolor

Date	Mintage	F	VF	XF	Unc	BU
2010 Proof	5,000	Value: 55.00				

KM# 391 2 DOLLARS
31.1030 g., 0.9990 Silver 0.9989 oz. ASW, 40.7 mm. **Ruler:** Elizabeth II **Subject:** Yamal **Rev:** Gas and Oil exploration in multicolor

Date	Mintage	F	VF	XF	Unc	BU
2010 Proof	5,000	Value: 55.00				

KM# 408 2 DOLLARS
31.1030 g., 0.9990 Silver 0.9989 oz. ASW, 40.7 mm. **Ruler:** Elizabeth II **Series:** Russian Transport **Obv:** Head with tiara right **Rev:** Bus in multicolor

Date	Mintage	F	VF	XF	Unc	BU
2010 Proof	15,000	Value: 60.00				

KM# 409 2 DOLLARS
31.1030 g., 0.9990 Silver 0.9989 oz. ASW, 40.7 mm. **Ruler:** Elizabeth II **Subject:** Russian Transport **Obv:** Head with tiara right **Rev:** Trolley Bus in multicolor

Date	Mintage	F	VF	XF	Unc	BU
2010 Proof	15,000	Value: 60.00				

KM# 410 2 DOLLARS
31.1030 g., 0.9990 Silver 0.9989 oz. ASW, 40.7 mm. **Ruler:** Elizabeth II **Subject:** Russian Transport **Obv:** Head with tiara right **Rev:** Metro in color

Date	Mintage	F	VF	XF	Unc	BU
2010 Proof	15,000	Value: 60.00				

KM# 411 2 DOLLARS
31.1030 g., 0.9990 Silver 0.9989 oz. ASW, 40.7 mm. **Ruler:** Elizabeth II **Subject:** Russian Transport **Obv:** Head with tiara right **Rev:** Tram in color

Date	Mintage	F	VF	XF	Unc	BU
2010 Proof	15,000	Value: 60.00				

KM# 416 2 DOLLARS
28.2800 g., 0.9250 Silver 0.8410 oz. ASW, 38.61 mm. **Ruler:** Elizabeth II **Obv:** Head with tiara right **Rev:** Kirovo Chepetsk

Date	Mintage	F	VF	XF	Unc	BU
2010 Proof	2,000	Value: 75.00				

KM# 424 2 DOLLARS
56.5600 g., 0.9250 Silver 1.6820 oz. ASW, 41.6x55.6 mm. **Ruler:** Elizabeth II **Subject:** Faberge Imperial Eggs - Clover Leaf **Obv:** Head with tiara right above opened egg **Rev:** Egg on stand in color **Shape:** Vertical oval

Date	Mintage	F	VF	XF	Unc	BU
2010 Proof	7,000	Value: 125				

KM# 431 2 DOLLARS
1.0000 g., 0.9000 Silver 0.0289 oz. ASW, 12 mm. **Ruler:** Elizabeth II **Subject:** Tadeusz Kosciuszko **Obv:** Head with tiara right **Rev:** Head left, signature below

Date	Mintage	F	VF	XF	Unc	BU
2010 Proof	5,000	Value: 50.00				

KM# 442 2 DOLLARS
25.0000 g., 0.9250 Silver 0.7435 oz. ASW, 38.61 mm. **Ruler:** Elizabeth II **Subject:** Twelve days of Christmas **Rev:** Partridge in a pear tree

Date	Mintage	F	VF	XF	Unc	BU
2010 Proof	1,500	Value: 60.00				

KM# 443 2 DOLLARS
25.0000 g., 0.9250 Silver 0.7435 oz. ASW, 38.61 mm. **Ruler:** Elizabeth II **Subject:** Twelve days of Christmas **Rev:** Turtle dove

Date	Mintage	F	VF	XF	Unc	BU
2010 Proof	1,500	Value: 60.00				

KM# 444 2 DOLLARS
25.0000 g., 0.9250 Silver 0.7435 oz. ASW, 38.61 mm. **Ruler:** Elizabeth II **Subject:** Twelve days of Christmas **Rev:** French hen

Date	Mintage	F	VF	XF	Unc	BU
2010 Proof	1,500	Value: 60.00				

KM# 445 2 DOLLARS
25.0000 g., 0.9250 Silver 0.7435 oz. ASW **Ruler:** Elizabeth II **Subject:** Twelve days of Christmas **Rev:** Calling bird

Date	Mintage	F	VF	XF	Unc	BU
2010 Proof	1,500	Value: 60.00				

KM# 446 2 DOLLARS
25.0000 g., 0.9250 Silver 0.7435 oz. ASW, 38.61 mm. **Ruler:** Elizabeth II **Subject:** Twelve days of Christmas **Rev:** Golden rings

Date	Mintage	F	VF	XF	Unc	BU
2010 Proof	1,500	Value: 60.00				

KM# 447 2 DOLLARS
25.0000 g., 0.9250 Silver 0.7435 oz. ASW, 38.61 mm. **Ruler:** Elizabeth II **Subject:** Twelve days of Christmas **Rev:** Geese a laying

Date	Mintage	F	VF	XF	Unc	BU
2010 Proof	1,500	Value: 60.00				

KM# 448 2 DOLLARS
25.0000 g., 0.9250 Silver 0.7435 oz. ASW, 38.61 mm. **Ruler:** Elizabeth II **Subject:** Twelve days of Christmas **Rev:** Swans a swimming

Date	Mintage	F	VF	XF	Unc	BU
2010 Proof	1,500	Value: 60.00				

KM# 449 2 DOLLARS
25.0000 g., 0.9250 Silver 0.7435 oz. ASW, 38.61 mm. **Ruler:** Elizabeth II **Subject:** Twelve days of Christmas **Rev:** Maids a milking

Date	Mintage	F	VF	XF	Unc	BU
2010 Proof	1,500	Value: 60.00				

KM# 450 2 DOLLARS
25.0000 g., 0.9250 Silver 0.7435 oz. ASW, 38.61 mm. **Ruler:** Elizabeth II **Subject:** Twelve days of Christmas **Rev:** Ladies dancing

Date	Mintage	F	VF	XF	Unc	BU
2010 Proof	1,500	Value: 60.00				

KM# 451 2 DOLLARS
25.0000 g., 0.9250 Silver 0.7435 oz. ASW, 38.61 mm. **Ruler:** Elizabeth II **Subject:** Twelve days of Christmas **Rev:** Lords a leaping

Date	Mintage	F	VF	XF	Unc	BU
2010 Proof	1,500	Value: 60.00				

KM# 452 2 DOLLARS
25.0000 g., 0.9250 Silver 0.7435 oz. ASW, 38.61 mm. **Ruler:** Elizabeth II **Subject:** Twelve days of Christmas **Rev:** Pipers piping

Date	Mintage	F	VF	XF	Unc	BU
2010 Proof	1,500	Value: 60.00				

KM# 453 2 DOLLARS
25.0000 g., 0.9250 Silver 0.7435 oz. ASW, 38.61 mm. **Ruler:** Elizabeth II **Subject:** Twelve days of Christmas **Rev:** Drummers drumming

Date	Mintage	F	VF	XF	Unc	BU
2010 Proof	1,500	Value: 60.00				

KM# 457 2 DOLLARS
31.1030 g., 0.9990 Silver 0.9989 oz. ASW, 38.61 mm. **Ruler:** Elizabeth II **Subject:** Bulgarian theme roses - Survachka **Rev:** Figure-8 floral arangement

Date	Mintage	F	VF	XF	Unc	BU
2010 Proof	3,000	Value: 55.00				

KM# 458 2 DOLLARS
31.1030 g., 0.9990 Silver 0.9989 oz. ASW, 38.61 mm. **Ruler:** Elizabeth II **Subject:** Bulgarian rose **Rev:** Top view into colored pink rose, gilt border

Date	Mintage	F	VF	XF	Unc	BU
2010	6,000	Value: 50.00				

KM# 459 2 DOLLARS
31.1030 g., 0.9990 Silver 0.9989 oz. ASW, 38.61 mm. **Ruler:** Elizabeth II **Subject:** Bulgarian rose theme - Martenitsa **Rev:** tassle like device

Date	Mintage	F	VF	XF	Unc	BU
2010 Proof	3,000	Value: 55.00				

KM# 460 2 DOLLARS
31.1030 g., 0.9990 Silver 0.9989 oz. ASW, 38.61 mm. **Ruler:** Elizabeth II **Rev:** Saint Peter icon

Date	Mintage	F	VF	XF	Unc	BU
2010 Proof	2,000	Value: 60.00				

KM# 461 2 DOLLARS
31.1030 g., 0.9990 Silver 0.9989 oz. ASW, 38.61 mm. **Ruler:** Elizabeth II **Rev:** Saint Paul icon

Date	Mintage	F	VF	XF	Unc	BU
2010 Proof	2,000	Value: 60.00				

KM# 550 2 DOLLARS
Silver, 40 mm. **Ruler:** Elizabeth II **Subject:** Korean War, 60th Anniversary **Rev:** Soldier in multicolor

Date	Mintage	F	VF	XF	Unc	BU
2010 Proof	2,000	Value: 70.00				

KM# 372 2 DOLLARS
31.1050 g., 0.9990 Silver 0.9990 oz. ASW, 37.1x31.9 mm. **Ruler:** Elizabeth II **Subject:** Hello Kitty **Shape:** Heart with ribbon

Date	Mintage	F	VF	XF	Unc	BU
2010 Proof	Est. 3,000	Value: 50.00				

KM# 507 2 DOLLARS
31.1000 g., 0.9990 Silver 0.9988 oz. ASW, 40.7 mm. **Ruler:** Elizabeth II **Subject:** Love is precious **Rev:** Two pink flamingos within heart

Date	Mintage	F	VF	XF	Unc	BU
2011 Proof	20,000	Value: 50.00				

KM# 521 2 DOLLARS
31.1000 g., 0.9990 Silver 0.9988 oz. ASW **Ruler:** Elizabeth II **Subject:** The Evangelists - St. Mathew and angel **Rev:** Icon in color

Date	Mintage	F	VF	XF	Unc	BU
2011 Proof	2,000	Value: 60.00				

KM# 522 2 DOLLARS
31.1000 g., 0.9990 Silver 0.9988 oz. ASW **Ruler:** Elizabeth II **Subject:** The Evangelists - St Mark with lion **Rev:** Icon in color

Date	Mintage	F	VF	XF	Unc	BU
2011 Proof	2,000	Value: 60.00				

KM# 523 2 DOLLARS
31.1000 g., 0.9990 Silver 0.9988 oz. ASW **Ruler:** Elizabeth II **Subject:** The Evangelists - Luke and oxen **Rev:** Icon in color

Date	Mintage	F	VF	XF	Unc	BU
2011 Proof	2,000	Value: 60.00				

KM# 524 2 DOLLARS
31.1000 g., 0.9990 Silver 0.9988 oz. ASW **Ruler:** Elizabeth II **Subject:** The Evangelists - John and eagle **Rev:** Icon in color

Date	Mintage	F	VF	XF	Unc	BU
2011 Proof	2,000	Value: 60.00				

KM# 525 2 DOLLARS
31.1000 g., 0.9990 Silver 0.9988 oz. ASW **Ruler:** Elizabeth II **Subject:** Eternal Love **Rev:** Two white doves within flora and scrolls

Date	Mintage	F	VF	XF	Unc	BU
2011 Proof	5,000	Value: 50.00				

KM# 563 2 DOLLARS
31.1050 g., 0.9990 Silver 0.9990 oz. ASW **Ruler:** Elizabeth II **Subject:** Pirates of the Caribbean - Blackbeard **Obv:** Head with crown right **Rev:** Blackbeard in multicolor

Date	Mintage	F	VF	XF	Unc	BU
2011 Proof	2,000	Value: 70.00				

KM# 564 2 DOLLARS
31.1050 g., 0.9990 Silver 0.9990 oz. ASW **Ruler:** Elizabeth II **Series:** Pirates of the Caribbean - Bartholomew Roberts **Obv:** Head with crown right **Rev:** Bartholomew Roberts in multicolor

Date	Mintage	F	VF	XF	Unc	BU
2011 Proof	2,000	Value: 70.00				

KM# 565 2 DOLLARS
31.1050 g., 0.9990 Silver 0.9990 oz. ASW **Ruler:** Elizabeth II **Subject:** Pirates of the Caribbean - Henry Avery **Obv:** Head with crown right **Rev:** Henry Avery in multicolor

Date	Mintage	F	VF	XF	Unc	BU
2011 Proof	2,000	Value: 70.00				

KM# 566 2 DOLLARS
3.1050 g., 0.9990 Silver 0.0997 oz. ASW **Ruler:** Elizabeth II **Subject:** Pirates of the Caribbean - Calico Jack **Obv:** Head with crown right **Rev:** Calico Jack and two ladies in multicolor

Date	Mintage	F	VF	XF	Unc	BU
2011 Proof	2,000	Value: 70.00				

KM# 567 2 DOLLARS
31.1050 g., 0.9990 Silver 0.9990 oz. ASW **Ruler:** Elizabeth II **Subject:** Legends of the Air **Obv:** Head with crown right **Rev:** B-2 Spirit Stealth Bomber in color

Date	Mintage	F	VF	XF	Unc	BU
2011 Proof	2,000	Value: 60.00				

KM# 568 2 DOLLARS
31.1050 g., 0.9990 Silver 0.9990 oz. ASW **Ruler:** Elizabeth II **Subject:** Legends of the Air **Obv:** Head with crown right **Rev:** F-16 Fighting Falcon

Date	Mintage	F	VF	XF	Unc	BU
2011 Proof	2,000	Value: 60.00				

KM# 569 2 DOLLARS
31.1050 g., 0.9990 Silver 0.9990 oz. ASW **Ruler:** Elizabeth II **Subject:** Legends of the Air **Obv:** Head with crown right **Rev:** AH-64D Apache Longbow in color

Date	Mintage	F	VF	XF	Unc	BU
2011 Proof	2,000	Value: 60.00				

KM# 570 2 DOLLARS
31.1050 g., 0.9990 Silver 0.9990 oz. ASW **Ruler:** Elizabeth II **Subject:** Legends of the Air **Obv:** Head with crown right **Rev:** B-52 Stratofortress Bomber

Date	Mintage	F	VF	XF	Unc	BU
2011 Proof	2,000	Value: 60.00				

KM# 573 2 DOLLARS
31.1050 g., 0.9990 Silver 0.9990 oz. ASW, 38.61 mm. **Ruler:** Elizabeth II **Subject:** First crossing of the Simpson Desert, 75th Anniversary **Obv:** Head with crown right **Rev:** Ted Colson in color

Date	Mintage	F	VF	XF	Unc	BU
2011 Proof	2,000	Value: 75.00				

KM# 589 2 DOLLARS
31.1030 g., 0.9990 Silver 0.9989 oz. ASW, 33x55 mm. **Ruler:** Elizabeth II **Subject:** Kagaya Art Zodiac - Leo

Date	Mintage	F	VF	XF	Unc	BU
2011 Proof	8,000	Value: 80.00				

KM# 590 2 DOLLARS
31.1030 g., 0.9990 Silver 0.9989 oz. ASW, 33x55 mm. **Ruler:** Elizabeth II **Subject:** Kagaya Art Zodiac - Virgo

Date	Mintage	F	VF	XF	Unc	BU
2011 Proof	8,000	Value: 80.00				

KM# 591 2 DOLLARS
31.1030 g., 0.9990 Silver 0.9989 oz. ASW, 33x55 mm. **Ruler:** Elizabeth II **Subject:** Kagaya Art Zodiac - Libra **Shape:** Vertical rectangle

Date	Mintage	F	VF	XF	Unc	BU
2011 Proof	8,000	Value: 80.00				

KM# 592 2 DOLLARS
31.1030 g., 0.9990 Silver 0.9989 oz. ASW, 33x55 mm. **Ruler:** Elizabeth II **Subject:** Kagaya Art Zodiac - Scorpio **Shape:** Vertical rectangle

Date	Mintage	F	VF	XF	Unc	BU
2011 Proof	8,000	Value: 80.00				

KM# 593 2 DOLLARS
31.1030 g., 0.9990 Silver 0.9989 oz. ASW, 33x55 mm. **Ruler:** Elizabeth II **Subject:** Kagaya Art Zodiac - Sagittarius **Shape:** Vertical rectangle

Date	Mintage	F	VF	XF	Unc	BU
2011 Proof	8,000	Value: 80.00				

KM# 601 2 DOLLARS
31.1030 g., 0.9990 Silver 0.9989 oz. ASW, 40.7 mm. **Ruler:** Elizabeth II **Subject:** Love Forever **Obv:** Head with crown right **Rev:** Two doves in flight, two golden rings, word Forever in many languages in background

Date	Mintage	F	VF	XF	Unc	BU
2011 Proof	20,000	Value: 65.00				

KM# 602 2 DOLLARS
31.1030 g., 0.9990 Silver 0.9989 oz. ASW, 40.7 mm. **Ruler:** Elizabeth II **Subject:** Supersonic Transport - TU-144 **Rev:** Plane color image

Date	Mintage	F	VF	XF	Unc	BU
2011 Proof	8,000	Value: 65.00				

KM# 603 2 DOLLARS
31.1030 g., 0.9990 Silver 0.9989 oz. ASW, 40.7 mm. **Ruler:** Elizabeth II **Subject:** Supersonic Transport - Concorde **Rev:** Plane color image

Date	Mintage	F	VF	XF	Unc	BU
2011 Proof	8,000	Value: 65.00				

KM# 639 2 DOLLARS
31.1350 g., 0.9990 Silver 1.0000 oz. ASW, 27x47 mm. **Ruler:** Elizabeth II **Subject:** Orthodox shrines, Holy Trinity **Obv:** Head with crown right **Rev:** Five saints seated around table, partially gilt and colored **Edge:** Plain **Shape:** Vertical rectangle, convex

Date	Mintage	F	VF	XF	Unc	BU
2011 Proof	Est. 3,000	Value: 100				

KM# 640 2 DOLLARS
31.1350 g., 0.9990 Silver 1.0000 oz. ASW, 27x47 mm. **Ruler:** Elizabeth II **Subject:** Orthodox Shrines, Christ Pantokrator **Obv:** Head with crown right **Rev:** Christ facing holding gospels, partially gilt and colored **Edge:** Plain **Shape:** Vertical rectangle, convex

Date	Mintage	F	VF	XF	Unc	BU
2011 Proof	3,000	Value: 100				

KM# 642 2 DOLLARS

31.1050 g., 0.9990 Silver 0.9990 oz. ASW, 55x33 mm. **Ruler:** Elizabeth II **Obv:** Head with crown right **Rev:** First man in space, multicolor **Shape:** rectangle

Date	Mintage	F	VF	XF	Unc	BU
2011 Proof	5,000	—	—	—	—	100

KM# 643 2 DOLLARS

31.1050 g., 0.9990 Silver 0.9990 oz. ASW, 55x33 mm. **Ruler:** Elizabeth II **Obv:** Head with crown right **Rev:** First space walk

Date	Mintage	F	VF	XF	Unc	BU
2011 Proof	5,000	Value: 100				

KM# 663 2 DOLLARS

31.1050 g., 0.9990 Silver 0.9990 oz. ASW, 40 mm. **Ruler:** Elizabeth II **Subject:** Star Wars - C3PO and R2D2

Date	Mintage	F	VF	XF	Unc	BU
2011 Prooflike	Est. 7,500	—	—	—	—	120

KM# 664 2 DOLLARS

31.1050 g., 0.9990 Silver 0.9990 oz. ASW, 40 mm. **Ruler:** Elizabeth II **Subject:** Star Wars - Darth Vader

Date	Mintage	F	VF	XF	Unc	BU
2011 Prooflike	Est. 7,500	—	—	—	—	120

KM# 665 2 DOLLARS

31.1050 g., 0.9990 Silver 0.9990 oz. ASW, 40 mm. **Ruler:** Elizabeth II **Subject:** Star Wars - Emperor Palpatine

Date	Mintage	F	VF	XF	Unc	BU
2011 Prooflike	Est. 7,500	—	—	—	—	120

KM# 666 2 DOLLARS

31.1050 g., 0.9990 Silver 0.9990 oz. ASW, 40 mm. **Ruler:** Elizabeth II **Subject:** Star Wars - Death Star

Date	Mintage	F	VF	XF	Unc	BU
2011 Prooflike	Est. 7,500	—	—	—	—	120

KM# 667 2 DOLLARS

31.1050 g., 0.9990 Silver 0.9990 oz. ASW, 40 mm. **Ruler:** Elizabeth II **Subject:** Star Wars - Han Solo and Chewbacca

Date	Mintage	F	VF	XF	Unc	BU
2011 Prooflike	Est. 7,500	—	—	—	—	120

KM# 668 2 DOLLARS

31.1050 g., 0.9990 Silver 0.9990 oz. ASW, 40 mm. **Ruler:** Elizabeth II **Subject:** Star Wars - Luke Skywalker and Princess Leia

Date	Mintage	F	VF	XF	Unc	BU
2011 Prooflike	Est. 7,500	—	—	—	—	120

KM# 669 2 DOLLARS

31.1050 g., 0.9990 Silver 0.9990 oz. ASW, 40 mm. **Ruler:** Elizabeth II **Series:** Star Wars - Stormtrooper

Date	Mintage	F	VF	XF	Unc	BU
2011 Prooflike	Est. 7,500	—	—	—	—	120

KM# 670 2 DOLLARS

31.1050 g., 0.9990 Silver 0.9990 oz. ASW, 40 mm. **Ruler:** Elizabeth II **Subject:** Star Wars - Obi-Wan Kenobi and Yoda

Date	Mintage	F	VF	XF	Unc	BU
2011 Prooflike	Est. 7,500	—	—	—	—	120

KM# 671 2 DOLLARS

31.1050 g., 0.9990 Silver 0.9990 oz. ASW, 40 mm. **Ruler:** Elizabeth II **Subject:** Anne Geddes - Boy

Date	Mintage	F	VF	XF	Unc	BU
2011 Prooflike	3,000	—	—	—	—	100

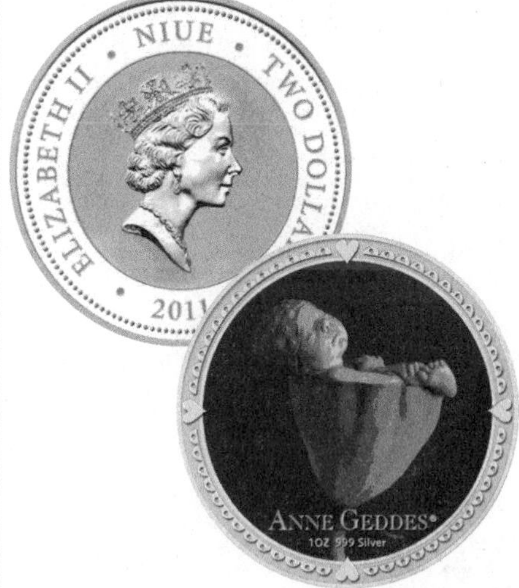

KM# 672 2 DOLLARS

31.1050 g., 0.9990 Silver 0.9990 oz. ASW, 40 mm. **Ruler:** Elizabeth II **Subject:** Anne Geddes - Girl

Date	Mintage	F	VF	XF	Unc	BU
2011 Prooflike	3,000	—	—	—	—	100

KM# 673 2 DOLLARS
15.5500 g., 0.9250 Silver 0.4624 oz. ASW, 35 mm. **Ruler:** Elizabeth II **Rev:** Mexican redknee tarantula in color

Date	Mintage	F	VF	XF	Unc	BU
2011	1,250	—	—	—	—	125

KM# 692 2 DOLLARS
31.1050 g., 0.9990 Silver 0.9990 oz. ASW, 38.61 mm. **Ruler:** Elizabeth II **Obv:** Head with crown right **Rev:** Virgin Mary with arms outstretched in color **Edge:** Reeded

Date	Mintage	F	VF	XF	Unc	BU
2011 Proof	3,000	Value: 100				

KM# 736 2 DOLLARS
56.5600 g., 0.9250 Silver 1.6820 oz. ASW, 41.6x55.6 mm. **Ruler:** Elizabeth II **Subject:** Imperial Faberge Egg - Pansy Egg **Obv:** Head right in filigree, open egg below **Rev:** Pansy flowers around closed egg **Shape:** Vertical oval

Date	Mintage	F	VF	XF	Unc	BU
2011 Proof	7,000	Value: 200				

KM# 802 2 DOLLARS
31.1000 g., 0.9990 Silver 0.9988 oz. ASW, 40.7 mm. **Ruler:** Elizabeth II **Rev:** School children playing with globe

Date	Mintage	F	VF	XF	Unc	BU
2011 Proof	Est. 6,000	Value: 100				

KM# 883 2 DOLLARS
10.0000 g., 0.9250 Silver 0.2974 oz. ASW, 32 mm. **Ruler:** Elizabeth II **Rev:** Earth in color

Date	Mintage	F	VF	XF	Unc	BU
2011 Proof	—	Value: 75.00				

KM# 884 2 DOLLARS
12.0000 g., 0.9250 Silver 0.3569 oz. ASW, 35x35 mm. **Ruler:** Elizabeth II **Subject:** Elements - Air

Date	Mintage	F	VF	XF	Unc	BU
2011 Proof	—	Value: 75.00				

KM# 885 2 DOLLARS
12.0000 g., 0.9250 Silver 0.3569 oz. ASW **Ruler:** Elizabeth II **Subject:** Elements - Water **Shape:** 35x35

Date	Mintage	F	VF	XF	Unc	BU
2011 Proof	—	Value: 85.00				

KM# 886 2 DOLLARS
12.0000 g., 0.9250 Silver 0.3569 oz. ASW, 35x35 mm. **Ruler:** Elizabeth II **Subject:** Elements - Land

Date	Mintage	F	VF	XF	Unc	BU
2011 Proof	—	Value: 85.00				

KM# 887 2 DOLLARS
12.0000 g., 0.9250 Silver 0.3569 oz. ASW, 35x35 mm. **Ruler:** Elizabeth II **Subject:** Elements - Fire

Date	Mintage	F	VF	XF	Unc	BU
2011 Proof	—	Value: 85.00				

KM# 888 2 DOLLARS
56.5600 g., 0.9250 Silver 1.6820 oz. ASW, 41.6x56.6 mm. **Ruler:** Elizabeth II **Subject:** Faberge egg - Dutchess of Marlboro egg **Shape:** Vertical oval

Date	Mintage	F	VF	XF	Unc	BU
2011 Proof	—	Value: 100				

KM# 889 2 DOLLARS
31.1050 g., 0.9990 Silver 0.9990 oz. ASW, 40.7 mm. **Ruler:** Elizabeth II **Obv:** Corwned head rigth, eternal flame and wreath below **Rev:** WWII Russian Victory celebrations in color

Date	Mintage	F	VF	XF	Unc	BU
2011 Proof	5,000	Value: 85.00				

KM# 594 2 DOLLARS
31.1030 g., 0.9990 Silver 0.9989 oz. ASW, 33x55 mm. **Ruler:** Elizabeth II **Subject:** Kagaya Art Zodiac - Capricorn **Shape:** Vertical rectangle

Date	Mintage	F	VF	XF	Unc	BU
2012 Proof	8,000	Value: 80.00				

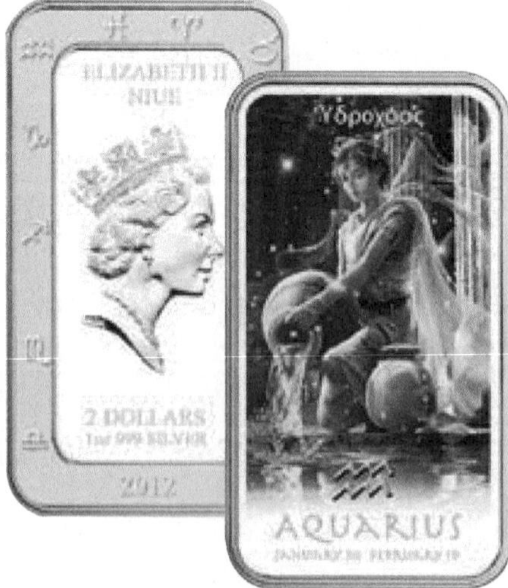

KM# 595 2 DOLLARS
31.1030 g., 0.9990 Silver 0.9989 oz. ASW, 33x55 mm. **Ruler:** Elizabeth II **Subject:** Kagaya Art Zodiac - Aquarius **Shape:** Vertical rectangle

Date	Mintage	F	VF	XF	Unc	BU
2012 Proof	8,000	Value: 80.00				

KM# 596 2 DOLLARS
31.1030 g., 0.9990 Silver 0.9989 oz. ASW, 33x55 mm. **Ruler:** Elizabeth II **Subject:** Kagaya Art Zodiac - Pisces **Shape:** Vertical rectangle

Date	Mintage	F	VF	XF	Unc	BU
2012 Proof	8,000	Value: 80.00				

KM# 597 2 DOLLARS
31.1030 g., 0.9990 Silver 0.9989 oz. ASW, 33x55 mm. **Ruler:** Elizabeth II **Subject:** Kagaya Art Zodiac - Aries **Shape:** Vertical rectangle

Date	Mintage	F	VF	XF	Unc	BU
2012 Proof	8,000	Value: 80.00				

KM# 598 2 DOLLARS
31.1030 g., 0.9990 Silver 0.9989 oz. ASW, 33x55 mm. **Ruler:** Elizabeth II **Subject:** Kagaya Art Zodiac - Taurus **Shape:** Vertical rectangle

Date	Mintage	F	VF	XF	Unc	BU
2012 Proof	8,000	Value: 80.00				

KM# 599 2 DOLLARS
31.1030 g., 0.9990 Silver 0.9989 oz. ASW, 33x55 mm. **Ruler:** Elizabeth II **Subject:** Kagaya Art Zodiac - Gemini **Shape:** Vertical rectangle

Date	Mintage	F	VF	XF	Unc	BU
2012 Proof	8,000	Value: 80.00				

KM# 600 2 DOLLARS
31.1030 g., 0.9990 Silver 0.9989 oz. ASW, 33x55 mm. **Ruler:** Elizabeth II **Subject:** Kagaya Art Zodiac - Cancer **Shape:** Vertical rectangle

Date	Mintage	F	VF	XF	Unc	BU
2012 Proof	8,000	Value: 80.00				

KM# 638 2 DOLLARS
31.1050 g., 0.9990 Silver 0.9990 oz. ASW, 40.7 mm. **Ruler:** Elizabeth II **Obv:** Head with crown right **Rev:** H.M.S. Titanic sailing right within compass points

Date	Mintage	F	VF	XF	Unc	BU
2012 Proof	2,229	Value: 225				

KM# 675 2 DOLLARS
28.2800 g., Copper-Nickel, 38.61 mm. **Ruler:** Elizabeth II **Rev:** Crowned state flowers **Edge:** Reeded

Date	Mintage	F	VF	XF	Unc	BU
2012	—	—	—	—	—	25.00

KM# 675a 2 DOLLARS
28.2800 g., 0.9250 Silver 0.8410 oz. ASW, 38.61 mm. **Ruler:** Elizabeth II **Rev:** Crowned state flowers

Date	Mintage	F	VF	XF	Unc	BU
2012 Proof	19,500	Value: 80.00				

KM# 676 2 DOLLARS
31.1050 g., 0.9990 Silver 0.9990 oz. ASW, 40.7 mm. **Ruler:** Elizabeth II **Rev:** Florida alligator, gilt **Edge:** Reeded

Date	Mintage	F	VF	XF	Unc	BU
2012 Proof	2,500	Value: 80.00				

KM# 677 2 DOLLARS
31.1050 g., 0.9990 Silver 0.9990 oz. ASW, 40.7 mm. **Ruler:** Elizabeth II **Subject:** Year of the Dragon **Rev:** Dragon

Date	Mintage	F	VF	XF	Unc	BU
2012 Proof	2,500	Value: 80.00				

KM# 691 2 DOLLARS
31.1050 g., 0.9990 Silver 0.9990 oz. ASW, 27x47 mm. **Ruler:** Elizabeth II **Subject:** Orthodox Shrines **Rev:** Faith, Hope and Charity and their mother, Sofia **Edge:** Plain

Date	Mintage	F	VF	XF	Unc	BU
2012 Proof	3,000	Value: 100				

KM# 693 2 DOLLARS
31.1050 g., 0.9990 Silver partially gilt 0.9990 oz. ASW, 38.61 mm. **Ruler:** Elizabeth II **Rev:** Feng Shui - two Koi Carp gilt

Date	Mintage	F	VF	XF	Unc	BU
2012 Proof	10,000	Value: 100				

KM# 694 2 DOLLARS
31.1050 g., 0.9990 Silver 0.9990 oz. ASW **Ruler:** Elizabeth II **Subject:** Nickelodeon's Sponge Bob **Rev:** Sponge Bob **Shape:** Square

Date	Mintage	F	VF	XF	Unc	BU
2012 Proof	100,000	Value: 75.00				

KM# 695 2 DOLLARS
31.1050 g., 0.9990 Silver 0.9990 oz. ASW **Ruler:** Elizabeth II **Subject:** Nickelodeon's Sponge Bob **Rev:** Patrick Star **Shape:** Square

Date	Mintage	F	VF	XF	Unc	BU
2012 Proof	100,000	Value: 75.00				

KM# 696 2 DOLLARS
31.1050 g., 0.9990 Silver 0.9990 oz. ASW **Ruler:** Elizabeth II **Subject:** Nickelodeon's Sponge Bob **Rev:** Sandy Cheeks **Shape:** Square

Date	Mintage	F	VF	XF	Unc	BU
2012 Proof	100,000	Value: 75.00				

KM# 697 2 DOLLARS
31.1050 g., 0.9990 Silver 0.9990 oz. ASW **Ruler:** Elizabeth II **Subject:** Nickelodeon's Sponge Bob **Rev:** Gary (snail) **Shape:** Square

Date	Mintage	F	VF	XF	Unc	BU
2012 Proof	100,000	Value: 75.00				

KM# 712 2 DOLLARS
31.1050 g., 0.9990 Silver 0.9990 oz. ASW, 40.7 mm. **Ruler:** Elizabeth II **Rev:** Dragon

Date	Mintage	F	VF	XF	Unc	BU
2012 Proof	50,000	Value: 50.00				

KM# 717 2 DOLLARS
31.1050 g., 0.9999 Silver 0.9999 oz. ASW, 40.7 mm. **Ruler:** Elizabeth II **Subject:** Star Wars - Battle Droid

Date	Mintage	F	VF	XF	Unc	BU
2012 Prooflike	10,000	—	—	—	—	125

KM# 718 2 DOLLARS
31.1050 g., 0.9990 Silver 0.9990 oz. ASW, 40.7 mm. **Ruler:** Elizabeth II **Subject:** Star Wars - Darth Maul

Date	Mintage	F	VF	XF	Unc	BU
2012 Prooflike	10,000	—	—	—	—	125

KM# 719 2 DOLLARS
31.1050 g., 0.9990 Silver 0.9990 oz. ASW, 40.7 mm. **Ruler:** Elizabeth II **Subject:** Star Wars - young Obi Wan Kenobi

Date	Mintage	F	VF	XF	Unc	BU
2012 Prooflike	10,000	—	—	—	—	125

KM# 720 2 DOLLARS
31.1050 g., 0.9990 Silver 0.9990 oz. ASW, 40.7 mm. **Ruler:** Elizabeth II **Subject:** Star Wars - Mace Windu

Date	Mintage	F	VF	XF	Unc	BU
2012 Prooflike	10,000	—	—	—	—	125

KM# 721 2 DOLLARS
31.1050 g., 0.9990 Silver 0.9990 oz. ASW, 40.7 mm. **Ruler:** Elizabeth II **Subject:** Star Wars - Yoda

Date	Mintage	F	VF	XF	Unc	BU
2012 Prooflike	10,000	—	—	—	—	125

KM# 722 2 DOLLARS
31.1050 g., 0.9990 Silver 0.9990 oz. ASW, 40.7 mm. **Ruler:** Elizabeth II **Subject:** Star Wars - Queen Amidala

Date	Mintage	F	VF	XF	Unc	BU
2012 Prooflike	10,000	—	—	—	—	125

KM# 723 2 DOLLARS
31.1050 g., 0.9990 Silver 0.9990 oz. ASW, 40.7 mm. **Ruler:** Elizabeth II **Subject:** Star Wars - Qui-Gon Jinn

Date	Mintage	F	VF	XF	Unc	BU
2012 Prooflike	10,000	—	—	—	—	125

KM# 724 2 DOLLARS
31.1050 g., 0.9990 Silver 0.9990 oz. ASW, 40.7 mm. **Ruler:** Elizabeth II **Subject:** Star Wars - young Anakin Skywalker

Date	Mintage	F	VF	XF	Unc	BU
2012 Prooflike	10,000	—	—	—	—	125

KM# 743 2 DOLLARS
15.5500 g., 0.9990 Silver 0.4994 oz. ASW, 33 mm. **Ruler:** Elizabeth II **Subject:** Year of the Dragon **Rev:** Dragon with pearl in color

Date	Mintage	F	VF	XF	Unc	BU
2012 Proof	8,000	Value: 50.00				

KM# 744 2 DOLLARS
31.1050 g., 0.9990 Silver 0.9990 oz. ASW, 45x31 mm. **Ruler:** Elizabeth II **Subject:** Year of the Dragon, Lucky Red dragon **Rev:** Red dragon lying down with rays in background **Shape:** Horizontal oval

Date	Mintage	F	VF	XF	Unc	BU
2012 Proof	4,000	Value: 100				

KM# 745 2 DOLLARS
31.1050 g., 0.9990 Silver 0.9990 oz. ASW, 45x31 mm. **Ruler:** Elizabeth II **Subject:** Year of the Dragon - Lucky Blue Dragon **Rev:** Blue dragon lying down, rays in background **Shape:** Horizontal oval

Date	Mintage	F	VF	XF	Unc	BU
2012 Proof	8,000	Value: 100				

KM# 746 2 DOLLARS
31.1050 g., 0.9990 Silver 0.9990 oz. ASW, 40.7 mm. **Ruler:** Elizabeth II **Subject:** Year of the Dragon - Lunar Fan Dragon **Rev:** Dragon seated left, colored lunar hand fan in background

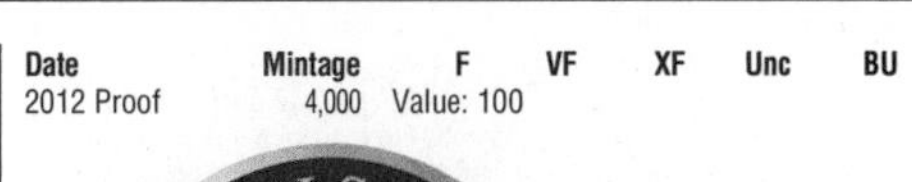

Date	Mintage	F	VF	XF	Unc	BU
2012 Proof	4,000	Value: 100				

KM# 756 2 DOLLARS
56.5600 g., 0.9250 Silver 1.6820 oz. ASW, 41.6x55.6 mm. **Ruler:** Elizabeth II **Subject:** Imperial Faberge Eggs - Bay Tree **Rev:** Bay tree **Shape:** Vertical oval

Date	Mintage	F	VF	XF	Unc	BU
2012 Proof	Est. 7,000	Value: 125				

KM# 762 2 DOLLARS
39.6000 g., 0.9250 Silver 1.1776 oz. ASW, 48.61 mm. **Ruler:** Elizabeth II **Subject:** Love Notes **Rev:** Cupid writing on central tablet

Date	Mintage	F	VF	XF	Unc	BU
2012 Proof	Est. 3,000	Value: 100				

KM# 782 2 DOLLARS
31.1050 g., 0.9990 Silver 0.9990 oz. ASW, 40.7 mm. **Ruler:** Elizabeth II **Subject:** WWII Nose Art - Yellow Rose

Date	Mintage	F	VF	XF	Unc	BU
2012	Est. 3,000	—	—	—	—	80.00

KM# 783 2 DOLLARS
31.1050 g., 0.9990 Silver 0.9990 oz. ASW, 40.7 mm. **Ruler:** Elizabeth II **Subject:** WWII Nose Art - Briefing Time

Date	Mintage	F	VF	XF	Unc	BU
2012	Est. 3,000	—	—	—	—	80.00

KM# 784 2 DOLLARS
31.1050 g., 0.9990 Silver 0.9990 oz. ASW, 40.7 mm. **Ruler:** Elizabeth II **Subject:** WWII Nose Art - Memphis Belle

Date	Mintage	F	VF	XF	Unc	BU
2012	Est. 3,000	—	—	—	—	80.00

KM# 795 2 DOLLARS
10.0000 g., 0.9250 Silver 0.2974 oz. ASW, 32 mm. **Ruler:** Elizabeth II **Subject:** Four seasons, central device **Rev:** Flowers, leaves and crystal

Date	Mintage	F	VF	XF	Unc	BU
2012 Proof	Est. 9,999	Value: 70.00				

KM# 796 2 DOLLARS
12.0000 g., 0.9250 Silver 0.3569 oz. ASW, 35x35 mm. **Ruler:** Elizabeth II **Subject:** Four seasons - Spring **Rev:** Springtime flora and crystal **Shape:** Irregular

Date	Mintage	F	VF	XF	Unc	BU
2012 Proof	Est. 9,999	Value: 70.00				

KM# 797 2 DOLLARS
12.0000 g., 0.9250 Silver 0.3569 oz. ASW, 35x35 mm. **Ruler:** Elizabeth II **Subject:** Four seasons - Summer **Rev:** Summer flora and crystal **Shape:** Irregular

Date	Mintage	F	VF	XF	Unc	BU
2012 Proof	Est. 9,999	Value: 70.00				

KM# 798 2 DOLLARS
12.0000 g., 0.9250 Silver 0.3569 oz. ASW, 35x35 mm. **Ruler:** Elizabeth II **Subject:** Four seasons - Autumn **Rev:** Autumn foilage and crystal **Shape:** Irregular

Date	Mintage	F	VF	XF	Unc	BU
2012 Proof	Est. 9,999	Value: 70.00				

KM# 799 2 DOLLARS
12.0000 g., 0.9250 Silver 0.3569 oz. ASW, 35x35 mm. **Ruler:** Elizabeth II **Subject:** Four seasons - Winter **Rev:** Winter foilage and crystal **Shape:** Irregular

Date	Mintage	F	VF	XF	Unc	BU
2012 Proof	Est. 9,999	Value: 70.00				

KM# 803 2 DOLLARS
31.1050 g., 0.9990 Silver 0.9990 oz. ASW, 40.7 mm. **Ruler:** Elizabeth II **Rev:** Great White Shark

Date	Mintage	F	VF	XF	Unc	BU
2012 Proof	5,000	Value: 120				

KM# 806 2 DOLLARS
31.1050 g., 0.9990 Silver 0.9990 oz. ASW, 27x47 mm. **Ruler:** Elizabeth II **Obv:** Crowned head left **Rev:** Katherina icom **Shape:** Vertical rectangle

Date	Mintage	F	VF	XF	Unc	BU
2012 Proof	2,000	Value: 100				

KM# 807 2 DOLLARS
31.1050 g., 0.9990 Silver 0.9990 oz. ASW, 27x47 mm. **Ruler:** Elizabeth II **Obv:** Crowned head right **Rev:** Rublov - Archangel Michael painting **Shape:** Vertical rectangle

Date	Mintage	F	VF	XF	Unc	BU
2012 Proof	3,000	Value: 100				

KM# 808 2 DOLLARS
31.1050 g., 0.9990 Silver 0.9990 oz. ASW, 27x47 mm. **Ruler:** Elizabeth II **Obv:** Crowned head right **Rev:** Rubov - Christ painting **Shape:** Vertical rectangle

Date	Mintage	F	VF	XF	Unc	BU
2012 Proof	3,000	Value: 100				

KM# 809 2 DOLLARS
31.1050 g., 0.9990 Silver 0.9990 oz. ASW, 27x47 mm. **Ruler:** Elizabeth II **Obv:** Crowned head right **Rev:** Rublov - Holy Trinity painting **Shape:** Vertical rectangle

Date	Mintage	F	VF	XF	Unc	BU
2012 Proof	3,000	Value: 100				

KM# 810 2 DOLLARS
31.1050 g., 0.9990 Silver 0.9990 oz. ASW, 27x47 mm. **Ruler:** Elizabeth II **Obv:** Corwned head right **Rev:** Rublov - Apostle Paul painting **Shape:** Vertical rectangle

Date	Mintage	F	VF	XF	Unc	BU
2012 Proof	3,000	Value: 100				

KM# 811 2 DOLLARS
31.1050 g., 0.9990 Silver 0.9990 oz. ASW, 27x47 mm. **Ruler:** Elizabeth II **Obv:** Crowned head right **Rev:** Mary and child **Shape:** Vertical rectangle

Date	Mintage	F	VF	XF	Unc	BU
2012 Proof	3,000	Value: 100				

KM# 812 2 DOLLARS
31.1050 g., 0.9990 Silver 0.9990 oz. ASW, 27x47 mm. **Ruler:** Elizabeth II **Obv:** Crowned head right **Rev:** Christ holding book **Shape:** Vertical rectangle

Date	Mintage	F	VF	XF	Unc	BU
2012 Proof	3,000	Value: 100				

KM# 813 2 DOLLARS
31.1050 g., 0.9990 Silver 0.9990 oz. ASW, 27x47 mm. **Ruler:** Elizabeth II **Obv:** Crowned head right **Rev:** God the father holding book, angels above **Shape:** Vertical rectangle

Date	Mintage	F	VF	XF	Unc	BU
2012 Proof	3,000	Value: 100				

KM# 814 2 DOLLARS
31.1050 g., 0.9990 Silver 0.9990 oz. ASW, 38.61 mm. **Ruler:** Elizabeth II **Obv:** Crowned head right **Rev:** Secret Evening, Christ and deciples around table **Edge:** Reeded

Date	Mintage	F	VF	XF	Unc	BU
2012 Proof	2,000	Value: 100				

KM# 818 2 DOLLARS
0.9990 Silver **Ruler:** Elizabeth II **Obv:** Crowned head right **Rev:** Saint facing right

Date	Mintage	F	VF	XF	Unc	BU
2012 Proof	500	Value: 100				

KM# 819 2 DOLLARS
0.9990 Silver **Ruler:** Elizabeth II **Obv:** Crowned head right **Rev:** Saint standing right

Date	Mintage	F	VF	XF	Unc	BU
2012 Proof	500	Value: 100				

KM# 820 2 DOLLARS
0.9990 Silver **Ruler:** Elizabeth II **Obv:** Crowned head right **Rev:** Saint standing right

Date	Mintage	F	VF	XF	Unc	BU
2012 Proof	500	Value: 100				

KM# 821 2 DOLLARS
0.9990 Silver **Ruler:** Elizabeth II **Obv:** Crowned head right **Rev:** Saint standing right

Date	Mintage	F	VF	XF	Unc	BU
2012 Proof	500	Value: 100				

KM# 822 2 DOLLARS
0.9990 Silver **Ruler:** Elizabeth II **Obv:** Crowned head right **Rev:** Christ facing

Date	Mintage	F	VF	XF	Unc	BU
2012 Proof	500	Value: 150				

KM# 823 2 DOLLARS
0.9990 Silver **Ruler:** Elizabeth II **Obv:** Crowned head right **Rev:** Saint standing left

Date	Mintage	F	VF	XF	Unc	BU
2012 Proof	500	Value: 100				

KM# 824 2 DOLLARS
0.9990 Silver **Ruler:** Elizabeth II **Obv:** Crowned head right **Rev:** Saint standing left

Date	Mintage	F	VF	XF	Unc	BU
2012 Proof	500	Value: 100				

KM# 825 2 DOLLARS
0.9990 Silver **Ruler:** Elizabeth II **Obv:** Crowned head right **Rev:** Saint standing left

Date	Mintage	F	VF	XF	Unc	BU
2012 Proof	500	Value: 100				

KM# 826 2 DOLLARS
0.9990 Silver **Ruler:** Elizabeth II **Obv:** Crowned head right **Rev:** Saint standing left

Date	Mintage	F	VF	XF	Unc	BU
2012 Proof	500	Value: 100				

KM# 836 2 DOLLARS
10.0000 g., 0.9250 Silver 0.2974 oz. ASW, 32 mm. **Ruler:** Elizabeth II **Obv:** Head with tiara right **Rev:** Palace gate

Date	Mintage	F	VF	XF	Unc	BU
2012 Proof	6,999	Value: 70.00				

KM# 837 2 DOLLARS
12.0000 g., 0.9250 Silver 0.3569 oz. ASW, 35x35 mm. **Ruler:** Elizabeth II **Obv:** Head with tiara right **Rev:** Palace façade **Shape:** Irregular

Date	Mintage	F	VF	XF	Unc	BU
2012 Proof	6,999	Value: 70.00				

KM# 838 2 DOLLARS
12.0000 g., 0.9250 Silver 0.3569 oz. ASW, 35x35 mm. **Ruler:** Elizabeth II **Obv:** Head with tiara right **Rev:** Tsar bust **Shape:** Irregular

Date	Mintage	F	VF	XF	Unc	BU
2012 Proof	6,999	Value: 70.00				

KM# 839 2 DOLLARS
12.0000 g., 0.9250 Silver 0.3569 oz. ASW, 35x35 mm. **Ruler:** Elizabeth II **Obv:** Head with tiara right **Rev:** Building view **Shape:** Irregular

Date	Mintage	F	VF	XF	Unc	BU
2012 Proof	6,999	Value: 70.00				

KM# 840 2 DOLLARS
12.0000 g., 0.9250 Silver 0.3569 oz. ASW, 35x35 mm. **Ruler:** Elizabeth II **Obv:** Head with tiara right **Rev:** Tsarina bust **Shape:** Irregular

Date	Mintage	F	VF	XF	Unc	BU
2012 Proof	6,999	Value: 70.00				

KM# 845 2 DOLLARS
28.2800 g., 0.9250 Silver 0.8410 oz. ASW, 41 mm. **Ruler:** Elizabeth II **Subject:** Wedding **Obv:** Head with tiara above present, hearts and rings **Rev:** Bridge and groom, rings and bouquet

Date	Mintage	F	VF	XF	Unc	BU
2012 Proof	Est. 15,000	Value: 100				

KM# 865 2 DOLLARS
31.1050 g., 0.9990 Silver 0.9990 oz. ASW, 40 mm. **Ruler:** Elizabeth II **Obv:** Crowned head right **Rev:** Great white shark

Date	Mintage	F	VF	XF	Unc	BU
2012 Proof	5,000	Value: 100				

KM# 866 2 DOLLARS
31.1050 g., 0.9990 Silver 0.9990 oz. ASW, 40.7 mm. **Ruler:** Elizabeth II **Subject:** Birds of Prey **Obv:** Crowned head right **Rev:** American Bald Eagle

Date	Mintage	F	VF	XF	Unc	BU
2012 Proof	5,000	Value: 100				

KM# 867 2 DOLLARS
31.1050 g., 0.9990 Silver 0.9990 oz. ASW, 40.7 mm. **Ruler:** Elizabeth II **Subject:** Birds of Prey **Obv:** Crowned head right **Rev:** Osprey

Date	Mintage	F	VF	XF	Unc	BU
2012 Proof	5,000	Value: 100				

KM# 871 2 DOLLARS
31.1050 g., 0.9990 Silver 0.9990 oz. ASW, 54x32 mm. **Ruler:** Elizabeth II **Obv:** Crowned head right **Rev:** Blue Iguana head and eye **Shape:** Horizontal oval

Date	Mintage	F	VF	XF	Unc	BU
2012 Proof	1,000	Value: 100				

KM# 872 2 DOLLARS
31.1050 g., 0.9990 Silver 0.9990 oz. ASW, 45 mm. **Ruler:** Elizabeth II **Obv:** Crowned head right **Rev:** Lotto ball mixer

Date	Mintage	F	VF	XF	Unc	BU
2012 Proof	1,000	Value: 100				

KM# 882 2 DOLLARS
56.5600 g., 0.9250 Silver 1.6820 oz. ASW, 41.6x55.6 mm. **Ruler:** Elizabeth II **Obv:** Head with tiara right above open egg **Rev:** Imperial Faberge Egg - 100th Anniversary of the Patriotic War of 1812 **Shape:** Vertical oval

Date	Mintage	F	VF	XF	Unc	BU
2012 Proof	Est. 7,000	Value: 125				

KM# 857 2 DOLLARS
31.1050 g., 0.9990 Silver 0.9990 oz. ASW, 40.7 mm. **Ruler:** Elizabeth II **Obv:** Crowned head right **Rev:** Transformers - OPTIMUS PRIME

Date	Mintage	F	VF	XF	Unc	BU
2013 Proof	5,000	Value: 100				

KM# 858 2 DOLLARS
31.1050 g., 0.9990 Silver 0.9990 oz. ASW, 40.7 mm. **Ruler:** Elizabeth II **Obv:** Crowned head right **Rev:** Transformers - Megatron

Date	Mintage	F	VF	XF	Unc	BU
2013 Proof	5,000	Value: 100				

KM# 859 2 DOLLARS
31.1050 g., 0.9990 Silver 0.9990 oz. ASW, 30.5x30.5 mm. **Ruler:** Elizabeth II **Obv:** Crowned head right **Rev:** Mr. Monopoly **Shape:** Square

Date	Mintage	F	VF	XF	Unc	BU
2013 Proof	5,000	Value: 125				

KM# 860 2 DOLLARS
31.1050 g., 0.9990 Silver 0.9990 oz. ASW, 30.5x30.5 mm. **Ruler:** Elizabeth II **Obv:** Crowned head right **Rev:** Monopoly Game pieces - car, top hat, thimble, dog, battleship **Shape:** Square

Date	Mintage	F	VF	XF	Unc	BU
2013 Proof	5,000	Value: 125				

KM# 870 2 DOLLARS
31.1050 g., 0.9990 Silver 0.9990 oz. ASW, 45x31 mm. **Ruler:** Elizabeth II **Obv:** Crowned head right **Rev:** Lunar Lucky Snake in color **Shape:** Horizontal oval

Date	Mintage	F	VF	XF	Unc	BU
2013 Proof	8,000	Value: 100				

KM# 785 3 DOLLARS
33.3000 g., 0.9250 Silver 0.9903 oz. ASW, 38.61 mm. **Ruler:** Elizabeth II **Subject:** Polish Radio, station 3 **Obv:** Head with tiara right **Rev:** Radio microphone and sound arcs

Date	Mintage	F	VF	XF	Unc	BU
2012 Proof	Est. 3,333	Value: 75.00				

KM# 295 5 DOLLARS
155.5000 g., 0.9990 Silver 4.9942 oz. ASW, 70 mm. **Ruler:** Elizabeth II **Subject:** Year of the Dog **Rev:** Multicolor dog

Date	Mintage	F	VF	XF	Unc	BU
2005 Proof	—	Value: 225				

KM# 266 5 DOLLARS
155.5000 g., 0.9990 Silver 4.9942 oz. ASW, 70 mm. **Ruler:** Elizabeth II **Subject:** Year of the Rooster **Rev:** Multicolor rooster standing right, sunrise

Date	Mintage	F	VF	XF	Unc	BU
2005 Proof	—	Value: 225				

KM# 272 5 DOLLARS
6.2200 g., 0.9990 Gold 0.1998 oz. AGW, 25 mm. **Ruler:** Elizabeth II **Subject:** Year of the Rooster

Date	Mintage	F	VF	XF	Unc	BU
2005 Proof	—	Value: 400				

KM# 273 5 DOLLARS
15.5500 g., 0.9990 Gold 0.4994 oz. AGW, 33 mm. **Ruler:** Elizabeth II **Subject:** Year of the Rooster

Date	Mintage	F	VF	XF	Unc	BU
2005 Proof	—	Value: 950				

KM# 333 5 DOLLARS
15.5000 g., 0.9170 Gold 0.4570 oz. AGW, 27 mm. **Ruler:** Elizabeth II **Subject:** Amber Road - Gdansk **Rev:** Nepture statue, castle, amber insert

Date	Mintage	F	VF	XF	Unc	BU
2007	—	—	—	—	—	850

KM# 191 5 DOLLARS
15.5000 g., 0.9000 Gold 0.4485 oz. AGW, 27 mm. **Ruler:** Elizabeth II **Subject:** Amber road **Obv:** Bust and Roman cart **Rev:** Kaliningrad Castle, Roman coin, Amber insert

Date	Mintage	F	VF	XF	Unc	BU
2008 Proof	2,000	Value: 850				

KM# 230 5 DOLLARS
62.2100 g., 0.9990 Silver 1.9980 oz. ASW, 50x32 mm. **Ruler:** Elizabeth II **Subject:** Battleship: Tripitz **Shape:** Rectangle

Date	Mintage	F	VF	XF	Unc	BU
2009	1,000	—	—	—	—	150

KM# 349 5 DOLLARS
15.5000 g., 0.9000 Gold 0.4485 oz. AGW, 27 mm. **Ruler:** Elizabeth II **Subject:** Amber Road - Elblag **Rev:** Amber insert

Date	Mintage	F	VF	XF	Unc	BU
2009 Proof	—	Value: 850				

KM# 364 5 DOLLARS
77.7000 g., 0.9990 Silver 2.4955 oz. ASW, 50x32 mm. **Ruler:** Elizabeth II **Rev:** Battleship Tirpitz sailing left **Shape:** Wavy rectangle

Date	Mintage	F	VF	XF	Unc	BU
2009 Proof	1,000	Value: 175				

KM# 250 5 DOLLARS
0.5000 g., 0.9990 Gold 0.0161 oz. AGW, 11 mm. **Ruler:** Elizabeth II **Rev:** Ned Kelly

Date	Mintage	F	VF	XF	Unc	BU
2010 Proof	—	Value: 65.00				

KM# 368 5 DOLLARS
15.5000 g., 0.9000 Gold 0.4485 oz. AGW, 27 mm. **Ruler:** Elizabeth II **Subject:** Amber road - Stare Hradisko **Rev:** Amber insert

Date	Mintage	F	VF	XF	Unc	BU
2010	2,000	—	—	—	—	850

KM# 376 5 DOLLARS
2.5000 g., 0.9990 Gold 0.0803 oz. AGW, 14x26.7 mm. **Ruler:** Elizabeth II **Subject:** Kitty **Shape:** Vertical rectangle

Date	Mintage	F	VF	XF	Unc	BU
2010 Proof	Est. 2,000	Value: 175				

KM# 377 5 DOLLARS
2.5000 g., 0.9990 Gold 0.0803 oz. AGW, 14x26.7 mm. **Ruler:** Elizabeth II **Subject:** Kiki Lala **Shape:** Vertical rectangle

Date	Mintage	F	VF	XF	Unc	BU
2010 Proof	Est. 2,000	Value: 175				

KM# 378 5 DOLLARS
2.5000 g., 0.9990 Gold 0.0803 oz. AGW, 14x26.7 mm. **Ruler:** Elizabeth II **Subject:** My Melo **Shape:** Vertical rectangle

Date	Mintage	F	VF	XF	Unc	BU
2010 Proof	Est. 2,000	Value: 175				

KM# 397 5 DOLLARS
15.5000 g., 0.9000 Gold 0.4485 oz. AGW, 27 mm. **Ruler:** Elizabeth II **Subject:** Amber Road - Carnuntum **Rev:** Arches, ancient coin, statue

Date	Mintage	F	VF	XF	Unc	BU
2010	2,000	Value: 850				

KM# 399 5 DOLLARS
15.5000 g., 0.9000 Gold 0.4485 oz. AGW, 27 mm. **Ruler:** Elizabeth II **Subject:** Amber Route - Szombathely **Rev:** Cathedral, ancient coin

Date	Mintage	F	VF	XF	Unc	BU
2010 Matte finish	2,000	Value: 850				

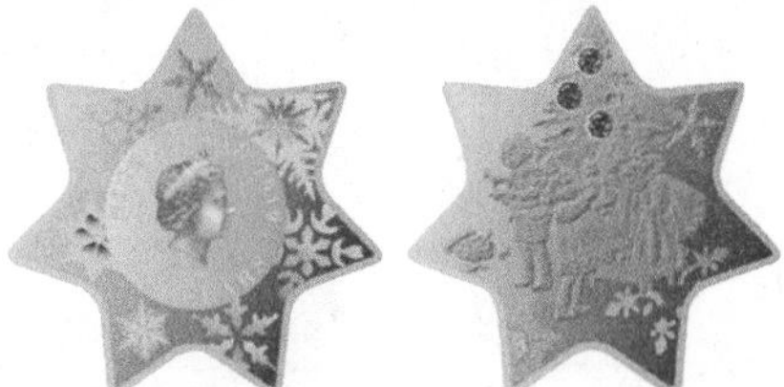

KM# 423 5 DOLLARS
15.5000 g., 0.9000 Gold 0.4485 oz. AGW, 27 mm. **Ruler:** Elizabeth II **Subject:** Christmas Star **Obv:** Head with tiara right, snowflakes around **Rev:** Three children and christmas tree, crystal insets

Date	Mintage	F	VF	XF	Unc	BU
2010 Proof	2,000	Value: 850				

KM# 430 5 DOLLARS
15.5000 g., 0.9000 Gold 0.4485 oz. AGW, 27 mm. **Ruler:** Elizabeth II **Obv:** Head with tiara right, wing enlargement as background **Rev:** Butterfly - Lycaena Virgaureae

Date	Mintage	F	VF	XF	Unc	BU
2010 Proof	1,000	Value: 850				

KM# 513 5 DOLLARS
50.0000 g., 0.9990 Silver 1.6059 oz. ASW, 35.2x35.2 mm. **Ruler:** Elizabeth II **Subject:** The three kings of 1936 **Obv:** Head with tiara right **Rev:** Busts left of George V, Edward VIII and George VI

Date	Mintage	F	VF	XF	Unc	BU
2011 Proof	2,500	Value: 100				

KM# 587 5 DOLLARS
27.0000 g., 0.9000 Gold 0.7812 oz. AGW, 27 mm. **Ruler:** Elizabeth II **Subject:** Amber Route - Aquileia **Rev:** Rhomulus and Remus suckling at she-wolf, amber insert

Date	Mintage	F	VF	XF	Unc	BU
2011	Est. 2,000	—	—	—	—	1,500

KM# 620 5 DOLLARS
1.0000 g., 0.9990 Gold 0.0321 oz. AGW, 12x8 mm. **Ruler:** Elizabeth II **Obv:** Head with crown right **Rev:** Baby tiger, diamond chip and paw print **Shape:** Rectangle

Date	Mintage	F	VF	XF	Unc	BU
2011 Proof	Est. 5,000	Value: 100				

KM# 623 5 DOLLARS
8.6000 g., 0.9000 Gold 0.2488 oz. AGW, 22 mm. **Ruler:** Elizabeth II **Obv:** Head with tiara right **Rev:** Dragon rearing upwards, paw to mouth

Date	Mintage	F	VF	XF	Unc	BU
2011 Proof	Est. 1,000	—	—	—	—	475

KM# 651 5 DOLLARS
25.0000 g., 0.9990 Silver 0.8029 oz. ASW, 40.6 mm. **Ruler:** Elizabeth II **Obv:** Head with tiara right **Rev:** Tasmanian tiger in lenticular 3-D **Edge:** Reeded

Date	Mintage	F	VF	XF	Unc	BU
2011 Proof	3,000	Value: 75.00				

KM# 689 5 DOLLARS
6.0000 g., 0.9990 Gold 0.1927 oz. AGW, 21 mm. **Ruler:** Elizabeth II **Subject:** Amber Route **Rev:** Map of European cities

Date	Mintage	F	VF	XF	Unc	BU
2011 Proof	999	Value: 400				

KM# 710 5 DOLLARS
6.0000 g., 0.9999 Gold 0.1929 oz. AGW, 21 mm. **Ruler:** Elizabeth II **Obv:** Ancient horsecart **Obv. Legend:** SZLAK BURSZTYNOWY **Rev:** Nepture statue, coin, mine building, amber insert **Rev. Legend:** Gdansk

Date	Mintage	F	VF	XF	Unc	BU
2011 Proof	999	Value: 400				

KM# 678 5 DOLLARS
40.0000 g., 0.9990 Silver 1.2847 oz. ASW, 29x47 mm. **Ruler:** Elizabeth II **Subject:** Year of the Dragon

Date	Mintage	F	VF	XF	Unc	BU
2012 Proof	—	Value: 100				

KM# 679 5 DOLLARS
40.0000 g., 0.9990 Silver 1.2847 oz. ASW, 29x47 mm. **Ruler:** Elizabeth II **Subject:** Year of the Dragon

Date	Mintage	F	VF	XF	Unc	BU
2012 Proof	—	Value: 100				

KM# 680 5 DOLLARS
40.0000 g., 0.9990 Silver 1.2847 oz. ASW, 29x47 mm. **Ruler:** Elizabeth II **Subject:** Year of the Dragon

Date	Mintage	F	VF	XF	Unc	BU
2012 Proof	—	Value: 100				

KM# 681 5 DOLLARS
40.0000 g., 0.9990 Silver 1.2847 oz. ASW, 29x47 mm. **Ruler:** Elizabeth II **Subject:** Year of the Dragon

Date	Mintage	F	VF	XF	Unc	BU
2012 Proof	—	Value: 100				

KM# 682 5 DOLLARS
40.0000 g., 0.9990 Silver 1.2847 oz. ASW, 29x47 mm. **Ruler:** Elizabeth II **Subject:** Year of the Dragon

Date	Mintage	F	VF	XF	Unc	BU
2012 Proof	—	Value: 100				

KM# 683 5 DOLLARS
40.0000 g., 0.9990 Silver 1.2847 oz. ASW, 29x47 mm. **Ruler:** Elizabeth II **Subject:** Year of the Dragon

Date	Mintage	F	VF	XF	Unc	BU
2012 Proof	—	Value: 100				

KM# 684 5 DOLLARS
40.0000 g., 0.9990 Silver 1.2847 oz. ASW, 29x47 mm. **Ruler:** Elizabeth II **Subject:** Year of the Dragon

Date	Mintage	F	VF	XF	Unc	BU
2012 Proof	—	Value: 100				

KM# 685 5 DOLLARS
40.0000 g., 0.9990 Silver 1.2847 oz. ASW, 29x47 mm. **Ruler:** Elizabeth II **Subject:** Year of the Dragon

Date	Mintage	F	VF	XF	Unc	BU
2012 Proof	—	Value: 100				

KM# 686 5 DOLLARS
40.0000 g., 0.9990 Silver 1.2847 oz. ASW, 29x47 mm. **Ruler:** Elizabeth II **Subject:** Year of the Dragon

Date	Mintage	F	VF	XF	Unc	BU
2012 Proof	—	Value: 100				

KM# 698 5 DOLLARS
0.5000 g., 0.9990 Gold 0.0161 oz. AGW, 11 mm. **Ruler:** Elizabeth II **Rev:** Ned Kelly standing, name vertically at left **Edge:** Reeded

Date	Mintage	F	VF	XF	Unc	BU
2012 Proof	5,000	Value: 75.00				

KM# 716 5 DOLLARS
1.2400 g., 0.9999 Gold 0.0399 oz. AGW, 13.92 mm. **Ruler:** Elizabeth II **Rev:** Dragon

Date	Mintage	F	VF	XF	Unc	BU
2012 Proof	5,000	Value: 125				

KM# 738 5 DOLLARS
155.5500 g., 0.9990 Silver 4.9958 oz. ASW, 65 mm. **Ruler:** Elizabeth II **Subject:** Vietnam War, 50th Anniversary of Australia's involvement **Rev:** Two soldiers with rifles on patrol, helicopter above

Date	Mintage	F	VF	XF	Unc	BU
2012 Proof	400	Value: 250				

KM# 748 5 DOLLARS
100.0000 g., 0.9990 Silver 3.2117 oz. ASW, 52.5x118 mm. **Ruler:** Elizabeth II **Subject:** DaVinci's Last Supper **Rev:** Bartholomew **Shape:** Vertical rectangle

Date	Mintage	F	VF	XF	Unc	BU
2012 Proof	750	Value: 150				

KM# 749 5 DOLLARS
100.0000 g., 0.9990 Silver 3.2117 oz. ASW, 52.5x118 mm. **Ruler:** Elizabeth II **Subject:** DaVinci's Last Supper **Rev:** James Minor and Andrew **Shape:** Vertical rectangle

Date	Mintage	F	VF	XF	Unc	BU
2012 Proof	750	Value: 150				

KM# 750 5 DOLLARS
100.0000 g., 0.9990 Silver 3.2117 oz. ASW, 52.5x118 mm. **Ruler:** Elizabeth II **Subject:** DaVinci's Last Supper **Rev:** Judas Iscariot, Peter and John **Shape:** Vertical rectangle

Date	Mintage	F	VF	XF	Unc	BU
2012 Proof	750	Value: 150				

KM# 751 5 DOLLARS
100.0000 g., 0.9990 Silver 3.2117 oz. ASW, 52.5x118 mm. **Ruler:** Elizabeth II **Subject:** DaVinci's Last Supper **Rev:** Jesus **Shape:** Vertical rectangle

Date	Mintage	F	VF	XF	Unc	BU
2012 Proof	750	Value: 150				

KM# 752 5 DOLLARS
100.0000 g., 0.9990 Silver 3.2117 oz. ASW, 52.5x118 mm. **Ruler:** Elizabeth II **Subject:** DaVinci's Last Supper **Rev:** Thomas, James the Greater, Philip **Shape:** Vertical rectangle

Date	Mintage	F	VF	XF	Unc	BU
2012 Proof	750	Value: 150				

KM# 753 5 DOLLARS
100.0000 g., 0.9990 Silver 3.2117 oz. ASW, 52.5x118 mm. **Ruler:** Elizabeth II **Subject:** DaVinci's Last Supper **Rev:** Matthew **Shape:** Vertical rectangle

Date	Mintage	F	VF	XF	Unc	BU
2012 Proof	750	Value: 150				

KM# 754 5 DOLLARS
100.0000 g., 0.9990 Silver 3.2117 oz. ASW, 52.5x118 mm. **Ruler:** Elizabeth II **Subject:** DaVinci's Last Supper **Rev:** Jude Thaddeus and Simon the Zealot **Shape:** Vertical rectangle

Date	Mintage	F	VF	XF	Unc	BU
2012 Proof	750	Value: 150				

KM# 774 5 DOLLARS
6.0000 g., 0.9999 Gold 0.1929 oz. AGW, 21 mm. **Ruler:** Elizabeth II **Subject:** Stare Hradisko **Obv:** Queen's head at left, two horse cart at right **Rev:** Celtic coin design and art

Date	Mintage	F	VF	XF	Unc	BU
2012 Proof	999	Value: 400				

KM# 776 5 DOLLARS
6.0000 g., 0.9000 Gold 0.1736 oz. AGW, 16.7x22.3 mm. **Ruler:** Elizabeth II **Subject:** Imperial Faberge Eggs - Coronation egg **Rev:** Egg and state coach

Date	Mintage	F	VF	XF	Unc	BU
2012 Proof	Est. 777	Value: 425				

KM# 780 5 DOLLARS
6.0000 g., 0.9999 Gold 0.1929 oz. AGW, 21 mm. **Ruler:** Elizabeth II **Subject:** Silk Route - Wroclaw **Obv:** Queen's head at left, two horse cart at right **Rev:** Old building at left, statue at right

Date	Mintage	F	VF	XF	Unc	BU
2012 Proof	Est. 999	Value: 400				

KM# 801 5 DOLLARS
6.0000 g., 0.9990 Gold 0.1927 oz. AGW, 21 mm. **Ruler:** Elizabeth II **Subject:** Szlak Bursztynowy - Szombathely **Rev:** Building, old coins and amber insert

Date	Mintage	F	VF	XF	Unc	BU
2012 Proof	Est. 999	Value: 400				

KM# 816 5 DOLLARS
62.2100 g., 0.9990 Silver 1.9980 oz. ASW, 50 mm. **Ruler:** Elizabeth II **Subject:** Napoleon and 1812, first design **Obv:** Crowned head right

Date	Mintage	F	VF	XF	Unc	BU
2012 Proof	999	Value: 150				

KM# 817 5 DOLLARS
62.2100 g., 0.9990 Silver 1.9980 oz. ASW, 50 mm. **Ruler:** Elizabeth II **Subject:** Napoleon, 2nd design **Obv:** Crowned head right

Date	Mintage	F	VF	XF	Unc	BU
2012 Proof	999	Value: 150				

KM# 842 5 DOLLARS
6.0000 g., 0.9999 Gold 0.1929 oz. AGW, 21 mm. **Ruler:** Elizabeth II **Obv:** Head with tiara at left, cart, map **Rev:** Ruins, statue, coin and amber insert **Rev. Legend:** CARNUNTUM

Date	Mintage	F	VF	XF	Unc	BU
2012 Proof	999	Value: 400				

KM# 844 5 DOLLARS
6.0000 g., 0.9999 Gold 0.1929 oz. AGW, 21 mm. **Ruler:** Elizabeth II **Subject:** Amber Route **Obv:** Head with tiara at left, cart, map **Rev:** She-wold statue, mosaic coin, amber insert **Rev. Legend:** AQUILEIA

Date	Mintage	F	VF	XF	Unc	BU
2012 Proof	999	Value: 400				

KM# 856 5 DOLLARS
6.0000 g., 0.9000 Gold 0.1736 oz. AGW, 16.7x22.3 mm. **Ruler:** Elizabeth II **Obv:** Head with tiara right above open egg **Rev:** Imperial Faberge Eggs - Cockerel **Shape:** Vertical oval

Date	Mintage	F	VF	XF	Unc	BU
2012 Proof	Est. 777	Value: 425				

KM# 124 10 DOLLARS
28.2800 g., 0.9250 Silver 0.8410 oz. ASW, 38.6 mm. **Ruler:** Elizabeth II **Subject:** Snoopy as an Ace **Obv:** Crowned head right **Rev:** Snoopy flying his dog house **Edge:** Reeded

Date	Mintage	F	VF	XF	Unc	BU
2001 Proof	10,000	Value: 35.00				

KM# 130 10 DOLLARS
28.2800 g., 0.9250 Silver 0.8410 oz. ASW, 38.6 mm. **Ruler:** Elizabeth II **Series:** Pokeman **Obv:** Crowned shield within sprigs **Rev:** Bulbasaur **Edge:** Reeded

Date	Mintage	F	VF	XF	Unc	BU
2001 Proof	10,000	Value: 35.00				

KM# 133 10 DOLLARS
28.2800 g., 0.9250 Silver 0.8410 oz. ASW, 38.6 mm. **Ruler:** Elizabeth II **Series:** Pokeman **Obv:** Crowned shield within sprigs **Rev:** Charmander **Edge:** Reeded

Date	Mintage	F	VF	XF	Unc	BU
2001 Proof	10,000	Value: 35.00				

KM# 136 10 DOLLARS
28.2800 g., 0.9250 Silver 0.8410 oz. ASW, 38.6 mm. **Ruler:** Elizabeth II **Series:** Pokeman **Obv:** Crowned shield within sprigs **Rev:** Meowth **Edge:** Reeded

Date	Mintage	F	VF	XF	Unc	BU
2001 Proof	10,000	Value: 35.00				

KM# 139 10 DOLLARS
28.2800 g., 0.9250 Silver 0.8410 oz. ASW, 38.6 mm. **Ruler:** Elizabeth II **Series:** Pokeman **Obv:** Crowned shield within sprigs **Rev:** Pikachu **Edge:** Reeded

Date	Mintage	F	VF	XF	Unc	BU
2001 Proof	10,000	Value: 35.00				

KM# 142 10 DOLLARS
28.2800 g., 0.9250 Silver 0.8410 oz. ASW, 38.6 mm. **Ruler:** Elizabeth II **Series:** Pokeman **Obv:** Crowned shield within sprigs **Rev:** Squirtle **Edge:** Reeded

Date	Mintage	F	VF	XF	Unc	BU
2001 Proof	10,000	Value: 35.00				

KM# 147 10 DOLLARS
28.2800 g., 0.9250 Silver 0.8410 oz. ASW, 38.6 mm. **Ruler:** Elizabeth II **Subject:** Pokémon Series **Obv:** Crowned shield within sprigs **Rev:** Pikachu **Edge:** Reeded

Date	Mintage	F	VF	XF	Unc	BU
2002PM Proof	10,000	Value: 35.00				

KM# 152 10 DOLLARS
28.2800 g., 0.9250 Silver 0.8410 oz. ASW, 38.6 mm. **Ruler:** Elizabeth II **Subject:** Pokémon Series **Obv:** Crowned shield within sprigs **Rev:** Pichu **Edge:** Reeded

Date	Mintage	F	VF	XF	Unc	BU
2002PM Proof	10,000	Value: 35.00				

KM# 157 10 DOLLARS
28.2800 g., 0.9250 Silver 0.8410 oz. ASW, 38.6 mm. **Ruler:** Elizabeth II **Subject:** Pokémon Series **Obv:** Crowned shield within sprigs **Rev:** Mewtwo **Edge:** Reeded

Date	Mintage	F	VF	XF	Unc	BU
2002PM Proof	10,000	Value: 35.00				

KM# 162 10 DOLLARS
28.2800 g., 0.9250 Silver 0.8410 oz. ASW, 38.6 mm. **Ruler:** Elizabeth II **Subject:** Pokémon Series **Obv:** Crowned shield within sprigs **Rev:** Entei **Edge:** Reeded

Date	Mintage	F	VF	XF	Unc	BU
2002PM Proof	10,000	Value: 35.00				

KM# 167 10 DOLLARS
28.2800 g., 0.9250 Silver 0.8410 oz. ASW, 38.6 mm. **Ruler:** Elizabeth II **Subject:** Pokémon Series **Obv:** Crowned shield within sprigs **Rev:** Celebi **Edge:** Reeded

Date	Mintage	F	VF	XF	Unc	BU
2002PM Proof	10,000	Value: 35.00				

KM# 274 10 DOLLARS
31.1050 g., 0.9990 Gold 0.9990 oz. AGW, 38.6 mm. **Ruler:** Elizabeth II **Subject:** Year of the Rooster

Date	Mintage	F	VF	XF	Unc	BU
2005 Proof	—	Value: 2,000				

KM# 254 10 DOLLARS
155.5000 g., 0.9990 Silver 4.9942 oz. ASW, 65 mm. **Ruler:** Elizabeth II **Subject:** Peanuts 60th Anniversary **Rev:** Peanut character heads around a central Snoopy

Date	Mintage	F	VF	XF	Unc	BU
2010 Prooflike	1,000	—	—	—	—	225

KM# 375 10 DOLLARS
100.0000 g., 0.9990 Silver 3.2117 oz. ASW, 64x54.2 mm. **Ruler:** Elizabeth II **Subject:** Kitty and friends **Shape:** Heart

Date	Mintage	F	VF	XF	Unc	BU
2010 Proof	Est. 1,000	Value: 150				

KM# 387 10 DOLLARS
155.5000 g., 0.9990 Silver 4.9942 oz. ASW, 65 mm. **Ruler:** Elizabeth II **Subject:** Miffy with cake

Date	Mintage	F	VF	XF	Unc	BU
2010 Proof	Est. 1,500	Value: 200				

KM# 815 10 DOLLARS
155.5500 g., 0.9990 Silver 4.9958 oz. ASW **Ruler:** Elizabeth II **Obv:** Crowned head right **Rev:** Secret Evening icon, Christ and deciples around table **Edge:** Reeded

Date	Mintage	F	VF	XF	Unc	BU
2012 Proof	500	Value: 450				

KM# 296 15 DOLLARS
500.0000 g., 0.9990 Silver 16.058 oz. ASW, 100 mm. **Ruler:** Elizabeth II **Subject:** Year of the Dog **Rev:** Multicolor dog

Date	Mintage	F	VF	XF	Unc	BU
2005 Proof	—	Value: 600				

KM# 267 15 DOLLARS
500.0000 g., 0.9990 Silver 16.058 oz. ASW, 100 mm. **Ruler:** Elizabeth II **Subject:** Year of the Rooster **Rev:** Multicolor rooster standing right, sunrise

Date	Mintage	F	VF	XF	Unc	BU
2005 Proof	—	Value: 600				

KM# 125 20 DOLLARS
1.2400 g., 0.9999 Gold 0.0399 oz. AGW, 13.9 mm. **Ruler:** Elizabeth II **Subject:** Snoopy as an Ace **Obv:** Crowned head right **Rev:** Snoopy flying his dog house **Edge:** Reeded

Date	Mintage	F	VF	XF	Unc	BU
2001 Proof	10,000	Value: 85.00				

KM# 148 20 DOLLARS
1.2400 g., 0.9999 Gold 0.0399 oz. AGW, 13.92 mm. **Ruler:** Elizabeth II **Subject:** Pokémon Series **Obv:** Crowned shield within sprigs **Rev:** Pikachu **Edge:** Reeded

Date	Mintage	F	VF	XF	Unc	BU
2002PM Proof	10,000	Value: 85.00				

KM# 153 20 DOLLARS
1.2400 g., 0.9999 Gold 0.0399 oz. AGW, 13.9 mm. **Ruler:** Elizabeth II **Subject:** Pokémon Series **Obv:** Crowned shield within sprigs **Rev:** Pichu **Edge:** Reeded

Date	Mintage	F	VF	XF	Unc	BU
2002PM Proof	10,000	Value: 85.00				

KM# 158 20 DOLLARS
1.2400 g., 0.9999 Gold 0.0399 oz. AGW, 13.92 mm. **Ruler:** Elizabeth II **Subject:** Pokémon Series **Obv:** Crowned shield within sprigs **Rev:** Mewtwo **Edge:** Reeded

Date	Mintage	F	VF	XF	Unc	BU
2002PM Proof	10,000	Value: 85.00				

KM# 163 20 DOLLARS
1.2400 g., 0.9999 Gold 0.0399 oz. AGW, 13.9 mm. **Ruler:** Elizabeth II **Subject:** Pokémon Series **Obv:** Crowned shield within sprigs **Rev:** Entei **Edge:** Reeded

Date	Mintage	F	VF	XF	Unc	BU
2002PM Proof	10,000	Value: 85.00				

KM# 168 20 DOLLARS
1.2400 g., 0.9999 Gold 0.0399 oz. AGW, 13.9 mm. **Ruler:** Elizabeth II **Subject:** Pokémon Series **Obv:** Crowned shield within sprigs **Rev:** Celebi **Edge:** Reeded

Date	Mintage	F	VF	XF	Unc	BU
2002PM Proof	10,000	Value: 85.00				

KM# 379 20 DOLLARS
0.9170 Gold, 13.9x16.7 mm. **Ruler:** Elizabeth II **Subject:** Hello Kitty **Shape:** Face **Note:** Center part to KM#380.

Date	Mintage	F	VF	XF	Unc	BU
2010 Proof	Est. 1,000	Value: 475				

KM# 255 25 DOLLARS
15.5500 g., 0.9990 Gold 0.4994 oz. AGW, 22 mm. **Ruler:** Elizabeth II **Subject:** Peanuts 60th Anniversary **Rev:** Snoopy dancing, Charlie Brown's zig-zag shirt pattern in background

Date	Mintage	F	VF	XF	Unc	BU
2010 Prooflike	1,000	—	—	—	—	950

KM# 388 25 DOLLARS
7.7700 g., 0.9990 Gold 0.2496 oz. AGW, 22 mm. **Ruler:** Elizabeth II **Subject:** Miffy with key

Date	Mintage	F	VF	XF	Unc	BU
2010 Proof	1,000	Value: 475				

KM# 715 25 DOLLARS
7.7800 g., 0.9999 Gold 0.2501 oz. AGW, 22 mm. **Ruler:** Elizabeth II **Rev:** Dragon

Date	Mintage	F	VF	XF	Unc	BU
2012 Proof	2,000	Value: 465				

KM# 846 25 DOLLARS
15.5000 g., 0.9999 Gold 0.4983 oz. AGW, 27 mm. **Ruler:** Elizabeth II **Obv:** Head with tiara at left, wreath **Rev:** Stanislaus Augustus head right

Date	Mintage	F	VF	XF	Unc	BU
2012 Proof	8,000	Value: 950				

KM# 268 30 DOLLARS
1000.0000 g., 0.9990 Silver 32.117 oz. ASW, 120 mm. **Ruler:** Elizabeth II **Subject:** Year of the Rooster **Rev:** Multicolor rooster standing right, sunrise

Date	Mintage	F	VF	XF	Unc	BU
2005 Proof	—	Value: 1,250				

KM# 297 30 DOLLARS
1000.0000 g., 0.9990 Silver 32.117 oz. ASW, 120 mm. **Ruler:** Elizabeth II **Subject:** Year of the Dog **Rev:** Multicolor dog

Date	Mintage	F	VF	XF	Unc	BU
2005 Proof	—	Value: 1,250				

KM# 380 30 DOLLARS
0.9170 Gold, 30 mm. **Ruler:** Elizabeth II **Subject:** Bears **Note:** Outer ring for KM#379

Date	Mintage	F	VF	XF	Unc	BU
2010 Proof	Est. 1,000	Value: 650				

KM# 742 30 DOLLARS
1000.0000 g., 0.9990 Silver 32.117 oz. ASW, 100 mm. **Ruler:** Elizabeth II **Subject:** Year of the Dragon **Rev:** Dragon with pearl in color

Date	Mintage	F	VF	XF	Unc	BU
2012 Proof	250	Value: 1,250				

KM# 788 30 DOLLARS
1000.0000 g., 0.9990 Silver 32.117 oz. ASW, 100 mm. **Ruler:** Elizabeth II **Subject:** Russian municipalities - Belgorod **Obv:** Head with crown right **Rev:** Statue, shield and building

Date	Mintage	F	VF	XF	Unc	BU
2012 Proof	—	Value: 1,300				

KM# 869 30 DOLLARS
1000.0000 g., 0.9990 Silver 32.117 oz. ASW, 100 mm. **Ruler:** Elizabeth II **Obv:** Crowned head right **Rev:** Coral Snake with chinese character above

Date	Mintage	F	VF	XF	Unc	BU
2013 Proof	300	Value: 1,000				

KM# 126 50 DOLLARS
3.1100 g., 0.9999 Gold 0.1000 oz. AGW, 17.9 mm. **Ruler:** Elizabeth II **Subject:** Snoopy as an Ace **Obv:** Crowned head right **Rev:** Snoopy flying his dog house **Edge:** Reeded

Date	Mintage	F	VF	XF	Unc	BU
2001 Proof	7,500	Value: 195				

KM# 149 50 DOLLARS
3.1100 g., 0.9999 Gold 0.1000 oz. AGW, 17.9 mm. **Ruler:** Elizabeth II **Subject:** Pokémon Series **Obv:** Crowned shield within sprigs **Rev:** Pikachu **Edge:** Reeded

Date	Mintage	F	VF	XF	Unc	BU
2002PM Proof	7,500	Value: 195				

KM# 154 50 DOLLARS
3.1100 g., 0.9999 Gold 0.1000 oz. AGW, 17.9 mm. **Ruler:** Elizabeth II **Subject:** Pokémon Series **Obv:** Crowned shield within sprigs **Rev:** Pichu **Edge:** Reeded

Date	Mintage	F	VF	XF	Unc	BU
2002PM Proof	7,500	Value: 195				

KM# 159 50 DOLLARS
3.1100 g., 0.9999 Gold 0.1000 oz. AGW, 17.9 mm. **Ruler:** Elizabeth II **Subject:** Pokémon Series **Obv:** Crowned shield within sprigs **Rev:** Mewtwo **Edge:** Reeded

Date	Mintage	F	VF	XF	Unc	BU
2002PM Proof	7,500	Value: 195				

KM# 164 50 DOLLARS
3.1100 g., 0.9999 Gold 0.1000 oz. AGW, 17.9 mm. **Ruler:** Elizabeth II **Subject:** Pokémon Series **Obv:** Crowned shield within sprigs **Rev:** Entei **Edge:** Reeded

Date	Mintage	F	VF	XF	Unc	BU
2002PM Proof	7,500	Value: 195				

KM# 169 50 DOLLARS
3.1100 g., 0.9999 Gold 0.1000 oz. AGW, 17.9 mm. **Ruler:** Elizabeth II **Subject:** Pokémon Series **Obv:** Crowned shield within sprigs **Rev:** Celebi **Edge:** Reeded

Date	Mintage	F	VF	XF	Unc	BU
2002PM Proof	7,500	Value: 195				

KM# 256 50 DOLLARS
15.5500 g., 0.9990 Gold 0.4994 oz. AGW, 30 mm. **Ruler:** Elizabeth II **Subject:** Peanuts 60th Anniversary **Rev:** Snoopy as a king

Date	Mintage	F	VF	XF	Unc	BU
2010 Prooflike	1,000	—	—	—	—	950

KM# 389 50 DOLLARS
15.5500 g., 0.9990 Gold 0.4994 oz. AGW, 30 mm. **Ruler:** Elizabeth II **Subject:** Miffy in flowers

Date	Mintage	F	VF	XF	Unc	BU
2010 Proof	Est. 1,000	Value: 950				

KM# 584 50 DOLLARS
250.0000 g., 0.9990 Silver 8.0293 oz. ASW, 67.35x90 mm. **Ruler:** Elizabeth II **Subject:** Russian Royal Family **Obv:** Nicholas II and family standing as Saints in the Othodox Church, head with tiara right below **Rev:** Oval portrait images of the Imperial family **Shape:** Vertical Oval

Date	Mintage	F	VF	XF	Unc	BU
2011 Proof	400	Value: 400				

KM# 702 50 DOLLARS
62.2000 g., 0.9999 Gold 1.9995 oz. AGW **Ruler:** Elizabeth II **Rev:** John Wycliff and Jan Hus

Date	Mintage	F	VF	XF	Unc	BU
2011 Proof	Est. 1,000	Value: 3,700				

KM# 714 50 DOLLARS
31.1050 g., 0.9999 Gold 0.9999 oz. AGW, 32 mm. **Ruler:** Elizabeth II **Rev:** Dragon

Date	Mintage	F	VF	XF	Unc	BU
2012 Proof	2,000	Value: 1,850				

KM# 777 50 DOLLARS
31.1000 g., 0.9999 Gold 0.9997 oz. AGW, 29.2x39 mm. **Ruler:** Elizabeth II **Subject:** Imperial Faberge Eggs - Corconation Egg **Rev:** Egg and state coach

Date	Mintage	F	VF	XF	Unc	BU
2012 Proof	Est. 333	Value: 2,000				

KM# 778 50 DOLLARS
250.0000 g., 0.9990 Silver 8.0293 oz. ASW, 67.35x90 mm. **Ruler:** Elizabeth II **Subject:** Imperial Faberge Eggs - Coronation Egg **Rev:** Egg and state coach

Date	Mintage	F	VF	XF	Unc	BU
2012 Proof	Est. 333	Value: 350				

KM# 791 50 DOLLARS
250.0000 g., 0.9990 Silver 8.0293 oz. ASW, 67.35x90 mm. **Ruler:** Elizabeth II **Subject:** Great Ukrainian Hetmans **Obv:** Seven shields around central head of Queen Elizabeth **Rev:** Seven busts around central shield **Shape:** Vertical oval

Date	Mintage	F	VF	XF	Unc	BU
2012 Proof	400	Value: 400				

KM# 793 50 DOLLARS
250.0000 g., 0.9250 Silver 7.4345 oz. ASW, 67.35x90 mm. **Ruler:** Elizabeth II **Subject:** Royal Hunting **Obv:** Saint on horseback **Rev:** Horseman with falcon **Shape:** Vertical oval

Date	Mintage	F	VF	XF	Unc	BU
2012 Proof	Est. 400	Value: 400				

KM# 827 50 DOLLARS
31.1050 g., 0.9999 Gold 0.9999 oz. AGW, 32 mm. **Ruler:** Elizabeth II **Obv:** Head in tiara at left, branches **Rev:** Head right of Stanislaus Augustus

Date	Mintage	F	VF	XF	Unc	BU
2012 Proof	Est. 16,000	Value: 1,775				

KM# 880 50 DOLLARS
250.0000 g., 0.9990 Silver 8.0293 oz. ASW, 90x67.35 mm. **Ruler:** Elizabeth II **Subject:** Russian Royal Charity **Obv:** Head with tiara at top center, four building façades around **Rev:** Oval portraits at left and right, church at center **Shape:** Horizontal oval

Date	Mintage	F	VF	XF	Unc	BU
2012 Proof	Est. 400	Value: 350				

KM# 127 100 DOLLARS
6.2200 g., 0.9999 Gold 0.1999 oz. AGW, 22 mm. **Ruler:** Elizabeth II **Subject:** Snoopy as an Ace **Obv:** Crowned head right **Rev:** Snoopy flying his dog house **Edge:** Reeded

Date	Mintage	F	VF	XF	Unc	BU
2001 Proof	5,000	Value: 400				

KM# 150 100 DOLLARS
6.2200 g., 0.9999 Gold 0.1999 oz. AGW, 22 mm. **Ruler:** Elizabeth II **Subject:** Pokémon Series **Obv:** Crowned shield within sprigs **Rev:** Pikachu **Edge:** Reeded

Date	Mintage	F	VF	XF	Unc	BU
2002PM Proof	5,000	Value: 400				

KM# 155 100 DOLLARS
6.2200 g., 0.9999 Gold 0.1999 oz. AGW, 22 mm. **Ruler:** Elizabeth II **Subject:** Pokémon Series **Obv:** Crowned shield within sprigs **Rev:** Pichu **Edge:** Reeded

Date	Mintage	F	VF	XF	Unc	BU
2002PM Proof	5,000	Value: 400				

KM# 160 100 DOLLARS
6.2200 g., 0.9999 Gold 0.1999 oz. AGW, 22 mm. **Ruler:** Elizabeth II **Subject:** Pokémon Series **Obv:** Crowned shield within sprigs **Rev:** Mewtwo **Edge:** Reeded

Date	Mintage	F	VF	XF	Unc	BU
2002PM Proof	5,000	Value: 400				

KM# 165 100 DOLLARS
6.2200 g., 0.9999 Gold 0.1999 oz. AGW, 22 mm. **Ruler:** Elizabeth II **Subject:** Pokémon Series **Obv:** Crowned shield within sprigs **Rev:** Entei **Edge:** Reeded

Date	Mintage	F	VF	XF	Unc	BU
2002PM Proof	5,000	Value: 400				

KM# 170 100 DOLLARS
6.2200 g., 0.9999 Gold 0.1999 oz. AGW, 22 mm. **Ruler:** Elizabeth II **Subject:** Pokémon Series **Obv:** Crowned shield within sprigs **Rev:** Celebi **Edge:** reeded

Date	Mintage	F	VF	XF	Unc	BU
2002PM Proof	5,000	Value: 400				

KM# 425 100 DOLLARS
93.3000 g., 0.9000 Gold 2.6996 oz. AGW, 41.6x55.6 mm. **Ruler:** Elizabeth II **Subject:** Imperial Faberge Egg - Coronation Egg **Obv:** Head with tiara right above opened egg **Rev:** Coronation egg and coach **Shape:** Vertical oval

Date	Mintage	F	VF	XF	Unc	BU
2010 Proof	222	Value: 5,000				

KM# 511 100 DOLLARS

31.1030 g., 0.9990 Gold 0.9989 oz. AGW, 38.61 mm. **Ruler:** Elizabeth II **Obv:** Head with tiara right **Rev:** Tasmanian tiger in color

Date	Mintage	F	VF	XF	Unc	BU
2011 Proof	200	Value: 2,000				

KM# 572 100 DOLLARS

93.3000 g., 0.9000 Gold 2.6996 oz. AGW, 41.6x55.6 mm. **Ruler:** Elizabeth II **Subject:** Imperial Faberge Egg **Obv:** Head with tiara right, open egg below **Rev:** Clover leaf floral egg on stand **Shape:** Vertical oval

Date	Mintage	F	VF	XF	Unc	BU
2011 Proof	222	Value: 5,000				

KM# 648 100 DOLLARS

93.3000 g., 0.9000 Gold 2.6996 oz. AGW, 41.6x55.6 mm. **Ruler:** Elizabeth II **Subject:** Imperial Easter Egg - Lilly **Obv:** Head with tiara right, open egg below **Rev:** Egg on stand, lillys around

Date	Mintage	F	VF	XF	Unc	BU
2011 Proof	Est. 222	Value: 5,000				

KM# 650 100 DOLLARS

50.0000 g., 0.9990 Silver partially gilt 1.6059 oz. ASW, 35.2 x 35.2 mm. **Ruler:** Elizabeth II **Obv:** Head with tiara right **Rev:** Three Kings of 1936 - George V, Edward VIII, George VI selectively gilt **Edge:** Reeded **Shape:** Square

Date	Mintage	F	VF	XF	Unc	BU
2011 Proof	1,500	Value: 160				

KM# 701 100 DOLLARS

139.5000 g., 0.9999 Gold 4.4844 oz. AGW, 50 mm. **Ruler:** Elizabeth II **Subject:** General Perina, Battle of Britain pilot **Rev:** Perina as pilot

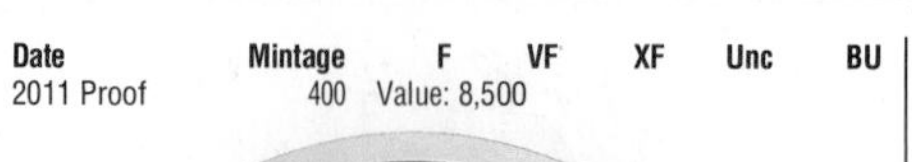

Date	Mintage	F	VF	XF	Unc	BU
2011 Proof	400	Value: 8,500				

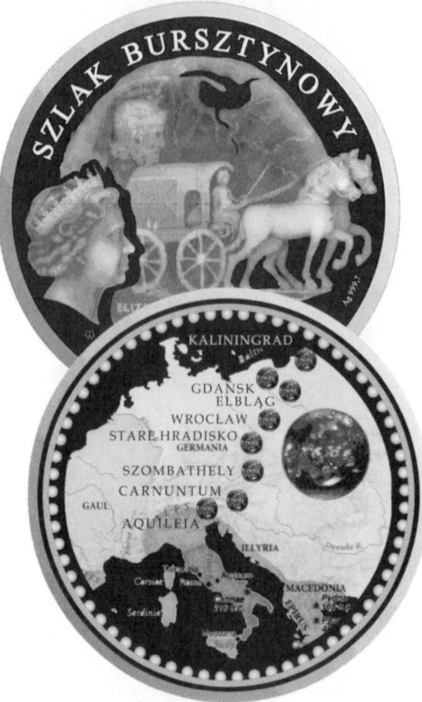

KM# 747 100 DOLLARS

400.0000 g., 0.9997 Silver gilt 12.855 oz. ASW, 90 mm. **Ruler:** Elizabeth II **Subject:** Szlak Bursztynowy **Obv:** Queen's head at left, Roman horse cart at right **Rev:** Map of central Europe, amber insert

Date	Mintage	F	VF	XF	Unc	BU
2011 Proof	245	Value: 500				

KM# 737 100 DOLLARS

31.1050 g., 0.9990 Gold 0.9990 oz. AGW, 38.61 mm. **Ruler:** Elizabeth II **Rev:** Tasmanian Wedge-Tailed Eagle **Edge:** Reeded and numbered

Date	Mintage	F	VF	XF	Unc	BU
2012 Proof	150	Value: 2,000				

KM# 755 100 DOLLARS

93.3000 g., 0.9000 Gold 2.6996 oz. AGW, 41.6x55.6 mm. **Ruler:** Elizabeth II **Subject:** Imperial Faberge Eggs - Duchess of Marlborough **Rev:** Serpent at bottom stem of egg **Shape:** Vertical oval

Date	Mintage	F	VF	XF	Unc	BU
2012 Proof	222	Value: 5,000				

KM# 834 100 DOLLARS

93.3000 g., 0.9000 Gold 2.6996 oz. AGW, 41.6x55.6 mm. **Ruler:** Elizabeth II **Obv:** Head with tiara above opened egg **Rev:** Imperial Faberge Eggs - Pansy Egg **Shape:** Vertical oval

Date	Mintage	F	VF	XF	Unc	BU
2012 Proof	222	Value: 4,850				

KM# 835 100 DOLLARS

93.3000 g., 0.9000 Gold 2.6996 oz. AGW, 41.6x55.6 mm. **Ruler:** Elizabeth II **Obv:** Head in tiara right above opened egg **Rev:** Imperial Faberge Egg - Bay Tree **Shape:** Vertical oval

Date	Mintage	F	VF	XF	Unc	BU
2012 Proof	222	Value: 4,850				

KM# 512 200 DOLLARS

62.2000 g., 0.9990 Gold 1.9977 oz. AGW, 35.2x35.2 mm. **Ruler:** Elizabeth II **Subject:** Three kings of 1935 **Obv:** Head with tiara right **Rev:** Head left of George V, Edward VIII and George VI

Date	Mintage	F	VF	XF	Unc	BU
2011 Proof	250	Value: 3,750				

KM# 649 200 DOLLARS

62.2100 g., 0.9990 Gold 1.9980 oz. AGW, 35.2x35.2 mm. **Ruler:** Elizabeth II **Obv:** Head with tiara right **Rev:** Three kings of 1936 - George V, Edward VIII, George VI in 3-D **Edge:** Reeded **Shape:** Square

Date	Mintage	F	VF	XF	Unc	BU
2011 Proof	75	Value: 4,000				

KM# 713 200 DOLLARS

155.5500 g., 0.9999 Gold 5.0003 oz. AGW **Ruler:** Elizabeth II **Rev:** Dragon

Date	Mintage	F	VF	XF	Unc	BU
2012 Proof	100	Value: 9,500				

KM# 740 200 DOLLARS

1000.0000 g., 0.9990 Silver 32.117 oz. ASW, 118.2x52.7 mm. **Ruler:** Elizabeth II **Obv:** Head with crown at left **Rev:** Two dragons flanking center ball **Shape:** Horizontal rectangle

Date	Mintage	F	VF	XF	Unc	BU
2012 Proof	1,800	Value: 1,250				

KM# 700 250 DOLLARS

348.5000 g., 0.9999 Gold 11.202 oz. AGW, 65 mm. **Ruler:** Elizabeth II **Rev:** Jan Amos Komensky seated at desk with globe

Date	Mintage	F	VF	XF	Unc	BU
2011 Proof	Est. 250	Value: 20,000				

KM# 405 3000 DOLLARS

500.0000 g., 0.9999 Gold 16.073 oz. AGW, 67.35x90 mm. **Ruler:** Elizabeth II **Subject:** Russian Royal Family **Obv:** Seven figures as Orthodox Saints, Elizabeth head with tiara below **Rev:** Oval portaits of Nicholas II and his family **Shape:** Vertical Oval

Date	Mintage	F	VF	XF	Unc	BU
2010 Proof	23	Value: 29,500				

KM# 588 3000 DOLLARS

500.0000 g., 0.9999 Gold 16.073 oz. AGW, 67.35x90 mm. **Ruler:** Elizabeth II **Subject:** Royal Hunting **Obv:** Russian saint on horseback, head with tiara right below, multicolor **Rev:** Russian figure on horseback with falcon, multicolor

Date	Mintage	F	VF	XF	Unc	BU
2011 Proof	40	Value: 29,500				

KM# 881 3000 DOLLARS

500.0000 g., 0.9999 Gold 16.073 oz. AGW, 90x67.35 mm. **Ruler:** Elizabeth II **Subject:** Russian Royal Charity **Obv:** Head with tiara at top center, four building façades around **Rev:** Vertical oval portraits flanking church **Shape:** Horizontal oval

Date	Mintage	F	VF	XF	Unc	BU
2012 Proof	Est. 30	Value: 29,500				

KM# 699 10000 DOLLARS

1000.0000 g., 0.9999 Gold 32.146 oz. AGW, 85 mm. **Ruler:** Elizabeth II **Rev:** Good Queen Ann seated on throne

Date	Mintage	F	VF	XF	Unc	BU
2011 Proof	Est. 150	Value: 58,500				

KM# 708 10000 DOLLARS

1000.0000 g., 0.9999 Gold 32.146 oz. AGW, 90 mm. **Ruler:** Elizabeth II **Obv:** Ancient horsecart **Obv. Legend:** SZLAK BURSZTYNOWY **Rev:** European map with cities, amber insert

Date	Mintage	F	VF	XF	Unc	BU
2011	Est. 12	Value: 60,000				

MINT SETS

KM#	Date	Mintage	Identification	Issue Price	Mkt Val
MS1	2009 (5)	20,000	KM#193-197	—	30.00
MS2	2010 (5)	10,000	KM#193-196, 198	—	30.00

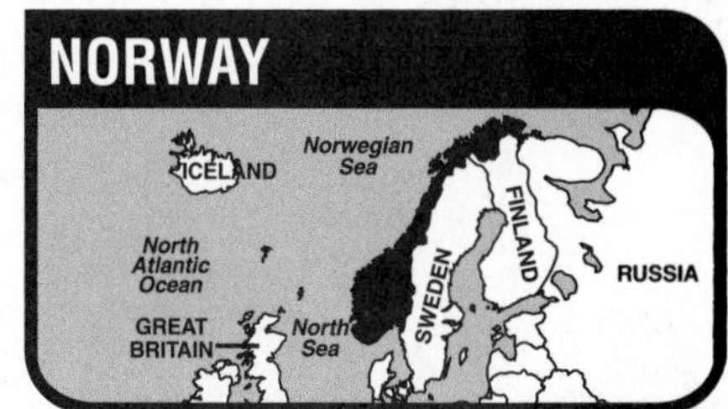

The Kingdom of Norway (*Norge, Noreg*), a constitutional monarchy located in northwestern Europe, has an area of 150,000sq. mi. (324,220 sq. km.), including the island territories of Spitzbergen (Svalbard) and Jan Mayen, and a population of *4.2 million. Capital: Oslo (Christiania). The diversified economic base of Norway includes shipping, fishing, forestry, agriculture, and manufacturing. Nonferrous metals, paper and paperboard, paper pulp, iron, steel and oil are exported.

RULER

Harald V, 1991-

MINT MARK

(h) - Crossed hammers – Kongsberg

MONETARY SYSTEM

100 Ore = 1 Krone

KINGDOM

DECIMAL COINAGE

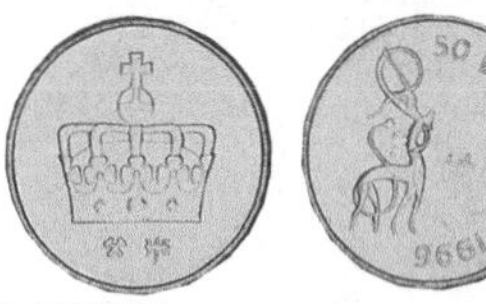

KM# 460 50 ORE

3.6000 g., Bronze, 18.5 mm. **Ruler:** Harald V **Obv:** Crown **Rev:** Stylized animal and value **Edge:** Plain **Designer:** Grazyna Jolanta Linday

Date	Mintage	VG	F	VF	XF	BU
2001 without star	16,848,250	—	—	—	—	0.50
2001 with star	13,291,750	—	—	—	1.00	3.00
2001 Proof	11,500	Value: 10.00				
2002	28,293,000	—	—	—	—	0.40
2002 Proof	11,500	Value: 10.00				
2003	15,522,000	—	—	—	—	0.40
2003 Proof	10,800	Value: 10.00				
2004	14,747,500	—	—	—	—	0.40
2004 Proof	8,550	Value: 10.00				
2005	4,954,500	—	—	—	—	0.40
2005 Proof	8,550	Value: 10.00				
2006	30,218,500	—	—	—	—	0.40
2006 Proof	8,550	Value: 10.00				
2007	20,110,500	—	—	—	—	0.40
2007 Proof	6,582	Value: 10.00				
2008	19,384,000	—	—	—	—	0.40
2008 Proof	7,091	Value: 10.00				
2009	9,897,000	—	—	—	—	0.40
2009 Proof	6,310	Value: 10.00				
2010	14,988,000	—	—	—	—	0.40
2010 Proof	5,119	Value: 10.00				
2011 11 in date reversed	8,300,000	—	—	—	—	0.40
2011 11 in date corrected	1,666,000	—	—	—	—	0.40
2011 Proof	4,142	Value: 10.00				

KM# 462 KRONE

4.3500 g., Copper-Nickel, 21 mm. **Ruler:** Harald V **Obv:** Crowned monograms form cross within circle with center hole **Rev:** Bird on vine above center hole date and value below

Date	Mintage	VG	F	VF	XF	BU
2001 without star	43,128,650	—	—	—	—	0.65
2001 with star	7,355,350	—	—	—	2.00	4.00
2001 Proof	11,500	Value: 10.00				
2002	21,313,000	—	—	—	—	0.65
2002 Proof	11,500	Value: 10.00				
2003	24,082,000	—	—	—	—	0.65
2003 Proof	10,800	Value: 10.00				
2004	25,142,500	—	—	—	—	0.65
2004 Proof	8,550	Value: 10.00				
2005	25,639,500	—	—	—	—	0.65
2005 Proof	8,550	Value: 10.00				
2006	63,120,500	—	—	—	—	0.65
2006 Proof	8,500	Value: 10.00				
2007	47,101,500	—	—	—	—	0.65
2007 Proof	6,582	Value: 10.00				
2008	46,040,000	—	—	—	—	0.65
2008 Proof	7,091	Value: 10.00				
2009	50,049,000	—	—	—	—	0.65

Date	Mintage	VG	F	VF	XF	BU
2009 Proof	6,310	Value: 10.00				
2010	40,021,000	—	—	—	—	0.65
2010 Proof	5,119	Value: 10.00				
2011	35,042,000	—	—	—	—	0.50
2011 Proof	4,142	Value: 10.00				
2012	—	—	—	—	—	0.50
2012 Proof	—	Value: 20.00				

KM# 463 5 KRONER
7.8500 g., Copper-Nickel, 26 mm. **Ruler:** Harald V **Subject:** Order of St. Olaf **Obv:** Hole at center of order chain **Rev:** Center hole divides sprigs, value above and date below **Edge:** Reeded

Date	Mintage	VG	F	VF	XF	BU
2001	480,000	—	—	—	—	2.50
2001 Proof	11,500	Value: 13.00				
2002	3,622,000	—	—	—	—	1.50
2002 Proof	11,500	Value: 13.00				
2003	816,000	—	—	—	—	1.50
2003 Proof	10,800	Value: 13.00				
2004	494,500	—	—	—	—	1.50
2004 Proof	8,550	Value: 14.00				
2005	494,500	—	—	—	—	2.00
2005 Proof	8,550	Value: 14.00				
2006	500,500	—	—	—	—	1.50
2006 Proof	8,500	Value: 14.00				
2007	9,152,000	—	—	—	—	1.50
2007 Proof	9,145,000	Value: 14.00				
2008	5,495,000	—	—	—	—	1.50
2008 Proof	7,091	Value: 14.00				
2009	10,014,000	—	—	—	—	1.50
2009 Proof	6,310	Value: 14.00				
2011	—	—	—	—	—	1.50
2012	—	—	—	—	—	1.50
2012 Proof	—	Value: 40.00				

KM# 457 10 KRONER
6.8000 g., Nickel-Brass, 24 mm. **Ruler:** Harald V **Obv:** Head right **Rev:** Stylized church rooftop, value and date **Edge:** Segmented reeding **Designer:** Ingrid Austlid Rise

Date	Mintage	VG	F	VF	XF	BU
2001 without star	9,854,000	—	—	—	—	3.50
2001 with star	10,000	—	—	—	—	50.00
2001 Proof	11,500	Value: 10.00				
2002	1,123,000	—	—	—	—	3.50
2002 Proof	11,500	Value: 10.00				
2003	946,500	—	—	—	—	3.50
2003 Proof	10,800	Value: 10.00				
2004	494,500	—	—	—	—	4.50
2004 Proof	8,550	Value: 10.00				
2005	457,500	—	—	—	—	4.50
2005 Proof	8,550	Value: 10.00				
2006	488,500	—	—	—	—	3.50
2006 Proof	8,500	Value: 10.00				
2007	467,500	—	—	—	—	3.50
2007 Proof	6,582	Value: 10.00				
2008	565,508	—	—	—	—	3.50
2008 Proof	—	Value: 10.00				
2009	469,000	—	—	—	—	3.50
2009 Proof	6,310	Value: 10.00				
2010	—	—	—	—	—	3.50
2010 Proof	—	Value: 10.00				
2011	—	—	—	—	—	3.00
2012	—	—	—	—	—	3.00
2012 Proof	—	Value: 50.00				

KM# 482 10 KRONER
6.8000 g., Nickel-Brass, 24 mm. **Ruler:** Harald V **Subject:** Henrik Vergeland **Obv:** Head right **Rev:** Spectacles and vertical signature

Date	Mintage	F	VF	XF	Unc	BU
2008	4,620,638	—	—	—	—	3.50
2008 Proof	7,091	Value: 10.00				

KM# 483 10 KRONER
6.8000 g., Nickel-Brass, 24 mm. **Ruler:** Harald V **Subject:** Ole Bull 100th Anniversary of Birth **Obv:** Head right **Rev:** Bust and music score **Edge:** Segmented reeding

Date	Mintage	F	VF	XF	Unc	BU
2010	974,000	—	—	—	—	3.00
2010 Proof	5,119	Value: 10.00				

KM# 484 10 KRONER
6.8000 g., Nickel-Brass, 24 mm. **Ruler:** Harald V **Subject:** Norway's first University, 200th Anniversary **Obv:** Head right **Rev:** Column

Date	Mintage	F	VF	XF	Unc	BU
2011	2,996,000	—	—	—	—	3.00
2011 Proof	4,142	Value: 10.00				

KM# 453 20 KRONER
9.9000 g., Nickel-Brass, 27.5 mm. **Ruler:** Harald V **Obv:** Head right **Rev:** Value above 1/2 ancient boat **Designer:** Ingrid Austlid Rise

Date	Mintage	VG	F	VF	XF	BU
2001	4,194,000	—	—	—	—	5.00
2001 with star	10,000	—	—	—	—	200
2001 Proof	11,500	Value: 25.00				
2002	18,218,000	—	—	—	—	5.00
2003	30,050,000	—	—	—	—	5.00
2003 Proof	11,100	Value: 25.00				
2005	544,500	—	—	—	—	5.00
2005 Proof	8,550	Value: 25.00				
2007	486,500	—	—	—	—	5.00
2007 Proof	6,582	Value: 25.00				
2008	474,000	—	—	—	—	5.00
2008 Proof	7,091	Value: 25.00				
2009	467,000	—	—	—	—	5.00
2009 Proof	6,310	Value: 25.00				

KM# 471 20 KRONER
9.9000 g., Nickel-Brass, 27.5 mm. **Ruler:** Harald V **Subject:** Niels Henrik Abel **Obv:** Head right **Rev:** Pair of glasses, dates and value within mathematical graphs **Edge:** Plain

Date	Mintage	F	VF	XF	Unc	BU
2002	2,230,000	—	—	—	5.50	12.00
2002 Proof	11,500	Value: 25.00				

KM# 478 20 KRONER
9.9000 g., Nickel-Brass, 27.5 mm. **Ruler:** Harald V **Subject:** First Norwegian Railroad **Obv:** Head right **Rev:** Railroad track switch and value **Edge:** Plain

Date	Mintage	F	VF	XF	Unc	BU
2004	490,500	—	—	—	5.50	20.00
2004 Proof	8,550	Value: 25.00				

KM# 479 20 KRONER
9.9000 g., Nickel-Brass, 27.5 mm. **Ruler:** Harald V **Obv:** Head right **Rev:** Henrik Ibsen caricature walking left, signature **Edge:** Plain

Date	Mintage	F	VF	XF	Unc	BU
2006	991,500	—	—	—	5.50	12.00
2006 Proof	8,500	Value: 10.00				

KM# 469 100 KRONER
33.6000 g., 0.9250 Silver 0.9992 oz. ASW, 39 mm. **Ruler:** Harald V **Subject:** Nobel Peace Prize Centennial **Obv:** Rampant crowned lion left holding axe **Rev:** Head left **Edge:** Plain

Date	Mintage	F	VF	XF	Unc	BU
2001 Proof	50,000	Value: 200				

KM# 472 100 KRONER
33.8000 g., 0.9250 Silver 1.0052 oz. ASW, 39 mm. **Ruler:** Harald V **Subject:** 1905 Independence from Sweden **Obv:** Three kings **Rev:** Farm field **Edge:** Plain

Date	Mintage	F	VF	XF	Unc	BU
2003 Proof	65,000	Value: 70.00				

KM# 474 100 KRONER
33.8000 g., 0.9250 Silver 1.0052 oz. ASW, 39 mm. **Ruler:** Harald V **Subject:** 1905 Liberation **Obv:** Three kings **Rev:** Off shore ocean oil well **Edge:** Plain

Date	Mintage	F	VF	XF	Unc	BU
2004 Proof	65,000	Value: 70.00				

KM# 476 100 KRONER
33.8000 g., 0.9250 Silver 1.0052 oz. ASW, 39 mm. **Ruler:** Harald V **Obv:** Three kings **Rev:** Circuit board **Edge:** Plain

Date	Mintage	F	VF	XF	Unc	BU
2005 Proof	72,000	Value: 70.00				

KM# 480 200 KRONER
16.8500 g., 0.9250 Silver 0.5011 oz. ASW, 32 mm. **Ruler:** Harald V **Subject:** Henrik Wergeland, 200th Birth Anniversary **Obv:** Head right **Rev:** Spectacles and signature

Date	Mintage	F	VF	XF	Unc	BU
2008 Proof	40,000	Value: 100				

KM# 481 200 KRONER
16.8500 g., 0.9250 Silver 0.5011 oz. ASW, 32 mm. **Ruler:** Harald V **Subject:** Knut Hamsun 150th Birth Anniversary **Obv:** Crowned shield **Rev:** Streppled portrait, novel text and signature

Date	Mintage	F	VF	XF	Unc	BU
2009 Proof	40,000	Value: 100				

KM# 485 200 KRONER
16.8500 g., 0.9250 Silver 0.5011 oz. ASW, 32 mm. **Ruler:** Harald V **Subject:** World Ski Championships, 2011 **Obv:** Head right **Rev:** Different types of skiers

Date	Mintage	F	VF	XF	Unc	BU
2011 Proof	40,000	Value: 100				

KM# 486 200 KRONER

16.8500 g., 0.9250 Silver 0.5011 oz. ASW, 32 mm. **Ruler:** Harald V **Obv:** Head right **Rev:** Various Athletics, Javelin, track, skating, snowboarding, table tennis.

Date	Mintage	F	VF	XF	Unc	BU
2011 Proof	40,000	Value: 100				

KM# 487 200 KRONER

16.8500 g., 0.9250 Silver 0.5011 oz. ASW, 32 mm. **Ruler:** Harald V **Subject:** Harold V and Queen Sonia, 75th Birthday **Obv:** Crowned shield **Obv. Legend:** KONGERIKET NORGE **Rev:** Heads 1/4 right of Harold and Sonia **Rev. Legend:** KONG HARALD V DRONNING SONJA 75 AR

Date	Mintage	F	VF	XF	Unc	BU
2012 Proof	40,000	Value: 100				

KM# 470 1500 KRONER

16.9600 g., 0.9170 Gold 0.5000 oz. AGW, 27 mm. **Ruler:** Harald V **Subject:** Nobel Peace Prize Centennial **Obv:** Head right **Rev:** Reverse design of the prize medal **Edge:** Plain

Date	Mintage	VG	F	VF	XF	BU
ND(2001) Matte Proof	7,500	Value: 1,200				

KM# 473 1500 KRONER

16.9600 g., 0.9170 Gold 0.5000 oz. AGW, 27 mm. **Ruler:** Harald V **Subject:** 1905 Liberation **Obv:** Three kings **Rev:** Various leaf types **Edge:** Plain

Date	Mintage	F	VF	XF	Unc	BU
2003 Proof	10,000	Value: 1,000				

KM# 475 1500 KRONER

16.9600 g., 0.9170 Gold 0.5000 oz. AGW, 27 mm. **Ruler:** Harald V **Subject:** 1905 Liberation **Obv:** Three kings **Rev:** Liquid drops on hard surface **Edge:** Plain

Date	Mintage	F	VF	XF	Unc	BU
2004 Proof	10,000	Value: 1,000				

KM# 477 1500 KRONER

16.9600 g., 0.9170 Gold 0.5000 oz. AGW, 27 mm. **Ruler:** Harald V **Obv:** Three kings **Rev:** Binary language **Edge:** Plain

Date	Mintage	F	VF	XF	Unc	BU
2005 Proof	10,000	Value: 1,000				

MINT SETS

KM#	Date	Mintage	Identification	Issue Price	Mkt Val
MS66	2001 (5)	17,000	KM453, 457, 460, 462, 463. Uncirculated set, souvenir version, Norwegian text	20.00	30.00
MS67	2001 (5)	—	KM#453, 457, 460, 462, 463 (Uncirculated Set, Souvenir Version, English text). Mintage included with MS66.	—	30.00
MS68	2001 (5)	30,000	KM453, 457, 460, 462, 463. Children's (Baby) set.	18.00	30.00
MS69	2001 (5)	2,000	KM453, 457, 460, 462, 463 plus medal.	27.00	27.00
MS70	2001 (5)	—	KM453, 457, 460, 462, 463. Uncirculated set, classic version (hard plastic case)	—	30.00
MS71	2002 (5)	55,000	KM#453, 457, 460, 462, 463, Uncirculated set, classic version (hard plastic case)	—	32.00
MS72	2002 (5)	9,893	KM#453, 457, 460, 462, 463 (Uncirculated Set, Souvenir Version, Norwegian text)	—	30.00
MS73	2002 (5)	—	KM#453, 457, 460, 462, 463 (Uncirculated Set, Souvenir Version, English text). Mintage included with MS72.	—	30.00
MS74	2002 (5)	—	KM#453, 457, 460, 462, 463 plus Silver medal Children's (Baby) Set	—	50.00
MS75	2003 (5)	55,000	KM#453, 457, 460, 462, 463, Uncirculated set, classic version (hard plastic case)	—	32.00
MS76	2003 (5)	20,000	KM#453, 457, 460, 462, 463 (Uncirculated Set, Souvenir Version)	—	30.00
MS77	2003 (5)	2,000	KM#453, 457, 460, 462, 463 plus Silver medal Children's (Baby) Set	—	50.00
MS78	2004 (5)	35,000	KM#457, 460, 462, 463, 478, (Uncirculated set, classic version (hard plastic case)	—	25.00
MS79	2004 (5)	6,000	KM#457, 460, 462, 463, 478 (Uncirculated Set, Souvenir Version)	—	30.00
MS80	2004 (5)	2,000	KM#457, 460, 462, 463, 478 plus Silver medal Children's (Baby) Set	—	50.00
MS81	2005 (5)	32,000	KM#453, 457, 460, 462, 463, Uncirculated set, classic version (hard plastic case)	—	25.00
MS82	2005 (5)	6,500	KM#453, 457, 460, 462, 463 (Uncirculated Set, Souvenir Version)	—	35.00
MS83	2005 (5)	—	KM#453, 457, 460, 462, 463 plus Child in Basket Silver medal (Children's (Baby) Set)	—	60.00
MS84	2005 (5)	2,005	KM#453, 457 (proof), 460, 462, 463 plus gilded Silver copy of medal issued for 1905 referendum, all coins minted on June 7, 2005 (Referendum Set)	—	450
MS85	2006 (5)	27,800	KM#457, 460, 462, 463, 479 Uncirculated Set, Classic Version (hard plastic case)	—	28.00
MS86	2006 (5)	5,450	KM#457, 460, 462, 463, 479 Uncirculated Set, Souvenir Version	—	30.00
MS87	2006 (5)	800	KM#457, 460, 462, 463, 479 plus Child in Basket 0.5 oz. 0.999 Silver Medal Children's (Baby) Set	—	65.00
MS88	2006 (5)	2,006	KM#457, 460, 462, 463, 479 plus Gold-plated Silver copy of 1906 King Haakon VII Coronation medal, all coins minted on June 22, 2006 (Coronation Set)	—	375
MS89	2007 (5)	10,000	KM#453, 457, 460, 462, 463 (Brilliant Uncirculated Set)	—	58.00
MS90	2007 (5)	26,135	KM#453, 457, 460, 462, 463 Uncirculated Set, Classic Version (hard plastic case)	—	30.00
MS91	2007 (5)	5,050	KM#453, 457, 460, 462, 463 (Uncirculated Set, Souvenir Version)	—	30.00
MS92	2007 (5)	835	KM#453, 457, 460, 462, 463 plus Child in Basket 0.5 oz. 9.999 Silver Medal Children's (Baby) Set	—	65.00
MS93	2007 (5)	2,007	KM#453, 457, 460, 462, 463 plus 0.999 Gold-plated 0.925 Silver medal, 32 mm., all coins minted on February 21, 2007 (King Harald V 70th Birthday Set)	—	700
MS94	2008 (5)	2,924	KM#453, 460, 462, 463, 482 (Brilliant Uncirculated Set)	—	58.00
MS95	2008 (5)	26,185	KM#453, 457, 460, 462, 463 Uncirculated Set, Classic Version (hard plastic case)	—	40.00
MS96	2008 (5)	5,000	KM#453, 457, 460, 462, 463 (Uncirculatd Set, Souvenir Version)	—	30.00
MS97	2008 (5)	600	KM#453, 457, 460, 462, 463 plus Child in Basket Silver medal Children's (Baby) Set	—	70.00
MS98	2009 (5)	2,271	KM#453, 457, 460, 462, 463 (Brilliant Uncirculated Set)	—	60.00
MS99	2009 (5)	23,400	KM#453, 457, 460, 462, 463 Uncirculated Set, Classic Version (hard plastic case)	—	30.00
MS100	2009 (5)	4,251	KM#453, 457, 460, 462, 463 (Uncirculated Set, Souvenir Version)	—	30.00
MS101	2009 (5)	675	KM#453, 457, 460, 462, 463 plus Child in Basket Silver medal Children's (Baby) Set	—	65.00
MS102	2010 (3)	1,673	KM#460, 462, 483 (Brilliant Uncirculated Set)	—	60.00
MS103	2010 (3)	21,926	KM#460, 462, 483 Uncirculated Set, Classic Version (hard plastic case)	—	35.00
MS104	2010 (3)	3,823	KM#460, 462, 463 (Uncirculated Set, Souvenir Version)	—	35.00
MS105	2010 (3)	460	KM#460, 462, 483 plus Child in Basket Silver medal (Children's (Baby) Set)	—	65.00
MS106	2011 (3)	1,073	KM#460, 462, 484 (Brilliant Uncirculated Set)	—	58.00
MS107	2011 (3)	18,436	KM#460, 462, 484 plus 325th Anniversary of the Norwegian Mint bimetallic medal (Uncirculated Set, Classic Version (hard plastic case)	—	38.00
MS108	2011 (3)	2,454	KM#460, 462, 484 (Uncirculated Set, Souvenir Version)	—	38.00
MS109	2011 (3)	466	KM#460, 462, 484 plus Child in Basket Silver medal (Children's (Baby) Set)	—	75.00
MS110	2012 (3)	2,000	KM#457, 462, 463 (Brilliant Uncirculated Set)	—	65.00
MS111	2012 (3)	25,000	KM#457, 462, 463 plus 200th Anniversary of the birth of Peter Christian Asbjornsen medal (Uncirculated Set, classic Version (hard plastic case)	—	35.00
MS112	2012 (3)	5,000	KM#457, 462, 463 (Uncirculated Set, Souvenir Version)	—	35.00
MS113	2012 (3)	1,500	KM#457, 462, 463 plus Child in Basket Silver medal (Children's (Baby) Set)	—	75.00

PROOF SETS

KM#	Date	Mintage	Identification	Issue Price	Mkt Val
PS16	2001 (5)	10,000	KM#453, 457, 460, 462, 463 (Classic Proof Set)	—	100
PS17	2001 (5)	1,500	KM#453, 457, 460, 462 463 plus medal (Exclusive Proof Set)	—	300
PS18	2002 (5)	10,000	KM#457, 460, 462, 463, 471, (Classic Proof Set)	—	125
PS19	2002 (5)	1,500	KM#457, 460, 462, 463, 471 plus medal (Exclusive Proof Set)	—	450
PS20	2003 (5)	10,000	KM#453, 457, 460, 462, 463, (Classic Proof Set)	—	100
PS21	2003 (5)	800	KM#453, 457, 460, 462, 463 plus 0.5833 Gold 100th Anniversary of the Birth of King Olav V medal (Exclusive Proof Set)	—	550
PS22	2004 (5)	7,800	KM#457, 460, 462, 463, 478, (Classic Proof Set)	—	100
PS23	2004 (5)	750	KM#457, 460, 462, 463, 478 plus Princess Ingrid Alexandra Gold medal (Exclusive Proof Set)	—	500
PS24	2005 (5)	7,800	KM#453, 457, 460, 462, 463, (Classic Proof Set)	—	100
PS25	2005 (5)	750	KM#453, 457, 460, 462, 463 plus 0.5833 Gold 7th June-9th June-13th August 1905 medal (Exclusive Proof Set)	—	500
PS26	2003-05 (6)	5,000	KM#472-477	—	3,300
PS27	2006 (5)	8,000	KM#457, 460, 462, 463, 479 (Classic Proof Set)	—	100
PS28	2006 (5)	500	KM#457, 460, 462, 463, 479 plus 3.295 g., 0.999 Platinum, 14.0 mm. medal (Exclusive Proof Set)	—	700
PS29	2007 (5)	6,182	KM#453, 457, 460, 462, 463 (Classic Proof Set)	—	100
PS30	2007 (5)	400	KM#453, 457, 460, 462, 463 plus proof 3.00 g., 0.585 Gold-0.265 Silver-0.150 Palladium, 14.0 mm. medal (Exclusive Proof Set)	—	700
PS31	2008 (5)	6,591	KM#453, 460, 462, 463, 482 (Classic Proof Set)	—	100
PS32	2008 (5)	500	KM#453, 460, 462, 463, 482 plus 3.00 g., 0.585 Gold-0.265 Silver-0.150 Palladium, 14.0 mm. Henrik Wergeland medal (Exclusive Proof Set)	—	700
PS33	2009 (5)	5,910	KM#453, 457, 460, 462, 463 (Classic Proof Set)	—	100
PS34	2009 (6)	400	KM#453, 457, 460, 462, 463, 481 plus 7.70 g., 0.585 Gold, 22.0 mm. 150th Anniversary of Birth of Knut Hamsun medal (Exclusive Proof Set)	—	750
PS35	2010 (3)	4,619	KM#460, 462, 483 plus medal (Classic Proof Set)	—	130
PS36	2010 (3)	500	KM#460, 462, 483 plus 7.70 g., 0.585 Gold, 22.0 mm. Liberation of Norway in 1945 medal (Exclusive Proof Set)	—	750
PS37	2011 (3)	3,642	KM#460, 462, 484 plus 325th Anniversary of the Norwegian Mint gilded medal (Classic Proof Set)	—	130
PS38	2011 (3)	500	KM#460, 462, 484 plus 7.70g., 0.85 Gold, 22.0mm. 100th Anniversary of Roald Amundsen's reaching the South Pole medal (Exclusive Proof Set)	—	850
PS39	2012 (3)	7,000	KM#457, 462, 463 (Classic Proof Set)	—	130
PS40	2012 (3)	500	KM#457, 462, 463 plus medal (Exclusive Proof Set)	—	800

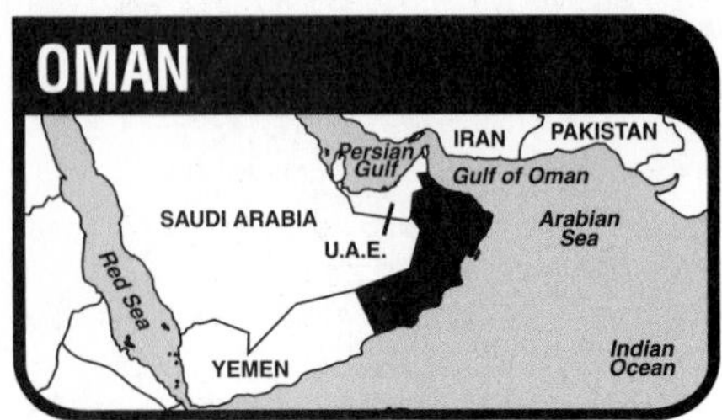

The Sultanate of Oman (formerly Muscat and Oman), an independent monarchy located in the southeastern part of the Arabian Peninsula, has an area of 82,030 sq. mi. (212,460 sq. km.) and a population of *1.3 million. Capital: Muscat. The economy is based on agriculture, herding and petroleum. Petroleum products, dates, fish and hides are exported.

RULER

Qaboos ibn al-Sa'id, AH1390-/1970AD-

SULTANATE

REFORM COINAGE

1972; 1000 Baisa = 1 Omani Rial

KM# 150 5 BAISA

2.6500 g., Bronze Clad Steel, 19 mm. **Ruler:** Qabus bin Sa'id AH1390-/1970AD- **Obv:** National arms **Rev:** Value and dates

Date	Mintage	F	VF	XF	Unc	BU
AH1429-2008	—	—	—	0.20	0.50	0.75

KM# 151 10 BAISA

4.0400 g., Bronze Clad Steel, 22.5 mm. **Ruler:** Qabus bin Sa'id AH1390-/1970AD- **Obv:** National arms **Rev:** Value with both dates

Date	Mintage	F	VF	XF	Unc	BU
AH1429-2008	—	—	—	0.30	0.75	1.00

KM# 152a 25 BAISA

2.6300 g., Nickel Clad Steel, 17.95 mm. **Ruler:** Qabus bin Sa'id AH1390-/1970AD- **Obv:** National arms **Rev:** Value with both dates **Edge:** Reeded

Date	Mintage	F	VF	XF	Unc	BU
AH1427-2007	—	—	—	0.35	0.90	1.25
AH1428-2008	—	—	—	0.35	0.90	1.25
AH1429-2009	—	—	—	0.35	0.90	1.25
AH1430-2010	—	—	—	0.35	0.90	1.25

KM# 152 25 BAISA

3.0300 g., Copper-Nickel, 18 mm. **Ruler:** Qabus bin Sa'id AH1390-/1970AD- **Obv:** National arms **Rev:** Value and both dates **Edge:** Plain

Date	Mintage	F	VF	XF	Unc	BU
AH1428-2008	—	—	0.15	0.35	0.90	1.25
AH1429-2009	—	—	0.15	0.35	0.90	1.25

KM# 153a 50 BAISA

5.5700 g., Nickel Clad Steel, 24 mm. **Ruler:** Qabus bin Sa'id AH1390-/1970AD- **Obv:** National arms **Rev:** Value with both dates **Edge:** Reeded

Date	Mintage	F	VF	XF	Unc	BU
AH1427-2007	—	—	—	0.60	1.50	2.00
AH1428-2008	—	—	—	0.60	1.50	2.00
AH1429-2009	—	—	—	0.60	1.50	2.00
AH1430-2010	—	—	—	0.60	1.50	2.00

KM# 153 50 BAISA

6.4000 g., Copper-Nickel, 24 mm. **Ruler:** Qabus bin Sa'id AH1390-/1970AD- **Obv:** National arms **Rev:** Value with both dates **Edge:** Reeded

Date	Mintage	F	VF	XF	Unc	BU
AH1429-2008	—	—	0.25	0.60	1.50	2.00

KM# 154 OMANI RIAL

28.2800 g., 0.9250 Silver 0.8410 oz. ASW, 38.6 mm. **Ruler:** Qabus bin Sa'id AH1390-/1970AD- **Subject:** 31st National Day and Environment Year **Obv:** National arms **Rev:** Multicolor map design **Edge:** Reeded

Date	Mintage	F	VF	XF	Unc	BU
2001	500	—	—	—	90.00	—
2001 Proof	105	Value: 150				

KM# 154a OMANI RIAL

37.8000 g., 0.9160 Gold 1.1132 oz. AGW, 38.6 mm. **Ruler:** Qabus bin Sa'id AH1390-/1970AD- **Subject:** 31st National Day and Environment Year **Obv:** National arms **Rev:** Multicolor map design **Edge:** Reeded

Date	Mintage	F	VF	XF	Unc	BU
2001	350	—	—	—	2,000	—
2001 Proof	105	Value: 2,200				

KM# 156 OMANI RIAL

28.2800 g., 0.9250 Silver 0.8410 oz. ASW, 38.7 mm. **Ruler:** Qabus bin Sa'id AH1390-/1970AD- **Series:** Environment Collection **Obv:** National arms **Rev:** Hoopoe bird standing right multicolor

Date	Mintage	F	VF	XF	Unc	BU
2002 Proof	1,000	Value: 75.00				

KM# 157 OMANI RIAL

28.2800 g., 0.9250 Silver 0.8410 oz. ASW, 38.7 mm. **Ruler:** Qabus bin Sa'id AH1390-/1970AD- **Series:** Environment Collection **Obv:** National arms **Rev:** Dolphin right multicolor

Date	Mintage	F	VF	XF	Unc	BU
2002 Proof	1,000	Value: 75.00				

KM# 158 OMANI RIAL

28.2800 g., 0.9250 Silver 0.8410 oz. ASW, 38.7 mm. **Ruler:** Qabus bin Sa'id AH1390-/1970AD- **Series:** Environment Collection **Obv:** National arms **Rev:** Turtle left multicolor

Date	Mintage	F	VF	XF	Unc	BU
2002 Proof	1,000	Value: 75.00				

KM# 159 OMANI RIAL

28.2800 g., 0.9250 Silver 0.8410 oz. ASW, 38.7 mm. **Ruler:** Qabus bin Sa'id AH1390-/1970AD- **Series:** Environment Collection **Obv:** National arms **Rev:** Flower multicolor

Date	Mintage	F	VF	XF	Unc	BU
2002 Proof	1,000	Value: 75.00				

KM# 160 OMANI RIAL

28.2800 g., 0.9250 Silver 0.8410 oz. ASW, 38.7 mm. **Ruler:** Qabus bin Sa'id AH1390-/1970AD- **Series:** Environment Collection **Obv:** National arms **Rev:** Ibex standing left multicolor

Date	Mintage	F	VF	XF	Unc	BU
2002 Proof	1,000	Value: 75.00				

KM# 161 OMANI RIAL

28.2800 g., 0.9250 Silver 0.8410 oz. ASW, 38.7 mm. **Ruler:** Qabus bin Sa'id AH1390-/1970AD- **Series:** Environment Collection **Obv:** National arms **Rev:** Butterfly multicolor

Date	Mintage	F	VF	XF	Unc	BU
2002 Proof	1,000	Value: 75.00				

KM# 162 OMANI RIAL

28.2800 g., 0.9250 Silver 0.8410 oz. ASW, 38.7 mm. **Ruler:** Qabus bin Sa'id AH1390-/1970AD- **Subject:** Population Census - December, 2003

Date	Mintage	F	VF	XF	Unc	BU
2003 Rare	—	—	—	—	—	—

KM# 155 OMANI RIAL

28.2800 g., 0.9250 Silver 0.8410 oz. ASW, 38.6 mm. **Ruler:** Qabus bin Sa'id AH1390-/1970AD- **Subject:** The Sindibad Voyage, 1980/1981 **Obv:** National arms **Rev:** Sailing ship below map within circle **Edge:** Reeded

Date	Mintage	F	VF	XF	Unc	BU
2003 Proof	—	Value: 65.00				

KM# 163 OMANI RIAL

28.2800 g., 0.9250 Silver 0.8410 oz. ASW, 38.7 mm. **Ruler:** Qabus bin Sa'id AH1390-/1970AD- **Subject:** 35th National Day **Obv:** Oman Map

Date	Mintage	F	VF	XF	Unc	BU
AH1427-2005	—	—	—	—	100	120

KM# 164 OMANI RIAL

28.2800 g., 0.9250 Silver 0.8410 oz. ASW, 38.7 mm. **Ruler:** Qabus bin Sa'id AH1390-/1970AD- **Subject:** 40th Anniversary of First Oil Export from Oman

Date	Mintage	F	VF	XF	Unc	BU
2007	—	—	—	—	90.00	100

KM# 165 OMANI RIAL

28.2800 g., 0.9250 Silver 0.8410 oz. ASW, 38.7 mm. **Ruler:** Qabus bin Sa'id AH1390-/1970AD- **Subject:** 29th GCC Summit held in Muscat in December 2008

Date	Mintage	F	VF	XF	Unc	BU
2008	—	—	—	—	100	120

KM# 166 OMANI RIAL

28.2800 g., 0.9250 Silver 0.8410 oz. ASW, 38.7 mm. **Ruler:** Qabus bin Sa'id AH1390-/1970AD- **Subject:** 19th Arabian Gulf Cup

Date	Mintage	F	VF	XF	Unc	BU
2008	—	—	—	—	250	—

KM# 168 OMANI RIAL

28.2800 g., 0.9990 Silver 0.9083 oz. ASW **Ruler:** Qabus bin Sa'id AH1390-/1970AD- **Subject:** Royal Opera House **Rev:** Building exterior

Date	Mintage	F	VF	XF	Unc	BU
2011 Proof	—	Value: 75.00				

KM# 169 OMANI RIAL

28.2800 g., 0.9990 Silver 0.9083 oz. ASW **Ruler:** Qabus bin Sa'id AH1390-/1970AD- **Subject:** Royal Opera House **Rev:** Violin, Tamboreen in color

Date	Mintage	F	VF	XF	Unc	BU
2011 Proof	—	Value: 75.00				

KM# 170 OMANI RIAL

28.2800 g., 0.9990 Silver 0.9083 oz. ASW **Ruler:** Qabus bin Sa'id AH1390-/1970AD- **Subject:** Royal Opera House **Rev:** Horns, flute and sax in color

Date	Mintage	F	VF	XF	Unc	BU
2011 Proof	—	Value: 75.00				

KM# 171 OMANI RIAL

Silver **Ruler:** Qabus bin Sa'id AH1390-/1970AD- **Subject:** Royal Opera House **Rev:** Tamboreen, horns and strings in color

Date	Mintage	F	VF	XF	Unc	BU
2011 Proof	—	Value: 75.00				

PAKISTAN

The Islamic Republic of Pakistan, located on the Indian subcontinent between India and Afghanistan, has an area of 310,404 sq. mi. (803,940 sq. km.) and a population of130 million. Capital: Islamabad. Pakistan is mainly an agricultural land although the industrial base is expanding rapidly. Yarn, textiles, cotton, rice, medical instruments, sports equipment and leather are exported.

TITLE

پاکستان

Pakistan

ISLAMIC REPUBLIC

DECIMAL COINAGE

100 Paisa = 1 Rupee

KM# 62 RUPEE

4.0000 g., Bronze, 20 mm. **Obv:** Head of Jinnah facing left **Rev:** Mosque above value **Edge:** Reeded

Date	Mintage	F	VF	XF	Unc	BU
2001	146,996,000	0.20	0.25	0.35	0.65	0.75
2002	192,252,000	0.20	0.25	0.35	0.65	0.75
2003	217,996,000	0.20	0.25	0.35	0.65	0.75
2004	162,210,000	0.20	0.25	0.35	0.65	0.75
2005	202,330,000	0.20	0.25	0.35	0.65	0.75
2006	113,135,000	0.20	0.25	0.35	0.65	0.75

KM# 67 RUPEE

1.7500 g., Aluminum, 20 mm. **Obv:** Head left **Rev:** Mosque

Date	Mintage	F	VF	XF	Unc	BU
2007	201,670,000	—	—	—	—	2.00
2008	97,953,000	—	—	—	—	2.00
2009	80,280,000	—	—	—	—	2.00
2010	100,000,000	—	—	—	—	2.00
2011	—	—	—	—	—	2.00
2012	—	—	—	—	—	2.00

KM# 64 2 RUPEES

5.0000 g., Nickel-Brass, 22.5 mm. **Obv:** Crescent, star and date above sprigs **Rev:** Value below mosque and clouds **Edge:** Reeded

Date	Mintage	F	VF	XF	Unc	BU
2001	85,444,000	0.20	0.30	0.45	0.85	1.00
2002	148,940,000	0.20	0.30	0.45	0.85	1.00
2003	125,220,000	0.20	0.30	0.45	0.85	1.00
2004	105,148,000	0.20	0.30	0.45	0.85	1.00
2005	98,912,000	0.20	0.30	0.45	0.85	1.00
2006	34,432,000	0.20	0.30	0.45	0.85	1.00

KM# 68 2 RUPEES

Aluminum **Obv:** Star and crescent, wheat ears below **Rev:** Mosque

Date	Mintage	F	VF	XF	Unc	BU
2007	100,848,000	—	—	—	—	2.00
2008	—	—	—	—	—	2.00
2009	100,000,000	—	—	—	—	2.00
2010	5,337,000	—	—	—	—	2.00
2011	—	—	—	—	—	2.00
2012	—	—	—	—	—	2.00
2013	—	—	—	—	—	2.00

KM# 65 5 RUPEES

6.5000 g., Copper-Nickel, 24 mm. **Obv:** Cresent, star and date above sprays **Rev:** Value within star design and sprigs **Edge:** Reeded

Date	Mintage	F	VF	XF	Unc	BU
2002	35,668,000	0.50	1.00	1.50	3.00	3.25
2003	138,566,000	0.50	1.00	1.50	3.00	3.25
2004	224,228,000	0.50	—	1.50	3.00	3.25
2005	148,248,000	0.50	—	—	3.00	3.25
2006	177,222,000	—	—	—	3.00	3.25

KM# 66 10 RUPEES
7.5000 g., Copper-Nickel, 27.5 mm. **Obv:** Cresent, star and date above sprays **Rev:** Flowers and inscription **Rev. Inscription:** Year of Fatima Jinnah **Edge:** Reeded

Date	Mintage	F	VF	XF	Unc	BU
2003	200,000	—	—	4.00	6.50	7.50

KM# 69 10 RUPEES
8.2500 g., Copper-Nickel, 27.5 mm. **Subject:** Benazir Bhutto **Obv:** Star and crescent, wheat wreath below **Rev:** Bust facing, Urdu script legend above

Date	Mintage	F	VF	XF	Unc	BU
2007	—	—	—	—	—	5.00
2008	300,000	—	—	—	—	5.00

KM# 70 10 RUPEES
8.2500 g., Copper-Nickel, 27.5 mm. **Subject:** Pakistan - China Friendship, 60 years of Peoples' Republic of China **Obv:** Crescent and star **Rev:** Pakistan and Chinese flags, clasped hands below

Date	Mintage	F	VF	XF	Unc	BU
2009	100,000	—	—	—	4.50	6.50

KM# 71 20 RUPEES
Copper-Nickel **Subject:** Pakistan-China Friendship, 60th anniversary

Date	Mintage	F	VF	XF	Unc	BU
2011	—	—	—	—	8.00	15.00

PALAU

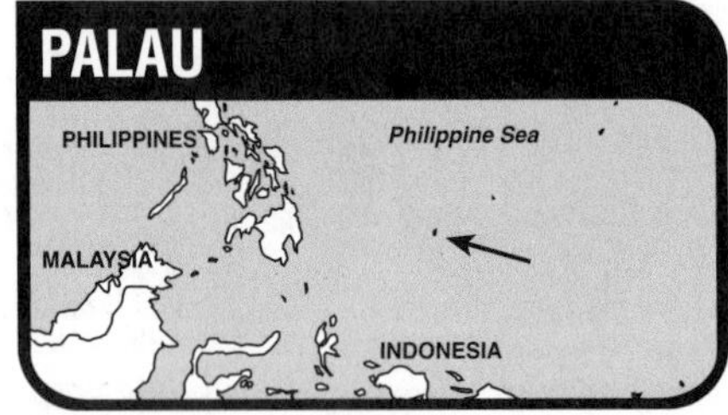

The Republic of Palau, a group of about 100 islands and islets, is generally considered a part of the Caroline Islands. It is located about 1,000 miles southeast of Manila and about the same distance southwest of Saipan and has an area of 179 sq. mi. and a population of 12,116. Capital: Koror.

REPUBLIC

MILLED COINAGE

KM# 86 DOLLAR
1.2441 g., 0.9999 Gold 0.0400 oz. AGW, 13.94 mm. **Subject:** Marine Life Protection **Obv:** Prone Mermaid **Rev:** Two fish

Date	Mintage	F	VF	XF	Unc	BU
2001 Proof	—	Value: 75.00				

KM# 87 DOLLAR
1.2441 g., 0.9999 Gold 0.0400 oz. AGW, 13.94 mm. **Subject:** Marine Life Protection **Obv:** Seated Mermaid with raised arm above value **Rev:** Two glittering fish

Date	Mintage	F	VF	XF	Unc	BU
2001 Proof	—	Value: 65.00				

KM# 88 DOLLAR
1.2441 g., 0.9999 Gold 0.0400 oz. AGW, 13.94 mm. **Subject:** Marine Life Protection **Obv:** Figurehead Mermaid and value **Rev:** Moorish Idol fish

Date	Mintage	F	VF	XF	Unc	BU
2001 Proof	—	Value: 75.00				

KM# 89 DOLLAR
1.2441 g., 0.9999 Gold 0.0400 oz. AGW, 13.94 mm. **Subject:** Marine Life Protection **Obv:** Figurehead Mermaid and value **Rev:** Moorish Idol fish

Date	Mintage	F	VF	XF	Unc	BU
2001 Proof	—	Value: 75.00				

KM# 60 DOLLAR
26.8000 g., Copper-Nickel, 37.2 mm. **Subject:** Marine Life Protection **Obv:** Seated Mermaid with raised arm above value **Rev:** Two glittering fish **Edge:** Reeded

Date	Mintage	F	VF	XF	Unc	BU
2001 Proof	—	Value: 30.00				

KM# 61 DOLLAR
26.8000 g., Copper-Nickel, 37.2 mm. **Subject:** Marine Life Protection **Obv:** Prone Mermaid above value **Rev:** Two glittering fish **Edge:** Reeded

Date	Mintage	F	VF	XF	Unc	BU
2001 Proof	—	Value: 32.50				

KM# 62 DOLLAR
26.8000 g., Copper-Nickel, 37.2 mm. **Subject:** Marine Life Protection **Obv:** Figurehead mermaid and value **Rev:** Moorish-Idol fish **Edge:** Reeded

Date	Mintage	F	VF	XF	Unc	BU
2001 Proof	—	Value: 30.00				

KM# 52 DOLLAR
26.8600 g., Copper-Nickel, 37.3 mm. **Subject:** Marine Life Protection **Obv:** Mermaid figurehead and value **Rev:** Multicolor jellyfish **Edge:** Reeded

Date	Mintage	F	VF	XF	Unc	BU
2001 Proof	—	Value: 30.00				

KM# 253 DOLLAR
1.2500 g., 0.9990 Gold 0.0401 oz. AGW, 13.9 mm. **Obv:** Mermaid body-surfing wave **Rev:** Blue angelfish

Date	Mintage	F	VF	XF	Unc	BU
2001 Proof	—	Value: 75.00				

KM# 254 DOLLAR
1.2400 g., 0.9990 Gold 0.0398 oz. AGW, 13.9 mm. **Obv:** Large breasted mermaid on beach **Rev:** Emperor Angelfish

Date	Mintage	F	VF	XF	Unc	BU
2001 Proof	—	Value: 75.00				

KM# 287 DOLLAR
35.0000 g., Copper-Nickel, 50 mm. **Obv:** National Arms **Rev:** Cut card corners, Queens of Hearts, Clubs

Date	Mintage	F	VF	XF	Unc	BU
ND (2001) Antique finish	—	—	—	—	—	10.00

KM# 288 DOLLAR
35.0000 g., Copper-Nickel, 50 mm. **Obv:** National arms **Rev:** Cut card corner, Queen of Spades, diamonds

Date	Mintage	F	VF	XF	Unc	BU
ND (2001) Antique finish	—	—	—	—	—	10.00

KM# 56 DOLLAR
26.8000 g., Copper-Nickel, 37.2 mm. **Subject:** Marine Life Protection **Obv:** Mermaid figurehead and value **Rev:** Multicolor fish scene **Edge:** Reeded

Date	Mintage	F	VF	XF	Unc	BU
2002 Proof	—	Value: 32.50				

KM# 57 DOLLAR
26.8000 g., Copper-Nickel, 37.2 mm. **Subject:** Marine Life Protection **Obv:** Mermaid figurehead on approaching ship **Rev:** Multicolor reflective fish scene under an acrylic layer **Edge:** Reeded

Date	Mintage	F	VF	XF	Unc	BU
2002 Proof	—	Value: 37.50				

KM# 63 DOLLAR
26.8000 g., Copper-Nickel, 37.2 mm. **Subject:** Marine Life Protection **Obv:** Figurehead mermaid and value **Rev:** Blue Tang Fish **Edge:** Reeded

Date	Mintage	F	VF	XF	Unc	BU
2002 Proof	—	Value: 37.50				

KM# 64 DOLLAR
26.8000 g., Copper-Nickel, 37.2 mm. **Subject:** Marine Life Protection **Obv:** Figurehead mermaid and value **Rev:** Multicolor whales **Edge:** Reeded

Date	Mintage	F	VF	XF	Unc	BU
2002 Proof	—	Value: 37.50				

KM# 65 DOLLAR
26.8000 g., Copper-Nickel, 37.2 mm. **Subject:** Marine Life Protection **Obv:** Mermaid washing hair and value **Rev:** Multicolor jellyfish **Edge:** Reeded

Date	Mintage	F	VF	XF	Unc	BU
2002 Proof	—	Value: 37.50				

KM# 90 DOLLAR
1.2441 g., 0.9999 Gold 0.0400 oz. AGW, 13.94 mm. **Subject:** Marine Life Protection **Obv:** Figurehead Mermaid and value **Rev:** Multicolor whales

Date	Mintage	F	VF	XF	Unc	BU
2002 Proof	—	Value: 75.00				

KM# 91 DOLLAR
1.2441 g., 0.9999 Gold 0.0400 oz. AGW, 13.94 mm. **Subject:** Marine Life Protection **Obv:** Figurehead Mermaid and value **Rev:** Pufferfish

Date	Mintage	F	VF	XF	Unc	BU
2002 Proof	—	Value: 75.00				

KM# 92 DOLLAR
1.2441 g., 0.9999 Gold 0.0400 oz. AGW, 13.94 mm. **Subject:** Marine Life Protection **Obv:** Seated Mermaid with both arms raised and value **Rev:** Jellyfish

Date	Mintage	F	VF	XF	Unc	BU
2002 Proof	—	Value: 75.00				

KM# 93 DOLLAR
1.2441 g., 0.9999 Gold 0.0400 oz. AGW, 13.94 mm. **Subject:** Marine Life Protection **Obv:** Figurehead Mermaid and value **Rev:** Blue Tang Fish

Date	Mintage	F	VF	XF	Unc	BU
2002 Proof	—	Value: 75.00				

KM# 94 DOLLAR
1.2441 g., 0.9999 Gold 0.0400 oz. AGW, 13.94 mm. **Subject:** Marine Life Protection **Obv:** Figurehead mermaid and value **Rev:** Lionfish

Date	Mintage	F	VF	XF	Unc	BU
2002 Proof	—	Value: 75.00				

KM# 95 DOLLAR
1.2441 g., 0.9999 Gold 0.0400 oz. AGW, 13.94 mm. **Subject:** Marine Life Protection **Obv:** Mermaid riding dolphin and value **Rev:** Starfish

Date	Mintage	F	VF	XF	Unc	BU
2003 Proof	—	Value: 75.00				

KM# 96 DOLLAR
1.2441 g., 0.9999 Gold 0.0400 oz. AGW, 13.94 mm. **Subject:** Marine Life Protection **Obv:** Seated Mermaid on shell and value **Rev:** Multicolor Orca **Edge:** Reeded Proof

Date	Mintage	F	VF	XF	Unc	BU
2003 Proof	—	Value: 75.00				

KM# 97 DOLLAR
1.2441 g., 0.9999 Gold 0.0400 oz. AGW, 13.94 mm. **Subject:** Marine Life Protection **Obv:** Mermaid under radiant sun and value **Rev:** Crab

Date	Mintage	F	VF	XF	Unc	BU
2003 Proof	—	Value: 75.00				

KM# 98 DOLLAR
1.2441 g., 0.9999 Gold 0.0400 oz. AGW, 13.94 mm. **Subject:** Marine Life Protection **Obv:** Mermaid riding turtle and value **Rev:** Two glittering fish

Date	Mintage	F	VF	XF	Unc	BU
2003 Proof	—	Value: 75.00				

KM# 66 DOLLAR
26.8000 g., Copper-Nickel, 37.2 mm. **Subject:** Marine Life Protection **Obv:** Mermaid under sun and value **Rev:** Orange crab **Edge:** Reeded

Date	Mintage	F	VF	XF	Unc	BU
2003 Proof	—	Value: 37.50				

KM# 67 DOLLAR
26.8000 g., Copper-Nickel, 37.2 mm. **Subject:** Marine Life Protection **Obv:** Mermaid riding turtle and value **Rev:** Two glittering fish **Edge:** Reeded

Date	Mintage	F	VF	XF	Unc	BU
2003 Proof	—	Value: 37.50				

KM# 68 DOLLAR
26.8000 g., Copper-Nickel, 37.2 mm. **Subject:** Marine Life Protection **Obv:** Seated Mermaid on shell and value **Rev:** Multicolor Orca **Edge:** Reeded

Date	Mintage	F	VF	XF	Unc	BU
2003 Proof	—	Value: 37.50				

KM# 69 DOLLAR
26.8000 g., Copper-Nickel, 37.2 mm. **Subject:** Marine Life Protection **Obv:** Mermaid playing shell guitar and value **Rev:** Green fish **Edge:** Reeded

Date	Mintage	F	VF	XF	Unc	BU
2003 Proof	—	Value: 37.50				

KM# 256 DOLLAR
Copper-Nickel, 38.6 mm. **Obv:** Mermaid on dolphin **Rev:** Red starfish - multicolor

Date	Mintage	F	VF	XF	Unc	BU
2003	—	—	—	—	—	25.00

KM# 70 DOLLAR
26.8000 g., Copper-Nickel, 37.2 mm. **Subject:** Marine Life Protection **Obv:** Seated Mermaid on rock and value **Rev:** School of blue fish **Edge:** Reeded

Date	Mintage	F	VF	XF	Unc	BU
2004 Proof	—	Value: 37.50				

KM# 71 DOLLAR
26.8000 g., Copper-Nickel, 37.2 mm. **Subject:** Marine Life Protection **Obv:** Side view of Mermaid facing right and value **Rev:** Clownfish **Edge:** Reeded

Date	Mintage	F	VF	XF	Unc	BU
2004 Proof	—	Value: 37.50				

KM# 72 DOLLAR
26.8000 g., Copper-Nickel, 37.2 mm. **Subject:** Marine Life Protection **Obv:** Mermaid flanked by dolphins **Rev:** Multicolor dolphin head **Edge:** Reeded

Date	Mintage	F	VF	XF	Unc	BU
2004 Proof	—	Value: 37.50				

KM# 123 DOLLAR
Copper-Nickel, 37.2 mm. **Subject:** Marine Life Protection **Obv:** Mermaid seated inside a giant conch shell **Rev:** Puffer fish **Edge:** Reeded

Date	Mintage	F	VF	XF	Unc	BU
2004 Proof	—	Value: 35.00				

KM# 124 DOLLAR
Copper-Nickel, 37.2 mm. **Subject:** Marine Life Protection **Obv:** Seated Mermaid **Rev:** Sea turtle **Edge:** Reeded

Date	Mintage	F	VF	XF	Unc	BU
2004 Proof	—	Value: 50.00				

KM# 99 DOLLAR
1.2441 g., 0.9999 Gold 0.0400 oz. AGW, 13.94 mm. **Subject:** Marine Life Protection **Obv:** Mermaid under radiant sun and value **Rev:** Clownfish

Date	Mintage	F	VF	XF	Unc	BU
2004 Proof	—	Value: 75.00				

KM# 100 DOLLAR
1.2441 g., 0.9999 Gold 0.0400 oz. AGW, 13.94 mm. **Subject:** Marine Life Protection **Obv:** Mermaid flanked by dolphins **Rev:** Multicolor dolphin head

Date	Mintage	F	VF	XF	Unc	BU
2004 Proof	—	Value: 75.00				

KM# 101 DOLLAR
1.2441 g., 0.9999 Gold 0.0400 oz. AGW, 13.94 mm. **Subject:** Marine Life Protection **Obv:** Mermaid sitting in a shell listening to a conch shell **Rev:** Sea Horse

Date	Mintage	F	VF	XF	Unc	BU
2005 Proof	—	Value: 75.00				

KM# 139 DOLLAR
26.8000 g., Copper-Nickel, 37.2 mm. **Subject:** Marine Life - Protection **Obv:** Mermaid fixing hair, dolphin jumping **Rev:** School of fish

Date	Mintage	F	VF	XF	Unc	BU
2005	—	—	—	—	—	37.50

KM# 140 DOLLAR
26.8000 g., Copper-Nickel, 37.2 mm. **Subject:** Marine Life - Protection **Obv:** Mermaid seated in shell, listening to shell **Rev:** Multicolor sea horse

Date	Mintage	F	VF	XF	Unc	BU
2005	—	—	—	—	—	37.50

KM# 141 DOLLAR
26.8000 g., Copper-Nickel **Subject:** Marine Life - Protection **Obv:** Mermaid and dolphin **Rev:** Multicolor fish scene

Date	Mintage	F	VF	XF	Unc	BU
2005	—	—	—	—	—	37.50

KM# 255 DOLLAR
Copper-Nickel, 38.6 mm. **Obv:** Mermaid seated on rock **Rev:** Stingray - multicolor

Date	Mintage	F	VF	XF	Unc	BU
2005	—	—	—	—	—	37.00

KM# 125 DOLLAR
Copper-Nickel, 37.2 mm. **Subject:** Marine Life Protection **Obv:** Mermaid with head tilted back **Rev:** Barracuda

Date	Mintage	F	VF	XF	Unc	BU
2006 Proof	—	Value: 37.50				

KM# 126 DOLLAR
Copper-Nickel, 37.2 mm. **Subject:** Marine Life Protection **Obv:** Two mermaids **Rev:** Parrot fish

Date	Mintage	F	VF	XF	Unc	BU
2006 Proof	—	Value: 50.00				

KM# 127 DOLLAR
Copper-Nickel, 37.2 mm. **Subject:** Marine Life Protection **Obv:** Mermaid swimming downward **Rev:** Hog Fish **Edge:** Reeded

Date	Mintage	F	VF	XF	Unc	BU
2006 Proof	—	Value: 32.50				

KM# 128 DOLLAR
Copper-Nickel, 37.2 mm. **Subject:** Marine Life Protection **Obv:** Seated mermaid with bird perched on outstretched hand **Rev:** Mahi Mahi **Edge:** Reeded

Date	Mintage	F	VF	XF	Unc	BU
2006 Proof	—	Value: 47.50				

KM# 129 DOLLAR
Copper-Nickel, 37.2 mm. **Subject:** Marine Life Protection **Obv:** Mermaid, sailing ship and sun **Rev:** Box Fish **Edge:** Reeded

Date	Mintage	F	VF	XF	Unc	BU
2006 Proof	—	Value: 45.00				

KM# 142 DOLLAR
20.0000 g., 0.9990 Silver 0.6423 oz. ASW **Obv:** Arms **Rev:** Snowflake with blue crystal **Shape:** 38.6

Date	Mintage	F	VF	XF	Unc	BU
2006 Proof	2,500	Value: 65.00				

KM# 334 DOLLAR
27.0000 g., Copper-Nickel, 38.61 mm. **Rev:** Eclectus Parrot head right

Date	Mintage	F	VF	XF	Unc	BU
2006 Proof	Est. 5,000	Value: 20.00				

KM# 335 DOLLAR
27.0000 g., Copper-Nickel, 38.61 mm. **Rev:** Fruit dove head right

Date	Mintage	F	VF	XF	Unc	BU
2006 Proof	Est. 5,000	Value: 20.00				

KM# 336 DOLLAR

27.0000 g., Copper-Nickel, 38.61 mm. **Rev:** Rainbow lorikeet head left

Date	Mintage	F	VF	XF	Unc	BU
2006 Proof	Est. 5,000	Value: 20.00				

KM# 257 DOLLAR

25.0000 g., 0.9250 Silver 0.7435 oz. ASW, 38.6 mm. **Obv:** Arms **Rev:** White pearl in shell **Shape:** Heart

Date	Mintage	F	VF	XF	Unc	BU
2006 Proof	500	Value: 125				

KM# 322 DOLLAR

0.5000 g., 0.9990 Gold 0.0161 oz. AGW, 11.8 mm. **Obv:** National arms **Rev:** Elephant shrew

Date	Mintage	F	VF	XF	Unc	BU
2006 Proof	—	Value: 90.00				

KM# 323 DOLLAR

0.5000 g., 0.9990 Gold 0.0161 oz. AGW, 11.8 mm. **Obv:** National arms **Rev:** Rhino beettle

Date	Mintage	F	VF	XF	Unc	BU
2006 Proof	—	Value: 90.00				

KM# 324 DOLLAR

0.5000 g., 0.9990 Gold 0.0161 oz. AGW, 11.8 mm. **Obv:** National arms **Rev:** Buffalo Weaver

Date	Mintage	F	VF	XF	Unc	BU
2006 Proof	—	Value: 90.00				

KM# 325 DOLLAR

0.5000 g., 0.9990 Gold 0.0161 oz. AGW, 11.8 mm. **Obv:** National arms **Rev:** Ant lion

Date	Mintage	F	VF	XF	Unc	BU
2006 Proof	—	Value: 90.00				

KM# 326 DOLLAR

0.5000 g., 0.9990 Gold 0.0161 oz. AGW, 11.8 mm. **Obv:** National arms **Rev:** Leopard tortoise

Date	Mintage	F	VF	XF	Unc	BU
2006 Proof	—	Value: 90.00				

KM# 144 DOLLAR

27.0000 g., 0.9250 Silver 0.8029 oz. ASW **Obv:** Shield **Rev:** Multicolor John Paul II waving

Date	Mintage	F	VF	XF	Unc	BU
2007 Proof	—	Value: 45.00				

KM# 145 DOLLAR

1.2440 g., 0.9990 Gold 0.0400 oz. AGW, 13.92 mm. **Subject:** Marine Life - Protection **Obv:** Neptune and mermaid seated on rocks **Rev:** Tropical fish

Date	Mintage	F	VF	XF	Unc	BU
2007 Proof	—	Value: 75.00				

KM# 150 DOLLAR

25.0000 g., 0.9250 Silver 0.7435 oz. ASW **Subject:** Pacific Wildlife **Obv:** Shield **Rev:** Multicolor seahorse

Date	Mintage	F	VF	XF	Unc	BU
2007 Proof	—	Value: 70.00				

KM# 116 DOLLAR

25.7300 g., Silver Plated Bronze, 38.6 mm. **Obv:** National arms **Rev:** Multicolor Pope John Paul II with cross **Edge:** Reeded

Date	Mintage	F	VF	XF	Unc	BU
2007 Proof	—	Value: 37.50				

KM# 118 DOLLAR

27.0000 g., Copper-Nickel, 38.61 mm. **Series:** Marine Life Protection **Obv:** Neptune reclining with trident, mermaid at his side **Obv. Legend:** REPUBLIC OF PALAU **Rev:** Multicolor Doctor Fish

Date	Mintage	F	VF	XF	Unc	BU
2007 Proof	5,000	Value: 35.00				

KM# 121 DOLLAR

27.0000 g., Copper-Nickel, 38.61 mm. **Obv:** Shield with Neptune holding trident, mermaid reclining at his side, RAINBOW'S / END below **Obv. Legend:** REPUBLIC OF PALAU **Rev:** Red racing car 3/4 left **Rev. Legend:** FERRARI - 60 YEARS ANNIVERSARY

Date	Mintage	F	VF	XF	Unc	BU
ND(2007) Proof	5,000	Value: 35.00				

KM# 120 DOLLAR

0.5000 g., 0.9990 Gold 0.0161 oz. AGW, 11.0 mm. **Obv:** Shield with Neptune holding trident, mermaid reclining at his side, RAINBOW'S / END below **Obv. Legend:** REPUBLIC OF PALAU **Shape:** 4-leaf clover **Note:** Uniface

Date	Mintage	F	VF	XF	Unc	BU
2007 Proof	25,000	Value: 50.00				

KM# 258 DOLLAR

25.0000 g., 0.9990 Silver 0.8029 oz. ASW **Subject:** Pacific Wildlife **Rev:** Seahorse - prism

Date	Mintage	F	VF	XF	Unc	BU
2007 Proof	—	Value: 50.00				

KM# 337 DOLLAR

0.5000 g., 0.9990 Gold 0.0161 oz. AGW, 11 mm. **Subject:** Christopher Columbus, 500th Anniversary **Rev:** Columbus' flagship, Santa Maria

Date	Mintage	F	VF	XF	Unc	BU
2007 Proof	—	Value: 75.00				

KM# 338 DOLLAR

1.2400 g., 0.9990 Gold 0.0398 oz. AGW, 13.92 mm. **Subject:** Easter, 2007 **Rev:** Christ's Resurrection

Date	Mintage	F	VF	XF	Unc	BU
2007 Proof	Est. 15,000	Value: 100				

KM# 339 DOLLAR

0.5000 g., 0.9990 Gold 0.0161 oz. AGW, 11 mm. **Subject:** Deutsche Bundesbank, 50th anniversary **Rev:** Pile of coins

Date	Mintage	F	VF	XF	Unc	BU
2007 Proof	—	Value: 75.00				

KM# 154 DOLLAR
26.8000 g., Copper-Nickel silver plated, 38.61 mm. **Subject:** 150th Anniversary of the Appriations **Obv:** Shield **Rev:** Statue of Our Lady of Lourdes and holy water vile

Date	Mintage	F	VF	XF	Unc	BU
2008 Proof	—	Value: 22.50				

KM# 155 DOLLAR
26.8000 g., Copper-Nickel, 37.2 mm. **Subject:** Dealer Button **Obv:** Shield **Rev:** Vegas Chips and cards, Ace of Clubs corner cut

Date	Mintage	F	VF	XF	Unc	BU
2008	—	—	—	—	—	15.00

KM# 156 DOLLAR
26.8000 g., Copper-Nickel, 37.2 mm. **Subject:** Dealer Buttons **Obv:** Shield **Rev:** Vegas Chips and cards, Ace of Diamonds corner cut

Date	Mintage	F	VF	XF	Unc	BU
2008	—	—	—	—	—	15.00

KM# 157 DOLLAR
26.8000 g., Copper-Nickel, 37.2 mm. **Subject:** Dear Buttons **Obv:** Shield **Rev:** Vegas Chips and cards, Ace of Heats corner cut

Date	Mintage	F	VF	XF	Unc	BU
2008	—	—	—	—	—	15.00

KM# 158 DOLLAR
26.8000 g., Copper-Nickel, 37.2 mm. **Obv:** Shield **Rev:** Vegas chips and cards, Ace of Spades corner cut

Date	Mintage	F	VF	XF	Unc	BU
2008	—	—	—	—	—	15.00

KM# 159 DOLLAR
1.2400 g., 0.9990 Gold 0.0398 oz. AGW, 13.9 mm. **Subject:** St. Francis of Assisi **Obv:** Shield **Rev:** Bust facing

Date	Mintage	F	VF	XF	Unc	BU
2008 Proof	—	Value: 75.00				

KM# 160 DOLLAR
1.2440 g., 0.9900 Gold 0.0396 oz. AGW, 13.9 mm. **Subject:** St, Francis of Assisi **Obv:** Shield **Rev:** Multicolor bust facing

Date	Mintage	F	VF	XF	Unc	BU
2008	—	—	—	—	—	80.00

KM# 161 DOLLAR
0.5000 g., 0.9990 Gold 0.0161 oz. AGW, 11 mm. **Obv:** Shield **Rev:** Multicolor poppy **Shape:** Irregular

Date	Mintage	F	VF	XF	Unc	BU
2008	—	—	—	—	—	60.00

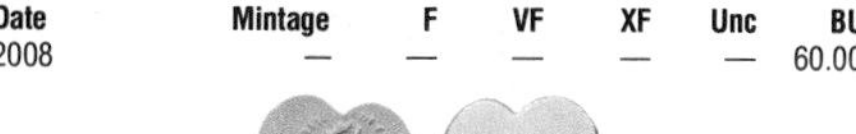

KM# 162 DOLLAR
0.5000 g., 0.9990 Gold 0.0161 oz. AGW, 11 mm. **Subject:** Everlasting love **Obv:** Shield **Rev:** Heart **Shape:** Heart

Date	Mintage	F	VF	XF	Unc	BU
2008	—	—	—	—	—	60.00

KM# 163 DOLLAR
1.2440 g., 0.9990 Gold 0.0400 oz. AGW **Subject:** Marine Life-Protection **Obv:** Neptune and mermaid seated on rock **Rev:** Grey reef shark

Date	Mintage	F	VF	XF	Unc	BU
2008 Proof	1,500	Value: 85.00				

KM# 164 DOLLAR
26.8000 g., Copper-Nickel, 37.2 mm. **Subject:** Endangered Wildlife **Obv:** Shield **Rev:** Multicolor Tiger shark

Date	Mintage	F	VF	XF	Unc	BU
2008	—	—	—	—	—	35.00

KM# 165 DOLLAR
26.8000 g., Copper-Nickel, 37.2 mm. **Subject:** Endangered Wildlife **Obv:** Shield **Rev:** Multicolor Hawksbill turtle

Date	Mintage	F	VF	XF	Unc	BU
2008	—	—	—	—	—	37.50

KM# 166 DOLLAR
26.8000 g., Copper-Nickel, 37.2 mm. **Subject:** Endangered Wildlife **Obv:** Shield **Rev:** Multicolored Regal angelfish swimming right

Date	Mintage	F	VF	XF	Unc	BU
2008 Proof	—	Value: 37.50				

KM# 167 DOLLAR
26.8000 g., Copper-Nickel, 37.2 mm. **Subject:** Endangered Wildlife **Obv:** Shield **Rev:** Multicolor Spiny lobster

Date	Mintage	F	VF	XF	Unc	BU
2008 Proof	—	Value: 30.00				

KM# 259 DOLLAR
0.5000 g., 0.9990 Gold 0.0161 oz. AGW, 11 mm. **Subject:** Sitting bull **Obv:** Shield **Rev:** Portrait facing

Date	Mintage	F	VF	XF	Unc	BU
2008 Proof	—	Value: 60.00				

KM# 449 DOLLAR
27.0000 g., Copper-Nickel, 38.61 mm. **Obv:** National arms **Rev:** Great white shark in color

Date	Mintage	F	VF	XF	Unc	BU
2008 Proof	—	Value: 35.00				

KM# 450 DOLLAR
27.0000 g., Copper-Nickel, 38.61 mm. **Subject:** Manfred Albrecht von Richtofen (The Red Baron) **Obv:** National arms **Rev:** Bust in oval below red tri-wing plane

Date	Mintage	F	VF	XF	Unc	BU
2008 Proof	—	Value: 75.00				

KM# 451 DOLLAR
25.0000 g., 0.9990 Silver 0.8029 oz. ASW, 38.61 mm. **Obv:** National arms **Rev:** Butterfly

Date	Mintage	F	VF	XF	Unc	BU
2008 Proof	—	Value: 80.00				

KM# 177 DOLLAR
1.2440 g., 0.9990 Gold 0.0400 oz. AGW, 13.9 mm. **Obv:** Shield **Rev:** Madonna and child

Date	Mintage	F	VF	XF	Unc	BU
ND(2009) Proof	25,000	Value: 80.00				

KM# 178 DOLLAR
1.2440 g., 0.9990 Gold 0.0400 oz. AGW, 13.9 mm. **Subject:** FIAA World Cup - South Africa **Obv:** Shield **Rev:** Soccer ball, South African flag and Water Buffalo

Date	Mintage	F	VF	XF	Unc	BU
2009 Proof	—	Value: 75.00				

KM# 222 DOLLAR
27.0000 g., Silver Plated Copper, 38.6 mm. **Rev:** Lighthouse of Alexandria, multicolor

Date	Mintage	F	VF	XF	Unc	BU
2009 Prooflike	5,000	—	—	—	—	20.00

KM# 223 DOLLAR
27.0000 g., Silver Plated Copper, 38.6 mm. **Rev:** Zeus statue, multicolor

Date	Mintage	F	VF	XF	Unc	BU
2009 Prooflike	—	—	—	—	—	20.00

KM# 224 DOLLAR
27.0000 g., Silver Plated Copper, 38.6 mm. **Rev:** Hanging Garden of Babylon, multicolor

Date	Mintage	F	VF	XF	Unc	BU
2009 Prooflike	5,000	—	—	—	—	20.00

KM# 225 DOLLAR
27.0000 g., Silver Plated Copper, 38.6 mm. **Rev:** Mausoleum, multicolor

Date	Mintage	F	VF	XF	Unc	BU
2009 Prooflike	5,000	—	—	—	—	20.00

KM# 226 DOLLAR
27.0000 g., Silver Plated Copper, 38.6 mm. **Rev:** Pyramids, multicolor

Date	Mintage	F	VF	XF	Unc	BU
2009 Prooflike	5,000	—	—	—	—	20.00

KM# 227 DOLLAR
27.0000 g., Silver Plated Copper, 38.6 mm. **Rev:** Artemis temple, multicolor

Date	Mintage	F	VF	XF	Unc	BU
2009 Prooflike	5,000	—	—	—	—	20.00

KM# 228 DOLLAR
27.0000 g., Silver Plated Copper, 38.6 mm. **Rev:** Colosus of Rhodes, multicolor

Date	Mintage	F	VF	XF	Unc	BU
2009 Prooflike	5,000	—	—	—	—	20.00

KM# 229 DOLLAR
27.0000 g., Silver Plated Copper, 38.6 mm. **Subject:** Ducati - Casey Stoner **Rev:** Motorcycle left, multicolor

Date	Mintage	F	VF	XF	Unc	BU
2009 Prooflike	2,008	—	—	—	—	25.00

KM# 230 DOLLAR
27.0000 g., Silver Plated Copper, 38.6 mm. **Subject:** Ducati - Troy Bayliss **Rev:** Motorcycle, multicolor

Date	Mintage	F	VF	XF	Unc	BU
2009 Prooflike	2,008	—	—	—	—	25.00

KM# 233 DOLLAR
27.0000 g., Copper-Nickel, 38.6 mm. **Subject:** Marine Life Protection **Obv:** Neptune standing, two mermaids below **Rev:** Lionfish, multicolor

Date	Mintage	F	VF	XF	Unc	BU
2009 Prooflike	5,000	—	—	—	—	25.00

KM# 234 DOLLAR
1.0000 g., 0.9990 Gold 0.0321 oz. AGW, 13.9 mm. **Subject:** Marine Life Protection **Rev:** Lionfish

Date	Mintage	F	VF	XF	Unc	BU
2009 Proof	25,000	Value: 70.00				

KM# 235 DOLLAR
0.5000 g., 0.9990 Gold 0.0161 oz. AGW, 11.8 mm. **Subject:** Augustus Aureus **Rev:** Head laureate right

Date	Mintage	F	VF	XF	Unc	BU
MMIX (2009)	15,000	—	—	—	—	40.00

KM# 236 DOLLAR
0.5000 g., 0.9990 Gold 0.0161 oz. AGW, 11.8 mm. **Subject:** Germanicus Dupondius **Rev:** General in quadriga right

Date	Mintage	F	VF	XF	Unc	BU
MMIX (2009)	15,000	—	—	—	—	40.00

KM# 237 DOLLAR
0.5000 g., 0.9990 Gold 0.0161 oz. AGW, 11.8 mm. **Subject:** Julius Caesar Denarius **Rev:** Head laureate right

Date	Mintage	F	VF	XF	Unc	BU
MMIX (2009)	15,000	—	—	—	—	40.00

KM# 238 DOLLAR
0.5000 g., 0.9990 Gold 0.0161 oz. AGW, 11.8 mm. **Subject:** Brutus Denarius **Rev:** Cap flanked by two daggers

Date	Mintage	F	VF	XF	Unc	BU
MMIX (2009)	15,000	—	—	—	—	40.00

KM# 239 DOLLAR
1.2400 g., 0.9990 Gold 0.0398 oz. AGW, 13.9 mm. **Subject:** Salesian Order, 150th Anniversary **Rev:** Don Bosco facing

Date	Mintage	F	VF	XF	Unc	BU
2009 Proof	15,000	Value: 75.00				

KM# 240 DOLLAR
0.5000 g., 0.9990 Gold 0.0161 oz. AGW, 11 mm. **Rev:** Pebbled **Shape:** 5-pointed star

Date	Mintage	F	VF	XF	Unc	BU
ND (2009)	25,000	—	—	—	—	40.00

KM# 241 DOLLAR
1.2400 g., 0.9990 Gold 0.0398 oz. AGW, 13.9 mm. **Subject:** Fontana de Trevi **Rev:** Trevi fountain and building facade

Date	Mintage	F	VF	XF	Unc	BU
2009 Proof	15,000	—	—	—	—	75.00

KM# 244 DOLLAR
0.5000 g., 0.9990 Gold 0.0161 oz. AGW, 11.8 mm. **Subject:** First didrachm **Rev:** Twins sucking at she-wolf

Date	Mintage	F	VF	XF	Unc	BU
MMIX (2009)	15,000	—	—	—	—	40.00

KM# 245 DOLLAR
0.5000 g., 0.9990 Gold 0.0161 oz. AGW, 11.8 mm. **Subject:** Claudius aureus **Rev:** Head laureate right

Date	Mintage	F	VF	XF	Unc	BU
MMIX (2009)	15,000	—	—	—	—	40.00

KM# 246 DOLLAR
0.5000 g., 0.9990 Gold 0.0161 oz. AGW, 11.8 mm. **Subject:** Tiberius aureus **Rev:** Head laureate right

Date	Mintage	F	VF	XF	Unc	BU
MMIX (2009)	15,000	—	—	—	—	40.00

KM# 247 DOLLAR
0.5000 g., 0.9990 Gold 0.0161 oz. AGW, 11.8 mm. **Subject:** Caligula aureus **Rev:** Head laureate right

Date	Mintage	F	VF	XF	Unc	BU
MMIX (2009)	15,000	—	—	—	—	40.00

KM# 260 DOLLAR
Silver Plated Copper, 30x30 mm. **Subject:** 2000th Anniversary Teutobury Forest Battle **Obv:** Shield **Rev:** Warrior in forest battle, multicolor **Shape:** Square

Date	Mintage	F	VF	XF	Unc	BU
MMIX (2009) Proof	2,500	Value: 30.00				

KM# 261 DOLLAR
25.0000 g., 0.9990 Silver 0.8029 oz. ASW, 38.6 mm. **Subject:** Pacific Wildlife **Obv:** Arms **Rev:** Barn Swallow - prism

Date	Mintage	F	VF	XF	Unc	BU
2009 Proof	2,500	Value: 50.00				

KM# 262 DOLLAR
25.0000 g., 0.9990 Silver 0.8029 oz. ASW, 38.6 mm. **Subject:** Pacific Wildlife **Obv:** Arms **Rev:** Gecko on rock - prism

Date	Mintage	F	VF	XF	Unc	BU
2009 Proof	2,500	Value: 50.00				

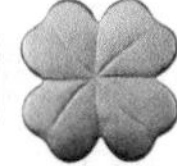

KM# 263 DOLLAR
0.5000 g., 0.9990 Gold 0.0161 oz. AGW, 11 mm. **Rev:** 4-leaf clover, green

Date	Mintage	F	VF	XF	Unc	BU
2009	—	—	—	—	—	65.00

KM# 269 DOLLAR
Copper-Nickel, 37.2 mm. **Subject:** Protect Wildlife - Angelfish **Rev:** Angelfish - Prisim

Date	Mintage	F	VF	XF	Unc	BU
2009	—	—	—	—	—	35.00

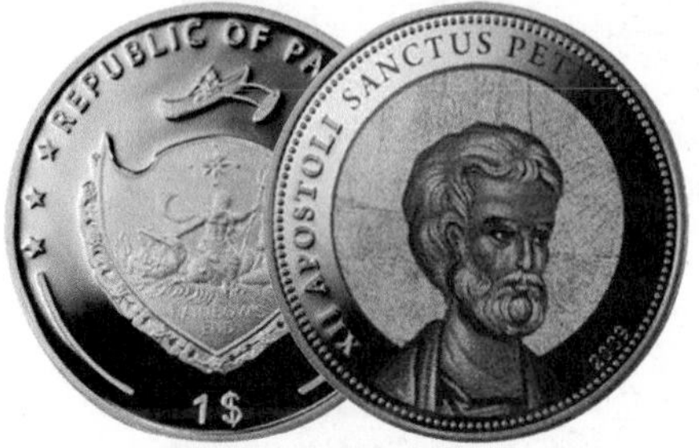

KM# 270 DOLLAR
Copper-Nickel, 37.2 mm. **Subject:** Apostles - Peter **Rev:** Multicolor icon image

Date	Mintage	F	VF	XF	Unc	BU
2009 Proof	1,000	Value: 25.00				

KM# 271 DOLLAR
Copper-Nickel, 37.2 mm. **Subject:** Apostles - James Minor **Rev:** Multicolor icon image

Date	Mintage	F	VF	XF	Unc	BU
2009 Proof	1,000	Value: 25.00				

KM# 272 DOLLAR
Copper-Nickel, 37.2 mm. **Subject:** Apostles - John **Rev:** Multicolor icon image

Date	Mintage	F	VF	XF	Unc	BU
2009 Proof	1,000	Value: 25.00				

KM# 273 DOLLAR
Copper-Nickel, 37.2 mm. **Subject:** Apostle - Simon **Rev:** Multicolor icon image

Date	Mintage	F	VF	XF	Unc	BU
2009 Proof	1,000	Value: 25.00				

KM# 274 DOLLAR
Copper-Nickel, 37.2 mm. **Subject:** Apostles - Matthaeus **Rev:** Multicolor icon image

Date	Mintage	F	VF	XF	Unc	BU
2009 Proof	1,000	Value: 25.00				

KM# 275 DOLLAR
Copper-Nickel, 37.2 mm. **Subject:** Apostles - Thomas **Rev:** Multicolor icon image

Date	Mintage	F	VF	XF	Unc	BU
2009 Proof	1,000	Value: 25.00				

KM# 276 DOLLAR
Copper-Nickel, 37.2 mm. **Subject:** Apostles - Judas Thaddaeus **Rev:** Multicolor icon image

Date	Mintage	F	VF	XF	Unc	BU
2009 Proof	1,000	Value: 25.00				

KM# 277 DOLLAR
Copper-Nickel, 37.2 mm. **Subject:** Apostles - Bartholomew **Rev:** Multicolor icon image

Date	Mintage	F	VF	XF	Unc	BU
2009 Proof	1,000	Value: 25.00				

KM# 278 DOLLAR
Copper-Nickel, 37.2 mm. **Subject:** Apostles - Philip **Rev:** Multicolor icon image

Date	Mintage	F	VF	XF	Unc	BU
2009 Proof	1,000	Value: 25.00				

KM# 279 DOLLAR
Copper-Nickel, 37.2 mm. **Subject:** Apostles - John Major **Rev:** Multicolor icon image

Date	Mintage	F	VF	XF	Unc	BU
2009 Proof	1,000	Value: 25.00				

KM# 280 DOLLAR
Copper-Nickel, 37.2 mm. **Subject:** Apostles - Andrew **Rev:** Multicolor icon image

Date	Mintage	F	VF	XF	Unc	BU
2009 Proof	1,000	Value: 25.00				

KM# 281 DOLLAR
Copper-Nickel, 37.2 mm. **Subject:** Apostles - Judas Iscariot **Rev:** Multicolor icon image

Date	Mintage	F	VF	XF	Unc	BU
2009 Proof	1,000	Value: 25.00				

KM# 282 DOLLAR
26.8000 g., Copper-Nickel, 37.2 mm. **Subject:** Endangered Wildlife - Orange Lined Tigerfish **Rev:** Multicolor fish left

Date	Mintage	F	VF	XF	Unc	BU
2009 Proof	—	Value: 37.50				

KM# 283 DOLLAR
26.8000 g., Copper-Nickel, 37.2 mm. **Subject:** Endangered Wildlife - Blue Grilled Angelfish **Rev:** Multicolor fish

Date	Mintage	F	VF	XF	Unc	BU
2009 Proof	—	Value: 37.50				

KM# 284 DOLLAR
26.8000 g., Copper-Nickel, 37.2 mm. **Subject:** Endangered Wildlife - Green Turtle **Rev:** Multicolor turtle

Date	Mintage	F	VF	XF	Unc	BU
2009 Proof	—	Value: 37.50				

KM# 285 DOLLAR
26.8000 g., Copper-Nickel, 37.2 mm. **Subject:** Endangered Wildlife - Sailfin Tang fish **Rev:** Multicolor fish right

Date	Mintage	F	VF	XF	Unc	BU
2009 Proof	—	Value: 37.50				

KM# 286 DOLLAR
26.8000 g., Copper-Nickel, 37.2 mm. **Subject:** Endangered Wildlife - Clown Trigger fish **Rev:** Multicolor fish left

Date	Mintage	F	VF	XF	Unc	BU
2009 Proof	—	Value: 37.50				

KM# 321 DOLLAR
0.5000 g., 0.9990 Gold 0.0161 oz. AGW, 11.8 mm. **Obv:** National arms **Rev:** Pamir, sail training vessel

Date	Mintage	F	VF	XF	Unc	BU
2009 Proof	25,000	Value: 90.00				

KM# 448 DOLLAR
27.0000 g., Copper-Nickel, 38.61 mm. **Obv:** National arms **Rev:** Two spotted fish in color

Date	Mintage	F	VF	XF	Unc	BU
2009 Proof	—	Value: 35.00				

KM# 266 DOLLAR
25.0000 g., 0.9250 Silver 0.7435 oz. ASW, 30x30 mm. **Subject:** Battle of Grimwald **Rev:** Vyautas and Jagiello busts **Shape:** Square

Date	Mintage	F	VF	XF	Unc	BU
2010 Proof	—	Value: 30.00				

KM# 267 DOLLAR
25.0000 g., 0.9990 Silver 0.8029 oz. ASW, 30x30 mm. **Subject:** Battle of Grunwald **Rev:** Warrior on horseback in color **Shape:** Square

Date	Mintage	F	VF	XF	Unc	BU
2010 Proof	2,500	Value: 35.00				

KM# 268 DOLLAR
25.0000 g., 0.9990 Silver 0.8029 oz. ASW, 30x30 mm. **Subject:** Battle of Grunwald **Rev:** Knight kneeling in color **Shape:** Square

Date	Mintage	F	VF	XF	Unc	BU
2010 Proof	2,500	Value: 35.00				

KM# 303 DOLLAR
0.5000 g., 0.9990 Gold 0.0161 oz. AGW, 11mm mm. **Obv:** National arms **Rev:** Teddy bear **Shape:** Irregular

Date	Mintage	F	VF	XF	Unc	BU
ND(2010)	25,000	—	—	—	—	75.00

KM# 307 DOLLAR
35.0000 g., Copper-Nickel, 50 mm. **Subject:** Hold Cards **Obv:** National arms **Rev:** King of Hearts and Clubs

Date	Mintage	F	VF	XF	Unc	BU
2010 Antique patina	5,000	—	—	—	—	25.00

KM# 308 DOLLAR
35.0000 g., Copper-Nickel, 50 mm. **Subject:** Hold Cards **Obv:** National arms **Rev:** King of Spades and Diamonds

Date	Mintage	F	VF	XF	Unc	BU
2010 Antique patina	5,000	—	—	—	—	25.00

KM# 309 DOLLAR
0.5000 g., 0.9999 Gold 0.0161 oz. AGW, 11.8 mm. **Obv:** National arms **Rev:** Nero coin

Date	Mintage	F	VF	XF	Unc	BU
2010	15,000	—	—	—	—	60.00

KM# 310 DOLLAR
0.5000 g., 0.9999 Gold 0.0161 oz. AGW, 11.8 mm. **Obv:** National arms **Rev:** Vespasian coin

Date	Mintage	F	VF	XF	Unc	BU
2010	15,000	—	—	—	—	60.00

KM# 311 DOLLAR
0.5000 g., 0.9990 Silver 0.0161 oz. ASW, 11.8 mm. **Obv:** National arms **Rev:** Titus coin

Date	Mintage	F	VF	XF	Unc	BU
2010	15,000	—	—	—	—	60.00

KM# 312 DOLLAR
0.5000 g., 0.9999 Gold 0.0161 oz. AGW, 11.8 mm. **Obv:** National arms **Rev:** Domitian coin

Date	Mintage	F	VF	XF	Unc	BU
2010	15,000	—	—	—	—	60.00

KM# 313 DOLLAR
27.0000 g., Silver Plated Copper, 38.61 mm. **Obv:** Mermaid **Rev:** Hammerhead shark color image

Date	Mintage	F	VF	XF	Unc	BU
2010 Prooflike	5,000	—	—	—	—	28.00

KM# 315 DOLLAR
1.0000 g., 0.9999 Gold 0.0321 oz. AGW, 13.92 mm. **Obv:** Mermaid **Rev:** Hammerhead sharks

Date	Mintage	F	VF	XF	Unc	BU
2010 Proof	25,000	Value: 100				

KM# 316 DOLLAR
27.0000 g., Silver Plated Copper, 35x35 mm. **Obv:** National arms **Rev:** Fernando Alonso and racecar in color

Date	Mintage	F	VF	XF	Unc	BU
2010 Prooflike	5,000	—	—	—	—	35.00

KM# 317 DOLLAR
0.5000 g., 0.9999 Gold 0.0161 oz. AGW, 11 mm. **Obv:** National arms **Rev:** Angel **Shape:** Irregular

Date	Mintage	F	VF	XF	Unc	BU
ND(2011)	15,000	—	—	—	—	50.00

KM# 327 DOLLAR
0.5000 g., 0.9990 Gold 0.0161 oz. AGW, 11.8 mm. **Obv:** National arms **Rev:** Romulus & Remus

Date	Mintage	F	VF	XF	Unc	BU
2010 Proof	15,000	Value: 50.00				

KM# 429 DOLLAR
Copper-Nickel, 38.61 mm. **Obv:** National arms **Rev:** Our Lady of Fatima statue in color at left, Pope benedict XVI at right

Date	Mintage	F	VF	XF	Unc	BU
2010 Proof	—	Value: 25.00				

KM# 445 DOLLAR
1.2400 g., 0.9990 Gold 0.0398 oz. AGW, 13.92 mm. **Obv:** Naitonal arms **Rev:** Mary, Joseph and Jesus **Rev. Legend:** CHRISTMAS

Date	Mintage	F	VF	XF	Unc	BU
2010 Proof	—	Value: 90.00				

KM# 405 DOLLAR
1.2400 g., 0.9990 Gold 0.0398 oz. AGW, 13.94 mm. **Obv:** Mermaid reclining on rock **Rev:** Anemone fish

Date	Mintage	F	VF	XF	Unc	BU
2011 Proof	—	Value: 90.00				

KM# 453 DOLLAR
25.0000 g., 0.9990 Silver 0.8029 oz. ASW, 38.61 mm. **Obv:** National arms **Rev:** Two striped fish

Date	Mintage	F	VF	XF	Unc	BU
2011 Proof	—	Value: 75.00				

KM# 340 DOLLAR
27.0000 g., Silver Plated Copper, 38.61 mm. **Subject:** John Paul II **Rev:** Visions at Fatima

Date	Mintage	F	VF	XF	Unc	BU
2011 Prooflike	2,500	—	—	—	—	22.00

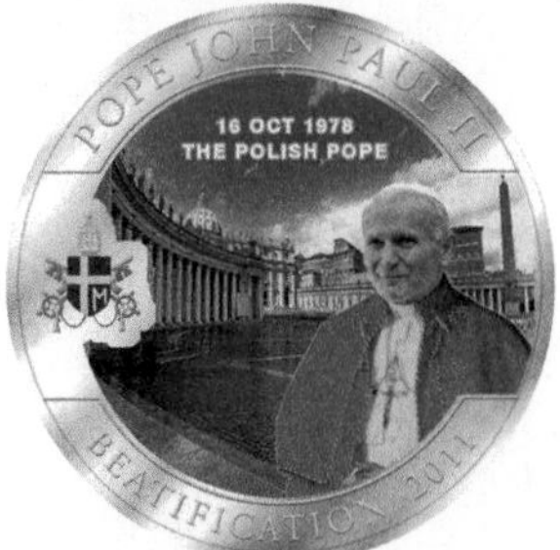

KM# 341 DOLLAR
27.0000 g., Silver Plated Copper, 38.61 mm. **Subject:** John Paul II **Rev:** Election as pope

Date	Mintage	F	VF	XF	Unc	BU
2011 Prooflike	2,500	—	—	—	—	22.00

KM# 342 DOLLAR
27.0000 g., Silver Plated Copper, 38.61 mm. **Subject:** John Paul II **Rev:** Death

Date	Mintage	F	VF	XF	Unc	BU
2011 Prooflike	2,500	—	—	—	—	22.00

KM# 343 DOLLAR
27.0000 g., Silver Plated Copper, 38.61 mm. **Subject:** John Paul II **Rev:** Anouncement as Venerable

Date	Mintage	F	VF	XF	Unc	BU
2011 Prooflike	2,500	—	—	—	—	22.00

KM# 344 DOLLAR
27.0000 g., Silver Plated Copper, 38.61 mm. **Subject:** John Paul II **Rev:** Miracle healing of a Sister

Date	Mintage	F	VF	XF	Unc	BU
2011 Prooflike	2,500	—	—	—	—	22.00

KM# 345 DOLLAR
27.0000 g., Silver Plated Copper, 38.61 mm. **Subject:** John Paul II **Rev:** Benedict VXI's pronouncement

Date	Mintage	F	VF	XF	Unc	BU
2011 Prooflike	2,500	—	—	—	—	22.00

KM# 346 DOLLAR
27.0000 g., Silver Plated Copper, 38.61 mm. **Subject:** John Paul II **Rev:** Opening the cause for sainthood

Date	Mintage	F	VF	XF	Unc	BU
2011 Prooflike	2,500	—	—	—	—	22.00

KM# 347 DOLLAR
27.0000 g., Silver Plated Copper, 38.61 mm. **Subject:** John Paul II **Rev:** Ceremony of Beautification

Date	Mintage	F	VF	XF	Unc	BU
2011 Prooflike	2,500	—	—	—	—	22.00

KM# 349 DOLLAR
0.5000 g., 0.9990 Gold 0.0161 oz. AGW, 11.8 mm. **Rev:** Roman Coin - Coliseum

Date	Mintage	F	VF	XF	Unc	BU
2011 Proof	—	Value: 55.00				

KM# 350 DOLLAR
0.5000 g., 0.9990 Gold 0.0161 oz. AGW, 11.8 mm. **Rev:** Roman Coin - Trajain

Date	Mintage	F	VF	XF	Unc	BU
2011 Proof	—	Value: 55.00				

KM# 351 DOLLAR
0.5000 g., 0.9990 Gold 0.0161 oz. AGW, 11.8 mm. **Rev:** Roman Coin - Hadrian

Date	Mintage	F	VF	XF	Unc	BU
2011 Proof	—	Value: 55.00				

KM# 352 DOLLAR
0.5000 g., 0.9990 Gold 0.0161 oz. AGW, 11.8 mm. **Rev:** Roman Coin - Marcus Aurillus

Date	Mintage	F	VF	XF	Unc	BU
2011 Proof	—	Value: 55.00				

KM# 370 DOLLAR
0.5000 g., 0.9990 Gold 0.0161 oz. AGW, 11.8 mm. **Obv:** National arms **Rev:** Diocletian coin

Date	Mintage	F	VF	XF	Unc	BU
2011	—	—	—	—	—	60.00

KM# 371 DOLLAR
0.5000 g., 0.9990 Gold 0.0161 oz. AGW, 11.8 mm. **Obv:** National arms **Rev:** Aurelian coin

Date	Mintage	F	VF	XF	Unc	BU
2011	—	—	—	—	—	60.00

KM# 372 DOLLAR
0.5000 g., 0.9990 Gold 0.0161 oz. AGW, 11.8 mm. **Obv:** National arms **Rev:** Caracalla coin

Date	Mintage	F	VF	XF	Unc	BU
2011	—	—	—	—	—	60.00

KM# 373 DOLLAR
0.5000 g., 0.9990 Gold 0.0161 oz. AGW, 11.8 mm. **Obv:** National arms **Rev:** Septimius Severus coin

Date	Mintage	F	VF	XF	Unc	BU
2011	—	—	—	—	—	60.00

KM# 406 DOLLAR
27.0000 g., Copper-Nickel, 38.6 mm. **Obv:** Mermaid reclining on rock **Rev:** Anemone fish in color

Date	Mintage	F	VF	XF	Unc	BU
2011	—	—	—	—	—	25.00

KM# 408 DOLLAR
27.0000 g., Copper-Nickel, 38.61 mm. **Obv:** National arms **Rev:** Harry Houdini bust at left, top had and wand at right

Date	Mintage	F	VF	XF	Unc	BU
2011	—	—	—	—	—	25.00

KM# 410 DOLLAR
0.5000 g., 0.9990 Gold 0.0161 oz. AGW, 11 mm. **Obv:** National arms **Rev:** Golden Butterfly **Shape:** Irregular

Date	Mintage	F	VF	XF	Unc	BU
ND(2011) Proof	—	Value: 85.00				

KM# 452 DOLLAR
25.0000 g., 0.9990 Silver 0.8029 oz. ASW, 38.61 mm. **Obv:** National arms **Rev:** Long nose hawk fish

Date	Mintage	F	VF	XF	Unc	BU
2011 Proof	—	Value: 75.00				

KM# 130 2 DOLLARS
10.0000 g., 0.9990 Silver 0.3212 oz. ASW, 30 mm. **Obv:** Shield with Neptune holding trident, mermaid reclining at his side **Obv. Legend:** REPUBLIC OF PALAU **Rev:** Red racing car 3/4 right **Rev. Legend:** FERRARI - 60 YEARS ANNIVERSARY

Date	Mintage	F	VF	XF	Unc	BU
ND(2007) Proof	2,500	Value: 45.00				

KM# 131 2 DOLLARS
10.0000 g., 0.9990 Silver 0.3212 oz. ASW, 30 mm. **Obv:** Shield with Neptune holding trident, mermaid reclining at his side **Obv. Legend:** REPUBLIC OF PALAU **Rev:** Red racing car 3/4 right **Rev. Legend:** FERRARI - 60 YEARS ANNIVERSARY

Date	Mintage	F	VF	XF	Unc	BU
ND(2007) Proof	2,500	Value: 45.00				

KM# 132 2 DOLLARS
10.0000 g., 0.9990 Silver 0.3212 oz. ASW, 30 mm. **Obv:** Shield with Neptune holding trident, mermaid reclining at his side **Obv. Legend:** REPUBLIC OF PALAU **Rev:** Red racing car front view **Rev. Legend:** FERRARI - 60 YEARS ANNIVERSARY

Date	Mintage	F	VF	XF	Unc	BU
ND(2007) Proof	2,500	Value: 45.00				

KM# 133 2 DOLLARS
10.0000 g., 0.9990 Silver 0.3212 oz. ASW, 30 mm. **Obv:** Shield with Neptune holding trident, mermaid reclining at his side **Obv. Legend:** REPUBLIC OF PALAU **Rev:** Looking down on red racing car approaching in turn **Rev. Legend:** FERRARI - 60 YEARS ANNIVERSARY

Date	Mintage	F	VF	XF	Unc	BU
ND(2007) Proof	2,500	Value: 45.00				

KM# 134 2 DOLLARS
10.0000 g., 0.9990 Silver 0.3212 oz. ASW, 30 mm. **Obv:** Shield with Neptune holding trident, reclining mermaid at his side **Obv. Legend:** REPUBLIC OF PALAU **Rev:** Front view of red racing car **Rev. Legend:** FERRARI - 60 YEARS ANNIVERSARY

Date	Mintage	F	VF	XF	Unc	BU
ND(2007) Proof	2,500	Value: 45.00				

KM# 135 2 DOLLARS
10.0000 g., 0.9990 Silver 0.3212 oz. ASW, 30.0 mm. **Obv:** Shield with Neptune holding trident, mermaid reclining at his side **Obv. Legend:** REPUBLIC OF PALAU **Rev:** Red racing car approaching 3/4 right **Rev. Legend:** FERRARI - 60 YEARS ANNIVERSARY

Date	Mintage	F	VF	XF	Unc	BU
ND(2007) Proof	2,500	Value: 45.00				

KM# 319 2 DOLLARS
15.5000 g., 0.9250 Silver 0.4609 oz. ASW, 35 mm. **Subject:** World of Insects **Obv:** National arms **Rev:** Large color dragon fly - Blue Eye Hawker

Date	Mintage	F	VF	XF	Unc	BU
2010 Proof	1,000	Value: 100				

KM# 375 2 DOLLARS
15.5000 g., 0.9250 Silver 0.4609 oz. ASW, 35 mm. **Subject:** Grasshopper

Date	Mintage	F	VF	XF	Unc	BU
2010 Proof	—	Value: 100				

KM# 353 2 DOLLARS
15.5000 g., 0.9990 Silver 0.4978 oz. ASW, 35 mm. **Subject:** Bible stories - Creation of the World

Date	Mintage	F	VF	XF	Unc	BU
2011 Proof	1,000	Value: 65.00				

KM# 354 2 DOLLARS
15.5000 g., 0.9990 Silver 0.4978 oz. ASW, 35 mm. **Subject:** Bible stories - Adam and Eve

Date	Mintage	F	VF	XF	Unc	BU
2011 Proof	1,000	Value: 65.00				

KM# 355 2 DOLLARS
15.5000 g., 0.9990 Silver 0.4978 oz. ASW, 35 mm. **Subject:** Bible stories - Cain and Abel

Date	Mintage	F	VF	XF	Unc	BU
2011 Proof	1,000	Value: 65.00				

KM# 356 2 DOLLARS
15.5000 g., 0.9990 Silver 0.4978 oz. ASW, 35 mm. **Subject:** Bible stories - 10 Commandments

Date	Mintage	F	VF	XF	Unc	BU
2011 Proof	1,000	Value: 65.00				

KM# 357 2 DOLLARS
15.5700 g., 0.9250 Silver 0.4630 oz. ASW, 35 mm. **Obv:** National arms **Rev:** Atelopus Certus, orange frog in color

Date	Mintage	F	VF	XF	Unc	BU
2011 Proof	500	Value: 85.00				

KM# 358 2 DOLLARS
151.5700 g., 0.9250 Silver 4.5074 oz. ASW, 35 mm. **Obv:** National arms **Rev:** Green frog in color

Date	Mintage	F	VF	XF	Unc	BU
2011 Proof	500	Value: 85.00				

KM# 359 2 DOLLARS
15.5700 g., 0.9250 Silver 0.4630 oz. ASW, 35 mm. **Obv:** National arms **Rev:** Atelopus Cerus, purple frog in color

Date	Mintage	F	VF	XF	Unc	BU
2011 Proof	500	Value: 85.00				

KM# 360 2 DOLLARS
15.5000 g., 0.9250 Silver 0.4609 oz. ASW, 35 mm. **Rev:** Bombus Latreille - Bumble bee in color

Date	Mintage	F	VF	XF	Unc	BU
2011 Proof	1,000	Value: 100				

KM# 361 2 DOLLARS
15.5700 g., 0.9250 Silver 0.4630 oz. ASW, 35 mm. **Rev:** John Paul II with cross croizer, doves

Date	Mintage	F	VF	XF	Unc	BU
2011 Proof	1,000	Value: 60.00				

KM# 362 2 DOLLARS
25.0000 g., 0.9250 Silver 0.7435 oz. ASW, 38.61 mm. **Obv:** National Arms **Rev:** Abu Simbel temple entrance with insert

Date	Mintage	F	VF	XF	Unc	BU
2011 Proof	999	Value: 100				

KM# 363 2 DOLLARS
25.0000 g., 0.9250 Silver 0.7435 oz. ASW, 41x31 mm. **Subject:** Opera - Carmen **Rev:** Couple kissing in color, two other opera scenes **Shape:** Rectangle

Date	Mintage	F	VF	XF	Unc	BU
2011 Proof	999	Value: 75.00				

KM# 366 2 DOLLARS
25.0000 g., 0.9250 Silver 0.7435 oz. ASW, 38.61 mm. **Subject:** Princess of the Sea **Rev:** Apricot pearl and shell

Date	Mintage	F	VF	XF	Unc	BU
2011 Proof	2,500	Value: 100				

KM# 409 2 DOLLARS
25.0000 g., 0.9250 Silver 0.7435 oz. ASW, 38.61 mm. **Obv:** National arms **Rev:** Harry Houdini bust at left, top had and wand at right

Date	Mintage	F	VF	XF	Unc	BU
2011 Proof	—	Value: 60.00				

KM# 442 2 DOLLARS
Silver, 38.61 mm. **Obv:** National arms **Rev:** Giant Prickly Stick Insect in color on flora

Date	Mintage	F	VF	XF	Unc	BU
2011 Proof	—	Value: 100				

KM# 426 2 DOLLARS
15.5000 g., Silver partially gilt, 35 mm. **Obv:** National arms **Rev:** Jansa Gora Monastery, Pope John Paul II, and rose

Date	Mintage	F	VF	XF	Unc	BU
2012 Proof	—	Value: 50.00				

KM# 433 2 DOLLARS
25.0000 g., 0.9250 Silver 0.7435 oz. ASW, 45x45 mm. **Obv:** National arms **Rev:** Winged heart **Shape:** Heart

Date	Mintage	F	VF	XF	Unc	BU
2012 Proof	—	Value: 55.00				

KM# 53 5 DOLLARS
25.0000 g., 0.9000 Silver 0.7234 oz. ASW, 37.2 mm. **Series:** Marine Life Protection **Obv:** Neptune **Rev:** Multicolor jellyfish **Edge:** Reeded

Date	Mintage	F	VF	XF	Unc	BU
2001 Proof	—	Value: 75.00				

KM# 75 5 DOLLARS
25.0000 g., 0.9000 Silver 0.7234 oz. ASW, 37.2 mm. **Subject:** Marine Life Protection **Obv:** Neptune behind Polynesian ship and value **Rev:** Moorish-Idol fish **Edge:** Reeded

Date	Mintage	F	VF	XF	Unc	BU
2001 Proof	—	Value: 75.00				

KM# 76 5 DOLLARS
Silver, 37.2 mm. **Subject:** Marine Life Protection **Obv:** Neptune riding seahorse and value **Rev:** Fish **Edge:** Reeded

Date	Mintage	F	VF	XF	Unc	BU
2001 Proof	—	Value: 75.00				

KM# 115 5 DOLLARS
25.0000 g., 0.9000 Silver 0.7234 oz. ASW, 37.2 mm. **Subject:** Marine Life Protection **Obv:** Neptune waist deep in water above value with mermaid to the left and behind **Rev:** Multicolor iridescent fish scene **Edge:** Reeded

Date	Mintage	F	VF	XF	Unc	BU
2001 Proof	—	Value: 70.00				

KM# 331 5 DOLLARS
25.0000 g., 0.9000 Silver 0.7234 oz. ASW, 38.61 mm. **Rev:** Angelfish

Date	Mintage	F	VF	XF	Unc	BU
2001 Proof	Est. 3,000	Value: 50.00				

KM# 332 5 DOLLARS
25.0000 g., 0.9000 Silver 0.7234 oz. ASW, 38.61 mm. **Rev:** Blowfish

Date	Mintage	F	VF	XF	Unc	BU
2002 Proof	Est. 3,000	Value: 55.00				

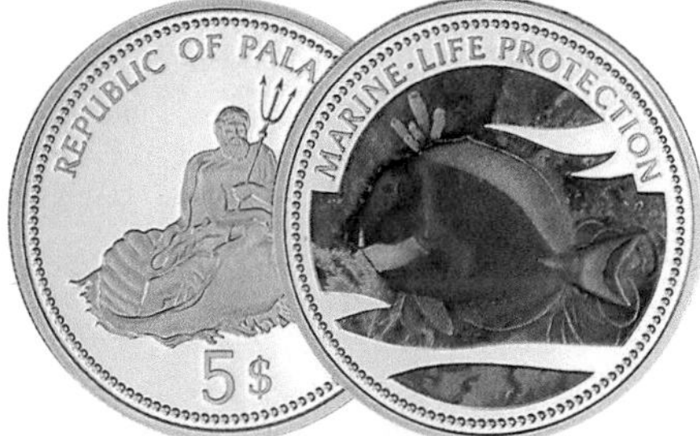

KM# 77 5 DOLLARS
25.0000 g., 0.9000 Silver 0.7234 oz. ASW, 37.2 mm. **Subject:** Marine Life Protection **Obv:** Neptune in shell boat **Rev:** Blue Tang Fish **Edge:** Reeded

Date	Mintage	F	VF	XF	Unc	BU
2002 Proof	—	Value: 75.00				

KM# 78 5 DOLLARS
25.0000 g., 0.9000 Silver 0.7234 oz. ASW, 37.2 mm. **Subject:** Marine Life Protection **Obv:** Neptune in sea chariot **Rev:** Multicolor whales **Edge:** Reeded

Date	Mintage	F	VF	XF	Unc	BU
2002 Proof	—	Value: 75.00				

KM# 79 5 DOLLARS
25.0000 g., 0.9000 Silver 0.7234 oz. ASW, 37.2 mm. **Subject:** Marine Life Protection **Obv:** Zeus and value **Rev:** Multicolor puffer fish **Edge:** Reeded

Date	Mintage	F	VF	XF	Unc	BU
2002 Proof	—	Value: 75.00				

KM# 80 5 DOLLARS
25.0000 g., 0.9000 Silver 0.7234 oz. ASW, 37.2 mm. **Subject:** Marine Life Protection **Obv:** Neptune standing behind Polynesian ship **Rev:** Multicolor Jellyfish **Edge:** Reeded

Date	Mintage	F	VF	XF	Unc	BU
2002 Proof	—	Value: 70.00				

KM# 102 5 DOLLARS
25.0000 g., 0.9000 Silver 0.7234 oz. ASW, 32 mm. **Subject:** Marine Life Protection **Obv:** Neptune in sea chariot with two merhorses **Rev:** Two multicolor reflective fish

Date	Mintage	F	VF	XF	Unc	BU
2002 Proof	—	Value: 60.00				

KM# 103 5 DOLLARS
25.0000 g., 0.9000 Silver 0.7234 oz. ASW, 32 mm. **Subject:** Marine Life Protection **Obv:** Neptune standing in waves **Rev:** Multicolor starfish

Date	Mintage	F	VF	XF	Unc	BU
2003 Proof	—	Value: 60.00				

KM# 104 5 DOLLARS
25.0000 g., 0.9000 Silver 0.7234 oz. ASW, 32 mm. **Subject:** Marine Life Protection **Obv:** Neptune standing in sea chariot **Rev:** Two multicolor reflective fish

Date	Mintage	F	VF	XF	Unc	BU
2003 Proof	—	Value: 60.00				

KM# 105 5 DOLLARS
25.0000 g., 0.9000 Silver 0.7234 oz. ASW, 32 mm. **Subject:** Marine Life Protection **Rev:** Multicolor Orca

Date	Mintage	F	VF	XF	Unc	BU
2003 Proof	—	Value: 60.00				

KM# 106 5 DOLLARS
25.0000 g., 0.9000 Silver 0.7234 oz. ASW, 32 mm. **Subject:** Marine Life Protection **Obv:** Neptune in sea chariot **Rev:** Multicolor Napoleon Fish

Date	Mintage	F	VF	XF	Unc	BU
2003 Proof	—	Value: 60.00				

KM# 333 5 DOLLARS
25.0000 g., 0.9000 Silver 0.7234 oz. ASW, 38.61 mm. **Rev:** Crab

Date	Mintage	F	VF	XF	Unc	BU
2003 Proof	Est. 3,000	Value: 55.00				

KM# 107 5 DOLLARS
25.0000 g., 0.9000 Silver 0.7234 oz. ASW, 32 mm. **Subject:** Marine Life Protection **Obv:** Neptune seated behind mermaid **Rev:** Multicolor school of sweetlips fish

Date	Mintage	F	VF	XF	Unc	BU
2004 Proof	—	Value: 60.00				

KM# 108 5 DOLLARS
25.0000 g., 0.9000 Silver 0.7234 oz. ASW, 32 mm. **Subject:** Marine Life Protection **Obv:** Standing Neptune and ship **Rev:** Multicolor Porcupine fish

Date	Mintage	F	VF	XF	Unc	BU
2004 Proof	—	Value: 75.00				

KM# 109 5 DOLLARS
25.0000 g., 0.9000 Silver 0.7234 oz. ASW, 32 mm. **Subject:** Marine Life Protection **Obv:** Neptune in sea chariot **Rev:** Multicolor Loggerhead turtle

Date	Mintage	F	VF	XF	Unc	BU
2004 Proof	—	Value: 75.00				

KM# 110 5 DOLLARS
25.0000 g., 0.9000 Silver 0.7234 oz. ASW, 32 mm. **Subject:** Marine Life Protection **Obv:** Neptune and merhorse **Rev:** Multicolor dolphin head

Date	Mintage	F	VF	XF	Unc	BU
2004 Proof	—	Value: 75.00				

KM# 81 5 DOLLARS
25.0000 g., 0.9000 Silver 0.7234 oz. ASW, 37.2 mm. **Subject:** Marine Life Protection **Obv:** Neptune with treasure chest **Rev:** Clownfish **Edge:** Reeded

Date	Mintage	F	VF	XF	Unc	BU
2004 Proof	—	Value: 75.00				

KM# 111 5 DOLLARS
25.0000 g., 0.9000 Silver 0.7234 oz. ASW, 32 mm. **Subject:** Marine Life Protection **Obv:** Neptune flanked by mermaids **Rev:** Multicolor sea horse

Date	Mintage	F	VF	XF	Unc	BU
2005 Proof	—	Value: 75.00				

KM# 113 5 DOLLARS
25.0000 g., 0.9000 Silver 0.7234 oz. ASW, 32 mm. **Subject:** Marine Life Protection **Obv:** Neptune flanked by mermaids **Rev:** Multicolor fish with ring-like stripes **Edge:** Reeded

Date	Mintage	F	VF	XF	Unc	BU
2005 Proof	—	Value: 75.00				

KM# 114 5 DOLLARS
25.0000 g., 0.9000 Silver 0.7234 oz. ASW, 32 mm. **Subject:** Marine Life Protection **Obv:** Neptune in shell boat talking to a dolphin **Rev:** Multicolor reef fish scene **Edge:** Reeded

Date	Mintage	F	VF	XF	Unc	BU
2006 Proof	—	Value: 75.00				

KM# 143 5 DOLLARS
25.0000 g., 0.9250 Silver with meteorite insert. 0.7435 oz. ASW **Subject:** Nantan Meteroite fall, May 1516 **Obv:** Shield **Rev:** Farmer and oxen plowing field, meteorite insert

Date	Mintage	F	VF	XF	Unc	BU
2006 Proof	2,500	Value: 100				

KM# 185 5 DOLLARS
24.8500 g., 0.9990 Silver 0.7981 oz. ASW, 38.6 mm. **Rev:** Black pearl oyster

Date	Mintage	F	VF	XF	Unc	BU
2006 Proof	2,500	Value: 300				

KM# 186 5 DOLLARS
25.0000 g., 0.9990 Silver 0.8029 oz. ASW, 38.61 mm. **Subject:** Pacific Wildlife **Rev:** Rainbow Lorikeet head left

Date	Mintage	F	VF	XF	Unc	BU
2006 Proof	5,000	Value: 55.00				

KM# 187 5 DOLLARS
25.0000 g., 0.9990 Silver 0.8029 oz. ASW, 38.61 mm. **Subject:** Pacific Wildlife **Rev:** Eclectus Parrot head right

Date	Mintage	F	VF	XF	Unc	BU
2006 Proof	5,000	Value: 55.00				

KM# 188 5 DOLLARS
25.0000 g., 0.9990 Silver 0.8029 oz. ASW, 38.61 mm. **Subject:** Pacific Wildlife **Rev:** Fruit dove head right

Date	Mintage	F	VF	XF	Unc	BU
2006 Proof	5,000	Value: 55.00				

KM# 189 5 DOLLARS
31.1050 g., 0.9990 Silver 0.9990 oz. ASW, 38.61 mm. **Subject:** One ounce of luck **Rev:** Four-leaf clover

Date	Mintage	F	VF	XF	Unc	BU
2006 Proof	5,000	Value: 70.00				

KM# 190 5 DOLLARS
25.0000 g., 0.9250 Silver 0.7435 oz. ASW, 38.61 mm. **Subject:** Dream Island **Rev:** Pacific island scene - beach, boat and sunset

Date	Mintage	F	VF	XF	Unc	BU
2006 Proof	5,000	Value: 50.00				

KM# 443 5 DOLLARS
25.0000 g., 0.9250 Silver 0.7435 oz. ASW, 38.61 mm. **Obv:** National arms **Rev:** Volcano, lava in color

Date	Mintage	F	VF	XF	Unc	BU
2006 Proof	—	Value: 100				

KM# 119 5 DOLLARS
25.0000 g., 0.9000 Silver 0.7234 oz. ASW, 38.61 mm. **Series:** Marine Life Protection **Obv:** Neptune reclining with trident, mermaid at his side **Obv. Legend:** REPUBLIC OF PALAU **Rev:** Multicolor Doctor Fish

Date	Mintage	F	VF	XF	Unc	BU
2007 Proof	1,500	Value: 120				

KM# 122 5 DOLLARS
25.0000 g., 0.5000 Silver 0.4019 oz. ASW, 38.61 mm. **Obv:** Shield with Neptune holding trident, mermaid reclining at his side, RAINBOW'S / End below **Obv. Legend:** REPUBLIC OF PALAU **Rev:** Red racing car 3/4 right **Rev. Legend:** FERRARI - 60 YEARS ANNIVERSARY

Date	Mintage	F	VF	XF	Unc	BU
ND(2007) Proof	2,500	Value: 75.00				

KM# 136 5 DOLLARS
25.0000 g., 0.9250 Silver 0.7435 oz. ASW, 38.61 mm. **Series:** Pacific Wildlife **Obv:** National arms **Obv. Legend:** REPUBLIC OF PALAU **Rev:** Saltwater Crocodile with green crystal eye

Date	Mintage	F	VF	XF	Unc	BU
2007 Proof	2,500	Value: 65.00				

KM# 151 5 DOLLARS
25.0000 g., 0.9250 Silver 0.7435 oz. ASW, 38.6 mm. **Subject:** Pacific Wildlife **Obv:** Shield **Rev:** Multicolor nautilus shell

Date	Mintage	F	VF	XF	Unc	BU
2007 Proof	—	Value: 70.00				

KM# 152 5 DOLLARS
25.0000 g., 0.9250 Silver 0.7435 oz. ASW **Subject:** Pacific Wildlife **Obv:** Shield **Rev:** Multicolor starfish

Date	Mintage	F	VF	XF	Unc	BU
2007 Proof	—	Value: 70.00				

KM# 153 5 DOLLARS
25.0000 g., 0.9250 Silver 0.7435 oz. ASW **Subject:** Good heavens! **Obv:** Multicolor devil and angel child **Shape:** Heart

Date	Mintage	F	VF	XF	Unc	BU
2007 Proof	2,500	Value: 65.00				

KM# 138 5 DOLLARS
24.7000 g., Silver, 38.6 mm. **Series:** Marine Life Protection **Obv:** National arms with Neptune and mermaid **Rev:** Pearl in oyster shell - multicolor **Edge:** Reeded

Date	Mintage	F	VF	XF	Unc	BU
2007 Proof	2,500	Value: 185				

KM# 428 5 DOLLARS
25.0000 g., 0.9990 Silver 0.8029 oz. ASW, 38.61 mm. **Obv:** Water Vial and National arms **Rev:** Statue of Mary at Lourds, Water Vial

Date	Mintage	F	VF	XF	Unc	BU
2007 Proof	5,000	Value: 100				

KM# 137 5 DOLLARS
24.7000 g., 0.9250 Silver 0.7345 oz. ASW, 38.5 mm. **Obv:** Outrigger canoe above shield **Obv. Legend:** REPUBLIC OF PALAU **Rev:** Pearl in colorized shell **Rev. Legend:** MARINE LIFE PROTECTION / Pearl of the sea **Edge:** Reeded

Date	Mintage	F	VF	XF	Unc	BU
2008 Proof	2,500	Value: 125				

KM# 168 5 DOLLARS
25.0000 g., 0.9250 Silver 0.7435 oz. ASW, 30x45 mm. **Obv:** Shield **Rev:** Don Quixote in armor **Shape:** Vertical oval

Date	Mintage	F	VF	XF	Unc	BU
2008 Proof	—	Value: 70.00				

KM# 169 5 DOLLARS
25.0000 g., 0.9250 Silver 0.7435 oz. ASW, 37.2 mm. **Subject:** Pacific Wildlife **Obv:** Shield **Rev:** Multicolor hologram, blue butterfly (Papilio Pericles)

Date	Mintage	F	VF	XF	Unc	BU
2008 Proof	2,500	Value: 60.00				

KM# 170 5 DOLLARS
25.0000 g., 0.9250 Silver 0.7435 oz. ASW, 37.2 mm. **Subject:** Pacific Wildlife **Obv:** Shield **Rev:** Multicolor sulphur butterfly (Hebomoia Leucippe)

Date	Mintage	F	VF	XF	Unc	BU
2008 Proof	2,500	Value: 60.00				

KM# 171 5 DOLLARS
25.0000 g., 0.9250 Silver 0.7435 oz. ASW, 37.2 mm. **Subject:** Pacific Wildlife **Obv:** Shield **Rev:** Multicolor hologram, butterfly

Date	Mintage	F	VF	XF	Unc	BU
2008 Proof	2,500	Value: 60.00				

KM# 172 5 DOLLARS
25.0000 g., 0.9250 Silver 0.7435 oz. ASW, 38.6 mm. **Subject:** Telescope, 400th Anniversary **Obv:** Shield **Rev:** Hans Lippersheg, lens insert

Date	Mintage	F	VF	XF	Unc	BU
2008 Matte finish	1,608	—	—	—	—	70.00

KM# 173 5 DOLLARS
25.0000 g., 0.9250 Silver 0.7435 oz. ASW, 38.6 mm. **Subject:** Telescope, 400th Anniversary **Obv:** Shield **Rev:** The Hubble Telescope, lens insert

Date	Mintage	F	VF	XF	Unc	BU
2008 Matte finish	1,608	—	—	—	—	70.00

KM# 174 5 DOLLARS
Copper-Nickel, 38.6 mm. **Subject:** Endangered Wildlife **Obv:** Shield **Rev:** Multicolor yellow fish

Date	Mintage	F	VF	XF	Unc	BU
2008 Proof	—	—	—	—	—	25.00

KM# 175 5 DOLLARS
25.0000 g., 0.9250 Silver 0.7435 oz. ASW, 38.6 mm. **Subject:** Everything for you **Obv:** Shield **Rev:** Multicolor, outstretched hand, ribbon above **Shape:** Heart

Date	Mintage	F	VF	XF	Unc	BU
2008 Proof	2,500	Value: 100				

KM# 192 5 DOLLARS
25.0000 g., 0.9250 Silver partially gilt 0.7435 oz. ASW, 30x45 mm. **Subject:** Illusion Autum Leaves **Rev:** Gilt leaf **Shape:** Oval

Date	Mintage	F	VF	XF	Unc	BU
2008 Proof	2,500	Value: 75.00				

KM# 447 5 DOLLARS
25.0000 g., 0.9250 Silver 0.7435 oz. ASW, 38.61 mm. **Subject:** 2008 Summer Olympics **Obv:** National arms **Rev:** Kyacker paddeling right

Date	Mintage	F	VF	XF	Unc	BU
2008 Proof	—	Value: 75.00				

KM# 179 5 DOLLARS
25.0000 g., 0.9250 Silver 0.7435 oz. ASW, 38.61 mm. **Subject:** Scent of Paradise **Obv:** Shield **Rev:** Multicolor open coconut, scented

Date	Mintage	F	VF	XF	Unc	BU
2009	2,500	—	—	—	—	65.00

KM# 180 5 DOLLARS
25.0000 g., 0.9250 Silver 0.7435 oz. ASW, 38.5 mm. **Subject:** Jewels of the Sea **Obv:** Shield **Rev:** Multicolor blue oyster with inset pearl

Date	Mintage	F	VF	XF	Unc	BU
2009 Proof	2,500	Value: 150				

KM# 181 5 DOLLARS
25.0000 g., 0.9250 Silver 0.7435 oz. ASW, 38.5 mm. **Subject:** Louis Braile, 200th Anniversary of Birth **Obv:** Shield **Rev:** Portrait of Braile

Date	Mintage	F	VF	XF	Unc	BU
2009 Matte finish	2,500	—	—	—	—	45.00

KM# 182 5 DOLLARS
25.0000 g., 0.9250 Silver 0.7435 oz. ASW **Subject:** Missing you **Obv:** Shield **Rev:** Two angels, multicolor, crystal insert **Shape:** Heart

Date	Mintage	F	VF	XF	Unc	BU
2009 Proof	2,500	Value: 55.00				

KM# 196 5 DOLLARS
25.0000 g., 0.9250 Silver 0.7435 oz. ASW, 38.61 mm. **Subject:** Pacific Wildlife **Rev:** Angelfish

Date	Mintage	F	VF	XF	Unc	BU
2009 Proof	2,500	Value: 60.00				

KM# 197 5 DOLLARS
25.0000 g., 0.9250 Silver 0.7435 oz. ASW, 38.61 mm. **Subject:** Pacific Wildlife **Rev:** Barn Swallow

Date	Mintage	F	VF	XF	Unc	BU
2009 Proof	2,500	Value: 60.00				

KM# 198 5 DOLLARS
25.0000 g., 0.9250 Silver 0.7435 oz. ASW, 38.61 mm. **Subject:** Pacific Wildlife **Rev:** Gecko

Date	Mintage	F	VF	XF	Unc	BU
2009 Proof	2,500	Value: 60.00				

KM# 199 5 DOLLARS
25.0000 g., 0.9250 Silver 0.7435 oz. ASW, 38.61 mm. **Subject:** Exceptional Animals **Rev:** Bird of Paradise

Date	Mintage	F	VF	XF	Unc	BU
2009 Proof	2,500	Value: 55.00				

KM# 200 5 DOLLARS
25.0000 g., 0.9250 Silver 0.7435 oz. ASW, 38.61 mm. **Subject:** Exceptional Animals **Rev:** Peacock

Date	Mintage	F	VF	XF	Unc	BU
2009 Proof	2,500	Value: 55.00				

KM# 201 5 DOLLARS
25.0000 g., 0.9250 Silver 0.7435 oz. ASW, 38.61 mm. **Subject:** Marine Life Protection **Rev:** Lionfish

Date	Mintage	F	VF	XF	Unc	BU
2009 Proof	1,500	Value: 65.00				

KM# 202 5 DOLLARS
25.0000 g., 0.9990 Silver 0.8029 oz. ASW, 38.61 mm. **Subject:** Fall of the Berlin Wall **Rev:** Brandenberg Gate, half with and half without wall

Date	Mintage	F	VF	XF	Unc	BU
2009 Proof	2,009	Value: 110				

KM# 203 5 DOLLARS
20.0000 g., 0.9250 Silver 0.5948 oz. ASW, 38.61 mm. **Rev:** Sail training vessel Pamir

Date	Mintage	F	VF	XF	Unc	BU
2009 Proof	2,500	Value: 70.00				

KM# 204 5 DOLLARS
25.0000 g., 0.9250 Silver 0.7435 oz. ASW, 38.61 mm. **Subject:** Wonders of the Ancient World **Rev:** Lighthouse at Alexandria

Date	Mintage	F	VF	XF	Unc	BU
2009 Proof	2,500	Value: 85.00				

KM# 205 5 DOLLARS
25.0000 g., 0.9250 Silver 0.7435 oz. ASW **Subject:** Wonders of the Ancient World **Rev:** Statue of Zeus

Date	Mintage	F	VF	XF	Unc	BU
2009 Proof	2,500	Value: 85.00				

KM# 206 5 DOLLARS
25.0000 g., 0.9250 Silver 0.7435 oz. ASW, 38.61 mm. **Subject:** Wonders of the Ancient World **Rev:** Hanging Gardens of Babylon

Date	Mintage	F	VF	XF	Unc	BU
2009 Proof	2,500	Value: 85.00				

KM# 207 5 DOLLARS
25.0000 g., 0.9250 Silver 0.7435 oz. ASW, 38.61 mm. **Subject:** Wonders of the Ancient World **Rev:** Mausoleum of Halicarnassus

Date	Mintage	F	VF	XF	Unc	BU
2009 Proof	2,500	Value: 85.00				

KM# 208 5 DOLLARS
25.0000 g., 0.9250 Silver 0.7435 oz. ASW, 38.61 mm. **Subject:** Wonders of the Ancient World **Rev:** Pyramids of Giza

Date	Mintage	F	VF	XF	Unc	BU
2009 Proof	2,500	Value: 85.00				

KM# 209 5 DOLLARS
25.0000 g., 0.9250 Silver 0.7435 oz. ASW, 38.61 mm. **Subject:** Wonders of the Ancient World **Rev:** Temple of Artemis

Date	Mintage	F	VF	XF	Unc	BU
2009 Proof	2,500	Value: 85.00				

KM# 210 5 DOLLARS
25.0000 g., 0.9250 Silver 0.7435 oz. ASW, 38.61 mm. **Subject:** Wonders of the Ancient World **Rev:** Colossus of Rhodes

Date	Mintage	F	VF	XF	Unc	BU
2009 Proof	2,500	Value: 85.00				

KM# 211 5 DOLLARS
25.0000 g., 0.9250 Silver 0.7435 oz. ASW, 38.6 mm. **Subject:** Flora and Mountains of the Alps **Rev:** Zugspitze and blue flower

Date	Mintage	F	VF	XF	Unc	BU
2009 Proof	2,500	Value: 65.00				

KM# 212 5 DOLLARS
25.0000 g., 0.9250 Silver 0.7435 oz. ASW, 38.61 mm. **Subject:** Flora and Mountains of the Alps **Rev:** Grossglockner and white flower

Date	Mintage	F	VF	XF	Unc	BU
2009 Proof	2,500	Value: 65.00				

KM# 213 5 DOLLARS
25.0000 g., 0.9250 Silver 0.7435 oz. ASW, 38.61 mm. **Subject:** Flora and Mountains of the Alps **Rev:** Matterhorn and pink flower

Date	Mintage	F	VF	XF	Unc	BU
2009 Proof	2,500	Value: 65.00				

KM# 214 5 DOLLARS
25.0000 g., 0.9250 Silver 0.7435 oz. ASW, 38.61 mm. **Subject:** Flora and Mountains of the Alps **Rev:** Dachstein and purple flower

Date	Mintage	F	VF	XF	Unc	BU
2009 Proof	2,500	Value: 65.00				

KM# 215 5 DOLLARS
25.0000 g., 0.9250 Silver 0.7435 oz. ASW, 38.61 mm. **Subject:** Flora and Mountains of the Alps **Rev:** Mont Blanc and orange flower

Date	Mintage	F	VF	XF	Unc	BU
2009 Proof	2,500	Value: 65.00				

KM# 216 5 DOLLARS
25.0000 g., 0.9250 Silver 0.7435 oz. ASW, 38.61 mm. **Subject:** Flora and Mountains of the Alps **Rev:** Watzmann and purple flower

Date	Mintage	F	VF	XF	Unc	BU
2009 Proof	2,500	Value: 65.00				

KM# 217 5 DOLLARS
25.0000 g., 0.9250 Silver 0.7435 oz. ASW, 38.61 mm. **Subject:** Flora and Mountains of the Alps **Rev:** Oetscher and yellow flower

Date	Mintage	F	VF	XF	Unc	BU
2009 Proof	2,500	Value: 65.00				

KM# 218 5 DOLLARS
25.0000 g., 0.9250 Silver 0.7435 oz. ASW, 38.61 mm. **Subject:** Flora and Mountains of the Alps **Rev:** Piz Buin and pink flower

Date	Mintage	F	VF	XF	Unc	BU
2009 Proof	2,500	Value: 65.00				

KM# 242 5 DOLLARS
20.0000 g., 0.9250 Silver 0.5948 oz. ASW, 38.6 mm. **Subject:** Finnish icebreaker Tarmo **Rev:** Ship left in ice pack

Date	Mintage	F	VF	XF	Unc	BU
2009 Proof	2,500	Value: 65.00				

KM# 264 5 DOLLARS
25.0000 g., 0.9250 Silver 0.7435 oz. ASW, 38.61 mm. **Subject:** Treasures of the World - Emeralds **Rev:** Mule mine cart and emerald insert

Date	Mintage	F	VF	XF	Unc	BU
2009 Antique	2,000	Value: 85.00				

KM# 265 5 DOLLARS
25.0000 g., 0.9250 Silver 0.7435 oz. ASW, 38.6 mm. **Obv:** Arms **Rev:** Our Lady of the Gate of Dawn, partially gilt

Date	Mintage	F	VF	XF	Unc	BU
2009 Proof	1,000	Value: 75.00				

KM# 432 5 DOLLARS
25.0000 g., 0.9250 Silver 0.7435 oz. ASW, 45x45 mm. **Obv:** National arms **Rev:** Ladybug in color on flora **Rev. Legend:** Good Luck & Prosperity **Shape:** Heart

Date	Mintage	F	VF	XF	Unc	BU
2009 Proof	2,500	Value: 65.00				

KM# 248 5 DOLLARS
25.0000 g., 0.9250 Silver 0.7435 oz. ASW, 38.6 mm. **Subject:** Marine Life Protection **Rev:** Blue freshwater pearl set within multicolor shell

Date	Mintage	F	VF	XF	Unc	BU
2010 Proof	2,500	Value: 85.00				

KM# 249 5 DOLLARS
25.0000 g., 0.9250 Silver 0.7435 oz. ASW, 38.6 mm. **Subject:** Scent of Paradise - Sea breeze fragrance **Rev:** Female surfboarder in multicolor wave

Date	Mintage	F	VF	XF	Unc	BU
2010	2,500	—	—	—	—	65.00

KM# 289 5 DOLLARS
25.0000 g., 0.9250 Silver 0.7435 oz. ASW, 38.61 mm. **Obv:** National arms **Rev:** St. Basil's Cathedral in color

Date	Mintage	F	VF	XF	Unc	BU
2010 Proof	2,500	Value: 60.00				

KM# 290 5 DOLLARS
25.0000 g., 0.9250 Silver 0.7435 oz. ASW, 38.61 mm. **Obv:** National arms **Rev:** Statue of Liberty in color

Date	Mintage	F	VF	XF	Unc	BU
2010 Proof	2,500	Value: 60.00				

KM# 291 5 DOLLARS
25.0000 g., 0.9250 Silver 0.7435 oz. ASW, 38.61 mm. **Obv:** National arms **Rev:** Kiyomizu Temple in color

Date	Mintage	F	VF	XF	Unc	BU
2010 Proof	2,500	Value: 60.00				

KM# 292 5 DOLLARS
25.0000 g., 0.9250 Silver 0.7435 oz. ASW, 38.61 mm. **Obv:** National arms **Rev:** Neuschwanstein Castle in color

Date	Mintage	F	VF	XF	Unc	BU
2010 Proof	2,500	Value: 60.00				

KM# 293 5 DOLLARS
25.0000 g., 0.9250 Silver 0.7435 oz. ASW, 38.61 mm. **Obv:** National arms **Rev:** Mt. Everest and Meconopsis betonicifolia in color

Date	Mintage	F	VF	XF	Unc	BU
2010 Proof	250	Value: 60.00				

KM# 294 5 DOLLARS
25.0000 g., 0.9250 Silver 0.7435 oz. ASW, 38.61 mm. **Obv:** National arms **Rev:** Mt. Kilimanjaro and Protea kilimandscharica in color

Date	Mintage	F	VF	XF	Unc	BU
2010 Proof	2,500	Value: 60.00				

KM# 295 5 DOLLARS
25.0000 g., 0.9250 Silver 0.7435 oz. ASW, 38.61 mm. **Obv:** National arms **Rev:** Mt. Elbrus and Rhododendron in color

Date	Mintage	F	VF	XF	Unc	BU
2010 Proof	2,500	Value: 60.00				

KM# 296 5 DOLLARS
25.0000 g., 0.9250 Silver 0.7435 oz. ASW, 38.61 mm. **Obv:** National arms **Rev:** Carstensz Pyramid and Orchidacae in color

Date	Mintage	F	VF	XF	Unc	BU
2010 Proof	2,500	Value: 60.00				

KM# 297 5 DOLLARS
25.0000 g., 0.9250 Silver 0.7435 oz. ASW, 38.61 mm. **Obv:** National arms **Rev:** Mount McKinley and Anaphalis margaritacea in color

Date	Mintage	F	VF	XF	Unc	BU
2010 Proof	2,500	Value: 60.00				

KM# 298 5 DOLLARS
25.0000 g., 0.9250 Silver 0.7435 oz. ASW, 38.61 mm. **Obv:** National arms **Rev:** Mt. Aconcagua and Aechmea distichantha in color

Date	Mintage	F	VF	XF	Unc	BU
2010 Proof	2,500	Value: 60.00				

KM# 299 5 DOLLARS
25.0000 g., 0.9250 Silver 0.7435 oz. ASW, 38.61 mm. **Obv:** National arms **Rev:** Mt. Vinson and Colobanthus quitensis in color

Date	Mintage	F	VF	XF	Unc	BU
2010 Proof	2,500	Value: 60.00				

KM# 300 5 DOLLARS
25.0000 g., 0.9250 Silver 0.7435 oz. ASW, 38.61 mm. **Obv:** National arms **Rev:** Mt. Elger and Arnica montana in color

Date	Mintage	F	VF	XF	Unc	BU
2010 Proof	2,500	Value: 60.00				

KM# 301 5 DOLLARS
25.0000 g., 0.9250 Silver 0.7435 oz. ASW, 38.61 mm. **Obv:** National arms **Rev:** Ayers Rock and Calytrix longiflora in color

Date	Mintage	F	VF	XF	Unc	BU
2010 Proof	2,500	Value: 60.00				

KM# 302 5 DOLLARS

25.0000 g., 0.9250 Silver 0.7435 oz. ASW, 38.61 mm. **Obv:** National arms **Rev:** Mt. Alpspitze and Campanula alpina in color

Date	Mintage	F	VF	XF	Unc	BU
2010 Proof	2,500	Value: 60.00				

KM# 306 5 DOLLARS

25.0000 g., 0.9250 Silver 0.7435 oz. ASW, 38.61 mm. **Obv:** Naitonal arms **Rev:** Christmas star above winter home scene in color

Date	Mintage	F	VF	XF	Unc	BU
2010 Proof	2,500	Value: 60.00				

KM# 314 5 DOLLARS

25.0000 g., 0.9250 Silver 0.7435 oz. ASW, 38.61 mm. **Obv:** National arms **Rev:** Hammerhead shark in color image

Date	Mintage	F	VF	XF	Unc	BU
2010 Proof	1,500	Value: 70.00				

KM# 379 5 DOLLARS

25.0000 g., 0.9250 Silver 0.7435 oz. ASW, 38.61 mm. **Obv:** National arms **Rev:** Acropolis in color

Date	Mintage	F	VF	XF	Unc	BU
2010 Proof	2,500	Value: 50.00				

KM# 388 5 DOLLARS

25.0000 g., 0.9250 Silver 0.7435 oz. ASW **Obv:** National arms **Rev:** Angkor Wat in color **Shape:** 38.61

Date	Mintage	F	VF	XF	Unc	BU
2010 Proof	2,500	Value: 50.00				

KM# 389 5 DOLLARS

25.0000 g., 0.9250 Silver 0.7435 oz. ASW, 38.61 mm. **Obv:** National arms **Rev:** Statues of Easter Island in color

Date	Mintage	F	VF	XF	Unc	BU
2010 Proof	2,500	Value: 50.00				

KM# 390 5 DOLLARS

25.0000 g., 0.9250 Silver 0.7435 oz. ASW, 38.61 mm. **Obv:** National arms **Rev:** Eiffel Tower in color

Date	Mintage	F	VF	XF	Unc	BU
2010 Proof	2,500	Value: 50.00				

KM# 430 5 DOLLARS

25.0000 g., 0.9250 Silver 0.7435 oz. ASW, 38.61 mm. **Obv:** National arms **Rev:** Gem engraver cutting saphire on wheel

Date	Mintage	F	VF	XF	Unc	BU
2010 Antique patina	2,000	—	—	—	75.00	—

KM# 446 5 DOLLARS

25.0000 g., 0.9250 Silver 0.7435 oz. ASW, 38.61 mm. **Subject:** Mother Theresa of Calcutta, 100th Anniversary of Birth **Obv:** National arms **Rev:** Mother Theresa at left, blue color design of Sister's of Charity order habbit in field

Date	Mintage	F	VF	XF	Unc	BU
2010 Proof	—	Value: 80.00				

KM# 365 5 DOLLARS

25.0000 g., 0.9250 Silver 0.7435 oz. ASW, 38.61 mm. **Subject:** Cuddley Bear **Rev:** Teddy bear patch

Date	Mintage	F	VF	XF	Unc	BU
2011 Proof	—	Value: 75.00				

KM# 364 5 DOLLARS

25.0000 g., 0.9990 Silver 0.8029 oz. ASW **Subject:** Treasures of the World **Rev:** Mine scene, ruby insert

Date	Mintage	F	VF	XF	Unc	BU
2011 Antique patina	2,000	—	—	—	75.00	—

KM# 374 5 DOLLARS

25.0000 g., 0.9990 Silver 0.8029 oz. ASW, 30x38 mm. **Subject:** Oyster shell and pearl inset **Shape:** Irregular

Date	Mintage	F	VF	XF	Unc	BU
2011	2,000	—	—	—	—	450

KM# 376 5 DOLLARS

25.0000 g., 0.9250 Silver 0.7435 oz. ASW, 38.61 mm. **Obv:** National arms **Rev:** Potala Palace in color

Date	Mintage	F	VF	XF	Unc	BU
2011 Proof	2,500	Value: 50.00				

KM# 377 5 DOLLARS
25.0000 g., 0.9250 Silver 0.7435 oz. ASW, 38.61 mm. **Obv:** National arms **Rev:** Tower Bridge in color

Date	Mintage	F	VF	XF	Unc	BU
2011 Proof	2,500	Value: 50.00				

KM# 378 5 DOLLARS
25.0000 g., 0.9250 Silver 0.7435 oz. ASW, 38.61 mm. **Obv:** National arms **Rev:** Temple of Heaven in color

Date	Mintage	F	VF	XF	Unc	BU
2011 Proof	2,500	Value: 50.00				

KM# 380 5 DOLLARS
25.0000 g., 0.9250 Silver 0.7435 oz. ASW, 38.61 mm. **Obv:** National arms **Rev:** Stonehenge in color

Date	Mintage	F	VF	XF	Unc	BU
2011 Proof	2,500	Value: 50.00				

KM# 381 5 DOLLARS
25.0000 g., 0.9250 Silver 0.7435 oz. ASW, 38.61 mm. **Obv:** National arms **Rev:** Schonebrunn Palace in color

Date	Mintage	F	VF	XF	Unc	BU
2011 Proof	2,500	Value: 50.00				

KM# 382 5 DOLLARS
25.0000 g., 0.9250 Silver 0.7435 oz. ASW, 38.61 mm. **Obv:** National arms **Rev:** Chapel Bridge in color

Date	Mintage	F	VF	XF	Unc	BU
2011 Proof	2,500	Value: 50.00				

KM# 383 5 DOLLARS
25.0000 g., 0.9250 Silver 0.7435 oz. ASW, 38.61 mm. **Obv:** National arms **Rev:** Florence Cathedral

Date	Mintage	F	VF	XF	Unc	BU
2011 Proof	2,500	Value: 50.00				

KM# 384 5 DOLLARS
25.0000 g., 0.9250 Silver 0.7435 oz. ASW, 38.61 mm. **Obv:** National arms **Rev:** CN Tower in color

Date	Mintage	F	VF	XF	Unc	BU
2011 Proof	2,500	Value: 50.00				

KM# 385 5 DOLLARS
25.0000 g., 0.9250 Silver 0.7435 oz. ASW, 38.61 mm. **Obv:** National arms **Rev:** Timbuktu in color

Date	Mintage	F	VF	XF	Unc	BU
2011 Proof	2,500	Value: 50.00				

KM# 386 5 DOLLARS
25.0000 g., 0.9250 Silver 0.7435 oz. ASW, 38.61 mm. **Obv:** National arms **Rev:** Leaning Tower of Pisa in color

Date	Mintage	F	VF	XF	Unc	BU
2011 Proof	2,500	Value: 50.00				

KM# 387 5 DOLLARS
25.0000 g., 0.9250 Silver 0.7435 oz. ASW, 38.61 mm. **Obv:** National arms **Rev:** Sydney Opera House in color

Date	Mintage	F	VF	XF	Unc	BU
2011 Proof	2,500	Value: 50.00				

KM# 391 5 DOLLARS
25.0000 g., 0.9250 Silver 0.7435 oz. ASW, 38.61 mm. **Obv:** National arms **Rev:** Mount Rushmore in color

Date	Mintage	F	VF	XF	Unc	BU
2011 Proof	2,500	Value: 50.00				

KM# 392 5 DOLLARS
25.0000 g., 0.9250 Silver 0.7435 oz. ASW, 38.61 mm. **Obv:** National arms **Rev:** Persepolis - Shiraz in color

Date	Mintage	F	VF	XF	Unc	BU
2011 Proof	2,500	Value: 50.00				

KM# 393 5 DOLLARS
25.0000 g., 0.9250 Silver 0.7435 oz. ASW, 38.61 mm. **Obv:** National arms **Rev:** Alhambra in color

Date	Mintage	F	VF	XF	Unc	BU
2011 Proof	2,500	Value: 50.00				

KM# 397 5 DOLLARS
25.0000 g., 0.9250 Silver 0.7435 oz. ASW, 38.61 mm. **Obv:** National arms **Rev:** K-2 and flora in color

Date	Mintage	F	VF	XF	Unc	BU
2011 Proof	2,500	Value: 60.00				

KM# 398 5 DOLLARS
25.0000 g., 0.9250 Silver 0.7435 oz. ASW, 38.61 mm. **Obv:** National arms **Rev:** Mount Kenya and flora in color

Date	Mintage	F	VF	XF	Unc	BU
2011 Proof	2,500	Value: 60.00				

KM# 399 5 DOLLARS
25.0000 g., 0.9250 Silver 0.7435 oz. ASW, 38.61 mm. **Obv:** National arms **Rev:** Mount Logan and flora in color

Date	Mintage	F	VF	XF	Unc	BU
2011 Proof	2,500	Value: 60.00				

KM# 400 5 DOLLARS
25.0000 g., 0.9250 Silver 0.7435 oz. ASW, 38.61 mm. **Obv:** National arms **Rev:** Mount Tyree and flora in color

Date	Mintage	F	VF	XF	Unc	BU
2011 Proof	2,500	Value: 60.00				

KM# 401 5 DOLLARS
25.0000 g., 0.9250 Silver 0.7435 oz. ASW, 38.61 mm. **Obv:** National Arms **Rev:** Dyke-Tau and flora in color

Date	Mintage	F	VF	XF	Unc	BU
2011 Proof	2,500	Value: 60.00				

KM# 402 5 DOLLARS
25.0000 g., 0.9250 Silver 0.7435 oz. ASW, 38.61 mm. **Obv:** National arms **Rev:** Ojos del Salado and flora in color

Date	Mintage	F	VF	XF	Unc	BU
2011 Proof	2,500	Value: 60.00				

KM# 403 5 DOLLARS
25.0000 g., 0.9250 Silver 0.7435 oz. ASW, 38.61 mm. **Obv:** National arms **Rev:** Puncak Trikora and flora in color

Date	Mintage	F	VF	XF	Unc	BU
2011 Proof	2,500	Value: 60.00				

KM# 404 5 DOLLARS
25.0000 g., 0.9250 Silver 0.7435 oz. ASW, 38.61 mm. **Subject:** Scent of Paradise **Obv:** National arms **Rev:** Large insence burner in color

Date	Mintage	F	VF	XF	Unc	BU
2011 Proof	—	Value: 65.00				

KM# 431 5 DOLLARS
25.0000 g., 0.9250 Silver 0.7435 oz. ASW, 38.61 mm. **Obv:** National arms **Rev:** Miners and ruby

Date	Mintage	F	VF	XF	Unc	BU
2011 Matte finish	2,000	Value: 200				

KM# 434 5 DOLLARS
Silver Plated Copper, 35x35 mm. **Obv:** National arms **Rev:** Ferrari FI 2000 in color

Date	Mintage	F	VF	XF	Unc	BU
2011 Proof	—	Value: 40.00				

KM# 435 5 DOLLARS
Silver Plated Copper, 35x35 mm. **Obv:** National arms **Rev:** Ferrari 500 F-2

Date	Mintage	F	VF	XF	Unc	BU
2011 Proof	—	Value: 40.00				

KM# 436 5 DOLLARS
Silver Plated Copper, 45x45 mm. **Obv:** National arms **Rev:** Ferrari F-2007

Date	Mintage	F	VF	XF	Unc	BU
2011 Proof	—	Value: 40.00				

KM# 437 5 DOLLARS
Silver Plated Copper, 35x35 mm. **Obv:** National arms **Rev:** Ferrari 158 F-1

Date	Mintage	F	VF	XF	Unc	BU
2011 Proof	—	Value: 40.00				

KM# 438 5 DOLLARS
Silver Plated Copper, 35x35 mm. **Obv:** National arms **Rev:** Ferrari 246 F-1

Date	Mintage	F	VF	XF	Unc	BU
2011 Proof	—	Value: 40.00				

KM# 439 5 DOLLARS
Silver Plated Copper, 35x35 mm. **Obv:** National arms **Rev:** Ferrari D-50

Date	Mintage	F	VF	XF	Unc	BU
2011 Proof	—	Value: 40.00				

KM# 440 5 DOLLARS
Silver Plated Copper, 35x35 mm. **Obv:** National arms **Rev:** Ferrari 126 C-2

Date	Mintage	F	VF	XF	Unc	BU
2011 Proof	—	Value: 40.00				

KM# 441 5 DOLLARS
Silver Plated Copper, 35x35 mm. **Obv:** National arms **Rev:** Ferrari 312 T

Date	Mintage	F	VF	XF	Unc	BU
2011 Proof	—	Value: 40.00				

KM# 444 5 DOLLARS
25.0000 g., 0.9250 Silver 0.7435 oz. ASW, 38.61 mm. **Obv:** National arms **Rev:** Pear in white clam shell

Date	Mintage	F	VF	XF	Unc	BU
2011 Proof	—	Value: 125				

KM# 415 5 DOLLARS
25.0000 g., 0.9250 Silver 0.7435 oz. ASW, 38.61 mm. **Obv:** National arms **Rev:** Brandenburg Gate in color

Date	Mintage	F	VF	XF	Unc	BU
2012 Proof	2,500	Value: 80.00				

KM# 416 5 DOLLARS
25.0000 g., 0.9250 Silver 0.7435 oz. ASW, 38.61 mm. **Obv:** National arms **Rev:** Itsukushima Shrine in color

Date	Mintage	F	VF	XF	Unc	BU
2012 Proof	2,500	Value: 80.00				

KM# 417 5 DOLLARS
25.0000 g., 0.9250 Silver 0.7435 oz. ASW, 38.61 mm. **Obv:** National arms **Rev:** Palmyra ruins in color

Date	Mintage	F	VF	XF	Unc	BU
2012 Proof	2,500	Value: 80.00				

KM# 418 5 DOLLARS
25.0000 g., 0.9250 Silver 0.7435 oz. ASW, 38.61 mm. **Obv:** National arms **Rev:** St. Patrick's Cathedral, Dublin in color

Date	Mintage	F	VF	XF	Unc	BU
2012 Proof	2,500	Value: 80.00				

KM# 419 5 DOLLARS
25.0000 g., 0.9250 Silver 0.7435 oz. ASW, 38.61 mm. **Obv:** National arms **Rev:** Hagia Sophia in color

Date	Mintage	F	VF	XF	Unc	BU
2012 Proof	2,500	Value: 80.00				

KM# 420 5 DOLLARS
25.0000 g., 0.9250 Silver 0.7435 oz. ASW, 38.61 mm. **Obv:** National arms **Rev:** Vienna Ferris Wheel in color

Date	Mintage	F	VF	XF	Unc	BU
2012 Proof	2,500	Value: 80.00				

KM# 421 5 DOLLARS
25.0000 g., 0.9250 Silver 0.7435 oz. ASW, 38.61 mm. **Obv:** National arms **Rev:** Teotihuacan in color

Date	Mintage	F	VF	XF	Unc	BU
2012 Proof	2,500	Value: 80.00				

KM# 422 5 DOLLARS
25.0000 g., 0.9250 Silver 0.7435 oz. ASW, 38.61 mm. **Obv:** National arms **Rev:** Western Wall in color

Date	Mintage	F	VF	XF	Unc	BU
2012 Proof	2,500	Value: 80.00				

KM# 425 5 DOLLARS
25.0000 g., 0.9250 Silver 0.7435 oz. ASW, 38.61 mm. **Obv:** National arms **Rev:** Four leaf clover in green

Date	Mintage	F	VF	XF	Unc	BU
2012 Proof	—	Value: 100				

KM# 427 5 DOLLARS
Silver, 20x30 mm. **Obv:** Haliotis oyster shell, National arms **Rev:** Oyster shell with pearl and multicolors **Shape:** Irregular

Date	Mintage	F	VF	XF	Unc	BU
2012 Matte finish	—	Value: 150				

KM# 191 10 DOLLARS
62.2050 g., 0.9990 Silver 1.9979 oz. ASW, 50 mm. **Subject:** Tiffany Art **Rev:** Renaissance doorway

Date	Mintage	F	VF	XF	Unc	BU
2007 Matte Proof	999	Value: 1,200				

KM# 193 10 DOLLARS
62.2100 g., 0.9990 Silver 1.9980 oz. ASW, 50 mm. **Subject:** Tiffany Art **Rev:** Mannerism, staircase design

Date	Mintage	F	VF	XF	Unc	BU
2008 Matte Proof	999	Value: 900				

KM# 194 10 DOLLARS
62.2100 g., 0.9990 Silver 1.9980 oz. ASW, 42x42 mm. **Subject:** WWII Battleships **Rev:** Japan's Yamato

Date	Mintage	F	VF	XF	Unc	BU
2008 Proof	1,000	Value: 300				

KM# 195 10 DOLLARS
62.2100 g., 0.9990 Silver 1.9980 oz. ASW, 42x42 mm. **Subject:** WWII Battleships **Rev:** USS Missouri, gilt eagle above

Date	Mintage	F	VF	XF	Unc	BU
2008 Proof	1,000	Value: 175				

KM# 184 10 DOLLARS
62.2500 g., 0.9990 Silver 1.9993 oz. ASW, 42x42 mm. **Subject:** WWII Battleships **Obv:** Shield **Rev:** Bismarck, gilt Iron Cross above **Shape:** Square

Date	Mintage	F	VF	XF	Unc	BU
2009 Proof	—	Value: 165				

KM# 219 10 DOLLARS
62.2100 g., 0.9990 Silver 1.9980 oz. ASW, 50 mm. **Subject:** Tiffany Art **Rev:** Baroque facade

Date	Mintage	F	VF	XF	Unc	BU
2009 Matte Proof	—	Value: 600				

KM# 220 10 DOLLARS
62.2100 g., 0.9990 Silver 1.9980 oz. ASW, 50 mm. **Rev:** Amber insert

Date	Mintage	F	VF	XF	Unc	BU
2009 Matte Proof	2,500	Value: 400				

KM# 221 10 DOLLARS
62.2100 g., 0.9990 Silver 1.9980 oz. ASW, 42x42 mm. **Subject:** WWII Battleship **Rev:** Britains's HMS Prince of Wales, gilt Union Jack above

Date	Mintage	F	VF	XF	Unc	BU
2009 Proof	1,000	Value: 145				

KM# 250 10 DOLLARS
62.2000 g., 0.9990 Silver 1.9977 oz. ASW, 42x42 mm. **Subject:** Russian Battleship Marat **Rev:** Battleship sailing left

Date	Mintage	F	VF	XF	Unc	BU
2010 Proof	1,000	Value: 80.00				

KM# 252 10 DOLLARS
64.2100 g., 0.9990 Silver 2.0622 oz. ASW, 50 mm. **Subject:** Tiffany Art - Rococo **Obv:** Arms at lower right, glass insert **Rev:** Cherus at left, glass insert

Date	Mintage	F	VF	XF	Unc	BU
2010 Antique	999	—	—	—	—	650

KM# 304 10 DOLLARS
62.2100 g., 0.9250 Silver 1.8500 oz. ASW, 42x42 mm. **Obv:** National arms **Rev:** French Battleship Richelieu, gilt flag at top **Shape:** Square

Date	Mintage	F	VF	XF	Unc	BU
2010 Proof	1,000	Value: 100				

KM# 320 10 DOLLARS
62.2000 g., 0.9250 Silver 1.8497 oz. ASW, 55 mm. **Subject:** Sagrada Familia **Obv:** National arms **Rev:** Scenes from the Birth of Jesus, insert

Date	Mintage	F	VF	XF	Unc	BU
2010 Proof	2,500	Value: 115				

KM# 369 10 DOLLARS
62.2000 g., 0.9990 Silver partially gilt 1.9977 oz. ASW, 42x42 mm. **Rev:** Battleship H.M.A.S. Australia, gilt flag above **Shape:** Square

Date	Mintage	F	VF	XF	Unc	BU
2011 Proof	—	Value: 150				

KM# 318 10 DOLLARS
62.2100 g., 0.9990 Silver 1.9980 oz. ASW, 50 mm. **Subject:** Tiffany Glass **Obv:** National arms **Rev:** Theater box, red glass insert

Date	Mintage	F	VF	XF	Unc	BU
2011 Antique patina	999	—	—	—	—	175

KM# 367 10 DOLLARS
62.2000 g., 0.9990 Silver 1.9977 oz. ASW, 50 mm. **Subject:** Neuschwanstein Castle **Obv:** Exterior of Castle **Rev:** Interior of castle, insert

Date	Mintage	F	VF	XF	Unc	BU
2011 Antique finish	2,500	—	—	—	375	—

KM# 368 10 DOLLARS
62.2000 g., 0.9990 Silver 1.9977 oz. ASW, 50 mm. **Subject:** Tiffany Art - Manueline **Rev:** Glass insert

Date	Mintage	F	VF	XF	Unc	BU
2011 Antique finish	999	—	—	—	650	—

KM# 395 10 DOLLARS
62.2100 g., 0.9990 Silver 1.9980 oz. ASW, 42x42 mm. **Obv:** National arms **Rev:** RN Vittorio Veneto

Date	Mintage	F	VF	XF	Unc	BU
2011 Proof	1,000	Value: 110				

KM# 411 10 DOLLARS
62.2100 g., 0.9990 Silver 1.9980 oz. ASW, 42x42 mm. **Subject:** Saint Patrick's Cathedral, New York **Obv:** Interior nave view, window of St. Patrick **Rev:** Exterior cathedral spires, window of St. Patrick

Date	Mintage	F	VF	XF	Unc	BU
2011 Antique patina	1,000	—	—	—	—	250

KM# 412 10 DOLLARS
62.2100 g., 0.9990 Silver 1.9980 oz. ASW, 42x42 mm. **Obv:** Santiago de Compostela interior statues, window of St. John the Baptist **Rev:** Santiago de Compostela exterior view

Date	Mintage	F	VF	XF	Unc	BU
2011 Antique patina	1,000	—	—	—	—	275

KM# 413 10 DOLLARS
62.2100 g., 0.9990 Silver 1.9980 oz. ASW, 42x42 mm. **Obv:** St. Peter's Bascilica, window of the Holy Spirit **Rev:** St. Peter's Bascilica, window of the Holy Spirit

Date	Mintage	F	VF	XF	Unc	BU
2011 Antique patina	1,000	—	—	—	—	275

KM# 414 10 DOLLARS
62.2100 g., 0.9990 Silver 1.9980 oz. ASW, 42x42 mm. **Obv:** Brasilia Cathedral, esterior arches, blue window **Rev:** Brasilia Cathedral, figures, blue window

Date	Mintage	F	VF	XF	Unc	BU
2011 Antique patina	1,000	—	—	—	—	275

KM# 423 10 DOLLARS
62.2100 g., 0.9990 Silver 1.9980 oz. ASW, 50 mm. **Subject:** Tiffany Glass, Neoclassicism **Obv:** Archway, green glass insert **Rev:** Alcove, green glass insert

Date	Mintage	F	VF	XF	Unc	BU
2012 Antique patrina	999	—	—	—	—	625

KM# 424 10 DOLLARS
62.2100 g., 0.9990 Silver 1.9980 oz. ASW, 50 mm. **Obv:** Moscow Kremlin interior room, red glass insert **Rev:** Moscow Kremlin exterior, red glass insert

Date	Mintage	F	VF	XF	Unc	BU
2012 Antique patina	999	Value: 600				

KM# 176 20 DOLLARS
164.0000 g., 0.9990 Silver 5.2672 oz. ASW, 63 mm. **Obv:** Auto wheel cover **Rev:** Side sillouette of Corvette Z60

Date	Mintage	F	VF	XF	Unc	BU
2008 Proof	—	Value: 275				

KM# 183 500 DOLLARS
77.7000 g., 0.9990 Gold 2.4955 oz. AGW, 42x42 mm. **Obv:** Shield **Rev:** Battleship Bismark

Date	Mintage	F	VF	XF	Unc	BU
2009 Proof	77	Value: 4,500				

KM# 243 500 DOLLARS
77.7500 g., 0.9990 Gold 2.4971 oz. AGW, 42x42 mm. **Subject:** H.M.S. Prince of Wales **Rev:** Battleship right, Royal Navy flag above

Date	Mintage	F	VF	XF	Unc	BU
2009 Proof	77	Value: 4,500				

KM# 251 500 DOLLARS
77.7500 g., 0.9990 Gold 2.4971 oz. AGW, 42x42 mm. **Subject:** Battleship Marat **Rev:** Battleship sailing left

Date	Mintage	F	VF	XF	Unc	BU
2010 Proof	77	Value: 4,500				

KM# 305 500 DOLLARS
77.7500 g., 0.9999 Gold 2.4994 oz. AGW, 42x42 mm. **Obv:** National arms **Rev:** French battleship Richelieu **Shape:** Square

Date	Mintage	F	VF	XF	Unc	BU
2010 Proof	77	Value: 4,500				

KM# 394 500 DOLLARS
77.7500 g., 0.9990 Gold 2.4971 oz. AGW, 42x42 mm. **Obv:** National arms **Rev:** H.M.A.S. Australia

Date	Mintage	F	VF	XF	Unc	BU
2011 Proof	77	Value: 4,500				

KM# 396 500 DOLLARS
77.7000 g., 0.9990 Gold 2.4955 oz. AGW, 42x42 mm. **Obv:** National arms **Rev:** RN Vittorio Veneto

Date	Mintage	F	VF	XF	Unc	BU
2011 Proof	77	Value: 4,500				

PROOF SETS

KM#	Date	Mintage	Identification	Issue Price	Mkt Val
PS4	2007 (6)	2,500	KM#130-135	—	375

PANAMA

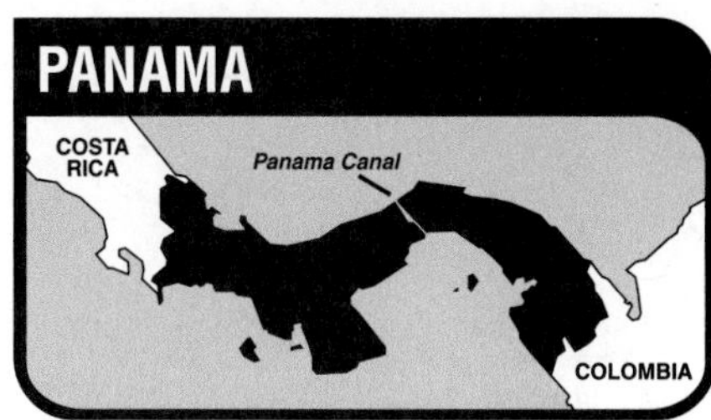

The Republic of Panama, a Central American country situated between Costa Rica and Colombia, has an area of 29,762 sq. mi. (78,200 sq. km.) and a population of *2.4 million. Capital: Panama City. The Panama Canal is the country's biggest asset; servicing world related transit trade and international commerce. Bananas, refined petroleum, sugar and shrimp are exported.

MONETARY SYSTEM

100 Centesimos = 1 Balboa

REPUBLIC

DECIMAL COINAGE

KM# 125 CENTESIMO

2.5000 g., Copper Plated Zinc, 19.05 mm. **Obv:** Written value **Obv. Legend:** REPUBLICA DE PANAMA **Rev:** Native Urraca bust left **Edge:** Plain

Date	Mintage	F	VF	XF	Unc	BU
2001(c)	160,000,000	—	—	—	0.25	0.50
2008(c)	—	—	—	—	0.25	0.50

KM# 133 5 CENTESIMOS

5.0000 g., Copper-Nickel, 21.15 mm. **Subject:** Sara Sotillo **Obv:** National coat of arms **Obv. Legend:** REPUBLICA DE PANAMA **Rev:** Head of Sotillo 3/4 right **Edge:** Plain

Date	Mintage	F	VF	XF	Unc	BU
2001(c)	8,000,000	—	—	—	0.25	0.75
2008(c)	—	—	—	—	0.25	0.75

KM# 127 1/10 BALBOA

2.2680 g., Copper-Nickel Clad Copper, 17.91 mm. **Obv:** National coat of arms **Obv. Legend:** REPUBLICA DE PANAMA **Rev:** Armored bust of Balboa left **Edge:** Reeded

Date	Mintage	F	VF	XF	Unc	BU
2001(c)	15,000,000	—	—	0.50	0.75	1.00
2008(c)	28,000,000	—	—	0.50	0.75	1.00

KM# 135 25 CENTESIMOS

5.6700 g., Copper-Nickel Clad Copper, 24.26 mm. **Obv:** National coat of arms **Obv. Legend:** REPUBLICA DE PANAMA **Rev:** Tower and Spanish ruins **Edge:** Reeded **Note:** Released in 2004

Date	Mintage	F	VF	XF	Unc	BU
2003(c)	6,000,000	—	—	0.50	2.00	3.00
2003(c) Proof	2,000	Value: 25.00				

KM# 136 25 CENTESIMOS

5.6700 g., Copper-Nickel Clad Copper, 24.26 mm. **Obv:** National coat of arms **Obv. Legend:** REPUBLICA DE PANAMA **Rev:** King's Bridge **Rev. Legend:** Puente Del Rey **Edge:** Reeded

Date	Mintage	F	VF	XF	Unc	BU
2005(c)	3,000,000	—	—	—	1.00	1.50
2005(c) Proof	2,000	Value: 14.00				

KM# 128 1/4 BALBOA

5.6700 g., Copper-Nickel Clad Copper, 24.26 mm. **Obv:** National coat of arms **Obv. Legend:** REPUBLICA DE PANAMA **Rev:** Armored bust of Balboa left **Edge:** Reeded

Date	Mintage	F	VF	XF	Unc	BU
2001(c)	12,000,000	—	—	0.35	0.75	1.50

KM# 137 1/4 BALBOA

5.6700 g., Copper-Nickel Clad Copper, 24.26 mm. **Subject:** Breast Cancer Awareness **Obv:** National coat of arms **Obv. Legend:** REPUBLICA DE PANAMA **Rev:** Ribbon **Rev. Legend:** Protegete Mujer **Edge:** Reeded

Date	Mintage	F	VF	XF	Unc	BU
2008(c)	14,000,000	—	—	—	0.75	1.00

Note: Also available in a laminated Breast Cancer Awareness pink bookmark

KM# 137a 1/4 BALBOA

5.6700 g., Copper-Nickel Clad Copper, 24.26 mm. **Subject:** Breast Cancer Awareness **Obv:** National coat of arms **Obv. Legend:** REPUBLICA DE PANAMA **Rev:** Pink Ribbon **Rev. Legend:** Protegete Mujer **Edge:** Reeded

Date	Mintage	F	VF	XF	Unc	BU
2008(c) Proof, pink colored ribbon	2,500	Value: 75.00				

Note: Pink ribbon proof issued in red plush case with black cardboard sleeve with printed pink ribbon

KM# 138 1/4 BALBOA

5.6700 g., Copper-Nickel Clad Copper, 24.26 mm. **Subject:** 50th Anniversary of the Children's Hospital **Obv:** National coat of arms **Obv. Legend:** REPUBLICA DE PANAMA **Rev:** Children's Hospital **Edge:** Reeded

Date	Mintage	F	VF	XF	Unc	BU
2008	6,000,000	—	—	—	1.00	2.00

KM# 138a 1/4 BALBOA

5.6700 g., Copper-Nickel Clad Copper, 24.26 mm. **Subject:** 50th Anniversary of the Children's Hospital **Obv:** National coat of arms **Obv. Legend:** REPUBLICA DE PANAMA **Rev:** Children's Hospital **Edge:** Reeded

Date	Mintage	F	VF	XF	Unc	BU
2008(c) Proof	1,000	Value: 35.00				

KM# 139 50 CENTESIMOS

11.3400 g., Copper-Nickel Clad Copper, 30.6 mm. **Subject:** Centenary of the National Bank of Panama **Obv:** National coat of arms **Obv. Legend:** REPUBLICA DE PANAMA **Rev:** BNP Building - Banco Nacional de Panama **Rev. Legend:** BANCO NACIONAL DE PANAMA CENTENARIO **Edge:** Reeded

Date	Mintage	F	VF	XF	Unc	BU
2009(c)	4,000,000	—	—	—	2.00	3.00

KM# 139a 50 CENTESIMOS

11.3400 g., Copper-Nickel Clad Copper, 30.6 mm. **Subject:** Centenary - National Bank of Panama **Obv:** National coat of arms **Obv. Legend:** REPUBLICA DE PANAMA **Rev:** BNP building - 1904-2004 **Rev. Legend:** BANCO NACIONAL DE PANAMA CENTENARIO **Edge:** Reeded

Date	Mintage	F	VF	XF	Unc	BU
2009(c) Proof	2,000	Value: 40.00				

KM# 129 1/2 BALBOA

11.3400 g., Copper-Nickel Clad Copper, 30.61 mm. **Obv:** National coat of arms **Obv. Legend:** REPUBLICA DE PANAMA **Rev:** Armored bust of Balboa left **Edge:** Reeded

Date	Mintage	F	VF	XF	Unc	BU
2001(c)	600,000	—	—	1.00	2.25	4.00
2008(c)	5,800,000	—	—	0.75	1.25	2.00

KM# 140 1/2 BALBOA

11.3400 g., Copper-Nickel Clad Copper, 30.61 mm. **Subject:** Convent of the Conception **Obv:** National arms **Rev:** Building ruins **Edge:** Reeded

Date	Mintage	F	VF	XF	Unc	BU
2010(c)	3,000,000	—	—	—	2.00	3.00

KM# 142 1/2 BALBOA

11.3400 g., Copper-Nickel Clad Copper, 30.61 mm. **Obv:** National arms **Obv. Legend:** REPUBLICA DE PANAMA / MEDIO BALBOA **Rev:** Crowned Hapsburg shield **Rev. Legend:** MONEDA DE 1580 / PANAMA VIEJO

Date	Mintage	F	VF	XF	Unc	BU
2011	3,000,000	—	—	—	2.00	3.00

KM# 143 1/2 BALBOA

11.3400 g., Copper-Nickel Clad Copper, 30.61 mm. **Subject:** Casa Reales

Date	Mintage	F	VF	XF	Unc	BU
2012	—	—	—	—	4.00	5.00

KM# 134 BALBOA

22.6800 g., Copper-Nickel Clad Copper, 38.1 mm. **Obv:** Bust of President Mireya Moscoso left, flanked by dates of her presidency **Rev:** Flag and canal scene **Edge:** Reeded

Date	Mintage	F	VF	XF	Unc	BU
2004(c)	348,000	—	—	1.50	4.50	12.00
2004(c) Proof	2,000	Value: 50.00				

KM# 141 BALBOA

7.2000 g., Bi-Metallic Brass center in Nickel ring, both plated on Stainless Steel core, 26.5 mm. **Obv:** National arms **Obv. Legend:** REPUBLICA DE PANAMA / date **Rev:** Balboa left **Rev. Legend:** VASCO NUNEZ DE BALBOA / UN BALBOA **Edge Lettering:** PANAMA (reeding) 1 BALBOA (reeding)

Date	Mintage	F	VF	XF	Unc	BU
2011	40,000,000	—	—	—	1.50	2.00

PAPUA NEW GUINEA

INDONESIA
Pacific Ocean
INDONESIA
Coral Sea
AUSTRALIA

The Independent State of Papua New Guinea occupies the eastern half of the island of New Guinea. It lies north of Australia near the equator and borders on West Irian. The country, which includes nearby Bismark archipelago, Buka and Bougainville, has an area of 178,260 sq. mi. (461,690 sq. km.) and a population of 3.7 million that is divided into more than 1,000 separate tribes, speaking more than 700 mutually unintelligible languages. Capital: Port Moresby. The economy is agricultural, and exports copra, rubber, cocoa, coffee, tea, gold and copper

Papua New Guinea is a member of the Commonwealth of Nations. Elizabeth II is Head of State, as Queen of Papua New Guinea.

CONSTITUTIONAL MONARCHY

Commonwealth of Nations

STANDARD COINAGE

KM# 1 TOEA

2.0000 g., Bronze, 17.65 mm. **Obv:** National emblem **Rev:** Butterfly and value **Edge:** Plain

Date	Mintage	F	VF	XF	Unc	BU
2001	—	—	—	0.25	1.00	10.00
2002	—	—	—	0.15	1.00	10.00
2004	—	—	—	0.10	1.00	10.00

KM# 2 2 TOEA

4.1000 g., Bronze, 21.6 mm. **Obv:** National emblem **Rev:** Lion fish **Edge:** Plain

Date	Mintage	F	VF	XF	Unc	BU
2001	—	—	—	0.30	0.75	2.50
2002	—	—	—	0.25	0.60	2.00
2004	—	—	—	0.15	0.45	1.25

KM# 3a 5 TOEA

2.5500 g., Nickel Plated Steel, 19.53 mm. **Obv:** National emblem **Rev:** Plateless turtle **Edge:** Reeded

Date	Mintage	F	VF	XF	Unc	BU
2002	—	—	—	0.50	1.25	2.50
2004	—	—	—	0.50	1.25	2.50
2005	—	—	—	0.40	1.00	2.00
2010	—	—	—	0.40	1.00	2.00

KM# 4 10 TOEA

5.6500 g., Copper-Nickel, 23.72 mm. **Obv:** National emblem **Rev:** Cuscus and value **Edge:** Reeded

Date	Mintage	F	VF	XF	Unc	BU
2001	—	—	—	—	1.50	2.00

KM# 4a 10 TOEA

5.1600 g., Nickel Plated Steel, 23.72 mm. **Obv:** National emblem **Rev:** Cuscus and value **Edge:** Reeded

Date	Mintage	F	VF	XF	Unc	BU
2002	—	—	—	0.80	2.00	3.00
2004	—	—	—	0.80	2.00	3.00
2005	—	—	—	6.00	1.50	3.00
2006	—	—	—	0.60	1.50	2.50
2009	—	—	—	0.60	1.50	2.50
2010	—	—	—	0.60	1.50	2.50

KM# 5a 20 TOEA

10.1300 g., Nickel Plated Steel, 28.65 mm. **Obv:** National emblem **Rev:** Bennett's Cassowary and value **Edge:** Reeded

Date	Mintage	F	VF	XF	Unc	BU
2004	—	—	—	0.80	2.00	3.00
2005	—	—	—	0.80	2.00	3.00
2006	—	—	—	0.60	1.50	2.50
2009	—	—	—	0.60	1.50	2.50
2010	—	—	—	0.60	1.50	2.50

KM# 53 50 TOEA

12.1000 g., Nickel Plated Steel, 30 mm. **Subject:** St. John's Ambulance, 50th Anniversary **Obv:** National emblem **Rev:** Ambulance corps logo **Shape:** 7-sided

Date	Mintage	F	VF	XF	Unc	BU
2007	—	—	—	—	4.00	5.00

KM# 54 50 TOEA

12.1000 g., Nickel Plated Steel, 30 mm. **Subject:** Bank of Papua New Guinea, 35th Anniversary **Obv:** National emblem **Rev:** Bank logo in colored central applique

Date	Mintage	F	VF	XF	Unc	BU
2008	—	—	—	—	4.00	5.00

KM# 6a KINA

14.6100 g., Nickel Plated Steel, 33.28 mm. **Obv:** Native design **Rev:** Two Salt Water Crocodiles **Edge:** Reeded

Date	Mintage	F	VF	XF	Unc	BU
2002	—	—	—	1.60	4.00	5.00
2004	—	—	—	1.40	3.50	4.50

KM# 6b KINA

11.1300 g., Nickel Plated Steel, 30 mm. **Obv:** Native design **Rev:** Two Salt Water Crocodiles **Edge:** Reeded

Date	Mintage	F	VF	XF	Unc	BU
2005	—	—	—	1.20	3.00	4.00
2010	—	—	—	1.20	3.00	4.00

KM# 51 2 KINA

12.2000 g., Bi-Metallic Aluminum-Bronze center in Copper-Nickel ring, 33.3 mm. **Subject:** Bank of Papua New Guinea, 35th Anniversary **Obv:** Bird of Paradise **Rev:** Bank logo **Edge:** Reeded

Date	Mintage	F	VF	XF	Unc	BU
2008	—	—	—	—	—	5.00

KM# 56 5 KINA
Silver, 38.61 mm. **Subject:** Railway re-opening, 50th Anniversary **Obv:** Bird of Paradise **Rev:** Steam train and mape of route

Date	Mintage	F	VF	XF	Unc	BU
2012 Proof	—	Value: 75.00				

The Republic of Paraguay, a landlocked country in the heart of South America surrounded by Argentina, Bolivia and Brazil, has an area of 157,048 sq. mi. (406,750 sq. km.) and a population of *4.5 million, 95 percent of whom are of mixed Spanish and Indian descent. Capital: Asuncion. The country is predominantly agrarian, with no important mineral deposits or oil reserves. Meat, timber, hides, oilseeds, tobacco and cotton account for 70 percent of Paraguay's export revenue.

During the Triple Alliance War (1864-1870) in which Paraguay faced Argentina, Brazil and Uruguay, Asuncion's ladies gathered in an Assembly on Feb. 24, 1867 and decided to give up their jewelry in order to help the national defense. The President of the Republic, Francisco Solano Lopez accepted the offering and ordered one twentieth of it be used to mint the first Paraguayan gold coins according to the Decree of the 11th of Sept.1867.

Two dies were made, one by Bouvet, and another by an American, Leonard Charles, while only the die made by Bouvet was eventually used.

MINT MARK
HF – LeLocle (Swiss)

REPUBLIC

REFORM COINAGE

100 Centimos = 1 Guarani

KM# 197 GUARANI
27.0000 g., 0.9250 Silver 0.8029 oz. ASW, 39.7 mm. **Subject:** 50th Anniversary of the Central Bank **Obv:** Naval gunship **Obv. Legend:** REPUBLICA DEL PARAGUAY **Obv. Inscription:** CAÑONERO PARAGUAY **Rev:** Bank building within circle **Rev. Legend:** BANCO CENTRAL DEL PARAGUAY **Edge:** Reeded

Date	Mintage	F	VF	XF	Unc	BU
2002 Proof	3,000	Value: 75.00				

KM# 199 GUARANI
26.8600 g., 0.9250 Silver 0.7988 oz. ASW, 40.03 mm. **Series:** 5th Ibero-America **Subject:** Encounter of the Two Worlds **Obv:** National arms in center with ten national arms in outer circle **Obv. Legend:** REPUBLICA DEL PARAGUAY **Rev:** Native in canoe with outline of South America in background at left, early sailing ship at lower right. **Rev. Legend:** ENCUENTRO DE DOS MUNDOS **Edge:** Reeded

Date	Mintage	F	VF	XF	Unc	BU
2002 Proof	—	Value: 60.00				

KM# 200 GUARANI
27.0000 g., 0.9250 Silver 0.8029 oz. ASW **Subject:** 60th Anniversary of Currency Reform **Obv:** National arms **Obv. Legend:** REPUBLICA DEL PARAGUAY **Rev:** Outline map of Paraguay **Edge:** Reeded

Date	Mintage	F	VF	XF	Unc	BU
2003 Proof	—	Value: 80.00				

KM# 201 GUARANI
26.9000 g., 0.9250 Silver 0.8000 oz. ASW, 40.04 mm. **Subject:** FIFA - XVIII World Football Championship - Germany 2006 **Obv:** National arms **Obv. Legend:** REPUBLICA DEL PARAGUAY **Rev:** Two opponents after ball **Rev. Legend:** COPA MUNDIAL DE LA FIFA - ALEMANIA **Edge:** Reeded

Date	Mintage	F	VF	XF	Unc	BU
2003 Proof	50,000	Value: 50.00				

KM# 202 GUARANI
27.0000 g., 0.9250 Silver 0.8029 oz. ASW **Subject:** FIFA - XVIII World Football Championship - Germany 2006 **Obv:** National arms **Obv. Legend:** REPUBLICA DEL PARAGUAY **Rev:** Ball in goal **Edge:** Reeded

Date	Mintage	F	VF	XF	Unc	BU
2004 Proof	50,000	Value: 50.00				

KM# 204 GUARANI
27.0000 g., 0.9250 Silver 0.8029 oz. ASW **Series:** 6th Ibero-America **Subject:** Encounter of the Two Worlds **Obv:** National arms in center with ten national arms in outer circle **Obv. Legend:** REPUBLICA DEL PARAGUAY **Rev:** Church of the Most Holy, Trinidad in Yaguarón **Rev. Legend:** ENCUENTRO DE DOS MUNDOS - IGLESIA DE LA SANTISIMA TRINIDAD **Edge:** Reeded

Date	Mintage	F	VF	XF	Unc	BU
2005 Proof	—	Value: 65.00				

KM# 191a 50 GUARANIES
Brass Plated Steel **Obv:** Uniformed bust facing **Rev:** Value above river dam **Note:** Magnetic

Date	Mintage	F	VF	XF	Unc	BU
2005	10,000,000	—	—	—	0.75	1.00

KM# 191b 50 GUARANIES
1.0100 g., Aluminum, 18.98 mm. **Obv:** Bust of Major General J.F. Estigarribia facing **Obv. Legend:** REPUBLICA DEL PARAGUAY **Rev:** Acaray River Dam **Rev. Inscription:** REPRESA ACARAY **Edge:** Plain **Note:** Reduced size

Date	Mintage	F	VF	XF	Unc	BU
2006	25,000,000	—	—	—	1.00	2.00
2008	—	—	—	—	1.00	2.00
2011	—	—	—	—	1.00	2.00

KM# 177a 100 GUARANIES
5.4500 g., Brass Plated Steel **Obv:** Bust of General Jose E. Dias facing **Obv. Legend:** REPUBLICA DEL PARAGUAY **Rev:** Ruins of Humaita **Rev. Inscription:** RUINAS DE HUMAITA 1865/70 **Note:** Reduced weight and thickness.

Date	Mintage	F	VF	XF	Unc	BU
2004	15,000,000	—	—	—	1.50	2.00
2005	10,000,000	—	—	—	1.50	2.00

KM# 177b 100 GUARANIES
3.6600 g., Nickel-Steel, 20.94 mm. **Obv:** Bust of General Jose E. Dias facing **Obv. Legend:** REPUBLICA DEL PARAGUAY **Rev:** Ruins of Humaita **Rev. Inscription:** RUINAS DE HUMAITA 1865/70 **Edge:** Plain

Date	Mintage	F	VF	XF	Unc	BU
2006	30,000,000	—	—	—	1.50	2.00
2007	25,000,000	—	—	—	1.50	2.00
2008	—	—	—	—	1.50	2.00
2011	—	—	—	—	1.50	2.00

KM# 195 500 GUARANIES
7.8200 g., Brass Plated Steel **Obv:** Head of General Bernardino Caballero facing **Obv. Legend:** REPUBLICA DEL PARAGUAY **Rev:** Bank above value within circle **Rev. Legend:** BANCO CENTRAL DEL PARAGUAY

Date	Mintage	F	VF	XF	Unc	BU
2002	15,000,000	—	—	—	2.50	3.00
2005	5,000,000	—	—	—	2.50	3.00

KM# 195a 500 GUARANIES
4.8000 g., Nickel-Steel, 23 mm. **Obv:** Head of General Bernardino Caballero facing **Obv. Legend:** REPUBLICA DEL PARAGUAY **Rev:** Bank above value in circle **Rev. Legend:** BANCO CENTRAL DEL PARAGUAY **Edge:** Plain

Date	Mintage	F	VF	XF	Unc	BU
2006	12,000,000	—	—	—	2.00	2.50
2007	25,000,000	—	—	—	2.00	2.50
2008	—	—	—	—	2.00	2.50
2011	—	—	—	—	2.00	2.50

KM# 198 MIL (1000) GUARANIES
6.0700 g., Nickel-Steel, 25 mm. **Obv:** Bust of Major General Francisco Solano Lopez facing **Obv. Legend:** REPUBLICA DEL PARAGUAY **Rev:** National Heroes Pantheon **Rev. Legend:** BANCO CENTRAL DEL PARAGUAY **Rev. Inscription:** PANTEON NACIONAL / DE LOS HEROES **Edge:** Plain

Date	Mintage	F	VF	XF	Unc	BU
2006	25,000,000	—	—	—	3.00	4.00
2007	35,000,000	—	—	—	3.00	4.00
2008	—	—	—	—	3.00	4.00

KM# 203 1500 GUARANIES
6.7000 g., 0.9990 Gold 0.2152 oz. AGW **Subject:** XVIII World Football Championship - Germany 2006 **Obv:** National arms **Obv. Legend:** REPUBLICA DEL PARAGUAY **Rev:** Ball in goal

Date	Mintage	F	VF	XF	Unc	BU
2004 Proof	25,000	Value: 450				

The Republic of Peru, located on the Pacific coast of South America, has an area of 496,225 sq. mi. (1,285,220sq. km.) and a population of *21.4 million. Capital: Lima. The diversified economy includes mining, fishing and agriculture. Fishmeal, copper, sugar, zinc and iron ore are exported.

MINT MARKS
L, LIMAE (monogram), Lima (monogram), LIMA = Lima

REPUBLIC

REFORM COINAGE

1991; 1/M Intis = 1 Nuevo Sol;
100 (New) Centimos = 1 Nuevo Sol

KM# 303.4 CENTIMO
1.8800 g., Brass, 15.9 mm. **Obv:** National arms, accent mark above "u" **Rev:** Without Braille dots, no Chavez **Edge:** Plain **Note:** LIMA monogram is mint mark.

Date	Mintage	F	VF	XF	Unc	BU
2001LIMA	—	—	—	—	0.25	0.40
2002LIMA	2,100,000	—	—	—	0.50	0.75
2004LIMA	2,000,000	—	—	—	0.50	0.75
2005LIMA	22,700,000	—	—	—	0.25	0.40
2006LIMA	19,700,000	—	—	—	0.25	0.40

KM# 303.4a CENTIMO
0.8200 g., Aluminum, 16 mm. **Obv:** National arms **Rev:** Value flanked by designs **Edge:** Plain **Note:** LIMA monogram is mint mark.

Date	Mintage	F	VF	XF	Unc	BU
2005LIMA	Inc. above	—	—	—	0.25	0.40
2006LIMA	19,200,000	—	—	—	0.50	0.75
2007LIMA	48,800,000	—	—	—	0.25	0.30
2008LIMA	63,800,000	—	—	—	0.25	0.30
2009LIMA	62,000,000	—	—	—	0.25	0.30
2010LIMA	73,000,000	—	—	—	0.25	0.30
2011LIMA	14,700,000	—	—	—	0.25	0.30

KM# 304.4 5 CENTIMOS
2.6900 g., Brass, 18 mm. **Obv:** National arms, accent above "u" **Rev:** Value flanked by designs. Without Braille dots, with accent above "e" **Edge:** Plain **Note:** LIMA monogram is mint mark.

Date	Mintage	F	VF	XF	Unc	BU
2001LIMA	—	—	—	—	0.35	0.50
2002LIMA	3,940,000	—	—	—	0.35	0.50
2005LIMA	8,900,000	—	—	—	0.35	0.50
2006LIMA	11,400,000	—	—	—	0.35	0.50
2007LIMA	12,800,000	—	—	—	0.35	0.50

KM# 304.4a 5 CENTIMOS
1.0200 g., Aluminum, 18 mm. **Obv:** National arms **Rev:** Value flanked by native designs **Edge:** Plain **Note:** LIMA monogram is mint mark.

Date	Mintage	F	VF	XF	Unc	BU
2007LIMA	12,400,000	—	—	—	0.35	0.50
2008LIMA	11,600,000	—	—	—	0.30	0.40
2009LIMA	20,000,000	—	—	—	0.30	0.40
2010LIMA	24,000,000	—	—	—	0.30	0.40
2011LIMA	36,000,000	—	—	—	0.30	0.40
2012LIMA	—	—	—	—	0.30	0.40

KM# 305.4 10 CENTIMOS
3.5000 g., Brass, 20.5 mm. **Obv:** National arms, accent above "u" **Rev:** Without braille dots, accent above "e" **Edge:** Plain **Note:** LIMA monogram is mint mark.

Date	Mintage	F	VF	XF	Unc	BU
2001LIMA	50,000,000	—	—	—	0.65	0.85
2002LIMA	37,420,000	—	—	—	0.65	0.85
2003LIMA	56,000,000	—	—	—	0.65	0.85
2004LIMA	27,500,000	—	—	—	0.65	0.85
2005LIMA	39,500,000	—	—	—	0.40	0.50
2006LIMA	54,200,000	—	—	—	0.40	0.50
2007LIMA	64,800,000	—	—	—	0.40	0.50
2008LIMA	79,400,000	—	—	—	0.40	0.50
2009LIMA	63,000,000	—	—	—	0.40	0.50
2010LIMA	82,000,000	—	—	—	0.40	0.50
2011LIMA	94,000,000	—	—	—	0.40	0.50
2012LIMA	—	—	—	—	0.40	0.50

KM# 306.4 20 CENTIMOS
4.4000 g., Brass, 23 mm. **Obv:** National arms, accent above "u" **Rev:** Without braille dots, accent above "e" **Edge:** Plain **Note:** LIMA monogram is mint mark.

Date	Mintage	F	VF	XF	Unc	BU
2001LIMA	13,000,000	—	—	—	0.85	1.20
2002LIMA	9,000,000	—	—	—	0.85	1.20
2003LIMA	2,000,000	—	—	—	1.00	1.25
2004LIMA	15,200,000	—	—	—	0.85	1.20
2006LIMA	3,700,000	—	—	—	0.75	1.00
2007LIMA	18,000,000	—	—	—	0.50	0.75
2008LIMA	24,300,000	—	—	—	0.50	0.75
2009LIMA	15,500,000	—	—	—	0.50	0.75
2010LIMA	25,000,000	—	—	—	0.50	0.75
2011LIMA	23,000,000	—	—	—	0.50	0.75
2012LIMA	—	—	—	—	0.50	0.75

KM# 307.4 50 CENTIMOS
5.4500 g., Copper-Nickel-Zinc, 22 mm. **Obv:** National arms, accent above "u" **Rev:** Without braille, accent above "e" **Edge:** Reeded **Note:** LIMA monogram is mint mark.

Date	Mintage	F	VF	XF	Unc	BU
2001LIMA	11,000,000	—	—	—	1.00	1.75
2002LIMA	12,000,000	—	—	—	1.50	1.75
2003LIMA	30,000,000	—	—	—	1.50	1.75
2004LIMA	6,000,000	—	—	—	1.50	1.75
2005LIMA	14,600,000	—	—	—	0.75	1.00
2006LIMA	24,200,000	—	—	—	0.75	1.00
2007LIMA	31,200,000	—	—	—	0.75	1.00
2008LIMA	36,200,000	—	—	—	0.75	1.00
2009LIMA	26,700,000	—	—	—	0.75	1.00
2010LIMA	5,180,000	—	—	—	0.75	1.00
2011LIMA	38,000,000	—	—	—	0.75	1.00
2012LIMA	—	—	—	—	0.75	1.00

KM# 307.3 50 CENTIMOS
5.4500 g., Copper-Nickel-Zinc, 22 mm. **Obv:** National arms within octagon **Rev:** Value flanked by sprig and monogram within octagon **Edge:** Reeded **Note:** LIMA monogram is mint mark.

Date	Mintage	F	VF	XF	Unc	BU
2001	—	—	—	—	1.50	1.75

KM# 308.4 NUEVO SOL
7.3200 g., Copper-Nickel-Zinc, 25.5 mm. **Obv:** National arms, accent above "u" **Rev:** Without braille, accent above "e" **Edge:** Reeded **Note:** LIMA monogram is mint mark.

Date	Mintage	F	VF	XF	Unc	BU
2001LIMA	10,000,000	—	—	—	2.50	3.00
2002LIMA	8,000,000	—	—	—	2.50	3.00
2003LIMA	5,000,000	—	—	—	2.50	3.00
2004LIMA	13,900,000	—	—	—	2.50	3.00
2005LIMA	14,600,000	—	—	—	1.25	1.50
2006LIMA	19,700,000	—	—	—	1.25	1.50
2007LIMA	36,700,000	—	—	—	1.25	1.50
2008LIMA	42,800,000	—	—	—	1.25	1.50
2009LIMA	34,330,000	—	—	—	1.25	1.50
2010LIMA	2,000,000	—	—	—	1.25	1.50
2011LIMA	23,000,000	—	—	—	1.25	1.50

KM# 329 NUEVO SOL
33.6250 g., 0.9250 Silver 0.9999 oz. ASW, 37 mm. **Subject:** 450th Anniversary - San Marcos University **Obv:** National arms **Rev:** University seal and building **Edge:** Reeded **Note:** LIMA monogram is mint mark.

Date	Mintage	F	VF	XF	Unc	BU
2001LIMA	Est. 5,000	—	—	—	—	65.00

KM# 330 NUEVO SOL
33.6250 g., 0.9250 Silver 0.9999 oz. ASW, 37 mm. **Subject:** 50th Anniversary - Numismatic Society of Peru **Obv:** National arms **Rev:** Stylized design within circle **Edge:** Reeded **Note:** LIMA monogram is mint mark.

Date	Mintage	F	VF	XF	Unc	BU
2001	Est. 1,000	—	—	—	—	65.00

KM# 331 NUEVO SOL

33.6250 g., 0.9250 Silver 0.9999 oz. ASW, 37 mm. **Subject:** 200th Anniversary - von Humboldt's visit to Peru **Obv:** National arms **Rev:** Seated figure 1/4 left **Edge:** Reeded **Note:** LIMA monogram is mint mark.

Date	Mintage	F	VF	XF	Unc	BU
2002LIMA	Est. 1,000	—	—	—	—	70.00

KM# 334 NUEVO SOL

27.0000 g., 0.9250 Silver 0.8029 oz. ASW, 40 mm. **Series:** Ibero-America **Obv:** National arms in center with ten national arms in outer circle **Obv. Legend:** BANCO CENTRAL DE RESERVA DEL PERÚ **Rev:** Ceramic - Indians in reed boats **Rev. Legend:** PERÚ **Edge:** Reeded

Date	Mintage	F	VF	XF	Unc	BU
2002(M) Proof	Est. 17,000	Value: 85.00				

KM# 332 NUEVO SOL

33.6250 g., 0.9250 Silver 0.9999 oz. ASW, 37 mm. **Subject:** 125th Anniversary of the Inmaculate Jesuitas - Lima College **Obv:** National arms **Rev:** Statue and 3/4 crowned shield **Edge:** Reeded **Note:** LIMA monogram is mint mark.

Date	Mintage	F	VF	XF	Unc	BU
2003LIMA	Est. 1,000	—	—	—	—	75.00

KM# 333 NUEVO SOL

33.6250 g., 0.9250 Silver 0.9999 oz. ASW, 37 mm. **Subject:** 180th Anniversary of Peru's Congress **Obv:** National arms **Rev:** Statue in front of building **Edge:** Reeded **Note:** LIMA monogram is mint mark.

Date	Mintage	F	VF	XF	Unc	BU
2003	Est. 1,000	—	—	—	—	75.00

KM# 335 NUEVO SOL

27.0000 g., 0.9250 Silver 0.8029 oz. ASW, 40 mm. **Subject:** FIFA World Cup Soccer **Obv:** Arms within wreath **Rev:** Action scene beneath globe **Edge:** Reeded

Date	Mintage	F	VF	XF	Unc	BU
2004(M) Proof	Est. 50,000	Value: 60.00				

KM# 339 NUEVO SOL

27.0000 g., 0.9250 Silver 0.8029 oz. ASW, 40 mm. **Series:** Ibero-America **Subject:** Lost city of the Incas **Obv:** National arms in center with ten national arms in outer ring **Obv. Legend:** BANCO CENTRAL DE RESERVA DEL PERÚ **Rev:** Village ruins **Rev. Legend:** MACHU PICCHU . PERÚ **Edge:** Reeded

Date	Mintage	F	VF	XF	Unc	BU
2005(Mo) Proof	Est. 17,000	Value: 85.00				

KM# 356 NUEVO SOL

33.6250 g., 0.9250 Silver 0.9999 oz. ASW, 37 mm. **Subject:** Lima Regatta Club, 130th Anniversary **Edge:** Reeded

Date	Mintage	F	VF	XF	Unc	BU
2005LIMA	Est. 1,000	—	—	—	—	65.00

KM# 357 NUEVO SOL

27.0000 g., 0.9250 Silver 0.8029 oz. ASW, 40 mm. **Series:** Ibero-American **Subject:** Volleyball **Rev:** Two volleyball players and net **Edge:** Reeded

Date	Mintage	F	VF	XF	Unc	BU
2007(Mo) Proof	Est. 14,000	Value: 85.00				

KM# 358 NUEVO SOL

33.6250 g., 0.9250 Silver 0.9999 oz. ASW, 37 mm. **Subject:** Lima-Huancayo Railway, 100th Anniversary **Rev:** Deisel and Steam trains in valley **Edge:** Reeded

Date	Mintage	F	VF	XF	Unc	BU
2008LIMA	Est. 1,000	—	—	—	—	65.00

KM# 359 NUEVO SOL

27.0000 g., 0.9250 Silver 0.8029 oz. ASW, 40 mm. **Series:** Ibero-American **Subject:** Historical coins of Peru

Date	Mintage	F	VF	XF	Unc	BU
2010(Mo) Proof	Est. 2,010	Value: 85.00				

KM# 340 NUEVO SOL

7.3200 g., Copper-Nickel-Zinc, 25.5 mm. **Series:** Wealth and Pride of Peru **Subject:** Tumi de Oro **Obv:** National arms **Rev:** Tumi de Oro **Edge:** Reeded

Date	Mintage	F	VF	XF	Unc	BU
2010Lima	10,000,000	—	—	—	2.50	3.00

KM# 341 NUEVO SOL

7.3200 g., Copper-Nickel-Zinc, 25.5 mm. **Series:** Wealth and Pride of Peru **Subject:** Sarcophagus of Karajia **Obv:** National arms **Rev:** Sarcophagus of Karajia **Edge:** Reeded

Date	Mintage	F	VF	XF	Unc	BU
2010LIMA	10,000,000	—	—	—	2.50	3.00

KM# 342 NUEVO SOL

7.3200 g., Copper-Nickel-Zinc, 25.5 mm. **Series:** Wealth and Pride of Peru **Obv:** National Arms **Rev:** Estela de Ramondi **Edge:** Reeded

Date	Mintage	F	VF	XF	Unc	BU
2010LIMA	10,000,000	—	—	—	2.50	3.00

KM# 345 NUEVO SOL

7.3000 g., Copper-Nickel-Zinc, 25.5 mm. **Obv:** National arms **Rev:** Chullpas de Sillustani ruins **Edge:** Reeded

Date	Mintage	F	VF	XF	Unc	BU
2011	10,000,000	—	—	—	2.50	3.00

KM# 346 NUEVO SOL

7.3200 g., Copper-Nickel-Zinc, 25.5 mm. **Series:** Wealth and Pride of Peru **Rev:** Monastery of Santa Catalina and plaza **Edge:** Reeded

Date	Mintage	F	VF	XF	Unc	BU
2011LIMA	10,000,000	—	—	—	2.50	3.00

KM# 360 NUEVO SOL

7.3200 g., Copper-Nickel-Zinc, 25.5 mm. **Obv:** National arms **Rev:** Machu Picchu ruins **Edge:** Reeded

Date	Mintage	F	VF	XF	Unc	BU
2011	10,000,000	—	—	—	2.00	3.00

KM# 361 NUEVO SOL

7.3200 g., Copper-Nickel-Zinc, 25.5 mm. **Obv:** National arms **Rev:** Gran Pajaten site

Date	Mintage	F	VF	XF	Unc	BU
2011	10,000,000	—	—	—	2.00	3.00

KM# 362 NUEVO SOL

7.3200 g., Copper-Nickel-Zinc, 25.5 mm. **Subject:** Piedra de Saywite **Obv:** National arms **Rev:** Monolith and animals and geometric designs **Edge:** Reeded

Date	Mintage	F	VF	XF	Unc	BU
2012	10,000,000	—	—	—	2.00	3.00

KM# 363 NUEVO SOL

7.3200 g., Copper-Nickel-Zinc, 25.5 mm. **Subject:** Fortaleza del Real Felipe **Obv:** National arms **Rev:** Fortress ruins **Edge:** Reeded

Date	Mintage	F	VF	XF	Unc	BU
2012	10,000,000	—	—	—	2.00	3.00

KM# 364 NUEVO SOL

7.3200 g., Copper-Nickel-Zinc, 25.5 mm. **Subject:** Templo del Sol Vilcashuaman **Obv:** National arms **Rev:** Temple ruins

Date	Mintage	F	VF	XF	Unc	BU
2012	10,000,000	—	—	—	2.00	3.00

KM# 365 NUEVO SOL

7.3200 g., Copper-Nickel-Zinc, 25.5 mm. **Obv:** National Arms **Rev:** Monolith of Kuntur Wasi **Edge:** Reeded

Date	Mintage	F	VF	XF	Unc	BU
2012	10,000,000	—	—	—	2.00	3.00

KM# 366 NUEVO SOL

7.3200 g., Copper-Nickel-Zinc, 25.5 mm. **Obv:** National arms **Rev:** Value within wreath

Date	Mintage	F	VF	XF	Unc	BU
2012	—	—	—	—	1.25	1.75

KM# 313 2 NUEVOS SOLES

5.6200 g., Bi-Metallic Nickel-Brass center in Stainless Steel ring, 22.2 mm. **Obv:** National arms within circle **Rev:** Stylized bird in flight to left of value within circle **Edge:** Plain **Note:** LIMA monogram is mint mark.

Date	Mintage	F	VF	XF	Unc	BU
2002LIMA	6,000,000	—	—	—	4.50	5.00
2003LIMA	5,000,000	—	—	—	4.50	5.00
2004LIMA	3,000,000	—	—	—	4.50	5.00
2005LIMA	6,000,000	—	—	—	2.00	2.50
2006LIMA	5,100,000	—	—	—	2.00	2.50
2007LIMA	7,000,000	—	—	—	2.00	2.50
2008LIMA	5,800,000	—	—	—	2.00	2.50
2009LIMA	7,000,000	—	—	—	2.00	2.50

KM# 343 2 NUEVOS SOLES

5.6200 g., Bi-Metallic Brass center in Stainless Steel ring, 22.38 mm. **Obv:** National Arms **Rev:** Hummingbird from the Inca Lines, large value at right

Date	Mintage	F	VF	XF	Unc	BU
2010LIMA	6,235,000	—	—	—	2.50	3.00
2011LIMA	17,000,000	—	—	—	2.50	3.00
2012LIMA	—	—	—	—	2.50	3.00

KM# 316 5 NUEVOS SOLES

6.6700 g., Bi-Metallic Nickel-Brass center in Stainless Steel ring, 24.32 mm. **Obv:** National arms within circle **Rev:** Stylized bird in flight to left of value within circle **Edge:** Reeded **Note:** LIMA monogram is mint mark.

Date	Mintage	F	VF	XF	Unc	BU
2001LIMA	5,000,000	—	—	—	6.50	7.00
2002LIMA	2,000,000	—	—	—	6.50	7.00
2004LIMA	—	—	—	—	6.50	7.00
2005LIMA	6,000,000	—	—	—	4.00	5.00
2006LIMA	5,500,000	—	—	—	4.00	5.00
2007LIMA	6,400,000	—	—	—	4.00	5.00
2008LIMA	9,900,000	—	—	—	4.00	5.00
2009LIMA	10,000,000	—	—	—	—	—

KM# 344 5 NUEVOS SOLES

6.6700 g., Bi-Metallic Brass center in Stainless Steel ring, 24.38 mm. **Obv:** National Arms **Rev:** Frigate bird from the Nasca lines, large value at right

Date	Mintage	F	VF	XF	Unc	BU
2010LIMA	6,000,000	—	—	—	5.00	6.00
2011LIMA	15,000,000	—	—	—	5.00	6.00
2012LIMA	—	—	—	—	5.00	6.00

PHILIPPINES

The Republic of the Philippines, an archipelago in the western Pacific 500 miles (805 km.) from the southeast coast of Asia, has an area of 115,830 sq. mi. (300,000 sq. km.) and a population of *64.9 million. Capital: Manila. The economy of the 7,000-island group is based on agriculture, forestry and fishing. Timber, coconut products, sugar and hemp are exported.

MINT MARKS

BSP - Bangko Sentral Pilipinas

M, MA - Manila

REPUBLIC

REFORM COINAGE

100 Sentimos = 1 Piso

KM# 273 SENTIMO

2.0000 g., Copper Plated Steel, 15.5 mm. **Obv:** Value and date **Rev:** Central bank seal within circle and gear design, 1993 (date Central Bank was established) below **Rev. Legend:** BANGKO SENTRAL NG PILIPINAS - 1993

Date	Mintage	F	VF	XF	Unc	BU
2001	—	—	—	—	0.10	0.15
2002	—	—	—	—	0.10	0.15
2004	—	—	—	—	0.10	0.15
2005	—	—	—	—	0.10	0.15
2006	—	—	—	—	0.10	0.15
2007	—	—	—	—	0.10	0.15
2008	—	—	—	—	0.10	0.15
2009	—	—	—	—	0.10	0.15
2011	—	—	—	—	—	0.50

KM# 268 5 SENTIMOS

1.9000 g., Copper Plated Steel, 15.5 mm. **Obv:** Numeral value around center hole **Rev:** Hole in center with date, bank and name around border, 1993 (date Central Bank was established) below **Rev. Legend:** BANGKO CENTRAL NG PILIPINAS - 1993 **Edge:** Plain

Date	Mintage	F	VF	XF	Unc	BU
2001	—	—	—	—	0.20	0.25
2002	—	—	—	—	0.20	0.25
2003	—	—	—	—	0.20	0.25
2004	—	—	—	—	0.50	1.00
2005	—	—	—	—	0.20	0.25
2006	—	—	—	—	0.20	0.25
2007	—	—	—	—	0.20	0.25
2008	—	—	—	—	0.20	0.25
2009	—	—	—	—	0.20	0.25
2010	—	—	—	—	0.20	0.25
2011	—	—	—	—	0.20	0.25
2012	—	—	—	—	0.20	0.25

KM# 270.1 10 SENTIMOS

2.5000 g., Copper Plated Steel, 17 mm. **Obv:** Value and date **Rev:** Central Bank seal within circle and gear design, 1993 (date Central Bank was established) below **Rev. Legend:** BANGKO SENTRAL NG PILIPINAS - 1993 **Edge:** Reeded

Date	Mintage	F	VF	XF	Unc	BU
2001	—	—	—	0.10	0.30	0.40
2002	—	—	—	0.10	0.30	0.40
2004	—	—	—	0.75	1.50	2.50
2005	—	—	—	0.10	0.30	0.40

KM# 270.2 10 SENTIMOS

2.5000 g., Copper Plated Steel, 17 mm. **Obv:** Value high on coin, different font, date **Rev:** Central Bank seal within circle and gear design **Rev. Legend:** BANGKO SENTRAL NG PILIPINAS - 1993 **Edge:** Reeded

Date	Mintage	F	VF	XF	Unc	BU
2006	—	—	—	0.10	0.30	0.40
2007	—	—	—	0.10	0.30	0.40
2008	—	—	—	0.10	0.30	0.40
2009	—	—	—	0.10	0.30	0.40
2010	—	—	—	0.10	0.30	0.40
2011	—	—	—	0.10	0.30	0.40
2012	—	—	—	0.10	0.30	0.40

KM# 271 25 SENTIMOS

3.8000 g., Brass, 20 mm. **Obv:** Value and date **Rev:** Central Bank seal within circle and gear design, 1993 (date Central Bank was established) below **Rev. Legend:** BANGKO SENTRAL NG PILIPINAS - 1993 **Edge:** Plain

Date	Mintage	F	VF	XF	Unc	BU
2001	—	—	0.10	0.25	0.60	0.80
2002	—	—	0.10	0.25	0.60	0.80
2003	—	—	0.10	0.25	0.60	0.80

KM# 271a 25 SENTIMOS

3.6000 g., Brass Plated Steel, 20 mm. **Obv:** Value and date **Rev:** Central Bank seal within circle and gear design **Rev. Legend:** BANGKO SENTRAL NG PILIPINAS - 1993 **Edge:** Plain

Date	Mintage	F	VF	XF	Unc	BU
2004	—	—	—	0.25	2.00	2.50
2005	—	—	—	0.25	1.00	1.25
2006	—	—	—	0.25	1.00	1.25
2007	—	—	—	0.25	1.00	1.25
2008	—	—	—	0.25	0.50	1.00
2009	—	—	—	0.25	0.50	1.00
2010	—	—	—	0.25	0.50	1.00
2011	—	—	—	0.25	0.50	1.00
2012	—	—	—	0.25	0.50	1.00

KM# 269 PISO

6.1000 g., Copper-Nickel, 24 mm. **Obv:** Head of Jose Rizal right, value and date **Rev:** Bank seal within circle and gear design, 1993 (date Central Bank was established) below **Rev. Legend:** BANGKO SENTRAL NG PILIPINAS - 1993 **Edge:** Reeded

Date	Mintage	F	VF	XF	Unc	BU
2001	—	—	0.25	0.50	1.25	1.75
2002	—	—	0.25	0.50	1.25	1.75
2003 Non Magnetic	—	—	—	—	—	11.00

KM# 269a PISO

5.4000 g., Nickel Plated Steel, 24 mm. **Obv:** Head of Jose Rizal right, value and date **Rev:** Bank seal within circle and gear design **Rev. Legend:** BANGKO SENTRAL NG PILIPINAS - 1993 **Edge:** Reeded

Date	Mintage	F	VF	XF	Unc	BU
2003	—	—	—	1.00	2.00	3.00
2004	—	—	—	0.45	5.00	7.00
2005	—	—	—	0.45	1.10	1.50
2006	—	—	—	0.45	1.10	1.50
2007	—	—	—	0.45	1.10	1.50
2008	—	—	—	0.45	1.10	1.50
2009	—	—	—	0.45	1.10	1.50
2010	—	—	—	0.45	1.10	1.50
2011	—	—	—	0.45	1.10	1.50
2012	—	—	—	0.45	1.10	1.50

KM# 284 PISO

5.3500 g., Nickel Plated Steel, 24 mm. **Subject:** Jose Rizal 150th Birth Anniversary **Edge:** Reeded

Date	Mintage	F	VF	XF	Unc	BU
2011	10,000,000	—	—	—	1.00	1.50

KM# 272 5 PISO

7.7000 g., Nickel-Brass, 27 mm. **Obv:** Head of Emilio Aguinaldo right, value and date within scalloped border **Rev:** Central Bank seal within circle and gear design within scalloped border, 1993 (date Central Bank was established) below **Rev. Legend:** BANGKO SENTRAL NG PILIPINAS - 1993 **Edge:** Plain

Date	Mintage	F	VF	XF	Unc	BU
2001BSP	—	—	1.00	2.00	3.00	4.50
2002	—	—	0.35	0.70	1.75	3.00
2003	—	—	0.35	0.70	1.75	3.00
2004	—	—	0.50	1.00	5.00	6.00
2005	—	—	0.35	0.70	1.75	4.00
2006	—	—	0.35	0.70	1.75	3.00
2007	—	—	0.35	0.70	1.75	3.00
2008	—	—	0.35	0.70	1.75	3.00
2009	—	—	0.35	0.70	1.75	3.00
2010	—	—	0.35	0.70	1.75	3.00
2011	—	—	0.35	0.70	1.75	3.00
2012	—	—	0.35	0.70	1.75	3.00

KM# 278 10 PISO

8.7000 g., Bi-Metallic Aluminum-Bronze center in Copper-Nickel ring, 26.5 mm. **Obv:** Conjoined heads right within circle **Rev:** Bank seal within circle and gear design, 1993 (date Central Bank was established) below **Rev. Legend:** BANGKO SENTRAL NG PILIPINAS - 1993 **Edge:** Segmented reeding

Date	Mintage	F	VF	XF	Unc	BU
2001	—	—	0.70	1.40	3.50	5.50
2002	—	—	0.60	1.20	2.00	3.00
2003	—	—	0.60	1.20	3.00	4.00
2004	—	—	0.80	2.00	5.00	8.00
2005	—	—	0.75	1.50	3.75	5.00
2006	—	—	0.60	1.20	3.00	4.00
2007	—	—	0.75	1.50	3.75	5.00
2008	—	—	0.75	1.50	3.75	5.00
2009	—	—	0.75	1.50	3.75	5.00
2010	—	—	0.75	1.50	3.75	5.00
2011	—	—	—	—	7.50	10.00
2012	—	—	0.75	1.50	3.75	5.00

MINT SETS

KM#	Date	Mintage	Identification	Issue Price	Mkt Val
MS39	2005 (7)	—	KM#268-273, 278 plus medal	10.00	15.00
MS40	2006 (7)	—	KM#268-273, 278	10.00	12.50
MS41	2009 (7)	—	KM#268-273, 278	25.00	30.00
MS42	2011 (7)	—	KM#268-273, 278 plus Rizal Medal	25.00	30.00

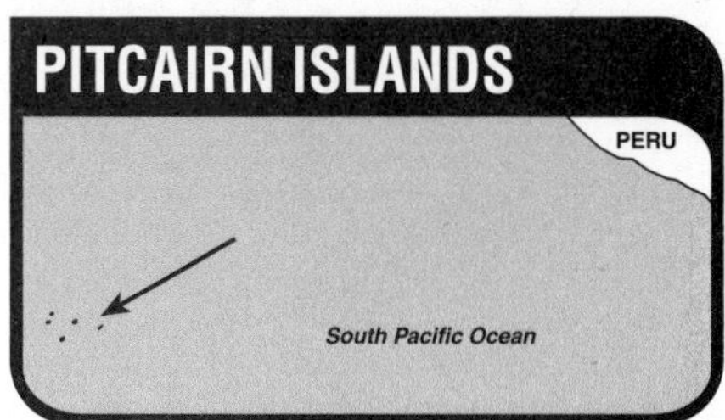

A small volcanic island, along with the uninhabited islands of Oeno, Henderson, and Ducie, constitute the British Colony of Pitcairn Islands. The main island has an area of about 2 sq. mi. (5 sq. km.) and a population of *68. It is located 1350 miles southeast of Tahiti. The islanders subsist on fishing, garden produce and crops. The sale of postage stamps and carved curios to passing ships brings cash income.

New Zealand currency has been used since July 10, 1967.

BRITISH COLONY

REGULAR COINAGE

KM# 54 5 CENTS

3.4000 g., Copper Plated Bronze, 19 mm. **Ruler:** Elizabeth II **Obv:** Head right **Rev:** Anchor from the H.M.A.V. Bounty

Date	Mintage	F	VF	XF	Unc	BU
2009	20,000	—	—	—	—	2.00
2010	20,000	—	—	—	—	2.00

KM# 55 10 CENTS

4.6000 g., Copper Plated Bronze, 22 mm. **Ruler:** Elizabeth II **Obv:** Head right **Rev:** Bell from H.M.A.V. Bounty **Edge:** Reeded

Date	Mintage	F	VF	XF	Unc	BU
2009	20,000	—	—	—	—	3.00
2010	20,000	—	—	—	—	3.00

KM# 56 20 CENTS

6.5000 g., Nickel Plated Bronze, 25 mm. **Ruler:** Elizabeth II **Obv:** Head right **Rev:** Bible from H.M.A.V. Bounty

Date	Mintage	F	VF	XF	Unc	BU
2009	20,000	—	—	—	—	5.00
2010	20,000	—	—	—	—	5.00

KM# 57 50 CENTS

8.0000 g., Copper-Nickel **Ruler:** Elizabeth II **Obv:** Head right **Rev:** Pitcairn Longboat

Date	Mintage	F	VF	XF	Unc	BU
2009	—	—	—	—	—	8.00
2010	—	—	—	—	—	8.00

KM# 14 DOLLAR

Copper-Nickel, 38.8 mm. **Ruler:** Elizabeth II **Obv:** Bust facing right **Rev:** Queen Mum, Elizabeth II and Margaret facing **Rev. Legend:** 80th Birthday of H.M. Queen Elizabeth II

Date	Mintage	F	VF	XF	Unc	BU
2006	—	—	—	—	10.00	12.00

KM# 58 DOLLAR

16.3000 g., Aluminum-Brass, 32 mm. **Ruler:** Elizabeth II **Obv:** Head right **Rev:** Cannon from H.A.M.V. Bounty **Edge:** Reeded

Date	Mintage	F	VF	XF	Unc	BU
2009	20,000	—	—	—	—	12.00
2010	20,000	—	—	—	—	12.00

KM# 45 2 DOLLARS

31.1050 g., 0.9990 Silver 0.9990 oz. ASW, 40.7 mm. **Ruler:** Elizabeth II **Subject:** Year of the Rat **Rev:** Multicolor rat seated right

Date	Mintage	F	VF	XF	Unc	BU
2008 Prooflike	30,000	—	—	—	—	85.00

KM# 46 2 DOLLARS

31.1050 g., 0.9990 Silver 0.9990 oz. ASW, 40.7 mm. **Ruler:** Elizabeth II **Rev:** Multicolor HMAV Bounty under full sail right

Date	Mintage	F	VF	XF	Unc	BU
2008 Prooflike	5,000	—	—	—	—	75.00

KM# 47 2 DOLLARS

31.1050 g., 0.9990 Silver Partially gilt 0.9990 oz. ASW, 40.7 mm. **Ruler:** Elizabeth II **Rev:** HMAV Bounty under full sail right

Date	Mintage	F	VF	XF	Unc	BU
2008 Proof	1,500	Value: 85.00				

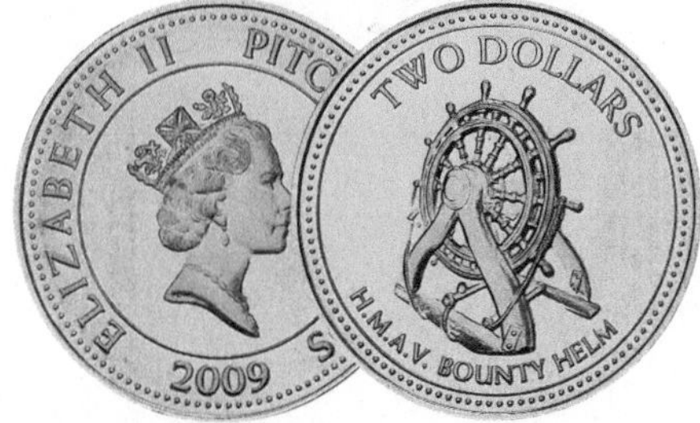

KM# 59 2 DOLLARS

19.5000 g., Aluminum-Brass, 35 mm. **Ruler:** Elizabeth II **Obv:** Head right **Rev:** Helm (wheel) from H.M.A.V. Bounty **Edge:** Seqmented reeding

Date	Mintage	F	VF	XF	Unc	BU
2009	20,000	—	—	—	—	15.00

KM# 51 2 DOLLARS

31.1050 g., 0.9990 Silver partially gilt 0.9990 oz. ASW, 40.7 mm. **Ruler:** Elizabeth II **Rev:** Captain William Bligh partially gilt

Date	Mintage	F	VF	XF	Unc	BU
2009 Proof	1,500	Value: 120				

KM# 67 2 DOLLARS

31.1050 g., Silver partially gilt, 40.7 mm. **Ruler:** Elizabeth II **Rev:** Ox striding right, gilt

Date	Mintage	F	VF	XF	Unc	BU
2009 Proof	15,000	Value: 85.00				

KM# 68 2 DOLLARS

31.1050 g., 0.9990 Silver 0.9990 oz. ASW, 40.7 mm. **Ruler:** Elizabeth II **Rev:** Ox striding right, color

Date	Mintage	F	VF	XF	Unc	BU
2009 Proof	15,000	Value: 85.00				

KM# 60 2 DOLLARS

Brass, 36 mm. **Ruler:** Elizabeth II **Rev:** H.M.A.V. Bounty at sail **Edge:** Segmented reeding

Date	Mintage	F	VF	XF	Unc	BU
2010	20,000	—	—	—	—	15.00

KM# 61 2 DOLLARS
15.5000 g., 0.9250 Silver 0.4609 oz. ASW, 35 mm. **Ruler:** Elizabeth II **Subject:** Deep sea fish **Rev:** Black sea devil (Melanocetus Johnsonii) in color

Date	Mintage	F	VF	XF	Unc	BU
2010 Proof	1,000	Value: 75.00				

KM# 62 2 DOLLARS
15.5500 g., 0.9250 Silver 0.4624 oz. ASW, 35 mm. **Ruler:** Elizabeth II **Subject:** Deep sea fish **Rev:** White spotted jellyfish in color

Date	Mintage	F	VF	XF	Unc	BU
2010 Proof	—	Value: 75.00				

KM# 63 2 DOLLARS
15.5500 g., 0.9250 Silver 0.4624 oz. ASW, 35 mm. **Ruler:** Elizabeth II **Subject:** Deep sea fish **Rev:** Laternfish (Mychtophios) in color

Date	Mintage	F	VF	XF	Unc	BU
2010 Proof	1,000	Value: 75.00				

KM# 65 2 DOLLARS
31.1050 g., 0.9990 Silver partially gilt 0.9990 oz. ASW, 40.7 mm. **Ruler:** Elizabeth II **Rev:** H.M.A.V. Bounty at sail, gilt

Date	Mintage	F	VF	XF	Unc	BU
2010 Proof	3,000	Value: 120				

KM# 66 2 DOLLARS
31.1050 g., 0.9990 Silver partially gilt 0.9990 oz. ASW, 40.7 mm. **Ruler:** Elizabeth II **Rev:** Fletcher Christian facing, partially gilt

Date	Mintage	F	VF	XF	Unc	BU
2010 Proof	3,000	Value: 120				

KM# 64 2 DOLLARS
31.1050 g., 0.9990 Silver 0.9990 oz. ASW, 40.7 mm. **Ruler:** Elizabeth II **Subject:** Alice in Wonderland **Rev:** March Hare within backward clock face

Date	Mintage	F	VF	XF	Unc	BU
2011 Proof	15,000	Value: 85.00				

KM# 69 2 DOLLARS
31.1050 g., 0.9990 Silver 0.9990 oz. ASW, 40.7 mm. **Ruler:** Elizabeth II **Rev:** Rabbit in snow, multicolor

Date	Mintage	F	VF	XF	Unc	BU
2011 Proof	15,000	Value: 125				

KM# 71 2 DOLLARS
15.5000 g., 0.9250 Silver 0.4609 oz. ASW, 35 mm. **Ruler:** Elizabeth II **Rev:** Cotylorhiza Tuberculata, Jellyfish in color

Date	Mintage	F	VF	XF	Unc	BU
2011 Proof	1,000	Value: 75.00				

KM# 72 2 DOLLARS
15.5000 g., 0.9250 Silver 0.4609 oz. ASW, 35 mm. **Ruler:** Elizabeth II **Rev:** Chrysaora Achlyos, black jellyfish in color

Date	Mintage	F	VF	XF	Unc	BU
2011 Proof	1,000	Value: 75.00				

KM# 73 2 DOLLARS
15.5000 g., 0.9250 Silver 0.4609 oz. ASW, 35 mm. **Ruler:** Elizabeth II **Rev:** Anoplogaster Cornuta, Fangtooth fish in color

Date	Mintage	F	VF	XF	Unc	BU
2011 Proof	1,000	Value: 75.00				

KM# 74 2 DOLLARS
15.5000 g., 0.9250 Silver 0.4609 oz. ASW, 35 mm. **Ruler:** Elizabeth II **Rev:** Melanostomias Biseriatus in color

Date	Mintage	F	VF	XF	Unc	BU
2011 Proof	1,000	Value: 75.00				

KM# 12 5 DOLLARS
31.1000 g., 0.9990 Silver with Mother-of-Pearl inset 0.9988 oz. ASW, 40 mm. **Ruler:** Elizabeth II **Series:** Save the Whales **Obv:** Crowned bust right **Obv. Legend:** ELIZABETH II • PITCAIRN ISLANDS **Rev:** Humpback Whale and date on mother-of-pearl inset **Edge:** Plain

Date	Mintage	F	VF	XF	Unc	BU
2002 Proof	2,000	Value: 95.00				

KM# 50 5 DOLLARS
1.2700 g., 0.9999 Gold 0.0408 oz. AGW, 13.92 mm. **Ruler:** Elizabeth II **Obv:** Crowned bust right **Obv. Legend:** Elizabeth II Pitcairn Islands **Rev:** Bounty Bible and ship

Date	Mintage	F	VF	XF	Unc	BU
2005 Proof	—	Value: 90.00				

KM# 48 10 DOLLARS
1.2440 g., 0.9999 Gold 0.0400 oz. AGW, 14 mm. **Ruler:** Elizabeth II **Rev:** HMAV Bounty under full sail right

Date	Mintage	F	VF	XF	Unc	BU
2008 Proof	10,000	Value: 165				

KM# 49 25 DOLLARS
7.7700 g., 0.9990 Gold 0.2496 oz. AGW, 22 mm. **Ruler:** Elizabeth II **Rev:** HMAV Bounty under full sail right

Date	Mintage	F	VF	XF	Unc	BU
2008 Proof	1,500	Value: 775				

MINT SETS

KM#	Date	Mintage	Identification	Issue Price	Mkt Val
MS1	2009 (6)	20,000	KM#54; 55; 56; 57; 58; 59	—	45.00
MS2	2010 (6)	20,000	KM#54; 55; 56; 57; 58; 60	—	45.00

The Republic of Poland, located in central Europe, has an area of 120,725 sq. mi. (312,680 sq. km.) and a population of *38.2 million. Capital: Warszawa (Warsaw). The economy is essentially agricultural, but industrial activity provides the products for foreign trade. Machinery, coal, coke, iron, steel and transport equipment are exported.

MINT MARKS

MV, MW, MW-monogram - Warsaw Mint, 1965-
CHI - Valcambi, Switzerland

Other letters appearing with date denote the Mintmaster at the time the coin was struck.

REPUBLIC

Democratic

REFORM COINAGE

100 Old Zlotych = 1 Grosz; 10,000 Old Zlotych = 1 Zloty

As far back as 1990, production was initiated for the new 1 Grosz - 1 Zlotych coins for a forthcoming monetary reform. It wasn't announced until the Act of July 7, 1994 and was enacted on January 1, 1995.

Y# 276 GROSZ

1.6400 g., Brass, 15.5 mm. **Obv:** National arms **Obv. Legend:** RZECZPOSPOLITA POLSKA **Rev:** Drooping oak leaf over value **Edge:** Reeded

Date	Mintage	F	VF	XF	Unc	BU
2001MW	210,000,020	—	—	—	0.10	0.20
2002MW	240,000,000	—	—	—	0.10	0.20
2003MW	250,000,000	—	—	—	0.10	0.20
2004MW	300,000,000	—	—	—	0.10	0.20
2005MW	375,000,000	—	—	—	0.10	0.20
2006MW	184,000,000	—	—	—	0.10	0.20
2007MW	330,000,000	—	—	—	0.10	0.20
2008MW	—	—	—	—	0.10	0.20
2009MW	—	—	—	—	0.10	0.20
2010MW	—	—	—	—	0.10	0.20
2011MW	—	—	—	—	0.10	0.20
2012MW	—	—	—	—	0.10	0.20

Y# 277 2 GROSZE

2.1300 g., Brass, 17.5 mm. **Obv:** National arms **Obv. Legend:** RZECZPOSPOLITA POLSKA **Rev:** Drooping oak leaves above value **Edge:** Plain

Date	Mintage	F	VF	XF	Unc	BU
2001MW	86,100,000	—	—	—	0.15	0.25
2002MW	83,910,000	—	—	—	0.15	0.25
2003MW	80,000,000	—	—	—	0.15	0.25
2004MW	100,000,000	—	—	—	0.15	0.25
2005MW	163,003,250	—	—	—	0.15	0.25
2006MW	105,000,000	—	—	—	0.15	0.25
2007MW	160,000,000	—	—	—	0.15	0.25
2008MW	—	—	—	—	0.15	0.25
2009MW	—	—	—	—	0.15	0.25
2010MW	—	—	—	—	0.15	0.25
2011MW	—	—	—	—	0.15	0.25
2012MW	—	—	—	—	0.15	0.25

Y# 278 5 GROSZY

2.5900 g., Brass, 19.5 mm. **Obv:** National arms **Obv. Legend:** RZECZPOSPOLITA POLSKA **Rev:** Value at upper left of oak leaves **Edge:** Segmented reeding

Date	Mintage	F	VF	XF	Unc	BU
2001MW	67,368,000	—	—	—	0.25	0.45
2002MW	67,200,000	—	—	—	0.25	0.45
2003MW	48,000,000	—	—	—	0.25	0.45
2004MW	62,500,000	—	—	—	0.25	0.45
2005MW	113,000,000	—	—	—	0.25	0.45
2006MW	54,000,000	—	—	—	0.25	0.45
2007MW	116,000,000	—	—	—	0.25	0.45
2008MW	—	—	—	—	0.25	0.45
2009MW	—	—	—	—	0.25	0.45
2010MW	—	—	—	—	0.25	0.45
2011MW	—	—	—	—	0.25	0.45
2012MW	—	—	—	—	0.25	0.45

Y# 279 10 GROSZY

2.5500 g., Copper-Nickel, 16.5 mm. **Obv:** National arms **Obv. Legend:** RZECZPOSPOLITA POLSKA **Rev:** Value within wreath

Date	Mintage	F	VF	XF	Unc	BU
2001MW	62,820,000	—	—	—	0.40	0.60
2002MW	10,500,000	—	—	—	0.40	0.60
2003MW	31,500,000	—	—	—	0.40	0.60
2004MW	70,500,000	—	—	—	0.40	0.60
2005MW	94,000,000	—	—	—	0.40	0.60
2006MW	40,000,000	—	—	—	0.40	0.60
2007MW	100,000,000	—	—	—	0.40	0.60
2008MW	—	—	—	—	0.40	0.60
2009MW	—	—	—	—	0.40	0.60
2010MW	—	—	—	—	0.40	0.60
2011MW	—	—	—	—	0.40	0.60
2012MW	—	—	—	—	0.40	0.60

Y# 280 20 GROSZY

3.2200 g., Copper-Nickel, 18.5 mm. **Obv:** National arms **Obv. Legend:** RZECZPOSPOLITA POLSKA **Rev:** Value within artistic design **Edge:** Reeded

Date	Mintage	F	VF	XF	Unc	BU
2001MW	41,980,001	—	—	—	0.65	0.85
2002MW	10,500,000	—	—	—	0.65	0.85
2003MW	20,400,000	—	—	—	0.65	0.85
2004MW	40,000,025	—	—	—	0.65	0.85
2005MW	37,000,000	—	—	—	0.65	0.85
2006MW	35,000,000	—	—	—	0.65	0.85
2007MW	68,000,000	—	—	—	0.65	0.85
2008MW	—	—	—	—	0.65	0.85
2009MW	—	—	—	—	0.65	0.85
2010MW	—	—	—	—	0.65	0.85
2011MW	—	—	—	—	0.65	0.85
2012MW	—	—	—	—	0.65	0.85

Y# 281 50 GROSZY

3.9400 g., Copper-Nickel, 20.5 mm. **Obv:** National arms **Obv. Legend:** RZECZPOSPOLITA POLSKA **Rev:** Value to right of sprig **Edge:** Reeded

Date	Mintage	F	VF	XF	Unc	BU
2008MW	—	—	—	—	1.00	1.25
2009MW	—	—	—	—	1.00	1.25
2010MW	—	—	—	—	1.00	1.25
2011MW	—	—	—	—	1.00	1.25
2012MW	—	—	—	—	1.00	1.25
2013MW	—	—	—	—	1.00	1.25

Y# 282 ZLOTY

5.0300 g., Copper-Nickel, 23 mm. **Obv:** National arms **Obv. Legend:** RZECZPOSPOLITA POLSKA **Rev:** Value within wreath **Edge:** Segmented reeding

Date	Mintage	F	VF	XF	Unc	BU
2008MW	—	—	—	—	1.75	2.00
2009MW	—	—	—	—	1.75	2.00
2010MW	—	—	—	—	1.75	2.00
2012MW	—	—	—	—	1.75	2.00
2013MW	—	—	—	—	1.75	2.00

Y# 408 2 ZLOTE

8.1500 g., Brass, 27 mm. **Subject:** Wieliczka Salt Mine **Obv:** Crowned eagle with wings open **Rev:** Ancient salt miners

Date	Mintage	F	VF	XF	Unc	BU
2001	500,000	—	—	3.50	7.00	12.00

Y# 410 2 ZLOTE

8.1500 g., Brass, 27 mm. **Subject:** Amber Route **Obv:** Crowned eagle with wings open **Rev:** Ancient Roman coin and map with route marked in stars

Date	Mintage	F	VF	XF	Unc	BU
2001	500,000	—	—	3.50	7.00	12.00

Y# 412 2 ZLOTE

8.1500 g., Brass, 27 mm. **Subject:** 15 Years of the Constitutional Court **Obv:** Crowned eagle with wings open **Rev:** Crowned eagle head and scale **Edge:** * NBP * eight times

Date	Mintage	F	VF	XF	Unc	BU
2001MW	500,000	—	—	—	3.00	5.00

Y# 414 2 ZLOTE

8.1500 g., Brass, 27 mm. **Obv:** Crowned eagle with wings open **Rev:** Butterfly **Edge:** * NBP * eight times

Date	Mintage	F	VF	XF	Unc	BU
2001MW	600,000	—	—	4.00	8.00	15.00

Y# 418 2 ZLOTE

8.1500 g., Brass, 27 mm. **Subject:** Cardinal Stefan Wyszynski **Obv:** Crowned eagle with wings open **Rev:** Bust left wearing mitre **Edge:** "NBP" eight times

Date	Mintage	F	VF	XF	Unc	BU
2001MW	1,200,000	—	—	—	3.00	5.00

Y# 421 2 ZLOTE

8.1500 g., Brass, 27 mm. **Subject:** Michal Siedlecki **Obv:** Crowned eagle with wings open **Rev:** Bust left and art work **Edge:** NBP eight times

Date	Mintage	F	VF	XF	Unc	BU
2001MW	600,000	—	—	—	3.00	5.00

Y# 422 2 ZLOTE

8.1500 g., Brass, 27 mm. **Subject:** Koledicy **Obv:** Crowned eagle with wings open **Rev:** Christmas celebration scene

Date	Mintage	F	VF	XF	Unc	BU
2001MW	600,000	—	—	—	3.00	5.00

Y# 423 2 ZLOTE

8.1500 g., Brass, 27 mm. **Subject:** Jan III Sobieski **Obv:** Crowned eagle with wings open **Rev:** Bust facing **Edge Lettering:** * NBP * eight times

Date	Mintage	F	VF	XF	Unc	BU
2001MW	500,000	—	—	3.50	7.00	12.00

Y# 426 2 ZLOTE

8.1500 g., Brass, 27 mm. **Subject:** Henryk Wieniawski **Obv:** Crowned eagle with wings open **Rev:** Bust left and violin **Edge Lettering:** * NBP * eight times

Date	Mintage	F	VF	XF	Unc	BU
2001MW	600,000	—	—	—	3.00	5.00

Y# 427 2 ZLOTE

8.1500 g., Brass, 27 mm. **Obv:** Crowned eagle with wings open **Rev:** European Pond Turtles **Edge Lettering:** * NBP * eight times

Date	Mintage	F	VF	XF	Unc	BU
2002MW	750,000	—	—	3.50	7.00	12.00

Y# 431 2 ZLOTE

8.1500 g., Brass, 27 mm. **Subject:** Bronislaw Malinowski **Obv:** Crowned eagle with wings open **Rev:** Bust facing and Trobriand Islanders **Edge Lettering:** * NBP * eight times

Date	Mintage	F	VF	XF	Unc	BU
2002MW	680,000	—	—	—	3.50	5.50

Y# 433 2 ZLOTE

8.1500 g., Brass, 27 mm. **Subject:** World Cup Soccer **Obv:** National arms **Rev:** Soccer players **Edge Lettering:** * NBP * eight times

Date	Mintage	F	VF	XF	Unc	BU
2002MW	1,000,000	—	—	—	3.00	5.00

Y# 439 2 ZLOTE

8.1000 g., Brass, 26.8 mm. **Subject:** August II (1697-1706, 1709-1733) **Obv:** National arms **Rev:** Head facing **Edge Lettering:** * NBP * eight times

Date	Mintage	F	VF	XF	Unc	BU
2002MW	620,000	—	—	—	4.00	7.00

Y# 440 2 ZLOTE

8.1500 g., Brass, 27 mm. **Subject:** Gen. Wladyslaw Anders **Obv:** Crowned eagle with wings open **Rev:** Uniformed bust facing and cross **Edge Lettering:** * NBP * eight times

Date	Mintage	F	VF	XF	Unc	BU
2002MW	680,000	—	—	—	3.00	5.00

Y# 443 2 ZLOTE

8.1500 g., Brass, 27 mm. **Subject:** Malbork Castle **Obv:** Crowned eagle with wings open **Rev:** Castle **Edge Lettering:** * NBP * eight times

Date	Mintage	F	VF	XF	Unc	BU
2002MW	680,000	—	—	—	3.00	5.00

Y# 444 2 ZLOTE

8.1500 g., Brass, 27 mm. **Subject:** Jan Matejko **Obv:** Denomination, crowned eagle and artist's palette **Rev:** Jester behind portrait **Edge Lettering:** * NBP * eight times

Date	Mintage	F	VF	XF	Unc	BU
2002MW	700,000	—	—	—	3.00	5.00

Y# 445 2 ZLOTE

8.1500 g., Brass, 27 mm. **Subject:** Eels **Obv:** Crowned eagle with wings open **Rev:** Two European eels **Edge Lettering:** * NBP * eight times

Date	Mintage	F	VF	XF	Unc	BU
2003MW	450,000	—	—	6.00	12.00	20.00

Y# 446 2 ZLOTE

7.7500 g., Brass, 27 mm. **Subject:** Children **Obv:** Children and square design above crowned eagle, date and value **Rev:** Children on square design **Edge Lettering:** * NBP * eight times **Note:** Center hole.

Date	Mintage	F	VF	XF	Unc	BU
2003MW	2,500,000	—	—	—	4.50	6.50

Y# 447 2 ZLOTE

8.1500 g., Brass, 27 mm. **Subject:** City of Poznan (Posen) **Obv:** Crowned eagle with wings open **Rev:** Clock face and tower flanked by goat heads **Edge Lettering:** * NBP * eight times

Date	Mintage	F	VF	XF	Unc	BU
2003MW	600,000	—	—	—	5.00	8.00

Y# 451 2 ZLOTE

8.1500 g., Brass, 27 mm. **Subject:** Easter Monday Festival **Obv:** Crowned eagle with wings open **Rev:** Festival scene **Edge Lettering:** * NBP * eight times

Date	Mintage	F	VF	XF	Unc	BU
2003MW	600,000	—	—	—	4.00	7.00

Y# 455 2 ZLOTE

8.1500 g., Brass, 27 mm. **Subject:** Petroleum and Gas Industry 150th Anniversary **Obv:** Crowned eagle with wings open **Rev:** Portrait and refinery **Edge Lettering:** * NBP * eight times

Date	Mintage	F	VF	XF	Unc	BU
2003MW	600,000	—	—	—	3.50	5.50

Y# 456 2 ZLOTE

8.1500 g., Brass, 27 mm. **Subject:** General B. S. Maczek **Obv:** Crowned eagle with wings open **Rev:** Military uniformed portrait **Edge Lettering:** * NBP * eight times

Date	Mintage	F	VF	XF	Unc	BU
2003MW	700,000	—	—	—	3.00	5.00

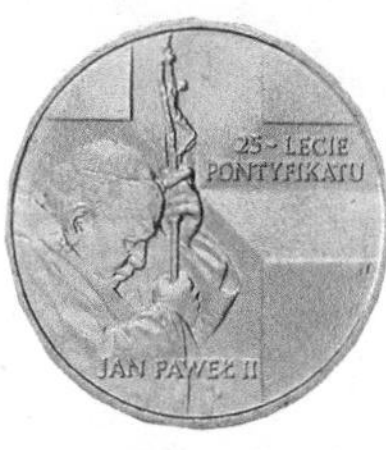

Y# 465 2 ZLOTE

8.1500 g., Brass, 27 mm. **Subject:** Pope John Paul II **Obv:** Small national arms at lower right with cross in background **Obv. Legend:** RZECZPOSPOLITA POLSKA **Rev:** Pope in prayer at left, cross in background **Edge Lettering:** * NBP * eight times

Date	Mintage	F	VF	XF	Unc	BU
2003MW	2,000,000	—	—	—	3.00	5.00

Y# 473 2 ZLOTE

8.1500 g., Brass, 27 mm. **Obv:** Crowned eagle with wings open **Rev:** Stanislaus Leszczywski **Edge Lettering:** * NBP * eight times

Date	Mintage	F	VF	XF	Unc	BU
2003MW	600,000	—	—	—	3.50	5.50

Y# 477 2 ZLOTE

8.1500 g., Brass, 27 mm. **Obv:** Crowned eagle with wings open and artist's palette **Rev:** Self portrait of Jacek Malczewski **Edge Lettering:** * NBP * eight times

Date	Mintage	F	VF	XF	Unc	BU
2003MW	600,000	—	—	—	3.50	5.50

Y# 479 2 ZLOTE

8.1500 g., Brass, 27 mm. **Subject:** 80th Anniversary of the Modern Zloty Currency **Obv:** Crowned eagle with wings open above value **Rev:** Bust left **Edge Lettering:** * NBP * eight times

Date	Mintage	F	VF	XF	Unc	BU
2004MW	800,000	—	—	—	3.00	5.00

Y# 481 2 ZLOTE

8.1500 g., Brass, 27 mm. **Subject:** Poland Joining the European Union **Obv:** Crowned eagle with wings open above value **Rev:** Map and stars **Edge Lettering:** * NBP * eight times

Date	Mintage	F	VF	XF	Unc	BU
2004MW	1,000,000	—	—	—	3.00	5.00

Y# 484 2 ZLOTE

8.1500 g., Brass, 27 mm. **Subject:** Dolnoslaskie (Lower Silesian) District **Obv:** Crowned eagle with wings open on map **Rev:** Silesian eagle on shield **Edge Lettering:** * NBP * eight times

Date	Mintage	F	VF	XF	Unc	BU
2004MW	700,000	—	—	—	4.00	6.00

Y# 485 2 ZLOTE

8.1500 g., Brass, 27 mm. **Subject:** Kujawsko-Pomorskie District **Obv:** Crowned eagle with wings open on map **Rev:** Shield with crowned half eagle and griffin **Edge Lettering:** * NBP * eight times

Date	Mintage	F	VF	XF	Unc	BU
2004MW	750,000	—	—	—	7.00	12.00

Y# 486 2 ZLOTE

8.1500 g., Brass, 27 mm. **Subject:** Lubuskie District **Obv:** Crowned eagle with wings open on map **Rev:** Shield with stag left **Edge Lettering:** * NBP * eight times

Date	Mintage	F	VF	XF	Unc	BU
2004MW	820,000	—	—	—	3.00	5.00

Y# 487 2 ZLOTE

8.1500 g., Brass, 27 mm. **Subject:** Lodzkie District **Obv:** Crowned eagle with wings open on map **Rev:** Shield with two creatures above an eagle **Edge Lettering:** * NBP * eight times

Date	Mintage	F	VF	XF	Unc	BU
2004MW	920,000	—	—	—	3.00	5.00

Y# 488 2 ZLOTE

8.1500 g., Brass, 27 mm. **Subject:** Malopolskie District **Obv:** Crowned eagle with wings open on map **Rev:** Shield with crowned eagle **Edge Lettering:** * NBP * eight times

Date	Mintage	F	VF	XF	Unc	BU
2004MW	920,000	—	—	—	3.00	5.00

Y# 489 2 ZLOTE

8.1500 g., Brass, 27 mm. **Subject:** Mazowieckie District **Obv:** Crowned eagle with wings open on map **Rev:** Eagle on shield **Edge Lettering:** * NBP * eight times

Date	Mintage	F	VF	XF	Unc	BU
2004MW	920,000	—	—	—	3.00	5.00

Y# 490 2 ZLOTE

8.1500 g., Brass, 27 mm. **Subject:** Podkarpackie District **Obv:** Crowned eagle with wings open on map **Rev:** Shield with iron cross above griffin and lion **Edge Lettering:** * NBP * eight times

Date	Mintage	F	VF	XF	Unc	BU
2004MW	920,000	—	—	—	3.00	5.00

Y# 491 2 ZLOTE

8.1500 g., Brass, 27 mm. **Subject:** Podlaskie District **Obv:** Crowned eagle with wings open on map **Rev:** Shield with Polish eagle above Lithuanian knight **Edge Lettering:** * NBP * eight times

Date	Mintage	F	VF	XF	Unc	BU
2004MW	900,000	—	—	—	3.00	5.00

Y# 492 2 ZLOTE

8.1500 g., Brass, 27 mm. **Subject:** Pomorskie District **Obv:** Crowned eagle with wings open on map **Rev:** Griffin on shield **Edge Lettering:** * NBP * eight times

Date	Mintage	F	VF	XF	Unc	BU
2004MW	900,000	—	—	—	3.00	5.00

Y# 493 2 ZLOTE

8.1500 g., Brass, 27 mm. **Subject:** Slaskie (Silesia) District **Obv:** Crowned eagle with wings open on map **Rev:** Eagle on shield **Edge Lettering:** * NBP * eight times

Date	Mintage	F	VF	XF	Unc	BU
2004MW	960,000	—	—	—	3.00	5.00

Y# 496 2 ZLOTE

8.1500 g., Brass, 27 mm. **Subject:** Warsaw Uprising 60th Anniversary **Obv:** Crowned eagle with wings open **Rev:** Resistance symbol on brick wall **Edge Lettering:** * NBP * eight times

Date	Mintage	F	VF	XF	Unc	BU
2004MW	900,000	—	—	—	3.00	5.00

Y# 499 2 ZLOTE

8.1500 g., Brass, 27 mm. **Obv:** Crowned eagle with wings open **Rev:** Gen. Stanislaw F. Sosabowski **Edge Lettering:** * NBP * eight times

Date	Mintage	F	VF	XF	Unc	BU
2004MW	850,000	—	—	—	3.00	5.00

Y# 501 2 ZLOTE

8.1500 g., Brass, 27 mm. **Subject:** Polish Police 85th Anniversary **Obv:** Crowned eagle with wings open **Rev:** Police badge **Edge Lettering:** * NBP * eight times

Date	Mintage	F	VF	XF	Unc	BU
2004MW	760,000	—	—	—	3.00	5.00

Y# 503 2 ZLOTE

8.1500 g., Brass, 27 mm. **Subject:** Polish Senate **Obv:** Crowned eagle with wings open **Rev:** Senate eagle and speaker's staff **Edge Lettering:** * NBP * eight times

Date	Mintage	F	VF	XF	Unc	BU
2004MW	760,000	—	—	—	3.00	5.00

Y# 505 2 ZLOTE

8.1500 g., Brass, 27 mm. **Obv:** Crowned eagle with wings open **Rev:** Aleksander Czekanowski (1833-1876) **Edge Lettering:** * NBP * eight times

Date	Mintage	F	VF	XF	Unc	BU
2004MW	700,000	—	—	—	3.00	5.00

Y# 507 2 ZLOTE

8.1500 g., Brass, 27 mm. **Obv:** National arms **Obv. Legend:** RZECZPOSPOLITA POLSKA **Rev:** Harvest fest couple in folk costume at left, large group in background at right **Rev. Legend:** DOZYNKI **Edge Lettering:** * NBP * eight times

Date	Mintage	F	VF	XF	Unc	BU
2004MW	850,000	—	—	—	3.00	5.00

Y# 509 2 ZLOTE

8.1500 g., Brass, 27 mm. **Subject:** Warsaw Fine Arts Academy Centennial **Obv:** Crowned eagle with wings open **Rev:** Painter's hands **Edge Lettering:** * NBP * eight times

Date	Mintage	F	VF	XF	Unc	BU
2004MW	850,000	—	—	—	3.00	5.00

Y# 516 2 ZLOTE

8.1500 g., Brass, 27 mm. **Subject:** Olympics **Obv:** Crowned eagle with wings open **Rev:** Ancient runners **Edge Lettering:** * NBP * eight times

Date	Mintage	F	VF	XF	Unc	BU
2004MW	1,000,000	—	—	—	3.00	5.00

Y# 607 2 ZLOTE

8.1500 g., Brass, 27 mm. **Obv:** National arms on outlined map **Obv. Legend:** RZECZPOSPOLITA POLSKA **Rev:** Region arms **Rev. Legend:** WOJEWODZTWO - OPOLSKIE **Edge Lettering:** * NBP * eight times

Date	Mintage	F	VF	XF	Unc	BU
2004MW	900,000	—	—	—	3.00	5.00

Y# 464 2 ZLOTE

8.1500 g., Brass, 27 mm. **Obv:** Crowned eagle with wings open **Rev:** Harbor Porpoises **Edge Lettering:** * NBP * eight times

Date	Mintage	F	VF	XF	Unc	BU
2004MW	800,000	—	—	3.50	7.00	12.00

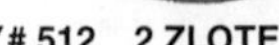

Y# 512 2 ZLOTE

8.1500 g., Brass, 27 mm. **Obv:** Crowned eagle with wings open and artist's palette **Rev:** Stanislaw Wyspianski (1869-1907) **Edge Lettering:** * NBP * eight times

Date	Mintage	F	VF	XF	Unc	BU
2004MW	900,000	—	—	—	3.00	5.00

Y# 514 2 ZLOTE

8.1500 g., Brass, 27 mm. **Obv:** National arms on outlined map **Rev:** Wojewodztwo-Lubelskie arms with stag on shield **Edge Lettering:** * NBP * eight times

Date	Mintage	F	VF	XF	Unc	BU
2004MW	820,000	—	—	—	—	7.50

Y# 283 2 ZLOTE

5.2100 g., Bi-Metallic Copper-Nickel center in Aluminum-Bronze ring, 21.5 mm. **Obv:** National arms within circle **Obv. Legend:** RZECZPOSPOLITA POLSKA **Rev:** Value flanked by oak leaves **Edge:** Plain

Date	Mintage	F	VF	XF	Unc	BU
2005MW	5,000,000	—	—	—	4.00	4.50
2006MW	5,000,000	—	—	—	4.00	4.50
2007MW	20,000,000	—	—	—	4.00	4.50
2008MW	—	—	—	—	4.00	4.50
2009MW	—	—	—	—	4.00	4.50
2010MW	—	—	—	—	4.00	4.50

Y# 520 2 ZLOTE

8.1500 g., Brass, 27 mm. **Obv:** National arms **Rev:** Owl perched on nest with owlets **Rev. Legend:** PUCHACZ - Bubo-bubo **Edge Lettering:** * NBP * eight times

Date	Mintage	F	VF	XF	Unc	BU
2005MW	990,000	—	—	—	4.00	7.00

Y# 521 2 ZLOTE

8.1500 g., Brass, 27 mm. **Obv:** Crowned eagle with wings open **Rev:** Ship within circle **Edge Lettering:** * NBP * eight times

Date	Mintage	F	VF	XF	Unc	BU
2005MW	920,000	—	—	—	3.50	5.50

Y# 522 2 ZLOTE

8.1500 g., Brass, 26.8 mm. **Subject:** Japan's Aichi Expo **Obv:** Crowned eagle with wings open **Rev:** Two cranes flying over Mt. Fuji with rising sun background **Edge Lettering:** * NBP * eight times

Date	Mintage	F	VF	XF	Unc	BU
2005MW	1,000,000	—	—	—	3.50	5.50

Y# 524 2 ZLOTE
8.1500 g., Brass, 27 mm. **Subject:** Obrony Jasnej Gory **Obv:** Crowned eagle with wings open **Rev:** Half length figure left and bombarded city scene **Edge Lettering:** * NBP * eight times

Date	Mintage	F	VF	XF	Unc	BU
2005MW	1,000,000	—	—	—	4.00	6.00

Y# 525 2 ZLOTE
8.1500 g., Brass, 27 mm. **Subject:** Pope John-Paul II **Obv:** National arms **Obv. Legend:** RZECZPOSPOLITA POLSKA **Rev:** Bust right at left, outline of St. Peter's Baslica at center right **Edge Lettering:** * NBP * eight times

Date	Mintage	F	VF	XF	Unc	BU
2005MW	4,000,000	—	—	—	4.00	6.00

Y# 527 2 ZLOTE
8.1500 g., Brass, 27 mm. **Obv:** Crowned eagle with wings open **Rev:** Bust 1/4 left with horse head and goose at left **Edge Lettering:** * NBP * eight times

Date	Mintage	F	VF	XF	Unc	BU
2005MW	850,000	—	—	—	3.00	5.00

Y# 528 2 ZLOTE
8.1500 g., Brass, 27 mm. **Obv:** Crowned eagle above wall **Rev:** Kolobrzeg Lighthouse **Edge Lettering:** * NBP * eight times

Date	Mintage	F	VF	XF	Unc	BU
2005MW	1,100,000	—	—	—	3.00	5.00

Y# 529 2 ZLOTE
8.1500 g., Brass, 27 mm. **Obv:** National arms above gateway **Rev:** Wioclawek Cathedral **Edge Lettering:** * NBP * eight times

Date	Mintage	F	VF	XF	Unc	BU
2005MW	1,100,000	—	—	—	3.00	5.00

Y# 530 2 ZLOTE
8.1500 g., Brass, 27 mm. **Obv:** National arms **Rev:** Bust of King Stanislaus Poniatowski right **Edge Lettering:** * NBP * eight times

Date	Mintage	F	VF	XF	Unc	BU
2005MW	990,000	—	—	—	3.00	5.00

Y# 541 2 ZLOTE
8.1500 g., Brass, 27 mm. **Obv:** Eagle, value, palette and paint brushes **Rev:** Painter Tadeusz Makowski **Edge Lettering:** * NBP * eight times

Date	Mintage	F	VF	XF	Unc	BU
2005MW	900,000	—	—	—	3.00	5.00

Y# 558 2 ZLOTE
8.1500 g., Brass, 27 mm. **Subject:** 60th Anniversary of WWII **Obv:** National arms **Edge Lettering:** * NBP * eight times

Date	Mintage	F	VF	XF	Unc	BU
2005MW	1,000,000	—	—	—	3.00	5.00

Y# 560 2 ZLOTE
8.1500 g., Brass, 27 mm. **Obv:** National arms on outline map **Obv. Legend:** RZECZPOSPOLITA POLSKA **Rev:** Region arms **Rev. Legend:** WOJEWOZTWO SWIETOKRZYSKIE **Edge Lettering:** * NBP * eight times

Date	Mintage	F	VF	XF	Unc	BU
2005MW	900,000	—	—	—	3.00	5.00

Y# 562 2 ZLOTE
8.1500 g., Brass, 27 mm. **Obv:** National arms **Rev:** Region Wielkopolskie **Edge Lettering:** * NBP * eight times

Date	Mintage	F	VF	XF	Unc	BU
2005MW	940,000	—	—	—	3.00	5.00

Y# 563 2 ZLOTE
8.1500 g., Brass, 27 mm. **Obv:** National arms on outlined map **Obv. Legend:** RZECZPOSPOLITA POLSKA **Rev:** Region arms **Rev. Legend:** WOJEWODZTWO ZACHODIOPOMORSKIE **Edge Lettering:** * NBP * eight times

Date	Mintage	F	VF	XF	Unc	BU
2005	—	—	—	—	3.00	5.00

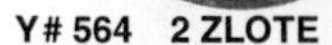

Y# 564 2 ZLOTE
8.1500 g., Brass, 27 mm. **Obv:** National arms **Rev:** City of Gniezno **Edge Lettering:** * NBP * eight times

Date	Mintage	F	VF	XF	Unc	BU
2005	1,250,000	—	—	—	3.00	5.00

Y# 565 2 ZLOTE
8.1500 g., Brass, 27 mm. **Obv:** National arms **Rev:** Solidarity **Edge Lettering:** * NBP * eight times

Date	Mintage	F	VF	XF	Unc	BU
2005MW	1,000,000	—	—	—	3.00	5.00

Y# 608 2 ZLOTE
8.1500 g., Brass, 27 mm. **Subject:** 500th Anniversary Birth of Nikolaja Reja **Obv:** National arms **Obv. Legend:** RZECZPOSPOLITA POLSKA **Rev:** Bust of Reja facing 3/4 right **Edge Lettering:** NBP eight times

Date	Mintage	F	VF	XF	Unc	BU
2005	850,000	—	—	—	3.00	5.00

Y# 614 2 ZLOTE
8.1500 g., Brass, 27 mm. **Obv:** National arms on outlined map **Obv. Legend:** RZECZPOSPOLITA POLSKA **Rev:** Region arms **Rev. Legend:** WOJEWÓDZTWO WARMINSKO - MAZURSKIE **Edge Lettering:** * NBP * eight times

Date	Mintage	F	VF	XF	Unc	BU
2005MW	900,000	—	—	—	3.00	5.00

Y# 753 2 ZLOTE
8.1500 g., Brass, 27 mm. **Subject:** Cizsyn **Rev:** Round tower

Date	Mintage	F	VF	XF	Unc	BU
2005MW	—	—	—	—	3.00	5.00

Y# 532 2 ZLOTE
8.1500 g., Brass, 27 mm. **Obv:** National arms **Rev:** St. John's Night dancer **Edge Lettering:** * NBP * eight times

Date	Mintage	F	VF	XF	Unc	BU
2006MW	1,000,000	—	—	—	2.50	4.00

Y# 534 2 ZLOTE
8.1500 g., Brass, 27 mm. **Obv:** National arms **Rev:** Alpine Marmot standing **Edge Lettering:** * NBP * eight times

Date	Mintage	F	VF	XF	Unc	BU
2006MW	1,400,000	—	—	—	3.00	6.00

Y# 543 2 ZLOTE

8.1500 g., Brass, 27 mm. **Obv:** Polish Eagle above castle gate **Rev:** Bochnia church **Edge Lettering:** * NBP * eight times

Date	Mintage	F	VF	XF	Unc	BU
2006MW	1,100,000	—	—	—	3.00	5.00

Y# 544 2 ZLOTE

8.1500 g., Brass, 27 mm. **Obv:** Polish Eagle above castle gate **Rev:** Chelm church **Edge Lettering:** * NBP * eight times

Date	Mintage	F	VF	XF	Unc	BU
2006MW	1,100,000	—	—	—	3.00	5.00

Y# 545 2 ZLOTE

8.1500 g., Brass, 27 mm. **Obv:** Polish Eagle above castle gate **Rev:** Chelmno Palace **Edge Lettering:** * NBP * eight times

Date	Mintage	F	VF	XF	Unc	BU
2006MW	1,100,000	—	—	—	3.00	5.00

Y# 546 2 ZLOTE

8.1500 g., Brass, 27 mm. **Obv:** Polish Eagle above castle gate **Rev:** Elblag tower **Edge Lettering:** * NBP * eight times

Date	Mintage	F	VF	XF	Unc	BU
2006MW	1,100,000	—	—	—	3.00	5.00

Y# 547 2 ZLOTE

8.1500 g., Brass, 27 mm. **Obv:** Polish Eagle above castle gate **Rev:** Castle **Rev. Legend:** KOSCIOL W. HACZOWIE **Edge Lettering:** * NBP * eight times

Date	Mintage	F	VF	XF	Unc	BU
2006MW	1,000,000	—	—	—	3.00	5.00

Y# 548 2 ZLOTE

8.1500 g., Brass, 27 mm. **Obv:** National arms above gateway **Rev:** Legnica tower and building **Edge Lettering:** * NBP * eight times

Date	Mintage	F	VF	XF	Unc	BU
2006MW	1,100,000	—	—	—	3.00	5.00

Y# 549 2 ZLOTE

8.1500 g., Brass, 27 mm. **Obv:** Polish Eagle above castle gate **Rev:** Pszczyna palace **Edge Lettering:** * NBP * eight times

Date	Mintage	F	VF	XF	Unc	BU
2006MW	1,100,000	—	—	—	3.00	5.00

Y# 550 2 ZLOTE

8.1500 g., Brass, 27 mm. **Obv:** Polish Eagle above castle gate **Rev:** Sandomierz palace **Edge Lettering:** * NBP * eight times

Date	Mintage	F	VF	XF	Unc	BU
2006MW	1,100,000	—	—	—	3.00	5.00

Y# 566 2 ZLOTE

8.1500 g., Brass, 27 mm. **Obv:** National arms **Rev:** City of Jaroslaw **Edge Lettering:** * NBP * eight times

Date	Mintage	F	VF	XF	Unc	BU
2006MW	1,200,000	—	—	—	3.00	5.00

Y# 569 2 ZLOTE

8.1500 g., Brass, 27 mm. **Obv:** National arms **Rev:** Castle Zagan **Edge Lettering:** * NBP * eight times

Date	Mintage	F	VF	XF	Unc	BU
2006MW	1,100,000	—	—	—	3.00	5.00

Y# 570 2 ZLOTE

815.0000 g., Brass, 27 mm. **Obv:** National arms above gateway **Rev:** City of Nysa **Edge Lettering:** * NBP * eight times

Date	Mintage	F	VF	XF	Unc	BU
2006MW	1,100,000	—	—	—	5.00	3.00

Y# 571 2 ZLOTE

8.1500 g., Brass, 27 mm. **Subject:** 30th Anniversary of June 1976 **Obv:** National arms **Edge Lettering:** * NBP * eight times

Date	Mintage	F	VF	XF	Unc	BU
2006MW	1,000,000	—	—	—	3.00	5.00

Y# 573 2 ZLOTE

8.1500 g., Brass, 27 mm. **Obv:** Polish eagle above wall **Rev:** Nowy Sacz church **Edge Lettering:** * NBP * eight times

Date	Mintage	F	VF	XF	Unc	BU
2006MW	1,100,000	—	—	—	3.00	5.00

Y# 574 2 ZLOTE

8.1500 g., Brass, 27 mm. **Subject:** 500th Anniversary of the Publication of the Statute by Laski **Obv:** National arms above value **Rev:** Jan Laski and book **Edge Lettering:** * NBP * eight times

Date	Mintage	F	VF	XF	Unc	BU
2006MW	1,000,000	—	—	—	3.00	5.00

Y# 575 2 ZLOTE

8.1500 g., Brass, 27 mm. **Subject:** Aleksander Gierymski (painter) **Obv:** Palette, brushes at left, national arms at right **Obv. Legend:** RZECZPOSPOLITA POLSKA **Rev:** Bust of Gierymski facing at left, coastline village in background **Edge Lettering:** * NBP * eight times

Date	Mintage	F	VF	XF	Unc	BU
2006MW	1,000,000	—	—	—	3.00	5.00

Y# 576 2 ZLOTE

8.1500 g., Brass, 27 mm. **Obv:** National arms **Rev:** Knight on horseback **Edge Lettering:** * NBP * eight times

Date	Mintage	F	VF	XF	Unc	BU
2006MW	1,000,000	—	—	—	3.00	5.00

Y# 580 2 ZLOTE

8.1500 g., Brass, 27 mm. **Obv:** Polish eagle above wall **Rev:** Kalisz building **Edge Lettering:** * NBP * eight times

Date	Mintage	F	VF	XF	Unc	BU
2006MW	1,100,000	—	—	—	3.00	5.00

Y# 582 2 ZLOTE

8.1500 g., Brass, 27 mm. **Obv:** National arms **Obv. Legend:** RZECZPOSPOLITA POLSKA **Rev:** Queen's head left as on KM-20, coin design from 1932 **Edge Lettering:** * NBP * eight times

Date	Mintage	F	VF	XF	Unc	BU
2006MW	1,000,000	—	—	—	3.00	5.00

Y# 605 2 ZLOTE
8.1500 g., Brass, 27 mm. **Obv:** National arms **Obv. Legend:** RZECZPOSPOLITA POLSKA **Rev:** Skier and marksman standing **Rev. Legend:** XX ZIMOWE IGAZYSKA OLIMPIJSKIE - TURYN **Edge Lettering:** * NBP * eight times

Date	Mintage	F	VF	XF	Unc	BU
2006MW	1,200,000	—	—	—	3.00	5.00

Y# 606 2 ZLOTE
8.1500 g., Brass, 27 mm. **Obv:** National arms **Obv. Legend:** RZECZPOSPOLITA POLSKA **Rev:** Large soccer ball with fancy linked date 2006 **Rev. Legend:** MISTRZOSTWA SWIATA W PItCE NOZNEJ NIEMCY - FIFA **Edge Lettering:** * NBP * eight times

Date	Mintage	F	VF	XF	Unc	BU
2006MW	1,200,000	—	—	—	3.00	5.00

Y# 609 2 ZLOTE
8.1500 g., Brass, 27 mm. **Subject:** 100th Anniversary - Warsaw School of Economics **Obv:** National arms **Obv. Legend:** RZECZPOSPOLITA POLSKA **Rev:** School facade **Rev. Legend:** SZKOLA CLOWNA HANDLOWA W WARSZAWIE **Rev. Inscription:** Large SGH **Edge Lettering:** * NBP * eight times

Date	Mintage	F	VF	XF	Unc	BU
2006MW	1,000,000	—	—	—	3.00	5.00

Y# 577 2 ZLOTE
8.1500 g., Brass, 27 mm. **Obv:** Crowned eagle **Rev:** Kwidzyn Castle **Edge Lettering:** * NBP * eight times

Date	Mintage	F	VF	XF	Unc	BU
2007MW	1,000,000	—	—	—	3.00	5.00

Y# 578 2 ZLOTE
8.1500 g., Brass, 27 mm. **Obv:** Crowned eagle **Rev:** Grey Seal and silhouette **Edge Lettering:** * NBP * eight times

Date	Mintage	F	VF	XF	Unc	BU
2007MW	1,000,000	—	—	—	4.00	7.00

Y# 586 2 ZLOTE
8.1500 g., Brass, 27 mm. **Subject:** 75th Anniversary Breaking the Enigma Code **Obv:** National arms **Obv. Legend:** RZECZPOSPOLITA POLSKA **Rev:** Enigma machine wheel **Edge Lettering:** * NBP * eight times

Date	Mintage	F	VF	XF	Unc	BU
2007MW	900,000	—	—	—	3.00	5.00

Y# 590 2 ZLOTE
8.1500 g., Brass, 27 mm. **Obv:** National arms **Obv. Legend:** RZECZPOSPOLITA POLSKA **Rev:** Bust of Domeyko facing **Rev. Legend:** IGNACY DOMEYKO 1802 - 1889 **Edge Lettering:** * NBP * eight times

Date	Mintage	F	VF	XF	Unc	BU
2007MW	900,000	—	—	—	3.00	5.00

Y# 592 2 ZLOTE
8.1500 g., Brass, 27 mm. **Subject:** History of Zloty **Obv:** Nike at left, obverse of 5 Zlotych, Y#18, national arms below **Obv. Legend:** RZECZPOLPOLITA POLSKA **Rev:** Spray at left of reverse of 5 Zlotych, Y# 18 **Edge Lettering:** * NBP * eight times

Date	Mintage	F	VF	XF	Unc	BU
2007MW	900,000	—	—	—	3.00	5.00

Y# 594 2 ZLOTE
8.1500 g., Brass, 27 mm. **Subject:** 750th Anniversary Municipality of Krakau **Obv:** National arms **Obv. Legend:** RZECZPOSPOLITA POLSKA **Rev:** Knight standing facing with spear and shield **Edge Lettering:** * NBP * eight times

Date	Mintage	F	VF	XF	Unc	BU
2007MW	900,000	—	—	—	3.00	5.00

Y# 591 2 ZLOTE
8.0300 g., Brass, 26.77 mm. **Subject:** 100th Anniversary Death of Konrad Korzeniowski **Obv:** National arms **Obv. Legend:** RZECZPOSPOLITA POLSKA **Rev:** Head of Korzeniowski facing slightly right at left, open book at lower center, sailing ship at right **Edge Lettering:** NBP repeated

Date	Mintage	F	VF	XF	Unc	BU
2007	—	—	—	—	3.00	4.00

Y# 610 2 ZLOTE
8.1500 g., Brass, 27 mm. **Subject:** Artic Explorers Antoni B. Dombrowolski and Henryk Arctowski **Obv:** National arms **Obv. Legend:** RZCEZPOSPOLITA POLSKA **Rev:** Explorer's bust facing at bottom, sailing ship in background **Edge Lettering:** * NBP * eight times

Date	Mintage	F	VF	XF	Unc	BU
2007MW	900,000	—	—	—	3.00	5.00

Y# 611 2 ZLOTE
8.1500 g., Brass, 27 mm. **Obv:** National arms **Obv. Legend:** RZECZPOSPOLITA POLSKA **Rev:** Ciezkozbrojny in armor, horseback left **Rev. Legend:** RYCERZ CIEZKOZBROJNY-XV **Edge Lettering:** * NBP * eight times

Date	Mintage	F	VF	XF	Unc	BU
2007MW	900,000	—	—	—	3.00	5.00

Y# 612 2 ZLOTE
8.1500 g., Brass, 27 mm. **Subject:** 70th Anniversary Death of Szymanowski **Obv:** National arms **Obv. Legend:** RZECZPOSPOLITA POLSKA **Rev:** Bust facing 3/4 right at left, music score in background **Rev. Legend:** ROCZNICA URODZIN KAROLA SYMANOWSKIEGO **Edge Lettering:** * NBP * eight times

Date	Mintage	F	VF	XF	Unc	BU
2007MW	900,000	—	—	—	3.00	5.00

Y# 613 2 ZLOTE
8.1500 g., Brass, 27 mm. **Obv:** National arms above gateway **Obv. Legend:** RZECZPOSPOLITA POLSKA **Rev:** Buildings **Rev. Legend:** STARGARD - SZCZECINSKI **Edge Lettering:** * NBP * eight times

Date	Mintage	F	VF	XF	Unc	BU
2007MW	1,000,000	—	—	—	3.00	5.00

Y# 615 2 ZLOTE
8.1500 g., Brass, 27 mm. **Obv:** National arms above gateway **Obv. Legend:** RZECZPOSPOLITA POLSKA **Rev:** Building with branches at left and right **Rev. Legend:** BRZEG **Edge Lettering:** * NBP * eight times

Date	Mintage	F	VF	XF	Unc	BU
2007MW	1,000,000	—	—	—	3.00	5.00

Y# 616 2 ZLOTE

8.1500 g., Brass, 27 mm. **Obv:** National arms above gateway **Obv. Legend:** RZECZPOSPOLITA POLSKA **Rev:** Church **Rev. Legend:** LOMZA **Edge Lettering:** * NBP alternating normal and inverted 4x

Date	Mintage	F	VF	XF	Unc	BU
2007MW	1,000,000	—	—	—	3.00	5.00

Y# 617 2 ZLOTE

8.1500 g., Brass, 27 mm. **Obv:** National arms above gateway **Obv. Legend:** RZECZPOSPOLITA POLSKA **Rev:** Church **Rev. Legend:** PLOCK **Edge Lettering:** * NBP * eight times

Date	Mintage	F	VF	XF	Unc	BU
2007MW	1,000,000	—	—	—	3.00	5.00

Y# 618 2 ZLOTE

8.1500 g., Brass, 27 mm. **Obv:** National arms above gateway **Obv. Legend:** RZECZPOSPOLITA POLSKA **Rev:** Church **Rev. Legend:** PRZEMYSL **Edge Lettering:** * NBP * eight times

Date	Mintage	F	VF	XF	Unc	BU
2007MW	1,000,000	—	—	—	3.00	5.00

Y# 619 2 ZLOTE

8.1500 g., Brass, 27 mm. **Obv:** National arms above gateway **Obv. Legend:** RZECZPOSPOLITA POLSKA **Rev:** Towered gateway **Rev. Legend:** RACIBÓRZ **Edge Lettering:** * NBP * eight times

Date	Mintage	F	VF	XF	Unc	BU
2007MW	1,000,000	—	—	—	3.00	5.00

Y# 620 2 ZLOTE

8.1500 g., Brass, 27 mm. **Obv:** National arms above gateway **Obv. Legend:** RZECZPOSPOLITA POLSKA **Rev:** Church **Rev. Legend:** SLUPSK **Edge Lettering:** NBP repeated

Date	Mintage	F	VF	XF	Unc	BU
2007MW	1,000,000	—	—	—	3.00	5.00

Y# 621 2 ZLOTE

8.1500 g., Brass, 27 mm. **Obv:** National arms above gateway **Obv. Legend:** RZECZPOSPOLITA POLSKA **Rev:** Church **Rev. Legend:** SWIDNICA **Edge Lettering:** * NBP * eight times

Date	Mintage	F	VF	XF	Unc	BU
2007MW	1,000,000	—	—	—	3.00	5.00

Y# 622 2 ZLOTE

8.1500 g., Brass, 27 mm. **Obv:** National arms **Obv. Legend:** RZECZPOSPOLITA POLSKE **Rev:** Town view **Rev. Legend:** MIASTO SREDNIOWIECZNE - W TORUNIU **Edge Lettering:** * NBP * eight times

Date	Mintage	F	VF	XF	Unc	BU
2007MW	900,000	—	—	—	3.00	5.00

Y# 623 2 ZLOTE

8.1500 g., Brass, 27 mm. **Obv:** National arms above gateway **Obv. Legend:** RZECZPOSPOLITA POLSKA **Rev:** Church **Rev. Legend:** GORZÓW WIELKOPOLSKI **Edge Lettering:** * NBP * eight times

Date	Mintage	F	VF	XF	Unc	BU
2007MW	1,000,000	—	—	—	3.00	5.00

Y# 624 2 ZLOTE

8.1500 g., Brass, 27 mm. **Obv:** National arms above gateway **Obv. Legend:** RZECZPOSPOLITA POLSKA **Rev:** Church at lower right, houses to left, fortress in upper background **Rev. Legend:** KLODZKO **Edge Lettering:** * NBP * eight times

Date	Mintage	F	VF	XF	Unc	BU
2007MW	1,000,000	—	—	—	3.00	5.00

Y# 625 2 ZLOTE

8.1500 g., Brass, 27 mm. **Obv:** National arms above gateway **Obv. Legend:** RZECZPOSPOLITA POLSKE **Rev:** Church **Rev. Legend:** TARNOW **Edge Lettering:** * NBP * eight times

Date	Mintage	F	VF	XF	Unc	BU
2007MW	1,000,000	—	—	—	3.00	5.00

Y# 626 2 ZLOTE

8.1500 g., Brass, 27 mm. **Subject:** Leon Wyczolkowski **Obv:** Artist's palette, brushes at left, national arms at right **Obv. Legend:** RZECZPOSPOLITA POLSKA **Rev:** Bust facing **Edge Lettering:** * NBP * eight times

Date	Mintage	F	VF	XF	Unc	BU
2007MW	900,000	—	—	—	3.00	5.00

Y# 627 2 ZLOTE

8.1500 g., Brass, 27 mm. **Obv:** National arms above flags **Obv. Legend:** RZECZPOSPOLITA POLSKA **Rev:** Peregrine Falcon perched on branch **Rev. Legend:** SOKOL WEDROWNY - Falco peregrinus **Edge Lettering:** * NBP * eight times

Date	Mintage	F	VF	XF	Unc	BU
2008MW	1,600,000	—	—	—	3.00	4.00

Y# 628 2 ZLOTE

8.1500 g., Brass, 27 mm. **Obv:** National arms above gateway **Obv. Legend:** RZECZPOSPOLITA POLSKA **Rev:** National arms ar upper left, Piotrków Tribunal building at lower right **Rev. Legend:** PIOTRKÓW - TRYBUNALSKI **Edge Lettering:** * NBP * eight times

Date	Mintage	F	VF	XF	Unc	BU
2008MW	1,100,000	—	—	0.90	2.25	3.00

Y# 629 2 ZLOTE

8.1500 g., Brass, 27 mm. **Subject:** 40th Anniversary "Rocznica" March **Obv:** National arms above value **Obv. Legend:** RZECZPOSPOLITA POLSKA **Rev:** University of Warsaw coat of arms above political protest marchers **Edge Lettering:** * NBP * eight times

Date	Mintage	F	VF	XF	Unc	BU
2008MW	1,400,000	—	—	0.90	2.25	3.00

Y# 630 2 ZLOTE

8.1500 g., Brass, 27 mm. **Obv:** National arms above gateway **Obv. Legend:** RZECZPOSPOLITA POLSKA **Rev:** Building **Rev. Legend:** LOWICZ **Edge Lettering:** * NBP * eight times

Date	Mintage	F	VF	XF	Unc	BU
2008MW	1,100,000	—	—	0.90	2.25	3.00

Y# 631 2 ZLOTE

8.1500 g., Brass, 27 mm. **Obv:** National arms above gateway **Obv. Legend:** RZECZPOSPOLITA POLSKA **Rev:** Monument **Rev. Legend:** KONIN **Edge Lettering:** * NBP * eight times

Date	Mintage	F	VF	XF	Unc	BU
2008MW	1,100,000	—	—	0.90	2.25	3.00

Y# 633 2 ZLOTE

8.1500 g., Brass, 27 mm. **Subject:** 65th Anniversary Warsaw Uprising **Obv:** National arms **Obv. Legend:** RZECZPOSPOLITA POLSKA **Rev:** Star of David in barbed wire, female freedom fighter at right. **Rev. Legend:** POWSTANIA W GETCIE WARSZAWSKIM 65. ROCZNICA **Edge Lettering:** * NBP * eight times

Date	Mintage	F	VF	XF	Unc	BU
2008MW	1,750,000	—	—	—	3.00	5.00

Y# 634 2 ZLOTE

8.1500 g., Brass, 27 mm. **Subject:** Zbigniew Herbert **Obv:** National arms **Obv. Legend:** RZECZPOSPOLITA POLSKA **Rev:** Head of Herbert right **Edge Lettering:** * NBP * eight times

Date	Mintage	F	VF	XF	Unc	BU
2008MW	1,510,000	—	—	—	3.00	4.00

Y# 638 2 ZLOTE

8.1500 g., Brass, 27 mm. **Subject:** Siberian Exiles **Obv:** National arms **Obv. Legend:** RZECZPOSPOLITA POLSKA **Rev:** Bleak forest **Rev. Inscription:** SYBIRACY **Edge Lettering:** * NBP * eight times

Date	Mintage	F	VF	XF	Unc	BU
2008MW	1,500,000	—	—	—	3.00	4.00

Y# 641 2 ZLOTE

8.1500 g., Brass, 27 mm. **Subject:** Kazimierz Dolny **Obv:** National arms **Obv. Legend:** RZECZPOSPOLITA POLSKA **Rev:** City view **Edge Lettering:** * NBP * eight times

Date	Mintage	F	VF	XF	Unc	BU
2008MW	1,380,000	—	—	—	3.00	4.00

Y# 644 2 ZLOTE

8.1500 g., Brass, 27 mm. **Subject:** 29th Olympic Games Beijing 2008 **Obv:** Eagle **Rev:** Two rowers in boat & a square **Edge Lettering:** * NBP * eight times

Date	Mintage	F	VF	XF	Unc	BU
2008	2,000,000	—	—	—	3.00	4.00

Y# 648 2 ZLOTE

8.1500 g., Brass, 27 mm. **Subject:** Polish Travellers & Explorers **Obv:** Eagle **Rev:** Bust of Bronislaw Pilsudski **Edge Lettering:** * NBP * eight times

Date	Mintage	F	VF	XF	Unc	BU
2008	1,100,000	—	—	—	3.00	4.00

Y# 650 2 ZLOTE

8.1500 g., Brass, 27 mm. **Subject:** 90th Anniversary of Regaining Freedom **Obv:** Eagle **Rev:** Order of Polonia Restituta **Edge Lettering:** * NBP * eight times

Date	Mintage	F	VF	XF	Unc	BU
2008	1,200,000	—	—	—	3.00	4.00

Y# 656 2 ZLOTE

8.1500 g., Brass, 27 mm. **Subject:** 450th Anniversary of the Polish Post **Obv:** Eagle **Rev:** Post rider on horse **Edge:** NBP

Date	Mintage	F	VF	XF	Unc	BU
2008	1,400,000	—	—	—	3.00	4.00

Y# 659 2 ZLOTE

8.1500 g., Brass, 27 mm. **Subject:** 400th Anniversary of Polish settlement in North America **Obv:** Eagle **Rev:** Man blowing glassware **Edge Lettering:** * NBP * eight times

Date	Mintage	F	VF	XF	Unc	BU
2008	1,200,000	—	—	—	3.00	4.00

Y# 662 2 ZLOTE

8.1500 g., Brass, 27 mm. **Subject:** 90th Anniversary of the Greater Poland Uprising **Obv:** Eagle **Rev:** Bust of Igancy Jan Paderewski, soldiers at bottom **Edge Lettering:** * NBP * eight times

Date	Mintage	F	VF	XF	Unc	BU
2008	1,100,000	—	—	—	3.00	4.00

Y# 663 2 ZLOTE

8.1500 g., Brass, 27 mm. **Subject:** Belsko - Biala **Obv:** National arms above gateway **Rev:** Building

Date	Mintage	F	VF	XF	Unc	BU
2008MW	—	—	—	—	3.00	4.00

Y# 670 2 ZLOTE

8.1500 g., Brass, 27 mm. **Subject:** Polish Cavalry **Obv:** National arms above value **Rev:** Hussar Knights, XVII Century

Date	Mintage	F	VF	XF	Unc	BU
2009MW	1,400,000	—	—	—	3.00	4.00

Y# 673 2 ZLOTE

8.1500 g., Brass, 27 mm. **Subject:** Supreme Chamber of Control, 90th Anniversary **Obv:** National arms above value **Rev:** Building

Date	Mintage	F	VF	XF	Unc	BU
2009MW	1,200,000	—	—	—	3.00	4.00

Y# 675 2 ZLOTE

8.1500 g., Brass, 27 mm. **Subject:** Central Banking, 180th Anniversary **Obv:** National arms above value **Rev:** Five coins

Date	Mintage	F	VF	XF	Unc	BU
2009MW	1,300,000	—	—	—	3.00	4.00

Y# 678 2 ZLOTE

8.1500 g., Brass, 27 mm. **Subject:** Green Lizards **Obv:** National arms above value **Rev:** Two green lizards on rocks (lacerta viridis) **Rev. Legend:** JASZCZURKA

Date	Mintage	F	VF	XF	Unc	BU
2009MW	1,700,000	—	—	—	3.00	4.00

Y# 680 2 ZLOTE

8.1500 g., Brass, 27 mm. **Subject:** General Elections of 1989 **Obv:** National arms above eagle **Rev:** Election notice within wreath

Date	Mintage	F	VF	XF	Unc	BU
2009MW	1,300,000	—	—	—	3.00	4.00

Y# 684 2 ZLOTE

8.1500 g., Brass, 27 mm. **Subject:** Czeslaw Niemen **Obv:** National arms above value **Rev:** Two dimensional facing portrait

Date	Mintage	F	VF	XF	Unc	BU
2009MW	1,400,000	—	—	—	3.00	4.00

Y# 687 2 ZLOTE

8.1500 g., Brass, 27 mm. **Subject:** Poets of the Warsaw uprising, 65th Anniversary **Obv:** National arms above eagle

Date	Mintage	F	VF	XF	Unc	BU
2009MW	1,400,000	—	—	—	3.00	4.00

Y# 690 2 ZLOTE

8.1500 g., Brass, 27 mm. **Subject:** First Cadre March **Obv:** National arms above value **Rev:** Military badge

Date	Mintage	F	VF	XF	Unc	BU
2009MW	1,000,000	—	—	—	3.00	4.00

Y# 692 2 ZLOTE

8.1500 g., Brass, 27 mm. **Subject:** Liquidation of Lodz Ghetto **Obv:** National arms above value **Rev:** Silhouette of Ghetto

Date	Mintage	F	VF	XF	Unc	BU
2009MW	1,000,000	—	—	—	3.00	4.00

Y# 694 2 ZLOTE

8.1500 g., Brass, 27 mm. **Subject:** Westerplatte **Obv:** National arms above value **Rev:** Three soldiers and map

Date	Mintage	F	VF	XF	Unc	BU
2009	1,400,000	—	—	—	3.00	4.00

Y# 697 2 ZLOTE

8.1500 g., Brass, 27 mm. **Subject:** Tatar Mountain Rescue **Obv:** National arms above value **Rev:** Mountain climber

Date	Mintage	F	VF	XF	Unc	BU
2009MW	1,400,000	—	—	—	3.00	4.00

Y# 700 2 ZLOTE

8.1500 g., Brass, 27 mm. **Subject:** Fr. Jerzy Popieluszko, 25th Anniversary of Murder **Obv:** National arms above value **Rev:** Portrait and candle memorial

Date	Mintage	F	VF	XF	Unc	BU
2009MW	1,500,000	—	—	—	3.00	4.00

Y# 703 2 ZLOTE

8.1500 g., Brass, 27 mm. **Subject:** Poles saving Jews **Obv:** National arms above value **Rev:** Broken brick wall

Date	Mintage	F	VF	XF	Unc	BU
2009MW	1,400,000	—	—	—	3.00	4.00

Y# 705 2 ZLOTE

8.1500 g., Brass, 27 mm. **Subject:** Wald Strzeminski **Obv:** Artist palette and National arms **Rev:** Portrait at left

Date	Mintage	F	VF	XF	Unc	BU
2009MW	1,300,000	—	—	—	3.00	4.00

Y# 707 2 ZLOTE

8.1500 g., Brass, 27 mm. **Subject:** Polish Underground **Obv:** National arms above value **Rev:** Monogram of resistance and map of Poland

Date	Mintage	F	VF	XF	Unc	BU
2009MW	1,000,000	—	—	—	3.00	4.00

Y# 709 2 ZLOTE

8.1500 g., Brass, 27 mm. **Subject:** Czestochowa **Rev:** Church

Date	Mintage	F	VF	XF	Unc	BU
2009MW	—	—	—	—	3.00	4.00

Y# 710 2 ZLOTE

8.1500 g., Brass, 27 mm. **Subject:** Jedrzejow Cistercian Monastery **Rev:** Church

Date	Mintage	F	VF	XF	Unc	BU
2009MW	—	—	—	—	3.00	4.00

Y# 711 2 ZLOTE

8.1500 g., Brass, 27 mm. **Subject:** Trzebnica **Rev:** Building

Date	Mintage	F	VF	XF	Unc	BU
2009MW	—	—	—	—	3.00	4.00

Y# 712 2 ZLOTE

8.1500 g., Brass, 27 mm. **Subject:** Liberation of Auschwitz **Obv:** National arms above value **Rev:** Three prisoners and camp gate sign

Date	Mintage	F	VF	XF	Unc	BU
2010MW	1,000,000	—	—	—	3.00	4.00

Y# 715 2 ZLOTE

8.1500 g., Brass, 27 mm. **Subject:** Vancouver Winter Olympics **Obv:** National arms above value **Rev:** Ski jump athlete

Date	Mintage	F	VF	XF	Unc	BU
2010MW	1,400,000	—	—	—	3.00	4.00

Y# 718 2 ZLOTE

8.1500 g., Brass, 27 mm. **Subject:** Imperial Guard **Obv:** National arms above value **Rev:** Napoleonic era mounted soldier

Date	Mintage	F	VF	XF	Unc	BU
2010MW	1,400,000	—	—	—	3.00	4.00

Y# 721 2 ZLOTE

8.1500 g., Brass, 27 mm. **Subject:** Katyn Crime **Obv:** National arms above value **Rev:** City name above cap

Date	Mintage	F	VF	XF	Unc	BU
2010MW	1,000,000	—	—	—	3.00	4.00

Y# 723 2 ZLOTE

8.1500 g., Brass, 27 mm. **Obv:** National arms above value **Rev:** Bat

Date	Mintage	F	VF	XF	Unc	BU
2010	—	—	—	—	3.00	4.00

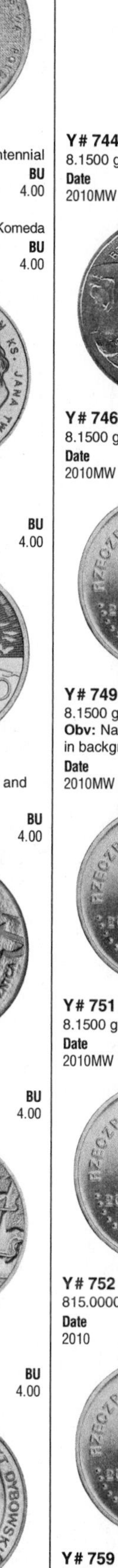

Y# 725 2 ZLOTE

8.1500 g., Brass, 27 mm. **Subject:** Polish Scouting Centennial

Date	Mintage	F	VF	XF	Unc	BU
2010MW	1,100,000	—	—	—	3.00	4.00

Y# 727 2 ZLOTE

8.1500 g., Brass, 27 mm. **Subject:** Popular Music - Krzyzt of Komeda

Date	Mintage	F	VF	XF	Unc	BU
2010MW	1,400,000	—	—	—	3.00	4.00

Y# 730 2 ZLOTE

8.1500 g., Brass, 27 mm. **Subject:** Jan Twardowski

Date	Mintage	F	VF	XF	Unc	BU
2010MW	1,000,000	—	—	—	3.00	4.00

Y# 732 2 ZLOTE

8.1500 g., Brass, 27 mm. **Subject:** Battles of Grunwald and Kluszyn

Date	Mintage	F	VF	XF	Unc	BU
2010MW	1,400,000	—	—	—	3.00	4.00

Y# 735 2 ZLOTE

8.1500 g., Brass **Subject:** Battle of Warsaw

Date	Mintage	F	VF	XF	Unc	BU
2010MW	1,200,000	—	—	—	3.00	4.00

Y# 737 2 ZLOTE

8.1500 g., Brass, 27 mm. **Subject:** August of 1980

Date	Mintage	F	VF	XF	Unc	BU
2010MW	1,400,000	—	—	—	3.00	4.00

Y# 742 2 ZLOTE

8.1500 g., Brass, 27 mm. **Subject:** Polish Explorers - Benedykt Dybowski

Date	Mintage	F	VF	XF	Unc	BU
2010MW Proof	1,200,000	—	—	—	3.00	4.00

Y# 744 2 ZLOTE

8.1500 g., Brass, 27 mm. **Subject:** Krzeszow

Date	Mintage	F	VF	XF	Unc	BU
2010MW	1,000,000	—	—	—	3.00	4.00

Y# 746 2 ZLOTE

8.1500 g., Brass, 27 mm. **Subject:** Arthur Grottger

Date	Mintage	F	VF	XF	Unc	BU
2010MW	1,300,000	—	—	—	3.00	4.00

Y# 749 2 ZLOTE

8.1500 g., Brass, 27 mm. **Subject:** Kalwaria Zebrzydowska **Obv:** National Arms above value **Rev:** Statue of Saint, Church in background

Date	Mintage	F	VF	XF	Unc	BU
2010MW	—	—	—	—	3.00	4.00

Y# 751 2 ZLOTE

8.1500 g., Brass, 27 mm. **Subject:** City of Warsaw

Date	Mintage	F	VF	XF	Unc	BU
2010MW	—	—	—	—	3.00	4.00

Y# 752 2 ZLOTE

815.0000 g., Brass, 27 mm. **Subject:** City of Trzemeszno

Date	Mintage	F	VF	XF	Unc	BU
2010	—	—	—	—	3.00	4.00

Y# 759 2 ZLOTE

8.1500 g., Brass, 27 mm. **Subject:** Gorlice **Obv:** National Arms above value **Rev:** City view

Date	Mintage	F	VF	XF	Unc	BU
2010	1,000,000	—	—	—	3.00	4.00

Y# 760 2 ZLOTE

8.1500 g., Brass, 27 mm. **Subject:** Miechow **Obv:** National Arms above value **Rev:** Building tower

Date	Mintage	F	VF	XF	Unc	BU
2010	1,000,000	—	—	—	3.00	4.00

Y# 761 2 ZLOTE

8.1500 g., Brass, 27 mm. **Subject:** Katowice **Obv:** National Arms above value **Rev:** Town factory view

Date	Mintage	F	VF	XF	Unc	BU
2010	1,000,000	—	—	—	3.00	4.00

Y# 762 2 ZLOTE

8.1500 g., Brass, 27 mm. **Subject:** Borsuk **Obv:** National Arms above value **Rev:** Eurasian Badgers

Date	Mintage	F	VF	XF	Unc	BU
2011	1,500,000	—	—	—	3.00	4.00

Y# 764 2 ZLOTE

8.1500 g., Brass, 27 mm. **Subject:** Zofia Stryjenska **Obv:** National arms, value and artist pallet with brushes **Rev:** Portrait facing

Date	Mintage	F	VF	XF	Unc	BU
2011	1,000,000	—	—	—	3.00	4.00

Y# 767 2 ZLOTE

8.1500 g., Brass, 27 mm. **Subject:** Independent Student's Union, 30th Anniversary

Date	Mintage	F	VF	XF	Unc	BU
2011MW	800,000	—	—	—	3.00	4.00

Y# 769 2 ZLOTE

8.1500 g., Brass, 27 mm. **Subject:** Smolensk plane crash

Date	Mintage	F	VF	XF	Unc	BU
2011MW	800,000	—	—	—	3.00	4.00

Y# 772 2 ZLOTE

8.1500 g., Brass, 27 mm. **Subject:** Beautification of Pope John Paul II **Obv:** Eagle **Rev:** Bust within rays

Date	Mintage	F	VF	XF	Unc	BU
2011MW	1,000,000	—	—	—	3.00	4.00

Y# 777 2 ZLOTE

8.1500 g., Brass, 27 mm. **Subject:** Poland's presidency of the Council of the European Union

Date	Mintage	F	VF	XF	Unc	BU
2011MW	800,000	—	—	—	3.00	4.00

Y# 780 2 ZLOTE

8.1500 g., Brass, 27 mm. **Subject:** History of the Polish Cavalry - Uhlan

Date	Mintage	F	VF	XF	Unc	BU
2011MW	1,000,000	—	—	—	3.00	4.00

Y# 783 2 ZLOTE

8.1500 g., Brass, 27 mm. **Subject:** Gdynia

Date	Mintage	F	VF	XF	Unc	BU
2011MW	800,000	—	—	—	3.00	4.00

Y# 784 2 ZLOTE

8.1500 g., Brass, 27 mm. **Subject:** Warsaw Pilgrimage to the Marian Shrine of Jasna Gora in Czestochowa, 300th Anniversary

Date	Mintage	F	VF	XF	Unc	BU
2011MW	800,000	—	—	—	3.00	4.00

Y# 785 2 ZLOTE

8.1500 g., Brass, 27 mm. **Subject:** Czeslaw Milosz

Date	Mintage	F	VF	XF	Unc	BU
2011MW	800,000	—	—	—	3.00	4.00

Y# 788 2 ZLOTE

8.1500 g., Brass, 27 mm. **Subject:** Mlawa

Date	Mintage	F	VF	XF	Unc	BU
2011MW	800,000	—	—	—	3.00	4.00

Y# 789 2 ZLOTE

8.1500 g., Brass, 27 mm. **Subject:** Ignacy Jan Paderewski

Date	Mintage	F	VF	XF	Unc	BU
2011MW	800,000	—	—	—	3.00	4.00

Y# 792 2 ZLOTE

8.1500 g., Brass, 27 mm. **Subject:** Silesian Uprising

Date	Mintage	F	VF	XF	Unc	BU
2011MW	800,000	—	—	—	3.00	4.00

Y# 794 2 ZLOTE

8.1500 g., Brass, 27 mm. **Subject:** Poznan

Date	Mintage	F	VF	XF	Unc	BU
2011MW	800,000	—	—	—	3.00	4.00

Y# 795 2 ZLOTE

8.1500 g., Brass, 27 mm. **Subject:** Society for the Protection of the Blind, 100th Anniversary

Date	Mintage	F	VF	XF	Unc	BU
2011MW	800,000	—	—	—	3.00	4.00

Y# 797 2 ZLOTE

8.1500 g., Brass, 27 mm. **Subject:** Ferdynand Ossendowski

Date	Mintage	F	VF	XF	Unc	BU
2011MW	900,000	—	—	—	3.00	4.00

Y# 799 2 ZLOTE

8.1500 g., Brass, 27 mm. **Subject:** Polonia Warszawa football club

Date	Mintage	F	VF	XF	Unc	BU
2011MW	800,000	—	—	—	3.00	4.00

Y# 801 2 ZLOTE

8.1500 g., Brass, 27 mm. **Subject:** Jeremi Przybora and Jerzy Wasowski

Date	Mintage	F	VF	XF	Unc	BU
2011MW	800,000	—	—	—	3.00	4.00

Y# 804 2 ZLOTE

8.1500 g., Brass, 27 mm. **Subject:** Lodz **Rev:** Building and architectural detail

Date	Mintage	F	VF	XF	Unc	BU
2011MW	—	—	—	—	3.00	4.00

Y# 805 2 ZLOTE

8.1500 g., Brass, 27 mm. **Subject:** Krakow **Rev:** Church along riverfront

Date	Mintage	F	VF	XF	Unc	BU
2011MW Proof	—	—	—	—	3.00	4.00

Y# 806 2 ZLOTE

8.1500 g., Brass, 27 mm. **Subject:** Kalisz **Rev:** Chruch

Date	Mintage	F	VF	XF	Unc	BU
2011MW	—	—	—	—	3.00	4.00

Y# 809 2 ZLOTE

8.1500 g., Brass, 27 mm. **Subject:** Christmas Charity Orchestra, 20th Anniversary **Rev:** Guitar with love hearts

Date	Mintage	F	VF	XF	Unc	BU
2012MW	—	—	—	—	3.00	4.00

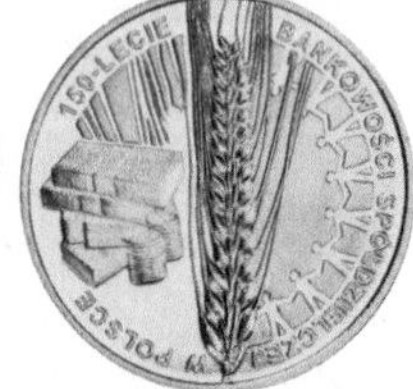

Y# 811 2 ZLOTE

8.1500 g., Brass, 27 mm. **Subject:** Cooperative banking in Poland, 150th Anniversary **Rev:** Stack of money and coins, wheat ear in center

Date	Mintage	F	VF	XF	Unc	BU
2012MW	—	—	—	—	3.00	4.00

Y# 813 2 ZLOTE

8.1500 g., Brass, 27 mm. **Subject:** Ulma, Baranek and Kowalski families **Rev:** Mother holding child

Date	Mintage	F	VF	XF	Unc	BU
2012MW	—	—	—	—	3.00	4.00

Y# 816 2 ZLOTE

8.1500 g., Brass, 27 mm. **Subject:** Polish Radio, 50th Anniversary

Date	Mintage	F	VF	XF	Unc	BU
2012MW	800,000	—	—	—	3.00	4.00

Y# 817 2 ZLOTE

8.1500 g., Brass, 27 mm. **Subject:** Stefan Banach

Date	Mintage	F	VF	XF	Unc	BU
2012MW	800,000	—	—	—	3.00	4.00

Y# 820 2 ZLOTE

8.1500 g., Brass, 27 mm. **Subject:** Blyskawica, destroyer

Date	Mintage	F	VF	XF	Unc	BU
2012MW	800,000	—	—	—	3.00	4.00

Y# 821 2 ZLOTE

8.1500 g., Brass, 27 mm. **Subject:** National Museum in Warsaw, 150th Anniversary

Date	Mintage	F	VF	XF	Unc	BU
2012	800,000	—	—	—	3.00	4.00

Y# 823 2 ZLOTE

8.1500 g., Brass, 27 mm. **Subject:** European Football Championships

Date	Mintage	F	VF	XF	Unc	BU
2012MW	1,000,000	—	—	—	3.00	4.00

Y# 832 2 ZLOTE

8.1500 g., Brass, 27 mm. **Subject:** London Olympics, 2012; Polish Team

Date	Mintage	F	VF	XF	Unc	BU
2012MW	1,000,000	—	—	—	3.00	4.00

Y# 835 2 ZLOTE

8.1500 g., Brass **Subject:** Krzemionki Opatowskie **Shape:** 27

Date	Mintage	F	VF	XF	Unc	BU
2012MW	800,000	—	—	—	3.00	4.00

Y# 837 2 ZLOTE

8.1500 g., Brass, 27 mm. **Subject:** Orzel, submarine

Date	Mintage	F	VF	XF	Unc	BU
2012MW	800,000	—	—	—	3.00	4.00

Y# 838 2 ZLOTE

8.1500 g., Brass, 27 mm. **Subject:** Boleslaw Prus

Date	Mintage	F	VF	XF	Unc	BU
2012MW	8,000,000	—	—	—	3.00	4.00

Y# 841 2 ZLOTE

8.1500 g., Brass, 27 mm. **Subject:** Dragon, light cruiser

Date	Mintage	F	VF	XF	Unc	BU
2012MW	800,000	—	—	—	3.00	4.00

Y# 842 2 ZLOTE

8.1500 g., Brass, 27 mm. **Subject:** Piotr Michalowski, painter

Date	Mintage	F	VF	XF	Unc	BU
2012MW	800,000	—	—	—	3.00	4.00

Y# 284 5 ZLOTYCH

6.5400 g., Bi-Metallic Aluminum-Bronze center in Copper-Nickel ring, 24 mm. **Obv:** National arms within circle **Obv. Legend:** RZECZPOSPOLITA POLSKA **Rev:** Value within circle flanked by oak leaves

Date	Mintage	F	VF	XF	Unc	BU
2008MW	—	—	—	—	7.00	8.00

Date	Mintage	F	VF	XF	Unc	BU
2009MW	—	—	—	—	7.00	8.00
2010MW	—	—	—	—	7.00	8.00

Y# 800 5 ZLOTYCH

7.0700 g., 0.9250 Silver 0.2102 oz. ASW, 24 mm. **Subject:** Polonia Warszawa football club

Date	Mintage	F	VF	XF	Unc	BU
2011MW Proof	50,000	Value: 30.00				

Y# 406 10 ZLOTYCH

14.1400 g., 0.9250 Silver 0.4205 oz. ASW **Subject:** Year 2001 **Obv:** Crowned eagle with wings open **Rev:** Printed circuit board

Date	Mintage	F	VF	XF	Unc	BU
2001MW Proof	35,000	Value: 75.00				

Y# 413 10 ZLOTYCH

14.1400 g., 0.9250 Silver 0.4205 oz. ASW, 32 mm. **Subject:** 15 Years of the Constitutional Court **Obv:** Crowned eagle suspended from a judge's neck chain **Rev:** Crowned eagle head and balance scale **Edge Lettering:** TRYBUNAL KONSTYTUCYJNY W SLUZBIE PANSTWA PRAWA

Date	Mintage	F	VF	XF	Unc	BU
2001MW Proof	25,000	Value: 65.00				

Y# 419 10 ZLOTYCH

14.1400 g., 0.9250 Silver 0.4205 oz. ASW, 32 mm. **Subject:** Cardinal Stefan Wyszynski **Obv:** Crowned eagle with wings open above ribbon **Rev:** Half length figure facing with raised hands **Edge Lettering:** 100 • ROCZNIA URODZIN

Date	Mintage	F	VF	XF	Unc	BU
2001MW Proof	60,000	Value: 30.00				

Y# 425 10 ZLOTYCH

14.2100 g., 0.9250 Silver 0.4226 oz. ASW, 32 mm. **Subject:** Jan III Sobieski **Obv:** Crowned eagle with wings open **Rev:** 3/4 armored bust facing with army in background **Edge:** Plain

Date	Mintage	F	VF	XF	Unc	BU
2001MW Proof	24,000	Value: 120				

Y# 458 10 ZLOTYCH

14.1400 g., 0.9250 Silver 0.4205 oz. ASW, 32 mm. **Obv:** Crowned eagle with wings open **Rev:** Jan Sobieski, half-length figure in armor standing **Edge:** Plain

Date	Mintage	F	VF	XF	Unc	BU
2001MW Proof	17,000	Value: 175				

Y# 459 10 ZLOTYCH

14.1400 g., 0.9250 Silver 0.4205 oz. ASW, 32 mm. **Obv:** Three violins **Rev:** Henryk Wieniawski **Edge:** Plain

Date	Mintage	F	VF	XF	Unc	BU
2001MW Proof	28,000	Value: 60.00				

Y# 460 10 ZLOTYCH

14.1400 g., 0.9250 Silver 0.4205 oz. ASW, 32 mm. **Obv:** Crowned eagle with wings open above fish **Rev:** Michal Siedlecki **Edge:** Plain

Date	Mintage	F	VF	XF	Unc	BU
2001MW Proof	26,000	Value: 60.00				

Y# 432 10 ZLOTYCH

14.1400 g., 0.9250 Silver 0.4205 oz. ASW, 32 mm. **Subject:** Bronislaw Malinowski **Obv:** Small crowned eagle with wings open to right of bust facing **Rev:** Trobriand Islands village scene **Edge Lettering:** etnolog, antropolog kultury

Date	Mintage	F	VF	XF	Unc	BU
2002MW Proof	33,500	Value: 35.00				

Y# 434 10 ZLOTYCH

14.1400 g., 0.9250 Silver 0.4205 oz. ASW, 32 mm. **Subject:** World Cup Soccer **Obv:** Crowned eagle with wings open **Rev:** Soccer player **Edge Lettering:** etnolog, antropolog kultury

Date	Mintage	F	VF	XF	Unc	BU
2002MW Proof	55,000	Value: 27.50				

Y# 435 10 ZLOTYCH

14.1400 g., 0.9250 Silver 0.4205 oz. ASW, 32 mm. **Subject:** World Cup Soccer **Obv:** Amber soccer ball inset entering goal net **Rev:** Two soccer players with amber soccer ball inset **Edge Lettering:** etnolog, antropolog kultury

Date	Mintage	F	VF	XF	Unc	BU
2002MW Proof	65,000	Value: 75.00				

Y# 437 10 ZLOTYCH

14.1400 g., 0.9250 Silver 0.4205 oz. ASW, 32 mm. **Subject:** Pope John Paul II **Obv:** Crowned eagle with wings open within two views of praying Pope **Rev:** Pope facing radiant Holy Door **Edge:** Plain

Date	Mintage	F	VF	XF	Unc	BU
2002MW Proof	80,000	Value: 45.00				

Y# 441 10 ZLOTYCH

14.2000 g., 0.9250 Silver 0.4223 oz. ASW, 32 mm. **Subject:** Gen. Wladyslaw Anders **Obv:** Crowned eagle with wings open, cross and multicolor flowers **Rev:** Uniformed bust right **Edge:** Plain

Date	Mintage	F	VF	XF	Unc	BU
2002MW Proof	40,000	Value: 120				

Y# 450 10 ZLOTYCH

14.1400 g., 0.9250 Silver 0.4205 oz. ASW, 32 mm. **Subject:** August II (1697-1706, 1709-1735) **Obv:** Crowned eagle with wings open **Rev:** Portrait and Order of the White Eagle **Edge:** Plain

Date	Mintage	F	VF	XF	Unc	BU
2002MW Proof	30,000	Value: 90.00				

Y# 453 10 ZLOTYCH

14.1400 g., 0.9250 Silver 0.4205 oz. ASW, 32 mm. **Subject:** Great Orchestra of Christmas Charity **Obv:** Large inscribed heart above crowned eagle with wings open **Rev:** Boy playing flute **Edge:** Plain

Date	Mintage	F	VF	XF	Unc	BU
2003MW Proof	47,000	Value: 45.00				

Y# 468 10 ZLOTYCH

14.1400 g., 0.9250 Silver 0.4205 oz. ASW, 32 mm. **Obv:** Tanks on battlefield **Rev:** General Maczek **Edge:** Plain

Date	Mintage	F	VF	XF	Unc	BU
2003MW Proof	44,000	Value: 35.00				

Y# 469 10 ZLOTYCH

14.1400 g., 0.9250 Silver 0.4205 oz. ASW, 32 mm. **Subject:** Gas and Oil Industry **Obv:** Crowned eagle and highway leading to city view **Rev:** Portrait and refinery **Edge:** Plain

Date	Mintage	F	VF	XF	Unc	BU
2003MW Proof	43,000	Value: 35.00				

Y# 474 10 ZLOTYCH

14.1400 g., 0.9250 Silver 0.4205 oz. ASW, 32 mm. **Obv:** Crowned eagle with wings open **Rev:** Stanislaus I and wife's portrait **Edge:** Plain

Date	Mintage	F	VF	XF	Unc	BU
2003MW Proof	45,000	Value: 35.00				

Y# 475 10 ZLOTYCH

14.1400 g., 0.9250 Silver 0.4205 oz. ASW, 32 mm. **Obv:** Crowned eagle with wings open **Rev:** Half-length figure of Stanislaus I with his wife in background **Edge:** Plain

Date	Mintage	F	VF	XF	Unc	BU
2003MW Proof	40,000	Value: 45.00				

Y# 448 10 ZLOTYCH

14.1400 g., 0.9250 Silver 0.4205 oz. ASW, 32 mm. **Subject:** City of Poznan (Posen) **Obv:** Old coin design and arched door **Rev:** Old coin design and city view **Edge:** Plain

Date	Mintage	F	VF	XF	Unc	BU
2003MW Proof	39,000	Value: 75.00				

Y# 480 10 ZLOTYCH
14.1400 g., 0.9250 Silver 0.4205 oz. ASW, 32 mm. **Subject:** 80th Anniversary of the Modern Zloty Currency **Obv:** Man wearing glasses behind crowned eagle with wings open **Rev:** Bust left **Edge:** Plain

Date	Mintage	F	VF	XF	Unc	BU
2004MW Proof	55,000	Value: 35.00				

Y# 482 10 ZLOTYCH
14.1400 g., 0.9250 Silver 0.4205 oz. ASW, 32 mm. **Subject:** Poland Joining the European Union **Obv:** Crowned eagle in blue circle with yellow stars **Rev:** Multicolor European Union and Polish flags **Edge:** Plain

Date	Mintage	F	VF	XF	Unc	BU
2004MW Proof	78,000	Value: 65.00				

Y# 497 10 ZLOTYCH
14.1400 g., 0.9250 Silver 0.4205 oz. ASW, 32 mm. **Subject:** Warsaw Uprising 60th Anniversary **Obv:** Crowned eagle and value on resistance symbol **Rev:** Polish soldier wearing captured German helmet **Edge:** Plain

Date	Mintage	F	VF	XF	Unc	BU
2004MW Proof	92,000	Value: 30.00				

Y# 500 10 ZLOTYCH
14.1400 g., 0.9250 Silver 0.4205 oz. ASW, 32 mm. **Obv:** Polish paratrooper badge **Rev:** Gen. Sosabowski and descending paratrooper **Edge:** Plain

Date	Mintage	F	VF	XF	Unc	BU
2004MW Proof	56,000	Value: 30.00				

Y# 502 10 ZLOTYCH
14.1400 g., 0.9250 Silver 0.4205 oz. ASW, 32 mm. **Subject:** Polish Police 85th Anniversary **Obv:** Crowned eagle with wings open **Rev:** Seal partially overlapping police badge **Edge:** Plain

Date	Mintage	F	VF	XF	Unc	BU
2004MW Proof	65,000	Value: 30.00				

Y# 506 10 ZLOTYCH
14.1400 g., 0.9250 Silver 0.4205 oz. ASW, 32 mm. **Obv:** Siberian landscape above crowned eagle and value **Rev:** Aleksander Czekanowski (1833-1876) **Edge:** Plain

Date	Mintage	F	VF	XF	Unc	BU
2004MW Proof	45,000	Value: 30.00				

Y# 510 10 ZLOTYCH
14.1400 g., 0.9250 Silver 0.4205 oz. ASW, 32 mm. **Subject:** Warsaw Fine Arts Academy Centennial **Obv:** Crowned eagle with wings open within city square **Rev:** Art studio, color painting on stand **Edge:** Plain

Date	Mintage	F	VF	XF	Unc	BU
2004MW Antique patina	75,000	Value: 30.00				

Y# 517 10 ZLOTYCH
14.1400 g., 0.9250 Silver 0.4205 oz. ASW, 32 mm. **Subject:** Olympics **Obv:** Crowned eagle with wings open and woman **Rev:** Fencers in front of Parthenon **Edge:** Plain

Date	Mintage	F	VF	XF	Unc	BU
2004MW Proof	70,000	Value: 30.00				

Y# 518 10 ZLOTYCH
14.1400 g., 0.9250 Silver 0.4205 oz. ASW, 32 mm. **Subject:** Olympics **Obv:** Crowned eagle with wings open within gold plated center **Rev:** Ancient athlete within gold plated circle **Edge:** Plain

Date	Mintage	F	VF	XF	Unc	BU
2004MW Proof	90,000	Value: 35.00				

Y# 523 10 ZLOTYCH
14.2300 g., 0.9250 Silver 0.4232 oz. ASW, 43.2 x 29.2 mm. **Subject:** Japan's Aichi Expo **Obv:** Monument **Rev:** Two cranes **Edge:** Plain **Shape:** Quarter of circle

Date	Mintage	F	VF	XF	Unc	BU
2005MW Proof	80,000	Value: 45.00				

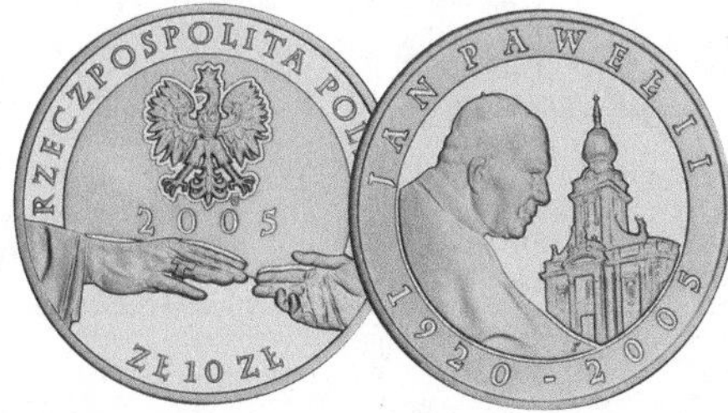

Y# 526 10 ZLOTYCH
14.1400 g., 0.9250 Silver partially gilt 0.4205 oz. ASW, 32.1 mm. **Obv:** Crowned eagle with wings open above date and grasping hands **Rev:** Gold plated bust right and church **Edge:** Plain

Date	Mintage	F	VF	XF	Unc	BU
2005MW Proof	—	Value: 30.00				

Y# 537 10 ZLOTYCH
14.1400 g., 0.9250 Silver 0.4205 oz. ASW, 32 mm. **Obv:** Horse drawn carriage **Rev:** Green duck at left and Konstanty Ildefons Galczynski in top hat at right **Edge:** Plain

Date	Mintage	F	VF	XF	Unc	BU
2005MW Proof	62,000	Value: 30.00				

Y# 539 10 ZLOTYCH
14.1400 g., 0.9250 Silver 0.4205 oz. ASW, 32 mm. **Obv:** Baptismal font and Polish eagle **Rev:** Pope John Paul II and St. Peter's Basilica **Edge:** Plain

Date	Mintage	F	VF	XF	Unc	BU
2005MW Proof	170,000	Value: 32.00				

Y# 552 10 ZLOTYCH
14.1400 g., 0.9250 Silver 0.4205 oz. ASW, 32 mm. **Obv:** Crowned eagle above value **Rev:** Stanislaw August Poniatowski and shadow **Edge:** Plain

Date	Mintage	F	VF	XF	Unc	BU
2005MW Proof	60,000	Value: 35.00				

Y# 553 10 ZLOTYCH
14.1400 g., 0.9250 Silver 0.4205 oz. ASW, 32 mm. **Obv:** Crowned eagle above value **Rev:** Stanislaw August Poniatowski and crowned monogram **Edge:** Plain

Date	Mintage	F	VF	XF	Unc	BU
2005MW Proof	60,000	Value: 35.00				

Y# 554 10 ZLOTYCH
14.1400 g., 0.9250 Silver 0.4205 oz. ASW, 32 mm. **Subject:** End of WWII 60th Anniversary **Obv:** Crowned eagle above soldier silhouettes and value **Rev:** City view in ruins above bird with green sprig **Edge:** Plain

Date	Mintage	F	VF	XF	Unc	BU
2005MW Proof	70,000	Value: 40.00				

Y# 568 10 ZLOTYCH

14.1400 g., 0.9250 Silver 0.4205 oz. ASW, 32 mm. **Obv:** Sail ship and obverse design of Y-31 **Rev:** Reverse design of Y-31 on radiant design **Edge:** Lettered

Date	Mintage	F	VF	XF	Unc	BU
2005MW Proof	61,000	Value: 35.00				

Y# 596 10 ZLOTYCH

14.1800 g., 0.9250 Silver 0.4217 oz. ASW, 32 mm. **Subject:** 500th Anniversary - Birth of M. Reja **Obv:** National arms in oval, value below **Obv. Legend:** RZECZPOSPOLITA POLSKA **Rev:** Bust of Reja 3/4 right **Rev. Legend:** 500. ROCZNICA URODZIN MIKOLAJA REJA **Edge:** Plain

Date	Mintage	F	VF	XF	Unc	BU
2005MW Proof	60,000	Value: 30.00				

Y# 556 10 ZLOTYCH

14.1400 g., 0.9250 Silver 0.4205 oz. ASW, 32 mm. **Subject:** 2006 Winter Olympics **Obv:** Small national arms at left, figure skating couple at center **Obv. Legend:** RZECZPOSPOLITA POLSKA **Rev:** Female figure skater **Rev. Legend:** XX ZIMOWE IGRZYSKA OLIMPIJSKIE **Edge:** Plain

Date	Mintage	F	VF	XF	Unc	BU
2006MW Proof	72,000	Value: 32.00				

Y# 599 10 ZLOTYCH

14.1800 g., 0.9250 Silver 0.4217 oz. ASW, 32 mm. **Series:** History of the Zloty **Obv:** National arms at upper left, 1932 dated 10 Zlotych obverse at lower right, building facade in background **Obv. Legend:** RZECZPOSPOLITA POLSKA **Rev:** Reverse of 1932 dated coin with head of Queen Jadwiga **Rev. Legend:** DZIEJE ZLOTEGO **Edge:** Plain

Date	Mintage	F	VF	XF	Unc	BU
2006MW Proof	61,000	Value: 40.00				

Y# 555 10 ZLOTYCH

14.1400 g., 0.9250 Silver 0.4205 oz. ASW, 32 mm. **Subject:** 2006 Winter Olympics **Obv:** Snow boarder above crowned eagle **Rev:** Snow boarder **Edge:** Plain

Date	Mintage	F	VF	XF	Unc	BU
2006MW Proof	71,400	Value: 30.00				

Y# 598 10 ZLOTYCH

14.1500 g., 0.9250 Silver 0.4208 oz. ASW, 32 mm. **Subject:** 30th Anniversary June 1976 **Obv:** National arms divides denomination, split railroad tracks below **Obv. Legend:** RZECZPOSPOLITA POLSKA **Rev:** 3/4 length woman standing with child, outlined row of shielded forces in background **Rev. Legend:** 30. ROCZNICA - CZERWCA 1976 **Edge:** Plain

Date	Mintage	F	VF	XF	Unc	BU
2006MW Proof	56,000	Value: 32.00				

Y# 754 10 ZLOTYCH

14.1400 g., Bi-Metallic, 32 mm. **Subject:** World Cup soccer **Obv:** Eagle within net **Rev:** Player kicking ball, sun

Date	Mintage	F	VF	XF	Unc	BU
2006 Proof	—	Value: 75.00				

Y# 600 10 ZLOTYCH

14.1000 g., 0.9250 Silver 0.4193 oz. ASW, 32 mm. **Subject:** 125th Anniversary - Birth of Szymanowskiego **Obv:** Piano keys at left, national arms on music score at right **Obv. Legend:** RZECZPOSPOLITA POLSKA **Rev:** Bust of Szymanowskiego 3/4 left, music composition at back of head and over upper body, dates as hologram at left **Rev. Legend:** 125. ROCZNICA URODZIN KAROLA SZYMANOWSKIEGO **Edge:** Plain

Date	Mintage	F	VF	XF	Unc	BU
2007MW Proof	55,000	Value: 35.00				

Y# 601 10 ZLOTYCH

14.3000 g., 0.9250 Silver 0.4253 oz. ASW, 14 mm. **Subject:** Arctic Explorers **Obv:** Sailing ship at center, national arms at right with denomination below **Obv. Legend:** RZECZPOSPOLITA POLSKA **Rev:** Busts of Henryk Arctowski and Antoni Dobrowolski facing, polar outline map at lower left **Edge:** Plain

Date	Mintage	F	VF	XF	Unc	BU
2007MW Proof	60,000	Value: 35.00				

Y# 602 10 ZLOTYCH

14.0500 g., 0.9250 Silver 0.4178 oz. ASW, 31.95 x 22.39 mm. **Obv:** Helmeted national arms, sword and denomination below **Obv. Legend:** RZECZPOSPOLITA - POLSKA **Rev:** Chivalrous knight on horseback jousting right **Rev. Inscription:** RYCERZ - CIEZKOZBROJNY **Edge:** Plain **Shape:** Rectangular

Date	Mintage	F	VF	XF	Unc	BU
2007MW Proof	57,000	Value: 45.00				

Y# 585 10 ZLOTYCH

14.1400 g., 0.9250 Silver 0.4205 oz. ASW, 32 mm. **Obv:** Mountains, Polish Eagle and value **Rev:** Ignacy Domeyko **Edge:** Plain

Date	Mintage	F	VF	XF	Unc	BU
2007MW Proof	55,000	Value: 32.00				

Y# 587 10 ZLOTYCH

14.1400 g., 0.9250 Silver 0.4205 oz. ASW, 32 mm. **Subject:** 75th Anniversary - Breaking the Enigma Code **Obv:** Polish Eagle on circuit board **Rev:** Segmented letters **Edge:** Lettered

Date	Mintage	F	VF	XF	Unc	BU
2007MW Proof	55,000	Value: 50.00				

Y# 589 10 ZLOTYCH

14.1400 g., 0.9250 Silver 0.4205 oz. ASW, 32 mm. **Obv:** Angel, Polish Eagle and obverse coin design of Y-18 **Rev:** Reverse coin design of Y-18 on wheat ears **Edge:** Plain

Date	Mintage	F	VF	XF	Unc	BU
2007MW Proof	57,000	Value: 40.00				

Y# 595 10 ZLOTYCH

14.1400 g., 0.9250 Silver 0.4205 oz. ASW, 32 mm. **Subject:** Munincipality of Krakow, 750th Anniversary **Obv:** City gate tower, national arms at lower right **Obv. Legend:** RZECZPOSPOLITA POLSKA **Rev:** Knight with shield standing facing

Date	Mintage	F	VF	XF	Unc	BU
2007MW Proof	58,000	Value: 50.00				

Y# 632 10 ZLOTYCH

14.1400 g., 0.9250 Silver 0.4205 oz. ASW, 32 mm. **Subject:** 40th Anniversary "Rocznica" March **Obv:** National arms at upper right, manuscript pages fluttering at left **Obv. Legend:** RZECZPOSPOLITA POLSKA **Rev:** Student protesters in front of gates of Warsaw University, military police in silhouette in foreground **Designer:** Andrzej Nowakowski

Date	Mintage	F	VF	XF	Unc	BU
2008MW Proof	118,000	Value: 50.00				

Y# 635 10 ZLOTYCH

14.1400 g., 0.9250 Silver 0.4205 oz. ASW, 32 mm. **Subject:** Zbigniew Herbert **Obv:** Bust of Herbert 3/4 right at left, national arms at lower right **Rev:** Statue of Nike **Edge:** Plain

Date	Mintage	F	VF	XF	Unc	BU
2008MW Proof	—	Value: 40.00				

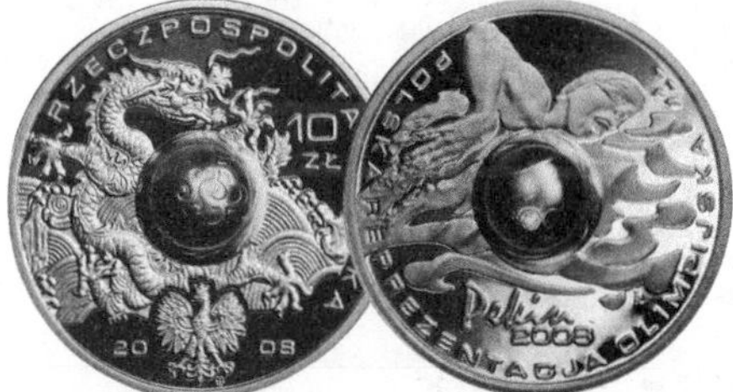

Y# 645 10 ZLOTYCH

14.4000 g., 0.9250 Silver with gilt center 0.4282 oz. ASW, 32 mm. **Subject:** The 29th Olympic Games Beijing 2008 **Obv:** Chinese ornament & dragon **Rev:** Swimmer **Designer:** Robert Kotowicz

Date	Mintage	F	VF	XF	Unc	BU
2008 Proof	140,000	Value: 50.00				

Y# 639 10 ZLOTYCH

14.1400 g., 0.9250 Silver 0.4205 oz. ASW, 32 mm. **Subject:** Siberian Exiles **Obv:** Small national arms at left, human outlines at right **Obv. Legend:** RZECZPOSPOLITA POLSKA **Rev:** Tree lines with imbedded triangular crystal below **Rev. Inscription:** SYBIRACY **Edge:** Plain **Designer:** Ewa Tyc-Karpinska

Date	Mintage	F	VF	XF	Unc	BU
2008MW Proof	135,000	Value: 35.00				

Y# 646 10 ZLOTYCH

14.1400 g., 0.9250 Silver 0.4205 oz. ASW, 32 mm. **Subject:** The 29th Olympic Games Beijing 2008 **Obv:** Square hole & an eagle **Rev:** Square hole & a windsurfer **Designer:** Urszula Walerzak

Date	Mintage	F	VF	XF	Unc	BU
2008 Proof	150,000	Value: 30.00				

Y# 649 10 ZLOTYCH

14.1400 g., 0.9250 Silver 0.4205 oz. ASW, 32 mm. **Subject:** Polish Travellers & Explorers **Obv:** Man & woman holding child **Rev:** Bust of Bronislaw Pilsudski

Date	Mintage	F	VF	XF	Unc	BU
2008 Proof	99,000	Value: 32.00				

Y# 655 10 ZLOTYCH

14.1400 g., 0.9250 Silver 0.4205 oz. ASW, 32 mm. **Subject:** 450th Anniversary of the Polish Post **Obv:** Eagle on top right, post stamp in center with man on horse **Rev:** Post courier **Designer:** Robert Kotowicz

Date	Mintage	F	VF	XF	Unc	BU
2008 Proof	135,000	Value: 35.00				

Y# 658 10 ZLOTYCH

14.1400 g., 0.9250 Silver 0.4205 oz. ASW, 32 mm. **Subject:** 400th Anniversary - Polish Settlement in North America **Obv:** Man blowing glassware left **Rev:** Man blowing glassware right **Designer:** Robert Kotowicz

Date	Mintage	F	VF	XF	Unc	BU
2008 Proof	126,000	Value: 35.00				

Y# 661 10 ZLOTYCH

14.1400 g., 0.9250 Silver 0.4205 oz. ASW, 32 mm. **Subject:** 90th Anniversary of the Greater Poland Uprising **Obv:** Eagle at top, Commander riding horse followed by soldiers **Rev:** Rose at left, Bust of Igancy Jan Paderewski at right **Designer:** Urszula Walerzak

Date	Mintage	F	VF	XF	Unc	BU
2008 Proof	107,000	Value: 40.00				

Y# 695 10 ZLOTYCH

14.1400 g., 0.9250 Silver 0.4205 oz. ASW, 32 mm. **Subject:** 70th Anniversary of the start of World War II **Obv:** Eagle and map of Nazi and Soviet invasion **Rev:** Planes dropping bombs on Wielun

Date	Mintage	F	VF	XF	Unc	BU
2009MW Proof	100,000	Value: 45.00				

Y# 671 10 ZLOTYCH

14.4000 g., 0.9250 Silver 0.4282 oz. ASW, 22x32 mm. **Obv:** Eagle, flag and armor **Rev:** Hussar Knights, XVII Century **Shape:** Vertical rectangle

Date	Mintage	F	VF	XF	Unc	BU
2009 Proof	100,000	Value: 50.00				

Y# 688 10 ZLOTYCH

14.1400 g., 0.9250 Silver Gold plated center in silver ring 0.4205 oz. ASW, 27 mm. **Subject:** Poets of the Uprising **Obv:** National arms **Rev:** Tadeusz Gajcy portrait

Date	Mintage	F	VF	XF	Unc	BU
2009MW Proof	100,000	Value: 45.00				

Y# 674 10 ZLOTYCH

14.1400 g., 0.9250 Silver 0.4205 oz. ASW, 32 mm. **Subject:** Supreme Chamber, 90th Anniversary **Obv:** Building **Rev:** Monogram hologram

Date	Mintage	F	VF	XF	Unc	BU
2009MW Proof	100,000	Value: 55.00				

Y# 676 10 ZLOTYCH

14.1400 g., 0.9250 Silver 0.4205 oz. ASW, 32 mm. **Subject:** Central Banking, 180th Anniversary **Obv:** National arms above building **Rev:** Portrait above banknote

Date	Mintage	F	VF	XF	Unc	BU
2009MW Proof	92,000	Value: 45.00				

Y# 681 10 ZLOTYCH

14.1400 g., 0.9250 Silver 0.4205 oz. ASW, 32 mm. **Subject:** General Elections of 1989 **Obv:** Eagle **Rev:** Pope John Paul II and Solidarity banner in color

Date	Mintage	F	VF	XF	Unc	BU
2009MW Proof	100,000	Value: 35.00				

Y# 685 10 ZLOTYCH

14.1400 g., 0.9250 Silver 0.4205 oz. ASW, 29x29 mm. **Subject:** Czeslaw Niemen **Obv:** National arms and large portrait **Rev:** Female crying **Shape:** Square

Date	Mintage	F	VF	XF	Unc	BU
2009MW Proof	100,000	Value: 45.00				

Y# 686 10 ZLOTYCH

14.1400 g., 0.9250 Silver 0.4205 oz. ASW, 32 mm. **Subject:** Cezeslaw Neiman **Obv:** National arms and portrait **Rev:** Abstract painting

Date	Mintage	F	VF	XF	Unc	BU
2009MW Proof	100,000	Value: 45.00				

Y# 689 10 ZLOTYCH

14.1400 g., 0.9250 Silver with gold plated ring 0.4205 oz. ASW, 32 mm. **Subject:** Poets of the uprising **Obv:** National arms **Rev:** Krzystof Baczynski portrait facing

Date	Mintage	F	VF	XF	Unc	BU
2009MW Proof	100,000	Value: 45.00				

Y# 691 10 ZLOTYCH

14.1400 g., 0.9250 Silver 0.4205 oz. ASW, 32 mm. **Subject:** First Cadre Company March **Obv:** National arms and eagle atop stelle monument **Rev:** Troops marching, song and music

Date	Mintage	F	VF	XF	Unc	BU
2009MW Proof	50,000	Value: 50.00				

Y# 698 10 ZLOTYCH

14.1400 g., 0.9250 Silver 0.4205 oz. ASW, 32 mm. **Series:** Tatar Rescues, 100th Anniversary **Obv:** National arms and logo colorized **Rev:** Mountains and figure of Karlowicz

Date	Mintage	F	VF	XF	Unc	BU
2009MW Proof	100,000	Value: 45.00				

Y# 701 10 ZLOTYCH

14.1400 g., 0.9250 Silver 0.4205 oz. ASW, 32 mm. **Subject:** Fr. Jerzy Popielosko, 25th Anniversary of Murder **Obv:** Rose on monument **Rev:** Statue and tear drop on map of Poland

Date	Mintage	F	VF	XF	Unc	BU
2009MW Proof	100,000	Value: 45.00				

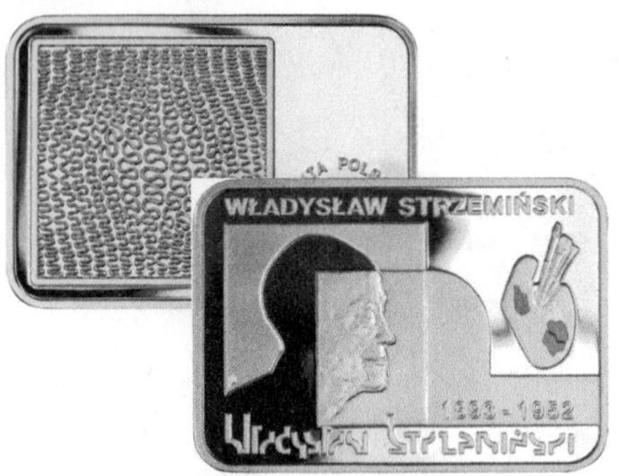

Y# 706 10 ZLOTYCH

28.2800 g., 0.9250 Silver 0.8410 oz. ASW, 40x28 mm. **Subject:** Wald Strzeminski **Obv:** Portrait and multicolor palette **Rev:** Artwork **Shape:** Rectangle

Date	Mintage	F	VF	XF	Unc	BU
2009MW Proof	100,000	Value: 45.00				

Y# 708 10 ZLOTYCH

14.1400 g., 0.9250 Silver 0.4205 oz. ASW, 32 mm. **Subject:** Polish Underground State **Obv:** National arms and monogram and cloth flag **Rev:** Figure and cloth flag

Date	Mintage	F	VF	XF	Unc	BU
2009MW Proof	50,000	Value: 55.00				

Y# 713 10 ZLOTYCH

14.1400 g., 0.9250 Silver 0.4205 oz. ASW, 32 mm. **Subject:** Auschwitz liberation **Obv:** National arms, camp sign and barbed wire fence **Rev:** Prisoner and barbed wire fence

Date	Mintage	F	VF	XF	Unc	BU
2010MW Proof	80,000	Value: 45.00				

Y# 716 10 ZLOTYCH

14.1400 g., 0.9250 Silver 0.4205 oz. ASW, 32 mm. **Subject:** Vancouver Winter Olympics **Obv:** Speedskaters **Rev:** Biathlon

Date	Mintage	F	VF	XF	Unc	BU
2010MW Proof	80,000	Value: 45.00				

Y# 719 10 ZLOTYCH

14.1400 g., 0.9250 Silver 0.4205 oz. ASW, 32x22 mm. **Subject:** Napoleonic Imperial Guard **Obv:** National arms and helmet **Rev:** Mounted Napoleonic Guard member **Shape:** Vertical rectangle

Date	Mintage	F	VF	XF	Unc	BU
2010MW Proof	100,000	Value: 45.00				

Y# 722 10 ZLOTYCH

14.1400 g., 0.9250 Silver 0.4205 oz. ASW, 32 mm. **Subject:** Katyn Crime **Obv:** National emblem and silhouette of a badge **Rev:** Field of crosses

Date	Mintage	F	VF	XF	Unc	BU
2010MW Antiqued	80,000	—	—	—	50.00	—

Y# 726 10 ZLOTYCH

14.1400 g., 0.9250 Silver 0.4205 oz. ASW, 32 mm. **Subject:** Polish Scouting Centennial

Date	Mintage	F	VF	XF	Unc	BU
2010MW Proof	90,000	Value: 30.00				

Y# 728 10 ZLOTYCH

14.1400 g., 0.9250 Silver 0.4205 oz. ASW, 32 mm. **Subject:** Popular Music - Marke Grechuta

Date	Mintage	F	VF	XF	Unc	BU
2010MW Proof	100,000	Value: 30.00				

Y# 729 10 ZLOTYCH

14.1400 g., 0.9250 Silver 0.4205 oz. ASW, 28.2x28.2 mm. **Subject:** Popular Music - Marek Grechuta **Shape:** Square

Date	Mintage	F	VF	XF	Unc	BU
2010MW Proof	100,000	Value: 35.00				

Y# 731 10 ZLOTYCH

14.1400 g., 0.9250 Silver 0.4205 oz. ASW, 32 mm. **Subject:** Jan Twardowski

Date	Mintage	F	VF	XF	Unc	BU
2010MW Proof	80,000	Value: 35.00				

Y# 733 10 ZLOTYCH

14.1400 g., 0.9250 Silver 0.4205 oz. ASW, 40x26 mm. **Subject:** Battles of Grunwald, Kluszyn **Shape:** Oval

Date	Mintage	F	VF	XF	Unc	BU
2010MW Proof	100,000	Value: 35.00				

Y# 738 10 ZLOTYCH

14.1400 g., 0.9250 Silver 0.4205 oz. ASW, 32 mm. **Subject:** August of 1980, 30th Anniversary

Date	Mintage	F	VF	XF	Unc	BU
2010MW Proof	100,000	Value: 35.00				

Y# 743 10 ZLOTYCH

14.1400 g., 0.9250 Silver 0.4205 oz. ASW, 32 mm. **Subject:** Polish Explorers - Benedykt Dybowski

Date	Mintage	F	VF	XF	Unc	BU
2010MW Proof	100,000	Value: 35.00				

Y# 745 10 ZLOTYCH

28.2800 g., 0.9250 Silver 0.8410 oz. ASW, 38.61 mm. **Subject:** Krzeszow

Date	Mintage	F	VF	XF	Unc	BU
2010MW Proof	80,000	Value: 40.00				

Y# 750 10 ZLOTYCH

14.1400 g., 0.9250 Silver 0.4205 oz. ASW, 40x26 mm. **Subject:** Battle of Grunwald **Shape:** Oval

Date	Mintage	F	VF	XF	Unc	BU
2010MW Proof	100,000	Value: 45.00				

Y# 758 10 ZLOTYCH

14.1400 g., 0.9250 Silver 0.4205 oz. ASW, 32 mm. **Subject:** Benedykt Dybowski **Obv:** Books **Rev:** Bust facing, map in background

Date	Mintage	F	VF	XF	Unc	BU
2010 Proof	60,000	Value: 55.00				

Y# 807 10 ZLOTYCH

14.1400 g., 0.9250 Silver 0.4205 oz. ASW, 32 mm. **Subject:** Krzystof Komeda **Rev:** Komeda and movie film real

Date	Mintage	F	VF	XF	Unc	BU
2010MW Proof	—	Value: 50.00				

Y# 808 10 ZLOTYCH

14.1400 g., 0.9250 Silver 0.4205 oz. ASW, 28.2x28.2 mm. **Subject:** Krzysztof Komeda **Shape:** Square

Date	Mintage	F	VF	XF	Unc	BU
2010MW Proof	—	Value: 50.00				

Y# 768 10 ZLOTYCH

14.1400 g., 0.9250 Silver 0.4205 oz. ASW, 32 mm. **Subject:** Independent Student's Union, 30th Anniversary

Date	Mintage	F	VF	XF	Unc	BU
2011MW Proof	50,000	Value: 30.00				

Y# 770 10 ZLOTYCH

14.1400 g., 0.9250 Silver 0.4205 oz. ASW, 32 mm. **Subject:** Smolensk plane crash

Date	Mintage	F	VF	XF	Unc	BU
2011MW Proof	30,000	Value: 30.00				

Y# 778 10 ZLOTYCH

14.1400 g., 0.9250 Silver 0.4205 oz. ASW, 32 mm. **Subject:** Poland's presidency of the Council of the European Union

Date	Mintage	F	VF	XF	Unc	BU
2011MW Proof	50,000	Value: 30.00				

Y# 781 10 ZLOTYCH

14.1400 g., 0.9250 Silver 0.4205 oz. ASW, 22.4x32 mm. **Subject:** History of the Polish Cavalry - Ulan of the Second Republic **Obv:** Eagle above military items: saddle, rifle, banners, lances and sword **Rev:** Cavalry officer on horseback **Shape:** Vertical rectangle

Date	Mintage	F	VF	XF	Unc	BU
2011MW Proof	50,000	Value: 50.00				

Y# 786 10 ZLOTYCH

14.1400 g., 0.9250 Silver 0.4205 oz. ASW, 32 mm. **Subject:** Czeslaw Milosz

Date	Mintage	F	VF	XF	Unc	BU
2011MW Proof	50,000	Value: 30.00				

Y# 790 10 ZLOTYCH

14.1400 g., 0.9250 Silver 0.4205 oz. ASW, 32 mm. **Subject:** Ignacy Jan Paderewski

Date	Mintage	F	VF	XF	Unc	BU
2011MW Proof	50,000	Value: 30.00				

Y# 793 10 ZLOTYCH

14.1400 g., 0.9250 Silver 0.4205 oz. ASW, 32 mm. **Subject:** Silesian Uprising

Date	Mintage	F	VF	XF	Unc	BU
2011MW Proof	50,000	Value: 30.00				

Y# 796 10 ZLOTYCH

14.1400 g., 0.9250 Silver 0.4205 oz. ASW, 32 mm. **Subject:** Society for the Protection of the Blind, 100th Anniversary

Date	Mintage	F	VF	XF	Unc	BU
2011MW Proof	50,000	Value: 35.00				

Y# 798 10 ZLOTYCH

14.1400 g., 0.9250 Silver 0.4205 oz. ASW, 32 mm. **Subject:** Ferdynand Ossendowski

Date	Mintage	F	VF	XF	Unc	BU
2011MW Proof	50,000	Value: 30.00				

Y# 802 10 ZLOTYCH
14.1400 g., 0.9250 Silver 0.4205 oz. ASW, 28.2x28.2 mm. **Subject:** Jeremi Przybora and Jerzy Wasowski **Shape:** Square

Date	Mintage	F	VF	XF	Unc	BU
2011MW Proof	50,000	Value: 30.00				

Y# 803 10 ZLOTYCH
14.1400 g., 0.9250 Silver 0.4205 oz. ASW, 32 mm. **Subject:** Jeremi Przybora and Jerzy Wasowski

Date	Mintage	F	VF	XF	Unc	BU
2011MW Proof	50,000	Value: 30.00				

Y# 810 10 ZLOTYCH
14.1400 g., 0.9250 Silver 0.4205 oz. ASW, 28.7x30 mm. **Subject:** Christmas Charity Orchestra, 20th Anniversary **Obv:** Piano keyboard **Rev:** Guitar with hearts **Shape:** Heart

Date	Mintage	F	VF	XF	Unc	BU
2012MW Proof	60,000	Value: 60.00				

Y# 812 10 ZLOTYCH
14.1400 g., 0.9250 Silver 0.4205 oz. ASW, 32 mm. **Subject:** Cooperative Banking in Poland, 150th Anniversary **Obv:** Eagle at left, bank building at right **Rev:** Pile of coin and banknotes at center, semi-circle of stick figures holding hands at right

Date	Mintage	F	VF	XF	Unc	BU
2012MW Proof	40,000	Value: 40.00				

Y# 818 10 ZLOTYCH
14.1400 g., 0.9250 Silver 0.4205 oz. ASW, 32 mm. **Subject:** Stefan Banach

Date	Mintage	F	VF	XF	Unc	BU
2012MW Proof	—	Value: 30.00				

Y# 822 10 ZLOTYCH
14.1400 g., 0.9250 Silver 0.4205 oz. ASW, 32 mm. **Subject:** National Museum in Warsaw, 150th Anniversary

Date	Mintage	F	VF	XF	Unc	BU
2012MW Proof	45,000	Value: 35.00				

Y# 824 10 ZLOTYCH
33.6200 g., 0.9250 Silver 0.9998 oz. ASW, 27.3x50 mm. **Subject:** European Football Championship **Shape:** Yin-Yang **Note:** A yin-Yang design, with the other half being a Ukraine 10 Hryvnia coin.

Date	Mintage	F	VF	XF	Unc	BU
2012MW Proof	5,000	Value: 50.00				

Y# 825 10 ZLOTYCH
14.1400 g., 0.9250 Silver 0.4205 oz. ASW, 28.8x28.8 mm. **Subject:** European Football Championship **Note:** Part of a four coin design.

Date	Mintage	F	VF	XF	Unc	BU
2012MW Proof	15,000	Value: 40.00				

Y# 826 10 ZLOTYCH
14.1400 g., 0.9250 Silver 0.4205 oz. ASW, 28.8x28.8 mm. **Subject:** European Football Championship **Note:** Part of a four coin design.

Date	Mintage	F	VF	XF	Unc	BU
2012MW Proof	15,000	Value: 40.00				

Y# 827 10 ZLOTYCH
14.1400 g., 0.9250 Silver 0.4205 oz. ASW, 28.8x28.8 mm. **Subject:** European Football Championships **Note:** Part of a four coin design.

Date	Mintage	F	VF	XF	Unc	BU
2012MW Proof	15,000	Value: 40.00				

Y# 828 10 ZLOTYCH
14.1400 g., 0.9250 Silver 0.4205 oz. ASW, 28.8x.28.8 mm. **Subject:** European Football Championships **Note:** Part of a four coin design.

Date	Mintage	F	VF	XF	Unc	BU
2012MW Proof	15,000	Value: 40.00				

Y# 833 10 ZLOTYCH
14.1400 g., 0.9250 Silver 0.4205 oz. ASW, 32 mm. **Subject:** London Olympics, 2012, Polish Team

Date	Mintage	F	VF	XF	Unc	BU
2012MW Proof	50,000	Value: 30.00				

Y# 839 10 ZLOTYCH
14.1400 g., 0.9250 Silver 0.4205 oz. ASW, 32 mm. **Subject:** Boleslaw Prus

Date	Mintage	F	VF	XF	Unc	BU
2012MW Proof	30,000	Value: 75.00				

Y# 409 20 ZLOTYCH
28.2800 g., 0.9250 Silver 0.8410 oz. ASW, 38.6 mm. **Subject:** Wieliezce Salt Mine **Obv:** Crowned eagle with wings open in center of rock **Rev:** Ancient salt miners **Edge:** Plain

Date	Mintage	F	VF	XF	Unc	BU
2001MW Proof	25,000	Value: 250				

Y# 411 20 ZLOTYCH
28.2800 g., 0.9250 Silver 0.8410 oz. ASW, 38.6 mm. **Subject:** Amber Route **Obv:** Crowned eagle and two ancient Roman silver cups **Rev:** Piece of amber mounted above an ancient Roman coin design and map with the route marked with stars **Edge:** Plain

Date	Mintage	F	VF	XF	Unc	BU
2001MW Antique finish	30,000	—	—	—	750	—

Y# 415 20 ZLOTYCH
28.2800 g., 0.9250 Silver 0.8410 oz. ASW, 38.6 mm. **Obv:** Crowned eagle with wings open flanked by flags **Rev:** European Swallowtail Butterfly **Edge:** Plain

Date	Mintage	F	VF	XF	Unc	BU
2001MW Proof	27,000	Value: 300				

Y# 424 20 ZLOTYCH
28.7700 g., 0.9250 Silver 0.8556 oz. ASW, 38.6 mm. **Subject:** Christmas **Obv:** Ornate city view **Rev:** Celebration scene including an attached zirconia star **Edge:** Plain

Date	Mintage	F	VF	XF	Unc	BU
2001MW Antique patina	55,000	—	—	—	225	—

Y# 428 20 ZLOTYCH
28.2800 g., 0.9250 Silver 0.8410 oz. ASW, 38.6 mm. **Obv:** Crowned eagle with wings open flanked by flags **Rev:** European Pond Turtles **Edge:** Plain

Date	Mintage	F	VF	XF	Unc	BU
2002 Proof	35,000	Value: 175				

Y# 442 20 ZLOTYCH
28.0500 g., 0.9250 Silver 0.8342 oz. ASW, 39.94x27.93 mm. **Subject:** Jan Matejko **Obv:** Seated figure with crowned eagle at lower right **Rev:** Head facing with multicolor artist's palette **Edge:** Plain **Shape:** Rectangle

Date	Mintage	F	VF	XF	Unc	BU
2002MW Proof	57,000	Value: 200				

Y# 457 20 ZLOTYCH
28.2800 g., 0.9250 Silver 0.8410 oz. ASW, 38.6 mm. **Obv:** National arms at lower left, castle complex in background **Rev:** Malborku castle, reddish-brown ceramic applique, **Rev. Legend:** ZAMEK W MALBORKU **Edge:** Plain

Date	Mintage	F	VF	XF	Unc	BU
2002MW Antique patina	51,000	—	—	—	100	—

Y# 449 20 ZLOTYCH
28.4700 g., 0.9250 Silver 0.8466 oz. ASW, 38.6 mm. **Obv:** Crowned eagle with wings open **Rev:** European Eels and world globe **Edge:** Plain

Date	Mintage	F	VF	XF	Unc	BU
2003MW Proof	—	Value: 250				

Y# 452 20 ZLOTYCH
28.2800 g., 0.9250 Silver 0.8410 oz. ASW, 38.6 mm. **Subject:** Easter Monday Festival **Obv:** Crowned eagle on lace curtain above lamb and multicolor Easter eggs **Rev:** Festival scene **Edge:** Plain

Date	Mintage	F	VF	XF	Unc	BU
2003MW Proof	44,000	Value: 100				

Y# 471 20 ZLOTYCH
28.2800 g., 0.9250 Silver 0.8410 oz. ASW, 40 x 40 mm. **Obv:** Standing Pope John Paul II **Rev:** Pope"s portrait **Edge:** Plain **Shape:** Square

Date	Mintage	F	VF	XF	Unc	BU
2003MW Proof	83,000	Value: 75.00				

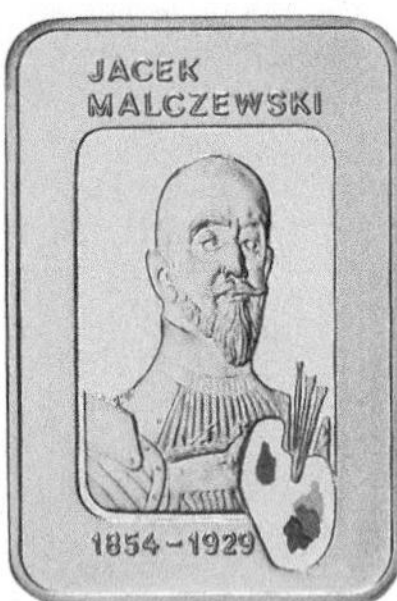

Y# 478 20 ZLOTYCH

28.2800 g., 0.9250 Silver 0.8410 oz. ASW, 27.93x39.94 mm. **Obv:** "Death" allegory closing an old man's eyes, national arms at lower right **Rev:** Self portrait of Jacek Malczewski, palette at lower right multicolor **Edge:** Plain **Shape:** Rectangle

Date	Mintage	F	VF	XF	Unc	BU
2003MW Proof	64,000	Value: 65.00				

Y# 498 20 ZLOTYCH

28.2800 g., 0.9250 Silver 0.8410 oz. ASW, 38.6 mm. **Subject:** Lodz Ghetto (1940-1944) **Obv:** Silhouette on wall **Rev:** Child with a pot **Edge:** Plain

Date	Mintage	F	VF	XF	Unc	BU
2004MW Matte	64,000	—	—	—	—	45.00

Y# 504 20 ZLOTYCH

28.2800 g., 0.9250 Silver 0.8410 oz. ASW, 38.6 mm. **Subject:** Polish Senate **Obv:** Crowned eagle above Senate chamber **Rev:** Senate eagle and speaker's staff **Edge:** Plain

Date	Mintage	F	VF	XF	Unc	BU
2004MW Proof	67,000	Value: 75.00				

Y# 508 20 ZLOTYCH

28.2800 g., 0.9250 Silver 0.8410 oz. ASW, 38.6 mm. **Obv:** Crowned eagle in harvest wreath **Rev:** Harvest fest parade **Edge:** Plain

Date	Mintage	F	VF	XF	Unc	BU
2004MW Proof	74,000	Value: 45.00				

Y# 513 20 ZLOTYCH

28.2800 g., 0.9250 Silver 0.8410 oz. ASW, 40x28 mm. **Obv:** Mother and children **Rev:** Stanislaw Wyspianski (1869-1907) **Edge:** Plain

Date	Mintage	F	VF	XF	Unc	BU
2004MW Proof	80,000	Value: 55.00				

Y# 515 20 ZLOTYCH

28.2800 g., 0.9250 Silver 0.8410 oz. ASW, 38.6 mm. **Obv:** National arms **Obv. Legend:** RZECZPOSPOLITA POLSKA **Rev:** 2 Harbor Porpoises **Rev. Legend:** MORSWIN - Phocoena phocoena **Edge:** Plain

Date	Mintage	F	VF	XF	Unc	BU
2004MW Proof	56,000	Value: 175				

Y# 531 20 ZLOTYCH

28.8400 g., 0.9250 Silver 0.8576 oz. ASW, 38.6 mm. **Obv:** Polish eagle above value **Rev:** Eagle Owl with nestlings **Edge:** Plain

Date	Mintage	F	VF	XF	Unc	BU
2005MW Proof	61,000	Value: 150				

Y# 542 20 ZLOTYCH

28.2800 g., 0.9250 Silver 0.8410 oz. ASW, 28 x 40 mm. **Obv:** Sneak thief stealing from a miser **Rev:** Painter Tadeusz Makowski **Edge:** Plain **Shape:** Rectangular

Date	Mintage	F	VF	XF	Unc	BU
2005MW Proof	70,000	Value: 60.00				

Y# 597 20 ZLOTYCH

28.5000 g., 0.9250 Silver 0.8475 oz. ASW, 38.5 mm. **Subject:** 350 Years, Defence of Góry **Obv:** National arms to right of outlined Góry **Obv. Legend:** RZECZPOSPOLITA POLSKA **Obv. Inscription:** Tutaj zawsze / bylismy woini / JAN PAWEL II **Rev:** 1/2 length figure of man at lower right, Góry under bombardment in background **Rev. Legend:** 350 - LECIE OBRONY JASNEJ GÓRY **Edge:** Lettered **Edge Lettering:** CZESTOCHOWA 2005 repeated three times

Date	Mintage	F	VF	XF	Unc	BU
2005MW Proof	69,000	Value: 55.00				

Y# 604 20 ZLOTYCH

28.1400 g., Silver, 39.95x27.97 mm. **Subject:** Aleksander Gierymski **Obv:** National arms at upper right, painting of elderly woman carrying baskets **Rev:** Bust of Gierymski facing at center, harbor scene at right, painter's palette at lower left multicolor **Edge:** Plain **Shape:** Rectangle

Date	Mintage	F	VF	XF	Unc	BU
2006MW Proof	66,000	Value: 65.00				

Y# 535 20 ZLOTYCH

28.8400 g., 0.9250 Silver 0.8576 oz. ASW, 38.6 mm. **Obv:** Polish eagle above value **Rev:** Alpine Marmot standing **Edge:** Plain

Date	Mintage	F	VF	XF	Unc	BU
2006MW Proof	60,000	Value: 125				

Y# 584 20 ZLOTYCH

28.4700 g., 0.9250 Silver 0.8466 oz. ASW, 38.6 mm. **Obv:** Polish Eagle on old wood **Rev:** Multi-color wood behind Haczowie church **Edge:** Plain

Date	Mintage	F	VF	XF	Unc	BU
2006MW Proof	—	Value: 60.00				

Y# 533 20 ZLOTYCH
28.8400 g., 0.9250 Silver 0.8576 oz. ASW, 38.6 mm. **Obv:** Polish eagle above value **Rev:** Multicolor holographic spider web **Edge:** Plain

Date	Mintage	F	VF	XF	Unc	BU
2006MW Proof	65,000	Value: 115				

Y# 579 20 ZLOTYCH
28.2800 g., 0.9250 Silver 0.8410 oz. ASW, 38.6 mm. **Obv:** Crowned eagle **Rev:** Two Grey Seal females and pup with two silhouettes in background **Edge:** Plain

Date	Mintage	F	VF	XF	Unc	BU
2007MW Proof	58,000	Value: 125				

Y# 603 20 ZLOTYCH
28.2500 g., 0.9250 Silver 0.8401 oz. ASW, 38.5 mm. **Subject:** Medieval Principality of Sredniowieczne in Torin **Obv:** City arms at right, national arms below walled city gate in background **Obv. Legend:** RZECZPOSPOLITA POLSKA **Rev:** City view **Rev. Legend:** MIASTO SREDNIOWIECZNE W TORUNIU **Edge:** Plain

Date	Mintage	F	VF	XF	Unc	BU
2007MW Proof	58,000	Value: 70.00				

Y# 636 20 ZLOTYCH
28.2800 g., 0.9250 Silver 0.8410 oz. ASW, 38.6 mm. **Subject:** 65th Anniversary Warsaw Ghetto Uprising **Obv:** Small national arms at left, flames, shattered wall **Obv. Legend:** RZECZPOSPOLITA POLSKA **Rev:** Tree, Star of David, wall in backgound **Rev. Inscription:** 65. ROCZNICA POWSTANIA / W GETCIE WARSZAWSKIM **Edge:** Plain

Date	Mintage	F	VF	XF	Unc	BU
2008MW Proof	—	Value: 60.00				

Y# 642 20 ZLOTYCH
28.2800 g., 0.9250 Silver 0.8410 oz. ASW, 38.61 mm. **Subject:** Kazimierez Dolny **Obv:** Part of a wall and an eagle **Rev:** Houses and a well **Designer:** Ewa Olszewska-Borys

Date	Mintage	F	VF	XF	Unc	BU
2008 Proof	125,000	Value: 50.00				

Y# 637 20 ZLOTYCH
28.2800 g., 0.9250 Silver 0.8410 oz. ASW, 38.61 mm. **Obv:** National arms **Obv. Legend:** RZECZPOSPOLITA POLSKA **Rev:** Peregrine Falcon by 2 chicks in nest at right **Rev. Legend:** SOKOL WEDROWNY - Falco peregrinus **Edge:** Plain

Date	Mintage	F	VF	XF	Unc	BU
2008MW Proof	107,000	Value: 80.00				

Y# 651 20 ZLOTYCH
28.2800 g., 0.9250 Silver 0.8410 oz. ASW, 38.61 mm. **Subject:** 90th Anniversary of Regaining Freedom **Obv:** War decoration left side, eagle top right **Rev:** 3 generals **Designer:** Ewa Olszewska-Borys

Date	Mintage	F	VF	XF	Unc	BU
2008 Proof	110,000	Value: 55.00				

Y# 679 20 ZLOTYCH
28.2800 g., 0.9250 Silver 0.8410 oz. ASW, 38.6 mm. **Subject:** Green Lizard **Obv:** National arms above value **Rev:** Two green lizards in nature

Date	Mintage	F	VF	XF	Unc	BU
2009MW Proof	100,000	Value: 45.00				

Y# 693 20 ZLOTYCH
28.2800 g., 0.9250 Silver 0.8410 oz. ASW, 38.6 mm. **Subject:** Liquidation of the Lotz Ghetto **Obv:** New oak sprig amongst broken bricks **Rev:** Oak tree, bare and with leaves, star of David within

Date	Mintage	F	VF	XF	Unc	BU
2009MW Antiqued	50,000	—	—	—	45.00	—

Y# 704 20 ZLOTYCH
28.2800 g., 0.9250 Silver 0.8410 oz. ASW, 38.6 mm. **Subject:** Honoring Poles who saved the Jews **Obv:** National arms above broken brick wall **Rev:** Three portraits

Date	Mintage	F	VF	XF	Unc	BU
2009MW Proof	100,000	Value: 40.00				

Y# 724 20 ZLOTYCH
28.2800 g., 0.9250 Silver 0.8410 oz. ASW, 38.61 mm. **Subject:** Lesser Horseshoe Bat

Date	Mintage	F	VF	XF	Unc	BU
2010MW Proof	100,000	Value: 37.50				

Y# 736 20 ZLOTYCH
28.2800 g., 0.9250 Silver 0.8410 oz. ASW, 38.6 mm. **Subject:** Battle of Warsaw **Rev:** Battle scene in color

Date	Mintage	F	VF	XF	Unc	BU
2010MW Proof	100,000	Value: 40.00				

Y# 747 20 ZLOTYCH
28.2800 g., 0.9250 Silver 0.8410 oz. ASW, 28x40 mm. **Subject:** Arthur Grottger

Date	Mintage	F	VF	XF	Unc	BU
2010MW Proof	100,000	Value: 40.00				

Y# 763 20 ZLOTYCH
28.2800 g., 0.9250 Silver 0.8410 oz. ASW, 38.6 mm. **Subject:** Borsuk **Obv:** National Arms above value **Rev:** Eurasian Badgers

Date	Mintage	F	VF	XF	Unc	BU
2011 Proof	80,000	Value: 60.00				

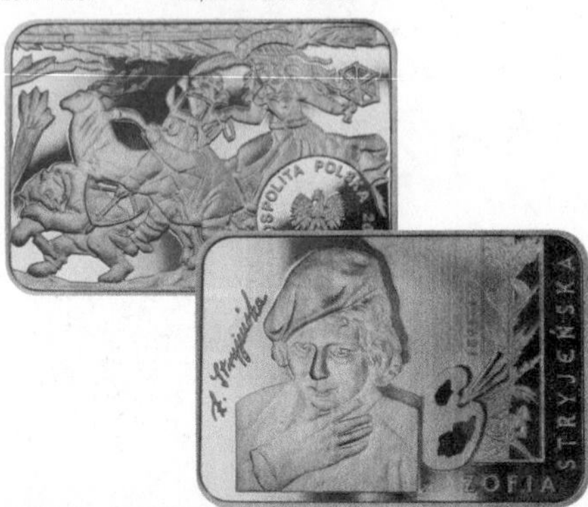

Y# 765 20 ZLOTYCH
28.2800 g., 0.9250 Silver 0.8410 oz. ASW, 40x28 mm. **Subject:** Zofia Stryjenska **Obv:** Horseback scene, National Arms at right **Rev:** Portrait with artist pallet with brushes **Shape:** Rectangle

Date	Mintage	F	VF	XF	Unc	BU
2011 Proof	50,000	Value: 55.00				

Y# 771 20 ZLOTYCH
28.2800 g., 0.9250 Silver 0.8410 oz. ASW, 38.61 mm. **Subject:** Smolensk plane crash

Date	Mintage	F	VF	XF	Unc	BU
2011MW Proof	—	Value: 50.00				

Y# 773 20 ZLOTYCH
14.1400 g., 0.9250 Silver 0.4205 oz. ASW, 38.61 mm. **Subject:** John Paul II Beautification **Rev:** Pope waving, earth in background in color

Date	Mintage	F	VF	XF	Unc	BU
2011MW Proof	80,000	Value: 50.00				

Y# 814 20 ZLOTYCH
28.2800 g., 0.9250 Silver 0.8410 oz. ASW, 38.61 mm. **Subject:** Ulma, Baranek and Kowalski families **Obv:** Fields and town view **Rev:** Family faces seen thru broken fenceboards

Date	Mintage	F	VF	XF	Unc	BU
2012MW Antique patina	40,000	—	—	—	50.00	—

Y# 829 20 ZLOTYCH
28.2800 g., 0.9250 Silver 0.8410 oz. ASW, 36.2x36.2 mm. **Subject:** European Football Championships

Date	Mintage	F	VF	XF	Unc	BU
2012MW Proof	35,000	Value: 75.00				

Y# 836 20 ZLOTYCH
28.2800 g., 0.9250 Silver 0.8410 oz. ASW, 38.61 mm. **Subject:** Krzemionki Opatowskie

Date	Mintage	F	VF	XF	Unc	BU
2012MW Proof	45,000	Value: 75.00				

Y# 843 20 ZLOTYCH
28.2800 g., 0.9250 Silver 0.8410 oz. ASW, 40x28 mm. **Subject:** Piotr Michalowski, painter **Shape:** Rectangle

Date	Mintage	F	VF	XF	Unc	BU
2012MW Proof	30,000	Value: 75.00				

Y# 682 25 ZLOTYCH
1.0000 g., 0.9000 Gold 0.0289 oz. AGW, 12 mm. **Subject:** General Elections of 1989 **Obv:** National arms above value **Rev:** Solidarity logo

Date	Mintage	F	VF	XF	Unc	BU
2009MW Proof	40,000	Value: 65.00				

Y# 740 25 ZLOTYCH
1.0000 g., 0.9000 Gold 0.0289 oz. AGW, 12 mm. **Subject:** Constitutional Tribunal

Date	Mintage	F	VF	XF	Unc	BU
2010MW Proof	10,000	Value: 75.00				

Y# 774 25 ZLOTYCH
1.0000 g., 0.9000 Gold 0.0289 oz. AGW, 12 mm. **Subject:** John Paul II Beatification

Date	Mintage	F	VF	XF	Unc	BU
2011MW Proof	10,000	Value: 75.00				

Y# 739 30 ZLOTYCH
1.7000 g., 0.9000 Gold 0.0492 oz. AGW, 16 mm. **Subject:** August of 1980

Date	Mintage	F	VF	XF	Unc	BU
2010MW Proof	50,000	Value: 100				

Y# 702 37 ZLOTYCH

1.7500 g., 0.9000 Gold 0.0506 oz. AGW, 16 mm. **Subject:** Fr. Jorzy Popieluszko, 25th Anniversary of Murder **Obv:** National arms above large 37 **Rev:** Many hands holding crosses

Date	Mintage	F	VF	XF	Unc	BU
2009MW Proof	60,000	Value: 100				

Y# 652 50 ZLOTYCH

3.1300 g., Gold, 18 mm. **Subject:** 90th Annniversary of Regaining Freedom **Obv:** Tomb of the unknown soldier **Rev:** Mounted Commander-In-Chief Jósef Pilsudski **Designer:** Ewa Olszewska-Borys

Date	Mintage	F	VF	XF	Unc	BU
2008 Proof	8,800	Value: 125				

Y# 416 100 ZLOTYCH

8.0000 g., 0.9000 Gold 0.2315 oz. AGW, 21 mm. **Subject:** Wladyslaw I (1320-33) **Obv:** Crowned eagle with wings open **Rev:** Crowned bust facing **Edge:** Plain

Date	Mintage	F	VF	XF	Unc	BU
2001MW Proof	2,000	Value: 875				

Y# 417 100 ZLOTYCH

8.0000 g., 0.9000 Gold 0.2315 oz. AGW, 21 mm. **Subject:** Boleslaw III (1102-1138) **Obv:** Crowned eagle with wings open **Rev:** Pointed crowned bust facing **Edge:** Plain

Date	Mintage	F	VF	XF	Unc	BU
2001MW Proof	2,000	Value: 875				

Y# 462 100 ZLOTYCH

8.0000 g., 0.9000 Gold 0.2315 oz. AGW, 21 mm. **Obv:** Crowned eagle with wings open **Rev:** Jan Sobieski III **Edge:** Plain

Date	Mintage	F	VF	XF	Unc	BU
2001MV Proof	2,200	Value: 875				

Y# 436 100 ZLOTYCH

8.0000 g., 0.9000 Gold 0.2315 oz. AGW, 21 mm. **Subject:** World Cup Soccer **Obv:** Crowned eagle with wings open and world background **Rev:** Soccer player **Edge:** Plain

Date	Mintage	F	VF	XF	Unc	BU
2002MW Proof	4,500	Value: 450				

Y# 429 100 ZLOTYCH

8.0000 g., 0.9000 Gold 0.2315 oz. AGW, 21 mm. **Obv:** Crowned eagle with wings open **Rev:** Crowned bust facing **Edge:** Plain

Date	Mintage	F	VF	XF	Unc	BU
2002MW Proof	2,400	Value: 875				

Y# 430 100 ZLOTYCH

8.0000 g., 0.9000 Gold 0.2315 oz. AGW, 21 mm. **Obv:** Crowned eagle with wings open **Rev:** Crowned bust 1/4 left **Edge:** Plain

Date	Mintage	F	VF	XF	Unc	BU
2002MW Proof	2,200	Value: 875				

Y# 454 100 ZLOTYCH

8.0000 g., 0.9000 Gold 0.2315 oz. AGW, 21 mm. **Obv:** Crowned eagle with wings open **Rev:** Uniformed bust 1/4 left **Edge:** Plain

Date	Mintage	F	VF	XF	Unc	BU
2003MW Proof	2,000	Value: 1,000				

Y# 466 100 ZLOTYCH

8.0000 g., 0.9000 Gold 0.2315 oz. AGW, 21 mm. **Subject:** 750th Anniversary - City Charter **Obv:** Door knocker and church **Rev:** Clock face and tower **Edge:** Plain

Date	Mintage	F	VF	XF	Unc	BU
2003MW Proof	2,100	Value: 750				

Y# 467 100 ZLOTYCH

8.0000 g., 0.9000 Gold 0.2315 oz. AGW, 21 mm. **Obv:** Crowned eagle with wings open **Rev:** Kazimierz IV (1447-1492) **Edge:** Plain

Date	Mintage	F	VF	XF	Unc	BU
2003MW Proof	2,300	Value: 750				

Y# 476 100 ZLOTYCH

8.0000 g., 0.9000 Gold 0.2315 oz. AGW, 21 mm. **Obv:** Crowned eagle with wings open **Rev:** Stanislaus I and eagle **Edge:** Plain

Date	Mintage	F	VF	XF	Unc	BU
2003MW Proof	2,500	Value: 750				

Y# 494 100 ZLOTYCH

8.0000 g., 0.9000 Gold 0.2315 oz. AGW, 21 mm. **Obv:** Crowned eagle with wings open **Rev:** King Przemysl II (1295-1296) **Edge:** Plain

Date	Mintage	F	VF	XF	Unc	BU
2004MW Proof	3,400	Value: 550				

Y# 495 100 ZLOTYCH

8.0000 g., 0.9000 Gold 0.2315 oz. AGW, 21 mm. **Obv:** Crowned eagle with wings open **Rev:** King Zygmunt I (1506-1548) **Edge:** Plain

Date	Mintage	F	VF	XF	Unc	BU
2004MW Proof	3,400	Value: 550				

Y# 540 100 ZLOTYCH

8.0000 g., 0.9000 Gold 0.2315 oz. AGW, 21 mm. **Obv:** St. Peters Basilica dome **Rev:** Pope John Paul II and baptismal font **Edge:** Plain

Date	Mintage	F	VF	XF	Unc	BU
2005MW Proof	18,700	Value: 450				

Y# 581 100 ZLOTYCH

8.0000 g., 0.9000 Gold 0.2315 oz. AGW, 21 mm. **Obv:** Line of soccer players on soccer ball surface with Polish eagle in one of the sections **Rev:** Two soccer players **Edge:** Plain

Date	Mintage	F	VF	XF	Unc	BU
2006MW Proof	—	Value: 450				

Y# 640 100 ZLOTYCH

8.0000 g., 0.9000 Gold 0.2315 oz. AGW, 21 mm. **Subject:** Siberian Exiles **Obv:** Small national arms at left, bleak forest at right **Obv. Legend:** RZECZPOSPOLITA POLSKA **Rev:** Grieving mother with child by tree at lower right, building in background at left **Rev. Legend:** SYBIRACY

Date	Mintage	F	VF	XF	Unc	BU
2008MW Proof	12,000	Value: 450				

Y# 657 100 ZLOTYCH

8.0000 g., 0.9000 Gold 0.2315 oz. AGW, 21 mm. **Subject:** 400th Anniversary of Polish Settlement in North America **Obv:** Eagle in center against wind rose. Outline of Europe & North America. **Rev:** Center wind rose surrounded by 4 men working

Date	Mintage	F	VF	XF	Unc	BU
2008 Proof	9,500	Value: 450				

Y# 665 100 ZLOTYCH

8.0000 g., 0.9000 Gold 0.2315 oz. AGW, 21 mm. **Subject:** Poles in the US, 400th Anniversary **Obv:** National Arms, North America and Europe map, compass **Rev:** Four glass maker views

Date	Mintage	F	VF	XF	Unc	BU
2008MW Proof	9,500	Value: 450				

Y# 699 100 ZLOTYCH

8.0000 g., 0.9000 Gold 0.2315 oz. AGW, 21 mm. **Subject:** Tatar Rescue, 100th Anniversary **Obv:** Figure of Mariusz Zaruski **Rev:** Mountains and reszue helicopter image

Date	Mintage	F	VF	XF	Unc	BU
2009MW Proof	10,000	Value: 450				

Y# 714 100 ZLOTYCH

8.0000 g., 0.9000 Gold 0.2315 oz. AGW, 21 mm. **Subject:** Auschwitz liberation **Obv:** Prisoner and railroad track entrance **Rev:** Buildings

Date	Mintage	F	VF	XF	Unc	BU
2010MW Proof	8,000	Value: 450				

Y# 741 100 ZLOTYCH

8.0000 g., 0.9000 Gold 0.2315 oz. AGW, 21 mm. **Subject:** Constitutional Tribunal

Date	Mintage	F	VF	XF	Unc	BU
2010MW Proof	5,000	Value: 450				

Y# 766 100 ZLOTYCH

8.0000 g., 0.9000 Gold 0.2315 oz. AGW, 21 mm. **Subject:** Smolensk plane crash **Rev:** President Lech Kaczynski and wife Maria

Date	Mintage	F	VF	XF	Unc	BU
2011 Proof	—	Value: 475				

Y# 775 100 ZLOTYCH

8.0000 g., 0.9000 Gold 0.2315 oz. AGW, 21 mm. **Subject:** John Paul II Beatification

Date	Mintage	F	VF	XF	Unc	BU
2011MW Proof	8,000	Value: 450				

Y# 779 100 ZLOTYCH

8.0000 g., 0.9000 Gold 0.2315 oz. AGW, 21 mm. **Subject:** Poland's presidency of the Council of the European Union

Date	Mintage	F	VF	XF	Unc	BU
2011MW Proof	4,000	Value: 500				

Y# 830 100 ZLOTYCH

8.0000 g., 0.9000 Gold 0.2315 oz. AGW, 21 mm. **Subject:** European Football Championships

Date	Mintage	F	VF	XF	Unc	BU
2012MW Proof	4,000	Value: 500				

Y# 407 200 ZLOTYCH

15.2000 g., 0.9000 Tri-Metallic Gold with Palladium center, Gold with Silver ring, Gold with Copper outer limit 0.4398 oz., 27 mm. **Subject:** Year 2001 **Obv:** Crowned eagle with wings open within a swirl **Rev:** Couple looking into the future **Edge:** Plain

Date	Mintage	F	VF	XF	Unc	BU
2001MW Proof	4,000	Value: 900				

Y# 420 200 ZLOTYCH

15.5000 g., 0.9000 Gold 0.4485 oz. AGW, 27 mm. **Subject:** Cardinal Stefan Wyszynski **Obv:** Pillar divides arms and eagle **Rev:** Bust left within arch **Edge Lettering:** 100 ROCZNIA URODZIN

Date	Mintage	F	VF	XF	Unc	BU
2001MW Proof	4,500	Value: 850				

Y# 463 200 ZLOTYCH

15.5000 g., 0.9000 Gold 0.4485 oz. AGW, 27 mm. **Obv:** Standing violinist **Rev:** Henryk Wieniawski **Edge Lettering:** XII MIEDZYNARODOWY KONKURS SKRZYPCOWY IM HENRYKA WIENIAWSKIEGO

Date	Mintage	F	VF	XF	Unc	BU
2001MW Proof	2,000	Value: 1,150				

Y# 438 200 ZLOTYCH

15.5000 g., 0.9000 Gold 0.4485 oz. AGW, 27 mm. **Subject:** Pope John Paul II **Obv:** Bust left and small eagle with wings open **Rev:** Pope facing radiant Holy Door **Edge:** Plain

Date	Mintage	F	VF	XF	Unc	BU
2002MW Proof	5,000	Value: 1,200				

Y# 470 200 ZLOTYCH

15.5000 g., 0.9000 Gold 0.4485 oz. AGW, 27 mm. **Subject:** Gas and Oil Industry **Obv:** Crowned eagle, oil wells and refinery **Rev:** Scientist at work **Edge:** Plain

Date	Mintage	F	VF	XF	Unc	BU
2003MW Proof	2,100	Value: 1,250				

Y# 472 200 ZLOTYCH

15.5000 g., 0.9000 Gold 0.4485 oz. AGW, 27 mm. **Obv:** Standing Pope John Paul II **Rev:** Seated Pope **Edge:** Plain

Date	Mintage	F	VF	XF	Unc	BU
2003MW Proof	4,900	Value: 1,300				

Y# 483 200 ZLOTYCH

15.5000 g., 0.9000 Gold 0.4485 oz. AGW, 27 mm. **Subject:** Poland Joining the European Union **Obv:** Polish euro coin design elements **Rev:** Polish euro coin design elements **Edge:** Plain

Date	Mintage	F	VF	XF	Unc	BU
2004MW Proof	4,400	Value: 850				

Y# 511 200 ZLOTYCH

15.5000 g., 0.9000 Gold 0.4485 oz. AGW, 27 mm. **Subject:** Warsaw Fine Arts Academy Centennial **Obv:** Campus view **Rev:** Statue and building **Edge:** Plain

Date	Mintage	F	VF	XF	Unc	BU
2004MW Proof	5,000	Value: 850				

Y# 519 200 ZLOTYCH

15.5000 g., 0.9000 Gold 0.4485 oz. AGW, 27 mm. **Subject:** Olympics **Obv:** Woman and crowned eagle **Rev:** Ancient runners painted on pottery **Edge:** Plain

Date	Mintage	F	VF	XF	Unc	BU
2004MW Proof	6,000	Value: 850				

Y# 538 200 ZLOTYCH

15.5000 g., 0.9000 Gold 0.4485 oz. AGW, 27 mm. **Obv:** Horse drawn carriage **Rev:** Konstanty Ildefons Galczynski in top hat **Edge:** Plain

Date	Mintage	F	VF	XF	Unc	BU
2005MW Proof	3,500	Value: 900				

Y# 536 200 ZLOTYCH

15.5000 g., 0.9000 Gold 0.4485 oz. AGW, 27 mm. **Obv:** Chopin **Rev:** Nagoya Castle roof tops and Mt. Fuji **Edge:** Plain **Note:** Aichi Expo Japan

Date	Mintage	F	VF	XF	Unc	BU
2005MW Proof	4,200	Value: 875				

Y# 672 200 ZLOTYCH

15.5000 g., 0.9000 Gold 0.4485 oz. AGW, 27 mm. **Obv:** Helmet and breastplate **Rev:** Knight of the 15th Century

Date	Mintage	F	VF	XF	Unc	BU
2007 Proof	10,500	Value: 850				

Y# 643 200 ZLOTYCH

15.5000 g., 0.9000 Gold 0.4485 oz. AGW, 27 mm. **Subject:** Zbigniew Herbert **Obv:** Eagle and Zbigniew Herbert **Rev:** Mounted statue of Marcus Aurelius **Designer:** Dominika Karpinska-Kopiec

Date	Mintage	F	VF	XF	Unc	BU
2008 Proof	11,200	Value: 850				

Y# 647 200 ZLOTYCH

15.5000 g., 0.9000 Gold 0.4485 oz. AGW, 27 mm. **Series:** The 29th Olympic Games Beijing 2008 **Obv:** Two kites and an eagle **Rev:** Female pole vault jumper **Designer:** Robert Kotowicz

Date	Mintage	F	VF	XF	Unc	BU
2008 Proof	—	Value: 850				

Y# 653 200 ZLOTYCH

15.5000 g., 0.9000 Gold 0.4485 oz. AGW, 27 mm. **Subject:** 90th Anniversary of Regaining Freedom **Obv:** Tomb of the unknown soldier **Rev:** Mounted Commander-In-Chief Jozef Pilsudski **Designer:** Ewa Olszewska-Borys

Date	Mintage	F	VF	XF	Unc	BU
2008 Proof	10,000	Value: 850				

Y# 654 200 ZLOTYCH

15.5000 g., 0.9000 Gold 0.4485 oz. AGW, 27 mm. **Subject:** 450 years of the Polish Post **Obv:** Eagle right, bottom against post stamp **Rev:** Horse with rider crossing bridge **Designer:** Robert Kotowicz

Date	Mintage	F	VF	XF	Unc	BU
2008 Proof	11,000	Value: 850				

Y# 660 200 ZLOTYCH

15.5000 g., 0.9000 Gold 0.4485 oz. AGW, 27 mm. **Subject:** 90th Anniversary of the Greater Poland Uprising **Obv:** Eagle at left, eagle at right with chain **Rev:** Charging cavalrymen and German soldiers firing at them **Designer:** Urszula Walerzak

Date	Mintage	F	VF	XF	Unc	BU
2008 Proof	9,400	Value: 850				

Y# 664 200 ZLOTYCH

15.5000 g., 0.9000 Gold 0.4485 oz. AGW, 27 mm. **Subject:** Warsaw Ghetto **Obv:** Building on fire, Naitonal arms **Rev:** Face looking out from broken brick wall

Date	Mintage	F	VF	XF	Unc	BU
2008MW Proof	12,000	Value: 850				

Y# 696 200 ZLOTYCH

15.1500 g., 0.9000 Gold 0.4384 oz. AGW, 27 mm. **Obv:** Eagle and statue, flames in background **Rev:** Stefan Starzonski, Warsaw Mayor; Burning of the Clock Tower

Date	Mintage	F	VF	XF	Unc	BU
2009 Proof	10,500	Value: 850				

Y# 677 200 ZLOTYCH

15.5000 g., 0.9000 Gold 0.4485 oz. AGW, 27 mm. **Subject:** Central Banking, 180th Anniversary **Obv:** National arms above crowned shield **Rev:** Building and portrait

Date	Mintage	F	VF	XF	Unc	BU
2009MW Proof	8,500	Value: 850				

Y# 683 200 ZLOTYCH

15.5000 g., 0.9000 Gold 0.4485 oz. AGW, 27 mm. **Subject:** General election of 1989 **Obv:** National arms above shipyard scene **Rev:** Lech Walesa silhouette before crowd

Date	Mintage	F	VF	XF	Unc	BU
2009MW Proof	10,000	Value: 850				

Y# 717 200 ZLOTYCH

15.5000 g., 0.9000 Gold 0.4485 oz. AGW, 27 mm. **Subject:** Vancouver Winter Olympics **Obv:** Downhill skiing **Rev:** Cross Country skiing

Date	Mintage	F	VF	XF	Unc	BU
2010MW Proof	8,000	Value: 850				

Y# 720 200 ZLOTYCH

15.5000 g., 0.9000 Gold 0.4485 oz. AGW, 27 mm. **Subject:** Napoleonic Imperial Guard **Obv:** Pile of arms **Rev:** Galloping guardsman

Date	Mintage	F	VF	XF	Unc	BU
2010MW Proof	10,500	Value: 850				

Y# 734 200 ZLOTYCH

15.5000 g., 0.9000 Gold 0.4485 oz. AGW, 27 mm. **Subject:** Battles of Grunwald and Kluszyn

Date	Mintage	F	VF	XF	Unc	BU
2010MW Proof	10,500	Value: 850				

Y# 782 200 ZLOTYCH

15.5000 g., 0.9000 Gold 0.4485 oz. AGW, 27 mm. **Subject:** Polish Cavalry - Uhlan **Edge Lettering:** 22.4x32

Date	Mintage	F	VF	XF	Unc	BU
2011MW Proof	5,000	Value: 875				

Y# 787 200 ZLOTYCH

15.5000 g., 0.9000 Gold 0.4485 oz. AGW, 27 mm. **Subject:** Czeslaw Milosz

Date	Mintage	F	VF	XF	Unc	BU
2011MW Proof	4,000	Value: 875				

Y# 791 200 ZLOTYCH

15.5000 g., 0.9000 Gold 0.4485 oz. AGW, 27 mm. **Subject:** Ignacy Jan Paderewski

Date	Mintage	F	VF	XF	Unc	BU
2011MW Proof	3,000	Value: 900				

Y# 819 200 ZLOTYCH

15.5000 g., 0.9000 Gold 0.4485 oz. AGW, 27 mm. **Subject:** Stefan Banach

Date	Mintage	F	VF	XF	Unc	BU
2012MW Proof	4,000	Value: 875				

Y# 834 200 ZLOTYCH

15.5000 g., 0.9000 Gold 0.4485 oz. AGW, 27 mm. **Subject:** London Olympics, 2012, Polish Team

Date	Mintage	F	VF	XF	Unc	BU
2012MW Proof	5,000	Value: 875				

Y# 840 200 ZLOTYCH

15.5000 g., 0.9000 Gold 0.4485 oz. AGW, 27 mm. **Subject:** Boleslaw Prus

Date	Mintage	F	VF	XF	Unc	BU
2012MW Proof	3,000	Value: 900				

Y# 831 500 ZLOTYCH
62.2000 g., 0.9990 Gold 1.9977 oz. AGW, 40 mm. **Subject:** European Football Championships

Date	Mintage	F	VF	XF	Unc	BU
2012MW Proof	1,000	Value: 3,750				

Y# 776 1000 ZLOTYCH
93.3000 g., 0.9990 Gold 2.9965 oz. AGW, 50 mm. **Subject:** John Paul II Beautification

Date	Mintage	F	VF	XF	Unc	BU
2011MW Proof	500	Value: 5,750				

GOLD BULLION COINAGE

Y# 292 50 ZLOTYCH
3.1000 g., 0.9999 Gold 0.0997 oz. AGW, 18 mm. **Obv:** Crowned eagle with wings open, all within circle **Rev:** Golden eagle

Date	Mintage	F	VF	XF	Unc	BU
2002	500	—	—	—	BV	220
2004	2,000	—	—	—	BV	200
2006	1,600	—	—	—	BV	200
2007	2,000	—	—	—	BV	200
2008	—	—	—	—	BV	200

Y# 293 100 ZLOTYCH
7.7800 g., 0.9999 Gold 0.2501 oz. AGW, 22 mm. **Obv:** Crowned eagle with wings open, all within circle **Rev:** Golden eagle

Date	Mintage	F	VF	XF	Unc	BU
2002	800	—	—	—	BV	475
2004	1,000	—	—	—	BV	475
2006	900	—	—	—	BV	475
2007	1,500	—	—	—	BV	475
2008	—	—	—	—	BV	475

Y# 294 200 ZLOTYCH
15.5000 g., 0.9000 Gold 0.4485 oz. AGW, 27 mm. **Obv:** Crowned eagle with wings open within beaded circle **Rev:** Golden eagle

Date	Mintage	F	VF	XF	Unc	BU
2002	1,000	—	—	—	BV	850
2004	1,000	—	—	—	BV	850
2006	900	—	—	—	BV	850
2007	1,500	—	—	—	BV	850
2008	—	—	—	—	BV	850

Y# 295 500 ZLOTYCH
31.1035 g., 0.9999 Gold 0.9999 oz. AGW **Obv:** Crowned eagle with wings open within beaded circle **Rev:** Golden eagle

Date	Mintage	F	VF	XF	Unc	BU
2002	1,000	—	—	—	BV	1,850
2004	2,500	—	—	—	BV	1,850
2006	600	—	—	—	BV	1,850
2007	2,500	—	—	—	BV	1,850
2008	—	—	—	—	BV	1,850

MINT SETS

KM#	Date	Mintage	Identification	Issue Price	Mkt Val
MS5	2007 (11)	2,000	Y#276-284, 465, 525, mixed date set - 1995-2007	39.95	37.50

PORTUGAL

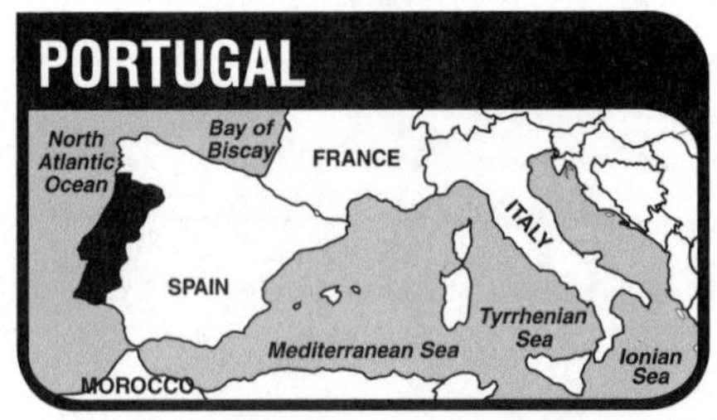

The Portuguese Republic, located in the western part of the Iberian Peninsula in southwestern Europe, has an area of 35,553 sq. mi. (92,080 sq. km.) and a population of *10.5 million. Capital: Lisbon. Portugal's economy is based on agriculture, tourism, minerals, fisheries and a rapidly expanding industrial sector. Textiles account for 33% of the exports and Portuguese wine is world famous. Portugal has become Europe's number one producer of copper and the world's largest producer of cork.

RULER
Republic, 1910 to date

MONETARY SYSTEM
100 Cents = 1 Euro

REPUBLIC

DECIMAL COINAGE

KM# 631a ESCUDO
4.6000 g., 0.9167 Gold 0.1356 oz. AGW, 16 mm. **Subject:** Last Escudo **Obv:** Design above shield with "Au" above top left corner of shield **Rev:** Flower design above value **Edge:** Plain

Date	Mintage	F	VF	XF	Unc	BU
2001INCM	50,000	—	—	—	235	250

KM# 634.1 20 ESCUDOS
6.9000 g., Copper-Nickel, 26.5 mm. **Obv:** Shield divides date with value below **Obv. Legend:** REPUBLICA PORTUGUESA **Rev:** Nautical windrose **Designer:** Euclides Vaz

Date	Mintage	F	VF	XF	Unc	BU
2001INCM	Est. 250,000	—	—	—	2.75	3.50

KM# 733 500 ESCUDOS
13.9600 g., 0.5000 Silver 0.2244 oz. ASW, 30.1 mm. **Subject:** Porto, European Culture Capital **Obv:** National arms and value **Rev:** Stylized design **Edge:** Reeded

Date	Mintage	F	VF	XF	Unc	BU
2001INCM	—	—	—	—	8.50	9.50
2001INCM Proof	10,000	Value: 60.00				

KM# 733a 500 ESCUDOS
Gold **Subject:** Porto, European Culture Capital **Obv:** National arms and value **Rev:** Stylized design **Edge:** Reeded

Date	Mintage	F	VF	XF	Unc	BU
2001INCM Proof	5,000	Value: 550				

KM# 734 1000 ESCUDOS
26.9500 g., 0.5000 Silver 0.4332 oz. ASW, 40 mm. **Obv:** National arms and value **Obv. Legend:** REPUBLICA PORTUGUESA 2001 **Rev:** Soccer ball within net **Rev. Legend:** 10º Campeonato Europeu de Futebol - UEFA Euro 2004 Portugal **Edge:** Reeded

Date	Mintage	F	VF	XF	Unc	BU
2001INCM	50,000	—	—	—	17.50	18.50
2001INCM Proof	—	Value: 75.00				

EURO COINAGE

European Union Issues

KM# 740 EURO CENT
2.3000 g., Copper Plated Steel, 16.25 mm. **Obv:** Royal seal of 1134 with country name and cross **Rev:** Value and globe **Edge:** Plain

Date	Mintage	F	VF	XF	Unc	BU
2002	278,106,172	—	—	—	0.35	0.50
2002 Proof	15,000	Value: 7.00				
2003	50,000	—	—	—	0.35	0.50
2003 Proof	15,000	Value: 7.00				
2004	75,000,000	—	—	—	0.35	0.50
2004 Proof	15,000	Value: 7.00				
2005	40,000,000	—	—	—	0.35	0.50
2005 Proof	10,000	Value: 7.00				
2006	30,000,000	—	—	—	0.35	0.50
2006 Proof	3,000	Value: 7.00				
2007	105,000,000	—	—	—	0.35	0.50
2007 Proof	2,500	Value: 7.00				
2008	75,000,000	—	—	—	0.35	0.50
2008 Proof	3,500	Value: 7.00				
2009	60,000,000	—	—	—	0.35	0.50
2009 Proof	4,000	Value: 7.00				
2010	15,000,000	—	—	—	0.35	0.50
2010 Proof	4,500	Value: 7.00				
2011	20,000,000	—	—	—	0.35	0.50
2011 Proof	4,500	Value: 7.00				
2012	—	—	—	—	0.35	0.50
2012 Proof	4,500	Value: 7.00				
2013	—	—	—	—	0.35	0.50
2013 Proof	—	Value: 7.00				

KM# 741 2 EURO CENT

3.0600 g., Copper Plated Steel, 18.75 mm. **Obv:** Royal seal of 1134 with country name and cross **Rev:** Value and globe **Edge:** Grooved

Date	Mintage	F	VF	XF	Unc	BU
2002	324,376,590	—	—	—	0.50	0.65
2002 Proof	15,000	Value: 9.00				
2003	50,000	—	—	—	—	2.50
Note: In sets only						
2003 Proof	15,000	Value: 9.00				
2004	1,000,000	—	—	—	0.50	0.65
2004 Proof	15,000	Value: 9.00				
2005	10,000,000	—	—	—	0.50	0.65
2005 Proof	10,000	Value: 9.00				
2006	1,000,000	—	—	—	0.50	0.65
2006 Proof	3,000	Value: 9.00				
2007	10,000,000	—	—	—	0.50	0.65
2007 Proof	2,500	Value: 9.00				
2008	35,000,000	—	—	—	0.50	0.65
2008 Proof	3,500	Value: 9.00				
2009	45,000,000	—	—	—	0.50	0.65
2009 Proof	4,000	Value: 9.00				
2010	10,000,000	—	—	—	0.50	0.65
2010 Proof	4,500	Value: 9.00				
2011	30,000,000	—	—	—	0.50	0.65
2011 Proof	4,500	Value: 9.00				
2012	—	—	—	—	0.50	0.65
2012 Proof	4,500	Value: 9.00				
2013	—	—	—	—	0.50	0.65
2013 Proof	—	Value: 9.00				

KM# 742 5 EURO CENT

3.9200 g., Copper Plated Steel, 21.25 mm. **Obv:** Royal seal of 1134 with country name and cross **Rev:** Value and globe **Edge:** Plain

Date	Mintage	F	VF	XF	Unc	BU
2002	234,512,047	—	—	—	0.75	1.00
2002 Proof	15,000	Value: 10.00				
2003	50,000	—	—	—	—	4.00
Note: In sets only						
2003 Proof	15,000	Value: 10.00				
2004	40,000,000	—	—	—	0.75	1.00
2004 Proof	15,000	Value: 10.00				
2005	30,000,000	—	—	—	0.75	1.00
2005 Proof	10,000	Value: 10.00				
2006	20,000,000	—	—	—	0.75	1.00
2006 Proof	3,000	Value: 10.00				
2007	25,000,000	—	—	—	0.75	1.00
2007 Proof	2,500	Value: 10.00				
2008	25,000,000	—	—	—	0.75	1.00
2008 Proof	3,500	Value: 10.00				
2009	25,000,000	—	—	—	0.75	1.00
2009 Proof	4,000	Value: 10.00				
2010	5,000,000	—	—	—	0.75	1.00
2010 Proof	4,500	Value: 10.00				
2011	25,000,000	—	—	—	0.75	1.00
2011 Proof	4,500	Value: 10.00				
2012	—	—	—	—	0.75	1.00
2012 Proof	4,500	Value: 10.00				
2013	—	—	—	—	0.75	1.00
2013 Proof	—	Value: 10.00				

KM# 743 10 EURO CENT

4.1000 g., Brass, 19.75 mm. **Obv:** Royal seal of 1142, country name in circular design **Rev:** Value and map **Edge:** Reeded

Date	Mintage	F	VF	XF	Unc	BU
2002	220,289,835	—	—	—	0.75	1.00
2002 Proof	15,000	Value: 12.00				
2003	6,332,000	—	—	—	1.00	1.50
2003 Proof	15,000	Value: 12.00				
2004	1,000,000	—	—	—	1.50	2.00
2004 Proof	15,000	Value: 12.00				
2005	1,000,000	—	—	—	1.50	2.00
2005 Proof	10,000	Value: 12.00				
2006	1,000,000	—	—	—	1.50	2.00
2006 Proof	3,000	Value: 12.00				
2007	21,500	—	—	—	1.50	2.00
2007 Proof	2,500	Value: 12.00				

KM# 763 10 EURO CENT

4.1000 g., Brass, 19.75 mm. **Obv:** Royal seal of 1142, country name in circular design **Rev:** Relief map of Western Europe, stars, lines and value **Edge:** Reeded

Date	Mintage	F	VF	XF	Unc	BU
2008	1,000,000	—	—	—	1.50	2.00
2008 Proof	3,500	Value: 12.00				
2009	10,000,000	—	—	—	1.50	2.00
2009 Proof	4,000	Value: 12.00				
2010	—	—	—	—	1.50	2.00
2010 Proof	4,500	Value: 12.00				
2011	—	—	—	—	1.50	2.00
2011 Proof	4,500	Value: 12.00				
2012	—	—	—	—	1.50	2.00
2012 Proof	4,500	Value: 12.00				
2013	—	—	—	—	1.50	2.00
2013 Proof	—	Value: 12.00				

KM# 744 20 EURO CENT

5.7400 g., Brass, 22.25 mm. **Obv:** Royal seal of 1142, country name in circular design **Rev:** Value and map **Edge:** Notched

Date	Mintage	F	VF	XF	Unc	BU
2002	147,411,038	—	—	—	1.00	1.25
2002 Proof	15,000	Value: 14.00				
2003	9,493,600	—	—	—	1.25	1.50
2003 Proof	15,000	Value: 14.00				
2004	1,000,000	—	—	—	1.50	2.00
2004 Proof	15,000	Value: 14.00				
2005	25,000,000	—	—	—	1.50	2.00
2005 Proof	10,000	Value: 14.00				
2006	20,000,000	—	—	—	1.50	2.00
2006 Proof	3,000	Value: 14.00				
2007	21,500	—	—	—	1.50	2.00
2007 Proof	2,500	Value: 14.00				

KM# 764 20 EURO CENT

5.7400 g., Brass, 22.25 mm. **Obv:** Royal seal of 1142, country name in circular design **Rev:** Relief map of Western Europe, stars, lines and value **Edge:** Notched

Date	Mintage	F	VF	XF	Unc	BU
2008	1,000,000	—	—	—	1.50	2.00
2008 Proof	3,500	Value: 14.00				
2009	20,000,000	—	—	—	1.50	2.00
2009 Proof	4,000	Value: 14.00				
2010	5,000,000	—	—	—	1.50	2.00
2010 Proof	4,500	Value: 14.00				
2011	10,000,000	—	—	—	1.50	2.00
2011 Proof	4,500	Value: 14.00				
2012	—	—	—	—	1.50	2.00
2012 Proof	4,500	Value: 14.00				
2013	—	—	—	—	1.50	2.00
2013 Proof	—	Value: 14.00				

KM# 777 1/4 EURO

1.5600 g., 0.9990 Gold 0.0501 oz. AGW, 14 mm. **Series:** Portugal Universal **Subject:** King Alfons I, the Conqueror **Obv:** National arms, value **Obv. Legend:** REPÚBLICA PORTUGUESA **Rev:** Stylized 3/4 length armored figure standing facing **Rev. Legend:** D. AFONSO HENRIQUES **Edge:** Reeded **Note:** Each coin is numbered.

Date	Mintage	F	VF	XF	Unc	BU
2006	30,000	—	—	—	—	145

KM# 826 1/4 EURO

1.5600 g., 0.9990 Gold 0.0501 oz. AGW, 14 mm. **Subject:** Anthony of Padua

Date	Mintage	F	VF	XF	Unc	BU
2007	30,000	—	—	—	—	125

KM# 827 1/4 EURO

1.5600 g., 0.9990 Gold 0.0501 oz. AGW, 14 mm. **Subject:** King Denis

Date	Mintage	F	VF	XF	Unc	BU
2008	30,000	—	—	—	—	125

KM# 787 1/4 EURO

1.5600 g., 0.9990 Gold 0.0501 oz. AGW, 14 mm. **Subject:** Vasco da Gama

Date	Mintage	F	VF	XF	Unc	BU
2009	20,000	—	—	—	125	—

KM# 794 1/4 EURO

1.5600 g., 0.9990 Gold 0.0501 oz. AGW, 14 mm. **Subject:** Luis Vaz de Camoes

Date	Mintage	F	VF	XF	Unc	BU
2010	15,000	—	—	—	—	145

KM# 805 1/4 EURO

1.5600 g., 0.9990 Gold 0.0501 oz. AGW, 14 mm. **Subject:** Fr. António Vieira **Obv:** National arms **Rev:** Linear portrait of Vieira

Date	Mintage	F	VF	XF	Unc	BU
2011	10,000	—	—	—	—	125

KM# 807 1/4 EURO

1.5600 g., 0.9990 Gold 0.0501 oz. AGW, 14 mm. **Subject:** Spain and Portugal's accession to the European Union, 25th Anniversary **Designer:** João Duarte

Date	Mintage	F	VF	XF	Unc	BU
2011	12,500	—	—	—	—	125

KM# 814 1/4 EURO

1.5600 g., 0.9990 Gold 0.0501 oz. AGW, 14 mm. **Subject:** Carlos Seixas, composer **Obv:** National arms **Rev:** Head facing, name at left, dates at right **Designer:** Rui Vasquez

Date	Mintage	F	VF	XF	Unc	BU
2012	15,000	—	—	—	—	145

KM# 745 50 EURO CENT

7.8000 g., Brass, 24.25 mm. **Obv:** Royal seal of 1142, country name in circular design **Rev:** Value and map **Edge:** Reeded

Date	Mintage	F	VF	XF	Unc	BU
2002	151,947,133	—	—	—	1.50	2.00
2002 Proof	15,000	Value: 16.00				
2003	10,353,000	—	—	—	1.50	2.00
2003 Proof	15,000	Value: 16.00				
2004	1,000,000	—	—	—	2.50	3.00
2004 Proof	15,000	Value: 16.00				
2005	1,000,000	—	—	—	2.50	3.00
2005 Proof	10,000	Value: 16.00				
2006	1,000,000	—	—	—	2.50	3.00
2006 Proof	3,000	Value: 16.00				
2007	21,500	—	—	—	2.50	3.00
2007 Proof	2,500	Value: 16.00				

KM# 765 50 EURO CENT

7.8000 g., Brass, 24.25 mm. **Obv:** Royal seal of 1142, country name in circular design **Rev:** Relief map of Western Europe, stars, lines and value **Edge:** Reeded

Date	Mintage	F	VF	XF	Unc	BU
2008	5,000,000	—	—	—	2.50	3.00
2008 Proof	3,500	Value: 16.00				
2009	20,000,000	—	—	—	2.50	3.00
2009 Proof	4,000	Value: 16.00				
2010	20,000,000	—	—	—	2.50	3.00
2010 Proof	4,500	Value: 16.00				
2011	—	—	—	—	2.50	3.00
2011 Proof	4,500	Value: 16.00				
2012	—	—	—	—	2.50	3.00
2012 Proof	4,500	Value: 16.00				
2013	—	—	—	—	2.50	3.00
2013 Proof	—	Value: 16.00				

KM# 746 EURO

7.5000 g., Bi-Metallic Copper-Nickel center in Nickel-Brass ring, 23.25 mm. **Obv:** Royal seal of 1144, country name in looped design **Rev:** Value and map **Edge:** Segmented reeding

Date	Mintage	F	VF	XF	Unc	BU
2002	100,228,135	—	—	—	2.00	2.50
Note: Variety in the edge milling, 28 or 29.						
2002 Proof	15,000	Value: 18.00				
2003	16,206,875	—	—	—	2.00	2.50

Date	Mintage	F	VF	XF	Unc	BU
2003 Proof	15,000	Value: 18.00				
2004	20,000,000	—	—	—	2.00	2.50
2004 Proof	15,000	Value: 18.00				
2005	20,000,000	—	—	—	2.00	2.50
2005 Proof	10,000	Value: 18.00				
2006	20,000,000	—	—	—	2.00	2.50
2006 Proof	3,000	Value: 18.00				
2007	4,935,400	—	—	—	2.00	2.50
2007 Proof	2,500	Value: 18.00				

KM# 766 EURO

7.5000 g., Bi-Metallic Copper-Nickel center in Nickel-Brass ring, 23.25 mm. **Obv:** Royal seal of 1144, country name in looped design **Rev:** Relief map of Western Europe, stars, lines and value **Edge:** Segmented reeding

Date	Mintage	F	VF	XF	Unc	BU
2008	5,000,000	—	—	—	2.75	3.50
2008 Proof	3,500	Value: 18.00				
2009	20,000,000	—	—	—	2.75	3.50
2009 Proof	4,000	Value: 18.00				
2010	20,000,000	—	—	—	2.75	3.50
2010 Proof	4,500	Value: 18.00				
2011	5,000,000	—	—	—	2.75	3.50
2011 Proof	4,500	Value: 18.00				
2012	—	—	—	—	2.75	3.50
2012 Proof	4,500	Value: 18.00				
2013	—	—	—	—	2.75	3.50
2013 Proof	—	Value: 18.00				

KM# 828 1-1/2 EURO

10.0000 g., Copper-Nickel, 26.5 mm. **Subject:** Internaitonal Medical Care **Obv:** National Arms **Rev:** AMI logo

Date	Mintage	F	VF	XF	Unc	BU
2008	300,000	—	—	—	10.00	12.50

KM# 828a 1-1/2 EURO

8.0000 g., Copper-Nickel, 26.5 mm. **Subject:** International Medical Assistance **Obv:** National arms **Rev:** AMI logo

Date	Mintage	F	VF	XF	Unc	BU
2008 Special Unc.	50,000	—	—	—	20.00	25.00

KM# 828b 1-1/2 EURO

10.0000 g., 0.9250 Silver 0.2974 oz. ASW, 26.5 mm. **Subject:** International Medical Assistance **Obv:** National arms **Rev:** AMI logo

Date	Mintage	F	VF	XF	Unc	BU
2008 Proof	5,000	Value: 60.00				

KM# 788 1-1/2 EURO

10.3700 g., 0.9990 Gold 0.3331 oz. AGW, 26.5 mm. **Subject:** Numismatics - Marabitino of Sancho II **Obv:** Cross of shields **Rev:** King on horseback

Date	Mintage	F	VF	XF	Unc	BU
2009 Proof	2,500	Value: 650				

KM# 789 1-1/2 EURO

Copper-Nickel, 26.5 mm. **Obv:** Numismatics - Marabitino of Sancho II

Date	Mintage	F	VF	XF	Unc	BU
2009 Proof	150,000	—	—	—	5.00	6.00

KM# 795 1-1/2 EURO

8.0000 g., Copper-Nickel, 26.5 mm. **Subject:** Against Famine

Date	Mintage	F	VF	XF	Unc	BU
2010	100,000	—	—	—	5.00	6.00
2010INCM Special Unc.	100,000	—	—	—	—	10.00

KM# 795a 1-1/2 EURO

10.0000 g., 0.9250 Silver 0.2974 oz. ASW, 26.5 mm. **Subject:** Against Famine

Date	Mintage	F	VF	XF	Unc	BU
2010 Proof	5,000	Value: 55.00				

KM# 747 2 EURO

8.5000 g., Bi-Metallic Nickel-Brass center in Copper-Nickel ring, 25.75 mm. **Obv:** Royal seal of 1144, country name in looped design **Rev:** Value and map **Edge:** Reeding over castles and shields

Date	Mintage	F	VF	XF	Unc	BU
2002	61,930,775	—	—	—	3.50	4.00
2002 Proof	15,000	Value: 22.00				
2003	5,979,750	—	—	—	4.25	5.00
2003 Proof	15,000	Value: 22.00				
2004	1,000,000	—	—	—	5.50	6.00
2004 Proof	15,000	Value: 22.00				
2005	1,000,000	—	—	—	5.50	6.00
2005 Proof	10,000	Value: 22.00				
2006	1,000,000	—	—	—	5.50	6.00
2006 Proof	3,000	Value: 22.00				
2007	21,500	—	—	—	5.50	6.00
2007 Proof	2,500	Value: 22.00				

KM# 771 2 EURO

8.5000 g., Bi-Metallic Nickel-Brass center in Copper-Nickel ring, 25.75 mm. **Subject:** 50th Anniversary Treaty of Rome **Obv:** Open treaty book **Rev:** Large value at left, modified outline of Europe at right **Edge:** Reeded and lettered

Date	Mintage	F	VF	XF	Unc	BU
2007	1,500,000	—	—	—	4.50	6.00
2007 Prooflike	15,000	—	—	—	—	12.50
2007 Proof	5,000	Value: 25.00				

KM# 772 2 EURO

8.5000 g., Bi-Metallic Nickel-Brass center in Copper-Nickel ring, 25.75 mm. **Subject:** European Union President **Obv:** Large tree, small national arms at lower left **Obv. Inscription:** POR / TV / GAL **Rev:** Large value at left, revised map of Europe at right **Edge:** Reeded with repeated symbols

Date	Mintage	F	VF	XF	Unc	BU
2007	1,250,000	—	—	—	4.50	6.00
2007 Prooflike	15,000	—	—	—	—	12.50
2007 Proof	5,000	Value: 25.00				

KM# 767 2 EURO

8.5200 g., Bi-Metallic Nickel-Brass center in Copper-Nickel ring, 25.7 mm. **Obv:** Royal seal of 1144, country name in looped design **Rev:** Relief map of Western Europe, stars, lines and value **Edge:** Reeding over castles and shields

Date	Mintage	F	VF	XF	Unc	BU
2008 In sets only	—	—	—	—	—	6.00
2008 Proof	3,500	Value: 22.00				
2009 In sets only	—	—	—	—	—	6.00
2009 Proof	4,000	Value: 22.00				
2010	—	—	—	—	—	6.00
2010 Proof	4,500	Value: 22.00				
2011	—	—	—	—	—	6.00
2011 Proof	4,500	Value: 22.00				
2012	—	—	—	—	—	6.00
2012 Proof	4,500	Value: 22.00				
2013	—	—	—	—	—	6.00
2013 Proof	—	Value: 22.00				

KM# 784 2 EURO

8.5000 g., Bi-Metallic Nickel-Brass center in Copper-Nickel ring, 25.75 mm. **Subject:** Declaration of Human Rights, 60th Anniversary **Obv:** Seal above field

Date	Mintage	F	VF	XF	Unc	BU
2008	1,000,000	—	—	—	4.00	5.00
2008 Proof	10,000	Value: 25.00				

KM# 785 2 EURO

8.5000 g., Bi-Metallic Nickel-Brass center in Copper-Nickel ring, 25.75 mm. **Subject:** European Monetary Union, 10th Anniversary **Obv:** Stick figure and Euro symbol

Date	Mintage	F	VF	XF	Unc	BU
2009	1,250,000	—	—	—	6.00	12.00
2009 Proof	15,000	Value: 25.00				

KM# 786 2 EURO

8.5000 g., Bi-Metallic Nickel-Brass center in Copper-Nickel ring, 25.75 mm. **Subject:** Lusofonia Games **Rev:** Figure with long flowing ribbon

Date	Mintage	F	VF	XF	Unc	BU
2009	1,275,000	—	—	—	—	5.00
2009 Proof	10,000	Value: 25.00				

KM# 796 2 EURO

8.5000 g., Bi-Metallic Nickel-Brass center in Copper-Nickel ring, 25.75 mm. **Subject:** Portuguese Republic, 100th Anniversary

Date	Mintage	F	VF	XF	Unc	BU
2010	1,265,000	—	—	—	6.00	7.00
2010 Proof	10,000	Value: 20.00				

KM# 804 2 EURO

8.5000 g., Bi-Metallic Nickel-Brass center in Copper-Nickel ring, 25.75 mm. **Subject:** Fernão Mendes Pinto, 500th Anniversary of Birth **Obv:** Sailing ship right

Date	Mintage	F	VF	XF	Unc	BU
2011	500,000	—	—	—	6.00	7.00
2011 Special Unc.	12,500	—	—	—	—	9.00
2011 Proof	7,500	Value: 25.00				

KM# 812 2 EURO

8.5000 g., Bi-Metallic Nickel-Brass center in Copper-Nickel ring, 25.75 mm. **Subject:** Euro circulation, 10th Anniversary **Obv:** Euro symbol on globe, childlike images around

Date	Mintage	F	VF	XF	Unc	BU
2012	500,000	—	—	—	6.00	7.00
2012 Special Unc.	10,000	—	—	—	—	9.00
2012 Proof	10,000	Value: 25.00				

KM# 813 2 EURO

8.5000 g., Bi-Metallic Nickel-Brass center in Copper-Nickel ring, 25.75 mm. **Subject:** Guimarães, European Cultural Capital **Obv:** Stylized cross and castle

Date	Mintage	F	VF	XF	Unc	BU
2012	500,000	—	—	—	6.00	7.00
2012 Special Unc.	10,000	—	—	—	—	9.00
2012 Proof	10,000	Value: 25.00				

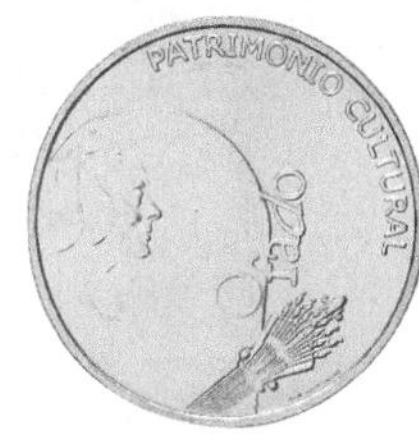

KM# 783 2-1/2 EURO

9.8500 g., Copper-Nickel, 28 mm. **Obv:** Small national arms on stringed instrument at right **Rev:** Fado musician at lower left **Edge:** Coarse reeding

Date	Mintage	F	VF	XF	Unc	BU
2008	150,000	—	—	—	6.00	9.00

KM# 783a 2-1/2 EURO

12.0000 g., 0.9250 Silver 0.3569 oz. ASW, 28 mm. **Obv:** Small national arms on stringed instrument at right **Rev:** Fado musician at lower left

Date	Mintage	F	VF	XF	Unc	BU
2008 Proof	20,000	Value: 60.00				

KM# 790 2-1/2 EURO

10.0000 g., Copper-Nickel, 28 mm. **Subject:** Bejing Olympics

Date	Mintage	F	VF	XF	Unc	BU
2008	487,500	—	—	—	6.00	7.00

KM# 790a 2-1/2 EURO

12.0000 g., 0.9250 Silver 0.3569 oz. ASW, 28 mm. **Subject:** Bejing Olympics

Date	Mintage	F	VF	XF	Unc	BU
2008 Proof	12,500	Value: 60.00				

KM# 824 2-1/2 EURO

10.0000 g., Copper-Nickel, 28 mm. **Subject:** UNESCO - World Historic Site, Porto **Obv:** National arms **Rev:** Bridge and town view

Date	Mintage	F	VF	XF	Unc	BU
2008	80,000	—	—	—	10.00	15.00

KM# 824a 2-1/2 EURO

12.0000 g., 0.9250 Silver 0.3569 oz. ASW, 28 mm. **Subject:** UNESCO Historic Site - Porto **Obv:** National arms **Rev:** Bridge and town view

Date	Mintage	F	VF	XF	Unc	BU
2008 Proof	5,000	Value: 60.00				

KM# 825 2-1/2 EURO

10.0000 g., Copper-Nickel, 28 mm. **Subject:** UNESCO Historic Site - Wine region of Alto Douro **Obv:** National arms and river **Rev:** Terraced fields

Date	Mintage	F	VF	XF	Unc	BU
2008 80000	—	—	—	—	10.00	12.50

KM# 825a 2-1/2 EURO

12.0000 g., 0.9250 Silver 0.3569 oz. ASW, 28 mm. **Subject:** UNESCO historic sites - Wine region of Alto Douro **Obv:** National arms and river **Rev:** Terraced fields

Date	Mintage	F	VF	XF	Unc	BU
2008 Proof	5,000	Value: 60.00				

KM# 792 2-1/2 EURO

Copper-Nickel, 28 mm. **Subject:** UNESCO Heritage Site - Hieronymites Monastery **Obv:** Arched cieling design, National arms **Rev:** Façade detail

Date	Mintage	F	VF	XF	Unc	BU
2009	150,000	—	—	—	6.00	7.00

KM# 791 2-1/2 EURO

Copper-Nickel, 28 mm. **Subject:** Portugese Literature **Obv:** Portrait of Fernando António Nogueira de Seabra, and text **Rev:** Stylized portrait of Luis Vaz de Camões and lines

Date	Mintage	F	VF	XF	Unc	BU
2009	150,000	—	—	—	6.00	7.00

KM# 791a 2-1/2 EURO

12.0000 g., 0.9250 Silver 0.3569 oz. ASW, 28 mm. **Subject:** Portuguese Literature

Date	Mintage	F	VF	XF	Unc	BU
2009 Proof	14,000	Value: 60.00				

KM# 791b 2-1/2 EURO

15.5500 g., 0.9990 Gold 0.4994 oz. AGW, 28 mm. **Subject:** Portuguese Literature

Date	Mintage	F	VF	XF	Unc	BU
2009 Proof	2,500	Value: 950				

KM# 792a 2-1/2 EURO

12.0000 g., 0.9250 Silver 0.3569 oz. ASW, 28 mm. **Subject:** UNESCO World Heritage Site - Hieronymites Monastery **Obv:** Arched ceiling design, National arms **Rev:** Façade detail

Date	Mintage	F	VF	XF	Unc	BU
2009 Proof	5,000	Value: 60.00				

KM# 793 2-1/2 EURO

10.0000 g., Copper-Nickel, 28 mm. **Obv:** National arms, rope splice below **Rev:** UNESCO World Heritage Site - Belém

Date	Mintage	F	VF	XF	Unc	BU
2009	150,000	—	—	—	6.00	7.00

KM# 793a 2-1/2 EURO

12.0000 g., 0.9250 Silver 0.3569 oz. ASW, 28 mm. **Subject:** UNESCO - World Heritage Site - Belém **Obv:** Naitonal arms, rope splice below **Rev:** Fortress

Date	Mintage	F	VF	XF	Unc	BU
2009 Proof	5,000	Value: 60.00				

KM# 797a 2-1/2 EURO

12.0000 g., 0.9250 Silver 0.3569 oz. ASW, 28 mm. **Subject:** FIFA Soccer - South Africa

Date	Mintage	F	VF	XF	Unc	BU
2010INCM Proof	12,500	Value: 55.00				

KM# 797 2-1/2 EURO

10.0000 g., Copper-Nickel, 28 mm. **Subject:** FIFA Soccer - South Africa

Date	Mintage	F	VF	XF	Unc	BU
2010INCM	120,000	—	—	—	6.00	7.00

KM# 798 2-1/2 EURO

10.0000 g., Copper-Nickel, 28 mm. **Subject:** Palace Square, Lisbon

Date	Mintage	F	VF	XF	Unc	BU
2010INCM	120,000	—	—	—	6.00	7.00

KM# 798a 2-1/2 EURO

12.0000 g., 0.9250 Silver 0.3569 oz. ASW, 28 mm. **Subject:** Palace Square, Lisbon

Date	Mintage	F	VF	XF	Unc	BU
2010INCM Proof	15,000	Value: 55.00				

KM# 798b 2-1/2 EURO

15.5500 g., 0.9990 Gold 0.4994 oz. AGW, 28 mm. **Subject:** Palace Square, Lisbon

Date	Mintage	F	VF	XF	Unc	BU
2010INCM Proof	2,500	Value: 950				

KM# 800 2-1/2 EURO

10.0000 g., Copper-Nickel, 28 mm. **Subject:** Torres Defence Line, 200th Anniversary

Date	Mintage	F	VF	XF	Unc	BU
2010INCM	—	—	—	—	6.00	7.00

KM# 800a 2-1/2 EURO

12.0000 g., 0.9250 Silver 0.3569 oz. ASW, 28 mm. **Subject:** Torres Defence Line, 200th Anniversary

Date	Mintage	F	VF	XF	Unc	BU
2010INCM Proof	—	Value: 55.00				

KM# 801 2-1/2 EURO

10.0000 g., Copper-Nickel, 28 mm. **Subject:** UNESCO World Cultural Heritage site - Coa Valley

Date	Mintage	F	VF	XF	Unc	BU
2010INCM	120,000	—	—	—	6.00	7.00

KM# 801a 2-1/2 EURO

12.0000 g., 0.9250 Silver 0.3569 oz. ASW, 28 mm. **Subject:** UNESCO World Cultural Heritage Site - Coa Valley

Date	Mintage	F	VF	XF	Unc	BU
2010INCM Proof	5,000	—	—	—	—	—

KM# 806 2-1/2 EURO

10.0000 g., Copper-Nickel, 28 mm. **Subject:** European explorers **Obv:** National arms, tree branch and Chinese characters **Rev:** Two portraits **Designer:** Baiba Shime

Date	Mintage	F	VF	XF	Unc	BU
2011	100,000	—	—	—	—	7.00

KM# 806a 2-1/2 EURO

12.0000 g., 0.9250 Silver 0.3569 oz. ASW, 28 mm. **Subject:** European explorers **Obv:** National arms, tree branch and Chinese characters **Rev:** Two portraits **Designer:** Baiba Shime

Date	Mintage	F	VF	XF	Unc	BU
2011 Proof	—	Value: 55.00				

KM# 806b 2-1/2 EURO

15.5500 g., 0.9990 Gold 0.4994 oz. AGW, 28 mm. **Subject:** European explorers **Obv:** National arms, tree branch, Chinese characters **Rev:** Two portraits **Designer:** Baiba Shime

Date	Mintage	F	VF	XF	Unc	BU
2011 Proof	—	Value: 950				

KM# 809 2-1/2 EURO

10.0000 g., Copper-Nickel, 28 mm. **Subject:** Army College, 100th Anniversary **Obv:** National arms and sword **Rev:** Sword and cadet cap

Date	Mintage	F	VF	XF	Unc	BU
2011	100,000	—	—	—	—	7.00

KM# 809a 2-1/2 EURO

12.0000 g., 0.9250 Silver 0.3569 oz. ASW, 28 mm. **Subject:** Army College, 100th Anniversary **Obv:** National arms and sword **Rev:** Sword and cadet cap **Designer:** José Viriato

Date	Mintage	F	VF	XF	Unc	BU
2011 Proof	—	Value: 55.00				

KM# 810 2-1/2 EURO

10.0000 g., Copper-Nickel, 28 mm. **Subject:** Pico Island, Azores. Wine growing landscape **Obv:** National arms and tree **Rev:** Grape leaf and vine fields

Date	Mintage	F	VF	XF	Unc	BU
2011	100,000	—	—	—	—	7.00

KM# 810a 2-1/2 EURO

12.0000 g., 0.9250 Silver 0.3569 oz. ASW, 28 mm. **Subject:** Pico Island, Azores, Wine growing landscape **Obv:** National arms and tree **Rev:** Wine leaf, wine fields in background

Date	Mintage	F	VF	XF	Unc	BU
2011 Proof	3,000	Value: 55.00				

KM# 815 2-1/2 EURO

10.0000 g., Copper-Nickel, 28 mm. **Subject:** José Malhoa **Obv:** Female model at left, national arms at right **Rev:** Malhoa half-length figure with artist pallet and brushes **Designer:** Paula Lourenço

Date	Mintage	F	VF	XF	Unc	BU
2012	100,000	—	—	—	—	6.00

KM# 815a 2-1/2 EURO

12.0000 g., 0.9250 Silver 0.3569 oz. ASW, 28 mm. **Subject:** José Malhoa **Obv:** Female model seated at left, national arms at right **Rev:** Malhoa half-length figure standing with artist pallet and brushes **Designer:** Paula Lourenço

Date	Mintage	F	VF	XF	Unc	BU
2012 Proof	10,000	Value: 55.00				

KM# 815b 2-1/2 EURO

15.5500 g., 0.9990 Gold 0.4994 oz. AGW, 28 mm. **Subject:** José Malhoa **Obv:** Female model seated at left, national arms at right **Rev:** Malhoa half-length figure standing wiht artist pallet and brushes **Designer:** Paula Lourenço

Date	Mintage	F	VF	XF	Unc	BU
2012 Proof	1,500	Value: 950				

KM# 816 2-1/2 EURO

10.0000 g., Copper-Nickel, 28 mm. **Subject:** Portugual's participation in 2012 London Olympics **Obv:** National arms and laurel branch **Rev:** Two judo players, geometric pattern **Designer:** José João de Brito

Date	Mintage	F	VF	XF	Unc	BU
2012	300,000	—	—	—	—	10.00

KM# 816a 2-1/2 EURO

12.0000 g., 0.9250 Silver 0.3569 oz. ASW, 28 mm. **Subject:** Portugal's participation in 2012 London Olympics **Obv:** National arms and laurel branch **Rev:** Judo players, geometric pattern **Designer:** José João de Brito

Date	Mintage	F	VF	XF	Unc	BU
2012 Proof	5,000	Value: 55.00				

KM# 816b 2-1/2 EURO

Bi-Metallic 3.1 g. Gold center in 12 g. Silver ring, 28 mm. **Subject:** Portugal's participation in 2012 London Olympics **Obv:** National arms and laurel branch **Rev:** Judo players and geometric pattern **Designer:** José João de Brito

Date	Mintage	F	VF	XF	Unc	BU
2012 Proof	2,500	Value: 600				

KM# 819 2-1/2 EURO

12.0000 g., Copper-Nickel, 28 mm. **Subject:** Guimarães - UNESCO World Heritage site **Obv:** National arms and city plan **Rev:** Linear architectural representations **Designer:** Antónia Marinho

Date	Mintage	F	VF	XF	Unc	BU
2012	100,000	—	—	—	—	25.00

KM# 819a 2-1/2 EURO

12.0000 g., 0.9250 Silver 0.3569 oz. ASW, 28 mm. **Subject:** Guimarães - UNESCO World Heritage site **Obv:** National arms, linear city plan **Rev:** Linear architectural renderings **Designer:** António Marinho

Date	Mintage	F	VF	XF	Unc	BU
2012 Proof	3,000	Value: 55.00				

KM# 749 5 EURO

14.0000 g., 0.5000 Silver 0.2250 oz. ASW, 30 mm. **Subject:** 150th Anniversary - First Portuguese Postage Stamp **Obv:** National arms and value within partial stamp design **Rev:** Partial postal stamp design **Edge:** Reeded

Date	Mintage	F	VF	XF	Unc	BU
2003INCM	300,000	—	—	—	22.50	30.00

KM# 749a 5 EURO

14.0000 g., 0.9250 Silver 0.4163 oz. ASW, 30 mm. **Obv:** National arms and value within partial stamp design **Rev:** Partial postal stamp design

Date	Mintage	F	VF	XF	Unc	BU
2003INCM	20,000	—	—	—	—	30.00
2003INCM Proof	20,000	Value: 55.00				

KM# 749b 5 EURO

17.5000 g., 0.9166 Gold 0.5157 oz. AGW, 30 mm. **Obv:** National arms and value within partial stamp design **Rev:** Partial postal stamp design

Date	Mintage	F	VF	XF	Unc	BU
2003INCM Proof	10,000	Value: 1,000				

KM# 754 5 EURO

14.0000 g., 0.5000 Silver 0.2250 oz. ASW, 30 mm. **Subject:** Convent of Christ **Obv:** National arms above value flanked by designs **Rev:** Ornate convent window **Edge:** Reeded

Date	Mintage	F	VF	XF	Unc	BU
2004INCM	300,000	—	—	—	30.00	32.50

KM# 754a 5 EURO

14.0000 g., 0.9250 Silver 0.4163 oz. ASW, 30 mm. **Subject:** Convent of Christ **Obv:** National arms above value flanked by designs **Rev:** Ornate convent window **Edge:** Reeded

Date	Mintage	F	VF	XF	Unc	BU
2004INCM Proof	10,000	Value: 60.00				

KM# 755 5 EURO

14.0000 g., 0.5000 Silver 0.2250 oz. ASW, 30 mm. **Subject:** Historic City of Evora **Obv:** National arms and value on city map silhouette **Rev:** Architectural highlights **Edge:** Reeded

Date	Mintage	F	VF	XF	Unc	BU
2004INCM	300,000	—	—	—	30.00	32.50

KM# 755a 5 EURO

14.0000 g., 0.9250 Silver 0.4163 oz. ASW, 30 mm. **Subject:** Historic City of Evora **Obv:** National arms and value on city map silhouette **Rev:** Architectural highlights **Edge:** Reeded

Date	Mintage	F	VF	XF	Unc	BU
2004INCM Proof	10,000	Value: 60.00				

KM# 762 5 EURO

14.0000 g., 0.5000 Silver 0.2250 oz. ASW, 30 mm. **Subject:** 800th Anniversary Birth of Pope John XXI **Obv:** National arms at lower right with archways in backgound **Obv. Legend:** REPUBLICA PORTUGUESA **Rev:** 1/2 length figure of Pope facing at right with staff dividing dates, small shield at left **Edge:** Reeded

Date	Mintage	F	VF	XF	Unc	BU
2005INCM	300,000	—	—	—	30.00	32.50

KM# 762a 5 EURO

14.0000 g., 0.9250 Silver 0.4163 oz. ASW, 30 mm. **Subject:** 800th Anniversary Birth of Pope John XXI **Obv:** National arms at lower right with archways in backgound **Obv. Legend:** REPUBLICA PORTUGUESA **Rev:** 1/2 length figure of Pope facing at right with staff dividing dates, small shield at left **Edge:** Reeded

Date	Mintage	F	VF	XF	Unc	BU
2005INCM Proof	15,000	Value: 65.00				

KM# 762b 5 EURO

17.5000 g., 0.9167 Gold 0.5157 oz. AGW, 30 mm. **Subject:** 800th Anniversary Birth of Pope John XXI **Obv:** National arms at lower right, archways in background **Obv. Legend:** REPUBLICA PORTUGUESA **Edge:** Reeded

Date	Mintage	F	VF	XF	Unc	BU
2005INCM Proof	7,500	Value: 1,000				

KM# 760 5 EURO

14.0000 g., 0.5000 Silver 0.2250 oz. ASW, 30 mm. **Obv:** National arms within circle **Obv. Legend:** REPUBLICA POTUGUESA **Rev:** Angra do Heroismo - Azores Terceira, emblem above **Rev. Legend:** CENTRO HISTÓRICO DE ANGRA DO HEROISMA **Edge:** Reeded

Date	Mintage	F	VF	XF	Unc	BU
2005	300,000	—	—	—	30.00	32.50

KM# 760a 5 EURO

14.0000 g., 0.9250 Silver 0.4163 oz. ASW, 30 mm. **Obv:** National arms within circle **Obv. Legend:** REPUBLICA PORTUGUESA **Rev:** Angra do Heroisma - Azores Terceira, emblem above **Rev. Legend:** CENTRO HISTÓRICO DE ANGRA DO HEROISMA **Edge:** Reeded

Date	Mintage	F	VF	XF	Unc	BU
2005 Proof	15,000	Value: 60.00				

KM# 761 5 EURO

14.0000 g., 0.5000 Silver 0.2250 oz. ASW, 30 mm. **Obv:** Design divides national arms and value **Obv. Legend:** REPUBLICA PORTUGUESA **Rev:** Batalha monastery and emblem **Rev. Legend:** MONTEIRO DA BATALHA **Edge:** Reeded

Date	Mintage	F	VF	XF	Unc	BU
2005	300,000	—	—	—	30.00	32.50

KM# 761a 5 EURO

14.0000 g., 0.9250 Silver 0.4163 oz. ASW, 30 mm. **Obv:** Design divides national arms and value **Obv. Legend:** REPUBLICA PORTUGUESA **Rev:** Batalha monastery and emblem **Rev. Legend:** MONTEIRO DA BATALHA **Edge:** Reeded

Date	Mintage	F	VF	XF	Unc	BU
2005 Proof	15,000	Value: 60.00				

KM# 769 5 EURO

14.0000 g., 0.5000 Silver 0.2250 oz. ASW, 30 mm. **Subject:** UNESCO - Cultural preservation **Obv:** National arms above value **Obv. Legend:** REPUBLICA PORTUGUESA **Rev:** Outlined view **Rev. Legend:** PAISAGEM CULTURAL DE SINTRA **Edge:** Reeded

Date	Mintage	F	VF	XF	Unc	BU
2006INCM	82,000	—	—	—	30.00	32.50

KM# 769a 5 EURO

14.0000 g., 0.9250 Silver 0.4163 oz. ASW, 30 mm. **Subject:** UNESCO - Cultural preservation **Obv:** National arms above value **Obv. Legend:** REPUBLICA PORTUGUESA **Rev:** Outlined view **Rev. Legend:** PAISAGEM CULTURAL DE SINTRA **Edge:** Reeded

Date	Mintage	F	VF	XF	Unc	BU
2006INCM Proof	6,000	Value: 60.00				

KM# 779 5 EURO

14.0000 g., 0.5000 Silver 0.2250 oz. ASW **Subject:** Alcobaça Monastery **Obv:** National arms **Obv. Legend:** REPÚBLICA PORTUGUESA **Edge:** Reeded

Date	Mintage	F	VF	XF	Unc	BU
2006INCM	82,000	—	—	—	25.00	27.50

KM# 779a 5 EURO

14.0000 g., 0.9250 Silver 0.4163 oz. ASW **Subject:** Alcobaça Monestary **Obv:** National arms **Obv. Legend:** REPÚBLICA PORTUGUESA **Edge:** Reeded

Date	Mintage	F	VF	XF	Unc	BU
2006INCM Proof	6,000	Value: 60.00				

KM# 782 5 EURO

13.9500 g., 0.5000 Silver 0.2242 oz. ASW, 30 mm. **Series:** UNESCO - World Heritage **Subject:** National Forest Reserve in Madeira Nature Park **Obv:** National arms **Obv. Legend:** REPÚBLICA PORTUGUESA **Rev:** Foliage with small UNESCO World Heritage logo at lower right **Rev. Legend:** FLORESTA LAURISSILVA DA MADEIRA **Edge:** Reeded

Date	Mintage	F	VF	XF	Unc	BU
2007INCM	75,000	—	—	—	25.00	27.50

KM# 782a 5 EURO

14.0000 g., 0.9250 Silver 0.4163 oz. ASW, 30 mm. **Series:** UNESCO - World Heritage **Subject:** National Forest Reserve in Madeira Nature Park **Obv:** National arms **Obv. Legend:** REPÚBLICA PORTUGUESA **Rev:** Foliage with small UNESCO World Heritage logo at lower right **Rev. Legend:** FLORESTA LAURISSILVA DA MADEIRA **Edge:** Reeded

Date	Mintage	F	VF	XF	Unc	BU
2007INCM Proof	6,000	Value: 65.00				

KM# 770 5 EURO

14.0000 g., 0.5000 Silver 0.2250 oz. ASW, 30 mm. **Subject:** World Scouting Centennial **Obv:** Portuguese Arms, World Scouting emblem **Obv. Legend:** REPUBLICA PORTUGUESA 1907-2007 CENTENARIO DO ESCUTISMO MUNDIAL **Rev:** Linear portrait of Lord Robert Baden-Powell **Rev. Legend:** UM MUNDO UMA PROMESA **Edge:** Reeded **Designer:** Joao Calvino

Date	Mintage	F	VF	XF	Unc	BU
ND(2007)	70,000	—	—	—	25.00	27.50

KM# 770a 5 EURO

14.0000 g., 0.9250 Silver 0.4163 oz. ASW, 30 mm. **Subject:** World Scouting Centennial **Obv:** National arms, World Scouting emblem **Obv. Legend:** REPUBLICA PORTUGUESA 1907 - 2007 CENTENARIO DO ESCUTISMO MUNDIAL **Rev:** Linear portrait of Lord Robert Baden-Powell **Rev. Legend:** UM MUNDO UMA PROMESA **Edge:** Reeded **Designer:** Joao Calvina

Date	Mintage	F	VF	XF	Unc	BU
ND(2007) Proof	10,000	Value: 60.00				

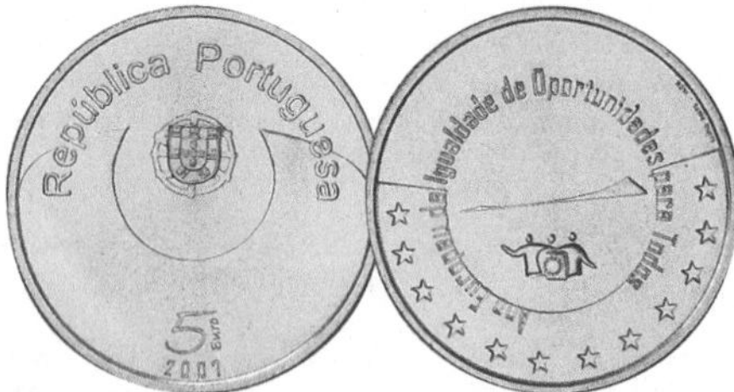

KM# 781 5 EURO

14.0400 g., 0.5000 Silver 0.2257 oz. ASW, 30 mm. **Subject:** Equal Opportunities **Obv:** Small national arms above moon shaped arc **Obv. Legend:** República Portuguesa **Rev:** Small 3 persons logo above 12 stars along rim **Rev. Legend:** Ano Europeu da Igualdade de Oportunidades para Todos **Edge:** Reeded

Date	Mintage	F	VF	XF	Unc	BU
2007INCM	70,000	—	—	—	25.00	27.50

KM# 781a 5 EURO

14.0000 g., 0.9250 Silver 0.4163 oz. ASW, 30 mm. **Subject:** Equal Opportunities **Obv:** Small national arms above moon shaped arc **Obv. Legend:** República Portuguesa **Rev:** Small 3 persons logo above 12 stars along rim **Rev. Legend:** Ano Europeu da Igualdade de Oportunidades para Todos **Edge:** Reeded

Date	Mintage	F	VF	XF	Unc	BU
2007INCM Proof	7,500	Value: 65.00				

KM# 802 5 EURO
14.0000 g., Copper-Nickel, 30 mm. **Subject:** Numismatic Treasurers - Justo of John II

Date	Mintage	F	VF	XF	Unc	BU
2010INCM	150,000	—	—	—	12.00	15.00

KM# 802a 5 EURO
15.5500 g., 0.9990 Gold 0.4994 oz. AGW, 30 mm. **Subject:** Numismatic Treasurers - Justo of John II

Date	Mintage	F	VF	XF	Unc	BU
2010INCM Proof	2,500	Value: 950				

KM# 817 5 EURO
14.0000 g., Copper-Nickel, 30 mm. **Subject:** Numismatic Treasurers - João V **Obv:** Bust right **Rev:** Crowned arms **Designer:** Rui Vasquez

Date	Mintage	F	VF	XF	Unc	BU
2012L	150,000	—	—	—	—	25.00

KM# 817a 5 EURO
15.5500 g., 0.9990 Gold 0.4994 oz. AGW, 30 mm. **Subject:** Numismatic Treasurers - João V **Obv:** Bust right **Rev:** Crowned shield

Date	Mintage	F	VF	XF	Unc	BU
2012 Proof	—	Value: 950				

KM# 811 7.5 EURO
18.5000 g., Copper-Nickel, 33 mm. **Subject:** Numismatic Treasurers - Manuel I **Obv:** Short cross **Rev:** National Arms in center of dourble ring legend

Date	Mintage	F	VF	XF	Unc	BU
2011 Proof	100,000	Value: 35.00				

KM# 811a 7.5 EURO
23.3300 g., 0.9990 Gold 0.7493 oz. AGW, 33 mm. **Subject:** Numismatic Treasurers - Manuel I **Obv:** Short Cross **Rev:** Crowned national shield within double ring legend

Date	Mintage	F	VF	XF	Unc	BU
2011 Proof	—	Value: 1,425				

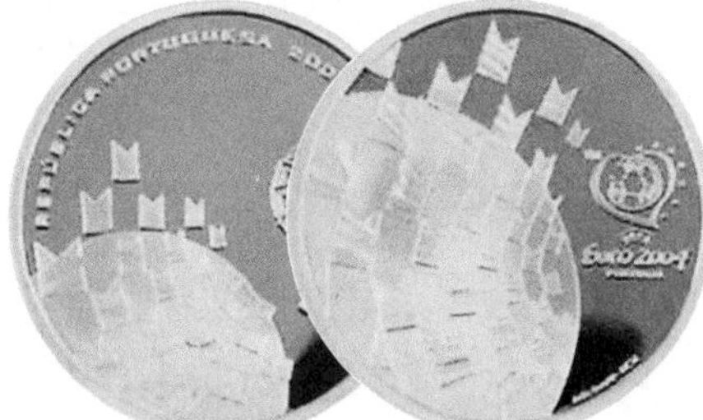

KM# 750 8 EURO
21.1000 g., 0.5000 Silver 0.3392 oz. ASW, 36 mm. **Obv:** National arms, value and flag-covered globe **Rev:** Flag-covered globe and "Euro 2004" soccer games logo **Edge:** Reeded

Date	Mintage	F	VF	XF	Unc	BU
2003INCM	1,500,000	—	—	—	35.00	37.50

KM# 750a 8 EURO
31.1000 g., 0.9250 Silver 0.9249 oz. ASW, 36 mm. **Obv:** National arms, value and flag-covered globe **Rev:** Flag-covered globe and "Euro 2004" soccer games logo

Date	Mintage	F	VF	XF	Unc	BU
2003INCM Prooflike	30,000	—	—	—	—	100
2003INCM Proof	15,000	Value: 165				

KM# 750b 8 EURO
31.1000 g., 0.9166 Gold 0.9165 oz. AGW, 36 mm. **Obv:** National arms, value and flag-covered globe **Rev:** Flag-covered globe and "Euro 2004" soccer games logo

Date	Mintage	F	VF	XF	Unc	BU
2003INCM Proof	10,000	Value: 1,850				

KM# 751 8 EURO
21.1000 g., 0.5000 Silver 0.3392 oz. ASW, 36 mm. **Obv:** National arms and value below many bubbles **Rev:** "Euro 2004" soccer games logo below many hearts **Edge:** Reeded

Date	Mintage	F	VF	XF	Unc	BU
2003INCM	1,500,000	—	—	—	35.00	37.50

KM# 751a 8 EURO
31.1000 g., 0.9250 Silver 0.9249 oz. ASW, 36 mm. **Obv:** National arms and value below many bubbles **Rev:** "Euro 2004" soccer games logo below many hearts

Date	Mintage	F	VF	XF	Unc	BU
2003INCM Prooflike	—	—	—	—	—	100
2003INCM Proof	15,000	Value: 165				

KM# 751b 8 EURO
31.1000 g., 0.9166 Gold 0.9165 oz. AGW, 36 mm. **Obv:** National arms and value below many bubbles **Rev:** "Euro 2004" soccer games logo below many hearts

Date	Mintage	F	VF	XF	Unc	BU
2003INCM Proof	10,000	Value: 1,850				

KM# 752 8 EURO
21.1000 g., 0.5000 Silver 0.3392 oz. ASW, 36 mm. **Obv:** National arms and value **Rev:** "Euro 2004" soccer games logo in center with partial text background **Edge:** Reeded

Date	Mintage	F	VF	XF	Unc	BU
2003INCM	1,500,000	—	—	—	35.00	37.50

KM# 752a 8 EURO
31.1000 g., 0.9250 Silver 0.9249 oz. ASW, 36 mm. **Obv:** National arms and value **Rev:** "Euro 2004" soccer games logo in center with partial text background

Date	Mintage	F	VF	XF	Unc	BU
2003INCM Prooflike	—	—	—	—	—	100
2003INCM Proof	15,000	Value: 165				

KM# 752b 8 EURO
31.1000 g., 0.9166 Gold 0.9165 oz. AGW, 36 mm. **Obv:** National arms and value **Rev:** "Euro 2004" soccer games logo in center with partial text background

Date	Mintage	F	VF	XF	Unc	BU
2003INCM Proof	10,000	Value: 1,850				

KM# 753 8 EURO
21.2200 g., 0.5000 Silver 0.3411 oz. ASW, 36 mm. **Subject:** Expansion of the European Union **Obv:** Radiant national arms and value **Rev:** European map **Edge:** Reeded

Date	Mintage	F	VF	XF	Unc	BU
2004INCM	300,000	—	—	—	25.00	27.50

KM# 753a 8 EURO
31.1000 g., 0.9250 Silver 0.9249 oz. ASW, 36 mm. **Subject:** Expansion of the European Union **Obv:** Radiant national arms and value **Rev:** European map **Edge:** Reeded

Date	Mintage	F	VF	XF	Unc	BU
2004INCM Proof	35,000	Value: 60.00				

KM# 756 8 EURO
21.0000 g., 0.5000 Silver 0.3376 oz. ASW, 36 mm. **Subject:** Euro 2004 Soccer **Obv:** National arms **Rev:** Stylized goal keeper **Edge:** Reeded

Date	Mintage	F	VF	XF	Unc	BU
2004INCM	1,500,000	—	—	—	25.00	27.50

KM# 756a 8 EURO
31.1000 g., 0.9250 Silver 0.9249 oz. ASW, 36 mm. **Subject:** Euro 2004 Soccer **Obv:** National arms **Rev:** Stylized goal keeper **Edge:** Reeded

Date	Mintage	F	VF	XF	Unc	BU
2004INCM	30,000	—	—	—	—	80.00
2004INCM Proof	15,000	Value: 150				

KM# 756b 8 EURO
31.1000 g., 0.9166 Gold 0.9165 oz. AGW, 36 mm. **Subject:** Euro 2004 Soccer **Obv:** National arms **Rev:** Stylized goal keeper **Edge:** Reeded

Date	Mintage	F	VF	XF	Unc	BU
2004INCM Proof	10,000	Value: 1,850				

KM# 757 8 EURO
21.0000 g., 0.9250 Silver 0.6245 oz. ASW, 36 mm. **Subject:** Euro 2004 Soccer **Obv:** National arms **Rev:** Face of player making shot **Edge:** Reeded

Date	Mintage	F	VF	XF	Unc	BU
2004INCM	1,500,000	—	—	—	25.00	27.50

KM# 757a 8 EURO
31.1000 g., 0.9250 Silver 0.9249 oz. ASW, 36 mm. **Subject:** Euro 2004 Soccer **Obv:** National arms **Rev:** Face of player making a shot **Edge:** Reeded

Date	Mintage	F	VF	XF	Unc	BU
2004INCM	30,000	—	—	—	—	80.00
2004INCM Proof	15,000	Value: 150				

KM# 757b 8 EURO
31.1000 g., 0.9166 Gold 0.9165 oz. AGW, 36 mm. **Subject:** Euro 2004 Soccer **Obv:** National arms **Rev:** Face of player making a shot **Edge:** Reeded

Date	Mintage	F	VF	XF	Unc	BU
2004INCM Proof	10,000	Value: 1,850				

KM# 758 8 EURO
21.0000 g., 0.5000 Silver 0.3376 oz. ASW, 36 mm. **Subject:** Euro 2004 Soccer **Obv:** National arms **Rev:** Symbolic explosion of a goal **Edge:** Reeded

Date	Mintage	F	VF	XF	Unc	BU
2004INCM	1,500,000	—	—	—	25.00	27.50

KM# 758a 8 EURO
31.1000 g., 0.9250 Silver 0.9249 oz. ASW, 36 mm. **Subject:** Euro 2004 Soccer **Obv:** National arms **Rev:** Symbolic explosion of a goal **Edge:** Reeded

Date	Mintage	F	VF	XF	Unc	BU
2004INCM	30,000	—	—	—	—	80.00
2004INCM Proof	15,000	Value: 150				

KM# 758b 8 EURO
31.1000 g., 0.9166 Gold 0.9165 oz. AGW, 36 mm. **Subject:** Euro 2004 Soccer **Obv:** National arms **Rev:** Symbolic explosion of a goal **Edge:** Reeded

Date	Mintage	F	VF	XF	Unc	BU
2004INCM Proof	10,000	Value: 1,850				

KM# 773 8 EURO
21.0000 g., 0.5000 Silver 0.3376 oz. ASW, 36 mm. **Subject:** 60th Anniversary End of WW II **Obv:** Quill pens horizontal at left center, national arms at lower righr **Obv. Inscription:** REPÚBLICA PORTUGUESA **Rev:** Four quill pens upright, outlined map of Europe in background **Rev. Inscription:** FIM DA II GUERRA MUNDIAL **Edge:** Reeded

Date	Mintage	F	VF	XF	Unc	BU
2005INCM	300,000	—	—	—	30.00	32.50

KM# 773a 8 EURO
31.1000 g., 0.9250 Silver 0.9249 oz. ASW, 36 mm. **Subject:** 60th Anniversary End of WW II **Obv:** Quill pens horizontal at left center, national arms at lower right **Obv. Inscription:** REPÚBLICA PORTUGUESA **Rev:** Four quill pens upright, outlined map of Europe in background **Rev. Inscription:** FIM DA II GUERRA MUNDIAL **Edge:** Reeded

Date	Mintage	F	VF	XF	Unc	BU
2005INCM Proof	35,000	Value: 70.00				

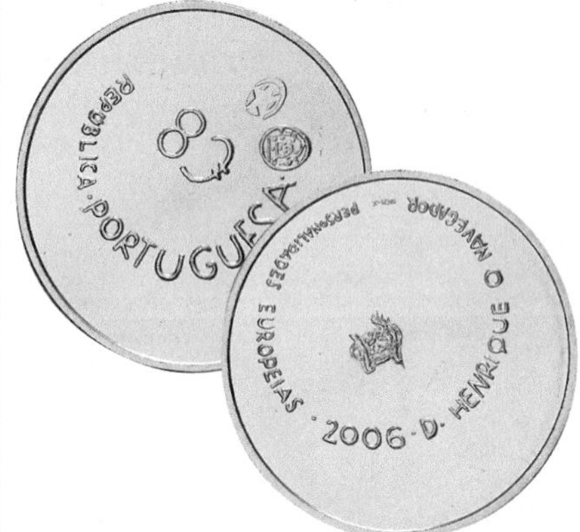

KM# 776 8 EURO
20.8000 g., 0.5000 Silver 0.3344 oz. ASW, 36 mm. **Series:** Famous Europeans **Subject:** Prince Henry the Navigator **Obv:** Small national arms and shield **Obv. Legend:** REPÚBLICA PORTUGUESA **Rev:** Tiny bust 3/4 right **Edge:** Reeded

Date	Mintage	F	VF	XF	Unc	BU
2006INCM	100,000	—	—	—	30.00	32.50

KM# 776a 8 EURO
31.1000 g., 0.9250 Silver 0.9249 oz. ASW, 36 mm. **Series:** Famous Europeans **Subject:** Prince Henry the Navigator **Obv:** Small national arms and shield **Obv. Legend:** REPÚBLICA PORTUGUESA **Rev:** Tiny bust 3/4 right **Edge:** Reeded

Date	Mintage	F	VF	XF	Unc	BU
2006INCM Proof	35,000	Value: 65.00				

KM# 778 8 EURO

21.0000 g., 0.5000 Silver 0.3376 oz. ASW, 36 mm. **Subject:** 150th Anniversary Railroad Lisbon - Carregado **Obv:** National arms on wavy flag **Obv. Legend:** REPÚBLICA PORTUGUESA **Rev:** Vertical railroad track divides two shields **Rev. Legend:** 150 ANOS DA PRIMEIRA LINHA FERREA LISBOA CARREGADO **Edge:** Reeded

Date	Mintage	F	VF	XF	Unc	BU
2006INCM	100,000	—	—	—	32.50	35.00

KM# 778a 8 EURO

31.1000 g., 0.9250 Silver 0.9249 oz. ASW, 36 mm. **Subject:** 150th Anniversary Railroad Lisbon - Carregado **Obv:** National srms on wavy flag **Obv. Legend:** REPÚBLICA PORTUGUESA **Rev:** Vertical railroad track divides two shields **Rev. Legend:** 150 ANOSDA PRIMEIRA LINHA FERREA LISBOA CARREGADO **Edge:** Reeded

Date	Mintage	F	VF	XF	Unc	BU
2006INCM Proof	35,000	Value: 75.00				

KM# 822 8 EURO

21.0000 g., 0.5000 Silver 0.3376 oz. ASW, 36 mm. **Subject:** Early flying inventions - the Passarola of Bartolomeu de Gusmão **Obv:** Large value and small national arms **Rev:** Schematic of flying machine

Date	Mintage	F	VF	XF	Unc	BU
2007	70,000	—	—	—	20.00	25.00

KM# 822a 8 EURO

31.1050 g., 0.9250 Silver 0.9250 oz. ASW, 36 mm. **Subject:** Early flying inventions - the Passarola of Bartolomeu de Gusmão **Obv:** Large value, small national arms **Rev:** Schematic of early flying machine

Date	Mintage	F	VF	XF	Unc	BU
2007 Proof	25,000	Value: 65.00				

KM# 748 10 EURO

27.0000 g., 0.5000 Silver 0.4340 oz. ASW, 40 mm. **Subject:** Nautica **Obv:** National arms within circle of assorted shields **Rev:** Sailing ship and sextant **Edge:** Reeded

Date	Mintage	F	VF	XF	Unc	BU
2003INCM	350,000	—	—	—	22.50	25.00

KM# 748a 10 EURO

27.0000 g., 0.9250 Silver 0.8029 oz. ASW, 40 mm. **Obv:** National arms within circle of assorted shields **Rev:** Sailing ship and sextant **Edge:** Reeded

Date	Mintage	F	VF	XF	Unc	BU
2003INCM Proof	10,000	Value: 70.00				

KM# 759 10 EURO

27.0000 g., 0.5000 Silver 0.4340 oz. ASW, 40 mm. **Subject:** Olympics **Obv:** National arms above stylized value **Rev:** Stylized sail above Olympic rings **Edge:** Reeded

Date	Mintage	F	VF	XF	Unc	BU
2004INCM	350,000	—	—	—	25.00	27.50

KM# 759a 10 EURO

27.0000 g., 0.9250 Silver 0.8029 oz. ASW, 40 mm. **Subject:** Olympics **Obv:** National arms above stylized value **Rev:** Stylized sail above Olympic rings **Edge:** Reeded

Date	Mintage	F	VF	XF	Unc	BU
2004INCM Proof	15,000	Value: 65.00				

KM# 768 10 EURO

27.0000 g., 0.5000 Silver 0.4340 oz. ASW, 40 mm. **Subject:** Arquitectura e Monumentos - Sé do Porto **Obv:** National arms above value in circle of multi-national coats of arms **Rev:** Church facade **Edge:** Reeded

Date	Mintage	F	VF	XF	Unc	BU
2005INCM	—	—	—	—	—	30.00
2005INCM Proof	300,000	Value: 75.00				

KM# 820 10 EURO

27.0000 g., 0.5000 Silver 0.4340 oz. ASW, 40 mm. **Subject:** Iberoamerican series - Architecture **Rev:** Façade of the Cathedral Sé de Porto

Date	Mintage	F	VF	XF	Unc	BU
2005	30,000	—	—	—	30.00	35.00

KM# 820a 10 EURO

27.0000 g., 0.9250 Silver 0.8029 oz. ASW, 40 mm. **Subject:** Iberoamerican Series - Architecture **Rev:** Façade of Cathedral of Sé do Porto

Date	Mintage	F	VF	XF	Unc	BU
2005 Proof	12,000	Value: 115				

KM# 774 10 EURO

27.0000 g., 0.5000 Silver 0.4340 oz. ASW, 40 mm. **Subject:** XVIII World Championship Football Games - Germany 2006 **Obv:** National arms above stadium **Obv. Legend:** REPÚBLICA PORTUGUESA **Rev:** Circular legend above sticks representing stadium fans **Rev. Legend:** CAMPEONATO DO MUNDO DE FUTEBOL FIFA ALEMANHA 2006 **Edge:** Reeded

Date	Mintage	F	VF	XF	Unc	BU
2006INCM	100,000	—	—	—	37.50	40.00

KM# 774a 10 EURO

27.0000 g., 0.9250 Silver 0.8029 oz. ASW, 40 mm. **Subject:** XVIII World Championship Football Games - Germany 2006 **Obv:** National arms above stadium **Obv. Inscription:** REPÚBLICA PORTUGUESA **Rev:** Circular legend above sticks representing stadium fans **Edge:** Reeded

Date	Mintage	F	VF	XF	Unc	BU
2006INCM Proof	25,000	Value: 85.00				

KM# 775 10 EURO

27.0000 g., 0.5000 Silver 0.4340 oz. ASW, 40 mm. **Subject:** 20th Anniversary of Spain and Portugal's membership in the European Union **Obv:** National arms **Obv. Legend:** REPÚBLICA PORTUGUESA **Rev:** Viaduct, outlined map of Europe above **Rev. Legend:** ADESÃO AS COMUNIDADES EUROPIAS **Edge:** Reeded

Date	Mintage	F	VF	XF	Unc	BU
2006INCM	100,000	—	—	—	27.50	30.00

KM# 775a 10 EURO

27.0000 g., 0.9250 Silver 0.8029 oz. ASW, 40 mm. **Subject:** 20th Anniversary of Spain and Portugal's membership in European Union **Obv:** National arms **Obv. Legend:** REPÚBLICA PORTUGUESA **Rev:** Viaduct, outlined map of Europe above **Rev. Legend:** ADESÃO AS COMUNIDADES EUROPIAS **Edge:** Reeded

Date	Mintage	F	VF	XF	Unc	BU
2006INCM Proof	25,000	Value: 70.00				

KM# 821 10 EURO

27.0000 g., 0.5000 Silver 0.4340 oz. ASW, 40 mm. **Subject:** Iberoamerican Series - Olympics **Rev:** Warrior running, two modern runners

Date	Mintage	F	VF	XF	Unc	BU
2007	100,000	—	—	—	25.00	30.00

KM# 821a 10 EURO

27.0000 g., 0.9250 Silver 0.8029 oz. ASW, 40 mm. **Subject:** Iberoamerican Series - Olympics **Rev:** Ancient warrior running, two modern runners

Date	Mintage	F	VF	XF	Unc	BU
2007 Proof	12,000	Value: 115				

KM# 823 10 EURO

27.0000 g., 0.5000 Silver 0.4340 oz. ASW, 40 mm. **Subject:** Sailing World Cup - Cascais **Obv:** National arms and stylized sails and waves **Rev:** Stylized sails and waves

Date	Mintage	F	VF	XF	Unc	BU
2007	70,000	—	—	—	25.00	30.00

KM# 823a 10 EURO

27.0000 g., 0.9250 Silver 0.8029 oz. ASW, 40 mm. **Subject:** World Sailing Championships - Cascais **Obv:** National arms and stylized sails and waves **Rev:** Stylized sails and waves

Date	Mintage	F	VF	XF	Unc	BU
2007 Proof	7,500	Value: 75.00				

KM# 803 10 EURO

27.0000 g., 0.9250 Silver 0.8029 oz. ASW, 40 mm. **Subject:** The Escudo

Date	Mintage	F	VF	XF	Unc	BU
2010INCM	100,000	—	—	—	32.50	35.00

KM# 803a 10 EURO

27.0000 g., 0.5000 Silver 0.4340 oz. ASW, 40 mm. **Subject:** The Escudo

Date	Mintage	F	VF	XF	Unc	BU
2010INCM Proof	12,000	Value: 85.00				

KM# 808 10 EURO

27.0000 g., Copper-Nickel, 40 mm. **Subject:** Spain and Portugal's accession to the European Union, 25th Anniversary **Designer:** João Duarte

Date	Mintage	F	VF	XF	Unc	BU
2011	100,000	—	—	—	—	7.00

KM# 808a 10 EURO

27.0000 g., 0.9250 Silver 0.8029 oz. ASW, 40 mm. **Subject:** Spain and Portugal's accession to the European Union, 25th Anniversary **Designer:** João Duarte

Date	Mintage	F	VF	XF	Unc	BU
2011 Proof	6,000	Value: 55.00				

KM# 818 10 EURO

27.0000 g., Copper-Nickel, 40 mm. **Subject:** Ibero-American series, 20th Anniversary **Obv:** National arms in center of other countries arms **Rev:** Stylized sails **Designer:** Espiga Pinto

Date	Mintage	F	VF	XF	Unc	BU
2012	100,000	—	—	—	—	25.00

KM# 818a 10 EURO

27.0000 g., 0.9250 Silver 0.8029 oz. ASW, 40 mm. **Subject:** Ibero-American series, 20th Anniversary **Obv:** National arms at center of other national arms **Rev:** Stylized sails **Designer:** Espiga Pinto

Date	Mintage	F	VF	XF	Unc	BU
2012 Proof	10,000	Value: 55.00				

MINT SETS

KM#	Date	Mintage	Identification	Issue Price	Mkt Val
MS32	2002 (8)	50,000	KM#740-747	—	50.00
MS33	2003 (8)	50,000	KM#740-747	—	50.00
MS34	2004 (8)	50,000	KM#740-747	—	45.00
MS35	2005 (8)	30,000	KM#740-747	—	45.00
MS36	2006 (8)	12,500	KM#740-747	—	45.00

PROOF SETS

KM#	Date	Mintage	Identification	Issue Price	Mkt Val
PS45	2002 (8)	15,000	KM#740-747	—	120
PS46	2003 (8)	15,000	KM#740-747	—	110
PS47	2004 (8)	15,000	KM#740-747	—	110
PS48	2005 (8)	10,000	KM#740-747	—	110
PS49	2006 (8)	3,000	KM#740-747	—	110
PS50	2007 (8)	2,500	KM#740-747	—	300
PS51	2008 (8)	3,500	KM#740-742, 763-767	—	150
PS52	2009 (8)	4,000	KM#740-742, 763-767	—	150
PS53	2010 (8)	4,500	KM#740-742, 763-767	—	100
PS54	2011 (8)	3,500	KM#740-742, 763-767	—	100

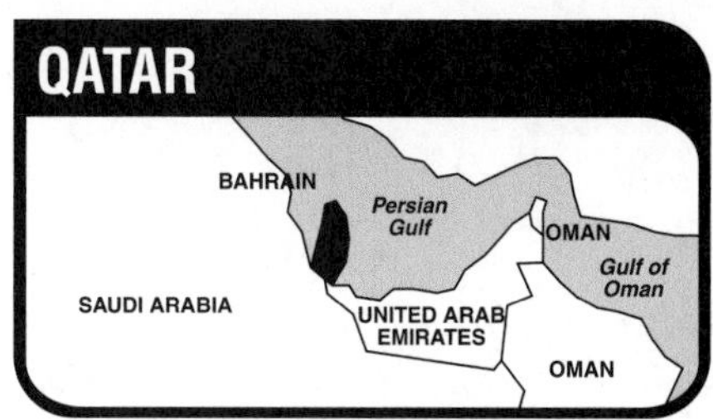

The State of Qatar, an emirate in the Persian Gulf between Bahrain and Trucial Oman, has an area of 4,247sq. mi. (11,000 sq. km.) and a population of *469,000. Capital: Doha. Oil is the chief industry and export.

TITLES

Daulat Qatar

RULERS

Al-Thani Dynasty

Hamad bin Khalifah, 1995-

MONETARY SYSTEM

100 Dirhem = 1 Riyal

STATE

STANDARD COINAGE

KM# 69 DIRHAM

Copper Plated Silver, 15 mm. **Ruler:** Hamad bin Khalifa **Obv:** National Arms **Rev:** Value

Date	Mintage	F	VF	XF	Unc	BU
AH1429-2008	—	—	—	—	—	—

KM# 12 5 DIRHAMS

3.7500 g., Bronze, 21.9 mm. **Ruler:** Hamad bin Khalifa **Obv:** National arms **Rev:** Value **Edge:** Plain

Date	Mintage	F	VF	XF	Unc	BU
AH1427-2006	—	—	—	0.35	0.90	1.25

KM# 13 10 DIRHAMS

7.5000 g., Bronze, 27 mm. **Ruler:** Hamad bin Khalifa **Obv:** National arms **Rev:** Value **Edge:** Plain

Date	Mintage	F	VF	XF	Unc	BU
AH1427-2006	—	—	—	0.60	1.50	2.00

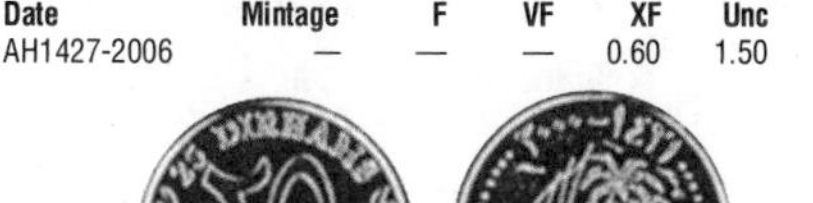

KM# 8 25 DIRHAMS

3.5000 g., Copper-Nickel, 20 mm. **Ruler:** Hamad bin Khalifa **Obv:** National arms **Rev:** Value **Rev. Legend:** STATE OF QATAR **Edge:** Reeded

Date	Mintage	F	VF	XF	Unc	BU
AH1424-2003	—	—	0.30	0.65	1.50	2.50

KM# 14 25 DIRHAMS

3.5000 g., Copper-Nickel, 20 mm. **Ruler:** Hamad bin Khalifa **Obv:** National arms **Rev:** Value **Edge:** Reeded

Date	Mintage	F	VF	XF	Unc	BU
AH1427-2006	—	—	—	0.75	1.85	2.50
AH1429-2008	—	—	—	0.75	1.85	2.50
AH1433-2012	—	—	—	0.75	1.85	2.50

KM# 14a 25 DIRHAMS

Nickel Plated Steel, 20 mm. **Ruler:** Hamad bin Khalifa **Obv:** National Arms **Rev:** Value

Date	Mintage	F	VF	XF	Unc	BU
AH1429-2008	—	—	—	—	1.50	3.00

KM# 9 50 DIRHAMS

6.5000 g., Copper-Nickel, 25 mm. **Ruler:** Hamad bin Khalifa **Obv:** National arms **Rev:** Value **Edge:** Reeded

Date	Mintage	F	VF	XF	Unc	BU
AH1424-2003	—	—	—	—	2.00	3.00

KM# 15 50 DIRHAMS

6.5000 g., Copper-Nickel, 25 mm. **Ruler:** Hamad bin Khalifa **Obv:** National arms **Rev:** Value **Edge:** Reeded

Date	Mintage	F	VF	XF	Unc	BU
AH1427-2006	—	—	—	0.80	2.00	2.75
AH1429-2008	—	—	—	0.80	2.00	2.75
AH1433-2012	—	—	—	0.80	2.00	2.75

KM# 15a 50 DIRHAMS

6.5000 g., Nickel Plated Steel, 25 mm. **Ruler:** Hamad bin Khalifa **Obv:** National Arms **Rev:** Value

Date	Mintage	F	VF	XF	Unc	BU
AH1429-2008	—	—	—	—	2.25	4.50

KM# 16 RIYAL

Aluminum-Bronze **Ruler:** Hamad bin Khalifa **Subject:** 15th Asian Games **Obv:** Arms above value **Rev:** Multicolor Fox on Bicycle, cartoon character

Date	Mintage	F	VF	XF	Unc	BU
2006	—	—	—	—	—	25.00

KM# 34 RIYAL

Aluminum-Bronze, 38.74 mm. **Ruler:** Hamad bin Khalifa **Subject:** 15th Asian Games **Obv:** Arms **Rev:** Multicolor mascot with flag

Date	Mintage	F	VF	XF	Unc	BU
2006	25,000	—	—	—	—	25.00

KM# 35 RIYAL

Aluminum-Bronze, 38.74 mm. **Ruler:** Hamad bin Khalifa **Subject:** 15th Asian Games **Obv:** Arms **Rev:** Multicolor mascot kicking soccer ball

Date	Mintage	F	VF	XF	Unc	BU
2006	25,000	—	—	—	—	25.00

KM# 36 RIYAL

Aluminum-Bronze, 38.74 mm. **Ruler:** Hamad bin Khalifa **Subject:** 15th Asian Games **Obv:** Arms **Rev:** Three multicolor torches

Date	Mintage	F	VF	XF	Unc	BU
2006	25,000	—	—	—	—	25.00

KM# 37 RIYAL

Aluminum-Bronze, 38.74 mm. **Ruler:** Hamad bin Khalifa **Subject:** 15th Asian Games **Obv:** Arms **Rev:** Two figures with linked arms

Date	Mintage	F	VF	XF	Unc	BU
2006	25,000	—	—	—	—	25.00

KM# 38 RIYAL

Aluminum-Bronze, 38.74 mm. **Ruler:** Hamad bin Khalifa **Subject:** 15th Asian Games **Obv:** Arms **Rev:** Figure with outstretched arms

Date	Mintage	F	VF	XF	Unc	BU
2006	25,000	—	—	—	—	25.00

KM# 25 10 RIYALS

31.1035 g., 0.9990 Silver 0.9990 oz. ASW, 40.5 mm. **Ruler:** Hamad bin Khalifa **Subject:** 15th Asian Games **Obv:** Arms **Rev:** Runner trailing green color

Date	Mintage	F	VF	XF	Unc	BU
2006 Proof	25,000	Value: 110				

KM# 26 10 RIYALS

31.1035 g., 0.9990 Silver 0.9990 oz. ASW, 40.5 mm. **Ruler:** Hamad bin Khalifa **Subject:** 15th Asian Games **Obv:** Arms **Rev:** Cyclist trailing red color

Date	Mintage	F	VF	XF	Unc	BU
2006 Proof	25,000	Value: 110				

KM# 27 10 RIYALS

31.1035 g., 0.9990 Silver 0.9990 oz. ASW, 40.5 mm. **Ruler:** Hamad bin Khalifa **Subject:** 15th Asian Games **Obv:** Arms **Rev:** Soccer player legs on green color

Date	Mintage	F	VF	XF	Unc	BU
2006 Proof	25,000	Value: 110				

KM# 28 10 RIYALS

31.1035 g., 0.9990 Silver 0.9990 oz. ASW, 40.5 mm. **Ruler:** Hamad bin Khalifa **Subject:** 15th Asian Games **Obv:** Arms **Rev:** Ribbon dancer trailing red color

Date	Mintage	F	VF	XF	Unc	BU
2006 Proof	25,000	Value: 110				

KM# 29 10 RIYALS

31.1035 g., 0.9990 Silver 0.9990 oz. ASW, 40.5 mm. **Ruler:** Hamad bin Khalifa **Subject:** 15th Asian Games **Obv:** Arms **Rev:** Karate contestants and dark yellow color

Date	Mintage	F	VF	XF	Unc	BU
2006 Proof	25,000	Value: 110				

KM# 30 10 RIYALS

31.1035 g., 0.9990 Silver 0.9990 oz. ASW, 40.5 mm. **Ruler:** Hamad bin Khalifa **Subject:** 15th Asian Games **Obv:** Arms **Rev:** Swimmer in aqua colored water

Date	Mintage	F	VF	XF	Unc	BU
2006 Proof	25,000	Value: 110				

KM# 31 10 RIYALS

31.1035 g., 0.9990 Silver 0.9990 oz. ASW, 40.5 mm. **Ruler:** Hamad bin Khalifa **Subject:** 15th Asian Games **Obv:** Arms **Rev:** Table tennis player and orange-brownish color

Date	Mintage	F	VF	XF	Unc	BU
2006 Proof	25,000	Value: 110				

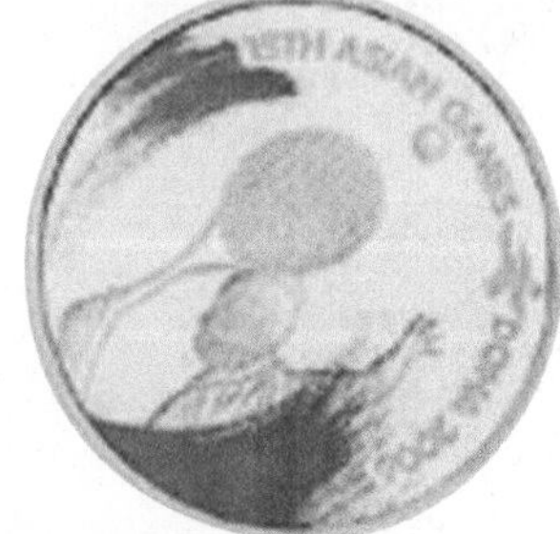

KM# 32 10 RIYALS

31.1035 g., 0.9990 Silver 0.9990 oz. ASW, 40.5 mm. **Ruler:** Hamad bin Khalifa **Subject:** 15th Asian Games **Obv:** Arms **Rev:** Tennis player and aqua color

Date	Mintage	F	VF	XF	Unc	BU
2006 Proof	25,000	Value: 110				

KM# 33 10 RIYALS

31.1035 g., 0.9990 Silver 0.9990 oz. ASW, 40.5 mm. **Ruler:** Hamad bin Khalifa **Subject:** 15th Asian Games **Obv:** Arms **Rev:** Volleyball player trailing purple color

Date	Mintage	F	VF	XF	Unc	BU
2006 Proof	25,000	Value: 110				

KM# 40 100 RIYALS

24.0000 g., 0.9250 Silver 0.7137 oz. ASW, 37 mm. **Ruler:** Hamad bin Khalifa **Subject:** Yousif al Sharif **Obv:** Wing desing **Rev:** Male bust

Date	Mintage	F	VF	XF	Unc	BU
2002 Proof	—	—	—	—	—	—

KM# 42 100 RIYALS

100.0000 g., 0.9990 Silver 3.2117 oz. ASW, 80 mm. **Ruler:** Hamad bin Khalifa **Subject:** Doha Cultural festival

Date	Mintage	F	VF	XF	Unc	BU
2003 Proof	—	—	—	—	—	—

KM# 17 100 RIYALS

Gold **Ruler:** Hamad bin Khalifa **Subject:** 15th Asian Games **Obv:** Arms above value **Rev:** Games mascot Fox on Bicycle cartoon character

Date	Mintage	F	VF	XF	Unc	BU
2006 Proof	Est. 10,000	Value: 550				

KM# 18 100 RIYALS

17.0000 g., 0.9200 Gold 0.5028 oz. AGW, 31 mm. **Ruler:** Hamad bin Khalifa **Obv:** Arms **Rev:** Central Bank building **Edge:** Reeded

Date	Mintage	F	VF	XF	Unc	BU
2006 Proof	300	Value: 1,500				

KM# 19 100 RIYALS

10.0000 g., 0.9999 Gold 0.3215 oz. AGW, 24.5 mm. **Ruler:** Hamad bin Khalifa **Subject:** 15th Asian Games **Obv:** Arms **Rev:** Khalifa Stadium **Edge:** Reeded

Date	Mintage	F	VF	XF	Unc	BU
2006 Proof	—	Value: 650				

KM# 20 100 RIYALS

10.0000 g., 0.9999 Gold 0.3215 oz. AGW, 24.5 mm. **Ruler:** Hamad bin Khalifa **Subject:** 15th Asian Games **Obv:** Arms **Rev:** Two oryxes head-butting **Edge:** Reeded

Date	Mintage	F	VF	XF	Unc	BU
2006 Proof	—	Value: 650				

KM# 21 100 RIYALS

10.0000 g., 0.9999 Gold 0.3215 oz. AGW, 24.5 mm. **Ruler:** Hamad bin Khalifa **Subject:** 15th Asian Games **Obv:** Arms **Rev:** Falcon bust **Edge:** Reeded

Date	Mintage	F	VF	XF	Unc	BU
2006 Proof	—	Value: 650				

KM# 22 100 RIYALS

10.0000 g., 0.9999 Gold 0.3215 oz. AGW, 24.5 mm. **Ruler:** Hamad bin Khalifa **Subject:** 15th Asian Games **Obv:** Arms **Rev:** Coffee pot **Edge:** Reeded

Date	Mintage	F	VF	XF	Unc	BU
2006 Proof	—	Value: 650				

KM# 23 100 RIYALS

10.0000 g., 0.9999 Gold 0.3215 oz. AGW, 24.5 mm. **Ruler:** Hamad bin Khalifa **Subject:** 15th Asian Games **Obv:** Arms **Rev:** Radiant sun **Edge:** Reeded

Date	Mintage	F	VF	XF	Unc	BU
2006 Proof	—	Value: 650				

KM# 76 100 RIYALS

22.2400 g., 0.9250 Silver 0.6614 oz. ASW, 37 mm. **Ruler:** Hamad bin Khalifa **Subject:** 2008 Arab States Stamp Exhibition **Obv:** National Arms **Rev:** Two profiles right

Date	Mintage	F	VF	XF	Unc	BU
2008 Proof	1,000	Value: 90.00				

KM# 77 100 RIYALS

22.2400 g., 0.9250 Silve\r 0.6614 oz. ASW, 37 mm. **Ruler:** Hamad bin Khalifa **Subject:** Central Municipal Council, 10th Anniversary **Obv:** National Arms in color **Rev:** Democracy House in color

Date	Mintage	F	VF	XF	Unc	BU
2009 Proof	—	—	—	—	—	—

KM# 78 100 RIYALS

Silver **Ruler:** Hamad bin Khalifa **Subject:** 10th Gulf Cooperation Council Banking Conference

Date	Mintage	F	VF	XF	Unc	BU
2011 Proof	—	Value: 60.00				

KM# 47 200 RIYALS

Gold **Ruler:** Hamad bin Khalifa **Subject:** al Wabra Wildlife Preservation, 50th Anniversary **Rev:** Blue headed macaw

Date	Mintage	F	VF	XF	Unc	BU
2003 Proof	240	—	—	—	—	—

KM# 67 200 RIYALS

0.9990 Silver, 40 mm. **Ruler:** Hamad bin Khalifa **Subject:** Doha Cultural Festival **Obv:** Wing emblem **Rev:** Four men seated under archway

Date	Mintage	F	VF	XF	Unc	BU
2004 Proof	—	—	—	—	—	—

KM# 79 200 RIYALS

Silver gilt **Ruler:** Hamad bin Khalifa **Subject:** 10th Gulf Cooperation Council Banking Conference

Date	Mintage	F	VF	XF	Unc	BU
2011 Proof	—	Value: 100				

KM# 11 250 RIYALS

Silver **Ruler:** Hamad bin Khalifa **Subject:** 4th WTO Conference **Obv:** National arms **Rev:** WTO logo, value, date, and legend in English and Islamic

Date	Mintage	F	VF	XF	Unc	BU
AH1422 (2001) Proof	1,000	Value: 650				

KM# 41 250 RIYALS

31.0000 g., 0.9990 Gold 0.9956 oz. AGW, 37 mm. **Ruler:** Hamad bin Khalifa **Subject:** Yousif al Sharif **Obv:** Wing design **Rev:** Male bust

Date	Mintage	F	VF	XF	Unc	BU
2002 Proof	—	—	—	—	—	—

KM# 55 250 RIYALS

120.0000 g., 0.9990 Silver 3.8541 oz. ASW, 60 mm. **Ruler:** Hamad bin Khalifa **Subject:** al Wabra Wildlife Preservation, 50th Anniversary **Rev:** Dama gazelle

Date	Mintage	F	VF	XF	Unc	BU
2003 Proof	1,800	Value: 250				

KM# 43 250 RIYALS

100.0000 g., 0.9990 Silver partially gilt 3.2117 oz. ASW, 80 mm. **Ruler:** Hamad bin Khalifa **Subject:** Doha Cultural festival

Date	Mintage	F	VF	XF	Unc	BU
2003 Proof	1,000	Value: 250				

KM# 44 250 RIYALS

120.0000 g., 0.9990 Silver 3.8541 oz. ASW, 60 mm. **Ruler:** Hamad bin Khalifa **Subject:** al Wabra Wildlife Preservation, 50th Anniversary **Rev:** Blue headed macaw in color

Date	Mintage	F	VF	XF	Unc	BU
2003 Proof	1,800	Value: 250				

KM# 45 250 RIYALS

120.0000 g., 0.9990 Silver 3.8541 oz. ASW, 60 mm. **Ruler:** Hamad bin Khalifa **Subject:** al Wabra Wildlife Preservation, 50th Anniversary **Rev:** bird in color

Date	Mintage	F	VF	XF	Unc	BU
2003 Proof	1,800	Value: 250				

KM# 46 250 RIYALS
120.0000 g., 0.9990 Silver 3.8541 oz. ASW, 60 mm. **Ruler:** Hamad bin Khalifa **Subject:** al Wabra Wildlife Preservation, 50th Anniversary **Rev:** Macaw in color

Date	Mintage	F	VF	XF	Unc	BU
2003 Proof	1,800	Value: 250				

KM# 53 250 RIYALS
120.0000 g., 0.9990 Silver 3.8541 oz. ASW, 60 mm. **Ruler:** Hamad bin Khalifa **Subject:** al Wabra Wildlife Preservation, 50th Anniversary **Rev:** Gazelle

Date	Mintage	F	VF	XF	Unc	BU
2003 Proof	1,800	Value: 250				

KM# 54 250 RIYALS
120.0000 g., 0.9990 Silver 3.8541 oz. ASW, 60 mm. **Ruler:** Hamad bin Khalifa **Subject:** al Wabra Wildlife Preservation, 50th Anniversary **Rev:** Sommering gazelle

Date	Mintage	F	VF	XF	Unc	BU
2003 Proof	1,800	Value: 250				

KM# 56 250 RIYALS
120.0000 g., 0.9990 Silver 3.8541 oz. ASW, 60 mm. **Ruler:** Hamad bin Khalifa **Subject:** al Wabra Wildlife Preservation, 50th Anniversary **Rev:** Stilt gazelle

Date	Mintage	F	VF	XF	Unc	BU
2003 Proof	1,800	Value: 250				

KM# 65 250 RIYALS
120.0000 g., 0.9990 Silver 3.8541 oz. ASW, 60 mm. **Ruler:** Hamad bin Khalifa **Subject:** National Council for Culture, Arts and Heritage, 5th Anniversary **Obv:** Bust 1/4 left **Rev:** Text and emblem

Date	Mintage	F	VF	XF	Unc	BU
2003 Proof	1,000	Value: 300				

KM# 70 250 RIYALS
120.0000 g., 0.9990 Silver 3.8541 oz. ASW, 60 mm. **Ruler:** Hamad bin Khalifa **Subject:** National Council for Culture, Arts and Heritage

Date	Mintage	F	VF	XF	Unc	BU
2006 Proof	—	Value: 250				

KM# 39 300 RIYALS
1000.0000 g., 0.9990 Silver 32.117 oz. ASW, 100.0 mm. **Ruler:** Hamad bin Khalifa **Obv:** National arms **Obv. Legend:** STATE OF QATAR **Rev:** Sports montage around game's logo **Rev. Inscription:** 15TH ASIAN GAMES / DOHA 2006 **Edge:** Plain

Date	Mintage	F	VF	XF	Unc	BU
2006 Proof	5,000	Value: 1,250				

KM# 68 1000 RIYALS
0.9990 Gold, 40 mm. **Ruler:** Hamad bin Khalifa **Subject:** Doha Coultural Festival **Obv:** Wing design **Rev:** Four men seated under archway

Date	Mintage	F	VF	XF	Unc	BU
2004 Proof	—	—	—	—	—	—

KM# 48 2000 RIYALS
Gold **Ruler:** Hamad bin Khalifa **Subject:** al Wabra Wildlife Preservation, 50th Anniversary **Rev:** bird

Date	Mintage	F	VF	XF	Unc	BU
2003 Proof	240	—	—	—	—	—

KM# 72 2000 RIYALS
40.6400 g., 0.9250 Silver 1.2086 oz. ASW, 50 mm. **Ruler:** Hamad bin Khalifa **Subject:** National Day **Obv:** National Arms in color **Rev:** State of Qatar, National arms in color

Date	Mintage	F	VF	XF	Unc	BU
2007 Proof	500	Value: 900				

KM# 73 2000 RIYALS
40.6400 g., 0.9250 Silver 1.2086 oz. ASW, 50 mm. **Ruler:** Hamad bin Khalifa **Subject:** National Day **Obv:** National Arms in color **Rev:** Qatar Central Bank, National arms in color

Date	Mintage	F	VF	XF	Unc	BU
2007 Proof	500	Value: 900				

KM# 49 5000 RIYALS
Gold **Ruler:** Hamad bin Khalifa **Subject:** al Wabra Wildlife Preservation, 50th Anniversary **Rev:** macaw

Date	Mintage	F	VF	XF	Unc	BU
2003 Proof	240	—	—	—	—	—

KM# 57 5000 RIYALS
Gold **Ruler:** Hamad bin Khalifa **Subject:** al Wabra Wildlife Preservation, 50th Anniversary **Rev:** Gazelle

Date	Mintage	F	VF	XF	Unc	BU
2003 Proof	240	—	—	—	—	—

KM# 58 5000 RIYALS
Gold **Ruler:** Hamad bin Khalifa **Subject:** al Wabra Wildlife Preservation, 50th Anniversary **Rev:** Sommering Gazelle

Date	Mintage	F	VF	XF	Unc	BU
2003 Proof	240	—	—	—	—	—

KM# 59 5000 RIYALS
Gold **Ruler:** Hamad bin Khalifa **Subject:** al Wabra Wildlife Preservation, 50th Anniversary **Rev:** Dama Gazelle

Date	Mintage	F	VF	XF	Unc	BU
2003 Proof	240	—	—	—	—	—

KM# 60 5000 RIYALS
Gold **Ruler:** Hamad bin Khalifa **Subject:** al Wabra Wildlife Preservation, 50th Anniversary **Rev:** Stilt Gazelle

Date	Mintage	F	VF	XF	Unc	BU
2003 Proof	240	—	—	—	—	—

KM# 66 5000 RIYALS
160.0000 g., 0.9990 Gold 5.1388 oz. AGW, 60 mm. **Ruler:** Hamad bin Khalifa **Subject:** National Council for Culture, Arts and Heritage, 5th Anniversary **Obv:** Bust 1/4 left **Rev:** Text and emblem

Date	Mintage	F	VF	XF	Unc	BU
2003 Proof	500	—	—	—	—	9,750

KM# 71 5000 RIYALS
160.0000 g., 0.9990 Gold 5.1388 oz. AGW, 60 mm. **Ruler:** Hamad bin Khalifa **Subject:** National Council for Culture, Arts and Heritage

Date	Mintage	F	VF	XF	Unc	BU
2006 Proof	—	—	—	—	—	—

KM# 50 10000 RIYALS
Platinum APW **Ruler:** Hamad bin Khalifa **Subject:** al Wabra Wildlife Preservation, 50th Anniversary **Rev:** Blue headed macaw

Date	Mintage	F	VF	XF	Unc	BU
2003 Proof	120	—	—	—	—	—

KM# 51 10000 RIYALS
Platinum APW **Ruler:** Hamad bin Khalifa **Subject:** al Wabra Wildlife Preservation, 50th Anniversary **Rev:** bird

Date	Mintage	F	VF	XF	Unc	BU
2003 Proof	120	—	—	—	—	—

KM# 52 10000 RIYALS
Platinum APW **Ruler:** Hamad bin Khalifa **Subject:** al Wabra Wildlife Preservation, 50th Anniversary **Rev:** Macaw

Date	Mintage	F	VF	XF	Unc	BU
2003 Proof	120	—	—	—	—	—

KM# 61 10000 RIYALS
Platinum APW **Ruler:** Hamad bin Khalifa **Subject:** al Wabra Wildlife Preservation, 50th Anniversary **Rev:** Gazelle

Date	Mintage	F	VF	XF	Unc	BU
2003 Proof	120	—	—	—	—	—

KM# 62 10000 RIYALS
Platinum APW **Ruler:** Hamad bin Khalifa **Subject:** al Wabra Wildlife Preservation, 50th Anniversary **Rev:** Sommering gazelle

Date	Mintage	F	VF	XF	Unc	BU
2003 Proof	120	—	—	—	—	—

KM# 63 10000 RIYALS
Platinum APW **Ruler:** Hamad bin Khalifa **Subject:** al Wabra Wildlife Preservation, 50th Anniversary **Rev:** Dama gazelle

Date	Mintage	F	VF	XF	Unc	BU
2003 Proof	120	—	—	—	—	—

KM# 64 10000 RIYALS
Platinum APW **Ruler:** Hamad bin Khalifa **Subject:** al Wabra Wildlife Preservation, 50th Anniversary **Rev:** Stilt gazelle

Date	Mintage	F	VF	XF	Unc	BU
2003 Proof	120	—	—	—	—	—

KM# 24 10000 RIYALS
1000.0000 g., 0.9999 Gold 32.146 oz. AGW, 75.3 mm. **Ruler:** Hamad bin Khalifa **Subject:** 15th Asian Games **Obv:** Arms **Rev:** Radiant sun **Edge:** Reeded **Note:** Illustration reduced.

Date	Mintage	F	VF	XF	Unc	BU
2006 Proof	—	Value: 57,500				

KM# 74 10000 RIYALS
70.1600 g., 0.9160 Gold 2.0661 oz. AGW, 50 mm. **Ruler:** Hamad bin Khalifa **Subject:** National Day **Obv:** National Arms **Rev:** State of Qatar, National Arms

Date	Mintage	F	VF	XF	Unc	BU
2007 Proof	500	Value: 4,500				

KM# 75 10000 RIYALS
70.1600 g., 0.9160 Gold 2.0661 oz. AGW, 50 mm. **Ruler:** Hamad bin Khalifa **Subject:** National Day **Obv:** National Arms **Rev:** Qatar Central Bank, National Arms

Date	Mintage	F	VF	XF	Unc	BU
2007 Proof	500	Value: 4,500				

Romania (formerly the Socialist Republic of Romania), a country in southeast Europe, has an area of 91,699 sq. mi. (237,500 sq. km.) and a population of 23.2 million. Capital: Bucharest. Machinery, foodstuffs, raw minerals and petroleum products are exported. Heavy industry and oil have become increasingly important to the economy since 1959. Romania joined the European Union in January 2007.

MONETARY SYSTEM
100 Bani = 1 Leu

REPUBLIC

STANDARD COINAGE

KM# 115 LEU
2.5200 g., Copper Plated Steel, 19 mm. **Obv:** Value flanked by sprigs **Rev:** Shield divides date

Date	Mintage	F	VF	XF	Unc	BU
2002 Proof	1,500	Value: 5.00				
2003 Proof	2,000	Value: 5.00				
2004 Proof	2,000	Value: 5.00				
2005	—	—	—	—	1.00	—
2005 Proof	—	Value: 6.00				
2006 Proof	1,000	Value: 6.00				

KM# 114 5 LEI
3.3000 g., Nickel Plated Steel, 21 mm. **Obv:** Value flanked by oak leaves **Rev:** Shield divides date **Edge:** Plain

Date	Mintage	F	VF	XF	Unc	BU
2002 Proof	1,500	Value: 5.00				
2003 Proof	2,000	Value: 5.00				
2004 Proof	—	Value: 5.00				
2005 Proof	—	Value: 5.00				

KM# 116 10 LEI
4.7000 g., Nickel Clad Steel, 23 mm. **Obv:** Value within sprigs **Rev:** Shield divides date **Edge:** Plain

Date	Mintage	F	VF	XF	Unc	BU
2002 Proof	1,500	Value: 6.00				
2003 Proof	2,000	Value: 6.00				

KM# 109 20 LEI
5.0000 g., Brass Clad Steel, 24 mm. **Obv:** Crowned bust of Prince Stefan Cel Mare facing, flanked by dots **Rev:** Value and date within half sprigs and dots **Edge:** Plain **Designer:** Constantin Dumitrescu **Note:** Date varieties exist.

Date	Mintage	F	VF	XF	Unc	BU
2002 Proof	1,500	Value: 7.50				
2003 Proof	2,000	Value: 7.50				

KM# 159 50 LEI
15.5510 g., 0.9990 Silver 0.4995 oz. ASW, 31.1 mm. **Series:** Romanian Aviation **Obv:** AVIONUL VUIA 1 - 1906 airplane **Rev:** Traian Vuia **Edge:** Plain **Shape:** Octagonal

Date	Mintage	F	VF	XF	Unc	BU
2001 Proof	500	Value: 165				

KM# 160 50 LEI
15.5510 g., 0.9990 Silver 0.4995 oz. ASW, 31.1 mm. **Series:** Romanian Aviation **Obv:** Avionul Coanda 1910, world's first (?) jet airplane **Rev:** Portrait of Henri Coanda **Edge:** Plain **Shape:** Octagonal

Date	Mintage	F	VF	XF	Unc	BU
2001 Proof	500	Value: 165				

KM# 161 50 LEI
15.5510 g., 0.9990 Silver 0.4995 oz. ASW, 27 mm. **Series:** Romanian Aviation **Obv:** IAR CV-11 airplane **Rev:** Elie Carafoli **Edge:** Plain **Shape:** Octagonal

Date	Mintage	F	VF	XF	Unc	BU
2001 Proof	500	Value: 165				

KM# 110 50 LEI
5.9000 g., Brass Clad Steel, 26 mm. **Obv:** Bust left flanked by dots **Rev:** Sprig divides date and value **Edge:** Plain **Designer:** Vasile Gabor

Date	Mintage	F	VF	XF	Unc	BU
2002 Proof	1,500	Value: 8.00				
2003 Proof	2,000	Value: 8.00				

KM# 167 50 LEI
15.5510 g., 0.9990 Silver 0.4995 oz. ASW, 29.5 mm. **Subject:** National Parks: Retezat **Obv:** National arms in triangular design **Rev:** Chamois **Edge:** Plain **Shape:** Rounded triangle

Date	Mintage	F	VF	XF	Unc	BU
2002 Proof	500	Value: 200				

KM# 168 50 LEI
15.5510 g., 0.9990 Silver 0.4995 oz. ASW, 29.5 mm. **Subject:** National Parks: Pictrosul Mare **Obv:** National arms in triangular design **Rev:** Eagle **Edge:** Plain **Shape:** Rounded triangle

Date	Mintage	F	VF	XF	Unc	BU
2002 Proof	500	Value: 200				

KM# 169 50 LEI
15.5510 g., 0.9990 Silver 0.4995 oz. ASW, 29.5 mm. **Subject:** National Parks: Piatra Craiului **Obv:** National arms in triangular design **Rev:** Lynx **Edge:** Plain **Shape:** Rounded triangle

Date	Mintage	F	VF	XF	Unc	BU
2002 Proof	500	Value: 200				

KM# 186 50 LEI
15.5510 g., 0.9990 Silver 0.4995 oz. ASW, 27 mm. **Subject:** Birds **Obv:** Stylized water drop **Rev:** Dalmatian Pelicans within circle **Edge:** Plain

Date	Mintage	F	VF	XF	Unc	BU
2003 Proof	500	Value: 100				

KM# 187 50 LEI
15.5510 g., 0.9990 Silver 0.4995 oz. ASW, 27 mm. **Subject:** Birds **Obv:** Stylized water drop **Rev:** Great Egret within circle **Edge:** Plain

Date	Mintage	F	VF	XF	Unc	BU
2003 Proof	500	Value: 100				

KM# 188 50 LEI
15.5510 g., 0.9990 Silver 0.4995 oz. ASW, 27 mm. **Subject:** Birds **Obv:** Stylized water drop **Rev:** Common Kingfisher within circle **Edge:** Plain

Date	Mintage	F	VF	XF	Unc	BU
2003 Proof	500	Value: 100				

KM# 111 100 LEI
8.7500 g., Nickel Plated Steel, 29 mm. **Obv:** Bust with headdress 1/4 right **Rev:** Value within sprigs **Edge Lettering:** ROMANIA **Designer:** Vasile Gabor

Date	Mintage	F	VF	XF	Unc	BU
2002 Proof	1,500	Value: 8.00				
2003 Proof	2,000	Value: 8.00				
2004 Proof	2,000	Value: 8.00				
2005	—	—	—	—	2.50	—
2005 Proof	2,000	Value: 9.00				
2006 Proof	1,000	Value: 9.00				

KM# 165 100 LEI
1.2240 g., 0.9990 Gold 0.0393 oz. AGW, 13.9 mm. **Subject:** History of Gold - "The Apahida Eagle" **Obv:** National arms in ornamental circle above value **Edge:** Plain

Date	Mintage	F	VF	XF	Unc	BU
2003 Proof	2,000	Value: 125				

KM# 198 100 LEI
1.2440 g., 0.9990 Gold 0.0400 oz. AGW, 13.93 mm. **Obv:** National arms in wreath **Obv. Legend:** ROMANIA **Rev:** Medieval helmet - "COIF POIANA COTOFENESTI" **Edge:** Reeded

Date	Mintage	F	VF	XF	Unc	BU
2003 Proof	—	Value: 100				

KM# 166 100 LEI
1.2240 g., 0.9990 Gold 0.0393 oz. AGW, 14 mm. **Subject:** History of Gold - Engolpion **Obv:** National arms and country name above two stylized birds and value **Rev:** Jeweled double headed eagle pendant

Date	Mintage	F	VF	XF	Unc	BU
2004 Proof	1,000	Value: 165				

KM# 170 500 LEI
6.2200 g., 0.9990 Gold 0.1998 oz. AGW, 11.75 mm. **Subject:** History of Gold - Treasure of Pietroasa **Rev:** "Big Clip" of Pietroasa

Date	Mintage	F	VF	XF	Unc	BU
	250	—	—	—	—	700

KM# 171 500 LEI
6.2200 g., 0.9990 Gold 0.1998 oz. AGW, 11.75 mm. **Subject:** History of Gold - Treasure of Pietroasa **Rev:** "Medium Clip" of Pietroasa

Date	Mintage	F	VF	XF	Unc	BU
2001	250	—	—	—	—	700

KM# 172 500 LEI
6.2200 g., 0.9990 Gold 0.1998 oz. AGW, 11.75 mm. **Subject:** History of Gold - Treasure of Pietroasa **Rev:** 12-sided golden bowl

Date	Mintage	F	VF	XF	Unc	BU
2001	250	—	—	—	—	700

KM# 173 500 LEI
6.2200 g., 0.9990 Gold 0.1998 oz. AGW, 11.75 mm. **Subject:** History of Gold - Treasure of Pietroasa **Rev:** Pitcher

Date	Mintage	F	VF	XF	Unc	BU
2001	250	—	—	—	—	700

KM# 176 500 LEI
6.2200 g., 0.9990 Gold 0.1998 oz. AGW, 23.2 mm. **Subject:** Christian Monuments **Rev:** Mogosoaia Palace **Shape:** Square

Date	Mintage	F	VF	XF	Unc	BU
2001	250	—	—	—	—	550

KM# 145 500 LEI
3.7000 g., Aluminum, 25 mm. **Obv:** Shield within sprigs **Rev:** Value within 3/4 wreath **Edge:** Lettered **Edge Lettering:** ROMANIA (three times)

Date	Mintage	F	VF	XF	Unc	BU
2001	—	—	—	0.75	2.00	—
2002 Proof	1,500	Value: 7.00				
2003 Proof	2,000	Value: 7.00				
2004 Proof	2,000	Value: 7.00				
2005	—	—	—	—	3.00	—
2005 Proof	1,000	Value: 8.00				
2006	—	—	—	—	3.00	—
2006 Proof	—	Value: 8.00				

KM# 174 500 LEI
6.2200 g., 0.9990 Gold 0.1998 oz. AGW, 23.2 mm. **Subject:** Christian Monuments **Rev:** Bistritz Monastery

Date	Mintage	F	VF	XF	Unc	BU
2002	250	—	—	—	—	550

KM# 175 500 LEI
6.2200 g., 0.9990 Gold 0.1998 oz. AGW, 23.2 mm. **Subject:** Christian Monuments **Rev:** Coltea Church

Date	Mintage	F	VF	XF	Unc	BU
2002	250	—	—	—	—	550

KM# 177 500 LEI
31.1030 g., 0.9990 Silver 0.9989 oz. ASW, 37 mm. **Subject:** 150th Anniversary - Birth of Ciprian Porumbescu, Composer **Obv:** Partial piano and violin left of National arms and value **Rev:** Portrait and musical score **Edge:** Plain

Date	Mintage	F	VF	XF	Unc	BU
2003 Proof	500	Value: 160				

KM# 178 500 LEI
31.1030 g., 0.9990 Silver 0.9989 oz. ASW, 37 mm. **Subject:** 500th Anniversary - Establishment of Bishopric of Ramnic **Obv:** National arms and value above inscription **Rev:** Bishopric's coat-of-arms **Edge:** Plain

Date	Mintage	F	VF	XF	Unc	BU
2003 Proof	500	Value: 160				

KM# 179 500 LEI
31.1030 g., 0.9990 Silver 0.9989 oz. ASW, 37 mm. **Subject:** Romanian Numismatic Society Centennial **Obv:** Cornucopia pouring forth coins, value below **Rev:** Minerva and torch **Rev. Legend:** CENTENARUL SOCIETATII NUMISMATICE ROMANE, 1903-2003 **Edge:** Plain

Date	Mintage	F	VF	XF	Unc	BU
2003 Proof	1,000	Value: 150				

KM# 180 500 LEI
31.1030 g., 0.9990 Silver 0.9989 oz. ASW, 37 mm. **Subject:** 140th Anniversary - University of Bucharest **Obv:** Vertical inscription divides National arms, value and date at left. University emblem at right **Obv. Inscription:** ROMANIA **Rev:** Cameo at right and crowned arms at left above University Building **Rev. Inscription:** Upper: UNIVERSITATEA DIN BUCURESTI / 140 DE ANI; Lower: INTEMEIATA LA 1864 DE / AL IOAN CUZA **Edge:** Plain

Date	Mintage	F	VF	XF	Unc	BU
2004 Proof	500	Value: 180				

KM# 193 500 LEI

31.1035 g., 0.9990 Silver 0.9990 oz. ASW, 37 mm. **Subject:** 150th Anniversary - Birth of Anghel Saligny **Obv:** Arms at left above Cernavoda bridge, inscription, date, and value below **Obv. Inscription:** PODUL DE LA CERNAVODA **Rev:** Bust of bridge builder Anghel Saligny half right, life dates at right, his signature below at left **Edge:** Plain

Date	Mintage	F	VF	XF	Unc	BU
2004 Proof	500	Value: 350				

KM# 163 500 LEI

31.1030 g., 0.9990 Silver 0.9989 oz. ASW, 37 mm. **Subject:** Christian Feudal Art Monuments **Obv:** National arms, date and value at left, belfry tower of church at right **Rev:** Cotroceni Monastery church **Edge:** Plain **Shape:** 10-sided

Date	Mintage	F	VF	XF	Unc	BU
2004 Proof	500	Value: 150				

KM# 164 500 LEI

31.1030 g., 0.9990 Silver 0.9989 oz. ASW, 37 mm. **Subject:** Christian Feudal Art Monuments **Obv:** National arms, bell and value **Rev:** St. Trei Ierarhi church in Iasi **Edge:** Plain **Shape:** 10-sided

Date	Mintage	F	VF	XF	Unc	BU
2004 Proof	500	Value: 150				

KM# 218 500 LEI

31.1050 g., 0.9990 Gold 0.9990 oz. AGW, 35 mm. **Subject:** Union of the Principalities of Moldavia and Wallachia, 150th Anniversary

Date	Mintage	F	VF	XF	Unc	BU
2009 Proof	250	Value: 1,900				

KM# 153 1000 LEI

2.0000 g., Aluminum, 22 mm. **Subject:** Constantin Brancoveanu **Obv:** Value above shield within lined circle **Rev:** Bust with headdress facing **Edge:** Plain with serrated sections

Date	Mintage	VG	F	VF	XF	Unc
2001	—	—	—	—	0.25	2.50
2002	—	—	—	—	0.25	2.50
2002 Proof	1,500	Value: 12.00				
2003	—	—	—	—	0.25	2.50
2003 Proof	2,000	Value: 12.00				
2004	—	—	—	—	0.25	2.50
2004 Proof	2,000	Value: 12.00				
2005	—	—	—	—	0.25	2.50
2005 Proof	—	Value: 13.00				
2006 Proof	1,000	Value: 13.00				

KM# 156 1000 LEI

15.5510 g., 0.9990 Gold 0.4995 oz. AGW, 27 mm. **Subject:** 1900th Anniversary of the First Roman-Dacian War **Obv:** Traian's column and shield **Rev:** Monument divides cameos **Edge:** Plain

Date	Mintage	VG	F	VF	XF	Unc
2001 Proof	500	Value: 950				

KM# 181 2000 LEI

25.0000 g., Bi-Metallic .999 Silver, 10g center in .999 Gold, 15g ring, 35 mm. **Subject:** Ion Heliade Radulescu (1802-1872) **Obv:** Lyre at left, national arms at right in divided circle design **Rev:** Ion Heliade Radulescu above signature **Edge:** Reeded

Date	Mintage	F	VF	XF	Unc	BU
2002 Proof	500	Value: 1,000				

KM# 158 5000 LEI

2.5000 g., Aluminum, 24 mm. **Obv:** Value and country name **Rev:** Sprig divides date and shield **Edge:** Plain **Shape:** 12-sided

Date	Mintage	F	VF	XF	Unc	BU
2001	—	—	—	—	0.50	—
2002	—	—	—	—	0.50	—
2002 Proof	1,500	Value: 15.00				
2003	—	—	—	—	0.25	—
2003 Proof	2,000	Value: 15.00				
2004	—	—	—	—	0.25	—
2004 Proof	2,000	Value: 16.00				
2005	—	—	—	—	0.25	—
2005 Proof	2,000	Value: 17.00				
2006 Proof	1,000	Value: 17.00				

KM# 162 5000 LEI

31.1035 g., 0.9990 Gold 0.9990 oz. AGW, 35 mm. **Subject:** Constantin Brancusi 125th Anniversary of Birth **Obv:** National arms, value and sculpture **Rev:** Bearded portrait and signature **Edge:** Plain

Date	Mintage	F	VF	XF	Unc	BU
2001 Proof	500	Value: 2,250				

KM# 183 5000 LEI

31.1030 g., 0.9990 Gold 0.9989 oz. AGW, 35 mm. **Subject:** Ion Luca Caragiale, playright (1852-1912) **Obv:** National arms, value and masks of Comedy and Tragedy **Rev:** Portrait **Edge:** Plain

Date	Mintage	F	VF	XF	Unc	BU
2002 Proof	250	Value: 2,500				

KM# 184 5000 LEI

31.1030 g., 0.9990 Gold 0.9989 oz. AGW, 35 mm. **Subject:** Bran Castle (1378-2003) **Obv:** Two coats of arms on shield above value **Rev:** Castle view **Edge:** Plain

Date	Mintage	F	VF	XF	Unc	BU
2003 Proof	250	Value: 2,000				

KM# 185 5000 LEI

31.1030 g., 0.9990 Gold 0.9989 oz. AGW, 35 mm. **Subject:** Stephen the Great **Obv:** National arms, value above coin design in wall **Rev:** Portrait of Stephen and Putna Monastery

Date	Mintage	F	VF	XF	Unc	BU
2004 Proof	250	Value: 2,000				

REFORM COINAGE - 2005

10,000 Old Leu = 1 New Leu

KM# 189 BAN

2.4000 g., Brass Plated Steel, 16.8 mm. **Subject:** Monetary Reform of 2005 **Obv:** National arms flanked by stars **Rev:** Value **Edge:** Plain

Date	Mintage	F	VF	XF	Unc	BU
2005	—	—	—	—	0.30	0.50
2005 Proof	—	Value: 2.50				
2006	—	—	—	—	0.30	0.50
2006 Proof	—	Value: 2.50				
2007	—	—	—	—	0.30	0.50
2007 Proof	—	Value: 2.50				
2008	—	—	—	—	0.30	0.50
2008 Proof	—	Value: 2.50				
2009	—	—	—	—	0.30	0.50
2009 Proof	—	Value: 2.50				
2010	—	—	—	—	0.30	0.50
2010 Proof	—	Value: 2.50				
2011	—	—	—	—	0.30	0.50
2011 Proof	—	Value: 2.50				
2012	—	—	—	—	0.30	0.50

KM# 190 5 BANI

2.8000 g., Copper Plated Steel, 18.25 mm. **Subject:** Monetary Reform of 2005 **Obv:** National arms flanked by stars **Obv. Legend:** ROMANIA **Rev:** Value **Edge:** Reeded

Date	Mintage	F	VF	XF	Unc	BU
2005	—	—	—	—	0.50	0.75
2005 Proof	—	Value: 5.00				
2006	—	—	—	—	0.50	0.75
2006 Proof	—	Value: 5.00				
2007	—	—	—	—	0.50	0.75
2007 Proof	—	Value: 5.00				
2008	—	—	—	—	0.50	0.75
2008 Proof	—	Value: 5.00				
2009	—	—	—	—	0.50	0.75
2009 Proof	—	Value: 5.00				
2010	—	—	—	—	0.50	0.75
2010 Proof	—	Value: 5.00				
2011	—	—	—	—	0.50	0.75
2011 Proof	—	Value: 5.00				
2012	—	—	—	—	0.50	0.75

KM# 191 10 BANI
4.0000 g., Nickel Plated Steel, 20.4 mm. **Subject:** Monetary Reform of 2005 **Obv:** National arms flanked by stars **Obv. Legend:** ROMANIA **Rev:** Value **Edge:** Segmented reeding

Date	Mintage	F	VF	XF	Unc	BU
2005	—	—	—	—	0.65	0.85
2005 Proof	—	Value: 7.00				
2006	—	—	—	—	0.60	0.80
2006 Proof	—	Value: 7.00				
2007	—	—	—	—	0.50	0.75
2007 Proof	—	Value: 7.00				
2008	—	—	—	—	0.50	0.70
2008 Proof	—	Value: 7.00				
2009	—	—	—	—	0.50	0.70
2009 Proof	—	Value: 7.00				
2010	—	—	—	—	0.50	0.70
2010 Proof	—	Value: 7.00				
2011	—	—	—	—	0.50	0.70
2011 Proof	—	Value: 7.00				
2012	—	—	—	—	0.50	0.70

KM# 192 50 BANI
6.1000 g., Nickel-Brass, 23.75 mm. **Subject:** Monetary Reform of 2005 **Obv:** National arms flanked by stars **Obv. Legend:** ROMANIA **Rev:** Value **Edge:** Lettered **Edge Lettering:** ROMANIA twice

Date	Mintage	F	VF	XF	Unc	BU
2005	—	—	—	—	0.85	1.00
2005 Proof	—	Value: 10.00				
2006	—	—	—	—	0.75	0.85
2006 Proof	—	Value: 10.00				
2007	—	—	—	—	0.65	0.75
2007 Proof	—	Value: 10.00				
2008	—	—	—	—	0.65	0.75
2008 Proof	—	Value: 10.00				
2009	—	—	—	—	0.65	0.75
2009 Proof	—	Value: 10.00				
2010	—	—	—	—	0.65	0.75
2010 Proof	—	Value: 10.00				
2011	—	—	—	—	0.65	0.75
2011 Proof	—	Value: 10.00				
2012	—	—	—	—	0.65	0.75

KM# 259 50 BANI
6.1000 g., Nickel-Brass, 23.75 mm. **Subject:** Aurel Vlaicu

Date	Mintage	F	VF	XF	Unc	BU
2010	5,000,000	—	—	—	0.65	1.00
Note: Medal rotation						
2010 Proof	1,000	Value: 150				
Note: Medal rotation						
2010 Proof	5,000	Value: 25.00				
Note: Coin rotation						
2011 Proof	1,000	—	—	—	—	—
Note: Medal rotation						

KM# 260 50 BANI
6.1000 g., Nickel-Brass, 23.75 mm. **Subject:** King Batran

Date	Mintage	F	VF	XF	Unc	BU
2011	—	—	—	—	0.65	0.75

KM# 209 LEU
23.5000 g., Copper Plated Tombac, 37 mm. **Subject:** 140th Anniversary Founding Romanian Academy **Edge:** Plain

Date	Mintage	F	VF	XF	Unc	BU
2006 Proof	35	Value: 750				

KM# 220 LEU
23.5000 g., Copper Plated Tombac, 37 mm. **Subject:** Centennial - Birth of Mircea Eliade **Obv:** Shield and value **Rev:** Portrait facing **Edge:** Reeded

Date	Mintage	F	VF	XF	Unc	BU
2007 Proof	250	Value: 150				

KM# 223 LEU
23.5000 g., Copper Plated Tombac, 37 mm. **Subject:** Dimitrie Cantemir, (Prince of Moldavia 1710-1711), Scientist **Edge:** Reeded

Date	Mintage	F	VF	XF	Unc	BU
2007 Proof	250	Value: 150				

KM# 226 LEU
23.5000 g., Copper Plated Tombac, 37 mm. **Subject:** Stephan the Great **Edge:** Reeded

Date	Mintage	F	VF	XF	Unc	BU
2007 Proof	250	Value: 150				

KM# 199 LEU
23.5000 g., Copper Plated Tombac, 37 mm. **Subject:** 130th Anniversary of Proclamation of Independence **Obv:** Shield and "The Smardan Assault" painting by Nicolae Grigoresuv **Rev:** Meeting of the Parliament

Date	Mintage	F	VF	XF	Unc	BU
2007 Proof	130	Value: 250				

KM# 258 LEU
23.5000 g., Copper Plated Tombac, 37 mm. **Subject:** Bucharest, 550th Anniversary **Obv:** Vlad Tepes **Rev:** Buildings

Date	Mintage	F	VF	XF	Unc	BU
2009 Proof	250	Value: 150				

KM# 234 LEU
23.5000 g., Copper Plated Tombac, 37 mm. **Subject:** Nicolae Balcescu, 190th Anniversary of Birth

Date	Mintage	F	VF	XF	Unc	BU
2009 Proof	1,000	Value: 75.00				

KM# 261 LEU
23.5000 g., Copper Plated Tombac, 37 mm. **Subject:** Central Bank, 130th Anniversary

Date	Mintage	F	VF	XF	Unc	BU
2010 Proof	1,500	Value: 65.00				

KM# 208 5 LEI
31.1000 g., 0.9990 Silver 0.9988 oz. ASW, 37 mm. **Subject:** 100th Anniversary - Birth of Grigore Vasiliu-Birlic **Edge:** Plain

Date	Mintage	F	VF	XF	Unc	BU
2005 Proof	150	Value: 1,200				

KM# 210 5 LEI
31.1000 g., 0.9990 Silver 0.9988 oz. ASW, 37 mm. **Subject:** 140th Anniversary Founding Romanian Academy **Edge:** Plain

Date	Mintage	F	VF	XF	Unc	BU
2006 Proof	500	Value: 300				

KM# 212 5 LEI
31.1000 g., 0.9990 Silver 0.9988 oz. ASW, 37 mm. **Subject:** Christian Feudal Art - "Wooden Church from Ieud-Deal" **Obv:** Fragment of mural in Ieud Church depicting Isaac, Abraham and Jacob at top, inscription, value and date in lower half **Obv. Inscription:** ROMANIA **Rev:** Front view of Ieud Church against frosted background **Rev. Inscription:** BISERICA DE LEMN IEUD DEAL **Edge:** Plain **Designer:** Cristian Ciornci, Vasilc Gabor

Date	Mintage	F	VF	XF	Unc	BU
2006 Proof	500	Value: 170				

KM# 213 5 LEI
31.1030 g., 0.9990 Silver 0.9989 oz. ASW, 37 mm. **Subject:** 150th Anniversary - Establishment of the European Commission of the Danube **Edge:** Plain

Date	Mintage	F	VF	XF	Unc	BU
2006 Proof	500	Value: 170				

KM# 216 5 LEI
31.1030 g., 0.9990 Silver 0.9989 oz. ASW, 37 mm. **Subject:** Church fron Densus **Obv:** Christ icon on pillar at left, national shield at right **Rev:** Church at left, arch at right

Date	Mintage	F	VF	XF	Unc	BU
2006 Proof	500	Value: 160				

KM# 217 5 LEI
31.1030 g., 0.9990 Silver 0.9989 oz. ASW, 37 mm. **Subject:** Sibiu - European Capital of Culture **Obv:** 2 city towers in Sibiu at left, fortress wall connecting them, Potter's Tower in background, coat of arms at right **Obv. Inscription:** ROMANIA **Rev:** City of Sibiu's logo at bottom, 2 line inscription at left, 3 line inscription at right, 4 famous edifices at center **Rev. Inscription:** SIBIU / 2007 and CAPITALA / CULTURALA / EUROPEANA **Edge:** Plain

Date	Mintage	F	VF	XF	Unc	BU
2007 Proof	500	Value: 400				

KM# 221 5 LEI
15.5500 g., 0.9990 Silver 0.4994 oz. ASW, 30 mm. **Subject:** Centennial - Birth of Mircea Eliade **Obv:** Shield and value **Rev:** Portrait facing **Edge:** Reeded

Date	Mintage	F	VF	XF	Unc	BU
2007 Proof	250	Value: 300				

KM# 224 5 LEI
15.5500 g., 0.9990 Silver 0.4994 oz. ASW, 30 mm. **Subject:** Dimitrie Cantemir, (Prince of Moldavia 1710-1711), Scientist **Edge:** Reeded

Date	Mintage	F	VF	XF	Unc	BU
2007 Proof	250	Value: 300				

KM# 227 5 LEI
15.5000 g., 0.9990 Silver 0.4978 oz. ASW, 30 mm. **Subject:** Stephan the Great **Edge:** Reeded

Date	Mintage	F	VF	XF	Unc	BU
2007 Proof	250	Value: 300				

KM# 200 5 LEI
15.5500 g., 0.9990 Silver 0.4994 oz. ASW, 30 mm. **Subject:** 130th Anniversary of Proclamation of Independence **Obv:** Shield and "The Smardan Assault" painting by Nicolae Grigoresuv **Rev:** Meeting of the Parliament

Date	Mintage	F	VF	XF	Unc	BU
2007 Proof	130	Value: 500				

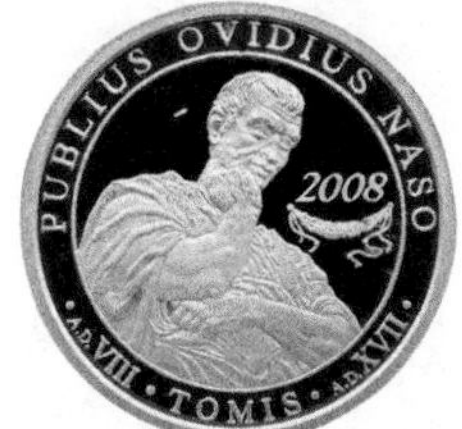

KM# 242 5 LEI
15.5500 g., 0.9990 Silver 0.4994 oz. ASW, 30 mm. **Subject:** Ovidivs Naso **Rev:** Half-length figure

Date	Mintage	F	VF	XF	Unc	BU
2008 Proof	500	Value: 170				

KM# 207 10 LEI
1.2240 g., 0.9990 Gold 0.0393 oz. AGW, 13.92 mm. **Subject:** History of Gold - The Persinari Hoard **Edge:** Reeded

Date	Mintage	F	VF	XF	Unc	BU
2005 Proof	1,000	Value: 200				

KM# 203 10 LEI
1.2240 g., 0.9990 Gold 0.0393 oz. AGW, 13.92 mm. **Subject:** Histoy of Gold - The Cuculeni Báiceni Hoard **Obv:** Romania's Coat of Arms with denomination **Rev:** Cheekpiece of the gold helmet in the Cucuteni-Baiceni hoard **Edge:** Reeded **Designer:** Cristian Ciornei

Date	Mintage	F	VF	XF	Unc	BU
2006 Proof	500	Value: 250				

KM# 229 10 LEI
31.1030 g., 0.9990 Silver 0.9989 oz. ASW, 37 mm. **Subject:** 50th Anniversary - Treaty of Rome **Edge:** Reeded

Date	Mintage	F	VF	XF	Unc	BU
2007 Proof	500	Value: 400				

KM# 240 10 LEI
31.1050 g., 0.9990 Silver 0.9990 oz. ASW, 37 mm. **Subject:** Petroleum Industry, 150th Anniversary **Rev:** Oil derrick and pump

Date	Mintage	F	VF	XF	Unc	BU
2007 Proof	500	Value: 150				

KM# 241 10 LEI
31.1050 g., 0.9990 Silver 0.9990 oz. ASW, 37 mm. **Subject:** Snagov Monastery **Rev:** Building and bust

Date	Mintage	F	VF	XF	Unc	BU
2007 Proof	500	Value: 170				

KM# 230 10 LEI
31.1000 g., 0.9990 Silver 0.9988 oz. ASW, 37 mm. **Subject:** 150th Anniversary of First Postage Stamp **Rev:** "Cap de Bour" (bull's head) stamp **Edge:** Reeded

Date	Mintage	F	VF	XF	Unc	BU
2008 Proof	1,000	Value: 175				

KM# 231 10 LEI
31.1030 g., 0.9990 Silver 0.9989 oz. ASW, 37 mm. **Subject:** 80th Anniversary Romanian Broadcasting Co. **Obv:** Radio Romania, years 1928 and 2008, coat of arms **Rev:** Radio set from 30's, logo of Radio Romania, headphones **Edge:** Reeded

Date	Mintage	F	VF	XF	Unc	BU
2008 Proof	500	Value: 300				

KM# 232 10 LEI
1.2440 g., 0.9990 Gold 0.0400 oz. AGW, 13.92 mm. **Subject:** Hoard of Hinova **Obv:** Romanian Coat of Arms, necklace parts **Rev:** Necklace parts, four bell shaped necklace parts, muff **Edge:** Reeded

Date	Mintage	F	VF	XF	Unc	BU
2008 Proof	500	Value: 135				

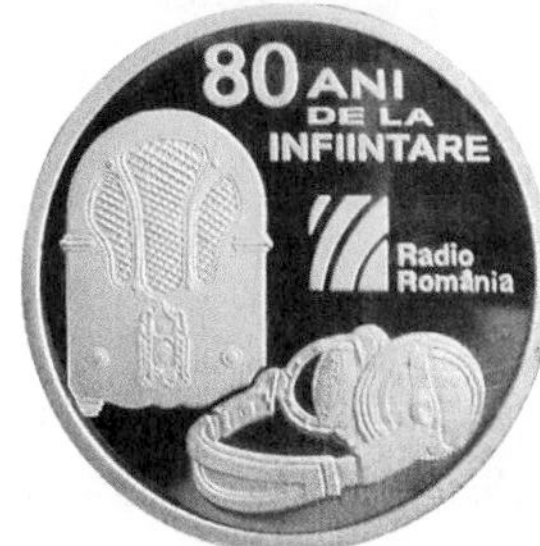

KM# 243 10 LEI
31.1050 g., 0.9990 Silver 0.9990 oz. ASW, 37 mm. **Subject:** Romanian Broadcast Company, 80th anniversary **Rev:** Radio and headset

Date	Mintage	F	VF	XF	Unc	BU
2008 Proof	500	Value: 250				

KM# 244 10 LEI
31.1050 g., 0.9990 Silver 0.9990 oz. ASW, 37 mm. **Subject:** Costin Kiritescu **Rev:** Bust facing

Date	Mintage	F	VF	XF	Unc	BU
2008 Proof	500	Value: 170				

KM# 245 10 LEI
31.1050 g., 0.9990 Silver 0.9990 oz. ASW, 37 mm. **Subject:** First printed book in Walachia, 500th Anniversary **Rev:** Building and printers at press

Date	Mintage	F	VF	XF	Unc	BU
2008 Proof	500	Value: 170				

KM# 246 10 LEI
31.1050 g., 0.9990 Silver 0.9990 oz. ASW, 37 mm. **Subject:** Simon Barnutiu **Rev:** Bust facing

Date	Mintage	F	VF	XF	Unc	BU
2008 Proof	500	Value: 150				

KM# 247 10 LEI

31.1050 g., 0.9990 Silver 0.9990 oz. ASW, 37 mm. **Subject:** Cozia Monastery **Rev:** Church building

Date	Mintage	F	VF	XF	Unc	BU
2008 Proof	500	Value: 165				

KM# 248 10 LEI

31.1050 g., 0.9990 Silver 0.9990 oz. ASW, 37 mm. **Subject:** Sambata des Sus Monastery **Rev:** Church building

Date	Mintage	F	VF	XF	Unc	BU
2008 Proof	500	Value: 165				

KM# 249 10 LEI

31.1050 g., 0.9990 Silver 0.9990 oz. ASW, 37 mm. **Subject:** Voronet Monastery **Rev:** Church building

Date	Mintage	F	VF	XF	Unc	BU
2008 Proof	500	Value: 165				

KM# 236 10 LEI

31.1050 g., 0.9990 Silver 0.9990 oz. ASW, 37 mm. **Subject:** Nicolae Balcescu, 190th Anniversary of Birth

Date	Mintage	F	VF	XF	Unc	BU
2009 Proof	1,000	Value: 85.00				

KM# 250 10 LEI

31.1050 g., 0.9990 Silver 0.9990 oz. ASW, 37 mm. **Subject:** European Monitary Union, 10th Anniversary **Rev:** Stick figure and Euro symbol

Date	Mintage	F	VF	XF	Unc	BU
2009 Proof	1,000	Value: 150				

KM# 251 10 LEI

31.1050 g., 0.9990 Silver 0.9990 oz. ASW, 37 mm. **Subject:** Alexander Macedonski **Rev:** Bust left

Date	Mintage	F	VF	XF	Unc	BU
2009 Proof	500	Value: 150				

KM# 252 10 LEI

31.1050 g., 0.9990 Silver 0.9990 oz. ASW, 37 mm. **Subject:** Walachia's establishment as an Archdiocese, 650th Anniversary **Rev:** Archbishop and Cathedral

Date	Mintage	F	VF	XF	Unc	BU
2009 Proof	500	Value: 170				

KM# 253 10 LEI

31.1050 g., 0.9990 Silver 0.9990 oz. ASW, 37 mm. **Subject:** Statistical Office, 150th Anniversary **Rev:** Two busts and document

Date	Mintage	F	VF	XF	Unc	BU
2009 Proof	500	Value: 150				

KM# 254 10 LEI

31.1050 g., 0.9990 Silver 0.9990 oz. ASW, 37 mm. **Subject:** Bucharest - Giurgiv Railway, 150th Anniversary **Rev:** Steam train

Date	Mintage	F	VF	XF	Unc	BU
2009 Proof	500	Value: 170				

KM# 255 10 LEI

31.1050 g., 0.9990 Silver 0.9990 oz. ASW, 37 mm. **Subject:** Bucharest, 550th Anniversary **Rev:** Architectural elements

Date	Mintage	F	VF	XF	Unc	BU
2009 Proof	500	Value: 160				

KM# 256 10 LEI

31.1050 g., 0.9990 Silver 0.9990 oz. ASW, 37 mm. **Subject:** Constanta Harbor, 100th Anniversary **Rev:** Ship and buildings

Date	Mintage	F	VF	XF	Unc	BU
2009 Proof	500	Value: 160				

KM# 257 10 LEI

31.1050 g., 0.9990 Silver 0.9990 oz. ASW, 37 mm. **Subject:** Tropaeum Traiani, 1900th Anniversary **Rev:** Ancient Roman building, Emperor Trajan

Date	Mintage	F	VF	XF	Unc	BU
2009 Proof	500	Value: 150				

KM# 238 10 LEI

1.2400 g., 0.9990 Gold 0.0398 oz. AGW, 13.92 mm. **Subject:** History of Gold **Rev:** Gold collar from the Gepids hoard

Date	Mintage	F	VF	XF	Unc	BU
2010 Proof	500	Value: 90.00				

KM# 262 10 LEI

31.1050 g., 0.9990 Silver 0.9990 oz. ASW **Subject:** Central Bank, 130th Anniversary **Shape:** 37

Date	Mintage	F	VF	XF	Unc	BU
2010 Proof	3,000	Value: 75.00				

KM# 266 10 LEI

31.1050 g., 0.9990 Silver 0.9990 oz. ASW, 37 mm. **Subject:** Romanian Orthodox Church Patriarchs **Rev:** Miron Cristea

Date	Mintage	F	VF	XF	Unc	BU
2010 Proof	1,000	Value: 75.00				

KM# 267 10 LEI

31.1050 g., 0.9990 Silver 0.9990 oz. ASW, 37 mm. **Subject:** Romanian Orthodox Church Patriarchs **Rev:** Nicodim Munteanu

Date	Mintage	F	VF	XF	Unc	BU
2010	1,000	Value: 75.00				

KM# 268 10 LEI

31.1050 g., 0.9990 Silver 0.9990 oz. ASW, 37 mm. **Subject:** Romanian Orthodox Church Patriarchs **Rev:** Justinian Marina

Date	Mintage	F	VF	XF	Unc	BU
2010 Proof	1,000	Value: 75.00				

KM# 269 10 LEI

31.1050 g., 0.9990 Silver 0.9990 oz. ASW, 37 mm. **Subject:** Romanian Orthodox Church Patriarchs **Rev:** Justin Moisescu

Date	Mintage	F	VF	XF	Unc	BU
2010 Proof	1,000	Value: 75.00				

KM# 270 10 LEI

31.1050 g., 0.9990 Silver 0.9990 oz. ASW, 37 mm. **Subject:** Romanian Orthodox Church Patriarchs **Rev:** Teoctist Arapasu

Date	Mintage	F	VF	XF	Unc	BU
2010 Proof	1,000	Value: 75.00				

KM# 271 10 LEI

31.1050 g., 0.9990 Silver 0.9990 oz. ASW, 37 mm. **Subject:** Hariclea Darclee **Obv:** Opera House

Date	Mintage	F	VF	XF	Unc	BU
2010	1,000	Value: 75.00				

KM# 272 10 LEI

31.1050 g., 0.9990 Silver 0.9990 oz. ASW, 37 mm. **Subject:** August Treboniu Laurian, 200th Anniversary of Birth **Obv:** She-wolf and twins

Date	Mintage	F	VF	XF	Unc	BU
2010 Proof	1,000	Value: 75.00				

KM# 273 10 LEI

31.1050 g., 0.9990 Silver 0.9990 oz. ASW, 37 mm. **Subject:** Stefan Ciobotarasu, 100th Anniversary of Birth **Obv:** Movie Theater

Date	Mintage	F	VF	XF	Unc	BU
2010 Proof	1,000	Value: 75.00				

KM# 274 10 LEI

31.1050 g., 0.9990 Silver 0.9990 oz. ASW, 37 mm. **Obv:** Turboprop aircraft, 1910 **Rev:** Henri Coanda

Date	Mintage	F	VF	XF	Unc	BU
2010 Proof	1,000	Value: 75.00				

KM# 276 10 LEI

31.1050 g., 0.9990 Silver 0.9990 oz. ASW, 37 mm. **Subject:** Grigore Alexandrescu, 200th Anniversary of Birth

Date	Mintage	F	VF	XF	Unc	BU
2010 Proof	1,000	Value: 75.00				

KM# 277 10 LEI

1.2400 g., 0.9990 Gold 0.0398 oz. AGW, 13.92 mm. **Subject:** History of Gold - Church of Sfantul Nicolae

Date	Mintage	F	VF	XF	Unc	BU
2011 Proof	500	Value: 90.00				

KM# 279 10 LEI

31.1050 g., 0.9990 Silver 0.9990 oz. ASW, 37 mm. **Subject:** Letterpress printing in Romanian language, 450th Anniversary

Date	Mintage	F	VF	XF	Unc	BU
2011 Proof	500	Value: 140				

KM# 280 10 LEI

31.1050 g., 0.9990 Silver 0.9990 oz. ASW, 37 mm. **Subject:** George Bacovia, 130th Anniversary of Birth

Date	Mintage	F	VF	XF	Unc	BU
2011 Proof	500	Value: 140				

KM# 281 10 LEI

31.1050 g., 0.9990 Silver 0.9990 oz. ASW, 37 mm. **Subject:** Nicolae Milescu, 375th Anniversary of Birth

Date	Mintage	F	VF	XF	Unc	BU
2011 Proof	500	Value: 140				

KM# 282 10 LEI

31.1050 g., 0.9990 Silver 0.9990 oz. ASW, 37 mm. **Subject:** ASTRA, 150th Anniversary **Obv:** Andrei Saguna **Rev:** Timotei Cipariu, George Baritiu, Ioan Puscariu

Date	Mintage	F	VF	XF	Unc	BU
2011 Proof	500	Value: 140				

KM# 283 10 LEI

31.1050 g., 0.9990 Silver 0.9990 oz. ASW, 37 mm. **Subject:** Romanian Military, 150th Anniversary **Obv:** Alexandru Ioan Cuza **Rev:** Mounted officer before infantry

Date	Mintage	F	VF	XF	Unc	BU
2011 Proof	500	Value: 140				

KM# 285 10 LEI

1.2400 g., 0.9990 Gold 0.0398 oz. AGW, 13.92 mm. **Subject:** History of Gold - Chain with cross

Date	Mintage	F	VF	XF	Unc	BU
2011 Proof	500	Value: 90.00				

KM# 286 10 LEI

31.1050 g., 0.9990 Silver 0.9990 oz. ASW, 37 mm. **Subject:** Euro, 10th Anniversary **Obv:** Builting and map of Romania **Rev:** Euro as world Currency

Date	Mintage	F	VF	XF	Unc	BU
2012 Proof	500	Value: 150				

KM# 211 50 LEI

6.4500 g., 0.9000 Gold 0.1866 oz. AGW, 21 mm. **Subject:** 140th Anniversary Founding Romanian Academy **Edge:** Plain

Date	Mintage	F	VF	XF	Unc	BU
2006 Proof	35	Value: 3,000				

KM# 222 100 LEI

6.4500 g., 0.9000 Gold 0.1866 oz. AGW, 21 mm. **Subject:** Centennial - Birth of Mircea Eliade **Obv:** Shield and value **Rev:** Portrait facing **Edge:** Reeded

Date	Mintage	F	VF	XF	Unc	BU
2007 Proof	250	Value: 900				

KM# 225 100 LEI

6.4500 g., 0.9000 Gold 0.1866 oz. AGW, 21 mm. **Subject:** Dimitrie Cantemir, (Prince of Moldavia 1710-1711), Scientist **Edge:** Reeded

Date	Mintage	F	VF	XF	Unc	BU
2007 Proof	250	Value: 900				

KM# 228 100 LEI

6.4520 g., 0.9000 Gold 0.1867 oz. AGW, 21 mm. **Subject:** 550th Anniversary - Ascension Prince Stephen the Great into Moldavia **Edge:** Reeded

Date	Mintage	F	VF	XF	Unc	BU
2007 Proof	250	Value: 900				

KM# 201 100 LEI

6.4520 g., 0.9000 Gold 0.1867 oz. AGW, 21 mm. **Subject:** 130th Anniversary of Proclamation of Independence **Obv:** Shield and "The Smardan Assault" painting by Nicole Grigorescu **Rev:** Meeting of the Parliament

Date	Mintage	F	VF	XF	Unc	BU
2007 Proof	130	Value: 1,500				

KM# 235 100 LEI

6.4520 g., 0.9990 Gold 0.2072 oz. AGW, 21 mm. **Subject:** Battles of Marasti, Marasesti, Oituz 90th Anniversary **Obv:** Mausoleum of Marasesti **Rev:** Group of soldiers at Battle of Marasti

Date	Mintage	F	VF	XF	Unc	BU
2007 Proof	250	Value: 550				

KM# 264 100 LEI

6.4500 g., 0.9000 Gold 0.1866 oz. AGW, 21 mm. **Subject:** Eugeniu Carada, 100th Anniversary of Death

Date	Mintage	F	VF	XF	Unc	BU
2010 Proof	500	Value: 450				

KM# 275 100 LEI

6.4500 g., 0.9990 Gold 0.2072 oz. AGW, 21 mm. **Subject:** Maria Alexandria Victoria, 135th Anniversary of Birth

Date	Mintage	F	VF	XF	Unc	BU
2010 Proof	1,000	Value: 500				

KM# 284 100 LEI

6.4500 g., 0.9990 Gold 0.2072 oz. AGW, 21 mm. **Subject:** Wallachian uprising, 190th Anniversary **Rev:** Tudor Vladimirescu

Date	Mintage	F	VF	XF	Unc	BU
2011 Proof	500	Value: 500				

KM# 263 200 LEI

15.5500 g., 0.9990 Gold 0.4994 oz. AGW, 27 mm. **Subject:** Central Bank, 130th Anniversary

Date	Mintage	F	VF	XF	Unc	BU
2010 Proof	1,500	Value: 950				

KM# 265 200 LEI

15.5500 g., 0.9990 Gold 0.4994 oz. AGW, 27 mm. **Subject:** Romanian Orthodox Church

Date	Mintage	F	VF	XF	Unc	BU
2010 Proof	1,000	Value: 1,000				

KM# 278 200 LEI

15.5500 g., 0.9990 Gold 0.4994 oz. AGW, 27 mm. **Subject:** Cozia Monastery

Date	Mintage	F	VF	XF	Unc	BU
2011 Proof	250	Value: 1,300				

KM# 206 500 LEI

31.1000 g., 0.9990 Gold 0.9988 oz. AGW, 35 mm. **Subject:** 50th Anniversary - Death of George Enescu **Edge:** Plain

Date	Mintage	F	VF	XF	Unc	BU
2005 Proof	250	Value: 2,250				

KM# 194 500 LEI

31.1035 g., 0.9990 Silver 0.9990 oz. ASW, 37 mm. **Subject:** 125th Anniversary - National Bank **Obv:** National arms and coin design of 5 Lei dated 1880 **Rev:** Bank building **Edge:** Plain

Date	Mintage	F	VF	XF	Unc	BU
2005 Proof	—	Value: 1,000				

KM# 214 500 LEI

31.1030 g., 0.9990 Gold 0.9989 oz. AGW, 35 mm. **Subject:** 350th Anniversary - Establishment of the Patriarchal Cathedral **Edge:** Plain

Date	Mintage	F	VF	XF	Unc	BU
2006 Proof	250	Value: 3,000				

KM# 204 500 LEI

31.1035 g., 0.9990 Gold 0.9990 oz. AGW, 35 mm. **Subject:** Romania's Accession to European Union, January 1 2007 **Obv:** Romania's Coat of Arms surrounded by 12 stars of European Union **Rev:** Map of the European Union including Romania **Edge:** Plain **Designer:** Cristian Ciornei

Date	Mintage	F	VF	XF	Unc	BU
2007 Proof	250	Value: 3,000				

KM# 205 500 LEI

31.1035 g., 0.9990 Gold 0.9990 oz. AGW, 35 mm. **Subject:** Nicolae Balcescu (1819-1852) **Obv:** Romania's Coat of Arms and **Obv. Inscription:** Justice and Brotherhood **Rev:** Portrait of Nicolae Balcescu **Edge:** Plain

Date	Mintage	F	VF	XF	Unc	BU
2007 Proof	250	Value: 2,250				

KM# 215 500 LEI

31.1050 g., 0.9990 Gold 0.9990 oz. AGW, 35 mm. **Subject:** Statehood, 90th Anniversary **Obv:** Shield **Rev:** Crown

Date	Mintage	F	VF	XF	Unc	BU
2008 Proof	3,000	Value: 1,850				

KM# 219 500 LEI

31.1050 g., 0.9990 Gold 0.9990 oz. AGW, 35 mm. **Subject:** Carol I, 170th Anniversary of Birth

Date	Mintage	F	VF	XF	Unc	BU
2009 Proof	250	Value: 1,850				

KM# 233 500 LEI

31.1050 g., 0.9990 Gold 0.9990 oz. AGW, 35 mm. **Subject:** Bucharest, 550th Anniversary

Date	Mintage	F	VF	XF	Unc	BU
2009 Proof	—	Value: 1,850				

KM# 237 500 LEI

31.1050 g., 0.9990 Gold 0.9990 oz. AGW, 35 mm. **Subject:** Nicolae Balcescu, 190th Anniversary of Birth

Date	Mintage	F	VF	XF	Unc	BU
2009 Proof	—	Value: 1,850				

KM# 239 500 LEI

31.1050 g., 0.9990 Gold 0.9990 oz. AGW, 35 mm. **Subject:** Mihai Eminescu, 160th Anniversary of Birth

Date	Mintage	F	VF	XF	Unc	BU
2010 Proof	—	Value: 1,850				

MINT SETS

KM#	Date	Mintage	Identification	Issue Price	Mkt Val
MS6	2005 (4)	—	KM#189-192	—	50.00
MS4	2006 (4)	—	KM189-192, plus medal	—	75.00
MS5	2007 (4)	1,000	KM189-192, plus medal	—	60.00

PROOF SETS

KM#	Date	Mintage	Identification	Issue Price	Mkt Val
PS4	2001 (3)	500	KM#159, 160, 161	80.00	525
PS5	2002 (9)	1,500	KM#109-111, 114-116, 145, 153, 158	20.00	75.00
PS6	2003 (9)	2,000	KM#109-111, 114-116, 145, 153, 158	20.00	75.00
PS7	2003 (3)	500	KM#186, 187, 188	—	325
PS8	2004 (2)	500	KM#163, 164	—	325
PSA8	2004 (5)	—	KM#111, 115, 145, 153, 158	—	50.00
PS9	2005 (10)	—	KM#111, 115, 145, 153, 158, 189-192 plus medal	—	80.00
PS10	2006 (10)	—	KM#111, 115, 145, 153, 158, 189-192	—	80.00
PS11	2006 (3)	—	KM#209, 210, 211	—	4,050
PS12	2007 (3)	—	KM#220, 221, 222	—	1,350
PS13	2007 (3)	—	KM#223, 224, 225	—	1,350
PS14	2007 (3)	—	KM#226, 227, 228	—	1,350
PS15	2007 (5)	—	KM#189-192 plus Silver 75th Anniversary of Rodna Mountains National Park medal	—	50.00
PS17	2008 (4)	—	KM#189-192 plus silver medal Antipa Museum	—	50.00

RUSSIA

The Russia Federation, formerly the central power of the Union of Soviet Socialist Republics and now of the Commonwealth of Independent States occupies the northern part of Asia and the eastern part of Europe, has an area of 17,075,400 sq. km. Capital: Moscow. Exports include iron and steel, crude oil, timber, and nonferrous metals.

In the fall of 1991, events moved swiftly in the Soviet Union. Estonia, Latvia and Lithuania won their independence and were recognized by Moscow, Sept. 6. The Commonwealth of Independent States was formed Dec. 8, 1991 in Mensk by Belarus, Russia and Ukraine. It was expanded at a summit Dec. 21, 1991 to include 11 of the 12 remaining republics (excluding Georgia) of the old U.S.S.R.

RUSSIAN FEDERATION

Issued by the БАНК РОССИИ (Bank of Russia)

REFORM COINAGE

January 1, 1998

1,000 Old Roubles = 1 New Rouble

Y# 600 KOPEK

1.5000 g., Copper-Nickel Plated Steel, 15.5 mm. **Obv:** St. George **Obv. Legend:** БАНК РОССИИ **Rev:** Value above vine sprig **Edge:** Plain

Date	Mintage	F	VF	XF	Unc	BU
2001M	—	—	—	—	0.30	0.40
2001СП	—	—	—	—	0.30	0.40
2002M	—	—	—	—	0.30	0.40
2002СП	—	—	—	—	0.30	0.40
2003M	—	—	—	—	0.30	0.40
2003СП	—	—	—	—	0.30	0.40
2004M	—	—	—	—	0.30	0.40
2004СП	—	—	—	—	0.30	0.40
2005M	—	—	—	—	0.30	0.40
2005СП	—	—	—	—	0.30	0.40
2006M	—	—	—	—	0.30	0.40
2006СП	—	—	—	—	0.30	0.40
2007M	—	—	—	—	0.30	0.40
2007СП	—	—	—	—	0.30	0.40
2008M	—	—	—	—	0.30	0.40
2008СП	—	—	—	—	0.30	0.40
2009M	—	—	—	—	1.00	2.00
2009СП	—	—	—	—	1.00	2.00

Y# 601 5 KOPEKS

2.6000 g., Copper-Nickel Clad Steel, 18.5 mm. **Obv:** St. George **Obv. Legend:** БАНК РОССИИ **Rev:** Value above vine sprig **Edge:** Plain

Date	Mintage	F	VF	XF	Unc	BU
2001M	—	—	—	—	0.40	0.60
2001СП	—	—	—	—	0.40	0.60
2002	—	—	80.00	95.00	120	—
2002M	—	—	—	—	0.40	0.60
2002СП	—	—	—	—	0.40	0.60
2003	—	—	10.00	15.00	25.00	—
2003M	—	—	—	—	0.35	0.50
2003СП	—	—	—	—	0.35	0.50
2004M	—	—	—	—	0.35	0.50
2004СП	—	—	—	—	0.35	0.50
2005M	—	—	—	—	0.35	0.50
2005СП	—	—	—	—	0.35	0.50
2006M	—	—	—	—	0.35	0.50
2006СП	—	—	—	—	0.35	0.50
2007M	—	—	—	—	0.35	0.50
2007СП	—	—	—	—	0.35	0.50
2008M	—	—	—	—	0.35	0.50
2008СП	—	—	—	—	0.35	0.50
2009M	—	—	—	—	1.00	2.00
2009СП	—	—	—	—	1.00	2.00

Y# 602 10 KOPEKS

1.9500 g., Brass, 17.5 mm. **Obv:** St. George horseback right slaying dragon **Rev:** Value above vine sprig **Edge:** Reeded

Date	Mintage	F	VF	XF	Unc	BU
2001M	—	—	—	—	0.50	0.80
2001СП	—	—	—	—	0.50	0.80
2002M	—	—	—	—	0.50	0.80
2002СП	—	—	—	—	0.50	0.80
2003M	—	—	—	—	0.50	0.80
2003СП	—	—	—	—	0.50	0.80
2004M	—	—	—	—	0.50	0.80
2004СП	—	—	—	—	0.50	0.80
2005M	—	—	—	—	0.50	0.80
2005СП	—	—	—	—	0.50	0.80
2006M	—	—	—	—	0.50	0.80
2006СП	—	—	—	—	0.50	0.80

Y# 602a 10 KOPEKS

1.8500 g., Brass Clad Steel, 17.5 mm. **Obv:** St. George on horseback slaying dragon to right **Obv. Legend:** БАНК РОССИИ **Rev:** Denomination above vine sprig **Edge:** Plain

Date	Mintage	F	VF	XF	Unc	BU
2006M	—	—	—	—	0.50	0.80
2006СП	—	—	—	—	0.50	0.80
2007M	—	—	—	—	0.50	0.80
2007СП	—	—	—	—	0.50	0.80
2008M	—	—	—	—	0.50	0.80
2008СП	—	—	—	—	0.50	0.80
2009M	—	—	—	—	0.50	0.80
2009СП	—	—	—	—	0.50	0.80
2010M	—	—	—	—	0.50	0.80
2010СП	—	—	—	—	0.50	0.80
2011M	—	—	—	—	0.50	0.80
2012M	—	—	—	—	0.50	0.80

Y# 603 50 KOPEKS

2.9000 g., Brass, 19.5 mm. **Obv:** St. George on horseback slaying dragon right **Rev:** Value above vine sprig **Edge:** Reeded

Date	Mintage	F	VF	XF	Unc	BU
2001M Rare	—	—	—	5,000	—	—
2002M	—	—	—	—	1.50	3.00
2002СП	—	—	—	—	1.50	3.00
2003M	—	—	—	—	0.80	1.00
2003СП	—	—	—	—	0.80	1.00
2004M	—	—	—	—	0.80	1.00
2004СП	—	—	—	—	0.80	1.00
2005M	—	—	—	—	0.80	1.00
2005СП	—	—	—	—	0.80	1.00
2006M	—	—	—	—	0.80	1.00
2006СП	—	—	—	—	0.80	1.00

Y# 603a 50 KOPEKS

2.7500 g., Brass Clad Steel, 19.5 mm. **Obv:** St. George on horseback slaying dragon right **Rev:** Value above vine sprig **Edge:** Plain

Date	Mintage	F	VF	XF	Unc	BU
2006M	—	—	—	—	0.80	1.00
2006СП	—	—	—	—	0.80	1.00
2007M	—	—	—	—	0.80	1.00
2007СП	—	—	—	—	0.80	1.00
2008M	—	—	—	—	0.80	1.00
2008СП	—	—	—	—	0.80	1.00
2009M	—	—	—	—	0.80	1.00
2009СП	—	—	—	—	0.80	1.00
2010M	—	—	—	—	0.80	1.00
2010СП	—	—	—	—	0.80	1.00
2011M	—	—	—	—	0.80	1.00
2012M	—	—	—	—	0.80	1.00

Y# 745 ROUBLE

17.4000 g., 0.9000 Silver 0.5035 oz. ASW, 32.8 mm. **Obv:** Double-headed eagle within beaded circle **Rev:** Altai argalia sheep **Edge:** Reeded

Date	Mintage	F	VF	XF	Unc	BU
2001(sp) Proof	7,500	Value: 60.00				

Y# 746 ROUBLE

17.4000 g., 0.9000 Silver 0.5035 oz. ASW, 32.8 mm. **Obv:** Double-headed eagle within beaded circle **Rev:** Beavers **Edge:** Reeded

Date	Mintage	F	VF	XF	Unc	BU
2001(sp) Proof	7,500	Value: 60.00				

Y# 604 ROUBLE

3.2500 g., Copper-Nickel-Zinc, 20.5 mm. **Obv:** Double-headed eagle **Rev:** Value **Edge:** Reeded

Date	Mintage	F	VF	XF	Unc	BU
2001M Rare	—	—	—	—	—	—

Y# 731 ROUBLE
3.2100 g., Copper-Nickel, 20.7 mm. **Obv:** Double-headed eagle **Rev:** Stylized design above hologram **Edge:** Reeded

Date	Mintage	F	VF	XF	Unc	BU
2001СПМД	100,000,000	—	—	—	1.50	2.00

Y# 732 ROUBLE
17.4300 g., 0.9000 Silver 0.5043 oz. ASW, 32.8 mm. **Subject:** Sturgeon **Obv:** Double-headed eagle within beaded circle **Rev:** Sakhalin sturgeon and other fish **Edge:** Reeded

Date	Mintage	F	VF	XF	Unc	BU
2001 Proof	7,500	Value: 60.00				

Y# 758 ROUBLE
17.4400 g., 0.9000 Silver 0.5046 oz. ASW, 33 mm. **Obv:** Double-headed eagle within beaded circle **Rev:** Chinese Goral **Edge:** Reeded

Date	Mintage	F	VF	XF	Unc	BU
2002(sp) Proof	10,000	Value: 50.00				

Y# 759 ROUBLE
17.4400 g., 0.9000 Silver 0.5046 oz. ASW, 33 mm. **Obv:** Double-headed eagle within beaded circle **Rev:** Sei Whale **Edge:** Reeded

Date	Mintage	F	VF	XF	Unc	BU
2002(sp) Proof	10,000	Value: 50.00				

Y# 760 ROUBLE
17.4400 g., 0.9000 Silver 0.5046 oz. ASW, 33 mm. **Subject:** Golden Eagle **Obv:** Double-headed eagle within beaded circle **Rev:** Golden Eagle with nestling **Edge:** Reeded

Date	Mintage	F	VF	XF	Unc	BU
2002(sp) Proof	10,000	Value: 50.00				

Y# 833 ROUBLE
3.2500 g., Copper-Nickel-Zinc, 20.5 mm. **Obv:** Two headed eagle above curved bank name and date, denomination above **Rev:** Value and flower **Edge:** Reeded

Date	Mintage	F	VF	XF	Unc	BU
2002(m) Mint sets only	15,000	—	—	—	—	—
2002(sp) Mint sets only	15,000	—	—	—	—	—
2003(sp)	15,000	—	—	300	400	500
2005(m)	—	—	—	—	2.00	3.00
2005(sp)	—	—	—	—	2.00	3.00
2006(m)	—	—	—	—	2.00	3.00
2006(sp)	—	—	—	—	2.00	3.00
2007(m)	—	—	—	—	2.00	3.00
2007(sp)	—	—	—	—	2.00	3.00
2008(m)	—	—	—	—	2.00	3.00
2008(sp)	—	—	—	—	2.00	3.00
2009(m)	—	—	—	—	2.00	3.00
2009(sp)	—	—	—	—	2.00	3.00

Y# A834 ROUBLE
7.7800 g., 0.9250 Silver 0.2314 oz. ASW, 25 mm. **Subject:** St. Petersburg **Obv:** Double-headed eagle within beaded circle **Rev:** Angel on steeple of Cathedral in fortress

Date	Mintage	F	VF	XF	Unc	BU
2002 Proof	5,000	Value: 25.00				

Y# 770 ROUBLE
8.5300 g., 0.9250 Silver 0.2537 oz. ASW, 25 mm. **Subject:** Ministry of Education **Obv:** Double-headed eagle within beaded circle **Rev:** Seedling within open book **Edge:** Reeded

Date	Mintage	F	VF	XF	Unc	BU
2002(m) Proof	3,000	Value: 50.00				

Y# 771 ROUBLE
8.5300 g., 0.9250 Silver 0.2537 oz. ASW, 25 mm. **Subject:** Ministry of Finances **Obv:** Double-headed eagle within beaded circle **Rev:** Caduceus in monogram **Edge:** Reeded

Date	Mintage	F	VF	XF	Unc	BU
2002(sp) Proof	3,000	Value: 50.00				

Y# 772 ROUBLE
8.5300 g., 0.9250 Silver 0.2537 oz. ASW, 25 mm. **Subject:** Ministry of Economic Development **Obv:** Double-headed eagle within beaded circle **Rev:** Crowned double-headed eagle with cornucopia and caduceus **Edge:** Reeded

Date	Mintage	F	VF	XF	Unc	BU
2002(sp) Proof	3,000	Value: 50.00				

Y# 773 ROUBLE
8.5300 g., 0.9250 Silver 0.2537 oz. ASW, 25 mm. **Subject:** Ministry of Foreign Affairs **Obv:** Double-headed eagle within beaded circle **Rev:** Crowned two-headed eagle above crossed sprigs **Edge:** Reeded

Date	Mintage	F	VF	XF	Unc	BU
2002(sp) Proof	3,000	Value: 50.00				

Y# 774 ROUBLE
8.5300 g., 0.9250 Silver 0.2537 oz. ASW, 25 mm. **Subject:** Ministry of Internal Affairs **Obv:** Double-headed eagle within beaded circle **Rev:** Crowned two-headed eagle with round breast **Edge:** Reeded

Date	Mintage	F	VF	XF	Unc	BU
2002(sp) Proof	3,000	Value: 50.00				

Y# 775 ROUBLE
8.5300 g., 0.9250 Silver 0.2537 oz. ASW, 25 mm. **Subject:** Ministry of Justice **Obv:** Double-headed eagle within beaded circle **Rev:** Crowned double-headed eagle with column on breast shield **Edge:** Reeded

Date	Mintage	F	VF	XF	Unc	BU
2002(sp) Proof	3,000	Value: 50.00				

Y# 776 ROUBLE
8.5300 g., 0.9250 Silver 0.2537 oz. ASW, 25 mm. **Subject:** Russian Armed Forces **Obv:** Double-headed eagle within beaded circle **Rev:** Double-headed eagle with crowned top pointed breast shield **Edge:** Reeded

Date	Mintage	F	VF	XF	Unc	BU
2002(m) Proof	3,000	Value: 50.00				

Y# 835 ROUBLE
7.7800 g., 0.9250 Silver 0.2314 oz. ASW, 25 mm. **Subject:** St. Petersburg **Obv:** Double-headed eagle within beaded circle **Rev:** Sphinx

Date	Mintage	F	VF	XF	Unc	BU
2002 Proof	5,000	Value: 25.00				

Y# 836 ROUBLE
7.7800 g., 0.9250 Silver 0.2314 oz. ASW, 25 mm. **Subject:** St. Petersburg **Obv:** Double-headed eagle within beaded circle **Rev:** Small ship

Date	Mintage	F	VF	XF	Unc	BU
2002 Proof	5,000	Value: 25.00				

Y# 837 ROUBLE
7.7800 g., 0.9250 Silver 0.2314 oz. ASW, 25 mm. **Subject:** St. Petersburg **Obv:** Double-headed eagle within beaded circle **Rev:** Lion

Date	Mintage	F	VF	XF	Unc	BU
2002 Proof	5,000	Value: 25.00				

Y# 838 ROUBLE
7.7800 g., 0.9250 Silver 0.2314 oz. ASW, 25 mm. **Subject:** St. Petersburg **Obv:** Double-headed eagle within beaded circle **Rev:** Horse sculpture

Date	Mintage	F	VF	XF	Unc	BU
2002 Proof	5,000	Value: 25.00				

Y# 839 ROUBLE
7.7800 g., 0.9250 Silver 0.2314 oz. ASW, 25 mm. **Subject:** St. Petersburg **Obv:** Double-headed eagle within beaded circle **Rev:** Griffin

Date	Mintage	F	VF	XF	Unc	BU
2002 Proof	5,000	Value: 25.00				

Y# 814 ROUBLE
17.4000 g., 0.9000 Silver 0.5035 oz. ASW, 32.8 mm. **Obv:** Double-headed eagle within beaded circle **Rev:** Arctic foxes **Edge:** Reeded

Date	Mintage	F	VF	XF	Unc	BU
2003(sp) Proof	10,000	Value: 35.00				

Y# 816 ROUBLE

17.4000 g., 0.9000 Silver 0.5035 oz. ASW, 32.8 mm. **Obv:** Double-headed eagle within beaded circle **Rev:** Pygmy Cormorant drying its wings **Edge:** Reeded

Date	Mintage	F	VF	XF	Unc	BU
2003(sp) Proof	10,000	Value: 35.00				

Y# 815 ROUBLE

17.4000 g., 0.9000 Silver 0.5035 oz. ASW, 32.8 mm. **Obv:** Double-headed eagle within beaded circle **Rev:** Chinese Softshell turtle **Edge:** Reeded

Date	Mintage	F	VF	XF	Unc	BU
2003(sp) Proof	10,000	Value: 40.00				

Y# 828 ROUBLE

17.2800 g., 0.9000 Silver 0.5000 oz. ASW, 33 mm. **Obv:** Two headed eagle within beaded circle **Rev:** Amur Forest Cat on branch **Edge:** Reeded

Date	Mintage	F	VF	XF	Unc	BU
2004(sp) Proof	10,000	Value: 35.00				

Y# 1029 ROUBLE

16.8000 g., 0.9250 Silver 0.4996 oz. ASW, 32.8 mm. **Subject:** The Great Bustard

Date	Mintage	F	VF	XF	Unc	BU
2004 Proof	—	Value: 35.00				

Y# 881 ROUBLE

17.2800 g., 0.5000 Silver 0.2778 oz. ASW, 32.8 mm. **Obv:** Double-headed eagle within beaded circle **Rev:** Rush Toad **Edge:** Reeded

Date	Mintage	F	VF	XF	Unc	BU
2004 Proof	—	Value: 60.00				

Y# 882 ROUBLE

16.8100 g., 0.4999 Silver 0.2702 oz. ASW, 32.8 mm. **Obv:** Double-headed eagle within beaded circle **Rev:** Two Marbled Murrelet sea birds **Edge:** Reeded

Date	Mintage	F	VF	XF	Unc	BU
2005 Proof	—	Value: 35.00				

Y# 883 ROUBLE

16.8100 g., 0.4999 Silver 0.2702 oz. ASW, 32.8 mm. **Obv:** Double-headed eagle within beaded circle **Rev:** Asiatic Wild Dog **Edge:** Reeded

Date	Mintage	F	VF	XF	Unc	BU
2005 Proof	—	Value: 35.00				

Y# 884 ROUBLE

16.8100 g., 0.4999 Silver 0.2702 oz. ASW, 32.8 mm. **Obv:** Double-headed eagle within beaded circle **Rev:** Volkhov Whitefish **Edge:** Reeded

Date	Mintage	F	VF	XF	Unc	BU
2005 Proof	—	Value: 35.00				

Y# 916 ROUBLE

8.5300 g., 0.9250 Silver 0.2537 oz. ASW, 25 mm. **Obv:** Double-headed eagle **Rev:** Russian Navy Emblem **Edge:** Reeded

Date	Mintage	F	VF	XF	Unc	BU
2005 Proof	10,000	Value: 25.00				

Y# 917 ROUBLE

8.5300 g., 0.9250 Silver 0.2537 oz. ASW, 25 mm. **Obv:** Double-headed eagle **Rev:** Russian Marine circa 1705 **Edge:** Reeded

Date	Mintage	F	VF	XF	Unc	BU
2005 Proof	10,000	Value: 25.00				

Y# 918 ROUBLE

8.5300 g., 0.9250 Silver 0.2537 oz. ASW, 25 mm. **Obv:** Double-headed eagle **Rev:** Russian Marine circa 2005 **Edge:** Reeded

Date	Mintage	F	VF	XF	Unc	BU
2005 Proof	10,000	Value: 25.00				

Y# 981 ROUBLE

15.5500 g., 0.9250 Silver 0.4624 oz. ASW, 33 mm. **Obv:** Double headed eagle **Rev:** Mongolian Gazelle **Edge:** Reeded

Date	Mintage	F	VF	XF	Unc	BU
2006 Proof	—	Value: 65.00				

Y# 1058 ROUBLE

33.9000 g., 0.9250 Silver 1.0081 oz. ASW, 39 mm. **Subject:** Swan Goose

Date	Mintage	F	VF	XF	Unc	BU
2006 Proof	—	Value: 45.00				

Y# 1059 ROUBLE

33.9000 g., 0.9250 Silver 1.0081 oz. ASW, 39 mm. **Subject:** Ussury Clawed Newt

Date	Mintage	F	VF	XF	Unc	BU
2006 Proof	—	Value: 45.00				

Y# 1069 ROUBLE

7.7800 g., 0.9250 Silver 0.2314 oz. ASW, 22.6 mm. **Subject:** Airborne Troops

Date	Mintage	F	VF	XF	Unc	BU
2006 Proof	—	Value: 25.00				

Y# 1070 ROUBLE

7.7800 g., 0.9250 Silver 0.2314 oz. ASW, 22.6 mm. **Subject:** Airborne Troops

Date	Mintage	F	VF	XF	Unc	BU
2006 Proof	—	Value: 25.00				

Y# 1071 ROUBLE
7.7800 g., 0.9250 Silver 0.2314 oz. ASW, 22.6 mm. **Subject:** Airborne Troops

Date	Mintage	F	VF	XF	Unc	BU
2006 Proof	—	Value: 25.00				

Y# 1072 ROUBLE
7.7800 g., 0.9250 Silver 0.2314 oz. ASW, 22.6 mm. **Subject:** Submarine Forces

Date	Mintage	F	VF	XF	Unc	BU
2006 Proof	—	Value: 25.00				

Y# 1073 ROUBLE
7.7800 g., 0.9250 Silver 0.2314 oz. ASW, 22.6 mm. **Subject:** Submarine Forces

Date	Mintage	F	VF	XF	Unc	BU
2006 Proof	—	Value: 25.00				

Y# 1074 ROUBLE
7.7800 g., 0.9250 Silver 0.2314 oz. ASW, 22.6 mm. **Subject:** Submarine Forces

Date	Mintage	F	VF	XF	Unc	BU
2006 Proof	—	Value: 25.00				

Y# 961 ROUBLE
15.5500 g., 0.9250 Silver 0.4624 oz. ASW, 33 mm. **Obv:** Double headed eagle **Rev:** Red banded snake **Edge:** Reeded

Date	Mintage	F	VF	XF	Unc	BU
2007 Proof	—	Value: 35.00				

Y# 962 ROUBLE
15.5500 g., 0.9250 Silver 0.4624 oz. ASW, 33 mm. **Obv:** Double headed eagle **Rev:** Pallid Harrier in flight

Date	Mintage	F	VF	XF	Unc	BU
2007 Proof	—	Value: 65.00				

Y# 1109 ROUBLE
33.9000 g., 0.9250 Silver 1.0081 oz. ASW, 39 mm. **Subject:** Ringed seal

Date	Mintage	F	VF	XF	Unc	BU
2007 Proof	—	Value: 45.00				

Y# 1110 ROUBLE
7.7800 g., 0.9250 Silver 0.2314 oz. ASW, 33 mm. **Subject:** Space Force

Date	Mintage	F	VF	XF	Unc	BU
2007 Proof	—	Value: 30.00				

Y# 1112 ROUBLE
33.9000 g., 0.9250 Silver 1.0081 oz. ASW, 3 mm. **Subject:** Space Force

Date	Mintage	F	VF	XF	Unc	BU
2007 Proof	—	Value: 40.00				

Y# 1111 ROUBLE
7.7800 g., 0.9250 Silver 0.2314 oz. ASW, 33 mm. **Subject:** Space Force

Date	Mintage	F	VF	XF	Unc	BU
2007 Proof	—	Value: 30.00				

Y# 833a ROUBLE
3.0000 g., Nickel Plated Steel, 20.5 mm. **Obv:** Two headed eagle above curved bank name and date, denomination above **Rev:** Value and flower

Date	Mintage	F	VF	XF	Unc	BU
2009ММД	—	—	—	—	0.75	1.50
2009СПМД	—	—	—	—	0.75	1.50
2010ММД	—	—	—	—	0.75	1.50
2010СПМД	—	—	—	—	2.00	3.00
2011ММД	—	—	—	—	0.75	1.50
2012ММД	—	—	—	—	0.75	1.50

Y# 1204 ROUBLE
16.8000 g., 0.9250 Silver 0.4996 oz. ASW, 33 mm. **Subject:** Air Force

Date	Mintage	F	VF	XF	Unc	BU
2009 Proof	—	Value: 30.00				

Y# 1205 ROUBLE
16.8000 g., 0.9250 Silver 0.4996 oz. ASW, 33 mm. **Subject:** Air Force

Date	Mintage	F	VF	XF	Unc	BU
2009 Proof	—	Value: 30.00				

Y# 1206 ROUBLE
16.8000 g., 0.9250 Silver 0.4996 oz. ASW, 33 mm. **Subject:** Air Force

Date	Mintage	F	VF	XF	Unc	BU
2009 Proof	—	Value: 30.00				

Y# 1244 ROUBLE
7.7800 g., 0.9250 Silver 0.2314 oz. ASW, 33 mm. **Subject:** Armored Forces **Rev:** Crowned eagle emblem

Date	Mintage	F	VF	XF	Unc	BU
2010 Proof	—	Value: 30.00				

Y# 1245 ROUBLE
7.7800 g., 0.9250 Silver 0.2314 oz. ASW, 33 mm. **Subject:** Armored Force **Rev:** Tank advancing left

Date	Mintage	F	VF	XF	Unc	BU
2010 Proof	—	Value: 30.00				

Y# 1246 ROUBLE
7.7800 g., 0.9250 Silver 0.2314 oz. ASW, 33 mm. **Subject:** Armored Force **Rev:** Tank advancing right

Date	Mintage	F	VF	XF	Unc	BU
2010 Proof	—	Value: 30.00				

Y# 1253 ROUBLE

7.7800 g., 0.9250 Silver 0.2314 oz. ASW, 22.6 mm. **Subject:** Russian Aviation

Date	Mintage	F	VF	XF	Unc	BU
2010 Proof	—	Value: 30.00				

Y# 1254 ROUBLE

7.7800 g., 0.9250 Silver 0.2314 oz. ASW, 33 mm. **Subject:** Russian Aviation

Date	Mintage	F	VF	XF	Unc	BU
2010 Proof	—	Value: 30.00				

Y# 1302 ROUBLE

7.7800 g., 0.9250 Silver 0.2314 oz. ASW, 25 mm. **Subject:** Russian Aviation **Rev:** TU-144 flying right, color tracer

Date	Mintage	F	VF	XF	Unc	BU
2011 Proof	5,000	Value: 30.00				

Y# 1303 ROUBLE

7.7800 g., 0.9250 Silver 0.2314 oz. ASW, 25 mm. **Subject:** Russian Aviation **Rev:** U-2 biplane in flight left, color tracer

Date	Mintage	F	VF	XF	Unc	BU
2011 Proof	5,000	Value: 30.00				

Y# 1310 ROUBLE

7.7800 g., 0.9250 Silver 0.2314 oz. ASW, 25 mm. **Subject:** Strategis Missile Forces **Rev:** Emblem with crowned double ehaded eagle

Date	Mintage	F	VF	XF	Unc	BU
2011 Proof	5,000	Value: 30.00				

Y# 1311 ROUBLE

7.7800 g., 0.9250 Silver 0.2314 oz. ASW, 25 mm. **Subject:** Strategic Missile Forces **Rev:** Mobile missile system

Date	Mintage	F	VF	XF	Unc	BU
2011 Proof	5,000	Value: 30.00				

Y# 1312 ROUBLE

7.7800 g., 0.9250 Silver 0.2314 oz. ASW, 25 mm. **Subject:** Strategic Missile Forces **Rev:** Missile system against mountian background

Date	Mintage	F	VF	XF	Unc	BU
2011 Proof	5,000	Value: 30.00				

Y# 1355 ROUBLE

7.7800 g., 0.9250 Silver 0.2314 oz. ASW, 25 mm. **Subject:** Russian Aviation

Date	Mintage	F	VF	XF	Unc	BU
2012 Proof	5,000	Value: 30.00				

Y# 1356 ROUBLE

7.7800 g., 0.9250 Silver 0.2314 oz. ASW, 25 mm. **Subject:** Russian Aviation

Date	Mintage	F	VF	XF	Unc	BU
2012 Proof	5,000	Value: 30.00				

Y# 1375 ROUBLE

8.5300 g., 0.9250 Silver 0.2537 oz. ASW, 25 mm. **Subject:** Court of Arbitration

Date	Mintage	F	VF	XF	Unc	BU
2012 Proof	3,000	Value: 35.00				

Y# 605 2 ROUBLES

5.1000 g., Copper-Nickel-Zinc, 23 mm. **Obv:** Double-headed eagle **Rev:** Value and vine sprig **Edge:** Segmented reeding

Date	Mintage	F	VF	XF	Unc	BU
2001M Rare	—	—	—	—	—	—

Y# 730 2 ROUBLES

17.0000 g., 0.9250 Silver 0.5055 oz. ASW, 33 mm. **Subject:** V.I. Dal **Obv:** Double-headed eagle **Rev:** Portrait, book, signature, figures **Edge:** Reeded

Date	Mintage	F	VF	XF	Unc	BU
2001(m) Proof	7,500	Value: 60.00				

Y# 675 2 ROUBLES

5.1000 g., Copper-Nickel, 23 mm. **Subject:** Yuri Gagarin **Obv:** Value and date to left of vine sprig **Rev:** Uniformed bust facing **Edge:** Segmented reeding

Date	Mintage	F	VF	XF	Unc	BU
2001	—	—	100	125	175	—
2001ММД	10,000,000	—	—	—	2.00	4.00
2001СПМД	10,000,000	—	—	—	2.00	4.00

Y# 1002 2 ROUBLES

16.8100 g., 0.9250 Silver 0.4999 oz. ASW, 33 mm. **Subject:** V. I. Dal. 200th Anniversary of birth

Date	Mintage	F	VF	XF	Unc	BU
2001 Proof	—	Value: 30.00				

Y# 742 2 ROUBLES

17.0000 g., 0.9250 Silver 0.5055 oz. ASW, 33 mm. **Subject:** Zodiac Signs **Obv:** Double-headed eagle within beaded circle **Rev:** Leo **Edge:** Reeded

Date	Mintage	F	VF	XF	Unc	BU
2002(m) Proof	20,000	Value: 35.00				

Y# 834 2 ROUBLES

5.1000 g., Copper-Nickel-Zinc, 23 mm. **Obv:** Two headed eagle above curved bank name and date, denomination above **Rev:** Value and flower **Edge:** Segmented reeding

Date	Mintage	F	VF	XF	Unc	BU
2002ММД Mint sets only	15,000	—	—	—	—	—
2002СПМД Mint sets only	15,000	—	—	—	—	—
2003ММД	15,000	—	—	300	400	500
2006ММД	—	—	—	—	4.00	5.00
2006СПМД	—	—	—	—	4.00	5.00
2007ММД	—	—	—	—	4.00	5.00
2007СПМД	—	—	—	—	4.00	5.00
2008ММД	—	—	—	—	4.00	5.00
2008СПМД	—	—	—	—	4.00	5.00
2009ММД	—	—	—	—	4.00	5.00
2009СПМД	—	—	—	—	4.00	5.00

Y# 747 2 ROUBLES

17.0000 g., 0.9250 Silver 0.5055 oz. ASW, 33 mm. **Subject:** Zodiac Signs **Obv:** Double-headed eagle within beaded circle **Rev:** Virgo and stars **Edge:** Reeded

Date	Mintage	F	VF	XF	Unc	BU
2002(m) Proof	20,000	Value: 30.00				

Y# 761 2 ROUBLES

17.0000 g., 0.9250 Silver 0.5055 oz. ASW, 33 mm. **Subject:** Zodiac Signs **Obv:** Double-headed eagle within beaded circle **Rev:** Capricorn **Edge:** Reeded

Date	Mintage	F	VF	XF	Unc	BU
2002(sp) Proof	20,000	Value: 35.00				

Y# 762 2 ROUBLES

17.0000 g., 0.9250 Silver 0.5055 oz. ASW, 33 mm. **Subject:** Zodiac Signs **Obv:** Double-headed eagle within beaded circle **Rev:** Sagittarius **Edge:** Reeded

Date	Mintage	F	VF	XF	Unc	BU
2002(sp) Proof	20,000	Value: 30.00				

Y# 766 2 ROUBLES

17.0000 g., 0.9250 Silver 0.5055 oz. ASW, 33 mm. **Subject:** Zodiac Signs **Obv:** Double-headed eagle within beaded circle **Rev:** Scorpion **Edge:** Reeded

Date	Mintage	F	VF	XF	Unc	BU
2002(m) Proof	20,000	Value: 35.00				

Y# 768 2 ROUBLES
17.0000 g., 0.9250 Silver 0.5055 oz. ASW, 33 mm. **Subject:** Zodiac Signs **Obv:** Double-headed eagle **Rev:** Balance scale **Edge:** Reeded

Date	Mintage	F	VF	XF	Unc	BU
2002(sp) Proof	20,000	Value: 30.00				

Y# 793 2 ROUBLES
17.0000 g., 0.9250 Silver 0.5055 oz. ASW, 33 mm. **Subject:** L.P. Orlova **Obv:** Double-headed eagle **Rev:** Head facing **Edge:** Reeded

Date	Mintage	F	VF	XF	Unc	BU
2002(m) Proof	10,000	Value: 40.00				

Y# 803 2 ROUBLES
17.1000 g., 0.9250 Silver 0.5085 oz. ASW, 32.8 mm. **Subject:** Zodiac signs **Obv:** Double-headed eagle within beaded circle **Rev:** Pisces **Edge:** Reeded

Date	Mintage	F	VF	XF	Unc	BU
2003(sp) Proof	20,000	Value: 50.00				

Y# 804 2 ROUBLES
17.1000 g., 0.9250 Silver 0.5085 oz. ASW, 32.8 mm. **Subject:** Zodiac signs **Obv:** Double-headed eagle within beaded circle **Rev:** Aquarius **Edge:** Reeded

Date	Mintage	F	VF	XF	Unc	BU
2003(m) Proof	20,000	Value: 35.00				

Y# 820 2 ROUBLES
17.0000 g., 0.9250 Silver 0.5055 oz. ASW, 33 mm. **Subject:** Zodiac Signs **Obv:** Double-headed eagle within beaded circle **Rev:** Cancer Crayfish **Edge:** Reeded

Date	Mintage	F	VF	XF	Unc	BU
2003(sp) Proof	20,000	Value: 50.00				

Y# 840 2 ROUBLES
16.8100 g., 0.9250 Silver 0.4999 oz. ASW, 33 mm. **Rev:** Guil Yarovsky

Date	Mintage	F	VF	XF	Unc	BU
2003(m) Proof	10,000	Value: 40.00				

Y# 841 2 ROUBLES
16.8100 g., 0.9250 Silver 0.4999 oz. ASW, 33 mm. **Rev:** Fedor Tyutchev

Date	Mintage	F	VF	XF	Unc	BU
2003(sp) Proof	10,000	Value: 40.00				

Y# 844 2 ROUBLES
17.0000 g., 0.9250 Silver 0.5055 oz. ASW, 33 mm. **Subject:** Zodiac Signs **Obv:** Double-headed eagle within beaded circle **Rev:** Aries

Date	Mintage	F	VF	XF	Unc	BU
2003 Proof	20,000	Value: 25.00				

Y# 845 2 ROUBLES
17.0000 g., 0.9250 Silver 0.5055 oz. ASW, 33 mm. **Subject:** Zodiac Signs **Obv:** Double-headed eagle within beaded circle **Rev:** Taurus

Date	Mintage	F	VF	XF	Unc	BU
2003 Proof	20,000	Value: 25.00				

Y# 846 2 ROUBLES
17.0000 g., 0.9250 Silver 0.5055 oz. ASW, 33 mm. **Subject:** Zodiac Signs **Obv:** Double-headed eagle within beaded circle **Rev:** Gemini

Date	Mintage	F	VF	XF	Unc	BU
2003 Proof	20,000	Value: 22.50				

Y# 842 2 ROUBLES
16.8100 g., 0.9250 Silver 0.4999 oz. ASW, 33 mm. **Rev:** V. P. Tchkalov

Date	Mintage	F	VF	XF	Unc	BU
2004(m) Proof	7,000	Value: 50.00				

Y# 843 2 ROUBLES
16.8100 g., 0.9250 Silver 0.4999 oz. ASW, 33 mm. **Rev:** Mikhail Glinka

Date	Mintage	F	VF	XF	Unc	BU
2004(m) Proof	7,000	Value: 50.00				

Y# 1021 2 ROUBLES
16.8000 g., 0.9250 Silver 0.4996 oz. ASW, 33 mm. **Subject:** Sini Rerikh, 100th Anniversary of Birth

Date	Mintage	F	VF	XF	Unc	BU
2004 Proof	—	Value: 60.00				

Y# 897 2 ROUBLES
17.0000 g., 0.9250 Silver 0.5055 oz. ASW, 33 mm. **Obv:** Double-headed eagle **Rev:** Gemini twins **Edge:** Reeded

Date	Mintage	F	VF	XF	Unc	BU
2005 Proof	20,000	Value: 30.00				

Y# 899 2 ROUBLES
17.0000 g., 0.9250 Silver 0.5055 oz. ASW, 33 mm. **Obv:** Double-headed eagle **Rev:** Cancer Crayfish **Edge:** Reeded

Date	Mintage	F	VF	XF	Unc	BU
2005 Proof	20,000	Value: 50.00				

Y# 901 2 ROUBLES
17.0000 g., 0.9250 Silver 0.5055 oz. ASW, 33 mm. **Obv:** Double-headed eagle **Rev:** Leo lion **Edge:** Reeded

Date	Mintage	F	VF	XF	Unc	BU
2005 Proof	20,000	Value: 50.00				

Y# 905 2 ROUBLES
17.0000 g., 0.9250 Silver 0.5055 oz. ASW, 33 mm. **Obv:** Double-headed eagle **Rev:** Mikhail Sholokhov with pen in hand **Edge:** Reeded

Date	Mintage	F	VF	XF	Unc	BU
2005 Proof	10,000	Value: 40.00				

Y# 909 2 ROUBLES
17.0000 g., 0.9250 Silver 0.5055 oz. ASW, 33 mm. **Obv:** Double-headed eagle **Rev:** Peter Klodt viewing man and horse statue **Edge:** Reeded

Date	Mintage	F	VF	XF	Unc	BU
2005 Proof	10,000	Value: 40.00				

Y# 914 2 ROUBLES
17.0000 g., 0.9250 Silver 0.5055 oz. ASW, 33 mm. **Obv:** Double-headed eagle **Rev:** Virgo standing lady **Edge:** Reeded

Date	Mintage	F	VF	XF	Unc	BU
2005 Proof	20,000	Value: 30.00				

Y# 919 2 ROUBLES
17.0000 g., 0.9250 Silver 0.5055 oz. ASW, 33 mm. **Obv:** Double-headed eagle **Rev:** Libra - 2 stylized birds forming a balance scale **Edge:** Reeded

Date	Mintage	F	VF	XF	Unc	BU
2005 Proof	20,000	Value: 50.00				

Y# 921 2 ROUBLES
17.0000 g., 0.9250 Silver 0.5055 oz. ASW, 33 mm. **Obv:** Double-headed eagle **Rev:** Scorpio scorpion **Edge:** Reeded

Date	Mintage	F	VF	XF	Unc	BU
2005 Proof	20,000	Value: 50.00				

Y# 926 2 ROUBLES
17.0000 g., 0.9250 Silver 0.5055 oz. ASW, 33 mm. **Obv:** Double-headed eagle **Rev:** Sagittarius the archer **Edge:** Reeded

Date	Mintage	F	VF	XF	Unc	BU
2005 Proof	20,000	Value: 50.00				

Y# 928 2 ROUBLES
17.0000 g., 0.9250 Silver 0.5055 oz. ASW, 33 mm. **Obv:** Double-headed eagle **Rev:** Capricorn as half goat and fish **Edge:** Reeded

Date	Mintage	F	VF	XF	Unc	BU
2005 Proof	20,000	Value: 50.00				

Y# 930 2 ROUBLES
17.0000 g., 0.9250 Silver 0.5055 oz. ASW, 33 mm. **Obv:** Double-headed eagle **Rev:** Pisces as catfish and sturgeon **Edge:** Reeded

Date	Mintage	F	VF	XF	Unc	BU
2005 Proof	20,000	Value: 50.00				

Y# 932 2 ROUBLES
17.0000 g., 0.9250 Silver 0.5055 oz. ASW, 33 mm. **Obv:** Double-headed eagle **Rev:** Aries ram **Edge:** Reeded

Date	Mintage	F	VF	XF	Unc	BU
2005 Proof	20,000	Value: 50.00				

Y# 934 2 ROUBLES
17.0000 g., 0.9250 Silver 0.5055 oz. ASW, 33 mm. **Obv:** Double-headed eagle **Rev:** Taurus bull **Edge:** Reeded

Date	Mintage	F	VF	XF	Unc	BU
2005 Proof	20,000	Value: 50.00				

Y# 936 2 ROUBLES
17.0000 g., 0.9250 Silver 0.5055 oz. ASW, 33 mm. **Obv:** Double-headed eagle **Rev:** Aquarius water carrier **Edge:** Reeded

Date	Mintage	F	VF	XF	Unc	BU
2005 Proof	20,000	Value: 30.00				

Y# 1054 2 ROUBLES
16.8000 g., 0.9250 Silver 0.4996 oz. ASW, 33 mm. **Subject:** O. K. Antonov, 100th Anniversary of Birth

Date	Mintage	F	VF	XF	Unc	BU
2006 Proof	—	Value: 50.00				

Y# 1055 2 ROUBLES
16.8000 g., 0.9250 Silver 0.4996 oz. ASW, 33 mm. **Subject:** M. A. Vrubel, 150th Anniversary of Birth

Date	Mintage	F	VF	XF	Unc	BU
2006 Proof	—	Value: 50.00				

Y# 1056 2 ROUBLES
16.8000 g., 0.9250 Silver 0.4996 oz. ASW, 33 mm. **Subject:** A. A. Ivanov, 200th Anniversary of Birth

Date	Mintage	F	VF	XF	Unc	BU
2006 Proof	—	Value: 50.00				

Y# 1057 2 ROUBLES

16.8000 g., 0.9250 Silver 0.4996 oz. ASW, 33 mm. **Subject:** D. D. Shostakovich, 100th Anniversary of Birth

Date	Mintage	F	VF	XF	Unc	BU
2006 Proof	—	Value: 50.00				

Y# 967 2 ROUBLES

17.0000 g., 0.9250 Silver 0.5055 oz. ASW, 33.0 mm. **Subject:** 100th Anniversary Birth of Gerasimov **Obv:** Two-headed eagle **Rev:** Gerasimov recreating a man's face **Rev. Legend:** М. М. ГЕРАСИМОВ

Date	Mintage	F	VF	XF	Unc	BU
2007(m) Proof	10,000	Value: 45.00				

Y# 968 2 ROUBLES

17.0000 g., 0.9250 Silver 0.5055 oz. ASW, 33.0 mm. **Subject:** 150th Anniversary Birth of Tsiolkovsky **Rev:** Bust of Tsiolkovsky 3/4 right at left, scheme of two flight vehicles with earth in background at upper right **Rev. Legend:** К. Э. ЦИОЛКОВСКИЈ **Edge:** Reeded

Date	Mintage	F	VF	XF	Unc	BU
2007(m) Proof	10,000	Value: 45.00				

Y# 1104 2 ROUBLES

16.8000 g., 0.9250 Silver 0.4996 oz. ASW, 33 mm. **Subject:** S.P. Korolyov, 100th Anniversary of Birth

Date	Mintage	F	VF	XF	Unc	BU
2007 Proof	—	Value: 50.00				

Y# 1105 2 ROUBLES

16.8000 g., 0.9250 Silver 0.4996 oz. ASW, 33 mm. **Subject:** V.M. Bekhterev, 150th Anniversary of Birth

Date	Mintage	F	VF	XF	Unc	BU
2007 Proof	—	Value: 50.00				

Y# 1106 2 ROUBLES

16.8000 g., 0.9250 Silver 0.4996 oz. ASW, 33 mm. **Subject:** L. Euler, 300th Anniversary of Birth

Date	Mintage	F	VF	XF	Unc	BU
2007 Proof	—	Value: 50.00				

Y# 1107 2 ROUBLES

16.8000 g., 0.9250 Silver 0.4996 oz. ASW, 33 mm. **Subject:** V. P. Soloviev - Sedoy, 100th Anniversary of Birth

Date	Mintage	F	VF	XF	Unc	BU
2007 Proof	—	Value: 50.00				

Y# 979 2 ROUBLES

15.5500 g., 0.9250 Silver 0.4624 oz. ASW, 33 mm. **Obv:** Double headed eagle **Rev:** Black caped marmot **Edge:** Reeded

Date	Mintage	F	VF	XF	Unc	BU
2008 Proof	—	Value: 45.00				

Y# 980 2 ROUBLES

15.5500 g., 0.9250 Silver 0.4624 oz. ASW, 33 mm. **Obv:** Double headed eagle **Rev:** Shemaya fish **Edge:** Reeded

Date	Mintage	F	VF	XF	Unc	BU
2008 Proof	—	Value: 50.00				

Y# 1131 2 ROUBLES

16.8000 g., 0.9250 Silver 0.4996 oz. ASW, 33 mm. **Subject:** L. D. Landau, 100th Anniversary of Birth

Date	Mintage	F	VF	XF	Unc	BU
2008 Proof	—	Value: 70.00				

Y# 1132 2 ROUBLES

16.8000 g., 0.9250 Silver 0.4996 oz. ASW, 33 mm. **Subject:** V. P. Glushko, 100th Anniversary of Birth

Date	Mintage	F	VF	XF	Unc	BU
2008 Proof	—	Value: 55.00				

Y# 1133 2 ROUBLES

16.8000 g., 0.9250 Silver 0.4996 oz. ASW, 33 mm. **Subject:** D. F. Oistrakh, 100th Anniversary of Birth

Date	Mintage	F	VF	XF	Unc	BU
2008 Proof	—	Value: 55.00				

Y# 1134 2 ROUBLES

16.8000 g., 0.9250 Silver 0.4996 oz. ASW, 33 mm. **Subject:** I. M. Frank. 100th Anniversary of Birth

Date	Mintage	F	VF	XF	Unc	BU
2008 Proof	—	Value: 55.00				

Y# 1135 2 ROUBLES

16.8000 g., 0.9250 Silver 0.4996 oz. ASW, 33 mm. **Subject:** N. N. Nosoc, 100th Anniversary of Birth

Date	Mintage	F	VF	XF	Unc	BU
2008 Proof	—	Value: 55.00				

Y# 1136 2 ROUBLES

16.8000 g., 0.9250 Silver 0.4996 oz. ASW, 33 mm. **Subject:** V. I. Nemirovich, 100th Anniversary of Birth

Date	Mintage	F	VF	XF	Unc	BU
2008 Proof	—	Value: 50.00				

Y# 1137 2 ROUBLES

16.8000 g., 0.9250 Silver 0.4996 oz. ASW, 33 mm. **Subject:** E. V. Vuchetich, 100th Anniversary of Birth

Date	Mintage	F	VF	XF	Unc	BU
2008 Proof	—	Value: 50.00				

Y# 1146 2 ROUBLES

16.8000 g., 0.9250 Silver 0.4996 oz. ASW, 33 mm. **Subject:** Emperor Dragon Fly

Date	Mintage	F	VF	XF	Unc	BU
2008 Proof	—	Value: 45.00				

Y# 834a 2 ROUBLES

5.0000 g., Nickel Plated Steel, 23 mm. **Obv:** Two headed eagle above curved bank name and date, denomination above **Rev:** Value and flower **Edge:** Segmented reeding

Date	Mintage	F	VF	XF	Unc	BU
2009ММД	—	—	—	—	0.50	0.75
2009СПМД	—	—	—	—	0.50	0.75
2010ММД	—	—	—	—	0.50	0.75
2010СПМД	—	—	—	—	0.50	0.75
2011ММД	—	—	—	—	0.50	0.75
2012ММД	—	—	—	—	0.50	0.75

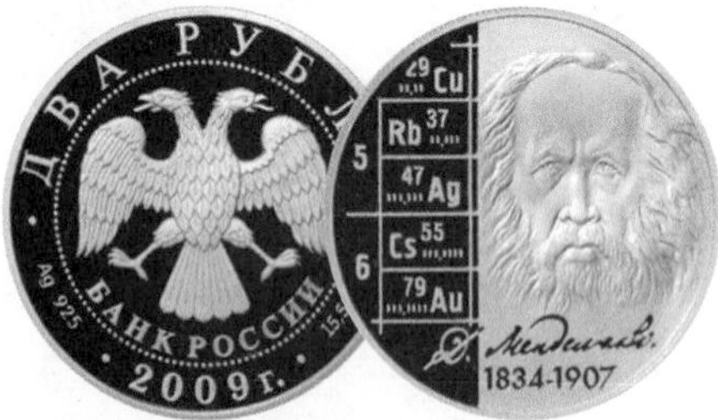

Y# 1158 2 ROUBLES

16.8000 g., 0.9250 Silver 0.4996 oz. ASW, 33 mm. **Subject:** D. I. Mendeleyev, 175th Anniversary of Birth

Date	Mintage	F	VF	XF	Unc	BU
2009 Proof	—	Value: 50.00				

Y# 1190 2 ROUBLES

16.8000 g., 0.9250 Silver 0.4996 oz. ASW, 33 mm. **Subject:** A. V. Koltsov, 200th Anniversary of Birth

Date	Mintage	F	VF	XF	Unc	BU
2009 Proof	—	Value: 50.00				

Y# 1191 2 ROUBLES

16.8000 g., 0.9250 Silver 0.4996 oz. ASW, 33 mm. **Subject:** A. N. Voronikhin, 250th Anniversary of Birth

Date	Mintage	F	VF	XF	Unc	BU
2009 Proof	—	Value: 60.00				

Y# 1192 2 ROUBLES

16.8000 g., 0.9250 Silver 0.4996 oz. ASW, 33 mm. **Subject:** G. S. Ulanova, 100th Anniversary of Birth

Date	Mintage	F	VF	XF	Unc	BU
2009 Proof	—	Value: 60.00				

Y# 1193 2 ROUBLES

16.8000 g., 0.9250 Silver 0.4996 oz. ASW, 33 mm. **Subject:** L. I. Yashin, Soccer player

Date	Mintage	F	VF	XF	Unc	BU
2009 Proof	—	Value: 55.00				

Y# 1194 2 ROUBLES

16.8000 g., 0.9250 Silver 0.4996 oz. ASW, 33 mm. **Subject:** E. I. Beskov, Soccer player

Date	Mintage	F	VF	XF	Unc	BU
2009 Proof	—	Value: 55.00				

Y# 1195 2 ROUBLES

16.8000 g., 0.9250 Silver 0.4996 oz. ASW, 33 mm. **Subject:** E. A. Stresov, Soccer player

Date	Mintage	F	VF	XF	Unc	BU
2009 Proof	—	Value: 55.00				

Y# 1196 2 ROUBLES

16.8000 g., 0.9250 Silver 0.4996 oz. ASW, 33 mm. **Subject:** V. M. Bobrov, Hockey player

Date	Mintage	F	VF	XF	Unc	BU
2009 Proof	—	Value: 55.00				

Y# 1197 2 ROUBLES

16.8000 g., 0.9250 Silver 0.4996 oz. ASW, 33 mm. **Subject:** A. N. Maltzev, Hockey player

Date	Mintage	F	VF	XF	Unc	BU
2009 Proof	—	Value: 55.00				

Y# 1198 2 ROUBLES

16.8000 g., 0.9250 Silver 0.4996 oz. ASW, 33 mm. **Subject:** V. B. Kharlamov, Hockey player

Date	Mintage	F	VF	XF	Unc	BU
2009 Proof	—	Value: 55.00				

Y# 1216 2 ROUBLES

16.8000 g., 0.9250 Silver 0.4996 oz. ASW, 33 mm. **Subject:** N. I. Pirogov, 200th Anniversary of Birth

Date	Mintage	F	VF	XF	Unc	BU
2010 Proof	—	Value: 55.00				

Y# 1217 2 ROUBLES

16.8000 g., 0.9250 Silver 0.4996 oz. ASW, 33 mm. **Subject:** I. I. Levitan, 150th Anniversary of Birth

Date	Mintage	F	VF	XF	Unc	BU
2010 Proof	—	Value: 55.00				

Y# 1218 2 ROUBLES

16.8000 g., 0.9250 Silver 0.4996 oz. ASW, 33 mm. **Subject:** G. S. Ulanova, 100th Anniversary of Birth

Date	Mintage	F	VF	XF	Unc	BU
2010 Proof	—	Value: 55.00				

Y# 1248 2 ROUBLES

16.8000 g., 0.9250 Silver 0.4996 oz. ASW, 33 mm. **Subject:** Sika Deer

Date	Mintage	F	VF	XF	Unc	BU
2010 Proof	—	Value: 45.00				

Y# 1249 2 ROUBLES
16.8000 g., 0.9250 Silver 0.4996 oz. ASW, 33 mm. **Subject:** Short tailed albatross

Date	Mintage	F	VF	XF	Unc	BU
2010 Proof	—	Value: 45.00				

Y# 1250 2 ROUBLES
16.8000 g., 0.9250 Silver 0.4996 oz. ASW, 33 mm. **Subject:** Gjursa

Date	Mintage	F	VF	XF	Unc	BU
2010 Proof	—	Value: 45.00				

Y# 1307 2 ROUBLES
20.3500 g., 0.9250 Silver 0.6052 oz. ASW, 33 mm. **Subject:** Year of Russian Culture and Language in Italy **Obv:** St. George slaying dragon **Rev:** St. Nicholas church in Bari

Date	Mintage	F	VF	XF	Unc	BU
2011 Proof	10,000	Value: 60.00				

Y# 1319 2 ROUBLES
15.5500 g., 0.9250 Silver 0.4624 oz. ASW, 33 mm. **Subject:** M.M. Botvinnik **Rev:** Chess player and board

Date	Mintage	F	VF	XF	Unc	BU
2011 Proof	3,000	Value: 70.00				

Y# 1320 2 ROUBLES
15.5500 g., 0.9250 Silver 0.4624 oz. ASW, 33 mm. **Subject:** A.I. Raykin **Rev:** Portrait left **Edge:** Reeded

Date	Mintage	F	VF	XF	Unc	BU
2011 Proof	3,000	Value: 70.00				

Y# 1325 2 ROUBLES
16.8100 g., 0.9250 Silver 0.4999 oz. ASW, 33 mm. **Subject:** I.A. Goncharov, 200th Anniversary of Birth **Rev:** Half-length figure seated reading

Date	Mintage	F	VF	XF	Unc	BU
2012 Proof	5,000	Value: 60.00				

Y# 1326 2 ROUBLES
16.8100 g., 0.9250 Silver 0.4999 oz. ASW, 33 mm. **Subject:** P.A. Stolypin, 150th Anniversary of Birth **Rev:** Half-length figure standing in cap and with hands behind back

Date	Mintage	F	VF	XF	Unc	BU
2012 Proof	5,000	Value: 60.00				

Y# 1327 2 ROUBLES
16.8100 g., 0.9990 Silver 0.5399 oz. ASW, 33 mm. **Subject:** M.V. Nesterov, 150th Anniversary of Birth

Date	Mintage	F	VF	XF	Unc	BU
2012 Proof	3,000	Value: 60.00				

Y# 1328 2 ROUBLES
16.8100 g., 0.9250 Silver 0.4999 oz. ASW, 33 mm. **Subject:** I.N. Kramskoy, 175th Anniversary of Birth **Rev:** Portrait painting in color

Date	Mintage	F	VF	XF	Unc	BU
2012 Proof	5,000	Value: 60.00				

Y# 1329 2 ROUBLES
16.8100 g., 0.9250 Silver 0.4999 oz. ASW, 33 mm. **Subject:** A.I. Vasilyev, 270th Anniversary of Birth

Date	Mintage	F	VF	XF	Unc	BU
2012 Proof	5,000	Value: 60.00				

Y# 1357 2 ROUBLES
16.8000 g., 0.9250 Silver 0.4996 oz. ASW, 33 mm. **Subject:** Alpine Weasel

Date	Mintage	F	VF	XF	Unc	BU
2012 Proof	5,000	Value: 55.00				

Y# 1358 2 ROUBLES
16.8000 g., 0.9250 Silver 0.4996 oz. ASW, 33 mm. **Subject:** Yellow-billed Loon

Date	Mintage	F	VF	XF	Unc	BU
2012 Proof	5,000	Value: 55.00				

Y# 1359 2 ROUBLES
16.8000 g., 0.9250 Silver 0.4996 oz. ASW, 33 mm. **Subject:** Emerald Rosalia Beetle

Date	Mintage	F	VF	XF	Unc	BU
2012 Proof	5,000	Value: 55.00				

Y# 1361 2 ROUBLES
16.8000 g., 0.9250 Silver 0.4996 oz. ASW, 33 mm. **Subject:** M.G. Isakova, skater

Date	Mintage	F	VF	XF	Unc	BU
2012 Proof	3,000	Value: 60.00				

Y# 1362 2 ROUBLES
16.8000 g., 0.9250 Silver 0.4996 oz. ASW, 33 mm. **Subject:** L.P. Skoblikova, skater

Date	Mintage	F	VF	XF	Unc	BU
2012 Proof	3,000	Value: 60.00				

Y# 1363 2 ROUBLES
16.8000 g., 0.9250 Silver 0.4996 oz. ASW, 33 mm. **Subject:** E.R. Grishin, skater

Date	Mintage	F	VF	XF	Unc	BU
2012 Proof	3,000	Value: 60.00				

Y# 1391 2 ROUBLES
5.0000 g., Nickel Plated Steel, 23 mm. **Subject:** War of 1812, 200th Anniversary

Date	Mintage	F	VF	XF	Unc	BU
2012	5,000,000	—	—	—	1.00	2.00

Y# 1392 2 ROUBLES
Nickel Plated Steel, 23 mm. **Subject:** General Field-Marshal M.I. Kutuzov

Date	Mintage	F	VF	XF	Unc	BU
2012ММД	5,000,000	—	—	—	1.00	2.00

Y# 1393 2 ROUBLES
Nickel Plated Steel, 23 mm. **Subject:** General Field Marshal M.B. Barklay de Tolly

Date	Mintage	F	VF	XF	Unc	BU
2012ММД	5,000,000	—	—	—	1.00	2.00

Y# 1394 2 ROUBLES
Nickel Plated Steel, 23 mm. **Subject:** Infantry General P.I. Bagration

Date	Mintage	F	VF	XF	Unc	BU
2012ММД	5,000,000	—	—	—	1.00	2.00

Y# 1395 2 ROUBLES
Nickel Plated Steel, 23 mm. **Subject:** Calvary General L.L. Benningsen

Date	Mintage	F	VF	XF	Unc	BU
2012ММД	5,000,000	—	—	—	1.00	2.00

Y# 1396 2 ROUBLES

Nickel Plated Steel, 23 mm. **Subject:** General Field-Marshal P.H. Witgenstein

Date	Mintage	F	VF	XF	Unc	BU
2012ММД	5,000,000	—	—	—	1.00	2.00

Y# 1397 2 ROUBLES

Nickel Plated Steel, 23 mm. **Subject:** Lieutenant General D.V. Davidov

Date	Mintage	F	VF	XF	Unc	BU
2012ММД	5,000,000	—	—	—	1.00	2.00

Y# 1398 2 ROUBLES

Nickel Plated Steel, 23 mm. **Subject:** Infantry General, D.S. Dohkturov

Date	Mintage	F	VF	XF	Unc	BU
2012ММД	5,000,000	—	—	—	1.00	2.00

Y# 1399 2 ROUBLES

Nickel Plated Steel, 23 mm. **Subject:** Staff Captain N.A. Durova

Date	Mintage	F	VF	XF	Unc	BU
2012ММД	5,000,000	—	—	—	1.00	2.00

Y# 1400 2 ROUBLES

Nickel Plated Steel, 23 mm. **Subject:** Infantry General A.P. Yermolov

Date	Mintage	F	VF	XF	Unc	BU
2012ММД	5,000,000	—	—	—	1.00	2.00

Y# 1401 2 ROUBLES

Nickel Plated Steel, 23 mm. **Subject:** Kozhina Vasilisa, organizer of the partisan movement

Date	Mintage	F	VF	XF	Unc	BU
2012ММД	5,000,000	—	—	—	1.00	2.00

Y# 1402 2 ROUBLES

Nickel Plated Steel, 23 mm. **Subject:** Major General A.I. Kutaisov

Date	Mintage	F	VF	XF	Unc	BU
2012ММД	5,000,000	—	—	—	1.00	2.00

Y# 1403 2 ROUBLES

Nickel Plated Steel, 23 mm. **Subject:** Infantry General M.A. Miloradovich

Date	Mintage	F	VF	XF	Unc	BU
2012ММД	5,000,000	—	—	—	1.00	2.00

Y# 1404 2 ROUBLES

Nickel Plated Steel, 23 mm. **Subject:** Infantry General A.I. Osterman-Tolstoi

Date	Mintage	F	VF	XF	Unc	BU
2012ММД	5,000,000	—	—	—	1.00	2.00

Y# 1405 2 ROUBLES

Nickel Plated Steel, 23 mm. **Subject:** Calvary General N.N. Rayevsky

Date	Mintage	F	VF	XF	Unc	BU
2012ММД	5,000,000	—	—	—	1.00	2.00

Y# 1406 2 ROUBLES

Nickel Plated Steel, 23 mm. **Subject:** Calvary General M.I. Platov

Date	Mintage	F	VF	XF	Unc	BU
2012ММД	5,000,000	—	—	—	1.00	2.00

Y# 1407 2 ROUBLES

Nickel Plated Steel, 23 mm. **Subject:** Tsar Alexander I

Date	Mintage	F	VF	XF	Unc	BU
2012ММД	5,000,000	—	—	—	1.00	2.00

Y# 677 3 ROUBLES

34.8800 g., 0.9000 Silver 1.0092 oz. ASW, 39 mm. **Subject:** 225 Years - Bolshoi Theater **Obv:** Double-headed eagle **Rev:** Standing figures facing **Edge:** Reeded

Date	Mintage	F	VF	XF	Unc	BU
2001 Proof	7,500	Value: 65.00				

Y# 680 3 ROUBLES

34.8800 g., 0.9000 Silver 1.0092 oz. ASW, 39 mm. **Subject:** 40th Anniversary of Manned Space Flight - Yuri Gagarin **Obv:** Double-headed eagle **Rev:** Uniformed bust holding dove **Edge:** Reeded

Date	Mintage	F	VF	XF	Unc	BU
2001 Proof	7,500	Value: 65.00				

Y# 682 3 ROUBLES

34.8800 g., 0.9000 Silver 1.0092 oz. ASW, 39 mm. **Subject:** Siberian Exploration **Obv:** Double-headed eagle **Rev:** Men riding horses, deer and sleds **Edge:** Reeded

Date	Mintage	F	VF	XF	Unc	BU
2001 Proof	5,000	Value: 80.00				

Y# 733 3 ROUBLES

34.8800 g., 0.9000 Silver 1.0092 oz. ASW, 39 mm. **Subject:** 200th Anniversary of Navigation School **Obv:** Double-headed eagle **Rev:** Navigational tools and building **Edge:** Reeded

Date	Mintage	F	VF	XF	Unc	BU
2001 Proof	5,000	Value: 80.00				

Y# 734 3 ROUBLES

34.8800 g., 0.9000 Silver 1.0092 oz. ASW, 39 mm. **Subject:** First Moscow Savings Bank **Obv:** Double-headed eagle **Rev:** Beehive above building within circle **Edge:** Reeded

Date	Mintage	F	VF	XF	Unc	BU
2001 Proof	17,500	Value: 45.00				

Y# 735 3 ROUBLES

34.8800 g., 0.9000 Silver 1.0092 oz. ASW, 39 mm. **Subject:** State Labor Savings Bank **Obv:** Double-headed eagle **Rev:** Dam, passbook and tractor **Edge:** Reeded

Date	Mintage	F	VF	XF	Unc	BU
2001 Proof	17,500	Value: 45.00				

Y# 736 3 ROUBLES

34.8800 g., 0.9000 Silver 1.0092 oz. ASW, 39 mm. **Subject:** Savings Bank of the Russian Federation **Obv:** Double-headed eagle **Rev:** Chevrons above building **Edge:** Reeded

Date	Mintage	F	VF	XF	Unc	BU
2001 Proof	17,500	Value: 45.00				

Y# 737 3 ROUBLES

34.8800 g., 0.9000 Silver 1.0092 oz. ASW, 39 mm. **Subject:** 10th Anniversary - Commonwealth of Independent States **Obv:** Double-headed eagle **Rev:** Hologram below logo **Edge:** Reeded

Date	Mintage	F	VF	XF	Unc	BU
2001 Proof	7,500	Value: 55.00				

Y# 738 3 ROUBLES

34.8800 g., 0.9000 Silver 1.0092 oz. ASW, 39 mm. **Subject:** Olympics **Obv:** Double-headed eagle **Rev:** Cross-country skiers **Edge:** Reeded

Date	Mintage	F	VF	XF	Unc	BU
2002 Proof	25,000	Value: 50.00				

Y# 744 3 ROUBLES

34.8800 g., 0.9000 Silver 1.0092 oz. ASW, 39 mm. **Subject:** St. John's Nunnery, St. Petersburg **Obv:** Double-headed eagle **Rev:** Nunnery and cameo **Edge:** Reeded

Date	Mintage	F	VF	XF	Unc	BU
2002 Proof	5,000	Value: 60.00				

Y# 778 3 ROUBLES

34.8800 g., 0.9000 Silver 1.0092 oz. ASW, 39 mm. **Subject:** Kideksha **Obv:** Double-headed eagle **Rev:** Three churches on river bank **Edge:** Reeded

Date	Mintage	F	VF	XF	Unc	BU
2002(sp) Proof	10,000	Value: 60.00				

Y# 779 3 ROUBLES

34.8800 g., 0.9000 Silver 1.0092 oz. ASW, 39 mm. **Subject:** Iversky Monastery, Valdaiy **Obv:** Double-headed eagle **Rev:** Building complex on an island in Lake Valdaiy **Edge:** Reeded

Date	Mintage	F	VF	XF	Unc	BU
2002(sp) Proof	10,000	Value: 60.00				

Y# 780 3 ROUBLES

34.8800 g., 0.9000 Silver 1.0092 oz. ASW, 39 mm. **Subject:** Miraculous Savior Church **Obv:** Double-headed eagle **Rev:** Church with separate bell tower **Edge:** Reeded

Date	Mintage	F	VF	XF	Unc	BU
2002(m) Proof	5,000	Value: 60.00				

Y# 781 3 ROUBLES

34.8800 g., 0.9000 Silver 1.0092 oz. ASW, 39 mm. **Subject:** Works of Dionissy **Obv:** Double-headed eagle **Rev:** "The Crucifix" **Edge:** Reeded

Date	Mintage	F	VF	XF	Unc	BU
2002(sp) Proof	10,000	Value: 45.00				

Y# 755 3 ROUBLES

34.8800 g., 0.9000 Silver 1.0092 oz. ASW, 39 mm. **Subject:** Admiral Nakhimov **Obv:** Double-headed eagle **Rev:** Monument, Admiral with cannon and naval battle scene **Edge:** Reeded

Date	Mintage	F	VF	XF	Unc	BU
2002(sp) Proof	10,000	Value: 45.00				

Y# 787 3 ROUBLES

34.8800 g., 0.9000 Silver 1.0092 oz. ASW, 39 mm. **Subject:** World Cup Soccer **Obv:** Double-headed eagle **Rev:** Soccer ball within circle of players **Edge:** Reeded

Date	Mintage	F	VF	XF	Unc	BU
2002(sp) Proof	25,000	Value: 40.00				

Y# 756 3 ROUBLES

34.8800 g., 0.9000 Silver 1.0092 oz. ASW, 39 mm. **Subject:** Hermitage **Obv:** Double-headed eagle **Rev:** Statues and arch **Edge:** Reeded

Date	Mintage	F	VF	XF	Unc	BU
2002(sp) Proof	10,000	Value: 50.00				

Y# 885 3 ROUBLES

34.8000 g., 0.9000 Silver 1.0069 oz. ASW, 38.7 mm. **Subject:** City of Pskov 1100th Anniversary **Obv:** Double-headed eagle **Rev:** Walled city view **Edge:** Reeded

Date	Mintage	F	VF	XF	Unc	BU
2003(sp) Proof	—	Value: 55.00				

Y# 801 3 ROUBLES

34.8000 g., 0.9000 Silver 1.0069 oz. ASW, 38.7 mm. **Subject:** Veborg **Obv:** Double-headed eagle **Rev:** Sailing ships and buildings **Edge:** Reeded

Date	Mintage	F	VF	XF	Unc	BU
2003(sp) Proof	10,000	Value: 55.00				

Y# 802 3 ROUBLES

34.7500 g., 0.9000 Silver 1.0055 oz. ASW, 38.7 mm. **Subject:** Lunar Calendar **Obv:** National emblem **Rev:** Mountain goat in crescent **Edge:** Reeded

Date	Mintage	F	VF	XF	Unc	BU
2003(m) Proof	15,000	Value: 50.00				

Y# 805 3 ROUBLES

34.8400 g., 0.9000 Silver 1.0081 oz. ASW, 38.8 mm. **Subject:** Zodiac signs **Obv:** Double-headed eagle within beaded circle **Rev:** Leo **Edge:** Reeded

Date	Mintage	F	VF	XF	Unc	BU
2003(m) Proof	30,000	Value: 50.00				

Y# 806 3 ROUBLES

34.7400 g., 0.9000 Silver 1.0052 oz. ASW, 38.8 mm. **Subject:** St. Daniel's Monastery **Obv:** Double-headed eagle **Rev:** Statue and monastery **Edge:** Reeded

Date	Mintage	F	VF	XF	Unc	BU
2003(m) Proof	10,000	Value: 50.00				

Y# 807 3 ROUBLES

34.7400 g., 0.9000 Silver 1.0052 oz. ASW, 38.8 mm. **Subject:** World Biathlon Championships **Obv:** Double-headed eagle **Rev:** Rifleman and archer on skis **Edge:** Reeded

Date	Mintage	F	VF	XF	Unc	BU
2003(m) Proof	7,500	Value: 60.00				

Y# 808 3 ROUBLES

34.7400 g., 0.9000 Silver 1.0052 oz. ASW, 38.8 mm. **Obv:** Double-headed eagle **Rev:** Monastery **Edge:** Reeded

Date	Mintage	F	VF	XF	Unc	BU
2003(m) Proof	10,000	Value: 50.00				

Y# 809 3 ROUBLES

34.7400 g., 0.9000 Silver 1.0052 oz. ASW, 38.8 mm. **Subject:** First Kamchatka Expedition **Obv:** Double-headed eagle **Rev:** Natives, fish and ship **Edge:** Reeded

Date	Mintage	F	VF	XF	Unc	BU
2003(sp) Proof	10,000	Value: 80.00				

Y# 810 3 ROUBLES

34.7400 g., 0.9000 Silver 1.0052 oz. ASW, 38.8 mm. **Subject:** Zodiac signs **Obv:** Double-headed eagle within beaded circle **Rev:** Virgo **Edge:** Reeded

Date	Mintage	F	VF	XF	Unc	BU
2003(sp)	30,000	Value: 40.00				

Y# 811 3 ROUBLES

34.7400 g., 0.9000 Silver 1.0052 oz. ASW, 38.8 mm. **Subject:** Zodiac signs **Obv:** Double-headed eagle within beaded circle **Rev:** Libra **Edge:** Reeded

Date	Mintage	F	VF	XF	Unc	BU
2003(m) Proof	30,000	Value: 45.00				

Y# 812 3 ROUBLES

34.7400 g., 0.9000 Silver 1.0052 oz. ASW, 38.8 mm. **Subject:** Diveyevsky Monastery **Obv:** Double-headed eagle **Rev:** Cameo above churches **Edge:** Reeded

Date	Mintage	F	VF	XF	Unc	BU
2003(sp) Proof	10,000	Value: 50.00				

Y# 813 3 ROUBLES

34.7400 g., 0.9000 Silver 1.0052 oz. ASW, 38.8 mm. **Subject:** Zodiac Signs **Obv:** Double-headed eagle within beaded circle **Rev:** Scorpio **Edge:** Reeded

Date	Mintage	F	VF	XF	Unc	BU
2003(m) Proof	30,000	Value: 40.00				

Y# 847 3 ROUBLES
34.5600 g., 0.9000 Silver 1.0000 oz. ASW, 39 mm. **Rev:** St. Trinity Monastery

Date	Mintage	F	VF	XF	Unc	BU
2003(sp) Proof	10,000	Value: 50.00				

Y# 848 3 ROUBLES
34.5600 g., 0.9000 Silver 1.0000 oz. ASW, 39 mm. **Subject:** Zodiac Signs **Obv:** Double-headed eagle within beaded circle **Rev:** Sagittarius

Date	Mintage	F	VF	XF	Unc	BU
2003(sp) Proof	30,000	Value: 40.00				

Y# 849 3 ROUBLES
34.5600 g., 0.9000 Silver 1.0000 oz. ASW, 39 mm. **Subject:** Zodiac Signs **Obv:** Double-headed eagle within beaded circle **Rev:** Capricorn

Date	Mintage	F	VF	XF	Unc	BU
2003(m) Proof	30,000	Value: 40.00				

Y# 1012 3 ROUBLES
33.9000 g., 0.9250 Silver 1.0081 oz. ASW, 39 mm. **Subject:** Year of the Goat

Date	Mintage	F	VF	XF	Unc	BU
2003 Proof	—	Value: 50.00				

Y# 850 3 ROUBLES
34.5600 g., 0.9000 Silver 1.0000 oz. ASW, 39 mm. **Subject:** Lunar Calendar **Rev:** Monkey

Date	Mintage	F	VF	XF	Unc	BU
2004(m) Proof	15,000	Value: 45.00				

Y# 851 3 ROUBLES
34.5600 g., 0.9000 Silver 1.0000 oz. ASW, 39 mm. **Subject:** Zodiac Signs **Obv:** Double-headed eagle within beaded circle **Rev:** Aquarius

Date	Mintage	F	VF	XF	Unc	BU
2004(sp) Proof	30,000	Value: 40.00				

Y# 852 3 ROUBLES
34.5600 g., 0.9000 Silver 1.0000 oz. ASW, 39 mm. **Rev:** Tomsk

Date	Mintage	F	VF	XF	Unc	BU
2004(m) Proof	8,000	Value: 60.00				

Y# 853 3 ROUBLES
34.5600 g., 0.9000 Silver 1.0000 oz. ASW, 39 mm. **Subject:** Zodiac Signs **Obv:** Double-headed eagle within beaded circle **Rev:** Pisces

Date	Mintage	F	VF	XF	Unc	BU
2004(m) Proof	30,000	Value: 40.00				

Y# 854 3 ROUBLES
34.5600 g., 0.9000 Silver 1.0000 oz. ASW, 39 mm. **Rev:** Epiphany Cathedral, Moscow

Date	Mintage	F	VF	XF	Unc	BU
2004(m) Proof	8,000	Value: 60.00				

Y# 855 3 ROUBLES
34.5600 g., 0.9000 Silver 1.0000 oz. ASW, 39 mm. **Subject:** Zodiac Signs **Obv:** Double-headed eagle within beaded circle **Rev:** Aries

Date	Mintage	F	VF	XF	Unc	BU
2004(sp) Proof	30,000	Value: 40.00				

Y# 856 3 ROUBLES
34.5600 g., 0.9000 Silver 1.0000 oz. ASW, 39 mm. **Rev:** Soccer

Date	Mintage	F	VF	XF	Unc	BU
2004(sp) Proof	10,000	Value: 45.00				

Y# 857 3 ROUBLES
34.5600 g., 0.9000 Silver 1.0000 oz. ASW, 39 mm. **Subject:** Zodiac Signs **Obv:** Double-headed eagle within beaded circle **Rev:** Taurus

Date	Mintage	F	VF	XF	Unc	BU
2004(sp) Proof	30,000	Value: 40.00				

Y# 858 3 ROUBLES
34.5600 g., 0.9000 Silver 1.0000 oz. ASW, 39 mm. **Rev:** Olympic torch

Date	Mintage	F	VF	XF	Unc	BU
2004(m) Proof	20,000	Value: 50.00				

Y# 859 3 ROUBLES
34.5600 g., 0.9000 Silver 1.0000 oz. ASW, 39 mm. **Subject:** Zodiac Signs **Obv:** Double-headed eagle within beaded circle **Rev:** Gemini

Date	Mintage	F	VF	XF	Unc	BU
2004(m) Proof	30,000	Value: 40.00				

Y# 860 3 ROUBLES
34.5600 g., 0.9000 Silver 1.0000 oz. ASW, 39 mm. **Subject:** Zodiac Signs **Obv:** Double-headed eagle within beaded circle **Rev:** Cancer

Date	Mintage	F	VF	XF	Unc	BU
2004(sp) Proof	30,000	Value: 40.00				

Y# 861 3 ROUBLES
34.5600 g., 0.9000 Silver 1.0000 oz. ASW, 39 mm. **Rev:** Church of the Sign of the Holy Mother of God

Date	Mintage	F	VF	XF	Unc	BU
2004(m) Proof	8,000	Value: 60.00				

Y# 862 3 ROUBLES
34.5600 g., 0.9000 Silver 1.0000 oz. ASW, 39 mm. **Rev:** Transfiguration icon

Date	Mintage	F	VF	XF	Unc	BU
2004(m) Proof	8,000	Value: 60.00				

Y# 863 3 ROUBLES
34.5600 g., 0.9000 Silver 1.0000 oz. ASW, 39 mm. **Rev:** Peter I's monetary reform

Date	Mintage	F	VF	XF	Unc	BU
2004(sp) Proof	8,000	Value: 75.00				

Y# 1013 3 ROUBLES
33.9000 g., 0.9250 Silver 1.0081 oz. ASW, 39 mm. **Subject:** 2nd Kamchatka Expedition, 1733-43

Date	Mintage	F	VF	XF	Unc	BU
2004 Proof	—	Value: 65.00				

Y# 1015 3 ROUBLES
33.9000 g., 0.9250 Silver 1.0081 oz. ASW, 39 mm. **Subject:** Theophanes the Greek

Date	Mintage	F	VF	XF	Unc	BU
2004 Proof	—	Value: 65.00				

Y# 1020 3 ROUBLES
33.9000 g., 0.9250 Silver 1.0081 oz. ASW, 39 mm. **Subject:** Church of the Virgin Nativity in Gordniya

Date	Mintage	F	VF	XF	Unc	BU
2004 Proof	—	Value: 65.00				

Y# 1022 3 ROUBLES
33.9000 g., 0.9250 Silver 1.0081 oz. ASW, 39 mm. **Subject:** Reindeer

Date	Mintage	F	VF	XF	Unc	BU
2004 Proof	—	Value: 70.00				

Y# 892 3 ROUBLES
33.9400 g., 0.9250 Silver 1.0093 oz. ASW, 39 mm. **Obv:** Double-headed eagle **Rev:** Rooster and crescent moon **Edge:** Reeded

Date	Mintage	F	VF	XF	Unc	BU
2005 Proof	15,000	Value: 50.00				

Y# 893 3 ROUBLES
33.9400 g., 0.9250 Silver 1.0093 oz. ASW, 39 mm. **Subject:** 60th Anniversary - Victory Over Germany **Obv:** Double-headed eagle **Rev:** Soldier and wife circa 1945 **Edge:** Reeded

Date	Mintage	F	VF	XF	Unc	BU
2005 Proof	35,000	Value: 40.00				

Y# 903 3 ROUBLES
33.9400 g., 0.9250 Silver 1.0093 oz. ASW, 39 mm. **Obv:** Double-headed eagle **Rev:** St. Nicholas Cathedral in Kaliningrad **Edge:** Reeded

Date	Mintage	F	VF	XF	Unc	BU
2005 Proof	10,000	Value: 55.00				

Y# 904 3 ROUBLES
33.9400 g., 0.9250 Silver 1.0093 oz. ASW, 39 mm. **Obv:** Double-headed eagle **Rev:** Kropotkin Metro Station in Moscow **Edge:** Reeded

Date	Mintage	F	VF	XF	Unc	BU
2005 Proof	10,000	Value: 55.00				

Y# 906 3 ROUBLES
33.9400 g., 0.9250 Silver 1.0093 oz. ASW, 39 mm. **Subject:** Helsinki Games **Obv:** Double-headed eagle **Rev:** Stylized track and field athletes **Edge:** Reeded

Date	Mintage	F	VF	XF	Unc	BU
2005 Proof	10,000	Value: 50.00				

Y# 908 3 ROUBLES
33.9400 g., 0.9250 Silver 1.0093 oz. ASW, 39 mm. **Obv:** Double-headed eagle **Rev:** Virgin Monastery in Raifa, Tatarstan **Edge:** Reeded

Date	Mintage	F	VF	XF	Unc	BU
2005 Proof	10,000	Value: 45.00				

Y# 910 3 ROUBLES
33.9400 g., 0.9250 Silver 1.0093 oz. ASW, 39 mm. **Obv:** Double-headed eagle **Rev:** Kazan Theater Building **Edge:** Reeded

Date	Mintage	F	VF	XF	Unc	BU
2005 Proof	10,000	Value: 50.00				

Y# 923 3 ROUBLES
33.9400 g., 0.9250 Silver 1.0093 oz. ASW, 39 mm. **Subject:** 625th Anniversary - Battle of Kulikovo **Obv:** Double-headed eagle **Rev:** Carved Lion and Griffin between opposing armies **Edge:** Reeded

Date	Mintage	F	VF	XF	Unc	BU
2005 Proof	10,000	Value: 50.00				

Y# 955 3 ROUBLES
33.9400 g., 0.9250 Silver 1.0093 oz. ASW, 39 mm. **Subject:** Moscow's Lomonosov University **Obv:** Two headed eagle **Rev:** Lomonosov statue before university building and Moscow skyline **Edge:** Reeded

Date	Mintage	F	VF	XF	Unc	BU
2005(m) Proof	10,000	Value: 45.00				

Y# 1038 3 ROUBLES
33.9000 g., 0.9250 Silver 1.0081 oz. ASW, 39 mm. **Subject:** I. V. Russakov, House of Culture

Date	Mintage	F	VF	XF	Unc	BU
2005 Proof	—	Value: 50.00				

Y# 1039 3 ROUBLES
33.9000 g., 0.9250 Silver 1.0081 oz. ASW, 39 mm. **Subject:** Novosibirsk State Academic Opera & Ballet

Date	Mintage	F	VF	XF	Unc	BU
2005 Proof	—	Value: 60.00				

Y# 1040 3 ROUBLES
33.9000 g., 0.9250 Silver 1.0081 oz. ASW, 39 mm. **Subject:** Year of the dog

Date	Mintage	F	VF	XF	Unc	BU
2006 Proof	—	Value: 65.00				

Y# 1041 3 ROUBLES
33.9000 g., 0.9250 Silver 1.0081 oz. ASW, 39 mm. **Subject:** Parliament, 100th Anniversary

Date	Mintage	F	VF	XF	Unc	BU
2006 Proof	—	Value: 65.00				

Y# 1046 3 ROUBLES
33.9000 g., 0.9250 Silver 1.0081 oz. ASW, 39 mm. **Subject:** Tretyakov State Gallery, 150th Anniversary

Date	Mintage	F	VF	XF	Unc	BU
2006 Proof	—	Value: 65.00				

Y# 1048 3 ROUBLES
33.9000 g., 0.9250 Silver 1.0081 oz. ASW, 39 mm. **Subject:** Russia Savings

Date	Mintage	F	VF	XF	Unc	BU
2006 Proof	—	Value: 65.00				

Y# 1052 3 ROUBLES
33.9000 g., 0.9250 Silver 1.0081 oz. ASW, 39 mm. **Subject:** State Bank Building, Nizhny Novgorod

Date	Mintage	F	VF	XF	Unc	BU
2006 Proof	—	Value: 60.00				

Y# 1060 3 ROUBLES
33.9000 g., 0.9250 Silver 1.0081 oz. ASW, 39 mm. **Subject:** Moscow's Kremlin and Red Square

Date	Mintage	F	VF	XF	Unc	BU
2006 Proof	—	Value: 70.00				

Y# 1065 3 ROUBLES
33.9000 g., 0.9250 Silver 1.0081 oz. ASW, 39 mm. **Subject:** XX Winter Olympics, Torino

Date	Mintage	F	VF	XF	Unc	BU
2006 Proof	12,500	Value: 95.00				

Y# 1066 3 ROUBLES
33.9000 g., 0.9250 Silver 1.0081 oz. ASW, 39 mm. **Subject:** FIFA World Cup, Germany

Date	Mintage	F	VF	XF	Unc	BU
2006 Proof	—	Value: 75.00				

Y# 966 3 ROUBLES
33.9400 g., 0.9250 Silver 1.0093 oz. ASW, 39 mm. **Subject:** 250th Anniversary Academy of the Arts **Obv:** Two-headed eagle **Rev:** Relief image of Minerva group **Rev. Legend:** РОССИЈСКАЯ - АКАДЕМИЯ ХУДОЖЕСТВ **Edge:** Reeded

Date	Mintage	F	VF	XF	Unc	BU
2007(m) Proof	10,000	Value: 55.00				

Y# 1080 3 ROUBLES
33.9000 g., 0.9250 Silver 1.0081 oz. ASW, 39 mm. **Subject:** International Arctic Year

Date	Mintage	F	VF	XF	Unc	BU
2007 Proof	—	Value: 65.00				

Y# 1086 3 ROUBLES
33.9000 g., 0.9250 Silver 1.0081 oz. ASW, 39 mm. **Subject:** Academy of Arts, 250th Anniversary

Date	Mintage	F	VF	XF	Unc	BU
2007 Proof	—	Value: 65.00				

Y# 1087 3 ROUBLES
33.9000 g., 0.9250 Silver 1.0081 oz. ASW **Subject:** First Artificial Earth Satellite, 50th Anniversary

Date	Mintage	F	VF	XF	Unc	BU
2007 Proof	—	Value: 60.00				

Y# 1088 3 ROUBLES
33.9000 g., 0.9250 Silver 1.0081 oz. ASW, 39 mm. **Subject:** Andrew Rublyov

Date	Mintage	F	VF	XF	Unc	BU
2007 Proof	—	Value: 60.00				

Y# 1092 3 ROUBLES
33.9000 g., 0.9250 Silver 1.0081 oz. ASW, 39 mm. **Subject:** Bashkira, 450th Anniversary of annexation by Russia

Date	Mintage	F	VF	XF	Unc	BU
2007 Proof	—	Value: 60.00				

Y# 1100 3 ROUBLES
33.9000 g., 0.9250 Silver 1.0081 oz. ASW, 39 mm. **Subject:** Nevyansk inclined tower, Sverdlorsk Region

Date	Mintage	F	VF	XF	Unc	BU
2007 Proof	—	Value: 65.00				

Y# 1103 3 ROUBLES
33.9000 g., 0.9250 Silver 1.0081 oz. ASW, 39 mm. **Subject:** Kazan Railway Station, Moscow

Date	Mintage	F	VF	XF	Unc	BU
2007 Proof	—	Value: 55.00				

Y# 1114 3 ROUBLES
33.9000 g., 0.9250 Silver 1.0081 oz. ASW, 39 mm. **Subject:** Year of the Rat

Date	Mintage	F	VF	XF	Unc	BU
2007 Proof	—	Value: 60.00				

Y# 1113 3 ROUBLES
33.9000 g., 0.9250 Silver 1.0081 oz. ASW, 39 mm. **Subject:** Year of the Bull

Date	Mintage	F	VF	XF	Unc	BU
2008 Proof	—	Value: 60.00				

Y# 1115 3 ROUBLES
33.9000 g., 0.9250 Silver 1.0081 oz. ASW, 39 mm. **Subject:** Russian Postage Stamp - 150th Anniversary of Introduction

Date	Mintage	F	VF	XF	Unc	BU
2008 Proof	—	Value: 65.00				

Y# 1118 3 ROUBLES
33.9000 g., 0.9250 Silver 1.0081 oz. ASW, 39 mm. **Subject:** I. M. Schenov Medical Academy, 250th Anniversary

Date	Mintage	F	VF	XF	Unc	BU
2008 Proof	—	Value: 65.00				

Y# 1119 3 ROUBLES
33.9000 g., 0.9250 Silver 1.0081 oz. ASW, 39 mm. **Subject:** Udmurtiya, 450th Anniversary of annexation into Russia

Date	Mintage	F	VF	XF	Unc	BU
2008 Proof	—	Value: 60.00				

Y# 1124 3 ROUBLES
33.9000 g., 0.9250 Silver 1.0081 oz. ASW, 39 mm. **Subject:** Cathedral of St. Demetrius, Vladimir

Date	Mintage	F	VF	XF	Unc	BU
2008 Proof	—	Value: 65.00				

Y# 1126 3 ROUBLES
33.9000 g., 0.9250 Silver 1.0081 oz. ASW, 39 mm. **Subject:** N. I. Sevastyanov, House of Trade Unions

Date	Mintage	F	VF	XF	Unc	BU
2008 Proof	—	Value: 60.00				

Y# 1127 3 ROUBLES
33.9000 g., 0.9250 Silver 1.0081 oz. ASW, 39 mm. **Subject:** Cathedral of the Nativity of our Lady, Snetogorsk

Date	Mintage	F	VF	XF	Unc	BU
2008 Proof	—	Value: 60.00				

Y# 1128 3 ROUBLES
33.9000 g., 0.9250 Silver 1.0081 oz. ASW, 39 mm. **Subject:** Assumption Church (Admiralty's)

Date	Mintage	F	VF	XF	Unc	BU
2008 Proof	—	Value: 60.00				

Y# 1129 3 ROUBLES
33.9000 g., 0.9250 Silver 1.0081 oz. ASW, 39 mm. **Subject:** St. Nicholas Cathedral, Yakutsk

Date	Mintage	F	VF	XF	Unc	BU
2008 Proof	—	Value: 65.00				

Y# 1130 3 ROUBLES
33.9000 g., 0.9250 Silver 1.0081 oz. ASW, 39 mm. **Subject:** St. Vladimir Cathedral, Zadonsk

Date	Mintage	F	VF	XF	Unc	BU
2008 Proof	—	Value: 65.00				

Y# 1138 3 ROUBLES
33.9000 g., 0.9250 Silver 1.0081 oz. ASW, 39 mm. **Subject:** European Beaver

Date	Mintage	F	VF	XF	Unc	BU
2008 Proof	—	Value: 60.00				

Y# 1147 3 ROUBLES
33.9000 g., 0.9250 Silver 1.0081 oz. ASW, 39 mm. **Subject:** Kamchatka Volcano

Date	Mintage	F	VF	XF	Unc	BU
2008 Proof	—	Value: 60.00				

Y# 1150 3 ROUBLES
33.9000 g., 0.9250 Silver 1.0081 oz. ASW, 39 mm. **Subject:** World walking Race Cup, Cheboksary

Date	Mintage	F	VF	XF	Unc	BU
2008 Proof	—	Value: 60.00				

Y# 1151 3 ROUBLES
16.8000 g., 0.9250 Silver 0.4996 oz. ASW, 39 mm. **Subject:** City of Moscow

Date	Mintage	F	VF	XF	Unc	BU
2008 Proof	—	Value: 25.00				

Y# 1152 3 ROUBLES

33.9000 g., 0.9250 Silver 1.0081 oz. ASW, 39 mm. **Subject:** 29th Summer Olympics Bejing

Date	Mintage	F	VF	XF	Unc	BU
2008 Proof	—	Value: 60.00				

Y# 1180 3 ROUBLES

33.9000 g., 0.9250 Silver 1.0081 oz. ASW, 39 mm. **Subject:** St. George the Victorious

Date	Mintage	F	VF	XF	Unc	BU
2009	280,000	—	—	—	—	60.00
2010	500,000	—	—	—	—	60.00

Y# 992 3 ROUBLES

33.9000 g., 0.9250 Silver 1.0081 oz. ASW, 39 mm. **Subject:** Year of the Bull **Obv:** Double headed eagle **Rev:** Stylized bull

Date	Mintage	F	VF	XF	Unc	BU
2009 Proof	—	Value: 50.00				

Y# 1159 3 ROUBLES

33.9000 g., 0.9250 Silver 1.0081 oz. ASW, 39 mm. **Subject:** Moon research, 50th Anniversary

Date	Mintage	F	VF	XF	Unc	BU
2009 Proof	—	Value: 60.00				

Y# 1161 3 ROUBLES

33.9000 g., 0.9250 Silver 1.0081 oz. ASW, 39 mm. **Subject:** Russian Currency

Date	Mintage	F	VF	XF	Unc	BU
2009 Proof	—	Value: 60.00				

Y# 1166 3 ROUBLES

33.9000 g., 0.9250 Silver 1.0081 oz. ASW, 39 mm. **Subject:** A. P. Chekhov, 150th Anniversary of Birth

Date	Mintage	F	VF	XF	Unc	BU
2009 Proof	—	Value: 70.00				

Y# 1170 3 ROUBLES

33.9000 g., 0.9250 Silver 1.0081 oz. ASW, 39 mm. **Subject:** Kalmyk Peoples, 400th Anniversary of annexation into Russia

Date	Mintage	F	VF	XF	Unc	BU
2009 Proof	—	Value: 60.00				

Y# 1173 3 ROUBLES

33.9000 g., 0.9250 Silver 1.0081 oz. ASW, 39 mm. **Subject:** N. V. Gogol, 200th Anniversary of Birth

Date	Mintage	F	VF	XF	Unc	BU
2009 Proof	—	Value: 60.00				

Y# 1177 3 ROUBLES

33.9000 g., 0.9250 Silver 1.0081 oz. ASW, 39 mm. **Subject:** Poltava Battle, 300th Anniversary

Date	Mintage	F	VF	XF	Unc	BU
2009 Proof	—	Value: 65.00				

Y# 1182 3 ROUBLES

33.9000 g., 0.9250 Silver 1.0081 oz. ASW, 39 mm. **Subject:** Vitebsky Railway Station, St. Petersburg

Date	Mintage	F	VF	XF	Unc	BU
2009 Proof	—	Value: 60.00				

Y# 1183 3 ROUBLES

33.9000 g., 0.9250 Silver 1.0081 oz. ASW, 39 mm. **Subject:** Tula Kremlin

Date	Mintage	F	VF	XF	Unc	BU
2009 Proof	—	Value: 60.00				

Y# 1185 3 ROUBLES

33.9000 g., 0.9250 Silver 1.0081 oz. ASW, 39 mm. **Subject:** Odygitriya Church

Date	Mintage	F	VF	XF	Unc	BU
2009 Proof	—	Value: 60.00				

Y# 1188 3 ROUBLES

33.9000 g., 0.9250 Silver 1.0081 oz. ASW, 39 mm. **Subject:** Intercession Cathedral, Voronezsh

Date	Mintage	F	VF	XF	Unc	BU
2009 Proof	—	Value: 60.00				

Y# 1189 3 ROUBLES
33.9000 g., 0.9250 Silver 1.0081 oz. ASW, 39 mm. **Subject:** Tales of the Russian People

Date	Mintage	F	VF	XF	Unc	BU
2009 Proof	—	Value: 60.00				

Y# 1199 3 ROUBLES
33.9000 g., 0.9250 Silver 1.0081 oz. ASW, 39 mm. **Subject:** Veliklу Novgorod

Date	Mintage	F	VF	XF	Unc	BU
2009 Proof	—	Value: 60.00				

Y# 1207 3 ROUBLES
33.9000 g., 0.9250 Silver 1.0081 oz. ASW, 39 mm. **Subject:** Fauna - Bear

Date	Mintage	F	VF	XF	Unc	BU
2009 Proof	—	Value: 60.00				

Y# 1208 3 ROUBLES
33.9000 g., 0.9250 Silver 1.0081 oz. ASW, 39 mm. **Series:** Year of the Tiger

Date	Mintage	F	VF	XF	Unc	BU
2009 Proof	—	Value: 60.00				

Y# 1214 3 ROUBLES
31.1050 g., 0.9990 Silver 0.9990 oz. ASW **Subject:** St. George the Victorious

Date	Mintage	F	VF	XF	Unc	BU
2010 Proof	—	Value: 55.00				

Y# 1219 3 ROUBLES
33.9000 g., 0.9250 Silver 1.0081 oz. ASW, 39 mm. **Subject:** Savior's Transfiguration Cathedral, Bolkhov

Date	Mintage	F	VF	XF	Unc	BU
2010 Proof	—	Value: 55.00				

Y# 1220 3 ROUBLES
33.9000 g., 0.9250 Silver 1.0081 oz. ASW, 39 mm. **Subject:** Vovnushki Battle tower

Date	Mintage	F	VF	XF	Unc	BU
2010 Proof	—	Value: 55.00				

Y# 1221 3 ROUBLES
16.8000 g., 0.9250 Silver 0.4996 oz. ASW, 39 mm. **Subject:** Holy Trinity Church, St. Petersburg

Date	Mintage	F	VF	XF	Unc	BU
2010 Proof	—	Value: 80.00				

Y# 1222 3 ROUBLES
33.9000 g., 0.9250 Silver 1.0081 oz. ASW, 39 mm. **Subject:** Round Square, Petrozavodsk

Date	Mintage	F	VF	XF	Unc	BU
2010 Proof	—	Value: 55.00				

Y# 1228 3 ROUBLES
33.9000 g., 0.9250 Silver 1.0081 oz. ASW, 39 mm. **Subject:** Bank of Russia, 150th Anniversary

Date	Mintage	F	VF	XF	Unc	BU
2010 Proof	—	Value: 60.00				

Y# 1232 3 ROUBLES
33.9000 g., 0.9250 Silver 1.0081 oz. ASW, 39 mm. **Subject:** UNESCO Heritage Site - Yaroslav

Date	Mintage	F	VF	XF	Unc	BU
2010 Proof	—	Value: 60.00				

Y# 1237 3 ROUBLES
33.9000 g., 0.9250 Silver 1.0081 oz. ASW, 39 mm. **Subject:** A. P. Chekhov, 200th Anniversary of Birth

Date	Mintage	F	VF	XF	Unc	BU
2010 Proof	—	Value: 65.00				

Y# 1241 3 ROUBLES
31.1000 g., 0.9250 Silver 0.9249 oz. ASW, 39 mm. **Subject:** Great Patriotic War, 65th Anniversary

Date	Mintage	F	VF	XF	Unc	BU
2010 Proof	—	Value: 55.00				

Y# 1242 3 ROUBLES
33.9000 g., 0.9250 Silver 1.0081 oz. ASW, 39 mm. **Subject:** Great Patriotic War, 65th Anniversary

Date	Mintage	F	VF	XF	Unc	BU
2010 Proof	—	Value: 55.00				

Y# 1243 3 ROUBLES
33.9000 g., 0.9250 Silver 1.0081 oz. ASW, 39 mm. **Subject:** Great Patriotic War, 65th Anniversary

Date	Mintage	F	VF	XF	Unc	BU
2010 Proof	—	Value: 55.00				

Y# 1247 3 ROUBLES
33.9000 g., 0.9250 Silver 1.0081 oz. ASW, 39 mm. **Subject:** Year of the Rabbit

Date	Mintage	F	VF	XF	Unc	BU
2010 Proof	—	Value: 50.00				

Y# 1251 3 ROUBLES
33.9000 g., 0.9250 Silver 1.0081 oz. ASW, 39 mm. **Subject:** EAEC, 10th Anniversary

Date	Mintage	F	VF	XF	Unc	BU
2010 Proof	—	Value: 60.00				

Y# 1252 3 ROUBLES
33.9000 g., 0.9250 Silver 1.0081 oz. ASW, 39 mm. **Subject:** EAEC, National Costumes

Date	Mintage	F	VF	XF	Unc	BU
2010 Proof	—	Value: 55.00				

Y# 1265 3 ROUBLES
31.1000 g., 0.9250 Silver 0.9249 oz. ASW **Subject:** Russian Census

Date	Mintage	F	VF	XF	Unc	BU
2010 Proof	—	Value: 55.00				

Y# 1269 3 ROUBLES
16.8000 g., 0.9250 Silver 0.4996 oz. ASW, 33 mm. **Subject:** I. K. Rodnina, Figure skater

Date	Mintage	F	VF	XF	Unc	BU
2010 Proof	—	Value: 40.00				

Y# 1270 3 ROUBLES
16.8000 g., 0.9250 Silver 0.4996 oz. ASW, 33 mm. **Subject:** A. G. Zaitsev, figure skater

Date	Mintage	F	VF	XF	Unc	BU
2010 Proof	—	Value: 40.00				

Y# 1271 3 ROUBLES
16.8000 g., 0.9250 Silver 0.4996 oz. ASW, 33 mm. **Subject:** L. A. Pakhomova, Figure skater

Date	Mintage	F	VF	XF	Unc	BU
2010 Proof	—	Value: 40.00				

Y# 1272 3 ROUBLES
16.8000 g., 0.9250 Silver 0.4996 oz. ASW, 33 mm. **Subject:** A. G. Gorshkov, Figure skater

Date	Mintage	F	VF	XF	Unc	BU
2010 Proof	—	Value: 40.00				

Y# 1273 3 ROUBLES
33.9000 g., 0.9250 Silver 1.0081 oz. ASW, 39 mm. **Subject:** 39th World Chess Olympics

Date	Mintage	F	VF	XF	Unc	BU
2010 Proof	—	Value: 55.00				

Y# 1282 3 ROUBLES
31.1050 g., 0.9990 Silver 0.9990 oz. ASW, 39 mm. **Subject:** Cathedral of the Virgin of Kazan and St. Sergiy of Radonezh, City of Kursk **Rev:** St. Sergius Kazansky Cathedral in Kursk **Edge:** Reeded

Date	Mintage	F	VF	XF	Unc	BU
2011СПМД Proof	7,500	Value: 80.00				

Y# 1285 3 ROUBLES
31.1050 g., 0.9250 Silver 0.9250 oz. ASW, 39 mm. **Rev:** Flag above five soldiers

Date	Mintage	F	VF	XF	Unc	BU
2011 Proof	3,000	Value: 75.00				

Y# 1287 3 ROUBLES
31.1050 g., 0.9990 Silver 0.9990 oz. ASW, 39 mm. **Rev:** U.A. Gagarian agains background of stars and earth in color **Edge:** Reeded

Date	Mintage	F	VF	XF	Unc	BU
2011 Proof	7,500	Value: 100				

Y# 1289 3 ROUBLES
31.1050 g., 0.9990 Silver 0.9990 oz. ASW, 39 mm. **Rev:** Female in national costume and wildlife native to Buryat flanking

Date	Mintage	F	VF	XF	Unc	BU
2011 Proof	3,000	Value: 80.00				

Y# 1293 3 ROUBLES
31.1050 g., 0.9250 Silver 0.9250 oz. ASW, 39 mm. **Subject:** 2014 Winter Olympics - Sochi - Biathlon **Rev:** Athlethe on skies with rifle, pitsunda pinecone in color at lower right

Date	Mintage	F	VF	XF	Unc	BU
2014 (2011) Proof	35,000	Value: 75.00				

Y# 1294 3 ROUBLES
31.1050 g., 0.9250 Silver 0.9250 oz. ASW, 39 mm. **Subject:** 2014 Winter Olympics - Sochi - Alpine Skiing **Rev:** Mountain skier and magnolia in color at lower right

Date	Mintage	F	VF	XF	Unc	BU
2014 (2011) Proof	35,000	Value: 90.00				

Y# 1295 3 ROUBLES
31.1050 g., 0.9250 Silver 0.9250 oz. ASW, 39 mm. **Subject:** 2014 Winter Olympics - Sochi - Figure Skater **Rev:** Figure skater and Voronov snowdrop in color at lower right

Date	Mintage	F	VF	XF	Unc	BU
2014 (2011) Proof	35,000	Value: 90.00				

Y# 1296 3 ROUBLES
31.1050 g., 0.9250 Silver 0.9250 oz. ASW, 39 mm. **Subject:** 2014 Winter Olympics - Sochi - Hockey **Rev:** Hockey player and branch of cork oak in color at lower left

Date	Mintage	F	VF	XF	Unc	BU
2014 (2011) Proof	35,000	Value: 90.00				

Y# 1315 3 ROUBLES
31.1050 g., 0.9250 Silver 0.9250 oz. ASW, 39 mm. **Rev:** Three children picking flowers and drawing

Date	Mintage	F	VF	XF	Unc	BU
2011 Proof	5,000	Value: 65.00				

Y# 1316 3 ROUBLES
31.1050 g., 0.9250 Silver 0.9250 oz. ASW, 39 mm. **Subject:** The Great Silk Way **Rev:** Camel rider against a background of desert ruins

Date	Mintage	F	VF	XF	Unc	BU
2011 Proof	5,000	Value: 70.00				

Y# 1330 3 ROUBLES
31.1050 g., 0.9250 Silver 0.9250 oz. ASW, 39 mm. **Subject:** Temple of the Sanctifier Martin the Confessor in Moscow

Date	Mintage	F	VF	XF	Unc	BU
2012 Proof	5,000	Value: 65.00				

Y# 1331 3 ROUBLES
31.1050 g., 0.9250 Silver 0.9250 oz. ASW, 39 mm. **Subject:** Kolotsky Assumption Monastery, Mozhaisk District of Moscow Region

Date	Mintage	F	VF	XF	Unc	BU
2012 Proof	5,000	Value: 65.00				

Y# 1332 3 ROUBLES
31.1050 g., 0.9250 Silver 0.9250 oz. ASW, 39 mm. **Subject:** Luzhetsky Ferapontov Monastery, Mozhaisk, Moscow region

Date	Mintage	F	VF	XF	Unc	BU
2012 Proof	5,000	Value: 65.00				

Y# 1333 3 ROUBLES
31.1050 g., 0.9250 Silver 0.9250 oz. ASW, 39 mm. **Subject:** Transfiguration Cathedral, Belozersk, Vologda region

Date	Mintage	F	VF	XF	Unc	BU
2012 Proof	5,000	Value: 65.00				

Y# 1334 3 ROUBLES
31.1050 g., 0.9250 Silver 0.9250 oz. ASW, 39 mm. **Subject:** Cathedral of the Saint Virgin's Nativity, Vladimir region

Date	Mintage	F	VF	XF	Unc	BU
2012 Proof	5,000	Value: 65.00				

Y# 1339 3 ROUBLES
31.1050 g., 0.9250 Silver 0.9250 oz. ASW, 39 mm. **Subject:** Millennium of the Unity of the Mordovian people within the Peoples of the Russian State

Date	Mintage	F	VF	XF	Unc	BU
2012 Proof	3,000	Value: 70.00				

Y# 1342 3 ROUBLES
31.1050 g., 0.9250 Silver 0.9250 oz. ASW, 39 mm. **Subject:** People's Volunteer Corps, 400th Anniversary

Date	Mintage	F	VF	XF	Unc	BU
2012 Proof	5,000	Value: 65.00				

Y# 1345 3 ROUBLES
31.1000 g., 0.9250 Silver 0.9249 oz. ASW, 39 mm. **Subject:** Russia's victory in the War of 1812

Date	Mintage
	5,000 Value: 65.00

Y# 1351 3 ROUBLES
31.1050 g., 0.9250 Silver 0.9250 oz. ASW, 39 mm. **Subject:** Pushkin State Museum of Fine Arts, Moscow, 100th Anniversary

Date	Mintage	F	VF	XF	Unc	BU
2012 Proof	5,000	Value: 65.00				

Y# 1353 3 ROUBLES
31.1050 g., 0.9250 Silver 0.9250 oz. ASW, 39 mm. **Subject:** UNESCO World Heritage Site

Date	Mintage	F	VF	XF	Unc	BU
2012 Proof	5,000	Value: 65.00				

Y# 1354 3 ROUBLES
31.1050 g., 0.9250 Silver 0.9250 oz. ASW, 39 mm. **Subject:** UNESCO World Heritage Site

Date	Mintage	F	VF	XF	Unc	BU
2012 Proof	5,000	Value: 65.00				

Y# 1364 3 ROUBLES
31.1000 g., 0.9250 Silver 0.9249 oz. ASW, 39 mm. **Subject:** European Judo Championship, Chelyabinsk

Date	Mintage	F	VF	XF	Unc	BU
2012 Proof	3,000	Value: 70.00				

Y# 1366 3 ROUBLES
31.1000 g., 0.9250 Silver 0.9249 oz. ASW, 39 mm. **Subject:** Year of the Snake

Date	Mintage	F	VF	XF	Unc	BU
2012 Proof	15,000	Value: 60.00				

Y# 1367 3 ROUBLES
31.1000 g., 0.9250 Silver 0.9249 oz. ASW, 39 mm. **Subject:** Origin of Russian Statehood, 1150th Anniversary

Date	Mintage	F	VF	XF	Unc	BU
2012 Proof	5,000	Value: 65.00				

Y# 1374 3 ROUBLES
31.1000 g., 0.9250 Silver 0.9249 oz. ASW, 39 mm. **Subject:** Russian language and literature in the French Republic and the French language and literature in the Russian Federation

Date	Mintage	F	VF	XF	Unc	BU
2012 Proof	5,000	Value: 65.00				

Y# 1377 3 ROUBLES
31.1000 g., 0.9250 Silver 0.9249 oz. ASW, 39 mm. **Subject:** Arms production in Tula, 300th Anniversary

Date	Mintage	F	VF	XF	Unc	BU
2012 Proof	5,000	Value: 65.00				

Y# 1379 3 ROUBLES
31.1000 g., 0.9250 Silver 0.9249 oz. ASW, 39 mm. **Subject:** Air Force, 100th Anniversary

Date	Mintage	F	VF	XF	Unc	BU
2012 Proof	3,000	Value: 65.00				

Y# 799 5 ROUBLES
6.4500 g., Copper-Nickel Clad Copper, 25 mm. **Obv:** Two headed eagle above curved bank name and denomination **Rev:** Value and flower **Edge:** Segmented reeding

Date	Mintage	F	VF	XF	Unc	BU
2002ММД In sets only	15,000	—	—	—	—	—
2002СПМД In sets only	15,000	—	—	—	—	—
2003ММД	15,000	—	—	150	200	250
2008ММД	—	—	—	—	3.00	4.00
2008СПМД	—	—	—	—	3.00	4.00
2009ММД	—	—	—	—	3.00	4.00
2009СПМД	—	—	—	—	4.00	5.00

Y# 829 5 ROUBLES
47.2400 g., Bi-Metallic .900 Silver 21.34g center in .900 Gold 25.9g ring, 39.5 mm. **Obv:** Double-headed eagle **Rev:** Uglich city view **Edge:** Reeded

Date	Mintage	F	VF	XF	Unc	BU
2004(sp) Proof	5,000	Value: 950				

Y# 1075 5 ROUBLES
Bi-Metallic Silver center in gold ring **Subject:** Bogolyvbovo Township

Date	Mintage	F	VF	XF	Unc	BU
2006 Proof	—	Value: 1,000				

Y# 1076 5 ROUBLES
47.2400 g., 0.9000 Silver .900 Silver 21.34g center in .900 Gold 25.9g ring 1.3669 oz. ASW, 39.5 mm. **Subject:** City of Turyev-Polsky

Date	Mintage	F	VF	XF	Unc	BU
2006 Proof	250	Value: 950				

Y# 1154 5 ROUBLES
47.2400 g., 0.9000 Silver .900 Silver 21.34g center in .900 Gold 25.9g ring 1.3669 oz. ASW, 39.5 mm. **Subject:** Pereslavl Zalessky

Date	Mintage	F	VF	XF	Unc	BU
2008 Proof	1,000	Value: 1,150				

Y# 1155 5 ROUBLES
47.2400 g., 0.9000 Silver .900 Silver 21.34g center in .900 Gold 25.9g ring 1.3669 oz. ASW, 39.5 mm. **Subject:** Alexandrov

Date	Mintage	F	VF	XF	Unc	BU
2008 Proof	—	Value: 1,150				

Y# 799a 5 ROUBLES
6.0000 g., Nickel Plated Steel, 25 mm. **Obv:** Two headed eagle above curved bank name and denomination **Rev:** Value and flower **Edge:** Segmented reeding

Date	Mintage	F	VF	XF	Unc	BU
2009ММД	—	—	—	—	2.00	3.00
2009СПМД	—	—	—	—	2.00	3.00
2010ММД	—	—	—	—	2.00	3.00
2010СПМД	—	—	—	—	4.00	5.00
2011ММД	—	—	—	—	2.00	3.00
2012ММД	—	—	—	—	2.00	3.00

Y# 1408 5 ROUBLES
6.0000 g., Nickel Plated Steel, 25 mm. **Subject:** Battle of Smolensk, War of 1812

Date	Mintage	F	VF	XF	Unc	BU
2012ММД	5,000,000	—	—	—	2.00	3.00

Y# 1409 5 ROUBLES
6.0000 g., Nickel Plated Steel, 25 mm. **Subject:** Battle of Borodino, War of 1812

Date	Mintage	F	VF	XF	Unc	BU
2012ММД	5,000,000	—	—	—	2.00	3.00

Y# 1410 5 ROUBLES
6.0000 g., Nickel Plated Steel, 25 mm. **Subject:** Battle of Tarutino, War of 1812

Date	Mintage	F	VF	XF	Unc	BU
2012ММД	5,000,000	—	—	—	2.00	3.00

Y# 1411 5 ROUBLES
6.0000 g., Nickel Plated Steel, 25 mm. **Subject:** Battle of Maloyaroslavets, War of 1812

Date	Mintage	F	VF	XF	Unc	BU
2012	5,000,000	—	—	—	2.00	3.00

Y# 1412 5 ROUBLES
6.0000 g., Nickel Plated Steel, 25 mm. **Subject:** Battle of Vyazma, War of 1812

Date	Mintage	F	VF	XF	Unc	BU
2012ММД	5,000,000	—	—	—	2.00	3.00

Y# 1413 5 ROUBLES
6.0000 g., Nickel Plated Steel, 25 mm. **Subject:** Battle of Krasnoye, War of 1812

Date	Mintage	F	VF	XF	Unc	BU
2012ММД	5,000,000	—	—	—	2.00	3.00

Y# 1414 5 ROUBLES
6.0000 g., Nickel Plated Steel, 25 mm. **Subject:** Battle of Berezina, War of 1812

Date	Mintage	F	VF	XF	Unc	BU
2012ММД	5,000,000	—	—	—	2.00	3.00

Y# 1415 5 ROUBLES
6.0000 g., Nickel Plated Steel, 25 mm. **Subject:** Battle of Kulm, War of 1812

Date	Mintage	F	VF	XF	Unc	BU
2012ММД	5,000,000	—	—	—	2.00	3.00

Y# 1416 5 ROUBLES
6.0000 g., Nickel Plated Steel, 25 mm. **Subject:** Battle of Leipzig, War of 1812

Date	Mintage	F	VF	XF	Unc	BU
2012ММД	5,000,000	—	—	—	2.00	3.00

Y# 1417 5 ROUBLES
6.0000 g., Nickel Plated Steel, 25 mm. **Subject:** Capture of Paris, War of 1812

Date	Mintage	F	VF	XF	Unc	BU
2012ММД	5,000,000	—	—	—	2.00	3.00

Y# 676 10 ROUBLES
8.2200 g., Bi-Metallic Copper-Nickel center in Brass ring, 27 mm. **Subject:** Yuri Gagarin **Obv:** Value with latent image in zero within circle and sprigs **Rev:** Helmeted bust 1/4 right **Edge:** Reeding over denomination

Date	Mintage	F	VF	XF	Unc	BU
2001ММД	10,000,000	—	—	—	4.00	5.00
2001СПМД	10,000,000	—	—	—	4.00	5.00

Y# 686 10 ROUBLES
1.6100 g., 0.9990 Gold 0.0517 oz. AGW, 12 mm. **Subject:** Bolshoi Theater 225 Years **Obv:** Double-headed eagle within circle **Rev:** Building above number 225 **Edge:** Reeded

Date	Mintage	F	VF	XF	Unc	BU
2001 Proof	3,000	Value: 110				

Y# 739 10 ROUBLES
8.2200 g., Bi-Metallic Copper-Nickel center in Brass ring, 27 mm. **Subject:** Ancient Towns - Derbent **Obv:** Value with latent image in zero within circle and sprigs **Rev:** Shield above walled city view **Edge:** Reeding over denomination

Date	Mintage	F	VF	XF	Unc	BU
2002ММД	5,000,000	—	—	—	4.00	5.00

Y# 740 10 ROUBLES

8.2200 g., Bi-Metallic Copper-Nickel center in Brass ring, 27 mm. **Subject:** Ancient Towns - Kostroma **Obv:** Value with latent image in zero within circle and sprigs **Rev:** Cupola, shield and river view **Edge:** Reeding over denomination

Date	Mintage	F	VF	XF	Unc	BU
2002СПМД	5,000,000	—	—	—	4.00	6.00

Y# 741 10 ROUBLES

8.2200 g., Bi-Metallic Copper-Nickel center in Brass ring, 27 mm. **Subject:** Ancient Towns - Staraya Russa **Obv:** Value with latent image in zero within circle and sprigs **Rev:** Shield and cathedral **Edge:** Reeding over denomination

Date	Mintage	F	VF	XF	Unc	BU
2002СПМД	5,000,000	—	—	—	4.00	6.00

Y# 748 10 ROUBLES

8.2200 g., Bi-Metallic Copper-Nickel center in Brass ring, 27 mm. **Subject:** Ministry of Education **Obv:** Value with latent image in zero within circle and sprigs **Rev:** Seedling within open book **Edge:** Reeding over denomination

Date	Mintage	F	VF	XF	Unc	BU
2002ММД	5,000,000	—	—	—	4.00	6.00

Y# 749 10 ROUBLES

8.2200 g., Bi-Metallic Copper-Nickel center in Brass ring, 27 mm. **Subject:** Ministry of Finance **Obv:** Value with latent image in zero within circle and sprigs **Rev:** Caduceus within monogram **Edge:** Reeding over denomination

Date	Mintage	F	VF	XF	Unc	BU
2002СПМД	5,000,000	—	—	—	4.00	6.00

Y# 750 10 ROUBLES

8.2200 g., Bi-Metallic Copper-Nickel center in Brass ring, 27 mm. **Subject:** Ministry of Economic Development and Trade **Obv:** Value with latent image in zero within circle and sprigs **Rev:** Crowned double-headed eagle with cornucopia and caduceus **Edge:** Reeding over denomination

Date	Mintage	F	VF	XF	Unc	BU
2002СПМД	5,000,000	—	—	—	4.00	6.00

Y# 751 10 ROUBLES

8.2200 g., Bi-Metallic Copper-Nickel center in Brass ring, 27 mm. **Subject:** Ministry of Foreign Affairs **Obv:** Value with latent image in zero within circle and sprigs **Rev:** Crowned double-headed eagle above crossed sprigs **Edge:** Reeding over denomination

Date	Mintage	F	VF	XF	Unc	BU
2002СПМД	5,000,000	—	—	—	5.00	6.00

Y# 752 10 ROUBLES

8.2200 g., Bi-Metallic Copper-Nickel center in Brass ring, 27 mm. **Subject:** Ministry of Internal Affairs **Obv:** Value with latent image in zero within circle and sprigs **Rev:** Crowned double-headed eagle with round breast shield **Edge:** Reeding over denomination

Date	Mintage	F	VF	XF	Unc	BU
2002ММД	5,000,000	—	—	—	5.00	6.00

Y# 753 10 ROUBLES

8.2200 g., Bi-Metallic Copper-Nickel center in Brass ring, 27 mm. **Subject:** Ministry of Justice **Obv:** Value with latent image in zero within circle and sprigs **Rev:** Crowned double-headed eagle with column on breast shield **Edge:** Reeding over denomination

Date	Mintage	F	VF	XF	Unc	BU
2002СПМД	5,000,000	—	—	—	4.00	6.00

Y# 754 10 ROUBLES

8.2200 g., Bi-Metallic Copper-Nickel center in Brass ring, 27 mm. **Subject:** Russian Armed Forces **Obv:** Value with latent image in zero within circle and sprigs **Rev:** Crowned double-headed eagle with crowned pointed top shield **Edge:** Reeding over denomination

Date	Mintage	F	VF	XF	Unc	BU
2002ММД	5,000,000	—	—	—	5.00	6.00

Y# 817 10 ROUBLES

8.3400 g., Bi-Metallic Copper-Nickel center in Brass ring, 27 mm. **Obv:** Value with latent image in zero within circle and sprigs **Rev:** Murom city view and tilted oval shields within circle **Edge:** Reeded and lettered

Date	Mintage	F	VF	XF	Unc	BU
2003(sp)	5,000,000	—	—	—	5.00	6.00

Y# 800 10 ROUBLES

8.4400 g., Bi-Metallic Copper-Nickel center in Brass ring, 27.1 mm. **Subject:** Pskov **Obv:** Value with latent image in zero within circle and sprigs **Rev:** Shield above walled city **Edge:** Reeding over lettering

Date	Mintage	F	VF	XF	Unc	BU
2003СПМД	5,000,000	—	—	—	5.00	6.00

Y# 818 10 ROUBLES

8.3400 g., Bi-Metallic Copper-Nickel center in Brass ring, 27 mm. **Obv:** Value with latent image in zero within circle and sprigs **Rev:** Kasimov city view and shield within circle **Edge:** Reeded and lettered

Date	Mintage	F	VF	XF	Unc	BU
2003СПМД	5,000,000	—	—	—	5.00	6.00

Y# 819 10 ROUBLES

8.3400 g., Bi-Metallic Copper-Nickel center in Brass ring, 27 mm. **Subject:** Dorogobuzh **Obv:** Value with latent image in zero within circle and sprigs **Rev:** Monument, city view and shield within circle **Edge:** Reeded and lettered

Date	Mintage	F	VF	XF	Unc	BU
2003ММД	5,000,000	—	—	—	5.00	6.00

Y# 824 10 ROUBLES

8.4600 g., Bi-Metallic Copper-Nickel center in Brass ring, 27.1 mm. **Subject:** Town of Ryazhsk **Obv:** Value with latent image in zero within circle and sprigs **Obv. Legend:** БАНК РОССИИ **Rev:** City view and crowned shield within circle **Edge:** Reeded and lettered

Date	Mintage	F	VF	XF	Unc	BU
2004ММД	—	—	—	—	5.00	6.00

Y# 825 10 ROUBLES

8.4600 g., Bi-Metallic Copper-Nickel center in Brass ring, 27.1 mm. **Subject:** Town of Dmitrov **Obv:** Value with latent image in zero within circle and sprigs **Obv. Legend:** БАНК РОССИИ **Rev:** City view and crowned shield within circle **Edge:** Reeded and lettered

Date	Mintage	F	VF	XF	Unc	BU
2004ММД	5,000,000	—	—	—	5.00	6.00

Y# 826 10 ROUBLES
8.4600 g., Bi-Metallic Copper-Nickel center in Brass ring, 27.1 mm. **Subject:** Town of Kem **Obv:** Value with latent image in zero within circle and sprigs **Obv. Legend:** БАНК РОССИИ **Rev:** City view and crowned shield within circle **Edge:** Reeded and lettered

Date	Mintage	F	VF	XF	Unc	BU
2004СПМД	5,000,000	—	—	—	5.00	6.00

Y# 827 10 ROUBLES
8.4000 g., Bi-Metallic Copper-Nickel center in Brass ring, 27 mm. **Subject:** Great Victory, 60th Anniversary **Obv:** Value with latent image in zero within circle and sprigs **Rev:** WWII eternal flame monument above date and sprig within circle **Edge:** Reeded and lettered

Date	Mintage	F	VF	XF	Unc	BU
2005ММД	30,000,000	—	—	—	5.00	6.00
2005СПМД	30,000,000	—	—	—	5.00	6.00

Y# 886 10 ROUBLES
8.2300 g., Bi-Metallic Copper-Nickel center in Brass ring, 27 mm. **Obv:** Value with latent image in zero within circle and sprigs **Rev:** Moscow coat of arms within circle **Edge:** Reeded and lettered

Date	Mintage	F	VF	XF	Unc	BU
2005ММД	10,000,000	—	—	—	5.00	6.00

Y# 887 10 ROUBLES
8.2300 g., Bi-Metallic Copper-Nickel center in Brass ring, 27 mm. **Obv:** Value with latent image in zero within circle and sprigs **Rev:** Leningrad Oblast coat of arms within circle **Edge:** Reeded and lettered

Date	Mintage	F	VF	XF	Unc	BU
2005СПМД	10,000,000	—	—	—	5.00	6.00

Y# 888 10 ROUBLES
8.2300 g., Bi-Metallic Copper-Nickel center in Brass ring, 27 mm. **Obv:** Value with latent image in zero within circle and sprigs **Rev:** Tverskaya arms within circle **Edge:** Reeded and lettered

Date	Mintage	F	VF	XF	Unc	BU
2005ММД	10,000,000	—	—	—	5.00	6.00

Y# 889 10 ROUBLES
8.2300 g., Bi-Metallic Copper-Nickel center in Brass ring, 27 mm. **Obv:** Value with latent image in zero within circle and sprigs **Rev:** Krasnodarskiy Kray coat of arms **Edge:** Reeded and lettered

Date	Mintage	F	VF	XF	Unc	BU
2005(m)	10,000,000	—	—	—	5.00	6.00

Y# 890 10 ROUBLES
8.2300 g., Bi-Metallic Copper-Nickel center in Brass ring, 27 mm. **Obv:** Value with latent image in zero within circle and sprigs **Rev:** Orlovskaya Oblast coat of arms within circle **Edge:** Reeded and lettered

Date	Mintage	F	VF	XF	Unc	BU
2005(m)	10,000,000	—	—	—	5.00	6.00

Y# 891 10 ROUBLES
8.2300 g., Bi-Metallic Copper-Nickel center in Brass ring, 27 mm. **Obv:** Value with latent image in zero within circle and sprigs **Rev:** Tatarstan Republic coat of arms within circle **Edge:** Reeded and lettered

Date	Mintage	F	VF	XF	Unc	BU
2005СПМД	10,000,000	—	—	—	5.00	6.00

Y# 943 10 ROUBLES
8.2300 g., Bi-Metallic Copper-Nickel center in Brass ring, 27.1 mm. **Obv:** Large value **Rev:** City of Kazan and arms

Date	Mintage	F	VF	XF	Unc	BU
2005СПМД	5,000,000	—	—	—	5.00	6.00

Y# 944 10 ROUBLES
8.2300 g., Bi-Metallic Copper-Nickel center in Brass ring, 27.1 mm. **Obv:** Large value **Rev:** City of Borovsk and arms

Date	Mintage	F	VF	XF	Unc	BU
2005СПМД	5,000,000	—	—	—	5.00	6.00

Y# 945 10 ROUBLES
8.2300 g., Bi-Metallic Copper-Nickel center in Brass ring, 27.1 mm. **Obv:** Large value **Rev:** City of Mzensk and shield

Date	Mintage	F	VF	XF	Unc	BU
2005ММД	5,000,000	—	—	—	5.00	6.00

Y# 946 10 ROUBLES
8.2300 g., Bi-Metallic Copper-Nickel center in Brass ring, 27.1 mm. **Obv:** Large value **Rev:** City of Kaliningrad and shield

Date	Mintage	F	VF	XF	Unc	BU
2005ММД	5,000,000	—	—	—	5.00	6.00

Y# 938 10 ROUBLES
8.2300 g., Bi-Metallic Copper-Nickel center in Brass ring, 27 mm. **Obv:** Value with latent image in zero within circle and sprigs **Rev:** Republic of Altai arms **Edge:** Lettered and reeded

Date	Mintage	F	VF	XF	Unc	BU
2006СПМД	10,000,000	—	—	—	5.00	6.00

Y# 939 10 ROUBLES
8.2300 g., Bi-Metallic Copper-Nickel center in Brass ring, 27 mm. **Obv:** Value with latent image in zero within circle and sprigs **Rev:** Chita Region arms **Edge:** Lettered and reeded

Date	Mintage	F	VF	XF	Unc	BU
2006СПМД	10,000,000	—	—	—	5.00	6.00

Y# 940 10 ROUBLES
8.2300 g., Bi-Metallic Copper-Nickel center in Brass ring, 27 mm. **Obv:** Value with latent image in zero within circle and sprigs **Rev:** Primorskij Kraj Maritime Territory coat of arms **Edge:** Lettered and reeded

Date	Mintage	F	VF	XF	Unc	BU
2006ММД	10,000,000	—	—	—	5.00	6.00

Y# 941 10 ROUBLES
8.2300 g., Bi-Metallic Copper-Nickel center in Brass ring, 27 mm. **Obv:** Value with latent image in zero within circle and sprigs **Rev:** Sakha (Yakutiya) Republic coat of arms **Edge:** Lettered and reeded

Date	Mintage	F	VF	XF	Unc	BU
2006СПМД	10,000,000	—	—	—	5.00	6.00

Y# 942 10 ROUBLES
8.2300 g., Bi-Metallic Copper-Nickel center in Brass ring, 27 mm. **Obv:** Value with latent image in zero within circle and sprigs **Rev:** Sakhalinskaya Oblast coat of arms **Edge:** Lettered and reeded

Date	Mintage	F	VF	XF	Unc	BU
2006ММД	10,000,000	—	—	—	5.00	6.00

Y# 947 10 ROUBLES
8.2300 g., Bi-Metallic Copper-Nickel center in Brass ring, 27.1 mm. **Obv:** Large value **Rev:** City of Belgorod and shield

Date	Mintage	F	VF	XF	Unc	BU
2006ММД	5,000,000	—	—	—	5.00	6.00

Y# 948 10 ROUBLES
8.2300 g., Bi-Metallic Copper-Nickel center in Brass ring, 27.1 mm. **Obv:** Large value **Rev:** City of Kargopol and shield

Date	Mintage	F	VF	XF	Unc	BU
2006ММД	5,000,000	—	—	—	5.00	6.00

Y# 949 10 ROUBLES
8.2300 g., Bi-Metallic Copper-Nickel center in Brass ring, 27.1 mm. **Obv:** Large value **Rev:** City of Turzhok and shield

Date	Mintage	F	VF	XF	Unc	BU
2006СПМД	5,000,000	—	—	—	5.00	6.00

Y# 963 10 ROUBLES
8.3000 g., Bi-Metallic Copper-Nickel center in Brass ring, 27 mm. **Obv:** Value with latent image in zero within circle and sprays **Rev:** Vologda church **Edge:** Reeded and lettered **Edge Lettering:** Denomination repeated

Date	Mintage	F	VF	XF	Unc	BU
2007ММД	2,500,000	—	—	—	5.00	6.00
2007СПМД	2,500,000	—	—	—	5.00	6.00

Y# 964 10 ROUBLES
8.3000 g., Bi-Metallic Copper-Nickel center in Brass ring, 27 mm. **Obv:** Value with latent image in zero within circle and sprays **Rev:** Veliky Ustyug city view **Edge:** Reeded and lettered **Edge Lettering:** Denomination repeated

Date	Mintage	F	VF	XF	Unc	BU
2007ММД	2,500,000	—	—	—	5.00	6.00
2007СПМД	2,500,000	—	—	—	5.00	6.00

Y# 965 10 ROUBLES
8.3000 g., Bi-Metallic Copper-Nickel center in Brass ring, 27 mm. **Obv:** Value with latent image in zero within circle and sprays **Rev:** Gdov church **Edge:** Reeded and lettered **Edge Lettering:** Denomination repeated

Date	Mintage	F	VF	XF	Unc	BU
2007ММД	2,500,000	—	—	—	5.00	6.00
2007СПМД	2,500,000	—	—	—	5.00	6.00

Y# 970 10 ROUBLES
8.5700 g., Bi-Metallic Copper-Nickel center in Brass ring, 27.08 mm. **Obv:** Value with latent image in zero within circle and sprays **Obv. Legend:** БАНК РОССИИ **Rev:** Rostovskaya Oblast arms **Edge:** Reeded and lettered **Edge Lettering:** Denomination repeated

Date	Mintage	F	VF	XF	Unc	BU
2007СПМД	10,000,000	—	—	—	4.00	6.00

Y# 971 10 ROUBLES
8.5700 g., Bi-Metallic Copper-Nickel center in Brass ring, 27.08 mm. **Obv:** Value with latent image in zero within circle and sprays **Obv. Legend:** БАНК РОССИИ **Rev:** Khakassia Republic arms **Edge:** Reeded and lettered **Edge Lettering:** Denomination repeated

Date	Mintage	F	VF	XF	Unc	BU
2007СПМД	10,000,000	—	—	—	5.00	6.00

Y# 972 10 ROUBLES
8.5700 g., Bi-Metallic Copper-Nickel center in Brass ring, 27.08 mm. **Obv:** Value with latent image in zero within circle and sprays **Obv. Legend:** БАНК РОССИИ **Rev:** Bashkortostan Republic arms **Edge:** Reeded and lettered **Edge Lettering:** Denomination repeated

Date	Mintage	F	VF	XF	Unc	BU
2007ММД	10,000,000	—	—	—	5.00	6.00

Y# 973 10 ROUBLES
8.5700 g., Bi-Metallic Copper-Nickel center in Brass ring, 27.08 mm. **Obv:** Value with latent image in zero within circle and sprays **Obv. Legend:** БАНК РОССИИ **Rev:** Archangelskaya Oblast arms **Edge:** Reeded and lettered **Edge Lettering:** Denomination repeated

Date	Mintage	F	VF	XF	Unc	BU
2007СПМД	10,000,000	—	—	—	5.00	6.00

Y# 974 10 ROUBLES
8.5700 g., Bi-Metallic Copper-Nickel center in brass ring., 27.08 mm. **Obv:** Value with latent image in zero within circle and sprays **Obv. Legend:** БАНК РОССИИ **Rev:** Novosibirskaya Oblast arms **Edge:** Reeded and lettered **Edge Lettering:** Denomination repeated

Date	Mintage	F	VF	XF	Unc	BU
2007ММД	10,000,000	—	—	—	5.00	6.00

Y# 993 10 ROUBLES
8.2300 g., Bi-Metallic Copper-Nickel center in Brass ring **Subject:** Lipetskaya Oblast

Date	Mintage	F	VF	XF	Unc	BU
2007ММД	10,000,000	—	—	—	2.00	3.50

Y# 975 10 ROUBLES
8.2000 g., Bi-Metallic Copper-Nickel center in Brass ring, 27.1 mm. **Obv:** Value with latent image in zero within circle and sprays **Obv. Legend:** БАНК РОССИИ **Rev:** Udmurtia Republic arms **Rev. Legend:** УДМУРТСКАЯ РЕСПУБЛИКА **Edge:** Reeded and lettered **Edge Lettering:** Denomination repeated

Date	Mintage	F	VF	XF	Unc	BU
2008ММД	5,000,000	—	—	1.00	2.00	3.00
2008СПМД	5,000,000	—	—	1.00	2.00	3.00

Y# 976 10 ROUBLES
8.2800 g., Bi-Metallic Copper-Nickel center in brass ring., 27.1 mm. **Series:** Ancient cities **Subject:** Vladimir **Obv:** Value with latent image in zero within circle and sprays **Obv. Legend:** БАНК РОССИИ **Rev:** Small shield at upper left above city view **Rev. Legend:** ВЛАДИМИР **Edge:** Reeded and lettered **Edge Lettering:** Denomination repeated

Date	Mintage	F	VF	XF	Unc	BU
2008ММД	2,500,000	—	—	1.00	2.00	3.00
2008СПМД	2,500,000	—	—	1.00	2.00	3.00

Y# 977 10 ROUBLES
8.2300 g., Bi-Metallic Copper-Nickel center in Brass ring, 27 mm. **Obv:** Value with latent image in zero within circle and sprays **Obv. Legend:** БАНК РОССИИ **Rev:** Astrakhanskaya Oblast arms **Edge:** Reeded and lettered **Edge Lettering:** Denomination repeated

Date	Mintage	F	VF	XF	Unc	BU
2008ММД	5,000,000	—	—	1.00	2.00	3.00
2008СПМД	5,000,000	—	—	1.00	2.00	3.00

Y# 978 10 ROUBLES
8.1600 g., Bi-Metallic Copper-Nickel center in brass ring, 27 mm. **Obv:** Value with latent image in zero within circle and sprays **Obv. Legend:** БАНК РОССИИ **Rev:** Sverdlovskaya Oblast arms **Edge:** Reeded and lettered **Edge Lettering:** Denomination repeated

Date	Mintage	F	VF	XF	Unc	BU
2008ММД	5,000,000	—	—	1.00	2.00	3.00
2008СПМД	5,000,000	—	—	1.00	2.00	3.00

Y# 986 10 ROUBLES
8.0800 g., Bi-Metallic Copper-Nickel center in Brass ring, 27 mm. **Rev:** Azov town view

Date	Mintage	F	VF	XF	Unc	BU
2008ММД	2,500,000	—	—	—	2.00	3.50
2008СПМД	2,500,000	—	—	—	2.00	3.50

Y# 991 10 ROUBLES
8.0800 g., Bi-Metallic Copper-Nickel center in Brass ring, 27 mm. **Rev:** Kabardino-Balkaria Republic Arms

Date	Mintage	F	VF	XF	Unc	BU
2008ММД	5,000,000	—	—	—	2.00	3.50
2008СПМД	5,000,000	—	—	—	2.00	3.50

Y# 994 10 ROUBLES
8.2300 g., Bi-Metallic Copper-Nickel center in Brass ring
Subject: Priozersk

Date	Mintage	F	VF	XF	Unc	BU
2008ММД	2,500,000	—	—	—	2.00	3.50
2008СПМД	2,500,000	—	—	—	2.00	3.50

Y# 995 10 ROUBLES
8.2300 g., Bi-Metallic Copper-Nickel center in Brass ring
Subject: Smolensk

Date	Mintage	F	VF	XF	Unc	BU
2008ММД	2,500,000	—	—	—	2.00	3.50
2008СПМД	2,500,000	—	—	—	2.00	3.50

Y# 998 10 ROUBLES
5.6300 g., Brass Plated Steel, 22 mm. **Obv:** Double headed eagle **Rev:** Value

Date	Mintage	F	VF	XF	Unc	BU
2009ММД	—	—	—	—	2.50	4.00
2010ММД	—	—	—	—	2.50	4.00
2010СПМД	—	—	—	—	2.50	4.00
2011ММД	—	—	—	—	2.50	4.00
2012ММД	—	—	—	—	2.50	4.00

Y# 982 10 ROUBLES
8.0800 g., Bi-Metallic Copper-Nickel center in Brass ring, 27 mm. **Rev:** Kaluga town view

Date	Mintage	F	VF	XF	Unc	BU
2009ММД	2,500,000	—	—	—	2.00	3.50
2009СПМД	2,500,000	—	—	—	2.00	3.50

Y# 983 10 ROUBLES
8.0800 g., Bi-Metallic Copper-Nickel center in Brass ring, 27 mm. **Rev:** Vyborg town view

Date	Mintage	F	VF	XF	Unc	BU
2009ММД	2,500,000	—	—	—	2.00	3.50
2009СПМД	2,500,000	—	—	—	2.00	3.50

Y# 984 10 ROUBLES
8.0800 g., Bi-Metallic Copper-Nickel center in Brass ring, 27 mm. **Rev:** Galich town view

Date	Mintage	F	VF	XF	Unc	BU
2009ММД	2,500,000	—	—	—	2.00	3.50
2009СПМД	2,500,000	—	—	—	2.00	3.50

Y# 985 10 ROUBLES
8.0800 g., Bi-Metallic Copper-Nickel center in Brass ring, 27 mm. **Rev:** Kalmykiya Republic arms

Date	Mintage	F	VF	XF	Unc	BU
2009ММД	5,000,000	—	—	—	2.00	3.50
2009СПМД	5,000,000	—	—	—	2.00	3.50

Y# 987 10 ROUBLES
8.0800 g., Bi-Metallic Copper-Nickel center in Brass ring, 27 mm. **Rev:** Adygeya Republic arms

Date	Mintage	F	VF	XF	Unc	BU
2009ММД	5,000,000	—	—	—	2.00	3.50
2009СПМД	5,000,000	—	—	—	2.00	3.50

Y# 988 10 ROUBLES
8.0800 g., Bi-Metallic Copper-Nickel center in Brass ring, 27 mm. **Rev:** Veliky Novgorod arms

Date	Mintage	F	VF	XF	Unc	BU
2009ММД	2,500,000	—	—	—	2.00	3.50
2009СПМД	2,500,000	—	—	—	2.00	3.50

Y# 989 10 ROUBLES
8.0800 g., Bi-Metallic Copper-Nickel center in Brass ring, 27 mm. **Rev:** Jewish Autonomous Oblast Arms

Date	Mintage	F	VF	XF	Unc	BU
2009ММД	5,000,000	—	—	—	2.00	3.50
2009СПМД	5,000,000	—	—	—	2.00	3.50

Y# 996 10 ROUBLES
8.0800 g., Bi-Metallic Copper-Nickel center in Brass ring
Subject: Komi Republic

Date	Mintage	F	VF	XF	Unc	BU
2009СПМД	10,000,000	—	—	—	2.00	3.50

Y# 997 10 ROUBLES
8.0800 g., Bi-Metallic Copper-Nickel center in Brass ring
Subject: Kirovskaya Oblast

Date	Mintage	F	VF	XF	Unc	BU
2009СПМД	10,000,000	—	—	—	2.00	3.50

Y# 1274 10 ROUBLES
8.0800 g., Bi-Metallic Copper-Nickel center in Brass ring, 27 mm. **Subject:** Russian Census

Date	Mintage	F	VF	XF	Unc	BU
2010	2,300,000	—	—	—	4.00	6.00

Y# 1275 10 ROUBLES
8.0800 g., Bi-Metallic Copper-Nickel center in Brass ring, 27 mm. **Subject:** Bryansk

Date	Mintage	F	VF	XF	Unc	BU
2010	10,000,000	—	—	—	4.00	6.00

Y# 1276 10 ROUBLES
8.0800 g., Bi-Metallic Copper-Nickel center in Brass ring, 27 mm. **Subject:** Yurevets, Ivanovo Region

Date	Mintage	F	VF	XF	Unc	BU
2010	10,000,000	—	—	—	4.00	6.00

Y# 1277 10 ROUBLES
8.0800 g., Bi-Metallic Copper-Nickel center in Brass ring, 27 mm. **Series:** Permskiy Krai

Date	Mintage	F	VF	XF	Unc	BU
2010	200,000	—	—	—	45.00	70.00

Y# 1278 10 ROUBLES
8.0800 g., Bi-Metallic Copper-Nickel center in Brass ring, 27 mm. **Subject:** Nenets Autonomous Region

Date	Mintage	F	VF	XF	Unc	BU
2010	1,950,000	—	—	—	4.00	6.00

Y# 1279 10 ROUBLES
8.0800 g., Bi-Metallic Copper-Nickel center in Brass ring, 27 mm. **Subject:** Chechen Republic

Date	Mintage	F	VF	XF	Unc	BU
2010	100,000	—	—	—	100	150

Y# 1280 10 ROUBLES
8.0800 g., Bi-Metallic Copper-Nickel center in Brass ring, 27 mm. **Subject:** Yamalo-Nenetskiy Autonomous Area

Date	Mintage	F	VF	XF	Unc	BU
2010	100,000	—	—	—	250	300

Y# 1283 10 ROUBLES
8.0800 g., Bi-Metallic Copper-Nickel center in Brass ring, 27 mm. **Rev:** Solikamsk town view

Date	Mintage	F	VF	XF	Unc	BU
2011СПМД	—	—	—	—	3.00	4.00

Y# 1284 10 ROUBLES
8.0800 g., Bi-Metallic Copper-Nickel center in Brass ring, 27 mm. **Rev:** Yelets city view

Date	Mintage	F	VF	XF	Unc	BU
2011СПМД	—	—	—	—	3.00	4.00

Y# 1292 10 ROUBLES
8.0800 g., Bi-Metallic Copper-Nickel center in Brass ring, 27 mm. **Rev:** Shield of the Republic of Buryatia

Date	Mintage	F	VF	XF	Unc	BU
2011СПМД	—	—	—	—	3.00	4.00

Y# 1305 10 ROUBLES
5.6300 g., Brass Plated Steel, 22 mm. **Subject:** Belgorod **Edge:** Segmented reeding

Date	Mintage	F	VF	XF	Unc	BU
2011СПМД	10,000,000	—	—	—	3.00	4.00

Y# 1308 10 ROUBLES
5.6300 g., Brass Plated Steel, 22 mm. **Subject:** Kursk city arms **Edge:** Segmented reeding

Date	Mintage	F	VF	XF	Unc	BU
2011СПМД	10,000,000	—	—	—	3.00	4.00

Y# 1309 10 ROUBLES
5.6300 g., Brass Plated Steel, 22 mm. **Subject:** Orel city arms

Date	Mintage	F	VF	XF	Unc	BU
2011	10,000,000	—	—	—	3.00	4.00

Y# 1313 10 ROUBLES
8.0800 g., Bi-Metallic Copper-Nickel center in Brass ring, 27 mm. **Rev:** Voronezh Region arms

Date	Mintage	F	VF	XF	Unc	BU
2011	10,000,000	—	—	—	3.00	4.00

Y# 1314 10 ROUBLES
5.6300 g., Brass Plated Steel, 22 mm. **Rev:** Vladikavkaz city arms **Edge:** Segmented reeding

Date	Mintage	F	VF	XF	Unc	BU
2011СПМД	10,000,000	—	—	—	3.00	4.00

Y# 1318 10 ROUBLES
5.6300 g., Brass Plated Steel, 22 mm. **Rev:** Malgobek city arms **Edge:** Segmented reeding

Date	Mintage	F	VF	XF	Unc	BU
2011СПМД	10,000,000	—	—	—	3.00	4.00

Y# 1323 10 ROUBLES
5.6300 g., Brass Plated Steel, 22 mm. **Rev:** Rzhev city arms **Edge:** Segmented reeding

Date	Mintage	F	VF	XF	Unc	BU
2011СПМД	10,000,000	—	—	—	3.00	4.00

Y# 1380 10 ROUBLES
8.0800 g., Bi-Metallic Copper-Nickel center in Brass ring, 27 mm. **Subject:** Belozersk, Vologda region

Date	Mintage	F	VF	XF	Unc	BU
2012	5,000,000	—	—	—	2.50	4.00

Y# 1381 10 ROUBLES
Brass Plated Steel, 22 mm. **Rev:** Voronezh city arms **Edge:** Segmented reeding

Date	Mintage	F	VF	XF	Unc	BU
2012СПМД	10,000,000	—	—	—	2.50	4.00

Y# 1382 10 ROUBLES

Brass Plated Steel, 22 mm. **Rev:** Luga city arms **Edge:** Segmented reeding

Date	Mintage	F	VF	XF	Unc	BU
2012СПМД	10,000,000	—	—	—	2.50	4.00

Y# 1383 10 ROUBLES

Brass Plated Steel, 22 mm. **Rev:** Polyarny city arms **Edge:** Segmented reeding

Date	Mintage	F	VF	XF	Unc	BU
2012СПМД	10,000,000	—	—	—	2.50	4.00

Y# 1384 10 ROUBLES

Brass Plated Steel, 22 mm. **Rev:** Rostov-on-Don city arms **Edge:** Segmented reeding

Date	Mintage	F	VF	XF	Unc	BU
2012СПМД	10,000,000	—	—	—	2.50	4.00

Y# 1385 10 ROUBLES

Brass Plated Steel, 22 mm. **Rev:** Tuapse city arms **Edge:** Segmented reeding

Date	Mintage	F	VF	XF	Unc	BU
2012СПМД	10,000,000	—	—	—	2.50	4.00

Y# 1386 10 ROUBLES

Brass Plated Steel, 22 mm. **Rev:** Velikiye Luki city arms **Edge:** Segmented reeding

Date	Mintage	F	VF	XF	Unc	BU
2012СПМД	10,000,000	—	—	—	2.50	4.00

Y# 1387 10 ROUBLES

Brass Plated Steel, 22 mm. **Subject:** Veliky Novgorod city arms

Date	Mintage	F	VF	XF	Unc	BU
2012	10,000,000	—	—	—	2.50	4.00

Y# 1388 10 ROUBLES

Brass Plated Steel, 22 mm. **Subject:** Dimitrov city arms

Date	Mintage	F	VF	XF	Unc	BU
2012	10,000,000	—	—	—	2.50	4.00

Y# 1389 10 ROUBLES

Brass Plated Steel, 22 mm. **Subject:** Origin of Russian Statehood, 1150th Anniversary

Date	Mintage	F	VF	XF	Unc	BU
2012	10,000,000	—	—	—	2.50	4.00

Y# 1390 10 ROUBLES

Brass Plated Steel, 22 mm. **Subject:** War of 1812, 200th Anniversary

Date	Mintage	F	VF	XF	Unc	BU
2012	10,000,000	—	—	—	2.50	4.00

Y# 678 25 ROUBLES

173.2900 g., 0.9000 Silver 5.0141 oz. ASW, 60 mm. **Subject:** Bolshoi Theater 225 Years **Obv:** Double-headed eagle **Rev:** Dancing couple scene **Edge:** Reeded **Note:** Illustration reduced.

Date	Mintage	F	VF	XF	Unc	BU
2001 Proof	2,000	Value: 350				

Y# 683 25 ROUBLES

173.2900 g., 0.9000 Silver 5.0141 oz. ASW, 60 mm. **Subject:** Siberian Exploration **Obv:** Double-headed eagle **Rev:** Standing king and river boats **Edge:** Reeded **Note:** Illustration reduced.

Date	Mintage	F	VF	XF	Unc	BU
2001 Proof	1,000	Value: 400				

Y# 794 25 ROUBLES

173.1300 g., 0.9000 Silver 5.0094 oz. ASW, 60.2 mm. **Subject:** Foundation of Russian Savings Banks **Obv:** Double-headed eagle **Rev:** Czar Nicholas I and document **Edge:** Reeded

Date	Mintage	F	VF	XF	Unc	BU
2001(m) Proof	10,500	Value: 275				

Y# 687 25 ROUBLES

3.2000 g., 0.9990 Gold 0.1028 oz. AGW, 16 mm. **Subject:** Bolshoi Theater **Obv:** Double-headed eagle **Rev:** Ballerina **Edge:** Reeded

Date	Mintage	F	VF	XF	Unc	BU
2001 Proof	2,500	Value: 200				

Y# 999 25 ROUBLES

169.0000 g., 0.9250 Silver 5.0258 oz. ASW, 60 mm. **Subject:** Bolshoi Theater, 225th Anniversary

Date	Mintage	F	VF	XF	Unc	BU
2001 Proof	—	Value: 350				

Y# 1000 25 ROUBLES

169.0000 g., 0.9250 Silver 5.0258 oz. ASW, 60 mm. **Subject:** Savings Bank

Date	Mintage	F	VF	XF	Unc	BU
2001 Proof	—	Value: 350				

Y# 1001 25 ROUBLES

169.0000 g., 0.9250 Silver 5.0258 oz. ASW, 60 mm. **Subject:** Siberia - Development and Exploration

Date	Mintage	F	VF	XF	Unc	BU
2001 Proof	—	Value: 350				

Y# 777 25 ROUBLES

173.2900 g., 0.9000 Silver 5.0141 oz. ASW, 60 mm. **Subject:** Czar Alexander I **Obv:** Double-headed eagle **Rev:** Head right and crowned double-headed eagle above document text **Edge:** Reeded **Note:** Illustration reduced.

Date	Mintage	F	VF	XF	Unc	BU
2002(m) Proof	1,500	Value: 400				

Y# 785 25 ROUBLES

173.2900 g., 0.9000 Silver 5.0141 oz. ASW, 60 mm. **Subject:** Admiral Nakhimov **Obv:** Double-headed eagle **Rev:** Admiral watching naval battle **Edge:** Reeded **Note:** Illustration reduced.

Date	Mintage	F	VF	XF	Unc	BU
2002(sp) Proof	2,000	Value: 350				

Y# 790 25 ROUBLES
173.2900 g., 0.9000 Silver 5.0141 oz. ASW, 60 mm. **Subject:** Hermitage **Obv:** Double-headed eagle **Rev:** Staircase viewed through doorway **Edge:** Reeded **Note:** Illustration reduced.

Date	Mintage	F	VF	XF	Unc	BU
2002(sp) Proof	2,000	Value: 350				

Y# 743 25 ROUBLES
3.2000 g., 0.9990 Gold 0.1028 oz. AGW, 16 mm. **Subject:** Zodiac Signs: **Obv:** Double-headed eagle within beaded circle **Rev:** Leo **Edge:** Reeded

Date	Mintage	F	VF	XF	Unc	BU
2002 Proof	10,000	Value: 200				

Y# 763 25 ROUBLES
3.2000 g., 0.9990 Gold 0.1028 oz. AGW, 16 mm. **Subject:** Zodiac Signs **Obv:** Double-headed eagle within beaded circle **Rev:** Capricorn **Edge:** Reeded

Date	Mintage	F	VF	XF	Unc	BU
2002(m)	10,000	—	—	—	—	200

Y# 764 25 ROUBLES
3.2000 g., 0.9990 Gold 0.1028 oz. AGW, 16 mm. **Subject:** Zodiac Signs **Obv:** Double-headed eagle within beaded circle **Rev:** Virgo **Edge:** Reeded

Date	Mintage	F	VF	XF	Unc	BU
2002(sp)	10,000	—	—	—	—	200

Y# 765 25 ROUBLES
3.2000 g., 0.9990 Gold 0.1028 oz. AGW, 16 mm. **Subject:** Zodiac Signs **Obv:** Double-headed eagle within beaded circle **Rev:** Sagittarius **Edge:** Reeded

Date	Mintage	F	VF	XF	Unc	BU
2002(SP)	10,000	—	—	—	—	200

Y# 767 25 ROUBLES
3.2000 g., 0.9990 Gold 0.1028 oz. AGW, 16 mm. **Subject:** Zodiac signs **Obv:** Double-headed eagle within beaded circle **Rev:** Scorpio **Edge:** Reeded

Date	Mintage	F	VF	XF	Unc	BU
2002(m)	10,000	—	—	—	—	200

Y# 769 25 ROUBLES
3.2000 g., 0.9990 Gold 0.1028 oz. AGW **Subject:** Zodiac Signs **Obv:** Double-headed eagle within beaded circle **Rev:** Libra **Edge:** Reeded

Date	Mintage	F	VF	XF	Unc	BU
2002(sp)	10,000	—	—	—	—	200

Y# 821 25 ROUBLES
3.2000 g., 0.9990 Gold 0.1028 oz. AGW, 16 mm. **Subject:** Zodiac signs **Obv:** Double-headed eagle within beaded circle **Rev:** Cancer **Edge:** Reeded

Date	Mintage	F	VF	XF	Unc	BU
2003(sp)	50,000	—	—	—	—	200

Y# 864 25 ROUBLES
172.8000 g., 0.9000 Silver 4.9999 oz. ASW, 60 mm. **Rev:** St. Sercius Monastery

Date	Mintage	F	VF	XF	Unc	BU
2003 Proof	2,000	Value: 350				

Y# 865 25 ROUBLES
172.8000 g., 0.9000 Silver 4.9999 oz. ASW, 60 mm. **Rev:** Shlisselburg

Date	Mintage	F	VF	XF	Unc	BU
2003(m) Proof	2,000	Value: 350				

Y# 866 25 ROUBLES
172.8000 g., 0.9000 Silver 4.9999 oz. ASW, 60 mm. **Rev:** Kamchatka

Date	Mintage	F	VF	XF	Unc	BU
2003	2,000	Value: 350				

Y# 1003 25 ROUBLES
169.0000 g., 0.9250 Silver 5.0258 oz. ASW, 60 mm. **Subject:** Aquarius

Date	Mintage	F	VF	XF	Unc	BU
2003 Proof	—	Value: 350				

Y# 1004 25 ROUBLES
169.0000 g., 0.9250 Silver 5.0258 oz. ASW, 60 mm. **Subject:** Pisces

Date	Mintage	F	VF	XF	Unc	BU
2003 Proof	—	Value: 350				

Y# 1005 25 ROUBLES
169.0000 g., 0.9250 Silver 5.0258 oz. ASW, 60 mm. **Subject:** Aries

Date	Mintage	F	VF	XF	Unc	BU
2003 Proof	—	Value: 350				

Y# 1006 25 ROUBLES
169.0000 g., 0.9250 Silver 5.0258 oz. ASW, 60 mm. **Subject:** Taurus

Date	Mintage	F	VF	XF	Unc	BU
2003 Proof	—	Value: 350				

Y# 830 25 ROUBLES
177.9600 g., 0.9000 Bi-Metallic .900 Silver 172.78g planchet with .900 Gold 5.18g insert 5.1492 oz., 60 mm. **Subject:** Monetary reform of Peter the Great **Obv:** Double-headed eagle **Rev:** Gold insert replicating the obverse and reverse designs of a 1704 one rouble coin **Edge:** Reeded **Note:** Illustration reduced.

Date	Mintage	F	VF	XF	Unc	BU
2004(sp) Proof	1,000	Value: 950				

Y# 867 25 ROUBLES
172.8000 g., 0.9000 Silver 4.9999 oz. ASW, 60 mm. **Rev:** Valaam Church

Date	Mintage	F	VF	XF	Unc	BU
2004	1,500	Value: 375				

Y# 1014 25 ROUBLES
169.0000 g., 0.9250 Silver 5.0258 oz. ASW, 60 mm. **Subject:** 2nd Kamchatka Expedition, 1733-43

Date	Mintage	F	VF	XF	Unc	BU
2004 Proof	—	Value: 350				

Y# 1019 25 ROUBLES
169.0000 g., 0.9250 Silver 5.0258 oz. ASW, 60 mm. **Subject:** Holy Trinity - St. Sergius Lavra in Sergiev Posad

Date	Mintage	F	VF	XF	Unc	BU
2004 Proof	—	Value: 350				

Y# 1023 25 ROUBLES
169.0000 g., 0.9250 Silver 5.0258 oz. ASW, 60 mm. **Subject:** Reindeer

Date	Mintage	F	VF	XF	Unc	BU
2004 Proof	—	Value: 350				

Y# 898 25 ROUBLES
3.2000 g., 0.9990 Gold 0.1028 oz. AGW, 16 mm. **Obv:** Double-headed eagle **Rev:** Gemini twins **Edge:** Reeded

Date	Mintage	F	VF	XF	Unc	BU
2005	10,000	—	—	—	—	200

Y# 900 25 ROUBLES
3.2000 g., 0.9990 Gold 0.1028 oz. AGW, 16 mm. **Obv:** Double-headed eagle **Rev:** Cancer crawfish **Edge:** Reeded

Date	Mintage	F	VF	XF	Unc	BU
2005 Proof	10,000	Value: 200				

Y# 902 25 ROUBLES
3.2000 g., 0.9990 Gold 0.1028 oz. AGW, 16 mm. **Obv:** Double-headed eagle **Rev:** Leo lion **Edge:** Reeded

Date	Mintage	F	VF	XF	Unc	BU
2005	10,000	—	—	—	—	220

Y# 915 25 ROUBLES
3.2000 g., 0.9990 Gold 0.1028 oz. AGW, 16 mm. **Obv:** Double-headed eagle **Rev:** Virgos standing lady **Edge:** Reeded

Date	Mintage	F	VF	XF	Unc	BU
2005 Proof	10,000	Value: 200				

Y# 920 25 ROUBLES
3.2000 g., 0.9990 Gold 0.1028 oz. AGW, 16 mm. **Obv:** Double-headed eagle **Rev:** Two stylized birds forming balance scale **Edge:** Reeded

Date	Mintage	F	VF	XF	Unc	BU
2005	10,000	—	—	—	—	220

Y# 922 25 ROUBLES
3.2000 g., 0.9990 Gold 0.1028 oz. AGW, 16 mm. **Obv:** Double-headed eagle **Rev:** Scorpio scorpion **Edge:** Reeded

Date	Mintage	F	VF	XF	Unc	BU
2005	10,000	—	—	—	—	220

Y# 927 25 ROUBLES
3.2000 g., 0.9990 Gold 0.1028 oz. AGW, 16 mm. **Obv:** Double-headed eagle **Rev:** Sagittarius the archer **Edge:** Reeded

Date	Mintage	F	VF	XF	Unc	BU
2005	10,000	—	—	—	—	220

Y# 929 25 ROUBLES
3.2000 g., 0.9990 Gold 0.1028 oz. AGW, 16 mm. **Obv:** Double-headed eagle **Rev:** Capricorn as half goat and fish **Edge:** Reeded

Date	Mintage	F	VF	XF	Unc	BU
2005	10,000	—	—	—	—	220

Y# 931 25 ROUBLES
3.2000 g., 0.9990 Gold 0.1028 oz. AGW, 16 mm. **Obv:** Double-headed eagle **Rev:** Pisces as catfish and sturgeon **Edge:** Reeded

Date	Mintage	F	VF	XF	Unc	BU
2005	10,000	—	—	—	—	220

Y# 933 25 ROUBLES
3.2000 g., 0.9990 Gold 0.1028 oz. AGW, 16 mm. **Obv:** Double-headed eagle **Rev:** Aries ram **Edge:** Reeded

Date	Mintage	F	VF	XF	Unc	BU
2005	10,000	—	—	—	—	220

Y# 935 25 ROUBLES
3.2000 g., 0.9990 Gold 0.1028 oz. AGW, 16 mm. **Obv:** Double-headed eagle **Rev:** Taurus bull **Edge:** Reeded

Date	Mintage	F	VF	XF	Unc	BU
2005	10,000	—	—	—	—	220

Y# 937 25 ROUBLES
3.2000 g., 0.9990 Gold 0.1028 oz. AGW, 16 mm. **Obv:** Double-headed eagle **Rev:** Aquarius water carrier **Edge:** Reeded

Date	Mintage	F	VF	XF	Unc	BU
2005	10,000	—	—	—	—	220

Y# 924 25 ROUBLES
169.0000 g., 0.9250 Silver 5.0258 oz. ASW, 60 mm. **Subject:** 625th Anniversary - Battle of Kulikovo **Obv:** Double-headed eagle **Rev:** Mounted warriors above and below crossed swords **Edge:** Reeded **Note:** Illustration reduced.

Date	Mintage	F	VF	XF	Unc	BU
2005 Proof	1,500	Value: 375				

Y# 1047 25 ROUBLES
169.0000 g., 0.9250 Silver 5.0258 oz. ASW, 60 mm. **Subject:** Tretyakov State Galler, 150th Anniversary

Date	Mintage	F	VF	XF	Unc	BU
2006 Proof	—	Value: 350				

Y# 1050 25 ROUBLES
169.0000 g., 0.9250 Silver 5.0258 oz. ASW, 60 mm. **Subject:** Malye Korely

Date	Mintage	F	VF	XF	Unc	BU
2006 Proof	—	Value: 350				

Y# 1051 25 ROUBLES
169.0000 g., 0.9250 Silver 5.0258 oz. ASW, 60 mm. **Subject:** Tikhvin Monastery, Dome of the Mother of God

Date	Mintage	F	VF	XF	Unc	BU
2006 Proof	—	Value: 350				

Y# 1053 25 ROUBLES
169.0000 g., 0.9250 Silver 5.0258 oz. ASW, 60 mm. **Subject:** Konevsky Monastery of St. Virgin's Nativity

Date	Mintage	F	VF	XF	Unc	BU
2006 Proof	—	Value: 350				

Y# 969 25 ROUBLES
169.0000 g., 0.9250 Silver 5.0258 oz. ASW, 60.00 mm. **Obv:** Two-headed eagle **Rev:** Vyatka St. Trifon Monastery of the Assumption, Kirov **Edge:** Reeded **Note:** Illustration reduced

Date	Mintage	F	VF	XF	Unc	BU
2007(sp) Proof	2,000	Value: 350				

Y# 1083 25 ROUBLES
169.0000 g., 0.9250 Silver 5.0258 oz. ASW, 60 mm. **Subject:** Russian Railways, 150th Anniversary

Date	Mintage	F	VF	XF	Unc	BU
2007 Proof	—	Value: 350				

Y# 1084 25 ROUBLES
169.0000 g., 0.9250 Silver 5.0258 oz. ASW, 60 mm. **Subject:** F. A. Golovin, first Order of St. Andrew awardee

Date	Mintage	F	VF	XF	Unc	BU
2007 Proof	—	Value: 350				

Y# 1101 25 ROUBLES
169.0000 g., 0.9250 Silver 5.0258 oz. ASW, 60 mm. **Subject:** St. Artemy Verkolsky Monastery, Arkhamgelsk

Date	Mintage	F	VF	XF	Unc	BU
2007 Proof	—	Value: 350				

Y# 1102 25 ROUBLES
169.0000 g., 0.9250 Silver 5.0258 oz. ASW, 60 mm. **Subject:** Pskov-Pechersky Holy Monastery of the Assumption

Date	Mintage	F	VF	XF	Unc	BU
2007 Proof	—	Value: 350				

Y# 1116 25 ROUBLES
169.0000 g., 0.9250 Silver 5.0258 oz. ASW, 60 mm. **Subject:** Goznak, 190th Anniversary

Date	Mintage	F	VF	XF	Unc	BU
2008 Proof	—	Value: 350				

Y# 1125 25 ROUBLES
169.0000 g., 0.9250 Silver 5.0258 oz. ASW, 60 mm. **Subject:** Astrakhan Kremlin

Date	Mintage	F	VF	XF	Unc	BU
2008 Proof	—	Value: 400				

Y# 1139 25 ROUBLES
169.0000 g., 0.9250 Silver 5.0258 oz. ASW, 60 mm. **Subject:** European Beaver

Date	Mintage	F	VF	XF	Unc	BU
2008 Proof	—	Value: 400				

Y# 1160 25 ROUBLES
168.0000 g., 0.9250 Silver 4.9960 oz. ASW, 60 mm. **Subject:** Alexander I Monument, 175th Anniversary

Date	Mintage	F	VF	XF	Unc	BU
2009 Proof	—	Value: 350				

Y# 1178 25 ROUBLES
168.0000 g., 0.9250 Silver 4.9960 oz. ASW, 60 mm. **Subject:** Poltava Battle, 300th Anniversary

Date	Mintage	F	VF	XF	Unc	BU
2009 Proof	—	Value: 350				

Y# 1184 25 ROUBLES
168.0000 g., 0.9250 Silver 4.9960 oz. ASW, 60 mm. **Subject:** Arkhangelskoye Museum

Date	Mintage	F	VF	XF	Unc	BU
2009 Proof	—	Value: 350				

Y# 1186 25 ROUBLES
168.0000 g., 0.9250 Silver 4.9960 oz. ASW, 60 mm. **Subject:** St. Trinity Monastery, Pensu Region

Date	Mintage	F	VF	XF	Unc	BU
2009 Proof	—	Value: 350				

Y# 1187 25 ROUBLES
168.0000 g., 0.9250 Silver 4.9960 oz. ASW, 60 mm. **Subject:** St. Nikolas Monastary, Staraya Ladoga

Date	Mintage	F	VF	XF	Unc	BU
2009 Proof	—	Value: 350				

Y# 1200 25 ROUBLES
168.0000 g., 0.9250 Silver 4.9960 oz. ASW, 60 mm. **Subject:** Veliklу Novgorod

Date	Mintage	F	VF	XF	Unc	BU
2009 Proof	—	Value: 350				

Y# 1223 25 ROUBLES
168.0000 g., 0.9250 Silver 4.9960 oz. ASW, 60 mm. **Subject:** Khmelita, Griboyedov family estate

Date	Mintage	F	VF	XF	Unc	BU
2010 Proof	—	Value: 350				

Y# 1224 25 ROUBLES
168.0000 g., 0.9250 Silver 4.9960 oz. ASW, 60 mm. **Subject:** Kirillo Belosersk Monastery

Date	Mintage	F	VF	XF	Unc	BU
2010 Proof	—	Value: 350				

Y# 1225 25 ROUBLES
168.0000 g., 0.9250 Silver 4.9960 oz. ASW, 60 mm. **Subject:** Alezxandro - Svirsky Monestary

Date	Mintage	F	VF	XF	Unc	BU
2010 Proof	—	Value: 350				

Y# 1226 25 ROUBLES
168.0000 g., 0.9250 Silver 4.9960 oz. ASW, 60 mm. **Subject:** Sanaksarsky Monestary

Date	Mintage	F	VF	XF	Unc	BU
2010 Proof	—	Value: 350				

Y# 1229 25 ROUBLES

168.0000 g., 0.9250 Silver 4.9960 oz. ASW, 60 mm. **Subject:** Bank of Russia, 150th Anniversary

Date	Mintage	F	VF	XF	Unc	BU
2010 Proof	—	Value: 350				

Y# 1233 25 ROUBLES

169.0000 g., 0.9250 Silver 5.0258 oz. ASW, 60 mm. **Subject:** UNESCO Heritage Site - Yaroslav

Date	Mintage	F	VF	XF	Unc	BU
2010 Proof	—	Value: 350				

Y# 1304 25 ROUBLES

155.5000 g., 0.9250 Silver 4.6243 oz. ASW, 60 mm. **Subject:** Virgin Mary Monastery, Kazan **Rev:** Icon in color and building complex

Date	Mintage	F	VF	XF	Unc	BU
2011 Proof	2,000	Value: 350				

Y# 1298 25 ROUBLES

10.0000 g., Copper-Nickel, 27 mm. **Subject:** 2014 Winter Olympics - Sochi **Obv:** Double-headed eagle, value below **Rev:** Mountain **Edge:** Reeded

Date	Mintage	F	VF	XF	Unc	BU
2011	10,000,000	—	—	—	—	8.00

Note: Value in card packaging is $40.

Y# 1306 25 ROUBLES

155.5000 g., 0.9250 Silver 4.6243 oz. ASW, 60 mm. **Subject:** Pavlovsky Palace and park **Rev:** Hilltop building, bridge in forefront, female statues flankings **Edge:** Reeded

Date	Mintage	F	VF	XF	Unc	BU
2011 Proof	1,500	Value: 300				

Y# 1317 25 ROUBLES

155.5000 g., 0.9250 Silver 4.6243 oz. ASW, 60 mm. **Subject:** Virgin's Saint Entrance Presentation Monastery, Optin **Rev:** Monastery buildings

Date	Mintage	F	VF	XF	Unc	BU
2011 Proof	2,000	Value: 300				

Y# 1321 25 ROUBLES

155.5000 g., 0.9250 Silver 4.6243 oz. ASW, 60 mm. **Subject:** Year of Italian Culture and Language in Russia **Rev:** Town vies of Sergiev Posad and Bari, Icon at center, Russian and Italian flags below in color

Date	Mintage	F	VF	XF	Unc	BU
2011 Proof	1,000	Value: 475				

Y# 1322 25 ROUBLES

155.5000 g., 0.9250 Silver 4.6243 oz. ASW, 60 mm. **Subject:** Kazan Cathedral, St. Petersburg **Rev:** Ariel view of Cathedral and plaza **Edge:** Reeded

Date	Mintage	F	VF	XF	Unc	BU
2011 Proof	1,500	Value: 400				

Y# 1335 25 ROUBLES

169.0000 g., 0.9250 Silver 5.0258 oz. ASW, 60 mm. **Subject:** Museum-Estate of V.D. Polenov, Tula region

Date	Mintage	F	VF	XF	Unc	BU
2012 Proof	2,000	Value: 325				

Y# 1336 25 ROUBLES

169.0000 g., 0.9250 Silver 5.0258 oz. ASW, 60 mm. **Subject:** Voskresensky New Jerusalem Monastery, Istra, Moscow region

Date	Mintage	F	VF	XF	Unc	BU
2012 Proof	2,000	Value: 350				

Y# 1337 25 ROUBLES
169.0000 g., 0.9250 Silver 5.0258 oz. ASW, 60 mm. **Subject:** Spaso-Borodinsky Monastery, Moscow region

Date	Mintage	F	VF	XF	Unc	BU
2012 Proof	2,000	Value: 365				

Y# 1338 25 ROUBLES
169.0000 g., 0.9250 Silver 5.0258 oz. ASW, 60 mm. **Subject:** Alexeevo-Akatov Monastery, Voronezh

Date	Mintage	F	VF	XF	Unc	BU
2012 Proof	1,500	Value: 400				

Y# 1343 25 ROUBLES
169.0000 g., 0.9250 Silver 5.0258 oz. ASW, 60 mm. **Subject:** People's Volunteer Corps, 400th Anniversary

Date	Mintage	F	VF	XF	Unc	BU
2012 Proof	1,000	Value: 425				

Y# 1346 25 ROUBLES
169.0000 g., 0.9250 Silver 5.0258 oz. ASW, 100 mm. **Subject:** Russia's victory in the War of 1812

Date	Mintage	F	VF	XF	Unc	BU
2012 Proof	2,000	Value: 375				

Y# 1347 25 ROUBLES
169.0000 g., 0.9250 Silver 5.0258 oz. ASW, 60 mm. **Subject:** Russia's victory in the War of 1812

Date	Mintage	F	VF	XF	Unc	BU
2012 Proof	2,000	Value: 350				

Y# 1352 25 ROUBLES
169.0000 g., 0.9250 Silver 5.0258 oz. ASW, 60 mm. **Subject:** Pushkin State Museum of Fine Arts, Moscow, 100th Anniversary

Date	Mintage
	2,000 Value: 350

Y# 1360 25 ROUBLES
169.0000 g., 0.9250 Silver 5.0258 oz. ASW, 60 mm. **Subject:** Asia-Pacific Economic Cooperation summit, Vladivostok **Rev:** APEC logo in color

Date	Mintage	F	VF	XF	Unc	BU
2012 Proof	1,000	Value: 425				

Y# 1372 25 ROUBLES
169.0000 g., 0.9250 Silver 5.0258 oz. ASW, 60 mm. **Subject:** Architecture

Date	Mintage	F	VF	XF	Unc	BU
2012 Proof	1,500	Value: 400				

Y# 1373 25 ROUBLES
169.0000 g., 0.9250 Silver 5.0258 oz. ASW, 60 mm. **Subject:** Architecture

Date	Mintage	F	VF	XF	Unc	BU
2012 Proof	1,500	Value: 400				

Y# 679 50 ROUBLES
8.7500 g., 0.9990 Gold 0.2810 oz. AGW, 22.6 mm. **Subject:** Bolshoi Theater **Obv:** Double-headed eagle within beaded circle **Rev:** Dueling figures **Edge:** Reeded

Date	Mintage	F	VF	XF	Unc	BU
2001 Proof	2,000	Value: 550				

Y# 684 50 ROUBLES
8.7500 g., 0.9000 Gold 0.2532 oz. AGW, 22.6 mm. **Subject:** Siberian Exploration **Obv:** Double-headed eagle within beaded circle **Rev:** Head with hat 1/4 right and boat **Edge:** Reeded

Date	Mintage	F	VF	XF	Unc	BU
2001 Proof	1,500	Value: 600				

Y# 757 50 ROUBLES
8.6444 g., 0.9000 Gold 0.2501 oz. AGW, 22.6 mm. **Subject:** Olympics **Obv:** Double-headed eagle within beaded circle **Rev:** Figure skater and flying eagle **Edge:** Reeded

Date	Mintage	F	VF	XF	Unc	BU
2002 Proof	3,000	Value: 575				

Y# 782 50 ROUBLES
7.8900 g., 0.9990 Gold 0.2534 oz. AGW, 22.6 mm. **Subject:** Works of Dionissy **Obv:** Double-headed eagle within beaded circle **Rev:** Half-length figure holding child flanked by double headed eagle and church **Edge:** Reeded

Date	Mintage	F	VF	XF	Unc	BU
2002(m) Proof	1,500	Value: 600				

Y# 786 50 ROUBLES
8.7500 g., 0.9000 Gold 0.2532 oz. AGW, 22.6 mm. **Subject:** Admiral Nakhimov **Obv:** Double-headed eagle within beaded circle **Rev:** Bust facing within circle above flags and anchor **Edge:** Reeded

Date	Mintage	F	VF	XF	Unc	BU
2002(sp) Proof	1,500	Value: 600				

Y# 788 50 ROUBLES
8.7500 g., 0.9000 Gold 0.2532 oz. AGW, 22.6 mm. **Subject:** World Cup Soccer **Obv:** Double-headed eagle within beaded circle **Rev:** Stylized player kicking soccer ball **Edge:** Reeded

Date	Mintage	F	VF	XF	Unc	BU
2002(m) Proof	3,000	Value: 575				

Y# 822 50 ROUBLES
7.8900 g., 0.9990 Gold 0.2534 oz. AGW, 22.6 mm. **Subject:** Zodiac Signs **Obv:** Double-headed eagle within beaded circle **Rev:** Virgo **Edge:** Reeded

Date	Mintage	F	VF	XF	Unc	BU
2003(sp)	30,000	—	—	—	—	475

Y# 823 50 ROUBLES
7.8900 g., 0.9990 Gold 0.2534 oz. AGW, 22.6 mm. **Subject:** Zodiac signs **Obv:** Double-headed eagle within beaded circle **Rev:** Libra **Edge:** Reeded

Date	Mintage	F	VF	XF	Unc	BU
2003(m)	30,000	—	—	—	—	475

Y# 868 50 ROUBLES
8.6400 g., 0.9000 Gold 0.2500 oz. AGW, 23 mm. **Rev:** Peter I monetary reform

Date	Mintage	F	VF	XF	Unc	BU
2003(m) Proof	1,500	Value: 600				

Y# 869 50 ROUBLES
8.6400 g., 0.9000 Gold 0.2500 oz. AGW, 23 mm. **Rev:** Ski race

Date	Mintage	F	VF	XF	Unc	BU
2003(m) Proof	1,500	Value: 600				

Y# 1007 50 ROUBLES
169.0000 g., 0.9250 Silver 5.0258 oz. ASW, 60 mm. **Subject:** Leo

Date	Mintage	F	VF	XF	Unc	BU
2003 Proof	—	Value: 475				

Y# 1008 50 ROUBLES

169.0000 g., 0.9250 Silver 5.0258 oz. ASW, 60 mm. **Subject:** Leo

Date	Mintage	F	VF	XF	Unc	BU
2003 Proof	—	Value: 475				

Y# 1009 50 ROUBLES

7.7900 g., 0.9990 Gold 0.2502 oz. AGW, 22.6 mm. **Subject:** Scorpion

Date	Mintage	F	VF	XF	Unc	BU
2003 Proof	—	Value: 475				

Y# 1010 50 ROUBLES

7.7800 g., 0.9990 Gold 0.2499 oz. AGW, 22.6 mm. **Subject:** Sagatarius

Date	Mintage	F	VF	XF	Unc	BU
2003 Proof	—	Value: 475				

Y# 1011 50 ROUBLES

7.7800 g., 0.9990 Gold 0.2499 oz. AGW, 22.6 mm. **Subject:** Capricorn

Date	Mintage	F	VF	XF	Unc	BU
2003 Proof	—	Value: 475				

Y# 870 50 ROUBLES

8.6400 g., 0.9000 Gold 0.2500 oz. AGW, 23 mm. **Rev:** Soccer player

Date	Mintage	F	VF	XF	Unc	BU
2004(sp) Proof	1,000	Value: 650				

Y# 871 50 ROUBLES

8.6400 g., 0.9000 Gold 0.2500 oz. AGW, 23 mm. **Rev:** Olympic athletes

Date	Mintage	F	VF	XF	Unc	BU
2004(m) Proof	2,000	Value: 550				

Y# 872 50 ROUBLES

8.6400 g., 0.9000 Gold 0.2500 oz. AGW, 23 mm. **Rev:** Virgin of the Son Icon

Date	Mintage	F	VF	XF	Unc	BU
2004(m) Proof	1,500	Value: 575				

Y# 1016 50 ROUBLES

7.7800 g., 0.9990 Gold 0.2499 oz. AGW, 22.6 mm. **Subject:** Theophanes the Greek

Date	Mintage	F	VF	XF	Unc	BU
2004 Proof	—	Value: 575				

Y# 1025 50 ROUBLES

7.7800 g., 0.9990 Gold 0.2499 oz. AGW, 22.6 mm. **Subject:** Reindeer

Date	Mintage	F	VF	XF	Unc	BU
2004 Proof	—	Value: 475				

Y# 1030 50 ROUBLES

7.7800 g., 0.9990 Gold 0.2499 oz. AGW, 22.6 mm. **Subject:** Aquarius

Date	Mintage	F	VF	XF	Unc	BU
2004 Proof	—	Value: 475				

Y# 1031 50 ROUBLES

7.7800 g., 0.9990 Gold 0.2499 oz. AGW, 22.6 mm.

Date	Mintage	F	VF	XF	Unc	BU
2004 Proof	—	Value: 475				

Y# 1032 50 ROUBLES

7.7800 g., 0.9990 Gold 0.2499 oz. AGW, 22.6 mm. **Subject:** Aries

Date	Mintage	F	VF	XF	Unc	BU
2004 Proof	—	Value: 475				

Y# 1033 50 ROUBLES

7.7800 g., 0.9990 Gold 0.2499 oz. AGW, 22.6 mm. **Subject:** Taurus

Date	Mintage	F	VF	XF	Unc	BU
2004 Proof	—	Value: 475				

Y# 1034 50 ROUBLES

7.7800 g., 0.9990 Gold 0.2499 oz. AGW, 22.6 mm. **Subject:** Gemni

Date	Mintage	F	VF	XF	Unc	BU
2004 Proof	—	Value: 475				

Y# 1035 50 ROUBLES

7.7800 g., 0.9990 Gold 0.2499 oz. AGW, 22.6 mm. **Subject:** Cancer

Date	Mintage	F	VF	XF	Unc	BU
2004 Proof	—	Value: 475				

Y# 894 50 ROUBLES

7.8900 g., 0.9990 Gold 0.2534 oz. AGW, 22.6 mm. **Subject:** 60th Anniversary - Victory Over Germany **Obv:** Double-headed eagle **Rev:** 60th Anniversary - Victory Over Germany medal **Edge:** Reeded

Date	Mintage	F	VF	XF	Unc	BU
2005 Proof	7,000	Value: 500				

Y# 907 50 ROUBLES

7.8900 g., 0.9990 Gold 0.2534 oz. AGW, 22.6 mm. **Subject:** Helsinki Games **Obv:** Double-headed eagle **Rev:** Stylized track and field athletes **Edge:** Reeded

Date	Mintage	F	VF	XF	Unc	BU
2005 Proof	1,500	Value: 575				

Y# 911 50 ROUBLES

7.8900 g., 0.9990 Gold 0.2534 oz. AGW, 22.6 mm. **Obv:** Double-headed eagle **Rev:** Kazan University Building **Edge:** Reeded

Date	Mintage	F	VF	XF	Unc	BU
2005 Proof	1,500	Value: 475				

Y# 1049 50 ROUBLES

7.7800 g., 0.9990 Gold 0.2499 oz. AGW, 22.6 mm. **Rev:** St. George the Victorious

Date	Mintage	F	VF	XF	Unc	BU
2006	150,000	—	—	—	—	475
2007	500,000	—	—	—	—	475
2008	630,000	—	—	—	—	475
2009	1,500,000	—	—	—	—	475
2010	640,000	—	—	—	—	475
2012	500,000	—	—	—	—	475
2012 Proof	10,000	Value: 500				

Y# 1063 50 ROUBLES

7.7800 g., 0.9990 Gold 0.2499 oz. AGW, 22.6 mm. **Subject:** Moscow's Kremlin and Red Square

Date	Mintage	F	VF	XF	Unc	BU
2006 Proof	—	Value: 600				

Y# 1067 50 ROUBLES

7.7800 g., 0.9990 Gold 0.2499 oz. AGW, 22.6 mm. **Subject:** XX Winter Olympics, Torino

Date	Mintage	F	VF	XF	Unc	BU
2006 Proof	—	Value: 550				

Y# 1068 50 ROUBLES

7.7800 g., 0.9990 Gold 0.2499 oz. AGW, 22.6 mm. **Subject:** FIFA World Cup, Germany

Date	Mintage	F	VF	XF	Unc	BU
2006 Proof	—	Value: 550				

Y# 1090 50 ROUBLES

7.7800 g., 0.9990 Gold 0.2499 oz. AGW, 22.6 mm. **Subject:** Andrew Rublyov

Date	Mintage	F	VF	XF	Unc	BU
2007 Proof	—	Value: 550				

Y# 1094 50 ROUBLES

7.7800 g., 0.9250 Gold 0.2314 oz. AGW, 22.6 mm. **Subject:** Bashkiria, 450th Anniversary of of annexation by Russia

Date	Mintage	F	VF	XF	Unc	BU
2007 Proof	—	Value: 550				

Y# 1097 50 ROUBLES

7.7800 g., 0.9990 Gold 0.2499 oz. AGW, 22.6 mm. **Subject:** Khakassia, 300th Anniversary of of annexation by Russia

Date	Mintage	F	VF	XF	Unc	BU
2007 Proof	—	Value: 550				

Y# 1121 50 ROUBLES

7.7800 g., 0.9990 Gold 0.2499 oz. AGW, 22.6 mm. **Subject:** Udmurtiya, 450th Anniversary of annexation into Russia

Date	Mintage	F	VF	XF	Unc	BU
2008 Proof	—	Value: 550				

Y# 1141 50 ROUBLES

7.7800 g., 0.9990 Gold 0.2499 oz. AGW, 22.6 mm. **Subject:** European Beaver

Date	Mintage	F	VF	XF	Unc	BU
2008 Proof	—	Value: 750				

Y# 1153 50 ROUBLES

7.7800 g., 0.9990 Gold 0.2499 oz. AGW, 22.6 mm. **Subject:** 29th Summer Olympics, Bejing

Date	Mintage	F	VF	XF	Unc	BU
2008 Proof	—	Value: 550				

Y# 1168 50 ROUBLES

7.7800 g., 0.9990 Gold 0.2499 oz. AGW, 22.6 mm. **Subject:** A. P. Chekhov, 150th Anniversary of Birth

Date	Mintage	F	VF	XF	Unc	BU
2009 Proof	—	Value: 550				

Y# 1172 50 ROUBLES

7.7800 g., 0.9990 Gold 0.2499 oz. AGW, 22.6 mm. **Subject:** Kalmyk Peoples, 400th Anniversary of annexation into Russia

Date	Mintage	F	VF	XF	Unc	BU
2009 Proof	—	Value: 550				

Y# 1175 50 ROUBLES

7.7800 g., 0.9990 Gold 0.2499 oz. AGW, 22.6 mm. **Subject:** N. V. Gogol, 200th Anniversary of Birth

Date	Mintage	F	VF	XF	Unc	BU
2009 Proof	—	Value: 550				

Y# 1202 50 ROUBLES

7.7800 g., 0.9990 Gold 0.2499 oz. AGW, 22.6 mm. **Subject:** Velikly Novgorod

Date	Mintage	F	VF	XF	Unc	BU
2009 Proof	—	Value: 550				

Y# 1230 50 ROUBLES

7.7800 g., 0.9990 Gold 0.2499 oz. AGW, 22.6 mm. **Subject:** Bank of Russia, 150th Anniversary

Date	Mintage	F	VF	XF	Unc	BU
2010 Proof	—	Value: 600				

Y# 1235 50 ROUBLES

7.7800 g., 0.9990 Gold 0.2499 oz. AGW, 22.6 mm. **Subject:** UNESCO Heritage Site - Yaroslav

Date	Mintage	F	VF	XF	Unc	BU
2010 Proof	—	Value: 550				

Y# 1239 50 ROUBLES

7.7800 g., 0.9990 Gold 0.2499 oz. AGW, 22.6 mm. **Subject:** A. P. Chekhov, 200th Anniversary of birth

Date	Mintage	F	VF	XF	Unc	BU
2010 Proof	—	Value: 600				

Y# 1286 50 ROUBLES

7.7800 g., 0.9990 Gold 0.2499 oz. AGW, 22.6 mm. **Rev:** Griffin with sword and shield above garland **Edge:** Reeded

Date	Mintage	F	VF	XF	Unc	BU
2011 Proof	750	Value: 600				

Y# 1291 50 ROUBLES

7.7800 g., 0.9990 Gold 0.2499 oz. AGW, 22.6 mm. **Rev:** Emblem of the Republic of Buryatia

Date	Mintage	F	VF	XF	Unc	BU
2011 Proof	1,000	Value: 650				

Y# 1300 50 ROUBLES
7.7800 g., 0.9990 Gold 0.2499 oz. AGW, 22.6 mm. **Subject:** 2014 Winter Olympics - Sochi **Rev:** Four-man Bobsled **Edge:** Reeded

Date	Mintage	F	VF	XF	Unc	BU
2014 (2011) Proof	20,000	Value: 500				

Y# 1301 50 ROUBLES
7.7800 g., 0.9990 Gold 0.2499 oz. AGW, 22.6 mm. **Subject:** 2014 Winter Olympics - Sochi - Curling **Rev:** Skip and sweeper with stones in play

Date	Mintage	F	VF	XF	Unc	BU
2014 (2011) Proof	20,000	Value: 500				

Y# 1341 50 ROUBLES
7.7800 g., 0.9990 Gold 0.2499 oz. AGW, 22.6 mm. **Subject:** Millennium of the Unity of the Mordovian people within the Peoples of the Russian State

Date	Mintage	F	VF	XF	Unc	BU
2012 Proof	100	Value: 750				

Y# 1349 50 ROUBLES
7.7800 g., 0.9990 Gold 0.2499 oz. AGW, 22.6 mm. **Subject:** Russia's victory in the War of 1812 **Rev:** Bust left

Date	Mintage	F	VF	XF	Unc	BU
2012 Proof	1,000	Value: 650				

Y# 1365 50 ROUBLES
7.7800 g., 0.9990 Gold 0.2499 oz. AGW, 22.6 mm. **Subject:** European Judo Championship, Chelyabinsk

Date	Mintage	F	VF	XF	Unc	BU
2012 Proof	750	Value: 675				

Y# 1369 50 ROUBLES
7.7800 g., 0.9990 Gold 0.2499 oz. AGW, 22.6 mm. **Subject:** Origin of Russian Statehood, 1150th Anniversary

Date	Mintage	F	VF	XF	Unc	BU
2012 Proof	1,500	Value: 575				

Y# 1376 50 ROUBLES
7.7800 g., 0.9990 Gold 0.2499 oz. AGW, 22.6 mm. **Subject:** Court of Arbitration

Date	Mintage	F	VF	XF	Unc	BU
2012 Proof	750	Value: 675				

Y# 795 100 ROUBLES
1111.1200 g., 0.9000 Silver 32.149 oz. ASW, 100 mm. **Subject:** The Bark Sedov **Obv:** Double-headed eagle **Rev:** Ship flanked by compass and cameo **Edge:** Reeded **Note:** Illustration reduced.

Date	Mintage	F	VF	XF	Unc	BU
2001(m) Proof	500	Value: 2,200				

Y# 681 100 ROUBLES
1111.1000 g., 0.9000 Silver 32.149 oz. ASW, 100 mm. **Subject:** 40th Anniversary of Manned Space Flight - Yuri Gagarin **Obv:** Double-headed eagle **Rev:** Astronaut and rocket in space **Edge:** Reeded **Note:** Illustration reduced.

Date	Mintage	F	VF	XF	Unc	BU
2001 Proof	750	Value: 2,000				

Y# 689 100 ROUBLES
1111.1000 g., 0.9000 Silver 32.149 oz. ASW, 100 mm. **Subject:** Bolshoi Theater 225 Years **Obv:** Double-headed eagle **Rev:** Casino gambling scene **Edge:** Reeded **Note:** Illustration reduced.

Date	Mintage	F	VF	XF	Unc	BU
2001 Proof	500	Value: 2,150				

Y# 685 100 ROUBLES
17.4500 g., 0.9000 Gold 0.5049 oz. AGW, 30 mm. **Subject:** Siberian Exploration **Obv:** Double-headed eagle within beaded circle **Rev:** Head and silhouette left, sailboat and other designs **Edge:** Reeded

Date	Mintage	F	VF	XF	Unc	BU
2001 Proof	1,000	Value: 1,150				

Y# 688 100 ROUBLES
15.7200 g., 0.9990 Gold 0.5049 oz. AGW, 30 mm. **Subject:** Bolshoi Theater 225 Years **Obv:** Double-headed eagle within beaded circle **Rev:** Three dancers with swords **Edge:** Reeded

Date	Mintage	F	VF	XF	Unc	BU
2001 Proof	1,500	Value: 1,100				

Y# 783 100 ROUBLES
1111.1200 g., 0.9000 Silver 32.149 oz. ASW, 100 mm. **Subject:** Works of Dionissy **Obv:** Double-headed eagle **Rev:** St. Ferapont Monastery in the center of a fresco covered cross **Edge:** Reeded **Note:** Illustration reduced.

Date	Mintage	F	VF	XF	Unc	BU
2002(sp) Prooflike	500	—	—	—	—	2,000

Y# 789 100 ROUBLES
1111.1200 g., 0.9000 Silver 32.149 oz. ASW, 100 mm. **Subject:** World Cup Soccer **Obv:** Double-headed eagle **Rev:** Soccer ball design with map and players **Edge:** Reeded **Note:** Illustration reduced.

Date	Mintage	F	VF	XF	Unc	BU
2002(sp) Proof	500	Value: 2,200				

Y# 791 100 ROUBLES
1111.1200 g., 0.9000 Silver 32.149 oz. ASW, 100 mm. **Subject:** Hermitage **Obv:** Double-headed eagle **Rev:** Statues and arches **Edge:** Reeded **Note:** Illustration reduced.

Date	Mintage	F	VF	XF	Unc	BU
2002(sp) Proof	1,000	Value: 1,800				

Y# 792 100 ROUBLES
17.4500 g., 0.9000 Gold 0.5049 oz. AGW, 30 mm. **Subject:** Hermitage **Obv:** Double-headed eagle within beaded circle **Rev:** Ancient battle scene sculpted on comb **Edge:** Reeded

Date	Mintage	F	VF	XF	Unc	BU
2002(sp) Proof	1,000	Value: 1,150				

Y# 873 100 ROUBLES
1111.1200 g., 0.9000 Silver 32.149 oz. ASW, 100 mm. **Rev:** St. Petersburg

Date	Mintage	F	VF	XF	Unc	BU
2003(m) Proof	1,000	Value: 2,000				

Y# 874 100 ROUBLES
17.4500 g., 0.9000 Gold 0.5049 oz. AGW, 30 mm. **Rev:** Petrozavodsk

Date	Mintage	F	VF	XF	Unc	BU
2003(m) Proof	1,000	Value: 1,150				

Y# 875 100 ROUBLES
17.4500 g., 0.9000 Gold 0.5049 oz. AGW, 30 mm. **Rev:** Kamchatka

Date	Mintage	F	VF	XF	Unc	BU
2003(sp) Proof	1,500	Value: 1,100				

Y# 832 100 ROUBLES
17.2800 g., 0.9000 Gold 0.5000 oz. AGW, 30 mm. **Subject:** 2nd Kamchatka Expedition **Obv:** Double-headed eagle **Rev:** Shaman and two seated men **Edge:** Reeded

Date	Mintage	F	VF	XF	Unc	BU
2004(sp) Proof	1,500	Value: 1,100				

Y# 831 100 ROUBLES
1000.0000 g., 0.9000 Silver 28.934 oz. ASW, 100 mm. **Obv:** Double-headed eagle **Rev:** Panel of icons painted by Theophanes the Greek **Edge:** Reeded **Note:** Illustration reduced.

Date	Mintage	F	VF	XF	Unc	BU
2004(sp) Proof	500	Value: 2,100				

Y# 876 100 ROUBLES
1111.1200 g., 0.9000 Silver 32.149 oz. ASW, 100 mm. **Rev:** Annunciation Cathedral Iconostasis

Date	Mintage	F	VF	XF	Unc	BU
2004(sp) Proof	500	Value: 2,200				

Y# 1024 100 ROUBLES
1000.0000 g., 0.9250 Silver 29.738 oz. ASW, 100 mm. **Subject:** Reindeer

Date	Mintage	F	VF	XF	Unc	BU
2004 Proof	—	Value: 1,850				

Y# 1026 100 ROUBLES
1000.0000 g., 0.9990 Silver 32.117 oz. ASW, 100 mm. **Subject:** Reindeer

Date	Mintage	F	VF	XF	Unc	BU
2004 Proof	—	Value: 2,000				

Y# 1036 100 ROUBLES
1046.0000 g., 0.9250 Silver 31.106 oz. ASW, 100 mm. **Subject:** Rostov

Date	Mintage	F	VF	XF	Unc	BU
2004 Proof	—	Value: 1,850				

Y# 895 100 ROUBLES
1083.7400 g., 0.9250 Silver 32.228 oz. ASW, 100 mm. **Subject:** 60th Anniversary Victory Over Germany **Obv:** Double-headed eagle **Rev:** Decorated locomotive returning soldiers circa 1945 **Edge:** Reeded **Note:** Illustration reduced.

Date	Mintage	F	VF	XF	Unc	BU
2005 Proof	2,000	Value: 1,850				

Y# 912 100 ROUBLES
1083.7400 g., 0.9250 Silver 32.228 oz. ASW, 100 mm. **Obv:** Double-headed eagle **Rev:** Kazan city view with mausoleums **Edge:** Reeded **Note:** Illustration reduced.

Date	Mintage	F	VF	XF	Unc	BU
2005 Proof	500	Value: 2,000				

Y# 925 100 ROUBLES
1083.7400 g., 0.9250 Silver 32.228 oz. ASW, 100 mm. **Subject:** 625th Anniversary - Battle of Kulikovo **Obv:** Double-headed eagle **Rev:** Battle of Kulikovo beginning scene **Edge:** Reeded **Note:** Illustration reduced.

Date	Mintage	F	VF	XF	Unc	BU
2005 Proof	500	Value: 2,000				

Y# 1078 100 ROUBLES
1046.0000 g., 0.9250 Silver 31.106 oz. ASW, 100 mm. **Subject:** Yuryev Polsky

Date	Mintage	F	VF	XF	Unc	BU
2006	—	Value: 1,850				

Y# 1044 100 ROUBLES
1046.0000 g., 0.9250 Silver 31.106 oz. ASW, 100 mm. **Subject:** Frigate Myr

Date	Mintage	F	VF	XF	Unc	BU
2006 Proof	—	Value: 1,750				

Y# 1061 100 ROUBLES
1046.0000 g., 0.9250 Silver 31.106 oz. ASW, 100 mm. **Subject:** Moscow's Kremlin and Red Square

Date	Mintage	F	VF	XF	Unc	BU
2006 Proof	—	Value: 1,750				

Y# 1077 100 ROUBLES
1046.0000 g., 0.9250 Silver 31.106 oz. ASW, 100 mm. **Subject:** Bogolyubovo Township

Date	Mintage	F	VF	XF	Unc	BU
2006 Proof	—	Value: 1,850				

Y# 1081 100 ROUBLES
1046.0000 g., 0.9250 Silver 31.106 oz. ASW, 100 mm. **Subject:** International Artic Year

Date	Mintage	F	VF	XF	Unc	BU
2007 Proof	—	Value: 1,850				

Y# 1085 100 ROUBLES
1046.0000 g., 0.9250 Silver 31.106 oz. ASW, 100 mm. **Subject:** Russian railways, 175th Anniversary

Date	Mintage	F	VF	XF	Unc	BU
2007 Proof	—	Value: 1,850				

Y# 1089 100 ROUBLES
1046.0000 g., 0.9250 Silver 31.106 oz. ASW, 100 mm. **Subject:** Andrew Rublyov

Date	Mintage	F	VF	XF	Unc	BU
2007 Proof	—	Value: 1,850				

Y# 1093 100 ROUBLES
169.0000 g., 0.9250 Silver 5.0258 oz. ASW, 60 mm. **Subject:** Bashkiria, 450th Anniversary of Annexation by Russia

Date	Mintage	F	VF	XF	Unc	BU
2007 Proof	—	Value: 400				

Y# 1096 100 ROUBLES
1046.0000 g., 0.9250 Silver 31.106 oz. ASW, 100 mm. **Subject:** Khakassia, 300th Anniversary of Annexation by Russia

Date	Mintage	F	VF	XF	Unc	BU
2007 Proof	—	Value: 1,850				

Y# 1120 100 ROUBLES
1046.0000 g., 0.9250 Silver 31.106 oz. ASW, 100 mm. **Subject:** Udmurtiya, 450th Anniversary of Annexation into Russia

Date	Mintage	F	VF	XF	Unc	BU
2008 Proof	—	Value: 1,850				

Y# 1140 100 ROUBLES
1046.0000 g., 0.9250 Silver 31.106 oz. ASW, 100 mm. **Subject:** European Beaver

Date	Mintage	F	VF	XF	Unc	BU
2008 Proof	—	Value: 1,850				

Y# 1142 100 ROUBLES
15.5600 g., 0.9990 Gold 0.4997 oz. AGW **Subject:** European Beaver

Date	Mintage	F	VF	XF	Unc	BU
2008 Proof	—	Value: 1,100				

Y# 1143 100 ROUBLES
1046.0000 g., 0.9250 Silver 31.106 oz. ASW, 100 mm. **Subject:** European Beaver

Date	Mintage	F	VF	XF	Unc	BU
2008 Proof	—	Value: 1,750				

Y# 1156 100 ROUBLES
1046.0000 g., 0.9250 Silver 31.106 oz. ASW, 100 mm. **Subject:** Pereslaval Zalessky

Date	Mintage	F	VF	XF	Unc	BU
2008 Proof	—	Value: 1,850				

Y# 1157 100 ROUBLES
1046.0000 g., 0.9990 Silver 33.594 oz. ASW, 100 mm. **Subject:** Alexandrov

Date	Mintage	F	VF	XF	Unc	BU
2008 Proof	—	Value: 2,000				

Y# 1148 100 ROUBLES
1046.0000 g., 0.9250 Silver 31.106 oz. ASW, 100 mm. **Subject:** Kamchatka Volcano

Date	Mintage	F	VF	XF	Unc	BU
2008 Proof	—	Value: 1,850				

Y# 1162 100 ROUBLES
168.0000 g., 0.9250 Silver 4.9960 oz. ASW, 60 mm. **Subject:** Russian Currency

Date	Mintage	F	VF	XF	Unc	BU
2009 Proof	—	Value: 400				

Y# 1163 100 ROUBLES
168.0000 g., 0.9250 Silver 4.9960 oz. ASW, 60 mm. **Subject:** Russian Currency

Date	Mintage	F	VF	XF	Unc	BU
2009 Proof	—	Value: 400				

Y# 1167 100 ROUBLES
168.0000 g., 0.9250 Silver 4.9960 oz. ASW, 60 mm. **Subject:** A. P. Chekhov, 150th Anniversary of Birth

Date	Mintage	F	VF	XF	Unc	BU
2009 Proof	—	Value: 400				

Y# 1171 100 ROUBLES
1046.0000 g., 0.9990 Silver 33.594 oz. ASW, 100 mm. **Subject:** Kalmyk Peoples, 400th Anniversary of annexation into Russia

Date	Mintage	F	VF	XF	Unc	BU
2009 Proof	—	Value: 2,000				

Y# 1174 100 ROUBLES
33.9000 g., 0.9250 Silver 1.0081 oz. ASW, 39 mm. **Subject:** N. V. Gogol, 200th Anniversary of Birth

Date	Mintage	F	VF	XF	Unc	BU
2009 Proof	—	Value: 60.00				

Y# 1179 100 ROUBLES
1048.0000 g., 0.9250 Silver 31.165 oz. ASW, 100 mm. **Subject:** Poltava Battle, 300th Anniversary

Date	Mintage	F	VF	XF	Unc	BU
2009 Proof	—	Value: 1,850				

Y# 1238 100 ROUBLES
1046.0000 g., 0.9250 Silver 31.106 oz. ASW, 100 mm. **Subject:** A. P. Chekhov, 200th Anniversary of Birth

Date	Mintage	F	VF	XF	Unc	BU
2010 Prooflike	—	—	—	—	—	1,850

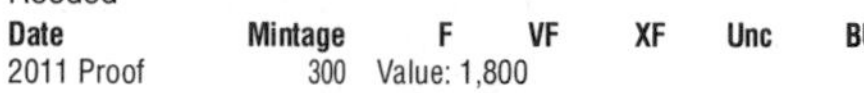

Y# 1290 100 ROUBLES
1000.0000 g., 0.9250 Silver 29.738 oz. ASW, 100 mm. **Rev:** Man playing stringed instrument, others in backbround **Edge:** Reeded

Date	Mintage	F	VF	XF	Unc	BU
2011 Proof	300	Value: 1,800				

Y# 1299 100 ROUBLES
1000.0000 g., 0.9250 Silver 29.738 oz. ASW, 100 mm. **Subject:** 2014 Winter Olympics - Sochi **Rev:** Montage of Russian winter sports

Date	Mintage	F	VF	XF	Unc	BU
2014 (2011) Proof	1,200	Value: 1,700				

Y# 1324 100 ROUBLES
15.5500 g., 0.9990 Gold 0.4994 oz. AGW, 30 mm. **Rev:** St. George the Victorious

Date	Mintage	F	VF	XF	Unc	BU
2012 Proof	10,000	Value: 1,000				

Y# 1340 100 ROUBLES
1111.1200 g., 0.9250 Silver 33.042 oz. ASW, 100 mm. **Subject:** Millennium of the Unity of the Mordovian people within the Peoples of the Russian State

Date	Mintage	F	VF	XF	Unc	BU
2012 Proof	300	Value: 2,000				

Y# 1344 100 ROUBLES
1111.1200 g., 0.9250 Silver 33.042 oz. ASW, 100 mm. **Subject:** People's Volunteer Corps, 400th Anniversary

Date	Mintage	F	VF	XF	Unc	BU
2012 Proof	500	Value: 2,000				

Y# 1368 100 ROUBLES
1111.1200 g., 0.9250 Silver 33.042 oz. ASW, 60 mm. **Subject:** Origin of the Russian Statehood, 1150th Anniversary

Date	Mintage	F	VF	XF	Unc	BU
2012 Prooflike	300	—	—	—	—	2,000

Y# 877 200 ROUBLES
3342.3899 g., 0.9000 Silver 96.710 oz. ASW, 130 mm. **Rev:** Peter I monetary reform

Date	Mintage	F	VF	XF	Unc	BU
2003(sp) Proof	300	Value: 5,250				

Y# 1027 200 ROUBLES
31.1050 g., 0.9990 Gold 0.9990 oz. AGW **Subject:** Reindeer

Date	Mintage	F	VF	XF	Unc	BU
2004 Proof	500	Value: 3,250				

Y# 1042 200 ROUBLES
31.1000 g., 0.9990 Gold 0.9988 oz. AGW **Subject:** Parliament, 100th Anniversary

Date	Mintage	F	VF	XF	Unc	BU
2006 Proof	750	Value: 2,000				

Y# 1062 200 ROUBLES
3138.0000 g., 0.9250 Silver 93.318 oz. ASW, 100 mm. **Subject:** Moscow's Kremlin and Red Square

Date	Mintage	F	VF	XF	Unc	BU
2006 Proof	200	Value: 6,500				

Y# 1144 200 ROUBLES
31.1050 g., 0.9990 Gold 0.9990 oz. AGW **Subject:** European Beaver

Date	Mintage	F	VF	XF	Unc	BU
2008 Proof	500	Value: 3,250				

Y# 1169 200 ROUBLES
31.1050 g., 0.9990 Gold 0.9990 oz. AGW **Subject:** A. P. Chekhov, 150th Anniversary of Birth

Date	Mintage	F	VF	XF	Unc	BU
2009 Proof	500	Value: 2,000				

Y# 1176 200 ROUBLES
3120.0000 g., 0.9250 Silver 92.783 oz. ASW, 100 mm. **Subject:** N. V. Gogol, 200th Anniversary of Birth

Date	Mintage	F	VF	XF	Unc	BU
2009 Proof	—	Value: 6,500				

Y# 1201 200 ROUBLES
31.1050 g., 0.9990 Gold 0.9990 oz. AGW **Subject:** Veliklу Novgorod

Date	Mintage	F	VF	XF	Unc	BU
2009 Proof	200	Value: 7,500				

Y# 1209 200 ROUBLES
31.1050 g., 0.9990 Gold 0.9990 oz. AGW **Series:** Speed Skating

Date	Mintage	F	VF	XF	Unc	BU
2009 Proof	500	Value: 2,000				

Y# 1210 200 ROUBLES
31.1000 g., 0.9990 Gold 0.9988 oz. AGW **Subject:** Ski Jumping

Date	Mintage	F	VF	XF	Unc	BU
2009 Proof	500	Value: 2,000				

Y# 1211 200 ROUBLES
31.1000 g., 0.9990 Gold 0.9988 oz. AGW **Subject:** Luge

Date	Mintage	F	VF	XF	Unc	BU
2009 Proof	500	Value: 2,000				

Y# 1213 200 ROUBLES
31.1050 g., 0.9990 Gold 0.9990 oz. AGW **Subject:** Figure Skating

Date	Mintage	F	VF	XF	Unc	BU
2009 Proof	500	Value: 2,000				

Y# 1212 200 ROUBLES
31.1050 g., 0.9990 Gold 0.9990 oz. AGW **Subject:** Biathlon

Date	Mintage	F	VF	XF	Unc	BU
2009 Proof	500	Value: 2,000				

Y# 1234 200 ROUBLES
3130.0000 g., 0.9250 Silver 93.080 oz. ASW **Subject:** UNESCO Heritage Site - Yaroslav

Date	Mintage	F	VF	XF	Unc	BU
2010 Proof	200	Value: 6,000				

Y# 1240 200 ROUBLES
31.1000 g., 0.9990 Gold 0.9988 oz. AGW **Subject:** A. P. Chekhov, 200th Anniversary of Birth

Date	Mintage	F	VF	XF	Unc	BU
2010 Proof	500	Value: 2,000				

Y# 1255 200 ROUBLES

31.1000 g., 0.9990 Gold 0.9988 oz. AGW **Subject:** Hockey

Date	Mintage	F	VF	XF	Unc	BU
2010 Proof	—	Value: 2,000				

Y# 1256 200 ROUBLES

31.1000 g., 0.9990 Gold 0.9988 oz. AGW **Subject:** Ski Race

Date	Mintage	F	VF	XF	Unc	BU
2010 Proof	500	Value: 2,000				

Y# 1257 200 ROUBLES

31.1000 g., 0.9990 Gold 0.9988 oz. AGW **Subject:** Nordic Combined

Date	Mintage	F	VF	XF	Unc	BU
2010 Proof	500	Value: 2,000				

Y# 1258 200 ROUBLES

31.1000 g., 0.9990 Gold 0.9988 oz. AGW **Subject:** Freestyle Skiing

Date	Mintage	F	VF	XF	Unc	BU
2010 Proof	500	Value: 2,000				

Y# 1259 200 ROUBLES

31.1000 g., 0.9990 Gold 0.9988 oz. AGW **Subject:** Short Track Speed Skating

Date	Mintage	F	VF	XF	Unc	BU
2010 Proof	500	Value: 2,000				

Y# 1260 200 ROUBLES

31.1000 g., 0.9990 Gold 0.9988 oz. AGW **Subject:** Curling

Date	Mintage	F	VF	XF	Unc	BU
2010 Proof	500	Value: 2,000				

Y# 1261 200 ROUBLES

31.1000 g., 0.9990 Gold 0.9988 oz. AGW **Subject:** Snowboarding

Date	Mintage	F	VF	XF	Unc	BU
2010 Proof	500	Value: 2,000				

Y# 1262 200 ROUBLES

31.1000 g., 0.9990 Gold 0.9988 oz. AGW **Subject:** Skeleton

Date	Mintage	F	VF	XF	Unc	BU
2010 Proof	500	Value: 2,000				

Y# 1263 200 ROUBLES

31.1000 g., 0.9990 Gold 0.9988 oz. AGW **Subject:** Bobsled

Date	Mintage	F	VF	XF	Unc	BU
2010 Proof	500	Value: 2,000				

Y# 1264 200 ROUBLES

31.1000 g., 0.9990 Gold 0.9988 oz. AGW **Subject:** Mountain Skiing

Date	Mintage	F	VF	XF	Unc	BU
2010 Proof	500	Value: 2,000				

Y# 1348 500 ROUBLES

5555.6001 g., 0.9250 Silver 165.21 oz. ASW **Subject:** Russia's victory in the War of 1812

Date	Mintage	F	VF	XF	Unc	BU
2012 Proof	50	Value: 6,000				

Y# 796 1000 ROUBLES

156.4000 g., 0.9990 Gold 5.0231 oz. AGW, 50 mm. **Subject:** The Bark Sedov **Obv:** Double-headed eagle **Rev:** Four-masted sailing ship **Edge:** Reeded

Date	Mintage	F	VF	XF	Unc	BU
2001(m) Proof	250	Value: 10,000				

Y# 878 1000 ROUBLES

156.4000 g., 0.9990 Gold 5.0231 oz. AGW, 50 mm. **Rev:** Cronstadt

Date	Mintage	F	VF	XF	Unc	BU
2003(m) Proof	250	Value: 10,000				

Y# 1037 1000 ROUBLES

1046.0000 g., 0.9250 Silver 31.106 oz. ASW, 100 mm. **Subject:** Uglich

Date	Mintage	F	VF	XF	Unc	BU
2004 Proof	—	Value: 1,750				

Y# 1045 1000 ROUBLES

1000.0000 g., 0.9990 Gold 32.117 oz. AGW, 100 mm. **Subject:** Frigate Myr

Date	Mintage	F	VF	XF	Unc	BU
2006 Proof	—	Value: 60,000				

Y# 1082 1000 ROUBLES

156.0000 g., 0.9990 Gold 5.0103 oz. AGW, 100 mm. **Subject:** International Artic Year

Date	Mintage	F	VF	XF	Unc	BU
2007 Proof	—	Value: 10,000				

Y# 1164 1000 ROUBLES

156.0000 g., 0.9990 Gold 5.0103 oz. AGW, 100 mm. **Subject:** Russian Currency

Date	Mintage	F	VF	XF	Unc	BU
2009 Proof	—	Value: 10,000				

Y# 1227 1000 ROUBLES

155.5000 g., 0.9990 Gold 4.9942 oz. AGW, 100 mm. **Subject:** Warship - Goto Predestination

Date	Mintage	F	VF	XF	Unc	BU
2010 Proof	—	Value: 10,000				

Y# 1281 1000 ROUBLES

155.5000 g., 0.9990 Gold 4.9942 oz. AGW, 50 mm. **Subject:** Beginning of Great Reforms - Abolition of Serfdom **Rev:** Man plowing, quill pen and signature on document

Date	Mintage	F	VF	XF	Unc	BU
2011ММД Proof	250	Value: 10,000				

Y# 1288 1000 ROUBLES

155.5000 g., 0.9990 Gold 4.9942 oz. AGW, 50 mm. **Rev:** U.A. Gagarin in spacesuit waving

Date	Mintage	F	VF	XF	Unc	BU
2011 Proof	500	Value: 10,000				

Y# 1297 1000 ROUBLES
155.5000 g., 0.9990 Gold 4.9942 oz. AGW, 50 mm. **Subject:** 2014 Winter Olympics - Sochi - Flora of Sochi **Rev:** Goddess Flora who's hair has plants of the Sochi region, female figure skater to right

Date	Mintage	F	VF	XF	Unc	BU
2014 (2011) Proof	600	Value: 10,000				

Y# 1418 1000 ROUBLES
155.5000 g., 0.9990 Gold 4.9942 oz. AGW, 100 mm. **Subject:** Battleship Ingermanland

Date	Mintage	F	VF	XF	Unc	BU
2012 Proof	500	Value: 10,000				

Y# 784 10000 ROUBLES
1001.1000 g., 0.9990 Gold 32.152 oz. AGW, 100 mm. **Subject:** Works of Dionissy **Obv:** Double-headed eagle **Rev:** Interior view of the carved portal of the Virgin of the Nativity Church **Edge:** Reeded **Note:** Illustration reduced.

Date	Mintage	F	VF	XF	Unc	BU
2002(sp) Proof	100	Value: 60,000				

Y# 879 10000 ROUBLES
1001.1000 g., 0.9990 Gold 32.152 oz. AGW, 100 mm. **Rev:** St. Petersburg area map

Date	Mintage	F	VF	XF	Unc	BU
2003 Proof	200	Value: 57,500				

Y# 1017 10000 ROUBLES
1000.0000 g., 0.9990 Gold 32.117 oz. AGW, 100 mm. **Subject:** Theophanes the Greek

Date	Mintage	F	VF	XF	Unc	BU
2004 Proof	—	Value: 60,000				

Y# 880 10000 ROUBLES
1001.1000 g., 0.9990 Gold 32.152 oz. AGW, 100 mm. **Rev:** Church of the Transfiguration of the Savior, Novgorod

Date	Mintage	F	VF	XF	Unc	BU
2004 Proof	100	Value: 60,000				

Y# 1028 10000 ROUBLES
1000.0000 g., 0.9990 Gold 32.117 oz. AGW, 100 mm. **Subject:** Reindeer

Date	Mintage	F	VF	XF	Unc	BU
2004 Proof	100	Value: 60,000				

Y# 896 10000 ROUBLES
1001.1000 g., 0.9990 Gold 32.152 oz. AGW, 100 mm. **Subject:** 60th Anniversary - Victory Over Germany **Obv:** Double-headed eagle **Rev:** Soldiers dishonoring captured Nazi flags and standards **Edge:** Reeded **Note:** Illustration reduced.

Date	Mintage	F	VF	XF	Unc	BU
2005 Proof	250	Value: 57,500				

Y# 913 10000 ROUBLES
1001.1000 g., 0.9990 Gold 32.152 oz. AGW, 100 mm. **Obv:** Two headed eagle **Rev:** Kazan Kremlin view **Edge:** Reeded **Note:** Illustration reduced.

Date	Mintage	F	VF	XF	Unc	BU
2005 Proof	150	Value: 58,000				

Y# 1043 10000 ROUBLES
1000.0000 g., 0.9990 Gold 32.117 oz. AGW, 100 mm. **Subject:** Parliament, 100th Anniversary

Date	Mintage	F	VF	XF	Unc	BU
2006 Proof	100	Value: 60,000				

Y# 1064 10000 ROUBLES
1000.0000 g., 0.9990 Gold 32.117 oz. AGW, 100 mm. **Subject:** Moscow's Kremlin and Red Square

Date	Mintage	F	VF	XF	Unc	BU
2006 Proof	—	Value: 60,000				

Y# 1091 10000 ROUBLES
1000.0000 g., 0.9990 Gold 32.117 oz. AGW, 100 mm. **Subject:** Andrew Rublyov

Date	Mintage	F	VF	XF	Unc	BU
2007 Proof	—	Value: 60,000				

Y# 1095 10000 ROUBLES
1000.0000 g., 0.9990 Gold 32.117 oz. AGW, 100 mm. **Subject:** Bashkiria, 450th Anniversary of Annexation by Russia

Date	Mintage	F	VF	XF	Unc	BU
2007 Proof	—	Value: 60,000				

Y# 1098 10000 ROUBLES
1000.0000 g., 0.9990 Gold 32.117 oz. AGW, 100 mm. **Subject:** Khakassia, 300th Anniversary of Annexation by Russia

Date	Mintage	F	VF	XF	Unc	BU
2007 Proof	—	Value: 60,000				

Y# 1122 10000 ROUBLES
1000.0000 g., 0.9990 Gold 32.117 oz. AGW, 100 mm. **Subject:** Udmurtiya, 450th Anniversary of Annexation into Russia

Date	Mintage	F	VF	XF	Unc	BU
2008 Proof	—	Value: 58,000				

Y# 1145 10000 ROUBLES
1000.0000 g., 0.9990 Gold 32.117 oz. AGW, 100 mm. **Subject:** European Beaver

Date	Mintage	F	VF	XF	Unc	BU
2008 Proof	—	Value: 58,000				

Y# 1149 10000 ROUBLES
1000.0000 g., 0.9990 Gold 32.117 oz. AGW, 100 mm. **Subject:** Kamchatka Volcano

Date	Mintage	F	VF	XF	Unc	BU
2008 Proof	—	Value: 58,000				

Y# 1203 10000 ROUBLES
1000.0000 g., 0.9990 Gold 32.117 oz. AGW, 100 mm. **Subject:** Velikly Novgorod

Date	Mintage	F	VF	XF	Unc	BU
2009 Proof	—	Value: 58,000				

Y# 1236 10000 ROUBLES
1000.0000 g., 0.9990 Gold 32.117 oz. AGW, 100 mm. **Subject:** UNESCO Heritage Site - Yaroslav

Date	Mintage	F	VF	XF	Unc	BU
2010 Prooflike	—	—	—	—	—	58,000

Y# 1370 10000 ROUBLES
1000.0000 g., 0.9990 Gold 32.117 oz. AGW, 100 mm. **Subject:** Origin of Russian Statehood, 1150th Anniversary

Date	Mintage	F	VF	XF	Unc	BU
2012 Prooflike	75	—	—	—	—	60,000

Y# 1371 10000 ROUBLES
1000.0000 g., 0.9990 Gold 32.117 oz. AGW, 100 mm. **Subject:** Sberbank, 170 Years

Date	Mintage	F	VF	XF	Unc	BU
2012 Prooflike	75	—	—	—	—	60,000

Y# 1117 25000 ROUBLES
1000.0000 g., 0.9990 Gold 32.117 oz. AGW, 100 mm. **Subject:** Goznak, 190th Anniversary

Date	Mintage	F	VF	XF	Unc	BU
2008 Proof	—	Value: 58,000				

Y# 1165 25000 ROUBLES
1000.0000 g., 0.9990 Gold 32.117 oz. AGW, 100 mm. **Subject:** Russian Currency

Date	Mintage	F	VF	XF	Unc	BU
2009 Proof	—	Value: 58,000				

Y# 1350 25000 ROUBLES
3000.0000 g., 0.9990 Gold 96.351 oz. AGW **Subject:** Russia's victory in the War of 1812

Date	Mintage	F	VF	XF	Unc	BU
2012 Proof	50	Value: 175,000				

Y# 1231 50000 ROUBLES
5000.0000 g., 0.9990 Gold 160.58 oz. AGW **Subject:** Bank of Russia, 150th Anniversary

Date	Mintage	F	VF	XF	Unc	BU
2010 Prooflike	—	—	—	—	—	285,000

MINT SETS

KM#	Date	Mintage	Identification	Issue Price	Mkt Val
MS44	2002 (7)	—	Y#600-603, 797-799, plus mint medal	7.50	15.00

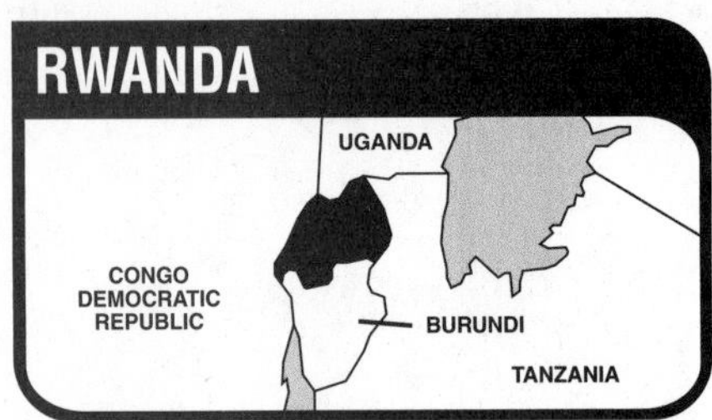

The Republic of Rwanda, located in central Africa between the Republic of the Congo and Tanzania, has an area of 10,169 sq. mi. (26,340 sq. km.) and a population of 7.3 million. Capital: Kigali. The economy is based on agriculture and mining. Coffee and tin are exported.

For earlier coinage see Belgian Congo, and Rwanda and Burundi.

MINT MARKS
(a) - Paris, privy marks only
(b) - Brussels, privy marks only

MONETARY SYSTEM
100 Centimes = 1 Franc

REPUBLIC

STANDARD COINAGE

KM# 22 FRANC
0.0700 g., Aluminum, 16 mm. **Obv:** National arms **Rev:** Sorghum plant **Edge:** Plain

Date	Mintage	F	VF	XF	Unc	BU
2003	—	—	—	0.25	0.65	1.00

KM# 23 5 FRANCS
2.9600 g., Brass Plated Steel, 20 mm. **Obv:** National arms **Rev:** Coffee plant **Edge:** Plain

Date	Mintage	F	VF	XF	Unc	BU
2003	—	—	—	0.25	0.65	1.00

KM# 33 5 FRANCS
2.9600 g., Brass Plated Steel, 20 mm. **Obv:** National arms **Rev:** Coffee plant **Rev. Legend:** BANKI NKURU YU RWANDA

Date	Mintage	F	VF	XF	Unc	BU
2009	—	—	—	0.25	0.65	1.00

KM# 24 10 FRANCS
5.0000 g., Brass Plated Steel, 23.9 mm. **Obv:** National arms **Rev:** Banana tree **Edge:** Plain

Date	Mintage	F	VF	XF	Unc	BU
2003	—	—	—	0.45	1.00	1.50
2009	—	—	—	0.45	1.00	1.50

KM# 34 10 FRANCS
5.0000 g., Brass Plated Steel, 23.9 mm. **Obv:** National arms **Rev:** Banana tree **Rev. Legend:** BANKI NKURU YU RWANDA

Date	Mintage	F	VF	XF	Unc	BU
2009	—	—	—	0.25	0.65	1.00

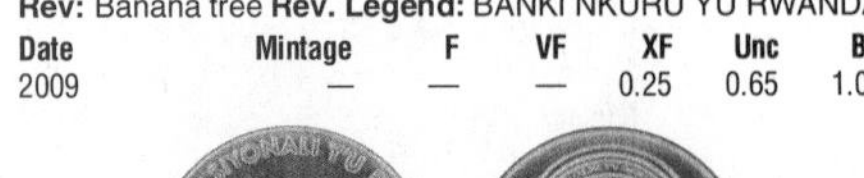

KM# 25 20 FRANCS
3.5000 g., Nickel Plated Steel, 20 mm. **Obv:** National arms **Rev:** Coffee plant seedling **Edge:** Reeded

Date	Mintage	F	VF	XF	Unc	BU
2003	—	—	—	—	1.75	2.00
2009	—	—	—	—	1.75	2.00

KM# 35 20 FRANCS
Nickel Plated Steel, 20 mm. **Obv:** National arms **Rev:** Coffee plant seedling **Rev. Legend:** BANKI NKURU YU RWANDA **Edge:** Reeded

Date	Mintage	F	VF	XF	Unc	BU
2009	—	—	—	—	1.75	2.00

KM# 26 50 FRANCS
5.8000 g., Nickel Plated Steel, 24 mm. **Obv:** National arms **Rev:** Ear of corn within husks **Edge:** Reeded

Date	Mintage	F	VF	XF	Unc	BU
2003(a)	—	—	—	—	2.50	4.00

KM# 36 50 FRANCS
5.8000 g., Nickel Plated Steel, 24 mm. **Obv:** National arms **Rev:** Ear of corn within husks **Rev. Legend:** BANKI NKURU YU RWANDA **Edge:** Reeded

Date	Mintage	F	VF	XF	Unc	BU
2009	—	—	—	—	2.50	4.00

KM# 32 100 FRANCS
Bi-Metallic Copper center in Copper-Nickel ring, 27 mm. **Obv:** National arms **Rev:** Value **Rev. Legend:** BANKI NKURU YU RWANDA

Date	Mintage	F	VF	XF	Unc	BU
2007	—	—	—	—	5.00	6.50

KM# 28 200 FRANCS
1.0000 g., 0.9990 Gold 0.0321 oz. AGW, 13.9 mm. **Subject:** 75th Birthday Dian Fossey **Obv:** National arms **Obv. Legend:** BANKI NASIYONALI Y'U RWANDA **Rev:** Fossey facing holding monkey **Edge:** Plain

Date	Mintage	F	VF	XF	Unc	BU
2007 Proof	15,000	Value: 85.00				

KM# 30 500 FRANCS
22.2000 g., 0.9000 Silver 0.6423 oz. ASW **Obv:** National arms **Obv. Legend:** BANQUE NATIONALE DU RWANDA **Rev:** Stalk of bananas on leaves

Date	Mintage	F	VF	XF	Unc	BU
2002(a) Proof	500	Value: 115				

KM# 31 500 FRANCS
22.2000 g., 0.9000 Silver 0.6423 oz. ASW **Subject:** Euro Parity **Obv:** Arms **Rev:** Plant

Date	Mintage	F	VF	XF	Unc	BU
2002 Proof	500	Value: 115				

KM# 27 500 FRANCS
20.0000 g., 0.9990 Silver 0.6423 oz. ASW, 38 mm. **Subject:** Olympic Games 2008 - Peking, marathon races **Obv:** National arms **Obv. Legend:** BANKI NASIYONALI Y'U RWANDA **Rev:** Three male marathon runners, Rwanda Olympic logo at right **Rev. Legend:** JEUX OLYMPIQUES **Edge:** Plain

Date	Mintage	F	VF	XF	Unc	BU
2006 Proof	—	Value: 110				

KM# 29 1000 FRANCS
93.3000 g., 0.9990 Silver And Gold 2.9965 oz., 65 mm. **Obv:** National arms **Obv. Legend:** BANKI NASIYONALI Y'U RWANDA **Rev:** Gilt elephant family of four with diamonds inset in eyes **Rev. Legend:** AFRICAN ELEPHANT **Edge:** Plain **Note:** Illustration reduced.

Date	Mintage	F	VF	XF	Unc	BU
2007	1,500	—	—	—	—	5,400
2007 Proof	500	Value: 5,800				

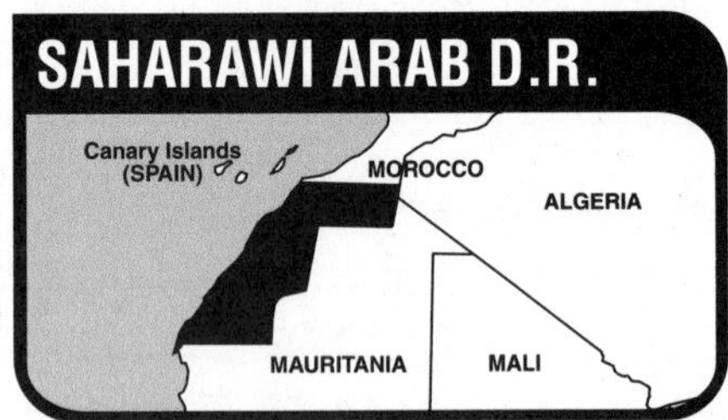

The Saharawi Arab Democratic Republic, located in northwest Africa has an area of 102,703 sq. mi. and a population (census taken 1974) of 76,425. Formerly known as Spanish Sahara, the area is bounded on the north by Morocco, on the east and southeast by Mauritania, on the northeast by Algeria, and on the west by the Atlantic Ocean. Capital: El Aaium. Agriculture, fishing and mining are the three main industries. Exports are barley, livestock and phosphates. The SADR is a "government in exile". It currently controls about 20% of its claimed territory, the former Spanish colony of Western Sahara; Morocco controls and administers the majority of the territory as its Southern Provinces. SADR claims control over a zone largely bordering Mauritania, described as "the Free Zone," although characterized by Morocco as a buffer zone.

DEMOCRATIC REPUBLIC

STANDARD COINAGE

KM# 54 1000 PESETAS
19.9400 g., 0.9990 Silver 0.6404 oz. ASW, 38.1 mm. **Obv:** National arms **Rev:** Soccer player and stadium **Edge:** Plain

Date	Mintage	F	VF	XF	Unc	BU
2002 Proof	—	Value: 35.00				

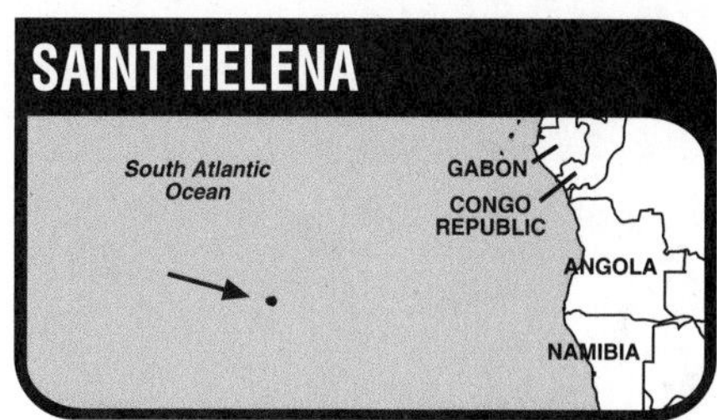

Saint Helena, a British colony located about 1,150 miles (1,850 km.) from the west coast of Africa, has an area of 47 sq. mi. (410 sq. km.) and a population of *7,000. Capital: Jamestown. Flax, lace, and rope are produced for export. Ascension and Tristan da Cunha are dependencies of Saint Helena.

MONETARY SYSTEM

100 Pence = 1 Pound

BRITISH COLONY

STANDARD COINAGE

KM# 19 50 PENCE

38.6000 g., Copper-Nickel, 38.6 mm. **Ruler:** Elizabeth II **Subject:** 75th Birthday of Queen Elizabeth II **Obv:** Crowned bust right **Rev:** Bust facing within circle and rose sprigs **Edge:** Reeded

Date	Mintage	VG	F	VF	XF	Unc
2001	—	—	—	—	—	8.00

KM# 19a 50 PENCE

28.2800 g., 0.9250 Silver 0.8410 oz. ASW, 38.6 mm. **Ruler:** Elizabeth II **Subject:** 75th Birthday of Queen Elizabeth II **Obv:** Crowned bust right **Rev:** Bust facing within circle and rose sprigs **Edge:** Reeded

Date	Mintage	F	VF	XF	Unc	BU
2001 Proof	10,000	Value: 45.00				

KM# 19b 50 PENCE

47.5400 g., 0.9166 Gold 1.4009 oz. AGW, 38.6 mm. **Ruler:** Elizabeth II **Subject:** 75th Birthday of Queen Elizabeth II **Obv:** Crowned bust right **Rev:** Bust facing within circle and rose sprigs **Edge:** Reeded

Date	Mintage	F	VF	XF	Unc	BU
2001 Proof	75	Value: 2,850				

KM# 20 50 PENCE

28.5500 g., Copper-Nickel, 38.6 mm. **Ruler:** Elizabeth II **Subject:** Queen Victoria's Death **Obv:** Crowned bust right **Rev:** Half-length figure facing and ship within circle **Edge:** Reeded

Date	Mintage	VG	F	VF	XF	Unc
2001	—	—	—	—	—	8.00

KM# 20a 50 PENCE

28.2800 g., 0.9250 Silver 0.8410 oz. ASW, 38.6 mm. **Ruler:** Elizabeth II **Subject:** Centennial - Death of Queen Victoria **Obv:** Crowned bust right **Rev:** Half-length figure facing and ship within circle **Edge:** Reeded

Date	Mintage	F	VF	XF	Unc	BU
2001 Proof	10,000	Value: 45.00				

KM# 20b 50 PENCE

47.5400 g., 0.9166 Gold 1.4009 oz. AGW, 38.6 mm. **Ruler:** Elizabeth II **Subject:** Centennial - Death of Queen Victoria **Obv:** Crowned bust right **Rev:** Half-length figure facing and ship within circle **Edge:** Reeded

Date	Mintage	F	VF	XF	Unc	BU
2001 Proof	100	Value: 2,800				

KM# 23 50 PENCE

28.2800 g., Copper-Nickel, 38.6 mm. **Ruler:** Elizabeth II **Subject:** 50th Anniversary - Queen Elizabeth II's Accession **Obv:** Crowned bust right **Rev:** Crown on pillow within circle **Edge:** Reeded

Date	Mintage	F	VF	XF	Unc	BU
ND(2002)	—	—	—	—	8.00	10.00

KM# 23a 50 PENCE

28.2800 g., 0.9250 Silver 0.8410 oz. ASW, 38.6 mm. **Ruler:** Elizabeth II **Subject:** 50th Anniversary - Queen Elizabeth's Accession **Obv:** Crowned bust right **Rev:** Crown on pillow within circle **Edge:** Reeded

Date	Mintage	F	VF	XF	Unc	BU
ND(2002) Proof	10,000	Value: 42.00				

KM# 24 50 PENCE

28.2800 g., Copper-Nickel, 38.6 mm. **Ruler:** Elizabeth II **Subject:** To Celebrate a Life of Duty, Dignity and Love, 1900-2002 **Obv:** Crowned bust right **Rev:** Conjoined busts right **Edge:** Reeded

Date	Mintage	F	VF	XF	Unc	BU
ND(2002)	—	—	—	—	8.00	10.00

KM# 24a 50 PENCE

28.2800 g., 0.9250 Silver 0.8410 oz. ASW, 38.6 mm. **Ruler:** Elizabeth II **Subject:** To Celebrate a Life of Duty, Dignity and Love, 1900-2002 **Obv:** Crowned bust right **Rev:** Conjoined busts right **Edge:** Reeded

Date	Mintage	F	VF	XF	Unc	BU
ND(2002) Proof	10,000	Value: 42.00				

KM# 25 50 PENCE

28.2800 g., Copper-Nickel, 38.6 mm. **Ruler:** Elizabeth II **Subject:** 500th Anniversary - Discovery of St. Helena **Obv:** Crowned bust right **Rev:** Half length figure right and ship above 1502 date **Edge:** Reeded

Date	Mintage	F	VF	XF	Unc	BU
ND(2002)	—	—	—	—	10.00	12.00

KM# 25a 50 PENCE

28.2800 g., 0.9250 Silver 0.8410 oz. ASW, 38.6 mm. **Ruler:** Elizabeth II **Subject:** 500th Anniversary - Discovery of St. Helena **Obv:** Crowned bust right **Rev:** Half length figure right and ship above 1502 date **Edge:** Reeded

Date	Mintage	F	VF	XF	Unc	BU
ND(2002) Proof	5,000	Value: 50.00				

KM# 26 50 PENCE

28.2800 g., Copper-Nickel, 38.6 mm. **Ruler:** Elizabeth II **Obv:** Crowned bust right **Rev:** Bust 1/4 left, ship HMS Paramour and a comet **Edge:** Reeded

Date	Mintage	F	VF	XF	Unc	BU
ND(2002)	—	—	—	—	10.00	12.00

KM# 26a 50 PENCE

28.2800 g., 0.9250 Silver 0.8410 oz. ASW, 38.6 mm. **Ruler:** Elizabeth II **Obv:** Crowned bust right **Rev:** Bust 1/4 left, ship HMS Paramour and a comet **Edge:** Reeded

Date	Mintage	F	VF	XF	Unc	BU
ND(2002) Proof	5,000	Value: 50.00				

KM# 27 50 PENCE

28.2800 g., Copper-Nickel, 38.6 mm. **Ruler:** Elizabeth II **Obv:** Crowned bust right **Rev:** Bust 1/4 right and the HMS Resolution **Edge:** Reeded

Date	Mintage	F	VF	XF	Unc	BU
ND(2002)	—	—	—	—	10.00	12.00

KM# 27a 50 PENCE

28.2800 g., 0.9250 Silver 0.8410 oz. ASW, 38.6 mm. **Ruler:** Elizabeth II **Obv:** Crowned bust right **Rev:** Bust 1/4 right and the HMS Resolution **Edge:** Reeded

Date	Mintage	F	VF	XF	Unc	BU
ND(2002) Proof	5,000	Value: 50.00				

KM# 28 50 PENCE

28.2800 g., Copper-Nickel, 38.6 mm. **Ruler:** Elizabeth II **Obv:** Crowned bust right **Rev:** Half length figure facing and the ship HMS Northumberland **Edge:** Reeded

Date	Mintage	F	VF	XF	Unc	BU
ND(2002)	—	—	—	—	10.00	12.00

KM# 28a 50 PENCE

28.2800 g., 0.9250 Silver 0.8410 oz. ASW, 38.6 mm. **Ruler:** Elizabeth II **Obv:** Queen Elizabeth II **Rev:** Napoleon and the ship HMS Northumberland **Edge:** Reeded

Date	Mintage	F	VF	XF	Unc	BU
ND(2002) Proof	5,000	Value: 50.00				

KM# 29 50 PENCE

28.2800 g., Copper-Nickel, 38.6 mm. **Ruler:** Elizabeth II **Obv:** Crowned bust right **Rev:** Four conjoined busts left plus the HMS Vanguard **Edge:** Reeded

Date	Mintage	F	VF	XF	Unc	BU
ND(2002)	—	—	—	—	8.00	10.00

KM# 29a 50 PENCE

28.2800 g., 0.9250 Silver 0.8410 oz. ASW, 38.6 mm. **Ruler:** Elizabeth II **Obv:** Crowned bust right **Rev:** Four conjoined busts left plus the HMS Vanguard **Edge:** Reeded

Date	Mintage	F	VF	XF	Unc	BU
ND(2002) Proof	5,000	Value: 45.00				

KM# 30 50 PENCE

28.2800 g., Copper-Nickel, 38.6 mm. **Ruler:** Elizabeth II **Subject:** 50th Anniversary of Queen Elizabeth's Coronation **Obv:** Crowned bust right **Rev:** Crowned Queen facing with scepter and orb **Edge:** Reeded

Date	Mintage	F	VF	XF	Unc	BU
ND(2003)	—	—	—	—	10.00	12.00

KM# 30a 50 PENCE

28.2800 g., 0.9250 Silver 0.8410 oz. ASW, 38.6 mm. **Ruler:** Elizabeth II **Subject:** 50th Anniversary - Queen Elizabeth's Coronation **Obv:** Crowned bust right **Rev:** Crowned Queen facing with scepter and orb **Edge:** Reeded

Date	Mintage	F	VF	XF	Unc	BU
ND(2003) Proof	5,000	Value: 50.00				

KM# 30b 50 PENCE

39.9400 g., 0.9166 Gold 1.1770 oz. AGW, 38.6 mm. **Ruler:** Elizabeth II **Subject:** 50th Anniversary of Queen's Coronation **Obv:** Crowned bust right **Rev:** Crowned Queen facing with scepter and orb **Edge:** Reeded

Date	Mintage	F	VF	XF	Unc	BU
ND(2003) Proof	50	Value: 2,500				

KM# 31 50 PENCE

28.2800 g., Copper-Nickel, 38.6 mm. **Ruler:** Elizabeth II **Subject:** 50th Anniversary of Coronation **Obv:** Crowned bust right **Rev:** Coronation implements **Edge:** Reeded

Date	Mintage	F	VF	XF	Unc	BU
ND(2003)	—	—	—	—	10.00	12.00

KM# 31a 50 PENCE

28.2800 g., 0.9250 Silver 0.8410 oz. ASW, 38.6 mm. **Ruler:** Elizabeth II **Subject:** 50th Anniversary - Queen Elizabeth II's Coronation **Obv:** Crowned bust right **Rev:** Coronation implements **Edge:** Reeded

Date	Mintage	F	VF	XF	Unc	BU
ND(2003) Proof	5,000	Value: 50.00				

KM# 31b 50 PENCE

39.9400 g., 0.9166 Gold 1.1770 oz. AGW, 38.6 mm. **Ruler:** Elizabeth II **Subject:** 50th Anniversary of Coronation **Obv:** Crowned bust right **Rev:** Coronation implements **Edge:** Reeded

Date	Mintage	F	VF	XF	Unc	BU
ND(2003) Proof	50	Value: 2,500				

PIEDFORT

KM#	Date	Mintage	Identification	Mkt Val
P3	ND(2002)	500	50 Pence. 0.9250 Silver. 56.5600 g. 38.6 mm. Reeded edge. Proof.	125

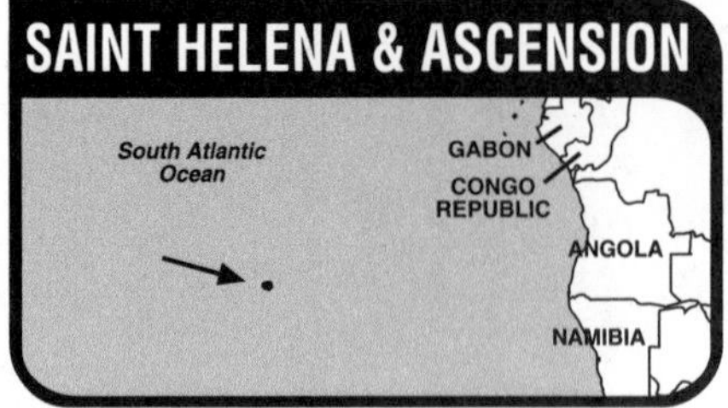

BRITISH OVERSEAS TERRITORY

STANDARD COINAGE

100 Pence = 1 Pound

KM# 13a PENNY

3.5000 g., Copper Plated Steel, 20.28 mm. **Ruler:** Elizabeth II **Obv:** Crowned head right **Rev:** Tuna above value **Edge:** Plain

Date	Mintage	F	VF	XF	Unc	BU
2003	—	—	—	0.15	0.35	0.75

KM# 12a 2 PENCE

Copper Plated Steel, 25.9 mm. **Ruler:** Elizabeth II **Obv:** Crowned head right **Rev:** Value below donkey

Date	Mintage	F	VF	XF	Unc	BU
2003	—	—	—	0.20	0.60	1.25
2006	—	—	—	0.20	0.60	1.25

KM# 22 5 PENCE

3.2500 g., Copper-Nickel, 18 mm. **Ruler:** Elizabeth II **Obv:** Crowned head right **Rev:** Giant tortoise

Date	Mintage	F	VF	XF	Unc	BU
2003	—	—	—	1.00	2.50	5.00
2006	—	—	—	1.00	2.50	5.00

KM# 23 10 PENCE

6.5000 g., Copper-Nickel, 24.5 mm. **Ruler:** Elizabeth II **Obv:** Crowned head right **Rev:** Dolphins

Date	Mintage	F	VF	XF	Unc	BU
2003	—	—	—	2.00	4.00	6.00
2006	—	—	—	2.00	4.00	6.00

KM# 55 10 PENCE

15.5500 g., 0.9990 Silver 0.4994 oz. ASW, 27 mm. **Ruler:** Elizabeth II **Obv:** Head with crown right **Rev:** Peacock displayed

Date	Mintage	F	VF	XF	Unc	BU
2012 Proof	Est. 20,000	Value: 32.50				

KM# 21 20 PENCE

5.0000 g., Copper-Nickel, 21.4 mm. **Ruler:** Elizabeth II **Obv:** Crowned head right **Rev:** Ebony flower **Shape:** 7-sided

Date	Mintage	F	VF	XF	Unc	BU
2003	—	—	—	0.75	1.50	2.50

KM# 56 20 PENCE

31.1050 g., 0.9990 Silver 0.9990 oz. ASW, 38.61 mm. **Ruler:** Elizabeth II **Obv:** Head with crown right **Rev:** Peacock displayed

Date	Mintage	F	VF	XF	Unc	BU
2012 Proof	Est. 20,000	Value: 55.00				

KM# 27 50 PENCE

8.0000 g., Copper-Nickel, 27.3 mm. **Ruler:** Elizabeth II **Obv:** Head with crown right **Rev:** Green Sea Turtle **Shape:** 7-sided

Date	Mintage	F	VF	XF	Unc	BU
2003	—	—	—	—	4.00	6.00
2006	—	—	—	—	4.00	6.00

KM# 57 50 PENCE

5.8300 g., 0.9990 Gold 0.1872 oz. AGW, 20 mm. **Ruler:** Elizabeth II **Obv:** Head with crown right **Rev:** Lion walking left, palm tree in background

Date	Mintage	F	VF	XF	Unc	BU
2012 Proof	Est. 3,250	Value: 400				

KM# 17 POUND

9.5000 g., Nickel-Brass, 22.5 mm. **Ruler:** Elizabeth II **Obv:** Crowned head right **Rev:** Sooty terns (Wideawake birds)

Date	Mintage	F	VF	XF	Unc	BU
2003	—	—	—	2.25	5.00	8.00
2006	—	—	—	2.25	5.00	8.00

KM# 58 POUND

11.6600 g., 0.9999 Gold 0.3748 oz. AGW, 26 mm. **Ruler:** Elizabeth II **Obv:** Head with crown right **Rev:** Lion advancing left, palm tree in background

Date	Mintage	F	VF	XF	Unc	BU
2012 Proof	3,250	Value: 725				

KM# 26 2 POUNDS

11.8100 g., Nickel-Brass, 28.3 mm. **Ruler:** Elizabeth II **Obv:** Crowned bust right **Rev:** National arms above value **Edge:** Reeded and lettered **Edge Lettering:** 500TH ANNIVERSARY

Date	Mintage	F	VF	XF	Unc	BU
2002	—	—	—	6.00	10.00	12.50

KM# 25 2 POUNDS

12.0000 g., Bi-Metallic Copper-Nickel center in Brass ring, 28.4 mm. **Ruler:** Elizabeth II **Obv:** Crowned bust right **Rev:** National Arms **Edge:** Reeded and lettered **Edge Lettering:** LOYAL AND FAITHFUL

Date	Mintage	F	VF	XF	Unc	BU
2003	—	—	—	9.00	15.00	17.50
2006	—	—	—	9.00	15.00	17.50

KM# 28 5 POUNDS

28.2800 g., 0.9250 Silver 0.8410 oz. ASW, 38.61 mm. **Ruler:** Elizabeth II **Obv:** Head with crown right **Rev:** Hawker Hurricane, emblem in color

Date	Mintage	F	VF	XF	Unc	BU
2008 Proof	20,000	Value: 55.00				

KM# 29 5 POUNDS

28.2800 g., 0.9250 Silver 0.8410 oz. ASW, 38.61 mm. **Ruler:** Elizabeth II **Obv:** Head with crown right **Rev:** Sir Douglas Bader

Date	Mintage	F	VF	XF	Unc	BU
2008 Proof	20,000	Value: 55.00				

KM# 30 5 POUNDS
28.2800 g., 0.9250 Silver 0.8410 oz. ASW, 38.61 mm. **Ruler:** Elizabeth II **Obv:** Head with crown right **Rev:** Spitfire, emblem in color

Date	Mintage	F	VF	XF	Unc	BU
2008 Proof	20,000	Value: 55.00				

KM# 31 5 POUNDS
28.2800 g., 0.9250 Silver 0.8410 oz. ASW, 38.61 mm. **Ruler:** Elizabeth II **Obv:** Head with crown right **Rev:** Johnnie Johnson, emblem in color

Date	Mintage	F	VF	XF	Unc	BU
2008 Proof	20,000	Value: 55.00				

KM# 32 5 POUNDS
28.2800 g., 0.9250 Silver 0.8410 oz. ASW, 38.61 mm. **Ruler:** Elizabeth II **Obv:** Head with crown right **Rev:** Mosquito, emblem in color

Date	Mintage	F	VF	XF	Unc	BU
2008 Proof	20,000	Value: 55.00				

KM# 33 5 POUNDS
28.2800 g., 0.9250 Silver 0.8410 oz. ASW, 38.61 mm. **Ruler:** Elizabeth II **Obv:** Head with crown right **Rev:** John Braham, emblem in color

Date	Mintage	F	VF	XF	Unc	BU
2008 Proof	20,000	Value: 55.00				

KM# 34 5 POUNDS
28.2800 g., 0.9250 Silver 0.8410 oz. ASW, 38.61 mm. **Ruler:** Elizabeth II **Obv:** Head with crown right **Rev:** Bomber Avro 698 Vulcan, emblem in color

Date	Mintage	F	VF	XF	Unc	BU
2008 Proof	20,000	Value: 55.00				

KM# 35 5 POUNDS
28.2800 g., 0.9250 Silver 0.8410 oz. ASW, 38.61 mm. **Ruler:** Elizabeth II **Obv:** Head with crown right **Rev:** Leonard Cheshire, emblem in color

Date	Mintage	F	VF	XF	Unc	BU
2008 Proof	20,000	Value: 55.00				

KM# 36 5 POUNDS
28.2800 g., 0.9250 Silver 0.8410 oz. ASW, 38.61 mm. **Ruler:** Elizabeth II **Obv:** Head with crown right **Rev:** Lancaster, emblem in color

Date	Mintage	F	VF	XF	Unc	BU
2008 Proof	20,000	Value: 55.00				

KM# 37 5 POUNDS
28.2800 g., 0.9250 Silver 0.8410 oz. ASW, 38.61 mm. **Ruler:** Elizabeth II **Obv:** Head with crown right **Rev:** Guy Penrose Gibson, emblem in color

Date	Mintage	F	VF	XF	Unc	BU
2008 Proof	20,000	Value: 55.00				

KM# 38 5 POUNDS
28.2800 g., 0.9250 Silver 0.8410 oz. ASW, 38.61 mm. **Ruler:** Elizabeth II **Obv:** Head with crown right **Rev:** Harrier, emblem in color

Date	Mintage	F	VF	XF	Unc	BU
2008 Proof	20,000	Value: 55.00				

KM# 39 5 POUNDS
28.2800 g., 0.9250 Silver 0.8410 oz. ASW, 38.61 mm. **Ruler:** Elizabeth II **Obv:** Head with crown right **Rev:** David Lord, emblem in color

Date	Mintage	F	VF	XF	Unc	BU
2008 Proof	20,000	Value: 55.00				

KM# 40 5 POUNDS
28.2800 g., 0.9250 Silver 0.8410 oz. ASW, 38.61 mm. **Ruler:** Elizabeth II **Obv:** Head with crown right **Rev:** The Gnat, emblem in color

Date	Mintage	F	VF	XF	Unc	BU
2008 Proof	20,000	Value: 55.00				

KM# 41 5 POUNDS
28.2800 g., 0.9250 Silver 0.8410 oz. ASW, 38.61 mm. **Ruler:** Elizabeth II **Obv:** Head with crown right **Rev:** Ray Hanna, emblem in color

Date	Mintage	F	VF	XF	Unc	BU
2008 Proof	20,000	Value: 55.00				

KM# 42 5 POUNDS
28.2800 g., 0.9250 Silver 0.8410 oz. ASW, 38.61 mm. **Ruler:** Elizabeth II **Obv:** Head with crown right **Rev:** SESA, emblem in color

Date	Mintage	F	VF	XF	Unc	BU
2008 Proof	20,000	Value: 55.00				

KM# 43 5 POUNDS
28.2800 g., 0.9250 Silver 0.8410 oz. ASW, 38.61 mm. **Ruler:** Elizabeth II **Obv:** Head with crown right **Rev:** Mick Mannock, emblem in color

Date	Mintage	F	VF	XF	Unc	BU
2008 Proof	—	Value: 55.00				

KM# 44 5 POUNDS
28.2800 g., 0.9250 Silver 0.8410 oz. ASW, 38.61 mm. **Ruler:** Elizabeth II **Obv:** Head with crown right **Rev:** Typhoon, emblem in color

Date	Mintage	F	VF	XF	Unc	BU
2008 Proof	20,000	Value: 55.00				

KM# 45 5 POUNDS
28.2800 g., 0.9250 Silver 0.8410 oz. ASW, 38.61 mm. **Ruler:** Elizabeth II **Obv:** Head with crown right **Rev:** Sir Hugh Trenchard, emblem in color

Date	Mintage	F	VF	XF	Unc	BU
2008 Proof	20,000	Value: 55.00				

KM# 59 5 POUNDS
28.2800 g., 0.9250 Silver 0.8410 oz. ASW, 38.61 mm. **Ruler:** Elizabeth II **Obv:** Head with tiara right **Rev:** Flags of Commonwealth nations on globe

Date	Mintage	F	VF	XF	Unc	BU
2012 Proof	—	Value: 55.00				

KM# 46 25 POUNDS
7.9800 g., 0.9167 Gold 0.2352 oz. AGW, 22 mm. **Ruler:** Elizabeth II **Obv:** Head with crown right **Rev:** Hurricane

Date	Mintage	F	VF	XF	Unc	BU
2008 Proof	500	Value: 500				

KM# 47 25 POUNDS
7.9800 g., 0.9167 Gold 0.2352 oz. AGW, 22 mm. **Ruler:** Elizabeth II **Obv:** Head with crown right **Rev:** Spitfire

Date	Mintage	F	VF	XF	Unc	BU
2008 Proof	500	Value: 500				

KM# 48 25 POUNDS
7.9800 g., 0.9167 Gold 0.2352 oz. AGW, 22 mm. **Ruler:** Elizabeth II **Obv:** Head with crown right **Rev:** Mosquito

Date	Mintage	F	VF	XF	Unc	BU
2008 Proof	500	Value: 500				

KM# 49 25 POUNDS
7.9800 g., 0.9167 Gold 0.2352 oz. AGW, 22 mm. **Ruler:** Elizabeth II **Obv:** Head with crown right **Rev:** Bomber Avro 698 Vulcan

Date	Mintage	F	VF	XF	Unc	BU
2008 Proof	500	Value: 500				

KM# 50 25 POUNDS
7.9800 g., 0.9167 Gold 0.2352 oz. AGW, 22 mm. **Ruler:** Elizabeth II **Obv:** Head with crown right **Rev:** Lancaster

Date	Mintage	F	VF	XF	Unc	BU
2008 Proof	500	Value: 500				

KM# 51 25 POUNDS
7.9800 g., 0.9167 Gold 0.2352 oz. AGW, 22 mm. **Ruler:** Elizabeth II **Obv:** Head with crown right **Rev:** Harrier

Date	Mintage	F	VF	XF	Unc	BU
2008 Proof	500	Value: 500				

KM# 52 25 POUNDS
7.9800 g., 0.9167 Gold 0.2352 oz. AGW, 22 mm. **Ruler:** Elizabeth II **Obv:** Head with crown right **Rev:** The Gnat

Date	Mintage	F	VF	XF	Unc	BU
2008 Proof	500	Value: 500				

KM# 53 25 POUNDS
7.9800 g., 0.9167 Gold 0.2352 oz. AGW, 22 mm. **Ruler:** Elizabeth II **Obv:** Head with crown right **Rev:** SESA

Date	Mintage	F	VF	XF	Unc	BU
2008 Proof	500	Value: 500				

KM# 54 25 POUNDS
7.9800 g., 0.9167 Gold 0.2352 oz. AGW, 22 mm. **Ruler:** Elizabeth II **Obv:** Head with crown right **Rev:** Typhoon

Date	Mintage	F	VF	XF	Unc	BU
2008 Proof	500	Value: 500				

SAMOA

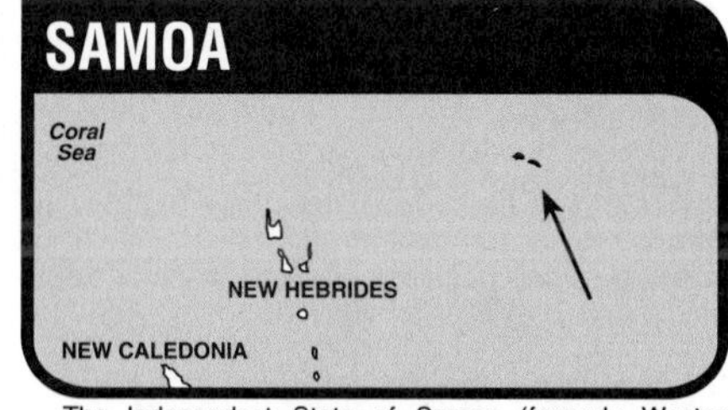

The Independent State of Samoa (formerly Western Samoa), located in the Pacific Ocean 1,600 miles (2,574 km.) northeast of New Zealand, has an area of 1,097 sq. mi. (2,860 sq. km.) and a population of *182,000. Capital: Apia. The economy is based on agriculture, fishing and tourism. Copra, cocoa and bananas are exported.

Samoa is a member of the Commonwealth of Nations. The Chief Executive is Chief of State. The prime minister is the Head of Government. The present Head of State, Malietoa Tanumafili II, holds his position for life. The Legislative Assembly will elect future Heads of State for 5-year terms.

Samoa, which had used New Zealand coinage, converted to a decimal coinage in 1967.

RULER
Malietoa Tanumafili II, 1962-2007
Tuiatua Tupua Tamasese Efi, 2007-

MONETARY SYSTEM
100 Sene = 1 Tala

CONSTITUTIONAL MONARCHY
Commonwealth of Nations

STANDARD COINAGE

KM# 131 5 SENE
2.8400 g., Copper-Nickel, 19.5 mm. **Obv:** Head left **Rev:** Pineapple and value **Edge:** Reeded **Note:** "Western" dropped from country name

Date	Mintage	F	VF	XF	Unc	BU
2002	—	—	—	0.30	0.50	0.75
2006	—	—	—	0.30	0.50	0.75
2010	—	—	—	0.30	0.50	0.75

KM# 167 5 SENE
Nickel Plated Steel

Date	Mintage	F	VF	XF	Unc	BU
2010	—	—	—	—	0.50	0.75

KM# 132 10 SENE
5.6500 g., Copper-Nickel, 23.6 mm. **Obv:** Head left **Rev:** Taro leaves and value **Edge:** Reeded **Note:** "Western" dropped from country name

Date	Mintage	F	VF	XF	Unc	BU
2002	—	—	—	0.45	0.75	1.00
2006	—	—	—	0.45	0.75	1.00
2010	—	—	—	0.45	0.75	1.00

KM# 168 10 SENE
2.7900 g., Nickel Plated Steel, 19 mm. **Obv:** President Efi bust 3/4 left **Rev:** Fautasi

Date	Mintage	F	VF	XF	Unc	BU
2010	—	—	—	—	0.75	1.00
2011	—	—	—	—	0.75	1.00

KM# 168a 10 SENE
3.5200 g., 0.9990 Silver 0.1131 oz. ASW, 19 mm. **Obv:** Efi portrait **Rev:** Fautasi

Date	Mintage	F	VF	XF	Unc	BU
2011 Proof	2,500	Value: 5.00				

KM# 133 20 SENE
11.4000 g., Copper-Nickel, 28.45 mm. **Obv:** Head left **Rev:** Breadfruits and value **Edge:** Reeded **Note:** "Western" dropped from country name

Date	Mintage	F	VF	XF	Unc	BU
2002	—	—	—	0.60	1.00	1.50
2006	—	—	—	0.60	1.00	1.50

KM# 169 20 SENE
3.6400 g., Nickel Plated Steel, 21 mm. **Obv:** Efi portrait 3/4 left **Rev:** Alpina Purpurata plant

Date	Mintage	F	VF	XF	Unc	BU
2010	—	—	—	—	1.00	1.50
2011	—	—	—	—	1.00	1.50

KM# 169a 20 SENE
4.6400 g., 0.9990 Silver 0.1490 oz. ASW, 21 mm. **Obv:** Efi portrait **Rev:** Alpinia purpurata

Date	Mintage	F	VF	XF	Unc	BU
2011 Proof	2,500	Value: 7.00				

KM# 134 50 SENE
14.1300 g., Copper-Nickel, 32.3 mm. **Obv:** Head left **Rev:** Banana tree and value **Edge:** Reeded **Note:** "Western" dropped from country name

Date	Mintage	F	VF	XF	Unc	BU
2002	—	—	—	1.00	1.75	2.00
2006	—	—	—	1.00	1.75	2.00
2010	—	—	—	1.00	1.75	2.00

KM# 170 50 SENE
5.4700 g., Nickel Plated Steel, 24.2 mm. **Obv:** Efi portrait 3/4 left **Rev:** Didunculus strigiostris - Columbidae bird right

Date	Mintage	F	VF	XF	Unc	BU
2010	—	—	—	—	1.75	2.00
2011	—	—	—	—	1.75	2.00

KM# 170a 50 SENE
6.9500 g., 0.9990 Silver 0.2232 oz. ASW, 24.2 mm. **Obv:** Efi portrait **Rev:** Columbidae right

Date	Mintage	F	VF	XF	Unc	BU
2011 Proof	2,500	Value: 9.50				

KM# 135 TALA
9.5000 g., Brass, 30 mm. **Obv:** Head left **Rev:** National arms above value and banner flanked by sprigs **Edge:** Reeded **Note:** "Western" dropped from country name

Date	Mintage	F	VF	XF	Unc	BU
2002	—	—	—	1.50	2.50	3.00
2006	—	—	—	1.50	2.50	3.00

KM# 180 TALA
0.8000 g., 0.9999 Gold 0.0257 oz. AGW, 11 mm. **Obv:** National arms **Rev:** Maya Calendar

Date	Mintage	F	VF	XF	Unc	BU
2008 Proof	10,000	Value: 75.00				

KM# 150 TALA
Goldine Plated Metal **Subject:** Thomas Mann **Obv:** Arms **Rev:** Bust facing

Date	Mintage	F	VF	XF	Unc	BU
2009	—	—	—	—	—	30.00

KM# 151 TALA
Goldine Plated Metal **Subject:** Hercules & Hydra

Date	Mintage	F	VF	XF	Unc	BU
2009	—	—	—	—	—	25.00

KM# 152 TALA
Goldine Plated Metal **Subject:** Alhambra

Date	Mintage	F	VF	XF	Unc	BU
2009	—	—	—	—	—	25.00

KM# 153 TALA
Goldine Plated Metal **Rev:** Golden horn

Date	Mintage	F	VF	XF	Unc	BU
2009	—	—	—	—	—	25.00

KM# 154 TALA
Goldine Plated Metal **Rev:** Sphinx

Date	Mintage	F	VF	XF	Unc	BU
2009	—	—	—	—	—	25.00

KM# 155 TALA
Goldine Plated Metal **Rev:** Kaiser Wilhelm II

Date	Mintage	F	VF	XF	Unc	BU
2009	—	—	—	—	—	25.00

KM# 156 TALA
Goldine Plated Metal **Rev:** Hagia Sophia

Date	Mintage	F	VF	XF	Unc	BU
2009	—	—	—	—	—	25.00

KM# 185 TALA
0.5000 g., 0.9990 Gold 0.0161 oz. AGW, 11 mm. **Obv:** National arms **Rev:** Barbarossa bust

Date	Mintage	F	VF	XF	Unc	BU
2009 Proof	10,000	Value: 50.00				

KM# 186 TALA
0.5000 g., 0.9990 Gold 0.0161 oz. AGW, 11 mm. **Obv:** National arms **Rev:** Marcus Tullius Cicero bust facing

Date	Mintage	F	VF	XF	Unc	BU
2009 Proof	10,000	Value: 50.00				

KM# 187 TALA
0.5000 g., 0.9990 Gold 0.0161 oz. AGW, 11 mm. **Obv:** National arms **Rev:** Marie Curie and atom design

Date	Mintage	F	VF	XF	Unc	BU
2009 Proof	10,000	Value: 50.00				

KM# 188 TALA
26.0300 g., Copper-Nickel plated silver, 38.61 mm. **Subject:** London Olympics, 2012 **Obv:** National arms **Rev:** White water kyacker

Date	Mintage	F	VF	XF	Unc	BU
2009 Proof	30,000	Value: 15.00				

KM# 189 TALA
0.5000 g., 0.9990 Gold 0.0161 oz. AGW, 11 mm. **Obv:** National arms **Rev:** Pallas Athene bust right

Date	Mintage	F	VF	XF	Unc	BU
2009 Proof	10,000	Value: 50.00				

KM# 190 TALA
0.5000 g., 0.9990 Gold 0.0161 oz. AGW, 11 mm. **Obv:** National arms **Rev:** Basilica of San Marco, Venice

Date	Mintage	F	VF	XF	Unc	BU
2009 Proof	10,000	Value: 50.00				

KM# 191 TALA
0.5000 g., 0.9999 Gold 0.0161 oz. AGW, 11 mm. **Obv:** National arms **Rev:** Thomas Mann bust facing

Date	Mintage	F	VF	XF	Unc	BU
2009 Proof	10,000	Value: 50.00				

KM# 171 TALA
6.0000 g., Aluminum-Bronze, 21.5 mm. **Rev:** Kava **Shape:** 7-sides

Date	Mintage	F	VF	XF	Unc	BU
2010	—	—	—	—	2.50	3.00
2011	—	—	—	—	2.50	3.00

KM# 174 TALA
0.5000 g., 0.9990 Gold 0.0161 oz. AGW, 11 mm. **Obv:** National arms **Rev:** Samoan Flying Fox (bat) in flight

Date	Mintage	F	VF	XF	Unc	BU
2010 Proof	10,000	Value: 75.00				

KM# 214 TALA
0.5000 g., 0.9990 Gold 0.0161 oz. AGW, 11 mm. **Obv:** National arms **Rev:** Nicolaus Copernicus bust at left, solar system

Date	Mintage	F	VF	XF	Unc	BU
2010 Proof	10,000	Value: 50.00				

KM# 215 TALA
0.5000 g., 0.9990 Gold 0.0161 oz. AGW, 11 mm. **Subject:** German Railways, 175th Anniversary **Obv:** National arms **Rev:** Early steam locomotive and modern high speed train

Date	Mintage	F	VF	XF	Unc	BU
2010 Proof	5,000	Value: 50.00				

KM# 216 TALA
0.5000 g., 0.9990 Gold 0.0161 oz. AGW, 11 mm. **Obv:** National arms **Rev:** Johannes Hevelius bust at right

Date	Mintage	F	VF	XF	Unc	BU
2010 Proof	10,000	Value: 50.00				

KM# 171a TALA
7.7700 g., 0.9990 Silver 0.2496 oz. ASW, 21.5 mm. **Obv:** Efi portrait **Rev:** Kava

Date	Mintage	F	VF	XF	Unc	BU
2011 Proof	2,500	Value: 12.00				

KM# 219 TALA
0.5000 g., 0.9990 Gold 0.0161 oz. AGW, 11 mm. **Obv:** National arms **Rev:** Pope John Paul II lat left holding cross croizer

Date	Mintage	F	VF	XF	Unc	BU
2011 Proof	10,000	Value: 50.00				

KM# 178 2 TALA
8.0000 g., Aluminum-Bronze, 25.6 mm. **Obv:** Efi portrait 3/4 right **Rev:** National arms **Shape:** Scalloped

Date	Mintage	F	VF	XF	Unc	BU
2011	—	—	—	—	5.00	8.00

KM# 193a 2 TALA
10.3700 g., 0.9990 Silver 0.3331 oz. ASW, 25.6 mm. **Obv:** Efi portrait **Rev:** National arms

Date	Mintage	F	VF	XF	Unc	BU
2011 Proof	2,500	Value: 18.00				

KM# 165 5 TALA
28.2800 g., 0.9250 Silver 0.8410 oz. ASW, 38.61 mm. **Obv:** National Arms **Rev:** Steam Locomotive centennial

Date	Mintage	F	VF	XF	Unc	BU
2007 Proof	Est. 5,000	Value: 75.00				

KM# 181 5 TALA
28.2800 g., 0.9250 Silver 0.8410 oz. ASW, 38.61 mm. **Obv:** National arms **Rev:** S.M.S. Bismark sailing right

Date	Mintage	F	VF	XF	Unc	BU
2008 Proof	5,000	Value: 75.00				

KM# 182 5 TALA
28.2800 g., 0.9250 Silver 0.8410 oz. ASW, 38.61 mm. **Subject:** Bejing Olympics, 2008 **Obv:** National arms **Rev:** Track runner

Date	Mintage	F	VF	XF	Unc	BU
2008 Proof	10,000	Value: 65.00				

KM# 166 5 TALA
31.1050 g., 0.9990 Silver 0.9990 oz. ASW, 38.6 mm. **Obv:** National arms **Rev:** John Paul II at right and as figure in flames

Date	Mintage	F	VF	XF	Unc	BU
2009 Proof	Est. 2,000	Value: 85.00				

KM# 179 5 TALA
31.1050 g., 0.9990 Silver 0.9990 oz. ASW, 38.61 mm. **Subject:** First pacific class locomotive **Obv:** National arms **Rev:** Badische IVf locomotive

Date	Mintage	F	VF	XF	Unc	BU
2009 Proof	5,000	Value: 75.00				

KM# 192 5 TALA
28.2800 g., 0.9250 Silver 0.8410 oz. ASW, 38.61 mm. **Subject:** German Railways, 175th Anniversary **Obv:** National arms **Rev:** BR-23 locomotive and V-80 locomotive

Date	Mintage	F	VF	XF	Unc	BU
2009 Proof	5,000	Value: 72.00				

KM# 194 5 TALA
28.2800 g., 0.9250 Silver 0.8410 oz. ASW, 38.61 mm. **Subject:** London Olympics, 2012 **Obv:** National arms **Rev:** White water kyacker

Date	Mintage	F	VF	XF	Unc	BU
2009 Proof	10,000	—	—	—	—	75.00

KM# 217 5 TALA
28.2800 g., 0.9250 Silver 0.8410 oz. ASW, 38.61 mm. **Subject:** German Railways, 175th Anniversary **Obv:** National arms **Rev:** Montage of locomotive and stations

Date	Mintage	F	VF	XF	Unc	BU
2010 Proof	5,000	Value: 75.00				

KM# 218 5 TALA
28.2800 g., 0.9250 Silver 0.8410 oz. ASW, 38.61 mm. **Obv:** National arms **Rev:** Lilienthal Glider

Date	Mintage	F	VF	XF	Unc	BU
2010 Proof	Est. 5,000	Value: 75.00				

KM# 137 10 TALA
31.1000 g., 0.9990 Silver with Mother-of-Pearl insert 0.9988 oz. ASW, 40 mm. **Series:** Save the Whales **Obv:** National arms above value and banner flanked by sprigs **Obv. Legend:** SAMOA I SISIFO **Rev:** Bowhead Whale on mother-of-pearl insert **Edge:** Plain

Date	Mintage	F	VF	XF	Unc	BU
2002 Proof	2,000	Value: 95.00				

KM# 139 10 TALA
31.4700 g., 0.9250 Silver 0.9359 oz. ASW **Subject:** XXVIII Summer Olympics - Athens **Obv:** National arms **Obv. Legend:** SAMOA I SISIFO **Rev:** Swimming - two divers

Date	Mintage	F	VF	XF	Unc	BU
2003 Proof	—	Value: 60.00				

KM# 146 10 TALA
1.2300 g., Gold, 13.89 mm. **Obv:** National arms **Obv. Legend:** SAMOA SISIFO **Rev:** Bust of Fletcher Christian 3/4 left at left, sailing ship "H. M. S. Bounty" at right **Edge:** Reeded

Date	Mintage	F	VF	XF	Unc	BU
2003 Proof	—	Value: 90.00				

KM# 140 10 TALA
1.2400 g., 0.9990 Gold 0.0398 oz. AGW **Series:** World Statesmen **Subject:** Mahatma Gandhi **Obv:** National arms **Obv. Legend:** SAMOA I SISIFO

Date	Mintage	F	VF	XF	Unc	BU
2003 Proof	—	Value: 90.00				

KM# 141 10 TALA
1.2400 g., 0.9990 Gold 0.0398 oz. AGW **Series:** World Statesmen **Subject:** Konrad Adenauer **Obv:** National arms **Obv. Legend:** SAMOA I SISIFO

Date	Mintage	F	VF	XF	Unc	BU
2003 Proof	—	Value: 90.00				

KM# 159 10 TALA
1.2400 g., 0.9990 Gold 0.0398 oz. AGW, 13.92 mm. **Obv:** National arms **Rev:** Theodore Roosevelt

Date	Mintage	F	VF	XF	Unc	BU
2003 Proof	Est. 2,000	Value: 90.00				

KM# 160 10 TALA
1.2400 g., 0.9990 Gold 0.0398 oz. AGW, 13.92 mm. **Obv:** National arms **Rev:** Winston Churchill

Date	Mintage	F	VF	XF	Unc	BU
2003 Proof	Est. 2,000	Value: 90.00				

KM# 161 10 TALA
1.2400 g., 0.9990 Gold 0.0398 oz. AGW, 13.92 mm. **Obv:** National arms **Rev:** Charles de Gaulle

Date	Mintage	F	VF	XF	Unc	BU
2003 Proof	Est. 2,000	Value: 90.00				

KM# 162 10 TALA
1.2400 g., 0.9990 Gold 0.0398 oz. AGW, 13.92 mm. **Obv:** National arms **Rev:** John F. Kennedy

Date	Mintage	F	VF	XF	Unc	BU
2003 Proof	Est. 2,000	Value: 90.00				

KM# 143 10 TALA
28.5800 g., Silver, 38.61 mm. **Obv:** National arms **Obv. Legend:** SAMOA I SISIFO **Rev:** Sailing ship "La Récherche" **Rev. Legend:** JEAN FRANCOIS GALAUP - COMTE DE LA PEROUSE **Edge:** Reeded

Date	Mintage	F	VF	XF	Unc	BU
2004 Proof	—	Value: 55.00				

KM# 142 10 TALA
1.2400 g., 0.9990 Gold 0.0398 oz. AGW **Subject:** Death of Pope John-Paul II **Obv:** National arms

Date	Mintage	F	VF	XF	Unc	BU
2005	15,000	—	—	—	—	75.00
2005 Proof	3,300	Value: 90.00				

KM# 163 10 TALA
1.2400 g., 0.9990 Gold 0.0398 oz. AGW, 13.92 mm. **Obv:** National arms **Rev:** 2006 FIFA World Cup Germany logo

Date	Mintage	F	VF	XF	Unc	BU
2005 Proof	Est. 25,000	Value: 90.00				

KM# 164 10 TALA
1.2400 g., 0.9990 Gold 0.0398 oz. AGW, 13.92 mm. **Obv:** National arms **Rev:** Pope Benedict XVI in robes and mitre giving blessing

Date	Mintage	F	VF	XF	Unc	BU
2006 Proof	—	Value: 90.00				

KM# 183 10 TALA
1.0000 g., 0.9999 Gold 0.0321 oz. AGW, 13.92 mm. **Obv:** National arms **Rev:** S.M.S. Bismark siling right

Date	Mintage	F	VF	XF	Unc	BU
2008 Proof	15,000	Value: 85.00				

KM# 184 10 TALA
1.2400 g., 0.9999 Gold 0.0399 oz. AGW, 13.92 mm. **Obv:** National arms **Rev:** Hans Christian Anderson bust right

Date	Mintage	F	VF	XF	Unc	BU
2008 Proof	10,000	Value: 100				

KM# 195 10 TALA
28.2800 g., 0.9990 Silver partially gilt 0.9083 oz. ASW, 38.61 mm. **Subject:** 10 Commandments - 1st Commandment **Obv:** National arms **Rev:** Two men worshiping a calf at an altar

Date	Mintage	F	VF	XF	Unc	BU
2009 Proof	5,000	Value: 75.00				

KM# 196 10 TALA
28.2800 g., 0.9250 Silver partially gilt 0.8410 oz. ASW, 38.61 mm. **Subject:** 10 Commandments - 2nd Commandment **Obv:** National arms **Rev:** Two men standing in the desert

Date	Mintage	F	VF	XF	Unc	BU
2009 Proof	5,000	Value: 75.00				

KM# 197 10 TALA
28.2800 g., 0.9250 Silver partially gilt 0.8410 oz. ASW, 38.61 mm. **Subject:** 10 Commandments - 3rd Commandment **Obv:** National arms **Rev:** Parents and child on a field

Date	Mintage	F	VF	XF	Unc	BU
2009 Proof	5,000	Value: 75.00				

KM# 198 10 TALA
28.2800 g., 0.9250 Silver partially gilt 0.8410 oz. ASW, 38.61 mm. **Subject:** 10 Commandments - 4th Commandment **Obv:** National arms **Rev:** Mother seated with child, father standing

Date	Mintage	F	VF	XF	Unc	BU
2009 Proof	5,000	Value: 75.00				

KM# 199 10 TALA
28.2800 g., 0.9250 Silver partially gilt 0.8410 oz. ASW, 38.61 mm. **Subject:** 10 Commandments - 5th Commandment **Obv:** National arms **Rev:** Man holding sword over kneeling man

Date	Mintage	F	VF	XF	Unc	BU
2009 Proof	5,000	Value: 75.00				

KM# 205 10 TALA
28.2800 g., 0.9250 Silver partially gilt 0.8410 oz. ASW, 38.61 mm. **Subject:** Charles Darwin, 200th Anniversary of Birth **Obv:** National arms **Rev:** Galapagos Island Finches

Date	Mintage	F	VF	XF	Unc	BU
2009 Proof	2,009	Value: 75.00				

KM# 206 10 TALA
28.2800 g., 0.9250 Silver partially gilt 0.8410 oz. ASW, 38.61 mm. **Subject:** Charles Darwin, 200th Anniversary of Birth **Obv:** National arms **Rev:** Galapagos Iguana

Date	Mintage	F	VF	XF	Unc	BU
2009 Proof	2,009	Value: 75.00				

KM# 207 10 TALA
28.2800 g., 0.9250 Silver partially gilt 0.8410 oz. ASW, 38.61 mm. **Subject:** Charles Darwin, 200th Anniversary of Birth **Obv:** National arms **Rev:** The H.M.R.S. Beagle and voyage map

Date	Mintage	F	VF	XF	Unc	BU
2009 Proof	2,009	Value: 75.00				

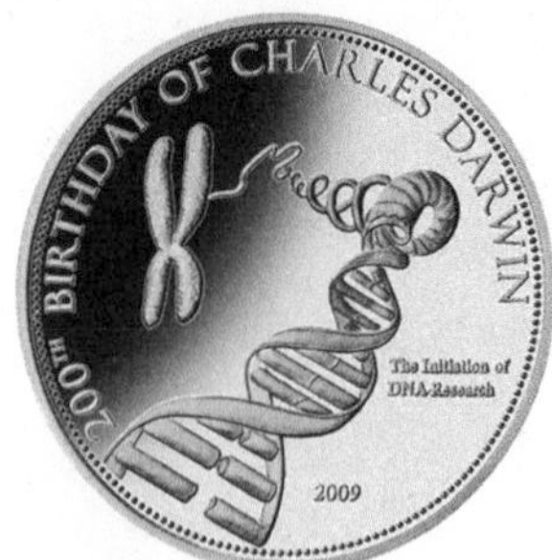

KM# 208 10 TALA
28.2800 g., 0.9250 Silver partially gilt 0.8410 oz. ASW, 38.61 mm. **Subject:** Charles Darwin, 200th Anniversary of Birth **Obv:** National arms **Rev:** DNA-Double helix and a chromosome

Date	Mintage	F	VF	XF	Unc	BU
2009 Proof	2,009	Value: 75.00				

KM# 209 10 TALA
28.2800 g., 0.9250 Silver partially gilt 0.8410 oz. ASW, 38.61 mm. **Subject:** Charles Darwin, 200th Anniversary of Birth **Obv:** National arms **Rev:** Galapagos Oldest Tortoise

Date	Mintage	F	VF	XF	Unc	BU
2009 Proof	2,009	Value: 75.00				

KM# 210 10 TALA
28.2800 g., 0.9250 Silver partially gilt 0.8410 oz. ASW, 38.61 mm. **Subject:** Charles Darwin, 200th Anniversary of Birth **Obv:** National arms **Rev:** Darwin portrait at left

Date	Mintage	F	VF	XF	Unc	BU
2009 Proof	2,009	Value: 75.00				

KM# 211 10 TALA
1.2400 g., 0.9999 Gold 0.0399 oz. AGW, 13.92 mm. **Obv:** National arms **Rev:** Nicolaus Copernicus bust and solar system

Date	Mintage	F	VF	XF	Unc	BU
2009 Proof	10,000	Value: 100				

KM# 212 10 TALA
1.2400 g., 0.9999 Gold 0.0399 oz. AGW, 13.92 mm. **Obv:** National arms **Rev:** Johannes Hevelius bust at right

Date	Mintage	F	VF	XF	Unc	BU
2009 Proof	5,000	Value: 100				

KM# 213 10 TALA
1.2400 g., 0.9990 Gold 0.0398 oz. AGW, 13.92 mm. **Obv:** National arms **Rev:** Marie Curie and atom symbol

Date	Mintage	F	VF	XF	Unc	BU
2009 Proof	5,000	Value: 100				

KM# 172 10 TALA

20.0000 g., 0.9250 Silver 0.5948 oz. ASW, 38.61 mm. **Obv:** National arms **Rev:** Sailing ship Preussen

Date	Mintage	F	VF	XF	Unc	BU
2010 Proof	2,500	Value: 75.00				

KM# 173 10 TALA

25.0000 g., 0.9250 Silver 0.7435 oz. ASW, 38.61 mm. **Obv:** National arms **Rev:** Samoan Flying Fox (bat) hanging, with colored eyes

Date	Mintage	F	VF	XF	Unc	BU
2010 Proof	2,500	Value: 75.00				

KM# 200 10 TALA

28.2800 g., 0.9990 Silver partially gilt 0.9083 oz. ASW, 38.61 mm. **Subject:** 10 Commandments - 6th Commandment **Obv:** National arms **Rev:** Man seated near half-naked reclining female

Date	Mintage	F	VF	XF	Unc	BU
2010 Proof	5,000	Value: 75.00				

KM# 201 10 TALA

28.2800 g., 0.9250 Silver partially gilt 0.8410 oz. ASW, 38.61 mm. **Subject:** 10 Commandments - 7th Commandment **Obv:** National arms **Rev:** Three men walking

Date	Mintage	F	VF	XF	Unc	BU
2010 Proof	5,000	Value: 75.00				

KM# 202 10 TALA

28.2800 g., 0.9990 Silver partially gilt 0.9083 oz. ASW, 38.61 mm. **Subject:** 10 Commandments - 8th Commandment **Obv:** National arms **Rev:** One man talking to another

Date	Mintage	F	VF	XF	Unc	BU
2010 Proof	5,000	Value: 75.00				

KM# 203 10 TALA

28.2800 g., 0.9990 Silver partially gilt 0.9083 oz. ASW, 38.61 mm. **Subject:** 10 Commandment - 9th Commandment **Obv:** National arms **Rev:** Female entering river to bathe, male watching from behind tree

Date	Mintage	F	VF	XF	Unc	BU
2010 Proof	5,000	Value: 75.00				

KM# 204 10 TALA

28.2800 g., 0.9250 Silver partially gilt 0.8410 oz. ASW, 38.61 mm. **Subject:** 10 Commandments - 10th Commandment **Obv:** National arms **Rev:** Temple building and man standing at right

Date	Mintage	F	VF	XF	Unc	BU
2010 Proof	5,000	Value: 75.00				

KM# 220 100 TALA

5.0000 g., 0.9999 Gold 0.1607 oz. AGW, 23.3x14 mm. **Obv:** Value and national arms **Rev:** Battlehsip Bismarck **Shape:** Rectangle

Date	Mintage	F	VF	XF	Unc	BU
2011 Proof	1,000	Value: 350				

KM# 221 100 TALA

5.0000 g., 0.9990 Gold 0.1606 oz. AGW, 23.3x14 mm. **Obv:** Value and national arms **Rev:** Battleship H.M.S. Hood **Shape:** Rectangle

Date	Mintage	F	VF	XF	Unc	BU
2011 Proof	1,000	Value: 350				

KM# 222 100 TALA

5.0000 g., 0.9990 Gold 0.1606 oz. AGW, 23.3x14 mm. **Obv:** Value and national arms **Rev:** Battleship U.S.S. Missouri **Shape:** Rectangle

Date	Mintage	F	VF	XF	Unc	BU
2011 Proof	1,000	Value: 350				

KM# 223 100 TALA

5.0000 g., 0.9999 Gold 0.1607 oz. AGW, 23.3x14 mm. **Obv:** Value and national arms **Rev:** Battleship S.M.S. Friedrich der Grosse **Shape:** Rectangle

Date	Mintage	F	VF	XF	Unc	BU
2011 Proof	1,000	Value: 350				

KM# 224 100 TALA

5.0000 g., 0.9999 Gold 0.1607 oz. AGW, 23.3x14 mm. **Obv:** Value and national arms **Rev:** Battleship Yamato **Shape:** Rectangle

Date	Mintage	F	VF	XF	Unc	BU
2011 Proof	1,000	Value: 350				

The Republic of San Marino, the oldest and smallest republic in the world is located in north central Italy entirely surrounded by the Province of Emilia-Romagna. It has an area of 24 sq. mi. (60 sq. km.) and a population of *23,000. Capital: San Marino. The principal economic activities are farming, livestock raising, cheese making, tourism and light manufacturing. Building stone, lime, wheat, hides and baked goods are exported. The government derives most of its revenue from the sale of postage stamps for philatelic purposes.

San Marino has its own coinage, but Italian and Vatican City coins and currency are also in circulation.

MINT MARKS

R - Rome

MONETARY SYSTEM

100 Centesimi = 1 Lira

REPUBLIC

STANDARD COINAGE

KM# 424 10 LIRE

1.6000 g., Aluminum, 23.3 mm. **Obv:** Three towers within circle **Rev:** Wheat stalks and value **Edge:** Plain

Date	Mintage	F	VF	XF	Unc	BU
2001R	—	—	—	—	0.35	0.50

KM# 425 20 LIRE

3.6000 g., Aluminum-Bronze, 21.8 mm. **Obv:** Three towers within circle **Rev:** Two dolphins and value **Edge:** Plain

Date	Mintage	F	VF	XF	Unc	BU
2001R	—	—	—	—	1.00	2.00

KM# 426 50 LIRE

4.5000 g., Copper-Nickel, 19 mm. **Obv:** Three towers within circle **Rev:** Tree and value **Edge:** Plain

Date	Mintage	F	VF	XF	Unc	BU
2001R	—	—	—	—	0.85	1.50

KM# 427 100 LIRE
4.5000 g., Copper-Nickel, 22 mm. **Obv:** Three towers within circle **Rev:** Grasping hands and value **Edge:** Plain and reeded sections

Date	Mintage	F	VF	XF	Unc	BU
2001R	—	—	—	—	1.25	2.00

KM# 428 200 LIRE
5.0000 g., Aluminum-Bronze, 24 mm. **Obv:** Three towers within circle **Rev:** Broken chain, leaves, vines and value **Edge:** Reeded

Date	Mintage	F	VF	XF	Unc	BU
2001R	—	—	—	—	1.50	2.50

KM# 429 500 LIRE
Bi-Metallic Aluminum-Bronze center in Stainless Steel ring, 25.8 mm. **Obv:** Three towers within circle **Rev:** Three different plant stalks and value **Edge:** Segmented reeding **Note:** 6.8 grams.

Date	Mintage	F	VF	XF	Unc	BU
2001R	—	—	—	—	3.00	3.50

KM# 430 1000 LIRE
8.8000 g., Bi-Metallic Stainless-Steel center in Aluminum-Bronze ring, 27 mm. **Obv:** Three towers within circle **Rev:** Value within circle of birds **Edge:** Segmented reeding

Date	Mintage	F	VF	XF	Unc	BU
2001R	—	—	—	—	7.50	10.00

KM# 431 5000 LIRE
18.0000 g., 0.8350 Silver 0.4832 oz. ASW, 32 mm. **Obv:** Three towers within circle **Rev:** Dove on laurel branch above value **Edge:** Reeded and plain sections

Date	Mintage	F	VF	XF	Unc	BU
2001R	—	—	—	—	22.50	27.50

KM# 436 5000 LIRE
18.0000 g., 0.8350 Silver 0.4832 oz. ASW, 32 mm. **Subject:** Last Lire Coinage **Obv:** Crowned arms within sprigs **Rev:** Feather above six old coin designs with value below, all within beaded border **Edge:** Lettered

Date	Mintage	F	VF	XF	Unc	BU
2001R Proof	20,000	Value: 25.00				

KM# 437 10000 LIRE
22.0000 g., 0.8350 Silver 0.5906 oz. ASW, 34 mm. **Subject:** Last Lire Coinage **Obv:** Crowned arms within sprigs **Rev:** Feather above six old coin designs with value below, all within star border **Edge:** Reeded and plain sections

Date	Mintage	F	VF	XF	Unc	BU
2001R Proof	20,000	Value: 42.00				

KM# 432 10000 LIRE
22.0000 g., 0.8350 Silver 0.5906 oz. ASW, 34 mm. **Subject:** Ferrari **Obv:** Crowned arms within sprigs **Rev:** Race car with "FERRARI" background **Edge:** Reeded and plain sections

Date	Mintage	F	VF	XF	Unc	BU
2001R Proof	20,000	Value: 45.00				

KM# 438 10000 LIRE
22.0000 g., 0.8350 Silver 0.5906 oz. ASW, 34 mm. **Subject:** 2nd International Chambers of Commerce Convention **Obv:** Crowned arms within sprigs **Rev:** Mercury running by a computer **Edge:** Segmented reeding

Date	Mintage	F	VF	XF	Unc	BU
2001R Proof	19,987	Value: 42.00				

KM# 433 1/2 SCUDO
1.6100 g., 0.9000 Gold 0.0466 oz. AGW, 13.8 mm. **Subject:** Cavaliere **Obv:** Crowned arms within sprigs **Rev:** Horse and rider **Edge:** Reeded

Date	Mintage	F	VF	XF	Unc	BU
2001R Proof	4,500	Value: 100				

KM# 434 SCUDO
3.2200 g., 0.9000 Gold 0.0932 oz. AGW, 16 mm. **Subject:** Tiziano **Obv:** Crowned arms within sprigs **Rev:** Bearded bust left **Edge:** Reeded

Date	Mintage	F	VF	XF	Unc	BU
2001R Proof	4,500	Value: 190				

KM# 435 2 SCUDI
6.4400 g., 0.9000 Gold 0.1863 oz. AGW, 21 mm. **Subject:** Flora **Obv:** Crowned arms within sprigs **Rev:** Bust 1/4 left and value **Edge:** Reeded

Date	Mintage	F	VF	XF	Unc	BU
2001R Proof	4,500	Value: 375				

KM# 457 2 SCUDI
6.4516 g., 0.9000 Gold 0.1867 oz. AGW, 21 mm. **Obv:** Crowned arms within sprigs **Rev:** Madonna and Child **Edge:** Reeded

Date	Mintage	F	VF	XF	Unc	BU
2002R Proof	2,950	Value: 375				

KM# 459 2 SCUDI
6.4516 g., 0.9000 Gold 0.1867 oz. AGW, 21 mm. **Obv:** Crowned arms within sprigs **Rev:** Nostradamus above value **Edge:** Reeded

Date	Mintage	F	VF	XF	Unc	BU
2003R Proof	7,500	Value: 375				

KM# 464 2 SCUDI
6.4516 g., 0.9000 Gold 0.1867 oz. AGW, 21 mm. **Subject:** The Domagnano Treasure **Obv:** Crowned arms within sprigs **Rev:** Gothic Eagle Brooch, 5 Mark coin of 1952 **Edge:** Reeded

Date	Mintage	F	VF	XF	Unc	BU
2004R Proof	6,494	Value: 375				

KM# 345 2 SCUDI
6.4500 g., 0.9000 Gold 0.1866 oz. AGW, 21 mm. **Subject:** Rotary International, 100th Anniversary **Rev:** Rotary emblem

Date	Mintage	F	VF	XF	Unc	BU
2005R Proof	4,249	Value: 425				

KM# 346 2 SCUDI
6.4500 g., 0.9000 Gold 0.1866 oz. AGW, 21 mm. **Subject:** General meeting of the heads of families, 100th Anniversary **Rev:** Three females with the fruits of democracy

Date	Mintage	F	VF	XF	Unc	BU
2006R Proof	2,821	Value: 425				

KM# 347 2 SCUDI
6.4500 g., 0.9000 Gold 0.1866 oz. AGW, 21 mm. **Subject:** Diplomatic relations with Japan, 50th Anniversary **Rev:** Shrine of Jinmu Tenno (1889) in Kashihara

Date	Mintage	F	VF	XF	Unc	BU
2007R Proof	7,536	Value: 425				

KM# 493 2 SCUDI
6.4100 g., 0.9000 Gold 0.1855 oz. AGW, 21 mm. **Subject:** Pompeo Batoni, 300th Anniversary of Brith **Obv:** Arms **Rev:** Batoni's "San Marino Risolleva la Republica"

Date	Mintage	F	VF	XF	Unc	BU
2008R Proof	2,100	Value: 375				

KM# 450 2 SCUDI
6.4500 g., 0.9000 Gold 0.1866 oz. AGW, 21 mm. **Subject:** Art treasures of San Marino **Rev:** Ceres Bronze Statue by Albert E. Carrier Belleuse

Date	Mintage	F	VF	XF	Unc	BU
2009R Proof	2,100	Value: 425				

KM# 451 2 SCUDI
6.4500 g., 0.9000 Gold 0.1866 oz. AGW, 21 mm. **Subject:** Art treasures of San Marino **Rev:** Justice with scales by Bernardino Mei

Date	Mintage	F	VF	XF	Unc	BU
2010R Proof	2,100	Value: 425				

KM# 517 2 SCUDI
6.4500 g., 0.9000 Gold 0.1866 oz. AGW, 21 mm. **Subject:** Christmas **Rev:** Nativity scene

Date	Mintage	F	VF	XF	Unc	BU
2011R Proof	1,600	Value: 475				

KM# 439 5 SCUDI
16.9655 g., 0.9166 Gold 0.4999 oz. AGW, 28 mm. **Subject:** San Marino's World Bank Membership **Obv:** Crowned arms within sprigs **Rev:** Orchid and bee within globe **Edge:** Reeded

Date	Mintage	F	VF	XF	Unc	BU
2001R Proof	4,000	Value: 950				

KM# 348 5 SCUDI
16.1300 g., 0.9000 Gold 0.4667 oz. AGW, 28 mm. **Subject:** Diplomatic relations with Japan, 50th Anniversary **Rev:** Jinmu Tenno

Date	Mintage	F	VF	XF	Unc	BU
2007R Proof	7,130	Value: 900				

EURO COINAGE

KM# 440 EURO CENT

2.2700 g., Copper Plated Steel, 16.2 mm. **Obv:** "Il Montale" **Rev:** Value and globe **Edge:** Plain

Date	Mintage	F	VF	XF	Unc	BU
2002R	125,000	—	—	—	—	40.00
2003R In sets only	70,000	—	—	—	—	42.00
2004R	1,500,000	—	—	—	—	20.00
2005R In sets only	70,000	—	—	—	—	20.00
2006R	2,730,000	—	—	—	8.00	12.00
2007R	—	—	—	—	8.00	12.00
2008R	—	—	—	—	8.00	12.00
2008R Proof	13,000	Value: 10.00				
2009R	—	—	—	—	8.00	12.00
2009R Proof	13,500	Value: 10.00				
2010R	—	—	—	—	8.00	12.00
2010R Proof	8,600	Value: 10.00				
2011R	—	—	—	—	8.00	12.00
2011R Proof	8,600	Value: 10.00				
2012R	—	—	—	—	8.00	12.00
2013R	—	—	—	—	8.00	12.00

KM# 441 2 EURO CENT

3.0300 g., Copper Plated Steel, 18.7 mm. **Obv:** Stefano Gallietti, Liberty fighter **Rev:** Value and globe **Edge:** Grooved

Date	Mintage	F	VF	XF	Unc	BU
2002R	125,000	—	—	—	—	40.00
2003R In sets only	70,000	—	—	—	—	42.00
2004R	1,395,000	—	—	—	—	20.00
2005R In sets only	150,000	—	—	—	—	20.00
2006R	2,730,000	—	—	—	8.00	12.00
2007R	—	—	—	—	8.00	12.00
2008R	—	—	—	—	8.00	12.00
2008R Proof	13,000	Value: 10.00				
2009R	—	—	—	—	8.00	12.00
2009R Proof	13,500	Value: 10.00				
2010R	—	—	—	—	8.00	12.00
2010R Proof	8,600	Value: 10.00				
2011R	—	—	—	—	8.00	12.00
2011R Proof	8,600	Value: 10.00				
2012R	—	—	—	—	8.00	12.00
2013R	—	—	—	—	8.00	12.00

KM# 442 5 EURO CENT

3.8600 g., Copper Plated Steel, 21.2 mm. **Obv:** "Guaita" tower **Rev:** Value and globe **Edge:** Plain

Date	Mintage	F	VF	XF	Unc	BU
2002R	125,000	—	—	—	—	40.00
2003R In sets only	70,000	—	—	—	—	42.00
2004R	1,000,000	—	—	—	—	20.00
2005R In sets only	70,000	—	—	—	—	20.00
2006R	2,880,000	—	—	—	8.00	12.00
2007R	—	—	—	—	8.00	12.00
2008R	—	—	—	—	8.00	12.00
2008R Proof	13,000	Value: 10.00				
2009R	—	—	—	—	8.00	12.00
2009R Proof	13,500	Value: 10.00				
2010R	—	—	—	—	8.00	12.00
2010R Proof	8,600	Value: 10.00				
2011R	—	—	—	—	8.00	12.00
2011R Proof	8,600	Value: 10.00				
2012R	—	—	—	—	8.00	12.00
2013R	—	—	—	—	8.00	12.00

KM# 443 10 EURO CENT

4.0700 g., Brass, 19.7 mm. **Obv:** Building Basilica del Santo Marinus **Rev:** Map and value **Edge:** Reeded

Date	Mintage	F	VF	XF	Unc	BU
2002R	125,000	—	—	—	—	40.00
2003R In sets only	70,000	—	—	—	—	42.00
2004R	180,000	—	—	—	—	22.00
2005R In sets only	70,000	—	—	—	—	22.00
2006R In sets only	65,000	—	—	—	—	20.00
2007R	—	—	—	—	—	18.00

KM# 482 10 EURO CENT

4.0700 g., Brass, 19.7 mm. **Obv:** Basilica de Santo Marinus facade **Rev:** Relief maps of Western Europe, value and stars

Date	Mintage	F	VF	XF	Unc	BU
2008R	—	—	—	—	8.00	12.00
2008R Proof	13,000	Value: 12.00				
2009R	—	—	—	—	8.00	12.00
2009R Proof	13,500	Value: 12.00				
2010R	—	—	—	—	8.00	12.00
2010R Proof	8,600	Value: 12.00				
2011R	—	—	—	—	8.00	12.00
2011R Proof	8,600	Value: 12.00				
2012R	—	—	—	—	8.00	12.00
2013R	—	—	—	—	8.00	12.00

KM# 444 20 EURO CENT

5.7300 g., Brass, 22.1 mm. **Obv:** St. Marinus from a portrait by van Guercino **Rev:** Map and value **Edge:** Notched

Date	Mintage	F	VF	XF	Unc	BU
2002R	267,400	—	—	—	18.00	20.00
2003R	430,000	—	—	—	15.00	18.00
2004R In sets only	70,000	—	—	—	15.00	18.00
2005R	310,000	—	—	—	15.00	18.00
2006R In sets only	70,000	—	—	—	15.00	18.00
2007R	—	—	—	—	14.00	16.00

KM# 483 20 EURO CENT

5.7300 g., Brass **Obv:** Saint holding Monte Titano **Rev:** Relief map of Western Europe, value and stars

Date	Mintage	F	VF	XF	Unc	BU
2008R	—	—	—	—	8.00	12.00
2008R Proof	13,000	Value: 15.00				
2009R	—	—	—	—	8.00	12.00
2009R Proof	13,500	Value: 15.00				
2010R	—	—	—	—	8.00	12.00
2010R Proof	8,600	Value: 15.00				
2011R	—	—	—	—	8.00	12.00
2011R Proof	8,600	Value: 15.00				
2012R	—	—	—	—	8.00	12.00
2013R	—	—	—	—	8.00	12.00

KM# 445 50 EURO CENT

7.8100 g., Brass, 24.2 mm. **Obv:** Fortress of San Marino **Rev:** Map and value **Edge:** Reeded

Date	Mintage	F	VF	XF	Unc	BU
2002R	230,400	—	—	—	20.00	22.50
2003R	415,000	—	—	—	17.50	20.00
2004R In sets only	70,000	—	—	—	17.50	20.00
2005R	179,000	—	—	—	17.50	20.00
2006R	343,880	—	—	—	15.00	18.00
2007R	—	—	—	—	14.00	16.00

KM# 484 50 EURO CENT

7.8000 g., Brass, 24.2 mm. **Obv:** Buildings on hill top **Rev:** Relief map of Western Europe, value and stars

Date	Mintage	F	VF	XF	Unc	BU
2008R	—	—	—	—	10.00	12.00
2008R Proof	13,000	Value: 13.00				
2009R	—	—	—	—	10.00	12.00
2009R Proof	13,500	Value: 13.00				
2010R	—	—	—	—	10.00	12.00
2010R Proof	8,600	Value: 13.00				
2011R	—	—	—	—	10.00	12.00
2011R Proof	8,600	Value: 13.00				
2012R	—	—	—	—	10.00	12.00
2013R	—	—	—	—	10.00	12.00

KM# 446 EURO

7.5000 g., Bi-Metallic Copper-Nickel center in Nickel-Brass ring, 23.25 mm. **Obv:** Crowned arms within sprigs and circle within star border **Rev:** Value and map **Edge:** Segmented reeding

Date	Mintage	F	VF	XF	Unc	BU
2002R	360,800	—	—	—	22.00	25.00
2003R In sets only	70,000	—	—	—	—	45.00
2004R	180,000	—	—	—	—	25.00
2005R In sets only	70,000	—	—	—	—	25.00
2006R In sets only	220,000	—	—	—	—	20.00
2007R	—	—	—	—	—	18.00

KM# 485 EURO

7.5000 g., Bi-Metallic Copper-Nickel center in Nickel-Brass ring, 23.25 mm. **Obv:** Covered arms within wreath and stars **Rev:** Relief map of Western Europe, value and stars **Edge:** Segmented reeding

Date	Mintage	F	VF	XF	Unc	BU
2008R	—	—	—	—	12.00	15.00
2008R Proof	13,000	Value: 15.00				
2009R	—	—	—	—	12.00	15.00
2009R Proof	13,500	Value: 15.00				
2010R	—	—	—	—	12.00	15.00
2010R Proof	8,600	Value: 15.00				
2011R	—	—	—	—	12.00	15.00
2011R Proof	8,600	Value: 15.00				
2012R	—	—	—	—	12.00	15.00

KM# 447 2 EURO

8.5000 g., Bi-Metallic Nickel-Brass center in Copper-Nickel ring, 25.75 mm. **Obv:** Government building **Rev:** Value and map **Edge:** Reeded with 2's and stars

Date	Mintage	F	VF	XF	Unc	BU
2002R	255,760	—	—	—	25.00	28.00
2003R In sets only	70,000	—	—	—	—	45.00
2004R In sets only	70,000	—	—	—	—	28.00
2005R In sets only	210,000	—	—	—	—	28.00
2006R In sets only	190,000	—	—	—	—	22.00
2007R	—	—	—	—	—	20.00

KM# 467 2 EURO

8.5000 g., Bi-Metallic Nickel-Brass center in Copper-Nickel ring, 25.75 mm. **Obv:** Crowned arms within sprigs **Rev:** Bartolomeo Borghesi **Edge:** Alternating stars and 2's

Date	Mintage	F	VF	XF	Unc	BU
2004R	110,000	—	—	—	135	150

KM# 469 2 EURO

8.5000 g., Bi-Metallic Nickel-Brass center in Copper-Nickel ring, 25.75 mm. **Obv:** Galileo Galilei at telescope

Date	Mintage	F	VF	XF	Unc	BU
2005R	130,000	—	—	—	135	150

KM# 478 2 EURO
8.5000 g., Bi-Metallic Nickel-Brass center in Copper-Nickel ring, 25.75 mm. **Subject:** Christopher Columbus, 500th Anniversary of Death **Obv:** Head of Columbus within border of stars **Rev:** Map and value

Date	Mintage	F	VF	XF	Unc	BU
2006R	120,000	—	—	—	100	125

KM# 481 2 EURO
8.5000 g., Bi-Metallic Nickel-Brass center in Copper-Nickel ring, 25.75 mm. **Subject:** Giuseppe Garibaldi, 200th Anniversary of Birth **Obv:** Half length bust facing **Rev:** Relief map of Western Europe, value and stars

Date	Mintage	F	VF	XF	Unc	BU
2007R	130,000	—	—	—	60.00	75.00

KM# 486 2 EURO
8.5000 g., Bi-Metallic Nickel-Brass center in Copper-Nickel ring, 25.75 mm. **Obv:** Palace **Rev:** Relief map of Western Europe, value and stars

Date	Mintage	F	VF	XF	Unc	BU
2008R	—	—	—	—	24.00	28.00
2008R Proof	13,000	Value: 20.00				
2009R	—	—	—	—	24.00	28.00
2009R Proof	13,500	Value: 20.00				
2010R	—	—	—	—	24.00	28.00
2010R Proof	8,600	Value: 20.00				
2011R	—	—	—	—	24.00	28.00
2011R Proof	8,600	Value: 20.00				
2012R	—	—	—	—	24.00	28.00
2013R	—	—	—	—	24.00	28.00

KM# 487 2 EURO
8.5000 g., Bi-Metallic Nickel-Brass center in Copper-Nickel ring, 25.75 mm. **Subject:** European Year of Intercultural Dialogue **Obv:** Five figures with arms outstretched, books below **Rev:** Relief map of Western Europe, value and stars

Date	Mintage	F	VF	XF	Unc	BU
2008R	130,000	—	—	—	70.00	90.00

KM# 490 2 EURO
8.5000 g., Bi-Metallic Nickel-Brass center in Copper-Nickel ring, 25.75 mm. **Subject:** Creativity and Innovation **Obv:** Chemical flasks and book

Date	Mintage	F	VF	XF	Unc	BU
2009R	—	—	—	—	45.00	55.00

KM# 494 2 EURO
8.5000 g., Bi-Metallic Nickel-Brass center in Copper-Nickel ring, 25.75 mm. **Subject:** Sandra Botticeli, 500th Anniversary of Death

Date	Mintage	F	VF	XF	Unc	BU
2010R	130,000	—	—	—	45.00	55.00

KM# 500 2 EURO
8.5000 g., Bi-Metallic Nickel-Brass center in Copper-Nickel ring, 25.75 mm. **Subject:** Hgiorgio Vasari, 500th Anniversary of Birth

Date	Mintage	F	VF	XF	Unc	BU
2011R	130,000	—	—	—	35.00	45.00

KM# 519 2 EURO
8.5000 g., Bi-Metallic Nickel-brass center in Copper-Nickel ring, 25.75 mm. **Obv:** Euro symbol

Date	Mintage	F	VF	XF	Unc	BU
2012R	125,000	—	—	—	35.00	45.00
2012R Proof	5,000	Value: 55.00				

KM# 448 5 EURO
18.0000 g., 0.9250 Silver 0.5353 oz. ASW, 32 mm. **Subject:** Welcome Euro **Obv:** Three plumed towers **Rev:** Circle of roses

Date	Mintage	F	VF	XF	Unc	BU
2002R Proof	37,000	Value: 75.00				

KM# 453 5 EURO
18.0000 g., 0.9250 Silver 0.5353 oz. ASW, 32 mm. **Subject:** 2004 Olympics **Obv:** Stylized three towers **Rev:** Ancient Olympians **Edge:** Reeded

Date	Mintage	F	VF	XF	Unc	BU
2003R Proof	37,742	Value: 50.00				

KM# 452 5 EURO
18.0000 g., 0.9250 Silver 0.5353 oz. ASW, 32 mm. **Obv:** National arms **Rev:** Allegorical depiction of Independence, Tolerance and Liberty

Date	Mintage	F	VF	XF	Unc	BU
2003R	70,000	—	—	—	35.00	40.00

KM# 458 5 EURO
18.0000 g., 0.9250 Silver 0.5353 oz. ASW, 32 mm. **Obv:** National arms **Rev:** Value behind Bartolomeo Borghesi

Date	Mintage	F	VF	XF	Unc	BU
2004R	70,000	—	—	—	30.00	35.00

KM# 462 5 EURO
18.0000 g., 0.9250 Silver 0.5353 oz. ASW, 32 mm. **Obv:** Three stylized plumed towers **Rev:** Two soccer players

Date	Mintage	F	VF	XF	Unc	BU
2004R Proof	29,673	Value: 45.00				

KM# 468 5 EURO
18.0000 g., 0.9250 Silver 0.5353 oz. ASW, 32 mm. **Obv:** Three towers **Rev:** Antonio Onofri and value

Date	Mintage	F	VF	XF	Unc	BU
2005R	70,000	—	—	—	30.00	35.00

KM# 511 5 EURO
18.0000 g., 0.9250 Silver 0.5353 oz. ASW, 32 mm. **Subject:** Winter Olympics, Turin **Rev:** Snowflake, snowman on skies

Date	Mintage	F	VF	XF	Unc	BU
2005R Proof	26,786	Value: 50.00				

KM# 472 5 EURO
18.0000 g., 0.9250 Silver 0.5353 oz. ASW, 32 mm. **Obv:** Portrait of Melchiorie Delfico

Date	Mintage	F	VF	XF	Unc	BU
2006R	65,000	—	—	—	30.00	35.00

KM# 476 5 EURO
18.0000 g., 0.9250 Silver 0.5353 oz. ASW, 32 mm. **Subject:** Andrea Mantegna, 500th Anniversary of Death **Obv:** Three towers **Rev:** Statue of soldier and naked female

Date	Mintage	F	VF	XF	Unc	BU
2006R Proof	18,986	Value: 40.00				

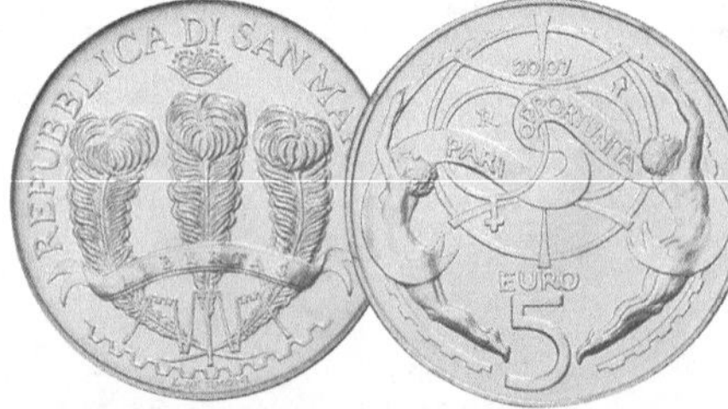

KM# 473 5 EURO
18.0000 g., 0.9250 Silver 0.5353 oz. ASW, 32 mm. **Subject:** Equal Opportunity between the sexes **Obv:** Three plumed towers **Obv. Legend:** REPUBLICA DI SAN MARINO **Rev:** Nude female at left, nude male at right, ribbon across symbols within circle above, value below **Rev. Inscription:** PARI OPPORTITA **Edge:** Reeded

Date	Mintage	F	VF	XF	Unc	BU
2007R	70,000	—	—	—	30.00	35.00

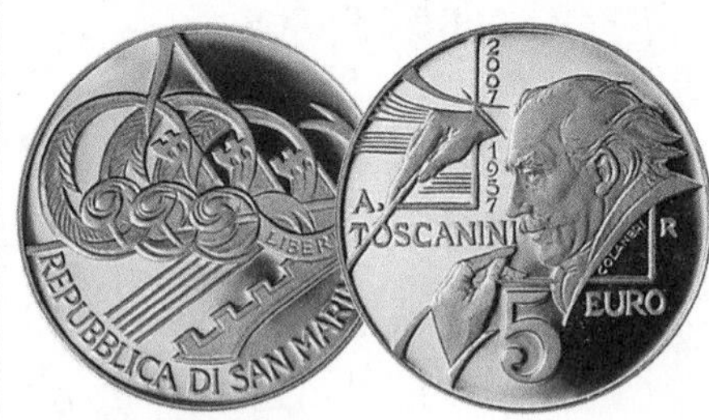

KM# 474 5 EURO
18.0000 g., 0.9250 Silver 0.5353 oz. ASW, 32 mm. **Subject:** 50th Anniversary Death of Toscanini **Obv:** Stylized national arms **Obv. Legend:** REPUBBLICA DI SAN MARINO **Rev:** Head of Toscanini left **Edge:** Reeded

Date	Mintage	F	VF	XF	Unc	BU
ND(2007)R Proof	17,736	Value: 40.00				

KM# 512 5 EURO
18.0000 g., 0.9250 Silver 0.5353 oz. ASW, 32 mm. **Rev:** Winds, land and sea

Date	Mintage	F	VF	XF	Unc	BU
2008R	50,000	—	—	—	30.00	35.00

KM# 513 5 EURO
18.0000 g., 0.9250 Silver 0.5353 oz. ASW, 32 mm. **Subject:** Summer Olympics, Peking **Rev:** Ribbon Dancer

Date	Mintage	F	VF	XF	Unc	BU
2008R Proof	21,000	Value: 45.00				

KM# 506 5 EURO
18.0000 g., 0.9250 Silver 0.5353 oz. ASW, 32 mm. **Subject:** Kepler **Obv:** Kepler bust and globe **Rev:** Planets orbit around central sun **Designer:** Maria Angela Cassol

Date	Mintage	F	VF	XF	Unc	BU
2009R Proof	13,400	Value: 50.00				

KM# 515 5 EURO
18.0000 g., 0.9250 Silver 0.5353 oz. ASW, 32 mm. **Subject:** Year of Astronomy **Obv:** Planets in orbit **Rev:** Planets in orbit, Astrolab

Date	Mintage	F	VF	XF	Unc	BU
2009R	50,000	—	—	—	30.00	35.00

KM# 495 5 EURO
18.0000 g., 0.9250 Silver 0.5353 oz. ASW, 32 mm. **Subject:** Shanghai Expo

Date	Mintage	F	VF	XF	Unc	BU
2010R Proof	10,000	Value: 65.00				

KM# 496 5 EURO
18.0000 g., 0.9250 Silver 0.5353 oz. ASW, 32 mm. **Subject:** Michelangelo Caravaggio, 500th Anniverdary of Death

Date	Mintage	F	VF	XF	Unc	BU
2010R	48,000	—	—	—	30.00	35.00

KM# 501 5 EURO
18.0000 g., 0.9250 Silver 0.5353 oz. ASW, 32 mm. **Subject:** European Discoveries **Obv:** Crowned coat of arms **Rev:** Busts of Antonio & Roberto Pazzaglia, Mt. Everest in background

Date	Mintage	F	VF	XF	Unc	BU
2011R Proof	10,000	Value: 50.00				

KM# 502 5 EURO
18.0000 g., 0.9250 Silver 0.5353 oz. ASW, 32 mm. **Subject:** First Manned Space Flight, 50th Anniversary

Date	Mintage	F	VF	XF	Unc	BU
2011R	48,000	—	—	—	30.00	35.00

KM# 518 5 EURO
18.0000 g., 0.9250 Silver 0.5353 oz. ASW, 32 mm. **Subject:** 509th Anniversary of man in space **Rev:** Gagarin and Shepard, Vostok I and Freedom 7 spacecraft

Date	Mintage	F	VF	XF	Unc	BU
2011R	—	—	—	—	30.00	35.00

KM# 520 5 EURO
18.0000 g., 0.9250 Silver 0.5353 oz. ASW, 32 mm. **Subject:** Giovanni Pascoli, 100th Anniversary of Death **Obv:** National arms **Rev:** Bust at right

Date	Mintage	F	VF	XF	Unc	BU
2012R Proof	40,000	Value: 35.00				

KM# 521 5 EURO
18.0000 g., 0.9250 Silver 0.5353 oz. ASW, 32 mm. **Subject:** Amerigo Vespucci, 500th Anniversary of Death **Obv:** National arms **Rev:** Vespucci standing holding astrolobe to the stars

Date	Mintage	F	VF	XF	Unc	BU
2012R Proof	12,000	Value: 55.00				

KM# 449 10 EURO
22.0000 g., 0.9250 Silver 0.6542 oz. ASW, 34 mm. **Subject:** Welcome Euro **Obv:** Three plumed towers **Rev:** Infant sleeping in flower

Date	Mintage	F	VF	XF	Unc	BU
2002R Proof	36,995	Value: 100				

KM# 454 10 EURO
22.0000 g., 0.9250 Silver 0.6542 oz. ASW, 34 mm. **Subject:** 2004 Olympics **Obv:** Three stylized towers **Rev:** Modern Olympians **Edge:** Segmented reeding

Date	Mintage	F	VF	XF	Unc	BU
2003R Proof	37,741	Value: 75.00				

KM# 463 10 EURO
22.0000 g., 0.9250 Silver 0.6542 oz. ASW, 34 mm. **Obv:** Three stylized plumed towers **Rev:** Two soccer players

Date	Mintage	F	VF	XF	Unc	BU
2004R Proof	29,617	Value: 70.00				

KM# 344 10 EURO
22.0000 g., 0.9250 Silver 0.6542 oz. ASW **Subject:** Uniformed National Military, 500th Anniversary **Obv:** National arms **Rev:** Soldier with flag

Date	Mintage	F	VF	XF	Unc	BU
2005R Proof	21,969	Value: 50.00				

KM# 477 10 EURO
22.0000 g., 0.9250 Silver 0.6542 oz. ASW, 34 mm. **Subject:** Antonio Canova **Obv:** Three towers **Rev:** The Three Graces

Date	Mintage	F	VF	XF	Unc	BU
2006R Proof	17,859	Value: 65.00				

KM# 475 10 EURO
22.0000 g., 0.9250 Silver 0.6542 oz. ASW, 34 mm. **Subject:** 100th Anniversary - Birthday of Giosuè Carducci **Obv:** Stylized national arms **Obv. Legend:** REPUBBLICA DI SAN MARINO **Rev:** 1/2 length figure of Carducci facing with quill pen in hand at table **Rev. Legend:** CARDUCCI **Edge:** Segmented reeding

Date	Mintage	F	VF	XF	Unc	BU
ND(2007)R Proof	14,615	Value: 55.00				

KM# 514 10 EURO
22.0000 g., 0.9250 Silver 0.6542 oz. ASW, 34 mm. **Subject:** Andrea Palladio, 500th Anniversary of Birth **Rev:** Building façade

Date	Mintage	F	VF	XF	Unc	BU
2008R Proof	17,000	Value: 65.00				

KM# 516 10 EURO
22.0000 g., 0.9250 Silver 0.6542 oz. ASW, 34 mm. **Subject:** Euro, 10th Anniversary

Date	Mintage	F	VF	XF	Unc	BU
2009R Proof	12,500	Value: 60.00				

KM# 497 10 EURO
22.0000 g., 0.9250 Silver 0.6542 oz. ASW, 34 mm. **Subject:** Robert Schumann, 200th Anniversary of Birth

Date	Mintage	F	VF	XF	Unc	BU
2010R Proof	10,000	Value: 55.00				

KM# 503 10 EURO
22.0000 g., 0.9250 Silver 0.6542 oz. ASW, 34 mm. **Subject:** Euro, 10th Anniversary **Obv:** Montage of partial coin designs

Date	Mintage	F	VF	XF	Unc	BU
2011R Proof	10,000	Value: 60.00				

KM# 522 10 EURO
22.0000 g., 0.9250 Silver 0.6542 oz. ASW, 34 mm. **Subject:** Aligi Sassu, 100th Birthday **Obv:** National arms **Rev:** Horse rearing up at left, bust at right

Date	Mintage	F	VF	XF	Unc	BU
2012R Proof	12,000	Value: 70.00				

KM# 460 20 EURO
6.4510 g., 0.9000 Gold 0.1867 oz. AGW, 21 mm. **Subject:** 1600th Anniversary of Ravenna **Obv:** National arms **Rev:** Bas-relief wall design **Edge:** Reeded

Date	Mintage	F	VF	XF	Unc	BU
2002R Proof	4,510	Value: 375				

KM# 455 20 EURO
6.4516 g., 0.9000 Gold 0.1867 oz. AGW, 21 mm. **Obv:** Three plumes **Rev:** Giotto's "Presentation of Jesus at the Temple" **Edge:** Reeded

Date	Mintage	F	VF	XF	Unc	BU
2003R Proof	7,281	Value: 375				

KM# 465 20 EURO
6.4510 g., 0.9000 Gold 0.1867 oz. AGW, 21 mm. **Obv:** Three plumes **Rev:** Marco Polo meeting Kublai Khan **Edge:** Reeded

Date	Mintage	F	VF	XF	Unc	BU
2004R Proof	5,885	Value: 375				

KM# 470 20 EURO
6.4510 g., 0.9000 Gold 0.1867 oz. AGW, 21 mm. **Subject:** International Day of Peace **Obv:** Stylized faces and leaves

Date	Mintage	F	VF	XF	Unc	BU
2005R Proof	3,914	Value: 375				

KM# 479 20 EURO
6.4500 g., 0.9000 Gold 0.1866 oz. AGW, 21 mm. **Subject:** Giovan Battista Belluzzi, 500th Birthday **Obv:** Crowned shield **Rev:** Fortification plan **Designer:** Guido Veroi

Date	Mintage	F	VF	XF	Unc	BU
2006R Proof	2,684	Value: 375				

KM# 507 20 EURO
6.4510 g., 0.9000 Gold 0.1867 oz. AGW

Date	Mintage	F	VF	XF	Unc	BU
2007R Proof	2,105	Value: 350				

KM# 491 20 EURO
6.4500 g., 0.9000 Gold 0.1866 oz. AGW **Subject:** Roman Antiquities **Obv:** Arms **Rev:** Small statue of Mercury

Date	Mintage	F	VF	XF	Unc	BU
2008R Proof	2,100	Value: 375				

KM# 509 20 EURO
6.4510 g., 0.9000 Gold 0.1867 oz. AGW, 21 mm.

Date	Mintage	F	VF	XF	Unc	BU
2009R Proof	2,000	Value: 350				

KM# 498 20 EURO
6.4510 g., 0.9000 Gold 0.1867 oz. AGW, 21 mm. **Subject:** Treasurers from San Marino - Wooden bust of St. Agata

Date	Mintage	F	VF	XF	Unc	BU
2010R Proof	2,000	Value: 375				

KM# 504 20 EURO
6.4510 g., 0.9000 Gold 0.1867 oz. AGW, 21 mm. **Subject:** Treasures from San Marino

Date	Mintage	F	VF	XF	Unc	BU
2011R Proof	1,600	Value: 375				

KM# 461 50 EURO
16.1290 g., 0.9000 Gold 0.4667 oz. AGW, 28 mm. **Subject:** 1600th Anniversary of Ravenna **Obv:** National arms **Rev:** Wall painting **Edge:** Reeded

Date	Mintage	F	VF	XF	Unc	BU
2002R Proof	4,510	Value: 900				

KM# 456 50 EURO
16.1290 g., 0.9000 Gold 0.4667 oz. AGW, 28 mm. **Obv:** Three plumes **Rev:** Giotto's "The Pentecost" **Edge:** Reeded

Date	Mintage	F	VF	XF	Unc	BU
2003R Proof	7,281	Value: 900				

KM# 466 50 EURO
16.1290 g., 0.9000 Gold 0.4667 oz. AGW, 28 mm. **Obv:** Three plumes **Rev:** Marco Polo **Edge:** Reeded

Date	Mintage	F	VF	XF	Unc	BU
2004R Proof	5,885	Value: 900				

KM# 471 50 EURO
16.1290 g., 0.9000 Gold 0.4667 oz. AGW, 28 mm. **Subject:** International Day of Peace **Obv:** Group of people gathering

Date	Mintage	F	VF	XF	Unc	BU
2005R Proof	3,914	Value: 900				

KM# 480 50 EURO
16.1300 g., 0.9000 Gold 0.4667 oz. AGW, 28 mm. **Subject:** Giovan Batista Belluzzi **Obv:** Crowned shield **Rev:** Bust right **Designer:** Guido Veroi

Date	Mintage	F	VF	XF	Unc	BU
2006R Proof	2,684	Value: 900				

KM# 508 50 EURO
16.1290 g., 0.9000 Gold 0.4667 oz. AGW, 28 mm.

Date	Mintage	F	VF	XF	Unc	BU
2007R Proof	2,105	Value: 900				

KM# 492 50 EURO
16.1300 g., 0.9000 Gold 0.4667 oz. AGW, 28 mm. **Subject:** Antiquities **Obv:** Arms **Rev:** Two bronze fibulae

Date	Mintage	F	VF	XF	Unc	BU
2008R Proof	2,100	Value: 900				

KM# 510 50 EURO
16.1300 g., 0.9000 Gold 0.4667 oz. AGW, 28 mm.

Date	Mintage	F	VF	XF	Unc	BU
2009R Proof	2,000	Value: 900				

KM# 499 50 EURO
16.1290 g., 0.9000 Gold 0.4667 oz. AGW, 28 mm. **Subject:** Treasurers from San Marino - Saint Marinus

Date	Mintage	F	VF	XF	Unc	BU
2010R Proof	2,000	Value: 900				

KM# 505 50 EURO
16.1290 g., 0.9000 Gold 0.4667 oz. AGW, 28 mm. **Subject:** Treasures from San Marino

Date	Mintage	F	VF	XF	Unc	BU
2011R Proof	1,600	Value: 900				

MINT SETS

KM#	Date	Mintage	Identification	Issue Price	Mkt Val
MS61	2001 (8)	2,000	KM424-431	18.00	50.00
MS62	2002 (8)	120,000	KM440 - 447	—	275
MS63	2003 (9)	—	KM#440-447, 452	55.00	350
MS64	2004 (9)	—	KM#440-447, 458	55.00	220
MS65	2005 (9)	—	KM#440-447, 468	55.00	225
MS66	2006 (9)	65,000	KM#440-447, 472	—	185
MS67	2007 (3)	—	KM#443, 444, 447	27.50	55.00
MS68	2007 (9)	—	KM#440-447, 473	120	160

PROOF SETS

KM#	Date	Mintage	Identification	Issue Price	Mkt Val
PS14	2001 (3)	4,500	KM433-435	179	500
PSA15	2001 (2)	—	KM#436, 437	—	70.00
PS15	2002 (2)	37,000	KM448-449	—	175
PS16	2002 (2)	4,550	KM#460-461	—	1,150
PS17	2003 (2)	7,300	KM#455-456	—	975
PS18	2004 (2)	7,300	KM#465-466	—	975
PS19	2005 (2)	5,300	KM#470-471	—	1,050
PS20	2008 (8)	13,000	KM#440-442, 482-486	—	135
PS21	2009 (8)	13,500	KM#440-443, 482-486	—	135
PS22	2010 (8)	8,600	KM#440-442, 482-486	—	135
PS23	2011 (8)	8,600	KM#440-442, 482-486	—	135

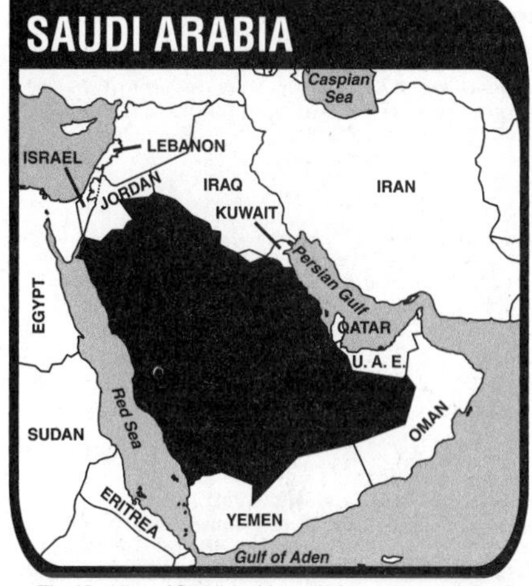

The Kingdom of Saudi Arabia, an independent and absolute hereditary monarchy comprising the former sultanate of Nejd, the old kingdom of Hejaz, Asir and Al Hasa, occupies four-fifths of the Arabian peninsula. The kingdom has an area of 830,000 sq. mi. (2,149,690 sq. km.) and a population of *16.1 million. Capital: Riyadh. The economy is based on oil, which provides 85 percent of Saudi Arabia's revenue.

TITLES

العربية السعودية

Al-Arabiya(t) as-Sa'udiya(t)

المملكة العربية السعودية

Al-Mamlaka(t) al-'Arabiya(t) as-Sa'udiya(t)

RULERS

al Sa'ud Dynasty

Fahad bin Abd Al-Aziz, AH1403-1426/1982-2005AD
Abdullah bin Abdul Aziz, AH1426-/2005AD

KINGDOM

REFORM COINAGE

5 Halala = 1 Ghirsh; 100 Halala = 1 Riyal

KM# 69 5 HALALA (Ghirsh)
Copper-Nickel **Ruler:** Abdullah bin Abdul Aziz AH1426-/2005-AD **Obv:** National emblem at center **Rev:** Legend above inscription in circle, dividing value, date below

Date	Mintage	F	VF	XF	Unc	BU
AH1430(2009)	—	—	0.30	0.60	1.50	2.00

KM# 62 10 HALALA (2 Ghirsh)
4.0000 g., Copper-Nickel, 21 mm. **Ruler:** Fahad Bin Abd Al-Aziz AH1403-1426/1982-2005AD **Obv:** National emblem at center, legend above and below **Rev:** Legend above inscription in circle dividing value, date below **Edge:** Reeded

Date	Mintage	F	VF	XF	Unc	BU
AH1423 (2002)	—	—	0.15	0.35	0.90	1.00

KM# 70 10 HALALA (2 Ghirsh)
Copper-Nickel **Ruler:** Abdullah bin Abdul Aziz AH1426-/2005-AD **Obv:** National emblem at center **Rev:** Legend above inscription in circle, dividing value, date below

Date	Mintage	F	VF	XF	Unc	BU
AH1430(2009)	—	—	0.30	0.60	1.50	2.50

KM# 63 25 HALALA (1/4 Riyal)
5.0000 g., Copper-Nickel, 23 mm. **Ruler:** Fahad Bin Abd Al-Aziz AH1403-1426/1982-2005AD **Obv:** National emblem at center, legend above and below **Rev:** Legend above inscription in circle dividing value, date below **Edge:** Reeded

Date	Mintage	F	VF	XF	Unc	BU
AH1423 (2002)	—	—	0.20	0.45	1.10	1.50

KM# 71 25 HALALA (1/4 Riyal)
Copper-Nickel **Ruler:** Abdullah bin Abdul Aziz AH1426-/2005-AD **Obv:** National emblem at center **Rev:** Legend above inscription in circle, divides value, date below

Date	Mintage	F	VF	XF	Unc	BU
AH1427 (2006)	—	—	0.20	0.45	1.10	1.50
AH1430 (2009)	—	—	0.20	0.45	1.10	1.50

KM# 64 50 HALALA (1/2 Riyal)
6.5000 g., Copper-Nickel, 26 mm. **Ruler:** Fahad Bin Abd Al-Aziz AH1403-1426/1982-2005AD **Obv:** National emblem at center, legend above and below **Rev:** Legend above inscription in circle dividing value, date below **Edge:** Reeded

Date	Mintage	F	VF	XF	Unc	BU
AH1423 (2002)	—	0.15	0.30	0.75	1.50	2.00

KM# 68 50 HALALA (1/2 Riyal)
6.5000 g., Copper-Nickel, 26 mm. **Ruler:** Abdullah bin Abdul Aziz AH1426-/2005-AD **Obv:** National emblem at center **Rev:** Legend above inscription in circle, dividing value, date below **Edge:** Reeded

Date	Mintage	F	VF	XF	Unc	BU
AH1427 (2006)	—	—	0.30	0.60	1.50	2.00
AH1428 (2007)	—	—	0.30	0.60	1.50	2.00
AH1431 (2010)	—	—	0.30	0.60	1.50	2.00

KM# 72 100 HALALA (1 Riyal)
Bi-Metallic Brass center in Copper-Nickel ring, 23 mm. **Ruler:** Abdullah bin Abdul Aziz AH1426-/2005-AD **Obv:** National emblem at center **Rev:** Legend above inscription, divides value, date below **Edge:** Reeded

Date	Mintage	F	VF	XF	Unc	BU
AH1427(2006)	—	—	0.45	0.90	2.25	3.00
AH1429(2008)	—	—	0.45	0.90	2.25	3.00

SERBIA

Serbia, a former inland Balkan kingdom has an area of 34,116 sq. mi. (88,361 sq. km.). Capital: Belgrade.

MINT MARKS
A - Paris
(a) - Paris, privy mark only
H - Birmingham
V - Vienna
БП - (BP) Budapest

MONETARY SYSTEM
100 Para = 1 Dinara

DENOMINATIONS
ПАРА = Para
ПАРЕ = Pare
ДИНАР = Dinar
ДИНАРА = Dinara

REPUBLIC

STANDARD COINAGE

KM# 34 DINAR
4.3400 g., Copper-Nickel-Zinc, 20 mm. **Obv:** National Bank emblem within circle **Rev:** Bank building and value **Edge:** Reeded

Date	Mintage	F	VF	XF	Unc	BU
2003	10,326,000	—	—	0.25	1.00	1.50
2004	25,038,000	—	—	0.25	1.00	1.50

KM# 39 DINAR
4.2600 g., Nickel-Brass, 20 mm. **Obv:** Crowned and mantled arms **Rev:** National Bank and value **Edge:** Segmented reeding

Date	Mintage	F	VF	XF	Unc	BU
2005	32,452,000	—	—	0.25	1.00	1.50
2006	39,550,000	—	—	0.25	1.00	1.50
2007	20,000,000	—	—	0.25	1.00	1.50
2008	10,093,000	—	—	0.25	1.00	1.50
2009	10,008,000	—	—	0.25	1.00	1.50

KM# 48 DINAR
4.2000 g., Copper Plated Steel, 20 mm. **Obv:** Arms **Rev:** National Bank and value

Date	Mintage	F	VF	XF	Unc	BU
2009	35,750,000	—	—	—	1.00	1.50
2010	30,600,000	—	—	—	1.00	1.50
2011	24,785,000	—	—	—	1.00	1.50

KM# 54 DINAR
20.0000 g., Copper Plated Steel, 20 mm. **Obv:** Arms, flat bottom crown above shield **Rev:** National Bank building and value

Date	Mintage	F	VF	XF	Unc	BU
2011	—	—	—	—	1.00	1.50
2012	—	—	—	—	1.00	1.50

KM# 35 2 DINARA
5.2400 g., Copper-Nickel-Zinc, 22 mm. **Obv:** National Bank emblem within circle **Rev:** Gracanica Monastery and value **Edge:** Reeded

Date	Mintage	F	VF	XF	Unc	BU
2003	15,216,000	—	—	0.50	2.00	2.50

KM# 46 2 DINARA
5.1500 g., Nickel-Brass, 22 mm. **Obv:** Crowned and mantled arms **Rev:** Gracanica Monastery and value **Edge:** Segmented reeding

Date	Mintage	F	VF	XF	Unc	BU
2006	15,385,500	—	—	0.50	2.00	2.50
2007	15,002,500	—	—	0.50	2.00	2.50
2008	10,093,000	—	—	0.50	2.00	2.50
2009	10,008,000	—	—	0.50	2.00	2.50

KM# 49 2 DINARA
5.0500 g., Copper Plated Steel, 22 mm. **Obv:** Arms **Rev:** Gracanica Monastery and value

Date	Mintage	F	VF	XF	Unc	BU
2009	27,845,000	—	—	0.50	2.00	2.50
2010	9,600,000	—	—	—	—	—
2011	12,400,000	—	—	—	—	—

KM# 55 2 DINARA
5.0500 g., Copper Plated Steel, 22 mm. **Obv:** Arms, flat bottom crown above shield **Rev:** Gracanica Monastery and value

Date	Mintage	F	VF	XF	Unc	BU
2011	—	—	—	—	2.00	2.50
2012	—	—	—	—	2.00	2.50

KM# 36 5 DINARA
6.2300 g., Copper-Nickel-Zinc, 22 mm. **Obv:** National Bank emblem within circle **Rev:** Krusedol Monastery and value **Edge:** Reeded

Date	Mintage	F	VF	XF	Unc	BU
2003	15,184,000	—	0.50	1.00	2.25	3.50

KM# 40 5 DINARA
6.1300 g., Nickel-Brass, 24 mm. **Obv:** Crowned and mantled arms **Rev:** Krusedol Monastery and value **Edge:** Segmented reeding

Date	Mintage	F	VF	XF	Unc	BU
2005	5,099,500	—	—	0.75	2.00	3.50
2006	10,372,500	—	—	0.75	2.00	3.50
2007	14,998,500	—	—	0.75	2.00	3.50
2008	15,093,500	—	—	0.75	2.00	3.50
2009	9,998,500	—	—	0.75	2.00	3.50
2010	15,005,000	—	—	0.75	2.00	3.50
2011	13,626,500	—	—	0.75	2.00	3.50

KM# 56 5 DINARA
Copper Plated Steel, 24 mm. **Obv:** Arms, flat bottom crown above shield **Rev:** Krusedol Monastery

Date	Mintage	F	VF	XF	Unc	BU
2011	—	—	—	—	2.25	3.50
2012	—	—	—	—	2.25	3.50

KM# 37 10 DINARA
7.7700 g., Copper-Nickel-Zinc, 26 mm. **Obv:** National Bank emblem within circle **Rev:** Studenica Monastery and value **Edge:** Reeded

Date	Mintage	F	VF	XF	Unc	BU
2003	15,166,500	—	0.50	1.00	2.50	3.50

KM# 41 10 DINARA
7.7700 g., Copper-Nickel-Zinc, 26 mm. **Obv:** Crowned and mantled arms **Rev:** Studenica Monastery and value **Edge:** Segmented reeding

Date	Mintage	F	VF	XF	Unc	BU
2005	5,099,500	—	—	0.75	2.25	4.00
2006	1,019,500	—	—	0.75	2.25	4.00
2007	1,050,500	—	—	0.75	2.00	4.00
2010	500,250	—	—	1.50	3.00	5.00
2011	500,250	—	—	1.50	3.00	5.00

KM# 51 10 DINARA
7.7700 g., Copper-Nickel-Zinc, 26 mm. **Subject:** 25th Summer Universiade, Belgrade **Obv:** Arms **Rev:** Logo

Date	Mintage	F	VF	XF	Unc	BU
2009	500,000	—	—	1.50	3.00	5.00

KM# 57 10 DINARA
7.7700 g., Copper-Nickel-Zinc, 26 mm. **Obv:** Arms, flat bottom crown above shield **Rev:** Studenica Monastery and value

Date	Mintage	F	VF	XF	Unc	BU
2011	—	—	—	—	2.25	4.00
2012	—	—	—	—	2.25	4.00

KM# 38 20 DINARA
9.0000 g., Copper-Nickel-Zinc, 28 mm. **Obv:** National Bank emblem within circle **Rev:** Temple of St. Sava and value **Edge:** Reeded

Date	Mintage	F	VF	XF	Unc	BU
2003	25,497,500	—	—	0.75	2.25	4.00

KM# 42 20 DINARA
9.0000 g., Copper-Nickel-Zinc, 28 mm. **Obv:** Crowned and mantled Serbian royal arms **Rev:** Nikola Tesla **Edge:** Segmented reeding

Date	Mintage	F	VF	XF	Unc	BU
2006	992,500	—	—	0.75	2.25	4.00

KM# 47 20 DINARA
9.0000 g., Copper-Nickel-Zinc, 28 mm. **Subject:** Dositej Obradovic, 1742-1811 **Obv:** National arms **Obv. Legend:** РЕПУБЛИКА СРБИЈА - REPUBLIKA SRBIJA **Rev:** Bust facing slightly left **Edge:** Segmented reeding

Date	Mintage	F	VF	XF	Unc	BU
2007	1,020,000	—	—	1.00	2.50	4.50

KM# 52 20 DINARA
9.0000 g., Copper-Nickel-Zinc, 28 mm. **Obv:** National arms **Rev:** Milutin Milankovic profile 3/4 left

Date	Mintage	F	VF	XF	Unc	BU
2009	494,500	—	—	—	2.00	3.50

KM# 53 20 DINARA
9.0000 g., Copper-Nickel-Zinc, 28 mm. **Obv:** National arms **Rev:** Ivo Andric

Date	Mintage	Good	VG	F	VF	XF
2011	500,000	—	—	—	—	2.00

KM# 43 1000 DINARA
13.0000 g., 0.9250 Silver 0.3866 oz. ASW, 30 mm. **Obv:** Crowned and mantled Serbian royal arms **Rev:** Nikola Tesla **Edge:** Segmented reeding

Date	Mintage	F	VF	XF	Unc	BU
2006 Proof	2,000	Value: 40.00				

KM# 44 5000 DINARA
3.4550 g., 0.9000 Gold 0.1000 oz. AGW, 20 mm. **Obv:** Crowned and mantled Serbian royal arms **Rev:** Nikola Tesla

Date	Mintage	F	VF	XF	Unc	BU
2006 Proof	2,000	Value: 200				

KM# 45 10000 DINARA
8.6400 g., 0.9000 Gold 0.2500 oz. AGW, 25 mm. **Obv:** Crowned and mantled Serbian royal arms **Rev:** Nikola Tesla

Date	Mintage	F	VF	XF	Unc	BU
2006 Proof	1,000	Value: 475				

MINT SETS

KM#	Date	Mintage	Identification	Issue Price	Mkt Val
MS1	2003 (5)	—	KM34-38	—	15.00
MS2	2005 (3)	—	KM39-41	—	10.00
MS3	2006 (5)	—	KM#39-42, 46	—	16.00

MINT SETS NON-STANDARD METALS

KM#	Date	Mintage	Identification	Issue Price	Mkt Val
MS4	2007 (5)	—	KM#39-42, 47	—	16.00

PROOF SETS

KM#	Date	Mintage	Identification	Issue Price	Mkt Val
PS1	2006 (3)	—	KM#43-45	—	725

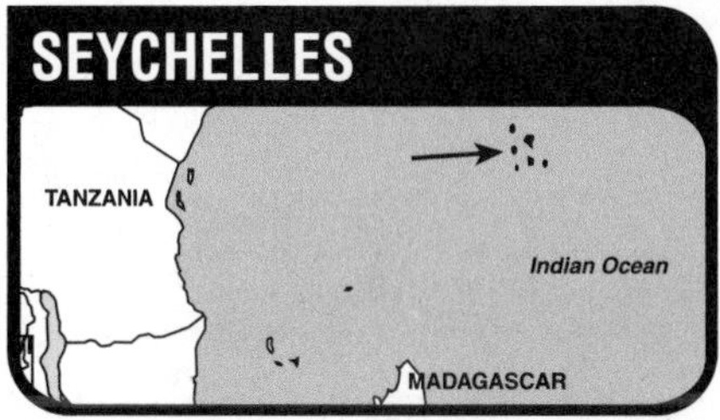

The Republic of Seychelles, an archipelago of 85 granite and coral islands situated in the Indian Ocean 600 miles (965 km.) northeast of Madagascar, has an area of 156 sq. mi. (455 sq. km.) and a population of *70,000. Among these islands are the Aldabra Islands, the Farquhar Group, and Ile Desroches, which the United Kingdom ceded to the Seychelles upon its independence. Capital: Victoria, on Mahe. The economy is based on fishing, a plantation system of agriculture, and tourism. Copra, cinnamon and vanilla are exported.

Seychelles is a member of the Commonwealth of Nations. The president is the Head of State and of the Government.

MINT MARKS
(sa) - M in oval – South African Mint Co.
(starting in 2000, not PM)
None - British Royal Mint

MONETARY SYSTEM
100 Cents = 1 Rupee

REPUBLIC

STANDARD COINAGE

KM# 46.2 CENT
1.4300 g., Brass, 16.03 mm. **Obv:** Altered coat of arms **Rev:** Mud Crab **Edge:** Plain

Date	Mintage	F	VF	XF	Unc	BU
2004	—	—	—	0.15	0.25	0.35

KM# 47.2 5 CENTS
2.0000 g., Brass, 18 mm. **Obv:** Altered coat of arms **Rev:** Tapioca plant

Date	Mintage	F	VF	XF	Unc	BU
2003	—	—	—	0.10	0.30	0.50

KM# 47a 5 CENTS
1.9700 g., Brass Plated Steel, 17.97 mm. **Obv:** National arms **Rev:** Tapioca plant **Edge:** Plain

Date	Mintage	F	VF	XF	Unc	BU
2007PM	—	—	—	0.10	0.30	0.50
2010PM	—	—	—	0.10	0.30	0.50

KM# 48.2 10 CENTS
3.3400 g., Brass, 21 mm. **Obv:** Altered coat of arms **Rev:** Yellowfin tuna **Edge:** Plain

Date	Mintage	F	VF	XF	Unc	BU
2003	—	—	0.10	0.35	1.00	1.50

KM# 48a 10 CENTS
3.3700 g., Brass Plated Steel, 21 mm. **Obv:** National arms **Rev:** Black parrot, value **Edge:** Plain

Date	Mintage	F	VF	XF	Unc	BU
2007PM	—	—	0.15	0.30	0.75	1.00

KM# 49a 25 CENTS
2.9700 g., Nickel Clad Steel, 18.9 mm. **Obv:** National arms **Rev:** Black Parrot and value **Edge:** Plain

Date	Mintage	F	VF	XF	Unc	BU
2003PM	—	—	—	0.40	1.00	1.25
2007PM	—	—	—	0.40	1.00	1.25
2010PM	—	—	—	0.40	1.00	1.25
2012PM	—	—	—	0.40	1.00	1.25

KM# 50.2 RUPEE
6.1800 g., Copper-Nickel, 25.46 mm. **Obv:** Altered coat of arms **Rev:** Triton Conch Shell **Edge:** Reeded

Date	Mintage	F	VF	XF	Unc	BU
2007	—	—	—	0.45	1.10	1.50
2010PM	—	—	—	0.45	1.10	1.50

KM# 118 5 RUPEES
28.2800 g., Copper-Nickel, 38.6 mm. **Subject:** John Paul II memorial **Obv:** National Arms **Rev:** John Paul II in mitre waving

Date	Mintage	F	VF	XF	Unc	BU
2005	—	—	—	—	8.00	10.00

KM# 119 5 RUPEES
28.2800 g., Copper-Nickel, 38.6 mm. **Obv:** National Arms **Rev:** Benedict XVI blessing crowd at St. Peter's Square

Date	Mintage	F	VF	XF	Unc	BU
2005	—	—	—	—	10.00	12.00

KM# 51.2 5 RUPEES
9.0000 g., Copper-Nickel, 29 mm. **Obv:** Altered arms **Rev:** Fruit tree divides value **Edge:** Reeded

Date	Mintage	F	VF	XF	Unc	BU
2007	—	—	—	0.70	1.75	2.25
2010	—	—	—	0.70	1.75	2.25

KM# 121 25 RUPEES
28.2800 g., 0.9250 Silver 0.8410 oz. ASW, 38.6 mm. **Obv:** National arms **Rev:** Benedict XVI blessing crowd at St. Peter's Square **Edge:** Reeded

Date	Mintage	F	VF	XF	Unc	BU
2005	—	Value: 55.00				

KM# 120 25 RUPEES
28.2800 g., 0.9250 Silver 0.8410 oz. ASW, 38.6 mm. **Obv:** National arms **Rev:** Description John Paul II in mitre waving **Edge:** Reeded

Date	Mintage	F	VF	XF	Unc	BU
2005 Proof	—	Value: 55.00				

KM# 122 250 RUPEES
6.2200 g., 0.9999 Gold 0.1999 oz. AGW, 22 mm. **Obv:** National arms **Rev:** Description John Paul II in mitre waving **Edge:** Reeded

Date	Mintage	F	VF	XF	Unc	BU
2005 Proof	—	Value: 400				

KM# 123 250 RUPEES
6.2200 g., 0.9999 Gold 0.1999 oz. AGW, 22 mm. **Obv:** National arms **Rev:** Benedict XVI blessing crowd at St. Peter's Square **Edge:** Reeded

Date	Mintage	F	VF	XF	Unc	BU
2005 Proof	—	Value: 400				

SHAWNEE TRIBAL NATION

SOVEREIGN NATION

MILLED COINAGE

KM# 1 DOLLAR
31.2000 g., 0.9999 Silver 1.0030 oz. ASW, 39 mm. **Obv:** Tribal seal **Obv. Legend:** THE SOVEREIGN NATION OF THE SHAWNEE TRIBE **Rev:** Bust of Chief Chief "Shooting Star" Tecumseh right **Edge:** Reeded

Date	Mintage	F	VF	XF	Unc	BU
2002	50,000	—	—	—	—	40.00
2002 Proof	20,000	Value: 55.00				

KM# 10 DOLLAR
124.4120 g., 0.9990 Silver 3.9958 oz. ASW

Date	Mintage	F	VF	XF	Unc	BU
2003 Proof	10,000	Value: 185				

KM# 3 DOLLAR
31.2000 g., 0.9999 Silver 1.0030 oz. ASW, 39 mm. **Obv:** Tribal seal **Obv. Legend:** THE SOVEREIGN NATION OF THE SHAWNEE TRIBE **Rev:** Lewis, Clark and Drouillard scouting **Edge:** Reeded

Date	Mintage	F	VF	XF	Unc	BU
2003	50,000	—	—	—	—	45.00
2003 Proof	20,000	Value: 55.00				

KM# 5 DOLLAR
31.2000 g., 0.9999 Silver 1.0030 oz. ASW, 39 mm. **Obv:** Tribal seal **Obv. Legend:** THE SOVEREIGN NATION OF THE SHAWNEE TRIBE **Rev:** Flag behing Indian Chief and Thomas Jefferson standing, eagle on shield at their feet **Edge:** Reeded

Date	Mintage	F	VF	XF	Unc	BU
2004	50,000	—	—	—	—	45.00
2004 Proof	20,000	Value: 55.00				

KM# 15 DOLLAR
31.3100 g., 0.9990 Silver 1.0056 oz. ASW, 40.6 mm. **Obv:** Tribal seal **Obv. Legend:** THE SOVEREIGN NATION OF THE SHAWNEE TRIBE **Rev:** Lewis, Clark, Dromillard and Sacagawea in a canoe **Rev. Legend:** EXPEDITION OF DISCOVERY **Edge:** Reeded

Date	Mintage	F	VF	XF	Unc	BU
2005	50,000	—	—	—	—	45.00
2005 Proof	20,000	Value: 55.00				

KM# 20 DOLLAR
31.2100 g., 0.9999 Silver 1.0033 oz. ASW, 40.6 mm. **Obv:** Tribal seal **Obv. Legend:** THE SOVEREIGN NATION OF THE SHAWNEE TRIBE **Rev:** 1/2 length figure of Tenskwatawa "the prophet" 3/4 left **Rev. Legend:** PROPHET TENSKWATAWA **Edge:** Reeded

Date	Mintage	F	VF	XF	Unc	BU
2006	50,000	—	—	—	—	45.00
2006 Proof	20,000	Value: 55.00				

KM# 24 DOLLAR
31.1050 g., 0.9990 Silver 0.9990 oz. ASW, 39 mm. **Subject:** Battle of the Wabash **Rev:** Indian warrior on horseback **Edge:** Reeded

Date	Mintage	F	VF	XF	Unc	BU
2007	50,000	—	—	—	—	50.00
2007 Proof	20,000	Value: 60.00				

KM# 26 DOLLAR
31.1050 g., 0.9990 Silver 0.9990 oz. ASW, 39 mm. **Subject:** Battle of Point Pleasant **Rev:** Indian warrior on horseback **Edge:** Reeded

Date	Mintage	F	VF	XF	Unc	BU
2008	50,000	—	—	—	—	50.00
2008 Proof	20,000	Value: 60.00				

KM# 28 DOLLAR
31.1050 g., 0.9990 Silver 0.9990 oz. ASW **Rev:** Battle of Fallen Timber

Date	Mintage	F	VF	XF	Unc	BU
2009	50,000	—	—	—	—	50.00
2009 Proof	20,000	Value: 60.00				

KM# 2 5 DOLLARS
6.2200 g., 0.9999 Gold 0.1999 oz. AGW, 20 mm. **Obv:** Arms **Obv. Legend:** THE SOVEREIGN NATION OF THE SHAWNEE TRIBE **Rev:** Bust of Tecumseh "Shooting Star" 3/4 left **Edge:** Reeded

Date	Mintage	F	VF	XF	Unc	BU
2002 Proof	5,000	Value: 400				

KM# 4 5 DOLLARS
6.2200 g., 0.9999 Gold 0.1999 oz. AGW, 22.5 mm. **Obv:** Arms **Obv. Legend:** THE SOVEREIGN NATION OF THE SHAWNEE TRIBE **Rev:** Bust of George Drouillard 3/4 right **Rev. Legend:** GEORGE DROUILLARD SIGN TALKER

Date	Mintage	F	VF	XF	Unc	BU
2003 Proof	5,000	Value: 400				

KM# 6 5 DOLLARS
6.2207 g., 0.9990 Gold 0.1998 oz. AGW, 22 mm. **Obv:** Arms **Obv. Legend:** THE SOVEREIGN NATION OF THE SHAWNEE TRIBE **Rev:** Sacagawea with child and horse **Edge:** Reeded

Date	Mintage	F	VF	XF	Unc	BU
2004 Proof	5,000	Value: 400				

KM# 16 5 DOLLARS
6.3000 g., 0.9999 Gold 0.2025 oz. AGW, 22.5 mm. **Obv:** Tribal seal **Obv. Legend:** THE SOVEREIGN NATION OF THE SHAWNEE TRIBE **Rev:** Sacagawea with papoose on horseback right **Rev. Legend:** EXPEDITION OF DISCOVERY **Edge:** Reeded

Date	Mintage	F	VF	XF	Unc	BU
2005 Proof	5,000	Value: 400				

KM# 21 5 DOLLARS
6.2500 g., 0.9999 Gold 0.2009 oz. AGW, 22.5 mm. **Obv:** Tribal seal **Obv. Legend:** THE SOVEREIGN NATION OF THE SHAWNEE TRIBE **Rev:** Bust of Chief Tecumseh 3/4 right **Rev. Legend:** TECVMSEH **Edge:** Reeded

Date	Mintage	F	VF	XF	Unc	BU
2006 Proof	5,000	Value: 400				

KM# 25 5 DOLLARS
6.2500 g., 0.9990 Gold 0.2007 oz. AGW **Rev:** Chief Blue Jacket

Date	Mintage	F	VF	XF	Unc	BU
2007 Proof	5,000	Value: 400				

KM# 27 5 DOLLARS
6.2500 g., 0.9990 Gold 0.2007 oz. AGW **Rev:** Chief Cornstalk

Date	Mintage	F	VF	XF	Unc	BU
2008 Proof	5,000	Value: 400				

KM# 29 5 DOLLARS
6.2500 g., 0.9990 Gold 0.2007 oz. AGW **Rev:** Chief Black-Hoof

Date	Mintage	F	VF	XF	Unc	BU
2009 Proof	5,000	Value: 400				

KM# 7 50 DOLLARS
15.5500 g., 0.9990 Gold 0.4994 oz. AGW **Rev:** George Drouillard

Date	Mintage	F	VF	XF	Unc	BU
2003 Proof	999	Value: 875				

KM# 11 50 DOLLARS
15.5500 g., 0.9990 Gold 0.4994 oz. AGW **Rev:** Sacagawea and child

Date	Mintage	F	VF	XF	Unc	BU
2004 Proof	—	Value: 875				

KM# 17 50 DOLLARS
15.5500 g., 0.9999 Gold 0.4999 oz. AGW, 30.1 mm. **Obv:** Tribal seal **Obv. Legend:** THE SOVEREIGN NATION OF THE SHAWNEE TRIBE **Rev:** Sacagawea with papoose on horseback right **Rev. Legend:** EXPEDITION OF DISCOVERY **Edge:** Reeded

Date	Mintage	F	VF	XF	Unc	BU
2005 Proof	999	Value: 875				

KM# 8 100 DOLLARS
30.9100 g., 0.9999 Gold 0.9936 oz. AGW, 38.9 mm. **Obv:** Tribal seal **Obv. Legend:** THE SOVEREIGN NATION OF THE SHAWNEE TRIBE **Rev:** Bust of "Sign Talker" 3/4 right **Rev. Legend:** GEORGE DROILLARD "SIGN TALKER" **Edge:** Milled

Date	Mintage	F	VF	XF	Unc	BU
2003 Proof	999	Value: 1,850				

KM# 12 100 DOLLARS
31.1050 g., 0.9990 Gold 0.9990 oz. AGW **Rev:** Sacagawea and child

Date	Mintage	F	VF	XF	Unc	BU
2004 Proof	—	Value: 1,850				

KM# 18 100 DOLLARS
31.1050 g., 0.9990 Gold 0.9990 oz. AGW **Rev:** Sacagawea and child on horseback

Date	Mintage	F	VF	XF	Unc	BU
2005 Proof	999	Value: 1,850				

KM# 23 100 DOLLARS
62.2100 g., 0.9990 Bi-Metallic 1 oz. gold and 1 oz. silver 1.9980 oz. **Rev:** Lewis and Clark

Date	Mintage	F	VF	XF	Unc	BU
2005 Proof	500	Value: 2,000				

KM# 9 500 DOLLARS
93.5000 g., 0.9999 Gold 3.0057 oz. AGW **Obv:** Tribal seal **Obv. Legend:** THE SOVEREIGN NATION OF THE SHAWNEE TRIBE **Rev:** Lewis, Clark and Drouillard scouting **Rev. Legend:** LEWIS • CLARK • DROUILLARD **Edge:** Reeded

Date	Mintage	F	VF	XF	Unc	BU
2003 Proof	300	Value: 5,800				

KM# 13 500 DOLLARS
15.5400 g., 0.9990 Platinum 0.4991 oz. APW, 30 mm. **Obv:** Tribal seal **Obv. Legend:** THE SOVEREIGN NATION OF THE SHAWNEE TRIBE **Rev:** Flag and shield between standing Chief and Thomas Jefferson **Rev. Legend:** EXPEDITION OF DISCOVERY **Edge:** Reeded

Date	Mintage	F	VF	XF	Unc	BU
2004 Proof	999	Value: 1,150				

KM# 23A 500 DOLLARS
15.5500 g., 0.9990 Platinum 0.4994 oz. APW **Rev:** Shawnee Chief and Thomas Jefferson standing

Date	Mintage	F	VF	XF	Unc	BU
2005 Proof	999	Value: 1,150				

KM# 14 1000 DOLLARS
31.0000 g., 0.9999 Platinum 0.9965 oz. APW, 38.7 mm. **Obv:** Tribal seal **Obv. Legend:** THE SOVEREIGN NATION OF THE SHAWNEE TRIBE **Rev:** Flag and shield between standing Chief and Thomas Jefferson **Rev. Legend:** EXPEDITION OF DISCOVERY **Edge:** Reeded

Date	Mintage	F	VF	XF	Unc	BU
2004 Proof	300	Value: 2,750				

KM# 22 1000 DOLLARS
31.1050 g., 0.9990 Platinum 0.9990 oz. APW **Rev:** Shawnee Chief and Thomas Jefferson standing

Date	Mintage	F	VF	XF	Unc	BU
2005 Proof	300	Value: 2,750				

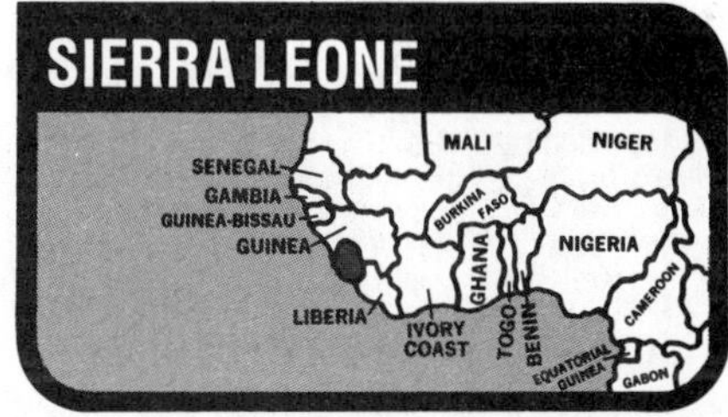

The Republic of Sierra Leone is located in western Africa between Guinea and Liberia, has an area of 27,699 sq. mi. (71,740 sq. km.) and a population of *4.1 million. Capital: Freetown. The economy is predominantly agricultural but mining contributes significantly to export revenues. Diamonds, iron ore, palm kernels, cocoa, and coffee are exported.

Sierra Leone is a member of the Commonwealth of Nations. The president is Chief of State and Head of Government.

MONETARY SYSTEM

Beginning 1964

100 Cents = 1 Leone

NOTE: Sierra Leone's official currency is the Leone. For previously listed Dollar Denominated Coinage, see the 5th Edition of Unusual World Coins.

REPUBLIC

STANDARD COINAGE

KM# 351 10 DOLLARS
28.2800 g., 0.9250 Silver 0.8410 oz. ASW, 38.61 mm. **Obv:** National arms **Rev:** Mountain Gorilla

Date	Mintage	F	VF	XF	Unc	BU
2011PM Proof	—	Value: 75.00				

KM# 295 20 LEONES
3.9200 g., Copper-Nickel, 21.7 mm. **Obv:** Value within fish and beaded circle **Rev:** Chimpanzee facing **Edge:** Plain

Date	Mintage	F	VF	XF	Unc	BU
2003	—	—	—	—	0.50	1.25

KM# 302 100 LEONES
28.2800 g., Copper-Nickel, 38.6 mm. **Subject:** 40th Anniversary - Bank of Sierra Leone **Obv:** Bank President Kabbah **Rev:** Lion **Edge:** Reeded

Date	Mintage	F	VF	XF	Unc	BU
ND (2004)PM	5,000	—	—	—	15.00	18.00

KM# 296 500 LEONES
7.2000 g., Bi-Metallic Stainless Steel center in Brass ring, 24 mm. **Obv:** Building within circle **Rev:** Bust with hat facing within circle **Edge:** Plain **Shape:** 10-sided

Date	Mintage	F	VF	XF	Unc	BU
2004	—	—	—	—	7.50	9.00

KM# 346 500 LEONES
28.2800 g., Bronze, 38.6 mm. **Subject:** 40th Anniversary - Bank of Sierra Leone **Obv:** Bank President Kabbah **Rev:** Lion, denomination as "Le 500" **Edge:** Reeded

Date	Mintage	F	VF	XF	Unc	BU
ND(2004)PM	10,000	—	—	—	15.00	18.00

DOLLAR DENOMINATED COINAGE

KM# 222 DOLLAR
28.4900 g., Copper-Nickel, 38.5 mm. **Series:** The Big Five **Obv:** National arms **Rev:** Rhino **Edge:** Reeded

Date	Mintage	F	VF	XF	Unc	BU
2001PM	—	—	—	—	12.50	15.00

KM# 225 DOLLAR
28.4900 g., Copper-Nickel, 38.6 mm. **Series:** The Big Five **Obv:** National arms **Rev:** Lion **Edge:** Reeded

Date	Mintage	F	VF	XF	Unc	BU
2001PM	—	—	—	—	10.00	15.00

KM# 228 DOLLAR
28.4900 g., Copper-Nickel, 38.6 mm. **Series:** The Big Five **Obv:** National arms **Rev:** Leopard **Edge:** Reeded

Date	Mintage	F	VF	XF	Unc	BU
2001PM	—	—	—	—	10.00	15.00

KM# 231 DOLLAR
28.4900 g., Copper-Nickel, 38.6 mm. **Series:** The Big Five **Obv:** National arms **Rev:** Elephants **Edge:** Reeded

Date	Mintage	F	VF	XF	Unc	BU
2001PM	—	—	—	—	10.00	15.00

KM# 234 DOLLAR
28.4900 g., Copper-Nickel, 38.6 mm. **Series:** The Big Five **Obv:** National arms **Rev:** Buffalo **Edge:** Reeded

Date	Mintage	F	VF	XF	Unc	BU
2001PM	—	—	—	—	10.00	15.00

KM# 237 DOLLAR
28.4900 g., Copper-Nickel, 38.5 mm. **Series:** The Big Five **Obv:** National arms **Rev:** All five animals **Edge:** Reeded

Date	Mintage	F	VF	XF	Unc	BU
2001PM	—	—	—	—	10.00	15.00

KM# 241.1 DOLLAR
28.5400 g., Copper-Nickel, 38.65 mm. **Series:** Big Cats **Obv:** National arms **Rev:** Male and female lions **Edge:** Reeded

Date	Mintage	F	VF	XF	Unc	BU
2001PM	—	—	—	—	12.50	15.00

KM# 241.2 DOLLAR
28.5400 g., Copper-Nickel, 38.65 mm. **Series:** Big Cats **Obv:** National arms **Rev:** Multi-colored male and female lions **Edge:** Reeded

Date	Mintage	F	VF	XF	Unc	BU
2001PM	—	—	—	—	15.00	17.50

KM# 242.1 DOLLAR
28.5400 g., Copper-Nickel, 38.65 mm. **Series:** Big Cats **Obv:** National arms **Rev:** Tiger **Edge:** Reeded

Date	Mintage	F	VF	XF	Unc	BU
2001PM	—	—	—	—	10.00	14.00

KM# 242.2 DOLLAR
28.5400 g., Copper-Nickel, 38.65 mm. **Series:** Big Cats **Obv:** National arms **Rev:** Multi-colored Tiger **Edge:** Reeded

Date	Mintage	F	VF	XF	Unc	BU
2001PM	—	—	—	—	15.00	17.50

KM# 243.1 DOLLAR
28.5400 g., Copper-Nickel, 38.65 mm. **Series:** Big Cats **Obv:** National arms **Rev:** Cheetah **Edge:** Reeded

Date	Mintage	F	VF	XF	Unc	BU
2001PM	—	—	—	—	12.50	15.00

KM# 243.2 DOLLAR
28.5400 g., Copper-Nickel, 38.65 mm. **Series:** Big Cats **Obv:** National arms **Rev:** Multi-colored Cheetah **Edge:** Reeded

Date	Mintage	F	VF	XF	Unc	BU
2001PM	—	—	—	—	15.00	17.50

KM# 244.1 DOLLAR
28.5400 g., Copper-Nickel, 38.65 mm. **Series:** Big Cats **Obv:** National arms **Rev:** Cougar **Edge:** Reeded

Date	Mintage	F	VF	XF	Unc	BU
2001PM	—	—	—	—	10.00	14.00

KM# 244.2 DOLLAR
28.5400 g., Copper-Nickel, 38.65 mm. **Series:** Big Cats **Obv:** National arms **Rev:** Multi-colored Cougar **Edge:** Reeded

Date	Mintage	F	VF	XF	Unc	BU
2001PM	—	—	—	—	15.00	17.50

KM# 245.1 DOLLAR
28.5400 g., Copper-Nickel, 38.65 mm. **Series:** Big Cats **Obv:** National arms **Rev:** Black panther **Edge:** Reeded

Date	Mintage	F	VF	XF	Unc	BU
2001PM	—	—	—	—	10.00	14.00

KM# 245.2 DOLLAR
28.5400 g., Copper-Nickel, 38.65 mm. **Series:** Big Cats **Obv:** National arms **Rev:** Multi-colored Black Panther **Edge:** Reeded

Date	Mintage	F	VF	XF	Unc	BU
2001PM	—	—	—	—	15.00	17.50

KM# 198 DOLLAR
28.2800 g., Copper-Nickel, 38.6 mm. **Subject:** Year of the Snake **Obv:** National arms **Rev:** Snake **Edge:** Reeded

Date	Mintage	F	VF	XF	Unc	BU
2001	—	—	—	—	10.00	14.00

KM# 206 DOLLAR
Copper-Nickel, 38.6 mm. **Subject:** P'an Ku **Obv:** National arms **Rev:** Dragon

Date	Mintage	F	VF	XF	Unc	BU
2001	—	—	—	—	10.00	14.00

KM# 214 DOLLAR
Copper-Nickel, 38.6 mm. **Subject:** P'an Ku **Obv:** National arms **Rev:** Dragon and three animals

Date	Mintage	F	VF	XF	Unc	BU
2001	—	—	—	—	10.00	14.00

KM# 256 DOLLAR
28.2800 g., Copper-Nickel, 38.6 mm. **Subject:** Year of the Horse **Obv:** National arms **Rev:** Horse **Edge:** Reeded

Date	Mintage	F	VF	XF	Unc	BU
2002	—	—	—	—	14.50	17.50

KM# 264 DOLLAR
28.2800 g., Copper-Nickel, 38.6 mm. **Subject:** RMS Titanic **Obv:** National arms **Rev:** Titanic at dock **Edge:** Reeded

Date	Mintage	F	VF	XF	Unc	BU
2002	—	—	—	—	10.00	12.00

KM# 268 DOLLAR
28.2800 g., Copper-Nickel, 38.6 mm. **Subject:** Queen's Golden Jubilee **Obv:** National arms **Rev:** Queen Elizabeth II and Prince Philip visiting blacksmiths in Sierra Leone **Edge:** Reeded

Date	Mintage	F	VF	XF	Unc	BU
2002	—	—	—	—	10.00	12.00

KM# 269 DOLLAR
28.2800 g., Copper-Nickel, 38.6 mm. **Subject:** Queen's Golden Jubilee **Obv:** National arms **Rev:** Queen, Prince Charles and Princess Anne **Edge:** Reeded

Date	Mintage	F	VF	XF	Unc	BU
2002	—	—	—	—	10.00	12.00

KM# 276 DOLLAR
28.2800 g., Copper-Nickel, 38.6 mm. **Subject:** British Queen Mother **Obv:** National arms **Rev:** Queen Mother with dog in garden **Edge:** Reeded

Date	Mintage	F	VF	XF	Unc	BU
2002	—	—	—	—	10.00	12.00

KM# 279 DOLLAR
28.2800 g., Copper-Nickel, 38.6 mm. **Subject:** Queen Mother **Obv:** National arms **Rev:** Queen Mother with daughters **Edge:** Reeded

Date	Mintage	F	VF	XF	Unc	BU
2002	—	—	—	—	10.00	12.00

KM# 282 DOLLAR
28.2800 g., Copper-Nickel, 38.6 mm. **Subject:** Queen's Golden Jubilee **Obv:** National arms **Rev:** Queen Elizabeth and a young Prince Charles **Edge:** Reeded

Date	Mintage	F	VF	XF	Unc	BU
2002	—	—	—	—	10.00	12.00

KM# 285 DOLLAR
28.2800 g., Copper-Nickel, 38.6 mm. **Subject:** Queen's Golden Jubilee **Obv:** National arms **Rev:** Queen Elizabeth and Prince Philip **Edge:** Reeded

Date	Mintage	F	VF	XF	Unc	BU
2002	—	—	—	—	10.00	12.00

KM# 288 DOLLAR
28.2800 g., Copper-Nickel, 38.6 mm. **Subject:** Olympics **Obv:** National arms **Rev:** Victory goddess Nike **Edge:** Reeded

Date	Mintage	F	VF	XF	Unc	BU
2003	—	—	—	—	10.00	12.00
2004	—	—	—	—	10.00	12.00

KM# 291 DOLLAR
28.2800 g., Copper-Nickel, 38.6 mm. **Subject:** Olympics **Obv:** National arms **Rev:** Ancient archer **Edge:** Reeded

Date	Mintage	F	VF	XF	Unc	BU
2003	—	—	—	—	10.00	12.00
2004	—	—	—	—	10.00	12.00

KM# 297 DOLLAR
28.2800 g., Copper-Nickel, 38.6 mm. **Obv:** National arms **Rev:** Nelson Mandela **Edge:** Reeded

Date	Mintage	F	VF	XF	Unc	BU
2004	—	—	—	—	15.00	16.50

KM# 300 DOLLAR
28.2800 g., Copper-Nickel, 38.6 mm. **Obv:** National arms **Rev:** Ronald Reagan **Edge:** Reeded

Date	Mintage	F	VF	XF	Unc	BU
2004	—	—	—	—	15.00	16.50

KM# 304 DOLLAR
28.4200 g., Copper-Nickel, 38.6 mm. **Obv:** National arms **Rev:** Giraffe **Edge:** Reeded

Date	Mintage	F	VF	XF	Unc	BU
2005	—	—	—	—	12.00	16.00

KM# 305 DOLLAR
28.4200 g., Copper-Nickel, 38.6 mm. **Obv:** National arms **Rev:** Crocodile **Edge:** Reeded

Date	Mintage	F	VF	XF	Unc	BU
2005	—	—	—	—	12.00	16.00

KM# 306 DOLLAR
28.4200 g., Copper-Nickel, 38.6 mm. **Obv:** National arms **Rev:** Hippo in water **Edge:** Reeded

Date	Mintage	F	VF	XF	Unc	BU
2005	—	—	—	—	12.00	16.00

KM# 345 DOLLAR
28.5000 g., Copper-Nickel, 38.58 mm. **Subject:** Death of Prince Rainier III **Obv:** National arms **Rev:** Bust left, small knight horseback right on neck **Edge:** Reeded

Date	Mintage	F	VF	XF	Unc	BU
2005	—	—	—	—	7.00	9.00

KM# 317 DOLLAR
Copper-Nickel **Series:** 60th Anniversary End of WW II **Subject:** Battle of El Alamein **Obv:** National arms **Obv. Legend:** REPUBLIC OF SIERRA LEONE **Rev:** Tank, plane and ground troops

Date	Mintage	F	VF	XF	Unc	BU
2005	—	—	—	—	10.00	12.00

KM# 316 DOLLAR
Copper-Nickel **Series:** 60th Anniversary End of WW II **Subject:** The Battle of the Atlantic **Obv:** National arms **Obv. Legend:** REPUBLIC OF SIERRA LEONE **Rev:** Plane and ship convoy

Date	Mintage	F	VF	XF	Unc	BU
2005	—	—	—	—	10.00	12.00

KM# 319 DOLLAR
Copper-Nickel **Series:** 60th Anniversary End of WW II **Subject:** The Battle of Berlin **Obv:** National arms **Obv. Legend:** REPUBLIC OF SIERRA LEONE **Rev:** Berlin city view, tank

Date	Mintage	F	VF	XF	Unc	BU
2005	—	—	—	—	10.00	12.00

KM# 315 DOLLAR
Copper-Nickel **Series:** 60th Anniversary End of WW II **Subject:** Battle of Britian **Obv:** National arms **Obv. Legend:** REPUBLIC OF SIERRA LEONE **Rev:** Planes in flight

Date	Mintage	F	VF	XF	Unc	BU
2005	—	—	—	—	10.00	12.00

KM# 318 DOLLAR
Copper-Nickel **Series:** 60th Anniversay End of WW II **Subject:** Battle of the Bulge **Obv:** National arms **Obv. Legend:** REPUBLIC OF SIERRA LEONE **Rev:** Forest battle scene

Date	Mintage	F	VF	XF	Unc	BU
2005	—	—	—	—	10.00	12.00

KM# 320 DOLLAR
Copper-Nickel **Series:** 60th Anniversary End of WW II **Subject:** The Heavy Water Raids **Obv:** National arms **Obv. Legend:** REPUBLIC OF SIERRA LEONE **Rev:** Troops on skies, factory in ruins

Date	Mintage	F	VF	XF	Unc	BU
2005	—	—	—	—	10.00	12.00

KM# 321 DOLLAR
Copper-Nickel **Obv:** National Arms **Rev:** Mountain Gorillia

Date	Mintage	F	VF	XF	Unc	BU
2005	—	—	—	—	12.00	16.00

KM# 322 DOLLAR
Copper-Nickel **Rev:** John Paul II head left, within ring of the Stations of the Cross

Date	Mintage	F	VF	XF	Unc	BU
2005	—	—	—	—	10.00	12.00

KM# 323 DOLLAR
Copper-Nickel **Rev:** Benedict XVI and St. Peter's

Date	Mintage	F	VF	XF	Unc	BU
2005	—	—	—	—	10.00	12.00

KM# 324 DOLLAR
Copper-Nickel **Obv:** National Arms **Rev:** Brontosaurus

Date	Mintage	F	VF	XF	Unc	BU
2006	—	—	—	—	14.00	16.00

KM# 308 DOLLAR
28.3700 g., Copper-Nickel, 38.5 mm. **Obv:** National arms **Rev:** Stegosaurus **Edge:** Reeded

Date	Mintage	F	VF	XF	Unc	BU
2006	—	—	—	—	14.00	16.00

KM# 309 DOLLAR
28.3700 g., Copper-Nickel, 38.5 mm. **Obv:** National arms **Rev:** Tyrannosaurus Rex **Edge:** Reeded

Date	Mintage	F	VF	XF	Unc	BU
2006	—	—	—	—	14.00	16.00

KM# 310 DOLLAR
28.3700 g., Copper-Nickel, 38.5 mm. **Obv:** National arms **Rev:** Triceratops **Edge:** Reeded

Date	Mintage	F	VF	XF	Unc	BU
2006	—	—	—	—	14.00	16.00

KM# 311 DOLLAR
28.3700 g., Copper-Nickel, 38.5 mm. **Obv:** National arms **Rev:** Lion **Edge:** Reeded

Date	Mintage	F	VF	XF	Unc	BU
2006	—	—	—	—	12.00	16.00

KM# 312 DOLLAR
28.3700 g., Copper-Nickel, 38.5 mm. **Obv:** National arms **Rev:** Dromedary Camel **Edge:** Reeded

Date	Mintage	F	VF	XF	Unc	BU
2006	—	—	—	—	12.00	16.00

KM# 313 DOLLAR
28.3700 g., Copper-Nickel, 38.63 mm. **Obv:** National arms **Rev:** Chimpanzee **Edge:** Reeded

Date	Mintage	F	VF	XF	Unc	BU
2006	—	—	—	—	12.00	16.00

KM# 314 DOLLAR

28.3700 g., Copper-Nickel, 38.5 mm. **Obv:** National arms **Rev:** Impala **Edge:** Reeded

Date	Mintage	F	VF	XF	Unc	BU
2006	—	—	—	—	12.00	16.00

KM# 326 DOLLAR

28.3700 g., Copper-Nickel, 38.5 mm. **Rev:** Cheetah

Date	Mintage	F	VF	XF	Unc	BU
2007	—	—	—	—	14.00	17.00

KM# 327 DOLLAR

28.3700 g., Copper-Nickel, 38.5 mm. **Rev:** Zebra

Date	Mintage	F	VF	XF	Unc	BU
2007	—	—	—	—	14.00	17.00

KM# 328 DOLLAR

28.3700 g., Copper-Nickel, 38.5 mm. **Rev:** Rhino

Date	Mintage	F	VF	XF	Unc	BU
2007	—	—	—	—	14.00	17.00

KM# 329 DOLLAR

28.3700 g., Copper-Nickel, 38.5 mm. **Obv:** Arms **Rev:** African elephant

Date	Mintage	F	VF	XF	Unc	BU
2007	—	—	—	—	15.00	18.00

KM# 347 DOLLAR

28.3700 g., Copper-Nickel, 38.6 mm. **Series:** Nocturnal Creatures of Africa **Obv:** National arms **Rev:** Duiker Antelope standing left, facing **Edge:** Reeded **Note:** Blackened finish.

Date	Mintage	F	VF	XF	Unc	BU
2008	—	—	—	—	17.50	20.00

KM# 348 DOLLAR

28.3700 g., Copper-Nickel, 38.6 mm. **Series:** Nocturnal Creatures of Africa **Obv:** National arms **Rev:** Bush Baby on tree limb **Edge:** Reeded **Note:** Blackened finish.

Date	Mintage	F	VF	XF	Unc	BU
2008	—	—	—	—	17.50	20.00

KM# 349 DOLLAR

28.3700 g., Copper-Nickel, 38.6 mm. **Series:** Nocturnal Creatures of Africa **Obv:** National arms **Rev:** Honey Badger **Edge:** Reeded **Note:** Blackened finish

Date	Mintage	F	VF	XF	Unc	BU
2008	—	—	—	—	17.50	20.00

KM# 350 DOLLAR

28.3700 g., Copper-Nickel, 38.6 mm. **Series:** Nocturnal Creatures of Africa **Obv:** National arms. **Rev:** Pygmy Hippopotamus in water facing **Edge:** Reeded **Note:** Blackened finish.

Date	Mintage	F	VF	XF	Unc	BU
2008	—	—	—	—	17.50	20.00

KM# 223 10 DOLLARS

28.2800 g., 0.9250 Silver 0.8410 oz. ASW, 38.6 mm. **Series:** The Big Five **Obv:** National arms **Rev:** Rhino and value within circle **Edge:** Reeded

Date	Mintage	F	VF	XF	Unc	BU
2001 Proof	—	Value: 45.00				

KM# 226 10 DOLLARS

28.2800 g., 0.9250 Silver 0.8410 oz. ASW, 38.6 mm. **Series:** The Big Five **Obv:** National arms **Rev:** Lion head and value within circle

Date	Mintage	F	VF	XF	Unc	BU
2001 Proof	Est. 10,000	Value: 45.00				

KM# 229 10 DOLLARS

28.2800 g., 0.9250 Silver 0.8410 oz. ASW, 38.6 mm. **Series:** The Big Five **Obv:** National arms **Rev:** Leopard and value within circle

Date	Mintage	F	VF	XF	Unc	BU
2001 Proof	Est. 10,000	Value: 45.00				

KM# 232 10 DOLLARS

28.2800 g., 0.9250 Silver 0.8410 oz. ASW, 38.6 mm. **Series:** The Big Five **Obv:** National arms **Rev:** Elephants and value within circle

Date	Mintage	F	VF	XF	Unc	BU
2001 Proof	Est. 10,000	Value: 45.00				

KM# 235 10 DOLLARS

28.2800 g., 0.9250 Silver 0.8410 oz. ASW, 38.6 mm. **Series:** The Big Five **Obv:** National arms **Rev:** Buffalo and value within circle

Date	Mintage	F	VF	XF	Unc	BU
2001 Proof	Est. 10,000	Value: 45.00				

KM# 238 10 DOLLARS

28.2800 g., 0.9250 Silver 0.8410 oz. ASW, 38.6 mm. **Series:** The Big Five **Obv:** National arms **Rev:** All five animals within circle

Date	Mintage	F	VF	XF	Unc	BU
2001 Proof	Est. 10,000	Value: 45.00				

KM# 246.1 10 DOLLARS

28.2800 g., 0.9250 Silver 0.8410 oz. ASW, 38.6 mm. **Series:** Big Cats **Obv:** National arms **Rev:** Male and female lions **Edge:** Reeded

Date	Mintage	F	VF	XF	Unc	BU
2001 Proof	10,000	Value: 45.00				

KM# 246.2 10 DOLLARS

28.2800 g., 0.9250 Silver 0.8410 oz. ASW, 38.6 mm. **Series:** Big Cats **Obv:** National arms **Rev:** Multi-colored male and female lions **Edge:** Reeded

Date	Mintage	F	VF	XF	Unc	BU
2001 Proof	—	Value: 55.00				

KM# 247.1 10 DOLLARS

28.2800 g., 0.9250 Silver 0.8410 oz. ASW, 38.6 mm. **Series:** Big Cats **Obv:** National arms **Rev:** Tiger **Edge:** Reeded

Date	Mintage	F	VF	XF	Unc	BU
2001 Proof	—	Value: 45.00				

KM# 247.2 10 DOLLARS

28.2800 g., 0.9250 Silver 0.8410 oz. ASW, 38.6 mm. **Series:** Big Cats **Obv:** National arms **Rev:** Multi-colored Tiger **Edge:** Reeded

Date	Mintage	F	VF	XF	Unc	BU
2001 Proof	—	Value: 55.00				

KM# 248.1 10 DOLLARS

28.2800 g., 0.9250 Silver 0.8410 oz. ASW, 38.6 mm. **Series:** Big Cats **Obv:** National arms **Rev:** Cheetah head facing **Edge:** Reeded

Date	Mintage	F	VF	XF	Unc	BU
2001 Proof	10,000	Value: 45.00				

KM# 248.2 10 DOLLARS

28.2800 g., 0.9250 Silver 0.8410 oz. ASW, 38.6 mm. **Series:** Big Cats **Obv:** National arms **Rev:** Multi-colored Cheetah head facing **Edge:** Reeded

Date	Mintage	F	VF	XF	Unc	BU
2001 Proof	—	Value: 55.00				

KM# 249.1 10 DOLLARS

28.2800 g., 0.9250 Silver 0.8410 oz. ASW, 38.6 mm. **Series:** Big Cats **Obv:** National arms **Rev:** Cougar **Edge:** Reeded

Date	Mintage	F	VF	XF	Unc	BU
2001 Proof	10,000	Value: 45.00				

KM# 249.2 10 DOLLARS

28.2800 g., 0.9250 Silver 0.8410 oz. ASW, 38.6 mm. **Series:** Big Cats **Obv:** National arms **Rev:** Multi-colored Cougar **Edge:** Reeded

Date	Mintage	F	VF	XF	Unc	BU
2001 Proof	—	Value: 55.00				

KM# 250.1 10 DOLLARS

28.2800 g., 0.9250 Silver 0.8410 oz. ASW, 38.6 mm. **Series:** Big Cats **Obv:** National arms **Rev:** Leopard **Edge:** Reeded

Date	Mintage	F	VF	XF	Unc	BU
2001 Proof	10,000	Value: 45.00				

KM# 199 10 DOLLARS

28.2800 g., 0.9250 Silver 0.8410 oz. ASW, 38.6 mm. **Subject:** Year of the Snake **Obv:** National arms **Rev:** Snake on bamboo **Edge:** Reeded

Date	Mintage	F	VF	XF	Unc	BU
2001 Proof	Est. 25,000	Value: 55.00				

KM# 207 10 DOLLARS

28.2800 g., 0.9250 Silver 0.8410 oz. ASW, 38.6 mm. **Subject:** P'an Ku **Obv:** National arms **Rev:** Dragon

Date	Mintage	F	VF	XF	Unc	BU
2001 Proof	Est. 5,000	Value: 55.00				

KM# 215 10 DOLLARS

28.2800 g., 0.9250 Silver 0.8410 oz. ASW, 38.6 mm. **Subject:** P'an Ku **Obv:** National arms **Rev:** Dragon and three animals

Date	Mintage	F	VF	XF	Unc	BU
2001 Proof	Est. 5,000	Value: 55.00				

KM# 250.2 10 DOLLARS

28.2800 g., 0.9250 Silver 0.8410 oz. ASW, 38.6 mm. **Series:** Big Cats **Obv:** National arms **Rev:** Multi-colored Leopard **Edge:** Reeded

Date	Mintage	F	VF	XF	Unc	BU
2001 Proof	—	Value: 55.00				

KM# 277 10 DOLLARS

28.2800 g., 0.9250 Silver Gold clad 0.8410 oz. ASW, 38.6 mm. **Subject:** British Queen Mother **Obv:** National arms **Rev:** Bust facing in garden with dog within sprigs **Edge:** Reeded

Date	Mintage	F	VF	XF	Unc	BU
2002 Proof	10,000	Value: 55.00				

KM# 280 10 DOLLARS

28.2800 g., 0.9250 Silver Gold clad 0.8410 oz. ASW, 38.6 mm. **Subject:** British Queen Mother **Obv:** National arms **Rev:** Conjoined busts facing within sprigs **Edge:** Reeded

Date	Mintage	F	VF	XF	Unc	BU
2002 Proof	10,000	Value: 55.00				

KM# 257 10 DOLLARS

28.2800 g., 0.9250 Silver 0.8410 oz. ASW, 38.6 mm. **Subject:** Year of the Horse **Obv:** National arms **Rev:** Horse divides circle **Edge:** Reeded

Date	Mintage	F	VF	XF	Unc	BU
2002 Proof	5,000	Value: 60.00				

KM# 265 10 DOLLARS

28.2800 g., 0.9250 Silver 0.8410 oz. ASW, 38.6 mm. **Subject:** RMS Titanic **Obv:** National arms **Rev:** Titanic at dock **Edge:** Reeded

Date	Mintage	F	VF	XF	Unc	BU
2002 Proof	10,000	Value: 55.00				

KM# 270 10 DOLLARS

28.2800 g., 0.9250 Silver Gold clad 0.8410 oz. ASW, 38.6 mm. **Subject:** Queen's Golden Jubilee **Obv:** National arms **Rev:** Queen Elizabeth II and Prince Philip visiting blacksmiths in Sierra Leone **Edge:** Reeded

Date	Mintage	F	VF	XF	Unc	BU
2002 Proof	10,000	Value: 55.00				

KM# 271 10 DOLLARS
28.2800 g., 0.9250 Silver Gold clad 0.8410 oz. ASW, 38.6 mm. **Subject:** Queen's Golden Jubilee **Obv:** National arms **Rev:** Queen Elizabeth II, Prince Charles and Princess Anne **Edge:** Reeded

Date	Mintage	F	VF	XF	Unc	BU
2002 Proof	10,000	Value: 52.00				

KM# 283 10 DOLLARS
28.2800 g., 0.9250 Silver Gold clad 0.8410 oz. ASW, 38.6 mm. **Subject:** Queen Elizabeth's Golden Jubilee **Obv:** National arms **Rev:** Queen and young Prince Charles **Edge:** Reeded

Date	Mintage	F	VF	XF	Unc	BU
2002 Proof	10,000	Value: 50.00				

KM# 286 10 DOLLARS
28.2800 g., 0.9250 Silver Gold clad 0.8410 oz. ASW, 38.6 mm. **Subject:** Queen Elizabeth's Golden Jubilee **Obv:** National arms **Rev:** Queen and Prince Philip **Edge:** Reeded

Date	Mintage	F	VF	XF	Unc	BU
2002 Proof	10,000	Value: 50.00				

KM# 292 10 DOLLARS
28.2800 g., 0.9250 Silver 0.8410 oz. ASW, 38.6 mm. **Subject:** Olympics **Obv:** National arms **Rev:** Ancient archer **Edge:** Reeded

Date	Mintage	F	VF	XF	Unc	BU
2003 Proof	10,000	Value: 50.00				
2004 Proof	10,000	Value: 50.00				

KM# 289 10 DOLLARS
28.2800 g., 0.9250 Silver 0.8410 oz. ASW, 38.6 mm. **Subject:** Olympics **Obv:** National arms **Rev:** Victory goddess Nike **Edge:** Reeded **Note:** The leone is the official currency of Sierra Leone

Date	Mintage	F	VF	XF	Unc	BU
2003 Proof	10,000	Value: 50.00				
2004 Proof	10,000	Value: 50.00				

KM# 298 10 DOLLARS
28.2800 g., 0.9250 Silver 0.8410 oz. ASW, 38.6 mm. **Obv:** National arms **Rev:** Nelson Mandela **Edge:** Reeded

Date	Mintage	F	VF	XF	Unc	BU
2004 Proof	10,000	Value: 55.00				

KM# 301 10 DOLLARS
28.2800 g., 0.9250 Silver 0.8410 oz. ASW, 38.6 mm. **Obv:** National arms **Rev:** Ronald Reagan **Edge:** Reeded

Date	Mintage	F	VF	XF	Unc	BU
2004 Proof	10,000	Value: 55.00				

KM# 307 10 DOLLARS
28.6200 g., 0.9250 Silver 0.8511 oz. ASW, 38.5 mm. **Obv:** National arms **Rev:** Giraffe **Edge:** Reeded

Date	Mintage	F	VF	XF	Unc	BU
2005 Proof	—	Value: 50.00				

KM# 339 10 DOLLARS
28.2800 g., 0.9250 Silver 0.8410 oz. ASW **Series:** 60th Anniversary of WW II **Subject:** Battle of Britain **Obv:** National arms **Obv. Legend:** REPUBLIC OF SIERRA LEONE **Rev:** Planes in flight

Date	Mintage	F	VF	XF	Unc	BU
2005 Proof	—	Value: 50.00				

KM# 340 10 DOLLARS
28.2800 g., 0.9250 Silver 0.8410 oz. ASW **Series:** 60th Anniversary End of WW II **Subject:** The Battle of the Atlantic **Obv:** National arms **Obv. Legend:** REPUBLIC OF SIERRA LEONE **Rev:** Plane and ship convoy

Date	Mintage	F	VF	XF	Unc	BU
2005 Proof	—	Value: 50.00				

KM# 341 10 DOLLARS
28.2800 g., 0.9250 Silver 0.8410 oz. ASW **Series:** 60th Anniversary End of WW II **Subject:** Battle of El Alamein **Obv:** National arms **Obv. Legend:** REPUBLIC OF SIERRA LEONE **Rev:** Tank, plane and ground troops

Date	Mintage	F	VF	XF	Unc	BU
2005 Proof	—	Value: 50.00				

KM# 342 10 DOLLARS
28.2800 g., 0.9250 Silver 0.8410 oz. ASW **Series:** 60th Anniversary End of WW II **Subject:** Battle of the Bulge **Obv:** National arms **Obv. Legend:** REPUBLIC OF SIERRA LEONE **Rev:** Forest battle scene

Date	Mintage	F	VF	XF	Unc	BU
2005 Proof	—	Value: 50.00				

KM# 343 10 DOLLARS
28.2800 g., 0.9250 Silver 0.8410 oz. ASW **Series:** 60th Anniversary End of WW II **Subject:** Battle of Berlin **Obv:** National arms **Obv. Legend:** REPUBLIC OF SIERRA LEONE **Rev:** Berlin city view, tank

Date	Mintage	F	VF	XF	Unc	BU
2005 Proof	—	Value: 50.00				

KM# 344 10 DOLLARS
28.2800 g., 0.9250 Silver 0.8410 oz. ASW **Series:** 60th Anniversary End of WW II **Subject:** The Heavy Water Raids **Obv:** National arms **Obv. Legend:** REPUBLIC OF SIERRA LEONE **Rev:** Troops on skies, factory in ruins

Date	Mintage	F	VF	XF	Unc	BU
2005 Proof	—	Value: 50.00				

KM# 330 10 DOLLARS
28.2800 g., 0.9250 Silver 0.8410 oz. ASW **Series:** Crown Jewels **Obv:** Arms **Obv. Legend:** REPUBLIC OF SIERRA LEONE **Rev:** Imperial State crown with ruby setting **Rev. Legend:** CROWN JEWELS **Edge:** Reeded

Date	Mintage	F	VF	XF	Unc	BU
2006 Proof	—	Value: 120				

KM# 331 10 DOLLARS
28.2800 g., 0.9250 Silver 0.8410 oz. ASW **Series:** Crown Jewels **Obv:** Arms **Obv. Legend:** REPUBLIC OF SIERRA LEONE **Rev:** Sword of State with sapphire setting **Rev. Legend:** CROWN JEWELS **Edge:** Reeded

Date	Mintage	F	VF	XF	Unc	BU
2006 Proof	—	Value: 120				

KM# 332 10 DOLLARS
28.2800 g., 0.9250 Silver 0.8410 oz. ASW **Series:** Crown Jewels **Obv:** Arms **Obv. Legend:** REPUBLIC OF SIERRA LEONE **Rev:** St. Edward's Crown with emerald setting **Rev. Legend:** CROWN JEWELS **Edge:** Reeded

Date	Mintage	F	VF	XF	Unc	BU
2006 Proof	—	Value: 120				

KM# 333 10 DOLLARS
28.2800 g., 0.9250 Silver 0.8410 oz. ASW **Series:** Crown Jewels **Obv:** Arms **Obv. Legend:** REPUBLIC OF SIERRA LEONE **Rev:** Orb and Sceptre with the cross with diamond setting **Rev. Legend:** CROWN JEWELS **Edge:** Reeded

Date	Mintage	F	VF	XF	Unc	BU
2006 Proof	—	Value: 120				

KM# 334 10 DOLLARS
Copper-Nickel **Subject:** 80th Birthday of Queen Elizabeth II **Obv:** Arms **Obv. Legend:** REPUBLIC OF SIERRA LEONE **Rev:** Elizabeth II seated giving Christmas message **Edge:** Reeded

Date	Mintage	F	VF	XF	Unc	BU
2006	—	—	—	—	16.50	18.50

KM# 334a 10 DOLLARS
28.2800 g., 0.9250 Silver 0.8410 oz. ASW **Subject:** 80th Birthday of Queen Elizabeth II **Obv:** Arms **Obv. Legend:** REPUBLIC OF SIERRA LEONE **Rev:** Elizabeth II seated giving Christmas Message **Edge:** Reeded

Date	Mintage	F	VF	XF	Unc	BU
2006 Proof	—	Value: 75.00				

KM# 335 10 DOLLARS
Copper-Nickel **Subject:** 80th Bithday of Queen Elizabeth II **Obv:** Arms **Obv. Legend:** REPUBLIC OF SIERRA LEONE **Rev:** Elizabeth II at 2002 Golden Jubilee celebrations in London, Concorde and Red Arrows doing flypass over Buckingham Palace **Edge:** Reeded

Date	Mintage	F	VF	XF	Unc	BU
2006	—	—	—	—	16.50	18.50

KM# 335a 10 DOLLARS
28.2800 g., 0.9250 Silver 0.8410 oz. ASW **Subject:** 80th Birthday of Queen Elizabeth Ii **Obv:** Arms **Obv. Legend:** REPUBLIC OF SIERRA LEONE **Rev:** Elizabeth II at 2002 Golden Jubilee celebrations in London, Concorde and Red Arrows doing flypass over Buckingham Palace **Edge:** Reeded

Date	Mintage	F	VF	XF	Unc	BU
2006 Proof	—	Value: 75.00				

KM# 336 10 DOLLARS
Copper-Nickel **Subject:** 80th Birthday of Queen Elizabeth II **Obv:** Arms **Obv. Legend:** REPUBLIC OF SIERRA LEONE **Rev:** Elizabeth II presenting 1966 Football World Cup to English team **Edge:** Reeded

Date	Mintage	F	VF	XF	Unc	BU
2006	—	—	—	—	16.50	18.50

KM# 336a 10 DOLLARS
28.2800 g., 0.9250 Silver 0.8410 oz. ASW **Subject:** 80th Birthday of Queen Elizabeth II **Obv:** Arms **Obv. Legend:** REPUBLIC OF SIERRA LEONE **Rev:** Elizabeth II presenting 1966 Football World Cup to English team **Edge:** Reeded

Date	Mintage	F	VF	XF	Unc	BU
2006 Proof	—	Value: 75.00				

KM# 337 10 DOLLARS
Copper-Nickel **Subject:** 80th Birthday of Queen Elizabeth II **Obv:** Arms **Obv. Legend:** REPUBLIC OF SIERRA LEONE **Rev:** Investiture of Charles as Prince of Wales in 1969 **Edge:** Reeded

Date	Mintage	F	VF	XF	Unc	BU
2006	—	—	—	—	16.50	18.50

KM# 337a 10 DOLLARS
0.9167 Silver **Subject:** 80th Birthday of Queen Elizabeth II **Obv:** Arms **Obv. Legend:** REPUBLIC OF SIERRA LEONE **Rev:** Investiture of Charles as Prince of Wales in 1969 **Edge:** Reeded

Date	Mintage	F	VF	XF	Unc	BU
2006 Proof	—	Value: 75.00				

KM# 338 10 DOLLARS
Copper-Nickel **Subject:** 10th Anniversary Death of Princess Diana **Obv:** Arms **Obv. Legend:** REPUBLIC OF SIERRA LEONE **Rev:** Diana with sons, Prince William and Prince Harry facing **Rev. Legend:** DIANA — PRINCESS OF WALES **Edge:** Reeded

Date	Mintage	F	VF	XF	Unc	BU
2007	—	—	—	—	16.50	18.50

KM# 338a 10 DOLLARS
28.2800 g., 0.9250 Silver 0.8410 oz. ASW **Subject:** 10th Anniversary Death of Princess Diana **Obv:** Arms **Obv. Legend:** REPUBLIC OF SIERRA LEONE **Rev:** Diana with sons, Prince William and Prince Harry facing **Rev. Legend:** DIANA — PRINCESS OF WALES **Edge:** Reeded

Date	Mintage	F	VF	XF	Unc	BU
2007 Proof	—	Value: 75.00				

KM# 200 20 DOLLARS
1.2441 g., 0.9990 Gold 0.0400 oz. AGW, 13.9 mm. **Subject:** Year of the Snake **Obv:** National arms **Rev:** Snake **Edge:** Reeded

Date	Mintage	F	VF	XF	Unc	BU
2001 Proof	Est. 50,000	Value: 85.00				

KM# 208 20 DOLLARS
1.2441 g., 0.9990 Gold 0.0400 oz. AGW, 13.9 mm. **Subject:** P'an Ku **Obv:** National arms **Rev:** Dragon

Date	Mintage	F	VF	XF	Unc	BU
2001 Proof	Est. 5,000	Value: 85.00				

KM# 216 20 DOLLARS
1.2441 g., 0.9990 Gold 0.0400 oz. AGW, 13.9 mm. **Subject:** P'an Ku **Obv:** National arms **Rev:** Dragon and three animals

Date	Mintage	F	VF	XF	Unc	BU
2001 Proof	Est. 5,000	Value: 85.00				

KM# 258 20 DOLLARS
1.2400 g., 0.9990 Gold 0.0398 oz. AGW, 13.92 mm. **Subject:** Year of the Horse **Obv:** National arms **Rev:** Horse **Edge:** Reeded

Date	Mintage	F	VF	XF	Unc	BU
2002 Proof	5,000	Value: 85.00				

KM# 272 30 DOLLARS
6.2200 g., 0.3750 Gold 0.0750 oz. AGW, 22 mm. **Subject:** Queen's Golden Jubilee **Obv:** National arms **Rev:** Queen Elizabeth II and Prince Philip **Edge:** Reeded

Date	Mintage	F	VF	XF	Unc	BU
2002 Proof	5,000	Value: 150				

KM# 273 30 DOLLARS
6.2200 g., 0.3750 Gold 0.0750 oz. AGW, 22 mm. **Subject:** Queen's Golden Jubilee **Obv:** National arms **Rev:** Queen Elizabeth II, Prince Charles and Princess Anne **Edge:** Reeded

Date	Mintage	F	VF	XF	Unc	BU
2002 Proof	5,000	Value: 150				

KM# 201 50 DOLLARS
3.1103 g., 0.9990 Gold 0.0999 oz. AGW, 18 mm. **Subject:** Year of the Snake **Obv:** National arms **Rev:** Snake **Edge:** Reeded

Date	Mintage	F	VF	XF	Unc	BU
2001 Proof	Est. 10,000	Value: 200				

KM# 209 50 DOLLARS
3.1103 g., 0.9990 Gold 0.0999 oz. AGW, 18 mm. **Subject:** P'an Ku **Obv:** National arms **Rev:** Dragon

Date	Mintage	F	VF	XF	Unc	BU
2001 Proof	Est. 5,000	Value: 200				

KM# 217 50 DOLLARS
3.1103 g., 0.9990 Gold 0.0999 oz. AGW, 18 mm. **Subject:** P'an Ku **Obv:** National arms **Rev:** Dragon and three animals

Date	Mintage	F	VF	XF	Unc	BU
2001 Proof	Est. 5,000	Value: 200				

KM# 266 50 DOLLARS
155.5500 g., 0.9999 Silver 5.0003 oz. ASW, 65 mm. **Subject:** RMS Titanic **Obv:** National arms **Rev:** Titanic at dock **Edge:** Reeded

Date	Mintage	F	VF	XF	Unc	BU
2002 Proof	2,000	Value: 220				

KM# 259 50 DOLLARS
3.1100 g., 0.9990 Gold 0.0999 oz. AGW, 18 mm. **Subject:** Year of the Horse **Obv:** National arms **Rev:** Horse **Edge:** Reeded

Date	Mintage	F	VF	XF	Unc	BU
2002 Proof	5,000	Value: 200				

KM# 202 100 DOLLARS
6.2200 g., 0.9990 Gold 0.1998 oz. AGW, 22 mm. **Subject:** Year of the Snake **Obv:** National arms **Rev:** Snake **Edge:** Reeded

Date	Mintage	F	VF	XF	Unc	BU
2001 Proof	—	Value: 380				

KM# 210 100 DOLLARS
6.2200 g., 0.9990 Gold 0.1998 oz. AGW, 22 mm. **Subject:** P'an Ku **Obv:** National arms **Rev:** Dragon

Date	Mintage	F	VF	XF	Unc	BU
2001 Proof	Est. 10,000	Value: 380				

KM# 218 100 DOLLARS
6.2200 g., 0.9990 Gold 0.1998 oz. AGW, 22 mm. **Subject:** P'an Ku **Obv:** National arms **Rev:** Dragon and three animals

Date	Mintage	F	VF	XF	Unc	BU
2001 Proof	Est. 10,000	Value: 380				

KM# 224 100 DOLLARS
6.2200 g., 0.9990 Gold 0.1998 oz. AGW, 22 mm. **Series:** The Big Five **Obv:** National arms **Rev:** Rhino **Edge:** Reeded

Date	Mintage	F	VF	XF	Unc	BU
2001 Proof	Est. 5,000	Value: 380				

KM# 227 100 DOLLARS
6.2200 g., 0.9990 Gold 0.1998 oz. AGW, 22 mm. **Series:** The Big Five **Obv:** National arms **Rev:** Lion

Date	Mintage	F	VF	XF	Unc	BU
2001 Proof	Est. 5,000	Value: 380				

KM# 230 100 DOLLARS
6.2200 g., 0.9990 Gold 0.1998 oz. AGW, 22 mm. **Series:** The Big Five **Obv:** National arms **Rev:** Leopard

Date	Mintage	F	VF	XF	Unc	BU
2001 Proof	Est. 5,000	Value: 380				

KM# 233 100 DOLLARS
6.2200 g., 0.9990 Gold 0.1998 oz. AGW, 22 mm. **Series:** The Big Five **Obv:** National arms **Rev:** Elephants

Date	Mintage	F	VF	XF	Unc	BU
2001 Proof	Est. 5,000	Value: 380				

KM# 236 100 DOLLARS
6.2200 g., 0.9990 Gold 0.1998 oz. AGW, 22 mm. **Series:** The Big Five **Obv:** National arms **Rev:** Buffalo

Date	Mintage	F	VF	XF	Unc	BU
2001 Proof	Est. 5,000	Value: 380				

KM# 239 100 DOLLARS
6.2200 g., 0.9990 Gold 0.1998 oz. AGW, 22 mm. **Series:** The Big Five **Obv:** National arms **Rev:** All five animals

Date	Mintage	F	VF	XF	Unc	BU
2001 Proof	Est. 5,000	Value: 380				

KM# 251 100 DOLLARS
6.2200 g., 0.9990 Gold 0.1998 oz. AGW, 22 mm. **Series:** Big Cats **Obv:** National arms **Rev:** Male and female lions **Edge:** Reeded

Date	Mintage	F	VF	XF	Unc	BU
2001 Proof	5,000	Value: 380				

KM# 252 100 DOLLARS
6.2200 g., 0.9990 Gold 0.1998 oz. AGW, 22 mm. **Series:** Big Cats **Rev:** Tiger **Edge:** Reeded

Date	Mintage	F	VF	XF	Unc	BU
2001 Proof	5,000	Value: 380				

KM# 253 100 DOLLARS
6.2200 g., 0.9990 Gold 0.1998 oz. AGW, 22 mm. **Series:** Big Cats **Rev:** Cheetah **Edge:** Reeded

Date	Mintage	F	VF	XF	Unc	BU
2001 Proof	5,000	Value: 380				

KM# 254 100 DOLLARS
6.2200 g., 0.9990 Gold 0.1998 oz. AGW, 22 mm. **Series:** Big Cats **Rev:** Cougar **Edge:** Reeded

Date	Mintage	F	VF	XF	Unc	BU
2001 Proof	5,000	Value: 380				

KM# 255 100 DOLLARS
6.2200 g., 0.9990 Gold 0.1998 oz. AGW, 22 mm. **Series:** Big Cats **Rev:** Black panther **Edge:** Reeded

Date	Mintage	F	VF	XF	Unc	BU
2001 Proof	5,000	Value: 380				

KM# 274 100 DOLLARS
6.2200 g., 0.9999 Gold 0.1999 oz. AGW, 22 mm. **Subject:** Queen's Golden Jubilee **Obv:** National arms **Rev:** Queen Elizabeth II and Prince Philip **Edge:** Reeded

Date	Mintage	F	VF	XF	Unc	BU
2002 Proof	2,002	Value: 380				

KM# 275 100 DOLLARS
6.2200 g., 0.9999 Gold 0.1999 oz. AGW, 22 mm. **Subject:** Queen's Golden Jubilee **Obv:** National arms **Rev:** Queen Elizabeth II, Prince Charles and Princess Anne **Edge:** Reeded

Date	Mintage	F	VF	XF	Unc	BU
2002 Proof	5,000	Value: 380				

KM# 284 100 DOLLARS
6.2200 g., 0.9999 Gold 0.1999 oz. AGW, 22 mm. **Subject:** Queen Elizabeth's Golden Jubilee **Obv:** National arms **Rev:** Queen and young Prince Charles **Edge:** Reeded

Date	Mintage	F	VF	XF	Unc	BU
2002 Proof	2,002	Value: 380				

KM# 287 100 DOLLARS
6.2200 g., 0.9999 Gold 0.1999 oz. AGW, 22 mm. **Subject:** Queen Elizabeth's Golden Jubilee **Obv:** National arms **Rev:** Queen and Prince Philip **Edge:** Reeded

Date	Mintage	F	VF	XF	Unc	BU
2002 Proof	2,002	Value: 380				

KM# 278 100 DOLLARS
6.2200 g., 0.9999 Gold 0.1999 oz. AGW, 22 mm. **Subject:** British Queen Mother **Obv:** National arms **Rev:** Queen Mother in garden with dog **Edge:** Reeded

Date	Mintage	F	VF	XF	Unc	BU
2002 Proof	2,000	Value: 380				

KM# 281 100 DOLLARS
6.2200 g., 0.9999 Gold 0.1999 oz. AGW, 22 mm. **Subject:** British Queen Mother **Obv:** National arms **Rev:** Queen Mother with daughters **Edge:** Reeded

Date	Mintage	F	VF	XF	Unc	BU
2002 Proof	2,000	Value: 380				

KM# 260 100 DOLLARS
6.2200 g., 0.9990 Gold 0.1998 oz. AGW, 22 mm. **Subject:** Year of the Horse **Obv:** National arms **Rev:** Horse **Edge:** Reeded

Date	Mintage	F	VF	XF	Unc	BU
2002 Proof	2,000	Value: 380				

KM# 290 100 DOLLARS
6.2200 g., 0.9999 Gold 0.1999 oz. AGW, 22 mm. **Subject:** Olympics **Obv:** National arms **Rev:** Victory goddess Nike **Edge:** Reeded

Date	Mintage	F	VF	XF	Unc	BU
2003 Proof	5,000	Value: 380				
2004 Proof	5,000	Value: 380				

KM# 293 100 DOLLARS
6.2200 g., 0.9999 Gold 0.1999 oz. AGW, 22 mm. **Subject:** Olympics **Obv:** National arms **Rev:** Ancient archer **Edge:** Reeded

Date	Mintage	F	VF	XF	Unc	BU
2003 Proof	5,000	Value: 380				
2004 Proof	5,000	Value: 380				

KM# 267 150 DOLLARS
1000.0000 g., 0.9999 Silver 32.146 oz. ASW, 85 mm. **Subject:** RMS Titanic **Obv:** National arms **Rev:** Titanic at dock **Edge:** Reeded

Date	Mintage	F	VF	XF	Unc	BU
2002 Proof	500	Value: 1,350				

KM# 203 250 DOLLARS
15.5118 g., 0.9990 Gold 0.4982 oz. AGW, 30 mm. **Subject:** Year of the Snake **Obv:** National arms **Rev:** Snake **Edge:** Reeded

Date	Mintage	F	VF	XF	Unc	BU
2001 Proof	Est. 5,000	Value: 950				

KM# 211 250 DOLLARS
15.5518 g., 0.9990 Gold 0.4995 oz. AGW, 30 mm. **Subject:** P'an Ku **Obv:** National arms **Rev:** Dragon

Date	Mintage	F	VF	XF	Unc	BU
2001 Proof	Est. 2,000	Value: 950				

KM# 219 250 DOLLARS
15.5518 g., 0.9990 Gold 0.4995 oz. AGW, 30 mm. **Subject:** P'an Ku **Obv:** National arms **Rev:** Dragon and three animals

Date	Mintage	F	VF	XF	Unc	BU
2001 Proof	Est. 2,000	Value: 950				

KM# 261 250 DOLLARS
15.5500 g., 0.9990 Gold 0.4994 oz. AGW, 30 mm. **Subject:** Year of the Horse **Obv:** National arms **Rev:** Horse **Edge:** Reeded

Date	Mintage	F	VF	XF	Unc	BU
2002 Proof	2,000	Value: 950				

KM# 204 500 DOLLARS
31.1035 g., 0.9990 Gold 0.9990 oz. AGW, 32.7 mm. **Subject:** Year of the Snake **Obv:** National arms **Rev:** Snake **Edge:** Reeded

Date	Mintage	F	VF	XF	Unc	BU
2001 Proof	Est. 1,000	Value: 1,850				

KM# 212 500 DOLLARS
31.1035 g., 0.9990 Gold 0.9990 oz. AGW, 32.7 mm. **Subject:** P'an Ku **Obv:** National arms **Rev:** Dragon

Date	Mintage	F	VF	XF	Unc	BU
2001 Proof	Est. 1,000	Value: 1,850				

KM# 220 500 DOLLARS
31.1035 g., 0.9990 Gold 0.9990 oz. AGW, 32.7 mm. **Subject:** P'an Ku **Obv:** National arms **Rev:** Dragon and three animals

Date	Mintage	F	VF	XF	Unc	BU
2001 Proof	Est. 1,000	Value: 1,850				

KM# 262 500 DOLLARS
31.1000 g., 0.9990 Gold 0.9988 oz. AGW, 32.7 mm. **Subject:** Year of the Horse **Obv:** National arms **Rev:** Horse **Edge:** Reeded

Date	Mintage	F	VF	XF	Unc	BU
2002 Proof	1,000	Value: 1,850				

KM# 294 500 DOLLARS
31.1000 g., 0.9999 Gold 0.9997 oz. AGW, 32.7 mm. **Obv:** National arms **Rev:** Multicolor Astro Boy cartoon **Edge:** Reeded

Date	Mintage	F	VF	XF	Unc	BU
2003 Proof	2,003	Value: 1,850				

KM# 299 500 DOLLARS
31.1035 g., 0.9999 Gold 0.9999 oz. AGW, 32.7 mm. **Obv:** National arms **Rev:** Nelson Mandela **Edge:** Reeded

Date	Mintage	F	VF	XF	Unc	BU
2004 Proof	—	Value: 1,850				

KM# 205 2500 DOLLARS
155.5175 g., 0.9990 Gold 4.9948 oz. AGW, 50 mm. **Subject:** Year of the Snake **Obv:** National arms **Rev:** Snake **Edge:** Reeded

Date	Mintage	F	VF	XF	Unc	BU
2001 Proof	Est. 250	Value: 9,250				

KM# 213 2500 DOLLARS
155.5175 g., 0.9990 Gold 4.9948 oz. AGW, 50 mm. **Subject:** P'an Ku **Obv:** National arms **Rev:** Dragon

Date	Mintage	F	VF	XF	Unc	BU
2001 Proof	Est. 250	Value: 9,250				

KM# 263 2500 DOLLARS
155.5100 g., 0.9990 Gold 4.9946 oz. AGW, 50 mm. **Subject:** Year of the Horse **Obv:** National arms **Rev:** Horse **Edge:** Reeded

Date	Mintage	F	VF	XF	Unc	BU
2002 Proof	250	Value: 9,250				

MINT SETS

KM#	Date	Mintage	Identification	Issue Price	Mkt Val
MS2	2006 (4)	—	KM# 334-337	65.00	75.00

PROOF SETS

KM#	Date	Mintage	Identification	Issue Price	Mkt Val
PS7	2006 (4)	—	KM# 330-333	450	480
PS8	2006 (4)	—	KM# 334a-337a	300	300

SINGAPORE

The Republic of Singapore, a member of the Commonwealth of Nations situated off the southern tip of the Malay peninsula, has an area of 224 sq. mi. (633 sq. km.) and a population of *2.7 million. Capital: Singapore. The economy is based on entrepôt trade, manufacturing and oil. Rubber, petroleum products, machinery and spices are exported.

The President is Chief of State. The prime minister is Head of Government.

MINT MARK
sm = ***"sm"*** - Singapore Mint monogram

MONETARY SYSTEM
100 Cents = 1 Dollar

REPUBLIC

STANDARD COINAGE

100 Cents = 1 Dollar

KM# 98a CENT
1.8100 g., 0.9250 Silver 0.0538 oz. ASW, 15.9 mm. **Obv:** National arms **Rev:** Value divides plants

Date	Mintage	F	VF	XF	Unc	BU
2001sm Proof	6,000	Value: 2.50				
2002sm Proof	6,300	Value: 2.50				

KM# 98 CENT
1.2400 g., Copper Plated Zinc, 15.9 mm. **Obv:** National arms **Rev:** Value divides plants **Edge:** Plain **Note:** Similar to KM#49 but motto ribbon on arms curves down at center.

Date	Mintage	F	VF	XF	Unc	BU
2001	40,101,738	—	—	—	0.10	0.15
2002	19,003,000	—	—	—	0.10	0.15
2003	—	—	—	—	0.10	0.15
2004	—	—	—	—	0.10	0.15
2005	—	—	—	—	0.10	0.15
2006	—	—	—	—	0.10	0.15
2007	—	—	—	—	0.10	0.15

KM# 99a 5 CENTS
2.0000 g., 0.9250 Silver 0.0595 oz. ASW, 16.75 mm. **Obv:** National arms **Rev:** Fruit salad plant

Date	Mintage	F	VF	XF	Unc	BU
2001sm Proof	6,000	Value: 2.75				
2002sm Proof	6,300	Value: 2.75				
2003sm Proof	4,900	Value: 2.75				
2004sm Proof	4,000	Value: 2.75				
2005sm Proof	3,250	Value: 2.75				

KM# 99 5 CENTS

1.5600 g., Aluminum-Bronze, 16.75 mm. **Obv:** National arms **Rev:** Fruit salad plant **Edge:** Reeded **Note:** Similar to KM#50 but motto ribbon on arms curves down at center.

Date	Mintage	F	VF	XF	Unc	BU
2001	13,101,738	—	—	—	0.20	0.30
2002	33,556,000	—	—	—	0.20	0.30
2003	16,508,980	—	—	—	0.20	0.30
2003 Proof	4,550	Value: 3.00				
2004	20,070,000	—	—	—	0.20	0.30
2004 Proof	3,500	Value: 3.00				
2005	70,061,981	—	—	—	0.20	0.30
2006 In sets only	53,214	—	—	—	0.50	—
2007	22,884,889	—	—	—	0.20	0.30
2008 In sets only	55,000	—	—	—	0.50	—
2009	19,850,000	—	—	—	0.20	0.30
2010sm	5,160,000	—	—	—	0.20	0.30
2011sm	—	—	—	—	0.20	0.30
2012sm	—	—	—	—	0.20	0.30

KM# 100a 10 CENTS

3.0500 g., 0.9250 Silver 0.0907 oz. ASW, 18.5 mm. **Obv:** National arms **Rev:** Star Jasmine plant **Edge:** Reeded

Date	Mintage	F	VF	XF	Unc	BU
2001sm Proof	6,000	Value: 4.00				
2002sm Proof	6,300	Value: 4.00				
2003sm Proof	4,900	Value: 4.00				
2004sm Proof	4,000	Value: 4.00				
2005sm Proof	3,250	Value: 4.00				

KM# 100 10 CENTS

2.6000 g., Copper-Nickel, 18.5 mm. **Obv:** National arms **Rev:** Star Jasmine plant **Edge:** Reeded **Note:** Similar to KM#51 but motto ribbon on arms curves down at center.

Date	Mintage	F	VF	XF	Unc	BU
2001	70,600,000	—	—	—	0.20	0.30
2002	61,670,000	—	—	—	0.20	0.30
2003	21,578,980	—	—	—	0.20	0.30
2003 Proof	4,550	Value: 4.00				
2004	59,670,000	—	—	—	0.20	0.30
2004 Proof	3,500	Value: 4.00				
2005	50,021,981	—	—	—	0.20	0.30
2006 In sets only	53,214	—	—	—	—	0.50
2007	50,054,889	—	—	—	0.20	0.30
2008 In sets only	55,000	—	—	—	—	0.50
2009	38,790,000	—	—	—	0.20	0.30
2010sm In sets only	Est. 40,000	—	—	—	0.20	0.50
2011sm	—	—	—	—	0.20	0.50
2012sm	—	—	—	—	0.20	0.50

KM# 101a 20 CENTS

5.2400 g., 0.9250 Silver 0.1558 oz. ASW, 21.36 mm. **Obv:** National arms **Rev:** Powder puff plant above value **Edge:** Reeded

Date	Mintage	F	VF	XF	Unc	BU
2001sm Proof	6,000	Value: 7.00				
2002sm Proof	6,300	Value: 7.00				
2003sm Proof	4,900	Value: 7.00				
2004sm Proof	4,000	Value: 7.00				
2005sm Proof	3,250	Value: 7.00				

KM# 101 20 CENTS

4.5000 g., Copper-Nickel, 21.36 mm. **Obv:** National arms **Rev:** Powder-puff plant above value **Edge:** Reeded **Note:** Similar to KM#52 but motto ribbon on arms curves down at center.

Date	Mintage	F	VF	XF	Unc	BU
2001	52,050,000	—	—	—	0.60	0.75
2002	48,120,000	—	—	—	0.60	0.75
2003	45,470,000	—	—	—	0.60	0.75
2003 Proof	4,550	Value: 5.00				
2004	44,870,000	—	—	—	0.60	0.75
2004 Proof	3,500	Value: 5.00				
2005 In sets only	61,981	—	—	—	—	1.00
2006	40,143,214	—	—	—	0.60	0.75
2007	30,144,889	—	—	—	0.60	0.75
2008 In sets only	55,000	—	—	—	—	1.00
2009	30,160,000	—	—	—	0.60	0.75
2010sm	Est. 10,030,000	—	—	—	0.60	0.75
2011sm	—	—	—	—	0.60	0.75
2012sm	—	—	—	—	0.60	0.75

KM# 102a 50 CENTS

8.5600 g., 0.9250 Silver 0.2546 oz. ASW, 24.66 mm. **Obv:** National arms **Rev:** Yellow Allamanda plant above value

Date	Mintage	F	VF	XF	Unc	BU
2001sm Proof	6,000	Value: 12.00				
2002sm Proof	6,300	Value: 12.00				
2003sm Proof	4,900	Value: 12.00				
2004sm Proof	1,900	Value: 12.00				
2005sm Proof	3,250	Value: 12.00				

KM# 102 50 CENTS

7.2900 g., Copper-Nickel, 24.66 mm. **Obv:** National arms **Rev:** Yellow Allamanda plant above value **Edge Lettering:** REPUBLIC OF SINGAPORE (lion's head) **Note:** Similar to KM#53 but motto ribbon on arms curves down at center.

Date	Mintage	F	VF	XF	Unc	BU
2001	30,020,000	—	—	—	0.75	1.00
2002	27,420,000	—	—	—	0.75	1.00
2003	23,650,000	—	—	—	0.75	1.00
2003 Proof	4,550	Value: 6.00				
2004	24,640,000	—	—	—	0.75	1.00
2004 Proof	3,500	Value: 6.00				
2005	25,057,981	—	—	—	0.75	1.00
2006 In sets only	53,214	—	—	—	—	1.25
2007	28,764,889	—	—	—	0.75	1.00
2008 In sets only	55,000	—	—	—	—	1.25
2009	12,390,000	—	—	—	0.75	1.00
2010	Est. 8,270,000	—	—	—	0.75	1.00
2011	—	—	—	—	0.75	1.00
2012sm	—	—	—	—	0.75	1.00

KM# 103a DOLLAR

8.0500 g., 0.9250 Silver 0.2394 oz. ASW, 22.4 mm. **Obv:** National arms **Rev:** Periwinkle flower

Date	Mintage	F	VF	XF	Unc	BU
2001sm Proof	6,000	Value: 15.00				
2002sm Proof	6,300	Value: 15.00				
2003sm Proof	4,900	Value: 15.00				
2004sm Proof	4,000	Value: 15.00				
2005sm Proof	3,250	Value: 15.00				

KM# 103 DOLLAR

6.3000 g., Aluminum-Bronze, 22.4 mm. **Obv:** National arms **Rev:** Periwinkle flower **Edge:** Reeded **Note:** Similar to KM#54 but motto ribbon on arms curves down at center.

Date	Mintage	F	VF	XF	Unc	BU
2001	40,941,738	—	—	—	1.50	2.25
2002	35,744,577	—	—	—	1.50	2.25
2003	31,968,980	—	—	—	1.50	2.25
2003 Proof	4,550	Value: 10.00				
2004	39,950,000	—	—	—	1.50	2.25
2004 Proof	3,500	Value: 10.00				
2005 In sets only	61,891	—	—	—	—	2.75
2006	63,053,214	—	—	—	1.50	2.25
2007 In sets only	54,889	—	—	—	—	2.75
2008	10,375,000	—	—	—	1.50	2.25
2009	21,750,000	—	—	—	1.50	2.25
2010sm In sets only	40,000	—	—	—	—	2.75
2011sm	—	—	—	—	1.50	2.75
2012sm	—	—	—	—	1.50	2.75

KM# 184a DOLLAR

8.5600 g., 0.9990 Silver 0.2749 oz. ASW, 24.7 mm. **Subject:** Old World Charm - Balestier **Obv:** Arms with supporters **Rev:** Old buildings **Note:** Colorized

Date	Mintage	F	VF	XF	Unc	BU
2004sm Proof	2,009	Value: 27.50				

KM# 190a DOLLAR

8.5600 g., 0.9990 Silver 0.2749 oz. ASW, 24.7 mm. **Subject:** Old World Charm - Jalan Besar **Note:** Colorized

Date	Mintage	F	VF	XF	Unc	BU
2004sm Proof	2,844	Value: 27.50				

KM# 191a DOLLAR

8.5600 g., 0.9990 Silver 0.2749 oz. ASW, 24.7 mm. **Subject:** Old World Charm - Joo Chiat **Note:** Colorized

Date	Mintage	F	VF	XF	Unc	BU
2004sm Proof	2,863	Value: 27.50				

KM# 184 DOLLAR

7.2900 g., Copper-Nickel, 24.7 mm. **Subject:** Old World Charm - Balestier **Obv:** Arms with supporters **Rev:** Old buildings **Edge:** Reeded

Date	Mintage	F	VF	XF	Unc	BU
2004sm Prooflike	3,486	—	—	—	—	10.00

KM# 190 DOLLAR

7.2900 g., Copper-Nickel, 24.7 mm. **Subject:** Old World Charm - Jalan Besar

Date	Mintage	F	VF	XF	Unc	BU
2004sm Prooflike	3,551	—	—	—	—	10.00

KM# 191 DOLLAR

Copper-Nickel, 24.6 mm. **Subject:** Old World Charm - Joo Chiat

Date	Mintage	F	VF	XF	Unc	BU
2004sm Prooflike	—	—	—	—	—	10.00

KM# 192 DOLLAR

7.2900 g., Copper-Nickel, 24.7 mm. **Subject:** Old World Charm - Tanjong Katong

Date	Mintage	F	VF	XF	Unc	BU
2004sm Prooflike	3,555	—	—	—	—	10.00

KM# 192a DOLLAR

0.9990 Silver, 24.7 mm. **Subject:** Old World Charm - Tanjong Katong

Date	Mintage	F	VF	XF	Unc	BU
2004sm Proof	2,263	Value: 27.50				

KM# 244 DOLLAR

18.0000 g., Copper-Nickel, 33 mm. **Series:** Urban Redevelopment **Obv:** National arms **Rev:** Anak Bukit

Date	Mintage	F	VF	XF	Unc	BU
2005sm Prooflike	2,620	Value: 12.00				

KM# 244a DOLLAR

17.3000 g., 0.9999 Silver 0.5561 oz. ASW, 33 mm. **Series:** Urban Redevelopment **Obv:** National arms **Rev:** Anak Bukit - multicolor

Date	Mintage	F	VF	XF	Unc	BU
2005sm Proof	2,450	Value: 45.00				

KM# 245 DOLLAR

18.0000 g., Copper-Nickel, 33 mm. **Series:** Urban Redevelopment **Obv:** National arms **Rev:** Coronation

Date	Mintage	F	VF	XF	Unc	BU
2005sm Prooflike	2,620	Value: 12.00				

KM# 245a DOLLAR

17.3000 g., 0.9999 Silver 0.5561 oz. ASW, 33 mm. **Series:** Urban Redevelopment **Obv:** National arms **Rev:** Coronation - multicolor

Date	Mintage	F	VF	XF	Unc	BU
2005sm Proof	790	Value: 45.00				

KM# 246 DOLLAR

18.0000 g., Copper-Nickel, 33 mm. **Series:** Urban Redevelopment **Obv:** National arms **Rev:** Jalan Leban and Casuarina Road

Date	Mintage	F	VF	XF	Unc	BU
2005sm Prooflike	2,620	Value: 12.00				

KM# 246a DOLLAR

17.0000 g., 0.9999 Silver 0.5465 oz. ASW, 33 mm. **Series:** Urban Redevelopment **Obv:** National arms **Rev:** Jalan Leban and Casuarina Road - multicolor

Date	Mintage	F	VF	XF	Unc	BU
2005sm Proof	790	Value: 45.00				

KM# 247 DOLLAR

18.0000 g., Copper-Nickel, 33 mm. **Series:** Urban Redevelopment **Obv:** National arms **Rev:** Springleaf

Date	Mintage	F	VF	XF	Unc	BU
2005sm Prooflike	2,620	Value: 12.00				

KM# 247a DOLLAR

17.3000 g., 0.9999 Silver 0.5561 oz. ASW, 33 mm. **Series:** Urban Redevelopment **Obv:** National arms **Rev:** Springleaf - multicolor

Date	Mintage	F	VF	XF	Unc	BU
2005sm Proof	2,450	Value: 45.00				

KM# 248 DOLLAR

18.0000 g., Copper-Nickel, 33 mm. **Series:** Urban Redevelopment **Obv:** National arms **Rev:** Thomson Village

Date	Mintage	F	VF	XF	Unc	BU
2005sm Prooflike	2,620	Value: 12.00				

KM# 248a DOLLAR

17.3000 g., 0.9999 Silver 0.5561 oz. ASW, 33 mm. **Series:** Urban Redevelopment **Obv:** National arms **Rev:** Thomson Village - multicolor

Date	Mintage	F	VF	XF	Unc	BU
2005sm Proof	800	Value: 45.00				

KM# 262a DOLLAR

17.3000 g., 0.9990 Silver 0.5556 oz. ASW, 33 mm. **Series:** Urban Redevelopment **Obv:** National arms **Rev:** Punggoi Point and Coney Island - multicolor

Date	Mintage	F	VF	XF	Unc	BU
2007sm Proof	2,289	Value: 32.50				

KM# 259 DOLLAR
Copper-Nickel **Series:** Urban Redevelopment **Obv:** National arms **Rev:** Changi Village - multicolor

Date	Mintage	F	VF	XF	Unc	BU
2007sm Prooflike	2,568	—	—	—	—	12.50

KM# 259a DOLLAR
17.3000 g., 0.9990 Silver 0.5556 oz. ASW, 33 mm. **Series:** Urban Redevelopment **Obv:** National arms **Rev:** Changi Village - multicolor

Date	Mintage	F	VF	XF	Unc	BU
2007sm Proof	976	Value: 37.50				

KM# 260 DOLLAR
Copper-Nickel **Series:** Urban Redevelopment **Obv:** National arms **Rev:** Pasir Ris Park - multicolor

Date	Mintage	F	VF	XF	Unc	BU
2007sm Prooflike	2,430	—	—	—	—	12.50

KM# 260a DOLLAR
17.3000 g., 0.9990 Silver 0.5556 oz. ASW, 33 mm. **Series:** Urban Redevelopment **Obv:** National arms **Rev:** Pasir Ris Park - multicolor

Date	Mintage	F	VF	XF	Unc	BU
2007sm Proof	936	Value: 37.50				

KM# 261 DOLLAR
Copper-Nickel **Series:** Urban Redevelopment **Obv:** National arms **Rev:** Pulau Ubin - multicolor

Date	Mintage	F	VF	XF	Unc	BU
2007sm Prooflike	2,408	—	—	—	—	12.50

KM# 261a DOLLAR
17.3000 g., 0.9990 Silver 0.5556 oz. ASW, 33 mm. **Series:** Urban Redevelopment **Obv:** National arms **Rev:** Pulau Ubin - multicolor

Date	Mintage	F	VF	XF	Unc	BU
2007sm Proof	2,327	Value: 32.50				

KM# 262 DOLLAR
Copper-Nickel **Series:** Urban Redevelopment **Obv:** National arms **Rev:** Punggoi Point and Coney Island - multicolor

Date	Mintage	F	VF	XF	Unc	BU
2007sm Prooflike	2,387	—	—	—	—	12.50

KM# 290 DOLLAR
Copper-Nickel **Obv:** Supported arms **Rev:** Multicolor Kent Ridge Park

Date	Mintage	F	VF	XF	Unc	BU
2008 Prooflike	2,250	Value: 10.00				

KM# 290a DOLLAR
17.3000 g., 0.9990 Silver 0.5556 oz. ASW **Obv:** Supported arms **Rev:** Multicolor Kent Ridge Park

Date	Mintage	F	VF	XF	Unc	BU
2008 Proof	850	Value: 37.50				

KM# 291 DOLLAR
Copper-Nickel **Obv:** Supported arms **Rev:** Multicolor Labrador Nature Reserve

Date	Mintage	F	VF	XF	Unc	BU
2008 Prooflike	2,250	Value: 10.00				

KM# 291a DOLLAR
17.3000 g., 0.9990 Silver 0.5556 oz. ASW **Obv:** Supported arms **Rev:** Multicolor Labrador Nature Reserve

Date	Mintage	F	VF	XF	Unc	BU
2008 Proof	850	Value: 37.50				

KM# 292 DOLLAR
Copper-Nickel **Obv:** Supported arms **Rev:** Multicolor Mount Faber Building

Date	Mintage	F	VF	XF	Unc	BU
2008 Prooflike	2,800	—	—	—	—	10.00

KM# 292a DOLLAR
17.3000 g., 0.9990 Silver 0.5556 oz. ASW **Obv:** Supported arms **Rev:** Multicolor Mount Faber Building

Date	Mintage	F	VF	XF	Unc	BU
2008 Proof	2,300	Value: 37.50				

KM# 293 DOLLAR
Copper-Nickel **Obv:** Supported arms **Rev:** Multicolor Telok Blangah Hill Park

Date	Mintage	F	VF	XF	Unc	BU
2008 Prooflike	2,300	—	—	—	—	10.00

KM# 293a DOLLAR
17.3000 g., 0.9990 Silver 0.5556 oz. ASW **Obv:** Supported arms **Rev:** Multicolor Telok Blangah Hill Park

Date	Mintage	F	VF	XF	Unc	BU
2008 Proof	2,200	Value: 37.50				

KM# 294 DOLLAR
0.3000 g., 0.9990 Gold 0.0096 oz. AGW, 7 mm. **Subject:** Year of the Ox **Obv:** Supported arms **Rev:** Ox

Date	Mintage	F	VF	XF	Unc	BU
2009	3,000	—	—	—	30.00	35.00

KM# 196 2 DOLLARS
Copper-Nickel **Subject:** Tribute to Healthcare Givers **Obv:** National arms **Rev:** Five 3/4 length people standing facing, clinic in background

Date	Mintage	F	VF	XF	Unc	BU
2003sm 32021 Prooflike		—	—	—	—	15.00

KM# 196a 2 DOLLARS
0.9990 Silver **Subject:** Tribute to Healthcare Givers **Obv:** National arms **Rev:** Five 3/4 length people standing facing, clinic in background

Date	Mintage	F	VF	XF	Unc	BU
2003sm Proof	5,200	Value: 60.00				

KM# 223 2 DOLLARS
20.0000 g., 0.9990 Silver 0.6423 oz. ASW, 38.70 mm. **Series:** Lunar **Subject:** Year of the Goat **Obv:** National arms **Rev:** Stylized goat standing right facing left

Date	Mintage	F	VF	XF	Unc	BU
2003sm Proof	2,000	Value: 60.00				

KM# 229 2 DOLLARS
20.0000 g., 0.9990 Silver 0.6423 oz. ASW, 38.7 mm. **Series:** Lunar **Subject:** Year of the Monkey **Obv:** National arms **Rev:** Stylized monkey sitting left

Date	Mintage	F	VF	XF	Unc	BU
2004sm Proof	2,180	Value: 60.00				

KM# 234 2 DOLLARS
20.0000 g., Copper-Nickel, 38.7 mm. **Series:** Lunar **Subject:** Year of the Rooster **Obv:** National arms **Rev:** Rooster standing right

Date	Mintage	F	VF	XF	Unc	BU
2005sm Prooflike	79,115	—	—	—	—	15.00

KM# 242 2 DOLLARS
Copper-Nickel **Subject:** 40th National Day Parade **Obv:** National arms **Rev:** Fireworks, parade in government plaza, multicolor

Date	Mintage	F	VF	XF	Unc	BU
2005sm Prooflike	5,443	Value: 15.00				

KM# 242a 2 DOLLARS
20.0000 g., 0.9999 Silver 0.6429 oz. ASW **Subject:** 40th National Day Parade **Obv:** National arms **Rev:** Fireworks, parade in government plaza

Date	Mintage	F	VF	XF	Unc	BU
2005sm Proof	4,204	Value: 60.00				

KM# 234a 2 DOLLARS
20.0000 g., 0.9999 Silver 0.6429 oz. ASW, 38.7 mm. **Series:** Lunar **Subject:** Year of the Rooster **Obv:** National arms **Rev:** Stylized rooster standing right

Date	Mintage	F	VF	XF	Unc	BU
2005sm Proof	4,879	Value: 42.50				

KM# 250 2 DOLLARS
20.0000 g., Copper-Nickel **Series:** Lunar **Subject:** Year of the Dog **Obv:** National arms **Rev:** Stylized dog standing left

Date	Mintage	F	VF	XF	Unc	BU
2006sm Prooflike	69,552	Value: 15.00				

KM# 250a 2 DOLLARS
20.0000 g., 0.9999 Silver 0.6429 oz. ASW **Series:** Lunar **Subject:** Year of the Dog **Obv:** National arms **Rev:** Stylized dog standing left

Date	Mintage	F	VF	XF	Unc	BU
2006sm Proof	4,500	Value: 60.00				

KM# 258 2 DOLLARS
Copper-Nickel **Subject:** 41st National Day **Obv:** National arms **Rev:** People in stadium, emblem - multicolor

Date	Mintage	F	VF	XF	Unc	BU
2006sm Prooflike	4,300	Value: 15.00				

KM# 258a 2 DOLLARS
20.0000 g., 0.9990 Silver 0.6423 oz. ASW **Subject:** 41st National Day **Obv:** National arms **Rev:** People in stadium, emblem - multicolor

Date	Mintage	F	VF	XF	Unc	BU
2006sm Proof	4,100	Value: 60.00				

KM# 264 2 DOLLARS
Copper-Nickel **Series:** Lunar **Subject:** Year of the Boar **Obv:** National arms **Rev:** Stylized boar running right

Date	Mintage	F	VF	XF	Unc	BU
2007sm Prooflike	63,930	—	—	—	—	12.00

KM# 193 2 DOLLARS
20.0000 g., Copper-Nickel, 38.70 mm. **Subject:** 42nd National Day Parade **Obv:** Arms with supporters **Obv. Legend:** SINGAPURA - SINGAPORE **Rev:** Colored overlay with four children above Marina Bay floating platform **Edge:** Reeded

Date	Mintage	F	VF	XF	Unc	BU
2007 Prooflike	6,400	—	—	—	—	13.50

KM# 193a 2 DOLLARS
20.0000 g., 0.9990 Silver 0.6423 oz. ASW, 38.70 mm. **Subject:** 42nd National Day Parade **Obv:** Arms with supporters **Obv. Legend:** SINGAPURA - SINGAPORE **Rev:** Colored overlay with four children above Marina Bay floating platform **Edge:** Reeded

Date	Mintage	F	VF	XF	Unc	BU
2007 Proof	6,150	Value: 42.50				

KM# 264a 2 DOLLARS
20.0000 g., 0.9990 Silver 0.6423 oz. ASW **Series:** Lunar **Subject:** Year of the Boar **Obv:** National arms **Rev:** Stylized boar running right

Date	Mintage	F	VF	XF	Unc	BU
2007sm Proof	6,000	Value: 45.00				

KM# 270 2 DOLLARS
20.0000 g., Copper-Nickel **Series:** Lunar **Subject:** Year of the Rat **Obv:** National arms **Rev:** Stylized rat lying left

Date	Mintage	F	VF	XF	Unc	BU
2008sm Prooflike	58,637	—	—	—	—	12.50

KM# 270a 2 DOLLARS
20.0000 g., 0.9990 Silver 0.6423 oz. ASW **Series:** Lunar **Subject:** Year of the Rat **Obv:** National arms **Rev:** Stylized rat lying left

Date	Mintage	F	VF	XF	Unc	BU
2008sm Proof	5,789	Value: 45.00				

KM# 287 2 DOLLARS
Copper-Nickel, 38.7 mm. **Subject:** Formula 1 - Singapore Grand Prix **Obv:** Supported arms **Rev:** Formula 1 racecar and skyline

Date	Mintage	F	VF	XF	Unc	BU
2008 Proof	7,000	Value: 10.00				

KM# 295 2 DOLLARS
Copper-Nickel **Subject:** Year of the Ox **Obv:** Supported arms

Date	Mintage	F	VF	XF	Unc	BU
2009 Prooflike	80,000	—	—	—	—	10.00

KM# 296 2 DOLLARS
20.0000 g., 0.9990 Silver 0.6423 oz. ASW **Subject:** Year of the Ox **Obv:** Supported arms **Rev:** Ox

Date	Mintage	F	VF	XF	Unc	BU
2009 Proof	6,000	Value: 37.50				

KM# 303 2 DOLLARS
Copper-Nickel, 38.7 mm. **Subject:** Independence, 44th Anniversary **Note:** Partially colorized

Date	Mintage	F	VF	XF	Unc	BU
2009 Prooflike	6,000	—	—	—	—	15.00

KM# 303a 2 DOLLARS
20.0000 g., 0.9990 Silver 0.6423 oz. ASW, 38.7 mm. **Series:** Indpendence, 44th Anniversary **Note:** Colorized

Date	Mintage	F	VF	XF	Unc	BU
2009 Proof	5,000	Value: 40.00				

KM# 104.1a 5 DOLLARS
8.2500 g., 0.9250 Silver 0.2453 oz. ASW, 23.3 mm. **Obv:** National arms **Rev:** Vanda Miss Joaquim flower and value within beaded circle

Date	Mintage	F	VF	XF	Unc	BU
1999sm Proof	9,200	Value: 25.00				
2001sm Proof	6,000	Value: 25.00				
2000sm Proof	8,900	Value: 25.00				
2002sm Proof	6,300	Value: 25.00				

KM# 104.2a 5 DOLLARS
8.2500 g., 0.9250 Silver 0.2453 oz. ASW, 23.3 mm. **Obv:** National arms, date and BCCS logo **Rev:** Vanda Miss Joaquim flower above value **Edge:** Plain

Date	Mintage	F	VF	XF	Unc	BU
2001sm Proof	6,000	Value: 25.00				
2002sm Proof	6,300	Value: 25.00				
2003sm Proof	4,900	Value: 25.00				
2004sm Proof	4,000	Value: 25.00				
2005sm Proof	3,250	Value: 25.00				
2006sm Proof	—	Value: 25.00				

KM# 104.2 5 DOLLARS
6.7000 g., Bi-Metallic Aluminumn-Bronze center in Copper-Nickel ring, 23.3 mm. **Obv:** National arms, date and BCCS logo **Rev:** Canda Miss Joaquim flower above value **Edge:** Plain **Note:** Date in hologram

Date	Mintage	F	VF	XF	Unc	BU
2001 In sets only	101,738	—	—	—	—	12.00
2002 In sets only	84,577	—	—	—	—	12.00
2003	—	—	—	—	—	12.00
2004	—	—	—	—	—	12.00
2005	—	—	—	—	—	12.00
2006	—	—	—	—	—	12.00

KM# 177a 5 DOLLARS
20.0000 g., 0.9250 Silver 0.5948 oz. ASW, 38.6 mm. **Subject:** Productivity Movement **Obv:** Arms with supporters **Rev:** Spiral design **Edge:** Reeded

Date	Mintage	F	VF	XF	Unc	BU
2001sm Proof	5,650	Value: 50.00				

KM# 177 5 DOLLARS
20.0000 g., Copper-Nickel, 38.6 mm. **Subject:** Productivity Movement **Obv:** Arms with supporters **Rev:** Spiral design **Edge:** Reeded

Date	Mintage	F	VF	XF	Unc	BU
2001sm	5,300	—	—	—	12.50	15.00

KM# 181 5 DOLLARS
20.0000 g., Copper-Nickel, 38.7 mm. **Subject:** Esplanade Theaters on the Bay **Obv:** Arms with supporters **Rev:** Stylized symbolic design **Edge:** Reeded

Date	Mintage	F	VF	XF	Unc	BU
2002sm	7,430	—	—	—	13.50	16.50

KM# 181a 5 DOLLARS
20.0000 g., 0.9990 Silver 0.6423 oz. ASW, 38.7 mm. **Subject:** Esplanade Theaters on the Bay **Obv:** Arms with supporters **Rev:** Stylized symbolic design **Edge:** Reeded

Date	Mintage	F	VF	XF	Unc	BU
2002sm Proof	6,540	Value: 45.00				

KM# 104.3 5 DOLLARS
6.7000 g., Bi-Metallic Aluminum-Bronze center in Copper-Nickel ring, 23.3 mm. **Obv:** National arms above latent image "MAS" **Rev:** Flower and value **Shape:** Scalloped

Date	Mintage	F	VF	XF	Unc	BU
2002sm	—	—	—	—	—	10.00
2003sm	—	—	—	—	—	10.00
2003sm Proof	4,550	Value: 15.00				
2004sm	—	—	—	—	—	10.00
2004sm Proof	3,500	Value: 15.00				
2005sm	—	—	—	—	—	10.00
2006sm	—	—	—	—	—	10.00
2007sm	—	—	—	—	—	10.00
2008sm	—	—	—	—	—	10.00
2009sm	—	—	—	—	—	10.00
2010sm	—	—	—	—	—	10.00
2011sm	—	—	—	—	—	10.00
2012sm	—	—	—	—	—	10.00

KM# 104.3a 5 DOLLARS
8.2500 g., 0.9250 Silver 0.2453 oz. ASW **Obv:** National arms above latent image "MAS or date" **Rev:** Flower and value **Shape:** Scalloped

Date	Mintage	F	VF	XF	Unc	BU
2003sm Proof	4,900	Value: 25.00				
2004sm Proof	4,000	Value: 25.00				
2005sm Proof	3,250	Value: 25.00				

KM# 194 5 DOLLARS
20.0000 g., 0.9990 Silver 0.6423 oz. ASW, 38.7 mm. **Obv:** Arms with supporters **Obv. Legend:** SINGAPURA - SINGAPORE **Rev:** Multicolor Singapore's skyline above world map, golden lion symbol below pointing to location of Singapore **Rev. Legend:** BOARD OF GOVERNORS ANNUAL MEETINGS • SINGAPORE 2006 • INTERNATIONAL MONETARY FUND • WORLD BANK GROUP •

Date	Mintage	F	VF	XF	Unc	BU
2006sm Proof	5,450	Value: 60.00				

KM# 256 5 DOLLARS
20.0000 g., 0.9990 Silver 0.6423 oz. ASW **Series:** Heritage Orchids **Obv:** National arms **Rev:** Vanda Tan Chay Yan - multicolor

Date	Mintage	F	VF	XF	Unc	BU
2006sm Proof	8,000	Value: 60.00				

KM# 257 5 DOLLARS
20.0000 g., 0.9990 Silver 0.6423 oz. ASW **Series:** Heritage Orchids **Obv:** National arms **Rev:** Aranda Majula - multicolor

Date	Mintage	F	VF	XF	Unc	BU
2006sm Proof	8,000	Value: 60.00				

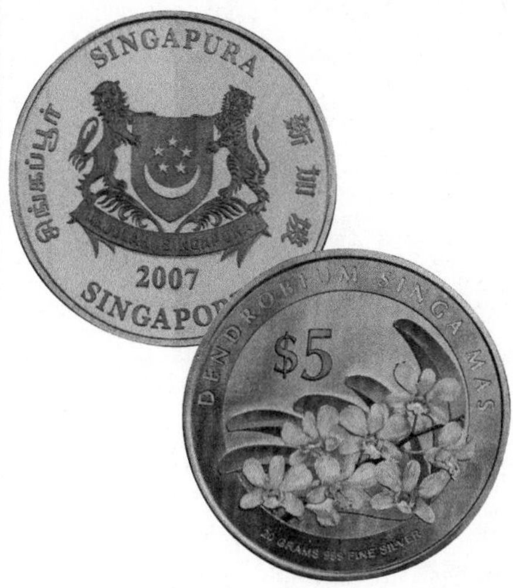

KM# 275 5 DOLLARS
20.0000 g., 0.9990 Silver 0.6423 oz. ASW, 38.7 mm. **Series:** Heritage Orchids **Obv:** National arms **Rev:** Dendrobium Singa Mas - multicolor

Date	Mintage	F	VF	XF	Unc	BU
2007sm Proof	8,000	Value: 45.00				

KM# 276 5 DOLLARS
20.0000 g., 0.9990 Silver 0.6423 oz. ASW, 38.7 mm. **Series:** Heritage Orchids **Obv:** National arms **Rev:** Vanda Mimi Palmar - multicolor

Date	Mintage	F	VF	XF	Unc	BU
2007sm Proof	8,000	Value: 45.00				

KM# 285 5 DOLLARS
20.0000 g., 0.9990 Silver 0.6423 oz. ASW, 38.6 mm. **Subject:** Heritage orchids **Obv:** Supported arms **Rev:** Multicolor yellow orchid - Oncidum Goldiana

Date	Mintage	F	VF	XF	Unc	BU
2008 Proof	8,000	Value: 45.00				

KM# 286 5 DOLLARS
20.0000 g., 0.9990 Silver 0.6423 oz. ASW, 38.6 mm. **Subject:** Heritage orchids **Obv:** Supported arms **Rev:** Multicolor pink orchid - Aranda Tay Swee Eng

Date	Mintage	F	VF	XF	Unc	BU
2008 Proof	8,000	Value: 45.00				

KM# 301 5 DOLLARS

20.0000 g., 0.9990 Silver 0.6423 oz. ASW **Subject:** Orchids of Singapore **Obv:** Arms **Rev:** Yellow flower - Spathoglottis Primrose

Date	Mintage	F	VF	XF	Unc	BU
2009 Proof	8,000	Value: 45.00				

KM# 302 5 DOLLARS

20.0000 g., 0.9990 Silver 0.6423 oz. ASW, 38.7 mm. **Subject:** Orchids of Singapore **Obv:** Arms **Rev:** Pink flower - Vanda Amy

Date	Mintage	F	VF	XF	Unc	BU
2009 Proof	8,000	Value: 45.00				

KM# 179 10 DOLLARS

28.0000 g., Copper-Nickel, 40.7 mm. **Series:** Lunar **Subject:** Year of the Snake **Obv:** National arms **Rev:** Stylized snake **Edge:** Reeded

Date	Mintage	F	VF	XF	Unc	BU
2001sm Prooflike	152,330	—	—	—	—	20.00

KM# 182 10 DOLLARS

28.0000 g., Copper-Nickel, 40.7 mm. **Series:** Lunar **Subject:** Year of the Horse **Obv:** National arms **Rev:** Stylized horse standing left **Edge:** Reeded

Date	Mintage	F	VF	XF	Unc	BU
2002sm Prooflike	128,666	—	—	—	—	20.00

KM# 225 10 DOLLARS

28.0000 g., Copper-Nickel, 40.7 mm. **Series:** Lunar **Subject:** Year of the Goat **Obv:** National arms **Rev:** Stylized goat standing right facing left

Date	Mintage	F	VF	XF	Unc	BU
2003sm Prooflike	103,047	—	—	—	—	20.00

KM# 187 10 DOLLARS

28.0000 g., Copper-Nickel, 40.7 mm. **Series:** Lunar **Subject:** Year of the Monkey **Obv:** National arms **Rev:** Stylized monkey sitting left **Edge:** Reeded

Date	Mintage	F	VF	XF	Unc	BU
2004sm Prooflike	100,000	—	—	—	—	20.00

KM# 189 10 DOLLARS

28.0000 g., Copper-Nickel, 40.7 mm. **Subject:** 10th Anniversary China-Singapore Suzhou Industrial Park **Obv:** National arms **Rev:** "Harmony" Sculpture **Edge:** Reeded

Date	Mintage	F	VF	XF	Unc	BU
2004sm Prooflike	3,511	—	—	—	—	20.00

KM# 189a 10 DOLLARS

20.0000 g., 0.9990 Silver 0.6423 oz. ASW, 40.7 mm. **Subject:** 10th Anniversary China-Singapore Suzhou Industrial Park **Obv:** National arms **Rev:** "Harmony" sculpture **Edge:** Reeded

Date	Mintage	F	VF	XF	Unc	BU
2004sm Proof	3,197	Value: 55.00				

KM# 240 10 DOLLARS

20.0000 g., Copper-Nickel, 40.7 mm. **Subject:** National University of Singapore **Obv:** National arms **Rev:** Person, globe and emblem

Date	Mintage	F	VF	XF	Unc	BU
2005sm Prooflike	12,264	—	—	—	—	22.50

KM# 240a 10 DOLLARS

20.0000 g., 0.9999 Silver 0.6429 oz. ASW, 38.7 mm. **Subject:** National University of Singapore **Obv:** National arms **Rev:** Person, globe and emblem

Date	Mintage	F	VF	XF	Unc	BU
2005sm Proof	5,293	Value: 60.00				

KM# 243 10 DOLLARS

31.1030 g., 0.9999 Silver with Gold 2.3g inlay 0.9998 oz. ASW **Subject:** 40th National Day parade **Obv:** National arms **Rev:** Fireworks, parade in government plaza

Date	Mintage	F	VF	XF	Unc	BU
2005sm Proof	756	Value: 245				

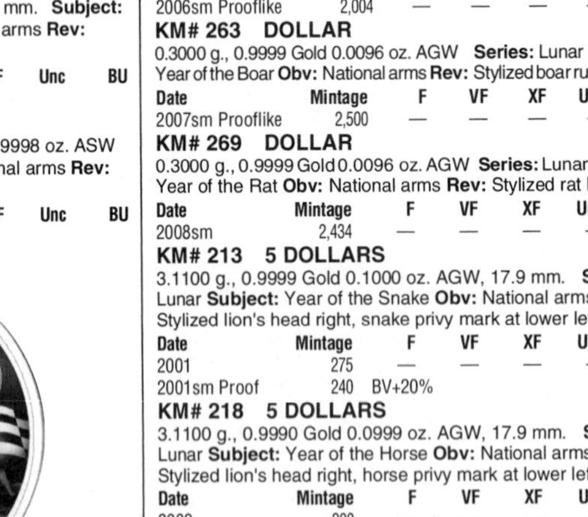

KM# 288 50 DOLLARS

20.0000 g., 0.9990 Silver 0.6423 oz. ASW **Subject:** Formula 1 - Singapore Grand Prix **Obv:** Supported arms **Rev:** Multicolor race car and skyline

Date	Mintage	F	VF	XF	Unc	BU
2008 Proof	5,000	Value: 40.00				

KM# 241 100 DOLLARS

31.1030 g., 0.9999 Gold 0.9998 oz. AGW, 33 mm. **Subject:** National University of Singapore **Obv:** National arms **Rev:** Person, globe and emblem

Date	Mintage	F	VF	XF	Unc	BU
2005sm Proof	244	Value: 1,850				

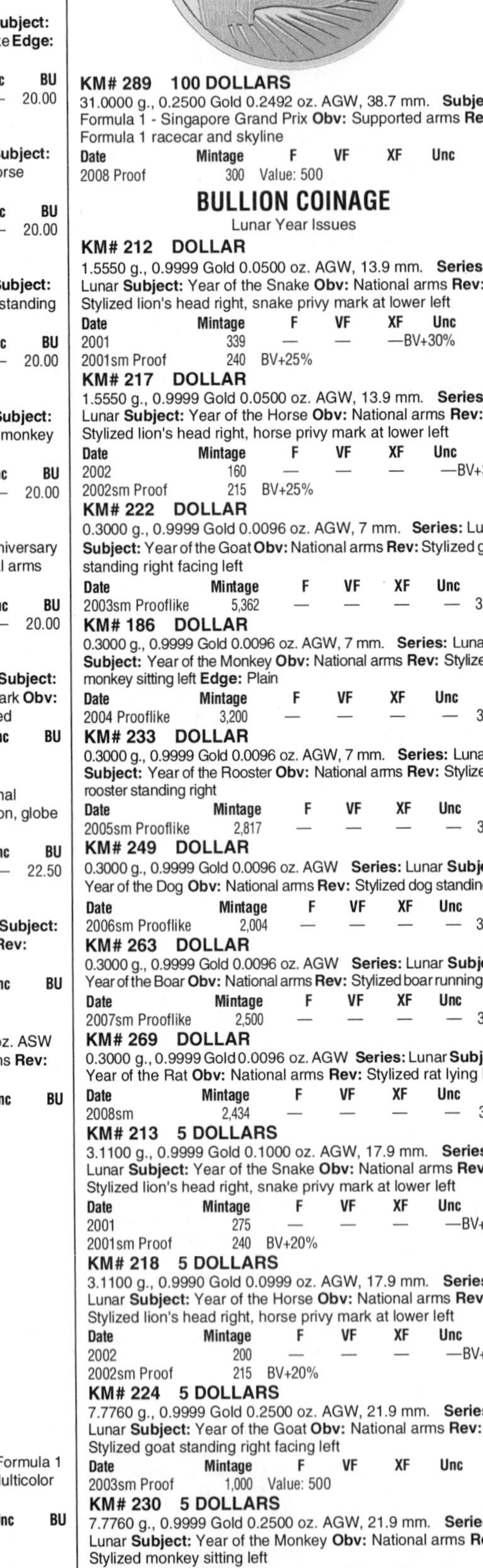

KM# 289 100 DOLLARS

31.0000 g., 0.2500 Gold 0.2492 oz. AGW, 38.7 mm. **Subject:** Formula 1 - Singapore Grand Prix **Obv:** Supported arms **Rev:** Formula 1 racecar and skyline

Date	Mintage	F	VF	XF	Unc	BU
2008 Proof	300	Value: 500				

BULLION COINAGE

Lunar Year Issues

KM# 212 DOLLAR

1.5550 g., 0.9999 Gold 0.0500 oz. AGW, 13.9 mm. **Series:** Lunar **Subject:** Year of the Snake **Obv:** National arms **Rev:** Stylized lion's head right, snake privy mark at lower left

Date	Mintage	F	VF	XF	Unc	BU
2001	339	—	—	—BV+30%		—
2001sm Proof	240	BV+25%				

KM# 217 DOLLAR

1.5550 g., 0.9999 Gold 0.0500 oz. AGW, 13.9 mm. **Series:** Lunar **Subject:** Year of the Horse **Obv:** National arms **Rev:** Stylized lion's head right, horse privy mark at lower left

Date	Mintage	F	VF	XF	Unc	BU
2002	160	—	—	—		—BV+30%
2002sm Proof	215	BV+25%				

KM# 222 DOLLAR

0.3000 g., 0.9999 Gold 0.0096 oz. AGW, 7 mm. **Series:** Lunar **Subject:** Year of the Goat **Obv:** National arms **Rev:** Stylized goat standing right facing left

Date	Mintage	F	VF	XF	Unc	BU
2003sm Prooflike	5,362	—	—	—	—	32.50

KM# 186 DOLLAR

0.3000 g., 0.9999 Gold 0.0096 oz. AGW, 7 mm. **Series:** Lunar **Subject:** Year of the Monkey **Obv:** National arms **Rev:** Stylized monkey sitting left **Edge:** Plain

Date	Mintage	F	VF	XF	Unc	BU
2004 Prooflike	3,200	—	—	—	—	32.50

KM# 233 DOLLAR

0.3000 g., 0.9999 Gold 0.0096 oz. AGW, 7 mm. **Series:** Lunar **Subject:** Year of the Rooster **Obv:** National arms **Rev:** Stylized rooster standing right

Date	Mintage	F	VF	XF	Unc	BU
2005sm Prooflike	2,817	—	—	—	—	32.50

KM# 249 DOLLAR

0.3000 g., 0.9999 Gold 0.0096 oz. AGW **Series:** Lunar **Subject:** Year of the Dog **Obv:** National arms **Rev:** Stylized dog standing left

Date	Mintage	F	VF	XF	Unc	BU
2006sm Prooflike	2,004	—	—	—	—	32.50

KM# 263 DOLLAR

0.3000 g., 0.9999 Gold 0.0096 oz. AGW **Series:** Lunar **Subject:** Year of the Boar **Obv:** National arms **Rev:** Stylized boar running right

Date	Mintage	F	VF	XF	Unc	BU
2007sm Prooflike	2,500	—	—	—	—	32.50

KM# 269 DOLLAR

0.3000 g., 0.9999 Gold 0.0096 oz. AGW **Series:** Lunar **Subject:** Year of the Rat **Obv:** National arms **Rev:** Stylized rat lying left

Date	Mintage	F	VF	XF	Unc	BU
2008sm	2,434	—	—	—	—	32.50

KM# 213 5 DOLLARS

3.1100 g., 0.9999 Gold 0.1000 oz. AGW, 17.9 mm. **Series:** Lunar **Subject:** Year of the Snake **Obv:** National arms **Rev:** Stylized lion's head right, snake privy mark at lower left

Date	Mintage	F	VF	XF	Unc	BU
2001	275	—	—	—		—BV+25%
2001sm Proof	240	BV+20%				

KM# 218 5 DOLLARS

3.1100 g., 0.9990 Gold 0.0999 oz. AGW, 17.9 mm. **Series:** Lunar **Subject:** Year of the Horse **Obv:** National arms **Rev:** Stylized lion's head right, horse privy mark at lower left

Date	Mintage	F	VF	XF	Unc	BU
2002	200	—	—	—		—BV+25%
2002sm Proof	215	BV+20%				

KM# 224 5 DOLLARS

7.7760 g., 0.9999 Gold 0.2500 oz. AGW, 21.9 mm. **Series:** Lunar **Subject:** Year of the Goat **Obv:** National arms **Rev:** Stylized goat standing right facing left

Date	Mintage	F	VF	XF	Unc	BU
2003sm Proof	1,000	Value: 500				

KM# 230 5 DOLLARS

7.7760 g., 0.9999 Gold 0.2500 oz. AGW, 21.9 mm. **Series:** Lunar **Subject:** Year of the Monkey **Obv:** National arms **Rev:** Stylized monkey sitting left

Date	Mintage	F	VF	XF	Unc	BU
2004sm Proof	1,426	Value: 500				

KM# 235 5 DOLLARS

7.7760 g., 0.9999 Gold 0.2500 oz. AGW, 21.9 mm. **Series:** Lunar **Subject:** Year of the Rooster **Obv:** National arms **Rev:** Stylized rooster standing right

Date	Mintage	F	VF	XF	Unc	BU
2005sm Proof	1,419	Value: 500				

KM# 251 5 DOLLARS

7.7750 g., 0.9999 Gold 0.2499 oz. AGW **Series:** Lunar **Subject:** Year of the Dog **Obv:** National arms **Rev:** Stylized dog standing left

Date	Mintage	F	VF	XF	Unc	BU
2006sm Proof	1,015	Value: 500				

KM# 265 5 DOLLARS

7.7750 g., 0.9999 Gold 0.2499 oz. AGW **Series:** Lunar **Subject:** Year of the Boar **Obv:** National arms **Rev:** Stylized boar running right

Date	Mintage	F	VF	XF	Unc	BU
2007sm Proof	1,060	Value: 500				

KM# 271 5 DOLLARS

7.7750 g., 0.9999 Gold 0.2499 oz. AGW **Series:** Lunar **Subject:** Year of the Rat **Obv:** National arms **Rev:** Stylized rat lying left

Date	Mintage	F	VF	XF	Unc	BU
2008sm Proof	1,200	Value: 500				

KM# 214 10 DOLLARS

7.7750 g., 0.9999 Gold 0.2499 oz. AGW, 21.9 mm. **Series:** Lunar **Subject:** Year of the Snake **Obv:** National arms **Rev:** Stylized lion's head right, snake privy mark at lower left

Date	Mintage	F	VF	XF	Unc	BU
2001	240	—	—	—		—BV+15%
2001sm Proof	240	BV+10%				

KM# 179a 10 DOLLARS

62.2060 g., 0.9990 Silver 1.9979 oz. ASW, 40.7 mm. **Series:** Lunar **Subject:** Year of the Snake **Obv:** National arms **Rev:** Stylized snake **Edge:** Reeded

Date	Mintage	F	VF	XF	Unc	BU
2001sm Proof	35,000	Value: 90.00				

KM# 219 10 DOLLARS

7.7750 g., 0.9999 Gold 0.2499 oz. AGW, 21.9 mm. **Series:** Lunar **Subject:** Year of the Horse **Obv:** National arms **Rev:** Stylized lion's head right, horse privy mark at lower left

Date	Mintage	F	VF	XF	Unc	BU
2002	180	—	—	—	—	525
2002sm Proof	215	Value: 475				

KM# 182a 10 DOLLARS

62.2060 g., 0.9990 Silver 1.9979 oz. ASW, 40.7 mm. **Series:** Lunar **Subject:** Year of the Horse **Obv:** National arms **Rev:** Stylized horse standing left **Edge:** Reeded

Date	Mintage	F	VF	XF	Unc	BU
2002sm Proof	35,000	Value: 90.00				

KM# 225a 10 DOLLARS

62.2060 g., 0.9990 Silver 1.9979 oz. ASW, 40.7 mm. **Series:** Lunar **Subject:** Year of the Goat **Obv:** National arms **Rev:** Stylized goat standing right facing left

Date	Mintage	F	VF	XF	Unc	BU
2003sm Proof	35,000	Value: 90.00				

KM# 185 10 DOLLARS

31.1040 g., 0.9999 Gold 0.9999 oz. AGW, 32.1 mm. **Subject:** 10th Anniversary China-Singapore Suzhou Industrial Park **Obv:** National arms **Rev:** "Harmony" Sculpture **Edge:** Lettered edge

Date	Mintage	F	VF	XF	Unc	BU
2004sm Proof	500	Value: 1,850				

KM# 187a 10 DOLLARS

62.2060 g., 0.9990 Silver 1.9979 oz. ASW, 40.7 mm. **Series:** Lunar **Subject:** Year of the Monkey **Obv:** National arms **Rev:** Stylized monkey sitting left **Edge:** Reeded

Date	Mintage	F	VF	XF	Unc	BU
2004sm Proof	35,000	Value: 90.00				

KM# 236 10 DOLLARS

62.2060 g., 0.9999 Silver 1.9997 oz. ASW, 45 mm. **Series:** Lunar **Subject:** Year of the Rooster **Obv:** National arms **Rev:** Stylized rooster standing right

Date	Mintage	F	VF	XF	Unc	BU
2005sm Proof	30,000	Value: 90.00				

KM# 252 10 DOLLARS

62.2030 g., 0.9990 Silver 1.9978 oz. ASW **Series:** Lunar **Subject:** Year of the Dog **Obv:** National arms **Rev:** Stylized dog standing left

Date	Mintage	F	VF	XF	Unc	BU
2006sm Proof	30,000	Value: 95.00				

KM# 266 10 DOLLARS

62.2060 g., 0.9990 Silver 1.9979 oz. ASW, 45 mm. **Series:** Lunar **Subject:** Year of the Boar **Obv:** National arms **Rev:** Stylized pigr running right - multicolor

Date	Mintage	F	VF	XF	Unc	BU
2007sm Proof	30,000	Value: 100				

KM# 272 10 DOLLARS
62.2060 g., 0.9990 Silver 1.9979 oz. ASW **Series:** Lunar **Subject:** Year of the Rat **Obv:** National arms **Rev:** Stylized rat lying left - multicolor

Date	Mintage	F	VF	XF	Unc	BU
2008sm Proof	20,000	Value: 110				

KM# 297 10 DOLLARS
62.2000 g., 0.9990 Silver 1.9977 oz. ASW **Subject:** Year of the Ox **Obv:** Supported arms **Rev:** Multicolor Ox

Date	Mintage	F	VF	XF	Unc	BU
2009 Proof	—	Value: 90.00				

KM# 215 20 DOLLARS
15.5520 g., 0.9999 Gold 0.4999 oz. AGW, 27 mm. **Series:** Lunar **Subject:** Year of the Snake **Obv:** National arms **Rev:** Stylized lion's head right, snake privy mark at lower left

Date	Mintage	F	VF	XF	Unc	BU
2001 169	169	—	—	—	—	BV+12%
2001sm 240 Proof	240	BV+12%				

KM# 220 20 DOLLARS
15.5520 g., 0.9999 Gold 0.4999 oz. AGW, 27 mm. **Series:** Lunar **Subject:** Year of the Horse **Obv:** National arms **Rev:** Stylized lion's head right, horse privy mark at lower left

Date	Mintage	F	VF	XF	Unc	BU
2002	165	—	—	—	—	BV+12%
2002sm Proof	215	BV+12%				

KM# 226 25 DOLLARS
155.5200 g., 0.9990 Silver 4.9949 oz. ASW, 65.00 mm. **Series:** Lunar **Subject:** Year of the Goat **Obv:** National arms **Rev:** Stylized goat standing right facing left

Date	Mintage	F	VF	XF	Unc	BU
2003sm Proof	250	Value: 300				

KM# 231 25 DOLLARS
155.5200 g., 0.9990 Silver 4.9949 oz. ASW, 65 mm. **Series:** Lunar **Subject:** Year of the Monkey **Obv:** National arms **Rev:** Stylized monkey sitting left

Date	Mintage	F	VF	XF	Unc	BU
2004sm Proof	250	Value: 300				

KM# 237 25 DOLLARS
155.5200 g., 0.9999 Silver 4.9994 oz. ASW, 65 mm. **Series:** Lunar **Subject:** Year of the Rooster **Obv:** National arms **Rev:** Stylized rooster standing right

Date	Mintage	F	VF	XF	Unc	BU
2005sm Proof	250	Value: 300				

KM# 253 25 DOLLARS
155.5150 g., 0.9990 Silver 4.9947 oz. ASW **Series:** Lunar **Subject:** Year of the Dog **Obv:** National arms **Rev:** Stylized dog standing right

Date	Mintage	F	VF	XF	Unc	BU
2006sm Proof	250	Value: 300				

KM# 267 25 DOLLARS
155.5150 g., 0.9990 Silver 4.9947 oz. ASW **Series:** Lunar **Subject:** Year of the Boar **Obv:** National arms **Rev:** Stylized boar running right

Date	Mintage	F	VF	XF	Unc	BU
2007sm Proof	250	Value: 300				

KM# 273 25 DOLLARS
155.5150 g., 0.9990 Silver 4.9947 oz. ASW **Series:** Lunar **Subject:** Year of the Rat **Obv:** National arms **Rev:** Stylized rat lying left

Date	Mintage	F	VF	XF	Unc	BU
2008sm Proof	250	Value: 300				

KM# 298 25 DOLLARS
155.5000 g., 0.9990 Silver 4.9942 oz. ASW **Subject:** Year of the Ox **Obv:** Supported arms **Rev:** Ox

Date	Mintage	F	VF	XF	Unc	BU
2009 Proof	—	Value: 300				

KM# 216 50 DOLLARS
31.1030 g., 0.9999 Gold 0.9998 oz. AGW, 32.1 mm. **Series:** Lunar **Subject:** Year of the Snake **Obv:** National arms **Rev:** Stylized lion's head right, snake privy mark at lower left

Date	Mintage	F	VF	XF	Unc	BU
2001	187	—	—	—	—	BV+9%
2001sm Proof	179	BV+9%				

KM# 221 50 DOLLARS
31.1030 g., 0.9999 Gold 0.9998 oz. AGW, 32.1 mm. **Series:** Lunar **Subject:** Year of the Horse **Obv:** National arms **Rev:** Stylized lion's head right, horse privy mark at lower left

Date	Mintage	F	VF	XF	Unc	BU
2002	165	—	—	—	—	BV+9%
2002sm Proof	160	BV+9%				

KM# 238 100 DOLLARS
31.1030 g., 0.9999 Gold 0.9998 oz. AGW, 33 mm. **Series:** Lunar **Subject:** Year of the Rooster **Obv:** National arms **Rev:** Stylized rooster standing right

Date	Mintage	F	VF	XF	Unc	BU
2005sm Proof	1,699	BV+10%				

KM# 254 100 DOLLARS
31.1030 g., 0.9999 Gold 0.9998 oz. AGW **Series:** Lunar **Subject:** Year of the Dog **Obv:** National arms **Rev:** Stylized dog standing left

Date	Mintage	F	VF	XF	Unc	BU
2006sm Proof	1,319	BV+10%				

KM# 268 100 DOLLARS
31.1030 g., 0.9999 Gold 0.9998 oz. AGW, 33 mm. **Series:** Lunar **Subject:** Year of the Boar **Obv:** National arms **Rev:** Stylized pig running right

Date	Mintage	F	VF	XF	Unc	BU
2007sm Proof	1,220	BV+10%				

KM# 274 100 DOLLARS
31.1030 g., 0.9999 Gold 0.9998 oz. AGW **Series:** Lunar **Subject:** Year of the Rat **Obv:** National arms **Rev:** Stylized rat lying left

Date	Mintage	F	VF	XF	Unc	BU
2008sm Proof	1,153	BV+10%				

KM# 299 100 DOLLARS
31.1050 g., 0.9990 Gold 0.9990 oz. AGW **Subject:** Year of the Ox **Obv:** Supported arms **Rev:** Ox

Date	Mintage	F	VF	XF	Unc	BU
2009 Proof	2,000	BV+10%				

KM# 239 200 DOLLARS
155.5200 g., 0.9999 Gold 4.9994 oz. AGW, 60 mm. **Series:** Lunar **Subject:** Year of the Rooster **Obv:** National arms **Rev:** Stylized rooster standing right

Date	Mintage	F	VF	XF	Unc	BU
2005sm Proof	84	Value: 9,750				

KM# 255 200 DOLLARS
155.1500 g., 0.9999 Gold 4.9875 oz. AGW **Series:** Lunar **Subject:** Year of the Dog **Obv:** National arms **Rev:** Stylized dog standing left

Date	Mintage	F	VF	XF	Unc	BU
2006sm Proof	50	Value: 9,750				

KM# 300 200 DOLLARS
155.5000 g., 0.9990 Gold 4.9942 oz. AGW, 60 mm. **Subject:** Year of the Ox **Obv:** Supported arms **Rev:** Ox

Date	Mintage	F	VF	XF	Unc	BU
2009 Proof	200	Value: 9,500				

KM# 178 250 DOLLARS
31.1035 g., 0.9990 Gold 0.9990 oz. AGW, 32.1 mm. **Subject:** Year of the Snake **Obv:** National arms **Rev:** Stylized snake **Edge:** Reeded

Date	Mintage	F	VF	XF	Unc	BU
2001sm Proof	3,775	BV+10%				

KM# 183 250 DOLLARS
31.1035 g., 0.9999 Gold 0.9999 oz. AGW, 32.1 mm. **Subject:** Year of the Horse **Obv:** National arms **Rev:** Horse **Edge:** Reeded

Date	Mintage	F	VF	XF	Unc	BU
2002sm Proof	3,199	BV+10%				

KM# 227 250 DOLLARS
31.1030 g., 0.9999 Gold 0.9998 oz. AGW, 32.1 mm. **Series:** Lunar **Subject:** Year of the Goat **Obv:** National arms **Rev:** Stylized goat standing right facing left

Date	Mintage	F	VF	XF	Unc	BU
2003sm Proof	2,390	BV+10%				

KM# 188 250 DOLLARS
31.1030 g., 0.9999 Gold 0.9998 oz. AGW, 32.1 mm. **Series:** Lunar **Subject:** Year of the Monkey **Obv:** National arms **Rev:** Stylized monkey sitting left **Edge:** Reeded

Date	Mintage	F	VF	XF	Unc	BU
2004sm Proof	2,535	BV+10%				

KM# 228 500 DOLLARS
155.5200 g., 0.9999 Gold 4.9994 oz. AGW, 55 mm. **Series:** Lunar **Subject:** Year of the Goat **Obv:** National arms **Rev:** Stylized goat standing right facing left

Date	Mintage	F	VF	XF	Unc	BU
2003sm Proof	62	Value: 9,750				

KM# 232 500 DOLLARS
155.5200 g., 0.9999 Gold 4.9994 oz. AGW, 55 mm. **Series:** Lunar **Subject:** Year of the Monkey **Obv:** National arms **Rev:** Stylized monkey sitting left

Date	Mintage	F	VF	XF	Unc	BU
2004sm Proof	76	Value: 9,750				

MINT SETS

KM#	Date	Mintage	Identification	Issue Price	Mkt Val
MS38A	2001 (7)	101,738	KM#98-103, 104.2	—	—
MS39	2002 (7)	84,577	KM#98-103, 104.3 Hongbao	—	15.00
MS40	2003 (6)	68,980	KM#99-103, 104.3 Hongbao	—	15.00
MS41	2004 (6)	70,000	KM#99-103, 104.3 Hongbao	—	15.00
MS42	2005 (6)	61,981	KM#99-103, 104.3 Hongbao	—	15.00
MS43	2006 (7)	53,214	KM#99-103, 104.3 Hongbao	—	15.00
MS44	2007 (6)	54,889	KM99-103, 104.3 Hongbao	10.78	15.00
MS45	2008 (6)	55,000	KM#99-103, 104.3	—	15.00
MS46	2009 (6)	60,000	KM#99-103, 104.3	—	15.00

PROOF SETS

KM#	Date	Mintage	Identification	Issue Price	Mkt Val
PS61	2001 (2)	3,000	KM#179-180 plus copper-nickel ingot	—	115
PS62	2001 (3)	2,000	KM#178-180 plus copper-nickel ingot	—	2,000
PS63	2001 (4)	—	KM#212-215	—	1,750
PS64	2001 (6)	—	KM#212-216, plus ingot	—	3,200
PS65	2001 (2)	2,001	KM#177, 177a	—	70.00
PS66	2001 (7)	6,000	KM#98a-103a, 104.2a	—	70.00
PS67	2002 (2)	3,000	KM#182, 182a	—	115
PS68	2002 (3)	2,000	KM#182, 182a, 183	—	2,000
PS69	2002 (2)	2,001	KM#181, 181a	—	65.00
PS70	2002 (3)	2,001	KM#181, 181a, 217	—	160
PS71	2002 (4)	—	KM#217-220	—	1,750
PS72	2002 (6)	—	KM#217-221 plus ingot	—	3,250
PS73	2002 (7)	6,300	KM#98a-103a, 104.2a	—	70.00
PS74	2003 (2)	2,003	KM#196, 196a	—	75.00
PS75	2003 (6)	4,900	KM#99a-103a, 104.3a	—	70.00
PS76	2003 (6)	1,000	KM#99a-103a, 104.3a	—	130
PS77	2003 (2)	88	KM#226, 228	—	10,050
PS78	2003 (2)	3,000	KM#225, 225a	—	115
PS79	2003 (3)	2,000	KM#225, 225a, 227	—	2,000
PS80	2004 (2)	1,000	KM#189, 189a	—	85.00
PS81	2004 (3)	88	KM#185, 189, 189a	—	1,950
PS82	2004 (6)	10,000	KM#98a-103a, 104.3a	—	70.00
PS83	2004 (2)	1,000	KM#184, 184a	—	40.00
PS84	2004 (2)	1,000	KM#190, 190a	—	40.00
PS85	2004 (2)	1,000	KM#191, 191a	—	40.00
PS86	2004 (2)	1,000	KM#192, 192a	—	40.00
PS87	2004 (4)	800	KM#184a, 190a-192a	—	110
PS88	2004 (8)	88	KM#184, 184a, 190, 190a, 191, 191a, 192, 192a	—	150
PS89	2004 (2)	80	KM#231, 232	—	10,050
PS90	2004 (2)	3,000	KM#187, 187a	—	110
PS91	2004 (3)	2,000	KM#187, 187a, 188	—	2,000
PS92	2005 (6)	3,250	KM#99a-103a, 104.3a	—	70.00
PS93	2005 (2)	3,000	KM#234, 236	—	110
PS94	2005 (2)	88	KM#237, 239	—	10,050

KM#	Date	Mintage	Identification	Issue Price	Mkt Val
PS95	2005 (3)	2,000	KM#234, 236, 238	—	2,000
PS97	2006 (2)	8,000	KM#256, 257	—	120
PS99	2007 (4)	800	KM#259a-262a	—	130
PS100	2007 (2)	8,000	KM#275, 276	90.00	90.00
PS101	2007 (2)	3,000	KM#193, 193a	65.00	65.00

PROOF-LIKE SETS (PL)

KM#	Date	Mintage	Identification	Issue Price	Mkt Val
PL1	2004 (4)	800	KM#184, 190, 191, 192	—	40.00
PL2	2007 (4)	800	KM#259-262	—	50.00

The Republic of Slovakia has an area of 18,923 sq. mi. (49,035 sq. km.) and a population of 4.9 million. Capital: Bratislava. Textiles, steel, and wood products are exported.

MINT MARK

Kremnica Mint

REPUBLIC

STANDARD COINAGE

100 Halierov = 1 Slovak Koruna (Sk)

KM# 17 10 HALIEROV

0.7200 g., Aluminum, 17 mm. **Obv:** Double cross on shield above inscription **Rev:** Church steeple **Edge:** Plain **Designer:** Drahomir Zobek

Date	Mintage	F	VF	XF	Unc	BU
2001	20,330,000	—	—	—	0.35	—
2001 Proof	12,500	Value: 2.50				
2002	37,640,000	—	—	—	0.35	—
2002 Proof	16,100	Value: 1.50				
2003 In sets only	3,000	—	—	—	—	2.50

KM# 17a 10 HALIEROV

2.8500 g., 0.9250 Silver 0.0848 oz. ASW, 17 mm.

Date	Mintage	F	VF	XF	Unc	BU
2004	4,000	—	—	—	—	10.00
2004 Proof	2,000	Value: 15.00				

KM# 18 20 HALIEROV

0.9500 g., Aluminum, 19.5 mm. **Obv:** Double cross on shield above inscription **Rev:** Krivan Mountain and value **Edge:** Reeded **Designer:** Drahomir Zobek

Date	Mintage	F	VF	XF	Unc	BU
2001	21,920,000	—	—	—	0.45	—
2001 Proof	12,500	Value: 2.50				
2002	36,300,000	—	—	—	0.45	—
2002 Proof	16,100	Value: 1.50				
2003 In sets only	3,000	—	—	—	—	2.50

KM# 18a 20 HALIEROV

3.8700 g., 0.9250 Silver 0.1151 oz. ASW, 19.5 mm.

Date	Mintage	F	VF	XF	Unc	BU
2004	4,000	—	—	—	—	15.00
2004	2,000	Value: 20.00				

KM# 35 50 HALIEROV

2.8000 g., Copper Plated Steel, 18.75 mm. **Obv:** Double cross on shield above inscription **Rev:** Devin watch tower and value **Edge:** Segmented reeding **Designer:** Drahomir Zobek

Date	Mintage	F	VF	XF	Unc	BU
2001	10,400,000	—	—	—	0.60	—
2001 Proof	12,500	Value: 2.50				
2002	11,000,000	—	—	—	0.60	—
2002 Proof	16,100	Value: 1.50				
2003	11,000,000	—	—	—	0.60	—
2004	16,500,000	—	—	—	0.60	—
2004 Proof	—	Value: 1.50				
2005	17,000,000	—	—	—	0.60	—
2006	22,050,000	—	—	—	0.60	—
2006 Proof	—	Value: 1.50				
2007	—	—	—	—	0.60	—
2008	—	—	—	—	0.60	—
2008 Proof	—	Value: 1.50				

KM# 12 KORUNA

3.8500 g., Bronze Plated Steel, 21 mm. **Subject:** 15th Century of Madonna and Child **Obv:** Double cross on shield above inscription **Rev:** Madonna holding child and value **Edge:** Milled **Designer:** Drahomir Zobek

Date	Mintage	F	VF	XF	Unc	BU
2001 In sets only	12,500	—	—	—	—	1.50
2001 Proof	—	Value: 3.00				
2002	11,000,000	—	—	—	0.75	—
2002 Proof	16,100	Value: 2.50				
2003 In sets only	14,000	—	—	—	—	1.50
2004 In sets only	—	—	—	—	—	1.50
2004 Proof	—	Value: 2.50				
2005	10,000,000	—	—	—	0.75	—
2005 Proof	—	Value: 2.50				
2006	9,605,000	—	—	—	0.75	—
2006 Proof	—	Value: 2.50				
2007	—	—	—	—	0.75	—
2008	—	—	—	—	0.75	—
2008 Proof	—	Value: 2.50				

KM# 13 2 KORUNA

4.4000 g., Nickel Plated Steel, 22.5 mm. **Obv:** Double cross on shield above inscription **Rev:** Venus statue and value **Designer:** Drahomir Zobek

Date	Mintage	F	VF	XF	Unc	BU
2001	10,668,000	—	—	—	0.85	—
2001 Proof	12,500	Value: 5.00				
2002	11,000,000	—	—	—	0.85	—
2002 Proof	16,100	Value: 2.50				
2003	11,000,000	—	—	—	0.85	—
2004 In sets only	—	—	—	—	—	2.00
2004 Proof	—	Value: 2.50				
2005 In sets only	—	—	—	—	—	2.00
2006 In sets only	—	—	—	—	—	2.00
2006 Proof	—	Value: 2.50				
2007 In sets only	—	—	—	—	—	2.00
2008 In sets only	—	—	—	—	—	2.00
2008 Proof	—	Value: 2.50				

KM# 14 5 KORUNA

5.4000 g., Nickel Plated Steel, 24.75 mm. **Obv:** Double cross on shield above inscription **Rev:** Celtic coin of BIATEC at upper left of value **Edge:** Milled **Designer:** Drahomir Zobek

Date	Mintage	F	VF	XF	Unc	BU
2001 In sets only	—	—	—	—	—	2.00
2001 Proof	12,500	Value: 6.00				
2002 Proof	16,100	Value: 5.00				
2003 In sets only	14,000	—	—	—	—	2.00
2004 In sets only	—	—	—	—	—	2.00
2004 Proof	—	Value: 5.00				
2005 In sets only	—	—	—	—	—	2.00
2006 In sets only	—	—	—	—	—	2.00
2006 Proof	—	Value: 5.00				
2007	—	—	—	—	1.50	—
2008 In sets only	—	—	—	—	—	2.00
2008 Proof	—	Value: 5.00				

KM# 11 10 KORUNA

6.6000 g., Aluminum-Bronze, 26.5 mm. **Obv:** Double cross on shield above inscription **Rev:** Bronze cross and value **Designer:** Drahomir Zobek

Date	Mintage	F	VF	XF	Unc	BU
2001 In sets only	—	—	—	—	—	4.00
2001 Proof	12,500	Value: 12.50				
2002 Proof	16,100	Value: 10.00				
2003	10,923,000	—	—	—	2.50	—
2004 In sets only	—	—	—	—	—	4.00
2004 Proof	—	Value: 10.00				
2005 In sets only	—	—	—	—	—	4.00
2006 In sets only	—	—	—	—	—	4.00
2006 Proof	—	Value: 10.00				
2007 In sets only	—	—	—	—	—	4.00
2008 In sets only	—	—	—	—	—	4.00
2008 Proof	—	Value: 10.00				

KM# 67 20 KORUN

24.4800 g., 0.9250 Silver 0.7280 oz. ASW, 27.1 x 50.6 mm. **Series:** Banknotes **Obv:** Prince Pribina (800-861) **Rev:** Nitra Castle **Edge:** Plain

Date	Mintage	F	VF	XF	Unc	BU
2003 Proof	6,000	Value: 60.00				

KM# 68 50 KORUN

26.6300 g., 0.9250 Silver 0.7919 oz. ASW, 28.2 x 52.8 mm. **Series:** Banknotes **Obv:** Saints Cyril and Methodius (814-885) **Rev:** Two hands **Edge:** Plain

Date	Mintage	F	VF	XF	Unc	BU
2003 Proof	6,000	Value: 65.00				

KM# 69 100 KORUN

28.8700 g., 0.9250 Silver 0.8585 oz. ASW, 29.3 x 55 mm. **Series:** Banknotes **Obv:** The Levoca Madonna **Rev:** St. James Church in Levoca **Edge:** Plain

Date	Mintage	F	VF	XF	Unc	BU
2003 Proof	—	Value: 75.00				

KM# 59 200 KORUN

20.0000 g., 0.7500 Silver 0.4822 oz. ASW, 34 mm. **Subject:** Alexander Dubcek **Obv:** Double cross on shield and tree **Rev:** Head left **Edge Lettering:** LUDSKOST SLOBODA DEMOKRACIA

Date	Mintage	F	VF	XF	Unc	BU
2001	12,800	—	—	—	—	25.00
2001 Proof	3,000	Value: 70.00				

Note: Unc. examples without edge lettering exist. Value $850.00.

KM# 60 200 KORUN

20.0000 g., 0.7500 Silver 0.4822 oz. ASW, 34 mm. **Subject:** Ludovit Fulla **Obv:** Modern art **Rev:** Head facing in national costume, value and dates **Edge:** Lettered **Designer:** Emil Fulka **Note:** 1,800 pieces melted.

Date	Mintage	F	VF	XF	Unc	BU
2002	11,300	—	—	—	—	25.00
2002 Proof	2,400	Value: 55.00				

KM# 62 200 KORUN

20.3500 g., 0.7500 Silver 0.4907 oz. ASW, 34 mm. **Subject:** UNESCO World Heritage site - Vlkolínec **Obv:** Log building and double cross on shield **Rev:** Wooden tower and value **Edge Lettering:** WORLD HERITAGE PATRIMONE MONDIAL **Designer:** Pavol Karoly **Note:** 900 pieces melted.

Date	Mintage	F	VF	XF	Unc	BU
2002	11,500	—	—	—	—	25.00
2002 Proof	2,800	Value: 55.00				

KM# 66 200 KORUN

20.0000 g., 0.7500 Silver 0.4822 oz. ASW, 34 mm. **Subject:** Jozef Skultety, Slovak linguist and historian **Obv:** Building below double cross within shield **Rev:** Head facing and value **Edge Lettering:** VYTRVALOST A VERNOST NARODNEMU IDEALU **Note:** 500 pieces uncirculated melted.

Date	Mintage	F	VF	XF	Unc	BU
2003	8,800	—	—	—	—	25.00
2003 Proof	2,700	Value: 55.00				

KM# 65 200 KORUN

20.0000 g., 0.7500 Silver 0.4822 oz. ASW, 34 mm. **Subject:** Imrich Karvas **Obv:** Building, national arms and value **Rev:** Portrait **Edge:** Lettered **Edge Lettering:** NARODOHOSPODAR HUMANISTA EUROPAN **Designer:** Miroslav Ronai **Note:** 500 pieces uncirculated melted.

Date	Mintage	F	VF	XF	Unc	BU
2003	9,800	—	—	—	—	25.00
2003 Proof	3,000	Value: 50.00				

KM# 70 200 KORUN

31.2100 g., 0.9250 Silver 0.9281 oz. ASW, 30.4 x 57.2 mm. **Series:** Banknotes **Obv:** Head facing and value **Rev:** 18th Century city view and value **Edge:** Plain

Date	Mintage	F	VF	XF	Unc	BU
2003 Proof	6,000	Value: 90.00				

KM# 75 200 KORUN

20.0000 g., 0.7500 Silver 0.4822 oz. ASW, 34 mm. **Obv:** Kempelen's Chess Machine (1770) **Rev:** Inventor Wolfgang Kemelen (1734-1804) above Bratislava city view **Edge Lettering:** VYNALEZCA - TECHNIK - KONSTRUKTER **Designer:** Miroslav Ronai

Date	Mintage	F	VF	XF	Unc	BU
2004	8,000	—	—	—	—	25.00
2004 Proof	3,200	Value: 50.00				

KM# 76 200 KORUN

20.0000 g., 0.7500 Silver 0.4822 oz. ASW, 34 mm. **Obv:** Church and town hall below double cross within shield **Rev:** Aerial view of Bardejov circa 1768 **Edge Lettering:** WORLD HERITAGE - PATRIMOINE MONDIAL **Designer:** Jan Cernaj

Date	Mintage	F	VF	XF	Unc	BU
2004	8,400	—	—	—	—	25.00
2004 Proof	3,600	Value: 50.00				

KM# 77 200 KORUN

18.0000 g., 0.9000 Silver 0.5208 oz. ASW, 34 mm. **Obv:** "The Segner Wheel" model **Rev:** Bust with fur hat facing within circle of designs **Edge Lettering:** VYNALEZCA - FYZIK - MATEMATIK - PEDAGOG **Designer:** Maria Poldaufova

Date	Mintage	F	VF	XF	Unc	BU
2004	10,500	—	—	—	—	25.00
2004 Proof	4,700	Value: 45.00				

KM# 78 200 KORUN

20.0000 g., 0.7500 Silver 0.4822 oz. ASW, 34 mm. **Subject:** Slovakian entry into the European Union **Obv:** Circle of stars in arch above national arms **Rev:** Map in arch above value **Edge Lettering:** ROZSIRENIE EUROPSKEJ UNIE O DESAT KRAJIN **Designer:** Patrik Kovacovsky

Date	Mintage	F	VF	XF	Unc	BU
2004	10,100	—	—	—	—	25.00
2004 Proof	4,700	Value: 45.00				

KM# 81 200 KORUN

18.0000 g., 0.9000 Silver 0.5208 oz. ASW, 34 mm. **Subject:** Leopold I Coronation 350th Anniversary **Obv:** Value and partial castle view **Rev:** Coin design of Leopold I in large size legend **Edge Lettering:** BRATISLAVSKE KORUNOVACIE **Designer:** Maria Poldaufova

Date	Mintage	F	VF	XF	Unc	BU
2005	8,900	—	—	—	—	25.00
2005 Proof	4,800	Value: 45.00				

KM# 82 200 KORUN

18.0000 g., 0.9000 Silver 0.5208 oz. ASW, 34 mm. **Subject:** Treaty of Pressburg **Obv:** Primate's Palace behind French military standard **Rev:** Napoleon and Francis I of Austria **Edge Lettering:** 26 DECEMBER. 5 MIVOSE AN 14 **Designer:** Pavel Karoly

Date	Mintage	F	VF	XF	Unc	BU
2005	5,100	—	—	—	—	25.00
2005 Proof	3,400	Value: 45.00				

KM# 87 200 KORUN

18.0000 g., 0.9000 Silver 0.5208 oz. ASW, 34 mm. **Subject:** 200th Anniversary Birth of Karol Kuzmány **Obv:** Small national arms at upper left, denomination at center **Obv. Inscription:** SLOVENSKÁ / REPUBLIKA **Rev:** Partial medallic head of Kuzmány facing

Date	Mintage	F	VF	XF	Unc	BU
2006	—	—	—	—	—	25.00
2006 Proof	—	Value: 55.00				

KM# 105 200 KORUN

18.0000 g., 0.9000 Silver 0.5208 oz. ASW, 34 mm. **Subject:** Josef M. Petzval, Physicist **Obv:** Lens **Rev:** Bust at left

Date	Mintage	F	VF	XF	Unc	BU
2007	4,700	—	—	—	—	25.00
2007 Proof	2,500	Value: 70.00				

KM# 88 200 KORUN

18.0000 g., 0.9000 Silver 0.5208 oz. ASW, 34 mm. **Subject:** 100th Anniversary Birth of Andrej Kmet **Obv:** Small national arms above stylized M-shaped memorial representing the Slovak Museum. **Obv. Legend:** SLOVENSKÁ REPUBLIKA **Rev:** Head of Kmet 3/4 left **Edge:** Lettered **Edge Lettering:** POZNÁVAJME KRAJE SVOJE A POZNÁME SAMYCH SEBA

Date	Mintage	F	VF	XF	Unc	BU
2008	8,500	—	—	—	—	25.00
2008 Proof	3,400	Value: 75.00				

KM# 56 500 KORUN
33.6300 g., 0.9250 Silver 1.0000 oz. ASW, 40 mm. **Subject:** Mala Fatra National Park **Obv:** National arms center of cross formed by beetles (Alpine Salyers) **Rev:** Orchid with mountain background **Edge Lettering:** OCHRANA PRIRODY A KRAJINY **Designer:** Patrik Kovacovsky **Note:** 400 pieces uncirculated melted.

Date	Mintage	F	VF	XF	Unc	BU
2001	10,200	—	—	—	—	90.00
2001 Proof	1,800	Value: 250				

KM# 57 500 KORUN
31.1035 g., 0.9990 Silver 0.9990 oz. ASW, 45 mm. **Subject:** Third Millennium **Obv:** "The Universe" **Rev:** Three hands **Edge:** Plain **Shape:** 3-sided **Designer:** Patrik Kovacovsky **Note:** 400 pieces uncirculated melted.

Date	Mintage	F	VF	XF	Unc	BU
2001	13,000	—	—	—	—	90.00
2001 Proof	4,000	Value: 185				

KM# 71 500 KORUN
33.6300 g., 0.9250 Silver 1.0000 oz. ASW, 31.5 x 59.4 mm. **Series:** Banknotes **Obv:** Head facing and value **Rev:** Bratislava Castle view and value **Edge:** Plain

Date	Mintage	F	VF	XF	Unc	BU
2003 Proof	6,000	Value: 100				

KM# 85 500 KORUN
33.6300 g., 0.9250 Silver 1.0000 oz. ASW, 40 mm. **Subject:** Slovensky Kras National Park **Obv:** 2 Rock buntings above value **Rev:** Dogs Tooth violet flowers in front of Karst cave interior view **Edge Lettering:** OCHRANA PRIRODY A KRAJINY **Designer:** Maria Poldaufova

Date	Mintage	F	VF	XF	Unc	BU
2005	8,500	—	—	—	—	55.00
2005 Proof	3,600	Value: 90.00				

KM# 84 500 KORUN
33.6300 g., 0.9250 Silver 1.0000 oz. ASW, 40 mm. **Subject:** Muranska Planina National Park **Obv:** Wildflowers and Muran castle ruins **Rev:** Two wild horses **Edge Lettering:** OCHRANA PRIRODY A KRAJINY [flower] **Designer:** Karol Licko

Date	Mintage	F	VF	XF	Unc	BU
2006	4,300	—	—	—	—	95.00
2006 Proof	2,800	Value: 200				

KM# 86 500 KORUN
33.6300 g., 0.9250 Silver 1.0000 oz. ASW, 40 mm. **Subject:** 450th Anniversary - Construction Fortress at Komárno **Obv:** Early ships, fortress in background, national arms at lower right **Obv. Legend:** SLOVENSKÁ REPUBLIKA **Rev:** Layout of fortress, horses in battle against Turks below **Rev. Legend:** PEVNOST - KOMÁRNO **Edge Lettering:** NEC ARTE NEC MARTE - COMORRA in relief

Date	Mintage	F	VF	XF	Unc	BU
2007	4,600	—	—	—	—	80.00
2007 Proof	2,600	Value: 250				

KM# 106 500 KORUN
33.6300 g., 0.9250 Silver 1.0000 oz. ASW, 40 mm. **Subject:** National Park - Low Tatra Mountains **Obv:** Mountains, flower and shield **Rev:** Bear in pine tree

Date	Mintage	F	VF	XF	Unc	BU
2008	4,300	—	—	—	—	75.00
2008 Proof	4,800	Value: 150				

KM# 63 1000 KORUN
62.2070 g., 0.9990 Silver 1.9979 oz. ASW, 43.6 x 43.6 mm. **Subject:** 10th Anniversary of Republic **Obv:** National arms between hands **Rev:** Value above map **Edge:** Segmented reeding **Shape:** Square **Designer:** Milos Vavro

Date	Mintage	F	VF	XF	Unc	BU
2003 Proof	10,000	Value: 150				

KM# 72 1000 KORUN
43.9100 g., 0.9250 Bi-Metallic .925 Silver 43.91g planchet with .999 Gold .28g insert 1.3058 oz., 32.6 x 61.6 mm. **Series:** Banknotes **Obv:** Head facing and value **Rev:** The Madonna Protector facing and church of Liptovske Sliace **Edge:** Plain **Note:** Illustration reduced.

Date	Mintage	F	VF	XF	Unc	BU
2003 Proof	6,000	Value: 175				

KM# 58 5000 KORUN
Tri-Metallic 31.1035, .999 Silver, 1.00 oz ASW with 6.22, .999 Gold, .20 oz AGW and .31, .999 Platinum, .10 oz. APW, 50 mm. **Series:** Third Millennium **Obv:** "The Universe" **Rev:** Three hands **Edge:** Plain **Shape:** Triangular **Designer:** Patrik Kovacovsky

Date	Mintage	F	VF	XF	Unc	BU
2001 Proof	8,000	Value: 500				

KM# 61 5000 KORUN
9.5000 g., 0.9000 Gold 0.2749 oz. AGW, 26 mm. **Subject:** Vlkolinec village - UNESCO historic site **Obv:** Enclosed communal well **Rev:** Window and fence **Edge:** Reeded **Designer:** Maria Poldaufova

Date	Mintage	F	VF	XF	Unc	BU
2002 Proof	7,200	Value: 575				

KM# 73 5000 KORUN
47.6340 g., 0.9250 Bi-Metallic .925 Silver 46.65g planchet with two .9999 Gold inserts .964g in total 1.4165 oz., 33.4 x 63.8 mm. **Series:** Banknotes **Obv:** Head facing and value **Rev:** Stefanik's grave monument **Edge:** Plain **Note:** Illustration reduced.

Date	Mintage	F	VF	XF	Unc	BU
2003 Proof	6,000	Value: 275				

KM# 80 5000 KORUN
9.5000 g., 0.9000 Gold 0.2749 oz. AGW, 26 mm. **Subject:** Bardejov - UNESCO historic site **Obv:** National arms and value left of Town Hall **Rev:** Zachariah in window frame left of St. Aegidius Church, Bardejov **Edge:** Reeded

Date	Mintage	F	VF	XF	Unc	BU
2004 Proof	9,000	Value: 575				

KM# 83 5000 KORUN
9.5000 g., 0.9000 Gold 0.2749 oz. AGW, 26 mm. **Subject:** Leopold I Coronation **Obv:** Mounted Herald with Bratislava Castile in background **Rev:** Leopold I and Crown of St. Stephan **Edge:** Reeded

Date	Mintage	F	VF	XF	Unc	BU
2005 Proof	7,500	Value: 575				

KM# 89 5000 KORUN
9.5000 g., 0.9000 Gold 0.2749 oz. AGW, 26 mm. **Subject:** 400th Anniversary Coronation of King Matthias II **Obv:** Cathedral and Bratislava castle **Obv. Legend:** SLOVENSKÁ - REPUBLIKA **Rev:** 1/2 length figure of Matthias II left, crown in lower foreground, towers of the St. Michael's Gate and franciscan Church in Bratislava in background **Rev. Legend:** KORUNOVÁCIA MATEJA II. / BRATISLAVA **Edge:** Reeded

Date	Mintage	F	VF	XF	Unc	BU
2008 Proof	4,050	Value: 575				

KM# 64 10000 KORUN
18.8350 g., Bi-Metallic 1.555g, .999 Palladium round center in a 15.55g, .900 Gold square, 29.5 x 29.5 mm. **Subject:** 10th Anniversary of the Republic **Obv:** Young head left within circular inscription above double cross within shield **Rev:** Bratislava castle above value **Edge:** Segmented reeding **Shape:** Square **Designer:** Ludmila Cvengrosova

Date	Mintage	F	VF	XF	Unc	BU
2003 Proof	6,000	Value: 1,250				

KM# 79 10000 KORUN
24.8828 g., Bi-Metallic .999 Gold 12.4414g 23mm round center in .999 Palladium 12.4414g pentagon, 40 mm. **Subject:** Slovakian entry into the European Union **Obv:** National arms above date in center **Rev:** European map with entry date **Edge:** Plain

Date	Mintage	F	VF	XF	Unc	BU
2004 Proof	7,200	Value: 1,200				

EURO COINAGE

European Union Issues

KM# 95 EURO CENT
2.3000 g., Copper Plated Steel, 16.25 mm. **Obv:** Krivan Peak in the Tatras, state emblem **Rev:** Denomination and globe

Date	Mintage	F	VF	XF	Unc	BU
2009	90,745,000	—	—	—	0.35	0.50
2009 Proof	13,300	Value: 15.00				
2010	30,000,000	—	—	—	0.35	0.50
2010 Proof	5,000	Value: 8.00				
2011	—	—	—	—	0.35	0.50
2011 Proof	6,000	Value: 6.00				
2012	—	—	—	—	—	0.50
2012 Proof	—	Value: 6.00				
2013	—	—	—	—	—	0.50
2013 Proof	—	Value: 6.00				

KM# 96 2 EURO CENT
3.0600 g., Copper Plated Steel, 18.75 mm. **Obv:** Krivan Peak in the Tatras, state emblem **Rev:** Denomination and globe **Edge:** Grooved

Date	Mintage	F	VF	XF	Unc	BU
2009	64,387,000	—	—	—	0.50	0.65
2009 Proof	13,300	Value: 15.00				
2010	50,063,000	—	—	—	0.50	0.65
2010 Proof	5,000	Value: 8.00				
2011	—	—	—	—	0.50	0.65
2011 Proof	6,000	Value: 6.00				
2012	—	—	—	—	—	0.65
2012 Proof	—	Value: 6.00				
2013	—	—	—	—	—	0.65
2013 Proof	—	Value: 6.00				

KM# 97 5 EURO CENT
3.9200 g., Copper Plated Steel, 21.25 mm. **Obv:** Krivan Peak in the Tatras - state emblem **Rev:** Denomination and globe

Date	Mintage	F	VF	XF	Unc	BU
2009	84,874,000	—	—	—	0.75	1.00
2009 Proof	13,300	Value: 15.00				
2010	—	—	—	—	0.75	1.00
2010 Proof	5,000	Value: 8.00				
2011	—	—	—	—	0.75	1.00
2011 Proof	6,000	Value: 6.00				
2012	—	—	—	—	0.75	1.00
2012 Proof	—	Value: 6.00				
2013	—	—	—	—	0.75	1.00
2013 Proof	—	Value: 6.00				

KM# 98 10 EURO CENT
4.1000 g., Brass, 19.75 mm. **Obv:** Bratislava Castle and state emblem **Rev:** Expanded relief map of European Union at left, denomination at right **Edge:** Reeded

Date	Mintage	F	VF	XF	Unc	BU
2009	74,717,000	—	—	—	0.75	1.00
2009 Proof	13,300	Value: 15.00				
2010	—	—	—	—	0.75	1.00
2010 Proof	5,000	Value: 8.00				
2011	—	—	—	—	0.75	1.00
2011 Proof	6,000	Value: 6.00				
2012	—	—	—	—	0.75	1.00
2012 Proof	—	Value: 6.00				
2013	—	—	—	—	0.75	1.00
2013 Proof	—	Value: 6.00				

KM# 99 20 EURO CENT
5.7400 g., Brass, 22.25 mm. **Obv:** Bratislava Castle and state emblem **Rev:** Expanded relief map of European Union at left, denomination at right **Edge:** Notched

Date	Mintage	F	VF	XF	Unc	BU
2009	66,519,000	—	—	—	1.00	1.25
2009 Proof	13,300	Value: 16.00				
2010	—	—	—	—	1.00	1.25
2010 Proof	5,000	Value: 10.00				
2011	—	—	—	—	1.00	1.25
2011 Proof	6,000	Value: 7.00				
2012	—	—	—	—	1.00	1.25
2012 Proof	—	Value: 7.00				
2013	—	—	—	—	1.00	1.25
2013 Proof	—	Value: 7.00				

KM# 100 50 EURO CENT
7.8000 g., Brass, 24.25 mm. **Obv:** Bratislava Castle and state shield **Rev:** Expanded relief map of European Union at left, denomination at right **Edge:** Reeded

Date	Mintage	F	VF	XF	Unc	BU
2009	59,317,000	—	—	—	1.25	1.50
2009 Proof	13,300	Value: 16.00				
2010	—	—	—	—	1.25	1.50
2010 Proof	5,000	Value: 10.00				
2011	—	—	—	—	1.25	1.50
2011 Proof	6,000	Value: 7.00				
2012	—	—	—	—	1.25	1.50
2012 Proof	—	Value: 7.00				
2013	—	—	—	—	1.25	1.50
2013 Proof	—	Value: 7.00				

KM# 101 EURO
7.5000 g., Bi-Metallic Copper-Nickel center in Nickel-Brass ring, 23.25 mm. **Obv:** Double cross in middle of three hills **Rev:** Value at left, expanded relief map of European Union at right **Edge:** Segmented reeding

Date	Mintage	F	VF	XF	Unc	BU
2009	46,777,000	—	—	—	2.50	2.75
2009 Proof	13,300	Value: 20.00				
2010	—	—	—	—	2.50	2.75
2010 Proof	5,000	Value: 15.00				
2011	—	—	—	—	2.50	2.75
2011 Proof	6,000	Value: 12.00				
2012	—	—	—	—	2.50	2.75
2012 Proof	—	Value: 12.00				
2013	—	—	—	—	2.50	2.75
2013 Proof	—	Value: 12.00				

KM# 102 2 EURO
8.5000 g., Bi-Metallic Nickel-Brass center in Copper-Nickel ring, 25.75 mm. **Obv:** Double cross on middle of three hills **Rev:** Value at left, expanded map of European Union at left

Date	Mintage	F	VF	XF	Unc	BU
2009	35,667,000	—	—	—	5.00	6.00
2009 Proof	13,300	Value: 25.00				
2010	—	—	—	—	5.00	6.00
2010 Proof	5,000	Value: 20.00				
2011	—	—	—	—	5.00	6.00
2011 Proof	6,000	Value: 15.00				
2012	—	—	—	—	5.00	6.00
2012 Proof	—	Value: 15.00				
2013	—	—	—	—	5.00	6.00
2013 Proof	—	Value: 15.00				

KM# 103 2 EURO
8.5000 g., Bi-Metallic Nickel-Brass center in Copper-Nickel ring, 25.75 mm. **Subject:** EMU 10th Anniversary **Obv:** Stick figure and large E symbol **Rev:** Expanded relief map of European Union at left, denomination at right

Date	Mintage	F	VF	XF	Unc	BU
2009	2,493,000	—	—	—	6.00	7.50
2009 Special Unc.	7,000	—	—	—	—	20.00

KM# 107 2 EURO
8.5000 g., Bi-Metallic Nickel-Brass center in Copper-Nickel ring, 25.75 mm. **Subject:** Freedom, 17 November 1989, 20th Anniversary **Obv:** Ringing Freedom bell

Date	Mintage	F	VF	XF	Unc	BU
2009	1,000,000	—	—	—	6.00	7.50
2009 Special Unc.	7,000	—	—	—	—	20.00
2009 Prooflike	1,000	—	—	—	—	175

KM# 114 2 EURO
8.5000 g., Bi-Metallic Nickel-Brass center in Copper-Nickel ring, 25.75 mm. **Subject:** Visegrad Group, 20th Anniversary

Date	Mintage	F	VF	XF	Unc	BU
2011	981,000	—	—	—	5.00	6.00
2011 Special Unc.	7,000	—	—	—	—	20.00

KM# 120 2 EURO
8.5000 g., Bi-Metallic Nickel-Brass center in Copper-Nickel ring, 25.75 mm. **Subject:** Euro coinage, 10th Anniversary **Obv:** Euro symbol on globe at center, child-like rendering around

Date	Mintage	F	VF	XF	Unc	BU
2012	1,000,000	—	—	—	6.00	8.00

KM# 108 10 EURO
18.0000 g., 0.9000 Silver 0.5208 oz. ASW, 34 mm. **Subject:** Aurel Stodola, 150th Anniversary of birth **Obv:** Turbo generator, national shield **Rev:** Portrait **Edge Lettering:** KONSTRUKTER - VYNALEZCA - PEDAGOG

Date	Mintage	F	VF	XF	Unc	BU
2009	10,100	—	—	—	—	50.00
2009 Proof	13,300	Value: 65.00				

KM# 110 10 EURO
18.0000 g., 0.9000 Silver 0.5208 oz. ASW, 34 mm. **Subject:** Wooden Churches of Carpathian Slovakia - UNESCO World Heritage site

Date	Mintage	F	VF	XF	Unc	BU
2010	—	—	—	—	—	50.00
2010 Proof	—	Value: 65.00				

KM# 111 10 EURO
18.0000 g., 0.9000 Silver 0.5208 oz. ASW, 34 mm. **Subject:** Martin Kukucin, 150th Anniversary of birth **Obv:** Landscape scene from Brac, "House on the hillside" **Rev:** Fortrait facing, cuckoo, signature **Edge Lettering:** PROZAIK - DRAMATIK - PUBLICISTA

Date	Mintage	F	VF	XF	Unc	BU
2010	9,900	—	—	—	—	50.00
2010 Proof	17,325	Value: 65.00				

KM# 115 10 EURO
18.0000 g., 0.9000 Silver 0.5208 oz. ASW, 34 mm. **Subject:** Zobor Documents, 900th Anniversary **Obv:** Two scribes **Rev:** Seal and partial document text

Date	Mintage	F	VF	XF	Unc	BU
2011	—	—	—	—	—	50.00
2011 Proof	—	Value: 65.00				

KM# 116 10 EURO
18.0000 g., 0.9000 Silver 0.5208 oz. ASW, 34 mm. **Subject:** Adoption of the memorandum of the Slovak Nation, 150th Anniversary **Designer:** Andrea Rolkova and Pavel Karoly

Date	Mintage	F	VF	XF	Unc	BU
2011	9,500	—	—	—	—	50.00
2011 Proof	9,100	Value: 65.00				

KM# 117 10 EURO
18.0000 g., 0.9000 Silver 0.5208 oz. ASW, 34 mm. **Subject:** Jan Cikker, 100th Anniversary of Birth **Designer:** Kliment Mitura

Date	Mintage	F	VF	XF	Unc	BU
2011	7,900	—	—	—	—	50.00
2011 Proof	8,900	Value: 65.00				

KM# 122 10 EURO
18.0000 g., 0.9000 Silver 0.5208 oz. ASW, 34 mm. **Subject:** Master Pavol of Levoca **Obv:** Female and shield **Rev:** Bearded male

Date	Mintage	F	VF	XF	Unc	BU
2012	7,400	—	—	—	—	50.00
2012 Proof	11,870	Value: 65.00				

KM# 123 10 EURO
18.0000 g., 0.9000 Silver 0.5208 oz. ASW, 34 mm. **Subject:** Chatam Sofer, 250th Anniversary of Birth **Obv:** City view of Bratislava **Rev:** Chatam Sofer, torah, menorah

Date	Mintage	F	VF	XF	Unc	BU
2012	5,800	—	—	—	—	50.00
2012 Proof	7,900	Value: 65.00				

KM# 124 10 EURO
18.0000 g., 0.9000 Silver 0.5208 oz. ASW, 34 mm. **Subject:** Anton Bernolak, 250th Anniversary of Birth **Obv:** Quill pen **Rev:** Bust facing

Date	Mintage	F	VF	XF	Unc	BU
2012	—	—	—	—	—	50.00
2012 Proof	—	Value: 65.00				

KM# 109 20 EURO
33.6300 g., 0.9250 Silver 1.0000 oz. ASW, 40 mm. **Subject:** National Park - Vel'ká Fatra **Obv:** Fora and national shield **Rev:** Falcon in flight over mountain peak **Edge Lettering:** OCHRANA PRÍRODY A KRAJINY **Designer:** Roman Lugar

Date	Mintage	F	VF	XF	Unc	BU
2009	9,900	—	—	—	—	55.00
2009 Proof	12,600	Value: 65.00				

KM# 112 20 EURO
33.6300 g., 0.9250 Silver 1.0000 oz. ASW, 40 mm. **Subject:** Poloniny National Park **Obv:** Mountainside and flowers **Rev:** Two wolves

Date	Mintage	F	VF	XF	Unc	BU
2010	—	—	—	—	—	50.00
2010 Proof	—	Value: 75.00				

KM# 118 20 EURO
33.6300 g., 0.9250 Silver 1.0000 oz. ASW, 40 mm. **Subject:** Historical Sites - Trnava **Designer:** Roman Lugar

Date	Mintage	F	VF	XF	Unc	BU
2011	8,150	—	—	—	—	60.00
2011 Proof	9,950	Value: 75.00				

KM# 121 20 EURO
33.6300 g., 0.9250 Silver 1.0000 oz. ASW, 40 mm. **Subject:** Historical towns - Trencin **Obv:** Castle, historical Roman inscription and National arms below **Rev:** Rendering of the Trencin historical preservation area

Date	Mintage	F	VF	XF	Unc	BU
2012	5,900	—	—	—	—	65.00
2012 Proof	7,500	Value: 80.00				

KM# 113 100 EURO
9.5000 g., 0.9000 Gold 0.2749 oz. AGW, 26 mm. **Subject:** Wooden Churches of Carpathian Slovakia - UNESCO Heritage Site **Obv:** Church of St. Francis of Assisi in Hervartov, belfry of the church in Hronsek and Church of St. Nicholas in Brodrzal **Rev:** Baroque altar of All Saints Church in Tvrdosin **Edge:** Reeded **Designer:** Kliment Mitura and Dalibor Schmidt

Date	Mintage	F	VF	XF	Unc	BU
2010 Proof	Est. 7,000	Value: 575				

KM# 119 100 EURO
9.5000 g., 0.9000 Gold 0.2749 oz. AGW, 26 mm. **Subject:** Prince Pribina Nitra, 1150th Anniversary of Death **Designer:** Ivan Rehak

Date	Mintage	F	VF	XF	Unc	BU
2011 Proof	6,800	Value: 575				

KM# 125 100 EURO
9.5000 g., 0.9000 Gold 0.2749 oz. AGW, 26 mm. **Subject:** Charles III, 300th Anniversary of Coronation **Obv:** City View **Rev:** Bust, crown of St. Stephen, Bratislava castle

Date	Mintage	F	VF	XF	Unc	BU
2012 Proof	—	Value: 575				

MINT SETS

KM#	Date	Mintage	Identification	Issue Price	Mkt Val
MS9	2001 (7)	—	KM#11.1-14, 17-18, 35, plus medal	—	20.00
MS10	2002 (7)	—	KM#11-1-14, 17-18, 35, plus medal	—	17.50
MS11	2003 (7)	—	KM#11.1-14, 17-18, 35, plus medal	—	15.00
MS12	2004 (7)	—	KM#11.1-14, 17, 18, 35 plus medal	—	12.00
MS13	2005 (7)	—	KM#11.1-14, 17, 18, 35 plus medal	—	12.00
MS14	2005 (6)	—	KM#11.1, 12-14, 35, Austrian 2005 KM#3088	—	10.00
MS15	2006 (7)	—	KM#11.1-14, 17, 18, 35 plus medal	—	12.00
MS16	2007 (7)	—	KM#11.1-14, 17, 18, 35 plus medal	—	12.00
MS17	2007 (5)	—	KM11.2, 12-14, 35. National parks	—	15.00
MS18	2007 (5)	—	KM#11.1, 12-14, 35	—	12.00
MS19	2007 (5)	—	KM#11.1, 12-14, 35. National parks packaging	—	15.00
MS20	2007 (5)	—	KM#11.1, 12-14, 35 and a bimetallic medal and cd. Set to commemorate musician Gejza Dusik	—	20.00
MS21	2009 (8)	87,100	KM#95-102.	—	25.00
MS22	2010 (8)	45,000	kM#95-102.	—	25.00
MS23	2011 (8)	25,000	KM#95-102.	—	25.00
MS24	2012 (8)	23,000	KM#95-102.	—	25.00

PROOF SETS

KM#	Date	Mintage	Identification	Issue Price	Mkt Val
PS2	2001 (7)	12,500	KM#11.1-14, 17-18, 35	—	35.00
PS3	2002 (7)	16,500	KM#11.1-14, 17-18, 35	—	25.00
PS4	2004 (7)	—	KM#11.1, 12-14, 35, silver strikes of 1993, KM#17-18	—	40.00
PS5	2006 (6)	—	KM#11.1, 12-14, 35 plus medal. 2006 Torino Winter Olympics	—	45.00
PS6	2008 (6)	—	KM#11.1, 12-14, 35 plus medal. 2008 Peking Olympics	—	45.00
PS7	2009 (9)	13,300	KM#95-102 plus medal	—	125
PS8	2010 (9)	5,000	KM#95-102 plus medal	—	80.00
PS9	2011 (9)	5,000	KM#95-102 plus CN medal	—	65.00
PS10	2011 (9)	1,000	KM#95-102 plus CN medal, wood box	—	350
PS11	2012 (9)	5,000	KM#95-102 plus medal.	—	65.00

The Republic of Slovenia is located northwest of Yugoslavia in the valleys of the Danube River. It has an area of 7,819 sq. mi. and a population of *1.9 million. Capital: Ljubljana. Agriculture is the main industry with large amounts of hops and fodder crops grown as well as many varieties of fruit trees. Sheep raising, timber production and the mining of mercury from one of the country's oldest mines are also very important to the economy. Slovenia joined the European Union in May 2004.

MINT MARKS

Based on last digit in date.
(K) - Kremnitz (Slovakia): open 4, upturned 5
(BP) - Budapest (Hungary): closed 4, down-turned 5

MONETARY SYSTEM

100 Stotinov = 1 Tolar
100 Euro Cents = 1 Euro

REPUBLIC

STANDARD COINAGE

100 Stotinow = 1 Tolar

KM# 7 10 STOTINOV

0.5500 g., Aluminum, 16 mm. **Obv:** Value within square **Rev:** Olm salamander **Edge:** Plain **Note:** Varieties exist.

Date	Mintage	F	VF	XF	Unc	BU
2001 In sets only	1,000	—	—	—	—	3.00
2001 Proof	800	Value: 5.00				
2002 In sets only	1,000	—	—	—	—	3.00
2002 Proof	800	Value: 5.00				
2003 In sets only	1,000	—	—	—	—	3.00
2003 Proof	800	Value: 5.00				
2004 In sets only	1,000	—	—	—	—	3.00
2004 Proof	800	Value: 5.00				
2005 In sets only	3,000	—	—	—	—	2.00
2005 Proof	1,000	Value: 5.00				
2006 In sets only	4,000	—	—	—	—	2.00
2006 Proof	1,000	Value: 5.00				

KM# 8 20 STOTINOV

0.7000 g., Aluminum, 18 mm. **Obv:** Value within square **Rev:** Barn owl and value **Edge:** Plain

Date	Mintage	F	VF	XF	Unc	BU
2001 In sets only	1,000	—	—	—	—	4.00
2001 Proof	800	Value: 6.00				
2002 In sets only	1,000	—	—	—	—	4.00
2002 Proof	800	Value: 6.00				
2003 In sets only	1,000	—	—	—	—	4.00
2003 Proof	800	Value: 6.00				
2004 In sets only	1,000	—	—	—	—	4.00
2004 Proof	500	Value: 6.00				
2005 In sets only	3,000	—	—	—	—	3.00
2005 Proof	1,000	Value: 6.00				
2006 In sets only	4,000	—	—	—	—	3.00
2006 Proof	1,000	Value: 6.00				

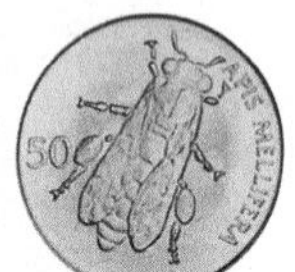

KM# 3 50 STOTINOV

0.8500 g., Aluminum, 20 mm. **Obv:** Value within square **Rev:** Bee and value **Edge:** Plain

Date	Mintage	F	VF	XF	Unc	BU
2001 In sets only	1,000	—	—	—	—	6.00
2001 Proof	800	Value: 7.50				
2002 In sets only	1,000	—	—	—	—	6.00
2002 Proof	800	Value: 7.50				
2003 In sets only	1,000	—	—	—	—	6.00
2003 Proof	800	Value: 7.50				
2004 In sets only	1,000	—	—	—	—	6.00
2004 Proof	500	Value: 12.00				
2005 In sets only	3,000	—	—	—	—	4.00
2005 Proof	1,000	Value: 7.00				
2006 In sets only	4,000	—	—	—	—	4.00
2006 Proof	1,000	Value: 7.00				

KM# 4 TOLAR

4.5000 g., Nickel-Brass, 22 mm. **Obv:** Value within circle **Rev:** Three brown trout **Rev. Legend:** SALMO TRUTTA FARIO **Edge:** Reeded **Note:** Date varieties exist: 1994 = closed or open "4"; 1995 = serif up and serif down in "5".

Date	Mintage	F	VF	XF	Unc	BU
2001	10,001,000	—	—	—	0.75	1.25
2001 Proof	800	Value: 7.50				
2002 In sets only	1,000	—	—	—	—	5.00
2002 Proof	800	Value: 7.50				
2003 In sets only	1,000	—	—	—	—	5.00
2003 Proof	800	Value: 7.50				
2004	10,001,000	—	—	—	0.75	1.25
2004 (K) In sets only	1,000	—	—	—	—	5.00
Note: 4 open to right						
2004 Proof	500	Value: 8.50				
2005 In sets only	3,000	—	—	—	—	4.00
2005 Proof	1,000	Value: 7.50				
2006 In sets only	4,000	—	—	—	—	4.00
2006 Proof	1,000	Value: 7.50				

KM# 5 2 TOLARJA

5.4000 g., Nickel-Brass, 24 mm. **Obv:** Value within circle **Rev:** Barn swallow in flight **Rev. Legend:** HIRUNDO RUSTICA **Edge:** Reeded **Note:** Date varieties exist: 1994 = closed or open "4"; 1995 = serif up and serif down in "5".

Date	Mintage	F	VF	XF	Unc	BU
2001	10,001,000	—	—	—	0.75	1.75
2001 Proof	800	Value: 8.50				
2002 In sets only	1,000	—	—	—	—	7.00
2002 Proof	800	Value: 8.50				
2003 In sets only	1,000	—	—	—	—	7.00
2003 Proof	800	Value: 8.50				
2004	10,001,000	—	—	—	0.75	1.50
2004 Proof	500	Value: 8.50				
2005 In sets only	3,000	—	—	—	—	7.00
2005 Proof	1,000	Value: 8.50				
2006 In sets only	4,000	—	—	—	—	7.00
2006 Proof	1,000	Value: 8.50				

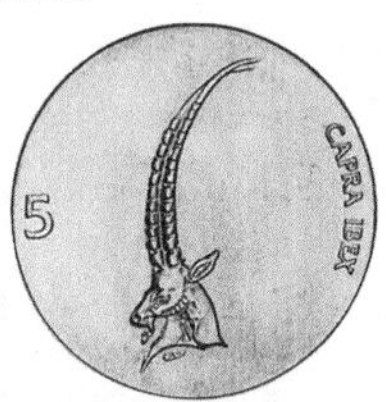

KM# 6 5 TOLARJEV

6.4400 g., Nickel-Brass, 26 mm. **Obv:** Value within circle **Rev:** Head and horns of ibex **Edge:** Reeded **Note:** Date varieties exist: 1994 = closed or open "4"; 1995 = serif up and serif down in "5".

Date	Mintage	F	VF	XF	Unc	BU
2001 In sets only	1,000	—	—	—	—	8.00
2001 Proof	800	Value: 10.00				
2002 In sets only	1,000	—	—	—	—	8.00
2002 Proof	800	Value: 10.00				
2003 In sets only	1,000	—	—	—	—	8.00
2003 Proof	800	Value: 10.00				
2004 In sets only	1,000	—	—	—	—	8.00
2004 Proof	500	Value: 15.00				
2005 In sets only	3,000	—	—	—	—	7.00
2005 Proof	1,000	Value: 10.00				
2006 In sets only	4,000	—	—	—	—	7.00
2006 Proof	1,000	Value: 10.00				

KM# 41 10 TOLARJEV

5.7500 g., Copper-Nickel, 24 mm. **Obv:** Value within circle **Rev:** Stylized rearing horse **Rev. Legend:** EQUUS **Edge:** Reeded

Date	Mintage	F	VF	XF	Unc	BU
2001	29,441,000	—	—	—	2.00	3.50
2001 Proof	800	Value: 12.00				
2002	10,037,000	—	—	—	2.00	3.50
2002 Proof	800	Value: 12.00				
2003 In sets only	1,000	—	—	—	—	5.00
2003 Proof	800	Value: 12.00				
2004	10,001,000	—	—	—	2.00	3.50
2004 Proof	500	Value: 12.00				
2005	6,003,000	—	—	—	2.00	3.50
2005 Proof	1,000	Value: 12.00				
2006	6,001,000	—	—	—	2.00	3.50
2006 Proof	1,000	Value: 12.00				

KM# 51 20 TOLARJEV

6.8500 g., Copper-Nickel, 24 mm. **Obv:** Value within circle **Rev:** White Stork **Rev. Legend:** CICONIA CICONIA **Edge:** Reeded

Date	Mintage	F	VF	XF	Unc	BU
2003	10,001,000	—	—	—	3.50	5.00
2003 Proof	800	Value: 15.00				
2004	10,001,000	—	—	—	3.00	5.00
2004 Proof	500	Value: 15.00				
2005	12,003,000	—	—	—	3.50	5.00
2005 Proof	1,000	Value: 15.00				
2006	4,004,000	—	—	—	3.50	5.00
2006 Proof	1,000	Value: 15.00				

KM# 52 50 TOLARJEV

8.0000 g., Copper-Nickel, 26 mm. **Obv:** Value within circle **Rev:** Stylized bull **Rev. Legend:** TAURUS TAURUS **Edge:** Segmented reeding

Date	Mintage	F	VF	XF	Unc	BU
2003	10,001,000	—	—	—	2.50	4.50
2003 Proof	800	Value: 12.00				
2004	5,001,000	—	—	—	2.50	4.50
2004 Proof	500	Value: 15.00				
2005	8,003,000	—	—	—	2.50	4.50
2005 Proof	1,000	Value: 12.00				
2006 In sets only	4,000	—	—	—	—	6.50
2006 Proof	1,000	Value: 12.00				

KM# 42 100 TOLARJEV

9.1000 g., Copper-Nickel, 28 mm. **Subject:** 10th Anniversary of Slovenia and the Tolar **Obv:** Value **Rev:** Tree rings and inscription **Edge:** Reeded

Date	Mintage	F	VF	XF	Unc	BU
2001	500,000	—	—	—	3.00	4.00
2001 Proof	800	Value: 10.00				

KM# 45 500 TOLARJEV

8.5400 g., Bi-Metallic Copper-Nickel center in Brass ring, 28.1 mm. **Subject:** Soccer **Obv:** Value **Rev:** Soccer player and radiant sun **Edge:** Reeded

Date	Mintage	F	VF	XF	Unc	BU
2002	500,000	—	—	—	5.50	7.50
2002 Proof	800	Value: 12.50				

KM# 50 500 TOLARJEV
8.7200 g., Bi-Metallic Copper-Nickel center in Brass ring, 27.9 mm. **Subject:** European Year of the Disabled **Obv:** Stylized wheelchair **Rev:** Value **Edge:** Reeded

Date	Mintage	F	VF	XF	Unc	BU
2003	200,000	—	—	—	6.00	8.00
2003 Proof	800	Value: 13.50				

KM# 57 500 TOLARJEV
8.6000 g., Bi-Metallic Copper-Nickel center in Brass ring, 28 mm. **Obv:** Value **Rev:** Profile left looking down within mathematical graph **Edge:** Reeded

Date	Mintage	F	VF	XF	Unc	BU
2004	200,000	—	—	—	6.00	8.00
2004 Proof	500	Value: 20.00				

KM# 63 500 TOLARJEV
8.6500 g., Bi-Metallic Copper-Nickel center in Brass ring, 27.9 mm. **Obv:** Perched falcon and value **Rev:** Horizontal line in center divides partial suns **Edge:** Reeded

Date	Mintage	F	VF	XF	Unc	BU
2005	103,000	—	—	—	6.25	8.50
2005 Proof	1,000	Value: 12.00				

KM# 65 500 TOLARJEV
8.6000 g., Bi-Metallic Copper-Nickel center in Brass ring, 28 mm. **Obv:** Value **Rev:** Anton Tomaz Linhart's silhouette above life dates **Edge:** Reeded

Date	Mintage	F	VF	XF	Unc	BU
2006	104,000	—	—	—	6.00	8.00
2006 Proof	1,000	Value: 12.00				

KM# 43 2000 TOLARJEV
15.0000 g., 0.9250 Silver 0.4461 oz. ASW, 32 mm. **Subject:** 10th Anniversary of Slovenia and the Tolar **Obv:** Value **Rev:** Tree rings and inscription **Edge:** Reeded

Date	Mintage	F	VF	XF	Unc	BU
2001 Proof	3,000	Value: 35.00				

KM# 46 2500 TOLARJEV
15.0000 g., 0.9250 Silver 0.4461 oz. ASW, 32 mm. **Subject:** Soccer **Obv:** Value **Rev:** Soccer player and radiant sun **Edge:** Reeded

Date	Mintage	F	VF	XF	Unc	BU
2002 Proof	2,500	Value: 35.00				

KM# 48 2500 TOLARJEV
15.0000 g., 0.9250 Silver 0.4461 oz. ASW, 32 mm. **Subject:** 35th Chess Olympiad **Obv:** Rearing horse and reflection **Rev:** Chess pieces in starting positions and reflection **Edge:** Reeded **Designer:** MNiljenko Licul and Jan Cernaj

Date	Mintage	F	VF	XF	Unc	BU
2002 Proof	1,000	Value: 45.00				

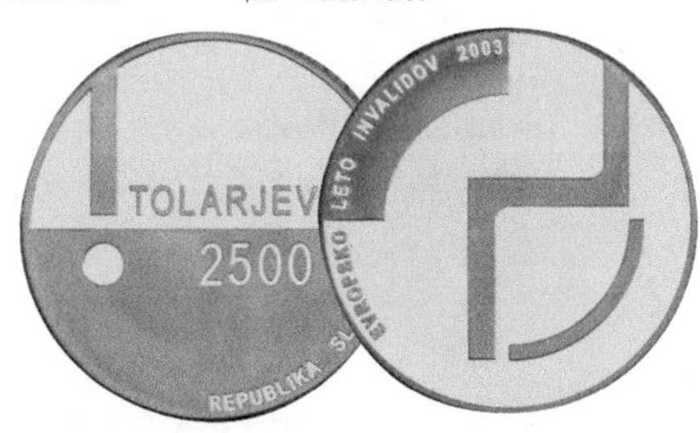

KM# 53 2500 TOLARJEV
15.0000 g., 0.9250 Silver 0.4461 oz. ASW, 32 mm. **Subject:** European Year of the Disabled **Obv:** Value **Rev:** Stylized wheel chair **Edge:** Reeded

Date	Mintage	F	VF	XF	Unc	BU
2003 Proof	1,500	Value: 42.00				

KM# 55 5000 TOLARJEV
15.0000 g., 0.9250 Silver 0.4461 oz. ASW, 32 mm. **Subject:** 60th Anniversary of the Slovenian Assembly **Obv:** Value in partial star design **Rev:** Dates in partial star design **Edge:** Reeded

Date	Mintage	F	VF	XF	Unc	BU
2003 Proof	1,500	Value: 42.00				

KM# 58 5000 TOLARJEV
15.0000 g., 0.9250 Silver 0.4461 oz. ASW, 32 mm. **Obv:** Value **Rev:** Facial profile left looking down within mathematical graph **Edge:** Reeded

Date	Mintage	F	VF	XF	Unc	BU
2004 Proof	1,500	Value: 50.00				

KM# 60 5000 TOLARJEV
15.0000 g., 0.9250 Silver 0.4461 oz. ASW, 32 mm. **Subject:** 1000th Anniversary Town of Bled **Obv:** Value **Rev:** Castle and towers silhouette **Edge:** Reeded

Date	Mintage	F	VF	XF	Unc	BU
2004 Proof	1,500	Value: 50.00				

KM# 62 5000 TOLARJEV
15.1000 g., 0.9250 Silver 0.4490 oz. ASW, 32 mm. **Subject:** Slovenian Film Centennial **Obv:** Value above a director's clapboard **Rev:** Film segment **Edge:** Reeded

Date	Mintage	F	VF	XF	Unc	BU
2005 Proof	—	Value: 47.50				

KM# 64 5000 TOLARJEV
15.1000 g., 0.9250 Silver 0.4490 oz. ASW, 32 mm. **Obv:** Perched falcon above value **Rev:** Diagonal center line divides partial suns **Edge:** Reeded

Date	Mintage	F	VF	XF	Unc	BU
2005 Proof	—	Value: 47.50				

KM# 91 5000 TOLARJEV
15.0000 g., 0.9250 Silver 0.4461 oz. ASW, 32 mm. **Subject:** 1000th Anniversary, mention of town of Bled, 2nd issue

Date	Mintage	F	VF	XF	Unc	BU
2006 Proof	1,000	Value: 55.00				

KM# 92 5000 TOLARJEV
15.0000 g., 0.9000 Silver 0.4340 oz. ASW, 32 mm. **Subject:** Anton Tomaz Linhart, 250th Anniversary of Birth **Rev:** Bust left

Date	Mintage	F	VF	XF	Unc	BU
2006 Proof	5,000	Value: 45.00				

KM# 93 5000 TOLARJEV
15.0000 g., 0.9250 Silver 0.4461 oz. ASW, 32 mm. **Subject:** Anton Askerc, 150th Anniversary of birth **Rev:** Bust left

Date	Mintage	F	VF	XF	Unc	BU
2006 Proof	5,000	Value: 45.00				

KM# 44 20000 TOLARJEV

7.0000 g., 0.9000 Gold 0.2025 oz. AGW, 24 mm. **Subject:** 10th Anniversary of Slovenia and the Tolar **Obv:** Value **Rev:** Tree rings and inscription **Edge:** Reeded

Date	Mintage	F	VF	XF	Unc	BU
2001 Proof	1,000	Value: 520				

KM# 47 20000 TOLARJEV

7.0000 g., 0.9000 Gold 0.2025 oz. AGW, 24 mm. **Subject:** World Cup Soccer **Obv:** Value **Rev:** Soccer player and rising sun **Edge:** Reeded

Date	Mintage	F	VF	XF	Unc	BU
2002 Proof	500	Value: 550				

KM# 49 20000 TOLARJEV

7.0000 g., 0.9000 Gold 0.2025 oz. AGW, 24 mm. **Subject:** 35th Chess Olympiad **Obv:** Rearing horse and reflection **Rev:** Chess pieces in starting positions and reflection **Edge:** Reeded

Date	Mintage	F	VF	XF	Unc	BU
2002 Proof	500	Value: 550				

KM# 54 25000 TOLARJEV

7.0000 g., 0.9000 Gold 0.2025 oz. AGW, 24 mm. **Subject:** European Year of the Disabled **Obv:** Value **Rev:** Stylized wheel chair **Edge:** Reeded

Date	Mintage	F	VF	XF	Unc	BU
2003 Proof	300	Value: 575				

KM# 56 25000 TOLARJEV

7.0000 g., 0.9000 Gold 0.2025 oz. AGW, 24 mm. **Subject:** 60th Anniversary of the Slovenian Assembly **Obv:** Value in partial star design **Rev:** Dates in partial star design **Edge:** Reeded

Date	Mintage	F	VF	XF	Unc	BU
2003 Proof	300	Value: 575				

KM# 59 25000 TOLARJEV

7.0000 g., 0.9000 Gold 0.2025 oz. AGW, 24 mm. **Subject:** 250th Anniversary of Jurij Vega's Birth **Obv:** Value **Rev:** Facial profile left looking down within mathematical graph **Edge:** Reeded

Date	Mintage	F	VF	XF	Unc	BU
2004 Proof	300	Value: 575				

KM# 61 25000 TOLARJEV

7.0000 g., 0.9000 Gold 0.2025 oz. AGW, 24 mm. **Subject:** 1000th Anniversary Town of Bled **Obv:** Value **Rev:** Castle and towers silhouette **Edge:** Reeded

Date	Mintage	F	VF	XF	Unc	BU
2004 Proof	300	Value: 575				

KM# 66 25000 TOLARJEV

7.0000 g., 0.9000 Gold 0.2025 oz. AGW, 24 mm. **Subject:** Centennial of Slovene Sokol Association **Obv:** Perched falcon above value **Rev:** Rising sun and reflection **Edge:** Reeded

Date	Mintage	F	VF	XF	Unc	BU
2005 Proof	1,000	Value: 520				

KM# 67 25000 TOLARJEV

7.0000 g., 0.9000 Gold 0.2025 oz. AGW, 24 mm. **Subject:** Centennial of Slovene Film **Obv:** Value above clapboard **Rev:** Film segment **Edge:** Reeded

Date	Mintage	F	VF	XF	Unc	BU
2005 Proof	1,000	Value: 520				

KM# 83 25000 TOLARJEV

7.0000 g., 0.9000 Gold 0.2025 oz. AGW, 24 mm. **Subject:** Anton Askerc **Edge:** Reeded

Date	Mintage	F	VF	XF	Unc	BU
2006 Proof	—	Value: 550				

KM# 84 25000 TOLARJEV

7.0000 g., 0.9000 Gold 0.2025 oz. AGW, 24 mm. **Subject:** Anton Tomaz Linhart **Edge:** Reeded

Date	Mintage	F	VF	XF	Unc	BU
2006 Proof	—	Value: 550				

KM# 90 25000 TOLARJEV

7.0000 g., 0.9000 Gold 0.2025 oz. AGW, 24 mm. **Subject:** 1000th Anniversary, Town of Bled mention, 2nd issue

Date	Mintage	F	VF	XF	Unc	BU
2006 Proof	500	Value: 550				

EURO COINAGE

KM# 68 EURO CENT

2.3000 g., Copper Plated Steel, 16.25 mm. **Obv:** White Stork **Obv. Legend:** SLOVENIJA, star between each letter **Rev:** Value and globe **Edge:** Plain

Date	Mintage	F	VF	XF	Unc	BU
2007	44,800,000	—	—	—	0.25	0.35
2008	148,000	—	—	—	0.25	0.35
2008 Proof	2,000	Value: 22.00				
2009	17,900,000	—	—	—	0.25	0.35
2010	70,000	—	—	—	0.25	0.35
2010 Proof	5,000	Value: 5.00				
2011	15,000	—	—	—	1.25	1.35
2011 Proof	2,000	Value: 15.00				
2012	—	—	—	—	0.25	0.35
2012 Proof	2,000	Value: 15.00				
2013	—	—	—	—	0.25	0.35

KM# 69 2 EURO CENT

3.0600 g., Copper Plated Steel, 18.75 mm. **Obv:** Princely stone of power in consciousness **Obv. Legend:** SLOVENIJA, star between each letter **Rev:** Value and globe **Edge:** Grooved

Date	Mintage	F	VF	XF	Unc	BU
2007	44,250,000	—	—	—	0.50	0.65
2008	148,000	—	—	—	0.50	0.65
2008 Proof	2,000	Value: 22.00				
2009	12,300,000	—	—	—	0.50	0.65
2010	70,000	—	—	—	0.50	0.65
2010 Proof	5,000	Value: 5.00				
2011	15,000	—	—	—	1.50	1.65
2011 Proof	2,000	Value: 15.00				
2012	—	—	—	—	0.50	0.65
2012 Proof	2,000	Value: 15.00				
2013	—	—	—	—	0.50	0.65

KM# 70 5 EURO CENT

3.9200 g., Copper Plated Steel, 21.25 mm. **Obv:** Sower of Seeds - and stars **Obv. Legend:** SLOVENIJA, star between each letter **Rev:** Value and globe **Edge:** Plain

Date	Mintage	F	VF	XF	Unc	BU
2007	43,800,000	—	—	—	0.75	1.00
2008	148,000	—	—	—	0.75	1.00
2008 Proof	2,000	Value: 22.00				
2009	100,000	—	—	—	0.75	1.00
2010	70,000	—	—	—	0.75	1.00
2010 Proof	5,000	Value: 5.00				
2011	15,000	—	—	—	1.50	2.00
2011 Proof	2,000	Value: 15.00				
2012	—	—	—	—	0.75	1.00
2012 Proof	2,000	Value: 15.00				
2013	—	—	—	—	0.75	1.00

KM# 71 10 EURO CENT

4.1000 g., Brass, 19.75 mm. **Obv:** Plecnik's unrealised plans for Parliament building **Obv. Legend:** SLOVENIJA, star between each letter **Rev:** Value and map **Edge:** Reeded

Date	Mintage	F	VF	XF	Unc	BU
2007	42,800,000	—	—	—	1.00	1.25
2008	148,000	—	—	—	1.00	1.25
2008 Proof	2,000	Value: 22.00				
2009	100,000	—	—	—	1.00	1.25
2010	70,000	—	—	—	1.00	1.25
2010 Proof	5,000	Value: 5.00				
2011	15,000	—	—	—	2.00	2.25
2011 Proof	2,000	Value: 15.00				
2012	—	—	—	—	1.00	1.25
2012 Proof	2,000	Value: 15.00				
2013	—	—	—	—	1.00	1.25

KM# 72 20 EURO CENT

5.7400 g., Brass, 22.25 mm. **Obv:** Two Lipizzaner horses prancing left **Obv. Legend:** SLOVENIJA, star between each letter **Rev:** Value and map **Edge:** Notched

Date	Mintage	F	VF	XF	Unc	BU
2007	37,250,000	—	—	—	1.25	1.50
2008	148,000	—	—	—	1.25	1.50
2008 Proof	2,000	Value: 8.00				
2009	100,000	—	—	—	1.25	1.50
2010	70,000	—	—	—	1.25	1.50
2010 Proof	5,000	Value: 28.00				
2011	15,000	—	—	—	2.25	2.50
2011 Proof	2,000	Value: 18.00				
2012	—	—	—	—	1.25	1.50
2012 Proof	2,000	Value: 18.00				
2013	—	—	—	—	1.25	1.50

KM# 73 50 EURO CENT

7.8000 g., Brass, 24.25 mm. **Obv:** Triglav Mountain (highest peak in Slovenia) and stars **Rev:** Value and map **Edge:** Reeded

Date	Mintage	F	VF	XF	Unc	BU
2007	32,400,000	—	—	—	1.50	2.00
2008	148,000	—	—	—	1.50	2.00
2008 Proof	2,000	Value: 8.00				
2009	100,000	—	—	—	1.50	2.00
2010	70,000	—	—	—	1.50	2.00
2010 Proof	5,000	Value: 28.00				
2011	15,000	—	—	—	2.50	3.00
2011 Proof	2,000	Value: 18.00				
2012	—	—	—	—	1.50	2.00
2012 Proof	2,000	Value: 18.00				
2013	—	—	—	—	1.50	2.00

KM# 74 EURO

7.5000 g., Bi-Metallic Copper-Nickel center in Nickel-Brass ring, 23.25 mm. **Obv:** Bearded Primoz Trubar **Rev:** Value and map **Edge:** Segmented reeding

Date	Mintage	F	VF	XF	Unc	BU
2007	29,750,000	—	—	—	2.50	3.50
2008	148,000	—	—	—	2.50	3.50
2008 Proof	2,000	Value: 35.00				
2009	100,000	—	—	—	2.50	3.50
2010	70,000	—	—	—	2.50	3.50
2010 Proof	5,000	Value: 15.00				
2011	15,000	—	—	—	3.50	4.50
2011 Proof	2,000	Value: 22.00				
2012	—	—	—	—	2.50	3.50
2012 Proof	2,000	Value: 22.00				
2013	—	—	—	—	2.50	3.50

KM# 75 2 EURO

8.5000 g., Bi-Metallic Nickel-Brass center in Copper-Nickel ring, 25.75 mm. **Obv:** France Preseren silhouette and signature **Rev:** Value and map **Edge:** Reeded and lettered

Date	Mintage	F	VF	XF	Unc	BU
2007	21,350,000	—	—	—	4.00	5.00
2008	148,000	—	—	—	4.00	5.00
2008 Proof	2,000	Value: 40.00				
2009	100,000	—	—	—	4.00	5.00
2010	70,000	—	—	—	4.00	5.00
2010 Proof	5,000	Value: 20.00				
2011	15,000	—	—	—	5.00	6.00
2011 Proof	2,000	Value: 28.00				
2012	—	—	—	—	4.00	5.00
2012 Proof	2,000	Value: 28.00				
2013	—	—	—	—	4.00	5.00

KM# 106 2 EURO

8.5000 g., Bi-Metallic Nickel-Brass center in Copper-Nickel ring, 25.75 mm. **Subject:** Treaty of Rome, 50th Anniversary

Date	Mintage	F	VF	XF	Unc	BU
2007	399,100	—	—	—	6.50	7.50
2007 Encased in a lucite block	990	—	—	—	—	10.00

KM# 80 2 EURO

8.5000 g., Bi-Metallic Nickel-Brass center in Copper-Nickel ring, 25.75 mm. **Subject:** 500th Anniversary Birth of Primoz Tubar **Obv:** Bust of Trubar left at right **Rev:** Large "2" at left, modified map of Europe at right **Edge:** Reeded

Date	Mintage	F	VF	XF	Unc	BU
2008	950,000	—	—	—	6.00	8.00
2008 Special Unc.	10,000	—	—	—	—	32.50
2008 Proof	40,000	Value: 45.00				

KM# 82 2 EURO

8.5000 g., Bi-Metallic Nickel-Brass center in Copper-Nickel ring., 25.75 mm. **Subject:** European Monetary Union, 10th Anniversary **Obv:** Stick figure and large E symbol **Rev:** Value at left, modified map of Europe at left

Date	Mintage	F	VF	XF	Unc	BU
2009	1,000,000	—	—	—	5.00	6.00
2009 Special Unc.	—	—	—	—	—	32.50
2009 Proof	—	Value: 40.00				

KM# 94 2 EURO

8.5000 g., Bi-Metallic Nickel-Brass center in Copper-Nickel ring, 25.75 mm. **Subject:** Ljubljana Botanical Gardens, 200th Anniversary

Date	Mintage	F	VF	XF	Unc	BU
2010	980,000	—	—	—	8.00	10.00
2010 Proof	20,000	Value: 50.00				

KM# 100 2 EURO

8.5000 g., Bi-Metallic Nickel-Brass center in Copper-Nickel ring, 25.75 mm. **Subject:** Franc Razman, 100th Anniversary of Birth

Date	Mintage	F	VF	XF	Unc	BU
2011	486,000	—	—	—	6.00	8.00
2011 Proof	14,000	Value: 50.00				

KM# 107 2 EURO

8.5000 g., Bi-Metallic Nickel-Brass center in Copper-Nickel ring, 25.75 mm. **Subject:** Euro Coinage, 10th Anniversary **Obv:** Euro symbol on globe, child-like renderings around

Date	Mintage	F	VF	XF	Unc	BU
2012	1,000,000	—	—	—	7.00	8.00
2012 Proof	1,000	Value: 25.00				

KM# 81 3 EURO

15.0000 g., Bi-Metallic Copper-Nickel center in Aluminum-Bronze ring, 32 mm. **Subject:** Six Month Term as President of the EU 2008 **Obv:** Field of stars representing EU membership **Rev:** Pinwheel

Date	Mintage	F	VF	XF	Unc	BU
2008	348,000	—	—	—	8.00	10.00
2008 Special Unc.	148,000	—	—	—	—	20.00
2008 Proof	4,000	Value: 165				

KM# 85 3 EURO

15.0000 g., Bi-Metallic Copper-Nickel center in Aluminum-Bronze ring, 32 mm. **Subject:** First Airplane flight in Slovenia by Edvard Rusjan, 100th Anniversary

Date	Mintage	F	VF	XF	Unc	BU
2009	300,000	—	—	—	8.00	10.00

KM# 95 3 EURO

15.0000 g., Bi-Metallic Copper-Nickel center in Aluminum-Bronze ring, 32 mm. **Subject:** UNESCO - World Book Capital, Ljubljana

Date	Mintage	F	VF	XF	Unc	BU
2010	—	—	—	—	—	10.00
2010 Proof	5,000	Value: 50.00				

KM# 101 3 EURO

7.5000 g., Bi-Metallic Copper-Nickel center in Aluminum-Bronze ring, 32 mm. **Subject:** Independence, 20th Anniversary

Date	Mintage	F	VF	XF	Unc	BU
2011	5,000	—	—	—	—	15.00
2011 Proof	4,000	Value: 110				

KM# 76 30 EURO

15.0000 g., 0.9250 Silver 0.4461 oz. ASW, 32 mm. **Subject:** 250th Anniversary Birth of Valentin Vodnik **Obv:** Value **Obv. Legend:** SLOVENIJA **Rev:** Large bust of Vodnik left

Date	Mintage	F	VF	XF	Unc	BU
2008 Proof	8,000	Value: 90.00				

KM# 78 30 EURO

15.0000 g., 0.9250 Silver 0.4461 oz. ASW, 32 mm. **Subject:** EU President **Obv:** EU membership stars **Obv. Legend:** SLOVENIJA **Rev:** Pinwheel 5-pointed star

Date	Mintage	F	VF	XF	Unc	BU
2008 Proof	8,000	Value: 150				

KM# 86 30 EURO

15.0000 g., 0.9250 Silver 0.4461 oz. ASW, 32 mm. **Subject:** First Airplane, 100th Anniversary

Date	Mintage	F	VF	XF	Unc	BU
2009 Proof	8,000	Value: 65.00				

KM# 88 30 EURO

15.0000 g., 0.9250 Silver 0.4461 oz. ASW, 32 mm. **Subject:** Zoran Music, painter

Date	Mintage	F	VF	XF	Unc	BU
2009 Proof	—	Value: 70.00				

KM# 96 30 EURO

15.0000 g., 0.9250 Silver 0.4461 oz. ASW, 32 mm. **Subject:** UNESCO - World Book Capital, Ljubljana

Date	Mintage	F	VF	XF	Unc	BU
2010 Proof	—	Value: 65.00				

KM# 98 30 EURO

15.0000 g., 0.9250 Silver 0.4461 oz. ASW, 32 mm. **Subject:** World Ski Jumping Championships, Planica

Date	Mintage	F	VF	XF	Unc	BU
2010 Proof	—	Value: 70.00				

KM# 102 30 EURO

15.0000 g., 0.9250 Silver 0.4461 oz. ASW, 32 mm. **Subject:** Independence, 20th Anniversary

Date	Mintage	F	VF	XF	Unc	BU
2011 Proof	—	Value: 65.00				

KM# 104 30 EURO

15.0000 g., 0.9250 Silver 0.4461 oz. ASW, 32 mm. **Series:** World Rowing Championships

Date	Mintage	F	VF	XF	Unc	BU
2011 Proof	—	Value: 65.00				

KM# 77 100 EURO

7.0000 g., 0.9000 Gold 0.2025 oz. AGW, 24 mm. **Subject:** 250th Anniversary Birth of Valentin Vodnik **Obv:** Value **Obv. Legend:** SLOVENIJA **Rev:** Large bust of Vodnik left

Date	Mintage	F	VF	XF	Unc	BU
2008 Proof	5,000	Value: 450				

KM# 79 100 EURO

7.0000 g., 0.9000 Gold 0.2025 oz. AGW, 24 mm. **Subject:** EU President **Obv:** EU membership stars **Obv. Legend:** SLOVENIJA **Rev:** Pinwheel 5-pointed star

Date	Mintage	F	VF	XF	Unc	BU
2008 Proof	5,000	Value: 650				

KM# 87 100 EURO

7.0000 g., 0.9000 Gold 0.2025 oz. AGW, 24 mm. **Subject:** First Airplane, 100th Anniversary

Date	Mintage	F	VF	XF	Unc	BU
2009 Proof	6,000	Value: 425				

KM# 89 100 EURO

7.0000 g., 0.9000 Gold 0.2025 oz. AGW, 24 mm. **Subject:** Zoran Music, painter

Date	Mintage	F	VF	XF	Unc	BU
2009 Proof	—	Value: 425				

KM# 97 100 EURO

7.0000 g., 0.9000 Gold 0.2025 oz. AGW, 24 mm. **Subject:** UNESCO - World Book Capital, Ljubljana

Date	Mintage	F	VF	XF	Unc	BU
2010 Proof	—	Value: 425				

KM# 99 100 EURO

7.0000 g., 0.9000 Gold 0.2025 oz. AGW, 24 mm. **Subject:** World Ski Jumping Championships, Planica

Date	Mintage	F	VF	XF	Unc	BU
2010 Proof	—	Value: 425				

KM# 103 100 EURO

7.0000 g., 0.9000 Gold 0.2025 oz. AGW, 24 mm. **Subject:** Independence, 20th Anniversary

Date	Mintage	F	VF	XF	Unc	BU
2011 Proof	—	Value: 425				

KM# 105 100 EURO

7.0000 g., 0.9000 Gold 0.2025 oz. AGW, 24 mm. **Subject:** World Rowing Championships

Date	Mintage	F	VF	XF	Unc	BU
2011 Proof	—	Value: 425				

MINT SETS

KM#	Date	Mintage	Identification	Issue Price	Mkt Val
MS10	2001 (7)	1,000	KM#3-8, 41	20.00	40.00
MS11	2002 (8)	1,000	KM#3-8, 41, 45	—	45.00
MS12	2003 (10)	1,000	KM#3-8, 41, 50-52	—	55.00
MS13	2004 (10)	1,000	KM#3-8, 41, 51, 52, 57	—	45.00
MS14	2005 (9)	3,000	KM#3-8, 41, 51, 52	25.00	45.00
MS15	2006 (10)	4,000	KM#3-8, 41, 51, 52, 65	25.00	50.00
MS16	2007 (8)	100,000	KM#68-75	—	50.00
MS17	2008 (9)	148,000	KM#68-75, 81	—	50.00
MS18	2009 (9)	100,000	KM#68-75, 85	—	50.00
MS19	2010 (10)	70,000	KM#68-75, 94, 95	—	75.00
MS20	2011 (10)	150,000	KM#68-75, 100, 101	—	100

PROOF SETS

KM#	Date	Mintage	Identification	Issue Price	Mkt Val
PS13	2001 (8)	800	KM#3-8, 41, 42	—	70.00
PS14	2002 (8)	800	KM#3-8, 41, 45	—	70.00
PS15	2003 (10)	800	KM#3-8, 41, 50-52	22.50	100
PS16	2004 (10)	500	KM#3-8, 41, 51-52, 57	—	120
PS17	2005 (10)	1,000	KM#3-8, 41, 51-52, 63	—	95.00
PS18	2006 (10)	1,000	KM#3-8, 41, 51-52, 65	—	95.00
PS19	2008 (9)	2,000	KM#68-75, 81	—	350
PS20	2010 (10)	5,000	KM#68-75, 94, 95	—	215
PS21	2011 (10)	2,000	KM#68-75, 100, 101	—	315

The Solomon Islands are made up of about 200 islands. They are located in the southwest Pacific east of Papua New Guinea, have an area of 10,983 sq. mi. (28,450 sq. km.) and a population of *552,000. Capital: Honiara. The most important islands of the Solomon chain are Guadalcanal (scene of some of the fiercest fighting of World War II), Malaitia, New Georgia, Florida, Vella Lavella, Choiseul, Rendova, San Cristobal, the Lord Howe group, the Santa Cruz islands, and the Duff group. Copra is the only important cash crop but it is hoped that timber will become an economic factor.

Solomon Islands is a member of the Commonwealth of Nations. Queen Elizabeth II is Head of State, as Queen of the Solomon Islands.

RULER

British

MONETARY SYSTEM

100 Cents = 1 Dollar

COMMONWEALTH NATION

STANDARD COINAGE

KM# 24 CENT

2.3000 g., Bronze Plated Steel, 17.53 mm. **Ruler:** Elizabeth II **Obv:** Crowned head right **Obv. Legend:** ELIZABETH II - SOLOMON ISLANDS **Rev:** Food bowl divides value **Edge:** Plain

Date	Mintage	F	VF	XF	Unc	BU
2005	—	—	—	—	0.35	0.75
2010	—	—	—	—	0.35	0.75

KM# 25 2 CENTS

Bronze Plated Steel, 21.6 mm. **Ruler:** Elizabeth II **Obv:** Crowned head right **Obv. Legend:** ELIZABETH II - SOLOMON ISLANDS **Rev:** Eagle spirit below value **Edge:** Plain

Date	Mintage	F	VF	XF	Unc	BU
2005	—	—	—	—	0.35	0.75
2006	—	—	—	—	0.35	0.75

KM# 26a 5 CENTS

Nickel Plated Steel, 19.4 mm. **Ruler:** Elizabeth II **Obv:** Crowned bust right **Obv. Legend:** ELIZABETH II - SOLOMON ISLANDS **Rev:** Value at left, native mask at center right

Date	Mintage	F	VF	XF	Unc	BU
2005	—	—	—	—	0.50	1.00

KM# 27a 10 CENTS

Nickel Plated Steel, 23.6 mm. **Ruler:** Elizabeth II **Subject:** Ngorieru **Obv:** Crowned head right **Obv. Legend:** ELIZABETH II - SOLOMON ISLANDS **Rev:** Sea spirit divides value **Edge:** Reeded

Date	Mintage	F	VF	XF	Unc	BU
2005	—	—	—	—	0.65	1.00

KM# 171a 10 CENTS

3.5200 g., Silver, 19 mm. **Ruler:** Elizabeth II **Rev:** Sea Spirit Ngorieru

Date	Mintage	F	VF	XF	Unc	BU
2012 Proof	—	Value: 5.00				

KM# 28 20 CENTS

11.2500 g., Nickel Plated Steel, 28.5 mm. **Ruler:** Elizabeth II **Obv:** Crowned head right **Obv. Legend:** ELIZABETH II - SOLOMON ISLANDS **Rev:** Malaita pendant design within circle, denomination appears twice in legend **Edge:** Reeded

Date	Mintage	F	VF	XF	Unc	BU
2005	—	—	—	—	0.85	1.25

KM# 172 20 CENTS

Nickel Plated Steel, 21 mm. **Ruler:** Elizabeth II **Rev:** Pendant from Malaita province

Date	Mintage	F	VF	XF	Unc	BU
2012	—	—	—	—	0.85	1.25

KM# 172a 20 CENTS

4.6400 g., Silver, 21 mm. **Ruler:** Elizabeth II **Rev:** Pendant from Malaita province

Date	Mintage	F	VF	XF	Unc	BU
2012 Proof	—	Value: 5.00				

KM# 29 50 CENTS

10.0000 g., Copper-Nickel, 29.5 mm. **Ruler:** Elizabeth II **Obv:** Crowned head right **Obv. Legend:** ELIZABETH II - SOLOMON ISLANDS **Rev:** Arms with supporters **Edge:** Plain **Shape:** 12-sided **Note:** Circulation type.

Date	Mintage	F	VF	XF	Unc	BU
2005	—	—	—	—	2.00	3.00

KM# 173 50 CENTS

Copper-Nickel, 24.2 mm. **Ruler:** Elizabeth II **Rev:** Eagle, wings open

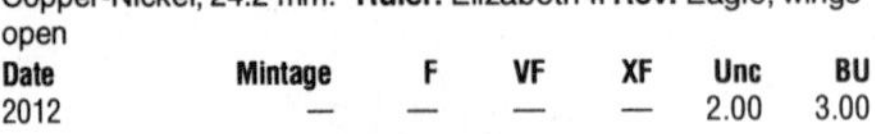

Date	Mintage	F	VF	XF	Unc	BU
2012	—	—	—	—	2.00	3.00

KM# 173a 50 CENTS

6.9500 g., Silver, 24.2 mm. **Ruler:** Elizabeth II **Rev:** Eagle, wings open

Date	Mintage	F	VF	XF	Unc	BU
2012 Proof	—	Value: 7.50				

KM# 72 DOLLAR

13.4500 g., Copper-Nickel, 30 mm. **Ruler:** Elizabeth II **Obv:** Crowned head right **Obv. Legend:** ELIZABETH II - SOLOMON ISLANDS **Rev:** Sea spirit statue divides value **Edge:** Plain **Shape:** 7-sided

Date	Mintage	F	VF	XF	Unc	BU
2005	—	—	—	—	2.50	4.00

KM# 159 DOLLAR

26.0000 g., Bronze, 38.61 mm. **Ruler:** Elizabeth II **Rev:** Archangel Michael in color

Date	Mintage	F	VF	XF	Unc	BU
2009 Proof	—	Value: 17.50				

KM# 160 DOLLAR

26.0000 g., Bronze, 38.61 mm. **Ruler:** Elizabeth II **Rev:** Archangel Raphael in color

Date	Mintage	F	VF	XF	Unc	BU
2009 Proof	—	Value: 17.50				

KM# 161 DOLLAR

26.0000 g., Bronze, 38.61 mm. **Ruler:** Elizabeth II **Rev:** Archangel Gabriel in color

Date	Mintage	F	VF	XF	Unc	BU
2009 Proof	—	Value: 17.50				

KM# 174 DOLLAR

Copper-Nickel, 21.5 mm. **Ruler:** Elizabeth II **Rev:** Spirit Nguzu Nguzu

Date	Mintage	F	VF	XF	Unc	BU
2012	—	—	—	—	2.50	4.00

KM# 174a DOLLAR

7.7700 g., Silver, 21.5 mm. **Ruler:** Elizabeth II **Rev:** Spirit Nguzu Nguzu

Date	Mintage	F	VF	XF	Unc	BU
2012 Proof	—	Value: 7.50				

KM# 83 2 DOLLARS

62.2700 g., 0.9990 Silver 1.9999 oz. ASW, 50.3 mm. **Subject:** Regional Assistance Mission to Solomon Islands **Obv:** Crowned head right **Rev:** Dove outline over multicolor islands in a sea of country names **Edge:** Reeded

Date	Mintage	F	VF	XF	Unc	BU
2005 Proof	2,500	Value: 95.00				

KM# 175 2 DOLLARS

Copper-Nickel, 25.6 mm. **Ruler:** Elizabeth II **Rev:** Bokolo, traditional money

Date	Mintage	F	VF	XF	Unc	BU
2012	—	—	—	—	4.00	6.00

KM# 175a 2 DOLLARS
10.3700 g., Silver, 25.6 mm. **Ruler:** Elizabeth II **Rev:** Bobolo, traditional money

Date	Mintage	F	VF	XF	Unc	BU
2012 Proof	—	Value: 10.00				

KM# 176 2 DOLLARS
Silver, 38.61 mm. **Ruler:** Elizabeth II **Subject:** Royal visit to the Solomon Islands **Obv:** Heas with tiara right **Rev:** Portraits of Prince Willam and Kate Middleton in color

Date	Mintage	F	VF	XF	Unc	BU
2012 Proof	—	Value: 75.00				

KM# 130 5 DOLLARS
25.0000 g., 0.9000 Silver 0.7234 oz. ASW **Ruler:** Elizabeth II **Rev:** Butterfly fish in color

Date	Mintage	F	VF	XF	Unc	BU
2001 Proof	—	Value: 65.00				

KM# 125 5 DOLLARS
Silver partially gilt, 38.6 mm. **Ruler:** Elizabeth II **Obv:** Head crowned right **Rev:** Mace and coronation scene

Date	Mintage	F	VF	XF	Unc	BU
2002 Proof	—	Value: 50.00				

KM# 113a 5 DOLLARS
28.2800 g., 0.9250 Silver partially gilt 0.8410 oz. ASW, 38.6 mm. **Ruler:** Elizabeth II **Obv:** Bust right gilt **Rev:** Orb

Date	Mintage	F	VF	XF	Unc	BU
2002 Proof	20,000	Value: 40.00				

KM# 113 5 DOLLARS
Copper-Nickel **Ruler:** Elizabeth II **Rev:** Orb

Date	Mintage	F	VF	XF	Unc	BU
2002	—	—	—	—	—	15.00

KM# 75 5 DOLLARS
28.2800 g., Copper-Nickel, 38.6 mm. **Obv:** Crowned head right **Rev:** F-117A Nighthawk Stealth fighter plane **Edge:** Reeded

Date	Mintage	F	VF	XF	Unc	BU
2003	—	—	—	—	8.00	10.00

KM# 76 5 DOLLARS
28.2800 g., Copper-Nickel, 38.6 mm. **Obv:** Crowned head right **Rev:** Concorde supersonic airliner **Edge:** Reeded

Date	Mintage	F	VF	XF	Unc	BU
2003	—	—	—	—	8.00	10.00

KM# 84 5 DOLLARS
31.1035 g., 0.9990 Silver 0.9990 oz. ASW, 38.6 mm. **Obv:** Maklouf's portrait of Elizabeth II **Rev:** Gold plated pig **Edge:** Reeded **Note:** Year of the Pig

Date	Mintage	F	VF	XF	Unc	BU
2007	10,000	—	—	—	—	50.00

KM# 85 5 DOLLARS
31.1035 g., 0.9990 Silver 0.9990 oz. ASW, 38.6 mm. **Obv:** Maklouf's portrait of Elizabeth II **Rev:** Dark red pig and piglet **Edge:** Reeded **Note:** Year of the Pig

Date	Mintage	F	VF	XF	Unc	BU
2007	10,000	—	—	—	—	50.00

KM# 119 5 DOLLARS
0.5000 g., 0.9990 Gold 0.0161 oz. AGW, 11 mm. **Ruler:** Elizabeth II **Subject:** For World Peace **Rev:** John Paul II and Mother Theresa

Date	Mintage	F	VF	XF	Unc	BU
2010 Proof	10,000	Value: 75.00				

KM# 123 5 DOLLARS
0.5000 g., 0.9990 Gold 0.0161 oz. AGW, 11 mm. **Ruler:** Elizabeth II **Rev:** Spotted Cuscus in tree

Date	Mintage	F	VF	XF	Unc	BU
2010 Proof	15,000	Value: 75.00				

KM# 126 5 DOLLARS
15.5500 g., 0.9990 Silver 0.4994 oz. ASW, 35 mm. **Ruler:** Elizabeth II **Rev:** Archangel Gabriel in color

Date	Mintage	F	VF	XF	Unc	BU
2011 Proof	2,000	Value: 75.00				

KM# 127 5 DOLLARS
15.5500 g., 0.9990 Silver 0.4994 oz. ASW, 35 mm. **Ruler:** Elizabeth II **Rev:** Auchangel Michael

Date	Mintage	F	VF	XF	Unc	BU
2011 Proof	—	Value: 75.00				

KM# 163 5 DOLLARS
0.5000 g., 0.9990 Gold 0.0161 oz. AGW, 11 mm. **Ruler:** Elizabeth II **Rev:** Manatee

Date	Mintage	F	VF	XF	Unc	BU
2011 Proof	10,000	Value: 60.00				

KM# 164 5 DOLLARS
0.5000 g., 0.9990 Gold 0.0161 oz. AGW, 11 mm. **Ruler:** Elizabeth II **Rev:** Great Wall of China

Date	Mintage	F	VF	XF	Unc	BU
2011 Proof	Est. 7,000	Value: 50.00				

KM# 165 5 DOLLARS
0.5000 g., 0.9990 Gold 0.0161 oz. AGW, 11 mm. **Ruler:** Elizabeth II **Rev:** Storehouse at Petra

Date	Mintage	F	VF	XF	Unc	BU
2011 Proof	Est. 7,000	Value: 50.00				

KM# 166 5 DOLLARS
0.5000 g., 0.9990 Gold 0.0161 oz. AGW, 11 mm. **Ruler:** Elizabeth II **Rev:** Christ statue in Rio de Janeiro

Date	Mintage	F	VF	XF	Unc	BU
2011 Proof	Est. 7,000	Value: 50.00				

KM# 167 5 DOLLARS
0.5000 g., 0.9990 Gold 0.0161 oz. AGW, 11 mm. **Ruler:** Elizabeth II **Rev:** Machu Picchu

Date	Mintage	F	VF	XF	Unc	BU
2011 Proof	Est. 7,000	Value: 50.00				

KM# 168 5 DOLLARS
0.5000 g., 0.9990 Gold 0.0161 oz. AGW, 11 mm. **Ruler:** Elizabeth II **Rev:** Stepped pyramid at Chichen Itza

Date	Mintage	F	VF	XF	Unc	BU
2011 Proof	Est. 7,000	Value: 50.00				

KM# 169 5 DOLLARS
0.5000 g., 0.9990 Gold 0.0161 oz. AGW, 11 mm. **Ruler:** Elizabeth II **Rev:** Colusem in Rome

Date	Mintage	F	VF	XF	Unc	BU
2011 Proof	Est. 7,000	Value: 50.00				

KM# 170 5 DOLLARS
0.5000 g., 0.9990 Gold 0.0161 oz. AGW, 11 mm. **Ruler:** Elizabeth II **Rev:** Taj Mahal

Date	Mintage	F	VF	XF	Unc	BU
2011 Proof	Est. 7,000	Value: 50.00				

KM# 131 10 DOLLARS
1.2400 g., 0.9990 Gold 0.0398 oz. AGW, 13.92 mm. **Ruler:** Elizabeth II **Rev:** Butterfly fish

Date	Mintage	F	VF	XF	Unc	BU
2001 Proof	—	Value: 90.00				

KM# 124 10 DOLLARS
28.3600 g., 0.9250 Silver 0.8434 oz. ASW, 38.6 mm. **Ruler:** Elizabeth II **Subject:** Olympics 2004 **Rev:** Runner, Sydney Opera House and Parthenon

Date	Mintage	F	VF	XF	Unc	BU
2004 Proof	—	Value: 50.00				

KM# 86 10 DOLLARS
28.3600 g., 0.9250 Silver 0.8434 oz. ASW, 38.6 mm. **Obv:** Crowned bust right **Obv. Legend:** ELIZABETH II - SOLOMON ISLANDS **Rev:** Bust of Mendana facing at left, early sailing ship at center - right **Rev. Legend:** ALVARO DE MENDANA **Edge:** Reeded

Date	Mintage	F	VF	XF	Unc	BU
2004 Proof	—	Value: 50.00				

KM# 140 10 DOLLARS
31.6350 g., 0.9990 Silver 1.0160 oz. ASW, 40 mm. **Ruler:** Elizabeth II **Subject:** 2006 FIFA World Cup, Germany **Obv:** Head with crown right **Rev:** Two players in color

Date	Mintage	F	VF	XF	Unc	BU
2005 Proof	Est. 5,000	Value: 65.00				

KM# 141 10 DOLLARS
1.2400 g., 0.9990 Gold 0.0398 oz. AGW, 13.92 mm. **Ruler:** Elizabeth II **Rev:** Prospector panning for gold

Date	Mintage	F	VF	XF	Unc	BU
2005 Proof	—	Value: 90.00				

KM# 142 10 DOLLARS
1.2400 g., 0.9990 Gold 0.0398 oz. AGW, 13.92 mm. **Ruler:** Elizabeth II **Subject:** John Lennon, 25th Anniversary of Death **Obv:** Head with crown right **Rev:** Lennon's head facing

Date	Mintage	F	VF	XF	Unc	BU
2005 Proof	—	Value: 90.00				

KM# 153 10 DOLLARS
7.7800 g., 0.5850 Gold 0.1463 oz. AGW, 25 mm. **Ruler:** Elizabeth II **Subject:** 2006 World Cup, Germany

Date	Mintage	F	VF	XF	Unc	BU
2006 Proof	—	Value: 325				

KM# 96 10 DOLLARS
1.2200 g., 0.9990 Gold 0.0392 oz. AGW, 14 mm. **Ruler:** Elizabeth II **Subject:** Wonders of the Ancient World **Obv:** Head right **Rev:** Mausoleum of Mauussollos of Halicarnassus

Date	Mintage	F	VF	XF	Unc	BU
2007 Proof	7,000	Value: 85.00				

KM# 97 10 DOLLARS
1.2200 g., 0.9990 Gold 0.0392 oz. AGW, 14 mm. **Ruler:** Elizabeth II **Subject:** Wonders of the Ancient World **Obv:** Head right **Rev:** Taj Mahal

Date	Mintage	F	VF	XF	Unc	BU
2007 7000	—	Value: 85.00				

KM# 98 10 DOLLARS
1.2200 g., 0.9990 Gold 0.0392 oz. AGW, 14 mm. **Ruler:** Elizabeth II **Subject:** Wonders of the Ancient World **Obv:** Head right **Rev:** Treasury at Petra

Date	Mintage	F	VF	XF	Unc	BU
2007 Proof	7,000	Value: 85.00				

KM# 99 10 DOLLARS
1.2200 g., 0.9990 Gold 0.0392 oz. AGW, 14 mm. **Ruler:** Elizabeth II **Subject:** Wonders of the Ancient World **Obv:** Head right **Rev:** Coliseum in Rome

Date	Mintage	F	VF	XF	Unc	BU
2007 Proof	7,000	Value: 85.00				

KM# 100 10 DOLLARS
1.2200 g., 0.9990 Gold 0.0392 oz. AGW, 14 mm. **Ruler:** Elizabeth II **Subject:** Wonders of the Ancient World **Obv:** Head right **Rev:** Inca's Machu Kicuhu

Date	Mintage	F	VF	XF	Unc	BU
2007 Proof	7,000	Value: 85.00				

KM# 101 10 DOLLARS
1.2200 g., 0.9990 Gold 0.0392 oz. AGW, 14 mm. **Ruler:** Elizabeth II **Subject:** Wonders of the Ancient World **Obv:** Head right **Rev:** Chichen Itza

Date	Mintage	F	VF	XF	Unc	BU
2007 Proof	7,000	Value: 85.00				

KM# 102 10 DOLLARS
1.2200 g., 0.9990 Gold 0.0392 oz. AGW, 14 mm. **Ruler:** Elizabeth II **Subject:** Wonders of the World **Obv:** Head right **Rev:** Great wall of China

Date	Mintage	F	VF	XF	Unc	BU
2007 Proof	7,000	Value: 85.00				

KM# 103 10 DOLLARS
1.2200 g., 0.9990 Gold 0.0392 oz. AGW, 14 mm. **Ruler:** Elizabeth II **Subject:** Wonders of the World **Rev:** Christ Statue in Rio

Date	Mintage	F	VF	XF	Unc	BU
2007 Proof	7,000	Value: 85.00				

KM# 154 10 DOLLARS
1.2400 g., 0.9990 Gold 0.0398 oz. AGW, 13.92 mm. **Ruler:** Elizabeth II **Rev:** Legendary chief of El Dorado sprinking water

Date	Mintage	F	VF	XF	Unc	BU
2008 Proof	—	Value: 90.00				

KM# 104 10 DOLLARS
1.2200 g., Gold, 14 mm. **Ruler:** Elizabeth II **Subject:** Seven Wonders of the World **Obv:** Head right **Rev:** Giza Pyramids

Date	Mintage	F	VF	XF	Unc	BU
2009 Proof	7,500	Value: 85.00				

KM# 105 10 DOLLARS
1.2200 g., 0.9990 Gold 0.0392 oz. AGW, 14 mm. **Ruler:** Elizabeth II **Subject:** Seven Wonders of the World **Obv:** Head right **Rev:** Colossus of Rhodes

Date	Mintage	F	VF	XF	Unc	BU
2009 Proof	7,500	Value: 85.00				

KM# 106 10 DOLLARS
1.2200 g., 0.9990 Gold 0.0392 oz. AGW, 14 mm. **Ruler:** Elizabeth II **Subject:** Seven Wonders of the World **Obv:** Head right **Rev:** Statue of Zeus at Olympia

Date	Mintage	F	VF	XF	Unc	BU
2009 Proof	7,500	Value: 85.00				

KM# 107 10 DOLLARS
1.2200 g., 0.9990 Gold 0.0392 oz. AGW, 14 mm. **Ruler:** Elizabeth II **Subject:** Seven Wonders of the World **Obv:** Head right **Rev:** Temple of Artemis at Ephesus

Date	Mintage	F	VF	XF	Unc	BU
2009 Proof	7,500	Value: 85.00				

KM# 108 10 DOLLARS
1.2200 g., 0.9990 Gold 0.0392 oz. AGW, 14 mm. **Ruler:** Elizabeth II **Subject:** Seven Wonders of the World **Obv:** Head right **Rev:** Hanging Gardens of Bablyon

Date	Mintage	F	VF	XF	Unc	BU
2009 Proof	7,500	Value: 85.00				

KM# 109 10 DOLLARS
1.2200 g., 0.9990 Gold 0.0392 oz. AGW, 14 mm. **Ruler:** Elizabeth II **Subject:** Seven Wonders of the World **Obv:** Head right **Rev:** Lighthouse at Alexandria

Date	Mintage	F	VF	XF	Unc	BU
2009 Proof	7,500	Value: 85.00				

KM# 110 10 DOLLARS
1.2200 g., 0.9990 Gold 0.0392 oz. AGW, 14 mm. **Ruler:** Elizabeth II **Subject:** Seven Wonders of the World **Obv:** Head right

Date	Mintage	F	VF	XF	Unc	BU
2009 Proof	7,500	Value: 85.00				

KM# 120 10 DOLLARS
20.0000 g., 0.9250 Silver 0.5948 oz. ASW, 38.61 mm. **Ruler:** Elizabeth II **Subject:** For World Peace **Rev:** John Paul II and Mother Theresa

Date	Mintage	F	VF	XF	Unc	BU
2010 Proof	2,500	Value: 75.00				

KM# 121 10 DOLLARS
20.0000 g., 0.9250 Silver 0.5948 oz. ASW, 38.61 mm. **Ruler:** Elizabeth II **Rev:** S.M.S. Gneisenau under full sail

Date	Mintage	F	VF	XF	Unc	BU
2010 Proof	2,500	Value: 75.00				

KM# 122 10 DOLLARS
25.0000 g., 0.9250 Silver 0.7435 oz. ASW, 38.61 mm. **Ruler:** Elizabeth II **Rev:** Spotted Cuscus in color with Swarovsky crystal eyes

Date	Mintage	F	VF	XF	Unc	BU
2010 Proof	2,500	Value: 65.00				

KM# 162 10 DOLLARS
20.0000 g., Silver, 38.61 mm. **Ruler:** Elizabeth II **Rev:** Manatee in color

Date	Mintage	F	VF	XF	Unc	BU
2011 Proof	2,500	Value: 55.00				

KM# 91 25 DOLLARS
31.1050 g., 0.9990 Silver 0.9990 oz. ASW, 38.6 mm. **Ruler:** Elizabeth II **Subject:** Don Everhart II **Obv:** Head right **Rev:** AN-225 Mriya

Date	Mintage	F	VF	XF	Unc	BU
2003 Proof	—	Value: 45.00				

KM# 90 25 DOLLARS
31.1050 g., 0.9990 Silver 0.9990 oz. ASW, 38.61 mm. **Ruler:** Elizabeth II **Obv:** Head right **Rev:** Wright Brother's 1903 Flyer

Date	Mintage	F	VF	XF	Unc	BU
2003 Proof	—	Value: 45.00				

KM# 92 25 DOLLARS
31.1050 g., 0.9990 Silver 0.9990 oz. ASW, 38.61 mm. **Ruler:** Elizabeth II **Obv:** Head right **Rev:** Spitfire

Date	Mintage	F	VF	XF	Unc	BU
2003 Proof	—	Value: 45.00				

KM# 114 25 DOLLARS
31.1050 g., 0.9990 Silver 0.9990 oz. ASW, 38.61 mm. **Ruler:** Elizabeth II **Rev:** NC 14716 China Clipper

Date	Mintage	F	VF	XF	Unc	BU
2003 Proof	—	Value: 65.00				

KM# 115 25 DOLLARS
31.1000 g., 0.9990 Silver 0.9988 oz. ASW, 38.6 mm. **Ruler:** Elizabeth II **Rev:** Messerschmitt ME 262

Date	Mintage	F	VF	XF	Unc	BU
2003 Proof	—	Value: 45.00				

KM# 132 25 DOLLARS
31.1050 g., 0.9990 Silver 0.9990 oz. ASW, 38.61 mm. **Ruler:** Elizabeth II **Rev:** Sikorsky VS 30

Date	Mintage	F	VF	XF	Unc	BU
2003 Proof	—	Value: 42.50				

KM# 133 25 DOLLARS
31.1050 g., 0.9990 Silver 0.9990 oz. ASW, 38.61 mm. **Ruler:** Elizabeth II **Rev:** Concorde

Date	Mintage	F	VF	XF	Unc	BU
2003 Proof	—	Value: 42.50				

KM# 134 25 DOLLARS
31.1050 g., 0.9990 Silver 0.9990 oz. ASW, 38.61 mm. **Ruler:** Elizabeth II **Rev:** Lockheed Martin F-117 Nighthawk

Date	Mintage	F	VF	XF	Unc	BU
2003 Proof	—	Value: 42.50				

KM# 135 25 DOLLARS
31.1050 g., 0.9990 Silver 0.9990 oz. ASW, 38.61 mm. **Ruler:** Elizabeth II **Rev:** Bell X 1

Date	Mintage	F	VF	XF	Unc	BU
2003 Proof	—	Value: 42.50				

KM# 136 25 DOLLARS
31.1050 g., 0.9990 Silver 0.9990 oz. ASW, 38.61 mm. **Ruler:** Elizabeth II **Rev:** De Havilland Comet

Date	Mintage	F	VF	XF	Unc	BU
2003 Proof	—	Value: 42.50				

KM# 137 25 DOLLARS
31.1050 g., 0.9990 Silver 0.9990 oz. ASW, 38.61 mm. **Ruler:** Elizabeth II **Rev:** AV 8B Harrier II

Date	Mintage	F	VF	XF	Unc	BU
2003 Proof	—	Value: 42.50				

KM# 138 25 DOLLARS
31.1050 g., 0.9990 Silver 0.9990 oz. ASW, 38.61 mm. **Ruler:** Elizabeth II **Rev:** Curtiss Jenny

Date	Mintage	F	VF	XF	Unc	BU
2003 Proof	—	Value: 42.50				

KM# 139 25 DOLLARS
31.1050 g., 0.9990 Silver 0.9990 oz. ASW, 38.61 mm. **Ruler:** Elizabeth II **Rev:** Douglas DC 3

Date	Mintage	F	VF	XF	Unc	BU
2003 Proof	—	Value: 42.50				

KM# 93 25 DOLLARS
31.1050 g., 0.9990 Silver 0.9990 oz. ASW **Ruler:** Elizabeth II **Subject:** Trafalgar **Obv:** Head right **Rev:** H.M.S. Victory

Date	Mintage	F	VF	XF	Unc	BU
2005 Proof	—	Value: 45.00				

KM# 90.1 25 DOLLARS
31.1000 g., 0.9990 Silver partially gilt 0.9988 oz. ASW, 38.61 mm. **Ruler:** Elizabeth II **Rev:** Wright flier of 1903

Date	Mintage	F	VF	XF	Unc	BU
2005 Proof	—	Value: 75.00				

KM# 92.1 25 DOLLARS
31.1050 g., 0.9990 Silver partially gilt 0.9990 oz. ASW, 38.61 mm. **Ruler:** Elizabeth II **Rev:** Spitfire

Date	Mintage	F	VF	XF	Unc	BU
2005 Proof	—	Value: 55.00				

KM# 114.1 25 DOLLARS
31.1050 g., 0.9990 Silver partially gilt 0.9990 oz. ASW, 38.61 mm. **Ruler:** Elizabeth II **Rev:** NC 14716 China Clipper

Date	Mintage	F	VF	XF	Unc	BU
2005 Proof	—	Value: 55.00				

KM# 91.1 25 DOLLARS
31.1050 g., 0.9990 Silver partially plated 0.9990 oz. ASW, 38.61 mm. **Ruler:** Elizabeth II **Rev:** Antonov AN-225 Mrija

Date	Mintage	F	VF	XF	Unc	BU
2005 Proof	—	Value: 55.00				

KM# 115.1 25 DOLLARS
31.1050 g., 0.9990 Silver partially gilt 0.9990 oz. ASW, 38.61 mm. **Ruler:** Elizabeth II **Rev:** Messerschmitt ME 262

Date	Mintage	F	VF	XF	Unc	BU
2005 Proof	—	Value: 55.00				

KM# 132.1 25 DOLLARS
31.1050 g., 0.9990 Silver partially gilt 0.9990 oz. ASW, 38.61 mm. **Ruler:** Elizabeth II **Rev:** Sikorsky VS 300

Date	Mintage	F	VF	XF	Unc	BU
2005 Proof	—	Value: 55.00				

KM# 133.1 25 DOLLARS
31.1050 g., 0.9990 Silver partially gilt 0.9990 oz. ASW, 38.61 mm. **Ruler:** Elizabeth II **Rev:** Concorde

Date	Mintage	F	VF	XF	Unc	BU
2005 Proof	—	Value: 55.00				

KM# 134.1 25 DOLLARS
31.1050 g., 0.9990 Silver partially gilt 0.9990 oz. ASW, 38.61 mm. **Ruler:** Elizabeth II **Rev:** Lockheed Martin F-117 Nighthawk

Date	Mintage	F	VF	XF	Unc	BU
2005 Proof	—	Value: 55.00				

KM# 135.1 25 DOLLARS
31.1050 g., 0.9990 Silver Partially gilt 0.9990 oz. ASW, 38.61 mm. **Ruler:** Elizabeth II **Rev:** Bell X1

Date	Mintage	F	VF	XF	Unc	BU
2005 Proof	—	Value: 55.00				

KM# 136.1 25 DOLLARS
31.1050 g., 0.9990 Silver partially gilt 0.9990 oz. ASW, 38.61 mm. **Ruler:** Elizabeth II **Rev:** De Havilland Comet

Date	Mintage	F	VF	XF	Unc	BU
2005 Proof	—	Value: 55.00				

KM# 137.1 25 DOLLARS
31.1050 g., 0.9990 Silver partially gilt 0.9990 oz. ASW, 38.61 mm. **Ruler:** Elizabeth II **Rev:** AV 8B Harrier II

Date	Mintage	F	VF	XF	Unc	BU
2005 Proof	—	Value: 55.00				

KM# 138.1 25 DOLLARS
31.1050 g., 0.9990 Silver partially gilt 0.9990 oz. ASW, 38.61 mm. **Ruler:** Elizabeth II **Rev:** Curtiss Jenny

Date	Mintage	F	VF	XF	Unc	BU
2005 Proof	—	Value: 55.00				

KM# 139.1 25 DOLLARS
31.1050 g., 0.9990 Silver partially gilt 0.9990 oz. ASW, 38.61 mm. **Ruler:** Elizabeth II **Rev:** Douglas DC 3

Date	Mintage	F	VF	XF	Unc	BU
2005 Proof	—	Value: 55.00				

KM# 143 25 DOLLARS
31.1050 g., 0.9990 Silver 0.9990 oz. ASW, 38.61 mm. **Ruler:** Elizabeth II **Subject:** Triere

Date	Mintage	F	VF	XF	Unc	BU
2005 Proof	—	Value: 55.00				

KM# 144 25 DOLLARS
31.1050 g., 0.9990 Silver 0.9990 oz. ASW, 38.61 mm. **Ruler:** Elizabeth II **Subject:** H.M.S. Mary Rose

Date	Mintage	F	VF	XF	Unc	BU
2005 Proof	—	Value: 55.00				

KM# 145 25 DOLLARS
31.1050 g., 0.9990 Silver 0.9990 oz. ASW, 38.61 mm. **Ruler:** Elizabeth II **Subject:** U.S.S. Bonhomme Richard

Date	Mintage	F	VF	XF	Unc	BU
2005 Proof	—	Value: 55.00				

KM# 146 25 DOLLARS
31.1050 g., 0.9990 Silver 0.9990 oz. ASW, 38.61 mm. **Ruler:** Elizabeth II **Subject:** H.M.S. Dorsetshire

Date	Mintage	F	VF	XF	Unc	BU
2005 Proof	—	Value: 55.00				

KM# 95 25 DOLLARS
31.1050 g., 0.9990 Silver partially gilt 0.9990 oz. ASW, 38.6 mm. **Ruler:** Elizabeth II **Obv:** Head right, partially gilt **Rev:** Queen Elizabeth II and WWII Red Cross Nurse, gilt 80 above.

Date	Mintage	F	VF	XF	Unc	BU
2006 Proof	—	Value: 50.00				

KM# 87 25 DOLLARS
0.9250 Silver **Ruler:** Elizabeth II **Obv:** Crowned bust right **Obv. Legend:** ELIZABETH II - SOLOMON ISLANDS **Rev:** 3/4 length figures of Elizabeth and Prince Philip facing

Date	Mintage	F	VF	XF	Unc	BU
2006 Proof	—	Value: 50.00				

KM# 87a 25 DOLLARS
31.1050 g., 0.9990 Silver partially gilt 0.9990 oz. ASW **Ruler:** Elizabeth II **Obv:** Head right, partially gilt **Rev:** Wedding of Elizabeth II and Philip. Gothic window behind, gilt 80 above.

Date	Mintage	F	VF	XF	Unc	BU
2006 Proof	—	Value: 50.00				

KM# 147 25 DOLLARS
31.1050 g., 0.9990 Silver 0.9990 oz. ASW, 38.61 mm. **Ruler:** Elizabeth II **Subject:** Turtle boat

Date	Mintage	F	VF	XF	Unc	BU
2006 Proof	—	Value: 55.00				

KM# 148 25 DOLLARS
31.1050 g., 0.9990 Silver 0.9990 oz. ASW, 38.61 mm. **Ruler:** Elizabeth II **Subject:** Ville de Paris

Date	Mintage	F	VF	XF	Unc	BU
2006 Proof	—	Value: 55.00				

KM# 149 25 DOLLARS
31.1050 g., 0.9990 Silver 0.9990 oz. ASW, 38.61 mm. **Ruler:** Elizabeth II **Subject:** Admiral Graf Spree

Date	Mintage	F	VF	XF	Unc	BU
2006 Proof	—	Value: 55.00				

KM# 150 25 DOLLARS
31.1050 g., 0.9990 Silver 0.9990 oz. ASW, 38.61 mm. **Ruler:** Elizabeth II **Subject:** H.M.S. Dreadnought

Date	Mintage	F	VF	XF	Unc	BU
2006 Proof	—	Value: 55.00				

KM# 151 25 DOLLARS
31.1050 g., 0.9990 Silver 0.9990 oz. ASW, 38.61 mm. **Ruler:** Elizabeth II **Subject:** U.S.S. Hornet

Date	Mintage	F	VF	XF	Unc	BU
2006 Proof	—	Value: 55.00				

KM# 152 25 DOLLARS
31.1050 g., 0.9990 Silver 0.9990 oz. ASW, 38.61 mm. **Ruler:** Elizabeth II **Subject:** Yamato

Date	Mintage	F	VF	XF	Unc	BU
2006 Proof	—	Value: 55.00				

KM# 116 25 DOLLARS
28.2800 g., 0.9250 Silver 0.8410 oz. ASW, 38.6 mm. **Ruler:** Elizabeth II **Rev:** Press clippings, soldier standing over field cross

Date	Mintage	F	VF	XF	Unc	BU
2008 Proof	—	Value: 50.00				

KM# 117 25 DOLLARS
28.2800 g., 0.9250 Silver 0.8410 oz. ASW, 38.6 mm. **Ruler:** Elizabeth II **Rev:** Battlefield

Date	Mintage	F	VF	XF	Unc	BU
2008 Proof	—	Value: 50.00				

KM# 118 25 DOLLARS
28.2800 g., 0.9250 Silver 0.8410 oz. ASW, 38.6 mm. **Ruler:** Elizabeth II **Rev:** Soldier overlooking beach

Date	Mintage	F	VF	XF	Unc	BU
2008 Proof	—	Value: 50.00				

KM# 155 25 DOLLARS
28.2800 g., 0.9250 Silver 0.8410 oz. ASW, 38.61 mm. **Ruler:** Elizabeth II **Subject:** Cannons

Date	Mintage	F	VF	XF	Unc	BU
2008 Proof	—	Value: 55.00				

KM# 156 25 DOLLARS
28.2800 g., 0.9250 Silver 0.8410 oz. ASW, 38.61 mm. **Ruler:** Elizabeth II **Subject:** Eastern Front

Date	Mintage	F	VF	XF	Unc	BU
2008 Proof	—	Value: 55.00				

KM# 157 25 DOLLARS
28.2800 g., 0.9250 Silver 0.8410 oz. ASW, 38.61 mm. **Ruler:** Elizabeth II **Subject:** Truce

Date	Mintage	F	VF	XF	Unc	BU
2008 Proof	—	Value: 55.00				

KM# 158 50 DOLLARS
155.5000 g., 0.9250 Silver 4.6243 oz. ASW, 65 mm. **Ruler:** Elizabeth II **Rev:** Poppy on war novel

Date	Mintage	F	VF	XF	Unc	BU
2008 Proof	Est. 150	Value: 225				

PROOF SETS

KM#	Date	Mintage	Identification	Issue Price	Mkt Val
PS13	2012 (5)	1,500	KM#171a-175a	—	—

SOMALIA

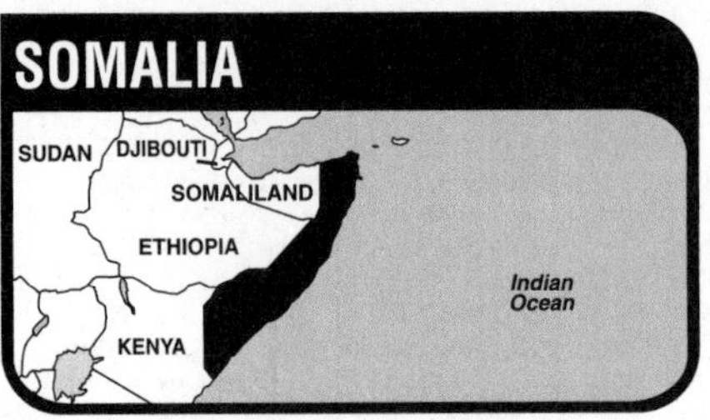

The Somali Republic consists of the former Italian Somaliland and is located on the coast of the eastern projection of the African continent commonly referred to as the "Horn". It has an area of 178,201 sq. mi. (461,657 sq. km.) and a population of *8.2 million. Capital: Mogadishu. The economy is pastoral and agricultural. Livestock, bananas and hides are exported.

The Northern Somali National Movement (SNM) declared a secession of the northwestern Somaliland Republic on May 17, 1991, which is not recognized by the Somali Democratic Republic.

TITLE
Al-Jumhuriya(t)as - Somaliya(t)

REPUBLIC OF SOMALIA

STANDARD COINAGE

KM# 45 5 SHILLING / SCELLINI
1.2900 g., Aluminum, 21 mm. **Series:** F.A.O. **Obv:** Crowned arms with supporters **Rev:** Elephant **Edge:** Plain

Date	Mintage	F	VF	XF	Unc	BU
2002	—	—	—	—	1.50	1.75

KM# 159 10 SHILLINGS
25.1500 g., Copper-Nickel, 38.66 mm. **Series:** Marine Life Protection **Obv:** National arms **Rev:** Two fish multicolor **Edge:** Reeded

Date	Mintage	F	VF	XF	Unc	BU
2003 Proof	—	Value: 10.00				

KM# 46 10 SHILLINGS / SCELLINI
1.2900 g., Aluminum, 21.9 mm. **Series:** F.A.O. **Obv:** Crowned arms with supporters **Rev:** Camel **Edge:** Plain

Date	Mintage	F	VF	XF	Unc	BU
2002	—	—	—	—	2.00	2.25

KM# 175 20 SHILLINGS
0.6200 g., 0.9990 Gold 0.0199 oz. AGW **Obv:** Arms **Rev:** Mom and baby elephant

Date	Mintage	F	VF	XF	Unc	BU
2007 Proof	—	Value: 50.00				

KM# 166 25 SHILLINGS
Silver **Obv:** Arms **Rev:** Mozart, multicolor

Date	Mintage	F	VF	XF	Unc	BU
2001	—	—	—	—	—	40.00

KM# 155 25 SHILLINGS
28.1000 g., Copper-Nickel, 38.73 mm. **Subject:** The Life of Pope John-Paul II **Obv:** National arms **Obv. Legend:** SOMALI REPUBLIC **Rev:** Pope John-Paul II in window at the Vatican **Edge:** Plain

Date	Mintage	F	VF	XF	Unc	BU
2004	—	—	—	—	6.00	7.00

KM# 156 25 SHILLINGS
28.1000 g., Copper-Nickel, 38.73 mm. **Subject:** Life of Pope John Paul II **Obv:** National arms **Obv. Legend:** SOMALI REPUBLIC **Rev:** Pope traveling in special vehicle **Edge:** Plain

Date	Mintage	F	VF	XF	Unc	BU
2004	—	—	—	—	6.00	7.00

KM# 157 25 SHILLINGS
28.1000 g., Copper-Nickel, 38.73 mm. **Subject:** The Life of Pope John-Paul II **Obv:** National arms **Obv. Legend:** SOMALI REPUBLIC **Rev:** Pope blessing Mother Teresa **Edge:** Plain

Date	Mintage	F	VF	XF	Unc	BU
2004	—	—	—	—	6.00	7.00

KM# 164 25 SHILLINGS
25.8000 g., Copper-Nickel, 38.77 mm. **Obv:** National arms **Obv. Legend:** SOMALI REPUBLIC **Rev:** Black rhinoceros walking left **Edge:** Reeded

Date	Mintage	F	VF	XF	Unc	BU
2006	—	—	—	—	12.00	14.00

KM# 165 25 SHILLINGS
25.8000 g., Copper-Nickel, 38.77 mm. **Obv:** National arms **Rev:** Red Kite perched on branch **Edge:** Reeded

Date	Mintage	F	VF	XF	Unc	BU
2006	—	—	—	—	12.00	14.00

KM# 103 25 SHILLINGS / SCELLINI
4.3700 g., Brass, 21.8 mm. **Subject:** Soccer **Obv:** Crowned arms with supporters **Rev:** Soccer player **Edge:** Plain

Date	Mintage	F	VF	XF	Unc	BU
2001	—	—	—	—	1.25	1.50

KM# 111 50 SHILLINGS
3.9000 g., Nickel Clad Steel, 21.9 mm. **Obv:** Crowned arms with supporters **Rev:** Mandrill **Edge:** Plain

Date	Mintage	F	VF	XF	Unc	BU
2002	—	—	—	—	0.85	1.25

KM# 161 50 SHILLINGS
1.2000 g., 0.9990 Gold 0.0385 oz. AGW, 13.88 mm. **Subject:** Gold of the Pharaohs **Obv:** National arms **Obv. Legend:** SOMALI REPUBLIC **Rev:** King Tutankhaman's death mask **Edge:** Reeded

Date	Mintage	F	VF	XF	Unc	BU
2002 Proof	—	Value: 80.00				

KM# 109 100 SHILLINGS
10.5000 g., 0.9990 Silver 0.3372 oz. ASW, 30.1 mm. **Subject:** Soccer **Obv:** Crowned arms with supporters **Rev:** Multicolor soccer player and Brandenburg Gate **Edge:** Reeded

Date	Mintage	F	VF	XF	Unc	BU
2001 Proof	—	Value: 25.00				

KM# 112 100 SHILLINGS
3.5400 g., Brass, 18.8 mm. **Obv:** Crowned arms with supporters above value **Rev:** Bust with headdress facing **Edge:** Plain

Date	Mintage	F	VF	XF	Unc	BU
2002	—	—	—	—	1.50	2.50

KM# 176 200 SHILLINGS
0.6200 g., 0.9990 Gold 0.0199 oz. AGW, 13.90 mm. **Obv:** Arms **Rev:** Elephant head left

Date	Mintage	F	VF	XF	Unc	BU
2005 Proof	—	Value: 60.00				

KM# 168 250 SHILLINGS
23.0000 g., 0.9250 Silver 0.6840 oz. ASW **Obv:** Arms **Rev:** Victoria, gothic crown

Date	Mintage	F	VF	XF	Unc	BU
2001 Proof	—	Value: 45.00				

KM# 169 250 SHILLINGS
23.0000 g., 0.9250 Silver 0.6840 oz. ASW **Obv:** Arms **Rev:** Soccer player, Brazil

Date	Mintage	F	VF	XF	Unc	BU
2002	—	—	—	—	—	45.00

KM# 158 250 SHILLINGS
20.0500 g., Silver, 38.59 mm. **Obv:** National arms **Obv. Legend:** SOMALI REPUBLIC **Rev:** Laureate bust of Julius Caesar 3/4 left **Edge:** Reeded

Date	Mintage	F	VF	XF	Unc	BU
2002 Proof	—	Value: 32.00				

KM# 162 250 SHILLINGS
1.2700 g., 0.9990 Gold 0.0408 oz. AGW, 13.90 mm. **Obv:** National arms **Obv. Legend:** SOMALI REPUBLIC **Rev:** Bust of Hans Rühmann facing **Edge:** Reeded

Date	Mintage	F	VF	XF	Unc	BU
2002 Proof	—	Value: 85.00				

KM# 110 250 SHILLINGS
31.1050 g., 0.9990 Silver 0.9990 oz. ASW, 40 mm. **Subject:** Queen of Sheba **Obv:** Crowned arms with supporters **Rev:** Crowned bust 1/4 right **Edge:** Reeded

Date	Mintage	F	VF	XF	Unc	BU
2002	—	—	—	—	35.00	40.00

KM# 160 250 SHILLINGS
20.5000 g., Silver, 38.56 mm. **Subject:** Wembley Goal - England 1966 **Obv:** National arms **Obv. Legend:** SOMALI REPUBLIC **Rev:** 3 soccer players at goal **Edge:** Reeded

Date	Mintage	F	VF	XF	Unc	BU
2003 Proof	—	Value: 28.00				

KM# 121 250 SHILLINGS
20.1200 g., Silver Plated Base Metal, 38.5 mm. **Obv:** Crowned arms with supporters **Rev:** Multicolor Pope John Paul II and mountains **Edge:** Reeded

Date	Mintage	F	VF	XF	Unc	BU
2005 Proof	—	Value: 16.50				

KM# 123 250 SHILLINGS
20.1200 g., Silver Plated Base Metal, 38.5 mm. **Obv:** Crowned arms with supporters **Rev:** Multicolor Pope John Paul II kissing bible **Edge:** Reeded

Date	Mintage	F	VF	XF	Unc	BU
2005 Proof	—	Value: 16.50				

KM# 125 250 SHILLINGS
20.1200 g., Silver Plated Base Metal, 38.5 mm. **Obv:** Crowned arms with supporters **Rev:** Multicolor Pope John Paul II with flowers **Edge:** Reeded

Date	Mintage	F	VF	XF	Unc	BU
2005 Proof	—	Value: 16.50				

KM# 127 250 SHILLINGS
20.1200 g., Silver Plated Base Metal, 38.5 mm. **Obv:** Crowned arms with supporters **Rev:** Multicolor Pope John Paul II saying mass **Edge:** Reeded

Date	Mintage	F	VF	XF	Unc	BU
2005 Proof	—	Value: 16.50				

KM# 129 250 SHILLINGS
20.1200 g., Silver Plated Base Metal, 38.5 mm. **Obv:** Crowned arms with supporters **Rev:** Multicolor Pope John Paul II with cardinals **Edge:** Reeded

Date	Mintage	F	VF	XF	Unc	BU
2005 Proof	—	Value: 16.50				

KM# 131 250 SHILLINGS
20.1200 g., Silver Plated Base Metal, 38.5 mm. **Obv:** Crowned arms with supporters **Rev:** Pope John Paul II with red vestments **Edge:** Reeded

Date	Mintage	F	VF	XF	Unc	BU
2005 Proof	—	Value: 16.50				

KM# 133 250 SHILLINGS
20.1200 g., Silver Plated Base Metal, 38.5 mm. **Obv:** Crowned arms with supporters **Rev:** Pope John Paul II in white with skull cap **Edge:** Reeded

Date	Mintage	F	VF	XF	Unc	BU
2005 Proof	—	Value: 16.50				

KM# 135 250 SHILLINGS
20.1200 g., Silver Plated Base Metal, 38.5 mm. **Obv:** Crowned arms with supporters **Rev:** Multicolor Pope John Paul II leaning head on staff **Edge:** Reeded

Date	Mintage	F	VF	XF	Unc	BU
2005 Proof	—	Value: 16.50				

KM# 137 250 SHILLINGS
20.1200 g., Silver Plated Base Metal, 38.5 mm. **Obv:** Crowned arms with supporters **Rev:** Multicolor Pope John Paul II with staff facing left **Edge:** Reeded

Date	Mintage	F	VF	XF	Unc	BU
2005 Proof	—	Value: 16.50				

KM# 139 250 SHILLINGS
20.1200 g., Silver Plated Base Metal, 38.5 mm. **Obv:** Crowned arms with supporters **Rev:** Multicolor Pope John Paul II with staff facing half right **Edge:** Reeded

Date	Mintage	F	VF	XF	Unc	BU
2005 Proof	—	Value: 16.50				

KM# 143 250 SHILLINGS
Copper-Nickel **Obv:** Crowned shield **Obv. Legend:** SOMALI REPUBLIC / 250 SHILLINGS **Rev:** Color applique, German Shephard **Rev. Legend:** YEAR OF THE DOG / 2006 **Edge:** Reeded

Date	Mintage	F	VF	XF	Unc	BU
2006	—	—	—	—	—	14.50

KM# 144 250 SHILLINGS
Copper-Nickel **Obv:** Crowned shield **Obv. Legend:** SOMALI REPUBLIC / 250 SHILLINGS **Rev:** Color applique, Dachsund **Rev. Legend:** YEAR OF THE DOG / 2006 **Edge:** Reeded

Date	Mintage	F	VF	XF	Unc	BU
2006	—	—	—	—	—	14.50

KM# 145 250 SHILLINGS
Copper-Nickel **Obv:** Crowned shield **Obv. Legend:** SOMALI REPUBLIC / 250 SHILLINGS **Rev:** Color applique, Yorkshire Terrier **Rev. Legend:** YEAR OF THE DOG / 2006 **Edge:** Reeded

Date	Mintage	F	VF	XF	Unc	BU
2006	—	—	—	—	—	14.50

KM# 146 250 SHILLINGS
Copper-Nickel **Obv:** Crowned shield **Obv. Legend:** SOMALI REPUBLIC / 250 SHILLINGS **Rev:** Color applique, Scottie (small white) **Rev. Legend:** YEAR OF THE DOG / 2006 **Edge:** Reeded

Date	Mintage	F	VF	XF	Unc	BU
2006	—	—	—	—	—	14.50

KM# 147 250 SHILLINGS

Copper-Nickel **Obv:** Crowned shield **Obv. Legend:** SOMALI REPUBLIC / 250 SHILLINGS **Rev:** Color applique, Wire-haired Terrier **Rev. Legend:** YEAR OF THE DOG / 2006 **Edge:** Reeded

Date	Mintage	F	VF	XF	Unc	BU
2006	—	—	—	—	—	14.50

KM# 148 250 SHILLINGS

Copper-Nickel **Obv:** Crowned shield **Obv. Legend:** SOMALI REPUBLIC / 250 SHILLINGS **Rev:** Color applique, Bulldog **Rev. Legend:** YEAR OF THE DOG / 2006 **Edge:** Reeded

Date	Mintage	F	VF	XF	Unc	BU
2006	—	—	—	—	—	14.50

KM# 149 250 SHILLINGS

Copper-Nickel **Obv:** Crowned shield **Obv. Legend:** SOMALI REPUBLIC / 250 SHILLINGS **Rev:** Color applique, Golden Retriever **Rev. Legend:** YEAR OF THE DOG **Edge:** Reeded

Date	Mintage	F	VF	XF	Unc	BU
2006	—	—	—	—	—	14.50

KM# 150 250 SHILLINGS

Copper-Nickel **Obv:** Crowned shield **Obv. Legend:** SOMALI REPUBLIC / 250 SHILLINGS **Rev:** Color applique, St. Bernard **Rev. Legend:** YEAR OF THE DOG / 2006 **Edge:** Reeded

Date	Mintage	F	VF	XF	Unc	BU
2006	—	—	—	—	—	14.50

KM# 151 250 SHILLINGS

Copper-Nickel **Obv:** Crowned shield **Obv. Legend:** SOMALI REPUBLIC / 250 SHILLINGS **Rev:** Color applique, Rottweiler **Rev. Legend:** YEAR OF THE DOG / 2006 **Edge:** Reeded

Date	Mintage	F	VF	XF	Unc	BU
2006	—	—	—	—	—	14.50

KM# 152 250 SHILLINGS

Copper-Nickel **Obv:** Crowned shield **Obv. Legend:** SOMALI REPUBLIC / 250 SHILLINGS **Rev:** Color applique, Basset Hound **Rev. Legend:** YEAR OF THE DOG / 2006 **Edge:** Reeded

Date	Mintage	F	VF	XF	Unc	BU
2006	—	—	—	—	—	14.50

KM# 153 250 SHILLINGS

Copper-Nickel **Obv:** Crowned shield **Obv. Legend:** SOMALI REPUBLIC / 250 SHILLINGS **Rev:** Color applique, Sheep Dog **Rev. Legend:** YEAR OF THE DOG / 2006 **Edge:** Reeded

Date	Mintage	F	VF	XF	Unc	BU
2006	—	—	—	—	—	14.50

KM# 154 250 SHILLINGS

Copper-Nickel **Obv:** Crowned shield **Obv. Legend:** SOMALI REPUBLIC / 250 SHILLINGS **Rev:** Color applique, Cocker Spaniel **Rev. Legend:** YEAR OF THE DOG / 2006 **Edge:** Reeded

Date	Mintage	F	VF	XF	Unc	BU
2006	—	—	—	—	—	14.50

KM# 170 250 SHILLINGS

Copper-Nickel Gilt, 38 mm. **Obv:** Arms in cartouche **Rev:** Gold mask of Tutankahamun, enameled

Date	Mintage	F	VF	XF	Unc	BU
2008	—	—	—	—	—	17.50

KM# 171 250 SHILLINGS

Copper-Nickel Gilt, 38 mm. **Obv:** Arms within cartouche **Rev:** Udjat eye, enameled

Date	Mintage	F	VF	XF	Unc	BU
2008	—	—	—	—	—	40.00

KM# 172 250 SHILLINGS

Copper-Nickel **Obv:** Arms within cartouche **Rev:** Statue of Ptah, enameled

Date	Mintage	F	VF	XF	Unc	BU
2008	—	—	—	—	—	20.00

KM# 173 250 SHILLINGS

Copper-Nickel Gilt, 38 mm. **Obv:** Arms in cartouche **Rev:** Jcarab Pectoral necklace, enameled

Date	Mintage	F	VF	XF	Unc	BU
2008	—	—	—	—	—	20.00

KM# 174 250 SHILLINGS

Copper-Nickel Gilt, 38 mm. **Obv:** Arms within cartouche **Rev:** Statue of Horus the Elder

Date	Mintage	F	VF	XF	Unc	BU
2008	—	—	—	—	—	20.00

KM# 122 500 SHILLINGS

18.8400 g., Silver Plated Base Metal, 34.1 mm. **Obv:** Crowned arms with supporters **Rev:** Multicolor Pope John Paul II and mountains **Edge:** Plain **Shape:** Square with round corners

Date	Mintage	F	VF	XF	Unc	BU
2005 Proof	—	Value: 16.50				

KM# 124 500 SHILLINGS

18.8400 g., Silver Plated Base Metal, 34.1 mm. **Obv:** Crowned arms with supporters **Rev:** Multicolor Pope John Paul II kissing bible **Edge:** Plain **Shape:** Square with round corners

Date	Mintage	F	VF	XF	Unc	BU
2005 Proof	—	Value: 16.50				

KM# 126 500 SHILLINGS

18.8400 g., Silver Plated Base Metal, 34.1 mm. **Obv:** Crowned arms with supporters **Rev:** Multicolor Pope John Paul II with flowers **Edge:** Plain **Shape:** Square with round corners

Date	Mintage	F	VF	XF	Unc	BU
2005 Proof	—	Value: 20.00				

KM# 128 500 SHILLINGS
18.1400 g., Silver Plated Base Metal, 34.1 mm. **Obv:** Crowned arms with supporters **Rev:** Multicolor Pope John Paul II saying mass **Edge:** Plain **Shape:** Square with round corners

Date	Mintage	F	VF	XF	Unc	BU
2005 Proof	—	Value: 16.50				

KM# 130 500 SHILLINGS
18.8400 g., Silver Plated Base Metal, 34.1 mm. **Obv:** Crowned arms with supporters **Rev:** Multicolor Pope John Paul II with cardinals **Edge:** Plain **Shape:** Square with round corners

Date	Mintage	F	VF	XF	Unc	BU
2005 Proof	—	Value: 16.50				

KM# 132 500 SHILLINGS
18.8400 g., Silver Plated Base Metal, 34.1 mm. **Obv:** Crowned arms with supporters **Rev:** Pope John Paul II with red vestments **Edge:** Plain **Shape:** Square with round corners

Date	Mintage	F	VF	XF	Unc	BU
2005 Proof	—	Value: 16.50				

KM# 134 500 SHILLINGS
18.8400 g., Silver Plated Base Metal, 34.1 mm. **Obv:** Crowned arms with supporters **Rev:** Pope John Paul II in white with skull cap **Edge:** Plain **Shape:** Square with round corners

Date	Mintage	F	VF	XF	Unc	BU
2005 Proof	—	Value: 16.50				

KM# 136 500 SHILLINGS
18.8400 g., Silver Plated Base Metal, 34.1 mm. **Obv:** Crowned arms with supporters **Rev:** Multicolor Pope John Paul II leaning head on staff **Edge:** Plain **Shape:** Square with round corners

Date	Mintage	F	VF	XF	Unc	BU
2005 Proof	—	Value: 16.50				

KM# 138 500 SHILLINGS
18.8400 g., Silver Plated Base Metal, 34.1 mm. **Obv:** Crowned arms with supporters **Rev:** Multicolor Pope John Paul II with staff facing left **Edge:** Plain **Shape:** Square with round corners

Date	Mintage	F	VF	XF	Unc	BU
2005 Proof	—	Value: 16.50				

KM# 140 500 SHILLINGS
18.8400 g., Silver Plated Base Metal, 34.1 mm. **Obv:** Crowned arms with supporters **Rev:** Multicolor Pope John Paul II with staff facing half right **Edge:** Plain **Shape:** Square with round corners

Date	Mintage	F	VF	XF	Unc	BU
2005 Proof	—	Value: 16.50				

KM# 181 1000 SHILLINGS
31.1050 g., 0.9990 Silver 0.9990 oz. ASW, 39 mm. **Obv:** Arms **Rev:** Heard of six elephants, multicolor

Date	Mintage	F	VF	XF	Unc	BU
2008	—	—	—	—	—	45.00

BULLION COINAGE

KM# 200 20 SHILLINGS
0.6200 g., 0.9990 Gold 0.0199 oz. AGW, 11 mm. **Rev:** Mother and baby elephant

Date	Mintage	F	VF	XF	Unc	BU
2007 Proof	20,000	Value: 50.00				

KM# 208 20 SHILLINGS
0.6200 g., 0.9990 Gold 0.0199 oz. AGW

Date	Mintage	F	VF	XF	Unc	BU
2008 Proof	20,000	Value: 50.00				

KM# 217 20 SHILLINGS
0.6200 g., 0.9990 Gold 0.0199 oz. AGW, 11 mm. **Rev:** Elephant advancing right, sunrise

Date	Mintage	F	VF	XF	Unc	BU
2009 Proof	20,000	Value: 50.00				

KM# 226 20 SHILLINGS
0.6200 g., 0.9990 Gold 0.0199 oz. AGW, 11 mm. **Rev:** Elephant advacning left, sunrise

Date	Mintage	F	VF	XF	Unc	BU
2010 Proof	20,000	Value: 50.00				

KM# 236 20 SHILLINGS
0.6200 g., 0.9990 Gold 0.0199 oz. AGW, 11 mm. **Rev:** Mother and baby elephant walking left, sun high up

Date	Mintage	F	VF	XF	Unc	BU
2011 Proof	20,000	Value: 50.00				

KM# 177 25 SHILLINGS
7.7800 g., 0.9990 Silver 0.2499 oz. ASW

Date	Mintage	F	VF	XF	Unc	BU
2007 Proof	2,000	Value: 15.00				

KM# 205 25 SHILLINGS
7.7800 g., 0.9990 Silver 0.2499 oz. ASW, 26 mm. **Rev:** Heard of six elephants

Date	Mintage	F	VF	XF	Unc	BU
2008 Proof	2,000	Value: 15.00				

KM# 214 25 SHILLINGS
7.7800 g., 0.9990 Silver 0.2499 oz. ASW, 26 mm. **Rev:** Elephant advancing right, sunrise

Date	Mintage	F	VF	XF	Unc	BU
2009 Proof	2,000	Value: 15.00				

KM# 223 25 SHILLINGS
7.7800 g., 0.9990 Silver 0.2499 oz. ASW, 26 mm. **Rev:** Elephant advacning left, sunrise

Date	Mintage	F	VF	XF	Unc	BU
2010 Proof	2,000	Value: 15.00				

KM# 232 25 SHILLINGS
7.7800 g., 0.9990 Silver 0.2499 oz. ASW, 26 mm. **Rev:** Mother and baby elephant walking left, sun high up

Date	Mintage	F	VF	XF	Unc	BU
2011	2,000	Value: 15.00				

KM# 178 50 SHILLINGS
15.5500 g., 0.9990 Silver 0.4994 oz. ASW, 32 mm.

Date	Mintage	F	VF	XF	Unc	BU
2007 Proof	2,000	Value: 30.00				

KM# 206 50 SHILLINGS
15.5500 g., 0.9990 Silver 0.4994 oz. ASW, 32 mm. **Rev:** Heard of six elephants

Date	Mintage	F	VF	XF	Unc	BU
2008 Proof	—	Value: 30.00				

KM# 209 50 SHILLINGS
1.2400 g., 0.9990 Gold 0.0398 oz. AGW, 13.92 mm. **Rev:** Heard of six elephants

Date	Mintage	F	VF	XF	Unc	BU
2008 Proof	10,000	Value: 100				

KM# 215 50 SHILLINGS
15.5500 g., 0.9990 Silver 0.4994 oz. ASW, 32 mm. **Rev:** Elephant advancing right, sunrise

Date	Mintage	F	VF	XF	Unc	BU
2009 Proof	2,000	Value: 30.00				

KM# 218 50 SHILLINGS
1.2400 g., 0.9990 Gold 0.0398 oz. AGW, 13.92 mm. **Rev:** Elephant advancing right, sunrise

Date	Mintage	F	VF	XF	Unc	BU
2009 Proof	10,000	Value: 100				

KM# 224 50 SHILLINGS
15.5500 g., 0.9990 Silver 0.4994 oz. ASW, 32 mm. **Rev:** Elephant advacning left, sunrise

Date	Mintage	F	VF	XF	Unc	BU
2010 Proof	2,000	Value: 30.00				

KM# 227 50 SHILLINGS
1.2400 g., 0.9990 Gold 0.0398 oz. AGW, 13.92 mm. **Rev:** Elephant advacning left, sunrise

Date	Mintage	F	VF	XF	Unc	BU
2010 Proof	10,000	Value: 100				

KM# 233 50 SHILLINGS
15.5500 g., 0.9990 Silver 0.4994 oz. ASW, 32 mm. **Rev:** Mother and baby elephant walking left, sun high up

Date	Mintage	F	VF	XF	Unc	BU
2011 Proof	2,000	Value: 30.00				

KM# 237 50 SHILLINGS
1.2400 g., 0.9990 Gold 0.0398 oz. AGW, 13.92 mm. **Rev:** Mother and baby elephant walking left, sun high up

Date	Mintage	F	VF	XF	Unc	BU
2011 Proof	10,000	Value: 100				

KM# 182 100 SHILLINGS
31.1050 g., 0.9990 Silver 0.9990 oz. ASW, 39 mm. **Obv:** Arms **Rev:** Mom and baby elephant

Date	Mintage	F	VF	XF	Unc	BU
2007	20,000	—	—	—	—	45.00
2007 Proof	5,000	Value: 55.00				

KM# 182a 100 SHILLINGS
31.1050 g., 0.9990 Silver partially gilt 0.9990 oz. ASW, 39 mm. **Rev:** Mother and baby elephant, partially gilt

Date	Mintage	F	VF	XF	Unc	BU
2007	3,000	—	—	—	—	50.00

KM# 180 100 SHILLINGS
31.1050 g., 0.9990 Silver 0.9990 oz. ASW, 39 mm. **Rev:** Mother and baby elephant, colored

Date	Mintage	F	VF	XF	Unc	BU
2007	5,000	—	—	—	—	50.00

KM# 203 100 SHILLINGS
31.1050 g., 0.9990 Silver 0.9990 oz. ASW, 39 mm. **Rev:** Heard of six elephants

Date	Mintage	F	VF	XF	Unc	BU
2008	20,000	—	—	—	—	35.00
2008 Proof	5,000	Value: 55.00				

KM# 203a 100 SHILLINGS
31.1050 g., 0.9990 Silver partially gilt 0.9990 oz. ASW, 39 mm. **Obv:** Arms **Rev:** Heard of six elephants

Date	Mintage	F	VF	XF	Unc	BU
2008	5,000	—	—	—	—	35.00

KM# 204 100 SHILLINGS
31.1050 g., 0.9990 Silver 0.9990 oz. ASW, 39 mm. **Rev:** Heard of six elephants, multicolored

Date	Mintage	F	VF	XF	Unc	BU
2008	5,000	—	—	—	—	50.00

KM# 212 100 SHILLINGS
31.1050 g., 0.9990 Silver 0.9990 oz. ASW, 39 mm. **Rev:** Elephant advancing right, sunrise

Date	Mintage	F	VF	XF	Unc	BU
2009	—	—	—	—	—	50.00
2009 Proof	5,000	Value: 55.00				

KM# 212a 100 SHILLINGS
31.1050 g., 0.9990 Silver partially gilt 0.9990 oz. ASW

Date	Mintage	F	VF	XF	Unc	BU
2009	5,000	—	—	—	—	55.00

KM# 213 100 SHILLINGS
31.1050 g., 0.9990 Silver 0.9990 oz. ASW, 39 mm. **Rev:** Elephant advancing right, sunrise, multicolor

Date	Mintage	F	VF	XF	Unc	BU
2009	5,000	—	—	—	—	55.00

KM# 221a 100 SHILLINGS
31.1050 g., 0.9990 Silver partially gilt 0.9990 oz. ASW

Date	Mintage	F	VF	XF	Unc	BU
2010	5,000	—	—	—	—	55.00

KM# 221 100 SHILLINGS
31.1050 g., 0.9990 Silver 0.9990 oz. ASW, 39 mm. **Rev:** Elephant advacning left, sunrise

Date	Mintage	F	VF	XF	Unc	BU
2010	—	—	—	—	—	50.00
2010 Proof	5,000	Value: 55.00				

KM# 222 100 SHILLINGS
31.1050 g., 0.9990 Silver 0.9990 oz. ASW, 39 mm. **Rev:** Elephant advacning left, sunrise, multicolor

Date	Mintage	F	VF	XF	Unc	BU
2010	5,000	—	—	—	—	55.00

KM# 230 100 SHILLINGS
31.1050 g., 0.9990 Silver 0.9990 oz. ASW, 39 mm. **Rev:** Mother and baby elephant walking left, sun high up

Date	Mintage	F	VF	XF	Unc	BU
2011	—	—	—	—	—	50.00
2011 Proof	5,000	Value: 55.00				

KM# 230a 100 SHILLINGS
31.1050 g., 0.9990 Silver partially gilt 0.9990 oz. ASW

Date	Mintage	F	VF	XF	Unc	BU
2011	5,000	—	—	—	—	55.00

KM# 231 100 SHILLINGS
31.1050 g., 0.9990 Silver 0.9990 oz. ASW, 39 mm. **Rev:** Mother and baby elephant walking left, sun high up, multicolor

Date	Mintage	F	VF	XF	Unc	BU
2011	5,000	—	—	—	—	55.00

KM# 188 200 SHILLINGS
0.6200 g., 0.9990 Gold 0.0199 oz. AGW

Date	Mintage	F	VF	XF	Unc	BU
2004 Proof	—	Value: 45.00				

KM# 194 200 SHILLINGS
0.6200 g., 0.9990 Gold 0.0199 oz. AGW

Date	Mintage	F	VF	XF	Unc	BU
2005 Proof	20,000	Value: 45.00				

KM# 179 200 SHILLINGS
62.2000 g., 0.9990 Silver 1.9977 oz. ASW, 50 mm.

Date	Mintage	F	VF	XF	Unc	BU
2007 Proof	—	Value: 100				

KM# 207 200 SHILLINGS
62.2000 g., 0.9990 Silver 1.9977 oz. ASW, 50 mm. **Rev:** Heard of six elephants

Date	Mintage	F	VF	XF	Unc	BU
2008 Proof	2,000	Value: 100				

KM# 216 200 SHILLINGS
62.2000 g., 0.9990 Silver 1.9977 oz. ASW, 50 mm. **Rev:** Elephant advancing right, sunrise

Date	Mintage	F	VF	XF	Unc	BU
2009	2,000	Value: 100				

KM# 225 200 SHILLINGS
62.2000 g., 0.9990 Silver 1.9977 oz. ASW, 50 mm. **Rev:** Elephant advacning left, sunrise

Date	Mintage	F	VF	XF	Unc	BU
2010 Proof	2,000	Value: 100				

KM# 234 200 SHILLINGS
62.2000 g., 0.9990 Silver 1.9977 oz. ASW, 50 mm. **Rev:** Mother and baby elephant walking left, sun high up

Date	Mintage	F	VF	XF	Unc	BU
2011 Proof	2,000	Value: 100				

KM# 185 250 SHILLINGS
7.7800 g., 0.9990 Silver 0.2499 oz. ASW

Date	Mintage	F	VF	XF	Unc	BU
2004 Proof	2,000	Value: 15.00				

KM# 191 250 SHILLINGS
7.7800 g., 0.9990 Silver 0.2499 oz. ASW

Date	Mintage	F	VF	XF	Unc	BU
2005 Proof	2,000	Value: 15.00				

KM# 197 250 SHILLINGS
7.7800 g., 0.9990 Silver 0.2499 oz. ASW

Date	Mintage	F	VF	XF	Unc	BU
2006 Proof	2,000	Value: 15.00				

KM# 186 500 SHILLINGS
15.5500 g., 0.9990 Silver 0.4994 oz. ASW, 32 mm. **Rev:** Elefant facing forward

Date	Mintage	F	VF	XF	Unc	BU
2004 Proof	2,000	Value: 30.00				

KM# 192 500 SHILLINGS
15.5500 g., 0.9990 Silver 0.4994 oz. ASW

Date	Mintage	F	VF	XF	Unc	BU
2005 Proof	—	Value: 30.00				

KM# 198 500 SHILLINGS
15.5500 g., 0.9990 Silver 0.4994 oz. ASW

Date	Mintage	F	VF	XF	Unc	BU
2006 Proof	2,000	Value: 30.00				

KM# 183 1000 SHILLINGS
31.1050 g., 0.9990 Silver 0.9990 oz. ASW

Date	Mintage	F	VF	XF	Unc	BU
2004	20,000	—	—	—	—	50.00
2004 Proof	5,000	Value: 55.00				

KM# 183a 1000 SHILLINGS
31.2700 g., 0.9990 Silver partially gilt 1.0043 oz. ASW, 38.54 mm. **Series:** African Wildlife **Obv:** National arms **Obv. Legend:** SOMALI REPUBLIC **Rev:** Elephant standing facing - gilt **Edge:** Reeded

Date	Mintage	F	VF	XF	Unc	BU
2004	—	—	—	—	—	55.00

KM# 184 1000 SHILLINGS
31.1050 g., 0.9990 Silver multicolored 0.9990 oz. ASW, 39 mm. **Rev:** Elephant facing forward, colored

Date	Mintage	F	VF	XF	Unc	BU
2004	5,000	—	—	—	—	55.00

KM# 189 1000 SHILLINGS
31.1050 g., 0.9990 Silver 0.9990 oz. ASW, 39 mm. **Rev:** Elephant profile left thrumpanting

Date	Mintage	F	VF	XF	Unc	BU
2005	20,000	—	—	—	—	50.00
2005 Proof	5,000	Value: 55.00				

KM# 189a 1000 SHILLINGS
31.1050 g., 0.9990 Silver partially gilt 0.9990 oz. ASW, 39 mm. **Rev:** Elephant profile left thrumpanting, partially gilt

Date	Mintage	F	VF	XF	Unc	BU
2005	3,000	—	—	—	—	55.00

KM# 190 1000 SHILLINGS
31.1050 g., 0.9990 Silver 0.9990 oz. ASW, 39 mm. **Obv:** Arms **Rev:** Elephant profile left thrumpanting, multicolor

Date	Mintage	F	VF	XF	Unc	BU
2005	5,000	—	—	—	—	45.00

KM# 195 1000 SHILLINGS
31.1050 g., 0.9990 Silver 0.9990 oz. ASW, 38 mm. **Obv:** Arms **Rev:** Elephant and mountain

Date	Mintage	F	VF	XF	Unc	BU
2006	20,000	—	—	—	—	45.00
2006 Proof	5,000	Value: 55.00				

KM# 195a 1000 SHILLINGS
31.1050 g., 0.9990 Silver partially gilt 0.9990 oz. ASW, 39 mm. **Rev:** Elephant, mountain, partially gilt

Date	Mintage	F	VF	XF	Unc	BU
2006	3,000	—	—	—	—	55.00

KM# 196 1000 SHILLINGS
31.1050 g., 0.9990 Silver 0.9990 oz. ASW, 39 mm. **Obv:** Arms **Rev:** Elephant, mountian in background. Multicolor

Date	Mintage	F	VF	XF	Unc	BU
2006	5,000	—	—	—	—	45.00

KM# 228 1000 SHILLINGS
31.1050 g., 0.9990 Gold 0.9990 oz. AGW, 38.6 mm. **Rev:** Elephant advacning left, sunrise

Date	Mintage	F	VF	XF	Unc	BU
2010	—	—	—	—	—	1,850

KM# 238 1000 SHILLINGS
31.1050 g., 0.9990 Gold 0.9990 oz. AGW, 38.6 mm. **Rev:** Mother and baby elephant walking left, sun high up

Date	Mintage	F	VF	XF	Unc	BU
2011	—	—	—	—	—	1,850

KM# 201 1500 SHILLINGS
155.5000 g., 0.9990 Gold 4.9942 oz. AGW, 65 mm. **Rev:** Mother and baby elephant

Date	Mintage	F	VF	XF	Unc	BU
2007 Proof	99	Value: 9,250				

KM# 210 1500 SHILLINGS
155.5000 g., 0.9990 Gold 4.9942 oz. AGW, 65 mm. **Rev:** Heard of six elephants

Date	Mintage	F	VF	XF	Unc	BU
2008 Proof	99	Value: 9,250				

KM# 219 1500 SHILLINGS
155.5000 g., 0.9990 Gold 4.9942 oz. AGW, 65 mm. **Rev:** Elephant advancing right, sunrise

Date	Mintage	F	VF	XF	Unc	BU
2009 Proof	99	Value: 9,250				

KM# 229 1500 SHILLINGS
155.5000 g., 0.9990 Gold 4.9942 oz. AGW, 65 mm. **Rev:** Elephant advacning left, sunrise

Date	Mintage	F	VF	XF	Unc	BU
2010 Proof	99	Value: 9,250				

KM# 239 1500 SHILLINGS
155.5000 g., 0.9990 Gold 4.9942 oz. AGW, 65 mm. **Rev:** Mother and baby elephant walking left, sun high up

Date	Mintage	F	VF	XF	Unc	BU
2011	99	Value: 9,250				

KM# 187 2000 SHILLINGS
62.2000 g., 0.9990 Silver 1.9977 oz. ASW, 50 mm. **Rev:** Elephant facing forward

Date	Mintage	F	VF	XF	Unc	BU
2004 Proof	2,000	Value: 100				

KM# 193 2000 SHILLINGS
62.2000 g., 0.9990 Silver 1.9977 oz. ASW

Date	Mintage	F	VF	XF	Unc	BU
2005 Proof	2,000	Value: 100				

KM# 199 2000 SHILLINGS
62.2000 g., 0.9990 Silver 1.9977 oz. ASW

Date	Mintage	F	VF	XF	Unc	BU
2006 Proof	2,000	Value: 100				

KM# 235 2000 SHILLINGS
1000.0000 g., 0.9990 Silver 32.117 oz. ASW, 100 mm. **Rev:** Mother and baby elephant walking left, sun high up

Date	Mintage	F	VF	XF	Unc	BU
2011	—	—	—	—	—	1,700

KM# 202 5000 SHILLINGS
1000.0000 g., 0.9990 Gold 32.117 oz. AGW

Date	Mintage	F	VF	XF	Unc	BU
2007 Proof	50	Value: 57,000				

KM# 211 5000 SHILLINGS
1000.0000 g., 0.9990 Gold 32.117 oz. AGW

Date	Mintage	F	VF	XF	Unc	BU
2008 Proof	50	Value: 57,000				

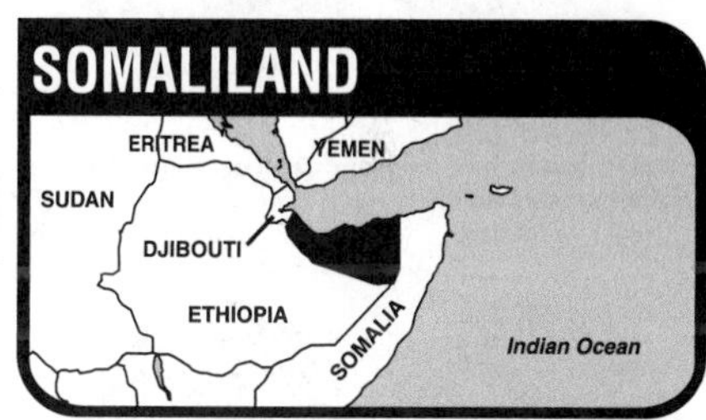

KM# 220 5000 SHILLINGS
1000.0000 g., 0.9990 Gold 32.117 oz. AGW **Rev:** Elephant advancing right, sunrise

Date	Mintage	F	VF	XF	Unc	BU
2009 Proof	50	Value: 57,000				

SOMALILAND

The Somaliland Republic consists of the former British Somaliland Protectorate and is located on the coast of the north-eastern projection of the African continent commonly referred to as the "Horn" on the southwestern end of the Gulf of Aden. Bordered by Ethiopia to the west and south and Somalia to the east. It has an area of 68,000* sq. mi. (176,000* sq. km). Capital: Hargeysa. It is mostly arid and mountainous except for the gulf shoreline.

The northern Somali National Movement (SNM) declared a secession of the Somaliland Republic on May 17, 1991, which is not recognized by the Somali Democratic Republic.

REPUBLIC

SHILLING COINAGE

KM# 4 5 SHILLINGS
1.4500 g., Aluminum, 21.9 mm. **Obv:** Value **Rev:** Bust of Sir Richard F. Burton - explorer, divides dates **Edge:** Plain

Date	Mintage	F	VF	XF	Unc	BU
2002	—	—	—	—	1.25	1.50

KM# 5 5 SHILLINGS
1.4500 g., Aluminum, 21.9 mm. **Obv:** Value **Rev:** Rooster **Edge:** Plain

Date	Mintage	F	VF	XF	Unc	BU
2002	—	—	—	—	1.00	1.25

KM# 19 5 SHILLINGS
1.2400 g., Aluminum, 22 mm. **Obv:** Elephant with calf walking right **Obv. Legend:** REPUBLIC OF SOMALILAND **Rev:** Value **Rev. Legend:** BAANKA SOMALILAND **Edge:** Plain

Date	Mintage	F	VF	XF	Unc	BU
2005	—	—	—	—	1.25	1.50

KM# 3 10 SHILLINGS
3.5100 g., Brass, 17.7 mm. **Obv:** Vervet Monkey **Rev:** Value **Edge:** Plain

Date	Mintage	F	VF	XF	Unc	BU
2002	—	—	—	—	0.65	1.25

KM# 7 10 SHILLINGS
4.8000 g., Stainless Steel, 24.9 mm. **Obv:** Value **Rev:** Aquarius the water carrier **Edge:** Plain

Date	Mintage	F	VF	XF	Unc	BU
2006	—	—	—	—	1.00	1.25

KM# 8 10 SHILLINGS
4.8000 g., Stainless Steel, 24.9 mm. **Obv:** Value **Rev:** Pisces the two fish **Edge:** Plain

Date	Mintage	F	VF	XF	Unc	BU
2006	—	—	—	—	1.00	1.25

KM# 9 10 SHILLINGS
4.8000 g., Stainless Steel, 24.9 mm. **Obv:** Value **Rev:** Aries the ram **Edge:** Plain

Date	Mintage	F	VF	XF	Unc	BU
2006	—	—	—	—	1.00	1.25

KM# 10 10 SHILLINGS
4.8000 g., Stainless Steel, 24.9 mm. **Obv:** Value **Rev:** Taurus the bull **Edge:** Plain

Date	Mintage	F	VF	XF	Unc	BU
2006	—	—	—	—	1.00	1.25

KM# 11 10 SHILLINGS
4.8000 g., Stainless Steel, 24.9 mm. **Obv:** Value **Rev:** Gemini twins **Edge:** Plain

Date	Mintage	F	VF	XF	Unc	BU
2006	—	—	—	—	1.00	1.25

KM# 12 10 SHILLINGS
4.8000 g., Stainless Steel, 24.9 mm. **Obv:** Value **Rev:** Cancer the crab **Edge:** Plain

Date	Mintage	F	VF	XF	Unc	BU
2006	—	—	—	—	1.00	1.25

KM# 13 10 SHILLINGS
4.8000 g., Stainless Steel, 24.9 mm. **Obv:** Value **Rev:** Leo the lion **Edge:** Plain

Date	Mintage	F	VF	XF	Unc	BU
2006	—	—	—	—	1.00	1.25

KM# 14 10 SHILLINGS
4.8000 g., Stainless Steel, 24.9 mm. **Obv:** Value **Rev:** Virgo as a winged woman **Edge:** Plain

Date	Mintage	F	VF	XF	Unc	BU
2006	—	—	—	—	1.00	1.25

KM# 15 10 SHILLINGS
4.8000 g., Stainless Steel, 24.9 mm. **Obv:** Value **Rev:** Libra balance scale **Edge:** Plain

Date	Mintage	F	VF	XF	Unc	BU
2006	—	—	—	—	1.00	1.25

KM# 16 10 SHILLINGS
4.8000 g., Stainless Steel, 24.9 mm. **Obv:** Value **Rev:** Scorpio the scorpion **Edge:** Plain

Date	Mintage	F	VF	XF	Unc	BU
2006	—	—	—	—	1.00	1.25

KM# 17 10 SHILLINGS
4.8000 g., Stainless Steel, 24.9 mm. **Obv:** Value **Rev:** Sagittarius the archer **Edge:** Plain

Date	Mintage	F	VF	XF	Unc	BU
2006	—	—	—	—	1.00	1.25

KM# 18 10 SHILLINGS
4.8000 g., Stainless Steel, 24.9 mm. **Obv:** Value **Rev:** Capricorn the goat **Edge:** Plain

Date	Mintage	F	VF	XF	Unc	BU
2006	—	—	—	—	1.00	1.25

KM# 6 20 SHILLINGS
3.8700 g., Stainless Steel, 21.8 mm. **Obv:** Value **Rev:** Greyhound dog **Edge:** Plain

Date	Mintage	F	VF	XF	Unc	BU
2002	—	—	—	—	1.00	1.50

KM# 2 1000 SHILLINGS
31.2700 g., 0.9990 Silver 1.0043 oz. ASW, 38.8 mm. **Obv:** Crowned arms with supporters **Rev:** Bust with hat 3/4 right **Edge:** Reeded

Date	Mintage	F	VF	XF	Unc	BU
2002	—	—	—	—	45.00	50.00

The Republic of South Africa, located at the southern tip of Africa, has an area of 471,445 sq. mi. (1,221,043 sq. km.) and a population of *30.2 million. Capitals: Administrative, Pretoria; Legislative, Cape Town; Judicial, Bloemfontein. Manufacturing, mining and agriculture are the principal industries. Exports include wool, diamonds, gold, and metallic ores.

The apartheid era ended April 27, 1994 with the first democratic election for all people of South Africa. Nelson Mandela was inaugurated President May 10, 1994, and South Africa was readmitted into the Commonwealth of Nations.

South African coins and currency bear inscriptions in tribal languages, Afrikaans and English.

MONETARY SYSTEM
100 Cents = 1 Rand

MINT MARKS
GRC + paw print = Gold Reef City Mint

REPUBLIC

STANDARD COINAGE

100 Cents = 1 Rand

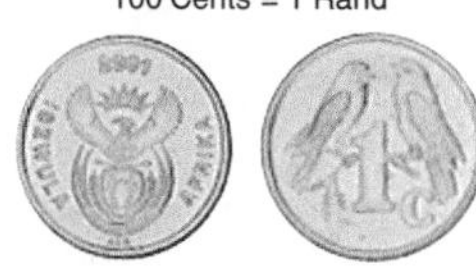

KM# 221 CENT

1.5000 g., Copper Plated Steel, 15 mm. **Obv:** New national arms **Obv. Legend:** ISEWULA AFRIKA **Rev:** Value divides two sparrows **Edge:** Plain

Date	Mintage	F	VF	XF	Unc	BU
2001	—	—	—	0.15	0.35	0.50
2001 Proof	3,678	Value: 5.00				

KM# 222 2 CENTS

3.0000 g., Copper Plated Steel, 18 mm. **Obv:** New national arms **Obv. Legend:** AFURIKA TSHIPEMBE **Rev:** Eagle with fish in talons divides value **Edge:** Plain **Designer:** A.L. Sutherland

Date	Mintage	F	VF	XF	Unc	BU
2001	—	—	—	—	0.50	0.75
2001 Proof	3,678	Value: 6.00				

KM# 223 5 CENTS

4.4200 g., Copper Plated Steel, 21 mm. **Obv:** New national arms **Obv. Legend:** AFRIKA DZONGA **Rev:** Value and Blue crane **Edge:** Plain

Date	Mintage	F	VF	XF	Unc	BU
2001	—	—	0.10	0.25	0.65	1.00
2001 Proof	—	Value: 5.00				

KM# 268 5 CENTS

4.5000 g., Copper Plated Steel, 21 mm. **Obv:** New national arms **Obv. Legend:** Ningizimu Afrika **Rev:** Value and Blue crane **Edge:** Plain

Date	Mintage	F	VF	XF	Unc	BU
2002	—	—	—	0.30	0.75	1.00
2002 Proof	3,250	Value: 5.00				

KM# 324 5 CENTS

4.5000 g., Copper Plated Steel, 21 mm. **Obv:** New national arms **Obv. Legend:** Afrika Dzonga **Rev:** Blue crane and denomination **Edge:** Plain

Date	Mintage	F	VF	XF	Unc	BU
2003	—	—	—	0.30	0.75	1.00
2003 Proof	2,909	Value: 5.00				

KM# 325 5 CENTS

4.5000 g., Copper Plated Steel, 21 mm. **Obv:** New national arms **Obv. Legend:** South Africa **Rev:** Value and Blue crane **Edge:** Plain

Date	Mintage	F	VF	XF	Unc	BU
2004	—	—	—	0.20	0.50	0.75
2004 Proof	1,935	Value: 5.00				

KM# 291 5 CENTS

4.5000 g., Copper Plated Steel, 21 mm. **Obv:** New national arms **Obv. Legend:** Aforika Borwa **Rev:** Value and Blue crane **Edge:** Plain

Date	Mintage	F	VF	XF	Unc	BU
2005	—	—	—	0.20	0.50	0.75
2005 Proof	—	Value: 5.00				

KM# 486 5 CENTS

4.5000 g., Copper Plated Steel, 21 mm. **Obv:** New National arms **Obv. Legend:** Afrika Borwa **Rev:** Blue crane and value

Date	Mintage	F	VF	XF	Unc	BU
2006	—	—	—	—	0.50	0.75
2006 Proof	—	Value: 5.00				

KM# 340 5 CENTS

4.5100 g., Copper Plated Steel, 21 mm. **Obv:** New national arms **Obv. Legend:** Suid- Afrika **Rev:** Value at left, Blue Crane at right **Edge:** Plain

Date	Mintage	F	VF	XF	Unc	BU
2007	—	—	—	0.20	0.50	0.75
2007 Proof	—	Value: 5.00				

KM# 440 5 CENTS

4.5000 g., Copper Plated Steel, 21 mm. **Obv:** New National arms **Obv. Legend:** uMzantsi Afrika **Rev:** Blue crane and value

Date	Mintage	F	VF	XF	Unc	BU
2008	—	—	—	—	0.75	1.00
2008 Proof	—	Value: 5.00				

KM# 464 5 CENTS

4.5000 g., Copper Plated Steel, 21 mm. **Obv:** National arms **Rev:** Value and Blue crane

Date	Mintage	F	VF	XF	Unc	BU
2009	—	—	—	—	0.50	0.75
2009 Proof	—	Value: 5.00				

KM# 493 5 CENTS

4.5000 g., Copper Plated Steel, 21 mm. **Obv:** National arms **Rev:** Value and Blue crane

Date	Mintage	F	VF	XF	Unc	BU
2010	—	—	—	—	0.75	1.00
2010 Proof	—	Value: 5.00				

KM# 500 5 CENTS

4.5000 g., Copper Plated Steel, 21 mm. **Obv:** National arms **Rev:** Blue crane and value

Date	Mintage	F	VF	XF	Unc	BU
2011	—	—	—	—	0.75	1.00
2011 Proof	—	Value: 5.00				

KM# 224 10 CENTS

2.0000 g., Bronze Plated Steel, 16 mm. **Obv:** New national arms **Obv. Legend:** AFRIKA DZONGA **Rev:** Arum Lily and value **Edge:** Reeded

Date	Mintage	F	VF	XF	Unc	BU
2001	—	—	—	0.30	0.60	1.00
2001 Proof	3,678	Value: 6.00				

KM# 269 10 CENTS

2.0000 g., Bronze Plated Steel, 16 mm. **Obv:** New national arms **Obv. Legend:** Afrika Dzonga **Rev:** Arum Lily and value **Edge:** Reeded

Date	Mintage	F	VF	XF	Unc	BU
2002	—	—	—	0.30	0.75	1.00
2002 Proof	3,250	Value: 6.00				

KM# 347 10 CENTS

2.0000 g., Bronze Plated Steel, 16 mm. **Obv:** New national arms **Obv. Legend:** South Africa **Rev:** Arum lily and value **Edge:** Reeded

Date	Mintage	F	VF	XF	Unc	BU
2003	—	—	—	0.30	0.75	1.00
2003 Proof	2,909	Value: 6.00				

KM# 326 10 CENTS
2.0000 g., Bronze Plated Steel, 16 mm. **Obv:** New national arms **Obv. Legend:** Aforika Borwa **Rev:** Arum lily and value **Edge:** Reeded

Date	Mintage	F	VF	XF	Unc	BU
2004	—	—	—	0.30	0.75	1.00
2004 Proof	1,935	Value: 6.00				

KM# 292 10 CENTS
2.0000 g., Bronze Plated Steel, 16 mm. **Obv:** New national arms **Obv. Legend:** Afrika Borwa **Rev:** Arum Lily and value **Edge:** Reeded

Date	Mintage	F	VF	XF	Unc	BU
2005	—	—	—	0.30	0.75	1.00
2005 Proof	—	Value: 6.00				

KM# 487 10 CENTS
2.0000 g., Bronze Plated Steel, 16 mm. **Obv:** National arms **Obv. Legend:** Suid-Afrika **Rev:** Arum lily and value **Edge:** Reeded

Date	Mintage	F	VF	XF	Unc	BU
2006	—	—	—	—	0.75	1.00
2006 Proof	—	Value: 6.00				

KM# 341 10 CENTS
2.0000 g., Bronze Plated Steel, 16 mm. **Obv:** New national arms **Obv. Legend:** uMzantsi - Afrika **Rev:** Alum lily and value **Edge:** Reeded

Date	Mintage	F	VF	XF	Unc	BU
2007	—	—	—	0.30	0.75	1.00
2007 Proof	—	Value: 6.00				

KM# 441 10 CENTS
2.0000 g., Bronze Plated Steel, 16 mm. **Obv:** National arms **Obv. Legend:** iNingizimu Afrika **Rev:** Arum lily and value **Edge:** Reeded

Date	Mintage	F	VF	XF	Unc	BU
2008	—	—	—	—	0.75	1.00
2008 Proof	—	Value: 8.00				

KM# 465 10 CENTS
2.0000 g., Copper Plated Steel, 16 mm. **Obv:** National arms **Rev:** Arum lily and value

Date	Mintage	F	VF	XF	Unc	BU
2009	—	—	—	—	0.75	1.00
2009 Proof	—	Value: 8.00				

KM# 494 10 CENTS
2.0000 g., Bronze Plated Steel, 16 mm. **Obv:** National arms **Rev:** Arum Lily and value

Date	Mintage	F	VF	XF	Unc	BU
2010	—	—	—	—	0.90	1.20
2010 Proof	—	Value: 7.00				

KM# 501 10 CENTS
2.0000 g., Bronze Plated Steel, 16 mm. **Obv:** National arms **Rev:** Arum lily and value

Date	Mintage	F	VF	XF	Unc	BU
2011	—	—	—	—	0.75	1.00
2011 Proof	—	Value: 6.00				

KM# 225 20 CENTS
3.5000 g., Bronze Plated Steel, 19 mm. **Obv:** New national arms **Obv. Legend:** AFERIKA BORWA **Rev:** Protea flower and value **Edge:** Reeded

Date	Mintage	F	VF	XF	Unc	BU
2001	—	—	—	0.35	0.90	1.20
2001 Proof	3,678	Value: 7.00				

KM# 270 20 CENTS
3.5000 g., Bronze Plated Steel, 19 mm. **Obv:** New national arms **Obv. Legend:** South Africa **Rev:** Protea flower and value **Edge:** Reeded

Date	Mintage	F	VF	XF	Unc	BU
2002	—	—	—	0.35	0.90	1.20
2002 Proof	3,250	Value: 7.00				

KM# 327 20 CENTS
3.5000 g., Bronze Plated Steel, 19 mm. **Obv:** New national arms **Obv. Legend:** Aforika Borwa **Rev:** Protea flower and value **Edge:** Reeded

Date	Mintage	F	VF	XF	Unc	BU
2003	—	—	—	0.35	0.90	1.20
2003 Proof	2,909	Value: 7.00				

KM# 328 20 CENTS
3.5000 g., Bronze Plated Steel, 19 mm. **Obv:** New national arms **Obv. Legend:** Afrika Borwa **Rev:** Protea flower and value **Edge:** Reeded

Date	Mintage	F	VF	XF	Unc	BU
2004	—	—	—	0.35	0.90	1.20
2004 Proof	1,935	Value: 7.00				

KM# 293 20 CENTS
3.5000 g., Bronze Plated Steel, 19 mm. **Obv:** New national arms **Obv. Legend:** Suid-Afrika **Rev:** Protea flower and value **Edge:** Reeded **Shape:** Round

Date	Mintage	F	VF	XF	Unc	BU
2005	—	—	—	0.35	0.90	1.20
2005 Proof	—	Value: 7.00				

KM# 488 20 CENTS
3.5000 g., Bronze Plated Steel, 19 mm. **Obv:** National arms **Obv. Legend:** uMzantsi Afrika **Rev:** Protea flower and value **Edge:** Reeded

Date	Mintage	F	VF	XF	Unc	BU
2006	—	—	—	—	0.90	1.20
2006 Proof	—	Value: 7.00				

KM# 342 20 CENTS
3.5000 g., Bronze Plated Steel, 19 mm. **Obv:** New national arms **Obv. Legend:** iNingizimu Afrika **Rev:** Protea flower and value **Edge:** Reeded

Date	Mintage	F	VF	XF	Unc	BU
2007	—	—	—	0.35	0.90	1.20
2007 Proof	—	Value: 7.00				

KM# 442 20 CENTS
3.5000 g., Bronze Plated Steel, 19 mm. **Obv:** National arms **Rev:** Protea flower and value **Edge:** Reeded

Date	Mintage	F	VF	XF	Unc	BU
2008	—	—	—	—	0.90	1.20
2008 Proof	—	Value: 7.00				

KM# 466 20 CENTS
3.5000 g., Bronze Plated Steel, 19 mm. **Obv:** National arms **Rev:** Protea flower and value

Date	Mintage	F	VF	XF	Unc	BU
2009	—	—	—	—	0.90	1.20
2009 Proof	—	Value: 7.00				

KM# 495 20 CENTS
3.5000 g., Bronze Plated Steel, 19 mm. **Obv:** National arms **Rev:** Protea flower and vlaue

Date	Mintage	F	VF	XF	Unc	BU
2010	—	—	—	—	0.90	1.50
2010	—	Value: 7.00				

KM# 502 20 CENTS
3.5000 g., Bronze Plated Steel, 19 mm. **Obv:** National arms **Rev:** Protea flower and value

Date	Mintage	F	VF	XF	Unc	BU
2011	—	—	—	—	0.90	1.20
2011 Proof	—	Value: 7.00				

KM# 226 50 CENTS
5.0000 g., Bronze Plated Steel, 22 mm. **Obv:** New national arms **Obv. Legend:** AFERIKA BORWA **Rev:** Strelitzia plant, value **Edge:** Reeded

Date	Mintage	F	VF	XF	Unc	BU
2001	1,152,000	—	—	0.50	1.20	1.60
2001 Proof	3,678	Value: 8.00				

KM# 271 50 CENTS
5.0000 g., Bronze Plated Steel, 22 mm. **Obv:** New national arms **Obv. Legend:** Aforika Borwa **Rev:** Strelitzia plant **Edge:** Reeded

Date	Mintage	F	VF	XF	Unc	BU
2002	16,000,000	—	—	0.50	1.20	1.60
2002 Proof	3,250	Value: 8.00				

KM# 287 50 CENTS
5.0000 g., Bronze Plated Steel, 22 mm. **Obv:** New national arms **Obv. Legend:** Afrika - Borwa **Rev:** Soccer player and value **Edge:** Reeded **Designer:** A. L. Sutherland

Date	Mintage	F	VF	XF	Unc	BU
2002	—	—	—	—	9.00	12.00

KM# 276 50 CENTS
5.0000 g., Bronze Plated Steel, 22 mm. **Obv:** New national arms **Obv. Legend:** Afrika - Borwa **Rev:** Cricket player diving towards the wicket, value below **Edge:** Reeded

Date	Mintage	F	VF	XF	Unc	BU
2003	11,749	—	—	—	9.00	12.00

KM# 329 50 CENTS

5.0000 g., Bronze Plated Steel, 22 mm. **Obv:** New national arms **Obv. Legend:** Aforika Borwa **Rev:** Cricket player diving towards the wicket **Edge:** Reeded **Designer:** A. L. Sutherland

Date	Mintage	F	VF	XF	Unc	BU
2003	—	—	—	—	9.00	12.00
2003 Proof	—	Value: 15.00				

KM# 330 50 CENTS

5.0000 g., Bronze Plated Steel, 22 mm. **Obv:** New national arms **Obv. Legend:** Afrika Borwa **Rev:** Strelitzia plant, value **Edge:** Reeded

Date	Mintage	F	VF	XF	Unc	BU
2003	—	—	—	0.50	1.60	1.20
2003 Proof	2,909	Value: 8.00				

KM# 331 50 CENTS

5.0000 g., Bronze Plated Steel, 22 mm. **Obv:** New national arms **Obv. Legend:** Suid Afrika **Rev:** Strelitzia plant, value **Edge:** Reeded

Date	Mintage	F	VF	XF	Unc	BU
2004	—	—	—	0.50	1.20	1.60
2004 Proof	1,935	Value: 8.00				

KM# 294 50 CENTS

5.0000 g., Bronze Plated Steel, 22 mm. **Obv:** New national arms **Obv. Legend:** uMzantsi Afrika **Rev:** Strelitzia plant, value **Edge:** Reeded

Date	Mintage	F	VF	XF	Unc	BU
2005	—	—	—	0.50	1.20	1.60
2005 Proof	—	Value: 8.00				

KM# 489 50 CENTS

5.0000 g., Bronze Plated Steel, 22 mm. **Obv:** National arms **Obv. Legend:** iNingizimu Afrika **Rev:** Strelitzia plant and value **Edge:** Reeded

Date	Mintage	F	VF	XF	Unc	BU
2006	—	—	—	—	1.20	1.60
2006 Proof	—	Value: 8.00				

KM# 343 50 CENTS

5.0000 g., Bronze Plated Steel, 22 mm. **Obv:** National arms **Obv. Legend:** iSewula Afrika **Rev:** Strelitzia plant and value **Edge:** Reeded

Date	Mintage	F	VF	XF	Unc	BU
2007	—	—	—	—	1.20	1.60
2007 Proof	—	Value: 8.00				

KM# 443 50 CENTS

5.0000 g., Bronze Plated Steel, 22 mm. **Obv:** National arms **Obv. Legend:** Afurika Tshipembe **Rev:** Strelitzia plant and value **Edge:** Reeded

Date	Mintage	F	VF	XF	Unc	BU
2008	—	—	—	—	1.20	1.60
2008 Proof	—	Value: 8.00				

KM# 467 50 CENTS

5.0000 g., Bronze Plated Steel, 22 mm. **Obv:** National arms **Rev:** Strelitzia plant

Date	Mintage	F	VF	XF	Unc	BU
2009	—	—	—	—	1.20	1.60
2009 Proof	—	Value: 8.00				

KM# 496 50 CENTS

5.0000 g., Bronze Plated Steel, 22 mm. **Obv:** National arms **Rev:** Strelitzia plant

Date	Mintage	F	VF	XF	Unc	BU
2010	—	—	—	—	1.20	1.60
2010 Proof	—	Value: 8.00				

KM# 503 50 CENTS

5.0000 g., Bronze Plated Steel, 22 mm. **Obv:** National arms **Rev:** Strelitzia plant and value

Date	Mintage	F	VF	XF	Unc	BU
2011	—	—	—	—	1.20	1.60
2011 Proof	—	Value: 10.00				

KM# 227 RAND

4.0000 g., Nickel Plated Copper, 20 mm. **Obv:** New national arms **Obv. Legend:** SUID-AFRIKA **Rev:** Springbok, value **Edge:** Segmented reeding

Date	Mintage	F	VF	XF	Unc	BU
2001	—	—	—	0.60	1.50	2.00
2001 Proof	3,678	Value: 10.00				

KM# 272 RAND

4.0000 g., Nickel Plated Copper, 20 mm. **Obv:** New national arms **Obv. Legend:** Suid-Afrika Afrika Borwa **Rev:** Springbok, value **Edge:** Segmented reeding

Date	Mintage	F	VF	XF	Unc	BU
2002	—	—	—	0.60	1.50	2.00
2002 Proof	3,250	Value: 10.00				

KM# 275 RAND

4.0000 g., Nickel Plated Copper, 20 mm. **Subject:** Johannesburg World Summit on Sustainable Development **Obv:** New national arms **Obv. Legend:** Suid-Afrika - Afrika Borwa **Rev:** World globe and logo **Edge:** Segmented reeding

Date	Mintage	F	VF	XF	Unc	BU
2002	—	—	—	—	12.00	18.00

KM# 332 RAND

4.0000 g., Nickel Plated Copper, 20 mm. **Obv:** New national arms **Obv. Legend:** uMzantsi Afrika Suid-Afrika **Rev:** Springbok, value **Edge:** Segmented reeding

Date	Mintage	F	VF	XF	Unc	BU
2003	—	—	—	0.60	1.50	2.00
2003 Proof	2,909	Value: 10.00				

KM# 333 RAND

4.0000 g., Nickel Plated Copper, 20 mm. **Obv:** New national arms **Obv. Legend:** iNingizimu Afrika - uMzantsi Afrika **Rev:** Springbok, value **Edge:** Segmented reeding

Date	Mintage	F	VF	XF	Unc	BU
2004	—	—	—	0.60	1.50	2.00
2004 Proof	1,935	Value: 10.00				

KM# 295 RAND

4.0000 g., Nickel Plated Copper, 20 mm. **Obv:** new national arms **Obv. Legend:** iSewula Afrika - iNingizimu Afrika **Rev:** Springbok, value **Edge:** Segmented reeding **Shape:** Round

Date	Mintage	F	VF	XF	Unc	BU
2005	—	—	—	0.60	1.50	2.00
2005 Proof	—	Value: 10.00				

KM# 490 RAND

4.0000 g., Nickel Plated Copper, 20 mm. **Obv:** National arms **Obv. Legend:** Afurika Tshipembe - iSewula Afrika **Rev:** Springbok and value

Date	Mintage	F	VF	XF	Unc	BU
2006	—	—	—	—	1.50	2.00
2006 Proof	—	Value: 10.00				

KM# 344 RAND

3.9300 g., Nickel Plated Copper, 19.94 mm. **Obv:** Natinal arms **Obv. Legend:** Ningizimu Afrika - Afurika Tshipemba **Rev:** Springbok leaping right **Edge:** segmented reeding

Date	Mintage	F	VF	XF	Unc	BU
2007	—	—	—	0.60	1.50	2.00
2007 Proof	—	Value: 10.00				

KM# 444 RAND

4.0000 g., Nickel Plated Copper, 20 mm. **Obv:** National arms **Obv. Legend:** Afrika-Dzonga - Ningizimu Afrika **Rev:** Springbok and value

Date	Mintage	F	VF	XF	Unc	BU
2008	—	—	—	—	2.00	2.75
2008 Proof	—	Value: 12.00				

KM# 468 RAND

4.0000 g., Nickel Plated Copper, 20 mm. **Obv:** National arms **Rev:** Spingbok

Date	Mintage	F	VF	XF	Unc	BU
2009	—	—	—	—	1.50	2.00
2009 Proof	—	Value: 10.00				

KM# 497 RAND

4.0000 g., Nickel Plated Copper, 20 mm. **Obv:** National arms **Rev:** Springbok right

Date	Mintage	F	VF	XF	Unc	BU
2010	—	—	—	—	1.50	2.00
2010 Proof	—	Value: 10.00				

KM# 508 RAND

3.1100 g., 0.9999 Gold 0.1000 oz. AGW, 16.5 mm. **Subject:** World Cup Soccer

Date	Mintage	F	VF	XF	Unc	BU
2010 Proof	—	Value: 200				

KM# 504 RAND

20.0000 g., Nickel Plated Copper, 20 mm. **Obv:** National arms **Rev:** Springbok and value

Date	Mintage	F	VF	XF	Unc	BU
2011	—	—	—	—	1.50	2.00
2011 Proof	—	Value: 10.00				

KM# 228 2 RAND
5.5000 g., Nickel Plated Copper, 23 mm. **Obv:** New national arms **Obv. Legend:** UMZANSTI AFRIKA **Rev:** Greater Kudu, value **Edge:** Segmented reeding **Designer:** A. L. Sutherland

Date	Mintage	F	VF	XF	Unc	BU
2001	3,600,000	—	—	0.80	2.00	3.00
2001 Proof	3,678	Value: 12.00				

KM# 273 2 RAND
5.5000 g., Nickel Plated Copper, 23 mm. **Obv:** New national arms **Obv. Legend:** iNingizimu Afrika - uMzantsi Afrika **Rev:** Greater Kudu, value **Edge:** Segmented reeding **Designer:** A.L. Sutherland

Date	Mintage	F	VF	XF	Unc	BU
2002	12,000,000	—	—	0.80	2.00	3.50
2002 Proof	3,250	Value: 12.00				

KM# 335 2 RAND
5.5000 g., Nickel Plated Copper, 23 mm. **Obv:** New national arms **Obv. Legend:** iNingizimu Afrika - iSewula Afrika **Rev:** Greater Kudu, value **Edge:** Segmented reeding **Designer:** A. L. Sutherland

Date	Mintage	F	VF	XF	Unc	BU
2003	5,000,000	—	—	0.80	2.00	3.50
2003 Proof	2,909	Value: 12.00				

KM# 336 2 RAND
5.5000 g., Nickel Plated Copper, 23 mm. **Obv:** New national arms **Obv. Legend:** Afurika Tshipembe / iSewula Afrika **Rev:** Greater Kudu, value **Edge:** Segmented reeding **Designer:** A. L. Sutherland

Date	Mintage	F	VF	XF	Unc	BU
2004	—	—	—	0.80	2.00	3.50
2004 Proof	1,935	Value: 12.00				

KM# 334 2 RAND
5.5000 g., Nickel Plated Copper, 23 mm. **Subject:** 10 Years of Freedom - 1994-2004 **Obv:** New national arms **Obv. Legend:** SOUTH / AFRICA **Rev:** Value, flag logo, people **Edge:** Segmented reeding **Note:** 5,885 issued in souveneir card.

Date	Mintage	F	VF	XF	Unc	BU
2004	—	—	—	0.80	2.00	2.75

KM# 296 2 RAND
5.5000 g., Nickel Plated Copper, 23 mm. **Obv:** New national arms **Obv. Legend:** Ningizimu Afrika - Afurika Tshipembe **Rev:** Greater Kudu, value **Edge:** Segmented reeding **Designer:** A. L. Sutherland

Date	Mintage	F	VF	XF	Unc	BU
2005	—	—	—	0.80	2.00	2.75
2005 Proof	—	Value: 12.00				

KM# 491 2 RAND
5.5000 g., Nickel Plated Copper, 23 mm. **Obv:** National arms **Obv. Legend:** Afrika-Dzonga - Ningizimo Afrika **Rev:** Greater kudu and value

Date	Mintage	F	VF	XF	Unc	BU
2006	—	—	—	—	2.00	2.75
2006 Proof	—	Value: 12.00				

KM# 345 2 RAND
5.5000 g., Nickel Plated Copper, 23 mm. **Obv:** National arms **Rev:** Greater Kudu

Date	Mintage	F	VF	XF	Unc	BU
2007	—	—	—	0.80	2.00	3.00
2007 Proof	—	Value: 15.00				

KM# 445 2 RAND
5.5000 g., Nickel Plated Copper, 23 mm. **Obv:** National arms **Obv. Legend:** Afrika-Dzonga - South Africa **Rev:** Kudu at center left, value at right **Edge:** Segmented reeding

Date	Mintage	F	VF	XF	Unc	BU
2008	—	—	—	0.80	2.00	2.75
2008 Proof	—	Value: 12.00				

KM# 469 2 RAND
5.5000 g., Nickel Plated Copper, 22 mm. **Obv:** National arms **Rev:** Greater Kudu

Date	Mintage	F	VF	XF	Unc	BU
2009	—	—	—	—	2.00	2.75
2009 Proof	—	Value: 12.00				

KM# 498 2 RAND
5.5000 g., Nickel Plated Copper, 23 mm. **Obv:** National arms **Rev:** Greater Kudu

Date	Mintage	F	VF	XF	Unc	BU
2010	—	—	—	—	2.00	2.75
2010 Proof	—	Value: 12.00				

KM# 505 2 RAND
5.5000 g., Nickel Plated Copper, 23 mm. **Obv:** Naitonal arms **Rev:** Kudo at center

Date	Mintage	F	VF	XF	Unc	BU
2011	—	—	—	—	2.00	2.75
2011 Proof	—	Value: 12.00				

KM# 229 5 RAND
7.0000 g., Nickel Plated Copper, 26 mm. **Obv:** New national arms **Obv. Legend:** ININGIZIMU AFRIKA **Rev:** Wildebeest, value **Edge:** Segmented reeding **Designer:** A.L. Sutherland

Date	Mintage	F	VF	XF	Unc	BU
2001	2,000,000	—	—	1.20	4.50	6.00
2001 CW	779	—	—	—	67.50	90.00
2001 Proof	3,678	Value: 15.00				

KM# 274 5 RAND
7.0000 g., Nickel Plated Copper, 26 mm. **Obv:** New national arms **Obv. Legend:** Afurika Tshipembe - Isewula Afrika **Rev:** Wildebeest, value **Edge:** Segmented reeding **Designer:** A.L. Sutherland

Date	Mintage	F	VF	XF	Unc	BU
2002	—	—	—	1.20	4.50	6.00
2002 CW	106	—	—	—	—	150
2002 Proof	3,250	Value: 15.00				

KM# 337 5 RAND
7.0000 g., Nickel Plated Copper, 26 mm. **Obv:** New national arms **Obv. Legend:** Afurika Tshipembe - Ningizimu Afrika **Rev:** Wildebeest, value **Edge:** Segmented reeding **Designer:** A. L. Sutherland

Date	Mintage	F	VF	XF	Unc	BU
2003	—	—	—	1.20	4.50	6.00
2003 Proof	2,909	Value: 15.00				

KM# 281 5 RAND
9.5000 g., Bi-Metallic Brass center in Copper-Nickel ring, 26 mm. **Obv:** New national arms **Obv. Legend:** Afrika-Dzonga - Ningizimu Afrika **Rev:** Wildebeest, value **Edge:** Security type with lettering **Edge Lettering:** "SARB R5" repeated ten times

Date	Mintage	F	VF	XF	Unc	BU
2004	—	—	—	1.20	5.00	6.50
2004 CW	3,243	—	—	—	—	22.50
2004 Proof	1,935	Value: 15.00				

KM# 297 5 RAND
9.5000 g., Bi-Metallic Brass center in Copper-Nickel ring, 26 mm. **Obv:** New national arms **Obv. Legend:** Afrika Dzonga - South Africa **Rev:** Wildebeest, value **Edge:** Security type with lettering **Edge Lettering:** "SARB R5" repeated ten times **Designer:** A. L. Sutherland

Date	Mintage	F	VF	XF	Unc	BU
2005	—	—	—	1.20	3.75	5.00
2005 CW	997	—	—	—	—	50.00
2005 Proof	—	Value: 15.00				

KM# 492 5 RAND
5.5000 g., Bi-Metallic Brass center in Copper-Nickel ring., 26 mm. **Obv:** National arms **Obv. Legend:** Aforika Borwa - South Africa **Rev:** Wildebeest and value

Date	Mintage	F	VF	XF	Unc	BU
2006	—	—	—	—	4.50	6.00
2006 Proof	—	Value: 12.00				

KM# 346 5 RAND
9.5000 g., Bi-Metallic Brass center in Copper-Nickel ring, 26 mm. **Obv:** National arms **Obv. Legend:** Aforika Borwa - Afrika Borwa **Rev:** Wildebeest and value **Edge:** Security type and lettered **Edge Lettering:** "SARB R5" repeated ten times **Designer:** A. L. Sutherland

Date	Mintage	F	VF	XF	Unc	BU
2007	—	—	—	1.20	3.00	4.00
2007 CW	—	—	—	—	—	22.50
2007 Proof	—	Value: 15.00				

KM# 446 5 RAND
9.5000 g., Bi-Metallic Brass center in Copper-Nickel ring, 26 mm. **Obv:** National arms **Rev:** Wildebeest rearing left

Date	Mintage	F	VF	XF	Unc	BU
2008	—	—	—	—	3.00	4.00
2008 CW	—	—	—	—	—	22.50
2008 Proof	—	Value: 12.00				

KM# 439 5 RAND
9.5000 g., Bi-Metallic Brass center in Copper-Nickel ring, 26 mm. **Subject:** Nelson Mandella, 90th Birthday **Obv:** National arms **Rev:** Bust facing

Date	Mintage	F	VF	XF	Unc	BU
2008	—	—	—	1.20	3.75	5.00
2008 Proof	—	Value: 15.00				

KM# 470 5 RAND
9.5000 g., Bi-Metallic Brass center in Copper-Nickel ring, 26 mm. **Obv:** National arms **Rev:** Wildebeest rearing left

Date	Mintage	F	VF	XF	Unc	BU
2009 CW	—	—	—	—	—	22.50
2009	—	—	—	—	3.00	4.00
2009 Proof	—	Value: 15.00				

KM# 499 5 RAND
9.5000 g., Bi-Metallic Brass center in Copper-Nickel ring, 26 mm. **Obv:** National arms **Rev:** Wildebeest rearing left

Date	Mintage	F	VF	XF	Unc	BU
2010	—	—	—	—	4.50	6.00
2010 CW	—	—	—	—	—	22.50
2010 Proof	—	Value: 15.00				

KM# 506 5 RAND
9.5000 g., Bi-Metallic Brass center in Copper-Nickel ring, 26 mm. **Obv:** National arms **Rev:** Wildebeest and value

Date	Mintage	F	VF	XF	Unc	BU
2011	—	—	—	—	4.50	6.00
2011 Proof	—	Value: 15.00				

KM# 507 5 RAND
9.5000 g., Bi-Metallic Brass center in Copper-Nickel ring, 26 mm. **Subject:** 90th Anniversary of the Rand **Obv:** National arms **Rev:** Old coin and bank note designs

Date	Mintage	F	VF	XF	Unc	BU
2011	—	—	—	—	4.50	7.00
2011 Proof	—	Value: 12.00				

GOLD BULLION COINAGE

KM# 105 1/10 KRUGERRAND
3.3930 g., 0.9170 Gold 0.1000 oz. AGW, 16.50 mm. **Obv:** Bust of Paul Kruger left **Obv. Legend:** SUID-AFRIKA - SOUTH AFRICA **Rev:** Springbok walking right divides date **Edge:** Reeded **Note:** 180 edge serrations for uncirculated, 220 serrations for proof

Date	Mintage	F	VF	XF	Unc	BU
2001	17,936	—	—	—	BV+15%	—
2001 Proof	4,058	Value: 200				
2002	12,890	—	—	—	BV+15%	—
2002 Proof	3,110	Value: 200				
2003	15,893	—	—	—	BV+15%	—
2003 Proof	1,893	Value: 200				
2004	—	—	—	—	BV+15%	—
2004 Proof	3,811	Value: 200				
2005	—	—	—	—	BV+15%	—
2005 Proof	—	Value: 200				
2006	—	—	—	—	BV+15%	—
2006 Proof	—	Value: 200				
2007	—	—	—	—	BV+15%	—
2007 Proof	4,400	Value: 200				
2008	—	—	—	—	BV+15%	—
2008 Proof	4,800	Value: 200				
2009	—	—	—	—	BV+15%	—
2009 Proof	6,000	Value: 200				
2010	—	—	—	—	BV+15%	—
2010 Proof	6,000	Value: 200				
2011	—	—	—	—	BV+15%	—
2011 Proof	—	Value: 200				
2012	—	—	—	—	BV+15%	—
2012 Proof	—	Value: 200				

KM# 106 1/4 KRUGERRAND
8.4820 g., 0.9170 Gold 0.2501 oz. AGW, 22 mm. **Obv:** Bust of Paul Kruger left **Obv. Legend:** SUID-AFRIKA - SOUTH AFRICA **Rev:** Springbok bounding right divides date **Edge:** Reeded **Note:** 180 edge serrations for uncirculated, 220 serrations for proof

Date	Mintage	F	VF	XF	Unc	BU
2001	10,607	—	—	—	BV+10%	—
2001 Proof	3,841	Value: 475				
2002	10,558	—	—	—	BV+10%	—
2002 Proof	2,442	Value: 475				
2003	11,468	—	—	—	BV+10%	—
2003 Proof	2,450	Value: 475				
2004	—	—	—	—	BV+10%	—
2004 Proof	4,570	Value: 475				
2005	—	—	—	—	BV+10%	—
2005 Proof	—	Value: 475				
2006	—	—	—	—	BV+10%	—
2006 Proof	—	Value: 475				
2007	—	—	—	—	BV+10%	—
2007 Proof	4,400	Value: 475				
2008	—	—	—	—	BV+10%	—
2008 Proof	4,800	Value: 475				
2009	—	—	—	—	BV+10%	—
2009 Proof	6,000	Value: 475				
2010	—	—	—	—	BV+10%	—
2010 Proof	6,000	Value: 475				
2011	—	—	—	—	BV+10%	—
2011 Proof	—	Value: 475				
2012	—	—	—	—	BV+10%	—
2012 Proof	—	Value: 475				

KM# 107 1/2 KRUGERRAND
16.9650 g., 0.9170 Gold 0.5001 oz. AGW, 27 mm. **Obv:** Bust of Paul Kruger left **Obv. Legend:** SUID-AFRIKA • SOUTH AFRICA **Rev:** Springbok walking right divides date **Edge:** Reeded **Note:** 180 edge serrations for uncirculated, 220 serrations for proof

Date	Mintage	F	VF	XF	Unc	BU
2001	6,429	—	—	—	BV+8%	—
2001 Proof	3,696	Value: 950				
2002	—	—	—	—	BV+8%	—
2002 Proof	2,295	Value: 950				
2003	11,588	—	—	—	BV+8%	—
2003 Proof	1,285	Value: 950				
2004	—	—	—	—	BV+8%	—
2004 Proof	3,288	Value: 950				
2005	—	—	—	—	BV+8%	—
2005 Proof	—	Value: 950				
2006	—	—	—	—	BV+8%	—
2006 Proof	—	Value: 950				
2007	—	—	—	—	BV+8%	—
2007 Proof	3,400	Value: 950				
2008	—	—	—	—	BV+8%	—
2008 Proof	3,300	Value: 950				
2009	—	—	—	—	BV+8%	—
2009 Proof	2,500	Value: 950				
2010	—	—	—	—	BV+8%	—
2010 Proof	2,500	Value: 950				
2011	—	—	—	—	BV+8%	—
2011 Proof	—	Value: 950				
2012	—	—	—	—	BV+8%	—
2012 Proof	—	Value: 950				

KM# 73 KRUGERRAND
33.9300 g., 0.9170 Gold 1.0003 oz. AGW, 32.7 mm. **Obv:** Bust of Paul Kruger left **Obv. Legend:** SUID — AFRIKA • SOUTH AFRICA **Rev:** Springbok walking right divides date **Edge:** Reeded **Note:** 180 edge serrations for uncirculated, 220 serrations for proof

Date	Mintage	F	VF	XF	Unc	BU
2001	5,889	—	—	—	—	BV+5%
2001 Proof	5,563	Value: 1,850				
2002	16,469	—	—	—	—	BV+5%
2002 Proof	3,531	Value: 1,850				
2003	47,789	—	—	—	—	BV+5%
2003 Proof	2,136	Value: 1,850				
2004	71,269	—	—	—	—	BV+5%
2004 Proof	3,492	Value: 1,850				
2004 W/MM Proof	500	Value: 1,850				
2005	—	—	—	—	—	BV+5%
2005 Proof	—	Value: 1,850				
2006	—	—	—	—	—	BV+5%
2006 Proof	—	Value: 1,850				
2007	—	—	—	—	—	BV+5%
2007 Proof	3,400	Value: 1,850				
2008	—	—	—	—	—	BV+5%
2008 Proof	3,300	Value: 1,850				
2009	—	—	—	—	—	BV+5%
2009 Proof	2,500	Value: 1,850				
2010	—	—	—	—	—	BV+5%
2010 Proof	2,500	Value: 1,850				
2011	—	—	—	—	—	BV+5%
2011 Proof	—	Value: 1,850				
2012	—	—	—	—	—	BV+5%
2012 Proof	—	Value: 1,850				

SILVER BULLION NATURA COINAGE

KM# 242 2-1/2 CENTS
1.4140 g., 0.9250 Silver 0.0420 oz. ASW, 16.3 mm. **Obv:** Crowned arms **Rev:** Dolphin **Edge:** Reeded

Date	Mintage	F	VF	XF	Unc	BU
2001 Proof	—	Value: 27.50				

KM# 480 2-1/2 CENTS
1.4140 g., 0.9250 Silver 0.0420 oz. ASW, 16.3 mm. **Obv:** Flower **Rev:** Vasco de Gama's ship "Sao Gabriel"

Date	Mintage	F	VF	XF	Unc	BU
2009 Proof	3,500	Value: 15.00				

KM# 243 5 CENTS
8.4560 g., 0.9250 Silver 0.2515 oz. ASW, 26.7 mm. **Series:** Wildlife - Power **Obv:** Water buffalo's head **Rev:** Two water buffalo heads within circle below value **Edge:** Reeded

Date	Mintage	F	VF	XF	Unc	BU
2001 Proof	1,853	Value: 40.00				

KM# 351 5 CENTS
8.4560 g., 0.9250 Silver 0.2515 oz. ASW, 26.7 mm. **Series:** Wildlife - Strength **Obv:** Elephant walking, facing **Rev:** Elephant 3/4 left bathing **Edge:** Reeded

Date	Mintage	F	VF	XF	Unc	BU
2002 Proof	2,425	Value: 30.00				

KM# 355 5 CENTS
8.4560 g., 0.9250 Silver 0.2515 oz. ASW, 26.7 mm. **Series:** Wildlife - Survivor **Obv:** New national arms **Rev:** 2 White Rhinoceros drinking at stream **Edge:** Reeded

Date	Mintage	F	VF	XF	Unc	BU
2003 Proof	1,870	Value: 40.00				

KM# 359 5 CENTS
8.4560 g., 0.9250 Silver 0.2515 oz. ASW, 26.7 mm. **Series:** Wildlife - The Legend **Obv:** New national arms **Rev:** Head of Leopard right drinking **Edge:** Reeded

Date	Mintage	F	VF	XF	Unc	BU
2004 Proof	—	Value: 40.00				

KM# 320 5 CENTS
8.4560 g., 0.9250 Silver 0.2515 oz. ASW, 27.12 mm. **Series:** Wildlife - African Wild Dog **Obv:** New national arms **Rev:** Painted Dog's head facing slightly left **Edge:** Reeded

Date	Mintage	F	VF	XF	Unc	BU
2005 Proof	1,500	Value: 40.00				

KM# 316 5 CENTS
8.4560 g., 0.9250 Silver 0.2515 oz. ASW, 27 mm. **Series:** Wildlife - Black-backed Jackal **Obv:** New national arms **Rev:** Black-backed jackal drinking **Edge:** Reeded

Date	Mintage	F	VF	XF	Unc	BU
2006 Proof	1,500	Value: 40.00				

KM# 363 5 CENTS
8.4560 g., 0.9250 Silver 0.2515 oz. ASW, 26.7 mm. **Series:** Wildlife - Kgalagadi Transfrontier Peace Park **Obv:** New national arms **Rev:** Local desert melons, value **Edge:** Reeded

Date	Mintage	F	VF	XF	Unc	BU
2007 Proof	—	Value: 40.00				

KM# 458 5 CENTS
8.4060 g., 0.9250 Silver 0.2500 oz. ASW, 27 mm. **Subject:** Richtersveld Transfrontier Park **Obv:** Arms **Rev:** Orbea Namaquensis succulant flower

Date	Mintage	F	VF	XF	Unc	BU
2008 Proof	2,200	Value: 30.00				

KM# 482 5 CENTS
8.4060 g., 0.9250 Silver 0.2500 oz. ASW, 27 mm. **Subject:** Maloti Drakensberg Transfrontier Project **Obv:** Arms **Rev:** Spiral Aloe Tree (aloe polyphylla)

Date	Mintage	F	VF	XF	Unc	BU
2009 Proof	3,700	Value: 25.00				

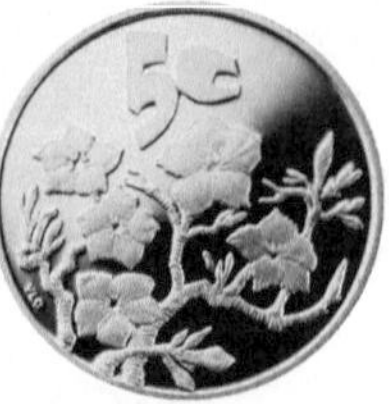

KM# 513 5 CENTS
8.4060 g., 0.9250 Silver 0.2500 oz. ASW, 27 mm.

Date	Mintage	F	VF	XF	Unc	BU
2011 Proof	—	Value: 40.00				

KM# 529 5 CENTS
8.4500 g., 0.9250 Silver 0.2513 oz. ASW, 27 mm. **Subject:** Great Mapungubwe Transfrontier Conservation Area **Obv:** National arms **Rev:** Baobab tree seed pod, sandstone landscape in background

Date	Mintage	F	VF	XF	Unc	BU
2012 Proof	—	Value: 25.00				

KM# 244 10 CENTS
16.8630 g., 0.9250 Silver 0.5015 oz. ASW, 32.7 mm. **Series:** Wildlife - Power **Obv:** Water buffalo's head **Rev:** Two water buffalo bulls fighting **Edge:** Reeded

Date	Mintage	F	VF	XF	Unc	BU
2001 Proof	1,989	Value: 65.00				

KM# 352 10 CENTS
16.8130 g., 0.9250 Silver 0.5000 oz. ASW, 38.3 mm. **Series:** Wildlife - Strength **Obv:** Elephant walking, facing **Rev:** 2 elephant heads facing each other **Edge:** Reeded

Date	Mintage	F	VF	XF	Unc	BU
2002 Proof	2,395	Value: 55.00				

KM# 356 10 CENTS
16.8130 g., 0.9250 Silver 0.5000 oz. ASW, 32.7 mm. **Series:** Wildlife - Survivor **Obv:** New national arms **Rev:** 2 Black Rhinoceros standing, facing **Edge:** Reeded

Date	Mintage	F	VF	XF	Unc	BU
2003 Proof	1,815	Value: 65.00				

KM# 360 10 CENTS
16.8130 g., 0.9250 Silver 0.5000 oz. ASW, 32.7 mm. **Series:** Wildlife - The Legend **Obv:** New national arms **Rev:** Leopard and impala above two leopard cubs playing **Edge:** Reeded

Date	Mintage	F	VF	XF	Unc	BU
2004 Proof	—	Value: 65.00				

KM# 321 10 CENTS
16.8130 g., 0.9250 Silver 0.5000 oz. ASW, 32.7 mm. **Series:** Wildlife - African Wild Dog **Obv:** New national arms **Rev:** Two Painted Dogs walking right **Edge:** Reeded

Date	Mintage	F	VF	XF	Unc	BU
2005 Proof	1,500	Value: 65.00				

KM# 317 10 CENTS
16.8630 g., 0.9250 Silver 0.5015 oz. ASW, 32.7 mm. **Series:** Wildlife - Black-backed Jackel **Obv:** New national arms **Rev:** Black-backed jackal chasing birds **Edge:** Reeded

Date	Mintage	F	VF	XF	Unc	BU
2006 Proof	1,500	Value: 65.00				

KM# 364 10 CENTS
16.8130 g., 0.9250 Silver 0.5000 oz. ASW, 32.7 mm. **Series:** Wildlife - Kgaladadi Transfrontier Peace Park **Obv:** New national arms **Rev:** Local tribe, value **Edge:** Reeded

Date	Mintage	F	VF	XF	Unc	BU
2007 Proof	—	Value: 65.00				

KM# 459 10 CENTS
16.8130 g., 0.9250 Silver 0.5000 oz. ASW, 32.7 mm. **Subject:** Richtersveld Transfrontier Park **Obv:** Arms **Rev:** Local Nama native and livestock

Date	Mintage	F	VF	XF	Unc	BU
2008 Proof	2,200	Value: 55.00				

KM# 483 10 CENTS
16.8130 g., 0.9250 Silver 0.5000 oz. ASW, 32.7 mm. **Subject:** Maloti Drakensberg Transfrontier Project **Obv:** Arms **Rev:** Native Basotho riding pony

Date	Mintage	F	VF	XF	Unc	BU
2009 Proof	3,700	Value: 45.00				

KM# 514 10 CENTS
16.8130 g., 0.9250 Silver 0.5000 oz. ASW, 32.7 mm.

Date	Mintage	F	VF	XF	Unc	BU
2011 Proof	—	Value: 65.00				

KM# 530 10 CENTS
16.8630 g., 0.9250 Silver 0.5015 oz. ASW, 32.82 mm. **Subject:** Great Mapungubwe Transfrontier Conservation Area **Obv:** National arms **Rev:** Golden Rhino and sandstone rock formations in background

Date	Mintage	F	VF	XF	Unc	BU
2012 Proof	—	Value: 65.00				

KM# 245 20 CENTS
33.7260 g., 0.9250 Silver 1.0030 oz. ASW, 38.3 mm. **Series:** Wildlife - Power **Obv:** Water buffalo's head **Rev:** Two water buffalo heads facing **Edge:** Reeded

Date	Mintage	F	VF	XF	Unc	BU
2001 Proof	1,902	Value: 85.00				

KM# 353 20 CENTS
33.7260 g., 0.9250 Silver 1.0030 oz. ASW, 38.3 mm. **Series:** Wildlife - Strength **Obv:** Elephant walking, facing **Rev:** Family of four elephants **Edge:** Reeded

Date	Mintage	F	VF	XF	Unc	BU
2002 Proof	2,435	Value: 75.00				

KM# 357 20 CENTS
33.7260 g., 0.9250 Silver 1.0030 oz. ASW, 38.3 mm. **Series:** Wildlife - Survivor **Obv:** New national arms **Rev:** White Rhinoceros mother with an offspring **Edge:** Reeded

Date	Mintage	F	VF	XF	Unc	BU
2003 Proof	1,930	Value: 85.00				

KM# 361 20 CENTS
33.7260 g., 0.9250 Silver 1.0030 oz. ASW, 38.3 mm. **Series:** Wildlife - The legend **Obv:** New national arms **Rev:** Leopard looking left, cub on branch behind her **Edge:** Reeded

Date	Mintage	F	VF	XF	Unc	BU
2004 Proof	—	Value: 85.00				

KM# 322 20 CENTS
33.7500 g., 0.9250 Silver 1.0037 oz. ASW, 38.67 mm. **Series:** Wildlife - African Wild Dog **Obv:** New National arms **Rev:** Three Painted Dogs **Edge:** Reeded

Date	Mintage	F	VF	XF	Unc	BU
2005 Proof	1,500	Value: 85.00				

KM# 318 20 CENTS
33.7260 g., 0.9250 Silver 1.0030 oz. ASW, 38.7 mm. **Series:** Wildlife - Black-backed Jackal **Obv:** National arms **Rev:** Two Black-backed jackals **Edge:** Reeded

Date	Mintage	F	VF	XF	Unc	BU
2006 Proof	1,500	Value: 85.00				

KM# 365 20 CENTS
33.7260 g., 0.9250 Silver 1.0030 oz. ASW, 38.3 mm. **Series:** Wildlife - Kgalagadi Transfrontier Peace Park **Obv:** New national arms **Rev:** Lion's head 3/4 right at left, meerkat standing with offspring at right, value **Edge:** Reeded

Date	Mintage	F	VF	XF	Unc	BU
2007 Proof	—	Value: 85.00				

KM# 460 20 CENTS
33.7250 g., 0.9250 Silver 1.0029 oz. ASW, 38.7 mm. **Subject:** Richtersveld Transfrontier Park **Obv:** Arms **Rev:** Two shy Kipspringer (Oreotragus oreotragos)

Date	Mintage	F	VF	XF	Unc	BU
2008 Proof	2,200	Value: 75.00				

KM# 484 20 CENTS
33.6200 g., 0.9250 Silver 0.9998 oz. ASW, 38.72 mm. **Subject:** Maloti Drakensberg Transfrontier Project **Obv:** Arms **Rev:** Cape griffon vulture

Date	Mintage	F	VF	XF	Unc	BU
2009 Proof	3,700	Value: 75.00				

KM# 515 20 CENTS
33.7260 g., 0.9250 Silver 1.0030 oz. ASW, 38.72 mm.

Date	Mintage	F	VF	XF	Unc	BU
2011 Proof	—	Value: 85.00				

KM# 531 20 CENTS
33.7260 g., 0.9250 Silver 1.0030 oz. ASW, 38.3 mm. **Subject:** Great Mapungubwe Transfrontier Conservation Area **Obv:** National arms **Rev:** Pel's Fishing Owl (scotopelia peli) and standstone rock formations in background

Date	Mintage	F	VF	XF	Unc	BU
2012 Proof	—	Value: 85.00				

KM# 246 50 CENTS
76.4020 g., 0.9250 Silver 2.2721 oz. ASW, 50 mm. **Series:** Wildlife - Power **Obv:** Water buffalo's head **Rev:** Water buffalo head, value **Edge:** Reeded

Date	Mintage	F	VF	XF	Unc	BU
2001 Proof	1,866	Value: 110				

KM# 354 50 CENTS
76.4020 g., 0.9250 Silver 2.2721 oz. ASW, 50 mm. **Series:** Wildlife - Strength **Obv:** Elephant walking, facing **Rev:** Elephant right with head raised **Edge:** Reeded

Date	Mintage	F	VF	XF	Unc	BU
2002 Proof	2,318	Value: 110				

KM# 358 50 CENTS
76.4020 g., 0.9250 Silver 2.2721 oz. ASW, 50 mm. **Series:** Wildlife - Survivor **Obv:** New national arms **Rev:** White Rhinoceros' head 3/4 right, value **Edge:** Reeded

Date	Mintage	F	VF	XF	Unc	BU
2003 Proof	1,918	Value: 110				

KM# 362 50 CENTS
76.4620 g., 0.9250 Silver 2.2738 oz. ASW, 50 mm. **Series:** Wildlife - The Legend **Obv:** New national arms **Rev:** Leopard facing snarling, two leopards at lower left **Edge:** Reeded

Date	Mintage	F	VF	XF	Unc	BU
2004 Proof	—	Value: 110				

KM# 323 50 CENTS
76.8600 g., 0.9250 Silver 2.2857 oz. ASW, 50.48 mm. **Series:** Wildlife - African Wild Dog **Obv:** New national arms **Rev:** Two painted Dog's heads facing **Edge:** Reeded

Date	Mintage	F	VF	XF	Unc	BU
2005 Proof	1,500	Value: 110				

KM# 319 50 CENTS
76.2520 g., 0.9250 Silver 2.2676 oz. ASW, 50 mm. **Series:** Wildlife - Black-backed Jackal **Obv:** New national arms **Rev:** Two black-backed jackals fighting over a carcass **Edge:** Reeded

Date	Mintage	F	VF	XF	Unc	BU
2006 Proof	1,500	Value: 110				

KM# 366 50 CENTS
76.4020 g., 0.9250 Silver 2.2721 oz. ASW, 50 mm. **Series:** Wildlife - Kgalagadi Transfrontier Peace Park **Obv:** New national arms **Rev:** Antelope running right **Edge:** Reeded

Date	Mintage	F	VF	XF	Unc	BU
2007 Proof	—	Value: 110				

KM# 461 50 CENTS
76.2520 g., 0.9250 Silver 2.2676 oz. ASW, 50 mm. **Subject:** Richtersveld Transfrontier Park **Obv:** Arms **Rev:** Giant aloe pillansii tree

Date	Mintage	F	VF	XF	Unc	BU
2008 Proof	2,200	Value: 110				

KM# 485 50 CENTS
76.2520 g., 0.9250 Silver 2.2676 oz. ASW, 50 mm. **Subject:** Maloti Drakensberg Transfrontier Project **Obv:** Arms **Rev:** Amphitheatre and Trukela River

Date	Mintage	F	VF	XF	Unc	BU
2009 Proof	3,700	Value: 100				

KM# 516 50 CENTS
76.4020 g., 0.9250 Silver 2.2721 oz. ASW, 50 mm.

Date	Mintage	F	VF	XF	Unc	BU
2011 Proof	—	Value: 110				

KM# 532 50 CENTS
76.4020 g., 0.9250 Silver 2.2721 oz. ASW, 50 mm. **Subject:** Great Mapungubwe Transfrontier Conservation Area **Obv:** National Arms **Rev:** Baobab Tree and sandstone landscape in background

Date	Mintage	F	VF	XF	Unc	BU
2012 Proof	—	Value: 110				

KM# 248 2 RAND
33.6260 g., 0.9250 Silver 1.0000 oz. ASW, 38.7 mm. **Obv:** New national arms **Rev:** Dolphins **Edge:** Reeded

Date	Mintage	F	VF	XF	Unc	BU
2001 Proof	2,987	Value: 80.00				

KM# 280 2 RAND
33.6260 g., 0.9250 Silver 1.0000 oz. ASW, 38.7 mm. **Obv:** New national arms **Rev:** Southern Right Whale **Edge:** Reeded

Date	Mintage	F	VF	XF	Unc	BU
2002 Proof	1,808	Value: 85.00				

KM# 286 2 RAND
33.6260 g., 0.9250 Silver 1.0000 oz. ASW, 38.7 mm. **Obv:** New national arms **Rev:** Martial and Bateleur Eagles **Edge:** Reeded

Date	Mintage	F	VF	XF	Unc	BU
2003 Proof	2,166	Value: 75.00				

KM# 284 2 RAND
33.6260 g., 0.9250 Silver 1.0000 oz. ASW, 38.7 mm. **Obv:** New national arms **Rev:** Verreaux's Eagle Owl face and value **Edge:** Reeded

Date	Mintage	F	VF	XF	Unc	BU
2004	—	—	—	—	50.00	55.00
2004 Proof	1,752	Value: 85.00				

KM# 372 2 RAND
33.6260 g., 0.9250 Silver 1.0000 oz. ASW, 38.7 mm. **Obv:** New national arms **Rev:** Three vultures **Edge:** Reeded

Date	Mintage	F	VF	XF	Unc	BU
2005 Proof	4,000	Value: 70.00				

KM# 374 2 RAND
33.6260 g., 0.9250 Silver 1.0000 oz. ASW, 38.7 mm. **Series:** Bird of Prey **Obv:** New national arms **Rev:** Two Secretary birds **Edge:** Reeded

Date	Mintage	F	VF	XF	Unc	BU
2006 Proof	4,000	Value: 75.00				

KM# 481 2 RAND
33.6260 g., 0.9250 Silver 1.0000 oz. ASW, 38.7 mm. **Obv:** Arms and country name **Rev:** Jan van Riebeeck's ship "Drommedaries"

Date	Mintage	F	VF	XF	Unc	BU
2009 Proof	3,500	Value: 55.00				

SILVER BULLION PROTEA COINAGE

KM# 282 2-1/2 CENTS
1.4140 g., 0.9250 Silver 0.0420 oz. ASW, 16.3 mm. **Obv:** Protea flower **Rev:** Southern Right Whale **Edge:** Plain

Date	Mintage	F	VF	XF	Unc	BU
2002 Proof	3,000	Value: 27.50				

KM# 285 2-1/2 CENTS
1.4140 g., 0.9250 Silver 0.0420 oz. ASW, 16.3 mm. **Obv:** Protea flower **Rev:** Martial and Bateleur Eagles **Edge:** Plain

Date	Mintage	F	VF	XF	Unc	BU
2003 Proof	—	Value: 25.00				

KM# 283 2-1/2 CENTS
1.4140 g., 0.9250 Silver 0.0420 oz. ASW, 16.3 mm. **Series:** Birds of Prey **Obv:** Protea flower **Rev:** Pearl Spotted Owlet **Edge:** Plain

Date	Mintage	F	VF	XF	Unc	BU
2004 Proof	2,000	Value: 25.00				

KM# 348 2-1/2 CENTS
1.4140 g., 0.9250 Silver 0.0420 oz. ASW, 16.3 mm. **Obv:** Protea flower **Obv. Legend:** SOUTH AFRICA **Rev:** Vulture alighting **Edge:** Plain

Date	Mintage	F	VF	XF	Unc	BU
2005 Proof	—	Value: 25.00				

KM# 349 2-1/2 CENTS
1.4140 g., 0.9250 Silver 0.0420 oz. ASW, 16.3 mm. **Obv:** Protea flower **Obv. Legend:** SOUTH AFRICA **Rev:** Head of Secretary bird **Edge:** Plain

Date	Mintage	F	VF	XF	Unc	BU
2006 Proof	—	Value: 25.00				

KM# 350 2-1/2 CENTS
1.4140 g., 0.9250 Silver 0.0420 oz. ASW, 16.3 mm. **Subject:** International Polar Year **Obv:** Protea flower **Obv. Legend:** SOUTH AFRICA **Rev:** Globe displaying South Pole **Edge:** Plain

Date	Mintage	F	VF	XF	Unc	BU
2007 Proof	—	Value: 25.00				

KM# 456 2-1/2 CENTS
1.4140 g., 0.9250 Silver 0.0420 oz. ASW, 16.3 mm. **Obv:** Flower **Rev:** Map of Antarctica

Date	Mintage	F	VF	XF	Unc	BU
2008 Proof	3,000	Value: 15.00				

KM# 231 RAND
15.0000 g., 0.9250 Silver 0.4461 oz. ASW, 32.7 mm. **Subject:** Tourism **Obv:** Protea flower **Rev:** Steam locomotive and flower **Edge:** Reeded

Date	Mintage	F	VF	XF	Unc	BU
2001	2,400	—	—	—	40.00	45.00
2001 Proof	1,784	Value: 65.00				

KM# 277 RAND
15.0000 g., 0.9250 Silver 0.4461 oz. ASW, 32.7 mm. **Subject:** Soccer **Obv:** Protea flower **Rev:** Goalkeeper in action **Edge:** Reeded

Date	Mintage	F	VF	XF	Unc	BU
2002	1,777	—	—	—	40.00	45.00
2002 Proof	1,250	Value: 65.00				

KM# 367 RAND
15.5500 g., 0.9250 Silver 0.4624 oz. ASW **Subject:** World Summit - Johannesburg **Obv:** Protea flower **Rev:** Globe **Edge:** Reeded

Date	Mintage	F	VF	XF	Unc	BU
2002	1,531	—	—	—	55.00	60.00
2002 Proof	1,413	Value: 75.00				

KM# 298 RAND
15.0500 g., 0.9250 Silver 0.4476 oz. ASW, 32.7 mm. **Obv:** Protea flower **Rev:** Cricket player **Edge:** Reeded

Date	Mintage	F	VF	XF	Unc	BU
2003	1,697	—	—	—	55.00	60.00
2003 Proof	1,250	Value: 75.00				

KM# 288 RAND
15.0000 g., 0.9250 Silver 0.4461 oz. ASW, 32.7 mm. **Subject:** 10th Anniversary of South African Democracy **Obv:** Protea flower **Rev:** Flora and fauna **Edge:** Reeded

Date	Mintage	F	VF	XF	Unc	BU
2004	3,427	—	—	—	35.00	40.00
2004 Proof	2,930	Value: 50.00				

KM# 368 RAND
15.0000 g., 0.9250 Silver 0.4461 oz. ASW, 32.7 mm. **Series:** Nobel Peace Prize Winners **Obv:** Protea flower **Rev:** Bust of Chief A. J. Luthuli facing at center, Luthuli seated at desk left at lower right **Edge:** Reeded

Date	Mintage	F	VF	XF	Unc	BU
2005	—	—	—	—	50.00	55.00
2005 Proof	—	Value: 65.00				

KM# 369 RAND
15.0000 g., 0.9250 Silver 0.4461 oz. ASW, 32.7 mm. **Series:** Nobel Peace prize Winners **Obv:** Protea flower **Rev:** 1/3 length figure of Archbishop Desmond Mpilo Tutu facing at right **Edge:** Reeded

Date	Mintage	F	VF	XF	Unc	BU
2006	—	—	—	—	60.00	65.00
2006 Proof	—	Value: 75.00				

KM# 370 RAND
15.0000 g., 0.9250 Silver 0.4461 oz. ASW, 32.7 mm. **Series:** Nobel Peace Prize Winners **Obv:** Protea flower **Rev:** Bust of De Klerk facing **Edge:** Reeded

Date	Mintage	F	VF	XF	Unc	BU
2007	—	—	—	—	55.00	60.00
2007 Proof	—	Value: 70.00				

KM# 371 RAND
15.5500 g., 0.9250 Silver 0.4624 oz. ASW, 32.7 mm. **Series:** Nobel Peace Prize Winners **Obv:** Protea flower **Rev:** Bust of Mandela facing **Edge:** Reeded

Date	Mintage	F	VF	XF	Unc	BU
2007	—	—	—	—	65.00	75.00
2007 Proof	—	Value: 95.00				

KM# 451 RAND
15.5500 g., 0.9250 Silver 0.4624 oz. ASW, 32.7 mm. **Obv:** Protea flower **Rev:** Ghandi portrait

Date	Mintage	F	VF	XF	Unc	BU
2008	—	—	—	—	—	25.00
2008 Proof	11,000	Value: 30.00				

KM# 475 RAND
15.5500 g., 0.9250 Silver 0.4624 oz. ASW, 32.7 mm. **Obv:** Protea flower **Rev:** Portraits of C. J. Langenhoven and N. L. de Villiers with musical score

Date	Mintage	F	VF	XF	Unc	BU
2009	—	—	—	—	—	25.00
2009 Proof	11,000	Value: 30.00				

SILVER BULLION CULTURE COINAGE

KM# 373 2 RAND
33.6260 g., 0.9250 Silver 1.0000 oz. ASW, 38.7 mm. **Subject:** 2006 FIFA World Cup Soccer - Germany **Obv:** New national arms **Rev:** Soccer ball above globe **Edge:** Reeded

Date	Mintage	F	VF	XF	Unc	BU
2005 Proof	50,000	Value: 60.00				

KM# 435 2 RAND
33.6260 g., 0.9250 Silver 1.0000 oz. ASW, 38.7 mm. **Subject:** 2010 World Cup

Date	Mintage	F	VF	XF	Unc	BU
2006	25,000	—	—	—	—	50.00

KM# 376 2 RAND
33.6260 g., 0.9250 Silver 1.0000 oz. ASW, 38.7 mm. **Subject:** International Polar Year **Obv:** New national arms **Rev:** Logo above globe **Edge:** Reeded

Date	Mintage	F	VF	XF	Unc	BU
2007 Proof	6,000	Value: 75.00				

KM# 377 2 RAND
33.6260 g., 0.9250 Silver 1.0000 oz. ASW, 38.7 mm. **Subject:** 2010 FIFA World Cup Soccer - South Africa **Obv:** New national arms **Rev:** Tower at left, animal heads at top. animal at right, soccer ball ar bottom **Edge:** Reeded

Date	Mintage	F	VF	XF	Unc	BU
2007 Proof	20,000	Value: 65.00				

KM# 437 2 RAND
33.6260 g., 0.9250 Silver 1.0000 oz. ASW, 38.7 mm. **Subject:** 2010 World Cup

Date	Mintage	F	VF	XF	Unc	BU
2008 Proof	—	Value: 60.00				

KM# 457 2 RAND
33.6260 g., 0.9250 Silver 1.0000 oz. ASW, 38.7 mm. **Obv:** Arms **Rev:** Polar ship "SA Sgulhas"

Date	Mintage	F	VF	XF	Unc	BU
2008 Proof	3,000	Value: 80.00				

GOLD BULLION NATURA COINAGE

KM# 517 2 RAND
7.7700 g., 0.9999 Gold 0.2498 oz. AGW, 22 mm.

Date	Mintage	F	VF	XF	Unc	BU
2011 Proof	—	Value: 475				

KM# 533 2 RAND
7.7700 g., 0.9999 Gold 0.2498 oz. AGW, 22 mm. **Subject:** Khoisan Heritage **Obv:** National Arms **Rev:** Incuse stone carving of an eland

Date	Mintage	F	VF	XF	Unc	BU
2012 Proof	—	Value: 475				

KM# 410 10 RAND
3.1107 g., 0.9999 Gold 0.1000 oz. AGW, 16.5 mm. **Series:** Natura **Obv:** Cheetah's head **Rev:** Cheetah drinking water **Edge:** Reeded

Date	Mintage	F	VF	XF	Unc	BU
2002 Proof	3,156	Value: 200				

KM# 414 10 RAND
3.1107 g., 0.9999 Gold 0.1000 oz. AGW, 16.5 mm. **Series:** Natura **Obv:** Male and female lion's heads **Rev:** Two lioness drinking water **Edge:** Reeded

Date	Mintage	F	VF	XF	Unc	BU
2003 Proof	4,233	Value: 200				

KM# 418 10 RAND
3.1107 g., 0.9999 Gold 0.1000 oz. AGW, 16.5 mm. **Series:** Natura **Obv:** Caracal's head and shoulders **Rev:** Caracal drinking water **Edge:** Reeded

Date	Mintage	F	VF	XF	Unc	BU
2004 Proof	1,809	Value: 210				

KM# 422 10 RAND
3.1107 g., 0.9999 Gold 0.1000 oz. AGW, 16.5 mm. **Series:** Natura **Obv:** Hippopotamus 1/2 way in water **Rev:** Hippopotamus deeply in water **Edge:** Reeded **Designer:** Aldrid Minnie

Date	Mintage	F	VF	XF	Unc	BU
2005 Proof	—	Value: 210				

KM# 426 10 RAND
3.1107 g., 0.9999 Gold 0.1000 oz. AGW, 16.5 mm. **Series:** Natura **Obv:** Giraffe's head and neck **Rev:** Giraffe drinking water **Edge:** Reeded

Date	Mintage	F	VF	XF	Unc	BU
2006 Proof	—	Value: 200				

KM# 430 10 RAND
3.1107 g., 0.9999 Gold 0.1000 oz. AGW, 16.5 mm. **Series:** Natura **Obv:** Forepart of Eland left **Rev:** Eland drinking water right **Edge:** Reeded **Designer:** Aldrid Minnie

Date	Mintage	F	VF	XF	Unc	BU
2007 Proof	—	Value: 200				

KM# 447 10 RAND
3.1100 g., 0.9990 Gold 0.0999 oz. AGW, 16.5 mm. **Obv:** Large elephant head and elephant family below **Rev:** One elephant eating, three elephants below **Designer:** C. Moses and N. van Niekerk

Date	Mintage	F	VF	XF	Unc	BU
2008 Proof	3,300	Value: 200				

KM# 471 10 RAND
3.1100 g., 0.9990 Gold 0.0999 oz. AGW, 16.5 mm. **Obv:** White rhino, silouette and forepart **Rev:** Two rhino foreparts facing left within large silouette

Date	Mintage	F	VF	XF	Unc	BU
2009 Proof	2,500	Value: 200				

KM# 509 10 RAND
3.1107 g., 0.9999 Gold 0.1000 oz. AGW, 16.5 mm.

Date	Mintage	F	VF	XF	Unc	BU
2011 Proof	—	Value: 210				

KM# 525 10 RAND
3.1170 g., 0.9999 Gold 0.1002 oz. AGW, 16.5 mm. **Subject:** Great Mapungubwe Transfrontier Conservation Area

Date	Mintage	F	VF	XF	Unc	BU
2012 Proof	—	Value: 210				

KM# 411 20 RAND
7.7770 g., 0.9999 Gold 0.2500 oz. AGW, 22 mm. **Series:** Natura **Obv:** Cheetah's head **Rev:** Cheetah family resting **Edge:** Reeded

Date	Mintage	F	VF	XF	Unc	BU
2002 Proof	2,548	Value: 510				

KM# 415 20 RAND
7.7770 g., 0.9999 Gold 0.2500 oz. AGW, 22 mm. **Series:** Natura **Obv:** Male and female lion's heads **Rev:** Lion family resting **Edge:** Reeded

Date	Mintage	F	VF	XF	Unc	BU
2003 Proof	2,799	Value: 510				

KM# 419 20 RAND
7.7770 g., 0.9999 Gold 0.2500 oz. AGW, 22 mm. **Series:** Natura **Obv:** Caracal's head and shoulders **Rev:** Caracal with cub standing right **Edge:** Reeded

Date	Mintage	F	VF	XF	Unc	BU
2004 Proof	1,407	Value: 520				

KM# 423 20 RAND
7.7770 g., 0.9999 Gold 0.2500 oz. AGW, 22 mm. **Series:** Natura **Obv:** Hippopotamus 1/2 way in water **Rev:** Mother and baby Hippopotamus grazing **Edge:** Reeded

Date	Mintage	F	VF	XF	Unc	BU
2005 Proof	—	Value: 520				

KM# 389 20 RAND
7.7770 g., 0.9999 Gold 0.2500 oz. AGW, 22 mm. **Series:** World Heritage Site **Subject:** Mapungubwe **Obv:** New national arms **Rev:** Rhinoceros standing right **Edge:** Reeded

Date	Mintage	F	VF	XF	Unc	BU
2005 Proof	1,000	Value: 520				

KM# 427 20 RAND
7.7770 g., 0.9999 Gold 0.2500 oz. AGW, 22 mm. **Series:** Natura **Obv:** Giraffe's head and neck **Rev:** Mother and baby giraffes grazing **Edge:** Reeded

Date	Mintage	F	VF	XF	Unc	BU
2006 Proof	—	Value: 520				

KM# 431 20 RAND
7.7770 g., 0.9999 Gold 0.2500 oz. AGW, 22 mm. **Series:** Natura **Obv:** Forepart of Eland left **Rev:** Mother Eland and calf grazing **Edge:** Reeded **Designer:** Aldrid Minnie

Date	Mintage	F	VF	XF	Unc	BU
2007 Proof	—	Value: 520				

KM# 448 20 RAND
7.7770 g., 0.9990 Gold 0.2498 oz. AGW, 22 mm. **Obv:** Large elephant head and elephant family below **Rev:** Two elephants fighting, three elephants below

Date	Mintage	F	VF	XF	Unc	BU
2008 Proof	3,300	Value: 510				

KM# 455 20 RAND
7.7700 g., 0.9990 Gold 0.2496 oz. AGW, 22 mm. **Subject:** Vredefort Dome **Obv:** Arms **Rev:** Meteorite

Date	Mintage	F	VF	XF	Unc	BU
2008 Proof	2,000	Value: 510				

KM# 472 20 RAND
7.7770 g., 0.9990 Gold 0.2498 oz. AGW, 22 mm. **Obv:** White rhino silouette and forepart **Rev:** Two rhinos walking forward within silhouette

Date	Mintage	F	VF	XF	Unc	BU
2009 Proof	2,500	Value: 510				

KM# 510 20 RAND
7.7700 g., 0.9999 Gold 0.2498 oz. AGW, 22 mm.

Date	Mintage	F	VF	XF	Unc	BU
2011 Proof	—	Value: 510				

KM# 526 20 RAND
7.7700 g., 0.9999 Gold 0.2498 oz. AGW, 22 mm.

Date	Mintage	F	VF	XF	Unc	BU
2012 Proof	—	Value: 510				

KM# 412 50 RAND
15.5530 g., 0.9999 Gold 0.5000 oz. AGW, 27 mm. **Series:** Natura **Obv:** Cheetah's head **Rev:** Cheetah attacking Impala **Edge:** Reeded

Date	Mintage	F	VF	XF	Unc	BU
2002 Proof	2,295	Value: 975				

KM# 416 50 RAND
15.5530 g., 0.9999 Gold 0.5000 oz. AGW, 27 mm. **Series:** Natura **Obv:** Male and female lion's heads **Rev:** Female and male lions playing **Edge:** Reeded

Date	Mintage	F	VF	XF	Unc	BU
2003 Proof	2,600	Value: 975				

KM# 420 50 RAND
15.5530 g., 0.9999 Gold 0.5000 oz. AGW, 27 mm. **Series:** Natura **Obv:** Caracal's head and shoulders **Rev:** Caracal eating prey **Edge:** Reeded **Designer:** Aldrid Minnie

Date	Mintage	F	VF	XF	Unc	BU
2004 Proof	1,327	Value: 1,000				

KM# 424 50 RAND
15.5530 g., 0.9999 Gold 0.5000 oz. AGW, 27 mm. **Series:** Natura **Obv:** Hippopotamus 1/2 way in water **Rev:** Hippopotamus submerged in water with head raised above, mouth wide open **Edge:** Reeded

Date	Mintage	F	VF	XF	Unc	BU
2005 Proof	—	Value: 1,000				

KM# 428 50 RAND
15.5530 g., 0.9999 Gold 0.5000 oz. AGW, 27 mm. **Series:** Natura **Obv:** Giraffe's head and neck **Rev:** Giraffe family walking left **Edge:** Reeded

Date	Mintage	F	VF	XF	Unc	BU
2006 Proof	—	Value: 1,000				

KM# 432 50 RAND
15.5530 g., 0.9999 Gold 0.5000 oz. AGW, 27 mm. **Series:** Natura **Obv:** Forepart of eland left **Rev:** Three eland running right **Edge:** Reeded

Date	Mintage	F	VF	XF	Unc	BU
2007 Proof	—	Value: 1,000				

KM# 449 50 RAND
15.5530 g., 0.9999 Gold 0.5000 oz. AGW, 27 mm. **Obv:** Large elephant and elephant family below **Rev:** Three elephants, one trumpeting, three elephants below

Date	Mintage	F	VF	XF	Unc	BU
2008 Proof	4,800	Value: 975				

KM# 473 50 RAND
15.5500 g., 0.9999 Gold 0.4999 oz. AGW, 27 mm. **Obv:** White rhino silhouette and forpart **Rev:** Two rhinos facing off within large silouette

Date	Mintage	F	VF	XF	Unc	BU
2009 Proof	4,000	Value: 975				

KM# 511 50 RAND
15.5530 g., 0.9999 Gold 0.5000 oz. AGW, 27 mm.

Date	Mintage	F	VF	XF	Unc	BU
2011 Proof	—	Value: 975				

KM# 527 50 RAND
15.5530 g., 0.9999 Gold 0.5000 oz. AGW, 27 mm.

Date	Mintage	F	VF	XF	Unc	BU
2012 Proof	—	Value: 975				

KM# 413 100 RAND
31.1070 g., 0.9999 Gold 1.0000 oz. AGW, 32.69 mm. **Series:** Natura **Obv:** Cheetah's head **Rev:** Cheetah posing **Edge:** Reeded

Date	Mintage	F	VF	XF	Unc	BU
2002 Proof	2,550	Value: 1,900				
2002 RSA logo Proof	496	Value: 2,000				

KM# 417 100 RAND
31.1070 g., 0.9999 Gold 1.0000 oz. AGW, 32.69 mm. **Series:** Natura **Obv:** Male and female lion's heads **Rev:** Snarling male and female lion's heads **Edge:** Reeded **Note:** L P RSA - LION PARK RSA.

Date	Mintage	F	VF	XF	Unc	BU
2003 Proof	2,758	Value: 1,900				
2003 L P RSA Proof	498	Value: 2,000				

KM# 421 100 RAND
31.1070 g., 0.9999 Gold 1.0000 oz. AGW, 32.69 mm. **Series:** Natura **Obv:** Caracal's head and shoulders **Rev:** Caracal crouching on branch left **Edge:** Reeded **Note:** C/C - CARACAL / CARACAL

Date	Mintage	F	VF	XF	Unc	BU
2004 Proof	1,405	Value: 1,900				
2004 C/C Proof	500	Value: 2,000				

KM# 425 100 RAND
31.1070 g., 0.9999 Gold 1.0000 oz. AGW, 32.69 mm. **Series:** Natura **Obv:** Hippopotamus 1/2 way in water **Rev:** Two hippopotami submerged in water, heads raised, mouths open faced in combat **Edge:** Reeded **Note:** MAPU - MAPUNGUBWE.

Date	Mintage	F	VF	XF	Unc	BU
2005 Proof	—	Value: 1,900				
2005 MAPU Proof	—	Value: 2,000				

KM# 429 100 RAND
31.1070 g., 0.9999 Gold 1.0000 oz. AGW, 32.69 mm. **Series:** Natura **Obv:** Giraffe's head and neck **Rev:** Head and neck view of giraffe eating tree leaves **Edge:** Reeded **Designer:** M. J. Scheepers **Note:** lpp/EWT - lion's paw print / EWT.

Date	Mintage	F	VF	XF	Unc	BU
2006 Proof	—	Value: 1,900				
2006 lpp/EWT Proof	—	Value: 2,000				

KM# 433 100 RAND
31.1070 g., 0.9999 Gold 1.0000 oz. AGW, 32.7 mm. **Series:** Natura **Obv:** Forepart of eland left **Rev:** Eland grazing left **Edge:** Reeded

Date	Mintage	F	VF	XF	Unc	BU
2007 Proof	—	Value: 1,900				

KM# 450 100 RAND
31.1070 g., 0.9990 Gold 0.9991 oz. AGW, 32.69 mm. **Obv:** Large elephant head and elephant family below **Rev:** Large elephant facing, three elephants below

Date	Mintage	F	VF	XF	Unc	BU
2008 Proof	4,800	Value: 1,900				

KM# 474 100 RAND
31.1070 g., 0.9990 Gold 0.9991 oz. AGW, 32.7 mm. **Obv:** White rhino silouette and forepart **Rev:** Rhino standing facing within large silhouette

Date	Mintage	F	VF	XF	Unc	BU
2009 Proof	4,000	Value: 1,900				

KM# 512 100 RAND
31.1070 g., 0.9999 Gold 1.0000 oz. AGW, 32.7 mm.

Date	Mintage	F	VF	XF	Unc	BU
2011 Proof	—	Value: 1,900				

KM# 528 100 RAND
31.1070 g., 0.9999 Gold 1.0000 oz. AGW, 32.7 mm.

Date	Mintage	F	VF	XF	Unc	BU
2012 Proof	—	Value: 1,900				

KM# 264 1/10 OUNCE
3.1107 g., 0.9999 Gold 0.1000 oz. AGW, 16.5 mm. **Series:** Natura **Obv:** Gemsbok's upper body **Rev:** Gemsbok drinking **Edge:** Reeded

Date	Mintage	F	VF	XF	Unc	BU
2001 Proof	3,498	Value: 210				

KM# 265 1/4 OUNCE
7.7770 g., 0.9999 Gold 0.2500 oz. AGW, 22 mm. **Series:** Natura **Obv:** Gemsbok's upper body **Rev:** Two Gemsbok bulls facing off **Edge:** Reeded

Date	Mintage	F	VF	XF	Unc	BU
2001 Proof	2,904	Value: 510				

KM# 266 1/2 OUNCE
15.5530 g., 0.9999 Gold 0.5000 oz. AGW, 27 mm. **Series:** Natura **Obv:** Gemsbok's upper body **Rev:** Gemsbok family grazing **Edge:** Reeded

Date	Mintage	F	VF	XF	Unc	BU
2001 Proof	2,754	Value: 975				

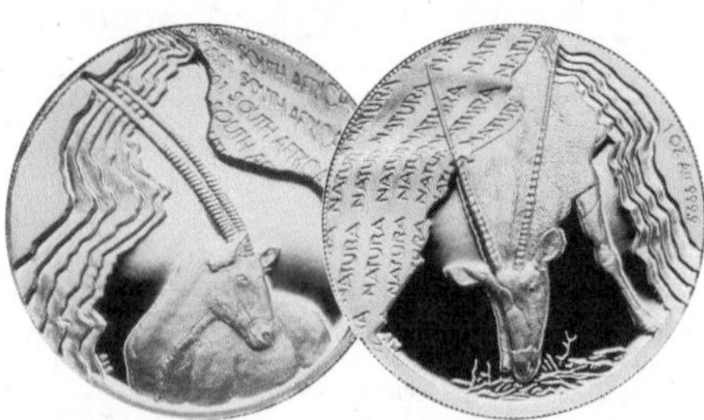

KM# 267 OUNCE
31.1070 g., 0.9999 Gold 1.0000 oz. AGW, 32.69 mm. **Series:** Natura **Obv:** Gemsbok's upper body **Rev:** Gemsbok grazing **Edge:** Reeded **Note:** ghCW - Gemsbok's head CW

Date	Mintage	F	VF	XF	Unc	BU
2001 Proof	3,104	Value: 1,900				
2001 Proof	491	Value: 2,000				

GOLD BULLION CULTURE COINAGE

KM# 247 RAND
3.1103 g., 0.9999 Gold 0.1000 oz. AGW, 16.5 mm. **Series:** Cultural **Obv:** New national arms **Obv. Legend:** UMZANTSI AFRIKA - SOUTH AFRICA **Rev:** Seated Sotho figure with headdress **Edge:** Reeded

Date	Mintage	F	VF	XF	Unc	BU
2001 Proof	236	Value: 275				

KM# 378 RAND
3.1103 g., 0.9999 Gold 0.1000 oz. AGW, 16.5 mm. **Series:** Cultural **Obv:** New national arms **Obv. Legend:** UMZANTSI AFRIKA - SOUTH AFRICA **Rev:** Three Xhosa tribe members **Edge:** Reeded

Date	Mintage	F	VF	XF	Unc	BU
2001 Proof	—	Value: 675				

KM# 379 RAND
3.1103 g., 0.9999 Gold 0.1000 oz. AGW, 16.5 mm. **Series:** Cultural **Subject:** Tswana Nation **Obv:** New national arms **Obv. Legend:** Aforika Borwa - South Africa **Rev:** Four tribe people standing **Edge:** Reeded

Date	Mintage	F	VF	XF	Unc	BU
2002 Proof	300	Value: 350				

KM# 380 RAND
3.1103 g., 0.9999 Gold 0.1000 oz. AGW, 16.5 mm. **Series:** Cultural **Obv:** New national arms **Obv. Legend:** Afrika-Dzonga - South Africa **Rev:** Tsonga tribe dancer and drummer **Edge:** Reeded

Date	Mintage	F	VF	XF	Unc	BU
2003 Proof	348	Value: 350				

KM# 381 RAND
3.1103 g., 0.9999 Gold 0.1000 oz. AGW, 16.5 mm. **Series:** Cultural **Obv:** New national arms **Obv. Legend:** Afurika Tshipembe - South Africa **Rev:** Six Venda tribe members crossing bridge **Edge:** Reeded

Date	Mintage	F	VF	XF	Unc	BU
2004 Proof	380	Value: 350				

KM# 382 RAND
3.1103 g., 0.9999 Gold 0.1000 oz. AGW, 16.5 mm. **Series:** Cultural **Obv:** New national arms **Obv. Legend:** iSewula Afrika - South Africa **Rev:** Ndebele woman standing, native print in background **Edge:** Reeded

Date	Mintage	F	VF	XF	Unc	BU
2005 Proof	1,000	Value: 210				

KM# 383 RAND
3.1103 g., 0.9999 Gold 0.1000 oz. AGW, 16.5 mm. **Series:** Cultural **Obv:** New national arms **Obv. Legend:** Ningizimu Afrika - South Africa **Rev:** 1/2 length figure of Ema-Swati Chief left at right **Edge:** Reeded

Date	Mintage	F	VF	XF	Unc	BU
2006 Proof	1,000	Value: 210				

KM# 385 RAND
3.1103 g., 0.9999 Gold 0.1000 oz. AGW, 16.5 mm. **Subject:** 2010 FIFA World Cup Soccer - South Africa **Obv:** New national arms **Obv. Legend:** SOUTH AFRICA **Rev:** Bird head at left facing animal at right, soccer ball at bottom **Edge:** Reeded

Date	Mintage	F	VF	XF	Unc	BU
2007 Proof	10,000	Value: 200				

KM# 384 RAND
3.1103 g., 0.9999 Gold 0.1000 oz. AGW, 16.5 mm. **Subject:** The Afrikaner Nation **Obv:** New national arms **Obv. Legend:** SOUTH AFRIKA **Rev:** Ox drawn wagon up hillside **Edge:** Reeded

Date	Mintage	F	VF	XF	Unc	BU
2007 Proof	—	Value: 210				

KM# 454 RAND
3.1100 g., 0.9990 Gold 0.0999 oz. AGW, 16.5 mm. **Obv:** Arms

Date	Mintage	F	VF	XF	Unc	BU
2008 Proof	1,000	Value: 210				

KM# 478 RAND
3.1100 g., 0.9990 Gold 0.0999 oz. AGW, 16.5 mm. **Subject:** Northern Sotho (Bapedi) peoples **Obv:** Arms **Rev:** Woman seated, cooking

Date	Mintage	F	VF	XF	Unc	BU
2009 Proof	1,000	Value: 210				

KM# 249 2 RAND
7.7770 g., 0.9999 Gold 0.2500 oz. AGW, 22 mm. **Obv:** New national arms **Rev:** Gondwana theoretical landmass and dinosaur **Edge:** Reeded

Date	Mintage	F	VF	XF	Unc	BU
2001 Proof	558	Value: 550				

KM# 386 2 RAND
7.7770 g., 0.9999 Gold 0.2500 oz. AGW, 22 mm. **Series:** World Heritage Site **Subject:** Robben Island **Obv:** New national arms **Rev:** Carved stone, island in background **Edge:** Reeded

Date	Mintage	F	VF	XF	Unc	BU
2002 Proof	999	Value: 550				

KM# 387 2 RAND
7.7770 g., 0.9999 Gold 0.2500 oz. AGW, 22 mm. **Series:** World heritage Site **Subject:** Greater St. Lucia Wetland Park **Obv:** New national arms **Rev:** Various birds **Edge:** Reeded

Date	Mintage	F	VF	XF	Unc	BU
2003 Proof	637	Value: 550				

KM# 388 2 RAND
7.7770 g., 0.9999 Gold 0.2500 oz. AGW, 22 mm. **Series:** World Heritage Park **Subject:** "Ukhahlamba" Drakensberg Park **Obv:** New national arms **Rev:** Early painting of animal and hunters **Edge:** Reeded

Date	Mintage	F	VF	XF	Unc	BU
2004 Proof	750	Value: 550				

KM# 390 2 RAND
7.7770 g., 0.9999 Gold 0.2500 oz. AGW, 22 mm. **Subject:** 2006 FIFA World Cup Soccer - Germany **Obv:** New national arms **Rev:** Soccer ball at center above partial globe within ornate border art **Edge:** Reeded

Date	Mintage	F	VF	XF	Unc	BU
2005 Proof	—	Value: 550				

KM# 391 2 RAND
7.7770 g., 0.9999 Gold 0.2500 oz. AGW, 22 mm. **Series:** World Heritage Site **Subject:** Cradle of Mankind **Obv:** New national arms **Rev:** Early man standing at upper left, ape's head at upper right, skull at lower left, value at lower right **Edge:** Reeded

Date	Mintage	F	VF	XF	Unc	BU
2006 Proof	1,000	Value: 520				

KM# 392 2 RAND
7.7770 g., 0.9999 Gold 0.2500 oz. AGW, 22 mm. **Subject:** 2006 FIFA World Cup Soccer - Germany **Obv:** New national arms **Rev:** Logo in ornate frame **Edge:** Reeded

Date	Mintage	F	VF	XF	Unc	BU
2006 Proof	15,000	Value: 510				

KM# 393 2 RAND
7.7770 g., 0.9999 Gold 0.2500 oz. AGW, 22 mm. **Series:** World Heritage Site **Subject:** Cape Floral **Obv:** New national arms **Rev:** Bird perched on branch at left, plant at center, land in distance **Edge:** Reeded

Date	Mintage	F	VF	XF	Unc	BU
2007 Proof	—	Value: 510				

KM# 394 2 RAND
7.7770 g., 0.9999 Gold 0.2500 oz. AGW, 22 mm. **Subject:** 2010 FIFA World Cup Soccer - South Africa **Obv:** New national arms **Rev:** Animal in ornate frame at left and right, small soccer ball at bottom below value **Edge:** Reeded

Date	Mintage	F	VF	XF	Unc	BU
2007 Proof	10,000	Value: 510				

KM# 479 2 RAND
7.7700 g., 0.9990 Gold 0.2496 oz. AGW, 22 mm. **Subject:** Richtersveld Cultural and Botanical Landscape **Obv:** Arms **Rev:** Native "haru on" hut and aloe pilansil tree

Date	Mintage	F	VF	XF	Unc	BU
2009 Proof	2,000	Value: 520				

GOLD BULLION PROTEA COINAGE

KM# 395 5 RAND
3.1107 g., 0.9999 Gold 0.1000 oz. AGW, 16.5 mm. **Subject:** 10th Anniversary Soccer "Bafana Bafana" **Obv:** Protea flower **Rev:** Two players running right **Edge:** Reeded

Date	Mintage	F	VF	XF	Unc	BU
2002 Proof	386	Value: 275				

KM# 397 5 RAND
3.1107 g., 0.9999 Gold 0.1000 oz. AGW, 16.5 mm. **Subject:** World Summit on Sustainable Development **Obv:** Protea flower **Rev:** Globe featuring Africa **Rev. Inscription:** prosperity **Edge:** Reeded

Date	Mintage	F	VF	XF	Unc	BU
2002 Proof	511	Value: 225				

KM# 278 5 RAND
3.1104 g., 0.9999 Gold 0.1000 oz. AGW, 16.5 mm. **Obv:** Protea flower **Rev:** Soccer player heading the ball **Edge:** Reeded

Date	Mintage	F	VF	XF	Unc	BU
2002 Proof	—	Value: 210				

KM# 399 5 RAND
3.1107 g., 0.9999 Gold 0.1000 oz. AGW, 16.5 mm. **Subject:** Cricket World Cup **Obv:** Protea flower **Rev:** Cricket ball striking stumps **Rev. Inscription:** Protea **Edge:** Reeded

Date	Mintage	F	VF	XF	Unc	BU
2003 Proof	925	Value: 210				

KM# 289 5 RAND
3.1100 g., 0.9999 Gold 0.1000 oz. AGW, 16.5 mm. **Subject:** 10th Anniversary of South African Democracy **Obv:** Protea flower **Rev:** Inscription covered flag **Edge:** Reeded

Date	Mintage	F	VF	XF	Unc	BU
2004 Proof	1,000	Value: 210				

KM# 401 5 RAND
3.1107 g., 0.9999 Gold 0.1000 oz. AGW, 16.5 mm. **Subject:** 10th Anniversay Democracy **Obv:** Protea flower **Rev:** Flag made of constitution **Edge:** Reeded **Note:** 10YF - circular 10 YEARS FREEDOM

Date	Mintage	F	VF	XF	Unc	BU
2004 Proof	2,089	Value: 375				
2004 10YF Proof	492	Value: 600				

KM# 403 5 RAND
3.1107 g., 0.9999 Gold 0.1000 oz. AGW, 16.5 mm. **Subject:** Nobel Prize Winners **Obv:** Protea flower **Rev:** Freedom Charter, Luthuli seated left at desk at lower right **Edge:** Reeded **Note:** FR - FREEDOM

Date	Mintage	F	VF	XF	Unc	BU
2005 Proof	2,000	Value: 210				
2005 FR Proof	—	Value: 600				

KM# 405 5 RAND
3.1107 g., 0.9999 Gold 0.1000 oz. AGW, 16.5 mm. **Subject:** Nobel Prize Winners **Obv:** Protea flower **Rev:** Cross, inscription **Edge:** Reeded

Date	Mintage	F	VF	XF	Unc	BU
2006 Proof	5,600	Value: 210				
2006 logo Proof	400	Value: 500				

KM# 407 5 RAND
3.1107 g., 0.9999 Gold 0.1000 oz. AGW, 16.5 mm. **Subject:** Nobel Prize winners **Obv:** Protea flower **Rev:** Extract from de Klerk's acceptance speech **Edge:** Reeded

Date	Mintage	F	VF	XF	Unc	BU
2007 Proof	8,000	Value: 210				
2007 dove Proof	—	Value: 700				

KM# 408 5 RAND
3.1107 g., 0.9999 Gold 0.1000 oz. AGW, 16.5 mm. **Subject:** Nobel Prize Winners **Obv:** Protea flower **Rev:** Extract from Mandela's acceptance speech **Edge:** Reeded

Date	Mintage	F	VF	XF	Unc	BU
2007 Proof	—	Value: 210				
2007 dove Proof	—	Value: 700				

KM# 452 5 RAND
3.1100 g., 0.9990 Gold 0.0999 oz. AGW, 16.5 mm. **Obv:** Protea flower **Rev:** Ghandi figure at prayer

Date	Mintage	F	VF	XF	Unc	BU
2008 Proof	8,000	Value: 210				

KM# 476 5 RAND
3.1100 g., 0.9990 Gold 0.0999 oz. AGW, 16.5 mm. **Obv:** Protea flower **Rev:** Portraits of C. J. Langenhoven and M. L. de Villiers with musical score

Date	Mintage	F	VF	XF	Unc	BU
2009 Proof	8,000	Value: 200				

KM# 396 25 RAND
31.1070 g., 0.9999 Gold 1.0000 oz. AGW, 32.69 mm. **Subject:** 10th Anniversary Soccer "Bafana Bafana" **Obv:** Protea flower **Rev:** Two players running left **Edge:** Reeded

Date	Mintage	F	VF	XF	Unc	BU
2002 Proof	137	Value: 1,950				
2002 flag/CW Proof	84	Value: 2,250				

KM# 398 25 RAND
31.1070 g., 0.9999 Gold 1.0000 oz. AGW, 32.69 mm. **Subject:** World Summit on Sustainable Development **Obv:** Protea flower **Rev:** Globe featuring Africa **Edge:** Reeded

Date	Mintage	F	VF	XF	Unc	BU
2002 Proof	421	Value: 1,900				

KM# 279 25 RAND
31.1035 g., 0.9999 Gold 0.9999 oz. AGW, 32.7 mm. **Obv:** Protea flower **Rev:** Soccer player kicking ball **Edge:** Reeded

Date	Mintage	F	VF	XF	Unc	BU
2002 Proof	492	Value: 1,900				

KM# 400 25 RAND
31.1070 g., 0.9999 Gold 1.0000 oz. AGW, 32.69 mm. **Subject:** Cricket World Cup **Obv:** Protea flower **Rev:** Batsman on one knee about to sweep the ball **Rev. Legend:** PROTEA **Edge:** Reeded

Date	Mintage	F	VF	XF	Unc	BU
2003 Proof	210	Value: 1,950				
2003 ball/RSA Proof	208	Value: 1,950				

KM# 402 25 RAND
31.1070 g., 0.9999 Gold 1.0000 oz. AGW, 32.69 mm. **Subject:** 10th Anniversary Democracy **Obv:** Protea flower **Rev:** Two heads of Mandela, one left, one facing, Union building in background **Edge:** Reeded **Note:** 10FP - 10/flag, people

Date	Mintage	F	VF	XF	Unc	BU
2004 Proof	6,000	Value: 3,000				
2004 10FP Proof	492	Value: 5,400				

KM# 404 25 RAND
31.1070 g., 0.9999 Gold 1.0000 oz. AGW, 32.69 mm. **Subject:** Nobel Prize Winners **Obv:** Protea flower **Rev:** Bust of Chief Albert Luthuli facing **Edge:** Reeded **Note:** FC - FREEDOM / CHARTER / 26 JUNE 1955

Date	Mintage	F	VF	XF	Unc	BU
2005 Proof	6,000	Value: 1,900				
2005 FC Proof	—	Value: 3,750				

KM# 406 25 RAND
31.1070 g., 0.9999 Gold 1.0000 oz. AGW, 32.69 mm. **Subject:** Nobel Prize Winners **Obv:** Protea flower **Rev:** Cross, bust of Archbishop Desmond Tutu right **Edge:** Reeded

Date	Mintage	F	VF	XF	Unc	BU
2006 Proof	7,600	Value: 1,900				
2006 logo Proof	400	Value: 2,600				

KM# 409 25 RAND
31.1070 g., 0.9999 Gold 1.0000 oz. AGW, 32.69 mm. **Subject:** Nobel Prize Winners **Obv:** Protea flower **Rev:** Busts of Mandela, de Klerk right **Edge:** Reeded **Note:** d-P - dove Peace

Date	Mintage	F	VF	XF	Unc	BU
2007 Proof	12,000	Value: 1,900				
2007 d-P Proof	—	Value: 2,750				

KM# 453 25 RAND
31.1070 g., 0.9990 Gold 0.9991 oz. AGW, 32.7 mm. **Obv:** Protea flower **Rev:** Ghandi profile at right

Date	Mintage	F	VF	XF	Unc	BU
2008 Proof	600	Value: 2,000				
2008 Proof	12,000	Value: 1,900				

KM# 477 25 RAND
31.1070 g., 0.9990 Gold 0.9991 oz. AGW, 32.7 mm. **Obv:** Protea flower **Rev:** Portraits of C. J. Langenhoven and M. L. de Villiers and musical score

Date	Mintage	F	VF	XF	Unc	BU
2009 Proof	11,000	Value: 1,900				

KM# 262 1/10 PROTEA
3.1107 g., 0.9999 Gold 0.1000 oz. AGW, 16.5 mm. **Subject:** Tourism **Obv:** Protea flower **Rev:** Lion's head facing, partial shield **Rev. Inscription:** PROTEA **Edge:** Reeded

Date	Mintage	F	VF	XF	Unc	BU
2001 Proof	1,076	Value: 210				

KM# 263 PROTEA
31.1070 g., 0.9999 Gold 1.0000 oz. AGW, 32.6 mm. **Subject:** Tourism **Obv:** Protea flower **Rev:** Child on sandy beach, Table Mountain in background, partial star at right **Rev. Inscription:** PROTEA **Edge:** Reeded

Date	Mintage	F	VF	XF	Unc	BU
2001 Proof	972	Value: 2,000				
2001 GRC(pp) Proof	196	Value: 2,500				

MINT SETS

KM#	Date	Mintage	Identification	Issue Price	Mkt Val
MS38	2002 (7)	—	KM#268-274 plus 1- and 2-cent medals	30.00	32.50
MS39	2001 (9)	5,577	KM#221-229	—	60.00
MS40	2002 (7)	3,886	KM#268-274	—	52.50
MS41	2002 (7)	1,640	KM#268-274, circulated coins	—	17.50
MS42	2003 (7)	2,602	KM#324, 327, 330, 332, 335, 337, 347	—	45.00
MS43	2003 (7)	1,380	KM#324, 327, 330, 332, 335, 337, 347, circulted coins	—	10.00
MS44	2004 (7)	1,948	KM#281, 325, 326, 328, 331, 333, 336	—	37.50
MS45	2004 (7)	1,131	KM#281, 325, 325, 328, 331, 333, 336, circulated coins	—	17.50
MS46	2004 (7)	325	KM#281, 325, 326, 328, 331, 333, 336, Baby	—	22.50
MS47	2004 (7)	23	KM#281, 325, 326, 328, 331, 333, 336, Wedding	—	22.50
MS48	2005 (7)	—	KM#291-297	—	30.00
MS49	2005 (7)	—	KM#291-297, circulated coins	—	15.00
MS50	2005 (7)	—	KM#291-297, Baby	—	23.00
MS51	2005 (7)	—	KM#291-297, Wedding	—	22.50
MS52	2006 (7)	—	KM#291-297	—	22.50
MS53	2006 (7)	—	KM#291-297, circulated coins	—	15.00
MS54	2006 (7)	—	KM#291-297, Baby	—	15.00
MS55	2006 (7)	—	KM#291-297, Wedding	—	15.00
MS56	2007 (7)	—	KM#340-346	—	22.50
MS57	2007 (7)	—	KM#340-346, circulated coins	—	15.00
MS58	2007 (7)	—	KM#340-346, baby	—	15.00
MS59	2007 (7)	—	KM#340-346, wedding	—	15.00

PIEFORT PROOF SETS (PPS)

KM#	Date	Mintage	Identification	Issue Price	Mkt Val
PS242	2007 (4)	—	KM#430-433, leatherette	—	3,000

PROOF SETS

KM#	Date	Mintage	Identification	Issue Price	Mkt Val
PS170	2002 (7)	—	KM#268-274 plus 1- and 2-cent medals	40.00	65.00
PS171	2005 (4)	1,500	KM#320-323	—	300
PS172	2001 (9)	3,678	KM#221-229	—	75.00
PS173	2001 (9)	—	KM#221-229 wedding	—	75.00
PS174	2002 (7)	—	KM#268-274	—	75.00
PS175	2002 (7)	330	KM#268-274, baby	—	75.00
PS176	2003 (7)	2,356	KM#324, 327, 330, 332, 335, 337, 347	—	65.00
PS177	2003 (7)	500	KM#324, 327, 330, 332, 335, 337, 347, baby	—	65.00
PS178	2003 (7)	53	KM#324, 327, 330, 332, 335, 337, 347, wedding	—	65.00
PS179	2004 (7)	1,935	KM#281, 325, 326, 328, 331, 333, 336	—	65.00
PS180	2004 (7)	326	KM#281, 325, 326, 328, 331, 333, 336, baby	—	65.00
PS181	2004 (7)	23	KM#281, 325, 326, 328, 331, 333, 336, wedding	—	65.00
PS182	2005 (7)	—	KM#291-297	—	65.00
PS183	2005 (7)	—	KM#291-297, baby	—	65.00
PS184	2005 (7)	—	KM#291-297, wedding	—	65.00
PS185	2006 (7)	—	KM#291-297	—	65.00
PS186	2006 (7)	—	KM#291-297, baby	—	65.00
PS187	2006 (7)	—	KM#291-297, wedding	—	65.00
PS188	2007 (7)	—	KM#340-346	—	65.00
PS189	2007 (7)	—	KM#340-346, baby	—	65.00
PS190	2007 (7)	—	KM#340-346, wedding	—	65.00
PS193	2001 (4)	411	KM#243-246, wooden case	—	375
PS194	2001 (4)	746	KM#243-246, velvet (med case)	—	300
PS195	2002 (3)	81	KM#234, 243, 351 (mixed dates)	—	110
PS196	2002 (3)	95	KM#235, 244, 352 (mixed dates)	—	185
PS197	2002 (3)	81	KM#236, 245, 353 (mixed dates)	—	250
PS198	2002 (3)	92	KM#237, 246, 354 (mixed dates)	—	335
PS199	2002 (4)	411	KM#351-354, wooden case	—	375
PS200	2002 (4)	746	KM#351-354, velvet lined case	—	275
PS201	2003 (4)	59	KM#234, 243, 351, 355 (mixed dates)	—	150
PS202	2003 (4)	47	KM#235, 244, 352, 356 (mixed dates)	—	250
PS203	2003 (4)	75	KM#236, 245, 353, 357 (mixed dates)	—	330
PS204	2003 (4)	62	KM#237, 246, 354, 358 (mixed dates)	—	450
PS205	2003 (4)	532	KM#355-358, wooden case	—	375
PS206	2003 (4)	1,029	KM#355-358, velvet lined case	—	300
PS207	2004 (5)	132	KM#234, 243, 351, 355, 359 (mixed dates)	—	200
PS208	2004 (5)	133	KM#235, 244, 352, 356, 360 (mixed dates)	—	325
PS209	2004 (5)	181	KM#236, 245, 353, 357, 361 (mixed dates)	—	450
PS210	2004 (5)	158	KM#237, 246, 354, 358, 362 (mixed dates)	—	555
PS211	2004 (4)	645	KM#359-362, wooden case	—	375
PS212	2004 (4)	454	KM#359-362, velvet lined case	—	300
PS213	2004 (4)	299	KM#359-362, plus 1/4 oz. medal	—	300
PS214	2005 (4)	—	KM#320-323, wooden case	—	300
PS215	2005 (4)	—	KM#320-323, velvet lined case	—	300
PS216	2006 (4)	—	KM#316-319, wooden case	—	300
PS217	2006 (4)	—	KM#316-319, velvet lined case	—	300
PS218	2007 (2)	—	KM#363-364, wooden case	—	150
PS219	2007 (2)	—	KM#363-364	—	105
PS223	2000 (4)	483	KM#258-261, prestige	—	3,500
PS224	2000 (4)	334	KM#258-261, leatherette	—	3,500
PS225	2001 (4)	691	KM#264-267	—	3,500
PS226	2001 (4)	985	KM#264-267, leatherette	—	3,500
PS227	2001 (4)	310	KM#264-267, special export	—	3,500
PS228	2002 (4)	698	KM#410-413, prestige	—	3,500
PS229	2002 (4)	529	KM#410-413, leatherette	—	3,500
PS230	2002 (4)	682	KM#410-413, special	—	3,500
PS231	2003 (4)	698	KM#414-417, prestige	—	3,500
PS232	2003 (4)	908	KM#414-417, leatherette	—	3,500
PS233	2003 (4)	722	KM#414-417, anniversary	—	3,500
PS234	2004 (4)	700	KM#418-421, prestige	—	3,525
PS235	2004 (4)	440	KM#418-421, leatherette	—	3,525
PS236	2004 (4)	125	KM#418-421, special export with silver African Continent	—	3,525
PS237	2005 (4)	—	KM#422-425, prestige	—	3,525
PS238	2005 (4)	—	KM#422-425, leatherette	—	3,525
PS239	2006 (4)	—	KM#426-429, prestige	—	3,500
PS240	2006 (4)	—	KM#426-429, leatherette	—	3,500
PS241	2007 (4)	—	KM#430-433, prestige	—	3,500

SPECIMEN SETS (SS)

KM#	Date	Mintage	Identification	Issue Price	Mkt Val
SS1	1994 (9)	5,508	KM#132-140	—	25.00
SS2	1995 (9)	4,956	KM#132-140	—	25.00
SS3	1996 (9)	5,766	KM#158-166	19.50	25.00
SS4	1997 (9)	4,236	KM#159-166, 170	—	25.00
SS5	1998 (9)	—	KM#159-166, 170	—	25.00
SS6	1999 (9)	—	KM#159-166, 170	—	25.00

S. GEORGIA & THE S. SANDWICH IS.

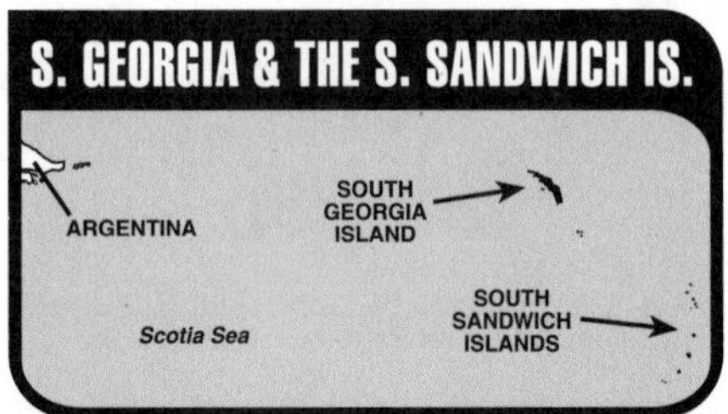

South Georgia and the South Sandwich Islands are a dependency of the Falkland Islands, and located about 800 miles east of them. South Georgia is 1,450 sq. mi. (1,770 sq. km.), and the South Sandwich Islands are 120 sq. mi. (311 sq. km.) Fishing and Antarctic research are the main industries. The islands were claimed for Great Britain in 1775 by Captain James Cook.

RULER

British since 1775

BRITISH OVERSEAS TERRITORY

STANDARD COINAGE

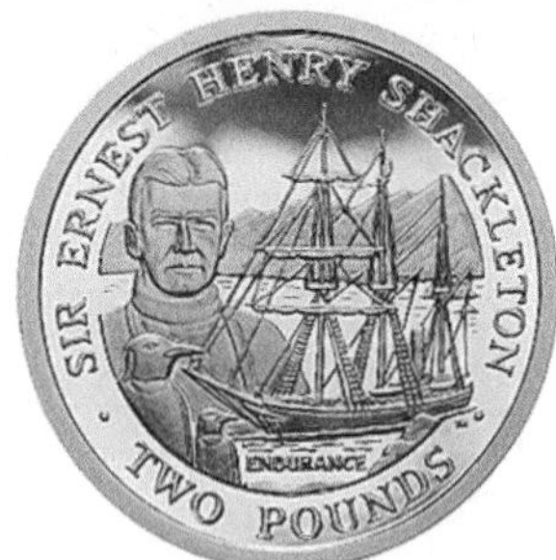

KM# 7 2 POUNDS
28.2800 g., Copper-Nickel, 38.61 mm. **Ruler:** Elizabeth II **Subject:** Sir Ernest H. Shackleton **Obv:** Crowned bust right **Rev:** Bust facing and ship "Endurance" **Edge:** Reeded

Date	Mintage	F	VF	XF	Unc	BU
2001PM	—	—	—	—	10.00	12.00

KM# 7a 2 POUNDS
28.2800 g., 0.9250 Silver 0.8410 oz. ASW, 38.61 mm. **Ruler:** Elizabeth II **Obv:** Crowned bust right **Rev:** Bust facing and ship "Endurance"

Date	Mintage	F	VF	XF	Unc	BU
2001PM Proof	Est. 10,000	Value: 50.00				

KM# 9 2 POUNDS
28.2800 g., Copper-Nickel, 38.61 mm. **Ruler:** Elizabeth II **Subject:** Sir Joseph Banks **Obv:** Crowned bust right **Rev:** Cameo and ship

Date	Mintage	F	VF	XF	Unc	BU
2001PM	—	—	—	—	10.00	12.00

KM# 9a 2 POUNDS
28.2800 g., 0.9250 Silver 0.8410 oz. ASW, 38.61 mm. **Ruler:** Elizabeth II **Obv:** Crowned bust right **Rev:** Ship and cameo

Date	Mintage	F	VF	XF	Unc	BU
2001PM Proof	Est. 10,000	Value: 50.00				

KM# 11 2 POUNDS
28.2800 g., Copper-Nickel, 38.6 mm. **Ruler:** Elizabeth II **Subject:** Queen Elizabeth II's Golden Jubilee **Obv:** Crowned bust right **Rev:** Young crowned bust right **Edge:** Reeded

Date	Mintage	F	VF	XF	Unc	BU
2002PM	—	—	—	—	10.00	12.00

KM# 11a 2 POUNDS
28.2800 g., 0.9250 Gold Plated Silver 0.8410 oz. ASW AGW, 38.6 mm. **Ruler:** Elizabeth II **Subject:** Queen Elizabeth II's Golden Jubilee **Obv:** Crowned bust right **Rev:** Young crowned bust right **Edge:** Reeded

Date	Mintage	F	VF	XF	Unc	BU
2002PM Proof	10,000	Value: 50.00				

KM# 13 2 POUNDS
28.2800 g., Copper-Nickel, 38.6 mm. **Ruler:** Elizabeth II **Subject:** Queen Elizabeth II's Golden Jubilee **Obv:** Crowned bust right **Rev:** Small crown above shield flanked by flower sprigs **Edge:** Reeded

Date	Mintage	F	VF	XF	Unc	BU
2002PM	—	—	—	—	10.00	12.00

KM# 13a 2 POUNDS
28.2800 g., 0.9250 Gold Plated Silver 0.8410 oz. ASW AGW, 38.6 mm. **Ruler:** Elizabeth II **Subject:** Queen Elizabeth II's Golden Jubilee **Obv:** Crowned bust right **Rev:** Small crown above shield flanked by flower sprigs **Edge:** Reeded

Date	Mintage	F	VF	XF	Unc	BU
2002PM Proof	10,000	Value: 50.00				

KM# 15 2 POUNDS
28.2800 g., Copper-Nickel, 38.6 mm. **Ruler:** Elizabeth II **Subject:** Diana, Princess of Wales - The Work Continues **Obv:** Crowned bust right **Rev:** Head 1/4 left **Edge:** Reeded

Date	Mintage	F	VF	XF	Unc	BU
2002PM	—	—	—	—	10.00	12.00

KM# 17 2 POUNDS
28.2800 g., Copper-Nickel, 38.6 mm. **Ruler:** Elizabeth II **Subject:** Prince William's 21st Birthday **Obv:** Crowned bust right **Rev:** Arms of Prince William of Wales **Edge:** Reeded

Date	Mintage	F	VF	XF	Unc	BU
2003PM	—	—	—	—	10.00	12.00

KM# 17a 2 POUNDS
28.2800 g., 0.9250 Silver 0.8410 oz. ASW, 38.6 mm. **Ruler:** Elizabeth II **Subject:** Prince William's 21st Birthday **Obv:** Crowned bust right **Rev:** Arms of Prince William of Wales **Edge:** Reeded

Date	Mintage	F	VF	XF	Unc	BU
2003PM Proof	—	Value: 50.00				

KM# 18 2 POUNDS
28.2800 g., Copper-Nickel, 38.6 mm. **Ruler:** Elizabeth II **Obv:** Crowned bust right **Rev:** Capt. Cook, ship and map **Edge:** Reeded

Date	Mintage	F	VF	XF	Unc	BU
2003PM	—	—	—	—	10.00	12.00

KM# 18a 2 POUNDS
28.2800 g., 0.9250 Silver 0.8410 oz. ASW, 38.6 mm. **Ruler:** Elizabeth II **Obv:** Crowned bust right **Rev:** Capt. Cook, ship and map **Edge:** Reeded

Date	Mintage	F	VF	XF	Unc	BU
2003PM Proof	—	Value: 50.00				

KM# 20 2 POUNDS
28.2800 g., Copper-Nickel, 38.6 mm. **Ruler:** Elizabeth II **Obv:** Crowned bust right **Rev:** Sir Ernest Shackleton and icebound ship **Edge:** Reeded

Date	Mintage	F	VF	XF	Unc	BU
2004PM	—	—	—	—	15.00	16.50

KM# 20a 2 POUNDS
28.2800 g., 0.9250 Silver 0.8410 oz. ASW, 38.6 mm. **Ruler:** Elizabeth II **Obv:** Crowned bust right **Rev:** Sir Ernest Shackleton and icebound ship **Edge:** Reeded

Date	Mintage	F	VF	XF	Unc	BU
2004PM Proof	10,000	Value: 50.00				

KM# 21 2 POUNDS
28.2800 g., Copper-Nickel, 38.6 mm. **Ruler:** Elizabeth II **Subject:** Centennial of Grytviken **Obv:** Crowned bust right **Rev:** Portrait above ship in harbor **Edge:** Reeded

Date	Mintage	F	VF	XF	Unc	BU
2004PM	—	—	—	—	15.00	16.50

KM# 21a 2 POUNDS
28.2800 g., 0.9250 Silver 0.8410 oz. ASW, 38.6 mm. **Ruler:** Elizabeth II **Subject:** Centennial of Grytviken **Obv:** Crowned bust right **Rev:** Portrait above ship in harbor **Edge:** Reeded

Date	Mintage	F	VF	XF	Unc	BU
2004PM Proof	—	Value: 50.00				

KM# 25 2 POUNDS
28.2800 g., Copper-Nickel, 38.61 mm. **Ruler:** Elizabeth II **Subject:** Marriage of Charles to Parker Bowles **Rev:** Arms of Prince of Wales

Date	Mintage	F	VF	XF	Unc	BU
2005PM	—	—	—	—	8.50	10.00

KM# 22 2 POUNDS
28.2800 g., Copper-Nickel, 38.61 mm. **Ruler:** Elizabeth II **Obv:** Elizabeth II **Rev:** Rockhopper Penguin and chick **Edge:** Reeded

Date	Mintage	F	VF	XF	Unc	BU
2006PM	—	—	—	—	12.00	14.00

KM# 23 2 POUNDS
28.2800 g., Copper-Nickel, 38.61 mm. **Ruler:** Elizabeth II **Obv:** Elizabeth II **Rev:** Elephant Seal and cub **Edge:** Reeded

Date	Mintage	F	VF	XF	Unc	BU
2006PM	—	—	—	—	10.00	12.00

KM# 24 2 POUNDS
28.2800 g., Copper-Nickel, 38.61 mm. **Ruler:** Elizabeth II **Obv:** Elizabeth II **Rev:** Humpback Whale and calf **Edge:** Reeded

Date	Mintage	F	VF	XF	Unc	BU
2006PM	—	—	—	—	8.50	12.00

KM# 26 2 POUNDS
28.2800 g., Copper-Nickel, 38.61 mm. **Ruler:** Elizabeth II **Subject:** Queen Elizabeth II's 80th Birthday **Rev:** Queen on horseback taking part in Trouping of the Color ceremony

Date	Mintage	F	VF	XF	Unc	BU
2006PM	—	—	—	—	8.50	10.00

KM# 26a 2 POUNDS
28.2800 g., 0.9250 Silver 0.8410 oz. ASW, 38.61 mm. **Ruler:** Elizabeth II **Subject:** Queen Elizabeth II's 80th Birthday **Rev:** Queen on horseback taking part in Trouping of the Color ceremony

Date	Mintage	F	VF	XF	Unc	BU
2006 Proof	25,000	Value: 75.00				

KM# 27 2 POUNDS
28.2800 g., Copper-Nickel, 38.61 mm. **Ruler:** Elizabeth II **Rev:** Pair of Grey-headed Albatros

Date	Mintage	F	VF	XF	Unc	BU
2006PM	—	—	—	—	8.50	12.00

KM# 28 2 POUNDS
28.2800 g., Copper-Nickel, 38.61 mm. **Ruler:** Elizabeth II **Subject:** Queen Elizabeth II's 80th Birthday **Rev:** 1953 Royal family

Date	Mintage	F	VF	XF	Unc	BU
2006PM	—	—	—	—	8.50	10.00

KM# 28a 2 POUNDS
28.2800 g., 0.9250 Silver 0.8410 oz. ASW, 38.61 mm. **Ruler:** Elizabeth II **Subject:** Queen Elizabeth II's 80th Birthday **Rev:** 1953 Royal family

Date	Mintage	F	VF	XF	Unc	BU
2006 Proof	25,000	Value: 75.00				

KM# 29 2 POUNDS
28.2800 g., Copper-Nickel, 38.61 mm. **Ruler:** Elizabeth II **Subject:** Queen Elizabeth's II 80th Birthday **Rev:** Wedding of Queen Elizabeth II and Prince Philip

Date	Mintage	F	VF	XF	Unc	BU
2006PM	—	—	—	—	8.50	10.00

KM# 29a 2 POUNDS
28.2800 g., 0.9250 Silver 0.8410 oz. ASW, 38.61 mm. **Ruler:** Elizabeth II **Subject:** Queen Elizabeth's 80th Birthday **Rev:** Wedding of Queen Elizabeth II and Prince Philip

Date	Mintage	F	VF	XF	Unc	BU
2006 Proof	25,000	Value: 75.00				

KM# 30 2 POUNDS
28.2800 g., Copper-Nickel, 38.61 mm. **Ruler:** Elizabeth II **Subject:** Queen Elizabeth II's 80th Birthday **Rev:** Queen in Garter robes

Date	Mintage	F	VF	XF	Unc	BU
2006PM	—	—	—	—	8.50	10.00

KM# 30a 2 POUNDS
28.2800 g., 0.9250 Silver 0.8410 oz. ASW, 38.61 mm. **Ruler:** Elizabeth II **Subject:** Queen Elizabeth II's 80th Birthday **Rev:** Queen in Garter robes

Date	Mintage	F	VF	XF	Unc	BU
2006 Proof	25,000	Value: 75.00				

KM# 31 2 POUNDS
28.2800 g., Copper-Nickel, 38.61 mm. **Ruler:** Elizabeth II **Rev:** Queen Elizabeth II 1926 (1953 portrait)

Date	Mintage	F	VF	XF	Unc	BU
2007PM	—	—	—	—	8.50	10.00

KM# 32 2 POUNDS
28.2800 g., Copper-Nickel, 38.61 mm. **Ruler:** Elizabeth II **Subject:** 25th Anniversary of Liberation **Rev:** Warship and helicopters

Date	Mintage	F	VF	XF	Unc	BU
2007PM	—	—	—	—	8.50	10.00

KM# 33 2 POUNDS
28.2800 g., Copper-Nickel, 38.61 mm. **Ruler:** Elizabeth II **Rev:** Trans Artic Expedition

Date	Mintage	F	VF	XF	Unc	BU
2007PM	—	—	—	—	8.50	10.00

KM# 34 2 POUNDS
28.2800 g., Copper-Nickel, 38.61 mm. **Ruler:** Elizabeth II **Subject:** International Polar Year **Rev:** Shackelton Expedition

Date	Mintage	F	VF	XF	Unc	BU
2007PM	—	—	—	—	8.50	10.00

KM# 48 2 POUNDS
28.2800 g., 0.9250 Silver 0.8410 oz. ASW **Ruler:** Elizabeth II **Rev:** King Penguin in color **Shape:** 38.61

Date	Mintage	F	VF	XF	Unc	BU
2007PM Proof	Est. 5,000	Value: 75.00				

KM# 35 2 POUNDS
28.2800 g., Copper-Nickel, 38.61 mm. **Ruler:** Elizabeth II **Rev:** Ernest Shacketon

Date	Mintage	F	VF	XF	Unc	BU
2007PM	—	—	—	—	8.50	10.00

KM# 36 2 POUNDS
28.2800 g., Copper-Nickel, 38.61 mm. **Ruler:** Elizabeth II **Rev:** James Cook

Date	Mintage	F	VF	XF	Unc	BU
2007PM	—	—	—	—	8.50	10.00

KM# 37 2 POUNDS
28.2800 g., Copper-Nickel, 38.6 mm. **Ruler:** Elizabeth II **Subject:** Diamond Wedding Anniversary **Obv:** Conjoined busts with Prince Philip right **Obv. Legend:** SOUTH GEORGIA & SOUTH SANDWICH ISLANDS **Rev:** Bust of Princess Elizabeth facing **Rev. Legend:** Diamond Wedding of H.M. Queen Elizabeth II & H.R.H. Prince Philip **Rev. Inscription:** THE BRIDE **Edge:** Reeded

Date	Mintage	F	VF	XF	Unc	BU
2007	—	—	—	—	15.00	16.50

KM# 37a 2 POUNDS
28.2800 g., 0.9250 Silver 0.8410 oz. ASW, 38.6 mm. **Ruler:** Elizabeth II **Subject:** Diamond Wedding Anniversary **Obv:** Conjoined busts with Prince Philip right **Obv. Legend:** SOUTH GEORGIA & SOUTH SANDWICH ISLANDS **Rev:** Bust of Princess Elizabeth facing **Rev. Legend:** Diamond Wedding of H.M. Queen Elizabeth II & H.R.H. Prince Philip **Rev. Inscription:** THE BRIDE **Edge:** Reeded

Date	Mintage	F	VF	XF	Unc	BU
2007 Proof	25,000	Value: 75.00				

KM# 38 2 POUNDS
28.2800 g., Copper-Nickel, 38.6 mm. **Ruler:** Elizabeth II **Subject:** Diamond Wedding Anniversary **Obv:** Conjoined busts with Prince Philip right **Obv. Legend:** SOUTH GEORGIA & SOUTH SANDWICH ISLANDS **Rev:** Bust of the bridegroom facing **Rev. Legend:** Diamond Wedding of H.M. Queen Elizabeth II & H.R.H. Prince Philip **Rev. Inscription:** THE BRIDEGROOM **Edge:** Reeded

Date	Mintage	F	VF	XF	Unc	BU
2007	—	—	—	—	15.00	16.50

KM# 38a 2 POUNDS
28.2800 g., 0.9250 Silver 0.8410 oz. ASW, 38.6 mm. **Ruler:** Elizabeth II **Subject:** Diamond Wedding Anniversary **Obv:** Conjoined busts with Prince Philip right **Obv. Legend:** SOUTH GEORGIA & SOUTH SANDWICH ISLANDS **Rev:** Bust of the bridegroom facing **Rev. Legend:** Diamond Wedding of H.M. Queen Elizabeth II & H.R.H. Prince Philip **Rev. Inscription:** THE BRIDEGROOM **Edge:** Reeded

Date	Mintage	F	VF	XF	Unc	BU
2007 Proof	25,000	Value: 75.00				

KM# 39 2 POUNDS
28.2800 g., Copper-Nickel, 38.6 mm. **Ruler:** Elizabeth II **Subject:** Diamond Wedding Anniversary **Obv:** Conjoined busts with Prince Philip right **Obv. Legend:** SOUTH GEORGIA & SOUTH SANDWICH ISLANDS **Rev:** 1/2 length figures of royal engaged couple looking at each other **Rev. Legend:** Diamond Wedding of H.M. Queen Elizabeth II & H.R.H. Prince Philip **Rev. Inscription:** ROYAL ENGAGEMENT • JULY • 10 • 1947 **Edge:** Reeded

Date	Mintage	F	VF	XF	Unc	BU
2007	—	—	—	—	15.00	16.50

KM# 39a 2 POUNDS
28.2800 g., 0.9250 Silver 0.8410 oz. ASW, 38.6 mm. **Ruler:** Elizabeth II **Subject:** Diamond Wedding Anniversary **Obv:** Conjoined busts with Prince Philip right **Obv. Legend:** SOUTH GEORGIA & SOUTH SANDWICH ISLANDS **Rev:** 1/2 length figures of royal engaged couple looking at each other **Rev. Legend:** Diamond Wedding of H.M. Queen Elizabeth II & H.R.H. Prince Philip **Rev. Inscription:** ROYAL ENGAGEMENT • JULY • 10 • 1947 **Edge:** Reeded

Date	Mintage	F	VF	XF	Unc	BU
2007 Proof	25,000	Value: 75.00				

KM# 40 2 POUNDS
28.2800 g., Copper-Nickel, 38.6 mm. **Ruler:** Elizabeth II **Subject:** Diamond Wedding Anniversary **Obv:** Conjoined busts with Prince Philip right **Obv. Legend:** SOUTH GEORGIA & SOUTH SANDWICH ISLANDS **Rev:** Marriage license, jubilant crowd scene **Rev. Legend:** Diamond Wedding of H.M. Queen Elizabeth II & H.R.H. Prince Philip **Rev. Inscription:** THE MARRIAGE LICENSE **Edge:** Reeded

Date	Mintage	F	VF	XF	Unc	BU
2007	—	—	—	—	15.00	16.50

KM# 40a 2 POUNDS
28.2800 g., 0.9250 Silver 0.8410 oz. ASW, 38.6 mm. **Ruler:** Elizabeth II **Subject:** Diamond Wedding Anniversary **Obv:** Conjoined busts with Prince Philip right **Obv. Legend:** SOUTH GEORGIA & SOUTH SANDWICH ISLANDS **Rev:** Marriage license, jubilant crowd scene **Rev. Legend:** Diamond Wedding of H.M. Queen Elizabeth II & H.R.H. Prince Philip **Rev. Inscription:** THE MARRIAGE LICENSE **Edge:** Reeded

Date	Mintage	F	VF	XF	Unc	BU
2007 Proof	25,000	Value: 75.00				

KM# 42 2 POUNDS
28.2800 g., Copper-Nickel, 38.61 mm. **Ruler:** Elizabeth II **Rev:** Four coinage portraits of Elizabeth II

Date	Mintage	F	VF	XF	Unc	BU
2008PM Proof	—	—	—	—	—	15.00

KM# 49 2 POUNDS
28.2800 g., Copper-Nickel, 38.61 mm. **Ruler:** Elizabeth II **Subject:** Royal Air Force, 90th Anniversary **Rev:** C 180 Hercules

Date	Mintage	F	VF	XF	Unc	BU
2008PM	—	—	—	—	—	15.00

KM# 41 2 POUNDS
28.2800 g., Copper-Nickel, 38.61 mm. **Ruler:** Elizabeth II **Subject:** The Nimrod Expedition **Rev:** Sailing ship stuck in ice

Date	Mintage	F	VF	XF	Unc	BU
2009PM	—	—	—	—	—	16.50

KM# 50 2 POUNDS
28.2800 g., Copper-Nickel, 38.61 mm. **Ruler:** Elizabeth II **Rev:** View of icebound sailing ship Terra Nova **Rev. Legend:** CENTENARY OF THE RACE TO THE SOUTH POLE

Date	Mintage	F	VF	XF	Unc	BU
2010PM	—	—	—	—	—	15.00

KM# 44 2 POUNDS
28.2800 g., Copper-Nickel, 38.6 mm. **Ruler:** Elizabeth II **Obv:** Bust with tiara right **Rev:** Prince Philip and Elizabeth II, half-length facing above diamond, rays at side

Date	Mintage	F	VF	XF	Unc	BU
2011PM	—	—	—	—	8.50	12.00

KM# 44a 2 POUNDS
28.2800 g., 0.9250 Silver 0.8410 oz. ASW, 38.6 mm. **Ruler:** Elizabeth II **Obv:** Bust with tiara right **Rev:** Prince Philip and Elizabeth II, half-lenght facing above diamond, rays at side

Date	Mintage	F	VF	XF	Unc	BU
2011PM Proof	—	Value: 75.00				

KM# 43 2 POUNDS
28.2800 g., Copper-Nickel, 38.61 mm. **Ruler:** Elizabeth II **Subject:** Frozen Planet **Obv:** Bust with tiara right **Rev:** King Pengiun and young

Date	Mintage	F	VF	XF	Unc	BU
2011PM	—	—	—	—	15.00	16.50

KM# 43a 2 POUNDS
28.2800 g., 0.9250 Silver 0.8410 oz. ASW, 38.61 mm. **Ruler:** Elizabeth II **Subject:** Frozen Planet **Rev:** King Penguin and young

Date	Mintage	F	VF	XF	Unc	BU
2011PM Proof	—	Value: 75.00				

KM# 51 2 POUNDS
28.2800 g., Copper-Nickel, 38.61 mm. **Ruler:** Elizabeth II **Subject:** Royal Wedding **Rev:** Royal Arms of Prince William

Date	Mintage	F	VF	XF	Unc	BU
2011PM	—	—	—	—	—	15.00

KM# 52 2 POUNDS
28.2800 g., Copper-Nickel, 38.61 mm. **Ruler:** Elizabeth II **Subject:** Elizabeth II, 60th Anniversary of reign **Rev:** Queen Mother and Princess Elizabeth

Date	Mintage	F	VF	XF	Unc	BU
2012PM	—	—	—	—	—	15.00

KM# 53 2 POUNDS
28.2800 g., Copper-Nickel, 38.61 mm. **Ruler:** Elizabeth II **Rev:** Elizabeth II delivering Christmas speach

Date	Mintage	F	VF	XF	Unc	BU
2012PM	—	—	—	—	—	15.00

KM# 54 2 POUNDS
28.2800 g., Copper-Nickel, 38.61 mm. **Ruler:** Elizabeth II **Subject:** Prince William and Kate Middleton, 1st Wedding Anniversary **Rev:** First Kiss on Buckingham Palace Balcony

Date	Mintage	F	VF	XF	Unc	BU
2012PM	—	—	—	—	—	15.00

KM# 45 4 POUNDS
1.2400 g., 0.9990 Gold 0.0398 oz. AGW, 13.92 mm. **Ruler:** Elizabeth II **Rev:** Rockhopper Penguin

Date	Mintage	F	VF	XF	Unc	BU
2006PM Proof	Est. 5,000	Value: 90.00				

KM# 46 4 POUNDS
1.2400 g., 0.9990 Gold 0.0398 oz. AGW, 13.92 mm. **Ruler:** Elizabeth II **Rev:** Henrik Johan Ibsen bust facing

Date	Mintage	F	VF	XF	Unc	BU
2006PM Proof	Est. 7,500	Value: 90.00				

KM# 19 10 POUNDS
155.5100 g., 0.9990 Silver 4.9946 oz. ASW, 65 mm. **Ruler:** Elizabeth II **Obv:** Crowned bust right **Rev:** Capt. Cook, ship and map **Edge:** Reeded

Date	Mintage	F	VF	XF	Unc	BU
2003PM Proof	2,003	Value: 225				

KM# 8 20 POUNDS
6.2200 g., 0.9999 Gold 0.1999 oz. AGW, 22 mm. **Ruler:** Elizabeth II **Obv:** Crowned bust right **Rev:** Sir Ernest H. Shackleton and ship **Edge:** Reeded

Date	Mintage	F	VF	XF	Unc	BU
2001PM Proof	Est. 2,000	Value: 425				

KM# 10 20 POUNDS
6.2200 g., 0.9999 Gold 0.1999 oz. AGW, 22 mm. **Ruler:** Elizabeth II **Obv:** Crowned bust right **Rev:** Sir Joseph Banks cameo and ship

Date	Mintage	F	VF	XF	Unc	BU
2001PM Proof	Est. 2,000	Value: 425				

KM# 16 20 POUNDS
6.2200 g., 0.9999 Gold 0.1999 oz. AGW, 22 mm. **Ruler:** Elizabeth II **Subject:** Princess Diana **Obv:** Crowned bust right **Rev:** Diana's portrait **Edge:** reeded

Date	Mintage	F	VF	XF	Unc	BU
2002PM Proof	—	Value: 425				

KM# 12 20 POUNDS
6.2200 g., 0.9990 Gold 0.1998 oz. AGW, 22 mm. **Ruler:** Elizabeth II **Subject:** Queen Elizabeth II's Golden Jubilee **Obv:** Crowned bust right **Rev:** Young crowned bust right **Edge:** Reeded

Date	Mintage	F	VF	XF	Unc	BU
2002PM Proof	2,002	Value: 425				

KM# 14 20 POUNDS
6.2200 g., 0.9990 Gold 0.1998 oz. AGW, 22 mm. **Ruler:** Elizabeth II **Subject:** Queen Elizabeth II's Golden Jubilee **Obv:** Crowned bust right **Rev:** National arms **Edge:** Reeded

Date	Mintage	F	VF	XF	Unc	BU
2002PM Proof	2,002	Value: 425				

KM# 47 20 POUNDS
6.2200 g., 0.9990 Gold 0.1998 oz. AGW, 22 mm. **Ruler:** Elizabeth II **Rev:** Henrik Johan Ibsen bust facing

Date	Mintage	F	VF	XF	Unc	BU
2006PM Proof	Est. 2,000	Value: 425				

The Kingdom of Spain, forming the greater part of the Iberian Peninsula of southwest Europe, has an area of 195,988 sq. mi. (504,714 sq. km.) and a population of 39.4 million including the Balearic and the Canary Islands. Capital: Madrid. The economy is based on agriculture, industry and tourism. Machinery, fruit, vegetables and chemicals are exported.

RULER
Juan Carlos I, 1975-

MINT MARK
(M) - Crowned "M" – Madrid

KINGDOM

DECIMAL COINAGE

100 Centimos = 1 Peseta

KM# 832 PESETA
0.5500 g., Aluminum, 14 mm. **Ruler:** Juan Carlos I **Obv:** Vertical line divides head left from value **Rev:** Crowned shield flanked by pillars with banner **Edge:** Plain

Date	Mintage	F	VF	XF	Unc	BU
2001	62,300,000	—	—	0.10	0.30	0.50

KM# 833 5 PESETAS
3.0000 g., Aluminum-Bronze, 17.5 mm. **Ruler:** Juan Carlos I **Obv:** Stylized JC I and date **Rev:** Value above stylized sailboats **Edge:** Plain

Date	Mintage	F	VF	XF	Unc	BU
2001	294,000,000	—	—	0.10	0.25	0.35

KM# 1013 25 PESETAS
4.2500 g., Aluminum-Bronze, 19.5 mm. **Ruler:** Juan Carlos I **Obv:** Center hole divides bust left and vertical letters **Rev:** Crowned above center hole, order collar at right, value at left **Edge:** Plain

Date	Mintage	F	VF	XF	Unc	BU
2001	91,200,000	—	—	—	2.00	2.50

KM# 1016 100 PESETAS
9.2500 g., Aluminum-Bronze, 24.5 mm. **Ruler:** Juan Carlos I **Subject:** 132nd Anniversary of the Peseta **Obv:** Head left **Rev:** Seated allegorical figure from an old coin design **Edge:** Fleur-de-lis repeated

Date	Mintage	F	VF	XF	Unc	BU
2001	142,800,000	—	—	—	2.25	2.75

KM# 924 500 PESETAS
12.0000 g., Aluminum-Bronze, 28 mm. **Ruler:** Juan Carlos I **Obv:** Conjoined heads of Juan Carlos and Sofia left **Rev:** Crowned shield flanked by pillars with banner, vertical value at right

Date	Mintage	F	VF	XF	Unc	BU
2001	3,300,000	—	—	—	7.00	9.00

KM# 1131 500 PESETAS
6.7300 g., Silver, 26.96 mm. **Ruler:** Juan Carlos I **Obv:** Minting equipment **Obv. Legend:** ESPAÑA **Rev:** Copy of Charles II silver Reales coin **Rev. Legend:** CASA DE LA MONEDA DE SEGOVIA **Edge:** Reeded **Note:** Aqueduct and crowned M mintmarks appear on obverse

Date	Mintage	F	VF	XF	Unc	BU
2001 Proof	20,000	Value: 20.00				

KM# 1017 2000 PESETAS
18.0000 g., 0.9250 Silver 0.5353 oz. ASW, 32.9 mm. **Ruler:** Juan Carlos I **Subject:** 132nd Anniversary of the Peseta **Obv:** Conjoined heads left **Rev:** Seated allegorical design from the 1869 Spanish coin series **Edge:** Plain

Date	Mintage	F	VF	XF	Unc	BU
2001	1,942,835	—	—	—	30.00	35.00

KM# 1038 2000 PESETAS
27.0000 g., 0.9250 Silver 0.8029 oz. ASW, 40 mm. **Ruler:** Juan Carlos I **Subject:** Segovia Mint's 500th Anniversary **Obv:** Hammer coining scene within beaded circle **Rev:** Segovia Mint 8 reales coin design of 1588 **Edge:** Reeded

Date	Mintage	F	VF	XF	Unc	BU
2001 Proof	15,000	Value: 55.00				

EURO COINAGE

European Union Issues

KM# 1040 EURO CENT
2.3000 g., Copper Plated Steel, 16.25 mm. **Ruler:** Juan Carlos I **Obv:** Cathedral of Santiago de Compostela **Rev:** Value and globe **Edge:** Plain

Date	Mintage	F	VF	XF	Unc	BU
2001(M)	130,900,000	—	—	—	0.25	0.30
2002(M)	141,100,000	—	—	—	0.25	0.30
2002(M) Proof	35,000	Value: 10.00				
2003(M)	670,500,000	—	—	—	0.25	0.30
2003(M) Proof	20,000	Value: 10.00				
2004(M)	206,700,000	—	—	—	0.25	0.30
2005(M)	444,200,000	—	—	—	0.25	0.30
2005(M) Proof	3,000	Value: 10.00				
2006(M)	383,900,000	—	—	—	0.25	0.35
2007(M)	—	—	—	—	0.25	0.35
2007(M) Proof	5,000	Value: 10.00				
2008(M)	—	—	—	—	0.25	0.35
2008(M) Proof	5,000	Value: 10.00				
2009(M)	—	—	—	—	0.25	0.35
2009(M) Proof	5,000	Value: 10.00				

KM# 1144 EURO CENT
2.3000 g., Copper Plated Steel, 16.25 mm. **Ruler:** Juan Carlos I **Obv:** Cathedral of Santiago de Compostela **Rev:** Value and globe

Date	Mintage	F	VF	XF	Unc	BU
2010	—	—	—	—	0.25	0.35
2010 Proof	—	Value: 10.00				

Date	Mintage	F	VF	XF	Unc	BU
2011	—	—	—	—	0.25	0.35
2011 Proof	—	Value: 10.00				
2012	—	—	—	—	0.25	0.35
2012 Proof	—	Value: 10.00				
2013	—	—	—	—	0.25	0.35
2013 Proof	—	Value: 10.00				

KM# 1041 2 EURO CENT

3.0600 g., Copper Plated Steel, 18.75 mm. **Ruler:** Juan Carlos I **Obv:** Cathedral of Santiago de Compostela **Rev:** Value and globe **Edge:** Grooved

Date	Mintage	F	VF	XF	Unc	BU
2001(M)	463,100,000	—	—	—	0.25	0.30
2002(M)	4,100,000	—	—	—	1.25	1.50
2002(M) Proof	35,000	Value: 10.00				
2003(M)	31,600,000	—	—	—	1.00	1.25
2003(M) Proof	20,000	Value: 10.00				
2004(M)	206,700,000	—	—	—	0.25	0.30
2005(M)	275,100,000	—	—	—	0.25	0.30
2005(M) Proof	3,000	Value: 10.00				
2006(M)	262,200,000	—	—	—	0.25	0.30
2007(M)	—	—	—	—	0.25	0.30
2007(M) Proof	5,000	Value: 10.00				
2008(M)	—	—	—	—	0.25	0.30
2008(M) Proof	5,000	Value: 10.00				
2009(M)	—	—	—	—	0.25	0.30
2009(M) Proof	5,000	Value: 10.00				

KM# 1145 2 EURO CENT

3.0600 g., Copper Plated Steel, 18.75 mm. **Ruler:** Juan Carlos I **Obv:** Cathedral of Santiago de Compostela **Rev:** Value and globe **Edge:** Grooved

Date	Mintage	F	VF	XF	Unc	BU
2010	—	—	—	—	0.25	0.30
2010 Proof	—	Value: 10.00				
2011	—	—	—	—	0.25	0.30
2011 Proof	—	Value: 10.00				
2012	—	—	—	—	0.25	0.30
2012 Proof	—	Value: 10.00				
2013	—	—	—	—	0.25	0.30
2013 Proof	—	Value: 10.00				

KM# 1042 5 EURO CENT

3.9200 g., Copper Plated Steel, 21.25 mm. **Ruler:** Juan Carlos I **Obv:** Cathedral of Santiago de Compostela **Rev:** Value and globe **Edge:** Plain

Date	Mintage	F	VF	XF	Unc	BU
2001(M)	216,100,000	—	—	—	0.50	0.60
2002(M)	8,300,000	—	—	—	1.00	1.50
2002(M) Proof	35,000	Value: 10.00				
2003(M)	327,600,000	—	—	—	0.50	0.60
2003(M) Proof	8,904	Value: 10.00				
2004(M)	258,700,000	—	—	—	0.40	0.50
2005(M)	411,400,000	—	—	—	0.40	0.50
2005(M) Proof	3,000	Value: 10.00				
2006(M)	142,800,000	—	—	—	0.40	0.50
2007(M)	—	—	—	—	0.40	0.50
2007(M) Proof	5,000	Value: 10.00				
2008(M)	—	—	—	—	0.40	0.50
2008(M) Proof	2,000	Value: 10.00				
2009(M)	—	—	—	—	0.40	0.50
2009(M) Proof	5,000	Value: 10.00				

KM# 1146 5 EURO CENT

3.9200 g., Copper Plated Steel, 21.25 mm. **Ruler:** Juan Carlos I **Obv:** Cathedral of Santiago de Compostela **Rev:** Value and globe

Date	Mintage	F	VF	XF	Unc	BU
2010	—	—	—	—	0.40	0.50
2010 Proof	—	Value: 10.00				
2011	—	—	—	—	0.40	0.50
2011 Proof	—	Value: 10.00				
2012	—	—	—	—	0.40	0.50
2012 Proof	—	Value: 10.00				
2013	—	—	—	—	0.40	0.50
2013 Proof	—	Value: 10.00				

KM# 1043 10 EURO CENT

4.1000 g., Brass, 19.75 mm. **Ruler:** Juan Carlos I **Obv:** Head of Cervantes with ruffed collar 1/4 left within star border **Rev:** Value and map **Edge:** Reeded

Date	Mintage	F	VF	XF	Unc	BU
2001(M)	160,100,000	—	—	—	0.60	0.75
2002(M)	113,100,000	—	—	—	0.60	0.75
2002(M) Proof	35,000	Value: 10.00				
2003(M)	292,500,000	—	—	—	0.75	0.90
2003(M) Proof	20,000	Value: 10.00				
2004(M)	121,900,000	—	—	—	0.40	0.50
2005(M)	321,300,000	—	—	—	0.40	0.50
2005(M) Proof	3,000	Value: 10.00				
2006(M)	91,800,000	—	—	—	0.40	0.50

KM# 1070 10 EURO CENT

4.1000 g., Brass, 19.75 mm. **Ruler:** Juan Carlos I **Obv:** Cervantes **Rev:** Relief map of Western Europe, stars, lines and value **Edge:** Reeded

Date	Mintage	F	VF	XF	Unc	BU
2007(M)	132,058,000	—	—	—	0.75	1.00
2007(M) Proof	5,000	Value: 12.00				
2008(M)	—	—	—	—	0.75	1.00
2008(M) Proof	5,000	Value: 12.00				
2009(M)	—	—	—	—	0.75	1.00
2009(M) Proof	5,000	Value: 12.00				

KM# 1147 10 EURO CENT

4.1000 g., Brass, 19.75 mm. **Ruler:** Juan Carlos I **Obv:** Cervantes bust at right **Rev:** Relief map of Western Europe, stars, lines and value **Edge:** Reeded

Date	Mintage	F	VF	XF	Unc	BU
2010	—	—	—	—	0.75	1.00
2010 Proof	—	Value: 12.00				
2011	—	—	—	—	0.75	1.00
2011 Proof	—	Value: 12.00				
2012	—	—	—	—	0.75	1.00
2012 Proof	—	Value: 12.00				
2013	—	—	—	—	0.75	1.00
2013 Proof	—	Value: 12.00				

KM# 1044 20 EURO CENT

5.7400 g., Brass, 22.25 mm. **Ruler:** Juan Carlos I **Obv:** Head of Cervantes with ruffed collar 1/4 left within star border **Rev:** Value and map **Edge:** Notched

Date	Mintage	F	VF	XF	Unc	BU
2001(M)	146,600,000	—	—	—	1.00	1.25
2002(M)	91,500,000	—	—	—	0.60	0.75
2002(M) Proof	35,000	Value: 12.00				
2003(M)	4,100,000	—	—	—	1.25	1.50
2003(M) Proof	20,000	Value: 12.00				
2004(M)	3,900,000	—	—	—	0.60	0.75
2005(M)	4,000,000	—	—	—	0.60	0.75
2005(M) Proof	3,000	Value: 12.00				
2006(M)	102,000,000	—	—	—	0.60	0.75

KM# 1071 20 EURO CENT

5.7400 g., Brass, 22.25 mm. **Ruler:** Juan Carlos I **Obv:** Cervantes **Rev:** Relief map of Western Europe, stars, lines and value **Edge:** Notched

Date	Mintage	F	VF	XF	Unc	BU
2007(M)	46,458,000	—	—	—	1.00	1.25
2007(M) Proof	5,000	Value: 12.00				
2008(M)	—	—	—	—	1.00	1.25
2008(M) Proof	2,000	Value: 12.00				
2009(M)	—	—	—	—	1.00	1.25
2009(M) Proof	5,000	Value: 12.00				

KM# 1148 20 EURO CENT

5.7400 g., Brass, 22.25 mm. **Ruler:** Juan Carlos I **Obv:** Cervantes bust at right **Rev:** Relief map of Western Europe, stars, lines and value **Edge:** Notched

Date	Mintage	F	VF	XF	Unc	BU
2010	—	—	—	—	1.00	1.25
2010 Proof	—	Value: 12.00				
2011	—	—	—	—	1.00	1.25
2011 Proof	—	Value: 12.00				
2012	—	—	—	—	1.00	1.25
2012 Proof	—	Value: 12.00				
2013	—	—	—	—	1.00	1.25
2013 Proof	—	Value: 12.00				

KM# 1045 50 EURO CENT

7.8000 g., Brass, 24.25 mm. **Ruler:** Juan Carlos I **Obv:** Head of Cervantes with ruffed collar 1/4 left within star border **Rev:** Value and map **Edge:** Reeded

Date	Mintage	F	VF	XF	Unc	BU
2001(M)	351,100,000	—	—	—	1.00	1.25
2002(M)	9,800,000	—	—	—	3.00	3.50
2002(M) Proof	35,000	Value: 12.00				
2003(M)	6,000,000	—	—	—	3.00	3.50
2003(M) Proof	20,000	Value: 12.00				
2004(M)	4,400,000	—	—	—	1.50	2.00
2005(M)	3,900,000	—	—	—	1.25	1.50
2005(M) Proof	3,000	Value: 12.00				
2006(M)	4,000,000	—	—	—	1.25	1.50

KM# 1072 50 EURO CENT

7.8000 g., Brass, 24.25 mm. **Ruler:** Juan Carlos I **Obv:** Cervantes **Rev:** Relief map of Western Europe, stars, lines and value **Edge:** Reeded

Date	Mintage	F	VF	XF	Unc	BU
2007(M)	3,958,000	—	—	—	1.25	1.50
2007(M) Proof	5,000	Value: 12.00				
2008(M)	—	—	—	—	1.25	1.50
2008(M) Proof	5,000	Value: 12.00				
2009(M)	—	—	—	—	1.25	1.50
2009(M) Proof	5,000	Value: 12.00				

KM# 1149 50 EURO CENT

7.8000 g., Brass, 24.25 mm. **Ruler:** Juan Carlos I **Obv:** Cervantes bust at right **Rev:** Relief map of Western Europe, stars, lines and value **Edge:** Reeded

Date	Mintage	F	VF	XF	Unc	BU
2010	—	—	—	—	1.25	1.50
2010 Proof	—	Value: 12.00				
2011	—	—	—	—	1.25	1.50
2011 Proof	—	Value: 12.00				
2012	—	—	—	—	1.25	1.50
2012 Proof	—	Value: 12.00				
2013	—	—	—	—	1.25	1.50
2013 Proof	—	Value: 12.00				

KM# 1046 EURO

7.5000 g., Bi-Metallic Copper-Nickel center in Nickel-Brass ring, 23.25 mm. **Ruler:** Juan Carlos I **Obv:** Head 1/4 left within circle and star border **Rev:** Value and map within circle **Edge:** Segmented reeding

Date	Mintage	F	VF	XF	Unc	BU
2001(M)	259,100,000	—	—	—	3.00	4.00
2002(M)	335,600,000	—	—	—	2.00	2.50
2002(M) Proof	23,000	Value: 15.00				
2003(M)	297,400,000	—	—	—	2.00	2.50
2003(M) Proof	20,000	Value: 15.00				

Date	Mintage	F	VF	XF	Unc	BU
2004(M)	9,870,000	—	—	—	2.00	2.50
2005(M)	77,800,000	—	—	—	2.00	2.50
2005(M) Proof	3,000	Value: 15.00				
2006(M)	101,600,000	—	—	—	2.00	2.50

KM# 1073 EURO
7.5000 g., Bi-Metallic Copper-Nickel center in Nickel-Brass ring, 23.25 mm. **Ruler:** Juan Carlos I **Obv:** King's portrait **Rev:** Relief map of Western Europe, stars, lines and value **Edge:** Segmented reeding

Date	Mintage	F	VF	XF	Unc	BU
2007(M)	150,558,000	—	—	—	3.00	3.50
2007(M) Proof	5,000	Value: 15.00				
2008(M)	—	—	—	—	3.00	3.50
2008(M) Proof	5,000	Value: 15.00				
2009(M)	—	—	—	—	3.00	3.50
2009(M) Proof	5,000	Value: 15.00				

KM# 1150 EURO
7.5000 g., Bi-Metallic Copper-Nickel center in Nickel-Brass ring, 23.25 mm. **Ruler:** Juan Carlos I **Obv:** King's portrait at right **Rev:** Relief map of Western Europe, stars, lines and value **Edge:** Segmented reeding

Date	Mintage	F	VF	XF	Unc	BU
2010	—	—	—	—	3.00	3.50
2010 Proof	—	Value: 15.00				
2011	—	—	—	—	3.00	3.50
2011 Proof	—	Value: 15.00				
2012	—	—	—	—	3.00	3.50
2012 Proof	—	Value: 15.00				
2013	—	—	—	—	3.00	3.50
2013 Proof	—	Value: 15.00				

KM# 1047 2 EURO
8.5000 g., Bi-Metallic Nickel-Brass center in Copper-Nickel ring, 25.75 mm. **Ruler:** Juan Carlos I **Obv:** Head 1/4 left within circle and star border **Rev:** Value and map within circle **Edge:** Reeding over stars and 2's

Date	Mintage	F	VF	XF	Unc	BU
2001(M)	140,200,000	—	—	—	4.50	5.00
2002(M)	164,000,000	—	—	—	3.50	4.00
2002(M) Proof	35,000	Value: 20.00				
2003(M)	44,500,000	—	—	—	4.50	5.00
2003(M) Proof	20,000	Value: 20.00				
2004(M)	4,100,000	—	—	—	4.50	5.00
2005(M)	4,000,000	—	—	—	4.50	5.00
2005(M) Proof	3,000	Value: 20.00				
2006(M)	4,000,000	—	—	—	4.50	5.00

KM# 1063 2 EURO
8.5000 g., Bi-Metallic Nickel-Brass center in Copper-Nickel ring, 25.75 mm. **Ruler:** Juan Carlos I **Obv:** Stylized half length figure of Don Quixote holding spear within circle and star border **Rev:** Value and map within circle **Edge:** Reeding over stars and 2's **Note:** Mint mark: Crowned M.

Date	Mintage	F	VF	XF	Unc	BU
2005	8,000,000	—	—	—	5.00	6.00
2005 Proof	3,000	Value: 25.00				

KM# 1074 2 EURO
8.5000 g., Bi-Metallic Nickel-Brass center in Copper-Nickel ring, 25.75 mm. **Ruler:** Juan Carlos I **Obv:** King's portrait **Rev:** Relief map of Western Europe, stars, lines and value **Edge:** Reeding over stars and 2's

Date	Mintage	F	VF	XF	Unc	BU
2007(M)	3,958,000	—	—	—	4.75	5.00
2007(M) Proof	5,000	Value: 20.00				
2008(M)	—	—	—	—	4.75	5.00
2008(M) Proof	5,000	Value: 20.00				
2009(M)	—	—	—	—	4.75	5.00
2009(M) Proof	5,000	Value: 20.00				

KM# 1130 2 EURO
8.5000 g., Bi-Metallic Nickel-Brass center in Copper-Nickel ring, 25.75 mm. **Ruler:** Juan Carlos I **Subject:** 50th Anniversary_ Treaty of Rome **Obv:** Open treaty book **Obv. Legend:** ESPAÑA **Rev:** Large value at left, modified outline of Europe at right **Edge:** Reeded with 2's and stars

Date	Mintage	F	VF	XF	Unc	BU
2007	7,935,000	—	—	—	7.00	9.00
2007(M) Special Unc.	60,000	—	—	—	—	20.00
2007(M) Proof	5,000	Value: 35.00				

KM# 1142.2 2 EURO
8.5000 g., Bi-Metallic Nickel-Brass center in Copper-Nickel ring, 25.75 mm. **Ruler:** Juan Carlos I **Subject:** European Monetary Unit, 10th Aniversary **Obv:** Stick figure and large E symbol **Edge:** Reeded with 2's and stars

Date	Mintage	F	VF	XF	Unc	BU
2009 Large Stars	—	—	—	—	40.00	45.00

KM# 1142.1 2 EURO
8.5000 g., Bi-Metallic Nickel-Brass center in Copper-Nickel ring, 25.75 mm. **Ruler:** Juan Carlos I **Subject:** European Monetary Unit, 10th Anniversary **Obv:** Stick figure and large E symbol **Rev:** Large value at left, modified map of Europe at right **Edge:** Reeded with 2's and stars

Date	Mintage	F	VF	XF	Unc	BU
2009 Small Stars	—	—	—	—	5.00	6.00
2009 Special Unc.	—	—	—	—	—	20.00
2009 Proof	—	Value: 35.00				

KM# 1151 2 EURO
8.5000 g., Bi-Metallic Nickel-Brass center in Copper-Nickel ring, 25.75 mm. **Ruler:** Juan Carlos I **Obv:** King's portrait at right **Rev:** Relief map of Western Europe, stars, lines and value **Edge:** Reeded with 2's and stars

Date	Mintage	F	VF	XF	Unc	BU
2010	—	—	—	—	4.75	5.00
2010 Proof	—	Value: 20.00				
2011	—	—	—	—	4.75	5.00
2011 Proof	—	Value: 20.00				
2012	—	—	—	—	4.75	5.00
2012 Proof	—	Value: 20.00				
2013	—	—	—	—	4.75	5.00
2013 Proof	—	Value: 20.00				

KM# 1152 2 EURO
8.5000 g., Bi-Metallic Nickel-Brass center in Copper-Nickel ring, 25.75 mm. **Ruler:** Juan Carlos I **Subject:** Cordoba - UNESCO Heritage site **Edge:** Reeded with 2's and stars

Date	Mintage	F	VF	XF	Unc	BU
2010	—	—	—	—	7.00	9.00
2010 Proof	5,000	Value: 25.00				

KM# 1184 2 EURO
8.5000 g., Bi-Metallic Nickel-Brass center in Copper-Nickel ring, 25.75 mm. **Ruler:** Juan Carlos I **Subject:** UNESCO Heritage Site - Granada **Obv:** The Alhambra **Edge:** Reeded with 2's and stars

Date	Mintage	F	VF	XF	Unc	BU
2011	8,000,000	—	—	—	7.00	9.00
2011 Proof	5,000	Value: 25.00				

KM# 1252 2 EURO
8.5000 g., Bi-Metallic Nickel-Brass center in Copper-Nickel ring, 25.75 mm. **Ruler:** Juan Carlos I **Subject:** Euro coinage, 10th Anniversary **Obv:** Euro symbol on globe at center, child-like rendering around

Date	Mintage	F	VF	XF	Unc	BU
2012	8,000,000	—	—	—	6.00	8.00
2012 Proof	—	Value: 25.00				

KM# 1153 5 EURO
13.5000 g., 0.9250 Silver 0.4015 oz. ASW, 33 mm. **Ruler:** Juan Carlos I **Subject:** Almeria

Date	Mintage	F	VF	XF	Unc	BU
2010 Proof	Est. 15,000	Value: 45.00				

KM# 1154 5 EURO
13.5000 g., 0.9250 Silver 0.4015 oz. ASW, 33 mm. **Ruler:** Juan Carlos I **Subject:** Huesca

Date	Mintage	F	VF	XF	Unc	BU
2010 Proof	Est. 15,000	Value: 45.00				

KM# 1155 5 EURO
13.5000 g., 0.9250 Silver 0.4015 oz. ASW, 33 mm. **Ruler:** Juan Carlos I **Subject:** Las Palmas G.C.

Date	Mintage	F	VF	XF	Unc	BU
2010 Proof	Est. 20,000	Value: 45.00				

KM# 1156 5 EURO
13.5000 g., 0.9250 Silver 0.4015 oz. ASW, 33 mm. **Ruler:** Juan Carlos I **Subject:** Santander

Date	Mintage	F	VF	XF	Unc	BU
2010 Proof	Est. 15,000	Value: 45.00				

KM# 1157 5 EURO
13.5000 g., 0.9250 Silver 0.4015 oz. ASW, 33 mm. **Ruler:** Juan Carlos I **Subject:** Avila

Date	Mintage	F	VF	XF	Unc	BU
2010 Proof	Est. 15,000	Value: 45.00				

KM# 1158 5 EURO
13.5000 g., 0.9250 Silver 0.4015 oz. ASW, 33 mm. **Ruler:** Juan Carlos I **Subject:** Albacete

Date	Mintage	F	VF	XF	Unc	BU
2010 Proof	Est. 15,000	Value: 45.00				

KM# 1159 5 EURO
13.5000 g., 0.9250 Silver 0.4015 oz. ASW, 33 mm. **Ruler:** Juan Carlos I **Subject:** Barcelona

Date	Mintage	F	VF	XF	Unc	BU
2010 Proof	Est. 25,000	Value: 45.00				

KM# 1160 5 EURO
13.5000 g., 0.9250 Silver 0.4015 oz. ASW, 33 mm. **Ruler:** Juan Carlos I **Subject:** Ceuta

Date	Mintage	F	VF	XF	Unc	BU
2010 Proof	Est. 15,000	Value: 45.00				

KM# 1161 5 EURO
13.5000 g., 0.9250 Silver 0.4015 oz. ASW, 33 mm. **Ruler:** Juan Carlos I **Subject:** Melilla

Date	Mintage	F	VF	XF	Unc	BU
2010 Proof	Est. 15,000	Value: 45.00				

KM# 1162 5 EURO
13.5000 g., 0.9250 Silver 0.4015 oz. ASW, 33 mm. **Ruler:** Juan Carlos I **Subject:** Madrid

Date	Mintage	F	VF	XF	Unc	BU
2010 Proof	—	Value: 45.00				

KM# 1163 5 EURO
13.5000 g., 0.9250 Silver 0.4015 oz. ASW, 33 mm. **Ruler:** Juan Carlos I **Subject:** Pamplona

Date	Mintage	F	VF	XF	Unc	BU
2010 Proof	Est. 15,000	Value: 45.00				

KM# 1164 5 EURO
13.5000 g., 0.9250 Silver 0.4015 oz. ASW, 33 mm. **Ruler:** Juan Carlos I **Subject:** Alicante

Date	Mintage	F	VF	XF	Unc	BU
2010 Proof	Est. 20,000	Value: 45.00				

KM# 1226 5 EURO
13.5000 g., 0.9250 Silver 0.4015 oz. ASW, 33 mm. **Ruler:** Juan Carlos I **Subject:** Oviedo

Date	Mintage	F	VF	XF	Unc	BU
2011 Proof	Est. 20,000	Value: 45.00				

KM# 1227 5 EURO
13.5000 g., 0.9250 Silver 0.4015 oz. ASW **Ruler:** Juan Carlos I **Subject:** Palma de Mallorca

Date	Mintage	F	VF	XF	Unc	BU
2011 Proof	Est. 20,000	Value: 45.00				

KM# 1228 5 EURO
13.5000 g., 0.9250 Silver 0.4015 oz. ASW, 33 mm. **Ruler:** Juan Carlos I **Subject:** Santa Cruz de Tenerife

Date	Mintage	F	VF	XF	Unc	BU
2011 Proof	Est. 20,000	Value: 45.00				

KM# 1229 5 EURO
13.5000 g., 0.9250 Silver 0.4015 oz. ASW, 33 mm. **Ruler:** Juan Carlos I **Subject:** Teruel

Date	Mintage	F	VF	XF	Unc	BU
2011 Proof	Est. 15,000	Value: 45.00				

KM# 1230 5 EURO
13.5000 g., 0.9250 Silver 0.4015 oz. ASW, 33 mm. **Ruler:** Juan Carlos I **Subject:** Bilbao

Date	Mintage	F	VF	XF	Unc	BU
2011 Proof	Est. 20,000	Value: 45.00				

KM# 1231 5 EURO
13.5000 g., 0.9250 Silver 0.4015 oz. ASW, 33 mm. **Ruler:** Juan Carlos I **Subject:** Cadiz

Date	Mintage	F	VF	XF	Unc	BU
2011 Proof	—	Value: 45.00				

KM# 1232 5 EURO
13.5000 g., 0.9250 Silver 0.4015 oz. ASW, 33 mm. **Ruler:** Juan Carlos I **Subject:** Logrono

Date	Mintage	F	VF	XF	Unc	BU
2011 Proof	Est. 15,000	Value: 45.00				

KM# 1233 5 EURO
13.5000 g., 0.9250 Silver 0.4015 oz. ASW, 33 mm. **Ruler:** Juan Carlos I **Subject:** Murcia

Date	Mintage	F	VF	XF	Unc	BU
2011 Proof	Est. 15,000	Value: 45.00				

KM# 1234 5 EURO
13.5000 g., 0.9250 Silver 0.4015 oz. ASW, 33 mm. **Ruler:** Juan Carlos I **Subject:** Donostia

Date	Mintage	F	VF	XF	Unc	BU
2011 Proof	—	Value: 45.00				

KM# 1235 5 EURO
13.5000 g., 0.9250 Silver 0.4015 oz. ASW, 33 mm. **Ruler:** Juan Carlos I **Subject:** Zaragoza

Date	Mintage	F	VF	XF	Unc	BU
2011 Proof	—	Value: 45.00				

KM# 1236 5 EURO
13.5000 g., 0.9250 Silver 0.4015 oz. ASW, 33 mm. **Ruler:** Juan Carlos I **Subject:** A Coruna

Date	Mintage	F	VF	XF	Unc	BU
2011 Proof	Est. 20,000	Value: 45.00				

KM# 1237 5 EURO
13.5000 g., 0.9250 Silver 0.4015 oz. ASW, 33 mm. **Ruler:** Juan Carlos I **Subject:** Badajoz

Date	Mintage	F	VF	XF	Unc	BU
2011 Proof	Est. 15,000	Value: 45.00				

KM# 1238 5 EURO
13.5000 g., 0.9250 Silver 0.4015 oz. ASW, 33 mm. **Ruler:** Juan Carlos I **Subject:** Cordoba

Date	Mintage	F	VF	XF	Unc	BU
2011 Proof	Est. 15,000	Value: 45.00				

KM# 1239 5 EURO
13.5000 g., 0.9250 Silver 0.4015 oz. ASW, 33 mm. **Ruler:** Juan Carlos I **Subject:** Girona

Date	Mintage	F	VF	XF	Unc	BU
2011 Proof	Est. 15,000	Value: 45.00				

KM# 1240 5 EURO
13.5000 g., 0.9250 Silver 0.4015 oz. ASW, 33 mm. **Ruler:** Juan Carlos I **Subject:** Leon

Date	Mintage	F	VF	XF	Unc	BU
2011 Proof	—	Value: 45.00				

KM# 1241 5 EURO
13.5000 g., 0.9250 Silver 0.4015 oz. ASW, 33 mm. **Ruler:** Juan Carlos I **Subject:** Lugo

Date	Mintage	F	VF	XF	Unc	BU
2011 Proof	Est. 15,000	Value: 45.00				

KM# 1242 5 EURO
13.5000 g., 0.9250 Silver 0.4015 oz. ASW, 33 mm. **Ruler:** Juan Carlos I **Subject:** Burgos

Date	Mintage	F	VF	XF	Unc	BU
2011 Proof	Est. 15,000	Value: 45.00				

KM# 1243 5 EURO
13.5000 g., 0.9250 Silver 0.4015 oz. ASW, 33 mm. **Ruler:** Juan Carlos I **Subject:** Caceres

Date	Mintage	F	VF	XF	Unc	BU
2011 Proof	Est. 15,000	Value: 45.00				

KM# 1244 5 EURO
13.5000 g., 0.9250 Silver 0.4015 oz. ASW, 33 mm. **Ruler:** Juan Carlos I **Subject:** Castellon de la Plana

Date	Mintage	F	VF	XF	Unc	BU
2011 Proof	Est. 15,000	Value: 45.00				

KM# 1245 5 EURO
13.5000 g., 0.9250 Silver 0.4015 oz. ASW, 33 mm. **Ruler:** Juan Carlos I **Subject:** Ciudad Real

Date	Mintage	F	VF	XF	Unc	BU
2011 Proof	Est. 15,000	Value: 45.00				

KM# 1048 10 EURO
27.0000 g., 0.9250 Silver 0.8029 oz. ASW, 40 mm. **Ruler:** Juan Carlos I **Subject:** Spanish Presidency of the European Union **Obv:** Head left **Rev:** Map of Europe **Edge:** Reeded

Date	Mintage	F	VF	XF	Unc	BU
2002 Proof	29,997	Value: 60.00				

KM# 1078 10 EURO
27.0000 g., 0.9250 Silver 0.8029 oz. ASW, 40 mm. **Ruler:** Juan Carlos I **Subject:** XIX Winter Olympics - Salt Lake City **Obv:** Head left **Obv. Legend:** JUAN CARLOS I REY DE ESPAÑA **Rev:** Cross country skier right, stylized snowflake at right **Rev. Legend:** JUEGOS OLIMPICOS DE - INVERNO 2002

Date	Mintage	F	VF	XF	Unc	BU
2002(M) Proof	17,703	Value: 60.00				

KM# 1079 10 EURO
27.0000 g., 0.9250 Silver 0.8029 oz. ASW, 40 mm. **Ruler:** Juan Carlos I **Subject:** XVII Football World Games 2002 - South Korea and Japan **Obv. Legend:** MUNDIAL DE FUTBOL/2002 - ESPAÑA **Rev:** Football against net

Date	Mintage	F	VF	XF	Unc	BU
2002(M) Proof	17,126	Value: 60.00				

KM# 1080 10 EURO
27.0000 g., 0.9250 Silver 0.8029 oz. ASW, 40 mm. **Ruler:** Juan Carlos I **Subject:** XVII Football World Games 2002 - South Korea and Japan **Obv. Legend:** MUNDIAL DE FUTBOL/2002 - ESPAÑA **Rev:** Glove

Date	Mintage	F	VF	XF	Unc	BU
2002(M) Proof	7,424	Value: 60.00				

KM# 1087 10 EURO
27.0000 g., 0.9250 Silver 0.8029 oz. ASW, 40 mm. **Ruler:** Juan Carlos I **Subject:** 100th Anniversary - Birth of Luis Cernuda **Obv:** Head left

Date	Mintage	F	VF	XF	Unc	BU
2002(M) Proof	25,000	Value: 60.00				

KM# 1088 10 EURO
27.0000 g., 0.9250 Silver 0.8029 oz. ASW, 40 mm. **Ruler:** Juan Carlos I **Subject:** 100th Anniversary - Birth of Rafael Alberti **Obv:** Head left **Obv. Legend:** JUAN CARLOS I REY DE ESPAÑA **Rev:** Bust of Alberti facing 3/4 right

Date	Mintage	F	VF	XF	Unc	BU
2002(M) Proof	25,000	Value: 60.00				

KM# 1082 10 EURO
27.0000 g., 0.9250 Silver 0.8029 oz. ASW, 40 mm. **Ruler:** Juan Carlos I **Subject:** 150th Anniversary Birth of Antonio Gaudí **Obv:** Bust of Gaudií at right **Obv. Legend:** Año Internacional **Rev:** Casa Milà

Date	Mintage	F	VF	XF	Unc	BU
2002(M) Proof	25,000	Value: 55.00				

KM# 1083 10 EURO
27.0000 g., 0.9250 Silver 0.8029 oz. ASW, 40 mm. **Ruler:** Juan Carlos I **Subject:** 150th Anniversary Birth of Antonio Gaudí **Obv:** Bust of Gaudí at right **Obv. Legend:** Año Internacional **Rev:** El Capricho

Date	Mintage	F	VF	XF	Unc	BU
2002(M) Proof	9,183	Value: 55.00				

KM# 1084 10 EURO
27.0000 g., 0.9250 Silver 0.8029 oz. ASW, 40 mm. **Ruler:** Juan Carlos I **Subject:** 150th Anniversary - Birth of Antonio Gaudí **Obv:** Bust of Gaudí at right **Obv. Legend:** Año Internacional **Rev:** Parque Güell

Date	Mintage	F	VF	XF	Unc	BU
2002(M) Proof	14,111	Value: 55.00				

KM# 1089 10 EURO
27.0000 g., 0.9250 Silver 0.8029 oz. ASW, 40 mm. **Ruler:** Juan Carlos I **Series:** Ibero-America V - ships **Obv:** Crowned arms in center circle, 10 participating country arms in outer circle **Obv. Legend:** JUAN CARLOS I REY DE ESPAÑA **Rev:** Galleon of the Spanish Armada **Rev. Legend:** ENCUENTRO DE DOS MUNDOS **Note:** Issued in 2003.

Date	Mintage	F	VF	XF	Unc	BU
2002(M) Proof	8,000	Value: 135				

KM# 1050 10 EURO
27.0000 g., 0.9250 Silver 0.8029 oz. ASW, 40 mm. **Ruler:** Juan Carlos I **Subject:** Annexation of Minorca **Obv:** Conjoined heads left **Rev:** Uniformed equestrians shaking hands flanked by ships **Edge:** Reeded **Note:** Mint mark: Crowned M.

Date	Mintage	F	VF	XF	Unc	BU
2002 Proof	8,693	Value: 100				

KM# 1076 10 EURO
27.0000 g., 0.9250 Silver 0.8029 oz. ASW, 40 mm. **Ruler:** Juan Carlos I **Subject:** FIFA World Cup **Obv:** Kings head left **Rev:** Goalie jumping for ball by net **Edge:** Reeded **Note:** Issued in 2004.

Date	Mintage	F	VF	XF	Unc	BU
2003(M) Proof	25,883	Value: 80.00				

KM# 1090 10 EURO
27.0000 g., 0.9250 Silver 0.8029 oz. ASW, 40 mm. **Ruler:** Juan Carlos I **Obv:** Conjoined heads left **Obv. Legend:** JUAN CARLOS I Y SOFIA **Rev:** Ediface of Parliament building in Madrid **Rev. Legend:** CONSTITUCION ESPAÑOLA

Date	Mintage	F	VF	XF	Unc	BU
2003(M) Proof	7,995	Value: 100				

KM# 1092 10 EURO
27.0000 g., 0.9250 Silver 0.8029 oz. ASW, 40 mm. **Ruler:** Juan Carlos I **Subject:** !st Anniversary of Euro **Obv:** Conjoined heads left **Obv. Legend:** PREMIER ANIVERSARIO EURO ? JUAN CARLOS I Y SOFIA **Rev:** Europa riding steer left

Date	Mintage	F	VF	XF	Unc	BU
2003(M) Proof	50,000	Value: 80.00				

KM# 1094 10 EURO
27.0000 g., 0.9250 Silver 0.8029 oz. ASW, 40 mm. **Ruler:** Juan Carlos I **Subject:** World Swimming Championship Games - Barcelona 2003 **Obv:** Head left **Obv. Legend:** JUAN CARLOS I REY DE ESPAÑA **Rev:** Swimmer doing the crawl right **Rev. Legend:** X FINA CAMPEONATOS DEL MUNDO DENATACION

Date	Mintage	F	VF	XF	Unc	BU
2003(M) Proof	5,470	Value: 90.00				

KM# 1052 10 EURO
27.0000 g., 0.9250 Silver 0.8029 oz. ASW, 40 mm. **Ruler:** Juan Carlos I **Obv:** Head left **Rev:** Sailing ship - De Eleano **Edge:** Reeded

Date	Mintage	F	VF	XF	Unc	BU
2003 Proof	12,486	Value: 90.00				

KM# 1053 10 EURO

27.0000 g., 0.9250 Silver 0.8029 oz. ASW, 40 mm. **Ruler:** Juan Carlos I **Obv:** Juan Carlos I **Rev:** Miguel Lopez de Legazpi **Edge:** Reeded

Date	Mintage	F	VF	XF	Unc	BU
2003 Proof	5,724	Value: 110				

KM# 1054 10 EURO

27.0000 g., 0.9250 Silver 0.8029 oz. ASW, 40 mm. **Ruler:** Juan Carlos I **Obv:** Head facing **Rev:** Seated female figure and Swan **Edge:** Reeded

Date	Mintage	F	VF	XF	Unc	BU
2004 Proof	17,597	Value: 90.00				

KM# 1055 10 EURO

27.0000 g., 0.9250 Silver 0.8029 oz. ASW, 40 mm. **Ruler:** Juan Carlos I **Obv:** Head facing **Rev:** Dali's painting "El gran masturbador" of 1929 **Edge:** Reeded

Date	Mintage	F	VF	XF	Unc	BU
2004 Proof	15,647	Value: 90.00				

KM# 1056 10 EURO

27.0000 g., 0.9250 Silver 0.8029 oz. ASW, 40 mm. **Ruler:** Juan Carlos I **Obv:** Head facing **Rev:** Dali's self portrait with bacon strip **Edge:** Reeded

Date	Mintage	F	VF	XF	Unc	BU
2004 Proof	18,290	Value: 90.00				

KM# 1059 10 EURO

27.0000 g., 0.9250 Silver 0.8029 oz. ASW, 40 mm. **Ruler:** Juan Carlos I **Obv:** Conjoined heads left **Rev:** Bust of St. James facing **Edge:** Reeded

Date	Mintage	F	VF	XF	Unc	BU
2004 Proof	12,214	Value: 90.00				

KM# 1060 10 EURO

27.0000 g., 0.9250 Silver 0.8029 oz. ASW, 40 mm. **Ruler:** Juan Carlos I **Obv:** Conjoined heads left within beaded circle **Rev:** Bust 1/4 left within beaded circle (1451-1504) **Edge:** Reeded

Date	Mintage	F	VF	XF	Unc	BU
2004 Proof	12,000	Value: 90.00				

KM# 1099 10 EURO

27.0000 g., 0.9250 Silver 0.8029 oz. ASW, 40 mm. **Ruler:** Juan Carlos I **Subject:** Expansion of the European Union **Obv:** Head left **Obv. Legend:** JUAN CARLOS I Y SOFIA **Rev:** Outlined map of European Union

Date	Mintage	F	VF	XF	Unc	BU
2004(M) Proof	41,448	Value: 80.00				

KM# 1101 10 EURO

27.0000 g., 0.9250 Silver 0.8029 oz. ASW, 40 mm. **Ruler:** Juan Carlos I **Subject:** XXVIII Summer Olympics - Athens 2004 **Obv:** Conjoined heads left **Obv. Legend:** JUAN CARLOS I Y SOFIA **Rev:** Broad jumper, outlined world map in backgound **Rev. Legend:** JUEGOS OLIMICOS

Date	Mintage	F	VF	XF	Unc	BU
2004(M) Proof	18,790	Value: 90.00				

KM# 1102 10 EURO

27.0000 g., 0.9250 Silver 0.8029 oz. ASW, 40 mm. **Ruler:** Juan Carlos I **Subject:** XVIII World Football games - Germany 2006 **Obv:** Head left **Obv. Legend:** JUAN CARLOS I REY DE ESPAÑA **Rev:** Goalie deflecting ball at net

Date	Mintage	F	VF	XF	Unc	BU
2004(M) Proof	50,000	Value: 80.00				

KM# 1097 10 EURO

27.0000 g., 0.9250 Silver 0.8029 oz. ASW, 40 mm. **Ruler:** Juan Carlos I **Subject:** Wedding of Prince Philip and Letizia Ortiz Rocasolano **Obv:** Conjoined heads left **Obv. Legend:** JUAN CARLOS I T SOFÍA **Rev:** Busts of wedding couple facing 3/4 right, crowned shield below **Rev. Legend:** FELIPE Y LETIZIA - 22.V.2004

Date	Mintage	F	VF	XF	Unc	BU
2004(M) Proof	40,367	Value: 55.00				

KM# 1104 10 EURO

27.0000 g., 0.9250 Silver 0.8029 oz. ASW, 40 mm. **Ruler:** Juan Carlos I **Obv:** Quixote seated reading a large book **Obv. Legend:** ESPAÑA - IV CENTENARIO DE LA PRIMERA EDICIÓN DE " EL QUIJOTE" **Rev:** Quixote being knocked off his horse by windmill blade **Rev. Legend:** LA AVENTURA - DE LOS - MOLINOS DE VIENTO

Date	Mintage	F	VF	XF	Unc	BU
2005(M) Proof	11,670	Value: 85.00				

KM# 1105 10 EURO
27.0000 g., 0.9250 Silver 0.8029 oz. ASW, 40 mm. **Ruler:** Juan Carlos I **Obv:** Quixote seated reading a large book **Obv. Legend:** ESPAÑA - IV CENTENARIO DE LA PREMERA EDICIÓN DE LA "EL QUIJOTE" **Rev:** Quixote thrusting his sword into an animal skin wine sack **Rev. Legend:** CON UNOS CUEROS DE VINO - BATALLA

Date	Mintage	F	VF	XF	Unc	BU
2005(M) Proof	7,902	Value: 85.00				

KM# 1106 10 EURO
27.0000 g., 0.9250 Silver 0.8029 oz. ASW, 40 mm. **Ruler:** Juan Carlos I **Obv:** Quixote seated reading a large book **Obv. Legend:** ESPAÑA - IV CENTENARIO DE LA PRIMERA EDICIÓN DE "EL QUIJOTE" **Rev:** Boy mounting a hobby horse with Quixote on it **Rev. Legend:** LA VENIDA DE CLAVAILEÑO CON...DILATADA AVENTURA

Date	Mintage	F	VF	XF	Unc	BU
2005(M) Proof	7,968	Value: 85.00				

KM# 1110 10 EURO
27.0000 g., 0.9250 Silver 0.8029 oz. ASW, 40 mm. **Ruler:** Juan Carlos I **Rev:** Crowned shield at left, head of Prince Philip at right **Rev. Legend:** XXV ANIVERSARIO - PREMIOS PRÍNCIPE DE ASTURIAS

Date	Mintage	F	VF	XF	Unc	BU
2005(M) Proof	12,845	Value: 90.00				

KM# 1109 10 EURO
27.0000 g., 0.9250 Silver 0.8029 oz. ASW, 40 mm. **Ruler:** Juan Carlos I **Series:** Ibero-America VI - Architecture **Obv:** Crowned arms in center circle, 10 participating country arms in outer circle **Obv. Legend:** JUAN CARLOS I REY DE ESPAÑA **Rev:** General Archives building of West Indes in Seville **Rev. Legend:** ENCUENTRO DE DOS MUNDOS

Date	Mintage	F	VF	XF	Unc	BU
2005(M) Proof	3,000	Value: 120				

KM# 1064 10 EURO
27.0000 g., 0.9250 Silver 0.8029 oz. ASW, 40 mm. **Ruler:** Juan Carlos I **Subject:** 2006 Winter Olympics **Obv:** Juan Carlos **Rev:** Skier **Edge:** Reeded

Date	Mintage	F	VF	XF	Unc	BU
2005 Proof	25,000	Value: 80.00				

KM# 1065 10 EURO
27.0000 g., 0.9250 Silver 0.8029 oz. ASW, 40 mm. **Ruler:** Juan Carlos I **Subject:** European Peace and Freedom **Obv:** Juan Carlos **Rev:** European map on clasped hands **Edge:** Reeded

Date	Mintage	F	VF	XF	Unc	BU
2005 Proof	29,231	Value: 90.00				

KM# 1114 10 EURO
27.0000 g., 0.9250 Silver 0.8029 oz. ASW, 40 mm. **Ruler:** Juan Carlos I **Subject:** 500th Anniversary Death of Columbus **Obv:** Bust of Columbus facing at right, astrolabe at lower left **Obv. Legend:** ESPAÑA **Rev:** Sailing ship "Santa Maria" **Rev. Legend:** CRISTOBAL COLON **Edge:** Reeded

Date	Mintage	F	VF	XF	Unc	BU
2006(M) Proof	9,960	Value: 100				

KM# 1115 10 EURO
27.0000 g., 0.9250 Silver 0.8029 oz. ASW, 40 mm. **Ruler:** Juan Carlos I **Subject:** 500th Anniversary - Death of Columbus **Obv:** Bust of Columbus facing at left, astrolabe at lower right **Obv. Legend:** ESPAÑA **Rev:** Sailing ship "Pinta" **Rev. Legend:** CRISTOBAL COLON **Edge:** Reeded

Date	Mintage	F	VF	XF	Unc	BU
2006(M) Proof	6,188	Value: 100				

KM# 1116 10 EURO
27.0000 g., 0.9250 Silver 0.8029 oz. ASW, 40 mm. **Ruler:** Juan Carlos I **Subject:** 500th Anniversary - Death of Columbus **Obv:** Bust of Columbus facing at right, astrolabe at lower left **Obv. Legend:** ESPAÑA **Rev:** Sailing ship "Niña" **Rev. Legend:** CRISTOBAL COLON **Edge:** Reeded

Date	Mintage	F	VF	XF	Unc	BU
2006(M) Proof	6,187	Value: 100				

KM# 1119 10 EURO
27.0000 g., 0.9250 Silver 0.8029 oz. ASW, 40 mm. **Ruler:** Juan Carlos I **Subject:** 20th Anniversay of Spain and Portugal membership in European Union **Obv:** Juan Carlos I **Rev:** Outlined map of Europe, bridge below **Rev. Legend:** ADHESIÓN A LAS COMUNIDADES EUROPEAS **Rev. Inscription:** ESPAÑA - PORTUGAL

Date	Mintage	F	VF	XF	Unc	BU
2006(M) Proof	11,100	Value: 70.00				

KM# 1120 10 EURO
27.0000 g., 0.9250 Silver 0.8029 oz. ASW, 40 mm. **Ruler:** Juan Carlos I **Rev:** Basketball player scoring in front of defender **Rev. Legend:** CAMPEONES DEL MUNDO - JAPÓN 2006

Date	Mintage	F	VF	XF	Unc	BU
2006(M) Proof	4,991	Value: 70.00				

KM# 1122 10 EURO
27.0000 g., 0.9250 Silver 0.8029 oz. ASW, 40 mm. **Ruler:** Juan Carlos I **Obv:** Head left **Obv. Legend:** JUAN CARLOS I REY DE ESPAÑA **Rev:** Charles I (V) standing facing 3/4 right in front of portal **Rev. Legend:** CAROLVS IMPERATOR

Date	Mintage	F	VF	XF	Unc	BU
2006(M) Proof	23,799	Value: 95.00				

KM# 1124 10 EURO
27.0000 g., 0.9250 Silver 0.8029 oz. ASW, 40 mm. **Ruler:** Juan Carlos I **Rev:** Two ornate portals **Rev. Legend:** V ANIVERSARIO DEL EURO

Date	Mintage	F	VF	XF	Unc	BU
2007 Proof	12,000	Value: 65.00				

KM# 1125 10 EURO
27.0000 g., 0.9250 Silver 0.8029 oz. ASW, 40 mm. **Ruler:** Juan Carlos I **Rev:** Stone arch bridge **Rev. Legend:** V ANIVERSARIO DEL EURO

Date	Mintage	F	VF	XF	Unc	BU
2007 Proof	12,000	Value: 65.00				

KM# 1126 10 EURO
27.0000 g., 0.9250 Silver 0.8029 oz. ASW, 40 mm. **Ruler:** Juan Carlos I **Rev:** Stone archway **Rev. Legend:** V ANIVERSARIO DEL EURO

Date	Mintage	F	VF	XF	Unc	BU
2007 Proof	12,000	Value: 65.00				

KM# 1132 10 EURO
27.0000 g., 0.9250 Silver 0.8029 oz. ASW, 40 mm. **Ruler:** Juan Carlos I **Obv:** Conjoined heads left **Obv. Legend:** JUAN CARLOS I Y SOFÍA - AÑO DE ESPAÑA EN CHINA **Rev:** Early silver "Pillar" reales coin with Chinese characters to left and right of pillars **Rev. Legend:** VTRAQUE VNVM

Date	Mintage	F	VF	XF	Unc	BU
2007 Proof	20,000	Value: 60.00				

KM# 1134 10 EURO
27.0000 g., 0.9250 Silver 0.8029 oz. ASW, 40 mm. **Ruler:** Juan Carlos I **Obv:** Head left **Obv. Legend:** JUAN CARLOS I REY DE ESPAÑA **Rev:** Basketball player shooting basket **Rev. Legend:** EUROBASKET 2007

Date	Mintage	F	VF	XF	Unc	BU
2007 Proof	12,000	Value: 80.00				

KM# 1141 10 EURO
27.0000 g., 0.9250 Silver 0.8029 oz. ASW, 40 mm. **Ruler:** Juan Carlos I **Subject:** Zaragoza Expo 2008

Date	Mintage	F	VF	XF	Unc	BU
2007 Proof	25,000	Value: 60.00				

KM# 1135 10 EURO
27.0000 g., 0.9250 Silver 0.8029 oz. ASW, 40 mm. **Ruler:** Juan Carlos I **Subject:** Treaty of Rome, 50th Anniversary **Obv:** Head left **Rev:** Map of Western Europe

Date	Mintage	F	VF	XF	Unc	BU
2007 Proof	15,000	Value: 60.00				

KM# 1137 10 EURO
27.0000 g., 0.9250 Silver 0.8029 oz. ASW, 40 mm. **Ruler:** Juan Carlos I **Subject:** El Cid 700th Anniversary **Obv:** Female standing before arches **Rev:** Monk writing

Date	Mintage	F	VF	XF	Unc	BU
2007 Proof	12,000	Value: 80.00				

KM# 1140 10 EURO
27.0000 g., 0.9250 Silver 0.8029 oz. ASW, 40 mm. **Ruler:** Juan Carlos I **Subject:** International Polar Year **Rev:** Ship left, outline map of Antartica in background

Date	Mintage	F	VF	XF	Unc	BU
2007 Proof	20,000	Value: 65.00				

KM# 1187 10 EURO
27.0000 g., 0.9250 Silver 0.8029 oz. ASW, 40 mm. **Ruler:** Juan Carlos I **Subject:** Expo Zaragoza **Rev:** Bridge

Date	Mintage	F	VF	XF	Unc	BU
2007	25,000	Value: 65.00				

KM# 1190 10 EURO
27.0000 g., 0.9250 Silver 0.8029 oz. ASW, 40 mm. **Ruler:** Juan Carlos I **Subject:** Velazquez

Date	Mintage	F	VF	XF	Unc	BU
2008 Proof	12,000	Value: 70.00				

KM# 1192 10 EURO
27.0000 g., 0.9250 Silver 0.8029 oz. ASW, 40 mm. **Ruler:** Juan Carlos I **Subject:** Soccer, European Champions

Date	Mintage	F	VF	XF	Unc	BU
2008 Proof	20,000	Value: 70.00				

KM# 1194 10 EURO
27.0000 g., 0.9250 Silver 0.8029 oz. ASW, 40 mm. **Ruler:** Juan Carlos I **Subject:** Numismatic Treasures - Hispano-Greek Pegasus

Date	Mintage	F	VF	XF	Unc	BU
2008 Proof	12,000	Value: 70.00				

KM# 1196 10 EURO
27.0000 g., 0.9250 Silver 0.8029 oz. ASW, 40 mm. **Ruler:** Juan Carlos I **Subject:** Olympic Sports - Sailing

Date	Mintage	F	VF	XF	Unc	BU
2008 Proof	—	Value: 60.00				

KM# 1199 10 EURO
27.0000 g., 0.9250 Silver 0.8029 oz. ASW, 40 mm. **Ruler:** Juan Carlos I **Subject:** War of Independence, 200th Anniversary Mamolita Malasanto

Date	Mintage	F	VF	XF	Unc	BU
2008 Proof	12,000	Value: 65.00				

KM# 1200 10 EURO
27.0000 g., 0.9250 Silver 0.8029 oz. ASW, 40 mm. **Ruler:** Juan Carlos I **Subject:** War of Independence, 200th Anniversary General Cortanas

Date	Mintage	F	VF	XF	Unc	BU
2008 Proof	12,000	Value: 65.00				

KM# 1201 10 EURO
27.0000 g., 0.9250 Silver 0.8029 oz. ASW, 40 mm. **Ruler:** Juan Carlos I **Subject:** War of Independence, 200th Anniversary El Tambor del Brue

Date	Mintage	F	VF	XF	Unc	BU
2008 Proof	20,000	Value: 80.00				

KM# 1203 10 EURO
27.0000 g., 0.9250 Silver 0.8029 oz. ASW, 40 mm. **Ruler:** Juan Carlos I **Subject:** Alphonse the wise

Date	Mintage	F	VF	XF	Unc	BU
2008 Proof	—	Value: 60.00				

KM# 1143 10 EURO
27.0000 g., 0.9250 Silver 0.8029 oz. ASW, 40 mm. **Ruler:** Juan Carlos I **Obv:** Head left **Rev:** Soccer player, ball and net

Date	Mintage	F	VF	XF	Unc	BU
2009 Proof	12,000	Value: 70.00				

KM# 1209 10 EURO
27.0000 g., 0.9250 Silver 0.8029 oz. ASW, 40 mm. **Ruler:** Juan Carlos I **Subject:** Dali Busto de mujer retraspective

Date	Mintage	F	VF	XF	Unc	BU
2009 Proof	10,000	Value: 75.00				

KM# 1210 10 EURO
27.0000 g., 0.9250 Silver 0.8029 oz. ASW, 40 mm. **Ruler:** Juan Carlos I **Subject:** Dali Retrato de Pablo Picasso and S. XXI

Date	Mintage	F	VF	XF	Unc	BU
2009 Proof	10,000	Value: 75.00				

KM# 1214 10 EURO
27.0000 g., 0.9250 Silver 0.8029 oz. ASW, 40 mm. **Ruler:** Juan Carlos I **Subject:** Philip II

Date	Mintage	F	VF	XF	Unc	BU
2009 Proof	18,000	Value: 80.00				

KM# 1216 10 EURO
27.0000 g., 0.9250 Silver 0.8029 oz. ASW, 40 mm. **Ruler:** Juan Carlos I **Subject:** World Cup Soccer, Africa

Date	Mintage	F	VF	XF	Unc	BU
2009 Proof	12,000	Value: 65.00				

KM# 1165 10 EURO
27.0000 g., 0.9250 Silver 0.8029 oz. ASW, 40 mm. **Ruler:** Juan Carlos I **Subject:** Numismatic Treasurers - Silver Shekel from Carthage, 3rd Century BC

Date	Mintage	F	VF	XF	Unc	BU
2010 Proof	10,000	Value: 75.00				

KM# 1169 10 EURO
27.0000 g., 0.9250 Silver 0.8029 oz. ASW, 40 mm. **Ruler:** Juan Carlos I **Subject:** Antoni Gaudi

Date	Mintage	F	VF	XF	Unc	BU
2010 Proof	10,000	Value: 75.00				

KM# 1171 10 EURO
27.0000 g., 0.9250 Silver 0.8029 oz. ASW, 40 mm. **Ruler:** Juan Carlos I **Subject:** EU Council Presidency

Date	Mintage	F	VF	XF	Unc	BU
2010 Proof	—	Value: 70.00				

KM# 1173 10 EURO
27.0000 g., 0.9250 Silver 0.8029 oz. ASW, 40 mm. **Ruler:** Juan Carlos I **Subject:** Holy Year 2010 - St. James the Elder

Date	Mintage	F	VF	XF	Unc	BU
2010 Proof	10,000	Value: 70.00				

KM# 1174 10 EURO
27.0000 g., 0.9250 Silver 0.8029 oz. ASW, 40 mm. **Ruler:** Juan Carlos I **Subject:** Shanghai Expo

Date	Mintage	F	VF	XF	Unc	BU
2010 Proof	10,000	Value: 70.00				

KM# 1175 10 EURO
27.0000 g., 0.9250 Silver 0.8029 oz. ASW, 40 mm. **Ruler:** Juan Carlos I **Subject:** Ibero-American Series - Historical Coins

Date	Mintage	F	VF	XF	Unc	BU
2010 Proof	12,000	Value: 70.00				

KM# 1176 10 EURO
27.0000 g., 0.9250 Silver 0.8029 oz. ASW, 40 mm. **Ruler:** Juan Carlos I **Subject:** FIFA World Cup - South Africa 2010

Date	Mintage	F	VF	XF	Unc	BU
2010 Proof	20,000	Value: 65.00				

KM# 1178 10 EURO
27.0000 g., 0.9250 Silver 0.8029 oz. ASW, 40 mm. **Ruler:** Juan Carlos I **Subject:** Francisco de Goya - The Clothed Maja

Date	Mintage	F	VF	XF	Unc	BU
2010 Proof	10,000	Value: 85.00				

KM# 1179 10 EURO
27.0000 g., 0.9250 Silver 0.8029 oz. ASW, 40 mm. **Ruler:** Juan Carlos I **Subject:** Francisco de Goya - The Grape Harvest

Date	Mintage	F	VF	XF	Unc	BU
2010 Proof	10,000	Value: 85.00				

KM# 1180 10 EURO
27.0000 g., 0.9250 Silver 0.8029 oz. ASW, 40 mm. **Ruler:** Juan Carlos I **Subject:** Francisco de Goya - Duel with Clubs

Date	Mintage	F	VF	XF	Unc	BU
2010 Proof	12,000	Value: 85.00				

KM# 1185 10 EURO
27.0000 g., 0.9250 Silver 0.8029 oz. ASW, 40 mm. **Ruler:** Juan Carlos I **Subject:** International Year of Chemistry **Rev:** Marie Curie

Date	Mintage	F	VF	XF	Unc	BU
2011 Proof	10,000	Value: 85.00				

KM# 1219 10 EURO
27.0000 g., 0.9250 Silver 0.8029 oz. ASW, 40 mm. **Ruler:** Juan Carlos I **Subject:** Spain-Portugal

Date	Mintage	F	VF	XF	Unc	BU
2011 Proof	10,000	Value: 70.00				

KM# 1220 10 EURO
27.0000 g., 0.9250 Silver 0.8029 oz. ASW, 40 mm. **Ruler:** Juan Carlos I **Subject:** Historic Spanish Coin, Ibero American series

Date	Mintage	F	VF	XF	Unc	BU
2011 Proof	—	Value: 75.00				

KM# 1223 10 EURO
27.0000 g., 0.9250 Silver 0.8029 oz. ASW, 40 mm. **Ruler:** Juan Carlos I **Subject:** Musillo-Bran Partov

Date	Mintage	F	VF	XF	Unc	BU
2011 Proof	10,000	Value: 90.00				

KM# 1224 10 EURO
27.0000 g., 0.9250 Silver 0.8029 oz. ASW, 40 mm. **Ruler:** Juan Carlos I **Subject:** Ribera-Jacdo

Date	Mintage	F	VF	XF	Unc	BU
2011 Proof	10,000	Value: 90.00				

KM# 1225 10 EURO
27.0000 g., 0.9250 Silver 0.8029 oz. ASW, 40 mm. **Ruler:** Juan Carlos I **Subject:** Zurbaram - Hercules

Date	Mintage	F	VF	XF	Unc	BU
2011 Proof	10,000	Value: 90.00				

KM# 1248 10 EURO
27.0000 g., 0.9250 Silver 0.8029 oz. ASW, 40 mm. **Ruler:** Juan Carlos I **Subject:** Orellana

Date	Mintage	F	VF	XF	Unc	BU
2011 Proof	12,000	Value: 65.00				

KM# 1250 10 EURO
27.0000 g., 0.9250 Silver 0.8029 oz. ASW, 40 mm. **Ruler:** Juan Carlos I **Subject:** Numismatic Treasurers - Elephant coin

Date	Mintage	F	VF	XF	Unc	BU
2011 Proof	10,000	Value: 65.00				

KM# 1217 10 EURO
27.0000 g., 0.9250 Silver 0.8029 oz. ASW, 40 mm. **Ruler:** Juan Carlos I **Subject:** Spain-Russia **Note:** The reverse design is the same as a Russian 3 Rouble

Date	Mintage	F	VF	XF	Unc	BU
2012 Proof	7,500	Value: 80.00				

KM# 1049 12 EURO
18.0000 g., 0.9250 Silver 0.5353 oz. ASW, 33 mm. **Ruler:** Juan Carlos I **Subject:** Spanish European Union Presidency **Obv:** Conjoined heads left **Rev:** Distorted star design **Edge:** Reeded

Date	Mintage	F	VF	XF	Unc	BU
2002	1,608,400	—	—	—	22.50	25.00
2002 Special select	—	—	—	—	—	30.00
2002 Proof	Est. 30,000	Value: 50.00				

KM# 1051 12 EURO
18.0000 g., 0.9250 Silver 0.5353 oz. ASW, 33 mm. **Ruler:** Juan Carlos I **Subject:** 25th Anniversary of Constitution **Obv:** Conjoined heads left **Rev:** National arms above denomination **Edge:** Plain

Date	Mintage	F	VF	XF	Unc	BU
2003	1,468,800	—	—	—	27.00	30.00
2003 Proof	19,346	Value: 40.00				

KM# 1069 12 EURO
18.0000 g., 0.9250 Silver 0.5353 oz. ASW, 33 mm. **Ruler:** Juan Carlos I **Obv:** Juan Carlos and Sofia **Rev:** Felipe and Letizia

Date	Mintage	F	VF	XF	Unc	BU
2004M	2,505,700	—	—	—	25.00	28.00

KM# 1095 12 EURO
18.0000 g., 0.9250 Silver 0.5353 oz. ASW, 32.93 mm. **Ruler:** Juan Carlos I **Subject:** 500th Anniversary - Death of Isabel **Obv:** Conjoined heads left **Obv. Legend:** JUAN CARLOS I Y SOFIA **Rev:** Bust of Isabella I left **Rev. Legend:** ISABEL I DE CASTILLA / 1481-1504 **Edge:** Plain

Date	Mintage	F	VF	XF	Unc	BU
2004(M)	1,496,100	—	—	—	27.00	30.00
2004(M) Proof	12,420	Value: 45.00				

KM# 1096 12 EURO
18.0000 g., 0.9250 Silver 0.5353 oz. ASW, 32.94 mm. **Ruler:** Juan Carlos I **Subject:** Wedding of Prince Philip and Letizia Ortiz Rocasolano **Obv:** Conjoined heads left **Obv. Legend:** JUAN CARLOS I Y SOFIA **Rev:** Busts of wedding couple facing 3/4 right **Rev. Legend:** FELIPE Y LETIZIA - 22.V.2004 **Edge:** Plain

Date	Mintage	F	VF	XF	Unc	BU
2004(M) Proof	27,655	Value: 25.00				

KM# 1067 12 EURO
18.0000 g., 0.9250 Silver 0.5353 oz. ASW, 33 mm. **Ruler:** Juan Carlos I **Subject:** Don Quixote **Obv:** Conjoined heads left **Rev:** Man seated on books **Edge:** Reeded

Date	Mintage	F	VF	XF	Unc	BU
2005	1,880,900	—	—	—	25.00	28.00

KM# 1113 12 EURO
18.0000 g., 0.9250 Silver 0.5353 oz. ASW, 32.95 mm. **Ruler:** Juan Carlos I **Subject:** 500th Anniversary - Death of Columbus **Obv:** Conjoined heads left **Obv. Legend:** JUAN CARLOS I Y SOFIA **Rev:** Bust of Columbus facing 3/4 right, latitude and longitude lines with three small sailing ships in background **Edge:** Plain

Date	Mintage	F	VF	XF	Unc	BU
2006(M)	1,379,600	—	—	—	25.00	28.00

KM# 1129 12 EURO
18.0000 g., 0.9250 Silver 0.5353 oz. ASW, 32 mm. **Ruler:** Juan Carlos I **Rev:** Hand with pen **Rev. Legend:** 50 ANIVERSARIO • TRATADO DE ROMA **Rev. Inscription:** EUROPA

Date	Mintage	F	VF	XF	Unc	BU
2007(M)	1,002,500	—	—	—	—	28.00
2007 Proof	20,000	Value: 35.00				

KM# 1195 12 EURO
18.0000 g., 0.9250 Silver 0.5353 oz. ASW, 33 mm. **Ruler:** Juan Carlos I **Subject:** International Year of Planet Earth

Date	Mintage	F	VF	XF	Unc	BU
2008 Proof	45,000	Value: 30.00				

KM# 1212 12 EURO
18.0000 g., 0.9250 Silver 0.5353 oz. ASW, 33 mm. **Ruler:** Juan Carlos I **Subject:** European Monetary Union, 10th Anniversary

Date	Mintage	F	VF	XF	Unc	BU
2009 Proof	20,000	Value: 30.00				

KM# 1172 12 EURO
18.0000 g., 0.9250 Silver 0.5353 oz. ASW, 33 mm. **Ruler:** Juan Carlos I **Subject:** EU Council Presidency

Date	Mintage	F	VF	XF	Unc	BU
2010 Proof	—	Value: 32.00				

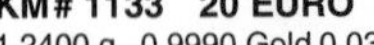

KM# 1133 20 EURO
1.2400 g., 0.9990 Gold 0.0398 oz. AGW, 13.92 mm. **Ruler:** Juan Carlos I **Obv:** National arms **Obv. Legend:** JUAN CARLOS I REY DE ESPAÑA - AÑO DE ESPAÑA EN CHINA **Rev:** Early silver "Pillar" reales coin with Chinese chopmarks

Date	Mintage	F	VF	XF	Unc	BU
2007 Proof	15,000	Value: 110				

KM# 1193 20 EURO
1.2400 g., 0.9990 Gold 0.0398 oz. AGW, 13.92 mm. **Ruler:** Juan Carlos I **Subject:** Numismatic Treasures - Roman Aureaus

Date	Mintage	F	VF	XF	Unc	BU
2008 Proof	12,000	Value: 120				

KM# 1206 20 EURO
1.2400 g., 0.9990 Gold 0.0398 oz. AGW, 13.92 mm. **Ruler:** Juan Carlos I **Subject:** Numismatic Treasurers - Spanish coin **Obv:** Obverse of 1609 gold coin **Rev:** Reverse of 1609 gold coin

Date	Mintage	F	VF	XF	Unc	BU
2009 Proof	12,000	Value: 120				

KM# 1166 20 EURO
1.2400 g., 0.9990 Gold 0.0398 oz. AGW, 13.92 mm. **Ruler:** Juan Carlos I **Subject:** Numismatic Treasurers - Tremis, King Leovigild (569-86)

Date	Mintage	F	VF	XF	Unc	BU
2010 Proof	12,000	Value: 120				

KM# 1177 20 EURO
1.2400 g., 0.9990 Gold 0.0398 oz. AGW, 13.92 mm. **Ruler:** Juan Carlos I **Subject:** FIFA World Cup - South Africa

Date	Mintage	F	VF	XF	Unc	BU
2010 Proof	20,000	Value: 115				

KM# 1183 20 EURO
18.0000 g., 0.9250 Silver 0.5353 oz. ASW, 33 mm. **Ruler:** Juan Carlos I **Subject:** FIFA World Cup Winners

Date	Mintage	F	VF	XF	Unc	BU
2010 Proof	12,000	Value: 60.00				

KM# 1218 20 EURO
1.2400 g., 0.9990 Gold 0.0398 oz. AGW **Ruler:** Juan Carlos I **Subject:** Span & Portugal **Shape:** 13.92

Date	Mintage	F	VF	XF	Unc	BU
2011 Proof	12,000	Value: 110				

KM# 1246 20 EURO
18.0000 g., 0.9250 Silver 0.5353 oz. ASW, 33 mm. **Ruler:** Juan Carlos I **Subject:** International Women's Day, 100th Anniversary

Date	Mintage	F	VF	XF	Unc	BU
2011 Proof	12,000	Value: 50.00				

KM# 1251 20 EURO
1.2400 g., 0.9990 Gold 0.0398 oz. AGW, 13.92 mm. **Ruler:** Juan Carlos I **Subject:** Numismatic Treasurers - Leovigild Gold

Date	Mintage	F	VF	XF	Unc	BU
2011 Proof	—	Value: 100				

KM# 1085 50 EURO
168.7500 g., 0.9250 Silver 5.0183 oz. ASW, 73 mm. **Ruler:** Juan Carlos I **Subject:** 150th Anniversary - Birth of Antonio Gaudí **Obv:** Bust of Gaudií at right **Obv. Legend:** Año Internacional **Rev:** Sagrada Familia

Date	Mintage	F	VF	XF	Unc	BU
2002(M) Proof	7,594	Value: 450				

KM# 1093 50 EURO
168.7500 g., 0.9250 Silver 5.0183 oz. ASW, 73 mm. **Ruler:** Juan Carlos I **Subject:** 1st Anniversary of Euro **Obv:** Conjoined heads left **Obv. Legend:** PREMIER ANIVERSARIO EURO • JUAN CARLOS I Y SOFÍA **Rev:** National arms at center surrounded by various items of architecture

Date	Mintage	F	VF	XF	Unc	BU
2003 Proof	5,554	Value: 500				

KM# 1057 50 EURO
168.7500 g., 0.9250 Silver with removeable gold plated silver insert 5.0183 oz. ASW, 73 mm. **Ruler:** Juan Carlos I **Obv:** Dali's "Dream State" painting **Rev:** Dali's "Rhinocerotic Disintegration..." painting **Edge:** Reeded

Date	Mintage	F	VF	XF	Unc	BU
2004 Proof	10,455	Value: 450				

KM# 1061 50 EURO
168.7300 g., 0.9250 Silver 5.0177 oz. ASW, 73 mm. **Ruler:** Juan Carlos I **Obv:** Crowned bust left(1451-1504) and castle within beaded circle **Rev:** Surrender of Grenada scene within beaded circle **Edge:** Reeded

Date	Mintage	F	VF	XF	Unc	BU
2004 Proof	3,158	Value: 500				

KM# 1107 50 EURO
168.7500 g., 0.9250 Silver 5.0183 oz. ASW, 73 mm. **Ruler:** Juan Carlos I **Obv:** 1/2 length figure of Miguel de Cervantes Saavedra facing writing in manuscript with quill pen **Obv. Legend:** ESPAÑA - IV CENTENARIO DE LA PRIMERA EDICIÓn DE "EL QUIJOTE" **Rev:** Quixote

Date	Mintage	F	VF	XF	Unc	BU
2005(M) Proof	5,795	Value: 450				

KM# 1117 50 EURO
168.7500 g., 0.9250 Silver 5.0183 oz. ASW, 73 mm. **Ruler:** Juan Carlos I **Subject:** 500th Anniversary - Death of Columbus **Obv:** Landing party at Guanahani **Obv. Legend:** ESPAÑA **Rev:** Columbus standing facing 3/4 left with right arm outstretched standing on outline of the northern part of South America **Rev. Legend:** CRISTOBAL COLON **Edge:** Plain

Date	Mintage	F	VF	XF	Unc	BU
2006(M) Proof	4,265	Value: 450				

KM# 1127 50 EURO
168.7500 g., 0.9250 Silver 5.0183 oz. ASW, 73 mm. **Ruler:** Juan Carlos I **Rev:** Euro seated on resting bull left **Rev. Legend:** V ANIVERSARIO DEL EURO

Date	Mintage	F	VF	XF	Unc	BU
2007 Proof	5,000	Value: 425				

KM# 1138 50 EURO
168.7500 g., 0.9250 Silver 5.0183 oz. ASW, 73 mm. **Ruler:** Juan Carlos I **Subject:** El Cid 700th Anniversary **Obv:** Statue of Rodrigo Diaz de Vivar in Burgas **Rev:** Two seated trumpeters

Date	Mintage	F	VF	XF	Unc	BU
2007 Proof	6,000	Value: 425				

KM# 1189 50 EURO
168.7500 g., 0.9250 Silver 5.0183 oz. ASW, 73 mm. **Ruler:** Juan Carlos I **Subject:** Velazquez

Date	Mintage	F	VF	XF	Unc	BU
2008 Proof	5,000	Value: 425				

KM# 1198 50 EURO
168.7500 g., 0.9250 Silver 5.0183 oz. ASW, 73 mm. **Ruler:** Juan Carlos I **Subject:** War of Independence, 200th Anniversary

Date	Mintage	F	VF	XF	Unc	BU
2008 Proof	5,000	Value: 425				

KM# 1205 50 EURO
168.7500 g., 0.9250 Silver 5.0183 oz. ASW, 73 mm. **Ruler:** Juan Carlos I **Subject:** Numismatic Treasurers - Spanish cim cuentim

Date	Mintage	F	VF	XF	Unc	BU
2009 Proof	6,000	Value: 450				

KM# 1208 50 EURO
168.7500 g., 0.9250 Silver 5.0183 oz. ASW, 73 mm. **Ruler:** Juan Carlos I **Subject:** Dali

Date	Mintage	F	VF	XF	Unc	BU
2009 Proof	5,000	Value: 450				

KM# 1181 50 EURO
168.7500 g., 0.9250 Silver 5.0183 oz. ASW, 73 mm. **Ruler:** Juan Carlos I **Subject:** Francisco de Goya - Witches' Sabbath

Date	Mintage	F	VF	XF	Unc	BU
2010 Proof	6,000	Value: 425				

KM# 1222 50 EURO
168.7500 g., 0.9990 Silver 5.4198 oz. ASW, 73 mm. **Ruler:** Juan Carlos I **Subject:** El Greco

Date	Mintage	F	VF	XF	Unc	BU
2011 Proof	5,000	Value: 425				

KM# 1077 100 EURO
6.7500 g., 0.9990 Gold 0.2168 oz. AGW, 23 mm. **Ruler:** Juan Carlos I **Obv:** Head left **Obv. Legend:** JUAN CARLOS I REY DE ESPAÑA **Rev:** Player running right kicking ball **Rev. Legend:** ALEMANIA 2006 at bottom **Note:** Issued in 2004.

Date	Mintage	F	VF	XF	Unc	BU
2003(M) Proof	8,230	Value: 600				

KM# 1103 100 EURO
6.7500 g., 0.9990 Gold 0.2168 oz. AGW, 23 mm. **Ruler:** Juan Carlos I **Subject:** XVIII World Football Games - Germany 2006 **Obv:** Head left **Obv. Legend:** JUAN CARLOS I REY DE ESPAÑA **Rev:** Goalie deflecting ball at net **Rev. Inscription:** COPA MUNDIAL DE LA FIFA

Date	Mintage	F	VF	XF	Unc	BU
2004(M) Proof	25,000	Value: 600				

KM# 1167 100 EURO
168.8800 g., 0.9250 Silver with gold plating 5.0222 oz. ASW, 73 mm. **Ruler:** Juan Carlos I **Subject:** Numismatic treasurers - The Centen, 100 Escudos, 1609

Date	Mintage	F	VF	XF	Unc	BU
2009 Proof	6,000	Value: 475				

KM# 1204 100 EURO
6.7500 g., 0.9990 Gold 0.2168 oz. AGW, 23 mm. **Ruler:** Juan Carlos I **Subject:** Numismatic Treasures - Spanish Escudo

Date	Mintage	F	VF	XF	Unc	BU
2009 Proof	—	Value: 425				

KM# 1215 100 EURO
6.7500 g., 0.9990 Gold 0.2168 oz. AGW, 23 mm. **Ruler:** Juan Carlos I **Subject:** World Cup Soccer, Africa

Date	Mintage	F	VF	XF	Unc	BU
2009 Proof	6,000	Value: 550				

KM# 1168 100 EURO
6.7500 g., 0.9990 Gold 0.2168 oz. AGW, 23 mm. **Ruler:** Juan Carlos I **Subject:** Numismatic Treasurers - Tremis, Suintila (621-31)

Date	Mintage	F	VF	XF	Unc	BU
2010 Proof	6,000	Value: 425				

KM# 1249 100 EURO
6.7500 g., 0.9990 Gold 0.2168 oz. AGW, 23 mm. **Ruler:** Juan Carlos I **Subject:** Numismatic Treasurers - Swinthila Gold

Date	Mintage	F	VF	XF	Unc	BU
2011 Proof	6,000	Value: 550				

KM# 1081 200 EURO
13.5000 g., 0.9990 Gold 0.4336 oz. AGW, 30 mm. **Ruler:** Juan Carlos I **Subject:** XVII Football World Games 2002 - South Korea and Japan **Obv. Legend:** MUNDIAL DE FUTBOL/2002 - ESPAÑA **Rev:** Ball hitting net

Date	Mintage	F	VF	XF	Unc	BU
2002(M) Proof	4,000	Value: 1,050				

KM# 1091 200 EURO
13.5000 g., 0.9990 Gold 0.4336 oz. AGW **Ruler:** Juan Carlos I **Obv:** Conjoined heads left **Obv. Legend:** JUAN CARLOS I Y SOFIA **Rev:** Ediface of Parliament Building in Madrid **Rev. Legend:** CONSTITUCION ESPANOLA

Date	Mintage	F	VF	XF	Unc	BU
2003(M) Proof	4,000	Value: 825				

KM# 1075 200 EURO
13.5000 g., 0.9990 Gold 0.4336 oz. AGW, 30 mm. **Ruler:** Juan Carlos I **Subject:** Birth of the Euro **Obv:** Spanish King and Queen left **Rev:** Mythological Europa riding on the back of a bull

Date	Mintage	F	VF	XF	Unc	BU
2003 Proof	20,000	Value: 1,050				

KM# 1062 200 EURO
13.5000 g., 0.9990 Gold 0.4336 oz. AGW, 30 mm. **Ruler:** Juan Carlos I **Obv:** Seated crowned figures on shield flanked by date and value **Rev:** Crowned busts facing each other on coin design **Edge:** Reeded

Date	Mintage	F	VF	XF	Unc	BU
2004 Proof	1,936	Value: 1,200				

KM# 1100 200 EURO
13.5000 g., 0.9990 Gold 0.4336 oz. AGW, 30 mm. **Ruler:** Juan Carlos I **Subject:** Expansion of the European Union **Obv:** Head left **Obv. Legend:** JUAN CARLOS I Y SOFIA **Rev:** Outlined map of the European Union

Date	Mintage	F	VF	XF	Unc	BU
2004(M) Proof	5,000	Value: 1,000				

KM# 1098 200 EURO
13.5000 g., 0.9990 Gold 0.4336 oz. AGW, 30 mm. **Ruler:** Juan Carlos I **Subject:** Wedding of Prince Philip and Letizia Ortiz Rocasolano **Obv:** Conjoined heads left **Obv. Legend:** JUAN CARLOS I Y SOFIA **Rev:** Busts of wedding couple facing 3/4 right at center left, crowned shield at right **Rev. Legend:** FELIPE Y LETIZIA - 22.V.2004

Date	Mintage	F	VF	XF	Unc	BU
2004(M) Proof	6,303	Value: 1,200				

KM# 1111 200 EURO
13.5000 g., 0.9990 Gold 0.4336 oz. AGW, 30 mm. **Ruler:** Juan Carlos I **Rev:** Crowned shield at left, head of Prince Philip left at right **Rev. Legend:** XXV ANIVERSAIO - PREMIOS PRÍNCIPE DE ASTURIAS

Date	Mintage	F	VF	XF	Unc	BU
2005(M) Proof	1,690	Value: 1,300				

KM# 1066 200 EURO
13.5000 g., 0.9990 Gold 0.4336 oz. AGW, 30 mm. **Ruler:** Juan Carlos I **Subject:** European Peace and Freedom **Obv:** Juan Carlos **Rev:** European map on clasped hands **Edge:** Reeded

Date	Mintage	F	VF	XF	Unc	BU
2005 Proof	2,350	Value: 1,100				

KM# 1123 200 EURO
13.5000 g., 0.9990 Gold 0.4336 oz. AGW, 30 mm. **Ruler:** Juan Carlos I **Obv:** Head left **Obv. Legend:** JUAN CARLOS I REY DE ESPAÑA **Rev:** Charles I (V) standing facing 3/4 right in front of portal **Rev. Legend:** CAROLVS IMPERATOR

Date	Mintage	F	VF	XF	Unc	BU
2006(M) Proof	3,500	Value: 1,050				

KM# 1136 200 EURO
13.5000 g., 0.9990 Gold 0.4336 oz. AGW, 30 mm. **Ruler:** Juan Carlos I **Subject:** Treaty of Rome, 50th Anniversary **Obv:** Head left **Rev:** Map of Western Europe

Date	Mintage	F	VF	XF	Unc	BU
2007 Proof	3,500	Value: 1,050				

KM# 1139 200 EURO
13.5000 g., 0.9990 Gold 0.4336 oz. AGW, 30 mm. **Ruler:** Juan Carlos I **Subject:** El Cid, 700th Anniversary **Obv:** Rodrigo Diaz de Vivar bust facing **Rev:** Knight on horseback within rectangle

Date	Mintage	F	VF	XF	Unc	BU
2007 Proof	3,500	Value: 1,050				

KM# 1188 200 EURO
13.5000 g., 0.9990 Gold 0.4336 oz. AGW, 30 mm. **Ruler:** Juan Carlos I **Subject:** Velazquez

Date	Mintage	F	VF	XF	Unc	BU
2008 Proof	3,500	Value: 1,050				

KM# 1191 200 EURO
13.5000 g., 0.9990 Gold 0.4336 oz. AGW, 30 mm. **Ruler:** Juan Carlos I **Subject:** Soccer, European Champions

Date	Mintage	F	VF	XF	Unc	BU
2008 Proof	4,000	Value: 1,050				

KM# 1202 200 EURO
13.5000 g., 0.9990 Gold 0.4336 oz. AGW, 30 mm. **Ruler:** Juan Carlos I **Subject:** Alphonse the Wise

Date	Mintage	F	VF	XF	Unc	BU
2008 Proof	3,500	Value: 1,050				

KM# 1213 200 EURO
13.5000 g., 0.9990 Gold 0.4336 oz. AGW, 30 mm. **Ruler:** Juan Carlos I **Subject:** Philip II

Date	Mintage	F	VF	XF	Unc	BU
2009 Proof	3,000	Value: 1,050				

KM# 1170 200 EURO
13.5000 g., 0.9990 Gold 0.4336 oz. AGW, 30 mm. **Ruler:** Juan Carlos I **Subject:** Antoni Gaudi

Date	Mintage	F	VF	XF	Unc	BU
2010 Proof	3,000	Value: 1,050				

KM# 1247 200 EURO
13.5000 g., 0.9990 Gold 0.4336 oz. AGW, 30 mm. **Ruler:** Juan Carlos I **Subject:** Orellana

Date	Mintage	F	VF	XF	Unc	BU
2011 Proof	3,000	Value: 1,050				

KM# 1112 300 EURO
Bi-Metallic .554 AGW Gold center in .343 ASW Silver ring, 40 mm. **Ruler:** Juan Carlos I **Subject:** XVIII World Championship Football Games - Germany 2006 **Obv:** Football player facing kicking ball **Obv. Legend:** ESPAÑA **Rev:** Football player kicking ball into net at foreground **Rev. Legend:** COPA MUNDIAL DE LA FIFA - ALEMANIA **Shape:** 12-sided

Date	Mintage	F	VF	XF	Unc	BU
2005(M) Proof	8,000	Value: 1,350				

KM# 1121 300 EURO
Bi-Metallic .554 AGW Gold center in .343 ASW Silver ring, 40 mm. **Ruler:** Juan Carlos I **Rev:** Basketball player facing tossing ball **Rev. Legend:** CAMPEONES DEL MUNDO - JAPÓN 2006 **Shape:** 12-sided

Date	Mintage	F	VF	XF	Unc	BU
2006(M) Proof	866	Value: 1,600				

KM# 1086 400 EURO
27.0000 g., 0.9990 Gold 0.8672 oz. AGW, 38 mm. **Ruler:** Juan Carlos I **Subject:** 150th Anniversary - Birth of Antonio Gaudí **Obv:** Bust of Gaudí at right **Obv. Legend:** Año Internacional **Rev:** Casa Batlló

Date	Mintage	F	VF	XF	Unc	BU
2002(M) Proof	3,000	Value: 2,000				

KM# 1058 400 EURO
27.0000 g., 0.9990 Gold 0.8672 oz. AGW, 38 mm. **Ruler:** Juan Carlos I **Obv:** Bust facing **Rev:** Dali's painting "Girl at the Window" **Edge:** Reeded

Date	Mintage	F	VF	XF	Unc	BU
2004 Proof	4,477	Value: 2,000				

KM# 1108 400 EURO
27.0000 g., 0.9990 Gold 0.8672 oz. AGW, 38 mm. **Ruler:** Juan Carlos I **Obv:** Quixote seated reading a large book **Obv. Legend:** ESPAÑA - IV CENTENARIO DE LA PRIMERA EDICIÓN DE "EL QUIJOTE" **Rev:** Quixote on horseback 3/4 right followed by his friend on a burro **Rev. Legend:** DON QUIJOTE DE LA MANCHA SANCHO PANZA

Date	Mintage	F	VF	XF	Unc	BU
2005(M) Proof	2,019	Value: 2,000				

KM# 1118 400 EURO
27.0000 g., 0.9990 Gold 0.8672 oz. AGW, 38 mm. **Ruler:** Juan Carlos I **Subject:** 500th Anniversary - Death of Columbus **Obv:** Columbus **Rev:** Audience with Ferdinand and Isabella

Date	Mintage	F	VF	XF	Unc	BU
2006(M) Proof	1,850	Value: 2,000				

KM# 1128 400 EURO
27.0000 g., 0.9990 Gold 0.8672 oz. AGW, 38 mm. **Ruler:** Juan Carlos I **Rev:** Large ring of stars around globe **Rev. Legend:** V ANIVERSARIO DEL EURO

Date	Mintage	F	VF	XF	Unc	BU
2007 Proof	3,000	Value: 2,000				

KM# 1197 400 EURO
27.0000 g., 0.9990 Gold 0.8672 oz. AGW, 38 mm. **Ruler:** Juan Carlos I **Subject:** War of Independence, 200th Anniversary

Date	Mintage	F	VF	XF	Unc	BU
2008 Proof	3,500	Value: 2,000				

KM# 1207 400 EURO
27.0000 g., 0.9990 Gold 0.8672 oz. AGW, 38 mm. **Ruler:** Juan Carlos I **Subject:** Dali

Date	Mintage	F	VF	XF	Unc	BU
2009 Proof	3,000	Value: 2,000				

KM# 1182 400 EURO
27.0000 g., 0.9990 Gold 0.8672 oz. AGW, 38 mm. **Ruler:** Juan Carlos I **Subject:** Francisco de Goya - Volaverunt

Date	Mintage	F	VF	XF	Unc	BU
2010 Proof	3,000	Value: 2,000				

KM# 1221 400 EURO
27.0000 g., 0.9990 Gold 0.8672 oz. AGW, 38 mm. **Ruler:** Juan Carlos I **Subject:** El Greco

Date	Mintage	F	VF	XF	Unc	BU
2011 Proof	3,000	Value: 2,000				

MINT SETS

KM#	Date	Mintage	Identification	Issue Price	Mkt Val
MS27	2000-2001 (8)	49,426	KM#832-833, 924, 991-992 (both dated 2000), 1012-1013, 1016	15.50	35.00
MS28	2002 (8)	99,301	KM#1040-1047	—	15.00
MS29	2003 (8)	149	KM#1040-1047	—	15.00
MS30	2004 (8)	43,000	KM#1040-1047	—	70.00
MS31	2005 (8)	49,923	KM#1040-1047	—	30.00
MS32	2006 (8)	49,996	KM#1040-1047	—	12.50
MS33	2007 (8)	—	KM#1040-1042, 1070-1074	—	30.00

PROOF SETS

KM#	Date	Mintage	Identification	Issue Price	Mkt Val
PS34	2002 (9)	23,000	KM#1040-1047, 1049	125	150
PS35	2003 (9)	8,904	KM#1040-1047, 1051	—	320
PS36	2005 (9)	3,000	KM#1040-1047, 1063	—	175
PS38	2007 (9)	1,800	KM#1040-1042, 1070-1074, 1130	—	150
PS39	2008 (8)	2,000	KM#1040-1042, 1070-1074	—	150
PS40	2009 (9)	5,000	KM#1040-1042, 1070-1074, 1142.1	—	150
PS41	2010 (9)	5,000	KM#1144-1150, 1152	—	150
PS42	2011 (9)	5,000	KM#1144-1151, 1184	—	150

SRI LANKA

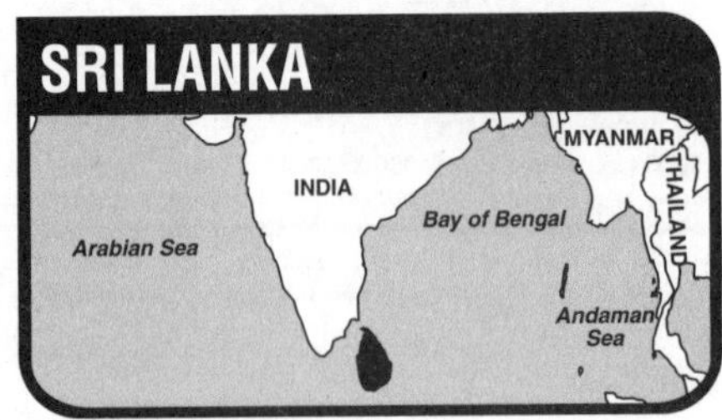

The Democratic Socialist Republic of Sri Lanka (formerly Ceylon) situated in the Indian Ocean 18 miles (29 km.) southeast of India, has an area of 25,332 sq. mi. (65,610 sq. km.) and a population of *16.9 million. Capital: Colombo. The economy is chiefly agricultural. Tea, coconut products and rubber are exported.

Sri Lanka is a member of the Commonwealth of Nations. The president is Chief of State. The prime minister is Head of Government. The present leaders of the country have reverted the country name back to Sri Lanka.

DEMOCRATIC SOCIALIST REPUBLIC

DECIMAL COINAGE

100 Cents = 1 Rupee

KM# 141a 25 CENTS
Nickel Clad Steel **Obv:** National arms **Rev:** Denomination **Edge:** Reeded

Date	Mintage	F	VF	XF	Unc	BU
2001	10,000,000	—	—	0.10	0.25	0.45
2002	10,000,000	—	—	0.10	0.25	0.45

KM# 141.2b 25 CENTS
1.1700 g., Copper Plated Steel, 16 mm. **Obv:** National arms **Rev:** Denomination

Date	Mintage	F	VF	XF	Unc	BU
2005	—	—	—	0.10	0.25	0.45
2006	—	—	—	0.10	0.25	0.45

KM# 135.2a 50 CENTS
Nickel Plated Steel, 21.5 mm. **Obv:** National arms **Rev:** Value above designs within wreath **Edge:** Reeded

Date	Mintage	F	VF	XF	Unc	BU
2001	30,000,000	—	0.10	0.25	0.65	1.00
2002	10,000,000	—	0.10	0.25	0.65	1.00
2004	—	—	0.10	0.25	0.65	1.00

KM# 135.2b 50 CENTS
2.4900 g., Copper Plated Steel, 17.92 mm. **Obv:** National arms **Rev:** Value above designs within wreath **Edge:** Reeded

Date	Mintage	F	VF	XF	Unc	BU
2005	—	—	—	0.25	0.60	1.00
2006	—	—	—	0.25	0.60	1.00
2009	—	—	—	0.25	0.60	1.00

KM# 166 RUPEE
7.1300 g., Copper-Nickel, 25.4 mm. **Subject:** Air Force's 50th Anniversary **Obv:** Badge of the Sri Lanka Air Force **Rev:** Two jets above propeller plane within circle **Edge:** Reeded

Date	Mintage	F	VF	XF	Unc	BU
2001 Proof	2,000	Value: 100				

KM# 136a RUPEE
Nickel Clad Steel **Obv:** National arms **Rev:** Inscription below designs within wreath **Edge:** Reeded

Date	Mintage	F	VF	XF	Unc	BU
2002	50,000,000	—	—	—	1.00	1.50
2004	—	—	—	—	1.00	1.50

KM# 136.3 RUPEE
3.6200 g., Brass Plated Steel, 20 mm. **Obv:** National emblem **Rev:** Inscription below designs within wreath **Edge:** Segmented reeding

Date	Mintage	F	VF	XF	Unc	BU
2005	—	—	—	—	0.75	1.00
2006	—	—	—	—	0.75	1.00
2008	—	—	—	—	0.75	1.00
2009	—	—	—	—	0.75	1.00
2011	—	—	—	—	0.75	1.00

KM# 147 2 RUPEES
8.2500 g., Copper-Nickel, 28.5 mm. **Obv:** National arms **Rev:** Value

Date	Mintage	F	VF	XF	Unc	BU
2001	10,000,000	—	0.30	0.60	1.35	1.75
2002	40,000,000	—	0.30	0.60	1.35	1.75
2004	—	—	0.30	0.60	1.35	1.75

KM# 167 2 RUPEES
8.2500 g., Copper-Nickel, 28.5 mm. **Subject:** Colombo Plan's 50th Anniversary **Obv:** Value within inscription above date **Rev:** Gear wheel **Edge:** Reeded

Date	Mintage	F	VF	XF	Unc	BU
2001	10,000,000	—	—	—	2.00	3.00

KM# 147a 2 RUPEES
7.0800 g., Nickel Clad Steel, 28.5 mm. **Obv:** National arms **Rev:** Value **Edge:** Reeded

Date	Mintage	F	VF	XF	Unc	BU
2005	—	—	—	0.45	1.10	1.50
2006	—	—	—	0.45	1.10	1.50
2007	—	—	—	0.45	1.10	1.50
2008	—	—	—	0.45	1.10	1.50
2009	—	—	—	0.45	1.10	1.50
2011	—	—	—	0.45	1.10	1.50
2012	—	—	—	0.45	1.10	1.50

KM# 178 2 RUPEES
7.0000 g., Nickel Plated Steel, 28.4 mm. **Subject:** Employees Provident Fund, 50th Anniversary **Obv:** Large 2 **Rev:** Open hands with image of tea pluckers, garment workers and office worker

Date	Mintage	F	VF	XF	Unc	BU
2008	2,000,000	—	—	—	1.35	1.75

KM# 184 2 RUPEES
7.0000 g., Nickel Plated Steel, 28.5 mm. **Obv:** Large value **Rev:** Large 60, Air Force emblem and historic aircraft circling

Date	Mintage	F	VF	XF	Unc	BU
2011	3,000,000	—	—	—	2.00	3.00
2011 Special Unc	500	—	—	—	—	15.00

KM# 148.2 5 RUPEES
9.5000 g., Nickel-Brass, 23.5 mm. **Obv:** National arms **Rev:** Value **Edge Lettering:** C.B.S.L.

Date	Mintage	F	VF	XF	Unc	BU
2002	30,000,000	—	0.35	0.65	2.00	2.75
2004	—	—	0.35	0.65	2.00	2.75

KM# 168 5 RUPEES
9.5200 g., Aluminum-Bronze, 23.4 mm. **Subject:** 250th Annniversary of the "Upasampada" Rite **Obv:** Value **Rev:** 1/2-length figure facing divides dates

Date	Mintage	F	VF	XF	Unc	BU
2003	4,000,000	—	—	—	3.00	4.50

KM# 169 5 RUPEES
9.5200 g., Aluminum-Bronze, 23.4 mm. **Subject:** 250th Anniversary - Upasampada **Obv:** Value **Rev:** Bust facing standing behind shield **Edge:** Reeded and lettered

Date	Mintage	F	VF	XF	Unc	BU
2003	4,000,000	—	—	—	3.00	4.50

KM# 148a 5 RUPEES
7.6700 g., Brass Plated Steel, 23.49 mm. **Obv:** National arms **Rev:** Value **Edge:** Reeded and Lettered **Edge Lettering:** CBSL repeated in various languages

Date	Mintage	F	VF	XF	Unc	BU
2005	—	—	—	0.75	1.85	2.50
2006	—	—	—	0.75	1.85	2.50
2008	—	—	—	0.75	1.85	2.50
2009	—	—	—	0.75	1.85	2.50
2011	—	—	—	0.75	1.85	2.50

KM# 170 5 RUPEES
7.6500 g., Brass Plated Steel, 23.5 mm. **Subject:** 2550th Anniversary of Buddha **Obv:** Value **Rev:** "Buddha Jayanthi", wheel above mountain **Edge:** Reeded and lettered

Date	Mintage	F	VF	XF	Unc	BU
2006	20,000,000	—	—	—	3.00	4.00

KM# 173 5 RUPEES
7.6500 g., Brass Plated Steel, 23.5 mm. **Subject:** Cricket World Cup

Date	Mintage	F	VF	XF	Unc	BU
2007	—	—	—	—	3.00	4.00

KM# 181 10 RUPEES
8.3600 g., Nickel Plated Steel, 26.4 mm. **Obv:** Sri Lanka ensign **Rev:** Large value **Shape:** 11-sided

Date	Mintage	F	VF	XF	Unc	BU
2009	—	—	—	—	1.50	2.50
2010	—	—	—	—	1.50	2.50
2011	—	—	—	—	1.50	2.50

KM# 186 10 RUPEES
8.3600 g., Nickel Plated Steel, 26.4 mm. **Subject:** Sambuddhatva Jayanti 2600 **Obv:** Large value **Rev:** 24 prong DharmaChakra (wheel of dochrine) **Shape:** 11-sided

Date	Mintage	F	VF	XF	Unc	BU
2011	1,500,000	—	—	—	—	2.50

KM# 180 200 RUPEES
11.9000 g., 0.9250 Silver 0.3539 oz. ASW, 28.4 mm. **Subject:** Customs Service, 200th Anniversary **Obv:** Proposed new Customs Building **Rev:** Customs Logo

Date	Mintage	F	VF	XF	Unc	BU
2009 Proof	3,000	Value: 55.00				

KM# 174 1000 RUPEES
Nickel Plated Steel **Subject:** Cricket World Cup

Date	Mintage	F	VF	XF	Unc	BU
2007	10,000	—	—	—	12.00	15.00

KM# 179 1000 RUPEES
Nickel Plated Steel, 28.5 mm. **Subject:** Employees Provident Fund, 50th Anniversary **Obv:** Large 1000 **Rev:** Open hands with image of tea pluckers, garment workers and office worker

Date	Mintage	F	VF	XF	Unc	BU
2008 Proof	1,200	Value: 150				

KM# 182 1000 RUPEES
Copper-Nickel, 27 mm. **Subject:** Sri Lanka Army - 60th Anniversay **Obv:** Army badge above value **Rev:** Soldier standing with flag, map of Sri Lanka in background, two smaller solders at right

Date	Mintage	F	VF	XF	Unc	BU
2009	—	—	—	—	20.00	25.00

KM# 182a 1000 RUPEES
Silver, 27 mm. **Subject:** Sri Lanka Army - 60th Anniversary **Obv:** Army badge above value **Rev:** Soldier standing with flag, map of Sri Lanka in background, two smaller solders at right

Date	Mintage	F	VF	XF	Unc	BU
2009 Proof	—	Value: 50.00				

KM# 185 1000 RUPEES
28.2800 g., 0.9250 Silver 0.8410 oz. ASW, 38.61 mm. **Subject:** Sambuddhatva Jayanti 2600 **Obv:** 24 prong Dharma Chakra (wheel of doctrine) **Rev:** Sri Maha Bo-Sapling bowl on a large pedistal

Date	Mintage	F	VF	XF	Unc	BU
2011 Proof	2,000	Value: 70.00				

KM# 171 1500 RUPEES
Silver **Subject:** 2550 Anniversary of Buddha

Date	Mintage	F	VF	XF	Unc	BU
2006 Proof	20,000	Value: 85.00				

KM# 172 2000 RUPEE
Silver **Subject:** 2550 Anniversary of Buddha

Date	Mintage	F	VF	XF	Unc	BU
2006 Proof	10,000	Value: 125				

KM# 183 5000 RUPEES
28.2800 g., 0.9250 Silver 0.8410 oz. ASW, 38.61 mm. **Subject:** Central Bank of Sri Lanka, 60th Anniversary **Obv:** Multicolor Central Bank crest at center **Rev:** Banyan tree **Edge:** Reeded

Date	Mintage	F	VF	XF	Unc	BU
2010 Proof	5,000	Value: 65.00				

SUDAN

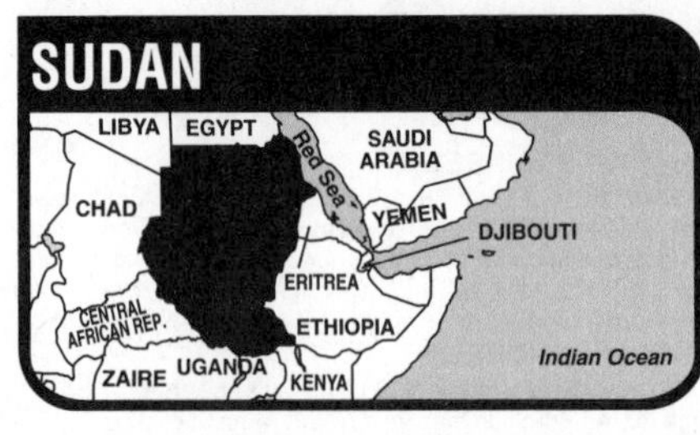

The Republic of the Sudan, located in northeast Africa on the Red Sea between Egypt and Ethiopia, has an area of 967,500 sq. mi. (2,505,810 sq. km.) and a population of *24.5 million. Capital: Khartoum. Agriculture and livestock raising are the chief occupations. Cotton, gum arabic and peanuts are exported.

REPUBLIC

REFORM COINAGE

100 Qurush (Piastres) = 1 Dinar
10 Pounds = 1 Dinar

KM# 119 5 DINARS
3.3500 g., Brass, 19 mm. **Obv:** Value **Rev:** Central Bank building

Date	Mintage	F	VF	XF	Unc	BU
AH1424-2003	—	—	0.75	1.50	3.00	5.00

KM# 120.1 10 DINARS
4.6800 g., Brass, 22 mm. **Rev:** Central Bank building, "a" above "n" at the left end of the Arabic inscription, 64 border beads

Date	Mintage	F	VF	XF	Unc	BU
AH1424-2003	—	—	1.00	2.00	3.50	6.00

KM# 120.2 10 DINARS
4.5600 g., Brass, 22 mm. **Obv:** Value **Rev:** Larger Central Bank building, "a" to right of "n" at the left end of the Arabic inscription, 72 border beads

Date	Mintage	F	VF	XF	Unc	BU
AH1424-2003	—	—	1.00	2.00	3.50	6.00

KM# 121 50 DINARS
Copper-Nickel, 24 mm. **Rev:** Central Bank building

Date	Mintage	F	VF	XF	Unc	BU
AH1423-2002	—	—	2.00	3.50	6.00	9.00

REFORM COINAGE

2005
100 Piastres = 1 Pound

KM# 126 PIASTRE (Ghirsh)
2.2500 g., Aluminum-Bronze, 16 mm. **Obv:** Clay pot **Obv. Legend:** CENTRAL BANK OF SUDAN **Rev:** Value

Date	Mintage	F	VF	XF	Unc	BU
2006	—	—	—	0.90	2.25	3.00

KM# 125 5 PIASTRES
2.8400 g., Brass, 18 mm. **Obv:** National arms **Rev:** Large value **Edge:** Reeded

Date	Mintage	F	VF	XF	Unc	BU
2006	—	—	—	1.20	3.00	4.00

KM# 122 10 PIASTRES
3.7000 g., Nickel, 20 mm. **Obv:** Pyramid **Obv. Legend:** CENTRAL BANK OF SUDAN **Rev:** Large value **Edge:** Reeded

Date	Mintage	F	VF	XF	Unc	BU
2006	—	—	—	1.25	3.00	4.00

KM# 124 20 PIASTRES
5.0000 g., Bi-Metallic Copper-Nickel center in Brass ring, 22 mm. **Obv:** Ankole Bull in right profile **Obv. Legend:** CENTRAL BANK OF SUDAN **Rev:** large value **Edge:** Reeded

Date	Mintage	F	VF	XF	Unc	BU
2006	—	—	—	1.20	3.00	4.00

KM# 123 50 PIASTRES
5.8200 g., Bi-Metallic Brass center in Copper-Nickel ring, 24 mm. **Obv:** Dove in flight **Obv. Legend:** CENTRAL BANK OF SUDAN **Rev:** Value **Edge:** Reeded

Date	Mintage	F	VF	XF	Unc	BU
2006	—	—	—	0.90	2.25	3.00

KM# 127 POUND
Nickel Plated Steel, 27 mm. **Obv:** Value **Rev:** Central Bank building

Date	Mintage	F	VF	XF	Unc	BU
2011	—	—	—	2.50	5.00	7.00

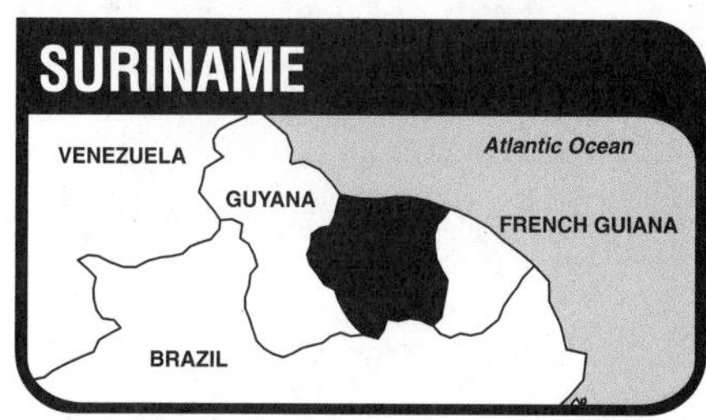

The Republic of Suriname also known as Dutch Guiana, located on the north central coast of South America between Guyana and French Guiana has an area of 63,037 sq. mi. (163,270 sq. km.) and a population of *433,000. Capital: Paramaribo. The country is rich in minerals and forests, and self-sufficient in rice, the staple food crop. The mining, processing and exporting of bauxite is the principal economic activity.

Lieutenants of Amerigo Vespucci sighted the Guiana coast in 1499. Spanish explorers of the 16th century, disappointed at finding no gold, departed leaving the area to be settled by the British in 1652. The colony prospered and the Netherlands acquired it in 1667 in exchange for the Dutch rights in Nieuw Nederland (state of New York). During the European wars of the 18th and 19th centuries, which were fought in part in the new world, Suriname was occupied by the British from 1781-1784 and 1796-1814.Suriname became an autonomous part of the Kingdom of the Netherlands on Dec. 15, 1954. Full independence was achieved on Nov. 25, 1975. In 1980, a coup installed a military government, which has since been dissolved.

MINT MARKS

(u) - Utrecht (privy marks only)

MONETARY SYSTEM

After January, 2004
1 Dollar = 100 Cents

REPUBLIC

MODERN COINAGE

KM# 11b CENT

2.5000 g., Copper Plated Steel, 18 mm. **Obv:** Arms with supporters within wreath **Rev:** Value divides date within circle **Edge:** Plain

Date	Mintage	F	VF	XF	Unc	BU
2004(u) In sets only	4,000	—	—	—	—	6.00
2005(u) In sets only	1,500	—	—	—	—	7.00
2006(u) In sets only	1,500	—	—	—	—	7.00
2007(u) In sets only	1,000	—	—	—	—	7.00
2008(u) In sets only	1,000	—	—	—	—	7.00
2009(u) In sets only	1,000	—	—	—	—	7.00
2010(u) In sets only	1,000	—	—	—	—	7.00
2011(u) In sets only	1,000	—	—	—	—	7.00

KM# 12.1b 5 CENTS

3.0000 g., Copper Plated Steel, 18 mm. **Obv:** Arms with supporters within circle **Rev:** Value divides date within circle **Edge:** Plain **Shape:** Square

Date	Mintage	F	VF	XF	Unc	BU
2004(u) In sets only	4,000	—	—	—	—	6.00
2005(u) In sets only	1,500	—	—	—	—	7.00
2006(u) In sets only	1,500	—	—	—	—	7.00
2007(u) In sets only	1,000	—	—	—	—	7.00
2008(u) In sets only	1,000	—	—	—	—	7.00
2009(u) In sets only	1,000	—	—	—	—	7.00
2010(u) In sets only	1,000	—	—	—	—	7.00
2011(u) In sets only	1,000	—	—	—	—	7.00

KM# 13a 10 CENTS

2.0000 g., Nickel Plated Steel, 16 mm. **Obv:** Arms with supporters within wreath **Rev:** Value and date within circle **Edge:** Reeded

Date	Mintage	F	VF	XF	Unc	BU
2004(u) In sets only	4,000	—	—	—	—	4.50
2005(u) In sets only	1,500	—	—	—	—	4.50
2006(u) In sets only	1,500	—	—	—	—	4.50
2007(u) In sets only	1,000	—	—	—	—	4.50
2008(u) In sets only	1,000	—	—	—	—	4.50
2009	—	—	—	0.50	1.00	2.00
2009(u) In sets only	1,000	—	—	—	—	4.50
2010(u) In sets only	1,000	—	—	—	—	4.50
2011(u) In sets only	1,000	—	—	—	—	4.50
2012	—	—	—	0.50	1.00	2.00

KM# 14a 25 CENTS

3.5000 g., Nickel Plated Steel, 20 mm. **Obv:** Arms with supporters within wreath **Rev:** Value and date within circle **Edge:** Reeded

Date	Mintage	F	VF	XF	Unc	BU
2004(u) In sets only	4,000	—	—	—	—	7.00
2005(u) In sets only	1,500	—	—	—	—	8.00
2006(u) In sets only	1,500	—	—	—	—	8.00
2007(u) In sets only	1,000	—	—	—	—	8.00
2008(u) In sets only	1,000	—	—	—	—	8.00
2009(u) In sets only	1,000	—	—	—	—	8.00
2010(u) In sets only	1,000	—	—	—	—	8.00
2011(u) In sets only	1,000	—	—	—	—	8.00

KM# 23 100 CENTS

5.6500 g., Copper-Nickel, 23 mm. **Obv:** Arms with supporters within wreath **Rev:** Value and date within circle **Edge:** Reeded

Date	Mintage	F	VF	XF	Unc	BU
2004(u) In sets only	4,000	—	—	—	—	7.00
2005(u) In sets only	1,250	—	—	—	—	8.00
2006(u) In sets only	1,500	—	—	—	—	8.00
2007(u) In sets only	1,000	—	—	—	—	8.00
2008(u) In sets only	1,000	—	—	—	—	8.00
2009(u) In sets only	1,000	—	—	—	—	8.00
2010(u) In sets only	1,000	—	—	—	—	8.00
2011(u) In sets only	1,000	—	—	—	—	8.00
2012	—	—	—	—	1.75	3.00

KM# 24 250 CENTS

9.5700 g., Copper-Nickel, 28 mm. **Obv:** Arms with supporters within wreath **Rev:** Value and date within circle

Date	Mintage	F	VF	XF	Unc	BU
2004(u) In sets only	4,000	—	—	—	—	8.00
2005(u) In sets only	1,250	—	—	—	—	10.00
2006(u) In sets only	1,500	—	—	—	—	10.00
2007(u) In sets only	1,000	—	—	—	—	10.00
2008(u) In sets only	1,000	—	—	—	—	10.00
2009(u) In sets only	1,000	—	—	—	—	10.00
2010(u) In sets only	1,000	—	—	—	—	10.00
2011(u) In sets only	1,000	—	—	—	—	10.00

KM# 65 $20

1.2442 g., 0.9990 Gold 0.0400 oz. AGW, 13.92 mm. **Subject:** Antony Nesty's 1988 Gold Medal win at Seoul Olympics, 20th Anniversary **Obv:** Arms with supporters **Rev:** Nesty swimming

Date	Mintage	F	VF	XF	Unc	BU
2008 Proof	5,000	Value: 85.00				

KM# 64 400 DOLLARS

7.9800 g., 0.9160 Gold 0.2350 oz. AGW, 22 mm. **Subject:** 30 Years of Independence **Obv:** Arms with supporters **Rev:** Man kissing flag **Edge:** Reeded

Date	Mintage	F	VF	XF	Unc	BU
2005 Proof	1,000	Value: 500				

KM# 66 500 DOLLARS

7.9800 g., 0.9160 Gold 0.2350 oz. AGW, 22 mm. **Subject:** Central Bank, 50th Anniversary **Obv:** Arms with supporters **Rev:** 50 jaar Central Bank van Suriname 1957-2007

Date	Mintage	F	VF	XF	Unc	BU
2007 Proof	1,000	Value: 475				

MINT SETS

KM#	Date	Mintage	Identification	Issue Price	Mkt Val
MS1	2004 (6)	4,000	KM#11b, 12.1b, 13a, 14a, 23, 24	25.00	40.00
MS2	2005 (6)	1,500	KM#11b, 12.1b, 13a-14a, 23-24	25.00	45.00
MS3	2006 (6)	1,500	KM#11b, 12.1b, 13a-14a, 23-24	25.00	45.00
MS4	2007 (6)	1,000	KM#11b, 12.1b, 13a-14a, 23-24	27.00	45.00
MS5	2008 (6)	1,000	KM#11b, 12.1b, 13a-14a, 23-24	27.00	45.00
MS6	2009 (6)	1,000	KM#11b, 12.1b, 13a, 14a, 23, 24	27.00	40.00
MS7	2010 (6)	1,000	KM#11b, 12.1b, 13a, 14a, 23, 24	27.00	45.00
MS8	2011 (6)	1,000	KM#11b, 12.1b, 13a, 14a, 23, 24	—	45.00

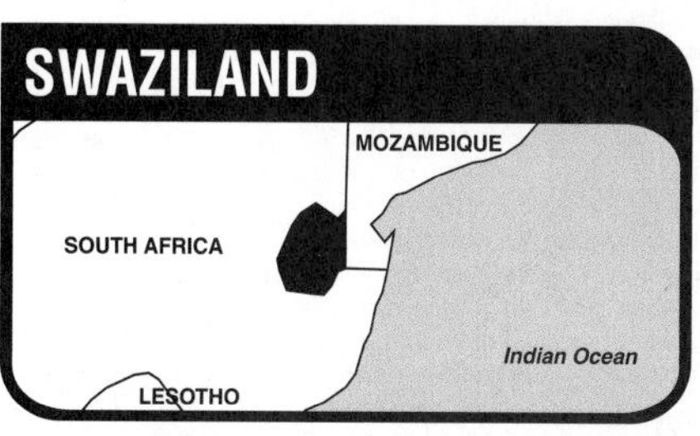

The Kingdom of Swaziland, located in southeastern Africa, has an area of 6,704 sq. mi. (17,360 sq. km.) and a population of *756,000. Capital: Mbabane (administrative); Lobamba (legislative). The diversified economy includes mining, agriculture, and light industry. Asbestos, iron ore, wood pulp, and sugar are exported.

The Kingdom is a member of the Commonwealth of Nations. King Mswati III is Head of State. The prime minister is Head of Government.

RULER

King Msawati III, 1986-

MONETARY SYSTEM

100 Cents = 1 Luhlanga
25 Luhlanga = 1 Lilangeni
(plural - Emalangeni)

KINGDOM

DECIMAL COINAGE

100 Cents = 1 Lilangeni (plural emelangeni)

KM# 48 5 CENTS

2.1000 g., Copper-Nickel, 18.5 mm. **Ruler:** King Msawati III **Obv:** Bust 3/4 right **Rev:** Arum lily and value **Edge:** Plain **Shape:** Scalloped

Date	Mintage	F	VF	XF	Unc	BU
2001	—	—	—	—	0.50	0.75
2002	—	—	—	—	0.50	0.75
2003	—	—	—	—	0.50	0.75
2005	—	—	—	—	0.50	0.75
2006	—	—	—	—	0.50	0.75
2007	—	—	—	—	0.50	0.75
2008	—	—	—	—	0.50	0.75
2009	—	—	—	—	0.50	0.75
2010	—	—	—	—	0.50	0.75

KM# 56 5 CENTS

Copper Plated Steel **Ruler:** King Msawati III

Date	Mintage	F	VF	XF	Unc	BU
2011	—	—	—	—	0.50	0.75

KM# 49 10 CENTS

3.6000 g., Copper-Nickel, 22 mm. **Ruler:** King Msawati III **Obv:** Bust 3/4 right **Rev:** Sugar cane and value **Edge:** Plain **Shape:** Scalloped

Date	Mintage	F	VF	XF	Unc	BU
2001	—	—	—	0.30	0.75	1.00
2002	—	—	—	0.30	0.75	1.00
2003	—	—	—	0.30	0.75	1.00
2005	—	—	—	0.30	0.75	1.00
2006	—	—	—	0.30	0.75	1.00
2007	—	—	—	0.30	0.75	1.00

KM# 57 10 CENTS
Copper Plated Steel **Ruler:** King Msawati III

Date	Mintage	F	VF	XF	Unc	BU
2011	—	—	—	0.30	0.75	1.00

KM# 50.2 20 CENTS
5.5200 g., Copper-Nickel, 25.2 mm. **Ruler:** King Msawati III **Obv:** Small bust 3/4 right **Rev:** Elephant head, value **Edge:** Plain **Shape:** Scalloped

Date	Mintage	F	VF	XF	Unc	BU
2001	—	—	—	0.35	0.90	2.25
2002	—	—	—	0.35	0.90	2.25
2003	—	—	—	0.35	0.90	2.25
2005	—	—	—	0.35	0.90	2.25

KM# 58 20 CENTS
Copper-Nickel **Ruler:** King Msawati III

Date	Mintage	F	VF	XF	Unc	BU
2011	—	—	—	0.35	0.90	2.25

KM# 52 50 CENTS
8.9000 g., Copper-Nickel, 29.45 mm. **Ruler:** King Msawati III **Obv:** Head 1/4 right **Rev:** Arms with supporters

Date	Mintage	F	VF	XF	Unc	BU
2001	—	—	—	—	3.75	4.50
2003	—	—	—	—	3.75	4.50
2005	—	—	—	—	3.75	4.50
2007	—	—	—	—	3.75	4.50

KM# 59 50 CENTS
Copper-Nickel **Ruler:** King Msawati III

Date	Mintage	F	VF	XF	Unc	BU
2011	—	—	—	—	3.75	4.50

KM# 45 LILANGENI
9.5000 g., Brass, 22.5 mm. **Ruler:** King Msawati III **Obv:** Head 1/4 right **Rev:** Bust facing

Date	Mintage	F	VF	XF	Unc	BU
2002	—	—	—	1.50	2.75	3.50
2003	—	—	—	1.50	2.75	3.50
2005	—	—	—	1.50	2.75	3.50
2008	—	—	—	1.50	2.75	3.50

KM# 60 LILANGENI
Brass **Ruler:** King Msawati III

Date	Mintage	F	VF	XF	Unc	BU
2011	—	—	—	—	3.75	4.50

KM# 46 2 EMALANGENI
5.0000 g., Brass **Ruler:** King Msawati III **Obv:** Head 1/4 right **Rev:** Lilies and value

Date	Mintage	F	VF	XF	Unc	BU
2003 sm. bust	—	—	—	—	3.75	4.25
2005	—	—	—	—	3.75	4.25
2008	—	—	—	—	3.75	4.25
2009	—	—	—	—	3.75	4.25

KM# 47 5 EMALANGENI
7.6000 g., Brass **Ruler:** King Msawati III **Obv:** Head 1/4 right **Rev:** Arms with supporters above value that divides date

Date	Mintage	F	VF	XF	Unc	BU
2003 sm. bust	—	—	—	—	6.00	7.00

KM# 54a 5 EMALANGENI
Gold **Ruler:** King Msawati III **Subject:** 40th Anniversary of Independence **Obv:** Head 1/4 right **Rev:** National arms at center

Date	Mintage	F	VF	XF	Unc	BU
2008 Proof, rare	100	—	—	—	—	—

KM# 55a 5 EMALANGENI
Gold **Ruler:** King Msawati III **Subject:** 40th Anniversary of Independence **Obv:** Head 1/4 right **Rev:** National arms at center

Date	Mintage	F	VF	XF	Unc	BU
2008 Proof, rare	100	—	—	—	—	—

KM# 55 5 EMALANGENI
7.6000 g., Brass, 27 mm. **Ruler:** King Msawati III **Subject:** 40th Birthday of King **Obv:** Head 1/4 right **Rev:** National arms at center

Date	Mintage	F	VF	XF	Unc	BU
2008	—	—	—	—	5.00	7.00

SWEDEN

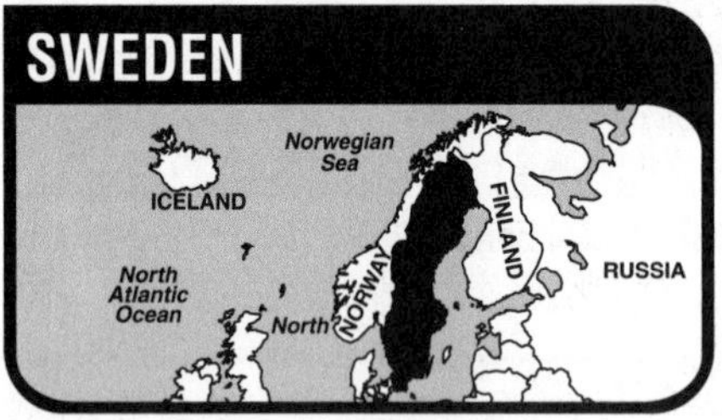

The Kingdom of Sweden, a limited constitutional monarchy located in northern Europe between Norway and Finland, has an area of 173,732 sq. mi. (449,960 sq. km.) and a population of *8.5 million. Capital: Stockholm. Mining, lumbering and a specialized machine industry dominate the economy. Machinery, paper, iron and steel, motor vehicles and wood pulp are exported.

RULER
Carl XVI Gustaf, 1973-

MINT OFFICIALS' INITIALS

Letter	Date	Name
B	1992-2005	Stefan Ingves
D	1986-2005	Bengt Dennis
SI	2006-	Stefan Ingves

MONETARY SYSTEM
100 Ore = 1 Krona

KINGDOM

REFORM COINAGE

1873 - present

KM# 878 50 ORE
3.7000 g., Bronze, 18.7 mm. **Ruler:** Carl XVI Gustaf **Obv:** Value **Rev:** Three crowns and date **Edge:** Reeded

Date	Mintage	F	VF	XF	Unc	BU
2001 B	30,120,532	—	—	0.10	0.15	0.25
2002 B	—	—	—	0.10	0.15	0.25
2003 H	—	—	—	0.10	0.15	0.25
2004 H	25,958,649	—	—	0.10	0.15	0.25
2005 H	—	—	—	0.10	0.15	0.25
2006 SI	—	—	—	0.10	0.15	0.25
2007 SI	—	—	—	0.10	0.15	0.25
2008 SI	—	—	—	0.10	0.15	0.25
2009 SI	—	—	—	0.10	0.15	0.25

KM# 894 KRONA
7.0000 g., Copper-Nickel, 25 mm. **Ruler:** Carl XVI Gustaf **Obv:** Head left **Rev:** Crown and value **Edge:** Reeded

Date	Mintage	F	VF	XF	Unc	BU
2001 B	23,905,454	—	—	—	0.65	1.00
2002 B	—	—	—	—	0.65	1.00
2003 H	—	—	—	—	0.65	1.00
2004 H	42,060,252	—	—	—	0.65	1.00
2005 H	—	—	—	—	0.65	1.00
2006	—	—	—	—	0.65	1.00
2007 B	—	—	—	—	0.65	1.00
2008	—	—	—	—	0.65	1.00

KM# 916 KRONA
7.0000 g., Copper-Nickel, 25 mm. **Ruler:** Carl XVI Gustaf **Subject:** Separation from Finland, 200 Anniversary **Obv:** Head left **Rev:** Horizontal sea waves **Edge:** Reeded

Date	Mintage	F	VF	XF	Unc	BU
2009	—	—	—	—	0.65	1.00

KM# 853a 5 KRONOR
9.6000 g., Copper-Nickel Clad Nickel, 28.5 mm. **Ruler:** Carl XVI Gustaf **Obv:** Crowned monogram **Rev:** Value

Date	Mintage	F	VF	XF	Unc	BU
2001 B	6,001,481	—	—	—	1.00	1.25
2002 B	—	—	—	—	1.00	1.25
2003 H	—	—	—	—	1.00	1.25
2004 H	6,732,730	—	—	—	1.00	1.25
2005 H	—	—	—	—	1.00	1.25
2006 H	—	—	—	—	1.00	1.25
2007 H	—	—	—	—	1.00	1.25
2008 H	—	—	—	—	1.00	1.25
2009 H	—	—	—	—	1.00	1.25

KM# 895 10 KRONOR
6.6000 g., Copper-Aluminum-Zinc, 20.5 mm. **Ruler:** Carl XVI Gustaf **Obv:** Head left **Rev:** Three crowns and value **Edge:** Segmented reeding

Date	Mintage	F	VF	XF	Unc	BU
2001 B	4,171,757	—	—	—	1.75	2.00
2002 B	—	—	—	—	1.75	2.00
2003 H	—	—	—	—	1.75	2.00
2004 H	9,045,581	—	—	—	1.75	2.00
2005 H	—	—	—	—	1.75	2.00
2006 SI	—	—	—	—	1.75	2.00
2007	—	—	—	—	1.75	2.00
2008	—	—	—	—	1.75	2.00
2009	—	—	—	—	1.75	2.00

KM# 910 50 KRONOR
22.0000 g., Aluminum-Bronze, 36 mm. **Ruler:** Carl XVI Gustaf **Subject:** 95th Anniversary - Birth of Astrid Lindgren **Obv:** Playful young girl **Rev:** Astrid Lindgren **Edge:** Plain

Date	Mintage	F	VF	XF	Unc	BU
ND (2002)	100,000	—	—	—	8.00	10.00

KM# 915 50 KRONOR

22.0000 g., Aluminum-Bronze, 36 mm. **Ruler:** Carl XVI Gustaf **Subject:** 150th Anniversary of Sweden's first postage stamp **Obv:** Winged letter flying over landscape **Rev:** Sweden's first postage stamp design **Edge:** Plain **Designer:** Annie Wildblad Jakubowski

Date	Mintage	F	VF	XF	Unc	BU
ND (2005)	100,000	—	—	—	8.00	10.00

KM# 896 200 KRONOR

27.2500 g., 0.9250 Silver 0.8104 oz. ASW, 36 mm. **Ruler:** Carl XVI Gustaf **Subject:** 25th Wedding Anniversary **Obv:** Conjoined busts left **Rev:** Crowned arms with supporters **Edge:** Plain **Designer:** Philip Nathan

Date	Mintage	F	VF	XF	Unc	BU
ND(2001)	50,000	—	—	—	40.00	50.00

KM# 908 200 KRONOR

27.2500 g., 0.9250 Silver 0.8104 oz. ASW, 36 mm. **Ruler:** Carl XVI Gustaf **Subject:** 750th Anniversary of Stockholm **Obv:** City seal with three towers and gate **Rev:** Three towers of city hall **Edge:** Plain **Designer:** Bo Thorén

Date	Mintage	F	VF	XF	Unc	BU
ND (2002) Proof	25,000	Value: 40.00				

KM# 902 200 KRONOR

27.2500 g., 0.9250 Silver 0.8104 oz. ASW **Ruler:** Carl XVI Gustaf **Subject:** 30th Anniversary of Reign **Designer:** Ernst Nordin

Date	Mintage	F	VF	XF	Unc	BU
2003	—	—	—	—	40.00	50.00

KM# 904 200 KRONOR

27.0000 g., 0.9250 Silver 0.8029 oz. ASW, 36 mm. **Ruler:** Carl XVI Gustaf **Subject:** 700th Anniversary, St. Birgitta **Obv:** Cross in circle above value **Rev:** St. Birgitta **Edge:** Plain **Designer:** Ernst Nordin

Date	Mintage	F	VF	XF	Unc	BU
ND (2003)	60,000	—	—	—	40.00	50.00

KM# 911 200 KRONOR

27.0000 g., 0.9250 Silver 0.8029 oz. ASW, 36 mm. **Ruler:** Carl XVI Gustaf **Subject:** Royal Palace in Stockholm 250th Anniversary **Obv:** Two antique keys over map **Rev:** Royal Palace in Stockholm **Edge:** Plain **Designer:** Annie Windblad Jakubowski

Date	Mintage	F	VF	XF	Unc	BU
ND (2004) Proof	35,000	Value: 40.00				

KM# 913 200 KRONOR

27.0000 g., 0.9250 Silver 0.8029 oz. ASW, 36 mm. **Ruler:** Carl XVI Gustaf **Subject:** 100th Anniversary of Dag Hammarskjöld **Obv:** Stylized flames **Rev:** Dag Hammarskjöld **Edge:** Plain **Designer:** Ernst Nordin

Date	Mintage	F	VF	XF	Unc	BU
ND (2005) Proof	35,000	Value: 40.00				

KM# 906 200 KRONOR

27.0300 g., 0.9250 Silver 0.8038 oz. ASW, 36 mm. **Ruler:** Carl XVI Gustaf **Subject:** Centennial of the end of the Union between Norway and Sweden **Obv:** Split disc **Rev:** Flag on pole and two clouds **Designer:** Annie Windblad Jakubowski

Date	Mintage	F	VF	XF	Unc	BU
2005	35,000	—	—	—	40.00	50.00

KM# 917 300 KRONOR

27.0300 g., 0.9250 Silver 0.8038 oz. ASW, 36 mm. **Ruler:** Carl XVI Gustaf **Subject:** Wedding of Princess Victoria and Daniel

Date	Mintage	F	VF	XF	Unc	BU
2010 Proof	—	Value: 50.00				

KM# 909 2000 KRONOR

12.0000 g., 0.9000 Gold 0.3472 oz. AGW, 26 mm. **Ruler:** Carl XVI Gustaf **Subject:** 750th Anniversary of Stockholm **Obv:** City seal with three towers and gate **Rev:** Three towers of city hall **Edge:** Plain **Designer:** Bo Thoréu

Date	Mintage	F	VF	XF	Unc	BU
ND (2002) Proof	5,000	Value: 600				

KM# 903 2000 KRONOR

12.0000 g., 0.9990 Gold 0.3854 oz. AGW **Ruler:** Carl XVI Gustaf **Subject:** 30th Anniversary of Reign **Designer:** Ernst Nordin

Date	Mintage	F	VF	XF	Unc	BU
2003	—	—	—	—	625	650

KM# 905 2000 KRONOR

12.0000 g., 0.9000 Gold 0.3472 oz. AGW, 26 mm. **Ruler:** Carl XVI Gustaf **Subject:** St. Birgitta's 700th Anniversary of birth **Obv:** Gothic letter B above value **Rev:** St. Birgitta **Edge:** Plain **Designer:** Ernst Nordin

Date	Mintage	F	VF	XF	Unc	BU
ND (2003)	8,000	—	—	—	625	650

KM# 912 2000 KRONOR

12.0000 g., 0.9000 Gold 0.3472 oz. AGW, 26 mm. **Ruler:** Carl XVI Gustaf **Subject:** Royal Palace in Stockholm 250th Anniversary **Obv:** Two antique keys over map **Designer:** Annie Windblad Jakubowski

Date	Mintage	F	VF	XF	Unc	BU
ND (2004) Proof	5,243	Value: 650				

KM# 914 2000 KRONOR

12.0000 g., 0.9000 Gold 0.3472 oz. AGW, 26 mm. **Ruler:** Carl XVI Gustaf **Subject:** 100th Anniversary of Dag Hammarskjöld **Obv:** Stylized flames **Rev:** Dag Hammarskjöld **Edge:** Plain **Designer:** Ernst Nordin

Date	Mintage	F	VF	XF	Unc	BU
ND (2005) Proof	5,000	Value: 650				

KM# 907 2000 KRONOR

12.0000 g., 0.9000 Gold 0.3472 oz. AGW, 26 mm. **Ruler:** Carl XVI Gustaf **Subject:** Centennial of the end of the Union between Norway and Sweden **Obv:** Split disc **Rev:** Flag pole dividing two clouds **Designer:** Annie Windblad Jakubowski

Date	Mintage	F	VF	XF	Unc	BU
2005	5,000	—	—	—	625	650

KM# 918 4000 KRONOR

12.0000 g., 0.9000 Gold 0.3472 oz. AGW, 26 mm. **Ruler:** Carl XVI Gustaf **Subject:** Wedding of Princess Victoria and Daniel

Date	Mintage	F	VF	XF	Unc	BU
2010 Proof	—	Value: 650				

MINT SETS

KM#	Date	Mintage	Identification	Issue Price	Mkt Val
MS107	2002 (4)	—	KM#853a, 878, 894, 895 plus medal	—	10.00

The Swiss Confederation, located in central Europe north of Italy and south of Germany, has an area of 15,941 sq. mi. (41,290 sq. km.) and a population of *6.6 million. Capital: Bern. The economy centers about a well-developed manufacturing industry. Machinery, chemicals, watches and clocks, and textiles are exported.

The Swiss Constitutions of 1848 and 1874 established a union modeled upon that of the United States.

MINT MARK

B – Bern

MONETARY SYSTEM

100 Rappen (Centimes) = 1 Franc

CONFEDERATION

DECIMAL COINAGE

KM# 46 RAPPEN

1.5000 g., Bronze, 16 mm. **Obv:** Cross **Rev:** Value and oat sprig **Edge:** Plain **Designer:** Josef Tannheimer

Date	Mintage	F	VF	XF	Unc	BU
2001B	1,522,000	—	—	—	0.50	1.00
2001B Proof	6,000	Value: 2.00				
2002B	2,024,000	—	—	—	0.50	1.00
2002B Proof	5,500	Value: 2.00				
2003B	1,522,000	—	—	—	0.50	1.00
2003B Proof	5,500	Value: 2.00				
2004B	1,526,000	—	—	—	0.50	1.00
2004B Proof	5,000	Value: 2.00				
2005B	1,524,000	—	—	—	0.50	1.00
2005B Proof	4,500	Value: 2.00				
2006B	26,000	—	—	—	—	135

Note: In sets only, circulation strikes not released

Date	Mintage	F	VF	XF	Unc	BU
2006B Proof	4,000	Value: 200				

KM# 26c 5 RAPPEN

1.8000 g., Aluminum-Bronze, 17.15 mm. **Obv:** Crowned head right **Rev:** Value within wreath **Edge:** Plain

Date	Mintage	F	VF	XF	Unc	BU
2001B	5,022,000	—	—	—	0.50	1.00
2001B Proof	6,000	Value: 2.00				
2002B	12,024,000	—	—	—	0.50	1.00
2002B Proof	6,000	Value: 2.00				
2003B	10,022,000	—	—	—	0.50	1.00
2003B Proof	5,500	Value: 2.00				
2004B	10,026,000	—	—	—	0.50	1.00
2004B Proof	5,000	Value: 2.00				
2005B	13,024,000	—	—	—	0.50	1.00
2005B Proof	4,500	Value: 2.00				
2006B	12,026,000	—	—	—	0.50	1.00
2006B Proof	4,000	Value: 2.00				
2007B	13,024,000	—	—	—	0.50	1.00
2007B Proof	4,000	Value: 2.00				
2008B	40,022,000	—	—	—	0.50	1.00
2008B Proof	4,000	Value: 2.00				
2009B	45,022,000	—	—	—	0.50	1.00
2009B Proof	4,000	Value: 2.00				
2010B	Est. 41,022,000	—	—	—	0.50	1.00
2010B Proof	Est. 4,000	Value: 2.00				
2011B	Est. 50,022,000	—	—	—	0.30	1.00
2011B Proof	Est. 4,000	Value: 2.00				
2012B	Est. 35,022,000	—	—	—	0.30	1.00
2012B Proof	Est. 4,000	Value: 2.00				
2013B	—	—	—	—	0.30	1.00
2013B Proof	—	Value: 2.00				

KM# 27 10 RAPPEN

3.0000 g., Copper-Nickel, 19.15 mm. **Obv:** Crowned head right **Obv. Legend:** CONFOEDERATIO HELVETICA **Rev:** Value within wreath **Edge:** Plain

Date	Mintage	F	VF	XF	Unc	BU
2001B	7,022,000	—	—	—	0.50	1.00
2001B Proof	6,000	Value: 2.00				
2002B	15,024,000	—	—	—	0.50	1.00
2002B Proof	6,000	Value: 2.00				
2003B	12,022,000	—	—	—	0.50	1.00
2003B Proof	5,500	Value: 2.00				
2004B	5,026,000	—	—	—	0.50	1.00
2004B Proof	5,000	Value: 2.00				
2005B	7,024,000	—	—	—	0.50	1.00
2005B Proof	4,500	Value: 2.00				
2006B	2,026,000	—	—	—	0.50	1.00
2006B Proof	4,000	Value: 2.00				
2007B	18,024,000	—	—	—	0.50	1.00
2007B Proof	4,000	Value: 2.00				
2008B	35,022,000	—	—	—	0.50	1.00
2008B Proof	4,000	Value: 2.00				
2009B	35,022,000	—	—	—	0.50	1.00
2009B Proof	4,000	Value: 2.00				
2010B	Est. 42,022,000	—	—	—	0.50	1.00
2010B Proof	Est. 4,000	Value: 2.00				
2011B	Est. 35,022,000	—	—	—	0.40	1.00
2011B Proof	Est. 4,000	Value: 2.00				
2012B	Est. 30,022,000	—	—	—	0.40	1.00
2012B Proof	Est. 4,000	Value: 2.00				
2013B	—	—	—	—	0.40	1.00
2013B Proof	—	Value: 2.00				

KM# 29a 20 RAPPEN

4.0000 g., Copper-Nickel, 21.05 mm. **Obv:** Crowned head right **Rev:** Value within wreath **Edge:** Plain

Date	Mintage	F	VF	XF	Unc	BU
2001B	7,022,000	—	—	—	1.00	2.00
2001B Proof	6,000	Value: 3.00				
2002B	12,024,000	—	—	—	1.00	2.00
2002B Proof	6,000	Value: 3.00				
2003B	10,022,000	—	—	—	1.00	2.00
2003B Proof	5,500	Value: 3.00				
2004B	10,026,000	—	—	—	1.00	2.00
2004B Proof	5,000	Value: 3.00				
2005B	6,024,000	—	—	—	1.00	2.00
2005B Proof	4,500	Value: 3.00				

Date	Mintage	F	VF	XF	Unc	BU
2006B	5,026,000	—	—	—	1.00	2.00
2006B Proof	4,000	Value: 3.00				
2007B	22,024,000	—	—	—	1.00	2.00
2007B Proof	4,000	Value: 3.00				
2008B	41,022,000	—	—	—	1.00	2.00
2008B Proof	4,000	Value: 3.00				
2009B	32,022,000	—	—	—	1.00	2.00
2009B Proof	4,000	Value: 3.00				
2010B	Est. 18,022,000	—	—	—	1.00	2.00
2010B Proof	Est. 4,000	Value: 3.00				
2011B	Est. 20,022,000	—	—	—	0.75	2.00
2011B Proof	Est. 4,000	Value: 3.00				
2012B	Est. 32,022,000	—	—	—	0.75	2.00
2012B Proof	Est. 4,000	Value: 3.00				
2013B	—	—	—	—	0.75	2.00
2013B Proof	—	Value: 3.00				

KM# 23a.3 1/2 FRANC

2.2000 g., Copper-Nickel, 18.2 mm. **Obv:** 23 Stars around figure **Rev:** Value within wreath **Edge:** Reeded **Designer:** A. Bovy

Date	Mintage	F	VF	XF	Unc	BU
2001B	6,022,000	—	—	—	2.50	3.50
2001B Proof	6,000	Value: 5.00				
2002B	2,024,000	—	—	—	2.50	3.50
2002B Proof	6,000	Value: 5.00				
2003B	2,022,000	—	—	—	2.50	3.50
2003B Proof	5,500	Value: 5.00				
2004B	2,026,000	—	—	—	2.50	3.50
2004B Proof	5,000	Value: 5.00				
2005B	1,024,000	—	—	—	2.50	3.50
2005B Proof	4,500	Value: 5.00				
2006B	2,025,000	—	—	—	2.50	3.50
2006B Proof	4,500	Value: 5.00				
2007B	18,024,000	—	—	—	2.00	3.00
2007B Proof	4,000	Value: 5.00				
2008B	25,022,000	—	—	—	2.00	3.00
2008B Proof	4,000	Value: 5.00				
2009B	27,022,000	—	—	—	2.00	3.00
2009B Proof	4,000	Value: 5.00				
2010B	Est. 27,022,000	—	—	—	2.00	3.00
2010B Proof	Est. 4,000	Value: 5.00				
2011B	Est. 15,022,000	—	—	—	1.50	3.00
2011B Proof	Est. 4,000	Value: 5.00				
2012B	Est. 20,022,000	—	—	—	1.50	3.00
2012B Proof	Est. 4,000	Value: 5.00				
2013B	—	—	—	—	1.50	3.00
2013B Proof	—	Value: 5.00				

KM# 24a.3 FRANC

4.4000 g., Copper-Nickel, 23.2 mm. **Obv:** 23 Stars around figure **Rev:** Value and date within wreath **Edge:** Reeded **Designer:** A. Bovy

Date	Mintage	F	VF	XF	Unc	BU
2001B	3,022,000	—	—	—	3.00	5.00
2001B Proof	6,000	Value: 7.00				
2002B	1,024,000	—	—	—	3.00	5.00
2002B Proof	6,000	Value: 7.00				
2003B	2,022,000	—	—	—	3.00	5.00
2003B Proof	5,500	Value: 7.00				
2004B	2,026,000	—	—	—	3.00	5.00
2004B Proof	5,000	Value: 7.00				
2005B	1,024,000	—	—	—	3.00	5.00
2005B Proof	4,500	Value: 7.00				
2006B	2,026,000	—	—	—	3.00	5.00
2006B Proof	4,000	Value: 7.00				
2007B	3,024,000	—	—	—	3.00	5.00
2007B Proof	4,000	Value: 7.00				
2008B	7,022,000	—	—	—	3.00	5.00
2008B Proof	4,000	Value: 7.00				
2009B	11,022,000	—	—	—	3.00	5.00
2009B Proof	4,000	Value: 7.00				
2010B	Est. 15,022,000	—	—	—	3.00	5.00
2010B Proof	Est. 4,000	Value: 7.00				
2011B	Est. 15,022,000	—	—	—	3.00	5.00
2011B Proof	Est. 4,000	Value: 7.00				
2012B	Est. 12,022,000	—	—	—	3.00	5.00
2012B Proof	Est. 4,000	Value: 7.00				
2013B	—	—	—	—	3.00	5.00
2013B Proof	—	Value: 7.00				

KM# 21a.3 2 FRANCS

8.8000 g., Copper-Nickel, 27.4 mm. **Obv:** 23 Stars around figure **Rev:** Value within wreath **Edge:** Reeded **Designer:** A. Bovy

Date	Mintage	F	VF	XF	Unc	BU
2001B	4,022,000	—	—	—	4.00	7.00
2001B Proof	6,000	Value: 10.00				
2002B	1,024,000	—	—	—	4.50	7.50
2002B Proof	6,000	Value: 10.00				
2003B	1,022,000	—	—	2.50	4.50	7.50
2003B Proof	5,500	Value: 10.00				
2004B	1,026,000	—	—	2.50	4.50	7.50
2004B Proof	5,000	Value: 10.00				
2005B	2,024,000	—	—	—	4.50	7.50
2005B Proof	4,500	Value: 10.00				
2006B	7,026,000	—	—	—	4.50	7.50
2006B Proof	4,000	Value: 10.00				
2007B	16,024,000	—	—	—	4.50	7.50
2007B Proof	4,000	Value: 10.00				
2008B	6,022,000	—	—	—	4.50	7.50
2008B Proof	4,000	Value: 10.00				
2009B	8,022,000	—	—	—	4.50	7.50
2009B Proof	4,000	Value: 10.00				
2010B	Est. 9,022,000	—	—	—	4.50	7.50
2010B Proof	Est. 4,000	Value: 10.00				
2011B	Est. 7,022,000	—	—	—	4.00	7.50
2011B Proof	Est. 4,000	Value: 10.00				
2012B	Est. 11,022,000	—	—	—	4.00	7.50
2012B Proof	Est. 4,000	Value: 10.00				
2013B	—	—	—	—	4.00	7.50
2013B Proof	—	Value: 10.00				

KM# 40a.4 5 FRANCS

13.2000 g., Copper-Nickel, 31.45 mm. **Obv:** William Tell right **Rev:** Shield flanked by sprigs **Edge:** DOMINUS PROVIDEBIT and 13 stars raised **Designer:** Paul Burkhard

Date	Mintage	F	VF	XF	Unc	BU
2001B	1,022,000	—	—	—	7.00	10.00
2001B Proof	6,000	Value: 15.00				
2002B	1,024,000	—	—	—	7.00	10.00
2002B Proof	6,000	Value: 15.00				
2003B	1,022,000	—	—	—	7.00	10.00
2003B Proof	5,500	Value: 15.00				
2004B	524,000	—	—	—	7.50	11.00
2004B Proof	5,000	Value: 15.00				
2005B	524,000	—	—	—	7.50	11.00
2005B Proof	4,500	Value: 15.00				
2006B	526,000	—	—	—	7.50	11.00
2006B Proof	4,000	Value: 15.00				
2007B	524,000	—	—	—	7.50	11.00
2007B Proof	4,000	Value: 15.00				
2008B	522,000	—	—	—	7.50	11.00
2008B Proof	4,000	Value: 15.00				
2009B	2,022,000	—	—	—	7.50	11.00
2009B Proof	4,000	Value: 15.00				
2010B	Est. 5,022,000	—	—	—	7.50	11.00
2010B Proof	Est. 4,000	Value: 15.00				
2011B	Est. 3,022,000	—	—	—	7.50	11.00
2011B Proof	Est. 4,000	Value: 15.00				
2012B	Est. 8,022,000	—	—	—	7.50	11.00
2012B Proof	Est. 4,000	Value: 15.00				
2013B	—	—	—	—	7.50	11.00
2013B Proof	—	Value: 15.00				

KM# 144 20 FRANCS

20.0000 g., 0.8350 Silver 0.5369 oz. ASW, 33 mm. **Subject:** Globi **Obv:** Swiss cross, legend, denomination & date **Obv. Legend:** CONFOEDERATIO HELVETICA **Rev:** Comic character Globi carying a cake with candles and legend **Rev. Legend:** GLOBI and ©Globi Verlag Zurich **Designer:** Roberet Lips

Date	Mintage	F	VF	XF	Unc	BU
2012	Est. 50,000	—	—	—	—	30.00
2012 Proof	Est. 7,000	Value: 65.00				

KM# 145 50 FRANCS

11.2900 g., 0.9000 Gold 0.3267 oz. AGW, 25 mm. **Subject:** Pro Juventute 100th Anniversary **Obv:** Swiss cross, legend, denomination and date **Obv. Legend:** CONFOEDERATIO HELVETICA **Rev:** Girl jumping rope, head of boy wearing cap **Rev. Legend:** PRO JUVENTUTE 1912-2012 and BRIGITTA G. L.

Date	Mintage	F	VF	XF	Unc	BU
2012 Proof	Est. 6,000	Value: 600				

COMMEMORATIVE COINAGE

KM# 92 5 FRANCS

15.0000 g., Bi-Metallic Nordic gold center in Copper-Nickel ring, 32.85 mm. **Subject:** Zurcher Sechselauten **Obv:** Value within circle **Rev:** Burning strawman within circle **Edge:** Reeded **Edge Lettering:** DOMINUS PROVIDEBIT (13 stars) **Designer:** John Grüniger

Date	Mintage	F	VF	XF	Unc	BU
2001B	170,000	—	—	—	8.00	12.00
2001B Proof	20,000	Value: 24.00				

KM# 98 5 FRANCS

15.0000 g., Bi-Metallic Nordic gold center in Copper-Nickel ring, 32.85 mm. **Subject:** Escalade 1602-2002 **Obv:** Value within circle **Rev:** Swirling ladders design within circle **Edge:** Reeded **Edge Lettering:** DOMINUS PROVIDEBIT (13 stars) **Designer:** P.A. Zuber

Date	Mintage	F	VF	XF	Unc	BU
2002B	130,000	—	—	—	8.00	12.00
2002B Proof	15,000	Value: 24.00				

KM# 103 5 FRANCS

15.0000 g., Bi-Metallic Nordic gold center in Copper-Nickel ring, 32.85 mm. **Subject:** Chalandamarz **Obv:** Value within circular inscription and designed wreath **Rev:** Boys shaking bells within 3/4 designed wreath **Edge:** Reeded **Edge Lettering:** DOMINUS PROVIDEBIT (13 stars) **Designer:** Gian Vonzun

Date	Mintage	F	VF	XF	Unc	BU
2003B	96,000	—	—	—	8.00	12.00
2003B Proof	12,000	Value: 24.00				

KM# 107 10 FRANCS

15.0000 g., Bi-Metallic Copper-Nickel center in Aluminum-Bronze ring, 32.85 mm. **Obv:** Value **Rev:** Matterhorn Mountain **Edge:** Segmented reeding **Designer:** Stephan Bundi

Date	Mintage	F	VF	XF	Unc	BU
2004B	94,976	—	—	—	—	22.00
2004B Proof	12,168	Value: 45.00				

KM# 111 10 FRANCS
15.0000 g., Bi-Metallic Copper-Nickel center in Aluminum-Bronze ring, 32.85 mm. **Obv:** Value **Rev:** Jungfrau mountain **Edge:** Segmented reeding **Designer:** Stephan Bundi

Date	Mintage	F	VF	XF	Unc	BU
2005B	77,791	—	—	—	—	18.00
2005B Proof	10,495	Value: 40.00				

KM# 114 10 FRANCS
15.0000 g., Bi-Metallic Copper-Nickel center in Aluminum-Bronze ring, 32.85 mm. **Obv:** Value **Rev:** Piz Bernina mountain **Edge:** Segmented reeding **Designer:** Stephan Bundi

Date	Mintage	F	VF	XF	Unc	BU
2006B	66,000	—	—	—	—	16.00
2006B Proof	9,000	Value: 40.00				

KM# 118 10 FRANCS
15.0000 g., Bi-Metallic Copper-Nickel center in Aluminum-Bronze ring, 32.85 mm. **Subject:** Swiss National Park **Obv:** Value **Rev:** Ibex **Edge:** Segmented reeding

Date	Mintage	F	VF	XF	Unc	BU
2007B	80,200	—	—	—	—	17.00
2007B Proof	10,300	Value: 40.00				

KM# 126 10 FRANCS
15.0000 g., Bi-Metallic Copper-Nickel center in Aluminum-Bronze ring, 32.85 mm. **Obv:** Small national arms **Obv. Legend:** CONFEDERATIO - HELVETICA **Rev:** Golden Eagle alighting **Rev. Legend:** PARK NATIONAL SUISSE **Edge:** Segmented reeding

Date	Mintage	F	VF	XF	Unc	BU
2008B	66,000	—	—	—	—	17.00
2008B Proof	10,300	Value: 40.00				

KM# 130 10 FRANCS
15.0000 g., Bi-Metallic Copper-Nickel center in Aluminum-Bronze ring, 32.85 mm. **Subject:** Swiss National Park **Obv:** Value **Rev:** Red deer

Date	Mintage	F	VF	XF	Unc	BU
2009B	49,000	—	—	—	—	49.00
2009B Proof	5,300	Value: 53.00				

KM# 134 10 FRANCS
15.0000 g., Bi-Metallic Copper-Nickel center in Aluminum-Bronze ring, 32.85 mm. **Subject:** Swiss National Park - Alpine Marmot **Obv:** Value **Rev:** Marmot

Date	Mintage	F	VF	XF	Unc	BU
2010B	Est. 94,000	—	—	—	—	17.00
2010B Proof	Est. 12,000	Value: 40.00				

KM# 138 10 FRANCS
15.0000 g., Bi-Metallic Copper-Nickel center in Aluminum-Bronze ring, 33 mm. **Subject:** Bern Onion Market **Obv:** Value **Rev:** Bear of Bern at left, woven plaits of onions at right **Edge:** Segmented reeding

Date	Mintage	F	VF	XF	Unc	BU
2011B	Est. 94,000	—	—	—	—	17.00
2011B Proof	Est. 12,000	Value: 40.00				

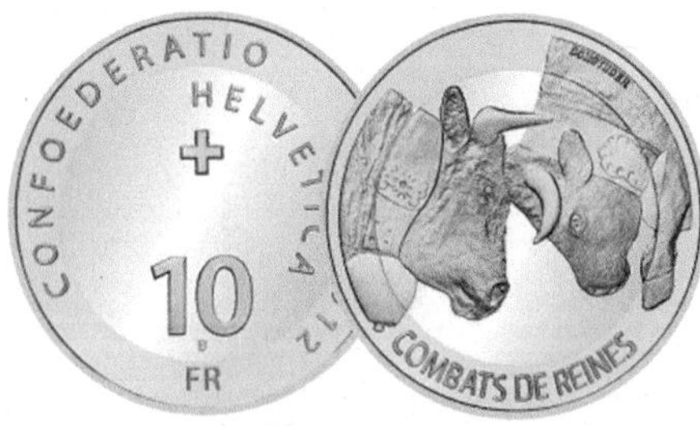

KM# 142 10 FRANCS
15.0000 g., Bi-Metallic Copper-Nickel center in Aluminum-Bronze ring, 33 mm. **Subject:** Bull fighting **Rev:** Two bull's heads butting

Date	Mintage	F	VF	XF	Unc	BU
2012B	Est. 94,000	—	—	—	—	17.00
2012B Proof	Est. 12,000	Value: 40.00				

KM# 93 20 FRANCS
20.0000 g., 0.8350 Silver 0.5369 oz. ASW, 32.8 mm. **Subject:** Mustair Cloister **Obv:** Church floor plan **Rev:** Cloister of Müstair **Edge Lettering:** DOMINUS PROVIDEBIT and 13 stars **Designer:** Hans-Peter von Ah

Date	Mintage	F	VF	XF	Unc	BU
2001B	50,076	—	—	—	26.00	30.00
2001B Proof	15,000	Value: 55.00				

KM# 94 20 FRANCS
20.0000 g., 0.8350 Silver 0.5369 oz. ASW, 32.8 mm. **Subject:** Johanna Spyri **Obv:** Value within handwritten background **Rev:** Bust facing **Edge Lettering:** DOMINUS PROVIDEBIT (13 stars) **Designer:** Silvia Goeschke

Date	Mintage	F	VF	XF	Unc	BU
2001B	60,364	—	—	—	26.00	30.00
2001B Proof	15,000	Value: 55.00				

KM# 99 20 FRANCS
20.0000 g., 0.8350 Silver 0.5369 oz. ASW, 32.8 mm. **Obv:** St. Gall and bear cub **Rev:** St. Gall Cloister **Edge Lettering:** DOMINUS PROVIDEBIT (13 stars) **Designer:** Hans-Peter von Ah

Date	Mintage	F	VF	XF	Unc	BU
2002B	35,895	—	—	—	26.00	30.00
2002B Proof	6,250	Value: 55.00				

KM# 100 20 FRANCS
20.0000 g., 0.8350 Silver 0.5369 oz. ASW, 32.8 mm. **Subject:** REGA **Obv:** Value, inscription and raised cross above rotating propeller **Rev:** Rescue helicopter in flight **Edge Lettering:** DOMINUS PROVIDEBIT (13 stars) **Designer:** Raphael Schenker

Date	Mintage	F	VF	XF	Unc	BU
2002B	37,314	—	—	—	26.00	30.00
2002B Proof	6,453	Value: 55.00				

KM# 101 20 FRANCS
20.0000 g., 0.8350 Silver 0.5369 oz. ASW, 32.8 mm. **Subject:** Expo '02 **Obv:** Value and date within circle **Rev:** Child at water's edge within beaded circle **Edge Lettering:** DOMINUS PROVIDEBIT (13 stars) **Designer:** Hervé Graumann

Date	Mintage	F	VF	XF	Unc	BU
2002B	51,899	—	—	—	26.00	30.00
2002B Proof	7,691	Value: 55.00				

KM# 104 20 FRANCS
19.9700 g., 0.8350 Silver 0.5361 oz. ASW, 32.8 mm. **Subject:** St. Moritz Ski Championships **Obv:** Value in snow storm **Rev:** Skier in snow storm **Edge Lettering:** DOMINUS PROVIDEBIT (13 stars) **Designer:** Claude Kuhn

Date	Mintage	F	VF	XF	Unc	BU
2003B	39,411	—	—	—	26.00	30.00
2003B Proof	6,471	Value: 55.00				

KM# 106 20 FRANCS
20.0000 g., 0.8350 Silver 0.5369 oz. ASW, 32.8 mm. **Subject:** Bern, Old Town **Obv:** Stylized clock tower and buildings **Rev:** Stylized aerial view of Berner Altstadt **Edge Lettering:** DOMINUS PROVIDEBIT **Designer:** Franz Fedier

Date	Mintage	F	VF	XF	Unc	BU
2003B	38,644	—	—	—	26.00	30.00
2003B Proof	5,909	Value: 55.00				

KM# 108 20 FRANCS
20.0000 g., 0.8350 Silver 0.5369 oz. ASW, 32.8 mm. **Obv:** Value **Rev:** The Three Castles of Bellinzona **Edge Lettering:** DOMINUS PROVIDEBIT **Designer:** Marco Prati

Date	Mintage	F	VF	XF	Unc	BU
2004B	29,697	—	—	—	26.00	30.00
2004B Proof	5,190	Value: 55.00				

KM# 109 20 FRANCS
20.0000 g., 0.8350 Silver 0.5369 oz. ASW, 32.8 mm. **Obv:** Value **Rev:** Chillon Castle and reflection **Edge Lettering:** DOMINUS PROVIDEBIT **Designer:** Jean-Benoît Lévy

Date	Mintage	F	VF	XF	Unc	BU
2004B	35,133	—	—	—	26.00	30.00
2004B Proof	5,670	Value: 55.00				

KM# 121 20 FRANCS
20.0000 g., 0.8350 Silver 0.5369 oz. ASW, 32.8 mm. **Subject:** FIFA Centennial **Obv:** Soccer ball with value at left **Rev:** Flower in center of cross

Date	Mintage	F	VF	XF	Unc	BU
2004B Proof only	14,041	Value: 150				

KM# 122 20 FRANCS
20.0000 g., 0.8350 Silver 0.5369 oz. ASW, 32.8 mm. **Subject:** Chapel Bridge Lucerne **Obv:** Value **Rev:** View of Chapel Bridge **Edge Lettering:** DOMINUS PROVIDEBIT

Date	Mintage	F	VF	XF	Unc	BU
2005B	44,359	—	—	—	26.00	30.00
2005B Proof	5,998	Value: 55.00				

KM# 112 20 FRANCS
20.0000 g., 0.8350 Silver 0.5369 oz. ASW, 32.8 mm. **Subject:** Geneva Motor Show **Obv:** Value **Rev:** Partial view of prototype car **Edge Lettering:** DOMINUS PROVIDEBIT **Designer:** Roger Pfund

Date	Mintage	F	VF	XF	Unc	BU
2005B	45,000	—	—	—	26.00	30.00
2005B Proof	6,000	Value: 55.00				

KM# 115 20 FRANCS
20.0000 g., 0.8350 Silver 0.5369 oz. ASW, 32.8 mm. **Obv:** Value **Rev:** 1906 Post Bus **Edge Lettering:** DOMINUS PROVIDEBIT **Designer:** Raphael Schenker

Date	Mintage	F	VF	XF	Unc	BU
2006B	40,000	—	—	—	26.00	30.00
2006B Proof	6,000	Value: 55.00				

KM# 117 20 FRANCS
20.0000 g., 0.8350 Silver 0.5369 oz. ASW, 32.8 mm. **Obv:** Value and legend **Rev:** Swiss Parliament Building **Edge Lettering:** DOMINUS PROVIDEBIT (13 stars) **Designer:** Benjamin Pfäffli

Date	Mintage	F	VF	XF	Unc	BU
2006B	35,000	—	—	—	25.00	30.00
2006B Proof	6,000	Value: 60.00				

KM# 119 20 FRANCS
20.0000 g., 0.8350 Silver 0.5369 oz. ASW, 32.8 mm. **Subject:** National Bank Centennial **Obv:** Value **Rev:** Partial face of Arthur Honegger (Composer) **Edge Lettering:** DOMINUS PROVIDEBIT

Date	Mintage	F	VF	XF	Unc	BU
2007B	41,747	—	—	—	25.00	30.00
2007B Proof	11,000	Value: 60.00				

KM# 124 20 FRANCS
20.0000 g., 0.8350 Silver 0.5369 oz. ASW, 32.8 mm. **Series:** Famous buildings **Subject:** Munot castle of Schaffhausen **Obv. Legend:** CONFEDERATIO - HELVETICA **Rev:** Two views of castle **Rev. Legend:** MUNOT **Designer:** Hansveli Holzer

Date	Mintage	F	VF	XF	Unc	BU
2007B	40,000	—	—	—	25.00	30.00
2007B Proof	5,000	Value: 60.00				

KM# 127 20 FRANCS

20.0000 g., 0.8350 Silver 0.5369 oz. ASW, 32.8 mm. **Subject:** 100th Anniversary Hockey **Obv:** Small national arms **Obv. Legend:** CONFEDERATIO - HELVETICA **Rev:** Two players, one about to swing at puck **Rev. Legend:** ICE HOCKEY 1908-2008

Date	Mintage	F	VF	XF	Unc	BU
2008B	46,000	—	—	—	25.00	30.00
2008B Proof	5,500	Value: 65.00				

KM# 128 20 FRANCS

20.0000 g., 0.8350 Silver 0.5369 oz. ASW, 32.8 mm. **Subject:** Vitznau-Rigi Cog Railway **Obv:** Value **Rev:** Modern locomotive descending, early locomotive ascending (inverted)

Date	Mintage	F	VF	XF	Unc	BU
2008B	Est. 50,000	—	—	—	25.00	30.00
2008B Proof	7,000	Value: 65.00				

KM# 131 20 FRANCS

20.0000 g., 0.8350 Silver 0.5369 oz. ASW, 32.8 mm. **Subject:** Swiss Museum of Transport, 50th Anniversary **Obv:** National arms and value **Rev:** Spiral of transport vehicles **Edge:** DOMINUS PROVIDEBIT

Date	Mintage	F	VF	XF	Unc	BU
2009B	50,000	—	—	—	25.00	30.00
2009B Proof	4,000	Value: 65.00				

KM# 132 20 FRANCS

20.0000 g., 0.8350 Silver 0.5369 oz. ASW, 32.8 mm. **Subject:** Brienz-Rothorn Railway **Obv:** Value **Rev:** Locomotive and railcar **Designer:** Bruno K. Zehnder

Date	Mintage	F	VF	XF	Unc	BU
2009B	50,000	—	—	—	25.00	30.00

KM# 135 20 FRANCS

20.0000 g., 0.8350 Silver 0.5369 oz. ASW, 32.8 mm. **Subject:** 100 Years Bernina Railway **Rev:** Steam train on viaduct

Date	Mintage	F	VF	XF	Unc	BU
2010B	Est. 50,000	—	—	—	30.00	35.00
2010B Proof	Est. 7,000	Value: 50.00				

KM# 136 20 FRANCS

20.0000 g., 0.8350 Silver 0.5369 oz. ASW, 32.8 mm. **Subject:** 100 Anniversary Death of Henry Dunant (Red Cross founder) **Rev:** Bust at left, flag

Date	Mintage	F	VF	XF	Unc	BU
2010B	Est. 50,000	—	—	—	30.00	35.00
2010B Proof	Est. 7,000	Value: 50.00				

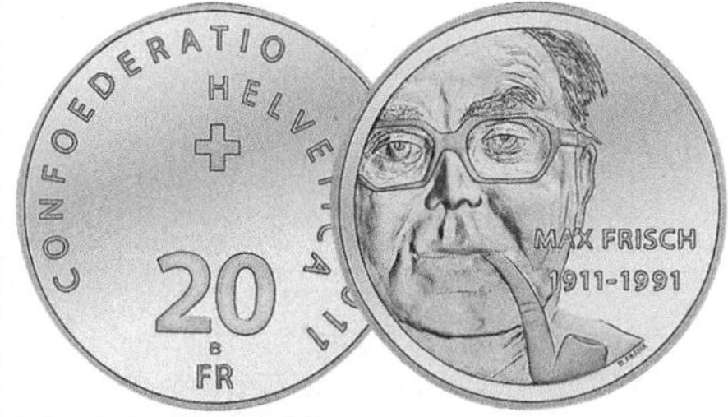

KM# 139 20 FRANCS

20.0000 g., 0.8350 Silver 0.5369 oz. ASW, 33 mm. **Subject:** Max Frisch, 100th Anniversary of Birth **Obv:** Value **Rev:** Facing portrait with pipe

Date	Mintage	F	VF	XF	Unc	BU
2011B	Est. 50,000	—	—	—	30.00	35.00
2011B Proof	Est. 7,000	Value: 50.00				

KM# 140 20 FRANCS

20.0000 g., 0.8350 Silver 0.5369 oz. ASW, 33 mm. **Subject:** Pilatus Railway **Obv:** Value, date and inscription "CONFOEDERATIO HELVETICA" **Rev:** Electric railway car climbing mountain and inscription "PILATUSBAHN" **Edge:** DOMINUS PROVIDEBIT (13 stars)

Date	Mintage	F	VF	XF	Unc	BU
2011B	Est. 50,000	—	—	—	30.00	35.00
2011B Proof	Est. 7,000	Value: 65.00				

KM# 143 20 FRANCS

20.0000 g., 0.8350 Silver 0.5369 oz. ASW, 33 mm. **Subject:** Jungfrau Railway

Date	Mintage	F	VF	XF	Unc	BU
2012B	50,000	—	—	—	30.00	35.00
2012B Proof	7,000	Value: 65.00				

KM# 95 50 FRANCS

11.2900 g., 0.9000 Gold 0.3267 oz. AGW, 25.1 mm. **Obv:** Landscape and value **Rev:** Heidi and goat running **Edge:** Lettered **Edge Lettering:** DOMINUS PROVIDEBIT (13 stars) **Designer:** Albrecht Schnider

Date	Mintage	F	VF	XF	Unc	BU
2001B Proof	3,967	Value: 700				

KM# 102 50 FRANCS

11.2900 g., 0.9000 Gold 0.3267 oz. AGW, 25.1 mm. **Subject:** Expo '02 **Obv:** Value **Rev:** Aerial view of 3 lakes landscape **Edge:** Lettered **Edge Lettering:** DOMINUS PROVIDEBIT (13 stars) **Designer:** Max Matter

Date	Mintage	F	VF	XF	Unc	BU
2002B Proof	4,856	Value: 650				

KM# 105 50 FRANCS

11.2900 g., 0.9000 Gold 0.3267 oz. AGW, 25.1 mm. **Obv:** Skier and value **Rev:** St. Moritz city view **Edge Lettering:** DOMINUS PROVIDEBIT (13 stars) **Designer:** Andreas His

Date	Mintage	F	VF	XF	Unc	BU
2003B Proof	4,000	Value: 650				

KM# 110 50 FRANCS

11.2900 g., 0.9000 Gold 0.3267 oz. AGW, 25.1 mm. **Obv:** Value **Rev:** Matterhorn Mountain **Edge Lettering:** DOMINUS PROVIDEBIT (13 stars) **Designer:** Stephan Bundi

Date	Mintage	F	VF	XF	Unc	BU
2004B Proof	7,000	Value: 700				

KM# 123 50 FRANCS

11.2900 g., 0.9000 Gold 0.3267 oz. AGW, 25.1 mm. **Subject:** FIFA Centennial **Obv:** FIFA depicting Wilhelm Tell **Rev:** Soccer ball on left value on right **Designer:** Joaquin Jimenez

Date	Mintage	F	VF	XF	Unc	BU
2004B Proof	10,000	Value: 900				

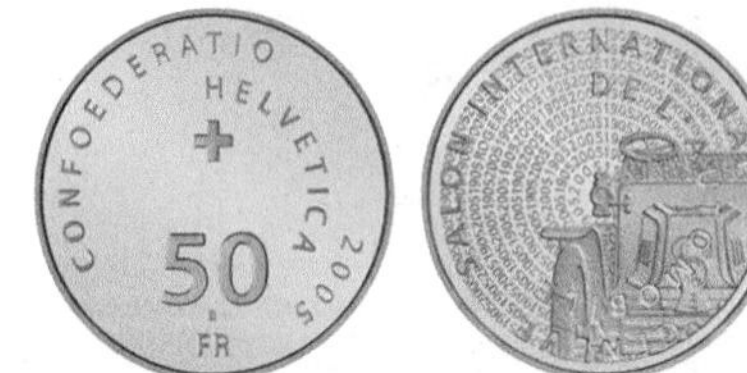

KM# 113 50 FRANCS

11.2900 g., 0.9000 Gold 0.3267 oz. AGW, 25.1 mm. **Subject:** Geneva Motor Show **Obv:** Value **Rev:** Partial view of an antique car **Edge Lettering:** DOMINUS PROVIDEBIT **Designer:** Roger Pfund

Date	Mintage	F	VF	XF	Unc	BU
2005B Proof	6,000	Value: 650				

KM# 116 50 FRANCS

11.2900 g., 0.9000 Gold 0.3267 oz. AGW, 25.1 mm. **Obv:** Value **Rev:** Swiss Guardsman **Edge Lettering:** DOMINUS PROVIDEBIT **Designer:** Rudolf Mirer

Date	Mintage	F	VF	XF	Unc	BU
2006B Proof	6,000	Value: 750				

KM# 120 50 FRANCS

11.2900 g., 0.9000 Gold 0.3267 oz. AGW, 25.1 mm. **Subject:** National Bank Centennial **Obv:** Value **Obv. Legend:** CONFEDERATIO - HELVETICA **Rev:** "Lumberjack" from painting by Ferdinand Hodler **Rev. Inscription:** SNB BNS + **Edge Lettering:** DOMINUS PROVIDEBIT

Date	Mintage	F	VF	XF	Unc	BU
2007B Proof	6,000	Value: 650				

KM# 129 50 FRANCS

11.2900 g., 0.9000 Gold 0.3267 oz. AGW, 25.1 mm. **Subject:** International Year of Planet Earth **Obv:** Value **Rev:** Dancing child with 3 globes above head, in hands and standing on one globe **Rev. Inscription:** DE LA PLANETE TERRE ANNEE INTERNATIONALE **Edge:** DOMINUS PROVIDEBIT **Designer:** Claude Sandoz

Date	Mintage	F	VF	XF	Unc	BU
2008B Proof	6,000	Value: 650				

KM# 133 50 FRANCS

11.2900 g., 0.9000 Gold 0.3267 oz. AGW, 25.1 mm. **Subject:** Pro Patria, 100th Anniversary **Obv:** Value **Edge:** DOMINUS PROVIDEBIT

Date	Mintage	F	VF	XF	Unc	BU
2009B Proof	6,000	Value: 650				

KM# 137 50 FRANCS

11.2900 g., 0.9000 Gold 0.3267 oz. AGW, 25.1 mm. **Subject:** 100th Anniversary Death of Alber Anker (Painter)

Date	Mintage	F	VF	XF	Unc	BU
2010B Proof	6,000	Value: 650				

KM# 141 50 FRANCS

11.2900 g., 0.9000 Gold 0.3267 oz. AGW, 25.1 mm. **Subject:** Bell for Ursli **Obv:** Value, date and inscription "CONFOEDERATIO HELVETICA" **Rev:** Boy holding bell and inscription "Schellen-Ursli" **Edge:** DOMINUS PROVIDEBIT

Date	Mintage	F	VF	XF	Unc	BU
2011B Proof	Est. 6,000	Value: 650				

ESSAIS

Swiss Shooting Thalers are listed online at www.NumisMaster.com

KM#	Date	Mintage	Identification	Mkt Val
E13	2001B	600	20 Francs. 0.8350 Silver. 20.0000 g. 33 mm. KM#93	300
E14	2002B	700	5 Francs. Bi-Metallic. 15.0000 g. 33 mm. KM#98	180
E15	2003B	700	5 Francs. Bi-Metallic. 15.0000 g. 33 mm. KM#103	200
E16	2004B	700	10 Francs. Bi-Metallic. 15.0000 g. 33 mm. KM#107.	300
E19	2005B	500	20 Francs. 0.8320 Silver. 20.0000 g. 33 mm. KM#112.	285
E20	2006B	500	20 Francs. 0.8350 Silver. 20.0000 g. 33 mm. KM#117.	285
E21	2007B	500	20 Francs. Silver. 20.0000 g. 33 mm. KM#119.	250
E22	2008B	700	10 Francs. Bi-Metallic. 15.0000 g. 33 mm. KM#126	200
E23	2009B	500	20 Francs. 0.8350 Silver. 20.0000 g. 33mm KM#132	220
E24	2010B	700	10 Francs. Bi-Metallic. 15.0000 g. 33 mm. KM#134	200

MINT SETS

KM#	Date	Mintage	Identification	Issue Price	Mkt Val
MS35	2001 (9)	21,532	KM#21a.3, 23a.3, 24a.3, 26c, 27, 29a, 40a.4, 46, 92 Zurich Sechselauten	—	40.00
MS36	2002 (9)	17,920	KM#21a.3, 23a.3, 24a.3, 26c, 27, 29a, 40a.4, 46, 98 Escalade	—	45.00
MS37	2002 (9)	1,974	KM#21a.3, 23a.3, 24a.3, 26c, 27, 29a, 40a.4, 46, 98, plus a medal. Baby mint set	—	220
MS38	2003 (9)	17,200	KM#21a.3, 23a.3, 24a.3, 26c, 27, 29a, 40a.4, 46, 103 Chalandamarz	—	50.00
MS39	2003 (8)	4,800	KM#21a.3, 23a.3, 24a.3, 26c, 27, 29a, 40a.2, 46 plus medal; Baby Mint Set	—	80.00
MS40	2004 (9)	16,000	KM#21a.3, 23a.3, 24a.3, 26c, 27, 29a, 40a.4, 46, 107 Matterhorn	—	80.00
MS41	2004 (8)	8,400	KM#21a.3, 23a.3, 24a.3, 26c, 27, 29a, 40a.2, 46 plus medal; Baby Mint Set	—	65.00
MS42	2005 (9)	15,279	KM#21a.3, 23a.3, 24a.3, 26c, 27, 29a, 40a.4, 46, 111 Jung Frau	—	40.00
MS43	2005 (8)	7,500	KM#21a.3, 23a.3, 24a.3, 26c, 27, 29a, 40a.2, 46 plus medal; Baby Mint Set	—	40.00
MS44	2006 (9)	16,000	KM#21a.3, 23a.3, 24a.3, 26c, 27, 29a, 40a.4, 46, 114 Piz Bernina	—	140
MS45	2006 (8)	2,000	KM#21a.3, 23a.3, 24a.3, 26c, 27, 29a, 40a.2, 46 plus medal; Jubilee Mint Set	—	450
MS46	2006 (8)	8,000	KM#21a.3, 23a.3, 24a.3, 26c, 27, 29a, 40a.2, 46 plus medal; Baby Mint Set	—	175
MS47	2007 (8)	16,000	KM#21a.3, 23a.3, 24a.3, 26c, 27, 29a, 40a.4, 118	—	45.00
MS48	2007 (7)	7,500	KM#21a.3, 23a.3, 24a.3, 26c, 27, 29a, 40a.2, plus medal; Baby Mint Set	—	45.00
MS49	2008 (8)	15,000	KM#21a.3, 23a.3, 24a.3, 26c, 27, 29a, 40a.4, 126	—	45.00
MS50	2008 (7)	7,000	KM#21a.3, 23a.3, 24a.3, 26c, 27, 29a, 40a.2, plus medal; Baby Mint Set	—	40.00
MS51	2009 (8)	13,500	KM#21a.3, 23a.3, 24a.3, 26c, 27, 29a, 40a4, 130.	—	50.00
MS52	2009 (7)	7,500	KM#21a.3, 23a.3, 24a.3, 26c, 27, 29a, 40a.2, plus medal; Baby Mint Set	—	40.00
MS53	2010 (8)	14,000	KM#21a.3, 23a.3, 24a.3, 26c, 27, 29a, 40a.2, 134	—	50.00
MS54	2010 (7)	8,000	KM#21a.3, 23a.3, 24a.3, 26c, 27, 29a, 40a.2, plus medal; Baby Mint Set	—	40.00
MS55	2011 (8)	14,000	KM#21a.3, 23a.3, 24a.3, 26c, 27, 29a, 40a.2, 138	—	50.00
MS56	2011 (7)	8,000	KM#21a.3, 23a.3, 24a.3, 26c, 27, 29a, 40a.2, plus medal; Baby Mint Set	—	40.00
MS58	2012 (7)	8,000	KM#21a.3, 23a.3, 24a.3, 26c, 27, 29a, 40a.4 plus medal. Baby Mint Set	—	40.00
MS67	2012 (8)	14,000	KM#21a.3, 23a.3, 24a.3, 26c, 27, 29a, 40a.4, 142	—	40.00

PROOF SETS

KM#	Date	Mintage	Identification	Issue Price	Mkt Val
PS30	2001 (9)	5,184	KM#21a.3, 23a.3, 24a.3, 26c, 27, 29a, 40a.4, 46, 92 Zurich Sechselauten	—	75.00
PS31	2002 (9)	4,518	KM#21a.3, 23a.3, 24a.3, 26c, 27, 29a, 40a.4, 46, 98 Escalade	—	80.00
PS32	2003 (9)	4,520	KM#21a.3, 23a.3, 24a.3, 26c, 27, 29a, 40a.4, 46, 103 Chatandamarz	—	80.00
PS33	2004 (9)	4,168	KM#21a.3, 23a.3, 24a.3, 26c, 27, 29a, 40a.4, 46, 107 Matterhorn	68.00	95.00
PS34	2005 (9)	3,783	KM#21a.3, 23a.3, 24a.3, 26c, 27, 29a, 40a.4, 46, 111	68.00	90.00
PS35	2006 (9)	4,000	KM#21a.3, 23a.3, 24a.3, 26c, 27, 29a, 40a.4, 46, 114	68.00	300
PS36	2007 (8)	4,000	KM#21a.3, 23a.3, 24a.3, 26c, 27, 29a, 40a.4, 118	68.00	85.00
PS37	2008 (8)	4,000	KM#21a.3, 23a.3, 24a.3, 26c, 27, 29a, 40a.4, 126	72.00	90.00
PS38	2009 (8)	4,000	KM#21a.3, 23a.3, 24a.3, 26c, 27, 29a, 40a.4, 130	75.00	90.00
PS39	2010 (8)	4,000	KM#21a.3, 23a.3, 24a.3, 26c, 27, 29a, 40a.4, 134	75.00	90.00
PS40	2011 (8)	4,000	KM#21a.3, 23a.3, 24a.3, 26c, 27, 29a, 40a.2, 138	—	90.00
PS41	2012 (8)	4,000	KM#21a.3, 23a.3, 24a.3, 26c, 27, 29a, 40a.4, 142	—	90.00

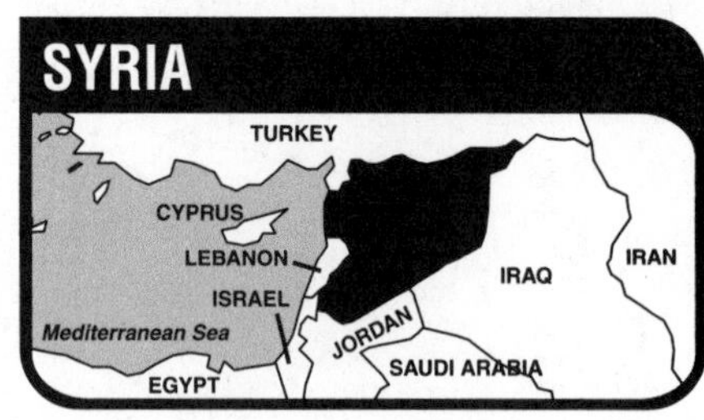

The Syrian Arab Republic, located in the Near East at the eastern end of the Mediterranean Sea, has an area of 71,498 sq. mi. (185,180 sq. km.) and a population of *12 million. Capital: Greater Damascus. Agriculture and animal breeding are the chief industries. Cotton, crude oil and livestock are exported.

TITLES

الجمهورية السورية

al-Jumhuriya(t) al-Suriya(t)

الجمهورية العربية السورية

al-Jumhuriya(t) al-Arabiya(t) as-Suriya(t)

SYRIAN ARAB REPUBLIC

STANDARD COINAGE

KM# 129 5 POUNDS

7.5300 g., Nickel Clad Steel, 24.5 mm. **Obv:** National arms within design and beaded border **Rev:** Old fort and latent image above value within design and beaded border **Edge:** Reeded and lettered **Edge Lettering:** CENTRAL BANK 5 SYP

Date	Mintage	F	VF	XF	Unc	BU
AH1424-2003	—	—	—	—	1.25	1.75

KM# 130 10 POUNDS

9.5300 g., Copper-Nickel-Zinc, 27.4 mm. **Obv:** National arms within beaded border **Rev:** Ancient ruins with latent image within beaded border **Edge Lettering:** 10 SYRIAN POUNDS

Date	Mintage	F	VF	XF	Unc	BU
AH1424-2003	—	—	—	—	2.50	3.50

KM# 131 25 POUNDS

8.4000 g., Bi-Metallic Copper-Nickel center in Nickel-Brass ring, 25 mm. **Obv:** National arms within beaded border **Rev:** Building and latent image within beaded border **Edge Lettering:** CENTRAL BANK OF SYRIA 25

Date	Mintage	F	VF	XF	Unc	BU
AH1424-2003	—	—	—	1.50	3.75	5.00

The Republic of Tajikistan (Tadjiquistan), was formed from those regions of Bukhara and Turkestan where the population consisted mainly of Tajiks. It is bordered in the north and west by Uzbekistan and Kyrgyzstan, in the east by China and in the south by Afghanistan. It has an area of 55,240 sq. miles (143,100 sq. km.) and a population of 5.95 million. It includes 2 provinces of Khudzand and Khatlon together with the Gorno-Badakhshan Autonomous Region with a population of 5,092,603. Capital: Dushanbe. Tajikistan was admitted as a constituent republic of the Soviet Union on Dec. 5, 1929. In August 1990 the Tajik Supreme Soviet adopted a declaration of republican sovereignty, and in Dec. 1991 the republic became a member of the CIS.

After demonstrations and fighting, the Communist government was replaced by a Revolutionary Coalition Council on May 7, 1992. Following further demonstrations President Nabiev was ousted on Sept. 7, 1992. Civil war broke out, and the government resigned on Nov. 10, 1992. On Nov. 30, 1992 it was announced that a CIS peacekeeping force would be sent to Tajikistan. A state of emergency was imposed in Jan. 1993. A ceasefire was signed in 1996 and a peace agreement signed in June 1997.

MONETARY SYSTEM

100 Drams = 1 Somoni

REPUBLIC

DECIMAL COINAGE

KM# 24 10 DIRAMS

3.0000 g., Copper-Brass, 20.5 mm. **Obv:** Coat of arms **Rev:** Large value with design

Date	Mintage	F	VF	XF	Unc	BU
2011	—	—	—	—	1.00	1.50

KM# 25 20 DIRAMS

4.5000 g., Copper-Brass **Obv:** Coat of arms **Rev:** Large value with design **Edge:** Reeded

Date	Mintage	F	VF	XF	Unc	BU
2011	—	—	—	—	1.50	2.00

KM# 23 5 DIRAMS

2.0000 g., Copper-Brass, 18 mm. **Obv:** Coat of arms **Rev:** Large value with design

Date	Mintage	F	VF	XF	Unc	BU
2011	—	—	—	—	0.50	0.75

KM# 26 50 DIRAMS

5.5000 g., Copper-Brass **Obv:** Coat of arms **Rev:** Large value with design **Edge:** Reeded

Date	Mintage	F	VF	XF	Unc	BU
2011	—	—	—	—	2.00	3.00

KM# 2.1 5 DRAMS

2.0000 g., Brass Clad Steel, 16.5 mm. **Obv:** Crown within 1/2 star border **Rev:** Small value within design **Edge:** Plain

Date	Mintage	F	VF	XF	Unc	BU
2001(sp)	—	—	—	—	0.50	0.75
2001(sp) Proof	—	Value: 2.50				

KM# 2.2 5 DRAMS

2.0000 g., Brass Clad Steel, 16.5 mm. **Obv:** Crown with 1/2 star border **Rev:** Large value within design

Date	Mintage	F	VF	XF	Unc	BU
2006(sp)	—	—	—	—	0.75	1.25

KM# 3.1 10 DRAMS

2.4000 g., Brass Clad Steel, 17.5 mm. **Obv:** Crown within 1/2 star border **Rev:** Small value within design **Edge:** Plain

Date	Mintage	F	VF	XF	Unc	BU
2001(sp)	—	—	—	—	0.75	1.00
2001(sp) Proof	—	Value: 3.00				

KM# 3.2 10 DRAMS

2.4000 g., Brass Clad Steel, 17.5 mm. **Obv:** Crown within 1/2 star border **Rev:** Large value within design

Date	Mintage	F	VF	XF	Unc	BU
2006(sp)	—	—	—	—	1.00	1.50

KM# 4.1 20 DRAMS

2.7000 g., Brass Clad Steel, 18.5 mm. **Obv:** Crown within 1/2 star border **Rev:** Small value within design **Edge:** Plain

Date	Mintage	F	VF	XF	Unc	BU
2001(sp)	—	—	—	—	1.00	1.25
2001(sp) Proof	—	Value: 3.75				

KM# 4.2 20 DRAMS

2.7000 g., Brass Clad Steel, 18.5 mm. **Obv:** Crown within 1/2 star border **Rev:** Large value within design

Date	Mintage	F	VF	XF	Unc	BU
2006(sp)	—	—	—	—	1.50	2.00

KM# 5.1 25 DRAMS

2.7600 g., Brass, 19 mm. **Obv:** Crown within 1/2 star border **Rev:** Small value within design **Edge:** Plain

Date	Mintage	F	VF	XF	Unc	BU
2001(sp)	—	—	—	—	1.50	1.75
2001(sp) Proof	—	Value: 5.00				

KM# 5.2 25 DRAMS

2.7600 g., Brass, 19 mm. **Obv:** Crown within 1/2 star border **Rev:** Large value within design

Date	Mintage	F	VF	XF	Unc	BU
2006(sp)	—	—	—	—	1.75	2.50

KM# 5.2a 25 DRAMS

2.7400 g., Brass Clad Steel, 19 mm. **Obv:** Crown within 1/2 star border **Rev:** Large value within design **Edge:** Reeded

Date	Mintage	F	VF	XF	Unc	BU
2006	—	—	—	—	2.00	3.00

KM# 6.1 50 DRAMS

3.6000 g., Brass, 21 mm. **Obv:** Crown within 1/2 star border **Rev:** Value within design **Edge:** Plain

Date	Mintage	F	VF	XF	Unc	BU
2001(sp)	—	—	—	—	2.00	3.00
2001(sp) Proof	—	Value: 7.00				

KM# 6.2 50 DRAMS

3.6000 g., Brass, 21 mm. **Obv:** Crown within 1/2 star border **Rev:** Large value within design

Date	Mintage	F	VF	XF	Unc	BU
2006(sp)	—	—	—	—	2.00	3.00

KM# 6.2a 50 DRAMS

3.4000 g., Brass Clad Steel, 21 mm. **Obv:** Crown within 1/2 star border **Rev:** Large value within design **Edge:** Reeded

Date	Mintage	F	VF	XF	Unc	BU
2006	—	—	—	—	2.00	3.00

KM# 7 SOMONI

5.2000 g., Copper-Nickel-Zinc, 24 mm. **Obv:** King's bust 1/2 right **Rev:** Value **Edge:** Segmented reeding

Date	Mintage	F	VF	XF	Unc	BU
2001(sp)	—	—	—	—	3.50	5.00
2001(sp) Proof	—	Value: 12.00				

KM# 12 SOMONI

5.2000 g., Copper-Nickel-Zinc, 24 mm. **Subject:** Year of Aryan Civilization **Obv:** National arms above value **Rev:** Ancient archer in war chariot **Edge:** Segmented reeding

Date	Mintage	F	VF	XF	Unc	BU
2006(sp)	100,000	—	—	—	3.50	5.00

KM# 13 SOMONI

5.2000 g., Copper-Nickel-Zinc, 24 mm. **Subject:** Year of Aryan Civilization **Obv:** National arms above value **Rev:** Two busts left **Edge:** Segmented reeding

Date	Mintage	F	VF	XF	Unc	BU
2006(sp)	100,000	—	—	—	3.50	5.00

KM# 19 SOMONI

20.0000 g., 0.9250 Silver 0.5948 oz. ASW, 35 mm. **Subject:** Year of Aryan Civilization **Obv:** National arms above value **Rev:** Ancient archer in war chariot **Edge:** Segmented reeding

Date	Mintage	F	VF	XF	Unc	BU
2006(sp) Proof	1,500	Value: 60.00				

KM# 18 SOMONI

20.0000 g., 0.9250 Silver 0.5948 oz. ASW, 24 mm. **Subject:** Year of Aryan Civilization **Obv:** National arms above value **Rev:** Two busts left **Edge:** Segmented reeding

Date	Mintage	F	VF	XF	Unc	BU
2006 Proof	1,500	Value: 60.00				

KM# 16 SOMONI
5.2000 g., Copper-Nickel-Zinc, 24 mm. **Subject:** 800th Anniversary Birth of Jaloliddini Rumi **Obv:** Small arms above value in cartouche **Rev:** 1/2 length figure facing **Edge:** Segmented reeding

Date	Mintage	F	VF	XF	Unc	BU
2007	—	—	—	—	3.50	5.00

KM# 27 SOMONI
5.2000 g., Copper-Nickel Plated Steel, 27 mm. **Obv:** Coat of arms **Rev:** Large value with design

Date	Mintage	F	VF	XF	Unc	BU
2011	—	—	—	—	3.50	5.00

KM# 8 3 SOMONI
6.3000 g., Copper-Nickel-Zinc, 25.5 mm. **Obv:** National arms **Rev:** Crown above value within design **Edge:** Lettered

Date	Mintage	F	VF	XF	Unc	BU
2001(sp)	—	—	—	—	5.00	7.00
2001(sp) Proof	—	Value: 18.00				

KM# 10 3 SOMONI
6.3000 g., Bi-Metallic Copper-Nickel center in Brass ring, 25.5 mm. **Subject:** 80th Year - Dushanbe City **Obv:** Value below arms within circle **Rev:** Statue in arch within circle

Date	Mintage	F	VF	XF	Unc	BU
2004(sp)	—	—	—	—	6.50	9.00

KM# 10a 3 SOMONI
6.9800 g., 0.9250 Silver 0.2076 oz. ASW, 25.5 mm. **Subject:** 80th Anniversary of Republic **Obv:** Value below arms within circle **Rev:** Statue in arch within circle

Date	Mintage	F	VF	XF	Unc	BU
2004 Proof	1,000	Value: 75.00				

KM# 14 3 SOMONI
6.3000 g., Bi-Metallic Copper-Nickel center in Brass ring, 25.5 mm. **Subject:** 2700th Anniversary of Kulyab **Obv:** National arms above value **Rev:** Kulyab city arms **Edge:** Lettered

Date	Mintage	F	VF	XF	Unc	BU
2006(sp)	100,000	—	—	—	6.00	7.50

KM# 20 3 SOMONI
26.0000 g., 0.9250 Silver 0.7732 oz. ASW, 39 mm. **Subject:** 2700th Anniversary of Kulyab **Obv:** National arms above value **Rev:** Kulyab city arms

Date	Mintage	F	VF	XF	Unc	BU
2006(sp) Proof	2,000	Value: 70.00				

KM# 9 5 SOMONI
7.0000 g., Copper-Nickel-Zinc, 26.5 mm. **Obv:** Turbaned head right **Rev:** Crown above value within design **Edge:** Segmented reeding with a star

Date	Mintage	F	VF	XF	Unc	BU
2001(sp)	—	—	—	—	7.50	9.00
2001(sp) Proof	—	Value: 25.00				

KM# 11 5 SOMONI
6.9400 g., Bi-Metallic Copper-Nickel center in Brass ring, 26.5 mm. **Subject:** 10th Anniversary - Constitution **Obv:** Arms above value within circle **Rev:** Flag and book within circle **Edge:** Lettered

Date	Mintage	F	VF	XF	Unc	BU
2004(sp)	—	—	—	—	7.50	10.00

KM# 11a 5 SOMONI
8.5500 g., 0.9250 Silver 0.2543 oz. ASW, 26.5 mm. **Subject:** 10th Anniversary - Constitution **Obv:** Arms above value within circle **Rev:** Flag and book within circle

Date	Mintage	F	VF	XF	Unc	BU
2004 Proof	2,000	Value: 65.00				

KM# 15 5 SOMONI
7.0000 g., Bi-Metallic Copper-Nickel center in Brass ring, 26.5 mm. **Subject:** 15th Anniversary of Independence **Obv:** National arms above value **Rev:** Government building **Edge:** Lettered

Date	Mintage	F	VF	XF	Unc	BU
2006(sp)	100,000	—	—	—	7.50	10.00

KM# 21 5 SOMONI
34.0000 g., 0.9250 Silver 1.0111 oz. ASW, 42 mm. **Subject:** 15th Anniversary of Independence **Obv:** National arms above value **Rev:** Government building

Date	Mintage	F	VF	XF	Unc	BU
2006(sp) Proof	2,000	Value: 75.00				

KM# 17 5 SOMONI
7.0000 g., Bi-Metallic Copper-Nickel center in Brass ring, 26.5 mm. **Subject:** 1150th Anniversary founding of Persian (Tajik) literature by Abuabdullo Rudaki **Obv:** National arms above value **Rev:** Bust of Rudaki left, scroll, feather pen

Date	Mintage	F	VF	XF	Unc	BU
2008	—	—	—	—	7.50	10.00

KM# 22 5 SOMONI
34.0000 g., 0.9250 Silver 1.0111 oz. ASW, 42 mm. **Subject:** 1150 Anniversary founding of Persian Literature by Abuabdullo Rudaki **Obv:** National arms above value **Rev:** Bust of Rudaki left, scroll, feather pen

Date	Mintage	F	VF	XF	Unc	BU
2008(sp) Proof	1,000	Value: 115				

MINT SETS

KM#	Date	Mintage	Identification	Issue Price	Mkt Val
MS1	2001 (8)	—	KM#2.1-6.1, 7-9	—	30.00

PROOF SETS

KM#	Date	Mintage	Identification	Issue Price	Mkt Val
PS1	2001 (8)	—	KM#2.1-6.1, 7-9	—	80.00

TANZANIA

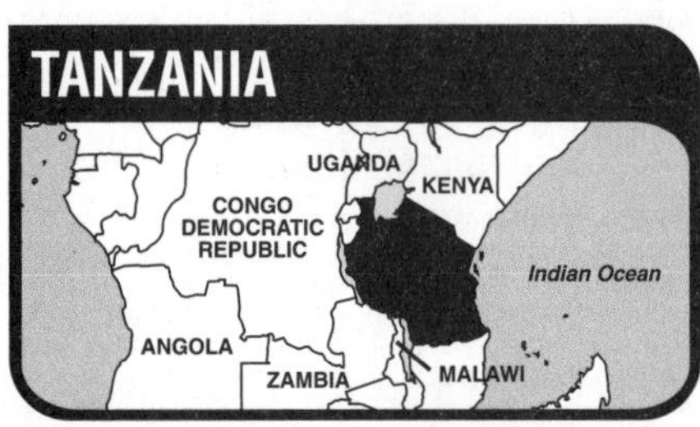

The United Republic of Tanzania, located on the east coast of Africa between Kenya and Mozambique, consists of Tanganyika and the islands of Zanzibar and Pemba. It has an area of 364,900 sq. mi. (945,090 sq. km.) and a population of *25.2 million. Capital: Dodoma. The chief exports are cotton, coffee, diamonds, sisal, cloves, petroleum products, and cashew nuts.

Tanzania is a member of the Commonwealth of Nations. The President is Chief of State.

REPUBLIC

STANDARD COINAGE

100 Senti = 1 Shilingi

KM# 34 200 SHILINGI
8.0000 g., Copper-Nickel-Zinc **Obv:** Head of Sheikh Karume 1/4 left within circle **Rev:** Two lions **Edge:** Segmented reeding

Date	Mintage	F	VF	XF	Unc	BU
2008	—	—	—	—	6.00	9.00

KM# 56 500 SHILLINGS
31.4600 g., 0.9250 Silver 0.9356 oz. ASW, 38.6 mm. **Obv:** Arms with supporters above value **Rev:** African dhow **Edge:** Reeded

Date	Mintage	F	VF	XF	Unc	BU
2001 Proof	—	Value: 45.00				

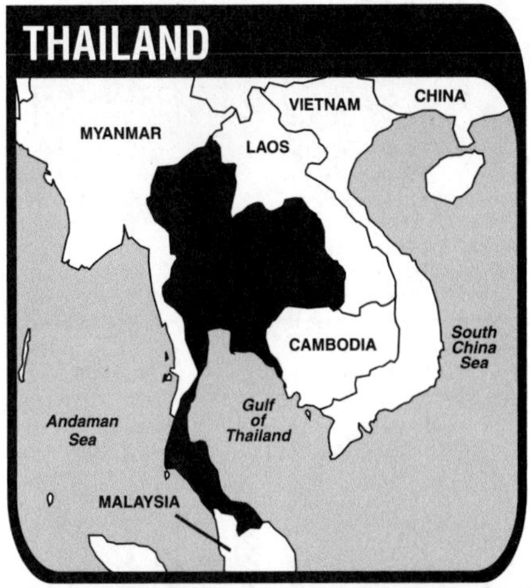

The Kingdom of Thailand (formerly Siam), a constitutional monarchy located in the center of mainland Southeast Asia between Burma and Laos, has an area of 198,457 mi. (514,000 sq. km.) and a population of *55.5 million. Capital: Bangkok. The economy is based on agriculture and mining. Rubber, rice, teakwood, tin and tungsten are exported.

The history of The Kingdom of Siam, the only country in south and Southeast Asia that was never colonized by an European power, dates from the 6th century A.D. when Thai people started to migrate into the area a process that accelerated with the Mongol invasion of China in the 13th century. After 400 years of sporadic warfare with the neighboring Burmese, King Taskin won the last battle in 1767. He founded a new capital, Dhonburi, on the west bank of the Chao Praya River. King Rama I moved the capital to Bangkok in 1782, thus initiating the so-called Bangkok Period of Siamese coinage characterized by Pot Duang money (bullet coins) stamped with regal symbols.

The Portuguese, who were followed by the Dutch, British and French, introduced the Thai to the Western world. Rama III of the present ruling dynasty negotiated a treaty of friendship and commerce with Britain in 1826, and in 1896 the independence of the kingdom was guaranteed by an Anglo-French accord.

In 1909 Siam ceded to Great Britain its suzerain rights over the dependencies of Kedah, Kelantan, Trengganu and Perlis, Malay states situated in southern Siam just north of British Malaya, which eliminated any British jurisdiction in Siam proper.

The absolute monarchy was changed into a constitutional monarchy in 1932.

On Dec. 8, 1941, after five hours of fighting, Thailand agreed to permit Japanese troops passage through the country to invade Northern British Malaysia. This eventually led to increased Japanese intervention and finally occupation of the country. On Jan. 25, 1942, Thailand declared war on Great Britain and the United States. A free Thai guerilla movement was soon organized to counteract the Japanese. In July 1943 Japan transferred the four northern Malay States back to Thailand. These were returned to Great Britain after peace treaties were signed in 1946.

DATING

Typical BE Dating

1 2 3 8

1244

Typical CS Dating

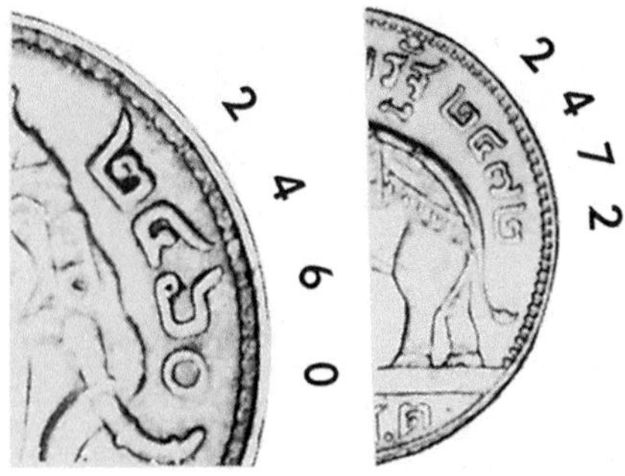

NOTE: Sometimes the era designator *BE* or *CS* will actually appear on the coin itself.

Denomination

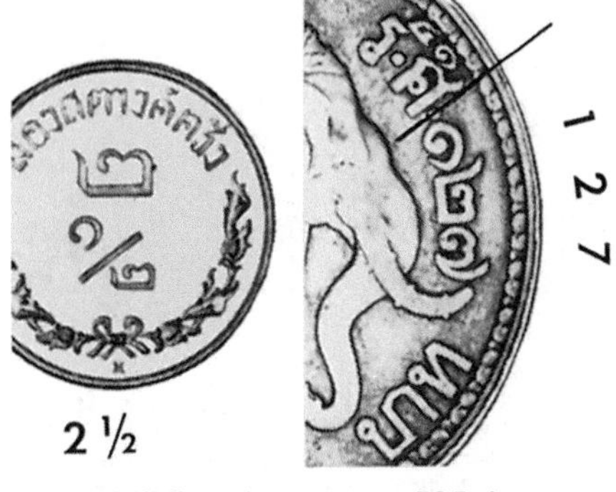

2 1/2

2-1/2 (Satang) **RS Dating**

DATE CONVERSION TABLES

B.E. date - 543 = A.D. date
Ex: 2516 - 543 = 1973
R.S. date + 1781 = A.D. date
Ex: 127 + 1781 = 1908
C.S. date + 638 = A.D. date
Ex 1238 + 638 = 1876

Primary denominations used were 1 Baht, 1/4 and 1/8 Baht up to the reign of Rama IV. Other denominations are much scarcer.

KINGDOM OF THAILAND

1939-

DECIMAL COINAGE

25 Satang = 1 Salung; 100 Satang = 1 Baht

Y# 186 SATANG

0.5000 g., Aluminum, 14.58 mm. **Ruler:** Rama IX **Obv:** Head left **Rev:** Haripunchai Temple, Lumpoon province **Edge:** Plain

Date	Mintage	F	VF	XF	Unc	BU
BE2544 (2001)	50,000	—	—	—	0.75	1.00
BE2545 (2002)	—	—	—	—	1.50	2.00
BE2546 (2003)	10,000	—	—	—	1.50	2.00
BE2547 (2004)	20,000	—	—	—	1.25	1.75
BE2548 (2005)	10,000	—	—	—	1.50	2.00
BE2549 (2006)	3,000	—	—	—	3.00	4.00
BE2550 (2007)	10,000	—	—	—	1.50	2.00

Y# 456 SATANG

0.5000 g., Aluminum, 15 mm. **Ruler:** Rama IX **Obv:** Bust left **Rev:** Haripunchai Temple, Lumpoon province

Date	Mintage	F	VF	XF	Unc	BU
BE2551 (2008)	—	—	—	—	1.50	2.00
BE2552 (2009)	10,000	—	—	—	1.50	2.00
BE2553 (2010)	10,000	—	—	—	1.50	2.00

Y# 208 5 SATANG

0.6000 g., Aluminum, 16 mm. **Ruler:** Rama IX **Obv:** Bust left **Rev:** Phra Patom Temple, Nakhon Pathom province **Edge:** Plain

Date	Mintage	F	VF	XF	Unc	BU
BE2544 (2001)	50,000	—	—	—	1.00	1.25
BE2546 (2003)	10,000	—	—	—	2.00	2.50
BE2547 (2004)	10,000	—	—	—	2.00	2.50
BE2548 (2005)	20,000	—	—	—	1.25	1.50
BE2549 (2006)	3,000	—	—	—	3.00	4.00
BE2550 (2007)	10,000	—	—	—	2.00	2.50

Y# 457 5 SATANG

0.6000 g., Aluminum, 16.5 mm. **Ruler:** Rama IX **Obv:** Bust left **Rev:** Phra Patom Temple, Nakhon Pathom province

Date	Mintage	F	VF	XF	Unc	BU
BE2551 (2008)	10,000	—	—	—	2.00	2.50
BE2552 (2009)	10,000	—	—	—	2.00	2.50
BE2553 (2010)	10,000	—	—	—	2.00	2.50

Y# 209 10 SATANG

0.8000 g., Aluminum, 17.5 mm. **Ruler:** Rama IX **Obv:** Young bust left **Rev:** Phra Tat Chungchum Temple, Sakon Nakhon province **Edge:** Plain

Date	Mintage	F	VF	XF	Unc	BU
BE2544 (2001)	50,000	—	—	—	1.00	1.50
BE2545 (2002)	—	—	—	—	2.00	2.50
BE2546 (2003)	10,000	—	—	1.00	2.00	2.50
BE2547 (2004)	20,000	—	—	—	0.75	1.75
BE2548 (2005)	10,000	—	—	1.00	2.00	2.50
BE2549 (2006)	3,000	—	—	2.00	4.00	5.00
BE2550 (2007)	10,000	—	—	1.00	2.00	2.50

Y# 458 10 SATANG

0.8000 g., Aluminum, 17.5 mm. **Ruler:** Rama IX **Obv:** Bust left **Rev:** Phra Tat Chungchum Temple, Sakon Nakhon province

Date	Mintage	F	VF	XF	Unc	BU
BE2551 (2008)	—	—	—	1.00	2.00	2.50
BE2552 (2009)	10,000	—	—	1.00	2.00	2.50
BE2553 (2010)	10,000	—	—	1.00	2.00	2.50

Y# 187 25 SATANG = 1/4 BAHT

1.9000 g., Aluminum-Bronze, 16 mm. **Ruler:** Rama IX **Obv:** Head left **Rev:** Mahathat Temple, Nakhon Si Thammarat province **Edge:** Reeded

Date	Mintage	F	VF	XF	Unc	BU
BE2544 (2001)	10,000	1.00	2.00	3.00	5.00	6.00
BE2545 (2002)	141,562,000	1.00	2.00	3.00	5.00	6.00
BE2546 (2003)	82,668,000	—	—	—	0.10	0.15
BE2547 (2004)	104,830,000	—	—	—	0.10	0.15
BE2548 (2005)	95,362,000	—	—	—	0.10	0.15
BE2549 (2006)	120,003,000	—	—	—	0.10	0.15
BE2550 (2007) r	180,000,000	—	—	—	0.10	0.15
BE2551 (2008) r	255,600	—	0.50	0.75	1.00	1.50
BE2552 (2009)	30,000	1.00	2.00	3.00	5.00	6.00

Y# 441 25 SATANG = 1/4 BAHT

1.9000 g., Copper Plated Steel, 16 mm. **Ruler:** Rama IX **Obv:** King's portrait **Rev:** Mahathat Temple, Nakhon Si Thammarat province

Date	Mintage	F	VF	XF	Unc	BU
BE2552 (2009)v	289,995,600	—	—	—	0.10	0.15
BE2553 (2010)v	220,000,000	—	—	—	0.10	0.15
BE2554 (2011)v	—	—	—	—	0.10	0.15
BE2555 (2012)v	—	—	—	—	0.10	0.15

Y# 203 50 SATANG = 1/2 BAHT

2.4000 g., Aluminum-Bronze, 18 mm. **Ruler:** Rama IX **Obv:** Head left **Rev:** Soi Suthep Temple, Chiang Mai province

Date	Mintage	F	VF	XF	Unc	BU
BE2544 (2001)	52,738,000	—	—	—	0.10	0.15
BE2545 (2002)	102,804,000	—	—	—	0.10	0.15
BE2546 (2003)	101,200,000	—	—	—	0.10	0.15

Date	Mintage	F	VF	XF	Unc	BU
BE2547 (2004)	79,596,000	—	—	—	0.10	0.15
BE2548 (2005)	99,920,000	—	—	—	0.10	0.15
BE2549 (2006)	130,803,000	—	—	—	0.10	0.15
BE2550 (2007)	24,905,000	—	—	—	0.10	0.15
BE2551 (2008)	27,163,509	—	—	—	0.10	0.15

Y# 442 50 SATANG = 1/2 BAHT

2.4000 g., Copper Plated Steel, 18 mm. **Ruler:** Rama IX **Obv:** King's portrait **Rev:** Doi Suthep Temple, Chiang Mai province

Date	Mintage	F	VF	XF	Unc	BU
BE2552 (2009)v	225,000,000	—	—	—	0.10	0.15
BE2553 (2010)v	118,536,000	—	—	—	0.10	0.15
BE2554 (2011)v	—	—	—	—	0.10	0.15
BE2555 (2012)	—	—	—	—	0.10	0.15

Y# 183 BAHT

3.4500 g., Copper-Nickel, 20 mm. **Ruler:** Rama IX **Obv:** Head left **Rev:** Phra Kaew Temple, Bangkok **Edge:** Reeded **Note:** Varieties exist.

Date	Mintage	F	VF	XF	Unc	BU
BE2544 (2001)	385,140,000	—	—	—	0.10	0.15
BE2545 (2002)	266,025,000	—	—	—	0.10	0.15
BE2546 (2003)	236,533,000	—	—	—	0.10	0.15
BE2547 (2004)	903,964,000	—	—	—	0.10	0.15
BE2548 (2005) wg	1,137,820,000	—	—	—	0.10	0.15
BE2549 (2006) v	778,061,000	—	—	—	0.10	0.15
BE2550 (2007) wg	614,866,877	—	—	—	0.10	0.15
BE2551 (2008)	660,307,123	—	—	—	0.10	0.15

Y# 443 BAHT

3.0000 g., Nickel Plated Steel, 20 mm. **Ruler:** Rama IX **Obv:** King's portrait **Rev:** Phra Kaew Temple, Bangkok **Edge:** Reeded

Date	Mintage	F	VF	XF	Unc	BU
BE2552 (2009)v	507,250,000	—	—	—	0.10	0.15
BE2553 (2010)v	551,853,000	—	—	—	0.10	0.15
BE2554 (2011)v	—	—	—	—	0.10	0.15
BE2555 (2012)v	—	—	—	—	0.10	0.15

Y# 444 2 BAHT

4.4000 g., Nickel Plated Steel, 21.75 mm. **Ruler:** Rama IX **Obv:** King's portrait **Rev:** Saket Temple, Bangkok

Date	Mintage	F	VF	XF	Unc	BU
BE2548 (2005)wg	60,000	—	—	—	0.20	0.25
BE2549 (2006)wg	107,872,500	—	—	—	0.20	0.25
BE2550 (2007)wg	232,105,100	—	—	—	0.20	0.25
BE2552 (2009)	50,370	—	—	2.00	4.00	6.00

Y# 445 2 BAHT

4.0000 g., Aluminum-Bronze, 21.75 mm. **Ruler:** Rama IX **Obv:** King's portrait **Rev:** Saket Temple, Bangkok

Date	Mintage	F	VF	XF	Unc	BU
BE2551 (2008)	10,004,000	—	—	0.15	0.30	0.40
BE2552 (2009)	244,741,000	—	—	—	0.20	0.25
BE2553 (2010)	137,228,000	—	—	—	0.20	0.25
BE2554 (2011)	—	—	—	—	0.20	0.25
BE2555 (2012)	—	—	—	—	0.20	0.25

Y# 219 5 BAHT

7.5000 g., Copper-Nickel Clad Copper, 24 mm. **Ruler:** Rama IX **Obv:** Head left **Rev:** Benchamabophit Temple, Bangkok **Edge:** Coarse reeding

Date	Mintage	F	VF	XF	Unc	BU
BE2544 (2001)	76,566,000	—	—	—	0.50	0.75
BE2545 (2002)	29,601,500	—	—	—	0.75	1.00
BE2546 (2003)	182,000	3.00	5.00	8.00	15.00	20.00
BE2547 (2004)	120,187,000	—	—	—	0.50	0.75
BE2548 (2005)	91,079,000	—	—	—	0.50	0.75
BE2549 (2006)	254,403,000	—	—	—	0.50	0.75
BE2550 (2007) dj	131,126,000	—	—	—	0.50	0.75
BE2551 (2008)	220,463,200	—	—	—	0.50	0.75

Y# 446 5 BAHT

6.0000 g., Copper-Nickel Clad Copper, 24 mm. **Ruler:** Rama IX **Obv:** King's portrait **Rev:** Benchamabophit Temp, Bangkok, Temple top does not break legend **Edge:** Coarse Reeding

Date	Mintage	F	VF	XF	Unc	BU
BE2551 (2008)	6,225,000	—	—	—	0.75	1.00
BE2552 (2009)	308,283,000	—	—	—	0.50	0.75
BE2553 (2010)	2,903,000	—	—	—	1.00	1.25
BE2554 (2011)	—	—	—	—	0.50	0.75
BE2555 (2012)	—	—	—	—	0.50	0.75

Y# 373 10 BAHT

8.5000 g., Bi-Metallic Aluminum-Bronze center in Copper-Nickel ring, 26 mm. **Ruler:** Rama IX **Subject:** Department of Lands, 100th Anniversary, February 17 **Obv:** Conjoined busts facing divides circle **Rev:** Department seal within circle **Edge:** Segmented reeding

Date	Mintage	F	VF	XF	Unc	BU
BE2544 (2001)	3,000,000	—	—	1.00	2.50	3.00

Y# 227 10 BAHT

8.5000 g., Bi-Metallic Aluminum-Bronze center in Copper-Nickel ring, 26 mm. **Ruler:** Rama IX **Obv:** Head left within circle **Rev:** Arun Temple (Temple of the Dawn), Bankok **Edge:** Segmented reeding **Note:** Varieties exist.

Date	Mintage	F	VF	XF	Unc	BU
BE2544 (2001)	2,060,000	—	0.75	2.00	5.00	6.00
BE2545 (2002)	61,333,000	—	—	—	2.25	2.75
BE2546 (2003)	49,292,000	—	—	—	2.25	2.75
BE2547 (2004)	62,689,000	—	—	—	2.25	2.50
BE2548 (2005)	111,491,000	—	—	—	2.00	2.50
BE2549 (2006) v	128,903,000	—	—	—	2.00	2.50
BE2550 (2007) v	130,202,000	—	—	—	2.00	2.50
BE2551 (2008)	179,165,360	—	—	—	2.00	2.50

Y# 387 10 BAHT

8.5000 g., Bi-Metallic Aluminum-Bronze center in Copper-Nickel ring, 26 mm. **Ruler:** Rama IX **Subject:** King's 75th Birthday, December 5 **Obv:** Head left **Rev:** Royal crown in radiant oval **Edge:** Segmented reeding

Date	Mintage	F	VF	XF	Unc	BU
BE2545 (2002)	7,500,000	—	—	1.00	2.00	2.75

Y# 381 10 BAHT

8.5000 g., Bi-Metallic Aluminum-Bronze center in Copper-Nickel ring, 26 mm. **Ruler:** Rama IX **Subject:** Irrigation Department, 100th Anniversary, June 13 **Obv:** Conjoined busts facing divides circle **Rev:** Department logo **Edge:** Segmented reeding

Date	Mintage	F	VF	XF	Unc	BU
BE2545 (2002)	3,000,000	—	—	1.00	2.00	2.75

Y# 382 10 BAHT

8.5000 g., Bi-Metallic Aluminum-Bronze center in Copper-Nickel ring, 26 mm. **Ruler:** Rama IX **Subject:** Department of Internal Trade, 60th Anniversary May 5 **Obv:** Head left **Rev:** Department logo **Edge:** Segmented reeding

Date	Mintage	F	VF	XF	Unc	BU
BE2545 (2002)	3,000,000	—	—	1.00	2.00	2.75

Y# 383 10 BAHT

8.5000 g., Bi-Metallic Aluminum-Bronze center in Copper-Nickel ring, 26 mm. **Ruler:** Rama IX **Subject:** Highway Department, 90th Anniversary, April 1 **Obv:** Conjoined busts facing divides circle **Rev:** Highway Department logo **Edge:** Segmented reeding

Date	Mintage	F	VF	XF	Unc	BU
BE2545 (2002)	3,000,000	—	—	1.00	2.00	2.75

Y# 384 10 BAHT

8.5000 g., Bi-Metallic Aluminum-Bronze center in Copper-Nickel ring, 26 mm. **Ruler:** Rama IX **Subject:** Vajira Medical Center, 90th Anniversary, January 2 **Obv:** Conjoined busts facing divides circle **Rev:** Hospital logo **Edge:** Segmented reeding

Date	Mintage	F	VF	XF	Unc	BU
BE2545 (2002)	3,500,000	—	—	1.00	2.00	2.75

Y# 385 10 BAHT

8.5000 g., Bi-Metallic Aluminum-Bronze center in Copper-Nickel ring, 26 mm. **Ruler:** Rama IX **Subject:** 20th World Scouting Jamboree **Obv:** Rama IX wearing a scouting uniform **Rev:** Jamboree log **Edge:** Segmented reeding

Date	Mintage	F	VF	XF	Unc	BU
BE2546 (2003)	3,000,000	—	—	1.00	2.00	2.75

Y# 405 10 BAHT

8.5000 g., Bi-Metallic Aluminum-Bronze center in Copper-Nickel ring, 26 mm. **Ruler:** Rama IX **Subject:** CITES World Meeting **Obv:** Bust 3/4 left within circle **Rev:** CITES logo **Edge:** Segmented reeding

Date	Mintage	F	VF	XF	Unc	BU
ND(2003)	Est. 3,000,000	—	—	1.00	2.00	2.75

Y# 400 10 BAHT

8.5000 g., Bi-Metallic Aluminum-Bronze center in Copper-Nickel ring, 26 mm. **Ruler:** Rama IX **Subject:** APEC 2003 Summit **Obv:** Head left **Rev:** APEC logo **Edge:** Segmented reeding

Date	Mintage	F	VF	XF	Unc	BU
BE2546-2003	1,000,000	—	—	1.00	2.25	3.00

Y# 409 10 BAHT

8.5000 g., Bi-Metallic Aluminum-Bronze center in Copper-Nickel ring, 26 mm. **Ruler:** Rama IX **Subject:** King Rama V, 150th Anniversary **Obv:** Bust of Rama V left **Rev:** Royal crown **Edge:** Segmented reeding

Date	Mintage	F	VF	XF	Unc	BU
BE2546 (2003)	3,600,000	—	—	1.00	1.80	2.50

Y# 391 10 BAHT

8.5000 g., Bi-Metallic Aluminum-Bronze center in Copper-Nickel ring, 26 mm. **Ruler:** Rama IX **Subject:** Inspector General's Department, 100th Anniversary, May 6 **Obv:** Head left within circle **Rev:** Department seal within circle and design **Edge:** Segmented reeding

Date	Mintage	F	VF	XF	Unc	BU
BE2546 (2003)	3,000,000	—	—	1.00	1.75	2.50

Y# 392 10 BAHT

8.5000 g., Bi-Metallic Aluminum-Bronze center in Copper-Nickel ring, 26 mm. **Ruler:** Rama IX **Subject:** Princess Galaniwattana, 80th Birthday, May 6 **Obv:** Bust 1/4 right **Rev:** Crowned emblem and value **Edge:** Alternating reeded and plain **Note:** This is the king's sister.

Date	Mintage	F	VF	XF	Unc	BU
BE2546 (2003)	2,000,000	—	—	1.00	1.75	2.50

Y# 396 10 BAHT

8.5000 g., Bi-Metallic Aluminum-Bronze center in Copper-Nickel ring, 26 mm. **Ruler:** Rama IX **Subject:** Government Savings Bank, 90th Anniversary, April 1 **Obv:** Uniformed bust facing within circle **Rev:** Bank emblem **Edge:** Segmented reeding

Date	Mintage	F	VF	XF	Unc	BU
BE2546 (2003)	2,000,000	—	—	1.00	2.00	2.75

Y# 411 10 BAHT

8.5000 g., Bi-Metallic Aluminum-Bronze center in Copper-Nickel ring, 26 mm. **Ruler:** Rama IX **Subject:** Royal Institute Board, 70th Anniversary **Obv:** 1/2 length civilian busts of 2 kings facing **Rev:** Royal Scholar Institute seal **Edge:** Segmented reeding

Date	Mintage	F	VF	XF	Unc	BU
BE2547 (2004)	2,000,000	—	—	1.00	1.80	2.50

Y# 412 10 BAHT

8.5000 g., Bi-Metallic Aluminum-Bronze center in Copper-Nickel ring, 26 mm. **Ruler:** Rama IX **Subject:** Queen's 72nd Birthday **Obv:** Bust of queen facing 3/4 left **Rev:** Royal seal **Edge:** Segmented reeding

Date	Mintage	F	VF	XF	Unc	BU
BE2547 (2004)	6,000,000	—	—	1.00	1.80	2.50

Y# 413 10 BAHT

8.5000 g., Bi-Metallic Aluminum-Bronze center in Copper-Nickel ring, 26 mm. **Ruler:** Rama IX **Subject:** IUCN World Conservation Congress **Obv:** Civilian bust 3/4 right **Rev:** IUCN logo **Edge:** Segmented reeding

Date	Mintage	F	VF	XF	Unc	BU
BE2547 (2004)	Est. 3,000,000	—	—	1.00	1.80	2.50

Y# 414 10 BAHT

8.5000 g., Bi-Metallic Aluminum-Bronze center in Copper-Nickel ring, 26 mm. **Ruler:** Rama IX **Subject:** Anti Drug Campaign **Obv:** Civilian bust left **Rev:** Tear drop shaped logo **Edge:** Segmented reeding

Date	Mintage	F	VF	XF	Unc	BU
BE2546 (2004)	3,000,000	—	—	—	1.80	2.50

Y# 415 10 BAHT

8.5000 g., Bi-Metallic Aluminum-Bronze center in Copper-Nickel ring, 26 mm. **Ruler:** Rama IX **Subject:** King Rama IV, 200th Anniversary **Obv:** Bust of Rama IV 3/4 right **Rev:** Royal seal **Edge:** Segmented reeding

Date	Mintage	F	VF	XF	Unc	BU
BE2547 (2004)	3,500,000	—	—	1.00	1.80	2.50

Y# 410 10 BAHT

8.5000 g., Bi-Metallic Aluminum-Bronze center in Copper-Nickel ring, 26 mm. **Subject:** Thammasat University, 70th Anniversary **Obv:** Civilian bust 3/4 left **Rev:** Thammasat University seal **Edge:** Segmented reeding

Date	Mintage	F	VF	XF	Unc	BU
BE2547 (2004)	3,000,000	—	—	1.00	1.80	2.50

Y# 416 10 BAHT

8.5000 g., Bi-Metallic Aluminum-Bronze center in Copper-Nickel ring, 26 mm. **Ruler:** Rama IX **Subject:** Army Transportation Corp, 100th Anniversary **Obv:** 2 King's military busts left **Rev:** Steering wheel, badge at center **Edge:** Segmented reeding

Date	Mintage	F	VF	XF	Unc	BU
BE2548 (2005)	3,000,000	—	—	1.00	1.80	2.50

Y# 402 10 BAHT

8.5000 g., Bi-Metallic Aluminum-Bronze center in Copper-Nickel ring, 26 mm. **Ruler:** Rama IX **Subject:** Department of the Treasury, 72nd Anniversary **Obv:** Bust 1/4 left within circle **Rev:** Treasury Department seal within circle **Edge:** Segmented reeding

Date	Mintage	F	VF	XF	Unc	BU
BE2548 (2005)	3,000,000	—	—	1.00	2.50	3.25

Y# 418 10 BAHT
8.5000 g., Bi-Metallic Aluminum-Bronze center in Copper-Nickel ring, 26 mm. **Ruler:** Rama IX **Subject:** 25th Asia-Pacific Scout Jamboree **Obv:** Rama IX in scout uniform 3/4 left **Rev:** Logo **Edge:** Segmented reeding

Date	Mintage	F	VF	XF	Unc	BU
BE2548 (2005)	3,000,000	—	—	1.00	1.80	2.50

Y# 424 10 BAHT
8.5000 g., Bi-Metallic Aluminum-Bronze center in Copper-Nickel ring, 26 mm. **Ruler:** Rama IX **Subject:** Prince Jaturon Ratsamee, 150th Anniversary of Birth **Obv:** Bust of Prince facing 3/4 right **Rev:** Radiant badge **Edge:** Segmented reeding

Date	Mintage	F	VF	XF	Unc	BU
BE2549(2006)	—	—	—	1.00	2.50	3.25

Y# 417 10 BAHT
8.5000 g., Bi-Metallic Aluminum-Bronze center in Copper-Nickel ring, 26 mm. **Ruler:** Rama IX **Subject:** Princess's Royal Cradle Ceremony **Obv:** Princess's baby head 3/4 left **Rev:** 4-line inscription **Edge:** Segmented reeding

Date	Mintage	F	VF	XF	Unc	BU
BE2548 (2006)	3,000,000	—	—	1.00	1.80	2.50

Y# 406 10 BAHT
8.5000 g., Bi-Metallic Aluminum-Bronze center in Copper-Nickel ring, 26 mm. **Ruler:** Rama IX **Subject:** 60th Anniversary of Reign **Obv:** Bust 1/4 left within circle **Rev:** Royal Crown on display **Edge:** Segmented reeding

Date	Mintage	F	VF	XF	Unc	BU
BE2549 (2006)	16,000,000	—	—	1.00	2.50	3.25

Y# 428 10 BAHT
8.5000 g., Bi-Metallic Aluminum-Bronze center in Copper-Nickel ring, 26 mm. **Ruler:** Rama IX **Subject:** Secretariat of the Cabinet, 72nd Anniversary **Obv:** Military bust 3/4 right **Rev:** Royal Cabinet seal **Edge:** Segmented reeding **Note:** Minted in 2005 but released in 2006.

Date	Mintage	F	VF	XF	Unc	BU
BE2547 (2004)	Est. 3,000,000	—	—	1.00	1.80	2.50

Y# 429 10 BAHT
8.5000 g., Bi-Metallic Aluminum-Bronze center in Copper-Nickel ring, 26 mm. **Ruler:** Rama IX **Subject:** Princess Petcharat, 80th Birthday **Obv:** Bust of Princess facing **Rev:** Royal seal of Princess **Edge:** Segmented reeding

Date	Mintage	F	VF	XF	Unc	BU
BE2548 (2006)	1,000,000	—	—	1.25	2.25	2.75

Y# 430 10 BAHT
8.5000 g., Bi-Metallic Aluminum-Bronze center in Copper-Nickel ring, 26 mm. **Ruler:** Rama IX **Subject:** Budget Inspection Department, 130th Anniversary **Obv:** Conjoined kings' busts left **Rev:** Ornate scale **Edge:** Segmented reeding

Date	Mintage	F	VF	XF	Unc	BU
BE2548 (2006)	Est. 3,000,000	—	—	1.00	1.80	2.50

Y# 431 10 BAHT
8.5000 g., Bi-Metallic Aluminum-Bronze center in Copper-Nickel ring, 26 mm. **Ruler:** Rama IX **Subject:** 60th Anniversary of Reign **Obv:** Bust 3/4 right **Rev:** Royal throne **Edge:** Segmented reeding

Date	Mintage	F	VF	XF	Unc	BU
BE2549 (2006)	16,000,000	—	—	1.00	1.80	2.50

Y# 432 10 BAHT
8.5000 g., Bi-Metallic Aluminum-Bronze center in Copper-Nickel ring, 26 mm. **Ruler:** Rama IX **Subject:** Department of Judge Advocate General, 100th Anniversary **Obv:** Conjoined kings' busts left **Rev:** Military emblem with scales of justice in background **Edge:** Segmented reeding

Date	Mintage	F	VF	XF	Unc	BU
BE2549 (2006)	3,000,000	—	—	1.00	1.80	2.50

Y# 425 10 BAHT
8.5000 g., Bi-Metallic Aluminum-Bronze center in Copper-Nickel ring, 26 mm. **Ruler:** Rama IX **Subject:** Royal Calvary Division, 100th Anniversary **Obv:** Conjoined kings' busts left **Rev:** Royal crown above emblem **Edge:** Segmented reeding

Date	Mintage	F	VF	XF	Unc	BU
BE2550 (2007)	3,000,000	—	—	1.00	1.75	2.50

Y# 426 10 BAHT
8.5000 g., Bi-Metallic Aluminum-Bronze center in Copper-Nickel ring, 26 mm. **Ruler:** Rama IX **Subject:** 1st Thai Commercial Bank, 100th Anniversary **Obv:** Conjoined kings' busts left **Rev:** Garuda Bird **Edge:** Segmented reeding

Date	Mintage	F	VF	XF	Unc	BU
BE2550 (2007)	5,000,000	—	—	1.00	1.75	2.50

Y# 433 10 BAHT
8.5000 g., Bi-Metallic Aluminum-Bronze center in Copper-Nickel ring, 26 mm. **Ruler:** Rama IX **Subject:** Queen's WHO Food Safety Award **Obv:** Queen's bust 3/4 right **Rev:** WHO emblem at upper left of inscription in sprays **Edge:** Segmented reeding

Date	Mintage	F	VF	XF	Unc	BU
BE2550 (2007)	5,000,000	—	—	1.00	1.75	2.50

Y# 434 10 BAHT
8.5000 g., Bi-Metallic Aluminum-Bronze center in Copper-Nickel ring, 26 mm. **Ruler:** Rama IX **Subject:** Medical Technology Department, 50th Anniversary **Obv:** Robed bust 3/4 right **Rev:** Oval medical seal **Edge:** Segmented reeding

Date	Mintage	F	VF	XF	Unc	BU
BE2550 (2007)	3,000,000	—	—	1.00	1.75	2.50

Y# 435 10 BAHT
8.5000 g., Bi-Metallic Aluminum-Bronze center in Copper-Nickel ring, 26 mm. **Ruler:** Rama IX **Subject:** UNIVERSIADE 2007 - World University Games **Obv:** Civilian bust 3/4 right **Rev:** Games logo **Edge:** Segmented reeding

Date	Mintage	F	VF	XF	Unc	BU
BE2550 (2007)	5,000,000	—	—	1.00	1.75	2.50

Y# 436 10 BAHT
8.5000 g., Bi-Metallic Aluminum-Bronze center in Copper-Nickel ring, 26 mm. **Ruler:** Rama IX **Subject:** Queen's 75th birthday **Obv:** Bust of Queen wearing tiara 3/4 left **Rev:** Queen's Royal seal **Edge:** Segmented reeding

Date	Mintage	F	VF	XF	Unc	BU
BE2550 (2007)	7,500,000	—	—	1.00	1.75	2.50

Y# 437 10 BAHT
8.5000 g., Bi-Metallic Aluminum-Bronze center in Copper-Nickel ring, 26 mm. **Ruler:** Rama IX **Subject:** IAAJS Conference - Bangkok **Obv:** Civilian bust 3/4 left **Rev:** Oval seal with scale above conference logo **Edge:** Segmented reeding

Date	Mintage	F	VF	XF	Unc	BU
BE2550 (2007)	3,000,000	—	—	1.00	1.75	2.50

Y# 438 10 BAHT

8.5000 g., Bi-Metallic Aluminum-Bronze center in Copper-Nickel ring, 26 mm. **Ruler:** Rama IX **Subject:** King's 80th birthday **Obv:** Royal bust 3/4 left **Rev:** Royal seal **Edge:** Segmented reeding

Date	Mintage	F	VF	XF	Unc	BU
BE2550 (2007)	18,000,000	—	—	1.00	1.75	2.50

Y# 439 10 BAHT

8.5000 g., Bi-Metallic Aluminum-Bronze center in Copper-Nickel ring, 26 mm. **Ruler:** Rama IX **Subject:** 24th SEA Games **Obv:** Civilian bust 3/4 left **Rev:** Games logo above inscription **Edge:** Segmented reeding

Date	Mintage	F	VF	XF	Unc	BU
BE2550 (2007)	3,000,000	—	—	1.00	1.75	2.50

Y# 440 10 BAHT

8.5000 g., Bi-Metallic Aluminum-Bronze center in Copper-Nickel ring, 26 mm. **Ruler:** Rama IX **Subject:** Siriraj Hospital, 120th Anniversary **Obv:** Conjoined kings' busts right **Rev:** Royal hospital's seal **Edge:** Segmented reeding

Date	Mintage	F	VF	XF	Unc	BU
BE2550 (2007)	3,000,000	—	—	1.00	1.75	2.50

Y# 459 10 BAHT

8.5000 g., Bi-Metallic Aluminum-Bronze center in Copper-Nickel ring, 26 mm. **Ruler:** Rama IX **Obv:** Head left **Rev:** Arun Temple (Temple of the Dawn), Bangkok

Date	Mintage	F	VF	XF	Unc	BU
BE2551 (2008)	18,450,000	—	—	—	2.00	2.75
BE2552 (2009)	59,107,733	—	—	—	2.00	2.75
BE2553 (2010)	1,953,000	—	—	—	2.00	2.75
BE2554 (2011)	—	—	—	—	2.00	2.75
BE2555 (2012)	—	—	—	—	2.00	2.75

Y# 460 10 BAHT

8.5000 g., Bi-Metallic Aluminum-Bronze center in Copper-Nickel ring, 26 mm. **Ruler:** Rama IX **Subject:** Thai Postal Service, 125th Anniversary **Obv:** Conjoined busts left **Rev:** Scroll with legend **Edge:** Segmented Reeding

Date	Mintage	F	VF	XF	Unc	BU
BE2551 (2008)	3,000,000	—	—	1.00	2.00	2.75

Y# 461 10 BAHT

8.5000 g., Bi-Metallic Aluminum-Bronze center in Copper-Nickel ring, 26 mm. **Ruler:** Rama IX **Subject:** National Research Council, 50th Anniversary **Obv:** Bust left **Rev:** Nucleus surrounded by electrons **Edge:** Segmented Reeding

Date	Mintage	F	VF	XF	Unc	BU
BE2552 (2009)	3,000,000	—	—	—	2.00	2.75

Y# 497 10 BAHT

Bi-Metallic Aluminum-bronze center in Copper-nickel ring, 26 mm. **Ruler:** Rama IX **Subject:** 120th Anniversary of the Department of Finance **Obv:** Conjoined heads facing left **Rev:** Seal of the Department of Finance (bird), inscription, value and date **Edge:** Segmented reeding

Date	Mintage	F	VF	XF	Unc	BU
BE2553 (2010)	1,000,000	—	—	—	2.00	2.50

Y# 498 10 BAHT

Bi-Metallic Aluminum bronze center in copper-nickel ring, 26 mm. **Ruler:** Rama IX **Subject:** 60th Anniversary of the Office of National Economic and Social Development **Obv:** Head of King Rama IX facing 1/4 right and inscriptions **Rev:** Seal of the Office of National Economic and Social Development (statue of three people), inscription, value and date

Date	Mintage	F	VF	XF	Unc	BU
BE2553 (2010)	—	—	—	—	2.00	2.50

Y# 504 10 BAHT

8.5000 g., Bi-Metallic Aluminum-Bronze center in Copper-Nickel ring, 26 mm. **Ruler:** Rama IX **Subject:** Princess Bejaratana, 84th Birthday **Rev:** Emblem

Date	Mintage	F	VF	XF	Unc	BU
BE2553 (2010)	—	—	—	—	2.00	2.75

Y# 374 20 BAHT

15.0000 g., Copper-Nickel, 32 mm. **Ruler:** Rama IX **Subject:** Chulalongkorn University 84th Anniversary March 26 **Obv:** Three conjoined busts right **Rev:** University emblem divides value **Edge:** Reeded

Date	Mintage	F	VF	XF	Unc	BU
BE2544 (2001)	800,040	—	—	2.00	3.50	5.00
BE2544 (2001) Proof	5,340	Value: 22.00				

Y# 375 20 BAHT

15.0000 g., Copper-Nickel, 32 mm. **Ruler:** Rama IX **Subject:** Civil Service Comission 72nd Anniversary April 1 **Obv:** Conjoined busts left **Rev:** Civil service emblem divides value **Edge:** Reeded

Date	Mintage	F	VF	XF	Unc	BU
BE2544 (2001)	500,000	—	—	2.00	3.50	5.00
BE2544 (2001) Proof	3,340	Value: 25.00				

Y# 393 20 BAHT

15.0000 g., Copper-Nickel, 32 mm. **Ruler:** Rama IX **Subject:** 80th Birthday of Princess Calyani Vadhani **Obv:** Bust 1/4 right **Rev:** Crowned emblem and value **Edge:** Reeded

Date	Mintage	F	VF	XF	Unc	BU
BE2546 (2003)	350,000	—	—	2.00	3.50	5.00
BE2546 (2003) Proof	3,200	Value: 17.50				

Y# 419 20 BAHT

15.0000 g., Copper-Nickel, 32 mm. **Ruler:** Rama IX **Subject:** 50th Anniversary of Audit Department of Cooperatives **Edge:** Reeded

Date	Mintage	F	VF	XF	Unc	BU
BE2545 (2002)	300,000	—	—	2.00	3.50	5.00
BE2545 (2002) Proof	3,000	Value: 17.50				

Y# 386 20 BAHT

15.0000 g., Copper-Nickel, 32 mm. **Ruler:** Rama IX **Subject:** Centennial of Thai Banknotes 2445-2545 **Obv:** Conjoined busts left **Rev:** Coat of arms in center of seal **Edge:** Reeded

Date	Mintage	F	VF	XF	Unc	BU
BE2545 (2002)	1,000,000	—	—	2.00	3.50	5.00
BE2545 (2002) Proof	40,000	Value: 17.50				

Y# 397 20 BAHT

15.0000 g., Copper-Nickel, 32 mm. **Ruler:** Rama IX **Subject:** Centennial of the National Police April 19 **Obv:** Conjoined busts left **Rev:** National Police emblem above banner **Edge:** Reeded

Date	Mintage	F	VF	XF	Unc	BU
BE2545 (2002)	600,000	—	—	2.00	3.50	5.00
BE2545 (2002) Proof	5,000	Value: 17.50				

Y# 398 20 BAHT

15.0000 g., Copper-Nickel, 32 mm. **Ruler:** Rama IX **Subject:** 50th Birthday of the Crown Prince July 28 **Obv:** Bust facing **Rev:** Crowned monogram **Edge:** Reeded

Date	Mintage	F	VF	XF	Unc	BU
BE2545 (2002)	300,000	—	—	2.00	3.50	5.00
BE2545 (2002) Proof	5,000	Value: 40.00				

Y# 388 20 BAHT

15.0000 g., Copper-Nickel, 32 mm. **Ruler:** Rama IX **Subject:** King's 75th Birthday December 5 **Obv:** Head left **Rev:** Royal crown in radiant oval **Edge:** Reeded **Note:** Minted and released in 2003.

Date	Mintage	F	VF	XF	Unc	BU
BE2545(2002)	1,200,000	—	—	2.00	3.50	5.00
BE2545(2002) Proof	16,000	Value: 17.50				

Y# 420 20 BAHT

15.0000 g., Copper-Nickel, 32 mm. **Ruler:** Rama IX **Subject:** 150th Anniversary, Birth of Rama V **Edge:** Reeded

Date	Mintage	F	VF	XF	Unc	BU
BE2546 (2003)	1,000,000	—	—	2.00	3.50	5.00
BE2546 (2003) Proof	26,000	Value: 18.00				

Y# 421 20 BAHT

15.0000 g., Copper-Nickel, 32 mm. **Ruler:** Rama IX **Subject:** Rama IV, 200th Anniversary of Birth **Obv:** King Rama IV **Edge:** Reeded

Date	Mintage	F	VF	XF	Unc	BU
BE2547 (2004)	500,000	—	—	2.00	3.50	5.00
BE2547 (2004) Proof	10,500	Value: 20.00				

Y# 422 20 BAHT

15.0000 g., Copper-Nickel, 32 mm. **Ruler:** Rama IX **Subject:** 72nd Anniversary of Queen's Birthday **Obv:** Head of Queen facing left **Edge:** Reeded

Date	Mintage	F	VF	XF	Unc	BU
BE2547 (2004)	600,000	—	—	2.00	3.50	5.00
BE2547 (2004) Proof	10,000	Value: 20.00				

Y# 462 20 BAHT

15.0000 g., Copper-Nickel, 32 mm. **Ruler:** Rama IX **Subject:** Rama IV, 200th Anniversary of Birth **Obv:** Bust 3/4 right **Rev:** Horizontal oval Royal seal **Edge:** Reeded

Date	Mintage	F	VF	XF	Unc	BU
BE2547 (2004)	500,000	—	—	2.00	4.00	6.00
BE2547 (2004) Proof	10,500	Value: 15.00				

Y# 423 20 BAHT

15.0000 g., Copper-Nickel, 32 mm. **Ruler:** Rama IX **Subject:** 50th Birthday of Princess Sirinahorn **Obv:** Head of Princess facing right **Edge:** Reeded

Date	Mintage	F	VF	XF	Unc	BU
BE2548 (2005)	650,000	—	—	2.00	4.00	6.00
BE2548 (2005) Proof	12,000	Value: 20.00				

Y# 403 20 BAHT

15.0000 g., Copper-Nickel, 32 mm. **Ruler:** Rama IX **Subject:** Department of the Treasury, 72nd Anniversary **Obv:** Bust 1/4 left **Rev:** Treasury Department seal **Edge:** Reeded

Date	Mintage	F	VF	XF	Unc	BU
BE2548 (2005)	300,000	—	—	2.00	4.00	6.00
BE2548 (2005) Proof	3,000	Value: 25.00				

Y# 471 20 BAHT

15.0000 g., Copper-Nickel, 32 mm. **Ruler:** Rama IX **Subject:** Centennial of the National Library **Obv:** Two busts, one facing left, one right **Rev:** Circle with inscription **Edge:** Reeded

Date	Mintage	F	VF	XF	Unc	BU
BE2548 (2005)	Est. 200,000	—	—	2.00	3.50	5.00

Y# 472 20 BAHT

15.0000 g., Copper-Nickel, 32 mm. **Ruler:** Rama IX **Subject:** Princess Rattana, 80th birthday **Obv:** Front facing portrait **Edge:** Reeded **Note:** Minted and released in 2006.

Date	Mintage	F	VF	XF	Unc	BU
BE2548 (2005)	200,000	—	—	2.00	3.50	5.00

Y# 474 20 BAHT

15.0000 g., Copper-Nickel, 32 mm. **Ruler:** Rama IX **Subject:** UN Development Program Award **Obv:** Head right **Rev:** Chalice on stand with legends **Edge:** Reeded

Date	Mintage	F	VF	XF	Unc	BU
BE2549 (2006)	2,200,000	—	—	2.00	3.50	5.00

Y# 407 20 BAHT

15.0000 g., Copper-Nickel, 32 mm. **Ruler:** Rama IX **Subject:** 60th Anniversary of Reign **Obv:** Head left **Rev:** Royal Crown on display **Edge:** Reeded

Date	Mintage	F	VF	XF	Unc	BU
BE2549 (2006)	5,600,000	—	—	2.00	4.00	6.00
BE2549 (2006) Proof	96,000	Value: 18.50				

Y# 473 20 BAHT

15.0000 g., Copper-Nickel, 32 mm. **Ruler:** Rama IX **Subject:** Royal Artificial Rain, 50th Anniversary **Obv:** Statue of King holding book and pencil **Rev:** Artificial rain wing symbol surrounded by rays and legend **Edge:** Reeded

Date	Mintage	F	VF	XF	Unc	BU
BE2549 (2006)	3,000,000	—	—	2.00	3.50	5.00

Y# 450 20 BAHT

15.0000 g., Copper-Nickel, 32 mm. **Ruler:** Rama IX **Subject:** King's 80th Birthday **Obv:** Bust left **Edge:** Reeded

Date	Mintage	F	VF	XF	Unc	BU
BE 2550 (2007)	5,800,000	—	—	2.00	3.50	5.00
BE 2550 (2007) Proof	95,000	Value: 15.00				

Y# 453 20 BAHT

15.0000 g., Copper-Nickel **Ruler:** Rama IX **Subject:** Queen's 75th Birthday **Obv:** Bust left **Edge:** Reeded **Shape:** 32

Date	Mintage	F	VF	XF	Unc	BU
BE 2550 (2007)	600,000	—	—	2.00	3.50	5.00
BE 2550 (2007) Proof	12,000	Value: 18.00				

Y# 475 20 BAHT

15.0000 g., Copper-Nickel, 32 mm. **Ruler:** Rama IX **Subject:** Princess Galyana Vadhana, 84th birthday **Obv:** Head left **Edge:** Reeded

Date	Mintage	F	VF	XF	Unc	BU
BE2550 (2007)	700,000	—	—	2.00	3.50	5.00
BE2550 (2007) Proof	8,400	Value: 18.00				

Y# 476 20 BAHT

15.0000 g., Copper-Nickel, 32 mm. **Ruler:** Rama IX **Subject:** Father of Thai heritage conservation **Obv:** Head left **Edge:** Reeded **Note:** Minted and released in 2008.

Date	Mintage	F	VF	XF	Unc	BU
BE2550 (2007)	500,000	—	—	2.00	3.50	5.00

Y# 495 20 BAHT

15.0000 g., Copper-Nickel, 32 mm. **Ruler:** Rama IX **Subject:** King Rama I, Father of Thai Trade **Obv:** Bust facing front and inscription **Rev:** Symbol, inscription, value and date **Edge:** Reeded **Note:** Minted and issued in BE2553

Date	Mintage	F	VF	XF	Unc	BU
BE2553 (2008)	500,000	—	—	—	3.50	4.00

Y# 464 20 BAHT

15.0000 g., Copper-Nickel, 32 mm. **Ruler:** Rama IX **Subject:** Princess Mother, 9th Cycle (108th Anniversary of Birth) **Obv:** Portrait facing left **Rev:** Emblem of Princess Mother Srinakarindra

Date	Mintage	F	VF	XF	Unc	BU
BE2551 (2008)	450,000	—	—	2.00	3.50	5.00
BE2551 (2008) Proof	5,500	Value: 20.00				

Y# 477 20 BAHT

15.0000 g., Copper-Nickel, 32 mm. **Ruler:** Rama IX **Subject:** WIPO Award **Obv:** Head left **Rev:** Award medal and legend **Edge:** Reeded **Note:** Minted and released in 2010

Date	Mintage	F	VF	XF	Unc	BU
BE2551 (2008)	500,000	—	—	2.00	3.50	5.00

Y# 499 20 BAHT

15.0000 g., Copper-Nickel, 32 mm. **Ruler:** Rama IX **Subject:** 100th Anniversary of Indra College **Obv:** Conjoined busts facing left **Rev:** Symbol, inscription, value and date **Edge:** Reeded **Note:** Minted and issued in BE2553

Date	Mintage	F	VF	XF	Unc	BU
BE2553 (2010)	500,000	—	—	—	3.50	4.00

Y# 506 20 BAHT

15.0000 g., Copper-Nickel, 32 mm. **Ruler:** Rama IX **Subject:** Princess Bejaratana, 84th Birthday

Date	Mintage	F	VF	XF	Unc	BU
RS2553 (2010)	—	—	—	—	3.50	5.00

Y# 404 50 BAHT

21.0000 g., Copper-Nickel, 36 mm. **Ruler:** Rama IX **Subject:** Air Force 50th Anniversary May 7 **Obv:** Uniformed bust facing **Rev:** Crowned wings within 3/4 wreath **Edge:** Reeded

Date	Mintage	F	VF	XF	Unc	BU
BE2546 (2003)	250,000	—	—	4.00	12.50	15.00

Y# 478 50 BAHT

21.0000 g., Copper-Nickel, 36 mm. **Ruler:** Rama IX **Subject:** National Intelligence Agency, 50th Anniversary **Obv:** Head right **Rev:** Emblem of the National Intelligence Agency **Edge:** Reeded **Note:** Minted and released in 2003.

Date	Mintage	F	VF	XF	Unc	BU
BE2547 (2004)	200,000	—	—	3.50	4.50	6.00

Y# 493 50 BAHT

Copper-Nickel, 36 mm. **Ruler:** Rama IX **Obv:** Head of infant facing right **Rev:** Design including chick, inscription, value and date **Edge:** Reeded

Date	Mintage	F	VF	XF	Unc	BU
BE2549 (2006)	450,000	—	—	—	4.50	6.00

Y# 479 50 BAHT

21.0000 g., Copper-Nickel, 36 mm. **Ruler:** Rama IX **Subject:** Technological Research **Obv:** Child's head right **Rev:** Small chicken at left, legends **Edge:** Reeded

Date	Mintage	F	VF	XF	Unc	BU
BE2549 (2006)	450,000	—	—	3.50	4.50	6.00

Y# 480 50 BAHT

21.0000 g., Copper-Nickel, 36 mm. **Ruler:** Rama IX **Subject:** Naval Academy, 100th Anniversary **Obv:** Conjoined heads left **Rev:** Symbol, inscriptions, value and date **Edge:** Reeded

Date	Mintage	F	VF	XF	Unc	BU
BE2549 (2006)	200,000	—	—	3.50	4.50	6.00

Y# 500 50 BAHT

21.0000 g., Copper-Nickel, 36 mm. **Ruler:** Rama IX **Subject:** 150th Anniversary of Thai Mint **Obv:** Conjoined busts facing 1/2 right and inscription **Rev:** Complex design, inscription, value and date **Edge:** Reeded

Date	Mintage	F	VF	XF	Unc	BU
BE2553 (2010)	150,000	—	—	—	4.50	6.00

Y# 501 50 BAHT

21.0000 g., Copper-Nickel, 36 mm. **Ruler:** Rama IX **Subject:** King's Seventh Cycle Ceremony **Obv:** Head of King facing 1/2 left **Rev:** Symbol, inscription, value and date **Edge:** Reeded

Date	Mintage	F	VF	XF	Unc	BU
BE2554 (2011)	Est. 3,000,000	—	—	—	4.50	6.00

Y# 389 600 BAHT

22.0000 g., 0.9250 Silver 0.6542 oz. ASW, 35 mm. **Ruler:** Rama IX **Subject:** King's 75th Birthday **Obv:** King's portrait **Rev:** Royal crown in radiant oval **Edge:** Reeded

Date	Mintage	F	VF	XF	Unc	BU
BE2545 (2002)	14,000	—	—	25.00	30.00	35.00
BE2545 (2002) Proof	3,000	Value: 70.00				

Y# 481 600 BAHT

22.0000 g., 0.9250 Silver 0.6542 oz. ASW, 35 mm. **Ruler:** Rama IX **Subject:** Crown Prince, 50th Birthday **Obv:** Crown Prince bust 1/4 facing left **Rev:** Crowned monogram **Edge:** Reeded

Date	Mintage	F	VF	XF	Unc	BU
BE2545 (2002)	5,000	—	—	40.00	50.00	55.00
BE2545 (2002) Proof	1,000	Value: 95.00				

Y# 394 600 BAHT

22.0000 g., 0.9250 Silver 0.6542 oz. ASW, 35 mm. **Ruler:** Rama IX **Subject:** 80th Birthday of Princess Calgani Vedhana **Obv:** Bust half right **Rev:** Crowned emblem and value **Edge:** Reeded

Date	Mintage	F	VF	XF	Unc	BU
BE2546 (2003)	4,500	—	—	35.00	45.00	50.00
BE2546 (2003) Proof	1,000	Value: 95.00				

Y# 482 600 BAHT

22.0000 g., 0.9250 Silver 0.6542 oz. ASW, 35 mm. **Ruler:** Rama V. 150th Anniversary of Birth **Obv:** Rama V bust left **Rev:** Royal Crown **Edge:** Reeded

Date	Mintage	F	VF	XF	Unc	BU
BE2546 (2003)	15,000	—	—	30.00	35.00	40.00
BE2546 (2003) Proof	4,600	Value: 85.00				

Y# 401 600 BAHT

22.1500 g., 0.9250 Silver 0.6587 oz. ASW, 35 mm. **Ruler:** Rama IX **Subject:** Queen's 72nd Birthday **Obv:** Crowned monogram **Rev:** Crowned bust of Queen 3/4 right **Edge:** Reeded

Date	Mintage	F	VF	XF	Unc	BU
BE2547 (2004)	12,000	—	—	30.00	35.00	40.00
BE2547 (2004) Proof	3,700	Value: 85.00				

Y# 463 600 BAHT

22.0000 g., 0.9250 Silver 0.6542 oz. ASW, 35 mm. **Ruler:** Rama IX **Subject:** King Rama IV, 200th Anniversary of Birth **Obv:** Bust right **Rev:** Horizontal oval **Edge:** Reeded

Date	Mintage	F	VF	XF	Unc	BU
BE2547 (2004)	12,000	—	—	40.00	45.00	60.00
BE2547 (2004) Proof	3,000	Value: 95.00				

Y# 467 600 BAHT

22.1500 g., 0.9250 Silver 0.6587 oz. ASW, 35 mm. **Ruler:** Rama IX **Subject:** Princess Petcharat, 80th Birthday **Obv:** Bust facing **Rev:** Princess' emblem

Date	Mintage	F	VF	XF	Unc	BU
BE2548 (2005)	—	—	—	40.00	55.00	60.00
BE2548 (2005) Proof	—	Value: 120				

Y# 427 600 BAHT

22.1500 g., 0.9250 Silver 0.6587 oz. ASW, 35 mm. **Ruler:** Rama IX **Subject:** Princess Maha Chakri Sirindhorn's 50th Birthday **Obv:** Bust right **Rev:** Oval **Edge:** Reeded

Date	Mintage	F	VF	XF	Unc	BU
BE2548 (2005)	15,000	—	—	35.00	45.00	40.00
BE2548 (2005) Proof	4,000	Value: 85.00				

Y# 484 600 BAHT

22.0000 g., 0.9250 Silver 0.6542 oz. ASW, 35 mm. **Ruler:** Rama IX **Subject:** Princess Rattana, 80th birthday **Obv:** Bust facing of Princess **Note:** Minted and released in 2006.

Date	Mintage	F	VF	XF	Unc	BU
BE2548 (2005)	3,500	—	—	40.00	55.00	60.00

Y# 408 600 BAHT

22.1500 g., 0.9250 Silver 0.6587 oz. ASW, 35 mm. **Ruler:** Rama IX **Subject:** 60th Anniversary of Reign **Obv:** Rama IX **Rev:** Royal cypher **Edge:** Reeded

Date	Mintage	F	VF	XF	Unc	BU
BE2549 (2006)	66,000	—	—	30.00	35.00	40.00
BE2549 (2006) Proof with colored hologram	16,000	Value: 90.00				

Y# 485 600 BAHT

22.0000 g., 0.9250 Silver 0.6542 oz. ASW **Ruler:** Rama IX **Subject:** Prince Royal Cradle Ceremony **Obv:** Prince's baby head left **Rev:** Four line legend **Edge:** Reeded

Date	Mintage	F	VF	XF	Unc	BU
BE2549 (2006)	10,000	—	—	40.00	45.00	50.00
BE2549 (2006) Proof	3,700	Value: 85.00				

Y# 502 800 BAHT

22.0000 g., 0.9250 Silver 0.6542 oz. ASW, 35 mm. **Ruler:** Rama IX **Subject:** King's 84th Birthday **Obv:** Head facing 1/4 left and inscription **Rev:** Symbol, value, date and inscription **Edge:** Reeded

Date	Mintage	F	VF	XF	Unc	BU
BE2554 (2003) Proof	100,000	Value: 55.00				

Y# 447 800 BAHT

22.0000 g., 0.9900 Silver 0.7002 oz. ASW, 35 mm. **Ruler:** Rama IX **Obv:** Bust left **Rev:** WHO logo and legend

Date	Mintage	F	VF	XF	Unc	BU
2005	Est. 6,500	—	—	—	40.00	45.00
2005 Proof	Inc. above	Value: 100				

Y# 486 800 BAHT

33.0000 g., 0.9250 Silver 0.9814 oz. ASW, 35 mm. **Ruler:** Rama IX **Subject:** King's 84th Birthday **Obv:** Head of Queen Sirikit facing right **Rev:** WHO emblem and four line English inscription **Edge:** Reeded

Date	Mintage	F	VF	XF	Unc	BU
BE2550 (2007)	6,500	—	—	—	35.00	40.00

Y# 451 800 BAHT

22.0000 g., 0.9900 Silver 0.7002 oz. ASW, 35 mm. **Ruler:** Rama IX **Subject:** King's 80th Birthday **Obv:** Bust left **Edge:** Reeded

Date	Mintage	F	VF	XF	Unc	BU
BE 2550 (2007)	80,000	—	—	—	35.00	40.00
BE 2550 (2007) Proof	28,000	Value: 75.00				

Y# 454 800 BAHT

22.0000 g., 0.9250 Silver 0.6542 oz. ASW, 35 mm. **Ruler:** Rama IX **Subject:** Queen's 75th Birthday **Obv:** Queen's bust left **Rev:** Queen's Royal Seal **Edge:** Reeded

Date	Mintage	F	VF	XF	Unc	BU
BE 2550 (2007)	12,000	—	—	—	35.00	40.00
BE 2550 (2007) Proof	4,000	Value: 75.00				

Y# 466 800 BAHT

22.0000 g., 0.9250 Silver 0.6542 oz. ASW, 35 mm. **Ruler:** Rama IX **Subject:** Princess Galyani Vadhana, 84th Birthday **Obv:** Bust facing right **Rev:** Princess' emblem

Date	Mintage	F	VF	XF	Unc	BU
BE2550 (2007)	11,500	—	—	—	35.00	40.00
BE2550 (2007) Proof	1,500	Value: 95.00				

Y# 465 800 BAHT

22.0000 g., 0.9250 Silver 0.6542 oz. ASW, 35 mm. **Ruler:** Rama IX **Subject:** Princess Mother, 9th Cycle (108th Birthday) **Obv:** Bust facing **Rev:** Princess Mother's emblem **Edge:** Reeded

Date	Mintage	F	VF	XF	Unc	BU
BE2551 (2008)	11,200	—	—	—	35.00	40.00
BE2551 (2008) Proof	1,500	Value: 95.00				

Y# 468 800 BAHT

22.0000 g., 0.9900 Silver 0.7002 oz. ASW, 35 mm. **Ruler:** Rama IX **Subject:** King's WIPO leader award **Obv:** Bust left **Rev:** Award medal and legned **Note:** Minted and released in 2010.

Date	Mintage	F	VF	XF	Unc	BU
BE2551 (2008) Proof	15,000	Value: 75.00				

Y# 507 800 BAHT

22.0000 g., 0.9250 Silver 0.6542 oz. ASW, 35 mm. **Ruler:** Rama IX **Subject:** Princess Bejaratana, 84th Birthday

Date	Mintage	F	VF	XF	Unc	BU
BE2553 (2010)	—	—	—	—	30.00	40.00

Y# 469 900 BAHT

31.1050 g., 0.9990 Silver 0.9990 oz. ASW, 40.6 mm. **Ruler:** Rama IX **Subject:** UNDP Human Development Lifetime Achievement Award **Obv:** King facing in multicolor applique **Rev:** Award bowl **Edge:** Reeded

Date	Mintage	F	VF	XF	Unc	BU
BE2549 (2006) Proof	200,000	Value: 75.00				

Y# 390 7500 BAHT

15.0000 g., 0.9000 Gold 0.4340 oz. AGW, 26 mm. **Ruler:** Rama IX **Subject:** King's 75th Birthday **Obv:** King's portrait **Rev:** Royal crown in radiant oval **Edge:** Reeded

Date	Mintage	F	VF	XF	Unc	BU
BE2545(2002)	6,000	—	—	—	800	825
BE2545(2002) Proof	1,200	Value: 850				

Y# 395 9000 BAHT

15.0000 g., 0.9000 Gold 0.4340 oz. AGW, 26 mm. **Ruler:** Rama IX **Subject:** 72nd Birthday of Queen **Obv:** Bust half right **Rev:** Crowned emblem and value **Edge:** Reeded

Date	Mintage	F	VF	XF	Unc	BU
BE2546 (2004)	6,000	—	—	—	800	825
BE2546 (2004) Proof	1,600	Value: 850				

Y# 490 9000 BAHT

15.0000 g., 0.4340 Gold 0.2093 oz. AGW, 26 mm. **Ruler:** Rama IX **Subject:** 150th Aniversary of the Birth of Rama V **Obv:** Bust of Rama V facing left and inscription **Rev:** Three symbols, inscription, value and date **Edge:** Reeded

Date	Mintage	F	VF	XF	Unc	BU
BE2546 (2003)	5,000	—	—	—	800	825
BE2546 (2003) Proof	1,500	Value: 900				

Y# 491 9000 BAHT

15.0000 g., 0.9000 Gold 0.4340 oz. AGW, 26 mm. **Ruler:** Rama IX **Subject:** Queen Sirikit's 72nd Birthday **Obv:** Bust of Queen facing 1/4 left and inscription **Rev:** Symbol honoring Queen Sirikit, inscription, value and date **Edge:** Reeded

Date	Mintage	F	VF	XF	Unc	BU
BE2547 (2004)	6,000	—	—	—	800	825
BE2547 (2004) Proof	1,600	Value: 900				

Y# 492 9000 BAHT

15.0000 g., 0.9000 Gold 0.4340 oz. AGW, 26 mm. **Ruler:** Rama IX **Subject:** 200th Anniversary of the Birth of King Rama IV **Obv:** Bust of King Rama IV facing 3/4 right and inscription **Rev:** Horizontal oval royal seal, inscription, value and date **Edge:** Reeded

Date	Mintage	F	VF	XF	Unc	BU
BE2547 (2004)	3,000	—	—	—	800	825
BE2547 (2004)	1,000	Value: 900				

Y# 488 9000 BAHT

15.0000 g., 0.9000 Gold 0.4340 oz. AGW, 26 mm. **Ruler:** Rama IX **Subject:** WHO Food Safety Award to Queen Sirikit **Obv:** Bust of Queen Sirikit right **Rev:** WHO emblem and legend **Edge:** Reeded

Date	Mintage	F	VF	XF	Unc	BU
BE2550 (2007) Proof	2,800	Value: 850				

Y# 494 12,000 BAHT

15.0000 g., 0.9000 Gold 0.4340 oz. AGW, 26 mm. **Ruler:** Rama IX **Subject:** 60th Anniversary of Reign **Obv:** Framed head facing 1/4 right **Rev:** Symbol of 60th Anniversary of Reign, value and date **Edge:** Reeded

Date	Mintage	F	VF	XF	Unc	BU
BE2551 (2008)	16,000	—	—	—	800	825
BE2551 (2008) Proof	9,600	Value: 900				

Y# 448 16,000 BAHT

15.0000 g., 0.9000 Gold 0.4340 oz. AGW, 26 mm. **Ruler:** Rama IX **Obv:** Bust of Queen Sirikit, right **Rev:** WHO logo and legend **Note:** Minted and issued in BE2550

Date	Mintage	F	VF	XF	Unc	BU
BE2585 (2005)	Est. 3,000	—	—	—	800	825
BE2548 (2005) Proof	Inc. above	Value: 850				

Y# 452 16,000 BAHT

15.0000 g., 0.9900 Gold 0.4774 oz. AGW, 26 mm. **Ruler:** Rama IX **Subject:** King's 80th Birthday **Obv:** Bust left **Rev:** Symbols, inscription, value and date **Edge:** Reeded

Date	Mintage	F	VF	XF	Unc	BU
BE2550 (2007)	16,800	—	—	—	870	900
BE2550 (2007) Proof	12,800	Value: 925				

Y# 455 16,000 BAHT

15.0000 g., 0.9000 Gold 0.4340 oz. AGW, 26 mm. **Ruler:** Rama IX **Subject:** Queen's 75th Birthday **Obv:** Bust left and inscription **Rev:** Symbol, inscription, value and date **Edge:** Reeded

Date	Mintage	F	VF	XF	Unc	BU
BE2550 (2007)	5,000	—	—	—	800	825
2550 (2007) Proof	2,000	Value: 850				

Y# 496 16,000 BAHT

15.0000 g., 0.9000 Gold 0.4340 oz. AGW, 26 mm. **Ruler:** Rama IX **Subject:** 108th Anniversary of the Birth of the Princess Mother **Obv:** Head of Princess Mother facing 1/4 left **Rev:** Symbol, inscription, value and date **Edge:** Reeded

Date	Mintage	F	VF	XF	Unc	BU
BE2551 (2008)	1,200	—	—	—	800	825
BE2551 (2008) Proof	400	Value: 1,000				

Y# 489 16,000 BAHT

15.0000 g., 0.9900 Gold 0.4774 oz. AGW, 26 mm. **Ruler:** Rama IX **Subject:** World Interlectural Propery Organization Award **Obv:** Head left **Rev:** Award Medal and legend **Edge:** Reeded **Note:** Minted and released in 2010.

Date	Mintage	F	VF	XF	Unc	BU
BE2551 (2008) Proof	2,000	Value: 875				

Y# 503 16,000 BAHT

15.0000 g., 0.9650 Gold 0.4654 oz. AGW, 26 mm. **Ruler:** Rama IX **Subject:** King's Seventh Cycle Ceremony **Obv:** Head of King facing 1/2 left **Rev:** Synmbol, inscription, value and date **Edge:** Reeded

Date	Mintage	F	VF	XF	Unc	BU
BE2554 (2011) Proof	Est. 25,000	Value: 1,000				

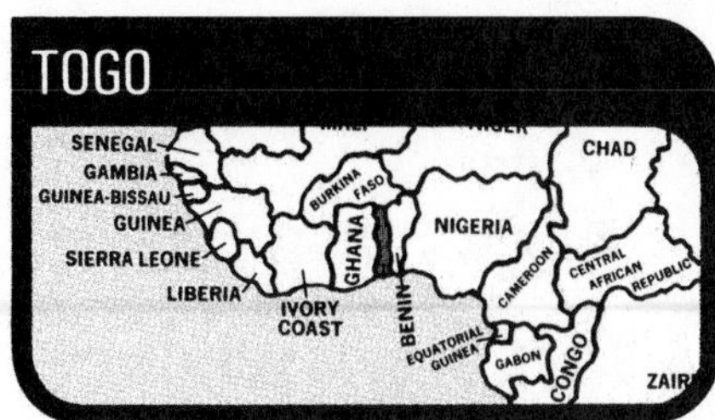

The Togolese Republic (formerly part of German Togoland), situated on the Gulf of Guinea in West Africa between Ghana and Benin, has an area of 21,622 sq. mi. (56,790 sq. km.) and a population of *3.4 million. Capital: Lome. Agriculture and herding, the production of dyewoods, and the mining of phosphates and iron ore are the chief industries. Copra, phosphates and coffee are exported.

MINT MARK

(a) - Paris, privy marks only

MONETARY SYSTEM

100 Centimes = 1 Franc

REPUBLIC

INSTITUT MONETAIRE STANDARD COINAGE

100 Centimes = 1 Franc

KM# 51 100 FRANCS

26.0000 g., Copper-Nickel, 38.6 mm. **Rev:** Blue sunbird, prism technology

Date	Mintage	F	VF	XF	Unc	BU
2010 Prooflike	2,500	—	—	—	—	25.00

KM# 52 100 FRANCS

26.0000 g., Copper-Nickel, 38.6 mm. **Rev:** Green bird, prism technology

Date	Mintage	F	VF	XF	Unc	BU
2010 Prooflike	2,500	—	—	—	—	25.00

KM# 53 100 FRANCS

26.0000 g., Copper-Nickel, 38.6 mm. **Rev:** Yellow bird, prism technology

Date	Mintage	F	VF	XF	Unc	BU
2010 Prooflike	2,500	—	—	—	—	25.00

KM# 62 100 FRANCS

Silver Plated Base Metal **Rev:** Prism lion standing left

Date	Mintage	F	VF	XF	Unc	BU
2011 Proof	5,000	Value: 40.00				

KM# 43 250 FRANCS

5.0000 g., 0.9990 Silver 0.1606 oz. ASW **Subject:** German President Horst Kohler **Obv:** National arms **Obv. Legend:** REPUBLIQUE TOGOLAISE **Rev:** Gilt figure

Date	Mintage	F	VF	XF	Unc	BU
2004 Proof	—	Value: 15.00				

KM# 29 500 FRANCS

7.0500 g., 0.9990 Silver 0.2264 oz. ASW, 30 mm. **Obv:** National arms above value **Rev:** Multicolor big cat **Edge:** Plain

Date	Mintage	F	VF	XF	Unc	BU
2001 Proof	—	Value: 35.00				

KM# 41 500 FRANCS

10.0000 g., 0.9990 Silver 0.3212 oz. ASW **Subject:** XVIII World Football Championship - Germany 2006 **Obv:** National arms **Obv. Legend:** REPUBLIQUE TOGOLAISE **Rev:** Two players, map of Germany in background

Date	Mintage	F	VF	XF	Unc	BU
2001 Proof	—	Value: 22.50				

KM# 60 500 FRANCS

15.0000 g., 0.9250 Silver 0.4461 oz. ASW, 30 mm. **Obv:** National arms **Rev:** Albrecht Durer portrait

Date	Mintage	F	VF	XF	Unc	BU
2003 Proof	—	Value: 25.00				

KM# 47 500 FRANCS

14.9700 g., 0.9250 Silver 0.4452 oz. ASW, 30 mm. **Obv:** Arms with supporters **Rev:** Full figures of Johann Wolfgang von Goethe and Friedrich von Schiller on pedestal facing

Date	Mintage	F	VF	XF	Unc	BU
2004 Proof	—	Value: 22.50				

KM# 44 500 FRANCS

7.0000 g., 0.9990 Silver 0.2248 oz. ASW **Subject:** German Chancellor Helmut Schmidt **Obv:** National arms **Obv. Legend:** REPUBLIQUE TOGOLAISE **Rev:** Gilt figue

Date	Mintage	F	VF	XF	Unc	BU
ND(2004) Proof	—	Value: 22.50				

KM# 65 500 FRANCS

15.5500 g., 0.9250 Silver 0.4624 oz. ASW, 35 mm. **Subject:** Greatest She-Warrior **Rev:** Zenobia standing, color ruins at left

Date	Mintage	F	VF	XF	Unc	BU
2011 Proof	1,000	Value: 65.00				

KM# 17 1000 FRANCS

14.9500 g., 0.9990 Silver 0.4802 oz. ASW, 35 mm. **Obv:** National arms **Obv. Legend:** REPUBLIQUE TOGOLAISE **Rev:** German sailing ship **Rev. Legend:** Adler von Lübeck **Edge:** Plain

Date	Mintage	F	VF	XF	Unc	BU
2001 Proof	—	Value: 50.00				

KM# 35 1000 FRANCS

14.7000 g., 0.9990 Silver 0.4721 oz. ASW, 36 mm. **Subject:** World Cup Soccer - Bern 1954 **Obv:** National arms **Rev:** Bust facing and tower **Edge:** Plain

Date	Mintage	F	VF	XF	Unc	BU
2001 Proof	—	Value: 40.00				

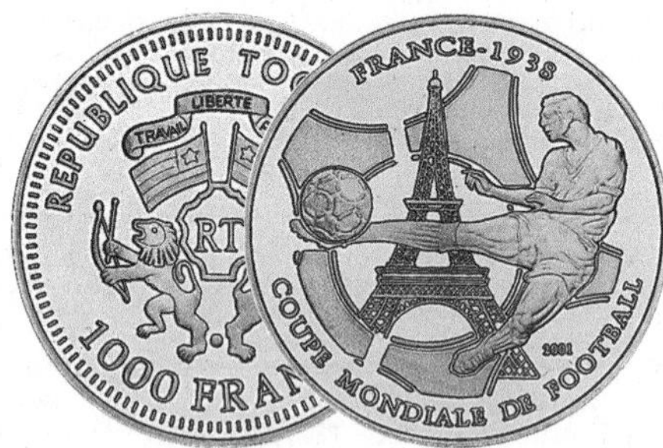

KM# 36 1000 FRANCS

19.9100 g., 0.9990 Silver 0.6395 oz. ASW, 38.1 mm. **Subject:** World Cup Soccer - France 1938 **Obv:** National arms **Rev:** Eiffel Tower behind soccer player kicking ball **Edge:** Reeded

Date	Mintage	F	VF	XF	Unc	BU
2001 Proof	—	Value: 40.00				

KM# 40 1000 FRANCS

14.9700 g., Silver, 35 mm. **Obv:** National arms **Obv. Legend:** REPUBLIQUE TOGOLAISE **Rev:** Imperial German sailing ship **Rev. Legend:** "PREUSSEN" **Edge:** Plain

Date	Mintage	F	VF	XF	Unc	BU
2001 Proof	—	Value: 40.00				

KM# 54 1000 FRANCS

15.0000 g., 0.9990 Silver 0.4818 oz. ASW, 36 mm. **Rev:** Multicolor Airbus 319 right

Date	Mintage	F	VF	XF	Unc	BU
2001 Proof	—	Value: 35.00				

KM# 37 1000 FRANCS

19.9700 g., 0.9990 Silver 0.6414 oz. ASW, 40 mm. **Subject:** World Cup Soccer - USA 1994 **Obv:** National arms **Obv. Legend:** REPUBLIQUE TOGOLAISE **Rev:** Soccer player kicking ball **Rev. Legend:** COUPE MONDIALE DE FOOTBALL **Edge:** Reeded

Date	Mintage	F	VF	XF	Unc	BU
2002 Proof	—	Value: 40.00				

KM# 55 1000 FRANCS

15.0000 g., 0.9990 Silver 0.4818 oz. ASW, 36 mm. **Rev:** Multicolor Douglas DC-4 and NY skyline

Date	Mintage	F	VF	XF	Unc	BU
2002 Proof	—	Value: 35.00				

KM# 56 1000 FRANCS

15.0000 g., 0.9990 Silver 0.4818 oz. ASW **Rev:** Multicolor Caravelle SE-210 before London skyline **Shape:** 36

Date	Mintage	F	VF	XF	Unc	BU
2002 Proof	—	Value: 35.00				

KM# 57 1000 FRANCS
15.0000 g., 0.9990 Silver 0.4818 oz. ASW, 36 mm. **Rev:** Multicolor Convair 440 at airport

Date	Mintage	F	VF	XF	Unc	BU
2003 Proof	—	Value: 35.00				

KM# 58 1000 FRANCS
15.0000 g., 0.9990 Silver 0.4818 oz. ASW, 36 mm. **Rev:** Multicolor McDonnell-Douglas MD-81 right

Date	Mintage	F	VF	XF	Unc	BU
2003 Proof	—	Value: 35.00				

KM# 34 1000 FRANCS
30.9200 g., 0.9990 Silver 0.9931 oz. ASW, 39 mm. **Obv:** Bust with headdress left within circle **Rev:** Gold plated baboon within circle **Edge:** Reeded **Note:** Date in Chinese numerals.

Date	Mintage	F	VF	XF	Unc	BU
2004 Proof	—	Value: 70.00				

KM# 39 1000 FRANCS
62.2400 g., 0.9999 Silver 2.0008 oz. ASW, 50 mm. **Subject:** Year of the Monkey **Obv:** Gold plated world globe **Rev:** Gold plated center with radiant holographic monkey within circle **Edge:** Reeded and lettered sections **Edge Lettering:** PAN ASIA BANK TAIWAN in English and Chinese **Note:** Date in Chinese numerals.

Date	Mintage	F	VF	XF	Unc	BU
2004 Proof	—	Value: 125				

KM# 38 1000 FRANCS
30.7300 g., 0.9990 Silver 0.9870 oz. ASW, 39 mm. **Subject:** Year of the Monkey **Obv:** Head with headdress 1/4 right within circle **Rev:** Gold plated baboon within circle **Edge:** Reeded **Note:** Note: Date in Chinese numerals.

Date	Mintage	F	VF	XF	Unc	BU
2004 Proof	—	Value: 70.00				

KM# 24 1000 FRANCS
31.1035 g., 0.9990 Silver 0.9990 oz. ASW, 40 mm. **Obv:** National arms **Obv. Legend:** REPUBLIQUE TOGOLAISE **Rev:** Incuse rendering of statue of Princess Kyninska of Sparta horseback left **Rev. Legend:** SPORTS - ANTIQUES **Edge:** Plain

Date	Mintage	F	VF	XF	Unc	BU
2004	2,500	—	—	—	—	65.00

KM# 25 1000 FRANCS
31.1035 g., 0.9990 Silver 0.9990 oz. ASW, 40 mm. **Obv:** National arms **Obv. Legend:** REPUBLIQUE TOGOLAISE **Rev:** Relief rendering of statue of Princess Kyninska of Sparta horseback right **Rev. Legend:** SPORTS - ANTIQUES **Edge:** Plain

Date	Mintage	F	VF	XF	Unc	BU
2004	2,500	—	—	—	—	65.00

KM# 26 1000 FRANCS
1.2440 g., 0.9999 Gold 0.0400 oz. AGW, 13.92 mm. **Obv:** National arms **Obv. Legend:** REPUBLIQUE TOGOLAISE **Rev:** Convex statue of Nike **Edge:** Plain

Date	Mintage	F	VF	XF	Unc	BU
2004 Proof	5,000	Value: 80.00				

KM# 59 1000 FRANCS
15.0000 g., 0.9990 Silver 0.4818 oz. ASW, 36 mm. **Rev:** Multicolor DeHaviland DH-89 biplane

Date	Mintage	F	VF	XF	Unc	BU
2004 Proof	—	Value: 35.00				

KM# 27 1000 FRANCS
1.2440 g., 0.9999 Gold 0.0400 oz. AGW, 13.92 mm. **Obv:** National arms **Obv. Legend:** REPUBLIQUE TOGOLAISE **Rev:** Concave statue of Nike **Edge:** Plain

Date	Mintage	F	VF	XF	Unc	BU
2004 Proof	5,000	Value: 80.00				

KM# 45 1000 FRANCS
Silver **Subject:** 170th Anniversary German Railroad, Nürnberg - Fürth **Obv:** National arms **Obv. Legend:** REPUBLIQUE TOGOLAISE **Rev:** Early steam locomotive "Adler"

Date	Mintage	F	VF	XF	Unc	BU
2005 Proof	—	Value: 55.00				

KM# 46 1000 FRANCS
1.2400 g., 0.9999 Gold 0.0399 oz. AGW **Subject:** 250th Anniversary Birth of Wolfgang Amadeus Mozart **Obv:** National arms **Obv. Legend:** REPUBLIQUE TOGOLAISE

Date	Mintage	F	VF	XF	Unc	BU
2006 Proof	—	Value: 85.00				

KM# 48 1000 FRANCS
25.0000 g., 0.9250 Silver 0.7435 oz. ASW, 38.6 mm. **Rev:** Blue sunbird, prism technology

Date	Mintage	F	VF	XF	Unc	BU
2010 Proof	2,500	Value: 60.00				

KM# 49 1000 FRANCS

25.0000 g., 0.9250 Silver 0.7435 oz. ASW, 38.6 mm. **Rev:** Green bird, prism technology

Date	Mintage	F	VF	XF	Unc	BU
2010 Proof	2,500	Value: 65.00				

KM# 50 1000 FRANCS

25.0000 g., 0.9250 Silver 0.7435 oz. ASW, 38.6 mm. **Rev:** Yellow bird, prism technology

Date	Mintage	F	VF	XF	Unc	BU
2010 Proof	2,500	Value: 55.00				

KM# 61 1000 FRANCS

25.0000 g., 0.9250 Silver partially plated 0.7435 oz. ASW, 38.61 mm. **Subject:** Year of the Tiger **Obv:** National arms **Rev:** Tiger, gilt

Date	Mintage	F	VF	XF	Unc	BU
2010 Proof	1,000	Value: 75.00				

KM# 63 1000 FRANCS

25.0000 g., 0.9250 Silver 0.7435 oz. ASW **Rev:** Prism Elephant

Date	Mintage	F	VF	XF	Unc	BU
2011 Proof	2,500	Value: 65.00				

KM# 64 1000 FRANCS

25.0000 g., 0.9250 Silver 0.7435 oz. ASW **Rev:** Prism Zebra

Date	Mintage	F	VF	XF	Unc	BU
2011 Proof	2,500	Value: 70.00				

KM# 42 2000 FRANCS

62.2000 g., 0.9990 Silver 1.9977 oz. ASW **Series:** Lunar **Subject:** Year of the Monkey **Obv:** World map **Obv. Legend:** REPUBLIQUE TOGOLAISE **Rev:** Monkey

Date	Mintage	F	VF	XF	Unc	BU
2004 Proof	—	Value: 145				

TOKELAU ISLANDS

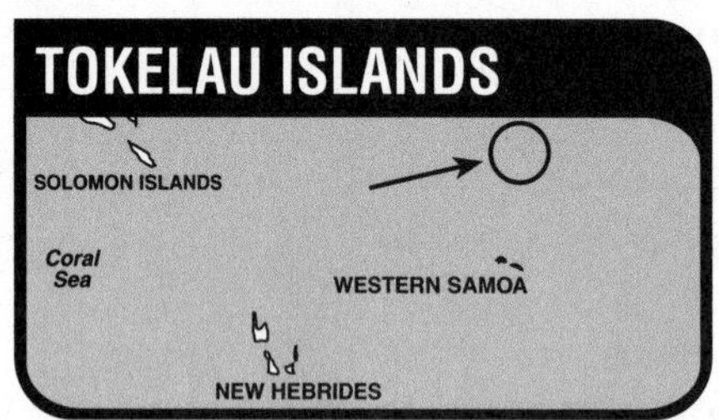

Tokelau or Union Islands, a New Zealand Territory located in the South Pacific 2,100 miles (3,379 km.) northeast of New Zealand and 300 miles (483 km.) north of Samoa, has an area of 4 sq. mi. (10 sq. km.) and a population of *2,000. Geographically, the group consists of four atolls - Atafu, Nukunono, Fakaofo and Swains – but the last belongs to American Samoa (and the United States claims the other three). The people are of Polynesian origin; Samoan is the official language. The New Zealand Minister for Foreign Affairs governs the islands; councils of family elders handle local government at the village level. The chief settlement is Fenuafala, on Fakaofo. It is connected by wireless technology with the offices of the New Zealand Administrative Center, located at Apia, Samoa. Subsistence farming and the production of copra for export are the main occupations. Revenue is also derived from the sale of postage stamps and, since 1978, coins.

Tokelau Islands issued its first coin in 1978, a "$1 Tahi Tala," Tokelauan for "One Dollar."

RULER

British

MINT MARK

PM - Pobjoy

NEW ZEALAND TERRITORY

STANDARD COINAGE

KM# 30 5 TALA

31.1000 g., 0.9990 Silver with Mother-of-Pearl inlay 0.9988 oz. ASW, 40 mm. **Series:** Save the Whales **Obv:** Crowned head right **Obv. Legend:** TOKELAU **Rev:** Fin Whale on mother of pearl insert **Edge:** Plain

Date	Mintage	F	VF	XF	Unc	BU
2002 Proof	2,000	Value: 95.00				

KM# 32 5 TALA

31.1000 g., 0.9990 Silver 0.9988 oz. ASW, 40 mm. **Ruler:** Elizabeth II **Obv:** Elizabeth II **Rev:** Capt. Smith and ship General Jackson **Edge:** Reeded

Date	Mintage	F	VF	XF	Unc	BU
2003 Proof	—	Value: 48.00				

KM# 47 5 TALA

Silver, 38.6 mm. **Ruler:** Elizabeth II **Subject:** Endangered Wildlife **Obv:** Head crowned right **Rev:** Pacific Boa around atree branch **Edge:** Reeded

Date	Mintage	F	VF	XF	Unc	BU
2003 Proof	—	Value: 50.00				

KM# 48 5 TALA

Silver, 38.6 mm. **Ruler:** Elizabeth II **Subject:** Olympics, 2004 **Obv:** Head crowned right **Rev:** Runner, swimmer and bicyalist **Edge:** Reeded

Date	Mintage	F	VF	XF	Unc	BU
2004 Proof	—	Value: 50.00				

KM# 33 5 TALA

28.6500 g., Silver, 38.60 mm. **Ruler:** Elizabeth II **Obv:** Crowned head right **Obv. Legend:** TOKELAU **Rev:** Sailing ship **Rev. Legend:** CUTTY SARK 1869 **Edge:** Reeded

Date	Mintage	F	VF	XF	Unc	BU
2005 Proof	—	Value: 45.00				

KM# 49 5 TALA

25.0000 g., 0.9250 Silver 0.7435 oz. ASW **Ruler:** Elizabeth II **Rev:** Roald Amundsen and jewel inset at South Pole

Date	Mintage	F	VF	XF	Unc	BU
2011 Proof	2,500	Value: 65.00				

KM# 46 10 TALA

1.2400 g., 0.9990 Gold 0.0398 oz. AGW, 13.92 mm. **Ruler:** Elizabeth II **Obv:** Crowned head right **Obv. Legend:** TOKELAU **Rev:** Two whales **Rev. Legend:** ENDANGERED WILDLIFE **Edge:** Reeded

Date	Mintage	F	VF	XF	Unc	BU
2003 Proof	—	Value: 85.00				

TONGA

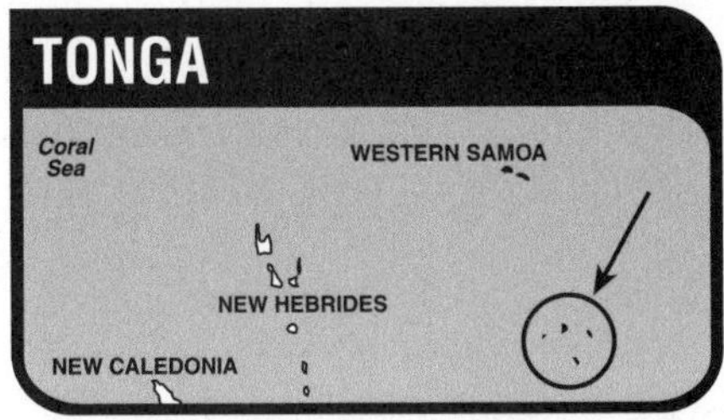

The Kingdom of Tonga (or Friendly Islands) is an archipelago situated in the southern Pacific Ocean south of Western Samoa and east of Fiji comprised of 150 islands. Tonga has an area of 270 sq. mi. (748 sq. km.) and a population of *100,000. Capital: Nuku'alofa. Primarily agricultural, the kingdom exports bananas and copra.

The monarchy is a member of the Commonwealth of Nations. King Siosa Tupou V is Head of State and Government.

RULER

King Taufa'ahau IV, 1965-2006
King Siosa Tupou V, 2006-2012

KINGDOM

DECIMAL COINAGE

100 Senti = 1 Pa'anga; 100 Pa'anga = 1 Hau

KM# 66a SENITI

Copper Plated Steel, 17.5 mm. **Ruler:** King Taufa'ahau Tupou IV **Series:** World Food Day **Obv:** Ear of corn **Obv. Legend:** TONGA **Rev:** Vanilla plant **Rev. Legend:** FAKALAHI ME'AKAI **Edge:** Plain

Date	Mintage	F	VF	XF	Unc	BU
2002	—	—	—	0.10	0.35	0.75
2003	—	—	—	0.10	0.35	0.75
2004	—	—	—	0.10	0.35	0.75

KM# 66 SENITI

1.8000 g., Bronze, 16.51 mm. **Ruler:** King Taufa'ahau Tupou IV **Series:** World Food Day **Obv:** Ear of corn **Rev:** Vanilla plant **Edge:** Plain

Date	Mintage	F	VF	XF	Unc	BU
2005	—	—	—	0.10	0.35	0.75
2006	—	—	—	0.10	0.35	0.75

KM# 67a 2 SENITI

Copper Plated Steel, 21 mm. **Ruler:** King Taufa'ahau Tupou IV **Series:** World Food Day **Obv:** Taro plants **Obv. Legend:** TONGA **Rev:** Paper doll cutouts form design in center circle of sprays **Rev. Legend:** PLANNED FAMILIES • FOOD FOR ALL

Date	Mintage	F	VF	XF	Unc	BU
2002	—	—	—	0.15	0.65	1.25
2003	—	—	—	0.15	0.65	1.25
2004	—	—	—	0.15	0.65	1.25

KM# 68a 5 SENITI

2.7900 g., Nickel Plated Steel, 19.39 mm. **Ruler:** King Taufa'ahau Tupou IV **Series:** World Food Day **Obv:** Hen with chicks **Obv. Legend:** TONGA **Rev:** Coconuts **Rev. Legend:** FAKALAHI ME'AKAI **Edge:** Reeded

Date	Mintage	F	VF	XF	Unc	BU
2002	—	—	—	0.25	0.75	1.35
2003	—	—	—	0.25	0.75	1.35
2004	—	—	—	0.25	0.75	1.35
2005	—	—	—	0.25	0.75	1.35

KM# 68 5 SENITI

2.8000 g., Copper-Nickel, 19.5 mm. **Ruler:** King Taufa'ahau Tupou IV **Series:** World Food Day **Obv:** Hen with chicks **Rev:** Coconuts above sprig **Edge:** Reeded

Date	Mintage	F	VF	XF	Unc	BU
2005	—	—	0.10	0.25	0.75	1.25

KM# 69a 10 SENITI

Nickel Plated Steel, 23.5 mm. **Ruler:** King Taufa'ahau Tupou IV **Series:** World Food Day **Obv:** Uniformed bust facing **Obv. Legend:** F • A • O - TONGA **Rev:** Banana tree **Rev. Legend:** FAKALAHI ME'AKAI

Date	Mintage	F	VF	XF	Unc	BU
2002	—	—	—	0.30	1.00	1.75
2003	—	—	—	0.30	1.00	1.75
2004	—	—	—	0.30	1.00	1.75
2005	—	—	—	0.30	1.00	1.75

KM# 70.1 20 SENITI

11.3000 g., Nickel Plated Steel, 28.5 mm. **Ruler:** King Taufa'ahau Tupou IV **Subject:** FAO - World Food Day **Obv:** Uniformed bust facing **Rev:** Yams

Date	Mintage	F	VF	XF	Unc	BU
2002	—	—	0.25	0.50	1.25	2.00
2003	—	—	0.25	0.50	1.25	2.00
2004	—	—	0.25	0.50	1.25	2.00

KM# 70a 50 SENITI

14.6000 g., Nickel Plated Steel, 32.5 mm. **Ruler:** King Taufa'ahau Tupou IV **Subject:** FAO - World Food Day **Obv:** Uniformed bust facing **Rev:** Tomato plants **Shape:** 12-sided

Date	Mintage	F	VF	XF	Unc	BU
2002	—	—	0.45	0.75	1.50	2.50
2003	—	—	0.45	0.75	1.50	2.50
2004	—	—	0.45	0.75	1.50	2.50

KM# 178 PA'ANGA

31.1000 g., 0.9990 Silver with Mother-of-Pearl inlay 0.9988 oz. ASW, 40 mm. **Ruler:** King Taufa'ahau Tupou IV **Series:** Save the Whales **Obv:** Crown within wreath above national arms within circle **Obv. Legend:** KINGDOM OF TONGA **Rev:** Right Whale on mother of pearl insert **Edge:** Plain

Date	Mintage	F	VF	XF	Unc	BU
2002 Proof	2,000	Value: 95.00				

KM# 182 PA'ANGA

31.4700 g., 0.9250 Silver 0.9359 oz. ASW **Ruler:** King Taufa'ahau Tupou IV **Subject:** 2004 Olympics **Obv:** National arms **Rev:** Kayak crew seen from above

Date	Mintage	F	VF	XF	Unc	BU
2003 Proof	—	Value: 65.00				

KM# 179 2 PA'ANGA

Silver **Ruler:** King Taufa'ahau Tupou IV **Subject:** King's 85th Birthday **Obv:** National arms

Date	Mintage	F	VF	XF	Unc	BU
2003 Proof	—	Value: 150				

TRANSNISTRIA

The Pridnestrovskaia Moldavskaia Respublica was formed in 1990, even before the separation of Moldavia from Russia. It has an area of 11,544 sq. mi. (29,900 sq. km.) and a population of 555,000. Capital: Tiraspol.

Transnistria (or Transdniestra) has a president, parliament, army and police forces, but as yet it is lacking international recognition.

MOLDAVIAN REPUBLIC

STANDARD COINAGE

1 Rublei = 100 Kopeek

KM# 50 5 KOPEEK

0.7000 g., Aluminum, 17.9 mm. **Obv:** Modified national arms **Obv. Legend:** ПРИДНЕСТРОВСКАЯ МОЛДАВСКАЯ РЕСПУБЛИКА **Rev:** Value flanked by wheat stalks. **Edge:** Plain **Note:** Prev. KM#2, 16.

Date	Mintage	F	VF	XF	Unc	BU
2005	—	—	—	0.20	0.50	0.65

KM# 51 10 KOPEEK

1.0000 g., Aluminum, 20 mm. **Obv:** Modified national arms **Obv. Legend:** ПРИДНЕСТРОВСКАЯ МОЛДАВСКАЯ РЕСПУБЛИКА **Rev:** Value flanked by wheat stalks **Edge:** Plain **Note:** Prev. KM#3, 17.

Date	Mintage	F	VF	XF	Unc	BU
2005	—	—	—	0.25	0.65	0.90

KM# 5 25 KOPEEK

2.1500 g., Aluminum-Bronze, 16.88 mm. **Obv:** National arms **Rev:** Value within sprays **Edge:** Plain

Date	Mintage	F	VF	XF	Unc	BU
2002	—	—	0.15	0.35	0.90	1.20

KM# 52 25 KOPEEK

Aluminum-Bronze, 16.9 mm. **Obv:** Modified national arms **Obv. Legend:** ПРИДНЕСТРОВСКАЯ МОЛДАВСКАЯ РЕСПУБЛИКА **Rev:** Value within sprays **Edge:** Plain **Note:** Prev. KM#18.

Date	Mintage	F	VF	XF	Unc	BU
2005	—	—	0.15	0.35	0.90	1.20

KM# 52a 25 KOPEEK

2.1000 g., Bronze Plated Steel, 16.9 mm. **Obv:** Modified national arms **Obv. Legend:** ПРИДНЕСТРОВСКАЯ МОЛДАВСКАЯ РЕСПУБЛИКА **Rev:** Value within sprays **Edge:** Plain **Note:** Prev. KM#5a; 18a.

Date	Mintage	F	VF	XF	Unc	BU
2005	—	—	0.15	0.35	0.90	1.20

KM# 53 50 KOPEEK

2.8000 g., Aluminum-Bronze, 19 mm. **Obv:** Modified national arms **Obv. Legend:** ПРИДНЕСТРОВСКАЯ МОЛДАВСКАЯ РЕСПУБЛИКА **Rev:** Value within sprays **Edge:** Plain **Note:** Prev. KM#4a; 19.

Date	Mintage	F	VF	XF	Unc	BU
2005	—	—	0.15	0.45	1.10	1.50

KM# 53a 50 KOPEEK

Bronze Plated Steel, 19 mm. **Obv:** Modified national arms **Obv. Legend:** ПРИДНЕСТРОВСКАЯ МОЛДАВСКАЯ РЕСПУБЛИКА **Rev:** Value within sprays **Edge:** Plain **Note:** Prev. KM#19a.

Date	Mintage	F	VF	XF	Unc	BU
2005	—	—	0.15	0.45	1.10	1.50

KM# 55 RUBLE

14.1400 g., 0.9250 Silver 0.4205 oz. ASW, 32 mm. **Obv:** National Arms **Rev:** Building with dome

Date	Mintage	F	VF	XF	Unc	BU
2005 Proof	500	Value: 125				

KM# 77 RUBLE

14.1400 g., 0.9250 Silver 0.4205 oz. ASW, 32 mm. **Obv:** National Arms **Rev:** Moth and caterpillar

Date	Mintage	F	VF	XF	Unc	BU
2006 Proof	1,000	Value: 145				

KM# 79 RUBLE

14.1400 g., 0.9250 Silver 0.4205 oz. ASW, 32 mm. **Obv:** Olympics - Turin **Rev:** Slalom

Date	Mintage	F	VF	XF	Unc	BU
2006 Proof	500	Value: 150				

KM# 95 3 RUBLYA

8.0000 g., 0.9000 Gold 0.2315 oz. AGW, 21 mm. **Obv:** National Arms **Rev:** Shield **Rev. Legend:** РЫБНИЦА

Date	Mintage	F	VF	XF	Unc	BU
2007 Proof	100	Value: 650				

KM# 97 3 RUBLYA

8.0000 g., 0.9000 Gold 0.2315 oz. AGW, 21 mm. **Obv:** National Arms **Rev:** Shield **Rev. Legend:** ТИРАСПОЛЪ

Date	Mintage	F	VF	XF	Unc	BU
2007 Proof	100	Value: 650				

KM# 110 3 RUBLYA

14.1400 g., 0.9250 Silver 0.4205 oz. ASW, 32 mm. **Obv:** National Arms **Rev:** Aquarius within zodiac emblems

Date	Mintage	F	VF	XF	Unc	BU
2007 Proof	100	Value: 285				

KM# 100 5 RUBLES
33.8500 g., 0.9250 Silver 1.0066 oz. ASW, 39 mm. **Obv:** National Arms **Rev:** Wooley mammoth

Date	Mintage	F	VF	XF	Unc	BU
2007 Proof	500	Value: 145				

KM# 101 5 RUBLES
33.8500 g., 0.9250 Silver 1.0066 oz. ASW, 39 mm. **Obv:** National Arms **Rev:** Moose

Date	Mintage	F	VF	XF	Unc	BU
2007 Proof	500	Value: 145				

KM# 134 5 RUBLES
33.8000 g., 0.9250 Silver 1.0052 oz. ASW, 39 mm. **Obv:** National Arms **Rev:** Woolly Mammoth (Archidiskodon Trogrnterii)

Date	Mintage	F	VF	XF	Unc	BU
2007 Proof	500	Value: 100				

KM# 112 10 RUBLEI
14.1400 g., 0.9250 Silver 0.4205 oz. ASW, 32 mm. **Obv:** National Arms **Rev:** Aquarius within circle of zodiac symbols

Date	Mintage	F	VF	XF	Unc	BU
2007 Proof	500	Value: 100				

KM# 102 10 RUBLEI
14.1400 g., 0.9250 Silver 0.4205 oz. ASW, 32 mm. **Obv:** National Arms **Rev:** Multicolor sprinter

Date	Mintage	F	VF	XF	Unc	BU
2007 Proof	500	Value: 100				

KM# 103 10 RUBLEI
14.1400 g., 0.9250 Silver 0.4205 oz. ASW, 32 mm. **Obv:** National Arms **Rev:** Multicolor female gymnast

Date	Mintage	F	VF	XF	Unc	BU
2007 Proof	500	Value: 100				

KM# 104 10 RUBLEI
14.1400 g., 0.9250 Silver 0.4205 oz. ASW, 32 mm. **Obv:** National Arms **Rev:** Multicolor runner, sports designs

Date	Mintage	F	VF	XF	Unc	BU
2007 Proof	500	Value: 100				

KM# 105 10 RUBLEI
14.1400 g., 0.9250 Silver 0.4205 oz. ASW, 32 mm. **Obv:** National Arms **Rev:** Multicolor javlin thrower

Date	Mintage	F	VF	XF	Unc	BU
2007 Proof	500	Value: 100				

KM# 106 10 RUBLEI
14.1400 g., 0.9250 Silver 0.4205 oz. ASW, 32 mm. **Obv:** National Arms **Rev:** Multicolor runner breaking tape at finish line

Date	Mintage	F	VF	XF	Unc	BU
2007 Proof	500	Value: 100				

KM# 107 10 RUBLEI
14.1400 g., 0.9250 Silver 0.4205 oz. ASW, 32 mm. **Obv:** National Arms **Rev:** Multicolor soccer player

Date	Mintage	F	VF	XF	Unc	BU
2007 Proof	500	Value: 100				

KM# 111 10 RUBLEI
14.1400 g., 0.9250 Silver 0.4205 oz. ASW, 32 mm. **Obv:** National Arms **Rev:** Constellation ophiuchus (man grasping serpant)

Date	Mintage	F	VF	XF	Unc	BU
2007 Proof	500	Value: 100				

KM# 125 10 RUBLEI
14.1400 g., 0.9250 Silver 0.4205 oz. ASW, 32 mm. **Obv:** National Arms **Rev:** Sturgeon fish

Date	Mintage	F	VF	XF	Unc	BU
2008 Proof	500	Value: 150				

KM# 126 10 RUBLEI
14.1400 g., 0.9250 Silver 0.4205 oz. ASW, 32 mm. **Obv:** National Arms **Rev:** Owl

Date	Mintage	F	VF	XF	Unc	BU
2008 Proof	500	Value: 165				

KM# 127 10 RUBLEI
14.1400 g., 0.9250 Silver 0.4205 oz. ASW, 32 mm. **Obv:** National Arms **Rev:** Flower

Date	Mintage	F	VF	XF	Unc	BU
2008 Proof	500	Value: 185				

KM# 128 10 RUBLEI
14.1400 g., 0.9250 Silver 0.4205 oz. ASW, 32 mm. **Obv:** National Arms **Rev:** Otter

Date	Mintage	F	VF	XF	Unc	BU
2008 Proof	500	Value: 190				

KM# 135 10 RUBLEI
14.1400 g., 0.9250 Silver 0.4205 oz. ASW, 32 mm. **Obv:** National Arms **Rev:** Lutra otter

Date	Mintage	F	VF	XF	Unc	BU
2008 Proof	5,000	Value: 85.00				

KM# 54 15 RUBLEI
156.4000 g., 0.9990 Gold 5.0231 oz. AGW, 50 mm. **Obv:** National Arms **Rev:** Building with dome

Date	Mintage	F	VF	XF	Unc	BU
2005 Proof, Rare	15	—	—	—	—	—

KM# 75 15 RUBLEI
156.4000 g., 0.9990 Gold 5.0231 oz. AGW, 15 mm. **Obv:** National Arms **Rev:** Building with tower

Date	Mintage	F	VF	XF	Unc	BU
2006 Proof, Rare	15	—	—	—	—	—

KM# 17 100 RUBLEI
14.1400 g., 0.9250 Silver 0.4205 oz. ASW, 32 mm. **Obv:** National Arms **Rev:** Cathedral of Ascension, Kitskany 1864

Date	Mintage	F	VF	XF	Unc	BU
2001 Proof	1,000	Value: 100				

KM# 10 100 RUBLEI
14.1400 g., 0.9250 Silver 0.4205 oz. ASW, 32 mm. **Obv:** National Arms **Rev:** D. Zielinskieg, chemist

Date	Mintage	F	VF	XF	Unc	BU
2001 Proof	1,000	Value: 70.00				

KM# 11 100 RUBLEI
14.1400 g., 0.9250 Silver 0.4205 oz. ASW, 32 mm. **Obv:** National Arms **Rev:** S. Berg, fish

Date	Mintage	F	VF	XF	Unc	BU
2001 Proof	1,000	Value: 70.00				

KM# 12 100 RUBLEI
14.1400 g., 0.9250 Silver 0.4205 oz. ASW, 32 mm. **Obv:** National Arms **Rev:** N.F. Skilfosowskieg, portrait at right

Date	Mintage	F	VF	XF	Unc	BU
2001 Proof	1,000	Value: 70.00				

KM# 13 100 RUBLEI
14.1400 g., 0.9250 Silver 0.4205 oz. ASW, 32 mm. **Obv:** National Arms **Rev:** M.F. Larionowa, bust, painter

Date	Mintage	F	VF	XF	Unc	BU
2001 Proof	1,000	Value: 70.00				

KM# 14 100 RUBLEI
14.1400 g., 0.9250 Silver 0.4205 oz. ASW, 32 mm. **Obv:** National Arms **Rev:** Cathedral in Tyraspol

Date	Mintage	F	VF	XF	Unc	BU
2001 Proof	1,000	Value: 80.00				

KM# 15 100 RUBLEI
14.1400 g., 0.9250 Silver 0.4205 oz. ASW, 32 mm. **Obv:** National Arms **Rev:** Cathedral XVII

Date	Mintage	F	VF	XF	Unc	BU
2001 Proof	1,000	Value: 100				

KM# 16 100 RUBLEI
14.1400 g., 0.9250 Silver 0.4205 oz. ASW, 32 mm. **Obv:** National Arms **Rev:** Cathedral 1800

Date	Mintage	F	VF	XF	Unc	BU
2001 Proof	1,000	Value: 100				

KM# 18 100 RUBLEI
14.1400 g., 0.9250 Silver 0.4205 oz. ASW, 32 mm. **Obv:** National Arms **Rev:** Cathedral 1825

Date	Mintage	F	VF	XF	Unc	BU
2001 Proof	1,000	Value: 100				

KM# 19 100 RUBLEI
14.1400 g., 0.9250 Silver 0.4205 oz. ASW, 32 mm. **Obv:** National Arms **Rev:** Church of St. Trinity, Rashkov 1778

Date	Mintage	F	VF	XF	Unc	BU
2001 Proof	1,000	Value: 100				

KM# 20 100 RUBLEI
14.1400 g., 0.9250 Silver 0.4205 oz. ASW, 32 mm. **Obv:** National Arms **Rev:** Cathedral XIX

Date	Mintage	F	VF	XF	Unc	BU
2001 Proof	1,000	Value: 100				

KM# 21 100 RUBLEI
14.1400 g., 0.9250 Silver 0.4205 oz. ASW, 32 mm. **Obv:** National Arms **Rev:** Cathedral 1784

Date	Mintage	F	VF	XF	Unc	BU
2001 Proof	1,000	Value: 100				

KM# 22 100 RUBLEI
14.1400 g., 0.9250 Silver 0.4205 oz. ASW, 32 mm. **Obv:** National Arms **Rev:** Cathedral 1854

Date	Mintage	F	VF	XF	Unc	BU
2001 Proof	1,000	Value: 100				

KM# 37 100 RUBLEI
14.1400 g., 0.9250 Silver 0.4205 oz. ASW, 32 mm. **Subject:** 10th Anniversary - Trans-Dniester Republican Bank **Obv:** National arms **Rev:** Colorized monogram within 3/4 wreath with "1992" at top **Edge:** Plain **Note:** Prev. KM#10.

Date	Mintage	F	VF	XF	Unc	BU
2002 Proof	500	Value: 90.00				

KM# 35 100 RUBLEI
14.1400 g., 0.9250 Silver 0.4205 oz. ASW, 32 mm. **Subject:** City of Tiraspol **Obv:** National arms **Rev:** Statue and buildings **Edge:** Plain **Note:** Prev. KM#7.

Date	Mintage	F	VF	XF	Unc	BU
2002 Proof	—	Value: 80.00				

KM# 36 100 RUBLEI
14.1400 g., 0.9250 Silver 0.4205 oz. ASW, 32 mm. **Subject:** City of Tiraspol **Obv:** National arms **Rev:** Cameo above fortress **Edge:** Plain **Note:** Prev. KM#8.

Date	Mintage	F	VF	XF	Unc	BU
2002 Proof	—	Value: 80.00				

KM# 38 100 RUBLEI
14.1600 g., 0.9250 Silver 0.4211 oz. ASW, 32 mm. **Subject:** K. K. Gedroets **Obv:** National arms **Rev:** Bust facing flanked by sprigs, beaker and book **Edge:** Plain **Note:** Prev. KM#9.

Date	Mintage	F	VF	XF	Unc	BU
2002 Proof	500	Value: 80.00				

KM# 40 100 RUBLEI
14.1400 g., 0.9250 Silver 0.4205 oz. ASW, 32 mm. **Obv:** National Arms **Rev:** Shield **Rev. Legend:** ТИРАСЛОЛБ

Date	Mintage	F	VF	XF	Unc	BU
2002 Proof	500	Value: 100				

KM# 41 100 RUBLEI
14.1400 g., 0.9250 Silver 0.4205 oz. ASW, 32 mm. **Obv:** National Arms **Rev:** Shield **Rev. Legend:** ГРНГОРКОПОЛL

Date	Mintage	F	VF	XF	Unc	BU
2002 Proof	500	Value: 100				

KM# 45 100 RUBLEI
14.1400 g., 0.9250 Silver 0.4205 oz. ASW, 32 mm. **Obv:** National Army **Rev:** Soccer Player

Date	Mintage	F	VF	XF	Unc	BU
2003 Proof	500	Value: 100				

KM# 43 100 RUBLEI
14.1400 g., 0.9250 Silver 0.4205 oz. ASW, 32 mm. **Obv:** National arms **Rev:** Hoopoe (Upupa Epops) bird on branch **Edge:** Plain **Note:** Prev. KM#11.

Date	Mintage	F	VF	XF	Unc	BU
2003 Proof	500	Value: 100				

KM# 42 100 RUBLEI
14.1400 g., 0.9250 Silver 0.4205 oz. ASW, 32 mm. **Obv:** National arms **Rev:** Shield flanked by sprigs **Edge:** Plain **Note:** Prev. KM#12.

Date	Mintage	F	VF	XF	Unc	BU
2003 Proof	500	Value: 75.00				

KM# 48 100 RUBLEI
14.1400 g., 0.9250 Silver 0.4205 oz. ASW, 32 mm. **Subject:** 80th Anniversary of Nationhood **Obv:** National arms **Rev:** Map and multicolor flag **Edge:** Plain **Note:** Prev. KM#13.

Date	Mintage	F	VF	XF	Unc	BU
2004 Proof	500	Value: 225				

KM# 44 100 RUBLEI
14.1400 g., 0.9250 Silver 0.4205 oz. ASW, 32 mm. **Obv:** National arms **Rev:** Doe and fawn flanked by trees **Edge:** Plain **Note:** Prev. KM#14.

Date	Mintage	F	VF	XF	Unc	BU
2004 Proof	1,000	Value: 225				

KM# 46 100 RUBLEI
14.1400 g., 0.9250 Silver 0.4205 oz. ASW, 32 mm. **Obv:** National Arms **Rev:** A.G. Rubinstein and music score

Date	Mintage	F	VF	XF	Unc	BU
2004 Proof	1,000	Value: 100				

KM# 47 100 RUBLEI
14.1400 g., 0.9250 Silver 0.4205 oz. ASW, 32 mm. **Obv:** National Arms **Rev:** JS Grousul

Date	Mintage	F	VF	XF	Unc	BU
2004 Proof	1,000	Value: 100				

KM# 60 100 RUBLEI
14.1400 g., 0.9250 Silver 0.4205 oz. ASW, 32 mm. **Obv:** National arms **Rev:** Eurasian Griffin bird on rock **Edge:** Plain **Note:** Prev. KM#15.

Date	Mintage	F	VF	XF	Unc	BU
2005 Proof	1,000	Value: 125				

KM# 56 100 RUBLEI
14.1400 g., 0.9250 Silver 0.4205 oz. ASW, 32 mm. **Obv:** National Arms **Rev:** Building with tower

Date	Mintage	F	VF	XF	Unc	BU
2005 Proof	500	Value: 110				

KM# 57 100 RUBLEI
14.1400 g., 0.9250 Silver 0.4205 oz. ASW, 32 mm. **Obv:** National Arms **Rev:** Zodiac - Capricorn

Date	Mintage	F	VF	XF	Unc	BU
2005 Proof	1,000	Value: 90.00				

KM# 58 100 RUBLEI
14.1400 g., 0.9250 Silver 0.4205 oz. ASW, 32 mm. **Obv:** National Arms **Rev:** Statue and long building

Date	Mintage	F	VF	XF	Unc	BU
2005 Proof	500	Value: 110				

KM# 59 100 RUBLEI
14.1400 g., 0.9250 Silver 0.4205 oz. ASW, 32 mm. **Obv:** National Arms **Rev:** Flag as book

Date	Mintage	F	VF	XF	Unc	BU
2005 Proof	500	Value: 180				

KM# 61 100 RUBLEI
14.1400 g., 0.9250 Silver 0.4205 oz. ASW, 32 mm. **Obv:** National Arms **Rev:** PP Werszygora

Date	Mintage	F	VF	XF	Unc	BU
2005 Proof	500	Value: 110				

KM# 62 100 RUBLEI
14.1400 g., 0.9250 Silver 0.4205 oz. ASW, 32 mm. **Obv:** National Arms **Rev:** Zodiac - Aquarius

Date	Mintage	F	VF	XF	Unc	BU
2005 Proof	500	Value: 90.00				

KM# 63 100 RUBLEI
14.1400 g., 0.9250 Silver 0.4205 oz. ASW, 32 mm. **Obv:** National Arms **Rev:** Zodiac - Pisces

Date	Mintage	F	VF	XF	Unc	BU
2005 Proof	500	Value: 90.00				

KM# 64 100 RUBLEI
14.1400 g., 0.9250 Silver 0.4205 oz. ASW, 32 mm. **Obv:** National Arms **Rev:** Zodiac - Aries

Date	Mintage	F	VF	XF	Unc	BU
2005 Proof	500	Value: 90.00				

KM# 65 100 RUBLEI
14.1400 g., 0.9250 Silver 0.4205 oz. ASW, 32 mm. **Obv:** National Arms **Rev:** Zodiac - Taurus

Date	Mintage	F	VF	XF	Unc	BU
2005 Proof	500	Value: 90.00				

KM# 66 100 RUBLEI
14.1400 g., 0.9250 Silver 0.4205 oz. ASW, 32 mm. **Obv:** National Arms **Rev:** Zodiac - Gemini

Date	Mintage	F	VF	XF	Unc	BU
2005 Proof	500	Value: 90.00				

KM# 67 100 RUBLEI
14.1400 g., 0.9250 Silver 0.4205 oz. ASW, 32 mm. **Obv:** National Arms **Rev:** Zodiac - Cancer

Date	Mintage	F	VF	XF	Unc	BU
2005 Proof	500	Value: 90.00				

KM# 68 100 RUBLEI
14.1400 g., 0.9250 Silver 0.4205 oz. ASW, 32 mm. **Obv:** National Arms **Rev:** Zodiac - Leo

Date	Mintage	F	VF	XF	Unc	BU
2005 Proof	500	Value: 90.00				

KM# 69 100 RUBLEI
14.1400 g., 0.9250 Silver 0.4205 oz. ASW, 32 mm. **Obv:** National Arms **Rev:** Zodiac - Virgo

Date	Mintage	F	VF	XF	Unc	BU
2005 Proof	500	Value: 90.00				

KM# 70 100 RUBLEI
14.1400 g., 0.9250 Silver 0.4205 oz. ASW, 32 mm. **Obv:** National Arms **Rev:** Zodiac - Libra

Date	Mintage	F	VF	XF	Unc	BU
2005 Proof	500	Value: 90.00				

KM# 71 100 RUBLEI
14.1400 g., 0.9250 Silver 0.4205 oz. ASW, 32 mm. **Obv:** National Arms **Rev:** Zodiac - Scorpio

Date	Mintage	F	VF	XF	Unc	BU
2005 Proof	500	Value: 90.00				

KM# 72 100 RUBLEI
14.1400 g., 0.9250 Silver 0.4205 oz. ASW, 32 mm. **Obv:** National Arms **Rev:** Zodiac - Sagittarius

Date	Mintage	F	VF	XF	Unc	BU
2005 Proof	500	Value: 90.00				

KM# 76 100 RUBLEI
14.1400 g., 0.9250 Silver 0.4205 oz. ASW, 32 mm. **Obv:** National Arms **Rev:** Lunar Year of the (fire) Dog

Date	Mintage	F	VF	XF	Unc	BU
2006 Proof	1,000	Value: 65.00				

KM# 78 100 RUBLEI
14.1400 g., 0.9250 Silver 0.4205 oz. ASW, 32 mm. **Obv:** National Arms **Rev:** Stag Beetle

Date	Mintage	F	VF	XF	Unc	BU
2006 Proof	500	Value: 285				

KM# 80 100 RUBLEI
14.1400 g., 0.9250 Silver 0.4205 oz. ASW, 32 mm. **Obv:** National Arms **Rev:** Biathlon

Date	Mintage	F	VF	XF	Unc	BU
2006 Proof	300	Value: 300				

KM# 81 100 RUBLEI
14.1400 g., 0.9250 Silver 0.4205 oz. ASW, 32 mm. **Subject:** Turin Olympics **Obv:** National Arms **Rev:** Ski Jump

Date	Mintage	F	VF	XF	Unc	BU
2006 Proof	200	Value: 325				

KM# 82 100 RUBLEI
14.1400 g., 0.9250 Silver 0.4205 oz. ASW, 32 mm. **Obv:** National Arms **Rev:** Town View - Tyraspol

Date	Mintage	F	VF	XF	Unc	BU
2006 Proof	500	Value: 110				

KM# 83 100 RUBLEI
14.1400 g., 0.9250 Silver 0.4205 oz. ASW, 32 mm. **Obv:** National Arms **Rev:** Town view Bendery

Date	Mintage	F	VF	XF	Unc	BU
2006 Proof	500	Value: 100				

KM# 84 100 RUBLEI
14.1400 g., 0.9250 Silver 0.4205 oz. ASW, 32 mm. **Obv:** Naational Arms **Rev:** Man in forest legend

Date	Mintage	F	VF	XF	Unc	BU
2006 Proof	1,000	Value: 85.00				

KM# 85 100 RUBLEI
14.1400 g., 0.9250 Silver 0.4205 oz. ASW, 32 mm. **Obv:** National Arms **Rev:** Legend - Fisherman in rowboat

Date	Mintage	F	VF	XF	Unc	BU
2006 Proof	1,000	Value: 85.00				

KM# 86 100 RUBLEI
14.1400 g., 0.9250 Silver 0.4205 oz. ASW, 32 mm. **Obv:** National Arms **Rev:** Legend dragon slayer

Date	Mintage	F	VF	XF	Unc	BU
2006 Proof	1,000	Value: 85.00				

KM# 87 100 RUBLEI
14.1400 g., 0.9250 Silver 0.4205 oz. ASW, 32 mm. **Obv:** National Arms **Rev:** Kossak

Date	Mintage	F	VF	XF	Unc	BU
2006 Proof	500	Value: 120				

KM# 88 100 RUBLEI
14.1400 g., 0.9250 Silver 0.4205 oz. ASW, 32 mm. **Obv:** National Arms **Rev:** General Bursak

Date	Mintage	F	VF	XF	Unc	BU
2006 Proof	500	Value: 120				

KM# 89 100 RUBLEI
14.1400 g., 0.9250 Silver 0.4205 oz. ASW, 32 mm. **Obv:** National Arms **Rev:** Multicolor baseball player hitting ball

Date	Mintage	F	VF	XF	Unc	BU
2006 Proof	500	Value: 100				

KM# 90 100 RUBLEI
14.1400 g., 0.9250 Silver 0.4205 oz. ASW, 32 mm. **Obv:** National Arms **Rev:** Cathedral of the Arch Angel Michael

Date	Mintage	F	VF	XF	Unc	BU
2006 Proof	500	Value: 100				

KM# 91 100 RUBLEI
14.1400 g., 0.9250 Silver 0.4205 oz. ASW, 32 mm. **Obv:** National Arms **Rev:** Sidor Bialy bust at right

Date	Mintage	F	VF	XF	Unc	BU
2006 Proof	300	Value: 175				

KM# 136 100 RUBLEI
14.1400 g., 0.9250 Silver 0.4205 oz. ASW, 32 mm. **Obv:** National Arms **Rev:** Monarch butterfly

Date	Mintage	F	VF	XF	Unc	BU
2006 Proof	1,000	Value: 60.00				

KM# 92 100 RUBLEI
14.1400 g., 0.9250 Silver 0.4205 oz. ASW, 32 mm. **Obv:** National Arms **Rev:** Seal impression, partially plated

Date	Mintage	F	VF	XF	Unc	BU
2006 Proof	300	Value: 175				

KM# 120 100 RUBLEI
14.1400 g., 0.9250 Silver 0.4205 oz. ASW, 32 mm. **Obv:** National Arms **Rev:** General Potiomkin

Date	Mintage	F	VF	XF	Unc	BU
2007 Proof	300	Value: 160				

KM# 96 100 RUBLEI
14.1400 g., 0.9250 Silver 0.4205 oz. ASW, 32 mm. **Obv:** National Arms **Rev:** Rybnitsa Shield **Rev. Legend:** PЫЪЦИUA

Date	Mintage	F	VF	XF	Unc	BU
2007 Proof	500	Value: 120				

KM# 113 100 RUBLEI
14.1400 g., 0.9250 Silver 0.4205 oz. ASW, 32 mm. **Obv:** National Arms **Rev:** Lunar year of the pig

Date	Mintage	F	VF	XF	Unc	BU
2007 Proof	300	Value: 160				

KM# 114 100 RUBLEI
14.1400 g., 0.9250 Silver 0.4205 oz. ASW, 32 mm. **Obv:** National Arms **Rev:** Castle view, 4 towers

Date	Mintage	F	VF	XF	Unc	BU
2007 Proof	500	Value: 120				

KM# 115 100 RUBLEI
14.1400 g., 0.9250 Silver 0.4205 oz. ASW, 32 mm. **Subject:** Soroky Fortress **Obv:** National Arms **Rev:** Castle view central tower and gate

Date	Mintage	F	VF	XF	Unc	BU
2007 Proof	500	Value: 120				

KM# 116 100 RUBLEI
14.1400 g., 0.9250 Silver 0.4205 oz. ASW, 32 mm. **Obv:** National Arms **Rev:** Zachary Czerega Kulis, ship at left

Date	Mintage	F	VF	XF	Unc	BU
2007 Proof	300	Value: 165				

KM# 117 100 RUBLEI
14.1400 g., 0.9250 Silver 0.4205 oz. ASW, 32 mm. **Subject:** Anton Goloway **Obv:** National Arms **Rev:** Bust facing

Date	Mintage	F	VF	XF	Unc	BU
2007 Proof	300	Value: 125				

KM# 118 100 RUBLEI
14.1400 g., 0.9250 Silver 0.4205 oz. ASW, 32 mm. **Obv:** National Arms **Rev:** Alexander Kuszer

Date	Mintage	F	VF	XF	Unc	BU
2007 Proof	500	Value: 115				

KM# 119 100 RUBLEI
14.1400 g., 0.9250 Silver 0.4205 oz. ASW, 32 mm. **Obv:** National Arms **Rev:** Field Marshal - Rumiancew-Zadunajski

Date	Mintage	F	VF	XF	Unc	BU
2007 Proof	300	Value: 125				

KM# 121 100 RUBLEI
14.1400 g., 0.9250 Silver 0.4205 oz. ASW, 32 mm. **Obv:** National Arms **Rev:** General Panin

Date	Mintage	F	VF	XF	Unc	BU
2007 Proof	300	Value: 125				

KM# 130 100 RUBLEI
14.1400 g., 0.9250 Silver 0.4205 oz. ASW, 32 mm. **Obv:** Naitonal Arms **Rev:** Tulip (Tulipa Biebersteiniana)

Date	Mintage	F	VF	XF	Unc	BU
2008 Proof	—	Value: 125				

KM# 131 100 RUBLEI
14.1400 g., 0.9250 Silver 0.4205 oz. ASW, 32 mm. **Obv:** National Arms **Rev:** Moldavian Metal Works shield

Date	Mintage	F	VF	XF	Unc	BU
2008 Proof	500	Value: 90.00				

KM# 132 100 RUBLEI
14.1400 g., 0.9250 Silver 0.4205 oz. ASW, 32 mm. **Obv:** National Arms **Rev:** Field Marshal Piotr Vitgenshtain

Date	Mintage	F	VF	XF	Unc	BU
2008 Proof	500	Value: 90.00				

KM# 133 100 RUBLEI
14.1400 g., 0.9250 Silver 0.4205 oz. ASW, 32 mm. **Obv:** National Arms **Rev:** Belgorod Dnestrovskaya Fortress

Date	Mintage	F	VF	XF	Unc	BU
2008 Proof	500	Value: 100				

KM# 129 100 RUBLEI
14.1400 g., 0.9250 Silver 0.4205 oz. ASW, 32 mm. **Subject:** Year of the Bull

Date	Mintage	F	VF	XF	Unc	BU
2009 Proof	500	Value: 100				

KM# 25 1000 RUBLEI
8.0000 g., 0.9000 Gold 0.2315 oz. AGW, 21 mm. **Obv:** National Arms **Rev:** 1800 Cathedral of God's Ascension

Date	Mintage	F	VF	XF	Unc	BU
2001 Proof	50	Value: 750				

KM# 23 1000 RUBLEI
8.0000 g., 0.9000 Gold 0.2315 oz. AGW, 21 mm. **Obv:** National Arms **Rev:** Church of the Blessed Virgins

Date	Mintage	F	VF	XF	Unc	BU
2001 Proof	50	Value: 750				

KM# 24 1000 RUBLEI
8.0000 g., 0.9000 Gold 0.2315 oz. AGW, 21 mm. **Obv:** National Arms **Rev:** Orthodox Church of the Virgin's Assumption

Date	Mintage	F	VF	XF	Unc	BU
2001 Proof	50	Value: 750				

KM# 26 1000 RUBLEI
8.0000 g., 0.9000 Gold 0.2315 oz. AGW, 21 mm. **Obv:** National Arms **Rev:** Cathedral of the Birth of Christ

Date	Mintage	F	VF	XF	Unc	BU
2001 Proof	50	Value: 750				

KM# 27 1000 RUBLEI
8.0000 g., 0.9000 Gold 0.2315 oz. AGW, 21 mm. **Rev:** Cathedral of the Transfiguration

Date	Mintage	F	VF	XF	Unc	BU
2001 Proof	50	Value: 750				

KM# 28 1000 RUBLEI
8.0000 g., 0.9000 Gold 0.2315 oz. AGW, 21 mm. **Obv:** National Arms **Rev:** Church of the Blessed Virgin's Birth

Date	Mintage	F	VF	XF	Unc	BU
2001 Proof	50	Value: 750				

KM# 29 1000 RUBLEI
8.0000 g., 0.9000 Gold 0.2315 oz. AGW, 21 mm. **Obv:** National Arms **Rev:** Church of the Transfiguration

Date	Mintage	F	VF	XF	Unc	BU
2001 Proof	50	Value: 750				

KM# 30 1000 RUBLEI
8.0000 g., 0.9000 Gold 0.2315 oz. AGW, 21 mm. **Obv:** National Arms **Rev:** Church of the Lifegiving Trinity

Date	Mintage	F	VF	XF	Unc	BU
2001 Proof	50	Value: 750				

KM# 31 1000 RUBLEI
8.0000 g., 0.9000 Gold 0.2315 oz. AGW, 21 mm. **Obv:** National Arms **Rev:** Orthodox Church to the Serbian Paraskeva (1854)

Date	Mintage	F	VF	XF	Unc	BU
2001 Proof	50	Value: 750				

KM# 32 1000 RUBLEI
8.0000 g., 0.9000 Gold 0.2315 oz. AGW, 21 mm. **Obv:** National Arms **Rev:** Church of Michael the Arch Angel in Stoiesti

Date	Mintage	F	VF	XF	Unc	BU
2001 Proof	50	Value: 750				

MINT SETS

KM#	Date	Mintage	Identification	Issue Price	Mkt Val
MS1	2005 (4)	—	KM#50, 51, 52a, 53.	—	20.00

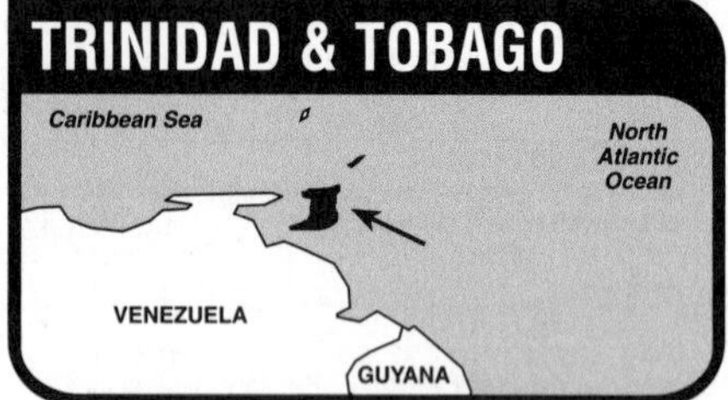

The Republic of Trinidad and Tobago is situated 7 miles (11 km.) off the coast of Venezuela, has an area of 1,981 sq. mi. (5,130 sq. km.) and a population of *1.2 million. Capital: Port-of-Spain. The island of Trinidad contains the world's largest natural asphalt bog. Birds of Paradise live on little Tobago, the only place outside of their native New Guinea where they can be found in a wild state. Petroleum and petroleum products are the mainstay of the economy. Petroleum products, crude oil and sugar are exported.

Trinidad and Tobago is a member of the Commonwealth of Nations. The President is Chief of State. The Prime Minister is Head of Government.

MONETARY SYSTEM
100 Cents = 1 Dollar

REPUBLIC

STANDARD COINAGE

KM# 29 CENT
1.9500 g., Bronze, 17.76 mm. **Obv:** National arms **Rev:** Hummingbird and value **Edge:** Plain

Date	Mintage	F	VF	XF	Unc	BU
2001	—	—	—	0.10	0.30	0.40
2002	—	—	—	0.10	0.30	0.40
2003	—	—	—	0.10	0.30	0.40
2005	—	—	—	0.10	0.30	0.40
2006	—	—	—	0.10	0.30	0.40
2007	—	—	—	0.10	0.30	0.40
2008	—	—	—	0.10	0.30	0.40
2009	—	—	—	0.10	0.30	0.40
2010	—	—	—	0.10	0.30	0.40
2011	—	—	—	0.10	0.30	0.40

KM# 30 5 CENTS
3.3100 g., Bronze, 21.2 mm. **Obv:** National arms **Rev:** Bird of paradise and value **Edge:** Plain

Date	Mintage	F	VF	XF	Unc	BU
2001	—	—	—	0.15	0.45	0.60
2002	—	—	—	0.15	0.45	0.60
2003	—	—	—	0.15	0.45	0.60
2004	—	—	—	0.15	0.45	0.60
2005	—	—	—	0.15	0.45	0.60
2006	—	—	—	0.15	0.45	0.60
2007	—	—	—	0.15	0.45	0.60
2008	—	—	—	0.15	0.45	0.60
2009FM	—	—	—	0.15	0.45	0.60
2010FM	—	—	—	0.15	0.45	0.60

KM# 31 10 CENTS
1.4000 g., Copper-Nickel, 16.2 mm. **Obv:** National arms **Rev:** Hibiscus and value **Edge:** Reeded

Date	Mintage	F	VF	XF	Unc	BU
2001	—	—	—	0.25	0.60	0.80
2002	—	—	—	0.25	0.60	0.80
2003	—	—	—	0.25	0.60	0.80
2004	—	—	—	0.25	0.60	0.80
2005	—	—	—	0.25	0.60	0.80
2006	—	—	—	0.25	0.60	0.80
2007	—	—	—	0.25	0.60	0.80
2008	—	—	—	0.25	0.60	0.80

KM# 32 25 CENTS
3.5000 g., Copper-Nickel, 20 mm. **Obv:** National arms **Rev:** Chaconia and value **Edge:** Reeded

Date	Mintage	F	VF	XF	Unc	BU
2001	—	—	—	0.30	0.75	1.00
2002	—	—	—	0.30	0.75	1.00
2003	—	—	—	0.30	0.75	1.00
2004	—	—	—	0.30	0.75	1.00
2005	—	—	—	0.30	0.75	1.00
2006	—	—	—	0.30	0.75	1.00
2007	—	—	—	0.30	0.75	1.00
2008	—	—	—	0.30	0.75	1.00

KM# 33 50 CENTS
7.0000 g., Copper-Nickel, 26 mm. **Obv:** National arms **Rev:** Kettle drums and value **Edge:** Reeded

Date	Mintage	F	VF	XF	Unc	BU
2003	—	—	—	1.00	2.00	4.00

KM# 63 10 DOLLARS
Copper-Nickel **Subject:** FIFA - XVIII World Football Championship - Soca Warriors - Germany 2006 **Obv:** Native hands playing steel drum, gilt **Rev:** Logo

Date	Mintage	F	VF	XF	Unc	BU
2006	—	—	—	5.00	12.00	35.00

KM# 64 100 DOLLARS
28.2800 g., 0.9250 Silver 0.8410 oz. ASW **Subject:** FIFA - XVIII World Football Championship - Soca Warriors - Germany 2006 **Obv:** Native hands playing steel drum, gilt **Rev:** Logo

Date	Mintage	F	VF	XF	Unc	BU
2006 Proof	—	Value: 70.00				

Tristan da Cunha is the principal island and group name of a small cluster of volcanic islands located in the South Atlantic midway between the Cape of Good Hope and South America, and 1,500 miles (2,414 km.) south-southwest of the British colony of St. Helena. The other islands are inaccessible, Gough, and the three Nightingale Islands. The group, which comprises a dependency of St. Helena, has a total area of 40 sq. mi. (104 sq. km.) and a population of less than 300. There is a village of 60 houses called Edinburgh. Potatoes are the staple subsistence crop.

MONETARY SYSTEM
100 Pence = 1 Pound

ST. HELENA DEPENDENCY

STANDARD COINAGE

KM# 27 1/2 PENNY
3.8300 g., Copper, 16.91 mm. **Ruler:** Elizabeth II **Obv:** Head with tiara right **Rev:** Snipe Eel **Edge:** Plain

Date	Mintage	F	VF	XF	Unc	BU
2008	—	—	—	—	0.75	1.00

KM# 28 PENNY
4.6300 g., Copper, 18.66 mm. **Ruler:** Elizabeth II **Obv:** Head with tiara right **Rev:** Crayfish **Edge:** Plain

Date	Mintage	F	VF	XF	Unc	BU
2008	—	—	—	—	1.20	1.60

KM# 29 2 PENCE
6.6000 g., Copper, 22.02 mm. **Ruler:** Elizabeth II **Obv:** Head with tiara right **Rev:** Violet Seasnail **Edge:** Plain

Date	Mintage	F	VF	XF	Unc	BU
2008	—	—	—	—	1.50	2.00

KM# 30 5 PENCE
3.7400 g., Copper-Nickel, 16.90 mm. **Ruler:** Elizabeth II **Obv:** Head with tiara right **Rev:** Sea Turtle **Edge:** Plain

Date	Mintage	F	VF	XF	Unc	BU
2008	—	—	—	—	1.80	2.40

KM# 31 10 PENCE
6.4900 g., Copper-Nickel, 22.03 mm. **Ruler:** Elizabeth II **Obv:** Head with tiara right **Rev:** Crab **Edge:** Plain

Date	Mintage	F	VF	XF	Unc	BU
2008	—	—	—	—	2.25	3.00

KM# 32 20 PENCE
6.1000 g., Aluminum-Bronze, 22.02 mm. **Ruler:** Elizabeth II **Obv:** Head with tiara right **Rev:** Orcha - Killer Whale **Edge:** Plain

Date	Mintage	F	VF	XF	Unc	BU
2008	—	—	—	—	3.00	4.00

KM# 33 25 PENCE
Bi-Metallic Aluminum-Bronze center in Copper-Nickel ring., 25.76 mm. **Ruler:** Elizabeth II **Obv:** Head with tiara right **Rev:** 2 Bottlenose Dolphins **Edge:** Plain

Date	Mintage	F	VF	XF	Unc	BU
2008	—	—	—	—	6.00	8.00

KM# 12 50 PENCE
29.1000 g., Copper-Nickel, 38.6 mm. **Ruler:** Elizabeth II **Subject:** Queen Elizabeth's 75th Birthday **Obv:** Crowned bust right **Rev:** Crowned bust facing **Edge:** Reeded

Date	Mintage	F	VF	XF	Unc	BU
2001	—	—	—	—	7.00	8.00

KM# 13 50 PENCE
29.6000 g., Copper-Nickel, 38.7 mm. **Ruler:** Elizabeth II **Subject:** Centennial of Queen Victoria's Death **Obv:** Crowned bust right **Rev:** Crown and veil on half-length figure of Queen Victoria facing left within oval circle **Edge:** Reeded

Date	Mintage	F	VF	XF	Unc	BU
2001	—	—	—	—	8.00	10.00

KM# 12a 50 PENCE
28.2800 g., 0.9250 Silver 0.8410 oz. ASW, 38.6 mm. **Ruler:** Elizabeth II **Subject:** Queen's 75th Birthday **Obv:** Crowned bust right **Rev:** Crowned bust facing **Edge:** Reeded

Date	Mintage	F	VF	XF	Unc	BU
2001 Proof	10,000	Value: 40.00				

KM# 12b 50 PENCE
47.5400 g., 0.9166 Gold 1.4009 oz. AGW, 38.6 mm. **Ruler:** Elizabeth II **Obv:** Crowned bust right **Rev:** Crowned bust facing

Date	Mintage	F	VF	XF	Unc	BU
2001 Proof	75	Value: 2,700				

KM# 13a 50 PENCE
28.2800 g., 0.9250 Silver 0.8410 oz. ASW, 38.6 mm. **Ruler:** Elizabeth II **Subject:** Centennial of Queen Victoria's Death **Obv:** Crowned bust right **Rev:** Crown and veil on half-length figure of Queen Victoria facing left within oval circle **Edge:** Reeded

Date	Mintage	F	VF	XF	Unc	BU
2001 Proof	10,000	Value: 50.00				

KM# 13b 50 PENCE
47.5400 g., 0.9166 Gold 1.4009 oz. AGW, 38.6 mm. **Ruler:** Elizabeth II **Subject:** Centennial of Queen Victoria's Death **Obv:** Crowned bust right **Rev:** Crown and veil on half-length figure of Queen Victoria facing left within oval circle **Edge:** Reeded

Date	Mintage	F	VF	XF	Unc	BU
2001 Proof	100	Value: 2,700				

KM# 41 CROWN
Copper-Nickel, 38.6 mm. **Ruler:** Elizabeth II **Obv:** Bust crowned right **Rev:** Conjoined busts left

Date	Mintage	F	VF	XF	Unc	BU
2005	—	—	—	—	—	20.00

KM# 43 CROWN
Copper-Nickel, 38.6 mm. **Ruler:** Elizabeth II **Obv:** Bust in tiara right **Rev:** Lord Nelson's bust 1/4 left

Date	Mintage	F	VF	XF	Unc	BU
2005	—	—	—	—	—	15.00

KM# 44 CROWN
Copper-Nickel, 38.6 mm. **Ruler:** Elizabeth II **Subject:** VE-Day, 60th Anniversary **Obv:** Bust in tiara right **Rev:** Ship, tank, two panes

Date	Mintage	F	VF	XF	Unc	BU
2005	—	—	—	—	—	15.00

KM# 14 CROWN
Copper-Nickel, 38.5 mm. **Ruler:** Elizabeth II **Obv:** Crowned bust right **Rev:** Pope John Paul II **Edge:** Reeded

Date	Mintage	F	VF	XF	Unc	BU
2005	—	—	—	—	8.50	12.00

KM# 14a CROWN
24.1200 g., 0.9250 Silver 0.7173 oz. ASW, 38.5 mm. **Ruler:** Elizabeth II **Obv:** Crowned bust right **Rev:** Pope John Paul II **Edge:** Reeded

Date	Mintage	F	VF	XF	Unc	BU
2005 Proof	—	Value: 45.00				

KM# 15 CROWN
25.0000 g., Copper-Nickel, 38.83 mm. **Ruler:** Elizabeth II **Series:** Privateering ships of the South Atlantic **Obv:** Crowned bust right **Obv. Legend:** ELIZABETH II — TRISTAN DA CUNHA **Rev:** Sailing ship "Tybalt" **Edge:** Reeded

Date	Mintage	F	VF	XF	Unc	BU
2006	—	—	—	—	8.50	12.00

KM# 16 CROWN
25.0000 g., Copper-Nickel, 38.83 mm. **Ruler:** Elizabeth II **Series:** Privateering ships of the South Atlantic **Obv:** Crowned bust right **Obv. Legend:** ELIZABETH II — TRISTAN DA CUNHA **Rev:** Sailing ship "Syren" **Edge:** Reeded

Date	Mintage	F	VF	XF	Unc	BU
2006	—	—	—	—	8.50	12.00

KM# 17 CROWN
25.0000 g., Copper-Nickel, 38.83 mm. **Ruler:** Elizabeth II **Series:** Privateering ships of the South Atlantic **Obv:** Crowned bust right **Obv. Legend:** ELIZABETH II — TRISTAN DA CUNHA **Rev:** Sailing ship "Pride of Baltimore" **Edge:** Reeded

Date	Mintage	F	VF	XF	Unc	BU
2006	—	—	—	—	8.50	12.00

KM# 18 CROWN
25.0000 g., Copper-Nickel, 38.83 mm. **Ruler:** Elizabeth II **Series:** Privateering ships of the South Atlantic **Obv:** Crowned bust right **Obv. Legend:** ELIZABETH II — TRISTAN DA CUNHA **Rev:** Sailing ship "Hornet" **Edge:** Reeded

Date	Mintage	F	VF	XF	Unc	BU
2006	—	—	—	—	8.50	12.00

KM# 19 CROWN
25.0000 g., Copper-Nickel, 38.83 mm. **Ruler:** Elizabeth II **Series:** Privateering ships of the South Atlantic **Obv:** Crowned bust right **Obv. Legend:** ELIZABETH II — TRISTAN DA CUNHA **Rev:** Sailing ship "Griffin" **Edge:** Reeded

Date	Mintage	F	VF	XF	Unc	BU
2006	—	—	—	—	8.50	12.00

KM# 20 CROWN

25.0000 g., Copper-Nickel, 38.83 mm. **Ruler:** Elizabeth II **Series:** Privateering ships of the South Atlantic **Obv:** Crowned bust right **Obv. Legend:** ELIZABETH II — TRISTAN DA CUNHA **Rev:** Sailing ship "Enterprise" **Edge:** Reeded

Date	Mintage	F	VF	XF	Unc	BU
2006	—	—	—	—	8.50	12.00

KM# 21 CROWN

25.0000 g., Copper-Nickel, 38.83 mm. **Ruler:** Elizabeth II **Series:** Privateering ships of the South Atlantic **Obv:** Crowned bust right **Obv. Legend:** ELIZABETH II — TRISTAN DA CUNHA **Rev:** Sailing ship "Columbus" **Edge:** Reeded

Date	Mintage	F	VF	XF	Unc	BU
2006	—	—	—	—	8.50	12.00

KM# 22 CROWN

25.0000 g., Copper-Nickel, 38.8 mm. **Ruler:** Elizabeth II **Series:** Privateering ships of the South Atlantic **Obv:** Crowned bust right **Obv. Legend:** ELIZABETH II — TRISTAN DA CUNHA **Rev:** Sailing ship "Chausseur" **Edge:** Reeded

Date	Mintage	F	VF	XF	Unc	BU
2006	—	—	—	—	8.50	12.00

KM# 23 CROWN

25.0000 g., Copper-Nickel, 38.8 mm. **Ruler:** Elizabeth II **Series:** Privateering ships of the South Atlantic **Obv:** Crowned bust right **Obv. Legend:** ELIZABETH II — TRISTAN DA CUNHA **Rev:** Sailing ship "Cabot" **Edge:** Reeded

Date	Mintage	F	VF	XF	Unc	BU
2006	—	—	—	—	8.50	12.00

KM# 24 CROWN

25.0000 g., Copper-Nickel, 38.8 mm. **Ruler:** Elizabeth II **Series:** Privateering ships of the South Atlantic **Obv:** Crowned bust right **Obv. Legend:** ELIZABETH II — TRISTAN DA CUNHA **Rev:** Sailing ship "Black Prince" **Edge:** Reeded

Date	Mintage	F	VF	XF	Unc	BU
2006	—	—	—	—	8.50	12.00

KM# 25 CROWN

25.0000 g., Copper-Nickel, 38.8 mm. **Ruler:** Elizabeth II **Series:** Privateering ships of the South Atlantic **Obv:** Crowned bust right **Obv. Legend:** ELIZABETH II — TRISTAN DA CUNHA **Rev:** Sailing ship "Argus" **Edge:** Reeded

Date	Mintage	F	VF	XF	Unc	BU
2006	—	—	—	—	8.50	12.00

KM# 26 CROWN

25.0000 g., Copper-Nickel, 38.8 mm. **Ruler:** Elizabeth II **Series:** Privateering ships of the South Atlantic **Obv:** Crowned bust right **Obv. Legend:** ELIZABETH II — TRISTAN DA CUNHA **Rev:** Sailing ship "True Blooded Yankee" **Edge:** Reeded

Date	Mintage	F	VF	XF	Unc	BU
2006	—	—	—	—	8.50	12.00

KM# 35 CROWN

Copper-Nickel, 38.75 mm. **Ruler:** Elizabeth II **Rev:** HMS Victory

Date	Mintage	F	VF	XF	Unc	BU
2008	—	—	—	—	—	15.00

KM# 36 CROWN

25.1800 g., Copper-Nickel **Ruler:** Elizabeth II **Obv:** HMS Belfast

Date	Mintage	F	VF	XF	Unc	BU
2008	—	—	—	—	—	15.00

KM# 37 CROWN

25.1800 g., Copper-Nickel, 38.75 mm. **Ruler:** Elizabeth II **Obv:** HMS Sceptre

Date	Mintage	F	VF	XF	Unc	BU
2008	—	—	—	—	—	15.00

KM# 38 CROWN

25.1800 g., Copper-Nickel, 38.75 mm. **Ruler:** Elizabeth II **Obv:** HMS Beagle

Date	Mintage	F	VF	XF	Unc	BU
2008	—	—	—	—	—	15.00

KM# 39 CROWN

28.1500 g., Copper-Nickel, 38.75 mm. **Ruler:** Elizabeth II **Obv:** HMS Dreadnought

Date	Mintage	F	VF	XF	Unc	BU
2008	—	—	—	—	—	15.00

KM# 34 CROWN

Copper-Nickel, 39 mm. **Ruler:** Elizabeth II **Obv:** Bust right **Rev:** Two whales

Date	Mintage	F	VF	XF	Unc	BU
2008	—	—	—	—	—	15.00

KM# 34a CROWN

Copper-Nickel, 38 mm. **Ruler:** Elizabeth II **Obv:** Head with tiara right **Rev:** 2 whales, multicolor

Date	Mintage	F	VF	XF	Unc	BU
2008	—	—	—	—	8.00	15.00

KM# 40 CROWN

28.1500 g., Copper-Nickel, 38.75 mm. **Ruler:** Elizabeth II **Rev:** H.M.S. Ark Royal

Date	Mintage	F	VF	XF	Unc	BU
2008	—	—	—	—	—	15.00

KM# 42 5 POUNDS

Silver **Ruler:** Elizabeth II **Rev:** St. George slaying dragon

Date	Mintage	F	VF	XF	Unc	BU
2008	—	—	—	—	45.00	50.00

KM# 45 5 POUNDS
Silver, 38.6 mm. **Ruler:** Elizabeth II **Obv:** Bust in tiara right **Rev:** Titles of the Queen

Date	Mintage	F	VF	XF	Unc	BU
2008 Proof	—	Value: 50.00				

PIEDFORT

KM#	Date	Mintage	Identification	Mkt Val
P1	2001	500	50 Pence. 0.9250 Silver. 56.5400 g. 38.6 mm.	100
P2	2001	500	50 Pence. 0.9250 Silver. 56.5600 g. 38.6 mm. Reeded edge. Proof KM-13a.	100

GOUGH ISLAND

DEPENDANCY

DECIMAL COINAGE

KM# 1 HALFPENNY
Copper Plated Steel, 17 mm. **Ruler:** Elizabeth II **Obv:** Bust right **Obv. Legend:** GOUGH ISLAND Tristan da Cunha **Rev:** Gough moorhen **Edge:** Plain

Date	Mintage	F	VF	XF	Unc	BU
2009	—	—	—	—	0.75	1.00

KM# 2 PENNY
Copper Plated Steel, 18.5 mm. **Ruler:** Elizabeth II **Obv:** Bust right **Obv. Legend:** GOUGH ISLAND Tristan da Cunha **Rev:** Pair of Sooty Albatross **Edge:** Plain

Date	Mintage	F	VF	XF	Unc	BU
2009	—	—	—	—	1.00	1.50

KM# 3 2 PENCE
Copper Plated Steel, 22 mm. **Ruler:** Elizabeth II **Obv:** Bust right **Obv. Legend:** GOUGH ISLAND Tristan da Cunha **Rev:** Pair of Antarctic Tern **Edge:** Plain

Date	Mintage	F	VF	XF	Unc	BU
2009	—	—	—	—	1.50	2.00

KM# 4 5 PENCE
Copper-Nickel Plated Steel, 17 mm. **Ruler:** Elizabeth II **Obv:** Bust right **Obv. Legend:** GOUGH ISLAND Tristan da Cunha **Rev:** Northern Rock Hopper Penguins **Edge:** Plain

Date	Mintage	F	VF	XF	Unc	BU
2009	—	—	—	—	2.00	2.50

KM# 5 10 PENCE
Copper-Nickel Plated Steel, 22 mm. **Ruler:** Elizabeth II **Obv:** Bust right **Obv. Legend:** GOUGH ISLAND Tristan da Cunha **Rev:** Giant Petrel on water **Edge:** Plain

Date	Mintage	F	VF	XF	Unc	BU
2009	—	—	—	—	3.00	3.50

KM# 6 20 PENCE
Brass, 22 mm. **Ruler:** Elizabeth II **Obv:** Bust right **Obv. Legend:** GOUGH ISLAND Tristan da Cunha **Rev:** Antarctic Skua **Edge:** Plain

Date	Mintage	F	VF	XF	Unc	BU
2009	—	—	—	—	4.50	5.00

KM# 7 25 PENCE
Bi-Metallic Brass center in Copper-Nickel ring, 25.8 mm. **Ruler:** Elizabeth II **Obv:** Bust right **Obv. Legend:** GOUGH ISLAND Tristan da Cunha **Rev:** Barn Owl **Edge:** Plain

Date	Mintage	F	VF	XF	Unc	BU
2009	—	—	—	—	8.00	9.00

KM# 8 CROWN
Copper-Nickel, 38.8 mm. **Ruler:** Elizabeth II **Obv:** Bust right **Obv. Legend:** GOUGH ISLAND Tristan da Cunha **Rev:** Peregrine Falcon **Edge:** Plain

Date	Mintage	F	VF	XF	Unc	BU
2009	—	—	—	—	12.00	14.00

STOLTENHOFF ISLAND

DEPENCENCY

DECIMAL COINAGE

KM# 1 HALFPENNY
Copper Plated Steel, 17 mm. **Ruler:** Elizabeth II **Obv:** Bust right **Rev:** Small sailboat - West Riding Tragedy Longboat

Date	Mintage	F	VF	XF	Unc	BU
2008	—	—	—	—	0.75	1.00

KM# 2 PENNY
Copper Plated Steel **Ruler:** Elizabeth II **Obv:** Bust right **Rev:** 18th century sailing ship - Portuguese Carrack type

Date	Mintage	F	VF	XF	Unc	BU
2008	—	—	—	—	1.00	1.50

KM# 3 2 PENCE
Copper Plated Steel, 21.5 mm. **Ruler:** Elizabeth II **Obv:** Bust right **Rev:** Three masted sailing ship - HMS Julia

Date	Mintage	F	VF	XF	Unc	BU
2008	—	—	—	—	1.50	2.00

KM# 4 5 PENCE
Copper-Nickel Plated Steel, 16 mm. **Ruler:** Elizabeth II **Obv:** Bust right **Rev:** Two masted sailing ship - HMS Beagle

Date	Mintage	F	VF	XF	Unc	BU
2008	—	—	—	—	2.00	2.50

M# 5 10 PENCE
Copper-Nickel Plated Steel, 21.5 mm. **Ruler:** Elizabeth II **Obv:** Bust right **Rev:** Three masted sailing ship - Blenden Hall

Date	Mintage	F	VF	XF	Unc	BU
2008	—	—	—	—	3.00	3.50

KM# 6 20 PENCE
Brass, 21.5 mm. **Ruler:** Elizabeth II **Obv:** Bust right **Rev:** Two masted sailing ship - HMS Satellite

Date	Mintage	F	VF	XF	Unc	BU
2008	—	—	—	—	4.50	5.00

KM# 7 25 PENCE
Bi-Metallic Brass center in Copper-Nickel ring, 25 mm. **Ruler:** Elizabeth II **Obv:** Bust right **Rev:** Sailing ship - Iron Barque West Riding

Date	Mintage	F	VF	XF	Unc	BU
2008	—	—	—	—	7.00	8.00

KM# 8 CROWN
Copper-Nickel, 39 mm. **Ruler:** Elizabeth II **Obv:** Bust right **Rev:** Sailing ship L'Heure du Berger

Date	Mintage	F	VF	XF	Unc	BU
2008	—	—	—	—	10.00	12.00

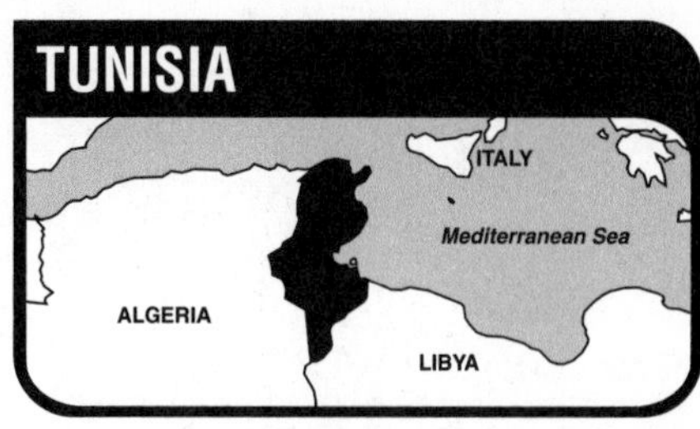

The Republic of Tunisia, located on the northern coast of Africa between Algeria and Libya, has an area of 63,170sq. mi. (163,610 sq. km.) and a population of *7.9 million. Capital: Tunis. Agriculture is the backbone of the economy. Crude oil, phosphates, olive oil, and wine are exported.

TITLES

المملكة التونسية

al-Mamlaka al-Tunisiya

الجمهورية التونسية

al-Jumhuriya al-Tunisiya

al-Amala al-Tunisiya
(Tunisian Protectorate)

REPUBLIC

DECIMAL COINAGE

1000 Millim = 1 Dinar

KM# 348 5 MILLIM
1.4900 g., Aluminum, 24 mm. **Obv:** Oak tree and dates **Rev:** Value within sprigs

Date	Mintage	F	VF	XF	Unc	BU
AH1425-2004	—	—	—	—	0.50	—
AH1426-2005	—	—	—	—	0.50	—

KM# 306 10 MILLIM
3.5000 g., Brass, 19 mm. **Obv:** Inscription and dates within inner circle of design **Rev:** Value in center of design **Edge:** Reeded

Date	Mintage	F	VF	XF	Unc	BU
AH1425-2004	—	—	0.15	0.25	0.50	—
AH1426-2005	—	—	0.15	0.25	0.50	—
AH1429-2008	—	—	0.15	0.25	0.50	—
AH1432-2011	—	—	0.15	0.25	0.50	—

KM# 307 20 MILLIM
4.5000 g., Brass, 22 mm. **Obv:** Inscription and dates within center circle of design **Rev:** Value within center of design

Date	Mintage	F	VF	XF	Unc	BU
AH1425-2004	—	—	—	0.50	0.80	—
AH1426-2005	—	—	—	0.50	0.80	—
AH1428-2007	—	—	—	0.50	0.80	—
AH1430-2009	—	—	—	0.50	0.80	—
AH1432-2011	—	—	—	0.50	0.80	—

KM# 308 50 MILLIM
6.0000 g., Brass, 25 mm. **Obv:** Inscription and dates within center circle of design **Rev:** Value in center of design

Date	Mintage	F	VF	XF	Unc	BU
AH1425-2004	—	—	0.65	0.85	1.25	—
AH1426-2005	—	—	0.65	0.85	1.25	—
AH1428-2007	—	—	0.65	0.85	1.25	—

KM# 309 100 MILLIM
7.5000 g., Brass, 27 mm. **Obv:** Inscription and dates within center circle of design **Rev:** Value in center of design

Date	Mintage	F	VF	XF	Unc	BU
AH1425-2004	—	—	1.25	1.50	2.00	—
AH1426-2005	—	—	1.25	1.50	2.00	—
AH1427-2006	—	—	1.25	1.50	2.00	—
AH1429-2008	—	—	1.25	1.50	2.00	—
AH1432-2011	—	—	1.25	1.50	2.00	—

KM# 346 1/2 DINAR
Copper-Nickel **Obv:** Shield within circle **Rev:** 2 hands with fruit and wheat sprig **Note:** Rim width varieties exist.

Date	Mintage	F	VF	XF	Unc	BU
AH1426-2005	—	—	1.00	2.50	4.50	—
AH1428-2007	—	—	1.00	2.50	4.50	—
AH1430-2009	—	—	1.00	2.50	4.50	—
AH1432-2011	—	—	1.00	2.50	4.50	—

KM# 347 DINAR
10.1000 g., Copper-Nickel, 28 mm. **Series:** F.A.O. **Obv:** Shield within circle **Rev:** Female half figure right

Date	Mintage	F	VF	XF	Unc	BU
AH1428-2007	—	—	2.00	4.00	7.50	—
AH1430-2009	—	—	2.00	4.00	7.50	—
AH1432-2011	—	—	2.00	4.00	7.50	—

KM# 330 5 DINARS
9.4060 g., 0.9000 Gold 0.2722 oz. AGW **Subject:** Anniversary of 7 Nov 1987 **Obv:** Shield **Rev:** Upstretched hand, flag **Note:** Arabic legends vary by year.

Date	Mintage	F	VF	XF	Unc	BU
2001-1421	40	—	—	—	650	700

KM# 329 5 DINARS
9.4060 g., 0.9000 Gold 0.2722 oz. AGW **Subject:** Anniversary of 7 Nov 1987 **Obv:** Shield **Rev:** Upstretched hand, flag **Note:** French legends vary by year.

Date	Mintage	F	VF	XF	Unc	BU
2001-1422	40	—	—	—	650	700

KM# 435 5 DINARS
9.4800 g., 0.9000 Gold 0.2743 oz. AGW, 22 mm. **Subject:** 7 November 1987, 15th Anniversary **Obv:** Shield **Rev:** Stylized dove **Note:** Arabic legends

Date	Mintage	F	VF	XF	Unc	BU
AH1423-2002 Proof	40	Value: 750				

KM# 436 5 DINARS
9.4800 g., 0.9000 Gold 0.2743 oz. AGW, 22 mm. **Subject:** 7 November 1987, 15th Anniversary **Obv:** Shield **Rev:** Stylized dove **Note:** French legends

Date	Mintage	F	VF	XF	Unc	BU
AH1423-2002 Proof	40	Value: 750				

KM# 443 5 DINARS
Bi-Metallic Silver center in Gold ring, 29 mm. **Subject:** 2nd Anniversary of Death **Obv:** Shield **Rev:** Head left

Date	Mintage	F	VF	XF	Unc	BU
AH1423-2002 Proof	750	Value: 375				

KM# 444 5 DINARS
10.0000 g., Bi-Metallic Copper-Nickel center in Copper ring, 29 mm. **Obv:** Shield **Rev:** Head left

Date	Mintage	F	VF	XF	Unc	BU
AH1423-2002	20,275,000	—	—	—	8.00	10.00

KM# 350 5 DINARS
10.0000 g., Bi-Metallic Copper-Nickel center in Aluminum-Bronze ring, 29 mm. **Obv:** National arms **Rev:** Former President Habib Bourguiba **Edge:** Segmented reeding **Shape:** 12-sided

Date	Mintage	F	VF	XF	Unc	BU
AH1423-2002	—	—	—	—	6.50	8.00

KM# 350a 5 DINARS
Bi-Metallic .925 Silver center in .900 gold ring, 29 mm. **Obv:** National arms **Rev:** Former President Habib Bourguiba **Edge:** 6 reeded and 6 plain sections **Shape:** 12-sided

Date	Mintage	F	VF	XF	Unc	BU
AH1423-2002 Proof	—	Value: 450				

KM# 445 5 DINARS
9.4800 g., 0.9000 Gold 0.2743 oz. AGW, 22 mm. **Subject:** 7 November 1987, 16th Anniversary **Obv:** Shield **Rev:** Hand with UN logo **Note:** Arabic legends

Date	Mintage	F	VF	XF	Unc	BU
AH1424-2003 Proof	40	Value: 750				

KM# 446 5 DINARS
9.4800 g., 0.9000 Gold 0.2743 oz. AGW, 22 mm. **Subject:** 7 November 1987, 16th Anniversary **Obv:** Shield **Rev:** Hand with UN logo **Note:** French legend

Date	Mintage	F	VF	XF	Unc	BU
AH1424-2003 Proof	40	Value: 750				

KM# 456 5 DINARS
9.4000 g., 0.9000 Gold 0.2720 oz. AGW, 22 mm. **Subject:** 7 November 1987, 17th Anniversary - Elections **Obv:** Shield **Rev:** Star and crescent and stylized flame **Note:** French legend

Date	Mintage	F	VF	XF	Unc	BU
AH1425-2004 Proof	40	Value: 750				

KM# 455 5 DINARS
9.4000 g., 0.9000 Gold 0.2720 oz. AGW, 22 mm. **Subject:** 7 November 1987, 17th Anniversary - Elections **Obv:** Shield **Rev:** Star and crescent and stylized flame **Note:** Arabic legend

Date	Mintage	F	VF	XF	Unc	BU
AH1425-2004 Proof	40	Value: 750				

KM# 465 5 DINARS
9.4000 g., 0.9000 Gold 0.2720 oz. AGW, 22 mm. **Subject:** 7 November 1987, 18th Anniversary **Obv:** Shield **Rev:** Globe in stylized ship **Note:** Arabic legend

Date	Mintage	F	VF	XF	Unc	BU
AH1426-2005 Proof	40	Value: 750				

KM# 466 5 DINARS
9.4000 g., 0.9000 Gold 0.2720 oz. AGW, 22 mm. **Subject:** 7 November 1987, 18th Anniversary **Obv:** Shield **Rev:** Globe in stylized ship **Note:** French legend

Date	Mintage	F	VF	XF	Unc	BU
AH1426-2005 Prook	40	Value: 750				

KM# 479 5 DINARS
9.4000 g., 0.9000 Gold 0.2720 oz. AGW, 22 mm. **Subject:** 7 November 1987, 19th Anniversary **Obv:** Shield **Rev:** Dove and atom **Note:** French legend

Date	Mintage	F	VF	XF	Unc	BU
AH1427-2006 Proof	40	Value: 750				

KM# 472 5 DINARS
24.0000 g., 0.9000 Silver 0.6944 oz. ASW, 35 mm. **Subject:** 50th Anniversary **Obv:** Shield **Rev:** Logo **Note:** Arabic legend

Date	Mintage	F	VF	XF	Unc	BU
AH1427-2006 Proof	900	Value: 125				

KM# 478 5 DINARS
9.4000 g., 0.9000 Gold 0.2720 oz. AGW, 22 mm. **Subject:** 7 November 1987, 19th Anniversary **Obv:** Shield **Rev:** Dove and atom **Note:** Arabic legends

Date	Mintage	F	VF	XF	Unc	BU
AH1427-2006 Proof	40	Value: 750				

KM# 473 5 DINARS
24.0000 g., 0.9000 Silver 0.6944 oz. ASW, 35 mm. **Subject:** 50th Anniversary **Obv:** Shield **Rev:** Logo **Note:** French legends

Date	Mintage	F	VF	XF	Unc	BU
AH1427-2006 Proof	100	Value: 225				

KM# 491 5 DINARS
9.4000 g., 0.9000 Gold 0.2720 oz. AGW, 22 mm. **Subject:** 7 November 1987, 20th Anniversary **Obv:** Head of Zine el Abidine Ben Ali right **Rev:** Two profiles, keyboard, satellite receiver **Note:** French legends

Date	Mintage	F	VF	XF	Unc	BU
AH1428-2007 Proof	40	Value: 750				

KM# 486 5 DINARS
24.0000 g., 0.9000 Silver 0.6944 oz. ASW, 35 mm. **Subject:** 50th Anniversary **Obv:** Shield **Rev:** Ship, scales of Justice **Note:** Arabic legend

Date	Mintage	F	VF	XF	Unc	BU
AH1428-2007 Proof	900	Value: 125				

KM# 490 5 DINARS
9.4000 g., 0.9000 Gold 0.2720 oz. AGW, 22 mm. **Subject:** 7 November 1987, 20th Anniversary **Obv:** Head of Zine el Abidne Ben Ali right **Rev:** Two profiles, keyboard, satellite receiver **Note:** Arabic legend

Date	Mintage	F	VF	XF	Unc	BU
AH1428-2007 Proof	43	Value: 750				

KM# 487 5 DINARS
24.0000 g., 0.9000 Silver 0.6944 oz. ASW, 35 mm. **Subject:** 50th Anniversary **Obv:** Shield **Rev:** Ship, scales of Justice **Note:** French legend

Date	Mintage	F	VF	XF	Unc	BU
AH1428-2007 Proof	100	Value: 225				

KM# 378 10 DINARS
38.0000 g., 0.9000 Silver 1.0995 oz. ASW **Subject:** 14th Anniversary 7 Nov and 19th Mediterranean Games **Edge:** Reeded

Date	Mintage	F	VF	XF	Unc	BU
AH1422-2001	—	—	—	—	275	—

KM# 341 10 DINARS
18.7700 g., 0.9000 Gold 0.5431 oz. AGW **Subject:** Anniversary - 7 Nov 1987 **Obv:** Shield **Rev:** Upstretched hand, flag **Note:** Arabic legends vary by year.

Date	Mintage	F	VF	XF	Unc	BU
2001-1422	40	—	—	—	1,025	1,050

KM# 430 10 DINARS
38.0000 g., 0.9000 Silver 1.0995 oz. ASW, 40 mm. **Subject:** 7 November 1987, 14th Anniversary **Obv:** Shield **Rev:** Open door **Note:** French legend

Date	Mintage	F	VF	XF	Unc	BU
AH1422-2001 Proof	400	Value: 150				

KM# 340 10 DINARS
18.7700 g., 0.9000 Gold 0.5431 oz. AGW **Subject:** Anniversary - 7 Nov 1987 **Obv:** Shield **Rev:** Upstretched hand, flag **Note:** French legends vary by year.

Date	Mintage	F	VF	XF	Unc	BU
2001-1422	40	—	—	—	1,025	1,050

KM# 438 10 DINARS
18.8000 g., 0.9000 Gold 0.5440 oz. AGW, 28 mm. **Subject:** 7 November 1987, 15th Anniversary **Obv:** Shield **Rev:** Stylized dove **Note:** French legends

Date	Mintage	F	VF	XF	Unc	BU
AH1423-2002 Proof	40	Value: 1,000				

KM# 379 10 DINARS
38.0000 g., 0.9000 Silver 1.0995 oz. ASW **Subject:** 15th Anniversary 7 Nov 1987 **Obv:** National arms **Edge:** Reeded

Date	Mintage	F	VF	XF	Unc	BU
AH1423-2002	—	—	—	—	275	—

KM# 433 10 DINARS
38.0000 g., 0.9000 Silver 1.0995 oz. ASW, 40 mm. **Subject:** 7 November 1987, 15th Anniversary **Obv:** Shield **Rev:** Stylized dove **Note:** Arabic legends

Date	Mintage	F	VF	XF	Unc	BU
AH1423-2002 Proof	490	Value: 150				

KM# 437 10 DINARS
18.8000 g., 0.9000 Gold 0.5440 oz. AGW, 28 mm. **Subject:** 7 November 1987, 15th Anniversary **Obv:** Shield **Rev:** Stylized dove **Note:** Arabic legends

Date	Mintage	F	VF	XF	Unc	BU
AH1423-2002 Proof	40	Value: 1,000				

KM# 380 10 DINARS
38.0000 g., 0.9000 Silver 1.0995 oz. ASW **Subject:** 16th Anniversary 7 Nov 1987 plus International Solidarity Fund **Obv:** National arms **Rev:** Large 16 with hands holding globe within the 6, banner which says International Solidarity Fund **Edge:** Reeded

Date	Mintage	F	VF	XF	Unc	BU
AH1424-2003	—	—	—	—	250	—
AH1424-2003 Proof	—	Value: 300				

KM# 452 10 DINARS
38.0000 g., 0.9000 Silver 1.0995 oz. ASW, 40 mm. **Subject:** 7 November 1987, 16th Anniversary **Obv:** Shield **Rev:** Large 16 and globe

Date	Mintage	F	VF	XF	Unc	BU
AH1423-2003 Proof	24	Value: 225				

KM# 447 10 DINARS
18.1800 g., 0.9000 Gold 0.5260 oz. AGW, 28 mm. **Subject:** 7 November 1987, 16th Anniversary **Obv:** Shield **Rev:** Hand with UN logo **Note:** Arabic legend

Date	Mintage	F	VF	XF	Unc	BU
AH1424-2003 Proof	40	Value: 1,000				

KM# 448 10 DINARS
18.1800 g., 0.9000 Gold 0.5260 oz. AGW, 28 mm. **Subject:** 7 November 1987, 16th Anniversary **Obv:** Shield **Rev:** Hand with UN logo **Note:** French legends

Date	Mintage	F	VF	XF	Unc	BU
AH1424-2003 Proof	40	Value: 1,000				

KM# 454 10 DINARS
38.0000 g., 0.9000 Silver 1.0995 oz. ASW, 40 mm. **Subject:** 7 November 1987, 17th Anniversary - Elections **Obv:** Shield **Rev:** Star and crescent and stylized flame **Note:** French legends

Date	Mintage	F	VF	XF	Unc	BU
AH1425-2004 Proof	24	Value: 225				

KM# 458 10 DINARS
18.8000 g., 0.9000 Gold 0.5440 oz. AGW, 28 mm. **Subject:** 7 November 1987, 17th Anniversary - Elections **Obv:** Shield **Rev:** Star and crescent adn stylized flame **Note:** French legend

Date	Mintage	F	VF	XF	Unc	BU
AH1425-2004 Proof	40	Value: 1,000				

KM# 457 10 DINARS
18.8000 g., 0.9000 Gold 0.5440 oz. AGW, 28 mm. **Subject:** 7 November 1987, 17th Anniversary - Elections **Obv:** Shield **Rev:** Star and crescent and stylized flame **Note:** Arabic legend

Date	Mintage	F	VF	XF	Unc	BU
AH1425-2004 Proof	40	Value: 1,000				

KM# 381 10 DINARS
38.0000 g., 0.9000 Silver 1.0995 oz. ASW **Subject:** 17th Anniversary of 7 Nov 1987 plus Elections of President and Parliament **Obv:** National arms **Edge:** Reeded

Date	Mintage	F	VF	XF	Unc	BU
AH1425-2004	—	—	—	—	275	—

KM# 453 10 DINARS
38.0000 g., 0.9000 Silver 1.0995 oz. ASW, 40 mm. **Subject:** 7 November 1987, 17th Anniversary - Elections **Obv:** Shield **Rev:** Star and crescent and stylized flame **Note:** Arabic legends

Date	Mintage	F	VF	XF	Unc	BU
AH1425-2004 Proof	375	Value: 150				

KM# 467 10 DINARS
18.8000 g., 0.9000 Gold 0.5440 oz. AGW **Subject:** 7 November 1987, 18th Anniversary **Obv:** Shield **Rev:** Globe in stylized ship **Shape:** 28 **Note:** Arabic legends

Date	Mintage	F	VF	XF	Unc	BU
AH1426-2005 Proof	40	Value: 1,000				

KM# 382 10 DINARS
38.0000 g., 0.9000 Silver 1.0995 oz. ASW **Subject:** 18th Anniversary of 7 Nov 1987 and Conference on Information in Tunis 2005 **Edge:** Reeded

Date	Mintage	F	VF	XF	Unc	BU
AH1426-2005	—	—	—	—	275	—

KM# 464 10 DINARS
38.0000 g., 0.9000 Silver 1.0995 oz. ASW, 40 mm. **Subject:** 7 November 1987, 18th Anniversary **Obv:** Shield **Rev:** Globe in stylized ship **Note:** Arabic legend

Date	Mintage	F	VF	XF	Unc	BU
AH1426-2005 Proof	431	Value: 150				

KM# 468 10 DINARS
18.8000 g., 0.9000 Gold 0.5440 oz. AGW, 28 mm. **Subject:** 7 November 1987, 18th Anniversary **Obv:** Shield **Rev:** Globe in stylized ship **Note:** French legend

Date	Mintage	F	VF	XF	Unc	BU
AH1426-2005 Proof	40	Value: 1,000				

KM# 463 10 DINARS
38.0000 g., 0.9000 Silver 1.0995 oz. ASW, 40 mm. **Subject:** 7 November 1987, 18th Anniversary **Obv:** Shield **Rev:** Globe in stylized ship **Note:** French legends

Date	Mintage	F	VF	XF	Unc	BU
AH1426-2005 Proof	50	Value: 175				

KM# 475 10 DINARS
18.8000 g., 0.9000 Gold 0.5440 oz. AGW, 28 mm. **Subject:** 50th Anniversary **Obv:** Shield **Rev:** Logo **Note:** French legends

Date	Mintage	F	VF	XF	Unc	BU
AH1427-2006 Proof	200	Value: 1,000				

KM# 477 10 DINARS
38.0000 g., 0.9000 Silver 1.0995 oz. ASW, 40 mm. **Subject:** 7 November 1987, 19th Anniversary **Obv:** Shield **Rev:** Dove and atom **Note:** French legend

Date	Mintage	F	VF	XF	Unc	BU
AH1427-2006 Profo	30	Value: 225				

KM# 481 10 DINARS
18.8000 g., 0.9000 Gold 0.5440 oz. AGW, 28 mm. **Subject:** 7 November 1987, 19th Anniversary **Obv:** Shield **Rev:** Dove and atom **Note:** French legend

Date	Mintage	F	VF	XF	Unc	BU
AH1427-2006 Proof	40	Value: 1,000				

KM# 476 10 DINARS
38.0000 g., 0.9000 Silver 1.0995 oz. ASW, 40 mm. **Subject:** 7 November 1987, 19th Anniversary **Obv:** Shield **Rev:** Dove and atom **Note:** Arabic legend

Date	Mintage	F	VF	XF	Unc	BU
AH1427-2006 Proof	300	Value: 150				

KM# 480 10 DINARS
18.8000 g., 0.9000 Gold 0.5440 oz. AGW, 28 mm. **Subject:** 7 November 1987, 19th Anniversary **Obv:** Shield **Rev:** Dove and atom **Note:** Arabic legend

Date	Mintage	F	VF	XF	Unc	BU
AH1427-2006 Proof	40	Value: 1,000				

KM# 383 10 DINARS
38.0000 g., 0.9000 Silver 1.0995 oz. ASW **Subject:** 50th Anniversary of Independence (12.3.1956) **Obv:** National arms **Rev:** Stylized bird, "50", crescent moon with stars

Date	Mintage	F	VF	XF	Unc	BU
AH1427-2006	—	—	—	—	275	—

KM# 383a 10 DINARS
19.0000 g., 0.9000 Gold 0.5498 oz. AGW **Subject:** 50th Anniversary of Independence

Date	Mintage	F	VF	XF	Unc	BU
AH1427-2006 Proof	600	Value: 1,000				

KM# 474 10 DINARS
18.8000 g., 0.9000 Gold 0.5440 oz. AGW, 28 mm. **Subject:** 50th Anniversary **Obv:** Shield **Rev:** Logo **Note:** Arabic legends

Date	Mintage	F	VF	XF	Unc	BU
AH1427-2006 Proof	1,800	Value: 950				

KM# 488 10 DINARS
18.8000 g., 0.9000 Gold 0.5440 oz. AGW, 28 mm. **Subject:** 50th Anniversary **Obv:** Shield **Rev:** Ship, scales of Justice **Note:** Arabic legend

Date	Mintage	F	VF	XF	Unc	BU
AH1428-2007 Proof	450	Value: 975				

KM# 492 10 DINARS
18.8000 g., 0.9000 Gold 0.5440 oz. AGW, 28 mm. **Subject:** 7 November 1987, 20th Anniversary **Obv:** Head of Zine El abidine Ben Ali right **Rev:** Two profiles, keyboard, satellite receiver **Note:** Arabic legend

Date	Mintage	F	VF	XF	Unc	BU
AH1428-2007 Proof	42	Value: 1,000				

KM# 489 10 DINARS
18.8000 g., 0.9000 Gold 0.5440 oz. AGW, 28 mm. **Subject:** 50th Anniversary **Obv:** Shield **Rev:** Ship, scales of Justice **Note:** French legend

Date	Mintage	F	VF	XF	Unc	BU
AH1428-2007 Proof	50	Value: 1,000				

KM# 493 10 DINARS
18.8000 g., 0.9000 Gold 0.5440 oz. AGW, 28 mm. **Subject:** 7 November 1987, 20th Anniversary **Obv:** Head of Zine El Abidine Ben Ali right **Rev:** Two profiles, keyboard, satellite receiver **Note:** French legends

Date	Mintage	F	VF	XF	Unc	BU
AH1428-2007 Proof	40	Value: 1,000				

KM# 396 50 DINARS
21.0000 g., 0.9000 Gold 0.6076 oz. AGW, 34 mm. **Subject:** 14th Anniversary 7 Nov 1987 and 19th Mediterranean Games **Edge:** Reeded **Note:** Arabic legends.

Date	Mintage	F	VF	XF	Unc	BU
AH1422-2001 Proof	—	Value: 1,200				

KM# 431 50 DINARS
21.0000 g., 0.9000 Gold 0.6076 oz. AGW, 34 mm. **Subject:** 7 November 1987, 14th Anniversary **Obv:** Shield **Rev:** Open door **Note:** French legends

Date	Mintage	F	VF	XF	Unc	BU
AH1422-2001 Proof	150	Value: 1,150				

KM# 397 50 DINARS
21.0000 g., 0.9000 Gold 0.6076 oz. AGW, 34 mm. **Subject:** 15th Anniversary of 7 Nov 1987 **Edge:** Reeded

Date	Mintage	F	VF	XF	Unc	BU
AH1423-2002 Proof	—	Value: 1,200				

KM# 440 50 DINARS
21.0000 g., 0.9000 Gold 0.6076 oz. AGW, 21 mm. **Subject:** 7 November 1987, 15th Anniversary **Obv:** Shileld **Rev:** Stylized dove

Date	Mintage	F	VF	XF	Unc	BU
AH1423-2002 Proof	80	Value: 1,250				

KM# 439 50 DINARS
21.0000 g., 0.9000 Gold 0.6076 oz. AGW, 34 mm. **Subject:** 7 November 1987, 15th Anniversary **Obv:** Shield **Rev:** Stylized dove **Note:** Arabic legend

Date	Mintage	F	VF	XF	Unc	BU
AH1423-2002 Proof	580	Value: 1,100				

KM# 450 50 DINARS
21.0000 g., 0.9000 Gold 0.6076 oz. AGW, 34 mm. **Subject:** 7 November 1987, 16th Anniversary **Obv:** Shield **Rev:** Hand with UN logo **Note:** French legends

Date	Mintage	F	VF	XF	Unc	BU
AH1424-2003 Proof	55	Value: 1,250				

KM# 449 50 DINARS
21.0000 g., 0.9000 Gold 0.6076 oz. AGW, 34 mm. **Subject:** 7 November 1987, 16th Anniversary **Obv:** Shield **Rev:** Hand with UN logo **Note:** Arabic legends

Date	Mintage	F	VF	XF	Unc	BU
AH1424-2003 Proof	545	Value: 1,100				

KM# 459 50 DINARS
21.0000 g., 0.9000 Gold 0.6076 oz. AGW, 34 mm. **Subject:** 7 November 1987, 17th Anniversary - Elections **Obv:** Shield **Rev:** Star and crescent and stylized flame **Note:** Arabic legend

Date	Mintage	F	VF	XF	Unc	BU
AH1425-2004 Proof	379	Value: 1,100				

KM# 398 50 DINARS
21.0000 g., 0.9000 Gold 0.6076 oz. AGW, 34 mm. **Subject:** 17th Anniversary of 7 Nov 1987 plus Elections of President and Parliament **Edge:** Reeded

Date	Mintage	F	VF	XF	Unc	BU
AH1425-2004 Proof	—	Value: 1,250				

KM# 460 50 DINARS
21.0000 g., 0.9000 Gold 0.6076 oz. AGW, 34 mm. **Subject:** 7 November 1987, 17th Anniversary - Elections **Obv:** Shield **Rev:** Star and crescent and stylized flame **Note:** French legend

Date	Mintage	F	VF	XF	Unc	BU
AH1425-2004 Proof	28	Value: 1,250				

KM# 470 50 DINARS
21.0000 g., 0.9000 Gold 0.6076 oz. AGW, 34 mm. **Subject:** 7 November 1987, 18th Anniversary **Obv:** Shield **Rev:** Globe and stylized ship **Note:** French legend

Date	Mintage	F	VF	XF	Unc	BU
AH1426-2005 Proof	45	Value: 1,250				

KM# 482 50 DINARS
21.0000 g., 0.9000 Gold 0.6076 oz. AGW, 34 mm. **Subject:** 7 November 1987, 19th Anniversary **Obv:** Shield **Rev:** Dove and atom **Note:** Arabic legend

Date	Mintage	F	VF	XF	Unc	BU
AH1427-2006 Proof	183	Value: 1,200				

KM# 483 50 DINARS
21.0000 g., 0.9000 Gold 0.6076 oz. AGW, 34 mm. **Subject:** 7 November 1987, 19th Anniversary **Obv:** Shield **Rev:** Dove and atom **Note:** French legends

Date	Mintage	F	VF	XF	Unc	BU
AH1427-2006 Proof	23	Value: 1,250				

KM# 432 100 DINARS
38.0000 g., 0.9000 Gold 1.0995 oz. AGW, 43 mm. **Subject:** 7 November 1987, 14th Anniversary **Obv:** Shield **Rev:** Open door **Note:** Arabic legend

Date	Mintage	F	VF	XF	Unc	BU
AH1422-2001 Proof	375	Value: 1,950				

KM# 412 100 DINARS
38.0000 g., 0.9000 Gold 1.0995 oz. AGW, 40 mm. **Subject:** 14th Anniversary of 7 Nov 1987 and 19th Mediterranean Games **Obv:** National arms **Rev:** Olympic rings divide 2 portals **Edge:** Reeded

Date	Mintage	F	VF	XF	Unc	BU
AH1422-2001 Proof	—	Value: 2,100				

KM# 441 100 DINARS
38.0000 g., 0.9000 Gold 1.0995 oz. AGW, 43 mm. **Subject:** 7 November 1987, 15th Anniversary **Obv:** Shield **Rev:** Stylized dove **Note:** Arabic legends

Date	Mintage	F	VF	XF	Unc	BU
AH1423-2002 Proof	380	Value: 1,950				

KM# 442 100 DINARS
38.0000 g., 0.9000 Gold 1.0995 oz. AGW, 43 mm. **Subject:** 7 November 1987, 15th Anniversary **Obv:** Sheild **Rev:** Stylized dove **Note:** French legend

Date	Mintage	F	VF	XF	Unc	BU
AH1423-2002 Proof	110	Value: 2,000				

KM# 352 100 DINARS
38.0000 g., 0.9000 Gold 1.0995 oz. AGW, 40 mm. **Subject:** United Nations **Obv:** National arms above value **Rev:** UN logo on stylized hand **Edge:** Reeded

Date	Mintage	F	VF	XF	Unc	BU
AH1424-2003 Proof	—	Value: 2,100				

KM# 451 100 DINARS
38.0000 g., 0.9000 Gold 1.0995 oz. AGW, 43 mm. **Subject:** 7 November 1987, 16th Anniversary **Obv:** Shield **Rev:** Hand with UN logo **Note:** French text

Date	Mintage	F	VF	XF	Unc	BU
AH1424-2003 Proof	53	Value: 2,100				

KM# 462 100 DINARS
38.0000 g., 0.9000 Gold 1.0995 oz. AGW, 43 mm. **Subject:** 7 November 1987, 17th Anniversary - Elections **Obv:** Shield **Rev:** Star and crescent and stylized flame **Note:** French legends

Date	Mintage	F	VF	XF	Unc	BU
AH1425-2004 Proof	44	Value: 2,100				

KM# 461 100 DINARS
38.0000 g., 0.9000 Gold 1.0995 oz. AGW, 43 mm. **Subject:** 7 November 1987, 17th Anniversary - Elections **Obv:** Shield **Rev:** Star and crescent and stylized flame **Note:** Arabic legend

Date	Mintage	F	VF	XF	Unc	BU
AH1425-2004 Proof	385	Value: 1,950				

KM# 469 100 DINARS
21.0000 g., 0.9000 Gold 0.6076 oz. AGW, 34 mm. **Subject:** 7 November 1987, 18th Anniversary **Obv:** Shield **Rev:** Globe in stylized ship **Note:** Arabic legend

Date	Mintage	F	VF	XF	Unc	BU
AH1426-2005 Proof	390	Value: 1,100				

KM# 413 100 DINARS
38.0000 g., 0.9000 Gold 1.0995 oz. AGW **Subject:** 18th Anniversary of 7 Nov 1987 and Conference on Information in Tunis 2005 **Edge:** Reeded

Date	Mintage	F	VF	XF	Unc	BU
AH1426-2005 Proof	—	Value: 2,100				

KM# 471 100 DINARS
38.0000 g., 0.9000 Gold 1.0995 oz. AGW, 43 mm. **Subject:** 7 November 1987, 18th Anniversary **Obv:** Shield **Rev:** Globe in stylized ship **Note:** French legends

Date	Mintage	F	VF	XF	Unc	BU
AH1426-2005 Proof	45	Value: 2,100				

KM# 485 100 DINARS
38.0000 g., 0.9000 Gold 1.0995 oz. AGW, 43 mm. **Subject:** 7 November 1987, 19th Anniversary **Obv:** Shield **Rev:** Dove and atom **Note:** French legend

Date	Mintage	F	VF	XF	Unc	BU
AH1427-2006 Proof	23	Value: 2,200				

KM# 484 100 DINARS
38.0000 g., 0.9000 Gold 1.0995 oz. AGW, 43 mm. **Subject:** 7 November 1987, 19th Anniversary **Obv:** Shield **Rev:** Dove and atom **Note:** Arabic legend

Date	Mintage	F	VF	XF	Unc	BU
AH1427-2006 Proof	212	Value: 2,000				

TURKEY

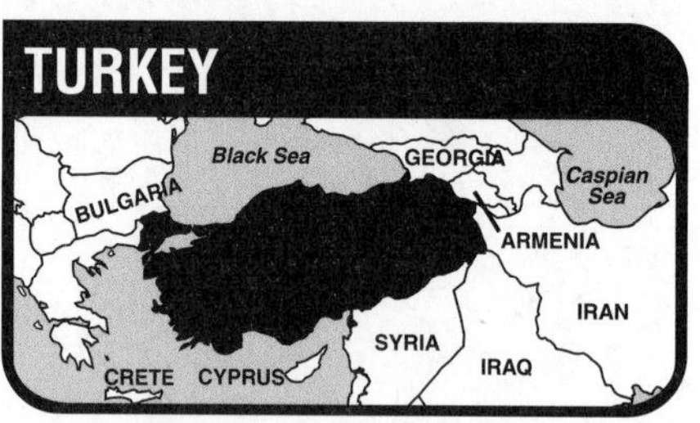

The Republic of Turkey, a parliamentary democracy of the Near East located partially in Europe and partially in Asia between the Black and the Mediterranean Seas, has an area of 301,382 sq. mi. (780,580 sq. km.) and a population of *55.4 million. Capital: Ankara. Turkey exports cotton, hazelnuts, and tobacco, and enjoys a virtual monopoly in meerschaum.

RULER
Republic, AH1341/AD1923-

Mint mark
"d" for darphane (meaning mint) is used on coins for overseas market.

REPUBLIC

DECIMAL COINAGE

40 Para = 1 Kurus; 100 Kurus = 1 Lira

KM# 1104 25000 LIRA (25 Bin Lira)
2.7000 g., Brass, 17 mm. **Obv:** Head left **Rev:** Value **Edge:** Plain

Date	Mintage	F	VF	XF	Unc	BU
2001	—	—	—	—	2.00	—
2002	—	—	—	—	2.00	—
2003	—	—	—	—	2.00	—

KM# 1105 50000 LIRA (50 Bin Lira)
3.2000 g., Copper-Nickel-Zinc, 17.75 mm. **Obv:** Head left within circle **Rev:** Value **Edge:** Plain

Date	Mintage	F	VF	XF	Unc	BU
2001	—	—	—	—	0.50	—
2002	—	—	—	—	0.50	—
2003	—	—	—	—	0.50	—
2004	—	—	—	—	0.50	—

KM# 1106 100000 LIRA (100 Bin Lira)
4.6000 g., Copper-Nickel-Zinc, 21 mm. **Obv:** Head with hat right within circle **Rev:** Value **Edge:** Plain

Date	Mintage	F	VF	XF	Unc	BU
2001	—	—	—	—	0.75	1.25
2002	—	—	—	—	0.75	1.25
2003	—	—	—	—	0.75	1.25
2004	—	—	—	—	0.75	1.25

KM# 1137 250000 LIRA
6.4200 g., Copper-Nickel-Zinc, 23.4 mm. **Obv:** Bust facing within circle **Rev:** Value **Edge Lettering:** "T.C." six times dividing reeded sections

Date	Mintage	F	VF	XF	Unc	BU
2002	—	—	—	—	1.00	1.50
2003	—	—	—	—	1.00	1.50
2004	—	—	—	—	1.00	1.50

KM# 1161 500000 LIRA
4.6000 g., Copper-Nickel, 21 mm. **Obv:** Value and date within sprigs **Rev:** One sheep **Edge:** Plain

Date	Mintage	F	VF	XF	Unc	BU
2002	—	—	—	—	2.00	3.00

KM# 1162 750000 LIRA
6.4000 g., Copper-Nickel, 23.5 mm. **Obv:** Value and date within sprigs **Rev:** Angora Ram **Edge:** Plain

Date	Mintage	F	VF	XF	Unc	BU
2002	—	—	—	—	3.00	4.00

KM# 1163 1000000 LIRA
12.0000 g., Copper-Nickel, 31.9 mm. **Obv:** Value and date within sprigs **Rev:** Turbaned bust 1/4 left divides dates **Edge:** Reeded

Date	Mintage	F	VF	XF	Unc	BU
2002	—	—	—	—	5.00	6.00

KM# 1170 1000000 LIRA
31.4200 g., 0.9250 Silver 0.9344 oz. ASW, 38.6 mm. **Subject:** Mevlana Celaleddin-I Rumi **Obv:** Value and date in wreath **Rev:** Turbaned bust **Edge:** Reeded

Date	Mintage	F	VF	XF	Unc	BU
2002 Proof	—	Value: 40.00				

KM# 1139.1 1000000 LIRA
11.8700 g., Bi-Metallic Brass center in Copper-Nickel ring, 32.1 mm. **Subject:** Foundation of the Mint **Obv:** Building and value within circle **Rev:** Legend and date inscription **Edge:** Plain **Note:** This coin type is produced by a machine outside the money museum at the Istanbul Mint. Visitors pay 1 mio lira, press a button and strike a coin with the actual date of their visit. Many other dates exist in unknown and unregistered quantities. Only Turkish months are on struck coins.

Date	Mintage	F	VF	XF	Unc	BU
Mayis 2002	—	—	—	—	5.00	6.00
Haziran 2002	—	—	—	—	5.00	6.00
Temmuz 2002	—	—	—	—	5.00	6.00
Agostos 2002	—	—	—	—	5.00	6.00
Eylul 2002	—	—	—	—	5.00	6.00
Ekim 2002	—	—	—	—	5.00	6.00
Kasim 2002	—	—	—	—	5.00	6.00
Aralik 2002	—	—	—	—	5.00	6.00

KM# 1139.2 1000000 LIRA
Bi-Metallic Brass center in Copper-Nickel ring., 32.1 mm. **Subject:** Foundation of the Mint **Obv:** Building and value within circle **Rev:** Legend and date inscription **Edge:** Plain **Note:** This coin type is produced by a machine outside the money museum at the Istanbul Mint. Visitors pay 1 mio lira, press a button and strike a coin with the actual date of their visit. Many other dates exist in unknown and unregistered quantities. The months are listed in both Turkish and English on struck coins.

Date	Mintage	F	VF	XF	Unc	BU
Ocak/January 2003	—	—	—	—	5.00	6.00
Subat/February 2003	—	—	—	—	5.00	6.00
Mart/March 2003	—	—	—	—	5.00	6.00
Nisan/April 2003	—	—	—	—	5.00	6.00
Mayis/May 2003	—	—	—	—	5.00	6.00
Haziran/June 2003	—	—	—	—	5.00	6.00

Date	Mintage	F	VF	XF	Unc	BU
Temmuz/July 2003	—	—	—	—	5.00	6.00
Agostos/August 2003	—	—	—	—	5.00	6.00
Eylul/September 2003	—	—	—	—	5.00	6.00
Ekim/October 2003	—	—	—	—	5.00	6.00
Kasim/November 2003	—	—	—	—	5.00	6.00
Aralik/December 2003	—	—	—	—	5.00	6.00

KM# 1110 5000000 LIRA
67.0000 g., Bronze, 50 mm. **Subject:** Children's Day **Obv:** Legend and inscription **Rev:** Dancing children **Edge:** Plain

Date	Mintage	F	VF	XF	Unc	BU
2001 Matte	1,583	—	—	—	35.00	—

KM# 1142 7500000 LIRA
31.2500 g., 0.9250 Silver 0.9293 oz. ASW, 38.5 mm. **Subject:** Cahit Arf, Turkish mathematician (1910-1997) **Obv:** Mathematical formula within circle **Rev:** 1/2-length figure facing **Edge:** Reeded

Date	Mintage	F	VF	XF	Unc	BU
2001 Proof	—	Value: 45.00				

KM# 1143 7500000 LIRA
31.2500 g., 0.9250 Silver 0.9293 oz. ASW, 38.5 mm. **Obv:** Ornamented circle design **Rev:** 1/2-length bust facing **Edge:** Reeded

Date	Mintage	F	VF	XF	Unc	BU
2001 Proof	—	Value: 45.00				

KM# 1144 7500000 LIRA
31.2500 g., 0.9250 Silver 0.9293 oz. ASW, 38.5 mm. **Subject:** Koca Yusuf Baspehlivan **Obv:** Two figures wrestling **Rev:** Portrait on circular background **Edge:** Reeded

Date	Mintage	F	VF	XF	Unc	BU
2001 Proof	—	Value: 42.50				

KM# 1120 7500000 LIRA
15.4000 g., 0.9250 Silver 0.4580 oz. ASW **Subject:** Bird Series - Saz Horozu **Obv:** Value and date within sprigs **Rev:** Purple swamphen on ground **Edge:** Plain **Shape:** 4-sided **Note:** 28.1 x 28.1mm

Date	Mintage	F	VF	XF	Unc	BU
2001 Proof	—	Value: 35.00				

KM# 1121 7500000 LIRA
15.4000 g., 0.9250 Silver 0.4580 oz. ASW **Subject:** Bird Series - Toy **Obv:** Value and date within sprigs **Rev:** Greater Bustard on ground **Edge:** Plain **Shape:** 4-sided **Note:** 28.1 x 28.1mm

Date	Mintage	F	VF	XF	Unc	BU
2001 Proof	—	Value: 35.00				

KM# 1122 7500000 LIRA
15.4000 g., 0.9250 Silver 0.4580 oz. ASW **Subject:** Bird Series - Yaz Ordegi **Obv:** Value and date within sprigs **Rev:** White-headed Duck on ground **Edge:** Plain **Shape:** 4-sided **Note:** 28.1 x 28.1mm

Date	Mintage	F	VF	XF	Unc	BU
2001 Proof	—	Value: 35.00				

KM# 1123 7500000 LIRA
15.4000 g., 0.9250 Silver 0.4580 oz. ASW **Subject:** Bird Series - Dikkuyruk **Obv:** Value and date within sprigs **Rev:** Marbled teal on water **Edge:** Plain **Shape:** 4-sided **Note:** 28.1 x 28.1mm

Date	Mintage	F	VF	XF	Unc	BU
2001 Proof	—	Value: 35.00				

KM# 1124 7500000 LIRA
15.4000 g., 0.9250 Silver 0.4580 oz. ASW **Subject:** Bird Series - Yesil Arikusu **Obv:** Value and date within sprigs **Rev:** Bee-eater on branch **Edge:** Plain **Shape:** 4-sided **Note:** 28.1 x 28.1mm

Date	Mintage	F	VF	XF	Unc	BU
2001 Proof	—	Value: 35.00				

KM# 1125 7500000 LIRA
15.4000 g., 0.9250 Silver 0.4580 oz. ASW **Subject:** Bird Series - Kucuk Karabatak **Obv:** Value and date within sprigs **Rev:** Three pygmy cormorants **Edge:** Plain **Shape:** 4-sided **Note:** 28.1 x 28.1mm

Date	Mintage	F	VF	XF	Unc	BU
2001 Proof	—	Value: 35.00				

KM# 1126 7500000 LIRA
15.4000 g., 0.9250 Silver 0.4580 oz. ASW **Subject:** Bird Series - Kizil Akbaba **Obv:** Value and date within sprigs **Rev:** Eurasian griffon **Edge:** Plain **Shape:** 4-sided **Note:** 28.1 x 28.1mm

Date	Mintage	F	VF	XF	Unc	BU
2001 Proof	—	Value: 35.00				

KM# 1127 7500000 LIRA
15.4000 g., 0.9250 Silver 0.4580 oz. ASW **Subject:** Bird Series - Sah Kartal **Obv:** Value and date within sprigs **Rev:** Eagles **Edge:** Plain **Shape:** 4-sided **Note:** 28.1 x 28.1mm

Date	Mintage	F	VF	XF	Unc	BU
2001 Proof	—	Value: 35.00				

KM# 1128 7500000 LIRA
15.4000 g., 0.9250 Silver 0.4580 oz. ASW **Subject:** Bird Series - Ala Sigireik **Obv:** Value and date within sprigs **Rev:** Rosy starling on ground **Edge:** Plain **Shape:** 4-sided **Note:** 28.1 x 28.1mm

Date	Mintage	F	VF	XF	Unc	BU
2001 Proof	—	Value: 35.00				

KM# 1129 7500000 LIRA
15.4000 g., 0.9250 Silver 0.4580 oz. ASW **Subject:** Bird Series - Izmir Yalicapkini **Obv:** Value and date within sprigs **Rev:** White-throated kingfisher on stump **Edge:** Plain **Shape:** 4-sided **Note:** 28.1 x 28.1mm

Date	Mintage	F	VF	XF	Unc	BU
2001 Proof	—	Value: 35.00				

KM# 1130 7500000 LIRA
15.4000 g., 0.9250 Silver 0.4580 oz. ASW **Subject:** Bird Series - Turac **Obv:** Value and date within sprigs **Rev:** Black francolin birds on the ground **Edge:** Plain **Shape:** 4-sided **Note:** 28.1 x 28.1mm

Date	Mintage	F	VF	XF	Unc	BU
2001 Proof	—	Value: 35.00				

KM# 1131 7500000 LIRA
15.4000 g., 0.9250 Silver 0.4580 oz. ASW **Subject:** Bird Series - Kelaynak **Obv:** Value and date within sprigs **Rev:** Two Bald Ibis birds on ground **Edge:** Plain **Shape:** 4-sided **Note:** 28.1 x 28.1mm

Date	Mintage	F	VF	XF	Unc	BU
2001 Proof	—	Value: 35.00				

KM# 1132 7500000 LIRA
15.4000 g., 0.9250 Silver 0.4580 oz. ASW **Subject:** Bird Series - Sakalli Akbaba **Obv:** Value and date within sprigs **Rev:** Bearded vulture **Edge:** Plain **Shape:** 4-sided **Note:** 28.1 x 28.1mm

Date	Mintage	F	VF	XF	Unc	BU
2001 Proof	—	Value: 35.00				

KM# 1133 7500000 LIRA
15.4000 g., 0.9250 Silver 0.4580 oz. ASW **Subject:** Bird Series - Tepeli Pelikan **Obv:** Value and date within sprigs **Rev:** Dalmatian pelican on rock **Edge:** Plain **Shape:** Square **Note:** 28.1 x 28.1mm

Date	Mintage	F	VF	XF	Unc	BU
2001 Proof	—	Value: 35.00				

KM# 1134 7500000 LIRA
15.4000 g., 0.9250 Silver 0.4580 oz. ASW **Subject:** Bird Series - Ishakkusu **Obv:** Value and date within sprigs **Rev:** European scops owl on branch **Edge:** Plain **Shape:** Square **Note:** 28.1 x 28.1mm

Date	Mintage	F	VF	XF	Unc	BU
2001 Proof	—	Value: 35.00				

KM# 1117 7500000 LIRA
31.4700 g., 0.9250 Silver 0.9359 oz. ASW **Subject:** Iznik Tabak **Obv:** Two peacocks within circle **Rev:** Iznik Tabak (Nicean pottery) 1570; Circle of flowers at center

Date	Mintage	F	VF	XF	Unc	BU
2001 Proof	1,349	Value: 50.00				

KM# 1135 7500000 LIRA
31.0300 g., 0.9250 Silver 0.9228 oz. ASW, 38.5 mm. **Subject:** Mevlana Celaleddin-i Rumi **Obv:** Dancer within circle **Rev:** Turbaned bust 3/4 right above dates **Edge:** Reeded

Date	Mintage	F	VF	XF	Unc	BU
2001 Proof	—	Value: 45.00				

KM# 1145 7500000 LIRA
15.6100 g., 0.9250 Silver 0.4642 oz. ASW, 27.9 x 38.6 mm. **Series:** Flowers **Obv:** Value and date within sprigs **Rev:** Paeonia turcica **Edge:** Reeded **Shape:** Oval

Date	Mintage	F	VF	XF	Unc	BU
2002 Proof	—	Value: 28.00				

KM# 1146 7500000 LIRA
15.6100 g., 0.9250 Silver 0.4642 oz. ASW, 27.9 x 38.6 mm. **Series:** Flowers **Obv:** Value and date within sprigs **Rev:** Orchis anatolica **Edge:** Reeded **Shape:** Oval

Date	Mintage	F	VF	XF	Unc	BU
2002 Proof	—	Value: 28.00				

KM# 1147 7500000 LIRA
15.6100 g., 0.9250 Silver 0.4642 oz. ASW, 27.9 x 38.6 mm. **Series:** Flowers **Obv:** Value and date within sprigs **Rev:** Iris pamphylica **Edge:** Reeded **Shape:** Oval

Date	Mintage	F	VF	XF	Unc	BU
2002 Proof	—	Value: 28.00				

KM# 1148 7500000 LIRA
15.6100 g., 0.9250 Silver 0.4642 oz. ASW, 27.9 x 38.6 mm. **Series:** Flowers **Obv:** Value and date within sprigs **Rev:** Gladiolus anatolicus **Edge:** Reeded **Shape:** Oval

Date	Mintage	F	VF	XF	Unc	BU
2002 Proof	—	Value: 28.00				

KM# 1149 7500000 LIRA
15.6100 g., 0.9250 Silver 0.4642 oz. ASW, 27.9 x 38.6 mm. **Series:** Flowers **Obv:** Value and date within sprigs **Rev:** Crocus sativus **Edge:** Reeded **Shape:** Oval

Date	Mintage	F	VF	XF	Unc	BU
2002 Proof	—	Value: 28.00				

KM# 1150 7500000 LIRA
15.6100 g., 0.9250 Silver 0.4642 oz. ASW, 27.9 x 38.6 mm. **Series:** Flowers **Obv:** Value and date within sprigs **Rev:** Campanula betulifolia **Edge:** Reeded **Shape:** Oval

Date	Mintage	F	VF	XF	Unc	BU
2002 Proof	—	Value: 28.00				

KM# 1151 7500000 LIRA
15.6100 g., 0.9250 Silver 0.4642 oz. ASW, 27.9 x 38.6 mm. **Series:** Flowers **Obv:** Value and date within sprigs **Rev:** Centaurea tchihatcheffii **Edge:** Reeded **Shape:** Oval

Date	Mintage	F	VF	XF	Unc	BU
2002 Proof	—	Value: 28.00				

KM# 1152 7500000 LIRA
15.6100 g., 0.9250 Silver 0.4642 oz. ASW, 27.9 x 38.6 mm. **Series:** Flowers **Obv:** Value and date within sprigs **Rev:** Tchihatchewia isatidea **Edge:** Reeded **Shape:** Oval

Date	Mintage	F	VF	XF	Unc	BU
2002 Proof	—	Value: 28.00				

KM# 1153 7500000 LIRA
15.6100 g., 0.9250 Silver 0.4642 oz. ASW, 27.9 x 38.6 mm. **Series:** Flowers **Obv:** Value and date within sprigs **Rev:** Linum anatolicum **Edge:** Reeded **Shape:** Oval

Date	Mintage	F	VF	XF	Unc	BU
2002 Proof	—	Value: 28.00				

KM# 1154 7500000 LIRA
15.6100 g., 0.9250 Silver 0.4642 oz. ASW, 27.9 x 38.6 mm. **Series:** Flowers **Obv:** Value and date within sprigs **Rev:** Cyclamen trochopteranthum **Edge:** Reeded **Shape:** Oval

Date	Mintage	F	VF	XF	Unc	BU
2002 Proof	—	Value: 28.00				

KM# 1155 7500000 LIRA
15.6100 g., 0.9250 Silver 0.4642 oz. ASW, 27.9 x 38.6 mm. **Series:** Flowers **Obv:** Value and date within sprigs **Rev:** Tulipa orphanidea **Edge:** Reeded **Shape:** Oval

Date	Mintage	F	VF	XF	Unc	BU
2002 Proof	—	Value: 28.00				

KM# 1156 7500000 LIRA
15.6100 g., 0.9250 Silver 0.4642 oz. ASW, 27.9 x 38.6 mm. **Obv:** Value and date within sprigs **Rev:** Stenbergia candida **Edge:** Reeded **Shape:** Oval

Date	Mintage	F	VF	XF	Unc	BU
2002 Proof	—	Value: 28.00				

KM# 1157 7500000 LIRA
15.6100 g., 0.9250 Silver 0.4642 oz. ASW, 27.9 x 38.6 mm. **Series:** Flowers **Obv:** Value and date within sprigs **Rev:** Arum maculatum **Edge:** Reeded **Shape:** Oval

Date	Mintage	F	VF	XF	Unc	BU
2002 Proof	—	Value: 28.00				

KM# 1118 10000000 LIRA
31.4700 g., 0.9250 Silver 0.9359 oz. ASW, 38.6 mm. **Subject:** Divrigi Ulu Camii **Obv:** Artwork within circle **Rev:** Ornate door at the Divrigi ulu Camii (Divrigi Great Mosque) built 1228 in Sivas Province **Edge:** Reeded

Date	Mintage	F	VF	XF	Unc	BU
2001 Matte	15,000	—	—	—	40.00	—

KM# 1159 10000000 LIRA
31.4200 g., 0.9250 Silver 0.9344 oz. ASW, 38.6 mm. **Subject:** Bogazici'nde Yalilar **Obv:** Value and date within sprigs **Rev:** Waterfront buildings **Edge:** Reeded

Date	Mintage	F	VF	XF	Unc	BU
2001 Proof	4,458	Value: 40.00				

KM# 1160 10000000 LIRA
31.4200 g., 0.9250 Silver 0.9344 oz. ASW, 38.6 mm. **Obv:** Turkish mint symbol within circle **Rev:** Mosque within surrounding buildings **Edge:** Reeded

Date	Mintage	F	VF	XF	Unc	BU
2002 Proof	2,106	Value: 45.00				

KM# 1140 10000000 LIRA
31.4600 g., 0.9250 Silver 0.9356 oz. ASW, 38.6 mm. **Subject:** 75th Anniversary of TRT (Türkiye Radyo Televizyon) **Obv:** Large mint mark and design within circle **Rev:** Radio microphone **Edge:** Reeded

Date	Mintage	F	VF	XF	Unc	BU
2002 Proof	—	Value: 45.00				

KM# 1265 150000000 LIRA
31.4900 g., 0.9250 Silver 0.9365 oz. ASW, 38.61 mm. **Subject:** 2006 FIFA World Cup **Obv:** Value within wreath **Rev:** Two scoccer players and globe **Edge:** Reeded

Date	Mintage	F	VF	XF	Unc	BU
2003 Proof	Est. 5,000	Value: 50.00				

REFORM DECIMAL COINAGE

2005
100,000 Old Lira = 1 New Lira

KM# 1164 NEW KURUS
2.7200 g., Aluminum-Bronze, 17 mm. **Obv:** Head of Atatürk left within circle **Rev:** Value **Edge:** Plain

Date	Mintage	F	VF	XF	Unc	BU
2005	148,419,560	—	—	—	0.15	0.20
2006	9,002,010	—	—	—	0.15	0.20
2007	5,357,000	—	—	—	0.15	0.20
2008	—	—	—	—	0.15	0.20

KM# 1165 5 NEW KURUS
2.9500 g., Copper-Nickel-Zinc, 17.1 mm. **Obv:** Head of Atatürk left within circle **Rev:** Value **Edge:** Plain

Date	Mintage	F	VF	XF	Unc	BU
2005	203,339,160	—	—	0.10	0.25	0.35
2006	202,253,310	—	—	0.10	0.25	0.35
2007	122,090,000	—	—	0.10	0.25	0.35
2008	—	—	—	0.10	0.25	0.35

KM# 1166 10 NEW KURUS
3.8300 g., Copper-Nickel-Zinc, 19.4 mm. **Obv:** Head of Atatürk with hat right within circle **Rev:** Value **Edge:** Plain

Date	Mintage	F	VF	XF	Unc	BU
2005	261,538,050	—	—	0.20	0.45	0.60
2006	196,717,510	—	—	0.20	0.45	0.60
2007	134,104,000	—	—	0.20	0.45	0.60
2008	—	—	—	0.20	0.45	0.60

KM# 1167 25 NEW KURUS
5.3000 g., Copper-Nickel-Zinc, 21.5 mm. **Obv:** Bust of Atatürk facing within circle **Rev:** Value **Edge:** Reeded

Date	Mintage	F	VF	XF	Unc	BU
2005	173,705,760	—	—	0.25	0.60	0.80
2006	67,803,010	—	—	0.30	0.75	1.00
2007	33,463,500	—	—	0.25	0.60	0.80
2008	—	—	—	0.25	0.60	0.80

KM# 1168 50 NEW KURUS
7.0000 g., Bi-Metallic Copper-Nickel center in Nickel-Brass ring, 23.8 mm. **Obv:** Head of Atatürk right within circle **Rev:** Value within circle **Edge:** Reeded

Date	Mintage	F	VF	XF	Unc	BU
2005	203,749,569	—	—	0.60	1.50	2.00
2006	45,089,010	—	—	0.60	1.50	2.00
2007	21,946,500	—	—	0.50	1.20	1.60
2008	—	—	—	0.50	1.20	1.60

KM# 1169 NEW LIRA
8.5000 g., Bi-Metallic Nickel-Bronze center in Copper-Nickel-Zinc ring, 26 mm. **Obv:** Bust of Atatürk 3/4 left within circle **Rev:** Value within circle **Edge:** Segmented reeding

Date	Mintage	F	VF	XF	Unc	BU
2005	305,235,560	—	—	—	2.25	3.00
2006	69,247,010	—	—	—	2.25	3.00
2007	56,498,200	—	—	—	2.25	3.00
2008	—	—	—	—	2.25	3.00

KM# 1171 5 NEW LIRA
12.0000 g., Bi-Metallic Brass center in Copper-Nickel ring, 32 mm. **Subject:** 23rd Universiade in red holder **Obv:** Stylized bird within circle **Rev:** Logo within circle **Designer:** Nesrin Ek

Date	Mintage	F	VF	XF	Unc	BU
ND (2005)	2,957	—	—	—	22.00	25.00

KM# 1172 5 NEW LIRA
12.0000 g., Bi-Metallic Copper-Nickel center in Brass ring, 32 mm. **Subject:** 23rd Universiade in blue holder **Obv:** Stylized bird within circle **Rev:** Logo within circle **Designer:** Nesrin Ek

Date	Mintage	F	VF	XF	Unc	BU
ND (2005)	2,900	—	—	—	22.00	25.00

KM# 1195 15 NEW LIRA
1.2400 g., 0.9990 Gold 0.0398 oz. AGW, 13.92 mm. **Subject:** Nemrud **Obv:** Value within wreath **Rev:** Two large statue heads **Designer:** Nesrin Ek **Note:** Dated 2003 but released in 2005

Date	Mintage	F	VF	XF	Unc	BU
2003	1,820	Value: 75.00				

KM# 1193 15 NEW LIRA
15.5500 g., 0.9250 Silver 0.4624 oz. ASW, 32 mm. **Obv:** Bird **Rev:** Logo **Designer:** Nesrin Ek

Date	Mintage	F	VF	XF	Unc	BU
2005 Proof	1,237	Value: 40.00				

KM# 1203 15 NEW LIRA
31.4700 g., 0.9250 Silver 0.9359 oz. ASW, 38.6 mm. **Subject:** Scouting in Turkey, 100th Anniversary **Obv:** Scout emblem, multicolor **Rev:** Flag, Scouts saluting, camp scene

Date	Mintage	F	VF	XF	Unc	BU
2007 Proof	1,414	Value: 50.00				

KM# 1180.1 20 NEW LIRA
23.5000 g., 0.9250 Silver 0.6988 oz. ASW, 38.6 mm. **Obv:** Value within sprigs and circle **Rev:** Angora Cat with plain eyes **Edge:** Reeded

Date	Mintage	F	VF	XF	Unc	BU
2005 Proof	5,000	Value: 60.00				

KM# 1180.2 20 NEW LIRA
23.5000 g., 0.9250 Silver 0.6988 oz. ASW, 38.6 mm. **Obv:** Value within sprigs and circle **Rev:** Angora cat with mismatched colored eyes **Edge:** Reeded

Date	Mintage	F	VF	XF	Unc	BU
2005 Proof	—	Value: 65.00				

KM# 1173 20 NEW LIRA
31.3600 g., 0.9250 Silver 0.9326 oz. ASW, 38.6 mm. **Obv:** Value within sprigs and circle **Rev:** Aegean Carpet **Edge:** Reeded

Date	Mintage	F	VF	XF	Unc	BU
2005 Proof	1,195	Value: 70.00				

KM# 1174 20 NEW LIRA

31.4300 g., 0.9250 Silver 0.9347 oz. ASW, 38.6 mm. **Obv:** Value within sprigs and circle **Rev:** Mostar Bridge **Edge:** Reeded

Date	Mintage	F	VF	XF	Unc	BU
2005 Proof	1,592	Value: 75.00				

KM# 1175 20 NEW LIRA

23.4500 g., 0.9250 Silver 0.6974 oz. ASW, 38.6 mm. **Obv:** Value within sprigs and circle **Rev:** Angora Goat **Edge:** Reeded

Date	Mintage	F	VF	XF	Unc	BU
2005 Proof	898	Value: 60.00				

KM# 1176 20 NEW LIRA

23.4600 g., 0.9250 Silver 0.6977 oz. ASW, 38.6 mm. **Obv:** Value within sprigs and circle **Rev:** Long-eared Desert Hedgehog **Edge:** Reeded

Date	Mintage	F	VF	XF	Unc	BU
2005 Proof	744	Value: 60.00				

KM# 1177 20 NEW LIRA

23.4100 g., 0.9250 Silver 0.6962 oz. ASW, 38.6 mm. **Obv:** Value within sprigs and circle **Rev:** Anatolian Mouflon **Edge:** Reeded

Date	Mintage	F	VF	XF	Unc	BU
2005 Proof	779	Value: 60.00				

KM# 1178 20 NEW LIRA

23.4300 g., 0.9250 Silver 0.6968 oz. ASW, 38.6 mm. **Obv:** Value within sprigs and circle **Rev:** Striped Hyena **Edge:** Reeded

Date	Mintage	F	VF	XF	Unc	BU
2005 Proof	778	Value: 60.00				

KM# 1179 20 NEW LIRA

23.4300 g., 0.9250 Silver 0.6968 oz. ASW, 38.6 mm. **Obv:** Value within sprigs and circle **Rev:** Hazel Dormouse **Edge:** Reeded

Date	Mintage	F	VF	XF	Unc	BU
2005 Proof	744	Value: 60.00				

KM# 1181 20 NEW LIRA

23.3700 g., 0.9990 Silver 0.7506 oz. ASW, 38.6 mm. **Obv:** Value within sprigs and circle **Rev:** Anatolian Leopard **Edge:** Reeded

Date	Mintage	F	VF	XF	Unc	BU
2005 Proof	855	Value: 60.00				

KM# 1182 20 NEW LIRA

23.2500 g., 0.9250 Silver 0.6914 oz. ASW, 38.6 mm. **Obv:** Value within sprigs and circle **Rev:** Turkish Kangal Dog **Edge:** Reeded

Date	Mintage	F	VF	XF	Unc	BU
2005 Proof	1,128	Value: 60.00				

KM# 1183 20 NEW LIRA

23.4600 g., 0.9250 Silver 0.6977 oz. ASW, 38.6 mm. **Obv:** Value within sprigs and circle **Rev:** Five-toed Jerboa **Edge:** Reeded

Date	Mintage	F	VF	XF	Unc	BU
2005 Proof	746	Value: 60.00				

KM# 1184 20 NEW LIRA

23.2600 g., 0.9250 Silver 0.6917 oz. ASW, 38.6 mm. **Obv:** Value within sprigs and circle **Rev:** Brown Bear **zEdge:** Reeded

Date	Mintage	F	VF	XF	Unc	BU
2005 Proof	802	Value: 60.00				

KM# 1185 20 NEW LIRA

23.5300 g., 0.9250 Silver 0.6997 oz. ASW, 38.6 mm. **Obv:** Value within sprigs and circle **Rev:** Desert Monitor **Edge:** Reeded

Date	Mintage	F	VF	XF	Unc	BU
2005 Proof	753	Value: 60.00				

KM# 1188 20 NEW LIRA

31.4700 g., 0.9250 Silver 0.9359 oz. ASW, 38.6 mm. **Subject:** Edirne Selimiye Mosque **Obv:** Value within wreath **Rev:** Mosque

Date	Mintage	F	VF	XF	Unc	BU
2005 Proof	1,660	Value: 55.00				

KM# 1189 20 NEW LIRA

31.4700 g., 0.9250 Silver 0.9359 oz. ASW, 38.6 mm. **Obv:** Crescent and star **Rev:** Large 85 above building

Date	Mintage	F	VF	XF	Unc	BU
2005 Proof	1,216	Value: 55.00				

KM# 1190 20 NEW LIRA

31.4700 g., 0.9250 Silver 0.9359 oz. ASW, 38.6 mm. **Subject:** Galatasaray Spor **Obv:** 100 above team mascot **Rev:** GS monogram

Date	Mintage	F	VF	XF	Unc	BU
2005 Proof	2,828	Value: 55.00				

KM# 1194 20 NEW LIRA

31.4700 g., 0.9250 Silver 0.9359 oz. ASW, 38.6 mm. **Subject:** Belt Maglova Cultural Heritage site **Obv:** Value within wreath **Rev:** Aqueduct

Date	Mintage	F	VF	XF	Unc	BU
2005 Proof	1,250	Value: 55.00				

KM# 1191 25 NEW LIRA

31.4700 g., 0.9250 Silver 0.9359 oz. ASW, 38.6 mm. **Subject:** Galatasaray Spor **Obv:** 100 above team mascot **Rev:** GS monogram, colored

Date	Mintage	F	VF	XF	Unc	BU
2005 Proof	1,250	Value: 85.00				

KM# 1196 25 NEW LIRA

31.4700 g., 0.9250 Silver 0.9359 oz. ASW, 38.6 mm. **Subject:** 800 year of Medical Education in Turkey **Obv:** Two snakes **Rev:** Figure **Designer:** Nesrin Ek

Date	Mintage	F	VF	XF	Unc	BU
2006 Proof	1,650	Value: 60.00				

KM# 1198 25 NEW LIRA

31.4700 g., 0.9250 Silver 0.9359 oz. ASW, 38.6 mm. **Subject:** Nevruz of Hatira **Obv:** Flower and rays **Rev:** Statue holding flames **Designer:** Betul U Urlu

Date	Mintage	F	VF	XF	Unc	BU
2006 Proof	1,300	Value: 85.00				

KM# 1199 25 NEW LIRA

31.4700 g., 0.9250 Silver 0.9359 oz. ASW, 38.6 mm. **Subject:** Hattat Hamid Aytac **Obv:** Design **Rev:** Bust facing **Designer:** Nesrin Ek

Date	Mintage	F	VF	XF	Unc	BU
2006 Proof	1,301	Value: 75.00				

KM# 1200 25 NEW LIRA

31.4700 g., 0.9250 Silver 0.9359 oz. ASW, 38.6 mm. **Subject:** T.C. Devlet Demiryollari, 150th Anniversary **Obv:** 150 above laural **Rev:** Building

Date	Mintage	F	VF	XF	Unc	BU
2006 Proof	1,950	Value: 55.00				

KM# 1201 25 NEW LIRA

31.4700 g., 0.9250 Silver 0.9359 oz. ASW, 38.6 mm. **Subject:** Mehmet Ersoy Akif, 70th Anniversary of death **Obv:** Scroll **Rev:** Linear portrait facing **Designer:** Nesrin Ek

Date	Mintage	F	VF	XF	Unc	BU
2006 Antiqued	1,500	—	—	—	55.00	—

KM# 1211 25 NEW LIRA

15.5500 g., 0.9250 Silver 0.4624 oz. ASW, 38.6x28 mm. **Obv:** Legend **Rev:** Zodiac - Pisces **Shape:** Oval

Date	Mintage	F	VF	XF	Unc	BU
2008 Proof	—	Value: 45.00				

KM# 1212 25 NEW LIRA

15.5500 g., 0.9250 Silver 0.4624 oz. ASW, 38.6x28 mm. **Obv:** Text **Rev:** Zodiac - Aquarius **Shape:** Oval

Date	Mintage	F	VF	XF	Unc	BU
2008 Proof	—	Value: 45.00				

KM# 1213 25 NEW LIRA

15.5500 g., 0.9250 Silver 0.4624 oz. ASW, 38.6x28 mm. **Obv:** Text **Rev:** Zodiac - Capricorn **Shape:** Oval

Date	Mintage	F	VF	XF	Unc	BU
2008 Proof	—	Value: 45.00				

KM# 1214 25 NEW LIRA

15.5500 g., 0.9250 Silver 0.4624 oz. ASW, 38.6x28 mm. **Obv:** Text **Rev:** Zodiac - Sagittarius **Shape:** Oval

Date	Mintage	F	VF	XF	Unc	BU
2008 Proof	—	Value: 45.00				

KM# 1215 25 NEW LIRA

15.5500 g., 0.9250 Silver 0.4624 oz. ASW, 38.6x28 mm. **Obv:** Text **Rev:** Zodiac - Libra **Shape:** Oval

Date	Mintage	F	VF	XF	Unc	BU
2008 Proof	—	Value: 45.00				

KM# 1216 25 NEW LIRA

15.5500 g., 0.9250 Silver 0.4624 oz. ASW, 38.6x28 mm. **Obv:** Text **Rev:** Zodiac - figure **Shape:** Oval

Date	Mintage	F	VF	XF	Unc	BU
2008 Proof	—	Value: 45.00				

KM# 1217 25 NEW LIRA

15.5500 g., 0.9250 Silver 0.4624 oz. ASW, 38.6x28 mm. **Obv:** Text **Rev:** Zodiac - Leo **Shape:** Oval

Date	Mintage	F	VF	XF	Unc	BU
2008 Proof	—	Value: 45.00				

KM# 1218 25 NEW LIRA

15.5500 g., 0.9250 Silver 0.4624 oz. ASW, 38.6x28 mm. **Obv:** Text **Rev:** Zodiac - Virgo **Shape:** Oval

Date	Mintage	F	VF	XF	Unc	BU
2008 Proof	—	Value: 45.00				

KM# 1219 25 NEW LIRA

15.5500 g., 0.9250 Silver 0.4624 oz. ASW, 38.6x28 mm. **Obv:** Text **Rev:** Zodiac - Gemeni **Shape:** Oval

Date	Mintage	F	VF	XF	Unc	BU
2008 Proof	—	Value: 45.00				

KM# 1220 25 NEW LIRA

15.5500 g., 0.9250 Silver 0.4624 oz. ASW, 38.6x28 mm. **Obv:** Text **Rev:** Zodiac - Taurus **Shape:** Oval

Date	Mintage	F	VF	XF	Unc	BU
2008 Proof	—	Value: 45.00				

KM# 1221 25 NEW LIRA

15.5500 g., 0.9250 Silver 0.4624 oz. ASW, 38.6x28 mm. **Obv:** Text **Rev:** Zodiac sign **Shape:** Oval

Date	Mintage	F	VF	XF	Unc	BU
2008 Proof	—	Value: 45.00				

KM# 1192 30 NEW LIRA

31.4700 g., 0.9250 Silver 0.9359 oz. ASW, 38.6 mm. **Subject:** Galatasaray Spor **Obv:** 100 above team mascot **Rev:** GS monogram colored and selective gold plating

Date	Mintage	F	VF	XF	Unc	BU
2005 Proof	1,106	Value: 55.00				

KM# 1197 30 NEW LIRA

23.3300 g., 0.9250 Silver partially gold plated 0.6938 oz. ASW, 38.61 mm. **Subject:** Solar Eclipse **Obv:** Turkey map with route of the eclipse **Rev:** Sun, gilt **Designer:** Nesrin Ek

Date	Mintage	F	VF	XF	Unc	BU
2006 Proof	2,475	Value: 100				

KM# 1204 30 NEW LIRA

31.4700 g., 0.9250 Silver 0.9359 oz. ASW, 38.6 mm. **Subject:** Bank of Sarfanbolu **Obv:** Building **Rev:** Landscape **Designer:** Nesrin Ek

Date	Mintage	F	VF	XF	Unc	BU
2007 Proof	1,312	Value: 70.00				

KM# 1205 30 NEW LIRA

31.4700 g., 0.9250 Silver 0.9359 oz. ASW, 38.6 mm. **Obv:** Crescent and star at center of four objects **Rev:** Knotted fabric pattern **Designer:** Ayse Sirin

Date	Mintage	F	VF	XF	Unc	BU
2007 Proof	1,210	Value: 55.00				

KM# 1206 30 NEW LIRA

31.4700 g., 0.9250 Silver 0.9359 oz. ASW, 38.6 mm. **Obv:** Crescent and star within four objects **Rev:** Twirling Dirvishes **Designer:** Leman Tin

Date	Mintage	F	VF	XF	Unc	BU
2007 Proof	1,224	Value: 55.00				

KM# 1207 30 NEW LIRA
31.4700 g., 0.9250 Silver 0.9359 oz. ASW, 38.6 mm. **Obv:** Crescent and star within four designs **Rev:** Twirling Dirvish and town facades around **Designer:** Sessile Beatris Kalayciyan

Date	Mintage	F	VF	XF	Unc	BU
2007 Proof	1,179	Value: 55.00				

KM# 1208 30 NEW LIRA
31.4700 g., 0.9250 Silver 0.9359 oz. ASW, 38.6 mm. **Obv:** Mosque **Rev:** Entranceway arch **Designer:** Nalan Yerl Bucak

Date	Mintage	F	VF	XF	Unc	BU
2007 Proof	1,222	Value: 70.00				

KM# 1222 30 NEW LIRA
10.0000 g., 0.9250 Silver 0.2974 oz. ASW, 22 mm. **Obv:** Seal within border **Rev:** Large seal rendering

Date	Mintage	F	VF	XF	Unc	BU
2008 Proof	—	Value: 30.00				

KM# 1210 35 NEW LIRA
23.2300 g., 0.9250 Silver 0.6908 oz. ASW, 38.6 mm. **Subject:** Antikabir, 70th Anniversary **Obv:** Value within wreath **Rev:** Antikabir building **Designer:** Tenkin Gulbasar

Date	Mintage	F	VF	XF	Unc	BU
2008 Proof	3,000	Value: 40.00				

KM# 1232 35 NEW LIRA
23.3300 g., 0.9250 Silver 0.6938 oz. ASW, 38.6 mm. **Obv:** Value within wreath **Rev:** Bust at left

Date	Mintage	F	VF	XF	Unc	BU
2008 Proof	—	Value: 40.00				

KM# 1233 35 NEW LIRA
23.3300 g., 0.9250 Silver 0.6938 oz. ASW, 38.6 mm. **Obv:** Classical design **Rev:** Mahmud of Kashgar at right

Date	Mintage	F	VF	XF	Unc	BU
2008 Proof	—	Value: 40.00				

KM# 1238 35 NEW LIRA
23.3300 g., 0.9250 Silver 0.6938 oz. ASW, 38.6 mm. **Obv:** Value within wreath **Rev:** Sultan on horseback **Designer:** Nesrin Ek

Date	Mintage	F	VF	XF	Unc	BU
2008 Proof	—	Value: 45.00				

KM# 1202 40 NEW LIRA
31.4700 g., 0.9250 Silver 0.9359 oz. ASW, 38.6 mm. **Subject:** Troy **Obv:** Linear design **Rev:** Stylized Trojan Horse **Designer:** Nalan Yerl Bucak

Date	Mintage	F	VF	XF	Unc	BU
2007 Proof	1,500	Value: 50.00				

KM# 1224 40 NEW LIRA
31.4700 g., 0.9990 Silver 1.0107 oz. ASW, 38.6 mm. **Obv:** Historic map **Rev:** Kyrgyzstan building

Date	Mintage	F	VF	XF	Unc	BU
2008 Antiqued	—	—	—	—	80.00	—

KM# 1225 40 NEW LIRA
31.4700 g., 0.9250 Silver 0.9359 oz. ASW, 38.6 mm. **Obv:** Village scene **Rev:** Large classical figure **Designer:** Nesrin Ek

Date	Mintage	F	VF	XF	Unc	BU
2008 Proof	—	Value: 80.00				

KM# 1227 40 NEW LIRA
31.4700 g., 0.9250 Silver 0.9359 oz. ASW, 38.6 mm. **Obv:** Building **Rev:** Seated figure

Date	Mintage	F	VF	XF	Unc	BU
2008 Proof	—	Value: 45.00				

KM# 1228 40 NEW LIRA
31.4700 g., 0.9250 Silver 0.9359 oz. ASW, 38.6 mm. **Obv:** Classical intricate design **Rev:** Mosque

Date	Mintage	F	VF	XF	Unc	BU
2008 Proof	—	Value: 45.00				

KM# 1229 40 NEW LIRA
31.4700 g., 0.9250 Silver 0.9359 oz. ASW, 38.6 mm. **Obv:** Head left above school building **Rev:** Monogram at center **Designer:** Nesrin Ek

Date	Mintage	F	VF	XF	Unc	BU
2008 Proof	—	Value: 45.00				

KM# 1230 40 NEW LIRA
31.4700 g., 0.9250 Silver 0.9359 oz. ASW, 38.6 mm. **Obv:** Large tower and acqueduct **Rev:** Classical scene **Designer:** Tekin Gulbasar

Date	Mintage	F	VF	XF	Unc	BU
2008 Proof	—	Value: 45.00				

KM# 1231 40 NEW LIRA
31.4700 g., 0.9250 Silver 0.9359 oz. ASW, 38.6 mm. **Obv:** Tortoise, seal and lighthouse in distance **Rev:** Lighthouse

Date	Mintage	F	VF	XF	Unc	BU
2008 Proof	—	Value: 45.00				

KM# 1234 40 NEW LIRA
23.3300 g., 0.9250 Silver 0.6938 oz. ASW, 38.6 mm. **Subject:** Vefs Sports Club, 100th Anniversary **Obv:** Club seal multicolor **Rev:** Large 100 and logo

Date	Mintage	F	VF	XF	Unc	BU
2008 Proof	—	Value: 45.00				

KM# 1235 40 NEW LIRA
31.4700 g., 0.9250 Silver 0.9359 oz. ASW, 38.6 mm. **Obv:** Ancient craft items **Rev:** Cave paintings

Date	Mintage	F	VF	XF	Unc	BU
2008 Proof	—	Value: 45.00				

KM# 1236 40 NEW LIRA
31.4700 g., 0.9250 Silver 0.9359 oz. ASW, 38.6 mm. **Obv:** Ancient map **Rev:** Uzbekistan mosque **Designer:** Tekin Gulbasar

Date	Mintage	F	VF	XF	Unc	BU
2008 Antiqued	—	—	—	—	40.00	45.00

KM# 1237 40 NEW LIRA
31.4700 g., 0.9250 Silver 0.9359 oz. ASW, 38.6 mm. **Obv:** Tower **Rev:** Tower **Designer:** Tekin Gulbasar

Date	Mintage	F	VF	XF	Unc	BU
2008 Proof	—	Value: 45.00				

KM# 1255 50 LIRA
36.0800 g., 0.9250 Silver 1.0730 oz. ASW, 38.6 mm. **Subject:** Sunlight **Obv:** Eastern Hemisphere logo **Rev:** Eastern Hemisphere in Sun

Date	Mintage	F	VF	XF	Unc	BU
2008 Proof	—	Value: 55.00				

KM# 1209 60 NEW LIRA
1.5000 g., 0.9160 Gold 0.0442 oz. AGW, 13.95 mm. **Obv:** Text **Rev:** Ancient pottery **Designer:** Nesrin Ek

Date	Mintage	F	VF	XF	Unc	BU
2007 Proof	1,925	Value: 85.00				

KM# 1223 100 NEW LIRA
7.2160 g., 0.9160 Gold 0.2125 oz. AGW, 22 mm. **Obv:** Seal within border **Rev:** Large seal

Date	Mintage	F	VF	XF	Unc	BU
2008 Proof	—	Value: 425				

KM# 1226 100 NEW LIRA
7.2160 g., 0.9160 Gold 0.2125 oz. AGW, 22 mm. **Obv:** Village scene **Rev:** Large classical figure

Date	Mintage	F	VF	XF	Unc	BU
2008 Proof	—	Value: 425				

REFORM DECIMAL COINAGE

2009

KM# 1272 NON-DENOMINATED
23.3300 g., Bronze **Subject:** European Youth Games, Trabzon **Shape:** 38.61

Date	Mintage	F	VF	XF	Unc	BU
2011 Antique patina	2,000	—	—	—	—	20.00

KM# 1273 NON-DENOMINATED
31.4700 g., 0.9250 Silver 0.9359 oz. ASW, 38.61 mm. **Subject:** European Youth Games, Trabzon

Date	Mintage	F	VF	XF	Unc	BU
2011 Proof	2,000	Value: 50.00				

KM# 1239 KURUS
Copper Plated Steel **Obv:** Head of Ataturk left **Rev:** Plant and value

Date	Mintage	F	VF	XF	Unc	BU
2009	—	—	—	—	0.30	0.50
2010	—	—	—	—	0.30	0.50
2011	—	—	—	—	0.30	0.50
2012	—	—	—	—	0.30	0.50

KM# 1240 5 KURUS
Brass **Obv:** Head of Ataturk left **Rev:** Value and traditional embroidery pattern

Date	Mintage	F	VF	XF	Unc	BU
2009	—	—	—	—	0.30	0.50
2010	—	—	—	—	0.30	0.50
2011	—	—	—	—	0.30	0.50
2012	—	—	—	—	0.30	0.50

KM# 1241 10 KURUS
Brass **Obv:** Head of Ataturk left **Rev:** Value

Date	Mintage	F	VF	XF	Unc	BU
2009	—	—	—	—	0.30	0.50
2010	—	—	—	—	0.30	0.50
2011	—	—	—	—	0.30	0.50
2012	—	—	—	—	0.30	0.50

KM# 1242 25 KURUS

Copper-Nickel **Obv:** Head of Ataturk left **Rev:** Value

Date	Mintage	F	VF	XF	Unc	BU
2009	—	—	—	—	0.50	0.75
2010	—	—	—	—	0.50	0.75
2011	—	—	—	—	0.50	0.75
2012	—	—	—	—	0.50	0.75

KM# 1243 50 KURUS

Bi-Metallic Brass center in Copper-Nickel ring **Obv:** Head of Atatürk left **Rev:** Value above suspension bridge **Edge:** Reeded

Date	Mintage	F	VF	XF	Unc	BU
2009	—	—	—	—	0.75	1.00
2010	—	—	—	—	0.75	1.00
2011	—	—	—	—	0.75	1.00

KM# 1244 LIRA

Bi-Metallic Copper-Nickel center in Brass ring **Obv:** Head of Atatürk left **Rev:** Value

Date	Mintage	F	VF	XF	Unc	BU
2009	—	—	—	—	3.00	5.00
2010	—	—	—	—	3.00	5.00
2011	—	—	—	—	3.00	5.00
2012	—	—	—	—	3.00	5.00

KM# 1249 LIRA

6.4000 g., Copper-Nickel, 23.5 mm. **Obv:** Lammergeier standing on rock **Rev:** Two eagles **Designer:** Nesrin Ek

Date	Mintage	F	VF	XF	Unc	BU
2009	120,000	—	—	—	4.50	6.00

KM# 1263 LIRA

8.3000 g., Bi-Metallic Copper-Nickel center in Brass ring, 26.15 mm. **Obv:** Value within wreath **Rev:** Elephant and calf

Date	Mintage	F	VF	XF	Unc	BU
2009	5,000	—	—	—	7.50	10.00

KM# 1264 LIRA

8.3000 g., Bi-Metallic Copper-Nickel center in Brass ring, 26.15 mm. **Obv:** Value within wreath **Rev:** Sea tortoise

Date	Mintage	F	VF	XF	Unc	BU
2009	5,000	—	—	—	7.50	10.00

KM# 1279 LIRA

Bi-Metallic Copper-nickel center in Brass ring, 26.15 mm. **Obv:** Value within wreath **Rev:** Cat's bust

Date	Mintage	F	VF	XF	Unc	BU
2010	—	—	—	—	7.50	10.00

KM# 1280 LIRA

Bi-Metallic Nickel center in Brass ring, 26.15 mm. **Obv:** Value within wreath **Rev:** Dog with puppet

Date	Mintage	F	VF	XF	Unc	BU
2010	—	—	—	—	7.50	10.00

KM# 1275 LIRA

8.3000 g., Bi-Metallic Brass center in Copper-Nickel ring, 26.15 mm. **Obv:** Value within wreath **Rev:** Lion advancing - Pathera leo persica

Date	Mintage	F	VF	XF	Unc	BU
2011	—	—	—	—	5.00	7.50

KM# 1276 LIRA

8.3000 g., Bi-Metallic Brass center in Copper-Nickel ring, 26.15 mm. **Obv:** Value within wreath **Rev:** Brown bear - Ursus arctos

Date	Mintage	F	VF	XF	Unc	BU
2011	11,000	—	—	—	5.00	7.50
2011 Proof	4,000	Value: 15.00				

KM# 1281 LIRA

Bi-Metallic Brass center in Copper-Nickel ring, 26.15 mm. **Obv:** Value within wreath **Rev:** 10th International Turkish Language Olympics

Date	Mintage	F	VF	XF	Unc	BU
2012	—	—	—	—	5.00	7.50

KM# 1282 LIRA

Bi-Metallic Brass center in Copper-Nickel ring, 26.15 mm. **Obv:** Value within wreath **Rev:** 150 Years of the Court

Date	Mintage	F	VF	XF	Unc	BU
2012	—	—	—	—	5.00	7.50

KM# 1283 LIRA

Bi-Metallic Brass Center in Copper-Nickel ring, 26.15 mm. **Obv:** Value within wreath **Rev:** Deer

Date	Mintage	F	VF	XF	Unc	BU
2012	—	—	—	—	5.00	7.50

KM# 1284 LIRA

Bi-Metallic Brass center in Copper-Nickel ring, 26.15 mm. **Obv:** Value within wreath **Rev:** Leopard

Date	Mintage	F	VF	XF	Unc	BU
2012	—	—	—	—	5.00	7.50

KM# 1250 10 LIRA

23.3300 g., Bronze, 38.6 mm. **Obv:** Scroll and inkwell **Rev:** Child's story **Edge:** Reeded **Designer:** Tekin Gulbasar

Date	Mintage	F	VF	XF	Unc	BU
2009 Antiqued	—	—	—	—	15.00	—

KM# 1258 20 LIRA

27.5000 g., Copper-Nickel, 38.6 mm. **Subject:** Year 1430 **Obv:** Inscription within rose wreath **Rev:** Interior of the Grand Mosque in Mecca **Designer:** Nesrin Ek

Date	Mintage	F	VF	XF	Unc	BU
2009 Antiqued	—	—	—	—	35.00	—

KM# 1266 20 LIRA

23.3300 g., Bronze, 38.61 mm. **Subject:** 25th Winter Sports Games - Hockey

Date	Mintage	F	VF	XF	Unc	BU
2011 Antique finish	3,000	—	—	—	—	20.00

KM# 1267 20 LIRA

23.3300 g., Brass, 38.61 mm. **Subject:** 25th Winter Sports Games - Hockey

Date	Mintage	F	VF	XF	Unc	BU
2011 Antique patina	3,000	—	—	—	—	20.00

KM# 1269 20 LIRA

23.3300 g., Bronze, 38.61 mm. **Subject:** 25th Winter Sports Games - Skiing

Date	Mintage	F	VF	XF	Unc	BU
2011 Antique patina	3,000	—	—	—	—	20.00

KM# 1270 20 LIRA

23.3300 g., Brass, 38.61 mm. **Subject:** 25th Winter Sports Games - Skiing

Date	Mintage	F	VF	XF	Unc	BU
2011 Antique patina	3,000	—	—	—	—	20.00

KM# 1278 20 LIRA

15.5500 g., 0.9250 Silver 0.4624 oz. ASW, 28x38.61 mm. **Subject:** Dolmabahce Clock Tower **Shape:** Vertical oval

Date	Mintage	F	VF	XF	Unc	BU
2011 Proof	—	Value: 50.00				

KM# 1247 50 LIRA

36.0000 g., 0.9250 Silver 1.0706 oz. ASW, 38.6 mm. **Obv:** Value within wreath **Rev:** Samsun 90th Anniversary

Date	Mintage	F	VF	XF	Unc	BU
2009 Proof	3,000	Value: 55.00				

KM# 1251 50 LIRA

36.0800 g., 0.9250 Silver 1.0730 oz. ASW, 38.6 mm. **Obv:** Scroll and inkwell **Rev:** Children's story character

Date	Mintage	F	VF	XF	Unc	BU
2009 Proof	—	Value: 40.00				

KM# 1252 50 LIRA
36.0800 g., 0.9250 Silver 1.0730 oz. ASW, 38.6 mm. **Subject:** Frederic Chopin, 200th Anniversary **Obv:** Piano and map of Europe **Rev:** Chopin's bust at left, piano at right, score in background **Designer:** Nalan Yerl Bucak

Date	Mintage	F	VF	XF	Unc	BU
2009	—	Value: 70.00				

KM# 1253 50 LIRA
36.0800 g., 0.9250 Silver 1.0730 oz. ASW, 38.6 mm. **Subject:** IMF Meeting, Istanbul **Obv:** Istanbul Skyline **Rev:** World Bank Group logo, multicolor **Designer:** Nesrin Ek

Date	Mintage	F	VF	XF	Unc	BU
2009 Proof	—	Value: 55.00				

KM# 1254 50 LIRA
36.0800 g., 0.9250 Silver 1.0730 oz. ASW, 38.6 mm. **Subject:** Water, source of life **Obv:** Eastern Hemisphere logo **Rev:** Clock hands, small amount of water, cracked and dried earth in rest of area

Date	Mintage	F	VF	XF	Unc	BU
2009 Proof	—	Value: 55.00				

KM# 1256 50 LIRA
36.0800 g., 0.9250 Silver 1.0730 oz. ASW, 38.6 mm. **Obv:** Eastern Hemisphere logo **Rev:** Small seedling within light blue colored water droplet, dried earth background

Date	Mintage	F	VF	XF	Unc	BU
2009 Antiqued	—	—	—	—	55.00	—

KM# 1257 50 LIRA
36.0800 g., 0.9250 Silver 1.0730 oz. ASW, 38.6 mm. **Obv:** Eastern Hemisphere logo **Rev:** Female face with hair forming waves and vine

Date	Mintage	F	VF	XF	Unc	BU
2009 Proof	—	Value: 55.00				

KM# 1259 50 LIRA
36.0000 g., 0.9250 Silver 1.0706 oz. ASW, 38.6 mm. **Subject:** Year 1430 **Obv:** Inscription within rose wreath **Rev:** Interior courtyard of Grand Mosque in Mecca **Designer:** Nesrin Ek

Date	Mintage	F	VF	XF	Unc	BU
2009 Proof	2,500	Value: 70.00				

KM# 1261 50 LIRA
36.0000 g., 0.9250 Silver 1.0706 oz. ASW, 38.6 mm. **Subject:** 150th Anniversary **Obv:** Multicolor shield and text **Rev:** Building facade **Designer:** Nesrin Ek

Date	Mintage	F	VF	XF	Unc	BU
2009 Proof	5,000	Value: 45.00				

KM# 1262 50 LIRA
36.0000 g., 0.9250 Silver 1.0706 oz. ASW, 38.6 mm. **Subject:** Chalabi clerks **Obv:** Symbol **Rev:** Classical figure seated

Date	Mintage	F	VF	XF	Unc	BU
2009 Proof	3,000	Value: 55.00				

KM# 1268 50 LIRA
31.4700 g., Silver, 38.61 mm. **Subject:** 25th Winter Sports Games - Hockey

Date	Mintage	F	VF	XF	Unc	BU
2011 Proof	3,000	Value: 50.00				

KM# 1271 50 LIRA
31.4700 g., 0.9250 Silver 0.9359 oz. ASW, 38.61 mm. **Subject:** 25th Winter Sports Games - Skiing

Date	Mintage	F	VF	XF	Unc	BU
2011 Proof	3,000	Value: 50.00				

KM# 1274 50 LIRA
31.4700 g., 0.9250 Silver 0.9359 oz. ASW, 38.61 mm. **Subject:** Hejaz Railway **Obv:** Railway route map from Turkey to Saudi Arabia **Rev:** Railway Station at Medina **Edge:** Reeded **Designer:** Nesrin Eksi Schnepf

Date	Mintage	F	VF	XF	Unc	BU
2011 Proof	3,000	Value: 85.00				

KM# 1277 50 LIRA
31.1000 g., 0.9250 Silver 0.9249 oz. ASW, 38.61 mm. **Subject:** Pergamon **Rev:** Ruins **Edge:** Reeded

Date	Mintage	F	VF	XF	Unc	BU
2012 Proof	2,000	Value: 75.00				

KM# 1245 50 NEW LIRA
36.0800 g., 0.9250 Silver 1.0730 oz. ASW, 38.6 mm. **Obv:** US and Turkish flags **Rev:** Barack Obama portrait facing **Designer:** Nesrin Ek

Date	Mintage	F	VF	XF	Unc	BU
2009 Proof	3,000	Value: 55.00				

KM# 1248 100 LIRA
1.5000 g., 0.9160 Gold 0.0442 oz. AGW, 13.95 mm. **Obv:** Classical orniament **Rev:** Hittite artifacts

Date	Mintage	F	VF	XF	Unc	BU
2009 Proof	—	Value: 95.00				

KM# 1246 200 LIRA
36.0800 g., 0.9160 Gold 1.0625 oz. AGW, 38.6 mm. **Obv:** US and Turkish flags **Rev:** Barack Obama portrait facing **Designer:** Nesrin Ek

Date	Mintage	F	VF	XF	Unc	BU
2009 Proof	1,000	Value: 1,850				

KM# 1260 200 LIRA
36.0000 g., 0.9160 Gold 1.0602 oz. AGW, 38.6 mm. **Obv:** Inscription within rose wreath **Rev:** Central courtyard of the Grand Mosque in Mecca **Designer:** Nesrin Ek

Date	Mintage	F	VF	XF	Unc	BU
2009 Proof	1,500	Value: 1,850				

GOLD BULLION COINAGE

Since 1943, the Turkish government has issued regular and deluxe gold coins in five denominations corresponding to the old traditional 25, 50, 100, 250, and 500 Kurus of the Ottoman period. The regular coins are all dated 1923, plus the year of the republic (e.g. 1923/40 = 1963), de Luxe coins bear actual AD dates. For a few years, 1944-1950, the bust of Ismet Inonu replaced that of Kemal Ataturk.

KM# 851 25 KURUSH
1.8041 g., 0.9170 Gold 0.0532 oz. AGW **Obv:** Head of Atatürk left **Rev:** Legend and date within wreath

Date	Mintage	F	VF	XF	Unc	BU
1923/78	—	—	—	BV	105	120
1923/79	—	—	—	BV	105	120
1923/70	—	—	—	BV	105	120
1923/71	—	—	—	BV	105	120
1923/72	—	—	—	BV	105	120
1923/73	—	—	—	BV	105	120
1923/74	—	—	—	BV	105	120
1923/75	—	—	—	BV	105	120
1923/76	—	—	—	BV	105	120
1923/77	—	—	—	BV	105	120

KM# 870 25 KURUSH
1.7540 g., 0.9170 Gold 0.0517 oz. AGW **Series:** Monnaie de Luxe **Obv:** Head of Atatürk left **Rev:** Country name and date in ornate monogram within circle of stars, floral border surrounds

Date	Mintage	F	VF	XF	Unc	BU
2001	—	—	—	BV	105	120
2002	—	—	—	BV	105	120
2003	—	—	—	BV	105	120
2004	—	—	—	BV	105	120
2005	—	—	—	BV	105	120
2006	—	—	—	BV	105	120
2007	—	—	—	BV	105	120
2008	—	—	—	BV	105	120
2009	—	—	—	BV	105	120
2010	—	—	—	BV	105	120

KM# 853 50 KURUSH
3.6083 g., 0.9170 Gold 0.1064 oz. AGW **Obv:** Head of Atatürk left **Rev:** Legend and date within wreath

Date	Mintage	F	VF	XF	Unc	BU
1923/78	—	—	—	BV	200	225
1923/79	—	—	—	BV	200	225
1923/80	—	—	—	BV	200	225
1923/81	—	—	—	BV	200	225
1923/82	—	—	—	BV	200	225
1923/83	—	—	—	BV	200	225
1923/84	—	—	—	BV	200	225
1923/85	—	—	—	BV	200	225
1923/86	—	—	—	BV	200	225
1923/87	—	—	—	BV	200	225

KM# 871 50 KURUSH
3.5080 g., 0.9170 Gold 0.1034 oz. AGW **Series:** Monnaie de Luxe **Obv:** Head of Kemal Atatürk left within circle of stars, wreath surrounds **Rev:** Country name and date in ornate monogram within circle of stars, floral border surrounds

Date	Mintage	F	VF	XF	Unc	BU
2001	—	—	—	BV	200	225
2002	—	—	—	BV	200	225
2003	—	—	—	BV	200	225
2004	—	—	—	BV	200	225
2005	—	—	—	BV	200	225
2006	—	—	—	BV	200	225
2007	—	—	—	BV	200	225
2008	—	—	—	BV	200	225
2009	—	—	—	BV	200	225
2010	—	—	—	BV	200	225

KM# 855 100 KURUSH
7.2160 g., 0.9170 Gold 0.2127 oz. AGW **Obv:** Head of Atatürk left **Rev:** Legend and date within wreath

Date	Mintage	F	VF	XF	Unc	BU
1923/78	—	—	—	BV	400	425
1923/79	—	—	—	BV	400	425
1923/80	—	—	—	BV	400	425
1923/81	—	—	—	BV	400	425
1923/82	—	—	—	BV	400	425
1923/83	—	—	—	BV	400	425
1923/84	—	—	—	BV	400	425
1923/85	—	—	—	BV	400	425
1923/86	—	—	—	BV	400	425
1923/87	—	—	—	BV	400	425

KM# 872 100 KURUSH
7.0160 g., 0.9170 Gold 0.2068 oz. AGW **Series:** Monnaie de Luxe **Obv:** Head of Atatürk left within circle of stars, wreath surrounds **Rev:** Country name and date in ornate monogram within circle of stars, floral border surrounds

Date	Mintage	F	VF	XF	Unc	BU
2001	—	—	—	—	BV	400
2002	—	—	—	—	BV	400
2003	—	—	—	—	BV	400
2004	—	—	—	—	BV	400
2005	—	—	—	—	BV	400
2006	—	—	—	—	BV	400
2007	—	—	—	—	BV	400
2008	—	—	—	—	BV	400
2009	—	—	—	—	BV	400
2010	—	—	—	—	BV	400

KM# 857 250 KURUSH
18.0400 g., 0.9170 Gold 0.5318 oz. AGW **Obv:** Head of Atatürk left **Rev:** Legend and date within wreath

Date	Mintage	F	VF	XF	Unc	BU
1923/78	—	—	—	BV	1,025	1,075
1923/79	—	—	—	BV	1,025	1,075
1923/80	—	—	—	BV	1,025	1,075
1923/81	—	—	—	BV	1,025	1,075
1923/82	—	—	—	BV	1,025	1,075
1923/83	—	—	—	BV	1,025	1,075
1923/84	—	—	—	BV	1,025	1,075
1923/85	—	—	—	BV	1,025	1,075
1923/86	—	—	—	BV	1,025	1,075
1923/87	—	—	—	BV	1,025	1,075

KM# 873 250 KURUSH
17.5400 g., 0.9170 Gold 0.5171 oz. AGW **Series:** Monnaie de Luxe **Obv:** Head of Atatürk left within circle of stars, wreath surrounds **Rev:** Country name and date in ornate monogram within circle of stars, floral border surrounds

Date	Mintage	F	VF	XF	Unc	BU
2001	—	—	—	BV	1,000	1,050
2002	—	—	—	BV	1,000	1,050
2003	—	—	—	BV	1,000	1,050
2004	—	—	—	BV	1,000	1,050
2005	—	—	—	BV	1,000	1,050
2006	—	—	—	BV	1,000	1,050
2007	—	—	—	BV	1,000	1,050
2008	—	—	—	BV	1,000	1,050
2009	—	—	—	BV	1,000	1,050
2010	—	—	—	BV	1,000	1,050

KM# 859 500 KURUSH
36.0800 g., 0.9170 Gold 1.0637 oz. AGW **Obv:** Head of Atatürk left **Rev:** Legend and date within wreath

Date	Mintage	F	VF	XF	Unc	BU
1923/78	—	—	—	BV	1,950	2,000
1923/79	—	—	—	BV	1,950	2,000
1923/80	—	—	—	BV	1,950	2,000
1923/81	—	—	—	BV	1,950	2,000
1923/82	—	—	—	BV	1,950	2,000
1923/83	—	—	—	BV	1,950	2,000
1923/84	—	—	—	BV	1,950	2,000
1923/85	—	—	—	BV	1,950	2,000
1923/86	—	—	—	BV	1,950	2,000
1923/87	—	—	—	BV	1,950	2,000

KM# 874 500 KURUSH
35.0800 g., 0.9170 Gold 1.0342 oz. AGW **Series:** Monnaie de Luxe **Obv:** Head of Atatürk left within circle of stars, wreath surrounds **Rev:** Country name and date in ornate monogram within circle of stars, floral border surrounds

Date	Mintage	F	VF	XF	Unc	BU
2001	—	—	—	BV	1,950	2,000
2002	—	—	—	BV	1,950	2,000
2003	—	—	—	BV	1,950	2,000
2004	—	—	—	BV	1,950	2,000
2005	—	—	—	BV	1,950	2,000
2006	—	—	—	BV	1,950	2,000
2007	—	—	—	BV	1,950	2,000
2008	—	—	—	BV	1,950	2,000
2009	—	—	—	BV	1,950	2,000
2010	—	—	—	BV	1,950	2,000

Turkmenistan, (formerly the Turkmen Soviet Socialist Republic) covers the territory of the Trans-Caspian Region of Turkestan, the Charjiui Vilayet of Bukhara and the part of Khiva located on the right bank of the Oxus. Bordered on the north by the Autonomous Kara-Kalpak Republic (a constituent of Uzbekistan), by Iran and Afghanistan on the south, by the Usbek Republic on the east and the Caspian Sea on the west. It has an area of 186,400 sq. mi. (488,100 sq. km.) and a population of 3.5 million. Capital: Ashkhabad (formerly Poltoratsk). Main occupation is agricultural products including cotton and maize. It is rich in minerals, oil, coal, sulphur and salt and is also famous for its carpets, Turkoman horses and Karakui sheep.

The Turkomans arrived in Trancaspia as nomadic Seluk Turks in the 11th century. It often became subjected to one of the neighboring states. Late in the 19th century the Czarist Russians invaded with their first victory at Kyzyl Arvat in 1877, arriving in Ashkhabad in 1882 resulting in submission of the Turkmen tribes. By March 18,1884 the Transcaspian province of Russian Turkestan was formed. During WW I the Czarist government tried to conscript the Turkmen; this led to a revolt in Oct. 1916 under the leadership of Aziz Chapykov. In 1918 the Turks captured Baku from the Red army and the British sent a contingent to Merv to prevent a German-Turkish offensive toward Afghanistan and India. In mid-1919 a Bureau of Turkestan Moslem Communist Organization was formed in Moscow hoping to develop one large republic including all surrounding Turkic areas within a Soviet federation. A Turkestan Autonomous Soviet Socialist Republic was formed and plans to partition Turkestan into five republics according to the principle of nationalities was quickly implemented by Joseph Stalin. On Oct. 27, 1924 Turkmenistan became a Soviet Socialist Republic and was accepted as a member of the U.S.S.R. on Jan. 29, 1925. The Bureau of T.M.C.O. was disbanded in 1934. In Aug. 1990 the Turkmen Supreme Soviet adopted a declaration of sovereignty followed by a declaration of independence in Oct. 1991 joining the Commonwealth of Independent States in Dec. A new constitution was adopted in 1992 providing for an executive presidency.

REPUBLIC

STANDARD COINAGE

100 Tenge = 1 Manat

KM# 25 500 MANAT
28.2800 g., 0.9250 Silver 0.8410 oz. ASW, 38.5 mm. **Subject:** 10th Anniversary of Independence **Obv:** Head of President Saparmyrat Nyyazow left within circle **Rev:** Monument divides dates within circle **Edge:** Reeded

Date	Mintage	F	VF	XF	Unc	BU
ND(2001) Proof	5,000	Value: 60.00				

KM# 41 500 MANAT
28.2800 g., 0.9250 Silver 0.8410 oz. ASW **Subject:** President's 61st Birthday **Obv:** National Flag

Date	Mintage	F	VF	XF	Unc	BU
2001	2,000	—	—	—	—	55.00

KM# 42 500 MANAT
28.2800 g., 0.9250 Silver 0.8410 oz. ASW **Subject:** President's 61st Birthday **Rev:** State arms

Date	Mintage	F	VF	XF	Unc	BU
2001	2,000	—	—	—	—	55.00

KM# 43 500 MANAT
28.2800 g., 0.9250 Silver 0.8410 oz. ASW **Subject:** Historical leaders **Rev:** Artogrul Grazy Turkmen (1191-1281)

Date	Mintage	F	VF	XF	Unc	BU
2001	100	—	—	—	—	55.00

KM# 44 500 MANAT
28.2800 g., 0.9250 Silver 0.8410 oz. ASW **Subject:** Historical leaders **Rev:** Oguz Khan Turkmen

Date	Mintage	F	VF	XF	Unc	BU
2001	1,000	—	—	—	—	55.00

KM# 45 500 MANAT
28.2800 g., 0.9250 Silver 0.8410 oz. ASW **Subject:** Historical leaders **Rev:** Gara Yusup Beg Turkmen

Date	Mintage	F	VF	XF	Unc	BU
2001	1,000	—	—	—	—	55.00

KM# 46 500 MANAT
28.2800 g., 0.9250 Silver 0.8410 oz. ASW **Subject:** Historical leaders **Rev:** Keymir Kor Turkmen

Date	Mintage	F	VF	XF	Unc	BU
2001	—	—	—	—	—	65.00

KM# 47 500 MANAT
28.2800 g., 0.9250 Silver 0.8410 oz. ASW **Subject:** Historical leaders **Rev:** Uzun Khasan Beg Turkmen

Date	Mintage	F	VF	XF	Unc	BU
2001	1,000	—	—	—	—	55.00

KM# 48 500 MANAT
28.2800 g., 0.9250 Silver 0.8410 oz. ASW **Subject:** Historical leaders **Rev:** Gorogly Beg Turkmen

Date	Mintage	F	VF	XF	Unc	BU
2001	1,000	—	—	—	—	55.00

KM# 49 500 MANAT
28.2800 g., 0.9250 Silver 0.8410 oz. ASW **Subject:** Historical leader **Rev:** Gorkut Ata Turkmen

Date	Mintage	F	VF	XF	Unc	BU
2001	1,000	—	—	—	—	55.00

KM# 50 500 MANAT
28.2800 g., 0.9250 Silver 0.8410 oz. ASW **Subject:** Historical leaders **Rev:** Muhammet Togrul Beg Turkmen

Date	Mintage	F	VF	XF	Unc	BU
2001	1,000	—	—	—	—	55.00

KM# 51 500 MANAT
Silver **Subject:** Historical leaders **Rev:** Muhammet Bayram Khan Turkmen

Date	Mintage	F	VF	XF	Unc	BU
2001	1,000	—	—	—	—	55.00

KM# 52 500 MANAT
28.2800 g., 0.9250 Silver 0.8410 oz. ASW **Subject:** Historical leaders **Rev:** Soltan Sawjar Turkmen

Date	Mintage	F	VF	XF	Unc	BU
2001	1,000	—	—	—	—	55.00

KM# 53 500 MANAT
28.2800 g., 0.9250 Silver 0.8410 oz. ASW, 46 mm. **Subject:** Historical writers **Obv:** State emblem **Rev:** Bust and Laurel branch **Rev. Legend:** Seyitnazar Seydi (1760-1830)

Date	Mintage	F	VF	XF	Unc	BU
2003	—	—	—	—	—	65.00

KM# 54 500 MANAT
28.2800 g., 0.9250 Silver 0.8410 oz. ASW **Subject:** Historical authors **Obv:** State emblem **Rev:** Bust and Laurel branch **Rev. Legend:** Mammetweli Kemine (1770-1840)

Date	Mintage	F	VF	XF	Unc	BU
2003	—	—	—	—	—	65.00

KM# 55 500 MANAT
28.2800 g., 0.5000 Silver 0.4546 oz. ASW, 46 mm. **Subject:** State emblem **Rev:** Bust and Laurel branch **Rev. Legend:** Mollanepes (1810-1862)

Date	Mintage	F	VF	XF	Unc	BU
2003	—	—	—	—	—	50.00

KM# 56 500 MANAT
28.2800 g., 0.9250 Silver 0.8410 oz. ASW, 46 mm. **Subject:** Historical authors **Obv:** State emblem **Rev:** Bust and Laurel branch **Rev. Legend:** Annagylyc Mataji (1824-1882)

Date	Mintage	F	VF	XF	Unc	BU
2003	—	—	—	—	—	65.00

KM# 62 500 MANAT
28.2800 g., 0.9250 Silver 0.8410 oz. ASW **Obv:** Bust left **Rev:** Wheat ears as rays

Date	Mintage	F	VF	XF	Unc	BU
2004	—	—	—	—	—	65.00

KM# 64 500 MANAT
28.2800 g., 0.9250 Silver 0.8410 oz. ASW **Obv:** Bust left **Rev:** Wheat ears forming rays

Date	Mintage	F	VF	XF	Unc	BU
2004	1,000	—	—	—	—	55.00

KM# 66 500 MANAT
28.2800 g., 0.9250 Silver 0.8410 oz. ASW **Subject:** 60th Anniversary of WWII **Obv:** State emblem **Rev:** Soldier standing, rays behind

Date	Mintage	F	VF	XF	Unc	BU
2005	1,000	—	—	—	—	65.00

KM# 68 500 MANAT
28.2800 g., 0.9250 Silver 0.8410 oz. ASW, 75 mm. **Subject:** President Nijazov, 60th Birthday **Obv:** State emblem **Rev:** Head left above tree design

Date	Mintage	F	VF	XF	Unc	BU
2005	—	—	—	—	—	65.00

KM# 40 1000 MANAT
7.9800 g., 0.9160 Gold 0.2350 oz. AGW, 28.28 mm. **Obv:** President Nyyazow **Rev:** Monument

Date	Mintage	F	VF	XF	Unc	BU
2001	1,000	—	—	—	—	1,800

KM# 57 1000 MANAT
47.6400 g., 0.9160 Gold 1.4029 oz. AGW, 46 mm. **Subject:** Historical authors **Obv:** State emblem **Rev:** Bust and Laurel branch **Rev. Legend:** Seyitnazar Seydi (1760-1830)

Date	Mintage	F	VF	XF	Unc	BU
2003	—	—	—	—	—	2,500

KM# 58 1000 MANAT
47.6400 g., 0.9160 Gold 1.4029 oz. AGW, 46 mm. **Subject:** Historical authors **Obv:** State arms **Rev:** Bust and laurel branch **Rev. Legend:** Mammetweli Kemine

Date	Mintage	F	VF	XF	Unc	BU
2003	—	—	—	—	—	2,500

KM# 59 1000 MANAT
47.6400 g., 0.9167 Gold 1.4040 oz. AGW, 46 mm. **Subject:** Historical authors **Obv:** State emblem **Rev:** Bust and laurel branch **Rev. Legend:** Mollanepes (1810-1862)

Date	Mintage	F	VF	XF	Unc	BU
2003	—	—	—	—	—	2,500

KM# 60 1000 MANAT
47.6400 g., 0.9160 Gold 1.4029 oz. AGW, 46 mm. **Subject:** Historical authors **Obv:** State emblem **Rev:** Bust and laurel branch **Rev. Legend:** Annagylyc Mataji (1824-1882)

Date	Mintage	F	VF	XF	Unc	BU
2003	—	—	—	—	—	2,500

KM# 61 1000 MANAT
28.2800 g., 0.9250 Silver 0.8410 oz. ASW **Subject:** 10th Anniversary of Reform

Date	Mintage	F	VF	XF	Unc	BU
2003	—	—	—	—	—	85.00

KM# 63 1000 MANAT
7.9800 g., 0.9160 Gold 0.2350 oz. AGW **Subject:** 100th Anniversary **Obv:** Bust left **Rev:** Wheat ears forming rays above

Date	Mintage	F	VF	XF	Unc	BU
2004	—	—	—	—	—	1,550

KM# 65 1000 MANAT
7.9800 g., 0.9160 Gold 0.2350 oz. AGW **Obv:** Bust left **Rev:** Wheat ears forming rays

Date	Mintage	F	VF	XF	Unc	BU
2004	250	—	—	—	—	1,550

KM# 67 1000 MANAT
47.5400 g., 0.9160 Gold 1.4000 oz. AGW **Subject:** 60th Anniversary of WWII **Obv:** State arms **Rev:** Soldier standing, rays behind

Date	Mintage	F	VF	XF	Unc	BU
2005	—	—	—	—	—	2,500

KM# 69 1000 MANAT
155.5000 g., 0.9990 Gold 4.9942 oz. AGW, 75 mm. **Subject:** President Nijazov Goth **Obv:** State emblem **Rev:** Head left above tree

Date	Mintage	F	VF	XF	Unc	BU
2005	—	—	—	—	—	9,000

KM# 70 1000 MANAT
28.2800 g., 0.9250 Silver 0.8410 oz. ASW **Subject:** Writings of President Nijazov

Date	Mintage	F	VF	XF	Unc	BU
2006	—	—	—	—	—	85.00

KM# 71 1000 MANAT
28.2800 g., 0.9250 Silver 0.8410 oz. ASW **Subject:** Writings of President Nijazov

Date	Mintage	F	VF	XF	Unc	BU
2006	—	—	—	—	—	85.00

KM# 72 1000 MANAT
28.2800 g., 0.9250 Silver 0.8410 oz. ASW **Subject:** Writings of President Nijazov

Date	Mintage	F	VF	XF	Unc	BU
2006	—	—	—	—	—	85.00

KM# 73 1000 MANAT
28.2800 g., 0.9250 Silver 0.8410 oz. ASW **Subject:** Writings of President Nijazov

Date	Mintage	F	VF	XF	Unc	BU
2006	—	—	—	—	—	85.00

KM# 74 1000 MANAT
28.2800 g., 0.9250 Silver 0.8410 oz. ASW **Subject:** Writings of President Nijazov

Date	Mintage	F	VF	XF	Unc	BU
2006	—	—	—	—	—	85.00

KM# 75 1000 MANAT
28.2800 g., 0.9250 Silver 0.8410 oz. ASW **Subject:** Writings of President Nijazov

Date	Mintage	F	VF	XF	Unc	BU
2006	—	—	—	—	—	85.00

REFORM COINAGE

January 1, 2009
5000 Old Manat = 1 New Manat
100 Tenge = 1 Manat

KM# 95 TENGE
Nickel Plated Steel, 16 mm. **Obv:** Spire over country map **Rev:** Denomination and date

Date	Mintage	F	VF	XF	Unc	BU
2009	—	—	—	—	0.50	0.75

KM# 96 2 TENGE
3.0000 g., Nickel Plated Steel, 18 mm. **Obv:** Spire over country map **Rev:** Denomination and date **Edge:** Reeded

Date	Mintage	F	VF	XF	Unc	BU
2009	—	—	—	—	0.75	1.00

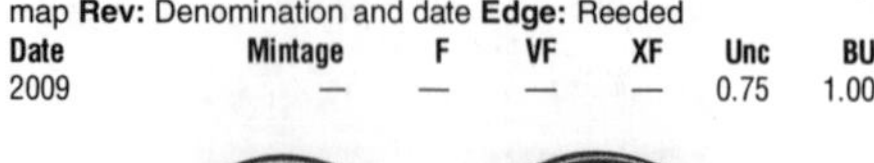

KM# 97 5 TENGE
Nickel Plated Steel, 20 mm. **Obv:** Spire over country map **Rev:** Denomination and date

Date	Mintage	F	VF	XF	Unc	BU
2009	—	—	—	—	1.00	1.25

KM# 98 10 TENGE
Brass, 22 mm. **Obv:** Spire over country map **Rev:** Denomination and date

Date	Mintage	F	VF	XF	Unc	BU
2009	—	—	—	—	1.50	1.75

KM# 99 20 TENGE
Brass, 23 mm. **Obv:** Spire over country map **Rev:** Denomination and date

Date	Mintage	F	VF	XF	Unc	BU
2009	—	—	—	—	2.50	3.00

KM# 100 50 TENGE
Brass, 26 mm. **Obv:** Spire over country map **Rev:** Denomination and date

Date	Mintage	F	VF	XF	Unc	BU
2009	—	—	—	—	3.00	3.50

KM# 103 MANAT
9.3000 g., Bi-Metallic Stainless-steel center in Brass ring, 27 mm. **Obv:** Spire over country map **Rev:** Denomination and date

Date	Mintage	F	VF	XF	Unc	BU
2010	—	—	—	—	4.00	5.00

KM# 104 2 MANAT
10.4000 g., Bi-Metallic Brass center in copper-nickel ring **Obv:** Spire over country map **Rev:** Value and date

Date	Mintage	F	VF	XF	Unc	BU
2010	—	—	—	—	7.00	8.00

TURKS & CAICOS ISLANDS

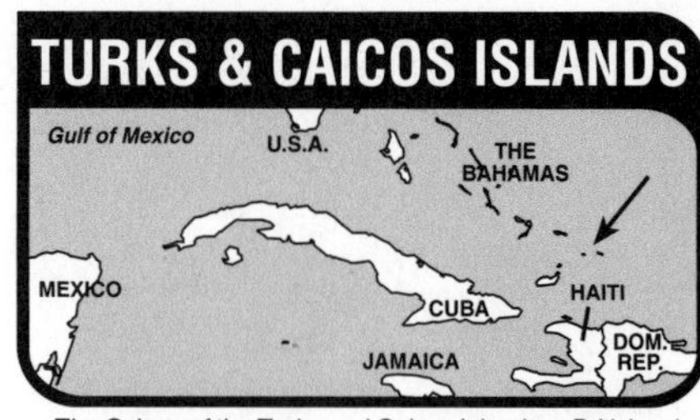

The Colony of the Turks and Caicos Islands, a British colony situated in the West Indies at the eastern end of the Bahama Islands, has an area of 166 sq. mi. (430 sq.km.) and a population of *10,000. Capital: Cockburn Town, on Grand Turk. The principal industry of the colony is the production of salt, which is gathered by raking. Salt, crayfish, and conch shells are exported.

RULER
British

MONETARY SYSTEM
1 Crown = 1 Dollar U.S.A.

BRITISH COLONY
STANDARD COINAGE

KM# 233 5 CROWNS
26.4300 g., Copper-Nickel, 39.2 mm. **Ruler:** Elizabeth II **Subject:** Royal Navy Submarines **Obv:** Head with tiara right **Rev:** Old and modern submarines **Edge:** Reeded

Date	Mintage	F	VF	XF	Unc	BU
2001	—	—	—	6.00	10.00	12.00

KM# 236 20 CROWNS
31.2000 g., 0.9990 Silver 1.0021 oz. ASW, 38.9 mm. **Obv:** Crowned head right **Rev:** Bust right facing divides dates **Edge:** Reeded

Date	Mintage	F	VF	XF	Unc	BU
2001 Proof	—	Value: 50.00				

KM# 245 20 CROWNS
31.1600 g., 0.9990 Silver 1.0008 oz. ASW, 39 mm. **Obv:** Crowned head right **Rev:** Richard II (1377-1399) **Edge:** Reeded

Date	Mintage	F	VF	XF	Unc	BU
2002 Proof	—	Value: 50.00				

KM# 246 20 CROWNS
Hafnium, 38.6 mm. **Ruler:** Elizabeth II **Subject:** H.M. Queen Elizabeth, The Queen Mother **Obv:** Crowned head right **Rev:** Crowned bust right within circle **Edge:** Reeded

Date	Mintage	F	VF	XF	Unc	BU
2002 Proof	—	Value: 145				

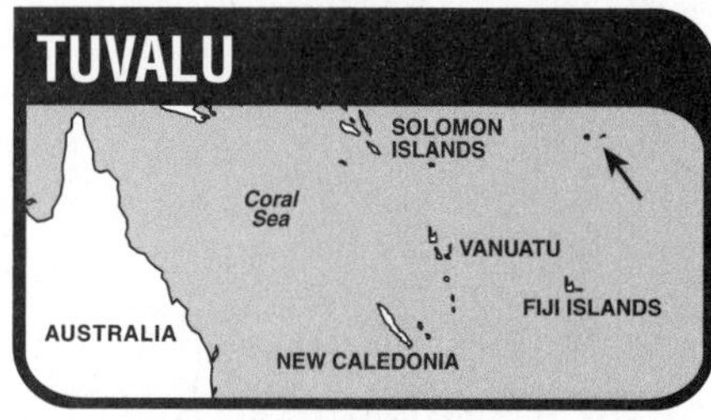

Tuvalu (formerly the Ellice or Lagoon Islands of the Gilbert and Ellice Islands), located in the South Pacific north of the Fiji Islands, has an area of 10 sq. mi. (26 sq.km.) and a population of *9,000. Capital: Funafuti. The independent state includes the islands of Nanumanga, Nanumea, Nui, Niutao, Viatupa, Funafuti, Nukufetau, Nukulailai and Nurakita. The latter four islands were claimed by the United States until relinquished by the Feb. 7, 1979, Treaty of Friendship signed by the United States and Tuvalu. The principal industries are copra production and phosphate mining.

Tuvalu is a member of the Commonwealth of Nations. Elizabeth II is Head of State as Queen of Tuvalu.

RULER
British, until 1978

MONETARY SYSTEM
100 Cents = 1 Dollar

CONSTITUTIONAL MONARCHY WITHIN THE COMMONWEALTH

STANDARD COINAGE

KM# 168 50 CENTS
15.5900 g., 0.9990 Silver 0.5007 oz. ASW, 36.6 mm. **Ruler:** Elizabeth II **Rev:** Two doves tying pink ribbon heart

Date	Mintage	F	VF	XF	Unc	BU
2011 Proof	2,500	Value: 50.00				

KM# 191 50 CENTS
15.5910 g., 0.9999 Silver 0.5012 oz. ASW, 36.6 mm. **Ruler:** Elizabeth II **Subject:** Forever Love **Rev:** Two koalas framed by heart shaped gum leaves and blossoms

Date	Mintage	F	VF	XF	Unc	BU
2012P Proof	7,500	Value: 60.00				

KM# 193 50 CENTS
15.5500 g., 0.9990 Silver 0.4994 oz. ASW, 30.6 mm. **Ruler:** Elizabeth II **Rev:** Baby dragon in color

Date	Mintage	F	VF	XF	Unc	BU
2012P Proof	—	Value: 90.00				

KM# 40 DOLLAR
20.0000 g., Brass, 38.7 mm. **Ruler:** Elizabeth II **Subject:** Dinosaurs **Obv:** Crowned head right **Rev:** Giganotosaurus **Edge:** Reeded **Note:** See KM#49.

Date	Mintage	F	VF	XF	Unc	BU
2002	50,000	—	—	—	18.00	22.00

KM# 41 DOLLAR
20.0000 g., Brass, 38.7 mm. **Ruler:** Elizabeth II **Subject:** Dinosaurs **Obv:** Crowned head right **Rev:** Dromaeosaurus **Edge:** Reeded **Note:** See KM#50.

Date	Mintage	F	VF	XF	Unc	BU
2002	50,000	—	—	—	18.00	22.00

KM# 43 DOLLAR
20.0000 g., Brass, 38.7 mm. **Ruler:** Elizabeth II **Subject:** Dinosaurs **Obv:** Crowned head right **Rev:** Stegosaurus **Edge:** Reeded **Note:** See KM#51.

Date	Mintage	F	VF	XF	Unc	BU
2002	50,000	—	—	—	18.00	22.00

KM# 42 DOLLAR
20.0000 g., Brass, 38.7 mm. **Ruler:** Elizabeth II **Subject:** Dinosaurs **Obv:** Crowned head right **Rev:** Seismosaurus **Edge:** Reeded **Note:** See KM#52.

Date	Mintage	F	VF	XF	Unc	BU
2002	50,000	—	—	—	18.00	22.00

KM# 149 DOLLAR
31.1030 g., 0.9990 Silver 0.9989 oz. ASW, 40.7 mm. **Ruler:** Elizabeth II **Subject:** Harry Potter **Rev:** Multicolor dementor

Date	Mintage	F	VF	XF	Unc	BU
2004	—	—	—	—	—	45.00

KM# 150 DOLLAR
31.1030 g., 0.9990 Silver 0.9989 oz. ASW, 40.7 mm. **Ruler:** Elizabeth II **Subject:** Harry Potter **Rev:** Multicolor owl

Date	Mintage	F	VF	XF	Unc	BU
2004	—	—	—	—	—	45.00

KM# 151 DOLLAR
31.1030 g., 0.9990 Silver 0.9989 oz. ASW, 40.7 mm. **Ruler:** Elizabeth II **Subject:** Harry Potter **Rev:** Multicolor color Harry Potter chasing snitch

Date	Mintage	F	VF	XF	Unc	BU
2004	—	—	—	—	—	45.00

KM# 53 DOLLAR
Silver **Ruler:** Elizabeth II **Obv:** Crowned head right **Rev:** 1955 Mercedes Benz 300 SL Gullwing

Date	Mintage	F	VF	XF	Unc	BU
2006 Proof	—	Value: 55.00				

KM# 54 DOLLAR
Silver **Ruler:** Elizabeth II **Obv:** Crowned head right **Rev:** 1963 Jaguar E-Type colorized

Date	Mintage	F	VF	XF	Unc	BU
2006 Proof	—	Value: 55.00				

KM# 55 DOLLAR
Silver **Ruler:** Elizabeth II **Obv:** Crowned head right **Rev:** 1969 Datsun 240Z

Date	Mintage	F	VF	XF	Unc	BU
2006 Proof	—	Value: 65.00				

KM# 58 DOLLAR
31.3100 g., 0.9990 Silver enameled 1.0056 oz. ASW, 40.51 mm. **Ruler:** Elizabeth II **Subject:** 400th Anniversary of First European Sighting of Australia **Obv:** Crowned bust right **Obv. Legend:** QUEEN ELIZABETH II **Rev:** Bust of Captain James Cook at left, his ship; "H.M.S. Endeavor" within ship's wheel **Rev. Inscription:** 1770 DISCOVERY - EASTERN AUSTRALIA **Edge:** Reeded

Date	Mintage	F	VF	XF	Unc	BU
2006 Proof	—	Value: 85.00				

KM# 59 DOLLAR
31.3100 g., 0.9990 Silver enameled 1.0056 oz. ASW, 40 mm. **Ruler:** Elizabeth II **Subject:** 400th Anniversary of First European Sighting of Australia **Obv:** Crowned bust right **Obv. Legend:** QUEEN ELIZABETH II **Rev:** Bust of Abel Jansoon Tasman at left, his Dutch ship within compass rose **Rev. Legend:** 1642 DISCOVERY OF VAN DIEMAN'S LAND **Edge:** Reeded

Date	Mintage	F	VF	XF	Unc	BU
2006 Proof	—	Value: 85.00				

KM# 60 DOLLAR
31.1050 g., 0.9990 Silver enameled 0.9990 oz. ASW, 40 mm. **Ruler:** Elizabeth II **Subject:** 400th Anniversary of First European Sighting of Australia **Obv:** Crowned bust right **Obv. Legend:** QUEEN ELIZABETH II **Rev:** Bust of William Dampier at right, his ship within wreath **Rev. Legend:** 1688 BRITISH DISCOVERY OF AUSTRALIA **Edge:** Reeded

Date	Mintage	F	VF	XF	Unc	BU
2006 Proof	—	Value: 85.00				

KM# 61 DOLLAR

31.3100 g., 0.9990 Silver enameled 1.0056 oz. ASW, 40 mm. **Ruler:** Elizabeth II **Subject:** 400th Anniversary of First European Sighting of Australia **Obv:** Crowned bust right **Obv. Legend:** QUEEN ELIZABETH II **Rev:** Dutch ship "Duyfken" within compas rose **Rev. Legend:** 1606 FIRST EUROPEAN DISCOVERY AUSTRALIA **Edge:** Reeded

Date	Mintage	F	VF	XF	Unc	BU
2006 Proof	—	Value: 85.00				

KM# 68 DOLLAR

31.1030 g., 0.9990 Silver 0.9989 oz. ASW, 40 mm. **Ruler:** Elizabeth II **Obv:** Crowned bust right **Obv. Legend:** QUEEN ELIZABETH II - TUVALU **Rev:** Red-back Spider, multicolor

Date	Mintage	F	VF	XF	Unc	BU
2006 Proof	5,000	Value: 285				

KM# 170 DOLLAR

31.1050 g., 0.9990 Silver 0.9990 oz. ASW, 40.6 mm. **Ruler:** Elizabeth II **Rev:** Lamborghini in color

Date	Mintage	F	VF	XF	Unc	BU
2006 Proof	—	Value: 65.00				

KM# 171 DOLLAR

31.1050 g., 0.9990 Copper Plated Silver 0.9990 oz., 40.6 mm. **Ruler:** Elizabeth II **Rev:** 1923 1/2 Penny of Australia, reverse

Date	Mintage	F	VF	XF	Unc	BU
2006 Proof	—	Value: 90.00				

KM# 62 DOLLAR

31.1035 g., 0.9990 Silver 0.9990 oz. ASW, 40.51 mm. **Ruler:** Elizabeth II **Obv:** Crowned bust right **Obv. Legend:** ELIZABETH II **Rev:** Multicolor Great White Shark **Edge:** Reeded

Date	Mintage	F	VF	XF	Unc	BU
2007 Proof	5,000	Value: 200				

KM# 63 DOLLAR

0.9990 Silver, 40 mm. **Ruler:** Elizabeth II **Series:** Fighting Ships of WW II **Obv:** Crowned bust right **Obv. Legend:** QUEEN ELIZABETH II - TUVALU **Rev:** USSR Sevastopol, multicolor water

Date	Mintage	F	VF	XF	Unc	BU
2007 Proof	1,500	Value: 75.00				

KM# 64 DOLLAR

0.9990 Silver, 40 mm. **Ruler:** Elizabeth II **Series:** Fighting Ships of WW II **Obv:** Crowned bust right **Obv. Legend:** QUEEN ELIZABETH II - TUVALU **Rev:** HMS Hood, multicolor water and smoke

Date	Mintage	F	VF	XF	Unc	BU
2007 Proof	1,500	Value: 75.00				

KM# 65 DOLLAR

0.9990 Silver, 40 mm. **Ruler:** Elizabeth II **Series:** Fighting Ships of WW II **Obv:** Crowned bust right **Obv. Legend:** QUEEN ELIZABETH II - TUVALU **Rev:** Bismarck, multicolor water and gun flashes

Date	Mintage	F	VF	XF	Unc	BU
2007 Proof	1,500	Value: 75.00				

KM# 66 DOLLAR

0.9990 Silver, 40 mm. **Ruler:** Elizabeth II **Series:** Fighting Ships of WW II **Obv. Legend:** QUEEN ELIZABETH II - TUVALU **Rev:** IJN Yamato, multicolor water and rising sun

Date	Mintage	F	VF	XF	Unc	BU
2007 Proof	1,500	Value: 75.00				

KM# 67 DOLLAR

0.9990 Silver, 40 mm. **Ruler:** Elizabeth II **Series:** Fighting Ships of WW II **Obv:** Crowned bust right **Obv. Legend:** QUEEN ELIZABETH II - TUVALU **Rev:** USS Missouri

Date	Mintage	F	VF	XF	Unc	BU
2007 Proof	1,500	Value: 75.00				

KM# 75 DOLLAR

31.1030 g., 0.9990 Silver 0.9989 oz. ASW, 40.6 mm. **Ruler:** Elizabeth II **Subject:** Early Governors of Australia **Obv:** Head right **Rev:** Multicolor Lahlan Macquarie

Date	Mintage	F	VF	XF	Unc	BU
2008 Proof	1,808	Value: 90.00				

KM# 71 DOLLAR

31.1030 g., 0.9990 Silver 0.9989 oz. ASW, 40.6 mm. **Ruler:** Elizabeth II **Subject:** Early Governors of Austrialia **Obv:** Head right **Rev:** Multicolor Arthur Phillip **Edge:** Reeded

Date	Mintage	F	VF	XF	Unc	BU
2008 Proof	1,808	Value: 90.00				

KM# 72 DOLLAR

31.1030 g., 0.9990 Silver 0.9989 oz. ASW, 40.6 mm. **Ruler:** Elizabeth II **Subject:** Early Governors of Australia **Obv:** Head right **Rev:** Multicolor John Hunter **Edge:** Reeded

Date	Mintage	F	VF	XF	Unc	BU
2008 Proof	1,808	Value: 90.00				

KM# 73 DOLLAR

31.1030 g., 0.9990 Silver 0.9989 oz. ASW, 40.6 mm. **Ruler:** Elizabeth II **Subject:** Early Governors of Australia **Obv:** Head right **Rev:** Multicolor Philip G. King

Date	Mintage	F	VF	XF	Unc	BU
2008 Proof	1,808	Value: 90.00				

KM# 74 DOLLAR

31.1030 g., 0.9990 Silver 0.9989 oz. ASW, 40.6 mm. **Ruler:** Elizabeth II **Subject:** Early Governors of Australia **Obv:** Head right **Rev:** Multicolor William Bligh **Edge:** Reeded

Date	Mintage	F	VF	XF	Unc	BU
2008 Proof	1,808	Value: 90.00				

KM# 76 DOLLAR

37.1080 g., 0.9990 Silver 1.1918 oz. ASW, 40.6 mm. **Ruler:** Elizabeth II **Obv:** Head right **Rev:** Multicolor Australian Lesser Blue-ringed Octopus **Edge:** Reeded

Date	Mintage	F	VF	XF	Unc	BU
2008 Proof	5,000	Value: 220				

KM# 81 DOLLAR

31.1050 g., 0.9990 Silver 0.9990 oz. ASW **Ruler:** Elizabeth II **Subject:** Motorcycles **Rev:** Indian Chief

Date	Mintage	F	VF	XF	Unc	BU
2008 Proff	—	Value: 80.00				

KM# 82 DOLLAR

31.1050 g., 0.9990 Silver 0.9990 oz. ASW **Ruler:** Elizabeth II **Subject:** Motorcycles **Rev:** BMW R12

Date	Mintage	F	VF	XF	Unc	BU
2008 Proof	—	Value: 80.00				

KM# 83 DOLLAR

31.1050 g., 0.9990 Silver 0.9990 oz. ASW **Ruler:** Elizabeth II **Subject:** Motorcycles **Rev:** BSA Gold Star DBD34

Date	Mintage	F	VF	XF	Unc	BU
2008 Proof	—	Value: 80.00				

KM# 84 DOLLAR

31.1050 g., 0.9990 Silver 0.9990 oz. ASW **Ruler:** Elizabeth II **Subject:** Motorcycles **Rev:** Norton - Commando 750

Date	Mintage	F	VF	XF	Unc	BU
2008 Proof	—	Value: 80.00				

KM# 85 DOLLAR

31.1050 g., 0.9990 Silver 0.9990 oz. ASW **Ruler:** Elizabeth II **Subject:** Motorcycles **Rev:** Honda CB760

Date	Mintage	F	VF	XF	Unc	BU
2008 Proof	—	Value: 80.00				

KM# 162 DOLLAR
31.1050 g., 0.9990 Silver 0.9990 oz. ASW, 40 mm. **Ruler:** Elizabeth II **Rev:** Charles Darwin, youthful multicolor portrait, older man portrait, ship Beagle.

Date	Mintage	F	VF	XF	Unc	BU
2009 Proof	—	Value: 75.00				

KM# 80 DOLLAR
31.1050 g., 0.9990 Silver 0.9990 oz. ASW **Ruler:** Elizabeth II **Subject:** Barbie, 50th Anniversary **Rev:** Barbie doll and drawing

Date	Mintage	F	VF	XF	Unc	BU
2009 Proof	20,000	Value: 60.00				

KM# 87 DOLLAR
31.1050 g., 0.9990 Silver 0.9990 oz. ASW, 40 mm. **Ruler:** Elizabeth II **Rev:** Saltwater Crocodile

Date	Mintage	F	VF	XF	Unc	BU
2009 Proof	—	Value: 175				

KM# 88 DOLLAR
31.1050 g., 0.9990 Silver 0.9990 oz. ASW **Ruler:** Elizabeth II **Subject:** Battle of Hastings **Rev:** Battle scene in multicolor

Date	Mintage	F	VF	XF	Unc	BU
2009 Proof	—	Value: 70.00				

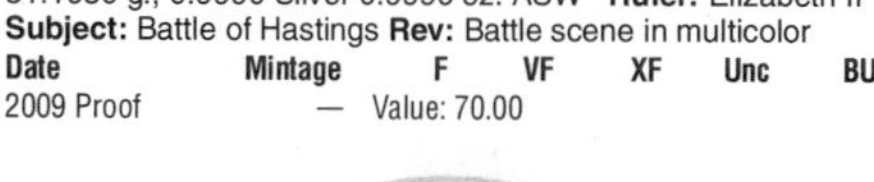

KM# 89 DOLLAR
31.1050 g., 0.9990 Silver 0.9990 oz. ASW, 40.6 mm. **Ruler:** Elizabeth II **Subject:** Battle of Cannae, 216 BC **Rev:** Battlefield scene, multicolor

Date	Mintage	F	VF	XF	Unc	BU
2009 Proof	5,000	Value: 70.00				

KM# 90 DOLLAR
31.1050 g., 0.9990 Silver 0.9990 oz. ASW **Ruler:** Elizabeth II **Subject:** Battle of Gettysburg **Rev:** Battlefield scene, multicolor

Date	Mintage	F	VF	XF	Unc	BU
2009 Proof	—	Value: 70.00				

KM# 91 DOLLAR
31.1050 g., 0.9990 Silver 0.9990 oz. ASW **Ruler:** Elizabeth II **Subject:** Battle of Balaklava, 1854 **Rev:** Battle scene, multicolor

Date	Mintage	F	VF	XF	Unc	BU
2009 Proof	—	Value: 70.00				

KM# 92 DOLLAR
31.1050 g., 0.9990 Silver 0.9990 oz. ASW **Ruler:** Elizabeth II **Subject:** Poltava, Peter the Great's 300th Anniversary **Rev:** Statue of Peter on horseback, multicolor battle scene

Date	Mintage	F	VF	XF	Unc	BU
2009 Proof	—	Value: 70.00				

KM# 94 DOLLAR
31.1050 g., 0.9990 Silver 0.9990 oz. ASW, 40.6 mm. **Ruler:** Elizabeth II **Subject:** Transformers **Rev:** Optimus Prime, multicolor

Date	Mintage	F	VF	XF	Unc	BU
2009 Proof	5,000	Value: 75.00				

KM# 95 DOLLAR
31.1050 g., 0.9990 Silver 0.9990 oz. ASW, 40.6 mm. **Ruler:** Elizabeth II **Subject:** Transformers **Rev:** Megatron, multicolor

Date	Mintage	F	VF	XF	Unc	BU
2009 Proof	5,000	Value: 75.00				

KM# 96 DOLLAR
31.1050 g., 0.9990 Silver 0.9990 oz. ASW, 40.6 mm. **Ruler:** Elizabeth II **Subject:** Fall of the Berlin Wall, 20th Anniversary **Rev:** Brandenburg gate, multicolor

Date	Mintage	F	VF	XF	Unc	BU
2009 Proof	5,000	Value: 65.00				

KM# 97 DOLLAR
31.1050 g., 0.9990 Silver 0.9990 oz. ASW, 40.6 mm. **Ruler:** Elizabeth II **Subject:** Golden Age of Piracy - Black Bart **Obv:** Head right **Rev:** Black Bart at left, multicolor treasure items at right

Date	Mintage	F	VF	XF	Unc	BU
2009 Proof	1,500	Value: 80.00				

KM# 98 DOLLAR
31.1050 g., 0.9990 Silver 0.9990 oz. ASW, 40.6 mm. **Ruler:** Elizabeth II **Subject:** Golden Age of Piracy - Black Beard **Obv:** Head right **Rev:** Black Beard at left, multicolor treasure chest at right

Date	Mintage	F	VF	XF	Unc	BU
2009 Proof	1,500	Value: 80.00				

KM# 99 DOLLAR
31.1050 g., 0.9990 Silver 0.9990 oz. ASW, 40.6 mm. **Ruler:** Elizabeth II **Subject:** Golden Age of Piracy - William Kidd **Obv:** Head right **Rev:** William Kidd at left, multicolor pistol and treasure map at right

Date	Mintage	F	VF	XF	Unc	BU
2009 Proof	1,500	Value: 80.00				

KM# 100 DOLLAR
31.1050 g., 0.9990 Silver 0.9990 oz. ASW, 40.6 mm. **Ruler:** Elizabeth II **Subject:** Golden Age of Piracy - Henry Morgan **Obv:** Head right **Rev:** Henry Morgan at left, multicolor kegs at right

Date	Mintage	F	VF	XF	Unc	BU
2009 Proof	1,500	Value: 80.00				

KM# 101 DOLLAR
31.1050 g., 0.9990 Silver 0.9990 oz. ASW, 40.6 mm. **Ruler:** Elizabeth II **Subject:** Golden Age of Piracy - Calico Jack **Obv:** Head right **Rev:** Calico jack at left, multicolor pirate flag at right

Date	Mintage	F	VF	XF	Unc	BU
2009 Proof	1,500	Value: 80.00				

KM# 102 DOLLAR
31.1050 g., 0.9990 Silver 0.9990 oz. ASW, 40.6 mm. **Ruler:** Elizabeth II **Subject:** Nikolai Gogol, 200th Anniversary of Birth **Obv:** Head right **Rev:** Bust at left, multicolor

Date	Mintage	F	VF	XF	Unc	BU
2009 Proof	6,000	Value: 60.00				

KM# 122 DOLLAR
31.1350 g., 0.9990 Silver 1.0000 oz. ASW, 40.6 mm. **Ruler:** Elizabeth II **Subject:** Mendelssohn

Date	Mintage	F	VF	XF	Unc	BU
2009P Proof	5,000	Value: 70.00				

KM# 123 DOLLAR
31.1350 g., 0.9990 Silver 1.0000 oz. ASW, 40.6 mm. **Ruler:** Elizabeth II **Subject:** Chopin

Date	Mintage	F	VF	XF	Unc	BU
2009P Proof	5,000	Value: 70.00				

KM# 133 DOLLAR
31.1350 g., 0.9990 Silver 1.0000 oz. ASW, 40.6 mm. **Ruler:** Elizabeth II **Subject:** Battle fo Poltava, 300th Anniversary **Rev:** Rearing horse

Date	Mintage	F	VF	XF	Unc	BU
2009P Proof	—	Value: 75.00				

KM# 93 DOLLAR
62.2100 g., 0.9990 Silver 1.9980 oz. ASW **Ruler:** Elizabeth II **Subject:** Battle of Marathon **Rev:** Pheidippides' run

Date	Mintage	F	VF	XF	Unc	BU
2010 Proof	5,000	Value: 95.00				

KM# 103 DOLLAR
31.1050 g., 0.9990 Silver 0.9990 oz. ASW, 40.6 mm. **Ruler:** Elizabeth II **Subject:** Anton Chekhov, 150th Anniversary of Birth **Obv:** Head right **Rev:** Chekhov multicolor portrait at left, comedy and tragedy masks at right

Date	Mintage	F	VF	XF	Unc	BU
2010 Proof	6,000	Value: 60.00				

KM# 104 DOLLAR
31.1050 g., 0.9990 Silver 0.9990 oz. ASW, 40 mm. **Ruler:** Elizabeth II **Subject:** Great River Journeys - The Rhine **Obv:** Head right **Rev:** Tour boat, color castle in background

Date	Mintage	F	VF	XF	Unc	BU
2010 Proof	1,500	Value: 90.00				

KM# 105 DOLLAR
31.1050 g., 0.9990 Silver 0.9990 oz. ASW, 40 mm. **Ruler:** Elizabeth II **Subject:** Great River Journeys - Volga **Obv:** Head right **Rev:** Tour boat and color river front view

Date	Mintage	F	VF	XF	Unc	BU
2010 Proof	1,500	Value: 90.00				

KM# 106 DOLLAR
31.1050 g., 0.9990 Silver 0.9990 oz. ASW, 40 mm. **Ruler:** Elizabeth II **Subject:** Great River Journeys - Yangtzee **Obv:** Head right **Rev:** Sail boat and color river gorge

Date	Mintage	F	VF	XF	Unc	BU
2010 Proof	1,500	Value: 90.00				

KM# 107 DOLLAR

31.1050 g., 0.9990 Silver 0.9990 oz. ASW, 40 mm. **Ruler:** Elizabeth II **Subject:** Great River Journeys - Mississippi **Obv:** Head right **Rev:** Delta Queen and multicolor New Orleans skyline

Date	Mintage	F	VF	XF	Unc	BU
2010 Proof	1,500	Value: 90.00				

KM# 108 DOLLAR

31.1050 g., 0.9990 Silver 0.9990 oz. ASW, 40 mm. **Ruler:** Elizabeth II **Subject:** Great River Journeys - The Nile **Obv:** Head right **Rev:** Dhow, classical sculpture, multicolor sandscape

Date	Mintage	F	VF	XF	Unc	BU
2010 Proof	1,500	Value: 90.00				

KM# 109 DOLLAR

31.1050 g., 0.9990 Silver 0.9990 oz. ASW, 40 mm. **Ruler:** Elizabeth II **Subject:** Ned Kelly - Outlaw **Obv:** Head right **Rev:** Ned Kelly multicolor - Reward Poster

Date	Mintage	F	VF	XF	Unc	BU
2010 Proof	1,880	Value: 90.00				

KM# 110 DOLLAR

31.1050 g., 0.9990 Silver 0.9990 oz. ASW, 40 mm. **Ruler:** Elizabeth II **Subject:** Ned Kelly - Armour **Obv:** Head right **Rev:** Ned Kelley's helmet in multicolor

Date	Mintage	F	VF	XF	Unc	BU
2010 Proof	1,880	Value: 90.00				

KM# 111 DOLLAR

31.1050 g., 0.9990 Silver 0.9990 oz. ASW, 40 mm. **Ruler:** Elizabeth II **Subject:** Ned Kelly - Siege **Obv:** Head right **Rev:** Ned Kelly in shoutout, multicolor

Date	Mintage	F	VF	XF	Unc	BU
2010 Proof	1,880	Value: 90.00				

KM# 112 DOLLAR

31.1050 g., 0.9990 Silver 0.9990 oz. ASW, 40 mm. **Ruler:** Elizabeth II **Subject:** Ned Kelly - Gallows **Obv:** Head right **Rev:** Ned Kelly standing at the gallows, multicolor

Date	Mintage	F	VF	XF	Unc	BU
2010 Proof	1,880	Value: 90.00				

KM# 113 DOLLAR

25.0000 g., 0.9250 Silver 0.7435 oz. ASW **Ruler:** Elizabeth II **Rev:** Sea horse facing left, Swarovski crystal chip eye **Shape:** 38.61

Date	Mintage	F	VF	XF	Unc	BU
2010 Proof	2,500	Value: 65.00				

KM# 114 DOLLAR

0.5000 g., 0.9990 Gold 0.0161 oz. AGW, 11 mm. **Ruler:** Elizabeth II **Rev:** Sea horse facing right

Date	Mintage	F	VF	XF	Unc	BU
2010 Proof	15,000	Value: 50.00				

KM# 115 DOLLAR

25.0000 g., 0.9250 Silver 0.7435 oz. ASW, 38.6 mm. **Ruler:** Elizabeth II **Subject:** Marine Life **Rev:** Hawksbill sea turtle, multicolor

Date	Mintage	F	VF	XF	Unc	BU
2010 Proof	2,500	Value: 50.00				

KM# 117 DOLLAR

31.1350 g., 0.9990 Silver 1.0000 oz. ASW, 40.6 mm. **Ruler:** Elizabeth II **Subject:** Ballet - Don Quixote **Rev:** Multicolor windmill scene

Date	Mintage	F	VF	XF	Unc	BU
2010P Proof	2,500	Value: 80.00				

KM# 118 DOLLAR

31.1350 g., 0.9990 Silver 1.0000 oz. ASW, 40.6 mm. **Ruler:** Elizabeth II **Subject:** Ballet - Sleeping Beauty **Rev:** Multicolor castle scene

Date	Mintage	F	VF	XF	Unc	BU
2010P Proof	2,500	Value: 80.00				

KM# 119 DOLLAR

31.1350 g., 0.9990 Silver 1.0000 oz. ASW, 40.6 mm. **Ruler:** Elizabeth II **Subject:** Ballet - Nutcracker **Rev:** Multicolor snow scene

Date	Mintage	F	VF	XF	Unc	BU
2010P Proof	2,500	Value: 80.00				

KM# 120 DOLLAR

31.1350 g., 0.9990 Silver 1.0000 oz. ASW, 40.6 mm. **Ruler:** Elizabeth II **Subject:** Ballet - Swan Lake **Rev:** Multicolor swan and lake scene

Date	Mintage	F	VF	XF	Unc	BU
2010P Proof	2,500	Value: 80.00				

KM# 121 DOLLAR

31.1350 g., 0.9990 Silver 1.0000 oz. ASW, 40.6 mm. **Ruler:** Elizabeth II **Subject:** Ballet - Cinderella **Rev:** Multicolor pumpkin coach scene

Date	Mintage	F	VF	XF	Unc	BU
2010P Proof	2,500	Value: 80.00				

KM# 124 DOLLAR

31.1350 g., 0.9990 Silver 1.0000 oz. ASW, 40.6 mm. **Ruler:** Elizabeth II **Subject:** Robert Schumann **Rev:** Bust, G-cleff and score

Date	Mintage	F	VF	XF	Unc	BU
2010P Proof	5,000	Value: 70.00				

KM# 125 DOLLAR

31.1350 g., 0.9990 Silver 1.0000 oz. ASW, 40.6 mm. **Ruler:** Elizabeth II **Subject:** Gustav Mahler

Date	Mintage	F	VF	XF	Unc	BU
2010P Proof	5,000	Value: 70.00				

KM# 127 DOLLAR

31.1350 g., 0.9990 Silver 1.0000 oz. ASW, 40.6 mm. **Ruler:** Elizabeth II **Subject:** Warrior - Legionary **Rev:** Multicolor Roman Legionary soldier standing

Date	Mintage	F	VF	XF	Unc	BU
2010P Proof	—	Value: 80.00				

KM# 128 DOLLAR

31.1350 g., 0.9990 Silver 1.0000 oz. ASW, 40.6 mm. **Ruler:** Elizabeth II **Subject:** Warrior - Viking **Rev:** Multicolor Viking

Date	Mintage	F	VF	XF	Unc	BU
2010P Proof	—	Value: 80.00				

KM# 129 DOLLAR

31.1350 g., 0.9990 Silver 1.0000 oz. ASW, 40.6 mm. **Ruler:** Elizabeth II **Subject:** Warrior - Knight **Rev:** Multicolor Knight

Date	Mintage	F	VF	XF	Unc	BU
2010P Proof	—	Value: 80.00				

KM# 130 DOLLAR

31.1350 g., 0.9990 Silver 1.0000 oz. ASW, 40.6 mm. **Ruler:** Elizabeth II **Subject:** Warrior - Samurai **Rev:** Multicolor Samurai

Date	Mintage	F	VF	XF	Unc	BU
2010P Proof	—	Value: 80.00				

KM# 131 DOLLAR

31.1350 g., 0.9990 Silver 1.0000 oz. ASW, 40 mm. **Ruler:** Elizabeth II **Subject:** "Banjo" Paterson Ballard - Man from Snowy River **Rev:** Multicolor cowboy chasing two horses

Date	Mintage	F	VF	XF	Unc	BU
2010P Proof	—	Value: 80.00				

KM# 134 DOLLAR

31.1350 g., 0.9990 Silver 1.0000 oz. ASW, 40.6 mm. **Ruler:** Elizabeth II **Rev:** Multicolor brown snake

Date	Mintage	F	VF	XF	Unc	BU
2010P Proof	—	Value: 185				

KM# 135 DOLLAR

31.1350 g., 0.9990 Silver 1.0000 oz. ASW, 40.6 mm. **Ruler:** Elizabeth II **Subject:** German Unification, 20th Anniversary **Rev:** Large 20, statues on Brandenburg gate

Date	Mintage	F	VF	XF	Unc	BU
2010P Proof	5,000	Value: 75.00				

KM# 136 DOLLAR
31.1350 g., 0.9990 Silver 1.0000 oz. ASW, 40.6 mm. **Ruler:** Elizabeth II **Subject:** Sir Charles Kingsford

Date	Mintage	F	VF	XF	Unc	BU
2010P Proof	—	Value: 75.00				

KM# 137 DOLLAR
31.1350 g., 0.9990 Silver 1.0000 oz. ASW, 40.6 mm. **Ruler:** Elizabeth II **Subject:** Working dogs **Rev:** Multicolor golden retreiver pups

Date	Mintage	F	VF	XF	Unc	BU
2010P Proof	—	Value: 85.00				

KM# 138 DOLLAR
31.1350 g., 0.9990 Silver 1.0000 oz. ASW, 40.6 mm. **Ruler:** Elizabeth II **Subject:** Man from Snowy River **Rev:** Multicolor group of horsemen

Date	Mintage	F	VF	XF	Unc	BU
2010P Proof	—	Value: 75.00				

KM# 139 DOLLAR
31.1350 g., 0.9990 Silver 1.0000 oz. ASW, 40.7 mm. **Ruler:** Elizabeth II **Subject:** Trucks - W900 **Rev:** Truck cab

Date	Mintage	F	VF	XF	Unc	BU
2010P Proof	—	Value: 75.00				

KM# 140 DOLLAR
31.1350 g., 0.9990 Silver 1.0000 oz. ASW, 40.6 mm. **Ruler:** Elizabeth II **Subject:** Trucks - Cascadia **Rev:** Multicolor truck cab

Date	Mintage	F	VF	XF	Unc	BU
2010P Proof	—	Value: 75.00				

KM# 141 DOLLAR
31.1350 g., 0.9990 Silver 1.0000 oz. ASW, 40.6 mm. **Ruler:** Elizabeth II **Subject:** Trucks - R500 **Rev:** Multicolor truck cab

Date	Mintage	F	VF	XF	Unc	BU
2010P Proof	—	Value: 75.00				

KM# 142 DOLLAR
31.1350 g., 0.9990 Silver 1.0000 oz. ASW, 40.6 mm. **Ruler:** Elizabeth II **Subject:** Trucks - GiGamax **Rev:** Multicolor truck cab

Date	Mintage	F	VF	XF	Unc	BU
2010P Proof	—	Value: 75.00				

KM# 143 DOLLAR
31.1350 g., 0.9990 Silver 1.0000 oz. ASW, 40.7 mm. **Ruler:** Elizabeth II **Subject:** Tanks - A22 Churchill **Rev:** Multicolor tank

Date	Mintage	F	VF	XF	Unc	BU
2010P Proof	—	Value: 75.00				

KM# 144 DOLLAR
31.1350 g., 0.9990 Silver 1.0000 oz. ASW **Ruler:** Elizabeth II **Subject:** Tanks - M-4 Sherman **Rev:** Multicolor tank **Shape:** 40.6

Date	Mintage	F	VF	XF	Unc	BU
2010P Proof	—	Value: 75.00				

KM# 145 DOLLAR
31.1350 g., 0.9990 Silver 1.0000 oz. ASW, 40.6 mm. **Ruler:** Elizabeth II **Subject:** Tanks - Type 97 Chi-Ha **Rev:** Multicolor tank

Date	Mintage	F	VF	XF	Unc	BU
2010P Proof	—	Value: 75.00				

KM# 146 DOLLAR
31.1350 g., 0.9990 Silver 1.0000 oz. ASW, 40.6 mm. **Ruler:** Elizabeth II **Subject:** Tanks - T-34 **Rev:** Multicolor tank

Date	Mintage	F	VF	XF	Unc	BU
2010P Proof	—	Value: 75.00				

KM# 147 DOLLAR
31.1350 g., 0.9990 Silver 1.0000 oz. ASW, 40.6 mm. **Ruler:** Elizabeth II **Subject:** Tanks - PzK pfw VI Tiger 1 **Rev:** Multicolor tank

Date	Mintage	F	VF	XF	Unc	BU
2010P Proof	—	Value: 75.00				

KM# 148 DOLLAR
13.9000 g., Aluminum-Bronze, 30.6 mm. **Ruler:** Elizabeth II **Rev:** Blackbeard standing, treasure chest at right

Date	Mintage	F	VF	XF	Unc	BU
2010P	—	—	—	—	—	15.00

KM# 126 DOLLAR
31.1350 g., 0.9990 Silver 1.0000 oz. ASW, 40.6 mm. **Ruler:** Elizabeth II **Subject:** Franz List

Date	Mintage	F	VF	XF	Unc	BU
2011P Proof	5,000	Value: 70.00				

KM# 163 DOLLAR
31.1350 g., 0.9990 Silver 1.0000 oz. ASW, 40.6 mm. **Ruler:** Elizabeth II **Subject:** Australia's extinct animals - Thylacine **Obv:** Head in diadem right **Rev:** Thylacine - Tasmanian tiger in multicolor

Date	Mintage	F	VF	XF	Unc	BU
2011P Proof	5,000	Value: 250				

KM# 165 DOLLAR
31.1050 g., 0.9990 Silver 0.9990 oz. ASW, 40.6 mm. **Ruler:** Elizabeth II **Obv:** Head with tiara right **Rev:** Australia's Box Jellyfish in color **Edge:** Reeded

Date	Mintage	F	VF	XF	Unc	BU
2011 Proof	5,000	Value: 120				

KM# 172 DOLLAR
31.1050 g., 0.9990 Silver 0.9990 oz. ASW, 40.6 mm. **Ruler:** Elizabeth II **Subject:** Franz Lizst, 200th anniversary of birth **Rev:** Lizst at left, G-cleft, 4 lines of score

Date	Mintage	F	VF	XF	Unc	BU
2011 Proof	—	Value: 80.00				

KM# 177 DOLLAR
13.8000 g., Aluminum-Bronze, 30.6 mm. **Ruler:** Elizabeth II **Subject:** Henry Morgan **Rev:** Morgan, ship, chest and barrels

Date	Mintage	F	VF	XF	Unc	BU
2011P	—	—	—	—	—	15.00

KM# 178 DOLLAR
13.8000 g., Aluminum-Bronze, 30.8 mm. **Ruler:** Elizabeth II **Subject:** Calico Jack **Rev:** Jack standing, ship, Skull and crossed-swords flag

Date	Mintage	F	VF	XF	Unc	BU
2011P	—	—	—	—	—	15.00

KM# 179 DOLLAR
13.8000 g., Aluminum-Bronze, 30.8 mm. **Ruler:** Elizabeth II **Subject:** Black Bart **Rev:** Bart at left, ship and cross

Date	Mintage	F	VF	XF	Unc	BU
2011P	—	—	—	—	—	15.00

KM# 180 DOLLAR
13.8000 g., Aluminum-Bronze, 30.8 mm. **Ruler:** Elizabeth II **Subject:** William Kidd **Rev:** Bust at left, ship, pistol and map

Date	Mintage	F	VF	XF	Unc	BU
2011P	—	—	—	—	—	15.00

KM# 181 DOLLAR
31.1350 g., 0.9990 Silver 1.0000 oz. ASW, 40.6 mm. **Ruler:** Elizabeth II **Subject:** Ships that changed the World **Rev:** Santa Maria under sail

Date	Mintage	F	VF	XF	Unc	BU
2011P Proof	5,000	Value: 75.00				

KM# 182 DOLLAR
31.1350 g., 0.9990 Silver 1.0000 oz. ASW, 40.6 mm. **Ruler:** Elizabeth II **Subject:** Ships that changed the World **Rev:** Golden Hind under sail

Date	Mintage	F	VF	XF	Unc	BU
2011P Proof	5,000	Value: 75.00				

KM# 183 DOLLAR
31.1350 g., 0.9990 Silver 1.0000 oz. ASW, 40.6 mm. **Ruler:** Elizabeth II **Subject:** Heroes and Villians **Rev:** Holmes and Moriarty

Date	Mintage	F	VF	XF	Unc	BU
2011P Proof	1,500	Value: 80.00				

KM# 184 DOLLAR
31.1350 g., 0.9990 Silver 1.0000 oz. ASW, 40.6 mm. **Ruler:** Elizabeth II **Subject:** Heroes and Villains **Rev:** van Helsing and Dracula

Date	Mintage	F	VF	XF	Unc	BU
2011P Proof	1,500	Value: 80.00				

KM# 185 DOLLAR
31.1350 g., 0.9990 Silver 1.0000 oz. ASW, 40.6 mm. **Ruler:** Elizabeth II **Subject:** Heroes and Villains **Rev:** Robin Hood and the Sherif

Date	Mintage	F	VF	XF	Unc	BU
2011P Proof	1,500	Value: 80.00				

KM# 186 DOLLAR
31.1350 g., 0.9990 Silver 1.0000 oz. ASW, 40.6 mm. **Ruler:** Elizabeth II **Subject:** Heros and Villains **Rev:** Peter Pan and Captain Hook

Date	Mintage	F	VF	XF	Unc	BU
2011P Proof	1,500	Value: 80.00				

KM# 187 DOLLAR
31.1350 g., 0.9990 Silver 1.0000 oz. ASW, 40.6 mm. **Ruler:** Elizabeth II **Subject:** Heroes and Villains **Rev:** Dr. Jeckel and Mr. Hyde

Date	Mintage	F	VF	XF	Unc	BU
2011P Proof	1,500	Value: 80.00				

KM# 195 DOLLAR
31.1350 g., 0.9990 Silver 1.0000 oz. ASW, 40.6 mm. **Ruler:** Elizabeth II **Subject:** Working dogs - Beagle

Date	Mintage	F	VF	XF	Unc	BU
2011 Proof	—	Value: 95.00				

KM# 196 DOLLAR
31.1350 g., 0.9990 Silver 1.0000 oz. ASW, 40.6 mm. **Ruler:** Elizabeth II **Subject:** Working dogs - Border Collie

Date	Mintage	F	VF	XF	Unc	BU
2011 Proof	—	Value: 75.00				

KM# 197 DOLLAR
31.1350 g., 0.9990 Silver 1.0000 oz. ASW, 40.6 mm. **Ruler:** Elizabeth II **Subject:** Working dogs - German Shepard

Date	Mintage	F	VF	XF	Unc	BU
2011 Proof	—	Value: 95.00				

KM# 198 DOLLAR
31.1350 g., 0.9990 Silver 1.0000 oz. ASW, 40.6 mm. **Ruler:** Elizabeth II **Subject:** Working dogs - Australian Cattle Dog

Date	Mintage	F	VF	XF	Unc	BU
2011 Proof	—	Value: 85.00				

KM# 202 DOLLAR
15.5000 g., 0.9250 Silver 0.4609 oz. ASW, 35 mm. **Ruler:** Elizabeth II **Subject:** Coral Protection **Rev:** Dendrocyra Cylindriclus, coral in color

Date	Mintage	F	VF	XF	Unc	BU
2011 Proof	1,000	Value: 65.00				

KM# 188 DOLLAR
31.1350 g., 0.9990 Silver 1.0000 oz. ASW, 40.6 mm. **Ruler:** Elizabeth II **Subject:** Ships that changed the World **Rev:** Mayflower at sail

Date	Mintage	F	VF	XF	Unc	BU
2012P Proof	5,000	Value: 100				

KM# 189 DOLLAR
31.1350 g., 0.9990 Silver 1.0000 oz. ASW, 40.6 mm. **Ruler:** Elizabeth II **Subject:** Ships that changed the World **Rev:** U.S.S. Constitution in sea battle

Date	Mintage	F	VF	XF	Unc	BU
2012P Proof	5,000	Value: 100				

KM# 190 DOLLAR
13.8000 g., Aluminum-Bronze, 30.6 mm. **Ruler:** Elizabeth II **Subject:** Year of the Dragon **Rev:** Baby Dragon in color

Date	Mintage	F	VF	XF	Unc	BU
2012P	10,000	—	—	—	—	15.00

KM# 192 DOLLAR
31.1350 g., 0.9990 Silver 1.0000 oz. ASW, 40.6 mm. **Ruler:** Elizabeth II **Rev:** R.M.S. Titanic sailing forward, tug at side

Date	Mintage	F	VF	XF	Unc	BU
2012P Proof	5,000	Value: 100				

KM# 194 DOLLAR
31.1350 g., 0.9990 Silver 1.0000 oz. ASW **Ruler:** Elizabeth II **Subject:** Wildlife in Need **Obv:** Head with tiara right **Rev:** Black rhinoceros and calf in color **Edge:** Reeded

Date	Mintage	F	VF	XF	Unc	BU
2012P Proof	5,000	Value: 100				

KM# 173 2 DOLLARS
Silver, 38.6 mm. **Ruler:** Elizabeth II **Subject:** Year of the Goat **Obv:** Head crowned right **Rev:** Two goats

Date	Mintage	F	VF	XF	Unc	BU
2003 Proof	—	Value: 50.00				

KM# 175 2 DOLLARS
31.1050 g., 0.9990 Silver 0.9990 oz. ASW, 38.6 mm. **Ruler:** Elizabeth II **Obv:** Head crowned right **Rev:** Harry Potter with wand raised, being followed by Dementor **Edge:** Reeded

Date	Mintage	F	VF	XF	Unc	BU
2004 Proof	—	Value: 55.00				

KM# 116 2 DOLLARS
1.2400 g., 0.9990 Gold 0.0398 oz. AGW, 13.92 mm. **Ruler:** Elizabeth II **Rev:** Los Reyes sailing ship

Date	Mintage	F	VF	XF	Unc	BU
2010 Proof	15,000	Value: 85.00				

KM# 169 2 DOLLARS
Gold, 13.9 mm. **Ruler:** Elizabeth II **Subject:** Marine life **Rev:** Sea horse

Date	Mintage	F	VF	XF	Unc	BU
2010 Proof	—	Value: 80.00				

KM# 174 3 DOLLARS
1.2240 g., 0.9990 Gold 0.0393 oz. AGW, 13.9 mm. **Ruler:** Elizabeth II **Subject:** Year of the Horse **Rev:** Horse galloping right

Date	Mintage	F	VF	XF	Unc	BU
2002 Proof	—	Value: 115				
2008 Proof	—	Value: 115				

KM# 158 3 DOLLARS
1.2240 g., 0.9990 Gold 0.0393 oz. AGW, 13.9 mm. **Ruler:** Elizabeth II **Rev:** Australian owl

Date	Mintage	F	VF	XF	Unc	BU
2005 Proof	—	Value: 85.00				
2006 Proof	—	Value: 85.00				
2007 Proof	—	Value: 85.00				

KM# 152 3 DOLLARS
1.2240 g., 0.9990 Gold 0.0393 oz. AGW, 13.9 mm. **Ruler:** Elizabeth II **Rev:** Multicolor mouse with heart

Date	Mintage	F	VF	XF	Unc	BU
2008	—	—	—	—	—	95.00

KM# 199 3 DOLLARS
1.2400 g., 0.9999 Gold 0.0399 oz. AGW, 14.5 mm. **Ruler:** Elizabeth II **Subject:** Lucky waving cat

Date	Mintage	F	VF	XF	Unc	BU
2011 Proof	2,000	Value: 125				

KM# 200 3 DOLLARS
1.2400 g., 0.9999 Gold 0.0399 oz. AGW, 14.5 mm. **Ruler:** Elizabeth II **Subject:** Lucky waving cats

Date	Mintage	F	VF	XF	Unc	BU
2011 Proof	2,000	Value: 125				

KM# 49 5 DOLLARS
62.5000 g., 0.9990 Silver 2.0073 oz. ASW, 49.9 mm. **Ruler:** Elizabeth II **Subject:** Dinosaurs **Obv:** Crowned head right **Rev:** Giganotosaurus **Edge:** Reeded

Date	Mintage	F	VF	XF	Unc	BU
2002 Proof	1,000	Value: 90.00				

KM# 50 5 DOLLARS
62.5000 g., 0.9990 Silver 2.0073 oz. ASW, 49.9 mm. **Ruler:** Elizabeth II **Subject:** Dinosaurs **Obv:** Crowned head right **Rev:** Dromaeosaurus **Edge:** Reeded

Date	Mintage	F	VF	XF	Unc	BU
2002 Proof	1,000	Value: 90.00				

KM# 51 5 DOLLARS
62.5000 g., 0.9990 Silver 2.0073 oz. ASW, 49.9 mm. **Ruler:** Elizabeth II **Subject:** Dinosaurs **Obv:** Crowned head right **Rev:** Stegosaurus **Edge:** Reeded

Date	Mintage	F	VF	XF	Unc	BU
2002 Proof	1,000	Value: 90.00				

KM# 52 5 DOLLARS
62.5000 g., 0.9990 Silver 2.0073 oz. ASW, 49.9 mm. **Ruler:** Elizabeth II **Subject:** Dinosaurs **Obv:** Crowned head right **Rev:** Seismosaurus **Edge:** Reeded

Date	Mintage	F	VF	XF	Unc	BU
2002 Proof	1,000	Value: 90.00				

KM# 159 15 DOLLARS
3.1110 g., 0.9990 Gold 0.0999 oz. AGW, 17.95 mm. **Ruler:** Elizabeth II **Rev:** Australian owl

Date	Mintage	F	VF	XF	Unc	BU
2005 Proof	—	Value: 185				
2006 Proof	—	Value: 185				
2007 Proof	—	Value: 185				

KM# 153 15 DOLLARS
3.1110 g., 0.9990 Gold 0.0999 oz. AGW, 17.95 mm. **Ruler:** Elizabeth II **Rev:** Multicolor mouse and golden egg

Date	Mintage	F	VF	XF	Unc	BU
2008	—	—	—	—	—	235

KM# 201 15 DOLLARS
3.1100 g., 0.9999 Gold 0.1000 oz. AGW, 18 mm. **Ruler:** Elizabeth II **Subject:** Lucky waving cat

Date	Mintage	F	VF	XF	Unc	BU
2011 Proof	2,000	Value: 225				

KM# 132 25 DOLLARS
7.7700 g., 0.9990 Gold 0.2496 oz. AGW, 22.6 mm. **Ruler:** Elizabeth II **Subject:** Ned Kelly **Rev:** Multicolor gun slinger and steel helmet

Date	Mintage	Good	VG	F	VF	XF
2010P Proof	1,000	Value: 600				

KM# 160 30 DOLLARS
6.2220 g., 0.9990 Gold 0.1998 oz. AGW, 21.95 mm. **Ruler:** Elizabeth II **Rev:** Australian owl

Date	Mintage	F	VF	XF	Unc	BU
2005 Proof	—	Value: 375				
2006 Proof	—	Value: 375				
2007 Proof	—	Value: 375				

KM# 176 30 DOLLARS
6.2200 g., 0.9990 Platinum 0.1998 oz. APW, 21.95 mm. **Ruler:** Elizabeth II **Subject:** Year of the Horse **Obv:** Head crowned right **Rev:** Horse galloping right

Date	Mintage	F	VF	XF	Unc	BU
2008 Proof	—	Value: 400				

KM# 154 30 DOLLARS
15.5540 g., 0.9990 Gold 0.4996 oz. AGW, 21.95 mm. **Ruler:** Elizabeth II **Rev:** Multicolor mouse and money bag

Date	Mintage	F	VF	XF	Unc	BU
2008	—	—	—	—	—	975

KM# 167 30 DOLLARS
6.2200 g., 0.9995 Platinum 0.1999 oz. APW **Ruler:** Elizabeth II **Rev:** Horse galloping right

Date	Mintage	F	VF	XF	Unc	BU
2008 Proof	—	Value: 500				

KM# 155 30 DOLLARS
6.2200 g., 0.9990 Gold 0.1998 oz. AGW, 21.95 mm. **Ruler:** Elizabeth II **Rev:** Cow seated with fans above

Date	Mintage	F	VF	XF	Unc	BU
2009	—	—	—	—	—	375

KM# 156 30 DOLLARS
6.2200 g., 0.9990 Gold 0.1998 oz. AGW, 21.95 mm. **Ruler:** Elizabeth II **Rev:** Cow standing with success symbol

Date	Mintage	F	VF	XF	Unc	BU
2009	—	—	—	—	—	375

KM# 157 30 DOLLARS
6.2200 g., 0.9990 Gold 0.1998 oz. AGW, 21.95 mm. **Ruler:** Elizabeth II **Rev:** Cow standing next to money bag

Date	Mintage	F	VF	XF	Unc	BU
2009	—	—	—	—	—	375

KM# 164 30 DOLLARS
6.2200 g., 0.9990 Gold 0.1998 oz. AGW **Ruler:** Elizabeth II **Obv:** Head crowned right **Rev:** Horse running right

Date	Mintage	F	VF	XF	Unc	BU
2010 Proof	—	Value: 400				

KM# 166 30 DOLLARS
6.2200 g., 0.9995 Gold 0.1999 oz. AGW **Ruler:** Elizabeth II **Rev:** Horse galloping right

Date	Mintage	F	VF	XF	Unc	BU
2010 Proof	—	Value: 400				

KM# 161 50 DOLLARS
15.5540 g., 0.9990 Gold 0.4996 oz. AGW, 30 mm. **Ruler:** Elizabeth II **Rev:** Australiam owl

Date	Mintage	F	VF	XF	Unc	BU
2005 Proof	—	Value: 925				
2006 Proof	—	Value: 925				
2007 Proof	—	Value: 925				

KM# 69 100 DOLLARS
Gold **Ruler:** Elizabeth II **Obv:** Crowned head right **Rev:** Red 1963 Corvette Sting Ray

Date	Mintage	F	VF	XF	Unc	BU
2006 Proof	250	Value: 1,850				

UGANDA

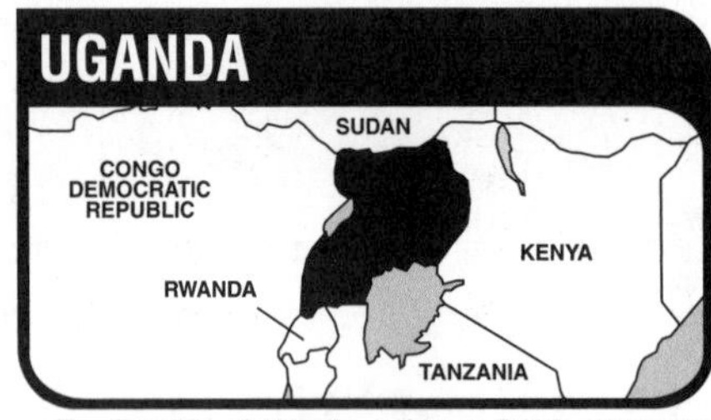

The Republic of Uganda, a former British protectorate located astride the equator in east-central Africa, has an area of 91,134 sq. mi. (236,040 sq. km.) and a population of *17 million. Capital: Kampala. Agriculture, including livestock, is the basis of the economy; there is some mining of copper, tin, gold and lead. Coffee, cotton, copper and tea are exported.

Uganda is a member of the Commonwealth of Nations. The president is Chief of State and Head of Government.

For earlier coinage refer to East Africa.

MONETARY SYSTEM
100 Cents = 1 Shilling

REPUBLIC

STANDARD COINAGE

KM# 66 50 SHILLINGS
4.0000 g., Nickel Plated Steel **Obv:** National arms **Rev:** Antelope head facing

Date	Mintage	F	VF	XF	Unc	BU
2003	—	—	—	—	1.00	1.25
2007	—	—	—	—	1.00	1.25

KM# 67 100 SHILLINGS
7.0000 g., Copper-Nickel, 26.9 mm. **Obv:** National arms **Rev:** African bull **Edge:** Reeded

Date	Mintage	F	VF	XF	Unc	BU
2003	—	—	—	—	1.50	1.75
2007	—	—	—	—	1.50	1.75
2008	—	—	—	—	1.50	1.75

KM# 129 100 SHILLINGS
3.5400 g., Stainless Steel, 23.98 mm. **Series:** Zodiac **Obv:** National arms **Rev:** Monkey with elf-like ears **Edge:** Plain

Date	Mintage	F	VF	XF	Unc	BU
2004	—	—	—	—	1.50	2.50

KM# 135 100 SHILLINGS
3.5400 g., Steel, 23.98 mm. **Series:** Zodiac **Obv:** National arms **Rev:** Ox **Edge:** Plain

Date	Mintage	F	VF	XF	Unc	BU
2004	—	—	—	—	1.50	2.50

KM# 136 100 SHILLINGS
3.5400 g., Steel, 23.98 mm. **Series:** Zodiac **Obv:** National arms **Rev:** Goat **Edge:** Plain

Date	Mintage	F	VF	XF	Unc	BU
2004	—	—	—	—	1.50	2.50

KM# 137 100 SHILLINGS
3.5400 g., Steel, 23.98 mm. **Series:** Zodiac **Obv:** National arms **Rev:** Horse **Edge:** Plain

Date	Mintage	F	VF	XF	Unc	BU
2004	—	—	—	—	1.50	2.50

KM# 138 100 SHILLINGS
3.5400 g., Steel, 23.98 mm. **Series:** Zodiac **Obv:** National arms **Rev:** Dragon **Edge:** Plain

Date	Mintage	F	VF	XF	Unc	BU
2004	—	—	—	—	1.50	2.50

KM# 139 100 SHILLINGS
3.5400 g., Steel, 23.98 mm. **Series:** Zodiac **Obv:** National arms **Rev:** Dog **Edge:** Plain

Date	Mintage	F	VF	XF	Unc	BU
2004	—	—	—	—	1.50	2.50

KM# 140 100 SHILLINGS
3.5400 g., Steel, 23.98 mm. **Series:** Zodiac **Obv:** National arms **Rev:** Tiger **Edge:** Plain

Date	Mintage	F	VF	XF	Unc	BU
2004	—	—	—	—	1.50	2.50

KM# 141 100 SHILLINGS
3.5400 g., Steel, 23.98 mm. **Series:** Zodiac **Obv:** National arms **Rev:** Snake **Edge:** Plain

Date	Mintage	F	VF	XF	Unc	BU
2004	—	—	—	—	1.50	2.50

KM# 142 100 SHILLINGS
3.5400 g., Steel, 23.98 mm. **Series:** Zodiac **Obv:** National arms **Rev:** Rooster **Edge:** Plain

Date	Mintage	F	VF	XF	Unc	BU
2004	—	—	—	—	1.50	2.50

KM# 143 100 SHILLINGS
3.5400 g., Steel, 23.98 mm. **Series:** Zodiac **Obv:** National arms **Rev:** Rabbit **Edge:** Plain

Date	Mintage	F	VF	XF	Unc	BU
2004	—	—	—	—	1.50	2.50

KM# 144 100 SHILLINGS
3.5400 g., Steel, 23.98 mm. **Series:** Zodiac **Obv:** National arms **Rev:** Rat **Edge:** Plain

Date	Mintage	F	VF	XF	Unc	BU
2004	—	—	—	—	1.50	2.50

KM# 145 100 SHILLINGS
3.5400 g., Steel, 23.98 mm. **Series:** Zodiac **Obv:** National arms **Rev:** Pig **Edge:** Plain

Date	Mintage	F	VF	XF	Unc	BU
2004	—	—	—	—	1.50	2.50

KM# 130 100 SHILLINGS
Steel, 23 mm. **Rev:** Type I of five different monkeys

Date	Mintage	F	VF	XF	Unc	BU
2004	—	—	—	—	1.75	2.75

KM# 131 100 SHILLINGS
Steel, 23 mm. **Rev:** Type II of five different monkeys

Date	Mintage	F	VF	XF	Unc	BU
2004	—	—	—	—	1.75	2.75

KM# 132 100 SHILLINGS
Steel, 23 mm. **Rev:** Type III of five different monkeys

Date	Mintage	F	VF	XF	Unc	BU
2004	—	—	—	—	1.75	2.75

KM# 133 100 SHILLINGS
Steel, 23 mm. **Rev:** Type IV of five different monkys

Date	Mintage	F	VF	XF	Unc	BU
2004	—	—	—	—	1.50	2.75

KM# 134 100 SHILLINGS
Steel, 23 mm. **Rev:** Type V of five different monkeys

Date	Mintage	F	VF	XF	Unc	BU
2004	—	—	—	—	1.75	2.75

KM# 188 100 SHILLINGS
3.5300 g., Nickel Plated Steel, 24 mm. **Series:** Zodiac **Obv:** National arms **Obv. Legend:** BANK OF UGANDA **Rev:** Head of a rat **Rev. Legend:** BANK OF UGANDA **Edge:** Plain

Date	Mintage	F	VF	XF	Unc	BU
2004	—	—	—	—	1.75	2.75

KM# 189 100 SHILLINGS
3.5300 g., Nickel Plated Steel, 24 mm. **Series:** Zodiac **Obv:** National arms **Obv. Legend:** BANK OF UGANDA **Rev:** Head of an ox **Rev. Legend:** BANK OF UGANDA **Edge:** Plain

Date	Mintage	F	VF	XF	Unc	BU
2004	—	—	—	—	1.75	2.75

KM# 190 100 SHILLINGS

3.5300 g., Nickel Plated Steel, 24 mm. **Series:** Zodiac **Obv:** National arms **Obv. Legend:** BANK OF UGANDA **Rev:** Head of a tiger **Rev. Legend:** BANK OF UGANDA **Edge:** Plain

Date	Mintage	F	VF	XF	Unc	BU
2004	—	—	—	—	1.75	2.75

KM# 191 100 SHILLINGS

3.5300 g., Nickel Plated Steel, 24 mm. **Series:** Zodiac **Obv:** National arms **Obv. Legend:** BANK OF UGANDA **Rev:** Head of a rabbit **Rev. Legend:** BANK OF UGANDA **Edge:** Plain

Date	Mintage	F	VF	XF	Unc	BU
2004	—	—	—	—	1.75	2.75

KM# 192 100 SHILLINGS

3.5300 g., Nickel Plated Steel, 24 mm. **Series:** Zodiac **Obv:** National arms **Obv. Legend:** BANK OF UGANDA **Rev:** Head of a dragon **Rev. Legend:** BANK OF UGANDA **Edge:** Plain

Date	Mintage	F	VF	XF	Unc	BU
2004	—	—	—	—	1.75	2.75

KM# 193 100 SHILLINGS

3.5300 g., Nickel Plated Steel, 24 mm. **Series:** Zodiac **Obv:** National arms **Obv. Legend:** BANK OF UGANDA **Rev:** Head and hood of Cobra snake **Rev. Legend:** BANK OF UGANDA **Edge:** Plain

Date	Mintage	F	VF	XF	Unc	BU
2004	—	—	—	—	1.75	2.75

KM# 194 100 SHILLINGS

3.5300 g., Nickel Plated Steel, 24 mm. **Series:** Zodiac **Obv:** National arms **Obv. Legend:** BANK OF UGANDA **Rev:** Head of a horse **Rev. Legend:** BANK OF UGANDA **Edge:** Plain

Date	Mintage	F	VF	XF	Unc	BU
2004	—	—	—	—	1.75	2.75

KM# 195 100 SHILLINGS

3.5300 g., Nickel Plated Steel, 24 mm. **Series:** Zodiac **Obv:** National arms **Obv. Legend:** BANK OF UGANDA **Rev:** Head of a goat **Rev. Legend:** BANK OF UGANDA **Edge:** Plain

Date	Mintage	F	VF	XF	Unc	BU
2004	—	—	—	—	1.75	2.75

KM# 196 100 SHILLINGS

3.5300 g., Nickel Plated Steel, 24 mm. **Series:** Zodiac **Obv:** National arms **Obv. Legend:** BANK OF UGANDA **Rev:** Head of a monkey **Rev. Legend:** BANK OF UGANDA **Edge:** Plain

Date	Mintage	F	VF	XF	Unc	BU
2004	—	—	—	—	1.75	2.75

KM# 197 100 SHILLINGS

3.5300 g., Nickel Plated Steel, 24 mm. **Series:** Zodiac **Obv:** National arms **Obv. Legend:** BANK OF UGANDA **Rev:** Forepart of a rooster **Rev. Legend:** BANK OF UGANDA **Edge:** Plain

Date	Mintage	F	VF	XF	Unc	BU
2004	—	—	—	—	1.75	2.75

KM# 198 100 SHILLINGS

3.5300 g., Nickel Plated Steel, 24 mm. **Series:** Zodiac **Obv:** National arms **Obv. Legend:** BANK OF UGANDA **Rev:** Head of a dog **Rev. Legend:** BANK OF UGANDA **Edge:** Plain

Date	Mintage	F	VF	XF	Unc	BU
2004	—	—	—	—	1.75	2.75

KM# 199 100 SHILLINGS

3.5300 g., Nickel Plated Steel, 24 mm. **Series:** Zodiac **Obv:** National arms **Obv. Legend:** BANK OF UGANDA **Rev:** Head of a pig **Rev. Legend:** BANK OF UGANDA **Edge:** Plain

Date	Mintage	F	VF	XF	Unc	BU
2004	—	—	—	—	1.75	2.75

KM# 200 100 SHILLINGS

Copper-Nickel **Subject:** Year of the Monkey **Obv. Legend:** BANK OF UGANDA **Rev:** Monkey swingging right

Date	Mintage	F	VF	XF	Unc	BU
2004	—	—	—	—	2.00	3.00

KM# 201 100 SHILLINGS

Copper-Nickel **Subject:** Year of the Monkey **Obv. Legend:** BANK OF UGANDA

Date	Mintage	F	VF	XF	Unc	BU
2004	—	—	—	—	2.00	3.00

KM# 202 100 SHILLINGS

Copper-Nickel **Subject:** Year of the Monkey **Obv. Legend:** BANK OF UGANDA **Rev:** Monkey right on all fours

Date	Mintage	F	VF	XF	Unc	BU
2004	—	—	—	—	2.00	3.00

KM# 203 100 SHILLINGS

Copper-Nickel **Subject:** Year of the Monkey **Obv. Legend:** BANK OF UGANDA **Rev:** Monkey seated left

Date	Mintage	F	VF	XF	Unc	BU
2004	—	—	—	—	2.00	3.00

KM# 204 100 SHILLINGS

Copper-Nickel **Subject:** Year of the Monkey **Obv. Legend:** BANK OF UGANDA **Rev:** Monkeys seated right, looking left over his shoulder

Date	Mintage	F	VF	XF	Unc	BU
2004	—	—	—	—	2.00	3.00

KM# 67a 100 SHILLINGS

7.0000 g., Nickel Plated Steel, 26.9 mm. **Obv:** National arms **Rev:** African bull **Edge:** Reeded

Date	Mintage	F	VF	XF	Unc	BU
2007	—	—	—	—	1.50	1.75
2008	—	—	—	—	1.50	1.75

KM# 68 200 SHILLINGS

8.0500 g., Copper-Nickel, 24.9 mm. **Obv:** National arms **Rev:** Cichlid fish above value and date **Edge:** Plain

Date	Mintage	F	VF	XF	Unc	BU
2003	—	—	—	—	2.00	3.00
2008	—	—	—	—	2.00	3.00

KM# 68a 200 SHILLINGS

8.0500 g., Nickel Plated Steel, 24.9 mm. **Obv:** National arms **Rev:** Cichlid fish above value and date

Date	Mintage	F	VF	XF	Unc	BU
2007	—	—	—	—	2.00	3.00
2008	—	—	—	—	2.00	3.00

KM# 69 500 SHILLINGS

9.0000 g., Nickel-Brass, 23.5 mm. **Obv:** National arms **Rev:** East African crowned crane head left **Edge:** Reeded

Date	Mintage	F	VF	XF	Unc	BU
2003	—	—	—	—	3.50	4.50
2008	—	—	—	—	3.50	4.50

KM# 77 1000 SHILLINGS

19.8400 g., Copper-Nickel, 38.6 mm. **Subject:** Colourful Big Five of Africa **Obv:** Arms with supporters **Rev:** Multicolor rhinocerous within stamp design in front of outlined African map **Edge:** Reeded

Date	Mintage	F	VF	XF	Unc	BU
2001 Proof	—	Value: 22.50				

KM# 78 1000 SHILLINGS

19.8400 g., Copper-Nickel, 38.6 mm. **Subject:** Colourful Big Five of Africa **Obv:** Arms with supporters **Rev:** Multicolor lion within stamp design in front of outlined African map **Edge:** Reeded

Date	Mintage	F	VF	XF	Unc	BU
2001 Proof	—	Value: 22.50				

KM# 79 1000 SHILLINGS

19.8400 g., Copper-Nickel, 38.6 mm. **Subject:** Coulourful Big Five of Africa **Obv:** Arms with supporters **Rev:** Multicolor water buffalo within stamp design in front of outlined African map **Edge:** Reeded

Date	Mintage	F	VF	XF	Unc	BU
2001 Proof	—	Value: 22.50				

KM# 80 1000 SHILLINGS

19.8400 g., Copper-Nickel, 38.6 mm. **Subject:** Colourful Big Five of Africa **Obv:** Arms with supporters **Rev:** Multicolor leopard within stamp design in front of outlined map **Edge:** Reeded

Date	Mintage	F	VF	XF	Unc	BU
2001 Proof	—	Value: 22.50				

KM# 81 1000 SHILLINGS

19.8400 g., Copper-Nickel, 38.6 mm. **Subject:** Colourful Big Five of Africa **Obv:** Arms with supporters **Rev:** Multicolor elephant within stamp design in front of outlined map **Edge:** Reeded

Date	Mintage	F	VF	XF	Unc	BU
2001 Proof	—	Value: 22.50				

KM# 173 1000 SHILLINGS

Silver **Subject:** XVII World Football Championship Games - Korea and Japan **Obv. Legend:** BANK OF UGANDA **Rev:** Football - gilt

Date	Mintage	F	VF	XF	Unc	BU
2001 Proof	—	Value: 28.00				

KM# 82 1000 SHILLINGS

24.8300 g., 0.9990 Silver 0.7975 oz. ASW, 38.6 mm. **Subject:** World of Football **Obv:** Arms with supporters **Rev:** Soccer ball globe **Edge:** Reeded

Date	Mintage	F	VF	XF	Unc	BU
2002 Proof	—	Value: 35.00				

KM# 83 1000 SHILLINGS

24.8300 g., 0.9990 Silver 0.7975 oz. ASW, 38.6 mm. **Subject:** World of Football **Obv:** Arms with supporters **Rev:** Soccer ball in net **Edge:** Reeded

Date	Mintage	F	VF	XF	Unc	BU
2002 Proof	—	Value: 32.50				

KM# 84 1000 SHILLINGS

24.8300 g., 0.9990 Silver 0.7975 oz. ASW, 38.6 mm. **Subject:** World of Football **Obv:** Arms with supporters **Rev:** Goalie catching ball, red kicker insert at right **Edge:** Reeded

Date	Mintage	F	VF	XF	Unc	BU
2002 Proof	—	Value: 32.50				

KM# 85 1000 SHILLINGS
24.8300 g., 0.9990 Silver 0.7975 oz. ASW, 38.6 mm. **Subject:** World of Football **Obv:** Arms with supporters **Rev:** Two players going after the ball, red runner insert at left **Edge:** Reeded

Date	Mintage	F	VF	XF	Unc	BU
2002 Proof	—	Value: 32.50				

KM# 86 1000 SHILLINGS
24.8300 g., 0.9990 Silver 0.7975 oz. ASW, 38.6 mm. **Subject:** World of Football **Obv:** Arms with supporters **Rev:** Player kicking ball, blue kicker insert at right **Edge:** Reeded

Date	Mintage	F	VF	XF	Unc	BU
2002 Proof	—	Value: 32.50				

KM# 101 1000 SHILLINGS
29.4400 g., Silver Plated Bronze (Specific gravity 8.8675), 38.5 mm. **Series:** Gorillas of Africa **Obv:** National arms **Rev:** Seated gorilla **Edge:** Reeded

Date	Mintage	F	VF	XF	Unc	BU
2002 Proof	—	Value: 12.50				
2003 Proof	—	Value: 12.00				

KM# 102 1000 SHILLINGS
29.4400 g., Silver Plated Bronze (Specific gravity 8.8675), 38.5 mm. **Series:** Gorillas of Africa **Obv:** National arms **Rev:** Gorilla eating **Edge:** Reeded

Date	Mintage	F	VF	XF	Unc	BU
2002 Proof	—	Value: 12.50				
2003 Proof	—	Value: 10.00				

KM# 103 1000 SHILLINGS
29.4400 g., Silver Plated Bronze (Specific gravity 8.8675), 38.5 mm. **Series:** Gorillas of Africa **Obv:** National arms **Rev:** Gorilla on all fours **Edge:** Reeded

Date	Mintage	F	VF	XF	Unc	BU
2002 Proof	—	Value: 12.50				
2003 Proof	—	Value: 10.00				

KM# 104 1000 SHILLINGS
29.4400 g., Silver Plated Bronze (Specific gravity 8.8675), 38.5 mm. **Series:** Gorillas of Africa **Obv:** National arms **Rev:** Gorilla female with infant **Edge:** Reeded

Date	Mintage	F	VF	XF	Unc	BU
2002 Proof	—	Value: 12.50				
2003 Proof	—	Value: 10.00				

KM# 106 1000 SHILLINGS
29.1600 g., Silver Plated Bronze (Specific gravity 8.8096), 38.6 mm. **Subject:** Marine Life **Obv:** Arms with supporters **Rev:** Multicolor sea horses **Edge:** Reeded

Date	Mintage	F	VF	XF	Unc	BU
2002 Proof	—	Value: 22.00				

KM# 107 1000 SHILLINGS
29.1600 g., Silver Plated Bronze (Specific gravity 8.8096), 38.6 mm. **Subject:** Marine Life **Obv:** Arms with supporters **Rev:** Multicolor Hammerhead sharks **Edge:** Reeded

Date	Mintage	F	VF	XF	Unc	BU
2002 Proof	—	Value: 22.00				

KM# 108 1000 SHILLINGS
29.1600 g., Silver Plated Bronze (Specific gravity 8.8096), 38.6 mm. **Subject:** Marine Life **Obv:** Arms with supporters **Rev:** Multicolor Stingray **Edge:** Reeded

Date	Mintage	F	VF	XF	Unc	BU
2002 Proof	—	Value: 22.00				

KM# 109 1000 SHILLINGS
29.1600 g., Silver Plated Bronze (Specific gravity 8.8096), 38.6 mm. **Subject:** Marine Life **Obv:** Arms with supporters **Rev:** Multicolor Seal **Edge:** Reeded

Date	Mintage	F	VF	XF	Unc	BU
2002 Proof	—	Value: 22.00				

KM# 110 1000 SHILLINGS
29.1600 g., Silver Plated Bronze (Specific gravity 8.8096), 38.6 mm. **Subject:** Marine Life **Obv:** Arms with supporters **Rev:** Multicolor sea turtle **Edge:** Reeded

Date	Mintage	F	VF	XF	Unc	BU
2002 Proof	—	Value: 22.00				

KM# 111 1000 SHILLINGS
29.1600 g., Silver Plated Bronze (Specific gravity 8.8096), 38.6 mm. **Subject:** Marine Life **Obv:** Arms with supporters **Rev:** Multicolor dolphins **Edge:** Reeded

Date	Mintage	F	VF	XF	Unc	BU
2002 Proof	—	Value: 22.00				

KM# 112 1000 SHILLINGS
29.1600 g., Silver Plated Bronze (Specific gravity 8.8096), 38.6 mm. **Subject:** Marine Life **Obv:** Arms with supporters **Rev:** Multicolor octopus **Edge:** Reeded

Date	Mintage	F	VF	XF	Unc	BU
2002 Proof	—	Value: 22.00				

KM# 113 1000 SHILLINGS
29.1600 g., Silver Plated Bronze (Specific gravity 8.8096), 38.6 mm. **Subject:** Marine Life **Obv:** Arms with supporters **Rev:** Multicolor red fish **Edge:** Reeded

Date	Mintage	F	VF	XF	Unc	BU
2002 Proof	—	Value: 22.00				

KM# 114 1000 SHILLINGS
29.1600 g., Silver Plated Bronze (Specific gravity 8.8096), 38.6 mm. **Subject:** Marine Life **Obv:** Arms with supporters **Rev:** Multicolor black fish with white dots **Edge:** Reeded

Date	Mintage	F	VF	XF	Unc	BU
2002 Proof	—	Value: 22.00				

KM# 115 1000 SHILLINGS
29.1600 g., Silver Plated Bronze (Specific gravity 8.8096), 38.6 mm. **Subject:** Marine Life **Obv:** Arms with supporters **Rev:** Multicolor yellow and black striped fish **Edge:** Reeded

Date	Mintage	F	VF	XF	Unc	BU
2002 Proof	—	Value: 22.00				

KM# 240 1000 SHILLINGS
Silver **Obv:** Arms **Rev:** Pope John Paul II bust facing

Date	Mintage	F	VF	XF	Unc	BU
2003 Proof	—	Value: 75.00				

KM# 105 1000 SHILLINGS
29.2000 g., Silver Plated Bronze (Specific gravity 9.0123), 38.6 mm. **Subject:** Pope John Paul II **Obv:** Arms with supporters **Rev:** Pope saying mass, design of Zambian 1000 Kwacha KM-160 **Edge:** Reeded **Note:** Muling error

Date	Mintage	F	VF	XF	Unc	BU
2003 Proof	—	Value: 300				

KM# 216 1000 SHILLINGS
Bronze **Subject:** Christmas **Obv. Legend:** BANK OF UGANDA **Rev:** Peace on Earth

Date	Mintage	F	VF	XF	Unc	BU
2004	500	—	—	—	—	50.00

KM# 75 2000 SHILLINGS
49.9000 g., 0.9990 Silver 1.6027 oz. ASW, 50 mm. **Subject:** Illusion: "Spirit of the Mountain" **Obv:** Crowned head right divides date above arms with supporters **Rev:** Landscape and tree that looks like a male portrait **Edge:** Reeded

Date	Mintage	F	VF	XF	Unc	BU
2001 Proof	—	Value: 75.00				

KM# 121 2000 SHILLINGS
25.0000 g., 0.9250 Silver 0.7435 oz. ASW, 38.6 mm. **Subject:** Queen Elizabeth's 75th Birthday **Obv:** Arms with supporters above crowned head right **Rev:** Queen accepting flowers from children **Edge:** Reeded

Date	Mintage	F	VF	XF	Unc	BU
2001 Proof	2,000	Value: 35.00				

KM# 100 2000 SHILLINGS
31.4000 g., 0.9990 Silver 1.0085 oz. ASW, 38.8 mm. **Obv:** Crowned head right divides date above arms with supporters **Rev:** Bust of Henry M. Stanley facing **Edge:** Reeded

Date	Mintage	F	VF	XF	Unc	BU
2002	—	—	—	—	40.00	45.00

KM# 177 2000 SHILLINGS
15.5500 g., 0.9990 Silver 0.4994 oz. ASW **Series:** Famous Places in China **Subject:** Mount Huangshan - Anhwei **Obv:** Two dragons **Obv. Legend:** BANK OF UGANDA

Date	Mintage	F	VF	XF	Unc	BU
2003 Proof	3,000	Value: 35.00				

KM# 178 2000 SHILLINGS
15.5500 g., 0.9990 Silver 0.4994 oz. ASW **Series:** Famous Places in China **Subject:** Zhangjiajie - Hunan **Obv:** Two dragons **Obv. Legend:** BANK OF UGANDA

Date	Mintage	F	VF	XF	Unc	BU
2003 Proof	3,000	Value: 35.00				

KM# 179 2000 SHILLINGS
15.5500 g., 0.9990 Silver 0.4994 oz. ASW **Series:** Famous Places in China **Subject:** Stone Forest - Yunnan **Obv:** Two dragons **Obv. Legend:** BANK OF UGANDA

Date	Mintage	F	VF	XF	Unc	BU
2003 Proof	3,000	Value: 35.00				

KM# 180 2000 SHILLINGS
15.5500 g., 0.9990 Silver 0.4994 oz. ASW **Series:** Famous Places in China **Subject:** Potala Palace - Lhasa, Tibet **Obv:** Two dragons **Obv. Legend:** BANK OF UGANDA

Date	Mintage	F	VF	XF	Unc	BU
2003 Proof	3,000	Value: 35.00				

KM# 181 2000 SHILLINGS
15.5500 g., 0.9990 Silver 0.4994 oz. ASW **Series:** Famous Places inChina **Subject:** Yangtse River Gorges **Obv:** Two dragons **Obv. Legend:** BANK OF UGANDA

Date	Mintage	F	VF	XF	Unc	BU
2003 Proof	3,000	Value: 35.00				

KM# 182 2000 SHILLINGS
31.1000 g., 0.9990 Silver 0.9988 oz. ASW **Series:** Chinese symbolism **Subject:** Harmony **Obv. Legend:** BANK OF UGANDA **Rev:** Dragon and phoenix

Date	Mintage	F	VF	XF	Unc	BU
2003 Proof	3,000	Value: 60.00				

KM# 183 2000 SHILLINGS
31.1000 g., 0.9990 Silver 0.9988 oz. ASW **Series:** Chinese symbolism **Subject:** Happiness **Obv. Legend:** BANK OF UGANDA **Rev:** Unicorn

Date	Mintage	F	VF	XF	Unc	BU
2003 Proof	3,000	Value: 60.00				

KM# 184 2000 SHILLINGS
31.1000 g., 0.9990 Silver 0.9988 oz. ASW **Series:** Chinese symbolism **Subject:** Health and long life **Obv. Legend:** BANK OF UGANDA **Rev:** Two cranes

Date	Mintage	F	VF	XF	Unc	BU
2003 Proof	3,000	Value: 60.00				

KM# 185 2000 SHILLINGS
31.1000 g., 0.9990 Silver 0.9988 oz. ASW **Series:** Chinese symbolism **Subject:** Success **Obv. Legend:** BANK OF UGANDA **Rev:** Carp

Date	Mintage	F	VF	XF	Unc	BU
2003 Proof	3,000	Value: 60.00				

KM# 186 2000 SHILLINGS
31.1000 g., 0.9990 Silver 0.9988 oz. ASW **Series:** Chinese symbolism **Subject:** Wealth **Obv. Legend:** BANK OF UGANDA **Rev:** Toad

Date	Mintage	F	VF	XF	Unc	BU
2003 Proof	3,000	Value: 60.00				

KM# 175 2000 SHILLINGS
15.5500 g., 0.9990 Silver 0.4994 oz. ASW **Series:** Famous Places in China **Subject:** Yugan Garden - Shanghai **Obv:** Two dragons **Obv. Legend:** BANK OF UGANDA

Date	Mintage	F	VF	XF	Unc	BU
2003 Proof	3,000	Value: 35.00				

KM# 176 2000 SHILLINGS
15.5500 g., 0.9990 Silver 0.4994 oz. ASW **Series:** Famous Places in China **Subject:** Tiger Hill Pagoda - Jiangsu **Obv:** Two dragons **Obv. Legend:** BANK OF UGANDA

Date	Mintage	F	VF	XF	Unc	BU
2003 Proof	3,000	Value: 35.00				

KM# 187 2000 SHILLINGS
4.0000 g., 0.9999 Gold 0.1286 oz. AGW **Series:** Guanyin **Subject:** Fulun **Obv:** Lotus blossom **Obv. Legend:** BANK OF UGANDA

Date	Mintage	F	VF	XF	Unc	BU
2003 Proof	—	Value: 245				

KM# 205 2000 SHILLINGS
Silver **Subject:** XXVIII Summer Olympics - Athens 2004 **Obv. Legend:** BANK OF UGANDA **Rev:** Sprinter

Date	Mintage	F	VF	XF	Unc	BU
2003 Proof	500	Value: 60.00				

KM# 210 2000 SHILLINGS
31.1000 g., 0.9990 Silver 0.9988 oz. ASW **Series:** Chinese symbolic floral New Year paintings **Subject:** Happiness **Obv. Legend:** BANK OF UGANDA **Rev:** Multicolor

Date	Mintage	F	VF	XF	Unc	BU
2004 Proof	2,000	Value: 60.00				

KM# 211 2000 SHILLINGS
31.1000 g., 0.9990 Silver 0.9988 oz. ASW **Series:** Chinese Dieties **Subject:** Happiness **Obv. Legend:** BANK OF UGANDA **Rev:** Fú - multicolor

Date	Mintage	F	VF	XF	Unc	BU
2004 Proof	2,000	Value: 60.00				

KM# 212 2000 SHILLINGS
31.1000 g., 0.9990 Silver 0.9988 oz. ASW **Series:** Chinese Deities **Subject:** Prosperity **Obv. Legend:** BANK OF UGANDA **Rev:** Lù - multicolor

Date	Mintage	F	VF	XF	Unc	BU
2004 Proof	2,000	Value: 60.00				

KM# 213 2000 SHILLINGS
31.1000 g., 0.9990 Silver 0.9988 oz. ASW **Series:** Chinese Dieties **Subject:** Health and Long Life **Obv. Legend:** BANK OF UGANDA **Rev:** Shòu - multicolor

Date	Mintage	F	VF	XF	Unc	BU
2004 Proof	2,000	Value: 60.00				

KM# 206 2000 SHILLINGS
31.1000 g., 0.9990 Silver 0.9988 oz. ASW **Series:** Chinese symbolic floral New Year paintings **Obv. Legend:** BANK OF UGANDA **Rev:** Carp and Lotus blossom - multicolor

Date	Mintage	F	VF	XF	Unc	BU
2004 Proof	2,000	Value: 60.00				

KM# 207 2000 SHILLINGS
31.1000 g., 0.9990 Silver 0.9988 oz. ASW **Series:** Chinese symbolic floral New Year paintings **Obv. Legend:** BANK OF UGANDA **Rev:** Deer - multicolor

Date	Mintage	F	VF	XF	Unc	BU
2004 Proof	2,000	Value: 60.00				

KM# 208 2000 SHILLINGS
31.1000 g., 0.9990 Silver 0.9988 oz. ASW **Series:** Chinese symbolic floral New Year paintings **Subject:** Abundance **Obv. Legend:** BANK OF UGANDA **Rev:** Fruit - multicolor

Date	Mintage	F	VF	XF	Unc	BU
2004 Proof	2,000	Value: 60.00				

KM# 209 2000 SHILLINGS
31.1000 g., 0.9990 Silver 0.9988 oz. ASW **Series:** Chinese symbolic floral New Year paintings **Subject:** Peace and prosperity **Obv. Legend:** BANK OF UGANDA **Rev:** Multicolor

Date	Mintage	F	VF	XF	Unc	BU
2004 Proof	2,000	Value: 60.00				

KM# 221 2000 SHILLINGS
Silver Plated Bronze **Series:** XIX World Football Championship - South Africa 2010 **Obv:** National arms **Obv. Legend:** BANK OF UGANDA **Rev:** Player about to kick

Date	Mintage	F	VF	XF	Unc	BU
2005 Proof	10,000	Value: 15.00				

KM# 222 2000 SHILLINGS
Silver Plated Bronze **Series:** XIX World Football Championship - South Afrika 2010 **Obv:** National arms **Obv. Legend:** BANK OF UGANDA **Rev:** Ball in net

Date	Mintage	F	VF	XF	Unc	BU
2005 Proof	10,000	Value: 15.00				

KM# 223 2000 SHILLINGS
Silver Plated Bronze **Series:** XIX World Football Championship - South Afrika 2010 **Obv:** National arms **Obv. Legend:** BANK OF UGANDA **Rev:** Player, map of Afrika

Date	Mintage	F	VF	XF	Unc	BU
2005 Proof	10,000	Value: 15.00				

KM# 224 2000 SHILLINGS
Silver Plated Bronze **Series:** XIX World Football Championship - South Afrika 2010 **Obv:** National arms **Obv. Legend:** BANK OF UGANDA **Rev:** Goalkeeper with ball

Date	Mintage	F	VF	XF	Unc	BU
2005 Proof	10,000	Value: 15.00				

KM# 225 2000 SHILLINGS
Silver Plated Bronze **Series:** XIX World Football Championship - South Afrika 2010 **Obv:** National arms **Obv. Legend:** BANK OF UGANDA **Rev:** Player and ball

Date	Mintage	F	VF	XF	Unc	BU
2005 Proof	10,000	Value: 15.00				

KM# 217 2000 SHILLINGS
31.1000 g., 0.9990 Silver 0.9988 oz. ASW **Obv:** Lotus blossom **Obv. Legend:** BANK OF UGANDA **Rev:** Guanyin - multicolor

Date	Mintage	F	VF	XF	Unc	BU
2005 Proof	2,000	Value: 75.00				

KM# 226 2000 SHILLINGS
40.0000 g., Bronze Gilt **Series:** Zodiac **Subject:** Year of the Dog **Obv:** Two dragons **Obv. Legend:** BANK OF UGANDA **Rev:** Three dogs - multicolor

Date	Mintage	F	VF	XF	Unc	BU
2006 Proof	—	Value: 45.00				

KM# 227 2000 SHILLINGS
40.0000 g., Bronze Gilt **Series:** Zodiac **Subject:** Year of the Dog **Obv:** Archaic Chinese characters **Obv. Legend:** BANK OF UGANDA **Rev:** Two dogs - multicolor

Date	Mintage	F	VF	XF	Unc	BU
2006 Proof	—	Value: 45.00				

KM# 227a 2000 SHILLINGS
31.1000 g., 0.9990 Silver 0.9988 oz. ASW **Series:** Zodiac **Subject:** Year of the Dog **Obv:** Archaic Chinese characters **Obv. Legend:** BANK OF UGANDA **Rev:** Two dogs - multicolor

Date	Mintage	F	VF	XF	Unc	BU
2006 Proof	3,000	Value: 75.00				

KM# 234 2000 SHILLINGS
31.1000 g., 0.9990 Silver 0.9988 oz. ASW **Series:** Zodiac **Subject:** Year of the Dog **Obv. Legend:** BANK OF UGANDA **Rev:** Tibet Terrier with pup surrounded by 10 symbols

Date	Mintage	F	VF	XF	Unc	BU
2006 Proof	3,000	Value: 75.00				

KM# 237 2000 SHILLINGS
31.1000 g., 0.9990 Silver 0.9988 oz. ASW **Series:** Zodiac **Subject:** Year of the Dog **Obv:** National arms **Obv. Legend:** BANK OF UGANDA **Rev:** Chow-chow as watchdog, gold bars, bat and flower

Date	Mintage	F	VF	XF	Unc	BU
2006 Proof	—	Value: 60.00				

KM# 172 5000 SHILLINGS
4.0000 g., 0.9999 Gold 0.1286 oz. AGW **Series:** Guanyin **Subject:** Chilian **Obv:** Lotus blossom **Obv. Legend:** BANK OF UGANDA

Date	Mintage	F	VF	XF	Unc	BU
2001 Proof	—	Value: 245				

KM# 87 5000 SHILLINGS
33.7300 g., 0.8500 Silver 0.9217 oz. ASW, 38.65 mm. **Subject:** "The Big Five" **Obv:** Arms with supporters **Rev:** Rhinoceros **Edge:** Reeded

Date	Mintage	F	VF	XF	Unc	BU
2002 Proof	—	Value: 65.00				

KM# 88 5000 SHILLINGS
33.7300 g., 0.8500 Silver 0.9217 oz. ASW, 38.65 mm. **Subject:** "The Big Five" **Obv:** Arms with supporters **Rev:** Lion **Edge:** Reeded

Date	Mintage	F	VF	XF	Unc	BU
2002 Proof	—	Value: 65.00				

KM# 89 5000 SHILLINGS
33.7300 g., 0.8500 Silver 0.9217 oz. ASW, 38.65 mm. **Subject:** "The Big Five" **Obv:** Arms with supporters **Rev:** Cape Buffalo **Edge:** Reeded

Date	Mintage	F	VF	XF	Unc	BU
2002 Proof	—	Value: 50.00				

KM# 90 5000 SHILLINGS
33.7300 g., 0.8500 Silver 0.9217 oz. ASW, 38.65 mm. **Subject:** "The Big Five" **Obv:** Arms with supporters **Rev:** Leopard **Edge:** Reeded

Date	Mintage	F	VF	XF	Unc	BU
2002 Proof	—	Value: 65.00				

KM# 91 5000 SHILLINGS
33.7300 g., 0.8500 Silver 0.9217 oz. ASW, 38.65 mm. **Subject:** "The Big Five" **Obv:** Arms with supporters **Rev:** Elephant **Edge:** Reeded

Date	Mintage	F	VF	XF	Unc	BU
2002 Proof	—	Value: 65.00				

KM# 96 5000 SHILLINGS
31.1035 g., 0.9990 Silver 0.9990 oz. ASW, 40.6 mm. **Subject:** Matthew Flinders **Obv:** Arms with supporters below crowned head right dividing date **Rev:** Multicolor bust half left at right with ship and harbor scene at left **Edge:** Plain **Shape:** Continent of Australia

Date	Mintage	F	VF	XF	Unc	BU
2002 Proof	2,500	Value: 55.00				

KM# 97 5000 SHILLINGS
31.1035 g., 0.9990 Silver 0.9990 oz. ASW, 40.6 mm. **Subject:** Matthew Flinders - H. M. S. Investigator **Obv:** Crowned head right divides date above arms with supporters **Rev:** Multicolor cameo at upper right of ship **Edge:** Plain **Shape:** Continent of Australia

Date	Mintage	F	VF	XF	Unc	BU
2002 Proof	2,500	Value: 55.00				

KM# 98 5000 SHILLINGS
31.1035 g., 0.9990 Silver 0.9990 oz. ASW, 40.6 mm. **Subject:** Matthew Flinders - Meeting at Encounter Bay **Obv:** Crowned head right divides date above arms with supporters **Rev:** Date and inscription divides multicolor busts facing **Edge:** Plain **Shape:** Continent of Australia

Date	Mintage	F	VF	XF	Unc	BU
2002 Proof	2,500	Value: 55.00				

KM# 99 5000 SHILLINGS
31.1035 g., 0.9990 Silver 0.9990 oz. ASW, 40.6 mm. **Subject:** Matthew Flinders - First Circumnavigation of Terra Australia - 1802 **Rev:** Multicolor bust right on Australian map showing his route around Australia **Edge:** Plain **Shape:** Continent of Australia

Date	Mintage	F	VF	XF	Unc	BU
2002 Proof	2,500	Value: 55.00				

KM# 174 5000 SHILLINGS
4.0000 g., 0.9999 Gold 0.1286 oz. AGW **Series:** Guanyin **Subject:** Fuyu **Obv:** Lotus blossom **Obv. Legend:** BANK OF UGANDA

Date	Mintage	F	VF	XF	Unc	BU
2002 Proof	—	Value: 245				

KM# 214 5000 SHILLINGS
4.0000 g., 0.9999 Gold 0.1286 oz. AGW **Series:** Guanyin **Subject:** Shile **Obv:** Lotus blossom **Obv. Legend:** BANK OF UGANDA

Date	Mintage	F	VF	XF	Unc	BU
2004 Proof	—	Value: 245				

KM# 220 5000 SHILLINGS
4.0000 g., 0.9999 Gold 0.1286 oz. AGW **Series:** Guanyin **Subject:** Songjing **Obv:** Lotus blossom **Obv. Legend:** BANK OF UGANDA

Date	Mintage	F	VF	XF	Unc	BU
2005 Proof	—	Value: 245				

KM# 235 6000 SHILLINGS
3.1100 g., 0.9999 Gold 0.1000 oz. AGW **Series:** Zodiac **Subject:** Year of the Dog **Obv. Legend:** BANK OF UGANDA **Rev:** Tibet Terrier with pup surrounded by 10 symbols

Date	Mintage	F	VF	XF	Unc	BU
2006 Proof	—	Value: 175				

KM# 228 6000 SHILLINGS
4.0000 g., 0.9999 Gold 0.1286 oz. AGW **Series:** Zodiac **Subject:** Year of the Dog **Obv:** Archaic Chinese characters **Obv. Legend:** BANK OF UGANDA **Rev:** Yorkshire Terrier and "Fú" - Happiness

Date	Mintage	F	VF	XF	Unc	BU
2006 Proof	14,000	Value: 235				

KM# 229 6000 SHILLINGS
4.0000 g., 0.9999 Gold 0.1286 oz. AGW **Series:** Zodiac **Subject:** Year of the Dog **Obv:** Archaic Chinese characters **Obv. Legend:** BANK OF UGANDA **Rev:** Yorkshire Terrier and "Lù" - Prosperity

Date	Mintage	F	VF	XF	Unc	BU
2006 Proof	14,000	Value: 235				

KM# 230 6000 SHILLINGS
4.0000 g., 0.9999 Gold 0.1286 oz. AGW **Series:** Zodiac **Subject:** Year of the Dog **Obv:** Archaic Chinese characters **Obv. Legend:** BANK OF UGANDA **Rev:** Yorkshire Terrier and "Shòu" - Health and Long Life

Date	Mintage	F	VF	XF	Unc	BU
2006 Proof	14,000	Value: 235				

KM# 238 6000 SHILLINGS
3.1100 g., 0.9999 Gold 0.1000 oz. AGW **Series:** Zodiac **Subject:** Year of the Dog **Obv:** National arms **Obv. Legend:** BANK OF UGANDA **Rev:** Chow-chow as watchdog, gold bars, bat and flower

Date	Mintage	F	VF	XF	Unc	BU
2006 Proof	—	Value: 175				

KM# 231 8000 SHILLINGS
8.0000 g., 0.9999 Gold 0.2572 oz. AGW **Series:** Zodiac **Subject:** Year of the Dog **Obv:** Archaic Chinese characters **Obv. Legend:** BANK OF UGANDA **Rev:** Yorkshire Terrier and "Fú" - Happiness

Date	Mintage	F	VF	XF	Unc	BU
2006 Proof	1,000	Value: 450				

KM# 232 8000 SHILLINGS
8.0000 g., 0.9999 Gold 0.2572 oz. AGW **Series:** Zodiac **Subject:** Year of the Dog **Obv:** Archaic Chinese characters **Obv. Legend:** BANK OF UGANDA **Rev:** Yorkshire Terrier and "Lù" - Prosperity

Date	Mintage	F	VF	XF	Unc	BU
2006 Proof	1,000	Value: 450				

KM# 215 10000 SHILLINGS
10.0000 g., 0.9999 Gold 0.3215 oz. AGW **Obv:** Lotus blossom **Obv. Legend:** BANK OF UGANDA **Rev:** Buddha

Date	Mintage	F	VF	XF	Unc	BU
2004 Proof	3,000	Value: 700				

KM# 278 10000 SHILLINGS
Bi-Metallic Copper-nickel ring, brass center **Obv:** Coat of Arms **Rev:** Crested crane circulating commemorative 50 years independence **Edge:** Reeded **Edge Lettering:** Incised in middle with text BOU 1000

Date	Mintage	F	VF	XF	Unc	BU
2012	—	—	—	—	4.50	6.00

KM# 76 12000 SHILLINGS
6.2207 g., 0.9999 Gold 0.2000 oz. AGW, 22 mm. **Subject:** Illusion: "Spirit of the Mountain" **Obv:** Crowned head right divides date above arms with supporters **Rev:** Landscape and tree that looks like a male portrait **Edge:** Reeded

Date	Mintage	F	VF	XF	Unc	BU
2001 Proof	—	Value: 375				

KM# 236 20000 SHILLINGS
15.5500 g., 0.9999 Gold 0.4999 oz. AGW **Series:** Zodiac **Subject:** Year of the Dog **Obv. Legend:** BANK OF UGANDA **Rev:** Tibet Terrier with pup surrounded by 10 symbols

Date	Mintage	F	VF	XF	Unc	BU
2006 Proof	—	Value: 900				

KM# 239 20000 SHILLINGS
15.5500 g., 0.9999 Gold 0.4999 oz. AGW **Series:** Year of the Dog **Obv:** National arms **Obv. Legend:** BANK OF UGANDA **Rev:** Chow-chow as watchdog, gold bars, bat and flower

Date	Mintage	F	VF	XF	Unc	BU
2006 Proof	—	Value: 900				

UKRAINE

Ukraine (formerly the Ukrainian Soviet Socialist Republic) is bordered by Russia to the east, Russia and Belarus to the north, Poland, Slovakia and Hungary to the west, Romania and Moldova to the southwest and in the south by the Black Sea and the Sea of Azov. It has an area of 233,088 sq. mi. (603,700 sq. km.) and a population of 51.9 million. Capital: Kyiv (Kiev). Coal, grain, vegetables and heavy industrial machinery are major exports.

Ukraine is a charter member of the United Nations and has inherited the third largest nuclear arsenal in the world.

MONETARY SYSTEM

(1) Kopiyka
(2) Kopiyky KOKH
(5 and up) Kopiyok KOIOK
100 Kopiyok = 1 Hrynia PBEH
100,000 Karbovanetsiv = 1 Hryni or Hryven)

REPUBLIC

REFORM COINAGE

September 2, 1996
100,000 Karbovanets = 1 Hryvnia
100 Kopiyok = 1 Hryvnia

KM# 6 KOPIYKA
1.5000 g., Stainless Steel, 16 mm. **Obv:** National arms **Rev:** Value within wreath **Edge:** Plain

Date	Mintage	F	VF	XF	Unc	BU
2001	—	—	—	0.35	0.75	—
2002	—	—	—	0.35	0.75	—
2003	—	—	—	0.35	0.75	—
2004	—	—	—	0.35	0.75	—
2005	—	—	—	0.35	0.75	—
2006	—	—	—	0.35	0.75	—
2007	—	—	—	0.35	0.75	—
2008	—	—	—	0.35	0.75	—
2008 Prooflike	5,000	—	—	—	—	3.00
2009	—	—	—	0.35	0.75	—
2010	—	—	—	0.35	0.75	—
2011	—	—	—	0.35	0.75	—
2011 Prooflike	5,000	—	—	—	—	1.50
2012	—	—	—	0.35	0.75	—
2012 Prooflike	5,000	—	—	—	—	1.50

KM# 4b 2 KOPIYKY
1.8000 g., Stainless Steel, 17.3 mm. **Obv:** National arms **Rev:** Value within wreath **Edge:** Plain

Date	Mintage	F	VF	XF	Unc	BU
2001	—	—	0.20	0.50	1.00	—
2002	—	—	0.20	0.50	1.00	—
2003	Est. 5,000	—	—	—	—	300
2004	—	—	0.20	0.50	1.00	—
2005	—	—	0.20	0.50	1.00	—
2006	—	—	—	0.50	1.00	—

Date	Mintage	F	VF	XF	Unc	BU
2007	—	—	—	0.50	1.00	—
2008	—	—	—	0.50	1.00	—
2008 Prooflike	5,000	—	—	—	—	3.00
2009	—	—	—	0.50	1.00	—
2010	—	—	—	0.50	1.00	—
2011	—	—	—	0.50	1.00	—
2011 Prooflike	5,000	—	—	—	—	1.50
2012	—	—	—	0.50	1.00	—
2012 Prooflike	5,000	—	—	—	—	1.50

KM# 7 5 KOPIYOK

4.3000 g., Stainless Steel, 23.91 mm. **Obv:** National arms **Rev:** Value within wreath **Edge:** Reeded

Date	Mintage	F	VF	XF	Unc	BU
2001 In sets only	10,000	—	—	—	—	10.00
2003	—	—	—	0.50	1.00	—
2004	—	—	—	0.50	1.00	—
2005	—	—	—	0.50	1.00	—
2006	—	—	—	0.50	1.00	—
2007	—	—	—	0.50	1.00	—
2008	—	—	—	0.50	1.00	—
2008 Prooflike	5,000	—	—	—	—	2.50
2009	—	—	—	0.50	1.00	—
2010	—	—	—	0.50	1.00	—
2011	—	—	—	5.00	1.00	—
2011 Prooflike	5,000	—	—	—	—	2.00
2012	—	—	—	5.00	1.00	—
2012 Prooflike	5,000	—	—	—	—	2.00

KM# 1.1b 10 KOPIYOK

1.7000 g., Aluminum-Bronze, 16.24 mm. **Obv:** National arms **Rev:** Value within wreath **Edge:** Reeded

Date	Mintage	F	VF	XF	Unc	BU
2001 In sets only	10,000	—	—	—	—	7.50
2002	—	—	0.60	1.25	2.50	—
2003	—	—	0.50	1.00	2.25	—
2004	—	—	0.50	1.00	2.25	—
2005	—	—	—	1.00	2.25	—
2006	—	—	—	1.00	2.25	—
2007	—	—	—	1.00	2.25	—
2008	—	—	—	1.00	2.25	—
2008 Prooflike	5,000	—	—	—	—	5.00
2009	—	—	—	1.00	2.00	—
2010	—	—	—	1.00	2.00	—
2011	—	—	—	1.00	2.00	—
2011 Prooflike	5,000	—	—	—	—	5.00
2012	—	—	—	1.00	2.00	—
2012 Prooflike	5,000	—	—	—	—	5.00

KM# 2.1b 25 KOPIYOK

2.9000 g., Aluminum-Bronze, 20.8 mm. **Obv:** National arms **Rev:** Value within wreath **Edge:** Segmented reeding

Date	Mintage	F	VF	XF	Unc	BU
2001	—	—	0.80	3.00	6.00	—
2003 Prooflike	Est. 5,000	—	—	—	—	300
2006	—	—	0.80	2.00	4.00	—
2007	—	—	0.80	2.00	4.00	—
2008	—	—	—	2.00	4.00	—
2008 Prooflike	5,000	—	—	—	—	8.00
2009	—	—	—	2.00	3.50	—
2010	—	—	—	2.00	3.50	—
2011	—	—	—	2.00	3.50	—
2011 Prooflike	5,000	—	—	—	—	8.00
2012	—	—	—	2.00	3.50	—
2012 Prooflike	5,000	—	—	—	—	8.00
2013	—	—	—	2.00	3.50	—

KM# 3.3b 50 KOPIYOK

4.2000 g., Aluminum-Bronze, 23 mm. **Obv:** National arms **Rev:** Five dots grouped in wreath to right of final letter 'K' in value **Edge:** Segmented reeding

Date	Mintage	F	VF	XF	Unc	BU
2001 In sets only	—	—	—	—	10.00	—
2003	Est. 5,000	—	—	—	300	—
2006	—	—	1.00	2.00	4.00	—
2007	—	—	1.00	2.00	4.00	—
2008	—	—	—	2.00	4.00	—
2008 Prooflike	5,000	—	—	—	—	8.00
2009	—	—	—	2.00	4.00	—
2010	—	—	—	2.00	4.00	—
2011	—	—	—	2.00	4.00	—
2011 Prooflike	5,000	—	—	—	—	8.00
2012	—	—	—	2.00	4.00	—
2012 Prooflike	5,000	—	—	—	—	8.00

KM# 8b HRYVNIA

6.9000 g., Aluminum-Bronze, 26 mm. **Obv:** National arms **Rev:** Value, sprigs and designs **Edge:** Lettered

Date	Mintage	F	VF	XF	Unc	BU
2001	—	—	—	2.50	4.50	—

KM# 8b.1 HRYVNIA

7.1000 g., Aluminum-Bronze, 26 mm. **Obv:** National arms **Rev:** Value, sprigs and designs **Edge:** Lettered

Date	Mintage	F	VF	XF	Unc	BU
2002	—	—	—	3.50	6.50	—
2003	—	—	—	2.50	4.50	—

KM# 208 HRYVNIA

6.8000 g., Aluminum-Bronze, 26 mm. **Subject:** 60th Anniversary - Victory over the Nazis **Obv:** National arms above value **Rev:** Uniform lapel with Soviet military medals group **Edge:** Lettered **Edge Lettering:** Date and denomination

Date	Mintage	F	VF	XF	Unc	BU
2004	5,000,000	—	—	—	5.00	—

KM# 209 HRYVNIA

6.7400 g., Aluminum-Bronze, 26 mm. **Obv:** National arms above value **Rev:** Half length figure of Volodymyr the Great facing holding church model building and staff **Edge:** Lettered **Edge Lettering:** Date and denomination

Date	Mintage	F	VF	XF	Unc	BU
2004	10,000,000	—	—	—	4.00	—
2005	—	—	—	—	3.00	—
2006	—	—	—	—	3.00	—
2008 Prooflike	5,000	—	—	—	—	12.50
2010	—	—	—	—	3.00	—
2011	—	—	—	—	3.00	—
2011 Prooflike, in sets only	5,000	—	—	—	—	12.50
2012	—	—	—	—	4.00	—
2012 Prooflike, in sets only	5,000	—	—	—	—	12.50

KM# 228 HRYVNIA

6.8000 g., Aluminum-Bronze, 26 mm. **Subject:** WW II Victory 60th Anniversary **Obv:** Value **Rev:** Soldiers in a "V" of search lights **Edge:** Reeded

Date	Mintage	F	VF	XF	Unc	BU
2005	5,000,000	—	—	—	5.00	—

KM# 654 HRYVNIA

31.1050 g., 0.9999 Silver 0.9999 oz. ASW, 38.6 mm. **Obv:** Logo of the Ukraine National Bank **Rev:** Archangel Michael **Edge:** Reeded

Date	Mintage	F	VF	XF	Unc	BU
2011	10,000	—	—	—	—	BV+40%
2012	20,000	—	—	—	—	BV+40%

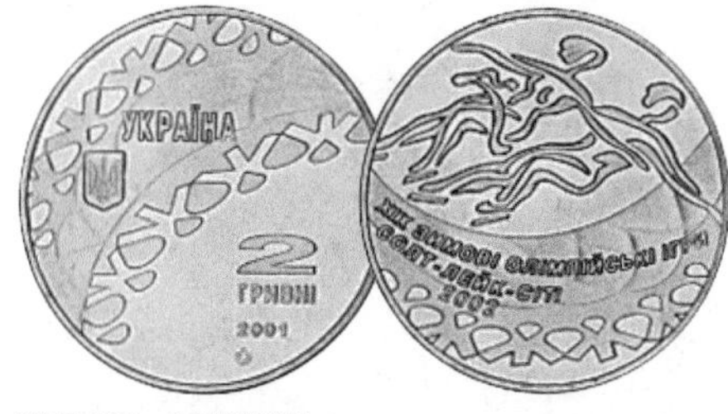

KM# 106 2 HRYVNI

12.8000 g., Copper-Nickel-Zinc, 31 mm. **Series:** Olympics - Salt Lake City, 2002 **Obv:** National arms, value and designs **Rev:** Stylized ice dancing couple **Edge:** Reeded

Date	Mintage	F	VF	XF	Unc	BU
2001	30,000	—	—	—	25.00	—

KM# 133 2 HRYVNI

12.8000 g., Copper-Nickel-Zinc, 31 mm. **Subject:** Kindness to Children **Obv:** National arms above value flanked by sprigs and doves **Rev:** Two children frolicking under fountain of knowledge **Edge:** Reeded

Date	Mintage	F	VF	XF	Unc	BU
2001	100,000	—	—	—	12.00	—

KM# 134 2 HRYVNI

12.8000 g., Copper-Nickel-Zinc, 31 mm. **Subject:** 5th Anniversary of Constitution **Obv:** National arms above value flanked by sprigs **Rev:** Building above book flanked by sprigs **Edge:** Reeded

Date	Mintage	F	VF	XF	Unc	BU
2001	30,000	—	—	—	30.00	—

KM# 111 2 HRYVNI

12.8000 g., Copper-Nickel-Zinc, 31 mm. **Series:** Flora and Fauna **Obv:** National arms and date divides wreath, value within **Rev:** Lynx and offspring **Edge:** Reeded

Date	Mintage	F	VF	XF	Unc	BU
2001	30,000	—	—	—	50.00	—

KM# 136 2 HRYVNI

12.8000 g., Copper-Nickel-Zinc, 31 mm. **Subject:** Mykolaiv Zoo **Obv:** Man running alongside large cat **Rev:** Twelve animals **Edge:** Reeded

Date	Mintage	F	VF	XF	Unc	BU
2001	30,000	—	—	—	40.00	—

KM# 137 2 HRYVNI

12.8000 g., Copper-Nickel-Zinc, 31 mm. **Subject:** Mykhailo Ostrohradskiy (Mathematician) **Obv:** National arms divides date and value divided by wavy line graph **Rev:** Head 1/4 left **Edge:** Reeded

Date	Mintage	F	VF	XF	Unc	BU
2001	30,000	—	—	—	17.00	—

KM# 138 2 HRYVNI

12.8000 g., Copper-Nickel-Zinc, 31 mm. **Subject:** Larix Polonica **Obv:** Value within wreath **Rev:** Pine branch with cone **Edge:** Reeded

Date	Mintage	F	VF	XF	Unc	BU
2001	30,000	—	—	—	45.00	—

KM# 139 2 HRYVNI

12.8000 g., Copper-Nickel-Zinc, 31 mm. **Subject:** Volodymyr Dal **Obv:** Books **Rev:** Head right **Edge:** Reeded

Date	Mintage	F	VF	XF	Unc	BU
2001	30,000	—	—	—	15.00	—

KM# 147 2 HRYVNI

12.8000 g., Copper-Nickel-Zinc, 31 mm. **Series:** Olympics - Salt Lake City, 2002 **Obv:** National arms and value on ice design **Rev:** Stylized hockey player **Edge:** Reeded

Date	Mintage	F	VF	XF	Unc	BU
2001	30,000	—	—	—	20.00	—

KM# 149 2 HRYVNI
12.8000 g., Copper-Nickel-Zinc, 31 mm. **Subject:** Mykhailo Drahomanov (Historian, Politician, etc.) **Obv:** National arms and value **Rev:** Bust right **Edge:** Reeded

Date	Mintage	F	VF	XF	Unc	BU
2001	30,000	—	—	—	15.00	—

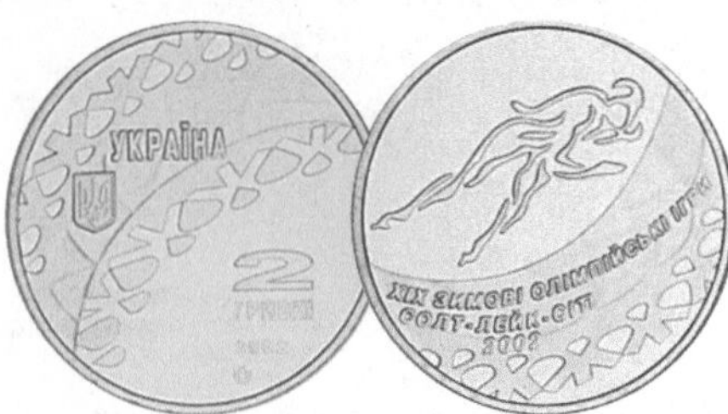

KM# 150 2 HRYVNI
12.8000 g., Copper-Nickel-Zinc, 31 mm. **Series:** Olympics - Salt lake City, 2002 **Obv:** National arms and value on ice design **Rev:** Speed skater **Edge:** Reeded

Date	Mintage	F	VF	XF	Unc	BU
2002	30,000	—	—	—	18.00	—

KM# 155 2 HRYVNI
12.8000 g., Copper-Nickel-Zinc, 31 mm. **Series:** Flora and Fauna **Obv:** National arms and date divides wreath, value within **Rev:** Eurasian Eagle Owl **Edge:** Reeded

Date	Mintage	F	VF	XF	Unc	BU
2002	30,000	—	—	—	60.00	—

KM# 156 2 HRYVNI
12.8000 g., Copper-Nickel-Zinc, 31 mm. **Subject:** Olympics - Athens, 2004 **Obv:** Two ancient figures above value **Rev:** Swimmer **Edge:** Reeded

Date	Mintage	F	VF	XF	Unc	BU
2002	30,000	—	—	—	—	18.00

KM# 166 2 HRYVNI
12.8000 g., Copper-Nickel-Zinc, 31 mm. **Subject:** Leonid Glibov, writer (1827-1893) **Obv:** National arms and value within scroll and wreath **Rev:** 1/2-length bust right **Edge:** Reeded

Date	Mintage	F	VF	XF	Unc	BU
2002	30,000	—	—	—	15.00	—

KM# 154 2 HRYVNI
12.8000 g., Copper-Nickel-Zinc, 31 mm. **Subject:** Mykola Lysenko (composer) **Obv:** Musical score and value **Rev:** Head 1/4 right **Edge:** Reeded

Date	Mintage	F	VF	XF	Unc	BU
2002	30,000	—	—	—	15.00	—

KM# 167 2 HRYVNI
12.8000 g., Copper-Nickel-Zinc, 31 mm. **Series:** Flora and Fauna **Obv:** National arms and date divides wreath, value within **Rev:** European Bison **Edge:** Reeded

Date	Mintage	F	VF	XF	Unc	BU
2003	50,000	—	—	—	30.00	—

KM# 168 2 HRYVNI
12.8000 g., Copper-Nickel-Zinc, 31 mm. **Obv:** National arms and date divides wreath, value within **Rev:** Long-snouted Sea Horse **Edge:** Reeded

Date	Mintage	F	VF	XF	Unc	BU
2003	50,000	—	—	—	30.00	—

KM# 169 2 HRYVNI
12.8000 g., Copper-Nickel-Zinc, 31 mm. **Subject:** Volodymyr Vernadskyi (academic) **Obv:** National arms, value and world globe **Rev:** Head on hand looking down **Edge:** Reeded

Date	Mintage	F	VF	XF	Unc	BU
2003	30,000	—	—	—	15.00	—

KM# 170 2 HRYVNI
12.8000 g., Copper-Nickel-Zinc, 31 mm. **Subject:** Volodymyr Korolenko (writer) **Obv:** National arms above book and value **Rev:** Bearded head 1/4 right above dates **Edge:** Reeded

Date	Mintage	F	VF	XF	Unc	BU
2003	30,000	—	—	—	15.00	—

KM# 171 2 HRYVNI
12.8000 g., Copper-Nickel-Zinc, 31 mm. **Subject:** Viacheslav Chornovil (politician) **Obv:** Arms with supporters within beaded circle **Rev:** Head 1/4 left **Edge:** Reeded

Date	Mintage	F	VF	XF	Unc	BU
2003	30,000	—	—	—	30.00	—

KM# 178 2 HRYVNI
1.2400 g., 0.9999 Gold 0.0399 oz. AGW, 13.92 mm. **Obv:** National arms flanked by dates within beaded circle **Rev:** Spotted Salamander divides beaded circle **Edge:** Plain

Date	Mintage	F	VF	XF	Unc	BU
2003	10,000	—	—	—	—	220

KM# 179 2 HRYVNI
12.8000 g., Copper-Nickel-Zinc, 31 mm. **Subject:** Singer Boris Gmyrya **Obv:** Value, arms ,date and musical symbol **Rev:** Head 1/4 left and dates **Edge:** Reeded

Date	Mintage	F	VF	XF	Unc	BU
2003	30,000	—	—	—	12.00	—

KM# 180 2 HRYVNI
12.8000 g., Copper-Nickel-Zinc, 31 mm. **Subject:** 70th Anniversary National Aviation University **Obv:** World globe behind national arms, value and date **Rev:** Wright Brothers biplane **Edge:** Reeded

Date	Mintage	F	VF	XF	Unc	BU
2003	30,000	—	—	—	20.00	—

KM# 181 2 HRYVNI
12.8000 g., Copper-Nickel-Zinc, 31 mm. **Subject:** Ostap Veresay (musician) **Obv:** Musical stringed instrument and ornamental design **Rev:** Bust facing playing stringed instrument **Edge:** Reeded

Date	Mintage	F	VF	XF	Unc	BU
2003	30,000	—	—	—	13.00	—

KM# 182 2 HRYVNI
12.8000 g., Copper-Nickel-Zinc, 31 mm. **Subject:** Olympics **Obv:** Two ancient women with seedlings **Rev:** Boxer **Edge:** Reeded

Date	Mintage	F	VF	XF	Unc	BU
2003	30,000	—	—	—	20.00	—

KM# 183 2 HRYVNI
12.8000 g., Copper-Nickel-Zinc, 31 mm. **Subject:** Vasyl Sukhomlynski (teacher) **Obv:** Children, books, value and national arms **Rev:** Head 1/4 right **Edge:** Reeded

Date	Mintage	F	VF	XF	Unc	BU
2003	30,000	—	—	—	13.00	—

KM# 184 2 HRYVNI
12.8000 g., Copper-Nickel-Zinc, 31 mm. **Subject:** Andriy Malyshko (poet) **Obv:** Ornamental shawl, national arms and value **Rev:** Head 1/4 right flanked by radiant sun and tree **Edge:** Reeded

Date	Mintage	F	VF	XF	Unc	BU
2003	30,000	—	—	—	13.00	—

KM# 201 2 HRYVNI
12.8000 g., Copper-Nickel-Zinc, 31 mm. **Subject:** Azov Dolphin **Obv:** National arms and date divides wreath, value within **Rev:** Harbor Porpoises **Edge:** Reeded

Date	Mintage	F	VF	XF	Unc	BU
2004	30,000	—	—	—	50.00	—

KM# 202 2 HRYVNI
12.8000 g., Copper-Nickel-Zinc, 31 mm. **Subject:** Football World Cup - 2006 **Obv:** Soccer ball in net **Rev:** Two soccer players **Edge:** Reeded

Date	Mintage	F	VF	XF	Unc	BU
2004	50,000	—	—	—	15.00	—

KM# 203 2 HRYVNI
12.8000 g., Copper-Nickel-Zinc, 31 mm. **Subject:** Serhiy Lyfar (ballet artist) **Obv:** Stylized dancer **Rev:** Head right **Edge:** Reeded

Date	Mintage	F	VF	XF	Unc	BU
2004	30,000	—	—	—	13.00	—

KM# 210 2 HRYVNI
12.8000 g., Copper-Nickel-Zinc, 31 mm. **Subject:** 170 Years of the Kyiv National University **Obv:** National arms in center above value dividing scientific items **Rev:** University building main entrance **Edge:** Reeded

Date	Mintage	F	VF	XF	Unc	BU
2004	50,000	—	—	—	13.00	—

KM# 211 2 HRYVNI
12.8000 g., Copper-Nickel-Zinc, 31 mm. **Subject:** Oleksander Dovzhenko (movie producer, writer) **Obv:** Boy standing in small boat **Rev:** Head facing **Edge:** Reeded

Date	Mintage	F	VF	XF	Unc	BU
2004	30,000	—	—	—	13.00	—

KM# 212 2 HRYVNI
12.8000 g., Copper-Nickel-Zinc, 31 mm. **Subject:** Mykola Bazhan (poet, translator) **Obv:** Winged pens and value **Rev:** Head 1/4 left **Edge:** Reeded

Date	Mintage	F	VF	XF	Unc	BU
2004	30,000	—	—	—	13.00	—

KM# 213 2 HRYVNI
12.8000 g., Copper-Nickel-Zinc, 31 mm. **Subject:** Mykhailo Kotsyubynsky (writer) **Obv:** Two reclining figures **Rev:** Head 1/4 right **Edge:** Reeded

Date	Mintage	F	VF	XF	Unc	BU
2004	30,000	—	—	—	13.00	—

KM# 214 2 HRYVNI
12.8000 g., Copper-Nickel-Zinc, 31 mm. **Subject:** Maria Zankovetska (actress) **Obv:** National arms, value and drawn curtain **Rev:** Hooded head 1/4 left **Edge:** Reeded

Date	Mintage	F	VF	XF	Unc	BU
2004	30,000	—	—	—	13.00	—

KM# 215 2 HRYVNI
12.8000 g., Copper-Nickel-Zinc, 31 mm. **Subject:** Mykhailo Maksymovych (historian, archaeologist) **Obv:** National arms above building and value **Rev:** Bust left **Edge:** Reeded

Date	Mintage	F	VF	XF	Unc	BU
2004	30,000	—	—	—	13.00	—

KM# 216 2 HRYVNI
12.8000 g., Copper-Nickel-Zinc, 31 mm. **Subject:** Mykhailo Deregus (painter) **Obv:** National arms and value on artists palette **Rev:** Head right **Edge:** Reeded

Date	Mintage	F	VF	XF	Unc	BU
2004	30,000	—	—	—	13.00	—

KM# 217 2 HRYVNI
12.8000 g., Copper-Nickel-Zinc, 31 mm. **Subject:** Nuclear Power Engineering of Ukraine **Obv:** National arms and value in atomic design **Rev:** Nuclear reactor **Edge:** Reeded

Date	Mintage	F	VF	XF	Unc	BU
2004	30,000	—	—	—	20.00	—

KM# 227 2 HRYVNI
1.2400 g., 0.9999 Gold 0.0399 oz. AGW, 13.92 mm. **Obv:** National arms divides dates within beaded circle **Rev:** Flying White Stork divides beaded circle **Edge:** Plain

Date	Mintage	F	VF	XF	Unc	BU
2004	10,000	—	—	—	—	220

KM# 330 2 HRYVNI
12.8000 g., Copper-Nickel-Zinc, 31 mm. **Subject:** 200th Anniversary of Kharkiv University **Obv:** National arms and atom **Rev:** University building and reflection **Edge:** Reeded

Date	Mintage	F	VF	XF	Unc	BU
2004	50,000	—	—	—	13.00	—

KM# 331 2 HRYVNI
12.8000 g., Copper-Nickel-Zinc, 31 mm. **Subject:** Ukraine National Academy of Law named after Yaroslav the Wise **Obv:** National arms above National Academy of Law arms and date **Rev:** Building **Edge:** Reeded

Date	Mintage	F	VF	XF	Unc	BU
2004	30,000	—	—	—	20.00	—

KM# 332 2 HRYVNI
12.8000 g., Copper-Nickel-Zinc, 31 mm. **Subject:** Yurii Fedkovych (poet, writer) **Obv:** National arms, value and man on horse **Rev:** Bust 1/4 right and dates **Edge:** Reeded

Date	Mintage	F	VF	XF	Unc	BU
2004	30,000	—	—	—	13.00	—

KM# 346 2 HRYVNI
12.8000 g., Copper-Nickel-Zinc, 31 mm. **Subject:** Boris Liatoshynsky (composer) **Obv:** Musical G Clef symbol and value below national arms **Rev:** Head 1/4 left **Edge:** Reeded

Date	Mintage	F	VF	XF	Unc	BU
2005	20,000	—	—	—	15.00	—

KM# 347 2 HRYVNI
12.8000 g., Copper-Nickel-Zinc, 31 mm. **Subject:** Volodymyr Filatov (surgeon) **Obv:** Light passing through the lens of an eye **Rev:** Head with cap facing **Edge:** Reeded

Date	Mintage	F	VF	XF	Unc	BU
2005	20,000	—	—	—	15.00	—

KM# 348 2 HRYVNI
12.8000 g., Copper-Nickel-Zinc, 31 mm. **Obv:** Books between stylized horsemen **Rev:** Ulas Samchuk **Edge:** Reeded

Date	Mintage	F	VF	XF	Unc	BU
2005	20,000	—	—	—	15.00	—

KM# 349 2 HRYVNI
12.8000 g., Copper-Nickel-Zinc, 31 mm. **Subject:** Pavlo Virsky (ballet artist) **Obv:** National arms in flower circle **Rev:** Bust right **Edge:** Reeded

Date	Mintage	F	VF	XF	Unc	BU
2005	20,000	—	—	—	15.00	—

KM# 350 2 HRYVNI
12.8000 g., Copper-Nickel-Zinc, 31 mm. **Obv:** Roses and grapes **Rev:** Poet Maksym Rylsky **Edge:** Reeded

Date	Mintage	F	VF	XF	Unc	BU
2005	20,000	—	—	—	15.00	—

KM# 351 2 HRYVNI
1.2400 g., 0.9999 Gold 0.0399 oz. AGW, 13.9 mm. **Obv:** National arms within beaded circle **Rev:** Scythian horseman depicted on golden plaque **Edge:** Plain

Date	Mintage	F	VF	XF	Unc	BU
2005	15,000	—	—	—	200	220

KM# 352 2 HRYVNI
12.8000 g., Copper-Nickel-Zinc, 31 mm. **Subject:** Serhiy Vsekhsviatsky (astronomer) **Obv:** "Solar Wind" depiction **Rev:** Head right **Edge:** Reeded

Date	Mintage	F	VF	XF	Unc	BU
2005	20,000	—	—	—	15.00	—

KM# 353 2 HRYVNI
12.8000 g., Copper-Nickel-Zinc, 31 mm. **Subject:** 50 Years of Kyivmiskbud **Obv:** National arms **Rev:** Buildings **Edge:** Reeded

Date	Mintage	F	VF	XF	Unc	BU
2005	20,000	—	—	—	20.00	—

KM# 354 2 HRYVNI
12.8000 g., Copper-Nickel-Zinc, 31 mm. **Subject:** 75 Years of Zhukovsky Aerospace University in Kharkiv **Obv:** Building divides book outline **Rev:** Airplane, computer monitor and books **Edge:** Reeded

Date	Mintage	F	VF	XF	Unc	BU
2005	30,000	—	—	—	18.00	—

KM# 356 2 HRYVNI
12.8000 g., Copper-Nickel-Zinc, 31 mm. **Subject:** Oleksander Korniychuk (writer, playright) **Obv:** Theatrical masks and feather **Rev:** Bust 1/4 right **Edge:** Reeded

Date	Mintage	F	VF	XF	Unc	BU
2005	20,000	—	—	—	15.00	—

KM# 357 2 HRYVNI
12.8000 g., Copper-Nickel-Zinc, 31 mm. **Obv:** National arms and date divides wreath, value within **Rev:** Sandy Mole Rat **Edge:** Reeded

Date	Mintage	F	VF	XF	Unc	BU
2005	60,000	—	—	—	20.00	—

KM# 359 2 HRYVNI
12.8000 g., Copper-Nickel-Zinc, 31 mm. **Obv:** National arms **Rev:** Tairov Wine Institute building and cameo **Edge:** Reeded

Date	Mintage	F	VF	XF	Unc	BU
2005	20,000	—	—	—	25.00	—

KM# 360 2 HRYVNI
12.8000 g., Copper-Nickel-Zinc, 31 mm. **Subject:** 300 Years to David Guramishvili (poet) **Obv:** Georgian and Ukrainian style ornamentation **Rev:** Head right **Edge:** Reeded

Date	Mintage	F	VF	XF	Unc	BU
2005	30,000	—	—	—	13.00	—

KM# 361 2 HRYVNI
12.8000 g., Copper-Nickel-Zinc, 31 mm. **Subject:** Dmytro Yavornytsky (historian, archaeologist, writer) **Obv:** National arms **Rev:** Bust 3/4 right **Edge:** Reeded

Date	Mintage	F	VF	XF	Unc	BU
2005	30,000	—	—	—	15.00	—

KM# 375 2 HRYVNI
12.8000 g., Copper-Nickel-Zinc, 31 mm. **Subject:** Oleksiy Alchevsky (banker) **Obv:** Steam train, factory, National arms and value **Rev:** Head with beard 1/4 right **Edge:** Reeded

Date	Mintage	F	VF	XF	Unc	BU
2005	20,000	—	—	—	25.00	—

KM# 376 2 HRYVNI
12.8000 g., Copper-Nickel-Zinc, 31 mm. **Subject:** Illia Mechnikov (biologist, Nobel prize laureate) **Obv:** Amoeba and National arms **Rev:** Bust with beard facing **Edge:** Reeded

Date	Mintage	F	VF	XF	Unc	BU
2005	20,000	—	—	—	25.00	—

KM# 377 2 HRYVNI
12.8000 g., Copper-Nickel-Zinc, 31 mm. **Subject:** Vsevolod Holubovych (politician) **Obv:** National arms **Rev:** Head 1/4 left **Edge:** Reeded

Date	Mintage	F	VF	XF	Unc	BU
2005	20,000	—	—	—	18.00	—

KM# 378 2 HRYVNI
12.8000 g., Copper-Nickel-Zinc, 31 mm. **Subject:** Volodymyr Vynnychenko (writer, politician) **Obv:** National arms **Rev:** Head facing **Edge:** Reeded

Date	Mintage	F	VF	XF	Unc	BU
2005	20,000	—	—	—	15.00	—

KM# 383 2 HRYVNI
12.8000 g., Copper-Nickel-Zinc, 31 mm. **Subject:** Kyiv National University of Economics **Obv:** National arms, value and graph **Rev:** University building **Edge:** Reeded

Date	Mintage	F	VF	XF	Unc	BU
2006	60,000	—	—	—	15.00	—

KM# 384 2 HRYVNI
12.8000 g., Copper-Nickel-Zinc, 31 mm. **Subject:** Viacheslav Prokopovych (historian, publist) **Obv:** National arms **Rev:** Bust facing **Edge:** Reeded

Date	Mintage	F	VF	XF	Unc	BU
2006	30,000	—	—	—	12.00	—

KM# 385 2 HRYVNI
12.8000 g., Copper-Nickel-Zinc, 31 mm. **Subject:** Heorhii Narbut (artist) **Obv:** Peasant couple **Rev:** Silhouette of standing figure on one leg facing right **Edge:** Reeded

Date	Mintage	F	VF	XF	Unc	BU
2006	30,000	—	—	—	12.00	—

KM# 386 2 HRYVNI
12.8000 g., Copper-Nickel-Zinc, 31 mm. **Subject:** Oleh Antonov (aircraft engineer) **Obv:** Large jet plane **Rev:** Bust 1/4 right **Edge:** Reeded

Date	Mintage	F	VF	XF	Unc	BU
2006	45,000	—	—	—	18.00	—

KM# 391 2 HRYVNI
12.8000 g., Copper-Nickel-Zinc, 31 mm. **Obv:** National arms above value in wreath **Rev:** Bush Katydid Grasshopper **Edge:** Reeded

Date	Mintage	F	VF	XF	Unc	BU
2006	60,000	—	—	—	20.00	—

KM# 398 2 HRYVNI
12.8000 g., Copper-Nickel-Zinc, 31 mm. **Subject:** Mykhailo Hrushevskyi **Obv:** National arms and value **Edge:** Reeded

Date	Mintage	F	VF	XF	Unc	BU
2006	45,000	—	—	—	12.00	—

KM# 408 2 HRYVNI
1.2400 g., 0.9999 Gold 0.0399 oz. AGW, 13.92 mm. **Subject:** Hedgehog **Obv:** National arms **Edge:** Plain

Date	Mintage	F	VF	XF	Unc	BU
2006	10,000	—	—	—	150	200

KM# 399 2 HRYVNI
12.8000 g., Copper-Nickel-Zinc, 31 mm. **Subject:** Serhii Ostapenko **Obv:** National arms **Edge:** Reeded

Date	Mintage	F	VF	XF	Unc	BU
2006	30,000	—	—	—	12.00	—

KM# 401 2 HRYVNI
12.8000 g., Copper-Nickel-Zinc, 31 mm. **Subject:** Economic University of Kharkiv

Date	Mintage	F	VF	XF	Unc	BU
2006	30,000	—	—	—	12.00	—

KM# 393 2 HRYVNI
12.8000 g., Copper-Nickel-Zinc, 31 mm. **Subject:** Mykola Strazhesko **Obv:** National arms and value **Edge:** Reeded

Date	Mintage	F	VF	XF	Unc	BU
2006	45,000	—	—	—	12.00	—

KM# 394 2 HRYVNI
12.8000 g., Copper-Nickel-Zinc, 31 mm. **Subject:** Volodymyr Chekhivsky **Obv:** National arms and value **Edge:** Reeded

Date	Mintage	F	VF	XF	Unc	BU
2006	30,000	—	—	—	12.00	—

KM# 395 2 HRYVNI
12.8000 g., Copper-Nickel-Zinc, 31 mm. **Subject:** Mykola Vasylenko **Obv:** National arms and value **Edge:** Reeded

Date	Mintage	F	VF	XF	Unc	BU
2006	30,000	—	—	—	13.00	—

KM# 396 2 HRYVNI
12.8000 g., Copper-Nickel-Zinc, 31 mm. **Subject:** Ivan Franko **Obv:** National arms and value **Edge:** Reeded

Date	Mintage	F	VF	XF	Unc	BU
2006	45,000	—	—	—	12.00	—

KM# 397 2 HRYVNI
12.8000 g., Copper-Nickel-Zinc, 31 mm. **Subject:** Dmytro Lutsenko **Obv:** National arms and value **Edge:** Reeded

Date	Mintage	F	VF	XF	Unc	BU
2006	30,000	—	—	—	12.00	—

KM# 400 2 HRYVNI
12.8000 g., Copper-Nickel-Zinc, 31 mm. **Subject:** Mykhailo Lysenko **Obv:** National arms and value **Edge:** Reeded

Date	Mintage	F	VF	XF	Unc	BU
2006	35,000	—	—	—	12.00	—

KM# 403 2 HRYVNI
1.2400 g., 0.9999 Gold 0.0399 oz. AGW, 13.92 mm. **Subject:** Ram **Obv:** National arms **Edge:** Plain

Date	Mintage	F	VF	XF	Unc	BU
2006	10,000	—	—	—	140	200

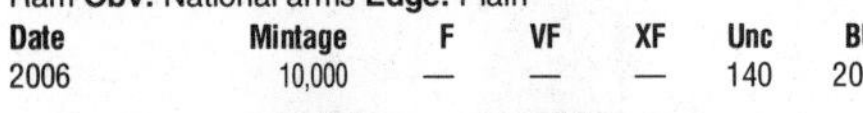

KM# 404 2 HRYVNI
1.2400 g., 0.9999 Gold 0.0399 oz. AGW, 13.92 mm. **Subject:** Bull **Obv:** National arms **Edge:** Plain

Date	Mintage	F	VF	XF	Unc	BU
2006	10,000	—	—	—	140	200

KM# 406 2 HRYVNI
1.2400 g., 0.9999 Gold 0.0399 oz. AGW, 13.92 mm. **Subject:** The Twins **Obv:** National arms **Edge:** Plain

Date	Mintage	F	VF	XF	Unc	BU
2006	10,000	—	—	—	140	200

KM# 428 2 HRYVNI
12.8000 g., Copper-Nickel-Zinc, 31 mm. **Subject:** Serhii Koroljov **Obv:** National arms **Edge:** Reeded

Date	Mintage	F	VF	XF	Unc	BU
2007	35,000	—	—	—	—	20.00

KM# 429 2 HRYVNI
12.8000 g., Copper-Nickel-Zinc, 31 mm. **Subject:** Les Kurbas **Obv:** National arms **Edge:** Reeded

Date	Mintage	F	VF	XF	Unc	BU
2007	35,000	—	—	—	—	12.00

KM# 430 2 HRYVNI
12.8000 g., Copper-Nickel-Zinc, 31 mm. **Subject:** Olexander Liapunov **Obv:** Small national arms above geometrical depiction of celestial mechanics graphics **Rev:** Large bust facing **Edge:** Reeded

Date	Mintage	F	VF	XF	Unc	BU
2007	35,000	—	—	—	—	12.00

KM# 431 2 HRYVNI
1.2400 g., 0.9999 Gold 0.0399 oz. AGW, 13.92 mm. **Subject:** Steppe Marmot **Obv:** National arms **Edge:** Plain

Date	Mintage	F	VF	XF	Unc	BU
2007	10,000	—	—	—	150	200

KM# 440 2 HRYVNI
12.8000 g., Copper-Nickel-Zinc, 31 mm. **Subject:** Ivan Ohienko **Obv:** Cross **Rev:** Head and hands clasped at prayer **Edge:** Reeded

Date	Mintage	F	VF	XF	Unc	BU
2007	35,000	—	—	—	—	12.00

KM# 441 2 HRYVNI
12.8000 g., Copper-Nickel-Zinc, 31 mm. **Subject:** Oleh Olzhych **Obv:** Chestnut leaf and stone path **Rev:** Bust facing **Edge:** Reeded

Date	Mintage	F	VF	XF	Unc	BU
2007	35,000	—	—	—	—	12.00

KM# 442 2 HRYVNI
12.8000 g., Copper-Nickel-Zinc, 31 mm. **Subject:** Donetsk Region 75th Anniversary **Obv:** Miner's lamp illuminating industrial plants **Rev:** Flag and 75 **Edge:** Reeded

Date	Mintage	F	VF	XF	Unc	BU
2007	35,000	—	—	—	—	20.00

KM# 443 2 HRYVNI
12.8000 g., Copper-Nickel-Zinc, 31 mm. **Subject:** Olena Teliha **Obv:** Scorched cherry blossom **Rev:** Bust facing **Edge:** Reeded

Date	Mintage	F	VF	XF	Unc	BU
2007	35,000	—	—	—	—	12.00

KM# 444 2 HRYVNI
12.8000 g., Copper-Nickel-Zinc, 31 mm. **Subject:** Orienteering **Obv:** Compass, star and benchmarks **Rev:** Runner **Edge:** Reeded

Date	Mintage	F	VF	XF	Unc	BU
2007	35,000	—	—	—	—	15.00

KM# 445 2 HRYVNI
12.8000 g., Copper-Nickel-Zinc, 31 mm. **Subject:** Ivan Bahrianji **Obv:** Book edge **Rev:** Bust facing, book edge **Edge:** Reeded

Date	Mintage	F	VF	XF	Unc	BU
2007	35,000	—	—	—	—	12.00

KM# 446 2 HRYVNI
12.8000 g., Copper-Nickel-Zinc, 31 mm. **Subject:** Petro Hryhorenko **Obv:** Sprout squeezing brick wall **Rev:** Head right **Edge:** Reeded

Date	Mintage	F	VF	XF	Unc	BU
2007	35,000	—	—	—	—	13.00

KM# 447 2 HRYVNI
12.8000 g., Copper-Nickel-Zinc, 31 mm. **Subject:** 90th Anniversary of 1st Government **Obv:** Parts of early 20th century bank notes and industrial elements **Rev:** Volodymyr Vynnychenko and ornamentation **Edge:** Reeded

Date	Mintage	F	VF	XF	Unc	BU
2007	35,000	—	—	—	—	13.00

KM# 448 2 HRYVNI
1.2400 g., 0.9990 Gold 0.0398 oz. AGW, 13.9 mm. **Subject:** Capricorn **Obv:** Elements of earth, air, water and fire **Rev:** Zodiac sign

Date	Mintage	F	VF	XF	Unc	BU
2007	10,000	—	—	—	140	200

KM# 450 2 HRYVNI
1.2400 g., 0.9990 Gold 0.0398 oz. AGW, 13.9 mm. **Subject:** Pisces **Obv:** Elements of earth, air, water and fire **Rev:** Zodiac sign, two fish

Date	Mintage	F	VF	XF	Unc	BU
2007	10,000	—	—	—	140	200

KM# 449 2 HRYVNI
1.2400 g., 0.9990 Gold 0.0398 oz. AGW, 13.9 mm. **Subject:** Aquarius **Obv:** Elements of earth, air, water and fire **Rev:** Zodiac sign, man pouring water

Date	Mintage	F	VF	XF	Unc	BU
2007	10,000	—	—	—	140	200

KM# 451 2 HRYVNI
1.2400 g., 0.9990 Gold 0.0398 oz. AGW, 13.9 mm. **Subject:** Scorpion **Obv:** Elements of earth, air, water and fire **Rev:** Zodiac sign

Date	Mintage	F	VF	XF	Unc	BU
2007	10,000	—	—	—	140	200

KM# 452 2 HRYVNI
1.2400 g., 0.9990 Gold 0.0398 oz. AGW, 13.9 mm. **Subject:** Sagitarius **Obv:** Elements of earth, air, water & fire **Rev:** Zodiac sign, archer

Date	Mintage	F	VF	XF	Unc	BU
2007	10,000	—	—	—	140	200

KM# 433 2 HRYVNI
12.8000 g., Copper-Nickel-Zinc, 31 mm. **Obv:** Small national arms at top, value in sprays with bird at left, butterfly at right **Rev:** Cinereous Vulture perched on nest with chick **Rev. Legend:** AEGYPIUS MONACHUS - ГРИФ ЧОРНИЙ **Edge:** Reeded

Date	Mintage	F	VF	XF	Unc	BU
2008	45,000	—	—	—	—	20.00

KM# 475 2 HRYVNI
12.8000 g., Copper-Nickel-Zinc, 31 mm. **Subject:** Vasyl Stus, Poet **Edge:** Reeded

Date	Mintage	F	VF	XF	Unc	BU
2008	35,000	—	—	—	—	12.00

KM# 476 2 HRYVNI
12.8000 g., Copper-Nickel-Zinc, 31 mm. **Subject:** Leo Landau **Edge:** Reeded

Date	Mintage	F	VF	XF	Unc	BU
2008	35,000	—	—	—	—	12.00

KM# 477 2 HRYVNI
12.8000 g., Copper-Nickel-Zinc, 31 mm. **Subject:** Sydir Holubovych **Edge:** Reeded

Date	Mintage	F	VF	XF	Unc	BU
2008	35,000	—	—	—	—	12.00

KM# 478 2 HRYVNI
12.8000 g., Copper-Nickel-Zinc, 31 mm. **Subject:** Kyiv Zoo, 100th Anniversary **Edge:** Reeded

Date	Mintage	F	VF	XF	Unc	BU
2008	50,000	—	—	—	—	15.00

KM# 479 2 HRYVNI
12.8000 g., Copper-Nickel-Zinc, 31 mm. **Subject:** Yevhen Petrushevych **Edge:** Reeded

Date	Mintage	F	VF	XF	Unc	BU
2008	35,000	—	—	—	—	12.00

KM# 481 2 HRYVNI
12.8000 g., Copper-Nickel-Zinc, 31 mm. **Subject:** Heorhii Voronyi **Edge:** Reeded

Date	Mintage	F	VF	XF	Unc	BU
2008	35,000	—	—	—	—	12.00

KM# 482 2 HRYVNI
1.2400 g., 0.9990 Gold 0.0398 oz. AGW, 13.9 mm. **Subject:** Skythian Gold (Goddess Api)

Date	Mintage	F	VF	XF	Unc	BU
2008	10,000	—	—	—	140	200

KM# 483 2 HRYVNI
1.2400 g., 0.9990 Gold 0.0398 oz. AGW, 13.9 mm. **Subject:** Zodiac **Rev:** Cancer

Date	Mintage	F	VF	XF	Unc	BU
2008	10,000	—	—	—	140	200

KM# 484 2 HRYVNI
1.2400 g., 0.9990 Gold 0.0398 oz. AGW, 13.9 mm. **Subject:** Zodiac **Rev:** Leo

Date	Mintage	F	VF	XF	Unc	BU
2008	10,000	—	—	—	140	200

KM# 485 2 HRYVNI
1.2400 g., 0.9990 Gold 0.0398 oz. AGW **Subject:** Virgo

Date	Mintage	F	VF	XF	Unc	BU
2008	10,000	—	—	—	140	200

KM# 486 2 HRYVNI
1.2400 g., 0.9990 Gold 0.0398 oz. AGW, 13.9 mm. **Subject:** Libra

Date	Mintage	F	VF	XF	Unc	BU
2008	—	—	—	—	140	200

KM# 487 2 HRYVNI
12.8000 g., Copper-Nickel-Zinc, 31 mm. **Subject:** Nataliia Vzhvii **Edge:** Reeded

Date	Mintage	F	VF	XF	Unc	BU
2008	35,000	—	—	—	—	12.00

KM# 488 2 HRYVNI
12.8000 g., Copper-Nickel-Zinc, 31 mm. **Subject:** Hryhorii Kvitka - Osnovianenko **Edge:** Reeded

Date	Mintage	F	VF	XF	Unc	BU
2008	35,000	—	—	—	—	12.00

KM# 489 2 HRYVNI
12.8000 g., Copper-Nickel-Zinc, 31 mm. **Subject:** Western Ukraine People's Repbulic, 90th Anniversary **Edge:** Reeded

Date	Mintage	F	VF	XF	Unc	BU
2008	35,000	—	—	—	—	12.00

KM# 490 2 HRYVNI
12.8000 g., Copper-Nickel-Zinc, 31 mm. **Subject:** Vasyl Symonenko **Edge:** Reeded

Date	Mintage	F	VF	XF	Unc	BU
2008	35,000	—	—	—	—	12.00

KM# 533 2 HRYVNI
12.8000 g., Copper-Nickel-Zinc, 31.0 mm. **Subject:** Pavlo Chubynskyi **Obv:** Folk music instruments **Obv. Legend:** НАЦІОНАЛЬНИЈ БАНК УКРА?НИ - 2 / ГРИВНІ / 2009 **Rev:** Chubynskyi's portrait **Rev. Legend:** ПАВЛО ЧУБИНСЬКИЈ - 1839-1884 **Edge:** Reeded

Date	Mintage	F	VF	XF	Unc	BU
2009	35,000	—	—	—	—	12.00

KM# 534 2 HRYVNI
12.8000 g., Copper-Nickel-Zinc, 31.0 mm. **Subject:** Andrii Livytskyi **Obv:** National Arms and value **Obv. Legend:** НАЦІОНАЛЬНИЈ БАНК УКРА?НИ - ДВІ ГРИВНІ **Rev:** Livytskyi's portrait **Rev. Legend:** АНДРІЈ ЛІВИЦЬКИЈ - 1879/1954 - ПРЕЗИДЕНТ УНР В ЕКЗИЛІ **Edge:** Reeded

Date	Mintage	F	VF	XF	Unc	BU
2009	35,000	—	—	—	—	12.00

KM# 535 2 HRYVNI
1.2400 g., 0.9990 Gold 0.0398 oz. AGW, 13.92 mm. **Subject:** Ukraine Fauna **Obv:** National Arms, value **Obv. Legend:** НАЦІОНАЛЬНИЈ БАНК УКРА?НИ - 2 ГРИВНІ **Rev:** Turtle **Rev. Legend:** ЧЕРЕПАХА - TESTUDINES

Date	Mintage	F	VF	XF	Unc	BU
2009	10,000	—	—	—	140	200

KM# 536 2 HRYVNI
12.8000 g., Copper-Nickel-Zinc, 31.0 mm. **Subject:** Borys Martos **Obv:** National Arms and value **Obv. Legend:** НАЦІОНАЛЬНИЈ БАНК УКРА?НИ - ДВІ ГРИВНІ **Rev:** Martos's portrait **Rev. Legend:** БОРИС МАРТОС **Edge:** Reeded

Date	Mintage	F	VF	XF	Unc	BU
2009	35,000	—	—	—	—	12.00

KM# 537 2 HRYVNI
12.8000 g., Copper-Nickel-Zinc, 31.0 mm. **Subject:** General Symon Petliura **Obv:** Two Military men holding wreath of a woman's profile **Obv. Legend:** НАЦІОНАЛЬНИЈ БАНК УКРА?НИ - 2 ГРИВНІ **Rev:** Petliura's portrait **Rev. Legend:** СИМОН ПЕТЛЮРА **Edge:** Reeded

Date	Mintage	F	VF	XF	Unc	BU
2009	35,000	—	—	—	—	15.00

KM# 538 2 HRYVNI
12.8000 g., Copper-Nickel-Zinc, 31 mm. **Subject:** Igor Sikorskyi, 100th Anniversary of birth **Obv:** Aircraft, National Arms, value **Obv. Legend:** НАЦІОНАЛЬНИЈ БАНК УКРА?НИ - 2 ГРИВНІ **Rev:** Sikorskyi portrait as an airman, Da Vinci drawing **Rev. Legend:** ІГОР СІКОРСЬКИЈ **Edge:** Reeded

Date	Mintage	F	VF	XF	Unc	BU
2009	35,000	—	—	—	—	15.00

KM# 539 2 HRYVNI
12.8000 g., Copper-Nickel-Zinc, 31 mm. **Subject:** Mykola Bogolijubov, physicist, 100th Anniversary of birth **Obv:** Diagram and formula, National Arms, value **Rev:** Bogolijubov's portrait **Edge:** Reeded

Date	Mintage	F	VF	XF	Unc	BU
2009	35,000	—	—	—	—	12.00

KM# 540 2 HRYVNI
12.8000 g., Copper-Nickel-Zinc, 31 mm. **Subject:** Volodymyr Ivasiuk, poet and singer **Obv:** Flower of Chervona Ruta, electrical musical instruments **Obv. Legend:** НАЦІОНАЛЬНИЈ БАНК УКРА?НИ - 2 / ГРИВНІ / 2009 **Rev:** Ivasiuk's portrait **Rev. Legend:** ВОЛОДИМИР ІВАСЮК **Edge:** Reeded

Date	Mintage	F	VF	XF	Unc	BU
2009	35,000	—	—	—	—	12.00

KM# 541 2 HRYVNI
12.8000 g., Copper-Nickel-Zinc, 31.0 mm. **Subject:** Bohdan-Igor Antonych, poet **Obv:** Figurative interpretation of Antonych's poetry **Obv. Legend:** НАЦІОНАЛЬНИЈ БАНК УКРА?НИ - 2 / ГРИВНІ **Rev:** Antonych's portrait **Rev. Legend:** БОГДАН-ІГОР АНТОНИЧ **Edge:** Reeded

Date	Mintage	F	VF	XF	Unc	BU
2009	35,000	—	—	—	—	12.00

KM# 542 2 HRYVNI
12.8000 g., Copper-Nickel-Zinc, 31.0 mm. **Subject:** Kost Levytskyi **Obv:** State Coat of Arms, issue year **Obv. Legend:** НАЦІОНАЛЬНИЈ БАНК УКРАІНИ - ДВІ ГРИВНІ **Rev:** Levytskyi bust **Rev. Legend:** КОСТЬ ЛЕВИЦЬКИЈ

Date	Mintage	F	VF	XF	Unc	BU
2009	35,000	—	—	—	—	12.00

KM# 551 2 HRYVNI
12.8000 g., Copper-Nickel-Zinc, 31.0 mm. **Subject:** Carpatho-Ukraine Republic, 70th Anniversary **Obv:** Carpathian ornamentation patterns, National Arms, value **Obv. Legend:** НАЦІОНАЛЬНИЈ БАНК УКРАІНИ - 2 / ГРИВНІ **Rev:** Transcarpathian holding flag with arms of Carpatho-Ukraine **Rev. Legend:** 70 / РОКІВ - ПРОГОЛОШЕННЯ КАРПАТСЬКОІ УКРАІНИ **Edge:** Reeded

Date	Mintage	F	VF	XF	Unc	BU
2009	35,000	—	—	—	—	14.00

KM# 571 2 HRYVNI
1.2400 g., 0.9990 Gold 0.0398 oz. AGW, 13.92 mm. **Subject:** Skythian Gold **Obv:** National Arms **Rev:** Scythian boar figure

Date	Mintage	F	VF	XF	Unc	BU
2009 Special Unc.	10,000	—	—	—	140	200

KM# 578 2 HRYVNI
12.8000 g., Copper-Nickel-Zinc, 31 mm. **Subject:** Zaporizhzhia Oblast **Obv:** Zaporizhzhia Arms **Rev:** Stone bana, Dnieper's waves and Dniporhes dam **Edge:** Reeded

Date	Mintage	F	VF	XF	Unc	BU
2009	45,000	—	—	—	—	13.00

KM# 572 2 HRYVNI
1.2400 g., 0.9990 Gold 0.0398 oz. AGW, 13.92 mm. **Obv:** National Arms **Rev:** Bee **Edge:** Plain

Date	Mintage	F	VF	XF	Unc	BU
2010 Special Unc.	10,000	—	—	—	140	200

KM# 576 2 HRYVNI
12.8000 g., Copper-Nickel-Zinc, 31 mm. **Subject:** Ukraine Ice Hockey, 100th Anniversary **Obv:** Golie before net, National Arms **Rev:** Old time and modern hockey players **Edge:** Reeded

Date	Mintage	F	VF	XF	Unc	BU
2010	35,000	—	—	—	—	13.00

KM# 580 2 HRYVNI
12.8000 g., Copper-Nickel-Zinc, 31 mm. **Subject:** Ivan Kozhedub **Obv:** La-7 aircraft in two searchlight beams **Rev:** Kozhedub's portrait and airfield **Edge:** Reeded

Date	Mintage	F	VF	XF	Unc	BU
2010	35,000	—	—	—	—	13.00

KM# 581 2 HRYVNI
12.8000 g., Copper-Nickel, 31 mm. **Subject:** Lviv Polytechnic National University, 165th Anniversary **Obv:** Arts and Sciences sculptures from main building **Rev:** University building façade

Date	Mintage	F	VF	XF	Unc	BU
2010	45,000	—	—	—	—	13.00

KM# 583 2 HRYVNI
12.8000 g., Copper-Nickel, 31 mm. **Subject:** Kharkiv Polytechnic Institute, 125th Anniversary **Obv:** Radio telescope and open book **Rev:** University building at right, symbols of science at left, oval portrait of V.L. Kyrpychov

Date	Mintage	F	VF	XF	Unc	BU
2010	50,000	—	—	—	—	13.00

KM# 585 2 HRYVNI
12.8000 g., Copper-Nickel, 31 mm. **Subject:** Ukraine Sovereignty, 20th Anniversary **Obv:** National flag in enamel within viburnum wreath **Rev:** Ukraine map within uneven background **Edge:** Reeded

Date	Mintage	F	VF	XF	Unc	BU
2010	35,000	—	—	—	—	18.00

KM# 593 2 HRYVNI
12.8000 g., Copper-Nickel, 31 mm. **Subject:** Flora and fauna **Obv:** National Arms and wreath **Rev:** Stipa Ucrainica, feather grass

Date	Mintage	F	VF	XF	Unc	BU
2010	35,000	—	—	—	—	13.00

KM# 603 2 HRYVNI
1.2400 g., 0.9990 Gold 0.0398 oz. AGW, 13.92 mm. **Obv:** National Arms **Rev:** Cranberry bush branch **Edge:** Plain

Date	Mintage	F	VF	XF	Unc	BU
2010	10,000	—	—	—	140	200

KM# 608 2 HRYVNI
12.8000 g., Copper-Nickel, 31 mm. **Subject:** Ukranian Medical Association, 100th Anniversary **Obv:** UMA Shield within wreath **Rev:** UMA in Lviv emblem (lion on cross) **Edge:** Reeded

Date	Mintage	F	VF	XF	Unc	BU
2010	35,000	—	—	—	—	15.00

KM# 612 2 HRYVNI
12.8000 g., Copper-Nickel-Zinc, 31 mm. **Subject:** Ivan Franko National University, Lviv, 350th Anniversary **Obv:** National arms, Statuary group, value **Rev:** Main University building façade

Date	Mintage	F	VF	XF	Unc	BU
2011	45,000	—	—	—	—	12.00

KM# 624 2 HRYVNI
1.2400 g., 0.9999 Gold 0.0399 oz. AGW, 13.92 mm. **Subject:** Scythian Gold **Obv:** National arms **Rev:** Scythian jewlery, gilt deer

Date	Mintage	F	VF	XF	Unc	BU
2011	10,000	—	—	—	100	150

KM# 636 2 HRYVNI
12.8000 g., Copper-Nickel-Zinc, 31 mm. **Subject:** CIS, 20th Anniversary **Obv:** National flag in color **Rev:** Commonwealth of Independent States emblem

Date	Mintage	F	VF	XF	Unc	BU
2011	30,000	Value: 15.00				

KM# 107 5 HRYVEN
9.4000 g., Bi-Metallic Brass center in Copper-Nickel ring, 28 mm. **Subject:** New Millennium **Obv:** Spiral design within circle **Rev:** Mother and child within circle **Edge:** Segmented reeding

Date	Mintage	F	VF	XF	Unc	BU
2001	50,000	—	—	—	32.00	—

KM# 112 5 HRYVEN
16.5400 g., Copper-Nickel-Zinc, 35 mm. **Subject:** Ostrozhska Academy **Obv:** Value, old writing and printing artifacts **Rev:** Seated figures, partial building and crowned arms with supporters **Edge:** Reeded

Date	Mintage	F	VF	XF	Unc	BU
2001	30,000	—	—	—	30.00	—

KM# 129 5 HRYVEN
16.5400 g., Copper-Nickel-Zinc, 35 mm. **Subject:** 10th Anniversary - National Bank **Obv:** National arms between two arches **Rev:** Large building central entrance **Edge:** Reeded

Date	Mintage	F	VF	XF	Unc	BU
2001	50,000	—	—	—	17.50	—

KM# 132 5 HRYVEN
16.5400 g., Copper-Nickel-Zinc, 35 mm. **Subject:** 10th Anniversary - National Independence **Obv:** Arms with supporters within beaded circle **Rev:** Building on map within beaded circle **Edge:** Reeded

Date	Mintage	F	VF	XF	Unc	BU
2001	100,000	—	—	—	15.00	—

KM# 135 5 HRYVEN
16.5400 g., Copper-Nickel-Zinc, 35 mm. **Subject:** 1100th Anniversary - Poltava **Obv:** National arms above value flanked by flower sprigs **Rev:** Buildings above shield **Edge:** Reeded

Date	Mintage	F	VF	XF	Unc	BU
2001	50,000	—	—	—	20.00	—

KM# 140 5 HRYVEN
9.4000 g., Bi-Metallic Brass center in Copper-Nickel ring, 28 mm. **Subject:** 10th Anniversary of Military forces **Obv:** Crossed maces, arms and date within wreath and circle **Rev:** Circle in center of cross within wreath and circle **Edge:** Reeded and plain sections

Date	Mintage	F	VF	XF	Unc	BU
2001	30,000	—	—	—	100	—

KM# 148 5 HRYVEN
16.5400 g., Copper-Nickel-Zinc, 35 mm. **Subject:** 400 Years of Krolevets **Obv:** National arms above gateway and value **Rev:** Krolivets city arms flanked by designs **Edge:** Reeded

Date	Mintage	F	VF	XF	Unc	BU
2001	30,000	—	—	—	50.00	—

KM# 151 5 HRYVEN
16.5400 g., Copper-Nickel-Zinc, 35 mm. **Subject:** City of Khotyn **Obv:** Value within arch above military fittings **Rev:** Castle below crowned shield **Edge:** Reeded

Date	Mintage	F	VF	XF	Unc	BU
2002	30,000	—	—	—	40.00	—

KM# 152 5 HRYVEN
16.5400 g., Copper-Nickel-Zinc, 35 mm. **Obv:** Sun and flying geese divides beaded circle **Rev:** "AN-225 Mrija" cargo jet divide beaded circle **Edge:** Reeded

Date	Mintage	F	VF	XF	Unc	BU
2002	30,000	—	—	—	80.00	—

KM# 158 5 HRYVEN
9.4300 g., Bi-Metallic Brass center in Copper-Nickel ring, 28 mm. **Subject:** 70th Anniversary of Dnipro Hydroelectric Power Station **Obv:** Turbine within circle **Rev:** Large dam within circle **Edge:** Reeded and plain sections

Date	Mintage	F	VF	XF	Unc	BU
2002	30,000	—	—	—	60.00	—

KM# 159 5 HRYVEN
16.5400 g., Copper-Nickel-Zinc, 35 mm. **Obv:** Arms with supporters within beaded circle **Rev:** Battle scene around Batig in 1652 divides beaded circle **Edge:** Reeded

Date	Mintage	F	VF	XF	Unc	BU
2002	30,000	—	—	—	30.00	—

KM# 163 5 HRYVEN
16.5400 g., Copper-Nickel-Zinc, 35 mm. **Subject:** Christmas **Obv:** National arms in star above value flanked by designed sprigs **Rev:** Christmas pageant scene **Edge:** Reeded

Date	Mintage	F	VF	XF	Unc	BU
ND(2002)	30,000	—	—	—	100	—

KM# 157 5 HRYVEN
16.5400 g., Copper-Nickel, 35 mm. **Subject:** 1100th Anniversary - City of Romny **Obv:** Sprigs divide national arms and value **Rev:** City view **Edge:** Reeded

Date	Mintage	F	VF	XF	Unc	BU
2002	30,000	—	—	—	40.00	—

KM# 200 5 HRYVEN
9.4000 g., Bi-Metallic Brass center in Copper-Nickel ring, 28 mm. **Obv:** Bandura strings over ornamental design **Rev:** Bandura divides circle and wreath **Edge:** Segmented reeding

Date	Mintage	F	VF	XF	Unc	BU
2003	30,000	—	—	—	25.00	—

KM# 172 5 HRYVEN
16.5400 g., Copper-Nickel-Zinc, 35 mm. **Subject:** Easter **Obv:** Circle of Easter eggs, national arms in center above value **Rev:** Religious celebration **Edge:** Reeded

Date	Mintage	F	VF	XF	Unc	BU
2003	50,000	—	—	—	50.00	—

KM# 173 5 HRYVEN
16.5400 g., Copper-Nickel-Zinc, 35 mm. **Subject:** Antonov AN-2 Biplane **Obv:** National arms sun face and flying geese divide beaded circle **Rev:** World's largest biplane divides beaded circle **Edge:** Reeded

Date	Mintage	F	VF	XF	Unc	BU
2003	50,000	—	—	—	25.00	—

KM# 185 5 HRYVEN
9.4000 g., Bi-Metallic Brass center in Copper-Nickel ring, 28 mm. **Subject:** 150th Anniversary of the Central Ukrainian Archives **Obv:** Value, signature and seal **Rev:** Hourglass divides books and circle **Edge:** Segmented reeding

Date	Mintage	F	VF	XF	Unc	BU
2003	30,000	—	—	—	15.00	—

KM# 186 5 HRYVEN
16.5400 g., Copper-Nickel-Zinc, 35 mm. **Subject:** 2500th Anniversary of the City of Yevpatoria **Obv:** National arms, date and value with partial sun background **Rev:** Ancient amphora and modern city view **Edge:** Reeded

Date	Mintage	F	VF	XF	Unc	BU
2003	30,000	—	—	—	40.00	—

KM# 187 5 HRYVEN
16.5400 g., Copper-Nickel-Zinc, 35 mm. **Subject:** 60th Anniversary - Liberation of Kiev **Obv:** Eternal flame monument **Rev:** Battle scene and map of the offense **Edge:** Reeded

Date	Mintage	F	VF	XF	Unc	BU
2003	30,000	—	—	—	25.00	—

KM# 204 5 HRYVEN
16.5400 g., Copper-Nickel-Zinc, 35 mm. **Subject:** 50th Anniversary - Pivdenne Space Design Office **Obv:** Satellite orbiting Earth **Rev:** Satellite above moonscape **Edge:** Reeded

Date	Mintage	F	VF	XF	Unc	BU
2004	30,000	—	—	—	17.00	—

KM# 205 5 HRYVEN
16.5400 g., Copper-Nickel-Zinc, 35 mm. **Subject:** 2500 Anniversary City of Balaklava **Obv:** National arms between two ancient ships **Rev:** Harbor view above pillar **Edge:** Reeded

Date	Mintage	F	VF	XF	Unc	BU
2004	30,000	—	—	—	25.00	—

KM# 218 5 HRYVEN
16.9400 g., 0.9250 Silver 0.5038 oz. ASW, 33 mm. **Obv:** National arms, value and atom **Rev:** Kharkiv University building **Edge:** Reeded

Date	Mintage	F	VF	XF	Unc	BU
2004 Proof	7,000	Value: 60.00				

KM# 219 5 HRYVEN
16.9400 g., 0.9250 Silver 0.5038 oz. ASW, 33 mm. **Obv:** National arms above value dividing scientific items **Rev:** Kiev University building main entrance **Edge:** Reeded

Date	Mintage	F	VF	XF	Unc	BU
2004 Proof	7,000	Value: 60.00				

KM# 220 5 HRYVEN
9.4300 g., Bi-Metallic BRASS center in COPPER-NICKEL ring, 28 mm. **Subject:** 50 Years of Ukraine's Membership in UNESCO **Obv:** National arms in center of sprigs and circle **Rev:** Building within sprigs and circle **Edge:** Segmented reeding

Date	Mintage	F	VF	XF	Unc	BU
2004	50,000	—	—	—	15.00	—

KM# 221 5 HRYVEN
16.5400 g., Copper-Nickel-Zinc, 35 mm. **Subject:** Ice Breaker "Captain Belousov" **Obv:** National arms on ship's wheel and anchor **Rev:** Ice breaker ship **Edge:** Reeded

Date	Mintage	F	VF	XF	Unc	BU
2004	30,000	—	—	—	16.00	—

KM# 222 5 HRYVEN
16.5400 g., Copper-Nickel-Zinc, 35 mm. **Subject:** Whit Sunday **Obv:** National arms in flower wreath above value flanked by sprigs **Rev:** Four dancing women and child **Edge:** Reeded

Date	Mintage	F	VF	XF	Unc	BU
2004	50,000	—	—	—	20.00	—

KM# 333 5 HRYVEN
9.4000 g., Bi-Metallic Brass center in Copper-Nickel ring, 28 mm. **Obv:** Horizontal lines across flowery design **Rev:** Cossack-style lyre within circle and wreath **Edge:** Segmented reeding

Date	Mintage	F	VF	XF	Unc	BU
2004	30,000	—	—	—	20.00	—

KM# 334 5 HRYVEN
16.5400 g., Copper-Nickel-Zinc, 35 mm. **Subject:** 250th Anniversary of Kirovohrad **Obv:** National arms above crossed cannons and value **Rev:** Arms with supporters above city view **Edge:** Reeded

Date	Mintage	F	VF	XF	Unc	BU
2004	30,000	—	—	—	20.00	—

KM# 335 5 HRYVEN
16.5400 g., Copper-Nickel-Zinc, 35 mm. **Subject:** 350 Years to Kharkiv **Obv:** Assumption Cathedral, value and national arms **Rev:** Kharkiv State Industrial Building complex **Edge:** Reeded

Date	Mintage	F	VF	XF	Unc	BU
2004	30,000	—	—	—	30.00	—

KM# 336 5 HRYVEN
9.4000 g., Bi-Metallic Brass center in Copper-Nickel ring, 28 mm. **Subject:** 50th Anniversary of Crimean Union With Ukraine **Obv:** National arms on wheat sheaf on map **Rev:** Crowned lion on shield flanked by pillars within rope wreath **Edge:** Segmented reeding

Date	Mintage	F	VF	XF	Unc	BU
2004	30,000	—	—	—	20.00	—

KM# 337 5 HRYVEN
16.5400 g., Copper-Nickel-Zinc, 35 mm. **Obv:** National arms on sun, flying geese divide beaded circle **Rev:** AN-140 Airliner divides beaded circle **Edge:** Reeded

Date	Mintage	F	VF	XF	Unc	BU
2004	50,000	—	—	—	15.00	—

KM# 362 5 HRYVEN
16.5400 g., Copper-Nickel-Zinc, 35 mm. **Obv:** National arms on sun with flying geese divide beaded circle **Rev:** AN-124 jet divides beaded circle **Edge:** Reeded

Date	Mintage	F	VF	XF	Unc	BU
2005	60,000	—	—	—	—	15.00

KM# 364 5 HRYVEN
16.5400 g., Copper-Nickel-Zinc, 35 mm. **Subject:** City of Korosten 1300th Anniversary **Obv:** National arms **Rev:** Ancient earring below modern building and bridge **Edge:** Reeded

Date	Mintage	F	VF	XF	Unc	BU
2005	30,000	—	—	—	—	18.00

KM# 365 5 HRYVEN
16.5400 g., Copper-Nickel-Zinc, 35 mm. **Subject:** City of Sumy 350th Anniversary **Obv:** National arms **Rev:** City view behind city arms **Edge:** Reeded

Date	Mintage	F	VF	XF	Unc	BU
2005	30,000	—	—	—	—	16.00

KM# 366 5 HRYVEN
16.5400 g., Copper-Nickel-Zinc, 35 mm. **Subject:** The Protection of the Virgin **Obv:** National arms on Cossack regalia **Rev:** Wedding scene **Edge:** Reeded

Date	Mintage	F	VF	XF	Unc	BU
2005	45,000	—	—	—	—	16.00

KM# 368 5 HRYVEN
16.5400 g., Copper-Nickel-Zinc, 35 mm. **Subject:** Sorochynsky Fair **Obv:** Busts facing each other flanked by sprigs **Rev:** Farmer with family in ox cart **Edge:** Reeded

Date	Mintage	F	VF	XF	Unc	BU
2005	60,000	—	—	—	—	16.00

KM# 379 5 HRYVEN
16.5400 g., Copper-Nickel-Zinc, 35 mm. **Subject:** 500th Anniversary - Kalmiuska Palanqua Cossack Settlement **Obv:** Cossack in ornamental frame and national arms **Rev:** Soldiers **Edge:** Reeded

Date	Mintage	F	VF	XF	Unc	BU
2005	30,000	—	—	—	—	18.00

KM# 380 5 HRYVEN
16.5400 g., Copper-Nickel-Zinc, 35 mm. **Subject:** Sviatohirsky Assumption Monastery **Obv:** Madonna and child flanked by angels **Rev:** Hillside monastery **Edge:** Reeded

Date	Mintage	F	VF	XF	Unc	BU
2005	45,000	—	—	—	—	16.00

KM# 387 5 HRYVEN
16.5400 g., Copper-Nickel-Zinc, 35 mm. **Subject:** Vernadsky Antarctic Station **Obv:** Flag and buildings **Rev:** Antarctica map within compass face **Edge:** Reeded

Date	Mintage	F	VF	XF	Unc	BU
2006	60,000	—	—	—	—	15.00

KM# 388 5 HRYVEN
16.9300 g., 0.9250 Silver 0.5035 oz. ASW, 33 mm. **Subject:** Year of the Dog **Obv:** Value on textile art **Rev:** Stylized dog **Edge:** Reeded

Date	Mintage	F	VF	XF	Unc	BU
2006 Proof	12,000	Value: 220				

KM# 389 5 HRYVEN
16.9300 g., 0.9250 Silver 0.5035 oz. ASW, 33 mm. **Subject:** Zodiac - Ram **Obv:** Sun face **Rev:** Ram **Edge:** Reeded

Date	Mintage	F	VF	XF	Unc	BU
2006 Proof	10,000	Value: 100				

KM# 390 5 HRYVEN
16.9300 g., 0.9250 Silver 0.5035 oz. ASW, 33 mm. **Subject:** Kyiv National University of Economics **Obv:** National arms, graph above value **Rev:** University building within circle **Edge:** Reeded

Date	Mintage	F	VF	XF	Unc	BU
2006 Proof	5,000	Value: 80.00				

KM# 402 5 HRYVEN
9.4200 g., Bi-Metallic Brass center in Copper-Nickel ring, 28 mm. **Obv:** Symbolic sound of music **Rev:** Tsimbal stringed musical instrument **Edge:** Segmented reeding

Date	Mintage	F	VF	XF	Unc	BU
2006	100,000	—	—	—	—	13.00

KM# 409 5 HRYVEN
16.5400 g., Copper-Nickel-Zinc, 35 mm. **Subject:** 10 Years of the Constitution of Ukraine **Obv:** National arms **Edge:** Reeded

Date	Mintage	F	VF	XF	Unc	BU
2006	30,000	—	—	—	—	20.00

KM# 411 5 HRYVEN
16.5400 g., Copper-Nickel-Zinc, 35 mm. **Subject:** 15 Years of Ukraine Independence **Obv:** National arms **Edge:** Reeded

Date	Mintage	F	VF	XF	Unc	BU
2006	75,000	—	—	—	—	13.00

KM# 413 5 HRYVEN
16.5400 g., Copper-Nickel-Zinc, 35 mm. **Subject:** 10 Years to the Currency Reform in Ukraine **Obv:** National arms **Edge:** Reeded

Date	Mintage	F	VF	XF	Unc	BU
2006	45,000	—	—	—	—	15.00

KM# 405 5 HRYVEN
16.8200 g., 0.9250 Silver 0.5002 oz. ASW, 33 mm. **Subject:** Bull **Obv:** National arms

Date	Mintage	F	VF	XF	Unc	BU
2006 Proof	10,000	Value: 100				

KM# 415 5 HRYVEN
16.5400 g., Copper-Nickel-Zinc, 35 mm. **Subject:** 750 Years of the City of L'viv **Obv:** National arms **Edge:** Reeded

Date	Mintage	F	VF	XF	Unc	BU
2006	60,000	—	—	—	—	15.00

KM# 416 5 HRYVEN
16.8200 g., 0.9250 Silver 0.5002 oz. ASW, 33 mm. **Subject:** Mykhailo Hrushevskyi **Obv:** National arms

Date	Mintage	F	VF	XF	Unc	BU
2006 Proof	5,000	Value: 80.00				

KM# 417 5 HRYVEN
16.8200 g., 0.9250 Silver 0.5002 oz. ASW, 33 mm. **Subject:** Dmytro Lutsenko **Obv:** National arms

Date	Mintage	F	VF	XF	Unc	BU
2006 Proof	3,000	Value: 95.00				

KM# 418 5 HRYVEN
16.8200 g., 0.9250 Silver 0.5002 oz. ASW, 33 mm. **Subject:** Ivan Franko **Obv:** National arms

Date	Mintage	F	VF	XF	Unc	BU
2006 Proof	5,000	Value: 80.00				

KM# 407 5 HRYVEN
16.8200 g., 0.9250 Silver 0.5002 oz. ASW, 33 mm. **Subject:** Gemini **Obv:** National arms

Date	Mintage	F	VF	XF	Unc	BU
2006 Proof	10,000	Value: 120				

KM# 420 5 HRYVEN
16.5400 g., Copper-Nickel-Zinc, 35 mm. **Subject:** Epiphany **Obv:** National arms **Edge:** Reeded

Date	Mintage	F	VF	XF	Unc	BU
2006	75,000	—	—	—	—	15.00

KM# 422 5 HRYVEN
16.5400 g., Copper-Nickel-Zinc, 35 mm. **Subject:** Saint Kyryl Church **Obv:** National arms

Date	Mintage	F	VF	XF	Unc	BU
2006	45,000	—	—	—	—	15.00

KM# 432 5 HRYVEN
16.5400 g., Copper-Nickel-Zinc, 35 mm. **Subject:** 100th Anniversary of "Motor Sich" **Obv:** Small national arms above falcon in flight with two globes in background **Rev:** Jet engine **Edge:** Reeded

Date	Mintage	F	VF	XF	Unc	BU
2007	45,000	—	—	—	—	15.00

KM# 419 5 HRYVEN
16.8200 g., 0.9250 Silver 0.5002 oz. ASW, 33 mm. **Subject:** Year of the Pig **Obv:** National arms **Edge:** Reeded

Date	Mintage	F	VF	XF	Unc	BU
2007 Proof	15,000	Value: 150				

KM# 453 5 HRYVEN
9.4000 g., Bi-Metallic Brass center in copper-nickel ring, 28 mm. **Subject:** Pure water is the source of life **Obv:** Drop of water in pond **Rev:** Man taking drink at waterfall

Date	Mintage	F	VF	XF	Unc	BU
2007	50,000	—	—	—	—	15.00

KM# 455 5 HRYVEN
9.4000 g., Bi-Metallic Brass center in copper-nickel ring, 28 mm. **Subject:** Organization Safety and Cooperation, 16th Annual Meeting **Obv:** State emblem and ornamentation **Rev:** Parliamentary Assemby Building in Kyiv

Date	Mintage	F	VF	XF	Unc	BU
2007	35,000	—	—	—	—	17.00

KM# 456 5 HRYVEN
16.5000 g., Copper-Nickel-Zinc, 35 mm. **Subject:** Odessa National Opera and Ballet, 120th Anniversary **Obv:** Ballet scene in oval **Rev:** Opera house in Odessa **Edge:** Reeded

Date	Mintage	F	VF	XF	Unc	BU
2007	35,000	—	—	—	—	15.00

KM# 457 5 HRYVEN
16.5000 g., Copper-Nickel-Zinc, 35 mm. **Subject:** Chernihiv, 1100th Anniversary **Obv:** Sword hilts and slate fragment **Rev:** Town view and open book **Edge:** Reeded

Date	Mintage	F	VF	XF	Unc	BU
2007	45,000	—	—	—	—	16.00

KM# 458 5 HRYVEN
9.4000 g., Bi-Metallic Brass center in copper-nickel ring, 28 mm. **Subject:** Buhai **Obv:** Sound waves as a baroque ornament **Rev:** Drum-like musical instrument

Date	Mintage	F	VF	XF	Unc	BU
2007	50,000	—	—	—	—	15.00

KM# 459 5 HRYVEN
16.5400 g., Copper-Nickel-Zinc, 35 mm. **Subject:** The Famine, Genocide of the Ukranian People **Obv:** Girl standing on fallow ground **Rev:** Stork within cross, candles in background **Edge:** Reeded

Date	Mintage	F	VF	XF	Unc	BU
2007	75,000	—	—	—	—	15.00

KM# 460 5 HRYVEN
16.5400 g., Copper-Nickel-Zinc, 35 mm. **Subject:** Crimean Resorts, 200th Anniversary **Obv:** Seaside Resort **Rev:** Felix De Searr and well **Edge:** Reeded

Date	Mintage	F	VF	XF	Unc	BU
2007	35,000	—	—	—	—	17.00

KM# 461 5 HRYVEN
15.5500 g., 0.9250 Silver 0.4624 oz. ASW, 33 mm. **Subject:** Capricorn **Obv:** Sun and seasons **Rev:** Zodiac sign

Date	Mintage	F	VF	XF	Unc	BU
2007 Proof	15,000	Value: 80.00				

KM# 462 5 HRYVEN
16.8200 g., 0.9250 Silver 0.5002 oz. ASW, 33 mm. **Subject:** Aquarius **Obv:** Sun and seasons **Rev:** Zodiac sign, man pouring water

Date	Mintage	F	VF	XF	Unc	BU
2007 Proof	15,000	Value: 80.00				

KM# 463 5 HRYVEN
16.8200 g., 0.9250 Silver 0.5002 oz. ASW, 33 mm. **Subject:** Pisces **Obv:** Sun and seasons **Rev:** Zodiac sign, two fish

Date	Mintage	F	VF	XF	Unc	BU
2007 Proof	15,000	Value: 80.00				

KM# 464 5 HRYVEN
16.8200 g., 0.9250 Silver 0.5002 oz. ASW, 33 mm. **Subject:** Scorpion **Obv:** Sun and seasons **Rev:** Zodiac sign, scorpion **Edge:** Reeded

Date	Mintage	F	VF	XF	Unc	BU
2007 Proof	15,000	Value: 80.00				

KM# 465 5 HRYVEN
16.8200 g., 0.9250 Silver 0.5002 oz. ASW, 33 mm. **Subject:** Sagittarius **Obv:** Sun and seasons **Rev:** Zodiac sign, archer

Date	Mintage	F	VF	XF	Unc	BU
2007 Proof	15,000	Value: 80.00				

KM# 531 5 HRYVEN
16.5400 g., Copper-Nickel, 35 mm. **Subject:** 1100th Aniversary of Perejaslav-Khmelnytskyi **Obv:** Parchment. **Obv. Legend:** НАЦІОНАЛЬНИЙ БАНК УКРА?НИ - 5 ГРИВЕНЬ / 2007 **Rev:** Old Rus cathedral, old Rus and Cossacks. **Rev. Legend:** ПЕРЕЯСЛАВ-ХМЕЛЬНИЦЬКИЈ - 1100

Date	Mintage	F	VF	XF	Unc	BU
2007	45,000	—	—	—	—	16.00

KM# 511 5 HRYVEN
16.5400 g., Copper-Nickel-Zinc, 35 mm. **Subject:** Rivne, 725th Anniversary **Edge:** Reeded

Date	Mintage	F	VF	XF	Unc	BU
2008	45,000	—	—	—	—	16.00

KM# 500 5 HRYVEN
16.5000 g., Copper-Nickel-Zinc, 35 mm. **Subject:** The Annunciation **Edge:** Reeded

Date	Mintage	F	VF	XF	Unc	BU
2008	45,000	—	—	—	—	16.00

KM# 501 5 HRYVEN
16.5000 g., Copper-Nickel-Zinc, 35 mm. **Subject:** Chernivtsi, 600th Anniversary **Edge:** Reeded

Date	Mintage	F	VF	XF	Unc	BU
2008	45,000	—	—	—	—	16.00

KM# 502 5 HRYVEN
16.5000 g., Copper-Nickel-Zinc, 35 mm. **Subject:** Sniatyn, 850th Anniversary **Edge:** Reeded

Date	Mintage	F	VF	XF	Unc	BU
2008	45,000	—	—	—	—	16.00

KM# 503 5 HRYVEN
16.8200 g., 0.9250 Silver 0.5002 oz. ASW, 33 mm. **Subject:** Year of the Rat **Rev:** Rat, diamond insert eye **Edge:** Reeded

Date	Mintage	F	VF	XF	Unc	BU
2008 Proof	15,000	Value: 100				

KM# 504 5 HRYVEN
16.8200 g., 0.9250 Silver 0.5002 oz. ASW, 33 mm. **Subject:** Cancer **Edge:** Reeded

Date	Mintage	F	VF	XF	Unc	BU
2008 Proof	15,000	Value: 80.00				

KM# 505 5 HRYVEN
16.8200 g., 0.9250 Silver 0.5002 oz. ASW, 33 mm. **Subject:** Roman Shukhevich, General **Edge:** Reeded

Date	Mintage	F	VF	XF	Unc	BU
2008 Proof	3,000	Value: 250				

KM# 506 5 HRYVEN
16.8200 g., 0.9250 Silver 0.5002 oz. ASW, 33 mm. **Subject:** Leo **Edge:** Reeded

Date	Mintage	F	VF	XF	Unc	BU
2008 Proof	15,000	Value: 80.00				

KM# 507 5 HRYVEN
16.8200 g., 0.9250 Silver 0.5002 oz. ASW, 33 mm. **Subject:** Virgo **Edge:** Reeded

Date	Mintage	F	VF	XF	Unc	BU
2008 Proof	15,000	Value: 80.00				

KM# 508 5 HRYVEN
16.8200 g., 0.9250 Silver 0.5002 oz. ASW, 33 mm. **Subject:** Libra **Edge:** Reeded

Date	Mintage	F	VF	XF	Unc	BU
2008 Proof	15,000	Value: 80.00				

KM# 509 5 HRYVEN
16.5400 g., Copper-Nickel-Zinc, 35 mm. **Subject:** State Arboretum "Trostianet-s", 175th Anniversary **Edge:** Reeded

Date	Mintage	F	VF	XF	Unc	BU
2008	45,000	—	—	—	—	15.00

KM# 510 5 HRYVEN
16.5400 g., Copper-Nickel-Zinc, 35 mm. **Subject:** Kievan Rus **Edge:** Reeded

Date	Mintage	F	VF	XF	Unc	BU
2008	45,000	—	—	—	—	15.00

KM# 512 5 HRYVEN
16.5400 g., Copper-Nickel-Zinc, 35 mm. **Subject:** Bohuslav, 975th Anniversary **Edge:** Reeded

Date	Mintage	F	VF	XF	Unc	BU
2008	45,000	—	—	—	—	14.00

KM# 513 5 HRYVEN
9.4000 g., Bi-Metallic Brass center in copper-nickel ring, 28 mm. **Subject:** Taras Shevchenko "Prosvita Society" 140th Anniversary

Date	Mintage	F	VF	XF	Unc	BU
2008	45,000	—	—	—	—	14.00

KM# 514 5 HRYVEN
16.8200 g., 0.9250 Silver 0.5002 oz. ASW, 33 mm. **Subject:** Mariya Prymachenko

Date	Mintage	F	VF	XF	Unc	BU
2008 Proof	5,000	Value: 80.00				

KM# 530 5 HRYVEN
16.8200 g., 0.9250 Silver 0.5002 oz. ASW, 33 mm. **Subject:** Year of the Ox **Obv:** National Arms and value **Rev:** Ox, rubies in eyes **Edge:** Reeded

Date	Mintage	F	VF	XF	Unc	BU
2009 Proof	20,000	Value: 80.00				

KM# 543 5 HRYVEN
16.8200 g., 0.9250 Silver 0.5002 oz. ASW, 33.0 mm. **Subject:** Nikolai Gogol **Obv:** Compositions of two main subjects of Gogol's work, National Arms, value **Obv. Legend:** НАЦІОНАЛЬНИЈ БАНК УКРАЇНИ - 5 ГРИВЕНЬ / 2009 **Rev:** Nikolai's portrait **Rev. Legend:** МИКОЛА ГОГОЛЬ

Date	Mintage	F	VF	XF	Unc	BU
2009 Proof	5,000	Value: 80.00				

KM# 544 5 HRYVEN
16.8200 g., 0.9250 Silver 0.5002 oz. ASW, 33.0 mm. **Subject:** Sholem Aleichem **Obv:** Conventionalized composition, book sheets, Aleichem's signet **Obv. Legend:** НАЦІОНАЛЬНИЈ БАНК УКРАЇНИ - 5 ГРИВЕНЬ / 2009 **Rev:** Aleichem's portrait **Rev. Legend:** МИР ВАМ - ШОЛОМ-АЛЕЈХЕМ - РАБИНОВИЧ ШОЛОМ

Date	Mintage	F	VF	XF	Unc	BU
2009 Proof	5,000	Value: 80.00				

KM# 545 5 HRYVEN
16.5400 g., Copper-Nickel-Zinc, 35.0 mm. **Subject:** Simferopol, 225th Anniversary **Obv:** Main railway station, National Arms **Obv. Legend:** НАЦІОНАЛЬНИЈ БАНК УКРА?НИ - 5 ГРИВЕНЬ 2009 **Rev:** City Coat of Arms, Architectural elements **Rev. Legend:** 225 / РОКІВ - СІМФЕРОПОЛЬ **Edge:** Reeded

Date	Mintage	F	VF	XF	Unc	BU
2009	45,000	—	—	—	—	16.00

KM# 546 5 HRYVEN
16.8200 g., 0.9250 Silver 0.5002 oz. ASW, 33 mm. **Subject:** Ivan Kotljarevskyi **Obv:** National Arms, boat, column and helmet **Obv. Legend:** НАЦІОНАЛЬНИЈ БАНК УКРАІНИ - П'ЯТЬ ГРИВЕНЬ **Rev:** Kotliarevskyi's portrait **Rev. Legend:** ...ПОКИ СОНЦЕ З НЕБА СЯЕ, ТЕБЕ НЕ ЗАБУДУТЬ! - ІВАН КОТЛЯРЕВСЬКИЈ

Date	Mintage	F	VF	XF	Unc	BU
2009 Proof	5,000	Value: 80.00				

KM# 547 5 HRYVEN
16.5400 g., Copper-Nickel-Zinc, 35 mm. **Subject:** Mykolaiv, 220th Anniversary **Obv:** Varvarivskyi Bridge, gull, ship, anchor **Obv. Legend:** НАЦІОНАЛЬНИЈ БАНК УКРА?НИ - П'ЯТЬ ГРИВЕНЬ **Rev:** Frigate Saint Nicholas, Architecture of Mykolaiv **Rev. Legend:** МИКОЛА?В - РІК ЗАСНУВАННЯ / 1789 **Edge:** Reeded

Date	Mintage	F	VF	XF	Unc	BU
2009	45,000	—	—	—	—	16.00

KM# 548 5 HRYVEN
9.4000 g., Bi-Metallic Brass center in Copper-Nickel ring, 28 mm. **Subject:** Council of Europe, 60th Anniversary **Obv:** Stars, map of Europe **Obv. Legend:** НАЦІОНАЛЬНИЈ БАНК УКРА?НИ - П'ЯТЬ ГРИВЕНЬ **Rev:** Council of Europe logo, stars **Rev. Legend:** COUNCIL OF EUROPE, CONSEIL DE EUROPE, РАДА ?ВРОПИ

Date	Mintage	F	VF	XF	Unc	BU
2009	45,000	—	—	—	—	15.00

KM# 549 5 HRYVEN
16.8200 g., 0.9250 Silver 0.5002 oz. ASW, 33.0 mm. **Subject:** Lviv National Medical University, 225th Anniversary **Obv:** Hippocratic Oath in Latin, National Arms, value **Obv. Legend:** НАЦІОНАЛЬНИЈ БАНК УКРАІНИ - 5 / ГРИВЕНЬ **Rev:** University building **Rev. Legend:** 225 / РОКІВ - ІМЕНІ / ДАНИЛА / ГАЛИЦЬКОГО - ЛЬВІВСЬКИЈ НАЦІОНАЛЬНИЈ МЕДИЧНИЈ УНІВЕРСИТЕТ

Date	Mintage	F	VF	XF	Unc	BU
2009 Proof	7,000	Value: 80.00				

KM# 550 5 HRYVEN
16.5400 g., Copper-Nickel-Zinc, 35 mm. **Subject:** T. H. Shevchenko National Museum, 60th Anniversary **Obv:** Kateryna painting, bandura, National Arms, value **Rev:** Museum bulding and portrait **Edge:** Reeded

Date	Mintage	F	VF	XF	Unc	BU
2009	30,000	—	—	—	—	15.00

KM# 553 5 HRYVEN
16.5400 g., Copper-Nickel-Zinc, 35 mm. **Subject:** Pysanka - Easter Egg decorating **Obv:** Easter eggs, National Arms, value **Rev:** Easter bread, eggs. **Edge:** Reeded

Date	Mintage	F	VF	XF	Unc	BU
2009	50,000	—	—	—	—	16.00

KM# 555 5 HRYVEN
16.5000 g., Copper-Nickel, 35 mm. **Subject:** Folk crafts of the Ukraine - Bokorash (Raftsmen) **Obv:** Two birds, Carpathian landscape, trees, cottages, logs **Obv. Legend:** НАЦІОНАЛЬНИЈ БАНК УКРА?НИ - 5 / ГРИВЕНЬ / 2009 **Rev:** Bokorash directing raft **Rev. Legend:** БОКОРАШ **Edge:** Reeded

Date	Mintage	F	VF	XF	Unc	BU
2009	45,000	—	—	—	—	15.00

KM# 557 5 HRYVEN
16.5400 g., Copper-Nickel, 35.0 mm. **Subject:** International Year of Astronomy **Obv:** Urania, planets, stars, solar system, National Arms, value **Obv. Legend:** НАЦІОНАЛЬНИЈ БАНК УКРА?НИ - 5 ГРИВЕНЬ **Rev:** Yurii Drohobych, International Year of Astronomy logo, artifacts **Rev. Legend:** МІЖНАРОДНИЈ / РІК / АСТРОНОМІ? **Edge:** Reeded

Date	Mintage	F	VF	XF	Unc	BU
2009	45,000	—	—	—	—	15.00

KM# 573 5 HRYVEN
16.5000 g., Copper-Nickel-Zinc, 35 mm. **Subject:** Ukrainian Folk crafts - Cartwright **Obv:** Wood cart and wheels **Rev:** Woodcraftsman hewing wood to make cart detail **Edge:** Reeded

Date	Mintage	F	VF	XF	Unc	BU
2009	45,000	—	—	—	—	15.00

KM# 567 5 HRYVEN
16.8200 g., 0.9250 Silver 0.5002 oz. ASW, 33 mm. **Subject:** Yevhen Paton **Obv:** Paton Bridge and the footbridge over Petrovska Alley **Rev:** Paton's portrait

Date	Mintage	F	VF	XF	Unc	BU
2010 Proof	5,000	Value: 80.00				

KM# 566 5 HRYVEN
16.8200 g., 0.9250 Silver 0.5002 oz. ASW, 33 mm. **Subject:** Ivan Puliui **Obv:** X-ray of jewelry portrait **Rev:** Puliui portrait and text

Date	Mintage	F	VF	XF	Unc	BU
2010 Proof	5,000	Value: 80.00				

KM# 568 5 HRYVEN
16.8200 g., 0.9250 Silver 0.5002 oz. ASW, 33 mm. **Subject:** Oksana Petrusenko **Obv:** Poppy flower and musical notation **Rev:** Bust facing

Date	Mintage	F	VF	XF	Unc	BU
2010 Proof	5,000	Value: 80.00				

KM# 569 5 HRYVEN
16.8200 g., 0.9250 Silver 0.5002 oz. ASW, 33 mm. **Subject:** Mykola Ivanovych Pyrohov, scientist and surgeon **Obv:** Sepulchral church erected over scientist's tomb **Rev:** Half length figure in apron holding surgical instruments

Date	Mintage	F	VF	XF	Unc	BU
2010 Proof	5,000	Value: 80.00				

KM# 577 5 HRYVEN
16.8200 g., 0.9250 Silver 0.5002 oz. ASW, 33 mm. **Subject:** Year of the tiger **Obv:** Vegitable ornamention pattern, National Arms **Rev:** Stylized playful tiger **Edge:** Reeded

Date	Mintage	F	VF	XF	Unc	BU
2010 Proof	20,000	Value: 80.00				

KM# 579 5 HRYVEN
16.5400 g., Copper-Nickel-Zinc, 35 mm. **Subject:** Kyiv National University Astronomical Observatory, 165th Anniversary **Obv:** Observatory building **Rev:** Telescope and night sky **Edge:** Reeded

Date	Mintage	F	VF	XF	Unc	BU
2010	45,000	—	—	—	—	15.00

KM# 582 5 HRYVEN
16.8200 g., 0.9250 Silver 0.5002 oz. ASW, 33 mm. **Subject:** Lviv Polytechnic National University, 165th Anniversary **Obv:** Arts and Science sculpture from main building **Rev:** University building façade

Date	Mintage	F	VF	XF	Unc	BU
2010 Proof	5,000	Value: 80.00				

KM# 584 5 HRYVEN
15.5500 g., 0.9250 Silver 0.4624 oz. ASW, 33 mm. **Subject:** Kharkiv Polytechnic Institute, 125th Anniversary **Obv:** Radio telescope and open book **Rev:** University building and oval portrait of V.L. Kyrpychov

Date	Mintage	F	VF	XF	Unc	BU
2010 Proof	5,000	Value: 80.00				

KM# 587 5 HRYVEN

16.5000 g., Copper-Nickel-Zinc, 35 mm. **Subject:** Folk Crafts - Weaver **Obv:** Spinning wheel and weaving products **Rev:** Woman working on a loom **Edge:** Reeded

Date	Mintage	F	VF	XF	Unc	BU
2010	45,000	—	—	—	—	15.00

KM# 589 5 HRYVEN

16.5000 g., Copper-Nickel-Zinc, 35 mm. **Subject:** UKranian spas **Obv:** Two cornucopiae and the Savior's Feast **Rev:** Peasants getting food gifts blessed **Edge:** Reeded

Date	Mintage	F	VF	XF	Unc	BU
2010	45,000	—	—	—	—	15.00

KM# 592 5 HRYVEN

16.5000 g., Copper-Nickel-Zinc, 35 mm. **Subject:** Lutsk, 925th Anniversary **Obv:** Entrance tower to town's castle **Rev:** City view from tower top, city carms above **Edge:** Reeded

Date	Mintage	F	VF	XF	Unc	BU
2010	45,000	—	—	—	—	15.00

KM# 598 5 HRYVEN

16.8200 g., 0.9250 Silver 0.5002 oz. ASW, 33 mm. **Subject:** Johann Georg Pinzel **Obv:** Buchach City hall **Rev:** Sculptor and angel

Date	Mintage	F	VF	XF	Unc	BU
2010 Proof	5,000	Value: 80.00				

KM# 599 5 HRYVEN

16.8200 g., 0.9250 Silver 0.5002 oz. ASW, 33 mm. **Subject:** Ivan Fedorov **Obv:** Apostol book page and large quill pin **Rev:** Ivan Fedorov portrait facing

Date	Mintage	F	VF	XF	Unc	BU
2010 Proof	5,000	Value: 80.00				

KM# 601 5 HRYVEN

16.5400 g., Copper-Nickel-Zinc, 35 mm. **Subject:** Maritime History **Obv:** Banner seperating compas rose and seal of the Zaporohian Host **Rev:** Cossack boat of the 18th century

Date	Mintage	F	VF	XF	Unc	BU
2010	45,000	—	—	—	—	15.00

KM# 604 5 HRYVEN

16.5000 g., Copper-Nickel-Zinc, 35 mm. **Subject:** Folk Crafts - Potter **Obv:** Pottery flanking central pattern **Rev:** Potter at wheel **Edge:** Reeded

Date	Mintage	F	VF	XF	Unc	BU
2010	45,000	—	—	—	—	15.00

KM# 653 5 HRYVEN

7.7800 g., 0.9999 Gold 0.2501 oz. AGW, 20 mm. **Obv:** Logo of the Ukraine National Bank **Rev:** Archangel Michael

Date	Mintage	F	VF	XF	Unc	BU
2011	3,000	—	—	—	—	550
2012	2,000	—	—	—	—	500

KM# 611 5 HRYVEN

16.8200 g., 0.9250 Silver 0.5002 oz. ASW, 33 mm. **Subject:** Pavlo Tychyna **Obv:** View of family homestead, mallow flowers, national arms **Rev:** Portrait with books **Edge:** lettered, incuse **Edge Lettering:** .925 15.55

Date	Mintage	F	VF	XF	Unc	BU
2011 Proof	5,000	Value: 80.00				

KM# 610 5 HRYVEN

16.8200 g., 0.9250 Silver 0.5002 oz. ASW, 33 mm. **Subject:** Year of the Cat **Obv:** National arms, value and floral design **Rev:** Playful cat with green alpinites in eyes **Edge:** Reeded

Date	Mintage	F	VF	XF	Unc	BU
2011 Proof	20,000	Value: 80.00				

KM# 613 5 HRYVEN

16.8200 g., 0.9250 Silver 0.5002 oz. ASW, 33 mm. **Subject:** Ivan Franko National University, Lviv, 350th Anniversary **Obv:** National arms, statuary group, value **Rev:** Main Building façade **Edge Lettering:** .925 15.55 (Mint logo)

Date	Mintage	F	VF	XF	Unc	BU
2011 Proof	7,000	Value: 80.00				

KM# 615 5 HRYVEN

16.5400 g., Copper-Nickel-Zinc, 35 mm. **Obv:** Blacksmith items, two birds **Rev:** Blacksmith at work **Edge:** Reeded

Date	Mintage	F	VF	XF	Unc	BU
2011	45,000	—	—	—	—	15.00

KM# 618 5 HRYVEN

16.8200 g., 0.9250 Silver 0.5002 oz. ASW, 33 mm. **Subject:** Heorhii Berehovyi **Obv:** Spacecraft launch, in orbit, sun **Rev:** Bust facing

Date	Mintage	F	VF	XF	Unc	BU
2011 Proof	5,000	Value: 90.00				

KM# 619 5 HRYVEN

16.5400 g., Copper-Nickel-Zinc, 35 mm. **Subject:** Taras Shevchenko, 150th Anniversary of Death **Obv:** Shevchenko's monument **Rev:** Portrait **Edge:** Reeded

Date	Mintage	F	VF	XF	Unc	BU
2011	35,000	—	—	—	—	15.00

KM# 620 5 HRYVEN

16.8200 g., 0.9250 Silver 0.5002 oz. ASW, 33 mm. **Subject:** Okeksandr Bohomolets **Obv:** Hands of an adult and child **Rev:** Portrait of Bohomolets

Date	Mintage	F	VF	XF	Unc	BU
2011 Proof	5,000	Value: 80.00				

KM# 621 5 HRYVEN

16.5400 g., Copper-Nickel-Zinc, 35 mm. **Subject:** Taras Shevchenko National Prize of Ukraine, 50th Anniversary **Obv:** Open book, quill, palette, brushes and National Arms **Rev:** Shevchenko Portrait **Edge:** Reeded

Date	Mintage	F	VF	XF	Unc	BU
2011	35,000	—	—	—	—	15.00

KM# 622 5 HRYVEN

16.5400 g., Copper-Nickel-Zinc, 35 mm. **Subject:** Constitution, 15th Anniversary **Obv:** National flag in color within wreath **Rev:** Book of the Constitution and Verkhjovna Rada building **Edge:** Reeded

Date	Mintage	F	VF	XF	Unc	BU
2011	30,000	—	—	—	—	16.00

KM# 623 5 HRYVEN

16.5400 g., Copper-Nickel-Zinc, 35 mm. **Subject:** Zbarazh, 800th Anniversary **Obv:** Jerusalem cross on wall of Our Saviour's Transfiguration Church **Rev:** Gate of the Zbarazh Castle **Edge:** Reeded

Date	Mintage	F	VF	XF	Unc	BU
2011	35,000	—	—	—	—	15.00

KM# 625 5 HRYVEN

16.5400 g., Copper-Nickel-Zinc, 35 mm. **Obv:** Baroque design from Church **Rev:** St. Andrew's Church **Edge:** Reeded

Date	Mintage	F	VF	XF	Unc	BU
2011	45,000	—	—	—	—	15.00

KM# 627 5 HRYVEN

16.5400 g., Copper-Nickel-Zinc, 35 mm. **Obv:** Couple in a dance **Rev:** Hopak folk dance **Edge:** Reeded

Date	Mintage	F	VF	XF	Unc	BU
2011	45,000	—	—	—	—	15.00

KM# 629 5 HRYVEN

16.5400 g., Copper-Nickel-Zinc, 35 mm. **Subject:** Independence, 20th anniversary **Obv:** National arms, rushnyks and portraits **Rev:** Legend **Edge:** Reeded

Date	Mintage	F	VF	XF	Unc	BU
2011	45,000	—	—	—	—	17.00

KM# 634 5 HRYVEN

16.8200 g., 0.9250 Silver 0.5002 oz. ASW, 33 mm. **Subject:** Mykhailo Yangel, 100th Anniversary of Birth **Obv:** Kosmos launch and satellite, earth in background **Rev:** Yangel portrait

Date	Mintage	F	VF	XF	Unc	BU
2011 Proof	5,000	Value: 90.00				

KM# 635 5 HRYVEN

16.8200 g., 0.9250 Silver 0.5002 oz. ASW, 33 mm. **Subject:** Liudmyla Vasylevska, 150th Anniversary of Birth **Obv:** Girl near the sea **Rev:** Vasylevska portrait

Date	Mintage	F	VF	XF	Unc	BU
2011 Proof	5,000	Value: 80.00				

KM# 638 5 HRYVEN

9.4000 g., Bi-Metallic, 28 mm. **Subject:** International year of Forests **Obv:** Conceptual tree **Rev:** Tree in leaf **Edge:** Segmented reeding

Date	Mintage	F	VF	XF	Unc	BU
2011	30,000	—	—	—	—	16.00

KM# 639 5 HRYVEN

16.8200 g., 0.9250 Silver 0.5002 oz. ASW, 33 mm. **Subject:** International Year of Forests **Obv:** Two birds sitting on branches **Rev:** Hand-like branches extended to the Sun

Date	Mintage	F	VF	XF	Unc	BU
2011 Antique finish	3,000	Value: 100				

KM# 645 5 HRYVEN

16.8200 g., 0.9250 Silver 0.5002 oz. ASW, 33 mm. **Subject:** Year of the Dragon **Obv:** National arms **Rev:** Dragon with orange zirconia crystals in eyes

Date	Mintage	F	VF	XF	Unc	BU
2011 Proof	20,000	Value: 80.00				

KM# 647 5 HRYVEN

16.5400 g., Copper-Nickel-Zinc, 35 mm. **Subject:** UEFA Euro 2012 Final Tournament **Obv:** Players superimposed on large 2012 in background **Rev:** UEFA logo and map of europe

Date	Mintage	F	VF	XF	Unc	BU
2011	100,000	—	—	—	—	15.00

KM# 648 5 HRYVEN

16.5400 g., 0.9250 Copper-Nickel-Zinc 0.4919 oz., 35 mm. **Subject:** UEFA Euro 2012 Final Tournament **Obv:** Two players wthin stadium **Rev:** Logo and map of Ukraine

Date	Mintage	F	VF	XF	Unc	BU
2011	100,000	—	—	—	—	15.00

KM# 649 5 HRYVEN

16.5400 g., Copper-Nickel-Zinc, 35 mm. **Subject:** UEFA Euro 2012 Final Tournament **Obv:** UEFA logo and map of the Ukraine **Rev:** Soccer plater and Lviv stadium

Date	Mintage	F	VF	XF	Unc	BU
2011	100,000	—	—	—	—	15.00

KM# 650 5 HRYVEN

16.5400 g., Copper-Nickel-Zinc, 35 mm. **Subject:** UEFA Euro 2012 Final Tournament **Obv:** UEFA logo and map of the Ukraine **Rev:** Two soccer players and Metalist Stadium, Kharkiv

Date	Mintage	F	VF	XF	Unc	BU
2011	100,000	—	—	—	—	15.00

KM# 651 5 HRYVEN

16.5400 g., Copper-Nickel-Zinc, 35 mm. **Subject:** UEFA Euro 2012 Final Tournament **Obv:** UEFA logo and map of the Ukraine **Rev:** Soccer player and Donbass Arena, Donetsk

Date	Mintage	F	VF	XF	Unc	BU
2011	100,000	—	—	—	—	15.00

KM# 655 5 HRYVEN

16.8200 g., 0.9250 Silver 0.5002 oz. ASW, 33 mm. **Subject:** Eugene Grebinka **Obv:** Cossack horseman **Rev:** Grebinka portrait

Date	Mintage	F	VF	XF	Unc	BU
2011 Proof	3,000	Value: 85.00				

KM# 515 10 HRYVNI

33.6220 g., 0.9250 Silver 0.9999 oz. ASW, 38.6 mm. **Subject:** The Annunciation **Edge:** Reeded

Date	Mintage	F	VF	XF	Unc	BU
2008 Proof	8,000	Value: 95.00				

KM# 113 10 HRYVEN
33.6220 g., 0.9250 Silver 0.9999 oz. ASW, 38.61 mm. **Subject:** Ivan Mazepa (Cossack leader) **Obv:** Arms with supporters within beaded circle **Rev:** Half figure divides beaded circle flanked by palace and oval shield **Edge:** Reeded

Date	Mintage	F	VF	XF	Unc	BU
2001 Proof	5,000	Value: 200				

KM# 114 10 HRYVEN
33.6220 g., 0.9250 Silver 0.9999 oz. ASW, 38.61 mm. **Subject:** Great Prince Yaroslav the Wise **Obv:** Value within grape wreath **Rev:** Mosaic head facing, half length figure facing holding scroll and dome building **Edge:** Reeded

Date	Mintage	F	VF	XF	Unc	BU
2001 Proof	3,000	Value: 1,400				

KM# 115 10 HRYVEN
33.6220 g., 0.9250 Silver 0.9999 oz. ASW, 38.61 mm. **Series:** Ukranian Flora and Fauna **Obv:** National arms and date divides wreath, value within **Rev:** Lynx with offspring **Edge:** Reeded

Date	Mintage	F	VF	XF	Unc	BU
2001 Proof	3,000	Value: 475				

KM# 130 10 HRYVEN
33.6220 g., 0.9250 Silver 0.9999 oz. ASW, 38.61 mm. **Subject:** 10th Anniversary - National Bank **Obv:** National arms and value between arches **Rev:** Large building entrance **Edge:** Reeded

Date	Mintage	F	VF	XF	Unc	BU
2001 Proof	3,000	Value: 250				

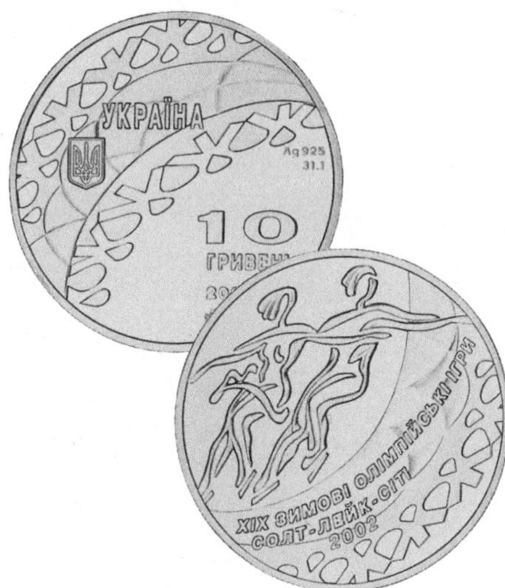

KM# 131 10 HRYVEN
33.6220 g., 0.9250 Silver 0.9999 oz. ASW, 38.61 mm. **Series:** Olympics **Obv:** National arms and value on ice **Rev:** Stylized ice dancing couple **Edge:** Reeded

Date	Mintage	F	VF	XF	Unc	BU
2001 Proof	15,000	Value: 100				

KM# 141 10 HRYVEN
33.6220 g., 0.9250 Silver 0.9999 oz. ASW, 38.61 mm. **Subject:** Flora and Fauna **Obv:** National arms and date divides wreath, value within **Rev:** Pine branch with cone **Edge:** Reeded

Date	Mintage	F	VF	XF	Unc	BU
2001 Proof	3,000	Value: 350				

KM# 142 10 HRYVEN
33.6220 g., 0.9250 Silver 0.9999 oz. ASW, 38.61 mm. **Subject:** Khan Palace in Bakhchisarai **Obv:** Value in arch **Rev:** Courtyard view **Edge:** Reeded

Date	Mintage	F	VF	XF	Unc	BU
2001 Proof	3,000	Value: 400				

KM# 143 10 HRYVEN
4.3110 g., 0.9000 Gold 0.1247 oz. AGW, 16 mm. **Subject:** 10 Years Independence **Obv:** National arms **Rev:** Parliament building on map **Edge:** Plain

Date	Mintage	F	VF	XF	Unc	BU
2001 Proof	3,000	Value: 1,100				

KM# 165 10 HRYVEN
33.6220 g., 0.9250 Silver 0.9999 oz. ASW, 38.61 mm. **Subject:** Olympics **Obv:** National arms and value on ice **Rev:** Stylized hockey player **Edge:** Reeded

Date	Mintage	F	VF	XF	Unc	BU
2001 Proof	15,000	Value: 100				

KM# 229 10 HRYVEN
33.6220 g., 0.9250 Silver 0.9999 oz. ASW, 38.61 mm. **Obv:** National arms and date divides wreath, value within **Rev:** Eurasian Eagle Owl on branch **Edge:** Reeded

Date	Mintage	F	VF	XF	Unc	BU
2002 Proof	3,000	Value: 650				

KM# 145 10 HRYVEN

33.6220 g., 0.9250 Silver 0.9999 oz. ASW, 38.61 mm. **Subject:** Ivan Sirko **Obv:** Arms with supporters within beaded circle **Rev:** Cossack battle scene divides beaded circle **Edge:** Reeded

Date	Mintage	F	VF	XF	Unc	BU
2002 Proof	3,000	Value: 400				

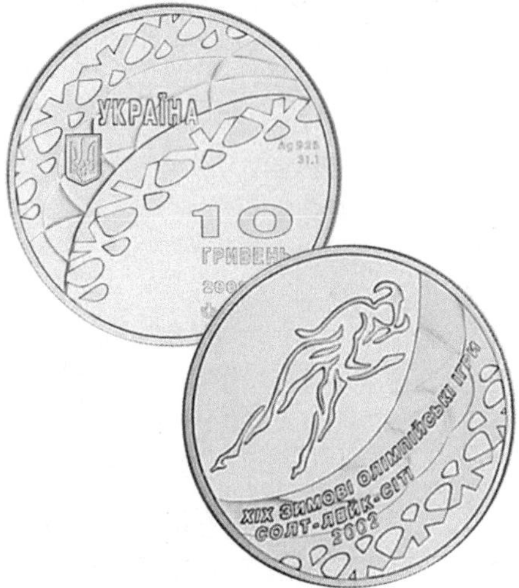

KM# 146 10 HRYVEN

33.6220 g., 0.9250 Silver 0.9999 oz. ASW, 38.61 mm. **Obv:** National arms and value on ice **Rev:** Stylized speed skater **Edge:** Reeded

Date	Mintage	F	VF	XF	Unc	BU
2002 Proof	3,000	Value: 150				

KM# 160 10 HRYVEN

33.9500 g., 0.9250 Silver 1.0096 oz. ASW, 38.61 mm. **Obv:** Value encircled by angels flanked by stars **Rev:** Steepled church and tower **Edge:** Reeded

Date	Mintage	F	VF	XF	Unc	BU
2002 Proof	3,000	Value: 375				

KM# 161 10 HRYVEN

33.6220 g., 0.9250 Silver 0.9999 oz. ASW, 38.61 mm. **Subject:** Grand Prince Vladimir Monomakh **Obv:** Value within jewelry design **Rev:** Bust holding book flanked by buildings and St. George **Edge:** Reeded

Date	Mintage	F	VF	XF	Unc	BU
2002 Proof	3,000	Value: 550				

KM# 162 10 HRYVEN

33.6220 g., 0.9250 Silver 0.9999 oz. ASW, 38.61 mm. **Subject:** Prince Svyatoslav **Obv:** Value in ornate design **Rev:** Armored half length figure facing **Edge:** Reeded

Date	Mintage	F	VF	XF	Unc	BU
2002 Proof	3,000	Value: 550				

KM# 164 10 HRYVEN

33.6220 g., 0.9250 Silver 0.9999 oz. ASW, 38.61 mm. **Subject:** Christmas **Obv:** National arms within star above value **Rev:** Christmas pageant scene **Edge:** Reeded

Date	Mintage	F	VF	XF	Unc	BU
2002 Proof	3,000	Value: 600				

KM# 176 10 HRYVEN

33.6220 g., 0.9250 Silver 0.9999 oz. ASW, 38.61 mm. **Subject:** Olympics **Obv:** Two ancient women with seedlings **Rev:** Swimmer **Edge:** Reeded

Date	Mintage	F	VF	XF	Unc	BU
2002 Proof	15,000	Value: 100				

KM# 177 10 HRYVEN

33.6220 g., 0.9250 Silver 0.9999 oz. ASW, 38.61 mm. **Subject:** Hetman Pylyp Orlik 1672-1742 **Obv:** Arms with supporters within beaded circle **Rev:** Standing figure facing holding scroll flanked by other standing figures **Edge:** Reeded

Date	Mintage	F	VF	XF	Unc	BU
2002 Proof	3,000	Value: 350				

KM# 198 10 HRYVEN

33.6220 g., 0.9250 Silver 0.9999 oz. ASW, 38.61 mm. **Obv:** National arms and date divides wreath, value within **Rev:** European bison **Edge:** Reeded

Date	Mintage	F	VF	XF	Unc	BU
2003 Proof	2,000	Value: 600				

KM# 189 10 HRYVEN
33.6220 g., 0.9250 Silver 0.9999 oz. ASW, 38.61 mm. **Subject:** Olympics **Obv:** Two ancient women with seedlings **Rev:** Boxer **Edge:** Reeded

Date	Mintage	F	VF	XF	Unc	BU
2003 Proof	15,000	Value: 100				

KM# 190 10 HRYVEN
33.6220 g., 0.9250 Silver 0.9999 oz. ASW, 38.61 mm. **Obv:** Fancy art work and sculpture **Rev:** Livadia Palace view **Edge:** Reeded

Date	Mintage	F	VF	XF	Unc	BU
2003 Proof	3,000	Value: 300				

KM# 191 10 HRYVEN
33.6220 g., 0.9250 Silver 0.9999 oz. ASW, 38.61 mm. **Obv:** National arms on sun, flying geese divides beaded circle **Rev:** Antonov AN-2 biplane divides beaded circle **Edge:** Reeded

Date	Mintage	F	VF	XF	Unc	BU
2003 Proof	3,000	Value: 320				

KM# 192 10 HRYVEN
33.6220 g., 0.9250 Silver 0.9999 oz. ASW, 38.61 mm. **Obv:** Easter eggs around arms above value **Rev:** Easter celebration **Edge:** Reeded

Date	Mintage	F	VF	XF	Unc	BU
2003 Proof	3,000	Value: 500				

KM# 193 10 HRYVEN
33.6220 g., 0.9250 Silver 0.9999 oz. ASW, 38.61 mm. **Obv:** Angels, national arms and value **Rev:** The protection of the Virgin Mary over the Pochayiv Lavra (Monastery) **Edge:** Reeded

Date	Mintage	F	VF	XF	Unc	BU
2003 Proof	Est. 8,000	Value: 200				

KM# 194 10 HRYVEN
33.6220 g., 0.9250 Silver 0.9999 oz. ASW, 38.61 mm. **Obv:** National arms and date divide wreath, value within **Rev:** Long-snouted seahorse **Edge:** Reeded

Date	Mintage	F	VF	XF	Unc	BU
2003 Proof	2,000	Value: 750				

KM# 195 10 HRYVEN
33.6220 g., 0.9250 Silver 0.9999 oz. ASW, 38.61 mm. **Subject:** Kyrylo Rozumovskyi (Cossack leader) **Obv:** Arms with supporters within beaded circle **Rev:** Half length figure 1/4 left within beaded circle **Edge:** Reeded

Date	Mintage	F	VF	XF	Unc	BU
2003 Proof	3,000	Value: 350				

KM# 196 10 HRYVEN
33.6220 g., 0.9250 Silver 0.9999 oz. ASW, 38.61 mm. **Subject:** Pavlo Polubotok (Cossack leader) **Obv:** Arms with supporters within beaded circle **Rev:** Half length figure within beaded circle **Edge:** Reeded

Date	Mintage	F	VF	XF	Unc	BU
2003 Proof	3,000	Value: 375				

KM# 197 10 HRYVEN
33.6220 g., 0.9250 Silver 0.9999 oz. ASW, 38.61 mm. **Obv:** Map, national arms and value **Rev:** Genoese Fortress in Sudak **Edge:** Reeded

Date	Mintage	F	VF	XF	Unc	BU
2003 Proof	3,000	Value: 300				

KM# 206 10 HRYVEN
33.9100 g., 0.9250 Silver 1.0084 oz. ASW, 38.61 mm. **Subject:** Azov Dolphin **Obv:** National arms and date divides wreath, value within **Rev:** Harbor Porpoises **Edge:** Reeded

Date	Mintage	F	VF	XF	Unc	BU
2004 Proof	8,000	Value: 150				

KM# 207 10 HRYVEN
33.9100 g., 0.9250 Silver 1.0084 oz. ASW, 38.61 mm. **Subject:** Football World Cup - 2006 **Obv:** Soccer ball in net **Rev:** Two soccer players **Edge:** Reeded

Date	Mintage	F	VF	XF	Unc	BU
2004 Proof	50,000	Value: 200				

KM# 223 10 HRYVEN
33.9100 g., 0.9250 Silver 1.0084 oz. ASW, 38.61 mm. **Obv:** National arms on sun, flying geese and value divides beaded circle **Rev:** AH-140 Airliner divides beaded circle **Edge:** Reeded

Date	Mintage	F	VF	XF	Unc	BU
2004 Proof	10,000	Value: 170				

KM# 224 10 HRYVEN
33.9100 g., 0.9250 Silver 1.0084 oz. ASW, 38.61 mm. **Subject:** Ice Breaker "Captain Belousov" **Obv:** National arms on ship's wheel and anchor **Rev:** Ice breaker ship **Edge:** Reeded

Date	Mintage	F	VF	XF	Unc	BU
2004 Proof	10,000	Value: 100				

KM# 225 10 HRYVEN
33.6220 g., 0.9250 Silver 0.9999 oz. ASW, 38.61 mm. **Subject:** Whit Sunday **Obv:** National arms within wreath above value flanked by sprigs **Rev:** Four women folk dancers and child **Edge:** Reeded

Date	Mintage	F	VF	XF	Unc	BU
2004 Proof	10,000	Value: 300				

KM# 339 10 HRYVEN
33.6220 g., 0.9250 Silver 0.9999 oz. ASW, 38.61 mm. **Subject:** Ostrozhsky Family **Obv:** Our Lady of Duben and Elias Icon **Rev:** Three cameos above crowned shield **Edge:** Reeded

Date	Mintage	F	VF	XF	Unc	BU
2004 Proof	3,000	Value: 270				

KM# 340 10 HRYVEN
33.6220 g., 0.9250 Silver 0.9999 oz. ASW, 38.61 mm. **Subject:** St. Yura Cathedral **Obv:** Statue of St. George on horse killing dragon **Rev:** Cathedral **Edge:** Reeded

Date	Mintage	F	VF	XF	Unc	BU
ND (2004) Proof	8,000	Value: 120				

KM# 342 10 HRYVEN
33.6220 g., 0.9250 Silver 0.9999 oz. ASW, 38.61 mm. **Subject:** Defense of Sevastopol 1854-56 **Obv:** National arms and value above fortifications map **Rev:** Cannon and ships **Edge:** Reeded

Date	Mintage	F	VF	XF	Unc	BU
2004 Proof	10,000	Value: 120				

KM# 343 10 HRYVEN
33.6220 g., 0.9250 Silver 0.9999 oz. ASW, 38.61 mm. **Subject:** Perejaslav Cossack Rada of 1654 **Obv:** National arms above value **Rev:** Standing figures facing **Edge:** Reeded

Date	Mintage	F	VF	XF	Unc	BU
2004 Proof	8,000	Value: 160				

KM# 358 10 HRYVEN
33.6220 g., 0.9250 Silver 0.9999 oz. ASW, 38.61 mm. **Subject:** Spalax Arenarius Reshetnik **Obv:** National arms and date divides wreath, value within **Rev:** Sandy mole rat **Edge:** Reeded

Date	Mintage	F	VF	XF	Unc	BU
2005 Proof	8,000	Value: 110				

KM# 367 10 HRYVEN
33.6220 g., 0.9250 Silver 0.9999 oz. ASW, 38.61 mm. **Subject:** The Protection of the Virgin **Obv:** National arms on Cossack regalia **Rev:** Wedding scene **Edge:** Reeded

Date	Mintage	F	VF	XF	Unc	BU
2005 Proof	8,000	Value: 150				

KM# 370 10 HRYVEN
33.6220 g., 0.9250 Silver 0.9999 oz. ASW, 38.61 mm. **Subject:** 60 Years UN Membership **Obv:** National arms, value and olive branch **Rev:** UN logo above partial globe **Edge:** Reeded

Date	Mintage	F	VF	XF	Unc	BU
2005 Proof	5,000	Value: 100				

KM# 371 10 HRYVEN
33.6220 g., 0.9250 Silver 0.9999 oz. ASW, 38.61 mm. **Subject:** National Anthem **Obv:** Musical score, national arms, value and date **Rev:** Coiled legend around holographic flower **Edge:** Reeded

Date	Mintage	F	VF	XF	Unc	BU
2005 Proof	3,000	Value: 300				

KM# 372 10 HRYVEN
33.6220 g., 0.9250 Silver 0.9999 oz. ASW, 38.61 mm. **Subject:** 100 Years of Olga Kobylianska Music and Drama Theatre in Chernivtsi **Obv:** Statue **Rev:** Theater **Edge:** Reeded

Date	Mintage	F	VF	XF	Unc	BU
2005 Proof	5,000	Value: 100				

KM# 373 10 HRYVEN
33.6220 g., 0.9250 Silver 0.9999 oz. ASW, 38.61 mm. **Subject:** Sviatohirsky Lavra Monastery **Obv:** Madonna and child flanked by angels **Rev:** Monastery on river bank **Edge:** Reeded

Date	Mintage	F	VF	XF	Unc	BU
2005 Proof	8,000	Value: 130				

KM# 381 10 HRYVEN
33.8600 g., 0.9250 Silver 1.0069 oz. ASW, 38.61 mm. **Subject:** Baturyn Hetman Capital City **Obv:** National arms within sun rays, value flanked by standing figures **Rev:** Four cameos and banner above city view **Edge:** Reeded

Date	Mintage	F	VF	XF	Unc	BU
2005 Proof	5,000	Value: 120				

KM# 382 10 HRYVEN
33.8600 g., 0.9250 Silver 1.0069 oz. ASW, 38.61 mm. **Subject:** Symyrenko Family **Obv:** Country name below national arms within sprigs **Rev:** Family tree **Edge:** Reeded

Date	Mintage	F	VF	XF	Unc	BU
2005 Proof	5,000	Value: 100				

KM# 392 10 HRYVEN
33.6220 g., 0.9250 Silver 0.9999 oz. ASW, 38.61 mm. **Obv:** National arms above value in wreath **Rev:** Grasshopper **Edge:** Reeded

Date	Mintage	F	VF	XF	Unc	BU
2006 Proof	8,000	Value: 150				

KM# 424 10 HRYVEN
33.6221 g., 0.9250 Silver 0.9999 oz. ASW, 38.61 mm. **Subject:** Chyhyryn **Obv:** National arms

Date	Mintage	F	VF	XF	Unc	BU
2006 Proof	5,000	Value: 120				

KM# 425 10 HRYVEN
33.6220 g., 0.9250 Silver 0.9999 oz. ASW, 38.61 mm. **Subject:** 10 Years of the Clearing House **Obv:** National arms

Date	Mintage	F	VF	XF	Unc	BU
2006 Proof	5,000	Value: 100				

KM# 410 10 HRYVEN
33.6220 g., 0.9250 Silver 0.9999 oz. ASW, 38.61 mm. **Subject:** 10 Years of the Constitution of Ukraine **Obv:** National arms

Date	Mintage	F	VF	XF	Unc	BU
2006 Proof	5,000	Value: 100				

KM# 421 10 HRYVEN
33.6200 g., 0.9250 Silver 0.9998 oz. ASW, 38.61 mm. **Subject:** Epiphany **Obv:** National arms **Edge:** Reeded

Date	Mintage	F	VF	XF	Unc	BU
2006 Proof	10,000	Value: 120				

KM# 423 10 HRYVEN
33.6220 g., 0.9250 Silver 0.9999 oz. ASW, 38.61 mm. **Subject:** Saint Kyryl Church **Obv:** National arms **Edge:** Reeded

Date	Mintage	F	VF	XF	Unc	BU
2006 Proof	8,000	Value: 120				

KM# 427 10 HRYVEN
33.6220 g., 0.9250 Silver 0.9999 oz. ASW, 38.61 mm. **Subject:** Twentieth Winter Olympic Games of 2006 **Obv:** National arms **Edge:** Reeded

Date	Mintage	F	VF	XF	Unc	BU
2006 Proof	5,000	Value: 100				

KM# 466 10 HRYVEN
33.6220 g., 0.9250 Silver 0.9999 oz. ASW, 38.6 mm. **Subject:** Odessa National Opera and Ballet, 120th Anniversary **Obv:** Interior view from stage **Rev:** Opera house in Odessa **Edge:** Reeded

Date	Mintage	F	VF	XF	Unc	BU
2007 Proof	5,000	Value: 100				

KM# 467 10 HRYVEN
33.6220 g., 0.9250 Silver 0.9999 oz. ASW, 38.61 mm. **Subject:** Ivan Bohun **Edge:** Reeded

Date	Mintage	F	VF	XF	Unc	BU
2007 Proof	5,000	Value: 110				

KM# 516 10 HRYVEN
33.6220 g., 0.9250 Silver 0.9999 oz. ASW, 38.61 mm. **Subject:** Black Griffin **Edge:** Reeded

Date	Mintage	F	VF	XF	Unc	BU
2008 Proof	7,000	Value: 120				

KM# 517 10 HRYVEN
33.6220 g., 0.9250 Silver 0.9999 oz. ASW, 38.61 mm. **Subject:** Sevastopol, 225th Anniversary **Edge:** Reeded

Date	Mintage	F	VF	XF	Unc	BU
2008 Proof	5,000	Value: 100				

KM# 518 10 HRYVEN
33.6220 g., 0.9250 Silver 0.9999 oz. ASW, 38.61 mm. **Subject:** Swallow's Nest **Edge:** Reeded

Date	Mintage	F	VF	XF	Unc	BU
2008 Proof	5,000	Value: 110				

KM# 519 10 HRYVEN
33.6220 g., 0.9250 Silver 0.9999 oz. ASW, 38.61 mm. **Subject:** Tereschenko Family **Edge:** Reeded

Date	Mintage	F	VF	XF	Unc	BU
2008 Proof	7,000	Value: 100				

KM# 520 10 HRYVEN
33.6220 g., 0.9250 Silver 0.9999 oz. ASW, 38.61 mm. **Subject:** Ukranian Swedish Alliances XVII-XVIII Century **Edge:** Reeded

Date	Mintage	F	VF	XF	Unc	BU
2008 Proof	5,000	Value: 110				

KM# 521 10 HRYVEN
33.6220 g., 0.9250 Silver 0.9999 oz. ASW, 38.61 mm. **Subject:** Hlukhiv **Edge:** Reeded

Date	Mintage	F	VF	XF	Unc	BU
2008 Proof	7,000	Value: 100				

KM# 522 10 HRYVEN
33.6220 g., 0.9250 Silver 0.9999 oz. ASW, 38.61 mm. **Subject:** UNESCO World Heritage Site - LVIV **Edge:** Reeded

Date	Mintage	F	VF	XF	Unc	BU
2008 Proof	5,000	Value: 120				

KM# 523 10 HRYVEN
33.6220 g., 0.9250 Silver 0.9999 oz. ASW, 38.61 mm. **Subject:** Cathedral in Buky Village **Edge:** Reeded

Date	Mintage	F	VF	XF	Unc	BU
2008 Proof	5,000	Value: 150				

KM# 532 10 HRYVEN
33.6220 g., 0.9250 Silver 0.9999 oz. ASW, 38.61 mm. **Subject:** Annunciation **Obv:** Conventionalized setting of the Gospel, lilies. **Obv. Legend:** НАЦІОНАЛЬНИЈ БАНК УКРАІНИ - 10 ГРИВЕНЬ **Rev:** Annunciation scene. **Rev. Legend:** БЛАГОВІЩЕННЯ **Edge:** Reeded

Date	Mintage	F	VF	XF	Unc	BU
2008 Proof	8,000	Value: 110				

KM# 556 10 HRYVEN
33.6220 g., 0.9250 Silver 0.9999 oz. ASW, 38.61 mm. **Subject:** Folk Crafts of the Ukraine - Bokorash (Raftsmen) **Obv:** Two birds, Carpathian landscape, trees, cottages, logs **Obv. Legend:** НАЦІОНАЛЬНИЈ БАНК УКРА?НИ - 10/ ГРИВЕНЬ/ 2009 **Rev:** Bokorash directing raft **Rev. Legend:** БОКОРАШ

Date	Mintage	F	VF	XF	Unc	BU
2009 Proof	Est. 10,000	Value: 100				

KM# 559 10 HRYVEN
33.6220 g., 0.9250 Silver 0.9999 oz. ASW, 38.61 mm. **Subject:** Surb Khach Monastery **Obv:** National Arms, vegitation ornament pattern **Obv. Legend:** НАЦІОНАЛЬНИЈ БАНК УКРАІНИ - ДЕСЯТЬ ГРИВЕНЬ **Rev:** Monastery buildings **Rev. Legend:** СТАРИЈ КРИМ - ВІРМЕНСЬКИЈ МОНАСТИР XIV СТ. - СУРБ ХАЧ **Edge:** Segmented reeding

Date	Mintage	F	VF	XF	Unc	BU
2009 Proof	Est. 10,000	Value: 95.00				

KM# 560 10 HRYVEN
33.6220 g., 0.9250 Silver 0.9999 oz. ASW, 38.61 mm. **Subject:** Battle of Konotop, 350th Anniversary **Obv:** Hetman's Insignia, Cossack arms and bandura, National Arms. **Obv. Legend:** НАЦІОНАЛЬНИЈ БАНК УКРАІНИ - 10 / ГРИВЬН **Rev:** Ivan Vyhovskyi with sabre, Cossacks, Konotop fortifications, banners. **Rev. Legend:** ПЕРЕМОГА В КОНОТОПСЬКІЈ БИТВІ - 350 РОКІВ

Date	Mintage	F	VF	XF	Unc	BU
2009 Proof	8,000	Value: 100				

KM# 561 10 HRYVEN
33.6220 g., 0.9250 Silver 0.9999 oz. ASW, 38.61 mm. **Subject:** Church of the Holy Spirit in Rogatyn **Obv:** Church Icon with candelabra flanking, National Arms **Rev:** Church facade

Date	Mintage	F	VF	XF	Unc	BU
2009 Proof	Est. 10,000	Value: 100				

KM# 562 10 HRYVEN
33.6220 g., 0.9250 Silver 0.9999 oz. ASW, 38.61 mm. **Subject:** Famous Ukranian Families - Galagan Family **Obv:** The family estate, National Arms, value **Rev:** Galagan's College building and three portraits

Date	Mintage	F	VF	XF	Unc	BU
2009 Proof	7,000	Value: 95.00				

KM# 563 10 HRYVEN
33.6220 g., 0.9250 Silver 0.9999 oz. ASW, 38.61 mm. **Subject:** Kiev Academy of Operatta Theater, 75th Anniversary **Obv:** Dance scene, National Arms, value **Obv. Legend:** НАЦІОНАЛЬНИЈ БАНК УКРАІНИ - 10 / ГРИВЬ / 2009 **Rev:** Theater building, operetta character silhouettes. **Rev. Legend:** КИЇВСЬКИЈ АКАДЕМІЧНИЈ ТЕАТР ОПЕРЕТИ - 75/РОКІВ

Date	Mintage	F	VF	XF	Unc	BU
2009 Proof	5,000	Value: 95.00				

KM# 574 10 HRYVEN
31.1000 g., 0.9250 Silver 0.9249 oz. ASW, 38.61 mm. **Subject:** Ukrainian folk craft - Cartwright **Obv:** Wagon and wheels **Rev:** Woodcraftsman hewing wood to make a cart detail **Edge:** Reeded

Date	Mintage	F	VF	XF	Unc	BU
2009	10,000	—	—	—	—	100

KM# 570 10 HRYVEN
31.1000 g., 0.9250 Silver 0.9249 oz. ASW, 38.6 mm. **Subject:** Pulyp Oriyk Constitution, 300th Anniversary **Obv:** Hetman and Cossack officials **Rev:** Pylyp Orlyk, quill pen and constitution

Date	Mintage	F	VF	XF	Unc	BU
2010 Proof	7,000	Value: 95.00				

KM# 575 10 HRYVEN
31.1000 g., 0.9250 Silver 0.9249 oz. ASW, 38.61 mm. **Subject:** Vancouver Winter Olympics **Obv:** Winter scene **Rev:** Snowflake, sport figures, downhill skier at left

Date	Mintage	F	VF	XF	Unc	BU
2010 Proof	8,000	Value: 95.00				

KM# 586 10 HRYVEN
31.1000 g., 0.9250 Silver 0.9249 oz. ASW, 38.61 mm. **Obv:** Icon of Our Lady of Zarvanytsia **Rev:** Cathedral of Our Lady of Zarvanytsia

Date	Mintage	F	VF	XF	Unc	BU
2010	7,000	Value: 95.00				

KM# 588 10 HRYVEN
31.1000 g., 0.9250 Silver 0.9249 oz. ASW, 38.61 mm. **Subject:** Folk Crafts - Weaving **Obv:** Spinning wheel and weaving products **Rev:** Woman working at a loom

Date	Mintage	F	VF	XF	Unc	BU
2010 Proof, Antique finish	10,000	Value: 100				

KM# 590 10 HRYVEN
31.1000 g., 0.9250 Silver 0.9249 oz. ASW, 38.61 mm. **Subject:** Ukraine Spas **Obv:** Two cornucopiae and Savior's fest **Rev:** Peasants getting food gifts blessed

Date	Mintage	F	VF	XF	Unc	BU
2010 Proof	—	Value: 100				

KM# 594 10 HRYVEN
31.1000 g., 0.9250 Silver 0.9249 oz. ASW, 38.61 mm. **Subject:** Flora and Fauna **Obv:** National Arms and wreath **Rev:** Stipa Ucrainica, feather grass

Date	Mintage	F	VF	XF	Unc	BU
2010 Proof	8,000	Value: 95.00				

KM# 600 10 HRYVEN
31.1000 g., 0.9250 Silver 0.9249 oz. ASW, 38.61 mm. **Subject:** Hetman Danylo Apostol **Obv:** National arms, Archangel Michael and Crowned lion (Symbols of Kyiv and Lviv) **Rev:** Danylo Apostol half length figure holding scep-tre

Date	Mintage	F	VF	XF	Unc	BU
2010 Proof	8,000	Value: 95.00				

KM# 605 10 HRYVEN
31.1000 g., 0.9250 Silver 0.9249 oz. ASW, 38.61 mm. **Subject:** Folk Crafts - Potter **Obv:** Pottery flanking central design **Rev:** Potter at wheel

Date	Mintage	F	VF	XF	Unc	BU
2010 Proof, Antique finish	10,000	Value: 100				

KM# 606 10 HRYVEN
31.1000 g., 0.9250 Silver 0.9249 oz. ASW, 38.6 mm. **Subject:** Tarnovskyi Family **Obv:** Mansion in Kachanivka, Chernihiv oblast **Rev:** Vasyl Tarnovskyi standing and oval portraits of Hryhorii and Vasyl.

Date	Mintage	F	VF	XF	Unc	BU
2010 Proof	10,000	Value: 95.00				

KM# 616 10 HRYVEN
33.6230 g., 0.9250 Silver 0.9999 oz. ASW, 38.61 mm. **Obv:** Blacksmith items, two little birds **Rev:** Blacksmith at work

Date	Mintage	F	VF	XF	Unc	BU
2011 Antique finish	10,000	—	—	—	—	110

KM# 626 10 HRYVEN
33.6230 g., 0.9250 Silver 0.9999 oz. ASW, 38.61 mm. **Obv:** Baroque element from the Church **Rev:** St. Andrew's Church

Date	Mintage	F	VF	XF	Unc	BU
2011 Proof	8,000	Value: 110				

KM# 628 10 HRYVEN
33.6230 g., 0.9250 Silver 0.9999 oz. ASW, 38.61 mm. **Obv:** Hopak dance **Rev:** Dancing Cossack

Date	Mintage	F	VF	XF	Unc	BU
2011 Proof	7,000	Value: 110				

KM# 632 10 HRYVEN
33.6230 g., 0.9250 Silver 0.9999 oz. ASW, 38.61 mm. **Subject:** Hryhorovych-Barskyi family **Obv:** Samson fountain in Kyiv **Rev:** Arms of the family

Date	Mintage	F	VF	XF	Unc	BU
2011 Proof	5,000	Value: 110				

KM# 641 10 HRYVEN
33.6230 g., 0.9250 Silver 0.9999 oz. ASW, 38.61 mm. **Subject:** UEFA Euro 2012 Final Tournament **Obv:** UEFA logo hologram and map of the Ukraine **Rev:** Two players, Olympic Stadium, Kyiv and city view

Date	Mintage	F	VF	XF	Unc	BU
2011 Proof	15,000	Value: 110				

KM# 642 10 HRYVEN
33.6230 g., 0.9250 Silver 0.9999 oz. ASW, 38.61 mm. **Subject:** UEFA Euro 2012 Final Tornament **Obv:** UEFA Euro 2012 Logo and map **Rev:** Player, city view and Livi Stadium

Date	Mintage	F	VF	XF	Unc	BU
2011 Proof	15,000	Value: 110				

KM# 643 10 HRYVEN
33.6230 g., 0.9250 Silver 0.9999 oz. ASW, 38.61 mm. **Subject:** UEFA Euro 2012 Final Tournament **Obv:** UEFA logo hologram and Map of Ukraine **Rev:** City view with two players

Date	Mintage	F	VF	XF	Unc	BU
2011 Proof	15,000	Value: 110				

KM# 644 10 HRYVEN
33.6230 g., 0.9250 Silver 0.9999 oz. ASW, 38.61 mm. **Subject:** UEFA Euro 2012 Final Tournament **Obv:** UEFA logo hologram and map of Ukraine **Rev:** Player with ball, Donbass Arena

Date	Mintage	F	VF	XF	Unc	BU
2011 Proof	15,000	Value: 110				

KM# 144 20 HRYVEN
67.2400 g., 0.9250 Silver 1.9996 oz. ASW, 50 mm. **Subject:** 10 Years Independence **Obv:** National arms **Rev:** Parliament building on map within beaded circle **Edge:** Segmented reeding

Date	Mintage	F	VF	XF	Unc	BU
2001 Proof	1,000	Value: 4,000				

KM# 174 20 HRYVEN
14.7000 g., Bi-Metallic .916 Gold center in .925 silver ring, 31 mm. **Subject:** "Kyiv Rus" Culture **Obv:** Old arms of Ukraine, Prince and a cathedral model in his hand and princess **Rev:** Old Rus earring **Edge:** Reeded and plain sections

Date	Mintage	F	VF	XF	Unc	BU
2001 Proof	2,000	Value: 1,000				

KM# 175 20 HRYVEN
14.7000 g., Bi-Metallic .916 Gold center in .925 Silver ring, 31 mm. **Subject:** Scythian Culture **Obv:** Warrior with a bowl in his hand and to the right, a Queen of Scythia **Rev:** Stylized horse flanked by pegasists **Edge:** Reeded and plain sections

Date	Mintage	F	VF	XF	Unc	BU
2001 Proof	2,000	Value: 1,200				

KM# 153 20 HRYVEN
67.2400 g., 0.9250 Silver 1.9996 oz. ASW, 50 mm. **Obv:** National arms on sun and flying geese divides beaded circle **Rev:** "AN-225 Mrija" cargo jet divides beaded circle **Edge:** Reeded and plain sections

Date	Mintage	F	VF	XF	Unc	BU
2002 Proof	2,002	Value: 1,200				

KM# 188 20 HRYVEN
67.2400 g., 0.9250 Silver 1.9996 oz. ASW, 50 mm. **Subject:** 60th Anniversary - Liberation of Kiev **Obv:** Eternal flame monument **Rev:** Map and battle scene **Edge:** Segmented reeding

Date	Mintage	F	VF	XF	Unc	BU
2003 Proof	2,000	Value: 400				

KM# 226 20 HRYVEN
67.2440 g., 0.9250 Silver 1.9997 oz. ASW, 50 mm. **Subject:** "Our Souls Do Not Die" **Obv:** National arms above value **Rev:** Bust of Taras Shevchenko facing flanked by standing figures **Edge:** Segmented reeding

Date	Mintage	F	VF	XF	Unc	BU
2004 Proof	4,000	Value: 250				

KM# 344 20 HRYVEN
67.2440 g., 0.9250 Silver 1.9997 oz. ASW, 50 mm. **Subject:** 2006 Olympic Games **Obv:** Woman holding flame and branch **Rev:** Six athletes around flame within square design **Edge:** Segmented reeding

Date	Mintage	F	VF	XF	Unc	BU
2004 Proof	5,000	Value: 200				

KM# 363 20 HRYVEN
67.2440 g., 0.9250 Silver 1.9997 oz. ASW, 50 mm. **Obv:** National arms on sun with flying geese divides beaded circle **Rev:** AN-124 jet plane divides beaded circle **Edge:** Segmented reeding

Date	Mintage	F	VF	XF	Unc	BU
2005 Proof	5,000	Value: 200				

KM# 369 20 HRYVEN
67.2440 g., 0.9250 Silver 1.9997 oz. ASW, 50 mm. **Subject:** Sorochynsky Fair **Obv:** Busts facing each other flanked by flower sprigs **Rev:** Farmer leading family in ox cart **Edge:** Segmented reeding

Date	Mintage	F	VF	XF	Unc	BU
2005 Proof	5,000	Value: 250				

KM# 374 20 HRYVEN
67.2440 g., 0.9250 Silver 1.9997 oz. ASW, 50 mm. **Subject:** 60th Anniversary of Victory in WWII **Obv:** Flying cranes divides value, date and national arms **Rev:** V-shaped searchlight beams filled with soldiers, order of the Patriotic War at bottom left **Edge:** Segmented reeding

Date	Mintage	F	VF	XF	Unc	BU
2005 Proof	5,000	Value: 200				

KM# 412 20 HRYVEN
67.2500 g., 0.9250 Silver 1.9999 oz. ASW, 50 mm. **Subject:** 15 Years of Ukraine Independency **Obv:** National arms

Date	Mintage	F	VF	XF	Unc	BU
2006 Proof	7,000	Value: 200				

KM# 468 20 HRYVEN
14.2300 g., Silver, 31 mm. **Subject:** Pure water is source of life **Obv:** Drop of water in pond **Rev:** Man taking drink from waterfall **Edge:** Segmented reeding

Date	Mintage	F	VF	XF	Unc	BU
2007 Prooflike	3,000	—	—	—	—	600

KM# 469 20 HRYVEN
67.2600 g., 0.9250 Silver 2.0002 oz. ASW, 50 mm. **Subject:** Chumaky's Way **Obv:** Hologram wheel at center of fiery spiral **Rev:** Merchant's carts under night sky

Date	Mintage	F	VF	XF	Unc	BU
2007 Proof	5,000	Value: 350				

KM# 470 20 HRYVEN
67.2500 g., 0.9250 Silver 1.9999 oz. ASW, 50 mm. **Subject:** The Famine, Genocide of the Ukranina People **Obv:** Girl standing on fallow ground, small green plant at left **Rev:** Swan at center of cross, candles in background

Date	Mintage	F	VF	XF	Unc	BU
2007 Antique finish	10,000	—	—	—	200	—

KM# 524 20 HRYVEN
67.2500 g., 0.9250 Silver 1.9999 oz. ASW, 50 mm. **Subject:** Kyiv, 1000th Anniversary of minting

Date	Mintage	F	VF	XF	Unc	BU
2008 Proof	5,000	Value: 250				

KM# 552 20 HRYVEN
67.2500 g., 0.9250 Silver 1.9999 oz. ASW, 50.0 mm. **Subject:** Republic of Carpatho-Ukraine - 70th Anniversary of proclamation **Obv:** Carpathian ornament patterns, National Arms, value **Obv. Legend:** НАЦІОНАЛЬНИЈ БАНК УКРАЇНИ - 20 / ГРИВНЬ **Rev:** Transcarpathian holding flag with the arms of the Carpatho-Ukraine **Rev. Legend:** 70 / РОКІВ - ПРОГОЛОШЕННЯ КАРПАТСЬКОІ УКРАІНИ

Date	Mintage	F	VF	XF	Unc	BU
2009 Proof	3,000	Value: 300				

KM# 554 20 HRYVEN
67.2500 g., 0.9250 Silver 1.9999 oz. ASW, 50 mm. **Subject:** Pysanka - Easter Egg decorating **Obv:** Ukrainian embroidered towels, eggs, Naitonal Arms, value **Rev:** Female pysanka maker ornamenting egg, young girl watching

Date	Mintage	F	VF	XF	Unc	BU
2009 Proof	8,000	Value: 250				

KM# 591 20 HRYVEN
62.2000 g., 0.9250 Silver partially gilt 1.8497 oz. ASW, 50 mm. **Subject:** Zymne Cloister **Obv:** Madonna icon partially gilt **Rev:** Zymne Cloister

Date	Mintage	F	VF	XF	Unc	BU
2010 Proof	5,000	—	—	—	—	250

KM# 596 20 HRYVEN
62.2000 g., 0.9250 Silver 1.8497 oz. ASW, 50 mm. **Subject:** Battle of Grunwald, 600th Anniversary **Obv:** Value within wreath, three armored hands holding horizontal sword **Rev:** Knights with spears on horseback in battle

Date	Mintage	F	VF	XF	Unc	BU
2010 Proof	5,000	Value: 200				

KM# 602 20 HRYVEN
62.2000 g., 0.9250 Silver 1.8497 oz. ASW, 50 mm. **Subject:** Maritime History **Obv:** Banner, compass rose and seal of Zaporozhin host **Rev:** Cossack boat of the 18th century

Date	Mintage	F	VF	XF	Unc	BU
2010 Proof	5,000	Value: 200				

KM# 652 20 HRYVEN
31.1050 g., 0.9999 Gold 0.9999 oz. AGW, 32 mm. **Subject:** Archangel Michael **Obv:** Logo of the Ukraine National Bank **Rev:** Archangel Michael **Edge:** Segmented reeding

Date	Mintage	F	VF	XF	Unc	BU
2011	1,500	Value: 2,100				
2012	5,000	Value: 2,000				

KM# 614 20 HRYVEN
67.2500 g., 0.9250 Silver 1.9999 oz. ASW, 50 mm. **Subject:** Lesya Ukrainka's "The Forest Song" **Obv:** Portrait **Rev:** Girl holding willow branch, boy in distance

Date	Mintage	F	VF	XF	Unc	BU
2011 Proof	4,000	Value: 200				

KM# 617 20 HRYVEN
67.2500 g., 0.9250 Silver 1.9999 oz. ASW, 50 mm. **Subject:** Peresopnytsia Gospels **Obv:** Gospel maker icon **Rev:** Four miniatures of the initial illustrations of each Gospel

Date	Mintage	F	VF	XF	Unc	BU
2011 Special Unc.	4,000	—	—	—	—	200

KM# 637 20 HRYVEN
67.2820 g., 0.9250 Silver 2.0008 oz. ASW, 50 mm. **Subject:** Ukrainian Railroads, 150th Anniversary **Obv:** Modern high-speed train **Rev:** Ukrainian railways logo, gilt

Date	Mintage	F	VF	XF	Unc	BU
2011 Proof	4,000	Value: 220				

KM# 640 20 HRYVEN
67.2820 g., 0.9250 Silver 2.0008 oz. ASW, 62.2 mm. **Subject:** UEFA Euro 2012 Final Tournament **Obv:** Holographic images of UEFA Euro 2012 logo **Rev:** Stadium

Date	Mintage	F	VF	XF	Unc	BU
2011 Proof	15,000	Value: 220				

KM# 426 50 HRYVEN
17.6300 g., 0.9000 Gold 0.5101 oz. AGW, 25 mm. **Subject:** Nestor - The Chronicler **Obv:** National arms

Date	Mintage	F	VF	XF	Unc	BU
2006 Proof	5,000	Value: 1,400				

KM# 525 50 HRYVEN
17.6300 g., 0.9000 Gold 0.5101 oz. AGW, 25 mm. **Subject:** Swallow's Nest Castle **Edge:** Plain

Date	Mintage	F	VF	XF	Unc	BU
2008 Proof	4,000	Value: 1,400				

KM# 526 50 HRYVEN
500.0000 g., 0.9999 Silver 16.073 oz. ASW **Subject:** Visit of Ecumenical Patriarch Bartholomew I

Date	Mintage	F	VF	XF	Unc	BU
2008 Proof	1,000	Value: 2,200				

KM# 564 50 HRYVEN
500.0000 g., 0.9990 Silver 16.058 oz. ASW, 85 mm. **Subject:** Mykola Hohol's stories - Evenings on a farm near Dykanka **Obv:** Hohol's portrait with quill, National arms, value **Rev:** Christmas star with yellow sapphire

Date	Mintage	F	VF	XF	Unc	BU
2009 Proof	Est. 1,500	Value: 2,500				

KM# 595 50 HRYVEN
17.6300 g., 0.9000 Gold 0.5101 oz. AGW, 25 mm. **Subject:** Ukrainian ballet **Obv:** Ballet shoes **Rev:** Ballet couple **Edge:** Plain

Date	Mintage	F	VF	XF	Unc	BU
2010 Proof	4,000	Value: 1,400				

KM# 609 50 HRYVEN
500.0000 g., 0.9990 Silver 16.058 oz. ASW, 85 mm. **Subject:** Cradle of the Ukrainian Cossacks **Obv:** Zaporizka Sich, historic site, shield and swords below **Rev:** Dovbysh (Cossack drummer) beating kettle drums, ornamental pattern

Date	Mintage	F	VF	XF	Unc	BU
2010 Proof	Est. 1,500	Value: 2,500				

KM# 631 50 HRYVEN
500.0000 g., 0.9990 Silver 16.058 oz. ASW, 85 mm. **Subject:** Independence, 20th Anniversary **Obv:** National arms, rushnyks, portraits **Rev:** Legend within wreath

Date	Mintage	F	VF	XF	Unc	BU
2011	1,000	—	—	—	—	2,500

KM# 633 50 HRYVEN
500.0000 g., 0.9990 Silver 16.058 oz. ASW, 85 mm. **Subject:** St. Sophia Cathedral, 1000th Anniversary **Obv:** St. Sophia Cathedral cupolas, model of XI century design **Rev:** Altar mural mosaics

Date	Mintage	F	VF	XF	Unc	BU
2011	1,000	—	—	—	—	2,500

KM# 199 100 HRYVEN
31.1000 g., 0.9000 Gold 0.8999 oz. AGW, 32 mm. **Subject:** Ancient Scythian Culture **Obv:** National arms above ornamental design and value within rope wreath **Rev:** Ancient craftsmen and jewelry **Edge:** Reeded

Date	Mintage	F	VF	XF	Unc	BU
2003 Proof	1,500	Value: 7,500				

KM# 345 100 HRYVEN
34.5594 g., 0.9000 Gold 1.0000 oz. AGW, 32 mm. **Subject:** The Golden Gate **Obv:** National arms above value between two stylized cranes **Rev:** Riders approaching castle gate **Edge:** Segmented reeding

Date	Mintage	F	VF	XF	Unc	BU
2004 Proof	2,000	Value: 5,000				

KM# 414 100 HRYVEN
1000.0000 g., 0.9990 Silver 32.117 oz. ASW, 100 mm. **Subject:** 10 Years to the Currency Reform in Ukraine **Obv:** National arms **Note:** Illustration reduced.

Date	Mintage	Good	VG	F	VF	XF
2006 Proof	1,501	Value: 6,500				

KM# 471 100 HRYVEN
34.5600 g., 0.9000 Gold 1.0000 oz. AGW, 32 mm. **Subject:** The Ostroh Bible **Obv:** Part of illumination on page **Rev:** Ivan Fedorov and Kostiantyn of Ostroth holding open bible

Date	Mintage	F	VF	XF	Unc	BU
2007 Proof	4,000	Value: 3,000				

KM# 527 100 HRYVEN
1000.0000 g., 0.9990 Silver 32.117 oz. ASW **Subject:** Kievan Rus

Date	Mintage	F	VF	XF	Unc	BU
2008 Proof	800	Value: 4,500				

KM# 558 100 HRYVEN
1000.0000 g., 0.9990 Silver 32.117 oz. ASW, 100 mm. **Subject:** International Year of Astronomy **Obv:** Solar System, armillary sphere, stars. **Obv. Legend:** НАЦІОНАЛЬНИЈ БАНК УКРАІНИ - 100 / ГРИВНЬ **Rev:** Galileo, stars, telescope, galaxies, observatory, Saturn (as the letter O). **Rev. Legend:** МІЖНАРОДНИЈ РІК АСТРОНОМІІ

Date	Mintage	F	VF	XF	Unc	BU
2009 Proof	Est. 700	Value: 4,500				

KM# 565 100 HRYVEN
34.5700 g., 0.9000 Gold 1.0003 oz. AGW, 32 mm. **Subject:** Ancient Site - Chersonesos Taurica **Obv:** Ancient ruins, coins, Naitonal Arms **Rev:** Ruins of ancient Chersonesos **Edge:** Segmented reeding

Date	Mintage	F	VF	XF	Unc	BU
2009 Proof	4,000	Value: 3,000				

KM# 597 100 HRYVEN
31.1000 g., 0.9000 Gold 0.8999 oz. AGW, 32 mm. **Subject:** Bosporan Kingdom **Obv:** Panticapaeum runins: classical columns, winged animals **Rev:** Panticapaeum stater, buildings, ancient sailing vessel

Date	Mintage	F	VF	XF	Unc	BU
2010 Proof	3,000	Value: 3,000				

KM# 630 100 HRYVEN
34.5600 g., 0.9000 Gold 1.0000 oz. AGW, 32 mm. **Subject:** Independence, 20th Anniversary **Obv:** National arms in center of rushnyks, Portraits around **Rev:** Legend within wreath

Date	Mintage	F	VF	XF	Unc	BU
2011 Proof	1,000	Value: 4,500				

KM# 646 500 HRYVEN
500.0000 g., 0.9999 Gold 16.073 oz. AGW, 80 mm. **Subject:** UEFA Euro 2012 Final Tournament **Obv:** Map of Europe, logo, tournament cities around **Rev:** Large and smaller images of players

Date	Mintage	F	VF	XF	Unc	BU
2011	Est. 500	—	—	—	—	47,000

MINT SETS

KM#	Date	Mintage	Identification	Issue Price	Mkt Val
MS2	2001 (8)	5,000	KM#1.1b, 2.1b, 3.3b, 4b, 6, 7, 8b, 129	—	150
MS3	2006 (8)	5,000	KM#1.1b, 2.1b, 3.3b, 4b, 6, 7, 8b, 411	—	30.00
MS4	2008 (7)	5,000	KM#1.1b, 2.1b, 3.3b, 4b, 6, 7, 209, prooflike	—	100
MS5	2011 (7)	5,000	KM#1.1b, 2.1b, 3.3b, 4b, 6, 7, 209. Prooflike	—	45.00
MS6	2012 (7)	5,000	KM#1.1b, 2.1b, 3.3b, 4b, 6, 7, 209. Prooflike	—	50.00

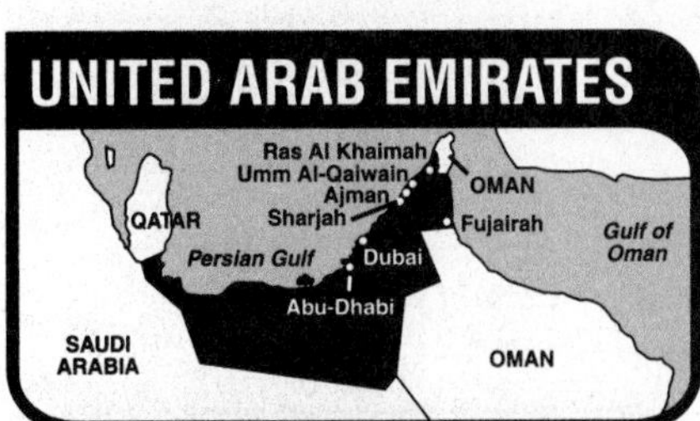

The seven United Arab Emirates (formerly known as the Trucial Sheikhdoms or States), located along the southern shore of the Persian Gulf, are comprised of the Sheikhdoms of Abu Dhabi, Dubai, al-Sharjah, Ajman, Umm al Qaiwain, Ras al-Khaimah and al-Fujairah. They have a combined area of about 32,000 sq. mi. (83,600 sq. km.) and a population of *2.1 million. Capital: Abu Zaby (Abu Dhabi). Since the oil strikes of 1958-60, the economy has centered about petroleum.

TITLES

الامارات العربية المتحدة

al-Imara(t) al-Arabiya(t) al-Muttahida(t)

UNITED EMIRATES

STANDARD COINAGE

KM# 2.2 5 FILS
Bronze **Series:** F.A.O. **Obv:** Value **Rev:** Fish above dates **Note:** Reduced size.

Date	Mintage	F	VF	XF	Unc	BU
AH1422-2001	—	—	—	0.15	0.30	1.50
AH1426-2005	—	—	—	0.15	0.30	1.50

KM# 3.2 10 FILS
Bronze, 19 mm. **Obv:** Value **Rev:** Arab dhow above dates **Note:** Reduced size.

Date	Mintage	F	VF	XF	Unc	BU
AH1422-2001	—	—	0.30	0.50	1.00	1.50
AH1425-2005	—	—	0.20	0.35	0.80	1.20

KM# 4 25 FILS
3.5000 g., Copper-Nickel, 20 mm. **Obv:** Value **Rev:** Gazelle above dates **Edge:** Reeded

Date	Mintage	F	VF	XF	Unc	BU
AH1425-2005	—	—	—	0.40	1.00	1.50
AH1428-2007	—	—	—	0.40	1.00	1.50
AH1428-2008	—	—	—	0.40	0.75	1.50
AH1432-2011	—	—	—	0.40	0.75	1.50

KM# 16 50 FILS
4.3000 g., Copper-Nickel, 21 mm. **Obv:** Value **Rev:** Oil derricks above dates **Shape:** 7-sided **Note:** Reduced size.

Date	Mintage	F	VF	XF	Unc	BU
AH1425-2005	—	—	—	0.70	1.50	2.50
AH1428-2007	—	—	—	0.50	1.50	2.00
AH1428-2008	—	—	—	0.50	1.50	2.00

KM# 49 DIRHAM

6.4000 g., Copper-Nickel, 24 mm. **Subject:** 25th Anniversary - Armed Forces Unification **Obv:** Value **Rev:** Heraldic eagle within rope wreath **Edge:** Reeded

Date	Mintage	F	VF	XF	Unc	BU
ND(2001) (2001)	250,000	—	—	1.00	5.00	6.00

KM# 51 DIRHAM

6.3300 g., Copper-Nickel, 24 mm. **Subject:** 50 Years of Formal Education **Obv:** Value **Rev:** Symbolic design **Edge:** Reeded

Date	Mintage	F	VF	XF	Unc	BU
ND (2003)	—	—	—	1.00	5.00	6.00

KM# 52 DIRHAM

6.4000 g., Copper-Nickel, 24 mm. **Subject:** Abu Dhabi National Bank 35th Anniversary **Obv:** Value **Rev:** Bank building tower divide dates within circle **Edge:** Reeded

Date	Mintage	F	VF	XF	Unc	BU
ND (2003)	—	—	—	1.00	4.50	6.00

KM# 54 DIRHAM

6.4000 g., Copper-Nickel, 24 mm. **Subject:** 40th Anniversary of Crude Oil Exports **Obv:** Value **Rev:** "ADCO" logo **Edge:** Reeded

Date	Mintage	F	VF	XF	Unc	BU
ND (2003)	—	—	—	1.00	4.50	6.00

KM# 73 DIRHAM

6.4000 g., Copper-Nickel, 23.93 mm. **Subject:** WBG & IMF meeting in Dubai 2003 **Obv:** Denomination **Rev:** Mosaic arc **Edge:** Reeded

Date	Mintage	F	VF	XF	Unc	BU
2003	250,000	—	—	1.00	7.00	9.00

KM# 74 DIRHAM

6.4000 g., Copper-Nickel, 24 mm. **Subject:** First Gulf Bank 25th Anniversary **Obv:** Value **Rev:** Bank logo **Edge:** Reeded

Date	Mintage	F	VF	XF	Unc	BU
ND(2004)	—	—	—	1.00	5.00	6.00

KM# 83 DIRHAM

6.4700 g., Copper-Nickel, 24.02 mm. **Subject:** Honoring Mother of Nations **Obv:** Large value **Rev:** Inscription in flower bud at center **Rev. Legend:** Sheikha Fatima Bint Mubarak **Edge:** Reeded

Date	Mintage	F	VF	XF	Unc	BU
2005	—	—	—	1.00	5.00	6.00

KM# 6.2 DIRHAM

6.4000 g., Copper-Nickel, 24 mm. **Obv:** Value **Rev:** Jug above dates **Edge:** Reeded **Note:** Reduced size.

Date	Mintage	F	VF	XF	Unc	BU
AH1425-2005	—	—	0.35	0.65	2.50	4.00
AH1426-2006	—	—	0.35	0.65	2.00	4.00
AH1428-2007	—	—	0.35	0.65	2.00	4.00

KM# 78 DIRHAM

6.4000 g., Copper-Nickel, 24 mm. **Obv:** Value **Obv. Legend:** UNITED ARAB EMIRATES **Rev:** Police badge in center **Rev. Legend:** DUABI POLICE GOLDEN JUBILEE **Edge:** Reeded

Date	Mintage	F	VF	XF	Unc	BU
ND(2006)	—	—	—	1.00	4.50	6.00

KM# 77 DIRHAM

6.3000 g., Copper-Nickel, 24 mm. **Obv:** Value **Rev:** Zakum Development Co. logo **Edge:** Reeded

Date	Mintage	F	VF	XF	Unc	BU
ND(2007)	—	—	—	1.00	4.50	6.00

KM# 76 DIRHAM

6.4000 g., Copper-Nickel, 24 mm. **Subject:** Sharjah International Airport, 75th Anniversary **Obv:** Value **Obv. Legend:** UNITED ARAB EMIRATES **Rev:** Three birds in flight under arc **Edge:** Reeded

Date	Mintage	F	VF	XF	Unc	BU
ND(2007)	—	—	—	1.00	4.00	5.00

KM# 84 DIRHAM

6.4000 g., Copper-Nickel, 24 mm. **Subject:** 10th Anniversary of the Hamdan Bin Rashed Award for Distinguished Academic Performance **Obv:** Large value **Rev:** 10 below pen with tip touching star **Edge:** Reeded

Date	Mintage	F	VF	XF	Unc	BU
ND(2007)	—	—	—	1.00	5.00	6.00

KM# 96 DIRHAM

6.4000 g., Copper-Nickel, 24 mm. **Subject:** U.A.E. Boy Scouts, 50th Anniversary **Obv:** Value at center **Rev:** Scout Fleur-de-lis within rope circle

Date	Mintage	F	VF	XF	Unc	BU
2007	—	—	—	1.00	5.00	7.00

KM# 79 DIRHAM

6.4300 g., Copper-Nickel, 24.03 mm. **Obv:** Value **Obv. Legend:** UNITED ARAB EMIRATES **Rev:** Large "30" and logo **Rev. Legend:** 30TH ANNIVERSARY OF THE 1ST LNG SHIPMENT **Rev. Inscription:** ADGAS **Edge:** Reeded

Date	Mintage	F	VF	XF	Unc	BU
ND(2007)	—	—	—	1.00	4.50	6.00

KM# 85 DIRHAM

6.4000 g., Copper-Nickel **Subject:** National Bank of Abu Dhabi, 40th Anniversary **Obv:** Large value **Obv. Legend:** UNITED ARAB EMIRATES **Rev:** Large stylized "40" **Edge:** Reeded

Date	Mintage	F	VF	XF	Unc	BU
ND(2008)	—	—	—	—	4.00	5.00

KM# 100 DIRHAM

6.4000 g., Copper-Nickel **Subject:** DIFC **Obv:** Large value **Obv. Legend:** UNITED ARAB EMIRATES **Rev:** DIFC (Dubai International Financial Centre) **Edge:** Reeded

Date	Mintage	F	VF	XF	Unc	BU
2009	—	—	—	—	4.00	5.00

KM# 101 DIRHAM

6.4000 g., Copper-Nickel **Subject:** World Environment Day **Obv:** Large value **Obv. Legend:** UNITED ARAB EMIRATES **Rev:** World Environment Day, Global map **Edge:** Reeded

Date	Mintage	F	VF	XF	Unc	BU
2012	—	—	—	—	4.00	5.00

KM# 102 DIRHAM

6.4000 g., Copper-Nickel **Subject:** 50th Anniversary 1st oil shipment **Obv:** Large value **Obv. Legend:** UNITED ARAM EMIRATES **Rev:** Oil derrick, commemorative text **Edge:** Reeded

Date	Mintage	F	VF	XF	Unc	BU
2012	—	—	—	—	4.00	5.00

KM# 6.3 DIRHAM

6.4000 g., Nickel Plated Steel, 24 mm. **Obv:** Value **Rev:** Jug above date **Edge:** Reeded **Note:** Reduced size. Magnetic, minted by Royal Canadian Mint

Date	Mintage	F	VF	XF	Unc	BU
AH1433-2012	—	—	0.35	0.65	2.00	4.00

KM# 47 50 DIRHAMS

40.2200 g., 0.9250 Silver 1.1961 oz. ASW, 40 mm. **Subject:** 25th Anniversary - Women's Union (1975-2000) **Obv:** Bust of President H. H. Sheikh Zayed bin Sultan Al Nahyan 7/8 right **Rev:** Stylized gazelle **Edge:** Reeded

Date	Mintage	F	VF	XF	Unc	BU
ND(2001) Proof	5,000	Value: 90.00				

KM# 59 50 DIRHAMS

40.0000 g., 0.9250 Silver 1.1895 oz. ASW, 40 mm. **Subject:** 25th Anniversary - Arab Bank of Investment and Foreign Trade **Edge:** Reeded

Date	Mintage	F	VF	XF	Unc	BU
ND(2001) Proof	2,000	Value: 100				

KM# 60 50 DIRHAMS

40.0000 g., 0.9250 Silver 1.1895 oz. ASW, 40 mm. **Subject:** 25th Anniversary - Armed Forces Unification **Edge:** Reeded

Date	Mintage	F	VF	XF	Unc	BU
ND(2001) Proof	10,000	Value: 85.00				

KM# 61 50 DIRHAMS
40.0000 g., 0.9250 Silver 1.1895 oz. ASW, 40 mm. **Subject:** 30th Anniversary - Al-Ain National Museum **Edge:** Reeded

Date	Mintage	F	VF	XF	Unc	BU
ND(2001) Proof	5,000	Value: 85.00				

KM# 62 50 DIRHAMS
40.0000 g., 0.9250 Silver 1.1895 oz. ASW, 40 mm. **Subject:** 25th Anniversary - University of the U.A.E. **Obv:** Bust of President H. H. Sheikh Zayed bin Sultan Al Nahyan 7/8 right **Rev:** Inscriptions **Edge:** Reeded

Date	Mintage	F	VF	XF	Unc	BU
ND(2002) Proof	5,000	Value: 85.00				

KM# 63 50 DIRHAMS
40.0000 g., 0.9250 Silver 1.1895 oz. ASW, 40 mm. **Subject:** Etisalat - Emirates Telecommunications, 25th Anniversary **Obv:** Value **Rev:** Stylized 25 **Edge:** Reeded

Date	Mintage	F	VF	XF	Unc	BU
ND(2002) Proof	5,000	Value: 90.00				

KM# 64 50 DIRHAMS
40.0000 g., 0.9250 Silver 1.1895 oz. ASW, 40 mm. **Subject:** Sheikh Hamdan bin Rashid al Maktoum Award for Medical Sciences **Obv:** Value **Rev:** Sheikh Hamdan bin Rashid al Maktoum bust 3/4 left **Edge:** Reeded

Date	Mintage	F	VF	XF	Unc	BU
ND(2002) Proof	2,000	Value: 100				

KM# 65 50 DIRHAMS
40.0000 g., 0.9250 Silver 1.1895 oz. ASW, 40 mm. **Subject:** Al Ahmadia School, 90th Anniversary **Obv:** Sheikh Rashid bin Saaed al Maktoum 3/4 left **Rev:** School building **Edge:** Reeded

Date	Mintage	F	VF	XF	Unc	BU
ND(2002) Proof	5,000	Value: 90.00				

KM# 67 50 DIRHAMS
40.0000 g., 0.9250 Silver 1.1895 oz. ASW, 40 mm. **Subject:** Administrative Development Institute, 20th Anniversary **Obv:** Sheikh Zayed bin Sultan al Nahyan bust 3/4 right **Rev:** Eagle **Edge:** Reeded

Date	Mintage	F	VF	XF	Unc	BU
ND(2002) Proof	2,000	Value: 120				

KM# 68 50 DIRHAMS
40.0000 g., 0.9250 Silver 1.1895 oz. ASW, 40 mm. **Subject:** U.A.E. Central Bank, 30th Anniversary **Obv:** Sheikh Zayed bin Sultan al Nahyan bust 3/4 right **Rev:** Sheikh Maktoum bin Rashid al Maktoum bust 3/4 right **Edge:** Reeded

Date	Mintage	F	VF	XF	Unc	BU
ND(2003) Proof	5,000	Value: 110				

KM# 69 50 DIRHAMS
40.0000 g., 0.9250 Silver 1.1895 oz. ASW, 40 mm. **Subject:** 58th Annual Meeting of the World Bank Group and the Int'l Money Fund **Obv:** Colored dots **Edge:** Reeded

Date	Mintage	F	VF	XF	Unc	BU
ND(2003) Proof	10,000	Value: 85.00				

KM# 50 50 DIRHAMS
40.0000 g., 0.9250 Silver 1.1895 oz. ASW, 40 mm. **Obv:** Value **Rev:** FIFA 2003 World Youth Soccer Championship **Edge:** Reeded

Date	Mintage	F	VF	XF	Unc	BU
ND(2003) Proof	—	Value: 95.00				

KM# 66 50 DIRHAMS
40.0000 g., 0.9250 Silver 1.1895 oz. ASW, 40 mm. **Subject:** Ministry of Finance and Industry ISO Certification **Obv:** Value **Rev:** Eagle at center **Edge:** Reeded

Date	Mintage	F	VF	XF	Unc	BU
ND(2003) Proof	3,000	Value: 110				

KM# 70 50 DIRHAMS
40.0000 g., 0.9250 Silver 1.1895 oz. ASW, 40 mm. **Subject:** 40th Anniversary - First Oil Export from Abu Dhabi Onshore Oil Fields (ADCO) **Obv:** Bust of President H. H. Sheikh Zayed bin Sultan Al Nayhan 3/4 right **Rev:** Logo **Edge:** Reeded

Date	Mintage	F	VF	XF	Unc	BU
ND(2004) Proof	—	Value: 300				

KM# 71 50 DIRHAMS
40.0000 g., 0.9250 Silver 1.1895 oz. ASW, 40 mm. **Subject:** 25th Anniversary - Sharjah City for Humanitarian Services (SCHS) **Edge:** Reeded

Date	Mintage	F	VF	XF	Unc	BU
ND(2005) Proof	—	Value: 120				

KM# 98 50 DIRHAMS
40.0000 g., 0.9250 Silver 1.1895 oz. ASW, 40 mm. **Subject:** Sheikha Fatima Birt Mubarak, Mother of the Nation

Date	Mintage	F	VF	XF	Unc	BU
2005 Proof	—	Value: 110				

KM# 82 50 DIRHAMS
40.0000 g., 0.9250 Silver 1.1895 oz. ASW, 40 mm. **Subject:** 25th Anniversary Emirates Banks Association **Obv:** Value **Obv. Legend:** UNITED ARAB EMIRATES **Rev:** Logo **Edge:** Reeded

Date	Mintage	F	VF	XF	Unc	BU
ND(2007) Proof	—	Value: 120				

KM# 95 50 DIRHAMS
40.0000 g., 0.9250 Silver 1.1895 oz. ASW, 40 mm. **Subject:** Hamdan Bin Rashed Award for Distinguished Academic Performance **Obv:** Denomination, legend above **Rev:** Pen with tip touching star, legend above **Edge:** Reeded **Note:** Issued 10th Anniversary of the Award

Date	Mintage	F	VF	XF	Unc	BU
ND(2008) Proof	—	Value: 700				

KM# 80 100 DIRHAMS
60.0000 g., 0.9250 Silver 1.7843 oz. ASW, 50 mm. **Obv:** Sheikh Zayed bin Sultan **Rev:** Sheikh Zayed Mosque

Date	Mintage	F	VF	XF	Unc	BU
2004 Proof	—	Value: 160				

KM# 97 100 DIRHAMS
60.0000 g., 0.9250 Silver 1.7843 oz. ASW, 50 mm. **Subject:** Sheikh Khalifa Ben Zayed, 1st Anniversary **Rev:** Emir's Palace

Date	Mintage	F	VF	XF	Unc	BU
2005 Proof	—	Value: 160				

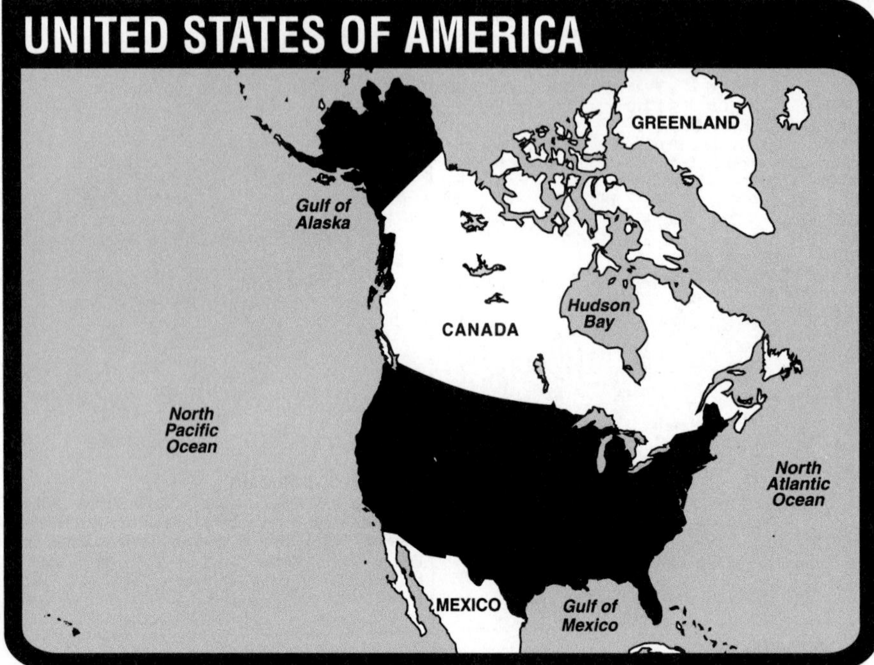

The United States of America as politically organized, under the Articles of Confederation consisted of the 13 original British-American colonies; New Hampshire, Massachusetts, Rhode Island, Connecticut, New York, New Jersey, Pennsylvania, Delaware, Virginia, North Carolina, South Carolina, Georgia and Maryland. Clustered along the eastern seaboard of North America between the forests of Maine and the marshes of Georgia. Under the Article of Confederation, the United States had no national capital: Philadelphia, where the "United States in Congress Assembled", was the "seat of government". The population during this political phase of America's history (1781-1789) was about 3 million, most of whom lived on self-sufficient family farms. Fishing, lumbering and the production of grains for export were major economic endeavors. Rapid strides were also being made in industry and manufacturing by 1775, the (then) colonies were accounting for one-seventh of the world's production of raw iron.

On the basis of the voyage of John Cabot to the North American mainland in 1497, England claimed the entire continent. The first permanent English settlement was established at Jamestown, Virginia, in 1607. France and Spain also claimed extensive territory in North America. At the end of the French and Indian Wars (1763), England acquired all of the territory east of the Mississippi River, including East and West Florida. From 1776 to 1781, the States were governed by the Continental Congress. From 1781 to 1789, they were organized under the Articles of Confederation, during which period the individual States had the right to issue money. Independence from Great Britain was attained with the American Revolution in 1776. The Constitution organized and governs the present United States. It was ratified on Nov. 21, 1788.

MINT MARKS

D – Denver, CO, 1906-present
P – Philadelphia, PA, 1793-present
S – San Francisco, CA, 1854-present
W - West Point, NY, 1984-present

BULLION COINS

Silver Eagle = $1.00
Gold 1/10 Ounce = $5.00
Gold ¼ Ounce = $10.00
Gold ½ Ounce = $25.00
Gold Ounce = $50.00
Platinum 1/10 Ounce = $10.00
Platinum ¼ Ounce = $25.00
Platinum ½ Ounce = $50.00
Platinum Ounce = $100.00

CIRCULATION COINAGE

CENT

Lincoln Cent

Lincoln Memorial reverse

KM# 201b • Copper Plated Zinc, 19 mm. • **Notes:** MS60 prices are for brown coins and MS65 prices are for coins that are at least 90% original red.

Date	Mintage	XF-40	MS-65	Prf-65
2001	4,959,600,000	—	3.00	—
2001D	5,374,990,000	—	3.00	—
2001S	3,099,096	—	—	3.50
2002	3,260,800,000	—	3.00	—
2002S	3,157,739	—	—	3.50
2002D	4,028,055,000	—	3.00	—
2003	3,300,000,000	—	3.50	—
2003D	3,548,000,000	—	3.50	—
2003S	3,116,590	—	—	3.50
2004	3,379,600,000	—	3.50	—
2004D	3,456,400,000	—	3.50	—
2004S	2,992,069	—	—	3.50
2005	3,935,600,000	—	2.50	—
2005 Satin Finish	Inc. above	—	4.00	—
2005D	3,764,450,000	—	2.50	—
2005D Satin Finish	Inc. above	—	4.00	—
2005S	3,273,000	—	—	3.50
2006	4,290,000,000	—	2.00	—
2006 Satin Finish	Inc. above	—	4.00	—
2006D	3,944,000,000	—	2.50	—
2006 Satin Finish	Inc. above	—	4.00	—
2006S	2,923,105	—	—	3.50
2007	—	—	2.00	—
2007 Satin Finish	—	—	4.00	—
2007D	—	—	2.00	—
2007 Satin Finish	—	—	4.00	—
2007S	—	—	—	3.50
2008	—	—	2.25	—
2008 Satin Finish	—	—	4.00	—
2008D	—	—	2.25	—
2008 Satin Finish	—	—	4.00	—
2008S	—	—	—	4.50

Lincoln Bicentennial

Bust right obverse Log cabin reverse

KM# 441 • 2.5000 g., **Copper Plated Zinc**, 19 mm. • **Rev. Designer:** Richard Masters and James Licaretz

Date	Mintage	XF-40	MS-65	Prf-65
2009P	284,400,000	—	1.50	—
2009D	350,400,000	—	1.50	—

KM# 441a • 3.3100 g., **Brass** • **Rev. Designer:** Richard Masters and James Licaretz

Date	Mintage	XF-40	MS-65	Prf-65
2009S	—	—	—	4.00

Lincoln seated on log reverse

KM# 442 • 2.5000 g., **Copper Plated Zinc**, 19 mm. • **Rev. Designer:** Charles Vickers

Date	Mintage	XF-40	MS-65	Prf-65
2009P	376,000,000	—	1.50	—
2009D	363,600,000	—	1.50	—

KM# 442a • 3.1100 g., **Brass**, 19 mm. • **Rev. Designer:** Charles Vickers

Date	Mintage	XF-40	MS-65	Prf-65
2009S	—	—	—	4.00

Lincoln standing before Illinois Statehouse reverse

KM# 443 • 2.5000 g., **Copper Plated Zinc**, 19 mm. • **Rev. Designer:** Joel Ishowitz and Don Everhart

Date	Mintage	XF-40	MS-65	Prf-65
2009P	316,000,000	—	1.50	—
2009D	336,000,000	—	1.50	—

KM# 443a • 3.1100 g., **Brass**, 19 mm. • **Rev. Designer:** Joel Iskowitz and Don Everhart

Date	Mintage	XF-40	MS-65	Prf-65
2009S	—	—	—	4.00

Capitol Building reverse

KM# 444 • 2.5000 g., **Copper Plated Zinc** • **Rev. Designer:** Susan Gamble and Joseph Menna

Date	Mintage	XF-40	MS-65	Prf-65
2009P	129,600,000	—	1.50	—
2009D	198,000,000	—	1.50	—

KM# 444a • 3.1100 g., **Brass**, 19 mm. • **Rev. Designer:** Susan Ganmble and Joseph Menna

Date	Mintage	XF-40	MS-65	Prf-65
2009S	—	—	—	4.00

Lincoln - Shield Reverse

KM# 468 • 2.5000 g., **Copper Plated Zinc**, 19 mm. • **Obv. Designer:** Victor D. Brenner **Rev. Designer:** Lyndall Bass and Joseph Menna

Date	Mintage	XF-40	MS-65	Prf-65
2010P	—	—	1.50	—
2010D	—	—	1.50	—
2010S	—	—	—	4.00
2011P	—	—	1.50	—
2011D	—	—	1.50	—
2011S	—	—	—	4.00
2012P	—	—	1.50	—
2012D	—	—	1.50	—
2012S	—	—	—	4.00
2013P	—	—	1.50	—
2013D	—	—	1.50	—
2013S	—	—	—	4.00

5 CENTS

Jefferson Nickel

KM# A192 • 5.0000 g., **Copper-Nickel**, 21.2 mm. • **Designer:** Felix Schlag **Edge Desc:** Plain

Date	Mintage	XF-40	MS-65	Prf-65
2001P	675,704,000	—	3.75	—
2001D	627,680,000	—	3.75	—
2001S	3,099,096	—	—	1.00
2002P	539,280,000	—	3.75	—
2002D	691,200,000	—	3.75	—
2002S	3,157,739	—	—	1.00
2003P	441,840,000	—	3.75	—
2003D	383,040,000	—	3.75	—
2003S	3,116,590	—	—	1.00

Jefferson - Westward Expansion - Lewis & Clark Bicentennial

Jefferson era peace medal design: two clasped hands, pipe and hatchet reverse

KM# 360 • 5.0000 g., **Copper-Nickel**, 21.2 mm. • **Obv. Designer:** Felix Schlag **Rev. Designer:** Norman E. Nemeth

Date	Mintage	MS-65	Prf-65
2004P	361,440,000	—	—
2004D	372,000,000	—	—
2004S	—	—	5.00

Lewis and Clark's Keelboat reverse

KM# 361 • 5.0000 g., **Copper-Nickel**, 21.2 mm. • **Obv. Designer:** Felix Schlag **Rev. Designer:** Al Maletsky

Date	Mintage	MS-65	Prf-65
2004P	366,720,000	1.50	—
2004D	344,880,000	1.50	—
2004S	—	—	5.00

Thomas Jefferson large profile right obverse American Bison right reverse

KM# 368 • 5.0000 g., **Copper-Nickel**, 21.2 mm. • **Obv. Designer:** Joe Fitzgerald and Don Everhart II **Rev. Designer:** Jamie Franki and Norman E. Nemeth

Date	Mintage	MS-65	Prf-65
2005P	448,320,000	1.50	—
2005P Satin Finish	1,160,000	4.00	—
2005D	487,680,000	1.50	—
2005D Satin Finish	1,160,000	4.00	—
2005S	—	—	6.50

Jefferson, large profile obverse Pacific coastline reverse

KM# 369 • 5.0000 g., **Copper-Nickel**, 21.2 mm. • **Obv. Designer:** Joe Fitzgerald and Don Everhart **Rev. Designer:** Joe Fitzgerald and Donna Weaver

Date	Mintage	MS-65	Prf-65
2005P	394,080,000	1.25	—
2005P Satin Finish	1,160,000	4.00	—
2005D	411,120,000	1.25	—
2005D Satin Finish	1,160,000	4.00	—
2005S	—	—	5.50

Jefferson large facing portrait - Enhanced Monticello Reverse

KM# 381 • 5.0000 g., **Copper-Nickel**, 21.2 mm. • **Obv. Designer:** Jamie N. Franki and Donna Weaver **Rev. Designer:** Felix Schlag and John Mercanti

Date	Mintage	MS-65	Prf-65
2006P	693,120,000	2.50	—
2006P Satin finish	847,361	4.00	—
2006D	809,280,000	2.50	—
2006D Satin finish	847,361	4.00	—
2006S	—	—	5.00
2007P	—	2.50	—
2007P Satin finish	895,628	4.00	—
2007D	—	2.50	—
2007D Satin finish	895,628	4.00	—
2007S	—	—	4.00
2008P	—	2.50	—
2008P Satin finish	745,464	4.00	—
2008D	—	2.50	—
2008D Satin finish	745,464	4.00	—
2008S	—	—	4.00
2009P	—	3.50	—
2009P Satin finish	784,614	4.00	—
2009D	—	1.75	—
2009D Satin finish	784,614	4.00	—
2009S	—	—	3.00
2010P	—	1.50	—
2010P Satin finish	—	4.00	—
2010D	—	1.50	—
2010D Satin finish	—	4.00	—
2010S	—	—	3.00
2011P	—	1.50	—
2011D	—	1.50	—
2011S	—	—	4.00
2012P	—	1.50	—
2012D	—	1.50	—
2012S	—	—	4.00
2013P	—	1.50	—
2013D	—	1.50	—
2013S	—	—	3.00

DIME

Roosevelt Dime

KM# 195a • 2.2680 g., **Copper-Nickel Clad Copper**, 17.91 mm. • **Designer:** John R. Sinnock **Notes:** The 1979-S and 1981-S Type II proofs have clearer mint marks than the Type I proofs of those years. On the 1982 no-mint-mark variety, the mint mark was inadvertently left off.

Date	Mintage	MS-65	Prf-65
2001P	1,369,590,000	2.75	—
2001D	1,412,800,000	2.75	—
2001S	2,249,496	—	3.75
2002P	1,187,500,000	2.75	—
2002D	1,379,500,000	3.00	—
2002S	2,268,913	—	2.50
2003P	1,085,500,000	3.00	—
2003D	986,500,000	3.00	—
2003S	2,076,165	—	2.60
2004P	1,328,000,000	3.00	—
2004D	1,159,500,000	3.00	—
2004S	1,804,396	—	4.75
2005P	1,412,000,000	2.75	—
2005P Satin Finish	—	4.00	—
2005D	1,423,500,000	2.75	—
2005D Satin Finish	—	4.00	—
2005S	—	—	2.60
2006P	1,381,000,000	2.50	—
2006P Satin Finish	—	4.00	—
2006D	1,447,000,000	2.50	—
2006D Satin Finish	—	4.00	—
2006S	—	—	2.50
2007P	—	2.00	—
2007P Satin Finish	—	3.00	—
2007D	—	2.00	—
2007D Satin Finish	—	3.00	—
2007S	—	—	2.50
2008P	—	1.25	—
2008 Satin Finish	—	2.50	—
2008D	—	1.25	—
2008 Satin Finish	—	2.50	—
2008S	—	—	2.50
2009P	—	1.25	—
2009 Satin Finish	—	1.00	—
2009D	—	1.25	—
2009 Satin Finish	—	1.00	—
2009S	—	—	2.50
2010P	—	4.00	—
2010P Satin Finish	—	2.00	—
2010D	—	4.00	—
2010D Satin Finish	—	2.00	—
2010S	—	—	2.50
2011P	—	4.00	—
2011D	—	4.00	—
2011S	—	—	2.50
2012P	—	4.00	—
2012D	—	4.00	—
2012S	—	—	2.50
2013P	—	4.00	—
2013D	—	4.00	—
2013S	—	—	2.50

KM# 195b • 2.5000 g., 0.9000 **Silver**, 0.0723 oz. ASW, 17.9 mm. • **Designer:** John R. Sinnock

Date	Mintage	Prf-65
2001S	849,600	5.00
2002S	888,826	5.00
2003S	1,090,425	4.75
2004S	—	5.00
2005S	—	5.00
2006S	—	4.50
2007S	—	6.00
2008S	—	6.50
2009S	—	6.75
2010S	—	6.75
2011S	—	6.75
2012S	—	6.75
2013S	—	6.75

QUARTER

50 State Quarters

Kentucky

KM# 322 • 5.6700 g., **Copper-Nickel Clad Copper**, 24.3 mm. •

Date	Mintage	MS-63	MS-65	Prf-65
2001P	353,000,000	1.00	6.50	—
2001D	370,564,000	1.00	7.00	—
2001S	3,094,140	—	—	4.00

KM# 322a • 6.2500 g., 0.9000 **Silver**, 0.1808 oz. ASW, 24.3 mm. •

Date	Mintage	MS-63	MS-65	Prf-65
2001S	889,697	—	—	9.50

New York

KM# 318 • 5.6700 g., **Copper-Nickel Clad Copper**, 24.3 mm. •

Date	Mintage	MS-63	MS-65	Prf-65
2001P	655,400,000	.80	5.50	—
2001D	619,640,000	.80	5.50	—
2001S	3,094,140	—	—	4.00

KM# 318a • 6.2500 g., 0.9000 **Silver**, 0.1808 oz. ASW, 24.3 mm. •

Date	Mintage	MS-63	MS-65	Prf-65
2001S	889,697	—	—	9.50

North Carolina

KM# 319 • 5.6700 g., **Copper-Nickel Clad Copper**, 24.3 mm. •

Date	Mintage	MS-63	MS-65	Prf-65
2001P	627,600,000	1.00	5.50	—
2001D	427,876,000	1.00	6.50	—
2001S	3,094,140	—	—	4.00

KM# 319a • 6.2500 g., 0.9000 **Silver**, 0.1808 oz. ASW, 24.3 mm. •

Date	Mintage	MS-63	MS-65	Prf-65
2001S	889,697	—	—	9.50

Rhode Island

KM# 320 • 5.6700 g., **Copper-Nickel Clad Copper**, 24.3 mm. •

Date	Mintage	MS-63	MS-65	Prf-65
2001P	423,000,000	.80	5.50	—
2001D	447,100,000	.80	6.00	—
2001S	3,094,140	—	—	4.00

KM# 320a • 6.2500 g., 0.9000 **Silver**, 0.1808 oz. ASW, 24.3 mm. •

Date	Mintage	MS-63	MS-65	Prf-65
2001S	889,697	—	—	9.50

Vermont

KM# 321 • 5.6700 g., **Copper-Nickel Clad Copper**, 24.3 mm. •

Date	Mintage	MS-63	MS-65	Prf-65
2001P	423,400,000	.80	6.50	—
2001D	459,404,000	.80	6.50	—
2001S	3,094,140	—	—	4.00

KM# 321a • 6.2500 g., 0.9000 **Silver**, 0.1808 oz. ASW, 24.3 mm. •

Date	Mintage	MS-63	MS-65	Prf-65
2001S	889,697	—	—	9.50

Indiana

KM# 334 • 5.6700 g., **Copper-Nickel Clad Copper**, 24.3 mm. •

Date	Mintage	MS-63	MS-65	Prf-65
2002P	362,600,000	.80	5.00	—
2002D	327,200,000	.80	5.00	—
2002S	3,084,245	—	—	2.30

KM# 334a • 6.2500 g., 0.9000 **Silver**, 0.1808 oz. ASW, 24.3 mm. •

Date	Mintage	MS-63	MS-65	Prf-65
2002S	892,229	—	—	8.50

Louisiana

KM# 333 • 5.6700 g., **Copper-Nickel Clad Copper**, 24.3 mm. •

Date	Mintage	MS-63	MS-65	Prf-65
2002P	362,000,000	.80	5.50	—
2002D	402,204,000	.80	6.00	—
2002S	3,084,245	—	—	2.30

KM# 333a • 6.2500 g., 0.9000 **Silver**, 0.1808 oz. ASW, 24.3 mm. •

Date	Mintage	MS-63	MS-65	Prf-65
2002S	892,229	—	—	8.50

Mississippi

KM# 335 • 5.6700 g., **Copper-Nickel Clad Copper**, 24.3 mm. •

Date	Mintage	MS-63	MS-65	Prf-65
2002P	290,000,000	.80	5.00	—
2002D	289,600,000	.80	5.00	—
2002S	3,084,245	—	—	2.30

KM# 335a • 6.2500 g., 0.9000 **Silver**, 0.1808 oz. ASW, 24.3 mm. •

Date	Mintage	MS-63	MS-65	Prf-65
2002S	892,229	—	—	8.50

Ohio

KM# 332 • 5.6700 g., **Copper-Nickel Clad Copper**, 24.3 mm. •

Date	Mintage	MS-63	MS-65	Prf-65
2002P	217,200,000	.80	5.50	—
2002D	414,832,000	.80	5.50	—
2002S	3,084,245	—	—	2.30

KM# 332a • 6.2500 g., 0.9000 **Silver**, 0.1808 oz. ASW, 24.3 mm. •

Date	Mintage	MS-63	MS-65	Prf-65
2002S	892,229	—	—	8.50

Tennessee

KM# 331 • 5.6700 g., **Copper-Nickel Clad Copper**, 24.3 mm. •

Date	Mintage	MS-63	MS-65	Prf-65
2002P	361,600,000	1.40	6.50	—
2002D	286,468,000	1.40	7.00	—
2002S	3,084,245	—	—	2.30

KM# 331a • 6.2500 g., 0.9000 **Silver**, 0.1808 oz. ASW, 24.3 mm. •

Date	Mintage	MS-63	MS-65	Prf-65
2002S	892,229	—	—	8.50

Alabama

KM# 344 • 5.6700 g., **Copper-Nickel Clad Copper**, 24.3 mm. •

Date	Mintage	MS-63	MS-65	Prf-65
2003P	225,000,000	.65	5.00	—
2003D	232,400,000	.65	5.00	—
2003S	3,408,516	—	—	2.30

KM# 344a • 6.2500 g., 0.9000 **Silver**, 0.1808 oz. ASW, 24.3 mm. •

Date	Mintage	MS-63	MS-65	Prf-65
2003S	1,257,555	—	—	8.50

Arkansas

KM# 347 • 5.6700 g., **Copper-Nickel Clad Copper**, 24.3 mm. •

Date	Mintage	MS-63	MS-65	Prf-65
2003P	228,000,000	.65	5.00	—
2003D	229,800,000	.65	5.00	—
2003S	3,408,516	—	—	2.30

KM# 347a • 6.2500 g., 0.9000 **Silver**, 0.1808 oz. ASW, 24.3 mm. •

Date	Mintage	MS-63	MS-65	Prf-65
2003S	1,257,555	—	—	8.50

Illinois

KM# 343 • 5.6700 g., **Copper-Nickel Clad Copper**, 24.3 mm. •

Date	Mintage	MS-63	MS-65	Prf-65
2003P	225,800,000	1.10	5.00	—
2003D	237,400,000	1.10	5.00	—
2003S	3,408,516	—	—	2.30

KM# 343a • 6.2500 g., 0.9000 **Silver**, 0.1808 oz. ASW, 24.3 mm. •

Date	Mintage	MS-63	MS-65	Prf-65
2003S	1,257,555	—	—	8.50

Maine

KM# 345 • 5.6700 g., **Copper-Nickel Clad Copper**, 24.3 mm. •

Date	Mintage	MS-63	MS-65	Prf-65
2003P	217,400,000	.65	5.00	—
2003D	213,400,000	.65	5.00	—
2003S	3,408,516	—	—	2.30

KM# 345a • 6.2500 g., 0.9000 **Silver**, 0.1808 oz. ASW, 24.3 mm. •

Date	Mintage	MS-63	MS-65	Prf-65
2003S	1,257,555	—	—	8.50

Missouri

KM# 346 • 5.6700 g., **Copper-Nickel Clad Copper**, 24.3 mm. •

Date	Mintage	MS-63	MS-65	Prf-65
2003P	225,000,000	.65	5.00	—
2003D	228,200,000	.65	5.00	—
2003S	3,408,516	—	—	2.30

KM# 346a • 6.2500 g., 0.9000 **Silver**, 0.1808 oz. ASW, 24.3 mm. •

Date	Mintage	MS-63	MS-65	Prf-65
2003S	1,257,555	—	—	8.50

Florida

KM# 356 • 5.6700 g., **Copper-Nickel Clad Copper**, 24.3 mm. •

Date	Mintage	MS-63	MS-65	Prf-65
2004P	240,200,000	.65	5.00	—
2004D	241,600,000	.65	5.00	—
2004S	2,740,684	—	—	2.30

KM# 356a • 6.2500 g., 0.9000 **Silver**, 0.1808 oz. ASW, 24.3 mm. •

Date	Mintage	MS-63	MS-65	Prf-65
2004S	1,775,370	—	—	8.50

Iowa

KM# 358 • 5.6700 g., **Copper-Nickel Clad Copper**, 24.3 mm. •

Date	Mintage	MS-63	MS-65	Prf-65
2004P	213,800,000	.65	5.00	—
2004D	251,800,000	.65	5.00	—
2004S	2,740,684	—	—	2.30

KM# 358a • 6.2500 g., 0.9000 **Silver**, 0.1808 oz. ASW, 24.3 mm. •

Date	Mintage	MS-63	MS-65	Prf-65
2004S	—	—	—	8.50

Michigan

KM# 355 • 5.6700 g., **Copper-Nickel Clad Copper**, 24.3 mm. •

Date	Mintage	MS-63	MS-65	Prf-65
2004P	233,800,000	.65	5.00	—
2004D	225,800,000	.65	5.00	—
2004S	2,740,684	—	—	2.30

KM# 355a • 6.2500 g., 0.9000 **Silver**, 0.1808 oz. ASW, 24.3 mm. •

Date	Mintage	MS-63	MS-65	Prf-65
2004S	1,775,370	—	—	8.50

Texas

KM# 357 • 5.6700 g., **Copper-Nickel Clad Copper**, 24.3 mm. •

Date	Mintage	MS-63	MS-65	Prf-65
2004P	278,800,000	.65	5.00	—
2004D	263,000,000	.65	5.00	—
2004S	2,740,684	—	—	2.30

KM# 357a • 6.2500 g., 0.9000 **Silver**, 0.1808 oz. ASW, 24.3 mm. •

Date	Mintage	MS-63	MS-65	Prf-65
2004S	1,775,370	—	—	8.50

Wisconsin

KM# 359 • 5.6700 g., **Copper-Nickel Clad Copper**, 24.3 mm. •

Date	Mintage	MS-63	MS-65	Prf-65
2004P	226,400,000	.65	5.00	—
2004D	226,800,000	.65	5.00	—
2004D Extra Leaf Low	Est. 9,000	135	190	—
2004D Extra Leaf High	Est. 3,000	175	285	—
2004S	—	—	—	2.30

KM# 359a • 6.2500 g., 0.9000 **Silver**, 0.1808 oz. ASW, 24.3 mm. •

Date	Mintage	MS-63	MS-65	Prf-65
2004S	1,775,370	—	—	8.50

California

KM# 370 • 5.6700 g., **Copper-Nickel Clad Copper**, 24.3 mm. •

Date	Mintage	MS-63	MS-65	Prf-65
2005P	257,200,000	.65	5.00	—
2005P Satin Finish	Inc. above	1.50	4.50	—
2005D	263,200,000	.65	5.00	—
2005D Satin Finish	Inc. above	1.50	4.50	—
2005S	3,262,960	—	—	2.30

KM# 370a • 6.2500 g., 0.9000 **Silver**, 0.1808 oz. ASW, 24.3 mm. •

Date	Mintage	MS-63	MS-65	Prf-65
2005S	1,679,600	—	—	8.50

Kansas

KM# 373 • 5.6700 g., **Copper-Nickel Clad Copper**, 24.3 mm. •

Date	Mintage	MS-63	MS-65	Prf-65
2005P	263,400,000	.65	5.00	—
2005P Satin Finish	Inc. above	1.50	4.50	—
2005D	300,000,000	.65	5.00	—
2005D Satin Finish	Inc. above	1.50	4.50	—
2005S	3,262,960	—	—	2.30

KM# 373a • 6.2500 g., 0.9000 **Silver**, 0.1808 oz. ASW, 24.3 mm. •

Date	Mintage	MS-63	MS-65	Prf-65
2005S	1,679,600	—	—	8.50

Minnesota

KM# 371 • 5.6700 g., **Copper-Nickel Clad Copper**, 24.3 mm. •

Date	Mintage	MS-63	MS-65	Prf-65
2005P	226,400,000	.65	5.00	—
2005P Satin Finish	Inc. above	1.50	4.50	—
2005D	226,800,000	.65	5.00	—
2005D Satin Finish	Inc. above	1.50	4.50	—
2005S	3,262,960	—	—	2.30

KM# 371a • 6.2500 g., 0.9000 **Silver**, 0.1808 oz. ASW, 24.3 mm. •

Date	Mintage	MS-63	MS-65	Prf-65
2005S	1,679,600	—	—	8.50

Oregon

KM# 372 • 5.6700 g., **Copper-Nickel Clad Copper**, 24.3 mm. •

Date	Mintage	MS-63	MS-65	Prf-65
2005P	316,200,000	.65	5.00	—
2005P Satin Finish	Inc. above	1.50	4.50	—
2005D	404,000,000	.65	5.00	—
2005D Satin Finish	Inc. above	1.50	4.50	—
2005S	3,262,960	—	—	2.30

KM# 372a • 6.2500 g., 0.9000 **Silver**, 0.1808 oz. ASW, 24.3 mm. •

Date	Mintage	MS-63	MS-65	Prf-65
2005S	1,679,600	—	—	8.50

West Virginia

KM# 374 • 5.6700 g., **Copper-Nickel Clad Copper**, 24.3 mm. •

Date	Mintage	MS-63	MS-65	Prf-65
2005P	365,400,000	.65	5.00	—
2005P Satin Finish	Inc. above	1.50	4.50	—
2005D	356,200,000	.65	5.00	—
2005D Satin Finish	Inc. above	1.50	4.50	—
2005S	3,262,960	—	—	2.30

KM# 374a • 6.2500 g., 0.9000 **Silver**, 0.1808 oz. ASW, 24.3 mm. •

Date	Mintage	MS-63	MS-65	Prf-65
2005S	1,679,600	—	—	8.50

Colorado

KM# 384 • 5.6700 g., **Copper-Nickel Clad Copper**, 24.3 mm. •

Date	Mintage	MS-63	MS-65	Prf-65
2006P	274,800,000	.65	5.00	—
2006P Satin Finish	Inc. above	1.50	4.50	—
2006D	294,200,000	.65	5.00	—
2006D Satin Finish	Inc. above	1.50	4.50	—
2006S	2,862,078	—	—	2.30

KM# 384a • 6.2500 g., 0.9000 **Silver**, 0.1808 oz. ASW, 24.3 mm. •

Date	Mintage	MS-63	MS-65	Prf-65
2006S	1,571,839	—	—	8.50

Nebraska

KM# 383 • 5.6700 g., **Copper-Nickel Clad Copper**, 24.3 mm. •

Date	Mintage	MS-63	MS-65	Prf-65
2006P	318,000,000	.65	5.00	—
2006P Satin Finish	Inc. above	1.50	4.50	—
2006D	273,000,000	.65	5.00	—
2006D Satin Finish	Inc. above	1.50	4.50	—
2006S	2,862,078	—	—	2.30

KM# 383a • 6.2500 g., 0.9000 **Silver**, 0.1808 oz. ASW, 24.3 mm. •

Date	Mintage	MS-63	MS-65	Prf-65
2006S	1,571,839	—	—	8.50

Nevada

KM# 382 • 5.6700 g., **Copper-Nickel Clad Copper**, 24.3 mm. •

Date	Mintage	MS-63	MS-65	Prf-65
2006P	277,000,000	.65	5.00	—
2006P Satin Finish	Inc. above	1.50	4.50	—
2006D	312,800,000	.65	5.00	—
2006D Satin Finish	Inc. above	1.50	4.50	—
2006S	2,862,078	—	—	2.30

KM# 382a • 6.2500 g., 0.9000 **Silver**, 0.1808 oz. ASW, 24.3 mm. •

Date	Mintage	MS-63	MS-65	Prf-65
2006S	1,571,839	—	—	8.50

North Dakota

KM# 385 • 5.6700 g., **Copper-Nickel Clad Copper**, 24.3 mm. •

Date	Mintage	MS-63	MS-65	Prf-65
2006P	305,800,000	.65	5.00	—
2006P Satin Finish	Inc. above	1.50	4.50	—
2006D	359,000,000	.65	5.00	—
2006D Satin Finish	Inc. above	1.50	4.50	—
2006S	2,862,078	—	—	2.30

KM# 385a • 6.2500 g., 0.9000 **Silver**, 0.1808 oz. ASW, 24.3 mm. •

Date	Mintage	MS-63	MS-65	Prf-65
2006S	1,571,839	—	—	8.50

South Dakota

KM# 386 • 5.6700 g., **Copper-Nickel Clad Copper**, 24.3 mm. •

Date	Mintage	MS-63	MS-65	Prf-65
2006P	245,000,000	.65	5.00	—
2006P Satin Finish	Inc. above	1.50	4.50	—
2006D	265,800,000	.65	5.00	—
2006D Satin Finish	Inc. above	1.50	4.50	—
2006S	2,862,078	—	—	2.30

KM# 386a • 6.2500 g., 0.9000 **Silver**, 0.1808 oz. ASW, 24.3 mm. •

Date	Mintage	MS-63	MS-65	Prf-65
2006S	1,571,839	—	—	8.50

Idaho

KM# 398 • 5.6700 g., **Copper-Nickel Clad Copper**, 24.3 mm. •

Date	Mintage	MS-63	MS-65	Prf-65
2007P	294,600,000	.65	5.00	—
2007P Satin finish	—	1.50	4.50	—
2007D	286,800,000	.65	5.00	—
2007D Satin finish	—	1.50	4.50	—
2007S	2,374,778	—	—	2.30

KM# 398a • 6.2500 g., 0.9000 **Silver**, 0.1808 oz. ASW, 24.3 mm. •

Date	Mintage	MS-63	MS-65	Prf-65
2007S	1,299,878	—	—	8.50

Montana

KM# 396 • 5.6700 g., **Copper-Nickel Clad Copper**, 24.3 mm.

Date	Mintage	MS-63	MS-65	Prf-65
2007 Satin Finish	—	1.50	4.50	—
2007 Satin Finish	—	1.50	4.50	—
2007P	257,000,000	.65	5.00	—
2007D	256,240,000	.65	5.00	—
2007S	2,374,778	—	—	2.30

KM# 396a • 6.2500 g., 0.9000 **Silver**, 0.1808 oz. ASW, 24.3 mm. •

Date	Mintage	MS-63	MS-65	Prf-65
2007S	1,299,878	—	—	8.50

Utah

KM# 400 • 5.6700 g., **Copper-Nickel Clad Copper**, 24.3 mm. •

Date	Mintage	MS-63	MS-65	Prf-65
2007P	255,000,000	.65	5.00	—
2007P Satin finish	—	1.50	4.50	—
2007D	253,200,000	.65	5.00	—
2007D Satin finish	—	1.50	4.50	—
2007S	2,374,778	—	—	2.30

KM# 400a • 6.2500 g., 0.9000 **Silver**, 0.1808 oz. ASW •

Date	Mintage	MS-63	MS-65	Prf-65
2007S	1,299,878	—	—	8.50

Washington

KM# 397 • 5.6700 g., **Copper-Nickel Clad Copper**, 24.3 mm. •

Date	Mintage	MS-63	MS-65	Prf-65
2007P	265,200,000	.65	5.00	—
2007P Satin Finish	—	1.50	4.50	—
2007D	280,000,000	.65	5.00	—
2007D Satin Finish	—	1.50	4.50	—
2007S	2,374,778	—	—	2.30

KM# 397a • 6.2500 g., 0.9000 **Silver**, 0.1808 oz. ASW, 24.3 mm. •

Date	Mintage	MS-63	MS-65	Prf-65
2007S	1,299,878	—	—	8.50

Wyoming

KM# 399 • 5.6700 g., **Copper-Nickel Clad Copper**, 24.3 mm. •

Date	Mintage	MS-63	MS-65	Prf-65
2007P	243,600,000	.65	5.00	—
2007P Satin finish	—	1.50	4.50	—
2007D	320,800,000	.65	5.00	—
2007 Satin finish	—	1.50	4.50	—
2007S	2,374,778	—	—	2.30

KM# 399a • 6.2500 g., 0.9000 **Silver**, 0.1808 oz. ASW, 24.3 mm. •

Date	Mintage	MS-63	MS-65	Prf-65
2007S	1,299,878	—	—	8.50

Alaska

KM# 424 • 5.6700 g., **Copper-Nickel Clad Copper**, 24.3 mm. •

Date	Mintage	MS-63	MS-65	Prf-65
2008P	251,800,000	.65	5.00	—
2008P Satin finish	—	1.50	4.50	—
2008D	254,000,000	.65	5.00	—
2008D Satin finish	—	1.50	4.50	—
2008S	2,100,000	—	—	2.30

KM# 424a • 6.2500 g., 0.9000 **Silver**, 0.1808 oz. ASW, 24.3 mm. •

Date	Mintage	MS-63	MS-65	Prf-65
2008S	1,200,000	—	—	8.50

Arizona

KM# 423 • 5.6700 g., **Copper-Nickel Clad Copper**, 24.3 mm. •

Date	Mintage	MS-63	MS-65	Prf-65
2008P	244,600,000	.65	5.00	—
2008P Satin finish	—	1.50	4.50	—
2008D	265,000,000	.65	5.00	—
2008D Satin finish	—	1.50	4.50	—
2008S	2,100,000	—	—	2.30

KM# 423a • 6.2500 g., 0.9000 **Silver**, 0.1808 oz. ASW, 24.3 mm. •

Date	Mintage	MS-63	MS-65	Prf-65
2008S	1,200,000	—	—	8.50

Hawaii

KM# 425 • 5.6700 g., **Copper-Nickel Clad Copper**, 24.3 mm. •

Date	Mintage	MS-63	MS-65	Prf-65
2008P	254,000,000	.65	5.00	—
2008P Satin finish	—	1.50	4.50	—
2008D	263,600,000	.65	5.00	—
2008D Satin finish	—	1.50	4.50	—
2008S	2,100,000	—	—	2.30

KM# 425a • 6.2500 g., 0.9000 **Silver**, 0.1808 oz. ASW, 24.3 mm. •

Date	Mintage	MS-63	MS-65	Prf-65
2008S	1,200,000	—	—	8.50

New Mexico

KM# 422 • 5.6700 g., **Copper-Nickel Clad Copper**, 24.3 mm. •

Date	Mintage	MS-63	MS-65	Prf-65
2008P	244,200,000	.65	5.00	—
2008P Satin finish	—	1.50	4.50	—
2008D	244,400,000	.65	5.00	—
2008D Satin finish	—	1.50	4.50	—
2008S	2,100,000	—	—	2.30

KM# 422a • 6.2500 g., 0.9000 **Silver**, 0.1808 oz. ASW, 24.3 mm. •

Date	Mintage	MS-63	MS-65	Prf-65
2008S	1,200,000	—	—	8.50

Oklahoma

KM# 421 • 5.6700 g., **Copper-Nickel Clad Copper**, 24.3 mm. •

Date	Mintage	MS-63	MS-65	Prf-65
2008P	222,000,000	.65	5.00	—
2008P Satin finish	—	1.50	4.50	—
2008D	194,600,000	.65	5.00	—
2008D Satin finish	—	1.50	4.50	—
2008S	2,100,000	—	—	2.30

KM# 421a • 6.2500 g., 0.9000 **Silver**, 0.1808 oz. ASW, 24.3 mm. •

Date	Mintage	MS-63	MS-65	Prf-65
2008S	1,200,000	—	—	8.50

DC and Territories

American Samoa

KM# 448 • 5.6700 g., **Copper-Nickel Clad Copper**, 24.3 mm. • **Rev. Designer:** Charles Vickers

Date	Mintage	MS-63	MS-65	Prf-65
2009P	42,600,000	.75	5.00	—
2009D	39,600,000	.75	5.00	—
2009S	—	—	—	3.75

KM# 448a • 6.2500 g., 0.9000 **Silver**, 0.1808 oz. ASW, 24.3 mm. •

Date	Mintage	MS-63	MS-65	Prf-65
2009S	—	—	—	7.75

District of Columbia

KM# 445 • 5.6700 g., **Copper-Nickel Clad Copper**, 24.3 mm. • **Rev. Designer:** Don Everhart

Date	Mintage	MS-63	MS-65	Prf-65
2009P	83,600,000	.75	5.00	—
2009D	88,800,000	.75	5.00	—
2009S	—	—	—	3.75

KM# 445a • 6.2500 g., 0.9000 **Silver**, 0.1808 oz. ASW, 24.3 mm. •

Date	Mintage	MS-63	MS-65	Prf-65
2009S	—	—	—	7.75

Guam

KM# 447 • 5.6700 g., **Copper-Nickel Clad Copper**, 24.3 mm. • **Rev. Designer:** James Licaretz

Date	Mintage	MS-63	MS-65	Prf-65
2009P	45,000,000	.75	5.00	—
2009D	42,600,000	.75	5.00	—
2009S	—	—	—	3.75

KM# 447a • 6.2500 g., 0.9000 **Silver**, 0.1808 oz. ASW, 24.3 mm. •

Date	Mintage	MS-63	MS-65	Prf-65
2009S	—	—	—	7.75

Northern Mariana Islands

KM# 466 • 5.6700 g., **Copper-Nickel Clad Copper**, • **Rev. Designer:** Pheve Hemphill

Date	Mintage	MS-63	MS-65	Prf-65
2009P	35,200,000	.75	5.00	—
2009D	37,600,000	.75	5.00	—
2009S	—	—	—	3.75

KM# 466a • 6.2500 g., 0.9000 **Silver**, 0.1808 oz. ASW •

Date	Mintage	MS-63	MS-65	Prf-65
2009S	—	—	—	7.75

Puerto Rico

KM# 446 • 5.6700 g., **Copper-Nickel Clad Copper**, 24.3 mm. • **Rev. Designer:** Joseph Menna

Date	Mintage	MS-63	MS-65	Prf-65
2009P	53,200,000	.75	5.00	—
2009D	86,000,000	.75	5.00	—
2009S	—	—	—	3.75

KM# 446a • 6.2500 g., 0.9000 **Silver**, 0.1808 oz. ASW, 24.3 mm. •

Date	Mintage	MS-63	MS-65	Prf-65
2009S	—	—	—	7.75

US Virgin Islands

KM# 449 • 5.6700 g., **Copper-Nickel Clad Copper**, 24.3 mm. • **Rev. Designer:** Joseph Menna

Date	Mintage	MS-63	MS-65	Prf-65
2009P	41,000,000	.75	5.00	—
2009D	41,000,000	.75	5.00	—
2009S	—	—	—	3.75

KM# 449a • 6.2500 g., 0.9000 **Silver**, 0.1808 oz. ASW, 24.3 mm. •

Date	Mintage	MS-63	MS-65	Prf-65
2009S	—	—	—	7.75

America the Beautiful

Grand Canyon National Park

KM# 472 • 5.6700 g., **Copper-Nickel Clad Copper**, 24.3 mm. •

Date	Mintage	MS-63	MS-65	Prf-65
2010P	—	.75	5.00	—
2010D	—	.75	5.00	—
2010S	—	—	—	3.75

KM# 472a • 6.2500 g., 0.9000 **Silver**, 0.1808 oz. ASW •

Date	Mintage	MS-63	MS-65	Prf-65
2010	—	—	—	7.75

Hot Springs, Ark.

KM# 469 • 5.6700 g., **Copper-Nickel Clad Copper**, 24.3 mm. •

Date	Mintage	MS-63	MS-65	Prf-65
2010P	—	.75	5.00	—
2010D	—	.75	5.00	—
2010S	—	—	—	3.75

KM# 469a • 6.2500 g., 0.9000 **Silver**, 0.1808 oz. ASW •

Date	Mintage	MS-63	MS-65	Prf-65
2010S	—	—	—	7.75

Mount Hood National Park

KM# 473 • 5.6700 g., **Copper-Nickel Clad Copper**, •

Date	Mintage	MS-63	MS-65	Prf-65
2010P	—	.75	5.00	—
2010D	—	.75	5.00	—
2010S	—	—	—	3.75

KM# 473a • 6.2500 g., 0.9000 **Silver**, 0.1808 oz. ASW •

Date	Mintage	MS-63	MS-65	Prf-65
2010	—	—	—	7.75

Yellowstone National Park

KM# 470 • 5.6700 g., **Copper-Nickel Clad Copper**, 24.3 mm. •

Date	Mintage	MS-63	MS-65	Prf-65
2010P	—	.75	5.00	—
2010D	—	.75	5.00	—
2010S	—	—	—	3.75

KM# 470a • 6.2500 g., 0.9000 **Silver**, 0.1808 oz. ASW •

Date	Mintage	MS-63	MS-65	Prf-65
2010	—	—	—	7.75

Yosemite National Park

KM# 471 • 5.6700 g., **Copper-Nickel Clad Copper**, 24.3 mm. •

Date	Mintage	MS-63	MS-65	Prf-65
2010P	—	.75	5.00	—
2010D	—	.75	5.00	—
2010S	—	—	—	3.75

KM# 471a • 6.2500 g., 0.9000 **Silver**, 0.1808 oz. ASW •

Date	Mintage	MS-63	MS-65	Prf-65
2010	—	—	—	7.75

Chickasaw National Recreation Area

KM# 498 • 5.6700 g., **Copper-Nickel Clad Copper**, 24 mm. •

Date	Mintage	MS-63	MS-65	Prf-65
2011P	—	.75	5.00	—
2011D	—	.75	5.00	—
2011S	—	—	—	3.75

KM# 498a • 6.2500 g., 0.9000 **Silver**, 0.1808 oz. ASW •

Date	Mintage	MS-63	MS-65	Prf-65
2011S	—	—	—	7.75

Gettysburg National Military Park

KM# 494 • 5.6700 g., **Copper-Nickel Clad Copper**, 24 mm. •

Date	Mintage	MS-63	MS-65	Prf-65
2011P	—	.75	5.00	—
2011D	—	.75	5.00	—
2011S	—	—	—	3.75

KM# 494a • 6.2500 g., 0.9000 **Silver**, 0.1808 oz. ASW •

Date	Mintage	MS-63	MS-65	Prf-65
2011S	—	—	—	7.75

Glacier National Park

KM# 495 • 5.6700 g., **Copper-Nickel Clad Copper**, 24 mm. •

Date	Mintage	MS-63	MS-65	Prf-65
2011P	—	.75	5.00	—
2011D	—	.75	5.00	—
2011S	—	—	—	3.75

KM# 495a • 6.2500 g., 0.9000 **Silver**, 0.1808 oz. ASW •

Date	Mintage	MS-63	MS-65	Prf-65
2011S	—	—	—	7.75

Olympic National Park

KM# 496 • 5.6700 g., **Copper-Nickel Clad Copper**, 24 mm. •

Date	Mintage	MS-63	MS-65	Prf-65
2011P	—	.75	5.00	—
2011D	—	.75	5.00	—
2011S	—	—	—	3.75

KM# 496a • 6.2500 g., 0.9000 **Silver**, 0.1808 oz. ASW •

Date	Mintage	MS-63	MS-65	Prf-65
2011S	—	—	—	7.75

Vicksburg National Military Park

KM# 497 • 5.6700 g., **Copper-Nickel Clad Copper**, 24 mm. •

Date	Mintage	MS-63	MS-65	Prf-65
2011P	—	.75	5.00	—
2011D	—	.75	5.00	—
2011S	—	—	—	3.75

KM# 497a • 6.2500 g., 0.9000 **Silver**, 0.1808 oz. ASW •

Date	Mintage	MS-63	MS-65	Prf-65
2011S	—	—	—	7.75

Acadia National Park

KM# 521 • 5.6700 g., **Copper-Nickel Clad Copper**, 24.3 mm. •

Date	Mintage	MS-63	MS-65	Prf-65
2012P	—	.75	5.00	—
2012D	—	.75	5.00	—
2012S	—	—	—	3.75

KM# 521a • 6.2500 g., 0.9000 **Silver**, 0.1808 oz. ASW, 24.3 mm. •

Date	Mintage	MS-63	MS-65	Prf-65
2012S	—	—	—	7.75

Chaco Culture National Historic Park

KM# 520 • 5.7100 g., **Copper-Nickel Clad Copper**, 24.3 mm. •

Date	Mintage	MS-63	MS-65	Prf-65
2012P	—	.75	8.00	—
2012D	—	.75	8.00	—
2012S	—	—	—	4.00

KM# 520a • 6.2500 g., 0.9000 **Silver**, 0.1808 oz. ASW, 24.3 mm. •

Date	Mintage	MS-63	MS-65	Prf-65
2012S	—	—	—	7.75

Denali National Park

KM# 523 • 5.6700 g., **Copper-Nickel Clad Copper**, 24.3 mm. •

Date	Mintage	MS-63	MS-65	Prf-65
2012P	—	.75	5.00	—
2012D	—	.75	5.00	—
2012S	—	—	—	3.75

KM# 523a • 6.2500 g., 0.9000 **Silver**, 0.1808 oz. ASW, 24.3 mm. •

Date	Mintage	MS-63	MS-65	Prf-65
2012S	—	—	—	7.75

El Yunque National Forest

KM# 519 • 5.6700 g., **Copper-Nickel Clad Copper**, 24.3 mm. •

Date	Mintage	MS-63	MS-65	Prf-65
2012P	—	.75	5.00	—
2012D	—	.75	5.00	—
2012S	—	—	—	3.75

KM# 519a • 6.2500 g., 0.9000 **Silver**, 0.1808 oz. ASW, 24.3 mm. •

Date	Mintage	MS-63	MS-65	Prf-65
2012S	—	—	—	7.75

Hawai'i Volcanoes National Park

KM# 522 • 5.6700 g., **Copper-Nickel Clad Copper**, 24.3 mm. •

Date	Mintage	MS-63	MS-65	Prf-65
2012P	—	.75	5.00	—
2012D	—	.75	5.00	—
2012S	—	—	—	3.75

KM# 522a • 6.2500 g., 0.9000 **Silver**, 0.1808 oz. ASW, 24.3 mm. •

Date	Mintage	MS-63	MS-65	Prf-65
2012S	—	—	—	7.75

Fort McHenry National Monument and Historic Shrine

KM# 545 • 5.6700 g., **Copper-Nickel Clad Copper**, 24.3 mm. •

Date	Mintage	MS-63	MS-65	Prf-65
2013P	—	.75	5.00	—
2013D	—	.75	5.00	—
2013S	—	—	—	3.75

KM# 545a • 6.2500 g., 0.9000 **Silver**, 0.1808 oz. ASW, 24.3 mm. •

Date	Mintage	MS-63	MS-65	Prf-65
2013S	—	—	—	7.75

Great Basin National Park

KM# 544 • 5.6700 g., **Copper-Nickel Clad Copper**, 24.3 mm. •

Date	Mintage	MS-63	MS-65	Prf-65
2013P	—	.75	5.00	—
2013D	—	.75	5.00	—
2013S	—	—	—	3.75

KM# 544a • 6.2500 g., 0.9000 **Silver**, 0.1808 oz. ASW, 24.3 mm. •

Date	Mintage	MS-63	MS-65	Prf-65
2013S	—	—	—	7.75

Mount Rushmore National Memorial

KM# 546 • 5.6700 g., **Copper-Nickel Clad Copper**, 24.3 mm. •

Date	Mintage	MS-63	MS-65	Prf-65
2013P	—	.75	5.00	—
2013D	—	.75	5.00	—
2013S	—	—	—	3.75

KM# 546a • 6.2500 g., 0.9000 **Silver**, 0.1808 oz. ASW, 24.3 mm. •

Date	Mintage	MS-63	MS-65	Prf-65
2013S	—	—	—	7.75

Perry's Victory and International Peace Memorial

KM# 543 • 5.6700 g., **Copper-Nickel Clad Copper**, 24.3 mm. •

Date	Mintage	MS-63	MS-65	Prf-65
2013P	—	.75	.50	—
2013D	—	.75	5.00	—
2013S	—	—	—	3.75

KM# 543a • 6.2500 g., 0.9000 **Silver**, 0.1808 oz. ASW, 24.3 mm. •

Date	Mintage	MS-63	MS-65	Prf-65
2013S	—	—	—	7.75

White Mountain National Forest

KM# 542 • 5.6700 g., **Copper-Nickel Clad Copper**, 24.3 mm. •

Date	Mintage	MS-63	MS-65	Prf-65
2013P	—	.75	5.00	—
2013D	—	.75	5.00	—
2013S	—	—	—	3.75

KM# 542a • 6.2500 g., 0.9000 **Silver**, 0.1808 oz. ASW, 24.3 mm. •

Date	Mintage	MS-63	MS-65	Prf-65
2013S	—	—	—	7.75

HALF DOLLAR

Kennedy Half Dollar

Regular design resumed reverse

KM# A202b • 11.3400 g., **Copper-Nickel Clad Copper**, 30.61 mm. • **Edge Desc:** Reeded **Notes:** KM#202b design and composition resumed. The 1979-S and 1981-S Type II proofs have clearer mint marks than the Type I proofs of those years.

Date	Mintage	MS-65	Prf-65
2001P	21,200,000	10.00	—
2001D	19,504,000	9.00	—
2001S	2,235,000	—	5.00
2002P	3,100,000	10.00	—
2002D	2,500,000	10.50	—
2002S	2,268,913	—	5.00
2003P	2,500,000	6.00	—
2003D	2,500,000	6.00	—
2003S	2,076,165	—	5.00
2004P	2,900,000	4.50	—
2004D	2,900,000	4.50	—
2004S	1,789,488	—	6.00
2005P	3,800,000	6.00	—
2005P Satin finish	1,160,000	8.00	—
2005D	3,500,000	5.00	—
2005D Satin finish	1,160,000	10.00	—
2005S	2,275,000	—	5.00
2006P	2,400,000	4.50	—
2006P Satin finish	847,361	12.00	—
2006D	2,000,000	4.50	—
2006D Satin finish	847,361	14.00	—
2006S	1,934,965	—	6.00
2007P	—	4.50	—
2007P Satin finish	—	8.00	—
2007D	—	4.50	—
2007D Satin finish	—	8.00	—
2007S	—	—	6.00
2008P	—	4.50	—
2008P Satin finish	—	8.50	—
2008D	—	4.50	—
2008D Satin finish	—	8.50	—
2008S	—	—	9.00
2009P	—	4.50	—
2009P Satin finish	—	8.50	—
2009D	—	4.50	—
2009D Satin finish	—	8.50	—
2009S	—	—	6.00
2010P	—	4.50	—
2010P Satin finish	—	8.50	—

Date	Mintage	MS-65	Prf-65
2010D	—	4.50	—
2010D Satin finish	—	8.50	—
2010S	—	—	13.00
2011P	—	4.50	—
2011D	—	4.50	—
2011S	—	—	9.00
2012P	—	4.50	—
2012D	—	4.50	—
2012S	—	—	9.00
2013P	—	4.50	—
2013D	—	4.50	—
2013S	—	—	9.00

KM# A202c • 12.5000 g., 0.9000 **Silver**, 0.3617 oz. ASW, 30.6 mm. • **Designer:** Gilroy Roberts

Date	Mintage	Prf-65
2001S	849,600	11.00
2002S	888,816	11.00
2003S	1,040,425	11.00
2004S	1,175,935	11.00
2005S	1,069,679	12.00
2006S	988,140	12.00
2007S	1,384,797	13.50
2008S	620,684	12.00
2009S	—	11.00
2010S	—	12.00
2011S	—	12.00
2012S	—	12.00
2013S	—	12.00

DOLLAR

Sacagawea Dollar

Sacagawea bust right, with baby on back obverse Eagle in flight left reverse

KM# 310 • 8.0700 g., **Copper-Zinc-Manganese-Nickel Clad Copper**, 26.5 mm. •

Date	Mintage	MS-63	MS-65	Prf-65
2000P	767,140,000	2.00	7.50	—
2000P Goodacre Presentation	5,000	—	575	—
2000D	518,916,000	2.00	11.00	—
2000D from Millennium Set	5,500	10.00	50.00	—
2000S	4,048,000	—	—	5.00
2001P	62,468,000	2.25	6.00	—
2001D	70,909,500	2.25	8.00	—
2001S	3,084,000	—	—	16.00
2002P	3,865,610	3.00	9.00	—
2002D	3,732,000	2.75	10.00	—
2002S	3,157,739	—	—	10.00
2003P	3,090,000	4.50	10.00	—
2003D	3,090,000	4.75	12.00	—
2003S	3,116,590	—	—	8.00
2004P	2,660,000	3.50	6.00	—
2004D	2,660,000	4.00	8.00	—
2004S	2,992,069	—	—	7.50
2005P	2,520,000	3.00	9.00	—
2005P Satin Finish	1,160,000	5.00	9.00	—
2005D	2,520,000	3.00	10.00	—
2005D Satin Finish	1,160,000	5.00	9.00	—
2005S	3,273,000	—	—	6.00
2006P	4,900,000	3.25	6.00	—
2006P Satin Finish	847,361	4.50	9.00	—
2006D	2,800,000	3.50	10.00	—
2006D Satin Finish	847,361	4.00	6.00	—
2006S	3,054,436	—	—	9.00
2007P	3,640,000	2.25	5.50	—
2007P Satin Finish	895,628	4.00	6.00	—
2007D	3,920,000	2.25	7.50	—
2007D Satin Finish	895,628	4.00	6.00	—
2007S	2,577,166	—	—	6.50
2008P	1,820,000	2.00	7.00	—
2008P Satin Finish	745,464	4.00	6.00	—
2008D	1,820,000	3.50	10.00	—
2008D Satin Finish	745,464	4.00	6.00	—
2008S	2,169,561	—	—	16.00

Native American female planting corn, beans and squash reverse

KM# 467 • 8.0700 g., **Copper-Zinc-Manganese-Nickel Clad Copper**, 26.5 mm. • Edge Lettering:E PLURIBUS UNUM, date, mint mark **Notes:** Date and mint mark on edge

Date	Mintage	MS-63	MS-65	Prf-65
2009P	37,380,000	2.00	5.00	—
2009 P Satin finish	784,614	4.00	7.00	—
2009D	33,880,000	2.00	5.00	—
2009D Satin finish	784,614	4.00	7.00	—
2009S	2,179,867	—	—	6.00

Hiawatha belt and bundle of five arrows reverse

KM# 474 • 8.0700 g., **Copper-Zinc-Manganese-Nickel Clad Copper**, 26.5 mm. • Edge Lettering:E PLURIBUS UNUM, date, mint mark **Notes:** Date and mint mark on edge

Date	Mintage	MS-63	MS-65	Prf-65
2010P	32,060,000	2.00	5.00	—
2010P Satin Finish	583,897	4.00	7.00	—
2010D	48,720,000	2.00	5.00	—
2010D Satin Finish	583,897	4.00	7.00	—
2010S	1,689,364	—	—	12.50

Hands passing peace pipe reverse

KM# 503 • 8.0700 g., **Copper-Zinc-Manganese-Nickel Clad Copper**, 26.5 mm. • **Obv. Designer:** Glenna Goodacre **Rev. Designer:** Richard Masters and Joseph Menna Edge Lettering:E PLURIBUS UNUM, date, mint mark **Notes:** Date and mint mark on edge

Date	Mintage	MS-63	MS-65	Prf-65
2011P	29,400,000	2.00	5.50	—
2011D	48,160,000	2.00	5.00	—
2011S	1,453,276	—	—	8.00

Horse and Native American profile facing left reverse

KM# 528 • 8.0700 g., **Copper-Zinc-Manganese-Nickel Clad Copper**, 26.5 mm. • Edge Lettering:E PLURIBUS UNUM, date, mint mark **Notes:** Date and mint mark on edge

Date	Mintage	MS-63	MS-65	Prf-65
2012P	28,000,000	2.00	7.00	—
2012D	3,080,000	2.00	7.00	—
2012S	—	—	—	12.50
2013P	—	2.00	5.50	—
2013D	—	2.00	5.00	—
2013S	—	—	—	8.00

Delaware Treaty of 1778

KM# 551 • 8.0700 g., **Copper-Zinc-Manganese-Nickel Clad Copper**, 26.5 mm. • Edge Desc:E PLURIBUS UNUM, date, mint mark **Notes:** Date and mint mark on edge.

Date	Mintage	MS-63	MS-65	Prf-65
2013P	—	2.00	3.00	—
2013D	—	2.00	3.00	—
2013S	—	—	—	5.00

Presidents

George Washington

KM# 401 • 8.0700 g., **Copper-Zinc-Manganese-Nickel Clad Copper**, 26.5 mm. • **Edge Lettering:**IN GOD WE TRUST date, mint mark E PLURIBUS UNUM **Notes:** Date and mint mark incuse on edge.

Date	Mintage	MS-63	MS-65	Prf-65
2007P	176,680,000	2.00	3.00	—
(2007) Plain edge error	Inc. above	175	275	—
2007P Satin Finish	895,628	2.00	4.00	—
2007D	163,680,000	2.00	3.00	—
2007D Satin Finish	895,628	2.00	4.00	—
2007S	3,883,103	—	—	3.00

James Madison

KM# 404 • 8.0700 g., **Copper-Zinc-Manganese-Nickel Clad Copper**, 26.5 mm. • **Edge Lettering:**IN GOD WE TRUST date, mint mark E PLURIBUS UNUM **Notes:** Date and mint mark incuse on edge.

Date	Mintage	MS-63	MS-65	Prf-65
2007P Satin Finish	895,628	2.00	4.00	—
2007P Satin Finish	895,628	2.00	4.00	—
2007P	84,560,000	2.00	3.00	—
2007D	87,780,000	2.00	3.00	—
2007S	3,876,829	—	—	3.00

John Adams

KM# 402 • 8.0700 g., **Copper-Zinc-Manganese-Nickel Clad Copper**, 26.5 mm. • **Edge Lettering:**IN GOD WE TRUST date, mint mark E PLURIBUS UNUM **Notes:** Date and mint mark incuse on edge.

Date	Mintage	MS-63	MS-65	Prf-65
2007P	112,420,000	2.00	3.00	—
2007P Double edge lettering	Inc. above	45.00	65.00	—
2007D Plain edge error	Inc. above	60.00	70.00	—
2007P Satin Finish	895,628	2.00	4.00	—
2007D	112,140,000	2.00	3.00	—
2007D Satin Finish	895,628	2.00	4.00	—
2007S	3,877,409	—	—	3.00

Thomas Jefferson

KM# 403 • 8.0700 g., **Copper-Zinc-Manganese-Nickel Clad Copper**, 26.5 mm. • **Edge Lettering:**IN GOD WE TRUST date, mint mark E PLURIBUS UNUM **Notes:** Date and mint mark incuse on edge.

Date	Mintage	MS-63	MS-65	Prf-65
2007P	100,800,000	2.00	3.00	—
2007P Satin Finish	895,628	2.00	4.00	—
2007D	102,810,000	2.00	3.00	—
2007D Satin Finish	895,628	2.00	4.00	—
2007S	3,877,573	—	—	3.00

Andrew Jackson

KM# 428 • 8.0700 g., **Copper-Zinc-Manganese-Nickel Clad Copper**, 26.5 mm. • **Edge Lettering:** IN GOD WE TRUST date, mint mark E PLURIBUS UNUM **Notes:** Date and mint mark incuse on edge.

Date	Mintage	MS-63	MS-65	Prf-65
2008P	61,180,000	2.00	3.00	—
2008P Satin Finish	745,464	2.00	4.00	—
2008D	61,070,000	2.00	3.00	—
2008D Satin Finish	745,464	2.00	4.00	—
2008S	3,000,000	—	—	4.00

James Monroe

KM# 426 • 8.0700 g., **Copper-Zinc-Manganese-Nickel Clad Copper**, Date and mint mark incuse on edge., 26.5 mm. • **Edge Lettering:** IN GOD WE TRUST date, mint mark E PLURIBUS UNUM

Date	Mintage	MS-63	MS-65	Prf-65
2008P	64,260,000	2.00	3.00	—
2008P Satin Finish	745,464	2.00	4.00	—
2008D	60,230,000	2.00	3.00	—
2008D Satin Finish	745,464	2.00	4.00	—
2008S	3,000,000	—	—	4.00

John Quincy Adams

KM# 427 • 8.0700 g., **Copper-Zinc-Manganese-Nickel Clad Copper**, 26.5 mm. • **Edge Lettering:** IN GOD WE TRUST date, mint mark E PLURIBUS UNUM **Notes:** Date and mint mark incuse on edge.

Date	Mintage	MS-63	MS-65	Prf-65
2008P	57,540,000	2.00	3.00	—
2008P Satin Finish	745,464	2.00	4.00	—
2008D	57,720,000	2.00	3.00	—
2008D Satin Finish	745,464	2.00	4.00	—
2008S	3,000,000	—	—	4.00

Martin van Buren

KM# 429 • 8.0700 g., **Copper-Zinc-Manganese-Nickel Clad Copper**, 26.5 mm. • **Edge Lettering:** IN GOD WE TRUST date, mint mark E PLURIBUS UNUM **Notes:** Date and mint mark incuse on edge.

Date	Mintage	MS-63	MS-65	Prf-65
2008P	51,520,000	2.00	3.00	—
2008P Satin Finish	745,464	2.00	4.00	—
2008D	50,960,000	2.00	3.00	—
2008D Satin Finish	745,464	2.00	4.00	—
2008S	3,000,000	—	—	4.00

James K. Polk

KM# 452 • 8.0700 g., **Copper-Zinc-Manganese-Nickel Clad Copper**, 26.5 mm. • **Edge Lettering:** E PLURIBUS UNUM, date, mint mark **Notes:** Date and mint mark on edge

Date	Mintage	MS-63	MS-65	Prf-65
2009P	46,620,000	2.00	3.00	—
2009P Satin Finish	784,614	2.00	4.00	—
2009D	41,720,000	2.00	3.00	—
2009D Satin Finish	784,614	2.00	4.00	—
2009S	2,224,827	—	—	3.00

John Tyler

KM# 451 • 8.0700 g., **Copper-Zinc-Manganese-Nickel Clad Copper**, 26.5 mm. • **Edge Lettering:** E PLURIBUS UNUM, date, mint mark **Notes:** Date and mint mark on edge.

Date	Mintage	MS-63	MS-65	Prf-65
2009P	43,540,000	2.00	3.00	—
2009P Satin Finish	784,614	2.00	4.00	—
2009D	43,540,000	2.00	3.00	—
2009D Satin Finish	784,614	2.00	4.00	—
2009S	2,224,827	—	—	3.00

William Henry Harrison

KM# 450 • 8.0700 g., **Copper-Zinc-Manganese-Nickel Clad Copper**, 26.5 mm. • **Edge Lettering:** E PLURIBUS UNUM, date, mint mark **Notes:** Date and mint mark on edge

Date	Mintage	MS-63	MS-65	Prf-65
2009P	43,260,000	2.00	3.00	—
2009P Satin Finish	784,614	2.00	4.00	—
2009D	55,160,000	2.00	3.00	—
2009P Satin Finish	784,614	2.00	4.00	—
2009S	2,224,827	—	—	3.00

Zachary Taylor

KM# 453 • 8.0700 g., **Copper-Zinc-Manganese-Nickel Clad Copper**, 26.5 mm. • **Edge Lettering:** E PLURIBUS UNUM, date, mint mark **Notes:** Date and mint mark on edge.

Date	Mintage	MS-63	MS-65	Prf-65
2009P	41,580,000	2.00	3.00	—
2009P Satin Finish	784,614	2.00	4.00	—
2009D	36,680,000	2.00	3.00	—
2009D Satin Finish	784,614	2.00	4.00	—
2009S	2,224,827	—	—	3.00

Abraham Lincoln

KM# 478 • 8.0700 g., **Copper-Zinc-Manganese-Nickel Clad Copper**, 26.5 mm. • **Edge Lettering:** E PLURIBUS UNUM, date, mint mark **Notes:** Date and mint mark on edge.

Date	Mintage	MS-63	MS-65	Prf-65
2010P	49,000,000	2.00	3.00	—
2010P	583,897	2.00	4.00	—
2010D	48,020,000	2.00	3.00	—
2010D	583,897	2.00	4.00	—
2010S	2,224,827	—	—	4.00

Franklin Pierce

KM# 476 • 8.0700 g., **Copper-Zinc-Manganese-Nickel Clad Copper**, 26.5 mm. • **Edge Lettering:** E PLURIBUS UNUM, date, mint mark **Notes:** Date and mint mark on edge.

Date	Mintage	MS-63	MS-65	Prf-65
2010P	38,220,000	2.00	3.00	—
2010P Satin finish	583,897	2.00	4.00	—
2010D	38,360,000	2.00	3.00	—
2010D	583,897	2.00	4.00	—
2010S	2,224,827	—	—	4.00

James Buchanan

KM# 477 • 8.0700 g., **Copper-Zinc-Manganese-Nickel Clad Copper**, 26.5 mm. • **Edge Lettering:** E PLURIBUS UNUM, date, mint mark **Notes:** Date and mint mark on edge.

Date	Mintage	MS-63	MS-65	Prf-65
2010P	36,820,000	2.00	3.00	—
2010P Satin Finish	583,897	2.00	4.00	—
2010D	36,540,000	2.00	3.00	—
2010D Satin Finish	583,897	2.00	4.00	—
2010S	2,224,827	—	—	4.00

Millard Filmore

KM# 475 • 8.0700 g., **Copper-Zinc-Manganese-Nickel Clad Copper**, 26.5 mm. • **Edge Lettering:** E PLURIBUS UNUM, date, mint mark **Notes:** Date and mint mark on edge.

Date	Mintage	MS-63	MS-65	Prf-65
2010P	37,520,000	2.00	3.00	—
2010P Satin Finish	583,897	2.00	4.00	—
2010D	36,960,000	2.00	3.00	—
2010D Satin Finish	583,897	2.00	4.00	—
2010S	2,224,827	—	—	4.00

Andrew Johnson

KM# 499 • 8.0700 g., **Copper-Zinc-Manganese-Nickel Clad Copper**, 26.5 mm. • **Edge Lettering:** E PLURIBUS UNUM, date, mint mark **Notes:** Date and mint mark on edge.

Date	Mintage	MS-63	MS-65	Prf-65
2011P	35,560,000	2.00	3.00	—
2011D	37,100,000	2.00	3.00	—
2011S	1,706,916	—	—	4.00

James Garfield

KM# 502 • 8.0700 g., **Copper-Zinc-Manganese-Nickel Clad Copper**, 26.5 mm. • **Edge Lettering:** E PLURIBUS UNUM, date, mint mark **Notes:** Date and mint mark on edge.

Date	Mintage	MS-63	MS-65	Prf-65
2011P	37,100,000	2.00	3.00	—
2011D	37,100,000	2.00	3.00	—
2011S	1,706,916	—	—	4.00

Rutherford B. Hayes

KM# 501 • 8.0700 g., **Copper-Zinc-Manganese-Nickel Clad Copper**, 26.5 mm. • **Edge Lettering:** E PLURIBUS UNUM, date, mint mark **Notes:** Date and mint mark on edge.

Date	Mintage	MS-63	MS-65	Prf-65
2011P	37,660,000	2.00	3.00	—
2011D	36,820,000	2.00	3.00	—
2011S	1,706,916	—	—	4.00

Ulysses S. Grant

KM# 500 • 8.0700 g., **Copper-Zinc-Manganese-Nickel Clad Copper**, 26.5 mm. • **Edge Lettering:** E PLURIBUS UNUM, date, mint mark **Notes:** Date and mint mark on edge.

Date	Mintage	MS-63	MS-65	Prf-65
2011P	38,080,000	2.00	3.00	—
2011D	37,940,000	2.00	3.00	—
2011S	1,706,916	—	—	4.00

Benjamin Harrison

KM# 526 • 8.0700 g., **Copper-Zinc-Manganese-Nickel Clad Copper**, 26.5 mm. • **Edge Lettering:** E PLURIBUS UNUM, date, mintmark **Notes:** Date at mint mark on edge

Date	Mintage	MS-63	MS-65	Prf-65
2012P	5,640,001	2.00	3.00	—
2012D	—	2.00	3.00	—
2012S	—	—	—	5.00

Chester A. Arthur

KM# 524 • 8.0700 g., **Copper-Zinc-Manganese-Nickel Clad Copper**, 26.5 mm. • **Edge Lettering:** E PLURIBUS UNUM, date, mintmark **Notes:** Date and mintmark on edge

Date	Mintage	MS-63	MS-65	Prf-65
2012P	6,020,000	2.00	3.00	—
2012D	4,060,000	2.00	3.00	—
2012S	—	—	—	5.00

Grover Cleveland, first term

KM# 525 • 8.0700 g., **Copper-Zinc-Manganese-Nickel Clad Copper**, 26.5 mm. • **Edge Lettering:** E PLURIBUS UNUM, date, mintmark **Notes:** Date and mint mark on edge

Date	Mintage	MS-63	MS-65	Prf-65
2012P	5,460,000	2.00	3.00	—
2012D	4,060,000	2.00	3.00	—
2012S	—	—	—	5.00

Grover Cleveland, second term

KM# 527 • 8.0700 g., **Copper-Zinc-Manganese-Nickel Clad Copper**, 26.5 mm. • **Edge Lettering:** E PLURIBUS UNUM, date, mintmark **Notes:** Date and mint mark on edge

Date	Mintage	MS-63	MS-65	Prf-65
2012P	10,680,000	2.00	3.00	—
2012D	3,920,000	2.00	3.00	—
2012S	—	—	—	5.00

Theodore Roosevelt

KM# 548 • 8.0700 g., **Copper-Zinc-Manganese-Nickel Clad Copper**, 26.5 mm. • **Edge Desc:** E PLURIBUS UNUM, date, mint mark **Notes:** Date and mint mark on edge.

Date	Mintage	MS-63	MS-65	Prf-65
2013P	—	2.00	3.00	—
2013D	—	2.00	3.00	—
2013S	—	—	—	5.00

William Howard Taft

KM# 549 • 8.0700 g., **Copper-Zinc-Manganese-Nickel Clad Copper**, 26.5 mm. • **Edge Desc:** E PLURIBUS UNUM, date, mint mark **Notes:** Date and mint mark on edge.

Date	Mintage	MS-63	MS-65	Prf-65
2013P	—	2.00	3.00	—
2013D	—	2.00	3.00	—
2013S	—	—	—	5.00

William McKinley

KM# 547 • 8.0700 g., **Copper-Zinc-Manganese-Nickel Clad Copper**, 26.5 mm. • **Edge Desc:** E PLURIBUS UNUM, date, mint mark **Notes:** Date and mint mark on edge.

Date	Mintage	MS-63	MS-65	Prf-65
2013P	—	2.00	3.00	—
2013D	—	2.00	3.00	—
2013S	—	—	—	5.00

Wodrow Wilson

KM# 550 • 8.0700 g., **Copper-Zinc-Manganese-Nickel Clad Copper**, 26.5 mm. • **Edge Desc:** E PLURIBUS UNUM, date, mint mark **Notes:** Date and mint mark on edge.

Date	Mintage	MS-63	MS-65	Prf-65
2013P	—	2.00	3.00	—
2013D	—	2.00	3.00	—
2013S	—	—	—	5.00

COMMEMORATIVE COINAGE

1982-PRESENT

All commemorative silver dollar coins of 1982-present have the following specifications: diameter — 38.1 millimeters; weight — 26.7300 grams; composition — 0.9000 silver, 0.7736 ounces actual silver weight. All commemorative $5 coins of 1982-present have the following specificiations: diameter — 21.6 millimeters; weight — 8.3590 grams; composition: 0.9000 gold, 0.242 ounces actual gold weight.

Note: In 1982, after a hiatus of nearly 20 years, coinage of commemorative half dollars resumed. Those designated with a 'W' were struck at the West Point Mint. Some issues were struck in copper-nickel. Those struck in silver have the same size, weight and composition as the prior commemorative half-dollar series.

HALF DOLLAR

U. S. CAPITOL VISITOR CENTER. KM# 323 Copper-Nickel Clad Copper 11.3400 g. **Obverse:** Capitol silouete, 1800 structure in detail **Reverse:** Legend within circle of stars **Obv. Designer:** Dean McMullen **Rev. Designer:** Alex Shagin and Marcel Jovine

Date	Mintage	MS-65	Prf-65
2001P	99,157	14.50	—
2001P	77,962	—	15.50

FIRST FLIGHT CENTENNIAL. KM# 348 Copper-Nickel Clad Copper 11.3400g. **Obverse:** Wright Monument at Kitty Hawk **Reverse:** Wright Flyer in flight **Obv. Designer:** John Mercanti **Rev. Designer:** Donna Weaver

Date	Mintage	MS-65	Prf-65
2003P	57,726	15.00	—
2003P	111,569	—	17.00

AMERICAN BALD EAGLE. KM# 438 Copper-Nickel Clad Copper 30.6 mm. 11.3400 g. **Obverse:** Two eaglets in nest with egg **Reverse:** Eagle Challenger facing right, American Flag in background **Obv. Designer:** Susan Gamble and Joseph Menna **Rev. Designer:** Donna Weaver and Charles Vickers

Date	Mintage	MS-65	Prf-65
2008S	120,180	12.50	—
2008S	222,577	—	14.00

U.S. ARMY. KM# 506 Copper-Nickel Clad Copper 30.6 mm. 11.3400 g. **Obverse:** Army contributions during peacetime, surveying, building a flood wall and space exploration **Reverse:** Continental soldier with musket **Obv. Designer:** Donna Weaver and Charles L. Vickers **Rev. Designer:** Thomas Cleveland and Joseph Menna

Date	Mintage	MS-65	Prf-65
2011D	39,461	69.00	—
2011	68,349	—	35.00

FIVE-STAR GENERALS - ARNOLD AND BRADLEY. KM# 554 Silver ASW.

Date	Mintage	MS-65	Prf-65
2013		50.00	—
2013		—	60.00

DOLLAR

CAPITOL VISITOR CENTER. KM# 324 Obv. Designer: Marika Somogyi **Rev. Designer:** John Mercanti **Obverse:** Original and current Capital facades **Reverse:** Eagle with sheild and ribbon

Date	Mintage	MS-65	Prf-65
2001P	66,636	40.80	—
2001P	143,793	—	40.80

NATIVE AMERICAN - BISON. KM# 325 Designer: James E. Fraser. **Obverse:** Native American bust right **Reverse:** Bison standing left

Date	Mintage	MS-65	Prf-65
2001D	197,131	165	—
2001P	272,869	—	169

2002 WINTER OLYMPICS - SALT LAKE CITY. KM# 336 Obv. Designer: John Mercanti **Rev. Designer:** Donna Weaver **Obverse:** Salt Lake City Olympic logo **Reverse:** Stylized skyline with mountains in background

Date	Mintage	MS-65	Prf-65
2002P	35,388	40.80	—
2002P	142,873	—	38.30

U.S. MILITARY ACADEMY AT WEST POINT - BICENTENNIAL. KM# 338 Obv. Designer: T. James Ferrell **Rev. Designer:** John Mercanti **Obverse:** Cadet Review flagbearers, Academy buildings in background **Reverse:** Academy emblems - Corinthian helmet and sword

Date	Mintage	MS-65	Prf-65
2002W	103,201	38.30	—
2002W	288,293	—	39.80

FIRST FLIGHT CENTENNIAL. KM# 349 Obv. Designer: T. James Ferrell **Rev. Designer:** Norman E. Nemeth **Obverse:** Orville and Wilbur Wright busts left **Reverse:** Wright Flyer over dunes

Date	Mintage	MS-65	Prf-65
2003P	53,761	40.80	—
2003P	193,086	—	46.80

LEWIS AND CLARK CORPS OF DISCOVERY BICENTENNIAL. KM# 363 Designer: Donna Weaver. **Obverse:** Lewis and Clark standing **Reverse:** Jefferson era clasped hands peace medal

Date	Mintage	MS-65	Prf-65
2004P	90,323	40.80	—
2004P	288,492	—	46.80

THOMAS A. EDISON - ELECTRIC LIGHT 125TH ANNIVERSARY. KM# 362 Obv. Designer: Donna Weaver **Rev. Designer:** John Mercanti **Obverse:** Edison half-length figure facing holding light bulb **Reverse:** Light bulb and rays

Date	Mintage	MS-65	Prf-65
2004P	68,031	40.80	—
2004P	213,409	—	41.80

JOHN MARSHALL, 250TH BIRTH ANNIVERSARY. KM# 375 Obv. Designer: John Mercanti **Rev. Designer:** Donna Weaver **Obverse:** Marshall bust left **Reverse:** Marshall era Supreme Court Chamber

Date	Mintage	MS-65	Prf-65
2005P	48,953	37.30	—
2005P	141,993	—	35.80

U.S. MARINE CORPS, 230TH ANNIVERSARY. KM# 376 Obv. Designer: Norman E. Nemeth **Rev. Designer:** Charles Vickers **Obverse:** Flag Raising at Mt. Suribachi on Iwo Jima **Reverse:** Marine Corps emblem

Date	Mintage	MS-65	Prf-65
2005P	130,000	48.00	—
2005P	370,000	—	52.50

BENJAMIN FRANKLIN, 300TH BIRTH ANNIVERSARY. KM# 387 Obv. Designer: Norman E. Nemeth **Rev. Designer:** Charles Vickers **Obverse:** Youthful Franklin flying kite **Reverse:** Revolutionary era "JOIN, or DIE" snake cartoon illustration

Date	Mintage	MS-65	Prf-65
2006P	58,000	40.80	—
2006P	142,000	—	45.00

BENJAMIN FRANKLIN, 300TH BIRTH ANNIVERSARY. KM# 388 Obv. Designer: Don Everhart II **Rev. Designer:** Donna Weaver **Obverse:** Bust 3/4 right, signature in oval below **Reverse:** Continental Dollar of 1776 in center

Date	Mintage	MS-65	Prf-65
2006P	58,000	40.80	—
2006P	142,000	—	51.00

SAN FRANCISCO MINT MUSEUM. KM# 394 Obv. Designer: Sherl J. Winter **Rev. Designer:** George T. Morgan **Obverse:** 3/4 view of building **Reverse:** Reverse of 1880s Morgan silver dollar

Date	Mintage	MS-65	Prf-65
2006S	65,609	40.80	—
2006S	255,700	—	40.80

CENTRAL HIGH SCHOOL DESEGREGATION. KM# 418 Obv. Designer: Richard Masters and Charles Vickers **Rev. Designer:** Don Everhart II **Obverse:** Children's feet walking left with adult feet in military boots **Reverse:** Little Rock's Central High School

Date	Mintage	MS-65	Prf-65
2007P	66,093	40.80	—
2007P	124,618	—	43.00

JAMESTOWN - 400TH ANNIVERSARY. KM# 405 Obv. Designer: Donna Weaver and Don Everhart II **Rev. Designer:** Susan Gamble and Charles Vickers **Obverse:** Two settlers and Native American **Reverse:** Three ships

Date	Mintage	MS-65	Prf-65
2007P	79,801	40.80	—
2007P	258,802	—	38.30

AMERICAN BALD EAGLE. KM# 439 Obv. Designer: Joel Iskowitz and Don Everhart II **Rev. Designer:** James Licaretz **Obverse:** Eagle with flight, mountain in background at right **Reverse:** Great Seal of the United States

Date	Mintage	MS-65	Prf-65
2008P	110,073	44.00	—
2008P	243,558	—	38.30

LINCOLN BICENTENNIAL. KM# 454 Obv. Designer: Justin Kunz and Don Everhart II **Rev. Designer:** Phebe Hemphill **Obverse:** 3/4 portrait facing right **Reverse:** Part of Gettysburg Address within wreath

Date	Mintage	MS-65	Prf-65
2009P	125,000	55.00	—
2009P	375,000	—	55.00

LOUIS BRAILLE BIRTH BICENTENNIAL. KM# 455 Obv. Designer: Joel Iskowitz and Phebe Hemphill **Rev. Designer:** Susan Gamble and Joseph Menna **Obverse:** Louis Braille bust facing **Reverse:** School child reading book in Braille, BRL in Braille code above

Date	Mintage	MS-65	Prf-65
2009P	82,639	38.50	—
2009P	135,235	—	38.30

AMERICAN VETERANS DISABLED FOR LIFE. KM# 479 Obv. Designer: Don Everhart II **Rev. Designer:** Thomas Cleveland and Joseph Menna **Obverse:** Soldier's feet, crutches **Reverse:** Legend within wreath

Date	Mintage	MS-65	Prf-65
2010W	77,859	40.80	—
2010W	189,881	—	42.30

BOY SCOUTS OF AMERICA, 100TH ANNIVERSARY. KM# 480 Obv. Designer: Donna Weaver **Rev. Designer:** Jim Licaretz **Obverse:** Cub Scout, Boy Scout and Venturer saluting **Reverse:** Boy Scouts of America logo

Date	Mintage	MS-65	Prf-65
2010P		38.50	—
2010P		—	42.00

MEDAL OF HONOR. KM# 504 Obv. Designer: James Licaretz **Rev. Designer:** Richard Masters and Phebe Hemphill **Obverse:** Medal of Honor designs for Army, Navy and Air Force awards **Reverse:** Army infantry doldier carrying another to safety

Date	Mintage	MS-65	Prf-65
2011S	44,769	46.50	—
2011S	112,850	—	43.50

U.S. ARMY. KM# 507 Obv. Designer: Richard Masters and Michael Gaudioso **Rev. Designer:** Susan Gamble and Don Everhart, II **Obverse:** Male and femlae soldier heads looking outward **Reverse:** Seven core values of the Army, Eagle from the great seal

Date	Mintage	MS-65	Prf-65
2011S		45.00	—
2011S		—	43.50

NATIONAL INFANTRY MUSEUM AND SOLDIER CENTER. KM# 529

Date	Mintage	MS-65	Prf-65
2012		—	—
2012		—	—

STAR-SPANGLED BANNER. KM# 530

Date	Mintage	MS-65	Prf-65
2012		—	—
2012		—	—

FIVE-STAR GENERALS - MARSHALL AND EISENHOWER. KM# 553

Date	Mintage	MS-65	Prf-65
2013		50.00	—
2013		—	60.00

GIRL SCOUTS OF THE USA, 100TH ANNIVERSARY. KM# 552

Date	Mintage	MS-65	Prf-65
2013		50.00	—
2013		—	60.00

$5 (HALF EAGLE)

CAPITOL VISITOR CENTER. KM# 326 Designer: Elizabeth Jones. **Obverse:** Column at right **Reverse:** First Capital building

Date	Mintage	MS-65	Prf-65
2001W	6,761	1,750	—
2001W	27,652	—	442

2002 WINTER OLYMPICS. KM# 337 Designer: Donna Weaver. **Obverse:** Salt Lake City Olympics logo **Reverse:** Stylized cauldron

Date	Mintage	MS-65	Prf-65
2002W	10,585	452	—
2002W	32,877	—	442

SAN FRANCISCO MINT MUSEUM. KM# 395 Obv. Designer: Charles Vickers and Joseph Menna **Rev. Designer:** Christian Gobrecht **Obverse:** Front entrance façade **Reverse:** Eagle as on 1860's $5. Gold

Date	Mintage	MS-65	Prf-65
2006S	16,230	442	—
2006S	41,517	—	442

JAMESTOWN - 400TH ANNIVERSARY. KM# 406 Obv. Designer: John Mercanti **Rev. Designer:** Susan Gamble and Norman Nemeth **Obverse:** Settler and Native American **Reverse:** Jamestown Memorial Church ruins

Date	Mintage	MS-65	Prf-65
2007W	18,843	442	—
2007W	47,050	—	442

AMERICAN BALD EAGLE. KM# 440 Obv. Designer: Susan Gamble adn Phebe Hemphill **Rev. Designer:** Don Everhart II **Obverse:** Two eagles on branch **Reverse:** Eagle with shield

Date	Mintage	MS-65	Prf-65
2008W	13,467	457	—
2008W	59,269	—	442

MEDAL OF HONOR. KM# 505 Obv. Designer: Joseph Menna **Rev. Designer:** Joel Iskowitz and Michael Gaudioso **Obverse:** 1861 Medal of Honor design for the Navy **Reverse:** Minerva standing with shield and Union flag, field artillery canon flanking

Date	Mintage	MS-65	Prf-65
2011S	8,251	585	—
2011S	18,012	—	500

U.S. ARMY. KM# 508 Obv. Designer: Joel Iskowitz and Phebe Hemphill **Rev. Designer:** Joseph Menna **Obverse:** Five Soldiers of different eras **Reverse:** Elements from the Army's emblem

Date	Mintage	MS-65	Prf-65
2011P	8,062	585	—
2011P	17,173	—	495

STAR-SPANGLED BANNER. KM# 531

Date	Mintage	MS-65	Prf-65
2012		—	—
2012		—	—

$10 (EAGLE)

FIRST FLIGHT CENTENNIAL. KM# 350 0.9000 Gold 0.4837 oz. AGW. 16.7180 g. **Obverse:** Orvile and Wilbur Wright busts facing **Reverse:** Wright flyer and eagle **Obv. Designer:** Donna Weaver **Rev. Designer:** Norman Nemeth

Date	Mintage	MS-65	Prf-65
2003P	10,129	1,050	—
2003W	21,846	—	893

$20 (DOUBLE EAGLE)

KM# 464 0.9990 Gold 0.999AGW. 27 mm. 31.1050 g. **Obverse:** Ultra high relief Liberty holding torch, walking forward **Reverse:** Eagle in flight left, sunrise in background **Designer:** Augustus Saint-Gaudens

Date	Mintage	MS-65	Prf-65
2009	115,178	2,750	—

AMERICA THE BEAUTIFUL SILVER BULLION

SILVER QUARTER

KM# 489 0.9990 **SILVER** 4.9958 oz. ASW. 155.5500 g. **Rev. Desc.:** Park Headquarters and fountain **Rev. Designer:** Don Everhart II and Joseph Menna

Date	Mintage	MS65	PRF65
2010	33,000	290	—
2010P Vapor Blast finish	27,000	250	—

KM# 490 0.9990 **SILVER** 4.9958 oz. ASW. 155.5500 g. **Rev. Desc.:** Old Faithful geyser and bison **Rev. Designer:** Don Everhart II

Date	Mintage	MS65	PRF65
2010	33,000	275	—
2010P Vapor Blast finish	27,000	240	—

KM# 491 0.9990 **SILVER** 4.9958 oz. ASW. 155.5500 g. **Rev. Desc.:** El Capitan, largest monolith of granite in the world **Rev. Designer:** Joseph Menna and Phebe Hemphill

Date	Mintage	MS65	PRF65
2010	33,000	275	—
2010P Vapor blast finish	27,000	225	—

KM# 492 0.9990 **SILVER** 4.9958 oz. ASW. 155.5500 g. **Rev. Desc.:** Grabarues above the Nankoweap Delta in Marble Canyon near the Colorado River **Rev. Designer:** Phebe Hemphill

Date	Mintage	MS65	PRF65
2010	33,000	250	—
2010P Vapor blast finish	26,019	225	—

KM# 493 0.9990 **SILVER** 4.9958 oz. ASW. 155.5500 g. **Rev. Desc.:** Mt. Hood with Lost Lake in the foreground **Rev. Designer:** Phebe Hemphill

Date	Mintage	MS65	PRF65
2010	33,000	275	—
2010P Vapor blast finish	25,318	200	—

KM# 513 0.9990 **SILVER** 4.9958 oz. ASW. 155.5500 g. **Rev. Desc.:** 72nd Pennsylvania Infantry Monumnet on the battle line of the Union Army at Cemetery Ridge **Rev. Designer:** Joel Iskowitz and Phebe Hemphill

Date	Mintage	MS65	PRF65
2011	126,700	200	—
2011P Vapor blast finish	24,625	190	—

KM# 514 0.9990 **SILVER** 4.9958 oz. ASW. 155.5500 g. **Rev. Desc.:** Northeast slope of Mount Reynolds **Rev. Designer:** Barbara Fox and Charles L. Vickers

Date	Mintage	MS65	PRF65
2011	126,700	200	—
2011P Vapor blast finish	20,503	190	—

KM# 515 0.9990 **SILVER** 4.9958 oz. ASW. 155.5500 g. **Rev. Desc.:** Roosevelt elk on a gravel river bar along the Hoh River, Mount Olympus in the background **Rev. Designer:** Susan Gambel and Michael Gaudioso

Date	Mintage	MS65	PRF65
2011	85,900	200	—
2011P Vapor blast finish	17,988	190	—

KM# 516 0.9990 **SILVER** 4.9958 oz. ASW. 155.5500 g. **Rev. Desc.:** U.S.S. Cairo on the Yazoo River **Rev. Designer:** Thomas Cleveland and Joseph menna

Date	Mintage	MS65	PRF65
2011	39,500	200	—
2011P Vapor blast finish	18,181	190	—

KM# 517 0.9990 **SILVER** 4.9958 oz. ASW. 155.5500 g. **Rev. Desc.:** Limestone Lincoln Bridge **Rev. Designer:** Donna Weaver and James Licaretz

Date	Mintage	MS65	PRF65
2011	29,700	200	—
2011P Vapor blast finish	16,386	190	—

KM# 536 0.9990 **SILVER** 4.9958 oz. ASW. 155.5500 g. **Rev. Desc.:** Coquin tree frog and Puerto Rico parrot

Date	Mintage	MS65	PRF65
2012	21,900	200	—
2012P Vapor blast finish	15,271	190	—

KM# 537 0.9990 **SILVER** 4.9949 oz. ASW. 155.5200 g. **Rev. Desc.:** Two elevated kivas at Chetro Ketl complex

Date	Mintage	MS65	PRF65
2012	20,000	200	—
2012P Vapor blast finish	12,679	190	—

KM# 538 0.9990 **SILVER** 4.9949 oz. ASW. 155.5200 g. **Rev. Desc.:** Bass Harbor Head Lighthouse

Date	Mintage	MS65	PRF65
2012	25,400	200	—
2012P Vapor blast finish	13,196	190	—

KM# 539 0.9990 **SILVER** 4.9949 oz. ASW. 155.5200 g. **Rev. Desc.:** Volcano erupting

Date	Mintage	MS65	PRF65
2012	20,000	200	—
2012P Vapor blast finish	13,789	190	—

KM# 540 0.9990 **SILVER** 4.9959 oz. ASW. 155.5520 g. **Rev. Desc.:** Dall sheep and Mount McKinley

Date	Mintage	MS65	PRF65
2012	20,000	200	—
2012P Vapor blast finish	10,180	190	—

KM# 556 0.9990 **SILVER** 4.9958 oz. ASW. 155.5500 g.

Date	Mintage	MS65	PRF65
2013	—	—	—
2013P Vapor blast finish	—	—	—

KM# 557 0.9990 **SILVER** 4.9958 oz. ASW. 155.5500 g.

Date	Mintage	MS65	PRF65
2013	—	—	—
2013 Vapor blast finish	—	—	—

KM# 558 0.9990 **SILVER** 4.9958 oz. ASW. 155.5500 g.

Date	Mintage	MS65	PRF65
2013	—	—	—
2013 Vapor blast finish	—	—	—

KM# 559 0.9990 **SILVER** 4.9958 oz. ASW. 155.5500 g.

Date	Mintage	MS65	PRF65
2013	—	—	—
2013	—	—	—

KM# 560 0.9990 **SILVER** 4.9958 oz. ASW. 155.5500 g.

Date	Mintage	MS65	PRF65
2013	—	—	—
2013 Vapor blast finish	—	—	—

AMERICAN EAGLE BULLION COINS

SILVER DOLLAR

KM# 273 0.9993 **SILVER** 0.9993 oz. ASW. 40.6mm. 31.1050 g. **Obv. Desc.:** Liberty walking left **Rev. Desc.:** Eagle with shield **Obv. Designer:** Adolph A. Weinman **Rev. Designer:** John Mercanti

Date	Mintage	MS65	PRF65
2001	9,001,711	30.40	—
2001W	746,398	—	63.00
2002	10,539,026	30.40	—
2002W	647,342	—	67.00
2003	8,495,008	30.40	—
2003W	747,831	—	67.00
2004	8,882,754	30.40	—
2004W	801,602	—	75.00
2005	8,891,025	30.40	—
2005W	816,663	—	63.00

Date	Mintage	MS65	PRF65
2006	10,676,522	31.60	—
2006W	1,093,600	—	63.00
2006P Reverse Proof	—	—	265
2006W Burnished Unc.	468,000	85.00	—
2006 20th Aniv. 3 pc. set	—	—	385
2007	9,028,036	30.60	—
2007W	821,759	—	63.00
2007W Burnished Unc.	690,891	34.40	—
2008	20,583,000	30.40	—
2008W Reverse of '07, U in United with rounded bottom.	—	475	—
2008	713,353	—	63.00
2008W Burnished Unc.	—	71.50	—
2009	30,459,000	30.40	—
2010	34,764,500	30.40	—
2010	—	—	63.00
2011	—	33.40	—
2011P Reverse Proof	100,000	—	285
2011S Unc.	100,000	285	—
2011W Burnished Unc.	100,000	50.00	—
2011W Proof	100,000	—	63.00
2012	—	30.40	—
2012 Reverse Proof	—	—	125
2012P Proof	—	—	90.00
2012W Burnished Unc.	—	55.00	—
2013	—	30.40	—
2013W Enhanced Unc.	—	55.00	—
2013W Reverse Proof	—	—	90.00
2013W Proof	—	—	63.00

GOLD $5

KM# 216 0.9167 **GOLD** 0.100AGW. 16.5mm. 3.3930 g. **Obv. Designer:** Augustus Saint-Gaudens **Rev. Designer:** Miley Busiek

Date	Mintage	MS65	PRF65
2001	269,147	185	—
2001W	37,530	—	190
2002	230,027	245	—
2002W	40,864	—	190
2003	245,029	185	—
2003W	40,027	—	190
2004	250,016	185	—
2004W	35,131	—	225
2005	300,043	185	—
2005W	49,265	—	225
2006	285,006	185	—
2006W	47,277	—	190
2006W Burnished Unc.	20,643	215	—
2007	190,010	185	—
2007W	58,553	—	190
2007W Burnished Unc.	22,501	175	—
2008	305,000	185	—
2008W	—	—	190
2008W Burnished Unc.	12,657	325	—
2009	27,000	185	—
2010	—	185	—
2010W	—	—	190
2011W	5,000	—	190
2011	—	185	—
2012W	—	—	190
2013W	—	—	190

GOLD $10

KM# 217 0.9167 **GOLD** 0.250AGW. 22mm. 8.4830 g. **Obv. Designer:** Augustus Saint-Gaudens **Rev. Designer:** Miley Busiek

Date	Mintage	MS65	PRF65
2001	71,280	434	—
2001W	25,613	—	453
2002	62,027	434	—
2002W	29,242	—	453
2003	74,029	434	—
2003W	30,292	—	453
2004	72,014	434	—
2004W	28,839	—	453
2005	72,015	434	—
2005W	37,207	—	453
2006	60,004	434	—
2006W	36,127	—	453
2006W Burnished Unc.	15,188	785	—
2007	34,004	434	—
2007W	46,189	—	453
2007W Burnished Unc.	12,786	990	—
2008	—	434	—
2008W	28,000	—	453
2008W Burnished Unc.	8,883	1,750	—
2009	27,500	434	—
2010	—	434	—
2010W	—	—	453
2011W	4,000	—	453
2011	—	434	—
2012	—	—	—

GOLD $25

KM# 218 0.9167 **GOLD** 0.500AGW. 27mm. 16.9660 g. **Obv. Designer:** Augustus Saint-Gaudens **Rev. Designer:** Miley Busiek

Date	Mintage	MS65	PRF65
2001	48,047	1,310	—
2001W	23,240	—	915
2002	70,027	995	—
2002W	26,646	—	915
2003	79,029	868	—
2003W	28,270	—	915
2004	98,040	868	—
2004W	27,330	—	915
2005	80,023	868	—
2005W	34,311	—	915
2006	66,004	871	—
2006W	34,322	—	915
2006W Burnished Unc.	15,164	1,650	—
2007	47,002	1,100	—
2007W	44,025	—	915
2007W Burnished Unc.	11,458	1,900	—
2008	61,000	871	—
2008W	27,800	—	915
2008W Burnished Unc.	15,683	1,650	—
2009	55,000	871	—
2010	—	868	—
2010W	—	—	915
2011W	2,000	—	915
2011	—	868	—
2012W	—	—	915
2013W	—	—	915

GOLD $50

KM# 219 0.9167 **GOLD** 10000AGW. 32.7mm. 33.9310 g. **Obv. Designer:** Augustus Saint-Gaudens **Rev. Designer:** Miley Busiek

Date	Mintage	MS65	PRF65
2001	143,605	1,659	—
2001W	24,555	—	1,725
2002	222,029	1,659	—
2002W	27,499	—	1,725
2003	416,032	1,659	—
2003W	28,344	—	1,725
2004	417,149	1,659	—
2004W	28,215	—	1,725
2005	356,555	1,659	—
2005W	35,246	—	1,725
2006	237,510	1,659	—
2006W	47,000	—	1,725
2006W Reverse Proof	10,000	—	2,550
2006W Burnished Unc.	45,912	1,885	—
2007	140,016	1,674	—
2007W	51,810	—	1,725
2007W Burnished Unc.	18,609	1,980	—
2008W	710,000	1,659	—
2008W	29,000	—	1,725
2008W Burnished Unc.	11,908	2,100	—
2008W Reverse of '07	—	—	—
2009	122,000	1,659	—
2010	—	1,659	—
2010W	—	—	1,725
2011	—	1,659	—
2011W	—	—	1,725
2011 Burnished Unc.	—	2,350	—
2012W	—	—	1,725
2013W	—	—	1,725

PLATINUM $10

KM# 327 0.9995 **PLATINUM** 0.0999 oz. 17mm. 3.1100 g. **Rev. Desc.:** Eagle in flight over Southwestern cactus desert **Obv. Designer:** John Mercanti

Date	Mintage	MS65	PRF65
2001W	12,174	—	223

KM# 283 0.9995 **PLATINUM** 0.0999 oz. 17mm. 3.1100 g. **Rev. Desc.:** Eagle flying right over sunrise **Obv. Designer:** John Mercanti **Rev. Designer:** Thomas D. Rogers Sr

Date	Mintage	MS65	PRF65
2001	52,017	178	—
2002	23,005	178	—
2003	22,007	178	—
2004	15,010	178	—
2005	14,013	178	—
2006	11,001	178	—
2006W Burnished Unc.	—	425	—
2007	13,003	285	—
2007W Burnished Unc.	—	265	—
2008	17,000	178	—
2008 Burnished Unc.	—	290	—

KM# 339 0.9995 **PLATINUM** 0.0999 oz. 17mm. 3.1100 g. **Rev. Desc.:** Eagle fishing in America's Northwest **Obv. Designer:** John Mercanti

Date	Mintage	MS65	PRF65
2002W	12,365	—	223

KM# 351 0.9995 **PLATINUM** 0.0999 oz. 17mm. 3.1100 g. **Rev. Desc.:** Eagle pearched on a Rocky Mountain Pine branch against a flag backdrop **Obv. Designer:** John Mercanti **Rev. Designer:** Al Maletsky

Date	Mintage	MS65	PRF65
2003W	9,534	—	250

KM# 364 0.9995 **PLATINUM** 0.0999 oz. 17mm. 3.1100 g. **Rev. Desc.:** Chester French, 1907. The sculpture is outside the N.Y. Customs House, now part of the Smithsonian's Museum of the American Indian **Obv. Designer:** John Mercanti

Date	Mintage	MS65	PRF65
2004W	7,161	—	455

KM# 377 0.9995 **PLATINUM** 0.0999 oz. 17mm. 3.1100 g. **Rev. Desc.:** Eagle with cornucopiae **Obv. Designer:** John Mercanti **Rev. Designer:** Donna Weaver

Date	Mintage	MS65	PRF65
2005W	8,104	—	265

KM# 389 0.9995 **PLATINUM** 0.0999 oz. 17mm. 3.1100 g. **Rev. Desc.:** Liberty seated writing between two columns **Obv. Designer:** John Mercanti

Date	Mintage	MS65	PRF65
2006W	10,205	—	223

KM# 414 0.9995 **PLATINUM** 0.0999 oz. 17mm. 3.1100 g. **Rev. Desc.:** Eagle with shield **Obv. Designer:** John Mercanti

Date	Mintage	MS65	PRF65
2007W	8,176	—	223

KM# 434 0.9995 **PLATINUM** 0.0999 oz. 17mm. 3.1100 g. **Rev. Desc.:** Justice standing before eagle **Obv. Designer:** John Mercanti

Date	Mintage	MS65	PRF65
2008W	8,176	—	495

KM# 460 0.9995 **PLATINUM** 0.0999 oz. 17mm. 3.1100 g. **Obv. Designer:** John Mercanti

Date	Mintage	MS65	PRF65
2009W	5,600	—	—

PLATINUM $25

KM# 328 0.9995 **PLATINUM** 0.2502 oz. 22mm. 7.7857 g. **Rev. Desc.:** Eagle in flight over Southwestern cactus desert **Obv. Designer:** John Mercanti

Date	Mintage	MS65	PRF65
2001W	8,847	—	452

KM# 284 0.9995 **PLATINUM** 0.2502 oz. 22mm. 7.7857 g. **Rev. Desc.:** Eagle in flight over sunrise **Obv. Designer:** John Mercanti **Rev. Designer:** Thomas D. Rogers Sr

Date	Mintage	MS65	PRF65
2001	21,815	441	—
2002	27,405	441	—
2003	25,207	441	—
2004	18,010	441	—
2005	12,013	441	—
2006	12,001	441	—
2006W Burnished Unc.	—	590	—
2007	8,402	441	—
2007W Burnished Unc.	—	590	—
2008	22,800	426	—
2008 Burnished Unc.	—	665	—

KM# 340 0.9995 **PLATINUM** 0.2502 oz. 22mm. 7.7857 g. **Rev. Desc.:** Eagle fishing in America's Northwest **Obv. Designer:** John Mercanti

Date	Mintage	MS65	PRF65
2002W	9,282	—	452

KM# 352 0.9995 **PLATINUM** 0.2502 oz. 22mm. 7.7857 g. **Rev. Desc.:** Eagle pearched on a Rocky Mountain Pine branch against a flag backdrop. **Obv. Designer:** John Mercanti **Rev. Designer:** Al Maletsky

Date	Mintage	MS65	PRF65
2003W	7,044	—	452

KM# 365 0.9995 **PLATINUM** 0.2502 oz. 22mm. 7.7857 g. **Rev. Desc.:** Chester French, 1907. The sculpture is outside the N.Y. Customs House, now part of the Smithsonian's Museum of the American Indian **Obv. Designer:** John Mercanti

Date	Mintage	MS65	PRF65
2004W	5,193	—	1,000

KM# 378 0.9995 **PLATINUM** 0.2502 oz. 22mm. 7.7857 g. **Rev. Desc.:** Eagle with cornucopiae **Obv. Designer:** John Mercanti **Rev. Designer:** Donna Weaver

Date	Mintage	MS65	PRF65
2005W	6,592	—	610

KM# 390 0.9995 **PLATINUM** 0.2502 oz. 22mm. 7.7857 g. **Rev. Desc.:** Liberty seated writing between two columns **Obv. Designer:** John Mercanti

Date	Mintage	MS65	PRF65
2006W	7,813	—	441

KM# 415 0.9995 **PLATINUM** 0.2502 oz. 22mm. 7.7857 g. **Rev. Desc.:** Eagle with shield **Obv. Designer:** John Mercanti

Date	Mintage	MS65	PRF65
2007W	6,017	—	441

KM# 435 0.9995 **PLATINUM** 0.2502 oz. 22mm. 7.7857 g. **Rev. Desc.:** Justice standing before eagle **Obv. Designer:** John Mercanti

Date	Mintage	MS65	PRF65
2008W	6,017	—	985

KM# 461 0.9995 **PLATINUM** 0.2502 oz. 22mm. 7.7857 g. **Obv. Designer:** John Mercanti

Date	Mintage	MS65	PRF65
2009W	3,800	—	—

PLATINUM $50

KM# 329 0.9995 **PLATINUM** 0.4997 oz. 27mm. 15.5520 g. **Rev. Desc.:** Eagle in flight over Southwestern cactus desert **Obv. Designer:** John Mercanti

Date	Mintage	MS65	PRF65
2001W	8,254	—	905

KM# 285 0.9995 **PLATINUM** 0.4997 oz. 27mm. 15.5520 g. **Rev. Desc.:** Eagle flying right over sunrise **Obv. Designer:** John Mercanti **Rev. Designer:** Thomas D. Rogers Sr

Date	Mintage	MS65	PRF65
2001	12,815	852	—
2002	24,005	852	—
2003	17,409	852	—
2004	13,236	852	—
2005	9,013	852	—
2006	9,602	852	—
2006W Burnished Unc.	—	905	—
2007	7,001	882	—
2007W Burnished Unc.	—	1,000	—
2008	14,000	852	—
2008W Burnished Unc.	—	1,200	—
2009	—	—	—

KM# 341 0.9995 **PLATINUM** 0.4997 oz. 27mm. 15.5520 g. **Rev. Desc.:** Eagle fishing in America's Northwest **Obv. Designer:** John Mercanti

Date	Mintage	MS65	PRF65
2002W	8,772	—	905

KM# 353 0.9995 **PLATINUM** 0.4997 oz. 27mm. 15.5520 g. **Rev. Desc.:** Eagle pearched on a Rocky Mountain Pine branch against a flag backdrop. **Obv. Designer:** John Mercanti **Rev. Designer:** Al Maletsky

Date	Mintage	MS65	PRF65
2003W	7,131	—	905

KM# 366 0.9995 **PLATINUM** 0.4997 oz. 27mm. 15.5520 g. **Rev. Desc.:** Chester French, 1907. The sculpture is outside the N.Y. Customs House, now part of the Smithsonian's Museum of the American Indian **Obv. Designer:** John Mercanti

Date	Mintage	MS65	PRF65
2004W	5,063	—	1,550

KM# 379 0.9995 **PLATINUM** 0.4997 oz. 27mm. 15.5520 g. **Rev. Desc.:** Eagle with cornucopiae **Obv. Designer:** John Mercanti **Rev. Designer:** Donna Weaver

Date	Mintage	MS65	PRF65
2005W	5,942	—	1,175

KM# 391 0.9995 **PLATINUM** 0.4997 oz. 27mm. 15.5520 g. **Rev. Desc.:** Liberty seated writing between two columns **Obv. Designer:** John Mercanti

Date	Mintage	MS65	PRF65
2006W	7,649	—	905

KM# 416 0.9995 **PLATINUM** 0.4997 oz. 27mm. 15.5520 g. **Rev. Desc.:** Eagle with shield **Obv. Designer:** John Mercanti

Date	Mintage	MS65	PRF65
2007W	22,873	—	905

KM# 436 0.9995 **PLATINUM** 0.4997 oz. 27mm. 15.5520 g. **Rev. Desc.:** Justice standing before eagle **Obv. Designer:** John Mercanti

Date	Mintage	MS65	PRF65
2008W	22,873	—	1,400

KM# 462 0.9995 **PLATINUM** 0.4997 oz. 27mm. 15.5520 g. **Obv. Designer:** John Mercanti

Date	Mintage	MS65	PRF65
2009	3,600	—	—

PLATINUM $100

KM# 330 0.9995 **PLATINUM** 0.9995 oz. 33mm. 31.1050 g. **Rev. Desc.:** Eagle in flight over Southwestern cactus desert **Obv. Designer:** John Mercanti

Date	Mintage	MS65	PRF65
2001W	8,969	—	1,809

KM# 286 0.9995 **PLATINUM** 0.9995 oz. 33mm. 31.1050 g. **Rev. Desc.:** Eagle in flight over sun rise **Obv. Designer:** John Mercanti **Rev. Designer:** Thomas D. Rogers Sr

Date	Mintage	MS65	PRF65
2001	14,070	1,704	—
2002	11,502	1,704	—
2003	8,007	1,704	—
2004	7,009	1,704	—
2005	6,310	1,704	—
2006	6,000	1,704	—
2006W Burnished Unc.	—	2,200	—
2007	7,202	1,749	—
2007W Burnished Unc.	—	2,100	—
2008	21,800	1,704	—
2008W Burnished Unc.	—	2,250	—

KM# 342 0.9995 **PLATINUM** 0.9995 oz. 33mm. 31.1050 g. **Rev. Desc.:** Eagle fishing in America's Northwest **Obv. Designer:** John Mercanti

Date	Mintage	MS65	PRF65
2002W	9,834	—	1,809

KM# 354 0.9995 **PLATINUM** 0.9995 oz. 33mm. 31.1050 g. **Rev. Desc.:** Eagle pearched on a Rocky Mountain Pine branch against a flag backdrop **Obv. Designer:** John Mercanti **Rev. Designer:** Al Maletsky

Date	Mintage	MS65	PRF65
2003W	8,246	—	1,826

KM# 367 0.9995 **PLATINUM** 0.9995 oz. 33mm. 31.1050 g. **Rev. Desc.:** Inspired by the sculpture "America" by Daniel Chester French, 1907. The sculpture is outside the N.Y. Customs House, now part of the Smithsonian's Museum of the American Indian **Obv. Designer:** John Mercanti **Rev. Designer:** Donna Weaver

Date	Mintage	MS65	PRF65
2004W	6,007	—	2,178

KM# 380 0.9995 **PLATINUM** 0.9995 oz. 33mm. 31.1050 g. **Rev. Desc.:** Eagle with cornucopiae **Obv. Designer:** John Mercanti **Rev. Designer:** Donna Weaver

Date	Mintage	MS65	PRF65
2005W	6,602	—	2,400

KM# 392 0.9995 **PLATINUM** 0.9995 oz. 33mm. 31.1050 g. **Rev. Desc.:** Liberty seated writing between two columns **Obv. Designer:** John Mercanti

Date	Mintage	MS65	PRF65
2006W	9,152	—	1,809

KM# 417 0.9995 **PLATINUM** 0.9995 oz. 33mm. 31.1050 g. **Rev. Desc.:** Eagle with shield **Obv. Designer:** John Mercanti

Date	Mintage	MS65	PRF65
2007W	8,363	—	1,809

KM# 437 0.9995 **PLATINUM** 0.9995 oz. 33mm. 31.1050 g. **Rev. Desc.:** Justice standing before eagle **Obv. Designer:** John Mercanti

Date	Mintage	MS65	PRF65
2008W	8,363	—	3,000

KM# 463 0.9995 **PLATINUM** 0.9994 oz. 33mm. 31.1020 g. **Rev. Desc.:** Four portraits **Obv. Designer:** John Mercanti

Date	Mintage	MS65	PRF65
2009W Proof	4,900	—	2,250

KM# 488 0.9990 **PLATINUM** 0.999 33mm. 31.1050 g. **Rev. Desc.:** Statue of Justice holding scales **Obv. Designer:** John Mercanti

Date	Mintage	MS65	PRF65
2010W	—	—	2,200

KM# 518 0.9995 **PLATINUM** 0.9995 oz. 33mm. 31.1050 g.

Date	Mintage	MS65	PRF65
2011W	10,299	—	1,658

KM# 541 0.9995 **PLATINUM** 0.9995 oz. 31.1050 g.

Date	Mintage	MS65	PRF65
2012	—	—	1,692

BISON BULLION COINAGE

GOLD $5

KM# 411 0.9999 **GOLD** 0.100AGW. 3.1100 g. **Obv. Desc.:** Indian Head right **Rev. Desc.:** Bison

Date	Mintage	MS65	PRF65
2008W	19,300	—	660
2008W	19,000	600	—

GOLD $10

KM# 412 0.9999 **GOLD** 0.2503 oz. AGW. 7.7857 g. **Obv. Desc.:** Indian Head right **Rev. Desc.:** Bison

Date	Mintage	MS65	PRF65
2008W	13,900	—	1,550
2008W	10,500	1,375	—

GOLD $25

KM# 413 0.9990 **GOLD** 0.4995 oz. AGW. 15.5520 g. **Obv. Desc.:** Indian Head right **Rev. Desc.:** Bison

Date	Mintage	MS65	PRF65
2008W	12,500	—	1,850
2008W	17,000	1,350	—

GOLD $50

KM# 393 0.9999 **GOLD** 0.9999 oz. AGW. 32mm. 31.1050 g. **Obv. Desc.:** Indian head right **Rev. Desc.:** **Designer:** James E. Fraser Bison standing left on mound

Date	Mintage	MS65	PRF65
2006W	246,267	—	1,795
2006W	337,012	1,659	—
2007W	136,503	1,659	—
2007W	58,998	—	1,795
2008W	189,500	1,659	—
2008W	19,500	3,200	—
2008W Moy Family Chop	—	—	3,950
2009W	—	1,659	—
2009W	—	—	1,765
2010W	49,374	—	1,795
2010	—	—	—
2011W	—	—	1,795
2011	—	—	—
2012W	—	—	—
2012	—	—	—

FIRST SPOUSE GOLD COINAGE

GOLD $10

KM# 407 0.9999 **GOLD** 0.4999 oz. AGW. 23.5mm. 15.5520 g. **Obv. Desc.:** Bust 3/4 facing **Rev. Desc.:** Martha Washington seated sewing **Obv. Designer:** Joseph Menna **Rev. Designer:** Susan Gamble and Don Everhart

Date	Mintage	MS65	PRF65
2007W	20,000	853	—
2007W	20,000	—	853

KM# 408 0.9999 **GOLD** 0.4999 oz. AGW. 26.5mm. 15.5520 g. **Obv. Desc.:** Bust 3/4 facing **Rev. Desc.:** Abigail Adams seated at desk writing to John during the Revolutionary War **Obv. Designer:** Joseph Menna **Rev. Designer:** Thomas Cleveland and Phebe Hemphill

Date	Mintage	MS65	PRF65
2007W	20,000	853	—
2007W	20,000	—	853

KM# 409 0.9999 **GOLD** 0.4999 oz. AGW. 26.5mm. 15.5520 g. **Obv. Desc.:** Bust design from coinage **Rev. Desc.:** Jefferson's tombstone **Obv. Designer:** Robert Scot and Phebe Hemphill **Rev. Designer:** Charles Vickers

Date	Mintage	MS65	PRF65
2007W	20,000	853	—
2007W	20,000	—	853

KM# 410 0.9999 **GOLD** 0.4999 oz. AGW. 26.5mm. 15.5520 g. **Obv. Desc.:** Bust 3/4 facing **Rev. Desc.:** Dolley standing before painting of Washington, which she saved from the White House **Obv. Designer:** Don Everhart **Rev. Designer:** Joel Iskowitz and Don Everhart

Date	Mintage	MS65	PRF65
2007W	12,500	853	—
2007W	18,300	—	853

KM# 430 0.9990 **GOLD** 0.4995 oz. AGW. 26.5mm. 15.5520 g. **Obv. Desc.:** Bust 3/4 facing right **Rev. Desc.:** Elizabeth standing before mirror **Obv. Designer:** Joel Iskowitz and Don Everhart **Rev. Designer:** Donna Weaver and Charles Vickers

Date	Mintage	MS65	PRF65
2008W	4,500	975	—
2008W	7,900	—	950

KM# 431 0.9990 **GOLD** 0.4995 oz. AGW. 26.5mm. 15.5520 g. **Obv. Desc.:** Bust 3/4 facing right **Rev. Desc.:** Lousia and son Charles before entrance **Obv. Designer:** Susan Gamble and Phebe Hemphill **Rev. Designer:** Joseph Menna

Date	Mintage	MS65	PRF65
2008W	4,200	1,175	—
2008W	7,400	—	1,125

KM# 432 0.9990 **GOLD** 0.4995 oz. AGW. 26.5mm. 15.5520 g. **Obv. Desc.:** Capped and draped bust left **Rev. Desc.:** Andrew Jackson on horseback right **Obv. Designer:** John Reich **Rev. Designer:** Justin Kunz and Don Everhart

Date	Mintage	MS65	PRF65
2008W	4,800	1,575	—
2008W	7,800	—	1,325

KM# 433 0.9990 **GOLD** 0.4995 oz. AGW. 26.5mm. 15.5520 g. **Obv. Desc.:** Seated Liberty with shiled **Rev. Desc.:** Youthful van Buren seated under tree, family tavern in distance **Obv. Designer:** Christian Gobrecht **Rev. Designer:** Thomas Cleveland and James Licaretz

Date	Mintage	MS65	PRF65
2008W	15,000	1,500	—
2008W	Inc. above	—	1,525

KM# 456 0.9990 **GOLD** 0.4995 oz. AGW. 15.5520 g. **Obv. Desc.:** Bust 3/4 left **Rev. Desc.:** Anna reading to her three children **Obv. Designer:** Donna Weaver and Joseph Menna **Rev. Designer:** Thomas Cleveland and Charles Vickers

Date	Mintage	MS65	PRF65
2009W	15,000	1,225	—
2009W	Inc. above	—	1,150

KM# 457 0.9990 **GOLD** 0.4995 oz. AGW. 15.5520 g. **Obv. Desc.:** Bust facing **Rev. Desc.:** Letitia and two children playing outside of Cedar Grove Plantation **Obv. Designer:** Phebe Hemphill **Rev. Designer:** Susan Gamble and Norm Nemeth

Date	Mintage	MS65	PRF65
2009W	15,000	1,525	—
2009W	Inc. above	—	1,325

KM# 458 0.9990 **GOLD** 0.4995 oz. AGW. 15.5520 g. **Obv. Desc.:** Bust facing **Rev. Desc.:** **Designer:** Joel Iskowitz and Don Everhart Julia and John Tyler dancing

Date	Mintage	MS65	PRF65
2009W	15,000	1,650	—
2009W	Inc. above	—	1,800

KM# 459 0.9990 **GOLD** 0.4995 oz. AGW. 15.5520 g. **Obv. Desc.:** Bust 3/4 right **Rev. Desc.:** **Designer:** Phebe Hemphill Sarah seated at desk as personal secretary to James Polk

Date	Mintage	MS65	PRF65
2009W	3,501	1,300	—
2009W	5,157	—	1,100

KM# 465 0.9990 **GOLD** 0.4995 oz. AGW. 15.5520 g. **Obv. Desc.:** Bust 3/4 left **Rev. Desc.:** Margaret Taylor nurses wounded soldier during the Seminole War **Obv. Designer:** Phebe Hemphill and Charles Vickers **Rev. Designer:** Mary Beth Zeitz and James Licaretz

Date	Mintage	MS65	PRF65
2009W	3,430	1,050	—
2009W	4,787	—	1,225

KM# 481 0.9990 **GOLD** 0.4985 oz. AGW. 15.5200 g. **Rev. Desc.:** Abigail Filmore placing books on library shelf **Obv. Designer:** Phebe Hemphill **Rev. Designer:** Susan Gamble and Joseph Menna

Date	Mintage	MS65	PRF65
2010W	15,000	1,300	—
2010W	Inc. above	—	1,025

KM# 482 0.9990 **GOLD** 0.4985 oz. AGW. 15.5200 g. **Rev. Desc.:** Jane Pierce seated on porch **Obv. Designer:** Donna Weaver and Don Everhart **Rev. Designer:** Donna Weaver and Charles Vickers

Date	Mintage	MS65	PRF65
2010W	3,333	1,000	—
2010W	4,843	—	1,225

KM# 483 0.9990 **GOLD** 0.4985 oz. AGW. 26.5mm. 15.5200 g. **Rev. Desc.:** Buchanan as clerk **Obv. Designer:** Christian Gobrecht **Rev. Designer:** Joseph Menna

Date	Mintage	MS65	PRF65
2010W	5,348	1,000	—
2010W	7,304	—	1,075

KM# 484 0.9990 **GOLD** 0.4985 oz. AGW. 15.5200 g. **Rev. Desc.:** Mary Lincoln visiting soldiers at hospital **Obv. Designer:** Phebe Hemphill **Rev. Designer:** Joel Iskowitz and Pheve Hemphill

Date	Mintage	MS65	PRF65
2010W	3,760	1,000	—

Date	Mintage	MS65	PRF65
2010W	6,904	—	975

KM# 509 0.9990 **GOLD** 0.4994 oz. AGW. 15.5500 g. **Obv. Desc.:** Bust of Eliza Johnson

Date	Mintage	MS65	PRF65
2011W	15,000	1,075	—
2011W	Inc. above	—	1,075

KM# 510 0.9990 **GOLD** 0.4995 oz. AGW. 26.5mm. 15.5520 g. **Obv. Desc.:** Bust of Julia Grant

Date	Mintage	MS65	PRF65
2011W	15,000	1,075	—
2011W	Inc. above	—	1,075

KM# 511 0.9990 **GOLD** 0.4995 oz. AGW. 15.5520 g. **Obv. Desc.:** Bust of Lucy Hayes

Date	Mintage	MS65	PRF65
2011W	15,000	1,325	—
2011W	3,826	—	1,075

KM# 512 0.9990 **GOLD** 0.4995 oz. AGW. 15.5520 g. **Obv. Desc.:** Bust of Lucretia Garfield

Date	Mintage	MS65	PRF65
2011W	15,000	1,325	—
2011W	3,521	—	1,075

KM# 561 0.9990 **GOLD** 0.4995 oz. AGW. 15.5520 g. **Obv. Desc.:** Bust of Ida McKinley

Date	Mintage	MS65	PRF65
2013W	—	950	—
2013W	—	—	1,000

KM# 562 0.9990 **GOLD** 0.4995 oz. AGW. 15.5520 g. **Obv. Desc.:** Bust of Edith Roosevelt

Date	Mintage	MS65	PRF65
2013W	—	950	—
2013W	—	—	1,000

KM# 563 0.9990 **GOLD** 0.4995 oz. AGW. 15.5520 g. **Obv. Desc.:** Bust of Helen Taft

Date	Mintage	MS65	PRF65
2013W	—	950	—
2013W	—	—	1,000

KM# 564 0.9990 **GOLD** 0.4995 oz. AGW. 15.5520 g. **Obv. Desc.:** Bust of Ellen Wilson

Date	Mintage	MS65	PRF65
2013W	—	950	—
2013W	—	—	1,000

KM# 565 0.9990 **GOLD** 0.4995 oz. AGW. 15.5520 g. **Obv. Desc.:** Bust of Edith Wilson

Date	Mintage	MS65	PRF65
2013W	—	950	—
2013W	—	—	1,000

KM# 532 0.9990 **GOLD** 0.4995 oz. AGW. 15.5520 g. **Obv. Desc.:** Alice Paul, suffragist

Date	Mintage	MS65	PRF65
2012W	2,021	1,050	—
2012W	2,802	—	1,075

KM# 533 0.9990 **GOLD** 0.4995 oz. AGW. 15.5520 g. **Obv. Desc.:** Francis Cleveland

Date	Mintage	MS65	PRF65
2012W	1,565	1,050	—
2012W	2,152	—	1,075

KM# 534 0.9990 **GOLD** 0.4995 oz. AGW. 15.5520 g. **Obv. Desc.:** Caroline Harrison

Date	Mintage	MS65	PRF65
2012W	942	1,050	—
2012W	1,380	—	1,075

KM# 535 0.9990 **GOLD** 0.4995 oz. AGW. 15.5520 g. **Obv. Desc.:** Francis Cleveland

Date	Mintage	MS65	PRF65
2012W	—	1,050	—
2012W	—	—	1,075

BULLION SETS

MINT SETS

Mint, or uncirculated, sets contain one uncirculated coin of each denomination from each mint produced for circulation that year. Values listed here are only for those sets sold by the U.S. Mint. Sets were not offered in years not listed. In years when the Mint did not offer the sets, some private companies compiled and marketed uncirculated sets. Mint sets from 1947 through 1958 contained two examples of each coin mounted in cardboard holders, which caused the coins to tarnish. Beginning in 1959, the sets have been packaged in sealed Pliofilm packets and include only one specimen of each coin struck for that year (both P & D mints). Listings for 1965, 1966 and 1967 are for "special mint sets," which were of higher quality than regular mint sets and were prooflike. They were packaged in plastic cases. The 1970 large-date and small-date varieties are distinguished by the size of the date on the coin. The 1976 three-piece set contains the quarter, half dollar and dollar with the Bicentennial design. The 1971 and 1972 sets do not include a dollar coin; the 1979 set does not include an S-mint-marked dollar. Mint sets issued prior to 1959 were double sets (containing two of each coin) packaged in cardboard with a paper overlay. Origional sets will always be toned and can bring large premiums if nicely preserved with good color.

Date	Sets Sold	Issue Price	Value
2001	1,066,900	14.95	9.50
2002	1,139,388	14.95	10.25
2003	1,002,555	14.95	8.25
2004	844,484	16.95	12.10
2005	—	16.95	8.50
2006	—	16.95	11.25
2007	—	—	22.50
2008	—	—	59.50
2009 18 piece clad set	—	—	24.50
2010 28 piece clad set	—	—	29.70
2010 14 piece clad	—	—	24.50
2011 14 piece clad set	532,059	—	33.00
2012 14 piece clad set	365,298	—	46.50

MODERN COMMEMORATIVE COIN SETS

American Buffalo

Date	Price
2001 2 coin set: 90% silver unc. & proof $1.; KM325.	330
2001 coin & currency set 90% unc. dollar & replicas of 1899 $5 silver cert.; KM325.	180

Capitol Visitor Center

Date	Price
2001 3 coin set: proof half, silver dollar, gold $5; KM323, 324, 326.	495

Winter Olympics - Salt Lake City

Date	Price
2002 2 coin set: proof 90% silver dollar KM336 & $5.00 Gold KM337.	465
2002 4 coin set: 90% silver unc. & proof $1, KM336 & unc. & proof gold $5, KM337.	925

Thomas Alva Edison

Date	Price
2004 Uncirculated silver dollar and light bulb.	55.00

Lewis and Clark Bicentennial

Date	Price
2004 Coin and pouch set.	65.00
2004 coin and currency set: Uncirculated silver dollar, two 2005 nickels, replica 1901 $10 Bison note, silver plated peace medal, three stamps & two booklets.	58.00
2004 Westward Journey Nickel series coin and medal set: Proof Sacagawea dollar, two 2005 proof nickels and silver plated peace medal.	40.00

Chief Justice John Marshall

Date	Price
2005 Coin and Chronicles set: Uncirculated silver dollar, booklet and BEP intaglio portrait.	57.00

U.S. Marine Corps

Date	Price
2005 Uncirculated silver dollar and stamp set.	63.00

Benjamin Franklin Tercentennary

Date	Price
2006 Coin and Chronicles set: Uncirculated "Scientist" silver dollar, four stamps, Poor Richards Almanac and intaglio print.	49.00

Central High School Desegregation

Date	Price
2007 Little Rock Dollar and medal set, KM#418	47.80

American Bald Eagle

Date	Price
2008 Proof half dollar, dollar and $5 gold, KM438, KM439, KM440	490
2008 Bald Eagle young collector's set; Half Dollar, KM#438	23.00

Louis Braille

Date	Price
Braille Education set, KM#455	43.50

PROOF SETS

Proof coins are produced through a special process involving specially selected, highly polished planchets and dies. They usually receive two strikings from the coin press at increased pressure. The result is a coin with mirrorlike surfaces and, in recent years, a cameo effect on its raised design surfaces.

Date	Sets Sold	Issue Price	Value
2001S 10 piece	2,249,498	19.95	12.75
2001S 5 quarter set	774,800	13.95	7.50
2001S Silver	849,600	31.95	45.80
2002S 10 piece	2,319,766	19.95	7.75
2002S 5 quarter set	764,419	13.95	4.50
2002S Silver	892,229	31.95	45.80
2003 X#207, 208, 209.2	—	44.00	28.75
2003S 10 piece	2,175,684	16.75	8.00
2003S 5 quarter set	1,225,507	13.95	3.60
2003S Silver	1,142,858	31.95	45.20
2004S 11 piece	1,804,396	22.95	9.10
2004S 5 quarter set	987,960	23.95	30.10
2004S Silver 11 piece	1,187,673	37.95	45.20
2004S Silver 5 quarter set	594,137	—	32.30
2005S American Legacy	—	—	79.50
2005S 11 piece	—	22.95	6.00
2005S 5 quarter set	—	15.95	35.00
2005S Silver 11 piece	—	37.95	46.20
2005S Silver 5 quarter set	—	23.95	32.30
2005S American Legacy	—	—	84.50
2006S 10 piece clad	—	22.95	10.75
2006S 5 quarter set	—	15.95	4.50
2006S Silver 10 piece	—	37.95	50.50
2006S Silver 5 quarter set	—	23.95	32.30
2006S American Legacy	—	—	81.00
2007S 5 quarter set	—	13.95	4.50
2007S Silver 5 quarter set	—	22.95	32.30
2007S 14 piece clad	—	—	16.50
2007S Silver 14 piece	—	—	51.20
2007S Presidential $ set	—	—	6.50
2007S American Legacy	—	—	120
2008 14 piece clad set	—	—	78.00
2008S 14 piece silver set	734,045	—	63.00
2008S Presidential $ set	—	—	11.00
2008S American Legacy	—	—	120
2008S 5 quarter clad set	—	22.95	47.50
2008S 5 quarter silver set	—	—	32.30
2009S 18 piece clad set	1,477,967	—	28.50
2009S 18 piece silver set	694,406	—	70.00
2009S Presidential $ set	627,925	—	8.25
2009S Lincoln Chronicle	—	—	135
2009S Lincoln 4 piece	—	—	15.50
2009S 6 quarter clad set	—	—	10.50
2009S 6 quarter silver set	—	—	36.60
2010S 14 piece clad set	1,103,950	—	72.00
2010S 14 piece silver set	583,912	—	71.50
2010S Presidential $ set	535,463	—	15.50
2010S 6 quarter set	276,335	—	32.00
2010S 5 quarter silver set	274,003	—	32.30
2011 6 quarter set	—	—	17.25
2011S 5 quarter silver set	147,005	—	49.50
2011S 14 piece silver set	572,247	—	77.00
2011S 5 quarter clad set	151,434	—	14.50
2011S Presidential $ set	299,161	—	20.00
2011S 14 piece clad set	1,095,318	—	44.00
2012S 5 quarter silver set	—	—	45.00
2012S 14 piece silver set	—	—	148
2012S 6 quarter set	—	—	20.00
2012S 14 piece clad set	—	—	77.00
2012S Presidential $ set	—	—	61.00

UNCIRCULATED ROLLS

Date	Cents	Nickels	Dimes	Quarters	Halves
2001P	3.75	4.75	7.75	—	16.50
2001D	2.00	6.50	7.25	—	16.00
2002P	2.00	4.00	7.25	—	20.00
2002D	3.25	4.10	7.25	—	20.00
2003P	3.35	7.50	7.00	—	22.50
2003D	2.00	3.50	7.00	—	19.50
2004P Peace Medal Nickel	1.75	6.75	7.00	—	30.00
2004D Peace Medal Nickel	2.50	7.00	7.00	—	30.00
2004P Keelboat Nickel	—	4.00	—	—	—
2004D Keelboat Nickel	—	3.50	—	—	—
2005P Bison Nickel	1.75	3.25	7.00	—	21.00
2005D Bison Nickel	2.75	3.25	7.00	—	21.00
2005P Ocean in view Nickel	—	3.25	—	—	—
2005D Ocean in view Nickel	—	3.25	—	—	—
2006P	2.75	3.25	8.50	—	29.00
2006D	1.75	3.25	8.50	—	29.00
2007P	1.75	3.50	8.00	—	21.00
2007D	1.75	3.50	7.75	—	21.00
2008P	1.75	3.75	8.00	—	24.50
2008D	1.75	3.75	7.50	—	25.50
2009P Log Cabin	2.00	23.00	13.50	—	18.50
2009D Log Cabin	2.15	13.50	13.50	—	18.50
2009P Log Splitter	1.75	—	—	—	—
2009D Log Splitter	1.75	—	—	—	—
2009P Professional	1.75	—	—	—	—
2009D Professional	1.75	—	—	—	—
2009P President	2.00	—	—	—	—
2009D President	2.00	—	—	—	—

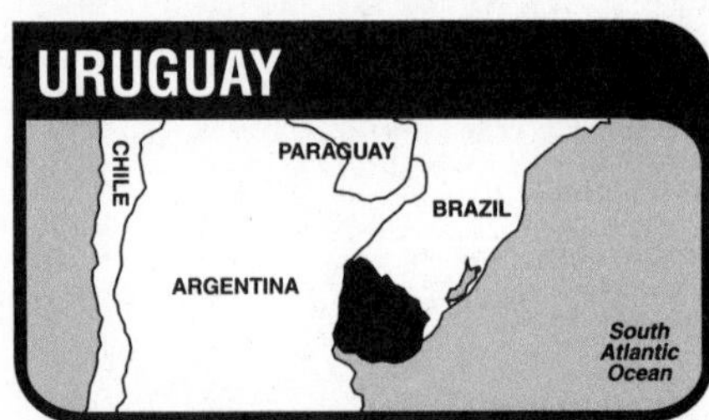

The Oriental Republic of Uruguay (so called because of its location on the east bank of the Uruguay River) is situated on the Atlantic coast of South America between Argentina and Brazil. This South American country has an area of 68,536 sq. mi. (176,220 sq. km.) and a population of *3 million. Capital: Montevideo. Uruguay's chief economic asset is the rich, rolling grassy plains. Meat, wool, hides and skins are exported.

MINT MARKS

(ba) – Buenos Aires
(br) – Acunaciones Espanolas S.A., Barcelona
(k) – Kremnica (Slovakia)
(m) - Madrid
Mo, (mo) and Mx - Mexico City
(p) – thunderbolt: Poissy, France
(rcm) – Royal Canadian Mint
(rj) – Rio de Janeiro
(sa) – Pretoria, South Africa
So, (so) – Santiago (Small o above S); (except 2007 2 Pesos Uruguayos)

REPUBLIC

REFORM COINAGE

March 1993

1,000 Nuevos Pesos = 1 Uruguayan Peso;
100 Centesimos = 1 Uruguayan Peso (UYP)

KM# 106 50 CENTESIMOS

3.0000 g., Stainless Steel, 21 mm. **Obv:** Bust of Artigas right **Obv. Legend:** REPUBLICA ORIENTAL DEL URUGUAY **Rev:** Value, date and sprig **Edge:** Plain **Note:** Coin rotation.

Date	Mintage	F	VF	XF	Unc	BU
2002(sa)	10,000,000	—	—	0.35	0.75	1.00
2005(m)	15,000,000	—	—	0.35	0.75	1.00
2008(k)	35,000,000	—	—	0.35	0.75	1.00
2009	—	—	—	0.35	0.75	1.00

KM# 103.2 UN PESO URUGUAYO

3.5000 g., Aluminum-Bronze, 20 mm. **Obv:** Bust of Artigas right **Obv. Legend:** REPUBLICA ORIENTAL DEL URUGUAY **Rev:** Value and date **Edge:** Plain **Note:** Medal rotation; left point of bust shoulder points at "P" in Republic.

Date	Mintage	F	VF	XF	Unc	BU
2005So	40,000,000	—	—	—	0.50	0.75
2007So	25,000,000	—	—	—	0.50	0.75

KM# 135 UN PESO URUGUAYO

3.5000 g., Brass Plated Steel, 20 mm. **Obv:** Arms in circle, date below **Obv. Legend:** REPUBLICA ORIENTAL DEL URUGUAY **Rev:** Mulita (armadillo) **Edge:** Plain

Date	Mintage	F	VF	XF	Unc	BU
2011(m)	20,000,000	—	—	—	0.50	0.60
2012	—	—	—	—	0.50	0.60

KM# 104.2 2 PESOS URUGUAYOS

4.5000 g., Aluminum-Bronze, 23 mm. **Obv:** Bust of Artigas right **Obv. Legend:** REPUBLICA ORIENTAL DEL URUGUAY **Rev:** Value and date **Edge:** Plain **Note:** Medal rotation. Left point of bust shoulder points at "P" in "Republic".

Date	Mintage	F	VF	XF	Unc	BU
2007So	25,000,000	—	—	0.75	1.50	2.00

Note: Minted at Paris with the So mintmark.

KM# 136 2 PESOS URUGUAYOS

4.5000 g., Brass Plated Steel, 23 mm. **Obv:** Arms in circle, date below **Obv. Legend:** REPUBLICA ORIENTAL DEL URUGUAY **Rev:** Carpincho **Edge:** Plain

Date	Mintage	F	VF	XF	Unc	BU
2011(m)	20,000,000	—	—	—	0.75	0.90

KM# 120.1 5 PESOS URUGUAYOS

6.3000 g., Aluminum-Bronze, 26 mm. **Obv:** Bust of Artigas right **Obv. Legend:** REPUBLICA ORIENTAL DEL URUGUAY **Rev:** Value **Edge:** Plain **Note:** Left point of bust shoulder points at "U" in "Republic".

Date	Mintage	F	VF	XF	Unc	BU
2003(ba)	15,150,000	—	—	—	2.50	3.00

KM# 120.2 5 PESOS URUGUAYOS

6.3000 g., Aluminum-Bronze, 26 mm. **Obv:** Bust of Antigas right **Obv. Legend:** REPUBLICA ORIENTAL DEL URUGUAY • **Rev:** Value, date **Note:** Left point of bust shoulder points at "P" in "Republic".

Date	Mintage	F	VF	XF	Unc	BU
2005So	30,000,000	—	—	—	2.50	3.00
2008So	20,000,000	—	—	—	2.50	3.00

KM# 137 5 PESOS URUGUAYOS

6.4000 g., Brass Plated Steel, 25.5 mm. **Obv:** Arms in circle, date below **Obv. Legend:** REPUBLICA ORIENTAL DEL URUGUAY **Rev:** Nandu **Edge:** Palin

Date	Mintage	F	VF	XF	Unc	BU
2011(l)	10,000,000	—	—	—	1.25	1.50

KM# 121 10 PESOS URUGUAYOS

10.4000 g., Bi-Metallic Aluminum-Bronze center in Stainless Steel ring, 28 mm. **Obv:** Artigas head right within circle **Rev:** Value above signature within circle **Edge:** Plain

Date	Mintage	F	VF	XF	Unc	BU
2000 (rcm)	40,000,000	—	—	—	3.50	5.00

Note: 5-pointed star on each side of date, issued 2006

KM# 134 10 PESOS URUGUAYOS

10.4000 g., Bi-Metallic Brass center, 28 mm. **Obv:** Oval arms, country name and date **Rev:** Puma walking left, sunrise in background and value

Date	Mintage	F	VF	XF	Unc	BU
2011(l)	10,000,000	—	—	—	2.00	2.50

KM# 139 50 PESOS URUGUAYOS

10.4000 g., Copper Plated Steel, 28 mm. **Subject:** Bicentennial of Uruguayan Independence **Obv:** Portrait of General Jose Artigas, country name and value **Rev:** Sun and rays and inscriptions "BICENTENARIO DE LOS HECHOS HISTORICOS" and "1811-2011" **Edge:** Reeded

Date	Mintage	F	VF	XF	Unc	BU
2011(k)	10,000,000	—	—	—	4.00	4.50

KM# 133 500 PESOS URUGAUAYOS

12.5000 g., 0.9000 Silver 0.3617 oz. ASW, 33 mm. **Subject:** Salto, 250th Anniversary **Obv:** Uruguay map with City of Salto location **Rev:** Emblem of the Department of Salto

Date	Mintage	F	VF	XF	Unc	BU
2006(u) Proof	10,000	Value: 25.00				

KM# 122 1000 PESOS URUGUAYOS

27.0000 g., 0.9250 Silver 0.8029 oz. ASW, 40 mm. **Subject:** XVIII World Championship Football - Germany 2006 **Obv:** National arms **Obv. Legend:** REPUBLICA ORIENTAL DEL URUGUAY **Rev:** Soccer player and value **Edge:** Reeded

Date	Mintage	F	VF	XF	Unc	BU
2003(m) Proof	—	Value: 50.00				

KM# 123 1000 PESOS URUGUAYOS

27.0000 g., 0.9250 Silver 0.8029 oz. ASW, 40 mm. **Subject:** XVIII World Championship Football - Germany 2006 **Obv:** National arms above date **Obv. Legend:** REPUBLICA ORIENTAL DEL URUGUAY **Rev:** Stylized soccer player and value **Edge:** Reeded

Date	Mintage	F	VF	XF	Unc	BU
2004(m) Proof	—	Value: 50.00				

KM# 125 1000 PESOS URUGUAYOS

27.0000 g., 0.9250 Silver 0.8029 oz. ASW, 40 mm. **Subject:** 100th Anniversary FIFA - 1930 Championship **Obv:** Football before net **Obv. Legend:** REPUBLICA ORIENTAL DEL URUGUAY **Rev:** Sun of national flag **Edge:** Reeded

Date	Mintage	F	VF	XF	Unc	BU
2004(m) Proof	—	Value: 45.00				

KM# 124 1000 PESOS URUGUAYOS

27.0000 g., 0.9250 Silver 0.8029 oz. ASW, 40 mm. **Subject:** XVIII World Championship Football - Germany 2006 **Obv:** National arms above date **Obv. Legend:** REPUBLICA ORIENTAL DEL URUGUAY **Rev:** FIFA trophy **Edge:** Reeded

Date	Mintage	F	VF	XF	Unc	BU
2005(m) Proof	—	Value: 50.00				

KM# 140 1000 PESOS URUGUAYOS

25.0000 g., 0.9000 Silver 0.7234 oz. ASW, 37 mm. **Subject:** Bicentennial of Uruguayan Independence **Obv:** Painting by Juan Luis Blanes of the surrender of Posadas at the battle of Las Piedras on May 18, 1811, country name and value **Rev:** Sun and rays and inscription "BICENTENARIO DE LOS HECHOS HISTORICOS" and "1811-2011" **Edge:** Reeded

Date	Mintage	F	VF	XF	Unc	BU
2011(k) Proof	5,000	Value: 80.00				

KM# 126 5000 PESOS URUGUAYOS

6.7500 g., 0.9250 Gold 0.2007 oz. AGW, 23 mm. **Subject:** 100th Anniversary FIFA - 1930 Championship **Obv:** Football **Obv. Legend:** REPUBLICA ORIENTAL DEL URUGUAY **Rev:** Tower of Homage in Montevideo **Edge:** Reeded

Date	Mintage	F	VF	XF	Unc	BU
2004(m) Proof	—	Value: 400				

KM# 127 5000 PESOS URUGUAYOS

6.7500 g., 0.9250 Gold 0.2007 oz. AGW, 23 mm. **Subject:** XVIII World Championship Football - Germany 2006 **Obv:** National arms **Obv. Legend:** REPUBLICA ORIENTAL DEL URUGUAY **Rev:** Stylized player and value **Edge:** Reeded

Date	Mintage	F	VF	XF	Unc	BU
2004(m) Proof	—	Value: 500				

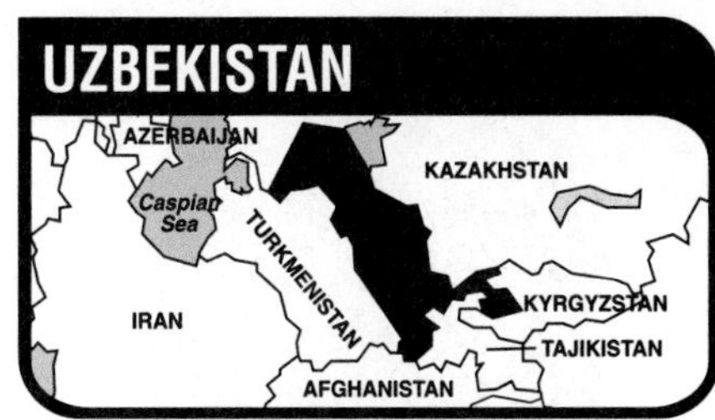

The Republic of Uzbekistan (formerly the Uzbek S.S.R.), is bordered on the north by Kazakhstan, to the east by Kirghizia and Tajikistan, on the south by Afghanistan and on the west by Turkmenistan. The republic is comprised of the regions of Andizhan, Bukhara, Dzhizak, Ferghana, Kashkadar, Khorezm (Khiva), Namangan, Navoi, Samarkand, Surkhan-Darya, Syr-Darya, Tashkent and the Karakalpak Autonomous Republic. It has an area of 172,741 sq. mi. (447,400 sq. km.) and a population of 20.3 million. Capital: Tashkent. Crude oil, natural gas, coal, copper, and gold deposits make up the chief resources, while intensive farming, based on artificial irrigation, provides an abundance of cotton.

MONETARY SYSTEM

100 Tiyin = 1 Som

REPUBLIC

STANDARD COINAGE

KM# 13 5 SOM

3.3500 g., Brass Plated Steel, 21.2 mm. **Obv:** National arms **Rev:** Value and map **Edge:** Plain

Date	Mintage	F	VF	XF	Unc	BU
2001	—	—	—	—	1.35	1.75

Note: 2 reverse map varieties known

KM# 14 10 SOM

2.7100 g., Nickel Clad Steel, 19.75 mm. **Obv:** National arms **Rev:** Value and map **Edge:** Plain

Date	Mintage	F	VF	XF	Unc	BU
2001	—	—	—	—	2.00	2.50

Note: 2 reverse map varieties exist

KM# 15 50 SOM

8.0000 g., Nickel Clad Steel, 26.2 mm. **Obv:** National arms **Rev:** Value and map **Edge:** Segmented reeding

Date	Mintage	F	VF	XF	Unc	BU
2001	—	—	—	1.20	3.00	4.00

KM# 16 50 SOM

7.9000 g., Nickel Clad Steel, 26.3 mm. **Subject:** 2700th Anniversary of Shahrisabz Town **Obv:** National arms **Rev:** Statue and ruins above value **Edge:** Segmented reeding

Date	Mintage	F	VF	XF	Unc	BU
2002	—	—	—	1.00	2.50	3.50

KM# 20 100 SOM

31.1000 g., 0.9990 Silver 0.9988 oz. ASW **Obv:** National arms **Obv. Legend:** O'ZBEKISTON MARKAZIY BANKI **Rev:** Amir-Timur Museum

Date	Mintage	F	VF	XF	Unc	BU
2001 Proof	1,000	Value: 225				

KM# 21 100 SOM

31.1000 g., 0.9990 Silver 0.9988 oz. ASW **Obv:** National Arms **Obv. Legend:** O'BEKISTON MARKAZY BANKI **Rev:** Toskent town hall

Date	Mintage	F	VF	XF	Unc	BU
2001 Proof	1,000	Value: 225				

KM# 22 100 SOM

31.1000 g., 0.9990 Silver 0.9988 oz. ASW **Obv:** National arms **Obv. Legend:** O'ZBEKISTON MARKAZIY BANKI **Rev:** World

Date	Mintage	F	VF	XF	Unc	BU
2001 Proof	1,000	Value: 225				

KM# 18 100 SOM

Bronze **Subject:** 500th Anniversary Death of 'Aliser Navoi **Obv:** National arms **Obv. Legend:** O'ZBEKISTON MARKAZIY BANKI **Rev:** 'Aliser Navoi

Date	Mintage	F	VF	XF	Unc	BU
2001	—	—	—	—	15.00	18.00

KM# 19 100 SOM

31.1000 g., 0.9990 Silver 0.9988 oz. ASW **Obv:** National arms **Obv. Legend:** O'ZBEKISTON MARKAZIY BANKI **Rev:** Parliament building in Toskent

Date	Mintage	F	VF	XF	Unc	BU
2001 Proof	1,000	Value: 225				

KM# 23 100 SOM

31.1000 g., 0.9990 Silver 0.9988 oz. ASW **Obv:** National arms **Obv. Legend:** O'ZBEKISTON MARKAZIY BANKI **Rev:** Football player

Date	Mintage	F	VF	XF	Unc	BU
2001 Proof	1,000	Value: 225				

KM# 24 100 SOM

31.1000 g., 0.9990 Silver 0.9988 oz. ASW **Obv:** National arms **Obv. Legend:** O'BEKISTON MARKAZIY BANKI **Rev:** Track runner

Date	Mintage	F	VF	XF	Unc	BU
2001 Proof	1,000	Value: 225				

KM# 25 100 SOM

31.1000 g., 0.9990 Silver 0.9988 oz. ASW **Obv:** National arms **Obv. Legend:** O'ZBEKISTON MARKAZIY BANKI **Rev:** Judo expert

Date	Mintage	F	VF	XF	Unc	BU
2001 Proof	1,000	Value: 225				

KM# 26 100 SOM

31.1000 g., 0.9990 Silver 0.9988 oz. ASW **Obv:** National arms **Obv. Legend:** O'ZBEKISTON MARKAZIY BANKI **Rev:** Tennis player

Date	Mintage	F	VF	XF	Unc	BU
2001 Proof	1,000	Value: 225				

KM# 27 100 SOM

31.1000 g., 0.9990 Silver 0.9988 oz. ASW **Obv:** National arms **Obv. Legend:** O'ZBEKISTON MARKAZIY BANKI **Rev:** Lenk monument in Timur

Date	Mintage	F	VF	XF	Unc	BU
2001 Proof	1,000	Value: 225				

KM# 28 100 SOM

31.1000 g., 0.9990 Silver 0.9988 oz. ASW **Obv:** National arms **Obv. Legend:** O'ZBEKISTON MARKAZIY BANKI **Rev:** Aliser Navoi monument

Date	Mintage	F	VF	XF	Unc	BU
2001 Proof	1,000	Value: 225				

KM# 29 100 SOM

31.1000 g., 0.9990 Silver 0.9988 oz. ASW **Obv:** National arms **Obv. Legend:** O'ZBEKISTON MARKAZIY BANKI **Rev:** Registan in Samarkand

Date	Mintage	F	VF	XF	Unc	BU
2001 Proof	1,000	Value: 225				

KM# 30 100 SOM

31.1000 g., 0.9990 Silver 0.9988 oz. ASW **Obv:** National arms **Obv. Legend:** O'BEKISTON MARKAZIY BANKI **Rev:** Bell tower in Toskent

Date	Mintage	F	VF	XF	Unc	BU
2001 Proof	1,000	Value: 225				

KM# 17 100 SOM

7.9200 g., Nickel Plated Steel, 26.95 mm. **Subject:** 10th Annniversary State Currency **Obv:** National arms **Obv. Legend:** O'ZBEKISTON MARKAZIV BANKI **Rev:** Sun rays over outlined map and value **Rev. Legend:** O'BEKISTON MILLIY VALYUTASIGA **Edge:** Lettered

Date	Mintage	F	VF	XF	Unc	BU
2004	—	—	—	—	12.50	15.00

KM# 31 100 SOM

7.9200 g., Nickel Plated Steel, 26.95 mm. **Subject:** Tashkent, 2200th Anniversary of settlement **Obv:** National arms **Rev:** Linear archway and monument in background

Date	Mintage	F	VF	XF	Unc	BU
2009	—	—	—	—	3.50	5.00

KM# 32 100 SOM

7.9200 g., Nickel Plated Steel, 26.95 mm. **Subject:** Tashkent, 2200th Anniversary of settlement **Obv:** National arms **Rev:** Monument

Date	Mintage	F	VF	XF	Unc	BU
2009	—	—	—	—	3.50	5.00

KM# 34.1 500 SOM

Copper-Nickel **Obv:** National emblem, sun disc behind eagle's head **Rev:** Building

Date	Mintage	F	VF	XF	Unc	BU
2011	—	—	—	—	—	15.00

KM# 34.2 500 SOM

Copper-Nickel **Obv:** National emblem, without sun disc behind eagle's head **Rev:** Building

Date	Mintage	F	VF	XF	Unc	BU
2011	—	—	—	—	—	15.00

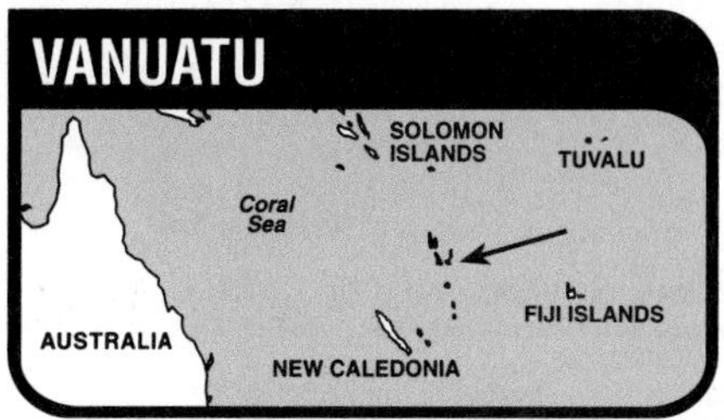

The Republic of Vanuatu, formerly New Hebrides Condominium, a group of islands located in the South Pacific 500 miles (800 km.) west of Fiji, were under the joint sovereignty of Great Britain and France. The islands have an area of 5,700 sq. mi. (14,760 sq. km.) and a population of 165,000, mainly Melanesians of mixed blood. Capital: Port-Vila. The volcanic and coral islands, while malarial land subject to frequent earthquakes, are extremely fertile, and produce copra, coffee, tropical fruits and timber for export.

The New Hebrides were discovered by Portuguese navigator Pedro de Quiros (sailing under orders by the King of Spain) in 1606, visited by French explorer Bougainville in 1768, and named by British navigator Capt. James Cook in 1774. Ships of all nations converged on the islands to trade for sandalwood, prompting France and Britain to relinquish their individual claims and declare the islands a neutral zone in 1878. The New Hebrides were placed under the control of a mixed Anglo-French commission of naval officers during the native uprisings of 1887, and established as a condominium under the joint sovereignty of France and Great Britain in 1906.

Vanuatu became an independent republic within the Commonwealth in July 1980. A president is Head of State and the Prime Minister is Head of Government.

MONETARY SYSTEM

Vatu to Present

REPUBLIC

STANDARD COINAGE

KM# 3 VATU

1.9900 g., Nickel-Brass, 16.95 mm. **Obv:** National arms **Rev:** Shell and value **Edge:** Plain

Date	Mintage	F	VF	XF	Unc	BU
2002	—	—	—	0.15	0.50	0.75

KM# 4 2 VATU

3.0000 g., Nickel-Brass, 20 mm. **Obv:** National arms **Rev:** Shell and value **Edge:** Plain

Date	Mintage	F	VF	XF	Unc	BU
2002	—	—	—	0.25	0.85	1.50

KM# 5 5 VATU

4.1000 g., Nickel-Brass, 23.5 mm. **Obv:** National arms **Rev:** Shell and value **Edge:** Plain

Date	Mintage	F	VF	XF	Unc	BU
2002	—	—	—	—	1.00	1.75
2009	—	—	—	—	1.00	1.75

KM# 45 10 VATU
Copper-Nickel silver plated **Obv:** Arms **Rev:** Multicolor butterfly (Papilio Toboroi)

Date	Mintage	F	VF	XF	Unc	BU
2006	2,500	—	—	—	—	32.00

KM# 50 10 VATU
Copper-Nickel silver plated **Obv:** Arms **Rev:** Multicolor butterfly (Delias Sagessa)

Date	Mintage	F	VF	XF	Unc	BU
2006	2,500	—	—	—	—	32.00

KM# 46 10 VATU
Copper-Nickel silver plated **Obv:** Arms **Rev:** Multicolor butterfly (Taenaris Catops)

Date	Mintage	F	VF	XF	Unc	BU
2006	2,500	—	—	—	—	32.00

KM# 47 10 VATU
Copper-Nickel silver plated **Obv:** Arms **Rev:** Multicolor Butterfly (Ornithoptera Priamus Urvillianus)

Date	Mintage	F	VF	XF	Unc	BU
2006	2,500	—	—	—	—	32.00

KM# 48 10 VATU
Copper-Nickel silver plated **Obv:** Arms **Rev:** Multicolor butterfly (Ornithoptera Paradisea)

Date	Mintage	F	VF	XF	Unc	BU
2006	2,500	—	—	—	—	32.00

KM# 49 10 VATU
Copper-Nickel silver plated **Obv:** Arms **Rev:** Multicolor butterfly (Cethosia Cydippe)

Date	Mintage	F	VF	XF	Unc	BU
2006	2,500	—	—	—	—	32.00

KM# 6 10 VATU
6.1000 g., Copper-Nickel, 23.95 mm. **Obv:** National arms **Rev:** Crab and value, palm trees **Edge:** Plain

Date	Mintage	F	VF	XF	Unc	BU
2009	—	—	—	0.35	1.25	2.80

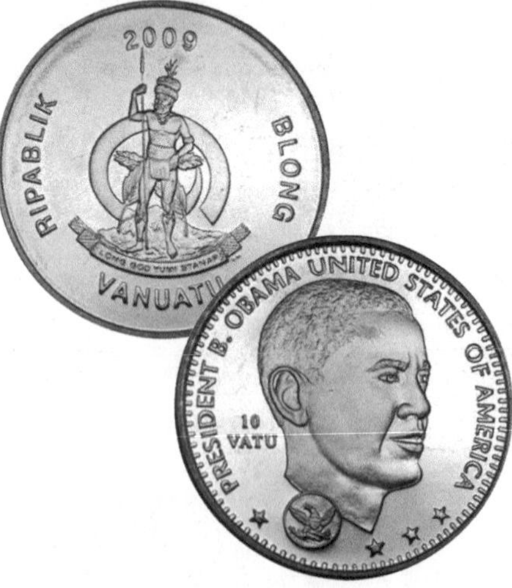

KM# 51 10 VATU
Copper-Nickel, 38.61 mm. **Subject:** Barack Obama **Obv:** National arms **Rev:** Profile right

Date	Mintage	F	VF	XF	Unc	BU
2009	—	—	—	—	—	14.00

KM# 59 10 VATU
26.0300 g., Silver Plated Copper-Nickel, 38.61 mm. **Subject:** Beach Volleyball **Obv:** National arms **Rev:** Two players going for ball at net

Date	Mintage	F	VF	XF	Unc	BU
2009 Proof	30,000	Value: 25.00				

KM# 65 10 VATU
27.0000 g., Silver Plated Copper, 38.61 mm. **Obv:** National arms **Rev:** Color image of John Paul II and Yaser Arafat

Date	Mintage	F	VF	XF	Unc	BU
2011 Proof	1,500	Value: 25.00				

KM# 66 10 VATU
27.0000 g., Silver Plated Copper, 38.61 mm. **Obv:** National arms **Rev:** Color image of John Paul II and Rabbi of Rome

Date	Mintage	F	VF	XF	Unc	BU
2011 Proof	1,500	Value: 25.00				

KM# 56 20 VATU
0.5000 g., 0.9990 Gold 0.0161 oz. AGW, 11 mm. **Obv:** National arms **Rev:** SMS Europa under full sail

Date	Mintage	F	VF	XF	Unc	BU
2008 Proof	10,000	Value: 75.00				

KM# 57 20 VATU
0.5000 g., 0.9990 Gold 0.0161 oz. AGW, 11 mm. **Obv:** National arms **Rev:** Sokrates head

Date	Mintage	F	VF	XF	Unc	BU
2009 Proof	10,000	Value: 75.00				

KM# 60 20 VATU
0.5000 g., 0.9990 Gold 0.0161 oz. AGW, 11 mm. **Obv:** National arms **Rev:** Pantheon

Date	Mintage	F	VF	XF	Unc	BU
2009 Proof	10,000	Value: 75.00				

KM# 67 20 VATU
0.5000 g., 0.9990 Gold 0.0161 oz. AGW, 11 mm. **Obv:** National arms **Rev:** Turtle drawn in sand

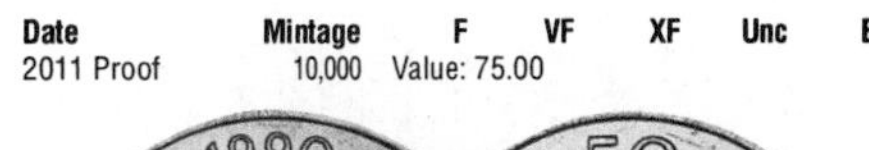

Date	Mintage	F	VF	XF	Unc	BU
2011 Proof	10,000	Value: 75.00				

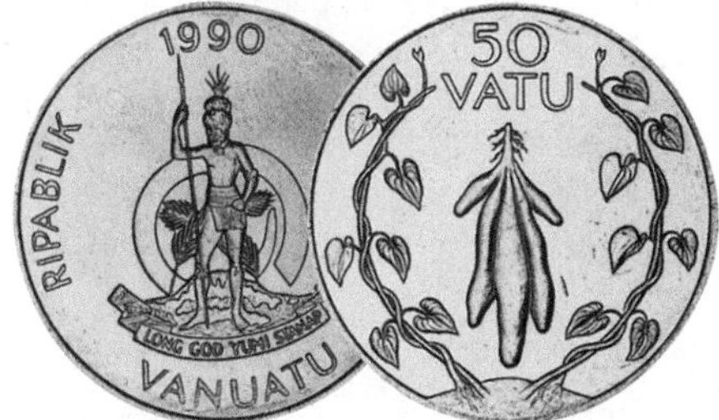

KM# 8 50 VATU
15.0000 g., Copper-Nickel, 32.9 mm. **Series:** F.A.O. **Obv:** National arms **Rev:** Tubers encircled by leafy vines, value above

Date	Mintage	F	VF	XF	Unc	BU
2002	—	—	—	—	2.00	3.00
2009	—	—	—	—	2.00	3.00

KM# 53 50 VATU
Silver, 38.6 mm. **Subject:** Olympics, 2004 **Obv:** National emblem **Rev:** Athlethe with torch, large torch, fragment of ancient vase

Date	Mintage	F	VF	XF	Unc	BU
2003 Proof	—	Value: 50.00				

KM# 38 50 VATU
28.3200 g., 0.9250 Silver 0.8422 oz. ASW, 38.6 mm. **Obv:** National arms **Obv. Legend:** RIPABLIK / VANUATU **Rev:** Early sailing ship center - left, stylized compass at right **Rev. Legend:** HISTORY OF SEAFARING / PEDRO FERNANDEZ DE QUIRÓS **Edge:** Reeded

Date	Mintage	F	VF	XF	Unc	BU
2005 Proof	—	Value: 45.00				

KM# 41 50 VATU
25.0000 g., 0.9000 Silver 0.7234 oz. ASW **Series:** Protection of Marine Life **Obv:** National arms **Rev:** Tiger Shark - multicolor

Date	Mintage	F	VF	XF	Unc	BU
2005 Proof	—	Value: 75.00				

KM# 55 50 VATU
1.2400 g., 0.9990 Gold 0.0398 oz. AGW, 13.92 mm. **Obv:** National arms **Rev:** Captain Kidd

Date	Mintage	F	VF	XF	Unc	BU
2005 Proof	15,000	Value: 150				

KM# 54 50 VATU
Silver, 38.6 mm. **Obv:** National emblem **Rev:** Two soccer players with large globe in background

Date	Mintage	F	VF	XF	Unc	BU
2006 Proof	—	Value: 60.00				

KM# 42 50 VATU
25.0000 g., 0.9000 Silver 0.7234 oz. ASW **Series:** Protection of Marine Life **Obv:** National arms **Rev:** Sea Turtle - multicolor

Date	Mintage	F	VF	XF	Unc	BU
2006 Proof	—	Value: 75.00				

KM# 43 50 VATU
25.0000 g., 0.9000 Silver 0.7234 oz. ASW **Series:** Protection of Marine Life **Obv:** National arms **Rev:** Sea Horse - multicolor

Date	Mintage	F	VF	XF	Unc	BU
2006 Proof	—	Value: 75.00				

KM# 52 50 VATU
Silver **Subject:** 2006 World Cup - Germany **Obv:** National arms **Rev:** 2 soccer players and globe

Date	Mintage	F	VF	XF	Unc	BU
2006 Proof	—	Value: 35.00				

KM# 58 50 VATU
28.2800 g., 0.9250 Silver 0.8410 oz. ASW, 38.61 mm. **Obv:** National Arms **Rev:** SMS Europa under full sail

Date	Mintage	F	VF	XF	Unc	BU
2008 Proof	5,000	Value: 75.00				

KM# 61 50 VATU
28.2800 g., 0.9250 Silver 0.8410 oz. ASW, 38.61 mm. **Subject:** Beach Volleyball **Obv:** National arms **Rev:** Two players at net going for ball

Date	Mintage	F	VF	XF	Unc	BU
2009 Proof	10,000	Value: 75.00				

KM# 62 50 VATU
1.0000 g., 0.9990 Gold 0.0321 oz. AGW, 13.92 mm. **Obv:** National arms **Rev:** Potala Palace **Note:** The denomination does not appear on either side.

Date	Mintage	F	VF	XF	Unc	BU
2009 Proof	10,000	Value: 125				

KM# 63 50 VATU
28.2800 g., 0.9250 Silver 0.8410 oz. ASW, 38.61 mm. **Obv:** National arms **Rev:** Shinkansen high speed train

Date	Mintage	F	VF	XF	Unc	BU
2009 Proof	5,000	Value: 75.00				

KM# 64 50 VATU
28.2800 g., 0.9250 Silver 0.8410 oz. ASW **Obv:** National arms **Rev:** The Gran, trans-Australia train **Shape:** 38.61

Date	Mintage	F	VF	XF	Unc	BU
2010 Proof	5,000	Value: 75.00				

KM# 68 50 VATU
31.1000 g., 0.9990 Silver 0.9988 oz. ASW, 40.6 mm. **Subject:** Royal Ascot Races **Obv:** National arms **Rev:** Horse race, grandstands, Elizabeth II and Prince Philip; partially colored

Date	Mintage	F	VF	XF	Unc	BU
2011 Proof	10,000	Value: 100				

KM# 69 50 VATU
20.0000 g., 0.9250 Silver 0.5948 oz. ASW, 38.61 mm. **Obv:** National arms **Rev:** TEE VT11.5 train, map of Europe above

Date	Mintage	F	VF	XF	Unc	BU
2011 Proof	5,000	Value: 75.00				

KM# 9 100 VATU
9.5500 g., Nickel-Brass, 23.9 mm. **Obv:** National arms **Rev:** Sprouting bulbs

Date	Mintage	F	VF	XF	Unc	BU
2002	—	—	—	—	3.00	4.00
2008	—	—	—	—	3.00	4.00

The State of the Vatican City, a papal state on the right bank of the Tiber River within the boundaries of Rome, has an area of 0.17 sq. mi. (0.44 sq. km.) and a population of *775. Capital: Vatican City.

Today the Pope exercises supreme legislative, executive and judicial power within the Vatican City, and the State of the Vatican City is recognized by many nations as an independent sovereign state under the temporal jurisdiction of the Pope, even to the extent of ambassadorial exchange. The Pope is of course, the head of the Roman Catholic Church.

PONTIFFS

John Paul II, 1978-2005
  Sede Vacante, April 2 - 19, 2005
Benedict XVI, 2005-2013
Frances, 2013 -

MINT MARK

R – Rome

MONETARY SYSTEM

100 Centesimi = 1 Lira (thru 2002)
100 Euro Cent = 1 Euro

DATING

Most Vatican coins indicate the regnal year of the pope preceded by the word *Anno* (or an abbreviation), even if the *anno domini* date is omitted.

CITY STATE

DECIMAL COINAGE

100 Centesimi = 1 Lira

KM# 331 10 LIRE

1.6000 g., Aluminum, 23.2 mm. **Ruler:** John Paul II **Obv:** Bust left **Rev:** Papal arms **Edge:** Plain **Designer:** Laura Cretara

Date	Mintage	F	VF	XF	Unc	BU
2001/XXIII	—	—	0.50	1.00	3.00	—

KM# 331a 10 LIRE

Gold, 23.2 mm. **Ruler:** John Paul II **Obv:** Benedict XV bust left **Rev:** Papal arms **Designer:** Laura Cretara **Note:** Struck in 2007.

Date	Mintage	F	VF	XF	Unc	BU
2001R Proof	499	Value: 2,000				

KM# 332 20 LIRE

3.5700 g., Brass, 21.2 mm. **Ruler:** John Paul II **Obv:** Bust left **Rev:** Papal arms **Edge:** Plain **Designer:** Laura Cretara

Date	Mintage	F	VF	XF	Unc	BU
2001/XXIII	—	—	0.50	1.00	3.00	—

KM# 332a 20 LIRE

Gold, 21.2 mm. **Ruler:** John Paul II **Obv:** Pius XI bust left **Rev:** Papal arms **Designer:** Laura Cretara **Note:** Struck in 2007.

Date	Mintage	F	VF	XF	Unc	BU
2001R Proof	499	Value: 2,000				

KM# 333 50 LIRE

4.5000 g., Copper-Nickel, 19.2 mm. **Ruler:** John Paul II **Obv:** Pius XII bust left **Rev:** Papal arms **Edge:** Plain **Designer:** Laura Cretara

Date	Mintage	F	VF	XF	Unc	BU
2001/XXIII	—	—	0.50	1.00	3.00	—

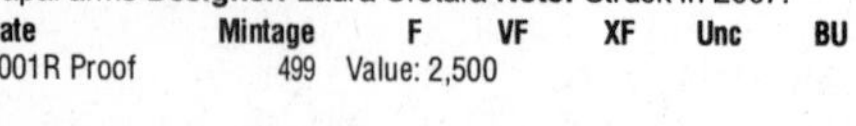

KM# 333a 50 LIRE

Gold, 19.2 mm. **Ruler:** John Paul II **Obv:** Pius XII bust left **Rev:** Papal arms **Designer:** Laura Cretara **Note:** Struck in 2007.

Date	Mintage	F	VF	XF	Unc	BU
2001R Proof	499	Value: 2,500				

KM# 334 100 LIRE

4.5000 g., Copper-Nickel, 22 mm. **Ruler:** John Paul II **Obv:** Bust left **Rev:** Papal arms within circle **Edge:** Reeded and plain sections **Designer:** Laura Cretara

Date	Mintage	F	VF	XF	Unc	BU
2001/XXIII	—	—	0.50	1.00	3.00	—

KM# 334a 100 LIRE

Gold, 22 mm. **Ruler:** John Paul II **Obv:** John XXIII bust left **Rev:** Papal arms **Designer:** Laura Cretara **Note:** Struck in 2007.

Date	Mintage	F	VF	XF	Unc	BU
2001R Proof	499	Value: 2,500				

KM# 335 200 LIRE

5.0000 g., Brass, 22 mm. **Ruler:** John Paul II **Obv:** Bust right **Rev:** Papal arms within circle **Edge:** Reeded **Designer:** Laura Cretara

Date	Mintage	F	VF	XF	Unc	BU
2001/XXIII	—	—	0.50	1.00	3.00	—

KM# 335a 200 LIRE

Gold, 22 mm. **Ruler:** John Paul II **Obv:** Paul VI bust right **Rev:** Papal arms **Designer:** Laura Cretara **Note:** Struck in 2007.

Date	Mintage	F	VF	XF	Unc	BU
2001R Proof	499	Value: 2,500				

KM# 336 500 LIRE

6.7700 g., Bi-Metallic Aluminum-Bronze center in Stainless steel ring, 25.7 mm. **Ruler:** John Paul II **Obv:** John Paul I head left **Rev:** Papal arms within circle **Edge:** Segmented reeding **Designer:** Laura Cretara

Date	Mintage	F	VF	XF	Unc	BU
2001/XXIII	—	—	—	3.50	7.00	—

KM# 336a 500 LIRE

Gold, 25.7 mm. **Ruler:** John Paul II **Obv:** John Paul I bust left **Rev:** Papal arms **Designer:** Laura Cretella

Date	Mintage	F	VF	XF	Unc	BU
2001R Proof	499	Value: 2,000				

KM# 337 1000 LIRE

8.8500 g., Bi-Metallic Copper-Nickel center in Brass ring, 26.9 mm. **Ruler:** John Paul II **Obv:** John Paul II bust left **Rev:** Papal arms **Edge:** Segmented reeding **Designer:** Laura Cretara

Date	Mintage	F	VF	XF	Unc	BU
2001/XXIII	—	—	—	5.50	9.00	—

KM# 337a 1000 LIRE

Gold, 26.9 mm. **Ruler:** John Paul II **Obv:** John Paul II bust left **Rev:** Papal arms **Designer:** Laura Cretella

Date	Mintage	F	VF	XF	Unc	BU
2001R Proof	499	Value: 2,000				

KM# 338 1000 LIRE

14.6000 g., 0.8350 Silver 0.3919 oz. ASW, 31.4 mm. **Ruler:** John Paul II **Subject:** Peace **Obv:** Stylized dove in front of globe **Rev:** Crowned shield **Edge Lettering:** +++ TOTVSTVVS +++ MMI

Date	Mintage	F	VF	XF	Unc	BU
2001/XXIII	—	—	—	20.00	40.00	—

KM# 338a 1000 LIRE

Gold, 31.4 mm. **Ruler:** John Paul II **Obv:** Stylized dove in front of globe **Rev:** Crowned arms

Date	Mintage	F	VF	XF	Unc	BU
2001R Proof	499	Value: 2,000				

KM# 339 2000 LIRE

16.0000 g., 0.8350 Silver 0.4295 oz. ASW, 31.4 mm. **Ruler:** John Paul II **Subject:** Dialog for Peace **Obv:** Bust right holding crozier **Rev:** Dove above crowd **Edge:** Reeded **Designer:** Floriano Bodini

Date	Mintage	F	VF	XF	Unc	BU
2001/XXIII	16,000	—	—	25.00	40.00	—
2001/XXIII Proof	8,000	Value: 45.00				

KM# 340 5000 LIRE

18.0000 g., 0.8350 Silver 0.4832 oz. ASW, 32 mm. **Ruler:** John Paul II **Subject:** Easter **Obv:** Kneeling Pope praying **Rev:** Standing figure flanked by clouds below dove **Edge:** Reeded and plain sections **Designer:** Floriano Bodini

Date	Mintage	F	VF	XF	Unc	BU
2001	—	—	—	30.00	45.00	—
2001/XXIII Proof	16,000	Value: 35.00				

KM# 390 50000 LIRE

7.5000 g., 0.9170 Gold 0.2211 oz. AGW, 23 mm. **Ruler:** John Paul II **Subject:** Religious symbols **Obv:** Bust right **Rev:** Cross

Date	Mintage	F	VF	XF	Unc	BU
2001//XXIIIR Proof	6,000	Value: 1,500				

KM# 391 100000 LIRE

15.0000 g., 0.9170 Gold 0.4422 oz. AGW, 28 mm. **Ruler:** John Paul II **Subject:** Religious symbols **Obv:** Bust right **Rev:** Chi rho with Alpha and Omega letters

Date	Mintage	F	VF	XF	Unc	BU
2001//XXIIIR Proof	6,000	Value: 2,000				

EURO COINAGE

KM# 341 EURO CENT

2.3000 g., Copper Plated Steel, 16.25 mm. **Ruler:** John Paul II **Obv:** Bust 1/4 left **Rev:** Value and globe **Edge:** Plain

Date	Mintage	F	VF	XF	Unc	BU
2002R	80,000	—	—	—	115	—
2002R Proof	9,000	Value: 175				
2003R In sets only	65,000	—	—	—	55.00	—
2003R Proof	13,000	Value: 145				
2004R In sets only	65,000	—	—	—	25.00	—
2004R Proof	13,000	Value: 145				
2005R In sets only	85,000	—	—	—	25.00	—
2005R Proof	16,000	Value: 140				

KM# 365 EURO CENT

2.3000 g., Copper Plated Steel, 16.25 mm. **Ruler:** Sede Vacante **Obv:** Arms of Cardinal Eduardo Martinez Somalo **Rev:** Value and globe

Date	Mintage	F	VF	XF	Unc	BU
MMV (2005)R In sets only	60,000	—	—	—	—	45.00

KM# 375 EURO CENT
2.3000 g., Copper Plated Steel, 16.25 mm. **Ruler:** Benedict XVI **Obv:** Pope's bust facing 3/4 right **Obv. Legend:** CITTA' DEL VATICANO **Rev:** Value and globe **Edge:** Plain

Date	Mintage	F	VF	XF	Unc	BU
2006R In sets only	85,000	—	—	—	—	12.00
2006R Proof	16,000	Value: 18.00				
2007R In sets only	85,000	—	—	—	—	12.00
2007R Proof	16,000	Value: 18.00				
MMVIII (2008)R In sets only	85,000	—	—	—	—	12.00
MMVIII (2008)R Proof	16,000	Value: 18.00				
2009R In sets only	85,000	—	—	—	—	12.00
2009R Proof	16,000	Value: 18.00				
2010R In sets only	94,000	—	—	—	—	12.00
2010R Proof	15,000	Value: 18.00				
2011R	94,000	—	—	—	—	12.00
2011R Proof	15,000	Value: 18.00				
2012R	84,000	—	—	—	—	12.00
2012R Proof	15,000	Value: 18.00				
2013R	85,000	—	—	—	—	12.00
2013R Proof	15,000	Value: 18.00				

KM# 342 2 EURO CENT
3.0600 g., Copper Plated Steel, 18.75 mm. **Ruler:** John Paul II **Obv:** Bust 1/4 left **Rev:** Value and globe **Edge:** Grooved

Date	Mintage	F	VF	XF	Unc	BU
2002R	80,000	—	—	—	115	—
2002R Proof	9,000	Value: 175				
2003R In sets only	65,000	—	—	—	55.00	—
2003R Proof	13,000	Value: 145				
2004R In sets only	65,000	—	—	—	25.00	—
2004R Proof	13,000	Value: 145				
2005R In sets only	85,000	—	—	—	25.00	—
2005R Proof	16,000	Value: 140				

KM# 366 2 EURO CENT
3.0600 g., Copper Plated Steel, 18.75 mm. **Ruler:** Sede Vacante **Obv:** Arms of Cardinal Eduardo Martinez Somalo **Rev:** Value and globe **Edge:** Grooved

Date	Mintage	F	VF	XF	Unc	BU
MMV (2005)R In sets only	60,000	—	—	—	—	42.00

KM# 376 2 EURO CENT
3.0600 g., Copper Plated Steel, 18.75 mm. **Ruler:** Benedict XVI **Obv:** Pope's bust facing 3/4 right **Obv. Legend:** CITTA' DEL VATICANO **Rev:** Value and globe **Edge:** Grooved

Date	Mintage	F	VF	XF	Unc	BU
2006R In sets only	85,000	—	—	—	—	15.00
2006R Proof	16,000	Value: 20.00				
2007R In sets only	85,000	—	—	—	—	15.00
2007R Proof	16,000	Value: 20.00				
MDVIII (2008)R In sets only	85,000	—	—	—	—	15.00
MDVIII (2008)R Proof	16,000	Value: 20.00				
2009R In sets only	85,000	—	—	—	—	15.00
2009R Proof	16,000	Value: 20.00				
2010R In sets only	94,000	—	—	—	—	15.00
2010R Proof	15,000	Value: 20.00				
2011R	94,000	—	—	—	—	15.00
2011R Proof	15,000	Value: 20.00				
2012R	84,000	—	—	—	—	15.00
2012R Proof	15,000	Value: 20.00				
2013R	85,000	—	—	—	—	15.00
2013R Proof	15,000	Value: 20.00				

KM# 343 5 EURO CENT
3.9200 g., Copper Plated Steel, 21.25 mm. **Ruler:** John Paul II **Obv:** Bust 1/4 left **Rev:** Value and globe **Edge:** Plain

Date	Mintage	F	VF	XF	Unc	BU
2002R	80,000	—	—	—	115	—
2002R Proof	9,000	Value: 175				
2003R In sets only	65,000	—	—	—	55.00	—
2003R Proof	13,000	Value: 145				
2004R In sets only	65,000	—	—	—	28.00	—
2004R Proof	13,000	Value: 145				
2005R In sets only	85,000	—	—	—	28.00	—
2005R Proof	16,000	Value: 140				

KM# 367 5 EURO CENT
3.9200 g., Copper Plated Steel, 21.25 mm. **Ruler:** Sede Vacante **Obv:** Arms of Cardinal Eduardo Martinez Somalo **Rev:** Value and globe

Date	Mintage	F	VF	XF	Unc	BU
MMV (2005)R In sets only	60,000	—	—	—	—	45.00

KM# 377 5 EURO CENT
3.9200 g., Copper Plated Steel, 21.25 mm. **Ruler:** Benedict XVI **Obv:** Pope's bust facing 3/4 right **Obv. Legend:** CITTA' DEL VATICANO **Rev:** Value and globe **Edge:** Plain

Date	Mintage	F	VF	XF	Unc	BU
2006R In sets only	85,000	—	—	—	—	16.50
2006R Proof	16,000	Value: 22.50				
2007R In sets only	85,000	—	—	—	—	16.50
2007R Proof	16,000	Value: 22.50				
MDVIII (2008)R In sets only	85,000	—	—	—	—	16.50
MDVIII (2008)R Proof	16,000	Value: 22.50				
2009R In sets only	85,000	—	—	—	—	16.50
2009R Proof	16,000	Value: 22.50				
2010R In sets only	94,000	—	—	—	—	16.50
2010R Proof	15,000	Value: 22.50				
2011R	94,000	—	—	—	—	16.50
2011R Proof	15,000	Value: 22.50				
2012R	84,000	—	—	—	—	16.50
2012R Proof	15,000	Value: 22.50				
2013R	85,000	—	—	—	—	16.50
2013R Proof	15,000	Value: 22.50				

KM# 344 10 EURO CENT
4.1000 g., Brass, 19.75 mm. **Ruler:** John Paul II **Obv:** Bust 1/4 left **Edge:** Reeded

Date	Mintage	F	VF	XF	Unc	BU
2002R	80,000	—	—	—	115	—
2002R Proof	9,000	Value: 175				
2003R In sets only	65,000	—	—	—	55.00	—
2003R Proof	13,000	Value: 145				
2004R In sets only	65,000	—	—	—	35.00	—
2004R Proof	13,000	Value: 145				
2005R In sets only	85,000	—	—	—	35.00	—
2005R Proof	16,000	Value: 140				

KM# 368 10 EURO CENT
4.1000 g., Brass, 19.75 mm. **Ruler:** Sede Vacante **Obv:** Arms of Cardinal Eduardo Martinez Somalo **Rev:** Map and value **Edge:** Reeded

Date	Mintage	F	VF	XF	Unc	BU
MMV (2005)R In sets only	60,000	—	—	—	—	48.00

KM# 378 10 EURO CENT
4.1000 g., Brass, 19.75 mm. **Ruler:** Benedict XVI **Obv:** Pope's bust facing 3/4 right **Obv. Legend:** CITTA' DEL VATICANO **Rev:** Map and value **Edge:** Reeded

Date	Mintage	F	VF	XF	Unc	BU
2006R In sets only	85,000	—	—	—	—	17.50
2006R Proof	16,000	Value: 25.00				
2007R In sets only	85,000	—	—	—	—	17.50
2007R Proof	16,000	Value: 25.00				

KM# 385 10 EURO CENT
4.1000 g., Brass, 19.75 mm. **Ruler:** Benedict XVI **Rev:** Relief map of Western Europe, stars, lines and value **Edge:** Reeded

Date	Mintage	F	VF	XF	Unc	BU
MMVIII (2008)R In sets only	85,000	—	—	—	—	17.50
MMVIII (2008)R Proof	16,000	Value: 25.00				
2009R In sets only	85,000	—	—	—	—	17.50
2009R Proof	16,000	Value: 25.00				
2010R In sets only	94,000	—	—	—	—	17.50
2010R Proof	15,000	Value: 25.00				
2011R	94,000	—	—	—	—	17.50
2011R Proof	15,000	Value: 25.00				
2012R	84,000	—	—	—	—	17.50
2012R Proof	15,000	Value: 25.00				
2013R	85,000	—	—	—	—	17.50
2013R Proof	15,000	Value: 25.00				

KM# 345 20 EURO CENT
5.7400 g., Brass, 22.25 mm. **Ruler:** John Paul II **Obv:** Bust 1/4 left **Rev:** Map and value **Edge:** Notched

Date	Mintage	F	VF	XF	Unc	BU
2002R	80,000	—	—	—	115	—
2002R Proof	9,000	Value: 175				
2003R In sets only	65,000	—	—	—	55.00	—
2003R Proof	13,000	Value: 145				
2004R In sets only	65,000	—	—	—	38.00	—
2004R Proof	13,000	Value: 145				
2005R In sets only	85,000	—	—	—	38.00	—
2005R Proof	16,000	Value: 140				

KM# 369 20 EURO CENT
5.7400 g., Brass, 22.25 mm. **Ruler:** Sede Vacante **Obv:** Arms of Cardinal Eduardo Martinez Somalo **Rev:** Map and value **Edge:** Notched

Date	Mintage	F	VF	XF	Unc	BU
MMV (2005)R In sets only	60,000	—	—	—	—	50.00

KM# 379 20 EURO CENT
5.7400 g., Brass, 22.25 mm. **Ruler:** Benedict XVI **Obv:** Pope's bust facing 3/4 right **Obv. Legend:** CITTA' DEL VATICANO **Rev:** Map and value **Edge:** Notched

Date	Mintage	F	VF	XF	Unc	BU
2006R In sets only	85,000	—	—	—	—	18.00
2006R Proof	16,000	Value: 28.00				
2007R In sets only	85,000	—	—	—	—	18.00
2007R Proof	16,000	Value: 28.00				

KM# 386 20 EURO CENT
5.7400 g., Brass, 22.25 mm. **Ruler:** Benedict XVI **Rev:** Relief map of Western Europe, stars, lines and value **Edge:** Notched

Date	Mintage	F	VF	XF	Unc	BU
MMVIII (2008)R In sets only	85,000	—	—	—	—	18.00
MMVIII (2008)R Proof	16,000	Value: 28.00				
2009R In sets only	85,000	—	—	—	—	18.00
2009R Proof	16,000	Value: 28.00				
2010R In sets only	94,000	—	—	—	—	18.00
2010R Proof	15,000	Value: 28.00				
2011R	94,000	—	—	—	—	18.00
2011R Proof	15,000	Value: 28.00				
2012R	84,000	—	—	—	—	18.00
2012R Proof	15,000	Value: 28.00				
2013R	85,000	—	—	—	—	18.00
2013R Proof	15,000	Value: 28.00				

KM# 346 50 EURO CENT
7.8000 g., Brass, 24.25 mm. **Ruler:** John Paul II **Obv:** Bust 1/4 left **Rev:** Map and value **Edge:** Reeded

Date	Mintage	F	VF	XF	Unc	BU
2002R	80,000	—	—	—	115	—
2002R Proof	9,000	Value: 175				
2003R In sets only	65,000	—	—	—	55.00	—
2003R Proof	13,000	Value: 145				
2004R In sets only	65,000	—	—	—	42.00	—
2004R Proof	13,000	Value: 145				
2005R In sets only	85,000	—	—	—	42.00	—
2005R Proof	16,000	Value: 140				

KM# 370 50 EURO CENT
7.8000 g., Brass, 24.25 mm. **Ruler:** Sede Vacante **Obv:** Arms of Cardinal Eduardo Martinez Somalo **Rev:** Map and value **Edge:** Reeded

Date	Mintage	F	VF	XF	Unc	BU
MMV (2005)R In sets only	60,000	—	—	—	—	55.00

KM# 380 50 EURO CENT
7.8000 g., Brass, 24.25 mm. **Ruler:** Benedict XVI **Obv:** Pope's bust facing 3/4 right **Obv. Legend:** CITTA' DEL VATICANO **Rev:** Map and value **Edge:** Reeded

Date	Mintage	F	VF	XF	Unc	BU
2006R In sets only	85,000	—	—	—	—	22.50
2006R Proof	16,000	Value: 35.00				
2007R In sets only	85,000	—	—	—	—	22.50
2007R Proof	16,000	Value: 35.00				

KM# 387 50 EURO CENT

7.8000 g., Brass, 24.25 mm. **Ruler:** Benedict XVI **Rev:** Relief map of Western Europe, stars, lines and value **Edge:** Reeded

Date	Mintage	F	VF	XF	Unc	BU
MMVIII (2008)R In sets only	85,000	—	—	—	—	32.50
MMVIII (2008)R Proof	16,000	Value: 40.00				
2009R In sets only	85,000	—	—	—	—	32.50
2009R Proof	16,000	Value: 40.00				
2010R In sets only	94,000	—	—	—	—	32.50
2010R Proof	15,000	Value: 40.00				
2011R	94,000	—	—	—	—	32.50
2011R Proof	15,000	Value: 40.00				
2012R	94,000	—	—	—	—	32.50
2012R Proof	15,000	Value: 40.00				
2013R	95,000	—	—	—	—	32.50
2013R Proof	15,000	Value: 40.00				

KM# 347 EURO

7.5000 g., Bi-Metallic Copper-Nickel center in Nickel-Brass ring, 23.25 mm. **Ruler:** John Paul II **Obv:** Bust 1/4 left **Rev:** Value and map **Edge:** Segmented reeding

Date	Mintage	F	VF	XF	Unc	BU
2002R	80,000	—	—	—	100	—
2002R Proof	9,000	Value: 185				
2003R In sets only	65,000	—	—	—	75.00	—
2003R Proof	13,000	Value: 145				
2004R In sets only	65,000	—	—	—	60.00	—
2004R Proof	13,000	Value: 145				
2005R In sets only	85,000	—	—	—	60.00	—
2005R Proof	16,000	Value: 140				

KM# 371 EURO

7.5000 g., Bi-Metallic Copper-Nickel center in Nickel-Brass ring, 23.25 mm. **Ruler:** Sede Vacante **Obv:** Arms of Cardinal Eduardo Martinez Somalo **Rev:** Value and map **Edge:** Segmented reeding

Date	Mintage	F	VF	XF	Unc	BU
MMV (2005)R In sets only	60,000	—	—	—	—	70.00

KM# 381 EURO

7.5000 g., Bi-Metallic Copper-Nickel center in Nickel-Brass ring., 23.25 mm. **Ruler:** Benedict XVI **Obv:** Pope's bust facing 3/4 right **Obv. Legend:** CITTA' - DEL VATICANO **Rev:** Value and map **Edge:** Segmented reeding

Date	Mintage	F	VF	XF	Unc	BU
2006R In sets only	85,000	—	—	—	—	25.00
2006R Proof	16,000	Value: 40.00				
2007R In sets only	85,000	—	—	—	—	25.00
2007R Proof	16,000	Value: 40.00				

KM# 388 EURO

7.5000 g., Bi-Metallic Copper-Nickel center in Nickel-Brass ring, 23.25 mm. **Ruler:** Benedict XVI **Rev:** Relief map of Western Europe, stars, lines and value **Edge:** Segmented reeding

Date	Mintage	F	VF	XF	Unc	BU
MMVIII (2008)R In sets only	85,000	—	—	—	—	25.00
MMVIII (2008)R Proof	16,000	Value: 40.00				
2009R In sets only	85,000	—	—	—	—	25.00
2009R Proof	16,000	Value: 40.00				
2010R In sets only	94,000	—	—	—	—	25.00
2010R Proof	15,000	Value: 40.00				
2011R	94,000	—	—	—	—	25.00
2011R Proof	15,000	Value: 40.00				
2012R	84,000	—	—	—	—	25.00
2012R Proof	15,000	Value: 40.00				
2013R	85,000	—	—	—	—	25.00
2013R Proof	15,000	Value: 40.00				

KM# 348 2 EURO

8.5000 g., Bi-Metallic Nickel-Brass center in Copper-Nickel ring, 25.75 mm. **Ruler:** John Paul II **Obv:** Bust 1/4 left **Rev:** Value and map **Edge:** Reeded with 2's and stars

Date	Mintage	F	VF	XF	Unc	BU
2002R	80,000	—	—	—	165	—
2002R Proof	9,000	Value: 215				
2003R In sets only	65,000	—	—	—	100	—
2003R Proof	13,000	Value: 185				
2004R In sets only	65,000	—	—	—	80.00	—
2004R Proof	13,000	Value: 185				
2005R In sets only	85,000	—	—	—	80.00	—
2005R Proof	16,000	Value: 180				

KM# 358 2 EURO

8.5000 g., Bi-Metallic Nickel-Brass center in Copper-Nickel ring, 25.75 mm. **Ruler:** John Paul II **Subject:** 75th Anniversary of the Founding of the Vatican City State **Obv:** St. Peter's Square within city walls, dates 1929-2004 **Rev:** Value and map **Edge:** Reeded with 2's and stars **Designer:** Luciana de Simoni

Date	Mintage	F	VF	XF	Unc	BU
2004R	85,000	—	—	—	25.00	—

KM# 372 2 EURO

8.5000 g., Bi-Metallic Nickel-Brass center in Copper-Nickel ring, 25.75 mm. **Ruler:** Sede Vacante **Obv:** Arms of Cardinal Eduardo Martinez Somalo **Rev:** Map and value **Edge:** Reeded with 2's and stars

Date	Mintage	F	VF	XF	Unc	BU
MMV (2005)R In sets only	60,000	—	—	—	—	75.00

KM# 374 2 EURO

8.5000 g., Bi-Metallic Nickel-Brass center in Copper-Nickel ring, 25.75 mm. **Ruler:** Benedict XVI **Subject:** World Youth Day **Obv:** Cologne Cathedral **Rev:** Value and Euro map **Edge:** Reeded with 2's and stars

Date	Mintage	F	VF	XF	Unc	BU
2005R	—	—	—	—	90.00	—

KM# 382 2 EURO

8.5000 g., Bi-Metallic Nickel-Brass center in Copper-Nickel ring, 25.75 mm. **Ruler:** Benedict XVI **Obv:** Pope's bust facing 3/4 right **Obv. Legend:** CITTA' - DEL VATICANO **Rev:** Value and map **Edge:** Reeded with 2's and stars

Date	Mintage	F	VF	XF	Unc	BU
2006R In sets only	85,000	—	—	—	—	28.00
2006R Proof	16,000	Value: 50.00				
2007R In sets only	85,000	—	—	—	—	28.00
2007R Proof	16,000	Value: 50.00				

KM# 394 2 EURO

8.5000 g., Bi-Metallic Nickel-Brass center in Copper-Nickel ring, 25.75 mm. **Ruler:** Benedict XVI **Subject:** Swiss guards, 500th Anniversary **Obv:** Swiss guard taking oath on flag **Rev:** Map and value **Edge:** Reeded with 2's and stars

Date	Mintage	F	VF	XF	Unc	BU
ND (2006)R	100,000	—	—	—	80.00	—

KM# 399 2 EURO

8.5000 g., Bi-Metallic Nickel-Brass center in Copper-Nickel ring, 25.75 mm. **Ruler:** Benedict XVI **Subject:** Pope Benedict's 80th Birthday **Obv:** Bust left **Rev:** Map and value **Edge:** Reeded with 2's and stars

Date	Mintage	F	VF	XF	Unc	BU
2007R	100,000	—	—	—	50.00	—

KM# 389 2 EURO

8.5000 g., Bi-Metallic Nickel-Brass center in Copper-Nickel ring, 25.75 mm. **Ruler:** Benedict XVI **Rev:** Relief map of Western Europe, stars, lines and value **Edge:** Reeded with 2's and stars

Date	Mintage	F	VF	XF	Unc	BU
MMVIII (2008)R In sets only	85,000	—	—	—	—	28.00
MMVIII (2008)R Proof	16,000	Value: 50.00				
2009R In sets only	85,000	—	—	—	—	28.00
2009R Proof	16,000	Value: 50.00				
2010R In sets only	94,000	—	—	—	—	28.00
2010R Proof	15,000	Value: 50.00				
2011R	94,000	—	—	—	—	28.00
2011R Proof	15,000	Value: 50.00				
2012R	84,000	—	—	—	—	25.00
2012R Proof	15,000	Value: 50.00				
2013R	85,000	—	—	—	—	25.00
2013R Proof	15,000	Value: 50.00				

KM# 404 2 EURO

8.5000 g., Bi-Metallic Nickel-Brass center in Copper-Nickel ring, 25.75 mm. **Ruler:** Benedict XVI **Obv:** St. Paul being blinded on reary horse **Rev:** Map and value **Edge:** Reeded with 2's and stars

Date	Mintage	F	VF	XF	Unc	BU
ND (2008)R	106,084	—	—	—	25.00	—

KM# 410 2 EURO

8.5000 g., Bi-Metallic Nickel-Brass center in Copper-Nickel ring, 25.75 mm. **Ruler:** Benedict XVI **Subject:** International Year of Astronomy **Rev:** Map and value **Edge:** Reeded with 2's and stars

Date	Mintage	F	VF	XF	Unc	BU
2009R	100,000	—	—	—	25.00	—

KM# 420 2 EURO

8.5000 g., Bi-Metallic Nickel-Brass center in Copper-Nickel ring, 25.75 mm. **Ruler:** Benedict XVI **Subject:** Year of the Priest **Edge:** Reeded with 2's and stars

Date	Mintage	F	VF	XF	Unc	BU
2010R	115,000	—	—	—	20.00	25.00

KM# 426 2 EURO

8.5000 g., Bi-Metallic Nickel-Brass center in Copper-Nickel ring, 25.75 mm. **Ruler:** Benedict XVI **Subject:** 26th World Youth Day **Obv:** Youth with Vatican City flags **Edge:** Reeded with 2's and stars

Date	Mintage	F	VF	XF	Unc	BU
2011R	98,000	—	—	—	—	20.00
2011R Special Unc.	11,500	—	—	—	—	28.00

KM# 435 2 EURO

8.5000 g., Bi-Metallic Nickel-Brass center in Copper-Nickel ring, 25.75 mm. **Ruler:** Benedict XVI **Subject:** 7th World Meeting of Families **Obv:** Family unit before Cathedral

Date	Mintage	F	VF	XF	Unc	BU
2012R	89,000	—	—	—	—	28.00
2012R Proof	—	Value: 50.00				

KM# 349 5 EURO
18.0000 g., 0.8350 Silver 0.4832 oz. ASW, 32 mm. **Ruler:** John Paul II **Subject:** 24th Anniversary of Reign **Obv:** Bust 1/4 left **Rev:** Allegorical female and bridge **Edge:** Lettered **Edge Lettering:** +++ TOTUS TUUS +++ MMII

Date	Mintage	F	VF	XF	Unc	BU
2002R Proof	10,000	Value: 125				

KM# 354 5 EURO
18.0000 g., 0.9250 Silver 0.5353 oz. ASW, 32 mm. **Ruler:** John Paul II **Subject:** Year of the Rosary **Obv:** Pope praying the rosary **Rev:** "Our Lady of Pompei" presenting rosaries to Saints Dominic and Catherine **Edge:** Reeded **Designer:** Roberto Mauri

Date	Mintage	F	VF	XF	Unc	BU
2003R Proof	10,000	—	—	—	65.00	—

KM# 359 5 EURO
18.0000 g., 0.9250 Silver 0.5353 oz. ASW, 32 mm. **Ruler:** John Paul II **Subject:** 150th Anniversary of the Proclamation of the Dogma of the Immaculate Conception **Obv:** Virgin Mary **Rev:** Two Papal coat of arms **Edge:** Reeded and plain sections **Designer:** Claudia Momoni

Date	Mintage	F	VF	XF	Unc	BU
2004R	13,000	—	—	—	60.00	—

KM# 373 5 EURO
18.0000 g., 0.9250 Silver 0.5353 oz. ASW, 32 mm. **Ruler:** Sede Vacante **Obv:** Dove within square **Rev:** Arms of Cardinal Eduardo Martinez Somalo **Edge:** Reeded **Designer:** Daniela Longo

Date	Mintage	F	VF	XF	Unc	BU
MMV (2005)R Proof	13,440	Value: 200				

KM# 383 5 EURO
18.0000 g., 0.9250 Silver 0.5353 oz. ASW, 32 mm. **Ruler:** Benedict XVI **Subject:** Life reborn **Obv:** Bust left **Rev:** Children playing among branches of an olive tree

Date	Mintage	F	VF	XF	Unc	BU
2005R Proof	13,000	Value: 100				

KM# 395 5 EURO
18.0000 g., 0.9250 Silver 0.5353 oz. ASW, 32 mm. **Ruler:** Benedict XVI **Subject:** World Day of Peace **Obv:** Half-length figure Benedict right in vestments with crozier **Rev:** St. Benedict of Nursia seated

Date	Mintage	F	VF	XF	Unc	BU
MMVI (2006)R Proof	14,160	Value: 90.00				

KM# 400 5 EURO
18.0000 g., 0.9250 Silver 0.5353 oz. ASW, 32 mm. **Ruler:** Benedict XVI **Subject:** World Day of Peace **Obv:** 1/2 length figure kneeling in prayer **Rev:** Standing St. Francis of Assissi, rays in background

Date	Mintage	F	VF	XF	Unc	BU
MMVII (2007)R Proof	13,693	Value: 55.00				

KM# 406 5 EURO
18.0000 g., 0.9250 Silver 0.5353 oz. ASW, 32 mm. **Ruler:** Benedict XVI **Subject:** World Youth Day - Sydney **Obv:** Pope right, blessing **Rev:** Sydney Harbor sites

Date	Mintage	F	VF	XF	Unc	BU
MMVIII (2008)R Proof	9,600	Value: 60.00				

KM# 415 5 EURO
18.0000 g., 0.9250 Silver 0.5353 oz. ASW, 32 mm. **Ruler:** Benedict XVI **Subject:** World day of Peace **Obv:** Bust right in prayer **Rev:** Candle, family

Date	Mintage	F	VF	XF	Unc	BU
2009R Proof	9,600	Value: 60.00				

KM# 421 5 EURO
18.0000 g., 0.9250 Silver 0.5353 oz. ASW, 32 mm. **Ruler:** Benedict XVI **Subject:** Migrants and Refugees **Obv:** Benedict standing facing in vestments and mitre **Rev:** Family scene **Designer:** Daniela Longo and Claudia Momoni

Date	Mintage	F	VF	XF	Unc	BU
2010R Proof	9,998	Value: 75.00				

KM# 427 5 EURO
18.0000 g., 0.9250 Silver 0.5353 oz. ASW, 32 mm. **Ruler:** Benedict XVI **Subject:** 44the World day of Peace **Obv:** Bust left **Rev:** Female standing

Date	Mintage	F	VF	XF	Unc	BU
2011R Proof	7,998	Value: 80.00				

KM# 429 5 EURO
18.0000 g., 0.9250 Silver 0.5353 oz. ASW, 32 mm. **Ruler:** Benedict XVI **Subject:** John Paul II beautification **Obv:** Bust facing of John Paul II **Rev:** Cherubs elevating Papal Arms of John Paul II

Date	Mintage	F	VF	XF	Unc	BU
2011R Proof	9,500	Value: 75.00				

KM# 436 5 EURO
18.0000 g., 0.9250 Silver 0.5353 oz. ASW, 32 mm. **Ruler:** Benedict XVI **Subject:** John Paul I, 100th Anniversary of Birth

Date	Mintage	F	VF	XF	Unc	BU
2012R Proof	8,999	Value: 90.00				

KM# 442 5 EURO
Silver **Ruler:** Sede Vacante **Obv:** Dove in flight **Rev:** Arms of Cardinal Tarciscio Bertone

Date	Mintage	F	VF	XF	Unc	BU
2013R Proof	—	Value: 50.00				

KM# 350 10 EURO
22.0000 g., 0.8350 Silver 0.5906 oz. ASW, 34 mm. **Ruler:** John Paul II **Subject:** 24th Anniversary of Reign **Obv:** Pope holding crucifix **Rev:** Risen Christ (Message of peace) **Edge:** Reeded **Designer:** Floriano Bodini

Date	Mintage	F	VF	XF	Unc	BU
2002R Proof	10,000	Value: 80.00				

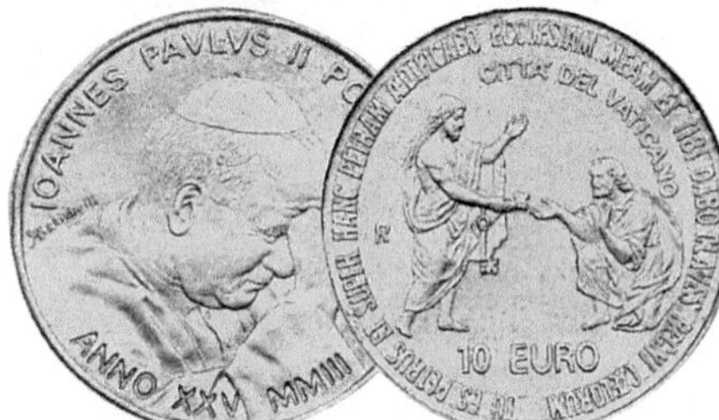

KM# 355 10 EURO
22.0000 g., 0.9250 Silver 0.6542 oz. ASW, 34 mm. **Ruler:** John Paul II **Subject:** 25th Anniversary of Reign **Obv:** Pope praying **Rev:** St. Peter receiving the keys of Earth and Heaven **Edge:** Reeded **Designer:** Amalia Mistichelli

Date	Mintage	F	VF	XF	Unc	BU
2003R Proof	10,000	Value: 80.00				

KM# 360 10 EURO
22.0000 g., 0.9250 Silver 0.6542 oz. ASW, 34 mm. **Ruler:** John Paul II **Obv:** Pope praying for peace **Rev:** Tree of Life rooted in virtues **Edge:** Reeded and plain sections **Designer:** Maria Carmela Colaneri

Date	Mintage	F	VF	XF	Unc	BU
2004R	13,000	—	—	—	90.00	—

KM# 384 10 EURO
22.0000 g., 0.9250 Silver 0.6542 oz. ASW **Ruler:** Benedict XVI **Subject:** Disciples of Emanaus **Obv:** Bust left **Rev:** Three men seated at table

Date	Mintage	F	VF	XF	Unc	BU
2006R Proof	13,000	Value: 215				

KM# 396 10 EURO
22.0000 g., 0.9250 Silver 0.6542 oz. ASW, 34 mm. **Ruler:** Benedict XVI **Subject:** St. Peter's Collonade, 350th Anniversary **Obv:** Collonade & Pope Benedict **Rev:** Collonade Schematics

Date	Mintage	F	VF	XF	Unc	BU
AN II MMVI (2006)R Proof	14,160	Value: 90.00				

KM# 401 10 EURO
22.0000 g., 0.9250 Silver 0.6542 oz. ASW, 34 mm. **Ruler:** Benedict XVI **Subject:** World Mission Day **Obv:** Bust right in ermine cape **Rev:** Blessed Mother Theresa of Calcutta and child

Date	Mintage	F	VF	XF	Unc	BU
AN III MVII (2007)R Proof	13,694	Value: 80.00				

KM# 407 10 EURO
22.0000 g., 0.9250 Silver 0.6542 oz. ASW, 34 mm. **Ruler:** Benedict XVI **Subject:** World Day of Peace **Obv:** Pope seated on chair in full robes and miter **Rev:** The Holy Family - Jesus, Mary, Joseph

Date	Mintage	F	VF	XF	Unc	BU
A VI MMVIII (2008)R Proof	9,602	Value: 95.00				

KM# 417 10 EURO
22.0000 g., 0.9250 Silver 0.6542 oz. ASW, 34 mm. **Ruler:** Benedict XVI **Subject:** Lateran Treaty, 80th Anniversary **Obv:** Bust right **Rev:** Rolled treaty with seal

Date	Mintage	F	VF	XF	Unc	BU
2009R Proof	9,602	Value: 95.00				

KM# 422 10 EURO
22.0000 g., 0.9250 Silver 0.6542 oz. ASW, 34 mm. **Ruler:** Benedict XVI **Subject:** 43rd World day of Peace **Obv:** Bust left **Rev:** Three figures **Designer:** Patrizio Daniele and Valerio de Seta

Date	Mintage	F	VF	XF	Unc	BU
2010R Proof	9,998	Value: 80.00				

KM# 428 10 EURO
22.0000 g., 0.9250 Silver 0.6542 oz. ASW, 34 mm. **Ruler:** Benedict XVI **Subject:** Benedict XVI's 60th Anniversary of Ordination **Obv:** Bust right **Rev:** Two fishermen hauling in net

Date	Mintage	F	VF	XF	Unc	BU
2011R Proof	7,998	Value: 90.00				

KM# 437 10 EURO
22.0000 g., 0.9250 Silver 0.6542 oz. ASW, 34 mm. **Ruler:** Benedict XVI **Subject:** 20th World Day of the Sick

Date	Mintage	F	VF	XF	Unc	BU
2012R Proof	8,999	Value: 90.00				

KM# 443 10 EURO
0.9170 Gold **Ruler:** Sede Vacante **Obv:** Dove in flight **Rev:** Arms of Cardinal Tarciscio Bertone

Date	Mintage	F	VF	XF	Unc	BU
2013R Proof	—	Value: 450				

KM# 361 20 EURO
6.0000 g., 0.9170 Gold 0.1769 oz. AGW, 21 mm. **Ruler:** John Paul II **Subject:** Roots of Faith **Rev:** Noah's Ark **Designer:** Floriano Bodini

Date	Mintage	F	VF	XF	Unc	BU
2002 Proof	2,800	Value: 1,200				

KM# 351 20 EURO
6.0000 g., 0.9166 Gold 0.1768 oz. AGW, 21 mm. **Ruler:** John Paul II **Rev:** Moses being found in floating basket **Edge:** Reeded **Designer:** Floriano Bodini

Date	Mintage	F	VF	XF	Unc	BU
2003R Proof	2,800	Value: 1,300				

KM# 363 20 EURO
6.0000 g., 0.9170 Gold 0.1769 oz. AGW, 21 mm. **Ruler:** John Paul II **Rev:** David slaying Goliath **Designer:** Floriano Bodini

Date	Mintage	F	VF	XF	Unc	BU
2004/XXVIIR Proof	3,050	Value: 1,200				

KM# 392 20 EURO
6.0000 g., 0.9160 Gold 0.1767 oz. AGW, 21 mm. **Ruler:** Benedict XVI **Subject:** Christian Initiation - Baptism **Obv:** Pope seated **Rev:** Fountain

Date	Mintage	F	VF	XF	Unc	BU
AN I MMV (2005)R Proof	3,046	Value: 600				

KM# 397 20 EURO
6.0000 g., 0.9160 Gold 0.1767 oz. AGW, 21 mm. **Ruler:** Benedict XVI **Subject:** Christian Initiation - Confirmation **Obv:** Bust right **Rev:** Bishop confirming three

Date	Mintage	F	VF	XF	Unc	BU
AN II MMVI (2006)R Proof	3,326	Value: 600				

KM# 402 20 EURO
6.0000 g., 0.9160 Gold 0.1767 oz. AGW, 21 mm. **Ruler:** Benedict XVI **Subject:** Christain Initiation - Eucharist **Obv:** Bust left in ermine cape **Rev:** Basket of fish and bread

Date	Mintage	F	VF	XF	Unc	BU
AN III (2007)R Proof	3,426	Value: 600				

KM# 408 20 EURO
6.0000 g., 0.9170 Gold 0.1769 oz. AGW, 21 mm. **Ruler:** Benedict XVI **Subject:** Vatican sculpture **Obv:** Pope right in mitre **Rev:** Torso of Belvedere

Date	Mintage	F	VF	XF	Unc	BU
AN IV MMVIII (2008)R Proof	2,930	Value: 500				

KM# 416 20 EURO
6.0000 g., 0.9170 Gold 0.1769 oz. AGW, 21 mm. **Ruler:** Benedict XVI **Subject:** Masterworks in the Vatican Collection **Rev:** John the Baptist with lamb on shoulders

Date	Mintage	F	VF	XF	Unc	BU
2009R Proof	2,934	Value: 550				

KM# 423 20 EURO
6.0000 g., 0.9170 Gold 0.1769 oz. AGW, 21 mm. **Ruler:** Benedict XVI **Subject:** Vatican Sculpture - Apollo Belvedere **Obv:** Large head profile left **Rev:** Statue of Apollo Belvedere

Date	Mintage	F	VF	XF	Unc	BU
2010R Proof	3,050	Value: 500				

KM# 431 20 EURO
6.0000 g., 0.9170 Gold 0.1769 oz. AGW, 21 mm. **Ruler:** Benedict XVI **Subject:** Pauline Chapel restoration **Obv:** Bust left **Rev:** Head

Date	Mintage	F	VF	XF	Unc	BU
2011R Proof	3,050	Value: 450				

KM# 433 20 EURO
26.0000 g., 0.9250 Silver 0.7732 oz. ASW, 36 mm. **Ruler:** Benedict XVI **Subject:** 10th Anniversary of the Vatican Euro **Rev:** St. Peter's Basilica

Date	Mintage	F	VF	XF	Unc	BU
2012R Proof	13,000	Value: 350				

KM# 438 20 EURO
6.0000 g., 0.9170 Gold 0.1769 oz. AGW, 21 mm. **Ruler:** Benedict XVI **Subject:** Restoration of the Pauline Chapel

Date	Mintage	F	VF	XF	Unc	BU
2012R Proof	3,000	Value: 400				

KM# 362 50 EURO
15.0000 g., 0.9170 Gold 0.4422 oz. AGW **Ruler:** John Paul II **Subject:** Roots of Faith **Rev:** Sacrifice of Abraham **Designer:** Floriano Bodini

Date	Mintage	F	VF	XF	Unc	BU
2002 Proof	2,800	Value: 2,200				

KM# 352 50 EURO
15.0000 g., 0.9166 Gold 0.4420 oz. AGW, 28 mm. **Ruler:** John Paul II **Rev:** Moses receiving the Ten Commandments **Edge:** Reeded **Designer:** Floriano Bodini

Date	Mintage	F	VF	XF	Unc	BU
2003R Proof	2,800	Value: 2,200				

KM# 364 50 EURO
15.0000 g., 0.9170 Gold 0.4422 oz. AGW **Ruler:** John Paul II **Rev:** Judgement of Solomon **Designer:** Floriano Bodini

Date	Mintage	F	VF	XF	Unc	BU
2004/XXVIIR Proof	3,050	Value: 2,200				

KM# 393 50 EURO
15.0000 g., 0.9160 Gold 0.4417 oz. AGW, 28 mm. **Ruler:** Benedict XVI **Subject:** Christian Initiation - Baptism **Obv:** Pope seated **Rev:** John baptising Christ

Date	Mintage	F	VF	XF	Unc	BU
AN I MMV (2005)R Proof	3,044	Value: 1,500				

KM# 398 50 EURO
15.0000 g., 0.9160 Gold 0.4417 oz. AGW, 28 mm. **Ruler:** Benedict XVI **Subject:** Christian Initiation - Confirmation **Obv:** Bust right **Rev:** Tongues of fire decending on Apostles

Date	Mintage	F	VF	XF	Unc	BU
AN II MMVI (2006)R Proof	3,324	Value: 1,500				

KM# 403 50 EURO
15.0000 g., 0.9160 Gold 0.4417 oz. AGW, 28 mm. **Ruler:** Benedict XVI **Subject:** Christian Initiation - Eucharist **Obv:** Bust left in ermine cape **Rev:** Scene of the Last Supper

Date	Mintage	F	VF	XF	Unc	BU
ANIII MMVII (2007)R Proof	—	Value: 1,500				

KM# 409 50 EURO
15.0000 g., 0.9170 Gold 0.4422 oz. AGW, 28 mm. **Ruler:** Benedict XVI **Subject:** Vatican sculpture **Obv:** Pope right in mitre **Rev:** The Pieta

Date	Mintage	F	VF	XF	Unc	BU
AN IV MMVIII (2008)R Proof	—	Value: 1,000				

KM# 418 50 EURO
15.0000 g., 0.9170 Gold 0.4422 oz. AGW, 28 mm. **Ruler:** Benedict XVI **Subject:** Masterworks in the Vatican Collection **Rev:** Hercules statue group

Date	Mintage	F	VF	XF	Unc	BU
2009R Proof	2,930	Value: 1,200				

KM# 424 50 EURO
15.0000 g., 0.9170 Gold 0.4422 oz. AGW, 28 mm. **Ruler:** Benedict XVI **Subject:** Vatican Sculpture - Augustus of Prima **Obv:** Large head profile left **Rev:** Statue of Augustus **Designer:** Orietta Rossi and Maria Carmela Colaneri

Date	Mintage	F	VF	XF	Unc	BU
2010R Proof	3,050	Value: 1,200				

KM# 432 50 EURO
15.0000 g., 0.9170 Gold 0.4422 oz. AGW, 28 mm. **Ruler:** Benedict XVI **Subject:** Pauline Chapel restoration **Obv:** Bust left **Rev:** Cruxifiction of St. Peter

Date	Mintage	F	VF	XF	Unc	BU
2011R Proof	2,700	Value: 950				

KM# 434 50 EURO
15.0000 g., 0.9170 Gold 0.4422 oz. AGW, 28 mm. **Ruler:** Benedict XVI **Subject:** 10th Anniversary of the Vatican Euro **Rev:** St. Peter's Basilica

Date	Mintage	F	VF	XF	Unc	BU
2012R Proof	2,000	Value: 1,000				

KM# 439 50 EURO
15.0000 g., 0.9170 Gold 0.4422 oz. AGW, 28 mm. **Ruler:** Benedict XVI **Subject:** Restoration of the Pauline Chapel

Date	Mintage	F	VF	XF	Unc	BU
2012R Proof	2,500	Value: 1,200				

KM# 405 100 EURO
30.0000 g., 0.9170 Gold 0.8844 oz. AGW, 35 mm. **Ruler:** Benedict XVI **Obv:** Bust left **Rev:** The Creator from the Sistine Chapel ceiling

Date	Mintage	F	VF	XF	Unc	BU
AN IV MMVIII (2008)R Proof	960	Value: 1,700				

KM# 419 100 EURO
30.0000 g., 0.9170 Gold 0.8844 oz. AGW, 35 mm. **Ruler:** Benedict XVI **Subject:** Sistine Chapel - Banishment from Eden

Date	Mintage	F	VF	XF	Unc	BU
2009R Proof	—	Value: 1,700				

KM# 425 100 EURO
30.0000 g., 0.9170 Gold 0.8844 oz. AGW, 35 mm. **Ruler:** Benedict XVI **Subject:** Sistine Chapel - Last Judgement **Obv:** Bust left **Rev:** Detail of the painting **Designer:** A. Masini

Date	Mintage	F	VF	XF	Unc	BU
2010R Proof	1,100	Value: 1,750				

KM# 430 100 EURO
30.0000 g., 0.9170 Gold 0.8844 oz. AGW, 35 mm. **Ruler:** Benedict XVI **Subject:** Raffaell painting **Obv:** Bust left in vestments and mitre **Rev:** Horseman and captive

Date	Mintage	F	VF	XF	Unc	BU
2011R Proof	1,100	Value: 1,650				

KM# 440 100 EURO
30.0000 g., 0.9170 Gold 0.8844 oz. AGW, 35 mm. **Ruler:** Benedict XVI **Rev:** Madonna of Foligno

Date	Mintage	F	VF	XF	Unc	BU
2012R Proof	999	Value: 2,300				

KM# 441 200 EURO
0.9170 Gold **Ruler:** Benedict XVI **Subject:** Theological Virtues - Faith

Date	Mintage	F	VF	XF	Unc	BU
2012R Proof	—	Value: 4,000				

MINT SETS

KM#	Date	Mintage	Identification	Issue Price	Mkt Val
MS107	2001 (8)	26,000	KM#331-338	21.25	200
MS108	2002 (8)	65,000	KM#341-348	12.00	975
MS109	2003 (8)	65,000	KM#341-348	15.00	500
MS110	2004 (8)	85,000	KM#341-348	16.50	335
MS111	2005 (8)	85,000	KM#341-348.	32.50	335
MS112	MMV (2005) (8)	60,000	KM#365-372 Sede Vacante	—	435
MS113	2006 (8)	—	KM#375-382	—	210
MS114	2007 (8)	—	KM#375-382	—	230
MS115	2008 (8)	85,000	KM#375-377, 385-389	45.00	165
MS116	2009 (8)	91,400	KM#375-377, 385-389	30.00	165
MS117	2010 (8)	94,000	KM#375-377, 385-389	30.00	150

PROOF SETS

KM#	Date	Mintage	Identification	Issue Price	Mkt Val
PS13	2001 (2)	—	KM#390, 391	—	1,350
PS15	2002 (8)	9,000	KM#341-348	75.00	1,450
PS16	2003 (8)	13,000	KM#341-348	78.00	1,200
PS17	2004 (8)	13,000	KM#341-348	—	1,200
PS18	2005 (8)	16,000	KM#341-348 plus silver medal	150	1,175
PS19	2006 (8)	16,000	KM#375-382 plus silver medal	—	375
PS20	2007 (8)	16,000	KM#375-382 plus silver medal	—	315
PS21	2008 (8)	16,000	KM#375-377, 385-389 plus silver medal	195	250
PS22	2009 (8)	15,000	KM#375-377, 385-389 plus silver medal	195	250
PS23	2010 (8)	15,000	KM#375-377, 385-389 plus silver medal	195	240
PS24	2010 (8)	300	KM#375-377, 385-389 plus gold medal	2,100	2,250

VENEZUELA

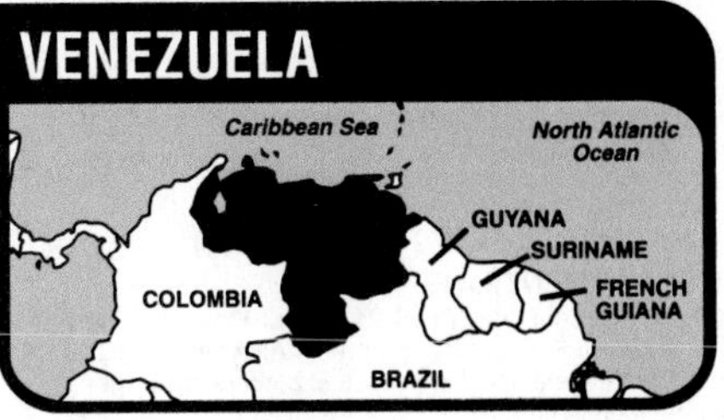

The Bolivarian Republic of Venezuela ("Little Venice"), located on the northern coast of South America between Colombia and Guyana, has an area of 352,145 sq. mi.(912,050 sq. km.) and a population of 20 million. Capital: Caracas. Petroleum and mining provide a significant portion of Venezuela's exports. Coffee, grown on 60,000 plantations, is the chief crop. Metalurgy, refining, oil, iron and steel production are the main employment industries.

GOVERNMENT
Republic, 1823-2000
Republic Bolivarian, 2000-

MINT MARKS
Maracay

REPUBLIC
Bolivariana

REFORM COINAGE
1896
100 Centimos = 1 Bolivar

Y# 80 10 BOLIVARES
2.3300 g., Nickel Clad Steel, 17 mm. **Obv:** National arms left of denomination **Obv. Legend:** REPÚBLICA BOLIVARIANA DE VENEZUELA **Rev:** Head of Bolívar left in 7-sided outline **Rev. Legend:** BOLÍVAR - LIBERTADOR **Edge:** Reeded

Date	Mintage	F	VF	XF	Unc	BU
2001	—	—	—	—	0.25	0.50
2002	—	—	—	—	0.25	0.50

Y# 80a 10 BOLIVARES
1.7390 g., Aluminum-Zinc, 16.92 mm. **Obv:** National arms and value **Obv. Legend:** REPÚBLICA BOLIVARIANA DE VENEZUELA **Rev:** Head of Bolívar left in 7-sided outline **Rev. Legend:** BOLÍVAR - LIBERTADOR **Edge:** Reeded

Date	Mintage	F	VF	XF	Unc	BU
2001	—	—	—	0.15	0.45	0.60
2002	—	—	—	0.15	0.45	0.60
2004	—	—	—	0.15	0.45	0.60

Y# 81 20 BOLIVARES
4.3200 g., Nickel Clad Steel, 20 mm. **Obv:** National arms left of denomination **Obv. Legend:** REPÚBLICA BOLIVARIANA DE VENEZUELA **Rev:** Head of Bolívar left in 7-sided outline **Rev. Legend:** BOLÍVAR - LIBERTADOR **Edge:** Plain

Date	Mintage	F	VF	XF	Unc	BU
2001	—	—	—	—	0.25	0.50
2002	—	—	—	—	0.25	0.50

Y# 81a.1 20 BOLIVARES
3.2650 g., Aluminum-Zinc, 20 mm. **Obv:** National arms and value with wavy based "2" **Obv. Legend:** REPÚBLICA BOLÍVARIANA DE VENEZUELA **Rev:** Head of Bolívar left in 7-sided outline **Rev. Legend:** BOLÍVAR - LIBERTADOR **Edge:** Plain

Date	Mintage	F	VF	XF	Unc	BU
2001	—	—	—	—	0.65	1.00

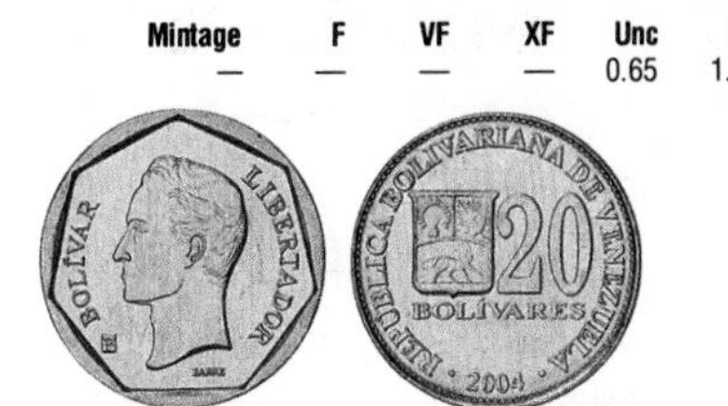

Y# 81a.2 20 BOLIVARES
3.2400 g., Aluminum-Zinc, 20 mm. **Obv:** National arms and value with flat based "2" **Obv. Legend:** REPÚBLICA BOLIVARIANA DE VENEZUELA **Rev:** Head of Bolívar left in 7-sided outline **Rev. Legend:** BOLÍVAR - LIBERTADOR **Edge:** Plain

Date	Mintage	F	VF	XF	Unc	BU
2002	—	—	—	0.25	0.60	0.80
2004	—	—	—	0.25	0.60	0.80

Y# 82 50 BOLIVARES
6.5800 g., Nickel Clad Steel, 23 mm. **Obv:** National arms left of denomination **Obv. Legend:** REPÚBLICA BOLIVARIANA DE VENEZUELA **Rev:** Head of Bolivar left in 7-sided outline **Rev. Legend:** BOLÍVAR - LIBERTADOR **Edge:** Reeded

Date	Mintage	F	VF	XF	Unc	BU
2001	—	—	—	0.30	0.75	1.00
2002	—	—	—	0.30	0.75	1.00
2004	—	—	—	0.30	0.75	1.00

Y# 83 100 BOLIVARES
6.8200 g., Nickel Clad Steel, 25 mm. **Obv:** National arms and value **Obv. Legend:** REPÚBUBLICA BOLIVARIANA DE VENEZUELA **Rev:** Head of Bolívar left in 7-sided ouline **Rev. Legend:** BOLÍVAR - LIBERTADO **Edge:** Plain

Date	Mintage	F	VF	XF	Unc	BU
2001	—	—	—	0.45	1.10	1.50
2002	—	—	—	0.45	1.10	1.50
2004	—	—	—	0.45	1.10	1.50

Y# 94 500 BOLIVARES
8.5000 g., Nickel Plated Steel, 28.4 mm. **Obv:** National arms and denomination **Obv. Legend:** REPÚBLICA BOLIVARIANA DE VENEZUELA **Rev:** Head of Bolívar left in 7-sided outline **Rev. Legend:** BOLÍVAR - LIBERTADOR **Edge:** Segmented reeding

Date	Mintage	F	VF	XF	Unc	BU
2004	—	—	—	0.60	1.50	2.00

Y# 85 1000 BOLIVARES
8.3500 g., Bi-Metallic Copper-Nickel center in Brass ring, 24 mm. **Obv:** National arms and value in center **Obv. Legend:** REPÚBLICA BOLIVARIANA DE VENEZUELA **Rev:** Head of Bolívar left **Rev. Legend:** BOLÍVAR - LIBERTADOR **Edge:** Lettered **Edge Lettering:** "BCV 1000" four times

Date	Mintage	F	VF	XF	Unc	BU
2005	9,000,000	—	—	0.90	2.25	3.00

REFORM COINAGE

2007

1000 Bolivares = 1 Bolivar Fuerte

Y# 87 CENTIMO

1.3600 g., Copper Plated Steel, 14.9 mm. **Obv:** National arms **Obv. Legend:** REPÚBLICA BOLIVARIANA DE VENEZUELA **Rev:** Eight stars at left, large value at right **Edge:** Reeded

Date	Mintage	F	VF	XF	Unc	BU
2007	—	—	—	—	0.25	0.35
Note: Many die rotation varieties exist.						
2009	—	—	—	—	0.25	0.35

Y# 88 5 CENTIMOS

2.0300 g., Copper Plated Steel, 16.9 mm. **Obv:** National arms **Obv. Legend:** REPÚBLICA BOLIVARIANA DE VENEZUELA **Rev:** Eight stars at left, large value at right **Edge:** Plain

Date	Mintage	F	VF	XF	Unc	BU
2007	—	—	—	—	0.50	0.75
2009	—	—	—	—	0.50	0.75

Y# 89 10 CENTIMOS

2.6200 g., Nickel Plated Steel, 18 mm. **Obv:** National arms **Obv. Legend:** REPÚBLICA BOLIVARIANA DE VENEZUELA **Rev:** Eight stars at left, large value at right **Edge:** Reeded

Date	Mintage	F	VF	XF	Unc	BU
2007	—	—	—	—	0.75	1.00
2009	—	—	—	—	0.75	1.00

Y# 90 12-1/2 CENTIMOS

3.9300 g., Nickel Plated Steel, 23 mm. **Obv:** National arms **Obv. Legend:** REPÚBLICA BOLIVARIANA DE VENEZUELA **Rev:** Large value, eight stars below in sprays **Edge:** Plain

Date	Mintage	F	VF	XF	Unc	BU
2007	—	—	—	—	1.50	1.75

Y# 91 25 CENTIMOS

3.8600 g., Nickel Plated Steel, 20 mm. **Obv:** National arms **Obv. Legend:** REPÚBLICA BOLIVARIANA DE VENEZUELA **Rev:** Eight stars at left, large value at center right **Edge:** Plain

Date	Mintage	F	VF	XF	Unc	BU
2007	—	—	—	—	2.00	2.50
2009	—	—	—	—	2.00	2.50

Y# 99 25 CENTIMOS

3.8600 g., Nickel Plated Steel, 20 mm. **Subject:** Independence, 200th Anniversary **Obv:** Legend **Rev:** Large value

Date	Mintage	F	VF	XF	Unc	BU
2010	—	—	—	—	2.50	3.00

Y# 92 50 CENTIMOS

4.3000 g., Nickel Plated Steel, 21.9 mm. **Obv:** National arms **Obv. Legend:** REPÚBLICA BOLIVARIANA DE VENEZUELA **Rev:** Eight stars at left, large value at center right **Edge:** Segmented reeding

Date	Mintage	F	VF	XF	Unc	BU
2007	—	—	—	—	3.00	3.50
2009	—	—	—	—	3.00	3.50

Y# 100 50 CENTIMOS

4.3000 g., Nickel Plated Steel, 21.9 mm. **Subject:** Banco Central, 70th Anniversary **Obv:** Legend **Rev:** Large vlaue

Date	Mintage	F	VF	XF	Unc	BU
2010	—	—	—	—	3.50	4.00

Y# 93 BOLIVAR

8.0400 g., Bi-Metallic Copper-Nickel center in Aluminum-Bronze ring, 24 mm. **Obv:** Eight stars at left of national arms, large value at right **Obv. Legend:** REPÚBLICA BOLIVARIANA DE VENEZUELA **Rev:** Head of Bolívar left **Edge:** Lettered **Edge Lettering:** "BCV 1" repeated

Date	Mintage	F	VF	XF	Unc	BU
2007	—	—	—	—	5.00	6.00
2009	—	—	—	—	5.00	6.00

Y# 101 50 BOLIVARES

31.1000 g., 0.9990 Silver 0.9988 oz. ASW, 38.6 mm. **Subject:** Banco Central, 70th Anniversary **Obv:** Legned **Rev:** Banco Central building

Date	Mintage	F	VF	XF	Unc	BU
2010 Proof	3,000	Value: 85.00				

Y# 102 50 BOLIVARES

0.9990 Gold **Subject:** Banco Central, 70th Anniversary **Obv:** Legend **Rev:** Banco Central building

Date	Mintage	F	VF	XF	Unc	BU
2010 Proof	—	Value: 2,000				

Y# 95 200 BOLIVARES

0.9990 Silver **Obv:** Flag **Rev:** Crowd outside building

Date	Mintage	F	VF	XF	Unc	BU
2010 Proof	—	Value: 85.00				

Y# 96 200 BOLIVARES

0.9990 Gold **Obv:** Flag **Rev:** Crowd before building

Date	Mintage	F	VF	XF	Unc	BU
2010 Proof	—	Value: 2,000				

Y# 97 200 BOLIVARES

0.9990 Silver **Obv:** Flag **Rev:** Francisco de Marianda

Date	Mintage	F	VF	XF	Unc	BU
2010 Proof	—	Value: 85.00				

Y# 98 200 BOLIVARES

0.9990 Gold **Obv:** Flag **Rev:** Francisco de Marianda

Date	Mintage	F	VF	XF	Unc	BU
2010 Proof	—	Value: 2,000				

VIET NAM

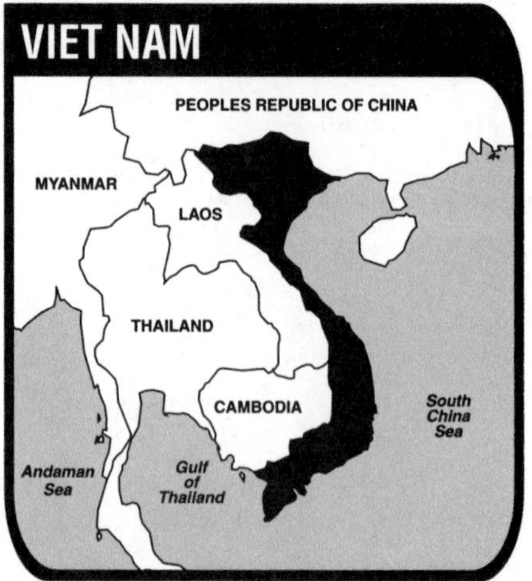

The Socialist Republic of Viet Nam, located in Southeast Asia west of the South China Sea, has an area of 127,300 sq. mi. (329,560 sq. km.) and a population of *66.8 million. Capital: Hanoi. Agricultural products, coal, and mineral ores are exported.

The activities of Communists in South Viet Nam led to the second Indochina war which came to a brief halt in 1973 (when a cease-fire was arranged and U.S. forces withdrew), but it didn't end until April 30, 1975 when South Viet Nam surrendered unconditionally. The two Viet Nams were reunited as the Socialist Republic of Viet Nam on July 2, 1976.

NOTE: For earlier coinage refer to French Indo-China or Tonkin.

SOCIALIST REPUBLIC

STANDARD COINAGE

KM# 71 200 DONG

3.1000 g., Nickel Clad Steel, 20.75 mm. **Obv:** National emblem **Rev:** Denomination

Date	Mintage	F	VF	XF	Unc	BU
2003	125,000,000	0.15	0.20	0.35	0.75	0.50

KM# 74 500 DONG

4.5000 g., Nickel Clad Steel, 21.86 mm. **Obv:** National emblem **Rev:** Denomination **Edge:** Segmented reeding

Date	Mintage	F	VF	XF	Unc	BU
2003	175,000,000	0.15	0.25	0.50	0.75	1.00

KM# 72 1000 DONG

3.7000 g., Brass Plated Steel, 19 mm. **Obv:** National emblem **Rev:** Bat De Pagoda in Hanoi **Edge:** Reeded

Date	Mintage	F	VF	XF	Unc	BU
2003	250,000,000	0.20	0.35	0.60	0.80	1.50

KM# 75 2000 DONG
5.0000 g., Brass Plated Steel, 23.5 mm. **Obv:** National emblem **Rev:** Highland Stilt House in Tay Nguyen above value **Edge:** Segmented reeding

Date	Mintage	F	VF	XF	Unc	BU
2003	—	—	—	—	2.25	2.75

KM# 64 5000 DONG
1.2441 g., 0.9999 Gold 0.0400 oz. AGW, 13.92 mm. **Subject:** Year of the Snake **Obv:** State emblem **Rev:** Sea snake **Edge:** Reeded

Date	Mintage	F	VF	XF	Unc	BU
2001	—	—	—	—	85.00	95.00

KM# 67 5000 DONG
1.2441 g., 0.9999 Gold 0.0400 oz. AGW, 13.9 mm. **Subject:** Year of the Horse **Obv:** State emblem **Rev:** Horse **Edge:** Reeded

Date	Mintage	F	VF	XF	Unc	BU
2002	28,000	—	—	—	75.00	85.00

KM# 73 5000 DONG
7.6000 g., Brass, 25 mm. **Obv:** National emblem **Rev:** Chua Mot Cot Pagoda in Hanoi

Date	Mintage	F	VF	XF	Unc	BU
2003	500,000,000	0.50	0.75	1.00	1.25	2.50

KM# 57 10000 DONG
20.0000 g., 0.9250 Silver 0.5948 oz. ASW, 38.7 mm. **Subject:** Year of the Snake **Obv:** State emblem above value **Obv. Legend:** "CONG HOA XA HOI CHU NGHIA VIET NAM" **Rev:** Sea snake **Rev. Legend:** "...VIET NAM" **Edge:** Reeded

Date	Mintage	F	VF	XF	Unc	BU
2001(S) Proof	3,500	Value: 85.00				

KM# 58 10000 DONG
20.0000 g., 0.9250 Silver 0.5948 oz. ASW **Subject:** Year of the Snake **Obv:** State emblem above value **Obv. Legend:** "CONG HOA XA HOI CHU NGHIA VIET NAM" **Rev:** Bamboo viper **Rev. Legend:** "...VIET NAM"

Date	Mintage	F	VF	XF	Unc	BU
2001(S) Proof	3,500	Value: 85.00				

KM# 59 10000 DONG
20.0000 g., 0.9250 Silver 0.5948 oz. ASW **Subject:** Year of the Snake **Obv:** State emblem above value **Obv. Legend:** "CONG HOA XA HOI CHU NGHIA VIET NAM" **Rev:** Multicolor holographic, cobra in center **Rev. Legend:** "...VIET NAM"

Date	Mintage	F	VF	XF	Unc	BU
2001(S) Proof	3,500	Value: 80.00				

KM# 61 10000 DONG
20.0000 g., 0.9990 Silver 0.6423 oz. ASW, 38.7 mm. **Subject:** Year of the Horse **Obv:** State emblem **Rev:** Horse with octagonal latent image **Edge:** Reeded

Date	Mintage	F	VF	XF	Unc	BU
2001 Proof	3,800	Value: 65.00				

Note: In proof set only

KM# 62 10000 DONG
20.0000 g., 0.9990 Silver 0.6423 oz. ASW, 38.7 mm. **Subject:** Year of the Horse **Obv:** State emblem **Rev:** Horse with multicolor accoutrements **Edge:** Reeded

Date	Mintage	F	VF	XF	Unc	BU
2001 Proof	3,800	Value: 75.00				

Note: In proof set only

KM# 63 10000 DONG
20.0000 g., 0.9990 Silver 0.6423 oz. ASW, 38.7 mm. **Subject:** Year of the Horse **Obv:** State emblem **Rev:** Multicolor holographic horse in center **Edge:** Reeded

Date	Mintage	F	VF	XF	Unc	BU
2001 Proof	3,800	Value: 75.00				

Note: In proof set only

KM# 76 10000 DONG
20.0000 g., 0.9990 Silver 0.6423 oz. ASW, 38.7 mm. **Obv:** State emblem **Rev:** Multicolored Grey-shanked Douc Langur monkey **Edge:** Reeded

Date	Mintage	F	VF	XF	Unc	BU
2004 Proof	6,200	Value: 70.00				

KM# 65 20000 DONG
7.7759 g., 0.9999 Gold 0.2500 oz. AGW, 22 mm. **Subject:** Year of the Snake **Obv:** State emblem **Rev:** Sea snake **Edge:** Reeded

Date	Mintage	F	VF	XF	Unc	BU
2001(S) Proof	—	Value: 525				

Note: Issued in a replica Faberge egg

KM# 68 20000 DONG
7.7759 g., 0.9999 Gold 0.2500 oz. AGW, 22 mm. **Subject:** Year of the Horse **Obv:** State emblem **Rev:** Horse **Edge:** Reeded

Date	Mintage	F	VF	XF	Unc	BU
2002 Proof	1,800	Value: 500				

KM# 66 50000 DONG
15.5518 g., 0.9999 Gold 0.4999 oz. AGW, 27 mm. **Subject:** Year of the Snake **Obv:** State emblem **Rev:** Multicolor holographic King Cobra **Edge:** Reeded

Date	Mintage	F	VF	XF	Unc	BU
2001(S) Proof	3,200	Value: 1,050				

KM# 69 50000 DONG
15.5518 g., 0.9999 Gold 0.4999 oz. AGW, 27 mm. **Subject:** Year of the Horse **Obv:** State emblem **Rev:** Multicolor holographic horse **Edge:** Reeded

Date	Mintage	F	VF	XF	Unc	BU
2002 Proof	3,800	Value: 1,000				

PROOF SETS

KM#	Date	Mintage	Identification	Issue Price	Mkt Val
PS4	2001(S) (3)	3,500	KM#57-59	120	250
PS5	2001(S) (2)	—	KM#59, 66	—	1,125
PS6	2001(S) (2)	—	KM#65-66	—	1,575
PS7	2002 (3)	3,800	KM#61-63	—	225

WEST AFRICAN STATES

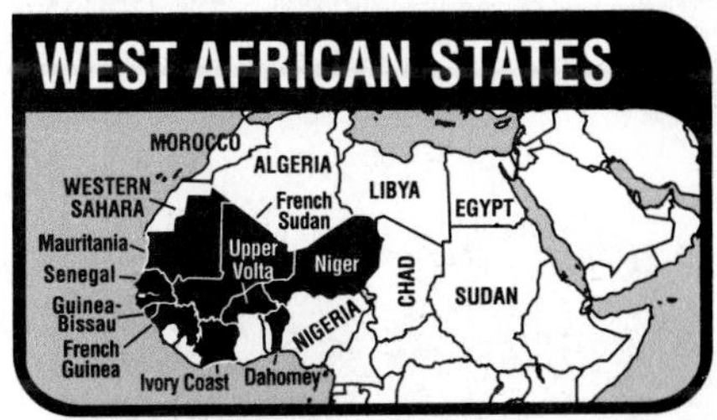

The West African States, a former federation of eight French colonial territories on the northwest coast of Africa, has an area of 1,831,079 sq. mi. (4,742,495 sq. km.) and a population of about 17 million. Capital: Dakar. The constituent territories were Mauritania, Senegal, Dahomey, French Sudan, Ivory Coast, Upper Volta, Niger and French Guinea.

The members of the federation were overseas territories within the French Union until Sept. of 1958 when all but French Guinea approved the constitution of the Fifth French Republic, thereby electing to become autonomous members of the new French Community. French Guinea voted to become the fully independent Republic of Guinea. The other seven attained independence in 1960. The French West Africa territories were provided with a common currency, a practice which was continued as the monetary union of the West African States which provides a common currency to the autonomous republics of Dahomey (now Benin), Senegal, Upper Volta (now Burkina Faso), Ivory Coast, Mali, Togo, Niger, and Guinea-Bissau.

For earlier coinage refer to Togo, and French West Africa.

MINT MARK
(a)- Paris, privy marks only

MONETARY SYSTEM
100 Centimes = 1 Franc

FEDERATION

STANDARD COINAGE

KM# 8 FRANC
1.6000 g., Steel **Obv:** Taku - Ashanti gold weight **Rev:** Value and date **Designer:** R. Joly

Date	Mintage	F	VF	XF	Unc	BU
2001(a)	—	—	—	0.10	0.35	0.60
2002(a)	—	—	—	0.10	0.35	0.60

KM# 2a 5 FRANCS
3.0000 g., Aluminum-Nickel-Bronze, 20 mm. **Obv:** Taku - Ashanti gold weight divides value **Rev:** Gazelle head facing

Date	Mintage	F	VF	XF	Unc	BU
2001(a)	—	—	0.10	0.20	0.40	0.60
2002(a)	—	—	0.10	0.20	0.40	0.60
2003(a)	—	—	0.10	0.20	0.40	0.60
2004(a)	—	—	0.10	0.20	0.40	0.60
2005(a)	—	—	0.10	0.20	0.40	0.60
2006(a)	—	—	0.10	0.20	0.40	0.60
2007(a)	—	—	—	0.20	0.40	0.60
2008(a)	—	—	—	0.20	0.40	0.60
2009(a)	—	—	—	0.20	0.40	0.60
2010(a)	—	—	—	0.20	0.40	0.60
2011(a)	—	—	—	0.20	0.40	0.60

KM# 10 10 FRANCS
4.0000 g., Aluminum-Bronze, 23.4 mm. **Series:** F.A.O. **Obv:** Taku - Ashanti gold weight divides value **Rev:** People getting water **Designer:** R. Joly

Date	Mintage	F	VF	XF	Unc	BU
2001(a)	—	—	0.25	0.50	1.25	1.50
2002(a)	—	—	0.25	0.50	1.25	1.50
2003(a)	—	—	0.25	0.50	1.25	1.50
2004(a)	—	—	0.25	0.50	1.00	1.50
2005(a)	—	—	0.25	0.50	1.00	1.50
2006(a)	—	—	0.25	0.50	1.00	1.50
2007(a)	—	—	—	0.50	1.00	1.50
2008(a)	—	—	—	0.50	1.00	1.50
2009(a)	—	—	—	0.50	1.00	1.50
2010(a)	—	—	—	0.50	1.00	1.50
2011(a)	—	—	—	0.50	1.00	1.50
2012(a)	—	—	—	0.50	1.00	1.50

KM# 9 25 FRANCS
7.9500 g., Aluminum-Bronze, 27 mm. **Series:** F.A.O. **Obv:** Taku - Ashanti gold weight divides value **Rev:** Figure filling tube **Note:** Mint mark position varieties exist.

Date	Mintage	F	VF	XF	Unc	BU
2001(a)	—	—	—	0.75	1.75	2.00
2002(a)	—	—	—	0.75	1.75	2.00
2003(a)	—	—	—	0.75	1.75	2.00
2004(a)	—	—	—	0.75	1.50	2.00
2005(a)	—	—	—	0.75	1.50	2.00
2006(a)	—	—	—	0.75	1.50	2.00
2007(a)	—	—	—	0.75	1.50	2.00
2008(a)	—	—	—	0.75	1.50	2.00
2009(a)	—	—	—	0.75	1.50	2.00
2010(a)	—	—	—	0.75	1.50	2.00
2011(a)	—	—	—	0.75	1.50	2.00
2012(a)	—	—	—	0.75	1.50	2.00

KM# 6 50 FRANCS
5.0000 g., Copper-Nickel, 22 mm. **Series:** F.A.O. **Obv:** Taku - Ashanti gold weight **Rev:** Value within mixed beans, grains and nuts **Designer:** R. Joly

Date	Mintage	F	VF	XF	Unc	BU
2001(a)	—	—	0.35	0.50	1.25	1.50
2002(a)	—	—	0.35	0.50	1.25	1.50
2003(a)	—	—	0.35	0.50	1.25	1.50
2004(a)	—	—	0.35	0.50	1.25	1.50
2005(a)	—	—	0.35	0.50	1.25	1.50
2006(a)	—	—	—	0.50	1.25	1.50
2007(a)	—	—	—	0.50	1.25	1.50
2009(a)	—	—	—	0.50	1.25	1.50
2010(a)	—	—	—	0.50	1.25	1.50
2011(a)	—	—	—	0.50	1.25	1.50
2012(a)	—	—	—	0.50	1.25	1.50

KM# 4 100 FRANCS
7.0700 g., Nickel, 26 mm. **Obv:** Taku - Ashanti gold weight **Rev:** Value within flowers **Edge:** Reeded **Designer:** R. Joly

Date	Mintage	F	VF	XF	Unc	BU
2001(a)	—	—	0.60	0.85	2.25	2.75
2002(a)	—	—	0.60	0.85	2.25	2.75
2003(a)	—	—	0.60	0.85	2.25	2.75
2004(a)	—	—	0.60	0.75	2.00	2.75
2005(a)	—	—	0.60	0.75	2.00	2.75
2006(a)	—	—	0.60	0.75	2.00	2.75
2009(a)	—	—	0.60	0.75	2.00	2.75
2010(a)	—	—	0.60	0.75	2.00	2.75
2012(a)	—	—	0.60	0.75	2.00	2.75

KM# 14 200 FRANCS
6.9000 g., Bi-Metallic Brass center in Copper-Nickel ring, 24.4 mm. **Obv:** Taku - Ashanti gold weight **Rev:** Agricultural produce and value **Edge:** Segmented reeding **Designer:** Raymond Joly

Date	Mintage	F	VF	XF	Unc	BU
2003	—	—	—	1.60	4.00	6.00
2004(a)	—	—	—	1.60	4.00	6.00
2005(a)	—	—	—	1.60	4.00	6.00
2010(a)	—	—	—	1.60	4.00	6.00

KM# 15 500 FRANCS
10.6000 g., Bi-Metallic Copper-Nickel center in Brass ring, 27.9 mm. **Obv:** Taku - Ashanti gold weight **Rev:** Agricultural produce and value **Edge:** Segmented reeding **Designer:** Raymond Joly

Date	Mintage	F	VF	XF	Unc	BU
2003	—	—	2.25	4.00	10.00	14.00
2004(a)	—	—	2.25	4.00	10.00	12.00
2005(a)	—	—	2.25	4.00	10.00	12.00
2010(a)	—	—	2.25	4.00	10.00	12.00

KM# 16 1000 FRANCS
22.2000 g., 0.9000 Silver 0.6423 oz. ASW **Obv:** Taku - Ashanti gold weight **Rev:** Agricultural produce above sprays surrounded by names of member countries

Date	Mintage	F	VF	XF	Unc	BU
2002(a) Proof	500	Value: 150				

KM# 17 1000 FRANCS
22.2000 g., 0.9000 Silver 0.6423 oz. ASW **Subject:** FIFA World Championship Football - Germany 2006 **Obv:** Player kicking ball, tree in background **Obv. Legend:** COUPE DU MONDE DE LA FIFA - ALLEMAGNE **Rev:** Agricultural produce above sprays surrounded by names of member countries

Date	Mintage	F	VF	XF	Unc	BU
2004(a) Proof	50,000	Value: 75.00				

YEMEN REPUBLIC

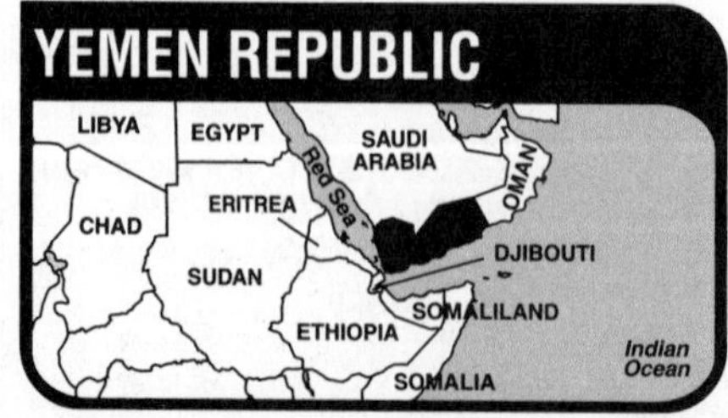

The Republic of Yemen, formerly Yemen Arab Republic and Peoples Democratic Republic of Yemen, is located on the southern coast of the Arabian Peninsula. It has an area of 205,020 sq. mi. (531,000 sq. km.) and a population of 12 million. Capital: San'a. The port of Aden is the main commercial center and the area's most valuable natural resource. Recent oil and gas finds and a developing petroleum industry have improved their economic prospects. Agriculture and local handicrafts are the main industries. Cotton, fish, coffee, rock salt and hides are exported.

On May 22, 1990, the Yemen Arab Republic (North Yemen) and Peoples Democratic Republic of Yemen (South Yemen) merged into a unified Republic of Yemen. Disagreements between the two former governments simmered until civil war erupted in 1994, with the northern forces of the old Yemen Arab Republic eventually prevailing.

TITLES

المملكة المتوكلية اليمنية

al-Mamlaka(t) al-Mutawakkiliya(t) al-Yamaniya(t)

REPUBLIC

MILLED COINAGE

KM# 26 5 RIYALS
4.5000 g., Stainless Steel, 22.9 mm. **Obv:** Denomination within circle **Rev:** Building **Shape:** 21-sided

Date	Mintage	F	VF	XF	Unc	BU
AH1421-2001	—	—	—	—	1.75	2.25
AH1425-2004	—	—	—	—	1.75	2.25

KM# 27 10 RIYALS
6.0500 g., Stainless Steel, 26 mm. **Obv:** Denomination within circle **Rev:** Bridge at Shaharah

Date	Mintage	F	VF	XF	Unc	BU
AH1424-2003	—	—	—	—	2.75	3.50
AH1430-2009	—	—	—	—	2.75	3.50

KM# 29 20 RIALS
7.1000 g., Bi-Metallic Brass plated Steel center in Stainless Steel ring, 29.85 mm. **Obv:** Value within circle **Rev:** Tree within circle **Edge:** Reeded

Date	Mintage	F	VF	XF	Unc	BU
AH1425-2004	—	—	—	—	4.00	5.00

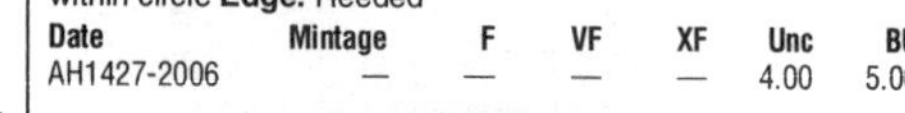

KM# 29a 20 RIALS
Stainless Steel, 29.85 mm. **Obv:** Value within circle **Rev:** Tree within circle **Edge:** Reeded

Date	Mintage	F	VF	XF	Unc	BU
AH1427-2006	—	—	—	—	4.00	5.00

KM# 30 500 RIALS
21.2500 g., Copper-Nickel-Zinc, 35.2 mm. **Subject:** City of San'a **Obv:** Value **Rev:** City gate below artwork **Edge:** Reeded

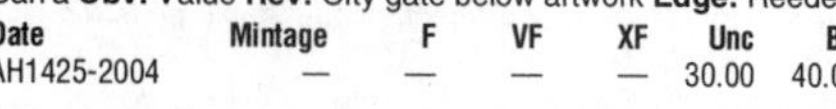

Date	Mintage	F	VF	XF	Unc	BU
AH1425-2004	—	—	—	—	30.00	40.00

KM# 32 500 RIALS
13.0000 g., Copper-Nickel gilt, 30 mm. **Subject:** City of San'a as Arab Cultural Capital **Note:** Pin added to reverse

Date	Mintage	F	VF	XF	Unc	BU
2004	—	—	—	—	40.00	50.00

KM# 31 1000 RIALS
73.3000 g., Pewter Antique silver finish, 60.3 mm. **Subject:** City of San'a **Obv:** Value **Rev:** City gate below artwork **Edge:** Plain **Note:** Illustration reduced.

Date	Mintage	F	VF	XF	Unc	BU
AH1425-2004	—	—	—	—	70.00	80.00

KM# 33 5000 RIALS
22.2000 g., 0.9000 Silver 0.6423 oz. ASW, 37 mm. **Subject:** President Ali Abdullah Saleh

Date	Mintage	F	VF	XF	Unc	BU
AH1424-2003	—	—	—	—	50.00	60.00

YUGOSLAVIA

The Federal Republic of Yugoslavia, formerly the Socialist Federal Republic of Yugoslavia, a Balkan country located on the east shore of the Adriatic Sea, has an area of 39,450 sq. mi. (102,173 sq. km.) and a population of 10.5 million. Capital: Belgrade. The chief industries are agriculture, mining, manufacturing and tourism. Machinery, nonferrous metals, meat and fabrics are exported.

The name Yugoslavia appears on the coinage in letters of the Cyrillic alphabet alone until formation of the Federated Peoples Republic of Yugoslavia in 1953, after which both the Cyrillic and Latin alphabets are employed. From 1965, the coin denomination appears in the 4 different languages of the federated republics in letters of both the Cyrillic and Latin alphabets.

MONETARY SYSTEM
100 Para = 1 Dinar

FEDERAL REPUBLIC
STANDARD COINAGE

KM# 180 DINAR
4.4000 g., Copper-Nickel-Zinc, 20 mm. **Obv:** National arms within circle **Rev:** Building **Edge:** Reeded

Date	Mintage	F	VF	XF	Unc	BU
2002	60,780,000	—	—	—	0.25	0.45

KM# 181 2 DINARA
5.2000 g., Copper-Nickel-Zinc, 21.9 mm. **Obv:** National arms within circle **Rev:** Church **Edge:** Reeded

Date	Mintage	F	VF	XF	Unc	BU
2002	71,053,000	—	—	—	0.30	0.50

KM# 182 5 DINARA
6.3000 g., Copper-Nickel-Zinc, 24 mm. **Obv:** National arms **Rev:** Domed building, denomination and date at left **Edge:** Reeded

Date	Mintage	F	VF	XF	Unc	BU
2002	30,966,000	—	—	—	1.25	1.50

ZAMBIA

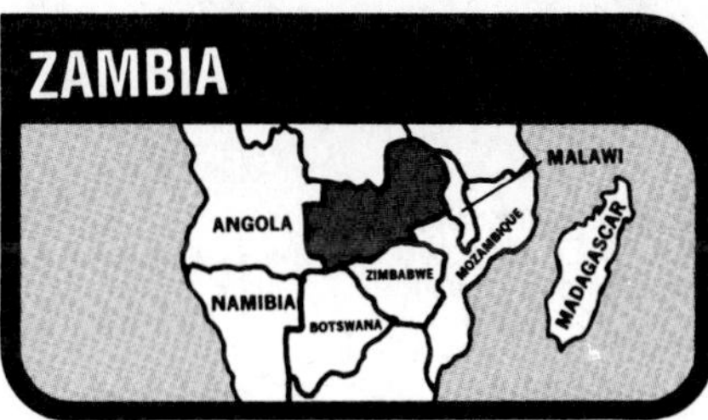

The Republic of Zambia (formerly Northern Rhodesia), a landlocked country in south-central Africa, has an area of 290,586 sq. mi. (752,610 sq. km.) and a population of*7.9 million. Capital: Lusaka. The economy of Zambia is based principally on copper, of which Zambia is the world's third largest producer. Copper, zinc, lead, cobalt and tobacco are exported. Zambia is a member of the Commonwealth of Nations. The President is the Head of State and the Head of Government.

REPUBLIC
DECIMAL COINAGE

100 Ngwee = 1 Kwacha

KM# 156 500 KWACHA
15.0000 g., 0.9990 Silver 0.4818 oz. ASW, 34.2 mm. **Subject:** Football World Champion - 1954 Germany **Obv:** Crowned head right within circle above arms with supporters and value **Rev:** Soccer game scene in front of Berlin Wall **Edge:** Plain

Date	Mintage	F	VF	XF	Unc	BU
2001 Proof	—	Value: 35.00				

KM# 174 500 KWACHA
15.0000 g., 0.9990 Silver 0.4818 oz. ASW, 34.2 mm. **Subject:** 1972 Munich Olympics **Obv:** Crowned head right above arms with supporters **Rev:** Torch runner in stadium **Edge:** Reeded

Date	Mintage	F	VF	XF	Unc	BU
2002 Proof	—	Value: 28.00				

KM# 87 1000 KWACHA
28.9100 g., Copper-Nickel, 38 mm. **Series:** Patrons of the Ocean **Obv:** Arms with supporters above crowned head right within circle **Rev:** Loggerhead sea turtle **Edge:** Reeded

Date	Mintage	F	VF	XF	Unc	BU
2001 Proof	—	Value: 17.00				

KM# 88 1000 KWACHA
28.9100 g., Copper-Nickel **Series:** Patrons of the Ocean **Obv:** Arms with supporters above crowned head right within circle **Rev:** Coelacanth

Date	Mintage	F	VF	XF	Unc	BU
2001 Proof	—	Value: 17.00				

KM# 89 1000 KWACHA
28.9100 g., Copper-Nickel **Series:** Patrons of the Ocean **Obv:** Arms with supporters above crowned head right within circle **Rev:** Sea horse and fish

Date	Mintage	F	VF	XF	Unc	BU
2001 Proof	—	Value: 17.00				

KM# 90 1000 KWACHA
28.9100 g., Copper-Nickel **Series:** Patrons of the Ocean **Obv:** Arms with supporters above crowned head right within circle **Rev:** Two dolphins

Date	Mintage	F	VF	XF	Unc	BU
2001 Proof	—	Value: 17.00				

KM# 181 1000 KWACHA
20.0300 g., Silver **Subject:** 75th Birthday Queen Elizabeth II **Obv:** Crowned head of Elizabeth II in circle, national arms below **Obv. Legend:** BANK OF ZAMBIA **Rev:** Bust of Elizabeth II facing wearing tiara **Edge:** Reeded

Date	Mintage	F	VF	XF	Unc	BU
2001 Proof	—	Value: 30.00				

KM# 74 1000 KWACHA
29.0000 g., Copper-Nickel, 40 mm. **Obv:** Crowned head right above arms with supporters divides date **Rev:** Dated calendar within circular design **Shape:** 7-sided

Date	Mintage	F	VF	XF	Unc	BU
2002 Proof-like	—	—	—	—	—	12.50
2003 Proof-like	—	—	—	—	—	12.50
2004 Proof-like	—	—	—	—	—	12.50

KM# 159 1000 KWACHA
31.2200 g., 0.9990 Silver 1.0027 oz. ASW, 38.6 mm. **Obv:** Crowned head right divides date above arms with supporters **Rev:** Bust 1/4 left **Edge:** Reeded

Date	Mintage	F	VF	XF	Unc	BU
2002	—	—	—	—	42.50	45.00

KM# 167 1000 KWACHA
25.0000 g., Copper-Nickel, 38.6 mm. **Subject:** 50th Anniversary of Elizabeth II's Coronation **Obv:** Crowned head right above arms with supporters **Rev:** Crown on pillow above crossed scepters **Edge:** Reeded

Date	Mintage	F	VF	XF	Unc	BU
ND(2003)	—	—	—	—	8.50	10.00

KM# 169 1000 KWACHA
25.0000 g., Copper-Nickel, 38.6 mm. **Obv:** Crowned head right above arms with supporters **Rev:** Prince William on jet ski **Edge:** Reeded

Date	Mintage	F	VF	XF	Unc	BU
2003	—	—	—	—	8.50	10.00

KM# 171 1000 KWACHA
25.0000 g., Copper-Nickel, 38.6 mm. **Obv:** Crowned head right above arms with supporters **Rev:** Crowned bust facing **Edge:** Reeded

Date	Mintage	F	VF	XF	Unc	BU
ND(2003)	—	—	—	—	8.50	10.00

KM# 172 1000 KWACHA
25.0000 g., 0.9250 Silver 0.7435 oz. ASW, 38.6 mm. **Obv:** Crowned head right above arms with supporters **Rev:** Crowned bust facing **Edge:** Reeded

Date	Mintage	F	VF	XF	Unc	BU
ND(2003) Proof	5,000	Value: 45.00				

KM# 160 1000 KWACHA
29.3000 g., Silver Plated Bronze (Specific gravity 9.099), 38.6 mm. **Subject:** Pope John Paul II **Obv:** National arms **Rev:** Pope saying mass **Edge:** Reeded **Note:** Specific gravity 9.099

Date	Mintage	F	VF	XF	Unc	BU
2003 Proof	—	Value: 20.00				

KM# 183 1000 KWACHA
7.7700 g., 0.9990 Silver 0.2496 oz. ASW, 26 mm. **Rev:** Elephant pair

Date	Mintage	F	VF	XF	Unc	BU
2003 Proof	2,000	Value: 18.00				

KM# 199 1000 KWACHA
Silver, 38 mm. **Subject:** Deadly Bugs **Obv:** National arms **Rev:** Harvest Ant in colored insert

Date	Mintage	F	VF	XF	Unc	BU
2010 Proof	—	Value: 40.00				

KM# 200 1000 KWACHA
Silver, 38 mm. **Subject:** Deadly Bugs **Obv:** National arms **Rev:** Giant Hornet in colored insert

Date	Mintage	F	VF	XF	Unc	BU
2010 Proof	—	Value: 40.00				

KM# 201 1000 KWACHA
Silver, 38 mm. **Subject:** Deadly Bugs **Obv:** National arms **Rev:** Mosquito in multicolor insert

Date	Mintage	F	VF	XF	Unc	BU
2010 Proof	—	Value: 40.00				

KM# 202 1000 KWACHA
Silver, 38 mm. **Subject:** Deadly Bugs **Obv:** National arms **Rev:** Scorpion

Date	Mintage	F	VF	XF	Unc	BU
2010 Proof	—	—	—	—	—	40.00

KM# 203 1000 KWACHA
Silver, 38 mm. **Subject:** Deadly Bugs **Obv:** National arms **Rev:** Tsetse Fly

Date	Mintage	F	VF	XF	Unc	BU
2010 Proof	—	Value: 40.00				

KM# 118 2000 KWACHA
31.1035 g., 0.9990 Silver 0.9990 oz. ASW, 38.6 mm. **Subject:** Centennial of the Anglo-Japanese Alliance **Obv:** Queen Elizabeth **Rev:** Fantasy Japanese coin design **Edge:** Reeded

Date	Mintage	F	VF	XF	Unc	BU
2002	500	—	—	—	80.00	85.00

KM# 184 2000 KWACHA
15.1500 g., 0.9990 Silver 0.4866 oz. ASW **Rev:** Elephant pair

Date	Mintage	F	VF	XF	Unc	BU
2003 Proof	2,000	Value: 30.00				

KM# 166 4000 KWACHA
25.0000 g., 0.9250 Silver 0.7435 oz. ASW, 38.6 mm. **Subject:** Queen Elizabeth's 75th Birthday **Obv:** Crowned head right above arms with supporters **Rev:** Bust with hat facing **Edge:** Reeded

Date	Mintage	F	VF	XF	Unc	BU
2001 Proof	2,000	Value: 40.00				

KM# 85 4000 KWACHA
25.1000 g., 0.9250 Silver 0.7464 oz. ASW, 37.9 mm. **Series:** Wildlife Protection **Obv:** Crowned head right below arms **Rev:** Lion head hologram **Edge:** Reeded **Note:** Lighter weight and smaller diameter than official specifications

Date	Mintage	F	VF	XF	Unc	BU
2001 Proof	—	Value: 60.00				

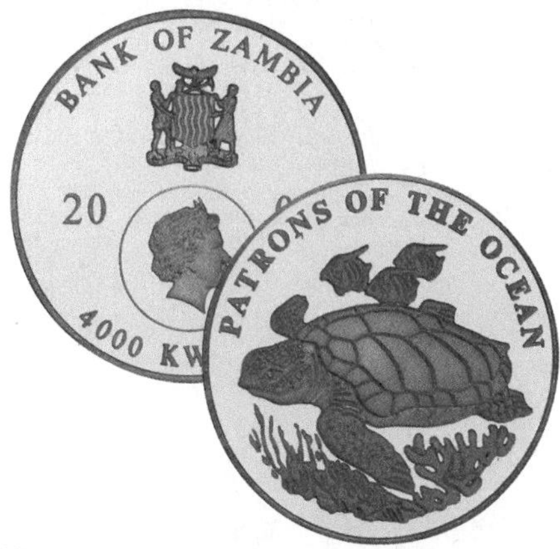

KM# 110 4000 KWACHA
20.0000 g., 0.9990 Silver 0.6423 oz. ASW, 37.9 mm. **Series:** Patrons of the Ocean **Obv:** Crowned head right within circle below arms with supporters **Rev:** Loggerhead sea turtle **Edge:** Reeded

Date	Mintage	F	VF	XF	Unc	BU
2001 Proof	—	Value: 32.00				

KM# 111 4000 KWACHA
20.0000 g., 0.9990 Silver 0.6423 oz. ASW **Series:** Patrons of the Ocean **Obv:** Crowned head right divides date below arms with supporters **Rev:** Coelacanth fish

Date	Mintage	F	VF	XF	Unc	BU
2001 Proof	—	Value: 38.00				

KM# 112 4000 KWACHA
20.0000 g., 0.9990 Silver 0.6423 oz. ASW **Series:** Patrons of the Ocean **Obv:** Crowned head right divides date below arms with supporters **Rev:** Sea horse and fish

Date	Mintage	F	VF	XF	Unc	BU
2001 Proof	—	Value: 35.00				

KM# 113 4000 KWACHA
20.0000 g., 0.9990 Silver 0.6423 oz. ASW **Series:** Patrons of the Ocean **Obv:** Crowned head right divides date below arms with supporters **Rev:** Two dolphins

Date	Mintage	F	VF	XF	Unc	BU
2001 Proof	—	Value: 38.00				

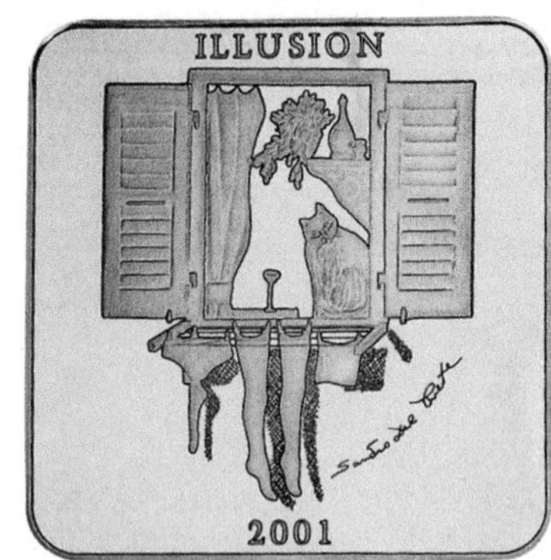

KM# 114 4000 KWACHA
50.0000 g., 0.9990 Silver 1.6059 oz. ASW **Subject:** Illusion **Obv:** Arms with supporters below crowned head right **Rev:** Cat within window **Edge:** Plain **Note:** 50x50mm

Date	Mintage	F	VF	XF	Unc	BU
2001 Proof	5,000	Value: 85.00				

KM# 175 4000 KWACHA
23.0000 g., 0.9990 Silver 0.7387 oz. ASW, 40 mm. **Obv:** Head with tiara right divides date above arms **Rev:** Dated calendar **Shape:** Seven-sided

Date	Mintage	F	VF	XF	Unc	BU
2002 Prooflike	—	—	—	—	—	45.00
2003 Prooflike	15,000	—	—	—	—	45.00
2004 Prooflike	5,000	—	—	—	—	45.00

KM# 168 4000 KWACHA
25.0000 g., 0.9250 Silver 0.7435 oz. ASW, 38.6 mm. **Subject:** 50th Anniversary of Elizabeth II's Coronation **Obv:** Crowned head right above arms with supporters **Rev:** Crown on pillow above crossed scepters **Edge:** Reeded

Date	Mintage	F	VF	XF	Unc	BU
ND(2003) Proof	5,000	Value: 45.00				

KM# 170 4000 KWACHA
25.0000 g., 0.9250 Silver 0.7435 oz. ASW, 38.6 mm. **Obv:** Crowned head right above arms with supporters **Rev:** Prince William on jet ski **Edge:** Reeded

Date	Mintage	F	VF	XF	Unc	BU
2003 Proof	5,000	Value: 45.00				

KM# 117 5000 KWACHA
31.3000 g., 0.9990 Silver 1.0053 oz. ASW, 38.6 mm. **Subject:** African Wildlife **Obv:** Arms with supporters **Rev:** Elephant mother and calf grazing on grass **Edge:** Reeded

Date	Mintage	F	VF	XF	Unc	BU
2001 Matte	—	—	—	—	42.00	45.00
2001 Proof	—	Value: 45.00				
Note: 50						

KM# 143 5000 KWACHA
28.8600 g., 0.9990 Silver 0.9269 oz. ASW, 38.5 mm. **Subject:** African Wildlife **Obv:** Arms with supporters **Rev:** Elephant **Edge:** Reeded

Date	Mintage	F	VF	XF	Unc	BU
2002 Matte	—	—	—	—	42.00	45.00
2002 Proof	—	Value: 50.00				

KM# 142 5000 KWACHA
28.6400 g., 0.9990 Silver 0.9198 oz. ASW, 38.5 mm. **Subject:** African Wildlife **Obv:** Queen Elizabeth's portrait above national arms and denomination **Rev:** Adult and juvenile elephants **Edge:** Reeded

Date	Mintage	F	VF	XF	Unc	BU
2002 Matte	—	—	—	—	42.00	45.00
2002 Proof	—	Value: 50.00				

KM# 165 5000 KWACHA
31.1000 g., 0.9990 Silver 0.9988 oz. ASW, 38.5 mm. **Obv:** Crowned bust right divides date **Rev:** Two African elephants **Edge:** Reeded

Date	Mintage	F	VF	XF	Unc	BU
2003 Matte	—	—	—	—	42.00	45.00
2003 Proof	—	Value: 50.00				

KM# 185 5000 KWACHA
31.1050 g., 0.9990 Silver 0.9990 oz. ASW **Rev:** Elephant pair

Date	Mintage	F	VF	XF	Unc	BU
2003 Proof	2,000	Value: 55.00				

KM# 186 5000 KWACHA
31.1050 g., 0.9990 Silver 0.9990 oz. ASW **Obv:** Head right **Rev:** Multicolor elephant pair

Date	Mintage	F	VF	XF	Unc	BU
2003 Proof	—	Value: 42.00				

KM# 187 5000 KWACHA
31.1050 g., 0.9990 Silver partially gilt 0.9990 oz. ASW, 40 mm. **Rev:** Elephant pair, partially gilt

Date	Mintage	F	VF	XF	Unc	BU
2003 Proof	—	Value: 50.00				

KM# 188 10000 KWACHA
62.2100 g., 0.9990 Silver 1.9980 oz. ASW, 50 mm. **Rev:** Two elephants

Date	Mintage	F	VF	XF	Unc	BU
2003 Proof	2,000	Value: 125				

KM# 94 40000 KWACHA
31.1035 g., 0.9999 Gold 0.9999 oz. AGW, 37.9 mm. **Series:** Wildlife Protection **Obv:** Arms with supporters above crowned head right **Rev:** Holographic lion head **Edge:** Reeded

Date	Mintage	F	VF	XF	Unc	BU
2001 Proof	—	Value: 1,750				

KM# 153.1 40000 KWACHA
47.5400 g., 0.9166 Gold 1.4009 oz. AGW, 39 mm. **Subject:** Queen Victoria **Obv:** Crowned head right within ornate frame divides date above arms with supporters **Rev:** Crowned veiled bust of Queen Victoria left **Edge:** Reeded

Date	Mintage	F	VF	XF	Unc	BU
2001 Proof	1	—	—	—	—	—

Note: Medallic die alignment

KM# 153.2 40000 KWACHA
47.5400 g., 0.9166 Gold 1.4009 oz. AGW, 39 mm. **Subject:** Queen Victoria **Obv:** Crowned head right within ornate frame divides date above arms with supporters **Rev:** Crowned veiled bust of Queen Victoria left **Edge:** Reeded

Date	Mintage	F	VF	XF	Unc	BU
2001 Matte	1	—	—	—	—	—

Note: Coin die alignment

KM# 154.1 40000 KWACHA
47.5400 g., 0.9166 Gold 1.4009 oz. AGW, 39 mm. **Subject:** Edward VII **Obv:** Crowned head right within ornate frame divides date above arms with supporters **Rev:** Crowned bust of King Edward VII right **Edge:** Reeded

Date	Mintage	F	VF	XF	Unc	BU
2001 Proof	1	—	—	—	—	—

Note: Medallic die alignment

KM# 154.2 40000 KWACHA
47.5400 g., 0.9166 Gold 1.4009 oz. AGW, 39 mm. **Subject:** Edward VII **Obv:** Crowned head right within ornate frame divides date above arms with supporters **Rev:** Crowned bust of King Edward VII right **Edge:** Reeded

Date	Mintage	F	VF	XF	Unc	BU
2001 Matte	1	—	—	—	—	—

Note: Coin die alignment

ZIMBABWE

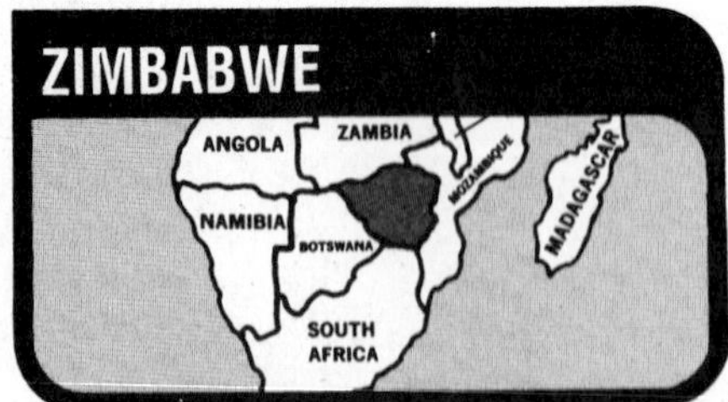

The Republic of Zimbabwe (formerly the Republic of Rhodesia or Southern Rhodesia), located in the east-central part of southern Africa, has an area of 150,804 sq. mi. (390,580 sq. km.) and a population of *10.1 million. Capital: Harare (formerly Salisbury). The economy is based on agriculture and mining. Tobacco, sugar, asbestos, copper, chrome, ore and coal are exported.

On April 18, 1980 pursuant to an act of the British Parliament, the colony of Southern Rhodesia became independent as the Republic of Zimbabwe, a member of the Commonwealth of Nations, until recently suspended.

MONETARY SYSTEM
100 Cents = 1 Dollar

MINT
Harare

REPUBLIC

DECIMAL COINAGE

KM# 3a 10 CENTS
Nickel Plated Steel, 20 mm. **Obv:** National emblem **Rev:** Baobab tree, value **Edge:** Plain **Mint:** Harare **Designer:** Jeff Huntly

Date	Mintage	F	VF	XF	Unc	BU
2001	—	—	0.15	0.30	0.75	1.00
2002	—	—	0.15	0.30	0.75	1.00
2003	—	—	0.15	0.30	0.75	1.00

KM# 4a 20 CENTS
Nickel Plated Steel, 23 mm. **Obv:** National emblem **Rev:** Birchenough Bridge over the Sabi River, value below **Edge:** Plain **Mint:** Harare **Designer:** Jeff Huntly

Date	Mintage	F	VF	XF	Unc	BU
2001	—	—	0.20	0.40	1.25	1.50
2002	—	—	0.20	0.40	1.25	1.50
2003	—	—	0.20	0.40	1.25	1.50

KM# 5a 50 CENTS
Nickel Plated Steel, 26 mm. **Obv:** National emblem **Rev:** Radiant sun rising, symbolic of independence, value **Edge:** Plain **Mint:** Harare **Designer:** Jeff Huntly

Date	Mintage	F	VF	XF	Unc	BU
2001	—	—	0.40	1.00	1.75	2.00
2002	—	—	0.40	1.00	1.75	2.00
2003	—	—	0.40	1.00	1.75	2.00

KM# 6a DOLLAR
Nickel Plated Steel, 29 mm. **Obv:** National emblem **Rev:** Zimbabwe ruins amongst trees, value **Edge:** Reeded **Mint:** Harare **Designer:** Jeff Huntly

Date	Mintage	F	VF	XF	Unc	BU
2001	—	—	1.00	1.50	2.50	3.00
2002	—	—	1.00	1.50	2.50	3.00
2003	—	—	1.00	1.50	2.50	3.00

KM# 12a 2 DOLLARS
Brass Plated Steel, 24.5 mm. **Obv:** National emblem **Rev:** Pangolin below value **Edge:** Reeded **Mint:** Harare

Date	Mintage	F	VF	XF	Unc	BU
2001	—	—	1.25	2.25	4.00	5.00
2002	—	—	1.25	2.25	4.00	5.00
2003	—	—	1.25	2.25	4.00	5.00

KM# 13 5 DOLLARS
9.0500 g., Bi-Metallic Nickel-plated-Steel center in Brass ring, 27.4 mm. **Obv:** National emblem **Rev:** Rhinoceros standing right **Edge:** Reeded **Mint:** Harare

Date	Mintage	F	VF	XF	Unc	BU
2001	—	—	—	—	5.00	6.00
2002	—	—	—	—	5.00	6.00
2003	—	—	—	—	5.00	6.00

KM# 14 10 DOLLARS
5.2000 g., Nickel Plated Steel, 21.5 mm. **Obv:** National emblem **Rev:** Water buffalo **Edge:** Reeded **Mint:** Harare

Date	Mintage	F	VF	XF	Unc	BU
2003	—	—	—	1.50	2.50	3.50

KM# 15 25 DOLLARS
7.3300 g., Nickel Plated Steel, 24.5 mm. **Obv:** National emblem **Rev:** Military monument **Edge:** Segmented reeding **Mint:** Harare

Date	Mintage	F	VF	XF	Unc	BU
2003	—	—	—	1.75	3.00	4.00